The Middle East and North Africa 1999

The Middle East and North Africa 1999

FORTY-FIFTH EDITION

EUROPA PUBLICATIONS LIMITED

Forty-Fifth Edition 1999

© **Europa Publications Limited 1998**
18 Bedford Square, London, WC1B 3JN, United Kingdom

Australia and New Zealand
James Bennett Library Services, 3 Narabang Way,
Belrose, NSW 2085, Australia

Japan
Maruzen Co Ltd, POB 5050, Tokyo International 100-31

British Library Cataloguing in Publication Data
The Middle East and North Africa—1999
1. Africa, North—Periodicals
961'. 048'05   DT160
ISBN 1-85743-047-6
ISSN 0076-8502

Library of Congress Catalog Card Number 48–3250

Typeset by UBL International and printed by Unwin Brothers Limited
The Gresham Press
Old Woking, Surrey
(Members of the MPG Information Division)
Bound by MPG Books Limited
Bodmin, Cornwall.
(All members of the Martins Printing Group)

FOREWORD

At the time of going to press, peace talks between the Palestinian and Israeli leaders, once again, have been resuscitated for sufficient time to dishearten optimists, following months of inactivity. US political initiatives in the region (examined here for the first time as a calendar of events) have been largely overshadowed by the domestic difficulties of the Clinton administration, thereby allowing the countries of the region greater freedom to assert their own political agendas on the international community, and prompting efforts by Iran to attempt a *rapprochement* with the West and by the region as a whole to secure wider support for an end to sanctions against Libya and Iraq.

The forty-fifth edition of THE MIDDLE EAST AND NORTH AFRICA provides a comprehensive discussion of the issues and interests involved in the peace process, as well as examining the historical perspectives of the topic. Meanwhile, mounting international concern with regard to the ferocity of the conflict between secular administrations and Islamist movements within a number of the featured countries (notably Algeria and Egypt) is represented here in a thoroughly revised and updated essay on The Islamist Movement in the Middle East and North Africa. In addition, expanded directories for each country include new information on broadcasting and communications and utilities, while a new introductory essay attempts to explain how the region's economies have been managed and/or mismanaged since indigenous water resources 'ran out' in the 1970s.

The Editor would once again, like to thank all the contributors for their articles and advice, and the various governmental and other organizations which have assisted in the revision of statistical and directory material in the new edition.

October 1998

ACKNOWLEDGEMENTS

The editors gratefully acknowledge the interest and co-operation of all the contributors to this volume, and of numerous national statistical and information offices, and government departments, as well as embassies in London and throughout the region, whose kind assistance in updating the material contained in THE MIDDLE EAST AND NORTH AFRICA is greatly appreciated.

We are particularly grateful for permission to make extensive use of material from the following sources: the UN *Statistical Yearbook, Demographic Yearbook, Industrial Commodity Statistics Yearbook, National Accounts Statistics and International Trade Statistics Yearbook*; the UNESCO *Statistical Yearbook*; the FAO *Production Yearbook, Yearbook of Forest Products* and *Yearbook of Fishery Statistics*; the ILO *Yearbook of Labour Statistics*; and the IMF's monthly *International Financial Statistics*. We are also grateful to the International Institute for Strategic Studies, 23 Tavistock Street, London, WC2E 7NQ, England, for the use of defence statistics from *The Military Balance 1997–98*; and to the Israeli embassy, London, for the use of two maps illustrating the disengagement agreements between Israel and Egypt (1974) and Israel and Syria.

The following publications have been of special value in providing regular coverage of the affairs of the Middle East and North Africa region: *Middle East Economic Digest*, The Invicta Press, Ashford, Kent, England; *IMF Survey*, Washington, DC, USA; *Keesing's Record of World Events*, Cambridge, England; and *Summary of World Broadcasts: Part 4, The Middle East*, BBC, Reading, England.

Our thanks also go to the following for particular assistance: Bank Markazi, Islamic Republic of Iran; Saudi Arabian Monetary Agency, Riyadh; United Nations Relief and Works Agency for Palestine Refugees in the Near East.

EXPLANATORY NOTE ON THE DIRECTORY SECTION

The Directory section of each chapter is arranged under the following headings, where they apply:

THE CONSTITUTION

THE GOVERNMENT
    HEAD OF STATE
    CABINET/COUNCIL OF MINISTERS
    MINISTRIES
    POLITICAL BUREAU OF PARTY

LEGISLATURE

POLITICAL ORGANIZATIONS

DIPLOMATIC REPRESENTATION

JUDICIAL SYSTEM

RELIGION

THE PRESS

PUBLISHERS

BROADCASTING AND COMMUNICATIONS
    TELECOMMUNICATIONS
    RADIO
    TELEVISION

FINANCE
    CENTRAL BANK
    STATE BANKS
    COMMERCIAL BANKS
    DEVELOPMENT BANKS
    INVESTMENT BANKS
    SAVINGS BANKS
    ISLAMIC BANKS
    FOREIGN BANKS
    STOCK EXCHANGE
    INSURANCE

TRADE AND INDUSTRY
    GOVERNMENT AGENCIES
    DEVELOPMENT ORGANIZATIONS
    CHAMBERS OF COMMERCE AND INDUSTRY
    INDUSTRIAL AND TRADE ASSOCIATIONS
    EMPLOYERS' ORGANIZATIONS
    PETROLEUM
    HYDROCARBONS
    UTILITIES
    MAJOR COMPANIES
    CO-OPERATIVES
    TRADE UNIONS

TRANSPORT
    RAILWAYS
    ROADS
    SHIPPING
    CIVIL AVIATION

TOURISM

DEFENCE

EDUCATION

CONTENTS

CONTENTS

THE CONTRIBUTORS

Simon Chapman. Editor of *The Middle East and North Africa*, 1989–97.

Dr Youssef Choueiri. Centre for Arab Gulf Studies, University of Exeter, England.

Alan J. Day. Editor of *The Annual Register,* London, England; former Joint Editor of the *Political Handbook of the World,* Binghamton University, New York, USA.

Michael James den Hartog. Graduate in Middle East Studies from the Universities of Exeter (England) and Nijmegen (The Netherlands). Nato Research Fellow at the Peace Research Centre (University of Nijmegen).

George Joffé. Deputy Director of the Royal Institute of International Affairs, London, England.

Richard I. Lawless. Emeritus Reader in Middle Eastern Studies, University of Durham, England.

Dr Kamil Mahdi. Director of Studies, Centre for Arab Gulf Studies, University of Exeter, England.

Malise Ruthven. Centre for the Study of Religions, University of Aberdeen, Scotland.

Rodney Wilson. Professor of Economics, University of Durham, England.

ABBREVIATIONS

AAHO	Afro-Asian Housing Organization
AAPSO	Afro-Asian People's Solidarity Organization
Acad.	Academy
AD	Algerian dinars
AD	anno Domini
ADB	African Development Bank
ADC	Aide-de-camp
AED	UAE dirhams
Admin.	Administrative, Administration, Administrator
Admin.-Gen	Administrator-General
Agric.	Agriculture
AH	anno Hegirae (year of the Hegira)
a.i.	ad interim
AIDS	Acquired Immunodeficiency Syndrome
AIWO	Agudath Israel World Organization
ALF	Arab Liberation Front
AM	Amplitude Modulation
a.m.	ante meridiem (before noon)
AOF	Afrique occidentale française (French West Africa)
Apdo	Apartado (Post Box)
API	American Petroleum Institute
approx.	approximately
apptd	appointed
ARE	Arab Republic of Egypt
AŞ	Anonim Şirketi (Joint-Stock Company)
Ass.	Assembly
Asscn	Association
Assoc.	Associate
Asst	Assistant
ATUC	African Trade Union Confederation
auth.	authorized
AUXERAP	Société auxiliaire de la régie du pétrole
Ave	Avenue
Avda	Avenida
BADEA	Banque arabe pour le développement economique en Afrique (Arab Bank for Economic Development in Africa)
BC	before Christ
b/d	barrels per day
BD	Bahrain dinars
Bd	Board
Bde	Brigade
Bldg	Building
Blvd	Boulevard
BP	Boîte Postale (Post Box)
br.(s)	branch(es)
Brig.	Brigadier
BST	British Standard Time
Bul.	Bulvar (Boulevard)
C	Centigrade
c.	circa
Cad.	Caddesi (Street)
CAFRAD	Centre africain de formation et de recherches administratives pour le développement
cap.	capital
Capt.	Captain
CARE	Co-operative for American Relief Everywhere
Cdre	Commodore
CE	Common era
cen.	central
CENTO	Central Treaty Organization
CEO	Chief Executive Officer
cf.	confer (compare)
Chair.	Chairman/person/woman
Cie	Compagnie (Company)
c.i.f.	cost, insurance and freight
C-in-C	Commander-in-Chief
circ.	circulation
CIS	Commonwealth of Independent States
cm	centimetre(s)
cnr	corner
c/o	care of
Co	Company
Col	Colonel

Comm.	Commission
Commdr	Commander
Commdt	Commandant
Commr	Commissioner
Conf.	Conference
Confed.	Confederation
Cons.-Gen.	Consul-General
COO	Chief Operating Officer
Corpn	Corporation
Cttee	Committee
cu	cubic
cwt	hundredweight
Del.	Delegate, Delegation
Dep.	Deputy
dep.	deposits
Dept	Department
Devt	Development
DFLP	Democratic Front for the Liberation of Palestine
Dir	Director
Div.	Division
DPA	Deutsche Presse-Agentur
Dr	Doctor
dwt	dead weight tons
E	East, Eastern
EC	European Community
ECOSOC	Economic and Social Council (UN)
ECU	European Currency Unit(s)
Ed.(s)	Editor(s)
edn	edition
EFTA	European Free Trade Association
e.g.	exempli gratia (for example)
est.	established; estimate(d)
excl.	excluding
EU	European Union
Exec.	Executive
F	Fahrenheit
f.	founded
FAO	Food and Agriculture Organization
FCM	Federation of Muslim Councillors
Fed.	Federal, Federation
FIDES	Fonds d'investissement pour le développement economique et sociale de la France d'outre-mer
Flt	Flight
FM	Frequency Modulation
fmr(ly)	former(ly)
f.o.b.	free on board
Fr.	Franc
ft	foot (feet)
g	gram(s)
GATT	General Agreements on Tariffs and Trade
GCC	Gulf Co-operation Council
GDA	Gas Distribution Administration
GDP	gross domestic product
Gen.	General
GHQ	General Headquarters
GMT	Greenwich Mean Time
GNP	gross national product
Gov.	Governor
Govt	Government
grt	gross registered ton(s)
GW	gigawatt(s)
GWh	gigawatt hour(s)
ha	hectare(s)
HE	His (or Her) Excellency, His Eminence
HIM	His Imperial Majesty
hl	hectolitre(s)
HM	His (or Her) Majesty
Hon.	Honorary; Honourable
HQ	Headquarters
HRH	His (or Her) Royal Highness
IAEA	International Atomic Energy Authority

ABBREVIATIONS

IATA	International Air Transport Association
ibid	ibidem (from the same source)
IBRD	International Bank for Reconstruction and Development
ICAO	International Civil Aviation Organization
ICATU	International Conference of Arab Trade Unions
ICFTU-AFRO	International Confederation of Free Trade Unions—African Regional Organization
IDA	International Development Association
i.e.	id est (that is to say)
IFC	International Finance Corporation
IISS	International Institute of Strategic Studies
ILO	International Labour Organization
IMF	International Monetary Fund
in(s)	inch(es)
Inc	Incorporated
incl.	include, including
Ind.	Independent
Insp.	Inspector
Inst.	Institute; Institution
Int.	International
IRF	International Road Federation
Is	Islands
ITU	International Telecommunications Union
ISIC	International Standard Industrial Classification
Jr	Junior
Jt	Joint
kg	kilogram(s)
KFAED	Kuwait Fund for Arab Economic Development
km	kilometre(s)
kV	kilovolt(s)
kW	kilowatt(s)
kWh	kilowatt hour(s)
lb	pound(s)
Legis.	Legislative
LNG	liquefied natural gas
LPG	liquefied petroleum gas
Lt	Lieutenant
Ltd	Limited
m	metre(s)
m.	million
Maj.	Major
Man.	Manager, Managing
MB	Bachelor of Medicine
MD	Doctor of Medicine
mem.(s)	member(s)
Mfg	Manufacturing
Mgr	Monseigneur, Monsignor
Mil.	Military
mm	millimetre(s)
MP	Member of Parliament
MSS	Manuscripts
Mt	Mount
MW	megawatt(s); medium wave
MWh	megawatt hour(s)
N	North, Northern
n.a.	not available
Nat.	National
NATO	North Atlantic Treaty Organization
NDRC	National Defence Research Council
NECCCRW	Near East Christian Council Committee for Refugee Work
n.e.s.	not elsewhere specified
NGLs	natural gas liquids
NGO(s)	non-governmental organization(s)
n.i.e.	not included elsewhere
no.	number
nr	near
nrt	net registered ton(s)
OAPEC	Organization of Arab Petroleum Exporting Countries
OAU	Organization of African Unity
OECD	Organization for Economic Co-operation and Development
OIC	Organization of the Islamic Conference
OPEC	Organization of the Petroleum Exporting Countries
Org.(s)	Organization(s)
oz	ounce(s)
p.	page
p.a.	per annum
Parl.	Parliament(ary)
PDFLP	Popular Democratic Front for the Liberation of Palestine
Perm.	Permanent
Perm. Rep.	Permanent Representative
PFLP	Popular Front for the Liberation of Palestine
PhD	Doctor of Philosophy
PLC	Public Limited Company
PLO	Palestine Liberation Organization
p.m.	post meridiem (after noon)
POB	Post Office Box
Pres.	President
Prof.	Professor
Propr	Proprietor
Pty	Proprietary
p.u.	paid up
publ.(s)	publication(s)
Publr	Publisher
q.v.	quod vide (to which refer)
RCC	Revolutionary Command Council (Iraq, Libya)
RCD	Regional Co-operation for Development
Rd	Road
RDA	Rassemblement démocratique africain
regd	registered
Rep.	Representative
Repub.	Republic
res	reserves
retd	retired
Rev.	Reverend
ro-ro	roll-on roll-off
S	South, Southern
SDR(s)	special drawing right(s)
Sec.	Secretary
Secr.	Secretariat
SITC	Standard International Trade Classification
Soc.	Society; Société
Sok.	Sokak (Street)
SpA	Società per Azioni (Limited Company)
sq	square (in measurements)
Sq.	Square
Sr	Senior
St	Saint; Street
Stn	Station
subs.	subscribed
Supt	Superintendent
Tapline	Trans-Arabian Pipeline Company
TAŞ	Türk Anonim Şirketi (Turkish Joint-Stock Company)
tel.	telephone
Treas.	Treasurer
trans.	translated; translation
TV	Television
TW	terawatt(s)
TWh	terawatt hour(s)
UA	Unit(s) of Account
UAE	United Arab Emirates
UAR	United Arab Republic
UBAF	Union des banques arabes et françaises
UHF	Ultra High Frequency
UK	United Kingdom
UN	United Nations
UNCTAD	United Nations Conference on Trade and Development
UNDOF	United Nations Disengagement Observer Force
UNDP	United Nations Development Programme
UNEF	United Nations Emergency Force
UNEP	United Nations Environment Programme
UNESCO	United Nations Educational, Scientific and Cultural Organization
UNFICYP	United Nations Peace-keeping Force in Cyprus
UNFPA	United Nations Population Fund
UNICEF	United Nations Children's Fund
UNIDO	United Nations Industrial Development Organization
UNIFIL	United Nations Interim Force in Lebanon
Univ.	University

ABBREVIATIONS

UNMEM	United Nations Middle East Mission	UTA	Union de Transports Aériens
UNRWA	United Nations Relief and Works Agency for Palestine Refugees in the Near East	VAT	Value Added Tax
UNSCOM	United Nations Special Commission	VHF	Very High Frequency
UNTSO	United Nations Truce Supervision Organization	vol.(s)	volume(s)
		VSO	Voluntary Service Overseas Limited
UPAF	Union Postale Africaine (African Postal Union)		
UP	University Press	W	West, Western
UPI	United Press International	WFTU	World Federation of Trade Unions
USA (US)	United States of America (United States)	WHO	World Health Organization
USIS	United States Information Services	WTO	World Trade Organization
USSR	Union of Soviet Socialist Republics	yr	year

TRANSCRIPTION OF ARABIC NAMES

The Arabic language is used over a vast area. Though the written language and the script are standard throughout the Middle East, the spoken language and also the pronunciation of the written signs exhibit wide variation from place to place. This is reflected, and even exaggerated, in the different transcriptions in use in different countries. The same words, names and even letters will be pronounced differently by an Egyptian, a Lebanese, or an Iraqi—they will be heard and transcribed differently by an Englishman, a Frenchman, or an Italian. There are several more or less scientific systems of transliteration in use, sponsored by learned societies and Middle Eastern governments, most of them requiring diacritical marks to indicate Arabic letters for which there are no Latin equivalents.

Arabic names occurring in the historical and geographical sections of this book have been rendered in the system most commonly used by British and American Orientalists, but with the omission of the diacritical signs. For the convenience of the reader, these are explained and annotated below. The system used is a transliteration—i.e. it is based on the writing, which is standard throughout the Arab world, and not on the pronunciation, which varies from place to place. In a few cases consistency has been sacrificed in order to avoid replacing a familiar and accepted form by another which, although more accurate, would be unrecognizable.

Consonants

d   represents two Arabic letters. The second, or emphatic *d*, is transliterated *ḍ*. It may also be represented, for some dialects, by *dh* and by *z*, e.g. Qāḍī, qadhi, qazi.

dh   in literary Arabic and some dialects, pronounced like English *th* in *this*. In many dialects pronounced *z* or *d*.

gh   A strongly guttural *g*—sometimes written *g*, e.g. Baghdād, Bagdad.

h   represents two Arabic letters. The second, more guttural *h*, is transliterated *ḥ*, e.g. Husain, Husein.

j   as English *j* in *John*, also represented by *dj* and *g*. In Egypt this letter is pronounced as a hard *g*, and may be thus transcribed (with *u* before *e* and *i*), e.g. Najib, Nadjib, Nagib, Naguib, Neguib.

kh   as *ch* in Scottish *loch*, also sometimes represented by *ch* and *h*, e.g. Khalīl, Chalil, Halil.

q   A guttural *k*, pronounced farther back in the throat. Also transcribed *ḳ*, *k*, and, for some dialects, *g*, e.g. Waqf, Waḳf, Wakf, waqf.

s   represents two Arabic letters. The second, emphatic *s*, is transliterated *ṣ*. It may also be represented by *ç*, e.g. Sāliḥ, Saleh, Çaleh.

sh   as in English *ship*. The French transcription *ch* is found in Algeria, Lebanon, Morocco, Syria and Tunisia, e.g. Shaikh, Sheikh, Cheikh.

t   represents two Arabic letters. The second, emphatic *t*, is transliterated *ṭ*.

th   in literary Arabic and some dialects, pronounced as English *th* in *through*. In many dialects pronounced *t* or *s*, e.g. Thābit, Tabit, Sabit.

w   as in English, but often represented by *ou* or *v*, e.g. Wādā, Vadi, Oued.

z   represents two Arabic letters. The second, or emphatic *z*, is transliterated *ẓ*. It may also be represented, for some dialects, by *dh* or *d*, e.g. Ḥāfiẓ, Hafidh, Hafid.

'   A glottal stop, as in Cockney *'li'l bo'ls'*. May also represent the sound transliterated ', a deep guttural with no English equivalent.

Vowels

The Arabic script only indicates three short vowels, three long vowels, and two diphthongs, as follows:

a   as in English *hat*, and often rendered *e*, e.g. balad, beled, emir, amir; with emphatics or gutturals usually pronounced as *u* in *but*, e.g. Khalīfa, Baghdād.

i   as in English *bit*. Sometimes rendered *e*, e.g. jihād, jehād.

u   as in English *good*. Often pronounced and written *o*, e.g. Muhammad, Mohammad.

In some Arabic dialects, particularly those of North Africa, unaccented short vowels are often omitted altogether, and long vowels shortened, e.g. Oued for Wādī, bled for balad, etc.

ā   Long *a*, variously pronounced as in *sand, dart* and *hall*.

ī   As *ee* in *feet*. In early books often rendered *ee*.

ū   As *oo* in *boot*. The French transcription *ou* is often met in English books, e.g. Maḥmūd, Mahmood, Mahmoud.

ai   Pronounced in classical Arabic as English *i* in *hide*, in colloquial Arabic as *a* in *take*. Variously transcribed as *ai, ay, ei, ey* and *ê*, e.g. sheikh, shaikh, shaykh, etc.

aw   Pronounced in classical Arabic as English *ow* in *town*, in colloquial Arabic as in *grow*. Variously rendered *aw, ew, au, ô, av, ev*, e.g. Tawfīq, Taufiq, Tevfik, etc.

Sun- and Moon-Letters

In Arabic pronunciation, when the word to which the definite article, *al*, is attached begins with one of certain letters called 'Sun-letters', the *l* of the article changes to the initial letter in question, e.g. *al-shamsu* (the sun) is pronounced *ash-shamsu*; *al-rajulu* (the man) is pronounced *ar-rajulu*. Accordingly, in this book, where the article is attached to a word beginning with a Sun-letter, it has been rendered phonetically.

There are 14 Sun-letters in the Arabic alphabet, which are transcribed as: d, dh, n, r, s, sh, t, th, z, zh (d, s, t and z, and their emphatic forms, ḍ, ṣ, ṭ and ẓ, are not differentiated in this book). The remaining 15 letters in the Arabic alphabet are known as 'Moon-letters'.

TURKISH ORTHOGRAPHY AND PRONUNCIATION

Turkish has been written in Roman characters since 1928. The following pronunciations are invariable:

c   hard *j*, as in *majority, jam*.

ç   *ch*, as in *church*.

g   hard *g*, as in *go, big*.

ğ   not voiced, or pronounced *y*; Ereğli is pronounced *erayly*.

ı   short vowel, as the second vowel of *'centre'*, or French *'le'*.

i   *i* sound of *Iran, bitter* (NOT as in *bite, might*).

o   *o*, as in *hot, boss*.

ö   *i* sound of *'birth'*, or French *'oeuvre'*.

u   as in *do, too*, German *'um'*.

ü   as in *burette*, German *'Hütte'*.

CALENDAR OF POLITICAL EVENTS IN THE MIDDLE EAST AND NORTH AFRICA, OCTOBER 1997–SEPTEMBER 1998

1997

OCTOBER

1 A number of Arab prisoners, including Sheikh Ahmad Yassin—one of the founders of Hamas, released from Israeli prisons, reportedly in exchange for the return of two Mossad agents who had been detained in Jordan following the attempted assassination of Hamas bureau chief, Khalid Meshaal.

8 Palestinian leader, Yasser Arafat, and Israeli Prime Minister, Binyamin Netanyahu, had their first direct discussions for eight months at the Erez check-point between Israel and the Gaza Strip.

9 Tunisian Council of Ministers reshuffled.

16 Elections to the Omani Consultative Council organized; 164 nominees elected from amongst 736 candidates—82 of whom were then appointed to the Council by Sultan Qaboos.

22 Kuwaiti Minister of Health resigned, citing personal reasons for his decision.

22–23 President Nelson Mandela of South Africa made a state visit to Libya, in defiance of US objections.

23 Local elections held in Algeria.

24 Local elections held in Morocco.

NOVEMBER

4 Parliamentary election conducted in Jordan; elections boycotted by Islamic parties; widespread allegations of electoral malpractice.

5 Greek Cypriot President Glavkos Klerides accepted the resignations of five DIKO party cabinet ministers; new ministers were appointed to serve until elections scheduled for February 1998.

12 Lebanese Government ordered the deployment of troops in the eastern Beka'a valley, in response to a campaign of civil disobedience (the 'revolution of the hungry') orchestrated by Sheikh Sobhi Tufayli, Hezbollah Secretary-General in 1989–91.

UN Security Council approved Resolution 1137, imposing a travel ban on senior Iraqi officials.

13 US members of UNSCOM weapons inspection team expelled from Iraq.

Diplomats from EU countries allowed to return to Iran, following compromise agreement.

14 Elections to the Chamber of Representatives conducted in Morocco.

16–18 Fourth Middle East and North Africa (MENA) economic conference convened in Doha, Qatar; widespread Arab boycott owing to participation of an Israeli delegation.

17 Seventy people (including 58 foreign tourists) killed by members of the Islamist Jama'at al-Islamiyah in Luxor, Egypt.

18 Minister of the Interior, Hassan Muhammad al-Alfi, replaced by head of state security, Habib Ibrahim el-Adli, in Egypt.

19–26 Nationwide demonstrations (often violent) organized by supporters of Ayatollah Khamenei in protest at the pronouncements of prominent dissident Ayatollah Montazeri.

21 UNSCOM inspectors allowed to return to Iraq, but prevented from inspecting presidential sites.

29 President Khatami of Iran appointed new Committee for Ensuring and Supervising the Implementation of the Constitution.

30 Israeli Cabinet agreed, in principle, to a partial withdrawal from the West Bank, but did not agree the timing or scale of such a withdrawal. The Cabinet also undertook to ceate a team of Ministers to decide which areas of the West should be permanently retained by Israel.

DECEMBER

4 UN Security Council extended the 'oil-for-food' agreement with Iraq for a further six months.

5 Indirect elections to the Chamber of Advisers conducted in Morocco.

Trial commenced of former Lebanese Forces commander Samir Geagea, in connection with the assassination of Prime Minister Rashid Karami in June 1987.

8 Four Jordanians executed in Iraq, following smuggling convictions, despite appeals by the Jordanian Government for the sentences to be commuted.

9–11 Eighth summit meeting of the Organization of the Islamic Conference (OIC) convened in Teheran, Iran.

10 King Hussein of Jordan expelled several Iraqi diplomats from Amman and recalled the Jordanian chargé d'affaires from Baghdad.

13 Announcement made that Cyprus was to begin EU accession talks in March 1998, prompting the administration of the 'Turkish Republic of Northern Cyprus' ('TRNC') to suspend participation in intercommunal talks.

16 Cabinet reshuffled in Oman.

Council of Oman (comprising the Consultative Council and a Council of State) established by decree.

19 Law presented to allow universal suffrage in Qatar.

25 An electoral college selected members for two-thirds of the seats in Algeria's new upper chamber, the Council of the Nation, from regional and municipal councils. The remaining 48 members were nominated by President Zéroual.

29 Libyan General People's Committee reshuffled.

1998

JANUARY

4 David Levy, the Israeli Minister of Foreign Affairs and leader of the Gesher party, resigned, and Gesher withdrew from the Government owing to the lack of progress on the peace process and the Government's indifference to the needs of low-income workers in Israel.

13–14 Iraq prevented UNSCOM from carrying out weapons inspections, claiming that the group's leader, former US marine officer Scott Ritter, was spying for the Central Intelligence Agency (CIA).

16 Turkish Constitutional Court ordered the closure of the Islamic Refah Partisi (Welfare Party, RP) and banned seven party members, including former Prime Minister Necmettin Erbakan, from political life for five years.

17 President Saddam Hussain of Iraq announced an end to all co-operation with UNSCOM until UN sanctions were ended.

Iraq's chargé d'affaires was killed in Amman, Jordan; speculation arose that Iraqi government agents were responsible but the Jordanian interior ministry announced the arrest of several Jordanians in connection with the incident, claiming that the crime was not politically motivated.

20 Cabinet reshuffled in Qatar.

Deputy Prime Minister and Minister of Education, Culture and Sport, Zevulun Hammer, died in Israel. Itzhak Levi was appointed Minister of Education, Culture and Sport, and also assumed Hammer's role as leader of the National Religious Party (NRP). Levi's previous responsibilities as Minister of Transport and Energy were taken over by NRP deputy Shaul Yahalom.

During a visit to the USA Israeli Prime Minister Netanyahu held talks with US President Clinton, at which he reportedly rejected US proposals for a second stage redeployment of 10%–15% of West Bank territory, proposing instead redeployment from no more than 9.5% of the territory.

30–31 At least eight people were killed as a reuslt of a confrontation in Lebanon's Beka'a valley, between supporters of Sheikh Sobhi Tufayli, recently expelled from Hezbollah, and local Hezbollah officials, and subsequent army intervention.

31 US Secretary of State, Madeleine Albright, visited the Middle East region and held talks with Prime Minister Netanyahu of Israel and Yasser Arafat of the Palestine National Authority (PNA), but failed to restart the peace process.

FEBRUARY

4 Abd ar-Rahman el-Youssoufi appointed Prime Minister of Morocco.

8 Rifaat al-Assad, the younger brother of President Assad of Syria, dismissed from his post as one of Syria's three Vice-Presidents.

8 and 15 Two rounds of presidential elections in Cyprus won by the incumbent President, Glavkos Klerides.

10 President Assad of Syria received the Iraqi Minister of Foreign Affairs in Damascus, the first time that he had met publicly with a senior Iraqi official since the early 1980s.

13 Riot police in Jordan suppressed pro-Iraqi demonstrations in the southern town of Ma'an; a number of arrests were made.

16 Report published by commission of investigation into Mossad's attempted assassination of Hamas chief Khalid Meshaal in September 1997; Israeli Prime Minister Netanyahu absolved of responsibility for the operation. Maj.-Gen. Danny Yatou, the head of Mossad, who had been severely criticized in the report, resigned and was replaced by Ephraim Halevy.

17 Jordanian Cabinet reshuffled.

21–24 Former Iranian President Rafsanjani became the first senior Iranian to visit Saudi Arabia since the 1979 Revolution.

22 UN Secretary-General Kofi Annan met Saddam Hussain in Baghdad; agreement was reached on a 'memorandum of understanding' with regard to weapons inspections.

23 EU ended a ban on high-level ministerial contacts between member states and Iran.

27 The International Court of Justice in The Hague ruled that it could hear Libya's complaint that the United Kingdom and the USA were acting unlawfully by insisting on the extradition of two men accused of bombing a Pan Am aircraft in 1988.

28 New Cypriot Government sworn in.

MARCH

2 UN Security Council adopted Resolution 1154, which threatened Iraq with the 'severest consequences' if it breached the terms of the February 'memorandum of understanding'.

4 The Knesset re-elected Ezer Weizman as President of Israel for a further five-year term.

5 UNSCOM inspectors returned to Iraq.

13 'TRNC' Minister of Labour and Housing resigned.

14 New Cabinet appointed in Morocco.

15 Council of Ministers in Kuwait resigned in protest at a forthcoming vote of 'no confidence' in the Minister of Information, Sheikh Sa'ud Nasir as-Sa'ud as-Sabah.

15–18 British Secretary of State for Foreign and Commonwealth Affairs, Robin Cook, visited the Middle East on a tour intended to raise the profile of the EU in the peace process. During his time in the region, Cook made a controversial visit to the Har Homa settlement in a disputed area of East Jerusalem.

22 New Kuwaiti Council of Ministers announced, including Sheikh Sa'ud Nasir as-Sa'ud as-Sabah as Minister of Oil.

29 The discovery in the West Bank of the body of Muhi ad-Din Sharif, a leader of the armed wing of Hamas, led to fears of reprisal attacks against Israel; however, Hamas members were later arrested for the murder, which was reportedly the result of an internal power struggle.

APRIL

1 Israel's 'inner' Security Cabinet voted unanimously to accept UN Security Council Resolution 425 (of March 1978) and withdraw from southern Lebanon, conditional upon Lebanese guarantees of the security of Israel's northern border. Lebanon continued to assert that Resolution 425 required an unconditional withdrawal from its territory, and refused to accede to Israel's terms for departure.

4 Mayor of Teheran, Gholamhossein Karbaschi, arrested in Iran on corruption charges.

16–21 British Prime Minister, Tony Blair, undertook a tour of the Middle East region during which he invited the Palestinian leader, Yasser Arafat, and the Israeli Prime Minister, Binyamin Netanyahu, to attend a 'summit' for peace in London, United Kingdom, in early May. During his visit Blair signed an EU-Palestinian security agreement.

22 New Constitutional Council installed in Algeria.

27 PNA Minister of Awqaf (Religious Endowments), Hassan Tahboob, died.

Iran and Saudi Arabia signed a comprehensive co-operation agreement.

UN Security Council voted not to review the sanctions regime against Iraq.

28 Yemeni Prime Minister, Faraj Said bin Ghanim, resigned following reported differences with President Saleh; Deputy Prime Minister and Minister of Foreign Affairs, Abd al-Karim al-Iryani, was appointed as his successor.

MAY

3 New Kuwaiti Minister of Higher Education appointed.

4–5 US Secretary of State, Madeleine Albright, held separate talks with the Israeli Prime Minister, Binyamin Netanyahu, and the Palestinian leader, Yasser Arafat, in London, United Kingdom. No significant progress was made and although both parties were invited to Washington, DC, for further talks, Netanyahu declined to attend since the talks were made conditional on Israeli support for a US plan for a 13.1% redeployment in the West Bank.

11 Iraqi Minister of Labour and Social Affairs, Abd al-Hamid Aziz Muhammad Salih as-Sayigh, was dismissed.

16 New Government, including three new ministers, appointed in Yemen.

24 First of four rounds of voting in Lebanon's first municipal elections since 1963.

26 Serious clashes erupted in East Jerusalem after a Jewish settler organization began construction work on a religious settlement on disputed territory in the Arab quarter of the city.

JUNE

21 Israeli Cabinet approved a draft plan to widen Jerusalem's municipal boundaries; the decision was condemned by the Palestinians, the Arab states and the international community.

Iranian Minister of the Interior, Abdollah Nuri, was impeached and dismissed, only to be appointed Vice-President in charge of Development and Social Affairs by President Khatami.

24 Palestinian leader, Yasser Arafat, accepted the resignation of his Cabinet (10 months after parliament had first demanded it).

28 Saadi Tuma-Abbas appointed Minister of Labour and Social Affairs in Iraq.

JULY

5 Maj.-Gen. Ali Aslan appointed as Syria's Chief of Staff of the Armed Forces, replacing Maj.-Gen. Hikmat ash-Shehabi, who had held the position since 1973.

Gen. Mahmoud ash-Shaqqa appointed as head of Syria's general intelligence directorate.

7 UN voted to upgrade the status of the PLO at the UN, despite objections from the USA and Israel, to allow the organization greater participation.

9 Jordanian Minister of Water and Irrigation, Mundhir Haddadin, resigned following a scandal involving contaminated drinking water and severe water shortages in Amman.

16–18 President Assad of Syria made a state visit to France, the first time since 1976 that he had ventured outside the Middle East (with the exception of his meetings, in Switzerland with US Presidents Carter and Clinton).

19–22 Israeli and Palestinian negotiators held their first direct peace talks for 16 months; however, the talks failed to secure agreement on redeployment.

21 Plans for elected municipal councils approved in Qatar; women to be allowed to vote.

22 Israeli Knesset gave preliminary parliamentary approval to a bill which would require a majority vote in the Knesset and a referendum to be held prior to allowing an Israeli withdrawal from either the Golan Heights or Jerusalem; this action was harshly condemned in Syria.

23 Sayed Abdolvahed Musavi-Lari, the former Vice-President in charge of Legal and Parliamentary Affairs, was appointed Minister of the Interior in Iran.

Former Mayor of Teheran Karbaschi was sentenced to five years' imprisonment and 60 lashes, having been found guilty on charges of corruption by an Iranian court; he was also fined and banned from holding public office for 20 years.

30 Turkish Grand National Assembly approved April 1999 as the date for the forthcoming legislative elections.

AUGUST

4 Key Turkish ministers resigned in preparation for the forthcoming elections.

5 Iraqi Council of Ministers suspended co-operation with UN weapons inspection teams; Saddam Hussein insisted that new terms and conditions should be negotiated.

Yasser Arafat announced a cabinet reshuffle within the PNA. Members of the legislature who had demanded the dismissal of key ministers for corruption and mismanagement were extremely critical of the reshuffle in which only one prominent cabinet member was removed from the Government. An additional 10 ministers were appointed, bringing the total to 28.

6 Hanan Ashrawi, the Minister of Higher Education, and Abd al-Jawad Saleh, Minister of State (and formerly Minister of Agriculture) resigned from the newly-formed Palestinian Cabinet, stating that the recent reshuffle had failed to address the internal problems of the PNA.

8 Eleven Iranian diplomats and more than 30 other Iranian nationals were reported missing following the capture, by Taliban troops, of the northern Afghan town of Mazar-e-Sharif.

9 UN Security Council endorsed a resolution to suspend periodic reviews of the sanctions regime against Iraq.

20 Jordanian Prime Minister al-Majali resigned and was replaced by Fayez at-Tarawneh; a cabinet reshuffle ensued.

27 UN Security Council resolution adopted in support of a US/British proposal to conduct a trial in the Netherlands for the two Libyans accused of bombing a Pan Am aircraft in 1988.

SEPTEMBER

2 Iranian Revolutionary Guards organized large-scale military exercises along the border with Afghanistan.

8 Yemeni Minister of Religious Endowments and Guidance, Ahmad Muhammad ash-Shami, resigned.

9–16 US special envoy to the Middle East, Dennis Ross, visited the region for the first time in four months, in an attempt to break the deadlock; no agreement was reached.

10 Bodies of several of the missing Iranian diplomats were discovered in Afghanistan.

14 Iraqi parliament voted to end all co-operation with UNSCOM unless the UN Security Council annulled its decision of 9 August.

15 Iran vowed to avenge the deaths of the diplomats murdered in Afghanistan, and placed its armed forces on full alert.

17 Agreement signed in Washington, DC, between the Iraqi Democratic Party of Kurdistan (DPK) and the Patriotic Union of Kurdistan (PUK), with the intention of establishing a regional parliament in northern Iraq.

24 Government of Prime Minister at-Tarawneh won a vote of confidence in Jordan's parliamentary lower house.

Iranian Government pledged formally to dissociate itself from the *fatwa* imposed on the British author Salman Rushdie in 1989.

28 At a US-mediated meeting in Washington, DC, the Palestinian and Israeli leaders agreed to attend a tripartite peace 'summit' in the USA in mid-October 1998.

PART ONE
General Survey

THE ISLAMIST MOVEMENT IN THE MIDDLE EAST AND NORTH AFRICA

MALISE RUTHVEN

Two decades after the proclamation of an Islamic revolution in Iran the Islamist political fervour afflicting the Middle East and North Africa shows little sign of abating. In Algeria the civil war between Islamists and the Government has devastated the country at the cost of more than 80,000 lives. In Egypt, where the Government, unlike Algeria, still appears to have the upper hand, the estimated casualty rate is much lower—about one-tenth of the Algerian figure—but the cost has been prodigious, with tourism, the country's largest foreign currency earner, devastated and the country's ancient Christian minority increasingly fearful of its future. In Gaza and the West Bank Islamic militants have adopted the 'rejectionist' position abandoned by the PLO since 1988, threatening to undermine the peace process – in ironic collusion with Jewish fundamentalists who also believe themselves to be acting on divine instructions. With Islamists already entrenched in Iran and Sudan and challenging for power in Algeria, alarm bells have been ringing on both sides of the Atlantic. Is a revitalized 'fundamentalist' Islam the new menace that will replace communism as the principal 'threat' to the secular, liberal, democratic values of the West?

This view, put forward among others by Samuel Huntington, the influential Harvard political scientist, and Willy Claes, the former Secretary-General of NATO, is based on the premise that the difference between 'Islamic' and 'Western' civilizations and value systems are as fundamental, in terms of economic management and social organization, as those which formerly divided the Eastern and Western blocs. It is seriously disputed by many leading scholars and journalists who argue that, despite its rhetorical excesses, the Islamist movement is not so much a 'threat' to the West or the regimes supported by it, as a reflection of a crisis – or series of crises – internal to the Islamic world. On closer inspection, these crises reveal themselves to be little different from those afflicting non-Islamic nations in the developing world.

In theory Islam is an inherently political religion. As well as being the bearer of divine revelation, the Prophet Muhammad founded a state which his successors, the caliphs, transformed into an empire stretching from the Atlantic to the Indus valley. Although the empire rapidly lost its political cohesion as rival claimants fought each other for the leadership, the elaboration of the laws derived from the Koran and the Hadith (reports of the sayings and deeds of the Prophet) by the 'ulama (specialists in the interpretations of texts) came to supply the unchallenged, and unchallengeable, rules of daily social life. After the first disputes, resulting in the split between Sunni and Shi'a, the Muslim ruler's legitimacy came to depend less on his lineage than his role as protector of the Umma, or Islamic community, and preserver of the Shari'a, divine law, according to the Koranic command to 'enjoin the good and forbid the evil'. Despite many regional variations, the application of the Shari'a over the course of fifteen centuries produced a remarkably homogenous international society, bound by common customs and procedures, which contrasted strikingly with the tribalism operating at the level of power politics. Islamic identity vis-à-vis the rest of the world became a matter of practice as much as belief; orthopraxy as distinct from orthodoxy. Whereas the Christian road to salvation was determined mainly by faith and moral outlook, Muslims, additionally, lived in a world of legal exactitude where rules were specified, together with the means of enforcing them.

Although comprehensive in theory, however, the system was never complete. In theory the rulers (sultans or emirs) ruled according to the Shari'a, with 'ulama support. In practice the 'ulama were often forced to acquiesce in the loss of their legal monopoly. Islamic law was supplemented by the decrees of rulers in substantial areas of commerce, taxation, public and criminal law. Moreover, since the qadis (Shari'a judges) were appointed by the rulers, they were powerless to enforce decisions that went against those rulers' interests. A de facto separation of politics and religion came into existence. However, it was not formally acknowledged by the religious establishment, which continued to uphold the principle that sovereignty belonged to God alone. A major consequence has been the continuance of 'Islam' as a political factor: for so long as the principle has continued to exist that Islam is a 'total way of life' that makes no distinction between God and Caesar, people have sought to realize the Islamic ideal through political action – or, to express the same idea more cynically, they have tried to achieve political power by exploiting Islam's rich symbolic repertoire.

The principal intellectual forbears of the modern fundamentalist or 'Islamist' political movements which would challenge governments from the Maghreb to Malaysia during the latter decades of the 20th century CE, were to be found in the Middle East and South Asia, with increasing cross-fertilization between the two regions. From the 18th century CE Islamic reformers, such as Shah Wali Ullah in India and Muhammad ibn Abd al-Wahhab in Arabia, had prepared the ground for a modernist movement by seeking to purge Islamic belief and ritual of the accretions and innovations acquired over the centuries, particularly the cults surrounding the Sufi walis or 'saints', living and dead. An Islam pruned of its medieval accretions was better able to confront the challenge of foreign power than a local cult bounded by the intercessional power of a particular saint or family of saints. The movements of resistance to European rule during the 19th century and early 20th century were led or inspired by renovators (mujaddids), most of them members of Sufi orders, who sought to emulate the Prophet Muhammad's example by purifying the religion of their day and waging war on corruption and infidelity.

Both modernists, like Sir Sayyid Ahmad Khan, founder of the Anglo-Oriental College (later University) of Aligarh in India, and reformers like Muhammad 'Abduh (d. 1906), founder of the Salafiyya movement in Egypt, were inspired by the same example. Their problem was not, as 'Abduh's patron Lord Cromer (virtual ruler of Egypt between 1882 and 1908) would argue, that 'reformed Islam is no longer Islam'; but rather that there was no institutional hierarchy comparable to a Christian priesthood through which theological and legal reforms could be effected. Reformist 'ulama like 'Abduh or his more conservative disciple, Rashid Rida, had no special authority through which they could impose their views and the 'ulama, for the most part, have remained unreconstructed traditionalists up to the present.

Rida became the first important advocate of a modernized Islamic state. He formulated his views during the crisis surrounding the abolition of the Ottoman Caliphate by Kemal Atatürk and the Turkish National Assembly in 1924, a move which, blamed on the colonial victors over the Ottoman Empire during the 1914–18 war, had led to a mass agitation among Muslims in India. Though originally a supporter of the Ottoman Caliphate, Rida came to accept its demise as a symptom of Muslim decadence; and while no advocate of secularism, he saw the Assembly's decision as a genuine expression of the Islamic principle of consultation (shura). The ideal caliph, according to Rida, was an independent interpreter of the Law (mujtahid) who would work in concert with the 'ulama. In the absence of a suitable candidate, and of 'ulama versed in the modern sciences, the best alternative was an Islamic state ruled by an enlightened élite in consultation with the people, and able to interpret the Shari'a and legislate when necessary.

Many of Rida's ideas were taken up by the most influential Sunni reform movement, the Muslim Brotherhood, founded in 1928 by Hassan al-Banna, an Egyptian schoolteacher. The Brotherhood's original aims were moral as much as political: it sought to reform society by encouraging Islamic observance and opposing western cultural influences, rather than by attempting to capture the state by direct political action. However, in the mounting crisis over Palestine during and after the Second World War the Brotherhood became increasingly radicalized. In 1948 the Egyptian Prime Minister, Nuqrashi Pasha, was assassinated by a Brotherhood member and Hassan al-Banna paid with his life in a retaliatory killing by the security services the following year.

The Brotherhood played a leading part in the disturbances that led to the overthrow of the Egyptian monarchy in 1952, but after the revolution it came into increasing conflict with the nationalist Government of Gamal 'Abdul Nasser. In 1954, after an attempt on Nasser's life, the Brotherhood was again suppressed, its members imprisoned, exiled or driven underground. It was during this period that the Brotherhood became internationalized, with affiliated movements springing up in Jordan, Syria, Sudan, Pakistan, Indonesia and Malaysia. In Saudi Arabia, under the vigorous leadership of Amir (later King) Faisal ibn 'Abdul 'Aziz, the Brotherhood found refuge, and political and financial support, with funds for the Egyptian underground and salaried posts for exiled intellectuals.

It was a radical member of the Brotherhood, Sayyid Qutb, executed in 1966 for an alleged plot to overthrow the Egyptian Government, who would prove to be the Arab world's most influential Islamist theorist. Some of Qutb's key ideas, however, are directly attributable to the Indian scholar and journalist, Abu'l 'Ala (Maulana) Maududi (1906–79), whose works became available in Arabic translation during the 1950s. One of Maududi's doctrines, in particular, would have a major impact on Islamic political movements. It was the idea that the struggle for Islam was not for the restoration of an ideal past, but for a principle vital to the here and now: the vice-regency of man under God's sovereignty. The *jihad* was therefore not just a defensive war for the protection of the Islamic territory or *Dar al-Islam*. It might also be waged against governments which prevent the preaching of true Islam, for the condition of *jahiliyya* (the state of ignorance before the coming of Islam) was to be found currently, in the here and now.

During his years in prison Qutb, who had spent some time in the USA as a member of an Egyptian educational delegation, wrote a comprehensive account of the modern *jahiliyya* in his book *Ma'alim fi'l-tariq* ('Signposts along the Road'):

'Today we are in the midst of a *jahiliyya* similar to or even worse than the *jahiliyya* that was 'squeezed out' by Islam. Everything about us is *jahiliyya*, the ideas of mankind and their beliefs, their customs and traditions, the sources of their culture, their arts and literature, and their laws and regulations. [This is true] to such an extent that much of what we consider to be Islamic culture and Islamic sources, and Islamic philosophy and Islamic thought . . . is nevertheless the product of that *jahiliyya*'.

Qutb advocated the creation of a new élite among Muslim youth that would fight the new *jahiliyya* as the Prophet had fought the old one. Like the Prophet and his Companions, this élite must choose when to withdraw from the *jahiliyya* and when to seek contact with it. His ideas set the agenda for Islamic radicals, not just in Egypt but throughout the Sunni Muslim world. Those influenced by them included Shukri Mustafa, a former Muslim Brotherhood activist and leader of a group known as *Takfir wa Hijra* ('excommunication and emigration') who followed the early Kharijites in designating their enemies (in this case the Government) as *kafirs* (infidels); Khalid Islambuli and Abd as-Salaam Farraj, executed for the murder of President Anwar Sadat in October 1981; and the *Hizb at-Tahrir* (Islamic Liberation Party), founded in 1952 by Sheikh Taqi ad-Din an-Nabahani (1910–1977), a graduate of al-Azhar whose writings lay down detailed prescriptions for a restored Caliphate.

While Qutb's writings remained an important influence on Islamic radicals or 'Islamists' from Algeria to Pakistan, a major boost to the movement came from Iran, where the Ayatollah Khomeini came to power after the collapse of the Pahlavi regime in February 1979. During the final two decades of the 20th century CE the Iranian revolution remained the inspiration for 'Islamists' from Morocco to Indonesia. Despite this universalist appeal, however, the revolution never succeeded in spreading beyond the confines of Shi'i communities and even among them its capacity to mobilize the masses remained limited. During the eight-year war that followed Iraq's invasion of Iran in 1980 the Iraqi Shi'is who form about 50% of the population conspicuously failed to support their co-religionists in Iran. The revolution did spread to Shi'i communities in Lebanon, Saudi Arabia, Bahrain, Afghanistan and Pakistan, but generally proved unable to cross the sectarian divide. The new Shi'i activism in these countries either stirred up sectarian conflicts or stimulated severe repression by Sunni governments (as in Iraq and Bahrain).

Within Iran the success of the revolution had rested on three factors usually absent from the Sunni world: the mixing of Shi'i and Marxist ideas among the radicalized urban youth during the 1970s; the autonomy of the Shi'i religious establishment which, unlike the Sunni *'ulama*, disposed of a considerable amount of social power as a body or 'estate'; and the eschatological expectations of popular Shi'ism surrounding the return of the Twelfth Imam.

The leading Shi'i exponent of Islam as a revolutionary ideology comparable to Marxism was 'Ali Shari'ati (d. 1977), a historian and sociologist who had been partly educated in Paris. Though without formal religious training, Shari'ati reached large numbers of youth from the traditional classes through his popular lectures at the Husayniyah Irshad, an informal academy which he established in Teheran. Shari'ati's teachings contain a rich mix of ideas in which theosophical speculations of mystics like Ibn al-'Arabi and Mulla Sadra were blended with the insights of Marx, Sartre, Camus and Fanon (whose friend he was and whose books he translated into Farsi). The result was an eclectic synthesis of Islamic and leftist ideas. God was virtually identified with the People, justifying revolutionary action in the name of Islam; the *kafirs* (infidels) excoriated in the Koran were identified with those who refused to take action against injustice. An outspoken critic of those members of the clergy who acquiesced in the Shah's tyranny, Shari'ati drew a distinction between the official Shi'ism of the Safavid dynasty (1501–1722), which made Shi'ism the state religion in Iran, and the 'revolutionary' commitment of such archetypical Shi'i figures as the Imams 'Ali and Husain and Abu Dharr al-Ghifari (a Companion of the Prophet often credited with having socialist principles). Shari'ati's ideas, disseminated through photocopies and audio tapes, provided a vital link between the student vanguard and the more conservative forces which brought down the Shah's regime. The latter were mobilized by Sayyid Ruhallah Khomeini, an Ayatollah or senior cleric from Qom who had come to prominence as the leading critic of Shah Muhammad Reza Pahlavi's 'White Revolution' during the early 1960s. This was a series of agricultural and social reforms which threatened the interest of the religious establishment, not least because the estates from which many of the *'ulama* drew their incomes were expropriated or divided up. Exiled to Najaf in Iraq, Khomeini developed his theory of government – the *Velayet-e-faqheh* (jurisconsult's trusteeship) – which radically broke with tradition by insisting that government be entrusted directly to the religious establishment:

'The slogan of the separation of religion and politics and the demand that Islamic scholars should not intervene in social or political affairs have been formulated and propagated by the imperialists; it is only the irreligious who repeat them. Were religion and politics separate at the time of the Prophet?'

Popular Shi'ism focuses on the martyred figures of 'Ali and Husain and the expected return of the Twelfth Imam to restore justice and peace in the world. These motifs were skilfully deployed in the mass demonstrations preceding the fall of the Shah in 1978/79. Though Khomeini never formally claimed to be the Hidden Imam, there can be no doubt that by allowing his followers to address him as 'Imam', a title normally reserved by Shi'is for the Imams of the Prophet's house (*Ahl al-bait*), Khomeini deliberately allowed popular eschatological expectations to work on his behalf.

Contrary to the view widely held in the West, however, Khomeini did not impose a fully 'Islamic' system of government (comparable, for example to Saudi Arabia, where the Government rules in accordance with the *Shari'a,* supplemented by royal decrees.) The 1979 Constitution is really a hybrid of Islamic and western liberal concepts. As the sociologist Sami Zubaida points out, there is a 'contradictory duality of sovereignties'. Article 6 refers to the 'sovereignty of the popular will' in line with democratic national states, but the principle of *Velayet-e-faqeh* gave sweeping powers to Khomeini as 'chief jurisconsult' or trustee. The Constitution is the keystone of a range of institutions, including the *majlis-e-shura* (consultative assembly) composed of elected members under the supervision of a *shura-e-nigahban* (council of guardians). Although the *Shari'a* is supposed to be the basis for all law and legislation, many of the civil codes from the previous regime were retained: there are three court systems, the *madani* (civil) courts, the *Shari'a* courts and the 'revolutionary courts' which handed out often arbitrary punishments by the *komitehs* or revolutionary guards. 'Islamization' was introduced in a number of areas. Women were forced to wear 'Islamic' clothing and removed from certain professions, including the law; interest-bearing loans were forbidden and education was altered to include Islamic doctrines. In practice the *shura-e-nigahban* proved an embarrassment by vetoing, as contrary to the *Shari'a,* various measures passed by the Majlis, including a major land reform. In January 1988 Khomeini ruled decisively in favour of the Majlis, pronouncing that the power of the Islamic state was comparable to that enjoyed by the Prophet Muhammad and took precedence over *Shari'a.* Now that the Islamic state had been won, religious obligations were 'secondary' to government decrees. By giving the state priority over Islamic law from within the religious tradition, Khomeini ironically initiated a process that could open the way to a *de facto* secular regime in which the power of the clergy as a separate estate was effectively neutralized. The reduced status of the Shi'i hierarchy became apparent on Khomeini's death in June 1989, with the election, by the *majlis-e-khobregan* (council of experts), of the then President, Ali Khamenei, as Khomeini's successor to the position of Wali Faqih, supreme jurisconsult. As Khamenei was only *hojatoleslam* at the time (i.e. a middle-ranking cleric), the choice in effect negated the revolution's most significant achievement, which had been to place government under the moral and juridical authority of the supreme spiritual leadership—known in Shi'i terminology as the *marja'iyya*, (after the highest clerical office, the *marja' at-taqlid*, source of imitation, of whom there are several). The succession was legitimized by an amendment to the Constitution which sanctioned the eventual separation of the *marja'iyya* as theological authority from the *velaya* (guardianship or legal authority), by allowing any faqih with 'scholastic qualifications for issuing religious decrees' to assume the leadership. The result was a divorce of political and religious functions at the highest level in blatant contradiction of Khomeini's doctrine. Since then Iran has witnessed an increasingly open conflict between the spiritual authority of the senior clergy and the politico-religious leadership exercised by the clerics actually in power. In January 1995, in an open letter to the authorities, Ayatollah Ruhani declared that life in Iran had become 'unbearable' for those who adhered to true Islamic principles. He felt he 'could not remain a spectator while Islam is violated daily' and the 'true religious leaders' were silenced in a country claiming to be an Islamic republic. He claimed that his home had been attacked by armed criminals who threatened to kill him unless he pledged allegiance to Khamenei; in July of the same year his residence was raided again and his son was arrested. Other senior clerics or their spokesmen, articulated similar views. Sayed Muhammad Qomi, a son of Ayatollah Sayed Hasan Qomi-Tabataba'i, asserted that state and religion were incompatible, and must be separated. Since governments were bound to commit immoral acts, it was counter to the interests of religion that they be run by clerics. The experience of Iran since 1979 had done damage to Islam and its religious leaders. 'Terrorism, torture, bombing, explosions and hostage-taking', which had no place in Islam, were now identified with it. The rule of the clerics had only brought disgrace to Islam. The same critique has been articulated even more forcefully by one of Iran's leading intellectuals, the philosopher Abd al-Karim Soroush, a professor at the University of Teheran. Adopting a view of religion in line with Western phenomenology, Soroush argues that religion, unlike ideology, cannot be cast in any one shape, but bears interpretations that vary in accordance with time and circumstance. Religion is richer, more comprehensive and more humane than mere ideology. It can generate weapons, instruments and ideals, but itself transcends all of these things. Imposing a fixed interpretation on religion—any religion— makes it rigid, superficial, dogmatic and one-dimensional. Khomeini's movement, according to Soroush, will not bear the 'appropriate fruits' unless his followers nurture 'a new understanding of the faith'. Soroush has been physically attacked on several occasions and has been subjected to harassment and intimidation by militants, such as the Ansar-e-Hezbollah, assumed to have links with Khamenei and the right-wing elements associated with the Society of Combatant Clergy (Jameh-e-Ruhaniyat Mobarez—JRM) in the Majlis. In May 1996, in an open letter to the then President Rafsanjani, Soroush accused the Ansar-e-Hezbollah, of 'fostering barbarism' with the 'covert support of various authorities'. Recent developments, however, indicate that Soroush is far from isolated, and that the political tide is moving in his direction. In April 1996 elections to the Majlis revealed a decline in support for the JRM and advanced the cause of its more liberal challengers, the pro-Rafsanjani Servants of Iran's Construction. An even more decisive shift in public opinion was demonstrated a year later, in May 1997, with the unexpected election of Sayed Muhammad Khatami to the presidency with a massive majority (more than 20m. votes to 7.2m.) over his leading rival, the Speaker of the Majlis, Ali Akbar Nateq Nouri. A former Minister of Culture and Islamic Guidance, noted for his support for the film industry, Khatami was supported by a broad coalition of forces, including industrialists, urban professionals, university students, educated women and technocrats. The right-wing elements surrounding Khamenei, however, are determined to retain their collective grip on power. In mid-1998 the conflict between conservatives and liberals, dogmatists and pragmatists, was raging in the Iranian courts, where the popular Mayor of Teheran, Gholamhossein Karbaschi, allegedly at Khamenei's instigation, was facing charges of embezzlement and corruption. (In July Karbaschi was sentenced to five years' imprisonment and 60 lashes. He was also fined and banned from public office for 20 years.)

The gap between the regime's Islamic rhetoric and its political realities has been demonstrated in one of the most sensitive cultural areas, namely gender and family life. In opposition and exile, Khomeini had opposed the female franchise introduced by the Shah and bitterly denounced the Family Protection Laws introduced in 1967 and 1976 which limited the rights of men in divorce cases, improved the rights of women and raised the age of marriage to 18. Khomeini declared that divorces obtained according to these laws would not be recognized and marriages subsequently contracted would be punished as adulterous. Chador-clad women were among the most active participants in the revolution: the rhetoric of the time stressed that 'true Islam' fully protected female rights, while granting them a dignity and status denied by Western 'sexploitation', which reduced them to the condition of prostitutes. After coming to power with much female support, however, the mullahs were in no position to remove the female franchise. Islamic legal practice was restored to the extent that the age of marriage for girls was lowered to 13, and in some cases to nine, the official age of maturity. However most of the provisions of the Shah's laws protecting the rights of women in marriage were retained. A new family law enacted in 1992 represents, in the view of the anthropologist Homa Hoodfar 'one of the most advanced marriage laws in the Middle East (after Tunisia and Turkey) without deviating from any of the major conventional assumptions of Islamic law'. At the same time, under clerical pressure, female employment in the public sector has been decreasing at a rate of 2% per year, and women are prevented by law from occupying certain senior offices of state. In May 1998 conservatives introduced two parliamentary bills (widely regarded as anti-feminist), that would outlaw press coverage of domestic violence, stifle criticism of laws affecting women and segregate medical services. While there was no certainty that the bills would succeed, their introduction demonstrated that in Iran, more than any other Middle Eastern country, the highly contentious issue of women's rights is being debated on the basis of contested interpretations of Islamic law, within the forum of an elected assembly. This may not be a fully fledged democracy according to Western models, but such open and public debate would be unthinkable in a conservative Islamic society such as that which prevails in Saudi Arabia.

Outside Iran, however, the factors that contributed to the Islamic revolution continued to sustain the Islamist movements, accounting for the continuing popularity of their ideologies. The collapse of communism and the failure of Marxism to overcome the stigma of 'atheism' made Islam seem an attractive ideological weapon against regimes grown increasingly corrupt, authoritarian and sometimes tyrannical. The rhetoric of national liberation, appropriated by monopolist ruling parties, became discredited as those parties failed to address fundamental economic and structural problems, and were increasingly seen to be controlled by tribal coteries or political cliques indifferent to the needs of the majority. In countries such as Egypt and Algeria, qualified successes achieved by governments in the field of education turned against them, as graduates from state universities found career opportunities blocked. As centres of opposition, the mosques enjoy privileged status, and the efforts of governments to subject them to state control are usually incomplete. If they close down 'rebel' mosques they merely confirm the charges of disbelief directed against them by their opponents. At the same time, the explosion of information technology and particularly the revolution in audio-visual communications undercut the authority of the literate élites. The effect of this has been twofold. While television and video expose ever-growing numbers of people to transgressive and often salacious images created by the Western entertainment and advertising industries, video and audio cassettes enable radical preachers to evade government controls on radio and television.

In many Middle Eastern countries an exponential leap in the rate of urbanization has decisively altered the cultural and demographic balance between urban and rural populations, creating a vast new proletariat of recently urbanized migrants susceptible to the messages of populist preachers and demagogues. The Islamist movements, through their welfare organizations, have been able to fill the gaps caused by government failure to deal with housing shortages and other social problems. Housing shortages are forcing young people to delay marriage in societies where extra-marital sexual activity is strictly taboo. The resulting frustration, it may be argued, accounts for the obsessive manner with which the Islamists seek to enforce their rigid sexual codes. Restrictions on government spending imposed by the IMF have tended to exacerbate housing and welfare problems by forcing cuts in social spending, leading to the withdrawal of the state from some areas and its replacement by Islamic welfare organizations and charitable associations. Such voluntary organizations have found generous sources of funds in Saudi Arabia and the Gulf. The Islamic financial sector, though tainted by the massive losses sustained by investors in Egypt, provides employment opportunities and an avenue for building networks of patronage, religious orthodoxy and political mobilization able to compensate for the disappearance of older communal bonds and patronage networks. With rapid urbanization and the growth of slums and shanty towns, the old systems have ceased to function, as sheikhs and notables, local and party leaders have become detached from their previous clients. The former nationalist rhetoric, whether Nasserist or Baathist, has been discredited. 'It is into this vacuum of organization and power', writes Sami Zubaida 'that the Islamic groups have stepped to impose their authority and discipline. The organization they impose is not one of popular participation. The activists and militants remain in charge, and the common people, to whom they provide services against modest payments, are considered as subjects of ethical reform, to be converted to orthodox conformity and mobilized in political support.'

Though inspired by local conditions, the international factors affecting the Islamist movement should not be ignored. Veterans of the Afghan war against the Soviet occupation have formed the core of armed Islamist groups in Algeria, Yemen and Egypt. At the height of the conflict there are said to have been between 10,000 and 12,000 *mujahidin* from Arab countries financed from mosques and private contributions in Saudi Arabia and the Gulf states. Many of them, ironically, are reported to have been trained by the US Central Intelligence Agency (CIA) in the camps of Gulbuddin Hekmatyar. Saudi influence also operates

at the religious or ideological level. Many of the Islamists active in Egypt and Algeria spent time in Saudi Arabia as teachers or exiles where they became converted to the rigid, puritanical version of Islam practised in that country. Thus a prominent (currently imprisoned) leader of the Front islamique du salut (FIS) in Algeria, Ali Belhadj, far from operating within the regional Maliki school of jurisprudence, which allows for considerable latitude of interpretation 'in the public interest', is trying to impose the rigid tenets of the Hanbali school prevailing in Saudi Arabia on the leadership of the FIS.

The responses of governments to the challenge of political Islam range from outright repression to co-optation and accommodation. In the Syrian city of Hama a rebellion by the Muslim Brotherhood in 1982 was suppressed by the Government of President Hafiz al-Assad at a human cost estimated at between 5,000 and 20,000 lives. In Algeria the army's cancellation of the second round of the national elections after the FIS won the first round in December 1991 led to an increasingly bloody civil war that came to resemble, in its barbarity and carelessness for the lives of non-combatants, the campaign fought by the French against Algerian nationalists nearly two generations earlier. Despite the intensified violence, which to date is thought to have cost some 80,000 lives, there is no clear conclusion in sight. Although it has organized meetings with some of its Islamist opponents, the Government has refused to countenance outside mediation by France, or by the European Union, initiatives which might present the possibility of an end to this terrible conflict on Europe's southern borders. The prospects for a solution have been undermined by internal divisions on both sides. On the Government side President Zéroual's freedom of manoeuvre has been restricted by the powerful faction of senior army generals known as the 'eradicators', headed by the Chief of Staff Lt-Gen. Muhammad Lamari, who favour a military solution; the Islamist cause is even more riven by factionalism, with increasingly bitter rivalry between the FIS and its military wing, the Armée islamique du salut (AIS) on one side, and the extremist Groupe islamique armé (GIA) on the other, as well as by divisions within the political leadership of the FIS.

A secret dialogue between the Government and the two FIS leaders Abbasi Madani and Ali Belhadj in the spring of 1995 ended in failure, with the Government blaming the FIS for reneging on a promise to abandon violence and for refusing 'to renounce installing an Islamic state'; for its part the FIS leadership-in-exile accused the Government of employing political blackmail against the two imprisoned leaders, as well as attempting to dictate who the FIS representative should be, in order to ensure their compliance. Following the failure of the talks, the Government sought to legitimize its own position and to discredit that of its Islamist opponents by holding presidential elections (the first multi-party elections since independence) to be followed by the creation of a new National Assembly. Despite a boycott by all the main opposition parties the strategy was successful to the extent that it improved the Government's international standing, securing victory with a convincing—if disputed—majority of 61% for President Zéroual. It did not, however, halt the escalating spiral of violence. The presidential elections took place in November 1995 under stringent security, following threats from the AIS and GIA. Although opposition leaders insisted that the electoral turnout did not exceed 37%, the Government claimed a turnout of more than 75% (about 12m. of just less than 16m. eligible voters). International observers noted that notwithstanding some inflation of the official figures, the turnout was still higher than the opposition was claiming. During the campaign registered opposition candidates including Mahfoud Nahnah, leader of the moderate Islamist Hamas party, were free to organize political rallies and to be critical of the Government in televised broadcasts. The relatively large showing for Nahnah, (25.6% against Zéroual's 61.0%, according to official figures) indicated that many FIS supporters had voted for him, though not in sufficient numbers to challenge the Government. Observers noted the high proportion of women voters, who had taken part in defiance of Islamist threats. Later, in an implicit acknowledgement of the set-back the elections had dealt the opposition, the FIS executive committee called for renewed negotiations between the Government and the 'effective opposition'.

Political advances towards participatory democracy and constitutional government, however, were vitiated by the deteriorating security situation, and by the spiralling cost in human lives in particular. The death toll among civilians, terrorists and armed forces since the conflict began in 1992 was unofficially estimated at 80,000 by mid-1998, about three times the official Government figure. In the complex and highly unstable patterns of terror and counter-terror, attributing responsibility for the massacres in which unarmed civilians have been the principal victims has become increasingly difficult. Initially, both of the armed Islamist organizations aimed to weaken the foundations of the state by striking at its economic infrastructure and its officials. Army officers, government employees and politicians were among the primary targets, as were religious functionaries who dared to condemn the insurgents' activities as being contrary to Islam. Increasingly, however, the GIA expanded its activity to embrace a much broader 'culture war', in which anything with 'Western' or 'secular' associations was liable to attack. The view that the education system serves an 'impious state' has resulted in the destruction of more than a thousand schools. Students have been warned to stay away, and occasionally schoolchildren have been attacked. Journalists and media personnel have also been targeted. In their war against the *'jahiliyya'* state, the Islamists have murdered hundreds of artists and journalists accused of collaborating with the enemy or of peddling Western 'filth'; technicians responsible for installing TV satellite dishes, through which Algerians can receive French and Italian programmes, have had their throats cut. Musicians specializing in the formerly popular *rai* music (a blend of Arabic music and Western rock) have been assassinated, along with other representatives of 'Western' or hybrid culture, including scientists, athletes and foreign personnel. The assault on 'Western' culture is seen by some observers as an attack on culture itself. One foreign journalist noted that the GIA's war against 'intellectuals' had begun to resemble 'not so much an Islamic uprising but a Khmer-Rouge style slaughter of the élite'. Women, particularly those suspected of having 'Western' educations, have been singled out for attack, along with all those who refuse to wear the veil. According to one secularist organization, the Algerian Rally of Democratic Women, more than 500 unveiled women and girls were murdered at random during the month of Ramadan (January–February) in 1995.

The counter-measures initiated by the army have been no less brutal, and in the distorted world where terrorism and counter-terrorism meet, accusations that sections of the armed forces have themselves perpetrated atrocities in order to 'discredit' the Islamists have become increasingly plausible. In a report on Algeria published in November 1997, Amnesty International confirmed that 'at least' 80,000 people had been killed since 1992. Noting that the Government blamed the violence on terrorist groups, the human rights organization drew attention to the fact that most of the attacks on unarmed villagers had occurred 'in areas around the capital in the most heavily militarized region of the country and often in close proximity to army barracks and security force outposts'. It also noted that 'on no occasion have the army and security forces intervened to stop or prevent the massacres, or to arrest those responsible'. In the case of the murders of some 300 people in three villages in the Blida region in August 1997, one of the worst incidents of the conflict so far, Amnesty noted that there were two military barracks within 6 km of the scene of the massacres, while there were security force posts within 'a few hundred yards'. The report concluded that 'at the very least' the Government was culpable for its failure to provide adequate protection for the population. It also suggested that there was a growing concern that death squads working in conjunction with elements in the security forces 'may have been responsible for some of the massacres'. In November 1997 a Paris newspaper, *Le Monde,* reported an interview with a senior Algerian officer known only as 'Hakim' who claimed that the Algerian secret services were resposible for many of the atrocities, including the murder of seven elderly French monks in May 1996—an act that prompted widespread outrage against the Islamists in France. He also claimed that two bomb explosions that killed eight people and wounded 143 in the Paris Metro in 1995 were planted at the instigation of Algerian military intelligence and Lt-Gen. Lamari.

In Tunisia the regime of President Zine al-Abidine Ben Ali, a former security chief, has taken a line that is now as uncompromising as Algeria's. The main Islamist party, an-Nahda ('Renaissance', formerly the Islamic Tendency Movement) has been banned along with all other parties based on religion, and its membership subjected to a ruthless campaign of repression leading to accusations of human rights abuses by Amnesty International and the UN Commission on Human Rights. The Government refuses to accept declarations by an-Nahda's leader, Rached Ghanouchi (currently in exile in the United Kingdom) that his party is committed to pluralism and representative government, although an-Nahda has joined with other, non-Islamist opposition parties in proposing a dialogue with the regime. Ghanouchi emphasizes that 'the Islamists should accept a democratic coalition rule that might encompass only part of their programme' while believing that, far from being incompatible, Islamic and Western values can accommodate each other. 'Once the Islamists are given a chance to comprehend the values of Western modernity, such as democracy and human rights, they will search within Islam for a place for these values.' Non-Islamic opposition parties, which won only six out of more than 4,000 seats in the municipal elections in May 1995 have accused the Government of using the struggle against the Islamists to reinforce its authoritarian powers. President Ben Ali, however, insists that he is not dealing with the Islamists by security methods alone, but is adopting policies 'which tackle the economic and social problems, by taking care of the poorer regions and helping the poorest sections of society'. In this he has been helped by Tunisia's relatively prosperous economy. Although commandos of the Algerian-based GIA claimed to have killed six Tunisian soldiers at a border post in 1995 (a report denied by the Tunisian Government, which claimed the soldiers had died in a car accident) the attack appears to have been an isolated incident. Stringent security measures, including roadblocks on all main routes leading to Algeria and the presence of undercover police officers on cross-border trains appear to have prevented the Algerian conflict from spilling over into Tunisia.

In Morocco, despite much higher levels of poverty and serious social problems, the Government has been more emollient. The principal Islamist leader, Abdl as-Salam Yassin, head of the banned *Al-Adl wa-'l Ihsan* (Justice and Charity movement) is technically under house arrest 'for his own protection' while 'judicial investigations' continue into his activities. However, he has been allowed to preach on at least one occasion, although the Government has insisted that he refrain from political statements. Islamic financial institutions have been refused licences. But compared to their Algerian counterparts, the Moroccan Islamists who, as elsewhere in the Arab world are active on university campuses, have taken a relatively moderate line, avoiding confrontation with the state or direct challenges to the authority of the monarch. According to one of Morocco's leading sociologists, there are at least 30 different Islamist groups in the country, but only four of them have a significant following and influence; security forces of the Ministry of the Interior constantly monitor their activities. Periodically weapons caches are discovered. In a few instances death sentences have been handed down by the courts. King Hassan II derives much legitimacy from his descent from the Prophet Muhammad and his caliphal title 'Commander of the Faithful'. The vast Hassan II mosque in Casablanca, completed in 1993 and one of the largest in the world, provides a tangible, if flamboyant symbol of the regime's Islamic credentials. Morocco's public discourse is replete with Islamic symbolism; more secure in its identity than its neighbours, there is less space in the 300-year-old kingdom for an 'Islamic alternative' that challenges the *status quo*.

In Jordan King Hussein, who also claims descent from the Prophet, has proved relatively successful in containing Islamic militancy within a parliamentary system. In the elections of November 1993 – the first multi-party elections for 36 years – an Islamist victory was confidently predicted until a change in the electoral rules was introduced, with the King's warm approval, substituting the plural voting system in multi-member constituencies for one limiting each voter to a single vote. The result was a reduction in representation of the Islamic Action Front (Muslim Brotherhood) in the National Assembly from 22 seats to 16. At the July 1997 elections, however, the main Islamist party, the Islamic Action Front, in common with other opposition parties, boycotted the poll in protest against the 1994 Peace Treaty between Jordan and Israel and censorship laws placing restrictions on Islamist publications. In March 1996 the leading Islamist, the former parliamentary deputy Leith Shbeilat, head of the Engineers' Association, and the Treaty's most outspoken critic, was sentenced to three years' imprisonment after being found guilty of 'slandering the royal family'. He had publicly criticized Queen Noor for weeping before the television cameras at the funeral of the assassinated Israeli Prime Minister, Itzhak Rabin. Six months later, in a conciliatory gesture to the opposition, Shbeilat was granted a royal pardon, the King personally driving him from Swaqa prison, 100 km south of Amman, to his mother's home in the capital.

In Israel, the Occupied Territories and the areas controlled by the Palestine National Authority (PNA), Hamas and its counterpart Islamic Jihad continued to challenge the authority of President Yasser Arafat. The Islamist movement was divided between rejectionists who sustained the 'armed struggle' and accommodationists who gave conditional support to Arafat in order to ensure an Israeli withdrawal from part of the Occupied Territories in accordance with the 1993 Oslo Accords. In the aftermath of the assassination of Prime Minister Itzhak Rabin by a right-wing Israeli extremist, in November 1995, the rejectionists appeared to gain the upper hand. A series of suicide bombings in Jerusalem, Ashkelon and Tel-Aviv (in which dozens of Israeli civilians were killed) helped to bring down the Labour Government of Rabin's successor, Shimon Peres, and elect the Likud coalition which, under Binyamin Netanyahu, effectively stalled the peace process by ending the 'freeze' on building new Jewish settlements. In order to appease the Israelis, Arafat was forced to clamp down on the rejectionists. While this appeared to confirm Islamist charges that he was, in effect, an Israeli stooge, the Hamas majority were prepared to bide their time, having no desire to take responsibility for an Israeli reoccupation of Palestinian territory. Hamas scored a moral victory when, following a bungled attempt by Israeli agents to murder one of its political advisers in Amman in September 1997, the Jordanian Government secured the release from an Israeli jail of its leader, Sheikh Ahmad Yassin, in exchange for returning the Mossad agents apprehended following the attempted assassination.

In Lebanon the militant Shi'i group Hezbollah, responsible for terrorism and kidnappings during the 1980's, provoked Israel to undertake an ill-considered minor invasion of southern Lebanon in 1996 which culminated in an Israeli rocket attack on a UN base at Qana, where more than 100 Lebanese refugees who had taken shelter there were killed.

In Egypt the Government initially adopted a broadly similar strategy to Jordan's, co-opting the moderates by allowing the Muslim Brotherhood to be represented through other parties in the National Assembly while seeking to eliminate the extremists by police methods. The more militant Islamist elements, led by Islamic Jihad and *Jama'ah al-Islamiyah*, active on university campuses since the 1970s, continued to wage a sporadic war of attrition against the regime, attacking Christians, government officials and foreign tourists. The violence was mainly concentrated in the southern part of the country, and was complicated by the still widely-practised tradition of blood-vengeance: when policemen, state officials or members of the Coptic minority were attacked or murdered, their families were honour-bound to respond in kind, and violence against the state rapidly became entangled in blood feuds. There were many reports of police officers taking hostage the relatives of Islamist fugitives, destroying their homes and burning their crops. In one of the worst incidents, near the southern village of Mallawi in May 1995, 24 people were killed and 18 others were wounded. Attacks on tourists were deliberately designed to cripple the country's economy by undermining its most important source of foreign currency. Tourists were also viewed as spies for Israel and the West, and a source of corruption. In an interview with Hisham Mubarak, an Egyptian Human Rights activist, Tal'at Fu'ad Qasim, a *Jama'ah* spokesman declared tourism in its present form to be 'an abomination', he went on to describe it as 'a means by which prostitution and AIDS are spread by Jewish women tourists', and 'a source of all manner of depravities, not

to mention a means of collecting information on the Islamic movement'. The campaign against tourism had the desired effect of crippling the industry. In April 1996 17 Greek tourists were killed and 15 others injured in an attack outside a Cairo hotel. In November 1997 68 tourists (mainly Swiss and Japanese) were shot dead outside the Temple of Queen Hatshepsut at Luxor in an attack that lasted for three full hours. As in April 1996, the *Jama'ah* accepted responsibility for the attack; however, they claimed that the casualties had been the result of bungling by the police; their intention having been to take the tourists hostage and attempt to force the release of a former head of the *Jama'ah's* governing council, currently serving a prison sentence for his involvement in the bombing of the World Trade Centre in New York in February 1993. Survivors of the massacre, however, rejected this excuse, stating that the gunmen, disguised as security officers, had begun firing automatic weapons at the tourists as soon as they arrived at the scene.

As the attack on the World Trade Center demonstrated, Islamists based in Egypt did not confine their attacks to Egyptian territory. In June 1995 President Mubarak's motorcade was attacked as he was driving from the airport to attend a conference of the Organization of African Unity in Addis Ababa, Ethiopia. Two Islamist organizations linked to the *Jama'ah* claimed responsibility. The following November at least 15 people were killed and 60 injured when a car bomb exploded in the Egyptian embassy compound in Islamabad, Pakistan. The Government's response to these attacks was to increase pressure not only on the militants, but also on so-called moderate elements within the mainstream Muslim Brotherhood. In 1994 moderate Islamists dominated the largest of the country's professional associations, including the medical, engineering and legal syndicates. The Government responded by introducing a 50% majority rule for elections to syndicates, hoping thereby to secure a secularist majority in future elections. In 1995 they took the additional step of granting the judiciary wide powers to supervise union elections, including the right to disqualify candidates. In the case of the engineers', doctors' and lawyers' unions where Islamists had been in control, secularists were able to use the new laws to reduce their influence or have them removed altogether. 'Grass roots' Brotherhood activists were arrested and detained, with dozens referred to military courts for rapid trials. The Government, however, took care to avoid making martyrs of the leadership: none of the Brotherhood's 15-member guidance council was arrested. Human rights organizations protested at the violation of civil rights. The judiciary in Egypt, however, is relatively independent, and contains its share of Islamist sympathizers at senior level. In a number of celebrated cases, the Egyptian courts became battle grounds for the culture wars conducted between the Islamists and their secular critics. In 1994 'The Emigrant', a semi-autobiographical film by a distinguished film-maker, Yusuf Shahin, loosely based on the story of Joseph, was withdrawn after an Islamist lawyer sued Shahin for offending Islamic sensibilities. In the most celebrated case of all, Nasir Hamid Abu Zayd, a professor of Arabic at the University of Cairo, was denied tenure and accused of apostasy after a colleague attacked his work in analysing the Koran from a literary-historical perspective. Not content with depriving Abu Zayd of his livelihood, some extreme Islamists demanded that his wife divorce him on the grounds that he was an 'apostate' who could not be married to a Muslim. While a lower court rejected their demands, a higher court ruled against Abu Zayd on appeal. The Abu Zayd case, which received widespread publicity, reveals the clear affinities between what might be called 'intellectual Islamism' and Protestant fundamentalism in the USA. American fundamentalists also object to the Bible being treated as a literary-historical text.

In Yemen the Islamist Yemeni Islah Party (YIP), consisting mainly of the northern Hashed tribe with support from the Muslim Brotherhood, strengthened its position after the 1994 civil war with the South. Their rather narrow tribal base, however, prevented the YIP from securing more than 53 seats in the legislative elections of April 1997, compared with the 187 seats secured by the governing General People's Congress (GPC).

Even Saudi Arabia, the most traditionalist and religiously observant of Muslim states was subjected to criticism from Islamist quarters, with the circulation of a manifesto in 1992 by mainly Nejdi *'ulama* complaining that the religious leaders were not sufficiently consulted by the Government, which, it complained, was 'inefficient, obsolete and corrupt in its upper reaches'. While the attack on princely corruption found an echo in some liberal circles, the ultra-traditionalist character of some of Saudi Arabia's religious protesters was evidenced by the fact that a leading member of the principal opposition group, the Committee for the Defence of Legal *(Shari'a)* Rights demanded that the whole of the country's Shi'ite minority be put to death.

In Bahrain where a Sunni dynasty rules over an underprivileged Shi'i majority, members of a group called Hezbollah Bahrain, recruited from Bahraini Shi'i students at Qom, in Iran, and trained in Lebanon, were arrested for plotting to overthrow the Government in June 1996; the culprits appeared on television, where they confessed to their crimes. In all the Gulf states, as in Saudi Arabia, economic stagnation resulting from the decline in oil prices meant there was less money to placate opposition with generous welfare provisions and expensive lifestyles. Discontent inevitably manifested itself in Islamic forms. In the United Arab Emirates the Government attempted to deflect criticisms directed at the privileged status of foreigners by announcing in February 1994 that a whole range of offences, including murder, manslaughter, theft, adultery and drugs offences, would henceforth be tried in *Shari'a* courts, regardless of whether they were committed by nationals or foreigners. In Kuwait Islamists in the National Assembly have been pressing for legislation to enforce greater adherence to the *Shari'a* as the only source of law and to outlaw coeducation in the University, where two-thirds of the student body is female. At elections to the National Assembly conducted in October 1996 Islamist candidates made a strong showing, securing 14 seats compared with the 19 seats secured by pro-Government factions.

The legitimacy of the territorial governments established after decolonization was always open to challenge on Islamic grounds. The new national states were in most cases being imposed on societies where the culture of public institutions was weak and where ties of kinship prevailed over allegiances to corporate bodies. In most Middle Eastern countries and many others beyond the Muslim heartlands, the ruling institutions fell victim to manipulation by factions based on kinship, regional or sectarian loyalties. Even when the army took power, as the only corporate group possessing internal cohesion, the élite corps buttressing the leadership were often drawn from a particular family, sect or tribe. In the period following decolonization the new élites legitimized themselves by appealing to nationalist goals. Their failure to 'deliver the goods' either economically or militarily (especially in the case of the states confronting Israel) led to an erosion of their popular bases and the rise of movements pledged to 'restore' Islamic forms of government after years of *jahiliyya* rule.

Following the collapse of communism, Islamism is likely to dominate the political discourse in Muslim lands for the foreseeable future. But for all the anxieties expressed in the West about a 'clash of civilizations' it seems unlikely to effect significant external political change. Existing Muslim states are locked into the international system. Despite the turbulence in Algeria and episodes of violence in Egypt there have been fewer violent changes of government in the Middle East since 1970 than in the preceding two decades when different versions of Arab nationalism competed for power. At the same time the political instability in Pakistan and the continuing conflict in Afghanistan demonstrate that 'Islam' in its current political or ideological forms is unable to transcend ethnic and sectarian divisions. The territorial state, though never formally sanctified by Islamic tradition, is proving highly resilient, not least because of the support it receives, militarily and economically, through the international system. For all the protests by Islamist movements that Saddam Hussein's invasion of Kuwait in August 1990 was a 'Muslim affair', the result of Operation Desert Storm (in which the Muslim armies of Morocco, Egypt, Pakistan, Syria and Saudi Arabia took part) demonstrated conclusively that where major economic and political interests are at stake, the *status quo* wins.

In the long term the globalization of culture through the revolution in communications technology must lead to a form of secularization in Muslim societies, not least because of the increasing availability of religious and cultural choice. A significant factor will be the presence of a large and growing Muslim diaspora educated in the West and able to rediscover in Islam a voluntary faith freed from the imperatives of enforcement, while finding an outlet for Islamic values through voluntary activity. Although the political currents of Shari'ati (exoteric) Islam appear to be in the ascendant, it is the pietistic and mystical traditions that promise to open up the 'straight path' *(sirat al mustaqim)* in the future. Both Maududi and Hassan al-Banna built pietism into their systems, believing that society must be converted before the state could be conquered. Though the militants and activists who followed them, obsessed with the corruption of governments and embittered by the appalling treatment many of them received at the hands of the state, have tended to focus on action, not least because killings and bombings are bound to attract attention in an international culture dominated by television, there is evidence that quietist versions of Islam are rapidly gaining ground. The *Tablighi Jama'at*, originally founded in India, has spread to more than 90 countries from Malaysia to Canada and is now becoming thoroughly internationalized. Though active in promoting the faith, it is explicitly non-political.

With globalization eroding the classic distinction between *Dar al-Islam* and *Dar al-Harb*, the coming decades could see a retreat from direct political action and a renewed emphasis on the personal and private aspects of faith. But so long as government corruption persists, and governments such as those of Egypt and Algeria find it more expedient to respond to the Islamist challenge by repression than reform, the Islamists, however inept their political programmes, will find a ready audience.

SELECT BIBLIOGRAPHY

Ahmed, Akbar S., and Donnan, Hastings (Eds). *Islam, Globalization and Postmodernity*. London, Routledge, 1994.

Al-Azmeh, Aziz. *Islams and Modernities*. London, Verso, 1993.

Beinin, Joel and Stork, Joe (Eds). *Political Islam: Essays from The Middle East Report*. London, Tauris, 1997.

Binder, Leonard. *Islamic Liberalism: A Critique of Development Ideologies*. Chicago, 1988.

Burgat, François, and Dowell, William. *The Islamic Movement in North Africa*. Austin, Texas, University of Texas Press, 1993.

Cantwell Smith, W. *Islam in Modern History*. Princeton University Press, 1957.

Choueiri, Youssef M. *Islamic Fundamentalism*. Boston, Twayne Books, 1990.

Cooper, John and Nettler, Ronald L. and Mahmoud, Mohamed (Eds). *Islam and Modernity: Muslim Intellectuals Respond*. London, Tauris, 1998.

Curtis, Michael (Ed.). *Religion and Politics in the Middle East*. Colorado, Westview, 1981.

Easterman, Daniel. *New Jerusalems: Reflections on Islam, Fundamentalism and the Rushdie Affair*. London, Grafton Books, 1993.

Eickelman, Dale F. and Piscatori, James. *Muslim Politics*. Princeton University Press, 1996.

Esposito, John L. (Ed.). *Islam and Development*. Syracuse University Press, 1980.

   (Ed.). *Voices of Resurgent Islam*. Oxford, 1983.

   The Islamic Threat: Myth or Reality? Oxford, 1993.

   (Ed.) *The Oxford Encyclopaedia of the Modern Islamic World*. Oxford University Press, 1995.

Gellner Ernest. *Postmodernism, Reason and Religion*. London, Routledge, 1992.

Gilsenan, Michael. *Recognizing Islam*. London, Croom Helm, 1982.

Heikal, Muhammad. *Autumn of Fury: The Assassination of Sadat*. London, André Deutsch, 1983.

Hourani, Albert. *Arabic Thought in the Liberal Age*. Oxford University Press, 1969.

Keddie, N. R. (Ed.). *Scholars, Saints and Sufis: Muslim Religious Institutions since 1500*. University of California Press, 1972.

Kepel, Gilles. *The Prophet and Pharaoh: Muslim Extremism in Egypt*. Trans. Jon Rothschild, London, Al Saqi Books, 1985.

Mernissi, Fatima. *Islam and Democracy – fear of the modern world*. London, Virago, 1993.

Mortimer, Edward. *Faith and Power: The Politics of Islam*. Faber, 1982.

Pipes, Daniel. *In the Path of God: Islam and Political Power*. New York Basic Books, 1983.

Piscatori, J. (Ed.). *Islam in the Political Process*. Cambridge University Press, 1983.

Islam in a World of Nation States. Cambridge, 1986.

Rahman, Fazlur. *Islam*. Chicago University Press, 1979.

Rippin, Andrew. *Muslims – Their Religious Beliefs and Practices*. Vol II, The Contemporary Period, London, Routledge, 1993.

Roy, Olivier. *The Failure of Political Islam*. London, I. B. Tauris, 1994.

Ruthven, Malise. *Islam in the World*. London, Penguin, 1991.

A Satanic Affair: Salman Rushdie and the Wrath of Islam. London, Hogarth, 1991.

Islam: A Very Short Introduction. Oxford University Press, 1997.

Sivan, Emmanuel. *Radical Islam: Medieval Theology and Modern Politics*. Yale University Press, 1985.

Third World Quarterly. Vol. 10, No. 2, *Islam and Politics*. April 1988.

Zubaida, Sami. *Islam, The People and The State: Essays on Political Ideas and Movements in the Middle East*. London, I. B. Tauris, 1993.

RECENT DEVELOPMENTS IN US POLICY TOWARDS THE MIDDLE EAST

GEORGE JOFFÉ

In mid-1997, *Time*, the US-based international weekly news magazine, published a triumphal issue celebrating US global dominance under the second Clinton administration. US beliefs in free market economics and liberal democracy were spreading throughout the world, it claimed, just as US demotic culture was being globalized. For its essayist, Charles Krauthammer, this was the just and deserved—if somewhat belated—reward for victory in the Cold War, in which the USA had led the free world against obscurantism and reaction. A unipolar world had emerged, dominated by the USA, which might not last, it was true, but which offered more hope to mankind than any other outcome.

THE NEW GLOBAL ARENA

This new-found confidence, in stark contrast to the general perceptions of US political commentators who had regularly belaboured the first Clinton administration for its failures and foreign policy mistakes, was to some extent justified, at least in a global context. The USA had successfully managed the transition from superpower hostility to some form of partnership with the new Russia that was slowly emerging under the unsteady hand of Boris Yeltsin. NATO had been preserved and enlarged, despite Russian opposition, thus ensuring a continued US role in Europe. The USA was still the supreme military power on the planet, capable of fighting two wars simultaneously, but determined not to commit its armed strength beyond the narrow realm of its national interest. This, in turn, was defined in ever more restrictive terms, as popular nationalist sentiment determined the Administration's objectives. Most importantly, the underlying diplomatic imperative had shifted away from rigid security to participation and control in a global economic market. Geo-economics, rather than geopolitics, was to be the focus of the future.

It was this transformation of the international economic agenda that had been the triumph of the first Clinton Administration, as it forced other states, particularly Japan, to accept its terms for the growth of world trade. The USA also paid ever-greater attention to the Pacific Rim and to its greatest potential economic rival, the People's Republic of China. Although Europe was the principal recipient of US investment—$225,000m. by 1993, compared with $60,000m. in East Asia—and European investment in the USA had reached $258,000m. in the same year, compared with only $100,000m. from East Asia, trade growth with China alone was dramatic. According to US trade figures, China's trade surplus with the USA (including re-exports via Hong Kong) increased from $6,000m. in 1989 to $23,000m. in 1993, and to $36,000m. in 1996, thus surpassing the surplus of Japan with the USA. Yet the Administration's policies had not been merely reactive. President Clinton had formulated a clear strategy, in which economic regions increasingly would co-operate within a regulated global arena, with an economically reinvigorated USA as its focus. He had forced the North American Free Trade Agreement (NAFTA) through a reluctant Congress; he had shepherded the transition of the General Agreement on Tariffs and Trade into the World Trade Organization (WTO); and he had overseen the birth of the Asia-Pacific Economic Co-operation (APEC). Economic regionalism was to be the first stage in economic globalization under US aegis. Within this new structure, US economic imperatives were to be of paramount importance—a situation which was to strain relations with Japan and Europe but which was to be eventually, if reluctantly, accepted. Whereas during the Cold War era, and even during the Bush interregnum, the Presidency had played the leading role in formulating and executing US foreign policy, President Clinton was forced increasingly to take account of congressional prejudices, and of the powerful lobbies and special-interest groups behind them that shape much of public opinion in the USA. This became particularly important in the wake of the Republican mid-term successes at congressional and gubernatorial elections in 1994, and the subsequent 'Contract for America' revolution engineered by the new Speaker of the House of Representatives, Newt Gingrich. Although the initiative collapsed two years later, it had wrought a major change in the way in which US foreign policy was initiated and articulated, with Congress participating with the Presidency and the Administration on more equal terms than in the past. Thus, US willingness to intervene physically in foreign conflict declined drastically, particularly after the Somalia fiasco in 1992/93. US support for the United Nations was also dramatically reduced, despite the enhanced role of the Security Council in the post-Cold War era—when, for a short period, it seemed set to operate as its founders had intended—as popular suspicion of the organization grew, it being viewed as increasingly anti-US and spendthrift. There was a similar radical decline in US willingness to fund foreign aid programmes—a development with which the Clinton administration sympathized, although this new radicalism did not extend, in practical terms, to the Middle East.

Yet, at the same time as this withdrawal from a wider global role, there were examples of increased US interventionism, again often at the instigation of Congress. Perhaps the most significant of these were the 1996 Helms-Burton Act, which warned foreign companies against conducting operations in Cuba, and the parallel D'Amato-Kennedy Act, which sought to impose sanctions against foreign concerns operating in Iran and Libya. The motivation behind such legislation appeared to be mounting intolerance of the so-called 'rogue states'; states which were accused of ignoring internationally-accepted principles of statehood, of supporting or initiating international terrorism and of imposing increasingly arrogant human rights and environmental agendas on foreign countries, with scant regard for local conditions. There was, in short, a growing—and peculiarly US—belief that the USA's distaste for such activities could be expressed through a legitimate extra-territorial extension to national legislation, not just at the federal level but also at the state and even the municipal level. Despite the fact that practical articulation of these attitudes increasingly began to emanate from Congress or subordinate elected bodies—not infrequently to the embarrassment of the Administration—the principles which these initiatives sought to defend were an integral part of the new diplomatic agenda espoused by the Clinton administrations. By 1997, in short, there seemed to be growing evidence that, despite the derision over foreign policy initiatives which had attended the first Clinton Presidency, there was indeed a coherent foreign policy platform for the US Administration. Furthermore, it was based on new assumptions about the post-Cold War world, although, inevitably, some continuity with the past was preserved. Perhaps the hesitancy of the early years of Clinton's tenure was, in part at least, a consequence of that continuity as much as it was the result of inexperience. Indeed the predominance of continuity should not be underestimated, particularly in the evolution of US policy towards the Middle East, and here, at least, the brash confidence of Krauthammer's *Time* essay seems somewhat misplaced.

THE MIDDLE EAST AND NORTH AFRICA IN THE NEW ERA

Certain themes have long informed US policy regarding these two adjacent regions which, until the 1990s, were often treated as a single unit—the Arab world and its eastern non-Arab outliers of Iran and Turkey. During the Cold War era, these themes were partly conditioned by the superpower confrontation, which often attributed increased significance to regional problems that might otherwise have attracted relatively little external attention. They were also affected, of course, by mounting Western dependence on hydrocarbon energy supplies from the region, an issue which, in turn, became integrated into the regional interests of the superpowers themselves. Of course the dominant theme was the Arab–Israeli conflict, although the US attitude to the issue had become one of almost unqualified support for Israel during the 1980s. During the same period the USA had displayed increasing antagonism towards Middle Eastern radicalism, particularly after the humiliation of the Carter administration by the Iranian revolution in 1979. There had also been a growing awareness that Western anxieties over energy dependence on the region, stimulated by the oil price crises of 1971–74 and of 1979–81, had been exaggerated and that, with the advent of significant non-OPEC oil supply to the international market, developments in the immediate future would be consumer-led.

The Bush legacy

The comprehensive victory of the US-led multinational coalition against Iraq following that country's invasion of Kuwait in August 1990, coupled with the decline in Soviet regional influence after 1985—when Mikhail Gorbachev came to power—until the collapse of the Soviet Union after August 1991, appeared to alter dramatically the dynamics of the Middle East theatre. Suddenly the USA, as the sole superpower, seemed poised to find solutions to regional problems that had long eluded Western statesmen. Arab states were dispirited or were allied to the USA; Israel had reluctantly accepted its dependence on US goodwill; and Western dependence on OPEC, in the short term at least, had been shown to be illusory. Dramatic changes had also taken place in the Middle East region. The Arab world was no longer a cohesive political and diplomatic unit—if, indeed, it had ever really been such. Instead, diplomatic activity was concentrated in sub-regional groups: the Gulf, the Levant, the North-east and Horn of Africa, and North Africa itself. Turkey and Iran were no longer isolated outliers; but well-placed to dominate a new non-Arab Middle East, equal in size to its Arab predecessor, comprising the newly-liberated states of the Caucasus and Central Asia and extending as far as Afghanistan and Pakistan. It was unclear which of Turkey or Iran would seek the leading role in the new region, or, indeed, whether they would co-operate over its future, although their resuscitation of the Regional Co-operation for Development group, as the Economic Co-operation Organization (ECO), alongside Pakistan, suggested that they might. Together with the Levant—where the USA remained acutely preoccupied with the future of Israel, both for domestic reasons and for reasons of atavistic regional strategy—and the Gulf—where the Bush administration's military victory allowed it to set the terms of the immediate post-war settlement—the new non-Arab Middle East was clearly going to be of interest to Washington. There were obvious strategic considerations in terms of restricting the revival of Russian imperialist ambitions and limiting the growth of Iranian regional influence. There were also the potential commercial interests presented by opportunities for hydrocarbon exploitation. Moreover, the geo-political significance of this area as a confluence of Russian, Chinese and other Asian interests was not overlooked. However, as the pressures of the Cold War era evaporated after 1990, so the strategic significance of the Western Mediterranean also declined: uninterrupted oil flows through the region were no longer subject to strategic threat from the Soviet Black Sea Fleet or from powers along the Southern Mediterranean rim; the Gulf War relieved Morocco and Tunisia of their roles as basing points for the US Rapid Deployment Force created by the Carter administration after the Iranian revolution; the readiness of the Arab world to contemplate peace with Israel marginalized Egypt's crucial role as a US ally in the region; the imperative of economic reform in North African states and the dominance of Europe as their major trading partner merely emphasized a growing US disinterest in them, notwithstanding Libya's designation as a 'rogue state' and (given the mounting crisis in Algeria) NATO consideration of a future southern flank policy.

The two regional issues for which US policy was actively formulated in the immediate aftermath of the Cold War era were Iraqi territorial aggression and the Middle East peace process. As one commentator pointed out at the time, the Iraqi annexation of Kuwait in 1990 was the final opportunity for

1980s-style Middle East policy, involving direct coercion and threats. The imposition of military controls and the maintenance of economic sanctions following the Gulf War—ostensibly to ensure that Iraq had abandoned any unconventional weapons development programmes and to force the Iraqi Government to halt the ill-treatment of Shi'a and Kurdish minorities, but in reality to hasten the end of the regime itself—were initiated by the US Government. These initiatives were supported by European allies, reluctantly accepted by Security Council partners (the USSR and China) and imposed on Arab clients, whether they agreed (Kuwait, Saudi Arabia and Bahrain), demurred (Syria, Egypt, Oman, the United Arab Emirates and Qatar) or disagreed (most of the remaining states in the Arab world). The US Administration's determination to maintain the sanctions regime was encouraged by massive domestic support, irrespective of the effects on the Iraqi population at large or of the growing evidence of their ineffectiveness in undermining the Iraqi regime. The Middle East peace process, on the other hand, was portrayed, and was understood, as something quite new in international diplomacy—an initiative which pointed to the way in which future conflict would be resolved. No solution was to be imposed on the belligerents and no plan was to be introduced. Instead, the USA would employ its regional and global prestige to initiate a process in which the participants would themselves set the terms of reference. The process, as defined by US Secretary of State James Baker, was complex. It would be 'twin-track' in nature, involving bilateral negotiations between states over concrete peace terms, and multilateral negotiations between all states concerned with regard to five themes that affected regional stability. One component of the bilateral negotiations involved the issue at the core of the conflict: the future relations between Israel and the Palestinians who had been the direct victims of its creation in 1948, and here an even more complex negotiating structure was established. In keeping with the aim of facilitating, rather than intervening in, the negotiating process—and recognizing that it would be easier to coerce the weaker side in the negotiating process—the USA conceded to Israeli demands concerning the form of the process itself, once the basic principle of 'land-for-peace' had been accepted in Tel-Aviv. Thus the Palestine Liberation Organization, recognized throughout the world since 1974 as the legitimate representative of the Palestinian people, was excluded from the process and, instead, only Israeli-approved representatives from the occupied territories of the West Bank and the Gaza Strip were allowed to participate. No agenda was predetermined, but was rather to be established through negotiation. Here, once again, Israel, with the stronger negotiating position, would be permitted largely to impose its own preferences. Undoubtedly such an approach was inevitable, since the Shamir Government was ferociously opposed to the very idea of a negotiated compromise. As the Israeli Premier himself later admitted, he would have prolonged the negotiations for ten years, if necessary, in order to transform demographic realities in the Occupied Territories irrevocably, and thereby render concessions irrelevant. In addition, every possible inducement to negotiate was offered to Israel by the USA, including $10,000m.-worth of loan guarantees to finance the resettlement of an estimated 1m. Jewish immigrants from Russia. When the Israeli Government redirected these funds towards Jewish settlement enlargement in the Occupied Territories the Bush administration did raise objections; however, restrictions on the extension of further loan guarantees were removed shortly before the President submitted himself (unsuccessfully) for re-election in 1992.

THE CLINTON ADMINISTRATION TAKES OFFICE

The Clinton administration thus inherited policy initiatives on the Gulf and the Middle East peace process, together with the personnel who had defined them. Clinton, however, had given little indication during the presidential election campaign of what his own approach to these issues would be. The appointment of Warren Christopher (an experienced observer of Middle East affairs) as the new Secretary of State, with Anthony Lake as head of the National Security Council, suggested a cautious approach. On the other hand, both the new President, and particularly his Vice-President—Al Gore, were open and ardent supporters of Israel's Zionist identity. Former American-Israeli Political Action Committee lobbyist Martin Indyk was promptly appointed special adviser on the Middle East at the National Security Council, although the majority of State Department personnel concerned with the Middle East—the so-called 'Baker's boys'—retained their posts.

Iraq and Iran

As far as Iraq was concerned, the Clinton administration promptly dashed all hopes of an early end to the sanctions regime. President Clinton seemed even more antagonistic towards the Iraqi leadership than his predecessor. Early confrontations over an assassination plot against former President Bush and threats against US aircraft in the air exclusion zones, together with Iraq's continued obstruction of the efforts of the United Nations Special Commission to oversee the dismantling of Iraq's proscribed weapons programmes, provoked an immediate US military response, and the Administration soon made it clear that any easing of the economic sanctions against Iraq would not be contemplated. It was a position that was maintained throughout the first Clinton presidency and was swiftly reinforced with an almost overt desire to see the Iraqi leader overthrown prior to the relaxation of sanctions. However, this stance attracted increasing criticism particularly abroad, where the sufferings of the Iraqi people were the subject of pointed anti-US comment. Even US disappointments such as the failed Iraqi coups of mid-1995 and the Iraqi Government's exploitation of the conflict between Kurdish factions in September 1996 to reassert its control over a large part of Iraqi Kurdistan (despite US threats) failed to prompt a change in policy direction. By the end of 1996 it was apparent that US policy with regard to Iraq had remained and would remain unchanged, provided President Clinton were re-elected for a second term.

While US policy towards Iraq was marked by resolute stasis, that with respect to Iran was characterized by a significant intensification of US disaffection. US involvement in the Gulf had traditionally sought to preserve a balance of power between the two dominant states in the region, Iran and Iraq, with the US Government supporting one to counter the potential role of the other. In the wake of the Iranian revolution in 1979, US support had been transferred, after an initial period of uncertainty, to Iraq, with diplomatic relations being restored in 1984 and the US navy effectively intervening in 1987 to support Iraq in the Iran–Iraq War. The Gulf War in 1990–91, of course, marked an end to US support for Iraq, support upon which Iraq's strategic mistake in invading Kuwait in August 1990 had been partly based. However, despite repeated attempts by the Rafsanjani Government in Teheran, after Ayatollah Khomeini's death in 1989, to convince the USA that it was seeking to improve relations with the West, including the 'Great Satan' itself, US resentment at past Iranian insults did not diminish. By 1992–93 US disapproval of the Islamic republic had been bolstered by mounting Israeli concerns that future threats to its security would originate in Iran, which had declared itself openly hostile to the peace process. (A proposed $10,000m. rearmament programme, announced by the Iranian Government in 1992, had prompted considerable alarm in Israel.) The USA responded with the controversial policy of 'dual containment', first enunciated in 1993 by Martin Indyk in the influential political journal, *Foreign Affairs*. This involved placing both Iran and Iraq outside of the international community with which the USA would entertain normal diplomatic relations and maintaining both the UN sanctions regime against Iraq, in operation since August 1990, and the unilateral 1984 US sanctions against Iran. The 1984 sanctions were tightened by presidential order in May 1995, thus aborting a proposed major petroleum agreement between the Iranian National Oil Company and CONOCO, a subsidiary of the US company, Du Pont. The presidential order proscribed all US trade and investment with Iran owing to that country's opposition to the Middle East peace process and alleged support for international terrorism. The order also signalled increased pressure on the USA's allies, particularly Japan and countries in Europe, to adopt similar measures in preference to the trade and investment links maintained by Japan (which depended on access to Iranian oil), and the European policy of 'critical dialogue'. Perhaps most importantly, this development persuaded pro-Israeli lobby groups and their supporters in Congress to consider extending the principle of US legal extra-territoriality towards the Middle East.

Libya, Lockerbie and terrorism

One of the themes that the first Clinton administration embraced—even more effectively than the Reagan administration—was the iniquity of international terrorism. Despite the fact that many of its own policies and diplomatic prejudices had intensified anti-US sentiment and pro-Islamist extremism in the Middle East, the Clinton administration, in support of the Israeli Government and, to a lesser extent, Arab governments facing similar threats, insisted that 'terrorism', in whatever form, would not be tolerated. The problem with such an attitude was that it ignored the degree to which Western, particularly US, policy initiatives might have contributed towards such extremism and the extent to which Western policy was perceived in the Middle East to be partial, particularly towards Israel. It also failed to treat non-Islamic extremism with the same distaste, so that Israel's 1993 and 1996 bombardments of southern Lebanon were actively supported by the Clinton administration, despite the lack of justification for them and the immense loss of life they caused. The policy nadir for many observers was reached in March 1996 when the USA and Egypt sponsored an international peace conference at Sharm esh-Sheikh to support the embattled Israeli Premier, Shimon Peres, then facing potential electoral defeat as a result of Hamas-inspired suicide bombings in Israel, to Western acclaim and widespread popular Arab derision. In response to US attitudes—for they hardly qualified as considered policies—Islamic hostility towards the USA intensified. This hostility, also, was in part the result of an inherited legacy of policy options as much as it was a consequence of the Clinton administration's own decisions. It had been the Reagan administration that had encouraged and armed Muslims to fight alongside the *mujahidin* in Afghanistan against the Soviet Union in the 1980s, and it had been the Bush Administration that had persuaded the Pakistani authorities to disband the militantly anti-Western guerrilla groups which had been created as a result. Their return to their countries of origin in the Middle East and North Africa had done much to polarize domestic confrontations there between government and Islamists, particularly in Egypt and Algeria.

Yet, beyond the issue of terrorism, the Clinton administration, in mid-term, seemed to be enunciating a more carefully considered attitude towards Islamic radicalism. US Under-Secretary of State Robert Pelletreau, who was responsible for human rights issues, made strenuous efforts, in 1995, to emphasize that the USA was increasingly willing to negotiate with Islamic radicals, provided they did not espouse violence. To the intense annoyance of the Algerian Government, Pelletreau met opposition leaders in Algiers, at a time when the political integrity of many of them had been severely compromised by accusations of their maintenance of contacts with Algeria's proscribed (at that time) Islamist movement, the Front islamique du salut (FIS). Unfortunately, the policy was not sustained owing to domestic disquiet, following attacks on US troops in Saudi Arabia by Islamist militants in November 1995 and June 1996.

In addition to US policy with regard to the conflict in Afghanistan and the Arab–Israeli peace process, other factors continued to contribute to anti-US sentiments among Islamist groups. One such factor was the continued presence of US forces in Saudi Arabia and the Gulf region and the associated restrictions imposed against Iraq. Not only was this offensive to many Muslims, in principle, but the high profile of US troops in the region inflamed radical Saudi opinion. The June 1996 bombing of a military housing complex at al-Khobar, near Dhahran (Saudi Arabia), which resulted in the deaths of 19 US personnel and injuries to a further 400 US, Bangladeshi and Saudi nationals, led to a more discreet US military presence there, but did little to diminish local feelings of anger and resentment, which were compounded by such developments as alleged US support for the Bahraini Government in exchange for berthing rights for the new US Fifth Fleet, specially created to patrol the Gulf. The aftermath of the December 1988 Lockerbie air disaster had also provoked considerable consternation in the region. In October 1991 charges of responsibility for the explosion on board the US Pan Am flight which was destroyed over the Scottish town of Lockerbie (with the deaths of all passengers and crew) were brought against two Libyan nationals. US demands that the two accused individuals should be deported to stand trial were supported by the United Kingdom and, less enthusiastically, by France, which was pursuing its own claims against Libya for the destruction of a UTA airliner over Niger the following September. The Libyan Government's refusal to hand over the two men, offering instead to organize a trial on neutral territory, led to UN Security Council sanctions being imposed against Libya in April 1992. Arab governments registered increasing disquiet with regard to Western policy on this issue, not least because of increased Israeli obduracy concerning the Arab-Israeli peace process. Such anxieties intensified and were echoed in Europe when, during 1996, US congressional leaders attempted to determine a new course of action for the Administration. Seizing on the example of the 1995 presidential order which proscribed US trade and investment with Iran, and inspired by the Reagan administration's attempts to block European investment in a Soviet gas pipeline project in the early 1980s, they attempted to hamper and even prevent Western economic links with Cuba, Libya and Iran. Senator D'Amato, who had repeatedly fulminated against Western companies dealing with Iran, was joined by Senator Kennedy in ensuring the successful passage through Congress of the secondary sanctions act which threatened to penalize any foreign company investing more than $40m. in energy projects in a number of prescribed states, including Iran and Libya. Although the President was invested with considerable latitude in bringing the proposed sanctions into operation, the newfound determination of the US Congress to affect Middle East policy formulation, irrespective of the consequences for US interests in the region, was unmistakable.

For President Clinton, however, this development posed a problem not of principle, but rather of timing. His Administration had already dissuaded Japan from making a $450m.-investment in Iran and had convinced China to abandon a similar project. Russia had been more obdurate, given its role in the proposed Iranian rearmament plan and its intention to refurbish nuclear reactors at Bushehr, although it did agree to cancel the sale of uranium centrifuge separators to Teheran. The US Administration was easily reconciled to the USA's right to act extra-territorially, but did recognize that this might adversely affect its relations with its Western partners and thus undermine the support its policies, particularly over the peace process in the Middle East, might receive. France had already expressed dissatisfaction with US policy regarding Lebanon and Iraq, and even the United Kingdom seemed increasingly uncomfortable with Western initiatives for peace in the Middle East.

The peace process and Israeli rejectionism

Increasingly, at least among Arab leaders, it was felt that a perceived partiality on the part of the Clinton administration with regard to a whole range of Middle East issues (notably Iraq, 'dual containment' and Libya) was threatening seriously to undermine compliance with, and support for the main thrust of US policy in the region, namely the furtherance of the peace process. In fact, the Clinton administration's involvement in the peace process has been as unproductive as its policies elsewhere in the region, largely because of a widely-accepted opinion that it has favoured Israel unfairly and been indifferent to the interests of other states in the region, including its own allies. Yet it inherited policies which, as far as peace in the Middle East was concerned, should have provided it with a major foreign policy triumph. The Administration's failure to capitalize on the political advantage it inherited from its predecessor arose from its inability to maintain the same distance from the process of negotiation. Instead of allowing parties to deal with each other directly, President Clinton and his advisers in the Administration (but not in the State Department) elected to intervene actively in the process. Admittedly, the negotiations had been close to deadlock after a year of fruitless discussion, first in Madrid and then in Washington; the President's intervention, however, brought them close to collapse. It was only the sudden revelation that parallel negotiations were being conducted between the Rabin Government (which had replaced the Shamir Government in Israel in June 1992 with the promise of movement towards peace) and the Palestine Liberation Organization in late August 1993 that revived the peace process itself. This

channel had been ignored by the USA and had been sponsored instead by Norway, making use of its own contacts with the Palestinian liberation movement which, weakened by its perceived support for Iraq during the Gulf War and its exclusion from the Madrid peace process, was anxious to place itself once more at centre-stage.

The Oslo process, as the new negotiating strategy was dubbed, comprised two stages. The initial agreement provided the Palestine Liberation Organization with rights of autonomy in the Gaza Strip and Jericho, with the promise of an extension of such rights over most of the West Bank and a close economic relationship with Israel. Then, in an agreed second stage—the 'final status' negotiations—after the new Palestinian autonomy authorities have been legitimized by elections, outstanding issues including the future of Jerusalem, the fate of the Jewish settlements in the Occupied Territories, the issue of Palestinian refugees (particularly those arising from the 1967 exodus) and the status of the new Palestinian entity were to be discussed. During 1993–97, despite a number of vicissitudes, this process moved slowly and hesitantly forward. Extremist opposition gave way to reluctant acquiescence on both sides; the process developed against a background of violence, but repeated Palestinian concession encouraged considerable hope that a genuine solution might be found. The political affinity between the Labour-led coalition Government in Israel and the Clinton administration was marked, and often resulted in increased US pressure on the Palestine National Authority to make additional concessions at critical moments in the negotiations—a development which provoked a degree of popular disenchantment with the process itself. Moreover, as the negotiations continued, Israeli ability to manipulate US support also increased, so that the USA's reputation as an even-handed broker was further undermined. Thus, in 1995, the US Congress supported the Israeli argument that Jerusalem should be the 'eternal, undivided capital of Israel'—a decision which the US Administration accepted, with the proviso that the proposed transfer of the US embassy to Jerusalem from Tel-Aviv should be delayed—despite the fact that such a decision ran counter to UN resolutions and to the original undertakings of the Oslo process, whereby nothing was to be done to alter the *status quo* before 'final status' negotiations began, theoretically in May 1996. Prior to this development the Clinton administration had already abandoned the long-held US position that Israeli settlements in the Occupied Territories were illegal under international law, in favour of the Israeli position that the territory itself was 'in dispute' rather than 'occupied'. The situation became critical in May 1996 when, despite open US support, Shimon Peres was forced from office at an election narrowly won by the Likud leader, Binyamin Netanyahu, who was openly hostile to the peace process. He argued that, instead of the Bush principle of 'land-for-peace' on which both the Oslo and the Madrid processes had been based, 'security' should become the precursor to 'peace'. Both Netanyahu and Clinton (who eventually came to accept the Israeli thesis) failed to note that the insecurity from which Israel was suffering, with bombings in March 1996 and the assassination of Premier Yitzhak Rabin in November 1995, had arisen as a direct result of a US policy of acquiescence to Israel at Palestinian expense, and from a continuing Israeli delusion that, despite its strength and international support, Israel was the victim of a Palestine Liberation Organization, now emasculated through repeated concession.

THE SECOND CLINTON ADMINISTRATION

Thus, the second Clinton administration, which took office at the start of 1997, inherited a situation in the Middle East at radical variance with the general air of self-congratulation in foreign affairs that attended the global sweep of US diplomacy. The Administration's three major regional initiatives—sanctions against Iraq, 'dual containment' and the peace process—came under increasing scrutiny during the first six months of the new Presidency. The nature of this scrutiny, furthermore, was not confined simply to issues of effectiveness but raised anxieties over the rationale behind, and justification for, the Administration's policy positions. In part, of course, such close examination owed much to the fact that Middle East policy, like the wider foreign policy field, was a continuum from Clinton's first term of office. Yet, this was not the sole explanation, for there was some internal movement in the policy-making process. One of the first changes implemented by the new Administration was the appointment of a new Secretary of State, to replace Warren Christopher, who had stepped down from the post. Although the President had expressed some interest in Senator George Mitchell, fresh from his success in Northern Ireland, administrative in-fighting prevented his appointment and the President chose instead the US ambassador at the United Nations, Madeleine Albright. She had proved to be an advocate of uncompromising policies, particularly towards Iraq, and had strongly opposed the continuation in office of the UN Secretary-General, Boutros Boutros-Ghali, after he had allowed the publication of a highly-critical UN report on Israeli actions in Lebanon in April 1996 which had resulted in the deaths of more than 100 civilians. Albright's appointment was viewed with little enthusiasm both in the Middle East and within the Washington policy-making establishment. Although Samuel Lewis, a former ambassador to Israel and a long-time member of the US State Department's Middle East peace process negotiating team, became National Security director, virtually all the other staff members were replaced. Martin Indyk was to be recalled from the US embassy in Israel to become Assistant Secretary of State for Near Eastern Affairs (although his return was delayed by a continuing crisis in the peace process itself) and the USA's special envoy to the region, Dennis Ross, became chief US negotiator for the peace process. Neither man was greatly admired or trusted among Palestinians or Arab leaders. Other new members of staff, such as Bruce Riedel, who was to be President Clinton's Special Assistant and the Senior Director for Near Eastern and South Asian Affairs, Richard Lebaron or Steve Grummon, apparently had little intrinsic interest in, or concern about, the peace process as such. As one commentator pointed out, the new appointees were interested only in 'process' and not in 'outcomes'. In other words, the actual result of the negotiating process was of little importance; the mere fact that negotiations were taking place was sufficient, even if the final outcome were to neglect virtually all Palestinian aspirations. It was a corollary of this attitude that if Israel objected to the conditions under which negotiations were taking place, it would fall to the Palestinians to make the necessary concessions to re-start the process, irrespective of where responsibility for the original disruption of the process might lie. Not surprisingly, the Palestinian leadership, backed by Palestinian public opinion, found such an approach unacceptable, despite the minimal Israeli concessions made with regard to evacuating Hebron, in the light of the crisis provoked by Netanyahu's decision to open to tourists an archaeological tunnel in the environs of the *Haram ash-Sharif* (Temple Mount) in September 1996.

There was little likelihood of active US intervention to force the pace of negotiations at a time when Palestinian disenchantment was becoming acute. Nor did it seem likely that there would be any significant change of policy towards Iraq or over 'dual containment' at this time. Yet, in both cases, as in other aspects of Middle East affairs, the situation was changing and new initiatives from the USA, given its enhanced global role, seemed essential. The question was whether the new Clinton Administration shared this perception, or whether its interest in future global economic relations, Russia, Latin America and the Pacific, had distracted it from an arena that seemed less and less important. US disinterest in the Middle East was the product of a certain objective reality. In terms of regional stability, Arab states such as Egypt or Algeria, both of which were considered by the Washington policy-making establishment to be 'pivotal states in the region' and which had appeared to be experiencing serious security crises, now appeared more stable. Economic integration with Europe was also proceeding swiftly, and those states which had not come to terms with the new political realities of the region—particularly the issue of peace with Israel—such as Syria, Iraq and Iran, appeared to be neutralized or isolated. Radicalism in the region also appeared to be abating, even over the stalled Middle East peace process, and Arab oil supplies to the West appeared to be assured, as non-OPEC supply continued to increase. In terms of US geo-economic priorities, therefore, the region seemed marginal; it was not a great security threat and it offered little in the way of significant economic potential. Only Turkey had been identified by the Clinton administration as one of 10 'big

emerging markets' towards which future US policy would be orientated. Furthermore, the Administration had every intention of perpetuating the Middle East and North Africa Economic Conference, established in 1993, as a vehicle for Israeli regional economic integration, despite growing Arab disenchantment.

'Dual containment'

Undoubtedly, pressure has been mounting since the beginning of the second Clinton administration for a reassessment of the policy of 'dual containment'. This has been particularly the case with respect to Iran, although US critics of the policy are increasingly aware that the USA will lose out to European, Japanese, Russian and Chinese competitors in Iraq, once sanctions are ended, unless initiatives are undertaken now. The US Administration has also had to confront the fact that its policies towards Iran have achieved little. In response, a series of initiatives have been formulated in an attempt to force a new policy direction, with support ranging from 'USA-Engage', a coalition of more than 400 US companies, to distinguished former statesmen and diplomats. It has been estimated by a presidential commission that, in 1995, US sanctions policies world-wide cost the US economy $15,000m.–$19,000m. in lost sales and affected 200,000–250,000 export-related jobs. US business interests were also anxious to see an end to the sanctions policies against Libya, where $2,000m. in US petroleum assets have been effectively frozen since 1987. In early May 1997 the prestigious *Council on Foreign Relations* in New York published a report by two former chairmen of the National Security Council, Zbigniew Brzeziński and Brent Scowcroft, and a former Assistant Secretary of State for Near Eastern Affairs, Richard Murphy, which warned that US policy in the Persian (Arabian) Gulf, Iran and Iraq had reached an impasse and that 'dual containment' had produced 'uneven results, not all of them positive from the point of view either of American interests, or those of our friends among the Gulf states'. According to the *Middle East Economic Survey* (April 28, 1997), their report advocates:

> . . . narrowing economic sanctions on Iraq and adopting a more flexible position towards Iran. It also advocates that American firms should negotiate with Iran and a post-Saddam Iraq, provided that no agreements are signed until sanctions are lifted. The report also calls upon Washington to draw up a Gulf policy distinct from the Arab-Israeli peace process, and encourage gradual and modest political and economic reforms in the GCC states.

Pressure was renewed in the wake of the presidential elections in Iran in May, which resulted in an overwhelming 70% endorsement for the moderate Muhammad Khatami against his conservative opponent, Ali Aqbar Nateq Nouri. US comment, led by Richard Murphy, underlined that change was taking place in Iran and that the USA could miss the opportunities presented by reform there if it did not generate a more flexible policy towards Teheran. Many observers also recognized that there were substantive obstacles to such a policy shift—US public opinion and suspicions of Iranian complicity in the al-Khobar bombing chief among them. None the less, the US Administration privately recognized that some gesture of conciliation was needed and, at the end of July 1997, withdrew its objections to a proposed pipeline from Turkmenistan to Turkey, via Iran. Although the new Secretary of State warned that this action should not be interpreted as a change in policy, and congressional opponents redoubled their efforts to prevent such change, it seemed undeniable that the policy of 'dual containment' would eventually have to be modified, at least as far as Iran was concerned. It remains to be seen to what extent the Clinton administration will prove flexible, and whether it will uncouple its Gulf policy from its stance on the Middle East peace process, as suggested by its more thoughtful critics. Change, however, does not seem inevitable with respect to Iraq. The Administration, having agreed in 1996 to the specific terms of UN Security Council Resolution 986 (1995) which allowed Iraq to sell up to $2,000m.-worth of oil every six months in order to purchase essential humanitarian supplies—food and medicines, in particular—thereafter insisted that the conditions attached to such sales should be as stringent as possible. The same reluctance to accept any significant or permanent easing of the sanctions regime against Iraq was manifest in UN Security Council Resolution 1111 (1997) which extended the food-for-oil regime in mid-1997. Despite the obvious need for essential supplies to ease the suffering of the Iraqi population, the Clinton administration is not prepared to concede to the removal of the sanctions regime until Saddam Hussein has been removed from power.

The problem here, as with the sanctions regime against Libya, is that the USA's obdurate refusal to countenance change is becoming less credible to its allies and opponents. Even Syria decided to restore links with Baghdad in 1997, despite the chronic tensions between the two states. Some of Washington's Gulf allies also warned that they could no longer support the sanctions, and Russia and China announced that they would consider signing oil contracts with Iraq in future, prompting concerns that French and Italian companies would flout the sanctions regime if Russia and China had already violated it.

The peace process
These difficulties seemed certain to be heightened by US attitudes towards the peace process and Israel. The antagonism between the Netanyahu Government and the Clinton administration was an open secret as was the President's annoyance at the Israeli premier's truculent indifference to US sensitivities. Initial US passivity at the start of 1997 gave way, in mid-year, to a renewed attempt to reactivate negotiations, following a catastrophic bombing in Jerusalem. Yet still no pressure was brought to bear on the Israeli Government to make concessions; instead the USA echoed Israeli demands that the Palestinians should intensify security measures as a first step to resumed negotiations. However, there was speculation that American Jewish opinion was now so disenchanted with the Netanyahu regime that it was prepared to support a toughening of official US attitudes over the peace process. Vice-President Al Gore, who intended to stand for presidential election in 2000, was apparently prepared to agree to this because he no longer feared a consequent adverse effect on his chances of election. There were also rumours that the USA was prepared to consider a redefinition of the peace process in which Jordan would play a greater role in an eventual solution, to the disadvantage of Yasser Arafat who was profoundly distrusted by Israel's Likud leadership.

The problem with such approaches was that they ignored the degree to which they might not be acceptable both to the Palestinians and to the wider Arab audience. Although an underlying assumption of both Israeli and US policy seems to have been a mistaken belief that public opinion in the Arab world could be ignored if Arab leaders could be coerced or persuaded to co-operate, this mistake was not made by Arab leaders themselves. They knew that political radicalism—whether Islamist or otherwise— would be encouraged by further concessions to Israeli sensitivities, and that US prestige in the Middle East had not been so low since the early 1980s. They also knew that, while Arab states had far fewer options to influence the regional diplomatic process than in the past, their freedom of movement was also circumscribed by domestic public opinion. Thus, for example, Egyptian politicians increasingly voiced scepticism over the peace process and sought to avoid open support for the USA, while Saudi Arabia openly voiced its own lack of conviction regarding US initiatives such as the Middle East and North Africa Economic Summit (due to be held in Qatar, but likely to face an Arab boycott). In short, given the scepticism of two states which had been the USA's principal allies in the region, the hopes of 1991 seemed likely to be frustrated in 1997 by a lack of US comprehension and by Israeli intolerance.

THE OUTLOOK
In geo-political terms, the regional outlook also appeared bleak. During 1996, Israel, with tacit US support, had forged a new alliance with Turkey. The Turkish military high command had supported such an initiative because of its dislike of the Islamist Erbakan Government which it forced from office in mid-1997, and because of mounting Arab antagonism towards its intervention in northern Iraq, which had become a redoubt for the Syrian-backed PKK Kurdish guerrilla movement. Arab states viewed this alliance as a new Israeli attempt at Arab encirclement, along the lines of the Ben Gurion 'periphery policy' of the 1950s and 1960s. There were also suspicions that Jordan, the recipient of renewed US support in the wake of its peace treaty with Israel, would form a third pillar of the new alliance configuration. These anxieties, together with Syria's realization that the Netanyahu Government would not cede the Golan Heights

as part of any peace agreement, led, in turn, to a new Middle East re-alignment. Links with Iran were strengthened during 1996 and tentative moves were made towards more permanent, if low-level, contacts with Iraq. At the same time, Egyptian support was courted and the Gulf states were served with proposals for an Arab common market linking Egypt, Syria and the six GCC states. In short, a new polarization of the Middle East seemed to be taking place.

Admittedly, the political arena has changed and the idea of a new, specifically anti-US alliance succeeding seems highly unlikely. Yet the new alliance was, in reality, another attempt to bring pressure to bear on the Clinton administration to modify its policies in the Middle East and to force Israel to behave more reasonably and realistically within the peace process. Implicit in the initiative was the argument that failure to realize this would only encourage recourse to the sole remaining alternative—a growth in non-state violence and increased instability in the region. This, in turn, was predicated to some extent on the assumption that the Middle East region continued to be important to Western strategy, at least as a source of energy. It is not clear, however, that such assumptions will prove to be justified. Middle East oil and gas is certainly significant, providing up to 43% of European imports of oil, a figure which rises, with the inclusion of North Africa, to around 63%. North Africa also provides up to 25% of Europe's gas requirements. US dependence is far lower and, although world demand seems likely to increase in the next decade so that the Middle East again becomes a crucial source of hydrocarbon energy, the Far East is expected to become the world's major consumer. Europe and the USA may turn to non-OPEC supplies of oil and gas, particularly in central Asia, where supplies will enter the Mediterranean and pass on to Europe and the USA via Turkey.

For the USA, therefore, the Middle East is an area of diminishing importance, particularly if threats from regional states can safely be ignored. That, for the foreseeable future, will be the case, since no Middle Eastern state would be prepared to risk the fate of Iraq. US concerns in the Middle East, therefore, will be concentrated on the future of Israel, provided the Persian Gulf remains secure—and there congressional demands for burden-sharing may well insist on a greater effort from Europe and Japan. Yet the issue of Israel is largely one stimulated by domestic policy concerns. It has been the effectiveness of the Israeli lobby in the USA that has ensured that Israel should continue to play such a crucial role in US foreign policy concerns, together with the continuing reauthentication of the memory of the Holocaust. It is certainly not Israel's strategic significance for, as a committed Israeli supporter in the USA has admitted, 'Israel is of limited military or economic importance to the United States . . . It is not a strategically vital state.' It is, rather, domestic sentiment which has ensured total official aid to Israel of $71,000m. by 1997, not to mention at least as much again from private and unofficial sources. Egypt, in return for its role in the peace process since 1979, has received a total of $49,000m. from the USA.

Yet the climate is changing. US public opinion is no longer prepared to fund foreign aid and, even if Israel remains an acute domestic concern in the USA, the present situation whereby Israel and Egypt consume some 30% of the entire US foreign affairs budget and 33%–43% of the foreign assistance budget, clearly cannot continue, and pressure for a definitive solution to the Arab–Israeli conflict and to the Palestinian issue will continue to be the touchstone of US policy towards the Middle East, for this reason if for no other. Congressional attitudes and lobby interests, however, are likely to ensure that Israeli imperatives will continue to dominate the peace agenda, even if the US Administration is concerned by the long-term implications of such pressures and the possible failure of the process as a consequence.

BIBLIOGRAPHY

Amuzegar, J. *Iran's Economy and the US Sanctions.* Middle East Journal, 51, 2, 1997.

Bahgat, G. *Beyond Sanctions: US Policy Towards Iraq.* International Relations, XIII, 4, 1997.

Clarke, D. L. *US Security Assistance to Egypt and Israel: Politically Untouchable?* Middle East Journal, 51, 2, 1997.

Cox, M. *US Foreign Policy After the Cold War: Superpower Without a Mission?* London. RIIA/Pinter, 1995.

Kaufman, B. I. *The Arab Middle East and the United States: inter-Arab Rivalry and Superpower Diplomacy.* New York. Twayne. 1996.

Watkins, E. *The Unfolding US Policy in the Middle East.* International Affairs, 73, 1, 1997.

CALENDAR OF US POLICY IN THE MIDDLE EAST AND NORTH AFRICA, 1997–98

1997

JANUARY

12 Carey Cavanaugh, a special envoy of the US Department of State, arrived in Nicosia, Cyprus, in an attempt to pacify increasingly belligerent relations between the Greek Cypriot and Turkish Cypriot authorities following the announcement by the Greek Cypriot Government, earlier in the month, that it planned to purchase an advanced missile system from Russia.

15 Agreement on Hebron was successfully negotiated between the Israeli and Palestinian authorities through US mediation; among the documents comprising the agreement was a letter signed by the outgoing US Secretary of State, Warren Christopher, in which the US Government's recognition of the paramountcy of Israel's security requirements was clearly detailed.

23–24 US Attorney-General, Janet Reno, and the Director of the US Federal Bureau of Investigation (FBI), Louis Freeh, both accused the Saudi authorities of not co-operating with their investigations into the deaths of US citizens in a bomb blast at the al-Khobar military housing complex in Saudi Arabia, in June 1996.

MARCH

3 Following a meeting with Palestinian leader, Yasser Arafat, in Washington, DC, US President Bill Clinton was critical of the Israeli Government's decision to commence construction of a new Jewish settlement (Har Homa) at Jabal Abu Ghunaym in East Jerusalem.

The US Department of State announced the creation of a new joint US-Palestinian commission.

7 The USA vetoed a draft resolution of the UN Security Council urging Israel to reconsider the decision to commence construction at Har Homa.

The Israeli Cabinet reluctantly agreed to a further 9% redeployment of troops from the West Bank, reportedly following intense pressure from the US Government.

25–28 The Saudi Minister of Defence and Civil Aviation led a ministerial delegation to Washington, DC, for talks with President Clinton and other prominent US officials. Discussions covered a wide range of topics including, reportedly, the possible supply by the USA of as many as 100 F-6 fighter aircraft to the Saudi Arabian defence forces.

26–28 The US special envoy to the Middle East, Dennis Ross, visited the region for talks with Israeli and Palestinian leaders, in an attempt to arrest a rapid deterioration in prospects for the peace process.

APRIL

10 The ruling of a German court that Iran's leaders were ultimately responsible for the assassination of Kurdish dissidents in Berlin in 1992, prompted the US Government to undertake a diplomatic initiative to convince EU member nations to adopt a more uncompromising attitude in their relations with Iran, and even advocated the imposition, by the EU, of economic sanctions against the regime.

15–18 Dennis Ross returned to Israel and the Palestinian autonomous regions in an attempt to reactivate the peace process; his efforts met with little success.

25 The USA voted against a successful resolution of the UN General Assembly (acting within the 'uniting for peace resolution' mechanism) urging the cessation of Israeli settlement activity in Jerusalem.

MAY

7–16 A visit to the Middle East by Dennis Ross again failed to reactivate the peace process.

9 The US Department of State announced that it was considering retaliatory action against Libya, following Col Qaddafi's breach of a 1992 UN Security Council resolution banning international flights to and from Libya, during an unannounced visit to Niger and Nigeria earlier in the month.

29 President Clinton expressed cautious optimism regarding US–Iranian relations, following the election of President Khatami in Iran.

JUNE

4 The appointment of the respected diplomat, Richard Holbrooke, as the US President's special envoy to Cyprus was widely interpreted as an attempt by the US Government to give increased priority to the negotiation of a peace on the island, and to improve relations between Greece and Turkey.

7 The USA voted against a successful UN General Assembly resolution to demand $1.7m. from the Israeli Government for damages inflicted by an Israeli rocket attack on a UN compound in Qana, Lebanon, in April 1996, in which more than 100 Lebanese civilians were killed.

10 The US House of Representatives approved a resolution which recognized Jerusalem as the undivided capital of Israel. The House also approved the allocation of $100m. to the costs of removing the US embassy in Israel from Tel-Aviv to Jerusalem.

JULY

8 Diplomatic pressure from the US Secretary of State helped to bring about the successful negotiation of a US-brokered 'convergence of views' document between Greece and Turkey. The document recognized the sovereign rights of both parties and renounced the use of force in the settlement of disputes.

16 The USA voted against a successful resolution of the UN General Assembly which urged the cessation of all Jewish settlement activity in the Occupied Territories.

30 The US Secretary of State, Madeleine Albright, announced an end to the ban on travel between the USA and Lebanon imposed in 1987.

AUGUST

6 Madeleine Albright delivered her first address on the Middle East in which she urged the Palestinians to improve security measures, and announced her readiness to visit the region as soon as an appreciable improvement in security had been achieved.

9–13 Dennis Ross visited the region to discuss security issues; following mediation of talks between Israeli and Palestinian security officers, the creation of a joint Israeli-Palestinian security forum, at which US intelligence organizations would also be represented, was announced.

SEPTEMBER

10 The US Department of State expressed concern at

unsubstantiated reports that the People's Republic of China and Russia were co-operating with Iranian attempts to build long-range nuclear missiles.

10–15 Madeleine Albright undertook her first official visit to the Middle East in her capacity as US Secretary of State. Albright visited Israel, the Palestinian autonomous regions, Syria, Egypt, Jordan, Lebanon and Saudi Arabia. Albright reiterated the US Government's concern at Palestinian terrorist activity, and urged the Israeli Government to 'freeze' settlement activity in East Jerusalem and release Palestine National Authority revenues which were being withheld in retaliation for recent suicide bombings in Jerusalem.

25 The third stage of a $1,100m.-Jordanian debt cancellation agreement was signed with the US Government.

29 The US Department of State condemned an announcement by the French energy company Total that it was part of a consortium, including Russian and Malaysian gas companies, that planned to co-operate with the National Iranian Oil Co in developing part of the South Pars gas field in Iran. The US authorities stated that the agreement would be fully examined within the context of the D'Amato-Kennedy Act (also known as the 'Iran-Libya sanctions act').

Following meetings with Palestinian and Israeli negotiators in New York, Madeleine Albright announced that direct peace talks were to resume between the two sides in early October.

OCTOBER

3 US Secretary of Defense, William Cohen, ordered the US aircraft carrier *Nimitz* to proceed immediately to the Persian (Arabian) Gulf at the head of a seven-ship fleet, following the violation, by Iranian aircraft, of the air exclusion zone over southern Iraq, in order to bomb two bases of the opposition Mujahidin-e-Khalq in that country (prompting Iraqi aircraft also to enter the zone in pursuit of the Iranian bombers).

8 The US Department of State announced that the Iranian anti-Government Mujahidin-e-Khalq had been placed on its list of proscribed terrorist organizations, thus preventing fundraising activities from taking place on US soil.

An unannounced meeting between Yasser Arafat and Binyamin Netanyahu, the first since February, took place at the Erez check-point between Gaza and Israel, according to arrangements made by Dennis Ross.

12–13 US Department of State co-ordinator for Cyprus, Thomas Miller, and President Clinton's special envoy to Cyprus, Richard Holbrooke, visited Ankara, Turkey, for talks with Prime Minister Mesut Yılmaz, in an attempt to reactivate negotiations over a peace settlement for Cyprus.

29 A US presidential spokesman described Iraqi demands that all US personnel should be withdrawn from the UN Special Commission (UNSCOM) weapons inspection teams operating in Iraq as 'unacceptable'.

NOVEMBER

6 A report in the US *International Herald Tribune* suggested that the recent purchase by the US Government of 21 MiG-29 fighter aircraft from Moldova had been prompted by speculation that the Iranian Government was considering buying them.

9 The US Government expressed disappointment that the Government of Kuwait had agreed a $200m.-arms purchase from the People's Republic of China in preference to 'the USA or another of its allies in the Gulf War coalition'.

10 In an address to the US Congress President Clinton announced that Syria and Lebanon had been removed from the US Government's list of nations considered to be involved in the illicit trafficking of drugs.

10–11 The US President's special envoy to Cyprus, Richard Holbrooke, attended meetings on the island with both

President Klerides and Rauf Denktaş, leader of the self-proclaimed 'Turkish Republic of Northern Cyprus' in an attempt to end the deadlock in negotiations for a settlement; Holbrooke flew on to Ankara for further discussion with the Turkish Prime Minister.

14 The US Government announced the dispatch of the aircraft carrier *George Washington* to the Persian (Arabian) Gulf (joining the *Nimitz*—see October), following the Iraqi Government's decision to expel six US UNSCOM inspectors from Iraq.

16 In an addresss to the fourth Middle East and North Africa (MENA) economic conference in Doha, Qatar, Madeleine Albright criticized the Israeli Government's repeated recourse to 'closure' of the West Bank and Gaza Strip as a punishment, blaming this policy for the worsening economic conditions of both areas.

20 Following a compromise agreement on the continuing work of US UNSCOM inspectors in Iraq, concluded as result of Russian intervention, President Clinton insisted that there would be no conditions attached to the return of the inspectors to their work and no tolerance of Iraq's failure to comply with all UN demands. At the same time, Clinton announced the dispatch of 32 additional aircraft to the Persian (Arabian) Gulf region.

26 In his annual report on weapons proliferation, the US Secretary of Defense, William Cohen, accused Iraq of deliberately misleading the UN with regard to its chemical weapons capabilities, and issued a warning that the USA was prepared to use considerable force to ensure that Iraq properly observed the terms of all UN resolutions relating to its weapons programme.

DECEMBER

5 Madeleine Albright met Binyamin Netanyahu in Paris, France, and urged him to make a prompt decision on troop redeployment on the West Bank.

15–16 President Clinton announced that he was 'encouraged' by a statement made by President Khatami of Iran which had advocated 'a thoughtful dialogue with the American people'. On the following day Clinton stated that the USA would not seek to change the position of Iran or of any Islamic state with regard to the peace process.

17–22 During a visit to the USA by the Turkish Prime Minister, Mesut Yılmaz, President Clinton declared US support for Turkey's application to join the EU, at the same time urging Yılmaz to seek to resolve outstanding disputes with Greece.

18 Following the Iraqi authorities' obstruction of UNSCOM inspectors' attempts to enter Iraqi presidential palaces, the US Government warned that further action might be necessary to force full Iraqi compliance with UN resolutions.

18 Madeleine Albright reiterated US recommendations for prompt action on redeployment during further talks with Binyamin Netanyahu in Paris.

1998

JANUARY

6–9 Dennis Ross visited Israel and the Palestinian autonomous regions. Further Israeli troop redeployment was discussed but no progress was made on this issue.

7 A joint naval exercise conducted by Turkish, Israeli and US forces in the Mediterranean caused disquiet in the region, and was strongly criticized by Iran, Iraq and Syria.

20 During a visit to the USA, Binyamin Netanyahu met President Clinton. Relations were reportedly strained; prior to the meeting, Netanyahu had conducted a series of high-profile meetings with Clinton's political opponents and Clinton had reportedly declined to invite Netanyahu to a formal White House lunch. During the meeting Clinton presented proposals for a phased Israeli withdrawal from the West Bank although no

mention was made of the extent of such a withdrawal. Yasser Arafat, who met Clinton two days later, had requested redeployment from at least 30% of West Bank territory, while Netanyahu reportedly refused to withdraw from more than 9.5% of the West Bank. The US Government urged a 'credible and significant' Israeli redeployment.

31 Madeleine Albright visited the Middle East, and held talks with Binyamin Netanyahu and Yasser Arafat, but failed to restart the peace process. During her visit to the region, she also visited Kuwait, Saudi Arabia, Bahrain and Egypt as part of a US diplomatic campaign to gain international support for air strikes against Iraq following the deterioration in relations between Iraq and UNSCOM weapons inspectors.

FEBRUARY

8–11 US Secretary of Defense, William Cohen, visited the six GCC states, but failed to gain support for US military intervention in Iraq. Of the six states, only Kuwait supported the use of force, with all six states strongly advocating a diplomatic solution.

MARCH

20 The question of sanctions against Libya was discussed at the UN. Libya put forward its case for an end to the sanctions, citing a recent decision by the International Court of Justice in The Hague that it was competent to consider the dispute between Libya, the USA and the United Kingdom over the location of the trial for the two suspects in the Lockerbie bomb case. The US and British permanent representatives to the UN, however, accused Libya of misrepresenting the facts of the case and advocated a continuance of the sanctions.

26–31 Dennis Ross visited Israel, the Palestinian autonomous regions and Egypt in an attempt to break the impasse on the issue of troop redeployment; little progress was made. Ross put forward US proposals for a 13.1% redeployment from the West Bank in exchange for security guarantees from the Palestinians. The Israeli Cabinet, however, had resolved on 23 March that it would not withdraw from more than 9% of West Bank territory, and claimed that the Palestinians had failed to honour their commitment to restrain the activities of Islamic militants.

APRIL

2 The US Department of State downgraded its warning to US citizens against travelling to Iran. (US citizens are now urged to defer such travel.)

27 The UN decided against reviewing sanctions against Iraq following the latest six-monthly UNSCOM report. The USA and the United Kingdom had earlier insisted on an automatic renewal of the sanctions package.

MAY

1–4 US Presidential envoy Richard Holbrooke visited Cyprus and held talks with President Klerides and Rauf Denktaş, leader of the self-proclaimed 'Turkish Republic of Northern Cyprus'. He failed, however, to make any progress on reactivating negotiations. A Russian peace plan was subsequently submitted to the UN Secretary-General, but was later rejected by Denktaş, who added that if Russia was committed to peace on the island, it should halt its planned missile sale to the Greek Cypriot Government.

4–5 Madeleine Albright held separate talks with Binyamin Netanyahu and Yasser Arafat in London, United Kingdom. No significant progress was made, and Albright announced that both parties had been invited to the White House on 11 May for further talks.

8–10 Dennis Ross visited the Middle East to try and broker an agreement prior to the planned Washington talks on 11 May. Binyamin Netanyahu reportedly would not discuss redeployment. The talks were, however, made conditional on Israeli backing of the US plan for a

13% redeployment and as a result Netanyahu declined to attend.

11 A meeting, held in Washington, DC, to discuss the peace process, was attended by President Clinton, Madeleine Albright, Dennis Ross, National Security Adviser Sandy Berger, and Assistant Secretary of State for the Near East, Martin Indyk. Albright agreed to remain in the USA (and not accompany Clinton on the first leg of a trip to Europe) and hold talks with Netanyahu during a pre-planned visit on 13–18 May.

12 Madeleine Albright delivered a speech praising the Palestinians for their 'constructive efforts' and acknowledging that they had made substantial changes in their negotiating position.

13–18 Binyamin Netanyahu visited the USA where he held meetings with Madeleine Albright and Dennis Ross, although little progress was made.

18 Madeleine Albright and Dennis Ross met Yasser Arafat in London, United Kingdom, and attempted to persuade him to accept 'refinements' to the redeployment plan.

22 Saudi Arabian Minister of the Interior, Prince Nayef ibn Abd al-Aziz as-Saʻud, announced that the bomb blast at the al-Khobar military housing complex in June 1996 had been carried out by Saudi nationals without foreign support. It was later reported that the USA was continuing to investigate a possible Iranian link and quoted a senior US official who had implied that the Saudi Government was trying not to implicate Iran to avoid jeopardizing recently-improved relations between the two countries.

26 During a visit to Cairo, Egypt, Yasser Arafat called for an Arab summit to discuss the stalled peace process. He later visited other Arab states to promote his idea; Israel dismissed the idea as a violation of the terms of the Oslo Accords which forbid the parties from seeking outside intervention in the peace process.

27 During a visit to Israel and the Palestinian autonomous regions the speaker of the US House of Representatives, Newt Gingrich, delivered a speech to the Israeli Knesset giving his public support to a plan to move the US embassy from Tel-Aviv to Jerusalem; the White House rejected his comments as provocative and undiplomatic.

30 During a news conference, President Clinton announced that he was encouraged by recent Iraqi co-operation with UNSCOM and that he expected to reduce the number of troops which had been deployed in the Gulf since the crisis developed in late 1997.

JUNE

4 Details of the US proposals for redeployment were leaked and published in the Israeli press. The Palestinians had agreed to the proposals, but the Israeli Government maintained that the proposed extent of the redeployment would undermine its national security.

15–19 Lebanese Prime Minister, Rafik Hariri, visited the USA and held talks with President Clinton and Madeleine Albright. Hariri reportedly told Clinton that both Lebanon and Syria would conclude a peace treaty with Israel within three months if Israel were to restart negotiations from the point at which the negotiations had broken down, and indicated that a joint Lebanese-Syrian initiative would be forthcoming.

17 Madeleine Albright gave a speech in which she called for a number of confidence-building measures between Iran and the USA. It was the first substantive US policy statement on Iran since the Iranian President's call for dialogue in January. President Clinton later reinforced Albright's comments saying he believed Iran was changing in a positive way and that his administration would support such changes. The Iranian Minister of Foreign Affairs, Kamal Kharrazi, welcomed these statements but urged the US Government to demonstrate an attitude of 'mutual respect and equality' if there was to be a real possibility of bilateral relations.

17 Assistant Secretary of State for the Near East, Martin Indyk, announced US financial support for 73 Iraqi opposition groups, and an opposition radio station, following authorization by the US Congress of US $33m. to organize opposition to the Iraqi regime.

21 The Israeli Cabinet approved a draft plan to widen Jerusalem's municipal boundaries. The draft had been widely criticized, a US Department of State spokesman having announced that it was 'extremely hard to understand why Israel would even consider taking such a provocative step at this sensitive time in the negotiations'.

27 The US *International Herald Tribune* reported that the US investigation of the bomb blast at the al-Khobar military housing complex in Saudia Arabia, in June 1996, had broken down over disagreements with the Saudi authorities; the report alleged that the Federal Bureau of Investigations (FBI) had withdrawn all but one of its investigators. The dispute appeared to centre on the involvement of Iran in the incident.

30 A US fighter plane fired a missile at a radar site in southern Iraq after the ground radar system reportedly 'locked on' to four British jets on a routine patrol over the southern air exclusion zone. Iraqi officials claimed the missile struck a point 18 km away from the nearest missile site. The USA sought to downplay the incident stating that there had been no evidence of troop movements and that it could have been an isolated incident.

JULY

19–22 The first direct peace talks for 16 months were held between Israel and the Palestinians. The talks failed to achieve agreement on redeployment, the Palestinians refused to accept less than the US-proposed 13% withdrawal which the Israelis maintained would threaten their security.

23 The US House of Representatives reduced aid to Egypt and Israel by US $100m. each, as part of a reduced foreign aid package for 1999.

SEPTEMBER

9–16 Dennis Ross visited Israel for the first time in four months in an attempt to break the deadlock. At the end of his visit no agreement had been reached; the Palestinians had accepted the US plan for a 13% withdrawal, but the Israelis could offer only a full 10% withdrawal and a further 3% partial withdrawal.

10 A joint US-British motion was passed at the UN suspending periodic reviews of sanctions on Iraq until that country resumes co-operation with the UNSCOM weapons inspectorate.

28 At a meeting in Washington, DC, Binyamin Netanyahu and Yasser Arafat agreed to a tripartite peace summit in the USA in mid-October. At the meeting, Netanyahu and Arafat appeared to make some progress on agreeing to the 13% withdrawal proposed by the USA.

WATER, 'VIRTUAL WATER' AND THE ECONOMIES OF THE MIDDLE EAST AND NORTH AFRICA

TONY ALLAN

It has often been argued that for many countries in arid regions like the Middle East and North Africa, where 'indigenous' water resources are insufficient to sustain national economies, water has become a highly-prized commodity and a potential source of armed conflict. Many prominent political commentators and politicians (including, recently, King Hussein of Jordan and former Secretary-General of the United Nations Boutros Boutros-Ghali) and fewer economists have warned of the threat to regional stability posed by the problems of water-deficit economies. Yet economies have been sustained and serious conflict has been avoided. In the case of the Middle East and North Africa, at least, water has been accessed from a global system, via trade; economic systems and not the clearly inadequate hydrological systems, have provided a solution to the region's water-supply problems. Water in the global trading system is known as 'virtual water'; this is the water embedded in key water-intensive commodities such as wheat. While there is good reason to suppose that, at least in terms of freshwater availability, there will be sufficient water to meet the needs of a future world population more than twice its current size, there remains a lack of reliable scientific projection as to the future capacity of the global freshwater system. In terms of demand, given that freshwater needs are driven by increased population, precise calculations are complicated by the vast range of future world population forecasts. This domain of uncertain information has given rise to both optimists, including the author and most economists, and pessimists, whose divergent interpretations owe much to the differing assumptions upon which their respective analyses are based. The issue is of particular importance to the peoples and political leaders of the Middle East and North Africa, given that the region's economies are already as dependent on global water as they are on their own renewable supplies. In the 1960s and 1970s there were attempts in the former Soviet Union to review the world's water balance; water availability and use have also been addressed. Since 1994 there has been a welcome and responsible attempt by the Food and Agriculture Organization (FAO) of the United Nations to examine the subjects of water availability for Africa and the Middle East and water utilization through irrigation, the major using sector. The publications provide first approximations that should be given prominence in order to allow the enhancement of the reliability of the data by progressive iteration. A balanced perspective on the population, water and food nexus from the International Food Policy Research Institute (IFPRI) identifies low, medium and high growth-rate scenarios for world population forecasts.

'In its 1996 study, the United Nations found that population growth between 1990 and 1995 was 1.48 per cent per year, rather than the 1.57 per cent projected in 1994. In light of this lower rate, the United Nations revised its projections for population growth in the next century, based on three different assumptions about the fertility of the world's women. The medium fertility model—the one usually considered the most likely—would put the world's population at 9.4 billion by 2050 (half a billion lower than the United Nations 1994 estimates). World population would continue to grow until 2200, according to this model, when it would stabilize at 10.73 billion.

The medium fertility model falls in the middle of a wide range of possible outcomes. Low fertility would result in a world population of 7.7 billion by 2200, whereas high fertility would mean 11.1 billion mouths to feed in 2200. These extremes are by no means unrealistic, and the population debate is far from over. . . . Public policy and individual behaviour, they say, will ultimately determine the world's population.'

The link between global water resources and the Middle East and North Africa

About the water of the Middle East and North Africa there is less scientific controversy; the region 'ran out' of water in the 1970s. The news of this important economic development was little reported. In the political world facts, including those on water, which are judged to have costly political consequences are easily ignored or dismissed as irrelevant. With selection and distortion of information often the norm in political processes it is predictable that discourses on the water resources of the Middle East and North Africa have often been misleading and confusing. For political leaders in the region political imperatives are more compelling than scientific facts. On the issue of water, these imperatives drive them to assert that their economies have not run out. Government ministers in Egypt in the mid-1990s maintained a vigorous public defence of their assertions that Egypt has sufficient water. The main reason for the discrepancy of interpretations of water sufficiency by scientists and politicians is the politicians' reluctance to specify their understanding of what 'sufficient' means. By 'sufficient', scientists mean sufficient 'indigenous' water to meet the total household requirements and agricultural (including water for food production), industrial and municipal needs of an economy. In most cases the politicians imply adherence to the same criteria as the scientists but in practice they are taking only a part of the 'total' needs into consideration. Without making their assumptions clear they are asserting that 'sufficient freshwater' is that volume necessary to sustain existing jobs in agriculture and industry and to meet municipal and industrial needs. For an economy such as Israel's this would account for only 25% of the water which would be needed for food self-sufficiency. For Egypt such a notion of sufficiency represents about 60% of the water needed for food self-sufficiency. For politicians in most of the countries in the region the food production gap resulting from the insufficiency of water has to be ignored, since to draw attention to the water and food shortfall could be politically destabilizing.

The particular importance of the Middle East *vis-à-vis* the water issue stems from its dubious distinction as the first major region in the world to 'run out' of water. The water demands of the populations of the Arabian Peninsula and much of Libya had exceeded the capacity of their water resources for food self-sufficiency by the 1950s. Israel and Palestine also 'ran out' of water in the 1950s, Jordan in the 1960s, and Egypt in the 1970s. The Maghreb countries have recently entered water deficit. The Tigris-Euphrates riparians have yet to fully utilize their water resources but will undoubtedly do so in the next couple of decades.

The major indicator of the scale of the water deficit of an economy is the level of its food imports, since the water required to raise food is what an economist would refer to as its 'dominant consumptive use'. This use dominates both in terms of the individual citizen and of the national economy. Water used by the agriculture sector exceeds tenfold the water employed by the industrial and municipal sectors combined. Each year an individual needs only 1 cu m of drinking water and between 50 and 100 cu m for other domestic uses, although a much lower actual level of use is not unusual in many rural communities in countries in other regions such as sub-Saharan Africa. In contrast, each year at least 1,000 cu m of water, either naturally occurring in soil profiles, or transported to the profiles by irrigation systems, is needed to meet the food requirements of that individual. At a national level, more than 90% of all official water budgets are devoted to the agricultural sector.

In the arid and semi-arid Middle East and North Africa the dominance of agricultural water demand is remarkable. There is little or no naturally occurring soil water, even in the winter when parts of the region do receive rainfall. By contrast, for economies located in temperate latitudes—in Europe and the humid tracts of North America for example—the issue of the relative demands of the agriculture and the industry (including services) sectors is of little consequence. In temperate latitudes crop production is almost entirely based on soil water which occurs naturally and is largely taken for granted. In these regions the huge volumes of water utilized by agriculture are not considered within the context of a national water budget. Such water is a free commodity. In the Middle East and North Africa, however, agricultural water is expensively won because of the costs of storage (in order to ensure timely availability) and distribution. In addition, mobilizing such volumes of water can be politically stressful both nationally, (owing to environmental impacts) and internationally, provoking riparian conflict.

Soil water and the economic efficiency of water use are crucial issues for the region. It is global soil water which balances the water budgets of all the economies of the Middle East and North Africa (with the arguable exception of Turkey) while the effective allocation of water among sectors in order to gain high returns and encourage high levels of employment is fundamental to economic and political stability.

The regional water shortfall and the global water surplus

The rate at which food imports have grown in the Middle East and North Africa since the 1970s appears to support the scientists' contentions that the region has 'run out' of water, given that the production of every ton of a food commodity such as wheat requires a water input of approximately one thousand times that volume. The trend in cereal imports reflects a reasonable approximation of the capacity or incapacity of an economy to meet its strategic food needs.

Meanwhile, the peoples of the region and their leaders do not need to recognize these resources and economic realities. Their interpretations of Middle East hydrological and economic contexts are based on now irrelevant past expectations; their perception of global hydrological and economic contexts is unsound. The Middle East's hydrological system is clearly less and less able to meet the rising demands being placed upon it, while the global hydrological system is in surplus, and evidently capable of meeting the most demanding element of global water demand—world food consumption. Assuming a medium water consumption rate of 1,500 cu m per person per year, global freshwater needs amount to some 8,250 m. cu m annually, a volume well within the estimated capacity of available global freshwater. At the regional level there can only be levels of pessimism regarding the future availability of water, at least for irrigated food production. There is some optimism with regard to future volumes of the region's freshwater, but this is based on non-scientific assumptions. On the other hand, optimism about the capacity to utilize the region's water more productively is justifiable, and it is on this aspect of water management that politicians and regional optimists focus, as do those with financial and consulting services to contribute from outside the region. At the global level there is uncertainty both about volumes of available freshwater and about the capacity to use the water effectively. In such circumstances there is evidence to support the arguments of both optimists and pessimists. Owing to the significant error margins of the statistics produced by the as yet inadequate models of potential global change, vastly differing views emerge concerning the capacity of the world's agricultural systems to raise food, which only serve to further complicate the debate. The pessimistic global freshwater scenario is persuasive if one accepts the following assumptions: the continuance of current or more extravagant (in terms of water use) patterns of food consumption by individuals; demographic transition based on estimates of maximum growth rates; static technology; totally inflexible international organizations and political institutions; and ineffective trading systems. If, however, it is assumed that communities can change their food consumption behaviour, global population growth will level off in the second half of the 21st century at some 10,000 m., sound economic policies can improve the productivity of water by ensuring that it is allocated to activities and crop production which yield high returns, advances in technology can significantly improve the productivity of water in food production, and that the mechanisms of international trade in staple foods continue to operate with proven effectiveness to ameliorate the uneven water endowments of the world's regions then one can conclude that the world's water and food futures are indeed uncertain but far from insecure. The contribution by the scientific community of best estimates of the status of existing soil water surpluses is crucial to a serious examination of the debate. Unfortunately these numbers are difficult to obtain because the concept of soil water availability is difficult to define and agree, and even if the concept were generally agreed, a method of comprehensive monitoring has yet to be defined. The particular insecurity of the Middle East and North Africa arises not just from its water resource endowment, but also from the inability of its governments and agriculture sectors, as well as international institutions, to adapt to the resource scarcity and take measures to find and mobilize substitutes.

It is important to stress that the types of adjustment anticipated by the water optimists cannot be achieved quickly. Even thirty years is a rather short transitional period for the necessary major adjustments in water policies to be developed in response to limited water availability. Effecting changes in the public perception of the value of water will take time. The associated political discourses enabling fundamental changes in water policies may take decades at least, so deeply-rooted are the belief systems, and so challenging any proposals that they should change, that politicians are loathe to contradict them, even though the implementation of such measures is essential for the stabilization of the political economy.

How is it that the theories of the pessimists and the optimists have evolved simultaneously yet are informed by such confusing and contradictory interpretations? There appear to be four main reasons, three concerning water supply and one related to water demand. In terms of supply, one must first acknowledge the diverse assumptions on surface and groundwater availability adopted by the two groups. Secondly, the most important variable of all, global soil water, is ignored by pessimists and little understood by the optimists. Thirdly, there is considerable imprecision in the estimates of the other important components of the global hydrological system, most particularly with regard to climatic change. Finally, with respect to demand there are so many factors affecting the requirements of a community for water that it is possible to extrapolate demands for water which differ hugely between the lowest and highest estimates; the optimists tend to invoke the former whereas the pessimists quote the latter.

Soil water and 'virtual water'

Soil water, located in the soil profiles of countries throughout the world, is perhaps the most crucial component of the water debate equation, and yet also the most frequently neglected by both optimists and pessimists. The neglect is especially true of the pessimists. Soil water and soil moisture rarely feature in their arguments, or if they do they generally refer to examples in some local irrigated circumstances and not to the pivotal role of naturally occurring soil water in feeding the world's future populations. If at least one-half of the water needed to feed the Middle East and North Africa's people in the 1990s lies in the soil profiles of temperate humid environments in North America, South America and Europe, it is surely derelict to ignore that water. This is not to discredit the inestimably important contributions of Lester Brown and Sandra Postel to international and local discourse on the state of the world's water resources. Their success in highlighting the urgency of achieving major shifts in perception and policy is extremely important. However, by discussing only surface water and groundwater, a very partial perspective on the waters of importance to human populations is presented. An analysis of the energy future of a hydrocarbon-deficient national economy would be as misleading if it neglected options to import oil and gas. Even more neglectful is the failure to emphasize properly the impressive international trading systems which transfer commodities requiring high water inputs from water surplus areas to water poor ones. In practice more water flows into the Middle East each year in this 'virtual' form, embedded in cereal imports, than is used for annual crop production in Egypt—Egypt being by far the most water-rich country in the arid part of the Middle East and North Africa.

Without wishing to contradict the concerns of the eco-pessimists and those afflicted with hydro-paranoia *vis-à-vis* the Middle East, it should be possible to enlighten those concerned by refocusing the analysis at a higher and more appropriate level, namely at the level of the international political economy. Here lie the answers to why economies operate as they do and why water policies are as they are in the Middle East and North Africa. Comprehensive explanations cannot be provided by narrow analysis of catchments and water budgets at national levels or even at regional levels. Catchment hydrologies do not represent the full range of options available to those managing a national economy. If national hydrological systems restrict economic options then politicians are obliged to find remedies in systems which do provide solutions. US water resource specialists have coined the term, the 'problemshed', to describe the 'catchment' or 'system' in which solutions can be found. National economies operate in international political economic systems — in problemsheds — and not just in hydrological systems — or watersheds. The shared and delimited catchment hydrologies, with their attendant troublesome international relations, are dangerously misleading frameworks of analysis. The existence of solutions in 'problemsheds' enable politicians to avoid the stresses of inter-riparian relations in the watershed.

Although many of the problems associated with water shortage in the Middle East and North Africa have been addressed successfully in the last quarter of the 20th century, certain recurrent frictions persist, most notably among the countries of the Jordan catchment. The initiatives of Turkey in the upper Tigris-Euphrates have also been the focus of considerable international attention. Meanwhile, many observers are predicting a new era of intense and possibly tense co-operation among the riparians of the Nile, following decades of inactivity.

The Jordan: Syria, Lebanon, Israel, Jordan and Palestine

The waters of the Jordan and the groundwater of the West Bank have long been issues of crucial importance for Israel, Jordan and Palestine. Peace talks conducted during 1993–94 between Jordan and Israel culminated in October 1994 with an agreement which included the provision of a phased 200 m. cu m of water per year for Jordan, to be allocated partly from current Israeli resources and partly from jointly-developed resources, and to be implemented in 50 m. cu m increments. The agreement was less favourable than Jordan had hoped but was acceptable in the context of a complex accord which established peace and also addressed territorial issues. Indeed, one of the unavoidable challenges for those involved in international negotiations over shared water resources is that discussions on water are always linked with other issues.

During the preliminary stages of the negotiations between the Israeli and Palestinian authorities which subsequently became known as the Oslo (1993) and Oslo II (1995) Accords, five crucial issues were identified: territory, Jerusalem, settlements, refugees and water. In the three difficult years since Oslo II the hand over of West Bank territory and the related issues of settlements have been prioritized. The status of Jerusalem is closely connected with the issues of settlement and territory, and will take its place at the top of the negotiating agenda in due course. Although water remains both a symbol of Palestinian national interest and an important current and future national resource, it is likely to be a foundation element in the co-operative relations between Israel and Palestine during and beyond the 'final status' negotiations. The emergence of water as a source of co-operation rather than long-term conflict owes much to the fact that the solution to the water problems of both Palestine and Israel lie beyond the water resources of the Jordan River and the West Bank. The principal water resource in terms of volume for all of these economies, both presently and in the future, lies outside the region, since their gross water needs can only be met by importing 'virtual water'. The ability to afford such imports is a problem of socio-economic development in which water plays a part, but is not determining; other production factors such as financial and human capital are the crucial determinants.

It is not yet clear to all Israelis that strong economies in the West Bank and Gaza are essential to a peaceful and secure future for Israel. However, a rapidly-growing minority is aware of the development pre-requisites for a comprehensive peace, and the discourse is being shaped slowly but favourably despite the high profile political manoeuvring over territory.

Although hopes for an Israeli agreement with both Syria and Lebanon were initially encouraged by speculation surrounding a possible Israeli withdrawal from southern Lebanon, by mid-1998 no resolution of the conflict was forthcoming and all sides remained firmly entrenched. The Golan Heights are considered by both Syrians and Israelis as crucial to the negotiation of a successful peace. Significant resources have been devoted to gaining and retaining the territory and considerable nationalist emotional energy has been expended in anticipating a new status for the tract and its water. The terrain is militarily strategic but the waters which flow from Golan into the upper Jordan River are of minor importance. They comprise only some 5% of current Israeli water use and about 1% of that of Syria. Owing to their location, the waters could not easily be used economically in Syria. The Baniyas tributary provides about 130 000 cu m of water per year; other Golan streams provide minor flows into Lake Tiberias. Certainly, in this instance, water poses no impediment to the negotiation of a settlement. Lebanon exports a similar quantity of water, via the Hasbani tributary, to the upper Jordan River. Despite its water surplus the Lebanese Government is by no means disposed to co-operate with Israel on this issue; it has often been alleged that Israel's original expansion into southern Lebanon was partly motivated by designs to divert the waters of the Litani River. The diplomatic distance between Lebanon and Israel is reinforced by the close relations between Syria and Lebanon. Any enhancement of Israel's water resources as a result of a *rapprochement* between Lebanon and Israel will require the approval of Syria. There is a good economic case for both parties to recognize the economic value of Lebanon's surplus water to its southern neighbour, but the political moment for such a recognition is not at hand. Although the Jordan riparians are among the region's most poorly-served with respect to water, the way that Israel, and, to a lesser extent, Jordan have surmounted the problem point the way to secure strategies of appropriate allocation and sound water re-use for all the Jordan riparians.

The Tigris-Euphrates system

The Tigris-Euphrates system is shared by Turkey, Syria, Iraq and Iran. The system is still in surplus in that use has yet to exhaust the water available. Turkey supplies more than 90% of the Euphrates' water and about one-half of the Tigris' flow. The remainder of the Tigris current originates in the Iranian tributaries.

Dam-building by Turkey during and since the 1970s has changed the regime of the Euphrates. The Keban (1975) and the Karakaya (1987) dams, each designed to store about 30 cu km of water, were part-financed by loans from the World Bank. Non-controversial power-generation and the control of flow were the stated purposes of these structures. The larger Atatürk Dam, with storage capacity of 46 cu km, was designed for consumptive water use in irrigation projects as well as for non-consumptive hydropower. The Atatürk reservoir filled in the early 1990s, and the project was financed by the Turkish Government, owing to a World Bank operating directive (OD 7.50) which states that structures that imply possible 'harmful' consequences for other riparians can only benefit from the Bank's concessionary financing if all potentially affected riparians approve the project. No such approval was forthcoming from Syria and Iraq. The hydrological impact of the reservoir on the Euphrates was easily predicted. The, albeit variable, flow of the river at the Turkish-Syrian border has decreased from some 30 cu km per year to just below 16 cu km per year. Since the mid-1970s an accumulated reduction in flow of about 150 cu km has resulted from filling reservoir storage, and evaporation from reservoirs at the three major, and other minor, structures. This accumulated reduction in flow is approximately equivalent to five years' total Euphrates' flow, or nine years of the 47% of flow which is the 500 cusec (cubic metres per second) average rate of flow promised to Syria by Turkey. Turkey argues that the flow is now reliable and assures its southern neighbours that the lower average flow will be guaranteed even after serious consumptive use of 10 or more cu km per year becomes the norm when associated irrigation projects are constructed and operational. Since the annual flow of the Euphrates was always unreliable, the average use of the flow by Syria and Iraq never exceeded an annual total of 15 cu km. Had Syria's irrigation projects undertaken in the 1970s proved more successful, then the consumptive use downstream of Turkey would have been greater. However, Syria is continuing to develop the irrigation potential of the Euphrates, diverting water to projects near Aleppo, where the soils are more productive than those in the Euphrates lowlands which proved so unrewarding in the 1970s.

Turkey has also initiated development projects for its Tigris waters which will almost certainly result in reductions in river flow and improvements in its reliability. The Tigris is of principal concern to Turkey and Iraq; Syria is only a minor riparian of the river, and the terrain makes the diversion of water into Syria costly. Iraq is the main beneficiary of the Tigris and any shortfall which might arise from the Euphrates as a result of Turkish upstream engineering could be made good by the development of the Tigris waters. Iraq, however, is in an extraordinary (if temporary) economic predicament. In July 1990, before the invasion of Kuwait, Iraq was importing 90% of its food requirements, implying that it was relying on imports for more than 90% of its water needs. In the context of the subsequent prolonged UN embargo imposed against Iraq there have been a number of significant shifts in Iraqi economic policy. Priority is now being given to food production, especially irrigated crops. However, the necessary emphasis being given to the use of land and water resources is undermined by a shortage of skilled farm labour; in the 1970s, accustomed to the spoils of the lucrative petroleum industry, Iraq came to rely heavily on Egyptian expatriates to operate its farms. The major water issue for Iraq is not the volume at its disposal—Iraq is almost as rich as Egypt in that respect, with a much smaller population—nor the quality of that water, but rather the intractable nature of its low-lying and saline soils and the absence, as yet, of appropriate rural institutions to mobilize the exceptional levels of expertise and technology needed to develop productive irrigation in such an unfriendly soil environment.

The Nile

The Nile has been of immense hydrological and economic importance to Egypt for thousands of years. The Nile waters are fundamental to Egypt's relations with the other riparian nations of the river. In the past Egyptian historical perspectives of the river and its tributaries have dominated riparian relations. The upstream riparians have become increasingly frustrated with the emphasis on precedent and what they regard as a biased perspective. In the early 1970s Egypt began to exhaust the water needed to meet all its food-raising, industrial and domestic needs. Since then it has met its burgeoning water requirements by importing 'virtual water'. The long established hydropolitical regime of the Nile Basin was based on two contrary objectives. The first was that of Egypt, supported by Sudan, and successfully sustained until the end of the 20th century, and was driven by the belief that there should be no impairment to the flow of Nile water to Egypt, since Egypt fully utilized all the water that arrived each year at Lake Nasser. The second objective, never successfully articulated by the upper riparians of the 'Blue' and the 'White' Nile regions was to assert their entitlement to some part of the flow of the upper tributaries.

Meanwhile, for the past three decades, discussions conducted under the auspices of the International Law Commission (ILC) of the United Nations on shared international freshwater have been taking place. In May 1997 the Commission's proposed convention on trans-national watercourses was agreed by the General Assembly of the United Nations. The deliberations of the Commission have been as principled as possible, but inevitably the pragmatism of the 1997 convention means that downstream interests such as those of Egypt and Sudan, as well as Syria and Israel (although their positions are complicated by being simultaneously upstream in some other watercourses), are being compromised to accommodate the upstream interests of riparians such as Ethiopia and the East African Lakes basin states in the Nile Basin, as well as Turkey in the Tigris-Euphrates system.

Just as the new international order evident since the demise of the former Soviet Union in 1990 has had a considerable impact on international relations in the Jordan basin, in the Nile basin also there is a perceptible shift in the level of discussion, the quality of the hydropolitical discourse and in the water-development initiatives being considered. There had been some basin-wide co-operation in the 1960s when the Hydromet Project, charged with the collection and sharing of hydrological data, was established by Nile Basin governments with international support. By the 1980s the project had foundered for a range of resource and organizational reasons. The potential for a new co-operative regime became evident in 1992 at three different levels of interaction: firstly, an annual meeting of regional water ministers was arranged; secondly, a twice-yearly TeccoNile (TAC since 1998) meeting of senior water resource engineers and planners from the respective riparian water ministries was instituted; thirdly, a series of annual meetings entitled Nile 2002 was inaugurated which involved representatives from the riparians as well as international specialists. In 1995 TeccoNile produced a Nile River Basin Action Plan (NRBAP) proposing that US $100m. be spent on projects to enhance basin-wide hydrological databases and other relevant capacity. For Egypt, this suited their goal of slow upstream development of Nile waters. The World Bank, along with a number of other international agencies, was asked to consider providing funding for the Plan. In December 1997 the proposal was reviewed by a panel of international water specialists and scientists and the response was significant for a number of reasons; although it was agreed that the concept of the basin could be useful in gaining some important water resource prizes—for example the storage of water upstream in places where it would not evaporate at the rate of three metres depth per year experienced at Lake Nasser—it was also noted that there were significant advantages in adopting planning scenarios at the sub-basin level, for example Egypt, the Sudan, Ethiopia and Eritrea for the Eastern ('Blue') Nile and other sub-basins in the Southern ('White') Nile. The panel also emphasized the need for sound economic principles as well as sound environmental principles to inspire all co-operative activity over Nile waters.

Some of these ideas and initiatives distinguish the 1990s from any previous decade. Whether the observed shifts in the level of hydropolitical activity and co-operation, as well as the new international water discourse, would have taken place without the change in the international order is impossible to establish. The evidence is very strong in the hydropolitics of both the Jordan basin and the Nile basin that the emergence of the single superpower in 1990 inspired a mixture of confidence and readiness to consider new positions, particularly on the part of stressed economies in Africa.

The economies of the Middle East and North Africa, and the governments responsible for them, have been fortunate that the emergence of the demographically-driven water shortages have occurred at a time when the global trading system is well able to handle such a growing deficit. The global trading system in grain can deliver 40,000m. cu m of water embedded in grain imports without any visible stress. No engineering system could mobilize one-tenth of that, and even then not with the flexibility of the trading system. It falls to those responsible for planning the appropriation of and/or access to the use of water for a nation's needs to take into account the status of the global soil water resources which have enabled the stress-free provision of water to the Middle East and North Africa since the 1970s. Information is not yet reliable on global soil moisture. For those with an inescapable need for flows of soil water via 'virtual water', the imperative to obtain best estimates of the volume of this water is clear. It is a paradox that the water pessimists may be wrong but their pessimism is a very useful political tool which can help the innovator to shift the eternally interdependent belief systems of the public and their politicians. The water optimists may be right but their optimism is dangerous because the notion enables politicians to treat water as a low policy priority, delay innovation and thereby appease those who perceive themselves to be prospering under the old order.

BIBLIOGRAPHY

ABARE (Australian Bureau of Agricultural and Resource Economics), *US grain policies and the world market*, ABARE policy monograph No 4, Canberra, Australian Government Publishing Service, 1989.

US agricultural policies on the eve of the 1995 farm bill, ABARE Policy Monograph No. 5, Canberra, Australian Government Publishing Service, Canberra, pp 195, 1995.

Allan, J. A., Overall perspectives on countries and regions, in Rogers, P. and Lydon, P. (Eds) *Water in the Arab World: perspectives and prognoses.* Cambridge, Massachusetts, Harvard University Press, pp 65–100, 1994.

The political economy of water [in the Jordan Basin]: reasons for optimism but long term caution, in Allan, J. A. and Court, J. H. O., *Water, peace and the Middle East, negotiating resources in the Jordan Basin,* London, Tauris Academic Studies, pp 75–94, 1996.

The Jordan Israel Peace Agreement–September 1994, Appendixes 1 and 2, in Allan, J. A., *Water, peace and the Middle East: negotiating resources in the Jordan Basin,* London, Tauris Academic Studies, pp 207–221, 1996.

The Israel-PLO Interim Agreement–September 1995, Appendixes 3 and 4, in Allan, J. A., *Water, peace and the Middle East: negotiating resources in the Jordan Basin,* London, Tauris Academic Studies, pp 223–240, 1996.

Allan, J. A. and Radwan, L., Perceptions of the value of water and water environments, *GeoForum.* Special issue edition by Allan, J. A. and Radwan, L. on the theme *Perceptions of the value of water and water environments,* 1998.

Arab Research Centre, Water, food and trade in the Middle East, Proceedings of a conference in Cairo convened by the Arab Research Centre and the Ministry of Agriculture and Land Reclamation, London, Arab Research Centre, 1995.

Bayazit M. and Avci, I., Water resources of Turkey: potential, planning, development and management, *Water Resources Development,* Vol 13, pp 443–452, 1997.

Brown, L, *Who will feed China: Wake-Up Call for a Small Planet?* Washington DC, World Watchmore Series, 1996.

Tough choices: facing the Challenge of Food Scarcity, Washington DC, World Watch Institute, Environmental Alert Series, 1996.

Brown, L. R. and Kane, H., *Full house: reassessing the Earth's Population Carrying Capacity,* Washington DC, World Watch Institute, Environmental Alert Series, 1995.

Conway, D, *The development of a grid-based hydrologic model of the Blue Nile and the sensitivity of Nile discharge to climate change,* PhD thesis, Climate Research Unit, University of East Anglia, UK, 1993.

Conway, D. and Hulme, M., Recent fluctuations in precipitation and runoff over the Nile sub-basins and their impact on Nile discharge. *Climate Change,* Vol. 25, 127–152, 1993.

The impacts of climate variability and future climate change in the Nile basin on water resources in Egypt, *Water Resources Development,* 12 (3) 277–296, 1996.

Conway, D., Krol, M., Alvamo, J. and Hulme, M., Future availability of water in 1996: the interaction of global, regional and basin scale driving forces in the Nile Basin, *Ambio* 25 (5) 336-342, 1996.

Dyson, T., Population growth and food production: recent global and regional trends, *Population and Development Review,* 1994.

FAO, *The water resources of Africa,* Rome, FAO, Land and Water Development Division, Aquistat programme, 1995.

Irrigation in Africa, Rome, FAO, Land and Water Development Division, Aquistat Programme, 1995.

Water resources of the Near East region: a review, Rome, FAO, Land and Water Development Division, Aquistat Programme, 1997.

Irrigation in the Near East region in figures, Water Reports No. 9, Rome, FAO, Land and Water Development Division, Aquistat Programme, 1997.

Feitelson, E., and Allan, J. A., The context and process of water policy transformation, *GeoForum,* 1998.

GEWEX, Monitoring soil water at the continental scale, GEWEX *Newsletter,* February 1997.

Gleick, P., An introduction to global freshwater issues, in Gleick, P. (Ed) *Water in crisis,* Oxford and New York, Oxford University Press, 1993.

Goleman, D., *Vital lies, simple truths,* London, Bloomsbury, 1997.

Higazi, Abd al-Aziz, Lecture in London at the Arab Research Centre, 1995.

Howell, P. P. and Allan, J. A., *The Nile: sharing a scarce resource,* Cambridge, Cambridge University Press, 1995.

IFPRI (International Food Production Research Institute), *China will remain a grain importer,* IFPRI Report, Washington, DC, 1997.

Global food security, IFPRI Report, Washington, DC, 1995.

Islam, N., *Population and food in the early 21st century: meeting future food demand of a rising population,* IFPRI report, Washington, DC, 1995.

Le Heron, R., *Globalized agriculture,* Oxford, Pergamon Press, 1993.

Le Heron, R. and Roche, M., A 'fresh' place in food's space, *Area,* 1995.

L'vovich, M. I., *Water resources in the future,* Moscow, Prosveshcheniye, 1969. (In Russian)

Water resources and their future, Moscow, Mysl' Publishing, 1974. (In Russian) US translation American Geophysical Union, Washington, DC, 1979.

McCaffrey, S., The 1997 United Nations Convention of the non-navigational uses of international watercourses, at the Second International Conference on *Water: legal and regulatory issues,* Dundee, CEPMLP, Dundee University, 1997.

Legal issues in the United Nations Convention on International Watercourses: prospects and pitfalls, paper delivered at World Bank Seminar on international watercourses, Washington, World Bank, 1997.

McCaffrey, S. and Sinjela, M., The United Nations Convention on International Watercourses, *American Journal of International Law,* Vol 92, 1998.

Postel, S., *Last oasis: facing water scarcity,* New York, Norton, 1997.

Rogers, P, Water in a future Middle East, in Rogers, P. and Lydon, P. (Eds) *Water in the Arab World: perspectives and prognoses,* Cambridge, Massachusetts, Harvard University Press, 1995.

Rosengrat, M. and Schleyer, R. G., *Vision for food, agriculture and environment,* A 2020 Vision IFPRI Paper, Washington, DC, 1995.

Shiklamanov, I. A. and Sokolov, A. A., Methodological basis of world water balance investigation and computation, in *Proceedings of the Hamburg Workshop,* IAHS Publication Bo. 148, pp 77–91, 1981.

Shiklamanov, I. A., Large-scale water transfer, in Rodda, J., (Ed.) *Facets of hydrology,* Vol II, London, John Wiley, pp 345–387, 1985.

Shiklomanov, I. A., 'Water consumption, water availability and large-scale water projects in the world', in *Proceedings of the international symposium on the impact of large water projects on the environment,* UNESCO, Paris, 21–31 October 1986.

Shiklamanov, I. A. and Markova, O. A., *Specific water availability of runoff transfers in the world,* Leningrad, Gidrometeoizdat, 1987.

World Bank, *World development report: the state in a changing world,* Washington, World Bank, 1997.

THE RELIGIONS OF THE MIDDLE EAST AND NORTH AFRICA

Islam

R. B. SERJEANT

Islam is a major world religion and the faith predominating throughout the Middle East (with the exception of Israel) and North Africa. There are substantial Christian minorities in some countries (e.g. Lebanon) and communities of oriental Jews and other faiths, for centuries integrated with the Muslim majority. Islam is not only a highly developed religious system, but also an established and distinctive culture embracing every aspect of human activity from theology, philosophy and literature to the visual arts and even the individual's routine daily conduct. Its characteristic intellectual manifestation, therefore, is in the field of Islamic law, the *Shari'a*. Though in origin a Semitic Arabian faith, Islam was also the inheritor of the legacy of classical Greek and Roman civilization and, in its major phase of intellectual, social and cultural development after its emergence from its Arabian womb, it was affected by Christian, Jewish and Persian civilization. In turn, Greek scientific and philosophical writings—in the form of direct translations into Arabic or as a principal element in the books of Arab scholars—began to enter medieval Europe in Latin renderings about the early 12th century from the brilliant intellectual circles of Islamic Spain, and formed a potent factor in the little Renaissance of western Europe.

Islamic civilization had, by about the 18th century, clearly lost its initiative to the ascendant West and has not since regained it. Today, however, certain oil-rich Arab states, notably Saudi Arabia and Kuwait, have made significant progress in the world of international finance and mercantilism, engaging in activities such as the provision of Islamic banking services, for which there has been an increase in demand over the last two decades.

HISTORY

The founder of the religion of Islam was the Prophet Muhammad b. 'Abdullah, born about AD 570, a member of the noble house of Hashim, belonging to the 'Abd Manaf clan, itself a part of the Quraish tribal confederation of Mecca. 'Abd Manaf may be described as semi-priestly since they had the privilege of certain functions during the annual pilgrimage to the Meccan Ka'ba, a cube-shaped temple set in the sacred enclave (*haram*). Quraish controlled this enclave which was maintained inviolate from war or killing, and they had established a pre-eminence and loose hegemony even, over many Arabian tribes which they had induced to enter a trading alliance extending over the main Arabian land routes, north and south, east and west. Muhammad clashed with the powerful Quraish leaders in Mecca (temple guardians, chiefs, merchant adventurers), when, aged about 40, he began to proclaim the worship of one God, Allah, as against their multiplicity of gods. The Quraish leaders were contemptuous of his mission.

While his uncle Abu Talib, head of the house of Hashim, lived, he protected Muhammad from physical harm, but after his death Muhammad sought protection from tribes outside Mecca. However, even after asking to remain quietly without preaching, they would not accept him and Thaqif of Taif (at-Ta 'if) drove him roughly away. Ultimately pilgrims of the Aws and Khazraj tribes of Yathrib (Medina), some 200 miles north of Mecca, agreed to protect him there, undertaking to associate no other god with Allah and accepting certain moral stipulations. Muhammad left Mecca with his Companion, Abu Bakr, in the year 622—this is the year of the *hijra* or hegira.

Arriving in Yathrib, Muhammad formed a federation or community (*umma*) of Aws and Khazraj known as the 'Supporters' (*Ansar*), followed by their Jewish client tribes, and the 'Emigrants' (*Muhajirun*—his refugee Quraish adherents) with himself as the ultimate arbiter of the *umma* as a whole. However, there remained a local opposition covertly antagonistic to him, the *Munafiqun*, rendered as 'Hypocrites'. Two internal issues had now to be fought by Muhammad—the enforcement of his position as theocratic head of the federation, and the acquisition of revenue to maintain his position; externally, he adopted an aggressive attitude towards the Meccan Quraish.

In Yathrib his disposal of the Jewish tribes who made common cause with the 'Hypocrites' improved his financial position. Muhammad overcame the Meccan Quraish more as a result of skilful political manoeuvre than of occasional armed clashes, and in year 8 he entered Mecca peacefully. He had previously declared Yathrib a sacred enclave (*haram*), renaming it Medina, the City (of the Prophet)—the two cities known as al-Haraman have become the holy land of Islam. Muhammad was conciliatory towards his defeated Quraish kinsmen, and after his success in Ta'if, south of Mecca, deputations came from the Arabian tribes to make terms with the Prophet—the heritor of the influence of the Meccan Quraish.

Early Islam

The two main tenets of Islam are embodied in the formula of the creed, 'There is no god but Allah and Muhammad is the Apostle of God'. Unitarianism (*tawhid*), as opposed to polytheism (*shirk*) or making partners with God, is Islam's basic principle, coupled with the authority conferred on Muhammad by God. Muhammad made little change to the ancient Arabian religion—he abolished idolatry but confirmed the pilgrimage to the Ka'ba; the Koran, the sacred Book in Arabic revealed to Muhammad for his people, lays down certain social and moral rules. Among these are the condemnation of usury or interest (*riba*) on loans and the prohibition of wine (*khamr*)—both ordinances have always been difficult to enforce. In many respects, the similarities between the old and new faiths enabled Arabia to embrace Islam with relative ease. While there is incontrovertible evidence of Muhammad's contact with Judaism, and even with Christianity, and the Koran contains versions of narrative known to the sacred books of these faiths, yet these are used to point purely Arabian morals. The limited social law laid down by the Koran is supplemented by a body of law and precept derived from the *Hadith* or Tradition of Muhammad's practice (*Sunna*) at Medina, and welded into the Islamic system, mainly in its second and third centuries.

Subsequent History

Immediately after Muhammad's death in 632, Abu Bakr, delegated by the Prophet to lead the prayer during his last indisposition, became his successor or Caliph. Some Medinan 'Supporters' had attempted a breakaway from Quraish overlordship but Abu Bakr adroitly persuaded them to accept his succession. Office in Arabia, generally speaking, is hereditary within a family group, though elective within that group, and Abu Bakr's action had taken no account of the claims of 'Ali, the Prophet's cousin and son-in-law. The house of Hashim, to which Muhammad and 'Ali belonged, was plainly aggrieved that a member of a minor Quraish clan, not of the 'house' (*Bait*) of their ancestor, Quṣaiy, the holder of religious offices in Mecca which he bequeathed to his descendants, should have snatched supreme power. Muhammad's Arabian coalition also weakened, the tribes particularly objecting to paying taxes to Medina, but Abu Bakr's uncompromising leadership reasserted cohesion. Expansionist thrusts beyond Arabia were undertaken during his Caliphate, continued under his successors 'Umar and 'Uthman, diverting tribal energies to profitable warfare in Mesopotamia, Palestine-Syria, Egypt and Persia. Muslim armies were eventually to conquer North Africa, much of Spain, parts of France, and even besiege Rome, while in the east they later penetrated to Central Asia and India.

During 'Uthman's tenure the pace of conquest temporarily slackened and the turbulent tribes, now settled in southern Iraq and Egypt, began to dispute the Caliph's disposal of plunder and revenue, maintaining that he favoured members of his own house unduly. A delegation of tribal malcontents from Egypt murdered 'Uthman in the holy city of Medina, and in the resultant confusion 'Ali, Muhammad's cousin, was elected Caliph with the support of the tribesmen responsible for murdering 'Uthman. This raised grave constitutional problems for the young Muslim state, and is regarded as the origin of the first and greatest schism in Islam.

If legitimist arguments were the sole consideration 'Ali's claims to succession would appear to be superior, but his claim had already been superseded by 'Uthman—whose father belonged to the Umaiya clan which had opposed Muhammad, but whose mother was of Hashim. 'Uthman naturally appointed Umaiya men loyal to him to commands in the Empire, notably Mu'awiya—the son of Abu Sufyan who had led Quraish opposition to Muhammad at Mecca, but was later reconciled with him—as governor of Syria. Mu'awiya demanded 'Uthman's murderers be brought to justice in accordance with the law, but 'Ali, unable to deliver the murderers from among his supporters, was driven by events to take up arms against Mu'awiya. When they clashed at Siffin, in Syria, 'Ali was forced, against his better judgement, to submit to the arbitration of the Koran and *Sunna*, thus automatically losing the position of supreme arbiter, inherited by the Caliphs from Muhammad. Although history is silent as to what the arbiters actually judged upon, it was most likely as to whether 'Ali had broken the law established by Muhammad, and that he was held to have sheltered unprovoked murderers. The arbiters deposed him from the Caliphial office, though historians allege trickery entered into their action.

'Ali shortly after was murdered by one of a group of his former supporters which had come out against the arbitration it had first urged upon him. This group, the Khawarij, is commonly held to be the forerunner of the Ibadis of Oman and elsewhere. Mu'awiya became Caliph and founder of the Umaiyad dynasty with its capital at Damascus. The ambitions of the Hashim house were not, however, allayed, and when Umaiyad troops slew 'Ali's son Husain at Karbala' in southern Iraq they created the greatest Shi'a martyr (see Religious Groupings, p. 29).

The house of Hashim also included the descendants of 'Abbas the Prophet's uncle, but 'Abbas had opposed Muhammad until late in his life. The 'Abbasids made common cause with the 'Ali-id Shi'a against the Umaiyads, but were evidently abler in the political field. In the Umaiyad empire the Arabian tribes formed a kind of military élite but were constantly at factious war with one another. The Hashimites rode to power on the back of a rebellion against the Umaiyads which broke out in Khurasan in eastern Persia, but it was the 'Abbasid branch of Hashim which assumed the Caliphate and ruled from the capital they founded at Baghdad.

The 'Abbasid Caliphate endured up to the destruction of Baghdad in 1258 by the devastating Mongol invaders of the eastern empire, but the Caliphs had long been mere instruments in the hands of Turkish and other mercenaries, and the unwieldy empire had fragmented into independent states which rose and fell, though they mostly conceded nominal allegiance to the 'Abbasid Caliphs.

The Mongol Ilkhanid sovereigns, now turned Muslim, were in turn displaced by the conquests of Tamerlane at the end of the 14th century. In fact the Islamic empire had largely been taken over by Turkic soldiery. The Mameluke or Slave rulers of medieval Egypt who followed the Aiyubid (Kurdish) dynasty of Salah ud-Din (Saladin) were mainly Turks or Circassians. It was they who checked the Mongol advance at 'Ain Jalut in Palestine (1260). The Ottoman Turks captured Constantinople in 1453, and took Egypt from the Mamelukes in 1516, subsequently occupying the Hijaz where the Ashraf, descendants of the Prophet, ruled in Mecca and Medina, under first Mameluke then Turkish suzerainty. In 1533 the Turks took Baghdad, and Iraq became part of the Ottoman Empire. The Ottoman Sultans assumed the title of Caliph—though in Islamic constitutional theory it is not easy to justify this. The Ottoman Caliphs endured until the Caliphate was abolished by Mustafa Kemal in 1924. The Turks have always been characterized by their adherence to Sunni orthodoxy.

Throughout history the 'Ali-ids have constantly asserted their right to be the Imams or leaders of the Muslim community—

this in the religious and political senses, since Islam is fundamentally theocratic. The Shi'a, or followers of 'Ali and his descendants, were in constant rebellion against the 'Abbasids and came to form a distinct schismatic group of legitimist sects—at one time the Fatimid Shi'a rulers of Egypt were near to conquering the main part of the Islamic world. The main Shi'a sects today are the Ithna'asharis, the Isma'ilis, and the near-orthodox Zaidis of Yemen. The Safavids who conquered Persia at the beginning of the 16th century brought it finally into the Shi'a fold. Sunni Hashimite dynasties flourish today in Jordan and Morocco as they did until fairly recently in Iraq and Libya, and the Shi'a Zaidi ruler of Yemen was only displaced in 1962. The main difference between Sunnis and Shi'a concerns the Imamate, i.e. the temporal and spiritual leadership of Islam; for Sunnis, while they respect the Prophet's house, do not consider the Imam must be a member of it—the Shi'a insist on an Imam of the descendants of 'Ali and Fatima his wife, the Prophet's daughter.

It has been too readily assumed that, during the later Middle Ages and long Turkish domination, the Islamic Middle East was completely stagnant. The shift in economic patterns after the discovery of the New World and the Cape route to India, coupled with widening Western intellectual horizons and the development of science and technology, did push European culture far ahead of the Muslim Middle East. It was confronted by a vigorous and hostile Christianity intent on proselytizing in its very homelands. Muslims had to face the challenge of the ideas and attitudes of Christian missionaries. Muslim thinkers like Muhammad 'Abduh (1849–1905) of Egypt and his school asserted that Islam had become heavily overlaid with false notions—hence its decline; like earlier reformers they were convinced that present difficulties could be resolved by reversion to an (idealized) pure, primitive Islam. Sometimes, in effect, this meant reinterpreting religious literature to suit attitudes and ideas of modern times—as for instance when the virtual prohibition of polygamy was identified in the restrictions which define the practice. Since the earlier modern days political leaders like Mustafa Kemal of Turkey have often taken drastic measures, secularizing the state itself even in the sensitive field of education, and accusing the more conservative forms of Islam of blocking progress. In recent years the Islamic Middle East has witnessed regimes ranging from the strong supporters of traditional Islam—like Saudi Arabia and Libya—to the anti-religious Marxist group which controlled Aden (the People's Democratic Republic of Yemen) until 1990. In Libya, nevertheless, Colonel Qaddafi has published *The Green Book*, embodying his personal solution (very socialist in tone) of problems of democracy and economics. Theocratic Shi'a Iran has a distinctive character of its own.

ISLAMIC LAW

Orthodox Sunni Islam finds its main expression in *Shari'a* law which it regards with great veneration. The Sunnis have crystallized into four schools or rites (*madhhab*), all of which are recognized as valid. Although in practice the adherents of one school can sometimes be at loggerheads with another, in modern times it is claimed that the law of any one of the rites can be applied to a case. The schools, named after their founders, are the Hanbali, regarded as the strictest, with adherents mainly in Saudi Arabia; the Shafi'is, the widest in extent with adherents in Egypt, Palestine-Syria, South Arabia and the Far East; the moderate Hanafi school which was the official rite of the Ottoman Turkish empire and to which most Muslims in the Indian sub-continent belong; and the Malikis of the North African states, Nigeria and Sudan. The Shi'ite sects have developed their own law, and give prominence to *ijtihad*, the forming of independent judgement, whereas the Sunnis are more bound by *taqlid* or following ancient models. However, as the law of Sunnis, the moderate Shi'a and the Ibadis is basically derived from the same sources, the differences are generally more of emphasis than principle.

The completely Islamic state as the theorists envisage it, run in conformity with the rules of the *Shari'a*, has probably never been achieved, and people's practice is often at variance with some or other requirements of *Shari'a*. The imprint of Islam is nevertheless unmistakably evident, in one way or another, on almost every country in this volume.

Civil Courts

In modern states of the Islamic world there exists, side by side with the *Shari'a* court (judging cases on personal status, marriage, divorce, etc.), the secular court which has a wide jurisdiction (based on Western codes of law) in civil and criminal matters. This court is competent to give judgment irrespective of the creed or race of the defendant.

Islamic Law as Applying to Minorities

In cases of minorities (Christian or Jewish) residing as a community in Muslim countries, spiritual councils are established where judgment is passed according to the law of the community, in matters concerning personal status, under the jurisdiction of the recognized head of that community.

Tribal Courts

In steppe and mountain areas of some countries a proportion of the population maintain tribal courts which administer law and justice in accordance with ancient custom and tribal procedure. Among tribes these courts are often more popular than *Shari'a* courts, because justice is swifter. Conciliation (*sulh*) is generally their objective. There is, nonetheless, constant pressure to eliminate customary practices where they are unequivocally seen to be contrary to Islamic principles.

Awqaf

In Muslim countries the law governing *awqaf* (singular, *waqf*) (called in North Africa *habous* (*hubus*)) is the law applied to religious and charitable endowments, trust and settlements. This important Islamic institution is administered in most Muslim countries by a special ministry of *awqaf*. *Awqaf*, or endowments, are pious bequests made by Muslims for the upkeep of religious institutions, public benefits, etc. Family *awqaf* provide an income partly for religious purposes and partly for the original donor's family.

SUFIS

In common with other religions where simple observance of a code of law and morals proves spiritually unsatisfying, some Muslims have turned to mysticism. From early times Islamic mystics existed known as Sufis, allegedly owing to their wearing a woollen garment. They seek complete identification with the Supreme Being, and annihilation of the self—the existence of which they term polytheism (*shirk*). The learned doctors of Islam often think ill of the Sufis, and indeed rogues and wandering mendicants found Sufism a convenient means of livelihood. Certain Sufi groups allowed themselves dispensations and, as stimulants, even used hashish and opium, which are not sanctioned by the Islamic moral code. The Sufis became organized in what are loosely called brotherhoods (*turuq*; singular, *tariqa*), and have to a large extent been incorporated into the structure of orthodox Islamic society. Some *turuq* induce ecstatic states by their performance of the *dhikr*, meaning, literally, the mentioning (of Allah). Today there is much disapproval of the more extravagant manifestations of the Sufis and in some places these have been banned entirely.

BELIEF AND PRACTICE

'Islam' means the act of submitting or resigning oneself to God, and a Muslim is one who resigns or submits himself to God. Muslims disapprove of the term 'Muhammadan' for the faith of Islam, since they worship Allah, and Muhammad is only the Apostle of Allah whose duty it was to convey revelation, though he is regarded as the 'Best of Mankind'. He is the Seal (*Khatam*) of the prophets, i.e. the ultimate Prophet in a long series in which both Moses and Jesus figure. They are revered, but, like Muhammad the Prophet, they are not worshipped.

Nearly all Muslims agree on acceptance of six articles of the faith of Islam: (i) Belief in God; (ii) in His angels; (iii) in His revealed books; (iv) in His Apostles; (v) in the Resurrection and Day of Judgement; and (vi) in His predestination of good and evil.

Faith includes works, and certain practices are obligatory on the believing Muslim. These are five in number:

1. The recital of the creed (*Shahada*)—'There is no god but God (Allah) and Muhammad is the Apostle of God.' This formula is embodied in the call to prayer made by the *muezzin* (announcer) from the minaret of the mosque before each of the five daily prayers.

2. The performance of the Prayer (*Salat*) at the five appointed canonical times—in the early dawn before the sun has risen above the horizon, in the early afternoon when the sun has begun to decline, later when the sun is about midway in its course towards setting, immediately after sunset, in the evening between the disappearance of the red glow in the west and bedtime. In prayer Muslims face towards the Ka'ba in Mecca. They unroll prayer mats and pray in a mosque (place of prostration), at home, or wherever they may be, bowing and prostrating themselves before God and reciting set verses in Arabic from the Koran. On Fridays it is obligatory for men to attend congregational Prayer in the central mosque of the quarter in which they live—women do not normally attend. On this occasion formal prayers are preceded by a sermon.

3. The payment of the legal alms (*Zakat*). In early times this contribution was collected by officials of the Islamic state, and devoted to the relief of the poor, debtors, travellers and to other charitable and state purposes, and it often became, in effect, a purely secular tax on crops. Nowadays the fulfilment of this religious obligation is left to the conscience of the individual believer. The *zakat* given at the breaking of the fast at the end of Ramadan, for example, is a voluntary gift of provisions.

4. The 30 days of the fast in the month of Ramadan, the ninth month in the lunar year. As the lunar calendar is shorter by 11 days than the solar calendar, Ramadan moves from the hottest to the coldest seasons of the solar year. It is observed as a fast from dawn to sunset each day by all adults in normal health, during which time no food or drink may be taken. The sick, pregnant women, travellers and children are exempt; some states exempt students, soldiers and factory workers. The fast ends with one of the two major Muslim festivals, 'Id al-Fitr.

5. The pilgrimage (*Hajj*) to Mecca. Every Muslim is obliged, circumstances permitting, to perform this at least once in his lifetime, and when accomplished he may assume the title, *Hajji*. More than two million pilgrims go each year to Mecca, but the holy cities of Mecca and Medina are prohibited to non-Muslims.

Before entering the sacred area around Mecca by the seventh day of Dhu'l-Hijja, the twelfth month of the Muslim year, pilgrims must don the *ihram*, consisting of two unseamed lengths of white cloth, indicating that they are entering a state of consecration and casting off what is ritually impure. The pilgrims circumambulate the Ka'ba seven times, endeavouring to kiss the sacred Black Stone. Later they run seven times between the nearby twin hills of Safa and Marwah (now covered in by an immense hall), thus recalling Hagar's desperate search for water for her child Ishmael (from whom the Arabs claim descent). On the eighth day of the month the pilgrims leave the city for Mina, a small town six miles to the east. Then, before sunrise of the next day, all make for the plain below Mount 'Arafat, some 12 miles east of Mecca, where they pass the day in prayers and recitation until sunset. This point is the climax of the pilgrimage when the whole gathering returns, first to Muzdalifah where it spends the night, then to Mina where pilgrims stone the devil represented by three heaps of stones (*jamra*). The devil is said to have appeared to Abraham here and to have been driven away by Abraham throwing stones at him. This day, the 10th of Dhu'l-Hijja, is 'Id al-Adha, the Feast of the Sacrifice, and the pilgrims sacrifice an animal, usually a sheep, and have their heads shaved by one of the barbers at Mina. They return to Mecca that evening. In recent years the increasing number of pilgrims arriving (especially by air) has presented the Saudi authorities, guardians of the Holy Places, with major problems of organization, supply, health and public order. In 1988, following the tragic events of July 1987, when 402 people, including 275 Iranian pilgrims, lost their lives in clashes between the Iranian and Saudi security forces, and in order to reduce overcrowding, the Saudi Government imposed national quotas for the numbers of pilgrims performing the *Hajj*. However, overcrowding has continued to present serious problems, and tragic incidents similar to that of 1988 have become worryingly frequent in recent years.

The Holy War (*Jihad*) against the infidel was the means whereby Arab Muslim rule made its immense expansion in the first centuries of Islam, but despite pressures to do so, it has never been elevated to form a sixth Pillar of Islam. Today some theologians interpret *jihad* in a less literal sense as the combating of evil, but it is significant that the Afghan guerrillas, who resisted the Soviet presence in their country, called themselves *mujahidin*, i.e. those who wage the *jihad* against the enemies of Islam.

The Koran (*Qur'an*, 'recital', 'reading') is for Muslims the very Word of God. The Koran consists of 114 chapters (*surah*) of uneven length, the longest coming first after the brief opening chapter called *al-Fatiha*. (The Koran is about as long as the New Testament). Al-Fatiha (The Opener) commences (as does every chapter) with the words, '*Bismillahi 'l-Rahmani 'l-Rahim*', 'In the name of God, the Compassionate, the Merciful', and forms part of the ritual five prayers (*salat*). Other special verses and chapters are also used on a variety of occasions, and, of course, Muslim children are taught to recite by heart a portion of the Koran or, preferably, the whole of it. The Koran has been the subject of vast written commentaries, but translation into other languages is not much approved by Muslims, though interlinear translations (a line of Koran underneath which is a line of translation) are used, and a number of modern translations into English and most other languages exist. The earlier (Meccan) chapters of the Koran speak of the unity of God and his wonders, of the Day of Judgement and Paradise, while the Medinan chapters tend to be occupied more with social legislation for marriage, divorce, personal and communal behaviour. The definitive redaction of the Koran was ordered by the Caliph 'Uthman (644–56).

HOLY PLACES

Mecca: Hijaz province of Saudi Arabia. Mecca is centred around the Ka'ba, the most venerated building in Islam, traditionally held to have been founded by Abraham, recognized by Islam also as a prophet. It stands in the centre of the vast courtyard of the Great Mosque and has the form of a cube; its construction is of local grey stone and its walls are draped with a black curtain embroidered with a strip of writing containing verses from the Koran. In the eastern corner is set the famous Black Stone. The enlarging of the Great Mosque commenced under the second Caliph 'Umar. Both the Ka'ba and Great Mosque have undergone many renovations, notably since 1952. Mecca is the centre of the annual pilgrimage from all Muslim countries.

Al-Medina (*The City*, i.e. of the Prophet): Hijaz province of Saudi Arabia. Medina, formerly called Yathrib, was created as a sacred enclave (*haram*) by Muhammad, who died there in the year 11 of the *hijra* and was buried in the Mosque of the Prophet. Close to his tomb are those of his companions and successors, Abu Bakr and 'Umar, and a little further away, that of his daughter Fatima. Frequently damaged, restored and enlarged, the mosque building was extensively renovated by the Saudi Government in 1955.

Jerusalem (Arabic *al-Quds* or *Bait al-Maqdis, The Hallowed/Consecrated*): West Bank (currently annexed by Israel). Jerusalem is Islam's next most holy city after al-Haraman (Mecca and Medina), not only because it is associated with so many pre-Islamic prophets, but because Muhammad himself is popularly held to have made the 'Night Journey' there. Jerusalem contains the magnificent Islamic shrine, the Dome of the Rock (688–91), built by the Caliph 'Abd al-Malik, and the famous al-Masjid al-Aqsa, severely damaged by arson a few years ago.

Hebron (Habrun): West Bank. The Mosque of Abraham, called al-Khalil, the 'Friend of God', is built over the tomb of Abraham, the Cave of Machpelah; it also contains the tombs of Sarah, Isaac, Rebecca, Jacob, and Leah. The shrine is revered by Muslims and Jews, and is also important to Christians.

Qairawan: Tunisia. The city is regarded as a holy place for Muslims, seven pilgrimages to the Great Mosque of Sidi 'Uqbah b. Nafi' (an early Muslim general who founded Qairawan as a base for the Muslim invaders of North Africa) being considered the equivalent of one pilgrimage to Mecca.

Muley Idris: Morocco. The shrine at the burial-place of the founder of the Idrisid dynasty in the year 687, at Walili, near Fez.

Every Middle Eastern country has a multitude of shrines and saints' tombs held in veneration, except Wahhabi states which consider saint cults to be polytheism (*shirk*). In Turkey, however, the policy of secularization led to Aya Sofya Mosque (St Sophia) being turned into a museum.

The following shrines are associated with the Shi'a or Legitimist sects of Islam.

Mashhad (Meshed): Iran. The city is famous for the shrine of Imam 'Ali ar-Rida/Riza, the eighth Imam of the Ithna'ashari group, which attracts some hundred thousand pilgrims each year. The shrine is surrounded by buildings with religious or historical associations.

Qom: Iran. A Shi'a centre, it is venerated as having the tomb of Fatima, the sister of Imam ar-Rida/Riza, and those of hundreds of saints and kings including Imams 'Ali b. Ja'far and Ibrahim, Shah Safi and Shah 'Abbas II. Following the Iranian Revolution it became the centre favoured by Ayatollah Khomeini.

Najaf: Iraq. Mashhad 'Ali, reputed to be constructed over the place where 'Ali b. Abi Talib, fourth Caliph, the cousin and son-in-law of Muhammad, is buried, is a most venerated Shi'a shrine, drawing many pilgrims.

Karbala': Iraq. The shrine of Husain b. 'Ali where, at Mashhad Husain, he was slain with most of his family, is today more venerated by the Shi'a than the Mashhad 'Ali. 'Ashoura Day (10th Muharram) when Husain was killed is commemorated by passion plays (*ta'ziya*) and religious processions during which the drama of his death is re-enacted with extravagant expressions of emotion.

Baghdad: Iraq. The Kazimain/Kadhimain Mosque is a celebrated Shi'a shrine containing the tomb of Musa al-Kazim/Kadhim, the seventh Imam of the Ithna'asharis.

RELIGIOUS GROUPINGS

Sunnis

The great majority, probably over 80% of Muslims, are Sunni, followers of the *Sunna*, i.e. the way, course, rule or manner of conduct of Prophet Muhammad; they are generally called 'Orthodox'. The Sunnis recognize the first four Caliphs (Abu Bakr, 'Umar, 'Uthman, 'Ali) as Rashidun, i.e. following the right course. They base their *Sunna* upon the Koran and 'Six Books' of Traditions, and are organized in four Orthodox schools or rites (*madhhab*), all of equal standing within the Orthodox fold. Many Muslims today prefer to avoid identification with any single school and simply call themselves Muslim or Sunni.

Wahhabis

The adherents of 'Wahhabism' strongly disapprove of this title by which they are known outside their own group, for they call themselves Muwahhidun or Unitarians. In fact they belong to the strict Hanbali school following its noted exponent, the 13th/14th century Syrian reformer Ibn Taimiyah. The founder of 'Wahhabism', Muhammad b. 'Abd al-Wahhab of Arabian Najd (1703–87), sought to return to the pristine purity of early Islam freed from all accretions and what he regarded as innovations contrary to its true spirit, such as saint worship, lax sexual practices, and superstition. His doctrine was accepted by the chief Muhammad b. Sa'ud of Dar'iya (near ar-Riyadh). Ibn Sa'ud and his son 'Abd al-'Aziz—who proved a capable general—conquered much of Arabia. Medina fell in 1804 and Mecca in 1806 to Sa'ud, son of 'Abd al-'Aziz, but after his death in 1814 the Wahhabis were gradually broken by the armies of the Pasha of Egypt, Muhammad 'Ali, acting nominally on behalf of the Ottoman Sultan of Turkey. After varying fortunes in the 19th century the Wahhabis emerged as an Arabian power in the opening years of the 20th century. By the close of 1925 they held the Holy Cities and Jeddah and are today the strongest power in the Arabian Peninsula. Though Wahhabism remains the strictest of the Orthodox groups, Saudi Arabia has made some accommodation to modern times.

The Turuq or Religious Orders

In many Middle Eastern countries the religious orders (*turuq*) have important political-cum-religious roles in society. There are the widely spread Qadiriya who, with Tijaniya, are found in North Africa, the Khatmiya in Sudan, the Rifa'iya in Egypt and Syria, to pick out a few at random. The West has no organizations exactly equivalent to these Sufi orders into which an individual has to be initiated, and in which, by dint of ascetic exercises and study, he may attain degrees of mystical enlightenment—this can also bring moral influence over his fellow men. The Orders may be Sunni or Shi'a; some few Orders are even so unconventional as to be hardly Islamic at all. Although Sufism is essentially uninterested in worldly politics, the *turuq* have, nonetheless, at times been drawn into the political arena. It was the Orthodox reformist Sanusi Order that played the most significant role in our time. The Grand Sanusi, Muhammad b. 'Ali, born at Mustaghanem in Algeria of a Sharif family, founded the first *zawiya* or lodge of the Sanusis in 1837. The Sanusi *tariqa* is distinguished for its exacting standards of personal morality. The Sanusis set up a network of lodges in Cyrenaica (Libya) and put up strong resistance to Italian colonization. The Grand Sanusi was recognized as King Idris of Libya in 1951, but lost his throne in the military revolt led by Colonel Qaddafi in 1969.

The Muslim Brothers (al-Ikhwan al-Muslimun)

Founded in Egypt by Hasan al-Banna in 1928, the career of the Muslim Brothers in Middle East political history has been active and often violent. Al-Banna considered westernizing influences and intellectual emancipation in Egypt to be weakening Islam, itself in decline since the ideal age of the first four Caliphs. So, the movement has a rigidity and intolerant attitude towards Christians and Jews, but this may even extend to other Muslim groups. Al-Banna was a member of a *tariqa* and the Brothers (*Ikhwan*) were initially organized along *tariqa* lines with a graded membership. This membership is not restricted to particular social classes but finds support especially among Azhar students, particularly those graduates of the Azhar who hold teaching and minor religious office. By 1939 the Brothers were one of the most important political groups in Egypt.

In 1944 a 'secret apparatus' was formed, rationalized as for the *jihad* in defence of Islam but used to defend the movement against the government. The *Ikhwan* became involved in acts of terrorism and murder, but in 1949 al-Banna himself was murdered by the political police. At first the *Ikhwan* supported the Egyptian revolution but, falling out with the republican government, they attempted the assassination of Nasser in 1954 following which he put down the society with a stern hand. The society opened branches in other Arab states—one of their emissaries was implicated in the 1948 Revolution in Yemen—and the movement flourishes in these states.

Ideologically the *Ikhwan* seeks a return to Islam and the *Shari'a*; it accepts all orthodox Islamic groups but it is anti-Qadiyani and Bahá'í. In Egypt it provided certain welfare projects and it has been active in publishing its views. A section of 'Muslim Sisters' was set up in 1933.

Shi'a

The Legitimist Shi'a pay allegiance to 'Ali as mentioned above. 'Ali's posterity, which must number at least hundreds of thousands scattered all over the Muslim world, are customarily called Sharifs if they trace descent to his son al-Hasan, and Saiyids if descended from al-Husain, but while the Sharifs and Saiyids, the religious aristocracy of Islam, traditionally are accorded certain privileges in Islamic society, not all are Shi'a, many being Sunnis. By the ninth century many strange sects and even pagan beliefs had become associated with the original Shi'a or Party of 'Ali, but these extremist sects called *ghulat* have mostly vanished except for a few, often practising a sort of quietism or dissimulation (*taqiyya*) for fear of persecution. All Shi'a accord 'Ali an exalted position, the extreme (and heretical) Shi'a at one time even according him a sort of divinity. Shi'ite Islam does not in the main differ on fundamental issues from the Sunni Orthodox since they draw from the same ultimate sources, but Shi'a *mujtahids* have, certainly in theory, greater freedom to alter the application of law since they are regarded as spokesmen of the Hidden Imam.

The Ithna'asharis (Twelvers)

The largest Shi'a school or rite is the Ithna'ashariya or Twelvers, acknowledging a succession of 12 Imams. From 1502 Shi'ism became the established school in Iran under the Safavid ruler Sultan Shah Isma'il who claimed descent from Musa al-Kazim (see below). There are also Ithna'ashariya in southern Iraq, al-Hasa, Bahrain and the Indian sub-continent.

The last Shi'a Imam, Muhammad al-Mahdi, disappeared in 878, but the Ithna'asharis believe he is still alive and will reappear in the last days before the Day of Judgement as the Mahdi (Guided One)—a sort of Messiah—who will rule personally by divine right.

The 12 Imams recognized by the Twelver, Ithna'ashari Shi'a are:

(1) 'Ali b. Abi Talib, cousin and son-in-law of the Prophet Muhammad.

(2) Al-Hasan, son of 'Ali.

(3) Al-Husain, second son of 'Ali.

(4) 'Ali Zain al-'Abidin, son of Husain.

(5) Muhammad al-Baqir, son of 'Ali Zain al-'Abidin.

(6) Ja'far as-Sadiq, son of Muhammad al-Baqir.

(7) Musa al-Kazim, son of Ja'far as-Sadiq.

(8) 'Ali ar-Rida, son of Musa al-Kazim.

(9) Muhammad at-Taqi, son of 'Ali ar-Rida.

(10) 'Ali an-Naqi, son of Muhammad at-Taqi.

(11) Al-Hasan az-Zaki, son of 'Ali an-Naqi, al-'Askari.

(12) Muhammad al-Mahdi, son of al-Hasan b. 'Ali, al-'Askari, known as al-Hujja, the Proof.

Isma'ilis

This group of the Shi'a does not recognize Musa al-Kazim as seventh Imam, but holds that the last Imam visible on earth was Isma'il, the other son of Ja'far as-Sadiq. For this reason they are also called the Sab'iya or Seveners. There is, however, much disagreement among the Seveners as to whether they recognized Isma'il himself as seventh Imam, or one of his several sons, and the Fatimids of Egypt (10th–12th centuries) in fact recognized a son of Isma'il's son Muhammad. Schismatic off-shoots from the Fatimid-Isma'ili group are the Druzes, the Musta'lians first settled in Yemen but now with their main centre in Bombay—where the Daudi section, under the chief 'missionary' (Da'i al-Du'a), is known as Bohoras, but who are properly called the Fatimi Taiyibi Da'wa, and the Nizari Isma'ilis of whom the Agha Khan is the spiritual head. These sects have a secret literature embodying their esoteric philosophies. Both groups are very active and a large Isma'ili Institute, sponsored by the Agha Khan, was opened in London in 1985. Small groups of Isma'ilis are to be found in north-west Syria, Iran, Afghanistan, East Africa and Zanzibar, and larger numbers in India and Pakistan.

'Alawis (Nusairis)

The 'Alawis believe Muhammad was a mere forerunner of 'Ali and that the latter was an incarnation of Allah. This Shi'a extremist sect established in the ninth century has also adopted practices of both Christian and pagan origin. Most of its members today live in north-west Syria.

Druze

The Druze are heretics, an offshoot of the Fatimid Isma'ilis (see above), established in Lebanon and Syria. Their name (Duruz) derives from ad-Darazi, a missionary of Persian origin who brought about the conversion of these Syrian mountaineers to the belief of the divine origin of the Fatimid Caliph al-Hakim. The origins of this sect and its subsequent expansion are still obscure. Hamza b. 'Ali, a Persian contemporary of ad-Darazi, is the author of several of the religious treatises of the Druze. This community acknowledges one God and believes that he has on many occasions become incarnate in man. His last appearance was in the person of the Fatimid Caliph al-Hakim (disappeared 1020). The Druze have played a distinctive role in the political and social life of their country and are renowned for their independence of character. They engaged ardently in *jihad* (holy war) against the Israeli invaders of Lebanon and their Christian allies. Druze morale is reinforced by the inspiration of the Islamic revolution in Shi'ite Iran.

Zaidis

The Zaidis are a liberal and moderate sect of the Shi'a, close enough to the Sunnis to call themselves the 'Fifth School' (*al-madhhab al-khamis*). Their name is derived from a grandson of al-Husain b. 'Ali called Zaid b. 'Ali whom they recognize as fifth Imam. They reject religious dissimulation (*taqiyya*) and are extremely warlike. Zaidism is the dominant school of Islam in Yemen, its main centres being San'a and Dhamar, but Shafi'is form roughly half the population.

Ibadis

The Ibadis are commonly held to have their origins in the Khawarij who dissociated themselves from 'Ali b. Abi Talib when he accepted arbitration in his quarrel with Mu'awiya, but this is open to question. They broke off early from the main stream of Islam and are usually regarded as heretics though with little justification. Groups of the sect, which has often suffered persecution, are found in Oman where Ibadism is the majority religion, Zanzibar, Libya and Algeria, mainly in the Mzab.

THE ISLAMIC REVIVAL

In a number of Muslim countries revivalist or reactionary Islamic movements are taking place. Islam makes no essential distinction between religion and politics so this affects not only the whole Muslim community but also those of other faiths residing in an Islamic state. In one sense it may be said that there is a common basis to the revival in all the Islamic states in that people believe that a reversion to an idealized Islamic community, or the substitution of the principles embodied in *Shari'a* law for the practice of a secular state, will resolve current problems and tensions. Each country, however, seems to differ as to what it expects the Islamic revival to react against. Since imported ideologies like socialism, communism, etc., have not solved political, social and economic problems besetting the Islamic world, in the popular return to the indigenous cultural heritage, Islam has tended to become the ideology of political opposition to existing political establishments and to be regarded as the means to link current development with the traditions of the past.

Saudi Arabia, the heartland of Islam, has always maintained a strict formal adherence to traditional Islam. The late King Faisal, though tactfully curbing the extreme tendencies of Saudi Arabia's Mutawwa' 'clergy', initiated and financed a policy of promoting Islam to counter President Nasser's alignment with socialist propaganda to subvert monarchic regimes elsewhere. King Faisal's initiative took the form of subsidizing the building of mosques in Muslim countries (and, later, also in Europe and other parts of the world), the publication of Islamic books and religious tracts, and the founding or support of such institutions as the Islamic Council of Europe.

In general, the concept of a 'permissive society' as promoted by certain Western elements, is rejected with distaste by all Muslim countries. Saudi Arabia's financial and moral strength has enabled it to take practical steps to pressure other Islamic states to conform, sometimes if they fear only to be out of line, to such Islamic prescriptions as the prohibition of liquor. Even in Egypt alcoholic beverages are not served at public occasions or in public places. On the other hand banks and insurance companies which depend on taking interest on loans, seem to be regarded as earning profit (*ribh*), which is lawful to a Muslim, not taking usury (*riba*), which is unlawful. Since the recent wide revivalist trend that has reasserted itself in Islamic countries, the ethics of banking have troubled the conscience of certain Muslim states, and experiments have been made with Islamic banks which, formally at least, avoid interest. A change-over to an Islamic banking system began in Iran in 1984. Colonel Qaddafi has also been making highly original experiments in the monetary field which he would regard as Islamic. To the West certain Islamic laws are repugnant, such as amputation of a hand for persistent theft, but the benefit in Saudi Arabia in compelling a high standard of honesty is undeniable—the penalty is probably not frequently inflicted. In Algeria the revival of conservative Islam was manifest in June 1990 with

the success in the local elections in the main cities of the Front islamique du salut (FIS). In May and June 1991 demonstrations and riots in Algiers by supporters of the FIS led to the dismissal of the Algerian Government by President Chadli, the postponement of the general election (which had been scheduled for 27 June) and the deployment of the army to restore order. After the FIS achieved an unassailable position in the first round of voting of the rescheduled general election in December 1991, the Algerian armed forces voted to stem its success by suspending the second round of voting and imposing a form of military rule. Algeria has subsequently fallen into a state close to civil war between the FIS and other militant Islamist groups and their supporters on the one hand, and the security forces on the other.

In Iran the motivation of Islamic reaction, as was symbolized by the Ayatollah (a high religious office) Khomeini, was in part that of the conservative, even chauvinistic, provinces against a secular monarch who introduced foreigners who brought with them Western manners distasteful to Islamic society. This found expression in the destruction of bars, cinemas, etc., the banning of music on the radio, and the attempt, by imposing the veil, to reverse the tide of female emancipation. Persecution of the Bahá'ís was reminiscent of the late 19th century. In 1982, all courts established prior to the Islamic Revolution of 1979 were abolished, and all laws not conforming with Islam were revoked. Although interest-free banking is being introduced, there are difficulties in applying Islamic law to economic policy as there seems to be fundamental disagreement on how to apply it. In practice, too, *Shari'a* penalties are not easy to enforce.

In Iran Khomeini aimed to return to the ideal 'Islamic' state as conceived by the Shi'a mullahs. The emphasis on the concept that the *ulema* (mullahs) have had trusteeship over the entire community deputed to them by the invisible Imam, has led to rule by them of a theocratic type, but Khomeini maintained that they must share in the Islamic ideology as interpreted by his group. Khomeini considered Islam's contemporary state as decadent and deviating from Islamic principles. He was critical of other Muslim governments, in part, as they were affected by Western influences, and his dictum, 'we should try hard to export our revolution to the world', though he considered this 'revolution' a spiritual, not a nationalistic one, had an aggressive overtone. The actions and practice of the new state have often been of an extremity rejected by Muslims and non-Muslims alike. Yet, if, on the one hand, some Muslim countries criticized the Khomeini regime for actions difficult to reconcile with the spirit of Islam, on the other there has been a widespread sentiment of sympathy among ordinary Muslims for the 'Islamic' government of Iran in its opposition to the 'Great Satan' USA, as supporter of Israel, etc.

The Turkey of Mustafa Kemal Atatürk aimed at a complete separation of religion and state—in this secular state women were accorded equal rights with men. It is now clear that secularization did not penetrate deeply into the urban and (particularly) the rural population. After the Second World War resentment against the Government for financial hardship was fanned by religious leaders, and ever increasing religious freedom has had to be conceded within the secular state. Many women have, illegally, resumed the veil. The upper classes tend to favour a secular state, but religious feeling combined with chauvinism are behind the popular revival of Islam. In legislative elections which took place in December 1995 the pro-Islamic Refah Partisi (RP) won the largest number of seats in the National Assembly, though not sufficient for it to govern alone. Its success was widely regarded as an expression of the electorate's disillusionment with the established political parties rather than an endorsement of Refah's Islamic policies, however. Indeed, in mid-1996 the RP leader, Necmettin Erbakan, assumed the premiership of the country at the head of a coalition administration but was forced to resign 12 months later following repeated accusations (proceeding chiefly from the armed forces) that he was attempting to undermine the secular State through the promotion of Islamist interests.

In no way was the interdependence of religion and politics in Islam better illustrated than in the condemnation of Israel by 40 Islamic states, over the question of Jerusalem, a city sacred to Muslims from which the Prophet made his celebrated Night Ascent to Heaven. Intensity of feeling over the Palestine issue varies in degree from one Islamic country to another and is often far overshadowed by local issues, but it remains everywhere a major obstacle to East-West understanding. Israel's invasion of Lebanon in 1982 and the horrific massacre perpetrated by a Christian Lebanese group at the Sabra and Chatila Palestinian refugee camps in Beirut, apparently with Israeli connivance, and the Israeli suppression of the Palestinian *intifada* (uprising) in the Occupied Territories, exacerbated an already tense situation, persuading the Islamic world at large of the West's underlying hostility. To many Muslims the attempt by President Saddam Hussain to link Iraq's occupation of Kuwait in August 1990 with the Israeli occupation of Arab territories was justifiable. The vigour with which Western governments reacted against the Iraqi occupation, having effectively condoned the Israeli occupations for so long, appeared to them to be blatant hypocrisy.

Arabs and Iranians frequently complain of the 'bad press' and distortion of their religion and politics in the West through ignorance or deliberate bias. Unfortunately, this has been compounded by the offence to Muslims caused by Salman Rushdie's novel *The Satanic Verses,* and by Western, and specifically American, actions against Iraq after the Gulf War. Muslims contrast the latter with the West's failure to halt Serbian aggression against the Bosnian Muslims.

A Muslim writer recently distinguished between 'Westernization' and 'modernization', describing the latter as broadly acceptable, except to a reactionary minority. If the distinction between the two is a little blurred, the idea has some validity. In general, however, the Islamic revival among ordinary Muslims is bound up with factors, simple conservatism apart, varying from country to country and class to class, and it may oppose either governments conducted on a secular basis, or those claiming to be 'Islamic'.

Christianity

DEVELOPMENT IN THE MIDDLE EAST

Christianity was adopted as the official religion of the Roman empire in AD 313, and the Christian Church came to be based on the four leading cities, Rome, Constantinople (capital from AD 330), Alexandria and Antioch. From the divergent development of the four ecclesiastical provinces there soon emerged four separate churches: the Roman Catholic or Latin Church (from Rome), the Greek Orthodox Church (from Constantinople), the Syrian or Jacobite Church (from Antioch) and the Coptic Church (from Alexandria).

Later divisions resulted in the emergence of the Armenian (Gregorian) Church, which was founded in the fourth century, and the Nestorian Church, which grew up in the fifth century in Syria, Mesopotamia and Iran, following the teaching of Nestorius of Cilicia (d. 431). From the seventh century onwards followers of St Maron began to establish themselves in northern Lebanon, laying the foundations of the Maronite Church.

Subsequently the Uniate Churches were brought into existence by the renunciation by formerly independent churches of doctrines regarded as heretical by the Roman Church and by the acknowledgement of Papal supremacy. These churches—the Armenian Catholic, the Chaldean (Nestorian) Catholic, Greek Catholic, the Coptic Catholic, the Syrian Catholic and the Maronite Church did, however, retain their Oriental customs and rites. The independent churches continued in existence alongside the Uniate Churches with the exception of the Maronites, who reverted to Rome.

HOLY PLACES

Bethlehem: Israeli-occupied West Bank. The traditional birthplace of Jesus is enclosed in the Basilica of the Nativity, revered also by Muslims. Christmas is celebrated here by the Roman and Eastern Rite Churches on 25 December, by the Greek Orthodox, Coptic and Syrian Orthodox Churches on 6 and 7 January, by the Ethiopian Church on 8 January, and by the Armenian Church on 19 January. The tomb of Rachel, important to the three faiths, is just outside the town.

Jerusalem: West Bank (but annexed by Israel). The most holy city of Christianity has been a centre for pilgrims since the

Middle Ages. It is the seat of the patriarchates of the Roman, Greek Orthodox and Armenian Churches, who share the custodianship of the Church of the Holy Sepulchre and who each own land and buildings in the neighbouring area.

The Church of the Holy Sepulchre stands on the hill of Golgotha in the higher north-western part of the Old City. In the central chamber of the church is the Byzantine Rotunda built by 12th century crusaders, which shelters the small shrine of the traditional site of the tomb. Here the different patriarchates exercise their rights in turn. Close by is the Rock of Calvary, revered as the site of the Crucifixion.

Most pilgrims devoutly follow the Way of the Cross leading from the Roman Praetorium through several streets of the Old City to the Holy Sepulchre. Franciscan monks, commemorating the journey to the Crucifixion, follow the course of this traditional route each Friday; on Good Friday this procession marks a climax of the Easter celebrations of the Roman Church.

Outside the Old City stands the Mount of Olives, the scene of Jesus' Ascension. At the foot of its hill is the Garden of Gethsemane which is associated with the vigil on the eve of the Crucifixion. The Cenaculum or traditional room of the Last Supper is situated on Mount Zion in Israel.

Nazareth: Israel. This town, closely associated with the childhood of Jesus, has been a Christian centre since the fourth century AD. The huge, domed Church of the Annunciation has recently been built on the site of numerous earlier churches to protect the underground Grotto of the Annunciation. Nearby the Church of St Joseph marks the traditional site of Joseph's workshop.

Galilee: Israel. Many of the places by this lake are associated with the life of Jesus: Cana, scene of the miracle of water and wine, which is celebrated by an annual pilgrimage on the second Sunday after Epiphany; the Mount of Beatitudes; Tabgha, scene of the multiplication of the loaves and fish; and Capurneum, scene of the healing of the Centurion's servant.

Mount Tabor: Israel. The traditional site of the Transfiguration, which has drawn pilgrims since the fourth century, is commemorated by a Franciscan Monastery and a Greek Basilica, where the annual Festival of the Transfiguration is held.

Jericho: Palestinian autonomous enclave. The scene of the baptism of Jesus; nearby is the Greek Monastery of St John the Baptist.

Nablus (*Samaria*): Palestinian autonomous enclave. This old town contains Jacob's Well, associated with Jesus, and the Tomb of Joseph.

Qubaibah (*Emmaus*): Jordan. It was near this town that two of the Disciples encountered Jesus after the Resurrection.

'Azariyyah (*Bethany*): Jordan. A town frequented by Jesus, the home of Mary and Martha, and the scene of the Raising of Lazarus.

Mount Carmel: Haifa, Israel. The Cave of Elijah draws many pilgrims, including Muslims and Druzes, who celebrate the Feast of Mar Elias on 20 July.

Ein Kerem: Israel. Traditional birthplace of John the Baptist, to whom a Franciscan church is dedicated; nearby is the church of the Visitation.

Ephesus: Turkey. The city, formerly a great centre of pagan worship, where Paul founded the first of the seven Asian Churches. The recently restored Basilica, built by Justinian, is dedicated to John the Evangelist, who legend claims died here; a fourth-century church on Aladag Mountain commemorating Mary's last years spent here now draws an annual pilgrimage in August.

Judaism

There are two main Jewish communities, the Ashkenazim and the Sephardim, the former from east, central and northern Europe, the latter from Spain, the Balkans, the Middle East and North Africa. The majority of immigrants into Israel were from the Ashkenazim, and their influence predominates there, though the Hebrew language follows Sephardim usage. There is no doctrinal difference between the two communities, but they observe distinct rituals.

HOLY PLACES

Wailing Wall: Jerusalem. This last remnant of the western part of the wall surrounding the courtyard of Herod's Temple, finally destroyed by the Romans in AD 70, is visited by devout Jews, particularly on the Fast Day of the ninth of Av, to grieve at the destruction of the First and Second Temples which had once stood on the same site.

Mount Zion: Israel. A hill south-west of the Old City of Jerusalem, venerated particularly for the tomb of David, acknowledged by Muslims as Abi Dawud (the Jebuzite hill on which David founded his Holy City is now known as Mount Ophel, and is in Jordan, just to the east of the modern Mount Zion). Not far from the foot of the hill are the rock-cut tombs of the family of King Herod.

Cave of Machpelah: Hebron, West Bank. The grotto, over which was built a mosque, contains the tombs of Abraham and Sarah, Isaac and Rebecca, Jacob and Leah.

Bethlehem: Israeli-occupied West Bank. The traditional tomb of Rachel is in a small shrine outside the town, venerated also by Muslims and Christians.

Mount Carmel: Israel. The mountain is associated with Elijah, whose Cave in Haifa draws many pilgrims. (See Christianity section).

Safad: Israel. Centre of the medieval Cabbalist movement, this city contains several synagogues from the 16th century associated with these scholars, and many important tombs, notably that of Rabbi Isaac Louria.

Meiron: Israel. The town contains the tombs of Shimon bar Yohai, reputed founder in the second century of the medieval Cabbalist movement, and his son Eleazer. A yearly Hassidic pilgrimage is held to the tomb to celebrate Lag Ba'Omer with a night of traditional singing and dancing in which Muslims also participate.

Tiberias: Israel. An ancient city containing the tombs of Moses Maimonides and Rabbi Meir Baal Harness. Famous as an historical centre of Cabbalist scholarship, it is with Jerusalem, Safad and Hebron, one of the four sacred cities of Judaism, and once accommodated a university and the Sanhedrin.

Other Communities

ZOROASTRIANS

Zoroastrianism developed from the teaching of Zoroaster, or Zarathustra, who lived in Iran some time between 700 and 550 BC. Later adopted as the official religion of the Persian empire, Zoroastrianism remained predominant in Iran until the rise of Islam. Many adherents were forced by persecution to emigrate, and the main centre of the faith is now Bombay, where they are known as Parsees. Technically a monotheistic faith, Zoroastrianism retained some elements of polytheism. It later became associated with fire-worship.

Yazd: Iran. This city was the ancient centre of the Zoroastrian religion, and was later used as a retreat during the Arab conquest. It contains five fire temples and still remains a centre for this faith, of which some 35,000 adherents live in Iran.

BAHÁ'ÍS

Bahá'ísm developed in the mid-19th century from Babism. The Bab, or Gateway (to Truth), Saiyid Ali Muhammad of Shiraz (1821–1850), was opposed to the corrupt Shi'a clergy in the Iran of his day and was executed in 1850. His remains were later taken to Haifa and buried in a mausoleum on the slopes of Mount Carmel. Mirza Husain Ali Bahá'ullah ('Splendour of Allah', 1817–1892), a follower of Babism, experienced a spiritual revelation while in prison and, in 1863, declared himself to be 'he whom Allah shall manifest' as predicted by the Bab. A member of the Persian nobility, he devoted his life to preaching against the corruption endemic in Persian society and as a result spent many years in exile. He died at Acre in Palestine in 1892 and is buried in a shrine adjacent to the mansion in which the Bab died, at Bahji, some miles north of Acre on the road to Beirut.

It was in the will and testament of Abdul Bahá, the eldest son and successor of Bahá'ullah that after his death (in 1921) the head of the Bahá'í faith would be Shoghi Effendi known as the Guardian of the Bahá'í faith ('Guardian of Allah's Command') and that he would be the 'President' of the Universal House of Justice which would be elected in due course. In fact Shoghi Effendi died in London in November 1957 after 36 years as Guardian but the Universal House of Justice was not elected from the Bahá'í world until 1963. The presidency was never assumed and there is no possibility of a second Guardian being appointed.

In 1846 the Babis declared their secession from Islam, and the Bahá'ís claim independence from all other faiths. They believe that the basic principles of the great religions of the world are in complete harmony and that their aims and functions are complementary. Other tenets include belief in the brotherhood of man, the opposition to racial and colour discrimination, the equality of the sexes, progress towards world peace, monogamy, chastity and the encouragement of family life. Bahá'ísm has no priesthood and discourages asceticism, monasticism and mystic pantheism. Most of Bahá'ísm's Middle Eastern adherents live in Iran and—on a temporary basis—Israel, but since the Islamic Revolution those in Iran have suffered from severe official persecution. More than 1m. Bahá'ís live in India and in fact there are now Bahá'ís in every country of the world with more than 150 national administrative bodies.

Haifa: Israel. Shrine and gardens of the Bab on Mount Carmel, world centre of the Bahá'í faith. Pilgrims visit the Bahá'í holy places in Haifa and in and around Acre. The Pilgrimage lasts for nine days and the pilgrimage period extends over the whole year with the exception of the months of August and September.

SAMARITANS

Mount Gerazim: Jordan. The mountain is sacred to this small sect, who celebrate Passover here. The Samaritan High Priest lives at Nablus.

ARAB–ISRAELI RELATIONS 1967–98

Updated for this edition by PAUL COSSALI

Based on an original article by MICHAEL ADAMS, with subsequent additions by DAVID GILMOUR, PAUL HARPER and STEVEN SHERMAN

Israel's decisive victory over the Arab states in the Six-Day War of 1967 raised hopes that at last it would be possible to reach a definitive settlement of the 19-year-old Arab–Israeli conflict. Instead it soon became apparent that the conflict had merely been complicated by the occupation of further Arab territory, the displacement of still more refugees and an aggravation of the sense of grievance felt by the Palestinians and now shared more widely than ever in the rest of the Arab world.

Once a cease-fire was in operation in June 1967, the UN Security Council's next step was to pass a resolution (No. 237, of 14 June 1967), calling on Israel to facilitate the return of the new refugees who had fled (and were still fleeing) from the areas occupied by Israel during the war. The resolution also called on Israel to ensure the safety, welfare and security of the inhabitants of the 'Occupied Areas'.

An emergency meeting of the UN General Assembly reiterated on 4 July the Security Council's call for the return of the refugees and on the same day it declared 'invalid' the Israeli annexation of the Arab sector of Jerusalem; but the Assembly failed to produce an agreed resolution for a settlement.

The deadlock became total when an Arab summit conference, held in Khartoum between 29 August and 3 September 1967, confirmed earlier decisions not to negotiate directly with Israel, not to accord it recognition and not to sign a peace treaty. The Israeli Government, for its part, announced its refusal to undertake any but direct negotiations; if no such negotiations developed, Israeli forces would maintain their occupation of the Arab territories conquered during the war.

RESOLUTION 242

In late 1967 the UN Security Council considered a number of draft resolutions which failed to gain approval, either because (according to supporters of the Arabs) they condoned the acquisition or occupation of territory by military force, or because (according to supporters of Israel) they contained no adequate guarantee of Israel's security. Finally, on 22 November 1967, the Security Council unanimously adopted Resolution 242 (see Documents on Palestine, p. 115), which was to be the basis of all peace initiatives during the next five years and which remains an important element in attempts to resolve the Palestinian question. By emphasizing the illegitimacy of the acquisition of territory by war, the resolution satisfied the demand of the Arabs and their supporter, the USSR, for an Israeli withdrawal. At the same time, by being less than categorical about the extent of that withdrawal, it was acceptable to the Israelis and their supporter, the USA. All the subsequent arguments which developed centred on the question of whether the Israelis, in return for a definitive peace treaty, should have the right to retain parts of the Arab territories occupied during the war.

PALESTINIAN RESISTANCE

In the immediate aftermath of the fighting, despite the Israeli Prime Minister's declaration on the eve of the war that Israel had no intention of annexing 'even one foot of Arab territory', the Israeli Knesset had legislated the 'reunification' of Jerusalem,* which in fact amounted to the annexation of the Arab sector of the city. This appeared to confirm Arab allegations of Israeli expansionism, and greatly encouraged the rise of a Palestinian resistance movement, already stimulated by the impotence of the Arab governments and the humiliation which the war had brought on the Arab world. When the Israelis began, as early as September 1967, to establish Jewish settlements in the Occupied Territories, support for the resistance movement became widespread in the Arab world. It was reinforced when the Israelis, after agreeing to allow the return of refugees (who

were still streaming eastward), closed the border again after only 14,000 of the 150,000 who had filed applications with the Red Cross had been allowed to re-enter Palestine.

The situation, then, was deteriorating even before Dr Gunnar Jarring, whom the Secretary-General had appointed as his Special Representative in accordance with Resolution 242, went to the Middle East at the end of 1967. During the first half of 1968 there were increasingly frequent breaches of the cease-fire along the Suez Canal (which remained blocked to traffic), while Palestinian guerrilla raids prompted costly Israeli reprisals in the Jordan valley. In July 1968, guerrillas of the Popular Front for the Liberation of Palestine (PFLP) carried out the first hijack operation in the Middle East, diverting an Israeli airliner to Algiers.

LEBANESE INVOLVEMENT

Israel, while not rejecting Resolution 242, said it could not be a substitute for specific agreements between the parties. When the UN General Assembly met in late 1968, Israel put forward a nine-point plan for a Middle East settlement which made no mention of withdrawal, but rather of 'a boundary settlement compatible with the security of Israel and the honour of the Arab states'. This produced no response from the Arab governments, which were shocked when President Johnson, at the height of the US election campaign, announced that the USA was considering the sale of *Phantom* aircraft to Israel. A month later Richard Nixon was elected as President Johnson's successor. The sale of 50 *Phantoms* to Israel was confirmed at the end of December and marked an important stage in the escalation of the arms race in the Middle East.

The day after the sale of the *Phantoms* was announced, Israeli commandos raided Beirut airport, in reprisal for an Arab guerrilla attack on an Israeli airliner in Athens, and destroyed 13 aircraft. This incident brought Lebanon directly into the Arab–Israeli confrontation. After the Security Council had unanimously condemned Israel for the raid, the Soviet Government took up an earlier French proposal for talks between the USSR, the USA, the United Kingdom and France to obtain agreement between the major powers over the implementation of Resolution 242.

At the beginning of February 1969, President Nasser of Egypt declared his willingness to enter into direct negotiations once Israeli forces had withdrawn from Arab territory. Mr Eshkol, the Prime Minister of Israel, stated his readiness to meet President Nasser and declared that Israel was prepared to be flexible about all the Occupied Territories except Jerusalem and the Golan Heights (captured from Syria in 1967). But, as the year wore on, sporadic fighting continued along both the Suez Canal and the Jordan fronts, until in July 1969 President Nasser publicly gave up hope of a peaceful settlement, forecasting that a long 'war of attrition' would be necessary to dislodge Israel from the Occupied Territories.

THE ROGERS PLAN

The quadripartite talks were suspended while Soviet and US representatives met separately. There was optimism when it appeared that a formula had been found for 'Rhodes-style' negotiations (after the talks conducted in Rhodes which led to the armistice agreements between Israel and the Arab states in 1949), but an Israeli suggestion that this would amount to direct negotiations prompted the Arabs to reject the formula. Instead, on 9 December 1969, the US Secretary of State, William Rogers, produced a set of proposals which came to be known as the Rogers Plan. This was an attempt to steer a middle course between the Arab view, that the Security Council resolution should be implemented *in toto* and did not require negotiation, and the Israeli preference for direct negotiations which would decide where the new borders should be drawn. The most

---

* For a discussion of the Jerusalem issue, *see* p. 98.

important aspect of the plan was that it made clear the US view that there should only be minor modifications of the pre-June 1967 boundaries. This ensured Israeli hostility to the plan, since, despite the insistence of the Israeli Minister of Foreign Affairs, Abba Eban, that 'everything is negotiable', it had now become clear that his cabinet colleagues were deeply divided on this crucial question.

In January 1970 Israel initiated a series of bombing raids (using the new US *Phantom* aircraft) on targets inside Egypt. General Dayan, Israel's Minister of Defence, announced at the beginning of February that the Israeli bombing attacks had three aims: to force the Egyptians to respect the cease-fire along the Suez Canal front, to prevent Egyptian preparations for a new war and to weaken the Egyptian regime. In practice, the raids had three results: they strengthened Egyptian support for President Nasser, they damaged Israel's international reputation and they provoked the USSR into providing further assistance to Egypt.

International concern over these developments led to a renewal of diplomatic efforts. Israel's requests for more *Phantoms* in early 1970 were not granted and it appeared that the immediate US objectives were to renew the cease-fire and to extract from the Israeli Government an undertaking to withdraw from the greater part of the Occupied Territories as part of an overall peace settlement. Israel made no public commitment to withdrawal, but its response in private was sufficiently encouraging for Mr Rogers to relaunch his proposals, with the backing of the four major powers. In a speech on 23 July 1970 President Nasser announced Egypt's acceptance of the US proposal for a renewal of the cease-fire, followed by negotiations through Dr Jarring for the implementation of Resolution 242. A week later, the Israeli Government, after receiving assurances on the future supply of arms from the USA, also agreed to the US proposal, with the provisos that Israel would never return to the pre-war boundaries and that none of its troops would be withdrawn from the cease-fire lines until a binding peace agreement had been signed.

The renewed cease-fire along the Suez Canal front came into operation on the night of 7/8 August. It was to last 90 days, during which the two sides were to engage in indirect negotiations through Dr Jarring. However, after a single meeting with Dr Jarring in New York, the Israeli representative was recalled and the Israeli Government protested that the cease-fire had been violated by the movement of Soviet missiles behind the Egyptian lines. Negotiations had not been renewed when a serious crisis in Jordan distracted the attention of all the parties concerned.

KING HUSSEIN AND THE PALESTINE GUERRILLAS

On 6 September 1970, Palestinian guerrillas of the PFLP hijacked two airliners and diverted them to a desert airfield near Zerqa, in Jordan. A third airliner was taken to Cairo and destroyed there. Three days later a fourth aircraft was hijacked and joined the two in Jordan, where the guerrillas demanded the release of a substantial number of Palestinians held prisoner in Israel, in exchange for some 300 hostages.

This episode proved the last straw for the Jordanian Government. During the previous two years, as the strength of the guerrilla movement increased, it had faced a dilemma. By allowing the guerrillas freedom of movement in Jordan, it had invited (and would continue to invite) retaliation from Israel in the form of ground and air raids which had depopulated the East Bank of the Jordan and caused severe casualties. If, however, the Government tried to control or suppress the activities of the guerrillas, it faced the possibility of civil war in Jordan.

The Palestine resistance movement, whose declared objective was the reconstitution in Palestine of a democratic state open to Jews and Arabs alike, opposed the idea of a political settlement with Israel implying the recognition and perpetuation of a Zionist state. King Hussein had accepted the Rogers Plan and was thus committed to the principle of a political settlement. So long as this was not in prospect, it had been possible for the King and the guerrillas to pursue their diverse objectives without coming into open conflict, but as soon as such a settlement became a serious possibility the uneasy coexistence between them was threatened. On several occasions in 1969

and 1970 the Jordanian Government and the guerrillas had come close to a confrontation, and after the renewal of the cease-fire in August 1970 and the acceptance by the Jordanian Government of the Rogers Plan, a clash became inevitable.

On 16 September King Hussein appointed a military Government in Jordan which the next day set about the liquidation of the resistance movement. After 10 days of heavy fighting in Amman, mediation efforts by other Arab governments, and in particular by President Nasser, brought about a truce, which was signed in Cairo on 27 September 1970. On the following day President Nasser suffered a heart attack and died almost immediately.

PRESIDENT SADAT AND THE CEASE-FIRE

There was both surprise and relief when the new President of Egypt, Anwar Sadat, showed himself willing to take up the pursuit of a settlement. He agreed to renew the cease-fire for 90 days and, after intensive consultations between Israeli and US leaders and the extension of American credits worth $500m., Israel agreed to return to the Jarring talks. As the cease-fire was expiring on 5 February 1971, President Sadat once more agreed to renew it, for 30 days, proposing that Israel should begin to withdraw its forces from the east bank of the canal, which Egypt would then be able to clear for navigation.

On 8 February Dr Jarring wrote to the Governments of Israel and Egypt, expressing his optimism about the desire of both parties for a settlement and inviting each of them to give firm commitments which would resolve the central deadlock. Israel, he suggested, should agree on certain stated conditions (providing guarantees for security and freedom of navigation) to withdraw to the international boundary between Egypt and the Palestine of the British Mandate. Egypt should give a parallel undertaking to conclude a peace agreement explicitly ending the state of belligerence and recognizing Israel's right to exist in peace and security. In other words, both parties were asked formally to accept the principal obligations imposed on them by Resolution 242.

The Egyptian reply gave the undertaking called for by Dr Jarring, provided that Israel did the same and agreed to withdraw its forces to the international border. Israel's reply stated firmly that, while it would be prepared to withdraw its forces to 'secure, recognized and agreed boundaries to be established in the peace agreement', it would in no circumstances withdraw to the pre-June 1967 lines. This embarrassed the US Government, which had first withheld and then granted military and economic assistance to Israel, in the attempt to persuade the Israeli Government to accept only 'minor rectifications' of the armistice lines. The USA made one further attempt when William Rogers urged Israel to accept international guarantees in place of territorial gains, adding that security did not 'necessarily require additions of territory' and that in the US view 'the 1967 boundary should be the boundary between Israel and Egypt'.

PROPOSAL FOR A 'PARTIAL SETTLEMENT'

The US Government took up instead President Sadat's suggestion of an Israeli withdrawal for some distance into Sinai to allow the reopening of the Suez Canal. But the new proposal for a partial settlement quickly became bogged down in arguments over the extent of the Israeli withdrawal and whether it should be seen as the first step to complete withdrawal. The arguments continued through most of 1971 until the proposal was finally dropped by the USA in November.

In December the UN General Assembly, in a resolution reaffirming the 'inadmissibility of the acquisition of territory by war' and calling for an Israeli withdrawal, also urged Israel to 'respond favourably' to the proposals made by Dr Jarring in February. Only seven states, including Israel, voted against the resolution and the USA, which had always voted in support of Israel on territorial questions, abstained, reflecting its view that Israel should withdraw from almost all of the Occupied Territories. The year ended with President Sadat in a dangerously weakened position. He had taken considerable risks in pursuit of a political settlement and had promised the Egyptian people that 1971 would be the 'year of decision'. He blamed the lack of progress on American 'political manoeuvring', and when 1972 (a US election year) began with the US Government promising Israel a further 42 *Phantom* and 90 *Skyhawk* aircraft, it seemed unlikely that a fresh US suggestion of indirect talks between Israel and Egypt in New York would be fruitful.

In February 1972 the Israelis launched a large-scale incursion into Lebanon, stating that its aim was the elimination of guerrilla bases near Israel's northern border. In June a further Israeli raid on Lebanon was condemned by the Security Council after more than 70 civilians had been killed or wounded.

In July 1972 President Sadat unexpectedly requested the withdrawal from Egypt of the Soviet advisers engaged in the reorganization of Egypt's defence system. This was interpreted as a final appeal to the US Government to bring pressure to bear on Israel to accept a settlement involving an Israeli withdrawal from Sinai.

In Europe, however, a reappraisal of Middle Eastern policy was taking place. This found expression in the annual Middle East debate in the General Assembly of the UN, when all the members of the European Community (EC), except Denmark, followed the lead of the UK (which entered the Community on 1 January 1973) and France in voting for a resolution strongly critical of Israel. (The USA again abstained.)

TERRORISM AND COUNTER-TERRORISM IN THE MIDDLE EAST

The cease-fire along the Suez Canal was maintained, but along the northern borders of Israel and Israeli-held territory there was a renewal of violence in the second half of 1972, accompanied by a mounting series of terrorist attacks by both Israelis and Palestinians in various parts of the world. In mid-1972, a number of Palestinian leaders were killed or seriously injured by explosive devices sent to them in Beirut. In September, during the Olympic Games in Munich, Palestinian guerrillas captured Israeli athletes and held them hostage in an attempt to obtain the release of Palestinians held captive in Israel. West German police, after promising the Palestinians safe conduct out of Germany, opened fire on them at Munich airport, whereupon the guerrillas killed the hostages and were themselves either killed or captured.

The Munich attack was followed by Israeli ground and air raids into Lebanon, which the Israeli Government held responsible for the activities of guerrillas whose bases (since their expulsion from Jordan in 1970 and 1971) were in the refugee camps of Beirut and elsewhere in Lebanon. Letter bombs were subsequently posted to Israeli representatives in various countries and representatives of the Palestine Liberation Organization (PLO) were attacked in Rome, Stockholm, Paris and Nicosia.

At the beginning of 1973 Mr Hafez Ismail (President Sadat's political adviser), King Hussein of Jordan and Mrs Golda Meir (the Israeli Prime Minister) visited Washington for talks with President Nixon. However, the frail hopes aroused by this were dashed when an Israeli attack on guerrilla installations in a refugee camp in northern Lebanon was followed within 24 hours by the shooting down by Israeli fighters of a Libyan airliner which had strayed over occupied Sinai. The two incidents provoked an unprecedented wave of criticism of Israel on the eve of Mrs Meir's arrival in Washington.

STALEMATE

In the autumn of 1973, the Arab–Israeli conflict appeared to be further from resolution than ever. Israel, confident that its military supremacy over the Arabs had increased, remained in control of all the territories it had occupied in 1967 and had established in these territories some 50 civilian and paramilitary settlements. The Egyptian and Jordanian Governments— though not yet the Syrian—had long since modified their earlier refusal to negotiate a settlement and had indicated their willingness to recognize the State of Israel; but they still refused to envisage a peace settlement which did not provide for the return of all the Occupied Territories. The UN, despite the passage every year of resolutions calling for an Israeli withdrawal, found all its efforts to devise a settlement blocked by Israel's refusal to relinquish its 1967 conquests.

More than ever, the key to the situation rested in the hands of the USA, which found itself isolated in support of Israel while becoming increasingly dependent on petroleum produced by the Arab states. The USA's allies, for whom dependence on Arab petroleum was already a fact, were increasingly impatient with the US Government's Middle East policy, which seemed to be aimed at maintaining Israel's overall supremacy without seeking any concessions from the Israeli Government over the Occupied Territories. The isolation of the USA was emphasized in the Security Council in the summer of 1973, when it vetoed a resolution put forward by eight non-aligned members, which was strongly critical of Israel's continued occupation of Arab territory. All the other Council members except the People's Republic of China, which abstained, voted affirmatively.

RENEWAL OF THE WAR

A surprise attack was launched on two fronts by the Egyptian and Syrian forces on 6 October 1973. Unusual activity behind the lines had been observed by Israeli and US intelligence agencies west of the Suez Canal and east of the cease-fire line on the Golan Heights; but the Israelis were convinced that the Egyptian army was incapable of the elaborate operation required to cross the canal and breach the chain of Israeli fortifications, known as the Bar-Lev line, on the east bank. This element of surprise won for the Egyptian and Syrian forces a substantial initial advantage on both fronts. This was enhanced by the fact that 6 October was Yom Kippur, the Day of Atonement in the Jewish calendar, when all public services were suspended, making it unusually difficult for the Israelis rapidly to mobilize their forces. By midnight on the first day of the war, 400 Egyptian tanks had crossed the canal, the Bar-Lev line had been outflanked and a massive Syrian tank attack beyond the Golan Heights had only been stemmed by a masterly rearguard action by greatly outnumbered Israeli armour, aided by air strikes.

During the next three weeks (despite the declaration of a UN-sponsored cease-fire on 22 October), the Syrians were driven back beyond the old cease-fire line and counter-attacking Israeli forces effected a westward crossing of the Suez Canal. At the end of the war, the military advantage lay with the Israelis, who had occupied a further area of Syrian territory and were threatening Damascus, while their units west of the canal had isolated an Egyptian army in Suez. However, largely as a result of the intervention of the Arab oil-producing states, the political objectives of the Arabs had been achieved and the whole context of the confrontation decisively altered.

By making unexpectedly efficient use of new weapons the Arab armies demonstrated that since 1967 they had significantly narrowed the (military) technological gap between themselves and Israel. They had exposed the fallacy on which Israeli strategy had been based since the Six-Day War: that the control of wide buffer zones (the territories occupied since 1967), together with the military supremacy of which it felt assured, rendered Israel immune to Arab attack. This assumption had encouraged the Israeli leaders to disregard the mounting pressure of world opinion calling for an Israeli withdrawal as the essential condition of a negotiated settlement with the Arabs.

THE PETROLEUM FACTOR

Soon after the outbreak of the war, there were calls within the Arab world to deny Middle East oil to the supporters of Israel. In October 1973 a meeting in Kuwait of representatives of the Arab oil producers resulted in an agreement to reduce output, while Abu Dhabi took the lead in halting the export of oil to the USA. In adopting and then intensifying these measures, the Arab oil-producing states displayed unexpected unity. This had an evident effect on the governments of western Europe, conscious of their dependence on the free flow of oil from the Middle East. On 6 November the nine member states of the EC endorsed a statement calling for an Israeli withdrawal from the territories occupied in 1967 and asserting that, while all states in the Middle East should enjoy the right to secure boundaries, the legitimate rights of the Palestinians should be taken into account in any settlement (see Documents on Palestine, p. 117). Israel accused the Europeans of giving in to Arab 'blackmail', but for several years the Europeans had been dissociating themselves from US policy and registering their growing impatience with Israel's intransigence.

AMERICAN INITIATIVE

The USA, which alone possessed the influence that could induce Israel to withdraw—and which now found itself inconvenienced much more by the oil embargo than it had anticipated—accepted its responsibility to bring about a settlement. The US Secretary of State, Dr Kissinger, now embarked on a dramatic series of visits to Middle Eastern capitals, out of which resulted disengagement agreements between Egypt and Israel (signed on 18 January 1974) and between Syria and Israel (signed on 30 May 1974). In the middle of June 1974 President Nixon, whose domestic position had become dangerously insecure after the Watergate scandal, embarked on a triumphant tour of the Middle East, forecasting a new era of co-operation between the USA and the Arab world, while reassuring Israel of continuing US support. This US initiative was generally well received, except by some Israelis who foresaw mounting pressure on Israel to make concessions inconsistent with its security, and by the extreme wing of the Palestinian resistance movement, which engaged in a series of terrorist attacks on targets in northern Israel in an effort to frustrate a settlement which did not guarantee Palestine's total liberation. Otherwise, President Nixon's visit revealed a strong desire on the part of the Arab governments to restore friendly relations with the USA. Diplomatic relations between Washington and Damascus were re-established and the embargo on the export of Arab oil to the USA was lifted.

CHANGE IN THE BALANCE OF POWER

This reconciliation was one of the most striking results of the October War; it was a reminder of the greatly increased influence of the Arab states so long as they continued to act in concert. Conversely, Israel's international position had been much weakened by the failure of its pre-war policies and by the revelation of the extent to which the rest of the world was dependent on Arab goodwill. The Government headed by Golda Meir was widely blamed both for provoking the October War by its policy of 'creeping annexation' and for being caught unawares when the war came. After winning a narrow victory in a general election at the end of 1973, Mrs Meir finally abandoned the attempt to rebuild her coalition in April 1974. She was succeeded as leader of the Labour Party and Prime Minister by Gen. Yitzhak Rabin, who had been Chief of Staff at the time of the 1967 war and later Israeli Ambassador in Washington. In the Arab world, the effect of the war was to strengthen the position of the regimes in Cairo and Damascus and to give new authority to King Faisal of Saudi Arabia, whose control of the greatest share of the oil reserves of the Middle East made him a dominant figure in Arab politics. The fact that the disengagement agreements involved small but significant Israeli withdrawals from Arab territory gave satisfaction throughout the Arab world, but the central problem of the future of the Palestinians remained unsolved. The difficulty of finding a solution acceptable both to Israel and to the PLO (which the Arab governments, meeting in Algiers in November 1973, had recognized as 'the sole legitimate representative of the Palestinian people') posed a continuing threat to the stability of the disengagement agreements of 1974.

Despite the new unity of the Arab world, the movement towards a settlement in the Middle East lost momentum during the second half of 1974 and a further outbreak of war seemed imminent at times. The disengagement agreements were honoured and UN forces were inserted between the combatants in Sinai and on the Golan front, but Syria and Israel exchanged mutual recriminations over the ill-treatment of prisoners and the destruction of the Syrian town of Quneitra by the Israelis on the eve of their withdrawal.

While the optimism generated by the disengagement agreements gave way to stalemate between the Arab governments and Israel, the Palestinians' central role in the conflict was strikingly endorsed. On 21 September 1974, the UN General Assembly voted to include 'the Palestine Question' on its agenda for the first time since the establishment of the State of Israel in 1948. (Only four Governments opposed this decision: Israel, the USA, the Dominican Republic and Bolivia.) On 14 October the General Assembly invited the PLO to take part in the debate and a month later the Chairman of the PLO, Yasser Arafat, outlined to the Assembly the PLO's design for a 'democratic, secular state' in Palestine in which Jews and Arabs would coexist on terms of equality, specifying that 'all Jews now living in Palestine who choose to live with us there in peace and without discrimination' were included in this design. At the end of October a meeting of Arab Heads of State in Rabat reiterated that the PLO was the 'sole legitimate representative of the Palestinian people', with the right to speak for the Palestinians at any future Middle East peace talks and to establish an independent national authority in any part of Palestine liberated from Israeli occupation.

These decisions greatly strengthened the hand of the Palestinians and the PLO. However, they also deepened the impasse over a settlement because the Israeli Government refused to have any dealings with the PLO, dismissing it as a terrorist organization. The PLO's position was also complicated by internal divisions over the objective which the organization should pursue. Although Yasser Arafat at the UN had spoken only of the PLO's goal of a unitary Palestine (which would mean the elimination of the State of Israel), he was under pressure from the Arab governments to accept the limited objective of a Palestinian state on the West Bank and the Gaza Strip, which could only be envisaged in the context of the recognition of Israel within its pre-1967 borders. A majority within the PLO appeared at the end of 1974 to be moving towards acceptance of this formula, but the minority rejected any thought of compromising the long-term goal of the total liberation of Palestine. This 'rejectionist front', with the backing of the Governments of Iraq and Libya, made it difficult for the PLO openly to align itself with those Arab governments (notably Egypt) which were prepared to exchange recognition of Israel for withdrawal from the territories occupied in 1967, including Arab Jerusalem, and the creation of a Palestinian state on the West Bank.

This was in effect the pattern for a settlement which had been envisaged in the Security Council's Resolution 242 and which had provided the basis for all the international initiatives undertaken between 1967 and 1973. These initiatives had failed because Israel, before October 1973, had felt confident of its ability to retain control of at least substantial parts of the Occupied Territories. The October War, by undermining this confidence, had highlighted Israel's dependence on US support; moreover, the initial efforts of Dr Kissinger immediately after the war had encouraged the Arabs to believe that US influence would at last be used to promote a settlement based on Israel's withdrawal.

ARAB IMPATIENCE

The Arab-US reconciliation, in which President Sadat had taken the lead and to which he totally committed himself during 1974, had failed by the end of the year to produce any results beyond the initial disengagement agreements. Apart from the tiny areas of territory conceded by Israel under those agreements, the Israeli occupation was maintained in Sinai, the Golan Heights (including the plateau up to the outskirts of Quneitra), the West Bank (including the Old City of Jerusalem) and the Gaza Strip, with no relaxation of the ban on political activity by the Arab population and other repressive measures. None of the Jewish settlements, of which about 50 had been established in the Occupied Territories before October 1973, had been given up; indeed the Israeli Government, under pressure from the right-wing opposition and the religious parties in the Knesset, continued to announce plans to extend Jewish settlement.

These developments caused growing impatience in the Arab world. When Dr Kissinger returned to the Middle East in March in an attempt to further the process of disengagement between Israel and Egypt, it was widely assumed that he had obtained prior assurances from both sides. However, after two weeks of intensive 'shuttle diplomacy' he had to admit failure when Israel refused to withdraw from the Mitla and Giddi passes in Sinai and from the oilfield at Abu Rudeis, without an explicit assurance of future non-aggression from President Sadat. The latter was clearly unrealistic, since it would have confirmed Arab suspicions that Egypt was prepared to abandon its allies for a separate peace with Israel. There was therefore little surprise when the US Secretary of State (and later President Ford) blamed Israeli obstinacy for the breakdown of the negotiations and announced that the USA would embark on a 'reassessment' of its Middle East policy. This was held to mean that Israel's latest request for increased military and economic aid from the USA would not be granted until Israel showed a more conciliatory attitude.

The breakdown of Dr Kissinger's mission coincided with the assassination in Riyadh of King Faisal of Saudi Arabia, whose prestige and authority had been greatly increased by his support for the Arab war effort during and after the October War. In May the Syrian Government unexpectedly agreed to renew for a further six months the mandate of the UN force separating the two sides on the Golan front, and on 5 June the Egyptian Government reopened the Suez Canal, eight years to the day after the outbreak of the war which had led to its closure in 1967.

FURTHER DISENGAGEMENT IN SINAI

On 21 August 1975 Dr Kissinger flew to Israel to promote a second disengagement agreement between Israel and Egypt. After two weeks of intensive negotiations Dr Kissinger persuaded Israel and Egypt to accept an agreement which was signed in Geneva on 4 September (see Documents on Palestine, p. 119). The new agreement provided for an Israeli withdrawal from the strategic Mitla and Giddi passes and the return to Egypt of the Abu Rudeis oilfields, on which Israel had depended for some 50% of its oil supplies since 1967. As in the first disengagement agreement, a UN buffer zone was established separating the Egyptian and Israeli forces. The most important new element was the provision for five electronic listening posts in this zone, of which one was to be manned by Egyptians, one by Israelis and the other three by a team of 200 US civilians who would monitor troop movements both east and west of the passes. Both sides undertook to respect the cease-fire and to resolve the conflict between them by peaceful means. Non-military cargoes in ships sailing to or from Israel were to be allowed through the Suez Canal and the agreement was to remain in force 'until superseded by a new agreement'.

The conclusion of this second agreement was considered a triumph for US diplomacy and it had significant effects on Egypt's relations with its Arab allies. Only Saudi Arabia, Sudan and (with reservations) Kuwait expressed approval of the agreement, which was criticized—most vehemently by the Syrians and the PLO—as a surrender to US and Israeli interests. The united Arab front presented during the October War was now seriously disrupted.

The agreement marked a further stage in the US-Egyptian *rapprochement* and the estrangement between Egypt and its former ally, the USSR. In October 1975 President Sadat made an official visit to Washington, while his repeated criticisms of the USSR led to a steady deterioration of relations culminating in Egypt's abrogation of the Soviet-Egyptian Treaty of Friendship in March 1976.

Syria now assumed the leadership of the Arab cause. President Assad found his position in the Arab world greatly strengthened and even succeeded in restoring close relations with King Hussein of Jordan, establishing a joint Syrian-Jordanian Command Council. In October 1975 he visited Moscow for talks with President Podgorny and other leaders and gained a promise of further arms supplies to counter the deliveries reaching Israel from the USA. At the end of November Syria's already considerable prestige as the most consistent defender of the rights of the Palestinians was enhanced when President Assad agreed to renew the mandate of the UN Disengagement Observer Force (UNDOF) on the Golan Heights, extracting in return a promise that the Security Council would hold a special debate on the Palestine question in January 1976, with the participation of the PLO.

PLO'S STANDING ENHANCED

This debate further strengthened the international position of the PLO. In November 1975 the UN General Assembly had adopted three resolutions concerning Palestine. The first had established a 20-nation committee to work out plans for the implementation of the Palestinian right 'to self-determination and national independence', the second invited the PLO to take part in all future UN debates on the Middle East, and the third denounced Zionism as 'a form of racism and racial discrimination'. (The last of these provoked an international storm of criticism in which the importance of the other two resolutions was widely overlooked.) A month later a US veto saved Israel from censure by the Security Council for a series of air raids on

targets in Lebanon in which 75 people were killed. When the Security Council debated the Palestine question in January 1976, the USA again used the veto to prevent the adoption of a resolution affirming the Palestinians' right to establish a state of their own and calling for an Israeli withdrawal from all the territories occupied since June 1967.

In January 1976 Western press reports suggested that US officials were in secret contact with Palestinian representatives, and the impression that a major change in US policy was in the offing was reinforced in March when the UN Security Council debated the question of Israeli policies in the Occupied Territories. Although the USA again exercised the veto to defeat a resolution, on Israel's behalf, its delegate strongly condemned Israel's establishment of 'illegal' settlements in Jerusalem and other occupied areas.

Israel's persistence in establishing these settlements was a major factor in provoking serious rioting all over the occupied West Bank and in Gaza during mid-1976. The riots had a decisive effect on the outcome of municipal elections organized by the Israeli occupation authorities in the West Bank in April. Instead of producing, as the Israelis had hoped, 'moderate' Palestinian leaders who would accept a measure of autonomy under continuing Israeli occupation, the elections demonstrated the strength of Palestinian nationalism and widespread support for the PLO.

CIVIL WAR IN LEBANON

The disunity in the Arab camp was highlighted by events in Lebanon, where armed clashes between Palestinian guerrillas and Christian militiamen in April 1975 led to a civil war which threatened to destroy the Lebanese state and almost provoked another Arab–Israeli confrontation. Attempts at mediation by the Arab League and by French and American emissaries failed to reconcile the warring parties, which, in turn, were supported by rival Arab interests. In January 1976, after nine months of heavy fighting, in which Palestinian guerrillas were drawn into a leftist alliance against the defenders of the conservative Christian establishment, the Syrian Government employed Syrian-based units of the Palestine Liberation Army to impose a cease-fire which was to be followed by a reform of the Lebanese political system. However, the cease-fire broke down in March, when Christian extremists, supporting President Franjiya, prevaricated over the implementation of the reform programme and the Druze leader of the leftist alliance tried to force the President's resignation.

Faced with a victory for the leftists and their Palestinian allies, which might provoke an Israeli military intervention in southern Lebanon, Syria used its influence to restrain the leftists, sending Syrian troops across the border at the end of May 1976, with tacit US approval. At the same time President Assad renewed the mandate of the UN force on the Golan front for a further six months.

In late 1976 the obstacles which had prevented any movement towards an Arab-Israeli settlement were removed. After repeated failures on the part of the Arab League to play an effective mediating role in Lebanon, determined efforts by the Saudi Arabian and Kuwaiti Governments brought about a restricted Arab summit meeting in Riyadh in October, at which the leaders of Egypt, Syria, Lebanon and the PLO agreed to the terms of a cease-fire. These were confirmed at a further meeting in Cairo on 26 October, and provided for the creation of a substantial Arab peace-keeping force which, within a month, had halted the savage fighting in Beirut, reopened the Beirut–Damascus road and occupied the main towns in the north and south of the country.

NEW ADMINISTRATION IN WASHINGTON

In the USA the President-elect, Jimmy Carter, had indicated his intention to take early action over the Middle East. Once more the Israelis found themselves under pressure both from the Arabs and from the USA. On 11 November 1976, the USA approved a unanimous 'consensus statement' by the Security Council which 'strongly deplored' Israel's actions in establishing settlements in the Occupied Territories and attempting to alter the demographic balance in Jerusalem. On 19 November the US Ambassador to Israel, speaking to the annual convention of B'nai B'rith in Jerusalem, said that 'unless Israel's professed willingness to return occupied territory is seen as more than mere rhetoric, the vicious circle of mutual mistrust cannot be broken'. On 24 November the USA joined 117 other nations in voting in the UN General Assembly (against the opposition of Israel and Costa Rica) to deplore Israel's refusal to allow the return of the Palestinian refugees who had left their homes in 1967.

In the occupied West Bank there was intermittent unrest throughout 1976. Demonstrations in Nablus, Ramallah and the Old City of Jerusalem in May and June were subdued by the Israeli security forces with exceptional violence. In October there were serious riots in Hebron over the respective rights of Jews and Arabs to pray in the mosque built over the Tombs of the Patriarchs. Israel's occupation policy was again condemned by the UN General Assembly on 20 December, following the publication of a report by the UN Special Committee for the Investigation of Israeli Practices in the Occupied Territories. The UN Human Rights Commission expressed 'grave concern' over the deteriorating situation in the Occupied Territories, and unanimously called on the Government of Israel to adhere to the terms of the Fourth Geneva Convention in its treatment of civilians.

Conscious of the growing tension in the Middle East and of the steadily increasing dependence of the Western world on Arab oil, the new US Administration moved swiftly to revive the Arab-Israeli peace process. In February President Carter dispatched his Secretary of State, Cyrus Vance, on a tour of the Middle East and invited Israeli and Arab leaders to visit him in Washington. During an interim period and as the prelude to a final peace agreement, the US President indicated that arrangements might be made to extend Israel's defence capability beyond its eventual legal frontiers. A week later President Carter stated, unexpectedly, that the final element in an Arab-Israeli settlement should be the creation of a 'homeland' for the dispossessed Palestinians.

ISRAELI GOVERNMENT RESIGNS

The renewed emphasis on the Palestinian aspect of the problem was unwelcome to the Israelis. The governing coalition was already under considerable internal pressure as a result of the difficult economic situation and the failure to devise any constructive policy for achieving peace with the Arabs; in addition, it had been undermined by a series of scandals involving leading figures in the Labour Party, which had dominated every government since the creation of the state. The most crucial issue facing the Government concerned the Occupied Territories and in particular the extent to which it should allow—or could control—Jewish settlement on the West Bank. The right-wing Likud coalition opposed any withdrawal from the West Bank, and Mr Rabin's Cabinet was divided on the issue; following a dispute with one of his coalition partners, Mr Rabin announced the Government's resignation. A general election was fixed for 17 May 1977.

ARAB GOVERNMENTS AND THE PLO

Once they had achieved a reconciliation between themselves and put an end to the war in Lebanon in late 1976, the Arab governments enlisted the help of the new US Administration in working towards a peace settlement with Israel. Their common position was that the Geneva conference should be reconvened, with the Palestinians participating, and that an overall settlement should be negotiated on the basis of an Israeli withdrawal to the 1967 borders and the establishment of a Palestinian state on the West Bank and the Gaza Strip. However, the PLO refused to renounce its objective of a unitary, 'secular, democratic state' in the whole of Palestine (which would replace the existing State of Israel), although PLO spokesmen did indicate their willingness to establish a state 'on any part of Palestine' from which the Israelis would withdraw.

Since the Israelis refused either to entertain the idea of an independent Palestinian state or to negotiate under any circumstances with the PLO (whether or not the PLO agreed to recognize the State of Israel), no accommodation appeared possible unless the US Government brought pressure to bear on Israel. This the Carter Administration was reluctant to do in the run-up to the Israeli general election, although there were indications that the USA was in contact with the PLO in an effort to persuade the Palestinians to modify their attitude.

RIGHT-WING VICTORY IN ISRAEL

The prospects for a negotiated Arab-Israeli settlement received a severe setback in May, when the elections in Israel resulted in an unexpected victory for the right-wing Likud grouping. The elections were fought mainly on domestic issues and the defeat of the ruling Labour Party was widely attributed to discontent over the economy and the series of scandals involving senior figures in the former administration. Likud, led by Menachem Begin (who, pre-1948, had been the leader of the terrorist organization, Irgun Zvai Leumi), was committed to maintaining Israeli rule over the whole of the occupied West Bank, on the grounds that it constituted part of Israel's divinely-ordained inheritance.

Faced with this challenge, President Carter invited the new Prime Minister of Israel to Washington and took steps to restate his own view of the prerequisites for a peace settlement in the Middle East and to obtain the acceptance of these by the USA's allies in Europe. A statement published at the end of June by the State Department reaffirmed US adherence to Security Council Resolution 242, stressing that a settlement had to involve Israeli withdrawal 'on all three fronts of the Middle East—that is, Sinai, Golan, West Bank and Gaza—and reiterating President Carter's belief in 'the need for a homeland for the Palestinians, whose exact nature should be negotiated between the parties'.

The theme of a Palestinian 'homeland' was taken up at a meeting of the heads of government of the EC in London. In a declaration published on 29 June 1977, the leaders of the nine members restated 'their view that a peace settlement should be based on Security Council Resolutions 242 and 338', adding that a solution to the Middle East conflict would be possible 'only if the legitimate right of the Palestinian people to give expression to its national identity is translated into fact, which would take into account the need for a homeland for the Palestinians'. The Declaration also said that representatives of 'the Palestinian people' must be included in peace negotiations.

When Mr Begin arrived in Washington in July 1977, he achieved an unexpected success with the US public, but it was clear that no serious attempt had been made in the talks between the two leaders to examine the basic conditions for a peace settlement. The US Administration was now intent on securing Palestinian participation in any peace negotiations, to which the Israeli Government was strenuously opposed. When the Secretary of State, Cyrus Vance, in the course of a tour of Middle Eastern capitals in August, was told by the Saudi Arabian Government that the PLO would accept Resolution 242 if it were amended to include provision for Palestinian self-determination, there was a moment of optimism in which Mr Carter spoke of the possibility that acceptance by the PLO of Resolution 242 might open the way to PLO participation in a reconvened Geneva peace conference. But Mr Vance's visit ended discouragingly in Israel, where Mr Begin's Government refused categorically to negotiate under any circumstances with the PLO or to consider the idea of a Palestinian 'homeland'. In any case, the PLO, sceptical about the terms of the proposed bargain, finally refused to amend its stance over Resolution 242 without firm assurances that it would receive in return something more substantial.

Within days of Mr Vance's departure, Israel announced that social services in the fields of education, health and welfare were to be extended to the Arab population of the West Bank and the Gaza Strip, which was widely interpreted as a step towards the annexation of these areas. This, and the decision to authorize three new Jewish settlements on the West Bank, caused an immediate consolidation of the PLO attitude and complicated still further the task of the USA in bringing the Israelis and the Arabs—including, if possible, the Palestinians—to the negotiating table.

When the Israeli Foreign Minister, Moshe Dayan, went to Washington in September 1977, he took with him draft proposals for a territorial settlement which envisaged the maintenance of the Israeli occupation throughout the West Bank and the Gaza Strip. These proposals expressed the continuing resolve of Mr Begin's Government not to agree to any step which could lead to the creation of an independent Palestinian state. The USA, by contrast, was apprehensive that anything which appeared to extinguish all hope of that ill-defined Palestinian 'homeland', would not merely ensure the continuation of Palestinian resistance but would also alienate those Arab governments on whose goodwill the USA was increasingly dependent.

Towards the end of September there was a fresh outbreak of fighting in southern Lebanon, with Israeli troops openly intervening across the border in support of right-wing forces and against the Palestinians. This prompted a US initiative, reluctantly accepted by the Israeli Government, to include Palestinian representatives in a joint Arab delegation to the peace conference in Geneva. Moshe Dayan emphasized that this did not mean that Israel was ready to abandon its attitude towards the PLO or its rejection of a Palestinian state. A joint Soviet-US statement published on 1 October 1977 called for a Middle East settlement that would ensure 'the legitimate rights of the Palestinians'. The use for the first time of this phrase by the US Government alarmed Israel and was taken by the Arabs as an indication that President Carter was prepared for the confrontation that had long been threatening with the Israeli Government and its powerful supporters in the USA. The prospect raised by the joint statement, however, that the two superpowers were prepared to collaborate again made a renewal of the Geneva Conference more likely and encouraged diplomatic activity, with even the PLO expressing its qualified acceptance of the Soviet-US statement as the basis for a reconvened peace conference.

PRESIDENT SADAT'S VISIT TO JERUSALEM

On 9 November 1977, in the course of a speech to the Egyptian Parliament in which he expressed impatience with the endless debates over procedural questions, President Sadat said that he would be willing to go to Jerusalem and to the Knesset itself to negotiate with Israel. Despite widely expressed scepticism, the suggestion was immediately taken up by the Israeli Prime Minister and pursued through intermediaries in the US embassies in Cairo, Beirut and Jerusalem. Resisting a rising tide of Arab disapproval, and despite the last-minute resignation of his Minister of Foreign Affairs, President Sadat flew to Jerusalem on 19 November 1977, and the next day made a dramatic appeal for peace in the Knesset and before the television cameras of the world.

This unexpected initiative was greeted with enthusiasm in the West, where it was regarded as a constructive break with the sterile attitudes of the past, and with incredulous delight by Israel, which glimpsed the prospect of an end to its dangerous isolation. Among the Arabs, however, while there were scattered expressions of approval and optimism, the general reaction of furious resentment left the Arab world in a state of unparalleled disunity, making it harder than ever to achieve a common platform on which to negotiate with Israel.

Nor did the euphoria which surrounded President Sadat in Jerusalem long survive his return to Cairo. It soon became apparent that his Israeli hosts had assumed—like his Arab critics—that President Sadat had despaired of achieving an overall settlement and had set himself the more limited objective of an Egyptian-Israeli peace treaty. The Israeli leaders were ready to withdraw from almost all Egyptian territory but they were not prepared to meet Mr Sadat's other demands for a complete withdrawal from all Arab territory occupied in 1967 and recognition of the Palestinian right to self-determination.

Serious negotiations were postponed until 25 December 1977, when Mr Begin flew to Ismailia for a summit meeting with President Sadat, at which the Israeli Prime Minister produced a set of proposals for the future of Sinai, the West Bank and the Gaza Strip. On the crucial question of the future of the Palestinians, Mr Begin offered only a limited form of self-rule for the population of the West Bank and the Gaza Strip, with Israel remaining in control of 'security and public order'. This was criticized in the Arab world as being merely a formula for the maintenance of the Israeli occupation.

President Sadat's position was made more difficult by a statement from President Carter apparently approving the Begin proposal for Palestinian 'self-rule'. When Mr Carter, in an evident attempt to repair the damage, altered the schedule of a foreign tour in order to meet Mr Sadat at Aswan, he took the opportunity to reiterate the need to recognize 'the legitimate rights of the Palestinian people' and to enable the Palestinians 'to participate in the determination of their own future'. Elsewhere in the Arab world, however, cynicism about an overall Arab-Israeli settlement was deepened by mistrust of Sadat's motives and by the apparent inconsistency of US policy.

The Ismailia summit meeting produced a commitment to bilateral talks on political and military questions affecting a settlement. The military talks opened in Cairo on 11 January 1978 and were at once complicated by a dispute over Israeli settlements in Sinai, which had been criticized as illegal by the International Commission of Jurists. This criticism was echoed by President Carter a week later and when the political talks opened in Jerusalem on 16 January they were interrupted after only 24 hours when President Sadat recalled the Egyptian delegation, saying that in view of Israel's insistence on retaining the settlements he saw no hope of reaching agreement.

ISRAELI INVASION OF SOUTH LEBANON

A visit by Mr Begin to Washington in March 1978 was delayed for a week after a terrorist raid near Tel-Aviv by Palestinian guerrillas operating from south Lebanon, in which 36 Israelis were killed. Israel mounted a major cross-border attack into southern Lebanon, initially to wipe out Palestinian guerrilla bases and establish a security belt along the Lebanese side of the frontier. After the USA hurriedly introduced a resolution in the UN Security Council calling for an Israeli withdrawal to be supervised by a UN force, the Israelis advanced further, and by the time a cease-fire finally came into effect on 20 March their forces were in occupation of the whole of south Lebanon as far as the Litani river, with the exception of the port of Tyre.

The Israeli invasion, which was accompanied by heavy and indiscriminate land, sea and air bombardments, provoked world-wide denunciation, especially as it became clear that an estimated 1,000 Lebanese civilians had been killed, in addition to some 200 guerrillas, and more than 200,000 refugees had been driven from their homes. When Mr Begin finally met President Carter on 20 March, the differences between them over the basic prerequisites of a Middle East peace settlement led to a confrontation which was barely masked by diplomatic protocol. Mr Begin returned from Washington to face a threat to his leadership in Israel, where there was dissension within the Cabinet.

There was friction over the role of the UN Interim Force in Lebanon (UNIFIL), whose mandate was to supervise the withdrawal of the Israeli army from southern Lebanon and to restore the authority of the Lebanese Government. The Israelis carried out a partial withdrawal at the end of April but insisted that they would maintain an armed presence in Lebanon until the UN force could ensure the security of northern Israel against attacks by Palestinian guerrillas. The PLO, which was determined not to relinquish its last area of operations, promised to co-operate with UNIFIL.

In May 1978 Mr Begin again visited Washington, where President Carter assured him that 'we will never waver in our absolute commitment to Israel's security'. However, two weeks later the US Senate authorized the sale of advanced fighter aircraft to Saudi Arabia. This decision clearly reflected US impatience with Mr Begin's stand on peace negotiations, and the importance the USA attached to retaining the friendship of Saudi Arabia, the leading oil producer in the Middle East.

When the Israelis withdrew the last of their forces from south Lebanon on 13 June, they refused to hand over their positions to UNIFIL but left them in the hands of Lebanese Christian militia units which had been collaborating with the Israelis against the Lebanese Government. This contributed to a crisis in Beirut at the beginning of July, when the Syrian-dominated Arab peace-keeping force attempted to impose its authority on the right-wing Christian militias.

The US Government, alarmed at the prospect of renewed Israeli intervention and of the final breakdown of the peace initiative launched by President Sadat in November 1977, exerted its influence to restrain both sides in Lebanon and persuaded the Israeli and Egyptian Governments to send their ministers of foreign affairs to a meeting in the United Kingdom, which took place at Leeds Castle on 18 July. When this meeting failed to narrow the gap between the two sides, President Sadat announced that he would not engage in further negotiations with Israel unless the Israeli Government changed its position. Faced with a deteriorating situation, President Carter took the unexpected step of inviting the Egyptian and Israeli leaders to meet him in a final attempt to break the deadlock at Camp David at the beginning of September 1978.

CAMP DAVID SUMMIT AND REACTIONS

The Camp David meeting, which lasted for 12 days and appeared more than once to be on the point of breaking down, ended on 17 September when President Carter made a triumphant appearance on television to announce that Mr Begin and President Sadat had signed two documents which together provided a framework for peace in the Middle East (see Documents on Palestine, p. 119). One of these dealt with the bilateral problems between Egypt and Israel, which the two leaders undertook to resolve by concluding within three months a peace treaty providing for an Israeli withdrawal from Sinai and the establishment of normal relations between the two countries. The other dealt with the wider question of the future of the West Bank and Gaza and provided for the election of a self-governing Palestinian authority to replace the existing Israeli military Government; once the authority was in being, there should be a transitional period of not more than five years, during which the inhabitants of the West Bank and Gaza would exercise autonomy; and finally, 'as soon as possible, but not later than the third year after the beginning of the transitional period', there should be negotiations to determine the final status of the West Bank and Gaza and to conclude a peace treaty between Israel and Jordan.

The Camp David agreements were greeted with a mixed reception by the participants. President Carter's own standing was greatly enhanced in the USA, where it was felt that his daring personal diplomacy had forced the Israeli and Egyptian leaders to make concessions. In Israel the agreements were greeted with more cautious approval, in the belief that Mr Begin had realized Israel's long-standing ambition to conclude a separate peace with Egypt without making any substantive concessions over Israel's right to maintain control of the West Bank and Gaza. In the Arab world, however, the agreements were regarded as proof that President Sadat had abandoned the Palestinians and his Arab allies. Even the Government of Saudi Arabia commented that the Camp David agreements constituted 'an unacceptable formula for a definitive peace', while the resignation of the Egyptian Minister of Foreign Affairs (who was at Camp David with President Sadat) showed that not even Egyptian opinion was whole-heartedly in favour of the Camp David formula.

The controversy within the Arab world centred on whether or not the agreements offered any real promise of eventual self-determination for the Palestinians. The advocates of the Camp David 'framework for peace' argued that if the Palestinians co-operated in the arrangements for a transitional period of self-rule they would set in motion a process which would be irreversible; that the end result of this process would be an independent Palestinian state; and that, if the Palestinians refused to co-operate, they would provide Israel with an excuse to perpetuate its occupation of the West Bank and Gaza. Critics argued that it was futile for Egypt to negotiate on behalf of the Palestinians over an issue on which the Palestinians themselves had not been consulted; that the arrangements for Palestinian autonomy outlined at Camp David were so imprecise as to be useless; that in any case Israel would hold a power of veto over their implementation and over the eventual future of the West Bank; and that Israel had no intention of ending its occupation or of allowing any development which might lead to Palestinian independence.

The last of these arguments was given greater credence in the immediate aftermath of the Camp David meeting by the actions of Mr Begin. On his return to Israel, he declared emphatically in the Knesset that Israel would not 'under any conditions or in any circumstances' allow the establishment of an independent Palestinian state, and that Israel would continue to create new settlements on the West Bank and would expect to maintain an armed presence there even after the end of the five-year transitional period.

ARAB OPPOSITION INTENSIFIES

In the circumstances it was not surprising that the US Secretary of State, Mr Vance, whom President Carter dispatched to the Middle East to enlist Arab support for the Camp David agreements, met with a frosty reception. The Governments of Jordan (whose co-operation would be necessary if the provisions for the West Bank were to be put into effect) and of Saudi Arabia (whose influence was important in shaping Arab opinion) both expressed serious reservations, while the more radical Arab governments, led by Syria acting in co-operation with the PLO, declared their rejection of the agreements.

So strong were the feelings aroused in the Arab world that they led to a reconciliation between the rival Baathist Governments of Iraq and Syria, and to a summit conference of all the Arab states (apart from Egypt) in Baghdad at the beginning of November 1978 to consider means of preventing the implementation of the Camp David agreements. After a fiery debate in which various proposals were aired for isolating Egypt and denying it economic aid, the Arab leaders agreed, at the insistence of Saudi Arabia, to delay implementation until Egypt should actually sign a peace treaty with Israel, thus allowing President Sadat the opportunity to reconsider a policy which would leave him totally dependent on the support of the USA. Further decisions by the Israelis to press ahead with their settlements in the West Bank led President Sadat to press for a revision of the Camp David agreements in order to link the provisions concerning the future of the West Bank more closely to those for a bilateral peace treaty between Egypt and Israel. In addition, President Sadat demanded that a specific timetable be adopted for the introduction of autonomy in the West Bank. This brought the peace-making process once again to a standstill, and the target date of 18 December (by which time the two sides had agreed at Camp David to sign a peace treaty) passed with the outstanding issues unresolved.

REVOLUTION IN IRAN

The disintegration of the Shah's regime in Iran at the end of 1978 had important repercussions throughout the Middle East. The suspension of oil exports from Iran, as a result of a strike in the oilfields, threatened an international energy crisis and cut off the most important source of Israel's oil supplies. It also became clear, even before the Shah went into exile on 15 January 1979, that whatever government might succeed him would give strong backing to the Palestinians.

These developments gave added urgency to the US desire to achieve at least a partial Arab-Israeli settlement, but reinforced the positions of all the possible participants. Israel insisted on an Egyptian undertaking in the draft peace treaty to guarantee them access to oil from Sinai after their evacuation of the peninsula. For President Sadat it became more necessary than ever to obtain some concession over the West Bank. Without such a concession it was less likely that Saudi Arabia or Jordan—let alone the other Arab states—would moderate their opposition to the Camp David peace formula.

PRESIDENT CARTER VISITS THE MIDDLE EAST

When a further ministerial meeting in Washington between Egypt and Israel failed to remove the remaining obstacles to an agreement, President Carter flew to the Middle East on 7 March 1979 in a final effort to persuade Egypt and Israel to sign the long-deferred peace treaty. Mr Carter returned to Washington to announce that 'we have now defined the major components of a peace treaty'; but before the treaty could be signed there were further acrimonious arguments about Israeli settlements on the West Bank, while opposition to the peace treaty on the part of even the most moderate Arab governments emphasized the isolation of Egypt.

ARAB BOYCOTT OF EGYPT

The attitude of Saudi Arabia was crucial, and the euphoria in the USA over the signing of the peace treaty—which finally took place in Washington on 26 March 1979 (see Documents on Palestine, p. 121)—was dispelled when Saudi Arabia made plain its opposition by attending a meeting of the Arab League in Baghdad at which a decision was taken to impose a political and economic boycott against Egypt. Arab ambassadors were recalled from Cairo, economic aid to Egypt was suspended and it was announced that the headquarters of the Arab League would be transferred from Cairo to Tunis. In agreeing to these measures and in subsequently severing diplomatic relations with Egypt, the Government of Saudi Arabia in effect chose to maintain solidarity with the rest of the Arab world at the expense of an open breach with the USA.

Arab opposition to the peace treaty focused on its failure to make any clear provision for Palestinian self-determination. President Sadat maintained that the treaty was the first step towards a comprehensive settlement which would restore Palestinian rights; but to the other Arabs it appeared to be a separate peace between Egypt and Israel which would restore Sinai to Egypt but would leave Israel in control of the rest of the Occupied Territories. That this was also the view of the Israeli Government seemed to be confirmed when Mr Begin, in a broadcast on Israel's Independence Day, reiterated that no border would ever again be drawn through 'the land of Israel' and that 'we shall never withdraw from the Golan Heights'.

THE AUTONOMY TALKS

Soon after the signing of the Egyptian-Israeli peace treaty the two countries began negotiations on the question of autonomy for the Palestinians in the Occupied Territories. The principal issue on which the two sides differed was the establishment of Israeli settlements in the Occupied Territories, which the Israeli Prime Minister, Mr Begin, insisted were in no way contrary to the Camp David Accords. When the Israeli Minister in Charge of Settlements, Ariel Sharon, announced plans at the end of May 1979 to build new settlements on the West Bank and in the Gaza Strip, the Egyptian Prime Minister, Mustapha Khalil, warned Israel that this would jeopardize the peace process. Shortly afterwards, on 12 June, the second round of talks ended with the two sides unable to agree on even the first principles of the autonomy plan.

On 4 September President Sadat went to Haifa to begin new talks with Mr Begin and announced that he was 'determined to spread the umbrella of peace to include the Palestinian people'. Bilateral agreements were made on the issues of border patrols, oil sales from Egypt to Israel, and the return of the Santa Caterina monastery to the Egyptians, but no progress was registered on the autonomy question. The two countries drifted still further apart a week later when the Israeli Government withdrew its ban on the purchase by Israeli citizens of Arab land in the Occupied Territories, an action immediately condemned by the US Government.

ISRAEL'S INTERNAL DISPUTES

In Israel, although the opposition movement, Peace Now, organized demonstrations against the establishment of more settlements in the Occupied Territories, a parliamentary committee in July 1979 approved plans to build 13 new settlements during the forthcoming 12 months. However, the Israeli Supreme Court ruled that the Elon Moreh settlement near Nablus was illegal. The ruling denied that the settlement served a necessary military function and ordered the expropriated land to be restored to its Arab owners. At the end of October an extremist nationalist party, Tehiya, was founded, its principal objective being the construction of Jewish settlements throughout the West Bank.

PALESTINIAN DIPLOMATIC GAINS

In mid-1979 there was speculation that the USA was making overtures to the PLO in order to bring it into the peace process. Although this was repeatedly denied by President Carter, the US Ambassador at the UN, Andrew Young, met the PLO observer, Zehdi Labib Terzi, in September. After strong protests from the Israelis, Young resigned, declaring that the USA's refusal to talk to the PLO was ridiculous.

Meanwhile, the PLO was making significant diplomatic headway in western Europe. In July Yasser Arafat had talks with Chancellor Kreisky of Austria and in September he was officially received by King Juan Carlos of Spain and his Prime Minister, Adolfo Suárez. At the UN General Assembly meeting later in the month, the Irish Minister of Foreign Affairs, Michael O'Kennedy, speaking on behalf of the EC, voiced strong criticism of current Israeli policy and mentioned, for the first time, the role of the PLO. In the same debate the British Foreign Secretary, Lord Carrington, called for an end to Israel's policy of settlement in the Occupied Territories and for a reversal of the decision to allow Israeli citizens to buy land there. In November the PLO was accorded 'political recognition' by the Italian Government and at the same time Arafat was received by the President and Prime Minister of Portugal. In addition, the PLO's spokesman on foreign affairs, Farouk Kaddoumi, held talks with the foreign ministers of Belgium, Italy and Greece.

UNREST IN THE WEST BANK

While Egypt and Israel made little progress on the autonomy question, the Palestinian population of the West Bank grew increasingly restless and frustrated. In February 1980 a new crisis arose when the Israeli Cabinet decided in principle to allow Jews to settle in the town of Hebron. This action was widely condemned in Israel and abroad and led to increased tension throughout the West Bank. Riots and demonstrations took place in a number of towns and in April a group of Jewish extremists mounted attacks in Ramallah. On 1 May a Palestinian youth was shot dead by an Israeli officer in Anabta, and the following day PLO guerrillas struck in Hebron and killed six Jewish settlers. The Israeli authorities reacted by destroying a number of houses near the scene of the ambush and deporting the mayors of Hebron and Halhul and the Qadi (religious leader) of Hebron.

NO PROGRESS TOWARDS REAL PEACE

The seizure of US embassy officials in Iran and the Soviet invasion of Afghanistan at the end of 1979 diverted international attention from the Arab–Israeli conflict and the USA concentrated its attention on the recovery of the hostages in Teheran. On 1 March 1980, however, the UN Security Council unanimously adopted a resolution (465 — see Documents on Palestine, p. 122) calling upon Israel to 'dismantle the existing settlements' and 'to cease, on an urgent basis, the establishment, construction and planning' of new ones. Two days later President Carter astonished the international community by retracting the affirmative US vote and announcing that it had been a mistake. The US vote, he said, had been 'approved with the understanding that all references to Jerusalem would be deleted', and he added: 'While our opposition to the establishment of the Israeli settlements is long-standing and well known . . . the call for dismantling was neither proper nor practical.' This retraction was widely seen as a surrender to the Zionist lobby by a US president needing votes in an election year.

As the autonomy negotiations showed little sign of progress, the EC sought new ways to break the deadlock. One idea was the suggestion that Resolution 242 should be amended to include a reference to the right of self-determination for the Palestinians. In February, during a visit to Bahrain, the Irish Minister of Foreign Affairs recognized the PLO and called for the establishment of a Palestinian state. In the course of an important tour of the Middle East in the following month, President Giscard d'Estaing of France supported the principle of self-determination for the Palestinians and spoke of the need to include the PLO in peace negotiations. In April the PLO's diplomatic success in Europe continued when Chancellor Kreisky of Austria officially recognized the PLO as the representative of the Palestinian people.

The USA made it clear that it disapproved of European attempts to intervene in the peace process. In March President Carter, under attack from the other presidential candidates for his inept handling of the Security Council vote, decided to make yet another attempt to mediate between Israel and Egypt. Although the two countries had exchanged ambassadors and some successes had been achieved on bilateral relations, their positions on the autonomy issue were as far apart as ever. Determined to make some progress before 26 May (the target date for the completion of the autonomy talks), President Carter invited President Sadat and Mr Begin to visit him separately in Washington during April. Nothing was achieved and at the beginning of May President Sadat announced that Egypt was suspending the negotiations indefinitely.

THE EUROPEAN INITIATIVE

Despite the opposition of Israel, Egypt and the USA, the EC countries finally produced their Middle East statement at a meeting in Venice on 13 June (see Documents on Palestine, p. 123). After criticism from the new US Secretary of State, Edmund Muskie, and a warning from President Carter that the USA would not hesitate to use its veto in the Security Council, the EC abandoned any attempt to introduce a resolution on Palestinian rights at the UN. However, they did go further than ever before in their support of Palestinian aspirations.

In the Venice statement, the EC declared, for the first time collectively, that the Palestinian people must be allowed 'to exercise fully its right to self-determination', and called for the PLO 'to be associated with the negotiations'. It also repeated its condemnations of Israeli settlements and any attempt to change the status of Jerusalem. Finally the EC announced its intention of consulting all the parties concerned, in order to determine the form of a European initiative.

EGYPTIAN–ISRAELI RELATIONS

The negotiations over Palestinian autonomy, which President Sadat had postponed in May 1980, were reopened in Washington in July. However, the parties' positions were as firmly entrenched as ever, and there was speculation that President Sadat had decided to resume the talks only in order to increase the chances of President Carter's re-election in the forthcoming US elections.

Meanwhile the so-called 'normalization' of relations between Egypt and Israel was moving forward at a slow pace. Although both countries had established embassies in each other's capitals and there were regular air-flights between the two, other agreements were taking a long time to implement.

WEST BANK NATIONALISM

Only a month after the mayors of Hebron and Halhul had been deported by the Israeli authorities, Jewish extremists placed bombs in the cars of three other West Bank mayors. Two of them were severely injured, including Bassam Shaka, the Mayor of Nablus, who lost both his legs. The attacks revealed the existence of a militant underground movement among Jewish settlers in the West Bank, which, in the ensuing weeks, issued death threats to Arabs and moderate Israelis, including Knesset members and prominent journalists. Tension increased as leading Palestinians, including Mayor Shaka, accused the Israeli Government of having links with the extremists. The Government's failure to investigate the crime properly, and the allegation that the head of the Shin Bet (Israel's internal security and intelligence service) had resigned because Mr Begin had refused to allow him to carry out an investigation of members of Gush Emunim (the main West Bank settlement organization), added substance to these suspicions.

PARTY RIVALRY IN ISRAEL

Opinion polls in Israel had long been predicting a disastrous defeat for Mr Begin's Government at the next general election, which had to be held before November 1981. Likud's unpopularity stemmed largely from its failure to solve the country's economic problems but during the early months of 1981 attention in Israel and abroad was focused on the parties' conflicting policies towards the Occupied Territories.

For electoral and other reasons, the Labour Party refused to define its policy towards the West Bank but it emphasized that it did not plan to annex the area. The Labour leader, Shimon Peres, seemed to favour the so-called 'Jordanian option', involving the return of the populated areas to Jordan but the retention of the Jordan Valley and various blocks of settlements. Although King Hussein of Jordan repeatedly declared that no such option existed and that he was not empowered to speak for the Palestinians, Labour politicians continued to think in terms of a partition of the West Bank.

The Likud Government was determined to make it impossible to implement this policy. In the months before the election, which was to be held in June 1981, the Likud coalition decided to launch a vast new settlement programme which an incoming Labour government would be unable to dismantle.

REAGAN ELECTED IN THE USA

The election of Ronald Reagan as President of the USA in 1980 was greeted enthusiastically in Israel but caused dismay in the Arab world. During the campaign Mr Reagan had made pro-Israeli statements that seemed excessive even for a US presidential candidate and his early appointments reflected the influence of his team of Zionist advisers. Nearly all of the Reagan appointees shared the feelings of the new Secretary of State, Alexander Haig, and the National Security Adviser, Richard Allen, who judged the Arab–Israeli conflict not on its own terms but in the context of the East–West confrontation. Dismay in the Arab world was increased by the new President's apparent ignorance of the issues; in an interview soon after taking office, Mr Reagan declared that the Israeli settlements were 'not illegal', thereby contradicting what had long been official US policy.

The US Administration soon made it clear that it regarded the European initiative as a hindrance to its own efforts in the Middle East. The USA's main preoccupation was not with the Palestinian question, but with the threat which it believed the USSR posed to the oil-rich Gulf. To counter this threat, the USA created a rapid deployment force able to intervene where necessary in the Gulf area. Although the Gulf Arabs denied the existence of a Soviet threat and declared their opposition to such a force, the USA went ahead with its plans to establish bases in Oman, Somalia and Kenya. In April 1981 Mr Haig visited Egypt, Israel, Jordan and Saudi Arabia, intent on convincing the conservative Arab regimes of the Soviet threat. Both Jordan and Saudi Arabia, two of the USA's closest allies in the Arab world, showed themselves to be highly sceptical about the Reagan Administration's new priorities, while Syria, the PLO and other forces in the region were even more critical of US policies.

FIGHTING ESCALATES IN LEBANON

At the beginning of March 1981 the Syrian and Lebanese Governments agreed to send regular units of the Lebanese army to join UNIFIL forces in southern Lebanon. This move was opposed by the Israeli-backed Lebanese rebel leader, Maj. Sa'ad Haddad, whose troops subsequently opened fire on UNIFIL positions. It was in response to this action and to attempts by the Phalangist Christian militia to strengthen its positions around the Lebanese town of Zahle that Syrian troops of the Arab Deterrent Force moved against the Maronite Christian positions in central Lebanon.

In early April Lebanon experienced its most serious fighting since the end of the civil war in 1976. The battles around Zahle were followed by fighting in Beirut and Baalbek and in the south between Haddad's forces and the Palestinians. After a truce during the week before Easter, Israel launched a series of attacks against the south. Renewed fighting broke out between the Syrians and the Phalangists on 27 April and the following day the Israeli air force shot down two Syrian helicopters. In response to this attack Syria deployed a number of SAM-6 anti-aircraft missiles to defend its positions in the Beka'a valley.

THE SYRIAN MISSILE CRISIS

Although the Syrian missiles were stationed deep inside Lebanon, far from the Israeli border, and fulfilled a defensive function, Mr Begin demanded their withdrawal because they limited Israel's ability to fly over its northern neighbour. Philip Habib, the US Special Envoy to the Middle East, made a series of visits to Jerusalem and Damascus during May in an attempt to draft a compromise formula to persuade Saudi Arabia to encourage the Syrians to modify their position. Instead, Saudi Arabia opened a round of inter-Arab negotiations aimed at reaching agreement on the main points of a comprehensive Lebanese settlement, which would then make it easier to solve the crisis caused by the missiles. The settlement envisaged was to be based on the conclusions of the Beiteddine conference of 1978 with provisions for the future relations between the Lebanese factions, between Syria and Lebanon, and between the Palestinians and the Lebanese Government. Meanwhile, inter-Arab relations, which had deteriorated since the beginning of the Iran–Iraq War, improved, and at a meeting of Arab ministers of foreign affairs, in Tunis on 23 May, Syria received the almost unanimous backing of the Arab world.

Hopes that Syria might accept a formula offered by the USA were frustrated by a new wave of Israeli attacks on Lebanon and by the further demands of Mr Begin, who insisted on the removal of anti-aircraft missiles inside Lebanon and a Syrian guarantee that Israeli aircraft would not be targeted while they were 'patrolling' Lebanon. In June Mr Begin warned that, if the USA failed to arrange the withdrawal of the missiles through diplomacy, Israel would remove them by force.

ISRAEL ATTACKS IRAQ

On 7 June 1981, with the Syrian missile crisis still unresolved, the Israelis bombed and destroyed the Iraqi nuclear plant near Baghdad. Mr Begin immediately claimed that the attack was justified on the grounds of self-defence, as Iraq would soon have had the capacity to produce nuclear bombs. However, the International Atomic Energy Agency (IAEA) in Vienna, which had recently inspected the plant, said that Iraq would not have had the means to make nuclear weapons for many years, a view supported by the Congressional research service in Washington. The IAEA pointed out that Iraq, unlike Israel, was a signatory of the Nuclear Non-Proliferation Treaty and that it had co-operated with the agency over safeguards.

The raid was criticized by governments all over the world, while in the UN Security Council, the United Kingdom and France demanded a 'firm resolution' condemning Israel. Even the Israeli opposition leader, Shimon Peres, accused Mr Begin of 'acting out of electoral considerations which ignore the national interest'. President Reagan responded by suspending the delivery of four F-16 aircraft to Israel until the US Congress had decided whether or not Israel had violated an agreement whereby US weapons were sold on condition they were not used in 'an act of aggression against any other state'. Nevertheless, the President made it clear where his sympathies lay when he stated that Israel had 'reason for concern' about Iraq's nuclear capacity.

BEGIN RETAINS POWER

The Israeli general elections, which took place on 30 June 1981, were the most violent in the country's history. The campaign was characterized by the Prime Minister's demagogic performances in front of huge crowds and by the physical attacks of his Likud supporters against members and property of the opposition Labour Party. Mr Begin's aggressive foreign policy obscured his Government's failures in tackling domestic problems and, in the elections, the Labour Party failed to gain the predicted huge victory. The results showed the two main parties to be evenly balanced, but it was soon clear that the Prime Minister would remain in power if he could persuade the various religious parties to join him in a coalition. This he achieved and a new Cabinet emerged, more homogeneous and uncompromising than its predecessor. The most significant appointment was that of Ariel Sharon, one of Israel's leading 'hawks', to the defence ministry.

Ten days after the elections, Israel launched a series of air strikes against Palestinian targets in southern Lebanon. Guerrillas belonging to the PLO retaliated with rocket and artillery attacks against settlements in Galilee and Israel, in turn, responded with further air strikes and with raids by sea-borne commandos. This time the targets included urban areas and in one strike against Beirut on 17 July more than 150 people were killed and 600 wounded. The international community was shocked by the action and the USA reacted by again suspending the delivery of F-16 aircraft to Israel and by making intensive attempts to bring about a cease-fire. While President Reagan's special envoy, Philip Habib, was trying to persuade Israel to accept a truce, Saudi Arabia was putting similar pressure on the Palestinians. A cease-fire finally came into effect on 24 July.

THE DEATH OF SADAT

In August 1981 President Sadat visited Washington for the first time since the election of President Reagan. Although the USA did not accept his suggestion that it should negotiate with the PLO, the visit was considered to be a diplomatic success. Yet, for all his popularity in the West, Sadat faced major problems inside Egypt.

During the summer there had been serious clashes between Copts and Muslim fundamentalists, and at the beginning of September some 1,700 people were arrested, a number of newspapers closed down and several foreign journalists expelled. Among those arrested were a large number of the President's political opponents who were neither Copts nor Muslim fundamentalists, which suggested that Sadat was using the religious clashes as a pretext to purge the opposition. A month after the arrests, however, President Sadat was assassinated by Muslim extremists at a military parade in Cairo. The large Western attendance at his funeral, which included three former US Presidents, presented a stark contrast to the lack of grief in evidence on the streets of the capital and indicated how much Sadat's popularity in his own country had declined as a result of his pro-Western stance on foreign policy.

EUROPE AND THE FAHD PLAN

The major diplomatic initiative of the second half of 1981 came from Saudi Arabia. The so-called 'Fahd Plan' was put forward by Crown Prince Fahd (see Documents on Palestine, p. 124). Although the USA reacted cautiously to the plan, European ministers of foreign affairs described it as 'extremely positive' and particularly welcomed Point Seven which, by guaranteeing 'the right of all states in the region to live in peace', indicated that Saudi Arabia was prepared to recognize Israel in return for a complete withdrawal from the Occupied Territories and the establishment of an independent Palestinian state.

Although Mr Begin described the Fahd Plan as a recipe for the destruction of Israel, the Europeans were quick to note its similarities to their own Venice Declaration of June 1980. By the end of the year, however, both plans had been virtually abandoned. Europe's initiative was wrecked when the French Minister of Foreign Affairs, Claude Cheysson, dissociated his Government from it during a visit to Israel and the Saudi plan collapsed at the end of November. Since its publication in August no member of the Arab League, apart from Libya, had rejected the Fahd Plan outright and even the PLO Chairman, Yasser Arafat, had expressed approval. The Saudi delegation went to the first Fez Arab summit in November confident, therefore, that it could win broad support for its proposals. However, a number of Arab states, led by Syria, were opposed to the plan, not so much for its content as for its timing. At Fez the opposition hardened and, rather than allow the summit to degenerate into a lengthy public quarrel, King Hassan of Morocco closed the meeting after only a few hours.

THE GOLAN ANNEXATION

In December 1981, while international attention was concentrated on the crisis in Poland, the Israeli Government decided to annex the Syrian Golan Heights. Overruling the more cautious minority in his Cabinet, on 14 December Mr Begin pushed through the Knesset a bill which extended Israeli laws, jurisdiction and administration to the territory Israel had occupied since 1967. The UN Security Council unanimously condemned the action and gave Israel two weeks to rescind its decision. When the Israeli Government refused to comply, the Security Council reconvened at the beginning of January 1982 in order to study what measures should be taken against Israel. Syria advocated a resolution calling for mandatory sanctions under Chapter Seven of the UN Charter but, in a bid to attract wider international support, Jordan introduced a milder resolution calling merely for voluntary sanctions against Israel. Even this was too harsh in the opinion of the USA, which vetoed the resolution, although at the same time stressing its opposition to the annexation.

THE USA WITHOUT A POLICY

After more than a year in office, the Reagan Administration, which had been lukewarm to the Fahd Plan and hostile to the European initiative, had still not made any proposals of its own. While ostensibly working towards a resumption of the autonomy talks between Egypt and Israel, and hoping that the Israeli withdrawal from Sinai in April 1982 would take place smoothly, the Administration's main concern remained the so-called 'Soviet threat'. It was primarily for strategic reasons that the USA made its two most important moves in the autumn of 1981: the sale of sophisticated radar aircraft (AWACS) to Saudi Arabia, which was endorsed by Congress after strong opposition from the Zionist lobby in October, and the signing of a 'memorandum of understanding' on defence co-operation with Israel on 30 November. However, this last agreement was suspended by the USA a fortnight later to show its disapproval of Israel's annexation of the Golan Heights; Begin reacted by verbally attacking the USA and repudiating the memorandum altogether.

ISRAEL WITHDRAWS FROM SINAI

Although President Mubarak of Egypt indicated soon after he succeeded Sadat that he wanted to improve his country's relations with the rest of the Arab world, it was clear that his immediate goal was the return of the last third of Sinai, which Israel was due to hand back in April 1982. Consequently, he was anxious to avoid any action which might offer Israel a pretext to continue the occupation. Within Israel there was much apprehension over the evacuation of Sinai and fears that it might lead to violence among the Jewish population.

In March, after months of hesitation, the Government finally ordered the army to move into the Yamit area and evict illegal settlers who had recently entered it. The withdrawal took place as scheduled on 25 April, and, in order not to antagonize Israel, Egypt recovered the key areas of Rafah and Sharm esh-Sheikh with as little ceremony as possible.

THE WEST BANK REVOLTS

For several months Israel had been trying to create an 'alternative' leadership among the inhabitants of the West Bank which would collaborate in imposing some form of limited autonomy on the Palestinians. With financial aid and military protection from Israel, a small number of 'village leagues' were established in a move to counter the radical nationalism of the urban leadership. Although the attempt was largely unsuccessful, it did provoke several of the West Bank's more radical mayors into refusing to collaborate with the Israeli administration. In response, on 18 March, the occupation authorities dismissed the Mayor of al-Bireh, Ibrahim Tawil, as well as the town's council.

The dismissals caused a three-day strike in East Jerusalem and the rest of the West Bank, which was later extended as a result of the harsh manner in which the Israeli army dealt with Palestinian demonstrators. Rioting took place in most West Bank towns and spread to the Gaza Strip. A week after the action taken against the al-Bireh town council, Israel issued summary dismissal orders against the Mayor of Ramallah, Karim Khalaf, and the Mayor of Nablus, Bassam Shaka. These dismissals provoked two weeks of the worst rioting the West Bank had yet seen, in which several Palestinians were killed.

ISRAEL'S 1982 INVASION OF LEBANON

The cease-fire on the Israel-Lebanon border, which had been arranged by the US Special Envoy Philip Habib in July 1981, held for less than a year. In May 1982 the Israeli air force struck at Palestinian positions inside Lebanon and PLO guerrillas retaliated by shelling Galilee. On 4 June, anti-PLO Arab gunmen shot and wounded the Israeli Ambassador to London, Shlomo Argov, and Israeli aircraft bombed targets in southern Lebanon and west Beirut. The PLO's subsequent bombardment of northern Israel—which did not result in loss of life—was the official pretext for an invasion the Israelis entitled 'Operation Peace for Galilee'. However, Gen. Sharon subsequently revealed that he had been planning the operation since becoming Minister of Defence in July 1981 and he had even visited Beirut secretly in January 1982, in preparation.

On 6 June the Israeli army, numbering some 30,000, brushed aside the UN forces in southern Lebanon and attacked Palestinian positions around Beaufort Castle and along the coast road to Tyre. While Israel's air force, backed up by the navy, bombed Beirut and other towns, infantry units were landed along the Lebanese coast. The Israelis captured Nabatiyah, Tyre, Sidon and Damour after massive bombardments which resulted in severe damage and thousands of civilian casualties. By 10 June Israeli troops had reached positions overlooking Beirut.

Syria, which had maintained some 30,000 troops in Lebanon since its intervention in 1976, tried to avoid being drawn into the war but on the fourth day of the invasion its forces clashed with the advancing Israelis. Although the battles on the ground never became as serious as in the 1973 war, Syria committed its air force against the Israelis and suffered a heavy defeat. On 11 June, under diplomatic pressure from the USA, Israel agreed to a cease-fire with Syria. However, fighting continued between Palestinian guerrillas and Israeli forces. During the siege of Beirut Sharon announced that the PLO should be expelled from the country and, if possible, destroyed altogether. As for Lebanon, Sharon's intention was to clear the Syrian troops out of Beirut and the centre of the country and to install a client regime drawn from the right-wing Phalangist Party.

THE SIEGE OF BEIRUT

The siege of Lebanon's capital began a week after the invasion and lasted almost two months. It was bombed almost continuously from land, sea and air from 13 June to 12 August. When the siege had ended two Lebanese newspapers, quoting government sources, calculated that since the beginning of the invasion 18,000 people had been killed and 30,000 wounded. About 85% of the casualties were civilians.

Israel's terms for ending the siege were that PLO forces in Beirut, numbering some 9,000 combatants, should surrender or leave the country, along with those Syrian troops still in the city, otherwise the Israeli army would force its way into Beirut and forcibly expel them. While US officials tried to negotiate an agreement with the PLO, the Israeli armed forces continued to bombard the city. They also cut off water and electricity supplies to west Beirut and prevented food and medical supplies from reaching its beleaguered population. Finally the PLO agreed to leave and on 21 August its guerrillas began their evacuation. By the end of the month the last Palestinian units had left the city that had been their headquarters since the Jordanian civil war 12 years earlier. Israel had achieved one of its principal objectives. A second goal was attained almost immediately when, on 23 August, the Lebanese National Assembly was persuaded to choose the right-wing, pro-Israeli, Phalangist commander, Bachir Gemayel, as the new President of Lebanon.

THE SABRA/CHATILA MASSACRE

The agreement governing the evacuation of the PLO from Beirut provided for the deployment of a multinational force to supervise the Palestinian withdrawal and to protect the inhabitants of Muslim west Beirut. On 25 August 1982 this force, composed of US, French and Italian soldiers, disembarked at Beirut. Only two weeks later, they began to withdraw, a fortnight earlier than provided for in the agreement.

On 14 September the President-elect, Bachir Gemayel, was killed by a bomb explosion at the Phalangist Party headquarters and a few hours later, in contravention of the evacuation agreement, the Israeli army moved into west Beirut. The day after the assassination Israeli officers held a meeting with local Phalangist commanders in which they agreed to help a force of Phalangist militiamen to 'clean up' the Palestinian refugee camps of Sabra and Chatila. On the evening of 16 September the Phalangists entered the camps and began the massacre which was to end in the death of as many as 2,000 refugees.

The outrage which the atrocity caused throughout the world eventually forced the Israeli Prime Minister to order an inquiry. In its report published in February 1983, the Israeli Commission of Inquiry criticized a number of leading Israelis including Begin, Sharon, the Minister of Foreign Affairs, Shamir, as well as high-ranking officers, such as the Chief of Staff, Eitan. Sharon was considered principally responsible for planning the operation; he resigned as Minister of Defence but Begin allowed him to remain in the Cabinet as a minister without portfolio.

TWO PEACE PLANS

On 1 September 1982 President Reagan announced a new plan to settle the Arab–Israeli conflict (see Documents on Palestine, p. 124). It was widely considered to be the work of the new Secretary of State, George Shultz, and it represented a significant change in US policy. While the Camp David accords had been ambiguous about the future of the territories occupied by Israel since 1967, the Reagan Plan envisaged their restoration to the Arabs. Nevertheless, at the same time the USA reaffirmed its opposition to the creation of a Palestinian state and proposed 'self-government in association with Jordan'.

The Reagan Plan was rejected by the Israeli Government, which immediately embarked on a new and more intensive programme of building settlements on the West Bank. A week after the announcement of the Reagan Plan, the Arab states, meeting again in Fez, countered with their own proposals (see Documents on Palestine, p. 124), which were almost identical to the Fahd Plan of the year before and called for the creation of a Palestinian state in the Occupied Territories. Point Seven of the proposals, which called on 'the United Nations Security Council to provide guarantees for peace between all states of the region . . .', implicitly recognized Israel's right to exist.

At the end of October King Hassan of Morocco led a delegation of Arab ministers of foreign affairs to Washington to explain their proposals to President Reagan. Although the US and Arab plans both envisaged the restoration of Arab rule over the Occupied Territories, they disagreed over the issue of who exactly would govern them. The crucial figure in the US strategy was King Hussein of Jordan, who visited Washington in December. Hussein was prepared to negotiate with the USA on the basis of the Reagan Plan only if he received a mandate to do so from the Palestinians. In January 1983 the King held talks with the PLO leader Yasser Arafat, aimed at establishing a joint Jordanian-Palestinian position and the following month the Palestine National Council (PNC) debated the matter in Algiers.

Although it was clear that Arafat and the Palestinian moderates were anxious to give Hussein the mandate he needed, there was strong opposition from some sections of the PNC, particularly from those groups backed by Syria. The PNC duly endorsed the Fez proposals and criticized the Reagan Plan without rejecting it outright. Although Arafat failed to achieve his objectives, discussions between Jordan and the PLO continued until King Hussein brought them to an end in April.

AMERICAN DIPLOMATIC EFFORTS

On 24 April 1983 the US Secretary of State George Shultz left for the Middle East, shortly after a bomb attack, apparently carried out by an unknown Shi'ite group, had destroyed the US Embassy in Beirut and left a large number of dead, including 17 US citizens. After a series of consultations with Arab and Israeli leaders, Shultz was able to persuade the Lebanese and Israeli Governments to sign an agreement on 17 May providing for the withdrawal of Israeli troops from Lebanon. Although Israel did not manage to secure some of the ambitious security demands it had been making earlier, the agreement did provide for the establishment of joint Israeli-Lebanese patrols operating inside the Lebanese border.

The Israeli Government had made clear at the time that any agreement to withdraw its troops from southern Lebanon was conditional on a commitment by Syria simultaneously to withdraw its army from the Beka'a valley. The Syrian Government, however, which had recently entered into a closer alliance with the USSR, quickly denounced an agreement that seemed to benefit only the USA and its allies, Israel and the Lebanese Government of Amin Gemayel (the brother of the late President-elect). Negotiations had neglected consideration of an Israeli withdrawal from the Syrian Golan Heights and the Occupied Territories of Palestine and President Assad, therefore, adopted an intransigent attitude. As an indication of Syrian policy, Assad supported a revolt by Palestinian dissidents inside Fatah (the Palestine National Liberation Movement) who were opposed to their leader Yasser Arafat's moderate, diplomatic approach. With the help of the Syrian army, the Fatah rebels under their extremist commander, Abu Musa, captured Palestinian loyalist positions in the Beka'a valley and in June Assad expelled Arafat from Syria.

The Israeli Government, meanwhile, was refusing to pull its army out of Lebanon without a simultaneous withdrawal by the Syrians—yet it was reluctant to leave its troops in occupation of so much Lebanese territory because of the toll being taken on them in attacks by Lebanese and Palestinian guerrillas. In Israel, demonstrations were held to demand the immediate withdrawal of Israeli troops. A year after the invasion the Government admitted that 500 soldiers had been killed in Lebanon and people began to question whether the war's objectives could justify such losses. It was in this atmosphere that the Israeli Government began to discuss proposals for a limited withdrawal to the Awali river north of Sidon.

THE ISRAELI WITHDRAWAL FROM BEIRUT

Growing factional violence in Lebanon during the summer of 1983 underlined the impracticability of both Israel's and the USA's plans for that country. A principal aim of Israel's invasion—the establishment of a strong central government closely allied to Israel—had clearly been abandoned when on 20 July the Israeli Cabinet decided, unilaterally, to pull back its forces behind the more easily defensible line of the Awali river. Simultaneously, a visit to Washington by President Gemayel left the US Administration with few illusions that the 17 May Lebanon/Israel agreement, which it had brokered, would ever be ratified, far less implemented. The sense of failure provoked the replacement of Philip Habib as special Middle East envoy by Robert McFarlane, and the announcement by Menachem Begin, on 28 August, of his intention to resign as Prime Minister. The situation in Lebanon deteriorated further (on 23 July the Druze leader Walid Joumblatt had announced the formation of a pro-Syrian coalition, the National Salvation Front, in opposition to the Gemayel Government). Any hope that without external support Gemayel's authority could be extended beyond the capital itself was dashed following Israel's sudden withdrawal to the Awali on 4 September, which precipitated a war between the Druze and the right-wing Christian forces. With Syrian logistical support, the Druze quickly gained the upper hand; their advance was checked only at Souk el-Gharb, a strategic mountain town overlooking Beirut, at which point the USA took the decision to intervene directly in the conflict with shelling by its offshore fleet of Druze- and Syrian-controlled territory.

AMERICAN INVOLVEMENT

The growing US involvement in the Lebanese conflict, with the concomitant danger of 'superpower' confrontation, alarmed not just the USA's European partners in the UNIFIL multinational force (MNF) but all levels of opinion in the USA itself, which was for the first time paying the price in American lives for its Middle East policy. The longer-term worry was that such involvement would destroy US credibility as the broker of a wider settlement of the Arab–Israeli conflict. On 26 July 1983 masked gunmen killed 3 Palestinian students and wounded 38 others in an attack on Hebron University. Then, on 2 August the US vetoed a UN Security Council resolution declaring the West Bank settlements illegal and condemning the violence against Palestinian civilians. Although, on 27 August, President Reagan declared the establishment of new Israeli settlements in the Occupied Territories to be 'an obstacle to peace', two days later the USA boycotted the UN International Conference on the Palestinian Question in Geneva, which was attended by 137 states, including its NATO allies in Europe.

BEGIN'S RESIGNATION

Any hopes that the resignation of Menachem Begin as Prime Minister on 30 August 1983 heralded a change in Israeli policies were banished when the Herut Party chose the even more uncompromising Minister of Foreign Affairs, Itzhak Shamir, to be his successor as leader of the party. Shamir, a veteran of the Jewish underground group, Lehi, allegedly gave the order for the assassination of UN mediator Count Folke Bernadotte in 1948, and had opposed the Camp David accords. Begin withheld his formal resignation until 15 September, giving Shamir time to form a viable Likud coalition. Sure of a narrow majority in the Knesset, Shamir was asked to form a government on 21 September.

THE INFLUENCE OF SYRIA

If Lebanon was the key to progress towards a wider settlement, it appeared to many observers that President Reagan believed that the civil war there could be settled in President Gemayel's favour through the exercise of US military might. This was despite efforts in the US Congress to invoke the 1973 War Powers Act requiring presidential consultations with Congress if US forces abroad faced 'imminent hostilities'. The impossibility of a force of 1,600 Marines with naval support sustaining the authority of Gemayel's Government, whose pleas to Israel for help against the Druze offensive had been dismissed, became increasingly clear in the aftermath of the fragile cease-fire agreed on 25 September 1983 through Saudi Arabian mediation. The terms of the cease-fire provided for a dialogue of national reconciliation with Syrian participation, in recognition of Syria's effective power of veto over decisions relating to the future of Lebanon.

There were signs too that Syria was seeking to extend its control over another key area of the Middle East conflict. On 29 July Yasser Arafat declared that Syrian and Libyan troops were involved in continuing clashes between pro- and anti-Arafat Palestinian factions in the Beka'a valley. Prolonged meetings of the PLO's Executive Committee and Central Council in Tunis in early August were unable to heal the rift in Palestinian ranks. Arafat managed to retain the loyalty, or at least the neutrality, of the more radical groupings such as the People's Front for the Liberation of Palestine (PFLP), led by George Habash, and the Democratic Front for the Liberation of Palestine (DFLP), led by Naif Hawatmeh, but was obliged in return to submit to the Central Council's denunciation of the Reagan Plan, something which the last PNC meeting had carefully avoided. The remaining pro-Arafat forces in Syrian-controlled northern Lebanon were steadily losing ground, and Arafat seemed to have decided to make his last stand with them when in mid-September he returned to the loyalist stronghold in the northern Lebanese port of Tripoli. This soon came under siege from Syrian and Palestinian forces.

With Syria dominating events in Lebanon and with the pro-Syrian Fatah dissidents led by Abu Musa apparently poised to inherit Arafat's leadership of the PLO, it seemed that any solution of the crisis must be acceptable in Damascus. The US Administration was forced belatedly to recognize Syria's influence and negotiations were initiated by special envoy Robert McFarlane through the Saudi Arabian Ambassador to the USA, Prince Bandar ibn Sultan. Much to the consternation of its European allies, however, the USA appeared unwilling to alter its perception of the conflict in Lebanon in terms of a Soviet threat to its interests in the region, a view in which it was encouraged by Syria's acquisition of Soviet long-range SS-21 missiles in early October. There was, equally, no hint of US readiness to put pressure on Israel over the issues necessary for Syrian acceptance of a peace settlement: Israeli withdrawal from southern Lebanon and, crucially, the inclusion of the Syrian Golan Heights, annexed by Israel in 1981, in any talks aimed at a wider settlement. Israel in turn applied its own leverage, threatening to close the bridges over the Awali river, now Lebanon's *de facto* line of partition. President Reagan's domestic position improved somewhat on 30 September 1983 with a Senate vote approving the deployment of US forces in Beirut for a further 18 months, but the precarious position of these forces made their withdrawal imperative before the 1984 presidential election campaign began in earnest.

SUICIDE BOMBINGS IN LEBANON

All the Reagan Administration's calculations were overturned on 23 October 1983 when simultaneous suicide bomb attacks destroyed the headquarters of the US and French contingents of the MNF in Beirut, killing 241 US marines and 58 French soldiers. Two extremist Shi'ite groups thought to have had links with a detachment of Iranian revolutionary guards stationed in Baalbek in eastern Lebanon claimed responsibility for the atrocities. Responsibility for the attacks, initially ascribed by the USA to Iran, was widened to include Syria and the USSR, all of whom vigorously denied any involvement. Although President Reagan was quick to reaffirm America's commitment to maintaining the marines in Lebanon—a determination echoed at a meeting of the ministers of foreign affairs of all four countries contributing to the MNF in Paris on 27 October—domestic opposition to his Middle East policy inevitably increased. In the case of the attack on the French forces, there was reason to believe it was linked with France's support for Iraq in the Iran–Iraq War; in the case of the USA the marines' deaths could not help but be attributed to its decision to intervene, as it appeared, directly on the side of Lebanon's Christian President against the largely Muslim opposition, and to the antipathy which US support for Israel had provoked among the Arabs at large. Israel's distancing itself from the US involvement in

Lebanon, as reaction to the bombings set in, was evidence of its sensitivity to the charge that by invading Lebanon it had set in motion the chain of events leading to the disaster. US resentment was evinced by the rejection of Israel's offer to help in treating the victims of the attack. Ten days before the Beirut attacks Israel had leaked secret US plans to arm and equip a Jordanian military force for possible intervention in a Gulf crisis. The leak led to the Senate Appropriations Committee vetoing the idea on 2 November and was a grave setback to the US-Jordanian dialogue, which was focused on King Hussein's willingness to revive talks with the Palestinians on the basis of the Reagan Plan.

The USA forged closer links with Israel after a bomb attack on Israel's military headquarters in Tyre which killed 60 people, including 32 Palestinians and Lebanese held captive there. Israeli planes immediately bombed Palestinian and Druze positions in the Chouf, and a 72-hour blockade of the occupied south was imposed. The USA seemed to be convinced by the Israeli Minister of Defence, Moshe Arens, that US setbacks in Lebanon were due to lack of co-ordination with Israeli forces there and it decided on a policy of 'strategic co-operation' with Israel. Syria, which Israel publicly held ultimately responsible for the Tyre attack, warned of 'aggressive US and Israeli intentions' and ordered a general mobilization of its forces on 7 November.

THE LEBANESE NATIONAL RECONCILIATION CONFERENCE

Despite the relative success of the organizers of the national reconciliation conference—which was convened in Geneva at the beginning of November—in persuading the protagonists, including the Syrian Minister of Foreign Affairs, Abd al-Halim Khaddam, to participate, Lebanon's internal strife persisted. The demand by the Syrians and their allies in the National Salvation Front for the abrogation of the 17 May agreement with Israel had prompted a compromise proposal whereby President Gemayel was to seek a substitute arrangement with the USA for securing Israeli withdrawal. The new US strategy (which coincided with the appointment on 3 November of a new special envoy for the Middle East, Donald Rumsfeld) of ever closer identification of its interests with those of Israel dictated the joint US-Israeli refusal to reconsider the unratified accord. President Gemayel's Christian constituency still had sufficient faith in US support and in the possibility of further Israeli military intervention on its side to resist changes to its constitutional privileges, and internal reconciliation made no progress. That US and Israeli strategies were coinciding more and more was demonstrated by a massive increase in US military aid to Israel, and in Lebanon, by further Israeli air raids on Syrian-controlled territory and a direct US–Syrian clash on 4 December in which two US planes were shot down.

ARAFAT'S DEPARTURE FROM TRIPOLI

The prestige which Syrian President Assad won in the Arab world as a result of his policy of confrontation with the USA was enhanced by Arab dismay at the US-Israeli accord. President Mubarak of Egypt, the USA's closest ally in the Arab world, described the accord as catastrophic and King Hussein of Jordan considered it a reward for Israeli intransigence. President Assad's apparent propaganda success in defying the USA was partly vitiated, however, by the bloody assault against forces loyal to Yasser Arafat in Tripoli, which by the end of November 1983 had claimed at least 500 lives. His evident determination to prevent Yasser Arafat from leaving the country alive was conditioned by the knowledge that, freed from the influence of hardline dissidents backed by Syria, the PLO Chairman would be in a position to try to forge a joint Jordanian-Palestinian alliance based on the Reagan Plan, a move repeatedly advocated by King Hussein. Although the PLO dissidents had initially attracted considerable sympathy, their collaboration with Syria against the loyalists swung opinion behind Arafat, especially in the Occupied Territories, and the struggle was increasingly seen as one for PLO independence from external control. Arafat's standing was enhanced on 24 November when six Israeli prisoners held by his forces in Tripoli were exchanged for 4,800 Palestinians and Lebanese imprisoned by Israel in southern Lebanon. Support for Arafat from many quarters, including the USSR, but especially from the Arab Gulf states, helped to secure a Saudi-Syrian-sponsored agreement to end the fighting on 24 November, in accordance with which Arafat and his supporters were to withdraw from Lebanon within two weeks. The UN Security Council agreed on 4 December to grant the ships evacuating Arafat's 4,000 supporters the protection of the UN flag, but naval attacks on Tripoli by Israel, and its refusal to guarantee the evacuation fleet safe passage, delayed its departure until 20 December.

ISRAEL'S DOMESTIC PROBLEMS

Israeli bombing raids continued against what were termed terrorist bases in Syrian-controlled Lebanon, inflicting heavy civilian casualties. Losses were also mounting from almost daily guerrilla attacks on Israeli forces in occupied southern Lebanon, where the overwhelmingly Shi'ite population had built up an increasingly effective military resistance movement. In addition, Israel was experiencing an economic crisis and record rates of inflation, which threatened the new Government of Itzhak Shamir. Huge debts had brought the country to the verge of bankruptcy and forced the new Minister of Finance, Yigal Cohen-Orgad, to devalue the shekel, slash subsidies on basic commodities and draw up an austerity package which included cuts in the hitherto sacred areas of defence and settlement. This, in turn, further endangered the ruling coalition's narrow majority in the Knesset, as the religious parties threatened to withdraw their support if the rapid colonization of the Occupied Territories was not sustained.

ARAFAT'S DIPLOMATIC INITIATIVES

On leaving Tripoli Arafat went to Egypt for a meeting with President Mubarak, becoming the first prominent Arab leader to go there since the signing of the Camp David accords. However, Egypt's continued commitment to the treaty was emphasized immediately after the meeting by the visit of a senior Egyptian official to Israel, the first of its kind since the 1982 invasion of Lebanon. Nevertheless, Arafat's visit was followed by the signing of an Egyptian-Jordanian trade protocol, a visit to Cairo by the Saudi Prince Talal ibn Abd al-Aziz, and, on 19 January 1984, by the decision of the Organization of the Islamic Conference to readmit Egypt to its ranks. The *de facto* ending of the Arab boycott of Egypt could, it was felt, provide the bridge for possible Arab–Israeli negotiations and the emergence of a moderate Arab alignment between Egypt, Jordan, the PLO and possibly Iraq. Syria, Libya and the PLO's left-wing factions vehemently denounced the *rapprochement* with Egypt and the burgeoning Jordan-PLO relationship. Although the Israeli Prime Minister, Itzhak Shamir, also denounced the Arafat-Mubarak meeting as a 'severe blow to the peace process', the US Administration welcomed it as a boost for the Reagan Plan.

In a move which was interpreted as preparing the constitutional ground for a joint Palestinian-Jordanian initiative, King Hussein decided on 5 January to reconvene the Jordanian Parliament (its representation theoretically divided between the East and the (occupied) West Banks of the Jordan), which had been suspended since 1974, (when the Rabat Arab summit accorded the PLO the status of sole representative of the Palestinian people), and had not actually convened since 1967.

DISQUIET AT THE USA'S ROLE IN LEBANON

The Reagan Administration in the USA refused to acknowledge the untenability of the position of US forces in Lebanon, despite warnings from US marine commanders in Beirut, mounting dissent on Capitol Hill, and public disquiet among the USA's European partners in the MNF, who in January 1984 announced partial withdrawals of their contingents. The difference between US and European perceptions of the Arab–Israeli conflict was illustrated on 11 January when the British Foreign Secretary, Sir Geoffrey Howe, called for a radical change in Israeli policies and urged Israel to negotiate with the PLO. The influence of the 1984 US presidential election campaign was already evident in dissuading the Reagan Administration from responding to the Arab peace initiative. A formal request from Egypt that 160 members of the PNC from the Occupied Territories be allowed to attend a proposed session of the Jordanian Parliament, aimed at securing a mandate for Arafat's progress towards a joint position with Jordan, was rejected by Israel, with no sign of US opposition.

THE WITHDRAWAL OF THE MULTINATIONAL FORCE FROM BEIRUT

Meanwhile US naval bombardments of anti-Gemayel forces in the hills overlooking Beirut prompted renewed attacks on the US contingent. At the beginning of February more than 200 people died in three days of continuous heavy fighting, the Lebanese Government resigned, and the Lebanese army disintegrated along sectarian lines. Druze militiamen from the mountains linked up with their Shi'ite allies in the southern suburbs of Beirut on 15 February 1984. The USA still refused to consider the one thing that might have halted the onslaught against Gemayel—the abrogation of the 17 May agreement—but it had clearly lost all control of events. Despite public avowals of support for the Gemayel Government and promises to keep US forces in the country, the decision had already been taken to 'redeploy' the marines even before President Reagan announced their withdrawal on 7 February. The next day the United Kingdom announced and completed the withdrawal of its token contribution to the MNF, followed by the Italian force on 20 February. The last US marines were evacuated from Beirut on 26 February, to be followed by the French in March, leaving the western sector of the city, as in the days before the Israeli invasion, under the control of Muslim and left-wing militias. On 5 March, bowing to Syrian influence, President Gemayel abrogated the 17 May Lebanon-Israel agreement in return for guarantees of internal security from President Assad.

THE CONSEQUENCES OF ISRAEL'S INVASION

The failure of Israel's 1982 invasion now became fully apparent. Far from securing a 'client regime' in Beirut, it had brought about the defeat of Israel's Christian allies, who had been forced to retreat into their traditional enclaves in east Beirut and around Jounieh. Abandoned by the USA, and with little prospect of further military support from Israel, there seemed little alternative to cantonization or a power-sharing deal with the Muslim majority. Meanwhile, the enormous cost of the Lebanese campaign in lives and resources appeared to have undermined Israel's security, rather than consolidate it. The death of the pro-Israeli militia commander, Maj. Sa'ad Haddad, on 15 January 1984, further disappointed Israel's hopes of creating a security zone along the Lebanese side of its northern border, and despite the setbacks suffered by the PLO in Lebanon, armed attacks against Israelis in Israel continued. In addition, the growth and increasing sophistication of a Jewish anti-Arab terrorist underground was both embarrassing the Government and threatening a backlash throughout the Arab and Muslim world. The Karp report, drawn up by a Ministry of Justice commission in May 1982, but suppressed until 8 February 1984, detailed the Government's failures to curb Jewish terrorism against Arab civilians. At the end of April Israeli security services finally acted, arresting some 30 people suspected of planting bombs on Arab buses. By that time the defection of the small Tami party from the ruling Likud coalition had led to the defeat of the Government in a vote to dissolve the Knesset and hold early elections, which were subsequently scheduled for 23 July. The lengthy trial of members of the Jewish terrorist underground, arrested in April, distracted attention from the election campaign, especially after it became known that some of the suspects, who were mainly Gush Emunim settlers but also included two army officers, had confessed to the 1980 assassination attempts on three Palestinian mayors in the West Bank and the previous year's attack on the Islamic college in Hebron. Their stated aim was to force a mass exodus of Palestinians from the Occupied Territories. The Government's own attitude toward the underground movement was called into question by a statement by a cabinet minister, Yuval Ne'eman, of the Tehiya party, who cited the bombing of the Palestinian mayors as having 'effectively paralysed the leading agitators' in the West Bank.

Abroad, Lebanon remained a cause for concern. On 4 April, a new commander, ex-Lebanese Army Col Antoine Lahad, was installed at the head of the militia in southern Lebanon, formerly led by Maj. Haddad, which the Israelis had reinforced and renamed the 'South Lebanon Army' (SLA). Israel's strategy was to remain in occupation of southern Lebanon until the SLA was capable of maintaining control there. However, neither Israel nor its surrogate force seemed capable of preventing a growing number of guerrilla attacks against the occupying army.

LEBANON'S GOVERNMENT OF NATIONAL RECONCILIATION

In Beirut, a new government of national unity installed at the end of April 1984 had resolved to secure Israel's complete and unconditional withdrawal. Comprising a delicate balance of Christians and Muslims achieved after a year's painstaking mediation on the part of Syria, the new Lebanese Cabinet included the Shi'ite leader Nabih Berri—an indication both of the rising influence of the Shi'ites and of how far the balance of power had shifted in favour of Lebanon's non-Christian communities (though Amin Gemayel retained the Presidency). Berri, leader of the Shi'ite Amal movement, which was spearheading the resistance to Israel in the south, joined the Government on the condition that he be made minister for the south, and his appointment signalled the first test of President Gemayel's pledge of 'support for the national resistance' given at the reconvened national reconciliation conference in Lausanne, Switzerland, in March. The new Prime Minister, Rashid Karami, a Sunni Muslim, confirmed the Government's intentions on 3 June by calling for the removal of Israel's 'liaison office' at Dbayye, in the Christian enclave north of Beirut. Israel's Likud Government was adamant that it would not leave southern Lebanon in the hands of a Syrian-influenced government in Beirut. The USA was unwilling to mediate between Lebanon and Israel to secure a withdrawal, even assuming that its participation would have been countenanced by Syria. On 10 June, during a tour of the Middle East, the UN Secretary-General, Javier Pérez de Cuéllar, quashed Israeli hopes that UN forces could act as a buffer north of Israel's lines, on the grounds that this would reinforce Lebanon's *de facto* partition. Israel, in turn, rejected the suggestion that UNIFIL could police Israel's northern border and ensure its security after an Israeli withdrawal. By the second anniversary of the invasion, the war in Lebanon had cost almost 600 Israeli lives, with 3,049 wounded—more than the total number of military and civilian casualties in the Six-Day War of 1967.

ISRAEL'S INCONCLUSIVE GENERAL ELECTION

In his election manifesto, Shimon Peres, who had been unanimously re-adopted on 12 April as leader of the opposition Labour Party, pledged to bring Israel's troops home within 'three to six' months of gaining power, and this appeared to be a crucial factor in his party's favour. However, the immediate concern of the Israeli voter as the election approached was the economy. With inflation reaching 15% a month, a balance-of-payments deficit of $5,000m., foreign debt of $23,000m. and a chronic shortage of foreign currency reserves, Israel was on the verge of bankruptcy; the occupation of Lebanon alone was costing the country an estimated $1m. a day.

At the election on 23 July, the major party groupings, Likud and the Labour Alignment, each secured just over one-third of the Knesset's 120 seats. The balance of power lay once again with the minority parties, which won the remaining 35 seats. The result confirmed the trend towards polarization in Israeli politics: the extreme right-wing Tehiya party increased its representation from three to five seats, and was joined on the far right by two members of the religious-nationalist Morasha party, which drew its support from the Gush Emunim movement, and by Rabbi Meir Kahane of the Kach party, who had campaigned on an openly racist platform. At the other political pole, Reserve General Matti Peled and Muhammad Mv'ari were elected as representatives of a newly formed Arab-Jewish coalition, the Progressive List for Peace, which called for dialogue with the PLO and the establishment of an independent Palestinian state in the Occupied Territories. The deadlock was resolved when Labour leader Shimon Peres was entrusted with forming the new Government after the factions in the political centre, Yahad and the National Religious Party, agreed to lend their support to Labour on condition that Peres formed a 'national unity' government with Likud. On 30 August Labour and Likud agreed to such an arrangement, with Peres as Prime Minister and Shamir as Minister of Foreign Affairs, their posts to be exchanged every two years. On 13 September the Knesset approved a bi-partisan Cabinet, completing the political rehab-

ilitation of Ariel Sharon, who was appointed Minister of Industry and Trade.

SYRIAN INFLUENCE IN LEBANON

In Lebanon, Syria was exercising unprecedented control over the Government in Beirut. On 18 June 1984 President Assad succeeded in sponsoring a Christian-Muslim power-sharing agreement, which included the implementation of a balanced security plan throughout Beirut, where local militias were to be disbanded and the port and airport re-opened. The plan was executed on 4 July, the army taking over positions in the city from the militias, including the hitherto intransigent Lebanese Forces (LF, the military wing of the Christian Phalangist Party), within hours. However, despite Syria's efforts, plans to extend the Lebanese army's deployment throughout the rest of the country made no headway, and renewed sectarian clashes threatened to reverse the progress that had been made, exposing Syria's inability to control its Druze and Shi'ite allies. Israel demonstrated its determination to thwart Syria's designs in Lebanon by a series of air raids on Druze- and Syrian-controlled areas and, on 10 September, an armoured column was deployed north of its lines on the Awali River into the Kharroub region to support Christian militias under attack from the Druze.

MOVES TOWARDS AN ISRAELI WITHDRAWAL FROM LEBANON

The new Government in Israel gave the first public indication that Israel had lost the political struggle for Lebanon; the hitherto rigid insistence on a simultaneous withdrawal of Syrian troops from the country was abandoned, and the Minister of Foreign Affairs, Shamir, said that Israel wanted the USA to mediate with Syria on a procedure for Israeli withdrawal. The US Assistant Secretary of State for Near East Affairs, Richard Murphy, visited Lebanon, Syria and Israel in September 1984, holding two rounds of talks with President Assad in Damascus, the first such US-Syrian contact and the first display of active US diplomacy in the region since the withdrawal of US forces from Beirut in February. Murphy followed in the footsteps of the UN Assistant Secretary-General, Brian Urquhart, who returned assured by all parties of their desire for UNIFIL to play a larger part in any settlement. However, Israel insisted that, though a withdrawal of forces need not be simultaneous, it should not be unilateral. Nevertheless, talks began under UN auspices on 8 November, at UNIFIL's headquarters in the Israeli-Lebanese border town of Naqoura, between military delegations from Israel and Lebanon, within the framework of the 1949 Armistice Commission.

DIPLOMATIC INITIATIVES ON PALESTINE

The new Israeli Government had also to contend with the nascent Arab 'peace alliance' between Yasser Arafat's wing of the PLO, Jordan and Egypt. Egypt's credibility in the Arab world and non-aligned movement was strengthened by its decision to restore full diplomatic relations with the USSR. However, it was King Hussein of Jordan's surprise decision on 25 September 1984 to restore diplomatic ties with Cairo, which first raised the possibility of talks between the new Israeli Government and a joint Jordanian-PLO delegation supported by Egypt. Yasser Arafat had been preoccupied by a long and difficult struggle to win the agreement of the various PLO factions to convene the PNC, which Arafat hoped would supply the Palestinian consensus for a joint peace strategy with Jordan. Amid signs of a thaw in relations between Syria and Arafat's mainstream PLO, and after mediation efforts by the USSR, the People's Democratic Republic of Yemen and Algeria, leaders of Fatah and the quadripartite Damascus-based Democratic Alliance, including the Popular Front for the Liberation of Palestine (PFLP) and the Democratic Front for the Liberation of Palestine (DFLP), met in Algiers on 18 April. Subsequently it was declared that the PFLP and DFLP had abandoned their opposition both to Arafat's leadership and to the dialogue with Jordan. Syria, however, remained opposed to any Damascus-based group attending a PNC meeting, and warned that those who did attend would not be allowed to return to Syria. The stalemate was finally broken on 14 October at a meeting in Tunis of the PLO Executive Committee, Fatah's Central Council and about 80 representatives of other Palestinian organizations, at which it was declared that the PNC must be convened before the end of November, and that 'the minority must accept the decision of the majority'. The 17th session of the PNC was duly scheduled for 22 November in Amman. On 9 October, President Mubarak visited the Jordanian capital, where a joint Egyptian-Jordanian strategy on Palestine was announced. Israel welcomed the new Egyptian-Jordanian relationship as helpful to peace, but Egypt, while welcoming the inauguration of Shimon Peres as Israel's Prime Minister, made it clear that its primary commitment was to the Arab world, and that it stood by its conditions for normalizing the frosty relations between them that had prevailed since Israel's invasion of Lebanon: namely, the initiation of steps to gain the confidence of the Palestinians living in areas under Israeli occupation, and talks on the disputed border strip of Taba on the Red Sea, which Israel continued to occupy after vacating Sinai in 1982. For his part, King Hussein dismissed speculation that a US-sponsored peace initiative along the lines of Camp David was in prospect when, on 10 October, he denounced Israeli Prime Minister Peres' call for direct negotiations between Jordan and Israel, explicitly excluding Palestinian involvement, as 'subterfuge and deception'.

REAGAN IS RETURNED TO THE WHITE HOUSE

In the USA the Administration concentrated on advancing the US-Israel strategic relationship. An unprecedented military exchange agreement between the countries' air forces was announced in early September 1984, and, during a visit to Israel in mid-October by the US Defense Secretary, Caspar Weinberger, details were released of the transfer of hitherto restricted US technology crucial to the development of Israel's *Lavi* fighter aircraft. To help Israel address its economic crisis the US also consented to transfer the whole of its $1,200m. annual civilian aid grant immediately, rather than in instalments.

As far as the Arab world was concerned, the US Administration appeared to be retreating into a defensive posture, as evinced by 'anti-terrorist' legislation drafted by the State Department in April. It was indisputable that the Reagan Administration had attracted an unprecedented degree of hostility in the Middle East. Threats of violence against and kidnappings of US citizens had led on 28 May to the recall of marines to protect the US Embassy in Beirut. Nevertheless, on 20 September a suicide bomb attack, responsibility for which was claimed by the Shi'ite Islamic Jihad (Holy War) organization, killed more than 20 people and accelerated the steady exodus of American diplomats, journalists and relief workers from Lebanon. Although, as a result of the intervention in Lebanon, more US citizens had been killed in international conflict than at any time since the Viet Nam war, seemingly no blame was attached to President Reagan, who was re-elected by a massive majority on 5 November.

FAILURE OF TALKS ON ISRAELI WITHDRAWAL

At the talks in Naqoura on Israel's withdrawal from Lebanon, Lebanon's demands included an unconditional Israeli withdrawal, the abolition of the SLA and $10,000m. in war reparations. Israel responded by threatening to withdraw unilaterally, without making provision for local security. The talks remained deadlocked, with Syria evidently refusing to give Israel any assurance of its security once its forces had withdrawn. The pressure was, nevertheless, increasing on Israel to withdraw. Guerrilla attacks on the Israeli army, the Israeli Defence Force (IDF), continued during the negotiations, and both the troops and the Israeli public were becoming increasingly frustrated at the high casualty toll. On 8 January 1985 Israel announced its withdrawal from the Naqoura talks; a week later, the Israeli Cabinet approved a three-phase unilateral withdrawal from Lebanon, which, Prime Minister Peres pledged, would be completed by July. Israel remained committed to intervening in Lebanon if it perceived a threat to its security, and to aiding 'friendly' militias and maintaining a security zone patrolled by the SLA on the Lebanese side of the border.

JORDANIAN-PALESTINIAN PARTNERSHIP

Matters elsewhere looked more promising in the wake of Arafat's success at the PNC meeting in Amman in late November 1984.

Although the PFLP and DFLP did not attend, they undertook not to approve the formation of an alternative organization, and the PLO succeeded in demonstrating its independence from Syria. In his address to the PNC, King Hussein laid down the guidelines for a new Arab approach to the peace process, consisting of a joint Jordanian-PLO initiative, based on UN Resolution 242 and the right of the Palestinian people to self-determination, in accordance with the principle of an exchange of territory for peace with Israel. The PNC, however, reiterated its rejection of Resolution 242, which refers to the Palestinians only as refugees, implicitly denying their right to self-determination and recognizing the State of Israel. Israel, which had always prohibited Palestinians living in areas under its occupation from attending the PNC, ignored King Hussein's proposals, nor did it respond to a statement by the Egyptian Minister of State for Foreign Affairs, Boutros-Ghali, expressing Egypt's willingness to back a new initiative in which Jordan and a delegation of West Bank and Gaza Palestinians would enter peace talks with Israel under a mandate from the PLO. In this, however, Egypt was not supported by either Jordan or the Palestinians, who made it clear that the PLO should be a full partner in any future peace negotiations. PLO-Jordanian relations were strengthened by a series of meetings between King Hussein and Yasser Arafat, culminating on 11 February in the signing in Amman of a PLO-Jordanian accord, which provided for Palestinian self-determination within the framework of a Jordanian-Palestinian confederation and for peace negotiations between all parties to the conflict, including the PLO, and the five permanent members of the UN Security Council. Israel promptly rejected the agreement.

The Amman agreement, which drew strong opposition from Syria and Arafat's PLO opponents, and was clearly a source of contention within the PLO Executive Committee itself, illustrated the urgency with which King Hussein and Yasser Arafat viewed the need to salvage the Occupied Territories for a future Palestinian homeland before Jewish settlement established a *de facto* extension of Israel. Despite pledges from the new Israeli Government to raise the quality of life for the Palestinians in the Occupied Territories, violence against the Arab population there persisted. Nor did the Labour component of the Government of national unity seem able or willing to halt the continued seizure of Palestinian land for Israeli settlement. On 10 February, a study by the US-financed West Bank Data Project found that, as of 1 January 1985, there were 42,500 Israeli settlers living on the occupied West Bank, double the figure of just two years earlier.

ISRAEL'S ECONOMIC CRISIS

The decision to spend more on colonizing the Occupied Territories drew protests from Israelis alarmed by soaring inflation and, for the first time in the country's history, widespread unemployment. A wages and prices 'freeze' agreed on 2 November 1984 between the Government and trades unions and employers temporarily checked the rise in inflation, but did not tackle the deep-rooted crisis in the economy. The Israeli shekel, having fallen to less than one five-hundredth of its 1977 value, was replaced for most practical purposes by the dollar. An Israeli economic delegation went to Washington at the end of December to request $4,100m. in aid in 1986, an increase of $1,500m. on the 1985 total approved by the US Congress just three months previously. Initially, the US Government insisted that any increase in aid should be conditional on the introduction of more rigorous measures to tackle the crisis. On 17 January, Israel and the USA finalized a free-trade agreement, and on 30 January President Reagan agreed to increase US military aid to Israel by $400m. to $1,800m. for the 1986 fiscal year. The same day, the Administration bowed to pressure from the pro-Israel lobby and delivered what appeared to be a deliberate snub to Saudi Arabia, its most important Arab ally. Less than two weeks before King Fahd was to pay a state visit to Washington, it was announced that the sale of 40 F-15 fighter bombers to Saudi Arabia had been postponed pending a review of US arms sales to the Middle East. King Fahd's appeal to the USA to revive the peace process was made in Washington on the same day (11 February) that Yasser Arafat and King Hussein signed the Amman agreement, but the USA continued to insist that the PLO explicitly accept UN Resolution 242 to secure participation in negotiations. The Arab initiative was complicated shortly afterwards when President Mubarak of Egypt launched proposals for direct talks between Israel and a Jordanian-Palestinian delegation, following preliminary discussions between the latter and the USA, a suggestion which clearly went beyond anything envisaged by King Hussein and Yasser Arafat. Mubarak's move, which drew sharp opposition from Syria and many Palestinians, as well as from the USSR, was cautiously welcomed by Israeli Prime Minister Peres, who said on 25 February that Israel would be willing to meet such a delegation provided it did not contain PLO members.

ISRAEL'S WITHDRAWAL FROM LEBANON

The first phase of Israel's withdrawal plan, the evacuation of the western seaboard from the Awali to the Litani, was accomplished peacefully in February 1985. Almost immediately, however, Shi'ite guerrillas stepped up their attacks. Israel launched a policy of 'Iron Fist' reprisal against villages suspected of harbouring guerrillas, storming scores of townships, killing and wounding their inhabitants, destroying houses and taking away hundreds of men to prison camps. The IDF clashed with UNIFIL forces protesting against the destruction of Shi'ite homes, and on 12 March, the USA vetoed a UN Security Council resolution, proposed by Lebanon, which condemned Israel's behaviour in southern Lebanon.

Israel's reprisal tactics did not have the desired effect: UN figures showed that in the first month in which the 'Iron Fist' policy operated, attacks on the IDF in Lebanon actually doubled. On 17 March, Israeli Prime Minister Peres announced that the withdrawal was to be accelerated and completed in 8–10 weeks. In late March elements of the LF, determined to salvage what they could from the retreat and the increasingly pro-Syrian policies pursued by the Gemayel Government, staged a revolt. Fighting in the capital and in the south between the Lebanese army and the Christian rebels soon degenerated into a general conflict between Christians and Muslims, which was accompanied by a fresh Israeli onslaught against Shi'ite villages in the occupied southern area. Israeli–Shi'ite antagonism was exacerbated by the news that, in contravention of the Geneva Convention, Israel had secretly transferred more than 1,000 Lebanese Shi'ite detainees to Israel, where the army Chief of Staff, General Moshe Levi, said they would remain imprisoned until 'the security situation improved'. The second phase of Israel's withdrawal (from the central and eastern sectors of southern Lebanon) was completed during April, as the sectarian fighting north of its lines intensified. Druze and Muslim militias took control of the main Sidon–Beirut highway on 28 April, overrunning many Christian villages whose inhabitants fled in their thousands towards the new Israeli lines. Israel, which at the beginning of May began fortifying its international border with Lebanon, made it clear that it would not intervene again to help the beleaguered Christians.

THE SUPPRESSION OF THE PLO IN BEIRUT

Meanwhile, in Beirut, Syria's two main militia allies in Lebanon, the Druze and the Shi'ite Amal, unleashed a violent *putsch* against the Sunni Murabitoun militia. The Sunni Prime Minister, Rashid Karami, resigned in protest on 17 April but was persuaded to remain in office. Significantly, the Murabitoun were the only force in Lebanon still supportive of Yasser Arafat's PLO. The determination of Syria and its Lebanese allies to prevent the resurgence of pro-Arafat Palestinian forces in Lebanon after the Israeli withdrawal, was ruthlessly demonstrated when troops of the Shi'ite Amal movement attacked the Palestinian refugee camps in Beirut on 20 May. The savagery of the assault, which claimed hundreds of Palestinian lives, led the hitherto pro-Syrian Palestinian factions in the camps to join forces with pro-Arafat fighters. As the third anniversary of Israel's invasion approached it appeared that a *pax Syriana* could be established in Lebanon after the Israelis had withdrawn if Syria could control its Lebanese allies and prevent the country dividing along sectarian lines into religious cantons.

ISRAEL'S CONTINUED REFUSAL TO NEGOTIATE WITH THE PALESTINIANS

On the wider front, the refusal of Israel and the USA to deal directly with the PLO remained the single greatest obstacle to all negotiations, including those on the basis of 'territory for peace' involving Israel, the Palestinians, Jordan and Egypt, proposed by King Hussein and President Mubarak. However, on 5 April the US Administration finally took a more active role, with visits to the Middle East by Assistant Secretary of State Richard Murphy and Secretary of State George Shultz. Neither Murphy nor Shultz, who toured the Middle East in April and May respectively, succeeded in resolving the central issue of Palestinian representation at peace talks, despite reports that, while in Jordan, the US Secretary of State had been presented with a list of Palestinians who were not PLO members for possible inclusion in a joint Jordanian-Palestinian delegation. Shultz was denied the economic pressure, which he could have brought to bear on Israel over the issue of Palestinian representation, when the US Administration finally decided to recommend to Congress, shortly before he left Washington, that Israel receive the additional \$1,500m. in emergency aid which it had requested. Israel's position hardened on 12 May when it announced that members of the PNC were also unacceptable as negotiating partners.

On 20 May three Israeli prisoners of war who had been held since the invasion of Lebanon by the hardline PFLP General Command, led by Ahmad Jibril, were exchanged for 1,150 Palestinians detained in Israel. The release of the Palestinian prisoners, some of them convicted terrorists, sparked a political storm in Israel, generating intense pressure on the Government to release Jews convicted of, or awaiting trial for, terrorist offences against Arabs. In an attempt to lend momentum to the peace initiative launched by the Jordan-PLO agreement, King Hussein went to Washington at the end of May 1985 to establish some form of international framework for his proposals. Radical quarters of the Arab world had already accused Jordan of seeking a separate deal with Israel, and King Hussein was clearly anxious to avoid the ostracism suffered by Egypt as a result of the Camp David treaty, preferring an international conference co-sponsored by both superpowers. By far the greatest obstacle to talks remained the issue of Palestinian representation. It was not until July that the PLO submitted to Jordan a list of names of 22 leading Palestinians for inclusion in a joint Jordanian-Palestinian delegation to meet US officials prior to the opening of wider negotiations involving Israel. Israel rejected the list (with two exceptions), calling for 'authentic Palestinian representatives' from the Occupied Territories, who had no direct links with the PLO.

ISRAEL COMPLETES ITS WITHDRAWAL

Israel announced the completion of its withdrawal from Lebanon on 10 June 1985, but its retention of an 8–10 km wide 'security zone' along the border inside Lebanon, policed by the Israeli-sponsored SLA and supported by smaller numbers of Israeli troops, proved a constant source of friction with UNIFIL, to the north.

Syria succeeded in sponsoring a cease-fire of sorts on 31 May in the battle for control of the Palestinian refugee camps in Beirut, after Shi'ite Amal militiamen had failed to subdue stubborn Palestinian resistance, but there was no foreseeable end to the sectarian violence. The rise of Lebanon's Shi'ite factions in particular (supported by Iran in certain cases), with their associated underground guerrilla groups, compounded the descent into anarchy, which extreme Islamic and anti-Western groups began increasingly to exploit. On 11 June a Jordanian airliner with 65 passengers on board was diverted by Shi'ites to Beirut, where the hostages were later released and the plane destroyed. Less than 48 hours later a US TWA airliner carrying 153 passengers including 43 US citizens was also hijacked, and flown between Beirut and Algiers (where 100 hostages were released) before landing for the third time in Beirut on 16 June. The USA responded with a build-up of naval forces off Lebanon, but the dispersal of the hostages in Shi'ite-controlled west Beirut precluded any US attempt to free them by force, putting pressure instead on Israel to accede to the hijackers' demands and release over 700 Lebanese Shi'ites being held in Israel. The intervention of President Assad of Syria resulted in the US hostages being freed unharmed (with the exception of one who had been killed when the plane was first seized) on 30 June. In return Israel released its Shi'ite prisoners in stages to avoid the impression of a surrender to terrorism. For the USA, the TWA hijacking was instrumental in diverting attention from a Middle East peace settlement to the immediate problem of combating terrorism.

Further Arab–Israeli violence on the occupied West Bank also threatened the prospects for negotiations. After the killing of two Israeli teachers, and of an occupation official, reprisal actions by Jewish settler groups were accompanied by additional security measures, including curfews, the closure of universities and newspapers, and detention without trial. Palestinians were also deported (a total of 26 in 1985)—a practice which Israel had discontinued in 1980 after widespread international criticism. The result was an escalation of violence by Arabs and Jews throughout August and September, at the end of which regular army troops were sent into occupied areas. The harassment of Palestinians by both the Israeli army and settler vigilantes was widespread, and there were signs that the Israeli coalition Government's right-wing Likud component was exploiting the unrest to sabotage the prospect of talks with a joint Jordanian-Palestinian delegation. Blaming PLO 'command centres' in Jordan for co-ordinating Palestinian resistance in the Occupied Territories, the Likud leader and Minister of Foreign Affairs Itzhak Shamir urged that Israel suspend diplomatic contacts so long as the PLO was allowed to maintain 'forward headquarters' on Jordanian soil. The future of the proposed talks was already in serious doubt after the failure of US Assistant Secretary of State Richard Murphy to meet members of a Jordanian-Palestinian delegation during his tour of the Middle East in mid-August.

Jordan was increasingly fearful of isolation within the Arab world, a fear heightened by the refusal of the Arab summit held in Casablanca on 7 August to endorse the aims of the Jordanian-Palestinian accord. This fear was somewhat allayed by the US decision, prior to King Hussein's visit to Washington on 30 September, to submit to Congress a $1,900m. arms deal with Jordan despite intense opposition to it from the Zionist lobby. Moreover, although US opposition to a meeting with PLO or PLO-associated Palestinians was as firm as ever, Jordanian hopes of progress were boosted in late September when the British Prime Minister, Margaret Thatcher, following her visits to Amman and Cairo, invited a Palestinian-Jordanian delegation (including two members of the PLO Executive Committee) to London for talks with the British Foreign Secretary, Sir Geoffrey Howe. Nevertheless, King Hussein was clearly insuring against the initiative's failure when, before leaving for the USA, he sanctioned the initial approaches in a *rapprochement* between Jordan and its main opponent in the Arab world, Syria.

ESCALATION OF VIOLENCE

On 1 October 1985, three days after King Hussein had arrived in the USA to address the UN General Assembly with an appeal for Arab–Israeli peace, Israeli jets bombed the PLO's headquarters in Tunis, killing 75 people, in retaliation for the killing of three Israelis by the PLO's élite Force 17 in Cyprus. The Israeli raid was condemned by the UN and by European leaders, but support for it from the White House as a 'legitimate response' to terrorism was a serious blow to US–Arab relations and to the USA's credibility as a peace-broker. Despite Jordanian and PLO pledges of continued commitment to the peace process, Arab anger over the affair clearly led to increased violence in the Israeli-occupied territories. Also on 7 October, four Palestinians succeeded in hijacking an Italian cruise liner, the *Achille Lauro*, with over 400 passengers and crew on board. The action was condemned by the PLO, which swiftly persuaded the hijackers to surrender themselves to the Egyptian authorities, but not before one passenger, an elderly American Jew, had been murdered. Egypt had agreed with the PLO that the hijackers would be flown to PLO headquarters in Tunis to stand trial, but the Egyptian airliner carrying them was intercepted *en route* by US fighter-planes and forced to land at a NATO base in Sicily. The US plan to take the hijackers, who were accompanied by the alleged mastermind of the operation, the leader of the Palestine Liberation Front, Muhammad Abu al-Abbas, to the USA for trial was thwarted by the Italians, who prevented the Americans from taking custody of the Palestinians and subsequently allowed Abu al-Abbas to leave the country on the grounds that he had not been actively involved in the hijack.

The political repercussions of the *Achille Lauro* affair set back the prospect of peace talks. In US and Israeli eyes, it further justified the exclusion of the PLO from the peace process for as long as it was involved in terrorism. On 21 October Jordan signed a three-point agreement with Syria which included a pledge not to seek a separate peace with Israel and was seen as a clear move away from the peace process based on Jordan's collaboration with Yasser Arafat, towards whom Syria and the Damascus-based PLO factions remained hostile.

With the peace process deadlocked, attention focused on the summit meeting between President Reagan and Mr Gorbachev on 19 November in Geneva. There was speculation that a new approach based on US-Soviet co-operation might result, but the summit meeting passed with no sign of any agreement on the Middle East, and the prospect of an international conference began to recede. One reason was the PLO's continued refusal to accede to the USA's precondition that it accept UN Resolution 242, renounce terrorism and recognize Israel. Jordanian impatience with the PLO mounted, as the reconciliation between King Hussein and President Assad of Syria proceeded apace; on 10 November King Hussein issued a statement accepting responsibility for the long period of poor relations with Syria and pledging an end to the activities of anti-Syrian elements based in Jordan. Syria did not conceal its view that the *rapprochement,* which continued with a meeting in Damascus between King Hussein and President Assad on 30–31 December, foreshadowed the end of the Jordan-PLO agreement. Yasser Arafat, despite warm support from Egypt during a visit to Cairo in mid-November, in the course of which the PLO leader renounced terrorist violence outside the Occupied Territories and against civilians, was becoming increasingly isolated. His position and the credibility of the PLO as a participant in peace talks was not improved by simultaneous terrorist attacks by Palestinians at Rome and Vienna airports on 27 December which killed 19 people (including five US citizens) and injured more than 100. Yet in the aftermath of the atrocities the US Administration, and the Government of Israel, whose El Al airline facilities had been the target of the attacks, for the first time made a distinction between the PLO, led by Arafat, and the dissident PLO splinter group (the Fatah Revolutionary Council), led by Abu Nidal, which was widely held to be responsible for the attacks. US and Israeli anger, and the threat of military retaliation, was directed almost exclusively toward Abu Nidal's alleged sponsor and protector, Libya, despite the more prominent links between the Abu Nidal group and Syria. The US Sixth Fleet was deployed off the Libyan coast, and on 7 January 1986 a package of anti-Libyan political and economic sanctions was announced by President Reagan, though European Governments refused to adopt them.

JORDAN RENOUNCES ITS AGREEMENT WITH THE PLO

During the first few weeks of 1986 it became clear that there was little prospect of progress in the Jordan-PLO peace initiative. A 12-day session of talks in January between King Hussein and Yasser Arafat, who came to Amman to reply to 'final' US terms for Palestinian participation in peace negotiations, collapsed without agreement. Although these terms represented a concession on the long-established US-Israeli position in that they entailed an invitation to the PLO to attend an international peace conference in return for the organization's acceptance of Resolution 242, this the PLO refused to do, unless the USA first recognized the Palestinian right to self-determination. No sooner had the Jordanian-Palestinian talks ended than the US Administration notified King Hussein that it was postponing indefinitely its request to Congress to sell advanced weaponry to Jordan, a sale which President Reagan had earlier said was 'essential to create the conditions for a lasting Middle East peace'. The Jordanian-PLO peace initiative was formally dissolved on 19 February, when King Hussein announced the end of political collaboration with the PLO leadership, strongly hinting that he would now seek a new partner in peace moves in the form of alternative representatives of the Palestinians. The principal reason given by King Hussein for the breakdown was the PLO's preoccupation with Palestinian self-determination at the expense of the 'liberation of the land' and its refusal to accept Resolution 242. The immediate effect was to raise

Arafat's standing among the considerable body of Palestinians who had suspected him of giving up the Palestinians' 'last card', by acknowledging Resolution 242, with its implicit recognition of Israel, in return for vague US promises of participation in peace talks. King Hussein's chances of finding alternative Palestinian representatives, who would have the backing of the majority of Palestinians and the Arab world at large, seemed slight.

THE TABA ISSUE

Israel's reaction to the collapse of the Jordan-PLO initiative was one of relief at avoiding a US-PLO dialogue and with it the threat of a split in the Government between the Labour bloc and the Likud faction, which was militantly opposed to any form of territorial concession. The fragile Israeli coalition Government had already been seriously threatened by the issue of Taba, the tiny coastal enclave claimed by both Egypt and Israel and outwardly the principal cause of the discord between the two, which had begun with the 1982 Israeli invasion of Lebanon. Prime Minister Peres, keen to improve relations with Egypt, was in favour of acceding to Egypt's demand to submit the issue to international arbitration, a course bitterly opposed by Likud leader Itzhak Shamir, a veteran critic of the Camp David treaty. Israel's overtures to Egypt were, however, undermined by its bombing of Tunis on 1 October, which President Mubarak denounced as a 'fatal blow' to peace; five days later seven Israeli tourists, including four children, were murdered by an Egyptian policeman in Sinai. Israeli-Egyptian contacts resumed in December, and on 14 January 1986 Peres succeeded in obtaining the Likud's approval to submit the Taba issue to arbitration. In return Egypt agreed to a series of measures to improve bilateral relations, including the return of Egypt's Ambassador to Tel Aviv. However, the expected improvement quickly became bogged down in low-level talks and Peres' hopes of a summit meeting with President Mubarak were not realized.

US-ISRAELI TIES

During his visit to Washington in early April the Israeli Prime Minister, Shimon Peres, proposed that the USA should support a 'Marshall Plan' (such as was employed to assist European recovery after World War II) for the Middle East—a $20,000m.–$30,000m. development fund, primarily designed to help Arab states affected by the sharp drop in the price of oil. The proposal was welcomed by US officials as worthy of serious consideration, despite the unlikelihood that Arab states would co-operate in any plan involving Israel, while the latter was in occupation of Arab territory. The positive US response to Peres' proposals underlined the strength of the US-Israeli alliance, despite two developments which were outwardly damaging to the relationship. First, on 24 November 1985 a US naval intelligence officer, Jonathan Pollard, was arrested by the FBI and charged with supplying classified documents to Israel. Then, in April 1986 a licensed Israeli arms dealer, retired Gen. Avraham Baram, was indicted in the USA for his part in a conspiracy to smuggle $2,500m. worth of advanced US weaponry, including tanks, missiles and fighter planes, to Iran. The indictment listed, among the items in the attempted sale, $800m. worth of arms that had been delivered to Israel as part of the US military aid programme.

On 17 January 1986 the USA invoked its veto in the UN Security Council to prevent the adoption of a resolution deploring Israel's behaviour in southern Lebanon, where the presence of Israeli troops remained a source of conflict. On 30 January the USA vetoed a draft resolution, which had won the support of all Council members with the exception of Thailand, condemning Israel's actions over Islamic holy places in Jerusalem, where religious extremists had provoked Palestinian rioting by attempting to establish a Jewish foothold in the compound of the al-Aqsa mosque (see article on The Jerusalem Issue, p. 98).

Shimon Peres was keen to gain credit for some progress in Arab-Israeli relations before surrendering power to Itzhak Shamir under the terms of their power-sharing agreement. With Egypt proving unco-operative, and King Hussein ignoring repeated Israeli appeals to proceed to peace talks independently of the PLO, in February Peres resorted to the idea of 'imposing' a limited autonomy on the Palestinian inhabitants of the Occupied Territories. As with similar attempts in the past, the 'unilateral autonomy' plan quickly foundered in the face of Palestinian opposition that united pro-Jordanian and pro-PLO leaders in the West Bank, who refused to countenance anything short of an end to Israeli occupation.

SYRIA REARMED

The dashing of peace prospects was followed by rising tension between Israel and Syria, which had been re-equipped militarily by the USSR to the point where its forces threatened Israel's long-standing military supremacy. On 19 November the Israeli air force had shot down two Syrian MiG fighters, reportedly in Syrian airspace. In response, Syria deployed SAM missiles in eastern Lebanon, a move denounced by Israel as a threat to its reconnaissance flights over that country. Its own threat to destroy the missile sites provoked a crisis which could have escalated into armed conflict, and which was only defused by US mediation. The underlying tension between the two countries remained and President Assad of Syria made a defiant speech reasserting Syria's determination to recover the Golan Heights 'annexed' to Israel in 1981. In turn, Israeli military analysts began to discuss the possibility of a pre-emptive Israeli attack to prevent Syria achieving military parity with Israel. In mid-April the Syrian Government accused Israel of responsibility for a series of terrorist bomb attacks inside Syria, which claimed many lives, while Israel charged Syria with sponsoring Arab terrorism in Europe.

THE USA CLASHES WITH LIBYA

US mediation in the Middle East was effectively ruled out by the Reagan Administration's preoccupation with combating terrorism, at the expense of tackling the fundamental causes of regional violence and instability. This narrowly-focused policy led to a military exchange between the USA and Libya, whose alleged sponsorship of international terrorism was apparently regarded by US policy-makers as the root cause of Middle East tension. On 24 March 1986, after SAM-5 missiles had been fired at US aircraft, fighter planes from the US Sixth Fleet in the Mediterranean sank four Libyan patrol vessels in the Gulf of Sirte and destroyed shore-based missile and radar facilities near the town of Sirte. The pretext for the incident was a US challenge to Libya's claim that the entire Gulf constituted Libyan territorial waters. Two weeks later a bomb exploded at a nightclub in West Berlin frequented by US servicemen, killing two people and injuring more than 200, in what the US Administration claimed was a Libyan-sponsored attack. In response US aircraft, including US air force bombers based in the United Kingdom, carried out air raids on Tripoli and Benghazi, which resulted in many civilian casualties, including members of Qaddafi's own family. The confrontation destroyed what little credibility the USA still had as a potential mediator in the Middle East conflict and many feared that, far from discouraging terrorism, the US action would encourage it.

THE VANUNU AFFAIR

The international media focused on Israel's nuclear weapons capability with the arrival in London, in October 1986, of Mordechai Vanunu, a former employee at the so-called 'textile factory' at Dimona in the Negev Desert in southern Israel. Vanunu claimed that he had worked as a technician at Dimona and that Israel had succeeded in developing thermonuclear weapons, and was stockpiling them there. The true nature of the Dimona plant had long been common knowledge in the West, in spite of official Israeli denials, yet the Israeli Government's first reaction to Vanunu's 'defection' was to prohibit Israeli papers from reporting the affair. Subsequently, Vanunu was lured to Rome by a female agent of Mossad, the Israeli external security service, which then kidnapped him and took him back to Israel to stand trial for treason.

SUPPORT FOR AN INTERNATIONAL PEACE CONFERENCE

Hopes of a revival in the peace process had been rekindled on 12 September 1986 when the Israeli Prime Minister, Shimon Peres, only a month before the scheduled transfer of power to coalition partner Itzhak Shamir, met President Mubarak of

Egypt in Alexandria. In a two-day summit, staged with the US and Israeli media very much in mind, the two leaders agreed, in principle, on the formation of a preparatory committee for an international conference to discuss the Arab–Israeli conflict. Such a conference, they agreed, should include the five permanent members of the UN Security Council, but the thorny issue of Arab, and particularly Palestinian, representation was left untouched. Support for an international conference grew to include King Hussein and the ministers of foreign affairs of the EC; the fact that clear backing, at least in principle, for such a conference had also been forthcoming from the USSR and the PLO, was a sign of both the range of possible delegates envisaged by the various parties concerned, and of how far the project was from becoming a reality since the two main protagonists, Israel and the PLO, were no nearer the required goal of mutual recognition.

SHAMIR ASSUMES THE PREMIERSHIP OF ISRAEL

In Israel, the major obstacle to an international conference was the assumption of power, on 16 October 1986, of Likud leader Itzhak Shamir, in accordance with the rotation agreement of September 1984 between the two main parties. Shamir unequivocally opposed such a conference. Shimon Peres, however, who became Minister of Foreign Affairs, made it quite clear that he had no intention of relinquishing the conference idea. Peres continued to promote the idea of an international conference, causing great embarrassment to Shamir. Indeed, Peres went to Egypt on 22 February to meet President Mubarak, and both leaders made repeated visits to Washington to secure the support of the US Administration. The coalition Government repeatedly teetered on the brink of disintegration, but Shimon Peres failed to secure the necessary support in the Knesset for his Labour bloc to carry a motion of 'no confidence' in the Government, which would have precipitated a general election. From Peres' point of view, however, the danger inherent in forcing a general election was that it might leave Likud in a position to form a coalition government which excluded Labour.

THE 'IRANGATE' SCANDAL

Having already seen its standing in the region plummet after a series of foreign-policy miscalculations, the final blow to the USA's credibility in Arab opinion came with the revelation, in November 1986, in the Lebanese magazine *Ash-Shira'*, of secret arms deals between Iran and the USA. The progressively more damaging disclosures which followed the publication of the article seriously undermined President Reagan's domestic popularity. It transpired that the arms contracts were brokered by Israeli arms merchants acting with the backing of the Israeli intelligence services and Government. From the perspective of links between Israel and Iran, the deal was not very unusual, Israel having been a major source of arms for Iran since the 1950s. On the other hand, the active part played by the USA, through its National Security Agency and with the clear knowledge and connivance of both President Reagan and many of his senior aides, was a stark contradiction of the USA's stated policy of not negotiating with regimes it held responsible for international terrorism. Israel originally convinced the USA of the desirability of the arms sales by claiming that they would help to bring about the release of a number of Western hostages held by Iranian-backed groups in Lebanon. An additional incentive was that the profits from the transaction could be used to circumvent US Congressional restrictions on aiding the Contra guerillas who were waging, by their own admission, a campaign of terror against the legitimate, but socialist, Government of Nicaragua.

The USA's traditional allies in the Arab world were dismayed by this further demonstration of the way in which supporters of Israel seemed to be able to sway US foreign policy so easily, even against the USA's own stated interests. Israel's success in persuading the USA to sell to Iran the very weapons systems that it had only recently refused to sell to Jordan, a staunch ally, made the Arab states' sense of betrayal even more acute.

THE POLLARD SPY CASE

At the beginning of March 1987, after a presidential commission had strongly criticized both President Reagan and Israel for

their parts in the 'Irangate' affair, more pressure was brought to bear on the Israeli-US relationship in the aftermath of the trial of Jonathan Pollard, a US citizen, and his wife. The couple were arrested in November 1985 and charged with spying for Israel. Although their conviction was widely expected, the severe sentences, announced on 4 March, were received with surprise. Jonathan Pollard was sentenced to life imprisonment, in spite of the expectation that, having spied for an ally of the USA, he would be treated more leniently. Pollard was a committed Zionist who was recruited as a spy during a visit to Israel. His work in US naval intelligence gave him access to vast quantities of classified information. Of particular interest to Israel was material concerning the defence facilities of the USA's allies in the Middle East and North Africa, including, it is believed, data which enabled the Israelis to carry out the bombing of the PLO headquarters in Tunis in October 1985. These revelations caused both astonishment and disillusionment in the pro-US Arab states. Although the deep-rooted and far-reaching nature of Israel's alliance with the USA had long been understood, and the support enjoyed by Israel in the US legislature and in successive administrations widely acknowledged, few of the Arab states were aware to what extent Israel had also succeeded in penetrating the upper echelons of the US intelligence establishment.

DEVELOPMENTS IN THE OCCUPIED TERRITORIES

In the Occupied Territories the cycle of repression and protest continued. The appointment by the Israeli military authorities of Arab mayors in three West Bank towns was interpreted as part of a policy to isolate the PLO in the territories by fostering a more moderate Palestinian constituency and an alternative, 'acceptable', Palestinian leadership, and coincided with Jordanian efforts to the same end. These included the announcement in August of a five-year development plan for the West Bank and the Gaza Strip involving projected expenditure of US $1,300m. This apparent coincidence of interests resulted in the arrest and deportation of Akram Haniya, Editor of the Jerusalem daily newspaper, *Ash-Sha'ab*. This action was regarded as a sop to Jordanian wishes—Haniya's hostility to Israel was no more threatening than that of any other newspaper editor in the Occupied Territories, but his aversion to King Hussein's plans in the West Bank clearly rankled with the Jordanian authorities. This episode was the prelude to a series of demonstrations by Palestinians and arrests by the military authorities, interspersed with acts of violence against Palestinian communities by Israeli settlers. December began with a number of clashes between the Israeli army and Palestinian demonstrators, the worst occurring at Bir Zeit University, where two students were shot dead. The subsequent closure of Bir Zeit, as well as an-Najah University in Nablus, brought no reduction in the level of Palestinian protests or in the consequent level of Israeli reprisals.

THE 'WAR OF THE CAMPS' SPREADS IN LEBANON

Lebanon continued to stumble from crisis to crisis in the second half of 1986. With sporadic fighting in the south between Israel's proxy SLA and the various Lebanese, mainly Shi'ite, forces opposing it, elements of the Maronite Lebanese Forces (LF) militia, opposed to President Gemayel, attempted a coup in east Beirut, which would have succeeded, but for the intervention of the Lebanese army. The failure of the coup was a blow to Syria's plans for a reconciliation of the many opposing forces in the country, for the Maronite forces loyal to President Gemayel remained the major stumbling block to a Syrian-brokered peace plan. In the south violent clashes flared up between Amal and PLO forces in and around Tyre and Sidon. Paralleled by the so-called 'war of the camps' in south Beirut, these clashes, which ushered in a prolonged period of conflict between the two forces, were a clear indication of the extent to which armed Palestinians from various PLO factions had re-established themselves in Lebanon, particularly in the Palestinian refugee camps. To the Syrians, this PLO revival, particularly in the number of fighters loyal to the leader of Fatah, Yasser Arafat, was another challenge to their hegemony over the country and to their bid to create an alternative PLO, independent of Arafat. Amal, as

Syria's closest ally in Lebanon, was the only Lebanese militia involved in this conflict, and Damascus relied on its ability to crush the resurgence of Palestinian military strength. Another source of concern for Syria was that pro- and anti-Arafat fighters made common cause in the defence of the camps, and their shared resentment of the Syrian role in suppressing the PLO threatened to cause a reconciliation. By December, with over 500 dead, there was no sign of any respite in the fighting in Tyre, Sidon and Beirut. The refugee camps at the core of the conflict were besieged, with essential supplies from outside effectively cut off.

THE WAVE OF ABDUCTIONS IN LEBANON

It was not until January 1987, however, that the Western news media turned its attention back to Lebanon, with the return to Beirut on 12 January of the Archbishop of Canterbury's special envoy, Terry Waite. The purpose of Waite's mission, against which he was strongly warned by both the British Ambassador and the Archbishop, was to negotiate the release of the 20 remaining Western hostages being held in Beirut. The kidnapping of foreigners had begun in Beirut in early 1984, and by the time of Waite's second visit more than 60 abductions had taken place, several of the hostages having been killed by their captors. No reliable figures are available for the numbers of Lebanese who had been kidnapped, many never to be seen again, since the civil war began. Waite himself disappeared on 21 January 1987 and remained in captivity until the end of 1991. Shi'a Muslims in the pay of Iran were believed to be responsible for his kidnapping.

Waite's disappearance, which was followed three days later by that of three US lecturers from the Beirut University College, provoked a strong response from the USA, whose Sixth Fleet was increasing its strength off the Lebanese coast. This deployment was backed up by calls for Westerners remaining in west Beirut to leave, as well as by strong criticism of the Iranian Government, which many held to be ultimately responsible for the kidnappings. Significantly, however, the group which held the three lecturers called itself 'Islamic Jihad for the Liberation of Palestine', and made its hostages' safe return dependent on Israel's release of 400 Arab prisoners. Whatever the true identity and motivation of the kidnappers, they drew attention to Israel's role in the Lebanese crisis, to the complexity of the problems affecting the Middle East, and the need to address the fundamental problem of Palestine, as a precondition of a wider settlement.

Israel's involvement in Lebanon was by no means confined to the security zone that it had established to the north of its northern border, policed by the SLA with support from Israeli troops. Israeli air raids on Palestinian targets around Tyre and Sidon continued, and were usually claimed to be retaliation for mortar and *katyusha* rocket attacks from south Lebanon into Galilee. On 2 January 1987 the Israelis intercepted a passenger ferry bound for the Maronite port of Jounieh from Larnaca, in Cyprus, accusing the LF of allowing PLO fighters to use the ferry to reach Lebanon and the Palestinian camps. This was neither the first time the Israelis had held up a Cyprus–Lebanon ferry, nor the first evidence of clandestine collaboration between Fatah and the Maronites loyal to President Gemayel. The Maronite leadership, presumably seeing little immediate prospect of relief from its traditional ally, Israel, sought instead to strengthen anti-Syrian forces in west Beirut.

SYRIAN TROOPS ASSERT THEIR AUTHORITY IN BEIRUT

Throughout January 1987, however, it became clear, as the 'war of the camps' continued, that the pro-Syrian nexus of Muslim forces in west Beirut was about to crumble. The Druze militia, the Sunni-dominated PSP militia and the Shi'ite-dominated Hezbollah and Lebanese Communist Party militias, had never shared Amal's enthusiasm for fighting the Palestinians. On several occasions the PSP had sent supplies into the camps and actively supported the besieged Palestinians. As a result, in February, open fighting broke out in Shi'ite areas between Amal and the Communists, supported by the PSP. Amal suffered a heavy defeat and this, coupled with increasingly heavy casualties sustained in the siege of Chatila and Bourj el-Barajneh, threatened Syria's position of influence in west Beirut, raising

the prospect of an alliance of PLO and leftist forces in control of the city. With Western media attention arousing widespread international sympathy for the plight of the besieged Palestinians, President Assad of Syria decided to act. On 22 February some 4,000 Syrian troops occupied west Beirut, put an end to the clashes between the rival militias and lifted the siege of the Palestinian camps in Beirut, though Syrian influence failed permanently to relieve those in the south of Lebanon, and Syrian troops stopped short of precipitating a confrontation with Hezbollah by entering the Shi'a-dominated southern suburbs of Beirut.

PLO REUNIFICATION

The 'war of the camps' in Beirut resulted in another serious blow to President Assad's regional plans. Faced with Amal's onslaught and besieged in poorly fortified refugee camps, the disparate factions of the PLO had no choice but to unite on the ground in order to protect the Palestinian population whose defence was their ultimate *raison d'être* in Lebanon. After months of mediation by Algeria, Libya and, perhaps most significantly, the USSR, factions representing the majority of the PLO were finally brought together in March 1987. The principal rebel groups, the Democratic Front for the Liberation of Palestine (DFLP), the Palestine Communist Party (PCP), the two wings of the Palestine Liberation Front and the largest left-wing group, the Popular Front for the Liberation of Palestine (PFLP), agreed to attend a session of the PNC, after agreement on key issues had been reached with Yasser Arafat. The PLO's reunification at the 18th session of the PNC in Algiers from 20–25 April appeared to signal an end to the post-1982 alignments within the movement. Resolutions adopted by the PNC confirmed the agreements between the factions made prior to the session. Under the agreements, Arafat undertook to abrogate the Amman accord between Jordan and the PLO and to downgrade co-operation with Egypt until that country formally rejected the Camp David agreements with Israel (the PFLP had initially demanded the immediate severing of links with Egypt); while the left-wing factions (principally the PFLP and the DFLP) endorsed Arafat's continued leadership of the movement, effectively emasculating the Syrian-backed Palestine National Salvation Front, based in Damascus.

The reunification caused genuine celebration among the Palestinians under Israeli rule, whose attempts at resistance had been severely limited by years of factional wrangling. It alienated the Arab front-line states, Jordan, Egypt and Syria, each of whom saw their future ability to manipulate the PLO seriously undermined. The Israeli leadership was evidently dismayed at the PNC's failure to relapse into internal division but, with the PLO thus isolated from the most important Arab states, Peres was able to predict a decline in its relevance to a solution of the Middle East conflict. Indeed, as far as the much-vaunted idea of a Middle East peace conference was concerned, the reunification of the PLO, which urged the rejection of the USA's terms for negotiation, specifically Resolution 242, if taken in isolation, underlined the problem of accommodating the PLO at such a conference. However, the PNC explicitly supported the idea of a conference, with the PLO as the sole representative of the Palestinians, a suggestion which remained unacceptable to Israel.

POLITICAL DEADLOCK IN ISRAEL

Frustration at Palestinian unity was reinforced by the bitter deadlock within Israeli politics. The Labour-Likud coalition Government of national unity had only managed to survive thus far because each party feared the consequences of fresh elections. Despite indications of a significant lead for Labour in opinion polls in early 1987, the party was unable to rally enough support in the divided Knesset to be sure of winning a vote to dissolve Parliament and force new elections. With the political parties divided on the fundamental issue of peace moves, polarization within Israeli society over the same issue was increasing. While Labour supporters became more and more frustrated with Prime Minister Shamir's dogged refusal in mid-1987 even to contemplate the possibility of an international conference, the Right grew increasingly contemptuous of what it saw as pandering to the Arabs with talk of 'land for peace'. The Labour leader Shimon Peres' visit to Washington in May confirmed the isolation of his Likud rival in the international arena. Peres' opinion of the form which a peace conference should take was given strong backing by US Secretary of State George Shultz, who, however, was unwilling to bring pressure to bear on the Israeli Prime Minister to take a more flexible line.

September 1987 brought a direct attack on the PLO's status in the USA. Bowing to Congressional pressure the US State Department arrogated to itself the right to close the PLO's observer mission at the UN, in New York, and the Palestine Information Office in Washington, in spite of objections from US human rights groups protesting against what they believed to be a denial of freedom of speech. The move came as a surprise to US allies in Europe, who saw it as counterproductive to a proposed peace conference. With increased diplomatic activity by the USSR, which led to an improvement in Soviet relations with Israel, the proposed international conference was beginning to gather momentum again. The crucial obstacle remained the position of Shamir's Likud party, which remained doggedly opposed to any form of conference conducted on the basis of an exchange of land for peace, and had not even conceded the notion of a conference with superpower or UN Security Council participation, whatever the terms of negotiation. With George Shultz's visit to Moscow in October expected to cover the Middle East, it was widely hoped that he might bring some pressure to bear on Shamir during a brief visit to Israel. In the event, however, his views failed to make any impression on Shamir. Besides, the USA's Middle East preoccupations were, at this time, focused on developments in the Iran–Iraq War, with the Arab–Israeli conflict of secondary importance.

ARAB PRIORITIES

Such preoccupations were also troubling the Arab states themselves. The Arab League summit meeting in Amman, in November 1987, had been convened primarily to consider the Iran–Iraq War, and the Palestine issue had been shuffled well down the agenda. Faced with the deepening involvement of Saudi Arabia and Kuwait in the war, it was hoped that the Amman summit would unite the Arab nations against Iran. In fact the summit was the first such gathering not to give the Palestine issue priority. Although the PLO's status as sole Palestinian representative was upheld, in spite of Syrian efforts to undermine it, it was only entrusted with joint responsibility, with Jordan and Syria, for drafting the meeting's Palestine resolution. With peace moves baulked and the Israelis seemingly entrenched in the Occupied Territories, there appeared to be little to distract Arab attention from Iran's perceived belligerence.

THE PALESTINIAN UPRISING

The events of the second week of December 1987 in the Gaza Strip and the West Bank took the international community by surprise. Thirteen Palestinian civilians were killed, 50 wounded and hundreds arrested in the most serious and sustained clashes between Palestinian youths and the Israeli army for many years. These clashes proved to be the beginning of what has become known as the *intifada* (uprising), a mass Palestinian demonstration against Israeli rule, which surprised none more than the Palestinians themselves by continuing into the 1990s. A number of factors clearly played a part in creating the conditions that led to a revolt on such a scale.

Ten days of serious clashes took place in Gaza in October, in which seven supporters of a resistance group new to the Occupied Territories, calling itself 'Islamic Jihad', were killed by the security forces. The very emergence of a radical fundamentalist group in Palestine was significant in itself; three of those killed had escaped from prison and returned to lead attacks on the Israelis and thereby greatly enhanced their popularity. As a result of this, the demonstrations which followed their deaths were particularly ferocious, but the Israelis were able eventually to restore order in the Strip. Indeed, the level of repression in the Occupied Territories was at its highest level for many years: a large number of Palestinians had been 'administratively' detained (i.e. without trial) during 1987, and deportations, house demolitions, and other repressive measures were beginning to try the Palestinians' collective patience. The Amman summit itself was, doubtless, another factor in driving the Palestinians to revolt. At the time it was being held, widespread demonstrations were taking place in the Occupied Territories to protest at Arafat's cold reception in the Jordanian capital. The heavy-handed Israeli response provoked further clashes.

The spark that actually ignited the *intifada*, however, appears to have been a traffic accident. On 8 December an Israeli army lorry crashed into a car queuing at the road-block on the Gaza Strip's northern frontier, crushing four Palestinians to death. Few people believed it was an accident, and the Gaza Strip erupted in violent demonstrations. Quickly spreading to Nablus, the West Bank's largest town, the scale of the uprising caught the Israelis quite unprepared. A panicked Israeli response— shooting on sight, harassing Muslim worshippers, attacking hospital patients and staff—was probably crucial in establishing and then maintaining the uprising's momentum. By the end of 1987, 28 Palestinians had been killed, the great majority in the Gaza Strip.

INTERNATIONAL REACTION TO THE INTIFADA

By mid-January 1988 it had become clear that what was under way in the Occupied Territories was a mass popular revolt. The Israelis had adopted a series of severely repressive measures (including curfews and travel bans), none of which had brought the recalcitrant Palestinians to heel. One of the uprising's most notable achievements in its earlier stages was to attract international press, particularly television, coverage which was unprecedentedly hostile to Israel. Western TV viewers were shown footage of Israeli troops firing live bullets and tear gas at Palestinian demonstrators; most spectacularly on 15 January, when the security forces invaded the precincts of the al-Aqsa mosque in Jerusalem, and attacked worshippers. Israel's attempts to restrict press access to areas of unrest merely provoked media fury, attracting further criticism from the Western press, which previously had generally been sympathetic towards Israel. Other Israeli countermeasures included the imposition of a curfew in towns, villages and refugee camps, which caused serious absenteeism of Palestinian workers from their jobs in Israel (an estimated 120,000 Palestinians from the Occupied Territories worked in Israel), adding economic hardship to Israel's difficulties. But the most disturbing aspect of the *intifada*, from Israel's viewpoint, was the emergence, as early as January 1988, of an underground leadership (the Unified National Leadership of the Uprising (UNLU)). The UNLU was composed of representatives of the various PLO factions and co-ordinated strikes and demonstrations. It issued regular, serialized communiqués which detailed day-to-day protest activities.

Lacking a coherent strategy in response to the uprising, the Israelis attempted various ways of undermining it. Apart from shooting at demonstrators (46 had been shot dead by 15 January), mass arrests and other collective punishments, nine Palestinians were served with deportation orders on 3 January (in the face of international opposition), and a concerted campaign against the Palestinian press was launched, including the arrest and detention of many journalists, the closure of newspapers and press bureaux, and the imposition of stricter than usual military censorship.

Faced with mounting international censure over the high number of Palestinian casualties, the Israeli Minister of Defence, Itzhak Rabin, issued new instructions to his troops in the Territories at the end of January. Firing live ammunition at demonstrators was to be superseded by the widespread use of CS tear-gas and indiscriminate, pre-emptive, beatings. The spate of savage assaults by club-wielding Israeli soldiers on unarmed Palestinians recorded by television cameras were merely part of a campaign that lasted three weeks.

Israel's reputation was suffering particular damage in the USA, most significantly among the American Jewish community, its staunchest and most crucial source of support. Shocked by extensive TV coverage of violent scenes, American Jewish leaders began to voice the community's discontent to their Israeli counterparts and to the US Government. The Reagan Administration was further spurred to action by the visit of President Mubarak of Egypt to Washington at the end of January. Mubarak emphasized the need for the US to re-engage itself in the peace process. As a result, the USA prepared for a foreign policy initiative in an area from which it would normally have remained aloof at the start of an election year.

Special envoy Philip Habib was dispatched to Amman on 30 January to seek consultation with King Hussein.

The Arabs too were by now keenly aware of the *intifada*. An extraordinary meeting of Arab ministers of foreign affairs in Tunis, in January, effectively reversed the previous deprioritization of the Palestine question, putting it back at the top of the Arab world's agenda. Such was the response to the uprising in the Occupied Territories that a special fund was set up, under PLO supervision, to which member states of the Arab League were to be obliged to contribute to 'ensure the continuation of the uprising'. EC Commissioner Claude Cheysson publicly condemned Israel's actions as 'shameful' and called for its 'evacuation' of the Occupied Territories. The incoming Chairman of the EC Council of Ministers, the West German Minister of Foreign Affairs, Hans Dietrich Genscher, caused further embarrassment to Israel by stating his intention to make the Middle East the priority of his foreign policy during his six-month 'presidency'. He made clear, with full EC backing, his intention to seek a role for Europe in pushing forward plans for an international peace conference under UN auspices.

THE SHULTZ PLAN

Herr Genscher's initiative (which led him to undertake visits to various regional capitals during his 'presidency') was, however, overshadowed by that of his US counterpart, Secretary of State George Shultz. Shultz made his first visit of the year to the Middle East on 25 February 1988, impelled not so much by an overriding desire to settle the region's problems as equitably as possible (his record in office contained no previous diplomatic successes of any note, relating to the Arab–Israeli conflict), as by pressure from within the USA, particularly the Jewish community, to do something to relieve the pressure on Israel which the *intifada* had brought about. His plan was outlined by the US Under-Secretary of State for Near Eastern and South Asian Affairs, Richard Murphy, on a preliminary visit to the region between 5 and 11 February. The plan proposed: a six-month period of negotiations, beginning on 1 May 1988, on the basis of UN Security Council Resolutions 242 and 338, between Israel and a joint Jordanian-Palestinian delegation, to determine a form of interim autonomy for the Occupied Territories, which would last for three years pending a permanent negotiated settlement; the provision in the interim agreement for an Israeli military withdrawal from the West Bank, and for municipal elections of Palestinian officials to be held during 1989; and negotiations on a final settlement, to be started by the end of 1988; both sets of negotiations to run concurrently with an international conference, involving the five permanent members of the UN Security Council and all other parties to the conflict, proceeding on the basis of UN Security Council Resolutions 242 and 338, but having no power to impose a settlement or veto any agreement reached in the separate Israeli-Jordanian-Palestinian negotiations. (See Documents on Palestine). The plan was fatally flawed. Some form of interim arrangement would clearly be a requirement of any peace plan, but the absence of PLO representation and the 'toothless' nature of the international conference would not endear Shultz's proposals to Arab governments, and the Israeli obstacle was well known. The time-scale for the plan's operation was an indication of the importance Washington attached to the peace process. However, another fundamental obstacle to the plan's acceptance was the Reagan Administration's lack of credibility in the Arab world. In the Arab view, the USA had done little or nothing in recent years to bring pressure to bear on Israel to reconsider its stance on peace negotiations—was it prepared to act differently now?

When Shultz visited the Middle East at the end of February to consult regional leaders, Israel's response to his plan, or, rather, the divided response of its two main leaders, was all too predictable: general endorsement, after some initial reservations, from Shimon Peres; outright rejection, after initial, hesitant interest, from Itzhak Shamir. For Shamir, the US plan had 'no prospect of implementation'; if Shultz pushed too hard for its implementation, Shamir believed, the Israeli Government would fall, and, given the new political climate engendered by the Palestinian uprising, Likud would win the ensuing election outright. Egypt and Syria stopped short of an outright rejection of the plan but Syria, in particular, gave no cause to suggest

that it would in any way support its implementation. Jordan pronounced itself sceptical that Israel would relinquish control over the Territories and reiterated its opposition to 'partial or interim solutions', though it welcomed the USA's acceptance on 1 March of the concept of the Palestinians' 'legitimate rights'. The UNLU interpreted the Shultz plan as an attempt to abort the uprising and halt the political momentum it was generating world-wide in favour of Palestinian national rights. The PLO rejected the plan outright, as it made no provision for the creation of a Palestinian state and did not recognize the PLO's right to be involved in the peace negotiations. So, when Shultz returned to the USA, following another visit to the region at the beginning of March, it was with virtually nothing to show for his peace initiative. In his absence US TV cameras had continued to record Israel's repressive measures to put down the uprising and the climate of sympathy for the Palestinians had not faded.

THE INTIFADA CONTINUES

In the Territories themselves, there had been no slackening in the intensity of the *intifada*. A total of 76 Palestinians had been shot dead by the end of February; others were beaten to death or killed by exposure to CS tear-gas. Fifteen were victims of the gas (over 80 aborted pregnancies were also attributed to the exposure of the mothers to the gas) following its use in confined spaces (narrow alleyways or even inside people's homes), in contravention of the manufacturer's recommendations. (The chemical was sold, and is used elsewhere, as a means of crowd dispersal in open areas. At the beginning of May the manufacturers eventually agreed to ban its sale to Israel.) Meanwhile, arrests, beatings, press restrictions, deportations, prolonged curfews, the forced opening of shops (closed according to strike instructions issued by the Palestinian underground leadership), and the closure of schools and colleges, all continued to be employed by the Israelis to contain the uprising.

NEW LEADERSHIP IN THE OCCUPIED TERRITORIES

In response, the Palestinians used a surprise weapon: unity. After its apparently spontaneous beginnings, it became clear to the Israeli authorities that the uprising was being carefully orchestrated. The degree of cohesion and co-ordination this gave to the various components of Palestinian society was unprecedented in its recent history. The solidarity engendered among Palestinians was the key factor in making the uprising viable on a prolonged basis. With clear support from Palestinians and Arabs inside pre-1967 Israel, and from many groups and individuals on the left of Israeli politics, the uprising had already made an indelible mark on Israeli society by March 1988.

Palestinian politics were also greatly affected. That the uprising was a spontaneous expression of popular frustration with Israel's rule and of the solidarity between Palestinian Christians and Muslims against Israel's oppression, was undeniable, but it marked a new departure in that the PLO leadership outside the Occupied Territories was not instrumental in organizing and sustaining it. After initial reports of differences between the PLO in Tunis and the underground leadership in the Territories, a working relationship between the two was quickly established, principally to ensure the passage of funds from outside into the Territories, but also to co-ordinate, as far as possible, the political strategy of the PLO as a whole. (The new leadership in the Territories was unequivocal in its allegiance to the PLO.)

At the end of March, the Israelis intensified their crackdown on the rebellion. Telephone links between the Occupied Territories and the outside world were severed; restrictions were placed on movement between districts within the Territories, and between the Territories and Israel and Jordan; a 24-hour curfew was imposed on the entire Gaza Strip for three successive days. The restrictions, which were primarily intended to prevent a massive Palestinian demonstration planned for Land Day on 30 March (commemorating the killing in 1976 of six Israeli Arabs demonstrating against Israeli land seizures), also included the suspension of fuel supplies and severe restrictions on press and media access. The arrest and detention without trial of suspected ringleaders was also stepped up. However, these measures only hardened Palestinian resolve. Local committees organized the distribution of food, fuel and other resources (as they also supervised strikes and the closure of shops, which the Israelis attempted to keep open by force, to preserve an appearance of normality), as well as taking responsibility for security after a mass resignation of Palestinian policemen, who had been threatened with reprisals for co-operating with the occupying power. Solidarity between Palestinian communities on both sides of the pre-1967 frontier was, if anything, strengthened.

With battle-lines thus, uncompromisingly, drawn, George Shultz returned to the Middle East in mid-April. However, his efforts were obstructed by Shamir's obstinacy, and hamstrung by his own unwillingness to bring pressure to bear on the Israeli Prime Minister. Despite a loss of interest in the Western media, engendered chiefly by the restrictions Israel had imposed on reporting in the Occupied Territories, the *intifada* continued. Shootings, beatings, tear-gassing and other less 'telegenic' acts of violence remained the Israelis' most visible means of combating the uprising. In addition, universities and schools were closed for four months, from April until the end of July; petrol supplies were periodically suspended; there were weeks of continuous night-time curfew throughout the Gaza Strip, and thousands of Palestinians were detained, many without trial, for six months, under martial law. By the end of July more than 290 Palestinians had been killed in the uprising and 28 deported. Fundamental changes had taken place in Palestinian society since the *intifada* began; old class divisions had begun to break down, as the West Bank's urban élite found itself as dependent on home-produced food as the poorest peasant families. In such a climate, Israeli repression alone could not break the popular will to continue the uprising, which was now a central fact in the life of every Palestinian in the Occupied Territories, and a rallying point for Palestinians throughout the diaspora.

THE ASSASSINATION OF 'ABU JIHAD'

On 16 April 1988, in Tunis, an Israeli assassination squad murdered Khalil al-Wazir (alias 'Abu Jihad'), Yasser Arafat's deputy as commander of the Palestine Liberation Army. In the wave of ensuing demonstrations in the Occupied Territories, 16 Palestinians were killed in a single day. The assassination prompted a *rapprochement* between Arafat and President Assad, who had been at odds since 'Abu Musa', a Fatah dissident, led a Syrian-backed revolt in Lebanon against Arafat's leadership of the PLO in 1983. On 25 April 1988 Arafat and President Assad met in Damascus, where 'Abu Jihad' was buried, to discuss their differences. It was Arafat's first visit to Syria since his expulsion in June 1983. However, any prospect of a further improvement in relations was nullified by the renewal, in May 1988, of attempts by Syrian-backed PLO guerrillas, led by 'Abu Musa', to drive Arafat loyalists out of the Palestinian refugee camps in Beirut.

At the beginning of June 1988 an extraordinary summit meeting of the Arab League was held in Algiers to discuss the *intifada* and Middle East peace moves. The final communiqué of the summit, endorsed by all 21 League members, effectively rejected the Shultz plan by demanding PLO participation in the proposed international peace conference and insisting on the Palestinians' right to self-determination and the establishment of an independent Palestinian state in the Occupied Territories (i.e. the principles of the 1982 Fez plan). The summit hailed the 'heroic' Palestinian uprising and pledged all necessary assistance (including an unspecified amount of financial aid) to sustain it.

JORDAN SEVERS TIES WITH THE WEST BANK

On 28 July 1988 Jordan cancelled a $1,300m. five-year development plan for the Occupied Territories, which had been launched in November 1986 but had failed to attract sufficient foreign funds. Then, two days later, King Hussein severed Jordan's 'administrative and legal links' with the West Bank, dissolving the House of Representatives (the lower house of the Jordanian National Assembly), where West Bank Palestinians occupied 30 of the 60 seats. The King explained that his actions were taken in accordance with the wishes of the PLO and the Arab League, as expressed in the resolutions of the Rabat summit of 1974, which recognized the PLO as the sole legitimate representative of the Palestinian people and which advocated the estab-

lishment of an independent Palestinian state in the West Bank, and in the peace plan proposed at the Fez summit of 1982. Commentators were quick to point out that King Hussein stopped short of actually repealing the annexation of the West Bank, which would have constituted a formal and irrevocable abrogation of Jordan's 38-year old ties with the region, while the dissolution of the House of Representatives would have little effect, as the Jordanian legislature had exerted little practical influence over affairs in the West Bank since the Israeli occupation in 1967.

King Hussein's decision to reduce Jordan's links with the West Bank was interpreted as partly a response to the Palestinian *intifada*, which had encouraged support amongst Palestinians for an independent Palestinian state, and partly as an attempt to persuade the PLO to accept responsibility for the Palestinian people and the peace process. It was suggested, however, that King Hussein considered the PLO constitutionally incapable of making the concessions necessary to the progress towards peace, and that the necessity of involving Jordan in any settlement would inevitably become apparent. In the short term, however, the effect of Jordan's actions was to strengthen the position of the Likud bloc (which had always ridiculed the Labour party's support for a Jordanian-Palestinian federation in the West Bank) in the period preceding the Israeli general election in November 1988. They also isolated the USA, whose peace initiatives, because they would not countenance negotiations involving the PLO, depended on Jordan's acting as interlocutor and forming part of a delegation representative of the Palestinians in any future peace talks.

To the PLO, King Hussein's move represented a considerable challenge. The Occupied Territories, with the exception of East Jerusalem, were now claimed *de jure* by no state as part of its sovereign territory, providing the PLO with an historic opportunity to assert sovereignty over a specific area. The PLO immediately began to make preparations regarding the issues of a provisional government and Palestinian statehood to be included on the agenda at the next session of the Palestine National Council in the autumn of 1988. In the Occupied Territories themselves, Jordan's severing of its ties with the West Bank was widely applauded. Communiqué No. 24 of the UNLU described the move as the *intifada's* 'greatest accomplishment'.

With Jordan's disengagement leaving the PLO the exclusive voice of Palestinian national aspirations, Yasser Arafat began to seek diplomatic support for a 'two-state' solution to the Arab–Israeli conflict. Addressing the European Parliament in Strasbourg on 12 September 1988, he sought the EC's active endorsement for the PLO's strategy. In his speech, he made a number of new concessions, stating that the PLO was ready to negotiate with Israel at an international peace conference on the basis of the UN Security Council's Resolutions 242 and 338, and to seek 'reciprocal recognition', whereby, in return for Israeli recognition of an independent Palestinian state, the PLO would accept Israel's right to security. Arafat also repeated his declaration, made in Cairo in 1985, which eschewed armed action outside the Occupied Territories. Armed struggle within the Territories remained, Arafat said, a justifiable option for the Palestinians, although firearms were only used in isolated instances.

POPULAR COMMITTEES OUTLAWED

However, the general tactic of demonstrations and stone-throwing continued unabated, as did the Israelis' counter-measures. Widespread demonstrations in Gaza on 14 August 1988 led to the imposition of a curfew throughout the Strip, and the protests spread to the West Bank during the following week. Here the two most immediate grievances were the deaths, by shooting, of two Palestinian political prisoners, and the deportation orders served on 25 activists on 17 August. The deportation orders provoked a spontaneous appeal for a three-day general strike in Nablus, Ramallah and Bethlehem. A military order (issued on the same day), outlawing the 'popular committees' (*lijan ash-sha'biya*), was of more far-reaching significance. Membership of the committees was declared to be an imprisonable offence, thus providing Israel with 'a more convenient legal means to deal with the institutionalization of the uprising', according to the Israeli Minister of Defence, Itzhak Rabin. The popular committees had been established at a very early stage of the uprising to organize day-to-day activities, such as the distribution of food and other supplies, agriculture, medical care, education and security. When the committees were forced underground, it became more difficult both for them to function and for the authorities to monitor and suppress their activities. The Israeli intelligence services therefore increased their efforts to infiltrate Palestinian organizations, while the Palestinians, in turn, intensified their campaign of exposing, and often executing, people known to have collaborated with the Israelis.

THE EFFECT OF THE INTIFADA ON PLO POLICY

Mass popular participation in 'grass-roots' organizations in the West Bank and Gaza had a major impact on PLO policy. The growth of the popular committees and the gradual, although partial, abrogation by Israeli state institutions of their role in the Territories encouraged Palestinian intellectuals to formulate ideas for the establishment of a provisional government for an independent Palestinian state. Despite the occupation, many national institutions had been established over the years, and, with the widening participation in the management of Palestinian society that was brought about by the *intifada*, they suggested the model for the structure of such a government. From a series of meetings of the Executive Committee of the PLO in August and September 1988, there emerged two basic proposals for debate at the meeting of the PNC in Algiers in November. The first was for the declaration of an independent state in the West Bank and Gaza, and advocated the establishment of a provisional government. The second recommended that the Occupied Territories be placed under the trusteeship of the UN, pending a settlement of the conflict.

DECLARATION OF PALESTINIAN INDEPENDENCE

The 19th session of the PNC, held in Algeria on 12–15 November 1988, brought together all the major factions of the PLO, including those based in Damascus. As expected, the PNC unilaterally declared the establishment of the independent State of Palestine, with its capital at Jerusalem. The UN General Assembly's Resolution 181 (see Documents on Palestine, p. 114) had provided the principle for Palestinian statehood in 1947, proposing the partition of Palestine into two states with defined borders. However, the declaration of independence left open the question of the new state's territory. The state was declared to be established, 'relying on the authority bestowed by international legitimacy as embodied in the resolutions of the United Nations since 1947', no mention being made of the specific details of any particular resolution, other than the principle of partition (and, thereby, a Palestinian state) in Resolution 181.

The UN General Assembly's Resolution 181 stipulated specific borders for two states in Palestine, while the UN Security Council's Resolution 242 of 1967 urged Israel to withdraw from territories occupied in the 1967 war. The borders that had been established by the 1948–49 Armistice Agreements between Israel, Egypt, Jordan, Lebanon and Syria, since they were 'dictated exclusively by military and not political considerations', gave Israel no technical right, under international law, to territories other than those designated by Resolution 181, which it had occupied in the hostilities of 1947–48. According to a strict interpretation of the international legal status of the former British mandated territory of Palestine, the declaration of an independent Palestinian state could have made reference to a specific territory, and many delegates representing the Occupied Territories at the PNC's 19th session urged such a move, and the creation of a provisional government. In the run-up to the meeting, however, there had been considerable disagreement within the PLO regarding the composition of such a government, and it was decided to refer the matter back to the Executive Committee for further consideration. The Executive Committee, it was decided, would function as an *ad hoc* government.

ACCEPTANCE OF RESOLUTION 242

Another source of controversy was the question of the UN Security Council's Resolution 242. For many years, the USA, supported by Israel, had demanded that the PLO should accept its provisions. However, since this Resolution sought 'respect

for the sovereignty, territorial integrity and political independence of every state in the area', such a concession would amount to recognition of the State of Israel. As the Fez Arab summit proposal of 1982, endorsed by the PLO, explicitly recognized Israel's existence, the PLO had already effectively recognized Israel. It had, furthermore, repeatedly stated its acceptance of all the pertinent UN resolutions. At the 19th session of the PNC in Algiers, Arafat and others within Fatah wanted to accept Resolution 242 'in isolation', in order to appease the USA and to spur it into action. However, left-wing factions within the wider Palestinian movement, as well as many Fatah cadres, forced the leadership to adopt a compromise formula: the PLO's acceptance of Resolution 242 was, in conjunction with Palestinian rights of self-determination and to international legality on the basis of UN resolutions, to provide the basis of an international peace conference. In a press conference at the end of the PNC session, Arafat was explicit: he sought acceptance of UN Security Council Resolution 242 as a mandate 'to actively pursue peace', and challenged the USA to respond to the PLO's overtures.

RESPONSES TO THE DECLARATION OF INDEPENDENCE

By the time that the 19th session of the PNC took place, the Israeli general election had resulted in a narrow victory (but not a clear parliamentary majority) for Itzhak Shamir's Likud party, while, in the USA, a Republican President had again been returned to power and the Democrats retained control of Congress. Shamir dismissed the results of the 19th PNC session as 'tactical moves devoid of any importance'. The response of the outgoing US Administration was more damaging. Invited to address the UN General Assembly in New York in December 1988, Yasser Arafat and his aides had to obtain visas to enter the USA. On the personal instructions of the US Secretary of State, George Shultz, the visas were denied. Elsewhere in the world, however, the PNC's declaration of independence encountered more favourable responses. By the time that Shultz had banned Arafat from entering the USA, more than 60 states, including two permanent members of the UN Security Council (China and the USSR), had recognized the State of Palestine. Although the 12 members of the EC had not recognized the new state, they welcomed the decisions of the 19th PNC session as a 'positive step forward', and continued, with the backing of the USSR, to support the PLO's appeal for the convening of an international peace conference.

ARAFAT ADDRESSES THE UN GENERAL ASSEMBLY

Arafat eventually addressed the UN General Assembly on 13 December 1988, the meeting having been relocated to Geneva, where he made a number of historic concessions. Inviting the 'leaders of Israel' to join him in reaching a peace agreement, Arafat presented the General Assembly with a three-point programme, the main proposals of which were that the UN Secretary-General should establish a preparatory committee for an international peace conference; that the Occupied Territories should be brought under the temporary supervision of UN forces, who would oversee Israel's withdrawal; and that there should be a comprehensive settlement, among the parties concerned, including Israel, at an international peace conference to be held on the basis of UN Security Council Resolutions 242 and 338. In his address, Arafat explicitly recognized Israel and rejected 'terrorism', as the USA had demanded.

Prime Minister Shamir of Israel, however, dismissed Arafat's address as a 'public relations exercise'. Its impact on the attitude of the USA towards the PLO was, nevertheless, alarming enough to persuade Shamir to disregard most of his party's differences with the Israeli Labour Party and to establish a new coalition government of national unity.

US RECOGNITION OF THE PLO

Although he found his Government almost completely isolated (in particular among its European allies) over its decision to ban Arafat from entering the USA, Shultz still refused to acknowledge that Arafat had conceded anything previously demanded of him by the USA. Following Arafat's address in Geneva, it required hours of intense Swedish diplomacy to detail the concessions asked of the PLO in words which the USA would find unambiguous. Even then, it took pressure from the incoming Administration of President-elect George Bush to convince Shultz. On 16 December 1988 the US Ambassador to Tunisia, Robert Pelletreau, held talks lasting 90 minutes with two representatives of the PLO. The USA had finally recognized the PLO. At the meeting, it was agreed that the dialogue should be maintained, and a second session of talks was planned for 20 January 1989. The PLO thus achieved its most important diplomatic breakthrough, although it did not necessarily expect any concrete advances in the peace process to follow quickly.

THE FIRST YEAR OF THE INTIFADA

In the Occupied Territories, the outcome of the 19th session of the PNC was greeted with widespread jubilation, and the declaration of independence was regarded as the greatest achievement of the *intifada*. The opening of a dialogue between the PLO and the USA was also widely perceived as a victory for the uprising, although many in the Occupied Territories feared that Arafat had conceded too much in return for too few guarantees. By the end of 1988, with more than 300 Palestinians shot dead and another 100 killed by other means in the first year of the uprising, a widespread pessimism had developed among the population of the Territories.

Apart from momentary lulls, there was no relaxation of the uprising. Palestinian protestors were still able to surprise the Israeli authorities by means of an underground network. Furthermore, despite the emergence of an autonomous Islamic fundamentalist group in Gaza (the Islamic Resistance Movement, allied to the Muslim Brotherhood and known by its Arab acronym, Hamas), both the UNLU and the people at large had managed to maintain unity of action and purpose. Israel's only real resort remained brute force.

The use of pre-emptive beatings to suppress the uprising, espoused by Israel's Minister of Defence, Itzhak Rabin, in the spring of 1988, gave way to the more widespread use of plastic and rubber bullets, many of which also contained lead, and which, contrary to official guidelines, were often discharged at very close range. On 18 December violent demonstrations erupted in Nablus after troops opened fire on a funeral procession, killing two people. The Israelis reacted severely and a further eight Palestinians were killed, and a curfew was imposed on the city for six consecutive days. By 16 January 1989 a total of 31 Palestinians had been killed, and more than 1,000 wounded, in confrontations with troops, as the indiscriminate firing of 'non-lethal' ammunition into crowds of demonstrators became commonplace. A further alarming development was the emergence of Israeli 'death-squads' which sought out, and attempted to liquidate, leaders of the uprising.

ISRAEL'S DIPLOMATIC INITIATIVE

Meanwhile, there were signs that Israel was preparing to announce a diplomatic initiative. Pressure from the USA and Europe, from both governments and Jewish communities, for Israel to redeem its image, together with condemnations of the high number of casualties, led to rumours that Prime Minister Shamir intended to reveal the initiative when he made his first visit to Washington since the election of President Bush.

However, even after the dialogue between the USA and the PLO had begun, and most Arab states had expressed support for Arafat's strategy, Shamir could still say, in January 1989, that 'nothing has changed' and that the 'Arab intention is the same: the destruction of Israel'. It was surprising, therefore, to learn that discussions had been taking place between Israeli officials and a prominent Jerusalem Palestinian, Faisal Husseini, the head of the Arab Studies Centre in Jerusalem, since the beginning of 1989. Despite this diplomatic initiative, there was no sign of an end to Israel's use of brutal methods to suppress the uprising. Indeed, discussions of Israeli concessions caused further problems for Palestinian communities in the form of attacks by Israeli settlers in the West Bank and Gaza. The death of a West Bank settler in February 1989 provoked a series of revenge attacks on the town of Qalqiliya and a raid on the village of Burin, near Nablus. It was alleged in the Knesset that a well-armed settlers' militia was operating in the West Bank. Further serious disturbances occurred in Rafah and Nablus at the end of February.

THE USSR ENDORSES THE PLO'S PROPOSALS

Diplomatic initiatives from the USA were slow to develop. A tour of the Middle East by the Soviet Minister of Foreign Affairs, Eduard Shevardnadze, in February 1989 emphasized the USA's inactivity, as he demonstrated, by his talks in Syria, Jordan, Egypt, Iran and Iraq, that the USSR was the only superpower able to talk freely to all parties to the Middle East conflict. With the exception of Israel's Likud party, all concerned agreed with Shevardnadze's proposal for the convening of an international peace conference.

THE USA CLARIFIES ITS POSITION

Despite a visit to Washington by the Israeli Minister of Foreign Affairs, Moshe Arens, in early March 1989, it became clear, when the dialogue between the USA and the PLO resumed, that the USA now accepted that the PLO was the only negotiating partner qualified to represent the Palestinians. However, several serious points of contention remained, in particular the purpose of the dialogue itself, which the PLO regarded as a prelude to wider negotiations and, eventually, an international peace conference. The USA rejected this notion.

During Arens' visit to Washington, the US Government hinted that Israel might eventually have to negotiate with the PLO, and pressure on Israel to formulate peace plans intensified. By the time that Prime Minister Shamir met President Bush in Washington on 6 April 1989, the details of his peace plan were widely known. Based largely on the proposals that Minister of Defence Rabin had presented, the plan offered 'free and democratic' elections in the Occupied Territories in return for the ending of the *intifada*. The elections, according to Shamir's plan, would produce a delegation to conduct negotiations with Israel for a permanent settlement. The USA gave its cautious approval to the plan, while Palestinians, both inside and outside the Territories, sought more specific details and attached a number of conditions to their acceptance of it. Israeli right-wing parties condemned the proposals and demanded a firmer suppression of the *intifada*.

THE VIOLENCE ESCALATES

April 1989 was one of the *intifada's* bloodiest months, with the death toll since the outbreak of the uprising exceeding 500. The worst atrocity of the uprising to date occurred on 7 April at the village of Nahalin, near Bethlehem. Members of the Israeli border police entered the village early in the morning and attacked people leaving a mosque, killing five and injuring more than 50. Violence in Gaza on 22–23 April left a further two people dead and 87 injured.

In Gaza, following demonstrations during the Islamic festival of Id al-Fitr, three Palestinians were shot dead, and more than 400 wounded, as troops fired 'plastic' bullets and canisters of CS tear-gas into crowds. On 8 May the territory was sealed off, with border crossings closed and telephone connections severed. An indefinite curfew was imposed, which continued until the end of the month, when the Israelis began to issue identity cards to all Gazans with a record of political activity, effectively denying them entry into Israel.

PALESTINIANS' RESPONSE TO ISRAEL'S PLAN FOR PEACE

These tougher measures were in accordance with Minister of Defence Rabin's warning, issued on 15 May 1989, when he threatened Palestinians with greater repression if they did not accept the Israeli Government's peace proposals. However, the leadership of the *intifada* and of the PLO in Tunis remained adamant that certain conditions must be satisfied before the plans could be accepted, although they did not reject the proposals outright. Full details of the Israeli peace plan were disclosed after its approval by the Knesset on 14 May. The plan was similar to the Camp David proposals in many respects. Its failure to clarify either who would be eligible to be a candidate or to vote in the proposed elections or the status of the residents of East Jerusalem; its reiteration of Israel's opposition to the creation of a Palestinian state and its proviso that no change in the status of the Territories could take place without the consent of the Israeli Government, all fell short of what was acceptable not only to the Palestinians and the USSR, but also to the EC states. However, the plan made too many concessions for right-wing opinion in Israel, and its announcement provoked threats by settlers to establish their own independent state on the West Bank if Israel ever agreed to relinquish the territory.

PRESSURE ON ISRAEL INCREASES

In early May 1989 Yasser Arafat was invited by President Mitterrand of France to make an official visit to Paris. The visit was a great success, especially after Arafat declared that the Palestinian National Charter had been superseded by the resolutions of the Algiers session of the PNC in November 1988. Israel was sufficiently disturbed by the success of Arafat's visit to Paris for Prime Minister Shamir to begin a European tour two weeks later, fearing, perhaps, that the PLO's publicity exercise might be repeated in other European capitals.

The USA was also beginning to give the Israeli Government cause for alarm. Shamir's visit to Washington had coincided with that of Egypt's President Mubarak, to whom President Bush had confided that the US Government shared Egypt's aim of ending Israel's occupation of the West Bank and Gaza. A warning by the USA that the time had come for Israel to renounce the idea of maintaining its control over the Territories, and the USA's description of the vision of a Greater Israel as 'unrealistic', caused further anxiety. The USA seemed to be gradually distancing itself from the policy of almost unquestioned support for Israel, which had characterized President Reagan's term of office. In July 1989, however, in order to appease critics of Israel's peace initiative within the Likud, Shamir agreed to a resolution which added four principles to the original plan. These clarified four areas of the initiative which had deliberately been left ambiguous to avoid alienating the USA and the PLO from the outset. They stipulated that residents of East Jerusalem would not be permitted to participate in the proposed elections in the West Bank and in Gaza; that violent attacks by Palestinians must cease before elections could be held in the Occupied Territories; that Jewish settlement should continue in the Territories and that foreign sovereignty should not be conceded in any part of Israel; and that the establishment of a Palestinian state west of the River Jordan was out of the question, as were negotiations with the PLO. In response the leadership of Israel's Labour Party recommended that the Party should withdraw from the coalition Government. At the end of July, however, it was reported that the Israeli Cabinet had voted in favour of endorsing the peace plan in its original form.

The *intifada* continued unabated throughout the summer of 1989. On 19 June the deportation of a further eight Palestinians was ordered, giving rise to more street protests, and in August the newly appointed commander of Israeli forces in the West Bank, Itzhak Mordechai, issued an order permitting troops to open fire on Palestinians who wore face masks during demonstrations. An increase in raids on Palestinian villages by the Israeli Defence Force (IDF), together with the deliberate targeting of organizers of the popular committees, contributed to a rising casualty toll.

In Gaza, meanwhile, a fierce battle of wills developed between the local population and the Israeli authorities over the introduction of new identity cards. The Israelis stipulated that possession of a new, computer-readable, magnetic identity card was necessary for all those travelling outside of the Gaza Strip. However, such cards would only be issued to those Palestinians who acquired security clearance and who could prove they were up-to-date with payment of taxes. As the majority of Gazans earned their living inside Israel, the Israeli authorities hoped that economic pressure would force them to accept the new identity cards. The popular committees responded by urging a boycott of the new identity cards, which were confiscated as soon as they were issued. By mid-July so few Gazans were reporting for work in Israel that employers pressurized the IDF into allowing some Gazans to leave the Gaza Strip without identity cards. However, fearing the financial hardships of a prolonged boycott, the UNLU eventually abandoned it.

Acts of communal resistance persisted in the West Bank. In Beit Sahour, a small Christian town near Bethlehem, residents had observed a total boycott of tax payments ever since the UNLU had first called for payments to the civil administration to be withheld. A six-week campaign to break the boycott was launched by the Israelis in 1989. It began with arrests, the imposition of lengthy curfews and the cutting of electricity and telephone lines, and ended with the blockading of the town and the confiscation of property in lieu of payment.

Despite the defiance in Beit Sahour and the struggle against the new identity cards in Gaza, there were signs that a combination of exhaustion and frustration at the lack of political return was fostering extremism. At the end of June 1989, a US aid worker was the victim of an unprecedented kidnapping in Gaza and two weeks later 14 people died when a young Palestinian seized control of an Israeli bus in which they were travelling and sent it crashing down a ravine.

MUBARAK'S ATTEMPT TO RESTART THE PEACE PROCESS

In mid-September 1989 President Mubarak attempted to restart the peace process by asking the Israeli Government to clarify 10 points concerning the procedure and substance of Prime Minister Shamir's peace plan. Mubarak sought commitment to the principle of exchanging land for peace and the participation of the residents of East Jerusalem in the plan's proposed election. At the same time, Mubarak offered to convene an early meeting of Israeli and Palestinian delegations to discuss the details of the election. The US Government had been privy to Mubarak's proposals since mid-July, but had cautioned against making them public in the hope that the Israeli Government would be able to sustain what was, after all, its own peace initiative. The fact that the US President George Bush had now permitted Mubarak to announce an initiative of his own revealed the US Government's ebbing faith in the Israeli Government.

The reaction of the Israeli Government to Mubarak's initiative was divided. The Labour leader Shimon Peres voiced his support, while Prime Minister Shamir stated his opposition and spoke of the need 'to fight off grave threats'. No formal rejection was sent to Cairo, but the Israeli Prime Minister was clearly irritated by the Egyptian Government's attempt to usurp his peace initiative. Both Mubarak and the US Secretary of State, James Baker, anxious not to further alienate the Israeli Prime Minister, insisted that the Egyptian proposal was merely a supplement to Shamir's plan, not a replacement. By mid-October, however, it was clear the USA was failing to persuade Likud to embrace the revised peace proposals. Prime Minister Shamir and the Israeli Minister of Foreign Affairs, Moshe Arens, did not regard Mubarak's 10 points as a basis for negotiations, nor would they agree to talks with a Palestinian delegation which had any connection whatsoever with the PLO. In a final attempt to keep the peace initiative alive, US Secretary of State James Baker put forward five proposals (the 'Baker plan') which aimed to remove Israeli objections. Essentially, Baker proposed that acceptance of Mubarak's 10 points should not be a precondition for participation in the Cairo talks and that the composition of the Palestinian delegation should be decided by the Governments of Israel, the USA and Egypt.

PLO'S FORMAL RESPONSE TO THE 'SHAMIR PLAN'

The 'Shamir plan' and the subsequent attempts to modify it aroused little enthusiasm in Palestinians or the PLO, who were convinced that Shamir had only conceived his peace initiative as a concession to the USA, and in order to pressurize the Palestinians. Moreover, the PLO believed that Mubarak's clarifications of the 'Shamir plan' still fell short of its own minimum negotiating position. At a meeting of the PLO's central council in Baghdad in October, the PLO stated that the negotiating team should be selected by the PLO and should comprise Palestinians from both inside the Occupied Territories and the Palestinian diaspora; and that the dialogue should be attended by the five permanent members of the UN Security Council and should constitute the preliminary stage in the convening of an international peace conference.

Although the gulf between the 'Baker plan' and the PLO's response appeared to be unbridgeable, the PLO was not keen to be seen to officially abandon a peace initiative which was being promoted by the USA. Privately, however, PLO officials complained that the USA was ignoring the need for the PLO to play a role in the peace process while, at the same time, seeking its support for the same process. All the more galling was the

USA's insistence that its endorsement of the peace process should be private rather than public so as not to deter Israel.

EXECUTION OF COLLABORATORS

Within the Occupied Territories opposition to the Baker proposals was widespread and was expressed in the underground communiqués of the UNLU. However, during the latter half of 1989 another issue drew the attention of the international media. The execution of Palestinians suspected of collaborating with the Israeli security forces had been accepted as necessary by most Palestinians, especially after it emerged that the Israelis had organized 'hit squads' of their own. During the second half of 1989, however, there was a dramatic increase in the killing of collaborators. Palestinian leaders began to fear that unless the killing was checked it might legitimize the use of violence to resolve factional disputes; they also recognized that the death of Palestinians at the hands of other Palestinians was a public relations disaster.

By the beginning of October 1989 the UNLU was urging the popular committees to show maximum restraint in their dealings with suspected collaborators. The activities of vigilante groups, such as the Red Eagles and the Black Panthers, were ultimately halted by the Israelis. However the widespread mourning and disturbances following the deaths of their members demonstrated to the UNLU and to the PLO that as the *intifada* approached the end of its second year, the political stalemate inside the Territories and the diplomatic impasse outside was strengthening the hand of radicals.

DIVISIONS WITHIN THE ISRAELI GOVERNMENT

There were few signs from Israel that the 'Baker plan' was improving the prospect of an Israeli-Palestinian dialogue in Cairo. Shimon Peres had signalled Labour's readiness to talk to a Palestinian delegation composed of deportees living outside the Occupied Territories as well as pro-PLO personalities from within the Territories. For Shamir, this was tantamount to talking to the PLO itself and he warned that Israel would boycott any talks with a delegation endorsed by the PLO. Moreover, in what amounted to a significant retreat from the terms of the original 'Shamir plan', the Israeli leadership demanded a guarantee that at any future meeting discussion would be confined to electoral procedure and would not address the question of a final settlement. In a visit to Washington in November Prime Minister Shamir failed to gain assurances on these questions, but did not face any real pressure from the US Government. In a private meeting with Shamir, President Bush reportedly criticized Israel's handling of the *intifada*, while Secretary of State James Baker called for Israel to show greater flexibility towards the peace process. Shortly before Shamir's visit, however, the USA had once again vetoed a UN Security Council resolution criticizing Israeli policy in the West Bank and in Gaza, and at the end of the visit Shamir was confident enough to declare that 'tensions had been relieved' by his trip.

In a letter to President Bush PLO chairman Yasser Arafat stated that Israeli intransigence was convincing Palestinians that Israel was not serious in its quest for peace and 'creating an atmosphere that rouses the radicals against the moderates'. The USA did not reply to the letter and, in a further rebuff, announced that it would cut funds to the UN's Food and Agriculture Organization if it co-operated with the PLO over agricultural development in the Occupied Territories.

Divisions in the Israeli Cabinet intensified in 1990. After returning from a visit to Cairo at the end of January, Shimon Peres announced that he had the support of the Labour Minister of Defence, Itzhak Rabin, for breaking up the Government if there was no progress on the issue of the Israeli-Palestinian dialogue. Shamir also faced pressure from right-wing elements within the Likud. At a meeting of Likud's central committee on 7 February 1990, the Minister of Trade, Ariel Sharon, the populist leader of the 'rejectionists', announced his resignation from the Cabinet. Sharon's resignation was ostensibly prompted by disagreement with Shamir over the 'Baker plan', but in reality it amounted to a thinly veiled bid for the party leadership. While Shamir managed to retain the support of the majority of Likud members within the Knesset, the attempted *putsch* weakened his authority. It was followed, a few days later, by the decision of Itzhak Modai to withdraw his Liberal faction

from Likud. On 21 February, with Shamir barely recovered from the dissent in his own ranks, Peres announced that he would give him two weeks to respond positively to the 'Baker plan' before withdrawing the Labour Party from the coalition. Moreover, the USA declared that further dilatory tactics by Israel might lead it to abandon the Middle East peace process altogether.

COLLAPSE OF THE COALITION

On 10 March 1990 Labour ministers walked out of a cabinet meeting after Shamir had refused to allow a vote on a proposal regarding the Cairo talks. Three days later, after Labour had stated its intention to vote with the opposition in favour of a 'no-confidence' motion against the Government, Shamir dismissed Peres from the Cabinet. The remaining Labour ministers immediately submitted their own resignations. In the ensuing 'no-confidence' debate, the small religious party, Shas, abstained, causing the collapse of the coalition. Israel's President Herzog granted Peres two weeks to form a Labour-led administration. Meanwhile Shamir would continue as 'caretaker' Prime Minister.

PROGRESS OF THE INTIFADA

The publication on 21 February of the US State Department's Country Reports on human rights indicated that despite the lower profile of the Palestinian *intifada* in 1989, its second year had been as bloody and intense as its first. The US report claimed that 304 Palestinians had been killed by Israeli soldiers and settlers in the year under review, while a further 128 suspected Palestinian collaborators had been killed by other Palestinians and 13 Israelis had died in *intifada* incidents. Up to 20,000 Palestinians had been wounded, 26 deported and 164 homes demolished or partially sealed. At the beginning of 1990 9,138 Palestinians, more than 2% of the adult male population, were being detained, more than 1,200 without charge or trial. The Palestinian universities remained closed throughout 1989 and the schools for many months.

Throughout 1989 the UNLU coalition had maintained an operational unity, although factional tension was increasing. Disputes concerned the PLO's pursuit of a diplomatic solution to the Middle East conflict and the short-term tactics of the *intifada*. In general, the PCP was prepared to give qualified support to Fatah, and sought to maintain the momentum of the *intifada*. The traditionally radical PFLP put the least faith in talks and moderation, and, unlike the PCP, favoured the steady escalation of strikes, street confrontations and civil disobedience. The DFLP occupied a position between that of the PCP and that of the PFLP. In the first quarter of 1990 disagreements between DFLP 'hardliners', led by Naif Hawatmeh, and a more pragmatic faction led by Yasser Abed Rabbo, caused a serious rift in the party.

Relations within the Occupied Territories between the nationalists of the UNLU and the fundamentalist grouping Hamas remained strained, although in some areas a *modus vivendi* was achieved. Gaza remained the stronghold of Hamas and of the more militant Islamic Jihad organization. The latter enjoyed a revival in 1989, having been weakened by arrests and deportations in 1988. It remained strongly opposed to the PLO's diplomacy.

EMIGRATION OF SOVIET JEWS TO ISRAEL

Following the USSR's relaxation of restrictions on Jewish emigration in 1989, a reported upsurge of anti-semitism in the Russian Republic and Washington's decision to reduce the number of visas it issued to Soviet Jews, 1990 offered the prospect of a huge increase in the emigration of Soviet Jews to Israel. Prime Minister Shamir claimed that up to 1m. Soviet emigrants might settle in Israel. More realistic estimates put the number at 150,000, but, whatever the figure, an influx of immigrants was regarded as a fillip for the Israeli right. Increased immigration helped counter the demographic argument used by those Israelis who favoured a withdrawal from the Occupied Territories and argued for increased 'colonization' of the West Bank and Gaza. Shamir commented on 14 January 1990, 'We will need a lot of room to absorb everyone and every immigrant will go where he wants . . . for a big immigration we will need a big and strong state'.

In Arab capitals and in the Occupied Territories the prospect of mass Jewish emigration to Israel, together with Shamir's statement, caused grave concern. King Hussein expressed a fear that the settlement of Jewish immigrants in the West Bank would presage the 'transfer' of the indigenous population to the East Bank, thus transforming the Hashemite Kingdom into a Palestinian state. Similar concern was expressed by the Arab League, which decided to send a high-level delegation to the superpowers and to the EC in order to discuss ways of reducing the flow of emigrants to Israel. Yasser Arafat conceded the right of Israel to accept Jewish refugees, but stated the PLO's opposition to the use of immigrants to perpetuate the occupation of the West Bank and Gaza. Within the Occupied Territories the UNLU urged the convening of an Arab summit meeting to debate the issue.

There was no clear evidence that Israel's Ministry of Immigrant Absorption was directing Soviet Jews to settle in the West Bank and in Gaza and only a small number were said to be considering making a home there. However, Israeli officials stated repeatedly that they would not discourage the new immigrants from settling in Judaea, Samaria and Gaza. Many of the new arrivals were already being directed to housing in occupied East Jerusalem. This caused considerable anger in the USA, from which Israel had requested an extra $400m. to facilitate the absorption of Jewish immigrants, at a time when Israeli intransigence over the peace process was straining US-Israeli relations. In a noticeable departure from the policy of the Reagan Administrations, President Bush stated his Administration's strong opposition not only to the settlement of Jews in the West Bank and in Gaza, but also in East Jerusalem. This pronouncement on what Israel regarded as its 'undivided and eternal' capital would certainly have provoked an acrimonious confrontation, had it not been for the collapse of the Likud-Labour coalition in March. A few weeks earlier, the leader of the Republican Party in the US Senate, Robert Dole, had attacked another 'sacred cow' of US-Israeli relations by suggesting that the USA's aid programme to eastern Europe should be financed by a 5% cut in aid to the five principal recipients of US aid, of which Israel was the major beneficiary.

LABOUR'S FAILURE TO FORM A NEW GOVERNMENT

By mid-April Peres' attempts to form a new government had failed, despite the Labour leader's determination to persuade the orthodox religious parties to lend their support to a new, Labour-dominated coalition. As the chance to form a new government passed back to Shamir, the Minister of Defence in the former Government, Itzhak Rabin, was reported to be considering challenging Shimon Peres for the leadership of the Labour Party. Meanwhile, both Peres' and Shamir's unseemly attempts to gain the support of the religious parties with lavish offers of cash and cabinet posts had prompted widespread disaffection among Israelis. On 7 April 100,000 people gathered in Tel-Aviv to call for an end to such political 'horsetrading' and for the reform of the country's electoral system.

FURTHER ESCALATION OF VIOLENCE

Soviet immigration, and the continuing controversy over Israeli settlement policy, was continuing to raise tension in the Occupied Territories. On 9 March violent protests against the settlement of Soviet Jews in East Jerusalem led to the killing of two young Palestinians. One month later attempts by a nationalist-religious group to settle in the Christian quarter of Jerusalem's Old City provoked violent confrontations with Israel's security forces. Palestinian anger was deepened by revelations that the Israeli Government had funded the settlers' fraudulent purchase of a building belonging to the Greek Orthodox Church.

By May 1990 the situation in the Occupied Territories was extremely volatile. On 20 May a uniformed Israeli approached a group of Palestinians congregating at a roadside labour market in Rishon le Zion. After checking their identity cards, he opened fire with an automatic rifle, killing eight of them and wounding 10 more. Demonstrations erupted and attempts at suppression by the army were ignored. By the end of that week more than 20 Palestinians had been killed and, for only the second time since December 1987, the *intifada* spilled over into Arab-populated regions inside Israel.

Following international criticism of Israel's response to the demonstrations, the US Government stated that it would consider an Arab-sponsored move to send UN observers to the Occupied Territories. At a specially convened session of the UN Security Council in Geneva Yasser Arafat accused Israel of attempted 'genocide' in the Occupied Territories. While no agreement was reached to send the UN observers to the Territories, Israel was now arguably more isolated than at any other time in its 42-year history. Further, and more predictable pressure came from the Arab summit meeting held in Baghdad at the end of May 1990 to discuss Soviet Jewish immigration to Israel and western hostility to Iraq's reported attempts to develop a nuclear capability. A bellicose Saddam Hussein reiterated his threat to unleash a chemical attack on Israel if the Israelis attacked Iraqi nuclear sites. The Jordanian delegation suggested that Israel was trying to engineer a war with Jordan as a means of expelling the Palestinian population from the West Bank. The USA was also criticized for its support of Israel and a pledge was made to honour a two-year-old promise of the Arab states to 'fund the *intifada*' at a rate of US $40m. per month.

NEW COALITION FORMED

The new Israeli coalition Government (an alliance of the Likud and small, right-wing religious groupings formed in early June 1990) was regarded as the least conciliatory in recent Israeli history, and unlikely to further the peace process. Rather, its very survival was dependent on its ability to appease those within the Knesset who sought to prevent any future dialogue between Israelis and Palestinians. A further setback to the peace process was the decision of the USA on 20 June to suspend its dialogue with the PLO after the PLO had failed satisfactorily to condemn an abortive attempt by the PLF (led by Muhammad Abbas—'Abu Abbas', a member of the PLO's Executive Committee) to land guerrillas on Israel's Mediterranean coast in May. At the same time, in a formal letter to Prime Minister Shamir, President Bush questioned the commitment of the new Israeli Government to the revival of the Middle East peace process. The first talks between representatives of the USA and the new Israeli Government were held in late July 1990.

IRAQ INVADES KUWAIT

Iraq's invasion of Kuwait in August 1990 was not regarded with the same sense of outrage in the Arab world as it was in the West. Although few Arabs condoned Iraq's occupation of Kuwait, there were many who admired the Iraqi President, Saddam Hussein. At a time of considerable disillusion with Western attitudes towards the emigration of Soviet Jews to Israel, and with the US Administration's decision to terminate its dialogue with the PLO, the militant rhetoric of the Iraqi leader and his promises to use Iraq's formidable military strength to confront Israeli expansionism had been favourably received by the Arab masses. Kuwait, on the other hand, was resented both for its prosperity and for its pro-Western outlook. As Arab Heads of State tried unsuccessfully to mediate between Iraq and Kuwait, two developments attracted popular support for Iraq. The first was Saddam Hussein's attempt to link Iraq's withdrawal from Kuwait to that of Israel from the Occupied Territories. The second was the decision of the USA to dispatch a large military force to the Gulf region in order, initially, to defend Saudi Arabia. What had begun as an act of aggression by one Arab state against another was now perceived by many Arabs as a confrontation between the forces of Arab nationalism and Western imperialism.

Many Palestinians, in particular, shared this perception. That the USA should act so swiftly to deter territorial conquest in Kuwait when it had effectively sustained such conquest in the areas occupied by Israel since 1967 was taken by Palestinians as proof of the West's hypocrisy and hostility to their cause. Saddam Hussein was swiftly championed as a saviour in the style of Nasser. By mid-August large pro-Iraqi demonstrations were taking place throughout the Occupied Territories and Jordan, and in the countries of the Maghreb.

THE POSITION OF THE PLO

The position of the PLO was far from clear at the outset of the new crisis in the Gulf. Privately, its leadership was said to be dismayed by the Iraqi invasion of Kuwait because it deflected attention from the *intifada* and created further divisions in the Arab world. However, the PLO's wish to broker an Arab solution to the crisis, together with its traditionally close ties to Iraq, made it reluctant to condemn the invasion. At the chaotic Arab summit meeting convened in Cairo on 10 August 1990 the PLO condemned Iraq's annexation of Kuwait, but abstained in the vote on whether to deploy a pan-Arab military force in Saudi Arabia. Furthermore, the PLO joined Jordan, Yemen, Tunisia and Algeria in denouncing the proposed deployment of US armed forces in the Gulf region.

On 19 August the PLO confirmed its opposition to the invasion of Kuwait in its first official statement on the crisis in the Gulf. Together with Libya and Jordan, it continued to attempt to act as a mediator, but with the US success in building an anti-Iraq coalition rapidly polarizing the Arab states, there was no sign of the consensus that was needed to make their proposals feasible. Instead, the concept of linkage of the Gulf conflict with the Palestinian question, popular support for Iraq and distrust of the USA all dictated that the PLO should align itself with Iraq. At the end of August 1990 Yasser Arafat issued a joint statement with the Iraqi leader in Baghdad, proclaiming that the Palestinians and the Iraqis were united in a common struggle against Israeli occupation and US military intervention in the Gulf. The political risks of such a firm alliance with Iraq were immense, but PLO officials argued that, given the mood of their constituency, they had no other option. Inside the Occupied Territories a special UNLU communiqué condemned the deployment of the US-led multinational force in Saudi Arabia and elsewhere in the Gulf region. It also upheld the rights of peoples to self-determination, but noticeably refrained from demanding Iraq's withdrawal from Kuwait.

The PLO's partisanship earned it the opprobrium of the West and alienated its principal financial supporters, Saudi Arabia and the Gulf states. Jordan, Yemen and Sudan, whose Governments were most hostile to Western military involvement in the Middle East, similarly had to endure the full weight of US and conservative Arab displeasure. Jordan, traditionally pro-Western and in the process of democratization, was subjected to particular criticism for having allowed a meeting of Arab nationalist and left-wing political parties to take place in Amman in mid-November 1990.

ISRAEL AS BENEFICIARY

Israel was one of the principal beneficiaries of the events which followed the invasion of Kuwait. It had until recently been internationally isolated for its procrastination over the peace process and the repression in the Occupied Territories; the Gulf crisis offered it the prospect of rehabilitation. Israeli leaders lost no time in restating their old claim that it was the lack of democracy in the Arab world, not Israel's occupation of Arab territory, which was the principal cause of instability in the region. The PLO's stance on the Iraqi invasion, they argued, conclusively validated their refusal to negotiate with it. Equally, the vociferous support in the West Bank and Gaza for Saddam Hussein confirmed Israel's wisdom in treading the path of diplomacy with caution, and maintaining its opposition to a Palestinian state.

Moreover, in President Bush's attempt to persuade Arab and majority Muslim states to participate in 'Operation Desert Shield', the codename for the deployment of the multinational force in Saudi Arabia, Israel also saw scope for political gain. The Israeli Prime Minister, Itzhak Shamir, understood that Israeli military action against Iraq, like its attack in 1981 on Iraq's nuclear reactor, would be disastrous for the USA: it would spell the end of Arab involvement in the multinational force, a political if not a military prerequisite for its success, and would also threaten a wider conflagration in the Middle East. Israel hinted that its restraint would be conditional upon its receiving certain guarantees from the USA: of increased military and economic aid, and of an easing of pressure with regard to the peace process. Israel's Minister of Defence, Moshe Arens, also made it clear that, from an Israeli point of view, the only acceptable conclusion to the crisis would be one that included the dismantling of the Iraqi military machine.

THE PRICE OF ISRAEL'S SUPPORT FOR THE USA

Just as the USA had to pay for Israel's passivity, so it had to offer inducements for Arab governments to participate in the multinational force. The Gulf states, potentially vulnerable to further Iraqi aggression, needed little persuasion to do so. Egypt, Syria and Morocco were also in favour of deploying armed forces in Saudi Arabia, the Governments of Syria and Egypt being deeply mistrustful of Baathist Iraq. However, it was the prospect of economic aid and of influence in any post-crisis settlement which ultimately persuaded them to dispatch troops to fight alongside Americans against fellow Arabs. President Assad of Syria, a longstanding radical, and hence the most unlikely of the coalition partners, certainly expected the crisis to be followed by moves to end the Israeli occupation of Arab, including Syrian, territory. President Mubarak of Egypt, who was anxious to see his country reinstated as the *primus inter pares* of the Arab world, aired the same concerns in discussions with his US and European counterparts.

The burden of conflicting expectations from Israel and the Arab states placed the USA in a delicate position. President Bush and the US Secretary of State, James Baker, had to avoid any linkage of the crisis in the Gulf with the Arab–Israeli conflict since this would effectively reward Saddam Hussain and displease Israel. At the same time they had to reassure the Arab world. Speaking in September 1990, President Bush agreed that sooner rather than later the Arab–Israeli conflict had to be resolved. Nevertheless he dismissed the possibility of an international conference on the issue in the near future. The EC states were more sensitive to Arab charges of hypocrisy over tackling the problems of the Middle East and hence to an implicit linkage of the occupation of Kuwait with other outstanding issues. During an emergency debate on the Gulf crisis in the British Parliament at the end of August 1990, members of all political parties spoke of the urgent need for a swift conclusion of the crisis, to be followed by the resolution of the Palestine problem. In an address to the UN General Assembly on 24 August, President Mitterrand of France proposed a timetable for the settlement of all the Middle East's problems. This would begin with an Iraqi declaration of intention to withdraw from Kuwait, but would also include direct dialogue between the concerned parties on the issues of Palestine, Lebanon and Israel's security. Moreover, at a meeting of EC ministers of foreign affairs in Paris in mid-September, the President of the EC Commission, Jacques Delors, warned Israel that once the Gulf crisis was over it would have to accept 'the legitimate rights of the Palestinians'. In addition, the Italian Minister of Foreign Affairs, Gianni de Michelis, who was acting as chairman of EC foreign policy meetings, informed his Israeli counterpart, the newly-appointed David Levy, that the Palestinians had a right to their own state.

EVENTS IN THE OCCUPIED TERRITORIES

Meanwhile, the Palestinian *intifada* continued, albeit with less intensity. Exhaustion, and the adoption of new tactics by Israel's Ministry of Defence, contributed to the decrease in activity. Israel's Minister of Defence, Moshe Arens, believed that intensive policing of population centres was largely counter-productive. Instead, he instructed the IDF to reduce its presence in the towns and villages of the West Bank and Gaza, and to redeploy troops on highways and at major road intersections. Fewer clashes and fewer Palestinian casualties resulted, but arrests and collective punishments continued. Palestinians were encouraged by Saddam Hussain's rhetoric, but the economic repercussions of the Gulf crisis were very damaging. Many Palestinian families relied on remittances from relatives working in Kuwait, and the loss of this income at a time when the population was already suffering economically, caused severe hardship. Factionalism was another source of concern for the Palestinian leadership. In September 1990 fierce disputes in Gaza and some towns of the West Bank, between the nationalists of Fatah and the fundamentalists of Hamas, led to ugly street brawls and at least one death. Divisions within the DFLP also resulted in a *de facto* split, prompting a struggle for the control of its various front organizations, such as trade unions, women's committees and press offices.

Yet even while international attention was firmly fixed on the huge military deployment in the Gulf, events in the Occupied

Territories continued to remind the world of the unresolved issue of Palestine. On 8 October 1990 at least 17 Palestinians were shot dead in the Old City of Jerusalem when a large crowd, protesting at an attempt by an extremist Israeli group to lay the symbolic cornerstone of the Third Temple on the Temple Mount, was indiscriminately fired on by Israeli security forces. News of the killings at Islam's third holiest shrine immediately precipitated a wave of protests which claimed a further three lives and left many injured. It was the bloodiest day yet of the *intifada*. Palestinian leaders in the Occupied Territories responded to the killings with an emotional appeal to the UN Security Council: 'We do not understand how oil in the Gulf can be more highly prized by you than Palestinian blood . . .' they wrote; 'we do not understand how the Security Council can ignore our pleas for protection when it is prepared to send troops to the Gulf region'. Moreover, the UNLU issued its most uncompromising communiqué so far, calling for a week of mourning and declaring that 'every soldier setting foot on the land of Palestine is a fair target to be liquidated'. Anxious to avoid charges of hypocrisy at such a sensitive time in Arab–US relations, the USA submitted a draft resolution to the UN Security Council condemning the Temple Mount killings. It also supported the decision of the UN Secretary-General to dispatch an investigative mission to Jerusalem. Although this fell short of the PLO's demand for UN protection for the population of the Occupied Territories, the USA's censure of Israel at the UN Security Council was significant for being the first vote of its kind for eight years. Predictably, Israel denounced the UN vote, and its decision to send a fact-finding mission to the Occupied Territories, as interference in its internal affairs. It declared that the UN representatives would only be admitted as 'tourists'. In an interview with the Israeli daily newspaper, *Ma'ariv,* Prime Minister Shamir castigated both President Bush and Secretary of State Baker for 'messing with Israel'. What they failed to understand, opined Shamir, 'is that Israel is Washington's only reliable ally'. The Arab League's own deliberations in Tunis on the Temple Mount killings ended in acrimony and confirmed the rift provoked by the Gulf crisis. A resolution which condemned the killings, but was also sharply critical of US bias towards Israel, was defeated by 11 votes to 10. In what was effectively a vote on the US military presence in the Gulf, only Morocco, facing mounting domestic criticism for having agreed to participate in the multinational force, confounded expectations by voting with the anti-US faction.

The killings of 8 October were followed by a spate of attacks by Palestinians on Israeli civilians and soldiers. The worst incidents occurred on 21 October, when three people were stabbed to death by a lone Palestinian in West Jerusalem, and at the beginning of December, when a series of attacks in Tel-Aviv claimed four lives and left several people injured. A number of Palestinians died in anti-Arab protests following the stabbings, and also in the violence precipitated by the assassination, in New York, of Rabbi Meir Kahane, the leader of the neo-fascist Kach movement. Nearly all the attacks by Palestinians were the work of individuals acting on their own initiative, although Hamas did claim responsibility for some of the murders in Tel-Aviv, and Islamic Jihad gave its wholehearted support to a 'revolution of knives'. The PLO factions were more ambivalent in their attitude towards the stabbings: Faisal Husseini denied that the stabbing of Israeli civilians had been sanctioned by the leadership of the *intifada*; the UNLU spoke only of the need to employ 'all forms of resistance'; and graffiti praising the use of knives was signed by both Fatah and the PFLP. Shortly after the incident on 21 October, the Israeli Ministry of Defence ordered all Palestinians from the Occupied Territories working in Israel to return to their homes. The borders were sealed for four days, after which the Minister of Defence, Moshe Arens, declared an intention to reduce the number of Palestinians working inside the 'Green Line' and to bar altogether those with a record of activism. The announcement was welcomed by some Palestinians as a further step towards redefining the 'Green Line'.

UN SECURITY COUNCIL RESOLUTION 678

The passing of UN Security Council Resolution No. 678 on 29 November 1990, which effectively authorized the use of military force against Iraq if it had not withdrawn from Kuwait by 15 January 1991, considerably increased tension in the region. In Israel the authorities completed the distribution of gas masks to the civilian population and issued instructions on civil defence against attacks with chemical weapons. Only belatedly did they decide to provide masks to limited areas of the West Bank. Iraq and Israel continued to exchange threats, while Jordanians and Palestinians expressed fears that Israel might use the pretext of military conflict in the Gulf to drive Palestinians from the West Bank into Jordan. Palestinian support for Saddam Hussain remained high during the weeks preceding the UN deadline for Iraq's withdrawal from Kuwait, while the PLO's relations with the USA's Arab allies continued to deteriorate. The leader of the PLF, 'Abu Abbas', warned that his organization would strike against Western targets if hostilities erupted. In mid-December Israel's Prime Minister travelled to Washington for his first meeting with the US President in more than a year. The proximity of the deadline set by UN Resolution 678 ensured that the encounter was cordial, despite a strong undercurrent of mutual distrust. Shamir sought and received assurances that the Gulf crisis would not be resolved at Israel's expense. However, no promises were made on the question of aid for the settlement of the 200,000 Soviet Jews who had emigrated to Israel during 1990, or on the sale of arms by the USA to Arab participants in the multinational force.

There was a resurgence of the *intifada* at the beginning of 1991. Seven Palestinians were killed in protests linked to the anniversary, on 1 January 1991, of the founding of Yasser Arafat's Fatah organization. On 6 January Saddam Hussain declared that the impending military conflict would be a 'battle for the sake of Palestine'. After the failure of meetings in Geneva on 9 January between the Iraqi Minister of Foreign Affairs, Tariq Aziz, and the US Secretary of State, war was generally accepted as inevitable.

IRAQ ATTACKS ISRAEL

On 19 January 1991, less than three days after the multinational force had begun a massive aerial bombardment of Iraq, Iraq launched an attack on Israel, employing adapted *Scud* missiles against Tel-Aviv and Haifa. The missiles were fitted with conventional, rather than chemical warheads, and although damage to buildings was considerable, casualties were light. Further attacks with *Scud* missiles on the nights of 20 and 22 January provoked panic, but resulted in only two deaths. The attacks drew immediate demands for retaliation from some senior Israeli military figures and politicians, but both the USA and the European members of the multinational force vigorously urged Israel to exercise restraint. Their concerns were obvious: while Arab states in the force had indicated that they would not be opposed to Israel taking appropriate and proportionate defensive action against an Iraqi attack, Syria and Egypt had made it quite clear that they could not remain aligned against Iraq if Israel were to attack it. Furthermore, Jordan had warned Israel that it would be forced to respond if there was any violation of its airspace. The US Administration backed its calls for restraint with an urgent airlift of *Patriot* anti-missile batteries to Tel-Aviv, and undertook to make the destruction of Iraq's mobile missile launchers a military priority. To be courted so attentively by the West after such a long period of soured relations was an agreeable novelty for Israel, and not one it had much incentive to jeopardize. Given the intensity of the bombing of Iraq, Israel's leaders were aware that any Israeli contribution to the campaign would be militarily insignificant as well as potentially catastrophic in political terms. Moreover, the Israeli Government knew that as long as the casualties from the *Scud* attacks remained minimal and chemical warheads were not employed, domestic pressure for retaliation would be containable. Shamir consequently assured the USA that there would be no unilateral retaliation by Israel. Immediate benefits were reaped from the policy of restraint: the USA indicated that it would provide funding for the development of Israel's antiballistic missile project, hitherto in some financial difficulty, while Germany promised up to US $1,000m. in military and economic aid. However, just as important for Israel's leaders was the wave of international sympathy for Israel which the Iraqi attacks provoked.

THE CONSEQUENCES OF IRAQ'S DEFEAT FOR THE PLO

Palestinians of the West Bank and Gaza endured a strict curfew for most of the duration of the war in the Gulf. The UNLU and Hamas instructed their supporters not to clash with the Israeli army during the curfew in order to avoid reprisals. Nevertheless, a number of people were shot and killed for curfew violations. The economic impact of the curfew was severe. According to Palestinian economists, losses to the local economy ranged from $150m.–$200m., equivalent to approximately 8% of the GDP of the Occupied Territories.

The decisive defeat of Iraq by the multinational force in February 1991 left the PLO demoralized and in its most vulnerable state for several years. As expected, the Gulf Co-operation Council (GCC) countries cut their funding to the PLO, thereby raising the prospect of financial crisis. It was also made clear in the USA and the Gulf that the best chance of improving relations lay in a change in the PLO leadership. Overtures were made by Saudi Arabia and other GCC member states to anti-Arafat Palestinian groups based in Damascus, but, given the political radicalism and the small following of these factions, it was difficult to imagine what Saudi Arabia hoped to achieve. Within the PLO itself there were a number of senior figures, for the most part identified with the conservative wing of Fatah, who had voiced criticism of the organization's support for Iraq and who could have formed the nucleus of a leadership acceptable to both Saudi Arabia and the USA. Yet the fact that the PLO had enjoyed overwhelming support among Palestinians for its stance on the Gulf crisis proved an important antidote to US and Arab hostility. The EC adopted a more pragmatic approach towards the PLO. At the conclusion of hostilities with Iraq it agreed to 'freeze' contacts at ministerial level. By the end of April 1991, however, the French Minister of Foreign Affairs, Roland Dumas, had met Yasser Arafat in Tripoli.

BAKER VISITS THE MIDDLE EAST

The Israeli Government drew comfort from the PLO's isolation, but was wary of the political pressures that might accompany the post-war search for a resolution of the Arab–Israeli conflict. As expected, US Secretary of State Baker undertook several tours of the Middle East in the weeks following the end of the war. He hoped to persuade Israel and the Arab states which had participated in the multinational force to move towards mutual recognition, and to win support for a regional peace conference, to be sponsored by the USA and the USSR. It soon became clear, however, that these propositions were not acceptable to either side. Although the Israeli Minister of Foreign Affairs, David Levy, indicated that Israel would give its approval to such a regional conference if it led directly to bilateral talks, and conceded that issues like the status of the Golan Heights could be negotiated, these were not views shared by Shamir and most of his colleagues within the Likud. Rebuking Levy, Shamir stated his opposition to Soviet involvement in the Middle East peace process. He also opposed negotiating the future of the Golan Heights or making goodwill gestures to the Palestinian population of the West Bank and Gaza, as urged by Baker, as long as the *intifada* continued. After the US Secretary of State had held talks with leading pro-PLO figures in East Jerusalem, Shamir warned that Israel did not consider any of them to be suitable partners for negotiation.

Israel's Arab neighbours expressed their own reservations about Baker's proposals. After lengthy talks with Baker in Damascus, Syrian officials reaffirmed that Syria would only attend a peace conference held under UN sponsorship and based on the implementation of UN Security Council Resolutions 242 and 338. Jordan and the PLO indicated that they were in full agreement with Syria. The PLO also voiced its suspicions that the concept of a regional conference had been promoted with the intention of normalizing Arab–Israeli relations and of avoiding the issue of Palestinian national rights. The PLO was relieved by the reluctance of the GCC states to open a dialogue with Israel. At the end of May 1991 PLO representatives made a rare visit to Damascus in order to discuss their common position with Syria on the peace process. Syrian officials also urged the PLO to readmit pro-Syrian Palestinian groups, including Fatah rebels from the 1983 revolt and the PFLP-GC, into the Organization.

Baker was reluctant to apportion blame for the lack of progress in his peace mission. However, the continued settlement of Soviet Jewish immigrants in the Occupied Territories angered the US Secretary of State enough for him to testify: 'I don't think there is any bigger obstacle to peace than the settlement activity that not only continues unabated but at an enhanced pace'. Further US pressure on Israel, regarded by much of the international community as essential if the opportunity for a peace agreement in the Middle East was not to be missed, did not materialize. Continued US arms supplies to Israel and the Gulf states, together with promises that the USA would guarantee Israel's regional military superiority, appeared to contradict President Bush's stated goal of working towards disarmament in the region, and heightened Arab cynicism about the US President's much-vaunted 'new world order'.

WORSENING CONDITIONS IN THE OCCUPIED TERRITORIES

There was little optimism in the Occupied Territories following the defeat of Iraq. After the lifting of the curfew many Palestinians discovered that they had lost their jobs in Israel to Soviet immigrants. Another series of knife attacks, including the killing of four women at a bus stop in Jerusalem in March 1991, prompted the Israeli authorities to impose further travel and employment restrictions. Only Palestinians with the requisite permits were allowed to enter Israel, including East Jerusalem. Those Palestinians fortunate enough to be issued with work permits had to be transported in buses to and from work by their employers. Those found working without permits faced fines or imprisonment. The result was soaring unemployment in the West Bank and in Gaza and the effective division of the West Bank into northern and southern zones. Concerns over the economic situation and continued Israeli settlement were raised in meetings with the US Secretary of State. There was debate within the Occupied Territories as to whether these meetings were appropriate, and the Palestinians who did meet Baker only did so after they had received the formal authorization of the PLO. Nevertheless, the US Administration's refusal to hold direct talks with the PLO led the organization's Communist and PFLP affiliates to boycott the meetings.

Adding to Palestinian gloom was uncertainty over the direction of the *intifada*. The killing and intimidation of Palestinians by other Palestinians, increasing criminal activity and further outbreaks of violence between followers of Hamas and the PLO factions were causing much public alarm. Several articles appeared in the Arab press in the first half of 1991, urging an end to the killing of suspected collaborators and a complete reappraisal of *intifada* tactics. Palestinian activists subsequently announced that strikes and demonstrations would be scaled down, and efforts made to control the masked fugitives responsible for most of the *intifada's* excesses. The use of firearms against military targets was widely predicted. Calls were made for greater democracy within the PLO, including elections to the PNC. Senior Communist Party officials also challenged the Palestinian leadership over its uncritical support for Iraq during the Gulf War and for having unrealistically raised Palestinian expectations of an Iraqi victory.

THE SYRIAN-LEBANESE TREATY

In May 1991 the Syrian and Lebanese Presidents signed a treaty of 'fraternity, co-operation and friendship', confirming Syria's dominant role in the affairs of its neighbour. Israel condemned the treaty as tantamount to a Syrian takeover of Lebanon and as a threat to its security. On 3 June the Israeli air force launched its heaviest raids on Lebanon since 1982. At least 20 people were killed and many injured in a series of attacks on Palestinian and Lebanese militia targets in the south of the country.

NEGOTIATIONS WITH SYRIA

Meanwhile PLO forces grouped around the Lebanese port of Sidon fell victim to the Lebanese Government's plan to disarm the country's militias and deploy the Lebanese army nationally. The attempts of PLO leaders to persuade the Lebanese Government that their forces should be exempt from the disarmament process, or at least that the process should be delayed until the rights of the country's Palestinian population had been formally safeguarded, were ignored. At the beginning of July, in a brief but bloody battle, units of the Lebanese army expelled PLO fighters from positions above Sidon. The defeated Palestinians withdrew to the refugee camps and were subsequently forced to give an undertaking to surrender their heavy weaponry. The circumstances surrounding the PLO's loss of its sole military stronghold in Lebanon fuelled speculation that Syria, deprived of its Soviet sponsor, had reached an understanding with the USA whereby the latter would tolerate Syria's control over Lebanese affairs in return for President Assad's backing for the Bush Administration's Middle East peace plans. Palestinians expressed suspicions that Damascus and the USA had been conspiring to ensure that the PLO remained militarily weakened and diplomatically isolated.

The extent to which the end of the cold war had pushed Syria to revise its foreign policy was underlined in dramatic fashion in mid-July. During US Secretary of State James Baker's fifth peace mission to the Middle East, it was announced that President Assad had acceded to US and Israeli conditions for the convening of a Middle East peace conference. Abandoning his long-held insistence that any conference on the Arab–Israeli dispute should have the coercive weight of the UN behind it, Assad gave his consent to a more symbolic gathering. Although based on UN Resolutions 242 and 338, this would only feature the UN in the role of an observer and would pave the way for direct negotiations between Israel and its Arab adversaries. Assad agreed to a joint Soviet-US chairing of the proposed conference with EC observers also present.

TOWARDS A PEACE CONFERENCE

The Syrian *volte face* was swiftly followed by Jordanian, Egyptian and Lebanese acceptance of the USA's proposals. Baker also received the backing of the G7 nations meeting in London, United Kingdom, and, more significantly, of Saudi Arabia. Saudi Arabia also gave its support to an Egyptian proposal that the Arab states should end their trade boycott of Israel in return for a 'freeze' on new settlements in the Occupied Territories, a gambit that Israel declined. Indeed, despite a *de facto* Arab capitulation to Shamir's conditions, the Israeli Government's attitude to the progress engineered by Baker was far from generous. The Israeli Cabinet endorsed Shamir's acceptance of the Baker conference proposals, but with the proviso that Israel hold a veto over the composition of any Palestinian negotiating team. Even this, however, failed to satisfy three right-wing members of the Cabinet, including Ariel Sharon, who voted against Israel's acceptance of the Baker formula. Moreover, in a pointed snub to both Arab states and the USA, which were hoping for a goodwill gesture from Israel in return for Arab flexibility, a new West Bank settlement was inaugurated less than two days after the cabinet meeting.

At the heart of Palestinian uncertainty over the proposed conference lay the issues of representation and settlement. It was accepted that the PLO would not participate officially and that Palestinians might have to be represented as part of a joint team with Jordan, but the threat of an Israeli veto of a Palestinian delegation that included East Jerusalem residents, led those Palestinians who had met with Baker to warn that they might not get popular backing for their attendance. They also demanded that the USA should apply pressure on Israel to halt settlement during negotiations, and that a letter of assurance be drafted on such issues as the USA's interpretation of UN resolutions and its commitment to mandatory international arbitration in the event of a deadlock in negotiations. Some PLO factions, notably the PFLP and the DFLP faction loyal to Naif Hawatmeh, rejected Palestinian participation outright. The PFLP issued a communiqué within the Occupied Territories calling the conference 'a conspiracy aimed at bypassing the PLO and Palestinian rights'. The fundamentalists of Hamas were even more forthright in their opposition, condemning the Baker proposals as a 'conference for selling land' and threatening any would-be participants. However, the two leading Palestinian participants in the Baker talks, Faisal Husseini and Hanan Ashrawi, made it clear that it would be the PLO which ultimately decided whether the Palestinians were represented at the conference.

It was clearly dangerous for the PLO to exclude itself from a process that might offer an opportunity to end the occupation of the West Bank and Gaza. However, the PLO was concerned that by giving approval to the peace conference it might be abdicating its role as the Palestinians' sole representative. There was also the sobering realization that the Organization could no longer rely on the support of Arab states for its own negotiating positions and that there was a real danger that a normalization of Arab–Israeli relations could be achieved without addressing the fundamentals of the Palestinian problem. Initiatives by the PLO, supported by Jordan, to organize a meeting with Arab front-line states in order to co-ordinate negotiating positions in the run-up to the conference, were rejected by Egypt and Syria.

At the end of August the PLO held a meeting in London, United Kingdom, attended by a number of Palestinian personalities from the Occupied Territories, to set guidelines for the letter of assurances from the USA that would facilitate Palestinian participation in the planned conference. The letter that Baker did finally present to Hanan Ashrawi in Amman did not fulfil all the Palestinian criteria for attending the conference, not least because Baker refused to contradict assurances he had already given to Israel. Arafat described the letter as 'a positive step, but one which fell short', referring to the fact that while Baker had clarified the US interpretations of the relevant UN resolutions and the status of East Jerusalem, which agreed with that of the Arabs, there was no mention of the USA's commitment to Palestinian self-determination nor any proposals for a resolution of the Jerusalem issue. Nor was there any suggestion that Baker would demand a 'freeze' on settlements in the Occupied Territories or allow the PLO to formally nominate the Palestinian delegation. Arafat left it to the PNC meeting in September to debate the question of Palestinian involvement in the peace conference. The Council's resolutions reiterated Palestinian commitment to the principle of autonomy, but such was the pressure on the PLO—from the USA and the Arab states—to accept the US proposals that by the end of September 1991 it was clear that the Palestinians would be sending representatives, albeit on terms that were far from satisfactory. Jordan, with which the Palestinians were now certain to form a joint delegation, had assured the PLO leader that it would fight for Palestinian objectives, but had also stressed that it would attend the conference whether these were achieved or not. Moreover, the failure in the Soviet Union of the attempted coup, which had been welcomed by some prominent Palestinians, removed any hopes that the USSR would counteract US authority in the Middle East.

SUSPENSION OF LOAN GUARANTEES

Israel, meanwhile, was engaged in its own battle of wills with the Bush Administration. The Likud Government had sought US $10,000m. in loan guarantees from the USA in order to help the settlement of immigrants from the USSR. However, in the run-up to the peace conference the combination of Bush's displeasure at the continuing settlement, and a desire not to offend Arab sensibilities, led the US President to ask Israel for a four-month delay in its formal submission for the loan guarantees. Bush also warned that if the loan request was approved by the US Congress, he would impose his veto. Shamir accepted the challenge and set Israel's formidable lobbying machine in motion. However, opinion polls in the USA suggested that an overwhelming majority of the public supported the Government's position and this was reflected in Congressional support for the President's stance. It was the first time since the Suez crisis that a US administration had made aid conditional on Israeli policy.

THE MADRID CONFERENCE

The peace conference, to be held in Madrid on 30 October 1991 (see Documents on Palestine, p. 128), was preceded by a series of inter-Arab meetings. Denied the Arab summit he had originally proposed, Arafat was nevertheless invited to talks in Cairo, Amman and Damascus—his first visit to the Syrian capital for eight years—where he was assured that there would be no Arab concessions until the question of territory was resolved. Faced with Israel's insistence that residents of East Jerusalem be barred from the Palestinian negotiating team, the PLO offered a compromise whereby the Palestinian delegation should include an advisory body made up largely of East Jerusalem residents. The USA supported this proposal, recognizing the advisers as an official part of the Palestinian delegation. Dr Haider Abdel Shafei, veteran chief of the Gaza Red Crescent Society, was named head of the negotiating team and Hanan Ashrawi was to be chief spokesperson. Faisal Husseini was in overall charge of the delegation which included supporters of Fatah, the Abed Rabbo faction of the DFLP, and the PCP as well as several independents. Shamir decided to head Israel's team himself, intimating that he did not trust the Minister of Foreign Affairs, David Levy, with such an important mission.

As Israel had never before attended a peace conference with its Arab neighbours, including the Palestinians, the Madrid conference generated intense media interest. In spite of the precedent, however, no real progress was made. During the three-day plenary session the Israeli delegation offered no prospect of an Israeli withdrawal from the Occupied Territories, while Arab Ministers of Foreign Affairs and Palestinians stated that there could be no peace without territorial compromise. Exchanges between Syria and Israel were particularly hostile and rapidly degenerated into mutual invective. Predictably their first round of bilateral talks, which followed the plenary sessions, ended in early deadlock, Syria's Minister of Foreign Affairs left Madrid repeating that Syria would not attend the proposed multilateral negotiations on regional issues until Israel committed itself to territorial concessions. Israel's talks with the other Arab delegations were more cordial but scarcely more productive. On the two principal issues of discussion, a venue and an agenda for the second round of talks, there was no agreement. Israeli officials demanded that the negotiations be held in the Middle East to emphasize the regional rather than the international nature of the process, and, for the opposite reason, the Arab states and the Palestinians insisted on a European venue. Only the Palestinian delegation had cause for satisfaction after the Madrid conference. It had won an early procedural victory by gaining the same (45 minute) period in which to make its representations as the other Arab delegations, and enjoyed public relations successes with eloquent and dignified articulations of the Palestinian case. Madrid was also significant for the Palestinian acceptance that self-determination should follow a period of autonomy in the Occupied Territories. However, the presence in Madrid of a high-level PLO delegation left little doubt that the Palestinian team was in close contact with the PLO.

The impression that the Palestinians had successfully exploited the opportunities afforded by the Madrid conference was reflected in several peace marches in the Occupied Territories. Some were tolerated by the Israeli army, but others ended in confrontation; a 15-year-old from Hebron became the one-thousandth casualty of the *intifada* when he was shot dead during a demonstration in support of the conference. However, the strong support for a general strike called by Hamas and the Popular and Democratic Fronts to protest against the conference underlined the strength of the radical opinion opposed to Palestinian participation in the peace talks. Meanwhile in southern Lebanon there were Israeli and SLA air strikes and artillery bombardments of Shi'ite and Palestinian positions, ostensibly in revenge for successful Palestinian and Hezbollah ambushes.

THE WASHINGTON CONFERENCE

The failure of the Arabs and Israelis to agree a venue or agenda for the next session of bilateral talks prompted James Baker to issue invitations for negotiations in Washington on 4 December 1991. A set of US guidelines suggesting how each delegation might conduct its negotiations was included with the invitations. However, while these efforts to maintain momentum in the peace process were largely welcomed by the Arab side, they were coolly received in Israel. Shamir announced that the Israeli delegation would not be going to Washington until five days after the scheduled opening of the talks. US disappointment was contrasted with satisfaction from Israeli government hardliners who applauded the 'revolt against American compulsion' and called on Shamir to take further steps to disrupt the peace process.

Israel's decision was interpreted in the Occupied Territories, as in the rest of the Arab world, as evidence of Shamir's contempt for the peace process. On the West Bank and in Gaza, it became increasingly difficult to convince the growing number of sceptics that there was any value in pursuing negotiations with an intransigent Israel. A decision by the USA to refuse US visas to several senior PLO figures who had played a covert role in Madrid further eroded Palestinian goodwill. Yasser Arafat tried to mobilize Arab support for a delayed attendance at the talks in solidarity with the PLO, but he was informed that the Arabs in general and the Palestinians in particular could not afford to be seen to disrupt the peace process. In the end the Palestinian delegation registered its disapproval by delaying its flight to Washington by 12 hours.

Israel's absence from the first days of the talks meant that the Arab delegations had to sit opposite empty chairs in the conference rooms. When the Israeli delegation did arrive, they immediately tried to undermine the Palestinian status as a delegation in their own right in Madrid by refusing to negotiate on Palestinian issues with a team that did not come under Jordanian auspices. As a result most of the time allocated for Israeli-Palestinian and Israeli-Jordanian talks was spent on procedural issues. The questions of a freeze on settlements in the Occupied Territories, interpretations of UN resolutions and the nature of interim autonomy in the Occupied Territories were barely discussed. Israeli talks with Syrian and Lebanese delegations also achieved very little. Israel's refusal to accept that Resolution 242 called on it to withdraw from occupied Arab territories continued to infuriate the Syrians. Lebanese-Israeli talks were less disorderly but threatened to founder on the Lebanese insistence that Resolution 425, calling for an Israeli withdrawal from Lebanese territory, was non-negotiable, and Israeli demands that it had to be discussed as part of the peace process. As the deadlock increased, the Arab delegation signalled that there was need of some form of US intervention. However, Baker had indicated that the USA would be adopting a 'hands-off' approach, commenting that the USA could not want peace more than the concerned parties themselves. For the Arabs this was tantamount to a surrender to Israeli obstructionism. 'If the Americans want us to talk to Israel without them . . . well, we have done', commented one Arab delegate, 'Without US intervention, however, they should have known success would be a long shot'. In New York, meanwhile, the UN General Assembly voted overwhelmingly to repeal its 1975 Resolution equating Zionism with racism. Several Arab states refused to participate in the vote.

EVENTS IN THE OCCUPIED TERRITORIES

Palestinian frustration was exacerbated by the accelerated settlement drive in the Occupied Territories. Indeed 1991 had been the most vigorous year for the building of settlements in nearly 25 years of occupation. Under the supervision of the Ministry of Housing, work had begun on 13,500 housing units in the Occupied Territories, excluding East Jerusalem, a 65% increase over all the units established in the previous 23 years. It was also reported that 13% of immigrants from the former USSR were being settled on occupied Arab lands, boosting the Israeli population in the territories to over 200,000. While the Washington talks were in progress a leaked report revealed that government approval had been given for a massive programme of Jewish colonization of Arab neighbourhoods in East Jerusalem. This was confirmed in mid-December, when a combined force of settlers and Israeli police took over several houses in the Silwan district of the city, evicting Palestinian families in the process. 'The Israelis are destroying the ground under our feet', commented Faisal Husseini on the effects of the settlement policy on his efforts to build support for the peace process. Israel's decision in early January 1992 to deport a further 12 Palestinians (reportedly in retaliation for the killing of a Jewish settler in Gaza) and to establish a settlers' civil guard in the West Bank and in Gaza, was further evidence that the Shamir Government was trying to provoke the Palestinians to withdraw from the peace talks, or, at least, to widen the rift between opponents and supporters of negotiation.

Clashes between Fatah and Hamas activists in Gaza and the West Bank became increasingly common as the *intifada* entered its fifth year. Despite appeals from PLO figures and community leaders for an end to the killing of collaborators, suspected informers were still stabbed and shot almost daily. In the refugee camps of Gaza and the nationalist strongholds of the

West Bank the knives and axes once carried in ceremonial fashion by masked activists were being replaced by pistols and automatic rifles. As predicted, there was an increase in armed attacks on settlers and soldiers at the beginning of 1992. In the most serious incident, in mid-February, three soldiers were bludgeoned to death in a raid on an army camp just inside the Green Line. Meanwhile, Israel's Ministry of Defence relied more heavily on the activities of undercover units to combat the *intifada*. An upsurge in what witnesses described as summary executions of Palestinian activists led journalists and human rights organizations to accuse Israel of operating Latin American-style death squads in the Occupied Territories.

Following the deportation orders in January, the Palestinians decided to postpone the sending of a delegation to the next round of bilateral talks in Washington. The other Arab delegations subsequently agreed to follow the Palestinian lead. The deportations also seemed to draw a more conciliatory line from the Bush Administration; visas, which had been refused to PLO members the previous month, were now granted. When the negotiations began on 16 January, Israel dropped its earlier objections to separate Palestinian representation, but refused to address the principal items on the Arab agenda, namely the interpretation of Resolution 242, borders, and settlements. The Palestinian delegation was told that the issue of settlements had no bearing on the autonomy details and could only be discussed when the final status of the territories had been decided. Arab frustration was compounded by the premature departure of the Israeli delegation. Israel's steadfast avoidance and obstruction of substantive negotiations created profound disillusion in Palestinian ranks; many believed that it was only to avoid alienating the USA while the question of loan guarantees was in the balance that Israel remained at the conference table. It was also recognized that US President Bush was unlikely to pressurize Israel into breaking the deadlock with an election due in November.

TALKS IN MOSCOW

The prospect of a negotiated settlement receded further in January 1992 when the far-right Moledet and Tehiya parties resigned from the Israeli Government in protest at discussion of Palestinian autonomy in the Occupied Territories. This left the Shamir Government without a majority in the Knesset and made an early election inevitable. Nevertheless, multilateral regional talks opened in Moscow at the end of January. With inter-Arab relations still strained in the wake of the 1991 Gulf War, it came as little surprise that they failed to agree on a coherent policy. Eleven states attended, a sufficient number for Israel to claim a diplomatic breakthrough, while Syria and Lebanon stuck to their earlier promise to observe a boycott of regional talks until progress had been made in the bilateral negotiations. The PLO, concerned at Arab disarray but determined to use the multilateral session to highlight the issue of Palestinian representation, sent a delegation composed of personalities from the West Bank and Gaza, Jerusalem and the diaspora. While conceding that representatives from the diaspora and Jerusalem could be included in some of the working groups that the conference was to establish—on the refugee problem for example—the USA only issued invitations to the plenary session to Palestinian delegates from Gaza and the West Bank. Believing that they had already made too many concessions, especially on the issue of representation, the Palestinian delegation refused to attend the talks. US Secretary of State Baker voiced his disappointment at the Palestinian decision and promised that diaspora Palestinians could be included in two of the five working groups scheduled to meet in the spring. The Palestinians had demanded free representation on all five, but could take some solace in the fact that their fears of Israeli and Arab participants taking steps towards normalizing relations were unfounded.

ESCALATION OF HOSTILITIES IN LEBANON

On 16 February 1992 the leader of the Lebanese Hezbollah, Sheikh Abbas Moussawi, was killed in an Israeli helicopter attack on his motorcade in southern Lebanon. Moussawi's wife, child and several bodyguards also died. Many observers were puzzled by the assassination; for all its anti-Israeli rhetoric Hezbollah had never launched attacks against targets inside

Israel, nor had there been a noticeable increase in raids on the IDF or its SLA allies in the Israeli security zone prior to the killing. One SLA spokesman even described Hezbollah as 'militarily insignificant'. Moreover, the killing halted negotiations to exchange Lebanese and Palestinian prisoners in return for news of Israeli servicemen missing in Lebanon. It also provoked an escalation of warfare in the south. Hezbollah rocket attacks on northern Israel were followed by heavy Israeli shelling of Shi'ite villages. Syria eventually persuaded Hezbollah to halt its salvoes, which led the organization to search for other means of retaliation. On 9 March Israel's chief security officer in Ankara was assassinated, and on 17 March a massive car-bomb wrecked the Israeli Embassy in Buenos Aires, Argentina, leaving 30 dead. Responsibility for both attacks was claimed by 'Islamic Jihad'.

The situation in Lebanon deepened the pessimism surrounding the peace process. The Israeli delegation arrived in Washington for the fourth round of bilateral talks in an unforgiving mood. At the end of February James Baker had finally ended speculation over Israel's request for $10,000m. in loan guarantees. He told Congress that they would not be granted unless there was a halt to new settlement activity in the Occupied Territories, a condition that Shamir had already rejected.

BILATERAL TALKS IN WASHINGTON

Negotiations over the form of Palestinian autonomy within the Occupied Territories confirmed the extent of the gulf between Israel and Arab/Palestinian aspirations. The Israeli delegates outlined a proposal which would maintain Israeli control over land, and guarantee the right of unlimited settlement and full responsibility for public order. There was no mention of elections with the implication that the limited administrative powers devolved to the Palestinians would be executed by official appointees. This contrasted with the Palestinian plan for a Palestinian interim self-governing authority along with the election of a legislative assembly, a halt to all settlement, a transfer of judicial and administrative power and the phased withdrawal of Israeli forces leading to Palestinian self-determination throughout the Occupied Territories. A US State Department spokesman described both positions as 'maximalist', but went on to criticize the Palestinians for trying to pre-empt the negotiations by declaring sovereignty as their goal. Although this criticism reflected the USA's longstanding opposition to a Palestinian nation, it was interpreted as an attempt to counterbalance the refusal to grant Israel's loan guarantees. Israel's outright rejection of territorial compromises left negotiations with Syria and Jordan in stalemate. Trying to negotiate with Israel, said a Syrian spokeswoman, was 'an exercise in futility'.

REACTIONS IN THE OCCUPIED TERRITORIES AND ISRAEL

Within the Occupied Territories there was further opposition to continued Palestinian involvement in the peace process. The PCP, renamed the Palestinian People's Party (PPP), had initially supported the Washington talks, but withdrew its backing during the fourth round after the Palestinian delegation had agreed to negotiate on the issue of autonomy without having secured Israel's prior agreement to a settlement 'freeze'. Yet more evidence of public opinion turning against the talks came in the elections to the Ramallah Chamber of Commerce in early March. Hamas supporters won a clear majority of seats despite the fact that Ramallah had a sizeable Christian majority and had long been considered as the stronghold of liberal, secular nationalism.

Party manoeuvring and infighting were also in evidence in Israel in the run-up to the general election. In February Shimon Peres was deposed as the leader of the Labour Party by his more hawkish, but equally veteran colleague, Itzhak Rabin. Rabin's reputation as a 'hardliner' on defence and security was widely regarded as a boost to the Labour Party's battle to win voters from Likud. Their fortunes were further enhanced by rifts within the Likud ranks. In a speech broadcast live on Israeli TV, the Minister of Foreign Affairs, David Levy, angered by what he claimed was a plot against his supporters during internal party elections, accused Likud of being 'racist'. Although he was dissuaded from resigning, Levy's vitriolic attack on his own party undoubtedly contributed to steady

Labour gains in the opinion polls. Meanwhile three parties of the centre-left, the Citizen Rights Movement, Shinui and Mapam, decided to merge their lists to form a new electoral bloc, Meretz.

The fifth round of the bilateral talks were held in Washington at the end of April, but were largely overshadowed by the Israeli election campaign. As predicted, the Israeli delegation arrived in Washington with a plan for phased municipal elections in the West Bank and in Gaza. The Palestinian delegation offered to consider the proposal, but reiterated its commitment to a nationally-elected legislative assembly. Hanan Ashrawi later described municipal elections as 'a dead-end'. There was also a suspicion among Palestinians that the Israeli offer was a Likud public relations exercise designed to win the moderate vote. Interestingly, those Palestinian factions which had raised the strongest objections to the autonomy negotiations—Hamas, the PFLP and DFLP—argued that municipal elections were a better option precisely because they did not commit Palestinians to the autonomy plan. Following its gains in the Ramallah Chamber of Commerce election, Hamas also viewed municipal elections as a welcome test of strength against a divided nationalist bloc. However, in elections to the Nablus Chamber of Commerce in mid-May, the nationalist bloc, standing as the National Muslim Coalition, won nine of the 12 seats contested.

There was an increase of violence associated with the *intifada* in the weeks leading up to the election. Four Palestinians were shot dead and 80 injured in Rafah on 7 April and several were killed in armed clashes during May. There was also a rise in the death-toll during demonstrations. The killing of an Israeli girl in a Tel-Aviv suburb at the end of May by a lone Palestinian was the catalyst for several nights of anti-Arab rioting and a government decision to further restrict the movement of Gazans into Israel; unemployment rates in some parts of the Gaza Strip were reported to exceed 50%. The stabbing of an Israeli settler in Gaza shortly afterwards was followed by widescale destruction of Palestinian crops and property.

In mid-June 1992 members of the Palestinian negotiating team travelled to Amman for a televised meeting with Yasser Arafat. Israeli government ministers condemned the meeting and demanded the arrest of the participants on their return. The USA made clear its firm opposition to such measures, leaving Israel's Minister of Police to make the somewhat lame threat of calling in the Palestinians concerned for questioning.

ELECTION VICTORY FOR LABOUR

A combination of public discontent over the economy, the state of relations with the USA, the plight of Russian immigrants and the lack of progress in the peace process, made Labour gains in the Israeli elections on 23 June inevitable. However, the extent of the Labour majority over the Likud, 44 seats to 32, exceeded most expectations. Meretz became the third largest party in the new Knesset with 12 seats, while the right-wing Tzomet Party, headed by the fiercely anti-clerical Rafael Eitan, made an unexpectedly strong showing and won eight seats. The right-wing Tehiya Party failed to win any seats. There was a slight drop in support for the orthodox religious parties and the Arab-dominated lists.

As expected, Meretz entered into partnership with Labour. The inclusion of the Sephardi Orthodox party, Shas, gave Rabin an overall majority, but an attempt to increase his majority and broaden his constituency by recruiting Tzomet into the coalition came to nothing. Former Labour leader Shimon Peres was appointed Minister of Foreign Affairs in the new Government, while Prime Minister Rabin retained the defence portfolio.

INITIAL REACTIONS TO RABIN

The USA and the EC, in the belief that only a Labour victory could keep the peace process alive, warmly welcomed the outcome of the election. The defeat of Shamir and the Likud was also greeted with relief in the Arab capitals where the attitude towards the new Israeli Government was one of official caution and unofficial optimism. The reaction of Palestinians was more equivocal. Those who had supported the peace negotiations saw Rabin's election as a positive development. But left-wing and Islamic factions feared that a Labour government would pave the way for an agreement on the autonomy proposals they so bitterly opposed. Relations between Fatah and Hamas supporters in particular grew more volatile following the election and,

in July, the Occupied Territories witnessed the worst round of internecine fighting in many years. Several people had been killed and scores injured in gun battles and street confrontations before an uneasy truce was brokered.

Rabin's initial comments on the peace process did little to reassure Palestinians. He stated that he would be willing to travel to any Arab capital to pursue peace negotiations, but stopped short of instituting the settlement 'freeze' the Palestinians had demanded. He promised a halt to the building of 'non-political' settlements, but insisted that all existing contracts would be honoured. This was positive enough for Egypt's President Mubarak to issue an invitation to Rabin to visit Cairo—the first visit by an Israeli Prime Minister for six years—and for the USA to intimate that it might release at least part of the $10,000m. in loan guarantees that Israel had requested. In mid-July James Baker began another round of 'shuttle' diplomacy in the Middle East in an effort to reactivate the peace process. In the wake of the Baker mission, Arab leaders, including the PLO, met in Damascus with Palestinians from the Occupied Territories in order to co-ordinate policy before a possible renewal of bilateral talks.

In mid-August Rabin travelled to the USA for a visit intended to restore US–Israeli relations to their traditional amicability after the frostiness of the Bush-Shamir years. The Israeli Prime Minister left Washington with pledges of further military aid and assurances of Israel's enhanced strategic importance to the USA in the post-cold war era. For his part, Rabin promised that the coming round of bilateral talks would achieve progress on substantive issues.

OPTIMISM AND DISAPPOINTMENT

Rabin's optimistic approach to the peace process was not shared by the Palestinians. There was disappointment that the new Israeli Government had refrained from implementing a complete 'freeze' on settlement in the Occupied Territories, and dismay at the USA's readiness to grant the $10,000m. in loan guarantees without such a policy change. Moreover, the goodwill measures that the Labour Government had announced prior to the resumption of negotiations—the rescinding of deportation orders against 11 Palestinians, the release of a small number of political prisoners and the reopening of some of the roads sealed during the *intifada*—were considered to be little more than political cosmetics. Government spokesmen in Jordan and Syria also expressed concern at the repercussions that the rapidly improved US–Israeli relations would have on the USA's supposed impartiality as co-sponsor of the peace process.

Despite Arab reservations, Israel's continued intimations that there was a real prospect of a breakthrough in the stalled peace process ensured that the mood before the sixth round of bilateral talks began in Washington was more sanguine than for some time. Delegates spoke of a 'positive new tone' and a constructive informality that previous encounters had lacked. However, by the end of the fourth week, the longest round of bilateral talks to date, the Arab parties described the negotiations as deadlocked. Syria's chief negotiator accused Rabin's Government of exhibiting 'exactly the same attitude and policy as Shamir'. His comments were provoked by Israel's insistence that Syria should commit itself to a full, normal peace with Israel before the issue of withdrawal from the Golan Heights could be discussed. The Palestinian delegation expressed similar frustration with its Israeli counterpart on the 'land for peace' issue. While the Palestinians insisted that the entire peace process—including discussions on Palestinian autonomy—should be guided by Resolution 242, the Israelis argued that UN resolutions were only applicable to negotiations on the ultimate status of occupied Arab land. Hanan Ashrawi, the chief Palestinian spokesperson, told journalists that Israel was still adhering to the notion of 'autonomy for the people but not the land'.

PEACE TALKS FOUNDER

The failure of the sixth round to produce tangible results strengthened the hand of Palestinian groups opposed to the peace process. Meeting in Damascus in mid-September 1992, 10 Palestinian organizations, four from within the PLO and six from outside, signed a memorandum urging a withdrawal from the Madrid process. A strike called by the 10 factions was widely observed in the Occupied Territories and caused clashes between Fatah and Hamas supporters. However, while pressure from the rejectionist group narrowed Arafat's field of manoeuvre and reflected the substantial opposition to further Palestinian involvement in the Washington talks, other developments encouraged the Palestinians to remain engaged. Israel's Minister of Justice announced his intention to repeal legislation outlawing contact between Israelis and Palestinians and the PLO, and economic controls were eased in order to allow a less restricted flow of capital to the Occupied Territories. One of the quietest periods in the *intifada* finally came to an end in mid-October when a hunger strike called by Palestinian prisoners in Israeli prisons prompted a series of violent protests in the Occupied Territories and a sharp rise in Palestinian deaths and injuries.

A meeting of the PLO's Central Committee was called by Arafat in October in order to obtain official approval for Palestinian participation in the seventh round of peace talks in Washington. Arafat achieved a minor victory in persuading the PFLP and DFLP to attend the meeting, although both factions refused to vote on the issue of participation and were bitter critics of the Palestinian negotiating position. Their opposition was intensified by reports that Israel was considering an exchange of land in return for peace with Syria. At a meeting of Arab foreign ministers in Amman, Jordan, in mid-October Syria refused to give assurances to its Jordanian and Palestinian colleagues that it would not conclude a separate Israeli-Syrian peace treaty, arguing that progress in the Israeli-Palestinian talks could take years. An angry Arafat cancelled a scheduled visit to Damascus.

The Israeli delegation travelled to Washington for the seventh round of bilateral talks buoyed by the USA's formal approval of the release of $10,000m. in loan guarantees, and with an apparent willingness to discuss 'withdrawal in the Golan' with its Syrian counterpart. However, the proximity of the US presidential election and an expected change to an unambiguously pro-Israeli administration ensured that the negotiations would be cautious. The Israeli-Lebanese dialogue was given a particular poignancy by artillery duels between the IDF and Hezbollah fighters that were prompted by the deaths of five Israeli soldiers in a land-mine explosion. Israel used the pretext of the fighting to try to persuade Lebanon to agree to the establishment of a joint military commission in the south of the country. Lebanon interpreted the offer as a ploy to legitimize Israel's occupation of the south and insisted that there could be no peace without a full Israeli withdrawal. After the Israeli delegation accused its Lebanese counterpart of 'abdicating responsibility to terrorists' and warned that they 'could make normal life impossible' for Lebanon, the Lebanese delegation walked out of the talks. The Israeli-Palestinian dialogue again foundered on disagreement over the applicability of UN resolutions to the interim negotiations on Palestinian autonomy in the Occupied Territories. Deadlock was only averted by Palestinian consent to a series of 'informal' talks on the substance of interim Palestinian autonomy. The Palestinian delegation was at pains to stress the exploratory nature of the talks for fear of being seen to give assent to discussions on the technicalities of autonomy before the broader political principles governing interim and final phase negotiations had been established. Israel's talks with Syria also disappointed. The Israeli delegation had come to Washington prepared to discuss territorial compromise in the Golan, but it rapidly became obvious that it would only commit itself to discussing a limited withdrawal. Talks with Syria were further soured by Israel's repeating of its earlier call that Syria should not hold out for a comprehensive resolution of Arab–Israeli disputes but should 'stand on its own'. Only in the talks between Israel and Jordan was there a modicum of success, with both parties agreeing on a provisional agenda for the next round of talks.

CLINTON ADMINISTRATION TAKES OVER IN USA

The seventh round of bilateral talks coincided with Bill Clinton's victory in the 1992 US presidential election. The outgoing Bush Administration was eager to bequeath a viable Middle East peace process to the new Administration and dutifully called for a resumption of talks in December. Not surprisingly, however, there was little enthusiasm for a further round of negotia-

tions before the formal inauguration of the new US President. The Palestinians, under mounting pressure from a sceptical constituency to protest at the lack of progress in, and general media indifference to, the peace process, were the most reluctant to attend. However, with the Arab states committed to returning to Washington, the Palestinians were left to register their unhappiness by sending a delegation of only four to deal with Israel's controversial proposals for Palestinian 'interim self-government'. The draft model for Palestinian autonomy envisaged a stratified system of authority in the Occupied Territories (excluding East Jerusalem); Israeli jurisdiction would be maintained over Israeli settlements, public lands would come under joint Palestinian-Israeli jurisdiction, and an Israeli-supervised Palestinian authority (whose composition and competence were to be negotiated) would govern private Palestinian lands and municipalities. While the Palestinian delegation was not in a position to reject the Israeli proposals outright, it argued that they would lead to the creation of a Palestinian Bantustan.

The inconclusive eighth round of Washington talks coincided with the fifth anniversary of the *intifada*. The character of the Palestinian uprising had changed considerably since its beginnings in Gaza. The popular committees that had served as the *intifada's* original dynamo had long since fallen victim to Israeli repression and factional infighting. The UNLU itself existed largely in name only and its bi-weekly communiqués no longer set the tone or tenor of resistance. Instead the activities of small armed groups had come to be viewed as the principal focus of the uprising. Many of these owed only nominal allegiance to identifiable political factions and some of their more dubious activities, especially the settling of political scores in the guise of eliminating collaborators, had led to heated debate and calls for the young gunmen to be restrained. However, with scant prospect of a breakthrough in the Washington talks, there was undeniable political capital to be made out of successful armed attacks against Israeli targets. Hamas, as self-appointed inheritor of the radical Palestinian mantle and an uncompromising opponent of the peace process, was the best placed, politically and militarily, to exploit the armed option. Bolstered by generous financial backing from Iran (which reportedly paid a bonus for every Israeli soldier killed), Hamas fighters embarked on a spectacular series of military operations. During two weeks in December four Israeli soldiers were killed in Hamas ambushes in Gaza and Hebron, and another was kidnapped inside Israel and later murdered (the IDF lost a further soldier to an Islamic Jihad gunman near Jenin in the same week).

DEPORTATION OF ALLEGED ISLAMIC ACTIVISTS

Rabin promised radical steps to counter the Islamist movement's military successes. On 16 and 17 December 1,600 alleged Hamas and Islamic Jihad activists were detained by the Israeli security forces. Some 413 of those arrested were subsequently transported to the Lebanese border and, with the approval of Israel's Supreme Court, expelled through Israel's security zone into south Lebanon. The Lebanese Government refused to accept the deportees, a stance which the Arab world unanimously applauded, leaving the displaced Palestinians to establish a makeshift refugee camp on a barren mountainside wedged between the IDF and Lebanese army front lines. Although Rabin explained that the deportees would be eligible to return to their homes after a two-year period, the mass expulsions elicited a chorus of international condemnation. The UN Security Council, affirming the inadmissibility of deportations under the Fourth Geneva Convention, unanimously passed Resolution 799 demanding the immediate safe return of the expelled Palestinians. UN Secretary-General Boutros Boutros-Ghali also warned Israel that he might ask the Security Council to take further measures if it did not comply with the UN Resolution. In the Occupied Territories, and particularly in Gaza, where the majority of the deportees originated, Rabin's action provoked another surge of violent street protests—six demonstrators were killed in Khan Yunis on 21 December alone.

The mainstream PLO appeared to benefit from the political and diplomatic repercussions of the deportations. Firstly, it was believed that the PLO would be able to extract significant concessions from Israel and the USA before sanctioning a Palestinian return to the negotiating table; secondly, in the opinion of some observers, Rabin's demonization of Hamas was effectively paving the way for a future Israeli-PLO dialogue; and thirdly the December events provided Yasser Arafat with an opportunity to manage his troublesome opposition. In reluctant admission of the PLO Chairman's stewardship of the Palestinian cause in times of crisis, Hamas and the Damascus-based rejectionists accepted invitations to a series of talks in Tunis. Although no real concessions were made by either side, with Arafat ignoring calls for a Palestinian withdrawal from the peace process, Hamas representatives agreed to work towards ending sectarian conflict and to co-ordinate activities with Fatah inside and outside the Occupied Territories. Hamas later signalled a significant revision of its maximalist position of settling for nothing less than an Islamic state in all of historical Palestine, by dropping objections to an independent state in part of Palestine.

US ATTEMPTS TO SAVE PEACE PROCESS

The deportations were a clear embarrassment for the new Clinton Administration. With the PLO and the Arab states urging the imposition of sanctions on Israel for non-compliance with Resolution 799, Clinton and his Secretary of State, Warren Christopher, persuaded Israel to take steps to defuse international unease over the expulsions. The Rabin Government subsequently announced that the expulsions had been an 'exceptional' measure and that the Palestinians would be allowed to return home before the end of 1993. It added that 101 of the deportees would be allowed back to the Occupied Territories immediately (this was rejected by the deportees' spokesman). Armed with the Israeli concessions, the USA embarked on a vigorous diplomatic campaign to persuade the six Third World members of the UN Security Council to abandon their support for sanctions against Israel. The USA argued that Israel had moved towards compliance with resolution 799 and that the imposition of sanctions would irreparably damage the fragile peace process. Madeleine Albright, the new US Ambassador to the UN, also warned that the USA would veto any move to impose sanctions. By 12 February 1993 the USA's heavy-handed diplomacy had borne fruit. The President of the UN Security Council issued a statement to the effect that there was to be no further debate on Resolution 799. He called on all parties 'to reinvigorate the Middle East peace process'. The UN decision caused glee in the Rabin Government, but confirmed the deep-seated Arab and Palestinian belief that Israel was immune to international law.

CHRISTOPHER TOURS MIDDLE EAST

In mid-February Warren Christopher made a tour of the Middle East with the primary intention of enticing the Palestinians and the front-line Arab states to resume talks in Washington. Syria and Lebanon were the easiest targets, since they had already indicated that they were prepared to separate the deportation issue from the peace process. However, Syria's President Assad went some way towards allaying Palestinian fears by stressing, in his talks with Christopher, that a separate Syrian-Israeli peace was impossible without a resolution of the Palestinian issue. Jordan proved to be less amenable to Christopher's urgings. It had said that it would not accept an invitation to Washington as long as the deportation issue was outstanding. This was not repeated by King Hussein in his talks with Christopher, but the Jordanian monarch left the US Secretary of State in no doubt that it would be almost impossible for a Jordanian delegation to attend the next round of talks if the Palestinians did not do so. It was clear, therefore, that the success or failure of the Christopher mission depended on the outcome of his meetings with the Palestinian peace team in Jerusalem. Initial reports suggested that progress had been made, and a six-point plan, designed to address Palestinian grievances, was agreed by the two sides. The outcome was a further letter of US assurances to the Palestinians. The Administration reiterated its commitment to Resolutions 242 and 338, stated its willingness to participate as a full partner in the peace talks, expressed opposition to deportation and settlement and affirmed its readiness to stand by assurances given by the previous Administration with regard to the peace process (most crucially the acknowledgement that East Jerusalem was occupied territory). Christopher also told the Palestinians that Israel would not resort to deportations in the future. However, while the Secretary of State flew back to the USA, the Palestinians waited in vain for a positive Israeli response

to the six points and a statement of principle on deportations. Instead, the Israeli media announced that the Palestinians would be attending the ninth round of talks on 20 April. Angered by subsequent US inaction and complaining bitterly that it was being taken for granted, the PLO ordered the Palestinian delegates to refuse an invitation to the talks. 'If Israel cannot comply with the six points,' commented one PLO official, 'then we cannot participate in the next round'.

PALESTINIANS RELUCTANTLY RETURN TO TALKS

The PLO's refusal to accept an invitation to the talks led to a series of inconclusive inter-Arab meetings and the postponement, at the end of March 1993, of any decision on whether to attend until further talks had been held with the US Administration. Privately the Palestinians had by now resigned themselves to the resumption of negotiations before the return of the deportees, but they insisted that they could not resume talks without major Israeli concessions on the issue of the deportations. The USA and Egypt's President Mubarak subsequently urged Rabin to adopt some confidence-building measures to smooth the way for Arab participation. The result was a declaration by Rabin that mass deportation was not government policy and a promise to allow the return of a small number of Palestinians expelled since 1967. In a departure from the Israeli Government's previously-held policy of refusing to allow Palestinians from East Jerusalem to participate in the negotiations, Rabin also announced that it no longer objected to Faisal Husseini becoming the official leader of the Palestinian delegation. This last point was regarded by some Palestinians, not least by Husseini himself, as an important gain and a sufficient concession for the Palestinian delegation to attend talks in Washington. However, for the majority of Palestinians, including delegation leader Haider Abdel Shafei, who had given an undertaking in his native Gaza that there would be no return to the talks while the deportees languished on a Lebanese hillside, Israel's concessions and the USA's promise to play a full and active role in the talks still fell short of the minimum required to enable them to return to Washington.

RENEWED VIOLENCE IN THE WEST BANK AND GAZA

Public opinion in the Occupied Territories remained firmly opposed to a retreat from commitments made to the deportees and had hardened as repression escalated in the West Bank and Gaza. Since the deportations there had been a dramatic increase in violent incidents in Gaza and the West Bank, with Palestinian deaths and injuries equalling those of the *intifada's* bloodiest months. The death of children had reached alarmingly high levels, as had summary executions of Palestinian fugitives by Israeli undercover units. Scores of homes were also being destroyed as the IDF adopted the controversial new tactic of targeting houses suspected of harbouring wanted Palestinians with rocket fire. Yet the militarization of occupation policy failed, as had mass expulsions, to halt anti-Israeli violence. Instead, the frequency of attacks and demonstrations in the Gaza Strip led some Israeli military figures to conclude that Gaza had been 'lost'. Each Israeli casualty drew appeals for stiffer policies to be applied in the Territories. Following the killing of two secondary school students in Jerusalem in March, Rabin ordered the closure of the Occupied Territories. Such a measure had been employed many times during the *intifada* but this time, Rabin stated, the West Bank and Gaza would be sealed for an indefinite period. Tens of thousands of Palestinians lost their livelihoods as a result. Pressure from Israeli employers eventually persuaded the Government to issue work permits for a few thousand Palestinians, but this still left many areas of Gaza and the West Bank in the grip of an economic catastrophe.

Against this background the PLO faced unenviable choices. Domestic animosity to the Middle East peace process was counterbalanced by pressure from the USA, the EC and Arab states for the PLO to resume talks. Syria paid official lip-service to Resolution 799, but it was eager to capitalize on its improving relations with the USA and sensed that there might be some movement on the Golan issue. Saudi Arabia also made it clear to the cash-starved PLO that restored relations and future funding would be contingent on Palestinian attendance at the ninth round of bilateral talks. Despite huge misgivings and against a chorus of protest from the Occupied Territories, Arafat finally consented to Palestinian participation in the ninth round, stating that 'We go to the negotiations because if we do not have a place on the political map we will not have a place on the geographical map either'. Another member of the PLO's old guard, Faruq Kaddoumi, called attendance 'the lesser of two evils'. The Palestinian peace delegates, who remained strongly opposed to Palestinian attendance at the talks, had to be ordered back to Washington. Hamas called the PLO's decision an act of 'treason' and severed contact with the Organization. A protest strike called by opposition factions shut down the Occupied Territories and precipitated a further round of bloody demonstrations.

Palestinian disarray immediately before the ninth round of bilateral talks fuelled Israeli intransigence. No promises were given on the return of the deportees, Rabin still refused to acknowledge that the West Bank and Gaza were 'Occupied Territories', in accordance with UN Security Council Resolution 242, and, despite the inclusion of Faisal Husseini in the Palestinian delegation, its Israeli counterpart continued to insist that East Jerusalem was not on the agenda. When, during the last days of negotiations, the USA submitted a draft proposal of principles in an attempt to break the deadlock and honour its earlier promise of playing a more active role in the negotiations, the Palestinian delegates complained that it was almost a carbon copy of Israeli positions. Further evidence of the USA's tilt towards Israel came in Assistant Secretary of State Edward Djerejian's testimony to a US Congress foreign affairs subcommittee on the Middle East in which he voiced no objections to the use of the unfrozen $10,000m. in loan guarantees to finance 'natural growth' of existing settlements in the Occupied Territories. A disgruntled Haider Abdel Shafei concluded at the end of the ninth round of bilateral talks that nothing had been accomplished. He said that the delegation would not return for further talks unless the PLO Chairman convened a session of either the PNC or the PLO's Central Council to assess the situation. This brought a sharp rejoinder from Faisal Husseini who said that the decision on whether to attend further talks rested with the PLO leadership. Rifts within Palestinian ranks grew wider with the resignation of the PNC's veteran speaker in protest at the direction of the peace process. 'Tragedies are befalling the Palestinian people', he said in his resignation address, 'and I do not want to be blamed for it'. There was little progress in the other bilateral talks. A claim by Israel's Minister of Foreign Affairs, Shimon Peres, that the Jordanian and Israeli delegations were on the brink of agreement was angrily denied by Jordan.

SOMBRE MOOD AT TENTH ROUND OPENING

The tenth round of bilateral negotiations opened in mid-June in quiet, almost ritualistic fashion and without Arab preconditions or expectations. Several Palestinian delegates, including Abdel Shafei, did not attend the talks but refrained from announcing an official boycott. The sense of Palestinian demoralization was deepened by comments made by the PLO Chairman to an Israeli newspaper to the effect that if Israel agreed to withdraw from Gaza and parts of the West Bank it would be proof of its implementation of Resolution 242. Arafat's statement was cited as evidence of the PLO leadership's abandonment of principle and absence of policy and led to calls for a complete re-evaluation of the Palestinian negotiating strategy. In a thinly-veiled attack on the PLO leader, Abdel Shafei also pleaded for democratization of the Organization. There was no progress in Washington to provide relief for the beleaguered Chairman. US efforts to produce a joint Israeli-Palestinian declaration of principles eventually led to the issuing of a draft proposal designed to constitute the new terms of reference for the peace talks. For the Palestinians the US document was an unacceptable departure from the assurances upon which their participation in the peace process was premised; firstly, because the USA insinuated that both Israel and the Palestinians had claims to sovereignty over the West Bank and Gaza; and secondly, because the issue of East Jerusalem was excluded from negotiations on interim self-government arrangements. The US proposals, Palestinian leaders agreed, were not even suitable as a starting point. Speculation that there might be progress between Israel and Syria was scotched after Rabin, under pressure from right-

wing Jewish settlers, rejected a Syrian offer of a 'total' peace in exchange for a 'total' withdrawal from the Golan Heights.

'OPERATION ACCOUNTABILITY'

At the end of July, following the killing of seven Israeli soldiers in south Lebanon by Hezbollah fighters, the IDF launched its severest bombardment of Lebanese territory since 1982. More than 55 villages were heavily damaged, 130 people, mainly civilians, were killed and 300,000 Lebanese fled north during the week-long assault. Hezbollah responded by firing salvoes of *Katyusha* rockets into northern Israel. These reportedly caused little damage and resulted in few casualties. Prime Minister Rabin code-named the IDF's action 'Operation Accountability' and stated that its purpose was to create a refugee crisis in Lebanon and thus pressurize Lebanon and Syria into taking action against Hezbollah. The deliberate targeting of civilians provoked harsh international condemnation. The UN Secretary-General, Boutros Boutros-Ghali, declared it 'deplorable that any government would consciously adopt policies that would lead to the creation of a new flow of refugees and displaced persons', sentiments that were echoed by Arab states and the European Union (EU—formerly EC). Fears that the fighting would deal a fatal blow to the faltering peace process prompted Syria and the USA to mediate an end to the hostilities and to arrange what was termed an 'understanding' between Israel and Hezbollah whereby the IDF would refrain from attacking civilian targets as long as Hezbollah fighters confined their military operations to Lebanese territory. Israel declared its attack on south Lebanon a success, but it quickly became evident that Hezbollah had not been entirely subdued by the IDF. Less than three weeks after the Israeli bombardment, nine Israeli soldiers killed in two ambushes carried out by Hezbollah fighters in Israel's security zone. Significantly, Israeli reprisals were confined to limited air strikes on Hezbollah bases in the Beka'a valley.

THE OSLO ACCORDS

Throughout the summer the political and financial crisis within the PLO deepened. Two prominent members of the PLO Executive Committee resigned before the beginning of the 11th round of bilateral talks in protest at Arafat's negotiating strategy; the resignation of Faisal Husseini, Saeb Erakat and Hanan Ashrawi from the Palestinian delegation was only averted by the PLO's acceptance of their demands for greater democratization of the decision-making process. Rumours of corruption and mismanagement of the Organization's finances caused further erosion of support for Arafat's leadership, as did the growing chorus of dissent from the Damascus-based Palestinian groups, independents and erstwhile Fatah supporters. With the prospect of the PLO's disintegration seeming ever more likely, a dramatic development at the end of August injected sudden energy into the peace process and promised to shift Arab–Israeli relations onto a more positive footing. It emerged that Israel and the PLO had been engaged in secret negotiations in the Norwegian capital, Oslo, and had reached agreement on mutual recognition and a plan for staged Palestinian autonomy in the West Bank and the Gaza Strip. The precise details of the autonomy agreement were purposefully vague, but according to initial press reports the key components of the 'Oslo Accords' were said to include an early withdrawal of Israeli forces from Gaza and the Jericho area; the redeployment of Israeli troops in other areas of the West Bank; the gradual transfer of power from the civil administration to a Palestinian authority; the creation of a Palestinian police force; and the election of a Palestinian Council. Permanent status negotiations were to begin within two years of the Israeli withdrawal from Gaza and Jericho, be concluded within five years and would address such issues as Jerusalem, borders, settlement, co-operation, security and refugees. The reaction of the Arab world to the nascent PLO-Israeli agreement was decidedly mixed, not least amongst Palestinians themselves. Arafat managed to secure majority support for the Accords from the Fatah Central Committee, but failed to persuade three of the movement's co-founders, Farouk Kaddoumi and Khalid and Hani Hassan, to give their backing. Hamas and the Damascus-based Palestinian groups denounced the agreement as a betrayal, an interpretation that was shared by the majority of Palestinian refugees in Lebanon who staged protest marches and decked their camps with the black flags of mourning. The prominent Palestinian writer, Edward Said, scorned the agreement for transforming the PLO from a national liberation movement to a municipal council. Within the Occupied Territories, many ordinary Palestinians, no doubt swayed by the attrition of the *intifada* years, expressed guarded approval of the plan. Nevertheless there was widespread concern among activists of all persuasions that the agreement represented a capitulation to Israeli demands and a dangerous journey into the unknown. Crucially, however, there was a strong consensus against the use of violence to settle inter-Palestinian differences. Gaining the support of the Arab world was as important for Arafat as winning over his domestic constituency and to this end the PLO Chairman embarked on a hurried tour of regional capitals at the beginning of September. President Mubarak predictably gave full support to the agreement, while Egyptian officials let it be known that Cairo had played a seminal role in securing the two sides' agreement. King Hussein of Jordan initially displayed considerable pique at the failure of the PLO to consult him over the details of its talks in Oslo, and the Jordanian press expressed official disquiet at a 'separate' Israeli-Palestinian peace. However, given the USA's endorsement of the Oslo Accords and Jordan's traditional, if cautious, advocacy of Israeli-Arab peace, it came as little surprise that Jordan soon expressed support for the PLO Chairman. On 4 September King Hussein told a press conference that the Oslo Accords were 'part of a process leading to the implementation of (Security Council Resolution) 242 . . . so I will emphasize our full support.' A day later the foreign ministers of the Gulf Co-operation Council (GCC) member states gave their qualified support to what was described as 'a first step towards the liberation of all occupied land, including Jerusalem.' President Assad of Syria proved to be far less amenable to the new developments. At various times during the peace process Syria had been accused of negotiating a separate peace deal with Israel regarding the Golan Heights. Revelations that the PLO was on the verge of concluding its own agreement with Israel prompted the government-controlled media in Syria to issue lengthy commentaries denouncing disunity within Arab ranks. During six hours of talks in Damascus, Arafat failed to persuade the Syrian President to endorse the Oslo Accords. Assad stressed that he believed the PLO's action had made the achievement of an Israeli withdrawal from the Golan Heights and southern Lebanon more difficult. These fears were shared by the Lebanese Prime Minster, Rafik Hariri, who was even more outspoken in his objections to the Israel-PLO deal. Addressing concerns that the Accords effectively froze the position of Palestinian refugees in Lebanon, he announced that 'under no circumstances whatsoever' would Palestinians be allowed to settle permanently in Lebanon.

The Israeli Cabinet unanimously approved the Oslo Accords on 30 August and early opinion polls suggested that there was a significant majority in the country in favour of the agreement. As government officials were quick to explain, there was little in the substance of the Oslo Accords to cause alarm in Israel. Withdrawal from the chaos of the Gaza Strip was broadly popular and dialogue with the PLO had become far more acceptable to the national psyche since the growth of Islamic fundamentalism. For the more hawkish and sceptical sectors of the Israeli population there was solace in the fact that, under the terms of the agreement, security for the West Bank and Gaza would remain an Israeli responsibility, and that the short-term future of Israeli settlements was assured. Agreement with the Palestinians also offered the prospect of an end to the Arab economic boycott of Israel and of normalized relations with the Arab world. The Likud opposition was largely unimpressed by Labour's arguments, however. It accused Prime Minister Rabin and Minister of Foreign Affairs Peres of laying the cornerstone of a Palestinian state and stated that if the Likud came to power it would refuse to honour the agreement. Representatives of the settler movement and of the extreme right-wing vowed to resort to civil disobedience in order to prevent the implementation of the Accords.

THE DECLARATION OF PRINCIPLES

The official signing of the Israeli-PLO Declaration of Principles took place on 13 September 1993 (see Documents on Palestine, p. 128) on the White House lawn in Washington. In front of 3,000 international guests Israeli Prime Minister Rabin declared: 'We the soldiers who have returned from the battle stained with blood, we who have fought against you the Palestinians, we say to you today in a loud and clear voice: "Enough blood and tears! Enough!" '. For his part, Yasser Arafat pleaded for 'courage and determination to continue the course of building coexistence and peace between us', and added, 'Our people do not consider the exercising of our right to self-determination could violate the rights of their neighbours or infringe on their security.' Significantly, however, it was the Israeli Minister of Foreign Affairs, Shimon Peres, and the PLO spokesman on foreign policy, Mahmud Abbas, who actually signed the Declaration documents. The ceremony was concluded by an embarrassed, but highly symbolic handshake between Arafat and Rabin. Support for the Oslo Accords had grown steadily in the Occupied Territories in the two weeks since the PLO-Israeli agreement had been made public and the day of the signing was marked by massive celebrations throughout the West Bank and the Gaza Strip. Detecting the shift, and fearful of its marginalization, Hamas revealed once again its pragmatic streak. While stressing its continued opposition to the Accords, it acknowledged that a new reality had been created which it would be foolish for it to ignore. It also agreed with Fatah that their respective demonstrations in favour of and in opposition to the Accords should be allowed to pass without interference. Contrary to the fears of Palestinians there were few reports of clashes between the two sides. Nevertheless, on the eve of the Washington ceremony Hamas sent a warning signal to the PLO and Israel when its gunmen ambushed and killed three Israeli soldiers on the edge of Gaza city; while in Beirut eight people were killed when units of the Lebanese army fired on a Hezbollah demonstration protesting against the PLO-Israeli agreement.

There were immediate and positive results from the signing of the Declaration of Principles for both Israel and the PLO. On 14 September Israeli Prime Minister Rabin was received in Morocco by King Hassan, in the first official visit by an Israeli Prime Minister to any Arab country other than Egypt. On the same day in Washington, Israeli and Jordanian representatives signed an agreement on an agenda for forthcoming negotiations between the two states. A number of issues of concern to Jordan were covered, including the return of Jordanian territory (adjoining the Dead Sea) occupied by Israel since the late 1960s; the fate of Palestinian refugees in Jordan; water rights; and a number of security issues. Jordan also committed itself not to threaten Israel by force and to work towards the removal of weapons of mass destruction from the Middle East. Meanwhile, Yasser Arafat was being feted by the media networks in the USA and enjoying the sort of rehabilitation in the eyes of the US public that would have been unthinkable only a few months previously. There was a developing awareness among all the parties who wished to see the peace process maintain its momentum that future progress depended on the ability of Arafat to demonstrate to his own constituency that the benefits of the deal outweighed its obvious shortcomings. Particularly important, PLO officials stressed, was the immediate commitment of the international community to the kind of substantial aid package that would be needed to revitalize the economy and to improve social conditions in the Occupied Territories. The Clinton Administration responded to these pleas by organizing a donors' conference in Washington that secured promises of $23,000m. in emergency aid for the West Bank and Gaza over the following five years; the EU and the USA pledged $600m. and $500m. respectively.

PLO LEADERSHIP CRISIS

Securing promises of substantial financial aid was an important fillip for the PLO Chairman in managing the scepticism with which the Oslo Accords were still regarded within PLO circles. In mid-October the PLO's Central Council met in Tunis to debate the Accords. The boycotting of the meeting by the Popular and Democratic Fronts (for the Liberation of Palestine) and the other opposition groups ensured that the ratification of the Accords was passed by a bigger majority (63 votes to 8 with 11 abstentions) than might have been expected. Yet, despite the margin of the victory, the Central Council session and subsequent meetings in Tunis were not the triumph that Arafat loyalists claimed. Delegates complained that there was little substantive discussion of the Accords and no attempt to map out a coherent negotiating strategy in the forthcoming talks with Israel over their implementation. Moreover, Arafat's autocratic handling of the meetings revived fears that the PLO Chairman lacked the requisite political skills to resist Israeli pressure to make further concessions, or for that matter to transform the Palestinian struggle from one of national liberation to one of nation building. Haider Abdel Shafei, the erstwhile chief Palestinian negotiator in the peace process, signalled his own lack of faith in the ability and motives of the PLO leadership by announcing his resignation from his post. The lack of confidence in the political leadership extended to the Damascus-based opposition, in particular to the PFLP and DFLP, which were widely criticized for boycotting the Tunis meetings and for their preference for sloganeering rather than establishing an alternative programme to the autonomy proposals. It also appeared increasingly obvious that the secular opposition was being outflanked and outmanoeuvred by Hamas. After the rejectionist PLO factions had announced their intentions to boycott a proposed Palestinian reconciliation conference in the Yemeni capital, San'a, Hamas informed Arafat that it would be attending. Behind the Islamic movement's contradictory pronouncements on its intended relationship with the new Palestinian authority (in contrast to the Popular and Democratic Fronts which insisted that they would have no dealings with the new autonomous Palestinian institutions) many observers claimed to detect a bid by Hamas to posit itself as the only credible opposition to the Arafat wing of the PLO.

FURTHER NEGOTIATIONS

Israeli-Palestinian negotiations on the implementation of the first stages of the Declaration of Principles began in Cairo and the Red Sea resort of Taba on 13 October. It quickly emerged during the first round of talks that there were several potentially serious obstacles to be overcome. Firstly, the Israeli and Palestinian delegations had widely differing definitions of what constituted the geographical area referred to as Jericho. According to the chief Palestinian negotiator, Nabil Sha'ath, Jericho referred to the old British Mandate Administrative Area comprising some 390 sq km and currently encompassing a number of Israeli settlements, as well as Arab villages. According to his Israeli counterpart, Gen. Amnon Shahak, the area in question was Jericho limited to its present municipal boundaries of a mere 25 sq km. More emotively, the two sides failed to agree on a timetable for the release of the estimated 11,000 Palestinian political prisoners in Israeli prisons. For the Palestinian side a comprehensive release of Palestinian prisoners was crucial to the maintenance of any degree of popular support for the autonomy plan. However, its request that Israel should draw up a timetable for release bore little fruit. Six hundred and seventeen prisoners were released on 25 October as a confidence-building measure. However, the majority of these were Fatah loyalists, leading one of the Palestinian negotiators to remark that they were 'trying to make peace between Palestinians and Israelis, not between Israel and a faction of the PLO'. Israel responded by saying that it would wait until the Palestinian police force was in place before releasing the majority of the detainees. Shortly afterwards it bowed to right-wing pressure and ended nearly all releases. The moratorium provoked one prominent Palestinian, Ziyad Abu Zayad, to tender his resignation from the negotiating team. The issue of border security proved just as intractable. From Israel's point of view this was its most sensitive domestic concern and, as such, the one area of the autonomy negotiations where it was least likely to compromise. On 1 November the Israeli delegation submitted proposals on security and the withdrawal of troops from the self-governing enclaves of Gaza and Jericho. These envisaged not so much the withdrawal of troops from Gaza as their redeployment in buffer zones around the Gaza Strip's Jewish settlements. They also proposed the retention of 20 checkpoints along the 1967 border to ensure the security of soldiers and settlers, and Israeli control over crossing points into and out of the autonomous enclaves. The Israeli proposals were condemned as unacceptable by Sha'ath, who withdrew the Palestinian delegation from the negotiations; it only returned after the Israeli delegation agreed

to revise its plans for the redeployment of the IDF in Gaza. Palestinian critics of the autonomy proposals commented that this early dispute over security went to the core of their dissatisfaction with the Declaration of Principles, namely its studied refusal to address the status of Jewish settlements. 'If Israelis and Palestinians can't agree that the settlements are illegal entities on our land,' commented one Gazan economist, 'then we are saying that in the Occupied Territories there are *de facto* two separate entities and that these are somehow equivalent. They are both legal or legitimate presences'. An inescapable corollary of this failure to define the status of the settlements was implicit acceptance of the long-held Israeli view that the West Bank and Gaza were not so much occupied territories as disputed ones.

VIOLENCE CONTINUES

Hopes that the signing of the Declaration of Principles would lead to a reduction in violent incidents in Gaza and the West Bank were also frustrated. In Gaza the impending transfer of power to a PLO authority gave rise to a secret feud within Fatah that claimed the lives of three top figures in the Organization, including that of As'ad Saftawi, a co-founder of the Fatah movement and its leading activist in Gaza. At the same time the IDF maintained its policy of pursuing wanted activists, killing and arresting gunmen of all political factions, including those identified as Fatah loyalists. Protests from the Palestinian negotiators that the targeting of activists was a violation of the spirit of the newly signed Accords failed to end the operations of Israeli undercover units. The killing of Hamas's senior military leader in Gaza in November gave rise to a massive increase in confrontations which were reignited two weeks later when a leading Fatah hawk, Ahmad Abu Rish, was shot dead by an Israeli undercover unit in Khan Yunis. Only a few days before his killing Abu Rish had received a much publicized amnesty from the Israeli authorities for obeying an Arafat directive and surrendering his weapon. His colleagues subsequently announced that they would resume their military operations unless Israel stopped pursuing wanted activists. Hamas, which was the principal target of the IDF's operations in Gaza, had never shown any sign of scaling down its attacks on Israeli targets. Despite the deaths and arrests of scores of its activists it continued to demonstrate that it was by far the most effective Palestinian military force in the Occupied Territories. Seemingly impervious to penetration by the Israeli security services, it was able to inflict regular casualties on both soldiers and settlers. Indeed, the killing of Jewish settlers by Palestinian gunmen during the autumn of 1993 produced fierce right-wing reprisals that escalated with every passing incident. Arguably more opposed to their Government's agreement with the PLO than the Islamists of Hamas, the settlers' desire to avenge attacks on their own community became intertwined with a desire to derail the negotiation process. Such was the scale of the assaults on Palestinian targets that Israeli newspapers started to refer to a 'Jewish *intifada*'. Right-wing spokesmen hinted darkly that as long as the twin provocations of Palestinian violence and government talks with the PLO existed, there was every likelihood of the re-emergence of the kind of settler underground movement that had operated during the late 1970s and early 1980s. At a nationalist rally in Jerusalem, settlers were urged to 'rise up against this government of iniquity, against the evil ruling over us', and were told that 'these are not days of peace but of war'. The warnings proved to be prophetic. In mid-December, after two settlers were killed in an attack by Hamas fighters near Hebron, Israeli gunmen shot dead three young Palestinian workers in retaliation.

CRISIS WITHIN FATAH

The cycle of violence made the prospect of an agreement on withdrawal from Gaza and Jericho by the 13 December deadline (as set down in the Declaration of Principles) increasingly unlikely. The main obstacles remained security and the size of the Jericho enclave. At a joint press conference in Cairo on 12 December, the Israeli and Palestinian negotiators announced their failure to meet the deadline. Rabin complained that the PLO Chairman 'lacked the inner strength' to reach an agreement, while the Israeli Chief of Staff, Gen. Ehud Barak, complained that it was unlikely that the IDF would hand over Gaza to the Palestinians as long as the PLO seemed unable to halt the violence there. Unlike Rabin, who appeared unperturbed by the delay and made a point of stating that the timetable laid out in the Declaration of Principles was not a rigid one, the PLO Chairman was visibly upset. And not without good reason. Failure to meet the deadline had further undermined dwindling support for the peace process—in the student council elections at Bir Zeit University, long regarded as a good indicator of Palestinian public opinion, Fatah had lost control of the student body to a coalition of rejectionist groups—and was an undoubted setback for the beleaguered Chairman. While he did receive grudging recognition for his refusal to accept Israel's proposals for the redeployment of the IDF to protect Jewish settlements in the Gaza Strip, this was small comfort when compared with the renewed chorus of criticism of the style and substance of his leadership. Calls for a clearer negotiating strategy and the democratization of the PLO were too loud to be ignored and compelled the PLO leader to accept demands for a dialogue with the nationalist opposition. Yet for some Fatah elements in Gaza patience with the PLO leadership had clearly run out. At the end of December three senior Fatah members resigned their posts in protest at the 'cronyism and favouritism' that had characterized political advancement in the Occupied Territories. They were articulating a concern of many Palestinians from within the Occupied Territories: that local cadres belonging to the *intifada* generation of activists were being marginalized by the imposition of political appointees from outside the Occupied Territories, and by 'salon spokesmen', with little experience of activism, from within. These were not new criticisms, but such a public airing of them at such a sensitive time pointed to an ever deepening crisis within the Fatah movement.

PLO RELATIONS WITH JORDAN

The PLO Chairman also had to contend with a crisis in the Organization's relationship with Jordan. While the PLO and Israel had been struggling to overcome their differences on the autonomy accords, Israel and Jordan had been making swift progress in their own talks in Washington. The claim, by an Israeli minister, that everything with Jordan 'is tied up and signed' hardly pleased the PLO leader. There was also strong annoyance with Jordan for signing a memorandum with Israel that allowed the opening of branches of Jordanian banks in the Occupied Territories during the interim period. According to the PLO, Jordan should have waited to sign an agreement with the new Palestinian authority, and by not doing so it had undermined Palestinian attempts to secure practical acknowledgement of Palestinian sovereignty. As a result, Arafat refused to sign an agreement that would have allowed Jordan's Central Bank to regulate monetary policies in the Occupied Territories during the interim period. The deadlock was finally broken in mid-January 1994 after a strong attack by the Jordanian monarch on the PLO's delaying tactics finally persuaded Arafat to dispatch Farouk Kaddoumi to Amman to sign an economic agreement. This allowed for the reopening of 20 branches of Jordanian banks closed in 1967 and confirmed the use of the Jordanian dinar in the Occupied Territories. The banks would be supervised by the Central Bank of Jordan until a Palestinian Central Bank was established.

SYRIAN REACTION

Syria, meanwhile, continued to smart at the perfidy of the Oslo Accords and at Jordan's apparently fruitful negotiations with Israel. King Hussein assured the Syrian leader that Jordan would not sign a separate deal with Israel, despite pressure to do so from Rabin and President Clinton of the USA. Nevertheless the feeling in Damascus remained one of perceived betrayal and injured pride, Syria regarding itself as the standard-bearer of Arab unity while all around the Arab world drifted into unprincipled accommodation with Israel. The USA's concern that Syrian isolation threatened to unbalance the peace process led to a summit meeting between the US and Syrian Presidents in Geneva, Switzerland, in January 1994. Assad stressed to Clinton that Syria could not consider a separate peace deal with Israel, and that he would not entertain a normalization of relations with Israel until Israel had committed itself to full withdrawal from the Golan Heights. Assad did, however, confirm that peace with Israel was Syria's goal and intimated that,

in return for an Israeli withdrawal from south Lebanon, the Syrian army would disarm Hezbollah. Fearing that the Clinton-Assad summit meeting was a dangerous step towards the rehabilitation of the Syrian President and a prelude to US pressure on Israel to make concessions over the Golan Heights, representatives of the Jewish settler movement delivered a letter of protest to the US Embassy in Tel-Aviv stating that any US interference would be harmful to the peace process. Despite claims that 90% of Israelis were opposed to withdrawal from the Golan Heights, a radio opinion poll revealed that nearly one-half of the 12,000 Israeli settlers there had considered moving back to the pre-1967 borders of Israel. Several of the more dovish members of the Israeli Cabinet, including the Deputy Minister of Foreign Affairs, Yosi Beilin, used the occasion of the Clinton-Assad meeting to concede that, given the proper security guarantees, Israel would have to withdraw from the Golan Heights. Rabin distanced himself from such remarks, preferring to allude to withdrawal in the Golan Heights rather than from the Golan Heights. Interestingly, however, the Israeli Prime Minister hinted at greater Israeli flexibility with the assessment that the 'extent of the withdrawal will be as the extent of the peace'.

RENEWED DISCUSSIONS

Yasser Arafat and the Israeli Minister of Foreign Affairs, Shimon Peres, met in Davos, Switzerland, in January 1994 for talks aimed at resolving the differences that were preventing the signing of an agreement on implementation of the Gaza-Jericho component of the Declaration of Principles. Sufficient progress was made for a resumption of talks in Cairo, Egypt, on 6 February. After three days of intense discussion it was announced that agreement had been reached on most of the issues that had been dividing the two sides. On the question of the control of border crossings between the autonomous zones and neighbouring states, it was agreed that Israel would maintain military control and have a veto over Palestinian visitors. The latter would be allowed to stay in Gaza and Jericho for a maximum period of four months only and would have to apply to the Israeli authorities for any extension of that time. The Palestinian presence at the borders was to be limited to flags, entry stamps, guards and immigration officials, although Israel acknowledged that the searching of Palestinian visitors would be largely a Palestinian responsibility. It was also agreed that the territory of Gaza would be divided into three zones; Israeli settlements and the Egyptian border area, which were to remain under Israeli control; a second area, encompassing the perimeter of the Israeli settlements and access roads, to be jointly patrolled; and the rest of the Gaza Strip, which was to be transferred to the new Palestinian authority. There was no resolution of the dispute over the precise size of the Jericho enclave, but Palestinian officials maintained that the 'size of Jericho will not be a problem in itself'.

PALESTINIAN REACTION

The agreement reached in Cairo was widely regarded as Palestinian capitulation to Israel's conception of what shape the interim autonomy period should take. In Damascus the 10 Palestinian rejectionist factions, grouped under the umbrella of the newly formed Alliance of Palestinian Forces (APF), condemned the new security arrangements and insisted that they would refuse to co-operate with the PLO or take part in elections scheduled for July 1994. The APF announced the formation of a new central council to rival that of the PLO and pledged an escalation of the *intifada*. The decision of the Palestinian rejectionists, together with continued Fatah infighting, was further evidence of the painful process of disintegration and realignment that was steadily transforming the face of Palestinian politics. In Gaza, which continued to be affected by both inter-Palestinian violence and Israeli–Palestinian clashes, there were reports that huge numbers of arms were being stockpiled for the purpose of settling political differences once the Israeli forces withdrew. The visibility and availability of weapons led to allegations that the IDF was encouraging future disorder in Gaza by ignoring the organized gun-running to the Strip.

THE HEBRON MASSACRE

The peace process suffered a dramatic setback on 25 February 1994 when Baruch Goldstein, an American-born adherent of the extremist Kach movement and resident of Kiryat Arba, carried out an armed attack on Palestinian worshippers in the Ibrahim Mosque in the centre of Hebron. Goldstein entered the mosque during early morning Ramadan prayers and sprayed the congregation with a hail of automatic gunfire. Twenty-nine people died before worshippers managed to overpower and kill their attacker. Palestinian fury at the massacre was heightened by reports that Israeli soldiers on duty at the mosque had contributed to the atrocity by failing to intercept Goldstein and by barring the doors of the mosque to fleeing worshippers. As news of the massacre spread, violent protests erupted throughout the Occupied Territories and among Arab communities inside Israel; a further 33 Palestinians were killed in the eight days following the massacre despite widespread curfews and massive troop deployment. The massacre and its bloody aftermath was roundly denounced in the Arab world. The Jordanian, Syrian and Lebanese Governments declared the suspension of their participation in the peace process. The Rabin Government responded to the events in Hebron by announcing its intention to set up a commission of inquiry and ordering the detention of a handful of known settler extremists. A ban was also declared on the Kach organization and its offshoot, Kahane Lives. These measures failed to mollify Palestinians, who asserted that only the disarming of settlers and the dismantling of the settlements could guarantee Palestinian security in the Occupied Territories. PLO spokesmen called for a revision of the Declaration of Principles to allow immediate discussion of the future of Israeli settlements and for the dispatch of an international protection force to the Occupied Territories, a suggestion that was endorsed by Arab states and the UN Secretary-General, but dismissed as 'neither particularly helpful or useful' by the USA. Several prominent PLO figures stated publicly that the removal of 400 or so militant settlers from the heart of Hebron was the *sine qua non* of the PLO's decision to restart talks with Israel. Both Hamas and Islamic Jihad vowed to take revenge for the Hebron massacre, a predictable response, but one that only added to the burden of pressure on the PLO leader. The massacre placed Arafat in a delicate position. Although it was believed that Hebron would allow the PLO Chairman to exact concessions from Israel in return for an early end to the Organization's suspension of participation in the autonomy negotiations, it was unlikely that Rabin would entertain the PLO's demands for immediate action against core settler interests. The Labour Government had little ideological affinity with 'hardline' settlers. However, Rabin recognized that they were valuable bargaining chips and that it would be a mistake to cash them in before the final status negotiations. Moreover, it was clear to Arafat that the best hope to bolster his own standing and to regain support for the peace process lay in demonstrating the benefits of the Oslo Accords by securing an early Israeli withdrawal from Gaza and Jericho. Any residual willingness of the PLO Chairman to hold out for Israeli concessions was also undermined by Syrian and Jordanian assurances to the USA that their withdrawal from the peace talks with Israel was only temporary. The somewhat surprising stance of the Syrian Government was explained by its Minister of Foreign Affairs as a response to the PLO's 'isolationist' approach and its refusal to co-ordinate its position with the front-line Arab states. But it was also clear that the USA had lobbied hard in Damascus for a Syrian return to the negotiating table, primarily as a means of putting pressure on the PLO to end its boycott of the talks. The USA similarly promised Jordan that it would lift the naval blockade of the Jordanian port of Aqaba (in place since the Iraqi invasion of Kuwait) as a reward for Amman's early resumption of talks with Israel. In the mean time, the USA maintained its pro-Israel diplomacy at the UN. US Ambassador Albright effectively delayed a vote on Resolution 904, which condemned the Hebron massacre and urged protection for Palestinians in the Occupied Territories, because the USA objected to the inclusion of paragraphs describing Jerusalem and the territories seized in 1967 as 'occupied Palestinian territory'. Resolution 904 was finally adopted by the Security Council on 10 March 1994, with the USA abstaining on two of its preambular paragraphs referring to occupied Palestinian territory. Albright justified the USA's abstentions on the ground that it did not wish to prejudice the course of the final status negotiations agreed upon in the Declaration of Principles. Nevertheless, Nasir el-Kidwa, the Palestinian observer at the UN, remarked that the USA's decision marked a disturbing departure from early US assurances that it regarded all of the 1967 territories as occupied. There was further Palestinian disappointment with Resolution 904's demand for their protection in the Occupied Territories. Instead of a UN armed force, as favoured by the PLO, the UN Security Council – again acting under US pressure – voted for a temporary observer force to be dispatched to Hebron. It was agreed that the force would not be under the control of the UN and that its mode of operations would be decided through negotiation between Israel and the PLO within the framework of the Declaration of Principles. Israel eventually agreed to the presence of 160 lightly armed, mainly Norwegian, observers operating under ultimate Israeli control. Their rather limited remit was 'to monitor Palestinian safety' and to aid the return of Hebron to 'normal life'.

RETALIATION BY HAMAS

By the beginning of April 1994 the PLO had agreed to resume negotiations with Israel despite the failure to secure the reassurances on settlements that PLO leaders had initially demanded. Its decision was perceived negatively by many Palestinians in the Occupied Territories, where dwindling goodwill towards the Oslo process was undergoing further erosion as a result of IDF security operations. Several people were killed in Hebron and a number of houses were destroyed by rocket fire in an army attempt to flush out Hamas gunmen. At the end of March six members of a pro-Arafat Fatah security team were shot dead in an ambush in Gaza. The latter incident forced an apology by the IDF and underlined a belief shared by many in the Israeli political establishment that urgent steps would have to be taken to reinforce Arafat's position and guarantee the viability of the peace process. The return of 47 Palestinian deportees, most of them senior PLO figures, was widely welcomed in the Occupied Territories. More importantly, the IDF began to redeploy its forces in response to news from Egypt that an agreement had been reached on the final issues dividing Israel and the PLO over the implementation of autonomy in the Gaza Strip and Jericho. However, even as the Oslo Accords were on the verge of being translated into reality, there came a deadly reminder of the fragility of that process. On 6 April 1994 a car bomb in the Israeli town of Afula killed seven Israelis and maimed scores of others, many of them schoolchildren. A week later five more people were killed in a similar outrage in Hadera. Hamas claimed responsibility for both attacks and claimed that they were in response to the Hebron massacre. Some 300 Islamic activists were rounded up after the bombings and the Occupied Territories were sealed off. The Hamas spokesman in Amman said his Organization would halt attacks on civilians in return for an end to the Israeli offensive. He also promised that Hamas would support a peace agreement with Israel in return for an Israeli withdrawal from all of the Palestinian territory occupied in 1967. The Hamas offer received no official reply from Israel except an appeal to Jordan to close down Hamas's offices on its territory. Israel was also highly critical of an agreement reached in Gaza between Hamas and Fatah that had been precipitated by an outbreak of armed clashes between the two factions. Both sides agreed to a month-long moratorium on the killing of collaborators and 'an end to violence in Palestinian society'. Commenting on Israel's criticism of its talks with Hamas, a Fatah spokesman rejoined that Fatah's dealings with Hamas to secure order in the Gaza Strip would be on the PLO's terms and not Rabin's. He added that 'Our decision to co-operate with Hamas is an internal Palestinian issue and does not concern any other side. Fatah and Hamas are in the same boat and we will not allow anyone to sink it.'

AUTONOMY IN GAZA AND JERICHO

Against a backdrop of weary anticipation and lawless confusion in Gaza, Israeli and Palestinian officials met in Cairo on 4 May 1994 for a signing ceremony to seal the successful conclusion of eight months of troubled talks on the implementation of an autonomy agreement for Gaza and Jericho. Yet, in ironic accordance with the problems that had bedevilled the negotiations from the start, the dignified proceedings turned to high farce when Arafat refused to sign one of the documents pertaining to the size of the Jericho enclave. A highly embarrassing moment for the assembled dignitaries and the Egyptian President was eventually resolved by a hasty adjournment and an agreement that Arafat would annotate the offending document with a comment to the effect that it was awaiting final agreement. On returning to Israel an outraged Rabin insinuated that the problems at the Cairo ceremony were symptomatic of the PLO Chairman's inability to provide leadership. Arafat was also reproached by members of the PLO Executive Committee for having failed to discuss the agreement about to be concluded with Israel at a meeting held just a few days before the Cairo signing. Many PLO executive members stayed away from Cairo in protest at Arafat's autocracy, while within the Occupied Territories deepening reservations over the style of Arafat's leadership and the substance of the agreement reached with Israel meant that the PLO Chairman experienced great difficulty in trying to persuade political figures to take seats on the 24-member Palestinian Autonomy Council, the body designed to oversee the implementation of the autonomy agreement. Nevertheless, the signing of the agreement in Cairo resulted in rapid change in Gaza and Jericho. The IDF hastened its withdrawal from centres of Palestinian population, and on 10 May the first contingent of the Palestinian police force arrived in Gaza. A further 400 arrived in Jericho a few days later. Israel had also announced the imminent release of 5,000 Palestinian detainees. On 13 May and 17 May, in Jericho and Gaza respectively, the IDF handed over its positions to the commanders of the Palestinian forces in simple ceremonies. The Chief of Palestinian Police Forces told crowds in Gaza that they were witnessing 'a historic day for the Palestinian people, the first step on the way to independence.' The following day, in the early hours of the morning, Israel evacuated its last position in Gaza city. Bitter memories of the occupation meant that even at this final hour there would be no dignity in the Israeli withdrawal. The departing troops left under a cloud of tear-gas and a shower of rocks and bottles, while tens of Palestinian gunmen joined members of the Palestinian police force in a deafening salute to the beginning of a somewhat different reality.

Finalization of the agreement on autonomy for Gaza and Jericho was met with scorn in Syria, where Arafat was widely perceived as having allowed the Palestinian national movement to be humiliated by Israel. Syria refused an invitation to attend the Cairo ceremony and the state-controlled media commented that, 'There can be no middle way. There can be no compromise over land and peace. Comprehensive peace in the Middle East depends on the return of all occupied land.' Syria's unwavering commitment to these principles was regarded by the USA as the principal obstacle to achieving a wider Middle East settlement. The US Secretary of State, Warren Christopher, was dispatched to the Middle East at the end of April and again in May in an attempt to reconcile the Syrian and Israeli positions. His mission proved largely fruitless. Rabin stated that he would entertain no greater compromise than a promise to dismantle some of the settlements on the Golan Heights and to make a phased withdrawal, over a number of years, from some areas of the Heights. This was unacceptable to President Assad, who insisted that a peace agreement had to be preceded by a total Israeli withdrawal from occupied Syrian territory accomplished within a one- to two-year period. Plans for a further visit by the US Secretary of State in June were abandoned after Rabin confirmed that negotiations with Syria were totally deadlocked and Syria reiterated that there was little purpose in further dialogue until Israel made a public pledge that its withdrawal from the Golan Heights would be total. Controversial Israeli military operations in Lebanon during May and June made it even less likely that Syria would soften its stance. On 22 May Mustafa ad-Dirani, a leader of the radical Iranian-backed Faithful Resistance Organization, was kidnapped by Israeli forces from the Beka'a valley. The raid, reminiscent of the abduction of Sheikh Obeid in 1989, was justified on the ground that ad-Dirani had information about the missing Israeli navigator, Ron Arad, who had been shot down over Lebanon in 1986. Ten days after ad-Dirani had been seized, Israeli aircraft were once again in action over Lebanon, attacking a Hezbollah

training camp in the Beka'a valley and killing, according to Israeli sources, 36 Hezbollah fighters and wounding more than one hundred. The attack was of questionable political value and it was regarded as an indication of a shift to the right in the governing Israeli Labour party.

In Gaza and Jericho there was widespread jubilation at the departure of Israeli troops and an end to the curfews and restrictions that had been part of daily existence during the years of the *intifada*. Israel's own relief at being rid of the security problem of Gaza was marred, only two days after the withdrawal, when two Israeli soldiers were shot dead by Islamic Jihad gunmen near the Erez border crossing to Israel. Significantly, the IDF did not pursue the gunmen into Palestinian-controlled territory, and while the PLO assured Israel that it would try to curb such actions, it insisted that the disarming of Palestinian groups could only take place within the framework of broad factional agreement. Nevertheless, the agreed joint patrols by Israeli and Palestinian security forces along the demarcation lines of authority in Gaza and Jericho appeared to function in a spirit of comparative harmony. A far greater worry for Palestinians than security co-ordination with Israel, and one that was only briefly masked by the general euphoria, was the financial and administrative chaos in Gaza. The difficulty Arafat was experiencing in recruiting appointees to the new Palestinian Autonomy Council — to be composed of 15 personalities from inside the Occupied Territories and nine from the Palestinian diaspora — resulted in the 3,000-strong police force operating in a judicial and legal vacuum. This situation was aggravated by the absence of properly constituted structures to co-ordinate and implement administrative change. The extent of the financial crisis was epitomized by the fact that the new police force was having to subsist on munitions donated by the local population. High unemployment levels made matters worse. Israel had placed a limit of 23,000 on the number of Gazan workers it was prepared to allow into Israel and had sealed its border completely in response to the killings at the Erez checkpoint. Under pressure from Israeli farmers, Rabin had also reneged on an earlier decision to allow the importation of Gazan agricultural produce into Israel. Further trouble loomed for the nascent Palestinian authority in Gaza with the prospect of having to pay the estimated 7,000 employees of the previous Israeli civilian administration. With little prospect of revenue from tax collection from a population for whom tax avoidance had been seen until now as a patriotic as well as a personal imperative, there were desperate pleas from the PLO for international aid. Palestinian economists had estimated that Palestinian self-rule would require an annual budget of $240m., with a maximum of $127m. likely to be raised in tax revenues. First year start-up costs were likely to be in the region of $600m., leaving a huge budgetary deficit. Although $2,300m. had been promised to the Palestinians at the international donors' conference held in Washington in October 1993, the international community was reluctant to disburse funds until the Palestinians had established proper accounting procedures and clear project proposals. The PLO rejoined that without immediate funds to set up a basic administrative structure—which the donors were reluctant to subsidize—it would be impossible to meet the international requirements. Arafat expressed his personal fury at the implications of corruption and mismanagement and stated that he would not visit the autonomous regions to take charge of the transition until pledges of aid were forthcoming. The Israeli media appeared to take delight in the discomfort of the PLO leader and cited the financial wrangling as further evidence of his unredeemable political shortcomings. However, for once, Arafat's brinkmanship appeared to pay off. In a series of tense meetings in Paris, France, in June the donor countries agreed to the immediate release of $42m. in aid, with at least one-quarter of this sum going to fund the setting up of the Palestinian administration—without the *quid pro quo* of detailed accounting. They also agreed to take measures to make up the shortfall to meet the expected 1994 deficit. There were also positive developments in the West Bank and Gaza. By the end of June most of the 24 places on the Autonomy Council had been filled, mostly by Arafat loyalists, but also by several quasi-independents and members of Fida, the faction of the DFLP led by Abed Rabbo. In Gaza the Palestinian police force had won an assurance from Hamas that the killing of collaborators would stop; and in Damascus the ageing leader of the PFLP, George Habash, marked a considerable softening of his organization's position on the new Palestinian authority by instructing his supporters 'not to take a negative stance towards the institutions that offer services during the interim phase.'

ARAFAT VISITS GAZA

The easing of the PLO's financial worries, coupled with criticism of the PLO Chairman's apparent hesitation in taking control of the Palestinian self-rule areas, was answered with a commitment by Arafat to make his long-awaited visit to the newly autonomous enclaves. On 1 July 1994, with little advance warning, the PLO leader crossed from Egypt into Gaza to step foot on Palestinian soil for the first time in 25 years. His reception was more muted than might have been expected for a returning leader who had for so many years been an international symbol of the Palestinian cause. Yet large crowds did gather both in Gaza city and in Jabalia refugee camp, birthplace of the *intifada*, to hear Arafat's address. There was little of note in either speech beyond the repeated pleas for Palestinian unity — directed principally at the Islamic opposition — and an acknowledgement that there was little popular enthusiasm for the Oslo Accords. Arafat reassured his audience that the Gaza and Jericho enclaves were the stepping-stones to an independent Palestinian state with Jerusalem as its capital. Similar sentiments were voiced two days later in Jericho. When the PLO Chairman ended his four-day visit to meet with Rabin and Peres in Paris, France, his aides announced that he would soon be returning 'for good' and that Gaza, rather than Jericho, would be the home of the new Palestinian administration. Arafat's visit had raised more questions than it had answered. Despite the affection extended to him, Arafat's performances failed to convince anybody that he possessed the requisite political skills to tackle the shortcomings of the autonomy accords or to build on their openings. The presence of the PLO Chairman in Gaza and Jericho had as much symbolic resonance on the boulevards of Tel-Aviv as in the alley-ways of Gaza. The return of a personality who for more than two decades had been demonized by politicians and the media alike, was seized on by the Israeli right wing as a focus to rally opposition to the Oslo Accords. A demonstration in Jerusalem organized by the nationalist right to protest at Arafat's visit ended as something of an 'own goal' for the Likud when some 10,000 demonstrators left the main rally and ran amok in East Jerusalem. Scenes of settlers and their supporters not only attacking Palestinians and their property, but also fighting running battles with the Israeli security forces, were a severe embarrassment for the struggling Likud leader, Binyamin Netanyahu. Rabin lambasted the settlers as the Israeli equivalent of Hamas, while the Likud quietly reflected that they had lost an opportunity to garner the moderate support needed to obstruct the PLO-Israeli agreement. Rabin's own fortunes were fortified in July with news that the orthodox Shas party would be rejoining the Labour coalition, as would Ye'ud, a splinter group from the right-wing Tzomet Party. There was no such comfort for Arafat. Shortly after returning to Gaza, the PLO leader became embroiled in the most serious incident of the Strip's two-month-old autonomy. In the early morning of 17 July a clash occurred at the Erez checkpoint between Palestinian labourers and units of the IDF trying to check that they possessed the correct documentation for entry into Israel. Pent-up frustrations at the slowness of the process led to a full-scale riot, with the Palestinian workers burning down an Israeli bus depot and Israeli soldiers attempting to restore order with live ammunition. There then followed a prolonged gun battle between members of the Palestinian police force and soldiers of the IDF. Two Palestinians were killed in the clash and 75 were injured; 18 Israeli soldiers also suffered gun-shot wounds. The mutual recriminations that followed failed to obscure the underlying tensions that had given the incident an air of inevitability. Firstly, rather than easing the process by which Palestinian workers gained employment in Israel, the advent of autonomy merely added to it a further tier of administrative bureaucracy. Secondly, the Erez violence confirmed the fears of Palestinians that the security arrangements agreed in Cairo had created a kind of Gaza gulag. Finally, the entire autonomy process appeared to be doomed to failure unless something could be done to address the perilous state of the Gazan economy. 'What happened in Gaza today,' the Palestinian Minister of Justice, Furaih Abu Middain, commented 'was a battle for a loaf of bread.' The Israeli decision to seal off the Strip in response to the violence was condemned as incendiary by Palestinian sources and cast a further shadow over impending negotiations on the implementation of the next phase of the autonomy accords.

ISRAELI–JORDANIAN RELATIONS IMPROVE

The depressed mood that characterized Israeli–Palestinian relations was thrown into sharp relief by dramatic progress in Israel's bilateral talks with Jordan. On 9 July 1994 King Hussein announced to the Jordanian National Assembly that he was prepared to meet the Israeli Prime Minister, and on 18 July Jordanian and Israeli negotiators sat at a table straddling the Israel-Jordan border to take part in the first bilateral talks to be held in the Middle East itself. The decision of the Jordanian monarch to make such a highly symbolic concession to Israel was widely interpreted as an exercise in pragmatic self-interest. Anxious to maintain the momentum for a comprehensive peace settlement in the Middle East, the USA had offered appealing incentives to King Hussein to move Israeli–Jordanian relations to the centre of the peace process. Not least among these was US President Clinton's promise that his Government would work towards the waiving of Jordan's $900m. debt to the USA, provide military assistance to Jordan and seek to persuade Saudi Arabia and the Gulf states to end their economic and political boycott of the Hashemite regime. An announcement by Shimon Peres in mid-July acknowledging the Golan Heights to be Syrian territory was seen as Israel's contribution to the wider US plan of muting Syrian criticism of Jordan's effective *coup de grâce* to the dying beast of Arab unity. That Jordan refrained from signing a full peace treaty with Israel did not disguise the fact that the normalization of Israeli–Jordanian relations was close. In Washington on 25 July King Hussein and Itzhak Rabin formally ended the state of belligerency between their two nations in a ceremony that underlined not only the understanding that had been a feature of Israeli–Jordanian relations for many years, but also the personal warmth that existed between King Hussein and Rabin, a quality that was visibly absent from relations between the Israeli Prime Minister and the PLO Chairman. With the exception of the extreme right-wing fringe of Israeli politics, the country met the formal end of the state of war with Jordan with general acclaim, and a feeling that the key issues of contention with Jordan, the sharing of water resources and the return of a small area of Jordanian territory seized by Israel in the late 1960s, could be easily resolved. Jordan's citizens were less sanguine. Fundamentalist and left-wing groups were critical of the *rapprochement*, while the majority of the population saw the overtures to Israel as the inevitable price that had to be paid if Jordan was to solve the problem it had created for itself in the aftermath of Iraq's invasion of Kuwait in 1990. Palestinian reaction, in contrast, was sharply critical. There were strong suspicions that Israel, the USA and Jordan were engaged in a concerted effort to isolate the PLO and prepare for a reassertion of Hashemite control over the West Bank, leaving the PLO Chairman as 'mayor of Gaza.' There was particular concern at the inclusion in the document signed by King Hussein and Itzhak Rabin in Washington of a paragraph acknowledging Jordan's 'special role' as guardian of the Muslim holy sites in Jerusalem. Assurances from King Hussein that there was no contradiction between Jordan reaching an understanding over guardianship of religious sites in East Jerusalem and Palestinian political sovereignty, failed to convince the PLO leadership. On 20 July the PLO retaliated against Jordan's perceived treachery by banning the sale and distribution of the pro-Jordanian daily, *An-Nahar*, in the autonomous enclaves. Arafat reportedly justified the decision on the ground that he could not 'tolerate any undermining of Palestinian national interest in the name of press freedom.' The irony of a Palestinian authority restricting Palestinian freedom of speech was not lost on anyone, least of all Israel. The Arab world responded to both the Israeli-Jordanian agreement and the PLO's quarrel with Jordan with a large measure of indifference, damning evidence, if such was still needed, that the Arab world could not muster sufficient enthusiasm even to pay lip-service to the notion of Arab solidarity. Of the region's principal powers, only Syria condemned Jordan's agreement with Israel, in a statement that was made much easier by an earlier refutation, by Rabin, of Shimon Peres' comment that Israel regarded the Golan Heights as Syrian territory.

ISRAELI-JORDANIAN PEACE TREATY

Israel's breakthrough in its relations with Jordan was succeeded by further diplomatic and political gains. On 1 September 1994 Morocco became only the second Arab nation to establish diplomatic ties with the Jewish state, while Tunisia announced that it would shortly be establishing its own links with Israel via the Belgian embassy in Tel-Aviv. At the end of the month the six GCC member states responded to US urgings and signalled the formal end of their long-standing economic boycott of companies trading with Israel. Meanwhile Jordanian and Israeli negotiators had reached agreement on outstanding disputes over territory and water. Israel acceded to the immediate diversion of 50 cu m from the Sea of Galilee to meet Jordanian water needs and, in order to aid the construction of flood reservoirs on the Rivers Jordan and Yarmouk, agreed to supply a further 50 cu m. The Israeli Government also recognized Jordanian sovereignty over contested border lands in return for a Jordanian commitment to lease back the territory to Israel. President Assad of Syria scorned this commitment as 'blasphemous', but despite his opposition and the resistance of Jordan's Islamic and leftist parties to the normalization of relations with their historic foe, King Hussein duly sealed the agreement with Israel on 26 October by signing a peace treaty with Itzhak Rabin in the presence of US President Clinton. Israel and Jordan opened their respective embassies in Amman and Tel-Aviv less than two months later. Peace with Jordan was broadly welcomed in Israel and met with overwhelming approval in the Knesset; only the three deputies of the right-wing Moledet party voted against ratification of the peace treaty with Jordan, with a handful of Likud 'diehards' abstaining. Equally indicative of Israel's rapidly improving relations with the Arab world was the presence of a large Israeli delegation at a regional economic summit meeting in Casablanca, Morocco, at the end of October. The meeting attracted 2,000 business and political leaders from the Arab world and their main Western trading partners and was designed to further the peace process by encouraging economic co-operation. Although the summit concluded with few substantive proposals, Israel's high-profile presence was celebrated at home as both a political and economic victory.

FURTHER DEADLOCK ON DECLARATION OF PRINCIPLES

The Palestinian reaction to the Israeli-Jordanian peace treaty was, predictably, less welcoming. Yasser Arafat was not invited to the signing ceremony, and unallayed Palestinian suspicions regarding Hashemite designs on Jerusalem led to the burning of King Hussein's portrait in demonstrations on the West Bank. It was also feared that, having achieved peace with Jordan, the Israeli Government would feel under less pressure to pursue negotiations with Arafat's Palestinian National Authority (PNA) on the implementation of the Declaration of Principles. Indeed, by the autumn of 1994 Israeli-Palestinian negotiations were effectively deadlocked. An early empowerment agreement had been reached between the Israeli Government and the PNA at the end of August for the transfer of control in the fields of education, tourism, taxation, health and social welfare from the Israeli civil administration to the PNA. However, this limited agreement was already several months behind the deadline stipulated in the Declaration of Principles and did nothing to resolve the serious differences preventing progress on the substantive issues of the interim phase negotiations. In Cairo, Egypt, Israeli negotiators emphasized that there could be no progress on IDF redeployment in the West Bank until they were satisfied that the Palestinian authorities had demonstrated an ability to curb the anti-Oslo violence of Islamist militants and PLO rejectionists. There were further disputes over the function and composition of an elected PNA authority. Itzhak Rabin reiterated a strong preference for a 24-member executive council whose legislative powers would be subject to an Israeli veto. Publicly, at least, PNA representatives argued for a 100-seat assembly with full executive and legislative authority. Without

such a formula Arafat realized that it would be increasingly difficult either to stem the tide of Palestinian disaffection with the course of the peace process or gain legitimacy for the PNA. There was already a growing conviction that the Palestinian negotiating team was being outmanoeuvred by its Israeli counterparts, and being drawn into a situation in which Israel's ostensible security concerns dominated the negotiating agenda. According to Palestinian sceptics the 'security' issue served a dual purpose for Israel. First, it trapped the PNA in the role of Israeli gendarme and hence ensured continuing Palestinian divisions. Secondly, the failure to reach agreement on arrangements for the interim period allowed the Israeli Government to postpone a confrontation with Jewish settlers in the West Bank, while providing a breathing space to pursue the infrastructural development—road building and settlement expansion—on the West Bank and around Arab Jerusalem that would create the necessary 'facts' to prejudice the course and outcome of the final status negotiations.

The fragility of the peace process and the character of the PNA's relationship with Israel was emphasized by a series of violent incidents towards the end of 1994. In mid-October an Israeli soldier, Nachshon Waxman, was kidnapped by Hamas militants demanding the release of 500 of their jailed comrades. Although there was no evidence that Waxman was being detained in the Gaza Strip or, indeed, that his kidnappers came from there, Rabin stated publicly that he held Arafat and the PNA responsible for the soldier's safety. Under mounting Israeli pressure, Arafat ordered his security forces to detain hundreds of known Hamas activists. However, it soon emerged that Waxman was in fact being held on the West Bank, where he and three of his captors died in a clumsily unsuccessful rescue operation by the IDF. Shortly after Waxman's killing Hamas struck again. Twenty-two Israelis were killed and tens were injured in the suicide bombing of a crowded Tel-Aviv bus. Rabin immediately ordered the sealing of the Gaza Strip and the West Bank, and, while he was more circumspect about blaming Arafat directly for the atrocity, he did urge the PNA to crush its Islamist opponents. He added that Israel reserved the right to intervene militarily in the Gaza Strip and on 2 November a leading member of Islamic Jihad in Gaza, Hani Abed, was blown up in his booby-trapped car. The killing bore all the hallmarks of an Israeli undercover operation and happened on the same day that Rabin stated that, while he was extending a hand of peace to Jordan, the other was 'pulling the trigger to hit the terrorists of Hamas and Islamic Jihad'. Jihad took revenge 10 days later with a suicide attack on an IDF checkpoint in Gaza that left three Israeli soldiers dead and several injured. Some 200 Jihad sympathizers were arrested by the Palestinian police in the aftermath of the attack, while Rabin again harangued the PLO Chairman about his duty to 'dry out the swamp of terrorism in Gaza'. There was little doubt that this ugly cycle of violence severely undermined the PNA. The forces of militant Islam gained considerable sympathy from being perceived as victims of Arafat's heavy-handedness in the same way as the readiness with which Arafat was seen to be doing Rabin's bidding served to increase the alienation of those ordinary Palestinians already frustrated at the absence of a tangible 'peace dividend'. The presence of scores of Hamas and Islamic Jihad cadres in Palestinian prisons, together with the swelling ranks of the various Palestinian security forces, also spelt the end of the delicate *modus vivendi* which the PNA had tried to construct with the Islamist opposition.

SPECULATION OVER THE GOLAN HEIGHTS

At various times during the second half of 1994 prominent members of the Israeli Cabinet hinted that Israel was prepared to make more extensive concessions regarding the Golan Heights than had hitherto been entertained by the Labour-led coalition. However, the Israeli Prime Minister reiterated that any Israeli withdrawal from the Heights would be both gradual and modest. The apparent disunity within the Israeli Government on policy towards Syria was widely interpreted as a ploy to test domestic opinion on territorial compromise, and to entice Syria into making concessions. If true, there was little evidence to suggest that President Assad was about to soften his own position. Despite the shuttle diplomacy of US Secretary of State Warren Christopher and face-to-face meetings in Washington between the Israeli and Syrian ambassadors to the USA, it was conceded that 'wide differences' still existed between the two Governments and official bilateral talks remained suspended. Rumour did, however, spur the leaders of the 13,000 Israeli settlers on the Golan Heights into launching a vigorous anti-withdrawal campaign. In TV adverts and rallies up and down the country the settlers and their supporters denounced what they described as Rabin's treachery in reneging on his election promise to maintain an Israeli presence on the Golan Heights. Particularly disturbing for the Labour Prime Minister was the fact that the Golan settlers enjoyed the backing of a significant section of the Labour establishment—seven Labour deputies tabled a bill that would have effectively ruled out withdrawal from the Golan Heights by making any change in the region's status subject to a 65% approval rating in a referendum. Opinion polls conducted in September also revealed that only 40% of the electorate would support a 'partial' withdrawal from the Golan Heights, while 35% opposed any withdrawal at all. This apparent lack of support in Israel for any compromise with Syria, together with a resurgence in the popularity of the Likud, led well-placed Israeli sources to suggest that Rabin would be happy to place the Golan issue on hold until the 1996 elections. This view gained in currency after visits to Damascus by US President Clinton and Warren Christopher in October and December only resulted in an Israeli-Syrian agreement to restart talks on the understanding that they would be characterized as an 'exchange of ideas' rather than 'negotiations'.

INTER-PALESTINIAN CONFLICT

Arafat's relations with his Islamist opponents seriously deteriorated on 18 November when units of the Palestinian police fired on demonstrators as they left a Gaza City mosque. Twelve people died and 200 were injured, most of them Islamists, in the initial shootings and the gunfights which followed. Pro-and anti-Arafat rallies in the immediate aftermath of the killings, which were characterized by mutual threats and recriminations, kept the political atmosphere at boiling-point in the Gaza Strip. However, a realization that further confrontations could well tip Gaza into the abyss of civil war served eventually to cool tempers. The Palestinian police were prudently absent from the funeral marches of those killed on 18 November, while newspaper editors and political independents, most notably Haider Abdel Shafei, gave support to hastily convened mediation committees. Their cause was aided in no small degree by the refusal of many Fatah cadres in Gaza to engage in the kind of provocation of Hamas in which the more ardent Arafat supporters in the West Bank had indulged. Arafat's own attempts to exploit the crisis beyond his Gaza headquarters proved only partially successful. By stressing the connection between civil unrest in Gaza and the dire economic situation there, he was able to persuade a conference of international donors in Brussels to promise an immediate aid package of $125m. and a further $23m. for infrastructural projects. However, the PLO Chairman found it far more difficult to exploit the Gaza crisis to wring the concessions he and the PNA needed so urgently from Israel. Central to Arafat's and wider Palestinian unease were the continuing signals that the Israeli Prime Minister, in contrast to the more conciliatory voices in the Cabinet, was intent on revising some of the fundamental articles of the Declaration of Principles. Speaking in mid-December, Rabin suggested that rather than completing its full withdrawal from Palestinian population centres in the West Bank prior to elections to the PNA, as stipulated in the Declaration of Principles, the IDF should redeploy only temporarily for the duration of the elections. The alternative, according to Rabin, was 'protracted negotiations' on the two issues. Arafat rejoined that the redeployment of the IDF would need to be completed by the eve of the elections, while one of the chief Palestinian negotiators stated that for Israel 'to come up with formulas and versions that contradict the Oslo Accords' would be 'the quickest way to destroy the peace process'. Events in the Gaza Strip and continued wrangling over the interpretation of the Declaration of Principles were thrown into sharp relief by the award of the Nobel prize for Peace to Arafat, Rabin and the Israeli Minister of Foreign Affairs, Shimon Peres. As with many other awards, the decision of the Nobel committee had caused controversy when it was initially

announced, but at the award ceremony in December it appeared particularly premature.

EXPANSION OF SETTLEMENTS

The sense of foreboding surrounding Israeli-Palestinian negotiations intensified at the beginning of 1995. On 2 January four Palestinian policemen were killed on the outskirts of Gaza City by Israeli soldiers who claimed that they had mistaken them for 'armed militants'. Yet this, the most serious breakdown to date in co-ordination between the Israeli and Palestinian security forces, was largely overshadowed by another furore over Israeli settlements. It was triggered by a decision of the settlement council of Efrat to expand its settlement on land adjoining the Palestinian village of Al-Khader and some 2 km away from the settlement itself. As Arab villagers and Israeli sympathizers confronted the bulldozers, Palestinian leaders protested that the expansion violated the Declaration of Principles. The Israeli Cabinet eventually devised a compromise solution that 'froze' building on the initial site but allowed for the construction of new housing on lands next to Efrat. The compromise failed to assuage the anger of the PNA, but it was powerless to effect a reversal of this or other incidences of land confiscation and settlement building that had occurred on the West Bank since the signing of the Declaration of Principles. The USA made it clear that it would not intervene in a dispute which it regarded as a local matter, to be dealt with within the framework of the programme. Yet this provided little comfort for the opponents of Israel's settlement- and road-building programme. Under the Declaration, the issue of settlements had been assigned to the final status negotiations and although a moratorium had been declared on the inauguration of new settlements, the expansion of existing ones had been implicitly accepted. Some 40,000 acres of Palestinian land had been confiscated since the signing of the Declaration of Principles, and construction had started on an additional 400 km of settlement roads. Their effect, in the words of Meron Benvenisti, a former deputy mayor of Jerusalem and a severe critic of the settlement programmes of successive Israeli governments, was to turn a 'huge expanse of the West Bank into a region in which it will be impossible to implement any final arrangement except by annexation to Israel'. Mahmud Abbas, Palestinian signatory of the Declaration of Principles in Washington, added: 'If the confiscation of Palestinian land is not stopped we will not find anything to negotiate over in the future'. That the continued settlement activity in the West Bank violated the spirit if not the letter of the Declaration of Principles was tacitly acknowledged by sections of the Israeli Cabinet. However, spokesmen for the Israeli Prime Minister explained that Rabin was too weak politically—polls at the beginning of 1995 showed the Labour-led coalition badly trailing its Likud rivals—to implement the next stage of the Declaration of Principles or to tackle settler interests directly. Instead, Rabin insisted, with strong backing from the USA, that the course of the peace process would be determined by Israel's assessment of the impact of the autonomy experiment on its security concerns. It was a formula that the Palestinian opponents of the Declaration of Principles continued to exploit.

THE BEIT LID BOMBINGS

On 22 January 1995 two Islamic Jihad suicide bombers killed 22 Israelis, most of them soliders, in a carefully planned attack at Beit Lid. Israel immediately sealed its borders with the Gaza Strip and the West Bank and arrested hundreds of Islamist activists. Rabin also gave his backing to a proposal to build a 228-mile long security fence in the West Bank that would 'physically segregate' Palestinians and Israelis. Yasser Arafat condemned the Beit Lid bombings and instructed his security forces to undertake a further and unpopular detention of Islamic Jihad cadres. The PNA leader attracted further criticism for his muted response to the security fence plan. Many Palestinians feared that the separation calls were inspired by a desire unilaterally to seize Palestinian territory around Israel's border settlements and thus pre-empt negotiations on the final status agreements. These concerns were aggravated on 25 January when the Israeli Cabinet committee for settlement voted in favour of the massive expansion of the Jewish satellite townships around Jerusalem. Attempts to limit the damage caused by the Beit Lid bombings produced few results. A beleaguered

Arafat met Rabin in Gaza City on 9 February in an attempt to have the closure of the Gaza Strip and the West Bank lifted, and to obtain assurances on the redeployment of troops in the West Bank. He achieved neither of his aims, leading one Palestinian negotiator to describe the peace process as having 'reached a state beyond that of collapse'. A meeting of Jordanian, Israeli, Egyptian and Palestinian representatives in Washington three days later proved no more fruitful for Arafat. US Secretary of State Christopher gave his seal of approval to the crippling security closure of the Gaza Strip and the West Bank by commenting that free movement into and out of the territories could not be expected until the problem of terrorism had been addressed. Confirming Arab and Palestinian fears that the USA's agenda was broadly the same as Israel's, Christopher refused to address the problem of Palestinian detainees and did not criticize Israel for its refusal to adhere to the timetable set out in the Declaration of Principles.

INCREASING ARAB DISILLUSIONMENT

The Palestinians were not the only Arab party to despair at the deadlock in the peace process. By the beginning of 1995 the Egyptian President was clearly exasperated with Israeli policy. Having enthusiastically played the role of the key Arab Government in achieving a comprehensive regional peace, and having invested considerable political capital in the outcome of the peace process, President Mubarak viewed Israel's obstructionism on fundamental issues as undermining his own regime. For Egypt to regain its place as leader of the Arab world, and for the Mubarak Government to erode support for Egypt's own violent Islamist opposition, Israel had to be seen to be dealing sensitively with Arab and Palestinian concerns. However, the Israeli Government's frequent humiliation of Arafat, its bellicose statements on Jerusalem and the ongoing concerns over the West Bank settlements strengthened Egypt's conviction that only by distancing itself from Israel could it ward off criticism that it was giving legitimacy to a process it was itself increasingly wary of. Egypt signalled the rapid deterioration in its relations with Israel through clear and public support for Syria's terms for an Israeli-Syrian peace, and by announcing that it would not sign the renewal of the 1970 Nuclear Non-Proliferation Treaty (NPT) unless Israel, a non-signatory and the only known nuclear power in the region, also undertook to adhere to it. This stance won the backing of Arab states but was greeted with annoyance by Israel. Gentle persuasion by the USA led Israel to make a minor concession, to the effect that it would sign the NPT once a comprehensive Middle East peace had been achieved. Such a peace, however, would have to include peace treaties with such arch foes as Iran, Iraq and Libya. This concession failed to impress President Mubarak. Emboldened by Arab support and by charges of hypocrisy against the USA for its failure to pressurize Israel, the Egyptian President disregarded the USA's urgings to reconsider Egypt's position on the NPT. On 20 April Egypt reiterated that it would withhold its signature to the extension of the NPT because of Israel's refusal to ratify the Treaty. However, further persuasion by the USA and its threats to withhold aid, led Egypt and the rest of the Arab states to agree to an extension of the NPT without Israel's signature. It was a victory for Israel, but one that emphasized its deteriorating relations with Egypt. An attempt by Israeli officials to blame the rift on the Egyptian Minister of Foreign Affairs, Amr Moussa, failed to disguise the fact that Egypt's position was symptomatic of wider Arab disaffection with the lack of reciprocity in Arab–Israeli relations. The evidence of the previous six months gave credence to the Syrian belief that separate deals with Israel and an absence of inter-Arab coordination made Israel's neighbours vulnerable to manipulation. It was feared that Israel would achieve integration into the Arab world without having to make a commitment to withdraw from the territories it occupied. This somewhat belated assessment provided the impetus for Jordan to seek better relations with the PNA. King Hussein and Yasser Arafat signed a general co-operation agreement on 27 January covering trade, currency, banking, communications and administrative affairs. The Jordanian Prime Minister also promised that in future Jordanian policy towards Israel would be guided by the aim of achieving Palestinian sovereignty over East Jerusalem. The *rapprochement* with the Palestinians signalled a shift in

Jordanian policy. Early in March the new Jordanian Minister of Foreign Affairs, Abdul Karim Kabariti, underlined Jordan's new priorities by warning Israel that the key to better Israeli-Jordanian relations lay in progress in negotiations with Syria and the Palestinians. In a meeting with US Secretary of State Christopher on 13 March King Hussein also admonished the US Administration for failing to honour pledges of increased economic and military assistance for Jordan. Without this promised assistance, the King argued, it would be difficult for him to persuade his subjects to see the value of peace with Israel. Moreover, Syria would be wary of any future US promises intended to encourage it to reach an agreement with Israel.

Israel gradually eased the restrictions it had imposed on Palestinians entering Israel following the Beit Lid bombings. Two months after the initial closure of its borders 20,000 workers were given permits to return to their jobs in Israel. This compared to 45,000 who had been working in Israel prior to the bombing and more than 100,000 who had worked in Israel before the Palestinian *intifada*. The presence in Israel of some 80,000 guest workers from Eastern Europe and Asia suggested that, despite the Gaza Strip's 50% unemployment rate, the Israeli Government had no plans to restore the number of Palestinians allowed to work in Israel to its pre-*intifada* level. The partial lifting of the blockade on Palestinian workers was agreed during talks between Arafat and Shimon Peres in Gaza on 9 March. An optimistic Peres described their meeting as a 'breakthrough', but this was not an assessment shared by Palestinian negotiators. Although Peres promised to open up a road corridor between the Gaza Strip and Jericho, and to initiate discussion in the Israeli Cabinet on the release of some of the 7,000 Palestinians still held in Israeli prisons, there was still no agreement on the outstanding issues of IDF redeployment and Palestinian elections. Rabin had earlier suggested that Israel would agree to a town-by-town redeployment in the West Bank, with the proviso that Arafat would have to curb terror attacks.

PNA ANTI-TERRORISM ACTIVITIES

Peres confirmed in his meeting with Arafat on 9 March that negotiations on redeployment might be completed by July 1995 as long as 'specific actions were taken by the Palestinians against terror'. Such warnings hardly seemed necessary. With the tacit approval of Israel and the USA, Yasser Arafat had presided over the expansion of security forces in the Gaza Strip to some 17,000 personnel organized into six separate, competing branches. In the period since the Beit Lid bombings and an attack by DFLP fighters on an IDF patrol on 6 February they had rounded up scores of activists opposed to the Declaration of Principles. Additionally, the PNA had set up special security courts which were administered by appointed security personnel. They were shortly to pass sentences of 25 years' imprisonment on members of the military wings of the Islamist opposition. Reports of the death in custody of Palestinian suspects and the routine torture of detainees provoked severe criticism from local and international human rights organizations. The harassment of journalists and the closure of opposition newspapers confirmed the increasingly authoritarian nature of the PNA regime. Arafat was also censured by former allies for his handling of negotiations with Israel, and in Gaza and the West Bank prominent independent activists had begun to seek support for a new political party committed to the democratization of the PNA. Especially troubling for the PLO leader was growing dissent from within his own Fatah ranks. At a stormy meeting of the Fatah central council in Tunis in late March Arafat came under strong pressure from erstwhile comrades-in-arms turned dissidents to suspend the peace process. Farouk Kaddoumi and Mahmoud Abbas, founder members of Fatah, argued that it would be a grave error to pursue talks with Israel until a new and more accountable negotiating strategy had been devised. Breaking ranks even further, Kaddoumi publicly accused Arafat of embezzlement and of surrounding himself with corrupt opportunists. The meeting ended in uproar, but not before Arafat had won a narrow mandate to continue with the autonomy negotiations, with the proviso that a committee be set up to monitor the course of the negotiations and that dialogue be initiated with the opposition. (The sense that the largest faction of the PLO was moving towards violent division was given added weight by a series of feuds and turf wars in the West Bank that led to several deaths and scores of injuries.) No sooner had Arafat survived the Tunis meetings than the PNA became embroiled in further crisis. On 2 April a massive explosion in a residential apartment block in Gaza City killed four Palestinians and injured 30 others. Among the dead were key figures of Hamas' military wing, the *Izz ad-Din-Qassam* Brigades. Hamas immediately accused the PNA authorities of collaborating with Israel in the bombing of the building. PNA representatives rejoined that the apartment had been blown up in an unsuccessful bomb-making operation. While Arafat's police produced a cache of arms and bomb-making equipment from the debris to support their claims, Hamas supporters demonstrated on the streets, vowing revenge for their slain comrades. On 9 April two suicide attacks on settlers and soldiers in Gaza left eight dead and more than 50 wounded. Hamas and Islamic Jihad claimed responsibility for the two operations. The Israeli Prime Minister ordered another closure of the West Bank and the Gaza Strip, a measure designed to deflect calls from right-wing political parties for an end to negotiations with the PNA over the extension of Palestinian autonomy in the West Bank. The closure did little to calm the rising passions in Gaza, however. Although Rabin confirmed that negotiations on the next phase of Palestinian self-rule would continue, there was little doubt that the events in Gaza had provided his Government with an opportunity to obtain both time and concessions from the embattled PNA. This was evidenced in Arafat's vetoing of a draft national reconciliation treaty brokered between the various leftist and Islamist opposition groups in Gaza. Arafat's aides stated that he had opposed the agreement because it did not contain a condition that the opposition should respect his agreements with Israel.

NO PROGRESS ON SYRIAN TRACK

Negotiations between Israel and Syria remained stalled during the spring of 1995. In the absence of progress, southern Lebanon once again became the arena for the pursuit of political objectives. Eighty attacks on IDF and SLA targets were reported during February, the highest monthly total for several years. Israel responded by subjecting the south Lebanese coast to a month-long blockade, an action that led to a loss of livelihood for some 1,800 Lebanese fishermen. On 31 March Israeli helicopter gunships attacked a car carrying a leading Hezbollah official, Rida Yasin. Both he and his companion died in an attack that was strongly reminiscent of the assassination of Hezbollah leader, Abbas Mussawi, in 1992. Hezbollah fighers retaliated with rocket attacks on targets in northern Israel. A further escalation of hostilities was only averted by the intervention of US Secretary of State Warren Christopher. In communications with the Israeli, Syrian and Lebanese leaders, he reminded the respondents of the agreements brokered in the wake of Israel's 'Operation Accountability' in 1993. The mediation of Warren Christopher reflected the high priority the Clinton Administration was giving to the Israeli-Syrian track of the peace process. The US President had stated that he hoped a peace agreement would be concluded between the two states prior to the 1996 elections in Israel and the USA. Mindful of the slow pace of negotiations he announced in March that a representative from the State Department would participate in the ambassadorial talks taking place in Washington. Conciliatory statements by the Israeli Prime Minister to Syria prompted rumours that more progress was being made in the negotiations than the terse official summaries suggested. It emerged, nevertheless, that this optimism was largely misplaced. However, having failed to reduce differences on the crucial issue of Israel's withdrawal from the Golan Heights, Christopher urged the Israeli and Syrian delegations to postpone these discussions and concentrate on what security arrangements would be satisfactory to them in the wake of an Israeli evacuation of the Golan Heights. This change in emphasis appeared to bear fruit. Emboldened by Shimon Peres' further references to the Heights as Syrian territory, President Assad hinted that he would be prepared to share the Golan's water resources with Israel in the event of the latter's evacuation. In June Syria also conceded that the demilitarized zones on either side of the new border would not have to be of equal size; until this point Syria had insisted on 'symmetry' in all security arrangements. Despite

these small shifts towards accommodation on security and water issues, there was little evidence of a breakthrough on the core issue of withdrawal. An opinion poll published in June indicated that 58% of the Israeli public remained opposed to a full withdrawal from the Golan in exchange for a comprehensive peace agreement with Syria. Disturbed by these findings, the Israeli Government repeated an earlier suggestion that an Israeli evacuation of land and settlements on the Golan Heights would have to be subject to a referendum. The idea was clearly irritating to the Syrian regime which saw it as evidence of Israel's unwillingness to give up the occupied land. Shimon Peres reassured Syria and the USA that, despite the pledge to hold a referendum, the Israeli Government was committed to its goal of peace with Syria. Supporters of Israel's continued presence on the Golan also found little comfort in the extent of opposition to withdrawal from the Heights. They were equally perturbed by Rabin's comment to the IDF's Golani Brigade that the Golan Heights was 'a tank land rather than a holy land'. In July three rebel Labour backbenchers sponsored legislation that sought to set a requirement of a majority of 70 in the 120-seat Knesset for any agreement to withdraw from the Golan. Rabin dismissed the proposed law as nonsense, adding that Israel had gone to war without such a mandate and could also make peace without one. The US ambassador, Martin Indyk, lobbied hard prior to the vote, pointing out that if the law was approved it would effectively destroy the chances of a peace agreement with Syria. At the end of July the Knesset voted 59-59 on a first reading of the proposed legislation. The Speaker cast his vote against and declared the bill defeated.

NEW SETTLEMENT PLANS

At the end of April 1995 Rabin expressed his support for a plan of the Ministry of Housing to construct 7,000 new homes in East Jerusalem and announced plans to confiscate 130 acres of Arab land to facilitate the project. The scale of the proposed construction and its prejudicial impact on final status negotiations on the future of Jerusalem caused an international furore. An irate Arafat authorized the tabling of a UN Security Council resolution demanding that the decision be annulled. He did, however, resist a call from Haider Abdel Shafei to 'shock international opinion' by withdrawing from the peace talks, insisting that there was no alternative to a continuation of dialogue. Shimon Peres attempted to ease the pressure on the PLO leader with several minor concessions—increasing the number of Palestinians allowed to work in Israel to 31,000, simplifying bureaucratic procedures for the entry of goods into the Gaza Strip, promising to hasten the release of 250 Palestinians held in Israeli detention. But, in view of Palestinian outrage at the construction proposals, Peres' clumsy attempt to make them more acceptable only added insult to injury. The US reaction was similarly anodyne. Madeleine Albright, the US Ambassador to the UN, admitted that the new housing units 'pose problems as far as the peace process is concerned', but added that the Security Council was an inappropriate forum for the discussion of the issue. On 17 May the USA once again used its veto at the UN to defeat a resolution which insisted that Israel should rescind its construction plan. All of the other 14 voting countries supported the resolution. It was the thirtieth time since 1972 that the USA had used its veto to prevent the censure of Israel. If developments in the Security Council were wholly predictable owing to the strong pro-Israeli bias of the Clinton Administration, what followed was not. With the PNA reluctant to take the lead in mobilizing opposition to the construction proposals, it was left to a late intervention by the six deputies of the Arab Democratic Party and the Communist-led Hadash coalition to obstruct the Israeli plans. The two parties submitted a motion of 'no-confidence' in the Rabin Government, in spite of warnings from Arafat not to do anything that would cause the Israeli coalition to fall. When it emerged that Likud, despite their strong support for the confiscations, intended to seize the chance to defeat the Labour coalition and that vigorous attempts to get other parties to abstain on the vote had failed, the Israeli Prime Minister was left with no option other than to suspend the plans to confiscate Arab land. The no-confidence motion was withdrawn immediately.

NEGOTIATIONS ON IDF REDEPLOYMENT

During June 1995 Israeli and Palestinian representatives outlined their respective positions on the next, long-delayed phase of Palestinian autonomy: the redeployment of Israeli troops in the West Bank and the related issue of Palestinian elections. Arafat summarized the official PNA position on 18 June: there would be no elections until the IDF withdrew from all population centres in the West Bank. This was loyal to the text of the Declaration of Principles but still at odds with Israel's own assessment of how stage two of the Declaration should be implemented. Advance warning of the rift was served by Rabin on 12 June when he commented that it would be impossible for Israel to reach agreement on redeployment by the target date of 1 July 1995 unless the PNA agreed to a partial redeployment of Israeli armed forces before the elections and further negotiations on full redeployment after them. The positions of the Israeli delegation involved in the redeployment talks were unveiled during June. A three-stage approach to the redeployment of the IDF was proposed. The first stage would involve the withdrawal of the IDF from towns and cities in the West Bank which were regarded as 'non problematic'. These would include Jenin, Nablus, Tulkarm and Qalqilya. The IDF had stated that withdrawal from these towns could be completed by November 1995 as long as it only involved a retreat to the municipal boundaries—refugee camps and villages outside the boundaries would remain under Israeli control. The second stage of the Israeli delegation's approach referred to towns such as Ramallah and Bethlehem, which were contentious in Israeli eyes because they were adjoined by large Israeli settlements. For this reason there could be no withdrawal from these towns until the completion of 110 km of settler roads, a project that would not be completed until May 1996. The third stage of the Israeli approach to redeployment referred to settlements, Israeli-declared state lands and the city of Hebron with its central colony of 400 settlers. According to Israeli officials there could be no withdrawal from these areas until the conclusion of the final status agreement. There were hints that the PNA leadership might accept the idea of a phased Israeli withdrawal, but only as long as it was guaranteed that the second stage of the redeployment would take place within two months of Palestinian elections. For many Palestinians, already weary with the delays to the implementation of autonomy, the Israeli proposals were too radical a departure from the Declaration of Principles to be entertained. As Israeli and Palestinian negotiators resumed their talks on the latest proposals it swiftly became obvious that no agreement would be reached before the target date of 1 July 1995. A later deadline of 25 July was set, but two days prior to this, in the midst of lengthy and secret negotiations, the PLO leader confirmed suspicions that the two sides were still some way from signing an agreement on the extension of Palestinian autonomy. On 25 July Hamas signalled its reaction to the impending agreement with the suicide bombing of a bus travelling through a Tel-Aviv suburb. Six Israelis were killed and dozens injured in the explosion. The prospect of an arrangement for withdrawal of the IDF from areas of the West Bank also led right-wing Israeli nationalists to stage land invasions and to occupy abandoned settlements throughout the occupied territory. Rabin ordered troops to break up the demonstrations leading to several days of clashes with settler groups and scores of arrests. On 21 August a suicide attack on a Jerusalem bus killed another five Israelis. Hamas's military wing immediately claimed that the female bomber responsible was one of its members and promised to carry out similar operations in the approach to the 1996 Israeli elections. The closure of the Gaza Strip and the West Bank followed, but it was accompanied by statements from Rabin that suggested that the talks on the second phase of the Oslo Accords (Oslo II), would be delayed rather than cancelled.

NEGOTIATIONS OVER OSLO II

As Palestinian and Israeli negotiators engaged in round the clock talks in the Red Sea resort of Taba, reports from the negotiations appeared to confirm Israeli and Palestinian pessimism: that an agreement on Oslo II would not be signed by the new target month of September 1995. The status of Hebron was cited as the principal obstacle. However, the submission by the Israeli Minister of Foreign Affairs, Shimon Peres, of a compromise proposal on the disputed city broke the deadlock and paved the way for a formal signing in Washington of an Israeli-Palestinian agreement on the interim stage of Oslo II. Under the terms agreed by the two sides, Israel committed itself to the withdrawal of the IDF from six of the seven main towns and the 440 villages of the West Bank. Civil authority was to be transferred to the PNA in these areas of Palestinian population, but Israel reserved the right to intervene militarily in the villages. Israel also agreed to the establishment of an elected 82-member Palestinian Council with executive and legislative powers. While this represented a more flexible approach, the Israeli Prime Minister insisted that no amendments could be made to existing legislation without prior Israeli approval. On the issue of Hebron, the Palestinian negotiators acceded to Israel's demands that the IDF preserve full or partial authority over 25%–30% of the city's municipal area. This included the Ibrahimi mosque and five locations in the city centre where Jewish settlers and religious students were housed. There was no definitive resolution of the fate of Palestinians in Israeli prisons. Instead, Israel undertook to free up to 2,200 prisoners prior to elections to the Palestinian Legislative Council and the remaining 3,000, somewhat cryptically, 'according to principles to be established separately'. However, Rabin remained adamant that there would be no freedom for those prisoners 'with Jewish blood on their hands'.

Palestinians were noticeably less enthusiastic in their response to the agreement reached at Taba than they had been two years previously, at the beginning of the Oslo process. This time there were no celebrations. A Hamas-inspired general strike shut down the city of Hebron on the day of the Washington signing and leaflets distributed by Islamists in the Gaza Strip and the West Bank castigated Arafat and declared the agreement null and void. In the refugee camps of Lebanon and Syria, Palestinians protested angrily at what they perceived as a further step towards marginalization. This rejection of the agreement was shared by their Arab hosts. Of Israel's neighbours, only Jordan was unconditional in its support for the Taba agreement. This contrasted sharply with King Hussein's initial hostility towards the first phase of the Oslo Accords (Oslo I) and appeared to confirm Jordan's increasing tendency to accommodate the USA's agenda for a Middle East peace. The Jordanian monarch's enthusiasm for the new agreement led to accusations in Arab circles that Jordan's improving relations with Israel and the USA had encouraged Israel to be less compromising in negotiations with the PNA.

The Israeli public's reaction to the Oslo II agreement, like that of the Palestinians, was characterized by indifference and resignation. Anti-Oslo II demonstrations organized by right-wing elements were unusually muted and poorly attended. The leader of the Likud party, Binyamin Netanyahu, initially refused to comment on a future Likud government's attitude towards Oslo II, but eventually conceded that his party would honour agreements between the Labour Party and the PNA. However, with obvious regard to his right-wing constituency, Netanyahu announced that he would renege on any clauses that might be considered harmful to Israel's security and added that the IDF would not refrain from pursuing 'terrorists' into areas of PNA control.

The Labour-led Government was also soon to prove that despite ongoing relations with Arafat's PNA, it had not adopted a more tolerant attitude towards more militant Palestinian factions. On 26 October 1995 Islamic Jihad leader, Fathi Shqaqi, was assassinated in the streets of the Maltese capital, Valetta. Although the Israeli Government refused to confirm or deny that it was behind Shqaqi's killing, it was widely acknowledged that the assassination showed signs of being a Mossad operation. Islamic Jihad cadres urged vengeance for the death of their leader and the news of the killing was followed by violent confrontations in towns of the West Bank. Elsewhere, however, the reaction to Shqaqi's death was decidedly low key. The Egyptian and Jordanian leaders declined to comment on the incident, while PNA spokesmen would go no further than to state that they would not be deflected from their commitment to the peace process. Hamas's reaction to the killing of an Islamist leader was also less strident than might have been expected. Unwilling to sour negotiations aimed at improving their relations with the PNA in the approach to elections to a

Palestinian Legislative Council, Hamas's Gaza-based leaders confined their official reaction to a restrained leaflet.

PHASED IDF REDEPLOYMENT BEGINS

In accordance with the Taba agreements, the IDF began its phased redeployment on the West Bank in mid-October 1995. The village of Salfit was the first Palestinian locality to be evacuated by Israeli troops and this was swiftly followed by other villages. On 25 October Jenin became the first West Bank town to be relinquished by the IDF. However, Palestinian relief at seeing the Israeli occupation lifted for the first time in nearly 30 years was tempered by the limitations of the autonomy. In many instances Israeli troops withdrew not much further than municipal boundaries, confirming opponents of the Oslo Accords in their belief that the new agreements represented not so much an ending of the occupation as its reorganization. Meanwhile, Arab and Israeli leaders gathered in New York to celebrate the 50th anniversary of the founding of the UN. In a speech to the General Assembly Arafat urged the UN to continue to support the Palestinian cause until the implementation of the Palestinians 'inalienable rights' and insisted that the Palestinians wished to live side by side with the Israeli people in two independent states. The Saudi Arabian Minister of Defence, Prince Sultan bin Abd al-Aziz, stated that a comprehensive and just peace would have to be concluded before the Arab world could countenance the normalization of diplomatic or economic relations with Israel. For his part, the Israeli Prime Minister thanked the international community for its support for the peace process and gave his undertaking that it would be pursued 'until we have brought peace to the region'.

ASSASSINATION OF RABIN

Rabin's ability to influence the course of the peace process was to be dramatically short-lived. On 4 November 1995 the Israeli Prime Minister was shot dead by a Jewish religious nationalist, Yigal Amir, as he was leaving a peace rally in Tel-Aviv. The assassination shocked Israeli society, not least because it had hitherto been unthinkable that a Jew would be responsible for the killing of the leader of the Jewish state. The Israeli internal security service, Shin Bet, came under severe criticism for its perceived complacency in not anticipating the threat of violence from the far right wing. This was particularly so given that Amir was well known on the extremist fringe of Israeli politics and his assassination plans were part of a wider conspiracy to attack Palestinian and pro-peace Israeli politicians, including Rabin's designated successor, Shimon Peres. While the manner and place of Rabin's death completed his metamorphosis from warrior to peacemaker and caused an outpouring of popular grief, it embarrassed the Israeli right wing. Likud leader Netanyahu was criticized for failing to distance himself from the increasingly rancourous verbal attacks on Rabin by the settler lobby and for thus contributing to the climate of opinion that made the assassination possible. Rabin's widow singled out the Likud leader as morally responsible for her husband's death. An opinion poll conducted in the immediate aftermath of the assassination revealed only 20% support for Netanyahu compared with 54% for Peres.

There were widely different reactions in the Arab world to Rabin's death. Oman and Qatar sent high ranking ministers to Rabin's Jerusalem funeral, at which both King Hussein of Jordan and Yasser Arafat paid effusive tribute to the memory of the Israeli premier. Damascus and Beirut offered no official comment on the killing, while in Lebanon Hezbollah and Palestinian fighters celebrated the death of an old foe with volleys of gunfire. Yet, despite the variety of responses to Rabin's killing there existed a widespread belief, and not just in the region of conflict, that the peace process was at a challenging juncture. There could be no doubting Rabin's importance to the Oslo process and his credibility with those sections of Israeli society that had traditionally opposed compromise with their Arab neighbours.

PERES BECOMES PRIME MINISTER

Whether his immediate successor, Shimon Peres, regarded as more dovish than his predecessor, possessed the political acumen to build a national consensus around the path taken by Rabin was the cause of much speculation. For Arafat's PNA there was comfort in the fact that the cornering of the Israeli right had created, albeit temporarily, a shift in the Israeli national consciousness and a mood that was far more hostile to settler interests in the West Bank and Gaza Strip. Syrian leaders noted that Peres' agenda was less strongly defined by security than Rabin's had been, and that the new Israeli Prime Minister was more amenable to their views on the Golan Heights. In talks with Western leaders Syrian officials reportedly expressed enthusiasm for a resumption of their deadlocked negotiations with Israel, sentiments that clearly elicited excitement in Washington and Jerusalem. In early December Peres visited Cairo and Amman before making his first official trip as Israeli Prime Minister to Washington. At each venue Peres stressed that his administration would be prioritizing efforts to achieve a breakthrough with Syria. However, in spite of Peres' assertion that 'a new chapter' was about to open in Israeli-Syrian relations, the resumption of negotiations in Washington at the end of December failed to achieve significant progress. The main obstacle remained Syria's insistence that UN resolutions, and hence Israel's withdrawal from the Golan Heights were the *sine qua non* of any agreement. Israeli demands for manned monitoring stations on the Golan Heights were rejected by Syria as a violation of its sovereignty and moves by Israel to tempt Damascus with joint economic and development initiatives proved no more successful. Hints from Washington that Syria's flexibility could lead to its removal from the US list of states which allegedly sponsored terrorism and therefore open the way for US aid, also left President Assad unmoved.

PALESTINIAN ELECTIONS

The IDF's redeployment on the West Bank had been completed by the end of 1995 and without serious disagreement. The way was now open for elections to the Palestinian Legislative Council. There was considerable uncertainty in the approach to the January 1996 poll as to which political factions would participate. The PFLP and the DFLP were quick to urge Palestinians to boycott the elections, a stance that was apparently dictated by their Damascus-based leaderships, but was opposed by many of the parties' cadres in Gaza who argued that a boycott would deprive Palestinians of a secular left-wing voice in the Council. For many observers the decision of the DFLP and the PFLP to boycott the elections without having developed a coherent alternative to the peace process was further evidence of their growing political irrelevance. Hamas' position on participation in the elections was initially more equivocal. Like all the other factions opposed to Arafat, it was highly critical of the first-past-the-post election system which seemed designed to guarantee the dominance of official Fatah candidates. However, a sizeable minority of pragmatists within Hamas was anxious to reach a *modus vivendi* with the PNA and called an early decision to boycott the elections 'unduly hasty and unwise'. The situation within Hamas was further complicated by the formation of a new Islamist party, the National Islamist Salvation Party (Khalas), formed to contest the election and including several personalities closely identified with the moderate caucus in Hamas. By mid-December it appeared that the 'hardliners' had won the debate within Hamas. The movement reiterated its decision to boycott the elections and most of the figures associated with Hamas and connected to Khalas sought to distance themselves from the latter. This was a setback for Arafat's long-standing efforts to drive a wedge between Hamas' political and military wings. Nevertheless talks between the two sides in Cairo at the end of the year did result in the issuing of a joint communiqué stressing the importance of national unity and the need for dialogue to resolve differences. Privately Hamas also promised to refrain from attacking Israeli targets until after the elections, but it also stated that there could be no question of the movement renouncing 'the armed struggle'. That the resumption of suicide attacks against Israel would be sooner rather than later was signalled by the assassination, on 4 January 1996, of Yahya Ayyash. Known by the *nom de guerre* the 'Engineer', Ayyash was thought to have organized the spate of Hamas bus bombings in Israel and was therefore a prime target for Israeli agents. Killed in Gaza by a booby-trapped mobile phone, Ayyash's funeral was attended by 100,000 Palestinians. The death of Ayyash at a time when Hamas had for several months observed a *de facto* cease-fire, was regarded within the movement as vindicating the position of the 'hardliners'. Hamas and Islamic Jihad concurred that retaliation for Ayyash's death was an inevitability.

Some 676 candidates contested the 88 seats in the Palestinian Legislative Council. In a separate poll to elect the President of the PNA, Yasser Arafat was opposed by a single candidate, Samiha Khalil, a veteran women's activist and Fatah dissident. The result of the presidential vote was never seriously in doubt, even without Arafat's supporters' control of the nascent Palestinian radio and TV stations and of much of the print media. His capture of 88% of the votes cast for the position of PNA President was largely anticipated. The election of the Legislative Council was more interesting, not least because of the extremely high turn-out—90% of the electorate in Gaza and 68% on the West Bank participated (interestingly only in localities that were fully or partially under Israeli control, Hebron and East Jerusalem, was there a low turn-out, of 35% and 40% respectively). As predicted, official Fatah candidates were successful, winning 50 of the Council seats. There was also a strong showing by independent candidates (many of them ex-Fatah cadres), who gained 35 seats. Haider Abdel Shafei, a former Washington negotiator, topped the poll in Gaza and in Jerusalem another independent activist, Hanan Ashrawi, came second to the incumbent Minister of Finance, Ahmed Quray. Overall, the results appeared to confirm the electorate's preference for candidates who had earned their political credentials through activism, as opposed to those who owed their position to Arafat's patronage. International observers declared the elections free and fair, an assessment that appeared to ignore not only Arafat's monopoly on media resources, but also widespread reports of ballot-rigging in the Hebron and Ramallah areas, and Israel's efforts to undermine Palestinian electioneering in Jerusalem. It led some commentators to conclude that the whole process had been rubber-stamped under pressure by a US Administration that was anxious to avoid further setbacks to the peace process. Yet, however flawed an excercise in democracy, the elections did represent a significant restructuring of Palestinian politics. They effectively signalled the end of Palestinian representation outside of the West Bank and the Gaza Strip, and with it a disintegration of the PLO institutions that had sustained the Palestinian struggle in the decades preceding the Oslo Accords. Exactly what the relationship would be between the Legislative Council and the Palestine National Council, theoretically the supreme decision-making body, was unclear. It seemed only a matter of time, nevertheless, before existing political forces realigned and transformed themselves into political parties.

RENEWED VIOLENCE AND SECURITY MEASURES

If the IDF's redeployment on the West Bank and the Palestinian elections were seen as proof of the workability of the peace process, what was shortly to occur provided that same process with its most serious test to date. On 25 February 1996, the second anniversary of the Ibrahimi mosque massacre, Palestinian suicide bombings in Jerusalem and Ashkelon, claimed the lives of 25 Israelis and wounded some 55 others. On 3 and 4 March a second wave of bombings in Tel-Aviv and Jerusalem left a further 32 Israelis dead and scores more injured. Hamas' military wing (the *Izz ad-Din Qassam* Brigades) claimed responsibility for the bombings, but a series of contradictory communiqués issued in the aftermath of the attacks appeared to suggest a growing split between the more moderate Gaza-based leadership of Hamas and a dissident military faction that owed allegiance to political radicals stationed abroad. Speculation regarding the bombers' motives identified revenge for the killing of Yahya Ayyash and a desire to hinder the peace process by wrecking Peres' electoral chances. Either way, the response of the PNA and the Israeli Government was wholly predictable. Having so clearly tied his political future to that of the Israeli Labour Party, it came as no surprise that Arafat instructed the forces of the PNA to ameliorate the discomfort of the Israeli leader. The risk of bloody internecine conflict prevented Arafat from acting to dismantle Hamas' institutional base, as Israeli and US leaders would have liked, but he did earn grudging approval for a massive wave of arrests of Hamas and Islamic Jihad members in the areas under his control. On 3 March, five Palestinian militias, including the *Izz ad-Din Qassam* Brigades

were officially outlawed by the PNA. On 6 March the PNA's Mahmud Abbas announced 'there is now no dialogue with either Hamas' political or military wings'. The Palestinian clampdown (as many as 12,000 Islamists were said to be in PNA custody by the end of March) was accompanied by Israel's announcement of an indefinite closure of the West Bank and Gaza Strip and restrictions on the movement of goods and people between autonomous areas on the West Bank. With the co-operation of the Palestinian security forces, the IDF also re-entered Palestinian villages to arrest suspects and several houses belonging to suspected Islamic militants were demolished in areas of Israeli control. However, despite Peres' and Arafat's co-ordinated attempts at damage limitation and the unequivocal condemnation of the bombings by a broad spectrum of Palestinian opinion, the suicide attacks heightened Israeli ambivalence towards the peace process. An opinion poll conducted shortly after the bombings revealed that the Likud leader had now overtaken his Labour rival, who had enjoyed a 30-point lead on becoming Prime Minister. Israeli observers suggested Netanyahu would have fared even better had Peres not been so uncompromising in his reaction to the spring's atrocities.

THE SHARM ESH-SHEIKH SUMMIT

In the wake of the suicide bomb attacks the US Administration sought to bolster the peace process and its vulnerable participants by organizing what was described as an anti-terrorism conference and a 'Summit of the Peacemakers' in the Egyptian resort of Sharm esh-Sheikh on 13 March. Twenty-seven nations were represented at the conference, including 12 Arab states, Israel and the nascent Palestinian entity. The conference concluded with a tame communiqué pledging the participants' support for the peace process and their commitment to combating terrorism. Iraq, Libya and Sudan were not invited to the conference. Syria and Lebanon declined their invitation, stating that the reconvening of the original Madrid peace conference would have been a more appropriate forum for discussion. Indeed, President Assad had already signalled his dissatisfaction with the state of the peace process by refusing publicly to condemn the Hamas bombings in Israel.

'OPERATION GRAPES OF WRATH'

With Israeli-Syrian peace talks deadlocked, the two states' proxy conflict in south Lebanon intensified. In a 16-day period in mid-March 1996 Hezbollah fighters killed six Israeli soldiers and wounded 27 others in and around Israel's self-declared security zone. At the end of the month Israeli tank fire killed two Lebanese civilians installing a water tank in the village of Yatar, prompting Hezbollah to fire rockets into northern Israel. On 8 April two Lebanese children were killed in an explosion on the edge of the security zone. Hezbollah blamed Israel for these attacks and fired more rockets into Galilee, wounding 13 people and sending hundreds more scurrying into air raid shelters. Three days later Shimon Peres announced the beginning of 'Operation Grapes of Wrath', and, in an attempt to deliver a fatal blow to Hezbollah's military capabilities, launched combined air and artillery strikes against targets in south Lebanon, Beirut and the Beka'a valley. In a development reminiscent of Israel's bombardment of the Lebanese south in 1993, IDF commanders warned the populations of Tyre and surrounding villages to leave their homes, sparking the displacement of an estimated 400,000 civilians northwards. During the following week Israeli forces expanded their area of attack. As well as firing thousands of shells at southern villages, Israel's navy bombarded the coast road south of Beirut and its air force struck against power-stations around Beirut and against the international airport, killing several Lebanese and Syrian troops. With few if any fixed positions to defend, Hezbollah's highly mobile guerrillas appeared largely unscathed by the Israeli onslaught and were able to continue firing *Katyusha* rockets into Israel. These caused panic in the northern settlements but little damage and no loss of life. One week into 'Operation Grapes of Wrath' it had become evident that Israeli forces had been unable to achieve their military objective of silencing Hezbollah, and that they would not be able to do so without the commitment of ground troops, an option that Peres could not sanction in view of the casualties this would inevitably entail. Politically, Peres was also beginning to regret his decision to intensify the conflict on the northern borders. The indiscriminate nature of the attacks had, temporarily at least, healed the sectarian divisions in Lebanon and united the country behind Hezbollah. As hundreds of Shi'a youth volunteered to join the ranks of the Islamist militia, their Sunni and Christian countrymen hailed it as Lebanon's most potent symbol of national resistance. Moreover, with the exception of the USA, which once again blocked attempts by the UN formally to condemn the Israeli action, the international community was vocal in its opposition to what was widely interpreted as a cynical electioneering excercise by the Israeli Prime Minister.

THE QANA MASSACRE AND THE SUBSEQUENT CEASE-FIRE

Peres' discomfort was magnified on 18 April 1996 when Israeli shells landed on a UN base at the village of Qana, killing 105 civilian refugees who had been sheltering there and wounding scores of others, including Fijian soldiers serving with the UN. Israel's claim that the shelling of Qana had been the result of technical and procedural errors was rejected in a report commissioned by the UN Secretary-General. Whatever the truth about the tragedy at Qana, it did galvanize diplomatic efforts to bring about a cease-fire between the warring parties. Following the massacre at Qana President Clinton dispatched the US Secretary of State on a seven-day assignment, travelling between Jerusalem and Damascus. However, his six-point plan for securing a cease-fire—which included the disarming of Hezbollah and a Lebanese-Syrian guarantee of security for Israel's northern border—was regarded as too hopelessly pro-Israel to survive exploration (the Syrian President pointedly snubbed Warren Christopher in Damascus). Eventually Israel and the USA were obliged to submit to proposals which developed through the diplomatic efforts of the French Minister of Foreign Affairs, Hervé de Charette. What emerged was a new 'understanding' between the warring parties—essentially a return to the *status quo ante*. Written, but unsigned, it stipulated the terms of engagement between the two sides to the conflict, principally that both parties would refrain from attacking civilians, that Hezbollah would not launch attacks from areas of civilian habitation and that Israel would not target civilian infrastructure. In addition, both parties agreed to retain the right of 'legitimate defence' within the understanding. The cease-fire was to be monitored by a group consisting of Lebanon, Israel, France, the USA and Syria. Most observers saw the cease-fire terms as a victory for the Arab side, in that Hezbollah's standing had been enhanced through its ability to emerge from the conflict undefeated. The Lebanese Prime Minister, Rafik Hariri, insisted that the resistance would continue. Three days after the cease-fire of 27 April Hezbollah fighters were once again attacking the IDF and the SLA in the security zone.

US–ISRAELI RELATIONS

With its Middle East policy now so firmly linked to the victory of the Labour Party in the forthcoming Israeli elections, the USA was determined to boost the fortunes of its ally in the wake of the 'Grapes of Wrath' débâcle. At the end of April 1996 the Israeli Prime Minister made an official visit to Washington where he was praised by and received the backing of President Clinton for his Lebanese adventure. He returned to Israel having obtained substantial US military and technological aid and promises to further develop mutual security, including the possible establishment of a formal defence treaty.

PALESTINIAN–ISRAELI RELATIONS

Yasser Arafat was also being urged to aid Peres' election campaign. On 24 April the PNC was convened in Gaza with the main intention of fulfilling Arafat's earlier promise to Rabin that the PNC would rescind those articles of the Palestinian Charter which denied Israel's right to exist. This the PNC dutifully approved by an overwhelming majority of 504 to 62. Arafat's control of the debate was underlined by the heavy defeat of a motion tabled by his opponents that urged the Council to oppose any amendment if Israel did not acknowledge the Palestinians' right to self-determination. 'I am very happy to have fulfilled my commitments,' was the comment of the PLO leader. A delighted Peres described the PNC's decision—

somewhat exaggeratedly—as 'the most significant ideological change in the Middle East in the last 100 years.' The *quid pro quo* for Arafat was the partial rehabilitation of the peace process in the aftermath of the suicide bombings and the crippling closure of the Palestinian territories. On 5 May Palestinian and Israeli negotiators met again in Taba to commence final status talks on issues such as settlements, Jerusalem, refugees, borders and the status of a future Palestinian entity. As expected, the impending Israeli elections led to a ceremonial inauguration, brief procedural discussion and a formal adjournment of the talks until after the formation of a new Israeli government.

ISRAELI ELECTIONS

Israelis voted on 29 May 1996 to elect a new Knesset. For the first time ever there was also a separate vote to elect the Prime Minister. The campaign of suicide bombings earlier in the year had eroded the massive lead the Labour leader had enjoyed over his Likud rival immediately following Rabin's assassination, and a close contest was predicted. The result was a win for Likud's Netanyahu by a margin of less than 1%, confirming the constancy of the left–right division of the Israeli electorate. Analysts attributed Netanyahu's victory partly to a dogged and opportunistic campaign that won the support of such diverse constituencies as the religious orthodox and the development town populations, and partly to a lacklustre performance by Peres. In the legislative elections the Likud's representation fell from 40 to 32 seats while the Labour Party lost 10 seats and its Meretz allies three. There was a particularly strong showing by the three religious parties, which captured 23 seats, and the Russian Immigrants' party, headed by the former Soviet dissident, Natan Scharansky, which won seven seats in the first election it had contested. Israel's Arab voters had voted overwhelmingly in favour of Peres to continue as Prime Minister, in spite of earlier threats to abstain because of the Israeli attack on Lebanon. In the Knesset Arab-dominated parties increased their representation from six to nine seats.

REACTION TO LIKUD VICTORY

The return to power of the Israeli right wing was viewed as little less than a disaster for the peace process. Netanyahu had long been associated with the nationalist 'hardliners' in the Likud and his pre-election pronouncements had included a commitment to treble the settler population of the West Bank and the expression of his total opposition to Palestinian self-determination and to any change to the status of Jerusalem. Sensitive to the international disquiet that had accompanied his victory, Netanyahu's first major speech (to an adoring Likud crowd) was moderate and conciliatory as he paid generous tribute to his defeated predecessor and pledged to continue the peace process. Yet, even if Netanyahu was ultimately more of a pragmatic opportunist than a nationalist ideologue, as many commentators suspected, nothing could disguise the disappointment in Western and Arab capitals at Peres' loss of office. Yasser Arafat, struggling to manage a $100m. budget deficit and the consequences of the 12-week closure of the PNA-ruled areas, was reported to be devastated by the Netanyahu victory, and not without good cause. For two years his policies had largely been predicated upon refraining from any course of action that would upset the electoral chances of Israel's Labour leaders. In the previous two months, and largely at Peres' bidding, Arafat had agreed to the delay of Israel's redeployment in Hebron, clamped down on dissent in the PNA, imprisoned nearly 1,000 Palestinians and unilaterally changed the Palestinian Charter. As his detractors now scornfully pointed out, the politics of acquiescence and accommodation had spectacularly backfired. Netanyahu, who refused to use the terms PNA or PLO, instructed a junior official at the Ministry of Foreign Affairs to inform Arafat's deputy, Mahmud Abbas, that a 'mechanism of contact' would be established in due course. The snub was deliberate. The Likud leader had already stated that he would not meet Arafat unless Israeli security deemed it necessary. As if this did not augur sufficiently badly for the future, Netanyahu went on to appoint the 'hardline' Ariel Sharon to head a ministry responsible for infrastructure development on the West Bank. The only comfort for Arafat and the PNA lay in Likud's ideological opposition to 'separation' and, hence, the prospect that there would be a gradual relaxation of the closure of the Occupied

Territories. Sources close to Israel's internal security services also pointed out that Netanyahu would be foolish to jeopardize the established sharing of information by Israeli and Palestinian intelligence chiefs.

Jordan and Egypt were relatively sanguine in their official responses to the changes in Israel, with both of their Government's adopting a 'wait-and-see' attitude to the Likud leader. Syria and Lebanon displayed a degree of grim satisfaction, seeing in Netanyahu's victory a vindication of their refusal to join those Arab states who had moved to build relations with the Jewish state. However, for neither Lebanon nor Syria was there any evidence that Netanyahu would advance bilateral relations. On the issue of Lebanon, the Likud leader differed little from his Labour predecessors. He had stated in his election campaign that Israel would maintain its security zone until the Lebanese army disarmed Hezbollah and assumed responsibility for security in the south. Netanyahu was notably more rigid in his views on the nature of Israeli–Syrian relations. There would be no withdrawal from the Golan Heights because it was vital to Israel's security. Given Assad's insistence that an Israeli withdrawal from occupied lands was a prerequisite for any peace deal between the two countries, it was predicted that Israeli–Syrian relations were about to enter a potentially dangerous new era.

ARAB SUMMIT IN CAIRO

There was sufficient trepidation in the Arab world over the implications of the change in government in Israel for the Egyptian and Syrian Presidents to organize an Arab summit meeting in Cairo on 21–23 June 1996. The first of its kind since the Iraqi invasion of Kuwait in 1990, the meeting was attended by all of the Arab states with the exception of an uninvited Iraq. Syria had wanted the summit to produce a commitment by the Arab states to make any moves towards the normalization of relations with Israel dependent upon progress being made in the peace process. Fear of the USA's reaction prevented the Syrian proposal from being adopted, but the summit's final communiqué did reiterate that peace should be based on Israel's withdrawal from Arab lands, and that if Israel reneged on any of the agreements it had so far signed under the terms of the Oslo Accords, then the Arab states would have to reconsider the steps they had taken in the peace process. A series of important bilateral meetings took place in the context of the summit in the Egyptian capital, the most noteworthy being between the Syrian President and the Jordanian and Palestinian leaders. King Hussein, perhaps least threatened by the Netanyahu victory, promised to support Syrian demands for an Israeli withdrawal from the Golan Heights, and agreed with Assad that they would continue their dialogue as a means of improving their strained relations. Similar sentiments were expressed at the conclusion of Palestinian-Syrian discussions.

HOPES FOR PROGRESS RECEDE

Fears of a slide towards greater instability in the region were partially borne out in the two months following the Israeli election. In south Lebanon Hezbollah attacks claimed the lives of 11 Israeli soldiers, and on the West Bank five settlers and three soldiers were killed in attacks blamed on the PFLP and Abu Musas's faction of Fatah. Both Damascus-based groups had for a number of years allowed Islamist groups to take the leading role in armed activities in the West Bank and Gaza Strip. Meanwhile the Netanyahu Government unveiled plans to establish eight new settlements in the West Bank in line with election promises to increase the settler population to 500,000 by the end of the millennium. A decision was also taken by the new Minister of Defence, Itzhak Mordechai, to reintroduce IDF undercover units to the West Bank and to expand their operations to include areas of PNA control. In mid-July one of these units was reported to be responsible for the killing of an Islamic Jihad activist in Ramallah, an area of the West Bank that according to the terms of Oslo II was supposed to be under exclusive Palestinian security control. The first contacts between the PNA and the Netanyahu Government also indicated that the future course of the peace process would not be smooth. Meeting Arafat on 19 July, the Israeli Minister of Foreign Affairs, David Levy, informed the PLO leader that there could be no progress on resolving the outstanding issues of the

interim phase period—principally the stalled redeployment in Hebron—until certain Israeli conditions were fulfilled. Levy detailed these as a halt to all PNA activity in Jerusalem, a moratorium on the release of Islamist suspects and the continued clamp down on terrorist activities. He also refused to set a date for the resumption of final status negotiations. The only concession that the Israeli Government was prepared to make was a verbal undertaking to increase by 10,000 to 35,000 the number of permits issued to Palestinians wanting to work in Israel.

During his first official visit to Washington as Israeli Prime Minister in mid-July 1966, Netanyahu did nothing to dispel Arab gloom or confirm Western hopes that he would reveal a more pragmatic bent. In a speech to the US Congress, Netanyahu dismissed the land-for-peace formula and stated instead that the resolution of the Middle East conflict must be based on security, reciprocity and democracy. Equally uncompromising were his comments on the future of Jerusalem and the prospects of peace with his northern neighbours. On talks with Syria he told reporters: 'I can tell you that the first item on my agenda would be the cessation of all terrorist attacks from Syrian-controlled areas in Lebanon, via Hezbollah, or for that matter other terrorist attacks from groups based in Syria'.

At the end of July the PLO leader made his first visit to Damascus since 1993. Given the mistrust and personal enmities that had soured Syrian–Palestinian relations for more than a decade, it was perhaps inevitable that the discussions between the two sides concluded with little more than a commitment to work towards future co-ordination. However, the arrival of the Jordanian monarch in the Syrian capital only a few days after Arafat had departed seemed to suggest that the changes in Israel were producing tentative moves by its Arab neighbours to establish less unilateral strategies of dealing with the Jewish state.

CONTACTS ARE RE-ESTABLISHED

Against a backdrop of mounting domestic unrest and cynicism with regard to the peace process, Arafat tried to persuade the Israeli Premier to meet for direct negotiations that would demonstrate that the Oslo process was again on track. Netanyahu remained aloof, judging correctly that delaying a resumption in the peace talks presented an opportunity to wring concessions from the PNA. By the end of July Palestinian negotiators were conceding that the agreements signed with the previous Labour Government on withdrawal from Hebron were open to revision. Equally controversially, Arafat bowed to Israeli demands that three Palestinian charitable institutions in Jerusalem, affiliated to the PNA, be closed down. Both developments laid Arafat open to criticism from a broad spectrum of Palestinian opinion, particularly when Netanyahu signalled that his Government would not be guided by notions of reciprocity. Just days after the Jerusalem closures, Israeli troops demolished a Palestinian centre for the disabled in Jerusalem's Old City (supposedly on the pretext that it had been built without a license) and announced that 900 new housing units would be built in a settlement near Ramallah. These were rebukes that the embattled Arafat could not afford to ignore. Declaring to the Legislative Council that 'Israel has declared war on us' he announced a four-hour general strike and warned that only a resumption of the *intifada* could end the current impasse with Israel. This latter announcement, together with a threat from President Mubarak to cancel November's Middle East and North Africa economic conference in Cairo unless Israel began to meet its Oslo commitments, aroused sufficient concern in Washington and in European capitals for the Israeli leader to calculate that it was no longer in his interests to distance himself from the PNA, and from the peace process.

On 4 September 1996 Prime Minister Netanyahu met the PLO Chairman at the Erez checkpoint between Israel and the Gaza Strip to discuss a resumption of the Oslo talks. There was evident relief, not least in Washington, that the meeting had finally taken place. US Secretary of State, Warren Christopher, applauded the Israeli Prime Minister for having crossed 'a psychological threshold'. But US approval and declarations from the two negotiating sides that the meeting had produced positive results, failed to disguise the largely symbolic nature of the encounter. The Israelis did commit themselves to resuming full contacts with the PNA, and to participation in a joint steering committee designed to direct implementation of the outstanding issues of Oslo's interim phase, yet when this committee first convened on 9 September in Jericho, there was an obvious divergence of opinion over the extent to which Israeli redeployment in Hebron could be renegotiated. In mid-September Arafat informed a meeting of Arab foreign ministers in Cairo that Israel was not committed to reaching consensus and that the peace process remained at a critical stage. On 23 September the Israeli Prime Minister announced that an ancient tunnel, running beneath the Muslim quarter of Jerusalem's Old City, alongside the al-Aqsa mosque, was to be reopened. Given the already strained nature of Israeli–Palestinian relations and the acute Palestinian and Muslim sensitivities to the perceived threat to Jerusalem and its Islamic holy sites, the tunnel judgement was widely interpreted as unnecessarily provocative. Arafat denounced the rehabilitation of the tunnel as 'a crime against our holy places' and, to a chorus of popular indignation and support, advocated protests against the 'Judaization of Jerusalem', effectively endorsing a return to the politics of the *intifada*; the crucial difference at this stage being the existence of a legitimate armed Palestinian security force.

PNA POLICE CLASH WITH IDF

On 25 September 1996 hundreds of Palestinian students, mobilized by the PNA and Arafat's Fatah movement, confronted IDF positions on the outskirts of Ramallah. For a while the furious exchange of rocks and rubber bullets recalled the early days of the *intifada*, but after Israeli troops resorted to live ammunition and made incursions into areas under Palestinian control, Palestinian police observers of the protest became full participants in the battle. The following day the West Bank and Gaza witnessed the worst violence since the occupation of 1967 as Israeli and Palestinian troops engaged in lengthy exchanges of gunfire; in Ramallah and Gaza the Israeli army used helicopter gunships to fire on Palestinian positions, while in Nablus Palestinian security forces and armed militants overran the Israeli-held site of Joseph's Tomb, killing six soldiers in the process. After three days of bloody clashes, 55 Palestinians had been killed and around one hundred more had been wounded. Fourteen Israeli soldiers had also died in the violence and Israeli tanks had been moved into positions around the areas of PNA control amid speculation that Netanyahu was about to order the reoccupation of Palestinian population centres. The prospect of a full-scale conflagration prompted the US President to interrupt campaigning for November's Presidential election and return to Washington. On 29 September President Clinton agreed to host a crisis summit between Arafat and Netanyahu and pledged his own participation in the talks. Invitations were also extended to the Jordanian and Egyptian leaders. In the West Bank and Gaza, meanwhile, Arafat ordered his forces to contain the demonstrations and to co-operate with the IDF who, in turn, imposed a closure of the major Palestinian population centres but refrained from further incursions. By the end of September only isolated incidents of violence were being reported from the West Bank and Gaza.

EUROPEAN REACTION

Internationally the crystallizing perception was that it was the Netanyahu Government's intransigence, rather than Arafat's manipulation, that was ultimately responsible for the latest débâcle. Amid reports that it intended to pursue a more proactive role in the peace process, the European Union (EU) emphasized its reservations concerning the policies of the Netanyahu Government by receiving the Palestinian leader in Luxembourg on the eve of the Washington summit. It was announced that negotiations would begin on a Euro-Palestinian trade agreement to accelerate the economic development of the West Bank and Gaza, and pledges of $30m. in immediate aid were made. Shortly afterwards EU foreign ministers issued a statement on the recent escalation of violence on the West Bank and in Gaza, in which the IDF was accused of deploying disproportionate force in dealing with the Palestinians. The statement went on to comment 'The EU recognizes that the recent incidents were precipitated by frustration and exasperation at the absence of any real progress in the peace process and .. firmly believes that the absence of such progress is the

root of the unrest.' The publication of the statement coincided with an announcement that the EU was for the first time to assign a special envoy to the Middle East. The eventual appointment of the Spanish diplomat, Miguel Moratinos, with a limited brief represented a defeat for a French-led attempt to have the post filled by a high-profile political personality with a wider ranging mandate.

THE WASHINGTON SUMMIT

Realistic expectations of the Washington mini-summit did not exceed an easing of tensions. The Egyptian President had declined an invitation to be present on the grounds that he doubted Israeli sincerity, while the looming US Presidential election effectively ruled out any significant political initiative from the Clinton Administration. Indeed Netanyahu had prefaced his appearance in Washington by insisting that the controversial Jerusalem tunnel would remain open and was unequivocal in attributing responsibility for the renewed violence to the PNA. Yet despite the lack of progress in Washington—the two sides committed themselves to little more substantive than continued talks over Hebron—Arafat was not despondent as he left the US capital. Temporarily, at least, his standing had been strengthened by the crisis. Opinion polls published in October revealed overwhelming Palestinian support for the stance adopted by the PNA and for the actions of the security forces during the tunnel crisis. In addition to reaping the benefits of European frustration with Israel's new Government, Arafat had also drawn strength from a rapid deterioration in relations between Jordan and Israel. The Jordanians had been deeply angered by the Israelis' unilateral decision to open the tunnel (the Jordanian-Israeli treaty of 1994 recognized Jordan's special relationship with Muslim holy sites in Jerusalem) and King Hussein was reported privately to have expressed severe criticism of Netanyahu's policies. In a subsequent interview with the Saudi newspaper, *Asharq al-Awsat*, King Hussein warned that Israel's failure to meet its commitments as established by the Oslo Accords was raising the spectre of war in the region. In a clear gesture of support for the Palestinian leader, King Hussein made his first visit to the West Bank since the Israeli occupation of 1967. Speaking at a joint news conference with Arafat, in Jericho, he described an unprecedented improvement in Jordanian–Palestinian relations.

ARAB–ISRAELI ECONOMIC RELATIONS

Israeli–Egyptian relations remained less than cordial. In mid-October 1996 President Mubarak announced that he would not meet with Netanyahu until redeployment in Hebron was agreed, although his earlier threat to cancel the Middle East and North Africa economic conference was quietly abandoned in the face of domestic economic interests and US opposition to such a move. Nevertheless, for Israeli delegates the conference presented few opportunities. The Egyptian Chamber of Commerce had urged its members to boycott Israeli business stands while Foreign Minister Musa told reporters that Israel's isolation was the 'natural reaction from people in the region' and that 'inter-Arab co-operation should be the base of all regional co-operation'. A plan to build a natural gas pipeline from Egypt (through Gaza) to Israel, first proposed in 1993, was postponed indefinitely by its Italian contractor, and a joint Egyptian-Jordanian-Israeli project for tourist development along the shared coastline of the Gulf of Aqaba became another victim of the soured atmosphere. (Earlier, on economic grounds, Israel had cancelled an agreement to buy gas exclusively from Qatar. The Qatari Government reacted by suspending moves towards normalization with Israel, thus isolating Oman as the only Gulf state continuing to develop trade links with Israel.)

DISCUSSIONS ON HEBRON

Whatever satisfaction Arafat derived from 'uniting the world against the Netanyahu Government' (his claim to the Palestinian Legislative Council), the formulation of a coherent strategy for future contact with the Israelis had become increasingly problematic given Palestinian expectations that their negotiators would now be resolute in resisting Israeli pressure to alter agreements already signed under the terms of the Oslo

Agreements. Discussions over the Hebron deployment were resumed and continued throughout the remainder of 1996 with the principal point of contention being the Israeli insistence that their troops should have the right to intervene militarily in the 20% of the city that would remain in Israeli hands following the initial redeployment. Under the terms of Oslo's interim agreement the IDF had preserved the right to enter Palestinian areas to 'bring an end to an act or incident' which threatened Israeli lives, but Netanyahu wanted this arrangement expanded to include, in the words of his chief media adviser, actions to 'pre-empt a terror attack as well as to pursue one.' There was little chance of Arafat agreeing to such a demand, given the support he had enjoyed internationally and locally in the wake of the September clashes. By the end of November, the Israeli Prime Minister was accusing his Palestinian interlocutors of deliberately delaying any agreement on Hebron in an attempt to increase international pressure on Israel to make further concessions. Mutual distrust deepened following an announcement on 19 November that 1,200 new housing units were to be built in the West Bank settlement of Emmanuel. The PNA reacted to the announcement by urging 'popular confrontation' against Israeli settlement policy, and organized a brief blockade of the Netzarim settlement in Gaza. The prospects for agreement on Hebron appeared to recede even further during December. On 10 December the Jerusalem District Planning Authority approved the construction of 110 housing units in a Palestinian district of East Jerusalem. The following day a Jewish settler and her young son were shot dead by members of the PFLP near the Jewish settlement of Beit El on the West Bank. At the funeral of the two victims, attended by the Israeli Prime Minister, settler leaders called for the immediate confiscation of land adjoining the settlement to make way for the building of 1,000 new homes. A belligerent Netanyahu seized on the mood of popular outrage and instructed his aides to draft a cabinet resolution calling for the expansion sought by the settlers. This decision attracted opposition from unexpected quarters. In addition to the predictable fury emanating from Arab capitals and protests from the EU, US officials also expressed their dismay. However it was the opposition of Israel's security chiefs, who warned that implementation of the Beit El scheme might lead to a repeat of the September clashes, coupled with the misgivings of Foreign Minister Levy and Defence Minister Mordechai, that persuaded the Israeli Premier to adopt a compromise on Beit El that involved a more modest expansion on land serving as an IDF base. Any goodwill that might have been engendered by this compromise was immediately eroded by an Israeli cabinet decision to reinstate subsidies and tax incentives to all settlements in the Occupied Territories by classifying them as 'national priority areas'. Clearly unimpressed by Netanyahu's assurances that the new ruling was largely symbolic and would not facilitate a new settlement initiative, US State Department spokesman, Nicholas Burns, expressed the Clinton Administration's view that '. . settlement activity is unhelpful, and settlement activity clearly complicates the peace process.' His concern was shared by former high ranking US officials who wrote to Netanyahu warning him 'not to take unilateral actions that would preclude a meaningful settlement and lasting peace.' The signatories of the letter included former Secretaries of State James Baker, Cyrus Vance and Lawrence Eagleburger as well as former national security advisers Brent Scowcroft, Frank Carlucci and Zbigniew Brezsinski.

On 15 December the Palestinian and Israeli leaders resumed contact and committed themselves to renewed talks on Hebron redeployment. Two weeks later a Jewish settler and off-duty soldier made an indiscriminate machine-gun attack on shoppers in Hebron's crowded central market, wounding eight Palestinians before being overpowered and disarmed by Israeli troops. The realization that the incident could have claimed many lives lent new urgency to the negotiations. In a secret meeting in Gaza on 5 January 1997 the outstanding issues surrounding Israel's security redeployment in Hebron were effectively agreed between Arafat and Netanyahu. Nevertheless, continuing disagreement on future redeployments elsewhere forestalled the public announcement of a Hebron deal. Instead the Israeli leader demanded that the deadline for Israel's final redeployment—from all West Bank territory except the settlements,

municipal Jerusalem and certain military locations—should be postponed until April 1999, rather than September 1997 as stipulated under the Oslo timetable.

AGREEMENT ON HEBRON

Arafat's unwillingness and effective inability to agree to this proposal meant that agreement on Hebron appeared as elusive as ever. Attempts by the US special envoy, Dennis Ross, to persuade the Palestinians to accommodate Netanyahu's request earned a swift rebuttal, and it fell to King Hussein of Jordan to broker a compromise. Travelling between Gaza and Tel-Aviv on 12 January the Jordanian monarch was able to secure Israeli and Palestinian acceptance of a proposal (originated by the Egyptian President) for Israel to complete its final West Bank redeployment by March 1998. The agreement was formalized by the signing of a protocol between Saeb Erakat and Dan Shomron, chief Palestinian and Israeli negotiators, on 15 January. Under the terms of the protocol Israel agreed to withdraw from 80% of the city of Hebron, while retaining control over a central enclave housing 400 settlers and their 20,000 Palestinian neighbours for an interim period of at least two years. In addition, Israel agreed to begin immediate discussion of outstanding interim issues of Oslo II, most notably the questions of Palestinian detainees, Gaza's airport and a West Bank–Gaza corridor. There was no mention of the earlier insistence of the IDF's right of pre-emptive operations in the self-rule areas. For its part, the PNA reiterated its commitments to combating 'terror', finalizing the revision of the Palestinian National Charter and confiscating illegal weapons in the areas under its control.

REACTION IN ISRAEL

A large majority of Knesset members supported the Hebron deal, as did the majority of Israel's population. The reaction of the nationalist right wing to the agreement also proved to be far more muted than their militant leaders had indicated. Attempts to disrupt the withdrawal through direct protest-action had been threatened but, in the event, failed to materialize. The Hebron agreement won the support of 11 of the 18 members of the Israeli Cabinet; of the seven dissenters only Binyamin Begin, the uncompromising Minister of Science, and son of the former Israeli Prime Minister, was prepared to express his opposition through resignation from the Government.

PALESTINIAN REACTION

The PNA leadership felt evident relief that the tortuous deliberations over Hebron had finally been concluded. There was satisfaction that the terms of the agreement were essentially in line with the Oslo Accords and that Arafat's strategy of internationalizing the negotiation process (and of discouraging Jordan from conducting a unilateral peace effort with Israel) had apparently been vindicated. The issue of Hebron had become for the Palestinians a crucial testing ground of relations with Likud. Palestinian concessions would have seriously undermined Arafat's position and made the Oslo process even more vulnerable to the revisionist intentions of the Israeli right wing. Nevertheless, while admitting that Palestinian negotiators had performed well in achieving the Hebron deal, sceptics of the Oslo process claimed that it was only mass participation in the September protests that had ultimately allowed Arafat to pursue such a course of inter-Arab co-operation and internationalization. Speaking to Arafat after he had addressed a large crowd in Hebron, Hamas leaders also adopted a conciliatory tone. Recognizing that the PLO Chairman was enjoying a rare moment of political success, they expressed disappointment with an agreement that left Israeli troops and settlers in control of the centre of Hebron, but promised that they would express their continued opposition to the Oslo Accords through 'democratic channels'.

DOMESTIC CRISIS FOR NETANYAHU

The optimism that had arisen from the January protocols proved to be short-lived. In Israel, at the end of January 1997, it was alleged that Netanyahu had supported the appointment as Attorney-General of a little-known lawyer, Roni Bar-On, on the understanding that Bar-On would ensure lenient treatment of Aryeh Der'i, the leader of the orthodox Shas party and coalition ally of the Likud, who was facing criminal proceedings on political and financial corruption charges. In return for leniency, it was reported, Shas party ministers were alleged to have pledged support for the Hebron withdrawal within the Cabinet. Bar-On resigned within 12 hours of his appointment; he was replaced by Elyaqim Rubenstein at the end of January. For a time, Netanyahu's impeachment seemed a distinct possibility, and this prospect exposed the growing rift between the nationalist 'hardliners' in government and the pragmatic ideologues grouped around the Prime Minister. Mindful of Netanyahu's vulnerability, and still irate at the Hebron withdrawal, the nationalist wing of the coalition threatened to bring down Netanyahu unless he agreed to a plan for the construction of a large new settlement on Palestinian-owned land to the southeast of Jerusalem. At the end of February 1997 the Ministerial Committee on Jerusalem approved the construction of a settlement (Har Homa) on the hilltop of Jabal Abu Ghunaim, just inside the municipal boundaries of Jerusalem. On completion Har Homa would house some 32,000 settlers in 6,500 housing units, and complete the ring of settlements around Arab East Jerusalem. In a palliative move, Netanyahu simultaneously announced that his Government was granting 3,015 building permits to Palestinians in East Jerusalem.

HAR HOMA

The Har Homa issue aroused a predictable storm of protest. The EU described the decision as a 'major obstacle to peace', while President Clinton, who had recently been effusive in his praise of Netanyahu's accomplishment over Hebron, expressed the opinion that, 'The important thing is for these people on both sides to be building confidence and working together and so I would have preferred the decision not to have been made because I don't think it builds confidence, I think it builds distrust and I wish it had not been made.' Palestinian reaction to Har Homa was predictably fierce, with PNA spokesmen warning that it spelled the end of the peace process and would usher in a new era of confrontation. The rhetoric softened, however, after the US cautioned against any repeat of September's armed clashes and the Israeli defence minister warned that contingency plans had been drawn up for invasion of the autonomous areas if violence proceeded from the Har Homa decision. Nevertheless, a series of marches and protest strikes were urged by political and community organizations throughout the West Bank and Gaza. These reportedly failed to win the full support of Arafat, whose preferred response to the crisis was to attempt the diplomatic isolation of the Israeli Government. The PNA leader consulted EU leaders, King Hassan of Morocco and the Egyptian and Jordanian leaders in quick succession. Arafat's relatively restrained response to Har Homa led to speculation, fermented in the Israeli media, that he had, at some time during negotiations with Israel, acquiesced to the construction of the settlement in return for swift progress on Israeli redeployments in the West Bank. Critics of Oslo repeated earlier assertions that what was happening at Har Homa was an inevitable consequence of the Accords' failure to curtail settlement activity during the interim period.

Following their success in helping to broker the Hebron agreement, the events surrounding Har Homa were received with alarm in Egypt and Jordan. On the day after the settlement was officially endorsed in Israel King Hussein wrote to the Israeli Prime Minister requesting his reappraisal of the decision and careful consideration of the consequences implicit in pursuing the project. To underline official Jordanian dissatisfaction, Crown Prince Hassan cancelled a scheduled visit to attend the inauguration of the Rabin Peace Centre at Tel-Aviv University. The Jordanian leader, however, stopped short of severing diplomatic links; Hussein had, after all, staked his regional policy on constructive engagement with Tel-Aviv. Yet the Jordanian monarch's perceived tolerance of Israeli provocation resulted in government policy that was severely at odds with a popular sentiment that was increasingly hostile to its country's relations with Israel under Netanyahu. Public feeling in Egypt was similarly pitched against the Jewish state. An ill-timed visit by Netanyahu to a Cairo trade fair in early March provoked overwhelming press hostility and the refusal of many prominent businessmen and intellectuals to accept invitations to be presented to the Israeli Prime Minister. On 7 March an EU-drafted UN resolution calling on Israel to refrain from settlement-building in East Jerusalem encountered the now customary US veto. Washington's new Ambassador to the UN, Bill Richardson, defended the use of the veto by stating that UN involvement in the current dispute could only serve to hinder progress.

Meanwhile, following lengthy cabinet discussion and considerable international pressure, Israel announced details of its first phase of West Bank troop redeployment, as required by the Oslo Accords and reaffirmed by the Hebron agreement. The Israeli proposal, which provided for the transfer of only 2% of 'new' West Bank territory to Palestinian control, was immediately rejected by the Palestinian negotiating team, which also challenged the level of total deployment quoted within the terms of the three-phase initiative. By 11 March negotiations had been suspended and all Palestinian officials had been instructed, by Arafat, to end all contacts with Israel. The deadline for the initiation of 'final status' talks, established by the Hebron agreement, was not observed by the Palestinians, who subsequently rejected an Israeli proposal to accelerate the timetable for the 'final status' negotiations, given that a satisfactory resolution of the outstanding provisions of Oslo II had yet to be achieved.

On 13 March seven Israeli schoolgirls visiting a border site in the Jordan Valley were killed when a Jordanian soldier sprayed their party with automatic gunfire. King Hussein condemned the massacre and curtailed an official visit in order to meet with the victims' families in Israel. His actions were widely applauded in Israel; less so in Jordan where his gesture was criticized as overly dramatic. Construction work on the Har Homa settlement began on 18 March 1997. On the following day a Palestinian suicide bomber killed three women at a café in Tel-Aviv. Hamas' military wing in Jerusalem claimed responsibility for the attack, but the organization's political leaders in Gaza denied involvement. The Israeli Government immediately accused Arafat of having given tacit approval to his Islamist opposition to renew terror attacks and urged the PNA authorities to rectify the situation. Twelve months previously the PNA had apprehended some 1,200 Islamist activists and sympathizers in the wake of a suicide bombing campaign, but on this occasion Arafat felt little compunction to respond so readily to Israeli demands. Arafat had made considerable efforts to build relations with Islamist organizations in the previous few months and was anxious not to antagonize this constituency with no prospect of reciprocity from Israel. Moreover, the issue of settlements had eroded residual support for the peace process in Palestinian communities and the prevalent mood was far less opposed to acts of violent resistance. Even Arafat's own Fatah faction was taking steps to distance itself from the policies of its nominal leader. On 23 March the Fatah Higher Committee in the West Bank called for an end to negotiations with Israel and an escalation of protests. There was an immediate response in the West Bank, particularly in Hebron, where there were prolonged clashes between Israeli soldiers and hundreds of demonstrators. Three Palestinian protesters were killed and more than 500 injured in the two weeks after the commencement of work at Har Homa.

ARAB FOREIGN MINISTERS' DECLARATION

Arab diplomatic protests were stepped up in response to the commencement of construction on Jabal Abu Ghunaim. The GCC foreign ministers' meeting in Riyadh, the Islamic summit in Islamabad and the ICO Jerusalem Committee meeting in Rabat all produced statements denouncing Israel's settlement activity. More tangible opposition was expressed at an Arab foreign ministers' meeting in Cairo at the end of the month when it was recommended that Arab League states should suspend involvement in multilateral negotiations with Israel, reassert the primary economic boycott and end moves towards normalization of relations, by closing down the representative offices through which they were conducted. (Morocco, Tunisia, Oman, Qatar and Mauritania all had trade or representative offices in Tel-Aviv.) As these recommendations were non-binding and did not apply to those states—Egypt, Jordan and the PNA—which had formal relations with Israel, it was unclear what practical import they would have. (The Omani Government did prohibit Israeli participation at a Muscat trade fair in early April.) A group of states led by Syria had urged the imposition of more severe measures against Israel and the convening of a special Arab summit to authorize them, but this proposal was vetoed by Cairo. There was little indication that the Netanyahu Government was unduly perturbed by the deterioration in relations with the Arab world. Although the previous Labour administration had regarded the development of closer relations with Arab states as a major dividend of the peace process, Israel's nationalist bloc had never been ideologically inclined to forge links with an Arab world that had long been held in cultural and political contempt.

DIPLOMATIC INITIATIVES

With the peace process effectively stalled over Har Homa and the issue of redeployment attention turned to Washington, and Arab hopes that Clinton's successful re-election would allow him the political freedom to adopt a more uncompromising stance in his dealings with Israel. While Dennis Ross's assessment of the prevailing mood in the Middle East was sufficiently pessimistic for him to recommend that the new Secretary of State Madeleine Albright should cancel plans for a tour of the region, Arab and Israel delegations beat a path to the White House. At the beginning of April the Jordanian monarch met Bill Clinton in Washington and expressed concerns that the precariousness of the current situation demanded that the USA play a more forthright role. However, Clinton replied that he was not willing to enforce an agreement. The end of King Hussein's visit coincided with the arrival in Washington of the Israeli Prime Minister. Netanyahu's visit was accompanied by an announcement that the USA was authorizing substantial new funds for Israel's anti-missile defence system, and no public expression of criticism of the Israeli leader was made by the US President. Their discussions, however, were described as 'frank', and privately Clinton aides revealed that the President had pressurized the Israeli leader to expedite a resumption of negotiations with the Palestinians by offering to suspend settlement in disputed areas, begin construction of Arab housing in Jerusalem and offer to negotiate on the next stage of redeployments. Netanyahu rejoined that under the terms of the Oslo Accords and the recent Hebron protocols Israel was under no obligation to move forward with the peace process while the Palestinians were failing to fulfil their 'security responsibilities'. This message was repeated to the PLO Chairman and the Palestinian delegation that held talks with US officials in Washington in mid-April. Arguing that the Palestinian side needed to undermine Israel's security argument, Clinton urged the Palestinians to renew security co-operation with Israel. Arafat duly complied, with an announcement that the PNA would 'temporarily' resume intelligence co-ordination.

INTER-PALESTINIAN PROBLEMS

Deaths and injuries were still occurring on much of the West Bank in continued demonstrations over Har Homa, and Arafat's decision on security was deeply unpopular, not least because the Israeli leader pointedly refused to make concessions in return. Hamas, who were judged to be the main target of intelligence-sharing, registered their anger by boycotting a conference aimed at building better relations between the PNA and the Palestinian opposition. Arafat was beset by mounting difficulties throughout May and June, including the economic problems associated with a burgeoning budget deficit. In addition, Arafat's Administration was severely undermined by allegations of widespread corruption and human rights abuses, and by a sustained strike by Palestinian teachers. Privately expressed hopes that domestic pressures would be relieved by the collapse of Netanyahu's Government were frustrated when investigation into the Der'i affair absolved the Israeli Prime Minister of any criminal wrongdoing. Instead Israeli–Palestinian relations further deteriorated into crisis after Israel accused the PNA of complicity in the murder of several Palestinians suspected of involvement in land sales to Israelis. PNA spokesmen denied the charge although one week prior to the first killing, the Authority's justice minister had stated that the selling of land to 'questionable land dealers' should become a capital offence.

ISRAELI RELATIONS WITH SYRIA AND LEBANON

Israel's relations with her northern neighbours had reverted to customary hostility following Syria's refusal to condemn Islamist attacks on Israeli civilian targets and the previous Israeli Administration's subsequent decision to suspend bilateral negotiations. In August 1996, an attempt by the Netanyahu Government to entice Syria into a 'Lebanon first' agreement was rebuffed, while Israeli consideration of a plan to double the number of Jewish settlers on the Golan through the building of a new township seemed to cast doubt on the sincerity of Netanyahu's stated readiness to resume negotiations with Damascus 'without preconditions'. Tension remained high between the two states in late 1996 when Syria deployed army units from the Lebanese coastal towns (as provided for by the Saudi-brokered Taif agreements between Lebanon and Syria) to the militarily sensitive area of the Beka'a valley. A substantial car-bomb attack in Damascus in late December that resulted in the deaths of a dozen people, and a machine-gun attack on a minibus transporting Syrian workers in Lebanon, were both attributed to Maronite elements working with Israel. Scores of Lebanese connected to the National Liberal Party, which had previously had close connections with Israeli intelligence services, were detained in the aftermath of the incidents. Netanyahu vehemently denied the charges of complicity in the attacks, while sections of the Israeli press carried ever more frequent stories of impending conflict with Syria, a proposition that was regarded as highly fanciful by most intelligence experts. Increasing security co-operation between Israel and Turkey, particularly the announcement in May 1997 of joint naval exercises with US warships in the Mediterranean, heightened Syrian concerns regarding territorial isolation and prompted renewed Syrian diplomatic efforts to persuade Arab states to block normalization with Israel. At the end of June Syria enlisted the support of Saudi Arabia in exerting pressure on Qatar to cancel the next post-Madrid economic summit due to take place in November with Israeli participation. The Saudi Crown Prince stated that the Kingdom would not be represented, a decision also taken by the UAE. Syrian moves to establish more cordial relations with Iraq (the two states agreed to reopen border crossings and resume limited trade in June) and its attempts to broker improved relations between Iran and Iraq, on the one hand, and Iran and Saudi Arabia on the other, were all interpreted as a response to the perceived threat of an Israeli-Turkish axis. Meanwhile, the war of attrition in southern Lebanon continued at differing rates of intensity but with no sign of cessation. The deaths of 73 Israeli servicemen in February, killed in a collision of helicopters while being transported to southern Lebanon, briefly provoked a debate on the future of Israel's presence in that country. Both left- and right-wing supporters in Israel argued that more was to be gained from abandoning the 'security zone' than maintaining it. However, this remained a minority opinion in the Knesset—a poll revealed that only 27 of the 120 deputies supported unilateral withdrawal—and was strongly opposed by Netanyahu and his defence minister. Reports also emerged that Israel had revised its counter-insurgency strategy with regard to Hezbollah and was relying more heavily on commando raids by élite parachute units. The IDF claimed this had been effective in disrupting Hezbollah's ability to engage in classic guerrilla warfare. However it did not prevent the Shi'a militia from continuing to inflict casualties on the IDF; 12 Israeli troops were killed in combat in southern Lebanon in the first half of 1997.

SPORADIC VIOLENCE CONTINUES

By the summer of 1997, and after months of stalled Israeli-Palestinian negotiations, many commentators were declaring the death of the Oslo process. Release from domestic scandal had fortified Netanyahu against US pressure to agree to the level of compromise on Har Homa that would facilitate the Palestinians' return to the negotiating table. However evidence of increasing US frustration with Israeli policy emerged in May with the leaking of a US intelligence report that claimed that many of the homes in Gaza's settlements and in the West Bank were lying empty. The report appeared seriously to undermine Netanyahu's principal public justification for continued settlement in the Occupied Territories, namely that land was needed to relieve Israel's chronic housing shortage. Netanyahu and settler leaders claimed the figures were groundless, but few doubted the accuracy of intelligence based on many years of field monitoring and satellite reconnaissance. Following the leak the Israelis agreed to two confidence building measures suggested by the Clinton Administration: allowing the construction of more Arab housing in Jerusalem and suspending the policy of demolishing dwellings built without a licence. On the crucial issue of halting work on the Har Homa settlement, however, there was little sign of compromise, cabinet 'hardliners' urging Netanyahu to ignore the pleas of the international community. The impasse ensured that the West Bank and Gaza remained in a state of high volatility. There were violent clashes in Gaza during May and June, provoked by settler attempts to encroach on neighbouring lands. Hebron also seemed to have descended into a state of permanent confrontation between stone throwing youths and Israeli troops and armed settlers. The appearance in the city at the end of June of crudely offensive anti-Islamic posters, prompted further large-scale unrest that provoked an Israeli ultimatum for the PNA to contain the protests or risk the reoccupation of the rest of the city. Two hundred unarmed Palestinian police were subsequently ordered onto the streets by Arafat to restore order. However, with the conflict in Hebron temporarily contained, another crisis arose when four Palestinian police-officers were arrested by Israeli troops outside Nablus on suspicion of planning attacks on Israeli targets. The discovery of a 'terror cell' was described by the Israeli defence minister as 'the gravest event since the Oslo Accords'. He also demanded the extradition of Jihad Masini, head of criminal investigations in Nablus, on suspicion of ordering an attack on a Jewish settler on 10 July. On 19 July Israel Radio reported that Ghaza Jabali, Arafat's police chief, had authorized actions against West Bank settlers and that Netanyahu had ordered his removal. Masini and Jabali denied the Israeli allegations, but after receiving instructions from Washington to treat the Israeli charges with 'the highest degree of seriousness', a number of Palestinian police-officers, including Masini, were detained for investigation. Their arrest coincided with the discovery by the Palestinian police of what they termed a Hamas 'bomb factory' in the West Bank town of Beit Sahur. In the same week, the announcement that a permit had been granted for the building of a Jewish settlement in the densely-populated Palestinian district of Ras al-Amud aroused considerable international concern.

NEW INITIATIVE THWARTED

A sense of impending crisis in the Occupied Territories led to renewed US efforts to formulate an initiative that would save the Oslo process. In mid-July Clinton dispatched Thomas Pickering, Under Secretary of State for Political Affairs, to meet with Israeli and Palestinian leaders. His presence in the region prompted speculation that Washington was close to securing the backing of both Israelis and Palestinians for a new proposal. Hopes were encouraged by a statement issued by the Israeli Prime Minister expressing his opposition to the building of the settlement in Ras al-Amud and an interior ministry announcement that the permit for construction had been temporarily suspended. On 28 July Israeli and Palestinian negotiators announced that they would resume formal talks on the Oslo Accords within one week. The nature of the formula that had broken the deadlock remained unclear but was thought to have involved the possibility of suspension of works at Har Homa for between three and six months. It was also announced that Dennis Ross would be making an imminent visit to the region with a new package of proposals. A sense of relief that the peace process might yet be salvaged proved to be short-lived. On 30 July two suicide bombers attacked West Jerusalem's Mahane Yehuda market. Thirteen Israelis were killed and scores were wounded in the double explosion, responsibility for which was claimed initially by Islamic Jihad and subsequently by Hamas' military wing. There was little chance that the fledgling attempts to revive the peace process would survive the scenes of carnage in Jerusalem. The proposed resumption of formal negotiations was cancelled, as was Ross's visit to the region. Netanyahu charged Arafat with responsibility for the atrocity for his failure effectively to combat Islamist extremism. He pointedly refused to accept a message of condolence from the PNA Chairman and instead ordered the sealing of the Palesti-

nian-controlled areas and the detention of suspected Islamist militants. Arafat aides described the measures as 'a declaration of war' on the Palestinian people. Despite the arrest of some Hamas and Islamic Jihad activists there was no immediate indication that the PNA was prepared to engage in the massive anti-activist campaign that Netanyahu declared to be the crucial prerequisite for both lifting of the siege and continuing the Oslo process.

The PLO Chairman's reluctance to accede to Israel's security demands was rooted in domestic vulnerability and ever-deepening mistrust of the Netanyahu Government. The day before the Jerusalem bombings, a report commissioned by the Legislative Council into the finances of the PNA had been presented and had concluded that corruption was endemic throughout the Authority. It recommended the dissolution of the existing executive and the prosecution of two Palestinian Ministers. Following an announcement by Israel that, in addition to the closure of the West Bank and Gaza, further sanctions were to be applied including the withholding of tax revenues for the PNA, the 'freezing' of Authority assets in Israeli banks and the obstruction of broadcasts from Palestinian TV and radio stations, there was little possibility that Arafat would risk further opprobrium and potential civil conflict by acquiescing with Israeli demands to dismantle the institutional base of his Islamic opposition. Instead he attempted to counter Israeli belligerence by taking steps to prevent further fracturing of his constituency. In mid-August he chaired a 'national unity' conference that was attended by representatives of both Hamas and Islamic Jihad. Although both organizations reiterated appeals for the PNA to abandon the Oslo process, their attendance at the conference was interpreted as a gesture of gratitude to Arafat for resisting Israeli demands for a crackdown on Islamist movements. The conference drew predictable criticism from the Netanyahu Government which accused the PLO Chairman of 'colluding with terrorists'.

Having expended considerable diplomatic energy in attempting to reactivate Israeli-Palestinian negotiations, the aftermath of the Jerusalem bombings was viewed with particular dismay by the Clinton administration. In mid-August 1997 the US Government announced that Secretary of State Albright was to undertake her first tour of the region. Arab expectations of the visit were decidedly low. Albright's diplomatic career had established a firmly pro-Israeli profile in the Arab world, and her consistent response to the suicide attacks had been to echo Israli demands for tighter security controls in the PNA-administered areas. However, greater encouragement was derived from the less partisan briefings of her spokesman, James Rubin who, despite condemning Hamas and Islamic Jihad as 'enemies of peace', was careful not to criticize Arafat's recent meetings with them and also let it be known that the US Government opposed the economic sanctions that Israel had imposed on the Arab populations of the West Bank and Gaza. For their part, Palestinian officials warned that the Albright visit would only provide the momentum for a resumption of the peace process if Israel's security concerns were not the Secretary of State's principal focus. Such hopes were largely frustrated by a triple suicide bombing in Jerusalem the week before Albright's arrival that claimed the lives of a further four Israelis and led to renewed demands from the Netanyahu Government for drastic action to be taken against Islamic militants. Albright repeatedly lent her voice to these calls in her first public statements in Jerusalem; however, she did go some way to addressing Arab concerns by criticizing Israel's withholding of Palestinian tax revenues and advising Israel against the 'unilateral actions' that were hindering the creation of a climate for peace. In Egypt Albright asserted that both the US and Egyptian Governments maintained that 'a permanent settlement must ensure real security for Israel and recognition of the legitimate rights of the Palestinian people'. Although such rhetorical flourishes won the Secretary of State guarded praise in some Arab quarters, Palestinian officials were less enthusiastic. They noted that there was 'a conspicuous dichotomy between our views and those of Albright on the concept of security and terrorism'. Even more worrying for Arafat and his loyalists, who had predicated their peace strategy on the expectation that the US Government would act as a guarantor of Israeli adherence to the terms of the Oslo Accords, Albright had pointedly discounted the possibility of a more interventionist role for the USA. Continuing Palestinian despondency was a stark contrast to the satisfaction of the Israeli Government that the US Secretary of State's visit had committed Netanyahu to little more than the release of funds illegally withheld from the PNA and the resumption of negotiations with the Palestinians in the USA later in the month.

THE MESHAAL INCIDENT

Jordanian relations with Israel were plunged into renewed crisis at the end of September 1997 following a bungled Mossad assassination attempt on Khalid Meshaal, a Jordanian citizen and head of the Hamas political bureau in Amman. Travelling with false Canadian passports, the two Israeli agents were overpowered on the streets of the Jordanian capital after they had injected Meshaal with a potentially lethal chemical agent. The Jordian Government threatened to try the two Israeli operatives for murder and to sever diplomatic relations with Israel unless an antidote to the poison was supplied. This was handed over immediately and probably saved Meshaal's life. Interviewed in the Arab press, King Hussein used the incident to launch a stinging attack on the Israeli Prime Minister and the role his Government had played in the search for a Middle East peace. Meanwhile, the Jordanian Government sought to undermine the gains made by its own Islamist opponents as a result of the Meshaal affair by exacting a high price for the return of the Israeli agents. The Government in Israel subsequently announced that it was to free from a lengthy prision sentence, Sheikh Ahmad Yassin, the founder and spiritual leader of the Hamas movement. Although Israeli and Jordanian officials denied that an agreement had been negotiated, Yassin's release was followed by the deportation of the Israeli agents, and the further release of Jordanian and Palestinian prisoners. On returning to his native Gaza the ailing Yassin was fêted by thousands of well-wishers and given an official reception by the PNA leadership. The scenes in Gaza did little to diminish the embarrassment that had been generated by the assassination attempt and by the ensuing rupture in relations with Jordan. Given Netanyahu's repeated demands for the PNA to apprehend and contain Hamas cadres, the release of the movement's leader by Israel could scarcely have been more ill-timed.

ISRAELI CASUALTIES IN LEBANON

September 1997 witnessed the most serious resurgence of violence in the conflict in southern Lebanon since the Israeli bombardments of April 1996. A series of clashes involving the SLA and Hezbollah militias resulted in a number of Lebanese civilian casualties and the launch of rocket attacks against northern Israel. Israel responded with air raids on Hezbollah and Palestinian targets, and the bombing of a power station providing electricity to the port of Sidon. On 5 September a party of Israeli commandos were ambushed by a combined Hezbollah, Amal and Lebanese army force while mounting a raid on territory north of the occupation zone. Twelve Israeli soldiers were killed and several were injured in the attack; two Lebanese soldiers and six Amal and Hezbollah militiamen also died during the IDF's evacuation of its wounded. The incident was significant not just for the number of Israeli casualties—the highest for more than a decade—but also because it illustrated a growing trend for regular Lebanese troops to engage the IDF and their SLA allies in battle. Further raids into Lebanon by Israeli forces on 12 and 13 September resulted in the deaths of six Lebanese soldiers and four Hezbollah fighters, and prompted a Lebanese army commander, Gen. Emile Lahoud, to state that 'the Lebanese army will confront Israel until all our land is liberated'. Five more Israeli troops were killed in action in Lebanon during September bringing the total number of IDF-SLA casualties during 1997 to 50 (compared to 48 Hezbollah deaths). Several reasons were advanced for the high number of casualties among Israeli and SLA forces. Defence commentators noted the deployment by Hezbollah of more sophisticated weaponry, particularly the *Sagar* missile, capable of penetrating the heavy armour of Israel's battle tanks. It was also suggested that Hezbollah had benefited from better intelligence; the activities of a 'double' agent were said to be behind the successful ambush of 5 September. Within Israel the mounting death toll in Lebanon provoked renewed public debate as to the wisdom of maintaining the occupation of the south. Yossi Beillin, a prominent member of the opposition Labour party earned a rebuke from the new party leader, Ehud Barak, for campaigning for an immediate withdrawal from Lebanon. The mothers of serving troops also launched protests in Tel-Aviv, while opinion polls suggested that some 60% of the Israeli population was in favour of evacuation.

THE SETTLEMENT AND DEPLOYMENT ISSUES

The long hiatus in negotiations over implementation of the Oslo Accords ended in late September 1997 when the Israeli foreign minister met with his Palestinian counterpart in the US capital. This meeting prefaced more substantive negotiations in October. The key areas of concern for the Palestinian negotiators remained the question of settlements, the opening of the Gaza harbour and seaport, and the timing and extent of the long overdue Israeli redeployment on the West Bank. The former issue remained the most contentious. In pre-meeting declarations the PLO Chairman restated his intention to seek a halt to all construction of Jewish settlements. Netanyahu's interpretation of Madeleine Albright's appeal for a suspension of 'unilateral steps' was predictably idiosyncratic. Speaking at a press conference in Jerusalem Netanyahu elaborated his own understanding of Albright's rubric—Israel would temporarily undertake not to inaugurate new settlements, but would proceed with planned construction in existing settlements (including Har Homa) so as to 'accommodate natural population growth'. Given this divergence over such a core issue and continued friction over Israel's security demands, observers on both sides predicted that a breakthrough in the forthcoming negotiations was unlikely. Their pessimism appeared to be justified. By November Palestinian officials were accusing Israel of miring the talks in procedural issues so as to avoid broaching the subject of Israeli redeployment and settlements. For his part, Netanyahu stated that he 'would not hand over any more land to the Palestinians without knowing in advance how the features of the 'final status' settlement would look'. This remained unacceptable to the Palestinian side, indeed the only satisfaction that the Palestinian delegation derived from its presence in Washington was the sign of increasing impatience towards Israel from within the US Department of State. Press reports revealed that Albright had 'lambasted' the Israeli premier over his perceived lack of sincerity towards the Oslo process. The lack of progress in Washington also determined that the 4th Middle East and North Africa economic conference in Qatar in mid-November, would not substantially advance the development of trade links and development opportunities between Israel and the Arab world. The Syrian Government, which had distanced itself completely from the multilateral forums of the peace process, urged the cancellation of the conference. Saudi Arabia, Morocco and the UAE, key US allies in the region, subsequently announced that they too would be boycotting the conference in response to Israeli policies. President Mubarak initially refused to commit Egypt to attendance or a boycott, his hesitation was linked to the hope that the Israeli Government would smooth the way for Egyptian participation by announcing substantive movement in the peace process. With no such development, and with domestic opinion crystalized against Israel, Mubarak announced that Egypt would join the boycott of the MENA conference. Despite overt and covert US pressure, only five Arab states (Jordan, Yemen, Kuwait, Oman and Mauritania) sent delegations to Doha. The absence of Egypt and Saudi Arabia inevitably deprived the conference of much political and economic—not to mention symbolic—import. Nevertheless, the conference attracted 2,000 participants from 65 countries; this rivalled the attendance at the previous year's summit in Cairo. American, Qatari and Israeli officials expressed satisfaction with the gathering. Jordan and Israel announced a commitment to a number of joint ventures including the establishment of an industrial park in the Jordanian city of Irbid.

Far from reactivating the peace process, Israeli-Palestinian negotiations were soon marginalized as policy statements in Israel accentuated the chasm between the two sides. At the end of November 1997 the Israeli Cabinet issued a memorandum which underlined the Government's desire to radically rework the Oslo process. While agreeing in principle to a further redeployment of the IDF on the West Bank, the cabinet paper stated that this could only be accomplished in stages, and after the fulfilment of two conditions. The first of these would be the PNA's meeting certain Israeli demands: the revision of the Palestinian National Charter, and an end to 'terrorism' and political activity in East Jerusalem. The second would be an assessment by government agencies of those areas of the Occupied Territories to be retained indefinitely by Israel and not made subject to negotiation in the 'final status' talks. This was in direct contravention of the Oslo Agreement. Happily for Arafat the Cabinet plan was rejected by Labour's Ehud Barak as 'totally irrelevant'. Of greater concern to the PNA was the response of the USA to Israel's posturing and the commitment of Secretary of State Albright to the provisions concerning redeployment as specified in the Oslo and Hebron interim agreements. As Palestinian officials pointed out, according to these agreements, three redeployments were due to be completed by mid-1998. After this date the only areas of the Occupied Territories to remain under Israeli control would be borders, East Jerusalem, settlements and specified military locations. Ahmad Tibi, one of Arafat's advisers, estimated these areas to comprise no more than 11% of West Bank territory, considerably less than the 55% being touted by some sections of the Israeli Government. In late December Albright flew to Europe to hold separate meetings with Netanyahu and Arafat in London and Paris, but neither these talks, nor a further trip to the Middle East by Dennis Ross in January 1998 achieved an appreciable shift in positions. Ross's visit coincided with the announcement by Israel of a major expansion to two settlements in the Occupied Territories and the resignation of Israel's Deputy Prime Minister and Minister of Foreign Affairs, David Levy. Although Levy's resignation was forced primarily by disagreements over the Government's budget proposals, he was regarded as one of the more liberal voices in the Israeli Cabinet. His departure (not to mention the growing influence of Ariel Sharon) reinforced fears that there would be no relaxation in Israel's uncompromising approach to brokering an agreement with the PNA on IDF withdrawals. Two weeks after the failed Ross mission, Arafat and Netanyahu returned to Washington to hold separate talks with the US Administration. Prior to his appointment at the White House, the Israeli leader held a series of meetings with leading Republicans, including the Speaker of the House of Representatives, Newt Gingrich, and representatives of the evangelical Christian movement—both fiercely pro-Israel and anti-Clinton. If these high-profile engagements were intended as a warning to the Clinton administration not to exert undue pressure on the Netanyahu Government, they proved to be barely necessary. With his presidency under threat from a rapidly-escalating sex scandal, this was hardly the occasion for Clinton to get involved in a diplomatic spat with the Israeli leader. In seven hours of meetings, described as 'attritional', Clinton failed to persuade Netanyahu to accept a new US initiative. This was thought to involve a phased Israeli redeployment from 12%–15% of the West Bank territory in return for Palestinian revision of the Charter and steps 'to fight terror and prevent violence' in the self-ruled areas. Netanyahu reportedly stated that his Cabinet would accept no more than a 9.5% withdrawal. Despite the fact that the US proposals represented far less than had been expected by the PNA only six months previously, Yasser Arafat was said to have reluctantly accepted the package. His decision was influenced, in part at least, by the possibility of Israeli rejection and Netanyahu's consequent diplomatic isolation. Netanyahu himself appeared unbowed by this eventuality. His supporters viewed the US trip as a diplomatic trimph—he had after all resisted the most modest of concessions. By contrast, Arafat's description of his meetings with Clinton as 'positive, fruitful and constructive' masked a deepening pessimism. For much of the wider Arab world also, the absence of real progress at meetings in the US capital signalled an end to hopes that the USA would be prepared to exert significant pressure on the Netanyahu Government.

ISRAELI INITIATIVE ON LEBANON

Since 1997 had been such a costly year for the Israelis in Lebanon, it was not surprising that the new year brought signs that the Netanyahu Government was prepared to respond to growing domestic unease with the human cost of the occupation. In an interview with a Lebanese daily newspaper, the Israeli Minister of Defence, Itzhak Mordechai, stated that Israel would

be prepared to consider a unilateral withdrawal from Lebanon in line with UN Security Council Resolution 425. He added that the withdrawal could only be undertaken if guarantees were forthcoming that the Lebanese army would be deployed to its southern border and would co-operate with the IDF in preventing 'terror and violence' against Israel. An Israeli foreign ministry briefing also urged the incorporation of the SLA into the regular Lebanese army in the same way that other militias had been absorbed at the end of the Lebanese civil war. Lebanon rejected the offer as unacceptable, a response that observers believed to be conditioned by Syria's long-held opposition to previous 'lebanon first' proposals mooted by the Israelis. In mid-January 1998 the Israeli press carried reports that senior Lebanese officials had contacted Yossi Beillin, the guiding force behind the newly-constituted 'Movement for a Peaceful Departure from Lebanon', and assured him that in the event of an Israeli withdrawal the Lebanese army would establish full sovereignty over the evacuated areas. In March the Israeli Prime Minister sought to secure international and regional backing for a more comprehensive version of the Mordechai proposals. This reiterated Israel's desire for a withdrawal, but stated that any return to the international borders would occur in phases and be conditional on the negotiation of security guarantees from the Lebanese Government. The plan received the backing of the US Government but was rejected by Damascus and Beirut. On 3 April the Lebanese Prime Minister, Rafik Hariri, accused Israel of rewriting Resolution 425 and of attempting to drive a wedge between Syria and Lebanon. He added that his country would not support a 'security before peace' proposal and indicated that there was no prospect of an amnesty being awarded to the higher ranking officers in the SLA. The Lebanese position received support from the French President, Jacques Chirac, who opined that Resolution 425 demanded a 'unilateral' and 'unconditional' withdrawal; this was also the majority opinion of the UN Security Council. After a closed meeting, the Council President, Hishashi Owada of Japan, reported that the body's consensus was that Security Council resolutions 'are mandatory and they should be implemented without pre-conditions'. Earlier the Iranian Minister of Foreign Affairs had stated that his Government believed Hezbollah should end its military campaign if Israel ended its occupation of southern Lebanon. He did, however, concur with the Syrian opinion that the Israeli proposal was 'a Zionist plot aimed at splitting the states in the region'. Later in the month the Lebanese President undertook a global tour to win international backing for his country's refusal to accept the Israeli initiative.

INCREASED EUROPEAN INVOLVEMENT

In January 1998 the European Commission issued a detailed review of the EU's Middle East policies. The report argued that, as the region's largest aid donor, the EU should play a more active role in Middle Eastern affairs, particularly in relation to the faltering peace process. The report was careful to acknowledge the leading role played by the US Administration, but at the same time the author of the report, European Commissioner Manuel Marin, was unusually explicit in apportioning blame for the political and economic failures of the previous 12 months. Marin stated that Israeli policies, and in particular the restrictions imposed on trade and economic activity, had undermined EU aid initiatives and were responsible for a severe economic decline in the Palestinian territories. This was, Marin pointed out, despite the injection of $1,200m. of EU funds into the Palestinian economy during 1993–97. Within days of the presentation of the report, the European Commission President, Jacques Santer, embarked on a seven-day tour of the Middle East, his first official visit to the region. The visit was designed to raise the profile of the EU in the region and was punctuated by frequent expressions of Europe's irritation with the policies of the Netanyahu Government. He levelled specific criticism at Israel for blocking the opening of the European-financed airport in Gaza. Having held talks with both Palestinian and Israeli leaders, he returned to Brussels accusing Netanyahu of generating 'contradictions' with regard to Israel's position. 'On the one hand, Prime Minister Netanyahu says he wants economic development in the Palestinian territories. On the other hand he won't allow the Palestinians to exploit their economic potential.' He also reiterated the European belief that Israel's security needs could best be assured by swift implementation of their obligations as laid down in the Oslo principles. Questioned as to what pressure the EU could bring to bear on the Israelis, Santer declared the Europeans 'powerless' to bring about a change in Israeli policies. He dismissed suggestions of sanctions being employed against Israel. European–Israeli relations deteriorated further in March, following the visit to the Middle East by the British Secretary of State for Foreign and Commonwealth Affairs, Robin Cook. Prior to the visit Cook had gained EU support for a British initiative to 'unblock the peace process'. In essence, the six-point British plan called for the Palestinians and Israelis to adhere to previously signed agreements. However, it also contained a specific appeal for Israel to implement substantial and credible redeployments on the West Bank and to 'freeze' all settlement activity. The proposals were dismissed by an Israeli Government spokesman as 'essentially Palestinian ideas' which only reinforced antipathy towards greater European involvement in the region. Cook's intended itinerary also raised Israeli hackles. A proposed visit to the site of the Har Homa settlement in the company of Faisal Husseini, the PNA's Minister with Responsibility for Jerusalem Affairs, was declared 'unacceptable' by Netanyahu. Cook eventually agreed to be escorted to Har Homa by Israel's Cabinet Secretary, David Naveh, a compromise that satisfied neither the Israelis nor the Palestinians. In the event, Cook's visit to Har Homa degenerated into an undignified spectacle as Israeli security personnel struggled to keep the British politician from being jostled by a crowd of right-wing settlers. Swiftly departing the scene, Cook travelled to East Jerusalem, where he met Faisal Husseini and laid a wreath to commemorate the Palestinian victims of the 1948 massacre at Deir Yassin. Netanyahu responded by cancelling an arranged dinner with Cook and cut short their scheduled meeting to a symbolic 15 minutes. The 15 EU foreign ministers issued a statement in support of Cook's visit, countering charges that it had irreparably damaged the chances of a more constructive EU role in the region. Netanyahu's refusal to pursue diplomatic channels in order to ease the strain on relations resulting from the visit suggested that the Israeli Prime Minister had seized on the incident as a way of scuppering the EU's political ambitions in the region.

RENEWED DEADLOCK

In early 1998, a renewed crisis in Washington's relations with Baghdad, occasioned by Saddam Hussain's refusal to allow UN weapons inspection teams free access to his presidential palaces, threw Arab dissatisfaction with the US Government's Middle East policy into sharp relief. The refusal of the Arab world to back US air strikes could be explained in part by the genuine desire to see an end to the hardships endured by ordinary Iraqis, but opposition to military action was also informed by a perception that the Clinton administration was overly indulgent of Israel's reluctance to meet its responsibilities. There were few signs during the early months of 1998 to suggest that the deadlock was about to be broken. Further visits to the Middle East by Madeleine Albright in February and Dennis Ross in March failed to sway Netanyahu from his earlier insistence that Israel would only accept a redeployment of less than 10%. He deemed the US proposals 'an imposed solution that is neither desirable nor viable'. While Netanyahu's stance was reported to be causing exasperation in Washington, it did not lead to the public condemnation of Israel demanded by the Arab world. Yasser Arafat, meanwhile, was taking great risks with his own constituency in order to appease the US Government. Arrests of Hamas cadres had resumed in areas under PNA control, and during the Iraqi crisis pro-Iraqi demonstrations were dispersed by the security forces (it was also reported that, following Israeli allegations that the PNA was secretly releasing imprisoned Islamists, Arafat organized a tour of prisons for the US Central Intelligence Agency (CIA) to demonstrate that those arrested remained incarcerated). More importantly, the PLO Chairman had remained committed to the unpublished, but widely reported US proposals to move the peace process forward. These proposals allegedly required Israel to redeploy from a further 13.1% of the West Bank's 'Area C' (under exclusive Israeli control) in three phases, and for 12% of this territory to be transferred to West Bank 'Area B' (under PNA civilian, but

Israeli security control) rather than 'Area A' (under exclusive PNA civilian and security control). An additional 12% of 'Area B' territory would be converted to 'Area A', as a form of compensation. The US initiative fell far short of the 30%–40% redeployment originally anticipated by the Palestinians, yet PNA spokesmen believed that Arafat had no other option but to remain committed to the proposal. Egypt and Jordan had already given their reluctant support to the plan and had convinced Arafat that the US ideas represented the most realistic chance of success with Netanyahu. The PNA leader was also aware that rejection of the agreement would jeopardize US support for a more substantial third redeployment. The Israeli Government had already made it known that they wanted the third redeployment cancelled or at best merged into the 'final status' talks.

Relations between the Jordanian Government and the Israeli authorities remained frosty following the attempted assassination of Khalid Meshaal. Prospects of a thaw receded in mid-March 1998 when Ariel Sharon reportedly threatened to attempt another assassination of the Hamas chief. Jordan's foreign ministry summoned the Israeli ambassador to demand an explanation of Sharon's comments; Sharon subsequently sent a letter to the Jordanian Government stating that his comments had been misunderstood and that Israel had no plans 'to attack Jordan or Jordanians'. In mid-April King Hussein and Prime Minister Netanyahu held an unscheduled meeting in Eilat to discuss the stalemate in the peace process. The details of the meeting were not revealed but the Jordanian monarch later commented that 'not all the results of the meeting had been positive'. In a letter sent to Netanyahu on the day after the talks, King Hussein urged Israel to accept the US formula for withdrawal and warned that if he failed to do so he would bear responsibility for the collapse of the peace process.

During a visit to the Middle East at the end of April 1998 the British Prime Minister, Tony Blair, invited Israeli, Palestinian and US leaders to peace talks in London to be conducted in May. All parties accepted the invitation which was presented, once again, as a last ditch attempt to salvage what remained of the peace process. Following two days of bilateral talks in London on 4 and 5 May, there was little sign that the joint efforts of Blair and Albright had persuaded the Israelis to accept the US proposals. At the end of the talks Tony Blair concluded, somewhat lamely, that there had been 'no breakthrough but no breakdown either'. Albright invited the Israeli and Palestinian leaders to meet President Clinton in Washington later in the month if Netanyahu could agree to the 13.1% redeployment. This was something that Netanyahu claimed his right-wing Cabinet colleagues were not prepared to countenance. He did, however, state that there were still issues to be explored with Albright, and in mid-May he flew to the USA. During his five-day trip to Washington and New York, Netanyahu once again displayed an adroit ability to manipulate the domestic US political scene. He argued his 'hardline' security agenda forcefully in the media, in the US Congress and to pro-Israeli lobby groups. He won both standing ovations and strong political backing from Republican representatives who were critical of the Clinton administration's 'bullying' of Israel. 'Congress,' claimed the Republican Chair of the Committee for International Relations, 'will continue to stand shoulder-to-shoulder with Israel regardless of the obstacles that others may place before her.' Meetings with Albright and Ross concentrated on a formula to bridge the gap between the US redeployment proposals and Netanyahu's insistence that a withdrawal from more than 9.5% of West Bank territory would conflict with Israel's security needs. Before he flew back to Israel to take part in his nation's 50th anniversary celebrations, Netanyahu suggested that his policy differences with the US Administration were diminishing. He refused to elaborate on the reasons for his optimism but there was speculation that a bridging formula may have been agreed. Two potential scenarios were advanced unofficially. The first envisaged the Israelis implementing a 9.5% redeployment and agreeing to honour the remaining percentage only after the Palestinians had met certain security obligations. The second, and more fancied scenario, involved the Israeli Government agreeing to the larger redeployment but demanding US support for a postponement of the all-important third deployment in compensation. If this was the case, it would be certain to cause a crisis within the PNA. Arafat had staked his negotiating strategy on the understanding, in accordance with the Oslo Accords, that he would be entering the 'final status' talks with at least 80% of the West Bank under his full or partial control. A postponement of the third redeployment would mean that these negotiations would begin with 60% of the West Bank under exclusive Israeli control. According to Hani al-Hassan of Fatah's central committee, this would inevitably lead to a 'final status' solution that involved the partitioning of the West Bank and the retention by Israel of 'around 45% of the territory'. This would be an arrangement, observed al-Hassan, 'that no Palestinian leader could endorse without falling'. The pessimism of the Fatah old guard was reflected in mounting frustration with regard to the peace process on the Palestinian streets. As Israelis were joyously marking the foundation of the Jewish State, Palestinians were marching through the streets of Gaza and the West Bank in officially sanctioned commemoration of the *Nabka*, the 'catastrophe' of 1948 that had led to their dispossession and dispersal. In a number of cities the thousands of demonstrators were joined by masked men carrying machine-guns and automatic rifles. Significantly, the majority of these were not the activists of Hamas and Islamic Jihad, but members of Arafat's increasingly estranged Fatah movement. In Nablus, the local leader of Hamas concluded a march by 15,000 people by firing a pistol into the air and calling for 'a new era of resistance'. Inevitably, several of the demonstrations erupted into violence as protesters vented their emotions on Israeli settlements and military positions. By the end of the day six Palestinians had been shot dead (five of them in Gaza) and scores had been wounded by live ammunition and rubber bullets.

THE JERUSALEM ISSUE

Updated for this edition by PAUL COSSALI

Based on an original article by Michael Adams, with subsequent additions by David Gilmour, Paul Harper and Steven Sherman

The Arab sector of Jerusalem, including the old walled city, was captured during the June War in 1967 by Israeli forces, which went on to occupy all the Jordanian territory lying west of the River Jordan. Theoretically, there was no difference in status between Jerusalem and the rest of the West Bank; both were occupied territory. In practice, Israel immediately removed the walls and barriers dividing the western (Israeli) and eastern (Arab) sectors of the city and at the end of June 1967 the Knesset passed legislation incorporating the Arab sector into a reunited Jerusalem under Israeli sovereignty. At the same time the boundaries of the municipal area of Jerusalem were greatly extended, reaching to near Bethlehem in the south and incorporating Kalandia airport (close to Ramallah) in the north.

Faced with Israel's effective annexation of the Arab sector, the UN General Assembly on 4 July 1967, ruled, by 99 votes to none, that the annexation was invalid and called on Israel not to take any measures to alter the status of the city. Ten days later the Assembly adopted a second resolution 'reiterating' the earlier one and 'deploring' Israel's failure to implement it.

Before the first of these resolutions was passed, the Israeli authorities had embarked on a series of structural alterations and demolitions in the Old City of Jerusalem, which aroused strong Arab protests and whose continuation was to lead to considerable international controversy. In clearing the area in front of the Western (Wailing) Wall, they expropriated 50 Arab families at very short notice and demolished their houses, while in the Jewish Quarter they dispossessed a further 200 Arab families. In all, and before the end of June 1967, some 4,000 Arabs in Jerusalem had lost their homes. In some cases, but not all, they were provided with alternative accommodation.

In November 1967 the UN Security Council passed its unanimous Resolution 242 setting out the basis for an overall settlement between Israel and its Arab neighbours. However, it was not until May 1968 that the Security Council passed its first resolution dealing specifically with the Jerusalem issue.

The resolution (No. 252 of 21 May 1968) deplored Israel's failure to comply with the two General Assembly resolutions of 4 and 14 July 1967, confirmed that any measures taken by Israel to alter the status of Jerusalem were invalid and called on Israel to rescind all such measures and to refrain from similar action in the future. The effect was only to increase the haste with which Israel set about changing the face of the city. Bulldozers had been at work on Mount Scopus since February, and soon the first of the new housing estates began to take shape beside the Nablus Road leading northwards out of Jerusalem. In the absence of any progress towards a peace settlement, it became clear that the Israeli Government intended to forestall, by establishing a physical presence in the Arab sector of Jerusalem, any future attempt to challenge its sovereignty over the whole of the municipal area.

Meeting again to consider the question in July 1969, the Security Council adopted, this time by a unanimous vote (in the previous year the USA had abstained from voting on the Jerusalem resolution), an even stronger resolution (No. 267 of 3 July 1969). Reaffirming its earlier stand and deploring 'the failure of Israel to show any regard' for the previous resolutions both of the General Assembly and of the Security Council, the Council 'censured in the strongest terms' all measures taken by Israel to change the status of Jerusalem, confirmed that all such measures were 'invalid' and again called on Israel to desist from taking any further action of a similar kind. Israel formally rejected the resolution and the Israeli Minister of Information stated in Jerusalem that it could not influence the 'facts' which had been intentionally created by Israel 'after due consideration of the political danger involved'.

The situation in Jerusalem itself was further aggravated in August 1969 by a disastrous fire in the al-Aqsa mosque, which at first sight appeared to confirm the fears of the Arabs for the safety of the Islamic and Christian shrines in the Old City.

Israeli investigations showed that the fire had been caused by a deranged Australian religious fanatic who was later brought to trial; but from that moment the concern of Muslim communities throughout the world reinforced the Arab sense of grievance at the loss of the Holy City.

In the following year Christian concern also began to make itself felt, especially after the publication of an Israeli 'master plan' for the future of Jerusalem. This plan envisaged the doubling of the Jewish population of the city by 1980 and an eventual total population of 900,000. An international conference of town planners, convoked by the Israeli municipal authorities at the end of 1970 to consider the plan, was almost unanimous in condemning its aesthetic implications. Early in 1971 a dispute also developed between the UN and the Israeli Government over the intention, announced in the master plan, to build another housing estate in the neighbourhood of Government House, the headquarters in Jerusalem of the UN. In March 1971 articles in the official Vatican newspaper L'Osservatore Romano and in the English Catholic weekly The Tablet revealed the strength of Catholic feeling over developments in the Holy City, and these feelings were strengthened when it became known that in the same month Israel had destroyed an Arab village on the hill of Nebi Samwil, north-west of Jerusalem, in preparation for the building on Arab land of yet another housing estate for immigrant Jews.

Israeli opinion was divided over the future of Jerusalem. Only a small minority of Israelis were in favour of relinquishing Israeli sovereignty over the Arab sector of the city, if negotiations for an overall settlement of the Arab–Israeli conflict should ever materialize. In the absence of any sign of such negotiations, the issue remained a hypothetical one and the Israeli Government made no secret of its determination to establish a hold on Jerusalem which would prove unbreakable. A further resolution by the Security Council (No. 298 of 25 September 1971—see Documents on Palestine, p. 108) was rejected by Israel as brusquely as the previous ones, and even the provision in the resolution that the Secretary-General, 'using such instrumentalities as he may choose', should report to the Council within 60 days on the implementation of the resolution, failed to achieve any result since the Secretary-General eventually had to report that he had been unable to execute his mission, for lack of co-operation from the Israeli authorities.

On purely aesthetic grounds, however, many Israelis were disturbed by the physical changes overtaking Jerusalem. Within five years of the June War of 1967 the construction of large housing estates had transformed the appearance of Mount Scopus, where the Old City (and the whole of the Arab sector) was dominated by a row of apartment blocks breaking the historic skyline. There were acute disagreements between the Mayor of Jerusalem and the ministers of housing and of tourism over some of the implications of this building programme, but continuing uncertainty over the prospects for a political settlement with the Arabs gave encouragement to the 'activists' in Israel, and the creation of 'facts' continued, in Jerusalem as in the rest of the Occupied Territories, throughout 1972 and most of 1973.

Anxiety over the future of Jerusalem and resentment at Israel's treatment both of the Arab population and of the physical fabric of the city played a part in provoking the Arab decision to resort to war in October 1973. In particular, these feelings influenced King Faisal to throw Saudi Arabia's weight behind the attempt to enforce Israel's withdrawal from the Occupied Territories, including Arab Jerusalem. Henceforth, the restoration of Arab sovereignty over the Old City became one of the principal conditions demanded by the Arabs for a comprehensive peace settlement with Israel.

Immediately after the October war political and economic conditions in Israel combined to slow down for a time the work of demolition and construction by which the face of the city was being transformed. In the course of 1974, however, the same general pattern as before was maintained, resulting in the steady eviction from the Old City of Arabs, whose houses were demolished and replaced by dwellings for Jewish immigrants. Between 1967 and 1977, 6,300 Arab residents of Jerusalem were evicted in this way from their homes in the Old City. Protests from the international community, stimulated by anxiety over the continuing exodus from Jerusalem of Christian Arabs, became more frequent but achieved only publicity.

Similar protests over excavations being conducted by the Israeli authorities in the vicinity of Islamic and Christian holy places in the Old City of Jerusalem brought to a head criticisms which had been voiced for more than five years within UNESCO. Recalling that urgent appeals previously addressed to the Israeli Government to suspend these excavations had been ignored, the Executive Board of UNESCO, in June 1974, voted 'to condemn the persistent violation by Israel of the resolutions and decisions adopted by the General Conference and the Executive Board'. In its turn the General Conference of UNESCO, meeting in November 1974, condemned Israel's attitude as 'contradictory to the aims of the Organization as laid down in its Constitution' and resolved to withhold assistance in the fields of education, science and culture until Israel agreed to respect previous conference resolutions in the matter.

The attitude previously expressed by both the Security Council and the General Assembly of the UN was reaffirmed in subsequent years despite the failure to obtain the compliance of the Government of Israel with existing resolutions. In a unanimous 'consensus statement' adopted on 11 November 1976, the Security Council 'strongly deplored' Israel's actions in the Occupied Territories, including Jerusalem; required Israel once more to 'desist forthwith from any action which tends to alter the status of Jerusalem'; and called on Israel to comply with the terms of the Geneva Convention on the Protection of Civilians in Wartime.

Jerusalem once again became a controversial issue in May 1980, when the ultra-nationalist Israeli Knesset (Parliament) member, Mrs Geula Cohen, tabled a bill in the Knesset with the object of confirming Jerusalem as Israel's indivisible capital. Despite strong protests from the Egyptian Government, which made it clear that it would not resume the peace negotiations on Palestinian autonomy (see Arab–Israeli Relations 1967–98) unless the bill was rejected, it was placed before a Knesset committee. Egypt was further antagonized when, on 23 June, the Israeli Prime Minister, Mr Begin, announced that he was moving his offices to the Arab sector of Jerusalem.

At a time when the USA was desperately trying to produce some compromise on the Jerusalem issue which would enable Israel and Egypt to resume the negotiations, the Knesset's legal committee voted in favour of giving a first reading of the bill confirming the annexed status of the Arab sector of Jerusalem. As the originator of the bill told *The Times* of London on 30 June: 'This Bill is designed to ensure that there will never be any compromise over the sovereignty of Jerusalem'.

Nevertheless, a debate taking place in the UN Security Council on the same day made it clear that this view would not be accepted by the international community. In a vote of 14 to none, with only the USA abstaining, the Security Council passed a resolution denying Israel the right either to change the status of Jerusalem or to declare the city to be its capital.

The action of the Security Council was followed by an emergency resolution in the UN General Assembly on 29 July 1980, which called upon Israel to withdraw completely and unconditionally from all territories occupied in 1967, including Jerusalem. The resolution (ES-7/2) was passed by 112 votes to 7, with 24 abstentions. The following day Israel enacted its 'basic law' proclaiming Jerusalem as its 'eternal capital'.

The Arab reaction to this law was swift and on 6 August 1980 Saudi Arabia and Iraq, the Middle East's two largest oil exporters, announced that they would break off economic and diplomatic relations with any country which recognized Jerusalem as Israel's capital. A fortnight later the Security Council adopted Resolution 478, which declared Israel's enactment of the 'basic law' to be a violation of international law and urged 'those states that have established diplomatic missions in Jerusalem to withdraw such missions from the Holy City'. The resolution was passed by 14 votes to none, with the USA

abstaining. In his speech during the debate the US Secretary of State, Edmund Muskie, berated the council for passing a 'series of unbalanced and unrealistic resolutions on Middle East issues'.

Shortly afterwards those Latin American countries with embassies in Jerusalem announced that they would be moving them to Tel-Aviv. They were Venezuela, Uruguay, Chile, Ecuador, El Salvador, Costa Rica, Haiti, Panama, Colombia and Bolivia. The only European country which retained its Ambassador in Jerusalem, the Netherlands, also decided to move to Tel-Aviv.

Jerusalem continued to figure prominently in international efforts to promote an overall settlement of the Arab–Israeli conflict: the European Community's (EC) Venice Declaration of 13 June 1980 (see Documents on Palestine, p. 123) rejected any unilateral actions designed to change the status of the city, and proposals adopted by the Fez Arab summit and a plan put forward by the Soviet President, Leonid Brezhnev, in September 1982 both urged an Israeli withdrawal from the eastern sector of the city and its inclusion in a future Palestinian state. The initiative of President Reagan, also announced in September 1982, confined itself to declaring that the city must remain undivided and its final status be negotiable. Every indication remained, however, that Israel was not deterred from its resolve to ensure in advance the city's ultimate status by pursuing an accelerated programme of 'Judaization'. To the south and east of the Old City, plans to complete the encirclement of the Arab population with high-rise, high-density housing complexes proceeded apace with the Neve Yaacov South, Gilo and Ma'aleh Edomin schemes, which were to comprise a total of 26,000 apartments. Over 10,000 dunums of land (1,000 dunums = 1 sq km) were seized for these schemes, virtually all of it expropriated from private Arab owners. In July 1981 the Knesset reaffirmed the designation of the whole of Jerusalem as Israel's 'eternal capital'.

The undiminished sensitivity to the issue of Arabs and the whole Islamic world was demonstrated following an indiscriminate gun attack on worshippers at the Dome of the Rock mosque by an Israeli soldier on 11 April 1982, in which two Arabs were killed and more than 30 wounded. The day of protest recommended by the Organization of the Islamic Conference was observed throughout the Islamic world, while a UN Security Council draft resolution condemning the attack and deploring 'any act or encouragement of destruction or penetration of the holy places, religious buildings and sites in Jerusalem' was vetoed by the USA, though otherwise gaining unanimous approval. The threat posed by Jewish religious extremists increased throughout 1983 with the emergence of a clandestine group calling itself 'Terror against Terror', which claimed responsibility for a series of bomb attacks on Islamic and Christian sites around Jerusalem, which fortunately resulted in few casualties and no deaths. This campaign culminated in January 1984 in an attempt to smuggle explosives into the al-Aqsa mosque, which was foiled at the last moment by security guards. The implications of the plot were particularly horrendous, not just because the attack had been timed to coincide with the congregation of thousands for Friday services on the following day but also because of evidence that the motivation of the group responsible, which was in possession of standard Israeli army-issue weapons, was to advance the reconstruction of the Jewish Temple by ridding the Temple Mount area of its 'encumbrance' of Islamic holy sites.

The dual threats to Jerusalem posed by Israeli settlement and Jewish religious fanaticism were overshadowed by another to the city's legal status, when it became clear that a number of countries, including, most importantly, the USA, were prepared to signal their acceptance of Israel's claim to the city as its sovereign capital by transferring their embassies from Tel-Aviv to Jerusalem. Discussion of such a move on the part of the USA began in Washington in February 1984 and the proposal rapidly gained momentum, winning the sponsorship of over 180 members of the House of Representatives and some 37 senators. The Reagan administration did not, however, lend its support to the move, and the Secretary of State, George Shultz, wrote to the Senate Foreign Relations Committee, describing the proposed legislation as 'damaging to the cause of peace' and contrary to the US position on Jerusalem of refusing 'to recognize unilateral acts by any party'. Such opposition was felt to spring more from fear of the anti-US backlash, which relocating the embassy would provoke throughout the Islamic world, than from respect for successive UN resolutions declaring East Jerusalem to be occupied territory, or for the Hague Convention of 1907 and the Geneva Civilians Convention of 1949, which held that purported annexations of territory occupied in war were a violation of international law (as treaties of the USA, both these conventions are parts of 'the Supreme Law of the Land' under Article VI of the US Constitution, and for the US Government to assent to or condone Israel's violation of them would be unconstitutional).

The extreme importance attached to the issue in Arab and Islamic quarters was illustrated again when, on 21 March, El Salvador followed Costa Rica's decision of 1982 to relocate its embassy in Jerusalem, a move which, it had been led to believe, would result in the pro-Israel lobby in Congress helping to clear the way for US military assistance programmes for El Salvador. A meeting of the Organization of the Islamic Conference in Fez in April, which spoke of the obligation to make Jerusalem an international, independent city open to all peoples and faiths, passed a resolution to the effect that member states should sever all diplomatic, economic and cultural relations with any country that moved its embassy to Jerusalem. Egypt made a similar declaration and duly severed diplomatic ties with El Salvador and Costa Rica on 22 April.

The US Administration remained firmly opposed to relocating its embassy in Israel to Jerusalem in the foreseeable future. US officials rejected as 'ridiculous' and potentially dangerous a formal statement issued on 4 April 1982 by leaders of the American Jewish Congress asserting that the status of the US Consulate in Jerusalem was 'intolerable' and undermined US interests in the Middle East. For its part, the Israeli Government stood by its claim that Jerusalem was Israel's 'eternal' capital, rejecting outright a proposal made by Pope John Paul II on 25 April for an internationally guaranteed status for Jerusalem in the interests of Christianity, Islam and Judaism.

Israeli settlement projects in the city proceeded apace in 1984 and 1985, with many thousands of new apartments being built and occupied within the boundary of annexed East Jerusalem. Just outside the municipal line, in the occupied West Bank, there was also rapid construction of the satellite towns of Efrat, south of Bethlehem, Ma'aleh Edomin to the east, and Givat Zeev to the north, which were designed to provide, in total, housing for over 50,000 Israelis. The completion of these new towns filled the last remaining gaps in the ring of settlements enclosing East Jerusalem as part of Israel's Metropolitan Plan, which aimed to achieve a Jewish majority of 120,000 over the Arab population in the Greater Jerusalem area by 1986.

The focus of the conflict over Jerusalem soon shifted back to the competing claims of possession of Jews and Muslims within the Old City. The increasing numbers of Jews settling in the Muslim Quarter, which before 1980 had housed no Jews at all, threatened to introduce strife into an area where relations between the two communities had long been exemplary. Cases of Jewish settlers intimidating Arab residents in order to establish proprietorial rights, and of Jewish-occupied buildings being illegally extended, greatly alarmed the Muslim population, who feared that the inroads could be the start of a campaign to expel the Old City's inhabitants. The new settlers, who, by mid-1985, numbered some 200 among the Muslim Quarter's 20,000 Arabs, were nearly all religious-nationalist extremists, openly dedicated to rebuilding the Jewish Temple on the site of the Muslim sanctuary and mosques, the Haram ash-Sharif. Traditionally, the controversy over the Temple Mount issue had been minimized by Jewish religious rulings forbidding Jews even to enter the area, but the encroachment by Jewish zealots on Muslim areas bordering on the shrine was a sign that this precept was now being challenged. In the Old City alone, seven *yeshivas* (Jewish religious colleges) had been set up expressly to study the issue of the Temple and how Jews could, once again, pray there.

In January 1986, members of the Israeli Knesset Interior Committee asked permission to visit the compound of al-Aqsa mosque on the Temple Mount, ostensibly to ensure that restoration work being undertaken by the Islamic authorities was not detrimental to the ancient remains of the Jewish Temple. Although it was known that the Knesset committee was acting

at the instigation of Jewish extremists, who had been attempting to establish a foothold in the mosque compound by conducting prayers there, the Islamic Awqaf department, entrusted with safeguarding the shrine, nevertheless gave permission for members of the committee to visit certain unused chambers beneath the al-Aqsa structure known to Jews as Solomon's Stables. On 7 January the Israeli parliamentarians arrived at the site accompanied by television crews and a number of religious and nationalist extremists, including the leader of the 'Temple Mount Faithful', a Jewish group dedicated to rebuilding the Temple in place of the al-Aqsa mosque. Islamic officials decided that the Israeli delegation intended a political demonstration of Jewish claims to the site rather than an inspection of restoration work, and refused it entry, whereupon members of the group, led by Knesset member Geula Cohen, of the extreme right-wing Tehiya Party, tried to force their way through. Calls for help were broadcast from the minarets of the Old City's mosques, and alarmed Muslims rushed to the site. The ensuing riot was controlled only by police escorting the Israeli group away and firing tear-gas into the crowd. A week later, despite an inspection of the site in the interim by the leader of the Knesset, Shlomo Hillel, and the Mayor of Jerusalem, Teddy Kollek, who testified that no structural changes had been made, the extremist group returned to the compound and attempted to pray inside it. More riots ensued, and were again dispersed by police using tear-gas.

The al-Aqsa riots were seized upon by Israeli nationalists as a vehicle for publicizing Jewish claims to the site, and there were signs that the Temple Mount was increasingly becoming a nationalist, as well as a religious issue in Israeli politics, in that it was a means of asserting Israeli sovereignty over what was internationally considered to be occupied territory. On 30 January the UN Security Council drafted a resolution strongly condemning Israel's 'provocative acts', which 'violated the sanctity of the sanctuary of the Haram ash-Sharif in Jerusalem' and constituted 'a serious obstruction to achieving a comprehensive, just and lasting peace in the Middle East'. The resolution, otherwise supported by all the Security Council members except Thailand, which abstained, was vetoed by the USA. Although the US Administration maintained its official position that East Jerusalem was occupied territory and that the ultimate status of the city should be determined through negotiation, it was clearly embarrassed by the resolution's reiteration of the UN's rejection of Israeli claims to sovereignty over the entire city. Despite the intense anger and alarm which was generated throughout the Arab and Muslim world by the perceived threat to Islam's third holiest shrine, Israel's Chief Rabbi, Mordechai Eliahu, shortly afterwards proposed the construction of a synagogue next to the mosques on Temple Mount. The proposed synagogue would be 'higher and more elevated' than the mosques of al-Aqsa and the Dome of the Rock, which would remain only 'to commemorate the Destruction' and the day when the Temple would be rebuilt.

There was a marked increase in tension in the Old City in the autumn of 1986, with acts of intimidation against Palestinians by religious zealots, as well as attacks against Israeli security personnel by Palestinians, occurring with greater frequency. The tension climaxed in November after the stabbing of a *yeshiva* student (one of a group of religious nationalists which had resorted to the violent intimidation of neighbouring Palestinian families in an effort to force them to abandon their homes in the Aqabat al-Khaldi quarter). The subsequent backlash from Israeli extremists shocked even Israeli officials. For several days they pursued a campaign of burning and looting Palestinian homes and shops, and assaulting individual Palestinians throughout the Old City. In the days following the violence, vigilante groups were created to warn and protect the community against the Israeli extremists.

While the level of violence diminished in the early part of 1987, the attitude of the Palestinian population in East Jerusalem continued to harden. Demands for protest action that were formerly heeded elsewhere in the Occupied Territories but only to a very limited extent in Jerusalem, began to win more active support. On Land Day in 1987, almost every shop in East Jerusalem closed in observance of the annual commemorative strike, marking a departure from previous years when few shopkeepers had been prepared to lose a day's takings, and a change in the political climate which prefigured confrontation on an increasing scale.

The sharpened nationalist consciousness of Palestinians in East Jerusalem progressively involved them in an extension of the running conflict between the people of the Occupied Territories and the Israeli authorities, which began in December 1987. Clashes in Jerusalem grew more frequent in 1987, and the Palestinian *intifada* (uprising), although it began in Gaza and spread to the West Bank, took root in Jerusalem as firmly as anywhere else. The city's historical status has made it a centre of Palestinian resistance, particularly for the Unified National Leadership of the Uprising (UNLU), whose organizational work has largely been conducted there. Israeli repression has been a little less in evidence in Jerusalem than elsewhere in the Occupied Territories, but arrests, beatings, deportations, curfews and other measures have all been employed there as well.

The city's central importance to the international community was underlined at the summit meeting of the Arab League in Amman (Jordan) in November 1987. Jerusalem was cited as a 'symbol of peace' and as the 'embodiment of the historic ties between the Muslim and Christian faiths'. This description was contained in a little-noticed passage of the official communiqué at the end of the summit in which King Hussein of Jordan, rather than the PLO, was mandated to undertake contacts with the Vatican on the Jerusalem issue.

During 1988, an election year in the USA, pronouncements on the subject of Jerusalem from presidential candidates were inevitable. Recommendations for the relocation of the US Embassy from Tel-Aviv to Jerusalem were frequently made in an attempt to gain Jewish support. All the candidates for the Democratic Party presidential nomination, with the exception of Jesse Jackson, promised to support such a relocation, if elected. Among the most ardent supporters of this move was Michael Dukakis who, having received the nomination of the Democratic Party in July 1988, was the favourite to succeed Ronald Reagan in the White House. As the November party conventions approached, there was a real fear in the Arab world of the election of a US President who would endorse the relocation of the US Embassy, conferring implicit US recognition of Israel's annexation of East Jerusalem. Such recognition had hitherto been withheld even by the Reagan administration— probably the most overtly pro-Israeli US Government since 1948. By the time George Bush had overtaken his Democratic rival in the polls, however, the danger of such a move had receded.

The peace proposals first put forward by the Israeli Government in April 1989 (see Arab–Israeli Relations 1967–98), while incorporating elections in the Occupied Territories, made no mention of the eligibility or otherwise of Palestinians in East Jerusalem to vote or stand as candidates in such elections. This question was repeatedly raised by those seeking to obtain more concessions from Israel in order to make the proposals more acceptable to Palestinians, but Israel's agreeing to allow the participation of residents of East Jerusalem would clearly have contradicted its formal annexation of the city in 1967.

At the 19th session of the Palestine National Council (PNC) in Algiers in November 1988, Jerusalem was named the capital of the newly declared independent state of Palestine, and in July 1989 was recognized as such by more than 60 countries.

Disagreements over the status of East Jerusalem and its residents continued to frustrate the progress of the various peace proposals put forward during 1989. The US Secretary of State James Baker's preference for 'constructive ambiguity'— keeping the peace agenda deliberately vague in order not to snare progress on controversial issues—was sorely tested by the Israeli Right's insistence that Palestinians from East Jerusalem be barred from prospective elections for the Occupied Territories. Moreover, after President Mubarak of Egypt had suggested that pre-election talks between an Israeli and a Palestinian delegation should be convened in Cairo, Israel's Prime Minister Shamir stated the opposition of the Likud to the inclusion of East Jerusalemites in the talks. Attempts by James Baker and Israel's Labour Party to coax Shamir into accepting a compromise formula, whereby Palestinians who had East Jerusalem identity papers but who lived in the West Bank would be allowed to participate in the talks, were unsuccessful.

Indeed, in what was widely interpreted as a move to emphasize his opposition to such a compromise, Shamir was said to have ordered the arrest in February 1990 of Faisal Husseini, a leading pro-PLO personality and East Jerusalem resident. The charge brought against Husseini—that he had supplied funds for the purchase of uniforms by the Palestine Popular Army—was as transparently ridiculous as his arrest was politically motivated. An international outcry forced Husseini's quick release and at a press conference he subsequently alleged that his arrest had been meant to discredit him in view of his association with the proposed Cairo talks.

There was little doubt that Shamir's refusal to compromise on the issue of East Jerusalem stemmed as much from tactical as from ideological imperatives. Endless debate over the details of Palestinian representation seemed the least damaging way for Israel to stifle the peace process. However, such delaying tactics risked frustrating the USA to such an extent that it would be compelled, against Secretary of State James Baker's wishes, to state its position on East Jerusalem. However, it was not the stalled peace process which finally led the US Administration to reveal its hand, but, rather, the issue of Soviet Jewish emigration to Israel. Angry that 10% of the new Jewish immigrants from the USSR were being settled in East Jerusalem, Bush unequivocally equated East Jerusalem with occupied territory during a telephone conversation with Prime Minister Shamir on 10 February 1990. One week later he commented that US foreign policy was opposed to any new settlements in either the West Bank or East Jerusalem.

While President Bush's comment marked a radical departure from the strong pro-Israeli sentiments of the Reagan administration, there were few signs that the Senate was about to abandon its traditional support for Israel. In March 1990 the Democrat-dominated chamber voted perfunctorily but overwhelmingly to recognise Jerusalem as the capital of Israel. Interestingly, the leader of the Republican minority in the Senate, Robert Dole, who had originally supported the Jerusalem resolution, but who was increasingly regarded as a stalking horse for a less slavish US foreign policy towards Israel, admitted that he had 'made a mistake' in voting for the resolution.

In 1989, as in 1988, the Palestinian *intifada* was waged with less ferocity in Jerusalem than in other cities in the West Bank and Gaza. Owing to the city's high profile and its importance to Israel's tourist industry, the Israelis were wary of employing the same kind of lethal force there as they did in Nablus or Gaza. The tactics of the security forces in Jerusalem were noticeably different from those employed elsewhere in the Occupied Territories. Whenever tension was high or a nationalist anniversary approached Israel was prepared to swamp Arab Jerusalem with huge numbers of police and border guards. Nevertheless, clashes between demonstrators and the security forces in and around the city claimed a number of lives during 1989. There were also frequent confrontations between Palestinians living in the eastern suburbs of Jerusalem and Israelis from the settlement of Ma'aleh Edomin. At the end of 1989 Israeli riot police violently dispersed a legitimate rally for peace held by Palestinians, Israelis and Europeans in the eastern half of the city. Many people, including several foreigners, suffered injury.

The influx of Soviet Jews into Israel at the beginning of 1990 was regarded with dismay by Palestinians living in Jerusalem. The settlement of the new immigrants on Jewish housing estates, built on confiscated Arab lands in the eastern half of the city, resulted in a significant increase in street confrontations during the early part of the year. At Easter a force of 120 Jewish religious nationalists forcibly occupied the St John's Hospice in the Christian quarter of the Old City, claiming they had purchased the building from an Armenian tenant for the sum of US \$1.8m., most of which had been supplied by the Israeli Government. The owner of the building, the Greek Orthodox Church, disputed the legality of the purchase and mounted an international campaign to have the 'settlers' removed. Anger among local Palestinian Christians was especially strong, not only because of the provocative timing of the action, but also because it was the first attempt by Israeli right-wingers to settle in the Christian quarter of Jerusalem. Demonstrations outside the Hospice by Greek Orthodox and Muslim clergy quickly developed into violent confrontations. The occupation of the Hospice was also condemned by the Israeli left and Jerusalem's Labour Mayor, Teddy Kollek, who reportedly threatened to resign unless the 'settlers' were evicted from the Hospice. While the Israeli courts eventually decided that most of the 'settlers' should leave the Hospice, 20 were given permission to remain until the ownership of the building was conclusively established.

The bloodiest incident yet of the Palestinian *intifada* occurred in Jerusalem on 8 October 1990, when members of the 'Temple Mount Faithful' (see above) made one of their periodic and highly conspicuous attempts to lay the symbolic cornerstone of the Third Temple at the al-Aqsa mosque. Both the Israeli police and the Palestinian population had been forewarned and prepared accordingly. The police refused the members of the 'Temple Mount Faithful' permission to enter the mosque compound, while Palestinians gathered at the site to defend it against the intruders. A full-scale riot rapidly developed. The paramilitary Border Guard opened fire indiscriminately on the crowds inside the compound and on medical staff called to treat casualties. By the time the violence had ceased, 17 Palestinians had been shot dead and many more had been injured. International condemnation, expressed in a unanimous UN Security Council resolution (supported by the USA), followed swiftly. However, a proposal to send a fact-finding mission to Jerusalem was rejected by the Israeli Government as interference in Israel's internal affairs. A commission of inquiry set up by the Israeli Government and chaired by an ex-General and former chief of Mossad known for his right-wing views, predictably absolved the security forces of responsibility for the bloodshed. In the months following the killings there was a spate of 'revenge' stabbings in West Jerusalem that claimed several Israeli lives and led to further anti-Arab violence. Many Palestinians employed in the West Bank either gave up their jobs or were forced to leave by gangs of right-wing vigilantes. Not since the early days of the occupation had the city appeared so divided.

The defeat of Iraq in the Gulf War in February 1991 by the multinational force led to a renewal of efforts to settle the Arab-Israeli conflict. The Israeli Government showed no signs of willingness to compromise on any of the substantive issues, arguably adopting its most intransigent stance on the issue of Jerusalem. Prime Minister Shamir took the opportunity of Jerusalem Day, the anniversary of the annexation of the city, to tell an audience of Soviet immigrants that 'Jerusalem has never been subject to negotiation. United Jerusalem is the capital of Israel'. This position was forcibly underlined by an ambitious programme of building for settlement in and around East Jerusalem, a policy that continued to exasperate both US President Bush and the US Secretary of State, James Baker. Furthermore, the confiscation of Arab property in the Muslim quarter of the Old City continued.

The dispute over the status of East Jerusalem and its Palestinian inhabitants initially threatened to obstruct the Arab-Israeli peace talks that began in Madrid in October 1991. Israel had made it clear to the USA that it regarded the participation in the talks of Palestinian residents of East Jerusalem as unacceptable because this would represent an implicit challenge to Israel's claim that the city was not occupied territory. Such a condition was unacceptable to the Palestinians, not only because it would have established the principle of an Israeli veto over Palestinian representation, but also because it would have made it even more difficult for the Palestinians to force the issue of Jerusalem onto the agenda. US Secretary of State James Baker assured the Palestinians that the USA did consider East Jerusalem to be occupied territory, but he cautioned that the Palestinians could not afford to be seen to be wrecking the peace talks by their inflexible attitude over representation. Similar warnings came from Egypt and Jordan and resulted in a compromise, supported by the USA and, somewhat reluctantly, by the PLO, whereby the official members of the Palestinian-Jordanian negotiating team would be accompanied by an advisory team composed primarily of East Jerusalem residents. At the Madrid conference and subsequent rounds of bilateral talks in Washington it became clear that the principal function of the advisory body was to co-ordinate negotiation tactics and positions with the PLO. In the course of the talks the meetings between East Jerusalem Palestinians and PLO representatives became more overt and there was pressure from the Israeli

establishment to bring charges against the offending Palestinians under anti-terrorism legislation which forbade such contact. But, although Faisal Husseini and Hanan Ashrawi were questioned by the police, US opposition restrained any further action.

The Palestinian delegation tried unsuccessfully to raise the subject of Jerusalem during various rounds of the peace process. James Baker's attitude towards the Arab-Israeli talks was that their continuation depended upon avoiding the more intractable problems until progress had been made in less controversial areas. As progress under the Shamir premiership was agonizingly slow, Jerusalem did not come onto the negotiation agenda.

In 1991 Israel began its most aggressive settlement building programme in the Occupied Territories since 1967. The settlement drive was concentrated in the West Bank and in Gaza, but included considerable building activity in and around Arab Jerusalem. A disturbing development for Palestinians were attempts to extend colonization to parts of the city hitherto regarded as exempt from them. In July 1991 security guards acting for a department of the Ministry of Housing took possession of a house in the Arab suburb of Sheikh Jarrah under orders from the Custodian of Absentee Property. Since the owners lived in the West Bank, the seizure set an ominous precedent by classifying West Bank residents as 'absentees'. On the eve of the Madrid conference, Jewish settlers occupied seven houses in the Silwan district outside the Old City walls, evicting a number of families in the process. Court action forced them to leave six of the houses, but the settlers returned in December, assured by Israel's Attorney General that he found nothing wrong with the settlers' titles to 20 houses in the district. These titles were based on the assertion that the properties had been owned by Jews in the 1930s. The Arab owners gained a temporary injunction for the eviction of some of the settlers, but the settlers appealed against this, guaranteeing a lengthy round of legal battles before ownership could be established. Jerusalem's Labour Mayor, Teddy Kollek, joined Palestinian leaders in condemning the settlers and their sponsors. The Government, he said, was sacrificing calm in the city 'on the altar of ideology'. Controversy over the Silwan incident was heightened by the leaking of a Ministry of Housing blueprint for extensive land expropriation in the Arab suburbs of the city.

The election of a Labour-led Government in Israel in July 1992 brought little hope that Jerusalem would be included on the agenda of the peace process. Although the new Government seemed sure to refrain from the ideological excesses of the Likud when it came to settlement in traditional Arab areas of East Jerusalem, Prime Minister Itzhak Rabin repeated that Israeli sovereignty over the whole of Jerusalem would remain non-negotiable if the peace talks were revived. His promise was borne out by Israel's continued refusal, during the sixth and subsequent rounds of the Middle East peace process, to discuss the issue of Jerusalem in negotiations on the period of interim self-rule for Palestinians in the Occupied Territories. Rabin's position received the unspoken support of the Bush administration when the latter declared that the USA would not deduct from the $10,000m. in loan guarantees recently released to Israel sums that were spent on financing settlement construction in East Jerusalem. This appeared to be a clear retreat from earlier assurances given to the Palestinian peace delegation on the US position regarding Jerusalem and was fundamental in strengthening Palestinian opposition to the peace process.

The election of Bill Clinton as President of the USA in late 1992 was greeted with some trepidation by the PLO. Both Clinton and his Vice-President, Al Gore, were regarded as committed Zionists. During the presidential campaign Gore had voiced his support for the transfer of the US Embassy to Jerusalem. Although such a step was highly unlikely, given sensitivities surrounding the peace process, Palestinians believed that the new US Administration would be reluctant to pressurize Israel into allowing Jerusalem onto the agenda of the bilateral negotiations. Attempts by Palestinian negotiators to extract from the USA a statement of principle regarding East Jerusalem produced conflicting signals. When US Secretary of State Warren Christopher visited East Jerusalem in the wake of the deportation affair (see Arab–Israeli Relations 1967–98) to try to establish grounds for a restart of the peace process, he reassured members of the Palestinian delegation that President

Clinton was committed to assurances on Jerusalem made by his predecessor—namely that it was considered to be occcupied territory. However, during the ninth and tenth rounds of bilateral talks in Washington in the spring and early summer of 1993, US negotiators supported Israel in its insistence that Jerusalem would not be discussed until final status negotiations took place some years hence. By the summer of 1993 the conflict over Jerusalem at the Washington talks was threatening to make progress on any other issue an impossibility.

Palestinians feared that the Rabin Government was adopting the same approach to negotiations on Jerusalem as the Shamir Government had towards the Occupied Territories as a whole, i.e. avoiding discussion of fundamental issues at the negotiating table while creating 'facts' on the ground. There was increasing evidence to support this view. In March 1993 Rabin sealed off the West Bank and Gaza from Israel proper, including annexed East Jerusalem, following the killing of two young Israelis by a Palestinian in West Jerusalem. As the cultural, political, geographical and economic capital of the Occupied Territories, the isolation of Jerusalem from the West Bank was extremely disruptive to Palestinian populations on both sides of the divide (it was possible for West Bank and Gaza residents to get permits to visit Jerusalem but these were reportedly very difficult to obtain). Most worrying from the Palestinian point of view were the political implications of the new measure. There was a widespread conviction that the closure heralded an attempt to cantonize the Occupied Territories and bring about the permanent separation of East Jerusalem from the West Bank. In June it was also revealed that, for the first time since 1967, there were more Israelis than Palestinians living in East Jerusalem.

The Declaration of Principles agreed in Oslo and signed by Yasser Arafat and Itzhak Rabin in September 1993 stipulated that issues relating to Jerusalem would be left until final status negotiations took place. Given the polarized positions of Palestinians and Israel on the future of the city, it was hardly surprising that discussion of Jerusalem would not take place during the interim negotiations. Palestinians were far less comfortable with this than their Israeli counterparts. A highly visible and ambitious programme of settlement and road building in and around the occupied east side of the city appeared as irrefutable confirmation that Israel was transforming East Jerusalem into a ghetto cut off from its West Bank hinterland. The rapid physical transformation suggested that by the time Jerusalem came on to the negotiation agenda, the proposed capital of a future Palestinian state would be dwarfed by a ring of Jewish suburbs and a major ring road. The deposition of the longstanding, moderate Labour Mayor, Teddy Kollek, in municipal elections in late 1993, and his replacement by the Likud candidate, Ehud Olmert, implied that this process of encirclement would be hastened. Kollek had tried to avoid a Likud victory in the municipal polls by appealing to Palestinians in East Jerusalem to vote. Significantly, however, the city's Arab population observed its customary boycott of Israeli elections: only 6% of Jerusalem's Palestinians exercised their voting rights.

Palestinians attempted to use the political space conferred by the legalization of the PLO to push their own claim to sovereignty over East Jerusalem. Orient House, once home to the Arab Studies centre, became the semi-official headquarters of the PLO in the Occupied Territories and there were moves to establish similar quasi-governmental offices in the city. This largely symbolic attempt to create the 'fact' of a Palestinian 'capital' was viewed with suspicion by the Israeli Government and the new Likud administration in the city. Indeed, public pronouncements by Israeli leaders about Jerusalem continued to be united by the common thread of a refusal to countenance any compromise on Israeli sovereignty. While the Israeli position was clear to the PLO, it was dismayed at what appeared to be a shift in the USA's policy towards Jerusalem. During the 1992 presidential campaign there had been unconfirmed rumours that Clinton and Gore had promised Jewish leaders that they would revise US policy on the status of Jerusalem by excluding reference to Jerusalem as occupied territory—a formulation that the USA had accepted in UN resolutions since 1971. However, during a UN Security Council vote on a resolution (No. 904) condemning the massacre of worshippers in Hebron, the USA abstained on a preambulary clause defining Jerusalem as occupied Palestinian territory and stated that if

the definition had been in an operative paragraph they would have voted against it. The US ambassador to the UN defended this apparent shift in policy by saying that Israel and the Palestinians had agreed, under the Declaration of Principles, to negotiate the city's final status and the Clinton administration did not wish to prejudice the outcome of those negotiations.

The conclusion of the first stage of the Declaration of Principles, with the redeployment of Israeli troops in Gaza and Jericho, once again focused attention on Jerusalem. The PLO Chairman was criticized in Israel when he appealed for a *jihad* to free Jerusalem. Although Arafat later attempted a clarification by insisting that he meant a peaceful crusade, his comment was acknowledged to be a public relations disaster. Israeli leaders responded to Arafat's gaffe with an offensive of their own. The Jerusalem municipality announced its intention to begin the process of demolishing an estimated 2,000 Arab dwellings in East Jerusalem that had been built without licences. Rabin, meanwhile, instructed his Government's legal experts to explore the possibility of drawing up legislation that would forestall the PLO's plans to develop its institutional base in East Jerusalem. A confidential cabinet report leaked to the Israeli press in July detailed plans to reinforce Israeli control of Jerusalem during the approach to the 1996 talks on the status of the city. It proposed the adoption of measures to stop the 'illegal' ingress of outsiders—presumably Arabs—to the city and the creation of job opportunities for Arabs outside the city boundaries. The inescapable conclusion was that the Israeli Government was trying to engineer a further change in the demographic balance, not just by settling Jews in the eastern half of the city, but also by trying to exclude its non-Jewish population.

Palestinian despondency over the developing battle for Jerusalem deepened with Israel's agreement, on 25 July, with Jordan to formally end the state of war that had existed between the two countries. One of the articles in the Israeli-Jordanian agreement acknowledged the special role of Jordan as guarding Muslim sites in Jerusalem. Responding to Palestinian objections to the implications of such an agreement, King Hussein stated that 'religious and political sovereignty over the holy city were two separate issues'. Further comments from Jordanian officials, that the motivation for the controversial clause was a desire to save the holy sites from Israeli control before the final status negotiations, failed to allay Palestinian fears that Jordan was being used by Israel to undermine Palestinian claims to sovereignty over East Jerusalem. Although the PLO had until this point declined to challenge Jordan's custodianship of the Muslim holy sites, King Hussein's agreement with Israel revived speculation that the Palestinians would work towards the creation of a Palestinian *waqf* (religious endowment fund) department to replace the existing Jordanian one. A furious Arafat insisted that only Palestinians could decide the fate of East Jerusalem and called a meeting of the Arab League to discuss the Jerusalem clause. There were also reports that King Hassan of Morocco had been asked to mediate between King Hussein and Arafat. Commentaries in the Arab press were generally critical of the Jordanian monarch's agreement with Israel on Jerusalem. Israel, meanwhile, appeared to take particular delight at the disarray. Speaking in Washington, Rabin commented, 'It wouldn't bother me at all if there is a little friction between Jordanians and Palestinians over Jerusalem.'

Israeli and Palestinian sensitivity over Jerusalem ensured that the city would continue to be an issue of contention between the Israeli Government and the Palestine National Authority (PNA) in the period leading up to final status talks. In September the World Bank was forced to cancel a donor's conference in Paris after Israel and the Palestinians became entangled in a bitter dispute over whether foreign aid for the PNA could be used to fund development projects in East Jerusalem. Israel adamantly refused to accept that such aid was authorized in the Declaration of Principles. Further controversy followed in November when the Turkish Prime Minister, Tansu Çiller, visited Orient House, the PNA's *de facto* headquarters in Jerusalem. The visit had not been approved by the Israeli Government and provoked strong protests. Israel insisted that any discussion on Palestinian self-rule had to take place in Gaza City or Jericho. Faisal Husseini, the principal Palestinian spokesperson on Jerusalem, whose office was located in Orient House, rejoined that what was being discussed with the Turkish

Prime Minister was the wider issue of the Middle East. The visit was followed by others from French, Czech and South African diplomats. The Israeli Government claimed that the Palestinians were trying to 'create facts' to prejudice the outcome of final status talks and stationed Israeli troops outside the building. In November a draft law to restrict PLO activity in Jerusalem was given its first reading in the Knesset and was passed on 26 December. This was despite the assertion, made by Shimon Peres in 1993 to his Norwegian counterpart, that 'All the Palestinian institutions of East Jerusalem, including the economic, social, educational and cultural . . . will be preserved. Needless to say, we will not hamper their activity; on the contrary, the fulfilment of this important mission is to be encouraged'.

By the end of the year it had also become apparent that Jordan would have to revise its position on Jerusalem. The clause it had signed with Israel concerning Hashemite custodianship of the Muslim Holy sites in the city was not popular on either bank of the River Jordan, largely because the rift that it had created in relations with the PLO was seen as divisive to Arab interests and only of benefit to Israel. More importantly, at a meeting of the Organization of the Islamic Conference in Casablanca in mid-December King Hussein spectacularly failed to win recognition of the Hashemite role in Jerusalem. Jordanian officials later conceded that they had mishandled the Jersulem issue with Israel and stated that defusing the conflict with the PLO over the city would become a priority. In January 1995 the Jordanian Minister of Foreign Affairs assured Arafat that Jordan would support all steps taken to ensure Palestinian sovereignty over the east of the city, and that the patronage of the holy sites was never intended to prejudice this eventuality. A mollified Arafat agreed not to raise the issue in a forthcoming visit to Jordan.

The construction of exclusively Jewish housing in East Jerusalem and around the city boundaries continued to provoke Palestinian and international concern. Commitment to the notion of a Jerusalem 'united under Israeli sovereignty' was once again underlined in the aftermath of the Bet Lid bombing when the Ministry of Housing won the Cabinet's support for the construction of an additional 5,000 housing units in the dormitory settlements of Greater Jerusalem. When the Meretz party leader enquired where the expanding Palestinian population of East Jerusalem was going to live, Rabin answered bluntly, 'I am worried about Israelis, not the Arabs'. It was left to her colleague, Yair Tzaban, to point out that of the 70,000 dunams of land in East Jerusalem, 23,000 had been confiscated since 1967. Of these expropriations, 85% had been of Arab land, but of the 35,000 apartments subsequently constructed, not one had been for Jerusalem's Arab citizens. 'Whoever thinks we can go on with this policy', commented Tzaban, 'is making a grave mistake'. It was not an opinion that would deflect Rabin from his drive to assert Israel's territorial and demographic domination. In April 1995 the Labour leader authorized the confiscation of a further 130 acres (500 dunams) of Arab land in Jerusalem and the construction of an additional 7,000 new homes. Ehud Olmert, the city's Likud Mayor expressed his warm support for the government plans, while his deputy stated that this was the first stage of a wider design to confiscate up to 4,400 dunams of East Jerusalem. The original expropriation proposals were eventually frozen following a threat by the Arab parties represented in the Knesset to bring down the Israeli Government. An earlier Security Council resolution demanding that Israel should rescind the land confiscation had been vetoed by the USA. The US Ambassador to the UN, Madeleine Albright, had defended the US action on the grounds that the issue was a local matter that would have to be resolved within the framework of the Declaration of Principles. The US veto was unremarkable and largely symptomatic of the increasingly pro-Israel bias informing the policies and discourse of both Democratic and Republican parties. The strongly Zionist views of the Clinton administration were well known; the US President had received 60% of his funding from Jewish sources and 80% of the Jewish vote in his 1992 campaign. What was more alarming from an Arab perspective was a movement among Republican leaders to co-ordinate their attempts to court the Jewish vote with a campaign to have the US Embassy in Israel moved from Tel-Aviv to Jerusalem. In February the Republican Speaker in the

US House of Representatives, Newt Gingrich, stated that he 'strongly favoured' moving the embassy. His comments prompted politicians in both the Senate and the House of Representatives to express support for his position. By May the leader of the Republicans in the House of Representatives, Bob Dole, who had recently argued in favour of a reduction in US aid to Israel, had garnered bipartisan support for a bill requiring the USA to build a new embassy in Jerusalem. Clinton's embarrassment at having to oppose the measure was pre-empted, for the time being, by Rabin's decidely lukewarm response to the Dole initiative. There were two reasons for this. Firstly, Rabin was concerned that such a gesture was untimely given the precarious state of negotiations on Palestinian autonomy. Secondly, and relatedly, the US Republicans' novel enthusiasm for the transfer of the embassy originated from the activities of Aipac, the most influential and increasingly intransigent pro-Israel lobby group. Ideologically Aipac had far more in common with the Israeli right than with the Labour party, and Rabin suspected that however welcome a transfer of embassy might be in theory, the sabotage of the autonomy talks was Aipac's hidden agenda.

An opinion poll published in June provided some comfort for Palestinians. It revealed that there was a significant decline in support among Jerusalem's Jewish citizens for the nationalist doctrine of exclusive Israeli sovereignty over Jerusalem. According to the findings, support for this notion had decreased from 57.4% in 1993 to 45.8%. There was a big difference in opinion between secular and religious voters, with the latter more strongly in favour of exclusive sovereignty. However, the preponderance of secular opinion nationally seemed to suggest that there was a greater readiness for some compromise with the Palestinians over the status of East Jerusalem than had previously been thought.

The PNA secured a small, but significant victory on the issue of Jerusalem during the negotiation of interim-phase agreements with Israel, within the framework of the Oslo Accords. According to a deal concluded by the two sides in the Egyptian resort of Taba in September 1995, the Palestinian villages on the municipal borders of the city were to enjoy the same status as the rest of the West Bank villages, i.e. civic authority and responsibility for 'public order' there would be transferred to the PNA, while Israel would remain in charge of 'overriding security'. Israel also agreed to allow residents of East Jerusalem to vote in the forthcoming elections to the Palestinian Legislative Council, and to stand as candidates provided they also had residency in the West Bank. In the view of one of the Palestinian negotiators at the Taba talks, the agreement on the Jerusalem villages meant that Israel's dream of a Greater Jerusalem had come to an end. Despite these concessions, Israel gave notice that it would not tolerate any PNA activity in East Jerusalem. As a prelude to the closure of Orient House, the unofficial PNA headquarters in the city, Israel's Chief of Police shut down three Palestinian institutions in the city (the Palestinian Health Council, Broadcasting Corporation and Bureau of Statistics). Arafat was able to forestall their closure by allowing the three institutions to sign declarations stating that they were independent of the PNA.

Meanwhile, US Senator Bob Dole, by now the leading Republican candidate for the US presidency, had won an overwhelming majority in the US Congress for his bill to have the US Embassy in Israel transferred from Tel-Aviv to Jerusalem by May 1999. The PNA reacted sharply to the decision, with Yasser Arafat angrily condemning the proposed move as 'incompatible with the spirit of the peace process'. President Bill Clinton's embarrassment at this transparent electioneering by his Republican rival was partially allayed when he secured a last-minute amendment to the bill. This allowed the US President to certify every six months that it would not be in the national interest to transfer the embassy. The certification could be used indefinitely and a White House spokesman insisted that Clinton would be using the waiver provision if he was still in office in 1999.

Palestinians were noticeably less enthusiastic about registering for the 1996 Legislative Council elections in Jerusalem than they were in the towns and villages of the West Bank and the Gaza Strip, despite the PNA urging them to do so. Their reluctance originated partly through fear that by registering to vote they would jeopardize their status as Jerusalem identity-card holders, and partly through lack of faith in a process that was being conducted under continued Israeli occupation. However, just as the PNA had a vested interest in ensuring that the turn-out for the elections to the Legislative Council was as high as possible, so Israel was happy to see as few Palestinians as possible take part. Israeli police established blockades to prevent candidates for Jerusalem's seven seats from canvassing during the election campaign and insisted on restricting polling stations to a number that Palestinians argued was far less than could realistically accommodate the expected number of voters. On 20 January 1996 some 40% of potential voters cast their ballots, a turn-out that was lower than in any other area of the territories occupied in 1967 except Hebron (significantly the only other Palestinian population centre also under partial Israeli control). This was a disappointment for the PNA, but the fact that Jerusalem had participated at all was declared by one of the successful Jerusalem candidates as signifying 'the beginning of the re-emerging of Jerusalem, legally, politically and structurally within the Palestinian system'.

In Israel's own prime-ministerial and legislative elections in May 1996 both the Labour and Likud leaders restated their commitment to a unified Jerusalem under Israeli sovereignty. Their pronouncements were given added resonance by the fact that the talks about to resume between Israel and the PNA on the final status of the territories occupied in 1967 would focus on the need to reconcile opposing claims to the Arab areas of Jerusalem. Despite the ritualized utterings of successive Labour leaders on the need to preserve Israeli domination of all sections of the city, the fact that a two-thirds majority of Labour Party members in Jerusalem were reportedly happy to accept something less than full Israeli sovereignty meant that most Palestinians supported Shimon Peres and the Labour Party. The victory of Likud and of Binyamin Netanyahu was received, not just by the Palestinians and Arab states, but by much of the international community as a setback to hopes of achieving a compromise on Jerusalem. Initial policy statements by the victorious Likud leader appeared to confirm the international pessimism. In his first meeting with Yasser Arafat, Israel's newly-appointed Minister of Foreign Affairs, David Levy, stated that the PNA would have to shut down all of its institutions in Jerusalem—including its headquarters, Orient House—before negotiations could be resumed on final status agreements. In a further statement of intent to limit the Palestinians room for manoeuvre in Jerusalem, the Israeli police summoned the seven PLC deputies who represented Jerusalem to question them about 'their political activity'. The seven refused to respond, claiming immunity under agreements previously signed between Israel and the PNA. In late June the Israeli press revealed plans for the seizure of large tracts of land belonging to two Palestinian villages with the purpose of building hundreds of new housing units, an industrial zone, a public park and a swimming pool. Observers pointed out that if the proposals proceeded, it would effectively mean the encirclement of East Jerusalem. Palestinians were angered again at the end of July when the Israeli High Court granted members of the extremist Jewish movement, the Temple Mount Faithful, permission to enter the compound of the al-Aqsa mosque. Hundreds of Palestinians converged on the scene and a bloody confrontation was only narrowly avoided. Commenting on the incident, the PNA's minister for waqf affairs declared: 'We know well that the hour of confrontation with the Jews is getting closer, and we must be willing to die and shed blood for our rights and for the holy places.'

Netanyahu underlined his Government's opposition to Palestinian attempts at institutional development in East Jerusalem with an order in late August 1996 for the closure of further institutions (including the Geographical Office and the Youth and Sports Department) loosely connected to the PNA. Just days after compliance with the order, Israeli bulldozers demolished a Palestinian centre for the elderly and handicapped in Jerusalem's Old City, on the grounds that the five-year-old building had been constructed without a licence. This development provoked strong protests from the PNA and from the city's Legislative Council members, who advocated a four-hour general strike to demonstrate opposition to the measure.

On 23 September 1996 the Likud Prime Minister announced the opening of the 500-m 'Hasmonean' tunnel that runs through the heart of the Old City, alongside the compound of the al-Aqsa mosque. Given the existing political climate and Muslim sensitivities over any perceived threat to Islamic holy sites, Netanyahu's decision was widely viewed as somewhat rash. King Hussein of Jordan, whose 1994 peace treaty with Israel recognized Hashemite custodianship of waqf property in the city, was extremely critical of Netanyahu's failure to consult or inform him regarding the move. Yasser Arafat, meanwhile, denounced the decision as a 'crime against our holy places' and he urged Palestinians to protest against what he termed the 'Judaization of Jerusalem'. The response was immediate and overwhelming. Three Palestinians were shot dead and more than 120 were injured after Friday prayer demonstrations at al-Aqsa on 27 September. Elsewhere in the Occupied Territories 52 Palestinians and 15 Israelis died in the bloodiest series of confrontations since the June War of 1967. While the scale of the violence unleashed in September injected an urgency into the peace process which had hitherto been lacking under the Netanyahu Government, there was no evidence of any reversal of Israel's policy of extending control over the east of the city, while denying Palestinians either the physical or the political space to preserve residual autonomy. In November 50 prominent Palestinians organized a sit-down demonstration outside Jerusalem's Interior Ministry to draw attention to two aspects of Israel's rule that they claimed were having a particularly insidious impact on the status and livelihoods of the city's Palestinian residents. The first of these was the 'general' closure imposed on the West Bank and Gaza in 1993. This had required non-resident Palestinians to obtain Israeli permission to enter the city and had effectively detached East Jerusalem from its Arab hinterland. Many of the city's businesses had subsequently relocated to the West Bank. The result, according to Palestinian economists, had been a 50% decline in trade among its merchants and steadily rising unemployment. Of equal concern to the protesters was an Interior Ministry policy of redefining the parameters under which Palestinians could live in Jerusalem. Since 1994 Palestinians' right of residency in Jerusalem had become increasingly determined by whether or not their so-called 'centre of life' was in the city. By the end of 1996 more than 1,000 Palestinians had been relieved of their rights of residency because they failed to meet this criterion. Many of these individuals were people who had moved to the West Bank in response to the economic downturn.

Construction of Jewish apartments in East Jerusalem continued at a steady pace. In December 1996 the Jerusalem District Housing Committee approved the construction of 132 housing units in the Palestinian village of Ras al-Amud, just outside the Old City walls. Financed by Irving Moskowitz, a Miami-based millionaire, and intended for Orthodox Jews, it had yet to receive ministerial sanction but was regarded as a particularly provocative proposal. According to the Israeli group Peace Now, who supported Palestinian opposition to the development, its inauguration would mean that for the first time since 1967 an Israeli government had 'decided to plan a settlement in the heart of a Palestinian neighbourhood.' While the international community was pondering the likely effect on the peace process of such a development, Prime Minister Netanyahu gave his support to the construction of a massive new settlement on Jabal Abu Ghunaym, a forested hilltop straddling the southeastern municipal borders of Jerusalem and belonging to the Palestinian town of Beit Sahur. Construction of the new development (Har Homa) which was expected to comprise 6,500 housing units, would represent the completion of Arab Jerusalem's encirclement by exclusively Jewish settlements. Despite united local and international opposition to Har Homa, work began on its construction in mid-March 1997. Under US pressure the Netanyahu Government also announced that it would be granting 3,015 building permits to Palestinians in East Jerusalem to ensure 'equal rights and development for Jews and Arabs' in the city. But this intended palliative did little to lessen Palestinian opposition to Har Homa. It was observed that the granting of permits would be conditional on infrastructural development in Palestinian areas, something for which successive Israeli governments had an extremely poor track record.

Yasser Arafat's PNA responded to the commencement of work on Har Homa by calling a halt to negotiations on the Oslo Accords. Arafat stated that their resumption would be conditional on suspension of the project. The US Administration also supported the international community's expression of opposition to Israeli settlements in East Jerusalem. Nevertheless, Washington vetoed a UN resolution condemning the Har Homa decision because its wording categorized East Jerusalem as occupied territory. This, according to the US ambassador to the UN, prejudged future Israeli-Palestinian negotiations on the final status of the city and was thus at odds with US policy. His remarks were considered disingenuous by many independent observers, since developments such as Har Homa, together with ongoing Jewish housing construction in other parts of East Jerusalem, were already creating the 'facts on the ground' that contravened the spirit, if not the letter, of the Oslo Accords.

With an increasing sense that the battle to preserve East Jerusalem as the future capital of an independent Palestinian state was being lost, there were belated signs of resistance. In April and May 1997 a campaign to raise US $100m. for real-estate development was conducted among Palestinian, Jordanian and Egyptian businessmen. In June Palestinian merchants also staged a one-day commercial strike in protest against tax raids initiated by Likud Mayor, Ehud Olmert, who claimed that the merchants owed the municipality $38m. In response, Palestinians claimed that their tax burden was too high, given that they comprised around 30% of the city's population but received only 7% of municipal funds. After the strike the Jerusalem Chamber of Commerce announced that it would maintain the tax boycott and would consider an indefinite strike if the raids continued.

The interruption to negotiations on the Oslo Accords caused by the Har Homa construction resulted in US pressure on the Netanyahu Government to take steps to ease tension over the settlement issue. In May 1997 Olmert announced a six-month moratorium on the demolition of unlicensed Palestinian dwellings in Jerusalem, and in July the Israeli Prime Minister declared his opposition to the controversial settlement of Ras al-Amud. This latter concession, together with reports that a temporary 'freeze' was being considered on the Har Homa development, was instrumental in an agreement by the Israeli Government and the PNA to restart formal negotiations suspended since March. The day after the announcement thirteen Israelis were killed in West Jerusalem's Mahane Yehuda market in a double suicide bombing by Islamist militants. Netanyahu immediately imposed a blockade of all PNA-controlled areas and announced that further negotiations on the Oslo Accords would be suspended until Arafat had satisfied Israeli demands for the apprehension of militant Islamist suspects. By the end of July the prospect of a solution to the Har Homa problem appeared to have receded. There were further suicide bombings in Jerusalem at the beginning of September. Three suspected Islamist bombers killed four Israelis and themselves in a co-ordinated attack in the west of the city.

The Jerusalem bomb attacks, and the deepening crisis in the Oslo peace process provided a sombre backdrop to the first official trip to the region by the new US Secretary of State Madeleine Albright. While in Israel in September 1997 she cautioned Israel against provocative settlement activity in the territories occupied by Israel in 1967. However within 48 hours of her leaving Israel, Jerusalem was once again the focus of media attention owing to settler action in the east of the city. On 14 September three Jewish families, escorted by armed settlers, occupied buildings in Ras al-Amud, an exclusively Palestinian village in East Jerusalem. The settler families claimed legitimacy of tenancy on the grounds that the buildings had been rented from Irving Moskowitz, a Miami-based financier who had initiated earlier plans for a settlement in the village and who had already bankrolled the activities of militant settlers in the Old City. Residents of the village however, fiercely disputed Moskowitz's claim to ownership of the occupied buildings. After the Government negotiated with lawyers representing Moskowitz, Netanyahu announced a 'compromise' deal to end the stand-off, whereby the Jewish families agreed to vacate the buildings on the understanding that they would be occupied by 10 *yeshiva* students. The agreement was savaged by Arafat and the Israeli peace movement and denounced as farcical. It sustained fears that the village would continue to be a target for settlers and their allies in the Israeli Government. The Israeli Minister of National Infrastructure, Ariel Sharon,

noted that the creation of a Jewish settlement in Ras al-Amud was critical if the Israeli state was to prevent 'Arab contiguity' between the Old City and the Palestinian villages that served as its hinterland. Palestinian–Israeli negotiations concerning the implementation of the Oslo Agreements, effectively stalled since the inauguration of work on the Har Homa project, remained deadlocked for much of 1997 and early 1998. Israel's refusal to undertake the scheduled redeployment of its forces in the West Bank was justified by the Israeli Government in terms of the continuing threat posed to Israel's security. However, there was also a widely-held belief that Netanyahu was hoping to secure an accelerated transition to 'final status' talks in which land settlements and the future of Jerusalem would be the most intractable issues for negotiation. Predictably, there was little sign that either Netanyahu's Government or the Labour opposition was prepared to countenance anything less than full Israeli sovereignty over the entire city. A corollary of this position was Israeli determination to undermine attempts by the PNA to develop an institutional base in the city. Indeed, a crucial pre-condition of the Netanyahu Government for moving towards redeployment in the West Bank was that the PNA end all political activity in East Jerusalem. Heightened political sensitivities over the Jerusalem issue were clearly underlined in March 1998 during a visit to the city by the British Secretary of State for Foreign and Commonwealth Affairs, Robin Cook. Cook's decision to visit the site of the Har Homa settlement provoked barely-concealed outrage from the Israeli Government; not only would the visit refocus world attention on Israel's settlement policy, but Cook announced that he intended to view the controversial building work in the company of Faisal Husseini, the Palestinian Minister with Responsibility for Jerusalem Affairs. Netanyahu declared such a visit 'unacceptable', and eventually it was agreed that the British politician would visit the site accompanied by Israel's cabinet secretary, a compromise that dismayed the Palestinians and appeared to do little to mollify Netanyahu. Cook was jeered and jostled at the site by right-wing settlers and was forced to make a swift retreat. However, the British politician later met Husseini in East Jerusalem where he laid a wreath to the victims of the 1948 massacre of Palestinians at Deir Yassin. Netanyahu reacted to the clear symbolism of Cook's itinerary by cancelling a planned dinner together, agreeing only to a brief 15-minute meeting with the visitor. At subsequent press conferences the Israeli Prime Minister promised 'thousands of homes in Har Homa'. For his part, Cook restated the position of the European Union. 'My visit to Har Homa was symbolic', he declared, 'one of the biggest obstacles to the peace process is the expansion of settlements . . . there has been no progress in the peace process since the decision to build Har Homa was made'.

If Cook's visit served to reinforce the Israeli Government's belief that they could expect little backing from Europe for their claim to exclusive sovereignty over Jerusalem, tours of the USA undertaken by Netanyahu in the first half of 1998 confirmed that there was no diminution in such support from US congressional leaders. Netanyahu won repeated standing ovations for a series of 'hardline' statements on Israeli attitudes towards relations with the Palestinians, none more enthusiastic than that which he received when he pledged that Israel would never give up a part of Jerusalem. In May, the city became the principal focus of Israel's 50th anniversary celebrations, during which time the city's West Bank borders were once again sealed to Palestinians. Large numbers of security personnel were deployed in the streets of Arab Jerusalem and the Old City to thwart Palestinian disruption of the celebrations. Nevertheless, serious rioting broke out in Arab quarters later in the month as Palestinians commemorated the *Nabka,* or 'catastrophe' of 1948 that had resulted in their dispossession.

On 23 May 1998 Israelis celebrated the 31st 'Jerusalem Day'. Sharing a platform with Irving Moskowitz, the Israeli Prime Minister reaffirmed his pledge that Jerusalem would remain united under Israeli sovereignty in perpetuity. The day also witnessed a march by some 13,000 Israeli troops through West Jerusalem, and symbolic attempts by right-wing extremist groups to occupy both the al-Aqsa mosque and Orient House. The following day members of the Ateret Kohanim movement (one of the most active settler organizations in East Jerusalem and largely funded by Moskowitz) began to lay the foundations of a new *yeshiva* in the Muslim quarter of the Old City. The site had originally housed a Palestinian charitable organization, but this had been one of the buildings demolished 21 months previously by the Jerusalem municipality on the grounds that they had been built without a licence. Ateret Kohanim had reportedly been interested in purchasing the site for several months and had been in illegal occupation since the beginning of May. Two days after the building work began, seven temporary homes had been erected and supplied with water and electricity. Although the construction work was patently illegal, since no building permit had been granted, the site was protected throughout by units of the paramilitary Border Police. Israeli radio also broadcast reports that the settlers had been encouraged to build on the plot by Ariel Sharon. On 26 May members of the Palestinian Legislative Council attempted to enter the building compound; the ensuing scuffles with the Border Police resulted in injury to several Palestinian politicians (including Faisal Husseini) and the destruction of one of the homes. Israel's internal security ministry subsequently announced that the Jerusalem municipality and the Israeli Antiquities Department had obtained a restraining order on further building—this announcement was made after the latter body had cautioned that the construction work was endangering the perimeter wall of the Old City. In discussions with local police chiefs and the Mayor of Jerusalem, Ehud Olmert, the settlers agreed to halt development on the site on the condition that their members would remain *in situ* to provide security for any excavation work carried out by the Antiquities Department. A tender would later be submitted by Ateret Kohanim to build a *yeshiva* and 12 apartments for 400 religious students. Expectation was high that the tender would be approved. Left-wing Israelis and Palestinians criticized the agreement, describing it as a capitulation to religious nationalism and a further significant setback to the peace process.

On 21 June 1998 the Israeli Cabinet approved a proposal to create a 'greater Jerusalem'. The plan envisaged the extension of the city's municipal boundaries westwards to incorporate Israeli commuter towns, and therefore guarantee a Jewish majority within the city. More controversially, the proposal also contained provision for the creation of an 'umbrella municipality' over eight Jewish settlements bordering the city but currently occupying the territories of the West Bank. These settlements would continue paying local property taxes and voting in their own jurisdictions but would fall under Jerusalem's municipal authority for certain services, including building and planning. The US Department of State described the plan as 'extremely provocative' and Ahmad Tibi, Yasser Arafat's economic adviser deemed it 'a total violation of the Oslo Agreement' and an attempt 'to annex Palestinian land'. Similar concerns were expressed by the European Union. Netanyahu responded to the mounting chorus of local and international criticism by stating that the proposal was 'entirely municipal, entirely administrative, with no political implications'.

DOCUMENTS ON PALESTINE

DECLARATION OF FIRST
WORLD ZIONIST CONGRESS

*The Congress, convened in Basle by Dr Theodor Herzl in August 1897, adopted the following programme.**

The aim of Zionism is to create for the Jewish people a home in Palestine secured by public law.

The Congress contemplates the following means to the attainment of this end:

1. The promotion on suitable lines, of the settlement of Palestine by Jewish agriculturists, artisans and tradesmen.

2. The organization and binding together of the whole of Jewry by means of appropriate institutions, local and general, in accordance with the laws of each country.

3. The strengthening of Jewish sentiment and national consciousness.

4. Preparatory steps towards obtaining government consent as are necessary, for the attainment of the aim of Zionism.

McMAHON CORRESPONDENCE†

Ten letters passed between Sir Henry McMahon, British High Commissioner in Cairo, and Sherif Husain of Mecca from July 1915 to March 1916. Husain offered Arab help in the war against the Turks if Britain would support the principle of an independent Arab state. The most important letter is that of 24 October 1915, from McMahon to Husain:

... I regret that you should have received from my last letter the impression that I regarded the question of limits and boundaries with coldness and hesitation; such was not the case, but it appeared to me that the time had not yet come when that question could be discussed in a conclusive manner.

I have realized, however, from your last letter that you regard this question as one of vital and urgent importance. I have, therefore, lost no time in informing the Government of Great Britain of the contents of your letter, and it is with great pleasure that I communicate to you on their behalf the following statement, which I am confident you will receive with satisfaction:

The two districts of Mersina and Alexandretta and portions of Syria lying to the west of the districts of Damascus, Homs, Hama and Aleppo cannot be said to be purely Arab, and should be excluded from the limits demanded.

With the above modification, and without prejudice to our existing treaties with Arab chiefs, we accept those limits.

As for those regions lying within those frontiers wherein Great Britain is free to act without detriment to the interest of her ally, France, I am empowered in the name of the Government of Great Britain to give the following assurances and make the following reply to your letter:

(1) Subject to the above modifications, Great Britain is prepared to recognize and support the independence of the Arabs in all the regions within the limits demanded by the Sherif of Mecca.

(2) Great Britain will guarantee the Holy Places against all external aggression and will recognize their inviolability.

(3) When the situation admits, Great Britain will give to the Arabs her advice and will assist them to establish what may appear to be the most suitable forms of government in those various territories.

(4) On the other hand, it is understood that the Arabs have decided to seek the advice and guidance of Great Britain only, and that such European advisers and officials as may be required for the formation of a sound form of administration will be British.

(5) With regard to the *vilayets* of Baghdad and Basra, the Arabs will recognize that the established position and interests of Great Britain necessitate special administrative arrangements in order to secure these territories from foreign aggression, to promote the welfare of the local populations and to safeguard our mutual economic interests.

I am convinced that this declaration will assure you beyond all possible doubt of the sympathy of Great Britain towards the aspirations of her friends the Arabs and will result in a firm and lasting alliance, the immediate results of which will be the expulsion of the Turks from the Arab countries and the freeing of the Arab peoples from the Turkish yoke, which for so many years has pressed heavily upon them....

ANGLO-FRANCO-RUSSIAN AGREEMENT
(SYKES—PICOT AGREEMENT)
April-May 1916

The allocation of portions of the Ottoman empire by the three powers was decided between them in an exchange of diplomatic notes. The Anglo-French agreement‡ dealing with Arab territories became known to Sherif Husain only after publication by the new Bolshevik government of Russia in 1917:

1. That France and Great Britain are prepared to recognize and protect an independent Arab State or a Confederation of Arab States in the areas (A) and (B) marked on the annexed map, under suzerainty of an Arab Chief. That in area (A) France, and in area (B) Great Britain shall have priority of right of enterprises and local loans. France in area (A) and Great Britain in area (B) shall alone supply foreign advisers or officials on the request of the Arab State or the Confederation of Arab States.

2. France in the Blue area and Great Britain in the Red area shall be at liberty to establish direct or indirect administration or control as they may desire or as they may deem fit to establish after agreement with the Arab State or Confederation of Arab States.

3. In the Brown area there shall be established an international administration of which the form will be decided upon after consultation with Russia, and after subsequent agreement with the other Allies and the representatives of the Sherif of Mecca.

4. That Great Britain be accorded

(a) The ports of Haifa and Acre;

(b) Guarantee of a given supply of water from the Tigris and the Euphrates in area (A) for area (B).

His Majesty's Government, on their part, undertake that they will at no time enter into negotiations for the cession of Cyprus to any third Power without the previous consent of the French Government.

5. Alexandretta shall be a free port as regards the trade of the British Empire and there shall be no discrimination in treatment with regard to port dues or the extension of special privileges affecting British shipping and commerce; there shall be freedom of transit for British goods through Alexandretta and over railways through the Blue area, whether such goods are going to or coming from the Red area, area (A) or area (B); and there shall be no differentiation in treatment, direct or indirect, at the expense of British goods on any railway or of British goods and shipping in any port serving the areas in question.

Haifa shall be a free port as regards the trade of France, her colonies and protectorates, and there shall be no differentiation in treatment or privilege with regard to port dues against

---

* Text supplied by courtesy of Josef Fraenkel.
† British White Paper, Cmd. 5957, 1939.

‡ E. L. Woodward and Rohan Butler (Eds.). *Documents on British Foreign Policy 1919–1939*. First Series, Vol. IV, 1919. London, HMSO, 1952.

French shipping and commerce. There shall be freedom of transit through Haifa and over British railways through the Brown area, whether such goods are coming from or going to the Blue area, area (A) or area (B), and there shall be no differentiation in treatment, direct or indirect, at the expense of French goods on any railway or of French goods and shipping in any port serving the areas in question.

6. In area (A), the Baghdad Railway shall not be extended southwards beyond Mosul, and in area (B), it shall not be extended northwards beyond Samarra, until a railway connecting Baghdad with Aleppo along the basin of the Euphrates will have been completed, and then only with the concurrence of the two Governments.

7. Great Britain shall have the right to build, administer and be the sole owner of the railway connecting Haifa with area (B). She shall have, in addition, the right in perpetuity and at all times of carrying troops on that line. It is understood by both Governments that this railway is intended to facilitate communication between Baghdad and Haifa, and it is further understood that, in the event of technical difficulties and expenditure incurred in the maintenance of this line in the Brown area rendering the execution of the project impracticable, the French Government will be prepared to consider plans for enabling the line in question to traverse the polygon formed by Banias-Umm Qais-Salkhad-Tall 'Osda-Mismieh before reaching area (B).

Clause 8 referred to customs tariffs.

9. It is understood that the French Government will at no time initiate any negotiations for the cession of their rights and will not cede their prospective rights in the Blue area to any third Power other than the Arab State or Confederation of Arab States, without the previous consent of His Majesty's Government who, on their part, give the French Government a similar undertaking in respect of the Red area.

10. The British and French Governments shall agree to abstain from acquiring and to withhold their consent to a third Power acquiring territorial possessions in the Arabian Peninsula; nor shall they consent to the construction by a third Power of a naval base in the islands on the eastern seaboard of the Red Sea. This, however, will not prevent such rectification of the Aden boundary as might be found necessary in view of the recent Turkish attack.

11. The negotiations with the Arabs concerning the frontiers of the Arab State or Confederation of Arab States shall be pursued through the same channel as heretofore in the name of the two Powers.

12. It is understood, moreover, that measures for controlling the importation of arms into the Arab territory will be considered by the two Governments.

BALFOUR DECLARATION

2 November 1917

Balfour was British Foreign Secretary, Rothschild the British Zionist leader.

Dear Lord Rothschild,

I have much pleasure in conveying to you on behalf of His Majesty's Government the following declaration of sympathy with Jewish Zionist aspirations, which has been submitted to and approved by the Cabinet.

'His Majesty's Government view with favour the establishment in Palestine of a national home for the Jewish people, and will use their best endeavours to facilitate the achievement of this object, it being clearly understood that nothing shall be done which may prejudice the civil and religious rights of existing non-Jewish communities in Palestine, or the rights and political status enjoyed by Jews in any other country.'

I should be grateful if you would bring this declaration to the knowledge of the Zionist Federation.

Yours sincerely,
Arthur James Balfour.

HOGARTH MESSAGE*

4 January 1918

The following is the text of a message which Commander D. G. Hogarth, CMG, RNVR, of the Arab Bureau in Cairo, was instructed on 4 January 1918 to deliver to King Husain of the Hijaz at Jeddah:

1. The *Entente* Powers are determined that the Arab race shall be given full opportunity of once again forming a nation in the world. This can only be achieved by the Arabs themselves uniting, and Great Britain and her Allies will pursue a policy with this ultimate unity in view.

2. So far as Palestine is concerned, we are determined that no people shall be subject to another, but—

(*a*) In view of the fact that there are in Palestine shrines, Wakfs and Holy places, sacred in some cases to Moslems alone, to Jews alone, to Christians alone, and in others to two or all three, and inasmuch as these places are of interest to vast masses of people outside Palestine and Arabia, there must be a special régime to deal with these places approved of by the world.

(*b*) As regards the Mosque of Omar, it shall be considered as a Moslem concern alone, and shall not be subjected directly or indirectly to any non-Moslem authority.

3. Since the Jewish opinion of the world is in favour of a return of Jews to Palestine, and inasmuch as this opinion must remain a constant factor, and, further, as His Majesty's Government view with favour the realization of this aspiration, His Majesty's Government are determined that in so far as is compatible with the freedom of the existing population, both economic and political, no obstacle should be put in the way of the realization of this ideal.

In this connection the friendship of world Jewry to the Arab cause is equivalent to support in all States where Jews have political influence. The leaders of the movement are determined to bring about the success of Zionism by friendship and co-operation with the Arabs, and such an offer is not one to be lightly thrown aside.

ANGLO-FRENCH DECLARATION†

7 November 1918

The object aimed at by France and Great Britain in prosecuting in the East the war let loose by the ambition of Germany is the complete and definite emancipation of the peoples so long oppressed by the Turks and the establishment of national Governments and Administrations deriving their authority from the initiative and free choice of the indigenous populations.

In order to carry out these intentions France and Great Britain are at one in encouraging and assisting the establishments of indigenous Governments and Administrations in Syria and Mesopotamia, now liberated by the Allies, and in the territories the liberation of which they are engaged in securing and recognizing these as soon as they are actually established.

Far from wishing to impose on the populations of these regions any particular institutions they are only concerned to ensure by their support and by adequate assistance the regular working of Governments and Administrations freely chosen by the populations themselves. To secure impartial and equal justice for all, to facilitate the economic development of the country by inspiring and encouraging local initiative, to favour the diffusion of education, to put an end to dissensions that have too long been taken advantage of by Turkish policy which the two Allied Governments uphold in the liberated territories.

---

* British White Paper, Cmd. 5964, 1939.

† Report of a Committee set up to consider Certain Correspondence between Sir Henry McMahon and the Sherif of Mecca in 1915 and 1916, 16 March 1939 (British White Paper, Cmd. 5974).

RECOMMENDATIONS OF
THE KING–CRANE COMMISSION‡

28 August 1919

The Commission was set up by President Wilson of the USA to determine which power should receive the Mandate for Palestine. The following are extracts from their recommendations on Syria:

1. We recommend, as most important of all, and in strict harmony with our Instructions, that whatever foreign administration (whether of one or more Powers) is brought into Syria, should come in, not at all as a colonising Power in the old sense of that term, but as a Mandatory under the League of Nations with the clear consciousness that 'the well-being and development' of the Syrian people form for it a 'sacred trust'.

2. We recommend, in the second place, that the unity of Syria be preserved, in accordance with the earnest petition of the great majority of the people of Syria.

3. We recommend, in the third place, that Syria be placed under one mandatory Power, as the natural way to secure real and efficient unity.

4. We recommend, in the fourth place, that Amir Faisal be made the head of the new united Syrian State.

5. We recommend, in the fifth place, serious modification of the extreme Zionist program for Palestine of unlimited immigration of Jews, looking finally to making Palestine distinctly a Jewish State.

(1) The Commissioners began their study of Zionism with minds predisposed in its favor, but the actual facts in Palestine, coupled with the force of the general principles proclaimed by the Allies and accepted by the Syrians have driven them to the recommendation here made.

(2) The Commission was abundantly supplied with literature on the Zionist program by the Zionist Commission to Palestine; heard in conferences much concerning the Zionist colonies and their claims; and personally saw something of what had been accomplished. They found much to approve in the aspirations and plans of the Zionists, and had warm appreciation for the devotion of many of the colonists, and for their success, by modern methods in overcoming great, natural obstacles.

(3) The Commission recognised also that definite encouragement had been given to the Zionists by the Allies in Mr Balfour's often-quoted statement, in its approval by other representatives of the Allies. If, however, the strict terms of the Balfour Statement are adhered to—favoring 'the establishment in Palestine of a national home for the Jewish people', 'it being clearly understood that nothing shall be done which may prejudice the civil and religious rights of existing non-Jewish communities in Palestine'—it can hardly be doubted that the extreme Zionist program must be greatly modified. For 'a national home for the Jewish people' is not equivalent to making Palestine into a Jewish State; nor can the erection of such a Jewish State be accomplished without the gravest trespass upon the 'civil and religious rights of existing non-Jewish communities in Palestine'. The fact came out repeatedly in the Commission's conference with Jewish representatives, that the Zionists looked forward to a practically complete dispossession of the present non-Jewish inhabitants of Palestine, by various forms of purchase.

In his address of 4 July 1918, President Wilson laid down the following principle as one of the four great 'ends for which the associated peoples of the world were fighting': 'The settlement of every question, whether of territory, of sovereignty, of economic arrangement, or of political relationship upon the basis of the free acceptance of that settlement by the people immediately concerned, and not upon the basis of the material interest or advantage of any other nation or people which may desire a different settlement for the sake of its own exterior influence or mastery.' If that principle is to rule, and so the wishes of Palestine's population are to be decisive as to what is to be done with Palestine, then it is to be remembered that the non-Jewish population of Palestine—nearly nine-tenths of the whole—are emphatically against the entire Zionist program. The tables show that there was no one thing upon which the population of Palestine were more agreed than upon this. To subject a people so minded to unlimited Jewish immigration, and to steady financial and social pressure to surrender the land, would be a gross violation of the principle just quoted, and of the people's rights, though it kept within the forms of law.

It is to be noted also that the feeling against the Zionist program is not confined to Palestine, but shared very generally by the people throughout Syria, as our conferences clearly showed. More then 72%—1,350 in all—of all the petitions in the whole of Syria were directed against the Zionist program. Only two requests—those for a united Syria and for independence—had a larger support. This general feeling was duly voiced by the General Syrian Congress in the seventh, eighth and tenth resolutions of their statement.

The Peace Conference should not shut its eyes to the fact that the anti-Zionist feeling in Palestine and Syria is intense and not lightly to be flouted. No British officer, consulted by the Commissioners, believed that the Zionist program could be carried out except by force of arms. The officers generally thought that a force of not less than 50,000 soldiers would be required even to initiate the program. That of itself is evidence of a strong sense of the injustice of the Zionist program, on the part of the non-Jewish populations of Palestine and Syria. Decisions requiring armies to carry out are sometimes necessary, but they are surely not gratuitously to be taken in the interests of serious injustice. For the initial claim, often submitted by Zionist representatives, that they have a 'right' to Palestine, based on an occupation of 2,000 years ago, can hardly be seriously considered.

There is a further consideration that cannot justly be ignored, if the world is to look forward to Palestine becoming a definitely Jewish State, however gradually that may take place. That consideration grows out of the fact that Palestine is the Holy Land for Jews, Christians, and Moslems alike. Millions of Christians and Moslems all over the world are quite as much concerned as the Jews with conditions in Palestine, especially with those conditions which touch upon religious feelings and rights. The relations in these matters in Palestine are most delicate and difficult. With the best possible intentions, it may be doubted whether the Jews could possibly seem to either Christians or Moslems proper guardians of the holy places, or custodians of the Holy Land as a whole.

The reason is this: The places which are most sacred to Christians—those having to do with Jesus—and which are also sacred to Moslems, are not only not sacred to Jews, but abhorrent to them. It is simply impossible, under those circumstances, for Moslems and Christians to feel satisfied to have these places in Jewish hands, or under the custody of Jews. There are still other places about which Moslems must have the same feeling. In fact, from this point of view, the Moslems, just because the sacred places of all three religions are sacred to them, have made very naturally much more satisfactory custodians of the holy places than the Jews could be. It must be believed that the precise meaning in this respect of the complete Jewish occupation of Palestine has not been fully sensed by those who urge the extreme Zionist program. For it would intensify, with a certainty like fate, the anti-Jewish feeling both in Palestine and in all other portions of the world which look to Palestine as the Holy Land.

In view of all these considerations, and with a deep sense of sympathy for the Jewish cause, the Commissioners feel bound to recommend that only a greatly reduced Zionist program be attempted by the Peace Conference, and even that, only very gradually initiated. This would have to mean that Jewish immigration should be definitely limited, and that the project for making Palestine distinctly a Jewish commonwealth should be given up.

There would then be no reason why Palestine could not be included in a united Syrian State, just as other portions of the country, the holy places being cared for by an international and inter-religious commission, somewhat as at present, under the oversight and approval of the Mandatory and of the League of Nations. The Jews, of course, would have representation upon this commission.

‡ US Department of State. *Papers Relating to the Foreign Relations of the United States. The Paris Peace Conference 1919.* Vol. XII. Washington, 1947.

ARTICLE 22 OF THE
COVENANT OF THE LEAGUE OF NATIONS

1. To those colonies and territories which as a consequence of the late War have ceased to be under the sovereignty of the States which formerly governed them and which are inhabited by peoples not yet able to stand by themselves under the strenuous conditions of the modern world, there should be applied the principle that the well-being and development of such peoples form a sacred trust of civilization and that securities for the performance of this trust should be embodied in this Covenant.

2. The best method of giving practical effect to this principle is that the tutelage of such peoples should be entrusted to advanced nations who by reason of their resources, their experience or their geographical position can best undertake this responsibility, and who are willing to accept it, and that this tutelage should be exercised by them as Mandatories on behalf of the League.

3. The character of the Mandate must differ according to the stage of the development of the people, the geographical situation of the territory, its economic conditions and other similar circumstances.

4. Certain communities formerly belonging to the Turkish Empire have reached a stage of development where their existence as independent nations can be provisionally recognized subject to the rendering of administrative advice and assistance by a Mandatory until such time as they are able to stand alone. The wishes of these communities must be a principal consideration in the selection of the Mandatory.

7. In every case of Mandate, the Mandatory shall render to the Council an annual report in reference to the territory committed to its charge.

8. The degree of authority, control, or administration to be exercised by the Mandatory shall, if not previously agreed upon by the Members of the League, be explicitly defined in each case by the Council.

9. A permanent Commission shall be constituted to receive and examine the annual reports of the Mandatories and to advise the Council on all matters relating to the observance of the Mandates.

MANDATE FOR PALESTINE*
24 July 1922

The Council of the League of Nations:

Whereas the Principal Allied Powers have agreed, for the purpose of giving effect to the provisions of Article 22 of the Covenant of the League of Nations to entrust to a Mandatory selected by the said Powers the administration of the territory of Palestine, which formerly belonged to the Turkish Empire, within such boundaries as may be fixed by them; and

Whereas the Principal Allied Powers have also agreed that the Mandatory should be responsible for putting into effect the declaration originally made on 2 November 1917 by the Government of His Britannic Majesty, and adopted by the said Powers, in favour of the establishment in Palestine of a National Home for the Jewish people, it being clearly understood that nothing should be done which might prejudice the civil and religious rights of existing non-Jewish communities in Palestine, or the rights and political status enjoyed by Jews in any other country; and

Whereas recognition has thereby been given to the historical connection of the Jewish people with Palestine and to the grounds for reconstituting their National Home in that country; and

Whereas the Principal Allied Powers have selected His Britannic Majesty as the Mandatory for Palestine; and

Whereas the Mandate in respect of Palestine has been formulated in the following terms and submitted to the Council of the League for approval; and

Whereas His Britannic Majesty has accepted the Mandate in respect of Palestine and undertaken to exercise it on behalf of

the League of Nations in conformity with the following provisions; and

Whereas by the afore-mentioned Article 22 (paragraph 8), it is provided that the degree of authority, control or administration to be exercised by the Mandatory, not having been previously agreed upon by the Members of the League, shall be explicitly defined by the Council of the League of Nations;

Confirming the said Mandate, defines its terms as follows:

ARTICLE 1. The Mandatory shall have full powers of legislation and of administration, save as they may be limited by the terms of this Mandate.

ARTICLE 2. The Mandatory shall be responsible for placing the country under such political, administrative and economic conditions as will secure the establishment of the Jewish National Home, as laid down in the preamble, and the development of self-governing institutions, and also for safeguarding the civil and religious rights of all the inhabitants of Palestine, irrespective of race and religion.

ARTICLE 3. The Mandatory shall, so far as circumstances permit, encourage local autonomy.

ARTICLE 4. An appropriate Jewish Agency shall be recognized as a public body for the purpose of advising and co-operating with the Administration of Palestine in such economic, social and other matters as may affect the establishment of the Jewish National Home and the interests of the Jewish population in Palestine, and, subject always to the control of the Administration, to assist and take part in the development of the country.

The Zionist organization, so long as its organization and constitution are in the opinion of the Mandatory appropriate, shall be recognized as such agency. It shall take steps in consultation with His Britannic Majesty's Government to secure the co-operation of all Jews who are willing to assist in the establishment of the Jewish National Home.

ARTICLE 5. The Mandatory shall be responsible for seeing that no Palestine territory shall be ceded or leased to, or in any way placed under the control of, the Government of any foreign Power.

ARTICLE 6. The Administration of Palestine, while ensuring that the rights and position of other sections of the population are not prejudiced, shall facilitate Jewish immigration under suitable conditions and shall encourage, in co-operation with the Jewish Agency referred to in Article 4, close settlement by Jews on the land, including State lands and waste lands not required for public purposes.

ARTICLE 7. The Administration of Palestine shall be responsible for enacting a nationality law. There shall be included in this law provisions framed so as to facilitate the acquisition of Palestinian citizenship by Jews who take up their permanent residence in Palestine.

ARTICLE 13. All responsibility in connection with the Holy Places and religious buildings or sites in Palestine, including that of preserving existing rights and of securing free access to the Holy Places, religious buildings and sites and the free exercise of worship, while ensuring the requirements of public order and decorum, is assumed by the Mandatory, who shall be responsible solely to the League of Nations in all matters connected herewith, provided that nothing in this Article shall prevent the Mandatory from entering into such arrangements as he may deem reasonable with the Administration for the purpose of carrying the provisions of this Article into effect; and provided also that nothing in this Mandate shall be construed as conferring upon the Mandatory authority to interfere with the fabric of the management of purely Moslem sacred shrines, the immunities of which are guaranteed.

ARTICLE 14. A special Commission shall be appointed by the Mandatory to study, define and determine the rights and claims in connection with the Holy Places and the rights and claims relating to the different religious communities in Palestine. The method of nomination, the composition and the functions of this Commission shall be submitted to the Council of the League for its approval, and the Commission shall not be appointed or enter upon its functions without the approval of the Council.

ARTICLE 28. In the event of the termination of the Mandate hereby conferred upon the Mandatory, the Council of the League

---

* British White Paper, Cmd. 1785.

of Nations shall make such arrangements as may be deemed necessary for safe-guarding in perpetuity, under guarantee of the League, the rights secured by Articles 13 and 14, and shall use its influence for securing, under the guarantee of the League, that the Government of Palestine will fully honour the financial obligations legitimately incurred by the Administration of Palestine during the period of the Mandate, including the rights of public servants to pensions or gratuities.

CHURCHILL MEMORANDUM*
3 June 1922

The Secretary of State for the Colonies has given renewed consideration to the existing political situation in Palestine, with a very earnest desire to arrive at a settlement of the outstanding questions which have given rise to uncertainty and unrest among certain sections of the population. After consultation with the High Commissioner for Palestine the following statement has been drawn up. It summarizes the essential parts of the correspondence that has already taken place between the Secretary of State and a Delegation from the Moslem Christian Society of Palestine, which has been for some time in England, and it states the further conclusions which have since been reached.

The tension which has prevailed from time to time in Palestine is mainly due to apprehensions, which are entertained both by sections of the Arab and by sections of the Jewish population. These apprehensions, so far as the Arabs are concerned, are partly based upon exaggerated interpretations of the meaning of the Declaration favouring the establishment of a Jewish National Home in Palestine, made on behalf of His Majesty's Government on 2 November 1917. Unauthorized statements have been made to the effect that the purpose in view is to create a wholly Jewish Palestine. Phrases have been used such as that Palestine is to become 'as Jewish as England is English.' His Majesty's Government regard any such expectation as impracticable and have no such aim in view. Nor have they at any time contemplated, as appears to be feared by the Arab Delegation, the disappearance or the subordination of the Arabic population, language or culture in Palestine. They would draw attention to the fact that the terms of the Declaration referred to do not contemplate that Palestine as a whole should be converted into a Jewish National Home, but that such a Home should be founded *in Palestine*. In this connection it has been observed with satisfaction that at the meeting of the Zionist Congress, the supreme governing body of the Zionist Organization, held at Carlsbad in September 1921, a resolution was passed expressing as the official statement of Zionist aims 'the determination of the Jewish people to live with the Arab people on terms of unity and mutual respect, and together with them to make the common home into a flourishing community, the upbuilding of which may assure to each of its peoples an undisturbed national development.'

It is also necessary to point out that the Zionist Commission in Palestine, now termed the Palestine Zionist Executive, has not desired to possess, and does not possess, any share in the general administration of the country. Nor does the special position assigned to the Zionist Organization in Article IV of the Draft Mandate for Palestine imply any such functions. That special position relates to the measures to be taken in Palestine affecting the Jewish population, and contemplates that the Organization may assist in the general development of the country, but does not entitle it to share in any degree in its Government.

Further, it is contemplated that the status of all citizens of Palestine in the eyes of the law shall be Palestinian, and it has never been intended that they, or any section of them, should possess any other juridical status.

So far as the Jewish population of Palestine are concerned, it appears that some among them are apprehensive that His Majesty's Government may depart from the policy embodied in the Declaration of 1917. It is necessary, therefore, once more to affirm that these fears are unfounded, and that the Declaration, re-affirmed by the Conference of the Principal Allied Powers at

San Remo and again in the Treaty of Sèvres, is not susceptible of change.

During the last two or three generations the Jews have recreated in Palestine a community, now numbering 80,000, of whom about one-fourth are farmers or workers upon the land. This community has its own political organs; an elected assembly for the direction of its domestic concerns; elected councils in the towns; and an organization for the control of its schools. It has its elected Chief Rabbinate and Rabbinical Council for the direction of its religious affairs. Its business is conducted in Hebrew as a vernacular language, and a Hebrew Press serves its needs. It has its distinctive intellectual life and displays considerable economic activity. This community, then, with its town and country population, its political, religious and social organizations, its own language, its own customs, its own life, has in fact 'national' characteristics. When it is asked what is meant by the development of the Jewish National Home in Palestine, it may be answered that it is not the imposition of a Jewish nationality upon the inhabitants of Palestine as a whole, but the further development of the existing Jewish community, with the assistance of Jews in other parts of the world, in order that it may become a centre in which the Jewish people as a whole may take, on grounds of religion and race, an interest and a pride. But in order that this community should have the best prospect of free development and provide a full opportunity for the Jewish people to display its capacities, it is essential that it should know that it is in Palestine as of right and not on sufferance. That is the reason why it is necessary that the existence of a Jewish National Home in Palestine should be internationally guaranteed, and that it should be formally recognized to rest upon ancient historic connection.

This, then, is the interpretation which His Majesty's Government place upon Declaration of 1917, and, so understood, the Secretary of State is of opinion that it does not contain or imply anything which need cause either alarm to the Arab population of Palestine or disappointment to the Jews.

For the fulfilment of this policy it is necessary that the Jewish community in Palestine should be able to increase its numbers by immigration. This immigration cannot be so great in volume as to exceed whatever may be the economic capacity of the country at the time to absorb new arrivals. It is essential to ensure that the immigrants should not be a burden upon the people of Palestine as a whole, and that they should not deprive any section of the present population of their employment. Hitherto the immigration has fulfilled these conditions. The number of immigrants since the British occupation has been about 25,000. . . .

REPORT OF PALESTINE ROYAL COMMISSION PEEL COMMISSION*
July 1937

The Commission under Lord Peel was appointed in 1936. The following are extracts from recommendations made in Ch. XXII:

Having reached the conclusion that there is no possibility of solving the Palestine problem under the existing Mandate (or even under a scheme of cantonization), the Commission recommend the termination of the present Mandate on the basis of Partition and put forward a definite scheme which they consider to be practicable, honourable and just. The scheme is as follows:

The Mandate for Palestine should terminate and be replaced by a Treaty System in accordance with the precedent set in Iraq and Syria.

Under Treaties to be negotiated by the Mandatory with the Government of Transjordan and representatives of the Arabs of Palestine on the one hand, and with the Zionist Organization on the other, it would be declared that two sovereign independent States would shortly be established—(1) an Arab State consisting of Transjordan united with that part of Palestine allotted to the Arabs, (2) a Jewish State consisting of that part of Palestine allotted to the Jews. The Mandatory would undertake to support any requests for admission to the League of Nations made by the Governments of the Arab and Jewish States. The Treaties would include strict guarantees for the

* Palestine, Correspondence with the Palestine Arab Delegation and the Zionist Organization (British White Paper, Cmd. 1700), pp. 17–21.

* *Palestine Royal Commission: Report*, 1937 (British Blue Book, Cmd. 5479).

protection of minorities. Military Conventions would be attached to the Treaties.

A new Mandate should be instituted to execute the trust of maintaining the sanctity of Jerusalem and Bethlehem and ensuring free and safe access to them for all the world. An enclave should be demarcated to which this Mandate should apply, extending from a point north of Jerusalem to a point south of Bethlehem, and access to the sea should be provided by a corridor extending from Jerusalem to Jaffa. The policy of the Balfour Declaration would not apply to the Mandated Area.

The Jewish State should pay a subvention to the Arab State. A Finance Commission should be appointed to advise as to its amount and as to the division of the public debt of Palestine and other financial questions.

In view of the backwardness of Transjordan, Parliament should be asked to make a grant of £2,000,000 to the Arab State.

WHITE PAPER†
May 1939

The main recommendations are extracted below:

10. . . . His Majesty's Government make the following declaration of their intentions regarding the future government of Palestine:

(i) The objective of His Majesty's Government is the establishment within ten years of an independent Palestine State in such treaty relations with the United Kingdom as will provide satisfactorily for the commercial and strategic requirements of both countries in the future. This proposal for the establishment of the independent State would involve consultation with the Council of the League of Nations with a view to the termination of the Mandate.

(ii) The independent State should be one in which Arabs and Jews share in government in such a way as to ensure that the essential interests of each community are safeguarded.

(iii) The establishment of the independent State will be preceded by a transitional period throughout which His Majesty's Government will retain responsibility for the government of the country. During the transitional period the people of Palestine will be given an increasing part in the government of their country. Both sections of the population will have an opportunity to participate in the machinery of government, and the process will be carried on whether or not they both avail themselves of it.

(iv) As soon as peace and order have been sufficiently restored in Palestine steps will be taken to carry out this policy of giving the people of Palestine an increasing part in the government of their country, the objective being to place Palestinians in charge of all the Departments of Government, with the assistance of British advisers and subject to the control of the High Commissioner. With this object in view His Majesty's Government will be prepared immediately to arrange that Palestinians shall be placed in charge of certain Departments, with British advisers. The Palestinian heads of Departments will sit on the Executive Council, which advises the High Commissioner. Arab and Jewish representatives will be invited to serve as heads of Departments approximately in proportion to their respective populations. The number of Palestinians in charge of Departments will be increased as circumstances permit until all heads of Departments are Palestinians, exercising the administrative and advisory functions which are at present performed by British officials. When that stage is reached consideration will be given to the question of converting the Executive Council into a Council of Ministers with a consequential change in the status and functions of the Palestinian heads of Departments.

(v) His Majesty's Government make no proposals at this stage regarding the establishment of an elective legislature. Nevertheless they would regard this as an appropriate constitutional development, and, should public opinion in Palestine hereafter show itself in favour of such a development, they will be prepared, provided that local conditions permit, to establish the necessary machinery.

(vi) At the end of five years from the restoration of peace and order, an appropriate body representative of the people of Palestine and of His Majesty's Government will be set up to review the working of the constitutional arrangements during the transitional period and to consider and make recommendations regarding the Constitution of the independent Palestine State.

(vii) His Majesty's Government will require to be satisfied that in the treaty contemplated by sub-paragraph (i) or in the Constitution contemplated by sub-paragraph (vi) adequate provision has been made for:

(a) the security of, and freedom of access to, the Holy Places, and the protection of the interests and property of the various religious bodies;

(b) the protection of the different communities in Palestine in accordance with the obligations of His Majesty's Government to both Arabs and Jews and for the special position in Palestine of the Jewish National Home;

(c) such requirements to meet the strategic situation as may be regarded as necessary by His Majesty's Government in the light of the circumstances then existing.

His Majesty's Government will also require to be satisfied that the interests of certain foreign countries in Palestine, for the preservation of which they are presently responsible, are adequately safeguarded.

(viii) His Majesty's Government will do everything in their power to create conditions which will enable the independent Palestine State to come into being within ten years. If, at the end of ten years, it appears to His Majesty's Government that, contrary to their hope, circumstances require the postponement of the establishment of the independent State, they will consult with representatives of the people of Palestine, the Council of the League of Nations and the neighbouring Arab States before deciding on such a postponement. If His Majesty's Government come to the conclusion that postponement is unavoidable, they will invite the co-operation of these parties in framing plans for the future with a view to achieving the desired objective at the earliest possible date.

14. . . . they believe that they will be acting consistently with their Mandatory obligations to both Arabs and Jews, and in the manner best calculated to serve the interests of the whole people of Palestine by adopting the following proposals regarding immigration:

(i) Jewish immigration during the next five years will be at a rate which, if economic absorptive capacity permits, will bring the Jewish population up to approximately one-third of the total population of the country. Taking into account the expected natural increase of the Arab and Jewish populations, and the number of illegal Jewish immigrants now in the country, this would allow for the admission, as from the beginning of April this year, of some 75,000 immigrants over the next five years. These immigrants would, subject to the criterion of economic absorptive capacity, be admitted as follows:

(a) For each of the next five years a quota of 10,000 Jewish immigrants will be allowed, on the understanding that a shortage in any one year may be added to the quotas for subsequent years, within the five-year period, if economic absorptive capacity permits.

(b) In addition, as a contribution towards the solution of the Jewish refugee problem, 25,000 refugees will be admitted as soon as the High Commissioner is satisfied that adequate provision for their maintenance is ensured, special consideration being given to refugee children and dependants.

(ii) The existing machinery for ascertaining economic absorptive capacity will be retained, and the High Commissioner will have the ultimate responsibility for deciding the limits of economic capacity. Before each periodic decision is taken, Jewish and Arab representatives will be consulted.

(iii) After the period of five years no further Jewish immigration will be permitted unless the Arabs of Palestine are prepared to acquiesce in it.

(iv) His Majesty's Government are determined to check illegal immigration, and further preventive measures are

---

† British White Paper, Cmd. 6019.

being adopted. The numbers of any Jewish illegal immigrants who, despite these measures, may succeed in coming into the country and cannot be deported will be deducted from the yearly quotas.

15. His Majesty's Government are satisfied that, when the immigration over five years which is now contemplated has taken place they will not be justified in facilitating, nor will they be under any obligation to facilitate, the further development of the Jewish National Home by immigration regardless of the wishes of the Arab population.

16. The Administration of Palestine is required, under Article 6 of the Mandate, 'while ensuring that the rights and position of other sections of the population are not prejudiced,' to encourage 'close settlement by Jews on the land,' and no restriction has been imposed hitherto on the transfer of land from Arabs to Jews. The Reports of several expert Commissions have indicated that, owing to the natural growth of the Arab population and the steady sale in recent years of Arab land to Jews, there is now in certain areas no room for further transfers of Arab land, whilst in some other areas such transfers of land must be restricted if Arab cultivators are to maintain their existing standard of life and a considerable landless Arab population is not soon to be created. In these circumstances, the High Commissioner will be given general powers to prohibit and regulate transfers of land. These powers will date from the publication of this statement of Policy and the High Commissioner will retain them throughout the transitional period.

17. The policy of the Government will be directed towards the development of the land and the improvement, where possible, of methods of cultivation. In the light of such development it will be open to the High Commissioner, should he be satisfied that the 'rights and position' of the Arab population will be duly preserved, to review and modify any orders passed relating to the prohibition or restriction of the transfer of land.

BILTMORE PROGRAMME*
11 May 1942

The following programme was approved by a Zionist Conference held in the Biltmore Hotel, New York City:

1. American Zionists assembled in this Extraordinary Conference reaffirm their unequivocal devotion to the cause of democratic freedom and international justice to which the people of the United States, allied with the other United Nations, have dedicated themselves, and give expression to their faith in the ultimate victory of humanity and justice over lawlessness and brute force.

2. This Conference offers a message of hope and encouragement to their fellow Jews in the Ghettos and concentration camps of Hitler-dominated Europe and prays that their hour of liberation may not be far distant.

3. The Conference sends its warmest greetings to the Jewish Agency Executive in Jerusalem, to the Va'ad Leumi, and to the whole Yishuv in Palestine, and expresses its profound admiration for their steadfastness and achievements in the face of peril and great difficulties. . . .

4. In our generation, and in particular in the course of the past twenty years, the Jewish people have awakened and transformed their ancient homeland; from 50,000 at the end of the last war their numbers have increased to more than 500,000. They have made the waste places to bear fruit and the desert to blossom. Their pioneering achievements in agriculture and in industry, embodying new patterns of co-operative endeavour, have written a notable page in the history of colonization.

5. In the new values thus created, their Arab neighbours in Palestine have shared. The Jewish people in its own work of national redemption welcomes the economic, agricultural and national development of the Arab peoples and states. The Conference reaffirms the stand previously adopted at Congresses of the World Zionist Organization, expressing the readiness and the desire of the Jewish people for full co-operation with their Arab neighbours.

6. The Conference calls for the fulfilment of the original purpose of the Balfour Declaration and the Mandate which

---

* Text supplied by courtesy of Josef Fraenkel.

'recognizing the historical connexion of the Jewish people with Palestine' was to afford them the opportunity, as stated by President Wilson, to found there a Jewish Commonwealth.

The Conference affirms its unalterable rejection of the White Paper of May 1939 and denies its moral or legal validity. The White Paper seeks to limit, and in fact to nullify Jewish rights to immigration and settlement in Palestine, and, as stated by Mr Winston Churchill in the House of Commons in May 1939, constitutes 'a breach and repudiation of the Balfour Declaration'. The policy of the White Paper is cruel and indefensible in its denial of sanctuary to Jews fleeing from Nazi persecution; and at a time when Palestine has become a focal point in the war front of the United Nations, and Palestine Jewry must provide all available manpower for farm and factory and camp, it is in direct conflict with the interests of the allied war effort.

7. In the struggle against the forces of aggression and tyranny, of which Jews were the earliest victims, and which now menace the Jewish National Home, recognition must be given to the right of the Jews of Palestine to play their full part in the war effort and in the defence of their country, through a Jewish military force fighting under its own flag and under the high command of the United Nations.

8. The Conference declares that the new world order that will follow victory cannot be established on foundations of peace, justice and equality, unless the problem of Jewish homelessness is finally solved.

The Conference urges that the gates of Palestine be opened; that the Jewish Agency be vested with control of immigration into Palestine and with the necessary authority for upbuilding the country, including the development of its unoccupied and uncultivated lands; and that Palestine be established as a Jewish Commonwealth integrated in the structure of the new democratic world.

Then and only then will the age old wrong to the Jewish people be righted.

UN GENERAL ASSEMBLY RESOLUTION ON THE FUTURE GOVERNMENT OF PALESTINE (PARTITION RESOLUTION)
29 November 1947

The General Assembly,

Having met in special session at the request of the mandatory Power to constitute and instruct a special committee to prepare for the consideration of the question of the future government of Palestine at the second regular session;

Having constituted a Special Committee and instructed it to investigate all questions and issues relevant to the problem of Palestine, and to prepare proposals for the solution of the problem, and

Having received and examined the report of the Special Committee (document A/364) including a number of unanimous recommendations and a plan of partition with economic union approved by the majority of the Special Committee,

Considers that the present situation in Palestine is one which is likely to impair the general welfare and friendly relations among nations;

Takes note of the declaration by the mandatory Power that it plans to complete its evacuation of Palestine by 1 August 1948;

Recommends to the United Kingdom, as the mandatory Power for Palestine, and to all other Members of the United Nations the adoption and implementation, with regard to the future government of Palestine, of the Plan of Partition with Economic Union set out below;

Requests that

(a) The Security Council take the necessary measures as provided for in the plan for its implementation;

(b) The Security Council consider, if circumstances during the transitional period require such consideration, whether the situation in Palestine constitutes a threat to the peace. If it decides that such a threat exists, and in order to maintain international peace and security, the Security Council should supplement the authorization of the General Assembly by taking measures, under Articles 39 and 41 of the Charter, to empower the United Nations Commission, as provided in this resolution, to exercise in Palestine the functions which are assigned to it by this resolution;

(*c*) The Security Council determine as a threat to the peace, breach of the peace or act of aggression, in accordance with Article 39 of the Charter, any attempt to alter by force the settlement envisaged by this resolution;

(*d*) The Trusteeship Council be informed of the responsibilities envisaged for it in this plan;

Calls upon the inhabitants of Palestine to take such steps as may be necessary on their part to put this plan into effect;

Appeals to all Governments and all peoples to refrain from taking any action which might hamper or delay the carrying out of these recommendations . . .

Official Records of the second session of the General Assembly, Resolutions, p. 131.

UN GENERAL ASSEMBLY RESOLUTION
194 (III)
11 December 1948

The resolution's terms have been reaffirmed every year since 1948.

11. . . . the refugees wishing to return to their homes and live at peace with their neighbours should be permitted to do so at the earliest practicable date, and that compensation should be paid for the property of those choosing not to return and for the loss of or damage to property which, under principles of international law or in equity, should be made good by the Governments or authorities responsible;

Official Records of the third session of the General Assembly, Part I, Resolutions, p. 21.

UN GENERAL ASSEMBLY RESOLUTION ON THE INTERNATIONALIZATION OF JERUSALEM
9 December 1949

The General Assembly,

Having regard to its resolution 181 (II) of 29 November 1947 and 194 (III) of 11 December 1948,

Having studied the reports of the United Nations Conciliation Commission for Palestine set up under the latter resolution,

I. Decides

In relation to Jerusalem,

Believing that the principles underlying its previous resolutions concerning this matter, and in particular its resolution of 29 November 1947, represent a just and equitable settlement of the question,

1. To restate, therefore, its intention that Jerusalem should be placed under a permanent international regime, which should envisage appropriate guarantees for the protection of the Holy Places, both within and outside Jerusalem, and to confirm specifically the following provisions of General Assembly resolution 181 (II): (1) The City of Jerusalem shall be established as a *corpus separatum* under a special international regime and shall be administered by the United Nations; (2) The Trusteeship Council shall be designated to discharge the responsibilities of the Administering Authority . . .; and (3) The City of Jerusalem shall include the present municipality of Jerusalem plus the surrounding villages and towns, the most eastern of which shall be Abu Dis; the most southern, Bethlehem; the most western, Ein Karim (including also the built-up area of Motsa); and the most northern, Shu'fat, as indicated on the attached sketchmap; . . . [*map not reproduced: Ed.*]

Official Records of the fourth session of the General Assembly, Resolutions, p. 25.

TEXT OF UN SECURITY COUNCIL RESOLUTION 242
22 November 1967

The Security Council,

Expressing its continued concern with the grave situation in the Middle East,

Emphasizing the inadmissibility of the acquisition of territory by war and the need to work for a just and lasting peace in which every state in the area can live in security,

Emphasizing further that all Member States in their acceptance of the Charter of the United Nations have undertaken a commitment to act in accordance with Article 2 of the Charter

1. *Affirms* that the fulfilment of Charter principles requires the establishment of a just and lasting peace in the Middle East which should include the application of both the following principles:

(i) Withdrawal of Israel armed forces from territories occupied in the recent conflict;

(ii) Termination of all claims or states of belligerency and respect for the acknowledgement of the sovereignty, territorial integrity and political independence of every State in the area and their right to live in peace within secure and recognized boundaries free from threats or acts of force.

2. *Affirms further* the necessity

(*a*) For guaranteeing freedom of navigation through international waterways in the area;

(*b*) For achieving a just settlement of the refugee problem;

(*c*) For guaranteeing the territorial inviolability and political independence of every State in the area, through measures including the establishment of demilitarized zones;

3. *Requests* the Secretary-General to designate a Special Representative to proceed to the Middle East to establish and maintain contacts with the States concerned in order to promote agreement and assist efforts to achieve a peaceful and accepted settlement in accordance with the provisions and principles in this resolution;

4. *Requests* the Secretary-General to report to the Security Council on the progress of the efforts of the Special Representative as soon as possible.

Source: UN Document S/RES/242 (1967).

UN SECURITY COUNCIL RESOLUTION ON JERUSALEM
25 September 1971

The resolution, No. 298 (1971), was passed nem. con., *with the abstention of Syria.*

The Security Council,

Recalling its resolutions 252 (1968) of 21 May 1968, and 267 (1969) of 3 July 1969, and the earlier General Assembly resolution 2253 (ES-V) and 2254 (ES-V) of 4 and 14 July 1967, concerning measures and actions by Israel designed to change the status of the Israeli-occupied section of Jerusalem,

Having considered the letter of the Permanent Representative of Jordan on this situation in Jerusalem and the reports of the Secretary-General, and having heard the statements of the parties concerned in the question,

Recalling the principle that acquisition of territory by military conquest is inadmissible,

Noting with concern the non-compliance by Israel with the above-mentioned resolutions,

Noting with concern also that since the adoption of the above-mentioned resolutions Israel has taken further measures designed to change the status and character of the occupied section of Jerusalem.

1. *Reaffirms* its resolutions 252 (1968) and 267 (1969);

2. *Deplores* the failure of Israel to respect the previous resolutions adopted by the United Nations concerning measures and actions by Israel purporting to affect the status of the City of Jerusalem;

3. *Confirms* in the clearest possible terms that all legislative and administrative actions taken by Israel to change the status of the City of Jerusalem, including expropriation of land and properties, transfer of populations and legislation aimed at the incorporation of the occupied section, are totally invalid and cannot change that status;

4. *Urgently calls upon* Israel to rescind all previous measures and actions and to take no further steps in the occupied section of Jerusalem which may purport to change the status of the City, or which would prejudice the rights of the inhabitants and

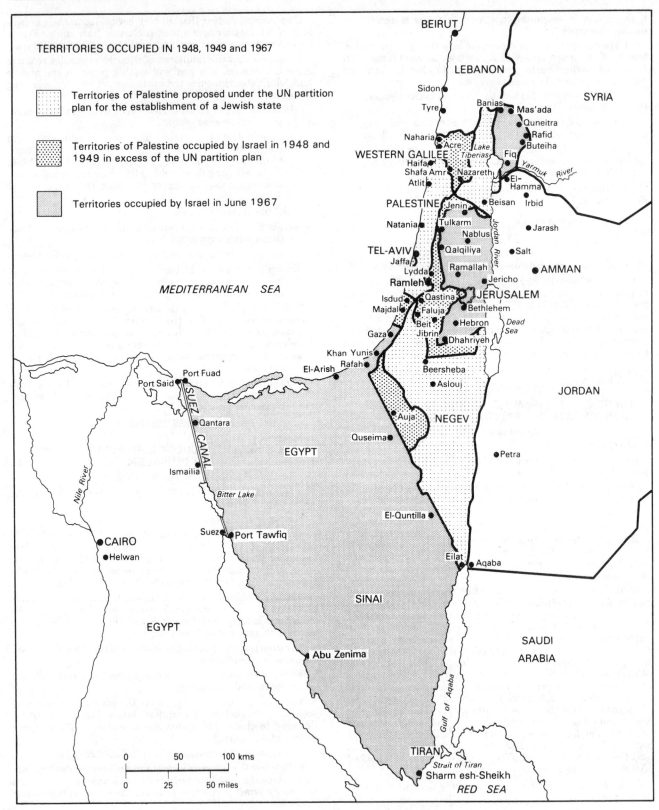

TERRITORIES OCCUPIED IN 1948, 1949 and 1967

Territories of Palestine proposed under the UN partition plan for the establishment of a Jewish state

Territories of Palestine occupied by Israel in 1948 and 1949 in excess of the UN partition plan

Territories occupied by Israel in June 1967

Territories occupied by Israel. See also map on page 118

the interests of the international community, or a just and lasting peace;

5. *Requests* the Secretary-General, in consultation with the President of the Security Council and using such instrumentalities as he may choose, including a representative or a mission, to report to the Council as appropriate and in any event within 60 days on the implementation of the present resolution.

Source: UN Document S/RES/298 (1971).

UN SECURITY COUNCIL RESOLUTION 338
22 October 1973

UN Resolutions between 1967 and October 1973 reaffirmed Security Council Resolution 242 (see above). In an attempt to end the fourth Middle East war, which had broken out between the Arabs and Israel on 6 October 1973, the UN Security Council passed the following Resolution:

The Security Council,

1. *Calls upon* all parties to the present fighting to cease all firing and terminate all military activity immediately, not later than 12 hours after the moment of the adoption of the decision, in the positions they now occupy;

2. *Calls upon* the parties concerned to start immediately after the ceasefire the implementation of Security Council Resolution 242 (1967) in all of its parts;

3. *Decides that,* immediately and concurrently with the ceasefire negotiations start between the parties concerned under appropriate auspices aimed at establishing a just and durable peace in the Middle East.

Source: UN Document PR/73/29 (1973).

UN SECURITY COUNCIL RESOLUTION 340
25 October 1973

The Security Council,

Recalling its Resolutions 338 (1973) of 22 October 1973 and 339 (1973) of 23 October 1973,

Noting with regret the reported repeated violations of the ceasefire in non-compliance with Resolutions 338 (1973) and 339 (1973),

Noting with concern from the Secretary-General's report that the UN military observers have not yet been enabled to place themselves on both sides of the ceasefire line,

1. *Demands* that an immediate and complete ceasefire be observed and that the parties withdraw to the positions occupied by them at 16.50 hours GMT on 22 October 1973;

2. *Requests* the Secretary-General as an immediate step to increase the number of UN military observers on both sides;

3. *Decides* to set up immediately under its authority a UN emergency force to be composed of personnel drawn from member states of the UN, except the permanent members of the Security Council, and requests the Secretary-General to report within 24 hours on the steps taken to this effect.

4. *Requests* the Secretary-General to report to the Council on an urgent and continuing basis on the state of implementation of this Resolution, as well as Resolutions 338 (1973) and 339 (1973);

5. *Requests* all member states to extend their full co-operation to the UN in the implementation of this Resolution, as well as Resolutions 338 (1973) and 339 (1973).

Source: UN Document PR/73/31 (1973).

DECLARATION OF EEC FOREIGN MINISTERS ON THE MIDDLE EAST SITUATION
6 November 1973

The Nine Governments of the European Community have exchanged views on the situation in the Middle East. While emphasizing that the views set out below are only a first contribution on their part to the search for a comprehensive solution to the problem, they have agreed on the following:

1. They strongly urge that the forces of both sides in the Middle East conflict should return immediately to the positions they occupied on 22 October in accordance with Resolutions 339

and 340 of the Security Council. They believe that a return to these positions will facilitate a solution to other pressing problems concerning prisoners of war and the Egyptian Third Army.

2. They have the firm hope that, following the adoption by the Security Council of Resolution 338 of 22 October, negotiations will at last begin for the restoration in the Middle East of a just and lasting peace through the application of Security Council Resolution 242 in all of its parts. They declare themselves ready to do all in their power to contribute to that peace. They believe that those negotiations must take place in the framework of the United Nations. They recall that the Charter has entrusted to the Security Council the principal responsibility for international peace and security. The Council and the Secretary-General have a special role to play in the making and keeping of peace through the application of Council Resolutions 242 and 338.

3. They consider that a peace agreement should be based particularly on the following points:

(i) the inadmissibility of the acquisition of territory by force;

(ii) the need for Israel to end the territorial occupation which it has maintained since the conflict of 1967;

(iii) respect for the sovereignty, territorial integrity and independence of every state in the area and their right to live in peace within secure and recognized boundaries;

(iv) recognition that in the establishment of a just and lasting peace account must be taken of the legitimate rights of the Palestinians.

Article 4 calls for the dispatch of peace-keeping forces to the demilitarized zones.

Source: *Bulletin of the European Communities Commission,* No. 10, 1973, p. 106.

EGYPTIAN-ISRAELI AGREEMENT ON DISENGAGEMENT OF FORCES IN PURSUANCE OF THE GENEVA PEACE CONFERENCE
(signed by the Egyptian and Israeli Chiefs of Staff, 18 January 1974)

This agreement was superseded by the second Egyptian-Israeli Disengagement Agreement signed in September 1975 (see p. 119 below) and then by the Peace Treaty between Egypt and Israel signed on 26 March 1979 (see p. 121 below). A map showing the boundaries of the first agreement is reproduced in this edition (p. 118) and the terms can be found in the 1975–76 edition of The Middle East and North Africa.

DISENGAGEMENT AGREEMENT BETWEEN SYRIAN AND ISRAELI FORCES
AND
PROTOCOL TO AGREEMENT ON UNITED NATIONS DISENGAGEMENT OBSERVER FORCE (UNDOF)
(signed in Geneva, Friday 31 May 1974)

(Annex A)

A. Israel and Syria will scrupulously observe the cease-fire on land, sea and air and will refrain from all military actions against each other, from the time of signing this document in implementation of the United Nations Security Council Resolution 338 dated 22 October 1973.

B. The military forces of Israel and Syria will be separated in accordance with the following principles:

1. All Israeli military forces will be west of a line designated line A on the map attached hereto (reproduced below), except in Quneitra (Kuneitra) area, where they will be west of a line A-1.

2. All territory east of line A will be under Syrian administration and Syrian civilians will return to this territory.

3. The area between line A and the line designated as line B on the attached map will be an area of separation. In this area will be stationed UNDOF established in accordance with the accompanying Protocol.

4. All Syrian military forces will be east of a line designated as line B on the attached map.

5. There will be two equal areas of limitation in armament and forces, one west of line A and one east of line B as agreed upon.

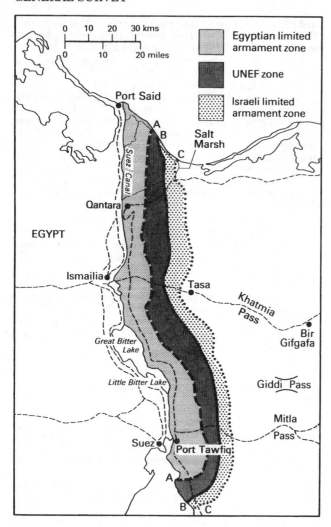

Disengagement Agreement of 18 January 1974 between Israel and Egypt.

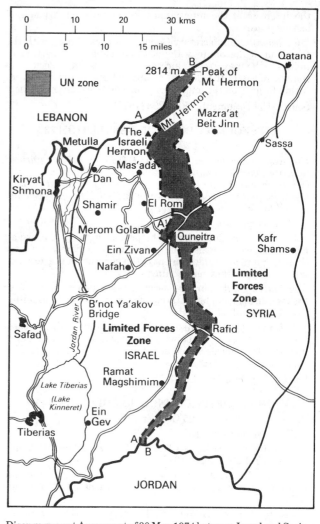

Disengagement Agreement of 30 May 1974 between Israel and Syria.

C.   In the area between line A and line A-1 on the attached map there shall be no military forces.

D.   *Paragraph D deals with practical details of signing and implementation.*

E.   Provisions of paragraphs A, B and C shall be inspected by personnel of the United Nations comprising UNDOF under the Agreement.

F.   *Paragraphs F and G deal with repatriation of prisoners and return of bodies of dead soldiers.*

H.   This Agreement is not a peace agreement. It is a step towards a just and durable peace on the basis of the Security Council Resolution 338 dated 22 October 1973.

A.   *Protocol to the Disengagement Agreement outlined the functions of the United Nations Disengagement Observer Force (UNDOF).*

RESOLUTION OF CONFERENCE OF ARAB HEADS OF STATE
Rabat, 28 October 1974

The Conference of the Arab Heads of State:

1.   *Affirms* the right of the Palestinian people to return to their homeland and to self-determination.

2.   *Affirms* the right of the Palestinian people to establish an independent national authority, under the leadership of the PLO in its capacity as the sole legitimate representative of the Palestine people, over all liberated territory. The Arab States are pledged to uphold this authority, when it is established, in all spheres and at all levels.

3.   *Supports* the PLO in the exercise of its national and international responsibilities, within the context of the principle of Arab solidarity.

4.   *Invites* the kingdom of Jordan, Syria and Egypt to formalize their relations in the light of these decisions and in order that they be implemented.

5.   *Affirms* the obligation of all Arab States to preserve Palestinian unity and not to interfere in Palestinian internal affairs.

Sources: *Le Monde: Problèmes Politiques et Sociaux,* 7 March 1975; *Arab Report and Record.*

UN GENERAL ASSEMBLY RESOLUTION 3236 (XXIX)
22 November 1974

The General Assembly,

Having considered the question of Palestine,

Having heard the statement of the Palestine Liberation Organization, the representative of the Palestinian people,

Having also heard other statements made during the debate,

Deeply concerned that no just solution to the problem of Palestine has yet been achieved and recognizing that the problem of Palestine continues to endanger international peace and security,

Recognizing that the Palestinian people is entitled to self-determination in accordance with the Charter of the United Nations,

Expressing its grave concern that the Palestinian people has been prevented from enjoying its inalienable rights, in particular its right to self-determination,

Guided by the purposes and principles of the Charter,

Recalling its relevant resolutions which affirm the right of the Palestinian people to self-determination,

1. *Reaffirms* the inalienable rights of Palestinian people in Palestine, including:

   (a) The right to self-determination without external interference;

   (b) The right to national independence and sovereignty;

2. *Reaffirms also* the inalienable right of the Palestinians to return to their homes and property from which they have been displaced and uprooted, and calls for their return;

3. *Emphasizes* that full respect for and the realization of these inalienable rights of the Palestinian people are indispensable for the solution of the question of Palestine;

4. *Recognizes* that the Palestinian people is a principal party in the establishment of a just and durable peace in the Middle East;

5. *Further Recognizes* the right of the Palestinian people to regain its rights by all means in accordance with the purposes and principles of the Charter of the United Nations;

6. *Appeals* to all States and international organizations to extend their support to the Palestinian people in its struggle to restore its rights, in accordance with the Charter;

7. *Requests* the Secretary-General to establish contacts with the Palestinian Liberation Organization on all matters concerning the question of Palestine;

8. *Requests* the Secretary-General to report to the General Assembly at its thirtieth session on the implementation of the present resolution;

9. *Decides* to include the item 'Question of Palestine' in the provisional agenda of its thirtieth session.

Source: UN Document BR/74/55 (1974).

SECOND INTERIM PEACE AGREEMENT BETWEEN EGYPT AND ISRAEL

(signed 4 September 1975)

This agreement was superseded by the Peace Treaty between Egypt and Israel signed on 26 March 1979 (see p. 121 below). A map showing the boundaries of the Second Interim Peace Agreement is reproduced in the 1979–80 edition and the terms can be found in the 1978–79 edition of The Middle East and North Africa.

DEVELOPMENTS 1975–78

At the 30th Meeting of the UN General Assembly in November 1975, General Assembly Resolution 3236 (XXIX) was reaffirmed and a 20-nation Committee (the Committee on Palestine Rights) was set up to report on the 'Exercise of the Inalienable Right of the Palestine People' by 1 June 1976.

At the UN Security Council a draft resolution which would have affirmed the rights of the Palestinian people to self-determination, including the right to establish an independent state, was vetoed by the USA on 26 January 1976. A Security Council draft resolution criticizing Israeli policies in East Jerusalem and on the West Bank of the Jordan was also vetoed by the USA on 25 March 1976.

The Committee on Palestine Rights presented its report in June 1976 and recommended that Israel should withdraw from all occupied territories by June 1977. A resolution in the Security Council, stemming from the report, affirmed the 'inalienable rights of the Palestinians' and called for the creation of a 'Palestine entity' in the West Bank and Gaza. This resolution was vetoed by the USA on 29 June 1976. The Committee on Palestine Rights then submitted its report to the UN General Assembly in November 1976 in the form of a resolution. The resolution (No. 20, of 24 November 1976) was adopted by a vote of 90 to 16 (30 members abstained; 10 were absent). The USA and 10 other Western countries (including the UK) opposed the resolution.

Other General Assembly resolutions in December 1976 called for the reconvening of the Geneva Middle East peace conference by March 1977 and the participation in the negotiations of the PLO. Neither of these resolutions was implemented.

After a meeting in London of the nine EC heads of government at the end of June 1977, a statement was issued reaffirming

earlier statements and stating that 'The Nine have affirmed their belief that a solution to the conflict in the Middle East will be possible only if the legitimate rights of the Palestinian people to give effective expression to its national identity is translated into fact, which would take into account the need for a homeland for the Palestinian people. . . . In the context of an overall settlement Israel must be ready to recognize the legitimate rights of the Palestinian people; equally, the Arab side must be ready to recognize the right of Israel to live in peace within secure and recognized boundaries'.

A UN General Assembly Resolution of 25 November 1977 (32/30) 'called anew' for the early convening of the Geneva Middle East peace conference.

A further UN General Assembly Resolution (33/29 of 7 December 1978) repeated the call for the convening of the Geneva Middle East peace conference. The main focus of attention, however, had now moved away from the UN. President Sadat of Egypt visited Jerusalem in November 1977, and after protracted negotiations, President Sadat and Menachem Begin first of all signed two agreements at Camp David in the USA under the auspices of the US President, Jimmy Carter, and subsequently signed a Peace Treaty in Washington on 26 March 1979. The Arab League Council, angry at Egypt's unilateral action, met in Baghdad on 27 March and passed a series of resolutions aimed at isolating Egypt from the Arab world.

CAMP DAVID: THE FRAMEWORK FOR PEACE IN THE MIDDLE EAST

Muhammad Anwar as-Sadat, President of the Arab Republic of Egypt, and Menachem Begin, Prime Minister of Israel, met with President Carter of the USA at Camp David from 5 September to 17 September 1978, and agreed on the following framework for peace in the Middle East. They invited other parties to the Arab-Israeli conflict to adhere to it.

Preamble:

The search for peace in the Middle East must be guided by the following:

The agreed basis for a peaceful settlement of the conflict between Israel and its neighbours is UN Security Council Resolution 242 in all its parts.

The historic initiative by President Sadat in visiting Jerusalem and the reception accorded to him by the Parliament, Government and people of Israel, and the reciprocal visit of Prime Minister Begin to Ismailia, the peace proposals made by both leaders, as well as the warm reception of these missions by the peoples of both countries, have created an unprecedented opportunity for peace which must not be lost if this generation and future generations are to be spared the tragedies of war.

The provisions of the Charter of the UN and the other accepted norms of international law and legitimacy now provide accepted standards for the conduct of relations between all states.

To achieve a relationship of peace, in the spirit of article 2 of the UN Charter, future negotiations between Israel and any neighbour prepared to negotiate peace and security with it, are necessary for the purpose of carrying out all the provisions and principles of Resolutions 242 and 338.

Peace requires respect for the sovereignty, territorial integrity and political independence of every state in the area and their right to live in peace within secure and recognized boundaries free from threats or acts of force. Progress toward that goal can accelerate movement towards a new era of reconciliation in the Middle East marked by co-operation in promoting economic development, in maintaining stability and in assuring security. . . .

Framework

Taking these factors into account, the parties are determined to reach a just, comprehensive and durable settlement of the Middle East conflict through the conclusion of peace treaties based on Security Council Resolutions 242 and 338 in all their parts. Their purpose is to achieve peace and good neighbourly relations. They recognize that, for peace to endure, it must involve all those who have been most deeply affected by the conflict. They therefore agree that this framework as appropriate is intended by them to constitute a basis for peace not only between Egypt and Israel but also between Israel and each of its other neighbours which is prepared to negotiate peace with Israel on this basis. With that objective in mind, they have agreed to proceed as follows:

A. West Bank and Gaza

1. Egypt, Israel, Jordan and the representatives of the Palestinian people should participate in negotiations on the resolution of the Palestinian problem in all its aspects to achieve that objective, negotiations relating to the West Bank and Gaza should proceed in three stages.

(A) Egypt and Israel agree that, in order to ensure a peaceful and orderly transfer of authority, and taking into account the security concerns of all the parties, there should be transitional arrangements for the West Bank and Gaza for a period not exceeding five years. In order to provide full autonomy to the inhabitants, under these arrangements the Israeli military government and its civilian administration will be withdrawn as soon as a self-governing authority has been freely elected by the inhabitants of these areas to replace the existing military government.

To negotiate the details of transitional arrangement, the Government of Jordan will be invited to join the negotiations on the basis of this framework. These new arrangements should give due consideration to both the principle of self-government by the inhabitants of these territories and to the legitimate security concerns of the parties involved.

(B) Egypt, Israel and Jordan will agree on the modalities for establishing the elected self-governing authority in the West Bank and Gaza. The delegations of Egypt and Jordan may include Palestinians from the West Bank and Gaza or other Palestinians as mutually agreed. The parties will negotiate an agreement which will define the powers and responsibilities of the self-governing authority to be exercised in the West Bank and Gaza. A withdrawal of Israeli armed forces will take place and there will be a redeployment of the remaining Israeli forces into specified security locations.

The negotiations shall be based on all the provisions and principles of UN Security Council Resolution 242. The negotiations will resolve, among other matters, the location of the boundaries and the nature of the security arrangements. The solution from the negotiations must also recognize the legitimate rights of the Palestinian people and their just requirements. In this way, the Palestinians will participate in the determination of their own future through:

(i) The negotiations among Egypt, Israel, Jordan and the representatives of the inhabitants of the West Bank and Gaza to agree on the final status of the West Bank and Gaza and other outstanding issues by the end of the transitional period.

(ii) Submitting their agreement to a vote by the elected representatives of the inhabitants of the West Bank and Gaza.

(iii) Providing for the elected representatives of the inhabitants of the West Bank and Gaza to decide how they shall govern themselves consistent with the provisions of their agreement.

(iv) Participating as stated above in the work of the committee negotiating the peace treaty between Israel and Jordan.

The agreement will also include arrangements for assuring internal and external security and public order. A strong local police force will be established, which may include Jordanian citizens. In addition, Israeli and Jordanian forces will participate in joint patrols and in the manning of control posts to assure the security of the borders.

(C) When the self-governing authority (administrative council) in the West Bank and Gaza is established and inaugurated, the transitional period of five years will begin. As soon as possible, but not later than the third year after the beginning of the transitional period, negotiations will take place to determine the final status of the West Bank and Gaza and its relationship with its neighbours, and to conclude a peace treaty between Israel and Jordan by the end of the transitional period. These negotiations will be conducted among Egypt, Israel, Jordan and the elected representatives of the inhabitants of the West Bank and Gaza.

Two separate but related committees will be convened; one committee, consisting of representatives of the four parties which will negotiate and agree on the final status of the West Bank and Gaza, and its relationship with its neighbours, and the second committee, consisting of representatives of Israel and representatives of Jordan to be joined by the elected representatives of the inhabitants of the West Bank and Gaza, to negotiate the peace treaty between Israel and Jordan, taking into account the agreement reached on the final status of the West Bank and Gaza.

2. All necessary measures will be taken and provisions made to assure the security of Israel and its neighbours during the transitional period and beyond. To assist in providing such security, a strong local police force will be constituted by the self-governing authority. It will be composed of inhabitants of the West Bank and Gaza. The police will maintain continuing liaison on internal security matters with the designated Israeli, Jordanian and Egyptian officers.

3. During the transitional period, the representatives of Egypt, Israel, Jordan and the self-governing authority will constitute a continuing committee to decide by agreement on the modalities of admission of persons displaced from the West Bank and Gaza in 1967, together with necessary measures to prevent disruption and disorder. Other matters of common concern may also be dealt with by this committee.

4. Egypt and Israel will work with each other and with other interested parties to establish agreed procedures for a prompt, just and permanent implementation of the resolution of the refugee problem.

B. Egypt-Israel

1. Egypt and Israel undertake not to resort to the threat or the use of force to settle disputes. Any disputes shall be settled by peaceful means in accordance with the provisions of article 33 of the Charter of the UN.

2. In order to achieve peace between them, the parties agree to negotiate in good faith with a goal of concluding within three months from the signing of this framework a peace treaty between them, while inviting the other parties to the conflict to proceed simultaneously to negotiate and conclude similar peace treaties with a view to achieving a comprehensive peace in the area. The framework for the conclusion of a peace treaty between Egypt and Israel will govern the peace negotiations between them. The parties will agree on the modalities and the timetable for the implementation of their obligations under the treaty.

Associated principles

1. Egypt and Israel state that the principles and provisions described below should apply to peace treaties between Israel and each of its neighbours—Egypt, Jordan, Syria and Lebanon.

2. Signatories shall establish among themselves relationships normal to states at peace with one another. To this end, they should undertake to abide by all the provisions of the Charter of the UN. Steps to be taken in this respect include:

(a) Full recognition.

(b) Abolishing economic boycotts.

(c) Guaranteeing that under their jurisdiction the citizens of the other parties shall enjoy the protection of the due process of law.

3. Signatories should explore possibilities for economic development in the context of final peace treaties, with the objective of contributing to the atmosphere of peace, co-operation, and friendship which is their common goal.

4. Claims commissions may be established for the mutual settlement of all financial claims.

5. The United States shall be invited to participate in the talks on matters related to the modalities of the implementation of the agreements and working out the time-table for the carrying out of the obligation of the parties.

6. The UN Security Council shall be requested to endorse the peace treaties and ensure that their provisions shall not be violated. The permanent members of the Security Council shall be requested to underwrite the peace treaties and ensure respect for their provisions. They shall also be requested to conform their policies and actions with the undertakings contained in this framework.

The second agreement signed at Camp David was a framework for the conclusion of a peace treaty between Egypt and Israel. The actual Treaty was signed on 26 March 1979, and is reproduced below.

THE PEACE TREATY BETWEEN EGYPT AND ISRAEL SIGNED IN WASHINGTON ON 26 MARCH 1979

The Government of the Arab Republic of Egypt and the Government of the State of Israel:

Preamble

Convinced of the urgent necessity of the establishment of a just, comprehensive and lasting peace in the Middle East in accordance with Security Council Resolutions 242 and 338:

Reaffirming their adherence to the 'Framework for Peace in the Middle East agreed at Camp David', dated 17 September 1978:

Noting that the aforementioned framework as appropriate is intended to constitute a basis for peace not only between Egypt and Israel but also between Israel and each of the other Arab neighbours which is prepared to negotiate peace with it on this basis:

Desiring to bring to an end the state of war between them and to establish a peace in which every state in the area can live in security:

Convinced that the conclusion of a treaty of peace between Egypt and Israel is an important step in the search for comprehensive peace in the area and for the attainment of the settlement of the Arab-Israeli conflict in all its aspects:

Inviting the other Arab parties to this dispute to join the peace process with Israel guided by and based on the principles of the aforementioned framework:

Desiring as well to develop friendly relations and co-operation between themselves in accordance with the UN Charter and the principles of international law governing international relations in times of peace:

Agree to the following provisions in the free exercise of their sovereignty, in order to implement the 'framework for the conclusion of a peace treaty between Egypt and Israel'.

Article I

1. The state of war between the parties will be terminated and peace will be established between them upon the exchange of instruments of ratification of this treaty.

2. Israel will withdraw all its armed forces and civilians from the Sinai behind the international boundary between Egypt and Mandated Palestine, as provided in the annexed protocol (annexed), and Egypt will resume the exercise of its full sovereignty over the Sinai.

3. Upon completion of the interim withdrawal provided for in Annex 1, the parties will establish normal and friendly relations, in accordance with Article II (3).

Article II

The permanent boundary between Egypt and Israel is the recognized international boundary between Egypt and the former Mandated Territory of Palestine, as shown on the map at Annex 2, without prejudice to the issue of the status of the Gaza Strip. The parties recognize this boundary as inviolable. Each will respect the territorial integrity of the other, including their territorial waters and airspace.

Article III

1. The parties will apply between them the provisions of the Charter of the UN and the principles of international law governing relations among states in times of peace.

In particular:

A. They recognize and will respect each other's sovereignty, territorial integrity and political independence.

B. They recognize and will respect each other's right to live in peace within their secure and recognized boundaries.

C. They will refrain from the threat of use of force, directly or indirectly, against each other and will settle all disputes between them by peaceful means.

2. Each party undertakes to ensure that acts or threats of belligerency, hostility, or violence do not originate from and are not committed from within its territory, or by any forces subject to its control or by any other forces stationed on its territory, against the population, citizens or property of the other party. Each party also undertakes to refrain from organizing, instigating, inciting, assisting or participating in acts or threats of belligerency, hostility, subversion or violence against the other party, anywhere, and undertakes to ensure that perpetrators of such acts are brought to justice.

3. The parties agree that the normal relationship established between them will include full recognition, diplomatic, economic and cultural relations, termination of economic boycotts and discriminatory barriers to the free movement of people and goods, and will guarantee the mutual enjoyment by citizens of the due process of law. The process by which they undertake to achieve such a relationship parallel to the implementation of other provisions of this treaty is set out in the annexed protocol (Annex 3).

Article IV

1. In order to provide maximum security for both parties on the basis of reciprocity, agreed security arrangements will be established including limited force zones in Egyptian and Israeli territory, and UN forces and observers, described in detail as to nature and timing in Annex 1, and other security arrangements the parties may agree upon.

2. The parties agree to the stationing of UN personnel in areas described in Annex 1, the parties agree not to request withdrawal of the UN personnel and that these personnel will not be removed unless such removal is approved by the Security Council of the UN, with the affirmative vote of the five members, unless the parties otherwise agree.

3. A joint commission will be established to facilitate the implementation of the treaty, as provided for in Annex 1.

4. The security arrangements provided for in paragraphs 1 and 2 of this article may at the request of either party be reviewed and amended by mutual agreement of the parties.

Article V

Article V deals with rights of passage of shipping through the Suez Canal, the Strait of Tiran and the Gulf of Aqaba.

Article VI

1. This treaty does not affect and shall not be interpreted as affecting in any way the rights and obligations of the parties under the Charter of the UN.

2. The parties undertake to fulfil in good faith their obligations under this treaty, without regard to action or inaction of any other party and independently of any instrument external to this treaty.

3. They further undertake to take all the necessary measures for the application in their relations of the provisions of the multilateral conventions to which they are parties. Including the submission of appropriate notification to the Secretary-General of the UN and other depositories of such conventions.

4. The parties undertake not to enter into any obligation in conflict with this treaty.

5. Subject to Article 103 of the UN Charter, in the event of a conflict between the obligations of the parties under the present treaty and any of their other obligations, the obligations under this treaty will be binding and implemented.

Article VII

1. Disputes arising out of the application or interpretation of this treaty shall be resolved by negotiations.

2. Any such disputes which cannot be settled by negotiations shall be resolved by conciliation or submitted to arbitration.

Article VIII

The parties agree to establish a claims commission for the mutual settlement of all financial claims.

Article IX

1. This treaty shall enter into force upon exchange of instruments of ratification.

2. This treaty supersedes the agreement between Egypt and Israel of September 1975.

3. All protocols, annexes, and maps attached to this treaty shall be regarded as an integral part hereof.

4. The treaty shall be communicated to the Secretary-General of the UN for registration in accordance with the provisions of Article 102 of the Charter of the UN.

Annex 1—military and withdrawal arrangements:

Israel will complete withdrawal of all its armed forces and civilians from Sinai within three years of the date of exchange of instruments of ratification of the treaty. The withdrawal will be accomplished in two phases, the first, within nine months, to a line east of Al Arish and Ras Muhammad; the second to behind the international boundary. During the three-year period, Egypt and Israel will maintain a specified military presence in four delineated security zones (see map), and the UN will continue its observation and supervisory functions. Egypt will exercise full sovereignty over evacuated territories in Sinai upon Israeli withdrawal. A joint commission will supervise the withdrawal, and security arrangements can be reviewed when either side asks but any change must be by mutual agreement.

Annex 2—maps.

Annex 3—normalization of relations:

Ambassadors will be exchanged upon completion of the interim withdrawal. All discriminatory barriers and economic boycotts will be lifted and, not later than six months after the completion of the interim withdrawal, negotiations for a trade and commerce agreement will begin. Free movement of each other's nationals and transport will be allowed and both sides agree to promote 'good neighbourly relations'. Egypt will use the airfields left by Israel near Al Arish, Rafah, Ras an-Naqb and Sharm ash-Shaikh, only for civilian aircraft. Road, rail, postal, telephone, wireless and other forms of communications will be opened between the two countries on completion of interim withdrawal.

Exchange of letters

Negotiations on the West Bank and Gaza—Negotiations on autonomy for the West Bank and Gaza will begin within one month of the exchange of the instruments of ratification. Jordan will be invited to participate and the Egyptian and Jordanian delegations may include Palestinians from the West Bank and Gaza, or other Palestinians as mutually agreed. If Jordan decides not to take part, the negotiations will be held by Egypt and Israel. The objective of the negotiations is the establishment of a self-governing authority in the West Bank and Gaza 'in order to provide full autonomy to the inhabitants'.

Egypt and Israel hope to complete negotiations within one year so that elections can be held as soon as possible. The self-governing authority elected will be inaugurated within one month of the elections at which point the five year transitional period will begin. The Israeli military Government and its civilian administration will be withdrawn, Israeli armed forces withdrawn and the remaining forces redeployed 'into specified security locations'.

MAIN POINTS OF THE RESOLUTIONS PASSED BY THE ARAB LEAGUE COUNCIL IN BAGHDAD ON 27 MARCH 1979

—To withdraw the ambassadors of the Arab states from Egypt immediately.

—To recommend the severance of political and diplomatic relations with the Egyptian Government. The Arab governments will adopt the necessary measures to apply this recommendation within a maximum period of one month from the date of the issue of this decision, in accordance with the constitutional measures in force in each country.

—To consider the suspension of the Egyptian Government's membership in the Arab League as operative from the date of the Egyptian Government's signing of the peace treaty with the Zionist enemy. This means depriving it of all rights resulting from that membership.

—To make the city of Tunis, capital of the Tunisian Republic, the temporary headquarters of the Arab League, its general secretariat, the competent ministerial councils and the permanent technical committees, as of the date of signing of the treaty between the Egyptian Government and the Zionist enemy. This shall be communicated to all international and regional organizations and bodies. They will also be informed that dealings with the Arab League will be conducted with its secretariat in its new temporary headquarters.

—To condemn the policy that the United States is practising regarding its role in concluding the Camp David agreements and the Egyptian-Israeli treaty.

The Arab League Council, at the level of Arab Foreign and Economy Ministers, has also decided the following:

—To halt all bank loans, deposits, guarantees or facilities, as well as all financial or technical contributions and aid by Arab Governments or their establishments to the Egyptian Government and its establishments as of the treaty-signing date.

—To ban the extension of economic aid by the Arab funds, banks and financial establishments within the framework of the Arab League and the joint Arab co-operation to the Egyptian Government and its establishments.

—The Arab governments and institutions shall refrain from purchasing the bonds, shares, postal orders and public credit loans that are issued by the Egyptian Government and its financial foundations.

—Following the suspension of the Egyptian Government's membership in the Arab League, its membership will also be suspended from the institutions, funds and organisations deriving from the Arab League.

—In view of the fact that the ill-omened Egyptian-Israeli treaty and its appendices have demonstrated Egypt's commitment to sell oil to Israel, the Arab states shall refrain from providing Egypt with oil and its derivatives.

—Trade exchanges with the Egyptian state and with private establishments that deal with the Zionist enemy shall be prohibited.

Source: *MEED Arab Report*, 11 April 1979, p. 9.

UN SECURITY COUNCIL RESOLUTION ON ISRAELI SETTLEMENTS

1 March 1980

The resolution, No. 465, was adopted unanimously by the 15 members of the Council. The USA repudiated its vote in favour of the resolution on 3 March 1980 (see below).

The Security Council, taking note of the reports of the Commission of the Security Council established under resolution 446 (1979) to examine the situation relating to the settlements in the Arab territories occupied since 1967, including Jerusalem, contained in documents S/13450 and S/13679,

—Taking note also of letters from the permanent representative of Jordan (S/13801) and the permanent representative of Morocco, Chairman of the Islamic Group (S/13802),

—Strongly deploring the refusal by Israel to co-operate with the Commission and regretting its formal rejection of resolutions 446 (1979) and 452 (1979),

—Affirming once more that the fourth Geneva Convention relative to the protection of civilian persons in time of war of 12 August 1949 is applicable to the Arab territories occupied by Israel since 1967, including Jerusalem,

—Deploring the decision of the Government of Israel to officially support Israeli settlement in the Palestinian and other Arab territories occupied since 1967,

—Deeply concerned over the practices of the Israeli authorities in implementing that settlement policy in the occupied Arab territories, including Jerusalem, and its consequences for the local Arab and Palestinian population,

—Taking into account the need to consider measures for the impartial protection of private and public land and property, and water resources,

—Bearing in mind the specific status of Jerusalem and, in particular, the need for protection and preservation of the unique spiritual and religious dimension of the holy places in the city,

—Drawing attention to the grave consequences which the settlement policy is bound to have on any attempt to reach a comprehensive, just and lasting peace in the Middle East,

—Recalling pertinent Security Council resolutions, specifically resolutions 237 (1967) of 14 June 1967, 252 (1968) of 21 May 1968, 267 (1969) of 3 July 1969, 271 (1969) of 15 September 1969 and 298 (1971) of 25 September 1971, as well as the consensus statement made by the President of the Security Council on 11 November 1976,

—Having invited Mr Fahd Qawasmah, Mayor of Al-Khalil (Hebron), in the occupied territories, to supply it with information pursuant to rule 39 of provisional rules of procedure,

1. Commends the work done by the Commission in preparing the report contained in document S/13679,

2. Accepts the conclusions and recommendations contained in the above-mentioned report of the Commission,

3. Calls upon all parties, particularly the Government of Israel, to co-operate with the Commission,

4. Strongly deplores the decision of Israel to prohibit the free travel of Mayor Fahd Qawasmah in order to appear before the Security Council, and requests Israel to permit his free travel to the United Nations headquarters for that purpose,

5. Determines that all measures taken by Israel to change the physical character, demographic composition, institutional structure or status of the Palestinian and other Arab territories occupied since 1967, including Jerusalem, or any part thereof, have no legal validity and that Israel's policy and practices of settling parts of its population and new immigrants in those territories constitute a flagrant violation of the Fourth Geneva Convention relative to the protection of civilian persons in time of war and also constitute a serious obstruction to achieving a comprehensive, just and lasting peace in the Middle East,

6. Strongly deplores the continuation and persistence of Israel in pursuing those policies and practices and calls upon the Government and people of Israel to rescind those measures, to dismantle the existing settlements and in particular to cease, on an urgent basis, the establishment, construction and planning of settlements in the Arab territories occupied since 1967, including Jerusalem,

7. Calls upon all states not to provide Israel with any assistance to be used specifically in connection with settlements in the occupied territories,

8. Requests the Commission to continue to examine the situation relating to settlements in the Arab territories occupied since 1967 including Jerusalem, to investigate the reported serious depletion of natural resources, particularly the water resources, with a view of ensuring the protection of those important natural resources of the territories under occupation, and to keep under close scrutiny the implementation of the present resolution,

9. Requests the Commission to report to the Security Council before 1 September 1980, and decides to convene at the earliest possible date thereafter in order to consider the report and the full implementation of the present resolution.

PRESIDENT CARTER'S STATEMENT REPUDIATING US VOTE IN SUPPORT OF UN SECURITY COUNCIL RESOLUTION 465

3 March 1980

I want to make it clear that the vote of the US in the Security Council of the UN does not represent a change in our position regarding the Israeli settlements in the occupied areas nor regarding the status of Jerusalem.

While our opposition to the establishment of the Israeli settlements is long-standing and well-known, we made strenuous efforts to eliminate the language in the resolution with reference to the dismantling of settlements. This call for dismantling was neither proper nor practical. We believe that the future disposition of the existing settlements must be determined during the current autonomy negotiations.

As to Jerusalem, we strongly believe that Jerusalem should be undivided with free access to the holy places for all faiths, and that its status should be determined in the negotiations for a comprehensive peace settlement.

The US vote in the UN was approved with the understanding that all references to Jerusalem would be deleted. The failure to communicate this clearly resulted in a vote in favour of the resolution rather than abstention.

EEC STATEMENT ON THE MIDDLE EAST

Issued in Venice, 13 June 1980

1. The heads of state and government and the ministers of foreign affairs held a comprehensive exchange of views on all aspects of the present situation in the Middle East, including the state of negotiations resulting from the agreements signed between Egypt and Israel in March 1979. They agreed that growing tensions affecting this region constitute a serious danger and render a comprehensive solution to the Israeli-Arab conflict more necessary and pressing than ever.

2. The nine member-states of the European Community consider that the traditional ties and common interests which link Europe to the Middle East oblige them to play a special role and now require them to work in a more concrete way towards peace.

3. In this regard, the nine countries of the Community base themselves on Security Council resolutions 242 and 338 and the positions which they have expressed on several occasions, notably in their declarations of 29 June 1977, 19 September 1978, 26 March and 18 June 1979, as well as the speech made on their behalf on 25 September 1979, by the Irish Minister of Foreign Affairs at the thirty-fourth United Nations General Assembly.

4. On the bases thus set out, the time has come to promote the recognition and implementation of the two principles universally accepted by the international community: the right to existence and to security of all the states in the region, including Israel, and justice for all the peoples which implies the recognition of the legitimate rights of the Palestinian people.

5. All of the countries in the area are entitled to live in peace within secure, recognized and guaranteed borders. The necessary guarantees for a peace settlement should be provided by the United Nations by a decision of the Security Council and, if necessary, on the basis of other mutually agreed procedures. The Nine declared that they are prepared to participate within the framework of a comprehensive settlement in a system of concrete and binding international guarantees, including (guarantees) on the ground.

6. A just solution must finally be found to the Palestinian problem, which is not simply one of refugees. The Palestinian people, which is conscious of existing as such, must be placed in a position, by an appropriate process defined within the framework of the comprehensive peace settlement, to exercise fully its right to self-determination.

7. The achievement of these objectives requires the involvement and support of all the parties concerned in the peace settlement which the Nine are endeavouring to promote in keeping with the principles formulated in the declaration referred to above. These principles apply to all the parties concerned, and thus the Palestinian people, and to the PLO, which will have to be associated with the negotiations.

8. The Nine recognize the special importance of the role played by the question of Jerusalem for all the parties concerned. The Nine stress that they will not accept any unilateral initiative designed to change the status of Jerusalem and that any agreement on the city's status should guarantee freedom of access for everyone to the holy places.

9. The Nine stress the need for Israel to put an end to the territorial occupation which it has maintained since the conflict of 1967, as it has done for part of Sinai. They are deeply convinced that the Israeli settlements constitute a serious obstacle to the peace process in the Middle East. The Nine consider that these settlements, as well as modifications in population and property in the occupied Arab territories, are illegal under international law.

10. Concerned as they are to put an end to violence, the Nine consider that only the renunciation of force or the threatened use of force by all the parties can create a climate of confidence

in the area, and constitute a basic element for a comprehensive settlement of the conflict in the Middle East.

11. The Nine have decided to make the necessary contacts with all the parties concerned. The objective of these contacts would be to ascertain the position of the various parties with respect to the principles set out in this declaration and in the light of the result of this consultation process to determine the form which such an initiative on their part could take.

Subsequent UN Resolutions (General Assembly Resolutions ES-7/2, 29 July 1980; Security Council Resolution 478, 20 August 1980; General Assembly Resolutions 35-169 and 35-207 of 15 and 16 December 1980, etc.) have reaffirmed earlier resolutions and condemned the Israeli 'Jerusalem Bill' of July 1980, which stated explicitly that Jerusalem should be for ever the undivided Israeli capital and seat of government, parliament and judiciary. A UN General Assembly Resolution of 6 February 1982, condemned Israel's annexation of the Golan Heights. UN Resolutions in June 1982 condemned the Israeli invasion of Lebanon, and called for the withdrawal of Israeli forces.

THE FAHD PLAN

In August 1981 Crown Prince Fahd of Saudi Arabia launched an 8-point peace plan for the Middle East. During the remainder of 1981 some Arab States showed their support, but failure to agree on the 'Fahd Plan' caused the break-up of the Fez Arab Summit in November only a few hours after it had opened. The plan is as follows:

1. Israel to withdraw from all Arab territory occupied in 1967, including Arab Jerusalem.

2. Israeli settlements built on Arab land after 1967 to be dismantled.

3. A guarantee of freedom of worship for all religions in holy places.

4. An affirmation of the right of the Palestinian Arab people to return to their homes, and compensation for those who do not wish to return.

5. The West Bank and Gaza Strip to have a transitional period under the auspices of the United Nations for a period not exceeding several months.

6. An independent Palestinian state should be set up with Jerusalem as its capital.

7. All states in the region should be able to live in peace.

8. The UN or member-states of the UN to guarantee carrying-out of these principles.

THE REAGAN PLAN

After the Israeli invasion of Lebanon in June 1982, and the consequent evacuation of the PLO from Beirut, the US Government made strenuous efforts to continue the Camp David peace process and find a permanent solution that would ensure peace in the Middle East. On 1 September 1982 President Reagan outlined the following proposals in a broadcast to the nation from Burbank, California:

'. . . First, as outlined in the Camp David accords, there must be a period of time during which the Palestinian inhabitants of the West Bank and Gaza will have full autonomy over their own affairs. Due consideration must be given to the principle of self-government by the inhabitants of the territories and to the legitimate security concerns of the parties involved.

The purpose of the 5-year period of transition, which would begin after free elections for a self-governing Palestinian authority, is to prove to the Palestinians that they can run their own affairs and that such Palestinian autonomy poses no threat to Israel's security.

The United States will not support the use of any additional land for the purpose of settlements during the transition period. Indeed, the immediate adoption of a settlement freeze by Israel, more than any other action, could create the confidence needed for wider participation in these talks. Further settlement activity is in no way necessary for the security of Israel and only diminishes the confidence of the Arabs that a final outcome can be freely and fairly negotiated.

I want to make the American position well understood: The purpose of this transition period is the peaceful and orderly

transfer of authority from Israel to the Palestinian inhabitants of the West Bank and Gaza. At the same time, such a transfer must not interfere with Israel's security requirements.

Beyond the transition period, as we look to the future of the West Bank and Gaza, it is clear to me that peace cannot be achieved by the formation of an independent Palestinian state in those territories. Nor is it achievable on the basis of Israeli sovereignty or permanent control over the West Bank and Gaza.

So the United States will not support the establishment of an independent Palestinian state in the West Bank and Gaza, and we will not support annexation or permanent control by Israel.

There is, however, another way to peace. The final status of these lands must, of course, be reached through the give-and-take of negotiations. But it is the firm view of the United States that self-government by the Palestinians of the West Bank and Gaza in association with Jordan offers the best chance for a durable, just and lasting peace.

We base our approach squarely on the principle that the Arab-Israeli conflict should be resolved through negotiations involving an exchange of territory for peace. This exchange is enshrined in UN Security Council Resolution 242, which is, in turn, incorporated in all its parts in the Camp David agreements. UN Resolution 242 remains wholly valid as the foundation stone of America's Middle East peace effort.

It is the United States' position that—in return for peace—the withdrawal provision of Resolution 242 applies to all fronts, including the West Bank and Gaza.

When the border is negotiated between Jordan and Israel, our view on the extent to which Israel should be asked to give up territory will be heavily affected by the extent of true peace and normalization and the security arrangements offered in return.

Finally, we remain convinced that Jerusalem must remain undivided, but its final status should be decided through negotiations.

In the course of the negotiations to come, the United States will support positions that seem to us fair and reasonable compromises and likely to promote a sound agreement. We will also put forward our own detailed proposals when we believe they can be helpful. And, make no mistake, the United States will oppose any proposal—from any party and at any point in the negotiating process—that threatens the security of Israel. America's commitment to the security of Israel is ironclad. And, I might add, so is mine.'

FEZ SUMMIT PEACE PROPOSAL

A further Fez Arab Summit was held in September 1982, and produced a set of peace proposals. The following excerpts are from the official English-language text of the final declaration on 9 September 1982, and are reproduced from American Arab Affairs, No 2:

I. The Israeli-Arab conflict:

The summit adopted the following principles:

1. The withdrawal of Israel from all Arab territories occupied in 1967 including Arab Al Qods (East Jerusalem).

2. The dismantling of settlements established by Israel on the Arab territories after 1967.

3. The guarantee of freedom of worship and practice of religious rites for all religions in the holy shrine.

4. The reaffirmation of the Palestinian people's right to self-determination and the exercise of its imprescriptible and inalienable national rights under the leadership of the Palestine Liberation Organization (PLO), its sole and legitimate representative, and the indemnification of all those who do not desire to return.

5. Placing the West Bank and Gaza Strip under the control of the United Nations for a transitory period not exceeding a few months.

6. The establishment of an independent Palestinian state with Al Qods as its capital.

7. The Security Council guarantees peace among all states of the region including the independent Palestinian state.

8. The Security Council guarantees the respect of these principles.

II. The Israeli aggression against Lebanon:

The summit was informed of the Lebanese Government's decision to put an end to the mission of the Arab deterrent forces in Lebanon. To this effect, the Lebanese and Syrian governments will start negotiations on measures to be taken in the light of the Israeli withdrawal from Lebanon.

JOINT JORDAN–PLO PEACE PROPOSALS

After a series of negotiations which began in January 1984, establishing a platform for joint action, King Hussein of Jordan and Yasser Arafat, Chairman of the PLO, announced their proposals for a Middle East peace settlement in Amman, on 23 February 1985. The failure of these proposals to further the peace process was acknowledged by King Hussein on 19 February 1986, when he abandoned Jordan's political collaboration with the PLO. The PLO did not formally abrogate the Amman agreement until the 18th session of the PNC in Algiers in April 1987. The following is the entire text of the joint agreement in an English-language version distributed by the Jordanian Government.

A PLAN OF JOINT ACTION

Proceeding from the spirit of the Fez summit resolutions approved by the Arab states and from UN resolutions on the Palestinian question, in accordance with international legitimacy, and proceeding from a common understanding on the building of a special relationship between the Jordanian and Palestinian peoples, the Government of the Hashemite Kingdom of Jordan and the Palestine Liberation Organization have agreed to work together with a view to a just and peaceful settlement of the Middle East crisis and to the termination of the occupation by Israel of the occupied Arab territories, including Jerusalem, on the basis of the following principles:

1. The return of all territories occupied in 1967 in exchange for a comprehensive peace, as stipulated in the resolutions of the United Nations and its Security Council.

2. The right of the Palestinian people to self-determination: in this respect the Palestinians will exercise their inalienable right to self-determination within the context of the formation of the proposed confederated states of Jordan and Palestine.

3. The solution of the Palestinian refugee problem in accordance with United Nations resolutions.

4. The solution of all aspects of the Palestinian question.

5. On this basis, negotiations should be undertaken under the auspices of an international conference to be attended by the five permanent members of the United Nations Security Council and all parties to the conflict, including the Palestine Liberation Organization, which is the sole legitimate representative of the Palestinian people, in the form of a joint delegation (a joint Jordanian–Palestinian delegation).

THE SHULTZ PLAN

At the beginning of February 1988 the Government of the USA announced a new plan for the resolution of the Palestine issue, which came to be known as the 'Shultz Plan', after the US Secretary of State, George Shultz. The presentation of the plan followed more than a year of diplomatic activity during which the idea of an international peace conference under the auspices of the UN, which had been agreed in principle by Shimon Peres, the Israeli Minister of Foreign Affairs, and King Hussein of Jordan, had won increasing support. The main provisions of the plan, as they were subsequently clarified, were for a six-month period of negotiations between Israel and a joint Jordanian / Palestinian delegation, to determine the details of a transitional autonomy arrangement for the West Bank and the Gaza Strip, which would last for three years; during the transitional period a permanent settlement would be negotiated by the Israeli and Jordanian / Palestinian delegations; both sets of negotiations would run concurrently with and, if necessary, with reference to, an international peace conference, involving the five permanent members of the UN Security Council and all the interested parties (including the Palestinians in a joint Jordanian / Palestinian delegation), which, like the separate Israeli-Jordanian / Palestinian negotiations, would be conducted on the basis of all the

participants' acceptance of UN Security Council resolutions 242 and 338, but would have no power to impose a settlement.

On 6 March 1988, the Israeli newspaper, Yedioth Aharonoth, published a photocopy of a letter from George Shultz to the Israeli Prime Minister, Itzhak Shamir, containing details of his peace proposals. The contents of the letter, identical versions of which were believed to have been delivered to the governments of Egypt, Jordan and Syria, were as follows:

Dear Mr. Prime Minister,

I set forth below the statement of understandings which I am convinced is necessary to achieve the prompt opening of negotiations on a comprehensive peace. This statement of understandings emerges from discussions held with you and other regional leaders. I look forward to the letter of reply of the government of Israel in confirmation of this statement.

The agreed objective is a comprehensive peace providing for the security of all the States in the region and for the legitimate rights of the Palestinian people.

Negotiations will start on an early date certain between Israel and each of its neighbors which is willing to do so. Those negotiations could begin by May 1, 1988. Each of these negotiations will be based on United Nations Security Council Resolutions 242 and 338, in all their parts. The parties to each bilateral negotiation will determine the procedure and agenda of their negotiation. All participants in the negotiations must state their willingness to negotiate with one another.

As concerns negotiations between the Israeli delegation and Jordanian-Palestinian delegation, negotiations will begin on arrangements for a transitional period, with the objective of completing them within six months. Seven months after transitional negotiations begin, final status negotiations will begin, with the objective of completing them within one year. These negotiations will be based on all the provisions and principles of the United Nations Security Council Resolution 242. Final status talks will start before the transitional period begins. The transitional period will begin three months after the conclusion of the transitional agreement and will last for three years. The United States will participate in both negotiations and will promote their rapid conclusion. In particular, the United States will submit a draft agreement for the parties' consideration at the outset of the negotiations on transitional arrangements.

Two weeks before the opening of negotiations, an international conference will be held. The Secretary-General of the United Nations will be asked to issue invitations to the parties involved in the Arab-Israeli conflict and the five permanent members of the United Nations Security Council. All participants in the conference must accept United Nations Security Council Resolutions 242 and 338, and renounce violence and terrorism. The parties to each bilateral negotiations may refer reports on the status of their negotiations to the conference, in a manner to be agreed. The conference will not be able to impose solutions or veto agreements reached.

Palestinian representation will be within the Jordanian-Palestinian delegation. The Palestinian issue will be addressed in the negotiations between the Jordanian-Palestinian and Israeli delegations. Negotiations between the Israeli delegation and the Jordanian-Palestinian delegation will proceed independently of any other negotiations.

This statement of understandings is an integral whole. The United States understands that your acceptance is dependent on the implementation of each element in good faith.

Sincerely yours,
George P. Shultz.

DECLARATION OF PALESTINIAN INDEPENDENCE

In November 1988, the 19th session of the Palestine National Council (PNC) culminated in the declaration 'in the name of God and the Palestinian Arab people' of the independent State of Palestine, with the Holy City of Jerusalem as its capital. The opportunity for the PLO to assert sovereignty over a specific area arose through the decision of King Hussein of Jordan, in July 1988, to sever Jordan's 'administrative and legal links' with the West Bank. The Declaration of Independence cited United Nations General Assembly Resolution 181 of 1947, which partitioned Palestine into two states, one Arab and one Jewish, as providing the legal basis for the right of the Palestinian Arab people to national sovereignty and independence. At the end of the session, the PNC issued a political statement. Details of the Declaration of Independence, and of the political statement, set out below, are taken from an unofficial English-language translation of the proceedings, distributed by the PLO.

'The National Council proclaims, in the name of God and the Palestinian Arab people, the establishment of the State of Palestine on our Palestinian land, with the Holy City of Jerusalem as its capital.

The State of Palestine is the state of Palestinians wherever they may be. In it they shall develop their national and cultural identity and enjoy full equality in rights. Their religious and political beliefs and their human dignity shall be safeguarded under a democratic parliamentary system of government built on the freedom of opinion; and on the freedom to form parties; and on the protection of the rights of the minority by the majority and respect of the decisions of the majority by the minority; and on social justice and equal rights, free of ethnic, religious, racial or sexual discrimination; and on a constitution that guarantees the rule of law and the independence of the judiciary; and on the basis of total allegiance to the centuries-old spiritual and civilizational Palestinian heritage of religious tolerance and coexistence.

The State of Palestine is an Arab state, an integral part of the Arab nation and of that nation's heritage, its civilization and its aspiration to attain its goals of liberation, development, democracy and unity. Affirming its commitment to the Charter of the League of Arab states and its insistence on the reinforcement of joint Arab action, the State of Palestine calls on the people of its nation to assist in the completion of its birth by mobilizing their resources and augmenting their efforts to end the Israeli occupation.

The State of Palestine declares its commitment to the principles and objectives of the United Nations, and to the Universal Declaration of Human Rights, and to the principles and policy of non-alignment.

The State of Palestine, declaring itself a peace-loving state committed to the principles of peaceful coexistence, shall strive with all states and peoples to attain a permanent peace built on justice and respect of rights, in which humanity's constructive talents can prosper, and creative competition can flourish, and fear of tomorrow can be abolished, for tomorrow brings nothing but security for the just and those who regain their sense of justice.

As it struggles to establish peace in the land of love and peace, the State of Palestine exhorts the United Nations to take upon itself a special responsibility for the Palestinian Arab people and their homeland; and exhorts the peace-loving, freedom-cherishing peoples and states of the world to help it attain its objectives and put an end to the tragedy its people are suffering by providing them with security and endeavouring to end the Israeli occupation of the Palestinian territories.

The State of Palestine declares its belief in the settlement of international and regional disputes by peaceful means in accordance with the Charter and resolutions of the United Nations; and its rejection of threats of force or violence or terrorism and the use of these against its territorial integrity and political independence or the territorial integrity of any other state, without prejudice to its natural right to defend its territory and independence.

The Palestine National Council resolves:

First: On the escalation and continuity of the *intifada*

A. To provide all the means and capabilities needed to escalate our people's *intifada* in various ways and on various levels to guarantee its continuation and intensification.

B. To support the popular institutions and organizations in the occupied Palestinian territories.

C. To bolster and develop the Popular Committees and other specialized popular and trade union bodies, including the attack group and the popular army, with a view to expanding their role and increasing their effectiveness.

D. To consolidate the national unity that emerged and developed during the *intifada*.

E. To intensify efforts on the international level for the release of the detainees, the repatriation of the deportees, and the

termination of the organized, official acts of repression and terrorism against our children, our women, our men, and our institutions.

F. To call on the United Nations to place the occupied Palestinian land under international supervision for the protection of our people and the termination of the Israeli occupation.

G. To call on the Palestinian people outside our homeland to intensify and increase their support, and to expand the family-assistance program.

H. To call on the Arab nation, its people, forces, institutions and governments, to increase their political, material and informational support of the *intifada*.

I. To call on all free and honorable people worldwide to stand by our people, our revolution, our *intifada* against the Israeli occupation, the repression, and the organized, fascist official terrorism to which the occupation forces and the armed fanatic settlers are subjecting our people, our universities, our institutions, our national economy, and our Islamic and Christian holy places.

Second: In the political field

Proceeding from the above, the Palestine National Council, being responsible to the Palestinian people, their national rights and their desire for peace as expressed in the Declaration of Independence issued on November 15, 1988; and in response to the humanitarian quest for international entente, nuclear disarmament and the settlement of regional conflicts by peaceful means, affirms the determination of the Palestine Liberation Organization to arrive at a political settlement of the Arab-Israeli conflict and its core, the Palestinian issue, in the framework of the UN Charter, the principles and rules of international legitimacy, the edicts of international law, the resolutions of the United Nations, the latest of which are Security Council Resolutions 605, 607 and 608, and the resolutions of the Arab summits, in a manner that assures the Palestinian Arab people's right to repatriation, self-determination and the establishment of their independent state on their national soil, and that institutes arrangements for the security and peace of all states in the region.

Towards the achievement of this, the Palestine National Council affirms:

1. The necessity of convening an international conference on the issue of the Middle East and its core, the Palestinian issue, under the auspices of the United Nations and with the participation of the permanent members of the Security Council and all parties to the conflict in the region, including, on an equal footing, the Palestine Liberation Organization, the sole legitimate representative of the Palestinian people; on the understanding that the international conference will be held on the basis of Security Council Resolutions 242 and 338 and the safeguarding of the legitimate national rights of the Palestinian people, foremost among which is the right to self-determination, in accordance with the principles and provisions of the UN Charter as they pertain to the right of peoples to self-determination, and the inadmissibility of the acquisition of others' territory by force or military conquest, and in accordance with the UN resolutions relating to the Palestinian issue.

2. The withdrawal of Israel from all the Palestinian and Arab territories it occupied in 1967, including Arab Jerusalem.

3. The annulment of all expropriation and annexation measures and the removal of the settlements established by Israel in the Palestinian and Arab territories since 1967.

4. Endeavouring to place the occupied Palestinian territories, including Arab Jerusalem, under the supervision of the United Nations for a limited period, to protect our people, to create an atmosphere conducive to the success of the proceedings of the international conference toward the attainment of a comprehensive political settlement and the achievement of peace and security for all on the basis of mutual consent, and to enable the Palestinian state to exercise its effective authority in these territories.

5. The settlement of the issue of the Palestinian refugees in accordance with the pertinent United Nations resolutions.

6. Guaranteeing the freedom of worship and the right to engage in religious rites for all faiths in the holy place in Palestine.

7. The Security Council shall draw up and guarantee arrangements for the security of all states concerned and for peace between them, including the Palestinian state.

The Palestine National Council confirms its past resolutions that the relationship between the fraternal Jordanian and Palestinian peoples is a privileged one and that the future relationship between the states of Jordan and Palestine will be built on confederal foundations, on the basis of the two fraternal peoples' free and voluntary choice, in consolidation of the historic ties that bind them and the vital interests they hold in common.

The National Council also renews its commitment to the United Nations resolutions that affirm the right of peoples to resist foreign occupation, imperialism and racial discrimination, and their right to fight for their independence; and it once more announces its rejection of terrorism in all its forms, including state terrorism, emphasizing its commitment to the resolutions it adopted in the past on this subject, and to the resolutions of the Arab summit in Algiers in 1988, and to UN Resolutions 42/159 of 1967 and 61/40 of 1985, and to what was stated in this regard in the Cairo Declaration of 7/11/85.

Third: In the Arab and international fields

The Palestine National Council emphasizes the importance of the unity of Lebanon in its territory, its people and its institutions, and stands firmly against the attempts to partition the land and disintegrate the fraternal people of Lebanon. It further emphasizes the importance of the joint Arab effort to participate in a settlement of the Lebanese crisis that helps crystallize and implement solutions that preserve Lebanese unity. The Council also stresses the importance of consecrating the right of the Palestinians in Lebanon to engage in political and informational activity and to enjoy security and protection; and of working against all the forms of conspiracy and aggression that target them and their right to work and live; and of the need to secure the conditions that assure them the ability to defend themselves and provide them with security and protection.

The Palestine National Council affirms its solidarity with the Lebanese nationalist Islamic forces in their struggle against the Israeli occupation and its agents in the Lebanese South; expresses its pride in the allied struggle of the Lebanese and Palestinian peoples against the aggression and toward the termination of the Israeli occupation of parts of the South; and underscores the importance of bolstering this kinship between our people and the fraternal, combative people of Lebanon.

And on this occasion, the Council addresses a reverent salute to the long-suffering people of our camps in Lebanon and its South, who are enduring the aggression, massacres, murder, starvation, air raids, bombardments and sieges perpetrated against the Palestinian camps and Lebanese villages by the Israeli army, air force and navy, aided and abetted by hireling forces in the region; and it rejects the resettlement conspiracy, for the Palestinians' homeland is Palestine.

The Council emphasizes the importance of the Iraq–Iran cease-fire resolution toward the establishment of a permanent peace settlement between the two countries and in the Gulf Region; and calls for an intensification of the efforts being exerted to ensure the success of the negotiations toward the establishment of peace on stable and firm foundations; affirming, on this occasion, the price of the Palestinian Arab people and the Arab nation as a whole in the steadfastness and triumphs of fraternal Iraq as it defended the eastern gate of the Arab nation.

The National Council also expresses its deep pride in the stand taken by the peoples of our Arab nation in support of our Palestinian Arab people and of the Palestine Liberation Organization and of our people's *intifada* in the occupied homeland; and emphasizes the importance of fortifying the bonds of combat among the forces, parties and organizations of the Arab national liberation movement, in defense of the right of the Arab nation and its peoples to liberation, progress, democracy and unity. The Council calls for the adoption of all measures needed to reinforce the unity of struggle among all members of the Arab national liberation movement.

The Palestine National Council, as it hails the Arab states and thanks them for their support of our people's struggle, calls on them to honour the commitments they approved at the summit conference in Algiers in support of the Palestinian people and their blessed *intifada*. The Council, in issuing this appeal, expresses its great confidence that the leaders of the Arab nation will remain, as we have known them, a bulwark of support for Palestine and its people.

The Palestine National Council reiterates the desire of the Palestine Liberation Organization for Arab solidarity as the framework within which the Arab nation and its states can organize themselves to confront Israel's aggression and American support of that aggression, and within which Arab prestige can be enhanced and the Arab role strengthened to the point of influencing international policies to the benefit of Arab rights and causes.

The Palestine National Council expresses its deep gratitude to all the states and international forces and organizations that support the national rights of the Palestinians; affirms its desire to strengthen the bonds of friendship and co-operation with the Soviet Union, the People's (Republic of) China, the other socialist countries, the non-aligned states, the Islamic states, the African states, the Latin American states and the other friendly states; and notes with satisfaction the signs of positive evolution in the positions of some West European states and Japan in the direction of support for the rights of the Palestinian people, applauds this development, and urges intensified efforts to increase it.

The National Council affirms the fraternal solidarity of the Palestinian people and the Palestine Liberation Organization with the struggle of the peoples of Asia, Africa and Latin America for their liberation and the reinforcement of their independence; and condemns all American attempts to threaten the independence of the states of Central America and interfere in their affairs.

The Palestine National Council expresses the support of the Palestine Liberation Organization for the national liberation movements in South Africa and Namibia . . . .

The Council notes with considerable concern the growth of the Israeli forces of fascism and extremism and the escalation of their open calls for the implementation of the policy of annihilation and individual and collective expulsion of our people from their homeland, and calls for intensified efforts in all areas to confront this fascist peril. The Council at the same time expresses its appreciation of the role and courage of the Israeli peace forces as they resist and expose the forces of fascism, racism and aggression, support our people's struggle and their valiant *intifada* and back our people's right to self-determination and the establishment of an independent state. The Council confirms its past resolutions regarding the reinforcement and development of relations with these democratic forces.

The Palestine National Council also addresses itself to the American people, calling on them all to strive to put an end to the American policy that denies the Palestinian people's national rights, including their sacred right to self-determination, and urging them to work toward the adoption of policies that conform to the Declaration of Human Rights and the international conventions and resolutions and serve the quest for peace in the Middle East and security for all its peoples, including the Palestinian people.

The Council charges the Executive Committee with the task of completing the formation of the Committee for the Perpetuation of the Memory of the Martyr-Symbol Abu Jihad, which shall initiate its work immediately upon the adjournment of the Council.

The Council sends its greetings to the United Nations Committee on the Exercise of the Inalienable Rights of the Palestinian People, and to the fraternal and friendly international and non-governmental institutions and organizations, and to the journalists and media that have stood and still stand by our people's struggle and *intifada*.

The National Council expresses deep pain at the continued detention of hundreds of combatants from among our people in a number of Arab countries, strongly condemns their continued detention, and calls upon those countries to put an end to these abnormal conditions and release those fighters to play their role in the struggle.

In conclusion, the Palestine National Council affirms its complete confidence that the justice of the Palestinian cause and of the demands for which the Palestinian people are struggling will continue to draw increasing support from honorable and free people around the world; and also affirms its complete confidence in victory on the road to Jerusalem, the capital of our independent Palestinian state.'

THE ISRAELI PEACE INITIATIVE

In May 1989 the Government of Israel approved a four-point peace initiative for a resolution of the Middle East conflict, the details of which had first been announced during a meeting between US President George Bush and Israeli Prime Minister, Itzhak Shamir, in Washington on 6 April. Based largely on peace proposals made by Israeli Defence Minister, Itzhak Rabin, in January 1989, the new plan followed increased international diplomatic pressure on Israel to respond to the uprising in the Occupied Territories with constructive action to end the conflict. The main proposals of the Israeli initiative were that elections should be held in the West Bank and Gaza Strip in order to facilitate the formation of a delegation of appropriate interlocutors (i.e. non-PLO representatives) to take part in negotiations on a transitional settlement, when a self-ruling authority might be established. The transitional period would serve as a test of co-operation and coexistence and would be followed by negotiations on a final agreement in which Israel would be prepared to discuss any option presented; that Israel, Egypt and the USA should reconfirm their commitment to the Camp David Agreements of 1979; that the USA and Egypt should seek to persuade Arab countries to desist from hostility towards Israel; and that an international effort should be made to solve the 'humanitarian issue' of the inhabitants of refugee camps in Judaea, Samaria and the Gaza Strip. In July 1989 four amendments to the Israeli peace initiative were approved by the central committee of the Likud. These stipulated that residents of East Jerusalem would not be allowed to take part in the proposed elections in the West Bank and Gaza; that violent attacks by Palestinians must cease before elections could be held in the Occupied Territories; that Jewish settlement should continue in the Territories and that foreign sovereignty should not be conceded in any part of Israel; and that the establishment of a Palestinian state west of the River Jordan was out of the question, as were negotiations with the PLO. At the end of July, however, the Israeli Cabinet once again endorsed the peace initiative in its original form.

In September 1989 President Mubarak of Egypt sought ten assurances from the Israeli Government with regard to its peace initiative: (i) a commitment to accept the results of the elections proposed by the peace initiative; (ii) the vigilance of international observers at the elections; (iii) the granting of immunity to all elected representatives; (iv) the withdrawal of the Israel Defence Force from the balloting area; (v) a commitment by the Israeli Government to begin talks on the final status of the Occupied Territories on a specific date within three to five years; (vi) an end to Jewish settlement activities in the Occupied Territories; (vii) a ban on election propaganda; (viii) a ban on the entry of Israelis into the Occupied Territories on the day of the proposed elections; (ix) permission for residents of East Jerusalem to participate in the elections; (x) a commitment by the Israeli Government to the principle of exchanging land for peace. Mubarak also offered to host talks between Palestinian and Israeli delegations prior to the holding of the elections, but a proposal by the Labour component of the Israeli Government to accept his invitation was rejected by Israel's 'inner' Cabinet in October 1989. In the same month the US Secretary of State, James Baker, put forward a series of unofficial proposals which aimed to give new impetus to the Israeli peace initiative and the subsequent clarification proposed by President Mubarak. On the basis of its understanding that a dialogue between Israeli and Palestinian delegations would take place, the USA, through the 'Baker plan', sought assurances that Egypt could not and would not substitute itself for the Palestinians in any future negotiations, and that both Israel and the Palestinians would take part in any future dialogue on the basis of the 'Shamir plan'.

THE 1991 MIDDLE EAST PEACE CONFERENCE

On 30 October 1991 the first, symbolic session of a Middle East peace conference, sponsored by the USA and the USSR and attended by Israeli, Syrian, Egyptian, Lebanese and Palestinian / Jordanian delegations, commenced in Madrid, Spain. The text of the invitation sent to the participants by the US and Soviet Presidents is reproduced from Al-Hayat, London

After extensive consultations with Arab states, Israel and the Palestinians, the US and the Soviet Union believe that an historic opportunity exists to advance the prospects for genuine peace throughout the region. The US and the Soviet Union are prepared to assist the parties to achieve a just, lasting and comprehensive peace settlement, through direct negotiations along two tracks, between Israel and the Palestinians, based on UN Security Council resolutions 242 and 338. The objective of this process is real peace.

Towards that end, the president of the US and the president of the USSR invite you to a peace conference, which their countries will co-sponsor, followed immediately by direct negotiations. The conference will be convened in Madrid on 30 October 1991.

President Bush and President Gorbachev request your acceptance of this invitation no later than 6.00pm Washington time, 23 October 1991, in order to ensure proper organisation and preparation of the conference.

Direct bilateral negotiations will begin four days after the opening of the conference. Those parties who wish to attend multilateral negotiations will convene two weeks after the opening of the conference to organise those negotiations. The co-sponsors believe that those negotiations should focus on regionwide issues such as arms control and regional security, water, refugee issues, environment, economic development, and other subjects of mutual interest.

The co-sponsors will chair the conference which will be held at ministerial level. Governments to be invited include Israel, Syria, Lebanon and Jordan. Palestinians will be invited and attend as part of a joint Jordanian-Palestinian delegation. Egypt will be invited to the conference as a participant. The EC will be a participant in the conference alongside the US and Soviet Union and will be represented by its presidency. The GCC will be invited to send its secretary-general to the conference as an observer, and GCC member states will be invited to participate in organising the negotiations on multilateral issues. The UN will be invited to send an observer, representing the secretary-general.

DECLARATION OF PRINCIPLES ON PALESTINIAN SELF-RULE

13 September 1993

The Government of the State of Israel and the Palestinian team (in the Jordanian-Palestinian delegation to the Middle East Peace Conference) (the 'Palestinian Delegation') representing the Palestinian people, agree that it is time to put an end to decades of confrontation and conflict, recognize their mutual legitimate and political rights, and strive to live in peaceful coexistence and mutual dignity and security and achieve a just, lasting and comprehensive peace settlement and historic reconciliation through the agreed political process.

Accordingly, the two sides agree to the following principles:

Article I

Aim of the negotiations

The aim of the Israeli-Palestinian negotiations within the current Middle East peace process is, among other things, to establish a Palestinian Interim Self-Government Authority, the elected Council, (the 'Council') for the Palestinian people in the West Bank and the Gaza Strip, for a transitional period not exceeding five years, leading to a permanent settlement based on Security Council Resolutions 242 and 338.

It is understood that the interim arrangements are an integral part of the overall peace process and that final status negotiations will lead to the implementation of Security Council Resolutions 242 and 338.

Article II

Framework for the interim period

The agreed framework for the interim period is set forth in the Declaration of Principles.

Article III

Elections

1. In order that the Palestinian people in the West Bank and Gaza Strip may govern themselves according to democratic principles, direct, free and general political elections will be held for the Council under agreed supervision and international observation, while the Palestinian police will ensure public order.

2. An agreement will be concluded on the exact mode and conditions of the elections in accordance with the protocol attached as Annex I, with the goal of holding the elections not later than nine months after the entry into force of this Declaration of Principles.

3. These elections will constitute a significant interim preparatory step toward the realization of the legitimate rights of the Palestinian people and their just requirements.

Article IV

Jurisdiction of the Council will cover West Bank and Gaza Strip territory, except for issues that will be negotiated in the permanent status negotiations. The two sides view the West Bank and the Gaza Strip as a single territorial unit, whose integrity will be preserved during the interim period.

Article V

Transitional period and permanent status negotiations

1. The five-year transitional period will begin upon the withdrawal from the Gaza Strip and Jericho area.

2. Permanent status negotiations will commence as soon as possible, but not later than the beginning of the third year of the interim period, between the Government of Israel and the Palestinian people representatives.

3. It is understood that these negotiations shall cover remaining issues, including Jerusalem, refugees, settlements, security arrangements, borders, relations and co-operation with other neighbours, and other issues of common interest.

4. The two parties agree that the outcome of the permanent status negotiations should not be prejudiced or pre-empted by agreements reached for the interim period.

Article VI

Preparatory transfer of powers and responsibilities

1. Upon the entry into force of this Declaration of Principles and the withdrawal from the Gaza Strip and Jericho area, a transfer of authority from the Israeli military government and its Civil Administration to the authorized Palestinians for this task, as detailed herein, will commence. This transfer of authority will be of preparatory nature until the inauguration of the Council.

2. Immediately after the entry into force of this Declaration of Principles and the withdrawal from the Gaza Strip and Jericho area, with the view to promoting economic development in the West Bank and Gaza Strip, authority will be transferred to the Palestinians in the following spheres: education and culture, health, social welfare, direct taxation, and tourism. The Palestinian side will commence in building the Palestinian police force, as agreed upon. Pending the inauguration of the Council, the two parties may negotiate the transfer of additional powers and responsibilities as agreed upon.

Article VII

Interim agreement

1. The Israeli and Palestinian delegations will negotiate an agreement on the interim period (the 'Interim Agreement').

2. The Interim Agreement shall specify, among other things, the structure of the Council, the number of its members, and the transfer of powers and responsibilities from the Israeli military government and its Civil Administration to the Council. The Interim Agreement shall also specify the Council's executive authority, legislative authority in accordance with Article IX below, and the independent Palestinian judicial organs.

3. The Interim Agreement shall include arrangements, to be implemented upon the inauguration of the Council, for the assumption by the Council of all of the powers and responsibilities transferred previously in accordance with Article VI above.

4. In order to enable the Council to promote economic growth, upon its inauguration, the Council will establish, among other things, a Palestinian Electricity Authority, a Gaza Sea Port Authority, a Palestinian Development Bank, a Palestinian Export Promotion Board, a Palestinian Environmental Authority, a Palestinian Land Authority and a Palestinian Water Administration Authority, and any other authorities agreed upon, in accordance with the Interim Agreement that will specify their powers and responsibilities.

5. After the inauguration of the Council, the Civil Administration will be dissolved, and the Israeli military government will be withdrawn.

Article VIII

Public order and security

In order to guarantee public order and internal security for the Palestinians of the West Bank and the Gaza Strip, the Council will establish a strong police force, while Israel will continue to carry the responsibility for defending against external threats, as well as the responsibility for overall security of the Israelis to protect their internal security and public order.

Article IX

Laws and military orders

1. The Council will be empowered to legislate, in accordance with the Interim Agreement, within all authorities transferred to it.

2. Both parties will review jointly laws and military orders presently in force in remaining spheres.

Article X

Joint Israeli-Palestinian liaison committee

In order to provide for a smooth implementation of this Declaration of Principles and any subsequent agreements pertaining to the interim period, upon the entry into force of this Declaration of Principles, a Joint Israeli-Palestinian Liaison Committee will be established in order to deal with issues requiring co-ordination, other issues of common interest, and disputes.

Article XI

Israeli-Palestinian co-operation in economic fields

Recognizing the mutual benefit of co-operation in promoting the development of the West Bank, the Gaza Strip and Israel, upon the entry into force of this Declaration of Principles, an Israeli-Palestinian Economic Co-operation Committee will be established in order to develop and implement in a co-operative manner the programmes identified in the protocols attached as Annex III and Annex IV.

Article XII

Liaison and co-operation with Jordan and Egypt

The two parties will invite the Governments of Jordan and Egypt to participate in establishing further liaison and co-operation arrangements between the Government of Israel and the Palestinian representatives, on one hand, and the Governments of Jordan and Egypt, on the other hand, to promote co-operation between them. These arrangements will include the constitution of a Continuing Committee that will decide by agreement on the modalities of the admission of persons displaced from the West Bank and Gaza Strip in 1967, together with necessary measures to prevent disruption and disorder. Other matters of common concern will be dealt with by this Committee.

Article XIII

Redeployment of Israeli forces

1. After the entry into force of this Declaration of Principles, and not later than the eve of elections for the Council, a redeploy-

ment of Israeli military forces in the West Bank and the Gaza Strip will take place, in addition to withdrawal of Israeli forces carried out in accordance with Article XIV.

2. In redeploying its military forces, Israel will be guided by the principle that its military forces should be redeployed outside the populated areas.

3. Further redeployments to specified locations will be gradually implemented commensurate with the assumption of responsibility for public order and internal security by the Palestinian police force pursuant to Article VIII above.

Article XIV

Israeli withdrawal from the Gaza Strip and Jericho area

Israel will withdraw from the Gaza Strip and Jericho area, as detailed in the protocol attached as Annex II.

Article XV

Resolution of disputes

1. Disputes arising out of the application or interpretation of this Declaration of Principles, or any subsequent agreements pertaining to the interim period, shall be resolved by negotiations through the Joint Liaison Committee to be established pursuant to Article X above.

2. Disputes which cannot be settled by negotiations may be resolved by a mechanism of conciliation to be agreed upon by the parties.

3. The parties may agree to submit to arbitration disputes relating to the interim period, which cannot be settled through conciliation. To this end, upon the agreement of both parties, the parties will establish an Arbitration Committee.

Article XVI

Israel-Palestinian co-operation concerning regional programs

Both parties view the multilateral working groups as an appropriate instrument for promoting a 'Marshall Plan,' the regional programs and other programs, including special programs for the West Bank and Gaza Strip, as indicated in the protocol atttached as Annex IV.

Article XVII

Miscellaneous provisions

1. This Declaration of Principles will enter into force one month after its signing.

2. All protocols annexed to this Declaration of Principles and Agreed Minutes pertaining thereto shall be regarded as an integral part hereof.

Annex 1—protocol on the mode and conditions of elections

1. Palestinians of Jerusalem who live there will have the right to participate in the election process, according to an agreement between the two sides.

2. In addition, the election agreement should cover, among other things, the following issues:

a. the system of elections,

b. the mode of the agreed supervision and international observation and their personal composition, and

c. rules and regulations regarding election campaign, including agreed arrangements for the organizing of mass media, and the possibility of licensing a broadcasting and TV station.

3. The future status of displaced Palestinians who were registered on 4th June 1967 will not be prejudiced because they are unable to participate in the election process due to practical reasons.

Annex 2—protocol on withdrawal of Israeli forces from the Gaza Strip and Jericho Area

1. The two sides will conclude and sign within two months from the date of entry into force of this Declaration of Principles, an agreement on the withdrawal of Israeli military forces from the Gaza Strip and Jericho area. This agreement will include comprehensive arrangements to apply in the Gaza Strip and the Jericho area subsequent to the Israeli withdrawal.

2. Israel will implement an accelerated and scheduled withdrawal of Israeli military forces from the Gaza Strip and Jericho area, beginning immediately with the signing of the agreement on the Gaza Strip and Jericho area and to be completed within a period not exceeding four months after the signing of this agreement.

3. The above agreement will include, among other things:

a. Arrangements for a smooth and peaceful transfer of authority from the Israeli military government and its Civil Administration to the Palestinian representatives.

b. structure, powers and responsibilities of the Palestinian authority in these areas, except, external security, settlements, Israelis, foreign relations, and other subjects mutually agreed upon.

c. Arrangements for assumption of internal security and public order by the Palestinian police force consisting of police officers recruited locally and from abroad (holding Jordanian passports and Palestinian documents issued by Egypt). Those who will participate in the Palestinian police force coming from abroad should be trained as police and police officers.

d. A temporary international or foreign presence, as agreed upon.

e. Establishment of a joint Palestinian-Israeli co-ordination and co-operation committee for mutual security purposes.

f. An economic development and stablization program, including the establishment of an Emergency Fund, to encourage foreign investment, and financial and economic support. Both sides will co-ordinate and co-operate jointly and unilaterally with regional and international parties to support these aims.

g. Arrangements for a safe passage for persons and transportation between the Gaza Strip and Jericho area.

4. The above agreement will include arrangements for co-ordination between both parties regarding passages:

a. Gaza – Egypt; and

b. Jericho – Jordan.

5. The offices responsible for carrying out the powers and responsibilities of the Palestinian authority under this Annex II and Article VI of the Declaration of Principles will be located in the Gaza Strip and in the Jericho area pending the inauguration of the Council.

6. Other than these agreed arrangements, the status of the Gaza Strip and Jericho area will continue to be an integral part of the West Bank and Gaza Strip, and will not be changed in the interim period.

PROTOCOL ON ISRAELI-PALESTINIAN CO-OPERATION IN ECONOMIC AND DEVELOPMENT PROGRAMS

The two sides agree to establish an Israeli-Palestinian Continuing Committee for Economic Co-operation, focusing, among other things, on the following:

1. Co-operation in the field of water, including a Water Development Program prepared by experts from both sides, which will also specify the mode of co-operation in the management of water resources in the West Bank and Gaza Strip, and will include proposals for studies and plans on water rights of each party, as well as on the equitable utilization of joint water resources for implementation in and beyond the interim period.

2. Co-operation in the field of electricity, including an Electricity Development Program, which will also specify the mode of co-operation for the production, maintenance, purchase and sale of electricity resources.

3. Co-operation in the field of energy, including an Energy Development Program, which will provide for the exploitation of oil and gas for industrial purposes, particularly in the Gaza Strip and in the Negev, and will encourage further joint exploitation of other energy resources. This Program may also provide for the construction of a Petrochemical industrial complex in the Gaza Strip and the construction of oil and gas pipelines.

4. Co-operation in the field of finance, including a Financial Development and Action Program for the encouragement of

international investment in the West Bank and the Gaza Strip, and in Israel, as well as the establishment of a Palestinian Development Bank.

5. Co-operation in the fields of transport and communications, including a Program, which will define guidelines for the establishment of a Gaza Sea Port Area, and will provide for the establishing of transport and communications lines to and from the West Bank and the Gaza Strip to Israel and to other countries. In addition, this Program will provide for carrying out the necessary construction of roads, railways, communications lines, etc.

6. Co-operation in the field of trade, including studies, and Trade Promotion Programs, which will encourage local, regional and inter-regional trade, as well as a feasiblity study of creating free trade zones in the Gaza Strip and in Israel, mutual access to these zones, and co-operation in other areas related to trade and commerce.

7. Co-operation in the field of industry, including industrial Development Programs, which will provide for the establishment of joint Israeli-Palestinian Research and Development Centers, will promote Palestinian-Israeli joint ventures, and provide guidelines for co-operation in the textile, food, pharmaceutical, electronics, diamonds, computer and science-based industries.

8. A program for co-operation in, and regulation of, labour relations and co-operation in social welfare issues.

9. A Human Resources Development and Co-operation Plan, providing for joint Israeli-Palestinian workshops and seminars, and for the establishment of joint vocational training centres, research institutes and data banks.

10. An Environmental Protection Plan, providing for joint and/or co-ordinated measures in this sphere.

11. A program for developing co-ordination and co-operation in the field of communication and media.

12. Any other programs of mutual interest.

PROTOCOL ON ISRAELI-PALESTINIAN CO-OPERATION CONCERNING REGIONAL DEVELOPMENT PROGRAMS

1. The two sides will co-operate in the context of the multilateral peace efforts in promoting a Development Program for the region, including the West Bank and the Gaza Strip, to be initiated by the G-7. The parties will request the G-7 to seek the participation in this program of other interested states, such as members of the Organization for Economic Co-operation and Development, regional Arab states and institutions, as well as members of the private sector.

2. The Development Program will consist of two elements:
   a) an Economic Development Program for the West Bank and the Gaza Strip;
   b) a Regional Economic Development Program

A. The Economic Development Program for the West Bank and the Gaza Strip will consist of the following elements:

(1) A Social Rehabilitation Program, including a Housing and Construction Program.

(2) A Small and Medium Business Development Plan.

(3) An Infrastructure Development Program (water, electricity, transportation and communications, etc.)

(4) A Human Resources Plan.

(5) Other programs.

B. The Regional Economic Development Program may consist of the following elements:

(1) The establishment of a Middle East Development Fund, as a first step, and a Middle East Development Bank, as a second step.

(2) The development of a joint Israeli-Palestinian-Jordanian Plan for co-ordinated exploitation of the Dead Sea area.

(3) The Mediterranean Sea (Gaza)—Dead Sea Canal.

(4) Regional Desalinization and other water development projects.

(5) A regional plan for agricultural development, including a co-ordinated regional effort for the prevention of desertification.

(6) Interconnection of electricity grids.

(7) Regional co-operation for the transfer, distribution and industrial exploitation of gas, oil and other energy resources.

(8) A regional Tourism, Transportation and Telecommunications Development Plan.

(9) Regional co-operation in other spheres.

3. The two sides will encourage the multilateral working groups, and will co-ordinate towards its success. The two parties will encourage international activities, as well as pre-feasibility and feasibility studies, within the various multilateral working groups.

AGREED MINUTES TO THE DECLARATION OF PRINCIPLES ON INTERIM SELF-GOVERNMENT ARRANGEMENTS

A. General Understandings and Agreements

Any powers and responsibilites transferred to the Palestinians pursuant to the Declaration of Principles prior to the inauguration of the Council will be subject to the same principles pertaining to Article IV, as set out in these Agreed Minutes below.

B. Specific Understandings and Agreements

Article IV

It is understood that:

1. Jurisdiction of the Council will cover West Bank and Gaza Strip territory, except for issues that will be negotiated in the permanent status negotiations: Jerusalem, settlements, military locations and Israelis.

2. The Council's jurisdiction will apply with regard to the agreed powers, responsibilities, spheres and authorities transferred to it.

Article VI (2)

It is agreed that the transfer of authority will be as follows:

(1) The Palestinian side will inform the Israeli side of the names of the authorized Palestinians who will assume the powers, authorities and responsibilities that will be transferred to the Palestinians according to the Declaration of Principles in the following fields: education and culture, health, social welfare, direct taxation, tourism, and any other authorities agreed upon.

(2) It is understood that the rights and obligations of these offices will not be affected.

(3) Each of the spheres described above will continue to enjoy existing budgetary allocations in accordance with arrangements to be mutually agreed upon. These arrangements also will provide for the necessary adjustments required in order to take into account the taxes collected by the direct taxation office.

(4) Upon the execution of the Declaration of Principles, the Israeli and Palestinian delegations will immediately commence negotiations on a detailed plan for the transfer of authority on the above offices in accordance with the above understandings.

Article VII (2)

The Interim Agreement will also include arrangements for co-ordination and co-operation.

Article VII (5)

The withdrawal of the military government will not prevent Israel from exercising the powers and responsibilities not transferred to the Council.

Article VIII

It is understood that the Interim Agreement will include arrangements for co-operation and co-ordination between the two parties in this regard. It is also agreed that the transfer of powers and responsibilities to the Palestinian police will be accomplished in a phased manner, as agreed in the Interim Agreement.

Article X

It is agreed that, upon the entry into force of the Declaration of Principles, the Israeli and Palestinian delegations will exchange the names of the individuals designated by them as members of the Joint Israeli-Palestinian Liaison Committee.

It is further agreed that each side will have an equal number of members in the Joint Committee. The Joint Committee will reach decisions by agreement. The Joint Committee may add other technicians and experts, as necessary. The Joint Committee will decide on the frequency and place or places of its meetings.

Annex II

It is understood that, subsequent to the Israeli withdrawal, Israel will continue to be responsible for external security, and for internal security and public order of settlements and Israelis. Israeli military forces and civilians may continue to use roads freely within the Gaza Strip and the Jericho area.

Article XVI

Israeli-Palestinian Co-operation Concerning Regional Programs

Both parties view the multilateral working groups as an appropriate instrument for promoting a 'Marshall Plan,' the regional programs and other programs, including special programs for the West Bank and Gaza Strip, as indicated in the protocol attached as Annex IV.

Article XVII

Miscellaneous Provisions

1. This Declaration of Principles will enter into force one month after its signing.

2. All protocols annexed to this Declaration of Principles and Agreed Minutes pertaining thereto shall be regarded as an integral part hereof.

THE CAIRO AGREEMENT ON THE GAZA STRIP AND JERICHO
4 May 1994

The Government of the State of Israel and the Palestine Liberation Organization (hereinafter 'the PLO'), the representative of the Palestinian people;

Preamble

Within the framework of the Middle East peace process initiated at Madrid in October 1991;

Reaffirming their determination to live in peaceful co-existence, mutual dignity and security, while recognizing their mutual legitimate and political rights;

Reaffirming their desire to achieve a just, lasting and comprehensive peace settlement through the agreed political process;

Reaffirming their adherence to the mutual recognition and commitments expressed in the letters dated September 9, 1993, signed by and exchanged between the Prime Minister of Israel and the Chairman of the PLO;

Reaffirming their understanding that the interim self-government arrangements, including the arrangements to apply in the Gaza Strip and the Jericho Area contained in this Agreement, are an integral part of the whole peace process and that the negotiations on the permanent status will lead to the implementation of Security Council Resolutions 242 and 338;

Desirous of putting into effect the Declaration of Principles on Interim Self-Government Arrangements signed at Washington, D.C. on September 13, 1993, and the agreed minutes thereto (hereinafter 'The Declaration of Principles'), and in particular the protocol on withdrawal of Israeli forces from the Gaza Strip and the Jericho Area:

Hereby agree to the following arrangements regarding the Gaza Strip and the Jericho Area:

Article I
Definitions

For the purpose of this Agreement:

a. The Gaza Strip and the Jericho Area are delineated on Map Nos. 1 and 2 attached to this Agreeement (*Maps not reproduced: Ed.*);

b. 'The settlements' means the Gush Katif and Erez settlement areas, as well as the other settlements in the Gaza Strip, as shown on attached Map No. 1;

c. 'The military installation area' means the Israeli military installation area along the Egyptian border in the Gaza Strip, as shown on Map No. 1; and

d. The term 'Israelis' shall also include Israeli statutory agencies and corporations registered in Israel.

Article II
Scheduled withdrawal of Israeli military forces

1. Israel shall implement an accelerated and scheduled withdrawal of Israeli military forces from the Gaza Strip and from the Jericho Area to begin immediately with the signing of this Agreement. Israel shall complete such withdrawal within three weeks from this date.

2. Subject to the arrangements included in the Protocol concerning withdrawal of Israeli military forces and security arrangements attached as Annex I, the Israeli withdrawal shall include evacuating all military bases and other fixed installations to be handed over to the Palestinian Police, to be established pursuant to Article IX below (hereinafter 'the Palestinian Police').

3. In order to carry out Israel's responsibility for external security and for internal security and public order of settlements and Israelis, Israel shall, concurrently with the withdrawal, redeploy its remaining military forces to the settlements and the military installation area, in accordance with the provisions of this Agreement. Subject to the provisions of this Agreement, this redeployment shall constitute full implementation of Article XIII of the Declaration of Principles with regard to the Gaza Strip and the Jericho Area only.

4. For the purposes of this Agreement, 'Israeli military forces' may include Israeli police and other Israeli security forces.

5. Israelis, including Israeli military forces, may continue to use roads freely within the Gaza Strip and the Jericho Area. Palestinians may use public roads crossing the settlements freely, as provided for in Annex I.

6. The Palestinian Police shall be deployed and shall assume responsibility for public order and internal security of Palestinians in accordance with this Agreement and Annex I.

Article III
Transfer of authority

1. Israel shall transfer authority as specified in this Agreement from the Israeli military government and its Civil Administration to the Palestinian Authority, hereby established, in accordance with Article V of this Agreement, except for the authority that Israel shall continue to excercise as specified in this Agreement.

2. As regards the transfer and assumption of authority in civil spheres, powers and responsibilities shall be transferred and assumed as set out in the Protocol concerning civil affairs attached as Annex II.

3. Arrangements for a smooth and peaceful transfer of the agreed powers and responsibilities are set out in Annex II.

4. Upon the completion of the Israeli withdrawal and the transfer of powers and responsibilities as detailed in Paragraphs 1 and 2 above and in Annex II, the Civil Administration in the Gaza Strip and the Jericho Area will be dissolved and the Israeli military government will be withdrawn. The withdrawal of the military government shall not prevent it from continuing to excercise the powers and responsibilities specified in this Agreement.

5. A joint Civil Affairs Co-ordination and Co-operation Committee (hereinafter 'the CAC') and two joint regional civil affairs subcommittees for the Gaza Strip and the Jericho Area respectively shall be established in order to provide for co-ordination and co-operation in civil affairs between the Palestinian Authority and Israel, as detailed in Annex II.

6. The offices of the Palestinian Authority shall be located in the Gaza Strip and the Jericho Area pending the inauguration of the council to be elected pursuant to the Declaration of Principles.

Article IV
Structure and composition of the Palestinian Authority

1. The Palestinian Authority will consist of one body of 24 members which shall carry out and be responsible for all the legislative and executive powers and responsibilities transferred to it under this Agreement, in accordance with this article, and shall be responsible for the excercise of judicial functions in accordance with Article VI, subparagraph 1.b of this Agreement.

2. The Palestinian Authority shall administer the departments transferred to it and may establish, within its jurisdiction, other departments and subordinate administrative units as necessary for the fulfilment of its responsibilities. It shall determine its own internal procedures.

3. The PLO shall inform the Government of Israel of the names of the members of the Palestinian Authority and any change of members. Changes in the membership of the Palestinian Authority will take effect upon an exchange of letters between the PLO and the Government of Israel.

4. Each member of the Palestinian Authority shall enter into office upon undertaking to act in accordance with this Agreement.

Article V
Jurisdiction

1. The authority of the Palestinian Authority encompasses all matters that fall within its territorial, functional and personal jurisdiction, as follows:

  a. The territorial jurisdiction covers the Gaza Strip and the Jericho Area territory, as defined in Article I, except for settlements and the military installation area.
  Territorial jurisdiction shall include land, subsoil and territorial waters, in accordance with the provisions of this Agreement.

  b. The functional jurisdiction encompasses all powers and responsibilities as specified in this Agreement. This jurisdiction does not include foreign relations, internal security and public order of settlements and the military installation area and Israelis, and external security.

  c. The personal jurisdiction extends to all persons within the territorial jurisdiction referred to above, except for Israelis, unless otherwise provided in this Agreement.

2. The Palestinian Authority has, within its authority, legislative, executive and judicial powers and responsibilities, as provided for in this Agreement.

3.a. Israel has authority over the settlements, the military installation area, Israelis, external security, internal security and public order of settlements, the military installation area and Israelis, and those agreed powers and responsibilities specified in this Agreement.

  b. Israel shall exercise its authority through its military government, which for that end, shall continue to have the necessary legislative, judicial and executive powers and responsibilities, in accordance with international law. This provision shall not derogate from Israel's applicable legislation over Israelis in personam.

4. The exercise of authority with regard to the electromagnetic sphere and airspace shall be in accordance with the provisions of this Agreement.

5. The provisions of this article are subject to the specific legal arrangements detailed in the Protocol concerning legal matters attached as Annex III. Israel and the Palestinian Authority may negotiate further legal arrangements.

6. Israel and the Palestinian Authority shall co-operate on matters of legal assistance in criminal and civil matters through the legal subcommittee of the CAC.

Article VI
Powers and responsibilities of the Palestinian Authority

1. Subject to the provisions of this Agreement, the Palestinian Authority, within its jurisdiction:

  a. has legislative powers as set out in Article VII of this Agreement, as well as executive powers;

  b. will administer justice through an independent judiciary:

  c. will have, inter alia, power to formulate policies, supervise their implementation, employ staff, establish departments, authorities and institutions, sue and be sued and conclude contracts; and

  d. will have, inter alia, the power to keep and administer registers and records of the population, and issue certificates, licenses and documents.

2.a. In accordance with the Declaration of Principles, the Palestinian Authority will not have powers and responsibilities in the sphere of foreign relations, which sphere includes the establishment abroad of embassies, consulates or other types of foreign missions and posts or permitting their establishment in the Gaza Strip or the Jericho Area, the appointment of or admission of diplomatic and consular staff, and the exercise of diplomatic functions.

  b. Notwithstanding the provisions of this paragraph, the PLO may conduct negotiations and sign agreements with states or international organizations for the benefit of the Palestinian Authority in the following cases only:

  (1) Economic agreements, as specifically provided in Annex IV of this Agreement;

  (2) Agreements with donor countries for the purpose of implementing arrangements for the provision of assistance to the Palestinian Authority;

  (3) Agreements for the purpose of implementing the regional development plans detailed in Annex IV of the Declaration of Principles or in agreements entered into in the framework of the multilateral negotiations; and

  (4) Cultural, scientific and education agreements.

  c. Dealings between the Palestinian Authority and representatives of foreign states and international organizations, as well as the establishment in the Gaza Strip and the Jericho Area of representative offices other than those described in subparagraph 2.a, above, for the purpose of implementing the agreements referred to in subparagraph 2.b above, shall not be considered foreign relations.

Article VII
Legislative powers of the Palestinian Authority

1. The Palestinian Authority will have the power, within its jurisdiction, to promulgate legislation, including basic laws, laws, regulations and other legislative acts.

2. Legislation promulgated by the Palestinian Authority shall be consistent with the provisions of this Agreement.

3. Legislation promulgated by the Palestinian Authority shall be communicated to a legislation subcommittee to be established by the CAC (hereinafter 'the Legislation Subcommittee'). During a period of 30 days from the communication of the legislation, Israel may request that the Legislation Subcommittee decide whether such legislation exceeds the jurisdiction of the Palestinian Authority or is otherwise inconsistent with the provisions of this Agreement.

4. Upon receipt of the Israeli request, the Legislation Subcommittee shall decide, as an initial matter, on the entry into force of the legislation pending its decision on the merits of the matter.

5. If the Legislation Subcommittee is unable to reach a decision with regard to the entry into force of the legislation within 15 days, this issue will be referred to a Board of Review. This Board of Review shall be comprised of two judges, retired judges or senior jurists (hereinafter 'Judges'), one from each side, to be appointed from a compiled list of three judges proposed by each.

6. Legislation referred to the Board of Review shall enter into force only if the Board of Review decides that it does not deal with a security issue which falls under Israel's responsibility, that it does not seriously threaten other significant Israeli interests protected by this Agreement and that the entry into force of the legislation could not cause irreparable damage or harm.

7. The Legislation Subcommitte shall attempt to reach a decision on the merits of the matter within 30 days from the date of the Israeli request. If this subcommittee is unable to

reach such a decision within this period of 30 days, the matter shall be referred to the joint Israeli-Palestinian Liaison Committee referred to in Article XV below (hereinafter 'the Liaison Committee'). This Liaison Committee will deal with the matter immediately and will attempt to settle it within 30 days.

8. Where the legislation has not entered into force pursuant to paragraphs 5 or 7 above, this situation shall be maintained pending the decision of the Liaison Committee on the merits of the matter, unless it has decided otherwise.

9. Laws and military orders in effect in the Gaza Strip or the Jericho Area prior to the signing of this Agreement shall remain in force, unless amended or abrogated in accordance with this Agreement.

Article VIII
Arrangements for security and public order

1. In order to guarantee public order and internal security for the Palestinians of the Gaza Strip and the Jericho Area, the Palestinian Authority shall establish a strong police force, as set out in Article IX below. Israel shall continue to carry the responsibility for defence against external threats, including the responsibility for protecting the Egyptian border and the Jordanian line, and for defence against external threats from the sea and from the air, as well as the responsibility for overall security of Israelis and settlements, for the purpose of safeguarding their internal security and public order, and will have all the powers to take the steps necessary to meet this responsibility.

2. Agreed security arrangements and co-ordination mechanisms are specified in Annex I.

3. A Joint Co-ordination and Co-operation committee for mutual security purposes (hereinafter 'the JSC'), as well as three joint district co-ordination and co-operation offices for the Gaza District, the Khan Younis District and the Jericho District respectively (hereinafter 'the DCOS') are hereby established as provided for in Annex I.

4. The security arrangements provided for in this Agreement and in Annex I may be reviewed at the requests of either party and may be amended by mutual agreement of the parties. Specific review arrangements are included in Annex I.

Article IX
The Palestinian Directorate of Police Force

1. The Palestinian Authority shall establish a strong police force, the Palestinian Directorate of Police Force (hereinafter 'the Palestinian Police'). The duties, functions, structure, deployment and composition of the Palestinian Police, together with provisions regarding its equipment and operation, are set out in Annex I, Article III. Rules of conduct governing the activities of the Palestinian Police are set out in Annex I, Article VIII.

2. Except for the Palestinian Police referred to in this article and the Israeli military forces, no other armed forces shall be established or operate in the Gaza Strip or the Jericho Area.

3. Except for the arms, ammunition and equipment of the Palestinian Police described in Annex I, Article III, and those of the Israeli military forces, no organization or individual in the Gaza Strip and the Jericho Area shall manufacture, sell, acquire, possess, import or otherwise introduce into the Gaza Strip or the Jericho Area any firearms, ammunition, weapons, explosives, gunpowder or any related equipment, unless otherwise provided for in Annex I.

Article X
Passages

Arrangements for co-ordination between Israel and the Palestinian Authority regarding the Gaza–Egypt and Jericho–Jordan passages, as well as any other agreed international crossings, are set out in Annex 1.

Article XI
Safe passage between the Gaza Strip and the Jericho Area

Arrangements for safe passage of persons and transportation between the Gaza Strip and the Jericho Area are set out in Annex I, Article IX.

Article XII
Relations between Israel and the Palestinian Authority

1. Israel and the Palestinian Authority shall seek to foster mutual understanding and tolerance and shall accordingly abstain from incitement, including hostile propaganda, against each other and, without derogating from the principle of freedom of expression, shall take legal measures to prevent such incitement by any organizations, groups or individuals within their jurisdiction.

2. Without derogating from the other provisions of this agreement, Israel and the Palestinian Authority shall co-operate in combating criminal activity which may affect both sides, including offences related to trafficking in illegal drugs and psychotropic substances, smuggling, and offences against property, including offences related to vehicles.

Article XIII
Economic relations

The economic relations between the two sides are set out in the Protocol on Economic Relations signed in Paris on April 29, 1994 and the appendixes thereto, certified copies of which are attached as Annex IV, and will be governed by the relevant provisions of this agreement and its annexes.

Article XIV
Human rights and the rule of law

Israel and the Palestinian Authority shall exercise their powers and responsibilities pursuant to this Agreement with due regard to internationally-accepted norms and principles of human rights and the rule of law.

Article XV
The Joint Israeli-Palestinian Liaison Committee

1. The Liaison Committee established pursuant to Article X of the Declaration of Principles shall ensure the smooth implementation of this Agreement. It shall deal with issues requiring co-ordination, other issues of common interest and disputes.

2. The Liaison Committee shall be composed of an equal number of members from each party. It may add other technicians and experts as necessary.

3. The Liaison Committee shall adopt its rules of procedure, including the frequency and place or places of its meetings.

4. The Liaison Committee shall reach its decision by agreement.

Article XVI
Liaison and Co-operation with Jordan and Egypt

1. Pursuant to Article XII of the Declaration of Principles, the two parties shall invite the governments of Jordan and Egypt to participate in establishing further Liaison and Co-operation Arrangements between the Government of Israel and the Palestinian Representatives on the one hand, and the governments of Jordan and Egypt on the other hand, to promote co-operation between them. These arrangements shall include the constitution of a Continuing Committee.

2. The Continuing Committee shall decide by agreement on the modalities of admission of persons displaced from the West Bank and the Gaza Strip in 1967, together with necessary measures to prevent disruption and disorder.

3. The Continuing Committee shall deal with other matters of common concern.

Article XVII
Settlement of differences and disputes

Any difference relating to the application of this agreement shall be referred to the appropriate co-ordination and co-operation mechanism established under this agreement. The provisions of Article XV of the Declaration of Principles shall apply to any such difference which is not settled through the appropriate co-ordination and co-operation mechanism, namely:

1. Disputes arising out of the application or interpretation of this agreement or any subsequent agreements pertaining to the

interim period shall be settled by negotiations through the Liaison Committee.

2. Disputes which cannot be settled by negotiations may be settled by a mechanism of conciliation to be agreed between the parties.

3. The parties may agree to submit to arbitration disputes relating to the interim period, which cannot be settled through conciliation. To this end, upon the agreement of both parties, the parties will establish an arbitration committee.

Article XVIII
Prevention of hostile acts

Both sides shall take all measures necessary in order to prevent acts of terrorism, crime and hostilities directed against each other, against individuals falling under the other's authority and against their property, and shall take legal measures against offenders. In addition, the Palestinian side shall take all measures necessary to prevent such hostile acts directed against the settlements, the infrastructure serving them and the military installation area, and the Israeli side shall take all measures necessary to prevent such hostile acts emanating from the settlements and directed against Palestinians.

Article XIX
Missing persons

The Palestinian Authority shall co-operate with Israel by providing all necessary assistance in the conduct of searches by Israel within the Gaza Strip and the Jericho Area for missing Israelis, as well as by providing information about missing Israelis. Israel shall co-operate with the Palestinian Authority in searching for, and providing necessary information about, missing Palestinians.

Article XX
Confidence-building measures

With a view to creating a positive and supportive public atmosphere to accompany the implementation of this agreement, and to establish a solid basis of mutual trust and good faith, both parties agree to carry out confidence-building measures as detailed herewith:

1. Upon the signing of this agreement, Israel will release, or turn over, to the Palestinian Authority within a period of 5 weeks, about 5,000 Palestinian detainees and prisoners, residents of the West Bank and the Gaza Strip. Those released will be free to return to their homes anywhere in the West Bank or the Gaza Strip. Prisoners turned over to the Palestinian Authority shall be obliged to remain in the Gaza Strip or the Jericho Area for the remainder of their sentence.

2. After the signing of this Agreement, the two parties shall continue to negotiate the release of additional Palestinian prisoners and detainees, building on agreed principles.

3. The implementation of the above measures will be subject to the fulfilment of the procedures determined by Israeli law for the release and transfer of detainees and prisoners.

4. With the assumption of Palestinian Authority, the Palestinian side commits itself to solving the problem of those Palestinians who were in contact with the Israeli authorities. Until an agreed solution is found, the Palestinian side undertakes not to prosecute these Palestinians or to harm them in any way.

5. Palestinians from abroad whose entry into the Gaza Strip and the Jericho Area is approved pursuant to this agreement, and to whom the provisions of this article are applicable, will not be prosecuted for offences committed prior to September 13, 1993.

Article XXI
Temporary international presence

1. The parties agree to a temporary international or foreign presence in the Gaza Strip and the Jericho Area (hereinafter 'the TIP'), in accordance with the provisions of this article.

2. The TIP shall consist of 400 qualified personnel, including observers, instructors and other experts, from 5 or 6 of the donor countries.

3. The two parties shall request the donor countries to establish a special fund to provide finance for the TIP.

4. The TIP will function for a period of 6 months. The TIP may extend this period, or change the scope of its operation, with the agreement of the two parties.

5. The TIP shall be stationed and operative within the following cities and villages: Gaza, Khan Younis, Rafah, Deir al-Balah, Jabalya, Absan, Beit Hanun and Jericho.

6. Israel and the Palestinian Authority shall agree on a special protocol to implement this article, with the goal of concluding negotiations with the donor countries contributing personnel within two months.

Article XXII
Rights, liabilities and obligations

1.a. The transfer of all powers and responsibilities to the Palestinian Authority, as detailed in Annex II, includes all related rights, liabilities and obligations arising with regard to acts or omissions which occurred prior to the transfer. Israel will cease to bear any financial responsibility regarding such acts or omissions and the Palestinian Authority will bear all financial responsibility for these and for its own functioning.

b. Any financial claim made in this regard against Israel will be referred to the Palestinian Authority.

c. Israel shall provide the Palestinian Authority with the information it has regarding pending and anticipated claims brought before any court or tribunal against Israel in this regard.

d. Where legal proceedings are brought in respect of such a claim, Israel will notify the Palestinian Authority and enable it to participate in defending the claim and raise any arguments on its behalf.

e. In the event that an award is made against Israel by any court or tribunal in respect of such a claim, the Palestinian Authority shall reimburse Israel the full amount of the award.

f. Without prejudice to the above, where a court or tribunal hearing such a claim finds that liability rests solely with an employee or agent who acted beyond the scope of the powers assigned to him or her, unlawfully or with willful malfeasance, the Palestinian Authority shall not bear financial responsibility.

2. The transfer of authority in itself shall not affect rights, liabilities and obligations of any person or legal entity, in existence at the date of signing of this Agreement.

Article XXIII
Final clauses

1. This Agreement shall enter into force on the date of its signing.

2. The arrangements established by this Agreement shall remain in force until and to the extent superseded by the Interim Agreement referred to in the Declaration of Principles or any other Agreement between the parties.

3. The five-year Interim Period referred to in the Declaration of Principles commences on the date of the signing of this Agreement.

4. The parties agree that, as long as this Agreement is in force, the security fence erected by Israel around the Gaza Strip shall remain in place and that the line demarcated by the fence, as shown on attached Map No. 1, shall be authoritative only for the purpose of this Agreement.

5. Nothing in this Agreement shall prejudice or pre-empt the outcome of the negotiations on the Interim Agreement or on the Permanent Status to be conducted pursuant to the Declaration of Principles. Neither party shall be deemed, by virtue of having entered into this Agreement, to have renounced or waived any of its existing rights, claims or positions.

6. The two parties view the West Bank and the Gaza Strip as a single territorial unit, the integrity of which will be preserved during the Interim Period.

7. The Gaza Strip and the Jericho Area shall continue to be an integral part of the West Bank and the Gaza Strip, and their

status shall not be changed for the period of this Agreement. Nothing in this Agreement shall be considered to change this status.

8. The preamble to this Agreement, and all Annexes, Appendices and Maps attached hereto, shall constitute an integral part hereof.

ISRAELI-PALESTINIAN INTERIM AGREEMENT ON THE WEST BANK AND THE GAZA STRIP

28 September 1995

The main provisions of the Israeli-Palestinian Interim Agreement on the West Bank and the Gaza Strip, signed in Washington, DC, USA, by Israel and the PLO on 28 September 1995 were as follows:

Israel agreed to begin redeploying its troops from the West Bank towns of Nablus, Ramallah, Jenin, Tulkarm, Kakilya and Bethlehem within 10 days of the signing of the Agreement, and to complete the redeployment within six months, after which elections to a Palestinian Council and for a Palestinian President were to be held, by late April 1996 at the latest. The Palestinian authorities were to assume full responsibility for security in the six above-mentioned towns. In the 400 surrounding villages Palestinians were to assume responsibility for civil authority, but Israeli troops would retain the freedom to act against potential attacks. A further 12,000 Palestinian policemen were to be deployed in the West Bank, bringing the total strength of the Palestinian security forces in the West Bank and the Gaza Strip to 30,000. In the West Bank town of Hebron Israel would effect only a partial withdrawal, and would maintain security in some 15% of the town occupied by 415 Jewish settlers. The Palestinian police force would assume responsibility for the rest of the town, but Israel would retain responsibility for access roads and for the Tomb of the Patriarch Abraham. There was also to be a temporary international presence in Hebron in order to reduce Arab-Jewish tension there. Until July 1997 Israel would retain control over a substantial area of the West Bank, including Jewish settlements, rural areas, military installations and the intersections of Palestinian roads with those used by Jewish settlers. After Palestinian elections Israel was to effect a second redeployment away from rural areas, to be completed by July 1997. However, Israel would retain control over Jewish settlements, military installations, Arab East Jerusalem and Jewish settlements around Jerusalem until a complete and final resolution of the Palestinian question, to be concluded by May 1999.

Israel and the PLO agreed that national Palestinian legislative elections should be held for an 82-member Palestinian Council. The Council would have extensive legislative power, but Israel would be able to veto any laws which it believed directly affected Israeli security interests. The 160,000 Palestinian residents of East Jerusalem would be allowed to vote in the elections, but would not be permitted to stand as candidates for election unless they had a second address in the West Bank or the Gaza Strip. The direct election of a Palestinian Executive President was to take place at the same time as the legislative elections.

Israel was to begin the release, in three phases, of up to 5,300 Palestinian prisoners, the first phase to begin immediately after the signing of the Agreement.

OIL IN THE MIDDLE EAST AND NORTH AFRICA

PETER BILD

Updated for this edition by SIMON CHAPMAN

INTRODUCTION

The strength of crude oil prices in the second half of 1996 led some oil industry forecasters to claim that a new trading range, one of US \$24–\$25, had established itself, compared with that of \$15–\$20 which had hitherto been regarded as the long-term, sustainable trend. Late in the year speculative articles began to examine the possible consequences for global economic growth if prices were to rise even higher and stay at that level. None predicted a global recession either directly caused or aggravated by high oil prices, but such recessions of both the present and the preceding two decades were nevertheless invoked as a warning of the possible consequences. Some 15 months later, by the end of March 1998, world markets for crude oil appeared to be on the verge of collapse. Saudi Arabia's marker crude, Arabian Light, for instance, was trading at its lowest level since 1986. Venezuela, generally considered to be OPEC's most extravagant quota-buster, had been instrumental, together with Saudi Arabia and Mexico, in obtaining the agreement of producers, both OPEC and non-OPEC alike, to begin to reduce supplies by 1.245m. barrels per day (b/d) from 1 April. To many observers this agreement, coming so soon after the formal revision of OPEC quotas in Jakarta, Indonesia, in November 1997, represented a significant step towards a free market in oil. But, for all its novelty, it was, initially at least, received with indifference by markets, and prices remained doggedly low. What were the factors behind the unexpected decline in the prices of crude oil?

The resumption of Iraqi supplies

One factor was the resumption, from 10 December 1996, of exports of Iraqi crude oil—the so-called 'oil-for-food' sales made under the terms of UN Security Council Resolution 986 of April 1995—for the first time (officially, at least) since the Gulf War of 1990–91. By April 1997 the 'basket price' for OPEC crude oils had fallen to about \$16 per barrel, compared to some \$24 per barrel at the end of 1996. It is important to note, however, that the imminence of Iraq's return to the market had probably supported prices in the second half, particularly the final quarter, of 1996, since some producers were thought to have prepared for it by restraining output. This, together with lower-than-anticipated output by some non-OPEC producers and low stocks world-wide, meant that prices were already at an artificially high level when Iraq's return to the market coincided with mild winter weather conditions in the northern hemisphere to bring about an unusually sharp adjustment. The conditions of UN Resolution 986 were another factor behind the weakening of prices in the first quarter of 1997: Iraqi oil exports were defined in terms of value rather than quantity. Consequently, every time oil prices weakened Iraq was able to increase the amount of oil it marketed.

As 1997 progressed it became clear that the resumption of Iraqi exports had introduced an element of volatility into an otherwise stable market. Iraq's periodic quarrels with the UN weapons inspectorate, for example, which had settled into a largely predictable pattern of confrontation, crisis and resentful compromise, now took on greater meaning as they began to combine with other market influences to strengthen or weaken the price of crude oil. The memorandum of agreement pertaining to UN Resolution 986 had to be renewed every six months (Iraq was allowed to sell \$2,000m.-worth of oil over 180 days, divided into two 90-day periods), and in June 1997 Iraq suspended its exports owing to a dispute with the UN regarding the distribution of revenues from the sales. The removal of the approximately 700,000 b/d, which Iraq had been exporting, immediately lifted prices from their lowest levels of the year. The longer Iraqi exports remained suspended, the greater the potential for disruption when they eventually resumed, since, in order to

achieve revenue targets in a shorter period of time, Iraq would have to increase the quantity it exported. Oil markets thus became subjected to speculation that Iraqi exports might resume, in July, at about twice the level recorded in December 1996–June 1997. According to the London-based Centre for Global Energy Studies (CGES), such a boost to OPEC output would lead to weaker prices in the third quarter of 1997. If, on the other hand, exports were delayed until the final quarter of the year, the CGES forecast increases to more than \$20 per barrel for some crudes. Iraqi exports thus began to exert a destabilizing influence on oil markets, although the contribution this made to the decline in prices in the first quarter of 1998 may have been exaggerated by some analysts. The main factor at work then was excess of supply, but on such a scale that, while the availability of Iraqi exports and the timing of their return to the market could make a bad situation worse, their suspension would do little to bring about any recovery.

Overproduction within OPEC

Supplies of crude oil were already regarded as more than adequate before the financial difficulties of some East Asian countries in late 1997 began to be perceived as an economic crisis, altering predictions of regional economic growth and reducing world demand for oil. The CGES, for example, had predicted an increase of some 2m. b/d, to 73.8m. b/d, in world demand in 1997, and suggested that this would be adequately covered by new supplies, especially non-OPEC supplies. In early and mid-1997 attention focused on the extent of overproduction within OPEC. According to the Paris-based International Energy Agency (IEA), OPEC production had reached 27.13m. b/d in April 1997, compared with the Organization's official quota of 25.03m. b/d. Other analysts estimated overproduction to be even higher. However, according to the BP *Statistical Review of World Energy,* global demand for oil had increased by 2.4% in 1996. Key producers, in particular Saudi Arabia, remained confident that demand in 1997 would exceed less assured expectations for the year. In its mid-year report the IEA referred to the continued strength of demand, led by economic growth in the USA, Asia and Latin America, but nevertheless forecast weaker prices and substantial growth in inventories in the second half of the year, unless there was a significant reduction in OPEC output. At the ministerial conference in Vienna in June 1997 OPEC's response to predictions of steady, if not strong, demand, adequate supplies and a weakening of prices was to renew its official production quota of 25.03m. b/d for a further six months. Attempts reportedly were made to obtain an agreement on the stricter observance of quotas, but these were unsuccessful. In spite of the scale of overproduction—generally estimated at about 2m. b/d in excess of the quota level—the failure to obtain such an agreement was dismissed as being of no great significance for prices during the second half of the year.

For the time being OPEC producers appeared to have assessed market conditions accurately. In the period June–October 1997 markets were influenced by the interplay between US summer demand for gasoline and the size of inventories, especially those of gasoline in the USA and of industrial oil in the countries of the Organization for Economic Co-operation and Development (OECD). Generally this had a positive effect on prices. In August the CGES forecast that the average price of the United Kingdom's Brent marker crude would be above \$19 per barrel in 1997 and that of OPEC crudes more than \$18.50 per barrel. The strength of European inventories, however, was regarded as likely to exert downward pressure on prices as the winter approached. The most important fundamental factor contributing to the stability of markets during the first three quarters of 1997 remained growing demand from the USA and Asia. In

October the IEA estimated that demand in the final quarter of the year and in the first quarter of 1998 would be some 2m. b/d higher than in the corresponding periods of 1996 and 1997. Since non-OPEC production, especially in the North Sea, had failed to match expectations, predictions of demand for OPEC crudes rose accordingly. In response, OPEC production was estimated to have risen to its highest level for 17 years, 27.62m. b/d, in September.

OPEC raises its quota

In view of what happened in early 1998, OPEC's decision, taken at the ministerial conference held in Jakarta, Indonesia, in November 1997, to raise, for the first time in four years, its production quota, to 27.5m. b/d from 1 January 1998, was subsequently described as a misjudgement. Without the benefit of hindsight, however, there appeared to be strong arguments in its favour. The producer states of the Persian (Arabian) Gulf that were the principal advocates of raising the quota—Saudi Arabia, in particular, but also Kuwait and the United Arab Emirates (UAE)—considered that, by abiding by their quotas (relatively speaking), they were not benefiting fully from growing world demand for oil. All three had costly production capacity to spare, yet they continued to forfeit market share to other OPEC members, especially Venezuela, with apparently fewer scruples about quota observance. At the time the decision was taken actual OPEC production was already estimated at about 28m. b/d, and was forecast to average some 27.5m. b/d in 1997. The crucial factor left out of the reckoning was the seriousness of the developing economic crisis in East Asia, the region which, in 1990–97, was estimated to have accounted for some 70% of growth in world demand for oil. Moreover, owing to changes in trading patterns and market share, this was precisely the area on which exports from the core Gulf producers had become concentrated. Almost as soon as OPEC took the decision to raise its quota, oil markets were caught in the pincers of increased production—or fear of it—and reduced Asian demand.

There was immediate concern that OPEC had misread conditions, the IEA noting that the raised quota appeared to have brought about a fundamental shift of mood on oil markets. According to the IEA, OPEC supplies were expected to rise by 500,000 b/d–1.1m. b/d as a result of the increase, and the mood that now prevailed was fear of an excess of supplies. The IEA itself forecast world oil demand at 76.1m. b/d in the first quarter of 1998 and demand for OPEC supplies at 27.1m. b/d. In early December the price of some crudes fell to their lowest level since June 1997, and from the beginning of January 1998 began to decline rapidly. That of Brent, the United Kingdom's marker crude, for instance, fell below $15 per barrel in the first week of 1998, compared with more than $17 per barrel in late December 1997. The increased OPEC quota was not the only factor behind these declines. Iraqi exports had again been suspended, but were now expected to resume. Winter weather in the northern hemisphere had been exceptionally mild, while data from the USA indicated that, contrary to expectations, stocks of some petroleum products had increased. By mid-January 1998 prices had fallen to their lowest levels for more than three years. Estimated growth in demand for oil in East Asia had by this time been revised downwards by some 300,000 b/d and, it was feared, would have to be revised downwards again if the regional economic crisis spread to India and China. At the end of January prices recovered temporarily as the likelihood of conflict in the Gulf increased owing to failure to achieve a resolution of Iraq's latest dispute with the UN over weapons inspections. However, the level of OPEC production remained a major concern. OPEC's decision, taken at a ministerial meeting in Vienna, Austria, on 26 January, to urge its members to comply with quotas was widely regarded as an inadequate response to the feared effect of the Far East economic crisis on demand for oil.

At the beginning of February 1998 Iraq began to exert a more negative influence on oil markets, following the announcement, by the UN Secretary-General, of a possible future increase in the value of Iraqi oil exports, from $2,000m. over six-month periods to $5,200m. Estimates of OPEC production published in the same month suggested that it had increased to more than 28m. b/d in December 1997 and January 1998. Meanwhile, the IEA once again reduced its forecast of world demand for oil in 1998 to take account of the decline in economic activity in East Asia. It was not until mid-February that the first signs of any action by producers to support prices emerged. By that time the price of UK Brent had fallen to below $14 per barrel. In late February falling Asian demand was reported to be causing increasing difficulties for Gulf producers, with European markets being sought for both crude and petroleum products that could not be sold in the Far East. By late March oil prices had fallen to their lowest levels for 10 years. Arabian Light, for instance, Saudi Arabia's marker crude, was trading below $10 per barrel. On 22 March a plan, initiated by Saudi Arabia, Venezuela and non-OPEC Mexico, was announced to reduce world oil supplies by some 2m. b/d from 1 April 1998. To summarize, the market conditions to which producers were attempting to co-ordinate a response were characterized by the following factors: forecasts that world production of oil would exceed demand by 1.5m. b/d–2m. b/d in 1998; a possible fall in East Asian demand of more than 300,000 b/d, whereas previous forecasts had predicted it to rise by some 1m. b/d in 1998; mild winter weather conditions in the northern hemisphere, which, together with surplus supplies, had increased fuel inventories at a time when they were usually drawn upon—according to the IEA, fuel inventories in the OECD countries were at their highest levels for 20 years—undermining future prices at the same time as spot prices; uncertainty as to whether the continuing reintegration of Iraq into world markets would support or weaken prices; the possibility of Iraqi exports approaching 2m. b/d by mid-1998; uncertainty about the level of non-OPEC output; OPEC production estimated at about 2m. b/d in excess of demand for it in January 1998 and, given the scale of overproduction, doubts about the Organization's ability to take effective action to reduce this.

In detail, the agreement announced on 22 March 1998 committed Saudi Arabia to reduce production by 300,000 b/d, Venezuela by 200,000 b/d and Mexico by 100,000 b/d. Kuwait and the UAE each undertook to implement reductions of 125,000 b/d. At a meeting of OPEC oil ministers in Vienna on 30 March, the reductions announced on 22 March were supplemented by a commitment by Norway to cut production by 100,000 b/d. In total, the agreement, if fully implemented, would reduce world production of oil by 1.5m. b/d, to which OPEC would contribute cuts totalling 1.245m. b/d and non-OPEC producers (Mexico, Oman, Norway and Egypt) 260,000 b/d. Oil markets responded positively to the initial announcement of the planned reductions, with crude prices rising by up to $2 per barrel. However, widespread scepticism remained about how effective the agreement would be, not least because of the failure of agreements concluded in similar circumstances in the past. Also, the agreement did not address the question of Iraqi production, and Iraq, having produced 1.8m. b/d in February, retained the potential to negate the confirmed reductions entirely. Even if the cuts could be effectively implemented, it was still estimated that supply would remain substantially in excess of demand. The agreement was regarded by many observers as a further step towards a free market in oil, especially as, if it were to collapse, OPEC producers which had hitherto observed their quotas would have no interest in restraining production while forfeiting market share.

In the first week of April 1998 oil prices fell back to the levels prevailing before 22 March. Doubts remained that the cuts announced in late March would be fully implemented. In mid-April UK Brent was trading at about $12.50 per barrel as markets remained oversupplied. In mid-May, however, prices rose in response to indications that OPEC producers were reducing output in line with their agreement. According to the IEA, world production had been reduced by about 1m. b/d in April, of which 800,000 b/d was contributed by reductions in OPEC output. Iraq was estimated to have increased its exports in April by some 160,000 b/d. Prices received further support from indications that Kuwait would back any agreement to reduce production further at the OPEC ministerial meeting on 24 June, and from reports of a recovery in Asian demand. However, at the end of the month reports that US stocks had risen to their highest levels for nearly five years stemmed the recovery and attention remained focused on the possibility of an agreement to implement further reductions at the OPEC ministerial meeting in late June.

For many observers, oil and money in the Middle East and North Africa mean the same thing. Inseparable they may be, but they are not the whole story. For all but the technical expert, it is the activities of governments, as represented by their politicians, civil servants and oil market experts, which constitute the history of oil. During the 1950s and 1960s, as the Middle East and North Africa came to dominate world supplies, this history was relatively simple: world demand for oil grew steadily and rapidly on the basis of low prices and rapid economic growth in the industrialized world. Although governments tried increasingly to become involved and to take more direct control of their economic destinies, it was the major international oil companies (the so-called 'seven sisters'), in concert with the governments of Europe and the USA, that played the key role. These companies assessed demand for oil products and balanced it internally with supplies that they both owned and controlled. The first 'oil shock' in 1973 changed the situation in two important ways. The quadrupling of prices, together with the embargoes and reductions in production imposed by Arab governments, focused the attention of Western governments on oil. The cost of oil imports became a major element in international monetary affairs, creating massive but unequal balance-of-payments deficits in the West. It also gave rise to fears that the 'petrodollars' of the newly-rich Middle Easterners would exacerbate monetary upheavals and vastly increase already existing inflationary pressures. The IEA, essentially a rich oil consumers' club, was set up in an atmosphere of hostility and confrontation. More significantly for the oil-producing states of the Middle East and North Africa today, the IEA caused the fragmentation of the hitherto integrated operations of the international oil companies, forcing governments with little experience in handling major international economic forces to deal with the consequences of their decisions on prices. The disintegration of the oil industry, as governments took control of production, coincided with huge, unprecedented reversals in the previously growing role of oil as the industrialized world's chief source of energy. High prices, combined with the widespread belief that 'rapacious' Middle Eastern governments would again hold the Western world to ransom, by raising prices *ad infinitum* or by cutting off supplies or both, provoked a new wave of exploration and development which brought oil on to world markets just as demand was dropping most steeply in the early 1980s. The spiralling price increases in 1979–81 (the second 'oil shock'), and the initially determined effort by OPEC members to keep them at a peak of almost 10 times their level of only 10 years previously led inevitably to the third 'oil shock' of 1986, when prices and revenues in real inflation-adjusted terms declined to well below their pre-1973 levels.

From a dominant position in 1973 when OPEC supplied 65% of the oil produced outside the centrally-planned economies, its share had declined to only 40% by 1985, the year in which OPEC finally abandoned its attempt to maintain oil prices at unrealistic levels. For the Middle East and North Africa, the loss in market share was even more drastic and was concentrated in the short period of six years from 1979 to 1985. From a peak of nearly 24m. b/d in 1979, the eight OPEC members in the Middle East and North Africa were forced by falling demand and the availability of new supplies to reduce production by almost one-half to 13m. b/d in 1985. At that level of production, control over world oil prices became ever more difficult to maintain.

Today's problems stem largely from that time and were exacerbated by Iraq's ill-fated Kuwaiti adventure. The peoples of the Middle East and North Africa, naturally, but unwisely, regarded their enormously enhanced revenues as the pattern for the future, spending and over-spending their annual revenues on gigantic domestic infrastructural and industrial development projects. Adapting to the loss of up to 80% of national income in the space of four or five years would have been a major trauma even if the governments in question had had the discipline and foresight to treat their 1980/81 income levels as the temporary boon they turned out to be. However, governments and whole nations had borrowed and invested in the belief that these income levels would be sustained into the future.

On a day-to-day level, it was the unwillingness of major oil companies to buy what they regarded as over-priced oil that forced OPEC members to wage an ultimately self-defeating price war, and it became politically convenient to blame the 'conspiracies' of Western companies and governments for the oil states' inability to sell as much crude as they had hoped, and at a price which they themselves had determined. While it is still true that relationships with the major international oil companies are the everyday reality for government officials charged with marketing crude oil, these relationships are a symptom rather than the cause of long-term developments. The time is past when the oil companies could be grouped together by the oil exporters as 'the enemy'. The reality that oil-exporting governments now recognize to a greater or lesser extent is that the market is impartial. They are also aware that the regulation of oil supplies is the only way they can influence the market. This, in turn, means that their relationships amongst themselves determine oil prices in the short- to medium-term. The 'enemy', if there is one, is within.

At the same time, in describing the geopolitics of the oil industry, it is easy to overlook the complexity of the everyday operations that take place out of sight of the general public. Producing, separating, treating, piping, storing, shipping, refining, marketing and distributing the oil are each major and complex industries in their own right, with their own economic rules and political logic. Equally, it is important to remember that it is the oil producers' resources which provide the framework for the operations of the oil industry.

Whilst it is true that the distribution of oil resources is the most important factor in determining the ultimate winners and losers in the 'oil game', the skill with which these resources are managed, the financial and political strengths and weaknesses of the countries involved are what makes the industry fascinating and crucial to all those who depend on oil. These strengths and weaknesses significantly augment or diminish the intrinsic value of naturally distributed resources. Nowhere in the world is this more true than in the Middle East and North Africa.

Oil is not the only thing that Middle Eastern and North African countries have in common. They have been linked (and sometimes divided) by permutations of religion, language, ethnic similarities, by conquest from within and without, and by the social and political legacy these conquerors have left behind. The unremitting thirst of the industrialized countries and their oil companies for the huge, though still unquantified, reserves of oil and gas is only the latest in a long line of 'Acts of God' and 'Acts of Man' to impinge on the countries of the Middle East and North Africa. With all they have in common, it would be natural to expect them to act in harmony, to imagine that oil producers would always think the same way about the important decisions and developments that confront them all in promoting and operating their oil industries, which are their major source of money and wealth. It is all the more puzzling, then, that so many major divisions should occur regarding policy. But those who are prepared to step back from their own political concerns in Europe and the USA and, simultaneously, to look more closely at the realities of the Middle Eastern and North African countries should not really be surprised by this. Common interests in Europe, which led to the establishment of the EC, sprang from the ravages of two hugely destructive wars in this century, but these same common interests have not prevented major policy disputes within the EC.

The diplomatic history that preceded the founding of OPEC in 1960 is an instructive pointer to the problems of today. It took the intervention of far-sighted statesmen from Venezuela to overcome the political and personal rivalries endemic to the Middle East to create OPEC in the first place, and for more than a decade after its establishment, even some of its more ardent admirers would have admitted, based on its apparent achievements, that it might as well never have been created. Today, in OPEC's 37th year, all of its members, particularly the Middle Eastern and North African countries, can point to impressive achievements and economic developments in which they have all shared. Likewise, they share many of the social and political problems that accompany economic upheavals. However, neither massive increases in monetary reserves, nor the subsequent devastating reduction in national income have been sufficient to overcome the obstacles to a common policy that all OPEC members recognize as being desirable. Within OPEC, the 'awkwardness' of the Arab countries, especially those in the Gulf, is a constant complaint of representatives of other countries. However, although they portray themselves as the victims of the Arab countries, their problem, in trying to reach agreements on oil prices or production, results from their own disunity rather than the unity of the Middle Eastern and North African countries.

The recent vicissitudes of the oil markets illustrate the need to look for the detailed national differences which lie beyond superficial similarities in the geological, social, political, economic and religious structures of the Middle Eastern and North African countries in order to understand their actions in the international arena.

As they entered the 1990s, the oil exporters of the Middle East and North Africa looked forward to healthier demand for their oil. 1988 and 1989 were eventful years, bringing both achievements and set-backs. They were years in which some long-standing problems were solved, but in which new problems also arose. Iraq agreed to abide by a production allocation equal to that of its erstwhile enemy Iran. However, the relief experienced by all oil exporters at the agreement of all 13 OPEC members to restrict output and observe a price target of $18 per barrel was shattered in the spring of 1989 when Kuwait declined to accept its quota within an overall production ceiling of 19.5m. b/d. Again, the stumbling block was a disagreement over policy objectives within the Middle Eastern and North African countries, rather than any clash between them and their counterparts in Asia, South America and West Africa. As prices began to weaken during the summer of 1989, after peaking at a level close to OPEC's official price target, many exporters felt they had almost exhausted all possibilities in their search for policies that all could accept.

It is worth recalling the geological, financial and political situations of the principal oil producers, which will continue to shape their attitudes on the fundamental questions facing oil exporters: what price should they aim to achieve in the short-, medium- and long-term, and to what extent are they prepared to achieve their objectives by reducing production? After the 'boom and bust' cycle of the period 1973–1986, producers are aware that the demand for oil is 'price elastic'. Sudden price increases do reduce the demand for oil, high prices do stimulate exploration, development and the production of new oil which competes with and replaces OPEC supplies. There were many economists and political leaders in the Middle East and North Africa who believed that oil's importance to the industrial economies was so great that it was immune to the conventional laws of supply and demand. Even though these laws are no longer in dispute, oil producers still respond to them in different ways.

For producers with relatively small remaining reserves, the long-term demand for and price of oil is of relatively little concern. Algeria, for example, can reasonably argue that it is not concerned that high oil prices may lead to exploitation of alternative sources of energy and/or alternative supplies of oil in twenty or thirty years' time. The same is true for Dubai and Qatar whose wealth depends on obtaining the highest possible price for their exports while resources last. On the other hand, Saudi Arabia, Kuwait, Iran, Iraq and Abu Dhabi, with a minimum of 100 years of oil reserves, regard excessively high prices as likely to deprive them of any source of revenue in the years ahead.

For all their cultural affinities, the perceived objectives of countries in the same reserves category differ in accordance with their domestic political systems.

The ability of those countries which possess high reserves of oil to accept lower prices at the expense of immediate income varies according to their financial strength and political stability. Kuwait's careful investment of its oil revenues over many years created an investment income comparable with its national income for oil exports. Saudi Arabia's decision in 1973 to build a modern physical infrastructure across its huge territory, its need to raise an enormously expensive army to defend its long borders with troublesome neighbours, and the financial needs of its ruling family have left it vulnerable to unexpected reductions in oil income. During the Iran–Iraq War, Iraq, which received massive financial support from Saudi Arabia and Kuwait, regarded lower prices as beneficial since they deprived Iran of the means to replace military equipment. Following the cease-fire declared in July 1988 both Iran and Iraq pursued a high-price policy in order to finance the rebuilding of their

shattered economies. In Iran the ascendancy of more pragmatic politicians has modified this policy such that reasonably high prices, together with the development of alternatives to crude petroleum, are now the main aim. Iraq's adventure in Kuwait, which was ostensibly motivated by Kuwait's persistent flouting of its OPEC quota, has left its economy in a state of collapse. Kuwait, having followed a path dictated almost entirely by self-interest, could have expected some retaliation from its less fortunate OPEC partners. The invasion by Iraq and its vicious policy of destruction went far beyond the avowed aim of bringing a recalcitrant OPEC partner back into line, giving the lie to assertions of regional solidarity.

OWNERSHIP OF THE INDUSTRY AND SUPPLY CONTRACTS

Concessions

Until the end of 1972 the bulk of the Middle East's and North Africa's output was produced under the traditional concession agreements. The first of the concessions was granted in 1901 in Iran by Muzaffareddin Shah to William Knox D'Arcy, in return for £20,000 in cash and the promise of a further £20,000 in shares. Oil was finally discovered in 1908 at Masjid-i-Sulaiman, and just before the beginning of the First World War, the Anglo-Persian Oil Company, which had been formed to take over the concession, began exports through the port of Abadan. (APOC was renamed the Anglo-Iranian Oil Company in 1935 and British Petroleum in 1954.)

During the 1920s and 1930s further concessions were granted in Iraq and in the states of the Arabian Peninsula—and in every case the concessionaire companies were made up chiefly by members of the seven major oil companies which have dominated the world oil business throughout this century. In approximate order of size these were: Standard Oil of New Jersey (which changed its name to Exxon in 1972 and markets its products in Europe under the name Esso), the Royal Dutch/Shell group, Texaco, Standard Oil of California (known as Socal and marketed as Chevron), Mobil, Gulf and British Petroleum. The only other company to participate in the early days was Compagnie Française des Pétroles (CFP—marketing as Total but known as Total-CFP since 1985), which is considerably smaller than the big seven, but is often regarded as an eighth major company because of the world-wide spread of its operations.

At first these companies held exclusive rights for drilling, production, sales, the ownership at the wellhead of all oil produced, and immunity from taxes and customs dues. The governments' receipts, apart from an initial downpayment and a rental, came either as a share of profits (which is how Iran's income was worked out until 1933, when Iran negotiated a fixed royalty plus share of company dividends formula) or as a fixed royalty of four gold shillings a ton (22 cents per barrel).

In view of the vast amounts of oil discovered during the 1930s and 1940s, and the extremely low cost of production, the Middle Eastern governments by the later 1940s no longer felt that the companies had been as generous as they had originally believed, and all aspects of the concessions came under attack. The main complaints, apart from criticism of the financial terms, were that the concessions were too large in area and their duration too long, that they were run almost entirely by foreign nationals, that the companies had appropriated for themselves a quasi-colonial authority, and that the host governments had no control over the amount of drilling carried out nor the volume of exports. The strength of the producers' feelings was only reinforced when Kuwait in 1948 and Saudi Arabia in 1949 granted concessions in their respective halves of the Neutral Zone (otherwise known as the Partitioned Zone) to independent US companies, Aminoil and Getty, on conditions which were very much more favourable than those obtained earlier from the Kuwait Oil Company (BP and Gulf) and Aramco (Exxon, Socal, Texaco and Mobil).

The major change in the financial terms of the concessions which followed did not, however, stem from events in the Middle East, but from Venezuela, where, after the first free elections in the country's history, the Acción Democrática party in November 1948 passed an income tax law giving the government 50% of the companies' profits. A year later Venezuela sent a delegation to the Gulf to explain the advantages of the new legislation, and the companies, realizing that such a revolutionary change could not be confined to one country, and that they would be able to deduct tax payments made abroad from tax paid in their home countries, promptly offered the same deal to the Middle Eastern governments. Under the new system, introduced in Saudi Arabia at the end of 1950 and in Iraq and Kuwait a few months later, the companies' 'profits', arrived at by deducting the production cost per barrel from the posted price, were divided equally between the companies and the governments. Assuming that no special discounts off the posted price were given, this arrangement increased the producers' revenue per barrel from 22 cents to about 80 cents.

The only country not to receive the 50-50 profit split at this time was Iran. Despite various revisions in concession terms during the inter-war years, relations between Anglo-Iranian and the Government were bedevilled not only by financial disputes, but also by the Iranian population's view of the company as the symbol of their country's subjugation to foreign influence and of Britain's colonial power—which had involved Iran being invaded in 1941 (so that the allies could secure a supply route to the Soviet armies in the Caucasus) and Reza Shah's deportation. In 1949, Anglo-Iranian and the Government resolved their differences in a Supplemental Agreement which gave Iran royalty and profit-sharing terms as good as those concluded in the Arab states 18 months later. But the Iranian National Assembly was dissatisfied with the deal, and during the following months, Dr Muhammad Mussadiq, the chairman of the Assembly's Oil Committee, managed to discredit the agreement totally. In December 1950, the Government, which had hoped that it would be able to solve the issue peacefully by negotiating minor revisions, was forced to renounce the agreement altogether. Anglo-Iranian immediately suggested further talks leading to a 50-50 settlement, while Mussadiq in February 1951 suggested nationalization, and, with Iran slipping into a state of internal chaos, the Shah on 1 May was forced to give his assent to the nationalization bill and appoint Mussadiq as Prime Minister.

Over the next two years, Mussadiq refused all compromise solutions offered to him, Iranian oil exports, embargoed by all the companies, rapidly ceased, and the economy collapsed. In July 1953, having tried to dismiss Mussadiq, the Shah was forced to flee to Rome; but within a few days, Mussadiq was overthrown by a coup, and the Shah returned. In subsequent negotiations, the principle of nationalization was recognized, but the National Iranian Oil Company (NIOC) was forced to grant a lease (which was a concession in all but name) incorporating the 50–50 profit split to Iranian Oil Participants (known as 'the Consortium') made up of BP, Shell, CFP and the five US majors—who were later obliged by the US Government to give a 5% shareholding to a group of US independents.

The Mussadiq debacle provided a reminder of the strength of the majors and although in 1961 the revolutionary Government of Gen. Kassem expropriated more than 99.5% of the concession held by the Iraq Petroleum Company group (BP, Shell, CFP, Exxon, Mobil and Gulbenkian), on the grounds that this area was not being exploited by the companies, no Middle Eastern government again nationalized an important productive operation until 1971—when Algeria seized a majority share of the local operations of CFP and the French State company, ERAP.

Partnerships, contracts and production sharing

Although, at the time, the nationalization of AIOC was a disaster for Iran, the dispute marked the end of the period in which Middle Eastern governments gave 75- or 95-year concessions, covering their whole country, to a single group. New concessions signed in the Arabian Peninsula states during the later 1950s and 1960s had a duration of 35 to 45 years, covered much smaller areas, and contained relatively tough terms, with bigger signature bonuses and provisions for the rapid relinquishment of acreage. Even in Libya, where the financial terms of the concessions let at the end of the 1950s were considerably more generous than those applying in the Gulf, the available acreage was divided among more than 10 different groups.

From 1957 the concession concept began to be replaced by new arrangements giving the state a degree of direct participation, and placing heavier financial burdens and greater risks on the companies. The first of the new arrangements was the partnership of Société Irano-Italienne des Pétroles (SIRIP) between the NIOC and the Italian state concern ENI. ENI's

subsidiary, AGIP, agreed to bear the whole exploration cost (only to be repaid half if oil was found), and undertook to spend not less than $22m. on exploration. It was arranged that half of any oil produced would be owned by NIOC and sold by AGIP on Iran's behalf, while half would be owned by the Italian company and taxed at the normal 50% rate—giving the government a 75-25 profit split, and valuable experience.

One year later Iran substantially improved its terms when it formed IPAC, a partnership with Amoco (a subsidiary of Standard Oil of Indiana). During the early 1960s and early 1970s, it signed further partnerships containing cash bonuses, production bonuses, minimum exploration guarantees and minimum development expenditure guarantees. Eventually four of the partnerships struck oil.

With certain variations Iran's example was followed in the allocation of new acreage by Saudi Arabia and Kuwait in the Neutral Zone, where in 1957, a few months after the formation of SIRIP, the two countries obtained a stake of 10% each when offshore acreage was let to a group of Japanese companies. Other countries that copied Iran were Kuwait, in leasing some of its own territory to Hispanoil (in an unsuccessful partnership with the Kuwaiti national oil company which was later abandoned), Egypt, and Algeria, which has applied partnerships to all areas let since 1973. In Qatar, Abu Dhabi, Tunisia and Kuwait (with its offshore areas granted to Shell), the governments have concluded carried interest arrangements, where acreage has been let originally as a concession, with the proviso that the state has the right to negotiate a shareholding once oil is discovered. In few cases have these ventures been successful, so the carried interest charges have seldom come into operation. In all countries, the tax terms have been adjusted to reflect current OPEC rates.

In 1966 Iran introduced the still more radical idea of service contracts, relinquishing Consortium acreage to a French group, SOFIRAN. Like the foreign companies in partnership arrangements, SOFIRAN agreed to bear the whole cost of exploration; but if oil was struck it was to be refunded completely, and NIOC was also to provide all development capital. NIOC was to be the sole owner of all oil produced, while the foreign contractor was to act as a broker for the national company on a commission of 2% of the realized price, being paid by the guaranteed purchase of between 35% and 45% of production at cost plus 2%. Of the difference between this sum and the realized price 50% was to be payable as income tax—though when oil was brought on stream the financial terms were to be adjusted.

After 1966 Iran signed a further seven service contracts, the last (in 1974) allowing the foreign companies to purchase about half of production at discounts of up to 5%. But only SOFIRAN brought oil on stream. Iraq signed three service contracts, which it later cancelled. One of these, involving ERAP, brought the Buzurgan, Abu Ghrab and Fuka fields on stream. None of the other Middle Eastern or North African states has concluded service contracts (service contractors should not be confused with ordinary foreign drilling contractors, such as Santa Fé and the South Eastern Drilling Company—SEDCO, which are employed on a straight fee basis by almost all oil companies and oil producing governments).

Not dissimilar to service contracts are 'production-sharing' arrangements, of a type pioneered by Indonesia. Production sharing arrangements have been concluded by Egypt (which invited Western companies to bid for new acreage in 1973, following a period in which oil exploration had been given over to the USSR), and by Libya in 1974. In the mid-1970s Syria signed a number of production-sharing agreements, allowing Western companies into the country for the first time since 1964. There are considerable variations in this type of agreement, but in most cases the foreign company is compensated for its share of expenditure in cash or kind, or by favourable tax terms, while production is divided in a ratio of between 75:25 and 85:15 in favour of the state.

After the Islamic Revolution in Iran, the new Government decided to end its four successful production partnerships—SIRIP, IPAC (with Amoco), LAPCO (with Arco, Murphy, Sun and Unocal) and IMINOCO (with AGIP, Phillips and the Indian Oil and Natural Gas Commission). The Government took over the foreign partners' shareholdings and in August 1980 announced that, in future, their operations were to be run by a new Continental Shelf Oil Company. This was to be supervised by a specially created directorate in the Ministry of Oil.

The drive for participation, and Algerian take-overs

In the 1960s producer governments sought participation in existing concessions. This idea was originally put by Saudi Arabia to Aramco in 1964, and in 1968 it was given formal voice in OPEC's Declaratory Statement of Petroleum Policy. Apart from being satisfactory on nationalist grounds, and giving the producers a more direct say in such matters as the relinquishment of acreage, the employment of nationals, production rates and investment in new capacity, the governments felt that participation would later enable them to mount their own crude oil sales operations, or expand their national companies downstream into tankering, refining and marketing. The producers, however, did not feel strong enough to press their claim until after the appearance of a seller's market and their success in the Teheran price negotiations of February 1971; and so it was not until OPEC's 25th Conference in Vienna in July 1971 that the members decided to call the companies to formal talks on participation.

By this time a precedent had already been set by Algeria. For political reasons Algeria had nationalized its US concessionaires and Shell in 1967, without causing itself economic harm. This left the French companies, CFP and ERAP, which were responsible for most of the country's production, and were in a special position under the 1965 Franco-Algerian Evian Agreement. Hopes of a satisfactory relationship under this agreement were not fulfilled, and in 1969, under the terms of the agreement, Algeria opened negotiations for higher prices. The talks were inconclusive, and in July 1970 Algeria increased its prices unilaterally. After further fruitless discussions, it seized 51% of the two French companies on 24 February 1971. France sponsored a highly effective boycott, but in June CFP settled its differences with the Government—Algeria agreeing to pay $60m. compensation, while CFP paid $40m. in backpayments and accepted a higher price. Five months later ERAP also came to terms, agreeing that compensation and backpayments should cancel each other out and entering into a minority partnership with Sonatrach in the Hassi Messaoud South field. In 1975 CFP agreed to extend its partnership with Sonatrach for a further five years, but ERAP allowed its agreement to lapse at the end of the year.

The take-over of CFP and ERAP was not directly related to the formal OPEC participation demand, being very much a Franco-Algerian affair, but it increased the confidence of the other producers when they began negotiations with the companies in Geneva in January 1972. The countries concerned in these negotiations were just the five Arab producers in the Gulf (Venezuela and Indonesia having already achieved a degree of participation or close involvement in the running of their oil industries, and Iran, Libya and Nigeria having made it clear that they would pursue their own negotiations), and in practice the talks were conducted by Sheikh Ahmad Zaki Yamani of Saudi Arabia, representing the producers, and Aramco, representing the companies. Yamani's initial demand was for an immediate 25% share rising to 51%, with compensation to be at net book value, and that part of the government share of production sold back to the companies should be priced between the posted price and the tax paid cost (government revenue plus production cost). The companies' counter-proposal, offering 50-50 joint ventures on new acreage, showed how big the gap between the two sides was at this point. In March, however, the companies agreed in principle to surrender 20% of their operations, and in October, by which time Iraq, having nationalized IPC five months earlier, was no longer concerned in the negotiations, an outline agreement was reached in New York.

The General Agreement of 1972

The details of the General Agreement on Participation were finalized in December 1972, and ratified by Saudi Arabia, Qatar and Abu Dhabi at the turn of the year. Under the Agreement the producers took an immediate 25% stake in the concessionaire companies. The earliest date for majority participation laid down was 1 January 1982, with the initial shareholding rising by 5% in 1978, 1979, 1980 and 1981 and by 6% in 1982. This timetable was designed to make for a smooth transition and to

enable all the companies to adjust their supply arrangements over the following decade.

The need to ease company problems also accounted for the complex arrangements for pricing and disposing of the states' 25% share of production. The 75% companies' entitlement, which became known as 'equity crude', remained subject to the provisions of the Teheran Agreement of February 1971, but the balance belonging to the producing states was divided into three categories, each priced in a different way. A small proportion of production (only 10% of the states' share or 2.5% of total output in 1973) the governments undertook to sell on the open market for whatever price they could get. The other two categories of crude were 'bridging crude' and 'phase-in crude', both priced at above the normal tax paid cost and both set to decline in volume as the states' direct sales were to increase. Within nine months of the General Agreement taking effect, however, the Gulf producers decided that both bridging and phase-in crude should be treated on the same basis, and priced at 93% of the posting—this being the price Saudi Arabia had obtained in the sale of its own 2.5% crude entitlement in May.

For compensation under the General Agreement the criterion adopted was 'updated book value' which took account of the cost of replacement of the companies' assets. This was a compromise between the producers' demand for compensation to be on a net book value basis (i.e. after depreciation) and the companies' efforts to obtain a formula which would repay them for some of the value of the proven reserves discovered in their concessions. In the event, the system adopted involved Saudi Arabia paying Aramco $500m., Abu Dhabi paying $162m. in almost equal parts to Abu Dhabi Marine Areas and the Abu Dhabi Petroleum Company, and Qatar paying $28m. to the Qatar Petroleum Company and $43m. to Shell.

Iraqi nationalization

Iraq ceased to have any involvement in the participation negotiations in 1972, when it nationalized the Iraq Petroleum Company. For 20 years relations between the government and the company had been poor. In the later 1950s, a dispute had arisen over the fact that IPC and its sisters, the Basra Petroleum Company in the south and the Mosul Petroleum Company in the north, had developed only a very minor part of their 160,000-square-mile concession. Combined with disagreements over the group's accounting procedures, this led to Law 80 of 1961 expropriating more than 99.5% of the group's acreage. The companies never accepted the expropriation and, although attempts were made to settle this and many other outstanding differences over the next 10 years, the two parties were forced to accept a position of stalemate, in which Iraqi production expanded very slowly.

In June 1971, as part of the agreement on Iraqi Mediterranean crude prices which followed the Teheran pact in February, the IPC group undertook to increase production, but in the following spring, the company found itself obliged to cut the throughput of its pipeline from Kirkuk to the Mediterranean terminals of Banias (Syria) and Tripoli (Lebanon). In a period of low Gulf/Europe freight rates, the high prices negotiated for all Mediterranean crudes in the previous years made it uneconomic for its owners to run the pipe at more than half capacity. The Iraqi Government claimed that the cut-back was politically motivated, and presented IPC with alternatives: either the company was to restore Kirkuk production to normal levels and hand the extra production over to the Government, or it was to surrender the field entirely and concentrate production on BPC's acreage in the south. This conflict was exacerbated by IPC's threats of legal action to prevent the sale of the Iraq National Oil Company's crude from North Rumaila (in expropriated BPC acreage), and by a number of old issues, including an Iraqi claim for royalty backpayments dating from 1964, which IPC had refused to pay until it received the compensation it was claiming for the acreage expropriated in 1971. On 31 May IPC presented its answers to the Iraqi ultimatum. These did not satisfy the government, and on the next day, IPC was nationalized. The affiliates, BPC and MPC, were not immediately affected.

In mid-July negotiations commenced, with Nadim Pachachi, then Secretary-General of OPEC, and M. Jean Duroc-Danner of CFP acting as mediators. IPC promptly announced that it would not pursue legal action against buyers of Kirkuk crude while mediation efforts were in progress, and Iraq was able to sell substantial amounts of oil—including a deal in February 1973 under which CFP agreed to take 23.75% of Kirkuk's output (equivalent to the company's stake in IPC) over 10 years. On 28 February 1973, IPC and the Government finally reached agreement. IPC accepted the expropriations of 1961 and the nationalization of the Kirkuk producing area, and at the same time handed over MPC and paid the Government $141m. of outstanding royalty backpayments. In return it was promised 15m. tons of oil in two batches in 1973 and 1974, and was given some assurance of the long-term security of its investment and growth of output from BPC's southern fields, where it agreed to more than double production from 640,000 b/d in 1972 to 1,626,000 b/d in 1976.

In the event, it was only seven months before BPC suffered the seizure, during the October war, of the holdings of Exxon and Mobil, and 60% of Shell's share (a proportion relating to the Dutch-registered part of the group) as a political gesture against the USA's and the Netherlands' association with Israel. Later the 5% share of the Participations and Explorations Corporations (owned by the Gulbenkian family) was seized on the grounds that the company was registered in Portugal, which was pursuing racist policies in Africa. Thereafter the Government watched the progress of the takeover negotiations in Saudi Arabia and Kuwait, and a few days after a final agreement had been signed in Kuwait, it nationalized the remaining Western-owned share in BPC. It then held negotiations with the BPC partners over compensation and supply arrangements.

Iranian Sales and Purchase Agreement

Although it was clear from the beginning of the Saudi Arabian-Aramco negotiations in January 1972 that Iran was not interested in the type of participation envisaged by the Gulf states, the Shah did not decide exactly what Iran would demand instead until early 1973. On 23 January the Shah gave the Consortium an ultimatum: Iran would not extend its lease, and the companies could either continue under existing arrangements until the expiry of their lease in 1979 and then become ordinary buyers under contract, or they could negotiate an entirely new agency agreement immediately. The Consortium opted for the latter plan, and, under the Iranian Sales and Purchase Agreement signed in Teheran in May, NIOC took formal control of the management of the Consortium's entire production operation and the Abadan refinery. The agreement laid down that NIOC would provide 60% of the capital for expanding production and that the companies would contribute 40% of the funds needed in the first five years (then expected to be the period of greatest expansion) in return for a 22 cents discount on their liftings.

Under the Sales and Purchase Agreement, though NIOC became owner/manager, the Consortium members established a service company, the Oil Service Company of Iran (OSCO), to carry out operations on NIOC's behalf for an initial period of five years, which could be renewed. NIOC undertook to raise total installed production capacity to 8m. b/d by October 1976. It was agreed that the national company would be entitled to take the oil needed for internal consumption and a 'stated quantity' for export, which was to rise from 200,000 b/d in 1973 to 1.5m. b/d in 1981, and therefore, except in certain cases of *force majeure*, would remain in the same proportion to total crude available for export as 1.5m. b/d represented to oil available for export in 1981. The balance of crude production went to the Consortium members, which were guaranteed security of supply for 20 years.

Libya asserts 51% control

Only weeks after OPEC had made its formal call for participation in July 1971, Libya, ever anxious to be first among the producers in militancy and to upstage any participation agreement negotiated by Saudi Arabia, announced that it would be interested in nothing less than an immediate 51% share. Four months later, at the beginning of December 1971, Libya nationalized outright BP's half-share of the Sarir field, but this was a purely political gesture (against alleged British connivance in the Iranian invasion of the Tunbs Islands some 24 hours before Britain's withdrawal from the Gulf)—and for the next year the Libyan Government made no move while it awaited the outcome of the participation negotiations in the Gulf.

Talks on Libya's demand for majority control began in early 1973, with the government adopting its usual policy of negotiating on a company by company basis; but they made no progress. In June Libya nationalized outright the American independent Nelson Bunker Hunt. This company had been BP's 50% partner in the Sarir field, and the government had chosen it for its first negotiations because it had no other source of oil outside the USA and seemed therefore to be especially vulnerable. Bunker Hunt, however, resisted hard. Being a private company it did not have shareholders to worry about and it was confident in the Libyan operators' secret agreement, under which the companies had promised to meet the supply commitments of any one of their number whose concession was expropriated. Col Qaddafi, the Libyan leader, correctly characterized the Bunker Hunt seizure as 'a warning to the companies to respond to the demands of the Libyan Arab Republic'. From circumstantial evidence it seems that Libya fully decided on nationalizing Bunker Hunt when it concluded that it would have no difficulty in selling the oil to markets apart from the Eastern bloc. This followed the judgment of a local court in Sicily which dismissed a suit brought by BP against the importers and refiners of its expropriated Sarir oil.

Following its nationalization of Bunker Hunt, the Libyan Government proceeded in August to seize 51% of Occidental's operations. Faced with the threat of having the rest of its assets seized and being deprived of its most vital source of oil outside the USA, Occidental announced its 'acquiescence' in the measure. For the other companies the significance of this 'acquiescence' lay in the fiscal terms. The companies had in fact been prepared to offer Libya a nominal 51% on the condition that the financial results gave parity with those deriving from the participation agreements with the Gulf producers and Nigeria—but this was not so in the terms settled with Occidental. Compensation was agreed on at book value, rather than the updated book value formula used in the Gulf, and the buy-back price was set above the posting, rather than between the posting and the tax paid cost.

Five days after the Occidental seizure, three independent companies in the Oasis group, Continental, Marathon and Amerada Hess, accepted a majority takeover on similar terms, though Shell, the only major in Oasis, did not comply. Then in September the Government announced 51% take-overs of all the other significant producing groups. Gelsenberg, a German concern in partnership with Mobil, and W. R. Grace, a small shareholder in the Esso Sirte venture, agreed to Libya's terms; but Atlantic Richfield (another partner in Esso Sirte) and the majors, Mobil, Esso (which held a concession on its own as well as the biggest share in Esso Sirte) and the Texaco-Socal company, Amoseas, joined Shell in resisting any sort of arrangement which might have undermined their participation agreements in the Gulf.

In February 1974 Libya seized all of the remaining assets of Texaco, Socal and Atlantic Richfield; and in the following month, Shell too was nationalized. Finally Mobil, in March, and Esso, in April, accepted the 51% seizure of the previous September.

Exxon and Mobil eventually withdrew from their concessions on their own initiative in November 1981 and April 1982. Exxon's liftings had stopped in the summer of 1981 and Mobil's liftings by the time of its withdrawal had fallen to only 10,000 b/d. Some months after its withdrawal Exxon negotiated an agreement with the Libyan Government whereby it received compensation for the assets of its two former concessionaires—Esso Sirte and Esso Standard Libya—at about 70% of net book value. The Libyans established the Sirte Oil Company, wholly owned by the National Oil Corporation, to run both operations formerly managed by Exxon. The W. R. Grace interest in the Sirte concession was unaffected.

Gulf states achieve 60% participation

The General Agreement on Participation concluded at the end of 1972 had satisfied the Kuwaiti Government, and had been signed by the Minister of Finance and Oil, Abd ar-Rahman Atiqi, at the beginning of January 1973; but the Kuwait National Assembly refused its approval. The determination of a handful of radicals opposed to the measure was fortified by Iraq's success in settling its dispute with IPC in February and by the signature of Iran's Sale and Purchase Agreement in May; and by the summer of 1973 it was clear that the Government would not, as it had originally hoped, be able to rally sufficient support to get the General Agreement accepted. On 13 June, the Ruler formally requested a revision of the accord, and during the autumn, when Libya announced its series of 51% take-overs, the other Gulf producers followed Kuwait's example. In November Sheikh Ahmad Zaki Yamani announced that Saudi Arabia would not accept a simple majority holding, and it was made clear early in 1974 that the Saudi Government would be negotiating a complete takeover of Aramco's operations.

Negotiations between the Kuwait Government and the Kuwait Oil Company shareholders, BP and Gulf, during the winter, resulted at the end of January in the state gaining a holding of 60%, which, after several months of further wrangling in the national assembly, was ratified on 14 May 1974. The new agreement was made valid from 1 January, meaning that the companies had conceded the principle of retroactivity on which they had held so firm in the past, and was to last for six years—though the Government reserved the right to call fresh negotiations at any point before the end of 1974. The compensation formula agreed was net book value (giving KOC $112m.), rather than updated book value, but there was no settlement of buy-back terms, with the volume and price of oil being left for more hard bargaining over the summer. In fact Kuwait did not conclude a buy-back deal with BP and Gulf until after it had rejected all bids put in for its 60% crude share at an auction in July. For the third quarter of the year, the Government then sold rather over 55% of its entitlement to the two companies at 94.8% of the posted price; and for the last quarter, BP and Gulf bought two-thirds of the state's crude at 93% of the posting.

Three months before the ratification of the Kuwaiti participation agreement, Qatar concluded a similar accord with its concessionaires (the Qatar Petroleum Company and Shell) in February, and in April it settled buy-back arrangements for the following six months. These involved the two companies purchasing 60% of the state entitlement (about 36% of total output) at 93% of the posted price—the same level as that agreed in September 1973 in the original modification of the terms of the General Agreement. Then in June, after the Kuwait ratification, Saudi Arabia concluded an 'interim' 60% participation agreement with Aramco though no details emerged about the buy-back arrangements. Finally, in September, Abu Dhabi negotiated a 60% share in the Abu Dhabi Petroleum Company and Abu Dhabi Marine Areas, backdated to the beginning of the year.

Aramco take-over negotiations

Although Saudi Arabia had decided to ask for more than a simple majority stake in Aramco in November 1973, it was not until early 1974 (shortly before the Government took 60% of Aramco as an interim measure in June) that it became clear that the Government sought a complete take-over. This was to be linked to sales and contracting arrangements similar to those agreed between Iran and the Consortium in May 1973. Within weeks the Government and Aramco were reported to be close to clinching the deal, but over the next six years changing circumstances in the Middle East, in Saudi Arabia and in the world oil market continually postponed the conclusion of an agreement.

There was an initial breakthrough in November 1974 when Aramco conceded the principle of a complete take-over, and during the following 18 months in successive rounds of negotiations general agreement was reached on all major practical issues. Indeed the two sides were said as much in an announcement made after talks in Panama City, Florida, in March 1976. It was reported at this time that compensation was to be a little more than $1,500m. for 75% of Aramco's assets (which had expanded considerably since 1973) at net book value. In due course part of this sum was transferred to the Aramco partners, bringing the compensation they had received for their assets up to the 60% level. It was also reported from Florida that the companies would continue to take the bulk of Saudi production; that they would be paid a fee of 15 cents a barrel for production operations plus six cents a barrel for new reserves discovered;

and that they would continue to put up part of the risk capital in exploration—only being refunded in the event of success.

During the four years that followed the announcement in Florida there were further rounds of negotiations, but an almost complete lack of news as to the substance of the talks. It was known that there were problems over the fees that Aramco would be paid: the four Aramco partners feared that under some of the formulae put forward their fees would not be big enough to cover their share of investment. On one occasion the companies were known to be objecting to a formula under which their fee would come out of a 75 cents per barrel margin allowed after deducting operating costs and payments to the government. This margin was supposed to cover exploration and the expansion of production capacity as well as the companies' fees.

Other problems centred on the companies' crude oil entitlements. The original understanding of 1976 and 1977 was that the Aramco partners should take up to 7.3m. barrels a day. But early in 1979 when Saudi Arabia's output was raised from the normal 8.5m. b/d to 9.5m. b/d in an attempt to stabilize the market in the aftermath of the Iranian Revolution, the companies' entitlement was increased for a short time to 8.1m. b/d. In 1980 this figure was cut to 7.2m. b/d, at which level it was maintained through the early part of 1981. For short periods during the three years from 1977 to 1980 the government cut Aramco's entitlement to below 7m. b/d—for different reasons on each occasion.

The Aramco partners always argued against short-term cuts in their entitlements, and in the longer term they were worried about their entitlements undergoing a progressive, permanent reduction. This seemed likely to be caused mainly by Saudi Arabia developing its own crude oil sales. It had long been Saudi policy to sell more oil directly to Third World countries and to the national oil companies of the industrial powers, rather than selling it through the integrated chains of the majors. (From just 190,000 b/d in 1973, Petromin's own sales by early 1981 had risen to some 2m. b/d.) It was also clear that the amounts of crude available to Aramco would gradually be reduced further by three other developments. These were the rise in domestic consumption, supplies to new export refineries, and allocations of 'incentive crude' being promised to foreign companies agreeing to invest in refineries and petrochemical plants in Saudi Arabia. An example of the volumes of crude involved in these deals—in this case applying to an Aramco partner—was provided by Mobil's commitment to invest in a petrochemical plant and a refinery at Yanbu. Over 15 years, beginning at the time of the project's start-up, Mobil was to receive 1,400m. barrels of oil, an average of 225,000 b/d. Although Exxon, Socal and Texaco were all involved in their own projects with the Saudi Government—albeit on a smaller scale than Mobil—most of the companies which concluded such deals in 1979 and 1980 were not Aramco partners. (In 1981 the Saudi Government announced that incentive crude would only be given to companies that had already signed agreements to participate in Saudi industrial projects. It was thought that the economics of Arabian industrialization had improved sufficiently since 1979 for prospective future partners not to need special incentives.)

In the background there was the further possibility of the Aramco partners' supplies being reduced by the government cutting production for internal or external political reasons—or because supplies from other producers had increased. A cutback was also thought likely to follow the government achieving its aim of stabilizing prices.

In 1980 the Aramco partners reckoned that if the Saudi Government were to return production to its 'normal' 8.5m. b/d 'ceiling', they would be lucky to receive 5m. b/d. (In practice, when Saudi production was reduced to 8.5m. b/d in November 1981, it was thought that the Aramco partners were getting 5.4m. b/d. This compared with some 6.5m. b/d–7.0m. b/d when the government was running production at 9m. or 10m. b/d, or more.) A cut-back in overall production to 5m. b/d, as advocated by the Saudi conservationists, would leave the Aramco partners with virtually no oil.

Both of the issues in dispute—the companies' fee and their crude entitlements—were apparently resolved early in 1980. In April the Saudi Government transferred to the companies the final instalment of compensation for their assets—$1,500m., in respect of the 40% share in Aramco retained by the companies since the second participation accord was reached in 1974. At the same time the government completed its take-over of the Ras Tanura refinery and natural gas liquids facilities, which had been excluded from the 60% participation deal and for several years after 1974 had remained 100% Aramco owned. The government then announced in April 1981 that it was taking 50% of Tapline, in which the Aramco partners each had the same shares as they had in Aramco itself. Exports via Tapline had been suspended for economic reasons in February 1975 and the pipeline had been used only sporadically since.

Exactly what commitments the government had given the companies on crude oil entitlements were not revealed. However, it was known that as of 1980 the Aramco partners were receiving a fee of 27 cents per barrel produced—though again there was no announcement of the details of the formula on which the fee was based. Nor was there any announcement on the form of the new state oil corporation which would hold the government's production assets; only the Ras Tanura refinery had been handed over to the existing state oil company, Petromin. Likewise nothing official was said about what arrangements were to be made by the Aramco partners to form a service company to run the industry on behalf of the new state corporation.

In practice, while the negotiations with Aramco were in progress the oil industry in Saudi Arabia was run as if the government had total control—in other words the government made decisions but the daily operations were managed by Aramco. The process of participation had involved the government's acquisition of the company's assets in Saudi Arabia and its decision-making powers over exploration, the development of production capacity and the volume and allocation of output. Technically Aramco remained (and remains) a wholly US-owned and US-registered company. Before the completion of the take-over it was part owner of the Saudi production operation; after the signing of the take-over agreement it was assumed in 1981 that its status would change to that of owner of a service company. For practical purposes within Saudi Arabia Aramco was seen both before and after the complete take-over as a giant foreign contractor and contract manager working for the government.

Take-over in Kuwait

Over a year before Aramco and the Saudi Government reached even the general agreement in Panama City on the major issues of the take-over, the initiative in the movement towards complete ownership of oil-producing operations in the Arabian Peninsula had been taken up by Kuwait, which announced on 5 March 1975 that as of that date it had taken over all assets of the Kuwait Oil Company and would be beginning negotiations to settle the terms with BP and Gulf retroactively. The Kuwaitis made it clear that they wanted a continuing relationship with the KOC owners, but that they felt quite capable of running the production operations themselves. Since geological and topographical conditions made Kuwaiti oil extremely cheap and easy to produce, and as the state had been fairly thoroughly explored and did not require large-scale new exploration or development work, the continued presence of the major companies was very much less necessary for Kuwait than it was for Saudi Arabia and Abu Dhabi, where there were large potentially oil-bearing areas still to be opened up. For this reason it was felt at the time of the announcement that Kuwait might have decided on a complete take-over after consultation with the other Gulf producers—wanting to use Kuwait's negotiations to gauge what conditions the major companies might be prepared to accept.

Successive rounds of negotiations, however, stuck on the problems of compensation, the service fee and credit terms, but at the beginning of December 1975 an agreement was announced. This involved: compensation of $66m.; a discount on the 93% of postings third party selling price of 15 cents per barrel reflecting BP's and Gulf's continuing provision of technical services and technical personnel, the large size of their purchases and their undertakings to buy Kuwait's bunker fuel and use Kuwaiti tankers; and commitments by BP to take an average of 450,000 b/d between 1 January 1976 and 1 April 1980 and by Gulf to take 500,000 b/d over the same period. The two companies received an option on a further 400,000 b/d. All

of these quantities were subject to the normal plus or minus 12.5% variations.

Since the completion of the take-over the special relationship between Gulf and BP and the Kuwaiti oil industry has been reduced virtually to nothing. As Kuwait has successfully Arabized many of the technical jobs in oil production and launched its own direct expatriate recruitment programmes to fill those jobs for which it has been unable to find experienced Arab personnel, the numbers seconded by BP and Gulf have fallen to a nominal level. The two companies' purchases of Kuwaiti crude were greatly reduced when their supply contracts were renegotiated in early 1980. Gulf took only 75,000 b/d at the official government selling price (GSP) under a two-and-a-half-year contract, while BP took 75,000 b/d at the GSP plus a further 75,000 b/d for one year (to 1 April 1981) at a premium price. When these contracts were negotiated the original 15 cents discount of 1975 was eliminated.

Beginning in early 1981, the main traditional customers for Kuwaiti crude, Gulf, BP and Shell (which had bought much of Gulf's entitlement in the old concession days), began further to reduce their purchases of Kuwaiti crude. Shell and BP opted out of their contracts altogether in November 1981, and Gulf in January 1982 cut its liftings to just 35,000 b/d.

Take-overs in the Lower Gulf

The take-over in Kuwait in 1975 opened the way for other producers to take 100% of their former concessionaires. Within days of the announcement in December 1975 Iraq nationalized the Basra Petroleum Company, and in February 1976 Kuwait began negotiations for the take-over of Aminoil in its half of the Neutral Zone (while stating that it did not intend to change the status of the Arabian Oil Company's operation offshore). Negotiations did not go well and in September 1977 Kuwait nationalized the company. For a few months a Kuwaiti Wafra Oil Company was established to run operations, until in April 1978 it was decided that KOC should take over the production operation and KNPC the Mina Abdullah refinery, which had processed Aminoil's entire output.

Starting in June 1976 Qatar negotiated the complete take-over of its two concessionaires, signing broadly similar agreements with QPC in September that year and, after a somewhat tougher series of talks, with Shell in February 1977. Compensation was calculated on the basis of net book value, involving the payment of $14m. for Shell's remaining assets and $18m. for QPC's; both companies established new contracting subsidiaries (Dukan Oil Services and Qatar Shell Service Company) to second personnel to run the industry for the state oil corporation; and both companies accepted a fee of 15 cents per barrel of oil produced. This fee, which compared with the Kuwaiti terms of a 15 cents per barrel discount on just that part of production sold back to BP and Gulf, reflected the much bigger oil company presence retained in Qatar. (These fees, although invariably referred to as being 15 cents, were in fact tied to the official government selling prices, which meant that by mid-1980 the fee had risen to 42 cents.) Furthermore it was agreed that Shell should be paid an unspecified lump sum bonus as a condition of its undertaking further exploration (for gas) for QGPC on a contracting basis.

The five-year operating agreements between the Qatar Government, the QPC group and Shell expired at the end of 1981 and early 1982. Dukan Oil Services and the Qatar Shell Service Company continued their work without interruption. It was assumed that the government would renegotiate the onshore contract with just one of QPC's shareholders—probably BP.

In Bahrain the government announced the take-over of the production operations of BAPCO in April 1978, the arrangement being backdated to the beginning of January. The Sitra refinery was left in the hands of BAPCO (owned by Caltex—50-50 Texaco and Socal) until May 1980, when the government took a stake of 60%.

In Abu Dhabi, meanwhile, the government made it clear that it felt that its big potential for further discoveries and the technical problems involved in its offshore production made it very much in the state's interest for the companies to retain an equity participation and that the 60–40 agreement would be maintained. Payment for the companies' services in Abu Dhabi came out of the margin between the GSP and the lower price, known as the tax paid cost, at which the companies got the 40% of their supplies represented by their equity stakes. (See prices section below.) In 1978 the companies' margin of their 40% crude entitlement worked out at 65 cents per barrel. With the oil price rises of 1979/80 this figure rose to $1.60, which the Abu Dhabi Government felt was excessive. It was therefore agreed in 1980 that the margin would be reduced to $1, which averaged over the full amount of production worked out at 40 cents per barrel.

The policy of retaining the concessionaire as a partner also applied in Oman. There were several reasons for this: the small size of the country's oil industry, its shortage of financial resources, the complexity of Oman's oil fields and the Sultanate's acute lack of trained manpower, which made the government reluctant to undertake any inessential commitments. In practice, the foreign company 'presence' in Oman was considerably bigger than in Abu Dhabi. Shell not only provided virtually all of the staff and did the purchasing of equipment, it also seemed to take many of the management decisions.

The end of the Iranian Consortium

In the true tradition of agreements of its type in the Middle East, it was not long before most of the Iranian Sales and Purchase Agreement became out of date. Whereas at one stage in 1973 the Shah had suggested that Iran's reserves might turn out to be more than 100,000m. barrels, in 1975 and 1976 it came to be realized quite suddenly that this was grossly over-optimistic. To add anything to the country's recoverable reserves beyond 65,000m. barrels, or even to recover that volume of oil, the Iranians realized that they would have to invest huge sums in a gas reinjection secondary recovery system.

At the end of 1975 the Consortium ceased contributing the 40% of development capital which it was supposed to invest under the Agreement, and in return NIOC reduced the Consortium's 22 cents per barrel discount to take account of interest accruing on the capital which NIOC saw itself as investing on the Consortium's behalf. Unsuccessful talks on a revision of the Agreement were held in late 1975 and early 1976. However, it was not until the beginning of 1978, after two years in which NIOC-Consortium relations had been further complicated by occasional big falls in Iranian production and by NIOC periodically lifting more than its share, that the two sides sat down to work out a complete replacement for the Agreement. After several rounds of difficult talks the negotiations were made irrelevant by the Iranian Revolution of February 1979.

The disturbances of the autumn that preceded the Revolution had disrupted production (which normally ran at just below 6m. b/d) and in January and February 1979 exports stopped altogether. Production ran at only 235,000 b/d, not even enough to meet domestic demand of 700,000 b/d. At the end of February, soon after the Ayatollah Khomeini had appointed his government, the NIOC Chairman, Hassan Nazih, announced that Iran was to have nothing to do with the Consortium ever again. It was reckoned that if Iran ran production at about two-thirds of its previous level, closing the more complex production areas and halting the development of its gas reinjection system, NIOC could carry out its work with minimal foreign assistance.

On 5 March exports started again, with production rising rapidly to over 4m. b/d, though this level was trimmed back by the beginning of May. It slowly emerged that government policy was not to allow production to exceed 4m. b/d, leaving about 3.3m. b/d for export. Later it was made known that the optimal production level was considered to be 3m. b/d, a figure which was still being quoted occasionally when the Iran–Iraq War broke out in the autumn of 1980. In practice during most of 1980 Iranian production ran at a level far below 3m. b/d.

Early sales contracts after the Revolution were with former direct customers of NIOC and the Consortium and former Consortium members, though by mid-May 1979 NIOC was talking to a number of entirely new companies. In total the Consortium members, who had been lifting 3.3m. b/d before the Revolution, got 1.1m. b/d, of which BP took 450,000 b/d and Shell 235,000 b/d. Up to 1.9m. b/d was allocated for about 50 other companies—some 30 of which had signed by mid-May—including among the biggest buyers old NIOC and Consortium customers such as Japan, Ashland, Petrofina (of Belgium), Amerada Hess and Marathon. All buyers soon found their contracts subject to

volume reductions, which NIOC made in order to have more crude available for new customers. As contracts came up for renewal the trend away from traditional customers continued. For a long period in late 1979 and 1980 the major companies stopped liftings entirely—partly because the premiums being charged by Iran were too high and partly because it was the policy of the companies (acting under pressure from the US Government) not to take Iranian oil while the American diplomats in Teheran were held hostage. A further disruptive element was introduced by the outbreak of the Iran–Iraq War in the autumn of 1980, which temporarily brought production to a standstill.

THE DEVELOPMENT OF PRICES

The 1940s and 1950s

In the years before the introduction of the 50-50 profit split in 1950 and 1951, when most producers received their revenues on the basis of the fixed royalty arrangements (22 cents per barrel) the development of prices was of only academic interest to the Middle Eastern governments. For all of the 1930s, and the first half of the 1940s, the pricing formula applied was the 'US Gulf Plus' system, which was worked out by the chairmen of Shell, Standard of New Jersey and Anglo-Persian when they drew up their famous cartel agreement at Achnacarry House in 1928. The US Gulf Plus system laid down that the price of oil in every export centre throughout the world should be the same as that obtaining in the Gulf of Mexico, but that the price at the point of delivery should be made up of the Gulf of Mexico price plus the cost of freight to that point from the Gulf of Mexico. It made no difference to the buyer where the oil actually came from. If a buyer in Bombay, for example, placed an order with a cartel company, the oil would probably be supplied from Persia, but he would still be charged the same freight cost as if the oil had been brought from the USA—and the saving, known as 'phantom freight', would go to the cartel company. This system could also work in reverse. A shipment of Persian oil to London, which was nearer to the US than to the Middle East, would still be priced at the Gulf of Mexico price plus freight from the Gulf of Mexico to London—leading to the company accepting an element of 'freight absorption'. The explanation for this peculiar system lay in the fact that the major companies, as a group, had their biggest and most valuable investments in the USA, and therefore had an interest in maintaining the biggest possible market for US oil.

Given that all of the other major companies and most of the larger US independents joined the cartel, the US Gulf Plus system operated successfully until near the end of the Second World War, when the British Government objected to paying phantom freight for bunker fuel supplied to the navy in the Indian Ocean, and forced the companies to institute a Persian Gulf base. Under the new system, crudes f.o.b. the Persian Gulf were given the same price as similar crudes f.o.b. the Gulf of Mexico, and at the point of delivery only real freight was levied on top. This resulted in crude oils from the two producing areas finding their natural markets (which met in the Mediterranean near Italy)—though if Middle East oil was landed in north-west Europe, the company would, of course, still have to bear an element of freight absorption if its oil was to be competitive.

It was not long, however, before the Persian Gulf Base system itself began to come under attack from the governments of the importing countries. Immediately after the war, the USA changed from being a big net exporter to being a small net importer (a position it maintained for the next 25 years), and as soon as domestic price controls were removed in 1946, prices in the Gulf of Mexico rose quickly. Persian Gulf prices followed automatically, and because the production cost of Middle Eastern oil was very much lower than that of Texan oil, the companies made enormous profits. Despite the freight disadvantage they were able to import Middle Eastern oil into the US and undercut domestic oil as far inland as the mid-West. In 1948 the companies, influenced in part by criticism from the US Government, lowered their Persian Gulf prices so that the delivered prices of Middle Eastern and Texan oil equalized at London; and in 1949 the US Government forced a further cut in the Persian Gulf so that the delivered prices of Texan and Middle Eastern oil were made to equalize at New York. This reduction, of course, affected only the profits of the companies in their sales to third parties, and made no difference to the profits down their integrated chain of affiliates.

The large profits made by the companies in this period were a major factor behind the Middle Eastern governments' demands in the late 1940s for better financial terms—demands which were met in 1950 and 1951 by the introduction of the 50-50 profit split (see 'Concessions' above). The new financial terms (which increased government revenues on Saudi Arabian Light from some $0.22 per barrel to about $0.80—depending on the fluctuations of prices in Texas) served to make the producers price-conscious. In retrospect they did not fail to notice that the price adjustments of the later 1940s had been to their disadvantage.

The producers also noticed soon after the introduction of 50-50 that the profit split was not quite as even as it seemed, because the companies were always able to press them into giving discounts and the marketing allowance (which was hardly justified when almost all production was sold to affiliates of the operator or to major companies under long-term contracts). In fact, Abdullah Tariki, the radical Saudi Arabian Minister of Oil during the 1950s, calculated soon after 50-50 came into force that the effective split of profits was 32-68 in favour of the companies.

Worse still, in the early 1950s, the price discrepancies between Texan, Venezuelan and Gulf crudes continued to expand, destroying the principle of the three crudes equalizing at New York. This ushered in a new era in which the price of Gulf crudes was to be determined by the supply and demand situation in Europe rather than in the USA—which directly or indirectly had been the basis for all quotations for Gulf crudes since 1929. The growing availability of production capacity in the Middle East, and increasing competition in the European market, led the companies to start giving their own discounts on the posted price for sales to third parties. It was at this stage that posted (or tax reference) prices and f.o.b. (or market) prices in the Gulf began to part company. Given that the 50-50 profit split was still worked out on the basis of the posting, this meant that the producer government's effective share of profits began to climb back towards the 50% it was always supposed to have been.

Then in 1957, after the closure of the Suez Canal, all prices went up—and although in the Middle East the increase was smaller than in Texas or Venezuela, the new price of $2.12 represented the highest posting for Saudi Arabian Light since 1948. These levels were maintained until February 1959, when there was a general reduction, in which Gulf crudes fell by more than the others. Two months later, the Venezuelan price was lowered again, and in August 1960, the Gulf price was reduced without any parallel reduction being made elsewhere. Thus the discrepancy between Arabian Light and Texan crude had expanded from zero in 1948 (when both crudes were priced at $2.68) to $1.20 in 1960—when Texan crude stood at $3.00 and the Saudi Arabian Light posting at $1.80.

From the point of view of the governments in the Middle Eastern capitals and Caracas, the price cuts of 1959 and 1960 (about which they were never consulted) were very damaging—affecting the size of their budgets and their development prospects. In April 1959, at the first Arab Petroleum Congress in Cairo (to which Iranian and Venezuelan representatives were invited as observers), the oil ministers of Saudi Arabia and Venezuela, Abdullah Tariki and Juan Pablo Pérez Alfonso, sponsored the formation of the Oil Consultation Commission. Then in September 1960, a month after the further reduction of Middle Eastern prices, the ministers of Iran, Iraq, Saudi Arabia, Kuwait and Venezuela met again in an atmosphere of crisis in Baghdad. The Oil Consultation Commission was already defunct, having met opposition from Iran and Iraq who objected to the inclusion of Egypt, and the ministers decided to create a permanent and stronger institution. The body that emerged was OPEC—the Organization of Petroleum Exporting Countries.

Since OPEC's formation, the original five members have been joined by Qatar in 1961, Libya and Indonesia in 1962, Abu Dhabi in 1967, Algeria in 1969, Nigeria in 1971, Ecuador in 1973 and Gabon—as an associate member in 1973 and a full member in 1975. The membership of Abu Dhabi was transferred to the UAE in 1974. In late 1992 Ecuador announced its decision

to exchange full for associate membership of the Organization. Gabon withdrew from OPEC at the end of 1996.

OPEC in the 1960s

At first the major companies ignored OPEC. In accordance with a resolution passed at the Organization's fourth conference in June 1962, the members addressed protests to the companies against the price cuts of August 1960, and demanded that prices be restored to their previous level. But the companies refused to enter into any collective negotiations, and in their individual replies they argued that the development of prices did not depend on their own will, but was determined by economic factors over which they had no control.

OPEC realized that the only way to restore posted prices would be to force up market prices, and this the producers decided would best be done by limiting the annual growth in their output. So over two years (from mid-1965 to mid-1967) the members worked out a joint production programme. In both years they overestimated the overall growth in demand for their oil, and at the same time certain members, notably Libya and Saudi Arabia, and, to a lesser extent, Iran, made no effort to keep within their quotas. The obvious conclusion was that in a period when prices were low enough to cause a tight budgeting condition in some states, those countries which were either new exporters and/or had big oil reserves and expensive development programmes, would not be willing to make a temporary sacrifice and await an improvement in the unit price of their oil, but would be tempted to increase revenues by maximizing the volume of their output.

However, OPEC did manage to increase its members' effective share of profits during the 1960s. First in 1963 the companies accepted a cut in the marketing allowance (which they were able to deduct as an expense before making the profit split) from some $0.01–$0.02, depending on arrangements in different states, to a uniform half-cent through the Gulf. Secondly, and more important, the Organization negotiated two agreements on the expensing of royalties. These agreements the Middle Eastern members saw as removing an anomaly in their fiscal arrangements, and as bringing their taxes into line with the system prevailing in Venezuela. Although the producers' revenues since 1950 had nominally been made up of a royalty of 12.5% of the posted price (as payment for the oil itself) and income tax (representing the 50% tax on the profits from the sale of this oil), payments made under the heading of royalties had always been totally deducted from tax. The producers, referring to the normal internationally accepted arrangements, under which the royalty payer was entitled to deduct the royalty only from his gross income when computing his tax liability, wanted royalties to be treated as an expense in their own countries also—and in 1964 this was what was agreed. As part of a package deal the companies received various further discounts on the posted price in respect of 'royalty expensing' and 'gravity differential'. These discounts were to be reduced each year—this process being accelerated by a second agreement in 1968, which arranged for the complete disappearance of the royalty expensing discount in 1972 and of the gravity allowance in 1975. Under the new system the companies deducted their production cost, the 12.5% royalty, and the applicable allowances and discounts from the posted price, then split the remainder 50-50, and then added the royalty on the government's share. For Arabian Light, the royalty expensing agreements and the reduction of the marketing allowance increased government take from $0.84 at the end of 1960 to about $0.90 in 1968.

The independents in Libya

It was not, however, OPEC's achievements in improving its members' share of profits that were to be of the greatest long-term significance for the oil industry in the 1960s. In 1957, oil had been found in Libya. Unlike the governments in the Gulf, Libya had not awarded all its acreage to a single group, and as the discoveries were brought on stream in the early 1960s, it became clear that some of the largest fields lay in concessions held by independent US companies. These companies had originally ventured out of the USA in the late 1940s with the intention of finding new supplies for their marketing operations at home, but when the US Government imposed import controls in 1959, they were forced either to launch themselves downstream in Europe, as Occidental (marketing as VIP or Oxy) and Continental (marketing as Conoco or Jet) did, or to sell their crude to others, as Marathon and Amerada Hess did.

Libya proved to be an ideal source of crude for such operations. Its oil yielded a high proportion of high value products such as gasoline and heating oils, and had a low sulphur content. The country's position gave its crude a big freight advantage over Gulf crudes (an advantage only enhanced by the closure of the Suez Canal in 1967), concession terms were uniquely generous, and for the first half of the decade the profit split was made not on posted prices, but on the much lower realized prices. In the mid-1960s these advantages were reduced when Libya seized the occasion of the first royalty expensing agreement as an opportunity to renegotiate its profit split on the basis of postings. The majors in Libya, who did not favour the independents having access to crude on terms so much more generous than those applying to their own production in the Gulf, agreed to Libya's request in 1965, but the independents only gave in in 1966, after a bitter struggle in which the government threatened to stop exports or nationalize their assets. Even with these new terms, Libyan crude was very competitive with Gulf crudes in Europe, because its posted prices, while higher than those in the Gulf, only partially reflected its freight advantage.

Given the relatively low price, Libyan production expanded extremely fast—from 20,000 b/d in 1962 to 3.3m. b/d in 1970—and throughout the decade prices in Europe fell. The majors' response to the independents' sales and marketing operations was to seek economies of scale in building ever larger tankers, refineries and storage and distribution facilities; but because larger units become most attractive when operated at near full capacity, this led the majors themselves to look for the highest possible market share, and led to an acceleration of price cutting. Although this process was most apparent at the downstream end of the industry, there was also an erosion of market prices in the Gulf, and because the existence of OPEC prevented a lowering of postings, the majors' margins were squeezed. The net earnings per barrel on the seven majors' eastern hemisphere operations dropped from $0.60 in 1958 to $0.33 in 1970, while the effective profit split in the Gulf climbed to about 70-30 in favour of the governments.

Teheran and Tripoli Agreements

In 1970 the marginal surpluses which had been so strong a feature of the previous decade suddenly disappeared. A combination of higher than expected demand as the Western economies entered a period of upturn, a shortage of tankers and a growing tightness of European refinery capacity, led to an unusually tight supply situation, which left the oil industry with very little flexibility to deal with any disruption which might occur in the Middle East.

These conditions coincided with a series of negotiations in Libya, where in January the new revolutionary regime of Col Qaddafi had started pursuing a claim, originally formulated by King Idris' government in 1969, for higher prices which would reflect the true freight advantage enjoyed by Libyan crude since the closure of the Suez Canal, and would incorporate a premium for the oil's high quality. During the early months of 1970, the government took a notably moderate stance, but negotiations made rather slow progress, and although it seemed that they might still be brought to a satisfactory conclusion, by the beginning of the summer the government's position had hardened. In part the regime's determination stemmed from an agreement in the spring to co-ordinate its efforts with Algeria, which was engaged in similar negotiations with its French concessionaires, but at the same time, Libya could see that its bargaining position as a short-haul supplier was being considerably strengthened by events in the tanker market. The economic upturn in Europe was resulting in a rapid rise in demand for industrial fuel oils of the type derived from the heavier Gulf crudes, and this additional pull on long-haul supplies increased the demand for tanker charters. The strain was only made worse by the loss of several of the new class of mammoth tankers in mysterious explosions early in the year; and in May the situation deteriorated further when a Syrian bulldozer broke Tapline, running from Saudi Arabia to the Mediterranean port of Sidon, and deprived the industry of 480,000 b/d of short-haul crude.

In the same month, Libya ordered Occidental, a particularly vulnerable independent which derived nearly a third of its earnings from its Libyan concession, to reduce its production. Whether this decision was made for conservation reasons, or because the government realized what chaos a further reduction in the supply of short-haul crude would cause, remains unclear—but, either way, Libya soon appreciated the value of production cuts as a lever in their price negotiations, and they quickly imposed further reductions on Occidental and on the other companies. By September, the industry had lost about 1m. b/d of Libyan production, and freight rates soared as extra supplies had to be brought in from the Gulf. One by one the companies surrendered—led, naturally, by Occidental and followed by the other independents in the Oasis group. The majors held out a bit longer, but finally Texaco and Socal broke ranks, and then Esso, Mobil and, eventually, Shell gave in too. The Libyans achieved a price rise of $0.30, rising to $0.40 over the next five years, and their tax rate rose from 50% to amounts varying from 54% to 58% in payment for what the government claimed should have been higher prices since 1965.

Although in theory these changes were made only to reflect the freight and quality advantages of Libyan crudes, the majors realized that they would be bound to result in higher prices in the Gulf, and they promptly decided to pay the Gulf producers a higher tax rate of 55% and an extra $0.09 on heavier crudes (which although normally regarded as of lower quality, were in particularly high demand in 1970). Then in December 1970, at OPEC's 21st Conference, in Caracas, the members decided that the Gulf countries should press for further price increases.

The oil industry, with the support of the consumer governments, formed itself into the united front combining majors, independents and European national companies. When talks with the producers' representatives began in Teheran in January 1971, the companies agreed in principle to a price revision, but insisted that negotiations should cover all OPEC states, so as to avoid the leap-frogging of the past few months. The companies were forced to concede this point and a parallel series of negotiations was begun in Libya. During the second half of January the gap between the Gulf producers and the companies gradually narrowed, but on 2 February the talks collapsed. OPEC then held an extraordinary conference, and all members resolved to legislate a price increase if the companies did not respond to their minimum demands by 15 February. But none of the parties wanted a confrontation, and one day before the OPEC deadline, the companies gave in. The producers were given: an immediate $0.33 basic increase, $0.02 for freight disparities, half a cent for every degree API by which any crude fell below 40° API, the elimination of all remaining discounts and allowances, and provision for prices to increase by 2.5% and $0.05 on 1 June 1971, and 1 January 1973, 1974 and 1975. This took 34° API Saudi Arabian Light from $1.80 to $2.18. In return, the companies were guaranteed that there would be no further claims until after 31 December 1975, no more leap-frogging if the Mediterranean producers concluded better terms, and no embargoes.

Later, in March, negotiations were resumed in Libya, and on 2 April an agreement was signed giving Libya $0.90, a uniform 55% tax rate, and provision for annual price increases of 2.5% and $0.07. Subsequent negotiations secured similar terms for Iraqi and Saudi crude arriving at Mediterranean terminals through the IPC pipe and Tapline.

The price explosion

It was hoped that the Teheran and Tripoli Agreements would give a full five years of price stability—but it was only months before they came under strain. In August 1971, President Nixon's decision to float the dollar (leading to a formal devaluation in December) produced OPEC claims for compensation—though in a notably moderate tone. The claim was settled on 20 January 1972, when the companies agreed in Geneva to an immediate price rise of 8.49% in the Gulf; and later, in May, after rather tougher negotiations, the same was agreed for Libya.

In February 1973 the dollar was devalued a second time by 10% and under the terms of the Geneva Agreement prices were duly raised by 5.8% on 1 April. The OPEC states were disappointed by the time the adjustment mechanism took to operate, and by the small size of their compensation, and, after a further series of discussions with the companies, on 1 June a second dollar compensation agreement was signed in Geneva. The producers obtained an 11.9% increase (which included the 5.8% increase in April plus compensation for the further slide in the dollar's parity during May) and it was agreed that prices would in future be adjusted monthly according to a weighted average movement of 11 major currencies against the dollar. This formula resulted in further rises in August and September and a reduction in October.

The companies presented the Geneva agreements as supplementary to the Teheran Agreement—although they both involved a significant rise in revenues, and could equally be characterized as a breach of the five-year price programme. Similarly, the participation arrangement negotiated in 1972 meant a significant increment in government receipts and a modification of the fiscal structure; and a still more drastic alteration came in September 1973 when Saudi Arabia agreed with Aramco that both categories of buy-back crude should be priced at 93% of postings—this being the price obtained by the Saudis in May at the first auction of their own direct crude entitlement.

In the summer of 1973, there were, however, much more fundamental forces undermining the Teheran Agreement. As production in the USA began to fall after 1970, the world's biggest consumer began to look to the eastern hemisphere not only to make up for its declining domestic output, but also for an annual increment in supplies that was nearly as big as the annual increase demanded by the whole of Western Europe. US imports from the Arab countries and Iran grew from 0.6m. b/d in 1971, to 1.0m. b/d in 1972, and to 1.7m. b/d in 1973. It was in 1973 that US demand became really noticeable in the Middle East, and prices on the open market began to rise accordingly.

The OPEC states profited from this situation in as much as they received bids close to postings for the small amounts of crude they were selling on the market themselves; but, with the fiscal terms applied to the bulk of their production still tied to modified 1971 prices, they were for the most part excluded from sharing in the boom, and the main benefit went to the companies. The producers calculated that the effective profit split had changed from about 80-20 in their favour at the time of the Teheran Agreement to about 64-36, and they suggested that the companies were making excessive profits, and that the whole set of prices negotiated two years earlier had become obsolete. These arguments were backed up by the producers pointing out that the small annual increments agreed at Teheran were not keeping up with the rate of world inflation.

At the OPEC conference in Vienna on 15 and 16 September the members agreed to call the companies to negotiations in the following month, and to seek a sizeable lump increase in posted prices to bring them sufficiently above market realizations to permit them to resume their function as a realistic tax reference, while establishing a mechanism whereby the desired differential between posted and realized prices could be maintained in future. The six Gulf members of the Organization began meetings with a company delegation in Vienna on 8 October, two days after the beginning of the Arab–Israeli October war, but the two sides' positions were far apart. The producers demanded an increase of some 70% and the companies offered only 20%. At the end of the week, the companies requested a fortnight's adjournment. The producers immediately held a meeting of their own, and decided to hold a conference in Kuwait four days later on 16 October 'to decide on a course of collective action to determine the true value of the oil they produced'.

When the producers met again, they quickly abandoned the idea of holding any further consultations with the companies, and raised their posted prices by 70%. For the Arabian Light 'marker' crude, the posting rose from $3.01 to $5.12, while government take went up by a slightly larger proportion from $1.77 to $3.05. Subsequently, Libya raised its price by 94% from $4.60 to $8.92, thereby widening further the differential between Gulf and Mediterranean crudes. The new prices were designed to be 40% above the market price for any given crude as determined by the direct sales of governments to third parties, and OPEC announced that the movement of prices would in future be determined for each quarter by actual market realizations. Both the size of the October increase and the fact that it was made unilaterally were unprecedented, and signalled the

final complete transfer of control over the price system, which until 1971 had been in the hands of the companies, into the hands of the producers—after a transitional three-and-a-half-year period of negotiated prices.

The price increase of 16 October was an important milestone in oil politics, but immediately, for the world economy, the meeting of Arab producers in Kuwait on the following day was far more cataclysmic. Gathering under the aegis of the Organization of Arab Petroleum Exporting Countries (OAPEC), they decided to use the 'oil weapon' in support of Egypt and Syria in their war with Israel. With Iraq opting out, the other nine members of OAPEC decided upon a policy of 5% cumulative monthly cuts in production from the levels of September—to continue until the political objective of Israeli withdrawal from the territories occupied in 1967 and the 'restoration of the rights of the Palestinians' had been achieved. The meeting was far from being an occasion of complete unanimity, and the decision on 5% cuts was taken with a degree of hesitancy on the part of some members and amounted to something of a compromise. But once the cuts had started, they escalated rapidly. Within days all of the Arab producers (including Iraq) placed embargoes on the USA and the Netherlands and reduced their production by equivalent additional amounts, while Saudi Arabia and Kuwait also incorporated the 5% reduction scheduled for November in their initial cut-back. Irritated by the lack of response from the West, the Arab producers then decided at a further meeting in Kuwait on 4 November to reduce output across the board by 25% of the September level, and gave notice of a further 5% cut in December. But in practice, the cut-back again turned out to be rather larger than it appeared to be on paper, and by the middle of November output in the two biggest Arab producers, Saudi Arabia and Kuwait, was down by between 30% and 40%.

With winter setting in, the Arab cuts had a dramatic effect on the market. Cargoes of Algerian and Nigerian short-haul crude fetched as much as $16 a barrel, and in December the National Iranian Oil Company, in an auction of its crude entitlement under the Sales and Purchase Agreement, sold oil at the staggering price of $17.40. In these conditions, the OPEC Economic Commission's search for a market price on which to base the quarterly revision of postings became impossible, and the views of company representatives, who suggested in November in a brief exchange in Vienna that no changes should be made until the market had become more stable, were discounted. When the Gulf producers met in Teheran on 22 December, the new price level set was an arbitrary one dictated largely by the Shah of Iran, who suggested a price of $14, while Sheikh Ahmad Zaki Yamani, the Saudi Oil Minister, argued for a price of about $7.50—though he did not, perhaps, put his plea for restraint as strongly as King Faisal would have wished. The other ministers gave Sheikh Yamani little backing, although they resented the way in which the Shah took control of the meeting, and it was eventually decided that the posted price should be increased by nearly 130% from $5.12 to $11.65—taking the government revenue from $3.05 to $7.00. The Libyan price rise which followed was rather more modest in percentage terms—from $8.92 to $15.76.

1974—changing the tax system

The OPEC conference at Geneva on 17–19 January 1974, revealed the full extent of Saudi Arabia's opposition to the price increase announced in the previous month—although in the conference chamber itself, Sheikh Yamani did not raise a formal objection. As it was, members endorsed the new prices while deciding on a three-month freeze. This was extended for a further quarter, after a rather tougher argument, at the next meeting in March.

Coinciding with the OPEC conference in March, was another review by the Arab states of their embargo policy. In effect the cuts had come to an end in December, when they announced that they would not be imposing a further 5% reduction in January, and reclassified most of the EC and Japan as 'favoured nations' for which they were prepared to run production as normal. But it was not until their meeting in March, by which time Dr Kissinger had arranged the Egyptian-Israeli disengagement, that they lifted the embargo on the USA (with Libya and Iraq temporarily dissenting) and only in July was the embargo on the Netherlands lifted. The resumption of normal exports to the USA was accompanied by a decision to restore output to September 1973 levels, and Saudi Arabia, with an eye on the coming price battle within OPEC, which it saw would not be settled without reference to actual market realizations, let it be known that it would raise its output somewhat above September levels.

Inevitably, market prices weakened over the following months. After the failure of several participation crude auctions and price cuts of up to $3 by non-Gulf producers, in August, in the biggest single sale of 1974, the Kuwaitis failed to sell any of their 60% of production at the 97% of postings demanded. For the third quarter of the year they subsequently sold rather over 55% of the oil on offer to BP and Gulf at 94.8% of postings.

As Saudi Arabia had hoped in March, the excess of supply assumed a critical importance in the struggle within OPEC over pricing policy. In June Sheikh Yamani indicated the size of the reduction sought when he formally proposed that the marker crude posting should be lowered by $2.50. But when OPEC held its third meeting of the year at Quito, Ecuador, in June, the other members argued for formulas which would have raised the cost of oil to the consumers by as much as $1.50. Saudi Arabia again threatened a unilateral lowering of prices, and a cheap auction of its participation crude entitlement, and the result was a stalemate in which it was decided (with Saudi Arabia dissenting) to increase the royalty rate on the companies' 40% crude entitlement (known as equity oil) from 12.5% to 14.5%.

Although within OPEC in the summer of 1974 a major battle was being fought over the level of postings, there was at the same time a considerable (and unopposed) increase in government take (and therefore in the cost of oil to the consumers) as a result of the 60% participation agreements, concluded in the middle of the year but backdated to the beginning of 1974. In that the states' participation crude was either sold back to the companies at a level well above the governments' take on equity crude, or was sold on the open market at roughly similar prices, the average government revenue over their whole production was increased, even though on participation crude the governments had to bear the production cost themselves. In 1973, under the 25% regime, the overall effect of participation was fairly small—increasing average government revenues by about $0.10 in the first nine months of the year and by $0.15/20 from September, when the 93% of postings buy-back price came into force. But in mid-1974, under the 60% participation regime, the weighted average revenue worked out, in theory, at some $2 above the government revenue on equity crude (which after the December 1973 increases was about $7.00). In practice, however, there were considerable variations between the different producers in the amount by which the weighted average revenue exceeded the take on equity crude, and in every case, the actual weighted average was lower than it appeared to be in theory. A relatively small factor in determining the variations between the states was the different percentages of postings (93% or 94.8%) charged to the companies for buy-back crude. Much more important was that, following the failure of their auctions (or, in Saudi Arabia's case, in the event of their not holding an auction), the governments kept part of their crude entitlement in the ground, and thus lowered the proportion of participation crude in their overall output, and reduced their weighted average revenues. In Kuwait, for instance, during the third quarter of the year, the ratio of the two types of crude was 65% equity and 35% participation.

One of the consequences of this dual pricing system was that the companies got their crude on average at a price well below that demanded by governments for their direct sales. The OPEC states realized that the companies' own sales of this relatively cheap crude to third parties were not only undercutting state prices and causing the failure of the auctions, but were also giving the companies large windfall profits. It was these problems that the producers tackled during the latter part of 1974. When OPEC held its fourth meeting of the year in Vienna on 12 and 13 September the members decided on a further increase in the royalty rate on equity crude to 16.67%, and an increase in the tax rate on equity crude from 55% to 65.65%. Saudi Arabia argued that these tax increases should have been accompanied by a cut in postings, and again declined to implement

the changes. It was only in the following month that Saudi Arabia, increasingly irritated by the companies' profits, decided to call on Aramco for back-payments to cover the Quito and Vienna tax adjustments.

In November Saudi Arabia took a more decisive step. A Saudi delegation held a meeting with the Qatar and Abu Dhabi oil ministers in Abu Dhabi and agreed with effect from the beginning of the month to raise the royalty rate on equity crude to 20% and the tax rate to 85%. At the same time $0.40 was cut from postings. This was meant to further narrow the gap between the weighted average cost of crude to the companies and the prices demanded at state sales—as well as reducing the impact of the changes on the consumers.

When OPEC met in Vienna for its fifth and final conference of 1974, on 13 and 14 December, the other members endorsed the new arrangements, and decided that from 1 January 1975 (the date to which it was assumed the final takeover of Aramco would be backdated) all of the Gulf states would apply the new weighted average cost to all of their production exported by their concessionaire companies, and that the new price levels should be frozen for nine months. The distinction between equity and participation crude, and the possibility of variations in the weighted average cost being caused by alterations in the ratio between the two crudes, therefore ceased to exist—even though the notion of a 40-60 split was still used to work out the new cost, known afterwards as the 'acquisition price'. The new single price system involved a big jump in government revenue, not only because it was based in part on the higher tax and royalty rates agreed at Abu Dhabi but also because it was based on a 40-60 equity-participation crude ratio which in practice had not existed before. The government revenue on the 'market' crude rose to $10.13, and the acquisition price for the companies to $10.25, reflecting the notional 'marker' production cost of $0.12. The gap between the acquisition price and the 93% of postings, $10.46, which remained the official sale price, was narrowed to $0.21.

Over the following years the acquisition price applied only in countries where the companies retained a 40% equity stake—which soon meant just Abu Dhabi and Saudi Arabia, among the bigger producers. In Kuwait and Qatar the former concessionaires got their crude at the government selling price (93% of postings) less a discount. This gave the companies a smaller margin than in Abu Dhabi and Saudi Arabia, which reflected the fact that in Kuwait and Qatar the companies were no longer investing capital. In Iran, where until the end of 1975 the companies continued to invest capital, the discount off the state selling price was bigger. In practice it was the state selling prices, in all countries, that became henceforth the important prices for OPEC.

Differentials—1975–78

December 1974 marked the end of the oil price explosion; in the space of 15 months government revenues and the cost of oil to the consumer had multiplied almost exactly five times. From then until 1 January 1979 there were only two OPEC price rises. One was agreed in Vienna in September 1975, when the state selling price was raised by 10%, and the other in Doha, in December 1976, when the majority of OPEC members raised their prices by a further 10%—causing a split with Saudi Arabia and the UAE.

During much of the four-year period 1975–78, demand was rather weak. There was something of a revival in the market in 1976, but in late 1977 and most of 1978 there was a serious glut caused by the new Mexican fields, Alaska and the North Sea, which had a significant impact on the world market at the same time. In these conditions OPEC members' attention became focused mainly on differentials—the different margins between crudes of different qualities in different locations. This problem was an important theme (sometimes the only theme) in at least half a dozen OPEC meetings: at Vienna in September and December 1975, Geneva in April 1976, Bali in May 1976, Stockholm in July 1977 and Caracas in December 1977.

Although ministers reached a flexible understanding on differential adjustments at the Bali meeting in May 1976, and periodically referred the matter to special committees (at Geneva in April 1976 and Stockholm in July 1977), the Organization could not agree on any comprehensive new system. Adjustments were made unilaterally, sometimes in accordance with guidelines laid down by one of the committees, but more often they took place when a state experienced a particularly embarrassing fall in demand, or when a price rise (in October 1975 or January 1977) produced an opportunity for producers to adjust their own crudes by implementing a fractionally bigger or smaller rise than that announced of the marker crude.

Apart from the differentials issue, OPEC meetings in 1975–78 were marked by quite frequent battles over price rises. Iraq and Libya were always numbered amongst the 'hawks' (often with Iran, Algeria and Nigeria), and Saudi Arabia generally stood as the single 'dove'—though sometimes it had the support of the UAE, Qatar and occasionally Kuwait. Although Saudi Arabia was forced to compromise in September 1975 and before Stockholm in July 1977, it succeeded in preventing rises at Bali, at Caracas in December 1977 and at Geneva in June 1978.

Other recurrent issues were production programming (the artificial limiting of output so as to influence the state of the market) and the protection of oil prices against the dollar's fluctuations. Saudi Arabia invariably rejected the idea of production programming, or even to discuss its own output, on which any programme would have hinged. On the matter of dollar compensation mechanisms, which was an issue in early 1975 (at Vienna and Libreville) and late 1977/early 1978, Saudi Arabia was less adamant, but still doubtful of the value of any of the formulas proposed.

OPEC split and reconciliation— December 1976–December 1977

The major event in OPEC—and the major confrontation over prices—in 1975–78 occurred at Doha in December 1976. Saudi Arabia, with the support of the UAE, refused to countenance the increases demanded by other OPEC members, ranging upwards from 10%, though it emerged later that had compromise been possible it would have been prepared to accept 7%. The outcome was that Saudi Arabia and the UAE opted for an immediate 5% increase for the whole of 1977, while the other members decided on 10% for the first six months of the year with an additional 5% to take effect on 1 July.

In part the Saudi policy at Doha stemmed from a hard-headed realization that the health of the OPEC economies is linked to that of the Western economies, and that inflation caused by oil price rises rebounds on the OPEC members; but at the same time there is no doubt that Saudi Arabia felt a genuine sense of responsibility for the West's economic well-being.

After the Doha meeting Saudi Arabia announced that it was raising its production ceiling from 8.5m. b/d to 10m. b/d, and immediately there were big drops in the production of some of the other states. Yet there was no increase in Saudi production at the beginning of the year; indeed output in January and February fell from the record levels of late 1976 (9.2m. b/d in December) to only 8.2m. b/d and 8.7m. b/d respectively. During the next four months, however, production rose, reaching over 10m. b/d at one point. There was some mystery surrounding the reasons for this performance. On one hand, it was suggested that the initial drop in output was caused either by the inevitable time-lag that would elapse before Saudi Arabia could sign up new customers or by Saudi Arabia realizing that the expansion of production might be more effective as a threat than as a *fait accompli*. On the other hand, there was evidence that Saudi Arabia had tried from the start to raise production to 10m. b/d but had been frustrated partly by bad weather preventing tankers loading, and partly by the realization that although it had rather more than 10m. b/d of capacity installed in hardware terms and was planning to expand this to some 12m. b/d by the end of the year, it did not have the personnel and management systems needed to maintain output at these levels.

Throughout the early months of 1977 attempts were made to heal the rift in OPEC. At quite an early stage it became clear that the 11 upper-tier countries would agree to a compromise involving Saudi Arabia and the UAE raising their prices by 5% in July and the rest at the same time forgoing their own scheduled 5% increase, but it was not until sometime in June that it emerged that Saudi Arabia would accept this formula. Some two weeks before the OPEC conference at Stockholm on 12 July, which it had been agreed should not be held unless a solution had been reached in advance, the two sides made their

compromise public. The Stockholm meeting itself concentrated on the issue of differentials. At the later meeting in Caracas in December 1977 prices remained frozen, not because of a consensus, but because Saudi Arabia managed to assemble behind it Iran, Kuwait, the UAE and Qatar.

The second oil crisis—1979

Despite the oil glut of most of 1978, relations between OPEC members improved from the middle of the year. On 6 and 7 May the ministers held an informal exchange of ideas on long-term strategy in Ta'if, Saudi Arabia. The relaxed atmosphere, free of the pressures of decision-making, was enhanced by the steps that Saudi Arabia was taking to cut its output. Late in 1977 it had reimposed its 8.5m. b/d ceiling, and in early 1978 it had decided to limit liftings of Arabian Light to not more than 65% of total liftings (compared with 72%–80% in 1975–77). The market, however, was unable to absorb the extra amounts of heavy crude that this ratio implied at prevailing production rates, so for the first nine months of the year Saudi output fell sharply.

The broad drift of the ministers' discussions at Ta'if assumed that the glut would begin to come to an end in later 1978 or 1979, that there would then be a period of balance in the market—how long a period depending on the consumers' growth rates and their success or failure at developing alternatives and conserving energy—and that at some point in the 1980s the world would return to conditions of shortage. In these circumstances it was felt that the market itself would look after oil prices and that OPEC might possibly orient itself to using its increased bargaining power for bringing about the new international economic order which had failed to emerge from the North-South dialogue in Paris. To study these questions the meeting established another ministerial committee composed of Saudi Arabia, Iran, Iraq, Kuwait, Venezuela (the five founder-members) and Algeria.

The turn-round in the market came much sooner than expected. At the end of October 1978 the strikes in Iran which were paralysing the Shah's regime began to affect oil production. During the next two months Iranian production varied between its norm of about 5.8m. b/d and 1.2m. b/d, but at the end of December it fell to 235,000 b/d (insufficient to meet domestic demand), at which point it remained until March 1979.

Up to the end of the year the companies made up the shortfall by increasing liftings elsewhere; Saudi output in December ran at a record 10m. b/d—it being permissible for Aramco to exceed the 8.5m. b/d limit for a month or so as long as it kept within it over the whole year. The Iranian crisis had no effect on the spot market. Nor did the crisis add much impetus to the OPEC meeting at Abu Dhabi on 16 and 17 December, when it was decided to raise prices for 1979 by 10% in quarterly instalments. These would bring the marker crude selling price from $12.70 in December 1978 to $14.54 in October 1979—a rise of 14.5% over nine months but an average increase for the year 1979 of 10%. What was remarkable was the storm of protest with which the rise was greeted by Western governments, which seemed to ignore the fact that the rise was extremely modest and followed a long period of price stability.

In the month that followed the OPEC meeting, spot market prices began to climb at a rate which was to destroy the price programme agreed at Abu Dhabi and, by mid-May, to cause the Western world to talk of a 'second oil crisis'. With Iranian exports halted the international oil industry was short of some 5m. b/d, which was only partially made up by Saudi Arabia raising its production ceiling from 8.5m. b/d to 9.5m. b/d and by smaller increases in Kuwait, Iraq and other producer countries. By the middle of February, at which point OPEC announced an extraordinary meeting to be held in Geneva at the end of March, spot prices for light Gulf crudes had risen to $21 and higher, involving premiums of above $7.50.

In February Abu Dhabi, Qatar, Libya, Kuwait, Iraq, Oman and the USSR (for its Western customers) imposed surcharges on their crudes of between 68 cents and $1.41 per barrel.

On 5 March Iran resumed oil exports, building up over the next two months to a production level of some 4m. b/d (which meant exports of 1.5m. b/d–2.0m. b/d less than before the Revolution). This caused the spot premiums to fall from their end-February peak of $23, but the market pressure for a rise was still impossible for Saudi Arabia to resist when OPEC met at Geneva on 26 and 27 March. All producers agreed to bring forward their scheduled 1979 last quarter increase to the second quarter (raising the marker to $14.55), and it was decided that producers could impose any additional surcharges they deemed 'justifiable in the light of their own circumstances'. Saudi Arabia added no premiums to its Light, Medium and Heavy crudes, but $1.14 to its high quality Berri crude. All of the other Gulf producers increased the surcharges they had imposed in February (on top of the new price levels), while the African producers raised their selling prices to the $17.50–$18.50 range.

In the middle of April it became known that Saudi Arabia was not maintaining its extra 1m. b/d of output in the second quarter, partly because it argued that the resumption of Iranian exports made this unnecessary, and partly, it was thought, to show its displeasure with the USA over the Egypt–Israel peace treaty. Shortly after this the effects of the Iranian stoppage began finally to feed through to the market, as oil companies cut back their deliveries. These developments set off in May another jump in the spot market price for light crudes, taking the price above the end-February level and then on to extraordinary levels in the region of $33 per barrel in mid-May. Nobody in the industry was surprised when the surge in the spot market was followed by two further rounds of leapfrogging increases—both led by Iran.

To try to lessen the pressure for higher prices, Saudi Arabia announced before the OPEC meeting in Geneva on 26 and 28 June 1979 that it was considering raising its output again. At the meeting the other members demanded further increases, which, if Saudi Arabia had co-operated, would have raised the marker crude to at least $20. Saudi Arabia, concerned at the recessionary influences that the oil price increases were having on the Western economies, sought to stabilize the price at a lower level of $17–$18. In the end OPEC reached an amicable compromise in which Saudi Arabia raised its marker price to $18 while the other members were allowed to impose surcharges up to $23.50. This figure was adopted for some of their crudes by Algeria, Libya, Nigeria and Venezuela. Soon after the meeting Saudi Arabia announced that it was raising production for the third quarter of 1979 by 1m. b/d to 9.5m. b/d.

It was not until September 1979 that Nigeria broke the $23.50 ceiling by imposing a further premium on the price of its crude— and so triggered yet another round of increases.

Saudi attempts to reunify prices— December 1979–September 1980

Saudi Arabia made a major attempt to restore order to the situation in December 1979, when it raised its crude prices by $6 per barrel, taking Arabian Light from $18 to $24. In doing this Saudi Arabia obviously hoped to set the stage for the unification of prices at the OPEC meeting in Caracas later in the month, but in the event, the Caracas meeting broke up in disarray. During January 1980 most OPEC members announced further increases backdated to the beginning of the year. Saudi Arabia felt that there would be no point in allowing their prices to fall further out of line with other members and so raised its own crudes by $2 per barrel. For the future they were encouraged by a softening of the spot market, caused by the downturn in economic activity in the industrialized world. Other producers, however, were not deterred from asking for even larger premiums and bonuses over and above their official prices on new crude sales contracts.

Saudi Arabia made another attempt to rationalize the price structure in May 1980, raising its prices by a further $2, taking Arabian Light to $28, effective from 1 April. This initiative, like its predecessor, failed. Within a week or so all other OPEC members—except Iran, which had already increased its second quarter prices—had matched the Saudi increase. When OPEC met at Algiers in early June the best that could be managed was an agreement to accept a two-tier price system. A theoretical marker price was set at $32 per barrel and on this basis producers of light crudes were allowed to charge differentials of up to $5. This established a new ceiling for OPEC prices of $37 but, in the following weeks, the price charged for Arabian Light stayed at $28. When the other producers realized that no changes would come from Saudi Arabia, they gradually raised

their prices in line with the new accord. The African producers put their best crudes at the $37 limit.

During the summer the market moved steadily in Saudi Arabia's favour. The Kingdom's production had stayed at 9.5m. b/d since the middle of 1979. At the same time the oil companies had continued to pay high prices, with premiums, for other producers' crude in spite of the over-supply that had begun to be obvious in the winter of 1979/80. By mid-1980 stocks in the industrialized world had risen to unprecedented levels, to the extent that the oil companies' storage facilities were simply unable to accommodate further crude. By September spot market prices for African crudes had fallen to some $5 below official levels, and OPEC production had dropped 1.5m. b/d below the 28.5m. b/d recorded early in the year.

It was against this background that OPEC held two meetings in Vienna in September 1980—a regular oil ministers' meeting and a tri-ministerial meeting of oil, finance and foreign ministers. The latter group was convened to discuss the Organization's 'long-term strategy'. This involved a formula for future price increases, a wide-ranging programme of aid to the Third World, a revived North-South dialogue between the industrial powers and the developing countries, and a further bilateral dialogue between OPEC and the industrialized countries—all subjects which the Organization had begun to study at the meeting held in Ta'if in May 1978. Given the state of the market, the Saudi delegation in Vienna was able to make what seemed to be real progress towards a reunification of prices and agreement on a proper system of differentials. It was agreed that the actual Arabian Light price should be raised $2 to $30 per barrel and that this should be regarded as the official marker price. It was accepted that other OPEC crudes, aligned on the theoretical $32 marker, should not be reduced but would remain frozen until the next OPEC conference in December.

Saudi Arabia argued strongly at the Vienna meeting that any price for Arabian Light of over $30 would be too high to serve as a starting point for the Organization's long-term price formula, which members were hoping to implement at the beginning of 1981. Noting that conservation and diversification measures in the industrialized world were at last beginning to bite, Saudi Arabia was concerned that anything over $30 as the starting point for escalation might permanently damage the world economy and cause an undesirably large drop in demand for OPEC crude. Arguing against Saudi Arabia, the more militant OPEC members refused to accept the $30 starting point because it would have involved a reduction of their existing prices. The eventual compromise, lobbied most strongly by Kuwait, was based on the idea that if the majority of members agreed to freeze their prices, the escalation formula would quite quickly bring the Saudi price up to their desired $32 starting point— possibly as soon as the end of the first quarter of 1981.

There remained the question of the details of the price formula. The 'draft plan' presented by the working group presided over by Sheikh Yamani envisaged quarterly price adjustments based on three indices: the exchange rates of the main industrial currencies, inflation in the industrial countries' consumer prices and export prices, and a GNP index reflecting the real rate of growth of the 10 biggest industrial countries. The purpose of the last index was to bring the price of OPEC oil gradually up to the price of the 'alternatives'—oil from tar sands, shales and coal. The plan also provided for the co-ordinated adjustment of production upwards and downwards to preserve the price structure in the face of serious glut or shortage, and for moderate one-off price increases in time of acute shortage.

Most of the OPEC members backed the draft plan and were broadly in sympathy with the Saudi stand. The dissenters were Algeria, Iran and Libya, which rejected the use of inflation and growth indices from the industrial nations in constructing the price escalation formula. They argued instead for an index based on the much higher growth rates of the OPEC members and on the inflation of OPEC's imports of industrial goods. As the tri-ministerial meeting proceeded there were indications that Algeria would be prepared to compromise with the majority— in which case it was thought that any further resistance by Libya or Iran would have little practical significance. This left only the issue of differentials. Here disagreements revolved around the Gulf producers' opinion that the $7 difference between African crudes and the new marker price of $30 were

$4–$4.50 too high. As with the differences over the structure of the long-term price formula there was some cautious optimism that the issue of differentials could be solved if there was the political will to do so.

Iran–Iraq War: renewed price discord

All optimism was destroyed at the end of September by the outbreak of the Iran–Iraq War, which soon led to the abandonment of the OPEC summit meeting. The two countries' attacks on each others' loading terminals and refineries led to a complete halt in exports and the removal of 4m. b/d from the international market. Iraq asked other producers to increase their output to compensate for the loss. In October the oil ministers of the four Arabian OPEC members met in Ta'if, Saudi Arabia, and agreed on a programme of increases, though given the 2m. b/d–2.5m. b/d surplus that had existed in the market before the war the amounts involved were modest. In all, the Arabian producers' output was raised by only some 1m. b/d of which some 700,000 b/d–800,000 b/d came from Saudi Arabia. This involved a new Saudi production level of 10.2m. b/d–10.3m. b/d. The extra Saudi crude was sold to state-owned oil companies of industrialized and developing countries at a $2 premium over the official Arabian Light price of $30. The production increases were not big enough to prevent a gradual rise in spot market prices. In November the Rotterdam price for Arabian Light rose to $40, and by the end of the month there were a few examples of Arabian Light and African oils being traded for between $42 and $43.

It was against this background that OPEC met again in Bali, Indonesia, in December 1980. In view of the renewed discord and the more buoyant state of the market, the more moderate OPEC members were pleased to achieve even a minimal degree of pricing order. The conference took a series of decisions very similar to those taken at the Algiers conference in June 1980. Saudi Arabia agreed to raise the price of Arabian Light by $2 to $32, and the conference as a whole set a theoretical marker crude price of $36—this being intended as the basis for increases in the prices of other crudes. A differentials limit of $5 was set, making an OPEC ceiling price of $41. Somewhat to the oil industry's surprise, in early January 1981 Kuwait, Qatar and Iraq raised their prices by $4 aligning them either side of the theoretical marker price of $36. Abu Dhabi raised its price for Murban crude by just $3 to $36.56. The African producers moved the prices of their light crudes to the $40–$41 range.

1981—Price reunification

During December 1980 both Iran and Iraq began exporting crude again. From the time lifting began both producers offered substantial discounts, nominally to offset the extra insurance premiums that tanker owners were obliged to pay for sailing their ships into a war zone. In response to the renewal of exports by the two countries, Abu Dhabi had promptly stopped its output of 80,000 b/d of war-relief crude, but Saudi Arabia maintained its output at 10.3m. b/d. This meant that the Kingdom was accounting for 43% of total OPEC output—a figure which it had never attained in the 1970s and which gave it unprecedented power within OPEC. Certainly in 1980 Saudi Arabia seemed much better equipped to dictate price levels to the other members of OPEC than it had been during the previous confrontation of 1977. In the circumstances it was inevitable that Iran's and Iraq's return to the market would lead to a general erosion of prices. In April and May several companies, including Atlantic Richfield in Nigeria, 'walked away' from their contracts. Qatar dropped its $6.50 premium.

As it approached the next OPEC conference, scheduled for 25 May 1981 in Geneva, Saudi Arabia felt confident of being able to persuade its fellow members, without too much difficulty, to accept a price 'freeze' for the rest of the year. Sheikh Yamani made it known before the meeting that the Kingdom would like the 'freeze' to be extended through 1982, to give the Western economies 'time to breathe and recover'. Saudi Arabia also wanted to move towards a unified price structure and revive the long-term strategy plan. This had been the subject of informal discussions which it had held with Kuwait, Nigeria, Algeria, Venezuela and Indonesia at a secret meeting in Geneva in February.

At the OPEC conference no progress was made towards reunification. A mooted compromise, which would have involved Saudi Arabia increasing its price by $2 to $34 and the other members lowering their theoretical marker price to the same figure proved unacceptable to the militants. Instead all members agreed to 'freeze' the theoretical marker price at $36 and the maximum OPEC price at $41 until the end of the year.

Most of the members at the conference—the exceptions being Saudi Arabia, Iran and Iraq—also agreed to cut their output by 10% in an attempt to reduce the surplus on world markets. This was important as the first occasion since the 1960s that OPEC had taken a decision on production levels. However, it was announced that the basis for the 10% cut was to be the output levels obtaining at the beginning of the year and, as most producers' output was running at well below these levels in May 1981, the actual reductions that resulted from the decision were not very large.

There was another abortive attempt to reunify prices at $34 when OPEC held a consultative meeting in Geneva in August. Events in the period immediately after the meeting, however, influenced OPEC attitudes. Saudi Arabia in September reduced its production to 9m. b/d–9.5m. b/d as a gesture of goodwill, while Nigeria, Indonesia, Gabon and Iraq all found that to maintain acceptable production levels they had unilaterally to cut their prices.

At the end of October, when OPEC gathered for its third Geneva meeting of 1981, the members were at least able to agree on reunification. As had been suggested at earlier meetings, the point of reunification was $34—a figure which involved Saudi Arabia increasing its price by $2 and the other members of OPEC cutting their prices by $1–$2. Saudi Arabia agreed to underpin the new price structure by restoring its production level to the traditional ceiling of 8.5m. b/d. Various loose ends concerning differentials were tied up at a meeting in Abu Dhabi in December. On this occasion there was a general lowering of the prices of both light and heavy crudes, to be effective from the beginning of 1982, which cut the average cost of OPEC crudes to consumers by some 50 cents per barrel.

OPEC's first production programme

Only weeks after the reunified price structure and the new, more realistic differentials had come into effect OPEC found itself facing the worst crisis in its history. The continuing recession in the industrialized countries and a run-down of stocks at a rate believed to be 4m. b/d cut demand for OPEC oil in February to just 20.5m. b/d. This compared with a forecast of 23m. b/d made before the new year. In response to the pressure of the market Iran in February made three price cuts totalling $4; North Sea prices were reduced by similar amounts to around $31 per barrel. The spot market price for Arabian Light fell to $28.50–$5.50 below the government selling price.

Slightly to the surprise of many outside the Organization, OPEC met the challenge fairly effectively. On 6 March 1982 Saudi Arabia made a further cut in its production to 7.5m. b/d. On the same day informal discussion by some of the OPEC ministers, attending an Arab conference in Doha, resulted in a tentative agreement that the production of OPEC as a whole should be limited to 18.5m. b/d, and that a full, extraordinary meeting of the Organization should be called two weeks later in Vienna.

The extraordinary meeting, on 19 and 20 March 1982, started badly. Individual members produced a series of inflated figures for what they regarded as their minimum acceptable production quotas. The total of all quotas initially demanded came to 21.9m. b/d, and Sheikh Yamani warned that if the OPEC nations were not serious in their defence of the $34 marker price, and allowed the market to degenerate into a free for all, Saudi Arabia would have no alternative but to go it alone, which would entail a whole barrage of competitive measures—reduction of the Arabian Light price to $24 per barrel, an increase in output to 10m. or 11m. b/d, and extensive sales of Saudi crude on the spot market. This glimpse of the abyss concentrated the minds of the other members wonderfully and caused them to agree on a realistic set of quotas involving an 18m. b/d ceiling. This was slightly below the ceiling which had been mentioned at Doha and some 1m. b/d below average first quarter production levels. The decision was accompanied by a further lowering of light crude prices in Africa and the Gulf, the establishment of a ministerial 'watchdog' committee to monitor the market and the implementation of the quotas, and an agreement that the 18m. b/d ceiling should be reviewed at the next ordinary conference in Quito in May.

The quotas agreed at the Vienna meeting, in millions of b/d, were as follows: Iraq 1.2, Iran 1.2, Saudi Arabia 7.5, Kuwait 0.65, Neutral Zone 0.3, UAE 1.0, Qatar 0.3, Nigeria 1.3, Libya 0.75, Algeria 0.65, Venezuela 1.5, Indonesia 1.3, Ecuador 0.2, Gabon 0.15. Immediately after the meeting Sheikh Yamani announced yet another cut in the Saudi production ceiling to 7m. b/d in April—0.5m. b/d below its quota level.

For three months following the Vienna meeting the OPEC production programme seemed to be working and prices on the spot market responded reassuringly by closing to official selling rates. At the next ordinary conference held in Quito on 20 and 21 May ministers expressed satisfaction with the success of the quota system. They decided to review the 17.5m. b/d ceiling later in the summer and there was some hope that it might be raised. By mid-June, however, it was clear that the limit on collective output had been exceeded. In that month production averaged nearly 18m. b/d despite the fact that Saudi Arabia's output was running well below its self-imposed ceiling at about 6m. b/d and Iraq, unable to export from the Gulf, was fulfilling little more than two-thirds of its quota. At the time the production programme was adopted Iran's attitude had seemed ambivalent and its participation doubtful. In the event it steadily increased its production from April onwards, stimulating exports through the offer of discounts of up to $3 and more below the officially agreed OPEC level. Its output had reached about 2.5m. b/d by July. Muhammad Gharazi, Iranian Minister of Oil, stated that the objective was 3m. b/d. Libya was estimated to be producing at a rate of 1.2m. b/d and in contracts had agreed to prices $2 below the official level. Because of their non-observance of the pact Venezuela declared that it would not be bound by the agreement. By the time the ministers gathered in Vienna for an extraordinary conference planned two months earlier the production programme was disintegrating. Chances of it being salvaged were not improved by Saudi Arabia's demand that the differential for the premium North African crudes should be increased from $1.50 to at least $3. This reflected the dissatisfaction of Saudi Arabia and the other Arab producers of the Gulf over the way in which their output was falling.

The fact that the extraordinary ministerial conference held on 9 and 10 July was suspended—rather than ended without any agreement—indicated the extent of its failure. Apart from a common commitment to the $34 reference price and recognition of the need to restrain production within a 17.5m. b/d ceiling, Iran, Libya and Algeria insisted that Saudi Arabia should further cut its production to accommodate other producers, in particular Iran. Saudi Arabia's response was that it still refused to discuss its level of output with other members and that it had already made substantial sacrifices. At a time when Libya and, to a lesser extent, Algeria were offering discounts in various forms off existing official prices, the Kingdom's insistence on widening differentials seemed a somewhat irrelevant, as well as disruptive, preoccupation. Above all, though, the belligerence of Iran, which had just previously taken the Gulf conflict into Iraq's territory, poisoned the atmosphere. Ministers dispersed comforted only by the strong expectation that demand for OPEC oil would revive in the second half of the year.

The willingness and ability of oil companies, banking on a price reduction, to run down stocks came as a surprise. OPEC production of about 18m. b/d in the third quarter and 19m. b/d in the fourth was too high to maintain the $34 reference price and Arabian producers grew restive. Meeting within the context of the Gulf Co-operation Council (GCC) made up of Saudi Arabia, Kuwait, the UAE, Qatar, Oman and Bahrain, they issued a thinly disguised threat of price cuts and increases in production by themselves if other exporters continued 'in their misguided actions'. The warning was evidently aimed at Britain, Norway and Mexico as well as OPEC recalcitrants.

OPEC's next biannual ministerial conference in Vienna from 18–20 December could do no more than agree that the $34 reference price should be defended and that collective output should be no more than 18.5m. b/d in 1983. Little progress was made on the allocation of production quotas, the elimination of discounting, and the correction of differentials. The lack of realism was clear from the fact that the initial quota nominations by individual members amounted to 23.4m. b/d. The possibility of the Gulf producers acting independently recurred but they decided against such a course.

A gathering in Bahrain on 23 January 1983 of oil ministers of the GCC, who were joined by their counterparts from Iraq, Indonesia, and Nigeria, paved the way for a full ministerial consultative meeting in Geneva on 23 and 24 January. Once again members failed to agree upon a concerted strategy in the face of a growing threat, although members moved a little closer to adoption of a new system of quotas. Once again the consultations were plagued by the issue of differentials and pressure from the Arab producers of the Gulf to obtain an accord on their increase. The central question, though, related to the $34 reference price. Saudi Arabia and its allies were clearly in favour of a cut to $30 per barrel.

The chief delegates of OPEC eventually reconvened in formal session in London on 6 March, though negotiations had been conducted continuously since mid-January. The common interest of producers looked imperilled in mid-February as, first, the British National Oil Corporation (BNOC) proposed to its customers a reduction in the top North Sea rate (in competition with the premium North African crudes) from $33.50 to $30.50 per barrel, and, then, a day later, Nigeria slashed its official selling rate from $35.50 to $30 in a bid to boost exports. Far from rising significantly there had been no recovery in demand for OPEC oil. On the contrary, destocking surged to a rate generally estimated at more than 4.5m. b/d during the first quarter of 1983, while members' output of oil and NGLs dropped to about 15.5m. b/d. The underlying desperation was, perhaps, best articulated by the Venezuelan Minister of Energy and Mines, who said on the third day of the conference: 'If we don't reach agreement this week we will meet in two months and be discussing $25 as a price'. The prospect of a general price collapse drew out reserves of endurance, as well as patience, from the delegates. The essential parts of the package finalized on 14 March were: a 15% cut in the reference price from $34 to $29 per barrel; a new production programme under a ceiling on collective output of 17.5m. b/d; and differentials on the bases set in March 1982.

Iran expressed strong reservations about the price cut, despite having previously given the biggest discounts to customers. It did so on principle and also, it seemed, as a ploy to secure a dispensation for acceptance by other members of a price for its own crudes below the OPEC structure. This was granted to take account of the higher insurance premiums and freight costs in respect of oil shipments from the Kharg Island terminal which had been the subject of periodic, if ineffective, Iraqi attacks in the continuing Gulf conflict. No limit was set but other members did not object to the announced $1.20 discount which more or less reflected the extra costs involved in shipping Iranian crude in March 1983.

The part of the agreement covering production caused the most trouble. Members appreciated from the outset the particular problems of Iran and Iraq—it was recognized that the latter could not fulfil its quota, but there was an understanding that Saudi Arabia and Kuwait would make up some of the difference. Three members caused particular difficulties as far as quotas were concerned. Saudi Arabia began by insisting on 6m. b/d for itself but, in the end, implicitly assented to produce no more than 5m. b/d without waiving its principle of refusing to participate in a production-sharing programme. The UAE held out to a late stage for 1.5m. b/d but ultimately agreed to an allocation of 1.1m. b/d. Venezuela, which demanded no less than 1.8m. b/d, settled in the end for 1.6725m. b/d. The quotas agreed, in millions of b/d, were as follows: Algeria 0.725, Ecuador 0.2, Gabon 0.15, Indonesia 1.3, Iran 2.4, Iraq 1.2, Kuwait 1.05, Libya 1.1, Nigeria 1.3, Qatar 0.3, UAE 1.1, Venezuela 1.6725, Saudi Arabia 5.0.

Where differentials were concerned, Nigeria posed one of the biggest problems confronting efforts to complete a satisfactory package, since it was politically impossible for the government of President Shagari, with an election looming, to revise upwards the price of Bonny Light in line with the $30.50 per barrel set by BNOC. The greatest danger to any new defence of a basic, albeit, lower price was a price-cutting war between Nigeria and the North Sea producers. The industry generally viewed the top Nigerian variety as being underpriced in comparison with its North Sea competitors. Algeria and Libya agreed to set the rate for their premium crudes at $30.50. In doing so they put themselves at a slight disadvantage. It was calculated that, if production limits were observed, each of the three would enjoy a fair share. In the mean time, the question of what constituted the right differential for premium grades and the Arabian Light reference price, in a constantly shifting market, remained unresolved.

OPEC's struggle to maintain stability

After the conclusion of their prices and production pact, the OPEC producers, the world's marginal suppliers of energy, not only had to face lower per-barrel revenues but also a depressed level of output at least until the summer of 1983 in order to maintain the value of their petroleum, the source of their livelihood.

Two months after the conclusion of the agreement there was optimism that the line could be held. Crucial, in this respect, was the fact that an official selling rate for North Sea oil compatible with OPEC's price structure was proposed by the BNOC and, after initial misgivings, accepted by the industry as a whole. Anything less than the $30 per barrel set for the Brent blend would have prompted retaliation from Nigeria and almost certainly set off a price-cutting war. The UK Government, with its ideological adherence to the principle of 'free-market forces', strenuously sought to avoid any impression that it had colluded with OPEC, but stressed its intention of doing nothing to destabilize market forces. Norway, as usual, aligned itself with Britain. The collaboration of Mexico, which had also been on the lower price tier, had previously been obtained by OPEC. Having emerged as the main single threat to the new price structure, the USSR raised its official selling rates closer to those of OPEC and trimmed back supplies after prices on the spot market rose in April 1983, as if finally alerted to the common danger facing all producers.

At the outset the new price structure together with the system of production controls looked fragile. By early summer, however, confidence had grown that the market was stabilizing and that the goal of balancing supply with demand could be achieved at the cost of short-term sacrifice. Iran and Libya had evidently overcome early resistance from customers to their new official price levels. There was a consensus that demand for OPEC oil would rise at least to between 18m. b/d and 20m. b/d in the last quarter from a level of only about 14.5m. b/d in the first quarter, depending on the rate of restocking and economic recovery. Thus, it was imperative that OPEC as a whole and its members individually should keep their nerve and discipline.

At first sight it was ironic that Britain, with exports of only about 600,000 b/d, should have assumed such a pivotal position in this crucial period. In fact, the importance attached to it, while essentially arising from the crucial relationship between North Sea and Nigerian prices, highlighted OPEC's loss of control over the world's oil market as a result of declining demand and competition from non-member producers.

After an initial period of uncertainty over OPEC's revised production-sharing agreement and doubts about its ability to maintain sufficient discipline, the market had strengthened considerably by the time that the Organization met for its next ministerial conference in Helsinki on 18 July. During the April–June (1983) quarter OPEC production of crude oil fell to about 16.7m. b/d as members made something like a concerted effort to discipline output and observe official prices. For that quarter Indonesia, Nigeria and the UAE exceeded their quotas by between 70,000 b/d and 100,000 b/d. However, there were no significant breaches of quota allocations as Saudi Arabia bore the brunt of slack demand during this period. Moreover, after Iran and Libya had withstood pressure from customers to concede discounts, price levels were successfully maintained.

With demand for OPEC oil clearly starting to grow it was hoped that economic recovery and an increase in the demand for oil might make it possible to raise the limit on output. As it was, however, OPEC output surged well above the ceiling to pass 19m. b/d, an average rate which was maintained until the end of the year. Indonesia was obviously in breach of its quota

of 1.3m. b/d with a rate of more than 1.4m. b/d during the second half of 1983. Iranian production probably ran at a rate 100,000 b/d or so above its 2.4m. b/d allocation. Kuwait also exceeded its quota of 1.05m. b/d with actual production of 1.2m. b/d or more. But, again, it was Saudi Arabia, the acknowledged 'swing producer' within OPEC (i.e. meeting any increase in demand for OPEC crude above the 17.5m. b/d ceiling or absorbing any drop below it), which was mainly responsible for the increase. At an estimated average of 5.87m. b/d its output during the July–December period was substantially higher than the 5m. b/d accorded it by other members of OPEC in the general understanding relating to the production-sharing programme of March 1983. This extra production would have accounted for about 60% of all OPEC output in excess of the 17.5m. b/d ceiling during the second half of 1983. Saudi Arabia had not, in fact, agreed to any limitation on its production, and at the end of the protracted London meeting in March 1983 it did no more than commit itself to being the Organization's 'swing producer'. The surge in its exports in the second half of 1983 coincided with the start of operations by NORBEC, a marketing company established to supplement the work of the state hydrocarbons corporation Petromin. When OPEC's market-monitoring committee called upon Saudi Arabia late in October 1983 to account for its high rate of output Riyadh's bland response was that the Kingdom could not perform its role as 'swing producer' if other members did not observe their quotas and price commitments. The Saudi statement also pointed to the oil being produced on behalf of Iraq (250,000 b/d from the Neutral Zone, shared with Kuwait, and 60,000 b/d from Saudi Arabia) to compensate it for the constraints on its exports imposed by the Iran–Iraq War, and to crude oil produced for storage rather than immediate sale so that, it was claimed, seasonal demand for natural gas could be met. There was some confusion, too, as to why Saudi Arabia was chartering a large number of supertankers and placing a considerable volume of crude in them. Initially, it was suggested that the oil was being stored because of the temporary shut-down of two offshore fields, Zuluf and Marjan, while they were being incorporated into the Kingdom's Master Gas System. Saudi Arabia sought to give the impression that the stockpile was not related to the possibility of a supply crisis resulting from the closure of the Strait of Hormuz or any other disruption of oil traffic. The cumulative total built up in floating storage by the end of 1983—just over 20m. barrels—was not sufficient to account for Saudi output over and above 5m. b/d.

The breakdown in OPEC discipline was seriously destabilizing the market again by the end of 1983 and when OPEC delegates met for a full ministerial conference in Geneva on 6 December the need to restore confidence in the market had become urgent.

The onus was on OPEC and the world was sceptical of its ability to defend the $29 per barrel reference price and the price structure relating to it. Even if there had been any scope for raising the ceiling the exercise would have been dangerous in the absence of an agreed mechanism for adjusting quotas and with the existence of conflicting quota claims. The UAE believed that it should have priority, and an increase in its allocation from 1.1m. b/d to 1.5m. b/d, if the ceiling was to be raised.

As early as July 1983 at the Helsinki meeting, Iran had given notice that it would demand a bigger quota at the Geneva conference and prior to it specified the increase being sought as 800,000 b/d in addition to the 2.4m. b/d accorded it under the London agreement of March 1983. Iraq, meanwhile, had voiced its claim for an increase from 1.2m. b/d to 1.8m. b/d. In any dispute over increased production the pleas of populous, debt-ridden Nigeria and Indonesia, two of the weakest links in the OPEC chain, could not be ignored. As it was, overproduction had pre-empted the possibility of lifting the ceiling and there was a strong argument for lowering it with percentage cuts in individual quotas. At the Geneva conference OPEC had little choice but to reaffirm the production ceiling and allocations agreed in London. Iran did press its claim for a bigger allocation at Saudi Arabia's expense, though not to the point of threatening a rupture. The Kingdom also came under fire from other members but Sheikh Ahmad Zaki Yamani, its Minister of Oil, did no more than promise privately that Saudi output would be restricted to a maximum of 5m. b/d without making it clear whether the pledge included oil produced on behalf of Iraq. Iran struck a discordant note by proposing that the $34 reference price should be restored because the $5 cut had not in any way stimulated demand but finally relented when other members agreed that a committee should be established to discuss the question.

OPEC and the world price structure looked very vulnerable to a further decline in prices on the spot market, and a chain reaction of price cuts by non-members eventually forcing Nigeria and perhaps others to give way. The United Kingdom again found itself in the pivotal position as it had in the spring of 1983 because of the close relationship between North Sea and North African crudes. The subsequent recommendation of the BNOC for unchanged prices in the first quarter of 1984, citing OPEC's production agreement as 'a sound basis for stability in the market', was couched in terms indicative of a general change of attitude on the part of the UK Government. It had watched the crisis early in 1983 with impassivity and little appreciation of the dangers involved. By the end of the year the implications for state revenue and the country's balance of payments were fully appreciated and reckoned to be more serious than any lapse in respect for free-market forces. At the same time the companies responsible for the greater part of production in the UK sector of the North Sea had come to appreciate that their interests lay in market stability and maintenance of the price structure. In the event BNOC obtained overwhelming acceptance for its proposal, with only two of its customers phasing out their contract options.

OPEC succeeded in pulling through the critical spring months without any serious price cutting, despite a fall in demand for members' crude. Output in the first quarter was estimated by the IEA to have averaged 17.8m. b/d. Saudi production, at about 5m. b/d, came more or less within the limit recognized by other OPEC members. Nigeria's production surged ahead to about 1.46m. b/d over the three months. Subsequently, output was reined in and Nigeria pledged not to seek a quota increase until the ministerial conference in July. The other main offender was Indonesia whose production averaged something like 1.5m. b/d. It, like Qatar, evidently resorted to giving some disguised discounts.

OPEC's collective output exceeded the 17.5m. b/d limit by a clear margin over the 12-month period following conclusion of the pact on production and prices but no precise figures were available. Indeed, the failure of member countries to report accurately made more difficult the job of the Organization's market monitoring committee, which was to supervise adherence to quotas. The IEA calculated average OPEC production from the beginning of April 1983 to the end of March 1984 at 18.1m. b/d (not including NGLs). That compared with an estimate of 17.67m. b/d for the production year 1982/83, when the average was depressed to a low point of less than 15.5m. b/d in the fourth quarter of the year (January–March). Members were not helped by the continued rundown of inventories, but early in 1984 severe winter weather in North America boosted demand. An unexpected bonus was the miners' strike in the United Kingdom which began in the spring of 1984, initially creating an extra demand for fuel oil of 200,000 b/d–300,000 b/d, and of as much as 600,000 b/d before the industrial dispute came to an end a year later. In the early part of 1984 there was also an unexplained fall in Soviet supplies. Rising tension in the Gulf also helped to sustain the market and to support prices in the early part of the year. The potential danger to oil traffic passing through the Strait of Hormuz had become apparent in the summer of 1983 when it became known that France was to provide Iraq with *Super Etendard* aircraft, capable of delivering the *Exocet* missiles already in its possession. These could be used to hit tankers loading at Kharg Island, Iran's main oil terminal, though it seemed they were not sufficiently effective to cause much damage there. In September 1983 Ayatollah Khomeini himself had said 'I warn oil states of the region, and the other countries which use oil in one way or the other, that the Government of Iran, exerting its utmost power, will oppose this aggression and is determined to block the Strait of Hormuz, thus obstructing the passage of a single drop of petroleum'. The danger became far more real as Iraq began to step up its attacks, with a fair measure of success, from February 1984 onwards, although Iran soon proved that it could maintain exports at something approaching its quota entitlement by offering the inducement of discounts and later by ferrying an increasing proportion of its output to Sirri Island in small tankers for onward shipment.

OPEC's production-monitoring scheme

The increase in oil demand, which became evident in the last quarter of 1983 following a decline totalling 20.5% from 1980 to 1984 in the industrialized world, as defined by membership of the OECD, was maintained in 1984 when it rose by 2.3% compared with the previous year, according to the calculations of the IEA. However, the rate of growth declined progressively during the year from 6.1% in the first quarter, to 3.4% in the second and third quarters and to 2.6% in the fourth. Disappointingly for OPEC, despite the general recovery of demand for oil throughout the OECD, it did not keep pace with economic growth in the industrialized world and the ratio of oil consumption to the Gross Domestic Product (GDP) of the OECD as a whole continued to fall as a result of further energy conservation and switching to coal, gas and electricity. Moreover, OPEC's share of the market in 1984 fell for the sixth year in succession. Its output of crude at about 17.2m. b/d, plus 1.3m. b/d of NGLs or condensates, was marginally up on 1983 but accounted for only 40.2% of estimated supplies to the world outside the Communist world compared with 41.2% in 1983, according to IEA estimates. Total non-OPEC supplies in 1984 rose from 26.1m. b/d to 27m. b/d.

Over 1984 as a whole OPEC's output of crude oil was just under 17.5m. b/d, marginally less than in the previous year, according to the most authoritative estimates. The IEA calculated OPEC output at 17.2m. b/d, or exactly the same rate as in 1983, not including condensates and NGLs, production of which, the agency calculated, had risen from 1.2m. b/d to 1.3m. b/d. The well-informed Petroleum Intelligence Weekly (PIW) put the OPEC rate for 1984 at 17.49m. b/d, including condensates, which would have amounted to 450,000 b/d–500,000 b/d. The Royal Dutch/Shell group figures gave a total for 1984 of 18.57m. b/d compared with 18.5m. b/d in 1983, including all condensates and NGLs.

In 1984 there were some significant changes in the national shares of total OPEC output. That of Saudi Arabia, including its 50% entitlement of almost exactly 200,000 b/d from the Neutral Zone shared with Kuwait, fell by about 8% to 4.64m. b/d, and Iran's by nearly 10% to 2.18m. b/d, according to PIW calculations. By contrast, Iraq's production rose by about 20% to about 1.2m. b/d, its full OPEC quota, as throughput via the pipeline to Ceyhan, the terminal on Turkey's south-east coast, rose to a capacity of 1m. b/d, with the remainder accounted for by domestic consumption and some 50,000 b/d of petroleum products transported by road to Aqaba, Jordan, for onward shipment. When the volume in excess of 300,000 b/d of 'war relief' crude produced on its behalf by Saudi Arabia and Kuwait (technically taking the latter above its quota) was taken into account, though, Iraq could be considered to have been the biggest violator of the prices and production pact. Nigeria was 100,000 b/d above its 1.3m. b/d allocation. Proportionately, Qatar was the biggest offender, with average output for the year running at no less than 400,000 b/d compared with a quota of 300,000 b/d. At about 250,000 b/d, Ecuador was 25% above its 200,000 b/d quota.

Rising consumption, which was evident in the winter of 1983/84 led OPEC to hope that it might be possible to raise the ceiling on output to as much as 19m. b/d for the last quarter of the year. The expectation was that, by then, demand for OPEC crude might amount to as much as 20m. b/d depending on the extent to which stocks were drawn down. In the mean time OPEC struggled, for the third summer in succession, to maintain its price structure and the related, all-important credibility in terms of the observance of production and pricing discipline. In the spring of 1984 the market had revived to the extent that spot rates for Brent blend, the North Sea reference crude, marginally exceeded its official selling rate of $30 per barrel at the end of April. It was strengthened by fears of serious disruption of supplies from the Gulf resulting from a continuation of Iraq's attacks on tankers lifting oil at Iran's Kharg Island terminal and from the possibility of serious Iranian retaliation following attacks on Kuwaiti and Saudi vessels in May.

International anxiety reached its highest point in mid-May, when the Saudi super-tanker *Yanbu Pride* was set ablaze by rocket fire from an Iranian aircraft only 30 miles from the Saudi coast. That was enough to send the price of Brent, now established as the all-important market indicator, soaring to $30.70 per barrel on the spot market. Orders for Saudi oil pumped through the Trans-Arabian pipeline (Tapline) rose from less than one-third of its 1.85m. b/d capacity, prior to the *Yanbu Pride* incident, to 1.5m. b/d in June. Iran had already threatened to prevent oil supplies leaving the Gulf via the Strait of Hormuz, through which a little over 20% (7m. b/d–8m. b/d) of supplies required by the non-Communist world were passing, if Iraqi military action prevented its own oil export industry from operating.

An increase in the use of the Tapline facility apart, it was reckoned that, in the event of the termination of supplies from the Gulf, other OPEC members would be able to provide 3.7m. b/d from idle capacity, while more than 500,000 b/d might be available from non-OPEC producers. In theory that would leave a shortfall in supply of up to 3m. b/d. The situation was potentially serious for Arab producers of the Gulf, as well as consumers, in view of the fact that a 2.5m. b/d shortfall over a period of a few months in 1970 sent spot rates soaring and led to the eventual doubling of official selling rates by the end of 1980 to the high point from which the subsequent deterioration in OPEC's fortunes began.

In the summer of 1984 there was no panic comparable to that experienced in 1979 and the concern over supplies proved to be short-lived. On the one hand, it was realized that Iran probably had not the capability to block the Strait of Hormuz by military means for more than a very brief period, if at all. Moreover, stocks were still at a high level, despite a steady rundown of company inventories since mid-1982. The stated readiness of the Reagan Administration to release oil from the US Strategic Petroleum Reserve of non-commercial stocks, then accounting for 80% or 400m. barrels, helped suppress any adverse speculation. In addition, there was the reassurance of the 55m.–60m. barrels which had been placed in floating storage by Saudi Arabia during the previous summer. Saudi Arabia had denied that the action was related to the possibility of the Strait of Hormuz being closed, but in the late summer of 1983 it did much to weaken the market, though little of the stored oil was released on to the market.

The oil market concluded that the situation was not as serious as first feared. The average spot rate for Brent fell below the official selling price in the last week of May. Having suffered a temporary reduction in oil liftings from Kharg Island, Iran moved rapidly to rectify the situation, offering discounts in the range of $2.50–$3.00 per barrel below the preferential rate relative to other Gulf crudes accorded it under the production and prices pact concluded by OPEC in March 1983. Exports quickly recovered to a level of 2.1m. b/d–2.2m. b/d, within its quota, with about another 700,000 b/d being used for domestic refining. It became evident that Qatar was far more flagrantly flouting the pact as its output rose above 400,000 b/d, stimulated by the offer of a discount of $1 or so below official selling prices.

A far more serious threat to the structure of the OPEC prices and production programme came from Nigeria, as it pressed for a rise in its quota to ease its grave financial and foreign exchange problems. There was the danger that Nigeria might go its own way, cutting its prices as it did in February 1983, which precipitated the OPEC crisis meeting in the following month and the traumatic $5 per barrel price reduction across the board. That was the main issue facing OPEC's 11–12 July ordinary mid-summer ministerial conference in Vienna, following a month which saw a steady decline in prices on the spot market. The unsatisfactory compromise reached at the conference was that Nigeria should be allowed an extra 100,000 b/d of output for August and 150,000 b/d for September with Saudi Arabia reducing its share to accommodate the increment. Yet, even at this stage there was optimism that there would be an appreciable rise in demand for OPEC oil in the latter half of the year.

OPEC's hopes were confounded. With available supplies greatly exceeding demand and, for the most part, selling at a discount on official prices, the market continued to sag. Saudi oil output surged to 5.5m. b/d in July and the OPEC total to over 18m. b/d. Largely as a result of these two factors the spot rate for Brent plummeted to $26.85–$26.95 at the end of the month. The crisis was such that Mr Alick Buchanan-Smith, British Minister of State for Energy, took the unprecedented step—given the UK's *laissez-faire* policy towards the oil industry—of writing to the eight largest operators in the North Sea urging them not to bring pressure on the BNOC to cut prices over the coming weeks. This, and subsequent clarification that Saudi output had been running at no more than 4.5m. b/d and that OPEC's output as a whole was more or less within its ceiling, did much to stabilize the market for a while.

It was becoming apparent that the growth in overall demand was slowing down, and OPEC crude output fell below 17m. b/d, with Saudi Arabia fulfilling its role as the 'swing producer', with its production falling below 4m. b/d, so that it seemed in September as if the market might be gaining some equilibrium. But with non-OPEC sources of supply progressively increasing, Nigeria raising its rate to 1.6m. b/d in October, and only a modest build-up of inventories, spot-market realizations began to sag again.

Even so, it was without any warning that OPEC found itself faced with a full-scale crisis in October, the market being thrown into panic with the news that Norway had offered its customers secret discounts on a month-by-month basis amounting to $1.35 per barrel off its Statjford crude for October and $1.05 for November. Already under some pressure from some customers (rather than the big suppliers) BNOC followed suit, cutting the rate for its Brent blend to $28.65 per barrel. Nigeria reacted predictably, leap-frogging the North Sea producers with a cut of $2 per barrel on its lighter varieties of crude and setting a price for Bonny Light (with which, in the spring of 1983, BNOC had managed to align Brent), to $28 per barrel, thereby threatening a vicious downward price spiral. Brent plummeted towards $26 per barrel on the spot market.

OPEC had no choice but to resist the downward trend set in motion by the North Sea producers and its recalcitrant member, Nigeria—any cut in per barrel revenues was not going to be offset by higher demand in the foreseeable future. Its response in consultations held in Geneva between six ministers on 22 October and the subsequent full extraordinary ministerial conference held from 29 to 31 October, was impressive. With remarkable speed, given the contortions which had been involved in apportioning output allocations in 1982 and 1983, it was decided to lower the ceiling on collective production to 16m. b/d (from the 17.5m. b/d set in spring 1982), and a new system of quotas was agreed upon. The limit was intended to be a temporary one, of unspecified duration, which would be lifted when the supply situation tightened up and spot-market prices came into line with official selling rates. Proportionately, Kuwait (14.3%), the UAE (13.6%), Saudi Arabia (an implied 12.9%, tacitly accepting the anticipated shortfall from Nigeria and a proportion of the cuts for Venezuela, Ecuador and Indonesia) and Libya (10.0%) agreed to the largest reductions in their output. In conformity with its traditional policy of refusing to allow its own output policy to be determined within the context of OPEC, Saudi Arabia made no formal commitment. The understanding was that it would not allow its rate to pass 4.353m. b/d, compared with 5m. b/d under the March 1983 pact. Nigeria's quota was left unchanged at 1.3m. b/d but it made it clear that it considered its entitlement to be no less than the 1.45m. b/d it was granted in September, and refused to rescind its $2 per barrel price cut bringing its prices back into line with those of other members. The Saudi and Kuwaiti chief delegates were confident that spot-market rates would come back into line with official selling rates before the end of the year and persuade Nigeria to conform. The new quotas (in millions of b/d, with the previous quotas in brackets) were as follows: Algeria 0.663 (0.725); Ecuador 0.183 (0.200); Gabon 0.137 (0.150); Indonesia 1.189 (1.300); Iran 2.300 (2.400); Iraq 1.200 (1.200); Kuwait 0.900 (1.050); Libya 0.990 (1.100); Nigeria 1.300 (1.300); Qatar 0.280 (0.300); Saudi Arabia 4.353 (5.000); UAE 0.950 (1.100); Venezuela 1.555 (1.675); total 16.0 (17.5).

No progress was made on the increasingly critical issue of OPEC's price differentials. By the late summer of 1984 it had become apparent that the defence of OPEC's crumbling price structure required a radical revision. Since they were last adjusted early in 1983, perhaps insufficiently for a system which had basically remained intact since 1979, rates had fallen glaringly out of line with market realities. In particular, the problem of a wide disparity between the prices of lighter crudes and those of the cheaper, heavier grades had become much too wide. This had been caused by the expansion of up-grading capacity in refineries world-wide to convert high gravity, sulphurous oil into premium products. The difficulties of the light producers were compounded by Saudi Arabia's decision to change the proportions of its export contract 'mix' from a blend of 20% Arabian Light, 20% Arabian Heavy and 60% Arabian Light, to 35%, 25% and 40% respectively. In the long term the switch was made in order to gear Saudi output to the level of its reserves, but the immediate purpose seemed, to producers dependent on lighter varieties, to be to ensure demand for the Kingdom's crude because it effectively lowered the price of the Kingdom's average barrel in the composite package from $28.08 to $27.55.

OPEC's October conference did no more than appoint a three-man committee, comprising a chairman, Sheikh Yamani of Saudi Arabia, and the chief delegates of the UAE and Libya, to deal with the problem of differentials. The consensus in the oil industry was that the gap between heavy and light crudes should be closed by no less than $1.50 per barrel to bring a measure of greater stability to the market. The conference which was held in Geneva in two sessions in December only marginally closed the gap of $4.50 between the $26 per barrel official selling price for Arabian Heavy and the $30.50 charged, notionally, for the premium varieties of Algeria and Libya. Algeria and Nigeria pressed for a reduction in the differential of as much as $2, to be achieved mainly by an increase in the price of the heavy crudes. Saudi Arabia adamantly opposed anything but a small increase in their rates and there was general reluctance in principle and some fierce opposition in practice to paring back the $29 per barrel price set in March 1983 for the Arabian Light reference or 'marker' crude, because such a cut would constitute a reduction in the price conceded in the face of market pressures. The interim decision, from which Algeria and Nigeria dissociated themselves, was for a 50 cents increase in the price of Arabian Heavy, and a 25 cents increase for Arabian Medium, with a reduction of 25 cents for the ultra-light Gulf crudes. This, in effect, was a 75 cents reduction in the differential, setting Abu Dhabi's Murban crude, the Gulf's top variety, at $29.31 per barrel. It left the premium North African grades of Algeria and Libya theoretically where they were before, while Nigeria, in practice, showed no sign of realigning its rates with the rest of OPEC. The price of an average barrel in Saudi Arabia's export package rose by 22 cents.

In the event a much more coherent system was evolved at the extraordinary ministerial conference held in Geneva from 28–30 January 1985. Ten members in all overcame the psychological barrier relating to Arabian Light (which had been OPEC's reference crude since 1973) by bringing its price down by $1 to $28 per barrel. The differential *vis-à-vis* the ultra light Gulf crudes was reduced to a maximum of 15 cents for Murban and Arabian Medium was switched back to its old level of $27.40 per barrel. It was agreed that Nigeria, because of its special problems in relation to the North Sea and its dire financial state, could keep Bonny Light at $28.65, the price which BNOC was still paying to its suppliers while suffering mounting losses in its sales of participation crude to third parties. It was calculated that the reduction in the average weighted OPEC price was 29 cents per barrel but that of the Saudi Arabian 'mix' was cut by 47 cents to $27.33.

Algeria, Libya and Iran dissociated themselves from the agreement, though this did not make much difference to its potential ability to stabilize the market. The greater part of Algeria's exports were in the form of refined products sold at spot-market-related prices. A large proportion of sales by Libya were accounted for by barter deals involving discounts which it was offering more directly to customers, anyway, in its efforts to maintain shipments and fulfil its quota. The fact that the official selling price of Algeria's Sahara blend remained at $30.50 per barrel and Libya's Brega blend at $30.40 was, therefore, somewhat notional. Despite its opposition to the majority agreement, however, Iran quickly adjusted its prices in line with those of the other producers. It set them for liftings from Sirri Island, to which it was transporting an increasing volume of oil

for onward transhipment, owing to buyers' inhibitions about lifting from the more vulnerable terminal at Kharg Island.

Another OPEC Monitoring Scheme

OPEC had, meanwhile, taken a major step towards enforcing more effectively the pact on production, pricing and sales. It was agreed at the 19–21 December 1984 conference session to establish a supervisory body, called the Ministerial Executive Council (MEC), under the chairmanship of Sheikh Yamani with the chief delegates of Venezuela, Nigeria, Indonesia and the UAE as the other participants. The far-reaching plan involved acquiescence by the 13 member states in an intrusion into their affairs and sovereignty unprecedented in the history of international organizations. The resolution empowered the council to employ independent auditors whom member states agreed to allow 'to check on member countries' petroleum sales, tanker nominations, shipments, pricing, quantities etc.' and 'to check the books, invoices, or any other documents that are deemed necessary by the firm in the fulfilment of its tasks'. Moreover, the brief of the council covered petroleum products and condensates as well as oil. Petroleum sales were also defined as covering barter deals, processing agreements, inter-governmental agreements, exchange and direct sales, equity oil, and all marketing arrangements—under most of which oil was disposed of at below official selling rates. The Dutch firm of auditors, KHG-Klynveld-Kraayenhof, was appointed before the end of January 1985. Although its role had been subsumed, OPEC's Market-Monitoring Committee continued.

In the second half of 1984 OPEC's output responded, despite varying degrees of indiscipline by nearly all members, to the slow-down in the short-lived growth in world demand and an actual decline in the preceding three months. The IEA calculated that collective production ran at 16.7m. b/d during the July–December period, well below the old ceiling. Not only was OPEC faced with increased supplies and greater price responsiveness to market pressures from its competitors but also by a large run-down of inventories in anticipation of cuts in official selling rates by the Organization. During the first quarter of 1985, with only a minimal build-up of 100,000 b/d by governments, the industrial stocks in the OECD area fell by no less than 2m. b/d.

In February 1985 the market strengthened, as a result of lower OPEC output and a measure of confidence arising from the revised differentials system and the new production-policing measures. Important short-term factors were a period of freezing weather in North America and Europe, together with a sudden shortfall in the availability of Soviet crude. The end of the UK miners' strike, however, removed 400,000 b/d–500,000 b/d in demand and, with a slump in demand forecast for the spring, OPEC needed support from other producers in its battle to hold the line. At the Geneva meeting in December 1984, Malaysia, Brunei and Egypt had encouragingly agreed to token cuts to show solidarity with OPEC, while Mexico repeated its commitment not to increase exports. On the critical North Sea front, however, hopes that the United Kingdom would try to hold Brent at $28.65 per barrel, with the aim of maintaining revenue and the value of sterling, were soon dashed.

In mid-March the British Government announced its decision to phase out the state-owned BNOC by July. The BNOC had, hitherto, purchased 51% of output from the UK sector and disposed of the critical volume (amounting to 700,000 b/d–800,000 b/d by 1985) which was not bought back by the larger companies with integrated operations and downstream (refining and marketing) interests. The implied threat of the abandonment of any form of structured-term pricing was soon realized as BNOC informed sellers that it would relate its prices to the spot market during its three-month period of phasing out. The announcement further depressed the market, which fell sharply at the end of April.

OPEC's prices and production discipline was still slack. Output in the first quarter of 1985 was reckoned by the IEA to have averaged 16.2m. b/d, just above the ceiling, having risen from 15.3m. b/d in January to 16.4m. b/d in February and fallen to 16.2m. b/d in March. There was evidence, though, that it was edging towards 16.5m. b/d by the end of April. Nigeria had not responded to the North Sea price cuts but its output, boosted by a series of new barter deals, was reckoned to be running at

1.7m. b/d. Four other members—Libya, Indonesia, the UAE and Ecuador—were exceeding their quotas, collectively by 400,000 b/d–450,000 b/d. Only the production below quota in Saudi Arabia and Iran was keeping production in check. Co-operation with the MEC had been reasonable. Nigeria refused access to the auditors until April, while Algeria refused to let them examine its production of condensates. The Council had made much slower progress than had been hoped: it was close to full monitoring of OPEC output, yet far from exposing the scale of price discounting.

OPEC was faced with the harsh fact that the $5 per barrel price cut of March 1983 had not stimulated any increase in demand for its members' own oil. The growth in consumption world-wide, such as it had been, had only benefited non-members whose own investment in exploration and development had been given a big boost by the scale of the second 1979–81 price escalation. Conservation and the substitution of oil by other sources of energy had established themselves, for the foreseeable future, as enduring features of the economic life of the industrialized world. The extent of the damage was reflected in the fall in OPEC output from a high point of over 31m. b/d in 1979 to about 18.5m. b/d (including NGLs) in 1984, a drop of 40%. In the same period OPEC's share of the market fell from 60% to 40%. New sources of energy emerged over the five years, contributing to the market the equivalent of about 20m. b/d of oil half of which was in the form of non-OPEC petroleum supplies.

In terms of financial resources, Saudi Arabia was best equipped to deal with the crisis. Kuwait, with its large investment income, was also well placed. The UAE and Qatar, though not without some painful belt-tightening, also looked capable of balancing budgets and payments. Overall, the Gulf producers, including Iran and Iraq with their export potential restricted by the war between them, had borne the brunt of the cuts in output over the years, with only 50% of capacity being utilized in 1985 compared with 65% of other members'. As far as the poorer members were concerned, though, the four producers of the area hitherto regarded as perpetually in surplus—Saudi Arabia, Kuwait, the UAE and Qatar—still enjoyed too great a share of the much-diminished cake, especially Saudi Arabia, with an effective quota over three times that conceded to Nigeria which had a population perhaps 15 times as large. This remained a cause of underlying tension. So, too, did the ideological commitment of Algeria and Iran to maintaining, officially, the highest possible price whatever they or other members did in practice (i.e. discounting).

Yet it was understood that no one would benefit by boosting oil exports by lowering prices, since the loss of per barrel revenues would generally cancel out any gain in sales volume and could risk a free-fall or even a collapse of prices. For OPEC, the main compensation had been the strength of the US dollar, the currency in which all oil prices are set. Owing to the remorseless rise in the value of the dollar from the end of 1982 to the beginning of 1985, western European countries, on average, were paying 13% more for their oil in local currency terms, with a roughly similar increase for Japan. At the same time, however, the appreciation of the dollar, alone, could have been responsible for reducing demand by 2m. b/d.

During the summer of 1985 it became increasingly clear that, on the one hand, OPEC would not be able to raise the 16m. b/d production ceiling, and that, on the other, several members could not live comfortably with their quotas under the pact agreed in 1984. The breakdown of even the pretence to a firm commitment to production discipline was brought about by Iraq's determination not to observe any restrictions on its oil exports, and by growing Saudi impatience over production quota violations by other members and the fall in its output level as a result of its strict adherence to official selling rates. (By mid-1985 it was the only member of OPEC respecting them fully.)

The erosion of the official price structure worsened despite the efforts of the MEC to eliminate abuses. When the MEC met in Ta'if, Saudi Arabia, in early June 1985, it was apparent that the auditors, Klynveld-Kraayenhof, were encountering obstacles from nearly all member states. At this point, however, respect for the ceiling was not the main problem. In the first half of 1985 collective OPEC output had been slightly above the ceiling, at 16.2m. b/d but in the second had dropped to around 15m. b/d, when Saudi Arabia's production averaged just under 3m.

b/d, compared with the maximum of 4.35m. b/d conceded under the revised 1984 production and prices pact. It had become clear that control of production was not, in itself, enough to strengthen the market, and drastic action on the issue of price was imperative. So-called 'net-back' deals, whereby prices for crude oil are related to current realizations for petroleum products on a spot-market basis, less agreed transportation and refining costs, assumed greater significance during 1985, having the effect of depressing prices further by locking them into a downward spiral of spot rates for products.

When OPEC met again in Vienna from 5–7 July, spot prices had fallen to a level $2–$3 per barrel below official selling rates, as output continued to stagnate. The need to restore a measure of credibility to official OPEC rates was more urgent than ever, and this meant resisting the drift towards market prices. Kuwait suggested that the ceiling should be adjusted on a seasonal basis, with a 7% reduction for the third quarter and a 7% increase for the fourth. For various reasons, five members opposed the Kuwaiti plan. In particular, Iraq gave notice that it not only wanted a bigger allocation but intended to pump to the full 500,000-b/d capacity of its new export outlet across Saudi Arabia via the new pipeline link which was scheduled for completion in August 1985. For the rest of OPEC and the oil market as a whole an important factor was the assertion by Saudi Arabia that it no longer considered itself to be the 'swing producer', and that it regarded the 4.35m. b/d conceded to it by the other members of OPEC, under the production-sharing pact of October 1984, as a 'fixed quota'.

At a subsequent consultative meeting in Vienna OPEC members agreed that they should cease direct discounting and phase out more involved price-cutting methods such as 'net-back' arrangements and counter-trade deals. The supervisory MEC was charged with contacting the governments of member states with a view to opening discussions on how this could be achieved.

At the next of OPEC's two annual ordinary conferences, in Geneva from 22–25 July, the majority of members agreed to a drop of 50 cents in the price of heavy Gulf crudes and to one of 20 cents in the prices of medium varieties, thus widening the differential between the former and ultra-light, North African crudes from $2.40 to $3 per barrel. The change reduced the weighted average official price for all OPEC crudes from $27.96 to $27.82 per barrel. Predictably, Algeria, Iran and Libya dissociated themselves from the majority decision, as they had done in the previous January, when a majority of 10 agreed to a lowering of the price for Arabian Light, then the essential reference for all other crudes, from $29 to $28 per barrel. It was doubtful whether the adjustment in price differentials would appreciably affect liftings of Saudi oil in the absence of a (totally unexpected) surge in demand. The triple alliance of Algeria, Iran and Libya, although they were dogged in their refusal to countenance any price cuts, were no respecters of the official rates. At this point, 70%–75% of OPEC exports were reckoned to be selling at rates conforming to the official structure but abuses were rapidly becoming more widespread.

Saudi Arabia's patience, meanwhile, was exhausted. The Kingdom's average output during the second quarter of 1985, including 50% of production from the Neutral Zone with Kuwait, ran at an average rate of something less than 3m. b/d, rather than the 3.8m. b/d that it could have expected on a pro rata basis under the quota system; and in May the rate of output fell to its lowest level for 20 years. The level of production officially regarded as necessary to cover the requirements of the 1984/85 budget was 3.85m. b/d, or the equivalent of $55,400m. at an average price of $27–$28 per barrel. By the time of the July 1985 meeting of OPEC, Saudi oil production was little more than 2m. b/d and, taking into account domestic consumption of about 800,000 b/d, sufficient to generate foreign exchange earnings from oil of only $11,000m.–$12,000m. As it was, the Saudi Government's revenue had fallen from a peak of $108,800m. in 1981/82 to $47,400m. in 1984/85, and it was becoming alarmed at the decline in economic activity, which was still very heavily dependent on state spending. The decision had almost certainly been made that the time had come for Saudi Arabia to cease making sacrifices on behalf of the other members of OPEC.

Saudi Arabia's decision to renounce the role of 'swing producer' and its determination to enjoy the maximum entitlement of

4.35m. b/d allowed it under the OPEC output sharing agreement became fully apparent in September. Saudi Arabia abandoned its previously strict adherence to official selling prices with three deals on a net-back basis with Exxon, Texaco and Mobil, involving 800,000 b/d. Almost simultaneously the Kingdom persuaded the United Kingdom to accept payment for 132 military aircraft, from early 1986 onwards, in the form of crude oil, following the precedent set in the summer of 1984 with Boeing and Rolls-Royce in respect of 747 'Jumbo' jets wanted by the Saudi Ministry of Defence. The far more significant development in Saudi policy, the reversion to net-back deals, remained officially unacknowledged. King Fahd stressed the Kingdom's continued belief in the need for discipline among OPEC members and for the observance of common accords. Nevertheless, he continued, the principle of free trade was crucial, and 'nobody should blame anyone else for breaking the rules in pursuit of his own interests if he believes he is compelled to do so'.

Saudi Arabia's categorical insistence on its full portion of OPEC's diminishing share of the oil market was, in itself, enough to ensure the failure of the next OPEC meeting, in Vienna, on 3–4 October, which, it was hoped, would agree upon a revised system of quotas satisfying those members claiming larger allocations. It was clear that increases would have to be at Saudi Arabia's expense. As it was, the ministerial conference had no choice but to reaffirm the ceiling on collective output of 16m. b/d, with the economic experts' optimum estimate of demand for OPEC crude amounting to only 15.6m. b/d, despite the onset of winter. The meeting foreshadowed the abandonment of any real effort to control production, despite the fact that discipline over output had become imperative if prices were to be maintained. Quota increments were requested by Ecuador, Iraq, Qatar and Gabon. Iran responded to the Iraqi demand by pledging to produce two barrels for each one produced by its enemy. The UAE warned that it, also, wanted a bigger quota. The issue was deferred until the next ordinary conference, which was scheduled for the end of 1985. The inescapable, though unvoiced conclusion, was that it was impossible to agree on any distribution of quotas under such a low ceiling. At this point, Sheikh Yamani spoke of the need for serious discussions with non-member producers if a collapse of the market was to be avoided.

In the event, prices held up surprisingly well until the end of November, when Arabian Light, at $27.95 per barrel, was close to its official selling rate of $28 and premium North African crudes were being quoted at over $30 per barrel. One reason for this short-lived resilience was seasonal demand and a build-up of stocks, which rose at a rate of 500,000 b/d during the fourth quarter of 1985 in the industrialized countries belonging to the OECD. Secondly, non-OPEC supplies did not rise. A third factor was the intensified campaign by Iraq to blockade Iran's oil exports, which was signalled by the low-level air raid on the Kharg Island oil terminal on 15 August, the first such attack since June 1984.

Analysts had been puzzled by Iraq's apparent unwillingness to make telling raids on the prime economic target and its concentration instead on the tankers shuttling oil to Sirri Island. It was not clear whether this restraint arose from subtle military or logistical factors, or from the persuasions of Iraq's major aid donors in the Gulf area, Saudi Arabia and Kuwait, which were anxious to prevent an escalation of the conflict which might involve them. The raid on Kharg Island temporarily reduced output from the terminal to only about one-half of the maximum export level of 1.6m. b/d, which was possible under Iran's 2.3m. b/d production quota. An increased number of Iraqi attacks from the air during the following months, aimed mainly at oil tanker traffic rather than the Kharg Island terminal, failed to have such a disruptive effect. The intensified campaign temporarily stabilized the spot market and forced Iran to consider various projects for reducing its dependence on Kharg Island. In practice, Iraq's failure to press home a potentially decisive advantage and Iran's resilience, enabled the latter to maintain the level of its exports, giving an output in the final quarter of the year of about 18.3m. b/d.

During the October–December quarter, OPEC output averaged rather more than 17.5m. b/d, far in excess of the optimum demand which had been estimated by the Organization's experts prior to the Vienna meeting in October. Saudi Arabia fulfilled

its quota as progressively it offered all its customers oil priced on a net-back basis. With the commissioning of its new pipeline facility Iraq was able to achieve a production rate of about 1.7m. b/d. Nigeria, whose output rose from 1.3m. b/d to 1.7m. b/d, was responsible for most of the remainder of the rise in collective output. Demand was greater than OPEC's experts had forecast but actual supplies were in excess of requirements. According to a subsequent estimate by the IEA, the surplus during the final quarter of 1985 was about 1m. b/d. Moreover, by the end of the year the surge in Gulf production had led to a substantial increase in stocks afloat which had yet to reach the market.

OPEC'S 'fair' market share policy

OPEC met again in Geneva on 7 December in a mood of growing desperation. Early in November, Sheikh Yamani had warned of the possibility of a 'price war', yet the decision of the Organization at the three-day meeting, 'to secure and defend a fair share of the world oil market', came as a surprise, and had enormous implications for prices. The 16m. b/d ceiling remained notionally in force and so, too, did official selling rates. In practice, the majority had abandoned them both in preference for a strategy aimed at forcing other producers to collaborate with OPEC in maintaining prices and to concede to them a part of their market share.

By the end of January 1986 the price of the North Sea Brent blend had fallen to $18.80 per barrel on the spot market. In the period from November 1985 to March 1986, prices on the spot market for widely traded crudes plummeted by between 60% and 75%, to their lowest level, in real terms, since 1973. Iran, Algeria and Libya had publicly dissociated themselves from the new policy, urging, instead, a reduction in OPEC output, in order to restore prices to former levels. The strategy being pursued by the majority, albeit with misgivings in some quarters, was very much the invention of Saudi Arabia, Kuwait and the UAE—three states with financial reserves large enough to cushion them against the effects of a period of drastically reduced per-barrel revenues. Others had no such safety net.

Nine days of arduous debate at the ministerial conference held in Geneva from 16–24 March failed to produce an agreement on what the level of OPEC production should be and how it should be shared. Iran, Algeria and Libya demanded a cut in production to 14m. b/d for the second quarter of 1986, but Saudi Arabia insisted that any such reduction would be contrary to the policy of regaining market share, and that there would be no possibility of members observing such a ceiling if they were unable to respect one of 16m. b/d or to agree on how to distribute output under the higher limit. The only agreement to be reached was with a group of non-member producers (Mexico, Egypt, Oman, Malaysia and Angola), who signed a memorandum of understanding on co-operation and committed themselves, in principle, to curbing their own output, with the implicit proviso that OPEC first establish a workable system of quotas.

The conference was adjourned and reconvened in Geneva on 15 April. After several days of tense discussion, the deadlock remained unbroken, but a clear majority of 10 had emerged in favour of maintaining the strategy of recovering a 'fair' market share. They agreed that an OPEC production rate of 16.3m. b/d in the third quarter of 1986 and 17.3m. b/d in the fourth, giving an average of 16.7m. b/d for 1986 as a whole, would be compatible with the aim of restoring market stability. Adamant that the prime objective should be the restoration of prices to $28 per barrel by the end of the year, Iran, Algeria and Libya dissociated themselves from the majority view, declaring that OPEC output should be limited to 14m. b/d, 14.5m. b/d and 16.8m. b/d for the second, third and fourth quarters, respectively.

There were practical reasons why these three countries should propose a policy of production restraint. Despite its promise to produce two barrels of oil for every extra Iraqi barrel, the intensification of Iraqi attacks on Iranian oil installations and on tanker traffic during the spring prevented Iran from producing much more than its quota allowed. Algeria was committed to respecting its quota, and Libya, meanwhile, looked as if it would face some marketing difficulties after the withdrawal of the five US companies (Occidental, Continental, Amerada Hess, Marathon and W. R. Grace) involved in exploration and production operations there, following the USA's identification of Libya as a promoter of international terrorism and its punitive air raids on Tripoli and Benghazi in April.

The critical question of quotas remained unresolved, and was deferred to the next ordinary ministerial conference in July. Following the marathon Geneva conference sessions, OPEC showed no sign of asserting any discipline. Collective OPEC output rose to about 17.5m. b/d in April, to about 18m. b/d in May and to more than 19m. b/d in the first two weeks of June, with Iran and Libya registering substantial increases in their production. So, too, did Saudi Arabia, which offered customers discounts ranging from 50 cents to $1.10 per barrel in order to maintain the level of liftings. Other producers, who had exceeded their quotas under the defunct 16m. b/d ceiling, continued to produce at these levels.

Saudi Arabia, Kuwait and the UAE seemed to want to inflict as much damage as possible on high-cost producers, in a bid to bring about the collaboration of the United Kingdom and Norway in OPEC's market-stabilization policy. By mid-1986, after six months of its application, they could derive some satisfaction from the fact that the strategy had had some tangible effect. Firstly, it was calculated that 800,000 b/d–900,000 b/d of capacity, mainly in the USA and Canada, had been closed down as a result of lower prices. Secondly, apart from the willingness, in principle, of five non-member exporters to co-operate with OPEC, the new Labour government in Norway, alarmed by the fall in state revenue and confronted by an economic crisis, suggested that it might be prepared to restrict the growth in the country's output provided that OPEC achieved a realistic system of production control. The British Government, however, remained dogged in its refusal to contemplate any intervention. Also, though at a considerable cost in pricing terms, OPEC had recovered some of its market share. According to the estimates of the IEA, OPEC's output of crude in the first half of 1986 was about 17.3m. b/d, a rise, which an increase in consumption of nearly 3% in the industrialized world, represented by members of the OECD, during the same period, helped to accommodate.

On 25 June OPEC oil ministers met on the Yugoslavian island of Brioni in another attempt to agree upon production levels and quotas. No progress was made towards agreement on a new quota system, although there was general agreement that the free-for-all should end. The demands of individual states totalled 20m.–21m. b/d, compared with IEA forecasts of demand for OPEC oil of 17.7m. b/d and 18.4m. b/d in the third and fourth quarters, respectively. Iran, Algeria and Libya continued to insist that the median price should be raised to $28 per barrel (OPEC's ultimate aim, officially) as soon as possible. It was recognised that the big surplus of supply overhanging the market, which had resulted from the June surge in OPEC production (19m. b/d—nearly 2m. b/d more than actual demand), would have an immediate, depressive effect on prices. Within a fortnight they had plummeted below $10 per barrel, the Brent blend falling to a nadir of $8.60. Early in July, Saudi Arabia's output soared to 5.7m. b/d, as it built up stocks in floating storage, in a move seemingly aimed at asserting more fully the Kingdom's influence over the market and OPEC, and collective production remained in excess of 18.5m. b/d well into July.

The reintroduction of quotas

The next OPEC meeting in Geneva on 28 July proved to be a turning point. It began with further talk about voluntary production cut-backs. By the fifth day of the conference the deadlock with Iraq, inevitably, proved to be an obstacle, with its refusal to join any production pact unless it was given parity with Iran. The impasse was surprisingly broken by Gholamreza Aqazadeh, Iran's Minister of Oil. He secretly proposed to Sheikh Ahmad Zaki Yamani, Saudi Arabia's Minister of Oil, that all members should return to the old quota system, under a ceiling of 16m. b/d (which had been determined in October 1984, and which had remained in force until the end of 1985), except for Iraq, which would be free to go its own way. In effect, the proposal set a limit for the 12 members, excluding Iraq, of 14.8m. b/d. Opposition from the UAE and Ecuador, which both demanded a larger share, had still to be overcome. Kuwait insisted that any evidence of quota violations by even one member would release the others from any obligation. As commitments had already been made to buyers, the proposal, if

approved, could not take effect until September. Moreover, at the insistence of Saudi Arabia, Kuwait, the UAE and Ecuador, the resolution adopted on 5 August stressed that 'this agreement is temporary and does not constitute a basis for any fair distribution of national quotas in any future negotiations thereon nor does it bear any prejudice on OPEC's appropriate and rightful production'. This qualification was enough to ensure that the next conference, in October, to decide on a definitive and permanent allocation of shares, would be a lengthy affair. Under the two-month interim pact the quotas (in millions of b/d) were as follows: Algeria 0.663, Ecuador 0.183, Gabon 0.137, Indonesia 1.189, Iran 2.300, Kuwait 0.999, Libya 0.999, Nigeria 1.300, Qatar 0.280, Saudi Arabia 4.353, UAE 0.950 and Venezuela 1.555; giving an OPEC total of nearly 17.1m. b/d during September and October, after taking into account estimated Iraqi production and 'war-relief crude' produced on its behalf from the Neutral Zone by Saudi Arabia and Kuwait, and assuming that the other 12 countries observed their quotas.

When the interim pact came into force the price of the United Kingdom's Brent blend had climbed to $14.45 per barrel. A significant boost to OPEC's attempts to stabilize the market was given by Norway, when the government there announced cuts in exports amounting to about 10% for November and December. Oman had previously showed solidarity with OPEC with a cut in output of 50,000 b/d and there was support for the interim agreement from some non-OPEC countries, including Mexico and Malaysia. The main threat to market stability came from within OPEC's own ranks, most seriously from the UAE. Dubai refused to contemplate any reduction in its output of about 380,000 b/d; while Abu Dhabi only trimmed its rate during September to 900,000 b/d, so that UAE production during that month was nearly 350,000 b/d above its quota. Ecuador and Gabon also exceeded their entitlements. Venezuela and Libya sold oil from stocks over and above their quotas which, they were to argue, related to production rather than exports. By the end of September Brent was selling at around $14 per barrel, having risen at one point to $16.

OPEC met again on 6 October with little scope for raising the production ceiling to satisfy the demands of some members for larger quotas. The majority were in favour of extending the two-month interim agreement until the end of the year. This was ruled out by Sheikh Yamani, who said a redistribution of quotas was 'absolutely essential'. The other matter to be settled was the GCC's insistence on the establishment of prices in a $17–$19 per barrel range. Some members, while not rejecting the objective, believed it better to concentrate on production control. The meeting proved to be the longest and most exhausting OPEC had ever held. Kuwait complicated and prolonged it by claiming a larger share of whatever production total was arrived at. In the past, it maintained, and especially at the time of the 1983 production pact, it had made bigger 'sacrifices' than any other member in accepting a lower share of the total production (5.6% under the existing formula). Kuwait wanted greater recognition for its substantial oil reserves, output capacity and historic production rate, in the form of a larger quota. There ensued lengthy discussions and argument over the proper criteria for determining the allocation of quotas. The deadlock was finally broken by a Saudi statement on 18 October that the Kingdom was willing, on two conditions, to adhere to its quota of 4.353m. b/d until the end of the year, 'in order to ease the obstacles facing' all members. The first condition was that minor upward adjustments in production should not total more than 200,000 b/d. The second was that 'the per barrel price should be set at not less than $18 and that everyone should adhere to this price'.

On 22 October agreement was reached on a complex formula under which a higher production ceiling for OPEC members (excluding Iraq) of 14.961m. b/d was set for November and one of 15.039m. b/d for December. The starting point for the calculation of quotas was the 16m. b/d ceiling set in Geneva in October 1984 (less the 1.2m. b/d then accorded Iraq). A 161,000 b/d overall increment was shared by the participating members in November. Kuwait was conceded the entire 78,000 b/d increase for December when the total was distributed thus (in millions of b/d): Algeria 0.669, Ecuador 0.221, Gabon 0.160, Indonesia 1.193, Iran 2.137, Kuwait 0.999, Libya 0.999, Nigeria 1.304, Qatar 0.300, Saudi Arabia 4.353, the UAE 0.950 and Venezuela 1.574.

On 31 October, King Fahd of Saudi Arabia dismissed Sheikh Yamani, who had been his Minister of Oil since March 1962. It is possible that he was a scapegoat for the financial consequences of OPEC's policy of recovering market share, regardless of the effect on prices. The ostensible reason for his dismissal, however, was his opposition to the King's demand for the immediate restoration of a fixed price of $18 or possibly $20 per barrel, and for a higher production quota for Saudi Arabia. Hisham Nazer, the Minister of Planning, and a known favourite of King Fahd, was appointed Acting Minister of Oil.

At Hisham Nazer's request, an emergency meeting of OPEC's pricing committee was convened in Quito on 14 November. It urged 'a prompt return to the system of fixing officially the prices for OPEC, as the appropriate means to restore to the Organization its capacity for controlling the price structure and maintaining the necessary stability in the world oil market. The committee also recommended that a reference price of $18 should not be fixed solely on the basis of 34° API Arabian Light (which Saudi Arabia, as it had previously made known, did not want to be the 'marker' crude) but on a 'basket' of seven crudes—Arabian Light, Dubai (UAE), Minas (Indonesia), Bonny Light (Nigeria), Saharan Blend (Algeria), Tia Juana Light (Venezuela) and Isthmus (Mexico).

During November the market strengthened with Britain's Brent crude, which commanded a premium of some 60 US cents over the chosen OPEC basket, averaging $14.40 per barrel, compared with $13.70 in October. OPEC output in November averaged about 16.5m. b/d. With the exception of the UAE, the output of the other 11 members party to the latest production pact was within their collective quota.

OPEC met in Geneva on 11 December, for its sixth conference of 1986, a year in which members suffered a drastic decline in oil revenue. All members were in favour of the $18 per barrel price target set by King Fahd but the majority were convinced that a reduction in the ceiling of 5%–10% would be necessary to achieve it. Iraq rejected a Saudi proposal that it should be given a quota of 1.466m. b/d. Final agreement was delayed by the Iranian demand that Iraq's expulsion from OPEC should be considered, and that a resolution should be adopted giving Iraq two months in which to reverse its decision not to participate in production agreements. Both measures were successfully opposed by the Arab members. The Arab producers opposed any censure of Iraq.

The result of the conference was an accord amongst the 12 on a 4.7% reduction in the limit on collective production from 15.039m. b/d in December, to 14.334m. b/d for the first half of 1987. A theoretical quota of 1.466m. b/d was allocated to Iraq, giving a notional ceiling for OPEC as a whole of 15.8m. b/d. It was agreed that fixed prices should be imposed from 1 February. Differential prices were fixed for the 17 most important crudes, apart from those in the basket, varying from $18.87 per barrel for Algeria's ultra-light Zarzaitine, to $16.67 for Kuwait's Export.

OPEC's new ceiling once again took into account certain factors which were becoming almost traditional: Iraq's refusal to participate in any production pact; the UAE's consistent violation of its quota; and the fact that, because of the Gulf conflict, Kuwait and Saudi Arabia refused to treat oil from the Neutral Zone produced on Iraq's behalf as contributing to their own output.

The cost of the 'price war'

Collective OPEC production in 1986, including NGLs, was 19.3m. b/d, compared with total consumption (outside the centrally planned economies of the Communist world) of 46.6m. b/d and supplies of 47.5m. b/d, according to IEA calculations. The discrepancy between consumption and supplies of 900,000 b/d was accounted for by the build-up of stocks largely caused by OPEC overproduction. Nevertheless, in terms of supply, OPEC increased its market share to 40.6%, compared with 37.7% in the previous year, thereby reversing the steady decline since 1979, when it was 61.7%. Non-OPEC supplies in 1986 were reckoned to be the same as in 1985, at 28.2m. b/d, with a 300,000 b/d decline in output by OECD member states, compensated for by a 300,000 b/d increase in net Communist (in practice Soviet) exports. Overall consumption rose by 1m. b/d, which could be partly attributed to lower oil prices, and a switch from other

fuels as a result, rather than to economic growth. These somewhat bald statistics did not in any way highlight the one success of the 'price war' that could be identified. The damage to the high-cost US industry became apparent when US production figures were published. They showed that output had declined by 8.5% from 9.12m. b/d in 1985 to 8.34m. b/d in 1986. OPEC tended to claim sole responsibility for this decline. In May 1987 Peter Holmes, Chairman of Shell Transport and Trading Company, suggested that the price collapse of 1986 might have accounted for losses of 'perhaps as much as 500,000 b/d', but he added that exploration activity in the USA had declined 'catastrophically'.

The reason for the effective abandonment of OPEC's 'fair' market share strategy at the meeting on Brioni in June 1986, despite the fact that its two leading proponents (Saudi Arabia and Kuwait) were still cushioned by substantial, if diminishing, financial reserves, was that it was proving too costly. Prior to the Brioni meeting OPEC experts had estimated the overall annual loss of revenue by the 13 members at $50,000m.–$60,000m. Despite a strengthening of prices in the second half of 1986 actual losses were probably much greater. For instance, the Royal Dutch/Shell group later estimated that the value of collective OPEC oil exports fell from $133,000m. in 1985 to $75,000m. in 1986, despite the fact that output was up by about 12%, and exports, in volume terms, by about 16%.

OPEC's efforts to control prices and production during 1987

OPEC's performance under the new agreement of December 1986 was sufficiently impressive to boost the price of Brent to $17.55 per barrel at the end of March 1987, compared with an average of $16.20 during February. Before the OPEC conference in Vienna in June, however, collective output rose to 17.3m. b/d, significantly in excess of demand, and there were signs of growing indiscipline. The UAE and Qatar, in particular, flagrantly exceeded their quotas. The prospect of 500,000 b/d of extra Iraqi pipeline capacity becoming available in September (in fact, the new Kirkuk-Ceyhan (Turkey) pipeline became operational in July 1987) overshadowed the future.

At least, however, when OPEC met again in Vienna, from 25–27 June (its first meeting of the year), prices on the spot market were more or less in line with official selling rates. This was very much to the satisfaction of Saudi Arabia and Kuwait, whose policy had largely been oriented to making oil competitive with other fuels and, thereby, to ensuring a future demand for their abundant reserves. The so-called 'price hawks' (Iran, Algeria and Libya) were not so happy with the outcome because of their anxiety to see the $28 per barrel level (which had effectively been abandoned in December 1986) restored as soon as possible and production levels kept at 15.8m. b/d. The result of the Vienna conference was an agreement on raising the limit on OPEC output by 800,000 b/d to 16.6m. b/d for the rest of the year. (Iraq, once again, refused to participate in the agreement.) The higher ceiling, incorporating an overall rise of about 5%, gave new quotas (including a notional figure for Iraq) as follows (in millions of b/d, with the previous quotas in brackets): Algeria 0.667 (0.635); Ecuador 0.221 (0.210); Gabon 0.159 (0.152); Indonesia 1.190 (1.133); Iran 2.369 (2.255); Iraq 1.540 (1.466); Kuwait 0.996 (0.948); Libya 0.996 (0.948); Nigeria 1.301 (1.238); Qatar 0.299 (0.285); Saudi Arabia 4.343 (4.133); the UAE 0.948 (0.902); Venezuela 1.571 (1.495); total 16.600 (15.800). A committee, composed of the oil ministers of Indonesia, Nigeria and Venezuela, was asked to visit member countries 'in order to motivate them to comply with the terms of the agreement'—meaning, in effect, persuading or cajoling quota violators to stop exceeding their entitlements. In practice, of course, no one expected collective output to be contained within a 16.6m. b/d ceiling. The level was calculated to be significantly lower than actual demand to make allowance for Iraq's likely output and quota violations by other members.

In mid-1987 OPEC was able to derive some comfort from the marked reduction in stocks, which had been built up to an inordinately high level by members' overproduction in the autumn and summer of 1986. It appeared, too, as if prices on the spot market would continue to be buoyed up by tension in the Gulf arising from the prospect of a military confrontation between the USA and Iran. The US Administration insisted on proceeding, in the face of congressional opposition, with its plan to protect Kuwaiti oil tankers reregistered under the US flag, in defence of the principle of freedom of shipping in international waters. In July it was reported that Iran, in what appeared to be a very ominous move, had finally begun to deploy Chinese-supplied *Silkworm* surface-to-sea missiles, with a range of 50 miles (80 km), in the vicinity of the Strait of Hormuz. It was also increasing its mine-laying operations around Kuwaiti coastal waters. Closure of the Strait of Hormuz would cut off supplies of more than one-third of OPEC output at its mid-1987 level, a shortfall which other members would be more than happy to make up.

Whilst a confrontation between the USA and Iran remained a matter of speculation, the Gulf conflict had made surprisingly little difference to the oil market, notwithstanding the sustained aggravation prompting Kuwait to seek assistance from the USSR, which chartered three supertankers to it, and then the USA.

In the face of repeated Iraqi air attacks (which were suspended for three weeks from 17 May when an Iraqi *Mirage* F-1 fighter plane mistakenly fired an *Exocet* missile at the *USS Stark*, killing 37 US sailors) Iran had managed to restore exports to the level of its OPEC quota by the spring of 1987. During 1986 Iraqi air raids had limited Iran's exports to little more than 1m. b/d. It was after Iraqi raids on the Iranian transhipment terminal at Sirri Island in August 1986 had reduced Iran's exports to 500,000 b/d (compared with 1.6m. b/d before) that Iran had begun its campaign of attacks against oil traffic to and from Kuwait. Kuwait was supporting Iraq financially in its war with Iran and selling oil on its behalf. What was probably a critical point in relation to the involvement of the superpowers in the Gulf and in prompting Kuwait's initial approach to the USA and the USSR came early in February 1987, when Lloyds of London announced that it was putting Kuwait on a par with Iraq and Iran with regard to insurance rates, charging a war premium of 3.75% of hull value on vessels using Kuwaiti ports, compared with 0.25% previously.

Iran criticized the Soviet decision to charter tankers to Kuwait (one of which struck a mine near the coast of Kuwait on 17 May—the same day as the *USS Stark* incident). On 29 April the Commander of the Iranian Navy warned that 'if there is any disruption in the movement of our ships and our imports and exports, this waterway would not be left open to any country. Subsequently, the Iranian Prime Minister proclaimed: 'everyone should know that we do not hesitate to make America's military presence in the region the target of our crushing blows'. The Iranian threat to close the Strait of Hormuz, first made in the autumn of 1983, when it became known that Iraq was to receive *Exocet* missiles, was once again being taken seriously. As the US Navy prepared to escort the reregistered Kuwaiti vessels in mid-July, any repercussions on the oil market and producers of the region from the heightened tension and looming confrontation in the Gulf were largely imponderable. There was general confidence that official selling rates of around $18 per barrel could be maintained, though it was realized that any serious development in the Gulf could send spot-market prices soaring, even if only briefly. The dangers of an Iranian-American confrontation were heightened on 24 July when the 400,000-dwt Ultra-Large Crude Carrier *Bridgeton*, one of the reflagged vessels, hit a mine near Farsi Island, when travelling in the first convoy to be escorted by the US Navy. Apparently undeterred by the prospect of conflict with the USA, Iran threatened to strike Kuwaiti onshore and offshore oil facilities with surface-to-surface missiles, if it continued to support Iraq in the Gulf conflict. Tension remained at a high level as the crude carrier *Texaco Caribbean* struck a mine in the Gulf of Oman off the coast of Fujairah on 10 August and another was discovered off Farsi Island, halting the progress of the second US-escorted convoy. Britain and France announced that they were reinforcing their naval forces in the region with minesweepers. Italy dispatched naval units, including minesweepers, which the Netherlands and Belgium also decided to send.

Nevertheless, with the escorting operation quickly established, the Iranian leadership made it clear that it wished to avoid a direct clash. As tension was defused, oil prices fell (prompting the OPEC committee meetings in September). Ironically, Iran enjoyed a period of just over six weeks, during which

its oil exports were totally unimpeded by the Iraqi Air Force. On 20 July the UN Security Council adopted Resolution 598, urging an immediate cease-fire and the withdrawal of forces to recognized pre-war international boundaries, and a negotiated end to all hostilities. Iraq accepted the resolution, and halted attacks against Iran's oil traffic and economic targets. It evidently did so under diplomatic pressure from the USA to the effect that the chances of a settlement could only be jeopardized by attacks on shipping. Iran's response to the resolution was ambivalent. It avoided outright rejection, not least because such a reaction could only encourage US-led moves towards international sanctions. Teheran insisted that the first priority was for an international tribunal to identify the original aggressor in the conflict. The USSR and China were both reluctant to support Western diplomatic efforts to impose an arms embargo against Iran, because of their concern about long-term relations with the Islamic Republic, which, they argued, should be given more time to comply with Resolution 598. Faced with what seemed to be Iranian temporizing, Iraqi patience wore thin. On 29 August it resumed attacks on vessels bound to and from Iranian ports within its declared maritime exclusion zone. There followed an unprecedented series of attacks, in which 17 vessels were damaged in a period of six days from 29 August to 3 September—eight by Iraq and seven by Iran. Iraq also resumed attacks on Iranian economic targets. As a result, Lloyds raised the war-risk premiums on the hulls of all vessels plying the waters of the Gulf by 50%.

The first direct clash in the Gulf itself between the USA and Iran came on 21 September when two US Navy helicopters attacked the Iranian vessel *Iran Ajr*, as it was laying mines in international waters. During September there was an intensification and a shift in direction as well. Of the 15 assaults mounted in September, 11 were on Saudi-directed traffic. Iraq stepped up its raids on Iranian oil traffic and in the most devastating attack yet, on 7 October, struck five chartered shuttle and storage tankers at the Larak Island export transhipment terminal, including the 256,263-dwt Cypriot-registered storage tanker *Shining Star,* and the 564,739-dwt *Seawise Giant,* the largest vessel in the world, both of which had to be written off as total losses. Iran came under more pressure as the US Navy sank three Iranian speedboats on the following day, alleging that they had fired on a US observation helicopter. On 15 October Iran fired two Chinese-manufactured *Silkworm* missiles from the Faw Peninsula, which it had occupied early in 1986, at the Liberian-registered, but US-owned, 275,932-dwt *Sungari* as it was waiting to load oil at Kuwait's Mina Ahmadi terminal. On the next day the US-flagged 81,283-dwt product carrier *Sea Island City*, was struck by a similar projectile off Kuwait's Shuaiba terminal. The US Navy's 'measured and appropriate response' was to destroy the two offshore oil platforms on the Rostam and Rakhsh oilfield, which it claimed were being used as bases from which to track and launch attacks against shipping. According to Iran, Rostam had been producing 20,000 b/d–25,000 b/d, and Rakhsh was being repaired having been bombed by Iraqi aircraft a year earlier. Iran retaliated on 22 October by firing another *Silkworm* missile at Kuwait's deep-water terminal at Sea Island. In practice Kuwait's capacity to export was not seriously affected—the main terminal at al-Ahmadi was out of range of the *Silkworm*.

Neither the USA nor Iran showed any inclination further to escalate hostilities. Iran's speedboat attacks increased but care was taken not to interfere with shipping escorted by US, west European or Soviet vessels. At the same time, Iraq intensified its raids on Iranian oil traffic with attacks taking an unprecedented toll during December. Over the year as a whole, the number of attacks increased by more than 50%. In 1987 there were 163 compared with 107 in 1986, 47 in 1985 and 71 in 1984, according to a report to the US Senate's Committee on Foreign Relations. Of the total, 76 were carried out by Iraq and 87 by Iran—a reversal of previous proportions.

The summit meeting of the Arab League held in Amman, Jordan, in November 1987, condemned Iran for its occupation of Iraqi territory, its negative attitude towards peace efforts, and the Mecca disturbances but refrained from recommending the severance of economic and diplomatic relations with Iran.

Iraqi military pressure on Iran's oil exports was the main factor cutting the volume of its actual production from something like 2.8m. b/d in August to 2m. b/d, or less, in October (when domestic consumption totalled an estimated 600,000 b/d). Another factor was the overwhelming vote in the US Congress banning imports of Iranian oil, which had reached 260,000 b/d in the January–August period. In August, France, in the midst of its diplomatic dispute with Iran, had taken a similar measure. The devastating raid on the Larak terminal was a particularly severe set-back. Early in November Lloyds List of London estimated that Iraqi air strikes had reduced the fleet of chartered tankers shuttling oil between Kharg and Larak island from 26 to 20, and the number actually owned by the Iranian National Tanker Company (INTC) from 12 to nine. The INTC was successful, however, in chartering six ultra large and very large crude carriers to ship oil from the Larak area for storage outside the war zone.

In the face of these difficulties Iran showed a resilience and flexibility in its selling arrangements which could only serve to undermine oil prices. Buyers were offered crude on a c.i.f., rather than an f.o.b., basis, delivered from floating storage near the major marketing areas. It offered Japanese customers discounts, which were the equivalent of $1 per barrel, based on spot-market rates for Oman and Dubai crude, in its attempts to sell an increasing volume of 'distress cargoes'. By mid-November it was estimated that there were as many as 20m. barrels of unsold Iranian crude in storage, mainly at Rotterdam, and another 14m. barrels at sea. The market was becoming awash with excess supplies from other producers, too. By December OPEC production was running at about 19m. b/d. The growing surplus had an inevitable impact on price levels. They slid ominously during November when the spot rate for the Brent blend fell to $17.37 in mid-month and was consistently below $18 throughout the month. As OPEC prepared for its end-of-year ministerial conference, it was clear that the price structure was coming under grave strain, largely as a result of the accumulated stresses of the Gulf conflict.

The meeting started amidst considerable despondency and scepticism as to what OPEC could and should do to stop the downward drift of prices from the $18 per barrel target, which had been set over a year before. Only six months before the issue had been whether OPEC could or should raise the reference price to a level higher than $18 per barrel. In general terms, the prospects for a successful meeting were blighted by deteriorating relations between Iran and Saudi Arabia, which would almost certainly make impossible the kind of compromises reached in August and December 1986, as well as June 1987. On the question of production OPEC was still divided between the 'hawks', seeking a lowering of the ceiling, and the Arab producers of the Gulf, who expressed confidence that demand could accommodate a higher limit. The OPEC Secretariat's assessment of future oil requirements was the most optimistic, with demand for members' crude in the second half of 1988 (assuming no change in the level of stocks) calculated at 18.4m. b/d. The minority on the Economic Commission Board (essentially the Arab states of the Gulf) estimated the requirement at 18.2m. b/d (assuming no change in stocks), while the majority put it at 17.6m. b/d (after a stock reduction of 300,000 b/d). The most pessimistic of the forecasts was almost identical to that of the IEA and closely in line with those of most major oil companies. True to form, Iran, at the outset, called for an increase in the reference price of at least $2.70 ($2.18 to compensate for the fall in the value of the dollar and 52 cents for inflation). The ritualistic demand received little sympathy from even the traditional 'price hawks' who fully appreciated that the burning priority was production restraint. On this front also Iran created initial turmoil and a fall in spot-market prices by threatening to opt out of any production pact that was agreed. That raised the possibility of only 11 of the 13 members subscribing to an agreement or, more intriguingly, of Iraq becoming party to an agreement while Iran excluded itself. In the run-up to the meeting Iraq had repeated its offer to participate in a production pact if it were given quota-parity with Iran, (i.e. a quota of 2.369m. b/d, compared with its notional quota of 1.54m. b/d). Such an arrangement would have set a more realistic upper limit on collective production of 15.89m. b/d; increasing the possibility that a market price of above $18 per barrel could be achieved if all members honoured their commitments. Moreover, as Iraq's sustained attacks on its enemy's oil exports effectively

limited Iran's production to 2.37m. b/d, an arrangement under which Iraq produced as much as Iran would actually have significantly lowered Iraq's output which, Baghdad had boasted, had reached no less than 2.83m. b/d in November, with the advantage of new pipeline capacity. As it was, Iraq's sincerity was never put to the test—Iran, once again, rejected outright the concept of parity. There was also vehement opposition from Venezuela which was not prepared to see any diminution of its percentage share. The only possible outcome of the meeting was a 'roll-over' (continuation) of the output sharing accord concluded in the previous June. Despite Iranian reluctance, the accord was renewed and the existing quotas of the 12 remained in force. The only difference was that any pretence about Iraq having a notional allocation was abandoned. The five-member ministerial committee on price monitoring was again empowered to call an extraordinary conference to restore stability if 'there was any significant change in market prices'.

At the December meeting OPEC seriously addressed the problem of over-production, to the extent that it rehired KHG-Klynveld-Kraayenhof, the Dutch auditing firm, to monitor members' production and exports. It had originally been appointed to undertake this task at the end of 1984, when its efforts were obstructed by several countries. At its second attempt, it was assured of better collaboration and it was agreed that the auditors would send teams to all member states simultaneously, to preclude prevarication. The UAE inevitably found itself cast in the role of principal quota violator. In the late summer its output had risen to a peak estimated at 1.9m. b/d (compared with a quota of 948,000 b/d), 1.5m. b/d accounted for by Abu Dhabi and 400,000 b/d by Dubai (which was beyond the purview of OPEC, anyway, because of the peculiar nature of the federation). UAE output subsequently fell to 1.6m. b/d–1.7m. b/d in November and December. After the December meeting, Abu Dhabi felt sufficiently chastened to order its operating companies to cut back by about 350,000 b/d, which effectively reduced the UAE's output to 900,000 b/d for a while. Sheikh Ali al-Khalifa as-Sabah, Kuwait's Minister of Oil, acknowledged that his country had been producing at a rate of 100,000 b/d–150,000 b/d above its quota. He attributed the excess to Iranian attacks against its oil tankers and the need to build up inventories outside the Gulf, as well as to its frustration with quota breaches by other members. Only after the meeting did it emerge that Saudi Arabia and Kuwait had agreed to resume supplies of 'war-relief crude' to Iraq at the full rate of 310,000 b/d.

According to revised calculations by the IEA, OPEC production had run at 18.9m. b/d during the last quarter of 1987. In the first half of 1988, it was clear, the price levels would not only depend on greater production discipline but also on the rate at which stocks were drawn down. The assumption was that they could come under heavy pressure in the second quarter of the year. Overall, however, there was optimism that demand for OPEC crude would rise in 1988. For instance, the Kuwaiti Minister of Oil predicted that over the year as a whole demand would be between 18.5m. b/d and 19m. b/d.

OPEC reaffirmed official selling prices based on the $18 reference level, but it was, in reality, on the verge of abandoning any real pretence or effort at maintaining them. The emphasis had switched decisively towards concentration on output control which, if effectively applied, would keep prices around $18 per barrel. Some producers—Iran, Iraq and Qatar—were already negotiating rates with their customers which were wholly and unashamedly market-related. A proportion of UAE output was priced in the same way, apart from the preferential treatment given to its equity partners. At their annual summit in Riyadh, on 26–29 December, the Heads of State of the GCC (Saudi Arabia, Kuwait, the UAE, Oman, Bahrain and Qatar) called on all OPEC members to abide by official prices. The ring of hollow hypocrisy about the appeal was confirmed shortly afterwards when it emerged that Saudi Arabia had been offering preferential prices to its four old US partners in the Aramco operation (Exxon, Mobil, Texaco, and Chevron) since the late summer. It conceded similar terms, based on spot rates for Dubai and Oman crude, to smaller US customers, and Japanese companies were demanding similar terms. By the end of March, Saudi Arabia was offering the market-related price formula to all contract volumes of 100,000 b/d. Other Gulf producers had no choice but to sell to US customers on a 'delivered' basis, linked to prices of Alaskan crude. From the beginning of January they met dogged resistance from Japanese customers, who were well cushioned by stocks, and were forced to give ground. By the spring, even Indonesia was selling to the Japanese at $1.56 below official prices. The respected Dr Fadhil ash-Shalabi, OPEC's Acting Secretary-General since 1982, publicly recognized in mid-March that the Organization was fighting a losing battle in trying to maintain official prices. He told the Arab Energy Conference in Baghdad that OPEC should revert to a system under which prices were allowed to fluctuate within a specified target range, using market-related formulae to sell quotas. The production ceiling would be lowered when rates fell within the agreed margin and raised when they exceeded it.

1988—no progress on prices or production

During January OPEC output dropped to about 17m. b/d. At the end of the month the spot rate for Brent blend had fallen to $16.25 per barrel, compared with $17.95 at the beginning. By the end of February Brent had dropped to only $14.77, despite the fact that collective production had averaged only 17.4m. b/d, with an estimated 500,000 b/d of Saudi Arabia's shipments and 300,000 b/d of Iran's in onshore storage overseas or in tankers. Throughout March the market remained weak, with the spot rate for North Sea crude dropping to a low point of $13.80 per barrel early in the month but recovering to $15.79 by its close. Over the first quarter, OPEC crude production averaged a modest 17.5m. b/d (well within the 15.06m. b/d ceiling after taking into account Iraq and oil production from the Neutral Zone sold on Iraq's behalf), as commercial stocks in the industrial world were drawn down at the rate of 1.9m. b/d, according to IEA calculations. After a hiatus at the turn of the year, when Syria attempted, unsuccessfully, to initiate a dialogue between Iran and the conservative Arab regimes of the Gulf, Iraq resumed attacks on Iranian oil and economic targets, while Iran retaliated against shipping on the Arab side of the Gulf. The new wave of attacks did not compare in intensity with the hostilities in the October–December period and, during the first quarter of 1988, the Gulf conflict was largely irrelevant to the oil market and, certainly, no salvation for prices. Indeed, it was indicative of the easing of tension that, early in February, Lloyds committee for rating war risk reduced premiums for oil and gas cargoes to and from Kuwait, Saudi Arabia, Bahrain and the UAE from 0.75% of hull value to 0.45%, and for other merchandise from 0.45% to 0.375%. The rate for all shipments to the Iranian port of Bandar Abbas was cut from 0.45% to 0.375%.

Despite a very 'significant change in market prices' in the early part of the year, it was not until 19 April that OPEC's price-monitoring committee met in Vienna. It did so mainly in response to an initiative by a group of non-member producers, Angola, the People's Republic of China, Egypt, Malaysia, Mexico and Oman. Mexico had indicated that the group would be prepared to cut its exports by 5% (equivalent to 183,000 b/d— including exports by Colombia, which took part in the group's preliminary discussions but which was not represented in the approach to OPEC) in return for a comparable reduction by OPEC. Mexico's Secretary of State for Energy, Mines and Industries emphasized that collaboration would have to be 'a long-term endeavour', the 'beginning of a new stage of co-operation'. Prior to the meeting of the committee Saudi Arabia did little to disguise its lack of enthusiasm for any such collaboration. Nevertheless, King Fahd took the opportunity to reaffirm his country's commitment to a price of $18 per barrel and at the same time attributed the weakness of prices in the market to discounts offered by other members, while denying that Saudi Arabia was offering any itself. Of the countries represented on the committee, Nigeria and Indonesia were reluctant to call a full ministerial emergency meeting in advance of the biannual ordinary conference, which was scheduled for June. Venezuela and Algeria, however, were strongly in favour of one. They were supported by Iran, which, though not represented on the committee, sent Hossain Ardebili, its Deputy Minister of Oil. His intervention was probably crucial. Surprisingly, Hisham Nazer, Saudi Arabia's Minister of Oil, consented to a full consultative meeting (which would automatically become an extraordinary conference if any decision was taken) and a joint session with the non-OPEC ('NOPEC', as it was dubbed by the media)

group immediately after it. Agreement was only reached after an intensive exchange between Arturo Hernández Grisanti, Venezuela's Minister of Energy and Mines, and Hisham Nazer. Mr Hernández accused Saudi Arabia of secretly aiming at a price of $15 per barrel, and was sharply critical of the price discounts that the Kingdom was known to be giving. Their confrontation was to set the scene for one of the most bitter OPEC conferences ever at the end of April. Before, it was convened, however, the chances for a reasonably amicable compromise were badly impaired by a further deterioration in relations between Saudi Arabia and Iran leading to the former severing diplomatic links on 26 April.

On the eve of the OPEC consultative conference, which began on 28 April, the proposal by six 'NOPEC' countries for a joint output reduction initiative with OPEC, received a polite but non-committal response from an OPEC ministerial committee. The 'NOPEC' delegation departed, leaving a senior Omani official to liaise with them on the outcome of the OPEC meeting. This, probably, was a tactical mistake, because it relieved OPEC members of any immediate pressure to reach a decision. The likelihood of an accord between the two groups was not great. Most OPEC members had been thinking in terms of matching barrel-for-barrel cuts, rather than of a reduction on the basis of a common percentage of total exports. (Saudi Arabia and Kuwait were known to have grave reservations about any lowering of the disrespected 15.06m. b/d ceiling.) On the second day of the conference, Algeria proposed that OPEC should respond to the 'NOPEC' proposal with an offer of a 300,000 b/d reduction (i.e. about 2.5% of current collective exports, compared with the 5% sought by the 'NOPEC' group), as a compromise. It was supported by seven other members leaving the Arab producers of the Gulf in a minority. Saudi Arabia produced a counter-proposal, to the effect that OPEC should match the non-members on a 183,000 b/d barrel-for-barrel basis but that the cut should be divided into 12 equal parts amongst the 12 members of the current production agreement. Hisham Nazer, the Saudi Oil Minister, defended the principle of equal distribution, according to which small producers like Gabon and Ecuador would have had to accept a disproportionately large reduction in their output, by saying that they should be made aware of what cutting back really meant. The proposal elicited more astonishment than support. The division of opinion over the 'NOPEC' offer remained, and the most that could be decided before the meeting ended on 2 May was to maintain contact with the group, with the aim of establishing the basis for long-term collaboration.

Prices dropped sharply in the aftermath of the meeting, with the Brent blend falling by 50 cents per barrel. At the same time OPEC was confronted with new, and potentially divisive issues relating to definitions of production. They were raised by Sheikh Ali al-Khalifa, the Kuwaiti chief delegate, largely as a result of the difficulties encountered by the Dutch auditing firm which had been re-engaged at the conference in December 1988. The most contentious issue concerned the definition of condensates, also known as NGLs, or gas which liquefies at the surface after being treated. KHG-Klynveld-Kraayenhof's study of the records of various member countries showed that, over the years, some of them had reclassified crude as condensates, production of which had been covered by none of OPEC's accords on output sharing. In retrospect, their exclusion was generally regarded as a mistake within OPEC but not one which could be rectified in the foreseeable future.

On the question of the reclassification of crude as condensates, Sheikh Ali al-Khalifa's attack was mostly directed at Venezuela. According to official figures published by the state oil corporation, Petróleos de Venezuela, Venezuela's output of condensates had increased from 17,000 b/d in 1982, to 142,000 b/d in 1987. Moreover, it was planned to increase to 190,000 b/d in 1988. Production of condensates by other members like Indonesia and Nigeria had also risen significantly. The auditors said in their report that Venezuela had defined condensates as NGLs with the American Petroleum Institute (API) gravity of 40.2° and above—an assertion which the Venezuelan delegation rejected. For their part, the auditors proposed defining condensates as all 'natural gas liquids and hydrocarbons with an API of 47° or higher, obtained from lease separators and field facilities when these are measured separately from crude oil'. Sheikh Ali al-

Khalifa pointed out that a number of important crude streams produced by member states were lighter than 40.20° API gravity, and that such a definition could put as much as 2m. b/d of OPEC supply outside the ambit of the production sharing system. Evidence was also produced that some members were excluding from their quotas so-called 'own use' oil, which was accounted for by industrial operations including refining. Sheikh Ali al-Khalifa calculated that, if such crude was excluded from quotas, it could add another 500,000 b/d–700,000 b/d to overall production. A special committee of experts was charged with drawing up a report on the problem of definition prior to the next OPEC ordinary ministerial conference in June.

OPEC's crude output was reckoned to have risen above 18.5m. b/d in May, compared with the modest 17.5m. b/d in the second quarter. From 11 to 16 May Iraq launched a punishing series of raids on Iran's Larak Island transhipment centre, hitting seven vessels, including the *Seawise Giant*, which was severely damaged again. But the raids did nothing to prevent the passage of the large volume of Iranian crude on the water in transit. Abu Dhabi apparently trimmed its allowable production by about 150,000 b/d in mid-May. In practice, however, making allowance for Iraq and production from the Neutral Zone, OPEC's rate of output was still some 500,000 b/d above the stipulated ceiling. In the circumstances a decision to roll-over the current agreement on quotas seemed to be a foregone conclusion. The pact seemed less tenable than ever, however, after Dr Mana bin Said al-Oteiba, the UAE Minister of Petroleum, walked out of the OPEC conference in Vienna on the second evening and flew to Rabat, Morocco, apparently to see his Head of State and the Ruler of Abu Dhabi, President Zaid. There he publicly repudiated the federation's quota of 948,000 b/d, saying that it could no longer accept so little. In a sense, his statement merely formalized the UAE's consistent violation of its allocation, which it had exceeded by 50% or more. Whilst disagreeing on forecasts for demand in the second half of 1988, Saudi Arabia and Kuwait threatened to flood the market with more than 1m. b/d of oil equivalent (in the form of condensates), unless the Organization agreed in December on precise technical definitions to distinguish between condensates and crude. Prior to the conference, at the experts' meeting, Venezuela had made a vigorous effort to convince other members that condensates could only be defined by certain reservoir characteristics and that neither specific gravity nor oil gas ratios should be the criteria. The majority seemed to believe that 'user oil' should be included in production. As long as members' behaviour was consistent, that question seemed relatively easy to solve. However, it looked as though the dispute over condensates would continue to be a far more contentious issue. After the conference, Sheikh Ali al-Khalifa said that any definition of what constituted condensates would have to be easily applicable and one which auditors could easily understand—suggesting that it would have to be fairly arbitrary in terms of its prescribed gravity. There was general recognition that the problem of Iraq's exclusion from the production-sharing system had to be dealt with but no progress was made towards solving it. Also, Saudi Arabia and Kuwait remained adamant that the 310,000 b/d, mostly from the Neutral Zone, which they were 'lending' to Iraq was (Iraq's) part of its quota, to be repaid at some future date, and that production from the territory as a whole was outside the pact.

In July, in the wake of the June conference, prices fell to around $14 per barrel, and, with stocks high, looked as though they would weaken further in the third quarter. Having failed to make positive progress towards (or even achieved a consensus in favour of) a collaborative production programme with the 'NOPEC' group, which might have stabilized prices, OPEC's $18 target seemed something of a chimera in mid-1988.

The acceptance, in July, by Iraq and Iran of UN cease-fire terms opened up new prospects for OPEC to take a firmer grip on oil supply. Iraq's freedom, for many years, to produce oil unconstrained by quota had been a major irritant to other oil exporters, in that it provided a precedent for overproduction. However, the prospects of peace also changed other policy attitudes among Iraq's neighbours, suggesting that there was now a possibility of a lasting OPEC accord and of meetings which would resolutely tackle the other issues which previous agreements had avoided. Iraq's self-exemption from quota curbs was not, however, the only obstacle to a production agreement to support prices.

Saudi Arabia, the world's largest oil exporter, whose support was crucial to the success of any agreement to regulate supply, had previously tended to temporize when other governments suggested that OPEC ministers should meet to suggest ways of reversing the price slide to an extraordinary conference of the whole group. Saudi Arabia disapproved of such meetings which tended, unfairly, in the view of its officials, to place the onus for restoring price stability on Saudi Arabia. The Saudi view was that it was the overproduction of other countries, mainly in the Arab Gulf, that was causing price weakness. Meetings of ministers simply focused international attention on Saudi Arabia's political weakness by highlighting its inability to persuade its smaller neighbours to observe OPEC discipline. Saudi Arabia's fear was that it would be asked, in effect, to sacrifice production to other exporters, both inside and outside the Middle East, in order to support prices. Its refusal to do so was based on its experience, in mid-1985, of being forced to cut its production to less than half of its official quota level while other producers continued to ignore quotas. However, as the cease-fire became a reality in July, Saudi Arabia reversed its opposition to an emergency meeting of OPEC's five-minister Pricing Committee, the group charged with convening the 13-nation conference if market prices were deviating too far from the official target. If Saudi Arabia, unlike other exporters, had been prepared to allow prices to slide rather than be put on a political spot, its ability to make up per barrel revenue losses with large scale overproduction was an option not open to many oil exporters. The threat of 'flooding' oil markets, with gains in volume compensating for price losses, was one that Saudi Arabia had used before, notably in 1986, and is a constant factor in oil politics.

With Saudi Arabia's agreement, five oil ministers met in Lausanne on 3 August. They were realistic enough to recognize there was little they could do until Iran and Iraq had begun to tackle directly the question of prisoners of war and the other outstanding issues which divided them. It was agreed that the Secretary-General of OPEC, the former Indonesian Minister of Oil, Dr Subroto, should try to act as an intermediary in an attempt to either persuade Iraq to relinquish its arbitrary demand for quota parity with Iran; or to press Iran to accept Iraq's claims in the interests of achieving a 13-nation agreement. The Lausanne session, despite the scepticism of market operators and some ministers, was ultimately to prove important in setting a politically realistic agenda for the 'reconstruction' of OPEC.

Saudi Arabian and Kuwaiti political and financial support for Iraq's war-effort also raised new difficulties for the oil-exporting countries. Iraq argued that the war with Iran had been fought not only for the sake of Iraq itself, but had also been important in maintaining the political, social and religious status quo in the face of Iran's destabilizing Islamic fundamentalism. If Iraq had failed to overcome or, at least, contain Iran, how long would it have been before Iran came to dominate the conservative Sheikhdoms of the Gulf? Along with direct financial support, Saudi Arabia and Kuwait agreed to 'lend' Iraq up to 330,000 b/d of oil exports from the shared Neutral Zone. In one respect, this was in response to justified Iraqi claims that it had lost long-standing and loyal crude oil customers when Iran destroyed its Gulf export facility at Fao in 1981. Saudi Arabia and Kuwait had prevailed upon other OPEC members to change the way quota production was defined and measured in such a way that crude oil exports 'loaned' to another country were attributed to the 'production' of the recipient. In this way, Saudi Arabia and Kuwait, which had already made the largest sacrifices, in both volume and percentage terms, to support falling oil prices, were able to produce their Neutral-Zone contribution to Iraq outside of their own allocations. Other OPEC members felt, with some justice, that their sales were being correspondingly reduced to balance finite demand, making them involuntary financial and political supporters of Iraq in its war with Iran. That situation was uncomfortable enough while Iraq was itself constrained by a quota. But in 1986, when OPEC reversed its market-share policy and reimposed quotas, Iraq refused to accept the quota allotted to it. This meant that the Neutral-Zone production of Saudi Arabia and Kuwait was now being attributed to no

OPEC member at all. Iran, Algeria and Libya, the traditional supporters of high prices and lower OPEC production, were outraged and gained the support of traditional moderates in accusing Kuwait and Saudi Arabia of adding to the market glut at a time when Iraq was not only producing more than its official quota, but even more than it was claiming as its rightful share.

This issue was also recognized in Lausanne as an important impediment to an overall production agreement. However, the five-minister Pricing Committee also demonstrated again that the Iran–Iraq conflict, together with the related Neutral Zone issue, was not the only regional problem impeding oil-exporter unity. The long-standing issue of overproduction by the UAE dominated the discussions at the Lausanne meeting. It had fallen to Dr Subroto to visit the President of the UAE, Sheikh Zayed, on behalf of OPEC, to seek assurances that the UAE would abide by the quota agreement which its Minister of Oil, Dr Mana Otaiba, had signed only weeks earlier. Market operators were as sceptical in public, as illustrated by a sharp drop in prices the day after the ministers had met, as other ministers were in private about the assurances that the UAE would always 'endeavour' to act in the best interests of OPEC as a whole. This lay oddly with the UAE's claim that its quota should be 1.5m. b/d, or more than 50% higher than that assigned by the rest of the group. While both Dr Subroto and the President of OPEC, the Nigerian Minister of Oil, Rilwanu Lukman, had to pretend to believe that the UAE would, in future, curtail output to the agreed level, the contradiction between its claim for a 1.5m. b/d quota and its assurances of co-operation, damaged market confidence.

The failure of the UAE to adhere to its quota was a mystery to many observers, since the UAE had one of the highest per capita oil incomes in the world. The origins of this failure lay in the fluctuating and uncertain relationship between Abu Dhabi and Dubai, the two leading Sheikhdoms in the federation, and in Dubai's refusal to accept federal (i.e. Abu Dhabi's) control over its oil policies and revenues. Dubai's adoption of an independent pricing policy had enabled it to maintain production at close to its 400,000 b/d capacity; Abu Dhabi had been put in the position of 'UAE swing producer'. This meant, in effect, that Abu Dhabi would have had to cut its production to the low level of 500,000 b/d, or less, in order to maintain the federation's output at its officially agreed level. This would have posed severe technical problems for its oilfield operators, which could have been overcome, had it not been for the financial contribution that Abu Dhabi was committed to making to the federal budget. With the relationship between individual rulers always uneasy, Abu Dhabi had in effect refused to cut its production to a level less than double that of Dubai, and, often, it had produced significantly more than that. The fault, as far as OPEC and its attempts to regulate production were concerned, lay with the decision to convert Abu Dhabi's 1967 membership to cover the whole of the UAE. The simple fact was that the Abu Dhabi and federal ministries had virtually no influence on Dubai's oil policy, making any quota for the UAE applicable only in theory. Whatever the historical background, the intra-emirate rivalry also provided a convenient excuse for Abu Dhabi to increase its revenue through bigger sales.

As prices continued to slide towards $10 a barrel (and below for some heavier Middle Eastern crude oils) ministers and Heads of State were in regular contact. However, with Iran and Iraq still unable to agree on quotas, as well as on territorial and other war-related issues, OPEC's Middle Eastern members increasingly took matters into their own hands and started to push up their production to compensate for lower prices, which were therefore subjected to further pressure. The UAE, Kuwait and lastly Saudi Arabia increased their exports, especially to the USA where Iraq had significantly increased its sales.

On 25 September the same five oil ministers who had met in Lausanne met in Madrid. Their decision to reconstitute OPEC's Long-Term Strategy Committee led to the addition to OPEC's steering group of three crucial Middle Eastern oil exporters: Iran, Iraq and Kuwait. Their statement, that a review of objectives and strategies in the context of current circumstances, *'especially concerning the price of oil and the production mechanism to support it'* was necessary, was a clear warning to all oil exporters that OPEC would either have to tackle outstanding issues, or give up all attempts to control prices and production.

The meeting of the wider group was seen as a necessary precursor to a full OPEC conference which would end the isolation of Iraq. Meanwhile, throughout October, Saudi Arabia, the UAE and Kuwait continued to boost output, as did other exporters, until the group was producing at levels as high as or even higher than they were at the peak of the 1986 price war. Saudi Arabia was demonstrating its unwillingness to carry the burden of price support at a time when other exporters were ignoring their obligations and showing that it could, unlike most other exporters, compensate in full, by higher sales, for any loss in revenue caused by lower prices.

With OPEC's eight-minister Pricing and Long-Term Strategy Committees due to meet again in Madrid on 20 October, the Arab Gulf countries grouped in the GCC (which included non-OPEC states) made their position clear when their oil ministers broke with their normal practice of steering clear of OPEC disputes. They issued a communiqué, in which they stated that their participation in a new production agreement for 1989 would be conditional on the 12 countries returning to and adhering to the agreed quotas which had been ignored since June, with the exception of Iraq, which would be given parity with Iran at 2.369m. b/d. The second, enlarged Madrid session on 20–22 October failed to overcome Iranian resistance to quota parity with Iraq, while Iraq remained adamant that it would accept nothing less than that. By the end of October, OPEC production had soared to over 22m. b/d, far in excess of what most analysts believed the market could absorb. The Gulf Arab states increased their production markedly and made it clear that they would not adhere to their official quotas unless there was total discipline. However, although prices were weak, they did not fall to the $5 per barrel level that some feared. The Madrid session was adjourned, rather than abandoned, until mid-November, when the full OPEC conference was due to assemble in Vienna. This reinforced the hope in the commercial oil industry that OPEC would, under pressure, find a solution. The result was that crude oil looked 'cheap' and was bought on that basis. More significantly, consumer demand for oil was increasing.

When the Long-Term Strategy Committee reassembled in Vienna on 17 November, there were signs that Iran had adopted a more flexible approach. A crucial consideration, both for Iran and for the other Middle Eastern countries which were anxious to reach an agreement, was the knowledge that Iraq had already commenced major pipeline expansion schemes across Saudi Arabia into the Red Sea and was repairing its Gulf export facilities which had been destroyed in the War. Unless Iraq agreed to adhere to its quota, it would be in the position to supply all of the likely increase in world demand for OPEC crude oil over the coming year and was likely to supply it anyway, if growth in demand declined, at the expense of other exporters' market share. The choice appeared to be simple: Iraq's demand for a quota of about 2.5m. b/d would have to be met, or Iraq would undermine the market for all other exporters with production of around 4m. b/d within the coming year. It required 10 days of tortuous negotiations to overcome the political problems that such a deal gave rise to within the faction-riven Iranian Government, and even so political sensitivities prevailed over economic sense in the agreement that was finally concluded. In resisting Iraq's demand for quota parity, Iran justified its stance by arguing that it would not relinquish its market share and insisted on retaining the same percentage of total allocations which it had been granted prior to 1986, when Iraq had last officially accepted an OPEC quota. Iranian delegates invited other OPEC members, notably Iraq's supporters in the Middle East, to sacrifice market share to Iraq if they so wished. The ploy was a subtle one. In the distribution that resulted, Iran's quota was 125,000 b/d higher than it would have been under the distribution proposed by the GCC. Iraq was granted the same amount while the other 11 members of OPEC sacrificed pro-rata 250,000 b/d out of the 18.5m. b/d ceiling agreed for the first half of 1989. Iran's Minister of Oil, Gholamreza Aqazadeh, who had sworn he would never sign an accord giving Iraq quota parity, flew home to consult his government colleagues, leaving a deputy to sign the OPEC resolution. Even then, the agreement almost collapsed at the eleventh hour when the Saudi Arabian Minister of Oil, Hisham Nazer, insisted that a 'floor price' of $15 should be incorporated into it. Suspicions, unfounded in 1988, but deriving from the price collapse of 1986, that Saudi Arabia actually wanted a lower price, led to opposition to this move, which Saudi Arabia believed would boost the market, even though it was unclear which producers would join Saudi Arabia in curtailing supplies if prices threatened to fall through the agreed 'floor-level'.

Very high production in November and December, after the OPEC agreement had been signed, but before the new 18.5m. b/d ceiling took effect, underlined that most exporters intended to abide by the letter of the agreement. Saudi Arabia increased production to 6m. b/d, the UAE produced more than double its allocation of 948,000 b/d and Kuwait, too, showed that it could easily produce and export up to 2m. b/d. In the final weeks of 1988, production reached 23m. b/d, 4.5m. above the ceiling agreed for the first six months of 1989, and 6m. b/d–7m. b/d in excess of the ceiling then officially still in force. It was feared that the rush to export ahead of the 1 January deadline would place huge stock in the hands of consumers, which they would draw upon in early 1989 in order to subject prices and sales to further pressure.

An 'audit' of each member's production, internal consumption and exports was agreed to buttress the agreement for the first six months of 1989, to be conducted once a month by officials from each of the 13 OPEC member states. However, it quickly became evident, as members claimed each month to have hit production and export targets almost to the barrel, that information was regarded as a tool to justify national policy stances, and not as the means of regulating the market which some had hoped for. The UAE, whose long-standing overproduction was well-known, declined to supply monthly data and sent no representatives to the agreed monthly meetings of experts. Its production did, however, decline sharply from the 23m. b/d peak of December. This fact, rather than continued 'cheating', became the focus of market attention. As it became clear that the demand for oil had surged ahead in late 1988 and was continuing to do so, oil prices strengthened to a level close to and, in some cases, above the official $18 per barrel target price.

In the first three months of 1989, OPEC and world oil markets received a morale booster from the activities of a loose collection of other exporters, in which Oman, a member of the GCC of Arab exporters, played a prominent role. Since 1986, Saudi Arabia and Kuwait had led an OPEC campaign for non-member oil-exporting countries to share the burden of market stabilization, and to curtail their growing, capacity-level production. Since 1983, the growing production and exports of non-OPEC members had been perceived as a major threat to price stability, with the pricing and production policy of the United Kingdom viewed as a major problem. With its high profile in world markets due to its transparent pricing, North Sea oil had posed a particular problem for Nigeria, one of OPEC's poorest members, with whose crude exports British and Norwegian supplies competed directly both in terms of quality and location. Attempts at political persuasion failed and the price war of 1986 was regarded as a means of forcing the British Government to abandon its inflexible stance with regard to oil production levels. However, the British Government refused to do so, despite the huge loss of government revenues and the damaging impact on the United Kingdom's balance of payments. However, Mexico agreed to reduce its exports by 5% and Norway reduced its planned increases by limiting output to 92.5% of its rising capacity. A meeting between non-OPEC ministers and the OPEC conference had failed in 1986, at the height of the crisis, to produce anything more than positive words. By 1988, when OPEC had managed to boost prices somewhat through its own efforts, an offer by non-OPEC ministers to reduce their exports by 5%, if OPEC members did likewise, was rebuffed by Saudi Arabia and Kuwait, since they felt that they had already reduced their production sufficiently.

On 27 January representatives of 13 non-OPEC oil exporters met with counterparts from six OPEC nations to indicate their willingness to support OPEC's efforts to stabilize prices. Saudi Arabia insisted that OPEC, by setting a ceiling of 18.5m. b/d for the first-half of 1989, had taken an important first step which should be matched by the non-members. Like many analysts, Saudi Arabian officials were sceptical about reports that demand for oil was rising rapidly, and they were deeply concerned about the possibility that prices would decline drasti-

cally in the traditionally weak April–June quarter. After a second meeting in London in late February, the non-OPEC governments announced that they would reduce exports by 5% (or freeze them at 5% below planned levels) for the April–June period at least. Although Mexico had initially played a major role in organizing the non-OPEC group, it was two countries from the Middle East and North Africa region, albeit with very different structures, that now played a major political role. Oman convened and chaired the first session, while the second was hosted by Egypt.

Market confidence that OPEC had solved the problems of its troublesome Middle Eastern and North African members was shaken when its eight-minister Price-Monitoring Committee met in late March, ostensibly to review how closely the membership had adhered to the agreement signed in November. Kuwait dramatically announced its intention of seeking a higher market-share for itself, the UAE and for the three smallest exporters, Gabon, Ecuador and Qatar. However, prices remained steady during April as supplies were reduced and demand continued to rise. In May, however, markets began to react to the disputes that were dividing traditional allies, and weaker prices led to a long, tense OPEC conference in early June.

When oil ministers reassembled on 1 June 1989, many were unable to believe that Kuwait would insist on a quota increase larger than the 5%–8% increase in the OPEC total which was under discussion for the second half of the year. However, they failed to take account of Kuwait's situation in early 1989, which was unique within OPEC. In percentage terms, it had made greater production sacrifices during the 1980s than any other OPEC member, despite having less financial interest than others in maintaining prices at a high level. Days of negotiations between Kuwait and the other OPEC members failed to reach an accommodation. Other governments' fear of the domestic political consequences of acceding to Kuwait's demands proved stronger, ultimately, than their desire to reach a compromise between Kuwait's claim for a quota of 1.35m. b/d and the 1.12m. b/d which it would have been allocated under a straight prorata distribution of the 20m. b/d ceiling which a majority thought reasonable to stabilize prices. Leaving no room for doubt about his intentions, Kuwait's Minister of Oil, Sheikh Ali Khalifa as-Sabah, proposed an amendment to the final OPEC resolution, exempting Kuwait from the agreed production quotas. To take account of the additional volume of Kuwaiti production, which was now regarded as inevitable (it had already been overproducing in May and June by some 800,000 b/d–900,000 b/d), the production ceiling was raised by only 1m. b/d to 19.5m. b/d, correspondingly reducing the extra volumes to which other members were entitled.

The 1990s—lost opportunities

The 1990s is a crucial decade for all oil exporters, especially for those with large reserves who are mainly in the Middle East and North Africa. Kuwait and Saudi Arabia have attempted to reduce their dependence on buyers of crude oil, beginning with the acquisition, in the 1970s, of control over their natural oil resources by buying into the downstream oil industry in Europe and the USA. While the reintegration of the oil industry is seen by many observers as inevitable and a force for stability, the restoration of direct ownership links between Middle Eastern producers and the refiners and distributors of oil products in the consuming countries may act as a counterweight to OPEC and the attempts to co-ordinate oil interests in the Middle East and North Africa. In September 1989, a meeting of OPEC's Long-Term Strategy Committee was due to attempt to solve the perennial problems of quota distribution, oil prices and the likely impact on oil producers of the growing 'environmentalist' movement in western consumer countries. In the event, the Long-Term Strategy Committee convened in Geneva from 23–27 September and, the eight permanent members being joined by ministers from all other OPEC adherents, a full-scale quota and pricing meeting took place. An interim report on long-term strategy talked airily about co-operation within OPEC, with non-OPEC producers and with consumers, but the meeting subsequently lapsed into the familiar pattern of proposal, counter-proposal, objection and final agreement on quotas. None of the participants appeared to be convinced that they would be adhered to. Iran called for a redistribution of quotas, to favour

Kuwait, the UAE, Ecuador and Gabon, within a ceiling of 21.5m. b/d. However, the call was rejected because of Libya's demand for parity with Kuwait, and the UAE's insistence on an even larger quota than Iran had proposed. The old prorata formula was revived, within a new ceiling of 20.5m. b/d, just 1m. b/d lower than the level set previously. Kuwait duly rejected its quota of 1.149m. b/d for the final quarter of 1989.

At the next full OPEC meeting, held on 25–28 November 1989, quotas were redistributed, with Kuwait being allocated 6.82% of total output compared with 5.61% previously. The production ceiling was raised to 22m. b/d, although most members regarded this as insignificant since the *de facto* level of production was already 24m. b/d. Iran, Algeria and Indonesia all relinquished quota shares in Kuwait's favour even though, given the parlous state of their economies, they were themselves probably more suitable candidates for increases. However, with Saudi Arabia refusing to make any concessions, someone had to give way to bring some semblance of peace. The immediate result was that the UAE, seeing how a rich member like Kuwait could achieve its aims by totally ignoring the needs of poorer members, felt obliged to follow suit. So the November 1989 agreement left the overall situation much as before, with Kuwait adhering to its quota, but the UAE producing 100% more than it had been allocated. Overall output continued to run at nearly 24m. b/d, apart from a dip in January 1990, when overproduction was limited to 830,000 b/d.

The hyperbole surrounding the new agreement had an unforeseen side-effect: the price of crude petroleum started to rise and by January 1990 it had reached its highest level for two years. To some extent this was prompted by optimistic demand estimates issued by OPEC, and by a closer adherence by members to their quotas. However, during January–May 1990, prices fell steadily, with discounting and 'new formula' pricing rife. The one thing that could have stabilized matters—adherence to quotas—was forgotten.

To a large extent, the first quarter of 1990 may go down in history as a period of lost opportunity for OPEC. World demand for oil rose slowly at a time when several non-OPEC producers were experiencing difficulties. The continued fall in US production, the problems facing the United Kingdom and Mexico and the inability of Soviet infrastructure to maintain oil-production levels all combined to open a sizeable gap in the market which OPEC producers could have filled. The rapid change of regime in virtually all Eastern European countries reinforced this trend. However, disputes between Middle Eastern producers once more resulted in overproduction and prices slumped. Moreover, despite professing concern over environmental issues, OPEC did not appear to have realized that the industrialized part of the world was becoming serious about eliminating the more noxious aspects of fossil-fuel use. The fact that the price of many oil products in consuming countries does not decline in line with declines in the price of crude oil also seemed to have gone unnoticed.

With the market behaving unpredictably, the meeting of the Ministerial Monitoring Committee, held on 16–17 March, took no action, hoping that the situation would become clearer before the next full OPEC meeting on 25 May. In the event, prices continued to decline, and overproduction continued to such an extent that, immediately before a further meeting of the Monitoring Committee, on 2 May, increasing numbers of tankers were being chartered to serve as floating storage in a glutted market. The next full OPEC meeting was thus postponed, first until June and then until late July.

At the meeting of the Monitoring Committee held on 2 May it was agreed to reduce production by 1.445m. b/d from an average level of 23.5m. b/d. This measure brought production to just within the previously agreed ceiling and had little more than a cosmetic effect on the market. Prices strengthened for a day or two, then resumed their steady downward slide. And while producers all willingly agreed to cut back their production, some weeks later the overall cut was only around half that which had been agreed.

The full OPEC meeting which began on 25 July 1990 took place in an atmosphere of increasing tension caused by Iraq's threats of military action against countries which failed to observe production quotas. Iraq had accused both the UAE and Kuwait of flouting their quotas and claimed, with reference to

a long-standing territorial dispute, that Kuwait had violated the Iraqi border in order to steal Iraqi oil. At the meeting Iraq sought to raise OPEC's minimum reference price to $25 per barrel, but in the event the ministerial council adopted a new price of $21 per barrel—which it hoped to achieve by the end of 1990—and fixed a new production ceiling of 22.5m. b/d for the remainder of 1990. Quotas for individual countries remained unchanged, except that of the UAE which was raised to 1.5m. b/d. The immediate effect of Iraq's invasion—and subsequent annexation—of Kuwait at the beginning of August, and of the economic sanctions imposed on Iraq by the UN in response to it, was the loss of about 8% of world oil production. By late August prices had risen to about $30 per barrel and OPEC members were divided over whether to increase production to compensate for the loss of supplies from Iraq and Kuwait.

Within a matter of weeks, however, many OPEC members had decided that it was in everybody's best interest to make good the 4.5m. b/d loss to the market. Saudi Arabia in particular pledged massive support for the reversal of Iraq's action, inviting foreign military assistance to defend its borders. It also raised its petroleum production considerably, partly to pay for such assistance and partly as a *quid pro quo*. Other OPEC members, mindful that non-OPEC sources might be used to make good the loss of Iraqi and Kuwaiti supplies, followed suit. Such non-OPEC action was not, in fact, immediately forthcoming, the option of marketing oil from the US Strategic Petroleum Reserve being withheld until the situation clarified. Similarly, the IEA declared that it would hold back its reserves until shortages were confirmed. Some non-OPEC producers raised their production, while planned closures for maintenance in areas such as the North Sea were postponed until the market stabilized.

The *de facto* raising of production by a number of OPEC member states duly became *de jure* on 29 August 1990, when 10 OPEC ministers of oil met in Vienna and agreed to compensate for 3.0m. b/d–3.5m. b/d of lost production. By this time the price of crude oil had risen to $32 per barrel. A further meeting took place on 12 December 1990 and it was agreed to continue with the suspension of quotas until the Iraqi–Kuwaiti conflict was resolved. Once it was resolved, it was decided that quotas would be brought back into force, with the target price of $21 per barrel being retained.

The next meeting of OPEC, on 12 March 1991, confirmed that whatever decisions OPEC took, the market remained the dominant force. Oil producers had by this time increased output to such an extent that, even as the loss of Iraqi and Kuwaiti production continued, prices had plummeted and storage capacity had become scarce. Pledges that the strategic reserves of consuming countries might be brought into use had acted as a spur. Saudi Arabian production peaked at more than 9m. b/d, while the UAE had raised its output to more than 2.5m. b/d.

With supplies abundant and demand moving from winter to summer levels, prices fell by about 50% from their peak of $32 per barrel. Saudi Arabia reduced production and by April 1991 the market had become more balanced, with prices having recovered to around $4 below the OPEC target price of $21 per barrel. The situation was more or less as it had been before Iraq's invasion of Kuwait. It was decided at the OPEC meeting on 12 March 1991 to reduce production by about 5%, from 23.4m. b/d to 22.298m. b/d. However, individual OPEC members had already taken account of falling demand and the true level of OPEC production was little above the newly targeted level. The cut was thus more apparent than real and had no effect on prices.

However, by formalizing new quotas the OPEC meeting of 12 March 1991 did allow most producers to maintain output at a level close to their production capacity. A further meeting was held on 4 June 1991 at which it was agreed to maintain the *status quo*. The quotas which had been set in March were to remain in force until September 1991, when a further meeting would decide whether any adjustments needed to be made. Ironically, Iraq's invasion of Kuwait, which had aimed to prevent the latter's persistent flouting of its OPEC quota, had had the effect of stabilizing the market, balancing supply with demand; but neither Iraq nor Kuwait were any longer in a position to take advantage of the new equilibrium.

The meeting of OPEC held on 24–26 September 1991 set a new production ceiling of 23.6m. b/d. In fact, OPEC production had averaged 23.636m. b/d during the first half of 1991, far above the production ceiling that had been agreed in March 1991; while in the second half of that year it had averaged 24.741m. b/d. Clearly, OPEC members were seeking to maximize their production regardless of their quota allocations, and prices remained far below the OPEC target price of $21 per barrel.

Kuwait recommenced production of oil in June 1991, increasing it gradually from 70,000 b/d to 550,000 b/d by the end of the year. It was clear that if Kuwait continued to restore capacity at this rate, then other OPEC producers would have to reduce theirs in order to accommodate it. At an interim meeting of OPEC held on 27 November 1991, it was agreed to reappraise the level of production within the Organization in February 1992. Meanwhile, however, the market began to dictate production levels. The situation was further complicated by a steep decline in production by the former Soviet republics, although this was offset by the continued economic recession in many consuming countries. As a result total demand for oil declined by 1.1% and it became clear that, without a voluntary reduction in production, the market would enforce a collapse in prices.

Before the OPEC meeting of February 1992 took place, nine of the 13 OPEC member states announced reductions in production totalling 400,000 b/d. Consequently there was little dissent when, at the meeting on 15 February, a new production quota of 22.982m. b/d was set. The new ceiling was opposed only by Saudi Arabia, whose official policy was now to seek quotas in accordance with production capacity.

In February 1992 Iraq was granted a production quota which, at 505,000 b/d, was sufficient to satisfy domestic demand. Kuwait was granted a quota of 812,000 b/d, although at the time it was unclear whether it would be able to achieve this level of production. Individual OPEC member states continued to abide by, or ignore, their production quotas as it suited them, but overall OPEC production remained more or less in line with the production ceiling as a result of market forces.

At the OPEC meeting held on 22 May 1992 ministers agreed, with some reservations, to maintain the production ceiling at 22.982m. b/d, although Kuwait was allowed to produce more than its previous quota of 812,000 b/d in order to compensate for production lost during the Iraqi occupation. Finally, the market met the wishes of almost all the OPEC member states. Increasing demand for oil for storage, for example, allowed Saudi Arabia, which had requested a higher quota, to continue to produce above the level of its formal quota. Iran had sought a reduction in the production ceiling in order to raise prices, and in fact increased demand raised spot market prices to close to the OPEC target price of $21 per barrel. However, the market remained exposed to factors that were beyond OPEC's control. Production by Russia and the United Kingdom, for instance, had begun to increase, while oil from recently-discovered fields in, for example, Colombia, increased the pressure on the cartel.

Spot prices continued to firm in the immediate aftermath of the OPEC meeting of 22 May 1992, and in late June reached their highest level for seven months. Factors influencing the market included the failure, on 22 June, of the UN and Iraq to reach any agreement on the resumption of Iraqi petroleum exports, and forecast higher demand for OPEC petroleum in the USA in the summer months. On the whole prices remained firm during July, August and the early weeks of September. By mid-September, however, when the Ministerial Monitoring Committee met in Geneva, concern was being expressed at the margin by which spot prices were failing to reach the target price of $21 per barrel, especially since market conditions were considered to be fundamentally favourable. By this time OPEC production was substantially in excess of the previously agreed level. Saudi Arabia, for instance, was reported to be producing, on average, 8.3m. b/d, compared with its allocation of 7.887m. b/d. Iranian production was also significantly above allocated level.

It was widely agreed that the statement issued at the conclusion of the Ministerial Monitoring Committee meeting contained no measures that were likely to raise prices to the target level. The statement indicated that OPEC's market share in the fourth quarter of 1992 should be 24.2m. b/d in order to achieve the target price, and reaffirmed OPEC's earlier decision to allow for additional, unspecified Kuwaiti production. However, some

analysts and OPEC ministers argued that the agreement would boost prices to the target level. Taking into account Kuwaiti production of 200,000 b/d, OPEC production was likely to be more than 24.4m. b/d during the final quarter of 1992. However, winter demand for OPEC oil was estimated at 25m. b/d–25.5m. b/d. Also at the September meeting Ecuador confirmed its withdrawal from OPEC with effect from November 1992, after which time it would enjoy 'associate status' of the Organization only.

As demand for OPEC crude oil rose, total production averaged some 24.75m. b/d in September. By early October demand had risen to such an extent that the Secretary-General of OPEC, Dr Subroto, dismissed the idea of reimposing quotas at the next OPEC meeting in November. Prices were reportedly sustained by forward winter demand and by continued political tension in the Middle East. However, as seasonal demand for oil began to reach its peak in early October, prices remained below the level that had been expected.

At the OPEC meeting held in November 1992 in Vienna measures were taken that were designed to remove some 400,000 b/d of OPEC crude from the market in December. These included the establishment of a total OPEC production level of slightly less than 24.6m. b/d for the first quarter of 1993; and the establishment of new production allocations for OPEC member states to take effect from 1 December 1992. It was also agreed to allow Kuwait to continue to produce more than its allocated level of crude.

By mid-December a feared collapse in the price of oil appeared to have been averted. By early January 1993, however, prices had fallen to almost the lowest levels recorded in 1992 as a result of weak demand and production that remained in excess of the levels agreed in Vienna the previous November. Indeed, it was reported that production by the 12 OPEC member states and Ecuador in December 1992 had averaged 25.27m. b/d, its highest level since 1980. During the remainder of January, with stock levels remaining high, prices continued to weaken and towards the end of the month the Saudi Arabian Minister of Oil suggested that member states should reduce their collective production by 1m. b/d in order to check the decline in prices, which had fallen from $21 per barrel to $17 per barrel over the previous four months.

At the next full OPEC meeting, held in Vienna in February, it was agreed to make pro rata reductions in production that would effectively remove almost 1.5m. b/d from the market. The reductions, which pertained to the second quarter of 1993, were to take effect from 1 March. However, OPEC's declared commitment to maintaining a production ceiling of 23.58m. b/d met with the strongest scepticism from most observers, who believed that the new agreement would only begin to support prices in mid-March when it would be clear whether or not it was being observed. It appeared that attention would be closely focused on Kuwaiti production in the second quarter. Kuwait had agreed, reluctantly, to reduce its output to 1.6m. b/d, but warned that the slightest non-observance by other OPEC member states would immediately cause it to produce at a claimed capacity level of 2.1m. b/d. Kuwait had reportedly only agreed to reduce its second-quarter production in exchange for a third-quarter allocation equal to that of other countries with similar production capacity, historical market share and quota. Above all, the agreement indicated that the pressures relieved by the loss of Kuwaiti production in the 1990–91 crisis in the Gulf now applied to the market once again.

By late February the price of crude petroleum had reached a three-month peak since it appeared that OPEC's biggest producers would observe the agreement of 16 February. Prices did, in fact, remain firm during March, even though it appeared that production had averaged between 24m. b/d–24.3m. b/d. This compared with estimated production of 25.35m. b/d in February and the reduction was greater than most observers had expected it to be. However, there was concern that Iran was continuing to produce above its allocated level and that such overproduction might cause Kuwait to flout its own allocated level of 1.6m. b/d. Observers also expressed fears that OPEC's efforts to support prices would be cancelled out if the industry failed to build up its stocks during the second quarter of 1993. At an unofficial meeting in Muscat, Oman, in mid-April the oil ministers of the OPEC member states determined to adhere more closely to the production levels allocated in February. OPEC's own estimate of total production in March was 23.8m. b/d, some 290,000 b/d in excess of the agreed ceiling.

At the beginning of May 1993 the market was reported to be broadly in balance and prices were steady though below the levels OPEC producers had hoped to achieve. According to one analyst, OPEC production had averaged 24.32m. b/d in April, with Saudi Arabia and Iran allegedly the main over-producers. Later in the month the CGES forecast that demand for OPEC oil would reach 25.3m. b/d in the third quarter of 1993. Fears were expressed that individual OPEC member states might be tempted to increase their production in pursuit of increased sales and greater revenue. The CGES suggested that additional demand for OPEC petroleum could be allocated on a pro rata basis, using the production agreement of February as a guide; or that extra demand could be shared according to each member state's sustainable capacity.

The spot price of a representative selection of OPEC crudes was reported to have averaged $18.20 per barrel in May, almost 1.5% lower than in April and March. Production in May was reportedly 230,000 b/d lower than in April, but, at an estimated 24.1m. b/d, still higher than OPEC's second-quarter output ceiling of 23.58m. b/d. Prices weakened during the approach to OPEC's next full ministerial meeting in June, in Geneva, not least because there was little confidence that the meeting would conclude a credible production agreement.

During June 1993 oil prices remained below the targeted level of $21 per barrel that OPEC had sought to achieve through the reintroduction—in all but name—of the quota system it had abandoned during the 1990–91 crisis in the Gulf, in the form of production allocations agreed by the member states. The problem, as far as the market was concerned, was that nobody involved in the industry believed that the member states would be able to summon sufficient discipline to observe the production ceiling of 23.58m. b/d introduced in February 1993 and extended, in June, to the third quarter of 1993. In its forecast of price trends for the year to June 1994 the CGES considered three possible developments, each based on the assumption that the supply of OPEC oil would continue to exceed demand for it: that OPEC would respond to demand by raising its production to 24.9m. b/d, in which case prices would remain below $19 per barrel; that OPEC would be able to hold production at or below 24.5m. b/d, in which case the CGES forecast that the average price for OPEC crude petroleum would reach $20.10 in the period April–June 1994; or, if OPEC were unable to exercise sufficient discipline and production rose to 25.2m. b/d in the third quarter of 1993, that the average price of OPEC crude would remain at or below $18.10 per barrel in October–December 1993, falling to $17.90 in April–June 1994.

The market had every reason to suspect that the OPEC member states would fail to observe their declared production target. Kuwait had begun to claim, with increasing insistence, an allocation that fully reflected its restored production capacity. At the OPEC ministerial meeting held in Geneva on 8–10 June 1993 Kuwait requested an official allocation of 2.16m. b/d for the third quarter of 1993, claiming that it had effectively been promised an increase in its allocation to 2m. b/d at the OPEC meeting in Vienna in February 1993. Saudi Arabia gave no indication of any willingness to renounce what it considered to be its right to one-third of total OPEC production, and Iran remained keen to maximize revenues by maximizing its production. The prospect of the removal of the UN's economic sanctions on Iraq remained distant, although Iraq had claimed, one year earlier, to have fully repaired all war damage to its oil production facilities and to have boosted its capacity. The vexed and potentially disruptive issue of quota parity between Iran and Iraq could thus be dismissed for the time being, and producing countries could concentrate on optimistic predictions of the increasing dependence of the large industrial countries on oil over the coming twenty years. Indeed, it had been argued that lower prices for oil since 1985 had acted in the interest of OPEC—and other—producers by discouraging research, investment in and development of alternative energy sources; and by making North American and North Sea fields less competitive, enabling OPEC to regain most of the markets it had lost after 1979.

In early July 1994 oil prices were strengthening in response to OPEC's decision, taken at a meeting of member states' oil ministers in mid-June, to freeze production at 24.52m. b/d for the remainder of 1994 and to cancel its regular September meeting. Another cause of firmer prices was growth in US demand, which was reported to have risen by some 1m. b/d since the beginning of 1994. Also, it appeared likely, owing to constraints on production in certain countries, that OPEC would be able to observe the production ceiling more easily than it had others in the past.

OPEC's decision consolidated a recovery in the price of world crude oil, which had risen by some 25% between the end of March and mid-May 1994. Factors involved in the recovery had included an upward revision in the forecast demand for crude oil in 1994 by the IEA; and a slight reduction, in April, in OPEC's total production of crude.

This recovery was in contrast to the trend that had prevailed for most of the previous 12 months. Indeed, OPEC's decision, in March 1994, to maintain production at 24.52m. b/d for the remainder of the year had led to fears of a collapse in the world price of oil and to speculation that OPEC might take emergency measures if prices fell any closer to $10 per barrel in the spring and summer. OPEC's inability to reduce surplus supplies to the market had been determined, in part, by Kuwait's unwillingness to accept a pro-rata cut in production, although all other OPEC states had indicated their readiness to act to reduce combined crude oil production by up to 10% for the second and third quarters of 1994. In 1993 OPEC production reportedly rose by 2.9% to an average of just under 25m. b/d, while world oil prices declined by some 30%. In December prices fell to their lowest level for five years as a consequence of OPEC's failure, in late November, to modify the production ceiling of 24.52m. b/d first fixed in September. This had initially provoked a positive reaction from the market, but prices subsequently fell owing to weak demand and doubts whether the OPEC member states would adhere to their individual quotas.

In late July 1994, prices were firm owing to OPEC member states' observance of the Organization's combined production quota, and to the loss of some Nigerian supplies after industrial action. By mid-August Nigerian production had declined by some 25% since the beginning of an oil workers' strike in June, and this factor had combined with a drop in Iranian production to support prices. During August OPEC producers did not attempt to compensate for the lost Nigerian production by raising their output, with the result that the distance between supply and demand continued to increase, contributing to an increase in the average price of crude oil during the second quarter of the year. During the third week of August the price of the OPEC 'basket' of crude oil was reported to have averaged $16.70 per barrel, about $0.40 higher than one year earlier. In the last week of August prices weakened as Nigerian production began to recover after the Government had ended the oil workers' strike.

Demand was expected to weaken during September as a result of the planned closure of refineries in the USA, Europe and Japan. This factor combined with Nigeria's wholehearted return to the market to put prices under pressure, and by the third week of the month they had fallen by about 15% from the levels achieved in August.

Prior to the OPEC ministerial conference in November 1994 there were optimistic forecasts of demand for OPEC oil for the rest of the year, and for 1995. According to the CGES, demand for OPEC crude for the whole of 1994 would increase, on average, by about 400,000 b/d, and would rise by a further 800,000 b/d in 1995.

At the OPEC ministerial conference in November the unanimous decision was taken to adhere to the existing level of production of 24.52m. b/d in the hope that this would cause prices to rise towards the desired level of $21 per barrel. The average price of OPEC crudes in October had been only $15.36 per barrel. At the ministerial meeting, when the decision on production levels was taken, OPEC's, output was above the quota level. Average production in November was estimated at 24.92m. b/d-25.1m. b/d. Most of the above-quota surplus was attributed to increases in Iranian and Venezuelan production. According to the Washington-based Petroleum Finance Corporation, OPEC's revenues were $121,000m. in 1994, compared with

$137,000m. in 1993. This indicated that average prices had been substantially lower in 1994 than in 1993.

At the beginning of 1995 prices remained firm despite further evidence of excessive production within OPEC and increased competition from non-OPEC suppliers. In January average OPEC production was estimated at 25m. b/d. The average price for OPEC crudes was $17 per barrel, compared with $16 per barrel in December 1994. This trend, which continued through the first quarter of the year, was attributed by the CGES to strong demand resulting from improving world economic conditions. OPEC producers nevertheless remained concerned about excessive production.

Prices remained stable in mid-March, but it was reported that increases achieved since production had been frozen at the beginning of 1995 had been cancelled out by the decline in the value of the US dollar in which world oil prices are denominated. OPEC production was reported to have risen further, to 25.1m. b/d, in February. In the final week of March prices rose to their highest level for the year owing to a combination of strong demand and uncertainty over whether the USA would succeed in imposing an embargo on sales of Libyan oil. These factors, combined with reduced production in Iran and Saudi Arabia in March, had, by mid-April, raised prices to more than $18 per barrel, their highest level since August 1994. At the beginning of May prices rose further during the approach to the imposition, by the USA, of a trade embargo against Iran. However, this rise was not sustained owing to lack of international support for the embargo.

The quota level agreed in November 1994 appeared to be under severe strain in May 1995 when, according to *Petroleum Intelligence Weekly*, output rose to 27.725m. b/d, the highest monthly production figure for three years. The increase was attributed to raised production in Saudi Arabia, Iran and Venezuela. At the ministerial meeting held in Vienna in June 1995 OPEC member states chose to retain the production quota of 24.52m. b/d for the remainder of the year.

By July, markets for oil were weak, prices having fallen to their lowest levels for the year earlier in the month. OPEC producers were reported to be increasingly concerned at the continued decline in their share of the market. Demand for crude petroleum had risen by some 10% over the preceding two years, but most of this had been met by non-OPEC suppliers. According to some estimates, OPEC production of crude oil was higher in July 1995 than in any of the previous six months, averaging 25.15m. b/d.

Speculation about the future marketing of Iraqi oil was responsible for a further weakening of prices in mid-August, amid predictions that weaker economic growth in the coming months would reduce demand for OPEC oil and that non-OPEC producers would capture most of the future growth in demand for oil that did occur. In mid-August, however, prices—especially those of US crudes—firmed as a result of potentially hostile Iraqi troop movements and of joint US-Jordanian military manoeuvres. Low US stocks were another factor. *Reuters* reported that OPEC production in August was at its highest level for 15 years, averaging 25.72m. b/d. Average OPEC production for the month was thus 1.2m. b/d higher than the quota level of 24.52m. b/d. *Reuters* reported that Saudi Arabia, Venezuela, Nigeria, Iran and the UAE all produced at more than their official quotas during August and speculated that such overproduction, if sustained, could place prices under pressure during the final quarter of 1995. During January–August 1995 the price of the OPEC 'basket' of crudes averaged $17 per barrel.

In late September OPEC estimated that demand for its members' oil would total 23.8m. b/d in the third quarter of 1995, some 200,000 b/d less than had previously been estimated. OPEC forecast that demand would total 25.6m. b/d in the final quarter of the year, a reduction of 300,000 b/d compared with OPEC's previous estimates. OPEC now estimated that demand for the year would average 25m. b/d.

In a report published in October the CGES recommended that OPEC should reduce production by at least 600,000 b/d if it was to limit the decline of prices in 1996. Such a reduction could only be achieved if current quotas were strictly observed. However, it was widely recognized that there was little possibility of this being realized: Venezuela, for example, was already overproducing by some 300,000 b/d. Prices nevertheless remained firm

in advance of the OPEC ministerial meeting in Vienna on 21 November, at which it was agreed to maintain production at its current level for a further six months from 1 January 1996. According to estimates by *Reuters*, OPEC production averaged 25.5m. b/d in October and 25.27m. b/d in November.

In a report published in December 1995, the IEA emphasized the warnings contained in the report published by the CGES in October (see above), forecasting a decline in demand for OPEC crude oil, from an average of 25.1m. b/d in 1995 to 24.6m. b/d in 1996. Stimulated by fundamental factors, however, demand in the northern hemisphere remained strong during December and into 1996. Prices declined slightly in the third week of January as a result of increased speculation regarding the return of Iraqi supplies to the market. Earlier predictions of a sharp decline in prices in 1996 seemed unlikely to be realized during the early part of the year as stocks—especially those in the USA—remained low, this factor combining with strong seasonal demand to support prices. According to the Washington-based Petroleum Finance Corporation, these factors were sufficient to maintain the market even if OPEC production were to rise as high as 26m. b/d.

Iraq's decision, announced on 24 January 1996, to reopen negotiations with the UN on the sale of a limited quantity of its oil had a depressing effect on prices, especially as OPEC was thought to have no strategy for dealing with the ultimate return of Iraqi supplies to the market. When the talks actually commenced on 6 February 1996 OPEC took the precaution of repeating that it would convene an extraordinary ministerial conference when an agreement was eventually reached between the UN and Iraq.

High seasonal demand continued to combine with low stocks to support prices during February, a process reinforced at the end of the month by the conclusion of the first round of negotiations between Iraq and the UN without agreement. The Iraqi issue continued to influence markets, however. In early March there were signs that Iraq was moving closer to accepting the UN's terms for a resumption of oil sales and there was widespread scepticism among observers that OPEC producers would be able, or, indeed, willing to reduce production to accommodate Iraqi supplies except in the event of a drastic decline in prices. The continued flouting of quotas was reported to have led to an increase in OPEC production to 26m. b/d in February.

Low stocks—again, principally in the USA—remained the major influence on the market and were regarded as responsible for prices rising to their highest level for five years on 20 March 1996. The continued failure of Iraq and the UN to make any progress in their negotiations was a further factor behind the rise. Prices appeared finally to peak in late April after US President Bill Clinton announced the decision to release 12m. barrels of oil from the US Strategic Petroleum Reserve over a six-month period in order to counter rises in the price of gasoline.

On 20 May 1996 the UN and Iraq concluded an agreement under the terms of which Iraq was permitted to sell $2,000m.-worth of petroleum over a 180-day period in order to finance the purchase of humanitarian supplies and UN operations in Iraq and in the three Kurdish governorates in the north of the country. Contrary to its own earlier expressed intentions, OPEC did not convene an emergency ministerial meeting in order to devise a strategy to accommodate Iraq's return to the market. Not surprisingly, however, it was Iraq that dominated the ordinary ministerial meeting of OPEC member states which commenced in Vienna on 5 June. There was speculation, prior to the meeting, that OPEC would instigate measures to curb overproduction by member states, but, in the event, no such action was taken. The OPEC production quota of 24.52m. b/d that had been in force during the first half of the year was merely renewed, with a supplementary allowance of 800,000 b/d which Iraq would need to sell, at prevailing price levels, in order to achieve the maximum revenue permitted under the agreement with the UN. The quota of 287,000 b/d for Gabon, which had left OPEC at the end of 1996, was withdrawn, leaving a final quota of 25.033m. b/d for the second half of 1996. Few observers considered the new quota to be realistic: in May OPEC production was estimated to have averaged 26m. b/d, rising above this level at the beginning of June. In view of this, already considerable overproduction, it was arguable that was the OPEC ministerial conference had done nothing that was likely to be effective to manage the return of Iraqi supplies to the market.

Prices nevertheless remained stable, as they had since the conclusion of the agreement between Iraq and the UN in May. It was announced in June that the OPEC monitoring committee was to be reconstituted and that it would monitor production in June, July and August before meeting for the first time in September 1996. Chaired by the Iranian Minister of Oil, Gholamreza Aqazadeh, with representatives from Libya and Nigeria, the committee pledged to take firm action against member states found to be in breach of their quotas, although no details were released of exactly how they might be penalized.

By the beginning of July 1996 it was clear that there was going to be some delay before Iraqi exports recommenced, the USA having rejected Iraq's proposed procedures on 27 June. From now almost until the end of 1996 prices were to rise consistently, mainly but not exclusively, in response to the delay in the implementation of the agreement between Iraq and the UN. The USA's rejection of Iraqi proposals, for example, bolstered prices which might otherwise have fallen as a result of predictions that supplies would be excessive in the second half of 1996. The delay of Iraq's return to the market continued to support prices in the second week of July when all other indications pointed to a market in balance. The price of Brent blend crude for immediate delivery—the reference price for the majority of crude petroleums—rose to $19.99 per barrel, its highest level since April. OPEC production was estimated to have amounted to 25.64m. b/d in June, some 600,000 b/d in excess of the expanded quota announced that month. OPEC reported that the 'basket' price of member states' crudes had averaged $18.83 per barrel in the first six months of 1996, compared with $16.86 per barrel in the whole of 1995.

At the beginning of August the continued failure of Iraq and the UN to establish the procedures for renewed sales of Iraqi petroleum remained the most important market-strengthening factor. Demand remained strong and it was estimated that OPEC production in July had totalled 25.86m. b/d. Saudi Arabia reportedly informed OPEC that, in spite of production in excess of its quota level, it had not marketed in excess of quota in that month. Prices continued to rise in the third week of August: in the middle of the month the Brent reference blend was fetching $21 per barrel, compared with an average price of $16 per barrel in August 1995; and analysts sought to explain why prices were doing precisely the opposite of what they had predicted they would do in the second half of the year. According to the CGES, low industrial stocks of petroleum were the most convincing explanation for the strength of petroleum markets at the end of August.

US missile attacks on Iraqi targets on 3 and 4 September 1996 raised oil prices to their highest levels since the 1991 conflict in the Persian (Arabian) Gulf. The USA's opposition to the resumption of Iraqi petroleum exports hardened and it appeared now that these exports would not commence before the end of 1996. Perceived shortages of heating oil in the USA and Europe began to assume more significance in forecasts of oil price development for the final quarter of the year. The possibility of shortages in the absence of Iraqi supplies lifted prices to their highest levels for the year in the second week of September as the renewed conflict between Iraq and the USA remained unresolved. In Europe the price of the Brent reference blend rose above $23 per barrel. The IEA, meanwhile, predicted that there would be a reduction in OPEC supplies in the third and fourth quarters and at the same time raised its estimate of demand for OPEC crudes in those periods by 700,000 b/d. According to the IEA, OPEC production amounted to 25.81m. b/d in August, a slight reduction compared with July.

With prices having risen by almost 30% since June and with many observers indicating the possibility of shortages before the end of 1996, it was no surprise that the OPEC monitoring committee, meeting in Vienna on 25 September, decided, in spite of the warning it had issued earlier in the year, to take no action against member states that continued to produce and to market oil well in excess of their quota levels. Prices were supported in early October by continued predictions of a shortage of heating oil in the northern hemisphere in the coming winter months, and by continued forecasts of strong demand in the final quarter of 1996. The IEA estimated OPEC production had amounted to 25.88m. b/d in September.

The market situation outlined above continued through the final quarter of the year. From December 1996 Iraq began to influence petroleum markets more directly. There was no dramatic weakening of prices when Iraqi exports finally recommenced on 10 December, but it soon became clear that the sanguine predictions voiced in the preceding months, that a new, higher trading range for petroleum had been established in response to favourable fundamental factors, were misplaced.

Oil Statistics
(compiled by the Editor)

CRUDE OIL PRODUCTION[1] (million barrels per day)

	1995	1996	1997
Middle East OPEC:			
Saudi Arabia	8.890	9.035	9.375
Kuwait	2.105	2.080	2.095
Neutral Zone[2]	0.430	0.483	0.530
Iran	3.695	3.710	3.730
Iraq	0.575	0.630	1.210
UAE—Abu Dhabi	1.832	1.954	2.000
UAE—Dubai	0.322	0.268	0.250
Qatar	0.460	0.570	0.695
North Africa OPEC:			
Libya	1.440	1.440	1.465
Algeria	1.320	1.395	1.440
Other OPEC:			
Venezuela	2.960	3.135	3.365
Nigeria	2.000	2.150	2.285
Indonesia	1.580	1.580	1.560
Other Middle East and North Africa:			
Oman	0.865	0.895	0.910
Bahrain	0.105	0.104	0.104
Syria	0.600	0.595	0.575
Egypt	0.930	0.900	0.880
Tunisia	0.090	0.090	0.090
Turkey	0.067	0.067	0.068
Yemen	0.350	0.355	0.385
Other producers:			
USA	8.320	8.295	8.255
Canada	2.400	2.480	2.560
Mexico	3.065	3.275	3.410
Ecuador	0.395	0.395	0.395
Trinidad and Tobago	0.140	0.140	0.135
Colombia	0.590	0.635	0.660
Argentina	0.750	0.815	0.845
Brazil	0.705	0.795	0.855
Brunei	0.175	0.165	0.165
India	0.790	0.770	0.790
Malaysia	0.725	0.735	0.730
Australia	0.585	0.620	0.670
United Kingdom	2.755	2.730	2.695
Norway	2.965	3.315	3.360
Ex-USSR	7.300	7.220	7.400
China, People's Rep.	2.990	3.170	3.210
Gabon	0.355	0.360	0.370
World total (incl. others)	67.945	69.870	72.215
OPEC total	27.530	28.330	29.920
Middle East and North Africa total	24.076	24.571	25.802

[1] Includes shale oil, oil sands and natural gas liquids.
[2] Shared equally between Saudi Arabia and Kuwait.
Source: Mainly BP, *Statistical Review of World Energy 1998*.

Conversion factors based on world average crude oil gravity:
1 long ton = 7.42 barrels
1 short ton = 6.63 barrels
1 metric ton = 7.30 barrels
1 barrel = 35 imperial gallons
1 barrel = 42 US gallons
To convert metric tons per year into b/d divide by 50.0
To convert long tons per year into b/d divide by 49.2

PROVEN PUBLISHED WORLD OIL RESERVES AS AT
1 JANUARY 1998 ('000 million barrels)

	Reserves	Years of production* at 1997 levels
Middle East and North Africa		
Saudi Arabia	261.5	79.5
Kuwait	96.5	†
Neutral Zone	5.0	n.a.
Iran	93.0	69.0
Iraq	112.5	†
UAE—Abu Dhabi	92.2	
UAE—Dubai	4.0	†
UAE—Sharjah	1.5	
Qatar	3.7	15.1
Oman	5.2	15.8
Bahrain	0.2	n.a.
Syria	2.5	12.0
Algeria	9.2	18.8
Libya	29.5	55.6
Egypt	3.8	12.2
Tunisia	0.3	9.4
Yemen	4.0	28.9
Middle East and North Africa total	**724.6**	**n.a.**

	Reserves	Years of production* at 1997 levels
Other leading producers		
Other OPEC		
Venezuela	71.7	59.5
Nigeria	16.8	20.2
Indonesia	5.0	9.0
Ecuador	2.1	14.8
Gabon	2.5	18.5
Total OPEC	**797.1**	**75.2**
Rest of World:		
USA	29.8	9.8.
Canada	6.8	9.2
Mexico	40.0	33.6
United Kingdom	5.0	5.2
Norway	10.4	8.6
Ex-USSR	65.4	24.7
Other Eastern Europe	2.1	n.a.
China, People's Repub.	24.0	20.5
World total	**1,037.6**	**40.9**

* Including crude oil, shale oil, oil sands and natural gas liquids.   † More than 100.

Sources: *Oil and Gas Journal,* December 1997; BP, *Statistical Review of World Energy 1998.*

Note: Reserve figures are subject to wide margins of error, and there are considerable differences between sources—including oil companies and governments. Proven reserves do not denote 'total oil in place', but only that proportion of the oil in a field that drilling has shown for certain to be there and to be recoverable with current technology and at present prices. Normally recoverable reserves amount to about a third of the oil in place. Because the potential of fields is continually being reassessed in the light of production experience and because the production characteristics of a field can (and often do) change as it gets older, proven reserves figures may sometimes be revised upwards or downwards by quite dramatic amounts without any new discoveries being made. Price rises tend inevitably to increase reserves figures by making small fields or more complex recovery techniques economic.

The only exception to the proven commercially recoverable reserves formula used in this table applies to the USSR figures, which, as reported by *Oil and Gas Journal,* refer to 'explored reserves', which include proved, probable and some possible reserves.

OILFIELDS IN THE MIDDLE EAST WITH RESERVES OF MORE THAN 5,000 MILLION BARRELS

		Year of discovery	Age of principal reservoirs	Estimated reserves ('000 million barrels)
Ghawar	Saudi Arabia	1948	Jurassic	83
Burgan	Kuwait	1948	Cretaceous	72
Safaniyah-Khafji	Saudi Arabia (Neutral Zone)	1951	Cretaceous	30
Rumaila	Iraq	1953	Cretaceous	20
Ahwaz	Iran	1958	Oligocene, Miocene, Cretaceous	17.5
Kirkuk	Iraq	1927	Oligocene-Eocene, Cretaceous	16
Marun	Iran	1964	Oligocene-Miocene	16
Gach Saran	Iran	1928	Oligocene-Miocene, Cretaceous	15.5
Agha Jari	Iran	1938	Oligocene-Miocene, Cretaceous	14
Abqaiq	Saudi Arabia	1940	Jurassic	12.5
Berri	Saudi Arabia	1964	Jurassic	12
Zakum	Abu Dhabi	1964	Cretaceous	12
Manifah	Saudi Arabia	1957	Cretaceous	11
Fereidoon-Marjan	Iran/Saudi Arabia	1966	Cretaceous	10
Bu Hasa	Abu Dhabi	1962	Cretaceous	9
Qatif	Saudi Arabia	1945	Jurassic	9
Khurais	Saudi Arabia	1957	Jurassic	8.5
Zuluf	Saudi Arabia	1965	Cretaceous	8.5
Raudhatain	Kuwait	1955	Cretaceous	7.7
Shayban	Saudi Arabia	1968	Cretaceous	7
Abu Safah	Saudi Arabia/Bahrain	1963	Jurassic	6.6
Asab	Abu Dhabi	1965	Cretaceous	6
Bab	Abu Dhabi	1954	Cretaceous	6
Umm Shaif	Abu Dhabi	1958	Jurassic	5

Source: *Oilfields of the World,* E.N. Tiratsoo (Scientific Press Ltd).

GOVERNMENT OIL REVENUES OF OPEC MEMBER COUNTRIES IN THE MIDDLE EAST AND NORTH AFRICA*
(million US dollars)

	1980	1981	1982	1983	1984	1985	1986	1987	1988	1989	1990	1991
Iran	13,286	12,053	19,233	19,255	12,255	13,115	7,183	10,515	8,170	14,000	15,240	19,300
Saudi Arabia† . .	105,813	116,183	75,534	42,809	34,243	24,180	16,975	19,271	20,500	16,000	40,700	47,900
Kuwait† . . .	17,678	13,790	8,827	9,736	10,740	9,817	6,378	7,520	6,295	9,250	5,800	1,100
Iraq	26,296	10,422	10,096	7,816	9,354	10,685	6,905	11,416	10,952	12,000	8,000	1,600
UAE	19,558	18,815	15,337	12,235	12,978	11,842	7,453	8,665	7,352	10,438	21,100	14,000
Qatar	5,406	5,350	4,108	3,110	4,386	3,068	1,720	1,829	1,709	1,800	2,000	2,200
Libya	21,378	15,254	12,769	11,909	10,631	9,962	5,787	6,011	5,169	5,000	9,000	8,800
Algeria. . . .	12,647	12,985	10,770	9,467	9,189	9,170	4,819	6,057	4,988	3,800	12,300	10,300

* Figures include income from refined products and natural gas liquids, except Saudi Arabian figures which exclude natural gas liquids. Figures for Algeria from 1990 include revenue from sales of natural gas.
† Including an equal share of revenue from Neutral Zone sales.

Sources: OPEC, to 1988; government and oil industry estimates from 1989.

NATURAL GAS IN THE MIDDLE EAST
AND NORTH AFRICA

CHRIS CRAGG

Revised for this edition by the Editor

The Middle East now accounts for more than 30% of the world's proven reserves of natural gas. With the addition of Algeria, Libya, Tunisia and Egypt, the figure is closer to 40%. This amounts to 54,670,000m. cu m (excluding Tunisia), according to a 1998 survey, but even this figure should be regarded as conservative. The eastern part of the region lies in a trend that most geologists now believe contains the bulk of Eurasia's hydrocarbons. This runs from the Yamal peninsular in Russian Siberia to the Caspian Sea, across the 'fertile crescent' into Saudi Arabia, and across the Red Sea towards Sudan. Proven reserves in the region, second only to those of Russia, have more than quadrupled since 1970. Indeed, since the mid-1980s they have risen by more than two-thirds, the additional amount alone sufficient for almost 8 years' of global gross consumption. At current levels of production, proven reserves in the Middle East could last well into the second century of the next millenium, and proven reserves underestimate potential reserves, sometimes by as much as a factor of two.

However, many countries, especially those on the shores of the Persian (Arabian) Gulf, have sufficient proven reserves to meet any short-term requirements and have simply not tried to discover more gas. Where this is not so, notably in Syria, Egypt, Yemen and Algeria, the search has continued successfully. In general, however, more attention has been paid to the expansion of domestic, western and eastern European and Japanese markets.

In spite of huge reserves, natural gas has until very recently been an under-utilized resource in much of the Middle East and North Africa. In contrast to oil, it was difficult to export, requiring either large pipeline systems or very expensive conversion into liquefied natural gas (LNG). Since in terms of volume, oil has a far greater thermal content than gas, gas produced far less reward than oil for a given capital expenditure. Local markets were generally dominated by oil burning, or did not exist. As a result, oil companies looking for oil and finding gas, shut in the gas and went elsewhere. Where gas was found with oil—'associated' gas—the oil was used and the gas flared. In 1973, Saudi Arabia was flaring as much as 86% of its gross production and its flare stacks were visible to the early astronauts. Some countries, notably Algeria, Libya and Abu Dhabi did export by liquefying the gas for European, American or Japanese consumption. Yet this was a formidable technical undertaking, requiring liquefaction plants to cool the gas to −165°C, each costing as much as US $2,000m., and special ships costing over $100m. Constructed in the late 1970s, these plants came into operation at an inopportune moment, since between 1979 and 1982 world gas consumption actually fell. In the USA, there was a huge surplus of domestically-produced gas, while in Europe, large volumes of Soviet gas from Siberia reached the market. Only the Japanese, with no resources of their own, remained faithful to their supplier in Abu Dhabi. Much of the extremely expensive Algerian LNG capacity became idle after a series of disputes with US distributors.

Many countries, however, perhaps motivated by this experience, began to realize the value of what was being flared. As a substitute for oil, gas could be burnt in power stations, desalination plants, and wherever heat was required. This, in an era of high oil prices, would free crude for export. As a result, the flaring of 'associated' gas was gradually cut, a process which, in the case of Saudi Arabia, required a major offshore and onshore gathering grid. By 1991 flaring in that country had been reduced to only 6% of total—greatly increased—production. Compared with 1983, when Saudi Arabia used some 4,000m. cu m of natural gas and flared 26,900m. cu m, in 1991 it used 32,000m.

cu m and flared only 4,400m. cu m. Iran, too, had realized the waste involved in flaring gas and had begun to use gas-reinjection techniques in order to assist the recovery of oil. In 1991, having increased its production of natural gas by 97% since 1983, Iran reinjected into the ground more gas than it had actually been using a decade earlier. In the Middle East and North Africa generally, however, flaring remained high, involving 52,420m. cu m in 1991—an amount almost double Norway's marketed production—compared with 43,840m. cu m in 1980. A sudden increase in 1991 was largely due to the tragedy of Kuwait, where the Iraqi invasion and subsequent war flared 96% of total production in that year. Over the same period, gross production in the region had increased by 110%. A greater achievement was to have found a commercial use for the gas. In 1991 the Middle East and North Africa used or exported some 179,760m. cu m of natural gas, more than double the level of consumption seven years earlier. Iran, Abu Dhabi, Saudi Arabia, Bahrain, Oman, Egypt, Libya and Qatar have all doubled domestic consumption of natural gas since the mid-1980s, water desalination plants, power-stations and even town distribution grids having been constructed near where the gas used to be flared. Equally, the development of the petrochemical and metal industries has increasingly utilized gas rather than oil. By 1991 the Middle East and North Africa had more gas-fired power-stations than both Western Europe and North America combined.

Natural gas is also a major petrochemical feedstock. With environmental awareness growing, the region has quickly realized the value of gas for production of methanol and, from it, methyl-tertiary-butyl ether (MTBE). With the search now on for cleaner fuels, methanol itself may one day become an important vehicle fuel and it requires a gas feedstock. In 1991, however, MTBE was in short supply as a gasoline octane enhancer, since lead was being phased out.

The increase in demand for natural gas has not only occurred in the countries that produce it. By 1991 the countries of the Middle East and North Africa were exporting 44,430m. cu m of natural gas, compared with only 2,300m. cu m a decade earlier. In 1990 Algeria, which had found it difficult to export natural gas in the early 1980s, received orders from Italy, Germany, Yugoslavia, Spain and France and had fully to utilize its previously idle LNG capacity. In addition, the capacity of the Transmediterranean pipeline to Italy via Libya had tripled between 1984 and 1991 and the construction of two new pipelines was planned. To the west, Spain and Morocco had agreed to begin constructing another pipeline to Spain, passing beneath the Strait of Gibraltar (see below). Algerian exports of natural gas had risen to 33,900m. cu m by 1991, compared with about 17,000m. cu m annually in the mid-1980s. Indeed, by 1992 European dependency on Algerian supplies had begun to cause alarm owing to political unrest in that country. Yet, with its rapidly increasing, youthful population, the Algerian Government could afford to reduce its exports. By late 1996 Algeria was supplying some 25% of gas imported into Europe and aimed to retain its market share in the face of future competition from Libya, which has supply contracts with Italy, and Egypt, whose potential first export market is Turkey (see below). It has been estimated that natural gas will meet about 25% of Europe's energy requirements in 2010, compared with 20% in 1996, of which some 50% will be imported. In late 1996 Algeria began to supply gas to Córdoba in southern Spain via the Maghreb-Europe pipeline which runs through Morocco and beneath the Strait of Gibraltar. Algerian exports of natural gas totalled about 38,000m. cu m in 1995 and it is planned to increase this to 60,000m. cu m. Algeria has begun actively to seek increased foreign investment in order to share the cost of developing its oil and gas industries, which was forecast at more than $17,000m. in 1996–2000.

Algeria is not alone in having come to regard exports of natural gas as a major source of revenue. In the Persian (Arabian) Gulf Abu Dhabi has long been a major supplier of LNG to Japan and plans to expand its production capacity. Qatar, which has huge offshore reserves—including 4,400,000m. cu m in a single field—has spent $3,500m. on constructing a LNG plant and export facilities which include an industrial port (at Ras Laffan), offshore platforms and ships to transport the LNG. This project, which was first conceived in the 1970s, was completed in 1997 and may eventually supply more than 6,000m. cu m of natural gas to Japanese electricity producers. A second LNG project was under way in early 1997, as was the expansion of associated petrochemicals programmes. In 1992 Oman announced similar plans to develop its LNG production capacity, in a deal with Shell, with the aim of exporting some 6,000m. cu m to Japan by 1999.

Iran plans to develop its South Pars field. The country has been interested in exporting natural gas since the fall of the Shah, as its proven reserves are greater than those of North America, South America and Europe combined. In fact, its proven resources are second only to those of the former USSR, and this after very little detailed exploration. Iranian domestic demand, while it is growing rapidly, uses only a tiny fraction of potential production. The problem for Iran has been transporting the gas. In 1991 a joint Pakistani-Iranian team completed a feasibility study on the construction of a trunk line from Iran to Pakistan. It is possible that Iran will be selling natural gas eastwards, perhaps even to India, by 2000. (Qatar, too, regards India as a market for its gas, foreseeing a submarine pipeline to its west coast.)

The question of constructing pipelines in the opposite direction is much more complex politically, but Iran's ambitions have been boosted by the collapse of the USSR. The USSR achieved its export links with western Europe with a system that took very little account of the real investment costs of the very long Siberian pipelines. These pipelines and the reserves that filled them were in poor condition, but the construction of new capacity was likely to be extremely expensive. The collapse of the communist system freed Eastern European countries and the republics of the former USSR to seek alternative suppliers of fuel. The implications of this geopolitical shift in the international gas business have yet to be fully understood. None the less, Iran now has two options for expanding its sales of natural gas in Europe. It can either conclude agreements with Turkey, or it can enter Eastern Europe through the Ukraine. In May 1997 Iran, Turkey and Turkmenistan agreed on plans to export as much as 30,000m. cu m of Turkmen gas to Turkey via Iran. This was in addition to plans to connect Turkey and Turkmenistan to the Iranian gas pipeline system.

If Iran appears likely to become a major exporter of natural gas in the 21st century, then the underlying reason is the increasing importance of gas to the global economy. Growth in world consumption has remained fairly steady (although a slight decrease was recorded in 1997) and 1,977.3m. tons of oil equivalent were consumed world-wide in 1997, compared with 1,581.0m. tons in 1987. The market for natural gas, in terms of energy equivalence, is about half the size of that for crude oil. Gas has a number of advantages over oil in an era of environmental concern. In contrast to coal or oil, gas produces less carbon dioxide on combustion and generally contains less sulphur. Any carbon tax thus discriminates against gas rather less than it does against rival fuels. In addition, the use of gas for generating electricity has greatly increased and will continue to increase because the fuel can be used in combined-cycle turbines. Such turbines generate power with a 50% rate of efficiency, compared with the 34% generally achieved by standard, single-cycle oil- or coal-fired power stations. The International Energy Agency (IEA) has forecast that the consumption of gas for power generation alone will increase from 32,000m. cu m in 1989 to at least 81,000m. cu m by 2000. Apart from nuclear energy, gas is the fuel best suited to this process. The only threat to this relatively new source of revenue to the region is likely to be internal consumption, which has been rising at a rate of 6% a year, if the impact of the invasion of Kuwait is ignored. The impact that this event and the Gulf War had on Iraqi supplies was considerable, since Iraqi gas is primarily associated with oil. Consequently, as Iraqi export sales of petroleum have been reduced, Iraq has lost its source of domestic gas supply. This has led to the necessity to produce crude oil and then return it back into the ground, simply to sustain the gas supply.

It is thus virtually certain that the role of Middle Eastern gas in world trade will grow, increasing exporters' revenues. However, the role of natural gas in many of the less fortunate Middle Eastern states should not be forgotten. Compared with Iran's resources, Jordan's reserves of 15,000m. cu m are minute, but gas from the al-Lisheh region now supplies 15% of Jordan's electricity, saving a considerable amount of foreign exchange. In Syria, where Shell has been remarkably successful at finding local supplies where none were previously believed to be, new reserves have rapidly been put to use for the production of electricity. In Egypt, in the western desert, offshore of Alexandria and in the Red Sea, small fields have all yielded quantities that would probably not have been developed in the Gulf region. These are now used to supply industry and an incipient Cairo gas distribution system. Since the mid-1980s pipeline development has doubled Egyptian consumption, but diligent exploration has discovered sufficient natural gas to produce a healthy reserves-to-production ratio. By late 1996 most Egyptian power stations were gas-fired, and the country had begun to consider the development of exports to Turkey. Meanwhile, Shell, Repsol and Norsk Hydro have invested some $750m. in the development of gas fields in the western desert. In September 1997 Amoco of the USA and Agip of Italy were involved in advanced negotiations with the Egyptian General Petroleum Corporation (EGPC) to develop new gas fields off the East Delta coast, including the construction of an export terminal for LNG.

The importance of natural gas to the future of the Middle East and North Africa has thus increased enormously since the early 1970s. A new appreciation of the fuel as clean-burning has created potential demand that will be a major element in the region's development over the next 20 years. In recognition of this, a new spirit of co-operation has developed. Unlike crude oil, the production of which is controlled by OPEC and thus dominated by the politics of oil pricing and the Organization's internal disputes, gas diplomacy is largely free of past east-west recriminations. The development of reserves, pipelines, liquefaction units and power plants in the region is being aided by Western multinational companies—Shell, Total, Agip, Elf and others—in a way that no longer applies in the oil business. Even Algeria, where the gas industry was formerly dominated by its state company, SONATRACH, requested inward investment in early 1992. Japanese trading groups, such as Mitsui and Mitsubishi, have also established a foothold in the industry. Gas remains a capital-intensive business and external assistance is required in both the financial and technical spheres. Yet, in contrast to oil, the development of gas resources and their exploitation seems to have an internationally binding effect. Gas supply is a central element in the Gulf Co-operation Council's plans for economic development. Iran trades with its northern neighbours. Trade in natural gas with Europe has made a major contribution to Algeria's economic development, and one which has been mutually beneficial. Despite their apparent vulnerability to civil commotion, the long gas pipelines that are beginning to spread across the region and on into Europe have become links that the beneficiaries are reluctant to break.

GAS: RESERVES AND PRODUCTION
(t.c.m. = trillion cu metres)

Country	Reserves 1 Jan. 1998 (t.c.m.)	Production 1997 (m. tons oil equivalent)
Saudi Arabia	5.4	39.5
Kuwait	1.5	8.5
Iran	22.9	38.7
Iraq	3.1	—
UAE	5.8	35.0
Qatar	8.5	12.5
Libya	1.3	5.7
Algeria	3.7	60.8
Nigeria	3.3	4.3
Indonesia	2.1	62.1
Venezuela	4.0	27.8
Ecuador	0.1	n.a.
USA	4.7	490.8
Canada	1.8	141.2
Mexico	1.8	29.8
UK	0.8	78.3
Norway	1.5	42.0
Netherlands	1.7	60.4
Italy	0.3	17.5
Germany	0.3	15.5
Russian Federation	48.1	477.9
Asia Pacific (excl. Indonesia)	7.0	154.4
World total (incl. others)	144.8	2,000.9
OPEC total	61.6	294.9
OPEC % World total	42.5	14.7

Source: BP, *Statistical Review of World Energy 1998*.

Notes: Figures in the Reserves column are for gas recoverable with present technology and at present prices. Figures for reserves of gas—like reserves of oil—may be subject to wide margins of error.

Definitions: Natural gas may be found on its own ('unassociated' gas) or with oil ('associated' gas). 'Associated' gas exists partly as a gas cap above the oil and partly dissolved in oil—it is the presence of gas under pressure in new oil fields which drives the oil to the surface. 'Associated' gas is unavoidably produced with oil and may be flared, reinjected or used as fuel.

Natural gas is a mixture of numerous hydrocarbons and varying amounts of inert gases, including nitrogen, carbon dioxide and sulphur compounds. (Gas containing large quantities of sulphur is know as *sour* gas; gas without sulphur is *sweet* gas.) By far the biggest component of all natural gas by volume (at least 75%) is methane, CH_4. Other components are ethane—C_2H_6, propane—C_3H_8, and butane—C_4H_{10}. All of these hydrocarbons are gases at normal temperatures and pressures. Suspended in the gas are various heavier hydrocarbons, pentane (C_5H_{12}), octane etc., which are liquids at normal temperatures and pressures. Gas with a relatively high proportion of propane, butane and the heavier hydrocarbons is known as *wet* gas. 'Associated' natural gas tends to be wetter than 'unassociated' gas.

Methane is the normal pipeline natural gas used for domestic and industrial purposes. It liquefies at very low temperatures (–160°C) and very high pressures, and in this condition is known as *liquefied natural gas,* LNG.

Ethane is either kept with methane and used as a fuel, or is separated and used as a feedstock for petrochemicals production. Ethane is not traded on its own internationally.

Propane and butane are used as cylinder gases for a large number of industrial and domestic purposes—camping gas and cigarette lighter gas is either propane or butane. The two gases liquefy at higher temperatures and lower pressures than methane. In their liquid state they are known as *liquefied petroleum gases*—LPGs.

Pentane and other heavier liquids are used for a variety of purposes, including the spiking of heavy crude oils and as petrochemical feedstocks. These hydrocarbons, liquid at normal temperatures and pressures, are known as *natural gasolines* or *condensate.*

Together, liquefied petroleum gases and natural gasolines are referred to as *natural gas liquids*—NGLs.

NATURAL GAS CONSUMPTION
(millions of metric tons of oil equivalent*)

	1995	1996	1997
USA	558.5	568.5	569.3
Canada	63.8	66.9	67.4
Mexico	26.7	28.1	29.5
North America Total	649.0	663.5	666.2
Belgium-Luxembourg	10.6	11.8	11.3
Netherlands	34.0	37.5	35.2
France	29.6	32.5	31.2
Germany	67.0	75.2	71.1
UK	65.4	76.4	77.2
Romania	21.6	21.8	19.6
Europe Total	340.5	378.6	375.4
Middle East	123.2	135.4	142.8
South and Central America	68.6	73.3	77.9
Africa	38.9	41.1	45.8
Australia	17.6	17.9	17.6
Japan	55.0	59.5	58.6
Former USSR	470.1	473.6	443.4
China, People's Republic	15.9	15.9	17.4
World Total	1,885.9	1,980.5	1,977.3

* One metric ton of oil equivalent = 1,120 cu m of gas.
Source: BP, *Statistical Review of World Energy 1998*.

ISLAMIC BANKING AND FINANCE

RODNEY WILSON

Revised for this edition by the Editor

The development of modern commercial banking has been relatively slow in the Middle East and, even today, most people do not use banks. To some extent this reflects the historical underdevelopment of the region as, for ordinary people, the monetarization of transactions has been a relatively recent phenomenon. In other Third World societies there were no moral objections to the replacement of barter with cash and credit transactions. Due to the Islamic code of ethics, however, there has been popular resistance to modern financial developments in many parts of the Muslim world, including the Middle East. Saudi Arabia, for example, did not issue its own notes until the 1960s, as before then gold and silver coins were the major instruments for transactions. Although most people no longer regard paper money as being un-Islamic, the use of cheques, commercial bank credit and other banking instruments are viewed with suspicion by many devout Muslims.

Arab-owned commercial banks were only founded in the Middle East in the 1920s, the first being Banque Misr of Egypt and the Arab Bank, a Palestinian institution. Most financial activity up until then was handled by foreign banks, and even banks such as the Ottoman Bank or the National Bank of Egypt were foreign-owned. As these banks were largely involved in trade finance or arranging government loans, they were not dealing directly with ordinary local Muslims. In any case, trade was often in the hands of non-Muslims; the Egyptian cotton trade, for example, being largely handled by foreigners resident in Alexandria. Hence, banks were regarded as institutions serving infidels, and not organizations with which the devout Muslim should become involved. This attitude has persisted, and despite the development of indigenous commercial banking, it tends to be only the more Westernized elements in Muslim societies which use modern banking services.

Principles of Islamic Finance

Perhaps the most widely known tenet of Islamic finance in the West is the prohibition of *riba*. What constitutes *riba* has long been the subject of debate amongst Islamic scholars. Some believe that *riba* refers to usury, whereas others believe that all interest is *riba*. Certainly, one Muslim objection to interest payments is on the grounds of equity. It is the poor and needy who are often forced to borrow, whereas the rich have surplus funds to save. Interest thus penalizes the poor and benefits the rich. To the devout Muslim this is anathema, as it results in hardship, and increasing social polarization. Such practices could not be tolerated in a community of believers.

A further objection to interest is that it corrupts the recipient. It is viewed as an unearned income, a reward without productive effort. Interest can be a deterrent to honest toil, as it may be tempting to rely on unearned income rather than working for a wage or salary. Western neo-classical economics sees interest as a reward for waiting or deferring consumption until a future time. The Protestant ethic which underlies Western capitalism regarded saving as virtuous. Time is treated as a type of commodity by Western economists, which has a price. There is believed to be a trade-off between earnings and leisure, and wages are a reward for foregoing leisure. Muslim scholars reject such notions. The just wage reflects the workers' contribution to society, not the time spent working. Time itself is valueless. Hence there can be no justification in a reward for time.

To the devout Muslim abstinence needs no material reward. The earth's bounty is to be used, but Allah demands certain sacrifices, such as fasting during the month of Ramadan. The rewards for such abstinence are spiritual, and the introduction of monetary incentives would only undermine the spiritual value of such practices. Furthermore, an incentive for saving may result in underconsumption, and a lack of effective demand in the economy. Hoarding is viewed as socially undesirable in

Muslim societies, as it can result in unemployment and idle capacity. In this sense Muslim ideals are consistent with Keynesian views on economic management. Currency must circulate, and the accumulation of the means of exchange for its own sake is seen as undesirable. In the view of Muslim economists, capitalism does not achieve the right balance. Too much power is vested in the suppliers of capital; and the loanable fund market is distorted. A market system is viewed as natural, it is capitalism that is unnatural.

Application of Islamic Ideals

Although there is little disagreement over the principles of Islamic finance, the interpretation of the prohibition of *riba* in practice has been subject to much greater controversy. Should the prohibition apply to all interest, or does it merely mean that interest rates should be constrained at moderate levels? Are interest charges for business loans permissible, as the borrowers are seeking to use their credit to generate profits? Are fixed interest loans preferable to those subject to interest rate variations, as at least the borrower knows the exact charges in advance, and there is no element of uncertainty? Finally under inflationary conditions, should interest rewards be allowed to compensate savers for the depreciation of the value of their savings? A prohibition of nominal interest to compensate for inflation would penalize lenders, and subsidize borrowers. It could be argued that the prohibition of *riba* applies to real interest, not nominal interest, as with inflation, a ban on the latter may result in negative real interest.

Most Islamic states in practice have tried to restrain nominal interest rates. As inflation results in social strains in any Muslim community, and also poses moral dilemmas, the control of price increases has been an important economic priority for Muslim governments. In the Middle East inflation has been a major worry in Turkey and Lebanon, and a cause of concern in Iran, Egypt and Syria. The consequences of inflation for nominal interest rates appalled the majority of devout Muslims. Double-figure nominal interest rates have become all too prevalent in these countries, and even when action against price rises has succeeded problems can remain. As there are some lags in adjustment, it is possible to have high real rates, especially as inflation starts to fall.

Some states, such as Saudi Arabia, have a prohibition on all interest payments and receipts under their Islamic laws. Arrangement fees and service charges are permitted, however, on bank loans, and in practice, as they are calculated on a percentage basis, they resemble interest in many respects. The service charges are fixed, however, and hence borrowers are not subject to the uncertainty over the future costs of debt-servicing which arises when interest rates vary. In Saudi Arabia most bank deposits are in current accounts which earn no income, but even deposits in savings accounts only earn a modest fixed return, not an interest receipt.

Modern Islamic Banking

In Islamic states where commercial banks are free to charge and receive interest, many Muslim businessmen felt obliged to participate in *riba* transactions, even though they felt a moral guilt in doing so. To overcome this dilemma of conscience, specifically Islamic banks were founded which could compete with conventional commercial banks but which adhered to Islamic principles. The movement was started in Pakistan in the 1950s, but soon spread to the Arab World, with the opening of the Mitr Ghams Savings Bank in Egypt in 1963, which later was superseded by the Nasser Social Bank. The impact of these institutions was modest, as the major state-owned banks continued to account for most of the banking business in Egypt. Nevertheless, the Nasser Social Bank attracted deposits from an influential group of pious farmer landlords, and backed some significant agro-industrial ventures.

It was, however, the devout Muslim merchants of the Gulf who were largely responsible for the subsequent rapid expansion of Islamic banking. These conservative merchants were reluctant to use the services of conventional commercial banks yet, with the rapid business expansion in the Gulf following the oil price rises of 1973–74, some type of financial intermediation was clearly needed. Institutions such as the Dubai Islamic Bank (founded 1975), the Kuwait Finance House (1977), and the Bahrain Islamic Bank (1979) were established to serve such clients, while at the same time avoiding *riba* transactions. There was some government encouragement, with the states taking a minority shareholding in each of the institutions, but most of the finance came from the merchants themselves, especially in the case of the Dubai Islamic Bank which is 80% privately owned.

The Islamic banks in the Gulf account for around 8% of total bank deposits. Although their role in Gulf finance is modest, the banks' market penetration is considered a success, given that they represent a new type of institution adopting innovative financial techniques. Although there have been set-backs, notably as a result of dealings in precious metals, the track record of the Islamic banks has been favourable so far, and the returns to investors have been competitive with those offered by more conventional banks. As most deposits are of modest amounts, the total number of depositors is higher than their share of total deposits indicates. Many customers maintain accounts with both the new Islamic banks and conventional commercial banks. In this sense the Islamic banks complement rather than replace conventional banks. Nevertheless, the ultimate objective for the Islamic banks is to provide a comprehensive range of banking services as a complete alternative to *riba* finance.

In terms of domestic market penetration, the Kuwait Finance House has been the most successful Islamic bank, accounting for almost one-fifth of total bank deposits in Kuwait. Its activities are more diverse than those of the commercial banks in Kuwait, as it is heavily involved in construction finance and housing loans, in addition to trade and commerce. The extent of its involvement in real estate means that, in many respects, it resembles a building society. Islamic services are provided in a modern fashion, with computerized accounts, fully automatic telling facilities and even Islamic credit cards. During Iraq's occupation of Kuwait in August 1990–February 1991, the Kuwait Finance House refused to remain open for business, unlike other Kuwaiti banks. Following the country's liberation, the Kuwait Finance House reopened, having gained much respect by its refusal to collaborate with the Iraqis in any way.

In Saudi Arabia there has been considerable support for Islamic banking, even though the Kingdom had no specifically Islamic banks until recently. As all banks in Saudi Arabia are supposed to operate according to Islamic principles, the Saudi Arabian Monetary Agency saw no need to license a specially designated Islamic bank. Indeed it was thought that granting such a licence would place the commercial banks in an invidious position. Hence the only Islamic financial institution in the Kingdom was the Jeddah-based Islamic Development Bank, but it is a development assistance agency, and not a bank which deals with the general public. Its principal aim is to provide *riba*-free finance for Islamic countries, especially those with low per caput income levels.

Money-lenders as Islamic Banks

Many Saudi citizens do not maintain accounts with the commercial banks in the Kingdom. Instead they resort to money-lenders and money-changers for their financial requirements. Some of these informal bankers offer a wide range of financial services, including the exchange of currency, the handling of overseas remittances, deposit facilities and loans. Interest is not earned on loans, which are often in kind rather than cash. For example, if a client needs some item of equipment, the money-lender will usually purchase it on behalf of the client, and then either collect instalments from the client, or else enter a leasing arrangement. In either case the payments over a period will exceed the initial cost of the item, the difference representing the money-lender's profit.

One Saudi Arabian money-lending and money-changing family, the ar-Rajhis, have grown to become one of the largest commercial financial institutions in the Kingdom. Their assets exceed US $9,300m. In 1997 Ar-Rajhi Banking and Investment Corporation was Saudi Arabia's most profitable bank, with an 8% increase in profits, to $347m. The bank's profitability owes much to its substantial non-interest bearing deposits. All of the business has been built up on the basis of *riba*-free transactions. In 1983 there were pressures on the ar-Rajhis to register as a commercial bank, as, unlike the other banks, they did not hold reserves with the Saudi Arabian Monetary Agency and were completely unregulated. Rather than register as a conventional commercial bank, the ar-Rajhis decided to seek Islamic banking status, as they claimed their business methods conformed to Koranic principles in any case.

There was some hesitation on the part of the Saudi Arabian Monetary Agency, given the implications for the other banks and the problems in acting as a lender of the last resort for this type of financial institution. In the end, however, the Saudi Arabian Monetary Agency decided to license the ar-Rajhis officially in 1985 as deposit-takers and exchange dealers, largely in order to help safeguard the stability of the domestic financial system. In 1988 the ar-Rajhis decided to increase their capital base by becoming a public company and sold one-half of their shares outside the family. Although the Monetary Agency is not obliged to act as lender of the last resort with respect to institutions such as the ar-Rajhis, it is widely believed that it would if the need arose. It is only the unregistered money-changers, who refuse to submit properly audited annual accounts, that lie outside the Monetary Agency's protective net. With the registration of the money-lenders as Islamic banks, the Monetary Agency has conceded that Islamic financial principles can be interpreted in different ways. Plurality exists as both the conventional commercial banks and the money-lenders claim to conform with Islamic principles, even though their methods of operation differ considerably.

Islamic Banks in International Markets

Prince al-Faisal as-Sa'ud of Saudi Arabia is one of the leading activists in the Islamic banking movement. Although he has not established a domestic banking operation within Saudi Arabia, he was the prime instigator of the Faisal Islamic Banks of Egypt and Sudan, both of which were founded in 1977. Both banks received some local deposits, but much of their funds for lending came from Saudi Arabia. Hence, in this sense, the institutions represented a vehicle for the intra-regional recycling of petroleum revenue to less affluent Muslim states. Prince al-Faisal as-Sa'ud, however, decided that it would be desirable to have an Islamic banking presence in Western financial markets. It was felt necessary to provide some mechanism whereby investors from Saudi Arabia and elsewhere in the Gulf could participate in Western markets on the basis of *riba*-free transactions. Consequently Dar al-Maal al-Islami, the House of Islamic Funds, was founded in Geneva, Switzerland, in 1981, with a paid-up capital of US $316m.

Despite some initial problems, and losses during the 1983/84 financial year, Dar al-Maal al-Islami seems to have established a sound deposit base, and is widening its lending and investment activities. The major difficulty has been to identify *riba*-free projects to back profitably in Western markets. There is no objection to dealing with institutions which participate in *riba* transactions, however, as long as the Islamic institution is not directly involved, though in the longer term it is hoped to avoid such dealings. In practice, Dar al-Maal al-Islami functions as a kind of investment company, deploying most of its funds in equity markets and in property, though it also holds short-term assets in the form of cash and commodities. It is the appropriate choice of liquid financial instruments which has caused greatest difficulty, as Islamic institutions cannot hold government bills or bonds which yield interest.

Constraints in Secular Societies

Problems inevitably arise when Islamic financial institutions operate in a non-Islamic environment. As the Islamic banks do not hold Western government securities as part of their liquid assets, they cannot be registered in Western Europe or the USA as fully-fledged commercial banks. Commodity holdings are not recognized as liquid assets, and the maintenance of a large proportion of non-earning cash reserves would substantially reduce the banks' returns on their assets. One possible solution in the West is to act as a kind of building society, lending to Muslims for house purchases. This approach has been adopted by First Path Financial Services of Michigan and Ontario, the leading Islamic retail financial institution in North America.

The Bank of England has been reluctant even to register the Islamic banks as licensed deposit-takers, largely owing to their inability to provide a guaranteed rate of return on deposits and a perceived opacity of transactions and procedures, and those operating in the United Kingdom are regarded as investment companies rather than banks. The lack of banking status has drawbacks. Islamic institutions cannot solicit for deposits from Muslim investors who reside in the United Kingdom, nor can they carry out normal banking operations. The Islamic financial institutions in London are mainly engaged in the finance of Euro-Arab trade. Clients of British banks exporting to the Islamic world are often referred to Islamic institutions in London. One new development has been for Western commercial banks to offer Islamic financial services to their Muslim clients. The Union Bank of Switzerland, for example, offers an Islamic investment fund. The Saudi International Bank in London offers Islamic trade finance and is also offering Islamic portfolio management services for clients of substantial means. The United Bank of Kuwait has opened a specialized Islamic Investment Banking Unit in London. It is now the leading provider of such services in Europe. Citibank has offered Islamic banking services since 1994, its Bahrain branch being the centre for these activities.

Indebtedness and the Shari'a Law

Sudden fluctuations in the world price for oil can result in vulnerable loan agreements and the creation of bad debts. Many borrowers argue that they should not be liable for interest payments when they fall into debt. The *Shari'a* courts have usually sided with the debtors rather than with the banks, and in Saudi Arabia there is some doubt if even service charges can be legally enforced.

In the United Arab Emirates the courts have ruled that simple interest is permissible, but that borrowers are not liable for compound interest payments. As the *Shari'a* law does not follow case precedent, there is much confusion about the situation. Commercial banks operating in the Gulf are increasingly reluctant to take debtors to court, and many are trying to reach out-of-court settlements by granting payment moratoriums. Rolling over credits is regarded as preferable to writing down the value of bank assets.

In order to avoid problems of this kind in the future the commercial banks in Saudi Arabia are now offering Islamic finance. Some, including the Kingdom's largest bank, the National Commercial, have opened separate branches for women, a move favoured by some Islamic theologians, who advocate the sexual segregation of finance in accordance with Islamic inheritance laws. The National Commercial Bank has also opened new Islamic branches, and converted some existing branches to Islamic branches. By 1998 46 of its 245 branches had been 'Islamized'. This is partly in response to clients' wishes, but also because, in the event of repayments failure, restitution can be more easily sought through the courts. Trade credit is granted through resale and leasing arrangements, and the profit-sharing principle covers medium- and long-term finance. It seems likely that an increasing proportion of commercial banking business in the Gulf will be 'Islamized', even though it requires much more work by the banks. The emphasis switches from mere risks appraisal, to the fuller evaluation of returns which is necessary with Islamic finance.

'Islamization' of Banking

In post-revolutionary Iran a major policy objective has been the 'Islamization' of the nation's institutions. In an Islamic society it is felt that all institutions should operate in accordance with Islamic principles, including banks and financial institutions. Merely permitting Islamic banks to operate alongside West-ernized commercial banks is unsatisfactory. In a society of believers there is no place for *riba* financial institutions, indeed the workings of commercial banks are an affront to the faithful.

Instead, to ensure conformity with Koranic ideas and the spirit of Shi'ism, the Teheran authorities have 'Islamized' the entire banking system which precludes the operation of commercial banks using principles of Western finance.

Iranian commentators have repeatedly attacked the Arab Islamic banking movement as a camouflage for capitalism. Merely using the word 'Islamic' does not change the nature of the banks themselves. The expression 'Islamic banking' is itself a contradiction in terms according to these critics. The word 'bank' comes from the Italian 'banco', meaning 'table', as, in the past, money-changers from Lombardy used to place money on a table. Such practices are inappropriate in Islamic financial transactions, which are based on trust. The word of a devout Muslim is believed, and he has no need to produce proof of his worth. This explains why even some Arab Islamic institutions are called houses rather than banks, the Kuwait Finance House and Dar al-Maal al-Islami (literally, Islamic House of Funds) being notable examples.

Merely providing interest-free transactions, though a welcome development, is insufficient, according to Iranian critics. Islamic financial institutions cannot be limited-liability companies as obligations between Muslims who enter transactions must be absolute. There can be no escape from personal liability, and institutions can have no personality of their own in any case.

Implementation of Islamic Financial Law

Iran's Islamic financial laws were passed by the Majlis (Islamic Consultative Assembly) in February 1984. They provided for the 'Islamization' of all Iran's financial institutions by 22 March 1985, although the implementation of the new regulations took four years to complete. Interest has been phased out of the system, and the banks now offer either interest-free current and savings deposits, or long-term investment deposits. With current account deposits customers can use chequing facilities, but only those with savings deposits are given preferential treatment with respect to loan applications. Incentives are also offered on savings deposits, including the possibility of a funded pilgrimage to Mecca. Those with long-term investment deposits cannot withdraw their funds without several months notice, but they are entitled to share in the bank's profits, in accordance with the Islamic *mudaraba* (speculation) system. Borrowers are encouraged to enter into partnership arrangements with the banks, under which they share any profits which arise as a result of the investments which the bank has financed. The partnership arrangement may be only in respect of one project which the bank backs, or it may be with the business as a whole. In the case of a limited partnership the profits shared are only those which arise from the specific project for which funds have been obtained. Under a full partnership arrange-ment all profits are shared. Machinery purchases are often financed by the bank purchasing the item required on behalf of the client, who repays by instalments. In this case the ownership is transferred on payment of the first instalment. An alternative arrangement is leasing conditioned to purchase, whereby the ownership is only transferred when the final instalment is paid.

Under the Islamic banking laws banks may also finance trade through forward purchases on a client's behalf. There is a distinction drawn between such purchases and futures trading, which is regarded as speculative, and therefore prohibited. Under a forward purchase the bank pays for the commodity being traded on behalf of the import agent or wholesaler, who will repay the bank when he resells the merchandise to the retailer or final customer. The Arab Islamic banks have similar resale contracts, the time period for this type of credit typically being 90 or 180 days.

Employee Attitudes

In practice, in Iran, there has been some opposition to the new laws from existing bankers, and many bank employees are less than enthusiastic about the new systems. To facilitate implementation the banks have been reorganized into three groups, Melat, Melli and Tejarat. A Council of Money and Credit Regulation has been established to supervise the banking system, the Council consisting of representatives from the banks themselves, independent financial experts, and religious advi-sors (two of whom are mullahs). The Central Bank retains its executive role, but the Council is responsible for bank policy,

MAJOR ISLAMIC BANKS (1997)

Institution	Country	Date of foundation	Paid-up capital (million US $)
Bahrain Islamic Bank	Bahrain	1979	35.0
Bahrain Islamic Investment Company	Bahrain	1981	14.0
Bank Islam Malaysia	Malaysia	1983	80.0
Al-Baraka Group	Saudi Arabia/ Bahrain	1982	54.0
Beit Ettamouil Saudi Tounsi	Tunisia	1984	50.0
Dar al-Maal al-Islami	Switzerland	1981	316.0
Dubai Islamic Bank	UAE	1975	74.0
Faisal Islamic Bank of Bahrain	Bahrain	1982	85.0
Faisal Islamic Bank of Egypt	Egypt	1977	132.0
Faisal Islamic Bank of Sudan	Sudan	1977	30.0
Faisal Islamic Bank of Turkey	Turkey	1985	6.0
International Islamic Bank	Bangladesh	1983	19.0
International Investor	Kuwait	1992	1,000.0
Islamic Development Bank	Saudi Arabia	1975	2,200.0
Jordan Islamic Bank for Finance & Investment	Jordan	1978	56.0
Kuwait Finance House	Kuwait	1977	229.0
Kuwait Finance House (Turkey)	Turkey	1983	20.0
Nasser Social Bank	Egypt	1972	29.0
Qatar Islamic Bank	Qatar	1983	43.0
Ar-Rajhi Bank	Saudi Arabia	1985	1,091.0
Saudi-Philippine Islamic Development Bank	Saudi Arabia	1982	5.0
Tadamon Islamic Bank	Sudan	1983	9.0

and the implementation of the new code. In 1994 it was announced that foreign banks could operate in Iran again, and not be confined solely to maintaining representative offices. It remains to be seen how they will be regulated under the Islamic banking laws.

The Arab Islamic financial institutions have had fewer personnel problems. All of the staff recruited by the Islamic banks are practising Muslims, apart from some employees in Europe. Many are experienced bankers, who took salary cuts to join the new institutions, because they wished to work in an Islamic environment, and refrain from participation in *riba* transactions. Their attitude is extremely positive, and they are genuinely seeking to make Islamic principles work. The bank employees view their jobs as part of their religious devotion and there is little doubt that in many respects a voluntary system of Islamic banking is preferable to compulsion.

Monetary Policy Issues

Islamic financial principles are not only applicable to banking activity, but also to government finance and management of the economy at the national level. The prohibition of *riba* precludes the use of interest-rate changes as an instrument of monetary policy. Islamic economists believe it is unfair to penalize borrowers by raising interest rates merely for the sake of demand management, when the problems which resulted in such an action were not the fault of individual borrowers. Hence, even in Muslim economies where interest is permitted, it is felt desirable to keep rates stable, and preferably at low levels. Other instruments of monetary policy can be used, including control of the money supply, and the regulation of bank lending through reserve requirements and special deposits. Indeed a strict monetary policy is thought to be essential in order to keep inflation under control. High and unpredictable rates of price increase result in social strains and uncertainty which can undermine the cohesion of Islamic societies.

Many Islamic economists urge balanced budgets, as, if government expenditure exceeds tax receipts, borrowing becomes necessary. If resort is made to bill or bond issues this implies the government is dependent on *riba* finance, an undesirable state of affairs for any government in the Islamic world. In Saudi Arabia the authorities have attempted to avoid interest by issuing government securities at a discount below their redeemable value. The difference represents the return to purchasers of the securities. A large number of Islamic economists object to this practice, however, as the yield on the securities resembles interest. Indeed the price at which this type of Saudi Government security has been traded has been influenced by interest-rate developments in Western markets. This is a result of the openness of the Kingdom's economy, and the ease with which foreign assets can be substituted for domestic assets.

Fiscal Policy Constraints

The public sector borrowing requirement can of course be controlled through fiscal policy, by restraining government expenditure or increasing taxation. The governments of many of the poorer Islamic states find great difficulty in restraining expenditure, especially on items such as food subsidies, given the pressing social needs. Many face a dilemma, as the reduction of the food subsidies results in inflationary pressures, which cause Islamic critics to assert that they are penalizing the poor, and are acting contrarily to the spirit of Islamic brotherhood. On the other hand if the subsidies are maintained, the governments are forced to borrow, not only from their own citizens, but also from Western infidels, or non-believers.

In the poorer Islamic states the tax base is extremely restricted, as most of the population do not earn enough to pay income tax, and purchase taxes on basic commodities would penalize the needy. Import duties usually constitute the major source of government revenue, except in the oil-exporting states. Islamic law provides for *zakat*, a type of wealth tax, which is on the statutes of all Muslim countries. This is levied annually on both businesses and individuals at a rate of 2.5% of their total net value. *Zakat* is a unique tax, as contributions are entirely voluntary, but most believers pay, as it is regarded as one of the five central obligations of the Islamic faith.

In countries such as Saudi Arabia, *zakat* collection is encouraged, and the funds are collected by a special ministry, which uses the revenue for social purposes. *Zakat* has to be administered separately from other tax revenue, and cannot be used for general government spending, even on development projects. For this reason some governments have done little to encourage *zakat*. In Iran, under the Shah, many of the bazaar merchants paid *zakat*, but not to the secular Teheran authorities. Instead they paid *zakat* to local relief agencies organized by the mullahs through the local mosques. Most of the revenue was used to help poor rural immigrants to the cities who had difficulty in finding employment and who often lived in appalling conditions. Since the revolution the Islamic Government has taken over the administration of the tax, and there has been much debate about whether it should be made compulsory given the great social problems inherited from the Shah's regime.

Islamic Investment

Perhaps the most interesting recent development has been the widening of the scope of Islamic finance to encompass equity investment. Such participatory finance is acceptable under the *Shari'a* law but until recently the major constraints have been the unacceptability of many western companies because of their involvement in *haram* activities such as alcohol or pork production and distribution. Drawing from the experience of the ethical investment movement in the West, criteria have now been established for Islamically-acceptable equity investment. Flemings, the British investment bank, launched its Oasis Fund in 1995, investing in companies world-wide, which are involved in *halal* activities. In Saudi Arabia the National Commercial Bank launched a Global Trading Fund in 1995 and the ar-Rajhi group established a Global Equity Fund in 1997, both of which are managed in accordance with the *Shari'a* law. The Faisal Islamic Bank of Bahrain initiated its Golden Equity Fund in 1997.

As a number of stock markets in the Middle East have acquired emerging-market status, including Istanbul, Amman, Cairo and Casablanca, this opens up further possibilities for Islamic equity investment in the Muslim world itself. Shares from these markets are already included in some emerging-market funds, and it should be possible to construct investment and unit trusts focused on these markets. Daily share price data for all these markets except for Cairo is available on-line. Recent privatizations in Turkey have increased the scale of the Istanbul market, and privatization in Egypt should help broaden and deepen the Cairo exchange. The Ibn Majid Emerging-Market Fund, jointly managed by International Investor of Kuwait and the Swiss Banking Corporation, invests in these exchanges.

Prospects for the Future

The prospects for Islamic finance were dealt several blows in the late 1980s, most notably the collapse in 1988 of the Egyptian Islamic investment house, Ar-Rayan, which was widely publicized. The Central Bank refused to intervene, thousands of small investors lost their savings and although Egypt's Islamic banks were not directly involved, confidence in the whole sector was shaken. This had implications well beyond Egypt, as did the difficulties of the Jordan Islamic Bank, which were caused by the effect on the Jordanian economy of the crisis in the Gulf in 1990/91.

Despite these reversals, the outlook for Islamic banking for the mid-1990s and beyond is encouraging. Islamic financial assets world-wide (including those held by insurance companies) amounted to an estimated US $80,000m. by 1998. Existing Islamic financial institutions are now well established and Islamic financial instruments are widely recognized as a viable alternative to *riba* finance. Investors in the Ar-Rayan company were eventually compensated by an anonymous Gulf source and confidence among depositors with Islamic banks in Egypt was restored. The four principal state-owned commercial banks in Egypt now offer Islamic banking facilities to their clients. These facilities have proved to be very successful, attracting 10% of total deposits in the Egyptian banking system within one year of their introduction. (New banking legislation enacted in Egypt in mid-1998 was expected to provide for the privatization of the country's four principal banks, and to prompt a period of acquisition, merger and increased competition.)

Recent political developments in the Gulf may favour Islamic finance. The unrest in Bahrain, a key financial centre in the Gulf, has brought a political response, but it also makes the authorities there and in Saudi Arabia more concerned than ever to emphasize their own Islamic credentials. This can be done with little controversy in the economic and banking sphere, by accepting and even encouraging Islamic finance. Financial 'Islamization' may be seen as preferable to political 'Islamization', and as a way of meeting at least some of the aspirations of citizens of the Gulf.

By mid-1998 future prospects for Islamic banking were continuing to improve. A number of new Islamic banks were launched in the region during 1997, including two in Bahrain and one in Abu Dhabi. It was also reported that new banks were to open shortly in Dubai and Kuwait. In addition, two large conventional banks in the region (Arab Bank and Arab Banking Corporation) and one foreign bank (ABN-Amro) have recently announced the creation of Islamic subsidiaries. The prospects for Islamic

banking outlets abroad were also encouraged by speculation, in mid-1998, that banking legislation would soon be enacted in the USA which would supersede the 1933 'Glass-Steagall' Banking Act, and thereby facilitate the establishment of truly Islamic banks there. Expansion in both the scale and the scope of the sector was predicted for the end of the decade following significant developments in the mid-1990s. During 1992–96 the combined total assets of the Gulf's three most successful Islamic banks increased by some 28%, compared with a 19% increase in the combined total assets of the region's 10 largest commercial banks. In 1996 the level of return on assets of the Islamic banks was almost double that of the 10 commercial banks taken as a whole. The financial contribution of the Kuwait Finance House to the ambitious Equate chemical plant project in Kuwait has also demonstrated the possibilities for Islamic financing of large development projects. Other interesting proposals for the sector include the possible future use of equity for long-term financing.

SELECT BIBLIOGRAPHY

Abdeen, Adnan M., and Shook, Dale N. *The Saudi Financial System in the Context of Western and Islamic Finance*. Chichester, John Wiley, 1984.

Ali, S. Nazim, and Ali, Naseem N. *Information Sources on Islamic Banking and Economics*. London, Kegan Paul International, 1994.

Beaugé, Gilbert, (Ed.). *Les Capitaux de l'Islam*. Paris, Presses du CNRS, 1990.

Chapra, M. Umer. *Islam and the Economic Challenge*. Leicester, Islamic Foundation, 1992.

Cunningham, Andrew. *Banking in the Middle East*. London, FT Finance, 1997.

Encyclopaedia of Islamic Banking and Insurance. London, Institute of Islamic Banking and Insurance, 1995.

Insurance in the Middle East. London, FT Finance, 1997.

Kazarian, Elias. *Islamic Banking in Egypt*. Lund Economic Studies, 1991.

Mallat, Chibli, (Ed.). *Islamic Law and Finance*. London, Graham and Trotman, 1988.

Mannan, Muhammad Abd al-. *Islamic Economics: Theory and Practice*. Sevenoaks, Hodder and Stoughton, 1986.

Mayer, Ann Elizabeth. 'Islamic Banking and Credit Policies in the Sadat Era: The Social Origins of Islamic Banking'. *Arab Law Quarterly*. Vol. 1, part 1, 1985.

Naqvi, Syed Nawab Haider. *Islam, Economics and Society*. London, Kegan Paul International, 1994.

Nomani, Farhad and Rahnema, Ali. *Islamic Economic Systems*. London, Zed Books, 1994.

Piccinelli, Gian Maria, (Ed.). *Banche Islamiche in Contesto Non-Islamico*. Rome, Istituto per l'Oriente, 1994.

Rodinson, Maxime. *Islam and Capitalism*. Harmondsworth, Penguin Books, 1979.

Roy, Delwin. *Islamic Banking. Middle Eastern Studies*. Vol. 27, 1991.

Sadeq, Abul Hasan M., (Ed.). *Financing Economic Development: Islamic and Mainstream Approaches*. Longman Malaysia, 1992.

Siddiqi, Muhammad, N. *Banking Without Interest*. Leicester, The Islamic Foundation, 1983.

Wilson, Rodney J. A. *Banking and Finance in the Arab Middle East*. London, Macmillan, 1983.

Islamic Business: Theory and Practice. London, Economist Intelligence Unit, Special Report No. 221, 1985.

'Islamic Banking—the Jordanian Experience'. *Arab Law Quarterly*. Vol. 2, part 3, 1987.

Islamic Financial Markets. London, Routledge, 1990.

CALENDARS, TIME RECKONING, AND WEIGHTS AND MEASURES

The Islamic Calendar

The Islamic era dates from 16 July 622, which was the beginning of the Arab year in which the *Hijra* ('flight' or migration) of the Prophet Muhammad (the founder of Islam), from Mecca to Medina (in modern Saudi Arabia), took place. The Islamic or *Hijri* Calendar is lunar, each year having 354 or 355 days, the extra day being intercalated 11 times every 30 years. Accordingly, the beginning of the *Hijri* year occurs earlier in the Gregorian Calendar by a few days each year. Dates are reckoned in terms of the *anno Hegirae* (AH) or year of the Hegira (*Hijra*). The Islamic year AH 1419 began on 28 April 1998.

The year is divided into the following months:

1. Muharram	30 days	7. Rajab	30 days
2. Safar	29 ,,	8. Shaaban	29 ,,
3. Rabia I	30 ,,	9. Ramadan	30 ,,
4. Rabia II	29 ,,	10. Shawwal	29 ,,
5. Jumada I	30 ,,	11. Dhu'l-Qa'da	30 ,,
6. Jumada II	29 ,,	12. Dhu'l-Hijja	29 or 30 days

The *Hijri* Calendar is used for religious purposes throughout the Islamic world and is the official calendar in Saudi Arabia. In most Arab countries it is used in conjunction with the Gregorian Calendar for official purposes, but in Turkey and Egypt the Gregorian Calendar has replaced it.

PRINCIPAL ISLAMIC FESTIVALS

New Year: 1st Muharram. The first 10 days of the year are regarded as holy, especially the 10th.

Ashoura: 10th Muharram. Celebrates the first meeting of Adam and Eve after leaving Paradise, also the ending of the Flood and the death of Husain, grandson of the Prophet Muhammad. The feast is celebrated with fairs and processions.

Mouloud or **Yum an-Nabi** (Birth of Muhammad): 12th Rabia I.

Leilat al-Meiraj (Ascension of Muhammad): 27th Rajab.

Ramadan (Month of Fasting).

Id al-Fitr or **Id as-Saghir** or **Küçük Bayram** (The Small Feast): Three days beginning 1st Shawwal. This celebration follows the constraint of the Ramadan fast.

Id al-Adha or **Id al-Kabir** or **Büyük Bayram** (The Great Feast, Feast of the Sacrifice): Four days beginning on 10th Dhu'l-Hijja. The principal Islamic festival, commemorating Abraham's sacrifice and coinciding with the pilgrimage to Mecca. Celebrated by the sacrifice of a sheep, by feasting and by donations to the poor.

Islamic Year	1418		1419		1420	
New Year	9 May	1997	28 April	1998	17 April	1999
Ashoura	18 May	1997	7 May	1998	26 April	1999
Mouloud	18 July	1997	7 July	1998	26 June	1999
Leilat al-Meiraj. . . .	28 Nov.	1997	17 Nov.	1998	6 Nov.	1999
Ramadan begins . . .	31 Dec.	1997	20 Dec.	1998	9 Dec.	1999
Id al-Fitr	30 Jan.	1998	19 Jan.	1999	8 Jan.	2000
Id al-Adha	8 April	1998	28 March	1999	16 March	2000

Note: Local determinations may vary by one day from those given here.

The Iranian Calendar

The Iranian Calendar, introduced in 1925, was based on the Islamic Calendar, adapted to the solar year. Iranian New Year (*Now Ruz*) occurs at the vernal equinox, which usually falls on 21 March in the Gregorian Calendar. In Iran it was decided to base the calendar on the coronation of Cyrus the Great, in place of the *Hijra*, from 1976, and the year beginning 21 March 1976 became 2535. During 1978, however, it was decided to revert to the former system of dating. The year 1377 began on 21 March 1998.

The Iranian year is divided into the following months:

1. Favardine	31 days	7. Mehr	30 days
2. Ordibehecht	31 ,,	8. Aban	30 ,,
3. Khordad	31 ,,	9. Azar	30 ,,
4. Tir	31 ,,	10. Dey	30 ,,
5. Mordad	31 ,,	11. Bahman	30 ,,
6. Chariver	31 ,,	12. Esfand	29 or 30 days

The Iranian Calendar is used for all purposes in Iran, except the determining of Islamic religious festivals, for which the lunar Islamic Calendar is used.

The Hebrew Calendar

The Hebrew Calendar is solar with respect to the year but lunar with respect to the months. The normal year has 353–355 days in 12 lunar months, but seven times in each 19 years an extra month of 30 days (*Adar II*) is intercalated after the normal month of Adar to adjust the calendar to the solar year. New Year (*Rosh Hashanah*) usually falls in September of the Gregorian calendar, but the day varies considerably. The year 5758 began on 2 October 1997, and 5759 begins on 21 September 1998.

The months are as follows:

1. Tishri	30 days	7. Nisan	30 days
2. Marcheshvan	29 or 30 days	8. Iyyar	29 ,,
3. Kislev	29 or 30 ,,	9. Sivan	30 ,,
4. Tebeth	29 days	10. Tammuz	29 ,,
5. Shebat	30 ,,	11. Ab	30 ,,
6. Adar	29 ,,	12. Ellul	29 ,,
(Adar II)	30 ,,		

The Hebrew Calendar is used to determine the dates of Jewish religious festivals only. The civil year begins with the month Tishri, while the ecclesiastical year commences on the first day of Nisan.

Standard Time

The table shows zones of standard time, relative to Greenwich Mean Time (GMT). Many of the individual countries adopt daylight saving time at certain times of year.

Traditional Arabic time is still widely used by the local population in Saudi Arabia except in most of the Eastern Province. This system is based on the local time of sunset, when timepieces are all set to 12.

GMT	One hour ahead	Two hours ahead	Three hours ahead	Three and one-half hours ahead	Four hours ahead
Algeria Morocco Spanish North Africa	Tunisia	Cyprus Egypt Israel Jordan Lebanon Libya Syria Turkey	Bahrain Iraq Kuwait Yemen	Iran	Oman Qatar United Arab Emirates

Note: Saudi Arabia uses solar time.

Weights and Measures

Principal weights and units of measurement in common use as alternatives to the metric and imperial systems.

WEIGHT

Unit	Country	Metric equivalent	Imperial equivalent
Hogga	Iraq	1.27 kg	2.8 lb
Maund	Yemen Saudi Arabia	37.29 kg	82.28 lb
Qintar (Kantar) or Buhar	Cyprus Egypt	228.614 kg 44.928 kg	504 lb 99.05 lb
Ratl or Rotl	Saudi Arabia Egypt	0.449 kg	0.99 lb
Uqqa or Oke	Cyprus Egypt	1.27 kg 1.245 kg	2.8 lb 2.751 lb
Yeni Okka	Turkey	1 kg	2.205 lb

LENGTH

Unit	Country	Metric equivalent	Imperial equivalent
Busa	Saudi Arabia	2.54 cm	1 in
Dirraa, Dra or Pic	Cyprus	60.96 cm	2 ft

CAPACITY

Unit	Country	Metric equivalent	Imperial equivalent
Ardabb or Ardeb	Saudi Arabia Egypt	198.024 litres	45.36 gallons
Kadah	Egypt Cyprus	2.063 litres 36.368 litres	3.63 pints 1 pint
Keila	Egypt	16.502 litres	3.63 gallons

AREA

Unit	Country	Metric equivalent	Imperial equivalent
Donum or Dunum	Cyprus Iraq Israel Jordan Syria Turkey	1,335.8 sq m 2,500 sq m 1,000 sq m 919.04 sq m	0.33 acre 0.62 acre 0.2471 acre 0.2272 acre
Feddan	Saudi Arabia Egypt	4,201 sq m	1.038 acres
Yeni Donum	Turkey	10,000 sq m (1 ha)	2.471 acres

Metric to Imperial Conversions

Metric units	Imperial units	To convert metric into imperial units multiply by:	To convert imperial into metric units multiply by:
Weight:			
Gram	Ounce (Avoirdupois)	0.035274	28.3495
Kilogram (kg)	Pound (lb)	2.204622	0.453592
Metric ton ('000 kg)	Short ton (2,000 lb)	1.102311	0.907185
	Long ton (2,240 lb)	0.984207	1.016047
	(The short ton is in general use in the USA, while the long ton is normally used in Britain and the Commonwealth.)		
Length			
Centimetre (cm)	Inch (in)	0.3937008	2.54
Metre (m)	Yard (=3 feet)	1.09361	0.9144
Kilometre (km)	Mile	0.62137	1.609344
Volume			
Cubic metre (cu m)	Cubic foot	35.315	0.0283
	Cubic yard	1.30795	0.764555
Capacity			
Litre	Gallon (=8 pints)	0.219969	4.54609
	Gallon (US)	0.264172	3.78541
Area			
Square metre (sq m)	Square yard	1.19599	0.836127
Hectare (ha)	Acre	2.47105	0.404686
Square kilometre (sq km)	Square mile	0.386102	2.589988

RESEARCH INSTITUTES
ASSOCIATIONS AND INSTITUTES STUDYING THE MIDDLE EAST AND NORTH AFRICA

(See also Regional Organizations—Education)

ALGERIA

Institut d'Etudes Arabes: Université d'Alger, 2 rue Didouche Mourad, Algiers.

Institut d'Etudes Orientales: Université d'Alger, 2 rue Didouche Mourad, Algiers; publ. *Annales.*

ARGENTINA

Facultad de Filosofía y Letras, Sección Interdisciplinaria de Estudios de Asia y Africa: Universidad de Buenos Aires, 25 de Mayo 221, 4° piso, 1002 Buenos Aires; tel. (1) 3347512; fax (1) 3432733; f. 1982; multidisciplinary research, seminars and lectures; Dir Prof. MARÍA ELENA VELA; publs *Temas de Africa y Asia* (2 a year).

ARMENIA

Institute of Oriental Studies of the National Academy of Sciences of Armenia: Pr. Marshal Bagranyan 24G, Yerevan 375019; tel. (8852) 583382; e-mail nhovanes@pnas.sci.am; f. 1971; Dir N. H. HOVHANNISIAN.

AUSTRALIA AND NEW ZEALAND

Australasian Middle East Studies Association: POB 64, Footscray 3011, Australia; Department of Semitic Studies, University of Sydney, N.S.W. 2006; tel. (2) 6922190; Pres. Dr A. SHBOUL; Past Pres. NEIL TRUSCOTT; publ. *Conference Proceedings.*

Programme in Middle East Studies: University of Western Australia, Nedlands, Western Australia 6009; tel. (8) 93802926; fax (8) 93801016; e-mail rgabby@ecel.uwa.edu.au; f. 1975 to promote, encourage and facilitate teaching, research and the dissemination of information on the Middle East; Dir Prof. R. GABBAY.

AUSTRIA

Afro-Asiatisches Institut in Wien: Türkenstrasse 3, A-1090 Vienna; tel. (1) 3105145; f. 1959; seminars, scholarship programmes and other cultural exchange between Africans and Asians in Vienna; Gen. Sec. CHRISTIAN GUGGENBERGER; Pres. Archbishop Dr CHRISTOPH SCHÖNBORN.

Institut für Orientalistik der Universität Wien: Spitalgasse 2-4, A-1090 Vienna; tel. (1) 427743401; fax (1) 42774934; e-mail orientalistik@univie.ac.at; f. 1886; library of 26,200 vols; Dir Prof. Dr MARKUS KÖHBACH; publs *Wiener Zeitschrift für die Kunde des Morgenlandes* (annually), *Türkologischer Anzeiger* (annually), *Archiv für Orientforschung* (annually).

AZERBAIJAN

Institute of Peoples of the Near and Middle East of the Academy of Azerbaijan: Pr. Narimanova 31, Baku 370143; f. 1958; Dir ZIYA MUSA BUNIYATOV.

BELGIUM

Centre d'Etudes et de Reserches Arabes: Université de l'Etat à Mons, 24 ave Champ de Mars, 7000 Mons; tel. (65) 373615; fax (65) 840631; e-mail h.safar@skynet.be; f. 1978; library of 2,000 vols; Dir Prof. H. SAFAR.

Centre pour l'Etude des Problèmes du Monde Musulman Contemporain: 44 ave Jeanne, 1050 Brussels; tel. (2) 6423359; f. 1957; Dir A. DESTREE; publs *Correspondance d'Orient-Etudes* and collections *Correspondance d'Orient* and *Le monde musulman contemporain—Initiations.*

Departement Oosterse en Slavische Studies: Faculteit Letteren, Katholieke Universiteit te Leuven, Blijde Inkomststraat 21, B—3000 Leuven; tel. (16) 324931; fax (16) 324932; e-mail oriental.studies@arts.kuleuven.ac.be; f. 1936; Pres. Prof. W. VANDE WALLE; 60 mems; publs *Orientalia Lovaniensia Analecta, Orientalia Lovaniensia Periodica, Bibliothèque du Muséon*

(1929–68), *Orientalia et Biblica Lovaniensia* (1957–68), *Inforient, Inforient-Reeks.*

Fondation Egyptologique Reine Elisabeth: Parc du Cinquantenaire, 10, B-1000 Brussels; tel. (2) 7417364; f. 1923 to encourage Egyptian studies; 1,450 mems; library of 90,000 vols; Pres. Comte D'ARSCHOT; Dirs M. J. BINGEN and H. DE MEULENAERE; publs *Chronique d'Egypte, Bibliotheca Aegyptiaca, Papyrologica Bruxellensia, Bibliographie Papyrologique sur fiches, Monumenta Aegyptiaca, Rites égyptiens, Papyri Bruxellenses Graecae, Monographies Reine Elisabeth.*

CUBA

Centro de Estudios de Africa y del Medio Oriente (Centre for African and Middle Eastern Studies): Avda 3ra, No 1805, entre 18 y 20, Miramar, Playa, Havana.

CYPRUS

PLO Research Centre: POB 5614, 16 Artemidos St, Strovolos, Nicosia; tel. (2) 429396; telex 4706; fax (2) 312104; fmrly in Beirut, Lebanon; f. 1965; studies Palestine question; Dir SABRI JIRYIS; publs *Shu'un Filastiniya* (Palestine Affairs, monthly) and various books and pamphlets on aspects of the Palestine problem.

CZECH REPUBLIC

Orientální ústav AV ČR (Oriental Institute AS CR): 182 08 Prague 8, Pod vodárenskou věží 4; tel. (2) 66052484; fax (2) 8585627; e-mail kolmas@orient.cas.cz; f. 1922; attached to Czech Academy of Sciences; Dir Prof. JOSEF KOLMAŠ; publs *Archív Orientální* (quarterly), *Nový Orient* (monthly).

DENMARK

Center for Mellemøst-Studier (Centre for Contemporary Middle East Studies): University of Odense, Campusvej 55, 5230 Odense M; tel. 66158600; fax 65931158; e-mail middleeast@av.dk; f. 1983; national centre for interdisciplinary research in cultures and societies of the contemporary Middle East; 9-member research team; library of 3,000 vols and 90 periodicals; Dir Prof. LARS ERSLEV ANDERSEN; publs *Mellemøst Information* (monthly in Danish) and a monographical series (semiannually).

Orientalsk Samfund (Orientalist Association): Carsten Niebuhr Institute of Near Eastern Studies, Shortsgade 17–19, 2300 Copenhagen S; tel. 35328900; f. 1915 to undertake the study and further the understanding of Oriental cultures and civilizations; 20 mems; Pres. Dr LEIF LIFFRIYN; Sec. Prof. J. P. ASMUSSEN; publ. *Acta Orientalia* (annually).

EGYPT

Academy of the Arabic Language: 15 Aziz Abaza St, Zamalek, Cairo; tel. (2) 3405931; fax (2) 3412002; e-mail aal@idsc. gov.eg; f. 1932; Pres. Dr AHMED SHAWKY DHEIF; Sec.-Gen. Dr AHMED SHAWKY DIEF; library of 60,000 vols and periodicals; publs *Review* (2 a year), books on reviving Arabic heritage, council and conference proceedings, biographies of members of Academy, lexicons and directories of scientific and technical terms.

American Research Center in Egypt Inc: 2 Midan Qasr ad-Dubarah, Garden City, Cairo; tel. (2) 3548239; fax (2) 3553052; and 30 East 20th St, Suite 401, New York, NY 10003-1310, tel. (212) 5296661; fax (212) 5296856; f. 1948 by American universities to promote research by US and Canadian scholars in all phases of Egyptian civilization, including archaeology, art history, humanities and social sciences; grants and fellowships available; 32 institutional mems and 1,250 individual mems; Pres. JANET JOHNSON; Vice-Pres. CHARLES D. SMITH; Cairo Dir MARK M. EASTON; New York Dir TERENCE WALZ; publs *Journal* (annually), *Newsletter* (quarterly).

Centre for Political and Strategic Studies: Al Ahram Foundation, al-Galaa St, Cairo; tel. (2) 755650; telex 20185; fax (2) 745888; f. 1968; research into international relations and politics; particular emphasis on Arab-Israeli relations; Dir Dr O. EL GHAZALI HARB; publs *The Arab Strategic Report* (quarterly), *The International Politics Magazine* (quarterly).

Institut Dominicain d'Etudes Orientales: Priory of theDominican Fathers, 1 Sharia Masna at-Tarabish, BP 18 Abbasiyah, 11381 Cairo; tel. (2) 4825509; fax (2) 2820682; e-mail ideo@link.com.eg; f. 1953; Dir Père REGIS MORELON; publ. *Mélanges* (annually).

Institut d'Egypte: 13 Sharia Sheikh Rihane, Cairo; f. 1798; studies literary, artistic and scientific questions relating to Egypt and neighbouring countries; 60 mems, 50 assoc. mems, 50 corresp., mems; library of 160,000 vols; Pres. Dr SULAIMAN HAZIEN; Sec. Gen. P. GHALIOUNGU; publs *Bulletin* (annually), *Mémoires* (irregular).

Institut Français d'Archéologie Orientale: 37 rue Sheikh Ali Youssef, BP 11562, Cairo; tel. (2) 3548248; fax (2) 3544635; e-mail cvelud@ifao.eg_net.net; f. 1880; excavations, research and publications; library of 60,000 vols; Dir of Studies CHRISTIAN VELUD; Dir Prof. NICOLAS GRIMAL; publs *Bulletin de l'Institut Français d'Archéologie Orientale, Annales Islamologiques*, etc.

Institute of Arab Research and Studies: 1 Tolombat St, POB 229, Cairo (Garden City); tel. (2) 3551648; telex 92642; fax (2) 3562543; f. 1953; research and studies into contemporary Arab affairs; international relations; library service; affiliated to the Arab League Educational, Cultural and Scientific Organization—ALECSO; Dir Prof. AHMAD YOUSUF AHMAD; publ. *Bulletin of Arab Research and Studies* (annual).

Middle East Research Centre: el-Khalifa el-Mahmoun St, Ain Shams University; tel. (2) 821117; telex 9470; Dir Prof. Dr MUHAMMAD REDA EL-EDET.

National Centre for Middle East Studies: 1 Kasr el-Nile St, Bab el-Louk, POB 18, 11513 Cairo; tel. (2) 770041; telex 22419; fax (2) 770063; f. 1989; research into peace process, arms control and conflict resolutions; Dir R. AHMAD ISMAIL FAKHR; publ. *Middle East Papers* (3 per year).

Société Archéologique d'Alexandrie: POB 815, 6 Mahmoud Mokhtar St, 21111 Alexandria; tel. and fax (3) 4820650; f. 1893; 248 mems; Pres. A. M. SADEK; Vice-Pres. YOUSSEF EL-GHERIANI; Treas. K. EL-ADM; publs *Bulletins, Mémoires, Monuments de l'Egypte Gréco-Romaine, Cahiers, Publications Spéciales, Archaeological and Historical Studies*.

Société Egyptienne d'Economie Politique, de Statistique et de Législation: BP 732, 16 ave Ramses, Cairo; f. 1909; 1,550 mems; 3,018 mems; library of 18,259 vols; Pres. Dr ATIF SIDKY; Sec.-Gen. Dr MAHMOUD HAFEZ GHANEM; Tech.-Secs Dr FATHI EL-MASSAFAWI and Dr SAKR AHMAD SAKR; publ. *Revue* (quarterly in Arabic, French and English).

Society for Coptic Archaeology: 222 ave Ramses, Cairo; tel. (2) 4824252; f. 1934; 360 mems; library of 15,000 vols; Pres. WASSIF BOUTROS GHALI; Sec.-Gen. Dr A. KHATER; Treas. AMIN F. ABD EN-NOUR; publs *Bulletin* (annually), *Fouilles, Bibliothèque d'Art et d'Archéologie, Textes et Documents*, etc.

FINLAND

Suomen Itämainen Seura (Finnish Oriental Society): c/o Department of Asian and African Studies, POB 13 (Meritullink 1B), SF-00014 University of Helsinki; fax (0) 1912094; f. 1917; 160 mems; Pres. Prof. ASKO PARPOLA; Sec. Prof. T. HARVIAINEN; publ. *Studia Orientalia*.

FRANCE

Centre des Hautes Etudes sur l'Afrique et l'Asie Modernes: 13 rue du Four, 75006 Paris; tel. (1) 44413880; fax (1) 40510358; f. 1936; Dir JEAN-PIERRE DOUMENGE; publs *Lettre d'Information* (4 a year), *Notes Africaines, Caraïbes et Asiatiques* (irregular).

Centre Interdisciplinaire d'Etudes et de Recherches sur les Relations Internationales au Moyen-Orient (Centre of Interdisciplinary Studies and Research on International Relations in the Middle East): Université de Rennes II Haute Bretagne, 6 ave Gaston Berger, 35043 Rennes Cedex; tel. 299335252.

Fondation Nationale des Sciences Politiques: 27 rue Saint-Guillaume, 75337 Paris Cedex 07; tel. (1) 45495050; fax (1) 44108450; f. 1945; Pres. RENÉ RÉMOND; Administrator R. DESCOINGS; Arab world section has research team of 5 mems; publs include *Maghreb-Machrek* (quarterly).

Institut d'Etudes Arabes et Islamiques: Université de la Sorbonne Nouvelle (Paris III), 13 rue de Santeuil, 75231 Paris Cedex 05; tel. (1) 45874139; Dir JEAN-PATRICK GUILLAUME.

Institut d'Etudes Iraniennes: Université de la Sorbonne Nouvelle (Paris III), 13 rue de Santeuil, 75231 Paris Cedex 05; tel. (1) 45874069; fax (1) 45874170; e-mail iran@univ_paris 3; f. 1947; Dir RICHARD YANN; publs *Travaux, Travaux et Mémoires* (series), *Studia Iranica* (journal), *Abstracta Iranica* (annual bibliography).

Institut d'Etudes Sémitiques: Institut d'Etudes Sémitiques, 11 place Marcelin-Berthelot, 75231 Paris Cedex 05; tel. (1) 44271051; fax (1) 44271109; e-mail 106357.2210@compuserve.com; f. 1930; Pres. J. TEIXIDOR: publ. *Semitica*.

Institut du Monde Arabe: 1 rue des Fossés Saint-Bernard, 75236 Paris Cedex 05; tel. (1) 40513838; telex 203832; fax (1) 43547645; f. 1980; Pres. CAMILLE CABANA.

Institut de Recherches et d'Etudes sur le Monde Arabe et Musulman (Institute of Research and Studies on the Arab and Muslim World): Université d'Aix-Marseille III, Maison de la Méditerranée, 3-5-7 ave Pasteur, 13617 Aix-en-Provence Cedex 1; tel. 442215988; fax 442215275; e-mail adiremam@univ_aix.fr.

Institut National des Langues et Civilisations Orientales: 2 rue de Lille, 75343 Paris Cedex 07; tel. (1) 49264200; fax (1) 49264299; internet http://www.inalco.fr; f. 1795; faculties of languages and civilizations of West Asia and Africa; the Far East, India and Oceania; Eastern Europe; North and Central America; library of 430,000 vols and 7,000 periodicals; c. 11,800 students, 300 teachers and lecturers; Pres. ANDRÉ BOURGEY; Vice-Pres. FRANCE BHATTACHARYA; Sec. Gen. CATHERINE DELAFOSSE; High International Studies (DHEI), Department of International Business (CPEI), Automatic Languages Treatment (TAL), Multilingual Engineering (IM); publs *Livret de l'Etudiant* (annually), various Oriental studies and periodicals.

Institut de Papyrologie: Université de Paris-Sorbonne, 1 rue Victor-Cousin, 75005 Paris; tel. (1) 40462645; Dir ALAIN BLANCHARD.

Société Asiatique: 3 rue Mazarine, 75006 Paris; tel. (1) 44414314; fax (1) 44414316; f. 1822; 700 mems; library of 100,000 vols; Pres. DANIEL GIMARET; Vice-Pres CHRISTIAN ROBIN, CAROLINE GYSS-VERMANDE; Secs J. L. BACQUE-GRAMMONT, C. LUBRANO DI CICCONE; publs *Journal Asiatique* (2 a year), *Cahiers de la Société Asiatique*.

GEORGIA

Institute of Oriental Studies of the Academy of Sciences of Georgia: Ul. G. Tsereteli 3, 380062 Tbilisi; tel. (8832) 233114; Dir T. V. GAMKRELIDZE.

GERMANY

Altorientalisches Seminar der Freien Universität Berlin: D-14195 Berlin, Bitterstr. 8–12; tel. (30) 8383347; fax (30) 8314252; f. 1950.

Deutsche Arbeitsgemeinschaft Vorderer Orient (DAVO): 20148 Hamburg, Mittelweg 150; tel. (40) 4132050; fax (40) 441484; e-mail doihh@uni_hamburg.de; internet http://www.rrz.uni_hamburg.de/DOI; consists of German research orgs into politics, economics and society of the Middle East; 36 mem. insts; Sec. Prof. Dr UDO STEINBACH.

Deutsche Morgenländische Gesellschaft: D-69120 Heidelberg, Im Neuenheimer Feld 330; tel. (6221) 548900; fax (6221) 544998; f. 1845; Sec. MANFRED HAKE; publs *Zeitschrift* (two a year), *Abhandlungen für die Kunde des Morgenlandes, Bibliotheca Islamica, Wörterbuch der Klassischen Arabischen Sprache, Beiruter Texte und Studien, Verzeichnis der orientalischen Handschriften in Deutschland*, etc.

Deutsches Orient-Institut: 20148 Hamburg, Mittelweg 150; tel. (40) 4132050; fax (40) 441484; e-mail doihh@uni_hamburg.de; internet http://www.rrz.uni_hamburg.de/DOI; f. 1960 from the Nah- und Mittelostverein e.V.; since 1965 has been affil. to Deutsches Übersee-Institut; devoted to research in politics, science and economics of Near and Middle East and provides a fortnightly press cutting service on the Middle East; Dir Prof. Dr UDO STEINBACH; publs *Nahost Jahrbuch* (annually), *Orient* (quarterly), *Mitteilungen* (irregular), *Schriften* (irregular).

Internationale Gesellschaft für Orientforschung: Orientalisches Seminar, J. W. Goethe-Universität, Postfach 11-1932, D-60054 Frankfurt/Main 11; f. 1948; 400 mems; Pres. Prof. R. SELLHEIM; publ. *Oriens* (annually).

Nah- und Mittelost Verein e.V. (German Near and Middle East Association): D20148 Hamburg, Mittelweg 151; tel. (40) 4503310; telex 212253; fax (40) 45033131; f. 1934; 600 mems; Chair. WERNER SCHOELTZKE.

Seminar für Orientalische Sprachen: Adenauerallee 102, D-53113 Bonn; tel. (228) 738415; fax (228) 738446; f. 1959 (1887 Berlin); University of Bonn, Near East Department; Prof. Dr W. SCHMUCKER.

INDIA

Asiatic Society of Bombay (Mumbai): Town Hall, Bombay 400 023; tel. 2660956; f. 1804 as Bombay Literary Society; 2,171 mems; to investigate and encourage sciences, arts and literature in relation to Asia; established the Dr P. V. Kane Research Institute for Oriental Studies in 1973 (later renamed the Dr P. V. Kane Institute for Post Graduate Studies and Research—affiliated to the University of Bombay); 2,811 mems; 235,000 vols; 2,357 MSS and 10,443 old coins; Pres. Dr D. R. SARDESAI; Hon. Sec. VIMAL SHAH; publs annual *Journal*, reports, critical annotated texts of rare Sanskrit and Pali MSS.

IRAN

British Institute of Persian Studies: Kucheh Alvand, Khiaban Dr Ali Shariati, Gholhak, POB 11365-6844, Teheran 19396; f. 1961; cultural institute, with emphasis on history and archaeology; 650 individual mems; library of more than 10,000 vols; Hon. Sec. Dr CHARLES MELVILLE; publ. *Iran* (annually).

Institute for Political and International Studies—IPIS: Shaheed Bahonar Ave, Shaheed Aghaii St, Tajrish, Teheran; POB 19395/1793, Teheran; tel. (21) 2571010; fax (21) 270964; f. 1983; research and information on international relations; emphasis on Middle East, Persian (Arabian) Gulf, and Central Asia; Dir Gen. ABBAS MALEKI; publs *Asyaye Markazi va Ghafgaz* (quarterly), *Iranian Journal of International Affairs* (quarterly), *Siayasat-e khariji* (quarterly).

IRAQ

Centre for Arab Gulf Studies: University of Basrah, POB 49, Basrah; tel. (40) 314657; fax (40) 213235; f. 1974; research into economics, politics, strategic issues, geography, history and culture in the Persian (Arabian) Gulf region; Dir Dr MUHAMMAD ABDULLAH ALAZAWI; publ. *Arab Gulf Journal* (quarterly).

Deutsches Archäologisches Institut: Hay al-Maarife 821/63, POB 2105, Alwiya, Baghdad; tel. 5431353.

Instituto Hispano-Arabe de Cultura: Hurriya Sq, Hay Babil 925/25/80, POB 2256, Alwiyah; tel. 7766045; f. 1958; Dir JUAN M. CASADO RAMOS.

Iraq Academy: Waziriyah, Baghdad; f. 1947 to maintain the Arabic language, to undertake research into Arabic history, Islamic heritage and the history of Iraq, and to encourage research in the modern arts and sciences; Pres. Dr SALEH A. AL-ALI; Sec.-Gen. Dr NOORI H. AL-QISSI; publ. *Bulletin of the Iraq Academy* (2 a year).

ISRAEL

The Academy of the Hebrew Language: POB 3449, Jerusalem 91034; tel. (2) 5632242; fax (2) 5617065; f. 1953; study and development of the Hebrew language and compilation of a historical dictionary; Pres. Prof. M. BAR-ASHER; publs *Zikhronot, Leshonenu* (quarterly), *Leshonenu La'am,* monographs and dictionaries.

Arab Studies Society: POB 20479, Jerusalem; tel. (2) 6273330; fax (2) 6286820; e-mail arabstudies@arabs.arabstudies; internet http://www.arabstudies.org; f. 1980 to promote Arabic culture

in general and Palestinian thought and culture in particular; works undertaken by 8 centres with 14 departments; library of more than 16,000 vols on Palestine and the Middle East; Chair FAISAL HUSSEINI; Gen. Dir ISHAQ BUDEIRI; publs more than 100 books on culture and history of Jerusalem and Palestine.

W. F. Albright Institute of Archaeological Research in Jerusalem: POB 19096, 26 Salah ed-Din, Jerusalem 91190; tel. (2) 6282131; fax (2) 6264424; f. 1900 by American Schools of Oriental Research; research in Syro-Palestinian archaeology, Biblical studies, Near Eastern history and languages; sponsors excavations; Pres. P. GERSTENBLITH; Dir S. GITIN.

Begin-Sadat Centre for Strategic Studies: Bar-Ilan University, Ramat-Gan 52900; tel. (3) 5318959; fax (3) 5359195; e-mail besa@ashur.cc.biu.ac.il; f. 1992; research on Middle Eastern security; conferences and workshops; Dir Prof. EFRAIM INBAR; publs *BESA Bulletin, BESA Colloquia on Strategy and Diplomacy, BESA Security and Policy Studies, The Middle East Review of International Affairs (MERIA)*.

The Ben-Zvi Institute for the Study of Jewish Communities in the East: POB 7660, 12 Abravanel St, Jerusalem 91076; tel. (2) 5639204; fax (2) 5638310; e-mail mahonzvi@hum.huji.ac.il; f. 1948; sponsors research in the history and culture of Jewish communities in the East; library of MSS and printed books; Chair. Prof. HAGGAI BEN SHAMMAI; publs *Sefunot, Pe'amim* (quarterly), and monographs.

Bertha von Suttner Research Program for Peace Studies and Conflict Resolution in the Middle East: University of Haifa, Mount Carmel, Haifa 31905; tel. (4) 8240111; fax (4) 8342104.

British School of Archaeology in Jerusalem: POB 19283, Jerusalem; tel. (2) 5828101; fax (2) 5323844; f. 1920; e-mail bsaj@vms.huji.ac.il; archaeological research and excavation; hostel and library; Chair. P. G. DE COURCY IRELAND; Dir R. P. HARPER; publ. *Levant.*

Couvent Saint Etienne des Pères Dominicains, Ecole Biblique et Archéologique Française: POB 19053, Jerusalem 91190; tel. (2) 6264468; fax (2) 6282567; e-mail ebaf@netvision.net.il; f. 1890; research, Biblical and Oriental studies, exploration and excavation in Palestine and Jordan; Dir Dr KEVIN McCAFFREY; library of 110,000 vols; publs *Revue Biblique, Etudes Bibliques, Cahiers annexes de la Bible de Jérusalem, Cahiers de la Revue Biblique, Bible de Jérusalem.*

Moshe Dayan Centre for Middle Eastern and African Studies/Shiloah Institute: Tel-Aviv University, Ramat Aviv, Tel-Aviv 69978; tel. (3) 640-9646; telex 342171; fax (3) 6415802; e-mail dayancen@ccsg.tav.ac.il; internet http://www.dayan.org; f. 1959; Dir Dr MARTIN KRAMER; publs *Middle East Contemporary Survey* (annually), also monographs, teaching aids, studies and occasional papers and computerized database on the Middle East; library e-mail dayanlib@ccsg.tav.ac.il.

Historical Society of Israel: POB 4179, Jerusalem 91041; tel. (2) 5637171; fax (2) 5662135; f. 1925 to promote the study of Jewish history and general history; 1,000 mems; Chair. Prof. YOSEF KAPLAN; Gen. Sec. ZVI YEKUTIEL; publ. *Zion* (quarterly).

Institute of Asian and African Studies: Hebrew University, Mount Scopus, Jerusalem 91905; tel. (2) 5883712; fax (2) 5322545; e-mail msjsai@pluto.mscc.huji.ac.il; f. 1926; studies of medieval and modern languages, culture and history of Middle East, Asia and Africa; Chair. Prof. SHAUL SHAKED; publs *Max Schloessinger Memorial Series, Jerusalem Studies in Arabic and Islam,* translation series and studies in classical Islam and Arabic language and literature.

Israel Exploration Society: POB 7041, 5 Avida St, Jerusalem 91070; tel. (2) 6257991; fax (2) 6247772; e-mail ies@vms.huji.ac.il; internet http://www.hum.huji.ac.il\ies; f. 1913; excavations and historical research, congresses and lectures; 4,000 mems; Chair. Prof. A. BIRAN; Dir J. AVIRAM; publs *Eretz-Israel* (Hebrew annual, with English summaries), *Qadmoniot* (Hebrew quarterly), *Israel Exploration Journal* (English quarterly), various books on archaeology (in Hebrew and English).

Israel Oriental Society: The Hebrew University, Jerusalem 91905; tel. (2) 5883633; f. 1949; lectures and symposia to study all aspects of contemporary Middle Eastern, Asian and African affairs; Pres. TEDDY KOLLEK; publs *Hamizrah Hehadash*

(Hebrew—with English summary—annual), *Oriental Notes and Studies* (1951–71).

Jaffee Center for Strategic Studies—JCSS: Tel-Aviv University, Ramat-Aviv, Tel-Aviv 69978; tel. (3) 6409200; fax (3) 6422404; f. 1977; research into Middle Eastern strategic affairs; Chair. MELVIN JAFFEE; Dir Prof. ZEEV MAOZ; publs *JCSS Bulletin* (2 a year), *The Middle East Military Balance*.

Jerusalem University College: POB 1276 Mt Zion, Jerusalem 91012; tel. (2) 671-8628; fax (2) 673-2717; f. 1957 as Institute of Holy Land Studies; Christian study centre, grad. and undergrad. in the history, languages, religions and cultures of Israel in the Middle Eastern Context; Pres. Dr SIDNEY DeWAAL; Academic Dean Dr PAUL WRIGHT.

Orientalisches Institut der Görres-Gesellschaft: Schmidt-Schule, POB 19424, Jerusalem; historical and archaeological studies.

Pontifical Biblical Institute: POB 497, 3 Paul Emile Botta St, Jerusalem 91004; tel. (2) 6252843; fax (2) 6241203; f. 1927; study of Biblical languages and Biblical archaeology, history, topography; in conjunction with Hebrew University of Jerusalem; seminar for post-graduate students, student tours; Dir Rev. JOHN R. CROCKER.

The Harry S. Truman Research Institute for the Advancement of Peace: Hebrew University, Mount Scopus, Jerusalem 91905; tel. (2) 882300; telex 26458; fax (2) 828076; f. 1966; conducts and sponsors social science and historical research, organizes conferences on Third-World and non-Western countries, with special emphasis on the Middle East; Dir Prof. MOSHE MA'OZ; publs works on the Middle East, Africa, Asia and Latin America.

Wilfrid Israel House for Oriental Art and Studies: Kibbutz Hazorea, Mobile Post Ha'amakim 30060; tel. (4) 899566; telex 471418; f. 1947; opened 1951 in memory of late Wilfrid Israel; a cultural centre for reference, study and art exhbns; houses Wilfrid Israel collection of Near and Far Eastern art and cultural materials; local archaeological exhibits from neolithic to Byzantine times; science and art library; Dir EHUD DOR; Curator for Far and Middle Eastern Art ORNA MERON; Curator for Archaeology RUTH GOSHEN.

ITALY

Istituto di Studi del Vicino Oriente: Dipartimento di Scienze Storiche, Archeologiche ed Antropologiche dell'Antichità, Sezione Vicino Oriente, Università degli Studi di Roma 'La Sapienza', P.le Aldo Moro, 5-00100 Rome; Dir Prof. PAOLO MATTHIAE.

Istituto Italiano per l'Africa e l'Oriente (IsIAO): via Ulisse Aldrovandi 16, Rome; tel. (06) 3216712; fax (06) 3225348; f. 1906; Pres. Prof. GHERARDO GNOLI; Dir-Gen. Dott. GIANCARLO GARGARUTI.

Istituto Italiano per il Medio ed Estremo Oriente (ISMEO): Palazzo Brancaccio, via Merulana 248, Rome; tel. (06) 4874273; telex 624163; fax (06) 4873138; f. 1933; Pres. Prof. GHERARDO GNOLI; publs *East and West* (quarterly), *Rome Oriental Series, Nuovo Ramusio, Archaeological Reports and Memoirs, Restorations*.

Istituto per l'Oriente C. A. Nallino: Via A. Caroncini 19, 00197 Rome; tel. (06) 8084106; fax (06) 8079395; e-mail ipo@mix.it; f. 1921 as L'istituto per l'Oriente; adopted current name in 1982 in honour of one of its founders, Carlo Alfonso Nallino; under supervision of the Ministry of Foreign Affairs; research into all aspects of bilateral and multilateral relations between Italy and the countries of the Near and Middle East; particular emphasis on law, society and immigration; library service; organizes courses on Arabic and Islamic culture; Pres. Prof. FRANCESCO CASTRO; publ. *Oriente Moderno* (monographic essays and bibliographical reviews).

Istituto per le relazioni tra l'Italia e i paesi dell'Africa, America Latina e Medio Oriente: via del Tritone 62B, 00187 Rome; tel. (06) 6792321; fax (02) 6797849; f. 1971; Pres. GILBERTO BONALUMI; publ. *Politica Internazionale* (6 a year Italian edition).

JAPAN

Ajia Keizai Kenkyusho (Institute of Developing Economies): 42 Ichigaya-Hommura-cho, Shinjuku-ku, Tokyo 162-8442; tel.

(3) 33534231; telex 32473; fax (3) 32268475; f. 1958; 254 mems; Chair. YŌTARŌ IIDA; Pres. KATSUHISA YAMADA; library of 351,595 vols; publs *Ajia Keizai* (Japanese, monthly), *The Developing Economies* (English, quarterly), occasional papers in English.

Chuto Chosakai (Middle East Institute of Japan): POB 1513, Shinjuku i-Land Tower, Tokyo 163-13; tel. (3) 53232145; fax (3) 53232148; f. 1960; Chair. WASUKE MIYAKE; publs *Chuto Kenkyu* (Journal of Middle Eastern Studies—monthly), *Chuto Nenkan* (Yearbook of Middle East and North Africa), *Newsletter*.

Nippon Oriento Gakkai (Society for Near Eastern Studies in Japan): Tokyo Tenrikyokan. 9, 1-chome, Kanda Nishiki-cho, Chiyoda-ku, Tokyo 101; tel. and fax (3) 32917519; f. 1954; about 910 mems; Pres. Dr HIDEO OGAWA; publs *Oriento* (Japanese, 2 a year), *Orient* (European languages annual).

JORDAN

Centre for Strategic Studies: University of Jordan, Amman; tel. (6) 5355667; fax (6) 5355515; e-mail uojcss@go.com.jo; f. 1984; research on strategic, political, economic and social issues concerning Jordan and the Middle East; Dir Dr MUSTAFA B. HAMARNEH.

LEBANON

Arab Institute for Research and Publishing: POB 11-5460; 3rd Floor, Carlton Tower Bldg, Saqiat el-Janzeer, Beirut; telex 40067; Gen. Man. MAHER KAYALI; works in Arabic and English.

Centre d'Etudes et de Recherches sur le Moyen-Orient contemporain (CERMOC): BP 2691, rue de Damas, Beirut; tel. (1) 640694; fax (1) 644857; POB 830413, Zahran, Amman, Jordan; Ambassade de France au Liban, Valise Diplomatique, 128 bis, rue de l'Université, 75531 Paris, France; f. 1977; 4 research fellows and 9 contractual researchers; university research and documentation institution; library specializes in human and social sciences concerning the Middle East; Dir JEAN HANNOYER; publs 40 books on contemporary Middle East.

Institut Français d'Archéologie du Proche Orient: rue de Damas, BP 11-1424, Beirut; tel. (1) 640698; fax (1) 644855; e-mail ifapo@lb.refer.org; Jordanian Section: BP 5348, Amman, Jordan; tel. (6) 611872; fax (6) 643840; Syrian Section: BP 3694, Damascus, Syria; tel. (11) 3338727; fax (11) 3325013; f. 1946; library of 45,000 vols (Bibliothèque Henri Seyrig); Dir J. M. DENTZER; publs *Syria, Revue d'Art et d'Archéologie* (annually), *Bibliothèque Archéologique et Historique*.

Institute for Palestine Studies, Publishing and Research Organization: POB 11-7164, Nsouli-Verdun St, Beirut; tel. and fax (1) 868387; telex 23317; e-mail ipsb10@calvacom.fr; 3501 M St, NW, POB 25301, Washington, DC 20007, USA; tel. (202) 3423990; fax (202) 3423927; e-mail jps@cais.com; 13 Hera St, POB 5658, Nicosia, Cyprus; tel. (2) 456165; fax (2) 456324; f. 1963; independent non-profit Arab research organization; to promote better understanding of the Palestine problem and the Arab-Israeli conflict; library of 30,000 vols, microfilm collection, private papers and archives; Hon. Chair. Dr CONSTANTINE ZURAYK; Chair. Dr HISHAM NASHABE; Exec. Sec. Prof. WALID KHALIDI; publs *Journal of Palestine Studies* (English, quarterly), *Revue d'études palestiniennes* (French, quarterly), *Majallat ad-Dirasat al-Filistiniyah* (Arabic, quarterly) and documentary series, reprints, research papers, etc.

Lebanese Center for Policy Studies—LCPS: Tayyar Center, Sin al-Fil, Beirut (international mailing address: POB 4101, Nicosia, Cyprus); tel. (1) 490561; fax (1) 601787; f. 1989; Arab-Western relations and Lebanese-Syrian relations; Pres. Dr ELIE A. SALEM; Dir of Studies Dr PAUL E. SALEM; Publs *The Beirut Review* (2 a year), *The Lebanon Report* (monthly).

THE NETHERLANDS

Assyriologisch Instituut der Rijksuniversiteit: Rijksuniversiteit Leiden, POB 9515, 2300 RA Leiden; tel. (71) 5272260; fax (71) 5272615; e-mail assyr@rullet.leidenuniv.nl; Dir Prof. Dr K. R. VEENHOF; publs *Altbabylonische Briefe in Umschrift und Übersetzung* (14 vols, continuing series), *Collection, Liagre Böhl Collection* (c. 3,000 cuneiform tablets) published in conjunction with the Netherlands Institute for the Near East, Leiden.

Middle East Research Associates: 116-III Lauriergracht, POB 10765, 1001 ET Amsterdam; Dir P. AARTS.

Netherlands Council for Trade Promotion (Netherlands Middle East Business Council): Bezuidenhoutseweg 181, POB 10, 2501 CA The Hague; tel. (70) 3441544; telex 32306; fax (070) 3853531; f. 1949; publs *Middle East Newsletter, Jordan Newsletter.*

Netherlands Institute for Archaeology and Arabic Studies: POB 20061, 2500 EB The Hague; e-mail niaasc@frcu.eun.eg; f. 1971; Dir Dr JOHANNES DEN HEIJER; library and publs in the field of Arabic and Coptic Studies.

Netherlands Institute for the Near East (*Nederlands Instituut voor het Nabije Oosten*): Witte Singel 25, POB 9515, 2300 RA Leiden; tel. (71) 272036; fax (71) 272038; e-mail beurs@rullet .leidenuniv.nl; Dir Prof. Dr J. DE ROOS; library of c. 35,000 vols and 600 periodicals; publs *Anatolica, Studia Francisci Scholten Memoriae dicata, Scholae de Buck, Publications de l'Institut historique et archéologique néerlandais de Stamboul, Bibliotheca Orientalis, Tabulae de Liagre Böhl, Studia de Liagre Böhl, Egyptologische Uitgaven* (monographs, 11th vol. in production), *Achaemenid History* (monographs).

PAKISTAN

Institute of Islamic Culture: 2 Club Rd, Lahore 3; tel. (42) 363127; f. 1950; Dir RASHID AHMAD JULLUNDHRI; Sec. MALIK FAIZ BAKHSH; publs *Al-Ma'arif* (quarterly), *Jamal* (annually) and about 200 publications on Islamic subjects in English and Urdu.

Islamic Research Institute: International Islamic University, POB 1035, Islamabad 44000; tel. (51) 850751; telex 54068; fax (51) 853360; e-mail dg-iri@iri-iiu.sdnpk.undp.org; f. 1960; conducts research in Islamic studies; organizes seminars and conferences on various aspects of Islam; library of 120,000 books and periodicals, 610 microfilms, 260 MSS, 1,035 photostats, 220 audio cassettes; Dir-Gen. Dr ZAFAR ISHAQ ANSARI; publs *Ad-Dirasat al-Islamiyah* (Arabic, quarterly), *Islamic Studies* (English, quarterly), *Fikr O-Nazar* (Urdu, quarterly), also monographs, reports, etc.

POLAND

Polskie Towarzystwo Orientalistyczne (Polish Oriental Society): Zarząd Główny, Śniadeckich 8, 00-656 Warsaw; tel. (2) 6282471; f. 1922; 200 mems; Pres. STANISŁAW KAŁUŻYŃSKI, ALEKSANDER DUBIŃSKI, CZESŁAW ZWIERZ; Sec. MAREK DZIEKAN; publ. *Przegląd Orientalistyczny* (quarterly).

Zakład Archeologii Śródziemnomorskiej (Research Centre for Mediterranean Archaeology): Pałac Staszica, (Room 33), Nowy Świat 72,00-330 Warsaw; f. 1956; 18 mems; Research Institute of Academy of Sciences; documentation and publication of Polish excavations in the Middle East and antiquities in Polish museums; Prof. KAROL MYŚLIWIEC, Prof. ZSOLT KISS; publs *Etudes et Travaux du Centre d'Archéologie Méditerranéenne, Palmyre, Nubia, Faras, Deir el-Bahari, Nea Paphos, Alexandrie, Corpus Vasorum Antiquorum, Corpus Signorum Imperii Romani.*

PORTUGAL

Instituto de Estudos Árabes e Islâmicos: Faculdade de Letras, Cidade Universitária, 1699 Lisbon; tel. (1) 7965162; fax (1) 7960063; f. 1966; library; 6 teachers; specializes in Arabic and Islamic studies; Dir A. DIAS FARINHA.

RUSSIA

Russian Centre for Strategic and International Studies: ul. Rozhdestvenka 12, 103753 Moscow; tel. (095) 9245150; telex 412157; fax (095) 4256237; f. 1991; research and training in international relations; Islamic studies, strategic and military studies, the Middle East and North Africa; Pres. VITALY V. NAUMKIN; Exec. Dir ALEKSANDR FILONIK.

SAUDI ARABIA

Arab Urban Development Institute: POB 6892, Riyadh 11452; tel. (1) 4802555; fax (1) 4802666; e-mail info@aud_ins.org; internet http://www.aud.ins.org; f. 1980; affiliated to the Arab Towns Organization; provides training, research, consultancy and documentation services to Arab cities and municipalities and members of ATO for improving the Arab city and preserving

its original character and Islamic cultural heritage; Dir-Gen. Eng. AHMED AS-SALLOUM; library of 78,440 vols and 630 periodicals; publs books and research papers.

Centre for Research and Islamic Economics: King Abd al-Aziz University, POB 16711, Jeddah 21474; tel. (2) 6952128; telex 401141; fax (2) 6952066; f. 1977; research into all aspects of Islamic economics; Dir Dr GHAZIOBAID MODANI.

SLOVAKIA

Institute of Asian and African Studies: Slovak Academy of Sciences, Klemensova 19, 813 64 Bratislava; tel. and fax (7) 326326; e-mail koholla@klemens.savba.sk; f. 1960; 14 mems; Dir Institute Dr V. KRUPA; publ. *Asian and African Studies* (2 a year).

SPAIN

Asociación Española de Orientalistas: Universidad Autónoma, Edificio Rectorado, Canto Blanco, 28049 Madrid; tel. (91) 3974112; f. 1965; publs *Boletín* (annually), etc.

Egyptian Institute of Islamic Studies: Francisco de Asis Méndez Casariego 1, Madrid 28002; tel. (91) 5639468; fax (91) 5638640; e-mail iegipcio@mundivia.es; internet http://www.em presas.mundivia.es/iegipcio; affiliated to Ministry of Higher Education, Cairo; f. 1950; Dir Dr SULAYMAN ABD AL-AZIM H. EL-ATTAR; publs *Magazine of the Egyptian Institute* and other educational books.

Instituto de Filología: Duque de Medinaceli 6, 28014 Madrid; tel. (91) 4290626; fax (91) 3690940; f. 1985 as a result of the amalgamation of four existing institutes (the Benito Arias Montano, Miguel Asin, Miguel de Cervantes and Antonio de Nebrija); six depts: Departamento de Estudios Arabes (four members), Departamento de Filología Biblica y de Oriente Antiguo (eight members), Departamento de Estudios Hebraicos (four members); Dir TERESA ORTEGA MONASTERIO; Sec. JULIO CÉSAR SUILS; publs *Sefarad* (review of Hebrew, Sephardic and Ancient Studies, 2 a year), *Alqantara* (review of Arab Studies, 2 a year) and books.

SWEDEN

Nordiska Afrikainstitutet (Nordic Africa Institute): POB 1703, SE-75147, Uppsala; tel. (18) 562200; fax (18) 695629; e-mail nai@nai.uu.se; f. 1962; research and documentation centre for contemporary African affairs, organizes seminars and publishes wide range of books and pamphlets in Swedish and English; library of 45,000 vols, 1,000 periodicals; Dir L. WOHLGE-MUTH; Head of Research LOUISE FREDÉN; publs *Seminar Proceedings, Research Reports, Discussion Papers, Africana, Annual Report, Current African Issues,* monographs and newsletters.

SWITZERLAND

Schweizerische Asiengesellschaft: Ostasiatisches Seminar der Universität Zürich, Zürichbergstr. 4, 8032 Zürich; tel. (1) 6343181; fax (1) 6344921; e-mail ofice@oas.unizh.ch; f. 1939; 224 mems; Pres. Prof. Dr E. KLOPFENSTEIN; publs *Asiatische Studien / Etudes Asiatiques* (4 a year), *Schweizer Asiatische Studien* (Monographien und Studienhefte).

SYRIA

Institut Français d'Etudes Arabes: BP 344, Damascus; tel. (11) 3330214; telex 412272; fax (11) 3327887; f. 1922; library of 55,000 vols, 980 periodicals; Dir DOMINIQUE MALLET; Head Librarian MICHEL NIETO; 48 scholars; publs *Bulletin d'Etudes Orientales* (annually, 47 vols published), monographs, translations and Arabic texts (158 vols published).

Near East Foundation: BP 427, Damascus.

TAJIKISTAN

Institute of Oriental Studies of Tajikistan: Ul. Parvin 8, Dushanbe; tel. (3772) 243010; Dir AKBAR TURSONOV.

TUNISIA

Institut des Belles Lettres Arabes: 12 rue Jamâa el-Haoua, 1008 Tunis BM; tel. (1) 560133; fax (1) 572683; f. 1930; cultural centre; Dir A. FERRE; publs *IBLA* (2 a year) and special studies.

TURKEY

British Institute of Archaeology at Ankara: Tahran Caddesi 24, Kavaklıdere, 06700 Ankara; tel. (312) 4275487; fax (312) 4280159; e-mail ingark-o@tr-net.net.tr; f. 1948; archaeological research and excavation; Dir Dr ROGER MATTHEWS; publs *Anatolian Studies* and *Anatolian Archaeology* (annually), *Occasional Publications*.

Deutsches Archäologisches Institut: Gümüşsuyu/Ayazpaşa Camii Sok. 48, TR-80090, İstanbul; tel. (212) 2440714; fax (212) 2523491; f. 1929; Dir Prof. Dr H. HAUPTMANN; publs *Istanbuler Mitteilungen* (annually), *Istanbuler Forschungen, Beihefte zu Istanbuler Mitteilungen*.

Institut Français d'Etudes Anatoliennes: Palais de France, PK 54, Beyoğlu, 80072 İstanbul; tel. (212) 2443327; fax (212) 2528091; f. 1930; 10 scientific mems; library of c. 20,000 vols; Dir STÉPHANE YERASIMOS; publs *Collection IFEA, Collection Varia Turcica, Collection Varia Anatolica, Anatolia Antiqua, Anatolia Moderna*.

Institute for Research on Economic Relations in Turkey, Europe and the Middle East: Dept of Economics, University of Istanbul, Beyazit; tel. (212) 5221489; telex 22062; fax (212) 5205473; Dir. E. MANISALI.

Netherlands Historical Archaeological Institute: Istiklâl Caddesi 393, Beyoğlu, İstanbul; tel. (212) 2939283; fax (212) 2513846; e-mail nlhai@superonline.com; f. 1958; library of 12,000 vols; Dir Dr H. E. LAGRO; publs *Publications de l'Institut Historique et Archéologique Néerlandais de Stamboul, Anatolica*.

Österreichisches Kulturinstitut Istanbul: Köybaşi Cad. 44, 80870 Yeniköy, İstanbul; tel. (212) 2237843; fax (212) 2233469; Dir Consul Dr ERWIN LUCIUS.

Türk Dil Kurumu (Turkish Language Institute): 217 Atatürk Bul, 06680 Ankara; tel. (312) 4286100; fax (312) 4285288; f. 1932; 40 mems; library of 28,000 vols; Pres. Prof. Dr AHMET B. ERCİLASUN; Vice-Pres. Prof. Dr HAMZA ZÜLFİKAR; publs *Türk Dili* (monthly), *Türk Dili Araştırmaları Yilliği-Belleten* (annually).

Türk Kültürünü Araştırma Enstitüsü (Institute for the Study of Turkish Culture): 17 Sokak No. 38, Bahçelievler, Ankara; tel. (312) 2133100; f. 1961; scholarly research into all aspects of Turkish culture; Dir Prof. Dr SÜKRÜ ELÇİN; publs *Türk Kültürü* (monthly), *Cultura Turcica* (annually), *Türk Kültürü Araştırmaları* (annually).

Türk Tarih Kurumu (Turkish Historical Society): Kızılay Sok. 1, 06100 Ankara; tel. (312) 3102368; fax (312) 3101698; e-mail yusuf@ttk.gov.tr; f. 1931; 40 mems; library of 210,000 vols; Pres. Prof. YUSUF HALAÇOĞLU; publs *Belleten* (3 a year), *Belgeler* (annually).

UNITED ARAB EMIRATES

Centre for Documentation and Research: Old Palace, POB 2380, Abu Dhabi; tel. (2) 345371; fax (2) 336059; f. 1968; attached to Ministry of Foreign Affairs; research, data collection and analysis on aspects of the Persian (Arabian) Gulf region; Dir MUHAMMAD MORSI ABDULLAH; publ. *Arabian Gulf Research Review* (quarterly).

UNITED KINGDOM

Arab Research Centre: 76/78 Notting Hill Gate, London, W11 3HS; tel. (171) 2212425; fax (171) 2215899; f. 1979; research into problems and issues concerning the Arab world; library of 27,000 vols; commissions writing of special papers; holds international symposia; Chair. ABD AL-MAJID FARID; Man. ALIA ARNALL; publs. *The Arab Researcher* (English and Arabic, quarterly).

British School of Archaeology in Iraq: 31–34 Gordon Sq., London, WC1H OPY.

Centre for Arab Gulf Studies: University of Exeter, Old Library Bldg, Prince of Wales Rd, Exeter, EX4 4JZ; tel. (1392) 264024; fax (1392) 264023; e-mail eagsdoc@ex.ac.uk; f. 1978 to promote research into the economy, society and modern history of the Arab Gulf (particularly Iraq, Yemen and countries of the GCC); extensive library; Dir Dr K. A. MAHDI.

Centre for Lebanese Studies: 59 Observatory St, Oxford, OX2 6EP; tel. (1865) 558465; fax (1865) 514317; e-mail shehadi @sable.ox.ac.uk; internet http://www.nonuniv.ox.ac.uk/CIS; Dir NADIM SHEHADI; Deputy Dir FIDAH NASRALLAH.

Centre for Middle Eastern and Islamic Studies: University of Durham, South End House, South Rd, Durham, DH1 3TG; tel. (191) 3742822; fax (191) 3742830; f. 1962; responsible for teaching undergraduate and postgraduate courses in Arabic, Persian, Turkish, Middle Eastern and Islamic studies; organizes seminars, lectures and conferences; documentation unit f. 1970 to monitor economic, social and political devts in the region with some 200,000 documents; publication programme of research monographs, occasional papers and bibliographies; Chair. Dr A. EHTESHAMI.

Centre of Middle Eastern Studies: Faculty of Oriental Studies, Sidgwick Ave, Cambridge CB3 9DA; tel. and fax (1223) 335103; e-mail oriental-mes@lists.cam.ac.uk; Dir Prof TARIF KHALIDI; publ. *Arabian Studies* (annually).

Council for the Advancement of Arab-British Understanding (CAABU): The Arab-British Centre, 21 Collingham Rd, London, SW5 0NU; tel. (171) 3738414; fax (171) 8352088; e-mail caabu@arab-british.u_net.com; f. 1967; Dir CYRIL D. TOWNSEND.

Egypt Exploration Society: 3 Doughty Mews, London, WC1N 2PG; tel. (171) 242 1880; fax (171) 404 6118; f. 1882; library of 4,500 vols; c. 3,000 mems; Chair. Prof. ALAN B. LLOYD; Hon. Sec. Dr ANTHONY LEAHY; publs *Bulletin of the Egypt Exploration Society, Excavation Memoirs, Archaeological Survey, Graeco-Roman Memoirs, Journal of Egyptian Archaeology, Texts from Excavations, Egyptian Archaeology*, etc.

Islamic Cultural Centre (and London Central Mosque): 146 Park Rd, London, NW8 7RG; tel. (171) 7243363; f. 1944 to provide information and guidance on Islam and Islamic culture and to provide facilities for Muslims residing in Great Britain; library of 10,000 vols in Arabic, English, Urdu and Persian; Dir-Gen. Dr HAMAD AL-MAJED.

Maghreb Studies Association: c/o The Executive Secretary, M. BEN-MADANI, 45 Burton St, London, WC1H 9AL; tel. (171) 388 1840; f. 1981; independent; to promote the study of, and interest in, the Maghreb; organizes lectures and conferences; issues occasional publications and co-operates with the periodical *The Maghreb Review* (q.v.); Chair. Prof. HÉDI BOURAOUI.

Middle East Association: Bury House, 33 Bury St, London, SW1Y 6AX; tel. (171) 839 2137; fax (171) 839 6121; f. 1961; an asscn for firms actively promoting UK trade with 20 Arab countries, plus Iran and Turkey; 300 mems; Dir-Gen. BRIAN CONSTANT; Sec. R. BROWN.

Middle East Centre: St Antony's College, 68 Woodstock Rd, Oxford, OX2 6JF; tel. (1865) 284780; fax (1865) 311475; e-mail eugene.rogen@sant.ox.ac.uk; f. 1958; Dir Dr EUGENE ROGEN; library of 34,000 vols and archive of private papers and photographs; publs St Antony's Middle East monographs.

Muslim Institute for Research and Planning: 109 Fulham Palace Rd, London, W6 8JA; tel. (181) 5631995; fax (181) 5631993; f. 1974; research and teaching programmes, academic and current affairs seminars, library of 6,000 vols; 800 mems; Dir Dr M. GHAYASUDDIN SIDDIQUI; publs *Crescent International* (2 a month), *Issues in the Islamic Movement* (annually). Supplies publications of the Muslim Parliament of Great Britain.

Oxford Centre for Islamic Studies: George St, Oxford OX1 2AR; tel. (1865) 278730; telex 83147; fax (1865) 248942; f. 1985; Dir Dr FARHAN A. NIZAMI; Reg. Dr DAVID G. BROWNING; publs *Journal of Islamic Studies* (2 a year).

Palestine Exploration Fund: 2 Hinde Mews, Marylebone Lane, London, W1M 5RR; tel. (171) 9355379; fax (171) 4867438; e-mail pefund@compuserve.com; f. 1865; 900 subscribers; Pres. The Archbishop of Canterbury; Exec. Sec. Dr R. L. CHAPMAN, III; Hon. Sec. J. M. C. BOWSHER; publ. *Palestine Exploration Quarterly*.

Royal Asiatic Society of Great Britain and Ireland: 60 Queen's Gardens, London, W2 3AF; tel. (171) 7244741; fax (171) 7064008; f. 1823 for the study of the history, sociology, institutions, customs, languages and art of Asia; approx. 900 mems; approx. 700 subscribing libraries; library of 100,000 vols and 1,500 MSS; branches in various Asian cities; Pres. Prof. F. ROBINSON; publs *Journal, Storey Bibliography of Persian Literature* and monographs.

Royal Society for Asian Affairs: 2 Belgrave Square, London, SW1X 8PJ; tel. (171) 2355122; fax (171) 2596771; e-mail info @rsaa.org.uk; internet http://www.rsaa.org.uk; f. 1901; 1,100 mems with past or present knowledge of the Middle East, Central Asia or the Far East; library of about 7,000 vols; Pres. Lord DENMAN; Chair. Sir DONALD HAWLEY; Sec. D. J. EASTON; publ. *Journal* (3 a year).

Saudi-British Society, The: 21 Collingham Rd, London, SW5 0NU; tel. (171) 3738414; fax (171) 8352088; non-political; Chair. Lord DENMAN; Sec. ANTHONY LEE.

School of African and Asian Studies: University of Sussex, Falmer, Brighton, Sussex, BN1 9QN; tel. (1273) 606755; fax (1273) 623572; Dean Dr D. ROBINSON.

School of Oriental and African Studies, University of London: Thornhaugh St, London, WC1H 0XG; tel. (171) 6372388; fax (171) 4363844; internet http://www.soas.ac.uk; f. 1916; library of over 750,000 vols and 2,750 MSS; Dir Sir TIM LANKESTER.

UNITED STATES OF AMERICA

America-Mideast Educational & Training Services, Inc (AMIDEAST): 1100 17th St, NW, Washington, DC 20036; tel. (202) 7850022; telex 440160; fax (202) 8226563; f. 1951; a private, non-profit organization promoting understanding and co-operation between Americans and the people of the Middle East and North Africa through programmes of education, development and information; offices in Washington DC, and Bahrain, Egypt, Jordan, Kuwait, Lebanon, Morocco, Tunisia, Yemen, the Israeli-occupied Territories and Syria; Pres. ROBERT S. DILLON; publs on education in the Middle East, *Advising Quarterly*, *AMIDEAST News* (quarterly), *Introduction to the Arab World* (educational videotape), and *Arab World Almanac* (three times per year).

American Oriental Society: Room 110D, Hatcher Graduate Library, University of Michigan, Ann Arbor, MI 48109-1205; f. 1842; 1,350 mems; library of 23,500 vols; Pres. STANLEY INSLER; Sec. JONATHAN RODGERS; publs *Journal* (quarterly), monograph series, essay series and offprint series.

American Schools of Oriental Research: 656 Beacon St, 5th Floor, Boston, MA 02215; tel. (617) 3536570; fax (617) 3536575; e-mail asora@bu.edu; f. 1900; 1,500 mems; support activities of independent archaeological institutions abroad: The Albright Institute of Archaeological Research, Jerusalem, Israel, the American Center of Oriental Research in Amman, Jordan, and the Cyprus American Archaeological Research Institute in Nicosia, Cyprus; Pres. JOE SEGER; publs *Newsletter* (quarterly), *Biblical Archaeologist* (quarterly), *Bulletin* (quarterly), *Journal of Cuneiform Studies* (quarterly), *Annual*.

Center for Contemporary Arab Studies: Georgetown University, Washington, DC 20057-1020; tel. (202) 6875793; fax (202) 6877001; f. 1975; Dir Dr BARBARA R. F. STOWASSER; Academic Dir Dr JUDITH TUCKER; publs on social, economic, political, cultural and development aspects of Arab World; publ. newsletter (four a year).

Center for Middle Eastern Studies: University of Chicago, 5828 S. University Ave, Chicago, IL 60637; tel. (773) 7028297; fax (773) 7022587; e-mail org-cmes@orgmail.uchicago.edu; f. 1965; research into medieval and modern cultures of North Africa and Western and Central Asia; Dir CORNELL H. FLEISCHER; Assoc. Dir JOHN E. WOODS.

Center for Middle Eastern Studies: Harvard University, 1737 Cambridge St, Cambridge, MA 02138; tel. (617) 4954055; fax (617) 4968584; e-mail mideast@fas.harvard.edu; research on Middle Eastern subjects and Islamic studies; Dir Prof. E. ROGER OWEN; Publs *Middle East Monograph Series*, *Harvard Middle Eastern and Islamic Review*.

Center for Middle Eastern Studies: The University of Texas at Austin, Austin, TX 78712; tel. (512) 4713881; telex 91087-41305; fax (512) 4717834; e-mail cmes@menic.utexas.edu; f. 1960; comprehensive interdisciplinary programme in area studies and languages of the Middle East, with some 50 affiliated faculties; offers graduate and undergraduate degrees in Middle Eastern studies; Dir Dr ABRAHAM MARCUS; publs books on the modern Middle East and translations of contemporary fiction and memoirs.

Center for Middle Eastern and North African Studies: University of Michigan, 1080 South University Ave, Suite 4640, Social Work Bldg, Ann Arbor, MI 48109-1106; tel. (734) 7640350; fax (734) 7648523; e-mail cmenas@umich.edu; f. 1961; research into the ancient, medieval and modern cultures of the modern Middle East and North Africa, Near Eastern languages and literature; library includes 301,884 vols on Middle East and North Africa; Dir Dr MICHAEL BONNER.

Gustave E. von Grunebaum Center for Near Eastern Studies: POB 951480, University of California, Los Angeles, 10286 Bunche Hall, Los Angeles, CA 90095; tel. (310) 8251181; fax (310) 2062406; f. 1957; social sciences, culture and language studies of the Near East since the rise of Islam; a growing programme of Ancient Near Eastern Studies; library of more than 250,000 vols and outstanding MSS collection in Arabic, Armenian, Hebrew, Judaeo-Persian, Persian and Turkish; annual publication of series of colloquia and of Levi Della Vida Award Conference volumes; 100 associated faculty members; Dir Dr IRENE A. BIERMAN; Assoc. Dir Dr OSMAN GALAL.

Hairenik Association, Inc: Boston, MA; f. 1899; Man. Editor Dr KEVORK DONOYAN; publs *Armenian Review, The Armenian Weekly, Hairenik Daily;* circ. 8,000.

Hoover Institution on War, Revolution and Peace: Stanford University, Stanford, CA 94305-6010; tel. (650) 7231754; telex 3722871; fax (650) 7231687; e-mail jajko@hoover.stanford .edu; internet http://www.hoover.stanford.edu; f. 1919; library of 1.7 m. vols and 4,500 archives on 20th-century history includes important collection of 125,000 vols and 150 archives on Middle East and North Africa; Dir J. RAISIAN; Middle East Dep. Curator E. A. JAJKO; publs about 20 books each year.

The Iran Foundation, Inc: New York, NY; project assistance relating to the advancement of health and education in Iran and other culturally related areas.

Institute for Mediterranean Affairs: 428 East 83rd St, New York, NY 10028; tel. (212) 9881725; established under charter of the University of the State of New York to evolve a better understanding of the historical background and contemporary political and socio-economic problems of the nations and regions that border on the Mediterranean Sea, with special reference to the Middle East and North Africa; 350 mems; Pres. Ambassador SEYMOUR M. FINGER; Dir SAMUEL MERLIN.

Joint Committee on the Near and Middle East: c/o Social Science Research Council, 605 Third Ave, New York, NY 10158; tel. (212) 6610280; fax (212) 3707896; the Committee administers (for pre-dissertation students who are citizens or permanent residents of the USA; for doctoral dissertation researchers who are either citizens or permanent residents of the USA, or for foreign students enrolled full-time in doctoral programmes in the USA) a programme of grants for research by individual scholars in the social sciences and humanities.

Middle East Center: University of Utah, Salt Lake City, UT 84112; tel. (801) 5816181; telex 3789459; fax (801) 5816183; f. 1960; co-ordinates programme in Middle East languages and area studies in 12 academic departments; BA, MA and PhD in Middle East Studies with area of concentration in Arabic, Hebrew, Persian, Turkish, anthropology, history and political science; annual summer programme for Utah educators in the Middle East, research and exchange agreements with several universities; pre-doctoral and teaching fellowships in Middle Eastern languages; library of 150,000 vols; Acting Dir Dr PETER SLUGETT.

Middle East Forum: Suite 600, 1920 Chestnut St, Philadelphia, PA 19103; tel. (215) 5699225; fax (215) 5699229; f. 1994; Dir DANIEL PIPES; Assoc. Dir AMY SHARGAL; publs *Middle East Quarterly, Middle East Wire*.

Middle East Institute: 1761 N St, NW, Washington, DC 20036; tel. (202) 7851141; fax (202) 3318861; f. 1946; promotes American understanding of the Middle East, North Africa, the Caucasus and Central Asia; the MEI is a non-profit making independent resource centre that sponsors classes in Arabic, Hebrew, Persian and Turkish, co-ordinates cultural presentations and an annual garden series, convenes political and economic programmes and an annual conference and conducts scholar-in-residence and college internship programmes; Keiser Library 25,000 vols; 1,300 mems; Pres. Hon. ROSCOE S. SUDDARTH; publs *Middle East Journal* (quarterly) and occasional books.

Middle East Institute: Columbia University, 1113 International Affairs Bldg, New York, NY 10027; f. 1954; a graduate training programme on the modern Middle East for students seeking professional careers as regional specialists, research into problems of economics, government, law, and international relations of the Middle East countries, and their languages and history; library of more than 150,000 vols in Middle East vernaculars and equally rich in Western languages, including Russian; Dir RICHARD W. BULLIET.

Middle East Policy Council: Suite 512, 1730 M St, NW, Washington, DC 20036; tel. (202) 2966767; telex 440506; fax (202) 2965791; publ. *Middle East Policy* (quarterly).

Middle East Studies Association of North America: University of Arizona, 1643 E. Helen St, Tucson, AZ 85721; tel. (520) 6215850; fax (520) 6269095; e-mail mesana@u.arizona.edu; internet http://www.mesa.arizona.edu; f. 1966 to promote high standards of scholarship and instruction in Middle East studies, to facilitate communication among scholars through meetings and publications, and to foster co-operation among persons and organizations concerned with the scholarly study of the Middle East since the rise of Islam; 2,400 mems; Pres. (1999) BARBARA STOWASSER; Exec. Dir ANNE H. BETTERIDGE; publs *International Journal of Middle East Studies* (quarterly), *Bulletin* (2 a year), *Newsletter* (4 a year), edited works and collections on the Middle East, etc.

Middle East Studies Center: Portland State Univ., POB 751, Portland, OR 97207; tel. (503) 7254074; fax (503) 7255320; e-mail jon@sab.misc.pdx.edu; f. 1959; Middle East language and area studies, Arabic, Hebrew, Persian and Turkish languages and literatures; contemporary Turkish studies and Islamic studies programme; area classes in history, political science, geography, anthropology and sociology; extensive outreach activities; Dir JON MANDAVILLE; Assoc. Dir MARTA COLBURN.

Near East Foundation: 342 Madison Ave, Suite 1030, New York, NY 10173-1030; tel. (212) 8670064; telex 226000; fax (212) 8670169; e-mail neareast95@aol.com; f. 1930; provides technical and financial assistance in support of locally-organized projects in agriculture and rural/community development in the Middle East and Africa; Chair. GEOFFREY A. THOMPSON; Pres. RICHARD C. ROBARTS; publs *Annual Report*.

Near Eastern Languages and Cultures, Department of: Indiana University, Bloomington, IN 47405; tel. (812) 8554323; fax (812) 8557500; courses in Arabic, Persian and Hebrew languages and literature, women's studies, history, civilization and religions of the region. Turkish available through the Department of Central Eurasian Studies; Chair. FEDWA MALTI-DOUGLAS.

Oriental Institute: 1155 East 58th St, Chicago, IL 60637; tel. (773) 7029514; fax (773) 702-9853; f. 1919; principally concerned with cultures and languages of the ancient Near East; extensive museum; affiliated to the University of Chicago; Dir WILLIAM M. SUMNER.

Program in Near Eastern Studies: Princeton University, Jones Hall, Princeton, NJ 08544; tel. (609) 2584272; fax (609) 2581242; f. 1947; research in all aspects of the modern Near East and North Africa; library of 340,000 vols; Dir HEATH W. LOWRY; publs *Princeton Studies on the Near East* (irregular), *Princeton Near East Papers* (irregular).

Semitic Museum: Harvard University, 6 Divinity Ave, Cambridge, Mass 02138; tel. (617) 4954631; fax (617) 4968904; f. 1889; sponsors exploration and research in Western Asia; contains collection of exhibits from ancient Near East; research collections open by appointment, museum open to general public; Dir LAWRENCE E. STAGER.

Washington Institute for Near East Policy: Suite 1050, 1828 L St, NW, Washington, DC 20036; tel. (202) 4520650; fax (202) 2235364; e-mail winep@access.digex.net; f. 1985; promotes scholarly research and informed debate on the Middle East; Chair. BARBI WEINBERG; Exec. Dir ROBERT SATLOFF; publs *Analytical Reports Series, Conference Proceedings, Policy Focus Series, Policy Paper Series,* also monographs.

VATICAN CITY

Pontificium Institutum Orientale (Pontifical Oriental Institute): 7 Piazza Santa Maria Maggiore, 00185 Rome; tel. (06) 4465589; fax (06) 4465576; f. 1917; library of 147,360 vols; Rector Rev. CLARENCE GALLAGHER; Sec. Rev. JAKOV KULIČ; publs *Orientalia Christiana Periodica, Orientalia Christiana Analecta, Concilium Florentinum (Documenta et Scriptores), Anaphorae Syriacae, Kanonika.*

SELECT BIBLIOGRAPHY

Books on the Middle East

See also bibliographies at end of relevant chapters in Part Three.

Abdel Malek, A. *La pensée politique arabe contemporaine*. Paris, Editions du Seuil, 1970.

Abed, George T. (Ed.). *The Palestinian Economy: Studies in Development under Prolonged Occupation*. London, Routledge, 1988.

   The Economic Viability of a Palestinian State. Washington, Institute for Palestine State, 1990.

Abir, Mordechai. *Oil, Power and Politics: Conflict in Arabia, The Red Sea and The Gulf*. London, Frank Cass, 1974.

Abu Jaber, Kamel S. *The Arab Baath Socialist Party*. New York, Syracuse University Press, 1966.

Abu-Lughod, Ibrahim (Ed.). *The Transformation of Palestine: Essays on the Development of the Arab-Israeli Conflict*. Evanston, Ill, Northwestern University Press, 1971.

Abu-Zahra, Nadia. *The Pure and Powerful: Studies in Contemporary Muslim Society*. Reading, Ithaca Press, 1997.

Aburish, Said. *Cry Palestine: Inside the West Bank*. London, Bloomsbury, 1991.

Acharya, Amitar. *US Military Strategy in the Gulf*. London, Routledge, 1989.

Adams, Michael and Mayhew, Christopher. *Publish it Not . . . the Middle East Cover-up*. London, Longman, 1975.

Addas, Claude. *Quest for the Red Sulphur: The Life of Ibn 'Arabi*. Cambridge, Islamic Texts Society, 1995.

Adelson, Roger. *London and the Invention of the Middle East: Money, Power and War 1902–1922*. New Haven, Yale University Press, 1995.

Afkhami, Mahnaz. *Faith and Freedom: Women's Human Rights in the Muslim World*. London, I. B. Tauris, 1996.

Ahmed, Akbar S. *Discovering Islam: making Sense of Muslim History and Society*. London, Routledge, 1989.

Ajami, Fouad. *The Arab Predicament: Arab Political Thought and Practice since 1967*. Cambridge University Press, 2nd edition, 1992.

Alderson, A. D. *The Structure of the Ottoman Dynasty*. New York, Oxford University Press, 1956.

al-Algosaibi, Ghazi. *The Gulf crisis—an attempt to understand*. London, Kegan Paul International, 1993.

Allan, J. A., and Mallat, Chibli (Eds). *Water in the Middle East: Legal, Political and Commercial Implications*. London, I. B. Tauris, 1995.

Allen, Richard. *Imperialism and Nationalism in the Fertile Crescent: Sources and Prospects of the Arab-Israeli Conflict*. London, Oxford University Press, 1975.

Anderson, Jack, and Boyd, James. *Oil: The Real Story Behind the World Energy Crisis*. London, Sidgwick and Jackson, 1984.

Arberry, A. J. (Ed.). *Religion in the Middle East*—Volume I, *Judaism and Christianity*, Volume II, *Islam and General Summary*. Cambridge University Press, 1969.

Ashtor, E. *A Social and Economic History of the Near East in the Middle Ages*. London, Collins, 1976.

Ayoob, M. (Ed.). *The Middle East in World Politics*. London, Croom Helm, 1981.

Ayubi, Nazih N. *Over-Stating the Arab State: Politics and Society in the Middle East*. London, I. B. Tauris, 1995.

Azzam, Salem (Ed.). *Islam and Contemporary Society: Islamic Council of Europe*. London, Longman, 1982.

Bailey, Sydney. *Four Arab-Israeli wars and the Peace Process*. London, Macmillan, 1990.

Barkey, Henri. *The Politics of Economic Reform in the Middle East*. London, Macmillan, 1993.

Barnaby, Frank. *The Invisible Bomb: The Nuclear Arms Race in the Middle East*. London, I. B. Tauris, 1989.

Baster, James. *The Introduction of Western Economic Institutions into the Middle East*. Royal Institute of International Affairs and Oxford University Press, 1960.

Behbehani, Hashim S. H. *China's Foreign Policy in the Arab World 1955–75*. Henley-on-Thames, Kegan Paul International, 1982.

Beinin, J. and Stork, J. *Political Islam*. London/New York, I. B. Tauris, 1997.

Bell, J. Bowyer. *The Long War, Israel and the Arabs since 1946*. Englewood Cliffs, NJ, 1969.

Bennis, Phyllis, and Moushabeck, Michael (Eds). *Beyond the Storm: A Gulf Crisis Reader*. Edinburgh, Canongate Press, 1992.

Berberoglu, Berch (Ed.). *Power and Stability in the Middle East*. London, Zed Books, 1989.

Berque, Jacques. *L'Islam au défi*. Paris, Gallimard, 1980.

Berque, Jacques and Charnay, J.-P. *Normes et valeurs dans l'Islam contemporaine*. Paris, Payot, 1966.

Bethell, Nicholas. *The Palestine Triangle*. London, André Deutsch, 1979.

Bidwell's Guides to Government Ministers, Vol. II, *The Arab World 1900–1972*. Compiled and edited by Robin Bidwell. London, Frank Cass, 1973.

Bill, J. and Springborg, R. *Politics in the Middle East*. London, HarperCollins, 4th Edition, 1994.

Binder, Leonard. *The Ideological Revolution in the Middle East*. New York, 1964.

Blake, Gerald H., and Drysdale, Alasdair. *The Middle East and North Africa: A Political Geography*. Oxford University Press, 1985.

Bonine, Michael E. (Ed.). *Population, poverty and politics in Middle Eastern cities*. University Press of Florida, 1997.

Boulares, Habib. *Islam: the Fear and the Hope*. London, Zed Books, 1991.

Boyd, Douglas A. *Broadcasting in the Arab World: A Survey of Radio and Television in the Middle East*. Philadelphia, Temple University Press, 1982.

Bregman, Ahron and El-Tahri, Jihan. *The Fifty Years War: Israel and the Arabs*. London, Penguin and BBC Books, 1998.

Brenchley, Frank. *Britain and the Middle East: an economic history, 1945–1987*. London, Lester Crook Academic Publishing, 1989.

Breslauer, George W. (Ed.). *Soviet Strategy in the Middle East*. London, Routledge, 1989.

Brittain, Victoria (Ed.). *The Gulf Between Us: The Gulf War and Beyond*. London, Virago, 1991.

Brockelmann, C. *History of the Islamic Peoples*. New York and London, 1947–48.

Brooks, Geraldine. *Nine Parts of Desire: The Hidden World of Islamic Women*. London, Hamish Hamilton, 1995.

Brown, Daniel. *Rethinking Tradition in Modern Islamic Thought*. Cambridge University Press, 1996.

Brown, Malcolm. *The Letters of T.E. Lawrence*. Oxford University Press, 1991.

Bull, General Odd. *War and Peace in the Middle East: the Experience and Views of a UN Observer*. London, Leo Cooper, 1976.

Bullard, Sir R. *Britain and the Middle East from the earliest times until 1952*. London, 1952.

Bulloch, John. *The Making of a War: The Middle East from 1967–1973*. London, Longman, 1974.

Bulloch, John, and Morris, Harvey. *The Gulf War*. London, Methuen, 1990.

Saddam's War. London, Faber & Faber, 1991.

Burgat, François. *Face to Face with Political Islam*. London, I. B. Tauris, 1997.

Burke, Edmond. *Struggle for Survival in the Modern Middle East*. London, I. B. Tauris, 1994.

Burrows, Bernard. *Footnotes in the Sand: the Gulf in Transition*. London, Michael Russell, 1991.

Butt, Gerald. *A Rock and a Hard Place: origins of Arab-Western conflict in the Middle East*. London, Harper Collins, 1994.

The Arabs: Myth and Reality. London, I. B. Tauris, 1998.

Calabrese, John. *China's changing relations with the Middle East*. London, Pinter, 1990.

Carré, Olivier. *L'Idéologie palestinienne de résistance*. Paris, Armand Colin, 1972.

Mystique et Politique. Paris, Presses de la Fondation nationale des sciences politiques and Editions du Cerf, 1984.

Carrère d'Encausse, Hélène. *La politique soviétique au Moyen-Orient, 1955–1975*. Paris, Presses de la Fondation Nationale des Sciences Politiques, 1976.

Cattan, Henry. *Palestine and International Law: The Legal Aspects of the Arab-Israeli Conflict*. London, Longman, 1973.

Jerusalem. London, Croom Helm, 1981 (Reissued, Gregg Revivals, 1994).

Cattan, J. *Evolution of Oil Concessions in the Middle East and North Africa*. New York, Oceana, Dobbs Ferry, 1967.

Chaliand, Gérard. *People Without a Country: The Kurds and Kurdistan*. London, Zed Press, 2nd edition, 1992.

Chevallier, Dominique, Guellouz, Azzedine and Miquel, André. *Les arabes, l'islam et l'europe*. Paris, Flammarion, 1991.

Chomsky, Noam. *Peace in the Middle East?: Reflections on Justice and Nationhood*. London, Collins, 1976.

The Fateful Triangle: The United States, Israel and the Palestinians. London, Pluto Press, 1983.

Pirates and Emperors: International Terrorism in the Real World. Armana Books, USA, 1990.

Choveiri, Youssef M. *Arab History and the Nation-State: A Study in Modern Arab Historiography 1820–1980*. London, Routledge, 1980.

Clarke, John I., and Fisher, W. B. (Ed.). *Populations of the Middle East and North Africa*. University of London Press, 1972.

Cleveland, William L. *A History of the Modern Middle East*. Oxford, Westview Press, 1994.

Cobban, Helena. *The Palestinian Liberation Organization: People, Power and Politics*. Cambridge University Press, 1984.

Cohen, Michael J. *Palestine: Retreat from the Mandate*. London, Elek Books, 1978.

Conrad, Lawrence J. (Ed.). *The Formation and Perception of the Modern Arab World, Studies by Marwan R. Buheiry*. Princeton, The Darwin Press, 1989.

Cook, M. A. (Ed.). *Studies in the Economic History of the Middle East*. Oxford University Press, 1970.

Cooley, John K. *Green March, Black September: The Story of the Palestinian Arabs*. London, Frank Cass, 1973.

Payback: America's Long War in the Middle East. London, Brassey's UK, 1992.

Coon, C. S. *Caravan: the Story of the Middle East*. New York, 1951, and London, 1952.

The Impact of the West on Social Institutions. New York, 1952.

Corbin, Henry. *History of Islamic Philosophy*. London, Kegan Paul International, 1992.

Cordesman, Anthony. *Weapons of mass destruction in the Middle East*. London, Brasseys, 1991.

Corm, Georges. *Fragmentation of the Middle East: the last thirty years*. London, Unwin Hyman, 1988.

Costello, V. F. *Urbanisation in the Middle East*. Cambridge University Press, 1977.

Courbage, Youssef and Fargues, Philippe. *Christians and Jews under Islam*. London, I. B. Tauris, 1997.

Crone, Patricia. *Meccan Trade and the Rise of Islam*. Oxford, Basil Blackwell, 1987.

Cudsi, Alexander, and Dessouki, Ali E. Hillal (Eds). *Islam and Power*. London, Croom Helm, 1981.

Curtiss, Richard H. *Stealth PACs: how Israel's American lobby took control of US-Middle East policy*. Washington, American Educational Trust, 1990.

Daftary, Farhad. *The Assassin Legends: Myths of the Isma'lis*. London, I. B. Tauris, 1995.

Daniel, Norman. *Islam and the West: The Making of an Image*. One World Publications, revised edition, 1993.

Islam, Europe and Empire. Edinburgh University Press, 1964.

Decobert, Christian. *Le mendiant et le combattant: l'institution de l'islam*. Paris, Editions du Seuil, 1991.

Dekmejian, R. H. *Islam in Revolution: fundamentalism in the Arab World*. New York, Syracuse University Press, 1995.

De la Billière, Peter. *Storm Command: a personal account of the Gulf War*. London, Harper Collins, 1992.

De Vore, Ronald M. (Ed.). *The Arab-Israeli Conflict: A Historical, Political, Social and Military Bibliography*. Oxford, Clio Press, 1977.

Dimbleby, Jonathan, and McCullin, Donald. *The Palestinians*. London, Quartet, 1970.

Dupuy, Trevor N. *Elusive Victory: The Arab-Israeli Wars 1947–1974*. London, MacDonald and Jane's, 1979.

Easterman, Daniel. *New Jerusalems—reflections on Islam, fundamentalism and the Rushdie affair*. London, Grafton Books, 1992.

Efrat, Moshe, and Bercovitch, Jacob. *Superpowers and Client States in the Middle East: The Imbalance of Influence*. London, Routledge, 1991.

Ehteshami, Anoushiravan, and Hinnebusch, Raymond. *Syria and Iran: Middle Powers in a Penetrated Regional System*. London, Routledge, 1997.

Ehteshami, Anoushiravan, and Nonneman, Gerd. *War and Peace in the Gulf: Domestic Politics and Regional Relations into the 1990s*. Reading, Ithaca Press, 1991.

Enayat, Hamid. *Modern Islamic Political Thought: The Response of the Shi'i and Sunni Muslims to the Twentieth Century*. London, Macmillan, 1982.

Encyclopaedia of Islam, The. 4 vols and supplement. Leiden, 1913–38 (Reissued, 9 vols, 1993).

Esposito, John L. (Ed.). *Voices of Resurgent Islam*. New York, Oxford University Press, 1983.

The Islamic Threat, Myth or Reality? New York, Oxford University Press Inc., 1992.

Ettinghausen, Richard. Books and Periodicals in Western Languages dealing with the Near and Middle East. Washington, Middle East Institute, 1952.

Fahmy, Mansour. *La condition de la femme en islam*. Paris, Editions Allia, 1991.

Field, Henry. *Bibliography on Southwestern Asia: VII, A Seventh Compilation*. University of Miami, 1962.

Field, Michael. *$100,000,000 a Day—Inside the World of Middle East Money*. London, Sidgwick and Jackson, 1975.

Inside the Arab World. London, John Murray, 1994.

Findlay, Allan M. *The Arab World*. London, Routledge, 1996.

Fisher, S. N. *Social Forces in the Middle East*. Ithaca, NY, Cornell University Press, 3rd edition, 1977.

The Middle East: A History. New York, McGraw-Hill, 4th edition, 1990.

Fisher, W. B. *The Middle East—a Physical, Social and Regional Geography*. London, 7th edition, 1978.

Frangi, Abdallah. *The PLO and Palestine*. London, Zed Press, 1984.

Freedman, Robert O. *Soviet Policy toward the Middle East since 1970*. New York, Praeger, 3rd edition, 1983.

Friedman, Thomas. *From Beirut to Jerusalem*. New York, Farrar, Straus and Giroux, 1989.

Frye, R. N. (Ed.). *The Near East and the Great Powers.* Cambridge, Mass, Harvard University Press, 1951; London, New York and Toronto, Oxford University Press, 1952.

Fuller, Graham E., and Lesser, Jan O. *A Sense of Siege: The Geopolitics of Islam and the West.* Boulder, Westview Press, 1995.

Gallagher, Nancy Elizabeth (Ed.). *Approaches to the History of the Middle East: Interviews with leading Middle East historians.* Reading, Garnet, 1995.

Gershoni, Israel and Jankowski, James (Eds) *Rethinking Nationalism in the Arab Middle East.* New York, Columbia University Press, 1998.

Gibb, H. A. R. *Mohammedanism.* London, 1949.

   Modern Trends in Islam. Chicago, 1947.

   Studies on the Civilisation of Islam. London, 1962.

Gibb, H. A. R., and Bowen, Harold. *Islamic Society and the West.* London, 2 vols, 1950, 1957.

Gilbar, Gad. *Population Dilemmas in the Middle East.* London, Frank Cass, 1997.

Gilbert, Martin. *The Arab-Israeli Conflict: Its History in Maps.* London, Weidenfeld and Nicolson, 1974 (reissued, Dent: International Publishing Services, 1993).

Gilmour, David. *The Dispossessed: The Ordeal of the Palestinians 1917–80.* London, Sidgwick & Jackson, 1980.

Gilsenan, Michael. *Recognizing Islam: Religion and Society in the Modern Middle East.* London, I. B. Tauris, 1990.

Gittings, John (Ed.). *Beyond the Gulf War: The Middle East and the New World Order.* London, Catholic Institute for International Relations, 1991.

Glassé, Cyril. *The Concise Encylopedia of Islam.* London, Stacey International, 1989.

Glubb, Lt-Gen. Sir John. *A Short History of the Arab Peoples.* London, Hodder and Stoughton, 1969.

Golan, Galia. *The Soviet Union and the Middle East Crisis.* Cambridge University Press, 1977.

Gomaa, Ahmed M. *The Foundation of the League of Arab States.* London, Longman, 1977.

Goodwin, Godfrey. *The Janissaries.* London, Saqi Books, 1997.

Gowers, Andrew, and Walter, Tony. *Behind the Myth: Yasir Arafat and the Palestinian revolution.* London, W.H. Allen, 1990.

Graz, Liesl. *The Turbulent Gulf.* London, I.B. Tauris, 1990.

Gresh, Alain, and Vidal, Dominique. *A–Z of the Middle East.* London, Zed Books, 1991.

Grossman, Mark. *Encyclopaedia of the Persian Gulf War.* Santa Barbara, California, ABC-Clio, 1996.

Grundwald, K., and Ronall, J. O. *Industrialisation in the Middle East.* New York, Council for Middle East Affairs, 1960.

Grunebaum, Gustave E. von (Ed.). *Unity and Variety in Muslim Civilisation.* Chicago, 1955.

   Islam: Essays on the Nature and Growth of a Cultural Tradition. London, Routledge and Kegan Paul, 1961.

   Modern Islam: the Search for Cultural Identity. London, 1962.

Guazzone, Laura. *The Islamist Dilemma.* Reading, Ithaca Press, 1995.

Halliday, Fred. *Islam and the Myth of Confrontation: Religion and Politics in the Middle East.* London, I. B. Tauris, 1995.

Halm, Heinz. *The Fatimids and their Traditions of Learning.* London, I. B. Tauris, 1997.

Halpern, Manfred. *The Politics of Social Change in the Middle East and North Africa.* New York, Princeton University Press, 1963.

Hardy, Roger. *Arabia after the Storm: internal stability of the Gulf Arab states.* London, Royal Institute of International Affairs, 1992.

Hare, William. *The Struggle for the Holy Land.* London, Madison Publishing, 1998.

Harris, Lillian Craig. *China Considers the Middle East.* London, I. B. Tauris, 1994.

Hart, Alan. *Arafat — Terrorist or Peacemaker?* London, Sidgwick and Jackson, 2nd edition, 1994.

Hartshorn, J. E. *Oil Companies and Governments.* London, Faber, 1962.

Hassan bin Talal, Crown Prince of Jordan. *A Study on Jerusalem.* London, Longman, 1980.

Hatem, M. Abdel-Kader. *Information and the Arab Cause.* London, Longman, 1974.

Hayes, J. R. (Ed.). *The Genius of Arab Civilisation: Source of Renaissance.* New York University Press, 3rd edition, 1992.

Hazard. *Atlas of Islamic History.* Oxford University Press, 1951.

Heikal, Mohammed. *Illusions of Triumph: An Arab View of the Gulf War.* London, Harper Collins, 1992.

Hershlag, Z. Y. *Introduction to the Modern Economic History of the Middle East.* Leiden, E. J. Brill, 2nd edition, 1980.

Herzog, Maj.-Gen. Chaim. *The War of Atonement.* London, Weidenfeld and Nicolson, 1975.

   The Arab-Israeli Wars. London, Arms and Armour Press, 1982.

Hewedy, Amin. *Militarisation and Security in the Middle East.* London, Pinter, 1989.

Higgins, Rosalyn. *United Nations Peacekeeping 1946–67: Documents and Commentary,* Volume I, *The Middle East.* Oxford University Press, 1969.

Hiro, Dilip. *Inside the Middle East.* London, Routledge and Kegan Paul, 1981.

   Islamic Fundamentalism. London, Paladin, 1988.

   The Longest War. London, Grafton Books, 1990.

   Dictionary of the Middle East. London, Macmillan, 1996.

   Sharing the Promised Land. An Interwoven Tale of Israelis and Palestinians. London, Hodder & Stoughton, 1996.

Hirst, David. *Oil and Public Opinion in the Middle East.* New York, Praeger, 1966.

   The Gun and the Olive Branch: the Roots of Violence in the Middle East. London, Faber, 1977.

Hirszowicz, Lukasz. *The Third Reich and the Arab East.* London, Routledge and Kegan Paul, 1966.

   A Short History of the Near East. New York, 1966.

   Makers of Arab History. London, Macmillan, 1968.

   Islam. A Way of Life. London, Oxford University Press, 1971.

Hoare, Ian and Tayar, Graham (Eds). *The Arabs. A handbook on the politics and economics of the contemporary Arab world.* London, BBC Publications, 1971.

Hodgkin, E. C. *The Arabs.* Modern World Series, Oxford University Press, 1966.

Holt, P. M. *Studies in the History of the Near East.* London, Frank Cass, 1973.

Holt, P. M., Lambton, A. K. S., and Lewis, B. (Eds.). *The Cambridge History of Islam.* Vol. I, *The Central Islamic Lands.* Cambridge University Press, 1970; Vol. II, *The Further Islamic Lands, Islamic Society and Civilization.* Cambridge University Press, 1971.

Hopwood, Derek (Ed.). *Studies in Arab History.* London, Macmillan, 1990.

Hourani, A. H. *Minorities in the Arab World.* London, 1947.

   A Vision of History. Beirut, 1961.

   Arabic Thought in the Liberal Age 1798–1939. Oxford University Press, 1962.

   Europe and the Middle East. London, Macmillan, 1980.

   The Emergence of the Modern Middle East. London, Macmillan, 1981.

   A History of the Arab Peoples. London, Faber and Faber, 1991.

   Islam in European Thought. Cambridge University Press, 1991.

Hoveyda, Fereydoun. *Que veulent les arabes?* Paris, Editions First, 1991.

Hudson, Michael C. *Arab Politics: The Search for Legitimacy.* New Haven and London, Yale University Press, 1977/78.

Hurewitz, J. C. *Unity and Disunity in the Middle East.* New York, Carnegie Endowment for International Peace, 1952.

Middle East Dilemmas. New York, 1953.

Diplomacy in the Near and Middle East. Vol. I, *1535–1914;* Vol. II, *1914–56.* Van Nostrand, 1956.

Soviet-American Rivalry in the Middle East (Ed.). London, Pall Mall Press, and New York, Praeger, 1969.

Middle East Politics: The Military Dimension. London, Pall Mall Press, 1969.

Al-Husari, Khaldun S. *Three Reformers; A Study in Modern Arab Political Thought.* Beirut, Khayats, 1966.

Hussein, Mahmoud. *Les Arabes au présent.* Paris, Editions Seuil, 1974.

Ibrahim, Saad Eddin. *The New Arab Social Order: A Study of the Social Impact of Oil Wealth.* Boulder, Colorado, Westview Press, 1982.

International Institute for Strategic Studies. *Sources of Conflict in the Middle East.* London, Adelphi Papers, International Institute for Strategic Studies, 1966.

Domestic Politics and Regional Security: Jordan, Syria and Israel. London, Gower, International Institute for Strategic Studies, 1989.

Ionides, Michael. *Divide and Lose: the Arab Revolt 1955–58.* London, Bles, 1960.

Irwin, I. J. *Islam in the Modern National State.* Cambridge University Press, 1965.

Isaak, David T., and Fesharaki, F. *OPEC, the Gulf and the World Petroleum Market.* London, Croom Helm, 1983.

Issawi, Charles. *An Economic History of the Middle East and North Africa.* London, Methuen, 1982.

Izzard, Molly. *The Gulf.* London, John Murray, 1979.

Jabbor, Suhayl J., and Conrad, Lawrence I. (Eds). *The Bedouins and the Desert: Aspects of Nomadic Life in the Arab East.* Albany, State University of New York Press, 1996.

Jaber, Faleh A. (Ed.) *Post-Marxism and the Middle East.* London, Saqi Books, 1997.

Janin, R. *Les églises orientales et les rites orientaux.* Paris, 1926.

Jansen, G. H. *Non-Alignment and the Afro-Asian States.* New York, Praeger, 1966.

Militant Islam. London, Pan Books, 1979.

Jansen, Johannes J. G. *The Dual Nature of Islamic Fundamentalism.* Ithaca, N.Y., Cornell University Press, 1997.

Jawad, Haifaa A. *The Middle East in the New World Order.* London, Macmillan, 1996.

Jerichow, A. and Simonsen, J. B. (Eds). *Islam in a Changing World and the Middle East.* Richmond, Surrey, Curzon Press, 1997.

Johnson, Nels. *Islam and the Politics of Meaning in Palestinian Nationalism.* Henley-on-Thames, Kegan Paul International, 1983.

Jones, David. *The Arab World.* New York, Hilary House, 1967.

Kandiyoti, Deniz (Ed.). *Gendering the Middle East: Emerging Perspectives.* London, I. B. Tauris, 1996.

Karpat, Kemal H. *Political and Social Thought in the Contemporary Middle East.* London, Pall Mall Press, 1968.

Katz, Mark N. *Russia and Arabia: Soviet Foreign Policy toward the Arabian Peninsula.* Baltimore and London, Johns Hopkins University Press, 1986.

Keay, John. *The Arabs: A Living History.* London, Harvill, 1983.

Kedourie, Elie. *England and the Middle East.* London, 1956.

The Chatham House Version and other Middle-Eastern Studies. London, Weidenfeld and Nicolson, 1970.

Arabic Political Memoirs and Other Studies. London, Frank Cass, 1974.

In the Anglo-Arab Labyrinth. 1976.

Islam in the Modern World and Other Studies. London, Mansell, 1980.

Towards a Modern Iran. 1980.

Kelly, J. B. *Eastern Arabian Frontiers.* London, Faber, 1963.

Arabia, the Gulf and the West: A Critical View of the Arabs and their Oil Policy. London, Weidenfeld and Nicolson, 1980.

Kemp, Geoffrey and Harkavy, Robert. *The Strategic Geography of the Changing Middle East.* Washington, DC, The Brookings Institution, 1996.

Kemp, Geoffrey and Pressman, Jeremy. *Point of No Return: The Deadly Struggle for Middle East Peace.* Washington, DC, The Brookings Institution, 1997.

Kerr, Malcolm. *The Arab Cold War 1958-1964.* Oxford University Press, 1965.

Khadouri, M. *Political Trends in the Arab World.* Baltimore, Johns Hopkins Press, 1970.

Khadouri, M., and Lievesny, H. J. (Eds). *Law in the Middle East,* Vol. I, Washington, 1955.

Khalil, Muhammad. *The Arab States and the Arab League* (historical documents). Beirut, Khayats.

Khouri, Fred J. *The Arab-Israeli Dilemma.* Syracuse/New York, 1968.

Khuri, Fuad I. *Imams and Emirs: state, religion and sects in Islam.* London, Saqi Books, 1990.

Tents and Pyramids. London, Saqi Books, 1992.

Kingsbury, R. C., and Pounds, N. J. G. *An Atlas of Middle Eastern Affairs.* New York, 1963.

Kingston, Paul W. T. *Britain and the Politics of Modernization in the Middle East, 1945–1958.* Cambridge University Press, 1996.

Kirk, George E. *The Middle East in the War.* London, 1953.

A Short History of the Middle East: from the Rise of Islam to Modern Times. New York, 1955.

Kliot, Norit. *Water Resources and Conflict in the Middle East.* London, Routledge, 1994.

Koch, Christopher. *Gulf Security in the Twenty-First Century.* London, I. B. Tauris, 1997.

Kreyenbroek, Philip G., and Sperl, Stefan (Eds). *The Kurds: a contemporary overview.* London, Routledge, 1992.

Kreutz, Andrej. *Vatican Policy on the Palestinian–Israeli Conflict: the struggle for the Holy Land.* London, Greenwood Press, 1990.

Kumar, Ravinder. *India and the Persian Gulf Region.* London, 1965.

Kurzman, Dan. *Genesis 1948: The First Arab/Israeli War.* London, Vallentine, Mitchell, 1972.

Kutschera, Chris. *Le mouvement national kurde.* Paris, Flammarion, 1979.

Lall, Arthur. *The UN and the Middle East Crisis.* New York/London, 1968.

Lapidus, Ira M. *A History of Islamic Societies.* Cambridge University Press, 1989.

Laqueur, W. Z. *Communism and Nationalism in the Middle East.* London and New York, 1957.

A History of Zionism. London, Weidenfeld and Nicolson, 1972.

The Struggle for the Middle East: The Soviet Union and the Middle East 1958-68. London, Routledge and Kegan Paul, 1969.

Confrontation: The Middle-East War and World Politics. London, Wildwood, 1974.

(Ed.) *The Middle East in Transition.* London, Routledge and Kegan Paul, 1958.

(Ed.) *The Israel-Arab Reader.* New York/London, Penguin Books, 4th Edition, 1984.

Lawrence, T. E. *The Seven Pillars of Wisdom.* London, 1935.

Lemarchand, Philippe (Ed.). *The Crescent of Crises: A Geopolitical Atlas of the Middle East and the Arab World.* Paris, Editions Complexe, 1995.

Lenczowski, George. *The Middle East in World Affairs.* Ithaca, N.Y., Cornell University Press, 4th Edition, 1980.

Oil and State in the Middle East. Cornell University Press, 1960.

Lesch, David W. (Ed.). *The Middle East and the United States: A Historical and Political Reassessment.* Boulder, Colorado, Westview Press, 1996.

Lewis, B. *The Arabs in History.* Oxford University Press, 6th edition, 1993.

Shaping of the Modern Middle East. New York, Oxford University Press, 1994.

Race and Colour in Islam. London, 1971.

Islam in History. Open Court Publishing Co., 2nd edition, 1992.

Islam to 1453. London, 1974.

Lieden, Karl. (Ed.). *The conflict of traditionalism and modernism in the Muslim Middle East.* Austin, Texas, 1969.

Lippman, Thomas W. *Understanding Islam: An Introduction to the Moslem World.* New York, New American Library, 1982.

Lloyd, Selwyn. *Suez 1956: A Personal Account.* London, Jonathan Cape, 1978.

Logan, William S. and White, Paul J. (Eds). *Remaking the Middle East.* Oxford, Berg, 1997.

Longrigg, S. H. *Oil in the Middle East.* London, 1954, 3rd edition, London 1968.

The Middle East: a Social Geography. London, 2nd revised edition, 1970.

Louis, William Roger. *The British Empire in the Middle East 1945–51.* Oxford University Press, 1984.

Maalouf, Amin. *The Crusades Through Arab Eyes.* Al-Saqi Books, 1984.

Mabro, Judy (Ed.). *Veiled Half-Truths: Western Travellers' Perceptions of Middle Eastern Women.* London, I. B. Tauris, 1992.

McCarthy, Justin. *The Population of Palestine.* New York, Columbia University Press, 1991.

Macdonald, Robert W. *The League of Arab States.* Princeton, Princeton University Press, 1965.

McDowall, David. *The Kurds: a nation denied.* London, Minority Rights Group, 1992.

Europe and the Arabs: discord and symbiosis. London, Royal Institute of International Affairs, 1992.

A Modern History of the Kurds. London, I. B. Tauris, 1997.

Maddy-Weitzmann, Bruce and Inbar, Efraim (Eds). *Religious Radicalism in the Greater Middle East.* London, Frank Cass, 1997.

Mallat, Chibli. *The Middle East into the Twenty-First Century: The Japan Lectures and other studies on the Arab-Israeli conflict, the Gulf crisis and political Islam.* Reading, Ithaca Press, 1996.

Mannin, Ethel. *A Lance for the Arabs.* London, 1973.

Mansfield, Peter. *The Ottoman Empire and Its Successors.* London, Macmillan, 1973.

(Ed.). *The Middle East: A Political and Economic Survey.* London, Oxford University Press, 5th edition, 1980.

The Arabs. Penguin, 5th edition, 1992.

Marlow, Louise. *Hierarchy and Egalitarianism in Islamic Thought.* Cambridge University Press, 1996.

Martin Muqoz, Gema (Ed.). *Islam, Modernism and the West: Cultural and Political Relations at the end of the Millennium.* London, I. B. Tauris, 1997.

Maull, Hanns, and Pick, Otto (Eds). *The Gulf War.* London, Pinter Publishers, 1989.

Meisami, J. S., and Starkey, Paul. *Encyclopaedia of Arabic Literature.* London, Routledge, 1995.

Menashiri, David (Ed.). *Central Asia meets the Middle East.* London, Frank Cass, 1998.

Mendelsohn, Everett. *A Compassionate Peace: a future for Israel, Palestine and the Middle East.* New York, The Noonday Press, 1989.

Michaelis, Alfred. *Wirtschaftliche Entwicklungsprobleme des Mittleren Ostens.* Kiel, 1960.

Mikdashi, Zuhayr. *The Community of Oil Exporting Countries.* London, George Allen and Unwin, 1972.

Miller, Davina. *Subverting Policy: British Arms Sales to Iran and Iraq.* London, Cassell, 1996.

Miquel, André. *Islam et sa civilisation.* Paris, 1968.

Momen, Moojan. *An Introduction to Shi'i Islam.* London, Yale University Press, revised edition, 1987.

Monroe, Elizabeth. *Britain's Moment in the Middle East 1914–71.* London, Chatto and Windus, new edition 1981.

Moore, John Norton. *The Arab-Israeli Conflict.* 4 vols. Princeton, Readings and Documents, 1976–92.

Morris, Claud. *The Last Inch: A Middle East Odyssey.* London, Kegan Paul International, 1996.

Mortimer, Edward. *Faith and Power: The Politics of Islam.* London, Faber, 1982.

Morzellec, Joëlle Le. *La question de Jérusalem devant l'Organisation des Nations Unies.* Brussels, Emile Bruylant, S.A., 1979.

Mosley, Leonard. *Power Play: The Tumultuous World of Middle East Oil 1890–1973.* London, Weidenfeld and Nicolson, 1973.

Mostyn, T. *Major Political Events in Iran, Iraq and the Arabian Peninsula 1945–1990.* Oxford/New York, Facts on File, 1991.

Munson, Henry Jr. *Islam and Revolution in the Middle East.* New Haven and London, Yale University Press, 1988.

Murakami, Masahiro. *Managing Water for Peace in the Middle East: Alternative Strategies.* Tokyo, United Nations University Press, 1996.

Nasr, Seyyed Hossein. *Science and Civilization in Islam.* Harvard (1968), revised edition, 1987.

Navias, Martin. *Going Ballistic: the build-up of missiles in the Middle East.* London, Brassey's, 1993.

Nevakivi, Jukka. *Britain, France and the Arab Middle East 1914–20.* Athlone Press, University of London, 1969.

Niblock, Tim, and Murphy, Emma. *Economic and Political Liberalism in the Middle East.* London, British Academic Press, 1993.

Nonneman, Gerd. *Development, Administration and Aid in the Middle East.* London, Routledge, 1988.

(Ed.) *The Middle East and Europe: The Search for Stability and Integration.* London, Federal Trust, 1993.

Nutting, Anthony. *The Arabs.* London, Hollis and Carter, 1965.

No End of a Lesson, The Story of Suez. London, Constable, 1967.

Nydell, Margaret K. *Understanding Arabs: A Guide for Westerners.* Yarmouth, Maine, Intercultural Press, 1992.

O'Ballance, Edgar. *The Third Arab-Israeli War.* London, Faber and Faber, 1972.

The Gulf War. London, Brassey's Defence Publishers, 1990.

Odell, Peter. *Oil and World Power.* London, Penguin, 1983.

Owen, Roger. *The Middle East in the World Economy 1800–1914.* I. B. Tauris (1972), revised edition, 1993.

State, Power and Politics in the making of the Modern Middle East. London, Routledge, 1992.

Oxford Regional Economic Atlas. *The Middle East and North Africa.* Oxford University Press, 1960.

Palmer, Alan. *The Decline and Fall of the Ottoman Empire.* London, John Murray, 1992.

Palumbo, Michael. *The Palestinian Catastrophe.* London, Faber, 1987.

Pantelides, Veronica S. *Arab Education 1956–1978: A Bibliography.* London, Mansell, 1982.

Pearson, J. D. (Ed.). *Index Islamicus.* Cambridge, 1967.

Pennar, Jaan. *The USSR and the Arabs: The Ideological Dimension.* London, Hurst, 1973.

Peters, F. E. *The Hajj: The Muslim pilgrimage to Mecca and the holy places.* Princeton University Press, 1995.

Piscatori, James P. (Ed.). *Islam in the Political Process.* Cambridge University Press, 1983.

Islam in a World of Nation-States. Cambridge University Press, 1986.

Playfair, Ian S. O. *The Mediterranean and the Middle East.* London, History of the Second World War, HMSO, 1966.

Poliak, A. N. *Feudalism in Egypt, Syria, Palestine and the Lebanon, 1250–1900.* London, Luzac, for the Royal Asiatic Society, 1939.

Polk, W. R. *The Arab World Today.* Harvard University Press, 1991.

(Ed. with Chambers, R. L.) *Beginnings of Modernization in the Middle East: the Nineteenth Century*. University of Chicago Press, 1969.

The Elusive Peace: The Middle East in the Twentieth Century. London, Frank Cass, 1980.

Porath, Y. *The Emergence of the Palestinian Arab National Movement 1918–1929*. London, Frank Cass, 1974.

Qubain, Fahim I. *Education and Science in the Arab World*. Baltimore, Johns Hopkins Press, 1967.

Raufer, Xavier. *Atlas Mondial de l'Islam Activiste*. Paris, Editions de la Table Ronde, 1991.

Richards, A. and Waterbury, J. *A Political Economy of the Middle East*. Boulder, Colorado, Westview Press (1990), 2nd edition (revised), 1996.

Ridgeway, James (Ed.). *The March to War*. New York, Four Walls Eight Windows, 1991.

Rikhye, Maj.-Gen. I. J. *The Sinai Blunder*. London, Frank Cass, 1980.

Rivlin, B., and Szyliowicz, J. S. (Eds). *The Contemporary Middle East – Tradition and Innovation*. New York, Random House, 1965.

Roberts, D. S. *Islam: A Concise Introduction*. New York, Harper and Row, 1982.

Robinson, Francis. *Atlas of the Islamic World since 1500*. London, Phaidon, 1983.

(Ed.) *The Cambridge Illustrated History of the Islamic World*. Cambridge University Press, 1996.

Rodinson, Maxime. *Islam and Capitalism*. France, 1965, England, 1974.

Muhammad. London, Penguin, 1974.

La fascination de l'Islam. Paris, Maspero, 1980.

The Arabs. University of Chicago Press (1981), revised edition, 1989.

Israel and the Arabs. London, Penguin, 1982.

Europe and the Mystique of Islam. London, I. B. Tauris, 1989.

Ro'i, Ya'acov. *The Limits of Power: Soviet Policy in the Middle East*. London, Croom Helm, 1978.

Ronart, Stephan and Nandy. *Concise Encyclopaedia of Arabic Civilization*. Amsterdam, 1966.

Rondot, Pierre. *The Destiny of the Middle East*. London, Chatto & Windus, 1960.

L'Islam. Paris, Prismes, 1965.

Rouhani, Fuad. *A History of OPEC*. London, Pall Mall Press, 1972.

Roy, Olivier. *The Failure of Political Islam*. London, I. B. Tauris, 1995.

Rubin, Barry M. *The Arab States and the Palestine Conflict*. New York, Syracuse University Press, 1981.

Ruthven, Malise. *Islam in the World*. Harmondsworth, Penguin (1984), revised edition, 1991.

A Satanic Affair: Salman Rushdie and the Rage of Islam. London, Chatto and Windus, 1990.

Sachar, Howard M. *Europe Leaves the Middle East 1936–1954*. London, Allen Lane, 1973.

Said, Edward W. *The Question of Palestine*. London, Routledge, 1979 (reissued, Vintage, 1992).

Covering Islam. London, Routledge, 1982.

Salame, G. *Democracy without Democrats? The Renewal of Politics in the Muslim World*. London/New York, I. B. Tauris, 1994.

Sardar, Ziauddin (Ed.). *Science and Technology in the Middle East*. Harlow, Longman, 1982.

Sauvaget, J. *Introduction à l'histoire de l'orient musulman*. Paris, 1943. 2nd edition re-cast by C. Cahen, University of California Press, 1965.

Savory, R. M. *Introduction to Islamic Civilization*. Cambridge University Press, 1976.

Sayigh, Fatallah. *Le Désert et la Gloire*. Paris, Editions Gallimard, 1993.

Sayigh, Yusif, A. *The Determinants of Arab Economic Development*. London, Croom Helm, 1977.

The Economies of the Arab World. London, Croom Helm, 1978.

Arab Oil Policies in the 1970s. London, Croom Helm, 1983.

Elusive Development: From Dependence to Self-Reliance in the Arab Region. London, Routledge, 1991.

Schimmel, Annemarie. *Islam: An Introduction*. State University of New York Press, 1992.

Scott Appleby, R. (Ed.). *Spokesmen for the Despised: Fundamentalist Leaders of the Middle East*. University of Chicago Press, 1997.

Seale, Patrick. *Abu Nidal: A Gun for Hire*. London, Hutchinson, 1992.

Searight, Sarah. *The British in the Middle East*. London, Weidenfeld and Nicolson, 1969.

Shaban, M. A. *The Abbasid Revolution*. Cambridge University Press, 1970.

Islamic History: A New Interpretation. 2 vols. Cambridge University Press, 1976–78.

Shadid, Muhammad K. *The United States and the Palestinians*. London, Croom Helm, 1981.

Shapland, Gregory. *Rivers of Discord: International Water Disputes in the Middle East*. London, C. Hurst and Co, 1997.

Sharabi, H. B. *Governments and Politics of the Middle East in the Twentieth Century*. London, Greenwood Press (1962), revised edition, 1987.

Nationalism and Revolution in the Arab World. New York, Van Nostrand, 1966.

Palestine and Israel: The Lethal Dilemma. New York, Pegasus Press, 1969.

Shiloah, Amnon. *Music in the World of Islam: A Socio-Cultural Study*. Aldershot, Scolar Press, 1995.

Shlaim, A. *War and Peace in the Middle East*. New York/London, Penguin Books, 1995.

Shlaim, A. and Sayigh, Y. (Eds). *The Cold War and The Middle East*. Oxford University Press, 1998.

Sid-Ahmad, Abd as-Salam, and Ehteshami, Anoushiravan (Eds). *Islamic Fundamentalism*. Boulder, Colorado, Westview Press, 1996.

Sid-Ahmad, Muhammad. *After the Guns Fell Silent*. London, Croom Helm, 1976.

Sivan, Emmanuel. *Radical Islam: Medieval Theology and Modern Politics*. Yale University Press, 1991.

Smith, W. Cantwell. *Islam and Modern History*. Toronto, 1957.

Sourdel, Dominique. *Medieval Islam*. London, Routledge and Kegan Paul, 1984.

Southern, R. W. *Western Views of Islam in the Middle Ages*. Oxford, 1957.

Stark, Freya. *Dust in the Lion's Paw*. London and New York, 1961.

Stevens, Georgina G. (Ed.). *The United States and the Middle East*. Englewood Cliffs, NJ, Prentice-Hall, 1964.

Stewart, Desmond. *The Middle East: Temple of Janus*. London, Hamish Hamilton, 1972.

Stewart, P. J. *Unfolding Islam*. Reading, Jehaca Press, 1995.

Stocking, G. W. *Middle East Oil. A Study in Political and Economic Controversy*. Nashville, Vanderbilt University Press, 1979.

Sumner, B. H. *Tsardom and Imperialism in the Far East and Middle East*. London, Oxford University Press, 1940.

Susser, Asher, and Shmuelevitz, Aryeh (Eds). *The Hashemites in the Modern Arab World: essays in honour of the late Professor Uriel Dann*. London, Frank Cass, 1995.

Talbot Rice, David. *Islamic Art*. London, Thames and Hudson, 1991.

Taylor, Alan R. *The Arab Balance of Power*. New York, Syracuse University Press, 1982.

Taylor, Trevor. *The Middle East in the International System: Lessons from Europe and Implications for Europe*. London, Royal Institute of International Affairs, 1997.

Thayer, P. W. (Ed.). *Tensions in the Middle East*. Baltimore, 1958.

Thomas, L. V., and Frye, R. N. *The United States and Turkey and Iran*. Cambridge, Massachusetts, 1951.

Tillman, Seth P. *The United States in the Middle East*. Hemel Hempstead, Indiana University Press, 1982.

Times Guide to the Middle East, The. Edited by P. Sluglett and M. Farouq-Sluglett. London, Times Books, revised edition, 1993.

Trevelyan, Humphrey (Lord). *The Middle East in Revolution*. London, Macmillan, 1970.

Trimingham, J. Spencer. *The Sufi Orders in Islam*. Oxford, Clarendon Press, 1971.

Tschirgi, Dan. *The American Search for Mideast Peace*. New York, Praeger, 1989.

Vassiliev, Alexei. *Russian Policy in the Middle East: from messianism to pragmatism*. Reading, Ithaca Press, 1993.

Vatikiotis, P. J. *Conflict in the Middle East*. London, George Allen and Unwin, 1971.

Islam and the State. London, Routledge, 1991.

Viorst, Milton. *Reaching for the Olive Branch: UNRWA and peace in the Middle East*. Washington, Middle East Institute, 1989.

Wadsman, P., and Teissedre, R.-F. *Nos politiciens face au conflict israélo arabe*. Paris, 1969.

Waines, David. *The Unholy War*. Wilmette, Medina Press, 1971.

An Introduction to Islam. Cambridge University Press, 1995.

Walker, Christopher J. *Armenia: The Survival of a Nation*. London, Croom Helm, 1980.

Warriner, Doreen. *Land and Poverty in the Middle East*. London, 1948.

Land Reform and Development in the Middle East: Study of Egypt, Syria and Iraq. London, 1962.

Watkins, Eric (Ed.). *The Middle East Environment: selected papers of the 1995 Conference of the British Society for Middle Eastern Studies*. Cambridge, St. Malo Press, 1995.

Watt, W. Montgomery. *Muhammad at Mecca*. Oxford, Clarendon Press, 1953.

Muhammad at Medina. Oxford, Clarendon Press (1956), revised edition, 1991.

Muhammad: Prophet and Statesman. Oxford University Press (1961), revised edition, 1974.

Muslim Intellectual — Al Ghazari. Edinburgh University Press, 1962.

Islamic Philosophy and Theology: an Extended Survey. Edinburgh University Press (1963), revised edition, 1995.

Islamic Political Thought: The Basic Concepts. Edinburgh University Press (1968), revised edition, 1987.

What is Islam? London, Longman, 2nd edition, 1979.

Weidenfeld, Werner and Janning, Josef and Behrendt, Sven. *Transformation in the Middle East and North Africa*. Gütersloh (Germany), Bertelsmann Foundation, 1997.

Wilson, Rodney. *Trade and Investment in the Middle East*. Macmillan Press, 1977.

Economic Development in the Middle East. London, Routledge, 1995.

Wolf, Aaron T. *Hydropolitics Along the Jordan River: Scarce Water and its Impact on the Arab-Israeli Conflict*. Tokyo, United Nations University Press, 1996.

Woolfson, Marion. *Prophets in Babylon: Jews in the Arab World*. London, Faber, 1980.

Wright, Clifford A. *Facts and Fables: the Arab Israeli conflict*. London, Kegan Paul International, 1989.

Yamani, Mai (Ed.). *Feminism and Islam: Legal and Literary Perspectives*. Reading, Ithaca Press, 1996.

Yapp, M. E. *The Near East since the First World War*. London, Longman, 1991.

Yergin, Daniel. *The Prize: the Epic Quest for Oil, Money and Power*. New York, Simon and Schuster (1990), revised edition, 1993.

Zahlan, Rosemarie Said. *The Making of the Modern Gulf States*. London, Unwin Hyman Ltd, 1989.

Zeine, Z. N. *The Struggle for Arab Independence*. Beirut, 1960.

Zouilaï, Kaddour. *Des voiles et des serrures: de la fermeture en islam*. Paris, L'Harmattan, 1991.

Books on North Africa

See also bibliographies at end of relevant chapters in Part Three.

Abun-Nasr, Jamil M. *A History of the Maghreb*. Cambridge University Press, 1972.

Allal El-Fassi. *The Independence Movements in Arab North Africa*. trans. H. Z. Nuseibeh. Washington, DC, 1954.

Amin, Samir. *L'Economie du Maghreb*. 2 vols Paris, Editions du Minuit, 1966.

The Maghreb in the Modern World. London, Penguin Books, 1971.

Balta, Paul. *Le Grand Maghreb*. Paris, Editions La Découverte, 1990.

Balta, Paul, and Rulleau, Claudine. *L'Algérie des algériens*. Paris, Editions Ouvrières, 1982.

Berque, Jacques. *Le Maghreb entre deux guerres*. 2nd edition, Paris, Editions du Seuil, 1967.

Bonnefous, Marc. *Le Maghreb: repères et rappels*. Editions du Centre des Hautes Etudes sur l'Afrique et l'Asie modernes de Paris, 1991.

Brace, R. M. *Morocco, Algeria, Tunisia*. Englewood Cliffs, N.J., Prentice-Hall, 1964.

Brown, Leon Carl (Ed.). *State and Society in Independent North Africa*. Washington, Middle East Institute, 1966.

Burgat, François. *The Islamic Movement in North Africa*. University of Texas, 1993.

Capot-Rey, R. *Le Sahara français*. Paris, 1953.

Centre d'Etudes des Relations Internationales. *Le Maghreb et la communauté economique européenne*. Paris, Editions FNSP, 1965.

Centre de Recherches sur l'Afrique Méditerranéenne d'Aix en Provence. *L'Annuaire de l'Afrique du Nord*. Paris, Centre Nationale de la recherche scientifique, annually.

Charbonneau, J. (Ed.). *Le Sahara français*. Paris, Cahiers Charles de Foucauld, No. 38, 1955.

Collinson, Sarah. *Shore to Shore: The Politics of Migration in Euro-Maghreb Relations*. London, Royal Institute of International Affairs, 1997.

Damis, John. *Conflict in Northwest Africa: The Western Sahara Dispute*. Stanford University, California, Hoover Institute Press, 1983.

Duclos, J., Leca, J., and Duvignaud, J. *Les nationalismes maghrébins*. Paris, Centre d'Etudes des Relations Internationales, 1966.

Economic Commission for Africa. *Main Problems of Economic Co-operation in North Africa*. Tangier, 1966.

Evers Rasander, E and Westerlund, David (Eds). *African Islam and Islam in Africa: Encounters Between Sufis and Islamists*. London, C. Hurst and Co, 1997.

Furlonge, Sir Geoffrey. *The Lands of Barbary*. London, Murray, 1966.

Gallagher, C. F. *The US and North Africa*. Cambridge, Massachusetts, 1964.

Gardi, René. *Sahara, Monographie einer grossen Wüste*. Berne, Kummerley and Frey, 1967.

Gautier, E. F. *Le Passé de l'Afrique du Nord*. Paris, 1937.

Germidis, Dimitri, with the help of Delapierre, Michel. *Le Maghreb, la France et l'enjeu technologique*. Paris, Editions Cujas, 1976.

Gordon, D. C. *North Africa's French Legacy 1954–62*. Harvard, 1962.

Hahn, Lorna. *North Africa: from Nationalism to Nationhood.* Washington, 1960.

Hermassi, Elbaki. *Leadership and National Development in North Africa.* University of California Press, 1973.

Heseltine, N. *From Libyan Sands to Chad.* Leiden, 1960.

Joffé, E. G. H. (Ed.). *North Africa: Nation, State and Region.* London, Routledge/University of London, 1993.

Julien, Ch.-A. *Histoire de l'Afrique du nord.* 2nd edition, 2 vols, Paris 1951–52.

L'Afrique du nord en marche. Paris, 1953.

History of North Africa: From the Arab Conquest to 1830. Revised by R. Le Tourneau. Ed. C. C. Stewart. London, Routledge and Kegan Paul, 1970.

Khaldoun, Ibn. *History of the Berbers.* Translated into French by Slane. 4 vols, Algiers, 1852–56.

Knapp, Wilfrid. *North West Africa: A Political and Economic Survey.* Oxford University Press, 3rd edition, 1977.

Le Tourneau, Roger. *Evolution politique de l'Afrique du nord musulmane.* Paris, 1962.

Liska, G. *The Greater Maghreb: From Independence to Unity?* Washington, DC, Center of Foreign Policy Research, 1963.

Marçais, G. *La Berberie musulmane et l'Orient au moyen age.* Paris, 1946.

Moore, C. H. *Politics in North Africa.* Boston, Little, Brown, 1970.

Mortimer, Edward. *France and the Africans, 1944–1960.* London, Faber, 1969.

Muzikár, Joseph. *Les perspectives de l'intégration des pays maghrébins et leur attitude vis-à-vis du marché commun.* Nancy, 1968.

Nickerson, Jane S. *Short History of North Africa.* New York, 1961.

Parrinder, Geoffrey. *Religion in Africa.* London, Pall Mall Press, 1970.

Polk, William R. (Ed.). *Developmental Revolution: North Africa, Middle East, South Asia.* Washington, DC, Middle East Institute, 1963.

Raven, Susan. *Rome in Africa.* London, Evans Brothers, 1970 (reissued, Routledge, 1993).

Robana, Abderrahma. *The Prospects for an Economic Community in North Africa.* London, Pall Mall, 1973.

Sahli, Mohamed Cherif. *Décoloniser l'histoire; introduction à l'histoire du Maghreb.* Paris, Maspero, 1965.

Schramm, Josef. *Die Westsahara.* Freilassing, Paunonia Verlag, 1969.

Shahin, Emad. *Political Ascent: Contemporary Islamic Movements in North Africa.* Boulder, Colorado, Westview Press, 1996.

Steel, R. (Ed.). *North Africa.* New York, Wilson, 1967.

Toynbee, Sir Arnold. *Between Niger and Nile.* Oxford University Press, 1965.

Trimingham, J. S. *The influence of Islam upon Africa.* London, Longmans, and Beirut, Libraire du Liban, 1968.

Tutsch, Hans E. *Nordafrika in Gärung.* Frankfurt, 1961.

From Ankara to Marrakesh. New York, 1962.

UNESCO. *Arid Zone Research,* Vol. XIX: *Nomades et Nomadisme au Sahara.* UNESCO, 1963.

Warren, Cline and Santmyer, C. *Agriculture of Northern Africa.* Washington, US Department of Agriculture, 1965.

Zartman, I. W. *Government and Politics in North Africa.* London, Greenwood Press, revised edition, 1978.

(Ed.) *Man, State and Society in the Contemporary Maghreb.* London, Pall Mall, 1973.

SELECT BIBLIOGRAPHY (PERIODICALS)

Al-Abhath. Published by American University of Beirut, POB 11-236/31, Beirut, Lebanon; tel. (1) 353465; telex 20801; fax (1) 4781995; e-mail publications@aub.edu.lb; f. 1948; Editor Farid el-Khazen; English and Arabic; annual on Middle East studies.

Acta Orientalia. Institute for the Comparative Research in Human Culture, POB 2832, Solli, 0204 Oslo, Norway; f. 1922; publ. under auspices of the Oriental Societies of Denmark, Finland, Norway, and Sweden; history, language, archaeology and religions of the Near and Far East; Editor Prof. Per Kvaerne; annually.

Acta Orientalia Academiae Scientiarum Hungaricae. H-1363 Budapest, POB 24, Hungary; f. 1950; text in English, French, German or Russian; Editor A. Sárközi; 3 a year.

Africa Contemporary Record. Africana Publishing Co, Holmes & Meier Publishers Inc, IUB Building, 30 Irving Place, New York, NY 10003, USA; tel. (212) 2544100; fax (212) 2544104; annual surveys, special essays and indices.

Africa Quarterly. Indian Council for Cultural Relations, Azad Bhavan, Indraprastha Estate, New Delhi 110002, India; tel. 3319309; telex 3166004; fax 3318647; f. 1961; Editor T. G. Ramamurthi; circ. 700.

Africa Review. Walden Publishing, 2 Market St, Saffron Walden, Essex, CB10 1HZ, England; tel. (1799) 521150; fax (1799) 524805; e-mail waldenpub@easynetco.uk; internet http://www.worldinformation.com; political and economic analysis; Editor Howard Hill; annually.

Africa Research Bulletins. Blackwell Publishers, 108 Cowley Road, Oxford, OX4 1JF, England; tel. (1392) 215655; f. 1964; monthly bulletins on (*a*) political and (*b*) economic subjects; Eds Pita Adams, Virginia Baily, Veronica Hoskins, Elizabeth Oliver.

Akhbar al-Alam al-Islami: Muslim World League, POB 537, Mecca al-Mukarramah; tel. (2) 5422733; telex 540009; fax (2) 5436619; Arabic; weekly.

Alam Attijarat (The World of Business). Johnston International Publishing Corpn (New York), Beirut, Lebanon; Arabic; business; Editor Nadim Makdisi; 10 a year.

Anatolian Studies. BIAA, Senate House, Malet St, London, WC1E 7HU, England; tel. and fax (171) 862-8734; f. 1948; annual of the British Institute of Archaeology at Ankara; Editor Dr Stephen Hill.

Anatolica. Netherlands Historical Archaeological Institute at İstanbul, Istiklâl Caddesi 393, İstanbul-Beyoğlu, Turkey; tel. 2939283; fax 2513846; e-mail nlhai@superonline.com; f. 1967; Editors B. Flemming, H. E. Lagro, J. J. Roodenberg, J. de Roos, D. J. W. Meijer, M. Özdoğan; annually.

Annales archéologiques Arabes Syriennes. Direction Générale des Antiquités et des Musées, University St, Damascus, Syria; tel. 2214854; telex 412491; f. 1951; archaeological and historical review; Dir-Gen. Dr Sultan Moheisen; annually.

Annuaire de l'Afrique du Nord. Edited by the Institut de recherches et d'études sur le Monde Arabe et Musulman, 3 & 5 ave Pasteur, 13617 Aix-en-Provence Cedex 1; tel. 442215988; telex 13100; fax 442215275; e-mail adiremam@univ-aix.fr; published by the Centre National de la Recherche Scientifique, CNRS Editions, 15 rue Malebranche, 75005 Paris, France; Editor Françoise Lorcerie; f. 1962; year-book contains special studies on current affairs, report on a collective programme of social sciences research on North Africa (Algeria, Libya, Mauritania, Morocco, Tunisia) and Maghrebis in Europe, chronologies, chronicles, documentation and bibliographies.

Annual Survey of African Law. Rex Collings Ltd, 'Chaceside', Coronation Rd, South Ascot, Berks, SL5 9LB, England; tel. (1344) 872453; fax (1344) 872858.

The Arab Economist. Centre for Economic, Financial and Social Research and Documentation SAL, Gefinor Tower, Clemenceau St, Bloc B-POB 11-6068, Beirut, Lebanon; f. 1969; Chair. Dr Chafic Akhras; monthly; circ. 7,300.

Arab Oil and Gas. The Arab Petroleum Research Centre, 7 ave Ingrès, 75016 Paris, France; tel. 145243310; fax 145201685; f. 1971; petroleum and gas; English and French; Editor Dr Nicolas Sarkis; 2 a month.

Arab Oil and Gas Directory. The Arab Petroleum Research Centre, 7 ave Ingrès, 75016 Paris, France; tel. 145243310; fax 145201685; f. 1974; English; annually.

Arab Political Documents. publ. by American University of Beirut, Beirut, Lebanon; f. 1963; Editor Yousuf Khoury; Arabic; compiles important political documents of the year in various Arab countries; annually.

Arab Studies Quarterly. Association of Arab-American University Graduates, Inc. (AAUG), POB 408, Normal, IL 61761-0408, USA; tel. (309) 4526588; fax (309) 4528335; f. 1976; Editor Jamal R. Nassar.

Arabia: The Islamic World Review. Crown House, Crown Lane, East Burnham, Bucks, SL2 3SG, England; tel. (12814) 5177; telex 847031; monthly.

Arabica. c/o Université de la Sorbonne Nouvelle, 13 rue de Santeuil, 75231 Paris Cedex 05, France; tel. (1) 45874139; Dir Mohammed Arkoun; 3 a year.

Aramco World. Aramco Services Co, Box 2106, Houston, TX 77252-2106, USA; non-political information—culture, natural history, economics, etc., of the Middle East; Editor Robert Arndt; bimonthly.

Aramtek Mideast Review. Aramtek Corporation, 122 East 42nd Street, Suite 3703, New York, NY 10017, USA; f. 1976; business news and features; USA Editor-in-Chief M. Handal; Man. Editor B. F. Ottaviani.

Archiv für Orientforschung. c/o Institut für Orientalistik der Universität Wien, Universitätsstrasse 7/V, A-1010 Vienna I, Austria; tel. (1) 427743401; fax (1) 42779434; e-mail michael .fursa@univie.ac.at; f. 1923; Editors Gerhard Selz, Hermann Hunger; annually.

Armenian Review. The Armenian Review Inc., 80 Bigelow Ave, Watertown, MA 02172, USA; tel. (617) 9264037; fax (617) 9261750; f. 1948; Editor Dr Hayg Oshagan; quarterly.

Asian Affairs. Royal Society for Asian Affairs, 2 Belgrave Square, London, SW1X 8PJ, England; tel. (171) 235-5122; fax (171) 259-6771; e-mail info@rsaa.org.uk; internet http://www.rsaa.org.uk; f. 1901; 3 a year.

L'Asie nouvelle. 94 rue St Lazare, 75442 Paris Cedex 09, France; tel. (1) 45266701; weekly and special issues; Dir André Roux.

Belleten. Türk Tarih Kurumu, Kızılay Sokak no. 1, 06100 Ankara, Turkey; tel. 3102368; fax 3101698; e-mail yusuf@ ttk.gov.tr; f. 1937; history and archaeology of Turkey; Editor Prof. Dr Yusuf Halaçoğlu; 3 a year.

The Bibliography of the Middle East. Publisher L. Farès, BP 2712, Damascus, Syria; annually.

Bibliotheca Orientalis. Published by Netherlands Institute for the Near East, Witte Singel 25, POB 9515, 2300 RA, Leiden, Netherlands; tel. (71) 272036; fax (71) 272038; e-mail beurs@ rullet.leidenuniv.nl; f. 1943; edited by J. de Roos, D. J. W. Meijer, H. J. A. de Meulenaere, A. van der Kooij, C. Nijland, J. J. Roodenberg, M. Stol; 3 double issues a year.

British Journal of Middle Eastern Studies. BRISMES Administrative Office, CMEIS, University of Durham, South Road, Durham DH1 3TG, England; tel. (191) 3747989; fax (191) 3742830; f. 1974 (as *British Society of Middle Eastern Studies Bulletin*); Editor Dr Adrian Gully, American University of Sharjah, POB 26666, Sharjah, United Arab Emirates; tel. (6) 585555; fax (6) 585858; e-mail gully@aus.ac.ae; internet http://www.dur.ac.uk/brismes; 2 a year.

Bulletin d'études orientales. Institut français d'études arabes, BP 344, Damascus, Syria; tel. (11) 3330214; fax (11) 3327887; f. 1922; annually (49 vols published).

Bulletin of the School of Oriental and African Studies. School of Oriental and African Studies, University of London, Thornhaugh Street, Russell Sq., London, WC1H 0XG, England; tel. (171) 637-2388; fax (171) 436-3844; publ. by Oxford University Press, Walton St, Oxford OX2 6DP; 3 a year.

Bulletin of Sudanese Studies. POB 321, Khartoum; Arabic; published by The Institute of African and Asian Studies, University of Khartoum, Sudan; tel. 75820; telex 22133; f. 1968; Editor Abdullahi Ali Ibrahim; 2 a year.

Les Cahiers de l'Orient. 60 rue des Cévennes, 75015 Paris, France; tel. (1) 40607311; f. 1986; published by CERPO (Centre of Near East Studies); review of Islamic and Arab affairs; quarterly.

Les Cahiers de Tunisie. Publ. by Faculté des sciences humaines et sociales de Tunis, 94 blvd de 9 Avril 1938, 1007 Tunis, Tunisia; tel. 260858; f. 1953; research in humanities; Dir Hédi Cherif; Editor-in-Chief Hassan Annabi; every six months.

Chuto Kenkyu (Journal of Middle Eastern Studies). The Middle East Institute of Japan, POB 1513, Shinjuku i-Land Tower, 163-13 Tokyo, Japan; tel. (3) 53232145; fax (3) 53232148; f. 1960; Editor Wasuke Miyake; monthly.

Le Commerce du Levant. Centre Azzam, Jdeidé-Metn, BP 90-1397, Beirut, Lebanon; tel. 899005; telex 40085; weekly.

Comunità Mediterranea. Lungotevere Flaminio 34, Rome, Italy; law and political science relating to Mediterranean countries; Pres. E. Bussi.

Crescent International. 300 Steelcase Rd West, Unit 8, Markham, ON L3R 2W2, Canada; tel. (905) 4749292; fax (905) 4749293; f. 1980; deals with Islamic movement throughout the world; 2 a month.

Dawat al-Haq. Muslim World League, POB 537, Mecca al-Mukarramah, Saudi Arabia; tel. (2) 5422733; telex 540009; fax (2) 5436619; Arabic; monthly.

Deutsche Morgenländische Gesellschaft; Zeitschrift. Seminar für Arabistik, Prinzenstr. 21, D-37073 Göttingen, Germany; tel. (551) 394398; fax (551) 399332; f. 1847; covers the history, languages and literature of the Orient; Editor Prof. Dr Tilman Nagel; 2 a year.

Developing Economies. Ajia Keizai Kenkyusho (Institute of Developing Economies), 42 Ichigaya Hommura-cho, Shinjuku-ku, Tokyo 162-8442, Japan; tel. (03) 33534231; telex 32473; fax (03) 32268475; f. 1962; English; quarterly.

L'Economiste Arabe. Centre d'études et de documentation économiques, financières et sociales, SAL, BP 6068, Beirut, Lebanon; Pres. Dr Chafic Akhras, Dir-Gen. Dr Sabbah al-Haj; monthly.

Europe Outremer. 178 quai L. Blériot, 75016 Paris, France; tel. (1) 46477844; f. 1923; economic and political material on French-speaking states of Africa; monthly.

France-Pays Arabes. 14 rue Augereau, 75007 Paris, France; tel. 145552752; fax 145512726; f. 1968; politics, economics and culture of the Arab world; Dir Lucien Bitterlin; monthly.

Grand Maghreb. BP 45, 38402 Saint-Martin-d'Hères, France; monthly.

Hamizrah Hehadash. Israel Oriental Society. The Hebrew University, Jerusalem, Israel; f. 1949; Hebrew with English summary; Middle Eastern, Asian and African affairs; Editor Jacob Landau.

Hesperis-Tamuda. Faculté des Lettres et des Sciences Humaines, Université Muhammad V, BP 1040, Rabat, Morocco; tel. (212) 7771989; fax (212) 7772068; f. 1921; history, anthropology, civilization of Maghreb and Western Islam, special reference to bibliography; Chief Editor B. Boutaleb; annually; circ. 2,000.

Ibla. Institut des belles lettres arabes, 12 rue Jamâa el-Haoua, 1008 Tunis BM, Tunisia; tel. 560133; fax 572683; f. 1937; 2 a year.

Indo-Iranian Journal. Kluwer Academic Publishers, POB 17, 3300 AA Dordrecht, Netherlands; tel. (78) 6392391; e-mail services@wkap.nl; f. 1957; Editors H. W. Bodewitz, J. W. de Jong and M. Witzel; quarterly.

Indo-Iranica. Iran Society, 12 Dr M. Ishaque Road, Calcutta 700016, India; tel. 299899; f. 1946; promotion of Persian studies

and Indo-Iranian cultural relations; Gen. Sec. and Man. Editor M. A. Majid; quarterly.

International Crude Oil and Product Prices. Middle East Petroleum and Economic Publications (Cyprus), POB 4940, 1355 Nicosia, Cyprus; tel. (02) 445431; telex 2198; fax (02) 474988; e-mail mees@spidernet.com.cy; f. 1971 (in Beirut); review and analysis of oil price trends in world markets; Publisher Basim W. Itayim; 2 a year.

International Journal of Middle East Studies. Cambridge University Press, The Edinburgh Bldg, Shaftesbury Road, Cambridge, CB2 2RU, England; tel. (1223) 312393; telex 817256; fax (1223) 315052; e-mail journals-marketing@cup.cam.ac.uk; Journal of the Middle East Studies Association of North America; first issue Jan. 1970; Editor Prof. R. Stephen Humphreys; 4 a year.

Iraq. British School of Archaeology in Iraq, 31–34 Gordon Sq., London, WC1H 0PY, England; f. 1932; annually.

Der Islam. D-20148 Hamburg, Rothenbaumchaussee 36, Germany; tel. (040) 41233180; fax (040) 41235674; 2 a year.

Islamic and Comparative Law Review. Dept of Law, Hamdard University, Tughlaqabad, New Delhi 110062, India; tel. (11) 6439685; f. 1981; Founder-Editor Tahir Mahmood; two a year.

Islamic Quarterly. The Islamic Cultural Centre, 146 Park Road, London, NW8 7RG, England; tel (171) 724-3363; fax (171) 724-0493; f. 1954; Editor Dr Hamad al-Majed; quarterly.

Israel and Palestine. POB 44, 75462 Paris Cedex 10, France; tel. (1) 48009660; fax (1) 48009645; f. 1971; Editor Maxim Ghilan; International Secretariat of the International Jewish Peace Union (IJPU); monthly.

Izvestia Rossiiskoi Akademii Nauk-Seriya Literatury i Yazyka. Russian Academy of Sciences, Moscow, Russia; tel. 2901709; f. 1852; 2 a month.

Jeune Afrique. Groupe Jeune Afrique, 51 ave des Ternes, Paris 17e, France; tel. (1) 47665242; telex 280674; f. 1960; Publisher Bechir ben Yahmed; weekly.

Journal of the American Oriental Society. American Oriental Society, 329 Sterling Memorial Library, Box 208236, Yale Station, New Haven, CT 06520, USA; tel. (313) 7474760; f. 1842; Ancient Near East, Inner Asia, South and Southeast Asia, Islamic Near East, and Far East; quarterly.

Journal Asiatique. Journal de la société asiatique, 3 rue Mazarine, 75006 Paris, France; f. 1822; Dir D. Matringe; covers all phases of Oriental research; 2 a year.

Journal of Indian Philosophy. Kluwer Academic Publishers, POB 17, 3300 AA Dordrecht, Netherlands; tel. (78) 6392392; e-mail services@wkap.nl; f. 1970; Editor Phyllis Granoff; quarterly.

Journal of the Institute of Muslim Minority Affairs. 46 Goodge St, London, W1P 1FJ, England; tel. (171) 636-6740; telex 296182; fax (171) 255-1473; f. 1976; Man. Editor Dr Saleha Mahmood; 2 a year.

Journal of Near Eastern Studies. Oriental Institute, University of Chicago, 1155 East 58th Street, Chicago, IL 60637, USA; tel (773) 7029540; telex 6871133; fax (773) 7029853; e-mail rbiggs@uchicago.edu; devoted to the Ancient and Medieval Near and Middle East, archaeology, languages, history, Islam; Editor R. Biggs.

Journal of Palestine Studies. 3501 M St, NW, Washington, DC 20007, USA; tel. (202) 3423990; fax (202) 3423927; e-mail jps@ipsjps.org; internet http://www.ipsjps.org; f. 1971; publ. by the University of California Press for the Inst. for Palestine Studies, Washington, DC; Palestinian affairs and the Arab-Israeli conflict; Editor Hisham Sharabi; Assoc. Editor Philip Mattar; circ. 3,600; quarterly.

Maghreb-Machrek-Monde-Arabe. Direction de la Documentation, Secrétariat général du gouvernement, La documentation française, 29–31 quai Voltaire, 75344 Paris Cedex 07, France; tel. 140157100; telex 204826; fax 140157230; e-mail mc-cosse@ladocfrancaise.gouv.fr; internet http://www.ladocfrancaise.gouv.fr; f. 1964; published with the assistance of the Fondation nationale des Sciences politiques and the Centre d'étude de l'Orient contemporain (University of Paris III); quarterly.

The Maghreb Review. 45 Burton St, London, WC1H 9AL, England; tel. (171) 388-1840; f. 1976; North African and Islamic studies from earliest times to the present; Editor Muhammad ben Madani; quarterly.

Maghreb-Sélection. IC Publications, 10 rue Vineuse, 75784 Paris Cedex 16, France; tel. 144308100; fax 144308111; e-mail rosenwal@pratique.fr; f. 1979; economic information about North Africa; weekly.

Majallat a-Rabita. Muslim World League, POB 537, Mecca al-Mukarramah, Saudi Arabia; tel. (2) 5422733; telex 540009; fax (2) 5436619; Arabic; monthly.

Marchés Arabes. IC Publications, 10 rue Vineuse, 75784 Paris Cedex 16, France; tel. 144308100; fax 144308111; e-mail rosenwal@pratique.fr; f. 1978; economic information about the Middle East; fortnightly.

Marchés Tropicaux et Mediterranéens. 190 blvd Haussmann, 75008 Paris, France; tel. 144959950; telex 641544; f. 1945; economics; Editor Serge Marpaud; weekly.

MEN Weekly. Middle East News Agency, Hoda Sharawi St, Cairo, Egypt; f. 1962; weekly news bulletin.

Le Message de l'Islam. BP 14155, 3899 Teheran, Iran; theoretical review of Iranian Islam; monthly.

The Middle East. 7 Coldbath Sq., London, EC1R 4LQ, England; tel. (171) 713-7711; fax (171) 713-7970; e-mail icpubs@dial.pipex.com; internet http://www.africaasia.com/icpubs; f. 1974; political, economic and cultural; Editor Pat Lancaster; Publr Ahmad Afif ben Yedder; circ. 17,292; monthly.

Middle East Business Intelligence. 717 D St, NW, Suite 300, Washington, DC 20004, USA; tel. (202) 6286900; fax (202) 6286618; newsletter of business opportunities; Publr William C. Hearn; 2 a month.

Middle East Contemporary Survey. Moshe Dayan Centre for Middle Eastern and African Studies, c/o Westview Press, 5500 Central Ave, Boulder, CO 80301, USA; tel. (303) 4443541; telex 239479; fax (303) 4493356; 12 Hid's Copse Rd, Cumnor Hill, Oxford, OX2 9JJ, England; tel. (1865) 865466; fax (1865) 862763; annual record of political developments, country surveys, special essays, maps, tables, notes, indices; Editors Ami Ayalon, Bruce Maddy-Weitzman.

Middle East Economic Digest. MEED Ltd, 21 John Street, London, WC1N 2BP, England; tel. (171) 470-6200; fax (171) 831-9537; e-mail ebi@meed.emap.co.uk; f. 1957; weekly report on economic, business and political developments; Publishing Dir Edmund O'Sullivan; Editor Peter Kemp.

Middle East Economic Survey. Middle East Petroleum and Economic Publications (Cyprus), POB 4940, 1355 Nicosia, Cyprus; tel. (2) 445431; telex 2198; fax (2) 474988; e-mail mees@spidernet.com.cy; f. 1957 (in Beirut); weekly review and analysis of petroleum, finance and banking, and political developments; Publr Basim W. Itayim; Editor Ian Seymour.

Middle East Events Bulletin. Centre of Near and Middle Eastern Studies, School of Oriental and African Studies—SOAS, University of London, Thornhaugh St, Russell Sq., London, WC1H 0XG, England; tel. (171) 323-6239; telex 291829; fax (171) 637-4248; e-mail lt@soas.ac.uk; English; Editor Sarah Stewart; monthly.

Middle East Executive Reports. 717 D Street, NW, Suite 300, Washington, DC 20004, USA; tel. (202) 6286900; fax (202) 6286618; legal and business guide to the Middle East; monthly; also publishes the *Arab Investors Sourcebook.*

Middle East Focus. Canadian Academic Foundation for Peace in the Middle East, 1057 Steeles Ave West, POB 81509, North York, ON M2R 3X1, Canada; tel. (416) 9639477; f. 1978; contemporary Middle Eastern issues; English; Editor Irving Abella; quarterly.

Middle East Insight. Suite 305, 1200 18th St, NW, Washington, DC 20036, USA; tel. (202) 4662146; fax (202) 4662147; e-mail mideast@dgs.dgsys.com; f. 1980; politics, economics and culture; English; Editor George Nader; 6 a year.

Middle East International. 21 Collingham Road, London, SW5 0NU, England; tel. (171) 373-5228; telex 8953551; fax (171) 370-5956; f. 1971; fortnightly; political and economic developments, book reviews; Editor Michael Wall.

The Middle East Journal. Middle East Institute, 1761 N Street, NW, Washington, DC 20036, USA; tel. (202) 7850191; fax (202)

3318861; journal in English devoted to the study of the modern Near East; f. 1947; Editor Mary-Jane Deeb; circ. 4,000; quarterly.

Middle East Military Balance. Jaffee Center for Strategic Studies, Tel-Aviv University, Ramat-Aviv, Tel-Aviv 69978, Israel; tel. (3) 6409200; fax (3) 6422404; English and Hebrew, Editor Shlomo Gazit; annual.

Middle East Monitor. Business Monitor International Ltd, 56–60 St. John St, London, EC1M 4DT, England; tel. (171) 608-3646; fax (171) 608-3620; monthly; economic and political brief; Editor John Roberts.

The Middle East Observer. 41 Sherif St, Cairo, Egypt; tel. (2) 3926919; fax (2) 3939732; f. 1954; economics; English; Editor Muhammad Abdullah Hesham A. Raouf; weekly.

Middle East Perspective. New York, USA; monthly newsletter on Eastern Mediterranean and North African affairs; Editor Dr Alfred Lilienthal.

Middle East Policy. Middle East Policy Council, 1730 M Street, NW, Suite 512, Washington, DC 20036, USA; tel. (202) 2966767; fax (202) 2965791; e-mail mepc@capitol.net; policy analysis; quarterly; Editor Anne Joyce.

Middle East Quarterly. Middle East Forum, Suite 600, 1920 Chestnut St, Philadelphia, PA 19103, USA; tel. (215) 5699225; fax (215) 5699229; f. 1994; English; Editor Daniel Pipes; quarterly.

Middle East Report. Room 518, 475 Riverside Drive, New York, NY 10115, USA; tel. (212) 8703281; f. 1971; Publisher James Paul; Editor Joe Stork; circ. 6,000; every 2 months.

Middle East Review. Walden Publishing Ltd, 2 Market St, Saffron Walden, Essex, CB10 1HZ, England; tel. (1799) 521150; fax (1799) 524805; e-mail waldenpub@easynet.co.uk; political and economic analysis; Man. Editor Rennie Campbell; annually.

Middle East Studies Association Bulletin. 200 LCI, Catholic University of America, Washington, DC 20064, USA; tel. (202) 3195999; fax (202) 3196267; Editor Jon Anderson; 2 a year.

Middle Eastern Studies. Frank Cass & Co Ltd, Newbury House, 890–900 Eastern Ave, Newbury Park, Ilford, Essex IG2 7HH; tel. (181) 599-8866; fax (181) 599-0984; e-mail 100067,1576@compuserve.com; f. 1964; Editor Sylvie Kedourie; 4 a year.

Mideast Report. 60 East 42nd Street, Suite 1433, New York, NY 10017, USA; political analysis, oil and finance and business intelligence.

The Muslim World. 77 Sherman Street, Hartford, CT 06105, USA; tel. (860) 509-9500; fax (860) 509-9539; f. 1911; Islamic studies in general and Muslim-Christian relations in past and present; Editors Ibrahim Abu-Rabi' and Jane I. Smith; quarterly.

The Muslim World League Journal. Press and Publications Department, Muslim World League, POBs 537 and 538, Mecca al-Mukarramah, Saudi Arabia; tel. (2) 5441622; telex 540009; fax (2) 5441622; Chief Editor Hamid Hassan ar-Raddadi; monthly in English.

Near East Report. 440 First St, NW, Suite 607, Washington, DC 20001, USA; tel. (202) 6395254; fax (202) 3474916; f. 1957; analyses US policy in the Middle East; Editor Raphael Danziger; circ. 55,000; bi-weekly.

New Outlook. 9 Gordon St, Tel-Aviv 63458, Israel; tel. (3) 236496; fax (3) 232492; f. 1957; Israeli and Middle Eastern Affairs; dedicated to Jewish-Arab rapprochement; Editor-in-Chief Chaim Shur; circ. 10,000; monthly.

Oil and Gas Journal. Penn Well Publishing Co, 1421 S. Sheridan, Tulsa, Oklahoma 74101, USA; tel. (918) 8353161; fax (918) 8329295; f. 1902; petroleum industry and business weekly; Editor John L. Kennedy; circ. 42,000.

Orient. German Orient Institute, 2 Hamburg 13, Mittelweg 150, Federal Republic of Germany; tel. (40) 4132050; fax (40) 441484; e-mail doihh@uni-hamburg.de; internet http://www.rrz.uni-hamburg.de/doi; f. 1960; current affairs articles in German and English; documents, book reviews and bibliographies; Editor Prof. Dr Udo Steinbach; quarterly.

Oriente Moderno. Istituto per l'Oriente C.A. Nallino, via A. Caroncini 19, 00197 Rome, Italy; tel. (6) 8084106; fax (6) 8079395; e-mail ipo@mix.it; f. 1921; articles, book reviews.

Palestine Affairs. POB 1691, Beirut, Lebanon; studies of Palestine problem; f. 1971; monthly in Arabic; Editor Bilal El-Hassan.

Persica. Netherlands-Iranian Society; c/o NINO, Witte Singel 24, POB 9515, 2300 RA Leiden, Netherlands; tel. (171) 272019; f. 1963; Editors E. During Caspers, J. de Bruijn, R. Hillenbrand, K. Kremer and C. Nijland; every 2 years.

Petroleum Economist. POB 105, Baird House, 15/17 St. Cross St, London, EC1N 8UN, England; tel. (171) 831-5588; fax (171) 831-4567; f. 1934; monthly in English; Editor Chris Skrebowski; circ. 5,500.

Petroleum Times Energy Report. Nexus Media Ltd, Nexos House, Azalea Drive, Swanley, Kent, BR8 8HY, England.

Politica Internazionale. Via del Tritone 62B, 00187 Rome, Italy; tel. (6) 6792321; fax (6) 6797849; publ. by Istituto per le relazioni tra Italia e i Paesi dell' Africa, America Latina e Medio Oriente; Italian edition (6 a year).

Pour la Palestine. 21 rue Voltaire, 75011 Paris, France; tel. (1) 43721579; fax (1) 43720725; f. 1979; monthly.

Revue d'assyriologie et d'archéologie orientale. Presses universitaires de France, 12 rue Jean-de-Beauvais, 75005 Paris, France; f. 1923; Dirs Paul Garelli, Pierre Amiet; 2 a year.

Revue des études islamiques. Librairie Orientaliste Paul Geuthner SA, 12 rue Vavin, 75006 Paris, France; f. 1927; Editors J. D. Sourdel and J. Sourdel-Thomine.

Revue d'études Palestiniennes. Published by l'Institut des études palestiniennes, POB 11-7164, Beirut, Lebanon; distributed by Les Editions de Minuit, 7 rue Bernard Palissy, 75006 Paris, France; tel. (1) 42225478; f. 1981; Chief Editor Elias Sanbar; quarterly.

Rivista Degli Studi Orientali. Dipartimento di Studi Orientali, Facoltà di Lettere, Università Degli Studi, 'La Sapienza', Rome, Italy; tel. (6) 49913562; fax (6) 4451209; Publr Giovanni Bardi; quarterly.

Rocznik Orientalistyczny. Instytut Orientalistyczny, Uniwersytet Warszawski, 00-927 Warszawa 64, Poland; f. 1915; Editor-in-Chief Edward Tryjarski; Sec. Marek M. Dziekan; 2 a year.

Royal Asiatic Society of Great Britain and Ireland Journal. 60 Queen's Gardens, London W2 3AF, England; tel. (171) 724-4742; fax (171) 706-4008; f. 1823; covers all aspects of Oriental research; Pres. Dr F. Robinson; Editor Dr D. O. Morgan; 3 a year.

Studia Arabistyczne i Islamistyczne. Zakład Arabistyki i Islamistyki, Instytut Orientalistyczny, Uniwersytet Warszawski, 00-927 Warszawa 64, Poland; f. 1993; Editor-in-Chief Janusz Danecki; Sec. Marek M. Dziekan; annually.

Studia Islamica, G. P. Maisonneuve et Larose, 15 rue Victor-Cousin, 75005 Paris, France; tel. (1) 44414930; fax (1) 43257741; f. 1953; Editors A. L. Udovitch and A. M. Turki; 2 a year.

Studies in Islam. Indian Institute of Islamic Studies, Panchkuin Road, New Delhi 110001, India; f. 1964; quarterly.

Sudanow. POB 2651, Khartoum, Sudan; tel. (0249) 77915; telex 22418; f. 1976; political, economic and cultural; Editor-in-Chief Ahmed Kamal ed-Din; circ. 7,000; monthly.

Sumer. State Antiquities and Heritage Organization, Karkh, Salihiya, Jamal abd an-Nasr St, Baghdad, Iraq; tel. 5376121; f. 1945; archaeological and historical; Chair. Editorial Bd Dr M. Said; annually.

At-Tijara al-Arabiya al-Inkleezya (World Arab Trade). Sahara Publications, 91 King Street, London, W6 9HW, England; tel. (181) 741-4921; telex 926493; f. 1947; Arabic; 6 a year.

Turcica. Publ. by Université des sciences humaines, Strasbourg, and Association pour le développement des études turques, EHESS, 54 blvd Raspail, 75006 Paris, France; tel. (1) 49542301; fax (1) 49542672; e-mail Etudes-turques@ehess.fr; f. 1971; all aspects of Turkish and Turkic culture; annually; Eds Prof. Gilles Veinstein and Paul Dumont.

Türk Kültürü Araştırmaları. T. K. Araştırma Enstitüsü, 17 Sokak No. 38 Bahçelievler, Ankara, Turkey; tel. (312) 2133100; f. 1964; scholarly articles in Turkish; Editor Dr Şükrü Elçin; annually.

Türkologischer Anzeiger (Turkology Annual). Oriental Institute of the University of Vienna; A-1010 Vienna I, Universitäts-strasse 7/V, Austria; tel. (1) 427743401; fax (1) 42779434; annually.

Al-Urdun al-jadid (New Jordan). POB 4856, Nicosia, Cyprus; Arabic; quarterly.

Vostok (*Orient*). Russian Academy of Sciences, ul. Spiridonovka 30/1, Moscow, Russia: tel. 2026650; f. 1955; Afro-Asian Societies past and present; Editor-in-Chief Dr L. B. Alayev; 6 a year.

The Washington Report on Middle East Affairs. POB 53062, Washington, DC 20009, USA; tel. (202) 9396050; fax (202) 2654574; e-mail wrmea@aol.com; internet http://www.washington-report.org; f. 1982; 8 a year.

Die Welt des Islams. (International Journal for the Study of Modern Islam.) Published by E. J. Brill, postbus 9000, 2300 PA, Leiden, Netherlands; tel. (71) 5353500; telex 39296; fax (71) 5317532; Orientalisches Seminar der Universität, Regina-Pacis-Weg 7, 53113 Bonn, Federal Republic of Germany; tel. (228) 737462; fax (228) 735601; f. 1913; contains articles in German, English and French on the contemporary Muslim world with special reference to literature; Editors Prof. Dr S. Wild (University of Bonn), Prof. Dr W. Ende (University of Freiburg), Prof. Dr M. Ursinus (University of Heidelberg).

Wiener Zeitschrift für die Kunde des Morgenlandes. Oriental Institute of the University of Vienna, A-1010 Vienna I, Universitätsstrasse 7/V, Austria; tel. (1) 401032599; fax (1) 4020533; f. 1887; Editors O. Prof. Dr Arne A. Ambros, O. Prof. Dr Hans Hirsch, O. Prof. Dr Markus Köhbach; annually.

PART TWO
Regional Organizations

THE UNITED NATIONS IN THE MIDDLE EAST AND NORTH AFRICA

Address: United Nations Plaza, New York, NY 10017, USA.
Telephone: (212) 963-1234; **fax:** (212) 963-4879; **internet:** http://www.un.org.

The United Nations (UN) was founded on 24 October 1945. The organization aims to maintain international peace and security and to develop international co-operation in economic, social, cultural and humanitarian problems. The principal organs of the UN are the General Assembly, the Security Council, the Economic and Social Council (ECOSOC), the International Court of Justice and the Secretariat. The General Assembly, which meets for three months each year, comprises representatives of all UN member states. The Security Council investigates disputes between member countries, and may recommend ways and means of peaceful settlement: it comprises five permanent members (the People's Republic of China, France, Russia, the United Kingdom and the USA) and 10 other members elected by the General Assembly for a two-year period. The Economic and Social Council comprises representatives of 54 member states, elected by the General Assembly for a three-year period: it promotes co-operation on economic, social, cultural and humanitarian matters, acting as a central policy-making body and co-ordinating the activities of the UN's specialized agencies. The International Court of Justice comprises 15 judges of different nationalities, elected for nine-year terms by the General Assembly and the Security Council: it adjudicates in legal disputes between UN member states.

Secretary-General of the United Nations: KOFI ANNAN (Ghana) (1997–2001)

MEMBER STATES IN THE MIDDLE EAST AND NORTH AFRICA

(with assessments for percentage contributions to UN budget for 1997, and year of admission)

Algeria	0.16	1962
Bahrain	0.02	1971
Cyprus	0.03	1960
Egypt	0.08	1945
Iran	0.45	1945
Iraq	0.14	1945
Israel	0.27	1949
Jordan	0.01	1955
Kuwait	0.19	1963
Lebanon	0.01	1945
Libya	0.20	1955
Morocco	0.03	1956
Oman	0.04	1971
Qatar	0.04	1971
Saudi Arabia	0.71	1945
Syria	0.05	1945
Tunisia	0.03	1956
Turkey	0.38	1945
United Arab Emirates	0.19	1971
Yemen	0.01	1947/67*

* The Yemen Arab Republic became a member of the UN in 1947, and the People's Democratic Republic of Yemen was admitted in 1967. The two countries formed the Republic of Yemen in 1990.

PERMANENT MISSIONS TO THE UNITED NATIONS

(with Permanent Representatives—August 1998)

Algeria: 326 East 48th St, New York, NY 10017; tel. (212) 750-1960; fax (212) 759-9538; e-mail dzaun@undp.org; ABDELLAH BAALI.

Bahrain: 2 United Nations Plaza, 25th Floor, New York, NY 10017; tel. (212) 223-6200; fax (212) 319-0687; e-mail bhrun@undp.org; JASSIM MOHAMMED BUALLAY.

Cyprus: 13 East 40th St, New York, NY 10016; tel. (212) 481-6023; fax (212) 685-7316; e-mail cypun@nygate.undp.org; SOTIRIOS ZACKHEOS.

Egypt: 36 East 67th St, New York, NY 10021; tel. (212) 879-6300; fax (212) 794-3874; e-mail egyun@undp.org; Dr NABIL A. ELARABY.

Iran: 622 Third Ave, 34th Floor, New York, NY 10017; tel. (212) 687-2020; fax (212) 867-7086; e-mail irnun@undp.org; HADI NEJAD-HOSSEINIAN.

Iraq: 14 East 79th St, New York, NY 10021; tel. (212) 737-4434; fax (212) 772-1794; e-mail irqun@undp.org; NIZAR HAMDOON.

Israel: 800 Second Ave, New York, NY 10017; tel. (212) 499-5510; fax (212) 499-5515; e-mail isrun@undp.org; DORE GOLD.

Jordan: 866 United Nations Plaza, Room 550–552, New York, NY 10017; tel. (212) 752-0135; fax (212) 826-0830; HASAN ABU-NIMAH.

Kuwait: 321 East 44th St, New York, NY 10017; tel. (212) 973-4300; fax (212) 370-1733; e-mail kwtun@undp.org; MOHAMMAD A. ABULHASAN.

Lebanon: 866 United Nations Plaza, Room 531–533, New York, NY 10017; tel. (212) 355-5460; fax (212) 838-2819; e-mail lbnun@undp.org; SAMIR MOUBARAK.

Libya: 309–315 East 48th St, New York, NY 10017; tel. (212) 752-5775; fax (212) 593-4787; ABUZED O. DORDA.

Morocco: 767 Third Ave, 30th Floor, New York, NY 10017; tel. (212) 421-1580; fax (212) 980-1512; e-mail marun@undp.org; AHMED SNOUSSI.

Oman: 866 United Nations Plaza, Suite 540, New York, NY 10017; tel. (212) 355-3505; fax (212) 644-0070; e-mail omnun@undp.org; SALIM BIN MUHAMMAD AL-KHUSSAIBY.

Qatar: 747 Third Ave, 22nd Floor, New York, NY 10017; tel. (212) 486-9335; fax (212) 758-4952; e-mail qatun@undp.org; NASSER BIN HAMAD AL-KHALIFA.

Saudi Arabia: 405 Lexington Ave, 56th Floor, New York, NY 10017; tel. (212) 697-4830; fax (212) 983-4895; e-mail sauun@undp.org; GAAFAR M. ALLAGANY (acting).

Syria: 820 Second Ave, 15th Floor, New York, NY 10017; tel. (212) 661-1313; fax (212) 983-4439; e-mail syrun@undp.org; Dr MIKHAIL WEHBE.

Tunisia: 31 Beekman Pl., New York, NY 10022; tel. (212) 751-7503; fax (212) 751-0569; e-mail tunun@undp.org; ALI HACHANI.

Turkey: 821 United Nations Plaza, 10th Floor, New York, NY 10017; tel. (212) 949-0150; fax (212) 949-0086; e-mail turkun@aol.com; VOLKAN VURAL.

United Arab Emirates: 747 Third Ave, 36th Floor, New York, NY 10017; tel. (212) 371-0480; fax (212) 371-4923; MOHAMMAD JASIM SAMHAN.

Yemen: 413 East 51st St, New York, NY 10022; tel. (212) 355-1730; fax (212) 750-9613; e-mail yemun@undp.org; ABDALLA SALEH AL-ASHTAL.

Observers

Asian-African Legal Consultative Committee: 404 East 66th St, Apt 12c, New York, NY 10021; tel. (212) 734-7608; e-mail 102077.27512@compuserve.com; K. BHAGWAT-SINGH.

Economic Co-operation Organization: c/o Permanent Mission of Pakistan to the UN, Pakistan House, 8 East 65th St, New York, NY 10021; tel. (212) 879-8600; fax (212) 744-7348.

International Committee of the Red Cross: 801 Second Ave, 18th Floor, New York, NY 10017; tel. (212) 599-6021; fax (212) 599-6009; e-mail mail@icrc.delnyc.org; SYLVIE JUNOD.

League of Arab States: 747 Third Ave, 35th Floor, New York, NY 10017; tel. (212) 838-8700; fax (212) 355-3909; MAHMOUD ABOUL-NASR.

Organization of the Islamic Conference: 130 East 40th St, 5th Floor, New York, NY 10016; tel. (212) 883-0140; fax (212) 883-0143; e-mail oicun@undp.org.

Palestine: 115 East 65th St, New York, NY 10021; tel. (212) 288-8500; fax (212) 517-2377; e-mail palestinun@aol.com; Dr NASSER AL-KIDWA.

GENERAL ASSEMBLY COMMITTEES CONCERNED WITH THE MIDDLE EAST

Committee on the Exercise of the Inalienable Rights of the Palestinian People: f. 1975; 23 members, elected by the General Assembly.

Special Committee on Peace-keeping Operations: f. 1965; 34 appointed members.

Economic Commission for Africa—ECA

Address: Africa Hall, POB 3001, Addis Ababa, Ethiopia.
Telephone: (1) 517200; **telex:** 21029; **fax:** (1) 512233; **e-mail:** ecainfo@un.org; **internet:** http://www.un.org/depts/eca.

The UN Economic Commission for Africa was founded in 1958 by a resolution of ECOSOC to initiate and take part in measures for facilitating Africa's economic development.

MEMBERS

Algeria	Eritrea	Niger
Angola	Ethiopia	Nigeria
Benin	Gabon	Rwanda
Botswana	The Gambia	São Tomé and
Burkina Faso	Ghana	Príncipe
Burundi	Guinea	Senegal
Cameroon	Guinea-Bissau	Seychelles
Cape Verde	Kenya	Sierra Leone
Central African	Lesotho	Somalia
Republic	Liberia	South Africa
Chad	Libya	Sudan
Comoros	Madagascar	Swaziland
Congo, Democratic	Malawi	Tanzania
Republic	Mali	Togo
Congo, Republic	Mauritania	Tunisia
Côte d'Ivoire	Mauritius	Uganda
Djibouti	Morocco	Zambia
Egypt	Mozambique	Zimbabwe
Equatorial Guinea	Namibia	

Organization

(August 1998)

COMMISSION

The Commission may only act with the agreement of the government of the country concerned. It is also empowered to make recommendations on any matter within its competence directly to the government of the member or associate member concerned, to governments admitted in a consultative capacity, and to the UN Specialized Agencies. The Commission is required to submit for prior consideration by ECOSOC any of its proposals for actions that would be likely to have important effects on the international economy.

CONFERENCE OF MINISTERS

The Conference, which meets every two years, is attended by ministers responsible for economic or financial affairs, planning and development of governments of member states, and is the main deliberative body of the Commission.

The Commission's responsibility to promote concerted action for the economic and social development of Africa is vested primarily in the Conference, which considers matters of general policy and the priorities to be assigned to the Commission's programmes, considers inter-African and international economic policy, and makes recommendations to member states in connection with such matters.

OTHER POLICY-MAKING BODIES

A Conference of Ministers of Finance and a Conference of Ministers responsible for economic and social development and planning meet in alternate years to formulate policy recommendations. Each is served by a committee of experts. Five intergovernmental committees of experts attached to the Subregional Development Centres (see below) meet annually and report to the Commission through a Technical Preparatory Committee of the Whole, which was established in 1979 to deal with matters submitted for the consideration of the Conference.

Seven other committees meet regularly to consider issues relating to the following policy areas: women and development; development information; sustainable development; human development and civil society; industry and private sector development; natural resources and science and technology; and regional co-operation and integration.

SECRETARIAT

The Secretariat provides the services necessary for the meeting of the Conference of Ministers and the meetings of the Commission's subsidiary bodies, carries out the resolutions and implements the programmes adopted there. It comprises an Office of the Executive Secretary and the following eight divisions: Food Security and Sustainable Development; Development Management; Development Information Services; Regional Co-operation and Integration; Programme Planning, Finance and Evaluation; Economic and Social Policy; Human Resources and System Management; Conference and General Services.

Executive Secretary: KINGSLEY Y. AMOAKO (Ghana).

SUBREGIONAL DEVELOPMENT CENTRES

Multinational Programming and Operational Centres (MULPOCs) were established, in 1977, to implement regional development programmes. In May 1997 the Commission decided to transform the MULPOCs into Subregional Development Centres (SRDCs) in order to enable member states to play a more effective role in the process of African integration and to facilitate the integration efforts of the other UN agencies active in the subregions. In addition, the SRDCs were to act as the operational arms of ECA at national and subregional levels: to ensure harmony between the objectives of subregional and regional programmes and those defined by the Commission; to provide advisory services; to facilitate subregional economic co-operation, integration and development; to collect and disseminate information; to stimulate policy dialogue; and to promote gender issues. In July 1997 it was reported that ECA intended to deploy 25% of its professional personnel in the SRDCs (up from 9%) and to allocate approximately 40% of its budget to the Centres. SRDCs are located in Yaoundé, Cameroon (serving eight countries in central Africa), Addis Ababa, Ethiopia (12 countries in east Africa), Lusaka, Zambia (11 countries in southern Africa), Niamey, Niger (15 countries in west Africa) and Tangier, Morocco (seven countries in north Africa).

Activities

The Commission's activities are designed to encourage sustainable socio-economic development in Africa and to increase economic co-operation among African countries and between Africa and other parts of the world. The Secretariat is guided in its efforts by major regional strategies including the Abuja Treaty establishing the African Economic Community signed under the aegis of the Organization of African Unity and the UN New Agenda for the Development of Africa covering the period 1991–2000. ECA's main programme areas for the period 1996–2001 were based on an Agenda for Action, which was announced by the OAU Council of Ministers in March 1995 and adopted by African heads of state in June, with the stated aim of 'relaunching Africa's economic and social development'. The five overall objectives were to facilitate economic and social policy analysis and implementation; to ensure food security and sustainable development; to strengthen development management; to harness information for development; and to promote regional co-operation and integration. In all its activities ECA aimed to promote the themes of capacity-building and of fostering leadership and the empowerment of women in Africa. In May 1998 ECA's African Centre for Women inaugurated a new Fund for African Women's Development to support capacity-building activities.

DEVELOPMENT INFORMATION SYSTEMS

The Pan-African Documentation and Information Service (PADIS) was established in 1980. The main objectives of PADIS are: to provide access to numerical and other information on African social, economic, scientific and technological development issues; to assist African countries in their efforts to develop national information handling capabilities through advisory services and training; to establish a data communication network to facilitate the timely use of information on development; and to design sound technical specifications, norms and standards to minimize technical barriers in the exchange of information. ECA is promoting the use of electronic systems to disseminate information throughout the region, under its commitment for the period 1996–2001 to harness information for development purposes. ECA aims to co-ordinate the implementation of the African Information Society Initiative (AISI), a framework for creating an information and communications infrastructure. In addition, ECA encourages member governments to liberalize the telecommunications sector and stimulate imports of computers in order to enable the expansion of information technology throughout Africa.

ECA also promotes the development and co-ordination of national statistical services in the region and undertakes the collection, evaluation and dissemination of statistical information. ECA's work in the field of statistics has been concentrated in five main areas: the African Household Survey Capability Programme, which aims to assist in the collection and analysis of demographic, social and economic data on households; the Statistical Training Programme for Africa, which aims to make the region self-sufficient in statistical personnel at all levels; the Technical Support Services, which provide technical advisory services for population censuses, demographic surveys and civil registration; the National Accounts Capability Programme, which aims at improving economic statistics generally by building up a capability in each country for the collection, processing and analysis of economic data; and the ECA-Regional Statistical Data Base, part of PADIS, which provides on-line statistical information to users. In 1997 ECA planned to upgrade its statistical database in order to provide a data services centre for the region.

ECA assists its member states in (i) population data collection and data processing; (ii) analysis of demographic data obtained from censuses or surveys; (iii) training demographers at the Regional Institute for Population Studies (RIPS) in Accra, Ghana, and at the Institut de formation et de recherche démographiques (IFORD) in Yaoundé, Cameroon; (iv) formulation of population policies and integrating population variables in development planning, through advisory missions and through the organization of national seminars on population and development; and (v) dissemination of information through its *Newsletter, Demographic Handbook for Africa,* the *African Population Studies* series and other publications. The strengthening of national population policies was an important element of ECA's objective of ensuring food security in African countries. The Ninth Joint Conference of African Planners, Statisticians and Demographers was held in March 1996, in Addis Ababa, Ethiopia.

DEVELOPMENT MANAGEMENT

ECA aims to assist governments, public corporations, universities and the private sector in improving their financial management; strengthening policy-making and analytical capacities; adopting measures to redress skill shortages; enhancing human resources development and utilization; and promoting social development through programmes focusing on youth, people with disabilities and the elderly. The Secretariat organizes training workshops, seminars and conferences at national, subregional and regional levels for ministers, public administrators and senior policy-makers, as well as for private and non-governmental organizations. ECA aims to increase the participation of women in economic development and incorporates this objective into its administrative activities and work programmes.

Following the failure to implement many of the proposals under the UN Industrial Development Decade for Africa (IDDA, 1980–90) and the UN Programme of Action for African Economic Recovery and Development (1986–90), a second IDDA was adopted by the Conference of African Ministers of Industry in July 1991. The main objectives of the second IDDA include the consolidation and rehabilitation of existing industries, the expansion of new investments, and the promotion of small-scale industries and technological capabilities. In June 1996 a conference, organized by ECA, was held in Accra, Ghana, with the aim of reviving private investment in Africa in order to stimulate the private sector and promote future economic development. The conference established a forum for African political leaders and business executives to discuss the development of capital markets in the region and to co-ordinate efforts in sectoral training and research.

In 1997 ECA hosted the first of a series of meetings on good governance, in the context of the UN system-wide Special Initiative on Africa. The second African Governance Forum (AGF II) was held in Accra, Ghana, in June 1998. The Forum focused on accountability and transparency, which participants agreed were essential elements in promoting development in Africa and should involve commitment from both governments and civil organizations. A third AGF was to be held in Mali, in 1999, to consider issues relating to conflict prevention, management and governance.

ECONOMIC AND SOCIAL POLICY

The Economic and Social Policy division concentrates on the following areas: economic policy analysis, social policy and poverty analysis, and the co-ordination and monitoring of special issues and programmes. Monitoring economic and social trends in the African region and studying the development problems concerning it are among the fundamental tasks of the Commission, while the special issues programme updates legislative bodies regarding the progress made in the implementation of initiatives affecting the continent. Every year the Commission publishes the *Survey of Economic and Social Conditions in Africa* and the *Economic Report on Africa.*

The Commission gives assistance to governments in general economic analysis, fiscal, financial and monetary management, trade liberalization, regional integration and planning. The ECA's work on economic planning has been broadened in recent years, in order to give more emphasis to macro-economic management in a mixed economy approach: a project is being undertaken to develop short-term forecasting and policy models to support economic management. The Commission has also undertaken a major study of the

informal sector in African countries. Special assistance is given to least-developed, land-locked and island countries which have a much lower income level than other countries and which are faced with heavier constraints. Studies are also undertaken to assist longer-term planning.

In May 1994 ECA ministers of economic and social development and of planning, meeting in Addis Ababa, adopted a *Framework Agenda for Building and Utilizing Critical Capacities in Africa.* The agenda aimed to identify new priority areas to stimulate development by, for example, strengthening management structures, a more efficient use of a country's physical infrastructure and by expanding processing or manufacturing facilities.

ECA aims to strengthen African participation in international negotiations. To this end, assistance has been provided to member states in the ongoing multilateral trade negotiations under the World Trade Organization; in the annual conferences of the IMF and the World Bank; in negotiations with the EU; and in meetings related to economic co-operation among developing countries. Studies have been prepared on problems and prospects likely to arise for the African region from the implementation of the Common Fund for Commodities and the Generalized System of Trade Preferences (both supervised by UNCTAD); the impacts of exchange-rate fluctuations on the economies of African countries; and on the long-term implications of different debt arrangements for African economies. ECA assists individual member states by undertaking studies on domestic trade, expansion of inter-African trade, transnational corporations, integration of women in trade and development, and strengthening the capacities of state-trading organizations. ECA encourages the diversification of production, the liberalization of cross-border trade and the expansion of domestic trade structures, within regional economic groupings, in order to promote intra-African trade. ECA also helps to organize regional and 'All-Africa' trade fairs.

In March/April 1997 the Conference of African Ministers of Finance, meeting in Addis Ababa, reviewed a new initiative of the World Bank and IMF to assist the world's 41 most heavily-indebted poor countries, of which 33 were identified as being in sub-Saharan Africa. While the Conference recognized the importance of the involvement of multilateral institutions in assisting African economies to achieve a sustainable level of development, it criticized aspects of the structural adjustment programmes imposed by the institutions and advocated more flexible criteria to determine eligibility for the new initiative.

In 1997, with regard to social policy, ECA was focusing upon improving the socio-economic prospects of women through the promotion of social and legal equality, increasing opportunities for entering higher education and monitoring the prevalence of poverty.

FOOD SECURITY AND SUSTAINABLE DEVELOPMENT

During 1991–92 reports were compiled on the development, implementation and sound management of environmental programmes at national, subregional and regional levels. ECA members adopted a common African position for the UN Conference on Environment and Development, held in June 1992. In 1995 ECA published its first comprehensive report and statistical survey of human development issues in African countries. The *Human Development in Africa Report,* which was to be published every two years, aimed to demonstrate levels of development attained, particularly in the education and child health sectors, to identify areas of concern and to encourage further action by policy-makers and development experts. In 1997 ECA was actively involved in the promotion of food security in African countries and the study of the relationship between population, food security, the environment and sustainable development.

PROGRAMME PLANNING, FINANCE AND EVALUATION

ECA provides guidance in the formulation of policies towards the achievement of Africa's development objectives to the policy-making organs of the UN and OAU. It contributes to the work of the General Assembly and other specialized agencies by providing an African perspective in the preparation of development strategies. In March 1996 the UN announced a system-wide Special Initiative on Africa to mobilize resources and to implement a series of political and economic development objectives over a 10-year period. ECA's Executive Secretary is the Co-Chair, with the Administrator of the UNDP, of the Steering Committee for the Initiative.

REGIONAL CO-OPERATION AND INTEGRATION

The Regional Co-operation and Integration Division administers the transport and communications and mineral and energy sectors, in addition to its activities concerning the Subregional Development Centres (SRDCs—see above), the integrated development of transboundary water resources, and facilitating and enhancing the process of regional economic integration.

The ECA was appointed lead agency for the second United Nations Transport and Communications Decade in Africa (UNTACDA II), comprising the period 1991–2000. The principal aim of UNTACDA II is the establishment of an efficient, integrated transport and communications system in Africa. The specific objectives of the programme include: (i) the removal of physical and non-physical barriers to intra-African trade and travel, and improvement in the road transport sector; (ii) improvement in the efficiency and financial viability of railways; (iii) development of Africa's shipping capacity and improvement in the performance of Africa's ports; (iv) development of integrated transport systems for each lake and river basin; (v) improvement of integration of all modes of transport in order to carry cargo in one chain of transport smoothly; (vi) integration of African airlines, and restructuring of civil aviation and airport management authorities; (vii) improvement in the quality and availability of transport in urban areas; (viii) development of integrated regional telecommunications networks; (ix) development of broadcasting services, with the aim of supporting socio-economic development; and (x) expansion of Africa's postal network. ECA is the co-ordinator, with the World Bank, of a regional Road Maintenance Initiative, which was launched in 1988. By early 1996 13 African countries were receiving assistance under the initiative, which sought to encourage a partnership between the public and private sectors to manage and maintain road infrastructure more efficiently and thus to improve country-wide communications and transportation activities. The third African road safety congress was held in April 1997, in Pretoria, South Africa. The congress, which was jointly organized by ECA and the OECD, aimed to increase awareness of the need to adopt an integrated approach to road safety problems. During 1998 transport activities were to include consideration of a new African air transport policy, workshops on port restructuring, and regional and country analyses of transport trends and reforms.

The Fourth Regional Conference on the Development and Utilization of Mineral Resources in Africa, held in March 1991, adopted an action plan that included the formulation of national mineral exploitation policies; and the promotion of the gemstone industry, small-scale mining and the iron and steel industry. ECA supports the Southern African Mineral Resources Development Centre in Dar-es-Salaam, Tanzania, and the Central African Mineral Development Centre in Brazzaville, Republic of the Congo, which provide advisory and laboratory services to their respective member states.

ECA's Energy Programme provides assistance to member states in the development of indigenous energy resources and the formulation of energy policies to extricate member states from continued energy crises. In 1997 ECA strengthened co-operation with the World Energy Council and agreed to help implement the Council's African Energy Programme.

ECA assists member states in the assessment and use of water resources and the development of river and lake basins common to more than one country. ECA encourages co-operation between

The United Nations in the Middle East and North Africa

countries with regard to water issues and collaborates with other UN agencies and regional organizations to promote technical and economic co-operation in this area. ECA has been particularly active in efforts to promote the integrated development of the water resources of the Zambezi river basin. During 1998 ECA planned to organize a meeting of the countries of the Zambezi basin, and was also committed to enhancing collaboration with sub-regional groupings for the development of other river basins and of Lake Victoria.

In all of its activities ECA aims to strengthen institutional capacities in order to support the process of regional integration, and aims to assist countries to implement existing co-operative agreements, for example by promoting the harmonization of macroeconomic and taxation policies and the removal of non-tariff barriers to trade.

BUDGET

For the two-year period 1998–99 ECA's regular budget, an appropriation from the UN budget, was an estimated US $89.6m.

PUBLICATIONS

Annual Report of the ECA.
Africa Index (2 a year).
African Population Newsletter (2 a year).
African Population Studies series (irregular).
African Socio-Economic Indicators (annually).
African Statistical Yearbook.
African Trade Bulletin (2 a year).
African Women Report (annually).
Compendium of Intra-African and Related Foreign Trade Statistics.
Demographic Handbook for Africa (irregular).
Devindex Africa (quarterly).
Directory of African Statisticians (every 2 years).
ECA Development Policy Review.
ECA Environment Newsletter (3 a year).
Flash on Trade Opportunities (quarterly).
Focus on African Industry (2 a year).
Human Development in Africa Report (every two years).
PADIS Newsletter (quarterly).
Report of the Executive Secretary (every 2 years).
Rural Progress (2 a year).
Statistical Newsletter (2 a year).
Survey of Economic and Social Conditions in Africa (annually).

Economic and Social Commission for Western Asia—ESCWA

Address: Riad el-Solh Sq., POB 11-8575, Beirut, Lebanon.
Telephone (1) 981301; **telex:** 216917; **fax:** (1) 981510; **internet:** http://www.escwa.org.lb.

The UN Economic Commission for Western Asia was established in 1974 by a resolution of the UN Economic and Social Council (ECOSOC), to provide facilities of a wider scope for those countries previously served by the UN Economic and Social Office in Beirut (UNESOB). The name 'Economic and Social Commission for Western Asia' (ESCWA) was adopted in 1985.

MEMBERS

Bahrain	Palestine
Egypt	Qatar
Iraq	Saudi Arabia
Jordan	Syria
Kuwait	United Arab Emirates
Lebanon	Yemen
Oman	

Organization

(August 1998)

COMMISSION

The sessions of the Commission (held every two years) are attended by representatives of member states, of UN bodies and specialized

agencies, of regional and intergovernmental organizations, and of other UN member states attending as observers.

TECHNICAL COMMITTEE

The Committee, formally the Standing Committee of the Programme, is the principal subsidiary body of the Commission and functions as its policy-making structure. Six specialized inter-governmental committees have been established to consider specific areas of activity, to report on these to the Technical Committee and to assist the Committee in formulating ESCWA's medium-term work programmes.

Statistical Committee: first session convened in 1995; to meet every two years.

Committee on Social Development: established in 1994; to meet every two years, from 1997.

Committee on Energy: established in 1995; to meet every two years, from 1997.

Committee on Water Resources: established in 1995; to meet annually, from 1997.

Committee on Transport: established in 1997; to meet every two years, from 1999.

Committee on Liberalization of Foreign Trade and Economic Globalization: established in 1997; to meet annually, from 1998.

SECRETARIAT

The Secretariat comprises an Executive Secretary, a Deputy Executive Secretary, a Senior Advisor and Secretary of the Commission, an Information Services Unit and a Programme Planning and Co-ordination Unit. ESCWA's technical and substantive activities are undertaken by the following divisions: energy, natural resources and environment; social development issues and policies; economic development issues and policies; sectoral issues and policies; statistics; and technical co-operation.

Executive Secretary: Dr HAZEM ABD EL-AZIZ EL-BEBLAWI (Egypt).

Activities

ESCWA is responsible for proposing policies and actions to support development and to further economic co-operation and integration in western Asia. ESCWA undertakes or sponsors studies of economic social and development issues of the region, collects and disseminates information, and provides advisory services to member states in various fields of economic and social development. It also organizes conferences and intergovernmental and export group meetings and sponsors training workshops and seminars.

Much of ESCWA's work is carried out in co-operation with other UN bodies, as well as with other international and regional organizations, for example the League of Arab States (q.v.) the Co-operation Council for the Arab States of the Gulf (q.v.) and the Organization of the Islamic Conference (OIC, q.v.).

ESCWA works within the framework of medium-term plans, which are divided into two-year programmes of action and priorities. The biennium 1994–95 was considered to be a transitional period during which the Commission restructured its work programme. This restructuring focused ESCWA activities from 15 to five sub-programmes. A further reorganization of the sub-programmes was implemented in 1997 to provide the framework for activities in the medium-term period 1998–2001.

MANAGEMENT OF NATURAL RESOURCES AND ENVIRONMENT

The main objective of the sub-programme was to promote regional co-ordination and co-operation in the management of natural resources, in particular water resources and energy, and the protection of the environment. The sub-programme aimed to counter the problem of an increasing shortage of freshwater resources and deterioration in water quality resulting from population growth, agricultural land-use and socio-economic development, by supporting measures for more rational use and conservation of water resources, and by promoting public awareness and community participation in water and environmental protection projects. In addition, ESCWA aimed to assist governments in the formulation and implementation of capacity-building programmes and the development of surface and groundwater resources.

ESCWA supports co-operation in the establishment of electricity distribution and supply networks throughout the region and promotes the use of alternative sources of energy and the development of new and renewable energy technologies. Similarly, ESCWA promotes the application of environmentally-sound technologies in order to achieve sustainable development, as well as measures to recycle resources, minimize waste and reduce the environmental impact of transport operations and energy use. Under the sub-programme ESCWA was to collaborate with national, regional and international organizations in monitoring and reporting on emerging environmental issues and to pursue implementation of Agenda 21, which was adopted at the June 1992 UN conference on Environment and Development, with particular regard to land and water resource management and conservation.

IMPROVEMENT OF THE QUALITY OF LIFE

ESCWA's key areas of activity in this sub-programme were population, human development, the advancement of women and human settlements, and, in particular, to pursue the implementation of recommendations relevant to the region of the four UN world conferences held on these themes during the mid-1990s.

ESCWA's objectives with regard to population were to increase awareness and understanding of links between population factors and poverty, human rights and the environment, and to strengthen the capacities of member states to analyse and assess demographic trends and migration. The main aim in the area of human development was to further the alleviation of poverty and to generate a sustainable approach to development through, for example, greater involvement of community groups in decision-making and projects to strengthen production and income-generating capabilities. The sub-programme incorporated activies to ensure all gender-related recommendations of the four world conferences could be pursued in the region, including support for the role of the family and assistance to organizations for monitoring and promoting the advancement of women. With regard to human settlements, the objectives of the sub-programme were to monitor and identify problems resulting from rapid urbanization and social change, to promote understanding and awareness of the problems and needs of human settlements, and to strengthen the capacity of governments in the region in formulating appropriate policies and strategies for sustainable human settlement development.

ECONOMIC DEVELOPMENT AND GLOBAL CHANGES

During the period 1998–2001 ESCWA aimed to support member states in their understanding of the process of globalization of the world economy and their participation in international trading negotiations and arrangements. ESCWA also aimed to strengthen the capacity of members in implementing economic reform policies, financial management and other structural adjustment measures, and to facilitate intra-regional trade, investment and capital movements.

CO-ORDINATION OF POLICIES AND HARMONIZATION OF NORMS AND REGULATIONS FOR SECTORAL DEVELOPMENT

This sub-programme was concerned with the harmonization of standards throughout the region in the areas of transport, industry, agriculture and technology. ESCWA aimed to promote co-operation among member states in transport and infrastructure policies and greater uniformity of safety and legal standards, the latter with a view to facilitating border crossings between countries in the region. ESCWA, similarly, aimed to assist local industries to meet regional and international standards and regulations, as well as to improve the competitiveness of industries through the development of skills and policies and greater co-operation with other national and regional support institutions. ESCWA strategies to develop the agricultural potential of member states included resource conservation activities, agricultural management, institution-building and harmonization of regulations and norms. In the field of technology the sub-programme was designed to strengthen the capabilities of member states, to promote the transfer of technologies, research and development activities, and to enhance collaboration in the production sector.

DEVELOPMENT, CO-ORDINATION AND HARMONIZATION OF STATISTICS AND INFORMATION

In the medium-term ESCWA aimed to develop the statistical systems of member states in order to improve the relevance and accuracy of economic and social data, and to implement measures to make the information more accessible to planners and researchers. ESCWA also intended to promote the comparability of statistics, through implementation of various standard international systems and programmes, particularly focusing on a series of national population and housing censuses scheduled to be conducted in the region in 2000.

BUDGET

ESCWA's share of the UN budget for the two years 1998–99 was US $49.5m., compared with $33.2m. for the previous biennium.

PUBLICATIONS

All publications are annual, unless otherwise indicated.

Agriculture and Development in Western Asia.
External Trade Bulletin of the ESCWA Region.
National Accounts Studies of the ESCWA Region.
Population Bulletin of the ESCWA Region.
Prices and Financial Statistics in the ESCWA Region.
Socio-economic Data Sheet (every 2 years).
Statistical Abstract.
Survey of Economic and Social Developments in the ESCWA Region.
Transport Bulletin.

United Nations Development Programme—UNDP

Address: One United Nations Plaza, New York, NY 10017, USA.
Telephone: (212) 906-5000; **fax:** (212) 826-2057; **internet:** http://www.undp.org.

The Programme was established in 1965 by the UN General Assembly. Its central mission is to help countries eradicate poverty and achieve a sustainable level of human development.

Organization

(August 1998)

UNDP is responsible to the UN General Assembly, to which it reports through the UN Economic and Social Council.

EXECUTIVE BOARD

The 36-member Executive Board is responsible for providing inter-governmental support to and supervision of the activities of UNDP and the UN Population Fund (UNFPA, of which UNDP is the governing body).

SECRETARIAT

Administrator: JAMES GUSTAVE SPETH (USA).

REGIONAL OFFICES

Headed by assistant administrators, the regional bureaux share the responsibility for implementing the programme with the Administrator's office. Within certain limitations, large-scale projects may be approved and funding allocated by the Administrator, and smaller-scale projects by the Resident Representatives, based in 136 countries.

Five regional bureaux, all at the Secretariat in New York, cover: Africa; Asia and the Pacific; the Arab states; Latin America and the Caribbean; and Europe and the Commonwealth of Independent States. There is also a Division for Global and Interregional Programmes.

Assistant Administrator and Director of the Regional Bureau for Arab States: SAAD ALFARARGI (Egypt).

FIELD OFFICES

In almost every country receiving UNDP assistance there is a country office, headed by the UNDP Resident Representative, who advises the government on formulating the country programme, sees that field activities are carried out, and acts as the leader of the UN team of experts working in the country. Resident Representatives are normally designated as co-ordinators for all UN operational development activities; the field offices function as the primary presence of the UN in most developing countries.

OFFICES OF UNDP REPRESENTATIVES IN THE MIDDLE EAST AND NORTH AFRICA

Algeria: 19 ave Chahid el-Quali, Mustapha Sayed, BP 823, Algiers 16000; tel. (2) 74-49-02; telex 66144; fax (2) 74-50-82.

Bahrain: Bldg 1083 Rd No 4225, Juffair 342, POB 26814, Manama; tel. 729922; telex 8337; fax 729922; e-mail fo.bhr@undp.org.

Cyprus: POB 5605, 1311 Nicosia; tel. (2) 303194; fax (2) 366125; e-mail fo.cyp@undp.org.

Egypt: World Trade Centre Bldg, 4th Floor, 1191 Corniche El-Nil St, Boulak, POB 982, Cairo; tel. (2) 5784840; telex 2034; fax (2) 5784847; e-mail fo.egy@undp.org.

Iran: United Nations Bldg, 185 Ghaem Magham Farahani Ave, POB 15875-4557, Teheran 15868; tel. (21) 8732812; telex 212397; fax (21) 8738864.

Iraq: Bldg No. 153, 102 Abi Nawas St, POB 2048 (Alwiyah), Baghdad; tel. (1) 887-2229; telex 212271; fax (1) 886-2523.

Jordan: Hirbawi Bldg, 'Obadah Ibn Al-Samet St, POB 35286, Amman; tel. (6) 5668177; telex 21654; fax (6) 5676582.

Kuwait: St No. 7, Block No. 12, Villa No. 145, Jabriya, POB 2993 Safat; tel. 5325968; telex 23138; fax 5325879; e-mail fo.kwt@undp.org.

Lebanon: POB 11–3216, UN House, Capt. Ali Ahmed Bldg, Bir Hassan (near Kuwaiti embassy), Beirut; tel. (1) 822146; fax (1) 603461; e-mail fo.leb@undp.org.

Libya: 67–71 Turkiya St, POB 358, Tripoli; tel. (21) 333-6297; telex 20582; fax (21) 333-0856.

Morocco: Immeuble de l'ONU, Angle ave Moulay Hassan et rue Assafi, Rabat; tel. (7) 703555; telex 31952; fax (7) 701566; e-mail fo.mor@undp.org.

Qatar: Fariq Bin Omran (near English Speaking School and Doha Players' Theatre), Box 3233, Doha; tel. 863260; fax 861552.

Saudi Arabia: POB 558, King Faysal St, Riyadh 11421; tel. (1) 465-3157; telex 401018; fax (1) 465-2087; e-mail fo.san@undp.org.

Syria: Abou Roumaneh 28, al-Jala'a St, POB 2317, Damascus; tel. (11) 3332440; telex 411123; fax (11) 3327764.

Tunisia: 61 blvd Bab Benat, BP 863, Tunis 1035; tel. (1) 5264-011; fax (1) 560-094; e-mail fo.tun@undp.org.

Turkey: 197 Atatürk Bul., 06680 Kavaklıdere, PK 407, Ankara; tel. (312) 4268113; telex 44584; fax (312) 4261372; e-mail fo.tur@undp.org.

United Arab Emirates: Sheikh Khalifa bin Shakhbout St, West 17/1 Villa no. 41, POB 3490, Abu Dhabi; tel. (2) 655600; telex 22727; fax (2) 650818; e-mail undp@emirates.net.ae.

Yemen: Al-Khorashi Bldg, opposite Awqaf Housing Complex, Shar'a Siteen, POB 551, San'a; tel. (1) 415505; telex 2234; fax (1) 4125411; e-mail fo.yem@undp.org.

There is also a UNDP office in the 'Occupied Palestinian Territories' (POB 51359, 4A Ya'kubi St, Jerusalem 91513; tel. 2-6277337; telex 25282; fax 2-6280089).

Activities

As the world's largest source of grant technical assistance in developing countries, UNDP works with more than 150 governments and 40 international agencies for faster economic growth and better standards of living throughout the world. Most of the work is undertaken in the field by the various United Nations agencies, or by the government of the country concerned. UNDP is committed to allocating some 87% of its core resources to low-income countries with an annual income per caput of less than US $750, while 60% of resources are allocated to the world's least-developed countries.

Assistance is mostly non-monetary, comprising the provision of experts' services, consultancies, equipment, and fellowships for advanced study abroad. In 1996 35% of spending on projects was for the services of experts, 25% was for subcontracts, 18% for equipment, 16% for training, and the remainder was for other costs, such as technical support. Most UNDP projects incorporate training for local workers. Developing countries themselves provide 50% or more of the total project costs in terms of personnel, facilities, equipment and supplies. In 1996 UNDP expenditure, on projects in the Arab states (i.e. excluding Cyprus, Iran and Turkey) amounted to US $61m., or 5% of the total field programme expenditure.

In June 1994 the Executive Board adopted a programme for change which focused on UNDP's role in achieving sustainable human development, an approach to economic growth that encompasses individual well-being and choice, equitable distribution of the benefits of development and conservation of the environment. Within this framework there were to be four priority objectives: poverty elimination; the expansion of employment opportunities; environmental regeneration; and the advancement and empowerment of women. A new Office of Evaluation and Strategic Planning was established to facilitate the restructuring required by these changes, while an Office of UN System Support and Services has been created to assist in unifying various UN agencies around the new framework for sustainable human development. The allocation of programming resources since 1994 has reflected UNDP's new agenda, with 39% of core funding directed towards poverty eradication and livelihoods for the poor, 32% to capacity-building and governance, and 21% to projects concerned with the environment and natural resources. Some 20% of total resources are allocated to promoting gender equality in all UNDP activities.

Approximately one-third of all UNDP programme resources support national efforts to ensure efficient governance and to build effective relations between the state, the private sector and civil society, which are essential to achieving sustainable development. UNDP undertakes assessment missions to help ensure free and fair elections and works to promote human rights, an accountable and competent public sector, a competent judicial system and decentralized government and decision-making. In July 1997 UNDP organized an International Conference on Governance for Sustainable Growth and Equity, which was held in New York, USA, and attended by more than 1,000 representatives of national and local authorities and the business and non-governmental sectors. At the Conference UNDP initiated a four-year programme to promote activities and to encourage new approaches in support of good governance. UNDP's Local Initiative Facility for Urban Environment (LIFE) undertakes small-scale environmental projects in low-income communities, in collaboration with local authorities and community-based groups.

LIFE was initiated at the UN Conference on Environment and Development, which was held in June 1992. UNDP supports the development of national programmes that emphasize the sustainable management of natural resources, for example through its Sustainable Energy Initiative, which promotes more efficient use of energy resources and the introduction of renewable alternatives to conventional fuels. UNDP is also concerned with forest management, the aquatic environment and sustainable agriculture and food security.

UNDP aims to help governments to reassess their development priorities and to design initiatives for sustainable development at a country-specific level. UNDP country offices support the formulation of national human development reports (NHDRs), which aim to facilitate activities such as policy-making, the allocation of resources and monitoring progress towards poverty eradication and sustainable development. By 1996 four countries in the Middle East and North African region (Cyprus, Egypt, Iraq and Turkey) had produced NHDRs. In addition, the preparation of Advisory Notes and Country Co-operation Frameworks help to highlight country-specific aspects of poverty eradication and national strategic priorities. Since 1990 UNDP has published an annual *Human Development Report*, incorporating a Human Development Index, which ranks countries in terms of human development, using three key indicators: life expectancy, adult literacy and basic income required for a decent standard of living. In 1997 a Human Poverty Index and a Gender-related Development Index, which assesses gender equality on the basis of life expectancy, education and income, were introduced into the Report for the first time.

In 1994 the Executive Board determined that UNDP should assume a more active and integrative role within the UN development system. This approach has been implemented by UNDP Resident Representatives, who aim to co-ordinate UN policies to achieve sustainable human development, in consultation with other agencies, in particular UNEP, FAO and UNHCR. In 1997 UNDP planned to allocate more resources to training and skill-sharing programmes in order to promote this co-ordinating role. UNDP is a co-sponsor, jointly with WHO, the World Bank, UNICEF, UNESCO and UNFPA, of a Joint UN Programme on HIV and AIDS, which became operational on 1 January 1996. UNDP was also to develop its role in co-ordinating activities following global UN conferences. In March 1995 government representatives attending the World Summit for Social Development, which was held in Copenhagen, Denmark, adopted the Copenhagen Declaration and a Programme of Action, which included initiatives to promote the eradication of poverty, to increase and reallocate official development assistance to basic social programmes and to promote equal access to education. With particular reference to UNDP, the Programme of Action advocated that UNDP support the implementation of social development programmes, co-ordinate these efforts through its field offices and organize efforts on the part of the UN system to stimulate capacity-building at local, national and regional levels. By 1996 a new Poverty Strategy Initiative was being implemented in more than 60 countries, while other activities were directed towards strengthening the private sectors in developing countries, in particular through the provision of financing for micro-enterprises, and creating the capacity for sound economic management and good governance. Following the UN Fourth World Conference on Women, held in Beijing, People's Republic of China, in September 1995, UNDP has led inter-agency efforts to ensure the full participation of women in all economic, political and professional activities, and has assisted with further situation analysis and training activities. (UNDP also created a Gender in Development Office to ensure that women participate more fully in UNDP-sponsored activities.) UNDP played an important role, at both national and international levels, in preparing for the second UN Conference on Human Settlements (Habitat II), which was held in Istanbul, Turkey, in June 1996. At the conference UNDP announced the establishment of a new facility, which was designed to promote private-sector investment in urban infrastructure. The facility was to be allocated inititial resources of US $10m., with the aim of generating a total of $1,000m. from private sources for this sector.

In February 1994 a new regional programme for the period 1994–96 was approved by a UNDP intergovernmental meeting of Arab states, that was convened in Yemen. The programme identified three new initiatives: incorporating human development issues into the region's development planning and resource allocation; an economic integration and trade initiative to improve the capacity for intra-regional trade; and promoting sustainable energy through public awareness programmes and the introduction of energy-saving techniques. UNDP supports a Mediterranean environmental technical assistance programme, which aims to promote the exchange of information between countries in the region and to focus resources on capacity-building and investment preparation projects.

In the mid-1990s UNDP expanded its role in countries in crisis and with special circumstances, working in collaboration with other UN agencies to promote relief and development efforts. In particular, UNDP was concerned to achieve reconciliation, reintegration and reconstruction in affected countries, as well as to support emergency interventions and manage the delivery of programme aid. In 1996 20 new special development initiatives were undertaken, including socio-economic rehabilitation in Lebanon and environmental improvements in areas of resettlement in Gaza and the West Bank. In addition, UNDP extended its Disaster Management Training Programme, in order, partly, to help countries meet the objectives of the International Decade for Natural Disaster Reduction (announced in 1990).

During 1996 UNDP implemented its first corporate communications and advocacy strategy, which aimed to generate public awareness of the activities of the UN system, to promote debate on development issues and to mobilize resources by increasing public and donor appreciation of UNDP. A series of national and regional workshops was held, while media activities focused on the publication of the annual *Human Development Report* and the International Day for the Eradication of Poverty, held on 17 October. UNDP aims to use the developments in information technology to advance its communications strategy and to disseminate guidelines and technical support throughout its country office network.

FINANCE

UNDP and its various funds and programmes (see below) are financed by the voluntary contributions of members of the United Nations and the Programme's participating agencies, as well as through cost-sharing by recipient governments and third-party donors. In 1996 total voluntary contributions amounted to US $2,186m., including $844m. to the Programme's core resources. In that year core expenditure on field programme activities amounted to $1,211m.

PUBLICATIONS

Annual Report.

Human Development Report (annually).

Choices (quarterly).

Co-operation South (quarterly).

Associated Funds and Programmes

UNDP is the central funding, planning and co-ordinating body for technical co-operation within the UN. Associated funds and programmes, financed separately by means of voluntary contributions, provide specific services through the UNDP network. In 1996 expenditure on projects carried out under the aegis of these funds and programmes amounted to US $263.3m.

CAPACITY 21

UNDP initiated Capacity 21 at the UN Conference on Environment and Development, which was held in June 1992, to support developing countries in preparing and implementing policies for sustainable development (i.e. the objectives of Agenda 21, which was adopted by the Conference). Capacity 21 promotes new approaches to development, through national development strategies, community-based management and training programmes. Programme expenditure in 1996 totalled US $7.4m.

GLOBAL ENVIRONMENT FACILITY—GEF

The GEF, which is managed jointly by UNDP, the World Bank and UNEP, began operations in 1991, with funding of US $1,500m. over a three-year period. Its aim is to support projects for the prevention of climate change, conserving biological diversity, protecting international waters, and reducing the depletion of the ozone layer in the atmosphere. UNDP is responsible for capacity-building, targeted research, pre-investment activities and technical assistance. UNDP also administers the Small Grants Programme of the GEF, which supports community-based activities by local non-governmental organizations. During the pilot phase of the GEF, in the period 1991–94, $242.5m. in funding was approved for 55 UNDP projects; by mid–1996 53 of these were being implemented. In March 1994 representatives of 87 countries agreed to provide $2,000m. to replenish GEF funds for a further three-year period from July of that year. Programme expenditure in 1996 amounted to $50.4m.

PROGRAMME OF ASSISTANCE TO THE PALESTINIAN PEOPLE—PAPP

PAPP is committed to strengthening newly-created institutions, to creating employment opportunities and to stimulating private and public investment in the area to enhance trade and export potential in the Israeli-occupied Territories and Palestinian autonomous areas. Examples of PAPP activities include the following: construction of sewage collection networks and systems in the northern Gaza Strip; provision of water to 500,000 people in rural and urban areas of the West Bank and Gaza; construction of schools, youth and health centres; support to vegetable and fish traders through the construction of cold storage and packing facilities; and provision of loans to strengthen industry and commerce. Field programme expenditure in 1996 totalled US $47.1m.

UNITED NATIONS CAPITAL DEVELOPMENT FUND—UNCDF

The Fund was established in 1966 and became fully operational in 1974. It invests in poor communities in least-developed countries by providing economic and social infrastructure, credit for both agricultural and small-scale entrepreneurial activities, and local development funds which encourage people's participation as well as that of local government in the planning and implementation of projects. UNCDF aims to promote the interests of women in community projects and to enhance their earning capacities. UNCDF programme expenditure totalled US $41.1m. in 1996. In that year income from voluntary contributions amounted to $34.8m.

Executive-Secretary: POUL GROSEN.

UNITED NATIONS DEVELOPMENT FUND FOR WOMEN—UNIFEM

UNIFEM, which became an associated fund of UNDP in 1985, is the UN's lead agency in addressing the issues relating to women in development and promoting the rights of women world-wide. The Fund provides direct financial and technical support to enable low-income women in developing countries to increase earnings, gain access to labour-saving technologies and otherwise improve the quality of their lives. It also funds activities that include women in decision-making related to mainstream development projects. UNIFEM has supported the preparation of national reports in 30 countries and used the priorities identified in these reports and in other regional initiatives to formulate a Women's Development Agenda for the 21st century. Through these efforts, UNIFEM played an active role in the preparation for the UN Fourth World Conference on Women, which was held in Beijing, People's Republic of China, in September 1995. Programme expenditure in 1996 totalled US $11m.

Director: NOELEEN HEYZER (Singapore).

OFFICE TO COMBAT DESERTIFICATION AND DROUGHT—UNSO

The Office was established following the conclusion, in October 1994, of the UN Convention to Combat Desertification in Those Countries Experiencing Serious Drought and/or Desertification, Particularly in Africa. It replaced the former UN Sudano-Sahelian Office (UNSO), while retaining the same acronym. UNSO is responsible for UNDP's role in desertification control and dryland management. Special emphasis is given to strengthening the environmental planning and management capacities of national institutions. During 1996 UNSO, in collaboration with other international partners, supported the implementation of the UN Convention in 43 designated countries. Programme expenditure in that year totalled US $6.1m.

Headquarters: Ave de la Résistance du 17 Mai, Immeuble de la Caisse Générale de Péréquation, Secteur 4, 01 BP 366, Ouagadougou 01, Burkina Faso; tel. 30-63-35; fax 31-05-81.

Director: SAMUEL NYAMBI.

UNITED NATIONS VOLUNTEERS—UNV

The United Nations Volunteers is an important source of middle-level skills for the UN development system, supplied at modest cost, particularly in the least-developed countries. Volunteers expand the scope of UNDP project activities by supplementing the work of international and host country experts and by extending the influence of projects to local community levels. UNV also supports technical co-operation within and among the developing countries by encouraging volunteers from the countries themselves and by forming regional exchange teams made up of such volunteers. The UN Short-term Advisory Programme, which is the private-sector development arm of UNV, has increasingly focused its attention on countries in the process of economic transition. The Programme completed 124 assignments in 18 countries in 1995. In addition to development activities UNV has become increasingly involved in areas such as peace-building, elections, human rights and community-based environmental programmes. In 1995 a total of 3,263 UNV specialists and field workers from 134 nations served in 139 countries. In 1996 programme expenditure totalled US $14.9m.

Executive Co-ordinator: BRENDA McSWEENEY.

Headquarters: Haus Carstanje, Bonn, Germany.

United Nations Environment Programme—UNEP

Address: POB 30552, Nairobi, Kenya.
Telephone: (2) 621234; **telex:** 22068; **fax:** (2) 226890; **internet:** http://www.unep.org.

The United Nations Environment Programme was established in 1972 by the UN General Assembly, following recommendations of the 1972 UN Conference on the Human Environment, in Stockholm, Sweden, to encourage international co-operation in matters relating to the human environment.

Organization

(August 1998)

GOVERNING COUNCIL

The main function of the Governing Council, which meets every two years, is to provide general policy guidelines for the direction and co-ordination of environmental programmes within the UN system. It comprises representatives of 58 states, elected by the UN General Assembly on a rotating basis.

SECRETARIAT

The Secretariat serves as a focal point for environmental action within the UN system.

Executive Director: Dr KLAUS TÖPFER (Germany).

REGIONAL OFFICES

Africa: POB 30552, Nairobi, Kenya; tel. (2) 624283; fax (2) 623928.
Europe: CP 356, 15 chemin des Anémones, 1219 Châtelaine, Geneva, Switzerland; tel. (22) 9799111; telex 415465; fax (22) 7973420.
West Asia: Sheikh Rashid Bldg, 1st Floor, Rd 2904, 329 Manama, Bahrain; tel. 276072; fax 276075; e-mail uneprowa@batelco.com.bh.

OTHER OFFICES

Convention on International Trade in Endangered Species of Wild Fauna and Flora (CITES): CP 456, 15 chemin des Anémones, 1219 Châtelaine, Geneva, Switzerland; tel. (22) 9799139; telex 415391; fax (22) 7973417; e-mail cites@unep.ch; Sec.-Gen. REUBEN OLEMBO (acting).

Co-ordinating Unit for the Mediterranean Action Plan (MEDU): Leoforos Vassileos Konstantinou 48, POB 18019, 11610 Athens, Greece; tel. (1) 7273100; fax (1) 7253196; e-mail unepmedu @unepmap.gr.

International Register of Potentially Toxic Chemicals (IRPTC): CP 356, 15 chemin des Anémones, 1219 Châtelaine, Geneva, Switzerland; tel. (22) 9799111; fax (22) 7973460; e-mail irptc@unep.ch; Dir JAMES B. WILLIS.

Secretariat of the Convention on Biological Diversity: World Trade Centre, 393 St Jacques St, Suite 300, Montréal, Québec, Canada HR7 1N9; tel. (514) 288-2220; fax (514) 288-6588; e-mail biodiv@mtl.net; Exec. Sec. CALESTOUS JUMA (until Oct. 1998).

Secretariat of the Multilateral Fund for the Implementation of the Montreal Protocol: 1800 McGill College Ave, 27th Floor, Montréal, Québec, Canada H3A 3J6; tel. (514) 282-1122; fax (514) 282-0068; e-mail secretariat@unmfs.org; Chief Dr OMAR EL-ARINI.

UNEP Arab League Liaison Office: 24 Iraq St, Mohandessin, Cairo, Egypt; tel. (2) 3361349; fax (2) 3370658.

UNEP Industry and Environment: Tour Mirabeau, 39–43, Quai André Citroen, 75739 Paris Cedex 15, France; tel. 1-44-37-14-50; fax 1-44-37-14-74; e-mail unepie@unep.fr; internet: http://www.une-pie.org/home.html; Dir JACQUELINE ALOISI DE LARDEREL.

UNEP International Environmental Technology Centre: 2-110 Ryokuchi koen, Tsurumi-ku, Osaka 530, Japan; tel. (6) 915-4580; fax (6) 915-0304; Dir JOHN WHITELAW.

UNEP Ozone Secretariat: POB 30552, Nairobi, Kenya; tel. (2) 623885; telex 22068; fax (2) 623913; e-mail ozoneinfo@unep.org; Exec. Sec. K. MADHAVA SARMA.

UNEP Secretariat of the Basel Convention: CP 356, 15 chemin des Anémones, 1219 Châtelaine, Geneva, Switzerland; tel. (22) 9799111; telex 415465; fax (22) 7973454; e-mail bulska@unep.ch; Exec. Sec. Dr I. RUMMEL-BULSKA.

UNEP Secretariat for the UN Scientific Committee on the Effects of Atomic Radiation: Vienna International Centre, Wagramerstrasse 5, 1400 Vienna, Austria; tel. (1) 21345-4330; telex 135612; fax (1) 21345-5902; e-mail bbennett@unov.un.at; Sec. B. BENNET.

UNEP/CMS (Convention on the Conservation of Migratory Species of Wild Animals) **Secretariat:** Martin-Luther-King-Str 8, 53175 Bonn, Germany; tel. (228) 8152401; fax (228) 8152449; e-mail cms@unep.de; internet: http://www.wcmc.org.uk/cms; Exec. Sec. ARNULF MÜLLER-HELMBRECHT.

Activities

UNEP aims to maintain a constant watch on the changing state of the environment; to analyse the trends; to assess the problems using a wide range of data and techniques; and to promote projects leading to environmentally sound development. It plays a catalytic and co-ordinating role within and beyond the UN system. Many UNEP projects are implemented in co-operation with other UN agencies, particularly UNDP, the World Bank group, FAO, UNESCO and WHO. About 45 intergovernmental organizations outside the UN system and 60 international non-governmental organizations have official observer status on UNEP's Governing Council, and, through the Environment Liaison Centre in Nairobi, UNEP is linked to more than 6,000 non-governmental bodies concerned with the environment. In September 1997 staff at UNEP headquarters numbered 329, and 287 at regional and other offices.

UNEP played a significant role in preparing for and conducting the UN Conference on Environment and Development (UNCED, or the 'Earth Summit'), which was held in Rio de Janeiro, Brazil, in June 1992. Agenda 21, a programme of activities to promote sustainable development, which was adopted at UNCED, reaffirmed UNEP's mandate and gave its Governing Council an enhanced role in the areas of policy guidance and development. The two-year 1994–95 programme was considered to be a transitional period for UNEP, during which its role and effectiveness as the UN's agency for environmental issues was re-evaluated. In May 1995 the Governing Council adopted a new programme of activities for the two-year period 1996–97, which aimed to incorporate the demands of Agenda 21 and achieve a more integrated approach to addressing environmental issues. UNEP's 12 previous sectoral subprogrammes were redesigned into the five main interdisciplinary areas of work listed below. Approaches to assessment and monitoring, formulation and evaluation of environment policy and management of environmental intitiatives (defined as priority actions by Agenda 21) were to be applied in all programme activities, in order to increase the efficacy of UNEP's work. The Governing Council resolved that UNEP should strengthen its co-operation partnerships with other UN agencies and regional, national and local institutions in order to benefit from their expertise and to address varying regional environmental concerns.

In February 1997 the Governing Council, at its 19th session, adopted a ministerial declaration on UNEP's future role and mandate, which recognized the organization as the principal UN body working in the field of the environment and as the leading global environmental authority, setting and overseeing the international environmental agenda. In June a Special Session of the UN General Assembly, referred to as the 'Earth Summit + 5', was convened to review the state of the environment and progress achieved in implementing UNCED's objectives. The meeting adopted a Programme for Further Implementation of Agenda 21 to intensify efforts in areas such as energy, freshwater resources and technology transfer. The meeting confirmed UNEP's essential role in advancing the Programme and as a global authority promoting a coherent legal and political approach to the environmental challenges of sustainable development.

SUSTAINABLE MANAGEMENT AND USE OF NATURAL RESOURCES

UNEP aims to promote the sustainable use of natural resources, in order to prevent degradation of the environment and natural ecosystems that results from intensified demands on land, water, marine and coastal resources.

UNEP estimates that one-third of the world's population will suffer chronic water shortages by 2025, owing to rising demand for drinking water as a result of growing populations, decreasing quality of water because of pollution and increasing requirements of industries and agriculture. Efforts to address these problems include

conducting a range of studies and assessments of river basins and regional seas, including the Nile River, the Caspian Sea and the Erhai Lake. In addition, UNEP provides scientific, technical and administrative support to facilitate the implementation and co-ordination of regional seas conventions and plans of action. UNEP promotes greater international co-operation in the management of river basins and coastal areas, and for the development of tools and guidelines to achieve the sustainable management of freshwater and coastal resources. In particular, UNEP aims to control land-based activities, principally pollution, which affect freshwater resources, marine biodiversity and the coastal ecosystems of small-island developing states. In November 1995 110 governments adopted a Global Programme of Action for the Protection of the Marine Environment from Land-based Activities. UNEP was to manage the Programme's Secretariat.

UNEP supports the sound management and conservation of biological resources, in order to maintain biological diversity and to achieve sustainable development. UNEP was instrumental in the drafting of a Convention on Biological Diversity (CBD), which was adopted by UNCED in order to preserve the immense variety of plant and animal species, in particular those threatened with extinction. The Convention entered into force at the end of 1993; the first conference of parties to the Convention was convened in November/December 1994, in Nassau, the Bahamas, and was attended by representatives of some 130 countries. UNEP supports co-operation for biodiversity assessment and management in selected developing regions and for the development of strategies for the conservation and sustainable exploitation of individual threatened species (e.g. the Global Tiger Action Plan). UNEP also provides assistance for the preparation of individual country studies and strategies to strengthen national biodiversity management and research. In November 1995 UNEP published a Global Diversity Assessment, which was presented as the first comprehensive study on biodiversity throughout the world. UNEP provides administrative and technical support to other national and international conventions, including the Convention on the Conservation of Migratory Species and the Convention on International Trade in Endangered Species of Wild Fauna and Flora (CITES).

In October 1994 87 countries, meeting under UN auspices, signed a Convention to Combat Desertification (see UNSO, p. 218), which aimed to provide a legal framework to counter the degradation of drylands. An estimated 75% of all drylands has suffered some land degradation, affecting approximately 1,000m. people in 110 countries. UNEP continues to support the implementation of the Convention, as part of its efforts to protect land resources. UNEP also aims to improve the assessment of dryland degradation and desertification in co-operation with governments and other international bodies, as well as identifying the causes of degradation and measures to overcome these.

SUSTAINABLE PRODUCTION AND CONSUMPTION

The use of inappropriate industrial technologies and the widespread adoption of unsustainable production and consumption patterns have been identified as being inefficient in the use of renewable resources and wasteful, in particular, in the use of energy. UNEP aims to develop new policy and management tools for governments and industry and to encourage the use of environmentally-sound technologies, in order to reduce pollution and the unsustainable use of natural resources. UNEP organizes conferences and training workshops to promote sustainable production practices and disseminates relevant information through the International Cleaner Production Information Clearing House.

UNEP provides institutional servicing to the Basel Convention on the Control of Transboundary Movements of Hazardous Wastes and their Disposal, which was adopted in 1989 with the aim of preventing the disposal of wastes from industrialized countries in countries that have no processing facilities. In March 1994 the second meeting of parties to the Convention agreed to ban exportation of hazardous wastes between OECD and non-OECD countries by the end of 1997. The amendment of the Convention required ratification by three-quarters of signatory states before it could enter into effect, and was not achieved by December 1997. The fourth full meeting of parties to the Convention, held in February 1998, attempted to clarify the classification and listing of hazardous wastes, which was expected to stimulate further ratifications. At that time the number of parties to the Convention had increased from 30 in 1992 to 117. UNEP also extends administrative support to the Vienna Convention for the Protection of the Ozone Layer (1985) and its 1987 Montreal Protocol, which provided for a 50% reduction in the production of chlorofluorocarbons (CFCs) by 2000. (An amendment to the Protocol was adopted in 1990, which required complete cessation of the production of CFCs by 2000 in industrialized countries and by 2010 in developing countries; these deadlines were advanced to 1996 and 2006 respectively, in November 1992.) A Multilateral Fund for the Implementation of the Montreal Protocol was established in June 1990, initially on an interim basis, to promote the use of suitable technologies and the transfer of technologies to developing countries. UNEP, UNDP, the World Bank and UNIDO are the sponsors of the Fund, which by early 1997 had financed 1,800 projects in 106 developing countries at a cost of US \$565m. In November 1996 the Fund was replenished, with commitments totalling \$540m. for the three-year period 1997–99. The OxonAction Programme of UNEP's industry and environment office works under the Fund to promote information exchange, training and technological awareness. Its objective is to strengthen the capacity of governments and industry in developing countries to undertake measures towards the cost-effective phasing-out of ozone-depleting substances.

UNEP encourages the development of alternative and renewable sources of energy. To achieve this, UNEP is supporting the establishment of a network of centres to research and exchange information of environmentally-sound energy technology resources. UNEP undertakes technical activities to support the implementation of the Framework Convention on Climate Change (FCCC), which was adopted at UNCED and entered into force in March 1994. The FCCC commits countries to submitting reports on measures being taken to reduce the emission of 'greenhouse gases' (i.e. carbon dioxide and other gases that have a warming effect on the atmosphere). The Convention recommended stabilizing these emissions at 1990 levels by 2000; however, this was not legally binding. At a full meeting of parties to the Convention, held in Kyoto, Japan, in December 1997, 38 industrial nations endorsed mandatory reductions of emissions of the six most harmful gases by an average of 5.2% from 1990 levels, between 2008 and 2012. The agreement was to enter into force on being ratified by countries representing 55% of the world's carbon dioxide emissions in 1990.

The realignment of UNEP activities, undertaken for the work programme 1996–97, addressed the concerns that unsustainable patterns of consumption and production, in particular in industrialized countries, were major contributing factors to the deterioration of the global environment. UNEP aims to adjust this situation by stimulating understanding and awareness of the relationship between production and consumption, and promoting dialogue among developed countries to attain an agreement on more sustainable forms of production.

A BETTER ENVIRONMENT FOR HUMAN HEALTH AND WELL-BEING

A guiding principle of Agenda 21 was that human beings were at the centre of concerns for sustainable development and that they were entitled to a healthy and productive life. The new UNEP sub-programme integrated its previous activities relating to health, human settlement and welfare with those concerned with toxic wastes and chemicals. UNEP continues to maintain the International Register of Potentially Toxic Chemicals (IRPTC). UNEP aims to facilitate access to data on chemicals and hazardous wastes, in order to assess and control health and environmental risks, by using the IRPTC as a clearing house facility of relevant information and by publishing information and technical reports on the impact of the use of chemicals. In 1996 UNEP, in collaboration with FAO, began to work towards promoting and formulating an international convention on prior informed consent (PIC) for hazardous chemicals in international trade, extending a voluntary PIC procedure of information exchange undertaken by more than 100 governments since 1991. A draft convention was concluded by an Intergovernmental Negotiating Committee in March 1998 and was scheduled to be open for signature in 1999. UNEP is also working towards a multilateral agreement to reduce and ultimately eliminate the manufacture and use of Persistent Organic Pollutants, which are considered to be a major global environmental hazard.

In conjunction with UNCHS (Habitat), UNDP, the World Bank and other regional organizations and institutions, UNEP promotes environmental concerns in urban planning and management through the Sustainable Cities Programme, as well as regional workshops on urban pollution and the impact of transportation systems. In January 1994 UNEP inaugurated an International Environmental Technology Centre (IETC), with offices in Osaka and Shiga, Japan, in order to strengthen the capabilities of developing countries and countries with economies in transition to promote environmentally-sound management of cities and fresh water reservoirs through technology co-operation and partnerships.

UNEP aims to reduce the risk to human populations of environmental change and emergencies. UNEP also aims to enhance accident prevention and emergency preparedness capabilities in all developing countries, for example through its APELL programme (Awareness and Preparedness for Emergencies at the Local Level). As part of its efforts to develop mechanisms to avoid and settle environmental disputes, UNEP participates in working groups in the Israeli-occupied Territories, under the Middle East peace process, and promotes greater regional co-operation in the management of shared natural resources in the Nile river basin, the Arctic and Antarctica.

GLOBALIZATION AND THE ENVIRONMENT

With the globalization of the world's economy UNEP has identified a need to enhance the assessment of the environmental impact of trade patterns and policies, at country and regional level, and to undertake legal analyses of the relationship between environmental laws and international trade regimes. UNCED recommended the need to integrate environmental issues into economic priorities as a prerequisite of sustainable development. UNEP operates a system of environmental valuation and environmental impact assessment, which it aims to promote through national guidelines and technical workshops. Other so-called environmental economic tools may be developed through environmental and natural resource accounting and the eco-labelling of country export products (i.e. identifying products with a high environmental quality profile). UNEP aims to promote the exchange of information relevant to this sector and to assist countries to develop additional sources of finance for environmentally sustainable development. UNEP, together with UNDP and the World Bank, is an implementing agency of the Global Environment. UNEP, together with UNDP and the World Bank, is an implementing agency of the Global Environment Facility (GEF), which was established in 1991 as a mechanism for international co-operation in projects concerned with biological diversity, climate change, international waters and depletion of the ozone layer. UNEP provides the secretariat for the Scientific and Technical Advisory Panel, which was established to provide expert advice on GEF programmes and operational strategies.

In order to complement the globalization process and the expanded environment agenda, UNEP supports the formulation and implementation of international and national legislation as environmental management tools. While it supports and helps co-ordinate the activities of the secretariats of international and regional conventions, UNEP is undertaking preliminary efforts to formulate a definitive international legal framework for sustainable development. At a national level UNEP assists governments to prepare environmental legislation and guidelines and to implement existing international conventions. Training workshops in various aspects of environmental law and its application are conducted.

UNEP aims to promote coherent decision-making, in the environment field, through its support for research and information exchange. It promotes the scientific research and review of key environmental issues and conducts workshops to develop policy recommendations. In 1996–97 UNEP aimed to integrate environmental concerns in the activities of international financial institutions and to encourage collaboration among these bodies.

GLOBAL AND REGIONAL SERVICING AND SUPPORT

UNEP has a major responsibility to identify and assess environmental issues of common concern, to alert the world community to these issues, to precipitate their resolution through international co-operation and to provide policy guidance for the direction and co-ordination of environmental programmes within the UN system. Under this subprogramme UNEP aims to fulfil its role and to deliver its programme of work through the basic institutional functions of environmental assessment, advisory services, public awareness and provision of information. The first Global Environment Outlook (GEO-1), which UNEP presented as an assessment of the state of the world's environment, was published in January 1997.

Through regional consultations and specialized centres worldwide, UNEP aims to develop and enhance frameworks, methodologies and indicators to achieve integrated environmental assessment and reporting. In particular, UNEP aims to strengthen early-warning mechanisms and region-specific assessment. UNEP is participating in the design of a Global Terrestrial Observing System, which was to be implemented by the GEF.

UNEP promotes and supports regional co-operation initiatives for environmental action by co-operation with regional banks, economic commissions and other organizations. In addition, UNEP provides policy and technical advice to governments in developing countries and countries with economies in transition for the integration of environmental considerations into national development plans.

Education and public awareness are critical for promoting sustainable development and improving the capacity of groups and individuals to address environmental issues. UNEP's public education campaigns and outreach programmes promote community involvement in environmental issues. Further communication of environmental concerns is undertaken through the media, an information centre service and special promotional events, including World Environment Day, photograph competitions and the awarding of the Sasakawa Prize to recognize distinguished service to the environment by individuals and groups.

UNEP's data and information services include a global resource information data-base (GRID), which converts data collected into information usable by decision-makers, and the INFOTERRA programme, which facilitates the exchange of environmental information through an extensive network of national 'focal points' (totalling 174 in early 1997), and the Environment and Natural Resource

REGIONAL ORGANIZATIONS

Information Networks (ENRIN), which UNEP aims to establish in every developing region. In 1996–97 UNEP aimed to integrate all its information resources in order to improve access to information and international environment information exchange. This was to be achieved through the design and implementation of UNEPNET, which was to operate throughout the UN system and be fully accessible through the world-wide information networks.

FINANCE

UNEP derives its finances from the regular budget of the United Nations and from voluntary contributions to the Environment Fund. UNEP's estimated budget for 1996–97 amounted to US \$9.9m. from the UN regular budget and \$90m. (with an additional supplementary appropriation of \$15m. if or when funds become available) from the Environment Fund. A budget of \$75m. has been approved for the 1998–99 work programme.

PUBLICATIONS

Report of the Executive Director (every 2 years).
APELL Newsletter (2 a year).
Cleaner Production Newsletter (2 a year).
Climate Change Bulletin (quarterly).

Connect (UNESCO-UNEP newsletter on environmental degradation, quarterly).
EarthViews (quarterly).
Environment Forum (quarterly).
Environmental Law Bulletin (2 a year).
Financial Services Initiative (2 a year).
GEF News (quarterly).
Global Biodiversity Assessment.
Global Environment Outlook (annually).
IETC Insight (3 a year).
Industry and Environment Review (quarterly).
Leave it to Us (children's magazine, 2 a year).
Managing Hazardous Waste (2 a year).
Nature et Faune / Wildlife and Nature (quarterly, with FAO).
Our Planet (6 a year).
OzoneAction Newsletter (quarterly).
Tiger Paper (quarterly, with FAO).
Tourism Focus (2 a year).
UNEP Update (monthly).
World Atlas of Desertification.
Studies, reports, legal texts, technical guidelines, etc.

United Nations High Commissioner for Refugees— UNHCR

Address: CP 2500, 1211 Geneva 2 dépôt, Switzerland.
Telephone: (22) 7398111; **telex:** 415740; **fax:** (22) 7319546; **internet:** http://www.unhcr.ch/.

The Office of the High Commissioner was established in 1951 to provide international protection for refugees and to seek durable solutions to their problems.

Organization
(August 1998)

HIGH COMMISSIONER

The High Commissioner is elected by the United Nations General Assembly on the nomination of the Secretary-General, and is responsible to the General Assembly and to the UN Economic and Social Council (ECOSOC).

High Commissioner: SADAKO OGATA (Japan).
Deputy High Commissioner: GERALD WALZER (Austria).

EXECUTIVE COMMITTEE

The Executive Committee of the High Commissioner's Programme, established by ECOSOC, gives the High Commissioner policy directives in respect of material assistance programmes and advice in the field of international protection. It meets once a year, usually in Geneva. It includes representatives of 53 states, both members and non-members of the UN.

ADMINISTRATION

Headquarters include the Executive Office, comprising the offices of the High Commissioner, the Deputy High Commissioner and the Assistant High Commissioner. The offices of Internal Oversight and of International Protection report directly to the Executive Office, as do the Secretariat, the Centre for Documentation and Research and the Department of Public Information. Refugee support services are undertaken by the divisions of Operations Support, Financial and Information Services and Human Resource Management. Operations are administered by the five regional bureaux covering Central, East and West Africa, Asia and the Pacific, Europe, the Americas and South-West Asia, the Middle East and North Africa. In November 1997 there were 249 offices in 122 countries.

Activities

The competence of the High Commissioner extends to any person who, owing to well-founded fear of being persecuted for reasons of race, religion, nationality or political opinion, is outside the country of his or her nationality and is unable or, owing to such fear or for reasons other than personal convenience, remains unwilling to accept the protection of that country; or who, not having a nationality and being outside the country of former habitual residence, is unable or, owing to such fear or for reasons other than personal convenience, is unwilling to return to it. Refugees who are assisted by other United Nations agencies, or who have the same rights or obligations as nationals of their country of residence, are outside the mandate of UNHCR.

In the early 1990s there was a significant shift in UNHCR's focus of activities. Increasingly UNHCR is called upon to support people who have been displaced within their own country, i.e. with similar needs to those of refugees but who have not crossed an international border. Operations involving internally displaced population may be undertaken only at the request of the UN Secretary-General or the General Assembly and with the consent of the country concerned. In addition, it is providing greater support to refugees who have returned to their country of origin, to assist their reintegration, and is working to enable the local community to support the returnees. At 1 January 1997 the refugee population world-wide totalled 13.20m., while UNHCR was concerned with a further 4.85m. internally displaced persons, 3.31m. returnees and 1.37m. others.

INTERNATIONAL PROTECTION

As laid down in the Statute of the Office, one of the two primary functions of UNHCR is to extend international protection to refugees. In the exercise of this function UNHCR seeks to ensure that refugees and asylum-seekers are protected against *refoulement* (forcible return), that they receive asylum, and that they are treated according to internationally recognized standards of treatment. UNHCR pursues these objectives by a variety of means which include promoting the conclusion and ratification by states of international conventions for the protection of refugees, particularly the 1951 UN Convention relating to the Status of Refugees, extended by a Protocol adopted in 1967. The Convention defines the rights and duties of refugees and contains provisions dealing with a variety of matters which affect their day-to-day lives. By November 1997 134 states had acceded to either the Convention or the Protocol, or both.

Palestine refugees in the region are under the care of UNRWA (q.v.).

ASSISTANCE ACTIVITIES

UNHCR assistance activities are divided into General Programmes, which include a Programme Reserve, a General Allocation for Voluntary Repatriation and an Emergency Fund, and Special Programmes. The latter are undertaken at the request of the UN General Assembly, the Secretary-General of the UN or member states, in response to a particular crisis.

The first phase of an assistance operation uses UNHCR's capacity of emergency preparedness and response. This enables UNHCR to address the immediate needs of refugees at short notice, for example, by employing specially trained emergency teams and maintaining stockpiles of basic equipment, medical aid and materials. A significant proportion of UNHCR expenditure is allocated to the next phase of an operation, providing 'care and maintenance' in stable refugee circumstances. This assistance can take various forms, including the provision of food, shelter, medical care and essential supplies. Also covered in many instances are basic services, including education and counselling. Whenever possible, measures of this kind are accompanied by efforts to encourage maximum levels of self-reliance among the refugee population.

As far as possible, assistance is geared towards the identification and implementation of durable solutions to refugee problems—this being the second statutory responsibility of UNHCR. Such solutions generally take one of three forms: voluntary repatriation, local integration and resettlement. Where voluntary repatriation is feasible, the Office assists refugees to overcome obstacles preventing their return to their country of origin. This may be done through negotiations with governments involved, or by providing funds either for the physical movement of refugees or for the rehabilitation of returnees once back in their own country.

When voluntary repatriation is not feasible, efforts are made to assist refugees to integrate locally and to become self-supporting in their countries of asylum. In cases where resettlement through emigration is the only viable solution to a refugee problem, UNHCR negotiates with governments in an endeavour to obtain resettlement opportunities, to encourage liberalization of admission criteria and to draw up special immigration schemes. During 1997 25,179 refugees were resettled under UNHCR auspices.

In the early 1990s UNHCR aimed to consolidate efforts to integrate certain priorities into its programme planning and implementation, as a standard discipline in all phases of assistance. The considerations include awareness of specific problems confronting refugee women, the needs of refugee children, the environmental impact of refugee programmes and long-term development objectives. In an effort to improve the effectiveness of its programmes UNHCR has initiated a process of delegating authority, as well as responsibility for operational budgets, to its regional and field representatives, increasing flexibility and accountability. In 1995 a new Inspection and Evaluation Service was established in order to strengthen UNHCR's capacity to review operational effectiveness and efficiency.

REGIONAL ASSISTANCE

From 1974 onwards UNHCR has acted as co-ordinator of the UN Humanitarian Programme of Assistance for Cyprus, assisting some 265,000 displaced persons on the island.

UNHCR co-ordinates humanitarian assistance for the estimated 165,000 Sahrawis registered as refugees in the Tindouf area of Algeria. Approximately 80,000 most vulnerable members of the Sahrawi refugee population receive direct assistance from UNHCR. In September 1997 an agreement was reached on implementing the 1991 Settlement Plan for the Western Sahara. Accordingly, UNHCR was to help organize the registration and safe return of up to 135,000 Sahrawi refugees who had been identified as eligible to vote in the referendum on the future of the territory, scheduled to be conducted in early December 1998. In addition, UNHCR was to facilitate the reintegration of the returnees and monitor their rehabilitation. The cost of the programme in 1998 was estimated by UNHCR to total US $50m.

From 1979, as a result of civil strife in Afghanistan, there was a massive movement of refugees from that country into Pakistan and Iran creating the world's largest refugee population, which reached a peak of almost 6.3m. in 1990. In April 1992, following the establishment of a new Government in Afghanistan, refugees began to return in substantial numbers (hitherto only a small number had returned under the UNHCR-administered repatriation programme). UNHCR supervised border crossings and routes of return in order to facilitate the process and to ensure the repatriation was voluntary. Within a six-month period more than 1.27m. Afghans returned from Pakistan and 300,000 from Iran. UNHCR continued to undertake projects to assist the reintegration of returnees into their communities and to supply them with food and other essential material assistance. During 1995 an estimated 153,000 Afghan refugees returned from Pakistan, despite an escalation of civil conflict, of whom 77,000 did so under a UNHCR repatriation programme, and 195,000 returned from Iran, including 92,000 with UNHCR assistance. From October 1996 renewed hostilities resulted in further large-scale population displacement, and in November UNHCR suspended its relief activities in the Afghan capital, Kabul, owing to mounting security concerns. Relief operations continued in other parts of the country. By November 1997 an estimated 3.9m. refugees had returned to Afghanistan since the repatriation programme was initiated in 1989, while some 2.7m. Afghans remained in camps in Iran, Pakistan, India and countries of the former USSR. At that time there were also 310,000 internally displaced persons in Afghanistan of concern to UNHCR. During 1997 UNHCR operated a pilot scheme to organize group repatriations to specific areas in Afghanistan,

under the protection of international observers. The programme was scheduled to be expanded in 1998, with additional transport and other welfare benefits granted to refugees and with a focus on reintegration projects in the returnees' home areas.

In March–May 1991, following the war against Iraq by a multinational force, and the subsequent Iraqi suppression of resistance in Kurdish areas in the north of the country, there was massive movement of some 1.5m., mainly Kurdish, refugees into Iran and Turkey. UNHCR was designated the principal UN agency to attempt to alleviate the crisis. In May the refugees began to return to Iraq in huge numbers and UNHCR assisted in their repatriation, establishing relief stations along their routes from Iran and Turkey. UNHCR provided winter shelter for those refugees encamped in northern Iraq. Following the war to liberate Kuwait UNHCR gave protection and assistance to Iraqis, Bidoons (stateless people) and Palestinians who were forced to leave that country.

In April 1994 UNHCR initiated a programme to provide food and relief assistance to Turkish Kurds who had fled into northern Iraq. In September 1996 fighting escalated among the Kurdish factions in northern Iraq. By the time a cease-fire agreement was concluded in November some 65,000 Iraqi Kurds had fled across the border into Iran. UNHCR, together with the Iranian Government, provided these new refugees with basic humanitarian supplies. By the end of the year, however, the majority of refugees had returned to Iraq, owing to poor conditions in the temporary settlements, security concerns at being located in the border region and pressure from the Iranian authorities. During 1996 UNHCR activities in northern Iraq focused on assisting the repatriation and reintegration of Iraqi refugees from Iran and on the protection and provision of humanitarian requirements to the Kurdish refugee populations in that region. Nevertheless, at the end of December, UNHCR announced its intention to withdraw from the Atroush camp, which housed an estimated 15,000 Turkish Kurds, following several breaches of security in the camp, and expressed its concern at the political vacuum in the region resulting from the factional conflict. UNHCR proceeded to transfer 4,000 people to other local settlements and to provide humanitarian assistance to those refugees who had settled closer to Iraqi-controlled territory but who had been refused asylum. At 31 December 1996 the refugee population in Iraq totalled 112,957, of whom 62,635 were Palestinians, 34,194 Iranians and 14,986 were from Turkey. In addition, there were 115,330 returnees and 32,000 displaced persons in Iraq of concern to UNHCR. At November 1997 there was still a substantial Iraqi refugee population in the region, totalling an estimated 630,000 in Iran, Pakistan, Saudi Arabia and other Middle Eastern countries. At that time Iran remained the principal country of asylum in the world, hosting some 2m. refugees, mainly from Afghanistan and Iraq.

In June 1992 people fleeing the civil war and famine in Somalia began arriving in Yemen in large numbers. UNHCR set up camps to accommodate some 50,000 refugees, providing them with shelter, food, water and sanitation. As a result of civil conflict in Yemen in mid-1994, a large camp in the south of the country was demolished and other refugees had to be relocated, while the Yemen authorities initiated a campaign of forcible repatriation. At December 1996 Yemen was hosting 53,546 refugees (including 43,871 Somalis), of whom 6,395 were receiving UNHCR assistance. During early 1998 the refugee population in Yemen expanded owing to the influx of Somalis fleeing the ongoing civil conflict and the effects of heavy flooding which had devastated areas in the south of that country.

Persons of concern to UNHCR in the Middle East and North Africa (at 31 December 1996, '000)*

Country	Refugees	Returnees	Internally displaced persons	Others of concern
Algeria . . .	190.3	—	—	—
Cyprus . . .	0.0	—	265.0	—
Iran . . .	2,030.4	—	—	—
Iraq . . .	113.0	115.3	32.0	—
Kuwait . . .	3.8	—	—	120.0†
Syria . . .	27.8	—	—	—
Yemen . . .	53.5	—	—	36.0‡

* The table shows only those countries where the total number of persons of concern to UNHCR amounted to more than 10,000. The figures are provided mostly by governments, based on their own methods of estimation. The data do not include Palestinian refugees, who come under the care of UNRWA (q.v.).
† Mainly Bidoons (Bedouin) and Palestinians with Jordanian identity documents.
‡ Comprises 30,000 Iraqi and 6,000 Sudanese asylum-seekers not formally recognized as refugees.

CO-OPERATION WITH OTHER ORGANIZATIONS

UNHCR works closely with other UN agencies, intergovernmental organizations and non-governmental organizations (NGOs) to increase the scope and effectiveness of its emergency operations. Within the UN system UNHCR co-operates, principally, with the World Food Programme in the distribution of food aid, UNICEF and the World Health Organization in the provision of family welfare and child immunization programmes and with the UN Development Programme in development-related activities and the preparation of guidelines for the continuum of emergency assistance to development programmes. UNHCR also has close working relationships with the International Committee of the Red Cross and the International Organization for Migration. In June 1994 a world conference was held in Oslo, Norway, attended by UNHCR and some 450 NGOs, at which a Declaration to consolidate their collaboration in humanitarian operations was adopted. In 1997 UNHCR implemented 931 projects in 131 countries in collaboration with 443 NGOs, enabling UNHCR to broaden the use of its resources while maintaining a co-ordinating role in the provision of assistance.

FINANCE

UNHCR administrative expenditure is financed under the United Nations regular budget. General Programmes of material assistance are financed from voluntary contributions made by governments, and also from non-governmental sources. The 1997 budget totalled US $1,189.8m., of which $452.6m. was allocated to General Programmes and $737.2m. to Special Programmes. In 1998 the General Programmes budget was $440m., of which $26m. was proposed for expenditure in North Africa and the Middle East.

PUBLICATIONS

Refugees (quarterly, in English, French, German, Italian, Japanese and Spanish).

UNHCR Handbook for Emergencies.

Refugee Survey Quarterly.

The State of the World's Refugees (every 2 years).

United Nations Peace-keeping Operations

Address: Department of Peace-keeping Operations, Room S-3727-B, United Nations, New York, NY 10017, USA.

Telephone: (212) 963-5055; **telex:** 420544; **fax:** (212) 963-4879; **internet:** http://www.un.org/Depts/dpko/.

United Nations peace-keeping operations have been conceived as instruments of conflict control. The UN has used these operations in various conflicts, with the consent of the parties involved, to maintain international peace and security, without prejudice to the positions or claims of parties, in order to facilitate the search for political settlements through peaceful means such as mediation and the good offices of the Secretary-General. Each operation has been established with a specific mandate, which requires periodic review by the Security Council. United Nations peace-keeping operations fall into two categories: peace-keeping forces and observer missions.

Peace-keeping forces are composed of contingents of military and civilian personnel made available by member states. These forces assist in preventing the recurrence of fighting, restoring and maintaining peace, and promoting a return to normal conditions. To this end, peace-keeping forces are authorized as necessary to undertake negotiations, persuasion, observation and fact-finding. They run patrols and interpose physically between the opposing parties. Peace-keeping forces are permitted to use their weapons only in self-defence.

Military observer missions are composed of officers (usually unarmed), who are made available, on the Secretary-General's request, by member states. A mission's function is to observe and report to the Secretary-General (who in turn informs the UN Security Council) on the maintenance of a cease-fire, to investigate violations and to do what it can to improve the situation.

Peace-keeping forces and observer missions must at all times maintain complete impartiality and avoid any action that might affect the claims or positions of the parties.

The UN's peace-keeping forces and observer missions are financed in most cases by assessed contributions from member states of the organization. During the 1990s, a significant expansion in the UN's peace-keeping activities has been accompanied by a perpetual financial crisis within the organization, as a result of the increased financial burden and some member states' delaying payment. At May 1997 outstanding assessed contributions to the peace-keeping budget amounted some US $1,600m.

UNITED NATIONS DISENGAGEMENT OBSERVER FORCE—UNDOF

Headquarters: Damascus, Syria.

Commander: Maj.-Gen. CAMERON ROSS (Canada).

UNDOF was established for an initial period of six months by a UN Security Council resolution in May 1974, following the signature in Geneva of a disengagement agreement between Syrian and Israeli forces. The mandate has since been extended by successive resolutions. The initial task of the Force was to take over territory evacuated in stages by the Israeli troops, in accordance with the disengagement agreement, to hand over territory to Syrian troops, and to establish an area of separation on the Golan Heights.

UNDOF continues to monitor the area of separation; it conducts fortnightly inspections of the areas of limited armaments and forces; uses its best efforts to maintain the cease-fire; and from time to time has undertaken activities of a humanitarian nature, such as arranging the transfer of prisoners and war-dead between Syria and Israel. The Force operates exclusively on Syrian territory.

At 31 May 1998 the Force comprised 1,064 troops from Austria, Canada, Japan and Poland. It is assisted by 80 UNTSO military observers (the Observer Group, Golan). The annual cost to the United Nations of the operation is approximately US $32.4m.

UNITED NATIONS INTERIM FORCE IN LEBANON—UNIFIL

Headquarters: Naqoura, Lebanon.

Commander: Maj.-Gen. JIOJE KONOUSE KONROTE (Fiji).

UNIFIL was established by a UN Security Council resolution in March 1978. The original mandate of the force was to verify the withdrawal of Israeli forces from southern Lebanon, to restore international peace and security, and to assist the Government of Lebanon in ensuring the return of its effective authority in the area. UNIFIL has also extended humanitarian assistance to the population of the area, particularly since the second Israeli invasion of Lebanon in 1982. By mid-1998 Security Council Resolution 425, requiring the unconditional withdrawal of Israeli troops from southern Lebanon, had yet to be implemented. In late March 1998 the Israeli Government announced that it recognized Resolution 425, although any withdrawal of its troops would be conditional on receiving security guarantees from the Lebanese authorities. A formal decision to this effect, adopted on 1 April, was rejected by the Lebanese and Syrian Governments. In April 1992, in accordance with its mandate, UNIFIL completed the transfer of part of its zone of operations to the control of the Lebanese army. UNIFIL maintains checkpoints and observation posts, which are designed to monitor movement on the principal roads and to deter hostilities. UNIFIL provides civilians with food, water, medical supplies, fuel and escorts to farmers. UNIFIL medical centres and mobile teams provide care to an average 3,000 civilian patients each month, and a field dental programme has been established.

In April 1996 Israel initiated a large-scale offensive against suspected targets pertaining to the Hezbollah militia in southern Lebanon. During the offensive Israeli artillery shells struck a UNIFIL base at Qana, which was temporarily being used to shelter civilians displaced by the hostilities, resulting in the deaths of more than 100 people. The UN Security Council condemned the attack and demanded the respect by all sides of UNIFIL's mandate and for the safety and freedom of movement of its troops. In May a UN inquiry concluded that the UN site had been deliberately targeted during the offensive, owing to the presence of Hezbollah activists in the camp. In June 1997 the UN General Assembly resolved that Israel should contribute US $1.8m. towards UNIFIL's operational costs, as compensation for the Qana incident.

At 31 May 1998 the Force comprised 4,520 troops (from nine countries), assisted by some 60 UNTSO military observers (the Observer Group, Lebanon), and other international and local civilian staff. The annual cost to the United Nations of the operation is approximately US $125.8m.

UNITED NATIONS IRAQ-KUWAIT OBSERVATION MISSION—UNIKOM

Headquarters: Umm Qasr, Kuwait.

Commander: Maj.-Gen. ESA KALERVO TARVAINEN (Finland).

UNIKOM was established by a UN Security Council resolution (initially for a six-month period) in April 1991, to monitor a 200-km demilitarized zone along the border between Iraq and Kuwait. The task of the mission was to deter violations of the border, to monitor the Khawr 'Abd Allah waterway between Iraq and Kuwait, and to prevent military activity within the zone. In February 1993 the Security Council adopted a resolution to strengthen UNIKOM and expand its mandate, following incursions into Kuwaiti territory by Iraqi personnel, in order to enable the use of physical action to prevent or redress violations of the demilitarized zone or the border between Iraq and Kuwait. In April the UN Secretary-General agreed to reinforce the mission's observer team and logistic support elements. UNIKOM provides technical support to other UN operations in the area, particularly the Iraq-Kuwait Boundary Demarcation Commission, and assisted with the relocation of Iraqi citizens from Kuwait, which was completed in February 1994.

At 31 May 1998 UNIKOM comprised 903 troops and support personnel and 194 military observers, assisted by 200 international and local civilian support staff. The annual cost to the United Nations of the mission is approximately US $59.2m. Two-thirds of the total cost of the mission are met by the Government of Kuwait.

UNITED NATIONS MISSION FOR THE REFERENDUM IN WESTERN SAHARA— MINURSO

Headquarters: El-Aaiún, Western Sahara.

Special Representative of the UN Secretary-General: CHARLES DUNBAR (USA).

Personal Envoy of the UN Secretary-General: JAMES BAKER, III (USA).

Chief Military Observer: Brig.-Gen. BERND LUBENIK (Austria).

In April 1991 the UN Security Council endorsed the establishment of MINURSO to verify a cease-fire in the disputed territory of Western Sahara (claimed by Morocco), which came into effect in September 1991, to secure the release of all Western Saharan political prisoners, to implement a programme of repatriation of Sahrawi refugees (in co-ordination with UNHCR), and to organize a referendum on the future of the territory. The referendum, originally envisaged for January 1992 was, however, postponed indefinitely. In 1992–93 the Secretary-General's Special Representative organized negotiations between the Frente Popular para la Liberación de Saguia el-Hamra y Río de Oro (Frente Polisario) and the Moroccan Government, who were in serious disagreement regarding criteria for eligibility to vote in the referendum (in particular, the Moroccan Government insisted that more than 100,000 members of ethnic groups who had been forced to leave the territory under Spanish rule prior to the last official census in 1974, the results of which were to be used as a basis for voter registration, should be allowed to participate in a referendum.) Nevertheless, in March 1993 the Security Council advocated that further efforts should be made to compile a satisfactory electoral list and to resolve the outstanding differences on procedural issues. An Identification Commission was consequently established to begin the process of voter registration, although this was obstructed by the failure of the Moroccan Government and the Frente Polisario to pursue political dialogue. In March 1994 the Security Council resolved that the Identification Commission should proceed with its work and the UN continued its efforts to obtain the co-operation of the two parties. The identification and registration operation was formally initiated in August; however, the process was complicated by the dispersed nature of the Western Saharan population and by a deterioration in diplomatic relations between Morocco and neighbouring Algeria, which hosts the majority of Sahrawi refugees. In December the Secretary-General expressed his intention to commence the transitional period of the settlement plan, during which time MINURSO was to oversee a reduction of Moroccan government troops in the region, a confinement of Frente Polisario forces, the release of political prisoners and the exchange of other prisoners and refugees, with effect from 1 June 1995. While this date was later reviewed, in June 1995 a Security Council mission visited the region to assess the referendum process. The mission recognized legitimate difficulties in conducting the indentification process; however, it urged all parties to co-operate with MINURSO and suggested that the future of the Mission would be reconsidered in the event of further delays. In December the UN Secretary-General reported that the identification of voters had stalled, owing to persistent obstruction of the process on the part of the Moroccan and Frente Polisario authorities. By May 1996 all efforts to resume the identification process had failed, owing to the ongoing dispute regarding the number of potentially eligible voters, as well as the Frente Polisario's insistence on reviewing those already identified (a demand rejected by Morocco). Three registration offices in Western Sahara and one in Mauritania were closed. At the end of that month the Security Council endorsed a recommendation of the Secretary-General to suspend the identification process, until all sides demonstrate their willingness to co-operate with the mission. In addition, the Security Council decided that MINURSO's operational capacity was to be reduced by 20%, with sufficient troops retained to monitor and verify the cease-fire. The Secretary-General's acting Special Representative pursued efforts to maintain political dialogue in the region; however, no significant progress was achieved in furthering the identification process. In early 1997 the new Secretary-General of the UN, Kofi Annan, attempted to revive the possibility of an imminent resolution of the dispute, amid increasing concerns that the opposing authorities were preparing for a resumption of hostilities in the event of a collapse of the existing cease-fire, and appointed James Baker, a former US Secretary of State, as his Personal Envoy to the region. In early June Baker obtained the support of Morocco and the Frente Polisario, as well as Algeria and Mauritania (which border the disputed territory), to conduct further negotiations in order to advance the referendum process. Direct talks between senior representatives of the Moroccan Government and the Frente Polisario authorities were initiated later in that month, in Lisbon, Portugal, under the auspices of the UN Special Representative, and attended by Algeria and Mauritania in an observer capacity. In September the two sides concluded an agreement which aimed to resolve the outstanding issues of contention and enable the referendum to be conducted in late 1998. The agreement included a commitment by both parties to identify eligible Sahrawi voters on an individual basis, in accordance with the results of the 1947 census, and a code of conduct to ensure the impartiality of the poll. In October 1997 the Security Council extended MINURSO's mandate to 20 April 1998. The Council also endorsed a recommendation of the Secretary-General to increase the strength of the mission, initially by 32 identification staff and 36 civilian police officers to work at up to nine identification centres. The process of voter identification resumed in December 1997. The timetable for the settlement plan envisaged the identification process as being completed by 31 May 1998, a final list of voters to be published, after a process of appeal, in late July, followed by a transitional period, under UN authority, during which all Sahrawi refugees were to be repatriated. The referendum was scheduled to be conducted on 7 December, and MINURSO was expected to withdraw from the region in January 1999. In January 1998 the Security Council approved the deployment of an engineering unit to support MINURSO in its demining activities. In April the Council extended MINURSO's mandate for a three-month period. At that time there were already significant delays apparent in the identification process, owing to ongoing disputes regarding the eligibility of members of three Saharan tribal groups. By the end of June 73,456 voters had been identified since December, bringing the total number of people identified since 1994 to 133,568. In July the Security Council extended MINURSO's mandate until 21 September, but warned that it would be terminated if either side significantly obstructed implementation of the settlement plan.

The Mission has headquarters in the north and south of the territory, and there is a liaison office in Tindouf, Algeria, in order to maintain contact with Polisario (which is based in Algeria) and the Algerian Government.

At 31 May 1998 MINURSO comprised 203 military observers, 123 troops and 78 civilian police officers. In June the UN General Assembly approved a budget of US $22m. for the Mission, to cover a four-month period from 1 July.

UNITED NATIONS PEACE-KEEPING FORCE IN CYPRUS—UNFICYP

Headquarters: Nicosia, Cyprus.

Special Adviser to the UN Secretary-General: DIEGO CÓRDOVEZ (Ecuador).

Deputy Special Representative of the UN Secretary-General and Chief of Mission: Dame ANNE HERCUS (New Zealand).

Commander: Maj.-Gen. EVERGISTO ARTURO DE VERGARA (Argentina).

UNFICYP was established in March 1964 by a UN Security Council resolution (for a three-month period, subsequently extended) to prevent a recurrence of fighting between the Greek and Turkish Cypriot communities, and to contribute to the maintenance of law and order and a return to normal conditions. The Force controls a 180-km buffer zone, established (following the Turkish intervention in 1974) between the cease-fire lines of the Turkish forces and the Cyprus National Guard. The Force also performs humanitarian functions, such as facilitating the supply of electricity and water across the cease-fire lines, and providing emergency medical services. In August 1996 serious hostilities between elements of the two communities in the UN-controlled buffer zone resulted in the deaths of two people and injuries to many others, including 12 UN personnel. Following further intercommunal violence, UNFICYP advocated the prohibition of all weapons and military posts along the length of the buffer zone. The Force also proposed additional humanitarian measures to improve the conditions of minority groups living in the two parts of the island. A new series of direct negotiations between the leaders of the two communities was initiated, under UN auspices, in July 1997.

At 31 May 1998 UNFICYP had an operational strength of 1,212 troops and 35 civilian police officers from nine countries, supported by 350 international and local civilian staff. The annual cost of maintaining the Force is estimated at US $43.0m., of which about one-half is met by assessed contributions from UN member states; the Government of Cyprus pays one-third of the total cost of the operation, while Greece contributes an estimated $6.5m.

UNITED NATIONS TRUCE SUPERVISION ORGANIZATION—UNTSO

Headquarters: Government House, Jerusalem.

Chief-of-Staff: Maj.-Gen. TIMOTHY R. FORD (Australia).

UNTSO was established initially to supervise the truce called by the UN Security Council in Palestine in May 1948 and has assisted in the application of the 1949 Armistice Agreements. Its activities have evolved over the years, in response to developments in the Middle East and in accordance with the relevant resolutions of the Security Council.

UNTSO observers assist the UN peace-keeping forces in the Middle East (see below), UNIFIL and UNDOF. UNTSO maintains a presence in Egypt, organized as Observer Group Egypt which has its headquarters at Ismailia, in the area of the Suez canal, and conducts patrols and operates outposts in the Sinai region. There is also a small detachment of observers in Beirut, Lebanon and liaison offices in Amman, Jordan and Gaza. UNTSO observers have been available at short notice to form the nucleus of other peace-keeping operations.

At 31 May 1998 UNTSO comprised 163 military observers, from 20 countries, who were supported by other international and local civilian staff. UNTSO expenditures are covered by the regular budget of the United Nations.

United Nations Relief and Works Agency for Palestine Refugees in the Near East—UNRWA

Addresses: Al Azhar Rd, POB 61, Gaza;
Bayader Wadi Seer, POB 140157, Amman, Jordan.
Telephone (Gaza): (7) 861196; **fax:** (7) 822552.
Telephone (Amman): (6) 826171; **telex:** 21170; **fax:** (6) 864151.

UNRWA began operations in 1950 to provide relief, health, education and welfare services for Palestine refugees in the Near East.

Organization

(August 1998)

UNRWA employs an international staff of about 180 and more than 20,000 local staff, mainly Palestine refugees. In mid-1996 the agency's headquarters were relocated, from Vienna, Austria, to Gaza. The Commissioner-General is appointed by the UN General Assembly, is the head of all UNRWA operations and is assisted by an Advisory Commission consisting of representatives of the governments of:

Belgium	Jordan	Turkey
Egypt	Lebanon	United Kingdom
France	Syria	USA
Japan		

Commissioner-General: PETER HANSEN (Denmark).

FIELD OFFICES

Each field office is headed by a director and has departments responsible for education, health and relief and social services programmes, finance, administration, supply and transport, legal affairs and public information.

Jordan: Al Zubeidi Bldg, Tla'a Al-Air, POB 484, Amman; tel. (6) 607194; telex 23402; fax (6) 685476.

Lebanon: POB 947, Beirut; tel. (1) 603437; fax (1) 603443.

Syria: POB 4313, Damascus; tel. (11) 6133035; fax (11) 6133047.

West Bank: Sheik Jarrah Qtr, POB 19149, Jerusalem; tel. (2) 890400; telex 26194; fax (2) 322714.

LIAISON OFFICES

Egypt: 2 Dar-el-Shifa St, Garden City, POB 277, Cairo; tel. (2) 354-8502; telex 94035; fax (2) 354-8504.

USA: Room DC 2-0550, United Nations, New York, NY 10017; tel. (212) 963-2255; telex 422311; fax (212) 935-7899.

Activities

SERVICES FOR PALESTINE REFUGEES

Since 1950 UNRWA has provided relief, health, education and social services for Palestine refugees in Lebanon, Syria, Jordan, the West Bank and the Gaza Strip. For UNRWA's purposes, a Palestine refugee is one whose normal residence was in Palestine for a minimum of two years before the 1948 conflict and who, as a result of the Arab–Israeli hostilities, lost his or her home and means of livelihood. To be eligible for assistance, a refugee must reside in one of the five areas in which UNRWA operates and be in need. A refugee's descendants who fulfil certain criteria are also eligible for UNRWA assistance. At 30 June 1996 UNRWA was providing essential services to 3,308,133 registered refugees (see table). Of these, an estimated 1,095,375 (approximately one-third) were living in 59 camps serviced by the Agency, while the remaining refugees had settled in the towns and villages already existing.

UNRWA's three principal areas of activity are education; health services; and relief and social services. More than 78% of the Agency's 1996 regular budget was devoted to these three operational programmes.

Education (under the technical supervision of UNESCO) accounted for 49% of UNRWA's 1996 budget. In the 1995/96 school year there were 421,854 pupils enrolled in 637 UNRWA schools (74 schools in Lebanon, 110 in Syria, 198 in Jordan, 100 on the West Bank and 155 in the Gaza Strip), and 13,140 educational staff. UNRWA also operated eight vocational and teacher-training centres, which provided a total of 4,624 training places. UNRWA awarded 943 scholarships for study at Arab universities in 1995/96. Technical co-operation for the Agency's education programme is provided by UNESCO.

Health services accounted for 18% of UNRWA's 1996 regular budget. At June 1996 there were 121 health units, of which 78 offered dental care, 120 offered family planning services and 108 offered special care. At that time annual patient visits to UNRWA medical units numbered 6.6m. UNRWA also operates a supplementary feeding programme, mainly for children, to combat malnutrition. Technical assistance for the health programme is provided by WHO.

Relief and social services accounted for 11% of UNRWA's regular budget for 1996. These services comprise the distribution of food rations, the provision of emergency shelter and the organization of welfare programmes for the poorest refugees (at June 1996 179,178 refugees, or 5.4% of the total registered refugee population, were eligible to receive special hardship assistance). In 1995/96 UNRWA's social services programme operated 68 women's centres and 30 community-based rehabilitation centres.

In order to encourage Palestinian self-reliance the Agency issues grants to ailing businesses and loans to families who qualify as special hardship cases. Between 1983 and early 1993 608 such grants and loans were made. In 1991 UNRWA launched an income generation programme, which was designed to combat rising unemployment, particularly in the Occupied Territories. By 30 June 1996 1,970 loans, with a total estimated value of US $9.8m., had been issued to new and existing Palestinian-owned enterprises.

AID TO DISPLACED PERSONS

After the renewal of Arab–Israeli hostilities in the Middle East in June 1967, hundreds of thousands of people fled from the fighting and from Israeli-occupied areas to east Jordan, Syria and Egypt. UNRWA provided emergency relief for displaced refugees and was additionally empowered by a UN General Assembly resolution to provide 'humanitarian assistance, as far as practicable, on an emergency basis and as a temporary measure' for those persons other than Palestine refugees who were newly displaced and in urgent need. In practice, UNRWA lacked the funds to aid the other displaced persons and the main burden of supporting them devolved on the Arab governments concerned. The Agency, as requested by the Government of Jordan in 1967 and on that Government's behalf, distributes rations to displaced persons in Jordan who are not registered refugees of 1948.

RECENT EMERGENCIES

Since 1982 UNRWA has managed a specially-funded operation in Lebanon, aimed at assisting refugees displaced by the continued civil conflict. In late 1986 and early 1987 fighting caused much destruction to Palestinian housing and UNRWA facilities in Lebanon, and an emergency relief operation was undertaken. In April 1996 UNRWA dispatched emergency supplies to assist some of the estimated 500,000 people displaced by renewed military activities in southern Lebanon.

Following the start of the Palestinian *intifada* (uprising) in December 1987 in the Israeli-occupied territories of the West Bank and the Gaza Strip, UNRWA provided expanded medical aid and relief to Palestinian residents in these areas.

In January 1991 (following the outbreak of war between Iraq and a multinational force whose aim was to enforce the withdrawal of Iraqi forces from Kuwait) the Israeli authorities imposed a curfew on Palestinians in the Israeli-occupied territories, and in February UNRWA began an emergency programme of food distribution to Palestinians who had thereby been prevented from earning a living. Following the conflict, Jordan absorbed more than 300,000 people fleeing Kuwait and other Gulf countries. Many of these people are eligible for UNRWA services.

In September 1992 an UNRWA mission was sent to Kuwait, following allegations of abuses of human rights perpetrated by the Kuwaiti authorities against Palestinian refugees living there. The mission was, however, limited to assessing the number of Palestinians from the Gaza Strip in Kuwait, who had been unable to obtain asylum in Jordan, since Jordan did not recognize Gazan identity documents.

Following the signing of the Declaration of Principles by the Palestine Liberation Organization and the Israeli Government in September 1993, UNRWA initiated a Peace Implementation Programme (PIP) to improve services and infrastructure for Palestinian refugees. In September 1994 the first phase of the programme (PIP I) was concluded after the receipt of US $93.2m. in pledged donations. PIP I projects included the construction of 33 schools and 24 classrooms and specialized education rooms, the rehabilitation of 4,700 shelters, the upgrading of solid waste disposal facilities throughout the Gaza Strip and feasibility studies for two sewerage systems. It was estimated that these projects created more than 5,500 jobs in the Gaza Strip for an average period of four months each. By mid-1996 the total number of PIP projects, including those under the second phase of the programme (PIP II), amounted to 276, while funds received or pledged to the Programme totalled $192.6m.

FINANCE

For the most part, UNRWA's income is composed of voluntary contributions, almost entirely from governments and the European Union, the remainder being provided by non-governmental organizations, business corporations and private sources.

As of January 1992 UNRWA adopted a biennial budgetary cycle. The general fund budget for 1994–95 amounted to US $632.3m., of which $552.8m. was to be in cash and $79.5m. in kind. The regular budget for 1996 amounted to $327.5m.

STATISTICS

Refugees Registered with UNRWA (30 June 1996)

Country								Number	% of total
Jordan	.	.	.	.	.	.	.	1,358,706	41.1
Gaza Strip	.	.	.	.	.	.	.	716,930	21.7
West Bank	.	.	.	.	.	.	.	532,438	16.1
Lebanon	.	.	.	.	.	.	.	352,668	10.7
Syria	.	.	.	.	.	.	.	347,391	10.5
Total	.	.	.	.	.	.	.	**3,308,133**	**100.0**

PUBLICATIONS

Annual Report of the Commissioner-General of UNRWA.

Palestine Refugees Today – the UNRWA Newsletter (2 a year).

UNRWA Accounts Summary (annually).

UNRWA – An Investment in People (every 2 years).

UNRWA News (monthly).

Catalogues of publications and audio-visual materials.

Food and Agriculture Organization—FAO

Address: Viale delle Terme di Caracalla, 00100 Rome, Italy.

Telephone: (06) 57051; **telex:** 625852; **fax:** (06) 5705-3152; **e-mail:** telex-room@fao.org; **internet:** http://www.fao.org.

FAO, the first specialized agency of the UN to be founded after the Second World War, was established in Québec, Canada, in October 1945. The Organization combats malnutrition and hunger and serves as a co-ordinating agency for development programmes in the whole range of food and agriculture, including forestry and fisheries. It helps developing countries to promote educational and training facilities and the creation of appropriate institutions.

Organization

(August 1998)

CONFERENCE

The governing body is the FAO Conference of member nations. It meets every two years, formulates policy, determines the Organization's programme and budget on a biennial basis, and elects new members. It also elects the Director-General of the Secretariat and the Independent Chairman of the Council. Every second year, FAO also holds conferences in each of its five regions (designated the Near East, Asia and the Pacific, Africa, Latin America and the Caribbean, and Europe).

COUNCIL

The FAO Council is composed of representatives of 49 member nations, elected by the Conference for staggered three-year terms. It is the interim governing body of FAO between sessions of the Conference. The most important standing Committees of the Council are: the Finance and Programme Committees, the Committee on Commodity Problems, the Committee on Fisheries, the Committee on Agriculture and the Committee on Forestry.

SECRETARIAT

The total number of staff at FAO headquarters in September 1997 was 2,465, of whom 67 were associate experts, while staff in field, regional and country offices numbered 1,967, including 133 associate experts. Work is supervised by the following Departments: Administration and Finance; General Affairs and Information; Economic and Social Policy; Agriculture; Forestry; Fisheries; Sustainable Development; and Technical Co-operation.

Director-General: JACQUES DIOUF (Senegal).

REGIONAL OFFICES

Regional Office for the Near East: 11 el-Eslah el-Zerai St, POB 2223, Dokki, Cairo, Egypt; tel. (2) 3316000; telex 21055; fax (2) 3495981; e-mail fao-rne@field.fao.org; Regional Rep. ATIF Y. BUKHARI.

Subregional Office for North Africa: BP 300, Tunis, Tunisia; tel. (1) 782686; telex 14994; fax (1) 791859; e-mail fao-tun@field.fao.org; Subregional Rep. BRAHIM AMOURI.

Activities

FAO aims to raise levels of nutrition and standards of living, by improving the production and distribution of food and other commodities derived from farms, fisheries and forests. FAO provides technical information, advice and assistance by disseminating information; acting as a neutral forum for discussion of food and agricultural issues; advising governments on policy and planning; and developing capacity directly in the field.

The 1997 FAO Conference, held in Rome in November, identified the following areas of activity as FAO priorities for 1998–99; the Special Programme for Food Security; transboundary animal and plant pests and diseases; forestry; the Codex Alimentarius code on food standards; and strengthening the Technical Co-operation Programme (which funds 15% of FAO's field programme expenditure). The Conference also endorsed FAO's 'TeleFood' initiative, a televised fund-raising event, broadcast to an estimated 500m. viewers in some 70 countries in October 1997. The initiative generated approximately US $2m. towards projects aimed at helping small-scale farmers to increase crop production, and was expected to take place on an annual basis in order to raise public awareness of the problems of hunger and malnutrition. In November 1996 FAO hosted the World Food Summit, which was held in Rome and was attended by heads of state and senior government representatives of 186 countries. Participants approved the Rome Declaration on World Food Security and the World Food Summit Plan of Action, with the aim of halving the number of people afflicted by undernutrition, at that time estimated to total 840m. world-wide, no later than 2015.

FAO's total field programme expenditure for 1996 was US $244m., compared with $264m. spent in 1995. An estimated 32% of field projects were in Africa, 23% in Asia and the Pacific, 11% in the Near East, 11% in Latin America and the Caribbean, 4% in Europe, and 19% were inter-regional or global.

AGRICULTURE

FAO's Field Programme provides training and technical assistance to enable small farmers to increase crop production, by a number of methods, including improved seeds and fertilizer use, soil conservation and reafforestation, better water resource management, upgrading storage facilities, and improvements in processing and marketing. Governments are advised on the conservation of genetic resources, on improving the supply of seeds, and on crop protection: animal and plant gene banks are maintained. In June 1996 representatives of more than 150 governments attending a conference in Leipzig, Germany, organized by FAO, adopted a Global Plan of Action to conserve and improve the use of plant genetic resources, in order to enhance food security throughout the world. The Plan included measures to strengthen the development of plant varieties and to promote the use and availability of local varieties and locally-adapted crops to farmers, in particular following a natural disaster, war or civil conflict. FAO's Special Programme for Food Security, which was initiated in 1994, was designed to assist target countries, i.e. low-income countries with a food deficit, to increase food production and productivity as rapidly as possible. This was to be achieved primarily through the widespread adoption by farmers of available improved production technologies, with emphasis on areas of high potential. At 31 March 1998 83 countries were categorized as 'low-income food-deficit', of which 42 were in Africa. By April of that year the Programme was operational in 30 countries, while preparations were under way for projects to be implemented in a further 37 of the targeted countries. A budget of US $10m. was allocated to the Programme for the two-year period 1998–99.

Plant protection, weed control and animal health programmes form an important part of FAO's work as farming methods become more intensive, and pests more resistant to control methods. In 1985 the FAO Conference approved an International Code of Conduct on the Distribution and Use of Pesticides, and in 1989 adopted an additional clause concerning 'Prior Informed Consent', whereby international shipments of newly banned or restricted pesticides should not proceed without the agreement of importing countries. Under the clause FAO aims to inform governments about the hazards of toxic chemicals and to encourage them to take proper measures to curb trade in highly toxic agrochemicals, while keeping the pesticides industry informed of control actions. In mid-1996 FAO publicized a new initiative which aimed to increase awareness of, and to promote international action on, obsolete and hazardous stocks of pesticides remaining throughout the world. By September 1997 22 pesticides and five industrial chemicals were subject to the PIC clause, and 154 countries were participating in the scheme. A central concept of FAO's plant protection programme is the Integrated Pest Management (IPM) strategy, which was initiated in 1988 in order to reduce over-reliance on pesticides. IPM principles include biological control methods, such as the introduction of natural predators to reduce pest infestation, crop rotation and the use of pest-resistant crop varieties. In mid-1995 FAO initiated a project, at the request of 16 Middle Eastern and North African Governments, to improve the development and use of IPM strategies at a local and national level throughout the region, and to improve their dissemination between the countries. FAO's Joint Division with the International Atomic Energy Agency (IAEA) tests controlled-release formulas of pesticides and herbicides that can limit the amount of agrochemicals needed to protect crops. The Joint FAO-IAEA Division is engaged in exploring biotechnologies and in developing non-toxic fertilizers (especially those that are locally available) and improved strains of food crops (especially from indigenous varieties). In animal production and health, the Joint Division has developed progesterone-measuring and disease-diagnostic kits, thousands of which are delivered to developing countries every year.

An Emergency Prevention System for Transboundary Animal and Plant Pests and Diseases (EMPRES) was established in 1994 to strengthen FAO's activities in the prevention, control and, where possible, eradication of highly contagious diseases and pests. EMPRES's initial priorities were locusts and rinderpest. During 1994 EMPRES published guidelines on all aspects of desert locust monitoring, commissioned an evaluation of recent control efforts and prepared a concept paper on desert locust management. FAO assumed responsibility for technical leadership and co-ordination of the Global Rinderpest Eradication Campaign, which aims to eradicate the disease, endemic in the area of the Horn of Africa, by 2010.

In November 1997 FAO initiated a Programme Against African Trypanosomiasis, which aimed to counter the parasitic disease, spread by the tsetse fly, which manifests itself as ngana in cattle and other animals and as sleeping sickness in humans, and is prevalent in almost one-third of Africa.

FISHERIES

FAO's Fisheries Department consists of a multi-disciplinary body of experts who are involved in every aspect of fisheries development from coastal surveys, improved production, processing and storage, to the compilation of statistics, development of computer databases, improvement of fishing gear, institution building and training. In March 1995 a ministerial meeting of fisheries adopted a Rome Consensus on World Fisheries, which identified a need for immediate action to eliminate overfishing and to rebuild and enhance depleting fish stocks. In November the FAO Conference adopted a Code of Conduct for Responsible Fishing, which incorporated many global fisheries and aquaculture issues (including fisheries resource conservation and development, fish catches, seafood and fish processing, commercialization, trade and research) to promote the sustainable development of the sector. FAO promotes aquaculture as a valuable source of animal protein, and as an income-generating activity for rural communities. In 1996/97 FAO participated in 21 technical consultations on the management of marine resources, strengthened work on aquatic genetic resources, and conducted studies to monitor the impact of 'El Niño', a periodic warming of the tropical Pacific Ocean, on aquaculture in Latin America and Africa.

FORESTRY

FAO focuses on the contribution of forestry to food security, on effective and responsible forest management and on maintaining a balance between the economic, ecological and social benefits of forest resources. FAO has helped to develop national forestry programmes and to promote the sustainable development of all types of forest. FAO's Forests, Trees and People Programme promotes the sustainable management of tree and forest resources, based on local knowledge and management practices, in order to improve the livelihoods of rural people in developing countries. A draft strategic plan for the sustainable management of trees and forests was formulated in 1997 and was expected to receive final endorsement in 1999. The main objectives of the draft plan were to maintain the environmental diversity of forests, to realise the economic potential of forests and trees within a sustainable framework, and to establish broad social networks of interested parties to manage and develop forest environments. During 1997 FAO helped to organize the Eleventh World Forestry Congress, which was held in Antalya, Turkey, in October.

PROCESSING AND MARKETING

An estimated 20% of all food harvested is lost before it can be consumed. FAO helps to reduce immediate post-harvest losses through the introduction of improved processing methods and storage systems. It also advises on the distribution and marketing of agricultural produce and on the selection and preparation of foods for optimum nutrition. Many of these activities form part of wider rural development projects. FAO continues to favour the elimination of export subsidies and related discriminatory practices, such as protectionist measures that hamper international trade in agricultural commodities. FAO has organized 18 regional workshops and 44 national projects in order to help member states to implement new World Trade Organization regulations, in particular with regard to agricultural policy, intellectual property rights, sanitary and phytosanitary measures, technical barriers to trade and the international standards of the Codex Alimentarius, and to consider the impact on member states of the ministerial decision concerning the possible negative effects of the reform programme on least-developed and net-food-importing developing countries. FAO evaluates new market trends and helps to develop improved plant and animal quarantine procedures. In November 1997 the FAO Conference adopted new guide-lines on surveillance and export certification systems in order to harmonize plant quarantine standards.

ENVIRONMENT

In April 1991 a Conference on Agriculture and the Environment was held in the Netherlands, organized jointly by FAO and the Netherlands Government. The alleviation of poverty was identified as being a major prerequisite for sustainable agricultural production. At the UN Conference on Environment and Development, held in Rio de Janeiro in June 1992, FAO participated in several working parties and supported the adoption of Agenda 21, a programme of activities to promote sustainable development. FAO was subsequently designated as the UN agency responsible for the chapters of Agenda 21 concerned with water resources, forests, fragile mountain ecosystems and sustainable agriculture and rural development.

NUTRITION

In December 1992 an International Conference on Nutrition was held in Rome, administered jointly by FAO and WHO. The Conference approved a World Declaration on Nutrition and a Plan of Action, aimed at promoting efforts to combat malnutrition as a development priority. Since the conference, more than 100 countries have formulated national plans of action for nutrition, many of which were based on existing development plans such as comprehensive food security initiatives, national poverty alleviation programmes and action plans to attain the targets set by the World Summit for Children in September 1990. By October 1995 several projects based on the national plans of action had been implemented in areas such as nutrition education, food quality and safety, micronutrient deficiency alleviation and nutrition surveillance.

FOOD SECURITY

FAO's food security policy aims to encourage the production of adequate food supplies, to maximize stability in the flow of supplies, and to ensure access on the part of those who need them. FAO was actively involved in the formulation of a Plan of Action on food security, adopted at the World Food Summit in November 1996, and was to be responsible for monitoring and promoting its implementation.

FAO's Global Information and Early Warning System (GIEWS), which became operational in 1975, monitors the crop and food outlook at global and national levels in order to detect emerging food supply difficulties and disasters and to ensure rapid intervention in countries experiencing food supply shortages. In 1996 the CIEWS conducted 30 missions to assess crops and food supply, and participated in a number of inter-agency surveillance programmes, mainly with the World Food Programme (WFP). At the end of 1997 FAO identified 37 countries, that were confronting acute food shortages and required exceptional and/or emergency food assistance, compared with 31 at the end of 1996.

FAO INVESTMENT CENTRE

The Investment Centre was established in 1964 to help countries prepare viable investment projects that would attract external financing. The Centre focuses its evaluation of projects on two fundamental concerns: the promotion of sustainable activities for land management, forestry development and environmental protection; and the alleviation of rural poverty. In 1996 41 projects were approved, representing a total investment of some US $2,500m.

EMERGENCY RELIEF

FAO works to rehabilitate agricultural production following natural and man-made disasters by providing emergency seed, tools, and technical and other assistance. In 1997 FAO's Special Relief Operations Service undertook emergency interventions in 34 countries, at a cost of more than US $60m. New projects approved in the first quarter of 1998 included assistance to farmers affected by earthquakes in Iran, crop protection in northern Iraq and assistance with implementation of the UN Security Council resolution to provide for the limited export of petroleum by Iraq in return for food and essential humanitarian supplies. Jointly with the United Nations, FAO is responsible for WFP (see below), which provides emergency food supplies and food aid in support of development projects.

INFORMATION

FAO functions as an information centre, collecting, analysing, interpreting and disseminating information through various media. It issues regular statistical reports, commodity studies, and technical manuals in local languages (see list of publications below). Other materials produced by the FAO include information booklets, reference papers, reports of meetings, training manuals and audiovisuals.

FAO compiles and co-ordinates an extensive range of international databases on agriculture, fisheries, forestry, food and statistics, the most important of these being AGRIS (the International Information System for the Agricultural Sciences and Technology) and CARIS (the Current Agricultural Research Information System). Statistical databases include the GLOBEFISH databank and electronic library, FISHDAB (the Fisheries Statistical Database), FORIS (Forest Resources Information System), and GIS (the Geographic Information System). In addition, AGROSTAT PC has been designed to provide access to updated figures in six agriculture-related topics via personal computer. In 1996 FAO established a World Agricultural Information Centre (WAICENT), which offers wide access to agricultural data through the internet.

FAO REGIONAL COMMISSIONS

Commission for Controlling the Desert Locust in the Near East: f. 1965 to carry out all possible measures to control plagues of the desert locust within the region and to reduce crop damage. Mems: 13 states.

Commission for Controlling the Desert Locust in North-West Africa: f. 1971 to promote research on control of the desert locust. Mems: 4 states.

General Fisheries Council for the Mediterranean—GFCM: f. 1952 to develop aquatic resources, to encourage and co-ordinate research in the fishing and allied industries, to assemble and publish information, and to recommend the standardization of scientific equipment, techniques and nomenclature. Mems: 19 states.

Near East Forestry Commission: f. 1953 to advise on formulation of forest policy and review and co-ordinate its implementation throughout the region; to exchange information and advise on technical problems. Mems: 20 states.

Near East Regional Commission on Agriculture: f. 1983 to conduct periodic reviews of agricultural problems in the region; to promote the formulation and implementation of regional and national policies and programmes for improving production of crops and livestock; to strengthen the production and management of crops, livestock, supporting services and research; to promote the transfer of technology and regional technical co-operation; and to provide guidance on training and manpower development. Mems: 15 states.

Near East Regional Economic and Social Policy Commission: f. 1983 to review developments relating to food, agriculture and food security; to recommend policies on agrarian reform and rural development; and to review and exchange information on food and nutrition policies and on agricultural planning. Mems: 15 states.

Regional Commission on Land and Water Use in the Near East: f. 1967 to review the current situation with regard to land and water use in the region; to identify the main problems concerning the development of land and water resources which require research and study and to consider other related matters. Mems: 21 states.

FINANCE

FAO's Regular Programme, which is financed by contributions from the member governments, covers the cost of FAO's Secretariat, its Technical Co-operation Programme (TCP) and part of the cost of several special action programmes. The budget for the two years 1997–98 amounted to US $650m. Much of FAO's Field Programme is funded from extra-budgetary sources. The single largest contributor is the United Nations Development Programme (UNDP), which in 1996 accounted for $47m., or 19%, of total Field Programme expenditure amounting to $244m. More important are the trust funds that come mainly from donor countries and international financing institutions. In 1996 they totalled $158m., or 65%, of Field Programme expenditure. FAO's contribution under the TCP was $36m., or 15% of expenditure in that year.

WORLD FOOD PROGRAMME—WFP

Address: Via Cesare Giulio Viola 68, Parco dei Medici, 00148 Rome, Italy.

Telephone: (06) 6513-1; **telex:** 626675; **fax:** (06) 6590-632; **e-mail:** wfpinfo@wfp.org; **internet:** http://www.wfp.org.

WFP is a joint UN-FAO effort to stimulate economic and social development through food aid and to provide emergency relief. It became operational in 1963.

Through its development activities, WFP aims to alleviate poverty in developing countries by promoting self-reliant families and communities. Food is supplied, for example, as an incentive in development self-help schemes, as part wages in labour-intensive projects of many kinds, particularly in the rural economy, but also in the industrial field, and in support of institutional feeding schemes where the emphasis is mainly on enabling the beneficiaries to have an adequate and balanced diet. Priority is given to vulnerable groups such as pregnant women and children. Some WFP projects are intended to alleviate the effects of structural adjustment programmes (particularly programmes which involve reductions in public expenditure and in subsidies for basic foods). At the end of 1996 WFP was supporting 174 development projects, with total commitments valued at US $1,994m.

In the early 1990s there was a substantial shift in the balance between emergency and development assistance provided by WFP, owing to the growing needs of victims of drought and other natural disasters, refugees and displaced persons. By 1994 two-thirds of all food aid was for relief assistance and one-third for development, representing a direct reversal of the allocations five years previously. In addition, there was a noticeable increase in aid given to those in need as a result of civil war, compared with commitments for victims of natural disasters. WFP maintains strategic stores of food and logistics equipment (at Nairobi, Kenya and Pisa, Italy) and supports eight field units, which undertake vulnerability analysis and mapping activities.

In 1996 WFP operational expenditure in the Middle East and North Africa amounted to US $129.8m., or 12.2% of total operational expenditure in that year, of which $92.6m. was for relief operations, $31.5m. was for development projects and $5.7m. was for extrabudgetary activities. New projects approved for the region in 1996 included the distribution of food rations to some 100,000 people affected by renewed military operations in southern Lebanon, the emergency provision of food to 6,000 refugees from Mali, based in Algeria, and aid for some 44,000 people affected by flooding in Yemen. WFP also approved operations to provide food to some 8,000 Somali refugees remaining in Yemen, to 80,000 vulnerable refugees from the Western Sahara based in Algeria, and to 388,000 Afghan and Iraqi refugees remaining in Iran. Other longer-term develop-

ment projects approved included a five-year commitment to support land improvement initiatives in Jordan, support for social welfare programmes in the Gaza Strip, with an estimated 50,000 beneficiaries over a one-year period, and a five-year project to enhance resource management and environmental protection in Egypt's western desert. In accordance with a Security Council resolution providing for the limited sale of petroleum by the Iraqi Government in exchange for the purchase of essential humanitarian supplies, which came into effect in December 1996, WFP was mandated to establish an observation system to ensure the fair and efficient distribution of food throughout the country. WFP was also required to transport and distribute the food supplies to local populations in the north of Iraq.

WFP Executive Director: Catherine A. Bertini (USA).

FAO PUBLICATIONS

Animal Health Yearbook.
Commodity Review and Outlook (annually).
Environment and Energy Bulletin.
Fertilizer Yearbook.
Food Outlook (quarterly).
Plant Protection Bulletin (quarterly).
Production Yearbook.
Quarterly Bulletin of Statistics.
The State of Food and Agriculture (annually).
The State of World Fisheries and Aquaculture (annually).
The State of the World's Forests (every two years).
Technical Co-operation Among Developing Countries Newsletter.
Trade Yearbook.
Unasylva (quarterly).
World Animal Review (two a year).
World Watch List for Domestic Animal Diversity.
Yearbook of Fishery Statistics.
Yearbook of Forest Products.
Commodity reviews; studies; manuals.

International Bank for Reconstruction and Development—IBRD, and International Development Association—IDA (World Bank)

Address: 1818 H St, NW, Washington, DC 20433, USA.

Telephone: (202) 477-1234; **telex:** 248423; **fax:** (202) 477-6391; **internet:** http://www.worldbank.org.

The IBRD was established on 27 December 1945. Initially it was concerned with post-war reconstruction in Europe; since then its aim has been to assist the economic development of member nations by making loans where private capital is not available on reasonable terms to finance productive investments. Loans are made either direct to governments, or to private enterprises with the guarantee of their governments. The 'World Bank', as it is commonly known, comprises the IBRD and the International Development Association (IDA), which was founded in 1960. The affiliated group of institutions, comprising the IBRD, the IDA, the International Finance Corporation (IFC, q.v.), the Multilateral Investment Guarantee Agency (MIGA, q.v.) and the International Centre for Settlement of Investment Disputes (ICSID) is referred to as the World Bank Group. Only members of the International Monetary Fund (IMF, q.v.) may be considered for membership in the Bank. Subscriptions to the capital stock of the Bank are based on each member's quota in the IMF, which is designed to reflect the country's relative economic strength. Voting rights are related to shareholdings.

Organization

(August 1998)

Officers and staff of the IBRD serve concurrently as officers and staff in the IDA. The World Bank has offices in New York, Paris, Brussels, London and Tokyo; regional missions in Nairobi (for eastern Africa), Abidjan (for western Africa), Bangkok (in Thailand) and Riga (in Latvia); and resident missions in 73 countries.

BOARD OF GOVERNORS

The Board of Governors consists of one Governor appointed by each member nation. Typically, a Governor is the country's finance minister, central bank governor, or a minister or an official of comparable rank. The Board normally meets once a year.

EXECUTIVE DIRECTORS

The general operations of the World Bank are conducted by a Board of 24 Executive Directors. Five Directors are appointed by the five members having the largest number of shares of capital stock, and the rest are elected by the Governors representing the other members. The President of the Bank is Chairman of the Board.

OFFICERS

President and Chairman of Executive Directors: James D. Wolfensohn (USA).

Vice-President, Middle East and North Africa Region: Kemal Dervis.

Activities

FINANCIAL OPERATIONS

The World Bank's primary objectives are the achievement of sustainable economic growth and the reduction of poverty in developing countries. In mid-1994 the World Bank Group published a review of its role and activities, and identified the following five major development issues on which it intended to focus in the future: the pursuit of economic reforms; investment in people, in particular through education, health, nutrition and family-planning programmes; the protection of the environment; stimulation of the private sector; and reorientation of government, in order to enhance the private sector by reforming and strengthening the public sector. The Bank compiles country-specific assessments and formulates country assistance strategies (CASs) to ensure that the Bank's own projects support and complement the programmes of the country concerned. Since 1987 the World Bank has accorded greater importance to the protection of the environment and in 1989/90 systematic 'screening' of all new projects was introduced, in order to assess their environmental impact.

IBRD loans are usually for a period of 20 years or less. Loans are made to governments, or must be guaranteed by the government concerned. IDA assistance is aimed at the poorer developing countries (i.e. those with a gross national product—GNP—per head of less than US $925 in 1996 dollars). Under IDA lending conditions, credits can be extended to countries whose balance of payments could not sustain the burden of repayment required for IBRD loans. Terms are more favourable than those provided by the IBRD; credits are for a period of 35–40 years, with a 'grace' period of 10 years, and carry no interest charges.

The IBRD's capital is derived from members' subscriptions to capital shares, the calculation of which is based on their quotas in the IMF (q.v.). In April 1988 the Board of Governors approved an increase of about 80% in the IBRD's authorized capital, to US $171,000m. At 30 June 1997 the total subscribed capital of the IBRD was $182,426m., of which the paid-in portion was $11,048m. (6.1%); the remainder is subject to call if required. Most of the IBRD's lendable funds come from its borrowing in world capital markets, and also from its retained earnings and the flow of repayments on its loans. Bank loans carry a variable interest rate, rather than a rate fixed at the time of borrowing.

IDA's development resources, consisting of members' subscriptions and supplementary resources (additional subscriptions and contributions), are replenished periodically by contributions from the more affluent member countries. In March 1996 representatives of more than 30 donor countries concluded negotiations for the 11th replenishment of IDA funds (and for a one-year interim fund), to finance the period July 1996–June 1999. New contributions over the three-year period were to amount to US $11,000m., while total funds available for lending, including past donor contributions, repayments of IDA credits and the World Bank's contributions, were to amount to $22,000m.

During the year ending 30 June 1997 US $914.8m., or 7.4% of World Bank assistance approved, was for the Middle East and North Africa (excluding Turkey): of the total, $145.2m. was in the form of IDA credits and $769.6m. in IBRD loans. In addition $83.5m. was committed, on IDA terms, from the Trust Fund for Gaza and the West Bank (see below). Some 20% of total Bank lending for the region was allocated to the agricultural sector; other main areas of support included water supply and sanitation, urban development and education.

The Bank has played a major role in promoting and co-ordinating international efforts in support of the Middle East peace process and in enhancing economic development throughout the region. Following agreement, in May 1994, on the implementation of the Declaration of Principles between Palestine and Israel, the Bank issued a report outlining an investment programme to assist Palestine in its transitional period to autonomous government: the Emergency Assistance Programme for the Occupied Territories was to cover a three-year period, with an investment budget of US $1,200m. pledged by the international community. Under the Programme, a Trust Fund for Gaza and the West Bank was established, in order to finance, on IDA terms, projects for the reconstruction and improvement of infrastructure, in particular education and health services. The Bank acts as the secretariat for the *Ad Hoc* Liaison Committee for the West Bank and Gaza, and for the joint Israeli–Jordan steering committee for the Jordan Rift Valley Development Programme. The Bank hosts annual meetings of a Consultative Group for the West Bank and Gaza, attended by donor governments and institutions, which considers projects for funding and reviews their implementation. In October 1996 the World Bank and the EU hosted an international conference, held in İstanbul, Turkey, to consider the privatization process in the Middle East and North Africa region and the participation of the private sector in major infrastructure projects. In the following month, at a regional economic 'summit' meeting, convened in Cairo, Egypt, the Bank declared its willingness to support the involvement of the private sector by reducing the perceived investment risks associated with such projects. In May 1997 the Bank sponsored a conference, held in Marrakech, Morocco, which aimed to promote economic development and regional competitiveness.

In September 1996 the World Bank/IMF Development Committee endorsed a joint initiative to assist heavily indebted poor countries (HIPCs) to reduce their debt burden, in cases where it impedes poverty reduction and economic growth. A new Trust Fund was established by the World Bank in November to finance the initiative. The Fund, consisting of an initial allocation of US $500m. from the IBRD surplus and other contributions from multilateral creditors, was to be administered by IDA. Of the 41 HIPCs identified by the Bank, only one country, Yemen, was in the Middle East and North Africa region.

TECHNICAL ASSISTANCE

The provision of technical assistance to member countries is a major component of Bank activities. The economic, sector and project analysis undertaken by the Bank in the normal course of its operations is the vehicle for considerable technical assistance. In addition, project loans and credits may include funds designated specifically for feasibility studies, resource surveys, management or planning advice, and training. Technical assistance (usually reimbursable) is also extended to countries that do not need Bank financial support e.g. for training and transfer of technology.

In 1992 the Bank established an Institutional Development Fund (IDF) to provide rapid, small-scale financial assistance, to a maximum value of US $500,000, for capacity-building initiatives. By the end of 1996 the Fund had approved a total of 345 grants for 108 countries.

ECONOMIC RESEARCH AND STUDIES

In the 1990s the World Bank's research, conducted by its own research staff, was increasingly concerned with providing information to reinforce the Bank's expanding advisory role to developing countries. Consequently the principal areas of current research focus on issues such as maintaining sustainable growth while protecting the environment and the poorest sectors of society, encouraging the development of the private sector, and reducing and decentralizing government activities. The Bank, together with UNDP, UNEP and the FAO, sponsors the Consultative Group on International Agricultural Research (CGIAR), which was formed in 1971 to raise financial support for research on improving crops and animal production in developing countries. CGIAR supports 16 research centres.

CO-OPERATION WITH OTHER ORGANIZATIONS

The World Bank co-operates closely with other UN bodies through consultations, meetings, and joint activities; co-operation with UNDP and WHO, in their programmes to improve health, nutrition and sanitation, is especially important. It collaborates with the IMF in implementing economic adjustment programmes in developing countries. The Bank holds regular consultations with the European Community and OECD on development issues, and the Bank-NGO Committee provides an annual forum for discussion with non-governmental organizations (NGOs). The Bank chairs meetings of donor governments and organizations for the co-ordination of aid to particular countries. The Bank also conducts co-financing and aid co-ordination projects with official aid agencies, export credit agencies and commercial banks. In April 1997 the World Bank signed a co-operation agreement with the World Trade Organization, in order to co-ordinate efforts to integrate developing countries into the global economy.

The World Bank administers the Global Environment Facility (GEF), which was established in 1990 in conjunction with UNDP and UNEP. The GEF became operational in 1991 for an initial three-year period, to provide grants to developing countries for measures that protect the environment. In March 1994 87 countries participating in the Facility agreed to restructure and replenish the GEF for a further three-year period from July of that year. Funds amounting to US $2,000m. were to be made available by 26 donor countries which would enable the GEF to act as the financial mechanism for the conventions on climate changes and biological diversity that were signed at the UN Conference on Environment and Development in June 1992. At 30 June 1997 the GEF portfolio comprised 69 projects, with financing of almost $675m., covering the following areas: biodiversity; climate change; the phase-out of ozone-depleting substances; and international waters. In November 33 donor countries committed themselves to a target figure of $2,750m. for the next replenishment of GEF funds.

In June 1995 the World Bank joined other international donors (including regional development banks, other UN bodies, Canada, France, the Netherlands and the USA) in establishing a Consultative Group to Assist the Poorest (CGAP), which was to channel funds to the most needy through grass-roots agencies. An initial credit of approximately US $200m. was committed by the donors. The Bank manages the CGAP Secretariat, which is responsible for the administration of external funding and for the evaluation and approval of project financing. In addition, the CGAP provides training and information services on microfinance for policy-makers and practitioners.

EVALUATION

The World Bank's Operations Evaluation Department studies and publishes the results of projects after a loan has been fully disbursed, so as to identify problems and possible improvements in future activities. Internal auditing is also carried out, to monitor the effectiveness of the Bank's operations and management.

In September 1993 the Bank's Board of Executive Directors agreed to establish an Independent Inspection Panel, consistent with the Bank's objective of improving project implementation and accountability. The Panel, which became operational in September 1994, was to conduct independent investigations and report on complaints concerning the design, appraisal and implementation of development projects supported by the Bank.

IBRD INSTITUTIONS

Economic Development Institute—EDI: founded in 1955. Training is provided for government officials at the middle and upper levels of responsibility who are concerned with development programmes and projects. The majority of courses are in economic and sector management and 'training of trainers', which aim to build up local capability to conduct projects courses in future. The Institute also produces training materials, and administers a fellowship scheme and the World Bank graduate scholarship programme (funded by the Government of Japan). EDI also organizes conferences, seminars and workshops, and is increasingly concerned with issues relating to good governance and with the development of human resources at all levels of society. In 1997 seminars on EDI's grass-roots management programme were held in Morocco and Tunisia. Dir AMNON GOLAN.

International Centre for Settlement of Investment Disputes—ICSID: founded in 1966 under the Convention of the Settlement of Investment Disputes between States and Nationals of Other States. The Convention was designed to encourage the growth of private foreign investment for economic development, by creating the possibility, always subject to the consent of both parties, for a Contracting State and a foreign investor who is a national of another Contracting State to settle any legal dispute that might arise out

of such an investment by conciliation and/or arbitration before an impartial, international forum. The governing body of the Centre is its Administrative Council, composed of one representative of each Contracting State, all of whom have equal voting power. The President of the World Bank is (*ex officio*) the non-voting Chairman of the Administrative Council.

At mid-1997 127 states had ratified the Convention to become ICSID member countries, with a further 14 states having signed the Convention. At that time 15 cases were pending before the Centre. Sec.-Gen. IBRAHIM F. I. SHIHATA.

PUBLICATIONS

Abstracts of Current Studies: The World Bank Research Program (annually).

Annual Report on Portfolio Performance.

Global Development Finance (annually).

Global Economic Prospects and Developing Countries (annually).

Research News (quarterly).

Staff Working Papers.

Transition (every 2 months).

Trends in Developing Economies (annually).

World Bank Annual Report.

World Bank Atlas (annually).

World Bank Economic Review (3 a year).

The World Bank and the Environment (annually).

World Bank News (2 a month).

World Bank Research Observer (2 a year).

World Development Indicators (annually).

World Development Report (annually).

World Tables (annually).

WORLD BANK OPERATIONS IN THE MIDDLE EAST AND NORTH AFRICA

IBRD Loans Approved, July 1996–June 1997 (US $ million)

Country	Purpose	Amount
Algeria	Rural employment	89.0
Jordan	Economic reform and business development	120.0
	Housing finance reform	20.0
Lebanon . . .	Water resources management and supply	53.1
	Power sector improvement	65.0
	Agricultural infrastructure development	31.0
	Road rehabilitation	42.0
Morocco . . .	Railways restructuring	85.0
	Employment and private sector enterprise project	23.0
Tunisia	Public sector management	80.0
	Urban sewerage	60.0*
	Natural resources management	26.5
	Economic competitiveness programme	75.0
Total		769.6

* Two loans for the same project.

IDA Credits Approved, July 1996–June 1997 (US $ million)

Country	Purpose	Amount
Egypt. . . .	Education enhancement programme	75.0
Yemen . . .	Community development	30.0
	Infrastructure rehabilitation and flood control	30.0
	Taiz water supply	10.2
Total		145.2

Source: *World Bank Annual Report 1997.*

International Finance Corporation—IFC

Address: 2121 Pennsylvania Ave, NW, Washington, DC 20433, USA.

Telephone: (202) 477-1234; **telex:** 248423; **fax:** (202) 477-6391; **internet:** http://www.ifc.org/.

IFC was founded in 1956 as an affiliate of the World Bank to encourage the growth of productive private enterprise and efficient capital markets in its member countries, particularly in the less-developed areas.

Organization

(August 1998)

IFC is a separate legal entity in the World Bank Group. Executive Directors of the World Bank also serve as Directors of IFC. The President of the World Bank is, *ex officio*, Chairman of the IFC Board of Directors, which has appointed him President of IFC. Subject to his overall supervision, the day-to-day operations of IFC are conducted by its staff under the direction of the Executive Vice-President.

PRINCIPAL OFFICERS

President: JAMES D. WOLFENSOHN (USA).

Executive Vice-President: JANNIK LINDBAEK (Norway), (from 1 January 1999) PETER L. WOICKE (Germany).

REGIONAL MISSIONS

The Middle East: World Trade Center, 1191 Corniche el-Nil, 12th Floor, Cairo, Egypt; tel. (2) 579-5353; telex 93110; fax (2) 579-2211; Regional Rep. MANUEL E. NÚÑEZ.

North Africa: 8 rue Kamal Mohamed, 12th Floor, Casablanca 20000, Morocco; tel. (2) 48-46-86; fax (2) 48-46-90; Regional Rep. MANSOUR KELADA-ANTOUN.

Activities

IFC provides financial support and advice for private sector ventures and projects, and assists governments to create conditions that stimulate the flow of domestic and foreign private savings and investment. Increasingly IFC has worked to mobilize additional capital from other financial institutions. In all its activities IFC is guided by three major principles:

(i) The catalytic principle. IFC should seek above all to be a catalyst in helping private investors and markets to make good investments.

(ii) The business principle. IFC should function like a business in partnership with the private sector and take the same commercial risks, so that its funds, although backed by public sources, are transferred under market disciplines.

(iii) The principle of the special contribution. IFC should participate in an investment only when it makes a special contribution that supplements or complements the role of market operators.

IFC's authorized capital is US $2,450m. At 30 June 1997 IFC's paid-in capital was $2,229m. The World Bank is the principal source of borrowed funds, but IFC also borrows from private capital markets. In 1996/97 total investments approved amounted to $6,722m. for 276 projects, compared with $8,118m. for 264 projects in the previous year. Of the total approved, $3,317m. was for IFC's own account, while $3,405m. was used in loan syndications and underwriting of securities issues and investment funds.

During the year ending 30 June 1997 IFC project financing approved for countries in the Middle East and North Africa was mainly concerned with the development and rehabilitation of financial sectors, tourism, industry and infrastructure. IFC supported a microenterprise credit initiative to strengthen the development of businesses in the West Bank and Gaza Strip and to boost employment and income opportunities. IFC technical assistance and advisory missions undertaken in the region during that year continued to focus on improving capital market institutions, privatization, management services, training and reviewing foreign investment laws and regulations.

IFC administers the Foreign Investment Advisory Service (FIAS), which provides advice to governments on attracting foreign investment. During 1997 FIAS completed a review of the investment environment in Yemen and helped to identify major obstacles to attracting foreign direct investment, while in the West Bank and Gaza FIAS continued to assist the authorities in developing a basic regulatory and institutional framework for private sector activities.

PUBLICATIONS

Annual Report.

Emerging Stock Markets Factbook (annually).

Global Agribusiness (series of industry reports).

Impact (quarterly).

Lessons of Experience (series).

Multilateral Investment Guarantee Agency—MIGA

Address: 1818 H Street, NW, Washington, DC 20433, USA.

Telephone: (202) 477-1234; **telex:** 248423; **fax:** (202) 477-6391; **internet:** http://www.miga.org/.

MIGA was founded in 1988, as an affiliate of the World Bank, to encourage the flow of investments for productive purposes among its member countries, especially developing countries, through the mitigation of non-commercial barriers to investment (especially political risk).

Organization

(August 1998)

MIGA is legally and financially separate from the World Bank. It is supervised by a Board of Directors.

President: JAMES D. WOLFENSOHN (USA).

Executive Vice-President: MOTOMICHI IKAWA (Japan).

Activities

The convention establishing MIGA took effect in April 1988. Authorized capital amounted to US $1,082m. In April 1998 MIGA's Board of Directors approved a capital increase of $1,000m. (including a $150m. grant transferred from the IBRD).

MIGA's purpose is to guarantee eligible investments against losses resulting from non-commercial risks, under four main categories:

transfer risk resulting from host government restrictions on currency conversion and transfer;

risk of loss resulting from legislative or administrative actions of the host government;

repudiation by the host government of contracts with investors in cases in which the investor has no access to a competent forum;

the risk of armed conflict and civil unrest.

Before guaranteeing any investment MIGA must ensure that it is commercially viable, contributes to the development process and will not be harmful to the environment. During the year to June 1997 MIGA issued 70 investment guarantee contracts. The amount of direct investment associated with the contracts totalled approximately US $4,700m., and created an estimated 4,000 jobs in 25 developing member states. Seven of the guarantee contracts were for projects in Algeria, Bahrain, Egypt and Saudi Arabia, which facilitated foreign investment valued at some $250m.

MIGA also provides policy and advisory services to promote foreign investment in developing countries and in transitional economies, and to disseminate information on investment opportunities. In October 1995 MIGA established a new network on investment opportunities, which connected investment promotion agencies (IPAs) throughout the world on an electronic information network. The so-called IPA*net* aimed to encourage further investments among developing countries, to provide access to comprehensive information on investment laws and conditions and to strengthen communications between governmental, business and financial associations and investors. A new internet-based facility, 'PrivatizationLink', was launched in 1998.

International Fund for Agricultural Development—IFAD

Address: Via del Serafico 107, 00142 Rome, Italy.
Telephone: (06) 54591; **telex:** 620330; **fax:** (06) 5043463; **e-mail:** ifad@ifad.org; **internet:** http://www.unicc.org/ifad.

Following a decision by the 1974 UN World Food Conference, IFAD was established in 1977 to fund rural development programmes specifically aimed at the poorest of the world's people. It began operations in January 1978.

Organization

(August 1998)

GOVERNING COUNCIL

Each member state is represented in the Governing Council by a Governor and an Alternate. Sessions are held annually with special sessions convened as required. The Governing Council elects the President of the Fund (who also chairs the Executive Board) by a two-thirds majority for a four-year term. The President is eligible for re-election.

EXECUTIVE BOARD

The Board consists of 18 members and 18 alternates, elected by the Governing Council, who serve for three years. The Executive Board is responsible for the conduct and general operation of IFAD and approves loans and grants for projects; it holds three regular sessions a year.

Following agreement on the fourth replenishment of the Fund's resources in February 1997, the governance structure of the Fund was amended. Former Category I countries (i.e. industrialized donor countries) were reclassified as List A countries and were awarded a greater share of the 1,800 votes in the Governing Council and Executive Board, in order to reflect their financial contributions to the Fund. Former Category II countries (petroleum-exporting developing donor countries) were reclassified as List B countries, while recipient developing countries, formally Category III countries, were termed as List C countries, and divided into three regional Sub-Lists. Where previously each category was ensured equal representation on the Executive Board, the new allocation of seats was as followes: eight List A countries, four List B, and two of each Sub-List C group of countries.

President and Chairman of Executive Board: FAWZI HAMAD AL-SULTAN (Kuwait).

Vice-President: JIM MOODY (USA).

Activities

The Fund's objective is to mobilize additional resources to be made available on concessional terms for agricultural development in developing member states. IFAD provides financing primarily for projects and programmes specifically designed to introduce, expand or improve food production systems and to strengthen related policies and institutions within the framework of national priorities and strategies. In allocating resources IFAD is guided by: the need to increase food production in the poorest food-deficit countries; the potential for increasing food production in other developing countries; and the importance of improving the nutritional level of the poorest people in developing countries and the conditions of their lives. All projects focus on those who often do not benefit from other development programmes: small-scale farmers, artisanal fishermen, nomadic pastoralists, women, and the rural landless.

IFAD is empowered to make both grants and loans. Under its Agreement, grants are limited to 5% of the resources committed in any one financial year. Loans are available on highly concessional, intermediate or ordinary terms. More than two-thirds of total IFAD lending is awarded on highly concessional terms, i.e. with no interest charges (although bearing an annual service charge of 0.75%) and a repayment period of 40 years. To avoid duplication of work, the administration of loans, for the purposes of disbursements and supervision of project implementation, is entrusted to competent international financial institutions, with the Fund retaining an active interest. During 1996 IFAD provided financing for some 40% of the costs of projects approved during that year, while the remainder was contributed by external donors, multilateral institutions and the recipient countries.

IFAD's development projects usually include a number of components, such as infrastructure (e.g. improvement of water supplies, small-scale irrigation and road construction); input supply (e.g. improved seeds, fertilizers and pesticides); institutional support (e.g. research, training and extension services); and producer incentives (e.g. pricing and marketing improvements). IFAD also attempts to enable the landless to acquire income-generating assets: by increasing the provision of credit for the rural poor, it seeks to free them from dependence on the unorganized and exploitative capital market and to generate productive activities.

From the late 1980s, increased emphasis was given to environmental conservation, in an effort to alleviate poverty that results from the deterioration of natural resources. In addition to promoting small-scale irrigation (which has proved more economically and ecologically viable than large-scale systems), projects include low-cost anti-erosion measures, land improvement, soil conservation, agro-forestry system, improved management of arid rangeland, and safe biological control of pests.

IFAD is a leading repository of knowledge, resources and expertise in the field of rural hunger and poverty alleviation. During 1995 a team established to review IFAD's activities focused on IFAD's role as an innovator, emphasizing the importance of pioneering practices and strategies that can be replicated, and of making its knowledge available to relevant agencies and governments. Through its technical assistance grants, IFAD aims to promote research and capacity-building in the agricultural sector. IFAD is financing efforts to improve the production of durum wheat in the dryland areas of West Asia and North Africa and is supporting the establishment of a regional animal surveillance and control network to identify and prevent outbreaks of livestock diseases in North Africa, the Middle East and the Arab Peninsula. In December 1994 the Executive Board approved financing for an agricultural management training programme in the Near East and North Africa, which aimed to improve the performance of agricultural projects and programmes, to increase awareness among decision-makers about administrative issues and to strengthen national training capacities. In 1996 preparations were undertaken for training programmes to be conducted in Morocco (for Algeria, Morocco and Tunisia), in Egypt (for Egypt and Sudan) and in Syria (for Jordan, Lebanon, the Palestinian territories and Syria).

By the end of 1996 IFAD's cumulative assistance to the Near East and North Africa region (including Djibouti, Somalia and Sudan) amounted to SDR 638.0m. for 72 projects in 17 countries. (The average value of the SDR—Special Drawing Right—in 1996 was US $1.45176.) During 1996 loans were approved to support the East Delta Newlands Agricultural Services Project in Egypt (SDR 17.3m.) and a rural development project in the Taourirt-Taforalt region of Morocco (SDR 13.5m.).

In October 1997 IFAD was appointed to administer the Global Mechanism of the Convention to Combat Desertification in those Countries Experiencing Drought and Desertification, Particularly in Africa, which entered into force in December 1996. The Mechanism was envisaged as a means of mobilizing and channelling resources for implementation of the Convention. A series of collaborative institutional arrangements was to be concluded between IFAD, UNDP and the World Bank in order to facilitate the effective functioning of the Mechanism.

FINANCE

IFAD's programme of work for 1996 envisaged loans and grants totalling SDR 304.3m., while the budget for administrative expenses amounted to US $52.5m. In February 1997 the Governing Council concluded an agreement on the fourth replenishment of the Fund's resources, amounting to $485m. over a three-year period.

PUBLICATIONS

Annual Report.
IFAD Update (3 a year).
Staff Working Papers (series).
The State of World Rural Poverty.

International Monetary Fund—IMF

Address: 700 19th St, NW, Washington, DC 20431, USA.

Telephone: (202) 623-7430; **telex:** 64111; **fax:** (202) 623-6701; **internet:** http://www.imf.org.

The IMF was established at the same time as the World Bank in December 1945.

Organization

(August 1998)

BOARD OF GOVERNORS

The highest authority of the Fund is exercised by the Board of Governors, on which each member country is represented by a Governor and an Alternate Governor. The Board normally meets annually, and an Interim Committee meets twice a year. The voting power of each country is related to its quota in the Fund.

BOARD OF EXECUTIVE DIRECTORS

The 24-member Board of Executive Directors is responsible for the day-to-day operations of the Fund. The USA, the United Kingdom, Germany, France, Japan and Saudi Arabia each appoint one Executive Director, while 16 of the remainder are appointed by groups of member countries sharing similar interests; there is also one Executive Director each from the People's Republic of China, Russia and Saudi Arabia.

OFFICERS

Managing Director: MICHEL CAMDESSUS (France).

First Deputy Managing Director: STANLEY FISCHER (USA).

Deputy Managing Directors: ALASSANE D. OUATTARA (Côte d'Ivoire); SHIGEMITSU SUGISAKI (Japan).

Director, African Department: EVANGELOS A. CALAMITSIS.

Director, Middle Eastern Department: PAUL CHABRIER.

Activities

The purposes of the IMF, as set out in the Articles of Agreement, are:

(i) To promote international monetary co-operation through a permanent institution which provides the machinery for consultation and collaboration on monetary problems.

(ii) To facilitate the expansion and balanced growth of international trade, and to contribute thereby to the promotion and maintenance of high levels of employment and real income and to the development of members' productive resources.

(iii) To promote exchange stability, to maintain orderly exchange arrangements among members, and to avoid competitive exchange depreciation.

(iv) To assist in the establishment of a multilateral system of payments in respect of current transactions between members and in the elimination of foreign exchange restrictions which hamper the growth of trade.

(v) To give confidence to members by making the general resources of the Fund temporarily available to them, under adequate safeguards, thus providing them with the opportunity to correct maladjustments in their balance of payments, without resorting to measures destructive of national or international prosperity.

(vi) In accordance with the above, to shorten the duration of and lessen the degree of disequilibrium in the international balances of payments of members.

In joining the Fund, each country agrees to co-operate with the above objectives, and the Fund monitors members' compliance by holding an annual consultation with each country, in order to survey the country's exchange rate policies and determine its need for assistance.

In accordance with its objective of facilitating the expansion of international trade, the IMF encourages its members to accept the obligations of Article VIII, Sections two, three and four, of the IMF Articles of Agreement. Members that accept Article VIII undertake to refrain from imposing restrictions on the making of payments and transfers for current international transactions and from engaging in discriminatory currency arrangements or multiple currency practices without IMF approval. By 30 June 1998 145 members had accepted Article VIII status.

RESOURCES

Members' subscriptions form the basic resource of the IMF. They are supplemented by borrowing. Under the General Arrangements to Borrow (GAB), established in 1962, the 'Group of Ten' industrialized nations (Belgium, Canada, France, Germany, Italy, Japan, the Netherlands, Sweden, the United Kingdom and the USA) and Switzerland (which became a member of the IMF in 1992, but which had been a full participant in the GAB from 1984) undertake to lend the Fund up to SDR 17,000m. (increased from SDR 6,400m. in December 1983) in their own currencies, so as to help meet the balance-of-payments requirements of any member of the group, or to meet requests to the Fund from countries with balance-of-payments problems that could threaten the stability of the international monetary system. In July 1983 the Fund entered into an agreement with Saudi Arabia, in association with the GAB, making available SDR 1,500m., and other borrowing arrangements were completed in 1984 with the BIS, the Saudi Arabian Monetary Agency, Belgium and Japan, making available a further SDR 6,000m.

In May 1996 GAB participants concluded an agreement in principle to expand the resources available for borrowing to SDR 34,000m., by securing the support of other countries with the financial capacity to support the international monetary system. The so-called New Arrangements to Borrow (NAB) was endorsed in September and approved by the Executive Board in January 1997. It was to enter into force, for an initial five-year period, as soon as the five largest potential creditors (of the anticipated 25 member countries and institutions participating in NAB) had approved the initiative and the total credit arrangement of participants endorsing the scheme had reached at least SDR 28,900m. While the GAB credit arrangement was to remain in effect, the NAB was expected to be the first facility to be activated in the event of the Fund requiring supplementary resources.

DRAWING ARRANGEMENTS

Exchange transactions within the Fund take the form of members' purchases (i.e. drawings) from the Fund of the currencies of other members for the equivalent amounts of their own currencies. Fund resources are available to eligible members on an essentially short-term and revolving basis to provide members with temporary assistance to contribute to the solution of their payments problems. Before making a purchase, a member must show that its balance of payments or reserve position make the purchase necessary. Apart from this requirement, reserve tranche purchases (i.e. purchases that do not bring the Fund's holdings of the member's currency to a level above its quota) are permitted unconditionally.

With further purchases, however, the Fund's policy of 'conditionality' means that a member requesting assistance must agree to adjust its economic policies, as stipulated by the IMF. All requests other than for use of the reserve tranche are examined by the Executive Board to determine whether the proposed use would be consistent with the Fund's policies, and a member must discuss its proposed adjustment programme (including fiscal, monetary, exchange and trade policies) with IMF staff. Purchases outside the reserve tranche are made in four credit tranches, each equivalent to 25% of the member's quota; a member must reverse the transaction by repurchasing its own currency (with SDRs or currencies specified by the Fund) within a specified time. A credit tranche purchase is usually made under a 'stand-by arrangement' with the Fund, or under the extended Fund facility. A stand-by arrangement is normally of one or two years' duration, and the amount is made available in instalments, subject to the member's observance of 'performance criteria'; repurchases must be made within three-and-a-quarter to five years. An extended arrangement is normally of three years' duration, and the member must submit detailed economic programmes and progress reports for each year; repurchases must be made within four-and-a-half to 10 years. A member whose payments imbalance is large in relation to its quota may make use of temporary facilities established by the Fund using borrowed resources, namely the 'enlarged access policy' established in 1981, which helps to finance stand-by and extended arrangements for such a member, up to a limit of between 90% and 110% of the member's quota annually. In October 1994 the Executive Board agreed to increase, for three years, the annual access limit under IMF regular tranche drawings, stand-by arrangements and extended Fund facility credits from 68% to 100% of a member's quota. In exceptional circumstances the access limit may be extended further.

During the year ending 30 April 1997 a stand-by arrangement totalling SDR 271.4m. was concluded with Egypt, while in the following financial year an extended Fund facility credit totalling SDR 105.9m. was made available to Yemen. At 30 April 1998 stand-by and extended Fund facility arrangements remained, additionally, in effect with Algeria and Jordan.

In addition, there are special-purpose arrangements, all of which are subject to the member's co-operation with the Fund to find an appropriate solution to its difficulties. The buffer stock financing facility (established in 1969) enables members to pay their contributions to the buffer stocks which are intended to stabilize primary commodity markets by drawing as much as 35% of their quota. The BSFF has not been used since 1984. In August 1988 the Fund established the compensatory and contingency financing facility (CCFF), which replaced and expanded the former compensatory financing facility, established in 1963. The CCFF provides compensation to members whose export earnings are reduced owing to circumstances beyond their control, or who are affected by excess costs of cereal imports. Contingency financing is provided, up to a maximum of 95% of quota, to help members maintain their efforts at economic adjustment even when affected by a sharp increase in interest rates or other externally-derived difficulties. In April 1992 the IMF disbursed SDR 178.6m. to Israel under the CCFF.

The structural adjustment facility (SAF) was established in 1986 to support medium-term macroeconomic adjustment and structural reforms in low-income developing countries on concessionary terms. Following the adoption of the enlarged enhanced structural adjustment facility (ESAF—see below) it was agreed that no further resources would be made available for SAF arrangements.

The ESAF, established in 1987, was to provide new resources to assist the adjustment efforts of, in particular, heavily-indebted countries. Eligible members must develop a three-year adjustment programme (with assistance given jointly by staff of the Fund and of the World Bank) to strengthen the balance-of-payments situation and foster sustainable economic growth. ESAF loans carry an interest rate of 0.5% per year and are repayable within 10 years, including a five-and-a-half-year grace period. Maximum access is set at 190% (255% in exceptional circumstances) of the member's quota. At 30 April 1997 35 ESAF arrangements were in effect, with commitments amounting to SDR 4,048m. Disbursements in the financial year 1996/97 amounted to SDR 705m., while cumulative SAF and ESAF disbursements to the end of April 1997 totalled SDR 7,172m. From April 1992 11 additional countries were eligible to borrow from the ESAF, including Egypt. In February 1994 a new period of operations of the ESAF became effective, following an agreement to enlarge the ESAF Trust (the funding source for ESAF arrangement). The terms and conditions of the new facility remain the same as those of the original ESAF, but the list of countries eligible for assistance was enlarged by six, to 78. (In January 1995 Eritrea became the 79th member eligible for ESAF assistance.) The new commitment period for lending from the ESAF Trust was to expire on 31 December 1996, while disbursements were to be made until 31 December 1999. In September 1996 the Interim Committee of the Board of Governors endorsed measures to finance the ESAF for a further five-year period, 2000–2004, after which the facility was to become self-sustaining. The interim period of the ESAF was to be funded mainly from bilateral contributions, but drawing on the Fund's additional resources as necessary. The ESAF was to support, through long-maturity loans and grants, IMF participation in a joint initiative, with the World Bank, to provide exceptional assistance to heavily indebted poor countries (HIPCs), in order to help them achieve a sustainable level of debt management. The initiative was formally approved at the September meeting of the Interim Committee, having received the support of the 'Paris Club' of international creditors which agreed to increase the relief on official debt from 67% to 80%.

In April 1997 the World Bank and the IMF announced that Uganda was to be the first beneficiary of the initiative. The IMF's share of the anticipated debt relief of US $338m. was to total $69m., effective from April 1998. (See also the World Bank, p. 229.) In September assistance was approved for Bolivia and Burkina Faso under the HIPC initiative. By April 1998 agreement had also been reached on the participation of Côte d'Ivoire, Guyana and Mozambique, while negotiations were underway for Guinea-Bissau and Mali to benefit from the initiative. Final country eligibility in the scheme is dependent on individual countries having implemented IMF economic and social reform programmes for a period of at least six years, and on the official creditors agreeing to contribute their proportion of debt relief.

SURVEILLANCE

Under its Articles of Agreement, the Fund is mandated to oversee the effective functioning of the international monetary system and to review the policies of individual member countries to ensure the stability of the exchange rate system. The Fund's main tools of surveillance are regular consultations, conducted by IMF staff with officials from member countries, and World Economic Outlook discussions, held, normally twice a year, by the Executive Board to access policy implications from a multilateral perspective and to monitor global developments. Following a rapid decline in the value of the Mexican peso in late 1994 and the ensuing financial crisis

MEMBERSHIP AND QUOTAS IN THE MIDDLE EAST AND NORTH AFRICA (million SDR)*

Country	Proposed quota under the Eleventh General Review	July 1998
Algeria	1,254.7	914.4
Bahrain	135.0	82.8
Cyprus	139.6	100.0
Egypt	943.7	678.4
Iran	1,497.2	1,078.5
Iraq	1,188.4	504.0†
Israel	928.2	666.2
Jordan	170.5	121.7
Kuwait	1,381.1	995.2
Lebanon	203.0	146.0
Libya	1,123.7	817.6
Morocco	588.2	427.7
Oman	194.0	119.4
Qatar	263.8	190.5
Saudi Arabia	6,985.5	5,130.6
Syria	293.6	209.9
Tunisia	286.5	206.0
Turkey	964.0	642.0
United Arab Emirates	611.7	392.1
Yemen	243.5	176.5

* The Special Drawing Right (SDR) was introduced in 1970 as a substitute for gold in international payments, and is intended eventually to become the principal reserve asset in the international monetary system. Its value (which was US $1.33156 at 30 June 1998 and averaged $1.37602 in 1997) is based on the currencies of the five largest exporting countries. Each member is assigned a quota related to its national income, monetary reserves, trade balance and other economic indicators; the quota approximately determines a member's voting power and the amount of foreign exchange it may purchase from the Fund. A member's subscription is equal to its quota. Under the Ninth General Review of quotas, which was completed in June 1990, an increase of 50% in total quotas (from SDR 90,000m. to SDR 135,200m.) was authorized. The increase entered into effect in November 1992; with additional contributions from countries that joined the IMF subsequent to June 1990, by 1 August 1997 total quotas amounted to SDR 145,300m. The Tenth General Review of Quotas was concluded, in December 1994, with no further increase of quotas. In February 1998 the Board of Governors adopted a resolution in support of an earlier decision of the Executive Board of an increase in total quotas of some 45%. The resolution completed the Eleventh General Review; however, the increase was only to enter into effect once member countries with at least 85% of total quotas (at December 1997) had consented to their new quotas and paid the subscription. Members were granted until January 1999 to complete this process.

† Figure is that determined under the Eighth General Review, given that Iraq had not paid for its quota increase under the Ninth Review by July 1998.

in that country, the IMF resolved to strengthen its surveillance activities. In April 1996 the IMF established the Special Data Dissemination Standard, which was intended to improve access to reliable economic statistical information for member countries that have, or are seeking, access to international capital markets. By 31 July 1997 42 countries had subscribed to the Standard. In March 1997 the Executive Board agreed to develop a General Data Dissemination System, to encourage all member countries to improve the production and dissemination of core economic data. In April 1997, in an effort to improve the value of surveillance by means of increased transparency, the Executive Board agreed to the release of Press Information Notices, following each member's Article IV consultation with the Board, on a voluntary basis.

TECHNICAL ASSISTANCE

Technical assistance is provided by special missions or resident representatives who advise members on every aspect of economic management. Assistance is provided by the IMF's various specialized departments and is becoming an increasingly important aspect of the Fund's relationship with its member countries. In particular, the expansion of the Fund's technical assistance activities during the early 1990s resulted from the increase in countries undergoing economic and systemic transformations. The IMF Institute, founded in 1964, trains officials from member countries in financial analysis and policy, balance-of-payments methodology and public finance: it also gives assistance to national and regional training centres. The IMF is co-sponsor of the Joint Vienna Institute, which was opened in the Austrian capital in October 1992 and which trains officials from former centrally-planned economies in various aspects of economic management and public administration. During 1996/97 a total of 1,182 people attended training courses or seminars at the IMF Institute or the Joint Vienna Institute, while some 1,110 senior officials participated in overseas training courses.

PUBLICATIONS

Annual Report.
Balance of Payments Statistics Yearbook.
Direction of Trade Statistics (quarterly, with yearbook).

Finance and Development (quarterly).
Government Finance Statistics Yearbook.
IMF Survey (2 a month).
International Financial Statistics (monthly, with yearbook).
Staff Papers (quarterly).
World Economic Outlook (2 a year).
Occasional papers, economic reviews, pamphlets, publications brochure.

United Nations Educational, Scientific and Cultural Organization—UNESCO

Address: 7 place de Fontenoy, 75352 Paris, France.
Telephone: 1-45-68-10-00; **telex:** 204461; **fax:** 1-45-67-16-90; **internet:** http://www.unesco.org.
UNESCO was established in 1946 'for the purpose of advancing, through the educational, scientific and cultural relations of the peoples of the world, the objectives of international peace and the common welfare of mankind'.

Organization

(August 1998)

GENERAL CONFERENCE

The supreme governing body of the Organization, the Conference meets in ordinary session once in two years and is composed of representatives of the member states.

EXECUTIVE BOARD

The Board, comprising 58 members, prepares the programme to be submitted to the Conference and supervises its execution; it meets twice or sometimes three times a year.

SECRETARIAT

Director-General: FEDERICO MAYOR (Spain).
Director of the Executive Office: GEORGES MALEMPRÉ (Belgium).

REGIONAL OFFICES

Regional Office for Education in the Arab States: POB 5244, Cité Sportive Ave, Beirut, Lebanon; tel. (1) 850075; fax (1) 824854; e-mail uhbei@unesco.org.
Regional Office for Science and Technology in the Arab States—ROSTAS: 8 Abdel Rahman Fahmy St, Garden City, Cairo, Egypt; tel. (2) 3543036; fax (2) 3545296; e-mail uhcai@unesco.org; Dir Dr ADNAN SHIHAB-ELDIN.
Regional Office for Social and Human Sciences in the Arab Region: POB 363, 12 rue de Rhodes, 1002 Tunis, Tunisia; tel. (1) 790947; telex 18409; fax (1) 791588; e-mail tunis@unesco.org; liaison office with the Arab League Educational, Cultural and Scientific Organization; Dir F. CARRILLO-MONTESINOS.
UNESCO Office—Amman: POB 2270, Wadi Saqra, Amman, Jordan; tel. (6) 5606559; fax (6) 5682183; e-mail uhamm@unesco.org; Dir ABDULQADER EL-ATRASH.
UNESCO Office—Doha: POB 3945, Doha, Qatar; tel. 867707; fax 867644; e-mail uhdoh@unesco.org; Dir A. MESHAL.
UNESCO Office—Rabat: BP 1777, 35 ave du 16 Novembre, Agdal, Rabat, Morocco; tel. (7) 670374; fax (7) 670375; Dir L. SALMAN EL-MADINI.

Activities in the Middle East and North Africa

UNESCO's overall work programme for 1998–99 comprised the following four major programmes: Education for All Throughout Life; the Sciences in the Service of Development; Cultural Development: Heritage and Creativity; and Communication, Information and Informatics. It also incorporated two transdisciplinary projects—Education for a Sustainable Future and Towards a Culture of Peace—with a combined budget of US $42.2m., which encompassed UNESCO's fundamental objectives of promoting peace, interna-

tional understanding, respect for human rights, and sustainable development, through education, training and awareness-generating activities. In implementing the work programme UNESCO was to target four priority groups, identified as being women, young people, African member states and least-developed countries.

EDUCATION

Since its establishment UNESCO has devoted itself to promoting education in accordance with principles based on democracy and respect for human rights.

In March 1990 UNESCO, with other UN agencies, sponsored the World Conference on Education for All. 'Education for All' was subsequently adopted as a guiding principle of UNESCO's contribution to development. The promotion of access to learning opportunities throughout an individual's life is a priority for UNESCO's 1996–2001 programme of activities: Education for All Throughout Life was a key element of the 1998–99 work programme and was allocated a budget of US $104.6m. UNESCO aims, initially, to foster basic education for all. The second part of its strategy is to renew and diversify education systems, including updating curricular programmes in secondary education, strengthening science and technology activities and ensuring equal access to education for girls and women. In December 1993 the heads of government of nine highly-populated developing countries (Bangladesh, Brazil, the People's Republic of China, Egypt, India, Indonesia, Mexico, Nigeria and Pakistan), meeting in Delhi, India, agreed to co-operate with the objective of achieving comprehensive primary education for all children and of expanding further learning opportunities of children and adults.

Within the UN system, UNESCO is responsible for providing technical assistance and educational services within the context of emergency situations. This includes providing education to refugees and displaced persons, as well as assistance for the rehabilitation of national education systems. In Palestine, UNESCO collaborates with UNRWA (q.v.) to assist with the training of teachers, educational planning and rehabilitation of schools.

UNESCO is concerned with improving the quality, relevance and efficiency of higher education. It assists member states in reforming their national systems, organizes high-level conferences for Ministers of Education and other decision-makers, and disseminates research papers. A World Conference on Higher Education was scheduled to be held in September/October 1998, prior to which UNESCO was organizing a series of regional meetings, focusing on access to higher education.

The International Institute for Educational Planning and the International Bureau of Education carry out training, research and the exchange of information on aspects of education.

SCIENCE AND SOCIAL SCIENCES

During 1998–99 UNESCO was to implement projects under the programme of the Sciences in the Service of Development, which aimed to foster the advancement, transfer and exchange of knowledge in the physical, natural, social and human sciences and to promote their application with the objective of improving the social and natural environment.

UNESCO has established various forms of intergovernmental co-operation concerned with the environmental sciences and research on natural resources, in order to support the recommendations of the June 1992 UN Conference on Environment and Development, and, in particular, the implementation of 'Agenda 21' to promote sustainable development. The International Geological Correlation Programme (IGCP), run jointly with the International Union of Geological Sciences, aims to improve and facilitate global research of geological processes. In the context of the International Decade for Natural Disaster Reduction (declared in 1990) UNESCO has conducted scientific studies of natural hazards and means of mitigating their effects and has organized several disaster-related workshops. The International Hydrological Programme (IHP) considers the scientific aspects of water resources assessment and management, while the Intergovernmental Oceanographic Commission (IOC), focuses on issues relating to oceans, shore-lines and marine resources, in particular the role of the ocean in climate and global systems. The IOC is actively involved in the establishment of a Global Coral Reef Monitoring Network, and in preparations for the 1998 International Year of the Ocean. An initiative on Environment and Development in Coastal Regions and in Small Islands is concerned with ensuring environmentally-sound and sustainable development by strengthening management of the following key areas: freshwater resources; the mitigation of coastline instability; biological diversity; and coastal ecosystem productivity. UNESCO's Man and the Biosphere Programme supports a worldwide network of biosphere reserves (comprising 377 sites in 85 countries in 1997), which aim to promote environmental conservation and research, education and training in biodiversity and problems of land use. Following the signing of the Convention to Combat Desertification in October 1994, UNESCO initiated an International Programme for Arid Land Crops, based on a network of existing institutions, including the Ben Gurion University of the Negev, in Israel, to assist implementation of the Convention. Also in 1994 UNESCO initiated an international research programme, the Management of Social Transformations, to promote capacity-building in social planning at all levels of decision-making.

The Regional Office for Science and Technology (ROSTAS) organizes courses and studies on the teaching of basic science, computer science, hydrology, oceanography, geophysics, soil biology, geomorphology and seismology. It provides regional seminars, training courses and consultancy missions. As part of its programmes in arid zone research, UNESCO has helped to establish research institutes in Iraq and Saudi Arabia, and has given financial aid to Egypt's Desert Research Institute.

In September 1996 UNESCO initiated a 10-year World Solar Programme, which aimed to promote the application of solar energy and to increase research, development and public awareness of all forms of ecologically-sustainable energy use.

In May 1997 the International Bioethics Committee, a group of specialists who meet under UNESCO auspices, approved a draft version of a Universal Declaration on the Human Genome and Human Rights, which aimed to provide ethical guide-lines for developments in human genetics. The Declaration, which identified some 100,000 hereditary genes as 'common heritage', was adopted by the UNESCO General Conference in November and committed states to promoting the dissemination of relevant scientific knowledge and co-operating in genome research. The November Conference also resolved to establish an 18-member World Commission on the Ethics of Scientific Knowledge and Technology to serve as a forum for the exchange of information and ideas and to promote dialogue between scientific communities, decision-makers and the public. UNESCO aims to improve the level of university teaching of the basic sciences through training courses, establishing national and regional networks and centres of excellence, and fostering co-operative research. UNESCO develops co-operative scientific and technological research programmes through the organization and support of scientific meetings and contacts with research institutions, and the establishment or strengthening of co-operative networks. With the International Council of Scientific Unions and the Third World Academy of Sciences, UNESCO operates a short-term fellowship programme in the basic sciences and an exchange programme of visiting lecturers. UNESCO also sponsors several research fellowships in the social sciences and promotes the rehabilitation of underprivileged urban areas, the research of socio-cultural factors affecting demographic change, and the study of family issues.

UNESCO aims to assist the building and consolidation of peaceful and democratic societies. An international network of institutions and centres involved in research on conflict resolution is being established to support the promotion of peace. Other training, workshop and research activities have been undertaken in countries that have suffered conflict. The Associated Schools Project (comprising some 3,000 institutions in 120 countries at October 1994) has, for more than 40 years, promoted the principles of peace, human rights, democracy and international co-operation through education. An International Youth Clearing House and Information Service (INFOYOUTH) aims to increase and consolidate the information available on the situation of young people in society, and to heighten awareness of their needs, aspirations and potential among public and private decision-makers. UNESCO's programme also focuses on the educational and cultural dimensions of physical education and sport and their capacity to preserve and improve health.

The struggle against all forms of discrimination is a central part of UNESCO's mission. It disseminates scientific information aimed at combating racial prejudice, works to improve the status of women and their access to education, and promotes equality between men and women.

CULTURE

In undertaking efforts to preserve the world's cultural and natural heritage UNESCO has attempted to emphasize the link between culture and development. The 1998–99 programme Cultural Development: Heritage and Creativity was to pursue UNESCO's objectives relating to the preservation and enhancement of cultural and natural heritage and promoting living cultures, in particular through the formulation of new national and international legislation (including an instrument on underwater cultural heritage), efforts to counter the illicit trafficking of cultural property and the promotion of all forms of creativity.

UNESCO encourages the translation and publication of literary works, publishes albums of art, and produces records, audiovisual programmes and travelling art exhibitions. It supports the development of book publishing and distribution, including the free flow of books and educational material across borders, and the training of editors and managers in publishing. During 1994–95 a pilot scheme to encourage reading, through the free distribution of Arabic literature in a serialized form, was initiated in Lebanon and Jordan. UNESCO is active in preparing and encouraging the enforcement of international legislation on copyright.

UNESCO's World Heritage Programme, inaugurated in 1978, aims to protect historic sites and natural landmarks of outstanding universal significance, in accordance with the 1972 UNESCO Convention Concerning the Protection of the World Cultural and Natural Heritage, by providing financial aid for restoration, technical assistance, training and management planning. By October 1997 there were 506 World Heritage Sites in 107 countries. UNESCO is assisting in the exploration of prehistoric sites in Libya, and in the preservation of sites and monuments in other countries, for example Carthage and Al-Qairawan in Tunisia, Fez in Morocco, Tyre in Lebanon and the Casbah of Algiers in Algeria. UNESCO has assisted Iraq in the establishment of a regional training centre for the conservation of cultural property in the Arab countries. In addition, UNESCO supports efforts for the collection and safeguarding of humanity's non-material heritage, including oral traditions, music, dance and medicine. In co-operation with the International Council for Philosophy and Humanistic Studies, UNESCO is compiling a directory of endangered languages.

UNESCO was the leading agency for promoting the UN's World Decade for Cultural Development (1988–97). In the framework of the World Decade UNESCO launched the Silk Roads Project, as a multidisciplinary study of the interactions among cultures and civilizations along the routes linking Asia and Europe. Other regional projects were undertaken to consider the dynamic process of dialogue and exchange in forming cultural identities, for example, a project to investigate the contributions of Arab culture to Latin American cultures through Spain and Portugal, and to promote creativity and cultural life.

In December 1992 UNESCO established the World Commission on Culture and Development to strengthen links between culture and development and to prepare a report on the issue.

COMMUNICATION, INFORMATION AND INFORMATICS

UNESCO's communications programme comprises three inter-related components concerned with the flow of information: a commitment to ensuring the wide dissemination of information, through the development of communications infrastructures and without impediments to freedom of expression or of the press; promotion of greater access to knowledge through international co-operation in the areas of information, libraries and archives; and efforts to harness informatics for development purposes and strengthen member states' capacities in this field. Within this framework, activities include assistance towards the development of legislation, training programmes and infrastructures for the media in countries where independent and pluralistic media are in the process of emerging; assistance, through professional organizations, in the monitoring of media independence, pluralism and diversity; promotion of exchange programmes and study tours, especially for young communications professionals from the least developed countries and central and eastern Europe; and improving access and opportunities for women in the media. In regions affected by conflict UNESCO supports efforts to establish and maintain an independent media service. Since September 1993 UNESCO has provided assistance for the establishment of the Palestinian Broadcasting Corporation and the modernization of the Palestinian News Agency. The strategy is largely implemented through an International Programme for the Development of Communication, which also channels funds, amounting to some US $3m. each year, to appropriate communication and media development projects, including the establishment of news agencies and newspapers and training editorial and technical staff.

The General Information Programme (PGI), which was established in 1976, provides a focus for UNESCO's activities in the fields of specialized information systems, documentation, libraries and archives. Under the PGI, UNESCO aims to facilitate the elaboration of information policies and plans to modernize libraries and archives services; to encourage standardization; to train information specialists; and to establish specialized information networks. The objectives of the programme are accomplished by improving access to scientific literature; the holding of national seminars on information policies; the furthering of pilot projects, and preservation and conservation efforts under the Records and Archives Management Programme (RAMP); and the training of users of library and information services. UNESCO is participating in the reconstruction of the ancient library at Alexandria, Egypt and in several national and regional projects to safeguard documentary heritage (for example, the Memory of the World Programme). PGI's mandate extends to trends and societal impacts of information technologies. In March 1997 the first International Congress on Ethical, Legal and Societal Aspects of Digital Information ('InfoEthics') was held, in Monte Carlo, Monaco. Also in March a regional InfoEthics congress, concerned with the interaction of the Islamic and Western cultures, was convened, in Morocco.

UNESCO supports the development of computer networking and the training of informatics specialists, in particular through its Intergovernmental Informatics Programme (IIP). IIP's priorities include training in informatics, software development and research, the modernization of public administration and informatics policies and the development of regional computer networks. A regional conference on the use of new information and communication technologies for development in the Arab States was held in May 1997.

FINANCE

UNESCO's activities are funded through a regular budget provided by member states and extrabudgetary funds from other sources, particularly UNDP, the World Bank, regional banks and other bilateral Funds-in-Trust arrangements. UNESCO co-operates with many other UN agencies and international non-governmental organizations.

UNESCO's Regular Programme budget for the two years 1998–99 was US \$544.4m., compared with \$518.4m. for the previous biennium.

PUBLICATIONS

(mostly in English, French and Spanish editions; Arabic, Chinese and Russian versions are also available in many cases)

UNESCO Statistical Yearbook.
UNESCO Courier (monthly, in 32 languages).
UNESCO Sources (monthly).
Copyright Bulletin (quarterly).
Museum International (quarterly).
International Social Science Journal (quarterly).
Nature and Resources (quarterly).
Prospects (quarterly review on education).
World Educational Report (every 2 years).
World Science Report (every 2 years).
Books, statistics, scientific maps and atlases.

World Health Organization—WHO

Address: ave Appia, 1211 Geneva 27, Switzerland.
Telephone: (22) 7912111; **telex:** 415416; **fax:** (22) 7910746; **internet:** http://www.who.ch/.

WHO was established in 1948 as the central agency directing international health work. Of its many activities, the most important single aspect is technical co-operation with national health administrations, particularly in the developing countries.

Organization
(August 1998)

WORLD HEALTH ASSEMBLY

The Assembly meets annually in Geneva; it is responsible for policy making, and the biennial programme and budget; it appoints the Director-General, admits new members and reviews budget contributions.

EXECUTIVE BOARD

The Board is composed of 32 health experts designated by, but not representing, their governments; they serve for three years, and the World Health Assembly elects 10 or 11 member states each year to the Board. It meets at least twice a year to review the Director-General's programme, which it forwards to the Assembly with any recommendations that seem necessary. It advises on questions referred to it by the Assembly and is responsible for putting into effect the decisions and policies of the Assembly. It is also empowered to take emergency measures in case of epidemics or disasters.

SECRETARIAT

Director-General: Dr Gro Harlem Brundtland (Norway).
Executive Directors: Dr Jie Chen (People's Republic of China), Dr Julio J. Frenk (Mexico), Dr David L. Heymann (USA), Ann Kern (Australia), Dr Poonam Khetrapal Singh (India), Dr Souad Lyagoubi-Ouahchi (Tunisia), Dr Michael Scholtz (Germany), Dr Olive Shisana (South Africa), Dr Yasuhiro Suzuki (Japan).
Regional Office for Africa: POB 6, Brazzaville, Republic of the Congo; tel. 83-91-11; telex 5217; fax 83-94-00; Dir Dr Ebrahim Malick Samba.
Regional Office for the Eastern Mediterranean: POB 1517, Alexandria 21511, Egypt; tel. (3) 4820223; telex 54028; fax (3) 4838916; e-mail emro@who.sci.eg; internet: http://www.who.sci.eg; Dir Dr Hussein Abd ar-Razzaq Gezairy.

Activities

WHO's objective is stated in the constitution as 'the attainment by all peoples of the highest possible level of health'.

It acts as the central authority directing international health work, and establishes relations with professional groups and government health authorities on that basis.

It supports, on request from member states, programmes to promote health, prevent and control health problems, control and eradicate disease, train health workers best suited to local needs and strengthen national health systems. Aid is provided in emergencies and natural disasters.

A global programme of collaborative research and exchange of scientific information is carried out in co-operation with about 1,000 leading national institutions. Particular stress is laid on the widespread communicable diseases of the tropics, and the countries directly concerned are assisted in developing their research capabilities.

It keeps diseases and other health problems under constant surveillance, promotes the exchange of information, formulates health regulations for international travel, and sets standards for the quality control of drugs, vaccines and other substances affecting health.

It collects and disseminates health data and carries out statistical analyses and comparative studies in such diseases as cancer, heart disease and mental illness.

It promotes improved environmental conditions, including housing, sanitation and working conditions. All available information on effects on human health of the pollutants in the environment is critically reviewed and published.

Co-operation among scientists and professional groups is encouraged, and the organization may propose international conventions and agreements. It assists in developing an informed public opinion on matters of health.

The WHO Regional Office for the Eastern Mediterranean works principally in the preparation of national and regional strategies for the achievement of Health for all by the year 2000 in the Eastern Mediterranean region, in accordance with the Global Strategy adopted by the World Health Assembly in May 1981. Primary health care is considered to be key to 'Health for all', with the following as minimum requirements:

Safe water in the home or within 15 minutes' walking distance, and adequate sanitary facilities in the home or immediate vicinity;

Immunization against diphtheria, pertussis, tetanus, poliomyelitis, measles and tuberculosis;

Local health care, including availability of at least 20 essential drugs, within one hour's travel;

Trained personnel to attend childbirth, and to care for pregnant mothers and children up to at least one year old.

In May 1998 the World Health Assembly agreed that a new global strategy should be effected, through regional and national health policies. The so-called 'Health for all in the 21st century' initiative was to build on the primary health care approach of the 'Health for all' strategy, but was to strengthen the emphasis on quality of life, equity in health and access to health services.

In July 1998 Dr Gro Harlem Brundtland officially took office as the new Director-General of WHO. She immediately announced an extensive reform of the organization, including restructuring the WHO technical programmes into nine groups, each headed by an Executive Director (see above). The groups were established within the framework of the following four main areas of activity: Building health populations and communities, comprising the groups Social change and mental health, Family and health services, and Sustainable development and healthy environments; Combating ill health, incorporating Communicable diseases and Non-communicable diseases; Sustained health, including the groups Evidence and information for policy and Health technology and drugs; and Internal support—reaching out, comprising General management, and External affairs and governing bodies. The final organization of each group was to be completed by 1 November.

The development of health manpower is given high priority in the region. Educational development and support forms a prominent feature of the Regional Office's work. It awards fellowships in health-related subjects. The Regional Arabic Programme issues training manuals and working guidelines.

DISEASE PREVENTION AND CONTROL

One of WHO's major achievements was the eradication of smallpox. Following a massive international campaign of vaccination and surveillance, begun in 1958 and intensified in 1967, this was declared to have been achieved in 1977. In May 1996 the World Health Assembly resolved that, pending a final endorsement, all remaining stocks of smallpox were to be destroyed on 30 June 1999, although doses of the smallpox vaccine were to be retained. In 1988 the World Health Assembly declared its commitment to the similar eradication of poliomyelitis by 2000; and in 1990 the Assembly resolved to eliminate iodine deficiency disorders (causing mental handicap) by 2000.

The objective of providing immunization for all children by 1990 was adopted by the World Health Assembly in 1977. Six diseases (measles, whooping cough, tetanus, poliomyelitis, tuberculosis and diphtheria) became the target of the Expanded Programme on Immunization (EPI), in which WHO, UNICEF and many other organizations collaborated. As a result of massive international and national efforts, the global immunization coverage increased from 20% in the early 1980s to the targeted rate of 80% by the end of 1990. This coverage signified that more than 100m. children in the developing world under the age of one had been successfully vaccinated against the targeted diseases, the lives of about 3m. children had been saved every year, and 500,000 annual cases of paralysis as a result of polio had been prevented. In 1992 the Assembly resolved to reach a new target of 90% immunization coverage with the six EPI vaccines; to introduce hepatitis B as a seventh vaccine and to introduce the yellow fever vaccine in areas where it occurs endemically. In September 1991 the Children's Vaccine Initiative (CVI) was launched, jointly sponsored by the Rockefeller Foundation, UNDP, UNICEF, WHO and the World Bank, to facilitate the development and provision of children's vaccines. The CVI has as its ultimate goal the development of a single oral immunization shortly after birth that will protect against all major childhood diseases.

WHO's Division of Diarrhoeal and Acute Respiratory Disease Control encourages national programmes aimed at reducing the estimated 3.5m. yearly childhood deaths as a result of diarrhoea, particularly through the use of oral rehydration therapy and preventive measures. The Division is also seeking to reduce deaths from pneumonia in infants through the use of a simple case-management strategy involving the recognition of danger signs and treatment with an appropriate antibiotic. In September 1997 WHO, in collaboration with UNICEF, formally launched a programme advocating the Integrated Management of Childhood Illness (IMCI), following successful regional trials in more than 20 developing countries during 1996–97. IMCI recognizes that pneumonia, diarrhoea, measles, malaria and malnutrition cause some 70% of the 11m. childhood deaths each year, and recommends screening sick children for all five conditions, in order to enable health workers to reach a more accurate diagnosis than may be achieved from the results of a single assessment. Simultaneous screening in such a way could avoid the provision of inadequate treatment and the excessive or inadequate use of drugs.

In 1995 WHO established the Division of Emerging, Viral and Bacterial ('Other Communicable') Diseases Surveillance and Control to strengthen the national and international capability to respond to the threats to public health from communicable diseases. The Division was to promote the development of national and international infrastructure and resources to recognize, monitor, prevent and control communicable diseases and emerging health problems, including antibiotic resistance. The Division aimed to promote applied research on the diagnosis, epidemiology, prevention and control of communicable diseases and emerging health problems. In

July 1996 WHO launched an interagency initiative to control an outbreak of cerebrospinal meningitis in Africa, which had caused some 15,000 deaths in the first half of that year. WHO provided technical assistance to enable countries to identify and control any outbreaks of the disease, including in Egypt, Morocco and Sudan, which had been seriously affected. In January 1997 an International Co-ordinating Group was established to ensure the optimum use and rapid provision of the 14m. doses of vaccine available for epidemic control in 1997, following the enormous demand of the previous year.

The Division of Control of Tropical Diseases provides member states with technical support to assist in the planning and implementation of control programmes, in particular of the following diseases: malaria, Chagas disease, schistosomiasis, filariasis (onchocerciasis and the lymphatic filariases), leishmaniasis, dengue haemorrhagic fever, sleeping sickness and dracunculiasis (Guinea worm disease). The Division formulates control strategies for global, regional or sub-regional application. Direct technical support is given to the design of realistic sustainable control programmes and to the integration of such programmes in the health services and the social and economic sectors of member countries. The Division takes part in mobilizing resources for disease control where needed, and co-ordinating national and international participation as appropriate. WHO's Special Programme for Research and Training in Tropical Diseases, sponsored jointly by WHO, UNDP and the World Bank, was established in 1975, and comprises a world-wide network of about 5,000 scientists working on the development of vaccines, new drugs, diagnostic kits, non-chemical insecticides and epidemiology and social and economic research on the target diseases. The programme aims to strengthen research institutions in developing countries, and to encourage participation by scientists from the countries most affected by tropical diseases. In January 1996 a new initiative to eliminate onchocerciasis became operational, with funding from the World Bank and with WHO as its executing agency. The African Programme for Onchocerciasis Control (APOC) aimed to benefit some 15m. people infected with the disease, which may cause blindness, in 16 participating African countries. APOC was to complement an existing control programme, initiated in 1974, which eliminated onchocerciasis as a major public health risk in 11 west African countries. In April 1998 WHO announced that the Onchocerciasis Control Programme in West Africa was to be terminated in 2002, by which time it was estimated that 40m. people would have been protected from the disease and 600,000 people prevented from developing blindness. WHO and the Regional Office in Africa proposed the establishment of a new surveillance organ to ensure rapid control of any future outbreak of the disease or of other infectious diseases. In January 1998 a new 20-year programme to eliminate lymphatic filariasis was initiated, with substantial funding from a major pharmaceutical company. A Ministerial Conference on Malaria, organized by WHO in October 1992 adopted a global strategy specifying requirements for effective control of the disease, which kills between 1.5m. and 2.7m. people every year and affects a further 300m.–500m. Preparations for a new African Initiative for Malaria Control in the 21st Century were underway in mid-1998. The Initiative was scheduled to be inaugurated in 1999, extending over 46 countries, and aimed to reduce the health, social and economic costs (estimated at US $2,000m. in 1997) of the disease in the region.

In December 1995 WHO's Global Programme on AIDS (Acquired Immunodeficiency Syndrome), which began in 1987, was concluded. A new Joint UN Programme on the human immunodeficiency virus (HIV) and AIDS—UNAIDS—became operational on 1 January 1996, sponsored jointly by WHO, the World Bank, UNICEF, UNDP, UNESCO and UNFPA. WHO established an Office of HIV/AIDS and Sexually-Transmitted Diseases in order to ensure the continuity of its global response to the problem, which included support for national control and education plans, improving the safety of blood supplies and improving the care and support of AIDS patients. In addition, the Office was to liaise with UNAIDS and to make available WHO's research and technical expertise. At December 1997 there were an estimated 30.7m. adults and children living with HIV/AIDS, compared with 22.6m. at the end of the previous year. During 1997 WHO and UNAIDS undertook a joint project of surveillance and analysis of the HIV/AIDS epidemic world-wide. The results were published in a report in June 1998.

In 1995 WHO established a Global Tuberculosis Programme to address the emerging challenges of the TB epidemic. According to WHO estimates, one-third of the world's population is infected with TB and more than 3m. people die from the disease each year, prompting WHO to declare TB a global emergency. WHO provides technical support to all member countries, with special attention being given to those with high TB prevalence, to establish effective national tuberculosis control programmes. WHO's strategy for TB control includes the use of DOTS (directly observed treatment, short-course), standardized treatment guide-lines, and result accountability through routine evaluation of treatment outcomes. Simultaneously, WHO is encouraging research with the aim of further disseminating DOTS, adapting it for wider use, developing new tools for prevention, diagnosis and treatment, and containing new threats such as the HIV/TB co-epidemic. In March 1997 it was announced that the use of DOTS in 10% of cases world-wide was resulting in the stabilization of the global epidemic. WHO predicted that an increased use of DOTS would prevent 10m. deaths within 10 years. Some 97 countries were implementing DOTS at the end of 1997. In March 1998 WHO identified Morocco and Oman among several countries successfully controlling TB through the use of DOTS, but at the same time criticized Iran, in addition to 15 other countries, as making inadequate progress in combating the disease.

WHO's Programme for the Promotion of Environmental Health undertakes a wide range of initiatives to tackle the increasing threats to health and well-being from a changing environment, especially in relation to air pollution, control of monitoring of water quality, sanitation, protection against radiation, management of hazardous waste, chemical safety and housing hygiene. The major part of WHO's technical co-operation in environmental health in developing countries is concerned with community water supply and sanitation. The Programme also gives prominence to the assessment of health risks from chemical, physical and biological agents. To contribute to the solution of environmental health problems associated with the rapid urbanization of cities in the developing world, the Programme was promoting globally in the 1990s the Healthy City approach that had been initiated in Europe. WHO is also working with other agencies to consider the implications on human health of global climate change.

WHO's Programmes for diabetes mellitus, chronic rheumatic diseases and asthma assist with the development of national programmes, based upon goals and targets for the improvement of early detection, care and reduction of long-term complications. They also monitor the global epidemiological situation and co-ordinate multinational research activities concerned with the prevention and care of non-communicable diseases. 'Inter-Health', a programme to combat non-communicable chronic diseases (such as those arising from an unhealthy diet) was initiated in 1990, with the particular aim of preventing an increase in the incidence of such diseases, and their related life-style determinants, in developing countries.

FOOD AND NUTRITION

WHO collaborates with FAO, WFP, UNICEF and other UN agencies in its activities relating to nutrition and food safety. In December 1992 an International Conference on Nutrition, co-sponsored by FAO and WHO, adopted a World Declaration on Nutrition and a Plan of Action designed to make the fight against malnutrition a development priority. In pursuing the objectives of the Declaration WHO promotes the elaboration of national plans of action for nutrition and aims to identify and support countries with high levels of malnutrition, which includes protein energy deficiencies, and deficiencies of iron, vitamin A and iodine. By January 1996 98 countries had formulated a national plan of action on nutrition. In collaboration with other international agencies, WHO is implementing a comprehensive strategy for promoting appropriate infant, young-child and maternal nutrition, and for dealing effectively with nutritional emergencies in large populations. Areas of emphasis include promoting health-care practices that enhance successful breast-feeding; appropriate complementary feeding; refining the use and interpretation of body measurements for assessing nutritional status; relevant information, education and training; and action to give effect to the 1981 International Code of Marketing of Breast-milk Substitutes. WHO's Food Safety Programme aims to eliminate risks, such as biological contaminants in foods which are a major cause of diarrhoea and malnutrition in children. WHO, together with FAO, establishes food standards (through the work of the Codex Alimentarius Commission) and evaluates food additives, pesticide residues and other contaminants and their implications for health.

DRUGS

The WHO Action Programme on Essential Drugs assists member countries to develop and implement national drug policies, in order to ensure the rational use of pharmaceuticals and the supply of essential drugs of good quality at low cost. In 1998 WHO published the 10th Model List of Essential Drugs, which identified 306 essential drugs. The Programme supports technical and operational research in the pharmaceutical sector and has a strong advocacy and information role on drug-related issues. WHO's Division of Drug Management and Policies provides information on international standards for the manufacture of pharmaceutical products in international trade, and advises national health agencies on the safety and efficacy of drugs, with particular regard to counterfeit and substandard products. WHO is also active in monitoring drug abuse and in developing effective approaches to the management of health problems resulting from substance abuse. In 1996 WHO published its first report on the tobacco situation worldwide. According to WHO about one-third of the world's population aged over 15 years smoke tobacco, which causes approximately 3m. deaths each year

(through lung cancer, heart disease, chronic bronchitis and other effects). In May the World Health Assembly approved a new five-year plan for the Programme on Tobacco or Health, including expansion of its public information activities and international research, and advocated that all member countries implement comprehensive tobacco control strategies.

WHO's Programme on Traditional Medicine encourages the incorporation of traditional health practices that have been evaluated as safe and effective into primary health care systems.

HEALTH PROMOTION

A Division of Health Promotion, Education and Communication was established in May 1994 to implement the priority assigned to health promotion in the Ninth General Programme of Work for the period 1996–2000. The Division promotes decentralized and community-based health programmes and is concerned with the challenge of population ageing and encouraging healthy life-styles and self-care. Several projects have been undertaken, in collaborations between WHO regional and country offices and other relevant organizations, including: the Global School Health Initiative, to bridge the sectors of health and education and to promote the health of school-age children; the Global Strategy for Occupational Health, to promote the health of the working population and the control of occupational health risks; Community-based Rehabilitation, which aimed to provide a more enabling environment for people with disabilities; and a communication strategy to provide training and support for health communications personnel and initiatives.

WHO's Division of Strengthening Health Services assists countries to expand and improve the functioning of their health infrastructure in order to ensure wider access to care, hospital services and health education. It works with countries to ensure continuity and quality of care at all levels, by well-trained health personnel. Under the UN's Special Initiative on Africa, launched in March 1996, WHO was mandated to co-ordinate international efforts to secure improvements in basic health care and to strengthen the management of health services and resources.

In March 1996 WHO's Centre for Health Development opened at Kobe, Japan. The Centre was to research health developments and other determinants to strengthen policy decision-making within the health sector.

EMERGENCY RELIEF

Through its Division of Emergency and Humanitarian Action WHO acts as the 'health arm' of UN relief efforts in response to emergencies and natural disasters. Its emergency preparedness activities include co-ordination, policy-making and planning, awareness-building, technical advice, training, publication of standards and guide-lines, and research. Its emergency relief activities include organizational support, the provision of emergency drugs and supplies and conducting technical emergency assessment missions. The Division's objective is to strengthen the national capacity of member states to reduce the adverse health consequences of disasters. In responding to emergency situations, WHO aims to develop projects and activities that will assist the national authorities concerned in rebuilding or strengthening their own capacity to handle the impact of such situations.

WHO assists UNRWA (q.v.) in providing healthcare to Palestinians living in the Occupied Territories. In October 1993, following a peace accord reached by Israel and Palestine in September, WHO launched an appeal for US $10m. to finance a technical assistance programme that was to implement the transfer of health services to a Palestinian self-governing authority, and provide for primary health care projects in the Occupied Territories. In May 1994 the World Health Assembly adopted a resolution to support the programme and to allocate the necessary funds to meet the urgent health needs of the Palestinian people.

In March 1996 a survey of health conditions in Iraq, published by WHO, generated concern at the impact on the population of the ongoing international trade embargo and, in particular, the widespread incidence of nutritional deficiencies and increasing infant mortality rates. Under the terms of Resolution 986 of the UN Security Council, which permitted the limited sale of petroleum by the Iraqi authorities in order to facilitate the purchase of essential humanitarian supplies, WHO was responsible for distributing medicines and medical supplies, for supervising the distribution of medicines by the Iraqi authorities in central and southern Iraq and for implementing an epidemiological surveillance network in the northern Kurdish provinces of Iraq. The distribution of medicines to an anticipated 600 hospitals and health centres was initiated in May 1997.

FINANCE

WHO's regular budget is provided by assessment of member states and associate members. An additional fund for specific projects is provided by voluntary contributions from members and other sources. Funds are received from the UNDP and from UNFPA for population programmes. The two-year budget for 1996–97 amounted to US $842.7m., with extra-budgetary funds expected to amount to $993.7m. during that period. In May 1997 the Assembly resolved to maintain the regular budget at $842.7m. for the 1998–99 biennium of which $157.4m. (or 18.7% of the total) was allocated to Africa and $90.2m. (10.7%) to the eastern Mediterranean region.

PUBLICATIONS

Full catalogue of publications supplied free on request.
Bulletin of WHO (6 a year).

International Digest of Health Legislation (quarterly).
Weekly Epidemiological Record.
WHO Drug Information (quarterly).
World Health (6 a year in several languages).
World Health Forum (quarterly, in several languages).
World Health Statistics Annual.
World Health Statistics Quarterly.
Series of technical reports.

Other UN Organizations Active in the Middle East and North Africa

OFFICE OF THE UNITED NATIONS SPECIAL CO-ORDINATOR IN THE OCCUPIED TERRITORIES—UNSCO

Address: POB 490, Government House, Jerusalem 91004.

Telephone: (7) 822746; fax (7) 820966.

UNSCO was established in June 1994 to support the Middle East peace process, in particular implementation of the Declaration of Principles with regard to interim arrangements for Palestinian self-rule (signed by the Israeli Government and the Palestine Liberation Organization in 1993), and to enhance the effectiveness of international donor assistance to the emerging autonomous areas. The Special Co-ordinator undertakes to co-ordinate UN programmes and agencies working in the region and organizes an annual inter-agency meeting. The Co-ordinator also co-chairs a Local Aid Co-ordination Committee to consider political and socio-economic developments affecting donor assistance and to identify priority areas for support.

Special Co-ordinator: CHINMAYA R. GHAREKHAN (India).

UNITED NATIONS CENTRE FOR HUMAN SETTLEMENTS—UNCHS (Habitat)

Address: POB 30030, Nairobi, Kenya.

Telephone: (2) 621234; **telex:** 22996; **fax:** (2) 624266; **e-mail:** webmaster@unchs.org; **internet:** http://www.unhabitat.org.

The Centre was established in 1978 to service the inter-governmental Commission on Human Settlements, and to serve as a focus for human settlements activities in the UN system. A Conference on Human Settlements (Habitat II) was held in İstanbul, Turkey, in June 1996.

Executive Director: Dr KLAUS TÖPFER (Germany) (acting).

UNITED NATIONS CHILDREN'S FUND—UNICEF

Address: 3 United Nations Plaza, New York, NY 10017, USA.

Telephone: (212) 326-7000; **telex:** 49620199; **fax:** (212) 888-7465; **e-mail:** webmaster@unicef.org; **internet:** http://www.unicef.org.

UNICEF was established in 1946 by the UN General Assembly as the UN International Children's Emergency Fund, to meet the emergency needs of children in post-war Europe and China. In 1950 its mandate was changed to emphasize programmes giving long-term benefits to children everywhere, particularly those in developing countries who are in the greatest need.

Executive Director: CAROL BELLAMY (USA).

Regional Office for the Middle East and North Africa: POB 811721, Amman, Jordan.

UNITED NATIONS CONFERENCE ON TRADE AND DEVELOPMENT—UNCTAD

Address: Palais des Nations, 1211 Geneva 10, Switzerland.

Telephone: (22) 9071234; **telex:** 412962; **fax:** (22) 9070057; **internet:** http://www.unctad.org.

UNCTAD was established in 1964. Its role is to promote international trade, particularly that of developing countries, with a view to accelerating economic development. UNCTAD is the principal organ of the UN General Assembly concerned with trade and development, and is the focal point within the UN system for integrated activities relating to trade, finance, technology, investment and sustainable development.

Secretary-General: RUBENS RICÚPERO (Brazil).

UNITED NATIONS INTERNATIONAL DRUG CONTROL PROGRAMME—UNDCP

Address: Vienna International Centre, Postfach 500, 1400 Vienna, Austria.

Telephone: (1) 213450; **telex:** 135612; **fax:** (1) 21345-5866; **e-mail:** undcp_hq@undcp.un.or.at; **internet:** http://www.undcp.org.

UNDCP was established in 1991, following a decision by the UN General Assembly, in order to enhance the effectiveness of the UN system for drug control and to provide leadership in the international control of drugs.

Executive Director: PINO ARLACCHI (Italy).

UNITED NATIONS POPULATION FUND—UNFPA

Address: 220 East 42nd St, New York, NY 10017, USA.

Telephone: (212) 297-5020; **telex:** 7607883; **fax:** (212) 557-6416; **internet:** http://www.unfpa.org.

Created in 1967 as the Trust Fund for Population Activities, the UN Fund for Population Activities (UNFPA) was established as a Fund of the UN General Assembly in 1972 and was made a subsidiary organ of the UN General Assembly in 1979, with the UNDP Governing Council designated as its governing body. In 1987 UNFPA's name was changed to the United Nations Population Fund (retaining the same acronym).

Executive Director: Dr NAFIS SADIK (Pakistan).

UN Specialized Agencies

INTERNATIONAL ATOMIC ENERGY AGENCY—IAEA

Address: Wagramerstrasse 5, POB 100, 1400 Vienna, Austria.

Telephone: (1) 20600; **telex:** 1-12645; **fax:** (1) 20607; **e-mail:** official.mail@iaea.org; **internet:** http://www.iaea.org/.

The Agency was founded in 1957 with the aim of enlarging the contribution of atomic energy to peace, health and prosperity throughout the world, through technical co-operation (assisting research on and practical application of atomic energy for peaceful uses) and safeguards (ensuring that materials and services provided by the Agency are not used for any military purpose).

Director-General: Dr MOHAMED EL-BARADEI (Egypt).

INTERNATIONAL CIVIL AVIATION ORGANIZATION—ICAO

Address: 999 University St, Montréal, PQ H5C 5H7, Canada.

Telephone: (514) 954-8219; **telex:** 05-24513; **fax:** (514) 954-6077; **e-mail:** icaohq@icao.org; **internet:** http://www.cam.org/icao.

ICAO was founded in 1947, on the basis of the Convention on International Civil Aviation, signed in Chicago, in 1944, to develop the techniques of international air navigation and to help in the planning and improvement of international air transport.

Secretary-General: RENATO CLAUDIO COSTA PEREIRA (Brazil).

Regional Office for the Middle East: Egyptian Civil Aviation Complex, Cairo Airport Rd, 11776 Cairo, Egypt.

INTERNATIONAL LABOUR ORGANIZATION—ILO

Address: 4 route des Morillons, 1211 Geneva 22, Switzerland.

Telephone: (22) 7996111; **telex:** 415647; **fax:** (22) 7988685; **internet:** http://www.ilo.org.

ILO was founded in 1919 to work for social justice as a basis for lasting peace. It carries out this mandate by promoting decent living standards, satisfactory conditions of work and pay and adequate employment opportunities. Methods of action include the creation of international labour standards; the provision of technical co-operation services; and training, education, research and publishing activities to advance ILO objectives.

Director-General: MICHEL HANSENNE (Belgium).

Regional Office for Africa: BP 3960, Abidjan 01, Côte d'Ivoire; tel. 32-27-16.

Regional Office for Arab States: POB 11-4088, Beirut, Lebanon; tel. (1) 371576; fax (1) 371573; e-mail beirut@ilo.org.lb.

INTERNATIONAL MARITIME ORGANIZATION—IMO

Address: 4 Albert Embankment, London, SE1 7SR, United Kingdom.

Telephone: (171) 735-7611; **telex:** 23588; **fax:** (171) 587-3210; **e-mail:** info@imo.org; **internet:** http://www.imo.org.

The Inter-Governmental Maritime Consultative Organization (IMCO) began operations in 1959, as a specialized agency of the UN to facilitate co-operation among governments on technical matters affecting international shipping. Its main aims are to improve the safety of international shipping, and to prevent pollution caused by ships. IMCO became IMO in 1982.

Secretary-General: WILLIAM A. O'NEIL (Canada).

INTERNATIONAL TELECOMMUNICATION UNION—ITU

Address: Place des Nations, 1211 Geneva 20, Switzerland.

Telephone: (22) 7305111; **telex:** 421000; **fax:** (22) 7337256; e-mail itumail@itu.int; **internet:** http://www.itu.int.

Founded in 1865, ITU became a specialized agency of the UN in 1947. It acts to encourage world co-operation in the use of telecommunication, to promote technical development and to harmonize national policies in the field.

Secretary-General: Dr PEKKA TARJANNE (Finland).

UNITED NATIONS INDUSTRIAL DEVELOPMENT ORGANIZATION—UNIDO

Address: Vienna International Centre, POB 300, 1400 Vienna, Austria.

Telephone: (1) 260260; **telex:** 135612; **fax:** (1) 2692669; **e-mail:** unido-pinfo@unido.org; **internet:** http://www.unido.org.

UNIDO began operations in 1967. It aims to promote sustainable and socially equitable industrial development in developing countries and in countries with economies in transition; encourages industrial partnerships between governments and the private sector and acts as a worldwide forum for industrial development; provides technical co-operation services.

Director-General: CARLOS ALFREDO MAGARIÑOS (Argentina).

UNIVERSAL POSTAL UNION—UPU

Address: Case postale, 3000 Berne 15, Switzerland.

Telephone: (31) 3503111; **telex:** 912761; **fax:** (31) 3503110; **e-mail:** ib.info@ib.upu.org; **internet:** http://ibis.ib.upu.org.

The General Postal Union was founded by the Treaty of Berne (1874), begining operations in July 1875. Three years later its name was changed to the Universal Postal Union. In 1948 UPU became a specialized agency of the UN. It aims to develop and unify the international postal service, to study problems and to provide training.

Director-General: THOMAS E. LEAVEY (USA).

WORLD INTELLECTUAL PROPERTY ORGANIZATION— WIPO

Address: 34 chemin des Colombettes, 1211 Geneva 20, Switzerland.

Telephone: (22) 3389111; **telex:** 412912; **fax:** (22) 7335428; **e-mail:** wipo.mail@wipo.int; **internet:** http://www.wipo.int.

WIPO was established in 1970. It became a specialized agency of the UN in 1974 concerned with the protection of intellectual property (e.g. industrial and technical patents and literary copyrights). WIPO formulates and administers treaties embodying international norms and standards of intellectual property, establishes model laws, and facilitates applications for the protection of inventions, trademarks etc. WIPO provides legal and technical assistance to developing countries and countries with economies in transition and advises countries on obligations under the World Trade Organization's agreement on Trade-Related Aspects of Intellectual Property Rights (TRIPS).

Director-General: Dr KAMIL IDRIS (Sudan).

WORLD METEOROLOGICAL ORGANIZATION—WMO

Address: 41 ave Giuseppe Motta, CP 2300, 1211 Geneva 2, Switzerland.

Telephone: (22) 7308111; **telex:** 414199; **fax:** (22) 7342326; **internet:** http://www.wmo.ch.

WMO started its activities in 1951, aiming to improve the exchange of information in the fields of meteorology, climatology and operational hydrology, and its applications.

Secretary-General: Prof. G.O.P. OBASI (Nigeria).

United Nations Information Centres

Algeria: BP 823, 19 ave Chahid el-Ouali, Mustapha Sayed, Algiers; tel. (2) 744902; telex (936) 66144; fax (2) 748505.

Bahrain: POB 26004, Villa 131, Rd 2803, Segaya 328, Manama; tel. (973) 231046; fax (973) 270749 (also covers Qatar and the United Arab Emirates).

Egypt: POB 982, World Trade Centre, 1191 Corniche El Nil, Boulak, Cairo; tel. (2) 769595; fax (2) 769393 (also covers Saudi Arabia).

Iran: POB 15875-4557, Ghaem Magham Farahani Ave 185, Teheran 15868; tel. (21) 8731534; telex 212397; fax (21) 2044523.

Jordan: POB 927115, 28 Abdul Hamid Sharaf St, Shmeisani, Amman; tel. (6) 5694351; telex 21691; fax (6) 5694981 (also covers Iraq).

Lebanon: POB 4656, Apt No 1, Fakhoury Bldg, Montée Bain Militaire, Ardati St, Beirut; tel. (1) 740231; fax (1) 740230 (also covers Kuwait and Syria).

Libya: POB 286, Muzzafar Al-Aftas St, Hay el-Andalous, Tripoli; tel. (21) 4777885; telex 20733; fax (21) 4777343; e-mail fo.lby@undp.org.

Morocco: BP 601, Angle Charia Ibnouzaid 6, Rabat; tel. (7) 68633; telex 32947; fax (7) 209776; e-mail rabat@ccmail.unicc.org.

Tunisia: BP 863, 61 blvd Bab-Benat, 1035 Tunis; tel. (1) 560203; telex 13777; fax (1) 568811.

Turkey: PK 407, 197 Atatürk Bul., Ankara; tel. (312) 4268113; telex 821-43684; fax (312) 4689719.

Yemen: POB 237, Handhal St, 4, Al-Boniya Area, San'a; tel. (1) 274000; fax (1) 274043.

ARAB FUND FOR ECONOMIC AND SOCIAL DEVELOPMENT—AFESD

Address: POB 21923, Safat, 13080 Kuwait.
Telephone: 4844500; **telex:** 22153; **fax:** 4815760.

Established in 1968 by the Economic Council of the Arab League, the Fund began its operations in 1974. It participates in the financing of economic and social development projects in the Arab states.

MEMBERSHIP

Twenty-one members (see table of subscriptions below).

Organization

(August 1998)

BOARD OF GOVERNORS

The Board of Governors consists of a Governor and an Alternate Governor appointed by each member of the Fund. The Board of Governors is considered as the General Assembly of the Fund, and has all powers.

BOARD OF DIRECTORS

The Board of Directors is composed of eight Directors elected by the Board of Governors from among Arab citizens of recognized experience and competence. They are elected for a renewable term of two years.

The Board of Directors is charged with all the activities of the Fund and exercises the powers delegated to it by the Board of Governors.

Director-General and Chairman of the Board of Directors: ABDLATIF YOUSUF AL-HAMAD.

FINANCIAL STRUCTURE

In 1982 the authorized capital was increased from 400m. Kuwaiti dinars (KD) to KD 800m., divided into 80,000 shares having a value of KD 10,000 each. At the end of 1997 paid-up capital was KD 663.04m.

SUBSCRIPTIONS (KD million, December 1997)*

Algeria	64.78		Oman		17.28
Bahrain	2.16		Palestine		1.10
Djibouti	0.02		Qatar		6.75
Egypt	40.50		Saudi Arabia		159.07
Iraq	31.76		Somalia		0.21
Jordan	17.30		Sudan		11.06
Kuwait	169.70		Syria		24.00
Lebanon	2.00		Tunisia		6.16
Libya	59.85		United Arab Emirates		28.00
Mauritania	0.82		Yemen		4.52
Morocco	16.00		**Total**		**663.04**

* 100 Kuwaiti dinars = US $328.5 (December 1997).

Activities

Pursuant to the Agreement Establishing the Fund (as amended in 1997 by the Board of Governors), the purpose of the Fund is to contribute to the financing of economic and social development projects in the Arab states and countries by:

1. Financing economic development projects of an investment character by means of loans granted on concessionary terms to governments and public enterprises and corporations, giving preference to projects which are vital to the Arab entity, as well as to joint Arab projects.

2. Financing private sector projects in member states by providing all forms of loans and guarantees to corporations and enterprises (possessing juridical personality), participating in their equity capital, and providing other forms of financing and the requisite financial, technical and advisory services, in accordance with such regulations and subject to such conditions as may be prescribed by the Board of Directors.

3. Forming or participating in the equity capital of corporations possessing juridical personality, for the implementation and financing of private sector projects in member states, including

the provision and financing of technical, advisory and financial services.

4. Establishing and administering special funds with aims compatible with those of the Fund and with resources provided by the Fund or other sources.

5. Encouraging, directly or indirectly, the investment of public and private capital in a manner conducive to the development and growth of the Arab economy.

6. Providing expertise and technical assistance in the various fields of economic development.

LOANS BY SECTOR, 1997

Sector	Amount (KD million)	%
Agriculture, livestock and fisheries	50.0	20.5
Transport and communications	34.5	14.1
Water and sewerage	31.5	12.9
Energy	44.6	18.3
Industry and mining	25.0	10.2
Other	58.5	24.0
Total	**244.1**	**100.0**

LOANS BY COUNTRY, 1997

Country	Project	Amount (KD million)
Algeria	Development of small- and medium-sized enterprises	10.0
	Mitigation of earthquake risks	3.5
Bahrain	Housing	15.0
	Water supply from Al-Hidd desalination and power facility	21.0
	Interconnection of Al-Hidd to the electricity network	10.0
Egypt	Construction of a steel factory	15.0
Lebanon	Higher education	23.0
Mauritania	Expansion of Nouakchott electricity-generating facility	4.6
	Urban water supply	3.5
	Electricity transmission from the Manantali hydroelectric facility	8.0
	Highway construction	3.5
Morocco	Construction of Dchar El Oued and Aït Messaoud dams	15.0
	Development of hydroelectric facilities at Dchar El Oued and Aït Messaoud dams	15.0
	Meknès water supply	7.0
	Improvements to domestic power grid for the Morocco-Spain electricity interconnection project	7.0*
Palestine	Improvements to Salah Eldin road	5.0
	Development of health services	3.0
	Rehabilitation of education services	3.0
Syria	Communications sector	26.0
Tunisia	Dam construction for irrigation schemes	22.0
	Support for vocational education and employment programmes	11.0
	Zarqa dam and irrigation projects	13.0
Total		**244.1**

* Supplementary loan.

The Fund co-operates with other Arab organizations such as the Arab Monetary Fund, the League of Arab States and OAPEC in preparing regional studies and conferences, and acts as the secretariat of the Co-ordination Group of Arab National and Regional Development Institutions. These organizations also work together to produce a *Unified Arab Economic Report*, which considers economic and social developments in the Arab states.

By the end of 1997 the Fund had made 355 loans for projects in 17 countries, since the beginning of its operations. The total value of these loans was KD 2,770m. Disbursements amounted to KD 1,612m. by the end of 1997.

During 1997 the Fund approved 22 loans totalling KD 244.1m. for projects in nine Arab countries (see table above).

The total number of technical assistance grants provided by the end of 1997 was 547, with a value of KD 60.8m. During 1997 41 new grants, totalling KD 4.9m., were approved, mainly for institutional support, infrastructure, training, feasibility studies and project preparation. Technical grants may be used to finance regional seminars and conferences and other general studies and research.

ARAB MONETARY FUND

Address: POB 2818, Abu Dhabi, United Arab Emirates.
Telephone: (2) 215000; **telex:** 22989; **fax:** (2) 326454.
The Agreement establishing the Arab Monetary Fund was approved by the Economic Council of Arab States in Rabat, Morocco, in April 1976 and entered into force on 2 February 1977.

MEMBERS

Algeria	Oman
Bahrain	Palestine
Djibouti	Qatar
Egypt	Saudi Arabia
Iraq*	Somalia*
Jordan	Sudan*
Kuwait	Syria
Lebanon	Tunisia
Libya	United Arab Emirates
Mauritania	Yemen
Morocco	

* From July 1993 loans to Iraq, Somalia and Sudan were suspended as a result of their failure to repay debts to the Fund totalling US $603m. By the end of 1997 the arrears amounted to some $762.4m.

Organization

(August 1998)

BOARD OF GOVERNORS

The Board of Governors is the highest authority of the Arab Monetary Fund. It formulates policies on Arab economic integration and liberalization of trade among member states. With certain exceptions, it may delegate to the Board of Executive Directors some of its powers. The Board of Governors is composed of a governor and a deputy governor appointed by each member state for a term of five years. It meets at least once a year; meetings may also be convened at the request of half the members, or of members holding half of the total voting power.

BOARD OF EXECUTIVE DIRECTORS

The Board of Executive Directors exercises all powers vested in it by the Board of Governors and may delegate to the Director-General such powers as it deems fit. It is composed of the Director-General and eight non-resident directors elected by the Board of Governors. Each director holds office for three years and may be re-elected.

DIRECTOR-GENERAL

The Director-General of the Fund is appointed by the Board of Governors for a renewable five-year term, and serves as Chairman of the Board of Executive Directors.

The Director-General supervises a Committee on Loans and a Committee on Investments to make recommendations on loan and investment policies to the Board of Executive Directors, and is required to submit an Annual Report to the Board of Governors.
Director-General and Chairman of the Board of Executive Directors: Dr JASSIM ABDULLAH AL-MANNAI.

FINANCE

The Arab Accounting Dinar (AAD) is a unit of account equivalent to 3 IMF Special Drawing Rights. (The average value of the SDR in 1997 was US $1.37602.)

Each member paid, in convertible currencies, 5% of the value of its shares at the time of its ratification of the Agreement and another 20% when the Agreement entered into force. In addition, each member paid 2% of the value of its shares in its national currency regardless of whether it is convertible. The second 25% of the capital was to be subscribed by the end of September 1979, bringing the

total paid-up capital in convertible currencies to AAD 131.5m. (SDR 394.5m.). An increase in requests for loans led to a resolution by the Board of Governors in April 1981, giving members the option of paying the balance of their subscribed capital. This payment became obligatory in July 1981, when total approved loans exceeded 50% of the already paid-up capital in convertible currencies. In April 1983 the authorized capital of the Fund was increased from AAD 288m. to AAD 600m. The new capital stock comprised 12,000 shares, each having the value of AAD 50,000. At the end of 1997 total paid-up capital was AAD 324.1m.

CAPITAL SUBSCRIPTIONS
(million Arab Accounting Dinars, 31 December 1997)

Member	Paid-up capital
Algeria	42.40
Bahrain	5.00
Djibouti	0.25
Egypt	32.00
Iraq	42.40
Jordan	5.40
Kuwait	32.00
Lebanon	5.00
Libya	13.44
Mauritania	5.00
Morocco	15.00
Oman	5.00
Palestine	2.16
Qatar	10.00
Saudi Arabia	48.40
Somalia	4.00
Sudan	10.00
Syria	7.20
Tunisia	7.00
United Arab Emirates	19.20
Yemen	15.40
Total	**324.09***

* Excluding Palestine's share, which was deferred by a Board of Governors' resolution in 1978.

Activities

The creation of the Arab Monetary Fund was seen as a step towards the goal of Arab economic integration. It assists member states in balance of payments difficulties, and also has a broad range of aims.

The Articles of Agreement define the Fund's aims as follows:

(*a*) to correct disequilibria in the balance of payments of member states;

(*b*) to promote the stability of exchange rates among Arab currencies, to render them mutually convertible, and to eliminate restrictions on current payments between member states;

(*c*) to establish policies and modes of monetary co-operation to accelerate Arab economic integration and economic development in the member states;

(*d*) to tender advice on the investment of member states' financial resources in foreign markets, whenever called upon to do so;

(*e*) to promote the development of Arab financial markets;

(*f*) to promote the use of the Arab dinar as a unit of account and to pave the way for the creation of a unified Arab currency;

(*g*) to co-ordinate the positions of member states in dealing with international monetary and economic problems; and (*h*) to provide a mechanism for the settlement of current payments between member states in order to promote trade among them.

The Arab Monetary Fund functions both as a fund and a bank. It is empowered:

(*a*) to provide short- and medium-term loans to finance balance of payments deficits of member states;

(*b*) to issue guarantees to member states to strengthen their borrowing capabilities;

(*c*) to act as intermediary in the issuance of loans in Arab and international markets for the account of member states and under their guarantees;

(*d*) to co-ordinate the monetary policies of member states;

(*e*) to manage any funds placed under its charge by member states;

(*f*) to hold periodic consultations with member states on their economic conditions; and

(*g*) to provide technical assistance to banking and monetary institutions in member states.

Loans are intended to finance an overall balance of payments deficit and a member may draw up to 75% of its paid-up subscription, in convertible currencies, for this purpose unconditionally (automatic loans). A member may, however, obtain loans in excess of this limit, subject to agreement with the Fund on a programme aimed at reducing its balance of payments deficit (ordinary and extended loans, equivalent to 175% and 250% of its quota respectively). From 1981 a country receiving no extended loans was entitled to a loan under the Inter-Arab Trade Facility (discontinued in 1989) of up to 100% of its quota. In addition, a member has the right to borrow up to 50% of its paid-up capital in order to cope with an unexpected deficit in its balance of payments resulting from a decrease in its exports of goods and services or a large increase in its imports of agricultural products following a poor harvest (compensatory loans). Over the period 1978–97, 103 loans were extended to 12 member countries.

Automatic and compensatory loans are repayable within three years, while ordinary and extended loans are repayable within five and seven years respectively. Loans are granted at concessionary and uniform rates of interest which increase with the length of the period of the loan. In 1988 the Fund's executive directors agreed to modify their policy on lending, placing an emphasis on the correction of economic imbalances in recipient countries.

At the end of 1997 total approved loans amounted to AAD 718.8m., of which AAD 694.2m. had been disbursed and AAD 487.5m. repaid. During 1997 the Fund approved three loans amounting to AAD 22.7m.

The Fund also provides technical assistance to its member countries. Such assistance is furnished through either the provision of experts to the country concerned or in the form of specialized training of officials of member countries. In view of the increased importance of this type of assistance, the Fund established, in 1988, the Economic Policy Institute (EPI) which offers regular training courses and specialized seminars for middle-level and senior staff, respectively, of financial and monetary institutions of the Arab countries.

TRADE PROMOTION

Arab Trade Financing Program (ATFP): POB 26799, Corniche Rd, Arab Monetary Fund Bldg, 7th Floor, Abu Dhabi, United Arab Emirates; tel. (2) 316999; telex 24166; fax (2) 316793; internet http://www.atfp.com; f. 1989 to develop and promote trade between Arab countries, and to enhance the competitive ability of Arab exporters; operates by extending lines of credit to Arab exporters and importers through national agencies (designated by the monetary authorities of Arab countries). The Arab Monetary Fund provided 50% of the ATFP's capital of US $500m., and participation was also invited from private and official Arab financial institutions and joint Arab/foreign institutions; paid-in cap. $454m. (June 1996); the ATFP, in accordance with a mandate of the Economic and Social Council of the Arab League, undertook to establish and to administer an Intra-Arab Trade Information Network (IATIN) Chief Exec. and Chair. of the Board Dr JASSIM ABDULLAH AL-MANNAI. Publs *Annual Report* (Arabic and English), *IATIN Quarterly Bulletin* (Arabic).

PUBLICATIONS

Annual Report.

Arab Countries: Economic Indicators (annually).

Cross Exchange Rates of Arab Currencies (annually).

Foreign Trade of Arab Countries (annually).

Joint Arab Economic Report (annually).

Money and Credit in Arab Countries.

National Accounts of Arab Countries (annually).

Balance of Payments and Public Debt of Arab Countries (annually).

AMF Publications Catalog (annually).

Policy and Management of Exchange Rates in the Arab Countries.

The Role of the State in the New Arab Economic Environment.

The Social Impact of Economic Reform on Arab Countries.

Reports on commodity structure (by value and quantity) of member countries' imports from and exports to other Arab countries.

LOANS APPROVED, 1997

Borrower	Type of loan	Amount (AAD million)
Djibouti	Ordinary	0.37
Jordan	Compensatory	2.66
Yemen	Extended	19.66
Total		22.68

LOANS APPROVED, 1978–97

Type of loan	Number of loans	Amount (AAD '000)
Automatic	53	257,775
Ordinary	11	104,566
Compensatory	11	72,485
Extended	17	219,206
Inter-Arab Trade Facility (cancelled in 1989)	11	64,730
Total	103	718,762

CO-OPERATION COUNCIL FOR THE ARAB STATES OF THE GULF

Address: POB 7153, Riyadh 11462, Saudi Arabia.
Telephone: (1) 482-7777; **telex:** 403635; **fax:** (1) 482-9089.
More generally known as the Gulf Co-operation Council (GCC), the organization was established on 25 May 1981 by six Arab states.

MEMBERS

Bahrain	Oman	Saudi Arabia
Kuwait	Qatar	United Arab Emirates

Organization

(August 1998)

SUPREME COUNCIL

The Supreme Council is the highest authority of the GCC, comprises the heads of member states and meets annually in ordinary session, and in emergency session if demanded by two or more members. The Presidency of the Council is undertaken by each state in turn, in alphabetical order. The Supreme Council draws up the overall policy of the organization; it discusses recommendations and laws presented to it by the Ministerial Council and the Secretariat General in preparation for endorsement. The GCC's charter provides for the creation of a commission for the settlement of disputes between member states, to be attached to and appointed by the Supreme Council. In December 1997 the Supreme Council authorized the establishment of a 30-member Consultative Council, appointed by member states, to act as an advisory body.

MINISTERIAL COUNCIL

The Ministerial Council consists of the foreign ministers of member states, meeting every three months, and in emergency session if demanded by two or more members. It prepares for the meetings of the Supreme Council, and draws up policies, recommendations, studies and projects aimed at developing co-operation and co-ordination among member states in various spheres.

SECRETARIAT GENERAL

The Secretariat assists member states in implementing recommendations by the Supreme and Ministerial Councils, and prepares reports and studies, budgets and accounts. The Secretary-General is appointed by the Supreme Council for a renewable three-year term. In March 1996 the Ministerial Council approved a proposal that, in future, the position of Secretary-General be rotated among member states, in order to ensure equal representation. Assistant Secretary-Generals are appointed by the Ministerial Council upon the recommendation of the Secretary General. All member states contribute in equal proportions towards the budget of the Secretariat.

Secretary-General: Sheikh Jamil Ibrahim Alhejailan (Saudi Arabia).

Assistant Secretary-General for Political Affairs: Dr Hamad Ali as-Sulayti (Bahrain).

Assistant Secretary-General for Economic Affairs: Dr Abdullah Saleh al-Khulayfi (Qatar).

Assistant Secretary-General for Military Affairs: Maj.-Gen. Faleh Abdullah ash-Shatti (Kuwait).

Activities

The GCC was set up following a series of meetings of foreign ministers of the states concerned, culminating in an agreement on the basic details of its charter on 10 March 1981. The Charter was signed by the six heads of state on 25 May. It describes the organization as providing 'the means for realizing co-ordination, integration and co-operation' in all economic, social and cultural affairs. A series of ministerial meetings subsequently began to put the proposals into effect.

ECONOMIC CO-OPERATION

In November 1982 GCC ministers drew up a 'unified economic agreement' covering freedom of movement of people and capital, the abolition of customs duties, technical co-operation, harmonization of banking regulations and financial and monetary co-ordination. At the same time GCC heads of state approved the formation of a

Gulf Investment Corporation, with capital of US $2,100m., to be based in Kuwait (see below). Customs duties on domestic products of the Gulf states were abolished in March 1983, and new regulations allowing free movement of workers and vehicles between member states were also introduced. A common minimum customs levy (of between 4% and 20%) on foreign imports was imposed in 1986. In May 1992 GCC trade ministers announced the objective of establishing a GCC common market by 2000. In September 1992 GCC ministers reached agreement on the application of a unified system of tariffs by March 1993. A meeting of the Supreme Council, held in December 1992, however, decided to mandate GCC officials to formulate a plan for the introduction of common external tariffs, to be presented to the Council in December 1993. Only the tax on tobacco products was to be standardized from March 1993, at a rate of 50%. (In June 1996 ministers agreed to increase the customs tariff on tobacco products to 70%, effective from 1 July 1997.) In April 1994 ministers of finance agreed to pursue a gradual approach to unifying tariffs, which was to be achieved according to a schedule over two to three years. In May 1998 finance ministers declared that the process of classifying items for the purposes of a unified external customs tariff was to be concluded by the end of that year.

In February 1987 the governors of the member states' central banks agreed in principle to co-ordinate their rates of exchange, and this was approved by the Supreme Council in November. It was subsequently agreed to link the Gulf currencies to a 'basket' of other currencies. In October 1990, following the Iraqi invasion of Kuwait, GCC Governments agreed to provide support for regional banks affected by the crisis. In April 1993 GCC central bank governors agreed to establish a joint banking supervisory committee, in order to devise rules for GCC banks to operate in other member states. They also decided to allow Kuwait's currency to become part of the GCC monetary system that was established following Iraq's invasion of Kuwait in order to defend the Gulf currencies. In December 1997 GCC heads of state authorized the guide-lines that had been formulated to enable national banks to establish operations in other GCC states. These were to apply only to banks established at least 10 years previously with a share capital of more than US $100m.

TRADE AND INDUSTRY

In 1982 a ministerial committee was formed to co-ordinate trade policies and development in the region. Technical subcommittees were established to oversee a strategic food reserve for the member states, and joint trade exhibitions (which were generally held every year until responsibility was transferred to the private sector in 1996). In November 1986 the Supreme Council approved a measure whereby citizens of GCC member states were enabled to undertake certain retail trade activities in any other member state, with effect from 1 March 1987. The ministerial committee in charge of trade also forms the board of directors of the GCC Authority for Standards and Metrology, which approves minimum standards for goods produced in or imported to the region.

In 1985 the Supreme Council endorsed a common industrial strategy for the GCC states. It approved regulations stipulating that priority should be given to imports of GCC industrial products, and permitting GCC investors to obtain loans from GCC industrial development banks. In November 1986 resolutions were adopted on the protection of industrial products, and on the co-ordination of industrial projects, in order to avoid duplication. In March 1989 the Ministerial Council approved the Unified GCC Foreign Capital Investment Regulations, which aimed to attract foreign investment and to co-ordinate investments amongst GCC countries. Further guidelines to promote foreign investment in the region were formulated during 1997. In December 1992 the Supreme Council endorsed Patent Regulations for GCC member states to facilitate regional scientific and technological research.

AGRICULTURE

A unified agricultural policy for GCC countries was endorsed by the Supreme Council in November 1985. Between 1983 and 1990 ministers also approved proposals for harmonizing legislation relating to water conservation, veterinary vaccines, insecticides, fertilizers, fisheries and seeds. A permanent committee on fisheries aims to co-ordinate national fisheries policies, to establish designated fishing periods and to undertake surveys of the fishing potential in the Arabian (Persian) Gulf. Co-operation in the agricultural sector also extends to consideration of the water resources in the region.

TRANSPORT, COMMUNICATIONS AND INFORMATION

During 1985 feasibility studies were undertaken on new rail and road links between member states, and on the establishment of a joint coastal transport company. A scheme to build a 1,700-km railway to link all the member states and Iraq (and thereby the European railway network) was postponed, owing to its high cost (estimated at US $4,000m.). In November 1993 ministers agreed to request assistance from the International Telecommunication Union on the establishment of a joint telecommunications network, which had been approved by ministers in 1986. The region's telecommunications systems were to be integrated through underwater fibre-optic cables and a satellite-based mobile telephone network. In the mid-1990s, GCC ministers of information began convening on a regular basis with a view to formulating a joint external information policy. In November 1997 GCC interior ministers approved a simplified passport system to facilitate travel between member countries.

ENERGY

In 1982 a ministerial committee was established to co-ordinate hydrocarbons policies and prices. Ministers adopted a petroleum security plan to safeguard individual members against a halt in their production, to form a stockpile of petroleum products, and to organize a boycott of any non-member country when appropriate. In December 1987 the Supreme Council adopted a plan whereby a member state whose petroleum production was disrupted could 'borrow' petroleum from other members, in order to fulfil its export obligations.

During the early 1990s proposals were formulated to integrate the electricity networks of the six member countries. In the first stage of the plan the networks of Saudi Arabia, Bahrain, Kuwait and Qatar would be integrated; those of the United Arab Emirates (UAE) and Oman would be interconnected and finally linked to the others in the second stage, to be completed by 2003. In December 1997 GCC heads of state declared that work should commence on the first stage of the plan, under the management of an independent authority. The estimated cost of the project was more than US $6,000m. However, it was agreed not to invite private developers to participate in construction of the grid, but that the first phase of the project be financed by member states (to contribute 35% of the estimated $2,000m. required), and by loans from commercial banking and international monetary institutions.

REGIONAL SECURITY

Although no mention of defence or security was made in the original charter, the summit meeting which ratified the charter also issued a statement rejecting any foreign military presence in the region. The Supreme Council meeting in November 1981 agreed to include defence co-operation in the activities of the organization: as a result, defence ministers met in January 1982 to discuss a common security policy, including a joint air defence system and standardization of weapons. In November 1984 member states agreed to form the Peninsula Shield Force for rapid deployment against external aggression, comprising units from the armed forces of each country under a central command to be based in Saudi Arabia.

In October 1987 (following an Iranian missile attack on Kuwait, which supported Iraq in its war against Iran) GCC ministers of foreign affairs issued a statement declaring that aggression against one member state was regarded as aggression against them all. In December the Supreme Council approved a joint pact on regional co-operation in matters of security. In August 1990 the Ministerial Council condemned Iraq's invasion of Kuwait as a violation of sovereignty, and demanded the withdrawal of all Iraqi troops from Kuwait. During the crisis and the ensuing war between Iraq and a multinational force which took place in January and February 1991, the GCC developed closer links with Egypt and Syria, which, together with Saudi Arabia, played the most active role among the Arab countries in the anti-Iraqi alliance. In March the six GCC nations, Egypt and Syria formulated the 'Declaration of Damascus', which announced plans to establish a regional peace-keeping force. The Declaration also urged the abolition of all weapons of mass destruction in the area, and recommended the resolution of the Palestinian question by an international conference. In June Egypt and Syria, whose troops were to have formed the largest proportion of the peace-keeping force, announced their withdrawal from the project, reportedly as a result of disagreements with the GCC concerning the composition of the proposed force and the remuneration involved. A meeting of ministers of foreign affairs of the eight countries took place in July, but agreed only to provide mutual military assistance when necessary. In June 1992 the GCC member states indicated that they had not completely abandoned the Declaration of Damascus, when they consented in principle to the convening of a summit conference on the pact, proposed by the Egyptian President. In September the signatories of the Damascus Declaration adopted a joint statement on regional questions, including the Middle East peace process and the dispute between the UAE and Iran (see below), but rejected an Egyptian proposal to establish a

series of rapid deployment forces which could be called upon to defend the interests of any of the eight countries. A meeting of GCC ministers of defence in November agreed to maintain the Peninsula Shield Force. In November 1993 GCC ministers of defence approved a proposal to expand the force from 8,000 to 17,000 troops and incorporate air and naval units. Ministers also agreed to strengthen the defence of the region by developing joint surveillance and early warning systems. A GCC military committee was established, and convened for the first time in April 1994, to discuss the implementation of the proposals. Joint military training exercises were conducted by forces of five GCC states (excluding Qatar) in northern Kuwait in March 1996. In December 1997 the Supreme Council approved plans that had been authorized by defence ministers in November for linking the region's military telecommunications networks and establishing a common early warning system.

In September 1992 the Ministerial Council endorsed the imposition by the USA, the United Kingdom, France and Russia of an air exclusion zone over southern Iraq in late August, which was designed to protect the population of that part of the country from attacks by the Iraqi armed forces. At the same meeting the Council expressed opposition to Iran's 'continued occupation' of islands claimed by the UAE: namely Abu Musa and the Greater and Lesser Tunb islands. In April 1993, Iran removed its restrictions on the movement of people to the island of Abu Musa, a development welcomed by the GCC states. Subsequently, the GCC has repeatedly confirmed its support for the UAE's sovereignty claim, condemned efforts by Iran to consolidate its presence on the islands and urged Iran to pursue peaceful means to end the dispute and refer the case to the International Court of Justice.

In late September 1992 a rift within the GCC was caused by an incident on the disputed border between Saudi Arabia and Qatar. Qatar's threat to boycott a meeting of the Supreme Council in December was allayed at the last minute as a result of mediation efforts by the Egyptian President. At the meeting, which was held in UAE, Qatar and Saudi Arabia agreed to establish a joint commission to demarcate the disputed border. The resolution of border disputes was the principal concern of GCC heads of state when they convened for their annual meeting in December 1994, in Bahrain. The Kuwaiti leader proposed the establishment of a GCC framework for resolving border disputes, consisting of bilateral negotiations between the concerned parties, mediated by a third GCC state.

In November 1994 a security agreement, to counter regional crime and terrorism, was concluded by GCC states. The pact, however, was not signed by Kuwait, which claimed that a clause concerning the extradition of offenders was in contravention of its constitution; Qatar did not attend the meeting, held in Riyadh, owing to its ongoing dispute with Saudi Arabia (see above). At the summit meeting in December GCC heads of state expressed concern at the increasing incidence of Islamic extremist violence throughout the region. In April 1995 GCC interior ministers convened to discuss ongoing civil unrest in Bahrain; the ministers collectively supported measures adopted by the Bahraini Government to secure political and civil stability. The continuing unrest in Bahrain and the involvement of the Iranian Government in Bahraini domestic affairs remained issues of concern for the GCC throughout 1995 and 1996.

During 1995 the deterioration of relations between Qatar and other GCC states threatened to undermine the Council's solidarity. In December Qatar publicly displayed its dissatisfaction at the appointment, without a consensus agreement, of Saudi Arabia's nominee as the new Secretary-General by failing to attend the final session of the Supreme Council, held in Muscat, Oman. However, at a meeting of ministers of foreign affairs in March 1996, Qatar endorsed the new Secretary-General, following an agreement on future appointment procedures, and reasserted its commitment to the organization. In June Saudi Arabia and Qatar agreed to reactivate a joint technical committee in order to finalize the demarcation of their mutual border. In December Qatar hosted the annual GCC summit meeting; however, Bahrain refused to attend, owing to Qatar's 'unfriendly attitude' and the long-standing territorial dispute over the Hawar islands. The issue dominated the meeting, which agreed to establish a four-member committee to resolve the conflicting sovereignty claims. In January 1997 the ministers of foreign affairs of Kuwait, Oman, Saudi Arabia and the UAE, meeting in Riyadh, formulated a seven-point memorandum of understanding to ease tensions between Bahrain and Qatar. The two countries refused to sign the agreement; however, in March both sides announced their intention to establish diplomatic relations at ambassadorial level.

In May 1997 the Ministerial Council, meeting in Riyadh, expressed concern at Turkey's cross-border military operation in northern Iraq and urged a withdrawal of Turkish troops from Iraqi territory. In December the Supreme Council reaffirmed the need to ensure the sovereignty and territorial integrity of Iraq. At the same time, however, the Council expressed concern at the escalation of tensions in the region, owing to Iraq's failure to co-operate with the UN Special Commission (UNSCOM). The Council also noted the opportunity to strengthen relations with Iran, in view of political developments in that country. In early 1998 tensions in the Gulf region continued to escalate. In mid-February the US Defense Secretary visited each of the GCC countries in order to generate regional support for any punitive military action against Iraq, given that country's obstruction of UN weapons inspectors. Kuwait was the only country to declare its support for the use of force (and to permit the use of its bases in military operations against Iraq), while other member states urged a diplomatic solution to the crisis. Qatar pursued a diplomatic initiative to negotiate directly with the Iraqi authorities, and in mid-February the Qatari Minister of Foreign Affairs became the most senior GCC government official to visit Iraq since 1990. The GCC supported an agreement concluded between the UN Secretary-General and the Iraqi authorities at the end of February, and urged Iraq to co-operate with UNSCOM in order to secure an end to the problem and a removal of the international embargo against the country. This position was reiterated at a meeting of the Ministerial Council in March, which also expressed concern at the lack of progress in the Middle East peace process and Iran's ongoing claim to sovereignty over the disputed islands (see above).

EXTERNAL RELATIONS

In June 1988 an agreement was signed by GCC and European Community (EC) ministers on economic co-operation (with effect from January 1990): the EC agreed to assist the GCC states in developing their agriculture and industry. A Joint Co-operation Council was established under the agreement, comprising EC and GCC ministers. In March 1990, at the first annual meeting of the Council, GCC and EC ministers of foreign affairs undertook to hold negotiations on a free-trade agreement. Discussions began in October, although any final accord would require the GCC to adopt a unified structure of customs duties. In early 1992 the agreement was jeopardized by the GCC's opposition to the EC's proposed tax on fossil fuels (in order to reduce pollution) which would have raised the price of a barrel of petroleum by an estimated US $10 by 2000. With the new US administration proposing a similar energy tax, in March 1993 GCC oil ministers threatened to restrict the supply of petroleum (the GCC countries control almost one-half of the world's petroleum reserves) in retaliation. In October 1995 a conference was held in Muscat, Oman, which aimed to strengthen economic co-operation between European Union (EU, as the restructured EC was now known) and GCC member states, and to promote investment in both regions. In April 1996 the Joint Council advocated the conclusion of free-trade negotiations by 1998. In December 1997 GCC heads of state condemned statements issued by the European Parliament, as well as by other organizations, regarding human rights issues in member states and insisted they amounted to interference in GCC judicial systems.

In December 1991 GCC ministers of finance and of foreign affairs approved the establishment of an Arab Development Fund, which aimed to create greater political and economic stability in the region, and in particular was intended to assist Egypt and Syria, as a reward for their active military part in the Gulf War and their major role in the security force envisaged by the Declaration of Damascus. The GCC made it clear that those countries and organizations which had supported Iraq during its occupation of Kuwait would not be beneficiaries of the new fund. A starting capital of US $10,000m. was originally envisaged for the Fund, although by mid-1992 only $6,500m. had been pledged, with reports that the project had been scaled down. In May 1993 ministers of finance from the GCC states, Egypt and Syria, meeting in Qatar, failed to agree on the level of contributions to the Fund.

In September 1994 GCC ministers of foreign affairs decided to end the secondary and tertiary embargo on trade with Israel. In February 1995 a ministerial meeting of signatories of the Damascus Declaration adopted a common stand, criticizing Israel for its refusal to renew the nuclear non-proliferation treaty. In December 1996 the foreign ministers of the Damascus Declaration states, convened in Cairo, requested the USA to exert financial pressure on Israel to halt the construction of settlements on occupied Arab territory.

In late June 1997 ministers of foreign affairs of the Damascus Declaration states agreed to pursue efforts to establish a free-trade zone throughout the region, which was to form the basis of a future Arab common market.

INVESTMENT CORPORATION

Gulf Investment Corporation (GIC): Joint Banking Center, Kuwait Real Estate Bldg, POB 3402, Safat 13035, Kuwait; tel. 2431911; telex 44002; fax 2448894; f. 1983 by the six member states of the GCC, each contributing US $350m. of the total capital of $2,100m.; total assets $10,245m., dep. $8,135m. (1995); investment chiefly in the Gulf region, financing industrial projects (including pharmaceuticals, chemicals, steel wire, aircraft engineering, aluminium, dairy produce and chicken-breeding). GIC provides merchant banking and financial advisory services, and in 1992 was appointed to advise the Kuwaiti Government on a programme of privatization. Chair. AHMED BIN HUMAID AT-TAYER; Gen. Man. HISHAM A. RAZZUQI. Publ. *The GIC Gazetteer* (annually).

Gulf International Bank: POB 1017, Al-Dowali Bldg, 3 Palace Ave, Manama 317, Bahrain; tel. 534000; fax 522633; f. 1976 by the six GCC states and Iraq; became a wholly-owned subsidiary of the GIC (without Iraqi shareholdings) in 1991; cap. US $450m., dep. $7,887.8m., total assets $9,523.9m. (Dec. 1997). Chair. IBRAHIM ABD AL-KARIM; Gen. Man. ABDULLAH AL-KUWAIZ.

PUBLICATIONS

GCC News (monthly).
Al-Ta'awun (periodical).

COUNCIL OF ARAB ECONOMIC UNITY

Address: POB 1, Mohammed Fareed, Cairo, Egypt.
Telephone: (2) 5755321; **fax:** (2) 5754090.
Established in 1957 by the Economic Council of the Arab League. The first meeting of the Council was held in 1964.

MEMBERS

Egypt	Palestine
Iraq	Somalia
Jordan	Sudan
Kuwait	Syria
Libya	United Arab Emirates
Mauritania	Yemen

Organization

(August 1998)

COUNCIL

The Council consists of representatives of member states, usually ministers of economy, finance and trade. It meets twice a year; meetings are chaired by the representative of each country for one year.

GENERAL SECRETARIAT

Entrusted with the implementation of the Council's decisions and with proposing work plans, including efforts to encourage participation by member states in the Arab Economic Unity Agreement. The Secretariat also compiles statistics, conducts research and publishes studies on Arab economic problems and on the effects of major world economic trends.

General Secretary: HASSAN IBRAHIM.

COMMITTEES

There are seven standing committees: preparatory, follow-up and Arab Common Market development; Permanent Delegates; budget; economic planning; fiscal and monetary matters; customs and trade planning and co-ordination; statistics. There are also seven *ad hoc* committees, including meetings of experts on tariffs, trade promotion and trade legislation.

Activities

A five-year work plan for the General Secretariat in 1986–90 was approved in December 1985. As in the previous five-year plan, it included the co-ordination of measures leading to a customs union subject to a unified administration; market and commodity studies; unification of statistical terminology and methods of data collection; studies for the formation of new joint Arab companies and federations; formulation of specific programmes for agricultural and industrial co-ordination and for improving road and railway networks.

ARAB COMMON MARKET

Members: Egypt, Iraq, Jordan, Libya, Mauritania, Syria and Yemen.

Based on a resolution passed by the Council in August 1964; its implementation is supervised by the Council and does not constitute a separate organization. Customs duties and other taxes on trade between the member countries were eliminated in annual stages, the process being completed in 1971. The second stage was to be the adoption of a full customs union, and ultimately all restrictions on trade between the member countries, including quotas, and restrictions on residence, employment and transport, were to be abolished. In practice, however, the trading of national products has not been freed from all monetary, quantitative and administrative restrictions.

Between 1978 and 1989, the following measures were undertaken by the Council for the development of the Arab Common Market:

Introduction of flexible membership conditions for the least developed Arab states (Mauritania, Somalia, Sudan and Yemen).

Approval in principle of a fund to compensate the least developed countries for financial losses incurred as a result of joining the Arab Common Market.

Approval of legal, technical and administrative preparations for unification of tariffs levied on products imported from non-member countries.

Formation of a committee of ministerial deputies to deal with problems in the application of market rulings and to promote the organization's activities.

Adoption of unified customs legislation and of an integrated programme aimed at enhancing trade between member states and expanding members' productive capacity.

MULTILATERAL AGREEMENTS

The Council has initiated the following multilateral agreements aimed at achieving economic unity:

Agreement on Basic Levels of Social Insurance.

Agreement on Reciprocity in Social Insurance Systems.

Agreement on Labour Mobility.

Agreement on Organization of Transit Trade.

Agreement on Avoidance of Double Taxation and Elimination of Tax Evasion.

Agreement on Co-operation in Collection of Taxes.

Agreement on Capital Investment and Mobility.

Agreement on Settlement of Investment Disputes between Host Arab Countries and Citizens of Other Countries.

JOINT VENTURES

A number of multilateral organizations in industry and agriculture have been formed on the principle that faster development and economies of scale may be achieved by combining the efforts of member states. In industries that are new to the member countries, Arab Joint Companies are formed, while existing industries are co-ordinated by the setting up of Arab Specialized Unions. The unions are for closer co-operation on problems of production and marketing, and to help companies deal as a group in international markets. The companies are intended to be self-supporting on a purely commercial basis; they may issue shares to citizens of the participating countries. The joint ventures are:

Arab Joint Companies (cap.=capital; figures in Kuwaiti dinars unless otherwise stated):

Arab Company for Drug Industries and Medical Appliances: POB 925161, Amman, Jordan; tel. (6) 821618; fax (6) 821649; f. 1976; cap. 60m.

Arab Company for Industrial Investment: POB 3385, Alwiyah, Baghdad, Iraq; tel. 718-9215; telex 212628; fax 718-0710; auth. cap. 150m.

Arab Company for Livestock Development: POB 5305, Damascus, Syria; tel. 666037; telex 11376; cap. 60m.

Arab Mining Company: POB 20198, Amman, Jordan; tel. (6) 663148; telex 21169; fax (6) 684114; cap. 120m.

Specialized Arab Unions and Federations:

Arab Co-operative Federation: POB 57640, Baghdad, Iraq; tel. (1) 888-8121; telex 2685.

Arab Federation of Chemical Fertilizers Producers: POB 23696, Kuwait.

Arab Federation of Engineering Industries: POB 509, Baghdad, Iraq; tel. 776-1101; telex 2724.

Arab Federation of Leather Industries: POB 2188, Damascus, Syria.

Arab Federation of Paper Industries: POB 5456, Baghdad, Iraq; tel. (1) 887-2384; telex 212205.

Arab Federation of Shipping: POB 1161, Baghdad, Iraq; tel. (1) 717-4540; telex 212695; fax (1) 717-7243; f. 1979; 16 mems.

Arab Federation of Textile Industries: POB 620, Damascus, Syria.

Arab Federation of Travel Agents: POB 7090, Amman, Jordan.

Arab Seaports Federation: Basrah, Iraq.

Arab Sugar Federation: POB 195, Khartoum, Sudan.

Arab Union for Cement and Building Materials: POB 9015, Damascus, Syria; tel. (11) 6665070; telex 412602; fax (11) 6621525; e-mail aucbm@go.com.jo; f. 1977; 18 mems.

Arab Union of Fish Producers: POB 15064, Baghdad, Iraq; tel. (1) 551-1261.

Arab Union of Food Industries: POB 13025, Baghdad, Iraq.

Arab Union of Land Transport: POB 926324, Amman, Jordan; tel. (6) 563153; telex 21118.

Arab Union of the Manufacturers of Pharmaceuticals and Medical Appliances: POB 81150, Amman 11181, Jordan; tel. (6) 4654306; telex 21528; fax (6) 4648141; f. 1986.

Arab Union of Railways: POB 6599, Aleppo, Syria; tel. (21) 220302; telex 331009.

General Arab Insurance Federation: POB 611, 11511 Cairo, Egypt; tel. (2) 5743177; telex 93141; fax (2) 762310; f. 1964.

PUBLICATIONS

Annual Bulletin for Arab Countries' Foreign Trade Statistics.
Annual Bulletin for Official Exchange Rates of Arab Currencies.
Arab Economic Unity Bulletin (2 a year).
Demographic Yearbook for Arab Countries.
Economic Report of the General Secretary (2 a year).
Guide to Studies prepared by Secretariat.
Progress Report (2 a year).
Statistical Yearbook for Arab Countries.
Yearbook for Intra-Arab Trade Statistics.
Yearbook of National Accounts for Arab Countries.

THE EUROPEAN UNION

The Mediterranean Policy of the European Union*

The European Community's scheme to negotiate a series of parallel trade and co-operation agreements encompassing almost all of the non-member states on the coast of the Mediterranean, known as the global policy for the Mediterranean, was formulated in 1972. Association agreements, intended to lead to customs union or the eventual full accession of the country concerned, had been signed with Greece in 1962, Turkey in 1964, and Malta in 1971, and a

fourth agreement was signed with Cyprus in 1972. Simple trade agreements with Spain, Portugal and Yugoslavia were all effective by September 1973. (Greece became a member of the Community in 1981, and Portugal and Spain did so in 1986.) During the 1970s a series of agreements, covering trade and economic co-operation, were concluded with the Arab Mediterranean countries and Israel, all of which established free access to EC markets for most industrial products, either soon or immediately. Access for agricultural products was facilitated, although some tariffs remained. For refined petroleum, cotton and phosphate fertilizers the EC imposed quotas for a transitional period on some of the Mediterranean countries. The principle of reciprocity (the granting of preferences in return) was not applied immediately in all of the co-operation agreements; in the association agreements, and some others, there were provisions for its introduction in the medium- or long-term future, should the economic progress of the Mediterranean country concerned

---

* The European Union was formally established on 1 November 1993 under the Treaty on European Union; prior to this it was known as the European Community (EC).

warrant this. In the event of a disturbance in a particular sector, or of economic decline in a particular region, the contracting party concerned was entitled to take protective action. Special organizations (Association or Co-operation Councils, comprising representatives of the Community and of the respective countries) were instituted to supervise the implementation of the agreements for each country.

Many of the agreements were accompanied by financial protocols stating the amount of each category of aid which the Mediterranean country would receive. Financial aid takes the form of direct grants, as well as loans from the European Investment Bank (EIB).

In 1982 the Commission formulated an integrated plan for the development of its own Mediterranean regions and recommended the adoption of a new policy towards the non-Community countries of the Mediterranean. This would include greater co-operation in helping to diversify agriculture, so as to avoid surpluses of items such as citrus fruits, olive oil and wine (which the Mediterranean countries all wished to export to the Community) and reduce the countries' dependence on imported food. The Commission also called for a return to the original principle of free access to the Community market for industrial goods from its Mediterranean neighbours, which had effectively been disregarded in the case of competitive imports of textiles, footwear and other goods, together with more efficient negotiating machinery to take action when problems arise.

In 1985 the Commission negotiated modifications in agreements with non-member Mediterranean countries to ensure that their exports of agricultural produce to the EC would not be adversely affected by the accession of Portugal and Spain to the Community at the beginning of 1986.

In December 1990, as part of the EC's new policy on the Mediterranean of providing greater financial assistance, the European Council approved ECU 2,075m. in loans and grants for the Maghreb and Mashreq countries and Israel, over the five-year period from November 1991. This amount was to include support for structural adjustment programmes, undertaken in conjunction with the IMF and the World Bank, and in particular to compensate for the adverse social effects of adjustment programmes. Particular emphasis was also to be placed on increasing production of food, promoting investment, the development of small- and medium-sized businesses, and protection of the environment.

In 1992 the EC began implementing a new Mediterranean policy, the basis of which was to be a consistent political approach for the development of the region. From 1 January 1993 the majority of agricultural exports from Mediterranean non-Community countries were granted exemption from customs duties. In June 1995 the European Council endorsed a programme to reform and strengthen the Mediterranean policy of the EU, on the basis of a strategic communication approved by the Commission in October 1994. The initiative envisaged the establishment of a Euro-Mediterranean Economic Area (EMEA) by the year 2010, preceded by a gradual liberalization of trade within the region through bilateral and other regional free trade arrangements. The so-called MEDA strategy also aimed to formulate common rules regarding intellectual property, company and banking laws and rules of origin, and to establish a fully-convertible currency. The Council agreed to allocate financial support amounting to ECU 4,685.5m. for the Maghreb and Mashreq agreement countries, as well as for Israel, Palestine, Cyprus, Malta, Turkey and Libya, for the period 1995–99. In November 1995 a ministerial conference of the EU member states, 11 Mediterranean non-member countries (excluding Libya) and the Palestine authorities, convened in Barcelona, Spain, endorsed the agreement on the EMEA and resolved to establish a permanent Euro-Mediterranean ministerial dialogue. The financial assistance, agreed by the Council in June, was to be directed to social and infrastructural projects, in accordance with an expansion in the scope of future co-operation. In a final Declaration ministers also endorsed commitments to uphold democratic principles and to pursue greater co-operation in the control of international crime, drugs-trafficking and illegal migration. In July 1996 the European Council adopted a MEDA Regulation, which provided a legal basis for EU co-operation with its Mediterranean partners, in particular for financial and technical measures to support structural reforms in those countries. A second Euro-Mediterranean Conference of ministers of foreign affairs was held in April 1997, in Malta, in order to review implementation of the partnership strategy. Also during 1997, Euro-Mediterranean sectoral conferences were held on investment issues and on good governance, in March, and on the environment, in November, while the first Euro-Mediterranean Energy Forum was convened in May.

Agreements with Countries in the Middle East and North Africa

THE MAGHREB COUNTRIES

A co-operation agreement between the EC and the Maghreb countries of Algeria, Morocco and Tunisia was signed in April 1976,

enabling the trade provisions to enter into effect in July of that year. The full agreement, which included economic and technical co-operation, was signed in January 1979. Under the agreement, industrial products were granted immediate duty free entry to the EC, while customs preferences were awarded for certain agricultural products. Restrictive quotas were, however, subsequently imposed on textile exports from the Maghreb, in order to protect the EC's domestic industry. In addition, conditions for migrant workers from the Maghreb countries were slightly improved under the agreement.

In January 1992 the European Parliament blocked ECU 438m. of grants and loans to Morocco for 1991–96 (under the fourth financial protocol with that country) in protest at Morocco's activities in Western Sahara, although the aid was released in October. Algeria's aid of ECU 350m. was to be conditional on progress towards democracy. Financial assistance of ECU 284m. was approved for Tunisia for 1991–96.

In June 1992 the EC approved a proposal to conclude new bilateral agreements with the Maghreb countries, incorporating the following components: political dialogue; economic, technical and cultural co-operation; financial co-operation; and the eventual establishment of a free trade area. An association agreement with Tunisia was signed in July 1995, which aimed to eliminate duties and other trade barriers on most products over a transitional 12-year period. In the short-term the agreement included an extension of the existing quota for exports of olive oil to the EU for a further four years, an increase of export quotas on potatoes, tomatoes and cut flowers, and greater access to European funds for investment and economic and industrial restructuring. In September 1996 the European Commission approved funding for Tunisia, under the MEDA Regulation (see above), totalling ECU 100m. for structural adjustment programmes and ECU 45m. for a professional development programme.

Morocco applied to join the EC in 1987; however, its application was rejected on the grounds that it is not a European country. In 1988 the EC reached an agreement with Morocco concerning fishing rights for the Spanish and Portuguese fleets in Moroccan waters (formerly subject to bilateral treaties). A new four-year fisheries agreement entered into effect in 1992. In October 1994 the EU and Morocco agreed to terminate the agreement one year early (i.e. with effect from 30 April 1995) as a result of a dispute concerning fishing licences and other incidents involving Moroccan and EU (mainly Spanish and Portuguese) fishing vessels. In November 1995, following extensive negotiations, the two sides concluded a new four-year fisheries accord, which established new levels of compensation to the Moroccan fishing industry and catch quotas to enable EU fleets again to operate in Moroccan waters. At the same time the two sides concluded an association agreement, which aimed to eliminate trade barriers in the industrial and service sectors over a 12-year period. The agreement provided greater preferential access for certain agricultural products, including citrus fruits and tomatoes. However, full liberalization of trade in agricultural goods was not to be considered until 2000. The agreement was signed in February 1996 and ratified, in June, by the European Parliament, with a request that the human rights situation in Morocco be closely monitored by the EU. In March 1997 the EU granted assistance worth ECU 120m. to support structural adjustment measures in Morocco.

The Community's relations with Algeria have been affected by political and civil instability in that country and by concerns regarding the government's respect for human rights and democratic principles. In December 1996 aid worth ECU 125m. was approved to support economic reform measures that the Algerian Government had agreed with the IMF. In March 1997 negotiations were initiated between the European Commission and representatives of the Algerian Government to conclude an association agreement, which would incorporate political commitments relating to respect for democratic principles and human rights. In early 1998 a fact-finding mission, comprising senior EU officials, visited Algeria, in response to concerns of an escalation of violence and unlawful killings in that country.

THE MASHREQ COUNTRIES

A co-operation agreement was signed by the EC with Egypt, Jordan and Syria in January 1977 and with Lebanon in April. Under the agreement, industrial products were granted tariff reductions of 80% until July 1977, and afterwards exempted from tariffs by the EC. Quantitative restrictions were removed as from January 1977. A wide range of tariff reductions were also granted for agricultural produce, varying between products from 30% to 80%.

In order to further economic and technical development in the Mashreq countries the EC approved a total of ECU 622m. for Egypt, Jordan and Lebanon to cover the period 1987–91. In November 1986 the EC imposed limited sanctions against Syria, in response to Syria's alleged involvement in international terrorism, and the disbursement of aid was not resumed until September 1987. Negotiations on assistance for Syria for 1987–91 (totalling ECU 146m.) were not concluded until late 1990.

Following the Iraqi invasion of Kuwait in August 1990, additional financial aid amounting to ECU 500m. was provided to Egypt and Jordan, which, together with Turkey, were the two countries most directly affected by the regional crisis. A further ECU 58m. in emergency aid was approved for the repatriation of refugees living in Egypt and Jordan. For 1991–96 assistance approved amounted to ECU 568m. for Egypt, ECU 126m. for Jordan, ECU 69m. for Lebanon and ECU 126m. for Syria.

In November 1994 the EU-Syria Co-operation Council convened for the first time since the 1977 agreement was signed. At the same time the General Affairs Council of the EU agreed to remove the embargo on the trade of armaments with Syria. In September 1996 EU funds amounting to ECU 18m. were granted to improve municipal services in four regional towns. Preliminary negotiations for the conclusion of an association agreement were initiated in July, although formal authorization to the European Commission to conclude an association agareement was only granted by EU heads of government in December 1997.

Negotiations between representatives of the EU and Egypt on the establishment of an association agreement were initiated in January 1995. However, progress was subsequently affected by opposition on the part of the Egyptian authorities to EU protection of its farm and processed food products. During 1997 aid totalling ECU 255m. was awarded under the MEDA Regulation to support a social development fund in Egypt, which aimed to counter poverty and create employment, and to upgrade primary education. In 1998 progress on the conclusion of an association agreement was further undermined by a provisional decision of the European Commission, adopted in March, to impose duties on imports of unbleached cotton from six countries, including Egypt, pending a final decision on the issue to be taken later in the year. In 1998 EU aid to Egypt was expected to include ECU 250m. for a three-year programme to modernize local industry.

Association agreement negotiations with Jordan commenced in July 1995 and with Lebanon in October. In September 1996 the European Commission approved ECU 100m. to support a structural adjustment programme in Jordan and ECU 38m. to help reform and strengthen administrative structures in Lebanon. An association agreement was formally concluded with Jordan in November 1997, providing for regular political dialogue, the gradual establishment of a free trade area and enhanced co-operation between the two parties.

ISRAEL

A co-operation agreement with Israel was signed in May 1975. In industrial sectors, according to the agreement, tariffs and related obstacles to free trade were to be removed on both sides. As regards agriculture, the EC reduced its tariffs substantially for products accounting for 85% of Israel's exports to the EC; these included products which the community had traditionally imported from Israel, for example some vegetables and fruit juices. An additional protocol on industrial, technical and financial co-operation was signed in February 1977.

In July 1991 additional aid of ECU 187.5m. was granted to Israel to alleviate the effects of the Gulf War that had followed Iraq's invasion of Kuwait. For 1991–96 loans to Israel amounting to ECU 82m. were approved.

In December 1993 the European Council authorized the Commission to commence negotiations for a new association agreement with Israel to replace that of 1975. The agreement, which aimed to strengthen trading relations and economic co-operation between the two sides and provided for more extensive political dialogue, was signed in November 1995 and approved by the European Parliament in February 1996. A separate agreement for further scientific and technical co-operation, enabling Israel's access to the Community's fourth framework programme (1994–98) on research and technological development, was signed in October 1995.

During 1998 diplomatic relations between Israel and the EU deteriorated, owing partly to Israel's inappropriate application of EU preferential trading arrangements by exporting agricultural products from Jewish settlements in the West Bank and Gaza, east Jerusalem and the Golan Heights (not recognized by the EU as being part of Israel) under Israeli licence. In May the Israeli Prime Minister insisted that any EU role in the Middle East peace process would be unacceptable if the European Commission proceeded with a threat to ban the disputed products from being imported into the EU. Additionally, the European Commission was critical of Israel's perceived obstruction of Palestinian trade, which had impeded implementation of the interim agreement between the EU and the Palestinian National Authority.

YEMEN

The co-operation agreement with Yemen, covering commercial, economic and development co-operation, was signed in October 1984. The agreement entered into force in January 1985, initially for a five-year period. In May 1989 the EC decided to intensify and diversify its co-operation with the Yemen Arab Republic. In June 1992 the European Council agreed to extend the original co-operation agreement to include the whole of the new Republic of Yemen (formed by the unification of the Yemen Arab Republic with the People's Democratic Republic of Yemen in 1990). During 1994 food aid and other Community projects in Yemen were suspended owing to civil conflict in that country, although ECU 1.2m. of humanitarian aid was delivered. In March 1995 the EU-Yemen Joint Co-operation Council convened for the first time since early 1993. A new co-operation agreement incorporating a political element (i.e. commitments to democratic principles and respect for human rights) was initialled by both sides in April 1997, and the draft agreement was signed in November. In April the European Commission provided substantial technical and financial support to assist the electoral process in Yemen.

CO-OPERATION COUNCIL FOR THE ARAB STATES OF THE GULF—GCC

A co-operation agreement with the GCC was signed in June 1988 and entered into force in January 1990. Negotiations on a full free-trade pact began in October, but it was expected that any agreement would involve transition periods of some 12 years for the reduction of European tariffs on 'sensitive products' (i.e. petrochemicals). In 1992–93 the agreement was jeopardized as a result of the GCC's opposition to an EC proposal to introduce a supplementary tax on petroleum, in order to reduce the use of pollutant-releasing fossil fuels as well as the failure of the GCC to adopt a unified tariff structure (see p. 246). While these issues continued to obstruct the conclusion of a new accord, in July 1995 an EU-GCC ministerial meeting, convened in Granada, Spain, agreed to establish a committee to facilitate dialogue between the two sides and to promote co-operation in other areas, such as cultural and scientific activities. In April 1996 the EU-GCC Joint Council advocated the conclusion of free trade negotiations by 1998.

IRAN

In April 1992 the EC held talks with Iran aimed at eventually concluding a co-operation agreement with that country. In December the Council of Ministers advocated that a 'critical dialogue' be pursued with Iran, owing to that country's importance to regional security. The two sides have subsequently held regular meetings; however, more extensive relations were prevented, owing to the EU's concerns regarding Iran's stance on the Middle East peace process, international terrorism, and human rights, in particular the situation of minorities in Iran and the death warrant imposed on a British author in 1989. In April 1997 the EU suspended its 'critical dialogue' with Iran, following a ruling by a German court that identified the Iranian authorities as responsible for ordering the assassination of four Kurdish dissidents in Berlin in 1992. The German and Dutch Governments withdrew their ambassadors from Iran and urged other EU countries to do the same. At the end of April a meeting of ministers of foreign affairs of EU countries confirmed the suspension of the dialogue but resolved that all diplomatic relations with Iran be upheld, in order to maintain the strong trading relationship between the two sides. This decision, however, was reversed when the Iranian Government refused to permit the German and Dutch ambassadors to return to their posts in Teheran. In November Iran agreed to readmit all EU ambassadors, and in February 1998 EU ministers of foreign affairs removed the ban on high-level contacts with Iran, in order to strengthen dialogue between the two sides. Foreign ministry officials conducted talks with the Iranian authorities in July, following a ministerial decision in June to initiate a 'comprehensive' dialogue with Iran.

CYPRUS

An association agreement with Cyprus came into effect in June 1973. Immediate tariff reductions were made by the EC of 70% in the industrial sector, 40% for citrus fruit and 100% for carob beans. From July 1977 onwards the EC granted duty-free entry to industrial goods from Cyprus, limited by tariff quotas in respect of man-made textiles and some garments. Since 1978 specific tariff reductions have been granted on fruit and vegetables. Tariffs on imports into Cyprus from the EC were generally reduced in annual stages, except in certain sectors, where the competition was felt to be harmful. Since 1978 Cyprus has been applying 35% tariff reductions on most Community products. In December 1987 the European Council adopted a protocol providing for the establishment of a full customs union, to be completed in two phases.

In July 1990 Cyprus made a formal application to join the EC. In June 1993 the European Commission approved the eligibility of Cyprus to join the Community. In December 1994 the European Council confirmed that Cyprus, together with Malta, were to be the next countries to be admitted to the EU. In accordance with an agreement concluded in March 1995, accession negotiations were to commence six months after the conclusion of the 1996 EU intergovernmental conference. In June 1995 the EU-Cyprus Association Council agreed to pursue a 'structured dialogue' as part of the pre-accession negotiations, and approved a new financial protocol, amounting to ECU 74m., for the period 1996–98. The first joint ministerial meeting was held in September 1995. During 1996 and 1997 the EU, together with the USA, undertook intensive diplomatic activities to broker a peace settlement, in order to facilitate Cyprus's accession to the EU as a single entity. In December 1997 the European Council adopted a framework for EU enlargement, which incorporated agreement on proceeding with Cyprus's application. Accession negotiations commenced on 31 March 1998; however, despite a compromise agreement between EU member states which enabled the talks to proceed as previously scheduled, incorporating a provision that the talks could be suspended, the Turkish Cypriot authorities refused an invitation to participate in the talks unless the EU extended full diplomatic recognition to the 'Turkish Republic of Northern Cyprus' ('TRNC').

TURKEY

An association agreement with Turkey was signed in September 1963. The preparatory phase of the agreement lasted from 1964 to 1973, during which preferences were given on agricultural products accounting for 40% of Turkey's exports to the EC: unmanufactured tobacco, dried raisins and figs, and nuts.

The transitional phase began in 1973, aiming to introduce a customs union by gradual stages over 12 to 22 years, depending on the product. The EC granted immediate duty and quota free access for industrial products, but placed restrictions on refined petroleum products and three textile products. The fourth financial protocol to the association agreement was to make available ECU 600m. for the period 1981–86 but, following the 1980 coup in Turkey, EC aid was suspended. A ministerial meeting was held in September 1986 to reactivate the association agreement. In April an agreement was reached determining levels of clothing imports from Turkey for 1986–88.

In April 1987 Turkey submitted a formal application for full membership of the EC. In 1989, however, the Commission stated that formal negotiations on Turkish membership could not take place until 1993, and that it would first be necessary for Turkey to restructure its economy, improve its observance of human rights, and harmonize its relations with Greece. The Commission undertook, however, to increase the EC's financial assistance for Turkey. In 1990 and 1991 additional assistance was provided for Turkey, as one of the countries directly affected by the crisis that followed the Iraqi invasion of Kuwait in August 1990, and to support Kurdish refugees who had fled from Iraq to Turkey.

In June 1992 the European Council agreed that relations with Turkey should be upgraded and in November a framework programme was adopted for the conclusion of a customs union. Discussions on the issue were pursued in 1993–94, and the Turkish Government undertook domestic economic reforms, to ensure that the customs union enter into effect on 1 January 1995. In December 1994 the EU-Turkey Association Council agreed to postpone the customs union, owing to persisting concerns regarding the Turkish Government's record on human rights, democracy and the rule of law. Negotiations to conclude the agreement in early 1995 were blocked by Greek opposition. Greece removed its veto on the customs union, having received assurance on the accession of Cyprus to the EU, and the agreement was signed at a meeting of the EU-Turkey Association Council in March. The customs union was ratified by the European Parliament in December, with a proviso that the human rights situation in Turkey, in particular the treatment of its Kurdish population, continue to be monitored, and entered into effect on 1 January 1996. Under the accord commercial barriers were to be eliminated and Turkey was to harmonize its laws to facilitate the flow of trade and investment between the two sides. A free trade agreement between the European Coal and Steel Community (ECSC—an integral part of the EU) and Turkey on products covered by the ECSC Treaty was signed in July and entered into force on 1 August. In April 1997 Turkey was assured that it would be considered on equal terms with any other country applying for membership of the EU, in spite of persisting concerns regarding human rights, the strength of influence of Islamic fundamentalism in the country and the situation in Cyprus. This policy was confirmed by a report of the European Commission, 'Agenda 2000', published in July, and by the European Council meeting, held in Luxembourg, in December. However, while the Luxembourg meeting confirmed Turkey's eligibility to join the EU, it failed to nominate that country as a candidate for admission (a status granted to 11 other countries). The Turkish Government declared the decision to be discriminatory and resolved to end all further political dialogue with the EU until Turkey's status, equal to all other aspirant members, had been restored. In March 1998 Turkey declined to attend the inaugural conference of heads of governments of EU and candidate countries,

which was intended as a permanent forum to be convened regularly throughout the enlargement process, and in May refused to participate in a scheduled meeting of the EU-Turkey Association Council. Ongoing efforts by the EU to improve relations with Turkey were hindered by the Greek Government's refusal to endorse a release of ECU 375m. in aid under the customs union agreement (which had been blocked since 1996).

Euro-Arab Dialogue

The 'Euro-Arab Dialogue' was begun in 1973, initially to provide a forum for discussion of economic issues: the principal organ was a General Committee, and about 30 working groups were set up to discuss specific issues and prepare projects, such as the creation of a Euro-Arab Centre for the Transfer of Technology. After the Egypt-Israel peace agreement in 1979 all activity was suspended at the request of the Arab League.

In December 1989 a meeting of ministers of foreign affairs of Arab and EC countries agreed to reactivate the Dialogue, entrusting political discussions to an annual ministerial meeting, and economic, technical, social and cultural matters to the General Committee of the Dialogue. However, meetings were suspended as a result of Iraq's invasion of Kuwait in August 1990; senior officials from the EC and Arab countries agreed in April 1992 to resume the Dialogue.

In 1992 the EC was involved in the Middle East peace negotiations, and participated in and chaired working groups on specific issues that formed part of the process. In September 1993, following the signing of an Israeli-PLO peace agreement, the EC committed ECU 33m. in immediate humanitarian assitance for the provision of housing, education and the development of small businesses in Jericho and the Gaza Strip. In addition, a five-year assistance programme for the period 1994–98 was proposed, which was to consist of ECU 500m. in grants and loans to improve the economic and social infrastructure in the Occupied Territories. The programme was to promote the Commission's declared commitment to support regional co-operation and development in order to consolidate the peace process. In May 1994 the Commission awarded ECU 10m. to support the establishment of a Palestinian police force in the Occupied Territories. In 1995 the EU granted additional aid amounting to ECU 10m. and dispatched a team of observers to support the electoral process in the Gaza Strip and the West Bank. Further aid totalling ECU 90m. was announced by the EU at an international conference of donors in January 1996. In October EU ministers of foreign affairs expressed concern at the adverse effect on the peace process resulting from Israeli activities in East Jerusalem and agreed to appoint a special envoy to the Middle East in order to strengthen EU involvement in promoting a peaceful settlement. In the following month ministers endorsed the appointment of Miguel Angel Moratinos, at that time Spain's ambassador to Israel, to the position. In July 1997 Moratinos successfully negotiated a meeting of the PLO leader, Yasser Arafat, and the Israeli Minister of Foreign Affairs, David Levy, who agreed to revive the peace talks, which had been suspended earlier in the year. In early 1998 the EU continued to attempt to facilitate the peace process, alongside the USA, the principal mediator in the region; however, its efforts were undermined by a deterioration in diplomatic relations with Israel. In March a mission by the British Secretary of State for Foreign and Commonwealth Affairs, representing the EU, provoked controversy when the Israeli Government objected to his meeting with senior Palestinian officials during a visit to the disputed Har Homa settlement in east Jerusalem. In addition, relations were adversely affected by the Israeli Government's failure to secure the opening of an international airport at Gaza (constructed largely with EU funds), and its trading activities (see above). An Interim Euro-Mediterranean Agreement on Trade and Co-operation was signed with the Palestinian authorities in January 1997 and entered into force on 1 July. The Agreement confirmed existing trade concessions, reduced further tariff levels for Palestinian exports to the EU and provided for the implementation of an association agreement within five years. A joint statement establishing regular political dialogue between the EU and PLO was concluded at the same time. In April 1998 the EU and the Palestinian National Authority signed a security co-operation agreement, which provided for regular meetings to promote joint efforts on security issues, in particular in combating terrorism.

In July 1994 representatives of the European Commission and the Arab League met to promote co-operation and good relations. During 1995 the Commission supported a Euro-Arab project to establish a central management training institute for business leaders in Granada, Spain. During 1997 the Commission undertook several co-operation projects with the Arab League and its specialized agencies in areas such as the environment, civil aviation, telecommunications, finance and management.

ISLAMIC DEVELOPMENT BANK

Address: POB 5925, Jeddah 21432, Saudi Arabia.

Telephone: (2) 6361400; **telex:** 601137; **fax:** (2) 6366871; **e-mail:** archives@isdb.org.sa; **internet:** http://www.isdb.org.sa.

The Bank is an international financial institution that was established following a conference of Ministers of Finance of member countries of the Organization of the Islamic Conference (OIC, q.v.), held in Jeddah in December 1973. Its aim is to encourage the economic development and social progress of member countries and of Muslim communities in non-member countries, in accordance with the principles of the Islamic *Shari'a* (sacred law). The Bank formally opened in October 1975.

MEMBERS

There are 52 members.

Organization

(August 1998)

BOARD OF GOVERNORS

Each member country is represented by a governor, usually its Minister of Finance, and an alternate. The Board of Governors is the supreme authority of the Bank, and meets annually.

BOARD OF EXECUTIVE DIRECTORS

The Board consists of 11 members, five of whom are appointed by the five largest subscribers to the capital stock of the Bank; the remaining six are elected by Governors representing the other subscribers. Members of the Board of Executive Directors are elected for three-year terms. The Board is responsible for the direction of the general operations of the Bank.

President of the Bank and Chairman of the Board of Executive Directors: Dr AHMED MOHAMED ALI.

Bank Secretary: Dr ABD AR-RAHIM OMRANA.

REGIONAL OFFICES

Kazakhstan: c/o Director, External Aid Co-ordination Dept, 93–95 Ablay-Khan Ave, 480091 Almaty; tel. (3272) 62-18-68; fax (3272) 69-61-52; Dir ZHANKYN KAKIMZKANOVA.

Malaysia: Level 11, Front Wing, Bank Industri, Jalan Sultan Ismail, POB 13671, 50818 Kuala Lumpur; tel. (3) 2946627; fax (3) 2946626; Dir Dr MUHAMMAD SIDDIK.

Morocco: 177 Ave John Kennedy, Souissi 10.15, POB 5003, Rabat; tel. (7) 757191; fax (7) 775726; Dir Dr MARWAN SEIFUDDIN.

FINANCIAL STRUCTURE

The authorized capital of the Bank is 6,000m. Islamic Dinars (divided into 600,000 shares, having a value of 10,000 Islamic Dinars each). The Islamic Dinar (ID) is the Bank's unit of account and is equivalent to the value of one Special Drawing Right of the IMF (SDR 1 = US $1.33156 at 30 June 1998).

Subscribed capital amounts to ID 4,000m.

Activities

The Bank adheres to the Islamic principle forbidding usury, and does not grant loans or credits for interest. Instead, its methods of project financing are: provision of interest-free loans (with a service fee), mainly for infrastructural projects which are expected to have a marked impact on long-term socio-economic development; provision of technical assistance (e.g. for feasibility studies); equity participation in industrial and agricultural projects; leasing operations, involving the leasing of equipment such as ships, and instalment sale financing; and profit-sharing operations. Funds not immediately needed for projects are used for foreign trade financing. Under the Import Trade Financing Operations (ITFO) scheme, funds are used for importing commodities for development purposes (i.e. raw materials and intermediate industrial goods, rather than consumer goods), with priority given to the import of goods from other member countries (see table). The Longer-term Trade Financing Scheme (LTTFS), introduced in 1987/88, provides financing for the export of non-traditional and capital goods. In addition, the Special Assistance Waqf Fund (which was established with effect from 7 May 1997, formally the Special Assistance Account) provides emergency aid and other assistance, with particular emphasis on education in Islamic communities in non-member countries. A Special Account

SUBSCRIPTIONS (million Islamic Dinars, as at July 1998)

Afghanistan	.	.	5.00	Malaysia	.	.	79.56
Albania	.	.	2.50	Maldives	.	.	2.50
Algeria	.	.	124.26	Mali	.	.	4.92
Azerbaijan	.	.	4.92	Mauritania	.	.	4.92
Bahrain	.	.	7.00	Morocco	.	.	24.81
Bangladesh	.	.	49.29	Mozambique	.	.	2.50
Benin	.	.	4.92	Niger	.	.	12.41
Brunei	.	.	12.41	Oman	.	.	13.78
Burkina Faso	.	.	12.41	Pakistan	.	.	124.26
Cameroon	.	.	12.41	Palestine	.	.	9.85
Chad	.	.	4.92	Qatar	.	.	49.23
Comoros	.	.	2.50	Saudi Arabia	.	.	997.17
Djibouti	.	.	2.50	Senegal	.	.	12.42
Egypt	.	.	49.23	Sierra Leone	.	.	2.50
Gabon	.	.	14.77	Somalia	.	.	2.50
The Gambia	.	.	2.50	Sudan	.	.	19.69
Guinea	.	.	12.41	Suriname	.	.	2.50
Guinea-Bissau	.	.	2.50	Syria	.	.	5.00
Indonesia	.	.	124.26	Tajikistan	.	.	2.50
Iran	.	.	349.97	Tunisia	.	.	9.85
Iraq	.	.	13.05	Turkey	.	.	315.47
Jordan	.	.	19.89	Turkmenistan	.	.	2.50
Kazakhstan	.	.	2.50	Uganda	.	.	12.41
Kuwait	.	.	496.64	United Arab			
Kyrgyzstan	.	.	2.50	Emirates	.	.	283.03
Lebanon	.	.	4.92	Yemen	.	.	24.81
Libya	.	.	400.00	**Total**	.	.	**3,761.27**

Operations approved, Islamic year 1417 (18 May 1996–6 May 1997)

Type of operation	Number of operations	Total amount (million Islamic Dinars)
Ordinary operations . . .	75	413.29
Project financing . .	59	407.64
Technical assistance .	16	5.65
Trade financing operations* .	88	713.99
Special assistance operations .	26	9.36
Total†	189	1,136.64

* Including ITFO, the LTTFS, and the Islamic Bank's Portfolio.
† Excluding cancelled operations.

for developed member countries aims to assist these countries by providing loans on concessionary terms. Loans financed by this Account are charged an annual service fee of 0.75%, compared with 2.5% for ordinary loans, and have a repayment period of 25–30 years, compared with 15–25 years.

By 6 May 1997 the Bank had approved a total of ID 3,399.57m. for project financing and technical assistance, a total of ID 9,209.52m. for foreign trade financing, and ID 373.37m. for special assistance operations, excluding amounts for cancelled operations. During the Islamic year 1417 (18 May 1996 to 6 May 1997) the Bank approved a total of ID 1,136.64m., for 189 operations.

The Bank approved 33 loans in the year ending 6 May 1997, amounting to ID 131.44m. (compared with 26 loans, totalling ID 79.16m., in the previous year). These loans supported projects concerned with infrastructural improvements, for example of roads, canals, water-supply and rural electrification, the construction of schools and health centres, and agricultural developments.

During AH 1417 the Bank approved 16 technical assistance operations for nine countries (as well as four regional projects) in the form of grants and loans, amounting to ID 5.65m.

Import trade financing approved during the Islamic year 1417 amounted to ID 421.98m. for 54 operations in eight member countries. By the end of that year cumulative import trade financing amounted to ID 7,912.49m., of which 39.1% was for imports of crude petroleum, 27.8% for intermediate industrial goods, 8.5% for vegetable oil and 5.8% for refined petroleum products. Financing approved under the Longer-term Trade Financing Scheme amounted to ID 44.83m. for 14 operations in five countries in AH 1417. In the same year the Bank's Portfolio for Investment and Development, established in AH 1407 (1986–87), approved 20 operations amounting to US $338m. (or approximately ID 247.18m.). Since its introduction, the Portfolio has approved 100 net financing operations in 18 member countries, amounting to $1,427m. (or ID 1,000.30m.).

During AH 1417 the Bank approved 26 special assistance operations, amounting to ID 9.36m., providing assistance primarily in the education and health sectors; of the total financing, 17 operations provided for Muslim communities in 11 non-member countries.

The Bank's scholarships programme sponsored 388 students from five member and 32 non-member countries during the year to 6 May 1997. The Merit Scholarship Programme, initiated in AH 1411 (1990–91), aims to develop scientific, technological and research capacities in member countries through advanced studies and/or research. Since the beginning of the programme 93 scholars from 35 member countries have been placed in academic centres of excellence in Australia, Europe and the USA. The Bank's Programme for Technical Co-operation aims to mobilize technical capabilities among member countries and to promote the exchange of expertise, experience and skills through expert missions, training, seminars and workshops. During AH 1417 60 projects were implemented under the programme. The Bank also undertakes the distribution of meat sacrificed by Muslim pilgrims: during the year meat from 414,319 animals was distributed to the needy in 27 countries.

Disbursements during the year ending 6 May 1997 totalled ID 546m., bringing the total cumulative disbursements since the Bank began operations to ID 9,064m.

The Bank's Unit Investment Fund became operational in 1990, with the aim of mobilizing additional resources and providing a profitable channel for investments conforming to *Shari'a*. The initial issue of the Fund was US $100m., which has subsequently been increased to $325m. The Fund finances mainly private-sector industrial projects in middle-income countries.

SUBSIDIARY ORGANS

Islamic Corporation for the Insurance of Investment and Export Credit—ICIEC: POB 15722, Jeddah 21454, Saudi Arabia; tel. (2) 6361400; telex 607509; fax (2) 6379504; e-mail iciec@

Project financing and technical assistance by sector, Islamic year 1417

Sector	Number of Operations	Amount (million Islamic Dinars)	%
Agriculture and agro-industry	20	97.97	23.7
Industry and mining . .	5	23.99	5.8
Transport and communications	11	73.15	17.7
Public utilities . . .	12	106.18	25.7
Social sectors	22	107.23	25.9
Other*	5	4.77	1.2
Total†	75	413.29	100.0

* Mainly approved amounts for Islamic banks.
† Excluding cancelled operations.

isdb.org.sa; internet http://www.isdb.org; f. 1994; aims to promote trade and the flow of investments among member countries of the OIC through the provision of export credit and investment insurance services; auth. cap. ID 100m., subscribed cap. ID 87.5m. (May 1997). Man. Dr ABDEL RAHMAN A. TAHA. Mems: 20 OIC member states.

Islamic Research and Training Institute: POB 9201, Jeddah 21413, Saudi Arabia; tel. (2) 6361400; telex 601137; fax (2) 6378927; f. 1982 for research enabling economic, financial and banking activities to conform to Islamic law, and to provide training for staff involved in development activities in the Bank's member countries. The Institute also organizes seminars and workshops, and holds training courses aimed at furthering the expertise of government and financial officials in Islamic developing countries. Dir Dr MABID ALI AL-JARHI. Publs *Annual Report, Islamic Economic Studies.*

PUBLICATION

Annual Report.

LEAGUE OF ARAB STATES

Address: POB 11642, Arab League Bldg, Tahrir Square, Cairo, Egypt.

Telephone: (2) 5750511; **telex:** 92111; **fax:** (2) 5775626.

The League of Arab States (more generally known as the Arab League) is a voluntary association of sovereign Arab states, designed to strengthen the close ties linking them and to co-ordinate their policies and activities and direct them towards the common good of all the Arab countries. It was founded in March 1945 (see Pact of the League, p. 258).

MEMBERS

Algeria	Lebanon	Somalia
Bahrain	Libya	Sudan
Comoros	Mauritania	Syria
Djibouti	Morocco	Tunisia
Egypt	Oman	United Arab
Iraq	Palestine*	Emirates
Jordan	Qatar	Yemen
Kuwait	Saudi Arabia	

* Palestine is considered an independent state, as explained in the Charter Annex on Palestine, and therefore a full member of the League.

Organization

(August 1998)

COUNCIL

The supreme organ of the Arab League, the Council consists of representatives of the member states, each of which has one vote, and a representative for Palestine. Unanimous decisions of the Council shall be binding upon all member states of the League; majority decisions shall be binding only on those states which have accepted them.

The Council may, if necessary, hold an extraordinary session at the request of two member states. Invitations to all sessions are extended by the Secretary-General. The ordinary sessions are presided over by representatives of the member states in turn.

The Council is supported by technical and specialized committees which advise on financial and administrative affairs, information affairs and legal affairs. In addition, specialized ministerial councils have been established to formulate common policies for the regulation and the advancement of co-operation in the following areas: information; home affairs; legal affairs; health; housing; social affairs; transport; the youth and sports sectors; environmental affairs; and telecommunications.

GENERAL SECRETARIAT

The administrative and financial offices of the League. The Secretariat carries out the decisions of the Council, and provides financial and administrative services for the personnel of the League. General departments comprise: the Bureau of the Secretary-General, Arab Affairs, Economic Affairs, International Affairs, Palestine Affairs, Legal Affairs, Military Affairs, Social and Cultural Affairs, Information Affairs and Financial and Administrative Affairs. In addition, there are Units for Internal Auditing and Institutional Development, a Documentation and Information Centre, Arab League Centres in Tunis and, for Legal and Judicial Research, in Beirut and a Principal Bureau for the Boycott of Israel, based in Damascus, Syria (see below).

The Secretary-General is appointed by the League Council by a two-thirds majority of the member states, for a five-year, renewable term. He appoints the Assistant Secretaries-General and principal officials, with the approval of the Council. He has the rank of ambassador, and the Assistant Secretaries-General have the rank of ministers plenipotentiary.

Secretary-General: Dr AHMAD ESMAT ABD AL-MEGUID (Egypt).

Assistant Secretaries-General:

Economic Affairs: Dr ABD AR-RAHMAN AS-SOUHAIBANI (Saudi Arabia).

Financial and Administrative Affairs: Dr ALI ABDULKARIM (Yemen).

Head of Arab League Centre, Tunis: NOUREDDINE HACHED (Tunisia).

Head of the Bureau of the Secretary-General: AHMAD IBRAHIM ADEL (Egypt).

Information Affairs: MUHAB MUQBEL (Egypt).

International Affairs: MUHAMMAD ZAKARIA ISMAIL (Syria).

Military Affairs: (vacant).

Palestine Affairs: SAID KAMAL (Palestine).

Social and Cultural Affairs: DHAW ALI SIWEDAN (Libya).

DEFENCE AND ECONOMIC CO-OPERATION

Groups established under the Treaty of Joint Defence and Economic Co-operation, concluded in 1950 to complement the Charter of the League.

Arab Unified Military Command: f. 1964 to co-ordinate military policies for the liberation of Palestine.

Economic and Social Council: to compare and co-ordinate the economic policies of the member states; supervises the activities of the Arab League's specialized agencies. The Council is composed of ministers of economic affairs or their deputies; decisions are taken by majority vote. The first meeting was held in 1953.

Joint Defence Council: supervises implementation of those aspects of the treaty concerned with common defence. Composed of foreign and defence ministers; decisions by a two-thirds majority vote of members are binding on all.

Permanent Military Commission: established 1950; composed of representatives of army general staffs; main purpose: to draw up plans of joint defence for submission to the Joint Defence Council.

ARAB DETERRENT FORCE

Created in June 1976 by the Arab League Council to supervise successive attempts to cease hostilities in Lebanon, and afterwards to maintain the peace. The mandate of the Force has been successively renewed. The Arab League Summit Conference in October 1976 agreed that costs were to be paid in the following percentage contributions: Saudi Arabia and Kuwait 20% each, the United Arab Emirates 15%, Qatar 10% and other Arab states 35%.

OTHER INSTITUTIONS OF THE LEAGUE

Other bodies established by resolutions adopted by the Council of the League:

Administrative Tribunal of the Arab League: f. 1964; began operations 1966.

Arab Fund for Technical Assistance to African Countries: f. 1975 to provide technical assistance for development projects by providing African and Arab experts, grants for scholarships and training, and finance for technical studies. Exec. Sec. HASSAN ABADI (Egypt).

Higher Auditing Board: comprises representatives of seven member states, elected every three years; undertakes financial and administrative auditing duties.

Investment Arbitration Board: examines disputes between member states relating to capital investments.

Special Bureau for Boycotting Israel: POB 437, Damascus, Syria; f. 1951 to prevent trade between Arab countries and Israel, and to enforce a boycott by Arab countries of companies outside the region that conduct trade with Israel. Commr-Gen. ZUHEIR AQUIL (Syria).

SPECIALIZED AGENCIES

All member states of the Arab League are also members of the Specialized Agencies, which constitute an integral part of the Arab League. (See also entries on the Arab Fund for Economic and Social Development, the Arab Monetary Fund, the Council of Arab Economic Unity and the Organization of Arab Petroleum Exporting Countries.)

Arab Academy for Science, Technology and Maritime Transport: POB 1029, Alexandria, Egypt; tel. (3) 5602366; telex 54160; fax (3) 5602144; f. 1975 as Arab Maritime Transport Academy; provides specialized training in marine transport, engineering, technology and management. Dir-Gen. Dr GAMAL EL-DIN MOUKHTAR. Publs *Maritime Research Bulletin* (monthly), *Journal of the Arab Academy for Science, Technology and Maritime Transport* (2 a year).

Arab Administrative Development Organization—ARADO: POB 2692 Al-Horreia, Heliopolis, Cairo, Egypt; tel. (2) 4175401; fax (2) 4175407; e-mail arado@idsc.gov.eg; f. 1961 (as Arab Organization of Administrative Sciences), although became operational in 1969; administration development, training, consultancy, research and studies, information, documentation; promotes Arab and international co-operation in administrative sciences; includes Arab Network of Administrative Information; 20 Arab state members; Library of 20,000 volumes, 380 periodicals. Dir-Gen. Dr AHMAD SAKR ASHOUR. Publs *Arab Journal of Administration* (biannual), *Management Newsletter* (quarterly), research series, training manuals.

Arab Atomic Energy Agency—AAEA: 4 rue Mouaouiya ibn Abi Soufiane, Al-Menzah 8, POB 402, 1004 Tunis, Tunisia; tel. (1) 709464; fax (1) 711330; e-mail aaea@aaea.org.tn; f. 1988 to co-ordinate research into the peaceful uses of atomic energy. Dir-Gen. Prof. Dr MAHMOUD FOUAD BARAKAT (Egypt). Publs *The Atom and Development* (quarterly), other publs in the field of nuclear sciences and their applications in industry, biology, medicine, agriculture and seawater desalination.

Arab Bank for Economic Development in Africa (Banque arabe pour le développement économique en Afrique—BADEA): Sayed Abdel-Rahman el-Mahdi Ave, POB 2640, Khartoum, Sudan; tel. (11) 773646; telex 22248; fax (11) 770600; e-mail badeadev@sudanet.net; f. 1973 by Arab League; provides loans and grants to African countries to finance development projects; paid-up cap. US $1,145.8m. (Dec. 1997). In 1997 the Bank approved loans and grants totalling $99.8m., and technical assistance amounting to $4.9m. By the end of 1997 total loans and grants approved since funding activities began in 1975 amounted to $1,730.5m. Subscribing countries: all countries of Arab League, except the Comoros, Djibouti, Somalia and Yemen; recipient countries: all countries of Organization of African Unity (q.v.), except those belonging to the Arab League. Chair. AHMED ABDALLAH AL-AKEIL (Saudi Arabia); Dir.-Gen. MEDHAT SAMI LOTFY (Egypt). Publs *Annual Report, Co-operation for Development,* Studies on Afro-Arab co-operation, periodic brochures.

Arab Centre for the Study of Arid Zones and Dry Lands — ACSAD: POB 2440, Damascus, Syria; tel. (11) 5323087; fax (11) 5323063; e-mail rudcsad@rusys.eg.net; f. 1971 to conduct regional research and development programmes related to water and soil resources, plant and animal production, agro-meteorology, and socio-economic studies of arid zones. The Centre holds conferences and training courses and encourages the exchange of information by Arab scientists. Dir-Gen. Dr HASSAN SEOUD.

Arab Industrial Development and Mining Organization: rue France, Zanagat Al Khatawat, POB 8019, Rabat, Morocco; tel. (7) 772600; telex 36763; fax (7) 772188; e-mail aidmo@arifonet.org.ma; internet http://www.arifonet.org.ma; f. 1990 by merger of Arab Industrial Development Organization, Arab Organization for Mineral Resources and Arab Organization for Standardization and Metrology. Dir-Gen. TALAAT BEN DAFER AL-DAFER. Publs *Arab Industrial Development* (monthly and quarterly newsletters).

Arab Labour Organization: POB 814, Cairo, Egypt; f. 1965 for co-operation between member states in labour problems; unification of labour legislation and general conditions of work wherever possible; research; technical assistance; social insurance; training, etc.; the organization has a tripartite structure: governments, employers and workers. Dir-Gen. BAKR MAHMOUD RASOUL (Iraq). Publs *ALO Bulletin* (monthly), *Arab Labour Review* (quarterly), *Legislative Bulletin* (annually), series of research reports and studies concerned with economic and social development issues in the Arab world.

Arab League Educational, Cultural and Scientific Organization—ALECSO: POB 1120, Tunis, Tunisia; tel. (1) 784-466; telex 18825; fax (1) 784-965; f. 1970 to promote and co-ordinate educational, cultural and scientific activities in the Arab region. Regional units: Arab Centre for Arabization, Translation, Authorship, and Publication—Damascus, Syria; Institute of Arab Manuscript—Cairo, Egypt; Institute of Arab Research and Studies—Cairo, Egypt; Khartoum Institute for Arabic Language—Khartoum, Sudan; and the Arabization Co-ordination Bureau—Rabat, Morocco. Dir-Gen. MOHAMED ALMILI IBRAHIMI (Algeria). Publs *Arab Journal of Culture, Arab Journal of Science, Arab Bulletin of Publications, Statistical Yearbook, Journal of the Institute of Arab Manuscripts, Arab Magazine for Information Science.*

Arab Organization for Agricultural Development: St no. 7, Al-Amarat, POB 474, Khartoum, Sudan; tel. (11) 472176; telex 22554; fax (11) 471402; e-mail aoad@sudanet.net; f. 1970; began operations in 1972 to contribute to co-operation in agricultural activities, and in the development of natural and human resources for agriculture; compiles data, conducts studies, training and food security programmes; includes Arab Institute of Forestry and Range, Arab Centre for Information and Early Warning, and Arab Centre for Agricultural Documentation. Dir-Gen. Dr YAHIA BAKOUR. Publs *Agricultural Statistics Yearbook, Annual Report on Agricultural Development, the State of Arab Food Security* (annually), *Agriculture and Development in the Arab World* (quarterly), *Accession Bulletin* (every 2 months), *AOAD Newsletter* (monthly in Arabic, quarterly in English).

Arab Satellite Communications Organization: POB 1038, Riyadh, 11431 Saudi Arabia; tel. (1) 464-6666; fax (1) 465-6983; f. 1976; operates the ARABSAT project, under which the first two satellites were launched in 1985, for the improvement of telephone, telex, data transmission and radio and television in Arab countries; a third satellite was launched in February 1992 with a 10-year operational life, and two more satellites were under construction in early 1993. Dir-Gen. SAAD IBN ABD AL-AZIZ AL-BADNA (Saudi Arabia).

Arab States Broadcasting Union—ASBU: POB 250, 1080 Tunis Cedex; 6 rue des Entrepreneurs, zone industrielle Charguia 2, Ariana Aéroport, Tunisia; tel. (1) 703854; telex 13398; fax (1) 704203; f. 1969 to promote Arab fraternity, co-ordinate and study broadcasting subjects, to exchange expertise and technical co-operation in broadcasting; conducts training and audience research. Mems: 21 Arab radio and TV stations and eight foreign associates. Sec.-Gen. RAOUF BASTI. Publ. *ASBU Review* (quarterly).

Inter-Arab Investment Guarantee Corporation: POB 23568, Safat 13096, Kuwait; tel. 4844500; telex 22562; fax 4815741; f. 1975; insures Arab investors for non-commercial risks, and export credits for commercial and non-commercial risks; undertakes research and other activities to promote inter-Arab trade and investment; authorized capital 25m. Kuwaiti dinars (Dec. 1995). Mems: 22 Arab governments. Dir-Gen. MAMOUN I. HASSAN. Publs *News Bulletin* (monthly), *Arab Investment Climate Report* (annually).

External Relations

ARAB LEAGUE OFFICES AND INFORMATION CENTRES ABROAD

Established by the Arab League to co-ordinate work at all levels among Arab embassies abroad.

Austria: Grimmelshausengasse 12, 1030 Vienna.

Belgium: 89 ave de l'Uruguay, 1000 Brussels.

China, Peoples's Republic: 14 Liang Male, 1-14-2 Tayuan Diplomatic Building, Beijing 100600.

Ethiopia: POB 5768, Addis Ababa.

France: 36 rue Fortuny, 75017 Paris.

Germany: Rheinallee 23, 53173 Bonn.

India: B-8/19 Vasant Vihar, New Delhi.

Italy: Piazzale delle Belle Arti 6, 00196 Rome.

Russia: 28 Koniouch Kovskaya, Moscow 132242.

Spain: Paseo de la Castellana 180, 60°, 28046 Madrid.

Switzerland: 9 rue du Valais, Geneva 1202.

Tunisia: 93 rue Louis Bray, el-Khadra, 1003 Tunis.

United Kingdom: 52 Green St, London W1Y 3RH.

USA: 1100 17th St, NW, Suite 602, Washington, DC 20036; 17 Third Ave, New York, NY 10017 (UN Office).

Record of Events

1945 Pact of the Arab League signed, March.

1946 Cultural Treaty signed.

1950 Joint Defence and Economic Co-operation Treaty.

1952 Agreements on extradition, writs and letters of request, nationality of Arabs outside their country of origin.

1953 Formation of Economic and Social Council.
Convention on the privileges and immunities of the League.

1954 Nationality Agreement.

1956 Agreement on the adoption of a Common Tariff Nomenclature.

1962 Arab Economic Unity Agreement.

1964 First Summit Conference of Arab kings and presidents, Cairo, January.
First meeting of Economic Unity Council, June. Arab Common Market approved by Arab Economic Unity Council, August.
Second Summit Conference welcomed establishment of Palestine Liberation Organization (PLO), September.

1965 Arab Common Market established, January.

1969 Fifth Summit Conference, Rabat. Call for mobilization of all Arab nations against Israel.

1977 Tripoli Declaration, December. Decision of Algeria, Iraq, Libya and Yemen PDR to boycott League meetings in Egypt in response to President Sadat's visit to Israel.

1979 Council meeting in Baghdad, March: resolved to withdraw Arab ambassadors from Egypt; to recommend severance of political and diplomatic relations with Egypt; to suspend Egypt's membership of the League on the date of the signing of the peace treaty with Israel; to transfer the headquarters of the League to Tunis; to condemn US policy regarding its role in concluding the Camp David agreements and the peace treaty; to halt all bank loans, deposits, guarantees or facilities, as well as all financial or technical contributions and aid to Egypt; to prohibit trade exchanges with the Egyptian state and with private establishments dealing with Israel.

1981 In November the 12th Summit Conference, held in Fez, Morocco, was suspended after a few hours, following disagreement over a Saudi Arabian proposal known as the Fahd Plan, which included not only the Arab demands on behalf of the Palestinians, as approved by the UN General Assembly, but also an implied *de facto* recognition of Israel.

1982 Twelfth Summit Conference reconvened, Fez, September: adopted a peace plan, which demanded Israel's withdrawal from territories occupied in 1967, and removal of Israeli settlements in these areas; freedom of worship for all religions in the sacred places; the right of the Palestinian people to self-determination, under the leadership of the PLO; temporary UN supervision for the West Bank and the Gaza Strip; the creation of an independent Palestinian state, with Jerusalem as its capital; and a guarantee of peace for all the states of the region by the UN Security Council.

1983 The summit meeting due to be held in November was postponed owing to members' differences of opinion concerning Syria's opposition to Yasser Arafat's chairmanship of the PLO, and Syrian support of Iran in the war against Iraq.

1984 In March an emergency meeting established an Arab League committee to encourage international efforts to bring about a negotiated settlement of the Iran–Iraq war. In May ministers of foreign affairs adopted a resolution urging Iran to stop attacking non-belligerent ships and installations in the Gulf region: similar attacks by Iraq were not mentioned.

1985 In August an emergency Summit Conference was boycotted by Algeria, Lebanon, Libya, Syria and the People's Democratic Republic of Yemen, while of the other 16 members only nine were represented by their heads of state. Two commissions were set up to mediate in disagreements between Arab states (between Jordan and Syria, Iraq and Syria, Iraq and Libya, and Libya and the PLO).

1986 In July King Hassan of Morocco announced that he was resigning as chairman of the next League Summit Conference, after criticism by several Arab leaders of his meeting with the Israeli Prime Minister earlier that month. A ministerial meeting, held in October, condemned any attempt at direct negotiation with Israel.

1987 An extraordinary Summit Conference was held in November, mainly to discuss the war between Iran and Iraq. Contrary to expectations, the participants (including President Assad of Syria) unanimously agreed on a statement expressing support for Iraq in its defence of its legitimate rights, and criticizing Iran for its procrastination in accepting the UN Security Council Resolution No. 598 of July 1987, which had recommended a cease-fire in the Iran–Iraq war and negotiations on a settlement of the conflict. The meeting also stated that the resumption of diplomatic relations with Egypt was a matter to be decided by individual states.

1988 In June a Summit Conference agreed to provide finance for the PLO to continue the Palestinian uprising in Israeli-occupied territories. It reiterated a demand for the convening of an international conference, attended by the PLO, to seek to bring about a peaceful settlement in the Middle East (thereby implicitly rejecting recent proposals by the US Government for a conference that would exclude the PLO).

1989 In January (responding to the deteriorating political situation in Lebanon) an Arab League mediation group, comprising six ministers of foreign affairs, began discussions with the two rival Lebanese governments on the possibility of a political settlement in Lebanon. At a Summit Conference, held in May, Egypt was readmitted to the League. The Conference expressed support for the chairman of the PLO, Yasser Arafat, in his recent peace proposals made before the UN General Assembly, and reiterated the League's support for proposals that an international conference should be convened to discuss the rights of Palestinians: in so doing, it accepted UN Security Council Resolutions 242 and 338 on a peaceful settlement in the Middle East and thus gave tacit recognition to the State of Israel. The meeting also supported Arafat in rejecting Israeli proposals for elections in the Israeli-occupied territories of the West Bank and the Gaza Strip. A new mediation committee, comprising the heads of state of Algeria, Morocco and Saudi Arabia, was established, with a six-month mandate to negotiate a cease-fire in Lebanon, and to reconvene the Lebanese legislature with the aim of holding a presidential election and restoring constitutional government in Lebanon. In September the principal factions in Lebanon agreed to observe a cease-fire, and the surviving members of the Lebanese legislature (originally elected in 1972) met at Taif, in Saudi Arabia, in October, and approved the League's proposed 'charter of national reconciliation' (see chapter on Lebanon).

1990 In May a Summit Conference, held in Baghdad, Iraq (which was boycotted by Syria and Lebanon), criticized recent efforts by Western governments to prevent the development of advanced weapons technology in Iraq. In August an emergency Summit Conference was held to discuss the invasion and annexation of Kuwait by Iraq. Twelve members (Bahrain, Djibouti, Egypt, Kuwait, Lebanon, Morocco, Oman, Qatar, Saudi Arabia, Somalia, Syria and the United Arab Emirates) approved a resolution condemning Iraq's action, and demanding the withdrawal of Iraqi forces from Kuwait and the reinstatement of the Government. The 12 states expressed support for the Saudi Arabian Government's invitation to the USA to send forces to defend Saudi Arabia; they also agreed to impose economic sanctions on Iraq, and to provide troops for an Arab defensive force in Saudi Arabia. The remaining member states, however, condemned the presence of foreign troops in Saudi Arabia, and their ministers of foreign affairs refused to attend a meeting, held at the end of August, to discuss possible solutions to the crisis. The dissenting countries also rejected the decision, taken earlier in the year, to return the League's headquarters from Tunis to Cairo. None the less, the official transfer of the League's headquarters to Cairo took place on 31 October. In November King Hassan of Morocco urged the convening of an Arab Summit Conference, in an attempt to find an 'Arab solution' to Iraq's annexation of Kuwait. However, the divisions in the Arab world over the issue meant that conditions for such a meeting could not be agreed.

1991 The first meeting of the Arab League since August 1990 took place in March, attended by representatives of all 21 member nations, including Iraq. Discussion of the recently-ended war against Iraq was avoided, in an attempt to re-establish the unity of the League. In September, despite deep divisions between member states, resulting from Iraq's invasion of Kuwait, particularly between Iraq and Kuwait, and Egypt and Jordan, it was agreed that a committee should be formed to co-ordinate Arab positions in preparation for the US-sponsored peace talks between Arab countries and Israel. (In the event, an *ad hoc* meeting, attended by Egypt, Jordan, Syria, the PLO, Saudi Arabia—representing the Gulf Co-operation Council (GCC), and Morocco—representing the Union of the Arab Maghreb, was held in October, prior to the start of the talks.) In December the League expressed solidarity with Libya, which was under international pressure to extradite two Libyan government agents who were suspected of involvement in the explosion which destroyed a US passenger aircraft over Lockerbie, United Kingdom, in December 1988.

1992 In early 1992 the League was involved in mediation efforts between the warring factions in Somalia to bring about a cease-fire. In March the League appointed a committee to seek to resolve the disputes betwen Libya and the USA, the United Kingdom and France over the Lockerbie explosion and the explosion which destroyed a French passenger aircraft over the Sahara (in Niger) in September 1989. The League condemned the UN's decision, at the end of March, to impose sanctions against Libya, and appealed for a negotiated solution. In September the League's Council issued a condemnation of Iran's alleged occupation of three islands in the Persian (Arabian) Gulf that were claimed by the United Arab Emirates, and decided to refer the issue to the United Nations.

1993 In April the Council approved the creation of a committee to consider the political and security aspects of water supply in Arab countries. In the same month the League pledged its commitment to the Middle East peace talks, but warned that Israel's continued refusal to repatriate the Palestinians who were stranded in Lebanon remained a major obstacle to the process. The League sent an official observer to the independence referendum in Eritrea, held in April. In September the Council admitted the Comoros as the 22nd member of the League. Following the signing of the Israeli-PLO peace accord in September the Council convened in emergency session, at which it approved the agreement, despite opposition from some members, notably Syria. In November it was announced that the League's boycott of commercial activity with Israel was to be maintained.

1994 The Council also considered the establishment of a regional court of justice, which had been discussed prior to the meeting by Arab ministers of foreign affairs. The League condemned a decision of the GCC, announced in late September, to end the secondary and tertiary trade embargo against Israel, by which member states refuse to trade with international companies which have investments in Israel. In September the Council endorsed a recommendation that the United Nations conduct a census of Palestinian refugees, in the

absence of any such action taken by the League. A statement issued by the League insisted that the embargo could be removed only on the decision of the Council.

1995 In January the League's Secretary-General advocated the creation of a free-trade area among Arab states in order, partly, to counter proposals for a regional market that would include Israel. In March Arab ministers of foreign affairs approved a resolution urging Israel to renew the Nuclear Non-Proliferation Treaty (NPT). The resolution stipulated that failure by Israel to do so would cause Arab states to seek to protect legitimate Arab interests by alternative means. At an extraordinary session of the Council, which was convened in early May, the League condemned a decision by Israel to confiscate Arab-owned land in East Jerusalem for resettlement, and requested that the UN Security Council consider the issue. Arab heads of state and government were scheduled to convene in emergency session later in that month to formulate a collective response to the action. However, the meeting was postponed, following an announcement by the Israeli Government that it was suspending its expropriation plans. In September the Council discussed plans for a regional court of justice and for an Arab Code of Honour to prevent the use of force in disputes between Arab states. The Council expressed its support for the Algerian Government in its efforts to combat Muslim separatist violence. In October the League was reported to be in financial difficulties, owing to the non-payment of contributions by seven member states. At that time undisputed arrears amounted to US $80.5m. In November the Arab League dispatched 44 observers to oversee elections in Algeria as part of an international monitoring team.

1996 In March, following protests by Syria and Iraq that extensive construction work in southern Turkey was restricting water supply in the region, the Council determined that the waters of the Euphrates and Tigris rivers be shared equitably between the three countries. In April an emergency meeting of the Council issued a further endorsement of Syria's position in the dispute with Turkey. The main objective of the meeting, which was convened at the request of Palestine, was to attract international attention to the problem of radiation from an Israeli nuclear reactor. The Council requested an immediate technical inspection of the site by the UN, and further demanded that Israel be obliged to sign the NPT to ensure the eradication of its nuclear weaponry. In June a Summit Conference was convened, the first since 1990, in order to formulate a united Arab response to the election, in May, of a new government in Israel and to the prospects for peace in the Middle East. The Conference, which was attended by heads of state of 13 countries and senior representatives of seven others (Iraq was excluded from the meeting in order to ensure the attendance of the Gulf member states), aimed to demonstrate the commitment of Arab states to the peace process. Israel was urged to honour its undertaking to withdraw from the Occupied Territories, including Jerusalem, and to respect the establishment of an independent Palestinian state, in order to ensure the success of the peace process. A final communiqué of the meeting warned that Israeli co-operation was essential to prevent Arab states' reconsidering their participation in the peace process and the re-emergence of regional tensions. Meanwhile, there were concerns over increasing inter-Arab hostility, in particular between Syria and Jordan, owing to the latter's relations with Israel and allegations of Syrian involvement in recent terrorist attacks against Jordanian targets. In early September the League condemned US missile attacks against Iraq as an infringement of that country's sovereignty. In addition, it expressed concern at the impact on Iraqi territorial integrity of Turkish intervention in the north of Iraq. Later in that month the League met in emergency session, following an escalation of civil unrest in Jerusalem and the Occupied Territories. The League urged the UN Security Council to prevent further alleged Israeli aggression against the Palestinians. In November the League criticized Israel's settlement policy, and at the beginning of December convened in emergency session to consider measures to end any expansion of the Jewish population in the West Bank and Gaza.

1997 On 1 March the Council met in emergency session, in response to the Israeli Government's decision to proceed with construction of a new settlement at Har Homa (Jabal Abu-Ghuneim) in East Jerusalem. The Council pledged its commitment to seeking a reversal of the decision and urged the international community to support this aim. At the end of March ministers of foreign affairs of Arab League states agreed to end all efforts to secure normal diplomatic relations with Israel (although binding agreements already in force with Egypt,

Jordan and Palestine were exempt) and to close diplomatic offices and missions while construction work continued in East Jerusalem. In addition, ministers recommended reactivating the economic boycott against Israel until comprehensive peace was achieved in the region and suspending Arab participation in the multilateral talks that were initiated in 1991 to further the peace process. Earlier in the year, in February, the Economic and Social Council ratified a programme to facilitate and develop inter-Arab trade through the reduction and eventual elimination of customs duties. The Council agreed to supervise the process and formally to review implementation of the programme twice a year. In June a 60-member delegation from the Arab League participated in an international mission to monitor legislative elections in Algeria. In the same month the League condemned Turkey's military incursion into northern Iraq and demanded a withdrawal of Turkish troops from Iraqi territory. In September ministers of foreign affairs of member states advocated a gradual removal of international sanctions against Libya, and agreed that member countries should permit international flights to leave Libya for specific humanitarian and religious purposes and when used for the purposes of transporting foreign nationals. Ministers also voted to pursue the decision, adopted in March, not to strengthen relations with Israel. Several countries urged a formal boycott of the forthcoming Middle East and North Africa economic conference, in protest at the lack of progress in the peace process (for which the League blamed Israel, which was due to participate in the conference). However, the meeting upheld a request by the Qatari Government, the host of the conference, and resolved that each member should decide individually whether to attend. In the event, only seven Arab League countries participated in the conference, which was held in Doha in mid-November, while the Secretary-General of the League decided not to attend as the organization's official representative. In November the League criticized the decision of the US Government to impose economic sanctions against Sudan. The League also expressed concern at the tensions arising from Iraq's decision not to co-operate fully with UN weapons inspectors, and held several meetings with representatives of the Iraqi administration in an effort to secure a peaceful conclusion to the impasse.

1998   In early 1998 the Secretary-General of the League condemned the use or threat of force against Iraq and continued to undertake diplomatic efforts to secure Iraq's compliance with UN Security Council resolutions. The League endorsed the agreement concluded between the UN Secretary-General and the Iraqi authorities in late February, and reaffirmed its commitment to facilitating the eventual removal of the international embargo against Iraq. A meeting of the Council of the Arab League in March, attended by ministers of foreign affairs of 16 member states, considered a range of issues including progress in the Middle East peace process, the need to promote Arabic aspects of life in Jerusalem and to prevent further Israeli expansion, measures to support Somali reconstruction, and the ongoing problem of Palestinian refugees. The Council rejected Israel's proposal to withdraw from southern Lebanon, which was conditional on the deployment by the Lebanese Government of extra troops to secure Israeli territory from attack, and, additionally, urged international support to secure Israel's withdrawal from the Golan Heights. The Council also urged the UN Security Council to review the international embargo against Libya. The League's Secretary-General later requested a removal of the sanctions, given developments in the process of bringing the suspected Lockerbie bombers to trial. In April Arab League ministers of the interior and of justice signed an agreement to strengthen Arab co-operation in the prevention of terrorism, incorporating security and judicial measures, such as extradition arrangements and the exchange of evidence. The agreement was to enter into effect 30 days after being ratified by at least seven member countries. In August the League denounced terrorist bomb attacks against the US embassies in Kenya and Tanzania. Nevertheless, it condemned US retaliatory military action, a few days later, against suspected terrorist targets in Afghanistan and Sudan, and endorsed a request by the Sudanese Government that the Security Council investigate the incident.

PUBLICATIONS

Arab Perspectives— Sh'oun Arabiyya (monthly).

Journal of Arab Affairs (monthly).

Bulletins of treaties and agreements concluded among the member states, essays, regular publications circulated by regional offices.

The Pact of the League of Arab States

(22 March 1945)

Article 1. The League of Arab States is composed of the independent Arab States which have signed this Pact.

Any independent Arab state has the right to become a member of the League. If it desires to do so, it shall submit a request which will be deposited with the Permanent Secretariat-General and submitted to the Council at the first meeting held after submission of the request.

Article 2. The League has as its purpose the strengthening of the relations between the member states; the co-ordination of their policies in order to achieve co-operation between them and to safeguard their independence and sovereignty; and a general concern with the affairs and interests of the Arab countries. It has also as its purpose the close co-operation of the member states, with due regard to the organization and circumstances of each state, on the following matters:

(a) Economic and financial affairs, including commercial relations, customs, currency, and questions of agriculture and industry.

(b) Communications: this includes railways, roads, aviation, navigation, telegraphs and posts.

(c) Cultural affairs.

(d) Nationality, passports, visas, execution of judgments, and extradition of criminals.

(e) Social affairs.

(f) Health problems.

Article 3. The League shall possess a Council composed of the representatives of the member states of the League; each state shall have a single vote, irrespective of the number of its representatives.

It shall be the task of the Council to achieve the realization of the objectives of the League and to supervise the execution of agreements which the member states have concluded on the questions enumerated in the preceding article, or on any other questions.

It likewise shall be the Council's task to decide upon the means by which the League is to co-operate with the international bodies to be created in the future in order to guarantee security and peace and regulate economic and social relations.

Article 4. For each of the questions listed in Article 2 there shall be set up a special committee in which the member states of the League shall be represented. These committees shall be charged with the task of laying down the principles and extent of co-operation. Such principles shall be formulated as draft agreements, to be presented to the Council for examination preparatory to their submission to the aforesaid states.

Representatives of the other Arab countries may take part in the work of the aforesaid committees. The Council shall determine the conditions under which these representatives may be permitted to participate and the rules governing such representation.

Article 5. Any resort to force in order to resolve disputes arising between two or more member states of the League is prohibited. If there should rise among them a difference which does not concern a state's independence, sovereignty, or territorial integrity, and if the parties to the dispute have recourse to the Council for the settlement of this difference, the decision of the Council shall then be enforceable and obligatory.

In such a case, the states between whom the difference has arisen shall not participate in the deliberations and decisions of the Council.

The Council shall mediate in all differences which threaten to lead to war between two member states, or a member state and a third state, with a view to bringing about their reconciliation.

Decisions of arbitration and mediation shall be taken by majority vote.

Article 6. In case of aggression or threat of aggression by one state against a member state, the state which has been attacked or threatened with aggression may demand the immediate convocation of the Council.

The Council shall by unanimous decision determine the measures necessary to repulse the aggression. If the aggressor is a member state, its vote shall not be counted in determining unanimity.

If, as a result of the attack, the government of the state attacked finds itself unable to communicate with the Council, that state's representative in the Council shall have the right to request the convocation of the Council for the purpose indicated in the foregoing paragraph. In the event that this representative is unable to communicate with the Council, any member state of the League shall have the right to request the convocation of the Council.

Article 7. Unanimous decisions of the Council shall be binding upon all member states of the League; majority decisions shall be binding only upon those states which have accepted them.

In either case the decisions of the Council shall be enforced in each member state according to its respective basic laws.

Article 8. Each member state shall respect the systems of government established in the other member states and regard them as exclusive concerns of those states. Each shall pledge to abstain from any action calculated to change established systems of government.

Article 9. States of the League which desire to establish closer co-operation and stronger bonds than are provided by this Pact may conclude agreements to that end.

Treaties and agreements already concluded or to be concluded in the future between a member state and another state shall not be binding or restrictive upon other members.

Article 10. The permanent seat of the League of Arab States is established in Cairo. The Council may, however, assemble at any other place it may designate.

Article 11. The Council of the League shall convene in ordinary session twice a year, in March and in September. It shall convene in extraordinary session upon the request of two member states of the League whenever the need arises.

Article 12. The League shall have a permanent Secretariat-General which shall consist of a Secretary-General, Assistant Secretaries, and an appropriate number of officials.

The Council of the League shall appoint the Secretary-General by a majority of two-thirds of the states of the League. The Secretary-General, with the approval of the Council, shall appoint the Assistant Secretaries and the principal officials of the League.

The Council of the League shall establish an administrative regulation for the functions of the Secretariat-General and matters relating to the Staff.

The Secretary-General shall have the rank of Ambassador and the Assistant Secretaries that of Ministers Plenipotentiary.

Article 13. The Secretary-General shall prepare the draft of the budget of the League and shall submit it to the Council for approval before the beginning of each fiscal year.

The Council shall fix the share of the expenses to be borne by each state of the League. This share may be reconsidered if necessary.

Article 14. (confers diplomatic immunity on officials).

Article 15. The first meeting of the Council shall be convened at the invitation of the head of the Egyptian Government. Thereafter it shall be convened at the invitation of the Secretary-General.

The representatives of the member states of the League shall alternately assume the presidency of the Council at each of its ordinary sessions.

Article 16. Except in cases specifically indicated in this Pact, a majority vote of the Council shall be sufficient to make enforceable decisions on the following matters:

(*a*) Matters relating to personnel.

(*b*) Adoption of the budget of the League.

(*c*) Establishment of the administrative regulations for the Council, the Committees, and the Secretariat-General.

(*d*) Decisions to adjourn the sessions.

Article 17. Each member state of the League shall deposit with the Secretariat-General one copy of every treaty or agreement concluded or to be concluded in the future between itself and another member state of the League or a third state.

Article 18. (deals with withdrawal).

Article 19. (deals with amendment).

Article 20. (deals with ratification).

ANNEX REGARDING PALESTINE

Since the termination of the last great war, the rule of the Ottoman Empire over the Arab countries, among them Palestine, which has become detached from that Empire, has come to an end. She has come to be autonomous, not subordinate to any other state.

The Treaty of Lausanne proclaimed that her future was to be settled by the parties concerned.

However, even though she was as yet unable to control her own affairs, the Covenant of the League (of Nations) in 1919 made provision for a regime based upon recognition of her independence.

Her international existence and independence in the legal sense cannot, therefore, be questioned, any more than could the independence of the Arab countries.

Although the outward manifestations of this independence have remained obscured for reasons beyond her control, this should not be allowed to interfere with her participation in the work of the Council of the League.

The states signatory to the Pact of the Arab League are therefore of the opinion that, considering the special circumstances of Palestine and until that country can effectively exercise its independence, the Council of the League should take charge of the selection of an Arab representative from Palestine to take part in its work.

ANNEX REGARDING CO-OPERATION WITH COUNTRIES WHICH ARE NOT MEMBERS OF THE COUNCIL OF THE LEAGUE

Whereas the member states of the League will have to deal in the Council as well as in the committees with matters which will benefit and affect the Arab world at large;

And whereas the Council has to take into account the aspirations of the Arab countries which are not members of the Council and has to work toward their realization;

Now therefore, it particularly behoves the states signatory to the Pact of the Arab League to enjoin the Council of the League, when considering the admission of those countries to participation in the committees referred to in the Pact, that it should do its utmost to co-operate with them, and furthermore, that it should spare no effort to learn their needs and understand their aspirations and hopes; and that it should work thenceforth for their best interests and the safeguarding of the future with all the political means at its disposal.

ORGANIZATION OF ARAB PETROLEUM EXPORTING COUNTRIES—OAPEC

Address: POB 20501, Safat 13066, Kuwait.

Telephone: 4844500; **telex:** 22166; **fax:** 4815747; **e-mail:** oapec@kuwait.net; **internet:** http://www.kuwait.net/~oapec.

OAPEC was established in 1968 to safeguard the interests of members and to determine ways and means for their co-operation in various forms of economic activity in the petroleum industry. In 1996 member states accounted for 25.7% of total world petroleum production.

MEMBERS

Algeria	Kuwait	Syria
Bahrain	Libya	United Arab Emirates
Egypt	Qatar	
Iraq	Saudi Arabia	

Organization

(August 1998)

MINISTERIAL COUNCIL

The Council consists normally of the ministers of petroleum of the member states, and forms the supreme authority of the Organization, responsible for drawing up its general policy, directing its activities and laying down its governing rules. It meets twice yearly, and may hold extraordinary sessions. Chairmanship is on an annual rotation basis.

EXECUTIVE BUREAU

Assists the Council to direct the management of the Organization, approves staff regulations, reviews the budget, and refers it to the Council, considers matters relating to the Organization's agreements and activities and draws up the agenda for the Council. The Bureau comprises one senior official from each member state. Chairmanship is by rotation. The Bureau convenes at least three times a year.

GENERAL SECRETARIAT

Secretary-General: ABD AL-AZIZ AT-TURKI (Saudi Arabia).

Besides the Office of the Secretary-General, there are four departments: Finance and Administrative Affairs, Information and Library, Technical Affairs and Economics. The last two form the Arab Centre for Energy Studies (which was established in 1983). At the end of 1997 there were 21 professional staff members and 30 general personnel at the General Secretariat.

JUDICIAL TRIBUNAL

The Tribunal comprises seven judges from Arab countries. Its task is to settle differences in interpretation and application of the OAPEC Agreement, arising between members and also between OAPEC and its affiliates; disputes among member countries on petroleum activities falling within OAPEC's jurisdiction and not under the sovereignty of member countries; and disputes that the Ministerial Council decides to submit to the Tribunal.

President: FARIS AL-WAGAYAN.

Registrar: Dr RIAD AD-DAOUDI.

Activities

OAPEC co-ordinates different aspects of the Arab petroleum industry through the joint undertakings described below. It co-operates with the League of Arab States and other Arab organizations, and attempts to link petroleum research institutes in the Arab states. It organizes or participates in conferences and seminars, many of which are held jointly with non-Arab organizations in order to enhance Arab and international co-operation.

OAPEC provides training in technical matters and in documentation and information. The General Secretariat also conducts technical and feasibility studies and carries out market reviews. It provides information through a library, 'databank' and the publications listed below.

The invasion of Kuwait by Iraq in August 1990, and the subsequent international embargo on petroleum exports from Iraq and Kuwait, severely disrupted OAPEC's activities. In December the OAPEC Council decided to establish temporary headquarters in Cairo while Kuwait was under occupation. The Council resolved to reschedule overdue payments by Iraq and Syria over a 15-year period, and to postpone the Fifth Arab Energy Conference from mid-1992 to mid-1994. The Conference was held in Cairo, Egypt, in May 1994, attended by OAPEC ministers of petroleum and energy, senior officials from nine other Arab states and representatives of regional and international organizations. The Sixth Conference was scheduled to be held in Damascus, Syria, in 1998. In June 1994 OAPEC returned to its permanent headquarters in Kuwait.

During 1995 the General Secretariat organized the 14th training programme relating to the fundamentals of the petroleum and gas industry, held in April, a workshop on the application of new technologies to the production of hydrocarbons, held in the Netherlands, in September, and a seminar on pipeline transportation of hydrocarbons in Arab countries, held in November. The Secretariat also convened a meeting of energy information specialists from the Arab countries, as part of its efforts to develop an integrated resource base, or 'databank' to serve the information needs of the sector throughout the region.

FINANCE

The 1998 budget, approved by the Council in December 1997, amounted to 1,447,000 Kuwaiti dinars (KD). In addition, a budget of 118,800 KD was approved for the Judicial Tribunal.

OAPEC-SPONSORED VENTURES

Arab Maritime Petroleum Transport Company—AMPTC: POB 22525, Safat 13086, Kuwait; tel. 4844500; telex 22180; fax 4842996; f. 1973 to undertake transport of crude petroleum, gas, refined products and petro-chemicals, and thus to increase Arab participation in the tanker transport industry; auth. cap. US $200m. Gen. Man. SULEIMAN AL-BASSAM.

Arab Petroleum Investments Corporation—APICORP: POB 448, Dhahran Airport 31932, Saudi Arabia; tel. (3) 864-7400; telex 870068; fax (3) 898-1883; f. 1975 to finance investments in petroleum and petrochemicals projects and related industries in the Arab world and in developing countries, with priority being given to Arab joint ventures. Projects financed include gas liquefaction plants, petrochemicals, tankers, oil refineries, pipelines, exploration, detergents, fertilizers and process control instrumentation; auth. cap. US $1,200m.; subs. cap. $460m. (31 Dec. 1996). Shareholders: Kuwait, Saudi Arabia and United Arab Emirates (17% each), Libya (15%), Iraq and Qatar (10% each), Algeria (5%), Bahrain, Egypt and Syria (3% each). Chair. ABDULLAH A. AZ-ZAID; Gen.-Man. Dr NUREDDIN FARRAG.

Arab Company for Detergent Chemicals—ARADET: POB 27864, el-Monsour, Baghdad, Iraq; tel. (1) 541-9893; telex 213675; f. 1981 to implement two projects in Iraq; APICORP and the Iraqi Government each hold 32% of shares in the co; auth. cap. 72m. Iraqi dinars.

Arab Petroleum Services Company—APSCO: POB 12925, Tripoli, Libya; tel. (21) 45861; telex 20405; fax (21) 3331930; f. 1977 to provide petroleum services through the establishment of companies specializing in various activities, and to train specialized personnel; auth. cap. 100m. Libyan dinars; subs. cap. 15m. Libyan dinars. Chair. AYYAD AD-DALI; Gen.-Man. ISMAIL AL-KORAITLI.

Arab Drilling and Workover Company: POB 680, Suani Rd, km 3.5, Tripoli, Libya; tel. (21) 800064; telex 20361; fax (21) 805945; f. 1980; auth. cap. 12m. Libyan dinars; Gen. Man. MUHAMMAD AHMAD ATTIGA.

Arab Geophysical Exploration Services Company—AGESCO: POB 84224, Airport Rd, Tripoli, Libya; tel. (21) 4804863; telex 20716; fax (21) 4803199; f. 1985; auth. cap. 12m. Libyan dinars; Gen. Man. AYYAD AD-DALI.

Arab Well Logging Company—AWLCO: POB 6225, Baghdad, Iraq; tel. (1) 541-8259; telex 213688; f. 1983; provides well-logging services and data interpretation; auth. cap. 7m. Iraqi dinars.

Arab Petroleum Training Institute—APTI: POB 6037, Al-Tajeyat, Baghdad, Iraq; tel. (1) 523-4100; telex 212728; fax (1) 521-0526; f. 1978 to provide instruction in many technical and managerial aspects of the oil industry. Since Dec. 1994 the Institute has been placed under the trusteeship of the Iraqi Government; the arrangement was scheduled to come to an end in Dec. 1998. Dir HAZIM A. AS-SULTAN.

Arab Shipbuilding and Repair Yard Company—ASRY: POB 50110, Hidd, Bahrain; tel. 671111; telex 8455; fax 670236; e-mail asryco@batelco.com.bh; f. 1974 to undertake repairs and servicing of vessels; operates a 500,000 dwt dry dock in Bahrain; two floating docks operational since 1992. Cap. (auth. and subs.) US $340m. Chair. Sheikh DAIJ BIN KHALIFA AL-KHALIFA; Chief Exec. MOHAMED M. AL-KHATEEB.

PUBLICATIONS

Annual Statistical Report.

Energy Resources Monitor (quarterly, Arabic).

OAPEC Monthly Bulletin (Arabic and English editions).

OAPEC Statistical Bulletin (Arabic and English editions).

Oil and Arab Co-operation (quarterly, Arabic).

Secretary-General's Annual Report (Arabic and English editions).

Papers, studies, conference proceedings.

ORGANIZATION OF THE ISLAMIC CONFERENCE—OIC

Address: Kilo 6, Mecca Rd, POB 178, Jeddah 21411, Saudi Arabia.
Telephone: (2) 680-0800; **telex:** 601366; **fax:** (2) 687-3568.

The Organization was formally established in May 1971, when its Secretariat became operational, following a summit meeting of Muslim heads of state at Rabat, Morocco, in September 1969, and the Islamic Foreign Ministers' Conference in Jeddah in March 1970, and in Karachi, Pakistan, in December 1970.

MEMBERS

Afghanistan	Iran	Qatar
Albania	Iraq	Saudi Arabia
Algeria	Jordan	Senegal
Azerbaijan	Kazakhstan	Sierra Leone
Bahrain	Kuwait	Somalia
Bangladesh	Kyrgyzstan	Sudan
Benin	Lebanon	Suriname
Brunei	Libya	Syria
Burkina Faso	Malaysia	Tajikistan
Cameroon	Maldives	Togo
Chad	Mali	Tunisia
The Comoros	Mauritania	Turkey
Djibouti	Morocco	Turkmenistan
Egypt	Mozambique	Uganda
Gabon	Niger	United Arab
The Gambia	Nigeria*	Emirates
Guinea	Oman	Uzbekistan
Guinea-Bissau	Pakistan	Yemen
Indonesia	Palestine	

* Nigeria renounced its membership of the OIC in May 1991; however, the OIC has not formally recognized this decision.
Note: Observer status has been granted to Bosnia and Herzegovina, the Central African Republic, Côte d'Ivoire, Guyana, the Muslim community of the 'Turkish Republic of Northern Cyprus', the Moro National Liberation Front (MNLF) of the southern Philippines, the United Nations, the Non-Aligned Movement, the League of Arab States, the Organization of African Unity, the Economic Co-operation Organization, the Union of the Arab Maghreb and the Co-operation Council for the Arab States of the Gulf.

Organization

(August 1998)

SUMMIT CONFERENCES

The supreme body of the Organization is the Conference of Heads of State, which met in 1969 at Rabat, Morocco, in 1974 at Lahore, Pakistan, and in January 1981 at Mecca, Saudi Arabia, when it was decided that summit conferences would be held every three years in future. Eighth Conference: Teheran, Iran, December 1997. The ninth Conference was to be held in Doha, Qatar, in 2000.

CONFERENCE OF MINISTERS OF FOREIGN AFFAIRS

Conferences take place annually, to consider the means for implementing the general policy of the Organization, although they may also be convened for extraordinary sessions.

SECRETARIAT

The executive organ of the Organization, headed by a Secretary-General (who is elected by the Conference of Ministers of Foreign Affairs for a four-year term, renewable only once) and four Assistant Secretaries-General (similarly appointed).

Secretary-General: AZEDDINE LARAKI (Morocco).

At the summit conference in January 1981 it was decided that an International Islamic Court of Justice should be established to adjudicate in disputes between Muslim countries. Experts met in January 1983 to draw up a constitution for the court, but by 1998 it was not yet in operation.

SPECIALIZED COMMITTEES

Al-Quds Committee: f. 1975 to implement the resolutions of the Islamic Conference on the status of Jerusalem (Al-Quds); it meets at the level of foreign ministers; maintains the Al-Quds Fund; Chair. King HASSAN II of Morocco.

Standing Committee for Economic and Commercial Co-operation (COMCEC): f. 1981; Chair. SÜLEYMAN DEMIREL (Pres. of Turkey).

Standing Committee for Information and Cultural Affairs (COMIAC): f. 1981; Chair. ABDOU DIOUF (Pres. of Senegal).
Standing Committee for Scientific and Technological Co-operation (COMSTECH): f. 1981; Chair. MOHAMMAD RAFIQ TARAR (Pres. of Pakistan).
Islamic Commission for Economic, Cultural and Social Affairs: f. 1976.
Permanent Finance Committee.

Other committees comprise the Committee of Islamic Solidarity with the Peoples of the Sahel, the Six-Member Committee on the Situation of Muslims in the Philippines, the Six-Member Committee on Palestine, the *ad hoc* Committee on Afghanistan, the OIC contact group on Bosnia and Herzegovina, and the OIC contact group on Jammu and Kashmir.

Activities

The Organization's aims, as proclaimed in the Charter that was adopted in 1972, are:

(i) To promote Islamic solidarity among member states;

(ii) To consolidate co-operation among member states in the economic, social, cultural, scientific and other vital fields, and to arrange consultations among member states belonging to international organizations;

(iii) To endeavour to eliminate racial segregation and discrimination and to eradicate colonialism in all its forms;

(iv) To take necessary measures to support international peace and security founded on justice;

(v) To co-ordinate all efforts for the safeguard of the Holy Places and support of the struggle of the people of Palestine, and help them to regain their rights and liberate their land;

(vi) To strengthen the struggle of all Muslim people with a view to safeguarding their dignity, independence and national rights; and

(vii) To create a suitable atmosphere for the promotion of co-operation and understanding among member states and other countries.

The first summit conference of Islamic leaders (representing 24 states) took place in 1969 following the burning of the Al Aqsa Mosque in Jerusalem. At this conference it was decided that Islamic governments should 'consult together with a view to promoting close co-operation and mutual assistance in the economic, scientific, cultural and spiritual fields, inspired by the immortal teachings of Islam'. Thereafter the foreign ministers of the countries concerned met annually, and adopted the Charter of the Organization of the Islamic Conference in 1972.

At the second Islamic summit conference (Lahore, Pakistan, 1974), the Islamic Solidarity Fund was established, together with a committee of representatives which later evolved into the Islamic Commission for Economic, Cultural and Social Affairs. Subsequently, numerous other subsidiary bodies have been set up (see below).

ECONOMIC CO-OPERATION

A general agreement for economic, technical and commercial co-operation came into force in 1981, providing for the establishment of joint investment projects and trade co-ordination. This was followed by an agreement on promotion, protection and guarantee of investments among member states. A plan of action to strengthen economic co-operation was adopted at the third Islamic summit conference in 1981, aiming to promote collective self-reliance and the development of joint ventures in all sectors. In May 1993 the OIC committee for economic and commercial co-operation, meeting in Istanbul, agreed to review and update the 1981 plan of action.

A meeting of ministers of industry was held in February 1982, and agreed to promote industrial co-operation, including joint ventures in agricultural machinery, engineering and other basic industries. The fifth summit conference, held in 1987, approved proposals for joint development of modern technology, and for improving scientific and technical skills in the less developed Islamic countries. In December 1988 it was announced that a committee of experts, established by the OIC, was to draw up a 10-year programme of assistance to developing countries (mainly in Africa) in science and technology.

CULTURAL CO-OPERATION

The Organization supports education in Muslim communities throughout the world, and was instrumental in the establishment of Islamic universities in Niger and Uganda (see below). It organizes seminars on various aspects of Islam, and encourages dialogue with the other monotheistic religions. Support is given to publications on Islam both in Muslim and Western countries.

In March 1989 the Conference of Ministers of Foreign Affairs denounced as an apostate the author of the controversial novel *The Satanic Verses* (Salman Rushdie), demanded the withdrawal of the book from circulation, and urged member states to boycott publishing houses that refused to comply.

HUMANITARIAN ASSISTANCE

Assistance is given to Muslim communities affected by wars and natural disasters, in co-operation with UN organizations, particularly UNHCR. The countries of the Sahel region (Burkina Faso, Cape Verde, Chad, The Gambia, Guinea, Guinea-Bissau, Mali, Mauritania, Niger and Senegal) receive particular attention as victims of drought. In April 1993 member states pledged US $80m. in emergency assistance for Muslims affected by the war in Bosnia and Herzegovina (see below for details of subsequent assistance).

POLITICAL CO-OPERATION

Since its inception the OIC has called for vacation of Arab territories by Israel, recognition of the rights of Palestinians and of the Palestine Liberation Organization (PLO) as their sole legitimate representative, and the restoration of Jerusalem to Arab rule. The 1981 summit conference called for a *jihad* (holy war—though not necessarily in a military sense) 'for the liberation of Jerusalem and the occupied territories'; this was to include an Islamic economic boycott of Israel. In 1982 Islamic ministers of foreign affairs decided to establish Islamic offices for boycotting Israel and for military co-operation with the PLO. The 1984 summit conference agreed to reinstate Egypt (suspended following the peace treaty signed with Israel in 1979) as a member of the OIC, although the resolution was opposed by seven states.

The fifth summit conference, held in January 1987, discussed the continuing Iran–Iraq war, and agreed that the Islamic Peace Committee should attempt to prevent the sale of military equipment to the parties in the conflict. The conference also discussed the conflicts in Chad and Lebanon, and requested the holding of a United Nations conference to define international terrorism, as opposed to legitimate fighting for freedom.

In August 1990 a majority of ministers of foreign affairs condemned Iraq's recent invasion of Kuwait, and demanded the withdrawal of Iraqi forces. In August 1991 the Conference of Ministers of Foreign Affairs obstructed Iraq's attempt to propose a resolution demanding the repeal of economic sanctions against the country. The sixth summit conference, held in Senegal in December 1991, reflected the divisions in the Arab world that resulted from Iraq's invasion of Kuwait and the ensuing war. Twelve heads of state did not attend, sending representatives, reportedly to register protest at the presence of Jordan and the PLO at the conference, both of which had given support to Iraq. Disagreement also arose between the PLO and the majority of other OIC members when it was proposed to cease the OIC's support for the PLO's *jihad* in the Arab territories occupied by Israel. The proposal, which was adopted, represented an attempt to further the Middle East peace negotiations.

In August 1992 the UN General Assembly approved a non-binding resolution, introduced by the OIC, that requested the UN Security Council to take increased action, including the use of force, in order to defend the non-Serbian population of Bosnia and Herzegovina (some 43% of Bosnians being Muslims) from Serbian aggression, and to restore its 'territorial integrity'. The OIC Conference of Ministers of Foreign Affairs, which was held in Jeddah, Saudi Arabia, in early December, demanded anew that the UN Security Council take all necessary measures against Serbia and Montenegro, including military intervention, in accordance with Article 42 of the UN Charter, in order to protect the Bosnian Muslims. In early February 1993 the OIC appealed to the Security Council to remove the embargo on armaments to Bosnia and Herzegovina with regard to the Bosnian Muslims, to allow them to defend themselves from the Bosnian Serbs, who were far better armed.

A report by an OIC fact-finding mission, which in February 1993 visited Azad Kashmir while investigating allegations of repression of the largely Muslim population of the Indian state of Jammu and Kashmir by the Indian armed forces, was presented to the 1993 Conference. The meeting urged member states to take the necessary measures to persuade India to cease the 'massive human rights violations' in Jammu and Kashmir and to allow the Indian Kashmiris to 'exercise their inalienable right to self-determination'. In September 1994 ministers of foreign affairs, meeting in Islamabad, Pakistan, urged the Indian Government to grant permission for an OIC fact-finding mission, and for other human rights groups, to visit Jammu and Kashmir (which it had continually refused to do) and to refrain from human rights violations of the Kashmiri people. The ministers agreed to establish a contact group on Jammu and

Kashmir, which was to provide a mechanism for promoting international awareness of the situation in that region and for seeking a peaceful solution to the dispute. In December OIC heads of state approved a resolution condemning reported human rights abuses by Indian security forces in Kashmir.

In July 1994 the OIC Secretary-General visited Afghanistan and proposed the establishment of a preparatory mechanism to promote national reconciliation in that country. In mid-1995 Saudi Arabia, acting as a representative of the OIC, pursued a peace initiative for Afghanistan and issued an invitation for leaders of the different factions to hold negotiations in Jeddah.

A special ministerial meeting on Bosnia and Herzegovina was held in July 1993, at which seven OIC countries committed themselves to making available up to 17,000 troops to serve in the UN Protection Force in the former Yugoslavia (UNPROFOR). The meeting also decided to dispatch immediately a ministerial mission to persuade influential governments to support the OIC's demands for the removal of the arms embargo on Bosnian Muslims and the convening of a restructured international conference to bring about a political solution to the conflict. At the end of September 1994 ministers of foreign affairs of nine countries constituting the OIC contact group on Bosnia and Herzegovina, meeting in New York, resolved to prepare an assessment document on the issue, and to establish an alliance with its Western counterpart (comprising France, Germany, Russia, the United Kingdom and the USA). The two groups met in Geneva, Switzerland, in January 1995. In December 1994 OIC heads of state, convened in Morocco, proclaimed that the UN arms embargo on Bosnia and Herzegovina could not be applied to the Muslim authorities of that Republic, and requested the support of the international community for the continued presence of a UN force in the area. The Conference also resolved to review economic relations between OIC member states and any country that supported Serbian activities. An aid fund was established, to which member states were requested to contribute between US $500,000 and $5m., in order to provide further humanitarian and economic assistance to Bosnian Muslims. In relation to wider concerns the conference adopted a Code of Conduct for Combating International Terrorism, in an attempt to control Muslim extremist groups. The code commits states to ensuring that militant groups do not use their territory for planning or executing terrorist activity against other states, in addition to states refraining from direct support or participation in acts of terrorism. In a further resolution the OIC supported the decision by Iraq to recognize Kuwait, but advocated that Iraq comply with all UN Security Council decisions.

In July 1995 the OIC contact group on Bosnia and Herzegovina (at that time comprising Egypt, Iran, Malaysia, Morocco, Pakistan, Saudi Arabia, Senegal and Turkey), meeting in Geneva, declared the UN arms embargo against Bosnia and Herzegovina to be 'invalid'. Several Governments subsequently announced their willingness officially to supply weapons and other military assistance to the Bosnian Muslim forces. In September a meeting of all OIC ministers of defence and foreign affairs endorsed the establishment of an 'assistance mobilization group' which was to supply military, economic, legal and other assistance to Bosnia and Herzegovina. In a joint declaration the ministers also demanded the return of all territory seized by Bosnian Serb forces, the continued NATO bombing of Serb military targets, and that the city of Sarajevo be preserved under a Muslim-led Bosnian Government. In November the OIC Secretary-General endorsed the peace accord for the former Yugoslavia, which was concluded, in Dayton, USA, by leaders of all the conflicting factions, and reaffirmed the commitment of Islamic states to participate in efforts to implement the accord. In the following month the OIC Conference of Ministers of Foreign Affairs, convened in Conakry, Guinea, requested the full support of the international community to reconstruct Bosnia and Herzegovina through humanitarian aid as well as economic and technical co-operation. Ministers declared that Palestine and the establishment of fully-autonomous Palestinian control of Jerusalem were issues of central importance for the Muslim world. The Conference urged the removal of all aspects of occupation and the cessation of the construction of Israeli settlements in the occupied territories. In addition, the final statement of the meeting condemned Armenian aggression against Azerbaijan, registered concern at the persisting civil conflict in Afghanistan, demanded the elimination of all weapons of mass destruction and pledged support for Libya (affected by the US trade embargo).

In December 1996 OIC ministers of foreign affairs, meeting in Jakarta, Indonesia, urged the international community to apply pressure on Israel in order to ensure its implementation of the terms of the Middle East peace process. The ministers reaffirmed the importance of ensuring that the provisions of the Dayton Peace Agreement for the former Yugoslavia were fully implemented, called for a peaceful settlement of the Kashmir issue, demanded that Iraq fulfil its obligations for the establishment of security, peace and stability in the region and proposed that an international conference on peace and national reconciliation in Somalia be convened. The ministers elected a new Secretary-General, Azeddine Laraki, who confirmed that the organization would continue to develop its role as an international mediator. In March 1997, at an extraordinary summit held in Pakistan, OIC heads of state and of government reiterated the organization's objective of increasing international pressure on Israel to ensure the full implementation of the terms of the Middle East peace process. An 'Islamabad Declaration' was also adopted, which pledged to increase co-operation between members of the OIC. In June both the OIC and the Islamic World League condemned the decision by the US House of Representatives to recognize Jerusalem as the Israeli capital. The Secretary-General of the OIC issued a statement rejecting the US decision as counter to the role of the USA as sponsor of the Middle East peace plan. In December OIC heads of state attended the eighth summit conference, held in Iran. The Teheran Declaration, issued at the end of the conference, demanded the 'liberation' of the Israeli-occupied territories and the creation of an autonomous Palestinian state. The conference also appealed for a cessation of the conflicts in Afghanistan, and between Armenia and Azerbaijan. It was requested that the UN sanctions against Libya be removed and that the US legislation threatening sanctions against foreign companies investing in certain countries (including Iran and Libya), introduced in July 1996, be dismissed as invalid. In addition, the Declaration encouraged the increased participation of women in OIC activities.

In early 1998 the OIC appealed for an end to the threat of US-led military action against Iraq arising from a dispute regarding access granted to international weapons inspectors. The crisis was averted following an agreement concluded between the Iraqi authorities and the UN Secretary-General in February. In March OIC ministers of foreign affairs, meeting in Doha, Qatar, requested an end to the international sanctions against Iraq. Additionally, the ministers urged all states to end the process of restoring normal trading and diplomatic relations with Israel until that country withdraws from the occupied territories and permits the establishment of an independent Palestinian state.

SUBSIDIARY ORGANS

International Commission for the Preservation of Islamic Cultural Heritage (ICPICH): POB 24, 80692 Beşiktaş, İstanbul, Turkey; tel. (212) 2591742; fax (212) 2584365; e-mail ircica@superonline.com; internet http://www.ircica.hypermart.net.ircica .html; f. 1982. Sec. Prof. Dr EKMELEDDIN İHSANOĞLU (Turkey).

Islamic Centre for the Development of Trade: Complexe Commercial des Habous, ave des FAR, BP 13545, Casablanca, Morocco; tel. (2) 314974; telex 46296; fax (2) 310110; e-mail icdt@icdt.org; internet http://www.icdt.org; f. 1983 to encourage regular commercial contacts, harmonize policies and promote investments among OIC mems. Dir BADRE EDDINE ALLALI. Publs *Tijaris: International and Inter-Islamic Trade Magazine* (quarterly), *Inter-Islamic Trade Report* (annual).

Islamic Institute of Technology (IIT): GPO Box 3003, Board Bazar, Gazipur, Dhaka, Bangladesh; tel. (2) 980-0960; telex 642739; fax (2) 980-0970; e-mail dg@iit.bangla.net; f. 1981 to develop human resources in OIC mem. states, with special reference to engineering, technology, tech. and vocational education and research; offers four-year degree courses, a three-year higher diploma, a one-year Masters degree, post-graduate diplomas, as well as short courses and seminars; capacity of 224 full-time and 57 part-time staff and 1,000 students; library of 18,000 vols. Dir-Gen. Prof. A. M. PATWARI. Publs *News Bulletin* (annually), calendar and announcements for admission, reports, human resources development series.

Islamic Jurisprudence Academy: Jeddah, Saudi Arabia; f. 1982. Sec.-Gen. Sheikh MOHAMED HABIB BELKHOJAH.

Islamic Solidarity Fund: c/o OIC Secretariat, POB 178, Jeddah 21411, Saudi Arabia; tel. (2) 680-0800; telex 601366; fax (2) 687-3568; f. 1974 to meet the needs of Islamic communities by providing emergency aid and the finance to build mosques, Islamic centres, hospitals, schools and universities. Chair. Sheikh NASIR ABDULLAH BIN HAMDAN; Exec. Dir ABDULLAH HERSI.

Islamic University of Niger: BP 11507, Niamey, Niger; tel. 723903; telex 8266; fax 733796; f. 1984; provides courses of study

in *Shar'ia* (Islamic law) and Arabic language and literature; also offers courses in pedagogy and teacher training; receives grants from Islamic Solidarity Fund and contributions from OIC member states; Rector Prof. ABDELALI OUDHRIRI.

Islamic University in Uganda: POB 2555, Mbale, Uganda; tel. (45) 33502; telex 66176; fax (45) 34452; e-mail iuiu@info.com.co.ug; Kampala Liaison Office: POB 7689, Kampala; tel. (41) 236874; fax (41) 254576; f. 1988 to meet the educational needs of Muslim populations in English-speaking African countries; mainly financed by OIC. Principal Officer Prof. MAHDI ADAMU.

Research Centre for Islamic History, Art and Culture (IRCICA): POB 24, Beşiktaş 80692, İstanbul, Turkey; tel. (212) 2591742; telex 26484; fax (212) 2584365; e-mail ircica@superonline .com; internet http://www.ircica.hypermart.net/ircica.html; f. 1980; library of 50,000 vols. Dir-Gen. Prof. Dr EKMELEDDIN İHSANOĞLU. Publ. *Newsletter* (3 a year).

Statistical, Economic and Social Research and Training Centre for the Islamic Countries: Attar Sok 4, GOP 06700, Ankara, Turkey; tel. (312) 4686172; telex 18944838; fax (312) 4673458; e-mail sesrtcic-f@servis.net.tr; f. 1978. Dir-Gen. ERDINÇ ERDÜN.

SPECIALIZED INSTITUTIONS

International Islamic News Agency (IINA): King Khalid Palace, Madinah Rd, POB 5054, Jeddah, Saudi Arabia; tel. (2) 665-8561; telex 601090; fax (2) 665-9358; e-mail iina@mail.gcc.com.bh; internet http:www.islamicnews.org; f. 1972. Dir-Gen. ABDULWAHAB KASHIF.

Islamic Development Bank: See p. 253.

Islamic Educational, Scientific and Cultural Organization (ISESCO): Hay Ryad, BP 2275, Rabat 10104, Morocco; tel. (7) 772433; telex 32645; fax (7) 777459; f. 1982. Dir-Gen. Dr ABDULAZIZ BIN OTHMAN AL-TWAIJRI. Publs *ISESCO Newsletter* (quarterly), *Islam Today* (2 a year), *ISESCO Triennial.*

Islamic States Broadcasting Organization (ISBO): POB 6351, Jeddah 21442, Saudi Arabia; tel. (2) 672-1121; telex 601442; fax (2) 672-2600; f. 1975. Sec.-Gen. HUSSEIN AL-ASKARY.

AFFILIATED INSTITUTIONS

International Association of Islamic Banks (IAIB): King Abdul-aziz St, Queen's Bldg, 23rd Floor, Al-Balad Dist, POB 23425, Jeddah 21426, Saudi Arabia; tel. (2) 643-1276; fax (2) 644-7239; f. 1977 to link financial institutions operating on Islamic banking principles; activities include training and research; mems: 192 banks and other financial institutions in 34 countries. Sec.-Gen. SAMIR A. SHAIKH.

Islamic Chamber of Commerce and Industry: POB 3831, Clifton, Karachi 75600, Pakistan; tel. (21) 5874756; telex 27272; fax (21) 5870765; e-mail icci@paknet3.ptc.pk; internet http://www .icci.org.pk/islamic/main.html; f. 1979 to promote trade and industry among member states; comprises nat. chambers or feds of chambers of commerce and industry. Sec.-Gen. AQEEL AHMAD AL-JASSEM.

Islamic Committee for the International Crescent: c/o OIC, Kilo 6, Mecca Rd, POB 178, Jeddah 21411, Saudi Arabia; tel. (2) 680-0800; telex 601366; fax (2) 687-3568; f. 1979 to attempt to alleviate the suffering caused by natural disasters and war. Sec.-Gen. Dr AHMAD ABDALLAH CHERIF.

Islamic Solidarity Sports Federation: POB 6040, Riyadh 11442, Saudi Arabia; tel. and fax (1) 482-2145; telex 404760; f. 1981. Sec.-Gen. Dr MOAMMAD SALEH GAZDAR.

Organization of Islamic Capitals and Cities (OICC): POB 13621, Jeddah 21414, Saudi Arabia; tel. (2) 698-1953; fax (2) 698-1053; e-mail oicc@compuserve.com; f. 1980 to promote and develop co-operation among OICC mems, to preserve their character and heritage, to implement planning guidelines for the growth of Islamic cities and to upgrade standards of public services and utilities in those cities. Sec.-Gen. OMAR ABDULLAH KADI.

Organization of the Islamic Shipowners' Association: POB 14900, Jeddah 21434, Saudi Arabia; tel. (2) 663-7882; telex 607303; fax (2) 660-4920; f. 1981 to promote co-operation among maritime cos in Islamic countries. Sec.-Gen. Dr ABDULLATIF A. SULTAN.

ORGANIZATION OF THE PETROLEUM EXPORTING COUNTRIES—OPEC

Address: Obere Donaustrasse 93, 1020 Vienna, Austria.

Telephone: (1) 211-12-0; **telex:** 134474; **fax:** (1) 214-98-27; **e-mail:** info@opec.org; **internet:** http://www.opec.org.

OPEC was established in 1960 to link countries whose main source of export earnings is petroleum; it aims to unify and co-ordinate members' petroleum policies and to safeguard their interests generally. The OPEC Fund for International Development is described on p. 267.

OPEC's share of world petroleum production was 40.2% in 1996 (compared with 44.6% in 1980 and 54.7% in 1974). It is estimated that OPEC members possess more than 75% of the world's known reserves of crude petroleum, of which about two-thirds are in the Middle East. In 1996 OPEC members possessed about 42.3% of known reserves of natural gas.

MEMBERS

Algeria	Kuwait	Saudi Arabia
Indonesia	Libya	United Arab Emirates
Iran	Nigeria	Venezuela
Iraq	Qatar	

Organization

(August 1998)

CONFERENCE

The Conference is the supreme authority of the Organization, responsible for the formulation of its general policy. It consists of representatives of member countries, who examine reports and recommendations submitted by the Board of Governors. It approves the appointment of Governors from each country and elects the Chairman of the Board of Governors. It works on the unanimity principle, and meets at least twice a year.

BOARD OF GOVERNORS

The Board directs the management of the Organization; it implements resolutions of the Conference and draws up an annual budget. It consists of one governor for each member country, and meets at least twice a year.

MINISTERIAL MONITORING COMMITTEE

The Committee (f. 1988) is responsible for monitoring price evolution and ensuring the stability of the world petroleum market. As such, it is charged with the preparation of long-term strategies, including the allocation of quotas to be presented to the Conference. The Committee consists of all national representatives, and is normally convened four times a year. A Ministerial Monitoring Sub-committee, reporting to the Committee on production and supply figures, was established in 1993.

ECONOMIC COMMISSION

A specialized body operating within the framework of the Secretariat, with a view to assisting the Organization in promoting stability in international prices for petroleum at equitable levels; consists of a Board, national representatives and a commission staff; meets at least twice a year.

SECRETARIAT

Secretary-General: Dr RILWANU LUKMAN (Nigeria).

Research Division: comprises three departments:

Data Services Department: Computer Section maintains and expands information services to support the research activities of the Secretariat and those of member countries. Statistics Section collects, collates and analyses statistical information and provides essential data for forecasts and estimates necessary for OPEC medium- and long-term strategies.

Energy Studies Department: Energy Section monitors, forecasts and analyses developments in the energy and petrochemical industries and their implications for OPEC, and prepares forecasts of demands for OPEC petroleum and gas. Petroleum Section assists the Board of the Economic Commission in determining the relative values of OPEC crude petroleum and gases and in developing alternative methodologies for this purpose.

Economics and Finance Department: Comprises the Economics Section and a Finance Section. Analyses and reports on economic and financial developments relevant to the world energy market and the deliberations of the Economic Commission Board and the Conference, including world trade, international monetary movements, Third World debt, the financial performance of petroleum companies and oil revenues of member states.

Division Head: Dr SHOKRI M. GHANEM.

Administration and Human Resources Department: Responsible for all organization methods, provision of administrative services for all meetings, personnel matters, budgets accounting and internal control; reviews general administrative policies and industrial relations practised throughout the oil industry; **Head:** ABBAS N. AFSHAR.

OPECNA and Information Department: Comprises the OPEC News Agency (OPECNA, f. 1980) and the Information Section. Responsible for a central public relations programme; production and distribution of publications, films, slides and tapes; and communication of OPEC objectives and decisions to the world at large. Operates a daily on-line news service; OPECNA daily bulletins are disseminated to more than 3,000 media outlets in some 80 countries; **Head:** FAROUK U. MUHAMMED (acting).

Legal Office: Provides legal advice, supervises the Secretariat's legal commitments, evaluates legal issues of concern to the Organization and member countries, and recommends appropriate action; **Head:** AHMED ABDULAZIZ.

Office of the Secretary-General: Provides the Secretary-General with executive assistance in maintaining contacts with governments, organizations and delegations, in matters of protocol and in the preparation for and co-ordination of meetings; **Head:** Dr NAFRIZAL SIKUMBANG.

Record of Events

1960   The first OPEC Conference was held in Baghdad in September, attended by representatives from Iran, Iraq, Kuwait, Saudi Arabia and Venezuela.

1961   Second Conference, Caracas, January. Qatar was admitted to membership; a Board of Governors was formed and statutes agreed.

1962   Fourth Conference, Geneva, April and June. Protests were addressed to petroleum companies against price cuts introduced in August 1960. Indonesia and Libya were admitted to membership.

1965   In July the Conference reached agreement on a two-year joint production programme, implemented from 1965 to 1967, to limit annual growth in output to secure adequate prices.

1967   Abu Dhabi was admitted to membership.

1969   Algeria was admitted to membership.

1970   Twenty-first Conference, Caracas, December. Tax on income of petroleum companies was raised to 55%.

1971   A five-year agreement was concluded in February between the six producing countries in the Gulf and 23 international petroleum companies (Teheran Agreement). Nigeria was admitted to membership.

1972   In January petroleum companies agreed to adjust petroleum revenues of the largest producers after changes in currency exchange rates (Geneva Agreement).

1973   OPEC and petroleum companies concluded an agreement whereby posted prices of crude petroleum were raised by 11.9% and a mechanism was installed to make monthly adjustments to prices in future (Second Geneva Agreement). Negotiations with petroleum companies on revision of the Teheran Agreement collapsed in October, and the Gulf states unilaterally declared 70% increases in posted prices, from US $3.01 to $5.11 per barrel.

     Thirty-sixth Conference, Teheran, December. The posted price was to increase by nearly 130%, from US $5.11 to $11.65 per barrel, from 1 January 1974. Ecuador was admitted to full membership and Gabon became an associate member.

1974   As a result of Saudi opposition to the December price increase, prices were held at current level for first quarter (and subsequently for the remainder of 1974). Abu Dhabi's membership was transferred to the United Arab Emirates (UAE). A meeting in June increased royalties charged to petroleum companies from 12.5% to 14.5% in all member states except

Saudi Arabia. A meeting in September increased governmental take by about 3.5% through further increases in royalties on equity crude to 16.67% and in taxes to 65.65%, except in Saudi Arabia.

1975   OPEC's first summit conference was held in Algiers in March. Gabon was admitted to full membership.
A ministerial meeting in September agreed to raise prices by 10% for the period until June 1976.

1976   The OPEC Special Fund for International Development was created in May.
In December 11 member states endorsed a rise in basic prices of 10% as of 1 January 1977, and a further 5% rise as of 1 July 1977. However, Saudi Arabia and the UAE decided to raise their prices by 5% only.

1977   Following an earlier waiver by nine members of the 5% second stage of the price increase, Saudi Arabia and the UAE announced in July that they would both raise their prices by 5%. As a result, a single level of prices throughout the organization was restored. Because of continued disagreements between the 'moderates', led by Saudi Arabia and Iran, and the 'radicals', led by Algeria, Libya and Iraq, the Conference, held in December, was unable to settle on an increase in prices.

1978   The June Conference agreed that price levels should remain stable until the end of the year. In December it was decided to raise prices in four instalments, in order to compensate for the effects of the depreciation of the US dollar. These would bring a rise of 14.5% over nine months, but an average increase of 10% for 1979.

1979   At an extraordinary meeting in March members decided to raise prices by 9%. In June the Conference agreed minimum and maximum prices which seemed likely to add between 15% and 20% to import bills of consumer countries. The December Conference agreed in principle to convert the OPEC Fund into a development agency with its own legal personality.

1980   In June the Conference decided to set the price for a marker crude at US $32 per barrel, and that the value differentials which could be added above this ceiling (on account of quality and geographical location) should not exceed $5 per barrel. The planned OPEC summit meeting in Baghdad in November was postponed indefinitely because of the Iran–Iraq war, but the scheduled ministerial meeting went ahead in Bali in December, with both Iranians and Iraqis present. A ceiling price of $41 per barrel was fixed for premium crudes.

1981   In May attempts to achieve price reunification were made, but Saudi Arabia refused to increase its US $32 per barrel price unless the higher prices charged by other countries were lowered. Most of the other OPEC countries agreed to cut production by 10% so as to reduce the surplus. An emergency meeting in Geneva in August again failed to unify prices, although Saudi Arabia agreed to reduce production by 1m. barrels per day (b/d). In October OPEC countries agreed to increase the Saudi marker price to $34 per barrel, with a ceiling price of $38 per barrel.

1982   The continuing world glut of petroleum forced prices below US $34 per barrel in some producer countries. In March an emergency meeting of petroleum ministers was held in Vienna and agreed (for the first time in OPEC's history) to defend the Organization's price structure by imposing an overall production ceiling of 18m. b/d. At the same time Saudi Arabia announced a reduction in its own production to 7m. b/d. In December the Conference agreed to limit OPEC production to 18.5m. b/d in 1983 but postponed the allocation of national quotas pending consultations among the respective governments.

1983   In January an emergency meeting of petroleum ministers, fearing a collapse in world petroleum prices, decided to reduce the production ceiling to 17.5m. b/d, but failed to agree on individual production quotas or on adjustments to the differentials in prices charged for the high-quality crude petroleum produced by Algeria, Libya and Nigeria compared with that produced by the Gulf States. In February Nigeria cut its prices to US $30 per barrel, following a collapse in its production. To avoid a 'price war' OPEC set the official price of marker crude at $29 per barrel, and agreed to maintain existing price differentials at the level agreed on in March 1982, with the temporary exception that the differentials for Nigerian crudes should be $1 more than the price of the marker crude. It also agreed to maintain the production ceiling of 17.5m. b/d and allocated quotas for each member country except Saudi Arabia, which was to act as a 'swing producer' to supply the balancing quantities to meet market requirements.

1984   In October the production ceiling was lowered to 16m. b/d. In December price differentials for light (more expensive) and heavy (cheaper) crudes were slightly altered in an attempt to counteract price-cutting by non-OPEC producers, particularly Norway and the United Kingdom.

1985   In January members (except Algeria, Iran and Libya) effectively abandoned the marker price system. During the year production in excess of quotas by OPEC members, unofficial discounts and barter deals by members, and price cuts by non-members (such as Mexico, which had hitherto kept its prices in line with those of OPEC) contributed to a weakening of the market.

1986   During the first half of the year petroleum prices dropped to below US $10 per barrel. In April ministers agreed to set OPEC production at 16.7m. b/d for the third quarter of 1986 and at 17.3m. b/d for the fourth quarter. Algeria, Iran and Libya dissented. Discussions were also held with non-member countries (Angola, Egypt, Malaysia, Mexico and Oman), which agreed to co-operate in limiting production, but the United Kingdom refused to reduce its petroleum production levels. In August all members, with the exception of Iraq (which demanded to be allowed the same quota as Iran and, when this was denied it, refused to be a party to the agreement), agreed upon a return to production quotas, with the aim of cutting production to 14.8m. b/d (about 16.8m. b/d including Iraq's production) for the ensuing two months. This measure resulted in an increase in prices to about $15 per barrel, and was extended until the end of the year. In December members (with the exception of Iraq) agreed to return to a fixed pricing system at a level of $18 per barrel as the OPEC reference price, with effect from 1 February 1987. OPEC's total production for the first half 1987 was not to exceed 15.8m. b/d.

1987   In June, with prices having stabilized, the Conference decided that production during the third and fourth quarters of the year should be limited to 16.6m. b/d (including Iraq's production). However, total production continued to exceed the agreed levels. In December ministers decided to extend the existing agreement for the first half of 1988, although Iraq, once more, refused to participate.

1988   By March prices had fallen below US $15 per barrel. In April non-OPEC producers offered to reduce the volume of their petroleum exports by 5% if OPEC members would do the same. Saudi Arabia, however, refused to accept further reductions in production, saying that existing quotas should first be more strictly enforced. In June the previous production limit (15.06m. b/d, excluding Iraq's production) was again renewed for six months, in the hope that increasing demand would be sufficient to raise prices. By October, however, petroleum prices were below $12 per barrel. OPEC members (excluding Iraq) were estimated to be producing about 21m. b/d. In November a new agreement was reached, limiting total production (including that of Iraq) to 18.5m. b/d, with effect from 1 January 1989. Iran and Iraq finally agreed to accept identical quotas.

1989   In June (when prices had returned to about US $18 per barrel) ministers agreed to increase the production limit to 19.5m. b/d for the second half of 1989. However, Kuwait and the UAE indicated that they would not feel bound to observe this limit. In September the production limit was again increased, to 20.5m. b/d, and in November the limit for the first half of 1990 was increased to 22m. b/d.

1990   In May those members that had been exceeding their quotas declared that they would reduce their production to the agreed limit, in response to a decline in prices of some 25% since the beginning of the year. By late June, however, it was reported that total production had decreased by only 400,000 b/d, and prices remained at about US$14 per barrel. In July Iraq threatened to take military action against Kuwait unless it reduced its petroleum production. In the same month OPEC members agreed to limit output to 22.5m. b/d. In August Iraq invaded Kuwait, and petroleum exports by the two countries were halted by an international embargo. Petroleum prices immediately increased to exceed $25 per barrel. Later in the month an informal consultative meeting of OPEC ministers placed the July agreement in abeyance, and permitted a temporary increase in production of petroleum, of between 3m. and 3.5m. b/d (mostly by Saudi Arabia, the UAE and Venezuela). In September and October prices fluctuated in response to political developments in the Gulf region, reaching a point in excess of $40 per barrel in early October, but falling to about $25 per barrel by the end of the month. In December a meeting of OPEC members voted to maintain the high levels of production and to reinstate the quotas that had been agreed in July, once the Gulf crisis was over. During the period August 1990–February 1991 Saudi Arabia increased its petroleum output from 5.4m. to 8.5m. b/d. Seven of the other OPEC states also produced in excess of their agreed quotas. It was estimated that OPEC producers' revenues from petroleum sales rose by 40% in 1990, owing to increased prices and panic buying by consumer countries.

1991 In the first quarter OPEC members were producing about 23m. b/d, and the average price of petroleum was US $19 per barrel, before dropping further to $17.5 per barrel in the second quarter. In an attempt to reach the target of a minimum reference price of $21 per barrel, ministers agreed in March to reduce production from 23m. b/d to 22.3m. b/d, although Saudi Arabia refused to return to its pre-August 1990 quota. In June ministers decided to maintain the ceiling of 22.3m. b/d into the third quarter of the year, since Iraq and Kuwait were still unable to export their petroleum. In September it was agreed that OPEC members' production for the last quarter of 1991 should be raised to 23.65m. b/d, and in November the OPEC Conference decided to maintain the increased production ceiling during the first quarter of 1992. From early November, however, the price of petroleum declined sharply, with demand less than anticipated as a result of continuing world recession and a mild winter in the northern hemisphere.

1992 The Ministerial Monitoring Committee, meeting in February, decided to impose a production ceiling of 22.98m. b/d with immediate effect. The agreement was, however, repudiated by both Saudi Arabia, which stated that it would not abide by its allocated quota of 7.9m. b/d, and Iran, unhappy that the production ceiling had not been set lower. In May it was agreed to continue the production restriction of 22.98m. b/d during the third quarter of 1992. Kuwait, which was resuming production in the wake of the extensive damage inflicted on its oil-wells by Iraq during the Gulf War, was granted a special dispensation to produce without a fixed quota. During the first half of 1992 member states' petroleum output consistently exceeded agreed levels, with Saudi Arabia and Iran (despite its stance on reducing production) the principal overproducers. In June, at the UN Conference on Environment and Development, OPEC's Secretary-General expressed its member countries' strong objections to the tax on fossil fuels (designed to reduce pollution) proposed by the EC. In September negotiations between OPEC ministers in Geneva were complicated by Iran's alleged annexation of Abu Musa and two other islands in the territorial waters of the UAE. However, agreement was reached on a production ceiling of 24.2m. b/d for the final quarter of 1992, in an attempt to raise the price of crude petroleum to the OPEC target of $21 per barrel. At the Conference, held in late November, Ecuador formally resigned from OPEC, the first country ever to do so, citing as reasons the high membership fee and OPEC's refusal to increase Ecuador's quota. The meeting agreed to restrict production to 24.58m. b/d for the first quarter of 1993 (24.46m. b/d, excluding Ecuador).

1993 In mid-February a quota was set for Kuwait for the first time since the onset of the Gulf crisis. Kuwait agreed to a quota of 1.6m. b/d (400,000 less than current output) from 1 March, on the understanding that it would be substantially increased in the third quarter of the year. The quota for overall production from 1 March was set at 23.58m. b/d. A Ministerial Monitoring Sub-committee was established to ensure compliance with quotas. In June OPEC ministers decided to 'roll over' the overall quota of 23.58m. b/d into the third quarter of the year. However, Kuwait rejected its new allocation of 1.76m. b/d, demanding a quota of at least 2m. In July discussions between Iraq and the UN on the possible supervised sale of Iraqi petroleum depressed petroleum prices to below $16 per barrel. The Monitoring Sub-committee urged member states to adhere to their production quotas (which were exceeded by a total of 1m. b/d in July). At the end of September an extraordinary meeting of the Conference was convened in Geneva. Members agreed on a raised production ceiling of 24.52m. b/d, to be effective for six months from 1 October. Kuwait accepted a quota of 2m. b/d, which brought the country back into the production ceiling mechanism. Iran agreed on an allocation of 3.6m. b/d, while Saudi Arabia consented to freeze production at current levels. The accord was intended effectively to lower production by ensuring that countries did not exceed their quotas, and thus boost petroleum prices which remained persistently low. In November the Conference rejected any further reduction in production. Prices subsequently fell below $14, owing partly to a decision by Iraq to allow the UN to monitor its weapons programme (a move that would consequently lead to a repeal of the UN embargo on Iraqi petroleum exports) and reached a low point of $12.87 per barrel.

1994 Prices remained depressed during the first quarter of the year. In March, ministers opted to maintain the output quotas, agreed in September 1993, until the end of the year, and urged non-OPEC producers to freeze their production levels. (Iraq failed to endorse the agreement, since it recognizes only the production agreement adopted in July 1990.) At the meeting Saudi Arabia resisted a proposal from Iran and Nigeria, both severely affected by declines in petroleum revenue, to reduce its production by 1m. b/d in order to boost prices. In June the Conference endorsed the decision to maintain the existing production ceiling, and attempted to reassure commodity markets by implying that the production agreement would remain in effect until the end of 1994. Ministers acknowledged that there had been a gradual increase in petroleum prices in the second quarter of the year, with an average basket price of $15.6 per barrel for that period. Political disruption in Nigeria, including a strike by petroleum workers, was considered to be the principal factor contributing to the price per barrel rising above $19 in August. In November OPEC ministers endorsed a proposal by Saudi Arabia to maintain the existing production quota, of 24.52m. b/d, until the end of 1995. At the Conference ministers elected Dr Rilwanu Lukman of Nigeria as the new Secretary-General, with effect from January 1995.

1995 In January it was reported that Gabon was reconsidering its membership of OPEC, owing to difficulties in meeting its budget contribution. During the first half of the year Gabon consistently exceeded its quota of 287,000 b/d, by 48,000 b/d, and the country failed to send a delegate to the ministerial Conference in June. At mid-1995 efforts were continuing in order to assess different options regarding the issue of membership subscriptions, including Gabon's proposal that they be linked to production; however, the problem remained unresolved. At the June Conference ministers expressed concern at OPEC's falling share of the world petroleum market. The Conference criticized the high level of North Sea production, by Norway and the United Kingdom, and urged collective production restraint in order to stimulate prices. In November the Conference agreed to extend the existing production quota, of 24.52m. b/d, for a further six months, in order to stabilize prices. During the year, however, output remained in excess of the production quotas, by between 500,000 b/d and 1.06m. b/d according to different estimates, and averaged some 25.58m. b/d.

1996 The possibility of a UN-Iraqi agreement permitting limited petroleum sales dominated OPEC concerns in the first half of the year and contributed to price fluctuations in the world markets. By early 1996 output by OPEC countries was estimated to be substantially in excess of quota levels; however, the price per barrel remained relatively buoyant (the average basket price reaching US $21 in March), owing largely to unseasonal cold weather in the northern hemisphere (stimulating demand). In May a memorandum of understanding was signed between Iraq and the UN to allow the export of petroleum, up to a value of $2,000m. over a six-month period, in order to fund humanitarian relief efforts within that country. In June the ministerial Conference agreed to increase the overall output ceiling by 800,000 b/d, i.e. the anticipated level of exports from Iraq in the first six months of the agreement. A proposal, endorsed by Iran, to raise the individual country quotas failed to win support, while a comprehensive reduction in output, in order to accommodate the Iraqi quota without adjusting the existing production ceiling, was also rejected, notably by Saudi Arabia and Venezuela. At the meeting Gabon's withdrawal from the Organization was confirmed. As a result of these developments, the new ceiling was set at 25.03m. b/d. It was agreed that, under the Monitoring Sub-committee, stricter efforts would be made to endorse the production agreement and to act against countries that persistently exceeded their quotas. Independent market observers expressed concern that, without any formal agreement to reduce overall production and given the actual widespread violation of the quota system, the renewed export of Iraqi petroleum would substantially depress petroleum prices. However, the markets remained stable as implementation of the UN-Iraqi agreement was delayed. In September the monitoring group acknowledged that members were exceeding their production quotas, but declined to impose any punitive measures (owing to the steady increase in petroleum prices). In late November the Conference agreed to maintain the existing production quota for a further six months. Also in November, Iraq accepted certain disputed technical terms of the UN agreement (for example, the freedom of movement of UN inspectors), enabling the export of petroleum to commence in December.

1997 During the first half of the year petroleum prices declined, reaching a low of US $16.7 per barrel in early April, owing to the Iraqi exports, depressed world demand and persistent overproduction. In June the Conference agreed to extend the existing production ceiling, of 25.03m. b/d, for a further six-month period. Member states resolved to adhere to their individual quotas in order to reduce the cumulative excess production of an estimated 2m. b/d; however, Venezuela, which (some sources claimed) was producing almost 800,000 b/d over its quota of 2.4m. b/d, declined to co-operate. An escalation in political tensions in the Gulf region in October, in particular Iraq's reluctance to co-operate with UN inspectors, prompted an increase in the price of crude petroleum to some $21.2 per barrel. Price fluctuations ensued, although there was a general downward trend. In November the OPEC Conference, meeting in Jakarta, approved a proposal by Saudi Arabia, to increase the overall production ceiling by some 10%, with effect from 1 January 1998, in order to meet the perceived stable world demand and to reflect more accurately current output levels. At the same time the Iranian Government announced its intention to increase its production capacity and maintain its share of the quota by permitting foreign companies to conduct petroleum exploration in Iran.

1998 At the start of the year there was widespread concern that the decision to increase production to 27.5m. b/d, coinciding with the prospect of a decline in demand from Asian economies that had been undermined by extreme financial difficulties and speculation that a new Iraqi agreement with the UN would provide for increased petroleum exports, was having an adverse effect on prices, which declined to US $14.78 per barrel in late January. A meeting of the Monitoring Sub-committee, in late January, urged members to implement production restraint and resolved to send a monitoring team to member states to encourage compliance with the agreed quotas. In February the UN Security Council approved a new agreement permitting Iraq to export petroleum valued at up to $5,200m. over a six-month period, although the Iraqi Government insisted that its production and export capacity was some $4,000m. Indonesia requested an emergency meeting of ministers to discuss this development and the ongoing decline in petroleum prices. Saudi Arabia rejected the proposal unless member states agreed to adhere to their

quotas, with particular reference to Venezuela, which was still OPEC's largest over-producer. In March Saudi Arabia, Venezuela and Mexico announced a joint agreement to reduce domestic production by 300,000 b/d, 200,000 b/d and 100,000 b/d respectively, with effect from 1 April, and agreed to co-operate in persuading other petroleum producing countries to commit to similar reductions. At the end of March an emergency ministerial meeting ratified the reduction proposals (the so-called 'Riyadh Pact'), which amounted to 1.245m. b/d pledged by OPEC members and 270,000 b/d by non-member states. Nevertheless, prices remained low, with over-production, together with lack of market confidence in member states' willingness to comply with the restricted quotas, an outstanding concern. In June Saudi Arabia, Venezuela and Mexico reached agreement on further reductions in output of some 450,000 b/d. Later in that month the OPEC Conference, having reviewed the market situation, agreed to implement a new reduction in total output of some 1.36m b/d, with effect from 1 July, reducing the total production target for OPEC members to 24.387m. b/d. Iran, which had been criticized for not adhering to the reductions agreed in March, confirmed that it would reduce output by 305,000 b/d. At the meeting, which was attended by senior officials from Mexico, Oman and Russia, Saudi Arabia proposed the establishment of a new *ad hoc* grouping of the world's largest petroleum producers, in order to monitor output and support price initiatives. In early August petroleum prices fell below $12 per barrel, reaching their lowest level since 1988. Saudi Arabia announced that it would commit to further production restrictions later in the year.

FINANCE

Total expenditure in 1997 amounted to 178.9m. Austrian Schillings.

PUBLICATIONS

Annual Report.
Annual Statistical Bulletin.
Monthly Oil Market Report.
OPEC Bulletin (monthly).
OPEC Review (quarterly).
Reports, information papers, press releases.

OPEC FUND FOR INTERNATIONAL DEVELOPMENT

Address: POB 995, 1011 Vienna, Austria.
Telephone: (1) 515-64-0; **telex:** 131734; **fax:** (1) 513-92-38.
The Fund was established by OPEC member countries in 1976.

MEMBERS
Member countries of OPEC (q.v.).

Organization
(August 1998)

ADMINISTRATION
The Fund is administered by a Ministerial Council and a Governing Board. Each member country is represented on the Council by its minister of finance. The Board consists of one representative and one alternate for each member country.
Chairman, Ministerial Council: Dr BAMBANG SUBIANTO (Indonesia).
Chairman, Governing Board: Dr SALEH AL-OMAIR (Saudi Arabia).
Director-General of the Fund: Dr YESUFU SEYYID ABDULAI (Nigeria).

FINANCIAL STRUCTURE
The resources of the Fund, whose unit of account is the US dollar, consist of contributions by OPEC member countries, and income received from operations or otherwise accruing to the Fund.
The initial endowment of the Fund amounted to US $800m. Its resources have been replenished three times, and have been further increased by the profits accruing to seven OPEC member countries through the sales of gold held by the International Monetary Fund. The pledged contributions to the OPEC Fund amounted to

$3,435.0m. at the end of 1997, and paid-in contributions totalled $2,860.2m.

Activities

The OPEC Fund for International Development is a multilateral agency for financial co-operation and assistance. Its objective is to reinforce financial co-operation between OPEC member countries and other developing countries through the provision of financial support to the latter on appropriate terms, to assist them in their economic and social development. The Fund was conceived as a collective financial facility which would consolidate the assistance extended by its member countries; its resources are additional to those already made available through other bilateral and multilateral aid agencies of OPEC members. It is empowered to:

(*i*) Provide concessional loans for balance-of-payments support;

(*ii*) Provide concessional loans for the implementation of development projects and programmes;

(*iii*) Make contributions and/or provide loans to eligible international agencies; and

(*iv*) Finance technical assistance and research through grants.

The eligible beneficiaries of the Fund's assistance are the governments of developing countries other than OPEC member countries, and international development agencies whose beneficiaries are developing countries. The Fund gives priority to the countries with the lowest income.

The Fund may undertake technical, economic and financial appraisal of a project submitted to it, or entrust such an appraisal to an appropriate international development agency, the executing national agency of a member country, or any other qualified agency. Most projects financed by the Fund have been co-financed by other development finance agencies. In each such case, one of the co-financing agencies may be appointed to administer the Fund's loan in association with its own. This practice has enabled the Fund to extend its lending activities to more than 104 countries over a short period of time and in a simple way, with the aim of avoiding duplication and complications. As its experience grew, the Fund increasingly resorted to parallel, rather than joint financing, taking up separate project components to be financed according to its rules and policies. In addition, it started to finance some projects completely on its own. These trends necessitated the issuance in 1982 of guidelines for the procurement of goods and services under the Fund's loans, allowing for a margin of preference for goods and services of local origin or originating in other developing countries: the general principle of competitive bidding is, however, followed by the Fund. The loans are not tied to procurement from Fund member countries or from any other countries. The margin of preference for goods and services obtainable in developing countries is allowed on the request of the borrower and within defined limits. Fund assistance in the form of programme loans has a broader coverage than project lending. Programme loans are used to stimulate an economic sector or sub-sector, and assist recipient countries in obtaining inputs, equipment and spare parts. Besides extending loans for project and programme financing and balance of payments support, the Fund also undertakes other operations, including grants in support of technical assistance and other activities (mainly research), and financial contributions to other international institutions.

OPEC FUND COMMITMENTS AND DISBURSEMENTS IN 1997 (US $ million)

	Commitments	Disbursements
Lending operations:	235.03	95.13
Project financing	210.30	91.25
Programme financing	24.73	3.88
Grant Programme	5.35	3.71
Technical assistance	2.13	1.77
Research and other activities	0.14	0.16
Emergency aid	2.02	1.58
Common Fund for Commodities	1.06	0.21
Total	240.37	98.85

The Fund's thirteenth lending programme, covering a two-year period effective from 1 January 1998, aimed, in particular, to target 71 developing countries. By the end of December 1997 the Fund had extended 752 loans since operations began in 1976, totalling US $3,825.5m., of which $2,808.0m. (or 73.4%) was for project financing, $724.2m. (18.9%) was for balance-of-payments support and $293.3m. (7.7%) was for programme financing.

Direct loans are supplemented by grants to support technical assistance, food aid and research. By the end of December 1997 446 grants, amounting to US $236.5m., had been extended, including $83.6m. to the Common Fund for Commodities (established by UNCTAD), and a special contribution of $20m. to the International Fund for Agricultural Development (IFAD). In addition, the Fund had committed $971.9m. to other international institutions by the end of 1997, comprising OPEC members' contributions to the resources of IFAD, and irrevocable transfers in the name of its members to the IMF Trust Fund. By the end of 1997 69.3% of total commitments had been disbursed.

During the year ending 31 December 1997 the Fund's total commitments amounted to US $240.4m. (compared with $161.5m. in 1996). These commitments included 33 project loans, amounting to $210.3m., and two loans to finance commodity import programmes in Guyana and Niger, totalling $24.7m. The largest proportion of project loans (24.3%) was to support improvements in the transportation sector in seven countries and included rehabilitation work at Durres Port in Albania, construction of a railway bridge in Bangladesh and road upgrading schemes in Bolivia, Kenya, Tanzania, Togo and the Philippines. The agriculture and agro-industry sector received 22.8% of loans, financing, amongst others, irrigated agriculture in Mauritania, Zimbabwe and Mali, rural development in Morocco and the construction of storage facilities in Cameroon, Chad and Syria. Education loans (19.6% of the total) aimed to help upgrade and strengthen teaching facilities in seven countries, namely Bosnia and Herzegovina, The Gambia, Kyrgyzstan, Madagascar, Myanmar, Nicaragua and Zambia. Five health projects (15.2%) were approved to build or rehabilitate hospitals and health centres in Egypt, Guatemala, Jordan, Malawi and Tajikistan. Loans for water supply and sewerage (4.8%) were awarded to Cape Verde, to improve sanitation and drinking water supplies in its tourist areas,

Project loans approved in 1997 (US $ million)

Region and country	Sector	Loans approved
Africa		102.50
Cameroon	Agriculture and agro-industry	4.85
Cape Verde	Water supply and sewerage	4.00
Chad	Agriculture and agro-industry	5.10
Egypt	Health	10.00
Eritrea	Water supply and sewerage	6.00
The Gambia	Education	1.50
Kenya	Transportation	5.00
Madagascar	Education	10.00
Malawi	Health	7.00
Mali	Agriculture and agro-industry	6.00
Mauritania	Agriculture and agro-industry	3.00
Morocco	Agriculture and agro-industry	7.05
Mozambique	Agriculture and agro-industry	10.00
Tanzania	Transportation	6.00
Togo	Transportation	6.00
Zambia	Education	5.00
Zimbabwe	Agriculture and agro-industry	6.00
Asia		75.80
Bangladesh	Transportation	15.00
Jordan	Health	5.00
Kyrgyzstan	Education	5.00
Myanmar	Education	5.80
Nepal	Telecommunications	8.00
Palestine	Other (community development)	10.00
Philippines	Transportation	10.00
Syria	Agriculture and agro-industry	6.00
Tajikistan	Health	5.00
Yemen	Other (social development fund)	6.00
Latin America		17.00
Bolivia	Transportation	4.00
Guatemala	Health	5.00
Nicaragua	Education	4.00
Peru	National development banks	4.00
Europe		15.00
Albania	Transportation	5.00
Bosnia and Herzegovina	Education	10.00
Total		210.30

and to Eritrea, to increase supplies of drinking water in the capital, Asmara. The telecommunications sector received one loan (3.8%) to expand Nepal's rural telephone network. In the sector of national development banks (1.9%), a line of credit worth $4m. was extended to Peru to encourage the growth of micro-enterprises. Two other loans (7.6%) were approved for the rehabilitation of Palestinian social and economic infrastructure and in support of Yemen's Social Fund for Development.

During 1997 the Fund approved US $5.35m. for 31 grants, of which $2.1m. was for technical assistance activities, $135,000 for research, $2.0m. in emergency assistance (extended to Bangladesh, Ethiopia, Indonesia, Iran, the Democratic People's Republic of Korea, Somalia, Venezuela and Viet Nam following natural disasters) and $1.1m. representing Myanmar's subscription to the Common Fund for Commodities.

PUBLICATIONS

Annual Report (in Arabic, English, French and Spanish).
OPEC Aid and OPEC Aid Institutions — A Profile (annually).
OPEC Fund Newsletter (3 a year).
Occasional books and papers.

OTHER REGIONAL ORGANIZATIONS

These organizations are arranged under the following sub-headings:

Agriculture
Commodities
Development and Economic Co-operation
Education, Arts and Sport
Finance and Economics
Government and Politics

Industrial Relations
Law
Medicine and Health
Post and Telecommunications
Religion and Welfare
Science and Technology

Social Sciences and Social
    Welfare
Trade and Industry
Transport

(See also lists of subsidiary bodies in the chapters on the main regional organizations, e.g. Council of Arab Economic Unity, League of Arab States, OIC, etc.; and the list of Research Institutes, p. 188.)

AGRICULTURE

Arab Authority for Agricultural Investment and Development—AAAID: POB 2102, Khartoum, Sudan; tel. 773752; telex 23017; fax 772600; f. 1976 to accelerate agricultural development in the Arab world and to ensure food security; acts principally by equity participation in agricultural projects, in Iraq, Sudan and Tunisia; auth. cap. US $500.0m., paid-in cap. $333.4m. (Dec. 1996). Mems: Algeria, Egypt, Iraq, Jordan, Kuwait, Mauritania, Morocco, Oman, Qatar, Saudi Arabia, Somalia, Sudan, Syria, Tunisia, United Arab Emirates. Pres. Dr YOUSIF ABD AL-LATIF ALSERKAL.

International Centre for Agricultural Research in the Dry Areas—ICARDA: POB 5466, Aleppo, Syria; tel. (21) 213433; telex 331206; fax (21) 213490; e-mail icarda@cgnet.com; internet http://www.cgiar.org/icarda/; f. 1977; aims to improve agricultural productivity, in particular in countries of west Asia and north Africa; activities include water management, cereal and legume improvement, farming systems improvement and recovery of degraded rangelands; member of the network of agricultural research centres supported by the Consultative Group on International Agricultural Research (CGIAR). Mems in 52 countries. Dir-Gen. Dr ADEL EL-BELTAGY. Publs *Annual Report, Faba Bean Information Service Newsletter* (2 a year), *Barley and Wheat Newsletter* (2 a year), *Lentil Experimental News Service Newsletter* (2 a year), *Caravan Newsletter*.

COMMODITIES

African Petroleum Producers' Association—APPA: BP 1097, Brazzaville, Republic of the Congo; tel. 83-64-38; telex 5552; fax 83-67-99; f. 1987 by African petroleum-producing countries to reinforce co-operation among regional producers and to stabilize prices; council of ministers responsible for the hydrocarbons sector of each country meets twice a year. Mems: Algeria, Angola, Benin, Cameroon, the Dem. Repub. of the Congo, Repub. of the Congo, Côte d'Ivoire, Egypt, Equatorial Guinea, Gabon, Nigeria. Presidency rotates. Publ. *APPA Bulletin* (2 a year).

International Grains Council: 1 Canada Sq., Canary Wharf, London, E14 5AE, United Kingdom; tel. (171) 513-1122; fax (171) 513-0630; e-mail igc-fac@igc.org.uk; internet http://www.igc.org.uk; f. 1949 as International Wheat Council, present name adopted in 1995; responsible for the admin. of the Grains Trade Convention of the International Grains Agreement, 1995; aims to further international co-operation in all aspects of trade in grains, to promote international trade in grains, and to secure the freest possible flow of this trade in the interests of mems, particularly developing mem. countries; and to contribute to the stability of the international grain market; acts as forum for consultations between mems, and provides comprehensive information on the international grain market and factors affecting it. Mems: 33 countries and the EU. Exec. Dir G. DENIS. Publs *World Grain Statistics* (annually), *Wheat amd Coarse Grain Shipments* (annually), *Report for the Fiscal Year* (annually), *Grain Market Report* (monthly).

International Olive Oil Council: Príncipe de Vergara 154, Madrid 28002, Spain; tel. (91) 5903638; fax (91) 5631263; e-mail iooc@mad.servicom.es; f. 1959 to administer the International Agreement on Olive Oil and Table Olives, the objectives of which are as follows: to promote international co-operation in connection with problems of the world economy for olive products; to prevent the occurrence of any unfair competition in the world olive products trade; to encourage the production and consumption of, and international trade in, olive products, and to reduce the disadvantages due to fluctuations of supplies on the market. Mems: of the 1986 Agreement (Fourth Agreement), as amended and extended, 1993: Algeria, Cyprus, Egypt, Israel, Lebanon, Morocco, Tunisia, Turkey, Yugoslavia (Serbia and Montenegro) and the 15 member countries of the EU. Dir FAUSTO LUCHETTI. Publs *Information Sheet* (fortnightly, French and Spanish), *OLIVAE* (5 a year, in English, French, Italian and Spanish), *National Policies for Olive Products* (annually), economic and technical studies, etc.

DEVELOPMENT AND ECONOMIC CO-OPERATION

African Training and Research Centre in Administration for Development (Centre africain de formation et de recherche administratives pour le développement—CAFRAD): Pavillon International, BP 310, Tangiers, Morocco; tel. (9) 942652; fax (9) 941415; e-mail cafradt@mail.sis.net.ma; f. 1964 by agreement between Morocco and UNESCO; undertakes research into administrative problems in Africa, documentation of results, provision of a consultation service for governments and organizations; holds frequent seminars; library of 20,000 vols. Mems: 27 African states. Pres. MESSAOUD MANSOURI; Dir-Gen. Dr M. A. WALI. Publs *Cahiers Africains d'Administration Publique* (2 a year), *African Administrative Studies* (2 a year), *Documents and Studies, Répertoire des Consultants, CAFRAD News* (3 a year in English, French and Arabic).

Afro-Asian Housing Organization—AAHO: POB 5623, 28 Ramses Ave, Cairo, Egypt; f. 1965 to promote co-operation between African and Asian countries in housing, reconstruction, physical planning and related matters. Mems: 18 countries. Sec.-Gen. HASSAN M. HASSAN (Egypt).

Afro-Asian Rural Reconstruction Organization—AARRO: Plot No. 2, State Guest House Complex (Near Chanakyapuri Telephone Exchange), Chanakyapuri, New Delhi 110021, India; tel. (11) 6877783; fax (11) 6115937; e-mail aarrohq@nde.vsnl.net.in; f. 1962 to act as catalyst for co-operative restructuring of rural life in Africa and Asia; to explore collectively opportunities for co-ordination of efforts for promoting welfare and eradicating hunger, thirst, disease, illiteracy and poverty amongst the rural people; and to assist the formation of organizations of farmers and other rural people. Activities include collaborative research on development issues; training; assistance in forming organizations of farmers and other rural people; the exchange of information; international conferences and seminars; and awarding 100 individual training fellowships at nine institutes in Egypt, India, Japan, the Republic of Korea and Taiwan. Mems: 11 African, 14 Asian and one African associate. Sec.-Gen. Dr BAHAR MUNIP. Publs *Annual Report, Rural Reconstruction* (2 a year), *AARRO Newsletter* (quarterly), conference and committee reports.

Arab Co-operation Council: Amman, Jordan; f. 1989 to promote economic co-operation between member states, including free movement of workers, joint projects in transport, communications and agriculture, and eventual integration of trade and monetary policies. Mems: Egypt, Iraq, Jordan, Yemen. Sec.-Gen. HELMI NAMRAR (Egypt).

Arab Gulf Programme for the United Nations Development Organizations—AGFUND: POB 18371, Riyadh 11415, Saudi Arabia; tel. (1) 441-6240; fax (1) 441-2963; e-mail agfund@khaleej.net.bh; f. 1981 to provide grants (not exceeding 50% of project costs) for projects in mother and child care undertaken by the United Nations, Arab non-governmental organizations and other international bodies, and to co-ordinate assistance by the nations of the Gulf; between 1981 and January 1996 AGFUND committed a total of over US $185m. for the benefit of 119 countries. Mems: Bahrain, Iraq, Kuwait, Oman, Qatar, Saudi Arabia, United Arab Emirates. Pres. HRH Prince TALAL IBN ABDUL AZIZ AL-SAUD.

Community of the Sahel-Saharan States Communauté des Etats du Sahel et du Sahara—COMESSA): Tripoli, Libya; f. 1997; aims to strengthen co-operation between signatory states; established a joint commission with the OAU, in 1998, to support mediation in the conflicts between Eritrea and Ethiopia; mems. Burkina Faso, Chad, Egypt, Libya, Mali, Niger, Sudan, Tunisia. Sec.-Gen. ALMADANI AL-AZHARI (Libya).

Developing Eight—D-8: Atik Ali Paşa Yalısı, Cırağan Cad. 80, Beşiktaş, İstanbul, Turkey; tel. (212) 2275610; fax (212) 2275613; inaugurated at a meeting of Heads of State in June 1997; aims to foster economic co-operation between member states and to strengthen the role of developing countries in the global economy; project areas include trade and industry, agriculture, human resources, telecommunications, rural development, and privatizations, banking and Islamic insurance. Second summit meeting scheduled to be convened in Dhaka, Bangladesh, in December 1997. Mems: Bangladesh, Egypt, Iran, Indonesia, Malaysia, Nigeria, Pakistan, Turkey.

Economic Co-operation Organization—ECO: 1 Golbou Alley, Kamranieh St, POB 14155-6176, Teheran, Iran; tel. (21) 283-1731; telex 213774; fax (21) 283-1732; f. 1985 (as successor to Regional Co-operation for Development, f. 1964); originally a tripartite arrangement (between Iran, Pakistan and Turkey) aiming to promote regional economic co-operation between member states; seven new members admitted in Nov. 1992; main areas of co-operation are transport (including the building of road and rail lines), telecommunications and post, trade and investment, energy (including the interconnection of power grids in the region), minerals and environmental issues, industry and agriculture, with long-term priorities defined in terms of action plans: the Quetta Plan of Action, the İstanbul Declaration, the Almaty Outline Plan and the Economic Co-operation Strategy. A joint Chamber of Commerce and Industry was established in 1990. The first summit meeting of heads of state of member countries was held in February 1992. The third ECO summit meeting held in Islamabad, Pakistan, in March 1995, endorsed decisions to establish an ECO Trade and Development Bank in İstanbul, a joint shipping company and airline in Iran and an ECO Reinsurance Company in Pakistan. The meeting also approved the establishment of an ECO Cultural Institute in Iran and an ECO Science Foundation in Pakistan, and agreed to strengthen co-operation among member states in the following areas: transport and communications; facilitating trade and investment; energy and ecology; and protection of the environment. The establishment of an ECO eminent persons group was endorsed by the meeting. An extraordinary meeting of the ECO Council of Ministers was held in Izmir, Turkey, in September 1996, at which member countries signed a revised Treaty of Izmir, the Organization's fundamental charter. An extraordinary summit meeting, held in Ashgabat, Turkmenistan, in May 1997, emphasized the importance of the development of the transport and communications infrastructure and the network of transnational pipelines in the ECO region. In May 1998, at the fifth summit meeting, held in Almaty, Kazakhstan, ECO heads of state signed a Transit Transport Framework Agreement and a memorandum of understanding to help counter cross-border trafficking of illegal goods. The meeting also agreed to establish an ECO Educational Institute in Ankara, Turkey. ECO works with several UN agencies and other international organizations in development-related activities and has been granted observer status at the UN and the OIC. Mems: Afghanistan, Azerbaijan, Iran, Kazakhstan, Kyrgyzstan, Pakistan, Tajikistan, Turkey, Turkmenistan, Uzbekistan; the 'Turkish Republic of Northern Cyprus' has been granted special guest status in the organization. Sec.-Gen. ONDER OZAR (Turkey).

Economic Research Forum for the Arab Countries, Iran and Turkey: Cairo, Egypt; f. 1993 to conduct in-depth economic research, compile an economic database for the region, and provide training; Dir HEBA HANDOUSSA (Egypt).

Indian Ocean Rim Association for Regional Co-operation—IOR-ARC: Mauritius; the first intergovernmental meeting of countries in the region to promote an Indian Ocean Rim initiative was convened in March 1995; charter to establish the Assoc. signed at a ministerial meeting in March 1997; aims to promote regional economic co-operation through trade, investment, infrastructure, tourism, science and technology. Mems: Australia, India, Indonesia, Kenya, Madagascar, Malaysia, Mauritius, Mozambique, Oman, Singapore, South Africa, Sri Lanka, Tanzania and Yemen. Interim Chair. PAUL RAYMOND BÉRENGER (Mauritius).

Union of the Arab Maghreb (Union du Maghreb arabe—UMA): 26–27 rue Okba, Agdal, Rabat, Morocco; tel. (7) 772668; telex 36488; fax (7) 772693; f. 1989; aims to encourage joint ventures and to create a single market; structure comprises a council of heads of state (meeting annually), a council of ministers of foreign affairs, a following committee, a consultative council of 30 delegates from each country, a UMA judicial court, and four specialized ministerial commissions. Chairmanship rotates annually between heads of state. By late 1994 joint projects that had been approved or were under consideration included: establishment of the Maghreb Investment and Foreign Trade Bank to fund joint agricultural and industrial projects (with a capital of US $500m.); free movement of citizens within the region; joint transport undertakings, including railway improvements and a Maghreb highway; the creation of a customs union; and the establishment of a 'North African Common Market'. The UMA represents member countries' interests in negotiations with the EU, Arab and African regional organizations, as well as other international organizations. In November 1992 member countries adopted a Maghreb charter on the protection of the environment. In April 1994, the Supreme Council, meeting in Tunis, adopted a resolution to undertake measures to establish a free trade zone. Mems: Algeria, Libya, Mauritania, Morocco, Tunisia. Sec.-Gen. MOHAMED AMAMOU (Tunisia).

EDUCATION, ARTS AND SPORT

Afro-Asian Writers' Association: 'Al Ahram' Bldg, Al-Gala'a St, Cairo, Egypt; tel (2) 5747011; telex 20185; fax (2) 5747023; f. 1958. Mems: writers' orgs in 50 countries. Sec.-Gen. LOTFI EL-KHOLY. Publs *Lotus Magazine of Afro-Asian Writings* (quarterly in English, French and Arabic), *Afro-Asian Literature Series* (in English, French and Arabic).

Alliance israélite universelle: 45 rue La Bruyère, 75425 Paris Cedex 09, France; tel. 1-55-32-88-55; fax 1-48-74-51-33; e-mail aiu@ imaginet.fr; f. 1860 to work for the emancipation and moral progress of the Jews; maintains 41 schools in the Mediterranean area and Canada; library of 120,000 vols. Mems: 8,000 in 14 countries. Pres. ADY STEG; Dir JEAN-JACQUES WAHL (France). Publs *Cahiers de l'Alliance Israélite Universelle* (3 a year), *The Alliance Review, Les Cahiers du Judaïsme* (quarterly).

Arab Bureau of Education for the Gulf States: POB 3908, Riyadh 11481, Saudi Arabia; tel. (1) 480-0555; fax (1) 480-2839; f. 1975; co-ordinates and promotes co-operation and integration among member countries in the fields of education, culture and science; aims to unify the educational systems of all Gulf Arab states. Specialized organs: Gulf Arab States' Educational Research Center (POB 25566, Safat, Kuwait), Council of Higher Education, Arabian Gulf University (opened in Bahrain in 1982). Mems: Governments of Bahrain, Kuwait, Oman, Qatar, Saudi Arabia and the United Arab Emirates. Dir-Gen. Dr ALI M. AL-TOWAGRY. Publs *Risalat Ul-Khaleej al-Arabi* (quarterly), *Arab Gulf Journal of Scientific Research* (2 a year).

Arab Sports Confederation: POB 62997, Riyadh, Saudi Arabia; tel. (1) 482-4927; telex 403099; fax (1) 482-3196; f. 1976 to encourage regional co-operation in sport. Mems: 20 national Olympic Committees, 38 Arab sports federations. Pres. Prince FAISAL BIN FAHD BIN ABD AL-AZIZ; Sec.-Gen. OTHMAN M. AL-SAAD.

Association of Arab Historians: POB 4085, Baghdad, Iraq; tel. (1) 443-8868; f. 1974. Mems: historians in 22 countries of the region. Sec.-Gen. Prof. MUSTAFA AN-NAJJAR. Publ. *Arab Historian.*

Association of Arab Universities: POB 401, Jubeyha, Amman, Jordan; tel. (6) 845131; telex 23855; fax (6) 832994; f. 1964. A scientific conference is held every 3 years; 1997: Sana'a, Yemen. Mems: 136 universities in 20 countries and territories. Sec.-Gen. Dr EHAB ISMAIL. Publs *Journal of AARU* (annually), *Directory of Arab Universities, Directory of Teaching Staff of Arab Universities.*

European Union of Arabic and Islamic Scholars (Union européenne d'Arabisants et d'Islamisants—UEAI): c/o Dipartimento di studi e ricerche su Africa e Paesi Arabi, Istituto Universitario Orientale, Palazzo Corigliano, Piazza San Domenico Maggiore 12, 80134 Naples, Italy; tel. (081) 5517840; fax (081) 5515386; f. 1962 to organize Congresses of Arabic and Islamic Studies; 1996 Congress: Leuven, Belgium, 1998 Congress: Halle, Germany. Mems: about 270 in 25 countries. Sec.-Gen. Prof. CARMELA BAFFIONI (Italy).

International Institute for Adult Education Methods: POB 19395/6194, Teheran, Iran; tel. (21) 6404272; fax (21) 6406940; f. 1968 by UNESCO and the Government of Iran; collects, analyzes and distributes information concerning the methods, media and techniques used in adult education programmes; maintains documentation service and library on adult education; arranges seminars. Dir GHOLAM ALI AFROOZ. Publ. *Adult Education and Development* (quarterly).

FINANCE

Arab Society of Certified Accountants: 23 Wadi el-Nil St, POB 96, Imbaba 12411 Mohandisseen, Cairo, Egypt; tel. (2) 3462951; fax (2) 3445729; f. 1987 as a professional body to supervise qualifications for Arab accountants and to maintain standards; organizes Arab International Accounting Conference (1998: Beirut, Lebanon). Mems in 21 countries. Pres. TALAL ABU GHAZALEH (Jordan). Publs *Arab Certified Accountant* (monthly), *ASCA Information Guide, International Accountancy Standards, International Audit Standards, Abu-Ghazaleh Dictionary of Accountancy.*

Union of Arab Banks (UAB): POB 2416, Beirut, Lebanon; tel. (1) 802968; fax (1) 867925; e-mail uab@cyberianet; f. 1972; aims to foster co-operation between Arab banks and to increase their efficiency; prepares feasibility studies for projects; 1992 Conference: Casablanca, Morocco.

Union of Arab Stock Exchanges and Securities Commissions: POB 22235, Safat 13083, Kuwait; tel. 2412991; fax 2420778; f. 1982 to develop capital markets in the Arab world; Sec.-Gen. SAFIQ AR-RUKEIBI (Kuwait).

GOVERNMENT AND POLITICS

Afro-Asian Peoples' Solidarity Organization—AAPSO: 89 Abdel Aziz al-Saoud St, POB 11559-61 Manial el-Roda, Cairo, Egypt;

tel. (2) 3636081; telex 92627; fax (2) 3637361; e-mail aapso@idsc.gov.eg; f. 1957 as the Organization for Afro-Asian Peoples' Solidarity; acts as a permanent liaison body between the peoples of Africa and Asia and aims to ensure their sovereignty, peace, disarmament and their economic, social and cultural development; congress held every four years (1992: Lebanon). Mems: 82 national committees and 10 European associates. Pres. Dr MORAD GHALEB; Sec.-Gen. NOURI ABD EL-RAZZAK (Iraq). Publs., *AAPSO Bulletin* (monthly), *Development and Socio-Economic Progress* (quarterly).

Arab Inter-Parliamentary Union: POB 4130, Damascus, Syria; tel. (11) 447654; fax (11) 234336; f. 1974; aims to strengthen dialogue between Arab parliamentarians to co-ordinate activities and representation at international forums. Mems from 15 countries. Chair. Dr MOHAMED JALAL ESSAID.

Parliamentary Association for Euro-Arab Co-operation: 21 Rue de la Tourelle, 1040 Brussels, Belgium; tel. (2) 231-13-00; fax (2) 231-06-46; e-mail paeac@medea.be; f. 1974 as an association of more than 650 parliamentarians of all parties from the national parliaments of 18 of the Council of Europe countries and from the European Parliament, to promote friendship and co-operation between Europe and the Arab world; Executive Committee (which has at least two members per country) holds annual meeting with Arab Parliamentary Union: the Euro-Arab Parliamentary Dialogue; works for the progress of the Euro-Arab Dialogue and a settlement in the Middle East which takes into account the national rights of the Palestinian people. Joint Chair. EDITHA LIMBACH (Germany), HENNING GJELLEROD (Denmark); Sec.-Gen. JEAN-MICHEL DUMONT (Belgium).

INDUSTRIAL RELATIONS

Arab Federation of Petroleum, Mining and Chemicals Workers: POB 5339, Tripoli, Libya; tel. (21) 608501; fax (21) 608989; f. 1961 to establish proper industrial relations policies and procedures for the guidance of all affiliated unions; promotes establishment of trade unions in the relevant industries in countries where they do not exist. Publs *Arab Petroleum* (monthly, in English, Arabic and French editions), specialized publications and statistics.

Arab Federation of Textile Workers: Al Fardaus St, POB 620, Damascus, Syria; tel. (11) 335592. Mems: eight organizations. Sec.-Gen. DAHER ABOU KHLEIF.

International Confederation of Arab Trade Unions—ICATU: POB 3225, Samat at-Tahir, Damascus, Syria; tel. (11) 459544; telex 411319; fax (11) 420323; f. 1956. Holds General Congress every four years. Mems: trade unions in 18 countries, and 12 affiliate international federations. Sec.-Gen. HASSAN JEMAM. Publ. *Al-Amal al-Arab* (monthly).

LAW

Arab Organization for Human Rights: 91 al-Marghany St, Heliopolis, Cairo, Egypt; tel. (2) 4181396; fax (2) 4185346; e-mail aohr@link.com.eg; f. 1983 to defend fundamental freedoms of citizens of the Arab states; assists political prisoners and their families; has consultative status with UN Economic and Social Council. General Assembly convened every three years; 1997: Rabat, Morocco. Mems in 16 regional and 14 other countries. Sec.-Gen. MOHAMMED FAYEK. Publs *Newsletter* (monthly), *Annual Report, The State of Human Rights in the Arab World, Nadwat Fikria* (series).

Asian-African Legal Consultative Committee: 27 Ring Rd, Lajpat Nagar-IV, New Delhi 110024, India; tel. (11) 6484265; fax (11) 6221344; f. 1956 to consider legal problems referred to it by member countries and to serve as a forum for Asian-African co-operation in international law and economic relations; provides background material for conferences, prepares standard/model contract forms suited to the needs of the region; promotes arbitration as a means of settling international commercial disputes; trains officers of member states. Mems: 44 states. Pres. Dr P. S. RAO (India); Sec.-Gen. TANG CHENGYUAN (China).

Union of Arab Jurists: POB 6026, al-Mansour, Baghdad, Iraq; tel. (1) 884-0051; fax (1) 884-9973; f. 1975 to safeguard the Arab legislative and judicial heritage; to facilitate contacts between Arab lawyers; to encourage the study of Islamic jurisprudence; and to defend human rights. Mems: national jurists associations in 15 countries. Sec.-Gen. Dr SHIBIB LAZIM AL-MALIKI. Publs *Al-Hukuki al-Arabi* (Arab Jurist), documents and studies.

MEDICINE AND HEALTH

International Federation of Red Cross and Red Crescent Societies: 17 Chemin des Crêts, Petit-Saconnex, CP 372, 1211 Geneva 19, Switzerland; tel. (22) 7304222; telex 412133; fax (22) 7330395; e-mail secretariat@ifrc.org; f. 1919 to prevent and alleviate human suffering and to promote humanitarian activities by national Red Cross and Red Crescent societies; conducts relief operations for refugees and victims of disasters, co-ordinates relief supplies and assists in disaster prevention; Sec.-Gen. GEORGE WEBER. Publs

Annual Report, Red Cross Red Crescent (quarterly), *Weekly News, World Disasters Report, Emergency Appeal.*

Middle East Neurosurgical Society: Neurosurgical Department, American University Medical Centre, POB 113-6044, Beirut, Lebanon; tel. (1) 353486; telex 20801; fax (1) 342517; e-mail gfhaddad@amb.edn.lb; f. 1958 to promote clinical advances and scientific research and to spread knowledge of neurosurgery and related fields among all members of the medical profession in the Middle East. Mems in 17 countries. Pres. Dr FUAD S. HADDAD; Sec. Dr GEDEON MOHASSEB.

POST AND TELECOMMUNICATIONS

Arab Permanent Postal Commission: c/o Arab League Bldg, Tahrir Sq., Cairo, Egypt; tel. (2) 5750511; fax (2) 5775626; f. 1952; aims to establish stricter postal relations between the Arab countries than those laid down by the Universal Postal Union, and to pursue the development and modernization of postal services in member countries. Publs *APU Bulletin* (monthly), *APU Review* (quarterly), *APU News* (annually).

Arab Telecommunications Union: POB 2397, Baghdad, Iraq; tel. (1) 555-0642; telex 212007; f. 1953 to co-ordinate and develop telecommunications between member countries; to exchange technical aid and encourage research; promotes establishment of new cable telecommunications networks in the region. Sec.-Gen. ABDUL JAFFAR HASSAN KHALAF IBRAHIM AL-ANI. Publs. *Arab Telecommunications Union Journal* (2 a year), *Economic and Technical Studies.*

RELIGION AND WELFARE

Bahá'í International Community: Bahá'í World Centre, POB 155, 31 001 Haifa, Israel; tel. (4) 8358394; telex 46626; fax (4) 8358522; f. 1844 in Persia to promote the unity of mankind and world peace through the teachings of the Bahá'í religion, which include the equality of men and women and the elimination of all forms of prejudice; maintains schools for children and adults worldwide, and maintains educational and cultural radio stations in the Americas; there are 31 Bahá'í Publishing Trusts in countries throughout the world. Governing body: The Universal House of Justice, consisting of nine members elected by 179 National Spiritual Assemblies. Mems in 131,933 centres worldwide. The Association for Bahá'í Studies (Ottawa, Canada) has affiliates in 27 countries. Sec.-Gen. ALBERT LINCOLN (USA); Deputy Sec.-Gen. MURRAY R. SMITH (New Zealand). Publs *The Bahá'í World* (annually), *La Pensée Bahá'íe* (quarterly), *World Order* (quarterly), *Opinioni Bahá'í* (quarterly), *One Country* (quarterly), *The Journal of Bahá'í Studies* (quarterly), *Herald of the South* (quarterly), *Bahá'í Briefe* (2 a year), *Andalib* (every 2 months).

Middle East Council of Churches: rue Makhoul, DEEB bldg, POB 5376, Beirut, Lebanon; tel. and fax (1) 344894; telex 22662; f. 1974. Mems: 24 churches in seven countries. Pres. Patriarch IGNATIUS ZAKKAI IWAS, Patriarch IGNATIUS IV, Rt Rev. SAMIR KAFITY, Archbishop YOUSUF EL-KHOURY; Gen. Sec. Rev. Dr RIAD JARJOUR. Publs *MECC News Report* (monthly), *Al Montada News Bulletin* (quarterly, in Arabic), *Courrier oecuménique du moyen-Orient* (quarterly), *MECC Perspectives* (3 a year).

Muslim World League (Rabita al-Alam al-Islami): POB 537, Mecca, Saudi Arabia; tel. (2) 5422733; telex 540009; fax (2) 5436619; e-mail mwlhq@aol.com; London office: 46 Goodge St, London W1, United Kingdom; tel. (171) 636-7568; telex 296182; f. 1962; aims to advance Islamic unity and solidarity, and to promote world peace and respect for human rights; provides financial assistance for Islamic education, medical care and relief work; has 26 offices throughout the world. Sec.-Gen. Dr ABDULLAH BIN SALEH AL-OBAID. Publs *Majalla al-Rabita* (monthly, Arabic), *Akhbar al-Alam al Islami* (weekly, Arabic), *Muslim World League Journal* (monthly, English), *Dawat al-Haq* (monthly, Arabic).

World Jewish Congress (Congrès Juif Mondial): 501 Madison Ave, New York, NY 10022, USA; tel. (212) 755-5770; fax (212) 755-5883; f. 1936 as a voluntary association of representative Jewish communities and organizations throughout the world, aiming to foster the unity of the Jewish people and to ensure the continuity and development of its religious, spiritual, cultural and social heritage. Mems: Jewish communities in 80 countries. Pres. EDGAR M. BRONFMAN; Sec.-Gen. ISRAEL SINGER. Publs *WJC Report* (New York), *Gesher* (Hebrew quarterly, Jerusalem), *Batfutstot* (Jerusalem), *Boletín Informativo OJI* (monthly, Buenos Aires).

SCIENCE AND TECHNOLOGY

African Organization of Cartography and Remote Sensing: BP 102, 16040 Hussein Dey, Algeria; tel. (2) 23-33-39; telex 65474; fax (2) 77-79-34; f. 1988 by amalgamation of African Association of Cartography and African Council for Remote Sensing; aims to encourage the development of cartography and of remote-sensing by satellites; organizes confs and other meetings, promotes establishment of training insts; maintains regional training centres in

Burkina Faso, Kenya, Nigeria and Tunisia. Mems: national cartographic institutions of 24 countries. Sec.-Gen. UNIS MUFTAH.

Federation of Arab Engineers: POB 6117, Baghdad, Iraq; tel. (1) 7762366; fax (1) 2434469; f. 1963 as Arab Engineering Union; a regional body of the World Federation of Engineering Organizations; co-operates with the Arab League, UNESCO and the other regional engineering federations. Holds a Pan-Arab conference on engineering studies every three years and annual symposia and seminars in different Arab countries. Mems: engineering asscns in 15 Arab countries; Sec.-Gen. GHASSAN A. RADHWAN.

Federation of Arab Scientific Research Councils: POB 13027, Al Karkh/Karadat Mariam, Baghdad, Iraq; tel. (1) 538-1090; telex 212466; f. 1976 to encourage co-operation in scientific research, to promote the establishment of new institutions and plan joint regional research projects. Mems: national science bodies, Governments of 15 countries. Sec.-Gen. Prof. TAHA AL-NUEIMI. Publs *Journal of Arab Scientific Research, Federation News*. Reports from conferences, seminars and workshops.

SOCIAL SCIENCES AND SOCIAL WELFARE

Arab Towns Organization—ATO: POB 68160, Kaifan, 71962, Kuwait; tel. 4849705; fax 4849322; e-mail ato@ato.net; f. 1967; aims to promote co-operation and the exchange of expertise with regard to urban administration; to improve the standard of municipal services and utilities in Arab towns; and to preserve the character and heritage of Arab towns. Administers an Institute for Urban Development (AUDI), based in Riyadh, Saudi Arabia, which provides training and research for municipal officers; the Arab Towns Development Fund, to provide financial assistance to help member towns implement projects; and the ATO Award, to encourage the preservation of Arab architecture. Mems: 413 towns. Dir-Gen. MOHAMMED ABDUL HAMID AS-SAQR; Sec.-Gen. ABD AL-AZIZ Y. AL-ADSANI. Publ. *Al-Madinah Al-Arabiyah* (every 2 months).

Centre for Social Science Research and Documentation for the Arab Region: Zamalek PO, Cairo, Egypt; tel. (2) 3472099; fax (2) 3470019; f. 1978 to encourage co-operation between regional research bodies; Mems: Egypt, Iraq, Kuwait, Saudi Arabia, Tunisia; Dir-Gen. Dr AHMAD M. KHALIFA. Publs *Newsletter* (3 a year), *Arab Comnet* (3 a year).

International Planned Parenthood Federation: Regional Office for the Arab World, 2 place Virgile, Notre Dame 1082, Tunis, Tunisia; tel. (1) 787743; telex 18106; fax (1) 789934; aims to advance education in family planning, to promote the use of family planning services through local voluntary associations, and to organize the training of service delivery providers. Member associations in Algeria, Bahrain, Egypt, Iraq, Jordan, Lebanon, Mauritania, Morocco, Palestine, Somalia, Sudan, Syria, Tunisia, Yemen. Regional Dir Dr MOHAMED BOUZIDI.

International Union for Oriental and Asian Studies: Közraktar u. 12A 11/2, 1093 Budapest, Hungary; f. 1951 by the 22nd International Congress of Orientalists under the auspices of UNESCO, to promote contacts between orientalists throughout the world, and to organize congresses, research and publications. Mems: in 24 countries. Sec.-Gen. Prof. GEORG HAZAL. Publs *Philologiae Turcicae Fundamenta, Materalien zum Sumerischen Lexikon, Sanskrit Dictionary, Corpus Inscriptionum Iranicarum, Linguistic Atlas of Iran,* *Matériels des parlers iraniens, Turcology Annual, Bibliographieegyptologique.*

Third World Forum: 39 Dokki St, POB 43, Orman, Cairo, Egypt; f. 1973 to link social scientists and others from the developing countries, to discuss alternative development policies and encourage research. Regional offices in Egypt, Mexico, Senegal and Sri Lanka. Mems: individuals in 52 countries. Chair. ISMAIL-SABRI ABDALLA.

TRADE AND INDUSTRY

Arab Iron and Steel Union—AISU: BP 4, route de Chéraga, Algiers, Algeria; tel. (2) 37-27-05; telex 71158; fax (2) 37-19-75; f. 1972 to develop commercial and technical aspects of Arab steel production by helping member associations to commercialize their production in Arab markets, guaranteeing them high quality materials and intermediary products, informing them of recent developments in the industry and organizing training sessions. Mems: 43 companies in 12 Arab countries. Gen.-Sec. MUHAMMAD LAID LACHGAR. Publs *AISU Annual Statistical Bulletin, Arab Steel Review* (monthly).

General Union of Chambers of Commerce, Industry and Agriculture for Arab Countries: POB 11-2837, Beirut, Lebanon; tel. (1) 814269; fax (1) 862841; e-mail gucciac@destination.com.lb; f. 1951 to foster Arab economic collaboration, to increase and improve production and to facilitate the exchange of technical information in Arab countries. Mems: chambers of commerce, industry and agriculture in 21 countries. Gen.-Sec. BURHAN DAJANI. Publs *Al-Omran al-Arabi* (every 2 months), *Arab Economic Report* (in Arabic and English), economic papers, proceedings of conferences and seminars.

Gulf Organization for Industrial Consulting—GOIC: POB 5114, Doha, Qatar; tel. 858888; telex 4619; fax 831465; f. 1976 by the Gulf Arab states to co-ordinate industrial development and encourage joint regional projects; undertakes feasibility studies, market diagnosis, assistance in policy-making, legal consultancies, project promotion, promotion of small and medium industrial investment profiles and technical training. Mems: member states of the Gulf Co-operation Council (q.v.). Sec.-Gen. Dr ABDUL RAHMAN A. AL-JAFARY (Saudi Arabia). Publs *GOIC Monthly Bulletin* (Arabic and English), *Al Ta' Awon al-Sinaie* (quarterly, in Arabic and English), *Annual Report*.

TRANSPORT

Arab Air Carriers' Organization—AACO: POB 13-5468, Beirut, Lebanon; tel. (1) 861297; fax (1) 603140; e-mail aaco@dn.net.lb; f. 1965 to co-ordinate and promote co-operation in the activities of Arab airline companies. Mems: 18 Arab air carriers. Pres. MOHAMED FAHIM RAYAN (Egypt); Sec.-Gen. ABDUL WAHAB TEFFAHA. Publs monthly statistical bulletins and research documents on aviation in the Arab world.

Arab Union of Railways: POB 6599, Aleppo, Syria; tel. (21) 220302; telex 331009; f. 1979 to stimulate and co-ordinate the development of Arab railways, particularly regional and international railway links. Mems: railway companies and organizations in Algeria, Egypt, Iraq, Jordan, Lebanon, Morocco, Palestine, Syria and Tunisia. Eighth symyposium: Beirut, Lebanon, 1997. Sec.-Gen. MOURHAF SABOUNI. Publs *As-Sikak al-Arabiye* (Arab Railways, quarterly), *Statistics of Arab Railways* (annually), glossary of railway terms in Arabic, French, English and German.

INDEX OF REGIONAL ORGANIZATIONS

(main references only)

PART THREE

Country Surveys

ALGERIA

Physical and Social Geography

Algeria is the largest of the three countries in north-west Africa that comprise the Maghreb, as the region of mountains, valleys and plateaux that lies between the sea and the Sahara desert is known. It is situated between Morocco and Tunisia, with a Mediterranean coastline of nearly 1,000 km and a total area of some 2,381,741 sq km, over four-fifths of which lies south of the Maghreb proper and within the western Sahara. Its extent, both from north to south and west to east, exceeds 2,000 km. The Arabic name for the country, el-Djezaïr (the Islands), is said to derive from the rocky islands along the coastline.

According to the census of April 1987, the population of Algeria was 23,038,942. The total had increased to 29,168,000, according to official estimates, by mid-1996. The great majority of the inhabitants reside in the northern part of the country, particularly along the Mediterranean coast where both the capital, Algiers or el-Djezaïr (population, not including suburbs, 1,483,000 in April 1987), and the second largest town, Oran or Ouahran (590,000), are located. Many settlements reverted to their Arabic names in 1981 (for the principal changes, see Statistical Survey, p. 321). The population is almost wholly Muslim. A majority speak Arabic and the remainder Berber, the language of the original inhabitants of the Maghreb. Many Algerians also speak French.

PHYSICAL FEATURES

The major contrast in the physical geography of Algeria is between the mountainous, relatively humid terrain of the north, which forms part of the Atlas mountain system, and the vast expanse of desert to the south, which is part of the Saharan tableland. The Atlas Mountains extend from south-west to north-east across the whole of the Maghreb. Structurally they resemble the 'Alpine' mountain chains of Europe and, like them, they came into existence during the Tertiary era. They remain unstable and liable to severe earthquakes, such as those which devastated el-Asnam in 1954 and 1980. The mountains consist of rocks, now uplifted, folded and fractured, that once accumulated beneath an ancestral Mediterranean sea. Limestone and sandstone are particularly extensive and they often present a barren appearance in areas where the topsoil and vegetation is thin or absent altogether.

In Algeria the Atlas mountain system is made up of three broad zones running parallel to the coast: the Tell Atlas, the High Plateaux and the Saharan Atlas. In the north, and separated from the Mediterranean only by a narrow and discontinuous coastal plain, is the complex series of mountains and valleys that comprise the Tell Atlas. Here individual ranges, plateaux and massifs vary in height from about 500 m to 2,500 m above sea-level and are frequently separated from one another by deep valleys and gorges which divide the country into self-contained topographic and economic units. Most distinctive of these are the massifs of the Great and Little Kabyle between Algiers and the Tunisian frontier, which have acted as mountain retreats where Berber ways of village life persist.

South of the Tell Atlas lies a zone of featureless plains known as the High Plateaux of the Shotts. To the west, near the Moroccan frontier, they form a broad, monotonous expanse of level terrain about 160 km across and more than 1,000 m above sea-level. They gradually narrow and descend eastward to end in the Hodna basin, a huge enclosed depression, the bottom of which is only 420 m above sea-level. The surface of the plateaux consists of alluvial debris from erosion of the mountains to the north and south. The plateaux owe their name to the presence of several vast basins of internal drainage, known as shotts, the largest of which is the Hodna basin. During rainy periods water accumulates in the shotts to form extensive shallow lakes which

give way, as the water is absorbed and evaporated, to saline mud flats and swamps.

The southern margin of the High Plateaux is marked by a series of mountain chains and massifs that form the Saharan Atlas. They are more interrupted than the Tell Atlas and present no serious barrier to communication between the High Plateaux and the Sahara. From west to east the chief mountain chains are the Ksour, Amour, Ouled Naïl, Ziban and Aurès. The latter is the most impressive massif in the whole Algerian Atlas system and includes the highest peak: Djebel Chelia, 2,328 m (7,638 ft). The relief of the Aurès is very bold, with narrow gorges cut between sheer cliffs surmounted by steep bare slopes, and to the east and north of the Hodna basin its ridges merge with the southernmost folds of the Tell Atlas. North-eastern Algeria forms, therefore, a compact block of high relief in which the two Atlas mountain systems cease to be clearly separated. Here there are a number of high plains studded with salt flats but their size is insignificant compared with the enormous shotts to the west.

CLIMATE AND VEGETATION

The climate of northernmost Algeria, including the narrow coastal plain and the Tell Atlas southward to the margin of the High Plateaux, is of 'Mediterranean' type with warm, wet winters and hot, dry summers. Rainfall varies from over 1,000 mm annually on some coastal mountains to less than 130 mm in sheltered, lee situations, and occurs mostly during the winter. Complete drought lasts for three to four months during the summer, when the notorious sirocco also occurs. It is a scorching, dry and dusty southerly wind blowing from the Sahara, and is known locally as the Chehili. It prevails for some 40 days a year over the High Plateaux but nearer the coast its duration is closer to 20 days. With the arrival of the sirocco, shade temperatures often rise rapidly to more than 40°C (104°F), while vegetation and crops, unable to withstand the intensity of evaporation, may die within a few hours. As a result of low and uneven rainfall combined with high rates of evaporation, the rivers of the Tell tend to be short and to suffer large seasonal variations in flow. Many dry out completely during the summer and are full only for brief periods following heavy winter rains. The longest perennially flowing river is the Oued Chélif, which rises in the High Plateaux and crosses the Tell to reach the Mediterranean Sea east of Oran.

Along the northern margin of the High Plateaux 'Mediterranean' conditions give way to a semi-arid or steppe climate in which summer drought lasts from five to six months and winters are colder and drier. Rainfall is limited to 200 mm–400 mm annually and tends to occur in spring and autumn rather than in winter. It is, moreover, variable from year to year, and under these conditions the cultivation of cereal crops without irrigation becomes unreliable. South of the Saharan Atlas annual rainfall decreases to below 200 mm and any regular cultivation without irrigation becomes impossible. There are no permanent rivers south of the Tell Atlas and any surface run-off following rain is carried by temporary watercourses towards local depressions, such as the shotts.

The soils and vegetation of northern Algeria reflect the climatic contrast between the humid Tell and the semi-arid lands farther south, but they have also suffered widely from the destructive effects of over-cultivation, over-grazing and deforestation. In the higher, wetter and more isolated parts of the Tell Atlas relatively thick soils support forests of Aleppo pine, cork-oak and evergreen oak, while the lower, drier, and more accessible slopes tend to be bare or covered only with thin soils and a scrub growth of thuya, juniper and various drought-resistant shrubs. Only a few remnants survive of the once extensive forests of Atlas cedar which have been exploited for timber and fuel since classical times. They are found chiefly above 1,500 m in the eastern Tell Atlas. South of the Tell there is very little woodland except in the higher and wetter parts of the Saharan Atlas. The surface of the High Plateaux is bare or covered only with scattered bushes and clumps of esparto and other coarse grasses.

SAHARAN ALGERIA

South of the Saharan Atlas, Algeria extends for over 1,500 km into the heart of the desert. Structurally, this huge area consists of a resistant platform of geologically ancient rocks against which the Atlas Mountains were folded. Over most of the area relief is slight, with occasional plateaux, such as those of Eglab, Tademaït and Tassili-n-Ajjer, rising above vast spreads of gravel, such as the Tanezrouft plain, and huge sand accumulations, such as the Great Western and Eastern Ergs. In the south-east, however, the great massif of Ahaggar rises to a height of 2,918 m (9,573 ft). Here, erosion of volcanic and crystalline rocks has produced a lunar landscape of extreme ruggedness. Southward from the Ahaggar the massifs of Adrar des Iforas and Aïr extend across the Algerian frontier into the neighbouring countries of Mali and Niger.

The climate of Saharan Algeria is characterized by extremes of temperature, wind and aridity. Daily temperature ranges reach 32°C, and maximum shade temperatures of over 55°C have been recorded. Sometimes very high temperatures are associated with violent dust storms. Mean average rainfall, although extremely irregular, is everywhere less than 130 mm, and in some of the central parts of the desert it falls to less than 10 mm. These rigorous conditions are reflected in the extreme sparseness of the vegetation and in a division of the population into settled cultivators, who occupy oases dependent on permanent supplies of underground water, and nomadic pastoralists who make use of temporary pastures which appear after rain.

History

Revised for this edition by RICHARD I. LAWLESS

EARLY HISTORY

The Berber people have comprised the majority of the population of this part of Africa since the earliest times. From 208 to 148 BC Numidia occupied most of present-day Algeria north of the Sahara. After the destruction of Carthage in 146 BC, Numidia, greatly reduced in extent, was transformed into a Roman vassal-state, while the rest of the area formed a loose confederacy of tribes, which maintained their independence by frequent revolt. After a brief period of Vandal dominance, Roman rule was restored in the provinces of Africa (modern Tunisia) and Numidia, and parts of the coast. Elsewhere, the Berber confederacies, centred in the Aurès and the Kabyle, maintained their independence.

The rise of Islam in Arabia was soon followed by its penetration of North Africa, the first Arab raids taking place about the middle of the seventh century. Qairawan (in present-day Tunisia) was founded by the Arabs in 670 as a base; the other towns remained under Byzantine control, and the Berber tribes set up a state centred on the eastern Maghreb. Increasing Arab immigration towards the end of the seventh century finally overcame Berber and Byzantine resistance, the Berbers gradually converted to Islam, and the whole of the area was incorporated into the Ummayad Empire. In 756 the Berbers freed themselves from the control of the recently established Abbasid Caliphate, and for the next three centuries power was disputed between various Arab dynasties and Berber tribes. After the invasion in c. 1050 of the Banu Hilal, a confederation of nomadic Arab tribes dislodged from Egypt, a period of anarchy ensued, but the Berber dynasty of the Almoravids, from Morocco, temporarily restored order in the area of modern Algiers and Oran. In c. 1147 the Almoravids were succeeded by the Almohads, who unified the whole of the Maghreb and Muslim Spain, bringing cultural and economic prosperity to North Africa. From the middle of the 13th century, however, the region entered a period of decline, both economic and in terms of its political influence, which persisted for more than two centuries.

In the closing years of the 15th century, the Spanish monarchy carried its crusade against Muslim power to North Africa, the fragmented political state of that area offering little resistance. On the death of Ferdinand of Castile in 1516, the Algerines sought the assistance of the Turkish corsair Aruj, who took possession of Algiers and several other towns and proclaimed himself Sultan. In 1518 he was succeeded by his brother Khayr ad-Din (Barbarossa), who placed all his territories under the nominal protection of the Ottoman Sultan. This decisive act may be said to mark the emergence of Algiers as a political entity. After numerous efforts to re-establish their position, the Spanish finally withdrew in 1541 and Algeria was left for three centuries to the Muslims. Power in Algiers lay in the hands of the dey and there was a rapid succession of deys, often due to assassinations. Each dey established his relationship with the Sultan by sending him tribute. Real power in Algiers was held by two bodies—the janissary corps and the guild of corsair captains. The Regency of Algiers reached its peak in the 17th century, the profitable trade of piracy bringing great wealth. Despite Turkish attempts to control the interior, several Berber tribes most distant from Algiers retained their independence. During the 18th century the growth of European sea power in the Mediterranean brought a period of decline to the littoral, while in the interior a period of relative economic prosperity ensued.

THE FRENCH CONQUEST

On 5 July 1830 Algiers fell to a French expedition, and the dey and most of the Turkish officials were sent into exile. The pretext for intervention was an insult offered by the dey to the French consul in 1827: the real cause was the pressing need of Polignac, the chief minister under Charles X, to secure some credit for his administration from the French public and to provide employment for the Napoleonic veterans. However, the Bourbon dynasty and its government were subsequently overthrown by revolution and Polignac's plan to hand over the rest of the country, and the decision on its future, to a European congress was abandoned. In Algeria the absence of any central authority increased the prestige of the tribal chiefs. In 1834, however, the French decided upon the further conquest and annexation of Algeria, and a governor-general was appointed.

Over the next quarter of a century, France pursued its conquest of Algeria, despite bitter opposition. Constantine, the last Turkish stronghold, was captured in 1837, and by 1841 French rule had been consolidated in most of the ports and their immediate environs. By 1844 most of the eastern part of Algeria was under French control, but in the west the conquerors encountered the formidable Abd al-Kadir, who claimed descent from the Prophet Muhammad. A skilful diplomat and military commander, he at first concluded treaties with the French, consolidating his position as leader of the Berber confederacies in the west. In 1839, however, he declared war on France and united Berbers and Arabs against the invaders. Resistance was maintained until 1847, when Abd al-Kadir was defeated by Gen. Bugeaud, the real architect of French rule in Algeria. During the late 1840s and 1850s, the tribes on the edge of the Sahara were pacified, while the conquest was effectively completed by the submission of the hitherto independent Berber confederacies of the Kabyle in 1857. Further rebellions were to occur, however, throughout the 19th century.

Meanwhile, a policy of colonization, with widespread confiscation of land and its transference to settler groups, had been adopted. Bugeaud had at first encouraged colonization in the coastal plains; after 1848 the influx of colonists was much increased, especially following the annexation of Alsace-Lorraine by Germany in 1871; further stimulus to colonization was provided by the widespread confiscation of lands after an unsuccessful Muslim rebellion in the same year. By that time the French settlers had become the dominant power in Algeria, owning much of the best land and initiating extensive agricultural development.

After the revolt of 1871, the situation was regularized by a new French administration under Thiers. A civil administration with the status of a French *département* was established for much of Algeria, while the amount of territory under military rule steadily declined. From 1871 to 1900 there was considerable economic development in Algeria and increasing European immigration, especially from Italy. A feature of this period was the growth of large-scale agricultural and industrial enterprises, which further concentrated power in the hands of the leaders of the settler groups. In 1900 Algeria secured administrative and financial autonomy, to be exercised through the so-called 'Financial Delegations', composed of two-thirds European and one-third Muslim members, which were empowered to set the annual budget and to raise loans for further economic development.

Within 70 years the Muslim people of Algeria had been reduced from relative prosperity to economic, social and cultural subordination. Some 3m. inhabitants had died, tribes had been disbanded and the traditional economy altered during the prolonged 'civilizing' campaigns. In particular, the production of wine for export had replaced the growing of cereals for domestic consumption. By contrast, the settlers enjoyed a high level of prosperity in the years before the First World War.

BIRTH OF NATIONALISM

The spirit of nationalism, which was spreading throughout the Middle East, emerged among Algerian Muslims after the First World War. Nationalist aspirations began to be voiced not only by Algerian veterans of the war in Europe but also by Algerians who had gone to France to study or work. In 1924 one of these students, Messali Hadj, in collaboration with the French Communist Party, founded in Paris the first Algerian nationalist newspaper; the link with the Communists was, however, severed in 1927. Messali Hadj and his movement were forced into hiding by the French Government, but reappeared in 1933 to sponsor a congress on the future of Algeria, which demanded full independence, the recall of French troops, the establishment of a revolutionary government, large-scale reforms in land ownership and the nationalization of industrial enterprises.

More moderate doctrines were advanced in the post-war years by an influential body of French-educated Muslims, formalized in 1930 as the Federation of Muslim Councillors. Under the leadership of Ferhat Abbas, this group urged integration with France on a basis of complete equality. The victory of the Popular Front in the French elections of 1936 gave rise to the hope that at least some of these aspirations might be peaceably achieved. However, the Blum-Viollet Plan, which would have granted full rights of citizenship to an increasing number of Algerian Muslims, was abandoned by the French Government as it was fiercely opposed by French settlers and the Algerian civil service.

The years immediately prior to the Second World War were characterized by growing nationalist discontent, in which Messali Hadj played a significant part with the formation of the Party of the Algerian People (PPA). The outbreak of war in 1939 suspended the nationalists' activities, but the war greatly strengthened their position. Although the Vichy administration in Algeria, strongly supported by the French settlers, was antipathetic to nationalist sentiment, the Allied landings in North Africa in 1942 provided an opportunity for the Algerian nationalists to present constitutional demands. In December a group led by Ferhat Abbas submitted to the French authorities and the Allied military command a memorandum demanding the post-war establishment of an Algerian constituent assembly, to be elected by universal suffrage. However, no demand was made for Algerian independence outside the French framework.

These proposals, to which the French authorities remained unresponsive, were followed early in 1943 by the 'Manifesto of the Algerian People', which demanded immediate reforms, including the introduction of Arabic as an official language and the end of colonization. Further proposals, submitted in May, envisaged the post-war creation of an Algerian state with a constitution to be determined by a constituent assembly, and anticipated an eventual North African Union, comprising Tunisia, Algeria and Morocco. The newly-established Free French administration in Algiers categorically rejected the Manifesto and the subsequent proposals.

Confronted by growing Muslim discontent, and following a visit to Algiers by Gen. Charles de Gaulle, a new statute for Algeria came into effect in March 1944. Membership of the French electoral college was opened to 60,000 Muslims, but there were still 450,000 European voters, and in the event only 32,000 Muslims registered to vote. The Muslim share of the seats in the *communes mixtes* was restricted to 40%. All further discussion of Algeria's future relationship with France was rejected.

Shortly afterwards, Ferhat Abbas founded the Friends of the Manifesto of Freedom (AML), which aimed to establish an autonomous Algerian republic linked federally with France. The movement was based mainly on the support of middle-class Muslims. The AML also gained a certain following among the masses, who comprised the main support of the PPA during 1944 and 1945.

FRENCH INTRANSIGENCE

All possibility of a gradually negotiated settlement was destroyed by blunders of post-war French policy and the opposition of the French settlers to any concessions to Muslim aspirations. Riots at Sétif in May 1945 were ruthlessly suppressed; it was estimated that 8,000–40,000 Muslims were killed. This suppression, the subsequent arrest of Ferhat Abbas and the dissolution of the AML convinced many nationalist leaders that force was the only means of gaining their objective.

Nevertheless, attempts to reach a compromise continued. In March 1946 Ferhat Abbas, released under an amnesty, launched the Democratic Union of the Algerian Manifesto (UDMA), with a programme providing for the creation of an autonomous, secular Algerian state within the French Union. Colonists were invited to join, but few did so. Despite successes in elections to the French Assembly, the UDMA failed to achieve its objectives. It withdrew from the Assembly in September and refused to participate in the next elections. The breach was filled by the more radical Movement for the Triumph of Democratic Liberties (MTLD), formed by Messali Hadj at the end of the war, which demanded the creation of a sovereign constituent assembly and the withdrawal of French troops.

In another attempt at compromise, the French Government introduced a new Constitution, adopted on 20 September 1947, granting French citizenship, and therefore the right to vote, to all Algerian citizens, both men and women, and recognizing Arabic as equal in status to French. The proposed new Algerian Assembly, however, was to be divided into two colleges, each of 60 members, one to represent the 1.5m. resident Europeans, the other the 9m. Algerian Muslims. Other provisions excluded any legislation contrary to the interest of the colonists.

The new Constitution was never fully brought into operation. Following MTLD successes in the municipal elections of October 1947, the elections to the Algerian Assembly were openly interfered with, many candidates being arrested, election meetings forbidden and polling stations improperly operated. As a result only one-quarter of the members returned to the second college in April 1948 belonged to the MTLD or the UDMA; the remainder, known as the 'Beni Oui Oui', were nominally independent, but easy to manipulate. Such methods continued to be employed in local and national elections during the next six years, as well as in the Algerian elections to the French National Assembly in June 1951. Some of the improvements that the 1947 Constitution envisaged were never put into effect. The aim was to destroy, or at least render harmless, opposition to French rule; the result was to compel the main forces of nationalism to operate clandestinely.

As early as 1947 several of the younger members of the MTLD had formed the 'Secret Organization' (OS), which collected arms and money and organized a network of cells throughout Algeria in preparation for armed insurrection and the establishment of a revolutionary government. Two years later the OS felt itself strong enough to launch a terrorist attack in Oran. The movement was subsequently discovered and most of its leaders were arrested. A nucleus survived, however, in the Kabyle region (ever a stronghold for dissident groups) and the organizer of the attack, Ahmed Ben Bella, escaped to Cairo in 1952.

A decisive split was opening in the ranks of the MTLD, and the veteran Messali Hadj, who now embraced nebulous doctrines of Pan-Arabism, was gradually losing control of the party organization to more activist members. In March 1954 nine former members of the OS formed the Revolutionary Council for Unity and Action (CRUA) to prepare for an immediate revolt against French rule.

WAR OF INDEPENDENCE

Plans for the insurrection were formulated at a series of CRUA meetings in Switzerland during March–October 1954. Algeria was divided into six *wilaya* (administrative districts) and a military commander was appointed for each. When the revolt was launched on 1 November the CRUA changed its name to the National Liberation Front (Front de libération nationale—FLN), its armed forces being known as the National Liberation Army (Armée de libération nationale—ALN). Beginning in the Aurès, by early 1955 the revolt had spread to the Constantine area, the Kabyle and the Moroccan frontier, west of Oran. By the end of 1956 the ALN was active throughout the settled areas of Algeria.

Ferhat Abbas and Ahmad Francis of the more moderate UDMA and the religious leaders of the *ulema* (Muslim scholar/lawyers) joined the FLN in April 1956, thereby integrating all sectors of Algerian nationalist feeling with the exception of Messali Hadj's Algerian National Movement (MNA). In August a secret congress of the FLN, convened at Soummam in the Kabyle, established a central committee and formed the National Council of the Algerian Revolution. A socialist programme for the future Algerian republic and plans for a terrorist offensive in Algiers were also approved.

Between September 1956 and June 1957 bomb explosions engineered by the FLN caused great loss of life. This terrorism was halted only by severe French repression of the Muslim population, including the use of torture and internment. Guerrilla activities continued but electrified barriers were erected along the Tunisian and Moroccan borders and ALN bands attempting to cross into Algeria suffered heavy losses.

In June 1957 the new Bourgès-Manoury administration in France introduced legislation to link Algeria indissolubly with France, but the measure was not approved. Following the Soummam conference, a joint Moroccan-Tunisian plan had been announced for the establishment of a North African federation linked with France. FLN leaders began negotiations in Morocco in October 1957. However, Ben Bella and his companions were kidnapped *en route* from Morocco to Tunisia, when the French pilot of their aircraft landed at Algiers. The French authorities could hardly ignore this *fait accompli*, and the hijacked leaders were arrested and interned in France. Neither the internment of FLN leaders nor the bombing by French aircraft, in February 1958, of the Tunisian border village of Sakhiet Sidi Youssif, in which 79 villagers were killed, weakened the resolve or the capacity of the FLN to continue fighting, and the failure of these desperate measures only made the possibility of French negotiations with the FLN more likely. This, in turn, provoked a violent reaction from the Europeans in Algeria (only about one-half of whom were of French origin).

In May 1958 the colonists rebelled and installed committees of public safety in the major Algerian towns. Supported by the army and exploiting the widespread fear of civil war, the colonists prompted the overthrow of the discredited Fourth French Republic and celebrated Gen. de Gaulle's return to power, in the belief that he would further their aim of complete integration of Algeria with France. Although de Gaulle intensified military action against the FLN, this was achieved only at the cost of increased terrorism in Algiers and of growing tension on the Tunisian and Moroccan borders. The FLN responded in August by establishing in Tunis the Provisional Government of the Algerian Republic (GPRA), headed by Ferhat Abbas, and including Ben Bella and the other leaders who had been interned in France. De Gaulle was already beginning to recognize the strength of Algerian nationalism and was moving cautiously towards accepting FLN demands.

NEGOTIATIONS AND THE COLONISTS' OPPOSITION

Initially de Gaulle's public statements on Algeria were vague. When he did make an unequivocal pronouncement in September 1959, which upheld the right of Algerians to determine their own future, the colonists reacted swiftly. In January 1960 they rebelled again, this time against de Gaulle, and erected barricades in Algiers. However, without the support of the army the insurrection collapsed within nine days. Provisional talks between French and FLN delegates took place in secret near Paris in mid-1960 but were inconclusive.

In November 1960 de Gaulle announced that a referendum was to be held on the organization of government in Algeria, pending self-determination, and in December he visited Algeria to prepare the way. In the referendum the electorate was asked to approve a draft law providing for self-determination and immediate reforms to give Algerians the opportunity to participate in government. There were mass abstentions from voting in Algeria, however, and in February 1961 new French approaches to the FLN were made through the President of Tunisia. Secret talks led to direct negotiations between French and FLN representatives at Évian, on the Franco-Swiss border. These began in May but foundered in August over the question of the Sahara and because of a French attack on the blockaded French naval base at Bizerta (Tunisia), which resulted in the deaths of 800–1,300 Tunisians.

Europeans in Algeria and sections of the French army, meanwhile, had formed the Secret Army Organization (OAS) to resist a negotiated settlement and the transfer of power from European hands. In April 1961 four generals, Challe, Zeller, Jouhaud and Salan, organized the seizure of Algiers, but this attempt at an army coup proved abortive, most regular officers remaining loyal to de Gaulle. Offensive operations against the Algerian rebels, which had been suspended when the Évian talks began, were resumed by the French Government, and fighting continued, although on a reduced scale. At the same time, the OAS initiated a campaign of indiscriminate terrorist violence against native Algerians. The Mayor of Évian had already been killed by an OAS bomb, and attacks were now also mounted in Paris.

Secret contacts between the French Government and the FLN were re-established in October 1961. Negotiations were resumed in December and in January 1962 in Geneva and Rome, the five members of the GPRA interned in France taking part through a representative of the King of Morocco. Meetings at ministerial level were held in strict secrecy in Paris in February and the final stage of the negotiations was concluded at Évian in mid-March with the signing of a cease-fire agreement and a declaration of future policy. The declaration provided for the establishment of an independent Algerian state after a transitional period, and for the safeguarding of individual rights and liberties. Other declarations issued subsequently dealt with the rights of French citizens in Algeria and with future Franco-Algerian co-operation. In the military sphere, France was to retain the naval base at Mers el-Kebir for 15 years and the nuclear testing site in the Sahara, together with various landing rights, for five years.

In accordance with the Évian agreements, a provisional Government was formed on 28 March 1962, with Abderrahman Farès as President and an executive composed of FLN members, other Muslims and Europeans. The USSR and many East European, African and Asian countries quickly gave *de jure* recognition to the GPRA.

The signing of the Évian agreements provoked renewed opposition by the OAS. A National Council of French Resistance in Algeria was formed, with Gen. Salan as Commander-in-Chief, and OAS commando units launched attacks on the Muslim population and on public buildings in an attempt to prompt a general breach of the cease-fire. After the failure of the OAS to establish an 'insurrectional zone' in the Orléansville (El-Asnam) area and the capture of Gen. Salan in April 1962, and with a renewal of FLN terrorist activity and reprisals, increasing numbers of Europeans began to leave Algeria for France. Secret negotiations between OAS leaders and the FLN, aimed at securing guarantees for the European population, revealed a division in the OAS, which heralded the virtual end of European terrorist activity. By late June more than one-half of the European population of Algeria had left the country.

The final steps towards Algerian independence were taken at a referendum on 1 July 1962 at which 91% of the electorate voted for independence. Algerian independence was proclaimed by Gen. de Gaulle on 3 July.

THE INDEPENDENT STATE

The achievement of power by the FLN revealed serious tensions within the Government, while the problems facing the new state after eight years of civil war were formidable.

The dominant position in the GPRA of the 'centralist' group, headed by Ben Khedda and comprising former members of the MTLD, was threatened by the release in March 1962 of the five GPRA members who had been detained in France—Ben Bella, Muhammad Khider, Muhammad Boudiaf, Aït Ahmad and Rabah Bitat. Boudiaf and Aït Ahmad rallied temporarily to the support of Ben Khedda, while the others formed yet another opposition faction besides that of Ferhat Abbas, who had been dropped from the GPRA leadership in 1961.

The ALN leadership was also split. The commanders of the main armed forces in Tunisia and Morocco were opposed to the politicians of the GPRA, and the commanders of the internal guerrilla groups were opposed to all external and military factions.

Serious differences emerged when the National Council of the Algerian Revolution met in Tripoli in May 1962 to consider policies for the new state. A commission headed by Ben Bella produced a programme which included large-scale agrarian reform, involving expropriation and the establishment of peasant co-operatives and state farms; a state monopoly of external trade; and a foreign policy aimed towards Maghreb unity, neutrality and anti-colonialism, especially in Africa. Despite the opposition of Ben Khedda's group, the Tripoli programme became the official FLN policy.

After independence, the GPRA Cabinet, with the exception of Ben Bella, flew to Algiers, where they installed themselves alongside the official Provisional Executive. Ben Khedda attempted to reassert control over the ALN by dismissing the Commander-in-Chief, Col Houari Boumedienne. Ben Bella, however, flew to Morocco to join Boumedienne, and in July 1962 they crossed into Algeria and established headquarters in Tlemcen, where Ben Bella instituted the Political Bureau as the chief executive organ of the FLN and a rival to the GPRA. After negotiations, he was joined by some of the GPRA leaders, leaving Ben Khedda isolated in Algiers, with Boudiaf and Aït Ahmad in opposition.

Several of the *wilaya* leaders, however, felt that, having provided the internal resistance, they represented the true current of the revolution, and they were opposed to the Political Bureau and Boumedienne. While ALN forces loyal to the Bureau occupied Constantine and Bône (Annaba) in the east in late July 1962, Algiers remained in the hands of the leadership of *wilaya* IV, who refused the Bureau entry. When Boumedienne's forces marched on Algiers from Oran in early September there were serious clashes with *wilaya* IV troops. Total civil war was averted, partly because of mass demonstrations against the fighting which were organized by the Algerian General Workers' Union (UGTA).

The struggle for power proved costly for Ben Khedda. Before the elections were held on 20 September 1962, one-third of the 180 candidates on the single list drafted in August had been purged (including Ben Khedda himself) and replaced with lesser-known figures. Although the elections failed to arouse much public enthusiasm, some 99% of the electorate were declared to have voted in favour of the proposed powers of the Constituent Assembly. The functions of the GPRA were transferred to the Assembly when it convened on 25 September, and Ferhat Abbas was elected its President. The Algerian Republic was proclaimed, and on the following day Ben Bella was elected Prime Minister. He subsequently appointed a Cabinet comprising his personal associates and former ALN officers.

BEN BELLA IN POWER

The new Government immediately acted to consolidate its position. Messali Hadj's PPA (formerly the MNA), the Algerian Communist Party, and Boudiaf's Party of the Socialist Revolution were all banned in November 1962; the *wilaya* system was abolished the following month, and, apart from the UGTA, all organizations affiliated to the FLN were brought firmly under control.

The economic plight of the country was severe. Some 90% (1m.) of the Europeans, representing virtually all the entrepreneurs, technicians, administrators, teachers, doctors and skilled workers, had left the country. Factories, farms and shops had closed, leaving 70% of the population unemployed. Public buildings and records had been destroyed by the OAS. At the end of the war, in which more than 1m. people had died, there had been 2m. in internment camps and 500,000 refugees in Tunisia and Morocco. An austerity plan was formulated in December 1962, and large loans and technical assistance from France, plus other emergency foreign aid, enabled the Government to remain in power.

By packing the first UGTA congress with FLN militants and unemployed, the FLN managed in January 1963 to gain control of the UGTA executive, which had been opposed to the dictatorial nature of the new Government. Decrees published in March legalized the workers' committees which, aided by the UGTA, had taken over the operation of many of the abandoned European estates in mid-1962; the remaining estates were nationalized in 1963. The system of workers' management, known as *autogestion*, under which the workers elected their own management board to work alongside a state-appointed director, became the basis of 'Algerian socialism'.

In April 1963 Ben Bella assumed the post of Secretary-General of the FLN. In August he secured the adoption by the Assembly of a draft constitution providing for a presidential regime, with the FLN as the sole political party. The new Constitution was approved by referendum and on 13 September Ben Bella was elected President for a period of five years, assuming the title of Commander-in-Chief of the Armed Forces as well as becoming Head of State and head of government. These moves towards dictatorial government aroused opposition. Ferhat Abbas, the leading proponent of a more liberal policy, resigned from the presidency of the Assembly and was subsequently expelled from the FLN. In the Kabyle, where discontent was accentuated by Berber regionalism, revolts were suppressed in 1963 and 1964.

BOUMEDIENNE TAKES OVER

On 19 June 1965 Ben Bella was deposed and arrested in a swift and bloodless military *coup d'état*, led by the Minister of Defence, Col Boumedienne, whose army had brought Ben Bella to power in 1962. In view of Algeria's economic plight and Ben Bella's dictatorial tendencies, many administrators and politicians did not oppose the coup. Moreover, Ben Bella's elimination of most of the traditional leaders, his repeated attacks on the UGTA and his failure to turn the FLN into a representative party left him without organized support when the army turned against him. Bereft of its leader, the FLN accepted the coup, and the UGTA, while expressing no real support for Boumedienne, did not oppose it.

Supreme political authority in Algeria passed to the Council of the Revolution, consisting mostly of military figures and presided over by Col Boumedienne. Under the Council's authority a new Government of 20 members was formed in July 1965, with Boumedienne as Prime Minister and Minister of Defence. Nine members of the Government, which included technocrats and members of the radical wing of the FLN, had held office under Ben Bella. To ensure a satisfactory relationship between the Government and the FLN, a five-man party secretariat under Cherif Belkacem was established shortly afterwards.

The aims of the new regime, as described by Boumedienne, were to remedy the abuses of personal power associated with Ben Bella, to end internal divisions, and to create an 'authentic socialist society' based on a sound economy. In international relations a policy of non-alignment was to be pursued and support for those struggling for freedom was to continue.

Apart from preparations for municipal elections, the regime made no attempt to secure a popular mandate, and the Algerian National Assembly remained in abeyance. New penal and civil legal codes were promulgated in 1966, the judiciary was 'Algerianized' and tribunals to try 'economic crimes', with powers to impose the death penalty, were created in July. New conditions of service and training schemes for public employees were introduced, with the aim of improving the standard of administration. In accordance with its socialist policies, the regime increased state participation in concerns previously left to private enterprise, particularly in the mining and insurance sectors. A National Bank of Algeria, specializing in short-term credit for the nationalized sector of the economy, was inaugurated in July. However, industrial activity continued at a low level and the country remained heavily dependent on foreign aid for industrial development. A new investment code, designed to attract both domestic and foreign capital and promulgated in September, contained assurances of indemnification in the event of nationalization.

CAUTION IN FOREIGN POLICY

The relationship with France, Algeria's main customer and the source of substantial assistance, remained of paramount importance. In 1966 agreements were signed which provided for French technical and educational assistance for 20 years, cancelled Algeria's pre-independence debts and reduced indebtedness to France to 400m. dinars. France was disturbed by the growing Soviet influence in Algeria. Soviet advisers played a leading role in the development of mining and industry, and the Algerian army received training and equipment from the USSR. However, French fears that the Soviet navy might be allowed to use the Mers el-Kebir base, handed over by France in January 1968, proved groundless. The French cultural influence remained: there were still French teachers, although the teaching of Arabic was extended in schools; large numbers of Algerians worked in France; there was a preference for such French consumer goods as were still imported; and France continued to give assistance, including training and equipment, to Algeria's armed forces.

Algerian involvement in the 'Six-Day War' between Israel and neighbouring Arab states in June 1967 was minimal. When the cease-fire came, however, there were demonstrations against Nasser's 'treason' and also against the USSR's lack of support for the Arab countries. At the Khartoum conference Algerian delegates advocated a people's war, and detachments of Algerian troops were maintained in the Suez Canal area until August 1970.

A highly critical, often openly hostile, attitude to the USA was maintained, and diplomatic relations were severed in 1967. Nevertheless, US petroleum technology was welcomed, as was investment in Algeria's oil industry; a contract to sell liquefied natural gas (LNG) to the USA was signed in 1969.

In Africa the Boumedienne Government adopted a consistently anti-colonial line, severing relations with the United Kingdom over Rhodesia in 1965 (but restoring them in 1968), and providing training and facilities for the liberation movements of southern Africa, as well as for the Eritrean Liberation Front and the National Liberation Front of Chad. A determined effort was made to improve relations with neighbouring countries in the Maghreb. In January 1969 President Boumedienne made his first official visit to Morocco, and in June frontier posts were reopened for the first time since 1963. In May 1970 the Algerian and Moroccan Governments signed an agreement to settle a long-standing border dispute and to co-operate on the question of the Spanish presence in North Africa. In mid-1972 further agreements were signed: one demarcating the Algerian–Moroccan border (ratified by Algeria in May 1973, but not by Morocco until 1989), the other providing for joint exploitation of the Gara-Djebilet mines in the border regions. An agreement with Mauritania was signed in December 1969, and a friendship treaty with Tunisia, agreeing on common borders, in January 1970. While Algeria welcomed the Libyan revolution in 1969, the subsequent orientation of the Libyan leaders towards Egypt and Sudan, rather than the Maghreb, was not conducive to close relations between the two regimes.

INTERNAL OPPOSITION OVERCOME

The new Government was opposed by certain left-wing ministers, such as Ali Yahia and Abd al-Aziz Zerdani, the UGTA, students, and sections of the army, notably the former *wilaya* leaders, all of whom feared the imposition of a technocratic and centralized socialism, different from the syndicalist concepts embodied in *autogestion*. Various members of the UGTA and of the Boumedienne administration were arrested following the suppression of an armed uprising in the Mitidja in December 1967. Boumedienne announced a series of selective dismissals in the FLN and the army, and appointed well-known supporters to vacant ministerial offices.

Opposition to Boumedienne, however, was by no means crushed. FLN attempts in February 1968 to impose a new loyal student committee at Algiers University provoked a strike by students and teachers, and there were numerous reports of guerrilla activity in the Aurès and the Kabyle. The Organization of Popular Resistance appeared to be active both in these areas and among students. In April Boumedienne escaped an assassination attempt in Algiers with minor injuries. However, some observers argued that the pardoning of as many as 100 political prisoners in November 1969 was indicative of the weakness of opposition to Boumedienne.

The second stage of the reform of governmental institutions (the first being the 1967 communal elections) was put into operation in May 1969, when elections were held for the 15 *wilaya* (administrative districts) and 72% of the electorate voted for candidates on a single FLN list.

RELATIONS WITH FRANCE

The consolidation of President Boumedienne's position in Algeria enabled him to adopt a more militant attitude towards France. Demands for increased revenues from Algerian petroleum resulted in dispute over the price to be paid by the French oil companies, and culminated in the decision to nationalize them. The two companies concerned, the Compagnie Française des Pétroles (CFP) and the Entreprise de Recherches et d'Activités Pétrolières (ERAP), were responsible for some two-thirds of Algeria's total production. In February 1971, following fruitless discussions with the French Government, Boumedienne announced the acquisition by the Algerian Government of a 51% holding in CFP and ERAP and the complete nationalization of the companies' gas and pipeline interests.

The French Government regarded this move as a breach of the 1965 agreement but could only ask for fair compensation. The subsequent Algerian offer was found unacceptable and in April 1971 France discontinued negotiations. It was announced that many French technicians and teachers were to leave Algeria, and attacks were made on some of the 700,000 Algerians in France. The French Government imposed a boycott against Algerian petroleum and tried to persuade other major consumers to do the same. Talks between the two French companies and SONATRACH, the Algerian state oil concern, were resumed, however, and agreements were reached in June and September under which the role of CFP and ERAP became that of minority partners of the Algerian state in return for guaranteed oil supplies. After approval by the two Governments an agreement, which also provided for compensation and reduced retrospective tax claims, was signed in December.

In April 1975 Valéry Giscard d'Estaing became the first French President to visit Algeria since independence. However, the goodwill that was generated by the visit quickly dissipated. French economic policies were resented by the Boumedienne Government, as they maintained an imbalance in trade between the two countries, and French support for, and provision of large quantities of arms to, Morocco, Algeria's potential enemy, during the Western Sahara dispute (see below) were regarded as a betrayal.

PALESTINE AND WESTERN SAHARA

The Boumedienne Government's stand on the Palestine question remained uncompromisingly militant. Algeria accepted neither the 1967 UN Resolution nor the cease-fire. When a further cease-fire was agreed in August 1970, Algerian troops were withdrawn from the Suez Canal. Radio stations of Palestine liberation movements expelled from Cairo in July 1970 were allowed to broadcast from Algiers and relations with Jordan were severed in June 1971 after the final destruction of Palestinian guerrilla bases in Jordan by King Hussein's forces. During the October War in 1973 Algeria actively encouraged African countries to sever relations with Israel. It participated fully with other Arab petroleum-producing states in reducing production and boycotting countries regarded as hostile to the Arab cause. Relations with Jordan were restored after the dispatch of Jordanian troops to the Syrian front, but Algeria continued to support the Palestinians against any Jordanian territorial claims. In December 1977 Algeria was one of the signatories of the Declaration of Tripoli, opposing President Sadat's attempts to negotiate with Israel, and in 1978 Algeria severed diplomatic relations with Egypt.

Despite the Government's policy towards Palestine and its support of almost any exiled foreign opposition group, Algeria was prepared to co-operate in the economic field with any state willing to do so. Fears that Algeria might fall under Soviet dominance proved groundless, although the USSR was a major source of military equipment. Despite disagreements with the USA over Viet Nam and the Palestinian question, full diplomatic relations were restored at the end of 1974 and trade between the two countries increased dramatically—by the end of 1977 the USA had replaced France as Algeria's leading trade partner.

From early 1975 a major confrontation developed with Morocco over the future of the Spanish Sahara. Algeria opposed Morocco's claim to the territory, advocating the founding of an independent Saharan state after decolonization. In May, at the International Court of Justice, Algeria appealed for genuine self-determination for the Saharans and denied any self-interest in the matter. When, in November, Spain agreed to hand over the territory to Morocco and Mauritania, Boumedienne protested vehemently and promised full support for the Polisario Front, the Saharan liberation movement. As Moroccan troops moved into the territory, now known as Western Sahara, Algeria mobilized part of its armed forces, and in January and February 1976 there were heavy clashes between units of the two armies in the territory, far from the Algerian border. In March Algeria recognized the Sahrawi Arab Democratic Republic, proclaimed by the Polisario Front. Both Morocco and Mauritania subsequently severed diplomatic relations with Algeria. The prospect of a full-scale war in Western Sahara quickly receded, especially as there was little enthusiasm for war among the Algerian population, but the Government continued to provide support and refuge for displaced persons and Polisario troops. Morocco and Mauritania refused to recognize the Polisario Front and interpreted all armed incursions into Western Sahara as Algerian attacks against their national territory. French bombing raids on Polisario troops, beginning in December 1977, were strongly condemned by Algeria, although the French Government declared that its intervention was solely for the protection of French citizens working in the area.

HOME AFFAIRS

In 1971 the Boumedienne Government initiated a programme of agrarian reform, known as the Agrarian Revolution. The reform was to proceed in three phases: the reallocation of state-owned and foreign land, the redistribution of private estates, and the transformation of the lives of the pastoral nomads. At the same time, the Government resolved to develop workers' control in industry and to reanimate the FLN as a radical force. Elected workers' councils slowly spread through nationalized industries, but the reorganization of the FLN was a failure, prompting the resignation of Kaid Ahmad, the party leader, in 1972. The initiative in promoting the Agrarian Revolution passed to a student *volontariat*. Boumedienne's determination to build a socialist society was resisted by conservative elements of the population, especially after the redistribution of private estates and the nationalization of food distribution. Conflict erupted in mid-1975 when there were clashes at Algiers University between students, supporting the Agrarian Revolution, and others, who wished to give priority to 'Arabization'.

The personal authority of Boumedienne increased in the 1970s. Following the death of Ahmad Medeghri in 1974 and Belkacem's dismissal from the Cabinet in 1975, Bouteflika was the only figure of comparable stature in the Government. Encouraged by the success of local and provincial elections since 1967 and 1969 respectively, Boumedienne announced in June 1975 that elections for a National Assembly and a President were to be held, and that a national charter would be drafted to provide the state with a new constitution.

Boumedienne's decision to consolidate the regime and his personal power provoked a resurgence of opposition, including the circulation, in March 1976, of a manifesto signed by, among others, Ferhat Abbas and Ben Khedda, both former presidents of the Algerian government-in-exile during the war of liberation. The manifesto criticized Boumedienne for his totalitarian rule and his fostering of a personality cult. The signatories were reportedly placed under house arrest.

In April 1976 the Algerian press began publication of the national charter, which, after public discussion, received the approval of 98.5% of the voters at a referendum in June. The essence of the charter was the irreversible commitment of Algeria to socialism, albeit a socialism specifically adapted to Third World conditions. The dominant role of the FLN was reasserted, but, as a concession to the conservatives, Islam was recognized as the state religion. In November a new Constitution, embodying the principles of the charter, was also approved by referendum, and in December Boumedienne was elected unopposed as President, with 99% of votes cast. To complete the new formal structure of power, the National People's Assembly of 261 members was elected in February 1977 from among 783 candidates selected by a committee of the FLN. Attempts were made to strengthen and enlarge the FLN: FLN officials were installed alongside local administrative officials to form the basis of a full party apparatus at all levels, and the mass organizations affiliated to the FLN (the unions of workers, peasants, war veterans, women and youth) held a series of congresses which was to culminate in a national FLN Congress (the first since 1964) in early 1979 (see below).

THE DEATH OF BOUMEDIENNE

Following a short illness, President Boumedienne died on 27 December 1978. During his illness there was speculation as to his successor, particularly since he had nominated neither a Vice-President nor a Prime Minister and was himself Minister of Defence (a post which had included, from 1977 onwards, direct supervision of the police and secret service) and Chief of Staff of the Armed Forces. As an interim measure, government was assumed by the Council of the Revolution, which by now consisted of only eight members. Although it had been given no official status in the 1976 Constitution, the Council declared that it would maintain continuity and protect existing institutions, and succeeded in bringing about a smooth transfer of power.

After Boumedienne's death, Rabah Bitat, the President of the National People's Assembly, was automatically sworn in as Head of State for a 45-day period. In late January 1979 the delayed FLN Congress was convened, with the double task of revitalizing the party and of choosing a presidential candidate. New statutes on party structure were adopted, whereby a Central Committee of 120–160 members and 30–40 advisory members, meeting at least once every six months, was to be elected by Congress and form the highest policy-making body not only of the party but of the country as a whole. The Committee was to select a party secretary-general who would automatically become the presidential candidate of the FLN, and therefore the sole presidential candidate. A political bureau of 17–21 members, nominated by the Secretary-General, would be elected by the Central Committee and be responsible to it. These structures superseded the Council of the Revolution, which was formally disbanded on 27 January.

CHADLI IN POWER

It was expected that the presidential candidate would be a member of the former Council, and the most likely choice appeared to be either Abd al-Aziz Bouteflika, the Minister for Foreign Affairs, or Muhammad Salah Yahiaoui, the administrative head of the FLN. The eventual choice, Col Ben Djedid Chadli, the commander of the Oran military district, was regarded as a compromise between the two. He was inaugurated as President on 9 February 1979, after his candidature had been approved by 94% of the electorate. He declared that he would uphold the policies of Boumedienne, the 'irreversible option' of socialism and 'national independence' in both political and economic spheres. It soon became clear that Chadli did not intend to monopolize power to the extent that Boumedienne had. For the first time since independence, a Prime Minister was named: Col Muhammad ben Ahmad Abd al-Ghani, who also kept his post as Minister of the Interior until January 1980. This nomination preceded constitutional changes, adopted by the National People's Assembly in June 1979, which made the appointment of a Prime Minister obligatory, and also reduced the President's term of office from six to five years, to coincide with five-yearly party congresses.

Within the first few months of his presidency, Chadli appeared to reject many of Boumedienne's doctrinaire policies. A new Government was formed, and Bouteflika was removed from the post of Minister of Foreign Affairs, which he had held for 15 years. Some of Boumedienne's political opponents were released from prison and it was announced that the former President, Ben Bella, had been freed, although it later transpired that he had merely been placed under a less stringent form of house arrest; he was finally freed from restrictions in October 1980. Exit visas for Algerians, compulsory since 1967, were abolished; income tax was reduced and restrictions on owning property were eased. In September 1979, however, a 'clean-up' campaign was mounted in Algiers and other cities. It was initially intended to improve the appearance of the streets in preparation for the 25th anniversary of the revolution, but was expanded to include the arrest and imprisonment of hundreds of 'social parasites' and a campaign against inefficiency and corruption. During 1980–81 the campaign was extended to the highest levels of state organizations, and numerous senior officials were arrested and tried by the Cour des Comptes for financial mismanagement.

In December 1979 the FLN Central Committee announced that Algeria would reduce its dependence on foreign financial and technical assistance, diversify its economic partners, and decrease its hydrocarbon exports in order to conserve these resources. The massive industrialization programme was to be reduced in scale and large state companies were to be reorganized into smaller units. Details of these changes were presented in a five-year plan adopted in June 1980. The emphasis of government policy was to shift from heavy industry to social areas, such as health, education and infrastructure, and raising agricultural production. The private sector was to be considerably liberalized.

FOREIGN POLICY UNDER CHADLI

During Chadli's presidency, Algerian foreign policy became more pragmatic and less determined by ideological considerations. Boumedienne's aim to present Algeria as one of the leaders of the Third World was abandoned, as was the policy of distracting attention from domestic problems by stridency abroad. He sought good relations with states of every political ideology and forged close links with conservatives without alienating radicals. Algeria, therefore, earned high regard as a mediator, and in October 1987 the country was elected to the UN Security Council for a two-year term beginning in January 1988.

Relations with other Arab states

Algeria under Chadli had no aspirations to leadership of the Arab world but worked for Arab unity and made attempts to mediate in disputes. The prestige that Chadli had gained was illustrated by his selection, together with that of King Hassan II of Morocco and King Fahd of Saudi Arabia, to form a Tripartite Arab Committee on Lebanon to pursue the decisions of the May 1989 Casablanca Arab summit meeting.

Diplomatic relations were restored with Egypt after a nine-year break in November 1988, and three months later Dr Esmat Abd al-Meguid became the first Egyptian minister to visit Algiers for 11 years. Algeria remained a staunch supporter of the Palestinian cause, and in June 1988 Chadli convened a special summit meeting to rally support for the *intifada* and provided a venue for the declaration of Palestinian statehood. Algeria strongly opposed the settlement of Soviet Jews in the West Bank region of Jordan, but Chadli declined to attend the Baghdad Arab summit meeting in person in May 1990 on the grounds that, without the participation of Syria, the meeting would be pointless.

Algeria, despite suspicions that it was covertly supporting its local Islamist fundamentalists, enjoyed friendly relations with the conservative Arab monarchies and co-operated with them in financial matters. Algeria also developed friendly diplomatic and commercial ties with Iran.

Relations with the superpowers

Whereas former President Boumedienne had restored diplomatic links with the USA while maintaining relations at a commercial level, Chadli sought to improve relations, with the aims of gaining higher levels of US investment and of promoting regional stability. Algeria played an important part in the negotiations over US hostages being detained in Iran, leading to their release in January 1981. However, relations with the USA became strained shortly afterwards when the US Government announced its decision to sell tanks to Algeria's then hostile neighbour, Morocco, and refused to agree to Algerian demands that the price of LNG (a major Algerian export) should be increased to a level of parity with the price of petroleum.

By 1985 relations with the USA had improved, and in April the two countries held a summit meeting in Washington, DC. This was the first official visit to the USA by an Algerian Head of State since independence. As a result of his visit, Chadli was successful in having Algeria removed from the list of countries that the US Government had declared 'ineligible' to purchase US military equipment. In order to balance this *rapprochement* with the USA, Chadli made an official visit to Moscow in March 1986. In October 1987 the USA expressed alarm when it was revealed that Algeria had agreed, in principle, to establish a political union with Libya. This agreement directly contravened the US policy of 'isolating' that country, and, after diplomatic pressure from the USA (in addition to opposition from within the Algerian Government), Chadli postponed the announcement of a treaty of political union with Libya.

Relations with France

After Chadli took office as President, relations with France began to improve. In September 1980 Algeria and France signed an agreement whereby the French Government provided incentives for the repatriation of some 800,000 Algerian workers and their dependants living in France, while Algeria released French bank assets which had been 'frozen' since independence. Following the election of a socialist government in France in 1981, relations became more cordial still. Gaston Defferre, the French Minister of the Interior, visited Algeria to discuss the problem of illegal immigration, and, shortly afterwards, President Mitterrand made an official visit. In February 1982 a dispute over the price of Algerian gas exports to France was settled, and in December Chadli made the first official visit to France by an Algerian Head of State since independence.

After the election of a right-wing French government in 1986, co-operation between France and Algeria was maintained. In September the French Prime Minister, Jacques Chirac, visited Algiers to discuss bilateral trade and foreign policy, although the positive aspects of his visit were vitiated by the announcement of proposals to introduce visa requirements for visitors from non-European Community (EC) countries to France, following a series of bombings in Paris. In October Algeria retaliated by introducing similar requirements for French visitors to Algeria. In the same month, however, France expelled 13 members of the Mouvement pour la démocratie en Algérie (MDA—founded by Ben Bella in 1984) and banned the MDA newspaper, *Al-Badil*, after Algerian security forces co-operated with France over the Paris bombings. In April 1987 the Algerian Government agreed to release the assets of former French settlers, which had been 'frozen' since independence, and subsequently allowed former French property-owners to sell their land in Algeria to the Algerian state, and French workers in Algeria to transfer their income to France. In return, the French Government agreed to provide financial assistance to Algeria for three years.

Relations deteriorated, however, during riots in Algiers in October 1988 (q.v.), as Algerian state-controlled newspapers accused the French media of exaggerating the unrest, and the Algerian Government criticized the French Minister of Co-operation for objecting to the severe measures taken against the rioters. However, in March 1989, during a visit to Algeria, President Mitterrand of France demonstrated his firm support for Chadli and his reforms. In June the Association for Franco-Algerian Friendship was founded, with the aim of strengthening links between the two countries.

In December 1990 relations between Algeria and France were subjected to renewed strain after Algeria issued a decree which designated Arabic as the country's official language, and which appeared to penalize the official use of French. In response, the French authorities appealed to Algerians to apply pressure on their Government to permit the continued official use of the French language. By May 1991 tensions appeared to have eased: France and Algeria concluded four petroleum agreements and French oil companies were granted two new concessions in the Sahara.

Co-operation with Spain

Until 1986 Algeria's relations with Spain had been circumspect, owing to Algerian suspicion of Spain's pro-Moroccan position in the Western Sahara conflict. In October 1986 the Spanish Government claimed that 'Txomin', the leader of the military wing of ETA (the Basque separatist movement), and a number of ETA supporters were living in Algeria, with the tacit approval of the Algerian Government. Algeria hastily denied any involvement with ETA and assured Spain that it would not allow the ETA members to engage in 'terrorist' activities. In December the Spanish Deputy Prime Minister visited Algeria and was reported to have met representatives of the Polisario Front. In the following month, Spain announced that it would incorporate Algeria into its programme of overseas military co-operation. The death of 'Txomin' in a road accident outside Algiers in February 1987 increased Spanish suspicions of the Algerian Government's stance regarding ETA. However, the tension was resolved by a pact, signed by the two countries in August, which allowed an Algerian security official to be stationed in Spain to monitor the activities of Algerian dissidents, in exchange for closer supervision of members of ETA in Algeria. In December an MDA activist was arrested by the Spanish authorities and expelled to Algeria. In April and May 1989 16 ETA members were expelled from Algeria, following the collapse of peace talks with the Spanish Government and a resumption of ETA violence in Spain. In December a Spanish company, Cepsa, signed a gas exploration and production agreement with the Algerian state monopoly SONATRACH. The reconciliation with Morocco removed political obstacles to the construction of a gas pipeline between Algeria and Spain.

Algeria and the 1990–91 Gulf crisis

Algeria condemned both the invasion of Kuwait by Iraq in August 1990, and the subsequent deployment of US and other Western armed forces in the Arabian peninsula. The Algerian Minister of Foreign Affairs, Sid-Ahmad Ghozali, advocated an 'Arab solution' to the conflict in the Persian (Arabian) Gulf region and deplored the UN's imposition of economic sanctions against Iraq. At the August 1990 summit meeting of Arab leaders, held in Cairo, President Chadli abstained in a vote to decide whether to deploy Arab forces alongside Western forces in Saudi Arabia.

President Chadli, both in a personal capacity and as the incumbent Chairman of the Union of the Arab Maghreb (UAM), made strenuous efforts to avert war in the Gulf region. In December 1990 he embarked on an extensive tour of the Middle East, but he denied that he was trying to arrange a summit meeting or that he had any particular plans to mediate in the conflict. At the conclusion of the hostilities between Iraq and the multinational force, the Algerian Minister of Foreign Affairs commended the resistance mounted by the Iraqi forces.

Moves towards Maghrebin unity

Although Algeria continued to support the Polisario Front in the Western Sahara conflict, Chadli was more interested in creating a 'Great Arab Maghreb', which would unify the five Maghrebin states politically and economically. In order to achieve this long-term goal, Chadli was prepared to display a greater flexibility than his predecessor with regard to Algeria's relations with Morocco and the Polisario Front.

Algeria's relations with other Maghrebin states improved considerably in the early 1980s. In 1979 Algeria assisted in negotiations with Mauritania over the withdrawal of its claim to Western Sahara. Mauritania signed a peace treaty in August, and Algeria resumed diplomatic relations. However, owing to the deadlock in Western Sahara, Algeria's relations with Morocco remained tense until 1983. In February of that year, as the culmination of a series of secret negotiations held since the death of Boumedienne, President Chadli and King Hassan of Morocco held a summit meeting on the Moroccan-Algerian border. A few months later restrictions on movements across the frontier were withdrawn.

In March 1983 Algeria and Tunisia signed the Maghreb Fraternity and Co-operation Treaty, which provided a framework for the creation of the Great Arab Maghreb. Unlike previous agreements made in the region, this treaty was not directed against neighbouring countries but was explicitly open to them to sign if they accepted the terms. At the same time, Algeria signed a treaty which delineated its borders with Tunisia, thus settling a 20-year old dispute between the two countries. At a meeting in April between representatives from Algeria, Morocco and Tunisia, it was agreed that further conferences would be held on Maghrebin unity, which Libya and Mauritania would be particularly welcome to attend. In December Mauritania signed the Maghreb Fraternity and Co-operation Treaty, and in April 1985, after three years of negotiations, it signed a border agreement with Algeria.

In the mid-1980s, however, Maghrebin unity became an increasingly remote ideal, owing to the deterioration of relations between the five nations. Algeria's relations with Libya became strained after Libya signed the Treaty of Oujda with Morocco in August 1984 and expelled Tunisian workers in 1985. Meanwhile, *rapprochement* with Morocco was hindered by Algeria's continuing support for the Polisario Front, and in July 1985 the Moroccan Minister of the Interior accused Algeria of training 'Moroccan terrorists' for operations against his Government. After Morocco had completed the construction of a new defensive wall on the borders of Western Sahara and Mauritania in April 1987, the Algerian Government expressed its concern that Mauritania might become involved in fighting between Moroccan troops and the Polisario Front.

In May 1987, however, President Chadli met King Hassan on the Moroccan-Algerian border, under the auspices of King Fahd of Saudi Arabia. The two leaders issued a joint communiqué, which stated that consultations to resolve bilateral differences would continue. Later in the month, the Algerian Government released 150 Moroccan soldiers, in exchange for 102 Algerian prisoners being held in Morocco.

Meanwhile, relations with Libya improved, following Chadli's meetings with the Libyan Secretary for Foreign Liaison, Dr Ali Abd as-Salim Treiki, in November 1985, and with Col Qaddafi in January 1986. Both Libya and Algeria reiterated their commitment to Maghreb unity and deplored the conflict over Western Sahara, demanding self-determination for the Sahrawi people. Following the US attack on Libya in April, Algeria unsuccessfully appealed for the convening of an emergency meeting of Arab nations. In an attempt to consolidate its good relations with Algeria, Libya advocated a union with Algeria in March and June. A year later, in June 1987, a proposal for political union between Libya and Algeria was submitted to Chadli by Col Qaddafi's deputy, Maj. Abd as-Salam Jalloud, during his visit to Algiers. After the visit, however, Algeria suggested that the Maghreb Fraternity and Co-operation Treaty already provided a framework for a new Algerian-Libyan relationship.

During late 1987 and early 1988 the process of achieving Maghrebin unity gathered momentum. In November 1987 Chadli received the Moroccan Minister of Foreign Affairs, and they discussed means of accelerating the development of the Great Arab Maghreb and of resolving the Western Sahara conflict. Maghreb unity also formed the agenda of a meeting between the Algerian, Mauritanian and Tunisian Ministers of Foreign Affairs in December, when hopes were again expressed that Libya might sign the Maghreb Fraternity and Co-operation Treaty. The restoration of diplomatic relations between Tunisia and Libya in the same month was viewed as a triumph of Algerian diplomacy. In January 1988, during a meeting in Tunis, Chadli and the new Tunisian President, Zine al-Abidine Ben Ali, issued directives to intensify bilateral co-operation, demanded a just resolution of the Western Sahara conflict, and pledged to work for regional stability and to hasten the creation of the Great Arab Maghreb. Chadli then visited Col Qaddafi, in an apparent attempt to persuade him to sign the Maghreb Fraternity and Co-operation Treaty, possibly in March, on the fifth anniversary of its inception. At a tripartite meeting in Tunis in February, Chadli, President Ben Ali and Col Qaddafi all expressed their determination to encourage co-operation between Maghreb countries and to work towards the creation of the Great Arab Maghreb.

In the hope that Libya would sign the Maghreb Fraternity and Co-operation Treaty (and with a view to the subsequent creation of a four-nation Great Arab Maghreb), Chadli aimed to isolate Morocco and thus force it to reach a settlement in the Western Sahara conflict. This would be a prelude to the eventual establishment of a complete five-nation Great Arab Maghreb. Faced with the collapse of this strategy (owing to Libya's failure to sign the treaty in March), and wishing to present a unified Maghreb front and to increase the number of 'moderate' Arab countries represented at the special Arab League summit which he had convened for June 1988 (see above), Chadli decided to seek the restoration of diplomatic relations with Morocco. Algerian officials made overtures towards Morocco, and in May the two countries announced the re-establishment of diplomatic relations at ambassadorial level. The Moroccan-Algerian border was opened in June, before the Arab League summit. It was reported that Algeria had offered to restore diplomatic relations if King Hassan agreed to attend the Arab League summit, and had withdrawn its insistence that Morocco should hold direct talks with the Polisario Front. At the summit King Hassan withdrew his former claim to Tindouf, and it became clear that Chadli was preparing to abandon the Western Sahara.

The creation of the Great Arab Maghreb became a reality in June 1988, when the first meeting of the five Heads of State of the Maghrebin countries was held in Algiers, following the conclusion of the Arab League summit. The five leaders issued a joint communiqué, which announced the creation of a Maghreb commission, comprising a delegation from each of the five countries, whose responsibility was to focus on the establishment of a semi-legislative, semi-consultative council to align legislation in the region, and to prepare joint economic projects. In late June Algeria and Libya agreed to hold referendums on a proposed union of the two countries. Unlike the proposals issued by Col Qaddafi in 1987 (which envisaged total merger), this revised proposal aimed merely to establish a federation between the two countries. President Chadli later announced that the Algerian referendum on the union would be held in 1989. In July 1988 Algeria and Morocco signed a co-operation agreement, and the two countries announced plans to harmonize their railway, postal and telecommunications systems. Later that month, the Maghreb commission met in Algiers and announced the creation of five working groups to examine areas of regional integration.

In August 1988 Morocco and the Polisario Front accepted a UN peace plan to settle the Western Sahara conflict. During the negotiations, it became apparent that Algeria's restoration of diplomatic relations with Morocco had forced Polisario, which was heavily dependent on Algerian support, to make concessions. (For a more detailed account of the Western Sahara conflict, see the chapter on Morocco.)

On 17 February 1989 the treaty creating the UAM was signed in Marrakesh, Morocco, by the leaders of Algeria, Libya, Mauritania, Morocco and Tunisia. Modelled on the EC, the UAM was formed principally to enable its members to negotiate with that body when it declared a single European market at the end of 1992. It was also intended to encourage trade and economic co-operation by allowing freedom of movement across frontiers. The treaty created a policy-making council of Heads of State, to meet every six months under an annually rotating chairman, and other administrative bodies, including a court, comprising 10 members, to consider disputes between member states. In June 1989 the five nations formed a joint parliament, and a defence clause prohibited aggression between the states.

During late 1989 and early 1990 Algeria became preoccupied with domestic and economic affairs and devoted little time to affairs in the Maghreb. Although in no way obstructive, it did not show the leadership that its strength and central position should have enabled it to extend and left much of the administration to Tunisia. At the same time, as was evident at the Tunis summit meeting in January 1990, its partners were increasingly concerned at its tolerance of an avowedly Islamic fundamentalist political party, the Front islamique du salut (FIS) and at the pace of its liberal reforms. In May Algeria hosted a meeting at which the UAM Ministers of Transport approved a draft

agreement to create a joint airline and to expand rail links to provide a continuous track from Tobruk (Libya) to Nouakchott (Mauritania).

Chadli earned the gratitude of Col Qaddafi in August 1989 by mediating an acceptable settlement of the dispute between Chad and Libya over the Aozou strip and also by attempting to allay US concerns about an alleged chemical weapons factory at Rabta in Libya. Relations with Morocco were complicated by deadlock in Western Sahara: Chadli continued to urge King Hassan to hold direct talks with the Polisario Front. Moroccan co-operation was vital for perhaps the most important of all Algeria's development projects, the gas pipeline to Western Europe. In February 1990 the Ministers of the Interior of the two countries signed agreements to co-operate in facilitating the movement of people and goods and in combating drugs-smuggling. It was agreed to promote co-operation between provincial and municipal authorities in the border regions.

In July 1990 the chairmanship of the UAM passed to Algeria. Later that month, at the third meeting of the UAM Heads of State, President Chadli outlined proposals to unify tariffs by 1992 and to create a full customs union by 1995. Six agreements were signed, providing for exchanges of agricultural products, the creation of a joint airline to operate initially alongside the national carriers, procedures to stop the spread of agricultural diseases, measures to encourage and guarantee investment, the ending of double taxation and the freedom of movement for goods and people. No agreement was reached on the choice of a Secretary-General for the UAM, nor on the location of its headquarters. The meeting issued a declaration of support for the Palestinian *intifada* and condemned the mass emigration of Soviet Jews to Israel.

CHANGES WITHIN THE FLN

During 1980 a general streamlining of the FLN took place, and the President's control over it was strengthened. In June, at an extraordinary congress of nearly 4,000 delegates, important changes in the party structure were initiated. The Political Bureau was now to consist of between seven and 11 members (having previously numbered between 17 and 21), and was to meet monthly instead of weekly. The President, as Secretary-General of the FLN, was empowered to select the members of the Political Bureau rather than merely to 'propose' them, although the choice would still be subject to the Central Committee's approval; he was also given freedom to make other changes in the party which he considered necessary. The reforms reinforced the President's position, and reduced the role of the Political Bureau to that of an advisory body. Chadli immediately reduced its membership to the new statutory minimum of seven. The Prime Minister, Col Abd al-Ghani, and several other ministers were removed from the Bureau, although it still represented a wide range of opinion. In addition, the number of FLN committees was reduced from 12 to five. Changes were also made in the wider membership of the FLN. The congress agreed that all officials of the UGTA and the other mass organizations must be members of the FLN. In this way members of 'unofficial' parties, such as the communist Parti d'avant-garde socialiste (PAGS—renamed Ettahaddi in 1993), would be excluded from official positions.

Further changes were made to the composition of the FLN's Political Bureau in July 1981, when its membership was increased to 10. Col Abd al-Ghani was reappointed, but Yahiaoui and Bouteflika, Chadli's rivals for the presidency in 1979, were removed, although they retained their membership of the Central Committee. In December Bouteflika was dismissed from the FLN Central Committee, as were three other senior members who had held important portfolios under Boumedienne. Legislative elections were held on 5 March 1982, when 72.7% of the electorate voted for FLN candidates. The membership of the National People's Assembly was increased to 281, of whom 55 were permanent members of the FLN.

At the fifth congress of the FLN, held in December 1983, Chadli was re-elected to the post of Secretary-General of the party, and became the sole candidate for the presidential elections, held on 12 January 1984. His candidature was endorsed by 95.4% of the electorate, and he was returned to office for another five years. Ten days after his re-election, President Chadli effected a major government reshuffle, and appointed a new Prime Minister, Abd al-Hamid Brahimi, formerly Minister of Planning.

MOVES TOWARDS LIBERALIZATION

Following public consultations and debate initiated by Chadli in February 1985, a new national charter was adopted at a special congress of the FLN, held in December. The charter's programme encouraged private enterprise and proposed a balance between socialism and Islam as the state ideology. In a referendum held in January 1986, in which 95.9% of the eligible population took part, 98.4% of the votes were cast in favour of the adoption of the new charter.

At a general election for the National People's Assembly on 26 February 1987, a record 87.9% of the electorate voted for FLN candidates. The number of seats was increased to 295, owing to demographic changes. The newly-elected Assembly comprised a larger number of younger, liberal deputies who were more likely to support Chadli's policy of liberalization.

In June 1987, in response to an increase in social unrest, a new Minister of the Interior was appointed and changes were made in the military hierarchy. In July, as part of its liberalization policy, the Government introduced legislation which permitted the formation of local organizations without prior consent from the authorities except where these were deemed to threaten Algeria's security or the policies of the revised national charter. 'National' organizations continued to require government approval. Even this relatively moderate measure aroused misgivings among 'conservative' deputies in the National People's Assembly, who feared that it might lead to the creation of alternative political organizations.

Meanwhile, Chadli accelerated the implementation of his policy to restructure and liberalize the economy. In July 1987 the National People's Assembly began to consider proposals that aimed to remove various state controls from agricultural co-operatives and public enterprises, in contrast to the collectivization of the 1970s, which was being increasingly criticized as inefficient. In accordance with this forthcoming legislation, during an extensive cabinet reshuffle in November, Chadli abolished the Ministry of Planning, which had previously supervised every aspect of Algeria's economy. The remaining functions of the ministry were assumed by a national Council of Planning, directly accountable to the Prime Minister, Brahimi. Chadli also took the opportunity to create a Ministry of Education and Training, in response to the growth in demand for employment and educational opportunities for young people.

However, the implementation of the new economic legislation, scheduled for 1988, was hindered by Algeria's complex bureaucratic procedures. In December 1987 Chadli announced a series of reforms intended to improve the efficiency of the country's administrative structures. Two measures to take immediate effect were the abolition of certain documents hitherto required by every citizen for each administrative procedure, and the instant application of legal decisions. In the short term, the Government was to introduce a single identity card, with a multiplicity of uses, and to appoint a national mediator to facilitate relations between the public and civil servants. In the medium term, measures were to be introduced in order to effect a complete reorganization of the administrative structure.

In February 1988, in preparation for the sixth FLN congress, Chadli appointed a national commission to evaluate Algeria's second Five-Year Development Plan, and to assist with the drafting of an appropriate economic plan for the 1990s. Later in February, Chadli announced several government changes whereby 'technocrat' ministers were appointed to preside over the more problematic sectors of the economy.

INTERNAL UNREST

In 1979 the Government encountered criticism from students, who boycotted classes to protest at the slow implementation of the policy of replacing French with Arabic. The students' demands were partly met by measures intended to accelerate the process of 'Arabization' in education, and 600 Arabic-speaking trainee magistrates were appointed. In May 1980 the FLN Central Committee announced that a co-ordinating body was to be established to encourage the use of Arabic, and that official newspapers should be printed in Arabic only. By the following year, many settlements had reverted to their Arabic names.

Protests against the suppression of the Berber language and culture continued in the early 1980s. These generally centred on the Kabyle, a region regarded for many years as having dangerously separatist intentions. Although some concessions were made (including the creation of chairs in Berber languages at the Universities of Tizi-Ouzou and Algiers and the provision of Berber radio programmes), President Chadli made it clear that he viewed the Berber demands as a threat to national unity. In 1981 a 'cultural charter' was proposed, which made provisions for the Berber culture as part of Algeria's national heritage. However, the charter received little approval; the discussions were accompanied by outbreaks of violence and had to be abandoned. Later, in September, the tension in the Kabyle was alleviated by the announcement that departments of popular literature and dialect were to be opened in Algiers, Constantine, Oran and Annaba (although not in Tizi-Ouzou).

Throughout 1985 there was increased activity among opposition groups. In June Ali Yahia Abdennour, the President of the unauthorized Algerian League of Human Rights (ALHR), was arrested and imprisoned for 11 months for forming an illegal organization. In July and August further members of the ALHR and the Association of the Sons of Chouhada, another unauthorized organization, were arrested. Clashes occurred in November in Tizi-Ouzou between public order forces and members of the Association of the Sons of Chouhada who were protesting against the arrests of fellow members. Following the theft of weapons and ammunition from an army barracks at Souma in August, several Islamist activists were arrested. In December 19 of Ben Bella's alleged supporters were imprisoned on charges of threatening state security.

In November 1986 four people were reportedly killed and 186 people arrested during three days of rioting in Constantine, which followed student protests against poor living conditions and inadequate tuition. In other parts of Algeria students and secondary school pupils held demonstrations against government attempts to reform the *baccalauréat* examination. Amid criticism, the 186 detainees were swiftly brought to trial and given severe sentences, ranging from two to eight years' imprisonment. Following the riots, the Chief of Staff of the Army, Gen. Mustafa ben Loucif, was discharged from his duties, and lost his deputy membership of the FLN. The ALHR became affiliated to the International League for Human Rights (ILHR) in December, but the leaders of the ALHR were later arrested and exiled to southern Algeria.

In 1987 the Government issued amnesties as part of its liberalization policy. In March 22 people were released from internal exile, including the leaders of the ALHR, and a branch of Amnesty International, a prominent human rights organization, was established in Algeria. The Algerian League for the Defence of Human Rights (ALDHR) was formed with government authorization in April, as a rival to the illegal ALHR. Following discussions between the Government and the ALDHR, the authorities released 186 people, imprisoned after the Constantine riots, and six members of the ALHR and two members of the Association of the Sons of Chouhada, imprisoned in 1985.

Nevertheless, the authorities continued to act vigorously against any signs of organized opposition which they considered to constitute a threat to the state. In January 1987 security forces shot dead Mustafa Bouiali, the leader, and three other members of the Islamist group responsible for the theft of weapons at Souma in 1985, who had been in hiding for 18 months. In June 12 people received prison sentences ranging from two to 10 years for distributing subversive literature and receiving funds from abroad, particularly from Libya and Ben Bella's MDA. The authorities also banned the leaders of the ALHR from leaving the country to attend a meeting of the ILHR. At the end of a trial in July, involving 202 defendants accused of involvement in the activities of Bouiali's Islamist group, four people received death sentences for plotting against the state, murder, armed attacks and robbery. Other defendants received sentences ranging from life to one year's imprisonment, while 15 people were acquitted. However, during a series of amnesties to commemorate the 25th anniversary of Algerian independence in August, the four death sentences were commuted to life imprisonment, and life sentences were reduced to 20 years in detention.

THE OCTOBER 1988 RIOTS

Boumedienne had insisted upon rigid state socialism controlled by an increasingly ponderous and corrupt bureaucracy and after his death his appointees fought to maintain their grip upon the state and the economy. The FLN had, however, abandoned any pretence to ideology or purpose beyond that of staying in power. In December 1987 President Chadli felt secure enough to introduce limited liberalization, giving more freedom to private enterprise and allowing managers in the public sector to make some decisions without reference to the bureaucracy. In June 1988 he reorganized the public sector by creating state-sponsored Trust Companies (Fonds de Participation) to which managers were to be accountable. The private sector was also allowed some access to foreign exchange. This economic restructuring was not extended to the political sphere, where the FLN continued to exercise complete control. In his speeches Chadli urged reform but seemed unable or unwilling to implement it.

Algeria had amassed a debt of some US $24,000m. and found the annual interest of $6,000m. an almost impossible burden, owing to the depressed price of oil and gas which traditionally accounted for 97% of the country's foreign exchange. The Government, for reasons of prestige and its unwillingness to accept the intervention of the World Bank, refused to reschedule the debt and instead reduced imports, 70% of which were foodstuffs. These became extremely scarce and expensive. The exposure of the economy to market forces while trying to service the huge debt precipitated an economic crisis. The increasing hardship and the sense of inequality produced a series of strikes from July onwards.

On the evening of 4 October 1988 as many as 5,000 youths destroyed shops selling luxury goods, and on the following day widespread looting occurred. Government buildings in Algiers were also targets for attack. On 6 October a state of emergency was declared, and a curfew was imposed in Algiers. The army, equipped with tanks, was deployed ruthlessly to suppress the disturbances, making no attempt to avoid civilian casualties. Special military courts were also established to punish the rioters. On 10 October Chadli, who had hitherto remained silent, promised to present a programme of reforms for debate when the violence, which had spread to Oran, Annaba and other towns, subsided. On 12 October the tanks were withdrawn. Officials stated that 159 people had been killed during the disturbances, but unofficial estimates indicated at least 500 deaths, while more than 3,500 had been arrested, some of whom were reported to have been tortured. The rioters, including a number expressing support for Ben Bella, had called themselves the Movement for Algerian Renewal. They were not Islamist activists, although fundamentalists did later participate in the disturbances; nor were they Berbers, who had their own grievances. On 15 October schools reopened; on the following day 500 minors, who had been detained, were freed, and the special courts were suspended. Stocks of food were released from warehouses to be sold, often at less than half the previous prices.

CONSTITUTIONAL REFORM

Young people were at the forefront of this uprising against the FLN. One-half of the Algerian people in their early twenties were unemployed, and there was widespread anger at the move towards an élitist education system. Little hostility was shown towards President Chadli himself; observers noted that the young people recognized his attempts to introduce reforms, despite the opposition of uncompromising elements within the FLN. Chadli exploited this sentiment by attempting to overcome vested interests and achieve reform. In late October 1988 he proposed that the identification of the state with the FLN be ended by allowing non-party candidates to contest elections. Furthermore, the Prime Minister would no longer be responsible to the President, who would stand above party politics, but to the National People's Assembly. To show that these measures would not be merely superficial, five days later Chadli dismissed his official FLN deputy, Muhammad Cherif Messaadia (a resolute opponent of reform, widely regarded as the most unpopular politician in the country), replacing him with the more liberal Abd al-Hamid Mehiri, who had been the Algerian Ambassador to France and Morocco. The head of internal security was also replaced. On 3 November the proposed reforms were approved at a referendum by 92.3% of the votes cast (by 83.1% of those eligible to vote).

In November 1988 Chadli dismissed the Prime Minister, Abd al-Hamid Brahimi, replacing him with Col Kasdi Merbah, who had been a chief of police under Boumedienne but had become a liberal Minister of Agriculture, allowing peasants to operate farms without state control, and a reforming Minister of Health. Merbah was considered to have more charisma and capacity for independent thought than his predecessor and he declared that he would form a cabinet of men of 'integrity, competence and efficiency' answerable to the National People's Assembly. Merbah announced proposals which laid emphasis on helping the young people, incorporating plans for an increase in expenditure on education, a building programme, wage rises from January 1989, a reduction in the duration of military service and a rise in taxes for the wealthy. Merbah's programme of reforms was submitted to the Assembly and, for the first time, the ensuing debate was broadcast live on television. The actions of 21 members of the Assembly in voting against the programme marked an even greater departure from precedent.

In late November 1988 a special two-day congress of the FLN accepted further reforms. Chadli was endorsed as the sole candidate for the presidency but he divorced himself from the party by relinquishing his post of Secretary-General to Abd al-Hamid Mehiri. It was decided that the FLN should revert to its former role as a forum for competing views, instead of the monolith that it had become under Boumedienne. It was agreed that independent candidates could contest elections, but the formation of other parties was forbidden, in order to exclude the Islamist activists. In early December Chadli instituted a reorganization of the army, replacing six military commanders. The army, which had played an important role in Algerian politics since independence, had been widely criticized by intellectuals and human rights activists for its violent suppression of the October riots. On 22 December Chadli was elected President for a third term of office, receiving 81% of the votes cast.

In early February 1989 a new draft Constitution was published. It completed the separation of the state from the FLN and permitted the 'creation of associations of a political nature', with certain restrictions. The 'irreversible commitment to socialism' of the previous Constitution was abandoned, while the army was entrusted with the sole task of defending the country and not of 'participating in the building of socialism'. The new Constitution emphasized individual and collective rights rather than those of 'the People' as a whole. Public-sector workers were given the right to strike. Executive, legislative and judicial functions were separated and no longer controlled by the party, but supervised by a Constitutional Council. The new draft was regarded as a complete break with the past, shifting Algeria from the socialist into the Western capitalist group of nations, and it was approved by referendum on 23 February by 73.4% of votes cast by 79% of the total electorate.

In March 1989 another significant reform of the political system was implemented. Senior army officers asked to be relieved of their duties as members of the FLN Central Committee, claiming that the army should be concerned exclusively with the defence of 'the superior interests of the nation and the free choice of the people'. After the turbulence of the past year, Chadli's task was to maintain control of the process of reform, but the Algerian people took advantage of a loosening of control and started to react against the inadequacy of their living conditions. In April there were demonstrations against sharp rises in food prices, and in May there were strikes and riots in protest against the slow pace of reform and the corrupt practices of local officials. The construction of just one-third of 90,000 projected dwellings, and the allocation of those through favouritism, led to an outbreak of violence in Souk Ahras in May. Army units were dispatched to the area to control the unrest, but poor housing conditions also prompted the blocking of roads and the seizure of the town hall in Didouche Mourad in September. In October more than 1,000 people deprived of drinking water for several days rioted in Sidi Aissa. Later in the month, after an earthquake had devastated Nador, further road blocks were mounted as a protest against the tardiness of government relief efforts.

TOWARDS MULTI-PARTY ELECTIONS

In early July 1989 the National People's Assembly approved a law on associations, revoking the ban on the formation of political parties. New parties were obliged to be licensed by the Ministry of the Interior, and were not to be externally financed or based exclusively on religious, professional or regional interest. At the same time, the Assembly adopted legislation reducing the role of the state in controlling the economy, thus increasing its exposure to market forces. Later in the same month, the Assembly adopted a new electoral law permitting opposition political parties to contest future elections and to occupy seats in the Assembly. Elections to the Assembly were to be held every five years, with one round of voting, after which the winning list of candidates in each multi-member constituency would take all the seats. For local and municipal elections the new electoral law stipulated that any party obtaining at least 50% of the votes in a multi-member constituency should take all the seats. If no party received 50% of the votes, the party with the largest share was to take one-half of the seats, while the remainder were to be divided proportionally among all the other parties that obtained more than 10% of the total vote. Other legislation adopted in July allowed greater investment in the economy by foreign companies and ended the state monopoly of the press while, controversially, leaving the principal newspapers under the control of the FLN.

In September 1989 President Chadli dismissed the Prime Minister, Col Kasdi Merbah, whom he regarded as insufficiently committed to the process of reform. Merbah was replaced by Mouloud Hamrouche (hitherto a senior official in the presidential office), who immediately declared his determination to end the identification of the party (i.e. the FLN) with the state, and to transform the country by means of dialogue with other political parties, trade unions and the public. In his new Council of Ministers Hamrouche retained only eight of his predecessor's appointees, replacing FLN officials and retired military officers with progressive politicians. Hamrouche abolished the Ministry of Information, which he regarded as incompatible with democracy. His programme, incorporating proposals for defending living standards while 'freeing public and private industry from all forms of obstacles', anti-inflation measures, educational reform, the introduction of free wage-bargaining and the encouragement of investment, was approved in the National People's Assembly, and endorsed by President Chadli, who declared the process of reform to be irreversible.

In response to complaints by newly-licensed political parties of insufficient opportunity for preparation, local and municipal elections, which had been scheduled to take place in December 1989, were postponed until June 1990. President Chadli welcomed the formation of parties representing diverse political persuasions, and by early 1990 more than 20 parties had been formally registered. They included the Parti social-démocrate (PSD), the communist PAGS, the FIS, the Berber Rassemblement pour la culture et la démocratie (RCD), the Front des forces socialistes (FFS—originally founded in 1963) and the strongly Islamist MDA.

In November 1989 some 5,000 members of the FLN attended an extraordinary party congress, at which widespread anxiety at the sudden onset of political pluralism was apparent. Many of the speeches made at the conference expressed nostalgia for the uncompromising leadership of Boumedienne, many of whose former lieutenants were elected to a new, enlarged central committee. The congress also revealed the strong Islamist sentiments of many party members. However, President Chadli and his Council of Ministers had not been marginalized in their enthusiastic espousal of political reform: the majority of a new politburo, elected at the end of December, were likewise in favour of change.

The amended Constitution of February 1989 gave public-sector workers the right to strike and they took such advantage of this provision that the number of strikes rose by 25% in the following 12 months, averaging 250 per month. In early 1990 students demonstrated against police brutality. Hundreds of thousands of women demonstrated in favour of the traditional Islamic role of women, after thousands of others had demonstrated against any reversion to such a role. There were reports of assaults on women wearing Western-style clothes, while an estimated 10,000 people in Oran demonstrated in support of the closure of brothels and of establishments selling alcohol. About 50,000 Berbers demonstrated in support of demands for an increase in the teaching of the Berber language.

Meanwhile, the Minister of the Economy, Ghazi Hidouci, expressed pessimism about the country's economic situation, indicating the difficulties of reform and urging all public-sector managers to increase their efforts. In order to stimulate the economy, he announced the ending of the distinction between the public and private sectors—both were to be open to investment. In March 1990 a joint-venture law was announced, foreign banks were permitted to open branches and a powerful Conseil de Monnaie et de Crédit was created to regulate the inflow and repatriation of capital.

Following a meeting of its central committee in March 1990, the FLN declared itself united. President Chadli even hinted that elections to the National People's Assembly might be brought forward from 1992, as the FIS demanded, and that he might consider 'coexisting' as President with an opposition government. However, the FLN was adversely affected by a statement from the former Prime Minister, Abd al-Hamid Brahimi, in which he alleged that government officials had received $26,000m. ($2,000m. more than the entire national debt) in bribes during the previous 10 years. The situation was not alleviated by Prime Minister Hamrouche's objection that the sum could not possibly have exceeded $2,000m. The FLN was further damaged by the allegation of a former government minister, Abubakr Belkaid, that mismanagement of gas development in the 1980s had cost the country $40,000m. in lost revenues; and by the demand of the FLN-affiliated trade union, the UGTA, for the abrogation of the law that permitted the establishment of rival unions. Meanwhile, rank-and-file members of the UGTA demonstrated against their leaders, accusing them of corruption, inactivity and subservience to the FLN.

In March 1990 the National People's Assembly approved amendments to the electoral law that had been introduced in July 1989. Under the amended law, a party gaining 50% or more of the votes in a multi-member constituency would no longer take all of the seats, which were to be divided proportionally instead. If no party gained a majority, the party gaining the most votes was to take one-half of the seats. Parties would need to gain only 7% of the total votes cast to achieve representation, rather than 10% as previously. The amendments to the electoral law were regarded as having been introduced to counter the perceived strength of the FIS in the approach to the municipal and local elections. The demands of opposition parties for a further postponement of the elections, so that they would have more time to prepare, were rejected, even though it was apparent that only the FLN and the FIS would be able to present candidates in all of Algeria's 48 *wilayat*. Even the FLN appeared unlikely to be able to contest all 1,539 council seats because in some localities conflicting elements within the party had been unable to agree on a candidate.

In April 1990 thousands of FIS supporters demonstrated in Algiers, demanding that the National People's Assembly should be dissolved within three months and that *Shari'a* (Islamic) law should be introduced. Out of concern that the strength of the FIS constituted a threat to democracy, the RCD organized a pro-democracy demonstration in May, in which tens of thousands were estimated to have participated. The election campaign began officially later in the month. On the final day of the campaign, in early June, the FIS rallied more than 100,000 of its supporters, in front of whom its leader, Abbasi Madani, warned the Algerian army not to attempt a military coup.

At the local elections held on 12 June 1990 the FIS received some 55% of the total votes cast and obtained a majority of seats in 853 municipalities and 32 *wilayat*, while the FLN, which obtained about 32% of the votes, retained control of 487 municipalities and 14 *wilayat*. Independent candidates won 11.7% of the votes in the municipal elections, the RCD 2.1% and the Parti national pour la solidarité et le développement (PNSD) 1.6%. In the elections to the *wilayat* the RCD gained control in 87 localities, and the PNSD in two.

While the success of the FIS was, to some extent, vitiated by a high rate of voter abstention—estimated at between 35% and 40%—and by a boycott of the elections by two main opposition parties, the MDA and the FFS—on the grounds that the Government should first have held elections to the National People's

Assembly—the scale of the victory that the FIS had achieved was remarkable, even unique, in the Arab world. Some Western observers claimed that it was the first occasion on which any Arab country had been allowed freely to express itself in a multi-party election. It was certainly the first time that an Islamist party had won a majority of the votes in such an election, and this achievement was particularly remarkable in Algeria, which had been widely regarded as one of the most secular, westernized countries in the Arab world.

THE AFTERMATH OF THE MUNICIPAL ELECTIONS OF JUNE 1990

Following its successes in the municipal elections of June 1990, the FIS demanded the dissolution of the National People's Assembly, to be followed by a general election contested by all political parties. At the same time, the FIS denied any aspiration to establish an Iranian-style Islamic republic in Algeria, or desire to oust President Chadli. The leader of the FIS, Abbasi Madani, issued a warning to the army not to attempt to cheat the party of its victory. Another senior figure in the FIS, Ali Belhadj, claimed that democracy was not an Islamic concept and demanded the introduction of *Shari'a* law in Algeria. From exile, the leader of the MDA, Ben Bella, claimed that the results of the municipal elections were 'an undeniable step forward'. Some observers believed that Chadli had deliberately given the FIS an opportunity to exercise limited local power so that it could discredit itself through dogmatism and inefficiency and destroy its chances of success in elections to the National People's Assembly.

It was uncertain, indeed, whether the inexperienced administrators of the FIS could implement large, expensive projects to provide housing and jobs and thus make Islamic municipal socialism succeed. There was no reduction in unemployment, and riots erupted in protest at the allegedly unfair distribution of food and subsequent shortages. In November 1990 some 5,000 FIS mayors and councillors marched on the presidential palace to demonstrate against 'politically-motivated' obstruction by government officials.

In the immediate aftermath of its poor performance in the municipal elections, the FLN denounced the use of religion for political ends and sought the co-operation of other political parties to safeguard democracy. The Prime Minister, Mouloud Hamrouche, rejected demands for his resignation and for the dissolution of the National People's Assembly, and promised that the process of reform would continue. However, by July 1990 it was clear that the FLN was too divided to implement further reforms. Hamrouche and four other government ministers, including the Minister of Foreign Affairs and the Minister of the Economy resigned from the FLN politburo in order to concentrate on affairs of state, distancing themselves from the party, which, Hamrouche believed, should renew itself free of governmental responsibilities. They were replaced in the politburo by young, university-educated professional men, rather than by veterans of the war of independence against France. One such veteran, Ben Khedda, founded a moderate Islamist party, El-Oumma (The Community), with the aim of gradually introducing *Shari'a* law into Algeria, without coercion. Another, Lakhdar Bentobbal, became honorary president of a new National Democratic Conference, in which the RCD, the PAGS and the PSD agreed to collaborate to contest the forthcoming elections to the National People's Assembly. In late July, in a cabinet reshuffle, President Chadli appointed Maj.-Gen. Khaled Nezzar, hitherto the Chief of Staff of the Armed Forces, as Minister of Defence. It was the first time since Boumedienne's seizure of power that the office had not been held by the President. Chadli also announced that elections to the National People's Assembly, which were not due to take place until 1992, would be held during the first four months of 1991. While the President declared that he was confident that Algeria's political parties would 'respect the rules of democracy', the newly-appointed Minister of Defence warned that the army might intervene in the event of unrest. Thousands of political prisoners, most of whom had been incarcerated after the riots of October 1988, were released.

The leader of the MDA, Ben Bella, returned to Algeria in September 1990 to a less enthusiastic welcome than had been anticipated. There was no response to his demands for the

Government to resign, for the creation of a 'united front', for a reduction in the number of opposition political parties and for unreserved support for Iraq in the Gulf crisis. The Government continued to implement its programme of economic reforms, which included plans to establish a stock market, to liberalize imports and to make the Algerian dinar fully convertible. The economic reform programme created further, more serious divisions within the FLN. One of the party's founders, the President of the National People's Assembly, Rabah Bitat, resigned, accusing Prime Minister Hamrouche of dismantling the public sector. The former Prime Minister, Abd al-Hamid Brahimi, also resigned from the FLN, complaining of a lack of democracy within the party.

In December 1990 the National People's Assembly passed a vote of confidence in favour of Prime Minister Hamrouche, the first such vote for 20 years. At the end of the month the Assembly approved a law stipulating that, after 1997, Arabic would become Algeria's official language and that the use of the French and Berber languages by private companies and by political parties would thereafter be subject to heavy fines. The new law was regarded as an attack on Algeria's Western-educated élite and the Berber people. In response, some 500,000 people demonstrated in Algiers against religious and political intolerance. The FIS regarded the adoption of the 'Arabization' law as a political triumph, but it no longer enjoyed a monopoly on 'Islamist activism'. There were now two new political parties which aimed to recruit people who were dissatisfied with the intolerance of the FIS and those who saw no incompatibility between Islam and liberal economics. Sheikh Abdullah Djaballah founded the Islamic Renaissance Movement (Nahdah), while Sheikh Mahfoud Nahnah founded Hamas. The FIS, which was also losing support to the MDA, claimed that these new parties had been sponsored by the Government. The FIS itself appeared to be suffering from divisions between Madani and Belhadj. While the latter urged his supporters to prepare to give military support to Iraq, Madani argued that military training should be restricted to the army and that the FIS should achieve power through electoral means.

By early 1991 increases in prices and the rate of unemployment were widely perceived to be the result of Hamrouche's economic policies. In March the UGTA organized a general strike, the first since independence, which was reported to have been extremely well supported. In response, Prime Minister Hamrouche announced a wide-ranging programme to improve economic efficiency and to satisfy the demands of the trades unions: child benefits, which had remained frozen for 29 years, were increased by 300% and it was announced that more than $1,500m. (14.5% of the national budget) was to be spent on subsidizing essential commodities in the current financial year.

In early April 1991 the Government announced that elections to the National People's Assembly would be held on 27 June and, at the same time, some major revisions to the country's electoral law were proposed. In constituencies where no candidate achieved an absolute majority in the first round of voting, second ballots were to be allowed. Campaigning in mosques and proxy voting were to be restricted. The number of constituencies was increased from 290 to 542. The FIS regarded all these changes to the electoral law as a deliberate ploy to reduce its chances of victory in the forthcoming elections. It also demanded that a presidential election should be held at the same time as elections to the National People's Assembly.

It appeared that some 40 political parties, including the first 'Green Party' in the Arab world, would contest the elections. However, the PAGS stated that there was insufficient time to prepare for the elections and declined to present candidates. Hamrouche, meanwhile, sought allies among the secular opposition parties and among moderate Muslims, letting it be known that, even in the event of an outright victory by the FLN, he would incorporate opposition leaders into the Government in the interest of national unity. Some 80% of the FLN's deputies in the National People's Assembly were omitted from the party's new lists of candidates.

The leaders of Algeria's Islamist political parties conferred and decided not to oppose each other's candidates. It was also agreed that the FIS should provide two-thirds of the Islamist candidates in the elections. However, Madani subsequently renounced this agreement and campaigned for changes to the electoral law, while the other Islamist parties attempted to avoid confrontation. When the electoral campaign commenced in May 1991, the founder of El-Oumma, Ben Khedda, announced that his party would not present any candidates, in order to avoid further division among Muslims. Conversely, Hamas presented 366 candidates, and the MDA 367. Altogether 5,000 candidates were nominated.

In mid-1991 Abbasi Madani appealed for an indefinite general strike in protest at the new electoral law, and demanded President Chadli's resignation. In response, about 40,000 people demonstrated in Algiers, and violence erupted when the police used tear-gas to disperse the crowds. Chadli warned that it might be necessary to use force to maintain public order so that the elections could be held. On 4 June the police opened fire on militant Islamist activists, allegedly killing at least five of them, while some 700 demonstrators were admitted to hospital, suffering from the effects of tear-gas. Other observers estimated that as many as 50 people had died in unrest around the country. On 5 June, after further violent incidents had occurred, Chadli declared a 'state of siege' and suspended the elections indefinitely. Tanks were deployed on the streets of Algiers, and a curfew was imposed. The army was authorized to ban strikes and 'subversive' literature, and to search buildings and control the distribution of food. In response to the intervention of the army, Madani announced that the FIS had reached an agreement with the Government and, claiming victory, abandoned the general strike.

The agreement between the FIS and the Government seemed to involve the removal of Mouloud Hamrouche, whose resignation had been announced earlier on 5 June 1991, and his replacement, as Prime Minister, by the Minister of Foreign Affairs, Sid-Ahmad Ghozali, who was a practising Muslim and a liberal. Ghozali promised that a presidential election and elections to the National People's Assembly would be held before the end of 1991. In mid-June, after having consulted opposition parties, Ghozali announced his Council of Ministers, which Madani welcomed for its political neutrality. It included two women, 21 newcomers to politics and the first Arab Minister for Human Rights. The new Minister of the Interior, Abd al-Latif Rahal, was a former diplomat with no known political links. Maj.-Gen. Nezzar retained the defence portfolio, and the army, rather than the Government, remained responsible for security, although its presence on the streets was quickly reduced. Ghozali's ambitious programme of reforms, which included the establishment of a Ministry of Small Business, was approved by a large majority in the National People's Assembly. On 28 June President Chadli announced his resignation from the FLN, in order to demonstrate the end of one-party rule, and Ben Bella declared that he would contest the forthcoming presidential election.

Tension nevertheless remained high, and there were further outbreaks of violence as the army began to remove FIS symbols which had replaced national insignia on municipal buildings. Caches of weapons were found, and later in June 1991 more than 40 people were killed, and over 350 wounded, in violent unrest. Belhadj seemed to be provoking the security forces, demanding their exclusion from parts of Algiers. On the night of 26–27 June tanks were redeployed on the streets of Algiers, and on 28 June, in his Friday sermon, Madani threatened to declare a *jihad* (holy war) if they were not withdrawn. On 30 June Madani, Belhadj and some 2,500 of their supporters (8,000, according to opponents of the Government) were arrested, and more weapons were seized. There were clashes in several places, ranging from Mostaganem in the west to Guelma on the Tunisian frontier, and in Djelfa on the edge of the Sahara, but by mid-July the army had begun to reduce its presence on the streets and more than half of those arrested had been provisionally released.

Despite pressure from the army, Chadli refused to proscribe the FIS, but during 30 June–2 July 1991 military personnel occupied its headquarters, thereby paralysing the party's communication network throughout the country. The Prime Minister announced that Madani and Belhadj would stand trial for 'fomenting, organizing, launching and leading an armed conspiracy against the security of the state', accusing them of seeking to establish a dictatorship. He added that general and presidential elections would be held as soon as possible and

announced a series of economic liberalization measures to combat 'poverty and misery' and to attract foreign investment. Muhammad Said, the acting leader of the FIS, was arrested while giving a news conference in early July, and there were signs of divisions within the party when moderates informed the Prime Minister that they wished to operate within the law. Fewer than 5% of FIS supporters responded to an appeal for a political strike, but a delegate conference re-elected Madani as leader of the FIS, and Belhadj as deputy leader.

In July 1991 Ghozali reorganized his Council of Ministers, distancing it still further from the FLN by dismissing the Minister of Justice, who had complained of the excessive power of the army. President Chadli severed his own formal connections with the party, and for the rest of the year maintained a low profile while Ghozali took the lead, declaring his readiness to meet representatives of the 51 political parties which by now existed, and to amend the electoral law. At a meeting between the Prime Minister and the political parties—boycotted by the FLN, the FIS, the PAGS and some others—no agreement on electoral reform was reached in three days of discussions, but Ghozali expressed hopes that it might still be possible to hold elections by the end of November. The meeting was adjourned for three weeks, during which the FLN elected a new politburo, which included former Prime Minister Hamrouche, and eight parties, including the MDA and Hamas, presented a joint plan to reduce the number of deputies in the National People's Assembly and to redraw constituency boundaries. When the meeting was reconvened, Prime Minister Ghozali agreed to these changes in the electoral law. Regarding an election as imminent, the FLN-dominated Assembly rejected a government proposal to reduce food subsidies, thus imperilling negotiations with the IMF. The Assembly also complained that there would be insufficient time to consider new electoral laws, and criticized individual ministers. On 29 September the 'state of siege', declared on 5 June, was repealed. At the same time, Abdelkader Hachani, the last prominent member of the Madani wing of the FIS, was arrested. The Minister of Human Rights stated that there were 357 political detainees awaiting trial in civilian prisons, and 99 held by the armed forces. A national conference of FIS representatives, held in early October, declared its aim to establish an Islamic state and its support for the imprisoned leaders of the FIS.

In mid-October 1991 the National People's Assembly approved amendments to the electoral law, establishing the number of single-member parliamentary constituencies at 430. (Changes to the electoral law that were adopted in April 1991 had never been implemented.) Other amendments concerned independent candidates, who would in future need to obtain only 300 (rather than 500) supporters of the candidacy, and the minimum age of parliamentary candidates, which was lowered from 35 to 28 years. President Chadli announced that the first round of voting in the general election would take place on 26 December, and that a second round of voting would be held on 16 January 1992 in constituencies where there had been no outright winner in the first round. Prime Minister Ghozali reshuffled his Council of Ministers, taking personal charge of the economy portfolio.

THE GENERAL ELECTION OF DECEMBER 1991

In October 1991 an estimated 60,000 people took part in an anti-FLN march, organized by the RCD, and 100,000–300,000 supporters of the FIS demonstrated for the establishment of an Islamic state without the formality of an election. The FIS threatened to boycott the election unless its leaders were released, but the threat was withdrawn and the party subsequently campaigned on extreme free-market policies, stating that it would end subsidies and state monopolies and allow the dinar to 'float' on foreign exchange markets. Prime Minister Ghozali admitted that the Algerian people were tired of 30 years of FLN rule and that 'the people don't trust us any more. We have lied to them too much'.

The 430 seats in the National People's Assembly were contested by 5,712 candidates representing 49 political parties and more than 1,000 independents. It was forecast that the FIS would obtain more than one-third of the votes (its leaders predicted at least 70%), and the FLN rather less, with the remaining one-third shared among the other parties. In the first round of voting in the general election, in which some 59% of the electorate participated, the FIS took an unassailable lead, winning 188 seats outright, although it had obtained just 3.2m. votes (1.5m. fewer than in the municipal elections) from an electorate of 13.3m. The FFS, led by Aït Ahmad, gained 25 seats, the FLN was humiliated with only 15 seats (although it won about half as many votes as the FIS), and independent candidates gained three seats. The FLN complained of intimidation and malpractice in 340 constituencies in which officials of FIS-controlled municipalities had distributed the voting slips. A second round of voting was required in 199 seats and the FIS needed to win only 20 to gain an absolute majority in the Assembly. Nahdah, Hamas and El-Oumma instructed their supporters to vote for the FIS against the FLN in the second round. However, the secular parties failed to declare their support for the FLN. President Chadli, faced with the choice of cancelling the elections or allowing them to proceed, indicated his willingness to 'cohabit' with an FIS government, but the FIS excluded the possibility of any sharing of power and demanded the appointment of Madani as Prime Minister and the holding of a presidential election. There were demonstrations urging the defence of democracy against an Iranian-style regime, and reports that mass emigration of intellectuals and women would follow an FIS victory.

THE MILITARY TAKE-OVER

On 4 January 1992 the National People's Assembly was dissolved by presidential decree. On 11 January, five days before the second round of the election was due to be held, President Chadli, apparently under intense pressure from military leaders, resigned in order 'to safeguard the interests of the country'. He had failed to persuade either the unemployed to desert the FIS and trust him to implement reforms or the armed forces to accept the inevitable result of the election. According to the Constitution, the President of the National People's Assembly, Abd al-Aziz Belkhadem, should have replaced Chadli on an interim basis for 45 days while a presidential election was held, but, as the Assembly had been dissolved, his status was uncertain. On 12 January the High Security Council, which comprised the Prime Minister, three senior generals and the Ministers of Justice and Foreign Affairs, appointed Abd al-Malek Benhabiles, the Chairman of the Constitutional Council, as acting Head of State (he was apparently unwilling to accept the position on a permanent basis), announced a 'state of exception' and cancelled the second round of the elections. Only a few tanks appeared on the streets, and for two days the FIS leaders refrained from comment.

On 14 January 1992 a five-member High Council of State (HCS) was appointed to operate as a collegiate presidency until the expiry of Chadli's term of office in December 1993. The leading figure in the Council was clearly Maj.-Gen. Nezzar, the Minister of Defence, but its Chairman was Muhammad Boudiaf, one of the leaders of the independence movement, who had been in exile in Morocco since quarrelling with Ben Bella in 1964. Although Boudiaf was untainted by the accusations of corruption against the old regime, his return was greeted without enthusiasm by the 75% of the population born after he had left the country. The other members of the HCS were the Minister of Human Rights, Ali Haroun, Sheikh Tejini Haddam, the Rector of the Paris Mosque, and Ali Kafi, the long-serving president of the war veterans' association and a member of the FLN establishment. Ghozali, although he remained Prime Minister, was not included. The constitutional legality of the Council was challenged by all the political parties, including the FLN. Both Boudiaf and Ghozali promised that elections would be held within two years.

On the first Friday after the resignation of Chadli, police turned worshippers away from mosques, but, amid claims that there had been 500 arrests, Hachani appealed to his followers not to give the authorities any excuse for more violent intervention. He gathered the 188 FIS deputies who had been elected in December 1991 as a 'shadow' Assembly, which demanded a return to legality.

Violence erupted in January 1992, when a soldier was killed, and two gendarmes were wounded, in a machine-gun attack on a police post 20 km from the capital; subsequent attacks at other checkpoints were also reported. The HCS took measures to undermine the municipalities, newspapers and mosques con-

trolled by the FIS, banned political speeches and assemblies and rearrested Hachani on a charge of inciting soldiers to desert. The remaining leaders again appealed for dialogue with the HCS, as the police fired on crowds gathering for prayer and hunted dissident prayer-leaders.

On 3 February 1992 the security forces took control of the FIS offices and those of the Islamic Labour Union, arresting a further 122 people, including moderates. In running battles in Batna, 14 people were killed as the army fired on demonstrators, and within three days the national total of those killed in clashes with the army exceeded 50. Tejini Haddam withdrew from the HCS, which, on the evening of 9 February, declared a 12-month state of emergency. The Minister of the Interior was empowered to open detention centres in the Sahara (which, within weeks, were holding 8,000 people), order house searches, ban marches, close public places, dissolve local authorities and order trial by military courts. On the following day Boudiaf, justifying these measures in the name of democracy, announced an economic programme which included plans for the provision of jobs and housing, improved supplies of food and medicines and a campaign against corruption. Opponents of the new regime retaliated by killing eight policemen, two of them inside a mosque. University students rioted, but the FIS abandoned a protest march when confronted by a huge deployment of troops. Three men who were rumoured to be members of Hezbollah, operating on the fringe of the FIS, were sentenced to death for murder, and in Batna 82 activists were sentenced to up to 20 years' imprisonment. The FIS, which claimed that 150 people had been killed and 30,000 detained since 'the junta' took over, and feared formal dissolution, made another appeal for talks. The FLN, meanwhile, showed signs of moderating its opposition to the new regime.

In mid-February 1992 Ghozali again reorganized his Council of Ministers. Maj.-Gen. Nezzar and the Minister of the Interior, Gen. Belkheir, retained their places, but several portfolios were eliminated, in favour of 'super-ministries'. One notable newcomer was Saeed Guechi (a founder member of the FIS who had left the party in June), who became Minister of Professional Training and Employment, while two other new ministers came from Islamic backgrounds. Ghozali announced that Algeria had obtained a loan of nearly $1,500m. from a consortium of 240 banks to refinance the foreign debt. He produced a 100-page action plan to address the country's economic problems: Algeria, which had once exported food, now had to import $2,000m.-worth per year; Algerian industry was operating at about one-half of full capacity because of lack of materials and spare parts; and about 1.5m. people were unemployed. The economy, Ghozali admitted, was in a disastrous state.

In early March 1992, at the request of Belkheir, a court ruled that the Government was entitled to dissolve the FIS for 'pursuing by subversive means goals that endanger public order'. Boudiaf promised radical reform, but this could not be introduced hastily. Further discontent followed considerable increases in the price of food; the cost of some items more than doubled in the first days of Ramadan (early March). It was estimated that about 14m. people (out of a population of slightly more than 25m.) were living in conditions of poverty. Bombs were found, local 'incidents' occurred daily, and the universities were closed. Arrests impaired local administration, as the FIS had controlled 32 regional and 853 local authorities, more than 400 of which were dissolved at the end of March. Belkheir announced the official number of dead since January as 103, of whom 31 had been members of the security forces, and estimated the number of arrests at 9,000. Amnesty International expressed concern at reported cases of torture. The FIS threatened that violence would not stop until a general election was held. The trials of Madani, Belhadj and Hachani were postponed until June, but Muhammad Said was sentenced to 10 years' imprisonment *in absentia*.

THE ASSASSINATION OF BOUDIAF

The constitutional position of Boudiaf was anomalous. Widely respected as a man of integrity but apparently appointed as a figurehead by a junta which had seized power, he began to give indications of a personal political agenda.

In April 1992 the HCS announced the creation of a National Human Rights Monitoring Centre, under the presidency of Abd ar-Razzek Barra, to replace the former Ministry of Human Rights; its 26 members were to report directly to Boudiaf. A 60-member National Consultative Council (NCC) was also appointed. Under the chairmanship of Redha Malek, it was to meet in the building of the former National People's Assembly and included women, journalists and intellectuals, but failed to find favour with opposition parties. A reference to combating corruption in Boudiaf's first speech was censored, but in April he again demonstrated political determination when Maj.-Gen. Mustafa Beloucif, a former senior defence ministry official, was charged before a military tribunal with the theft of millions of dinars. The HCS also ordered the FIS to surrender its headquarters and other buildings, as well as its newspapers, to the Government. After the loss of an appeal against the dissolution of the party, elements within the FIS advocated armed rebellion. Amid mounting violence, military courts in Ouargla and Blida condemned 16 FIS members to death.

At the beginning of June 1992, after dismissing an appeal by Mouloud Hamrouche for the formation of a national government, Boudiaf attempted to address the people directly, disregarding politicians, by appealing for the establishment of a National Patriotic Rally, with committees in every village and workplace, to prepare the way for a genuine multi-party democracy. Aït Ahmad and other opposition leaders denounced the proposal as a ruse to dragoon the masses into participation. Boudiaf also promised a constitutional review, the dissolution of the FLN and a presidential election. Moreover, he ordered the release of more than 2,000 FIS detainees, although operations against several hundred Islamist radicals in the mountains threatened to provoke civil war, with 700 people, including some 100 police personnel, having been killed in four months. Maj.-Gen. Nezzar promised 'implacable war', and there were accusations of a 'shoot-to-kill' policy against suspected opponents of the regime. Dissidents threatened to launch a *jihad* and to kill 1,000 policemen and magistrates from the end of June. On 27 June Abbasi Madani and Ali Belhadj were brought before a military court in Blida, accused of aggression and conspiracy against the state. Defence lawyers withdrew from the court, and the trial had to be adjourned until July.

On 29 June 1992, while opening a cultural centre in Annaba, Boudiaf was assassinated. Although the event was televised, it was by no means clear whether the assassination was the action of a lone killer or part of a conspiracy. The HCS declared seven days of mourning and cancelled planned celebrations to commemorate the 30th anniversary of independence on 5 July. It also ordered a commission of inquiry into the assassination, which was to announce its findings by the end of July. Islamist extremists applauded the killing but did not claim credit for it, and Boudiaf's widow stated that she did not believe them to have been responsible. Although the assassin had been seized on the spot, the motive for the killing remained a mystery. In December the commission's report was made available to the media with 76 of its 111 pages missing. The conclusion was that the killer had not acted alone but on behalf of an unspecified organization that was increasingly identified with the FLN. One of the demands of those taking part in a demonstration on 22 March 1993, the first permitted for over a year, was for the truth about the murder of Boudiaf to be published. It was not until June 1995 that Lt Lembarek Boumâarafi was sentenced to death for Boudiaf's murder. Little new information was revealed at the trial, and the authorities maintained that Boumâarafi had acted alone.

'WAR AGAINST THE ALGERIAN PEOPLE'

The shock of the assassination of Boudiaf did not reduce the violence which had begun within days of the military take-over. Documents found in Oran revealed that the police were a deliberate target of the militants. Senior officers were ambushed with their drivers and sometimes their families. It was estimated that by the end of December 1992 some 200 security officers had been killed since the imposition of the state of emergency: the number of members of the Mouvement islamique armé (MIA) who were killed in action seems to have been higher.

Whereas in the towns the MIA operated in small groups, in the mountainous countryside and on the borders of the Sahara they operated at considerable strength, co-ordinated by means of a clandestine radio station and fax machines. An FIS leaflet advocated a campaign of 'sabotage and fire', and power cables were destroyed and government buildings attacked. Some of the guerrillas who took part in these attacks were known to have fought as *Mujahidin* in Afghanistan and others were believed to have received training in Hezbollah camps in Lebanon. In June 1992 the Government denied that there had been mass desertions from the army, but admitted that a small number of soldiers had taken refuge in the mountains, where they were hunted by helicopters.

Forts and police stations were ransacked for arms, and the Government was particularly worried about disaffection in the armed forces as it became obvious that military supporters of the MIA remained at their posts to participate in the attacks. In December 1992 79 officers, privates and civilians were charged before a military court in Béchar with attempting subversion in the barracks of Oran and Sidi-Bel-Abbès, and in January 1993 19 of them were sentenced to death. The military court at Béchar, to which foreign observers were not admitted, sentenced a further seven soldiers to death in February. The death toll increased in March when sympathizers allowed guerrillas to enter the fort at Boughzoul, where they murdered 18 soldiers; after a hunt lasting a week, the alleged attackers were caught and 23 of them were killed.

The authorities had already shown themselves sensitive to press coverage of such incidents when, in January 1993, they closed the newspaper *El Watan* and arrested six journalists for 'premature reporting' of the murder of five gendarmes at Laghouat. They stated that security news could only be reported with the 'stamp of the competent services'. Since the announcement of an enabling decree in August, 10 newspapers had already been closed down.

The activities of the MIA were not directed solely against state employees. There were also deliberate attempts to damage the economy by deterring potential foreign investors. The most notorious of these was a bomb attack at Algiers airport in August 1992, in which nine people died and 120 were wounded. The Government denounced the attack as 'war against the Algerian people', promising to respond with 'draconian security'. At the same time, bombs were exploded near airline offices in Algiers and others, later, in Constantine. In September there were more bomb attacks at airline offices, and on the eve of the independence celebration a bomb was found near its centrepiece, the Martyrs' Memorial. The British and US Governments advised their nationals against visiting Algeria. In October two men were arrested in connection with the bombing at Algiers airport and in May 1993 54 defendants (26 *in absentia*) went on trial. For a time their lawyers boycotted the court but eventually 38 were condemned to death, bringing the number of death sentences pronounced since the beginning of the state of emergency to about 80.

Before the bomb explosion at Algiers airport, the HCS had offered to close the Saharan detention camps, from which 5,000 of the original 8,000 detainees had already been released before October. Instead, new security laws now came into force. In order to try 'terrorism and subversion', which were very loosely defined, three special courts, which recognized no right of appeal, were established. Membership of a terrorist organization was punishable by a sentence of up to 20 years' imprisonment, as was the sale of a firearm. Printing or copying a subversive document could result in a five-year sentence, as could identifying the judges or other officials of the special courts. The age of penal responsibility was lowered from 18 to 16. Reduced sentences were offered to those who surrendered during the following two months, and about 100 took advantage of this partial amnesty.

The number of arrests increased. There were 460 in one fortnight in October 1992 and 60 during a single day in November. Prime Minister Abd es-Salam, who had replaced Ghozali and appointed a new Council of Ministers in July, declared 'total war' on terrorism and stated that the time had come for the state to assume the offensive. A new offence of justifying terrorism was created, punishable by a minimum of five years' imprisonment. Amnesty International was to report a dramatic increase in the use of torture in subsequent months.

In December 1992 new measures were introduced, including the dissolution of local authorities still controlled by the FIS and the appointment of administrators chosen by the Government.

Similarly, mosques were forced to accept government-appointed preachers or risk closure. A curfew was imposed in Algiers and the six surrounding districts, where 60% of the entire population of the country lived. In January 1993 three state security courts were established with authority to impose harsh sentences including the death penalty. Later that month the first two Islamist terrorists were executed. Both of them were soldiers, and there was speculation about the extent of support for the Islamist cause within the lower ranks of the military. According to one report 500–800 junior and non-commissioned officers deserted in the early part of the year. More executions followed, including that of Hocine Abderramane, a close associate of Abbasi Madani. In February the HCS renewed indefinitely the state of emergency, and in May the curfew was extended to 10 further provinces. In April 1993 the HCS announced that since December 1992 some 200 terrorists had been killed, 3,800 arrested and a further 1,100 were being pursued. By mid-1993 some 400 Islamist militants had been killed and another 150 sentenced to death. Yet despite an intense assault by the authorities on militant Islam, the violence escalated. Terrorists targeted not just members of the security forces, but prominent public figures, local government officials, members of the judiciary, intellectuals, journalists, foreign nationals and ordinary civilians. The exiled FIS leadership continued to advocate armed struggle and the elimination of the junta in power and those who influenced it.

In February 1993 the Minister of Defence, Maj.-Gen. Nezzar, narrowly escaped death when a car-bomb exploded, and in March the former Minister of Education, Djilali Liabes, and two members of the NCC, were killed by gunmen. In August former Prime Minister Kasdi Merbah, together with his son, brother, driver and one of his bodyguards was assassinated. The Groupe islamique armé (GIA), a more radical rival of the MIA, claimed responsibility for the killing but an FIS statement denied any role in the assassination. Merbah had many enemies inside and outside the ruling establishment and there was intense speculation about the true identity of his assassins. Between March and June 1993 six leading intellectuals were murdered; many others were forced into hiding fearing for their lives. There were reports that Islamist militants were increasingly attacking economic targets such as the transport system, gas pipelines and factories, and carrying out arson attacks against schools. In late September Islamist militants began to target foreign nationals. Two French surveyors kidnapped by an armed gang near Tiaret, one of the strongholds of the GIA, were found dead in late September. The FIS again denied responsibility for these killings. The kidnapping of three French consular officials in October was reported to have provoked an exodus of some 3,000 foreign residents, including about 2,000 French nationals. The three officials were later released. The GIA claimed responsibility for the deaths of several foreign nationals, and warned all foreigners to leave the country by 30 November. By the end of December at least 24 foreigners had been killed and both France and the USA began withdrawing their nationals. In September the German Government had refused to extradite Rabah Kebir, the main spokesman for the FIS in Europe, and Ossama Madani, son of the imprisoned FIS leader, who had both been sentenced to death *in absentia* for their part in the bomb attack on Algiers airport in August 1992. In a statement made in December Rabah Kebir denied that the FIS was responsible for the attacks on foreigners, and declared that all those responsible for the killings in Algeria should be prosecuted.

The mass arrests and other repressive policies had seriously disrupted command structures within the FIS and new hierarchies emerged and attempted to gain control of the Islamist resistance within Algeria. Organizations such as the MIA of Abdelkader Chebouti and the GIA, well established in the Mitidja behind Algiers, and at Tiaret and Sidi-Bel-Abbès in the west of the country, recruited their guerrillas from the ranks of FIS militants but their leaders were unable to impose supreme authority on the armed opposition movement. In an attempt to overcome the disruption of the FIS caused by the arrest of its leaders, and to improve co-ordination between FIS militants in exile and those inside Algeria, in September 1993 a reorganization of the FIS leadership in exile was announced. The new executive was believed to include Rabah Kebir, Ossama Madani, Khareddin Kheraban, Anwar Haddam and Boujenaa Bounoua,

representing different factions of the movement. Rabah Kebir, having escaped house arrest and taken refuge in Germany, had served for some time as official spokesman for the FIS outside Algeria, but his role had been questioned by some FIS members. This new unified leadership was reported to have ordered an intensification of military operations in Algeria, but also to have demanded direct negotiations with the HCS.

Strict controls made it difficult to gauge the attitude of the ordinary population, but in mid-May 1993 demonstrations were officially sanctioned in Algiers, Oran and Constantine. In the capital a crowd estimated by the organizers at 1.5m. and by others at 100,000 demanded, in what was regarded as a genuine expression of opinion, that there should be no negotiation with terrorists. More than 500 councillors, members of the secularist RCD, resigned in protest at rumours that an amnesty would be granted to Islamist terrorists. A statement by FFS officials that the HCS was using Islamist fundamentalism as a pretext to prolong its hold on power was dismissed. In June the HCS urged a 'general mobilization against terrorism', but later in the month Abd es-Salam stated that he favoured dialogue with militants if they were not tainted with 'the cancer of terrorism': the 3m. Algerians who had voted for the FIS, he maintained, were not enemies, but citizens who had voted in good faith.

POLITICS AFTER BOUDIAF

There was speculation that Maj.-Gen. Nezzar would succeed Boudiaf as Chairman of the HCS, but he was not in good health and was apparently unwilling to make too obvious the military's control of the state. After conferring with party leaders (including Ben Bella, Aït Ahmad, Mehiri of the FLN and Sheikh Nahnah of Hamas), another member of the HCS, Ali Kafi, was nominated for the chairmanship on 2 July 1992. An experienced diplomat, Kafi was regarded as a figure-head, a man who enjoyed good relations with the army and who was a political foe of Chadli and Hamrouche. He pledged adherence to Boudiaf's programme, but showed no signs of carrying it out. The Chairman of the NCC, Redha Malek, also became a member of the HCS. One of the first actions of the new regime was to promote five senior officers to the rank of general.

Ghozali had resigned on 8 July 1992 in order to enable Kafi to appoint his own Prime Minister. He was succeeded by Belaid Abd es-Salam, who, for nearly 20 years after independence, had directed Algeria's petroleum and industrial policy. Abd es-Salam appointed a new Council of Ministers, retaining seven of Ghozali's ministers, but replacing Gen. Belkheir (whose management of the aftermath of the Boudiaf assassination had been much criticized) as Minister of the Interior by Muhammad Hardi, a former Secretary-General of the Ministry of Information, who was believed to have close links with the security services. Many of the new appointees were unknown technocrats, some of whom had previously served under Abd es-Salam. In October a reshuffle introduced three women and the first private businessman to serve in an Algerian Council of Ministers. In February 1993, in a more significant reshuffle, the professional diplomat Lakhdar Brahimi was replaced by Redha Malek—who had previously been engaged in negotiations with the non-Islamist opposition—as Minister of Foreign Affairs. He was said to have been given charge of the ministry as a friend of the new US Secretary of State and because Abd es-Salam wished to exert more control over foreign affairs. After a year in office the Prime Minister was deemed unpopular and was accused of being authoritarian and of seeking a return to the rigidities of the Boumedienne era; his long-term position was considered to be insecure.

The trial of Madani, Belhadj and other FIS leaders was held in July 1992, although the defendants boycotted the proceedings in protest at the exclusion of foreign observers. After two former Prime Ministers, Hamrouche and Ghozali, had testified, the court rejected the prosecution's demand for life imprisonment and pronounced sentences of 12 years' imprisonment instead. The verdict was greeted with immediate protest demonstrations and henceforward all government hints of readiness to negotiate with the FIS were met with the demand that the prisoners first be released.

The struggle to maintain itself in the face of armed resistance and the parlous state of the economy gave the HCS little opportunity to concentrate on other major problems—ending corruption and securing popular support. Many feared the influence of a corrupt 'mafia' of past and present officials. In November 1992 the Minister of Justice, Abd el-Hamed Mahi-Bahi, suspended several senior officials including the Prosecutor-General, the President of the court of Mostaganem (who was Chairman of the Judges' Syndicate) and other officials who had been appointed under the Chadli regime. There were rumours that Mahi-Bahi had been obstructed in his attempt to investigate official embezzlement as well as the murder of Boudiaf. The dismissed officials were also believed to have helped the military against the FIS, and a fortnight later, despite the reported support of Kafi and Abd es-Salam, Mahi-Bahi was dismissed and the suspended officials reinstated. However, in December 10 special magistrates were appointed to tackle corruption and in February 1993 Gen. Beloucif was sentenced to 15 years' imprisonment (and suffered the confiscation of property) for the theft of $6.4m.

In his first public statement as Prime Minister Abd es-Salam had refused to set a deadline for new elections, citing the need to revise the electoral rolls and to devise a procedure to eliminate the possibility of another victory for the FIS. Kafi, in his first public address, stated that he was aiming for a democratic system based on consensus; he subsequently promised to rebuild a modern, efficient state based on social justice. He blamed mismanagement in the Chadli era, referred to in the official press as 'the black decade', for poverty and inflation. At about the same time Abd es-Salam said that there was no possibility of elections taking place until the economy had recovered, and that such a recovery would take at least three years. On the anniversary of the military take-over, Kafi promised that a new Constitution would be drafted after consultation with groups not pledged to violence and that it would be pluralist and allow genuinely democratic elections. There would be a referendum on the balance of power between the President and the Government. Regarded as a further pretext for postponing elections, this proposal was greeted with scepticism as the largest political party, the FIS, was still banned and the second largest, the FFS, refused to have any contact with the regime, accusing the HCS of using instability as an excuse for retaining absolute power. Hamas hesitated, advocating involvement of the less extreme members of the FIS, while the RCD refused to commit itself. In March 1993, however, talks began, with Kafi meeting representatives of the war veterans' association, of which he was still President, and representatives of the FLN. A presidential communiqué stated that the talks had focused on enlarging and strengthening the NCC, on possible formulae for a 'transition' period, on the amendment of the Constitution to establish a better balance between the authorities and on the rationalization of institutions. In May Kafi promised a referendum before the end of the year on how a return to democracy should be managed. In June the HCS announced that it would dissolve itself in December, as originally proposed, and that there would follow a period of not more than three years by the end of which modern democracy with a free market economy would have been created.

In July 1993 Maj.-Gen. Nezzar, who had been reported to be suffering from poor health for some time, was replaced as Minister of Defence by Gen. Liamine Zéroual, although Nezzar remained a member of the HCS, and Gen. Muhammad Lamari, who since September 1992 had been responsible for organizing anti-terrorist units, was appointed Chief of Staff. These changes were preceded by a series of promotions of officers close to the HCS leadership.

On 21 August 1993 the HCS appointed the Minister of Foreign Affairs, Redha Malek, as Prime Minister in place of Belaid Abd es-Salam. Malek remained a member of the HCS. There had been speculation about the departure of Abd es-Salam since July and both the French and the US Governments, it was reported, had favoured the appointment of Malek. It was not until 4 September that the new Prime Minister announced his Government, and the delay was thought to reflect the deep divisions within the ruling establishment. Unlike his two predecessors, who had both assumed simultaneous responsibility for the economy portfolio, Malek, a former career diplomat, had no experience of economic affairs. He appointed Mourad Benachenhou, a former Algerian representative at the World Bank, as Minister of the Economy, signalling a return to the reform

programme. During a speech as his Government was inaugurated, Malek declared 'We will go to a free market economy with pragmatism, taking into account the particular needs of our society'. He also made it clear that he would not tolerate Islamist militancy. The Minister of Defence and Chief of Staff appointed in July retained their posts, and a senior army officer, Col Sélim Saadi, a former regional military commander who had held a number of ministerial posts in the early 1980s, was appointed as Minister of the Interior. It was thought that the military had instigated the replacement of the outgoing Minister of the Interior, Muhammad Hardi, a civilian, by a senior army officer; and that Saadi's appointment followed consultations with the senior officer corps over government policy on security. His appointment accelerated the reorganization of the security forces and the creation of a unified command between the military and police forces in order to combat Islamist violence. A diplomat, Muhammad Saleh Dembri, was appointed Minister of Foreign Affairs, and Ahmed Benbitour was promoted to Minister of Energy. Twelve ministers remained from the Abd es-Salam Government. Despite strong denials in Algiers, there were rumours of contacts between the HCS and exiled leaders of the FIS through intermediaries such as former President Ahmed Ben Bella, who was reported to have met Rabah Kebir and Anwar Haddam in Spain in September.

LIAMINE ZÉROUAL BECOMES HEAD OF STATE

The mandate of the HCS was scheduled to expire on 31 December 1993, and in October the formation of an eight-member National Dialogue Commission (NDC) was announced, which was to organize a gradual transition to an elected government. Three generals were appointed to the commission, Muhammad Touati, a councillor at the Ministry of Defence, Maj.-Gen. Tayeb Derradji, Inspector-General of Land Forces, and Gen. Ahmed Senhadji, Director-General of Military Infrastructure, bringing the military openly into the political process for the first time. But little progress was made by the NDC in its negotiations with opposition parties about the creation of a transitional regime. Leading opposition figures such as Aït Ahmad of the FFS and Ben Bella of the MDA withdrew from the negotiations, and both military and political leaders in the ruling establishment remained divided about overtures to the banned FIS. In mid-December the HCS issued a statement indicating that it would not disband itself until a new presidential body had been inaugurated. It proposed to hold a national dialogue conference in late January 1994 to choose a new collective leadership. The NDC recommended that FIS members who renounced violence and criminal activities should be allowed to participate, although the proscription of the party itself would remain in force. This approach appeared to have the support of some senior officers, while others, such as the Chief of Staff, Maj.-Gen. Muhammad Lamari, were firmly opposed to it. In response to the HCS statement, Rabah Kebir declared that there could only be dialogue if all political prisoners were released and the decrees imposing a state of emergency were revoked. The imprisoned leader, Ali Belhadj, had ordered that the FIS should have no contacts with the military-backed regime.

A draft document, circulated by the HCS to parties before the national dialogue conference, recommended a three-man presidency to replace the HCS and rule during a transitional period from 1994–96. The document also suggested the creation of a new consultative assembly of some 180 members, who would be appointed rather than elected. In mid-January 1994 the Government announced the release of almost 800 political prisoners held in two Saharan detention camps. Rabah Kebir welcomed the decision, but again demanded the release of all political prisoners, beginning with the FIS leadership.

In the event none of the main political parties, with the exception of Hamas, participated in the national dialogue conference in late January 1994. Efforts to persuade a few FIS members to participate failed and even the FLN and the RCD boycotted the meetings. There were threats of violence from the GIA against anyone participating in the conference. The two-day meeting, which it had been hoped would end the violence, was an abject failure. The possibility of a boycott by the leading political parties led the HCS to select Abdelaziz Bouteflika, Boumedienne's Minister of Foreign Affairs, as their first choice for the new Head of State, hoping that an internationally-known leader would command widespread support in the country. Bouteflika, however, declined the offer and is reported to have returned to Europe before the conference ended. A conflicting source, however, suggested that Bouteflika's candidature was contested—he had many enemies within the ruling establishment—and then rejected, representing a major defeat for the Nezzar, Belkheir, Gheziel and Mediene faction, which had nominated him. Subsequently the HCS named the Minister of Defence, Liamine Zéroual (a retired General), as Head of State and he was inaugurated on 31 January. An eight-man Higher Security Committee, mainly composed of senior army officers, is believed to have played an important part in Zéroual's selection. There was speculation that the Higher Security Committee would remain in existence to 'advise' on security matters. The NDC endorsed plans for a three-year transitional period leading to a presidential election and the appointment of a 180-member National Transition Council (NTC) to promote political consensus. Zéroual, one of the most respected members of the senior officer corps, was believed to share the views of those in the ruling élite who argued for dialogue with the Islamists to resolve the political crisis.

DIALOGUE FAILS

On his appointment as Head of State, Zéroual retained the defence portfolio, and the Council of Ministers under Redha Malek remained unchanged. In his first public statement the new President appealed for 'serious dialogue' to find a solution to the country's crisis and emphasized that the role of the army was to build 'national consensus'. In early February 1994 he declared that Algeria's problems could not be overcome only by addressing security issues, but that solutions had to be found to the country's economic and political difficulties. In response to Zéroual's appointment, the FIS leadership issued statements urging militants to limit their targets to members of the security forces rather than foreign nationals and Algerian civilians. Youcef Khatib, President of the NDC, admitted that it had contacts with FIS members inside the country and that these took place with the approval of the imprisoned leadership. The release in late February of Ali Djeddi and Abdelkader Boukhamkham, who represent the second tier in the FIS leadership below Madani, Belhadj and Hachani, was interpreted as an attempt to conciliate the FIS; but the FIS reaction remained contradictory. (On 1 March it was declared that Djeddi and Boukhamkham had been released 'against their will'.) Earlier in the year Anwar Haddam, one of the exiled leaders of the FIS based in the USA, described the radical GIA as 'the principal armed branch of the FIS'. In the past the FIS had tried to avoid overt support for the violent attacks perpetrated by armed Islamist groups. At the end of March Mihoub Mihoubi, the presidential spokesman, told the official Algérie Presse Service that Zéroual had met imprisoned Islamist leaders and obtained their assurance that the campaign of violence would end. According to the FIS, Zéroual had initiated contact with their movement at the end of 1993 before he became Head of State.

In March 1994 there were rumours of divisions within the military over Zéroual's efforts to establish dialogue with the Islamist opposition. After reports that dialogue with the FIS could endanger the unity of the armed forces and that a growing number of army officers were unhappy with Zéroual's overtures to the Islamist opposition, Gen. Lamari, the Chief of Staff, felt it necessary to issue a statement in mid-March reaffirming the army's confidence in Zéroual and 'his delicate mission'. It was also reported that Lamari had been given new powers confirming his position as number two in the new regime. In addition, *Asharq al-Awsat* reported that a number of senior officers believed to have opposed Lamari's appointment as Minister of Defence in January had been removed from their posts.

On 11 April 1994 Redha Malek resigned and Zéroual appointed Mokdad Sifi, the Minister of Equipment, as Prime Minister. Malek was known to be opposed to any compromise with the Islamist militants. He resigned the day after the Government agreed a new accord with the IMF opening the way for debt rescheduling, a move that was certain to renew tensions within the ruling establishment. The appointment of Sifi, a civil servant and technocrat, as Prime Minister, was interpreted by some observers as an attempt by Zéroual to increase his own direct involvement in government. When Sifi announced his new Government in April only 12 ministers retained their portfolios and the majority of those appointed were technocrats or senior civil servants. Changes included the departure of Sélim Saadi, a resolute opponent of the Islamist militants and a close associate of Redha Malek, from the Ministry of the Interior and the return of Sassi Lamouri to the highly sensitive Ministry of Religious Affairs. Saadi's replacement as Minister of the Interior was Abderrahmane Meziane Cherif, a former Governor of Algiers. Ministers with responsibility for implementing the Government's difficult economic programme demanded by the IMF accord were allocated new portfolios.

In May 1994, in what was regarded as an initiative of the President to strengthen his authority, Zéroual effected some major changes to senior posts in the military. Maj.-Gen. Khalifa Rahim was replaced as Commander of the Land Force by Maj.-Gen. Ahmed Gaïd, believed to be a close associate of Zéroual. A new head of the air force was appointed and there were changes to five out of the six *wilayat* or regional commanders. In the same month Zéroual inaugurated the NTC, an interim legislature of 200 appointed members, which was supposed to provide a forum for debate until legislative elections were held. Abdelkader Ben Salah was subsequently elected President of the NTC. Of the main political parties, only Hamas agreed to participate and was allocated five seats. Most of the 21 parties that agreed to take part were virtually unknown. Some 22 seats were set aside for the major parties, a gesture which seemed unlikely to encourage their participation in the new body which became the target of ridicule in the media.

Also in May 1994, in a move to promote dialogue with the Islamist militants and with other opposition groups, Zéroual appointed a group of six 'independent national figures'. They included former President Ahmed Ben Bella, Col Tahar Zbiri, the leader of a failed coup against Boumedienne in 1967, Col Muhammad Yahiaoui, a contender for the presidency after the death of Boumedienne, Haji Ben Alla, the former Speaker of the National People's Assembly, and two well-known socialists from the Boumedienne period, Muhammad Said Mazouzi and Ahmed Mahsas. The group was reported to have made contact with the two FIS leaders released earlier in the year, Ali Djeddi and Abdelkader Boukhamkham, but little progress appeared to have been made.

In August 1994 members of the FLN, the Parti du renouveau algérien (PRA), the MDA, Nahdah and Hamas participated in national dialogue with the Government; the FFS, Ettahaddi and the RCD boycotted the meetings. A further meeting held in early September focused on two letters sent to the President by Abbasi Madani, in which the imprisoned FIS leader agreed to respect the 1989 Constitution and the principle of the alternation of power and, while not explicitly renouncing violence, referred to the possibility of a 'truce'. In mid-September Zéroual announced the release of both Abbasi Madani and Ali Belhadj from prison and their transfer to house arrest in Algiers; three other leading Islamists were also freed. A government spokeswoman, Leila Aslaoui, a feminist and resolute opponent of dialogue with the Islamists, resigned in protest at their release; her husband had been killed by Islamist gunmen in the following month. A general strike was staged in September in the Kabyle as Berber activists protested at the prospect of national talks with 'Islamic fundamentalists', and demanded the official recognition of Tamazight, the Berber language.

Several factors were believed to have prompted the change in the intransigent stance of the FIS towards the military-backed regime, but the most important was presumed to have been its fear of marginalization by the extremist GIA. It was argued that the appalling acts of violence perpetrated by GIA guerrillas alarmed at least some of the FIS leaders who felt that it was not in their interest for the extremists to gain the dominant position. According to one source, Boukhamkham and Djeddi, the two FIS leaders released in early 1994, had produced a report in mid-1994 which highlighted the disarray existing throughout the rank and file of the organization, and the inability of those armed groups linked to the FIS to compete with the GIA in the scale and effectiveness of its military operations. The report concluded that unless major political initiatives were taken by the FIS leadership, the organization would be marginalized. Moreover, it was claimed that the MIA, renamed the Armée islamique du salut (AIS) in mid-1994, might not be under the control of the civilian wing of the FIS, frequently co-operated with the GIA, and had committed its share of nihilistic attacks and assassinations. After the transfer to house arrest of the two FIS leaders, the GIA reiterated its rejection of any cease-fire, reconciliation or dialogue, and threatened to kill Islamist leaders who participated in talks with the 'renegade' regime. However, two months earlier Anwar Haddam, the FIS spokesman in the USA, had issued a statement claiming that an agreement had been reached in May to merge the armed forces of the FIS with those of the GIA. A communiqué from Rabah Kebir in Germany, the most senior FIS spokesman in exile, immediately denied that any such merger had taken place. There was further confusion in August when the GIA announced that it was creating a 'provisional government' known as the 'caliphate' and named Haddam as Minister of Foreign Affairs, even though he had denied joining the GIA shortly after his statement. In September, after the official media claimed that GIA leader Abu-Abdallah Ahmad had been killed in clashes with the security forces, it was reported that Muhammad Said, a former university professor and senior FIS official who had apparently defected to the GIA, had been chosen as his successor, prompting speculation that the GIA might adopt a more moderate stance and seek greater credibility as a political movement. However, other reports stated that Said would remain with the FIS and named Abu-Khalil Mahfouz as the new GIA leader.

The transfer of Abbasi Madani and Ali Belhadj to house arrest failed to break the deadlock between the regime and the FIS. In late October 1994 Zéroual announced that neither Madani nor Belhadj were willing to renounce violence or participate in negotiations. Before his release, Madani had stated that he was willing to consider terminating the military campaign if certain conditions were met. Zéroual was unable to concede on a number of these points, namely rescinding the ruling which outlawed the FIS in order to restore the party to legality, and releasing all imprisoned FIS members and allowing its armed wing to participate in talks. Zéroual's ability to compromise was limited because of the objections of leading military figures opposed to negotiation with the Islamists, while the political leadership of the FIS was under pressure from radical militant groups opposed to any dialogue with the regime. In a speech on 31 October marking the 40th anniversary of the start of the War of Independence, Zéroual spoke of the failure of dialogue with the FIS and his decision to hold a presidential election in 1995, before the end of his mandate. He also used the occasion to announce the promotion of the Chief of Staff of the Army, Gen. Lamari, a leading opponent of dialogue with the Islamists, to Lt-Gen. and to the newly-created rank of General of the Army Corps, the highest position in the Algerian military.

THE SANT' EGIDIO PACT

The plan to hold a presidential election towards the end of 1995, announced by Zéroual in October 1994, was rejected by several leading legalized opposition parties and condemned by the exiled FIS leadership. In a surprise move the opposition parties seized the initiative and, after talks in Rome under the aegis of the Sant' Egidio Roman Catholic community in November 1994 and again in early January 1995, the main Algerian opposition parties agreed a 'platform for a national contract' presenting the basis for a negotiated end to the conflict and a return to democracy. The document was signed by representatives of the FIS, the FLN and the FFS (which between them won more than 80% of the votes in the first round of the general elections of December 1991), together with the MDA, Nahdah, the Parti des travailleurs (PT) and the ALDHR. (Hamas and the PRA sent representatives to the meeting in November.)

The Sant' Egidio pact made an urgent appeal to both parties in the conflict to end their hostilities and allow the restoration of civil peace. It recommended the establishment of a transitional government in which both the military-backed regime and the political parties would be represented, which would prepare the way for free multi-party elections as quickly as possible. All parties were asked to guarantee to respect the results of the elections. Before any negotiations, the participants appealed for the release of the FIS leadership and of all political detainees, the restoration of the FIS to legality, and an immediate end to

the use of torture and of attacks on civilians, foreigners and public property. The participants also agreed certain general principles including the renunciation of violence to achieve or retain power, respect for human rights, popular legitimacy, multi-party democracy and the alternation of power, and the guarantee of fundamental liberties. They recognized the importance of Islamic, Arab and Berber culture in Algeria and demanded that both the Arab and Berber languages be recognized as national languages. Finally they appealed for the withdrawal of the army from politics. Belhadj and Madani both endorsed the Sant' Egidio pact, whereas the GIA condemned it and reaffirmed its commitment to the establishment of a 'caliphate' by armed struggle.

The military-backed regime condemned the Sant' Egidio meeting even before it had begun, claiming foreign interference in its national affairs. Some days after the pact was announced a government spokesman categorically rejected its proposals. The French Minister of Foreign Affairs, Alain Juppé, expressed his disappointment, prompting some observers to detect a shift in the French Government's position from strong backing for the regime in Algeria to support for the process of dialogue. The Italian, Spanish and US Governments expressed support for the Rome talks. Whereas some analysts argued that the Sant' Egidio pact confirmed that the FIS was distancing itself from the Islamist radicals, anti-Islamist organizations in Algeria saw the pact as no more than a ploy by the Islamists to take power; with the army neutralized they would abandon all pretence at democracy and impose their intolerant rule. There was also criticism of the FLN and the FFS for their participation in the Rome meeting. The FLN was accused of attempting to discard its discredited image after 30 years of corrupt, single-party rule by forming an alliance with the Islamists against the military-backed regime in a mistaken bid to return to power. Other observers pointed to differences within the leadership of the FIS in their attitude towards a negotiated peace and in particular cast doubts on Belhadj's endorsement of the pact. In his sermons and in interviews before his arrest Belhadj had consistently rejected the ideal of pluralist democracy as impious and unislamic.

In the months following the Rome meeting there were efforts to consolidate the Sant' Egidio pact. These included a meeting organized in London in March 1995 by former Prime Minister Abd al-Hamid Brahimi, attended by most of the signatories of the pact. In late March Ali Djeddi, believed to be a moderate member of the FIS consultative council, pledged to persuade Islamist militants to surrender their arms, and in April Madani Merzak, a leading member of the AIS, published a long open letter addressed to all those involved in the conflict appealing for peace. A prominent figure in the FLN establishment, former Minister of Foreign Affairs Ahmad Taleb Ibrahimi, urged President Zéroual not to reject the pact but to make a 'historic concession' to resolve the conflict. At the beginning of March, in an interview with a Spanish newspaper, the Minister of Foreign Affairs, Muhammad Dembri, admitted that the Sant' Egidio pact contained potentially constructive proposals; however, in the following month he insisted that any proposal about dialogue should be presented in Algeria, and condemned the transfer of the debate abroad.

Meanwhile, President Zéroual continued to prepare for a presidential election. In April 1995 he attempted to regain the initiative by resuming talks with the legalized opposition parties (this time individually). Separate meetings were held between the President and the leaders of the FLN and the FFS, and Ben Bella of the MDA also responded positively to Zéroual's invitation, prompting speculation that the unity achieved at the Sant' Egidio meeting might prove short-lived. The FFS had previously refused to take part in any dialogue with the regime. Talks with the FLN and the FFS quickly collapsed, however, when Zéroual again refused to include the FIS in any dialogue. The FLN and the FFS agreed to take part in the presidential election only if the FIS was allowed to participate. The Government reiterated its demand that the FIS would have to renounce violence and accept the Constitution before it could participate in the election. In mid-April it was announced that the President would limit dialogue to the nine opposition parties that had agreed to participate in the presidential election on the Government's terms. In May the Government issued an electoral law decree prepared by the NTC stipulating that any candidate wishing to stand in the presidential election would first have to obtain 75,000 signatures, collected from at least 25 provinces, with a minimum of 1,500 signatures per province. Candidates would be obliged to sign a declaration stating that they respected the Constitution, rejected violence and agreed not to use Islam for partisan aims. (The decree was promulgated by the NTC in July.) It was announced that in preparation for the election Zéroual would continue bilateral meetings with six opposition parties: the FLN, the FFS, Hamas, Nahdah, the MDA, and the PNSD. There was speculation that unofficial talks were continuing between the Government and the FIS leadership. After being returned to prison in February, Madani and Belhadj were reported to have been placed under house arrest at the end of March. The two men were said to be held in separate residences west of Algiers, and were refused permission to meet with FIS supporters. However, in early June the Minister of the Interior, Abderrahmane Cherif, stated that the two men had been returned once again to prison. Nevertheless it was rumoured that contacts with the FIS leaders had been renewed and that discussions centred on the possibility of FIS support for the presidential election and on the restoration of the party to legality. In late June, in an interview with a French newspaper, Cherif expressed optimism that the violence would soon cease and that if the majority of Algerian people 'were for the FIS' in the forthcoming presidential election the Government would 'respect their decision'. In early July, following a series of bomb explosions across Algeria, Cherif was dismissed from his post and replaced by a technocrat, Mustapha Benmansour, a former Governor of Annaba *wilaya*. Some observers interpreted Cherif's dismissal as a gesture of goodwill towards the FIS, others as a concession to those in the regime who had been angered by the minister's comments in the French press. In his independence day speech in July the President reiterated his pledge to eradicate Islamist terrorism and violence by military force. On 11 July Sheikh Sahraoui, a co-founder of the FIS and leading spokesman in France for the Algerian opposition, was assassinated in Paris. Claims that the Algerian regime was responsible for the murder were strongly denied: most analysts believed the assassination to have been perpetrated by the GIA, as Sahraoui was reported to have been on a GIA list of FIS leaders condemned to death. In mid-July Zéroual issued a statement confirming the collapse of dialogue with the FIS. There were rumours that intransigent elements on both sides had opposed any compromise.

In April 1995 the Government made concessions to the Berberist movement when it concluded an agreement with the RCD, one branch of the Mouvement culturel berbère (MCB), to establish a government body to oversee the teaching of Tamazight in schools and universities and to promote its use in the official media. However the agreement failed to satisfy the MCB's original demand for Tamazight to be recognized as an official language alongside Arabic. The MCB remained divided in its response to the Government's offer and appealed for the continuation of its eight-month boycott of schools. According to official reports only one-half of the 800,000 school children and students on strike returned to their classes on 29 April.

THE DIRTY WAR

Despite the speculation about dialogue, the first months of Zéroual's presidency were marked by escalating violence in which the barbarous acts reported recalled the worst days of the struggle for independence. Certain towns such as Blida, Médéa, Tiaret and Chlef and entire neighbourhoods in some of the cities were virtually controlled by Islamist militants. Islamist attacks on government officials, judges, politicians, intellectuals, journalists and teachers continued while the murder of more foreign nationals led several countries to advise their citizens to leave. In February 1994 Muhammad Touali, a member of Ettahaddi, was killed, and in May Laïd Grine, a founder member of the Rassemblement arabe-islamique (a small moderate Islamist party), was murdered by unidentified assassins. A new underground group, the Force islamique du djihad armé emerged in February and claimed responsibility for the deaths of two people in February and March. Between March and May nine foreign nationals were killed, including a French nun and priest. In late March France advised all its citizens

whose presence was not essential to leave Algeria. The USA, the United Kingdom and Spain had already advised their nationals to leave. France subsequently closed almost all French schools and cultural centres in Algeria. Japan also advised its nationals in Algiers to leave. Attacks by armed Islamist groups on the security forces included an assault on the high security Tazoult prison near Batna in March, which resulted in the release of more than 1,000 political prisoners. There were reports in the French press that armed Islamist groups had become heavily involved in drugs-trafficking, the proceeds of which helped to finance much of their activities.

The security forces intensified their campaign against armed Islamist groups and resorted to air attacks, using napalm, punitive raids, torture and psychological warfare in their efforts to eradicate the militants. According to figures compiled by Agence France Presse, more than 600 alleged terrorists were killed between mid-March and mid-May, an indication of the scale of operations mounted by the security forces during the first half of 1994. In February the security forces claimed a major success when they killed Djafar al-Afghani, the leader of the GIA. The GIA's *majlis ash-shura*, or leadership council, immediately declared Abu-Abdallah Ahmad to be the group's new leader. In January the US human rights organization Middle East Watch condemned both the Government and the Islamist militants for human rights abuses. Their report claimed that during 1993 Algeria had carried out the highest number of judicial executions for politically motivated offences of any Arab state except Iraq.

In late June 1994 64 people were injured when two bombs exploded in Algiers during a march organized by the RCD. The GIA claimed responsibility and in their communiqué denounced 'the secular enemies of faith and religion'. On the eve of the G7 summit in Naples in early June, seven Italian sailors had their throats cut by suspected Islamist guerrillas while they slept on board a ship at the Algerian port of Djen-Djen. Exiled FIS leader Rabah Kebir publicly denounced the murders and expressed his condolences to the Italian Prime Minister. In July the ambassadors of Oman and Yemen in Algiers were kidnapped by members of the GIA—the first time Islamist guerrillas had targeted senior diplomats—but were subsequently released unharmed. According to Yemen's ambassador, the GIA had given them a letter in which the group stated that it was prepared to stop its terror campaign against foreign nationals if the regime released the imprisoned GIA leader Abd al-Hak Layada. Some 14 foreign nationals were killed in a single week in July, and, after three French gendarmes and two diplomats were shot by Islamists outside the French embassy in Algiers in August, the exodus of foreigners accelerated, and some countries closed their embassies in Algiers. After the transfer of Madani and Belhadj from prison to house arrest in September, the GIA intensified its military operations in an attempt to sabotage any political deal; 16 civilians were decapitated the following day in Tiaret and Médéa, and at the end of the month Cheb Hasni, one of Algeria's most popular singers, was killed in Oran. In the Kabyle, a region traditionally alienated from the regime but strongly opposed to the Islamist militants, Berber villagers began organizing their own armed patrols. In July, when a group of Islamists demanded weapons and food from the villagers of Igoujdal near Béjaia, they met with violent resistance, which resulted in the deaths of six guerrillas. The event was given prominence in the official media, and while some army officers were in favour of arming certain villages, others feared that in time the arms might be turned against the regime.

The Government admitted in September 1994 that 10,000 people had died in the conflict since early 1992. Amnesty International estimated the death toll at 20,000, half of them ordinary civilians. These figures almost certainly underestimated the actual number of fatalities as daily killings were not reported in the heavily-censored media. In addition to their campaign of assassinations, Islamist activists burnt down schools and colleges—the GIA has fiercely opposed coeducation—and instituted a reign of terror in areas under their control; anyone who violated Islamist decrees risked mutilation or murder. Women who refused to comply with the Islamists' 'code of behaviour' were especially vulnerable. However, army repression was harsh, particularly in popular quarters of Algiers and other large cities where many young men suspected of Islamist sympathies were tortured by the security forces and summarily executed. Death squads were reported to have emerged, which were responsible for conducting revenge killings of victims selected at random. It was also argued that the security forces might have penetrated the GIA sufficiently to be able to manipulate the group so that some of their operations served the interests of the regime.

Following the failure of dialogue with the Islamist opposition, the army embarked on the most extensive military operations of the conflict and, confident of eventual victory, appeared to have abandoned all restraint in its efforts to uncover suspected Islamist sympathizers and guerrilla units. In December 1994 President Zéroual told local officials that the state was determined to stem the violence by all available means. As evidence of the need for tougher measures, it was believed that the army had presented a report to the President in October, which stated that 283 military personnel had been killed between July and October, and that on average 25 members of the security forces were being killed every day. Some analysts argued that the main reason for the regime's new intransigence was that it could depend on the undivided support of France, fearful of the consequences of an Islamist victory in its former colony. Charles Pasqua, the French Minister of the Interior, enjoyed close links with the Algerian generals, and France was believed to be the main supplier of sophisticated military equipment to the regime for use in anti-guerrilla warfare (see below). In response to the regime's strategy of maximum force, the Islamist militants intensified their campaign of violence. In December GIA guerrillas hijacked an Air France airbus at Algiers airport and murdered three passengers before forcing the aircraft to fly to Marseilles, France, where it was stormed by French counter-terrorist police and the hijackers were killed. In retaliation, four Catholic priests, three French and one Belgian, were murdered by the GIA in the Kabyle. In January 1995 a car-bomb exploded in the centre of Algiers, killing 42 people and injuring more than 280. Both the AIS and the GIA claimed responsibility for the attack, which was the biggest terrorist operation since the conflict began. Also in January there were reports that German and Swiss intelligence services were concerned that FIS supporters in Europe were not just engaging in propaganda but were purchasing weapons, ammunition and explosives to ship to Algeria. In March several people were arrested in Belgium for preparing to ship arms to Algeria, probably to the GIA. The Islamists were believed to have imposed a 'war tax' on businesses in the Algerian community in Europe to raise funds for arms purchases.

In February 1995 the authorities announced that almost 100 prisoners, 81 of whom were Islamists, had been killed by the security forces during what was described as an attempted mass escape from Serkadji prison in Algiers. According to Islamist sources, however, the men were deliberately killed in an incident similar to one that took place at Berrouaghia prison in November 1994 when the authorities claimed that 60 prisoners had been killed while trying to escape. There were reports that many of those killed at Serkadji had been held in solitary confinement, casting doubts on the official version of a mass escape. The authorities rejected demands for an independent inquiry into both incidents. In March 1995, in what was believed to be a reprisal by the GIA for the deaths at Serkadji, a large car-bomb exploded in Algiers, injuring more than 60 people, most of them policemen and their families.

In February 1995 it was reported that the three special courts established in 1992 to try cases involving terrorism and sabotage had been abolished; in future such cases were to be considered by ordinary criminal courts. The special courts had been criticized for human rights abuses. In early 1995 the Minister of the Interior announced that he was preparing a law authorizing the inhabitants of isolated regions to create self-defence groups, claiming that some 10,000 'communal guards' had been armed during the previous six months. Opposition groups, notably the FFS, criticized the arming of civilians and urged the Government to retain responsibility for security matters. In March a former police chief, Muhammad Ouadah, was appointed to a new senior security post responsible for co-ordinating the Government's campaign against the Islamist militants. Later that month the security forces claimed to have killed as many as 1,300 GIA guerrillas in operations mounted in the Ain Defla,

Médéa and Jijel regions. The official media spoke of 'the decapitation of the GIA'. The major operation took place in the mountainous Ain Defla region where, according to press reports, the police ambushed some 900 GIA supporters as they gathered for a congress. However, other reports, including those from eye witnesses, stated that the police operation followed a mutiny at a large army barracks in the area. Although there seemed little doubt that the GIA suffered substantial losses in the operation, including some of its leaders, the security forces did not appear to have eliminated all Islamist groups from the Ain Defla region. Government statements that the Islamist militants had only 3,000–4,000 armed men in the whole country seriously underestimated their strength. The Islamist militants' ability to mount new operations was demonstrated in early April when an armed group occupied a television relay station at Ain Nsour in western Algeria and broadcast a 40-minute Islamist video. Also in April sabotage of water-pumping equipment affected supplies to the greater Algiers region. There was speculation, none the less, that because of the high casualties among commanders of local guerrilla units, it was proving increasingly difficult for the central leadership to maintain contact with, let alone control the activities of, their militants in the field.

In April 1995 security measures were reinforced in the four 'exclusion zones' at Ouargla, Laghouat, El Oued and Illizi established to protect Saharan petroleum and gas fields, which provided 95% of Algeria's export revenues. Nevertheless, in May five foreign nationals were killed by the GIA at the industrial zone of Bounoura close to Ghardaia. The five men were employed by the Algerian subsidiary of the US company Bechtel which was responsible for the construction of the Algerian section of the Maghreb–Europe gas pipeline. The murders, which received wide coverage in the international press, brought the number of foreign nationals killed since September 1993 to 82, of whom 29 were French. Prior to the incident the hydrocarbons sector had remained relatively free from guerrilla attacks—although damage to the country's infrastructure was estimated at $3,000m.—and the Saharan region as a whole had been less affected by the violence which had engulfed northern Algeria. In May 1995 police defused five bombs planted in an Algiers hotel where the leaders of Algeria's 48 provisional authorities were attending meetings about the forthcoming presidential election. In the months preceding the November election Algeria was witness to a series of car-bomb attacks across the country. Some 70 people were killed, and more than 450 were injured, between July and late October. The security forces, meanwhile, claimed to have killed more than 150 armed Islamists in July alone, and in the following months intensified their operations to 'eliminate' suspected Islamist militants. In September a former Minister of the Interior, Boubaker Belkaïd, was killed by Islamist activists. This was the third assassination of a high-ranking civil servant since early 1992.

IS THE FUTURE ISLAMIST?

Some observers predicted that the future of Algeria would be Islamist and that most people would accept this. It had been argued that the FIS leadership, unable to exert control over the armed extremists, might be content to let the army eradicate the GIA by force. According to this scenario, such a military victory would only be achieved at enormous human cost, and popular rage against state terrorism would force the army to negotiate a deal with the FIS. An FIS-led government would be inevitable and the army would be forced to return to its barracks. Whether the FIS would then seek to impose its model on all of Algerian society or make concessions to its opponents remained in doubt. The existence of the FFS, with strong support among the Berbers of the Kabyle determined to win recognition for their cultural and linguistic rights, was regarded as the best hope that the interests of democrats would not be ignored by the FIS or the army. The inevitability of Islamist rule was contested by others who were convinced that the Algerian people, horrified by the outrages committed by Islamist militants, had rejected the FIS and believed that Islamism could be eradicated by military force. The anti-Islamist tendency, which included professional associations, trade unions and feminist groups, stressed the profound changes that Algeria had undergone since December 1991, when the FIS won almost one-half of the votes cast in the first round of the general elections. They indicated that there had been a reduction in the level of support for Islamist guerrilla groups in both social and geographical terms. Islamist militants were certainly younger and were almost all recruited from among the unemployed urban youth. Although some observers believed that the army had forced the Islamist guerrillas to fall back to the major cities where they could wage their campaign only by assassinations, they still appeared to have access to an almost inexhaustible supply of recruits. The size of the guerrilla forces was difficult to determine: Western diplomatic sources in Algiers estimated them to number 10,000–15,000; other sources suggested that the GIA alone had more than 10,000 armed men, organized into 40 groups. The GIA appeared to be dominant in Algiers and central Algeria, and the AIS in the rest of the country. Some of the guerrillas operated in groups of around 15 men, others in bands of 150–200 men; their leadership changed every few months as leaders were killed in clashes with the security forces. For its part, the army, even though it numbered some 165,000 armed men, could only mobilize around 60,000 of these for anti-terrorist operations, which might explain why, despite their successes, the security forces had been unable to consolidate their control over areas won from the guerrillas. It was argued that success in rescheduling the country's foreign debt would enable the regime to open new lines of credit to purchase anti-terrorist equipment and increase its military capacity.

THE PRESIDENTIAL ELECTION, NOVEMBER 1995

In August 1995 President Zéroual announced that the first round of the presidential election would be held on 16 November. Observers from the UN, the Organization of African Unity (OAU) and the Arab League were to monitor the electoral process. In October it was announced that four candidates had qualified for the election: Zéroual; the staunchly anti-Islamist Saïd Saadi, Secretary-General of the RCD; Nourreddine Boukrouh, leader of the PRA; and Sheikh Mahfoud Nahnah, leader of Hamas, which had taken a pro-Government stance since the 1992 military take-over. Redha Malek, a former Prime Minister who had been regarded as Zéroual's most serious rival for the presidency, failed to obtain the necessary number of signatures and did not qualify as a candidate. Malek accused the security forces and government officials of obstructing his efforts to collect signatures. The three leading political parties, the FIS, the FLN and the FFS, urged voters to boycott the election. Notwithstanding their appeal, and threats by Islamist militants to turn the ballot-boxes into coffins, 75.7% of the electorate voted (according to official figures) at the election, which was held amidst tight security involving the deployment of some 300,000 soldiers, gendarmes, police and self-defence groups. An unexplained cessation in the violence had occurred during the two weeks immediately preceding the election, which may account in part for the high level of voter participation. The result of Algeria's first multi-party presidential election since independence was a clear victory for incumbent President Zéroual, who, according to official figures, gained 61.0% of the votes cast. In his electoral campaign he had promised peace, security and national reconciliation. Sheikh Mahfoud Nahnah came second with 25.6% of the votes polled, followed by Saïd Saadi (9.6%), and Nourreddine Boukrouh (3.8%).

The main legal opposition parties, together with the banned FIS, were forced to acknowledge the political implications of the election, and there were appeals for a renewal of dialogue. At his inauguration on 27 November 1995, Zéroual reiterated his commitment to national dialogue and pledged to hold pluralist legislative and municipal elections; however, he offered no precise timetable. He referred to the Islamists as 'misled youths' and vowed to continue to fight against 'the remnants of terrorist violence'. In January 1996 the FFS, weakened by the long absence of its leader, Aït Ahmad, and anxious to re-establish dominance in its Kabyle heartland, announced that it would end its boycott of the electoral process and was ready to participate in legislative elections. The party held its second national congress in March at which certain organizational changes were agreed. Aït Ahmad attended the congress and was given the title of president of the party. Seddik Debaili was appointed first secretary and Mustafa Bouhadef, who had led the party within Algeria since the military coup in 1992, became national secretary responsible for organization. But at the end of the congress

Aït Ahmad returned to his base in Switzerland (where he had been residing for security reasons), and rumours of in-fighting within the party persisted. At the FLN's central committee meeting in January Abdelhamid Mehri, a strong supporter of the 'national pact' who had led the party in its firm opposition to the Government, was forced to resign as Secretary-General and was replaced by Boualem Benhamouda, a minister under both Boumedienne and Chadli who narrowly defeated former Prime Minister Mouloud Hamrouche, the leader of the party's reformist wing. Benhamouda immediately sought to distance the party from the 'Rome group'. The FLN also indicated that it was prepared to contest elections. For their part, the RCD and Hamas hoped to take the place of their more powerful rivals, the FFS and the FIS. Some observers argued that the Government was actively manipulating the two major legal opposition parties, the FLN and the FFS, by exploiting their internal divisions in order to 'domesticate' them, and enable the FLN to assume the role of 'presidential party' in forthcoming legislative elections. The FLN, though greatly weakened, still retained many of its structures which could be used to mobilize a loyalist vote when parliamentary elections took place. These predictions appeared to be confirmed when the FLN leadership was publicly reconciled with Zéroual in February. The FLN elected a new political bureau in late February, which was believed to be sympathetic to the President.

Immediately after the presidential election, Rabah Kebir, the senior FIS spokesman in exile, acknowledged Zéroual's victory and appealed for new negotiations with the regime. These overtures were immediately condemned by another FIS spokesman, Anwar Haddam; however, in February 1996, at a press conference in Stockholm, Sweden, Haddam asked the Algerian Government to allow him to visit imprisoned FIS leader Abbasi Madani 'to unblock the situation'.

In April 1996 President Zéroual began three weeks of talks with more than 70 leaders of opposition parties, trade unions and social organizations, together with other influential personalities, in preparation for parliamentary elections. The FIS were excluded but other Islamists such as Sheikh Mahfoud Nahnah of Hamas and Sheikh Abdullah Djaballah of Nahdah were invited to the talks which also involved surviving leaders from the War of Independence, opponents of the late President Boumedienne, former Presidents Ahmed Ben Bella and Ali Kafi, and former Prime Ministers Belaid Abd es-Salam, Redha Malek and Mouloud Hamrouche. Former President Chadli was a notable exception and apparently was not invited to the talks.

In June 1996 President Zéroual announced that he would hold a referendum later in the year to seek approval for constitutional reforms in preparation for parliamentary elections which he reaffirmed would take place in 1997. The proposed constitutional reforms were presented in a memorandum sent to leading political figures and included the creation of a bicameral parliament in which some members of the upper chamber would be appointed rather than elected, a ban on political parties based on religion or language, and the introduction of voting by proportional representation. In July Zéroual embarked on a new round of talks with the main opposition parties and other associations, including the UGTA, culminating in a national conference in September to ratify his political reform programme. Both the FIS and the Islamist militias were excluded from the talks, despite appeals from most of the main legal opposition parties that the FIS should be included in the dialogue. The secret contacts that had been maintained for some years between the presidency and Abbasi Madani appeared to have come to an end. The proposed ban on political parties using religious symbolism was aimed primarily at preventing the FIS from returning to the political arena.

The main legal political parties indicated that they were in favour of parliamentary elections being held at the earliest possible opportunity. There was also widespread support for voting by proportional representation, which appeared likely to give parties such as the FFS, the FLN, Hamas and the RCD useful blocs of seats in the elected lower chamber, although no single party seemed likely to command a majority. However, considerable concern was expressed about the proposed upper house, to be called the Council of the Nation, composed of members appointed either directly or indirectly by the President. A presidential spokesman argued that it would widen the scope of national parliamentary representation, although to many its function appeared to be to control the elected chamber, thereby increasing the President's power and strengthening his position should a hostile lower house be elected. At that time a 'presidential majority' in the lower house seemed unlikely. The FLN, under its new leadership, had rallied to the President, but the party was deeply divided; Zéroual's only other allies were the newly-formed Alliance nationale républicaine, led by Redha Malek, and the PRA, although it was assumed that they would also be joined by Hamas and possibly Nahdah. The FFS, the RCD, the MDA, Ettahaddi and the PT, together with prominent individuals such as Abd al-Hamid Mehiri, the former FLN leader, Mouloud Hamrouche, the leader of the reformist wing of the FLN, and Ali Yahia Abdennour, President of the ALHR, argued that parliamentary elections should take place before the holding of a referendum in order to allow the elected assembly to draft the Constitution. Both the FFS, which had withdrawn from talks with the President in August 1996, and the RCD, angry at the Government's decision not to give official recognition to the Berber language, decided to boycott the referendum and refused to attend the Government-sponsored conference on national concord, held in September 1996. The conference, which was attended by some 1,000 delegates, endorsed a 'platforme de l'entente nationale', incorporating the President's proposals for reform. Delegates were given little opportunity to amend the proposals.

In October 1996 President Zéroual announced that the referendum to amend the 1989 Constitution would be held on 28 November, followed by general and local elections in 1997. In the weeks preceding the referendum, the Government launched a massive media campaign and during the voting more than 300,000 troops were deployed across the country. According to official sources, some 79.8% of the electorate participated in the referendum, of whom 85.8% voted in favour of the constitutional changes. A number of opposition parties denounced the results, claiming that they had been manipulated by the Government. Opposition to the proposed reforms was particularly strong in the Kabyle, where residents staged protests against the designation of Arabic as the only 'national language'.

On 31 December 1995 Mokdad Sifi was replaced as Prime Minister by Ahmed Ouyahia, a former diplomat who had served as President Zéroual's *chef du cabinet* since 1994. Ouyahia, aged 43, became the youngest premier since Algeria's independence. In the new Council of Ministers announced in January 1996 the main economic portfolios remained unchanged, while Hamas and the PRA were offered several portfolios. The new Council of Ministers also included, for the first time, a former member of the FIS, Ahmed Merani, who was appointed Minister of Religious Affairs. Merani was a founder member of the FIS but defected from the party after it was banned in 1992. Muhammad Dembri was replaced as Minister of Foreign Affairs by Ahmed Attaf, a junior minister and spokesman for the Sifi Government. Ouyahia announced that 'rigour and austerity' were the main characteristics of the Government's economic programme, and stated his commitment to eliminate corruption. In August Zéroual issued a decree promoting the Governor of Algiers to the rank of minister in order to address the urgent problems facing the capital. In a further cabinet reshuffle in September, Ahmed Benbitour, the Minister of Finance, and Mourad Benachenhou, the Minister of Industrial Restructuring and Participation, were replaced by allies of the Prime Minister. In October Ouyahia promised a further round of privatizations and public sector reforms.

THE GENERAL ELECTION OF JUNE 1997

In early 1997 a new political party, the Rassemblement national démocratique (RND), was created, with Abdelkader Bensalah, the President of the NTC, as its Chairman. The launch of the RND was delayed as the result of the assassination in late January of Abd al-Hak Benhamouda, the Secretary-General of the UGTA, who was to have been the new party's leader. Bensalah presented the RND as a centrist grouping with support throughout the country, and denied claims that it was a 'presidential' party. It brought together a range of anti-Islamist organizations, self-defence groups, trade unions and women's associations, and many of its leading members were drawn from the influential war veterans' association. The RND announced that

it would present candidates in all constituencies; its lists included Prime Minister Ouyahia and numerous other ministers. The party was given permission to use official buildings for its electoral campaign and also benefited from other public facilities, drawing accusations of favouritism from opposition parties. In February the leaders of the opposition parties agreed to the creation of an independent commission to monitor the forthcoming general election. All political parties were given until May to restructure their organizations to take account of new legislation or be dissolved. In order to comply with the ban on the use of religious symbolism, Hamas reluctantly agreed to change its name to the Mouvement de la société pour la paix (MSP). In March the NTC adopted an electoral law providing for voting by proportional representation.

At a meeting in Madrid, Spain, in April 1997, representatives of the main opposition parties, including the FIS, appealed for the opening of a 'dialogue for peace'. Although divided over whether or not to participate in the general election, the signatories of the 1995 Sant' Egidio pact (see above) reaffirmed their belief that only a political solution would bring the violence to an end. The Government, however, refused to make any concessions. At the Madrid forum, the official FIS spokesman in exile, Abdelkrim Ould Adda, not only condemned the 'blind repression' of the regime, but also denounced the violence committed by the GIA against the civilian population. The Algerian Government ignored requests from the FIS that it enter into dialogue with the banned opposition. Shortly before the election, President Zéroual officially dissolved the NTC and paid homage to those deputies allegedly killed by Islamist extremists. In the period preceding the election several opposition parties complained that the authorities were undermining their campaigns; by early June the commission monitoring the election had received 600 complaints of alleged abuse. Both the PT and the FFS were refused permission to broadcast on state television. Many analysts argued that the election was designed to strengthen Zéroual's position, while an editorial in a French daily newspaper, *Le Monde*, referred to 'an election without true debate for an assembly without real power'. The constitutional changes that came into effect in late 1996 effectively reduced the power of the National People's Assembly as in future any bill adopted by the Assembly would have to receive the support of two-thirds of the members of the Council of the Nation in order to become law. The Algerian authorities invited more than 40 countries and organizations to send representatives to monitor the election, but most of them declined.

Some 39 political parties qualified to take part in the election and more than 7,000 candidates contested the 380 seats in the National People's Assembly. The pro-Government press in Algeria reported a high rate of participation in the electoral campaign and referred to the energetic campaigning of the candidates. Other newspapers, however, insisted that most Algerians had little interest in the election and were more concerned about their daily livelihood than official discourse. For the first time eight seats in the Assembly were reserved for Algerians living abroad; however, in France the Government placed restrictions on the activities of political parties campaigning among the Algerian community and only the RND was given permission to hold public meetings. In Algeria the period preceding the election was marred by continued violence; there were almost daily bombings in Algiers in the week before the election, leaving 22 people dead and 120 injured.

According to the final official results (as revised by the Constitutional Council in mid-June), at the election to the National People's Assembly on 5 June 1997 the RND won 156 of the 380 seats contested, the MSP 69, the FLN 62, Nahdah 34, the FFS 20, the RCD 19, the PT four, and the remainder were taken by independent candidates and other small political groupings. The RND did not achieve an overall majority, although it was generally assumed that it could rely on the support of the FLN, which had allied itself more closely to the President since Boualem Benhamouda became its leader. The two Islamist parties, the MSP and Nahdah, won more than 100 seats in the Assembly and, according to official figures, they received over 20% of all votes cast. In contrast, the centre-left parties, especially the FFS, failed to gain as many seats as they had in the previous election. According to the authorities the level of voter participation was 65.5%, although less than one-half of eligible voters in Algiers took part in the election. Opposition parties insisted that the rate of participation had been lower than the official figures indicated and complained of numerous, repeated and deliberate abuses during the election. Sheikh Mahfoud Nahnah of the MSP was particularly critical and told the media that he had expected to win another 20 seats. A team of UN observers expressed reservations about the fairness of the electoral process.

In mid-June 1997 President Zéroual asked Ahmed Ouyahia (who had tendered his resignation following the general election) to form a new Government. Towards the end of the month Ouyahia announced the new Council of Ministers, comprising 30 ministers and ministers-delegate and eight secretaries of state; the FLN and the MSP each held seven portfolios, while the RND took the remainder. Meanwhile, the newly-elected National People's Assembly convened for the first time in mid-June. Also in June the Government formally dissolved seven political parties (including the MDA) for failing to comply with the new regulations concerning political associations. In July, following secret negotiations, Abbasi Madani, and another prominent FIS member, Abdelkader Hachani, were released. It was reported that a deal had been struck between the authorities and the FIS whereby the party would be restored to legality, but under a new name, and in return the FIS would renounce all forms of political violence, dissolve the AIS and end its armed struggle against the regime. It was rumoured that the negotiations led to a power struggle among the military chiefs, between Zéroual's faction and that of Gen. Lamari, the Chief of Staff of the Army and a well-known opponent of dialogue with the FIS. It was alleged that Zéroual would have been ousted in a *coup d'état* had he not received decisive support from the US authorities. The power struggle was temporarily resolved, and negotiations with the FIS proved inconclusive. Madani was once again placed under house arrest, and in October Zéroual declared that the file on the FIS was 'closed permanently'.

FURTHER DEMOCRATIZATION?

Elections to institute elected regional and municipal councils, which had not existed since 1992, were held in mid-October 1997: the RND won more than one-half of the seats contested. Seven other parties won seats in the regional councils and 33 in the municipal councils, notably the FLN and the MSP. According to official results, some 62.7% of the electorate participated in regional elections and 67.7% took part in municipal elections. The Government, which had invited the international media to witness the elections, expressed satisfaction at the result and sought to portray the polls as the final stage in the re-establishment of the democratic process in Algeria. All major political parties, including the FLN and the MSP, complained of widespread electoral fraud, and in the weeks following the elections opposition parties organized massive demonstrations on a scale not seen for many years. President Zéroual refused to annul the results and street protests continued. In late December an electoral college selected two-thirds of the seats in the new 144-member upper chamber, the Council of the Nation, from members of the regional and municipal councils: of the 96 seats, the RND took 80, the FLN 10, the FFS four and the MSP two. The remaining 48 members were nominated by Zéroual. Thenceforth, legislation drafted by the lower house, the National People's Assembly, would not be promulgated unless approved by two-thirds of members in the Council of the Nation. In April 1998 a new Constitutional Council was installed.

At the RND's first congress, held in April 1998, Abdelkader Bensalah announced his resignation as the party's president. Muhammad Tahar Benbaibeche was subsequently appointed as the RND Secretary-General, while the election of the party's president was postponed. In May the UGTA confirmed Abdelmadjid Sidi Said as its new Secretary-General; he was expected to preside over preparations for the UGTA's forthcoming conference. Despite considerable discontent among the union's rank and file, the conference was expected to express continued support for the Government. Also in May the authorities disbanded some 30 political groupings (notably including Ettahaddi and the PSD) as they did not satisfy legislation regarding political parties.

In July 1998 controversial legislation on the compulsory use of the Arabic language in public life came into effect. Although the law was promulgated in 1991 it had been suspended in 1992 for practical reasons by the Chairman of the HCS, Muhammad Boudiaf. In December 1996 the NTC revived the legislation and set the date for its implementation. Under the terms of the law, all documents produced by the administration, public enterprises, associations and the official media would have to be in Arabic. Thenceforth, anyone who signed a document in a language other than Arabic as part of their official duties would be subject to a fine. (Most ministries currently use French in their daily transactions.) In addition, all films and television programmes in a foreign language would have to be dubbed or translated into Arabic. Only institutions of higher education were given until 2000 to apply the law. The Berber-speaking Kabyle region remained fiercely opposed to the Government's 'arabization' policy. At a rally in Algiers organized by the RCD in early July to remember the Kabyle singer Lounes Matoub, who had been assassinated in June, the legislation was denounced. More than 1,000 people took part in the demonstration.

In mid-September 1998 President Zéroual announced that a presidential election would be held before March 1999, at least 21 months ahead of schedule. Although there were reports that Zéroual had been suffering from ill health, many analysts believed that the announcement was prompted primarily by the power struggle within the regime.

POLITICAL VIOLENCE CONTINUES

The presidential election in November 1995 did not bring an end to political violence, which continued to claim an estimated 100 victims every week. Within hours of President Zéroual's acceptance speech, Gen. Muhammad Boutighane, second in command of the navy and a personal friend of the President, was assassinated in a suburb of Algiers, and in December Col Boumezrague was murdered in central Algiers; both killings were attributed to the GIA. December saw a spate of car-bombs including an explosion in an Algiers suburb, which killed 15 people and injured 40 others. The Government estimated that during 1995 acts of sabotage by armed Islamist groups inflicted damage of more than $2,000m. Nevertheless, military analysts argued that the new strategies introduced by the security forces were more efficient than in the past, that anti-terrorist intelligence was better co-ordinated and that the self-defence groups, numbering some 18,000 men, had become increasingly integrated into the regime's security apparatus. They claimed that the security forces had made it more difficult for Islamist guerrilla bands to regroup and obtain weapons and that they had fragmented into small groups unable to mount operations against military convoys or major military targets. Islamist guerrillas were consequently forced to operate in groups of two or three people against a single victim, and increasingly favoured the use of car-bombs—the local press estimated that in the six weeks after the start of Ramadan in late January 1996 some 80 car-bombs had exploded. After the presidential election the internment camp in the Sahara for alleged Islamist militants was closed and its 640 remaining inmates were released. None the less, some 17,000 Algerians remained imprisoned, the majority without trial, for alleged terrorist activities. Meanwhile, the number of Islamist guerrillas surrendering to the authorities increased after the election, although not on a scale likely to inflict serious damage on the underground Islamist groups.

Local and international human rights organizations continued to condemn both the Islamist militants and the security forces for human rights abuses. Ali Yahia Abdennour, a veteran human rights activist, for example, claimed that some of the atrocities attributed to the GIA were actually perpetrated by the military to maintain an atmosphere of crisis for their own political ends, a view widely supported in the country. In March 1996 Amnesty International accused the security forces of resorting to torture, disappearances and extrajudicial executions, and alleged that many detainees were denied a fair trial. Particular alarm was expressed at the lack of an independent, public investigation into alleged human rights abuses and at the Government's failure to investigate the killings at Serkadji prison in February 1995 (see above). Journalists continued to experience violence and intimidation from Islamist militants and harassment by the authorities. In addition, a number of journalists were killed in the wave of car-bomb attacks in early 1996. For its part, the regime regularly banned newspapers for printing articles about security-related incidents, and arrested journalists on charges of libel or divulging security secrets. In February 1996 the Government tightened controls over the media, insisting that any stories relating to the violence had to be submitted to the censor unless they had been provided by the state news agency. In January the Mouvement des femmes démocrates was formed to campaign against the many abuses that Algerian women have suffered during the violence. The new party, led by Khalida Messaoudi, a well-known feminist, anti-Islamist and spokeswoman for Saïd Saadi, claimed that 343 women had been killed by Islamist militants since 1992. A pamphlet published by a group of women journalists in March 1996 to mark International Women's Day listed 600 'assassinations' of women and strongly criticized President Zéroual for not fulfilling his promises to improve conditions for Algerian women. In May the GIA murdered seven elderly French monks who had been kidnapped two months earlier from their monastery near Médéa. There were reports that the Algerian secret services had refused to collaborate with their French counterparts during efforts to secure the monks' release. Immediately after the murders, the French Government once again appealed to the remaining French citizens in Algeria to leave the country. There were further reports of in-fighting among Islamist militias, including the death in July of Djamel Zitouni, a GIA leader, in clashes between rival factions. In the following month the French Roman Catholic Bishop of Oran, Pierre Claverie, was assassinated by Islamist militants. In September Madani Merzak, the leader of the AIS, was reported to have condemned attacks against the civilian population and to have urged the Islamist guerrillas to unite under his command. On several occasions the AIS had insisted that it only perpetrated attacks on military or paramilitary targets. A month later a communiqué from Harakat al-Bakoun al-Ahd, a group formerly part of the GIA, condemned members of another faction, Takfir wa Hijra, composed of veterans of the Afghanistan war, for carrying out bloody attacks against the civilian population. In late October the Prime Minister, Ahmed Ouyahia, declared that the security forces were achieving considerable success in their campaign against the Islamist militias which he insisted received support from foreign organizations. Despite the determination of Algeria's security forces to eliminate the militants, and the deep divisions within the Islamist militias, Islamist groups continued to carry out car-bomb attacks, ambushes and offensives on infrastructure such as railway lines and power supplies. In December the GIA announced that its new leader was Slimane Maherzi, also known as Abou Djamil, a veteran of the war in Afghanistan. Government claims that the security situation was improving were undermined in January 1997 when there was a sharp upsurge in violence at the beginning of Ramadan; a series of bombs exploded in Algiers and other cities, and night attacks were launched on isolated villages. At least 180 people, most of them civilians, were killed in the first two weeks of Ramadan. After the assassination in late January of Abd al-Hak Benhamouda, the Secretary-General of the UGTA, there was speculation that his murder might not have been perpetrated by the GIA and that it might have been the result of in-fighting within the regime. Benhamouda had planned to leave the UGTA in order to lead the RND. It has been argued that at least some of the political violence in Algeria can be attributed to conflicts between different factions within the regime. The bombings in Algiers continued in the period preceding the general election, while reports emerged of attacks by GIA factions on villages, increasingly involving horrific ritualistic massacres. In April more than 90 people were slaughtered in one such massacre. Islamist militants continued to target the country's infrastructure; in late April more than 20 people were killed when a train was exploded on the Algiers–Blida railway line. The security forces claimed some successes, including the destruction of an important guerrilla base near Tizi-Ouzou in early April during which more than 100 Islamist militants were killed. However, renewed guerrilla attacks undermined the Government's claim that it was winning the battle against 'terrorism'. Some observers argued that there were indications that the Government was prepared to accept a

certain level of violence in the hope that internal divisions would weaken the guerrilla groups and that the horrific massacres of civilians attributed to Islamist extremists would alienate most Algerians. According to international sources, by mid-1997 at least 60,000 people had been killed since 1992, although analysts in Algeria indicated that the real figure could be double that number.

Meanwhile, the Government denied claims that many people arrested by the security forces were detained for long periods in secret detention centres. It was alleged that 15 such centres existed in Algiers alone. Several thousand people had simply disappeared, although not all of these 'disparitions' were attributed to the security forces. A report published in June 1997 by the Fédération international des ligues des droits de l'homme confirmed the systematic use of torture by the authorities against detainees suspected of membership of 'terrorist' groups, and arbitrary executions by the security forces of suspected Islamist militants. It alleged that many of these executions were perpetrated by self-defence groups, but that the regime invariably blamed them on the Islamists.

The cycle of violence intensified in mid-1997 when a series of massacres took place in villages to the south and west of Algiers in an area increasingly referred to as the 'triangle of death'. In some villages several hundred people—virtually the entire community—were slaughtered, including babies. Some victims had their throats cut or were burnt alive, and many were horribly mutilated. The security forces appeared unable or unwilling to prevent the bloodshed; on several occasions the military failed to assist the local population during attacks that took place in the vicinity of army barracks. Although the GIA was widely held responsible for the massacres, some claimed that most of the GIA factions had been infiltrated and some were controlled by military intelligence. It was also alleged that some massacres were perpetrated by army units disguised as Islamist guerrillas. Meanwhile, reports in the European press, based on allegations made by former members of the Algerian security services living in exile, claimed that the Algerian secret services were responsible for the bomb attacks in Paris in 1995 and the murder of seven Italian sailors at Djen-Djen in 1994 (see above). The allegations may have been made by rival military factions to discredit the head of the secret services, Gen. Tewfik Mediene, and his associates. In late August, following a night of slaughter in villages south of Algiers, Kofi Annan, the UN Secretary-General, angered the Algerian Government by suggesting that the UN might consider some form of intervention in Algeria in order to stem the violence. Abbasi Madani, who had recently been released from detention, responded by writing Annan an open letter offering to appeal for an immediate truce. Shortly afterwards Madani was once again confined to house arrest, and Annan did not repeat his suggestion of international intervention. Germany, the United Kingdom and Italy appealed for international action to be taken to resolve the conflict, but the Algerian authorities remained opposed to any form of international intervention or mediation in what it regarded as its internal affairs. In late September the AIS announced a unilateral cease-fire, effective from 1 October, in an attempt to expose members of the GIA as the principal perpetrators of the recent civilian massacres.

Further massacres took place in late December 1997 in the days preceding the start of Ramadan and continued during the holy month, during which more than 1,300 civilians were killed. As Ramadan began, independent reports claimed that more than 400 civilians were slaughtered in one night in villages near Relizane in the north-west of the country, where the AIS had been active before announcing a cease-fire. Massacres continued in the Relizane region and in one incident an entire village was razed to the ground: there were no survivors. Attacks also took place in other parts of the north-west, and in the Algiers region. International concern at the increasing scale of the violence in Algeria led to the dispatch of a ministerial delegation of the European Union (EU) to Algiers in late January 1998. Although the Algerian authorities reluctantly agreed to receive the delegation, the mission achieved little of substance. Algerian officials continued to reject all offers of foreign mediation or assistance for the victims of the violence and firmly opposed any form of independent inquiry into the massacres. The Government repeated its complaint that the European authorities were doing insufficient to contain the activities of Islamist networks operating in the EU. A delegation from the European Parliament visited Algiers in February but had limited success. Also in February the US-based Human Rights Watch announced that there was overwhelming evidence that the security forces were responsible for the disappearance of more than 1,000 people since 1992. In January Prime Minister Ouyahia declared that despite the recent massacres the authorities were close to defeating 'terrorism'. In answer to questions from leaders of parliamentary opposition parties, he stated that 26,536 people had been killed and 21,137 had been wounded in the conflict since the beginning of 1992. This was the first time that the authorities had released official figures for the death toll, which were considerably lower than those quoted by human rights organizations. In July a high-level UN 'fact-finding' mission was dispatched to Algeria to hold consultations with government officials and representatives of political parties and civil society; it was also permitted access to several sites of recent massacres and to Serkadji prison. The mission's report, released in September, stressed the need to reinforce civilian government in Algeria and to accelerate economic reforms. However, it was strongly criticized by Amnesty International for failing to address the human rights 'crisis'.

In early February 1998 official sources claimed that the GIA had suffered heavy casualties in clashes with the security forces, and the local press reported renewed fighting between the GIA and the AIS. In April it was reported that the security forces had arrested a number of local officials, including two mayors, and leaders of self-defence groups in Relizane, the scene of some of the country's worst massacres. According to local witnesses, two mass graves containing some 80 bodies had been discovered; Government supporters were suspected of perpetrating the killings. Officials stated that the Government had always admitted that some abuses were committed by its own forces, but insisted that these were exceptions. In late April there were reports that Islamist guerrillas had attacked a military post at Larba, near Algiers, killing 80 soldiers and capturing weaponry. In May the GIA was held responsible for two bomb attacks in Algiers in which more than 20 civilians were killed and many others were wounded.

FOREIGN RELATIONS AFTER THE 1992 COUP

The resignation of President Chadli and the blocking by the military of any advance towards a parliamentary system did not adversely affect Algeria's international relations. In those Arab countries that had their own problems with 'Islamic fundamentalists' it was generally welcomed. Soon after the coup the Minister of Foreign Affairs, Lakhdar Brahimi, visited the Persian (Arabian) Gulf to explain the motives behind it and to draw attention to his country's economic plight. Later Maj.-Gen. Nezzar went there to discuss co-operation on security matters. At a meeting of Arab Ministers of the Interior in Tunis in January 1993, Algeria, Egypt and Tunisia attempted to convince the other participants that terrorism resulting from extremism was a common concern. Egypt also took steps to ensure that Algeria was fully supportive of US peace initiatives. Only with Sudan did relations become strained as Algeria accused it of providing training for at least 500 Islamist guerrillas: the Algerian ambassador was recalled from Khartoum in December 1992. In September 1994 President Zéroual met Sudanese President Omar al-Bashir in Tripoli, Libya, where they were both attending the 25th anniversary celebration of the Libyan revolution. The Sudanese President and Libyan leader Col Qaddafi gave assurances that they would not support the Islamist militants in Algeria. Less than a year earlier, Qaddafi had declared that the Algerian Islamists were his 'friends'. In January 1995 Algeria protested vigorously to Yemen about a visit by FIS and GIA militants, who were believed to be receiving military training and indoctrination in camps operated by the Yemeni Islah Party (YIP), and, after an unsatisfactory response, recalled its ambassador from San'a. The inflammatory speeches of the YIP's leading ideologue, Sheikh Abd al-Majid Zindani, circulated on cassette in Algeria, where Zindani was considered to be the spiritual guide of the Islamists.

Iran had previously warned that force should not be used against the FIS, and declared the postponement of the second round of voting in the general election to be illegal. Prime Minister Ghozali claimed that he had evidence that Iran had given financial support to the FIS and that it had otherwise interfered in Algeria's internal affairs. As a protest, Algeria reduced its embassy staff in Teheran in November 1992 and severed relations completely in March 1993.

Algeria's North African neighbours did not disguise their relief that a possible fundamentalist take-over had been averted. Tunisia was one of the first countries to welcome the return to Algeria of Muhammad Boudiaf and frequent exchanges of visits and a ministerial declaration in April 1992 showed how closely the two Governments were co-operating.

Relations with Morocco fluctuated. Under Boudiaf, who had long been resident in that country, Algeria reduced still further its support for the Polisario Front, and collaborated in security matters, sending Gen. Belkheir to Marrakesh in March 1992. Subsequently, however, relations deteriorated to the extent that, in January 1993, King Hassan stated that it would have been better if the FIS had been allowed to take power in Algeria. There were angry press exchanges, and localized disputes over traffic temporarily closed the frontier. Later in the month, however, a long-overdue exchange of ambassadors took place and it was announced that work would start on the gas pipeline across Morocco to Spain, which was of prime economic importance to both countries. Border posts were reopened and aid to the Polisario Front, which had initially increased under Abd es-Salam, appeared to have been reduced again. Relations deteriorated again in 1994 during the trial in Algiers of Abd al-Hak Layada, believed to be the leader of the GIA. Layada, who had been extradited from Morocco in September 1993, stated that he had been contacted by senior Moroccan army officers and asked to eliminate certain members of the Moroccan opposition living in Algeria, together with the Secretary-General of the Polisario Front, Muhammad Abd al-Aziz. At a meeting of the OAU in August 1994 President Zéroual appeared to adopt a less flexible position on the Western Sahara and angered Morocco by referring to the disputed territory as 'an illegally occupied country'. In late August, after gunmen killed two Spanish tourists in Marrakesh, the Moroccan authorities alleged that two of the suspects sought were being paid by the Algerian secret services, which it accused of sponsoring terrorists to destabilize the country. Morocco imposed entry visas on Algerian nationals and others of Algerian origin, including French nationals, visiting Morocco. Two French nationals, one of Algerian origin, were arrested in Morocco in connection with the murders, and the Algerian community was targeted in the search for terrorists. In September the French police arrested alleged associates of the two men who were found in possession of FIS and GIA literature. The Algerian Government strongly denied that it was sponsoring terrorism against its neighbour, and in late August sealed its border with Morocco. By October the tension eased somewhat and, in a gesture of goodwill, Algeria appointed a permanent ambassador to Rabat. In the same month, the Moroccan Minister of Energy and Mines visited Algeria to attend the ceremony marking the formal start of work on the Maghreb–Europe gas pipeline (see Economy). The frontier remained closed, however, and visa requirements for Algerian nationals continued to be enforced. In December it was claimed that Algerian security forces had killed a Moroccan at one of the border posts. Senior-level talks later that month (during the summit of the Organization of the Islamic Conference held in Morocco) failed to make significant progress. Tensions intensified during 1995 with the re-emergence of differences over the disputed Western Sahara. In December King Hassan of Morocco expressed his anger at Algeria's 'involvement' in the Western Sahara dispute. Although reports suggest that the Algerian regime was no longer providing material support to Polisario, it remained sympathetic to their demands for self-determination, and President Zéroual himself was believed to have taken an active interest in the dispute. There was speculation that Algeria and Morocco were prepared to resolve their differences following a meeting in Rabat in December 1996 between the two countries' Ministers of the Interior.

President Zéroual attended the sixth UAM summit in Tunis in April 1994, at which Algeria assumed the UAM presidency for a 12-month period. At the meeting Zéroual declared Algeria's commitment to working towards Maghreb unity. However, the Libyan representative stated that unless the other UAM member states ceased to comply with UN sanctions against Libya, his country would leave the organization. In reply Zéroual expressed concern about 'the sufferings of the Libyan people' but carefully avoided any direct criticism of UN sanctions. Although Libya continued to attend UAM meetings, in January 1995 its representative stated that Col Qaddafi would not assume the presidency of the UAM and Algeria agreed to chair the organization for another six months. Rising tensions between Algeria and Morocco resulted in a demand from King Hassan in December for the suspension of UAM activities. The UAM heads of state summit planned for the end of the month was postponed, and in January 1996 the Tunisian and Mauritanian Ministers of Foreign Affairs, together with UAM Secretary-General Mohamed Amamou, held talks with Zéroual in Algiers to formulate an official reply to Morocco's demand.

In early 1995 security measures were increased along Algeria's border with Tunisia after an attack on a Tunisian border post by GIA guerrillas in February, during which six Tunisian border guards were killed. The Tunisian Government initially maintained that the guards were injured in a car accident; however it later admitted that they had been killed by Algerian Islamists.

In February 1995 the Algerian Minister of Foreign Affairs visited Libya shortly after the two countries had signed a co-operation agreement thought to reaffirm Libya's support for the Algerian Government in its struggle against Islamist militancy. In early 1996 the Algerian Minister of the Interior met the Libyan Secretary for Justice and Public Security to discuss co-operation in security issues, and there were reports that the Libyan administration had returned to the Algerian authorities some 500 Algerians, mainly members of the FIS, who had sought refuge in Libya after the 1992 coup.

Algeria has continued to maintain close relations with Mauritania. In April 1996 the two countries signed economic and social accords, and in July President Zéroual visited Nouakchott to hold talks with President Maawiya Ould Sid' Ahmed Taya.

During 1995 Algeria pursued a more active foreign policy aimed at strengthening its relations with the rest of Africa and the Arab world. In May Algeria signed two co-operation agreements with Iraq and in June President Zéroual made official visits to Egypt and Abu Dhabi (UAE). Addressing the OAU summit in Addis Ababa (Ethiopia) in June, Zéroual spoke of Algeria's role in Africa and his country's success in bringing about the reconciliation of the Tuareg and government forces in Mali. In June 1996 the Prime Minister of Jordan, Abdul-Karim Kabarati, visited Algiers to express King Hussein's support for President Zéroual's policies. The Iraqi Minister of Foreign Affairs also visited Algiers that month and held talks with Algerian ministers. There were reports that the two countries were discussing co-operation in hydrocarbons development. In October Zéroual visited China, Viet Nam and the Gulf states. During the first visit to Bahrain by an Algerian President, Zéroual expressed his full support for the Bahraini authorities in their struggle against 'terrorism'. Also in October, most Arab League members were represented at a security conference held in Algiers to formulate a common policy against Islamist militancy. In October 1997 Zéroual made an official visit to Saudi Arabia. There were unconfirmed reports that Saudi Arabia had been involved earlier in negotiations between the Algerian authorities and the FIS.

The need for foreign investment dominated Algeria's relations with the developed world and brought some useful dividends. In October 1992 a 20-year contract to supply gas was signed with Italy, following the signing of a similar accord with Spain. Japan made two loans to SONATRACH and in February it signed a contract to develop Saharan gas. Contracts were also signed with Portugal, Belgium and the USA and diplomatic relations established with Croatia, a possible customer for gas carried via the pipeline across Italy, for which the EC provided credits. In January British Petroleum had obtained a concession to prospect for gas in 6,000 sq km of the Tell Atlas and the company appeared to be making Algeria its principal base in the area. Fear of offending a Western government muted Algerian criticism of Germany's failure to extradite the FIS leader, Rabah Kebir. While there was a measure of agreement in principle among Western governments on providing Algeria with financial support, there was a reluctance to offer the regime political

backing. After a series of massacres of civilians in Algeria during 1997, which received extensive coverage in the Western media, there were more vociferous appeals for the international community to take action in order to stem the violence. The Algerian authorities, however, vigorously rejected any external mediation or intervention. While questions were raised in the West about the role of the Algerian Government in the recent bloodshed, Algerian officials criticized Western governments for allowing Islamist groups in their countries to raise funds to support 'terrorism' in Algeria.

Despite rumours that France, worried about the possibility of a fundamentalist Algeria, had prior knowledge of the military coup, and that it had even promised asylum to its leaders should it fail, the French Government disapproved of the subsequent harsh repression and did not wish to be identified too closely with an anti-Islamist Government. It was not until January 1993 that a senior figure, Roland Dumas, French Minister of Foreign Affairs, went to Algiers, where he admitted that there had been a widening gap between the two countries. However, he had 'very friendly and useful' talks with Kafi and, declaring that France wished to participate in the modernization of Algeria, he announced that it would grant commercial credits of 5,500m. francs. In June, after a visit to Paris by Redha Malek in the course of which he met both the French President and the Prime Minister, the French Government pledged to help Algeria to combat 'terrorism'.

After the right-wing Government of Edouard Balladur took office in early 1993, France became Algeria's leading supporter in the West and lent its political and economic backing to the military regime in its struggle to eradicate the Islamist underground and manage its severe economic problems, notably the burden of the country's large external debt. The French police continued to prosecute FIS cells in France which were accused of providing funds and weapons for Islamist militants in Algeria. Following the killing of five French embassy employees by suspected Islamist guerrillas at an embasssy housing compound in Algiers in August 1994, some 20 Algerians were arrested in different parts of France, accused of being Islamist militants, and interned at Folembray before most of them were expelled to Burkina Faso on the orders of the French Minister of the Interior. Several Frenchmen of Algerian origin were arrested by the French police in September in the Paris region, accused of being associates of the two suspects arrested in Morocco for the murder of two Spanish tourists in Marrakesh (see above). It was claimed that they were part of an Islamist cell—they had been found in possession of FIS and GIA literature—responsible for perpetrating terrorist acts. By the end of 1994 most of the Islamist networks in France had been dismantled and despite attempts by the French media to link Muslims, Islamism and violence, the vast majority of Algerians in France, and those of Algerian parentage, did not support the FIS; young people in particular were often indifferent to events in Algeria. One of the leading researchers on Muslims in France stressed that the efforts of organizations such as the Fraternité algérienne en France had been directed towards collecting money and weapons, not mobilizing the youth of the urban slums to form a fifth column in a new 'Algerian war'. Nevertheless, the tragic events in Algeria resulted in the formation of numerous non-political associations by ordinary Algerians resident in France dedicated to providing humanitarian assistance to their compatriots. In September 1994 the French embassy in Algiers announced that the issue of entry visas for France was provisionally suspended and that for security reasons applications previously dealt with by French consulates in Algeria would now be centralized in France. In early 1995 it was reported that the Bureau de Visas Algérie in Nantes was receiving 1,200–1,500 applications a day from Algerians seeking refuge in France but that only 10% were being granted.

During the approach to the 1995 French presidential election, there was considerable debate about differences within the French Government over policy on Algeria. Alain Juppé, the Minister of Foreign Affairs, insisted that he alone was responsible for French foreign policy and that the official policy on Algeria was to encourage democratic elections when conditions permitted. He expressed support for dialogue and for the Sant' Egidio pact. His powerful colleague, the Minister of the Interior, Charles Pasqua, was accused of using security issues in France to lead his own foreign policy, especially with regard to Algeria. Interviewed in October 1994 Pasqua condemned negotiations with the Islamist opposition, arguing that there were no 'moderate' Islamists, and he exploited the media by suggesting that should an Islamist government emerge in Algeria it would result in hundreds of thousands of people fleeing the country, the majority of whom would seek refuge in France. Confusion over French policy increased when François Léotard, the Minister of Defence, in an interview with a Saudi Arabian newspaper, criticized the Algerian regime and its inability to engage in successful negotiations with the opposition. At the same time there were reports, denied by the French Government, that France had approached Sudanese Islamist leader, Hassan at-Turabi, to assist in fostering *rapprochement* between the Algerian Government and the FIS. A report that a close associate of the French Minister of the Interior had met with exiled FIS leader Rabah Kebir in Germany was strongly denied by Pasqua.

In November 1994 the French press reported that 50 volunteer French military advisers were working in Algeria and that Prime Minister Balladur's inner cabinet had agreed to give the Algerian Government 'decisive help' in its struggle against Islamist violence. For some time there had been reports that France was supplying military equipment, especially helicopters, to the Zéroual regime and providing training for helicopter pilots. However, the French Prime Minister, Alain Juppé, denied that France was providing military aid to the Algerian Government. In January 1995, after the hijacking of an Air France aircraft by GIA guerrillas (see above), the GIA issued a statement declaring war on France because of its 'support to the oppressive regime, in addition to its military presence in Algeria'. In February relations between Algeria and France became strained when President Mitterrand proposed that the EU sponsor a peace conference on Algeria. Algeria denounced the proposal and recalled its ambassador from Paris. The French Government emphasized that the President's proposal was a personal one, not government policy, and within a week the ambassador returned to Paris. Between July and late October a total of seven people were killed, and more than 160 injured, in a series of bomb attacks across France, which were widely believed to have been perpetrated by the GIA. In September French police named a 24-year-old Algerian-born French resident, Khaled Kelkal, as a prime suspect in the bombing campaign. At the end of the month, following a large-scale operation to arrest him, Kelkal was shot and killed by French security forces as he attempted to escape. A second suspect, the Algerian-born Abdelkrim Deneche (resident in Sweden), was arrested and later released; in October the Swedish authorities rejected a French judicial ruling demanding Deneche's extradition. In October the GIA claimed responsibility for the wave of bomb attacks as retaliation for France's support for the Algerian regime. In November the French police made a number of arrests of alleged 'Islamic extremists' during a series of raids in Paris, Lyons and Lille. Weapons and bomb-making equipment were seized and the French Minister of the Interior claimed that the police action had prevented an imminent bomb attack on a market near the centre of Lille. Also in November the British police arrested two Algerians in London, Abdelkadir Benouif and Farouk Deneche, brother of Abdelkrim Deneche. Benouif, a long-term resident in the United Kingdom, was suspected of leading the GIA cell responsible for the bombing campaign in France. In mid-October President Zéroual cancelled a widely-publicized meeting in New York with the newly-elected French President, Jacques Chirac, in protest at France's 'malevolent' attitude towards Algeria. Both Presidents were attending the UN's 50th anniversary celebrations. President Chirac countered that the meeting had been 'postponed' as a reaction to his rejection of Zéroual's request for the meeting to receive extensive coverage in the mass media, as he had feared that such publicity might 'interfere' with Algeria's forthcoming presidential election. Franco–Algerian relations improved towards the end of the year with visits by Philippe Séguin, the President of the French National Assembly, to Algiers in December and by the new Algerian Minister of Foreign Affairs, Ahmed Attaf, to Paris in January 1996, his first official overseas engagement. In February 1996 a reciprocal investment agreement, delayed for some three years, was finalized in Paris. But in May Alain

Juppé again urged all French nationals remaining in Algeria to leave the country after seven French Trappist monks were murdered by the GIA in the Médéa area. As a result of the murders, Algeria's uneasy relations with France deteriorated. Nevertheless, the French Government concluded that its only option was to continue to offer discreet support to the Algerian authorities. In August France's Minister of Foreign Affairs, Hervé de Charette, became the first senior French minister to visit Algiers since 1993. He promised to work towards rebuilding relations with Algeria which he described as a key partner in France's foreign policy. But his visit was marred by the assassination of Pierre Claverie, the French Roman Catholic Bishop of Oran, shortly after the departure of the French delegation. Relations were further strained in December when Algerian Islamists were blamed for a bomb explosion on a Paris passenger train which resulted in the deaths of four people. Shortly after the bomb attack, the GIA threatened to renew its campaign of violence if the French Government did not sever its links with the Algerian administration. Following the election of a socialist government in France in 1997 there was speculation that the French authorities might adopt a more critical approach towards the Algerian regime. The incoming French Prime Minister, Lionel Jospin, was known to be a friend of Hocine Aït Ahmad of the opposition FFS. In October, when President Chirac announced his support for a peace initiative for Algeria devised by Romano Prodi, the Italian Prime Minister, Algeria's Minister of Foreign Affairs accused France of meddling in Algeria's internal affairs. Allegations in the media that members of the Algerian security services may have been responsible for the bomb attacks in Paris in mid-1995 further complicated bilateral relations. However, comments subsequently made by Hubert Védrine, the French Minister of Foreign Affairs, suggested that official policy towards Algeria remained unchanged. According to Védrine, France welcomed the holding of parliamentary elections in Algeria in mid-1997, and the consequent inclusion of opposition parties in the new legislative chambers. In addition, the 'Algerian crisis team', established by Jospin, was reported to have close links with Algerian security chiefs.

There was speculation, during 1994, that the Clinton administration in the USA was adjusting its policy towards Algeria and that, in order to avoid the mistakes made in Iran, it was preparing for a possible Islamist regime to assume power there in the future. The acting Secretary of State for Near Eastern Affairs, Mark Parris, admitted that US officials had held talks with exiled FIS officials and maintained that the FIS was not responsible for terrorist acts perpetrated by the GIA and other militant groups. In June President Clinton confirmed that there had been low-level contacts between US officials and the FIS in the USA and Germany and stated that his administration was not opposed to some form of power sharing between the Zéroual regime and 'dissident groups who are not involved in terrorism'. However, during 1995 the US administration appeared to change its attitude towards the FIS and to adopt a tougher policy on radical Islamists. It was reported that the National Security Council had taken over responsibility for US policy on Algeria and was influenced by analysts in the Pentagon who argued that Islamist forces could not win an overall victory over the Government. The US administration appeared to favour promoting links with legalized opposition parties in Algeria. Aït Ahmad of the FFS was received at the Department of State during a visit to the USA in June. In November Clinton congratulated President Zéroual on his election victory, describing the high turn-out as 'a significant development'. Clinton assured Zéroual of US support for all efforts towards national reconciliation and economic reform. However, in March 1996 relations became strained when the US Department of State issued its annual report on human rights which alleged that the Algerian security forces were responsible for dozens of killings and employed the use of torture. Nevertheless, later that month Robert Pelletreau, US Assistant Secretary of State, visited Algiers, the first visit by a senior US official since 1992, and reaffirmed his country's support for Zéroual's policy of dialogue. After the visit Algeria's official news agency spoke of the normalization of relations between the two countries and welcomed the fact that the US Department of State had ended contacts with FIS spokesman, Anwar Haddam. In December 1996 Haddam was taken into custody by US immigration officials pending his deportation. The Centre for Constitutional Rights based in New York also initiated legal proceedings against Haddam for alleged human rights violations. In late 1997 the US Government urged Algeria to allow UN investigators into the country after the series of massacres of civilians. In January 1998 a spokesman from the US Department of State announced that the US Government wanted the Algerian authorities to do more to protect its citizens while respecting the rule of law, but added that the USA had no plans to exert any pressure on the Algerian Government. Some human rights campaigners had appealed for restrictions on hydrocarbon imports from Algeria. The Clinton administration continued its policy of supporting the Zéroual regime as a bastion against militant Islam in the region.

In March 1996 Ahmed Attaf, the Algerian Minister of Foreign Affairs, attended the US-sponsored 'Summit of Peace-makers' in Egypt, an anti-terrorist summit meeting hastily arranged after a wave of suicide bomb attacks were launched against Israel. There was speculation that Algeria might begin to take a more active role in the Middle East peace process. In May reports in the Israeli press claimed that Algeria was engaged in discreet contacts with Israel as part of its campaign against Islamist militancy. In early 1997 Algeria denied reports that it was normalizing relations with Israel.

Despite a visit to Rome by Algerian Prime Minister Mokdad Sifi in June 1994, emphasizing the close links between Italy and Algeria, the Berlusconi administration appeared to be re-assessing its policy on Algeria. In July the Italian Minister of Foreign Affairs stated that the Algerian Government could not survive on foreign aid when it lacked legitimacy, and declared that the Italian Government was in favour of dialogue to broaden the base of the regime; however, he admitted that Islamist militants in Algeria and elsewhere in the Arab countries of the Mediterranean posed a direct threat to Italy. On a visit to Algeria in October, the Spanish Minister of Industry stated that the Spanish Government continued to offer political and economic support to the regime, but at the same time it encouraged dialogue with the Islamist opposition. The US, Italian and Spanish Governments all supported the Sant' Egidio meeting held in Rome in January 1995 which was attended by leading Algerian opposition parties, including the FIS. Relations with Italy became strained in January 1997 when an official of the Italian Ministry of Foreign Affairs proposed that the EU launch an initiative to stop the violence in Algeria and restore democracy. The proposal for a peace initiative was adopted by the Italian Prime Minister, Romano Prodi, in late 1997 and supported by France, but was strongly opposed by the Algerian authorities. Reports that members of the Algerian security services may have been responsible for the deaths of seven Italian seamen at an Algerian port in 1994 further strained relations between Italy and Algeria. The Italian Minister of Foreign Affairs, Prof. Lamberto Dini, declared that, if the allegations were substantiated, there would be reprisals against Algeria. Italy supported the EU mission to Algeria in January 1998.

In March 1996 Werner Hoyer, Germany's Secretary of State for Foreign Affairs, became the first senior German official to visit Algeria since 1989. The continued presence of FIS spokesman Rabah Kebir in Germany had strained relations between the two countries and reports in the Algerian press had even alleged that German security officials were favourable to the Islamists' cause and helped to support their networks. In April, however, the German authorities arrested a number of Algerians, including two sons of imprisoned FIS leader Abbasi Madani, and charged them with involvement in an organization smuggling arms and explosives from Germany to the GIA and AIS in Algeria. In June 1997 Madani's two sons were found guilty of the charges and sentenced to 28 and 32 months' imprisonment respectively. In October 1996 the German federal authorities failed in their second attempt to reverse a decision by a lower court granting Kebir refugee status. In late 1997 Dr Klaus Kinkel, Germany's Vice-Chancellor and Minister of Foreign Affairs, pledged his country's support for international action to resolve the conflict in Algeria. Kinkel was also a leading exponent of the EU's mission to Algeria in January 1998. On a visit to Algiers in May 1996 the Belgian Minister of Foreign Affairs expressed support for President Zéroual's political reforms and for Algeria's efforts to seek admission to the Euro-Mediterranean free-trade zone.

In December 1996 the EU agreed to begin talks on Algeria's admission to the Euro-Mediterranean free-trade zone. Discussions continued during early 1997 but were limited to establishing general principles. Both sides indicated that they hoped to enter into more detailed negotiations after the Algerian general election in June, which EU negotiators insisted had to be 'free and fair'. Officials from Algeria and the EU admitted that they expected the negotiations to be difficult, although Manuel Marín, the EU commissioner responsible for Mediterranean policy, indicated in April that he was hopeful that an agreement could be reached before the end of the year. In January 1998 the EU presidency expressed grave concern at the dramatic increase in violence in Algeria, and later that month sent an EU delegation of ministers from the United Kingdom, Luxembourg and Austria to Algiers. The Algerian authorities reluctantly agreed to receive the delegation, but continued to reject all forms of foreign intervention in the country's internal affairs. Despite growing unease in Europe at the escalating violence in Algeria, and concerns that the Algerian authorities might have been involved in the bloodshed, the EU appeared reluctant to antagonize the Algerian regime and risk jeopardizing member states' substantial economic interests in Algeria.

Economy

ALAN J. DAY

Revised for this edition by RICHARD I. LAWLESS

Algeria covers an area of 2,381,741 sq km (919,595 sq miles), of which a large part is desert. At the census of February 1977 the population (excluding Algerians abroad) was 16,948,000. At the census of April 1987 the population had reached 23,038,942, in addition to about 1m. Algerians living abroad (mainly in France). The overall population growth rate averaged 3.1% per annum during 1970–80 and 2.8% per annum in 1980–92. According to official estimates, the population grew by slightly less than 2% in 1996 to reach a total of 28.9m., the estimated populations of the main cities in 1996 being 3.1m. in the capital, Algiers (el-Djezaïr), 1.2m. in Oran (Ouahran), 1m. in Constantine (Qacentina) and 800,000 in Annaba. Official estimates indicated that the population totalled 29.3m. in January 1998 and that the annual rate of population growth had fallen to 1.7%. The proportion of the Algerian population living in urban areas increased from 40% in 1970 to 54% in 1992, the average urban growth rate having risen from 4.1% per annum during the 1970s to 4.9% per annum in 1980–92. Nearly 54% of Algerians were younger than 15 years of age in 1992. The average life expectancy at birth in 1992 was 67 years. The country is divided into 48 *wilayat* (departments) for administrative purposes.

Algeria has varied natural resources. In the coastal region are fertile plains and valleys, where profitable returns are made from cereals, wine, olives and fruit. The remainder of the country supports little agriculture, though in the mountains grazing and forestry produce a small income, and dates are cultivated in the oases of the Sahara. Mineral resources, in particular petroleum and natural gas, are abundant and dominate Algeria's export trade.

GOVERNMENT STRATEGY

After independence in 1962, Algerian governments sought to promote economic growth as a foundation for a future socialist society. They acquired either a complete or a controlling interest in most foreign-owned companies. In 1966 the Government nationalized foreign-owned mines, land which had been abandoned by Europeans at independence, and insurance companies. In 1971 it assumed control of the hydrocarbons sector. The hydrocarbons sector accounted for 32.0% of Algeria's gross domestic product (GDP) in 1996. In that year, according to estimates by the World Bank, Algeria's gross national product, measured at average 1994–96 prices, was US $43,726m., equivalent to $1,520 per head.

The Government's strategy for development traditionally involved a high degree of austerity, with heavy restrictions placed on the import of luxury and consumer goods. The first Four-Year Plan, covering the period 1970–73, emphasized the establishment of a capital-intensive sector, involving the hydrocarbons, iron and steel, chemical and engineering industries, and an annual growth rate of 9.7% was achieved. The second Plan, for 1974–77, aimed to establish a sound industrial base and also put emphasis on better agricultural methods, housing, health, job-creation and training. A high level of investment (40% of GDP) was maintained, and the Government aimed to achieve an average annual growth rate of 10%. Total expenditure, originally projected at AD 52,000m., was later increased to AD 110,000m., on the basis of increased income, owing to higher petroleum prices. The country's GDP grew by an average annual rate of 6%–6.5% in the 1970s, reaching AD 120,825m. in 1979.

During the 1980–84 planning period, total investment was estimated to have reached AD 345,000m. (nearly 14% below the Government's target figure), while GDP growth averaged 4.5% per year (compared with a planning target of 8.2% per year). Under a policy of gradual economic liberalization introduced during this planning period, light industries producing consumer goods were opened up to private investment, the private sector being responsible for an estimated AD 3,400m. of investment for the creation of 20,000 jobs (notably in the textile and leatherware industries). A new investment code was instituted in 1982 to stimulate private enterprise in areas such as retailing, hotels and catering, housing, handicrafts and light industry. Tax concessions were introduced to attract foreign partners into private-sector joint ventures. Within the state sector, efforts were made from 1981 to increase productivity and efficiency, notably by reorganizing 90 of Algeria's giant state corporations into 300 more specialized units, many with decentralized management away from Algiers.

The 1985–89 Development Plan, which required total investment of AD 550,000m., reflected the Government's new priorities for development, shifting investment away from industry and into agriculture and irrigation projects. Industry was to receive 32% of the total investment, compared with 38% in the previous Five-Year Plan. Agriculture and hydraulics were to receive 14% of investment, compared with 11% in 1980–84. About 30% of total investment spending in the Plan was allocated to social infrastructure, with projects for the development of housing, education, health and transport receiving particular emphasis. The targeting of these sectors reflected the need to satisfy the requirements of a rapidly expanding population, and to compensate for the imbalances of previous plans. More than one-half of the credits in the new Plan were to be allocated to the completion of existing projects.

The diversification of government revenue away from dependence on sales of crude petroleum to include refined products, natural gas and condensates—each contributing about one-quarter of total revenue by 1983—helped Algeria to adjust to the falls in OPEC-sponsored prices and quotas. During the 1985–89 Development Plan the Government aimed to increase non-hydrocarbon exports, particularly those of agricultural produce, other minerals and manufactured goods, which in 1984 accounted for only about 2% of total exports. In December 1985

a further slump in petroleum prices gave added urgency to the promotion of non-hydrocarbon exports. By 1988, however, revenue from the export of non-hydrocarbons had reached only AD 2,500m., just over 50% of the target figure. Meanwhile, the erosion of government income in 1986, as a result of the collapse in petroleum prices, had prevented the achievement of the investment targets of the 1985–89 Plan. Algeria entered this planning period with the highest foreign debt of any country in the Arab world (amounting to an estimated $18,500m. at the end of 1985), having financed many development projects through borrowings on the international capital markets since the 1970s. In 1986 Algeria borrowed from commercial banks to finance import spending; in 1987 it sought official export credit lines to finance imports; and in 1988/89 it had to raise major new medium- and long-term syndicated loans to finance current spending. Legislation enacted in December 1987 eased restrictions on commercial bank lending to private companies and opened the way for public-sector enterprises to adopt their own annual plans, to determine the prices of their products and to invest their profits freely. By mid-1989 three-quarters of Algeria's state-controlled enterprises, including banks, insurance companies and industrial, commercial and service organizations, had become autonomous *entreprises publiques économiques* (EPEs). Formal ownership of state shareholdings in EPEs was vested in eight state holding companies (*fonds de participation*), established in 1988 to take responsibility for different sectors (namely agriculture, fisheries and food; mining, hydrocarbons and hydraulics; equipment; construction; chemicals, petrochemicals and pharmaceuticals; electronics, telecommunications and computers; textiles, footwear and furnishings; and service industries). Regulations restricting access to convertible currency were modified in 1988 to attract investment in productive sectors and improve the export marketing capabilities of EPEs.

In June 1989 Algeria made its first ever use of IMF resources, securing a 12-month stand-by credit worth $187m. (to support the Government's economic programme) and a compensatory financing allocation of $378m. (to assist with trade financing). In 1990 the importation of goods for resale on the Algerian domestic market ceased to be a state monopoly. Foreign manufacturers and traders who established import businesses in Algeria were offered tax incentives to reinvest their profits in the country's production facilities. Under the old import rules there had been frequent supply shortages and widespread black-marketeering. Devaluation reduced the exchange rate of the dinar from around 8 dinars per US dollar at the end of 1990 to around 22 per dollar at the end of 1992. In June 1991 the IMF agreed to make $404m. of stand-by credit available in the period to March 1992, while the World Bank approved a $350m. structural adjustment loan to be disbursed in two instalments (the first of which was available immediately). In March 1992 a group of international banks, led by Crédit Lyonnais of France, agreed to refinance $1,457m. of Algeria's short-term commercial debt.

Prime Minister Sid-Ahmad Ghozali's announcement of a 'recovery programme' in February 1992 included details of recent economic statistics highlighting the seriousness of Algeria's current crisis. Reflecting the radical devaluation of the dinar, GDP had declined, in dollar terms, by 26.9% in 1991. GDP per head declined from $2,752 in 1987 to $1,607 in 1991. Production in 1991 was only 8% higher than in 1984 even though agricultural GDP and hydrocarbons output had risen substantially. Industrial production, in contrast, had fallen by 5.5% between 1987 and 1991. Consumer prices were increasing by about 28% a year. The debt-service ratio had risen from 35% in 1985 to 72.7% in 1991. Unemployment stood at 21% in 1991. Ghozali's recovery programme gave priority to key sectors of the economy, such as agriculture, public works and construction, which were targeted in a carefully structured import programme. Priority was also to be given to purchases of pharmaceuticals, essential consumer goods, food and spare parts. Ambitious plans were announced to develop small and medium-sized companies and to restructure public companies. While the programme envisaged a strong public sector at the centre of the economy, Ghozali favoured the private management of tourism, agriculture and trade. Financing the programme depended on the availability of international credit and success in attracting international petroleum companies to invest in the hydrocarbons sector.

In July 1992, addressing the nation for the first time since becoming Prime Minister, Belaid Abd es-Salam declared that Algeria had deviated from the principles of the revolution over the previous decade, and expressed strong reservations about Ghozali's economic reforms. He warned that a period of austerity lay ahead, stating that he intended to reduce imports to the bare minimum and close some factories, if necessary, in order to service the $25,000m.-foreign debt. He rejected debt rescheduling, devaluation and further trade liberalization. In September the Government imposed controls on imports, indicating that preference would be given in foreign exchange allocations to basic foods, spare parts and construction materials. In November the Government suspended indefinitely imports of luxury goods in order to conserve foreign exchange. Hydrocarbon earnings had fallen from AD 68,412m. ($3,096m.) in the second quarter of 1992 to AD 58,457m. ($2,645m.) in the third quarter, as a result of lower petroleum prices and changes in dollar exchange rates.

In August 1993 the decision of the High Council of State (HCS) to dismiss Abd es-Salam and to appoint Redha Malek resulted in a further change of economic policy. Mourad Benachenhou, formerly the Algerian representative at the World Bank and an advocate of debt rescheduling, was appointed Minister of the Economy in the new Government. It became clear that important decisions on economic policy would only be taken when the HCS, the Government and a majority of the conflicting pressure groups could agree on a suitable strategy. One of the new Government's first acts was to introduce an investment code whose implementation had been postponed during the Abd es-Salam premiership. The new code, intended to stimulate foreign and domestic private investment in areas outside the mining and hydrocarbons sectors (which were covered by separate legislation introduced in December 1991), provided protection for investors and offered them a range of tax and duty reductions for certain categories of investment. A new national investment agency, APSI (Agence de Promotion et de Suivi des Investissements), was established in November 1993 to accelerate investment applications.

In December 1993 talks recommenced with the IMF concerning a loan to be linked to an economic stabilization programme, and government statements indicated a return to a more liberal economic policy. Officials stated that there were plans to ease import controls and to dissolve the committee established under the previous Government to allocate hard currency. Negotiations with the IMF ended without agreement but resumed in January 1994. The economic situation was exacerbated by the depressed price of petroleum on world markets. In January 1994 Algeria ceased repayment of most of its medium- to long-term debt insured by European export credit agencies, including payments to its largest creditors. Talks on a stand-by loan from the IMF continued and, although the Government was still advocating bilateral rescheduling, most creditors were convinced that a 'Paris Club' of creditor governments rescheduling had become inevitable.

In March 1994 Algeria further reduced its forecast of export revenues for the current year, and in April the Government formally requested the 'Paris Club' to consider the rescheduling of up to $13,500m. of Algerian debt. In the same month the IMF approved a stand-by package for Algeria and requested donor agencies to provide substantial new loans over the next year. Over the next 12 months the IMF was to provide a $500m.-stand-by loan and a $300m.-compensatory and contingency financing facility. The IMF agreement committed Algeria to a number of reforms, including a 40% devaluation and a sharp increase in interest rates, which had already been implemented at the beginning of April.

In June 1994 the 'Paris Club' creditor governments agreed to refinance a total of about $5,400m. of sovereign debt incurred by Algeria up to September 1993, repayments to be rescheduled over a period of 15 years following a four-year grace period. (The Algerian Government had requested an eight-year grace period.) Finalization of the rescheduling arrangements was completed in March 1995. In July 1994 Saudi Arabia (not a 'Paris Club' member) rescheduled $500m. of official debt on similar terms. In October the Banque d'Algérie began talks with

the 'London Club' of banks to reschedule $3,200m. of long-term commercial debt (contracted by Algerian state-owned banks and by the state energy company SONATRACH). An agreement was reached in principle in May 1995 and finalized in July 1996 whereby repayments were rescheduled to start between September 1998 and September 2000.

In April 1994 Mourad Benachenhou became Minister of Industrial Restructuring and Participation with responsibility for managing the reform of the public sector as required by the new IMF programme. Later in the year the IMF indicated its approval of current government initiatives to contain the budget deficit and acknowledged that the overall performance of the economy in 1994 had to be seen against a background of escalating violence and political uncertainty which continued to discourage investment. Algeria's GDP declined by 1.8% in real terms in 1994 (the ninth consecutive year of negative growth), compared with a planning target of 3% positive growth. In January 1995 the World Bank approved a $150m. economic rehabilitation support loan to provide urgent assistance for current reform policies, including, in particular, privatization initiatives and the restructuring of public enterprises.

In February 1995 the IMF commenced talks with Algeria to agree a follow-up to the stand-by arrangement which was due to expire at the end of March. In May the IMF approved a $1,800m. three-year extended Fund facility for Algeria. The Government undertook to continue to pursue a wide-ranging programme of structural reforms, including privatization, rationalization of the public sector, trade liberalization, monetary and fiscal reforms to reduce inflation and encourage investment and private enterprise, and the elimination by the end of 1996 of subsidies on food and other commodities.

In advance of the IMF agreement, the Government had submitted a draft privatization law to public and private organizations for consultation purposes, and in January 1995 invited bids for five state-owned hotels as a pilot project for the privatization programme. Private capital participation had been permitted in public-sector companies since 1994 but no ownership transfer had actually taken place. A comprehensive privatization law was enacted in August 1995. Legislation was introduced later in the year to allow local councils to employ private contractors to manage water resources and related services.

Under a balance-of-payments support contract signed in May 1995, the European Union (EU) agreed to lend Algeria $268m. on conditions similar to those of the IMF. In July the 'Paris Club' creditor governments agreed to a refinancing of debts worth over $7,000m. Payments due between June 1995 and May 1997 were rescheduled over 15 years starting in 1999. Unlike the June 1994 'Paris Club' agreement, which dealt only with repayments of principal, the July 1995 agreement included some rescheduling of interest payments. Finalization of the rescheduling arrangements under this agreement was completed in July 1996. In April 1996 the World Bank approved a further loan of $300m. to support the Government's structural adjustment programme, together with a loan of $50m. in support of job-creation and other social welfare measures to offset some of the negative social effects of the adjustment programme. Higher agricultural output and stronger international petroleum prices contributed to a 3.8% increase in real GDP in 1995 (the first year of real growth since 1985).

To expedite the restructuring of public-sector enterprises, the system of ownership through *fonds de participation*, dating from 1988 (see above) was replaced in October 1996 by a new ownership structure. The former holding companies, which had been conceived as permanent fiduciary institutions, were replaced by 11 holding companies authorized not merely to hold shares in state enterprises but also to offer shares for sale and to take action to close 'non-performing' enterprises. Once they had fulfilled their roles as vehicles for the transfer of state assets to the private sector and into independent public companies, the holding companies would disappear.

The World Bank stated in February 1997 that a total of 138 public-sector 'industrial units' had so far been disposed of, although of these 87 were liquidated rather than sold as going concerns and 13 of the remainder were construction companies rather than industrial enterprises. The World Bank noted that a further 134 public-sector companies had been offered for sale, and that the Government's privatization programme was currently running somewhat ahead of the agreed schedule. The 134 companies in the most recent round of privatization offers included 60 industrial units (many of them individual plants owned by larger public enterprises) as well a commercial, agricultural and tourism companies. Some were offered for outright or partial sale, while others were tendered to the private sector on a management contract basis. The next round of privatizations was to focus on a list of 1,300 small and medium-sized companies.

In December 1996 the Government published a series of amendments to the August 1995 privatization law, designed to stimulate private-sector interest in the purchase of fully operational companies. Eligibility for privatization (hitherto limited to EPEs) was to be extended to enterprises controlled by Algerian local government bodies; purchasers were no longer to be required to take on a legal duty to maintain pre-privatization staffing levels (although financial incentives would be available to buyers who gave voluntary undertakings); mechanisms were to be introduced to facilitate sales of shares to retail investors as well as to corporate buyers, and to open up the possibility of direct share sales to companies' staff members; and the administration of the privatization process (including the pricing of share offers) was to become more flexible.

There was a fall in the end-year inflation rate to 15% in 1996, compared with 22% in 1995 and 39% in 1994, reflecting the economy's adjustment to more stable conditions after the large 1994 currency devaluation and the subsequent withdrawal of price subsidies. The dinar's end-year exchange rate against the US dollar (AD 24.10 in 1993, AD 42.90 in 1994 and AD 52.20 in 1995) underwent a relatively small decline to AD 56.20 in 1996. The freeing of prices had by early 1997 produced what the World Bank described as 'one of the most liberal trade regimes in the region'. Increases in both the volume and unit value of hydrocarbon exports, coupled with a record cereals harvest, gave Algeria a significant trade surplus and a positive current-account balance in 1996 and underpinned the achievement of 4% real GDP growth in that year. Most hydrocarbon exploration and production operations were relatively remote from centres of terrorist activity, which was not regarded as a major risk factor by petroleum companies operating in Algeria. Following the rescheduling agreements with foreign creditors, debt servicing as a proportion of export earnings (which had reached 76.3% in 1993, 47.0% in 1994 and 33.5% in 1995) fell to a more manageable level of 27.7% in 1996, when the country's total external indebtedness amounted to $33,260m. (of which $30,808m. was long-term public debt). Foreign-exchange reserves doubled during 1996 and were sufficient to cover six months' imports in the first quarter of 1997. A greatly reduced budget deficit was achieved in 1996, and the 1997 budget estimates (see Finance section below) were said by the Government to include an 'underlying surplus'.

Against these and other positive macroeconomic achievements had to be set the fact that the output of non-hydrocarbon industries fell by 8% in 1996, contributing to a rise in Algeria's official unemployment rate to 28.3% of the work-force. Over 56% of the unemployed were aged under 24 years and about 80% were aged under 30 years. The removal of price subsidies had caused hardship for the poorest sections of society, who were also those worst affected by acute housing shortages in Algiers and other urban centres. Given the continuing volatility of the internal security situation, the Government was fully aware in 1997 that many entrenched structural problems remained to be solved before Algeria could claim to have made a genuinely successful transition to a free-market economy. A government advisory body, the National Economic and Social Council, reported in early 1998 that GDP grew by only 1.2% in 1997, well below the official target of 5%, as a result of a 24% decline in agricultural production and a 7.2% fall in industrial output. Non-hydrocarbon exports fell by 50% in that year. The report presented a pessimistic outlook for the economy and warned that living standards were continuing to decline.

Following an agreement with the powerful Union Générale des Travailleurs Algériens (UGTA) in March 1998, it was reported that the Government had pledged to stop the closure of public-sector companies and promised to re-examine the position of some enterprises that had already been closed. The agreement was reached after a two-day strike, organized by the UGTA to protest against the high level of redundancies, resulting from the closure of many loss-making public-sector companies, and delays in the payment of salaries. In May Abdelkrim Harchaoui, the Minister of Finance, stated that Algeria would not seek to extend the IMF credit facility when it expired later that month, because the economy could be supported by private investment. He insisted, however, that the Government would continue to maintain fiscal discipline even though its economic policies would no longer be under the formal scrutiny of the IMF. Some financial analysts argued that, even though there had been an improvement in Algeria's macroeconomic situation, the Government would experience problems in raising finance cheaply from international capital markets. In mid-May Prime Minister Ahmed Ouyahia signed a decree listing the first 89 companies to be privatized from late June, affecting enterprises in the tourism, construction, services, agribusiness and transport sectors. The Government hoped to raise some $1,000m. from the sales, and further privatizations were anticipated. Since the 1995 privatization law, the Government's National Privatization Council had so far been unable to complete a successful sale; the new decree aimed to give impetus to the privatization programme. There had been an increase in private-sector investment, but mainly in the form of joint ventures between international manufacturing companies and public-sector enterprises, and new companies established by local investors.

AGRICULTURE

The agricultural sector employed 23.8% of Algeria's labour force in mid-1996, and accounted for 11.9% of GDP in that year. More than 90% of the land consists of arid plateaux, mountains or desert, supporting herds of sheep, goats or camels. Only the northern coastal strip, 100 km–200 km wide, is suitable for arable farming. There are about 7.6m. ha of cultivable land, representing less than one ha per rural inhabitant. Forests cover about 4.4m. ha. Most of the Sahara is devoted to semi-desert pasturage. The most valuable crop is the grape harvest, and wheat, barley and oats, grown for local consumption, cover a large area. Other crops include maize, sorghum, millet, rye, rice, citrus fruit, olives, figs, dates and tobacco.

Scarcity of food is an acute problem in Algeria. In 1969 the country was 73% self-sufficient in food. However, by 1986 it was importing 75% of its food requirements, and by 1990 produced only 25% of its domestic cereal requirements. In 1991 food and live animals comprised about 24% of total imports. The recovery programme announced by the Government in February 1992 drew attention to a dangerous level of dependence on strategic products such as cereals, animal feed and milk and stated that efforts to raise agricultural production were central to economic policy. Spending on imported foodstuffs amounted to $2,753m. (25.6% of total imports) in 1995 and $2,561m. (28.7% of total imports) in 1996.

AGRICULTURAL REFORM

By October 1963 state-owned farm land accounted for 2.7m. ha, roughly one-half of the cultivable land in Algeria. In May 1966 all remaining unoccupied property which had been evacuated by settlers was finally expropriated by the state; the land was turned into state farms run by workers' committees.

In mid-1971 President Boumedienne announced an agrarian reform programme which provided for the break-up of large, state-owned farms and their redistribution to families of landless peasants, or *fellahin*, who would be organized in co-operatives. The 1972 census showed that one-quarter of cultivable land was in the hands of 16,500 large landowners who represented only 3% of the total number of farmers. In 1973 the reform programme entered its second phase, that of redistributing over 650,000 ha of private land to 60,000 *fellahin*. Those receiving land were to be granted permanent use of it, on condition that they belonged to one of the new co-operatives. Through these they were to be given state loans and assistance in the form of seed, fertilizers and equipment. By early 1979, 22,000 absentee landowners had been obliged either to cultivate their land or to cede it to peasant farmers, and more than 6,000 agricultural co-operatives of various kinds had been established.

Following Boumedienne's death, there was a gradual change of priorities and the private sector was given new freedom to produce and market agricultural goods. The Chadli Government encouraged private, small-scale farmers by supplying equipment, loans and assistance. At the same time, investment in the agricultural infrastructure, particularly the construction of dams, was increased in an attempt to reduce the need for food imports. Moreover, to discourage rural drift (particularly among young people), farmers' earnings were more closely related to those of their industrial counterparts.

A new Banque de l'Agriculture et du Développement Rural (BADR) was established in 1982, expressly to serve the rural sector, whether socialist, state-owned or private. One of the BADR's first projects was a lending programme which aimed to make Algeria self-sufficient in eggs and poultry. In the same year, the Government relaxed price controls, allowing farmers to sell directly to markets or to private vendors and across *wilaya* boundaries. After 1983, farmers who brought desert land under cultivation automatically received a title to own the land. In 1987, in an attempt to increase efficiency and improve motivation, the Government introduced major reforms, whereby the *fellahin* were allowed to form autonomous collectives, comprising at least three members, and to lease land units, formed from the subdivision of the existing 3,347 co-operatives. The *fellahin* were to be allowed to transfer or trade their leases after five years, to control their own operations, to work directly with banks and to make a profit. The state, as owner of the land, was to restrict its role to the provision of aid and to mediation in disputes over land division. By October the reforms were being implemented in 41 *wilayat*, and by the end of the following year 3,000 state farms were controlled by private entrepreneurs. Meanwhile, subsidies on staple foods were drastically reduced. In January 1989 the Banque Nationale de Paris agreed to channel an agroindustrial loan of nearly $750m. for 1989 through the BADR. In 1990 the Government announced plans to encourage agricultural producers to form a new type of co-operative which would market goods directly, thereby promoting price competition between the co-operatives. A public fund to protect farmers against climatic and other disasters became operational in May. The fund guaranteed loans and other credits to small farmers affected by natural disasters. In the same month the Government released $107m. to support farmers affected by drought. State subsidies for agriculture totalled $1,000m. in 1990. In December 1994 the Government announced the creation of a lending agency, the Crédit Mutuel Agricole, to provide private-sector farmers with financial assistance, and measures to reschedule their outstanding debts. A land reform bill was presented to the National People's Assembly in January 1998 to allow the privatization of state-owned farms. Land reform was one of the measures insisted upon by the World Bank under its structural adjustment loan agreement with the Algerian Government. By clarifying land rights, the Government hoped to encourage greater investment in agriculture and create new jobs. Some 1.5m. ha of state-owned agricultural land was scheduled to be distributed to farmers during the following three years.

CROPS

Wines have been one of Algeria's principal agricultural exports since the time of the French. However, Algeria's annual output of wine declined from 8m. hl in the early 1970s to around 3m. hl by the end of the decade. The Government planned to maintain production at the latter level for the rest of the century, while developing the production of better-quality wines, which are more easily marketable in the EU. In the early 1980s annual production fell to less than 2m. hl, before recovering to 2.2m. hl in 1985. In 1989 Algeria produced only about 1m. hl of wine.

Production of cereals, grown principally in the Constantine, Annaba, Sétif and Tiaret areas, fluctuates considerably, largely as a result of drought, and grains have to be imported, particularly from Canada, France and the USA. Wheat and barley are the most important cereals. Yields are very low, at 26 cwt–32 cwt of wheat per ha, compared with average US yields of 70 cwt. Drought ravaged the 1993 harvest: total production of cereals was estimated to have been reduced to some 2m. metric tons from 3.2m. tons in 1992. In 1995 the harvest was badly affected by drought, producing only 2.1m. tons of cereals; however, in 1996 the cereals harvest totalled 4.6m. tons, including 2.8m. tons of wheat and 1.8m. tons of barley and oats. After a

serious drought, the Government announced that the 1997 cereals harvest would not exceed 1.1m. tons. Officials reported that 2.3m. ha of farmland (out of a total of 3.5m. ha) had been designated as drought-affected.

Olives are grown mainly in the western coastal belt and in the Kabyle. Production fluctuates because of the two-year flowering cycle of the olive. Production of olives totalled 313,000 tons in 1996. The citrus crop, grown in the coastal districts, totals 350,000–390,000 tons per year. Production of potatoes reached 1.5m. tons in 1996. About 250,000 tons of dried onions are produced annually. Algeria is the world's fifth largest producer of dates, the crop averaging 260,000 tons per year, some 80% of which are consumed locally. About 4,000 tons of tobacco are produced each year.

Overall agricultural output increased by 15% in volume in 1995 and by 12.0% in 1996. Agriculture provided 10.6% and 11.9% of GDP in 1995 and 1996, respectively. The average cereals yield in 1996 was 1.26 tons per ha, compared with 1.16 tons per ha in 1991.

LIVESTOCK, FORESTRY AND FISHING

Sheep, goats and cattle are raised, but great improvements are needed in stock-raising methods, grassland, control of disease and water supply if the increasing demand for meat is to be satisfied. The cost of raising milk production is prohibitive, and a high level of imports is likely to continue. By 1990 60% of milk requirements were imported. However, there has been a notable success in increasing production of white meat, in which the country was self-sufficient by 1984. About 1m. eggs, or one-half of total consumption, are imported annually. In September 1996 there were 1.2m. head of cattle, 17.6m. sheep and 2.9m. goats. Private farmers produce 90% of local meat.

The area covered by forests declined rapidly during 1970–90 in spite of the Government's plans to reafforest 364,000 ha in the 1985–89 Plan period. In 1975 work began to grow a 'green wall' of pines and cypresses 20 km wide, planted along 1,500 km on the northern edge of the Sahara from the Moroccan to the Tunisian frontier in order to arrest steady northward desertification. The project, which encountered numerous problems, also involved the construction of roads, reservoirs and plantations of fruit trees and vegetables.

The Government believes that Algeria is not exploiting its fishing potential and has attempted to increase the annual catch. The total catch in 1995 was 106,246 tons. In late 1994 it was announced that construction of a new fishing port at el-Kala would begin in 1995, with capacity for 29 trawlers, 34 sardine boats and at least 25 small fishing boats. The $10.5m. project is to include a 900-metre quay and ship repair facilities.

METALLIC MINERALS

Algeria has rich deposits of iron ore, phosphates, lead, zinc and antimony. Mining is controlled by the state enterprises that were created in 1983 by the restructuring of the former monopoly, SONAREM. A mining law, passed by the National People's Assembly in December 1991, allowed local private sector and foreign investment in the mining sector, which had been nationalized in 1966. The aim was to increase exploration and reverse declining production. Under the terms of the law, foreign companies could form joint ventures and benefit from tax concessions. The Office de Recherche Géologique et Minière was created to co-ordinate the various enterprises, state and private, involved in this sector. In September 1993 the Government authorized the allocation of mineral research permits to local companies and included for the first time enterprises from outside the mining sector.

Iron ore is mined at Beni-Saf, Zaccar, Timezrit and near the eastern frontier at Ouenza and Bou Khadra. The average grade of ore is 50%–60%. Production has fluctuated greatly since independence, reaching 2.1m. metric tons (metal content) in 1974, falling to 897,000 tons in 1981, and totalling 1.0m. tons in 1995. The deposits at Ouenza represent 75% of total production. Important deposits were found in 1975 at Djebel Bouari in Batna *wilaya*. Italy is the biggest customer, followed by the United Kingdom. Production of bituminous coal, mined at Colomb Béhar-Kenadza and Ksiksou, declined steadily from 153,000 tons in 1958 to about 5,000 tons in 1978. Production was estimated at 22,000 tons in 1995.

The main deposits of lead and zinc ores are at el-Abed, on the Algerian-Moroccan frontier, and at the Kherzet Youcef mine, in the Sétif region. Total zinc output (metal content) declined from 12,200 tons in 1988 to 3,000 tons in 1995, and deposits could be exhausted by the late 1990s. Production of lead in 1995 totalled 700 tons.

Exploitation of large phosphate deposits at Djebel-Onk, 340 km from Annaba, began in 1960. Total phosphate rock output was 757,000 tons in 1995. About one-half of phosphates produced is exported, mainly to France and Spain. Exports of phosphates earned AD 240m. ($27m.) in 1990.

Other mineral resources include tungsten, manganese, mercury, copper and salt. In January 1996 it was reported that mercury production was declining due to technical problems. The Entreprise Nationale des Métaux Non-Ferreux exported only 2,500 flasks in 1995 (compared with a capacity of 25,000 flasks a year). Production of marble at Bendjerah in Guelma amounted to 3,500 cu m in 1990. According to studies carried out by the state-owned Entreprise d'Exploitation des Mines d'Or (ENOR), gold deposits at Tirek and Amessmessa in the Haggar region are capable of producing yields of 25.1 grams per ton. Having failed to secure investment from outside Algeria, ENOR was in 1996 joined by SONATRACH, Société Algérienne d'Assurance and the Banque d'Algérie in a joint venture to develop the Tirek gold deposits.

ENERGY RESOURCES

Production of crude petroleum in the Algerian Sahara began, on a commercial scale, in 1958. The principal producing areas were at Hassi Messaoud, in central Algeria, and round Edjeleh-Zarzaitine in the Polignac Basin, near the Libyan frontier. Algeria's production of crude petroleum increased from 1.2m. metric tons in 1959 to 26m. tons per year in 1964 and 1965, with output limited by the capacity of the two pipelines to the coast, one from the eastern fields through Tunisia to La Skhirra, and the other from Hassi Messaoud to Béjaia on the Algerian coast. The Government established a state-controlled company, the Société Nationale pour la Recherche, la Production, le Transport, la Transformation et la Commercialisation des Hydrocarbures (SONATRACH), to be responsible for the construction of a third pipeline from Hassi Messaoud to Arzew on the coast. This pipeline came into operation in early 1966. In that year Algeria's production of crude petroleum was increased by substantial quantities from oilfields at Gassi Touil, Rhourde el-Baguel and Rhourde Nouss. Subsequent discoveries of petroleum were made at Nezla, Hoaud Berkaoui, Ouargla, Mesdar, el-Borma, Hassi Keskessa, Guellala, Tin Fouyé and el-Maharis. There were about 50 oilfields in operation in early 1989. Export pipelines link the oilfields to Algiers, to supply the refinery at el-Harrach, and to Skikda. Increased production of condensates and liquefied petroleum gas (LPG) prompted the construction of special pipelines to Arzew.

Output of crude petroleum peaked at around 1.2m. barrels per day (b/d) in 1979, representing over 92% of total Algerian oil production in that year. Thereafter output of crude petroleum was restricted in order to prolong the life of the oilfields and, after 1983, to conform to the production quotas set by OPEC. Production of other hydrocarbons, particularly gas, liquefied natural gas (LNG), natural gas liquids (NGL, a category which includes condensates) and refined products, assumed greater importance as a source of government revenues. By 1986 production of crude petroleum had decreased to an average of 670,000 b/d, mainly from the Hassi Messaoud oilfield, representing 56% of Algeria's total oil production in that year. By the mid-1990s, as new oilfields came into production, output began to rise. Crude output capacity was expected to increase from just under 1m. b/d in 1997 to 1.2m.–1.3m. b/d in 1998, according to official forecasts. In April 1998 Youcef Yousfi, the Minister of Energy and Mines, appealed for further cuts in global oil production, to restore prices, and announced that Algeria had reduced its average production of 890,000 b/d by 50,000 b/d from 1 April as part of OPEC's latest agreement. Algeria produces a light crude, with a low sulphur content, which is attractive to foreign refiners. Algeria's proven and recoverable petroleum reserves at the beginning of 1998 totalled 1,700m. tons, equivalent to 40 years' output at 750,000 b/d, Algeria's former annual OPEC quota. Algeria's OPEC quota was increased to 908,000 b/d from

January 1998. About 72% of Algeria's exports of crude petroleum go to Western Europe, and another 17% to North America.

Algeria had a total refining capacity of 464,000 b/d in January 1988, and by February 1989 capacity had risen to more than 470,000 b/d. The Government has complete control of the Algiers refinery (capacity 58,000 b/d) and of the domestic distribution network. The expansion of a small refinery at Hassi Messaoud was completed in 1979, and it has a capacity of about 23,000 b/d. There are other refineries at Arzew (built by a Japanese consortium and completed in June 1973; capacity 60,000 b/d) and Skikda (built by Snamprogetti of Italy and completed in March 1980; capacity 323,000 b/d). In 1996 Algerian refineries had an output capacity of around 590,000 b/d (22.5m. tons per year) of refined products. Algeria's domestic fuel prices were very low by international standards until March 1994, when the Government doubled the retail price of diesel fuel and petrol. In April 1995 the price of petrol for car-users was increased by 8%–11% as part of the Government's efforts to raise more revenue and control energy consumption.

In early 1989 the Government announced its intention to increase the efficiency of the energy sector through new exploration and the introduction of a market-related price structure; also, exports of value-added products, such as condensate and LPG, were to be increased at the expense of those of crude oil. In May 1991 Total of France and SONATRACH signed an agreement to develop condensate and LPG reserves in the Hamra field, 250 km from Hassi Messaoud.

In 1991 the Government established an organization to monitor energy strategy and projects. Its duties were to include approving oil-exploration concessions. Its members initially comprised the Minister for Industry and Mines, the Ministers of Commerce and Economic Affairs, the heads of SONATRACH and SONELGAZ and the Governor of the Central Bank.

At the end of 1997 Algeria's published proved reserves of natural gas—mostly unassociated with oilfields—totalled 3,700,000m. cu m, equivalent to 55 years' output at current rates. Most of the gas is in the Hassi R'Mel region, 400 km south of Algiers. The field was discovered in 1956, and is still considered to be one of the largest in the world. Unassociated gas is also found near In Amenas, Alrar, Gassi Touil, Rhourde Nouss, Tin Fouyé and In Salah. The Government has invested heavily in the development of these gas fields. Pipelines have been laid to the coast, to supply local gas distribution systems, and LNG has been exported since 1965. The export of dry natural gas to Italy began in 1983 following the inauguration of the Transmed pipeline (running from Algeria to Sicily via Tunisia and the Mediterranean). In 1996 Algeria's marketed production of natural gas (excluding gas flared or recycled) totalled 65,900m. cu m.

Before 1962 Algeria exported relatively small amounts of LNG from the Camel liquefaction plant at Arzew. The second phase of Algeria's gas development began in the early 1970s with the negotiation of major new export contracts with companies including the USA's Distrigas, Trunkline and El Paso, Belgium's Distrigaz, Enagas of Spain, and Italy's SNAM (a subsidiary of the Italian state energy group, Ente Nazionale Idrocarburi—ENI). Exports of LNG to the United Kingdom continued, and new contracts were signed with Gaz de France. The price of the gas to be delivered under the contracts was calculated according to the value of equivalent amounts of refined petroleum products (on a calorific basis). In 1978 there was a shift to a more aggressive pricing policy. The Government argued that the old pricing terms did not fully compensate Algeria for the massive investments in LNG facilities and transportation that it had made. The central feature of the change in Algerian gas policy was the demand that natural gas prices be linked to the then rapidly rising price of crude petroleum. The change in policy was strongly opposed by Algeria's customers, but the Government was able to persuade several clients to accept the terms, using various economic and political sanctions.

SONATRACH nevertheless lost several customers—El Paso in the USA, British Methane (after 1981) and Trunkline, which suspended purchases at the end of 1983. Other countries, such as the Federal Republic of Germany and Austria, considered buying Algerian gas, but then obtained cheaper supplies from the USSR and Norway. SONATRACH therefore became more flexible on the link between crude oil and gas prices in order to win new customers, while insisting on the existing index with current buyers. In April 1987 the US Panhandle Eastern Corpn, the parent company of Trunkline, agreed to resume shipments of Algerian LNG in late 1988. The price of deliveries was to be based on a flexible formula which would preserve SONATRACH's interests, while taking account of developments in the international market. In late 1987 Distrigas of Boston, USA, resumed shipments at the spot market price, after reaching a short-term agreement with SONATRACH in November. Distrigas had gone into liquidation under the US federal bankruptcy code in 1985, when its previous long-term contract with SONATRACH had proved to be too expensive. In February 1988 SONATRACH and Distrigas signed a 15-year contract, for the supply of LNG, whereby gas would be sold at 'market-responsive' prices. According to the terms of the contract, Distrigas was to pay for shipping and regasification, after which the gas would be sold at market prices and the profits divided on a ratio of 63:37 basis in SONATRACH's favour. In early 1988 SONATRACH reached similar long-term agreements with DEP of Greece and Botas of Turkey. Meanwhile, the signing of an agreement with Ruhrgas of the Federal Republic of Germany over purchases of LNG, discussed in late 1987, was delayed until January 1989. In 1991 a gas export agreement with ENI of Italy envisaged an increase of nearly 60% in the volume of SNAM's gas purchases from Algeria over the next 25 years.

In October 1992 Ente Nazionale per l'Energia Elettrica of Italy signed a 20-year supply contract with SONATRACH, starting in the last quarter of 1994, to lift 4,000m. cu m of gas annually through the enlarged Transmed pipeline and 1,000m. cu m–2,000m. cu m of LNG. The agreement helped to diversify gas exports and to strengthen Algeria's position in the Italian market. In January 1992 it was reported that Gaz de France had signed a series of new agreements with SONATRACH to extend its three gas supply contracts for another 10–15 years and that a new 10-year accord had been agreed. France is the major importer of Algerian LNG and, following the new agreement, annual imports could rise to more than 10,000m. cu m. In June 1992 SONATRACH signed a contract with Enagas of Spain to supply 6,000m. cu m of natural gas per year over 25 years via a new Maghreb-Europe pipeline (see below). In April 1994 the Portuguese consortium Transgas signed a 25-year contract with SONATRACH to take 2,500m. cu m of natural gas a year via the same pipeline. Under the terms of a co-operation agreement signed with SONATRACH in October 1994, ENI made a commitment to purchase 26,000m. cu m of natural gas a year by 1997, almost double the current amount. In late 1995 SONATRACH announced that it had signed an agreement to supply an extra 1,000m. cu m of LNG to Botas of Turkey in addition to the 2,000m. cu m already supplied. In May 1996 it was reported that Algeria's gas exports to the EU increased by 24% in 1995 to 1.6m. tons of oil equivalent, representing one-quarter of all EU gas imports. Algeria supplied one-half of Italy's natural gas imports in 1995.

In early 1990 contracts were signed for the renovation of gas liquefaction facilities at Skikda and Arzew which were constructed in the 1970s. In January 1992 it was reported that the GL1·K plant at Skikda was operating at about 55% of its annual capacity of 8,500m. cu m. The three plants at Arzew, GL1-Ž, GL2-Z and GL4-Z, with capacities of 10,580m. cu m, 10,700m. cu m and 1,400m. cu m, were operating at 60%, 85% and 90% of their respective capacities. In January 1996 SONATRACH announced that the renovation of the LNG units at Arzew and Skikda would raise total capacity to 30,000m. cu m per year and would generate additional revenue of up to $5,000m. The renovation programme, which was scheduled for completion in mid-1998, was expected to prolong the units' life by some 20 years. A major expansion of LPG production capacity was planned by SONATRACH for the late 1990s with the aim of raising LPG output from around 4.8m. tons in 1996 to 9.6m. tons in 2000.

The annual capacity of the Transmed gas pipeline between Algeria and Italy was due to increase from 16,000m. cu m to 24,000m. cu m during 1997 on completion of expansion work. Transport of gas through the pipeline was halted for four days in November 1997 after a fire was reported in one of the sections. SONATRACH denied reports that the incident was an act of sabotage by Islamist guerrillas. In November 1996 a new

Maghreb–Europe gas pipeline, running 1,365 km from Algeria to Spain via Morocco and the Mediterranean, carried its first supplies of Algerian dry gas to Spain. Portugal was linked to the pipeline in early 1997. Initially operating at a capacity of 7,000 cu m per year, the Maghreb–Europe line was expected to transport about 10,000m. cu m by 2000. In order to bring Algeria's expanded export pipeline capacity into full use there was a requirement to increase supplies from the Hassi R'Mel gasfield by building an additional 970-km 48-in trunkline within Algeria. In late 1997 the European Investment Bank (EIB) announced a $300m. loan for SONATRACH towards the $1,000m. project, known as the GR2 pipeline.

In 1970 the Algerian oil interests of Shell, Phillips, Elwerath and AMIF were nationalized, after protracted negotiations had failed to achieve agreement on tax reference prices, and SONATRACH thus became Algeria's largest producer. In 1971 Algeria nationalized French petroleum companies operating in the country, as well as pipeline networks and natural gas deposits. Later in the year President Boumedienne issued a decree banning concession-type agreements and laying down the conditions under which foreign oil companies could operate in Algeria. As a result, SONATRACH gained control of virtually all of Algeria's petroleum production, compared with only 31% in 1970. After 1979 SONATRACH attempted to bring foreign oil companies back to Algeria to explore, owing to its declining petroleum reserves. Some companies, such as Italy's Agip and France's Total, made small discoveries. In 1986 the Government passed a new oil exploration law, which offered better terms for foreign exploration companies, with the aim of encouraging those that had made discoveries to develop their finds. In addition, some new companies, including US oil firms, expressed an interest in acquiring rights to operate in Algerian concessions. In December 1987 Agip became the first foreign company to sign an exploration and production agreement with SONATRACH after the 1986 law. A further agreement was signed by the Spanish company Cepsa in January 1988, and a contract with the Australian group BHP Petroleum was concluded in December 1988. An agreement with the US company Anadarko Petroleum Corpn was signed in June 1989.

In December 1991 a new hydrocarbons law was promulgated, with the aim of encouraging greater participation by foreign companies in Algeria's oil and gas industry. It marked the most radical change in energy policy since the nationalizations in 1971. The legislation sought to stimulate exploration, but the most notable feature was that it allowed foreign companies to participate in existing oil fields in order to improve recovery rates and thus increase production. The Government hoped to encourage the participation of the major oil companies which were expected to pay substantial front-end bonuses in return for a share of the output. Equally significant was the fact that foreign companies would be allowed a stake in gas reserves discovered under exploration and production-sharing agreements, though not in existing fields. Previously gas had been a national monopoly and foreign companies had been excluded from benefiting from the discovery of gas in their oil acreage. New investment from the participation of foreign companies was regarded as essential to reverse falling output.

In July 1994 it was announced that negotiations were in progress with the US company Atlantic Richfield Co (Arco) on the terms of a $1,300m. enhanced oil recovery (EOR) contract to raise output in the Rhourde el-Baguel field. US firms were expected to take a leading role in future EOR contracts. Several contracts with international companies had been concluded in 1992–93 for new exploration work. In 1994 the Anadarko (Algeria) Petroleum Corpn of the USA announced plans to drill two more exploration wells in the Hassi Berkine field. Cepsa and Repsol of Spain and BHP Petroleum of Australia were also engaged in drilling projects. In late 1993 British Petroleum (BP) announced that it would drill its first exploration well in 1994 as part of a nine-year programme during which the company is committed to drill five wells. Despite the deteriorating security situation and the withdrawal of some expatriate staff and dependants, international petroleum companies stated that they were continuing operations. In January 1994 SONATRACH opened a second round of exploration bidding and announced that it was pursuing plans to allocate at least four new exploration permits; in May plans were announced to drill 51 exploration wells. In June Pluspetrol of Argentina signed an exploration agreement and in November a group of South Korean companies signed a contract to explore and drill wells in the central Illizi basin. In May 1995 Italy's Agip signed an exploration and production sharing agreement to undertake work in the Zemoul al-Kbar concession where three discoveries had already been made. Production facilities are under construction and a 230 km-pipeline is being built to link the new wells to the existing pipeline system. Total production will eventually rise to an estimated 60,000 b/d. The agreement also includes production tests at Agip's oil discovery at Rhourde Messaoud. In September 1994 Petro-Canada, which signed a 10-year exploration and production-sharing accord in April 1993, announced an oil and gas find in its Tinhrert acreage in the Illizi basin and in March 1995 sought approval to develop the field. In early 1995 Anadarko (Algeria) sought permission to develop two oil fields in the Hassi Berkine block following the announcement in December 1994 of a third oil discovery.

In December 1995 SONATRACH signed a gas exploration and production agreement with BP, the country's first gas production sharing agreement with a private company. Under the agreement, BP would undertake a two-year exploration and appraisal phase in the (as yet undeveloped) district 3 of the In Salah area. If the operation was successful, BP would develop the area and produce an estimated 10,000m. cu m of gas a year. On the basis of proven reserves, BP indicated that it was confident of producing an annual 5,000m. cu m with good prospects for a further 5,000m. cu m a year. Total reserves in the concession area were estimated at 286,000m. cu m. Development of the concession would involve drilling 200 wells and building a 48-in pipeline to Hassi R'Mel, requiring investment of some $3,500m., 65% of which was to be covered by BP and the remainder by SONATRACH. Production was due to commence in 2002–03 and the gas would be marketed by SONA-TRACH and BP under a 50:50 joint venture company. After the agreement with BP was signed, Exxon of the USA announced that it was to begin negotiations with the Government to develop a gas field in the In Salah area close to BP's concession. In January 1996 Total of France, together with Repsol of Spain, signed a production agreement with SONATRACH to develop the Tin Fouye Tabankort gas field, the second agreement of its kind between the state energy company and private investors. Development work would involve drilling 30–50 new wells, increasing production at the existing 30 wells, and constructing an LPG and condensate separation plant to process the wet gas from the Tin Fouye field. Some 35% of the cost of the project, estimated at $850m., would be met by Total, 30% by Repsol, and the remainder by SONATRACH. The field was expected to produce 18m. cu m of dry gas a day, 700,000 tons a year of LPG and 1m. tons a year of condensate. The estimated combined recoverable reserves were 1,000m. barrels of oil equivalent. Under the agreement, Total and Repsol would receive a share of the LPG and condensate production, while SONATRACH would take all the dry gas produced.

In March 1996 Arco signed a contract with SONATRACH to rehabilitate the Rhourde el-Baguel oil field, the country's second largest field, for which a preliminary agreement had been reached in July 1994 (see above). This was the country's first EOR scheme and involved the drilling of additional wells and the use of gas injection techniques to gradually increase production from 25,000 b/d to 125,000 b/d within 10 years. The field was expected to produce more than 500m. barrels over a period of 25 years. Arco would take 49% of the field's output. In October 1995 Anadarko Petroleum announced that it was proceeding with plans to develop the Hassi Berkine South field, including processing units and a 30 in-pipeline linking up with an existing pipeline used by Agip.

In November 1995 Mobil of the USA, which had signed a production sharing and exploration agreement in February, announced that it had found oil at its first exploration well and was evaluating the results to decide whether or not the discovery was commercial. In December Agip of Italy, which had signed a $25m.-exploration agreement with SONATRACH in May, discovered oil in the Zemoul el-Kbar concession in the Hassi Berkine North field. A second discovery was made in May 1996, and Agip planned to develop both wells and connect them to existing production facilities at the Bir Rebaa North field.

Production from the concession was to be increased from 46,000 b/d to 70,000 b/d. In March 1996 Cepsa of Spain announced that it was to develop a second field, the Rhourde el-Krouf field, in its Rhourde Yacoub concession with the aim of achieving production of 70,000 b/d by the end of the year. Estimated recoverable reserves at the field were 74m.–125m. barrels of light crude. Speaking in March 1996, the Minister of Energy and Mines, Amar Makhloufi, urged international oil companies to invest $3,500m. in hydrocarbon projects in the following five years. Algeria aimed to exploit all gas reserves and to increase oil production at many existing fields by as much as 50% by introducing enhanced oil recovery technology, similar to the project signed with Arco. Makhloufi stated that EOR projects being discussed with other companies, which had been deliberately suspended, would be re-opened in order to try and secure more deals in fields such as Rhourde el-Baguel. He said that $18,000m. was to be invested in the oil and gas industries in the following five years and that the Government hoped that as much as 20% might be covered by the private sector.

In January 1998 Oryx Energy, a US independent company, signed an exploration and production-sharing agreement with SONATRACH, whereby it would invest $28.8m. in exploration work in the Timissit region, south of Hassi Messaoud, over the following five years. By early 1998 there were 19 foreign oil companies with exploration and production-sharing contracts in Algeria. Anadarko (Algeria) announced a major investment programme in the country during 1998 to develop three oilfields and continue exploration work. In May Anadarko began producing oil at Hassi Berkine South, the company's first production in Algeria. Production was expected to increase from 60,000 b/d in mid-1998 to 180,000 b/d once the field has been developed fully. In April 1998 Cepsa of Spain announced investment of over $1,000m. to develop the Qoubba field, where production of 230,000 b/d was planned.

As a result of higher international prices for petroleum, Algeria's hydrocarbon exports rose to $12,630m. in 1996, but fell, in response to a decline in prices, to an estimated $12,380m. in 1997 and are forecast at $12,410m. for 1998. Revenue from hydrocarbon exports was projected to increase substantially by 2001, as new oilfields become productive, output from existing fields is augmented through EOR projects, and natural gas sales rise. By 2001 revenue from energy exports is projected to reach $16,000m. per year.

Following its establishment in 1963, SONATRACH expanded to become the largest, most complex and economically most important state company in Algeria. In May 1980 the Government decided that SONATRACH should be rationalized into smaller, specialized and more autonomous units. Thirteen such units were eventually formed, including SONATRACH itself. In January 1998 the National Energy Council, chaired by President Zéroual, approved a long-standing restructuring plan for SONA-TRACH, under which non-core activities were to be detached as separate companies, and the downstream oil and gas sector would be open to foreign investment. In March SONATRACH was converted into a joint-stock company by presidential decree, with a capital of AD 245,000m. ($4,100m.) entirely subscribed by the state. The company was to be headed by a director-general answerable to a board of directors chaired by the Minister of Energy and Mines. Foreign investors would not be allowed to have shares in SONATRACH, although the company would encourage foreign participation in both upstream and downstream projects.

In April 1989 Algeria's first nuclear reactor came into operation. Following international press speculation in April 1991 that the 15 MW nuclear reactor at Ain Oussera was for military use, officials of the Ministry of Research and Technology stressed its peaceful application and Algeria's willingness to allow an inspection by the International Atomic Energy Agency. At the inauguration of the reactor in December 1993, it was announced that Algeria would sign the nuclear non-proliferation treaty. In early 1990 plans to build a helium and nitrogen plant in Bethioua, near Arzew, were announced. The plant will produce 16m. cu m of liquid helium and 33,000 tons of liquid and gaseous nitrogen per year, mainly for export, utilizing gas from SONA-TRACH's LNG 2 plant at Arzew. Algeria has proven helium reserves of 6,000m. cu m.

HOUSING AND SOCIAL INFRASTRUCTURE

A key feature of the 1980–84 and the 1985–89 Development Plans, and a priority for the regime of President Chadli, was a concerted effort to address Algeria's chronic housing shortage. Additional expenditure was also allocated for other aspects of social infrastructure, notably health and education facilities, which, like housing, had been neglected in the 1970s. Under the 1985–89 Plan, 8% of total investment was allocated to transport infrastructure and nearly 16% to housing. More than 300,000 new homes were to be built and some 350,000 homes which had been started under the previous Plan were to be completed.

According to government estimates, at least 100,000 new homes were built in 1982–83. Building, traditionally the province of state concerns, was facilitated by two independent factors: firstly, the 30,000 and more homes believed to have been started—frequently without official permission—by the thriving private domestic construction industry; and, secondly, the prefabricated construction techniques which had been introduced by foreign companies under the aegis of the Office National de la Promotion de la Construction en Préfabrique (ONEP), a state concern founded in March 1982, following the successful use of imported prefabricated building techniques to repair earthquake damage in el-Asnam. By the end of that year, ONEP had signed contracts for its entire construction programme of almost 5m. sq m, at a total cost of almost $2,800m. It was the world's largest prefabricated construction programme and was chosen as a costly, but speedy and efficient, way of satisfying urgent demand. ONEP drew most of its contractors from France, Spain, Italy, Denmark, Belgium, the United Kingdom, Switzerland, Portugal and Sweden, financing the bulk of its work through export credits. The 1982 programme included 21,000 homes (about one-half of that number being attached to hospitals), 34 fully-equipped hospitals, 60 polyclinics, 83 vocational training centres, 41 technical schools, 122 secondary schools, six biological research centres and six university housing 'cities'. ONEP contractors worked directly for local *wilayat* (administrative districts) but negotiated through ONEP and received tax and customs dispensations.

Although prefabricated construction was, on average, almost half the cost of traditional methods, it drained Algeria's foreign exchange because of the high proportion of imported work. ONEP awarded no new contracts in 1983, and was finally disbanded in the following year. By then, traditional construction methods were being used to build most of the extra housing.

In 1983 the Government launched its other main scheme to expedite building, namely the use of foreign contractors under bilateral agreements with foreign governments. After the dissolution of ONEP, however, there was a general shift in government policy towards housing construction. Contracts were awarded to companies from Eastern Europe, often to accompany barter agreements, because they could complete the work more cheaply. The Government also urged local construction companies to become involved in the housing programme. Foreign companies were asked to form joint ventures with local companies if they wished to be awarded more work, but these requirements proved unpopular. After the collapse of petroleum prices in 1986, the Government began to search for cheaper methods of solving the housing crisis, encouraging local companies to undertake housing projects. The private sector was given more freedom to undertake developments on its own, and those who had built their houses illegally were offered an amnesty. However, the Government remained determined to prevent housing development on potential farming land. In 1989 it was estimated that about 100,000 new homes needed to be built each year in order to solve the housing crisis.

Announcing the outlines of the Government's recovery programme in February 1992, Prime Minister Ghozali stated that priority would be given to imports for public works and construction and that foreign participation would be encouraged in the production of construction materials. The Government's stated aim was to eliminate shanty towns, especially in the major cities. In April 1993 the World Bank approved a $200m.-loan to support the Government's emergency programme to build 130,000 public housing units. The EU also approved a parallel structural adjustment grant of ECU 70m. ($83m.) to finance imports needed for the construction of 100,000

social housing units. In July a loan was agreed with the Saudi Fund for Development to finance the construction of 2,000 homes in the Dar el-Beida and Bir Mourad Rais districts of Algiers. Following agreement on a new accord with Algeria in April 1994, the IMF asked other donors to concentrate additional funding on social spending projects, especially housing. Concern has been expressed that, as a result of the political crisis, Algeria's housing stock, much of which is old or, if recently built, of poor quality, is not being maintained. One option under consideration by the Government in 1996 was the introduction of an accommodation tax to raise AD 400m. for housing maintenance in Algiers. In April 1997 the Abu Dhabi Fund for Development approved a $20m. loan for housing projects.

A radical review of housing policy was in progress in early 1997 with a view to introducing reforms based on current IMF and World Bank criteria for structural adjustment loans. Agreement in principle with the World Bank was reached in March on an outline programme that envisaged a reform of the public-sector housing fund (Caisse Nationale d'Epargne et de Prévoyance—CNEP); privatization of state-run construction firms; privatization of the housing development sector, including the introduction of a mortgage market; and significant increases in rents for public-sector housing. In July the CNEP was restructured and converted into a state-owned commercial bank, the Banque de l'Habitat. In addition, the Government established two guarantee funds, the Société de Refinancement Hypothécaire and the Société de Garanties des Crédits Hypothécaires, to encourage other banks to lend money for property development. Both organizations were to act as insurance funds to reduce bad loan risks for banks lending for housing projects. In early 1998 the Ministry of Housing stated that it expected a significant increase in private investment in housing as a result of tax incentives and financial reforms targeted at this sector. Construction had begun in 1997 on 343,000 housing units financed largely by private households. Some 30 construction firms, including the state-owned Entreprise de Construction pour la Sidérurgie (COSIDER) and Entreprise Nationale de Réalisation des Travaux Sidérurgiques et Métallurgiques (REALSIDER), were among the first companies to be listed for privatization in May 1998.

In late 1997 a US company, Omnitek, signed a joint-venture agreement with COSIDER to build a factory in Algiers to produce prefabricated houses. In early 1998 it was reported that Royal Building Systems of Canada was to establish a similar plant with the capacity to produce 12,500 housing units per year.

TRANSPORT

At the start of the 1980s Algeria's state railway company, the Société Nationale des Transports Ferroviaires (SNTF), announced ambitious plans to double the length and the freight-carrying capacity of its 3,900-km network within 10 years. After 1985, however, SNTF revised its investment priorities in order to concentrate on the maintenance and upgrading of existing track and equipment. A local company was established in 1986 to implement the upgrading programme in co-operation with foreign firms, while most expansion projects were postponed or cancelled. In 1991 SNTF carried 58m. passengers and 12m. tons of freight. Rail routes within Algeria include Algiers–Oran, Béchar–Mohammedia (narrow-gauge), Mohammedia–Mostaganem, Algiers–Annaba, Constantine–Touggourt, Constantine–Skikda, Algiers–Tizi-Ouzou, Annaba–Tebessa and Djelfa–Blida (narrow-gauge). There are international rail links to Morocco and Tunisia.

In September 1994 the Government announced plans to restructure SNTF, including a proposed privatization of 12 subsidiary companies. Disagreements about corporate restructuring had earlier delayed the full utilization of a 1989 World Bank loan for railway projects. Contracts were awarded in 1996 for the construction of a 5.2-km tunnel at El-Achir, on the main east-west line between Constantine and Algiers, to be part-financed by an African Development Bank (ADB) loan approved in 1991. Completion of this project (which would reduce journey times considerably) was scheduled for 1999. Work to extend the Constantine–Touggourt line southwards to Ouargla and the oil town of Hassi Messaoud was proceeding at a very slow rate in mid-1996, by which time a total of 15 km of new track had been completed. Upgrading of the south-western (Béchar–Mohammedia) line, whose narrow-gauge track dated from 1912, was to be given high priority in the late 1990s. A long-standing (and repeatedly postponed) proposal to build a new east-west railway across the high plateaux of southern Algeria was in July 1996 again rejected for the foreseeable future because of the high cost of the project (an estimated $3,000m. at 1996 prices). The Government's most serious rail financing problem in 1996 arose out of the need to replace the 250 passenger carriages and 20 locomotives destroyed or damaged by Islamist guerrillas. In 1997 an Austrian railway equipment manufacturer announced plans to enter into a joint venture with an Algerian company within the framework of a 1986 Austrian–Algerian co-operation agreement which had latterly produced few new initiatives.

Construction of a proposed Algiers metro system began in the early 1980s but was suspended for some years, owing to financial constraints in the latter part of that decade. A limited resumption of work from 1989 had by 1992 produced only one km of completed tunnel because local contractors lacked modern tunnelling equipment, while the project organizers were not authorized to employ foreign contractors at this time. In 1995 a government initiative to attract international contractors to the metro project was unsuccessful, many potential bidders being deterred by the high level of terrorist activity in Algiers. In mid-1996 the Minister of Transport announced that plans to utilize foreign contractors had been abandoned 'for financial reasons' and that local firms would continue the project.

The national airline, Air Algérie, was restructured in 1984, with domestic routes being passed to the newly-formed Air Inter Services. Algeria purchased its first two European Airbus A310 aircraft in 1984. The number of passengers carried by Air Algérie fell from 4.2m. in 1986 to 3.7m. in 1991. The company's outstanding debt was calculated to have risen to AD 9,000m. in 1991 and debt due in 1992 equalled one-third of the company's turnover. The company's problems arose from the effects of devaluation, a reduction in traffic (due to the introduction of new visa regulations for Algerians visiting Europe) and increased operating costs. In 1991 Air Algérie raised its international fares by 50% and suspended its plans to spend an estimated $1,400m. on renewal of its aircraft fleet over the next 10 years. In 1992 a three-year reform programme, designed to improve the management and performance of the airline, was initiated. Air Algérie reported profits of $14.5m. in 1992, but in December 1994 the company's Director-General reported further losses of revenue, due to the security crisis and tougher visa restrictions imposed by France and other countries.

In September 1994, as part of a radical review of all state transport undertakings, the Government indicated its intention to reform the structure of Air Algérie in order to improve its efficiency and competitiveness as the Government moved towards its medium-term goal of opening up the air and sea transport sectors to private competition. Meanwhile, Air Algérie's aircraft purchase plans remained obstructed because of a lack of funds, the Government's stated preference in 1996 being for the airline to lease or charter additional aircraft while this remained a cost-effective option. In early 1998 it was reported that Air Algérie was in negotiations with international aircraft-leasing companies to lease nine new craft as the first part of a plan to renew all of its ageing medium-sized aeroplanes. In May 1997 plans were well advanced to create subsidiary companies to handle Air Algérie's non-core activities (including catering, cargo handling, distribution, security and the provision of petroleum industry chartering services), the intention being to leave the parent company free to concentrate on its primary passenger and freight transport operations. It was expected that the proposed subsidiaries would be opened up to private-sector investment, with Air Algérie itself remaining in state ownership. In early 1998 it was reported that the Government was preparing new legislation to allow the establishment of the country's first independent airline, owned jointly by Air Algérie and SONATRACH. The airline, which was expected to start operating later that year, would service the southern oilfields and have a capital of AD 700m. ($11.8m.).

Airport upgrading projects undertaken in the early 1990s included the construction of new runways at Tamanrasset, El-Achouet, Ain-Arnet and Hassi R'Mel and the completion of basic structural work on a new international terminal at Algiers Houari Boumedienne airport. However, funding was not available in 1996 to equip the terminal building and bring it into operation, the need for new facilities having become less pressing because of a decrease in passenger numbers (attributable to Algeria's internal security problems). In late 1996 the Government was examining the scope for negotiating a partnership agreement to attract overseas project finance for the terminal. In early 1998 the Minister of Transport stated that a further AD 15,000m. ($256m.), one-half in convertible currency, would be needed to complete the new airport.

In 1993 Japan's International Co-operation Agency completed a major survey of development priorities for the seaports of Algiers, Oran and Annaba. It recommended that facilities for unloading cereals and containers should be upgraded at the ports of Annaba and Oran. In 1991 the three ports handled 71% of all traffic: Algiers 32%, Annaba 23% and Oran 16%. A new port at Djen-Djen near Jijel would serve Algeria's first free-zone development, and was scheduled to open in 1998 (see Manufacturing below). In October 1995, as part of a World Bank scheme to reduce petroleum pollution in the southern Mediterranean, contractors were invited to bid for the supply and installation of maritime traffic control equipment at the ports of Algiers, Skikda and Arzew. In March 1996 Sci Costruzioni of Italy was awarded a $48m.-contract to expand Algiers port in co-operation with a local partner. The project was due to be completed in mid-2000.

In mid-1992 it was reported that the Government was to revive plans to build an east-west motorway system linking Annaba and Tlemcen and forming part of a trans-Maghreb motorway. About 100 km of the highway are currently operational and another 55 km are under construction, although completion could take another 20 years. In December 1993 the EIB made a loan of $24.2m. for a section of the 1,400-km trans-Algerian highway between Lakhdaria and Bouira, and an agreement for a further loan of $97m. was concluded in late 1994. In December 1995 the ADB agreed a loan of $39m. to finance the construction of a motorway to bypass Constantine. The new 11 km six-lane highway was to be integrated into the east-west motorway system. In 1996 a government study of the roads programme estimated that total spending of AD 227,000m. ($4,124m.) would be needed to complete a full renovation of existing roads, while AD 243,000m. ($4,415m.) would be required to complete the east-west motorway project. Available resources during 1996 (as allocated in that year's national budget) were AD 3,500m. for road reinforcement work, AD 2,000m. for rehabilitation work and AD 2,300m. for maintenance work.

Various transport companies, including the Société Nationale des Transports Routiers, were in the privatization list published by the Government in May 1998.

MANUFACTURING

Industrial development has long been a priority area of Algerian economic policy and the major investment effort in the 1970–73 Development Plan was devoted to this end. Under the 1974–77 Plan, industry received about 43.5% of total allocations. In the 1980–84 Plan it was allocated 38% of total investment, and 32% in the 1985–89 Plan.

At the time of independence the Algerian industrial sector was very small, being confined mainly to food processing, building materials, textiles and minerals. The departure of the French entailed loss of demand, capital and skill, thereby decelerating the industrialization process. Foreign firms became increasingly reluctant in the 1960s to invest in Algeria because of the danger of nationalization. By 1978 about 300 state-owned manufacturing plants had been established, but productivity was very low, with some factories operating at only 15%–25% of design capacity. The early 1980s were a time of increasing emphasis on productivity and efficiency, and nowhere more so than in the manufacturing sector. The restructuring of the state mechanical manufacturing and supply monopoly, SONACOME, into 11 smaller and, in theory, more efficient units appears to have helped output, as did profit-sharing schemes.

In 1983 the Government began to encourage foreign and domestic manufacturers to supply the larger *sociétés nationales*, such as SONACOME. Foreign companies would be junior partners to state concerns, but local businesses would receive the finance from state banks which was normally available to state concerns. The Government also sought to encourage companies to establish joint ventures, in order to stimulate foreign investment and to ensure closer working relations with foreign companies, thus enabling Algerian enterprises to monitor the progress of projects and gain a genuine transfer of technology.

In the late 1980s the Ministry of Light Industries considered that the basic network of small-scale manufacturing was complete, and it intended to concentrate in future on improving the integration of the sector. The private sector was to be given a greater role in setting up manufacturing industries, to process raw materials produced in the state sector. Instead of investing in new cement works, the ministry was to concentrate on increasing output at existing works, and to carry out small extensions to satisfy any increase in demand. Beyond 1990 the ministry planned to develop high technology industries, such as clock manufacturing, and intended to promote industries to integrate the sector, such as the manufacture of synthetic fibres. In early 1992 the Government announced radical measures to open state sector industries, which account for some 80% of industrial production, to local private and to foreign participation. Officials acknowledged that many state industries were operating at below 50% capacity, and recognized that, as income from hydrocarbons was not sufficient to finance the recovery of its industrial base, privatization was essential to provide investment and new markets as well as technology. The only exceptions would be industries classified as strategic, such as the Entreprise Nationale de Sidérurgie (SIDER), SONELGAZ and agroindustrial companies. After an audit of major state companies carried out as part of Algeria's World Bank structural adjustment programme, the following were identified as viable, if non-profit-making: Entreprise Nationale des Véhicules Industriels, Entreprise Nationale des Matériaux de Travaux Publics, Entreprise Nationale de Production de Matériel Agricole and Entreprise Nationale de Production de Matériel Hydraulique. In April 1994 a new ministry was created to oversee the restructuring of state companies as required by the agreements signed with the IMF in May 1994 and May 1995 (see Government Strategy).

According to a report by the Ministry of Industrial Restructuring and Participation in May 1996, four years of civil strife had reduced industrial capacity by 10%, but the decline was being stemmed, and industrial production fell by only 0.5% in 1995, compared with 8% in 1994. In a statement in mid-May the state-owned Entreprise Nationale de Distribution et de Commercialisation des Produits Pétroliers (NAFTAL) indicated that sabotage, allegedly by Islamist extremists, had inflicted damage totalling some AD 3,000m. to the company's facilities. NAFTAL reported a deficit of AD 11,700m. and demanded urgent government assistance.

Government efforts to attract foreign investment in the manufacturing industry met with only limited success, but in October 1997 Daewoo of South Korea signed a memorandum of understanding with the Ministry of Industry and Restructuring to invest some \$2,000m. over a five-year period, including acquiring a share of a range of state-owned manufacturing industries such as fertilizers, car assembly and electrical goods. However, progress with this investment programme (which represented more than twice the total foreign investment in the non-hydrocarbon sector over the previous three years) was threatened by South Korea's financial crisis which began in late 1997.

The iron and steel industry is crucial to the development of other industries. In 1988 the state-owned steel company, SIDER, announced proposals to increase output of long-steel products to meet 70%, rather than 30%, of local demand and thus reduce imports of steel, which total 1.9m.–2m. tons per year. Plans were also made to increase SIDER's annual flat-steel capacity to 1.8m. tons from 1.4m. tons. Huge investments have been made in the el-Hadjar complex at Annaba. Liquid steel output rose slightly from 830,000 tons in 1991 to 841,115 tons in 1992. According to SIDER's projections output should have reached 1.25m. tons, well below design capacity of 2m. tons. Exports of steel products in 1992 reached 281,949 tons. Metalsider, Algeria's first private steel maker, started operations in 1992. A merchant bar mill with a capacity of 100,000

tons a year commenced production in 1993 and a third bar/rod combination mill was due to commence operations in 1996. In April 1993 it was reported that Metalsider was seeking joint-venture partners to build a 1.5m.-ton-a-year direct-reduced iron plant.

Although ambitious plans have been announced to expand the country's petrochemical industries, technical and financial problems have hindered progress. A vast petrochemical complex at Skikda produces polyethylene, PVC, caustic soda and chlorine. In 1991 a project to build a high-density polyethylene plant at Skikda was announced, with a capacity of 130,000 tons a year. ENIP (Entreprise Nationale d'Industrie Pétrochimique) formed a joint venture company (Polymed) with Spain's Repsol Química to build the plant, but a series of problems delayed the start of construction work until June 1997. The plant was scheduled to come into operation by December 1999. In November 1991 it was reported that Rollechim Impianti of Italy together with ENIP and Entreprise Nationale de Raffinage de Pétrole had agreed to create a joint venture to build a petrochemicals plant at Skikda to produce 30,000 tons of orthoxylene, 71,000 tons of paraxylene and 25,000 tons of phthalic anhydride annually. There is a nitrogenous fertilizer plant at Arzew, utilizing natural gas, with an annual capacity of 800,000 tons, and a complex for the manufacture of intermediate petrochemical products. In May 1991 ENIP established a joint venture with Repsol of Spain and Rhône-Poulenc of France to build a polyester resins plant at Arzew with an annual production of 10,000 tons. In August 1991 Total of France, Ecofuel of Italy and SONATRACH confirmed plans to build a \$400m.-methyl tertiary butyl ether plant at Arzew, with an annual production capacity of 600,000 tons mainly for export to refineries in southern Europe. By July 1993 progress on the project had been limited, and it was reported that Total and Ecofuel were undecided about their continued participation. At Annaba, a plant for phosphate fertilizers, with an annual capacity of 550,000 tons, was opened in 1972 but has suffered from technical difficulties. A fertilizer complex began production in 1980, also at Annaba. New units starting up at Arzew and Annaba in 1981 and 1982, together with efforts to exploit existing productive capacity more fully, have provided a surplus of ammonium nitrate, phosphate fertilizers and urea for export.

Following a Government decision in January 1998 to open the downstream oil and gas sector to foreign investment, Prime Minister Ouyahia announced in March that the Government had started negotiations with several international companies wishing to invest in petrochemicals. In early 1998 a \$500m. joint venture was agreed between Fertiberia of Spain and SONATRACH, together with the Entreprise Publique Economique Asmidal and the Entreprise Nationale du Fer et du Phosphate (Ferphos) (state-owned fertilizer and phosphate companies), to produce fertilizers and ammonia products for the Algerian market and for export. Both Asmidal and Ferphos were to be opened to foreign investors under the privatization programme.

The assembly of industrial vehicles in Algeria began in 1974 at a plant in Rouiba, established by a state-run company in association with the French manufacturer Berliet. A large farm machinery complex went into production at Sidi-Bel-Abbès in 1976. The closure of a Renault assembly plant at Algiers in 1970 left Algeria with no car production capacity. In 1992 work began at Tiaret to build a Fiat car assembly plant, to be 64.4% owned by an Algerian public-sector company, Fatia, and 35.6% owned by Fiat of Italy. The plant would have the capacity to produce 30,000 Punto models each year. However, having suspended work on the nearly-completed factory for security reasons, Fiat said in late 1996 that in the current circumstances it was not possible to forecast a date for the resumption of the project. The company had meanwhile applied to the Italian export credit agency to extend the relevant project financing facilities (which expired in mid-1996) until the end of 1998. Tyres are manufactured near Algiers. The local manufacture of vehicle components by Algerian companies and joint ventures with other countries has been encouraged by the Government since 1987. A plant for the overhaul of Peugeot engines was established near Algiers in 1990 under an agreement with the French company. The importation of vehicles to meet Algeria's annual demand for about 100,000 cars and light vans was opened up to the private sector in 1990/91, allowing foreign manufacturers (including Peugeot, Renault, Fiat, Daewoo, Honda and Nissan) to establish local distribution agencies. Tax incentives were offered to encourage such manufacturers to make future investments in Algerian production facilities. As part of the 1997 agreement with Daewoo (see above), the South Korean company was reported to be in negotiations to acquire a 70% stake of the Société Nationale des Véhicules Industriels (SNVI), which manufactures industrial vehicles at Rouiba; however, the MAN group of Germany also expressed interest in acquiring part of the SNVI.

Other growth areas are the paper industry, textiles, electrical goods (including radio and television sets), flour milling and building materials. There are six cement works with a total installed capacity of about 9m. tons, but they have been operating at barely 50% of capacity. In July 1993 the four national cement companies created two new subsidiaries. The Société des Ciments de Tebessa was to manage the Tebessa factory, where there were plans to seek foreign capital for a project to double capacity. The Société de Maintenance et d'Equipment des Cimenteries was to deal with maintenance, subcontracting and the supply of parts to local cement companies. A pharmaceuticals industry was developed in Algeria after 1991, when international companies were encouraged to invest in local manufacturing facilities in return for licences to sell products on the local market. Several new joint ventures, including one between Rhône-Poulenc Rorer of France and the Entreprise Nationale de Production de Produits Pharmaceutiques (SAIDAL, the state-owned pharmaceutical company) were announced in early 1998. In 1992 the Caisse Française de Développement provided FF 160m. ($10.7m.) for the renovation of the Meftah asbestos cement plant, FF 35.4m. ($6.3m.) for upgrading the M'Sila aluminium plant and FF 19.6m. ($3.5m.) for reorganization and pollution reduction at the Ghazaouet zinc plant. In spite of all these efforts, it was estimated that total industrial production in 1991 was less than in 1984, while the country's population had increased by about 4m. Between the third quarter of 1995 and the third quarter of 1996 Algeria's official index of manufacturing output by public-sector enterprises outside the hydrocarbons sector fell from 70.8 to 59.9 (1989 = 100). In the first nine months of 1996 Algeria's production of iron and steel decreased by 18.7%, while output of chemical products declined by 17.1%. Output of building materials increased by 4.2% in response to strong demand for new housing units, and cement production rose by 11.6% (although cement plants continued to operate well below their full capacity).

The privatization offers announced by the Government during 1996 included a management contract for the SIDER steel mill; a management contract for the Ghardaia plant of the Entreprise Nationale de Tubes et de Transformation des Produits Plats (ENTTPP or ANABIB, the company supplying pipes for the Maghreb-Europe gas pipeline); a management contract for the Médéa plant of SAIDAL; the offer for sale of 17 textile manufacturing units currently owned by five state enterprises; management contracts for five cement units owned by two state enterprises; the offer for sale of six fertilizer units owned by the Asmidal company, with two further units offered on a management contract basis; and offers of shareholdings in several food companies, including the Office Régional des Produits Oléicoles (producing olive oil) and the Entreprise Nationale des Jus et Conserves Alimentaires (ENAJUC, producing fruit juice and other food products).

Algeria's first 'free zone' area for industrial development was due to open in 1998 on a site at Bellara, near Jijel international airport and 40 km from a new harbour. Basic infrastructure had previously been installed on the 500-ha site as part of a plan (otherwise unimplemented) to build a steel complex. The national investment agency APSI was in 1997 seeking an operator to manage the zone on a concession basis. Figures released by APSI in mid-1997 showed that foreign companies invested a total of AD 56,800m. ($989m.) in non-hydrocarbon sectors of the Algerian economy between November 1993 and May 1997.

TRADE

Algeria had a consistent foreign trade deficit, with the exception of small surpluses recorded in 1967 and 1968, until the huge increases in petroleum prices in 1973. Exports of petroleum and natural gas have transformed the pattern of Algerian exports, previously limited to agricultural products and some minerals—mainly wine, citrus fruit and iron ore. Hydrocarbons accounted for more than 95% of visible export earnings in 1996. Other exports include vegetables, tobacco, hides and skins, dates and phosphates. Prior to the liberalization of trading policy in the mid-1990s, the Government fixed an annual budget for imports and strictly controlled the import requirements of public-sector companies.

The visible trade account turned from a state of chronic deficit to surplus in 1974, alternating annually between deficit and surplus thereafter. Increases in the price of petroleum in 1979, however, put Algeria in credit and kept the trade balance in surplus. In order to preserve this surplus (which reached AD 16,500m. in 1985), the Government introduced new import controls. However, the sharp fall in the price of petroleum in 1986 resulted in a trade deficit of AD 6,567m. for that year. In 1987 the price of petroleum recovered slightly and there was a trade surplus of $2,413m. There was a trade surplus of $946m. in 1988. In 1990, although imports increased by almost 22%, exports increased further, by 42%. This produced a trade surplus of AD 11,497m., compared with a deficit of AD 1,835m. in 1989. A trade surplus of $4,107m. was recorded in 1991, although in 1992 the surplus declined to $2,489m., owing to a 12.6% rise in expenditure on imports. In February 1994 officials of the Ministry of Commerce stated that a ban on imports of consumer goods imposed by the Abd es-Salam Government in November 1992 had been lifted.

Algeria's overall trade balance (including trade in services as well as visible commodities) evolved as follows between 1993 and 1996. In 1993 there was a surplus of $756m. (imports $10,004m., exports $10,760m., including $9,760m. from hydrocarbons). In 1994 there was a deficit of $1,500m. (imports $11,090m., exports $9,590m., including $8,610m. from hydrocarbons). In 1995 there was a deficit of $1,260m. (imports $12,200m., exports $10,940m., including $9,370m. from hydrocarbons). In 1996 there was a surplus of $3,030m. (imports $11,240m., exports $14,270m., including $12,640m. from hydrocarbons). Foodstuffs accounted for 28.7% of visible imports in 1996 (25.6% in 1995); raw materials and semi-finished products constituted 26.3% of visible imports in 1996 (30.5% in 1995); capital equipment accounted for 33.5% of visible imports in 1996 (27.7% in 1995); and consumer goods constituted 11.5% of visible imports in 1996 (16.2% in 1995). By the end of 1996 all restrictions on external trade had been eliminated, allowing public and private importers to finance their transactions from their own foreign-exchange holdings or through official cash and credit lines. Full convertibility of the Algerian dinar was expected to be achieved by early 1998. At the end of 1996 Algerian customs statistics indicated that more than 25,000 private enterprises and about 300 public enterprises were involved in foreign trading operations. In 1997 the Government established an export promotion agency (PROMEX, to be funded out of the receipts from taxes on imported luxury goods) and introduced a range of financial incentives to stimulate the growth of non-hydrocarbon exports. In 1997 there was a trade surplus of $5,790m., with exports totalling $14,140m. and imports restricted to $8,350m. In September 1997 the ADB approved a 20-year loan of $215m. to pay for imports. In early 1998 it was reported that terms had been issued to enable Algerian exporters to draw on new short-term state credit insurance facilities.

Before independence France purchased 81% of Algeria's exports and provided 82% of its imports. In 1996 France remained Algeria's largest supplier of imports (with a 25.1% market share), but took only 12.9% of Algeria's 1996 exports. Hydrocarbons accounted for 96.3% of Algerian exports to France, while capital goods remained the single largest element in French exports to Algeria, followed by agroindustrial products and consumer goods. In April 1995 the French export agency, Coface, confirmed that it was continuing to provide normal cover for French export contracts despite the serious security situation in Algeria. The only modification to the agency's policy on Algeria concerned infrastructure projects which involved expatriate staff working in areas known to present a security problem. The agency, currently covering contracts worth $6,144m., was making every effort to ensure that projects in the oil and gas sector were covered in order to maintain Algeria's export capacity. Apart from France, Algeria's largest trading partners in 1996 were Italy (accounting for 20.8% of Algerian exports and supplying 9.2% of Algerian imports), the USA (15.5% of exports and 10.2% of imports), Spain (7.4% of exports and 12.6% of imports), Germany, Canada, Turkey, Belgium and the United Kingdom.

The finalization in July 1996 of debt rescheduling arrangements under the 1995 'Paris Club' and 'London Club' agreements (see Government Strategy section above) opened the way for a relaxation of export credit guarantee restrictions which had been introduced by several of Algeria's major trading partners. Agencies making announcements included Eximbank of the USA (short- and medium-term cover for Algerian public-sector importers resumed from August 1996); SACE of Italy (resumption of cover from late 1996, subject to strict conditions); the Belgian Government (reopening in November 1996 of a line of credit for Algerian transport projects, 'frozen' since 1994); and the United Kingdom's Export Credits Guarantee Department (resumption of cover for Algerian petroleum and gas projects from early 1997).

In February 1989 the Union of the Arab Maghreb (UAM) was formed by Algeria, Libya, Tunisia, Morocco and Mauritania. In January 1989 the Ministers of Industry of the Maghreb countries met to discuss industrial unity and economic integration; co-operation in the mining, textiles, electronics, domestic appliances, leather and construction industries is also under consideration. The UAM aims to establish a customs union and a single monetary exchange currency. The ultimate aim is to allow all members of the UAM to establish industries in each of the five countries. But despite a great deal of rhetoric little progress has been recorded to date (see History).

Negotiations for an association agreement between Algeria and the EU (to be broadly modelled on the EU's existing agreements with Morocco and Tunisia) were formally inaugurated in March 1997 and were expected to continue until at least 1999. With Algerian manufactures already having duty-free access to the EU, the main focus of the free-trade component of the negotiations was to be the phasing out of Algerian import duties on EU manufactures. Other issues to be discussed included economic co-operation, capital transfers, the establishment of companies, and social and cultural co-operation.

FINANCE

Before independence, Algeria was mostly dependent on France for its central banking and monetary system, though some of the usual central banking functions were carried out by the Banque d'Algérie. The Banque Centrale d'Algérie started its operations on 1 January 1963; it issues currency, regulates and licenses banks and supervises all foreign transactions. A state monopoly on all foreign financial transactions was imposed in November 1967; this followed a similar monopoly imposed on insurance in June 1966. State-run banks include the Banque Nationale d'Algérie, founded in 1966, traditionally service-sector based; Crédit Populaire d'Algérie, founded in 1966, strong in the construction sector; the Banque Extérieure d'Algérie, founded in 1967, dealing with foreign trade; the BADR, founded in 1982, providing finance for the agricultural sector; and the Banque de Développement Local, founded in 1985, which has traditionally provided loans for companies run by local government. Legislation on banking and credit was introduced in 1986 to define the role of these institutions and of the Central Bank, and to improve their project-assessment capabilities, as well as guaranteeing banking secrecy. In 1987 legislation was introduced to enable local commercial banks to provide credit directly to state-owned enterprises, as well as to private companies. The criteria for authorizing credit were modified, requiring the bank to assess a project primarily by its economic viability (including the company's ability to make repayments), rather than its social value. This legislation allowed banks to compete against each other for business, although they were not allowed to determine their own interest rates. In the same year the Conseil National de Crédit was established to supervise the implementation of the banking reforms and to determine the level of Algeria's foreign borrowing. In October 1988 banks were included in the group of more than 70 state-controlled companies which became

EPEs. The Banque Extérieure d'Algérie was the first state bank to become fully autonomous under the scheme.

Under the terms of the IMF accord signed in May 1995, five state-owned banks signed performance contracts of between one and three years with the Government in which they pledged to adhere to the Bank for International Settlements' standards, and to make their operations more transparent. The Government, for its part, will increase the banks' capital to help them restructure, but will phase out further subsidies over the contract period. The Ministry of Finance is to cease intervening in the running of the banks. The Government's aim is to prepare for privatization. In future the banks are to lessen their emphasis on lending and seek to expand their customer-base. In April 1996 the Minister of Finance, Ahmed Benbitour, announced that the Government was planning to restructure the five state-owned banks into five separate holdings, each with four subsidiaries specializing in financing areas such as leasing and equity participation. In March 1997 the Government announced that the first state bank to be opened up to private investment would be the Banque de Développement Local, which drew three-quarters of its current clients from small and medium-sized private businesses. The process of exchanging foreign currency—hitherto monopolized by the state banks—was opened up to the private sector in 1997. Following the drafting of regulations to permit private companies to enter the Algerian insurance market, a new insurance venture, Trust Algeria, was announced in mid-1997. Trust Insurance Co (of Bahrain) and Qatar General Insurance and Reinsurance Co were to hold 65% of the shares, while the remaining 35% was to be held by the state-owned Compagnie Algérienne d'Assurance.

Algeria has also formed joint institutions with other countries. In 1974 an Algerian-Libyan bank, the Banque Internationale Arabe, was opened in Paris to finance trade and investment between France and Arab countries. Possible joint financial institutions have been discussed with Kuwait, Saudi Arabia and the United Arab Emirates. The Banque de Coopération du Maghreb Arabe was established with Tunisia, in order to promote joint projects. In 1988 Algeria and Libya agreed to establish a joint bank, the Banque du Maghreb Arabe pour l'Investissement et du Commerce. In March 1990 a banking and investment law was approved which, for the first time since independence, permitted foreign investors, in most sectors, to own up to 100% of companies and to repatriate all of their profits. Foreign banks were to be allowed to establish representative branches. Three French banks had already opened 'liaison offices' in Algiers under the terms of earlier legislation. In June 1991 the Al-Baraka Bank of Algeria, the country's first joint-venture bank, opened. It was also Algeria's first Islamic bank, and the two partners are the local BADR and Dallah Al-Baraka of Jeddah. In June 1993 the Banque d'Algérie reported that legislation permitting the establishment of local private banks was in place and that applications to set up new institutions were being considered. The country's first local private bank, the Union Bank, was established in 1995 and recorded assets of AD 992m. ($16.6m.) at the end of 1996. Another two local private banks were authorized in early 1998: the El-Khalifa Bank, set up entirely by local investors, and the Mouna Bank, established in Oran. Also at the beginning of 1998 the Banque d'Algérie authorized a further three foreign financial institutions to open commercial banks in Algeria: Citibank of the USA, Société Générale of France and the Arab Banking Corpn of Bahrain. The central bank also ruled that, in future, new banks and financial institutions could be established without seeking its prior authorization.

In January 1996 the Government announced the creation of two new financial institutions, an interbank foreign exchange market, the Bourse des Valeurs Mobilières, and a monitoring organization to control the new Algiers stock exchange, the Commission d'Organisation et de Surveillance des Opérations de Bourse (Cosob). The interbank foreign exchange market is to set the dinar's rate of exchange, based on bidding for currency by banks, other financial institutions and authorized intermediaries, bringing to an end the flexible system of fixing the value of the dinar, introduced in October 1994 under the IMF stand-by agreement. All dinar and convertible currency transactions are to pass through the interbank market, but the central bank is to retain control over how the foreign exchange is used by intermediaries to prevent large imports of luxury and other consumer goods and undue capital flight. Non-hydrocarbon exports are expected to provide most of the receipts, and the size of the market is expected to increase in line with the growth of non-hydrocarbon exports, which are forecast to rise threefold by 1999. Cosob is co-ordinating the establishment of the market and represents Algeria's nascent investment industry abroad. The Ministry of Finance is examining ways of encouraging public saving through the stock exchange and the establishment of unit trusts and mutual funds. The new Algiers stock exchange began trading in February 1998 but was restricted to local investors until the introduction of government reforms to open it fully to foreign capital. Its first major operation was the launch of SONATRACH's five-year bond, Algeria's first domestic bond issue. The first equities were due to come into the market in mid-1998. A number of leading state companies were expected to seek listings.

Statistics published in 1994 revealed that Algeria's budget was in deficit by more than AD 74,000m. in 1992 and by AD 192,000m. in 1993. The 1992 budget had introduced new corporate, income and value-added taxes; provided for higher investment in agriculture, mining and energy; and sought to limit the impact of price rises on poor families, partly by maintaining price subsidies on 10 essential food items. The 1993 budget included sharply higher defence and internal security spending. The original budget estimates for 1994 provided for a deficit of AD 125,300m. (9.6% of forecast GDP). However, Algeria's 1994 currency devaluation, together with lower than expected world petroleum prices, contributed to an actual deficit of some AD 160,000m. in 1994. In 1995 the Government originally budgeted for a deficit of AD 148,400m. (8.3% of forecast GDP), but subsequently undertook to curb the deficit through tighter fiscal policies when it agreed a structural reform programme with the IMF in May 1995.

In 1996 the Government originally budgeted for a deficit of AD 99,400m. (revenue AD 749,200m., expenditure AD 848,600m.), and introduced various measures to improve revenues, including price increases for bread and petrol and steps to counter the evasion of an estimated AD 2,000m. of taxes each year. In the event, the actual deficit in 1996 was only about AD 31,500m., reflecting a rise in the average oil export price to $22 per barrel, compared with the Government's original estimate of $16.50 per barrel. Provisional outturn statistics for 1996 showed that AD 485,600m. had been raised in hydrocarbon taxes out of total revenue of AD 810,100m., while spending had totalled AD 841,600m. (slightly less than originally budgeted).

The 1997 budget provided for revenue of AD 829,400m. ($14,520m.), including AD 451,000m. from hydrocarbon taxes, and for expenditure of AD 914,100m. ($16,003m.), producing a deficit of AD 84,700m. ($1,483m.). However, the Government argued that there was in effect an underlying surplus of AD 7,400m., given that the expenditure total included an allowance for amortization of domestic debt (not included in previous years' budget calculations) and a once-only allocation of AD 78,000m. for a fund to restructure public-sector enterprises. The budget assumed an average 1997 petroleum export price of $17.50 per barrel and forecast an increase in the economic growth rate to 5% (compared with 4% in 1996), while the annual inflation rate was expected to fall to 10% (compared with an end-year rate of 15% in 1996). Capital spending was to be 10.3% higher than in 1996 and was to emphasize the completion of existing projects, while new projects would be required to demonstrate good growth potential. There was a reduction in the rate of value-added tax for companies. The 1997 budget was revised in August 1997, setting revenues at AD 881,500m. (of which AD 507,000m. was anticipated from oil and gas) and expenditure at AD 946,200m., giving a deficit of AD 64,700m. The 1998 budget, given parliamentary approval in December 1997, projected revenues of AD 901,500m. (of which AD 528,000m. was anticipated from oil and gas) and set expenditure at AD 980,200m., giving a deficit of AD 78,700m., representing 2.6% of GDP. Revenues from oil and gas were based on oil prices averaging $17 per barrel in 1998, a target which some analysts considered to be unrealistic. To balance a sharp increase in current expenditure in 1998, capital spending was reduced substantially.

During the 1970s Algeria borrowed heavily on the international markets to finance development, especially in its gas industry. Borrowing on the Euromarket, principally by SONATRACH, in one peak year, 1978, amounted to $2,515m. In 1979 total borrowing declined by almost one-third to around $2,000m. The total borrowing requirement for the 1980–84 Plan was estimated at $10,000m. Algeria avoided the Euromarkets during 1980–83, but after 1983 the country again began to borrow heavily on the international markets, owing to a steady erosion of its earnings from hydrocarbons. Algeria's return to the international capital markets in 1983 ended a period during which the Government had managed to effect a net repayment of its external debt. The OECD estimated that total external debt rose from $17,924m. at the end of 1983 to $25,757m. at the end of 1993. The cost of servicing the debt in the latter year was equivalent to 89% of Algeria's export earnings.

As detailed under the section on Government Strategy above, major reschedulings of sovereign debt (through the 'Paris Club' of 17 creditor governments) and of commercial debt (through the 'London Club' of creditor banks) had been completed by 1996, temporarily eliminating the short-term component within Algeria's external debt and leaving a total long-term debt of $30,800m. at the end of 1996. In 1995 the debt-servicing requirement as a proportion of export earnings was 44% (but would have been 85% without rescheduling); in 1996 it was 29% (but would have been 53% without rescheduling). Statistics published by the World Bank in mid-1996 gave Algeria's 'financing gap' for 1995 as $6,000m., which was covered by $3,770m. of 'Paris Club' rescheduling, $1,010m. of 'London Club' rescheduling and $1,220m. of balance-of-payments support from the IMF, World Bank and other sources. In 1996 a gap of $4,780m. was covered by 'Paris Club' rescheduling ($2,810m.), 'London Club' rescheduling ($920m.) and balance-of-payments support ($1,050m.). By 1998 the World Bank expected the financing gap to be below $1,000m., and to be covered by $560m. of 'Paris Club' rescheduling and $400m. of balance-of-payments support. The first repayment of Algeria's 'London Club' debt was made in March 1998. During 1998, as the grace period in the 'Paris Club' and 'London Club' rescheduling agreements neared their end, debt-service repayments were forecast to rise to $5,210m. In April 1998 the Banque d'Algérie announced that Algeria's total foreign debt stood at $31,222m. at the end of 1997, equivalent to 66.4% of GDP, down from 73.5% in 1996. In May Abdelkrim Harchaoui, the Minister of Finance, stated that, despite falling petroleum prices, external debt-servicing would not absorb more than 50% of foreign exchange reserves over the following three years.

According to IMF data, Algeria's foreign exchange reserves minus gold amounted to only $404m. in July 1991, as the Government came under pressure to meet debt repayments, but rose to $1,094m. in October. In June 1993 officials of the Banque d'Algérie stated that reserves had been increased to $2,000m., the highest level since 1986, as a result of the Government's austerity programme. By the end of 1993, however, they had decreased again to $1,510m. Subsequent end-year reserves levels were $2,640m. (1994), $2,110m. (1995) and $4,230m. (1996). At the end of June 1997 the reserves totalled $6,440m., representing around nine months' import cover. However, in May 1998 Harchaoui stated that foreign exchange reserves currently stood at $8,800m.

Statistical Survey

Source (unless otherwise stated): Office National des Statistiques, 8 rue des Moussebiline, BP 55, Algiers; tel. (2) 64-77-90; telex 52620.

Area and Population

AREA, POPULATION AND DENSITY

Area (sq km)	2,381,741*
Population (census results)†	
12 February 1977 (provisional)	16,948,000
20 April 1987	23,038,942
Population (official estimates at mid-year)†	
1994	27,902,000
1995	28,548,000
1996	29,168,000
Density (per sq km) at mid-1996	12.2

* 919,595 sq miles.

† Excluding Algerian nationals residing abroad, numbering an estimated 828,000 at 1 January 1978.

POPULATION BY WILAYA (ADMINISTRATIVE DISTRICT)

(provisional census results, April 1987)*

	Population
Adrar	216,931
el-Asnam (ech-Cheliff)	679,717
Laghouat	215,183
Oum el-Bouaghi (Oum el-Bouagul) . .	402,683
Batna	757,059
Béjaia	697,669
Biskra (Beskra)	429,217
Béchar	183,896
Blida (el-Boulaïda)	704,462
Bouira	525,460
Tamanrasset (Tamenghest)	94,219
Tébessa (Tbessa)	409,317
Tlemcen (Tilimsen)	707,453
Tiaret (Tihert)	574,786
Tizi-Ouzou	931,501
Algiers (el-Djezaïr)	1,687,579
Djelfa (el-Djelfa)	490,240
Jijel	471,319
Sétif (Stif)	997,482
Saida	235,240
Skikda	619,094
Sidi-Bel-Abbès	444,047
Annaba	453,951
Guelma	353,329
Constantine (Qacentina)	662,330
Médéa (Lemdiyya)	650,623
Mostaganem (Mestghanem)	504,124
M'Sila	605,578
Mascara (Mouaskar)	562,806
Ouargla (Wargla)	286,696
Oran (Ouahran)	916,678
el-Bayadh	155,494
Illizi	19,698
Bordj Bou Arreridj	429,009
Boumerdes	646,870
el-Tarf	276,836
Tindouf	16,339
Tissemsilt	227,542
el-Oued	379,512
Khenchela	243,733
Souk-Ahras	298,236
Tipaza	615,140
Mila	511,047
Ain-Defla	536,205
Naama	112,858
Ain-Temouchent	271,454
Ghardaia	215,955
Relizane	545,061
Total	22,971,558

* Excluding Algerian nationals abroad, estimated to total 828,000 at 1 January 1978.

PRINCIPAL TOWNS (estimated population at 1 January 1983)

Algiers (el-Djezaïr, capital) . .	1,721,607	Tlemcen (Tilimsen) .	146,089
		Skikda . . .	141,159
Oran (Ouahran) .	663,504	Béjaia . . .	124,122
Constantine (Qacentina) . .	448,578	Batna . . .	122,788
		El-Asnam (ech-Cheliff) . .	118,996
Annaba . .	348,322	Boufarik . .	112,000*
Blida (el-Boulaïda) .	191,314	Tizi-Ouzou . .	100,749
Sétif (Stif) . .	186,978	Médéa (Lemdiyya) .	84,292
Sidi-bel-Abbès . .	146,653		

* 1977 figure.

April 1987 (census results, not including suburbs): Algiers 1,483,000; Oran 590,000; Constantine 438,000.

BIRTHS AND DEATHS (UN estimates, annual averages)

	1980–85	1985–90	1990–95
Birth rate (per 1,000) . . .	40.6	33.9	29.1
Death rate (per 1,000) . . .	10.4	7.8	6.4

Expectation of life (UN estimates, years at birth, 1990–95): 67.1 (males 66.0; females 68.3).

Source: UN, *World Population Prospects: The 1994 Revision.*

1993 (provisional): Registered live births 776,000 (birth rate 28.8 per 1,000); Registered deaths 166,000 (death rate 6.2 per 1,000).

1994 (provisional): Registered live births 776,000 (birth rate 28.2 per 1,000); Registered deaths 180,000 (death rate 6.5 per 1,000).

Note: Figures refer to the Algerian population only and exclude live-born infants dying before registration of birth. Birth registration is estimated to be at least 90% complete, but death registration is incomplete.

ECONOMICALLY ACTIVE POPULATION (1987 census)*

	Males	Females	Total
Agriculture, hunting, forestry and fishing	714,947	9,753	724,699
Mining and quarrying . .	64,685	3,142	67,825
Manufacturing	471,471	40,632	512,105
Electricity, gas and water . .	40,196	1,579	41,775
Construction	677,211	12,372	689,586
Trade, restaurants and hotels .	376,590	14,399	390,990
Transport, storage and communications . .	207,314	9,029	216,343
Financing, insurance, real estate and business services . .	125,426	17,751	143,178
Community, social and personal services . . .	945,560	234,803	1,180,364
Activities not adequately defined .	149,241	83,718	232,959
Total employed . . .	3,772,641	427,183	4,199,824
Unemployed	1,076,018	65,260	1,141,278
Total labour force . . .	4,848,659	492,443	5,341,102

* Employment data relate to persons aged 6 years and over; those for unemployment relate to persons aged 16 to 64 years. Estimates have been made independently, so the totals may not be the sum of the component parts.

Mid-1996 (estimates in '000): Agriculture, etc. 2,153; Total labour force 9,041 (Source: FAO, *Production Yearbook*).

Agriculture

PRINCIPAL CROPS ('000 metric tons)

	1994	1995	1996
Wheat	714	1,500	2,800
Barley	234	585	1,690
Oats	15	53	110
Potatoes	716	1,200	1,500
Pulses	38	39	50
Rapeseed*	99	99	100
Olives	170	131	313
Tomatoes	695	859	718
Pumpkins, squash and gourds	100	100*	100*
Cucumbers and gherkins	40	41*	41*
Green chillies and peppers	80	133*	133*
Onions (dry)	248	314	313
Carrots	158	132	129
Other vegetables	424	423	424
Melons and watermelons	401	400*	400*
Grapes	120	159	132
Dates	317	285	361
Apples	49	64	74
Pears	36	37*	37*
Peaches and nectarines	36	45*	45*
Oranges	253	227	237
Tangerines, mandarins, clementines and satsumas	100	78	80
Apricots	43	43*	43*
Other fruits	130	125	124
Tobacco (leaves)	4	3	4

* FAO estimate(s).

Source: FAO, *Production Yearbook.*

LIVESTOCK ('000 head, year ending September)

	1994	1995	1996
Sheep	17,842	17,302	17,565
Goats	2,544	2,780	2,895
Cattle	1,269	1,267	1,228
Horses	67	67*	67*
Mules	81	82*	82*
Asses	226	230*	230*
Camels	114	115*	115*

* FAO estimate.

Poultry (million): 89 in 1994; 90 in 1995; 90 in 1996.

Source: FAO, *Production Yearbook.*

LIVESTOCK PRODUCTS ('000 metric tons)

	1994	1995	1996
Beef and veal	101	101	104
Mutton and lamb	169	170	175
Goat meat*	8	8	9
Poultry meat*	202	202	202
Other meat	9	10	9
Cows' milk*	530	530	530
Sheep's milk*	220	220	220
Goats' milk*	125	125	125
Poultry eggs*	150	150	150
Honey*	2	2	2
Wool:			
greasy*	50	50	50
clean*	26	26	26
Cattle hides*	13	13	13
Sheepskins*	29	26	27
Goatskins*	2	2	2

* FAO estimates.

Source: FAO, *Production Yearbook.*

Forestry

ROUNDWOOD REMOVALS ('000 cubic metres, excluding bark)

	1993	1994	1995
Sawlogs, veneer logs and logs for sleepers	90	64	40
Pulpwood	97	62	79
Other industrial wood	258	264	270
Fuel wood	2,035	2,081	2,128
Total	2,480	2,471	2,517

Sawnwood production ('000 cubic metres, incl. railway sleepers): 13 per year (FAO estimates) in 1980–95.

Source: FAO, *Yearbook of Forest Products.*

Fishing

('000 metric tons, live weight)

	1993	1994	1995
European pilchard (sardine)	67.3*	95.8*	59.0
Other fishes	29.6*	36.0*	44.3
Crustaceans and molluscs	5.0*	3.6*	3.0
Total catch	101.9	135.4	106.2
Inland waters	0.3	0.4	0.3
Mediterranean Sea	101.6	135.0	105.9

* FAO estimate.

Source: FAO, *Yearbook of Fishery Statistics.*

Mining

('000 metric tons, unless otherwise indicated)

	1993	1994	1995
Hard coal*	20	20	22
Crude petroleum	35,086	35,330	36,152
Natural gas (petajoules)	2,102	1,996	2,431
Iron ore:			
gross weight	2,311	2,016	2,000*
metal content	1,250	1,089	1,000†
Lead ores or concentrates‡	1.5	1.1	0.7†
Zinc concentrates‡	6.8	5.6	3.0†
Mercury (metric tons)	458	414†	292†
Phosphate rock	717	763	757
Salt (unrefined)	59	75	n.a.

* Provisional or estimated data.
† Data from the US Bureau of Mines.
‡ Figures refer to the metal content of ores or concentrates.

Sources: UN, *Industrial Commodity Statistics Yearbook* and *Monthly Bulletin of Statistics.*

Industry

SELECTED PRODUCTS ('000 metric tons, unless otherwise indicated)

	1993	1994	1995
Olive oil (crude)	22	14	15
Refined sugar	201	193	n.a.
Wine	65	50	57*
Beer ('000 hectolitres)	421	398	n.a.
Soft drinks ('000 hectolitres)	1,007	901	n.a.
Cigarettes (metric tons)	16,260	16,345	n.a.
Footwear—excl. rubber ('000 pairs)	7,171	6,467	n.a.
Nitrogenous fertilizers	80	62	n.a.
Phosphate fertilizers	204	179	n.a.
Naphthas†	4,400	4,500	4,400
Motor spirit (petrol)	2,469	2,907	2,576
Kerosene†	129	200	250
Jet fuel†	350	900	784
Distillate fuel oils	7,543	6,896	7,189
Residual fuel oils	5,827	5,810	5,535
Lubricating oils†	140	140	150
Petroleum bitumen (asphalt)†	240	250	260

— continued		1993	1994	1995
Liquefied petroleum gas:				
from natural gas plants	.	4,570	4,510	4,384
from petroleum refineries	.	430	520	510†
Cement	.	6,951	6,093	6,200†
Pig-iron for steel-making .	.	925	919	900‡
Crude steel (ingots) . .	.	798	772	827‡
Zinc—unwrought	.	29.7	20.1	24.0‡
Refrigerators for household use				
('000)	.	183	119	n.a.
Radio receivers ('000).	.	109	107	n.a.
Television receivers ('000)	.	157	94	n.a.
Buses and coaches—assembled				
(number)	.	596	468	n.a.
Lorries—assembled (number) .	.	2,304	1,230	n.a.
Electric energy (million kWh) .	.	19,415	19,888	19,714

* Data from FAO, *Quarterly Bulletin of Statistics*.
† Provisional or estimated data.
‡ Data from the US Bureau of Mines.

Source: mainly UN, *Industrial Commodity Statistics Yearbook*.

1996 ('000 metric tons): Olive oil 48; Wine 39.
1997 (FAO estimates, '000 metric tons): Olive oil 47; Wine 50.

(Source: FAO, *Quarterly Bulletin of Statistics*.)

Finance

CURRENCY AND EXCHANGE RATES

Monetary Units
100 centimes = 1 Algerian dinar (AD).

Sterling and Dollar Equivalents (31 May 1998)
£1 sterling = 95.26 dinars;
US $1 = 58.41 dinars;
1,000 Algerian dinars = £10.50 = $17.12.

Average Exchange Rate (dinars per US $)
1995   47.663
1996   54.749
1997   57.707

BUDGET ('000 million AD)*

Revenue		1994	1995	1996
Hydrocarbon revenue.	.	257.7	358.8	519.7
Export taxes	.	197.2	305.2	451.0
Domestic receipts	.	37.7	30.9	45.0
Dividends and entry rights .	.	22.8	22.7	23.7
Other revenue	.	176.5	242.1	305.1
Tax revenue	.	163.2	233.2	290.5
Taxes on income and profits	.	42.8	53.6	67.5
Taxes on goods and services	.	65.9	99.9	129.5
Customs duties	.	47.9	73.3	84.4
Non-tax revenue	.	13.3	8.9	14.6
Total	.	**434.2**	**600.9**	**824.8**

Expenditure†		1994	1995	1996
Current expenditure .	.	344.7	444.4	550.6
Personnel expenditure .	.	151.7	187.5	222.8
War veterans' pensions .	.	12.8	15.6	18.9
Material and supplies .	.	18.2	29.4	34.7
Current transfers .	.	120.9	149.7	185.2
Public services	.	42.3	55.5	69.9
Family allowances	.	14.1	24.5	36.4
Public works and social				
assistance. . .	.	11.8	13.6	14.2
Food subsidies .	.	30.9	18.3	11.9
Housing. . .	.	3.7	7.9	18.1
Interest payments .	.	41.1	62.2	89.0
Capital expenditure .	.	117.2	144.7	174.0
Total	.	**461.9**	**589.1**	**724.6**

* Figures refer to operations of the central Government, excluding special accounts. The balance (revenue less expenditure) on such accounts (in '000 million AD) was: 1.1 in 1994; −0.7 in 1995; 1.5 in 1996.
† Excluding net lending by the Treasury ('000 million AD): 7.0 in 1994; 2.4 in 1995; 2.4 in 1996. Also excluded are allocations to the Rehabilitation Fund ('000 million AD): 31.7 in 1994; 36.9 in 1995; 24.4 in 1996.

Source: IMF, *Algeria—Statistical Appendix* (October 1997).

CENTRAL BANK RESERVES (US $ million at 31 December)

	1995	1996	1997
Gold*	290	281	264
IMF special drawing rights . .	1	5	1
Foreign exchange . . .	2,004	4,230	8,046
Total	**2,295**	**4,516**	**8,311**

* Valued at SDR 35 per troy ounce.
Source: IMF, *International Financial Statistics*.

MONEY SUPPLY (million AD at 31 December)*

	1993	1994	1995
Currency outside banks . . .	211,310	222,990	249,770
Demand deposits at deposit money banks. . . .	188,930	196,450	210,780
Checking deposits at post office .	40,980	48,500	53,740
Private sector demand deposits at treasury	5,680	7,890	4,820
Total money (incl. others) . .	**450,320**	**485,650**	**520,290**

* Figures are rounded to the nearest 10 million dinars.
Source: IMF, *International Financial Statistics*.

COST OF LIVING (Consumer Price Index for Algiers; average of monthly figures; base: 1989 = 100)

	1994	1995	1996
Foodstuffs, beverages and tobacco	325.6	425.9	510.7
Clothing and footwear . . .	255.8	306.3	347.7
Housing costs	266.6	360.0	454.0
All items (incl. others) . . .	**303.8**	**394.4**	**468.2**

Source: IMF, *Algeria—Statistical Appendix* (October 1997).

NATIONAL ACCOUNTS

National Income and Product (million AD at current prices)

	1987	1988	1989
Compensation of employees .	125,754.4	137,647.5	156,145.1
Operating surplus . . .	92,417.5	99,899.8	142,711.2
Domestic factor incomes . .	**218,171.9**	**237,547.3**	**298,856.3**
Consumption of fixed capital .	32,525.2	32,621.8	33,050.1
Gross domestic product (GDP) at factor cost	**250,697.1**	**270,169.1**	**331,906.4**
Indirect taxes, *less* subsidies .	62,009.0	64,437.5	71,553.8
GDP in purchasers' values .	**312,706.1**	**334,606.6**	**403,460.2**
Net factor income from abroad	−7,267.7	−11,744.7	−13,178.4
Reinsurance (net) . . .	−76.0	—	—
Gross national product .	**305,362.4**	**322,861.9**	**390,281.8**
Less Consumption of fixed capital .	32,525.2	32,621.8	33,050.1
National income in market prices	**272,837.2**	**290,240.1**	**357,231.7**
Other current transfers from abroad (net)	2,358.2	2,067.7	3,850.4
National disposable income .	**275,195.4**	**292,307.8**	**361,082.1**

Expenditure on the Gross Domestic Product
('000 million AD at current prices)

	1994	1995	1996*
Government final consumption expenditure	247.1	309.7	356.4
Private final consumption expenditure . . .	825.6	1,097.4	1,318.4
Increase in stocks	41.7	52.4	−40.0
Gross fixed capital formation . .	426.2	580.0	690.7
Total domestic expenditure .	1,540.6	2,039.5	2,325.5
Exports of goods and services . .	349.4	539.8	791.1
Less Imports of goods and services .	418.6	612.7	614.6
GDP in purchasers' values . .	1,471.4	1,966.5	2,502.0

* Preliminary.

Source: IMF, *Algeria — Statistical Appendix* (October 1997).

Gross Domestic Product by Economic Activity
('000 million AD at current prices)

	1994	1995	1996
Agriculture, forestry and fishing .	140.5	190.0	271.9
Mining and quarrying* . . .	336.4	505.8	736.3
Manufacturing*	137.0	181.8	201.8
Energy (non-hydrocarbon) . .	15.2	23.8	34.4
Construction and public works .	166.9	200.7	233.5
Government services . . .	187.0	230.3	260.9
Non-government services . . .	354.5	453.4	550.9
Sub-total	1,352.3†	1,785.9	2,289.7
Import taxes and duties . .	122.4	180.6	212.3
GDP in purchasers' values .	1,474.7	1,966.5	2,502.0

* Processing of petroleum and natural gas is included in mining and excluded from manufacturing.
† Including adjustment.

Source: IMF, *Algeria — Statistical Appendix* (October 1997).

BALANCE OF PAYMENTS (US $ '000 million)

	1994	1995	1996
Exports of goods f.o.b. . . .	8.9	10.3	13.2
Imports of goods f.o.b. . . .	−9.2	−10.1	−9.1
Trade balance	−0.3	0.2	4.1
Exports of services . . .	0.7	0.7	0.8
Imports of services . . .	−1.9	−2.0	−2.2
Balance on goods and services .	−1.5	−1.1	2.7
Other income received . .	0.1	0.1	0.2
Other income paid . . .	−1.8	−2.3	−2.6
Balance on goods, services and income	−3.2	−3.3	0.3
Transfers (net)	1.4	1.1	0.9
Current balance . . .	−1.8	−2.2	1.2
Direct investment (net) . .	0.0	0.0	0.3
Official capital (net) . . .	−2.5	−3.9	−3.4
Short-term credit (net) . . .	−0.1	0.1	−0.2
Net errors and omissions . .	0.0	−0.2	0.0
Overall balance . . .	−4.4	−6.3	−2.1

Source: IMF, *Algeria — Statistical Appendix* (October 1997).

External Trade

Note: Data exclude military goods. Exports include stores and bunkers for foreign ships and aircraft.

PRINCIPAL COMMODITIES (distribution by SITC, US $ million)

Imports c.i.f.	1992	1993	1994
Food and live animals . . .	2,121.1	2,155.5	2,848.9
Dairy products and birds' eggs .	641.6	654.0	540.8
Milk and cream . . .	558.7	569.4	493.7
Cereals and cereal preparations .	772.8	904.2	1,324.1
Wheat and meslin (unmilled) .	320.9	353.8	602.4
Meal and flour of wheat, etc. .	231.8	281.3	323.2
Sugar, sugar preparations and honey	178.3	253.3	298.1
Sugar and honey . . .	177.3	253.3	297.3
Coffee, tea, cocoa and spices . .	165.8	113.9	336.7
Coffee and coffee substitutes .	56.9	105.8	308.2
Crude materials (inedible) except fuels	331.0	386.0	378.6
Animal and vegetable oils, fats and waxes	292.8	184.2	222.9
Fixed vegetable oils and fats . .	248.9	153.1	188.7
Chemicals and related products	922.3	895.4	1,027.0
Medicinal and pharmaceutical products	442.6	366.7	509.8
Medicaments (incl. veterinary) .	406.6	334.7	473.9
Basic manufactures . . .	1,859.6	1,905.6	2,087.4
Rubber manufactures . .	130.4	180.3	140.8
Non-metallic mineral manufactures	206.5	194.7	246.0
Iron and steel	824.2	740.3	913.6
Bars, rods, angles, shapes and sections	313.2	254.0	418.2
Bars and rods (excl. wire rod)	218.8	161.0	335.9
Tubes, pipes and fittings . .	271.3	224.8	325.3
Machinery and transport equipment	2,646.6	2,784.1	2,572.2
Power-generating machinery and equipment	199.5	355.6	398.5
Machinery specialized for particular industries . . .	418.0	241.2	232.9
General industrial machinery, equipment and parts . .	767.0	974.1	739.5
Heating and cooling equipment .	190.1	251.4	158.2
Telecommunications and sound equipment	179.0	135.9	134.1
Other electrical machinery, apparatus, etc. . . .	452.0	508.4	507.9
Switchgear, etc., and parts . .	122.7	164.0	217.3
Road vehicles and parts* . . .	394.1	351.7	348.2
Miscellaneous manufactured articles	306.9	299.9	321.8
Total (incl. others)	8,647.8	8,785.3	9,598.7

* Excluding tyres, engines and electrical parts.

Exports f.o.b.	1992	1993	1994
Mineral fuels, lubricants, etc. .	10,759.1	9,679.2	8,342.0
Petroleum, petroleum products, etc.	7,051.9	6,339.7	5,585.5
Crude petroleum oils, etc. .	4,806.7	4,448.7	3,924.5
Refined petroleum products .	2,161.2	1,828.8	1,617.0
Motor spirit (petrol) and other light oils	691.4	539.8	564.2
Gas oils (distillate fuels) . .	779.7	677.0	494.1
Residual fuel oils . .	669.1	587.8	485.2
Gas (natural and manufactured) .	3,643.6	3,329.9	2,677.6
Liquefied petroleum gases . .	2,574.8	2,198.8	1,773.9
Petroleum gases, etc., in the gaseous state . . .	1,068.7	1,131.0	903.7
Total (incl. others)	11,136.8	10,097.7	8,593.8

Source: UN, *International Trade Statistics Yearbook*.

PRINCIPAL TRADING PARTNERS (US $ million)*

Imports c.i.f.	1992	1993	1994
Austria	174.7	172.5	286.6
Belgium-Luxembourg . .	256.7	164.6	214.7
Brazil	41.0	79.4	126.4
Canada	179.5	120.0	156.5
China, People's Republic . .	157.1	248.0	383.1
France	2,097.0	2,240.6	2,376.3
Germany	752.2	469.1	517.1
Indonesia	55.2	216.5	240.2
Italy	1,242.4	952.1	931.4
Japan	385.0	375.9	254.0
Morocco	96.9	84.8	120.6
Netherlands	121.1	159.5	109.6
New Zealand . . .	59.1	96.7	76.9
Spain	832.2	926.2	901.3
Switzerland	87.4	69.8	91.8
Tunisia	123.7	122.5	138.5
Turkey	131.0	108.5	250.4
United Kingdom . . .	96.9	119.1	132.0
USA	954.2	1,311.5	1,371.9
Total (incl. others) . . .	8,647.8	8,785.3	9,598.7

Exports f.o.b.	1992	1993	1994
Austria	206.9	67.2	161.2
Belgium-Luxembourg . .	796.0	627.8	528.5
Brazil	351.0	443.8	195.2
Canada	33.2	158.2	174.1
France	2,037.8	1,688.6	1,326.2
Germany	524.0	504.2	524.8
Italy	2,414.6	2,219.7	1,535.1
Morocco	136.5	70.7	101.3
Netherlands	896.0	784.5	885.0
Portugal	157.8	284.7	285.0
Russia	126.2	126.3	40.0
Singapore	58.1	154.2	59.9
Spain	846.1	679.2	650.2
Tunisia	78.3	62.2	113.1
United Kingdom . . .	377.4	192.4	140.0
USA	1,553.4	1,608.7	1,414.0
Total (incl. others) . . .	11,136.8	10,097.7	8,593.8

* Imports by country of production; exports by country of last consignment.

Source: UN, *International Trade Statistics Yearbook*.

1995 (US $ million): Imports c.i.f. 10,250; Exports f.o.b. 10,240 (source: UN, *Monthly Bulletin of Statistics*).

Transport

RAILWAYS (traffic)

	1990	1991	1992
Passengers carried ('000) . . .	53,664	57,841	58,422
Freight carried ('000 metric tons) .	12,357	11,939	11,112
Passenger-km (million) . .	2,991	3,192	2,904
Freight ton-km (million) . .	2,690	2,710	2,523

ROAD TRAFFIC ('000 motor vehicles in use)

	1993	1994	1995
Passenger cars	1,547.8	1,555.8	1,562.1
Commercial vehicles . . .	926.0	930.8	933.1

Source: UN, *Statistical Yearbook*.

SHIPPING

Merchant Fleet (registered at 31 December)

	1994	1995	1996
Number of vessels . . .	148	151	151
Total displacement ('000 grt) .	935.8	980.5	982.5

Source: Lloyd's Register of Shipping, *World Fleet Statistics*.

International Sea-borne Freight Traffic (estimates, '000 metric tons)

	1991	1992	1993
Goods loaded	59,430	61,577	63,110
Goods unloaded	15,100	15,600	15,700

Source: UN Economic Commission for Africa, *African Statistical Yearbook*.

CIVIL AVIATION (traffic on scheduled services)

	1993	1994	1995
Kilometres flown (million) . .	36	36	31
Passengers carried ('000) . .	3,254	3,241	3,478
Passenger-km (million) . .	2,901	2,706	2,855
Total ton-km (million) . .	296	268	278

Source: UN, *Statistical Yearbook*.

Tourism

FOREIGN TOURIST ARRIVALS BY COUNTRY OF ORIGIN

	1994	1995	1996
France	38,581	26,349	35,214
Germany	2,416	1,398	1,467
Italy	8,788	2,791	2,541
Libya	11,014	7,698	6,349
Morocco	180,673	4,797	2,067
Spain	2,137	1,621	1,826
Tunisia	56,805	24,207	19,966
Total (incl. others) . . .	336,226	97,650	93,491

Source: Ministère du Tourisme et de l'Artisanat.

Communications Media

	1992	1993	1994
Radio receivers ('000 in use) . .	6,160	6,310	6,450
Television receivers ('000 in use) .	2,000	2,100	2,150
Telephones ('000 main lines in use)	962	1,068	1,122
Telefax stations (number in use) .	5,000	5,500*	4,138*
Mobile cellular telephones (subscribers)	4,781	4,781	1,348
Daily newspapers			
Number	5	n.a.	6
Average circulation ('000 copies)	1,000	n.a.	1,250

* Estimate.

Telephones (main lines in use, 1995): 1,176,000.
Telefax stations (estimated number in use, 1995): 5,200.
Mobile cellular telephones (subscribers, 1995): 4,691.

Sources: UNESCO, *Statistical Yearbook*, and UN, *Statistical Yearbook*.

Education

(1995/96)

	Institutions	Teachers	Pupils
Primary	17,186	169,010	4,617,000
Middle	2,921	98,187	1,691,561
Secondary	1,033	52,210	853,303

Source: Ministère de l'Education nationale.

Higher education (1994/95): Teachers 20,026; Students 298,767 (Source: UNESCO, *Statistical Yearbook*).

Directory

The Constitution

A new Constitution for the Democratic and People's Republic of Algeria, approved by popular referendum, was promulgated on 22 November 1976. The Constitution was amended by the National People's Assembly on 30 June 1979. Further amendments were approved by referendum on 3 November 1988, on 23 February 1989, and on 28 November 1996. The main provisions of the Constitution, as amended, are summarized below:

The preamble recalls that Algeria owes its independence to a war of liberation which led to the creation of a modern sovereign state, guaranteeing social justice, equality and liberty for all. It emphasizes Algeria's Islamic, Arab and Amazigh heritage, and stresses that, as an Arab Mediterranean and African country, it forms an integral part of the Great Arab Maghreb.

FUNDAMENTAL PRINCIPLES OF THE ORGANIZATION OF ALGERIAN SOCIETY

The Republic

Algeria is a popular, democratic state. Islam is the state religion and Arabic is the official national language.

The People

National sovereignty resides in the people and is exercised through its elected representatives. The institutions of the State consolidate national unity and protect the fundamental rights of its citizens. The exploitation of one individual by another is forbidden.

The State

The State is exclusively at the service of the people. Those holding positions of responsibility must live solely on their salaries and may not, directly or by the agency of others, engage in any remunerative activity.

Fundamental Freedoms and the Rights of Man and the Citizen

Fundamental rights and freedoms are guaranteed. All discrimination on grounds of sex, race or belief is forbidden. Law cannot operate retrospectively and a person is presumed innocent until proved guilty. Victims of judicial error shall receive compensation from the State.

The State guarantees the inviolability of the home, of private life and of the person. The State also guarantees the secrecy of correspondence, the freedom of conscience and opinion, freedom of intellectual, artistic and scientific creation, and freedom of expression and assembly.

The State guarantees the right to form political associations (on condition that they are not based on differences in religion, language, race, gender or region), to join a trade union, the right to strike, the right to work, to protection, to security, to health, to leisure, to education, etc. It also guarantees the right to leave the national territory, within the limits set by law.

Duties of Citizens

Every citizen must respect the Constitution, and must protect public property and safeguard national independence. The law sanctions the duty of parents to educate and protect their children, as well as the duty of children to help and support their parents. Every citizen must contribute towards public expenditure through the payment of taxes.

The National Popular Army

The army safeguards national independence and sovereignty.

Principles of Foreign Policy

Algeria subscribes to the principles and objectives of the UN. It advocates international co-operation, the development of friendly relations between states, on the basis of equality and mutual interest, and non-interference in the internal affairs of states.

POWER AND ITS ORGANIZATION

The Executive

The President of the Republic is Head of State, Head of the Armed Forces and responsible for national defence. He must be of Algerian origin, a Muslim and more than 40 years old. He is elected by universal, secret, direct suffrage. His mandate is for five years, and is renewable once. The President embodies the unity of the nation. The President presides over meetings of the Council of Ministers. He decides and conducts foreign policy and appoints the Head of Government, who is responsible to the National People's Assembly.

The Head of Government must appoint a Council of Ministers. He drafts, co-ordinates and implements his government's programme, which he must present to the Assembly for ratification. Should the Assembly reject the programme, the Head of Government and the Council of Ministers resign, and the President appoints a new Head of Government. Should the newly-appointed Head of Government's programme be rejected by the Assembly, the President dissolves the Assembly, and a general election is held. Should the President be unable to perform his functions, owing to a long and serious illness, the President of the Council of the Nation assumes the office for a maximum period of 45 days (subject to the approval of a two-thirds majority in the National People's Assembly and the Council of the Nation). If the President is still unable to perform his functions after 45 days, the Presidency is declared vacant by the Constitutional Council. Should the Presidency fall vacant, the President of the Council of the Nation temporarily assumes the office and organizes presidential elections within 60 days. He may not himself be a candidate in the election. The President presides over a High Security Council which advises on all matters affecting national security.

The Legislature

The legislature consists of the National People's Assembly and the Council of the Nation. The members of the National People's Assembly are elected by universal, direct, secret suffrage for a five-year term. Two-thirds of the members of the Council of the Nation are elected by indirect, secret suffrage from regional and municipal authorities; the remainder are appointed by the President of the Republic. The Council's term in office is six years; one-half of its members are replaced every three years. The deputies enjoy parliamentary immunity. The legislature sits for two ordinary sessions per year, each of not less than four months' duration. The commissions of the legislature are in permanent session. The two parliamentary chambers may be summoned to meet for an extraordinary session on the request of the President of the Republic, or of the Head of Government, or of two-thirds of the members of the National People's Assembly. Both the Head of Government and the parliamentary chambers may initiate legislation. Legislation must be deliberated upon respectively by the National People's Assembly and the Council of the Nation before promulgation. Any text passed by the Assembly must be approved by three-quarters of the members of the Council in order to become legislation.

The Judiciary

Judges obey only the law. They defend society and fundamental freedoms. The right of the accused to a defence is guaranteed. The Supreme Court regulates the activities of courts and tribunals, and the State Council regulates the administrative judiciary. The Higher Court of the Magistrature is presided over by the President of the Republic; the Minister of Justice is Vice-President of the Court. All magistrates are answerable to the Higher Court for the manner in which they fulfil their functions. The High State Court is empowered to judge the President of the Republic in cases of high treason, and the Head of Government for crimes and offences.

The Constitutional Council

The Constitutional Council is responsible for ensuring that the Constitution is respected, and that referendums, the election of the President of the Republic and legislative elections are conducted in accordance with the law. The Constitutional Council comprises nine members, of whom three are appointed by the President of the Republic, two elected by the National People's Assembly, two elected by the Council of the Nation, one elected by the Supreme Court and one elected by the State Council. The Council's term in office is six years; the President of the Council is appointed for a six-year term and one-half of the remaining members are replaced every three years.

The High Islamic Council

The High Islamic Council is an advisory body on matters relating to Islam. The Council comprises 15 members and its President is appointed by the President of the Republic.

Constitutional Revision

The Constitution can be revised on the initiative of the President of the Republic (subject to approval by the National People's Assembly and by three-quarters of the members of the Council of the Nation), and must be approved by national referendum. Should the Constitutional Council decide that a draft constitutional amendment does not in any way affect the general principles governing Algerian society, it may permit the President of the Republic to promulgate the amendment directly (without submitting it to referendum) if it has been approved by three-quarters of the members of both parliamentary chambers. Three-quarters of the members of both parliamentary chambers, in a joint sitting, may propose a constitutional amendment to the President of the Republic who may submit it to referendum. The basic principles of the Constitution may not be revised.

The Government

HEAD OF STATE

President and Minister of Defence: LIAMINE ZÉROUAL (appointed 30 January 1994; elected President 16 November 1995).

COUNCIL OF MINISTERS
(September 1998)

A coalition of the Rassemblement national démocratique (RND), the Front de libération nationale (FLN) and the Mouvement de la société pour la paix (MSP).

Prime Minister: AHMED OUYAHIA (RND).

Minister of Foreign Affairs: AHMED ATTAF (RND).

Minister of Justice: MUHAMMAD ADAMI (RND).

Minister of the Interior, Local Communities and the Environment : MUSTAPHA BENMANSOUR (RND).

Minister of Finance: ABDELKRIM HARCHAOUI (RND).

Minister of Energy and Mines: YOUCEF YOUSFI (RND).

Minister of Equipment and of National and Regional Development: ABDERRAHMANE BELAYAT (FLN).

Minister of Industry and Restructuring: ABEDELMAJID MENASRA (MSP).

Minister of War Veterans: SAÏD ABADOU (RND).

Minister of National Education: BOUBEKEUR BENBOUZID (RND).

Minister of Higher Education and Scientific Research: AMAR TOU (FLN).

Minister of Small and Medium-sized Enterprises: BOUGUERRA SOLTANI (MSP).

Minister of Health and Population: YAHIA GUIDOUM (RND).

Minister of Labour, Social Affairs and Vocational Training: HACÈNE LASKRI (RND).

Minister of Agriculture and Fisheries: BOULAHAOUADJEB BENALIA (FLN).

Minister of Tourism and Handicrafts: ABDELKADER BENGRINA (MSP).

Minister of Posts and Telecommunications: MUHAMMAD SALAH YOUYOU (RND).

Minister of Religious Affairs: BOUABDELLAH GHLAMALLAH (RND).

Minister of Housing: ABDELKADER BOUNEKRAF (FLN).

Minister of Transport: SID AHMED BOULIL (MSP).

Minister of Commerce: BAKHTI BELAIB (RND).

Minister of National Solidarity and the Family: RABEA MECHERNENE (RND).

Minister of Youth and Sports: MUHAMMAD AZIZ DEROUAZ (RND).

Minister of Communications and Culture, and Spokesman for the Government: HABIB CHAWKI HAMRAOUI (RND).

Minister of Parliamentary Affairs: MUHAMMAD KECHOUD (RND).

Minister Delegate to the Prime Minister in charge of the governorship of Algiers: CHERIF RAHMANI (RND).

Minister Delegate at the Office of the Prime Minister: AMAR ZEGRAR (RND).

Minister Delegate at the Office of the Prime Minister: ABDELKADER TAFFAR (RND).

Minister Delegate to the Minister of Finance in charge of the Budget: ALI BRAHITI (RND).

Minister Delegate to the Prime Minister in charge of Administrative Reform and the Civil Service: AHMED NOUI (RND).

Minister Delegate to the Minister of Foreign Affairs in charge of Co-operation and Maghreb Affairs: LAHCENE MOUSSAOUI (RND).

Secretary of State in charge of the Algerian Community Abroad: TEDJINI SALAOUANDJI (RND).

Secretary-General of the Government: MAHFOUD LACHEB.

In addition, there are seven Secretaries of State without independent portfolio (three from the MSP, three from the FLN and one from the RND).

MINISTRIES

Office of the President: Présidence de la République, el-Mouradia, Algiers; tel. (2) 69-15-15; telex 66044; fax (2) 69-15-95.

Office of the Prime Minister: rue Docteur Saâdane, Algiers; tel. (2) 73-23-40; telex 66066; fax (2) 71-79-27.

Ministry of Agriculture and Fisheries: 4 route des Quatre Canons, Algiers; tel. (2) 71-17-12; telex 66127; fax (2) 61-57-39.

Ministry of Commerce: rue Docteur Saâdane, Algiers; tel. (2) 73-23-40; telex 55273; fax (2) 73-54-18.

Ministry of Communications and Culture: Palais de la Culture, Les Annassers, Kouba, Algiers; tel. (2) 69-22-01; telex 65666; fax (2) 68-40-41.

Ministry of Defence: Les Tagarins, el-Biar, Algiers; tel. (2) 71-15-15; telex 66424; fax (2) 64-67-26.

Ministry of Energy and Mines: 80 ave Ahmed Ghermoul, Algiers; tel. (2) 67-33-00; telex 65092; fax (2) 65-27-83.

Ministry of Equipment and of National and Regional Development: BP 86, Ex Grand Séminaire, Kouba, Algiers; tel. (2) 58-65-50; telex 62560; fax (2) 58-50-38.

Ministry of Finance: Immeuble Maurétania, place du Pérou, Algiers; tel. (2) 71-13-66; telex 55073; fax (2) 73-42-76.

Ministry of Foreign Affairs: place Mohamed Seddik Benyahia, el-Mouradia, Algiers; tel. (2) 69-23-33; telex 66242; fax (2) 69-21-61.

Ministry of Health and Population: 125 rue Abd ar-Rahmane Laâla, el-Madania, Algiers; tel. (2) 68-29-00; telex 65316; fax (2) 66-24-13.

Ministry of Higher Education and Scientific Research: 11 rue Doudou Mokhtar, Algiers; tel. (2) 91-12-56; telex 61381; fax (2) 91-11-97.

Ministry of Housing: 137 rue Didouche Mourad, Algiers; tel. (2) 74-07-22; telex 66223; fax (2) 74-53-83.

Ministry of Industry and Restructuring: Immeuble le Colisée, 4 rue Ahmed Bey, Algiers; tel. (2) 60-11-44; telex 67947; fax (2) 69-32-35.

Ministry of the Interior, Local Communities and the Environment: 18 rue Docteur Saâdane, Algiers; tel. (2) 73-23-40; telex 66341; fax (2) 73-43-67.

Ministry of Justice: 8 place Bir Hakem, el-Biar, Algiers; tel. (2) 92-41-83; telex 61606; fax (2) 92-25-60.

Ministry of Labour, Social Affairs and Vocational Training: 14 blvd Mohamed Belouizdad, Algiers; tel. (2) 68-33-66; telex 65534; fax (2) 66-28-11.

Ministry of National Education: 8 ave de Pékin, Algiers; tel. (2) 69-20-98; telex 66638; fax (2) 60-67-57.

Ministry of Posts and Telecommunications: 4 blvd Krim Belkacem, Algiers; tel. (2) 71-12-20; telex 52020; fax (2) 71-76-84.

Ministry of Religious Affairs: 4 rue de Timgad, Hydra, Algiers; tel. (2) 60-85-55; telex 66118; fax (2) 60-09-36.

Ministry of Small and Medium-sized Enterprises: Immeuble le Colisée, 4 rue Ahmed Bey, Algiers; tel. (2) 23-97-11; fax (2) 69-72-73.

Ministry of Tourism and Handicrafts: 5 rue des Frères Ziata, el-Mouradia, 16000 Algiers; tel. (2) 60-59-60; telex 67758; fax (2) 59-06-64.

Ministry of Transport: 119 rue Didouche Mourad, Algiers; tel. (2) 74-06-99; telex 66137; fax (2) 74-33-95.

Ministry of War Veterans: 2 ave du Lt. Med Benarfa, el-Biar, Algiers; tel. (2) 92-23-55; telex 61370; fax (2) 92-35-16.

Ministry of Youth and Sports: 3 rue Mohamed Belouizdad, Algiers; tel. (2) 66-33-50; telex 65054; fax (2) 68-41-71.

President and Legislature

PRESIDENT

Presidential Election, 16 November 1995

Candidate	Votes	% of votes
LIAMINE ZÉROUAL	7,088,618	61.01
Sheikh MAHFOUD NAHNAH	2,971,974	25.58
SAÏD SAADI	1,115,796	9.60
NOURREDDINE BOUKROUH	443,144	3.81
Total*	11,619,532	100.00

* Excluding 467,749 spoilt votes.

ASSEMBLÉE NATIONALE POPULAIRE

President: ABDELKADER BENSALAH.

General Election, 5 June 1997

	Seats
Rassemblement national démocratique (RND) . . .	156
Mouvement de la société pour la paix (MSP) . . .	69
Front de libération nationale (FLN)	62
Nahdah	34
Front des forces socialistes (FFS)	20
Rassemblement pour la culture et la démocratie (RCD)	19
Independent	11
Parti des travailleurs (PT)	4
Parti républicain progressif (PRP)	3
Union pour la démocratie et les libertés (UDL) . .	1
Parti social-libéral (PSL)	1
Total	**380**

Constitutional amendments, approved by national referendum in November 1996, provided for the establishment of a second parliamentary chamber, the Council of the Nation. In late December 1997 two-thirds of the Council's 144 members were indirectly elected by regional and municipal authorities: the RND won 80 seats, followed by the FLN (10), the FFS (4) and the MSP (2). The remaining 48 members were appointed by the President of the Republic. The Chairman of the Council is BACHIR BOUMAAZA.

Political Organizations

Until 1989 the FLN was the only legal party in Algeria. The February 1989 amendments to the Constitution permitted the formation of other political associations, with some restrictions. The right to establish political parties was guaranteed by constitutional amendments in November 1996; however, political associations based on differences in religion, language, race, gender or region were proscribed. Some 39 political parties contested the legislative elections which took place in June 1997. The most important political organizations are listed below.

Alliance nationale républicaine: Algiers; f. 1995; anti-Islamist; Leader REDHA MALEK.

Front des forces socialistes (FFS): 56 ave Souidani Boudjemaâ, 16000 Algiers; tel. (2) 59-33-13; f. 1963; revived 1990; Leader HOCINE AÏT AHMAD.

Front islamique du salut (FIS): Algiers; f. 1989; aims to emphasize the importance of Islam in political and social life; formally dissolved by the Algiers Court of Appeal in March 1992; Leader ABBASI MADANI.

Front de libération nationale (FLN): 7 rue du Stade, Hydra, Algiers; tel. (2) 59-21-49; telex 53931; f. 1954; sole legal party until 1989; socialist in outlook, the party is organized into a Secretariat, a Political Bureau, a Central Committee, Federations, Kasmas and cells; under the aegis of the FLN are various mass political organizations, including the Union Nationale de la Jeunesse Algérienne (UNJA) and the Union Nationale des Femmes Algériennes (UNFA); Sec.-Gen. BOUALEM BENHAMOUDA.

Front national de renouvellement (FNR): Algiers; Leader ZINEDDINE CHERIFI.

Mouvement algérien pour la justice et le développement (MAJD): Villa Laibi, Lot. Kapiot No. 5, Bouzaréah, Algiers; tel. (2) 60-58-00; fax (2) 78-78-72; f. 1990; reformist party supporting policies of fmr Pres. Boumedienne; Leader ABD AL-KADER MERBAH.

Mouvement pour la démocratie et la citoyenneté (MDC): Tizi-Ouzou; f. 1997 by dissident members of the FFS; Leader SAÏD KHELIL.

Mouvement de la société pour la paix (MSP): 163 Hassiba Ben Bouali, Algiers; f. as Hamas; adopted current name in 1997; moderate Islamic party, favouring the gradual introduction of an Islamic state; Leader Sheikh MAHFOUD NAHNAH.

Nahdah: Algiers; fundamentalist Islamist group; Leader Sheikh ABDULLAH DJABALLAH.

Parti démocratique progressif (PDR): Algiers; f. 1990 as a legal party; Leader SACI MABROUK.

Parti national pour la solidarité et le développement (PNSD): Cité du 5 juillet 11, No. 22, Constantine; Leader MOHAMED CHERIF TALEB.

Parti du renouveau algérien (PRA): 29 rue des Frères Bouatik, el-Biar, Algiers; tel. (2) 56-62-78; Leader NOURREDDINE BOUKROUH.

Parti républicain progressif (PRP): 10 rue Ouahrani Abou-Mediêne, Cité Seddikia, Oran; tel. (5) 35-79-36; f. 1990 as a legal party; Sec.-Gen. SLIMANE CHERIF.

Parti des travailleurs (PT): Algiers; workers' party; Leader LOUISA HANOUNE.

Rassemblement pour la culture et la démocratie (RCD): 87A rue Didouche Mourad, Algiers; tel. (2) 73-62-01; telex 67256; fax (2) 73-62-20; f. 1989; secular party; advocates recognition of the Berber language, Tamazight, as a national language; Pres. SAÏD SAADI.

Rassemblement national démocratique (RND): Algiers; f. 1997; centrist party; Sec.-Gen. MUHAMMAD TAHAR BENBAIBECHE.

Union pour la démocratie et les libertés (UDL): Algiers; f. 1997; Leader ABDELKRIM SEDDIKI.

Diplomatic Representation

EMBASSIES IN ALGERIA

Angola: 14 rue Marie Curie, el-Biar, Algiers; tel. (2) 92-54-41; telex 61620; fax (2) 79-74-41; Ambassador: JOSÉ CÉSAR AUGUSTO.

Argentina: 26 rue Finaltieri, el-Biar, Algiers; tel. (2) 92-34-23; telex 55260; fax (2) 92-34-43; Ambassador: GERÓNIMO CORTES FUNES.

Austria: rue les Vergers, Villa 136, Bir Mourad Rais, Algiers; tel. (2) 56-26-99; telex 62302; fax (2) 56-73-52; Ambassador: CHRISTIAN BERLAKOVITS.

Belgium: 22 chemin Youcef Tayebi, el-Biar, Algiers; tel. (2) 92-24-46; telex 61365; fax (2) 92-50-36; Ambassador: DIRK LETTENS.

Benin: 36 Lot. du Stade, Birkhadem, Algiers; tel. (2) 56-52-71; telex 62307; Ambassador: LEONARD ADJIN.

Brazil: 10 chemin Laroussi Messaoud Les Glycines, BP 186, Algiers; tel. (2) 74-95-75; telex 67156; fax (2) 74-96-87; Ambassador: SÉRGIO THOMPSON-FLORES.

Bulgaria: 13 blvd Col Bougara, Algiers; tel. (2) 23-00-14; fax (2) 23-05-33; Ambassador: MARIN DIMITROV TODOROV.

Burkina Faso: 10 rue du Vercors, Air de France, el-Hammadia, Algiers; tel. (2) 94-26-77; telex 61200; fax (2) 94-25-35.

Cameroon: 34 rue Yahia Mazouni, 16011 el-Biar, Algiers; tel. (2) 92-11-24; telex 61356; fax (2) 92-11-25; Chargé d'affaires: Dr FRANCIS NGANTCHA.

Canada: BP 225, 16000 Alger-Gare, 27 bis rue des Frères Benhafid, Algiers; tel. (2) 69-16-11; fax (2) 69-39-20; Ambassador: JACQUES NOISEUX.

Chad: Villa No. 18, Cité DNC, chemin Ahmed Kara, Hydra, Algiers; tel. (2) 69-26-62; fax (2) 69-26-63; Ambassador: El-Hadj MAHAMOUD ADJI.

China, People's Republic: 34 blvd des Martyrs, Algiers; tel. (2) 69-27-24; telex 66193; fax (2) 69-29-62; Ambassador: LI QINGYU.

Congo, Democratic Republic: 5 rue Saint Georges, Kouba, Algiers; tel. (2) 59-12-27; telex 62545; Ambassador: IKAKI BOMELE MOLINGO.

Congo, Republic: 111 Parc Ben Omar, Kouba, Algiers; tel. (2) 58-68-00; telex 62433; Ambassador: PIERRE N'GAKA.

Côte d'Ivoire: Immeuble 'Le Bosquet', Le Paradou, BP 710 Hydra, Algiers; tel. (2) 69-23-78; telex 66152; fax (2) 69-36-83; Ambassador: GUSTAVE OUFFOUE-KOUASSI.

Cuba: 22 rue Larbi Alik, Hydra, Algiers; tel. (2) 69-21-48; telex 52963; fax (2) 69-32-81; Ambassador: RAFAEL POLANCO BRAHOJOS.

Czech Republic: BP 358, Villa Koudia, 3 chemin Ziryab, Algiers; tel. (2) 23-00-56; telex 66281; fax (2) 23-01-03; Chargé d'affaires a.i.: JOSEF BUZALKA.

Denmark: 12 ave Emile Marquis, Lot. Djenane el-Malik, 16035 Hydra, BP 384, 16000 Alger-Gare, Algiers; tel. (2) 69-27-55; telex 66270; fax (2) 69-28-46; Ambassador: HERLUF HANSEN.

Egypt: BP 297, 8 chemin Abdel-Kader Gadouche, 16300 Hydra, Algiers; tel. (2) 60-16-73; telex 66058; fax (2) 60-29-52; Ambassador: IBRAHIM YOUSSRI.

Finland: BP 256, 16035 Hydra, Algiers; tel. (2) 69-12-92; telex 66296; fax (2) 69-16-37; Ambassador: JAN GROOP.

France: chemin Abd al-Kader Gadouche, Hydra, Algiers; tel. (2) 69-24-88; telex 66076; fax (2) 69-13-69; Ambassador: ALFRED SIEFER-GAILLARDIN.

Gabon: BP 125, Rostomia, 21 rue Hadj Ahmed Mohamed, Hydra, Algiers; tel. (2) 69-24-00; telex 61282; fax (2) 60-25-46; Ambassador: YVES ONGOLLO.

Germany: BP 664, 165 chemin Sfindja, Algiers; tel. (2) 74-19-56; telex 56043; fax (2) 74-05-21; Ambassador: JOACHIM BROUDRÉ-GRÖGER.

Ghana: 62 rue des Frères Benali Abdellah, Hydra, Algiers; tel. (2) 60-64-44; telex 62234; fax (2) 69-28-56; Ambassador: GEORGE A. O. KUGBLENU.

Greece: 60 blvd Col Bougara, Algiers; tel. (2) 60-08-55; telex 66071; fax (2) 69-16-55; Ambassador: IOANNIS DRAKOULARAKOS.

Guinea: 43 blvd Central Saïd Hamdine, Hydra, Algiers; tel. (2) 60-06-11; telex 66208; fax (2) 60-04-68; Ambassador: MAMADY CONDÉ.

Guinea-Bissau: 17 rue Ahmad Kara, BP 32, Colonne Volrol, Hydra, Algiers; tel. (2) 60-01-51; telex 62210; fax (2) 60-97-25; Ambassador: JOSÉ PEREIRA BATISTA.

Holy See: 1 rue Noureddine Mekiri, 16090 Bologhine, Algiers (Apostolic Nunciature); tel. (2) 69-13-79; fax (2) 59-22-37; Apostolic Nuncio: Most Rev. AUGUSTINE KASUJJA, Titular Archbishop of Caesarea in Numidia.

Hungary: BP 68, 18 ave des Frères Oughlis, el-Mouradia, Algiers; tel. (2) 69-79-75; fax (2) 69-81-86; Chargé d'affaires: Dr LÁSZLÓ MÁRTON.

India: 14 rue des Abassides, el-Biar, 16030 Algiers; tel. (2) 92-34-44; telex 61526; fax (2) 92-40-11; e-mail eoialg.ist.cerist.dz; Ambassador: JAYANT PRASAD.

Indonesia: BP 62, 16 chemin Abdel-Kader Gadouche, 16070 el-Mouradia, Algiers; tel. (2) 69-20-11; telex 67912; fax (2) 69-39-31; Ambassador: LILLAHI GRAHANA SIDHARTA.

Iraq: 4 rue Abri Arezki, Hydra, Algiers; tel. (2) 69-31-25; telex 66098; fax (2) 69-10-97; Ambassador: ABD AL-KARIM AL-MULLA.

Italy: 18 rue Muhammad Ouidir Amellal, el-Biar, Algiers; tel. (2) 92-23-30; telex 61357; fax (2) 79-37-66; Ambassador: FRANCESCO DE COURTEN.

Japan: 1 chemin el-Bakri, el-Biar, Algiers; tel. (2) 91-20-04; telex 61389; fax (2) 91-20-46; Ambassador: YOSHIHISA ARA.

Jordan: 6 rue du Chenoua, Algiers; tel. (2) 60-20-31; telex 66089; Ambassador: KHALED ABIDAT.

Korea, Democratic People's Republic: 49 rue Hamlia, Bologhine, Algiers; tel. (2) 62-39-27; telex 61165; Ambassador: PAK HO IL.

Korea, Republic: 12 rue No 1 chemin des Crêtes, Hydra, Algiers; tel. (2) 69-36-20; fax (2) 69-16-03; Chargé d'affaires a.i.: SEE-YOUNG LEE.

Kuwait: chemin Abd al-Kader Gadouche, Hydra, Algiers; tel. (2) 59-31-57; telex 66628; Ambassador: YOUSSEFF ABDULLAH AL-AMIZI.

Lebanon: 9 rue Kaïd Ahmad, el-Biar, Algiers; tel. (2) 78-20-94; telex 61354; Ambassador: SALHAD NASRI.

Libya: 15 chemin Cheikh Bachir Ibrahimi, Algiers; tel. (2) 92-15-02; telex 52700; fax (2) 92-46-87; Ambassador: ABDEL-MOULA EL-GHADHBANE.

Madagascar: 22 rue Abd al-Kader Aouis, 16090 Bologhine, BP 65, Algiers; tel. (2) 95-03-74; fax (2) 95-17-76; Chargé d'affaires: MODESTE RANDRIANARIVONY.

Mali: Villa 16, Cité DNC/ANP, chemin Ahmed Kara, Algiers; tel. (2) 69-13-51; telex 66109; fax (2) 69-20-82; Ambassador: CHEICK S. DIARRA.

Malta: Bureau 24, Niv C, Hotel El Aurassi, Algiers; tel. (2) 63-19-74; telex 66371; Ambassador: ALFRED A. ZARB.

Mauritania: 107 Lot. Baranès, Air de France, Bouzaréah, Algiers; tel. (2) 79-21-39; telex 61455; fax (2) 78-42-74; Ambassador: SID AHMED OULD BABAMINE.

Mexico: BP 329, 21 rue du Commandant Amar Azzouz, el-Biar, Alger-Gare, Algiers; tel. (2) 92-40-23; telex 61641; fax (2) 92-34-51; Ambassador: HÉCTOR E. PÉREZ GALLARDO.

Morocco: 8 rue des Cèdres, el-Mouradia, Algiers; tel. (2) 69-14-08; telex 66159; fax (2) 69-29-00; Ambassador: ABDERRAZAK DOGHMI.

Netherlands: BP 72, 23 chemin Cheikh Bachir Ibrahimi, el-Biar, Algiers; tel. (2) 92-28-28; telex 61364; fax (2) 92-37-70; Ambassador: CORN. W. A. DE GROOT.

Niger: 54 rue Vercors Rostamia Bouzaréah, Algiers; tel. (2) 78-89-21; telex 61371; fax (2) 78-97-13; Ambassador: GOUROUZA OUMAROU.

Nigeria: BP 629, 27 bis rue Blaise Pascal, Algiers; tel. (2) 69-18-49; telex 61093; fax (2) 69-11-75; Ambassador: ALIYU MOHAMMED.

Oman: 53 rue Djamel Eddine, El Afghani, Bouzaréah, Algiers; tel. (2) 94-13-10; telex 61335; fax (2) 94-13-75; Ambassador: HELLAL AS-SIYABI.

Pakistan: BP 404, 62A Djenane el-Malik, Le Paradou, Hydra, Algiers; tel. (2) 69-37-81; telex 66277; fax (2) 69-22-12; e-mail pakembalg@ist.cerist.dz; Ambassador: M. ASLAM RIZVI.

Poland: 37 ave Mustafa Ali Khodja, el-Biar, Algiers; tel. (2) 92-25-53; telex 52562; fax (2) 92-14-35; Ambassador: ANDRZEJ MICHAL LUPINA.

Portugal: 7 rue Mohamed Khoudi, el-Biar, Algiers; tel. (2) 78-48-20; fax (2) 92-54-14; Ambassador: EDUARDO MANUEL FERNANDES.

Qatar: BP 118, 7 chemin Doudou Mokhtar, Algiers; tel. (2) 92-28-56; telex 66342; fax (2) 92-24-15; Ambassador: HOCINE ALI EDDOUSRI.

Romania: 24 rue Abri Arezki, Hydra, Algiers; tel. (2) 60-08-71; telex 66156; fax (2) 69-36-42; Ambassador: ÉMILIAN MANCIUR.

Russia: 7 chemin du Prince d'Annam, el-Biar, Algiers; tel. (2) 92-31-39; telex 61561; fax (2) 92-28-82; Ambassador: ALEKSANDR ADSENYONOK.

Saudi Arabia: 62 rue Med. Drafini, chemin de la Madeleine, Hydra, Algiers; tel. (2) 60-35-18; telex 61389; Ambassador: HASAN FAQQI.

Senegal: BP 379, Alger-Gare, 1 chemin Mahmoud Drarnine, Hydra, Algiers; tel. (2) 69-16-27; telex 67743; fax (2) 69-26-84; Ambassador: SAÏDOU NOUROU.

Slovakia: BP 84, 7 chemin du Ziryab, Didouche Mourad, 16006 Algiers; tel. (2) 22-01-31; fax (2) 23-00-51; Chargé d'affaires a.i.: TOMÁŠ FELIX.

Spain: 46 bis rue Mohamed Chabane, el-Biar, Algiers; tel. (2) 92-27-13; telex 61266; fax (2) 92-27-19; Ambassador: RICARDO ZALACAIN.

Sudan: 8 Shara Baski Brond, el-Yanabia, Bir Mourad Rais, Algiers; tel. (2) 60-95-35; fax (2) 69-30-19.

Sweden: rue Olof Palme, Nouveau Paradou, Hydra, Algiers; tel. (2) 69-23-00; telex 66046; fax (2) 69-19-17; Ambassador: GÖRAN WIDE.

Switzerland: BP 248, 27 blvd Zirout Youcef, 16000 Alger-Gare, Algiers; tel. (2) 73-73-10; telex 56042; fax (2) 73-81-58; Ambassador: ANDRÉ VON GRAFFENINED.

Syria: Domaine Tamzali, 11 chemin A. Gadouche, Hydra, Algiers; tel. (2) 91-20-26; telex 61368; fax (2) 91-20-30; Ambassador: ABEL-JABER ALDAHAK.

Tunisia: 11 rue du Bois de Boulogne, el-Mouradia, Algiers; tel. (2) 60-13-88; telex 66164; fax (2) 69-23-16; Ambassador: M'HEDI BACCOUCHE.

Turkey: Villa dar el Ouard, chemin de la Rochelle, blvd Col Bougara, Algiers; tel. (2) 69-12-57; telex 66244; fax (2) 69-31-61; Ambassador: UMIT PAMIR.

United Arab Emirates: BP 454, 19 rue des Frères Benhafid, Hydra, Algiers; tel. (2) 69-25-74; telex 67911; fax (2) 59-37-70; Ambassador: TARIQ AL-HAIDAN.

United Kingdom: BP 43, Résidence Cassiopée, Bâtiment B, 7 chemin des Glycines, 16000 Alger-Gare, Algiers; tel. (2) 23-00-68; telex 66151; fax (2) 23-00-67; Ambassador: FRANÇOIS GORDON.

USA: BP 549, 4 chemin Cheikh Bachir Ibrahimi, 16000 Alger-Gare, Algiers; tel. (2) 60-11-86; telex 66047; fax (2) 60-39-79; e-mail amembalg@ist.cerist.dz; Ambassador: CAMERON HUME.

Venezuela: BP 297, 3 impasse Ahmed Kara, Algiers; tel. (2) 69-38-46; telex 66642; fax (2) 69-35-55; Ambassador: EDUARDO SOTO-ALVAREZ.

Viet Nam: 30 rue de Chenoua, Hydra, Algiers; tel. (2) 69-27-52; telex 66053; Ambassador: TRAN XUAN MAN.

Yemen: Villa 19, Cité DNC, rue Ahmed Kara, Hydra, Algiers; tel. (2) 69-30-85; telex 66037; fax (2) 69-17-58; Ambassador: GASSEM ASKAR DJEBRANE.

Yugoslavia: BP 366, 7 rue des Frères Benhafid, Hydra, Algiers; tel. (2) 69-12-18; telex 66076; fax (2) 69-34-72; Chargé d'affaires a.i.: DIMITRIJE BABIĆ.

Judicial System

The highest court of justice is the Supreme Court (Cour suprême) in Algiers. Justice is exercised through 183 courts (tribunaux) and 31 appeal courts (cours d'appel), grouped on a regional basis. New legislation, promulgated in March 1997, provided for the eventual establishment of 214 courts and 48 appeal courts. The Cour des comptes was established in 1979. Algeria adopted a penal code in 1966, retaining the death penalty. In February 1993 three special courts were established to try suspects accused of terrorist offences; however, the courts were abolished in February 1995. Constitutional amendments, introduced in November 1996, provided for the establishment of a High State Court (empowered to judge the President of the Republic in cases of high treason, and the Head of Government for crimes and offences), and a State Council to regulate the administrative judiciary. In addition, a Conflicts Tribunal is to be established to adjudicate in disputes between the Supreme Court and the State Council.

Supreme Court: ave du 11 décembre 1960, Ben Aknoun, Algiers; tel. and fax (2) 92-44-89.

President of Supreme Court: A. NASRI.

Procurator-General: M. DAHMANI.

Religion

ISLAM

Islam is the official religion, and the whole Algerian population, with a few rare exceptions, is Muslim.

High Islamic Council: place Cheikh Abd al-Hamid ibn Badis, Algiers.

President of the High Islamic Council: ABDELMAJID MEZIANE.

CHRISTIANITY

The European inhabitants, and a few Arabs, are generally Christians, mostly Roman Catholics.

The Roman Catholic Church

Algeria comprises one archdiocese and three dioceses (including one directly responsible to the Holy See). In December 1996 there were an estimated 2,500 adherents in the country.

Bishops' Conference: Conférence Episcopale Régionale du Nord de l'Afrique, 13 rue Khélifa-Boukhalfa, 16000 Alger-Gare, Algiers; tel. (2) 74-41-22; fax (2) 73-41-78; f. 1985; Pres. Most Rev. HENRI TEISSIER, Archbishop of Algiers; Sec.-Gen. Fr ROMAN STÄGER.

Archbishop of Algiers: Most Rev. HENRI TEISSIER, Archevêché, 13 rue Khélifa-Boukhalfa, 16000 Alger-Gare, Algiers; tel. (2) 73-41-22; fax (2) 73-41-78.

Protestant Church

Protestant Church of Algeria: 31 rue Reda Houhou, 16000 Alger-Gare, Algiers; tel. and fax (2) 71-62-38; three parishes; 1,500 mems; Pastor Dr HUGH G. JOHNSON.

The Press

DAILIES

L'Authentique: Algiers; French.

Al-Badil: Algiers; relaunched 1990; MDA journal in French and Arabic; circ. 130,000.

Ach-Cha'ab (The People): 1 place Maurice Audin, Algiers; f. 1962; FLN journal in Arabic; Dir KAMEL AVACHE; circ. 24,000.

Al-Djeza'ir El-Youm: Algiers; Arabic; circ. 54,000.

Horizons: 20 rue de la Liberté, Algiers; tel. (2) 73-47-25; telex 66310; fax (2) 73-61-34; f. 1985; evening; French; circ. 35,000.

Al-Joumhouria (The Republic): 6 rue Bensenouci Hamida, Oran; f. 1963; Arabic; Editor BOUKHALFA BENAMEUR; circ. 20,000.

Le Journal: Algiers; f. 1992; French.

El Khabar: Maison de la Presse 'Tahar Djaout', 1 rue Bachir Attar, place du 1er mai, Algiers; tel. (2) 67-07-05; fax (2) 67-07-10; e-mail admin@elkhabar.com; f. 1990; Arabic; Gen. Man. CHERIF REZKI; circ. 200,000.

Liberté: 37 rue Larbi Ben M'Hidi, BP 178, Alger-Gare, Algiers; tel. (2) 69-25-88; fax (2) 69-35-46; internet http://www.liberte-algerie.com; French; independent; Dir-Gen. ABROUS OUTOUDERT.

Al-Massa: Maison de la Presse, Abdelkader Safir Kouba, Algiers; tel. (2) 59-54-19; fax (2) 59-64-57; f. 1977; evening; Arabic; circ. 45,000.

Le Matin: Maison de la Presse, 1 rue Bachir Attar, 16016 Algiers; tel. (2) 66-07-08; fax (2) 66-20-97; French.

Al-Moudjahid (The Fighter): 20 rue de la Liberté, Algiers; f. 1965; govt journal in French and Arabic; Dir ZOUBIR ZEMZOUM; circ. 392,000.

An-Nasr (The Victory): BP 388, Zone Industrielle, La Palma, Constantine; tel. (4) 93-92-16; f. 1963; Arabic; Editor ABDALLAH GUETTAT; circ. 340,000.

L'Opinion: Algiers; French.

Le Soir d'Algérie: Algiers; f. 1990; evening; independent information journal in French; Editors ZOUBIR SOUISSI, MAAMAR FARRAH.

La Tribune: Algiers; internet http://www.latribune-online.com; f. 1994; current affairs journal in French; Editor BAYA GACEMI.

El Watan: Maison de la Presse, 1 rue Bachir Attar, 16016 Algiers; tel. (2) 68-21-83; fax (2) 68-21-87; internet http://www.elwatan.com; French.

WEEKLIES

Algérie Actualité: 2 rue Jacques Cartier, 16000 Algiers; tel. (2) 63-54-20; telex 66475; f. 1965; French; Dir KAMEL BELKACEM; circ. 250,000.

Al-Hadef (The Goal): Constantine; tel. (4) 93-92-16; f. 1972; sports; French; Editor-in-Chief LARBI MOHAMED ABBOUD; circ. 110,000.

La Nation: Algiers; French; Editor SALIMA GHEZALI; circ. 60,000.

Révolution Africaine: 5 place Emir Abdelkader, 16400 Algiers; tel. (2) 64-04-71; telex 56126; fax (2) 61-19-96; current affairs journal in French; socialist; Dir FERRAH ABDELALI; circ. 50,000.

El Wadjh al-Akhar (The Other Face): Algiers; Arabic.

OTHER PERIODICALS

Al-Acala: 4 rue Timgad, Hydra, Algiers; tel. (2) 60-85-55; telex 66118; fax (2) 60-09-36; f. 1970; published by the Ministry of Religious Affairs; fortnightly; Editor MUHAMMAD AL-MAHDI.

Algérie Médicale: 3 blvd Zirout Youcef, Algiers; f. 1964; publ. of Union médicale algérienne; 2 a year; circ. 3,000.

Alouan (Colours): 119 rue Didouche Mourad, Algiers; f. 1973; cultural review; monthly; Arabic.

Bibliographie de l'Algérie: Bibliothèque Nationale d'Algérie, BP 127, Hamma el-Annasser, 16000 Algiers; tel. (2) 67-18-67; fax (2) 67-29-99; f. 1963; lists books, theses, pamphlets and periodicals published in Algeria; 2 a year; Arabic and French; Dir-Gen. MOHAMED AÏSSA OUMOUSSA.

Ach-Cha'ab ath-Thakafi (Cultural People): Algiers; f. 1972; cultural monthly; Arabic.

Ach-Chabab (Youth): Algiers; journal of the UNJA; bi-monthly; French and Arabic.

Al-Djeich (The Army): Office de l'Armée Nationale Populaire, 3 chemin de Gascogne, Algiers; f. 1963; monthly; Algerian army review; Arabic and French; circ. 10,000.

Journal Officiel de la République Algérienne Démocratique et Populaire: BP 376, Saint-Charles, Les Vergers, Bir Mourad Rais, Algiers; tel. (2) 54-35-06; telex 65180; fax (2) 54-35-12; f. 1962; French and Arabic.

Nouvelles Economiques: 6 blvd Amilcar Cabral, Algiers; f. 1969; publ. of Institut Algérien du Commerce Extérieur; monthly; French and Arabic.

Révolution et Travail: 1 rue Abdelkader Benbarek, place du 1er mai, Algiers; tel. (2) 66-73-53; telex 65051; fax (2) 65-82-21; journal of UGTA (central trade union) with Arabic and French editions; monthly; Editor-in-Chief LAKHDARI MOHAMED LAKHDAR.

Revue Algérienne du Travail: Algiers; f. 1964; labour publication; quarterly; French.

Ath-Thakafa (Culture): 2 place Cheikh ben Badis, Algiers; tel. (2) 62-20-73; f. 1971; every 2 months; cultural review; Editor-in-Chief CHEBOUB OTHMANE; circ. 10,000.

NEWS AGENCIES

Algérie Presse Service (APS): 4 rue Zouieche, Kouba, Algiers; tel. (2) 77-79-28; telex 66577; fax (2) 59-77-59; f. 1962.

Foreign Bureaux

Agence France-Presse (AFP): 6 rue Abd al-Karim el-Khettabi, Algiers; tel. (2) 63-62-01; telex 67427; Chief YVES LEERS.

Agencia EFE (Spain): 4 ave Pasteur, 15000 Algiers; tel. (2) 71-85-59; telex 66458; fax (2) 73-77-62; Chief MANUEL OSTOS LÓPEZ.

Agenzia Nazionale Stampa Associata (ANSA) (Italy): 4 ave Pasteur, Algiers; tel. (2) 63-73-14; telex 66467; fax (2) 61-25-84; Rep. CARLO DI RENZO.

Associated Press (AP) (USA): BP 769, 4 ave Pasteur, Algiers; tel. (2) 63-59-41; telex 67365; fax (2) 63-59-42; Rep. RACHID KHIARI.

Bulgarska Telegrafna Agentsia (BTA) (Bulgaria): Algiers; Chief GORAN GOTEV.

Informatsionnoye Telegrafnoye Agentstvo Rossii—Telegraf-noye Agentstvo Suverennykh Stran (ITAR—TASS) (Russia): 21 rue de Boulogne, Algiers; Chief KONSTANTIN DUDAREV.

Reuters (UK): Algiers; tel. (2) 74-70-53; telex 67756; fax (2) 74-53-75.

Rossiiskoye Informatsionnoye Agentstvo—Vesti (RIA—Vesti) (Russia): Algiers; Chief Officer YURII S. BAGDASAROV.

Xinhua (New China) News Agency (People's Republic of China): 32 rue de Carthage, Hydra, Algiers; tel. and fax (2) 69-27-12; telex 67950; Chief WANG LIANZHI.

Wikalat al-Maghreb al-Arabi (Morocco) and the Middle East News Agency (Egypt) are also represented.

Publishers

Entreprise Nationale du Livre (ENAL): 3 blvd Zirout Youcef, BP 49, Algiers; tel. and fax (2) 73-58-41; telex 53845; f. 1966 as Société Nationale d'Edition et de Diffusion, name changed 1983; publishes books of all types, and imports, exports and distributes printed material, stationery, school and office supplies; Pres. and Dir-Gen. HASSEN BENDIF.

Office des Publications Universitaires: 1 place Centrale de Ben Aknoun, Algiers; tel. (2) 78-87-18; telex 61396; publishes university textbooks.

Broadcasting and Communications

BROADCASTING

Radio

Arabic Network: transmitters at Adrar, Aïn Beïda, Algiers, Béchar, Béni Abbès, Djanet, El Goléa, Ghardaia, Hassi Messaoud, In Aménas, In Salah, Laghouat, Les Trembles, Ouargla, Reggane, Tamanrasset, Timimoun, Tindouf.

French Network: transmitters at Algiers, Constantine, Oran and Tipaza.

Kabyle Network: transmitter at Algiers.

Radio Algérienne: 21 blvd des Martyrs, Algiers; tel. (2) 59-07-00; fax (2) 60-58-14; govt-controlled; Dir-Gen. ABDELKADER LALMI.

Television

The principal transmitters are at Algiers, Batna, Sidi-Bel-Abbès, Constantine, Souk-Ahras and Tlemcen. Television plays a major role in the national education programme.

Télévision Algérienne: 21 blvd des Martyrs, Algiers; tel. (2) 60-23-00; fax (2) 60-19-22; Dir-Gen. BRAHIM BELBAHRI.

Finance

(cap. = capital; res = reserves; dep. = deposits; brs = branches; m. = million; amounts in Algerian dinars)

BANKING

Central Bank

Banque d'Algérie: 38 ave Franklin Roosevelt, Algiers; tel. (2) 23-02-32; telex 66499; fax (2) 23-01-50; f. 1963 as Banque Centrale d'Algérie; present name adopted 1990; cap. 40m.; bank of issue; Gov. ABDELOUAHAB KERAMANE; Sec.-Gen. FERHAT MECIBAH; 50 brs.

Nationalized Banks

Banque Extérieure d'Algérie (BEA): BP 344, Alger-Gare, 11 blvd Col Amirouche, Algiers; tel. (2) 71-12-52; telex 67488; fax (2) 63-93-34; f. 1967; cap. 1,600m., res 4,001m., total assets 318,420m. (Dec. 1994); chiefly concerned with energy and maritime transport sectors; Chair. MOHAMED BENHALIMA; Dir-Gen. HOCINE HANNACHI; 80 brs.

Banque du Maghreb Arabe pour l'Investissement et le Commerce: 21 blvd des Trois Frères Bouadou, Bir Mourad Rais, Algiers; tel. (2) 56-04-46; telex 62266; fax (2) 56-60-12; owned by the Algerian Govt (50%) and the Libyan Govt (50%); Pres. HAKIKI; Dir-Gen. IBRAHIM ALBISHARY.

Banque Nationale d'Algérie (BNA): 8 blvd Ernesto Ché Guévara, 16000 Alger-Gare, Algiers; tel. (2) 71-55-64; telex 61227; fax (2) 71-47-59; f. 1966; cap. 8,000m., res 10,227m., dep. 68,920m., total assets 228,892m. (Dec. 1995); specializes in industry, transport and trade sectors; Chair. and Man. Dir MUHAMMAD TERBECHE; 163 brs.

Al-Baraka Bank of Algeria (ABA): 11 rue Ahmed Kara, Saïd Hamdine, Hydra, Algiers; tel. (2) 69-32-76; telex 67928; fax (2) 59-01-68; f. 1991; Algeria's first Islamic financial institution; owned by the Jeddah-based Al-Baraka Investment and Development Co (50%) and the local Banque de l'Agriculture et du Développement Rural (BADR) (50%); Chair. MOHAMED TEWFIK AL-MAGHARIBI; Gen. Man. MOHAMED SEDDIK HAFID.

Crédit Populaire d'Algérie (CPA): BP 1031, 2 blvd Col Amirouche, 16000 Algiers; tel. (2) 64-96-60; telex 56061; fax (2) 64-97-29; f. 1966; cap. 13,600m. (Dec. 1996); specializes in light industry, construction and tourism; Chair. and Gen. Man. MADJID NASSOU; 117 brs.

Development Banks

Banque de l'Agriculture et du Développement Rural (BADR): BP 484, 17 blvd Col Amirouche, Algiers; tel. (2) 64-72-64; telex 66658; fax (2) 61-55-51; f. 1982; cap. 2,200m., res 1,942m., dep. 103,939m. (Dec. 1993); finance for the agricultural sector; Chair. and Man. Dir MOURAD DAMARDJI; 270 brs.

Banque Algérienne de Développement (BAD): 12 blvd Col Amirouche, Algiers; tel. (2) 73-89-50; telex 55220; fax (2) 74-51-36; f. 1963; cap. 100m. (1994), dep. 3,596.5m. (Dec. 1984); a public establishment with fiscal sovereignty; aims to contribute to Algerian economic development through long-term investment programmes; Chair. SASSI AZIZA; Dir-Gen. MUHAMMAD KERKEBANE; 4 brs.

Banque de Développement Local (BDL): 5 rue Gaci Amar, Staouéli, Wilaya de Tipaza; tel. (2) 39-28-01; telex 71171; fax (2) 39-23-51; f. 1985; regional devt bank; cap. and res 6,555.4m. (1996); Dir-Gen. MUHAMMAD MALEK; 14 brs.

Caisse Nationale d'Epargne et de Prévoyance (CNEP): 42 blvd Khélifa Boukhalfa, Algiers; tel. (2) 71-33-53; telex 65286; fax (2) 71-70-22; f. 1964; savings and housing bank; Dir-Gen. ABDELKRIM NAAS.

Private Banks

Mouna Bank: Oran; f. 1998.

Union Bank: Algiers; f. 1995; cap. 100m., total assets 992m. (Dec. 1996); principal shareholder Brahim Hadjas; Pres. SELIM BENATA.

Foreign Banks
(Representative offices)

Arab Banking Corpn (Bahrain): rue Didouche Mourad, Algiers; tel. (2) 74-91-13; telex 55373; fax (2) 74-74-88; Chief Rep. MUSTAPHA ACHOUR.

Beobanka ad (Yugoslavia): 12 rue Ali Azil, Algiers; tel. (2) 63-56-19; fax (2) 79-69-42.

Crédit Lyonnais SA (France): BP 268, 2 blvd Mohamed Khemisti, Algiers; tel. (2) 73-30-74; telex 56160; fax (2) 73-30-76; Dir PHILIPPE BRICQ.

Société Générale (France): BP 294, Villa No. 1, 2 rue le Paradou, Hydra, Algiers; tel. (2) 59-49-21; telex 66569; fax (2) 60-04-87; Dir JEAN-PAUL COURT.

STOCK EXCHANGE

The Algiers stock exchange began trading in February 1998, but was restricted to local investors until the introduction of government reforms to allow the participation of foreign investors.

INSURANCE

Insurance is a state monopoly; however, in 1997 regulations were drafted to permit private companies to enter the Algerian insurance market.

Caisse Nationale de Mutualité Agricole: 24 blvd Victor Hugo, Algiers; tel. (2) 73-46-31; telex 56033; fax (2) 73-31-07; f. 1972; Dir-Gen. YAHIA CHERIF BRAHIM; 47 brs.

Compagnie Algérienne d'Assurance: 48 rue Didouche Mourad, Algiers; tel. (2) 64-54-32; telex 56051; fax (2) 64-20-15; f. 1963 as a public corpn; Pres. ALI DJENDI.

Compagnie Centrale de Réassurance (CCR): 21 blvd Zirout Youcef, Algiers; tel. (2) 73-80-20; telex 55091; fax (2) 73-80-60; f. 1973; general; Chair. DJAMEL-EDDINE CHOUAÏB CHOUITER.

Société Nationale d'Assurances (SNA): 5 blvd Ernesto Ché Guévara, Algiers; tel. (2) 71-47-60; telex 61309; fax (2) 71-22-16; f. 1963; state-sponsored co; Pres. KACI AISSA SLIMANE; Chair. and Gen. Man. LATROUS AMARQ.

Trust Algeria: Algiers; f. 1997; 65% owned by Trust Insurance Co (Bahrain) and Qatar General Insurance and Reinsurance Co, 35% owned by Compagnie Algérienne d'Assurance.

Trade and Industry

DEVELOPMENT ORGANIZATIONS

Engineering Environment Consult (EEC): BP 395, Alger-Gare, 50 rue Khélifa Boukhalfa, Algiers; tel. (2) 73-33-90; telex 65153; fax (2) 73-24-81; e-mail eec@ist.cerist.dz; f. 1982; Dir-Gen. MUHAMMAD BENTIR.

Institut National de la Production et du Développement Industriel (INPED): 126 rue Didouche Mourad, Boumerdès; tel. (2) 41-52-50; telex 52488.

CHAMBERS OF COMMERCE

Chambre Française de Commerce et d'Industrie en Algérie (CFCIA): 1 rue Lieutenant Mohamed Touileb, Algiers; tel. (2) 73-28-28; fax (2) 63-75-33; f. 1965; Pres. JEAN-PIERRE DEQUEKER; Dir JEAN-FRANÇOIS HEUGAS.

Chambre Algérienne de Commerce et d'Industrie (CACI): BP 100, Palais Consulaire, rue Amilcar Cabral, Algiers; tel. (2) 57-55-55; telex 61345; fax (2) 57-70-25; f. 1980; Dir-Gen. MOHAMED CHAMI.

INDUSTRIAL AND TRADE ASSOCIATIONS

Association Nationale des Fabrications et Utilisateurs d'Emballages Métalliques: BP 245, rue de Constantine, Algiers; telex 64415; Pres. OTHMANI.

Entreprise Nationale de Développement des Industries Alimentaires (ENIAL): 2 rue Ahmed Aït Muhammad, Algiers; tel. (2) 76-51-42; telex 54816; Dir-Gen. MOKRAOUI.

Entreprise Nationale de Développement des Industries Manufacturières (ENEDIM): 22 rue des Fusillés, El Anasser, Algiers; tel. (2) 68-13-43; telex 65315; fax (2) 67-55-26; f. 1983; Dir-Gen. FODIL.

Entreprise Nationale de Développement et de Recherche Industriels des Matériaux de Construction (ENDMC): BP 78, 35000 Algiers; tel. (2) 41-50-70; telex 63352; f. 1982; Dir-Gen. A. TOBBAL.

Groupement pour l'Industrialisation du Bâtiment (GIBAT): BP 51, 3 ave Colonel Driant, 55102 Verdun, France; tel. 29-86-09-76; fax 29-86-20-51; Dir JEAN MOULET.

Institut Algérien de Normalisation et de Propriété Industrielle (INAPI): 5–7 rue Abou Hamou Moussa, 16000 Algiers; tel. (2) 63-51-80; telex 66409; fax (2) 61-09-71; f. 1973; Dir-Gen. DJENIDI BENDAOUD.

Institut National Algérien du Commerce Extérieur (COMEX): 6 blvd Anatole-France, Algiers; tel. (2) 62-70-44; telex 52763; Dir-Gen. SAAD ZERHOUNI.

Institut National des Industries Manufacturières (INIM): 35000 Boumerdès; tel. (2) 81-62-71; telex 68462; fax (2) 82-56-62; f. 1973; Dir-Gen. HOCINE HASSISSI.

State Trading Organizations

Since 1970 all international trading has been carried out by state organizations, of which the following are the most important:

Entreprise Nationale d'Approvisionnement en Bois et Dérivés (ENAB): BP 166, Alger-Gare, 2 blvd Muhammad V, Algiers; tel. (2) 63-85-32; telex 66470; fax (2) 61-10-89; wood and derivatives and other building materials; Dir-Gen. El-Hadj REKH-ROUKH.

Entreprise Nationale d'Approvisionnement en Outillage et Produits de Quincaillerie Générale (ENAOQ): 6 rue Amar Semaous, Hussein-Dey, Algiers; tel. (2) 77-45-03; telex 65566; tools and general hardware; Dir-Gen. ALI HOCINE.

Entreprise Nationale d'Approvisionnements en Produits Alimentaires (ENAPAL): Algiers; tel. (2) 76-10-11; telex 64278; f. 1983; monopoly of import, export and bulk trade in basic foodstuffs; brs in more than 40 towns; Chair. LAID SABRI; Man. Dir BRAHIM DOUA-OURI.

Entreprise Nationale d'Approvisionnement et de Régulation en Fruits et Légumes (ENAFLA): BP 42, 12 ave des Trois Frères Bouadou, Bir Mourad Rais, Algiers; tel. (2) 54-10-10; telex 62113; fax (2) 56-79-59; f. 1983; division of the Ministry of Commerce; fruit and vegetable marketing, production and export; Man. Dir RÉDHA KHELEF.

Office Algérien Interprofessionel des Céréales (OAIC): 5 rue Ferhat-Boussaad, Algiers; tel. (2) 73-26-01; telex 65056; fax (2) 73-22-11; f. 1962; monopoly of trade in wheat, rice, maize, barley and products derived from these cereals; Gen. Man. LAÏD TALAMALI.

Office National de la Commercialisation des Produits Viti-Vinicoles (ONCV): 112 Quai-Sud, Algiers; tel. (2) 73-72-75; telex 56063; fax (2) 73-72-97; f. 1968; monopoly of importing and exporting products of the wine industry; Man. Dir S. MEBARKI.

UTILITIES

Société Nationale de l'Electricité et du Gaz (SONELGAZ): 2 blvd Colonel Krim Belkacem, Algiers; tel. (2) 74-82-60; telex 66381; fax (2) 61-54-77; monopoly of production, distribution and transportation of electricity and transportation and distribution of natural gas; Gen. Man. AÏSSA ABDELKRIM BENGHANEM.

Electricity

Entreprise Nationale de Travaux d'Electrification: Villa Malwall, Ain d'Heb, Médéa; tel. (3) 50-61-27; telex 74061; f. 1982; study of electrical infrastructure; Dir-Gen. ABD AL-BAKI BELABDOUN.

Gas

Entreprise Nationale des Gaz Industriels (ENGI): BP 247, route de Baraki, Gué de Constantine, Algiers; tel. (2) 77-85-81; fax (2) 77-11-94; production and distribution of gas; Gen. Man. LAHOCINE BOUCHERIT.

HYDROCARBONS COMPANIES

Société Nationale pour la Recherche, la Production, le Transport, la Transformation et la Commercialisation des Hydrocarbures (SONATRACH): 10 rue du Sahara, Hydra, Algiers; tel. (2) 60-70-00; telex 62106; f. 1963; exploration, exploitation, transport and marketing of petroleum, natural gas and their products; Dir-Gen. ABDELMAJID ATTAR (acting).

In May 1980 SONATRACH was disbanded, and its functions were divided among 12 companies (including SONATRACH itself). The other 11 were:

Entreprise Nationale de Canalisation (ENAC): Algiers; tel. (2) 70-35-90; telex 42939; piping; Dir-Gen. HAMID MAZRI.

Entreprise Nationale de Distribution et de Commercialisation des Produits Pétroliers (NAFTAL): BP 73, route des Dusses, Cheraga, Algiers; tel. (2) 36-09-69; telex 53876; fax (2) 37-57-11; f. 1987; international marketing and distribution of petroleum products; Gen. Man. NORDINE CHEROUATY.

Entreprise Nationale d'Engineering Pétrolier (ENEP): 2 blvd Muhammad V, Algiers; tel. (2) 64-08-37; telex 66493; fax (2) 63-71-83; design and construction for petroleum-processing industry; Gen. Man. MUSTAPHA MEKIDECHE.

Entreprise Nationale de Forage (ENAFOR): BP 211, 30500 Hassi Messaoud, Algiers; tel. (2) 73-71-35; telex 44077; fax (2) 73-22-60; drilling; Dir-Gen. ABD AR-RACHID ROUABAH.

Entreprise Nationale de Génie Civil et Bâtiments (GCB): BP 23, route de Corso, Boudouaou, Algiers; tel. (2) 84-65-26; telex 68213; fax (2) 84-60-09; civil engineering; Dir-Gen. ABD EL-HAMID ZERGUINE.

Entreprise Nationale de Géophysique (ENAGEO): BP 140, Hassi Messaoud, Ouargla; tel. (9) 73-77-00; telex 42703; fax (9) 73-72-12; e-mail enageodg@ist.cerist.dz; geophysics; Dir-Gen. RABAH DJEDDI.

Entreprise Nationale des Grands Travaux Pétroliers (ENGTP): BP 09, Zone Industrielle, Reghaïa, Boumerdes; tel. (2) 85-24-50; telex 68150; fax (2) 85-14-70; f. 1980; major industrial projects; Dir-Gen. B. DRIAD.

Entreprise Nationale de la Pétrochimie (ENIP): BP 215, 21000 Skikda; tel. (8) 75-68-62; telex 87098; fax (8) 75-74-41; petrochemicals and fertilizers.

Entreprise Nationale des Plastiques et de Caoutchouc (ENPC): BP 452, rue des Frères Meslim, Aïn Turk, Sétif; tel. (5) 90-64-99; telex 86040; fax (5) 90-05-65; production and marketing of rubber and plastics; Dir-Gen. MAHIEDDINE ECHIKH.

Entreprise Nationale de Services Pétroliers (ENSP): BP 83, Hassi Messaoud, Ouargla; tel. (9) 73-73-33; telex 44026; fax (9) 73-82-01; oil-well services; Dir-Gen. A. GASMI.

Entreprise Nationale des Travaux aux Puits (ENTP): BP 71, In-Amenas, Illizi; telex 44052; oil-well construction; Dir-Gen. ABD AL-AZIZ KRISSAT.

NATIONALIZED INDUSTRIES

A large part of Algerian industry is nationalized. Following the implementation of an economic reform programme in the 1980s, however, more than 300 of the 450 nationalized companies had been transferred to the private sector by late 1990.

The following are some of the most important nationalized industries, each controlled by the appropriate ministry.

Centre National d'Etudes de Recherches Appliquées et de Travaux d'Art (CNERATA): BP 279, 114 rue de Tripoli, Hussein Dey, Algiers; tel. (2) 77-50-22; telex 65402; Gen. Man. REMILI SMIDA.

Entreprise des Eaux Minérales de l'Algérois: 21 rue Bellouchat Mouloud, Hussein Dey, Algiers; tel. (2) 23-13-94; telex 65424; fax (2) 23-14-01; mineral water, carbonated beverages and beer; Dir-Gen. RABAH CHENNOUFI.

Entreprise Nationale d'Ammeublement et de Transformation du Bois (ENATB): BP 18, route de Hassainia, Bouinan; tel. (3) 39-40-63; telex 72848; fax (3) 39-40-10; f. 1982; furniture and other wood products; Dir-Gen. ALI SLIMANI.

Entreprise Nationale d'Ascenseurs (ENASC): 86 rue Hassiba Ben Bouali, Algiers; tel. (2) 65-99-40; telex 65222; f. 1989; manufacture of elevators; Dir-Gen. MUHAMMAD FERRAH.

Entreprise Nationale de Bâtiments Industrialisés (BATI-METAL): BP 89, Ain Defla; tel. (3) 45-24-31; telex 53312; f. 1983; study and commercialization of buildings; Dir-Gen. ABD AL-KADER RAHAL.

Entreprise Nationale de la Cellulose et du Papier (CELPAP): BP 628, Mont Plaisir, 27000 Mostaganem; tel. (6) 26-28-75; telex 14048; fax (6) 26-31-00; f. 1985; pulp and paper; Chair. MUSTAPHA MERZOUK.

Entreprise Nationale de Charpentes et de Chaudronnerie (ENCC): BP 1547, 13 rue Marcel Cerdan, Oran; tel. (6) 33-29-32; telex 22107; f. 1983; manufacture of boilers; Dir-Gen. DRISS TANDJAOUI.

Entreprise Nationale de Commerce: 6–9 rue Belhaffat-Ghazali, Hussein Dey, Algiers; tel. (2) 77-43-20; telex 52063; monopoly of imports and distribution of materials and equipment; Dir-Gen. MUHAMMAD LAÏD BELARBIA.

Entreprise Nationale de Construction de Matériaux et d'Equipements Ferroviaires: BP 63, route d'El Hadjar, Annaba; tel. (8) 85-74-06; telex 81814; fax (8) 85-23-98; f. 1983; production, import and export of railway equipment; Dir-Gen. MELEK SALAH.

Entreprise Nationale de Développement et de Coordination des Industries Alimentaires (ENIAL): Bab Ezzouar, 5 route nationale, Algiers; tel. (2) 76-21-06; telex 64112; fax (2) 75-59-84; f. 1965; semolina, pasta, flour and couscous; Dir-Gen. YOUNSI HACHEMI.

Entreprise Nationale de Distribution du Matériel Electrique (EDIMEL): 4 et 6 blvd Muhammad V, Algiers; tel. (2) 63-70-82; telex 67161; f. 1983; distribution of electrical equipment; Dir-Gen. ABD AR-RAZAK KEBBAB.

Entreprise Nationale de Production de Produits Pharmaceutiques (SAIDAL): Aïn d'Heb, 26000 Médéa; tel. (3) 58-54-64; telex 74018; fax (3) 58-18-64; f. 1983; production of pharmaceuticals; Dir-Gen. ALI AOUN.

Entreprise Nationale de Produits Métalliques Utilitaires: BP 25, carrefour de Meftah, Oued Smar, Algiers; tel. (2) 51-65-12; telex 64524; fax (2) 51-68-44; f. 1983; manufacture of metal products; Dir-Gen. YACHIR EL HADI.

Entreprise Nationale de Produits Miniers Non-Ferreux et des Substances Utiles (ENOF): 31 rue Muhammad Hattab, Belfort; tel. (2) 76-62-42; telex 64161; f. 1983; production and distribution of minerals; Dir-Gen. HOCINE ANANE.

Entreprise Nationale des Appareils de Mesure et de Contrôle (AMC): BP 248, route de Djeinila, El Eulma; tel. (5) 87-34-24; telex 86843; fax (5) 87-49-72; f. 1984; production of measuring equipment; Dir-Gen. MOKHTAR TOUIMER.

Entreprise Nationale des Corps Gras (ENCG): 13 ave Mustapha Sayed el-Ouali, Algiers; tel. (2) 74-49-99; telex 66075; fax (2) 74-47-50; f. 1982 to replace SOGEDIA; oils, margarines, soaps and food packaging; Dir-Gen. SAÏD BOURAS.

Entreprise Nationale des Emballages en Papier et Cartons (ENEPAC): BP 490, route d'Alger, Bordj-Bou-Arreridj; tel. (5) 69-58-48; telex 86823; fax (5) 69-17-73; f. 1985; wrapping paper and cardboard containers.

Entreprise Nationale des Industries du Cable (ENICAB): BP 94, 62 blvd Salah Bouakouir, Algiers; tel. (2) 64-94-32; telex 66497; f. 1983; consortium of cable manufacturers; Dir-Gen. MUHAMMAD BELLAG.

Entreprise Nationale des Industries de Confection et de Bonneterie (ECOTEX): BP 324, Ihadaden, Béjaia; tel. (5) 21-28-84; telex 83030; fax (5) 22-00-08; consortium of textiles and clothing manufacturers; Dir-Gen. AMAR CHERIF.

Entreprise Nationale des Industries de l'Electroménager (EPE-ENIEM): BP 71A, Chikhi, Tizi-Ouzou; tel. (3) 21-87-45; telex 76031; fax (3) 21-87-44; consortium of manufacturers of household equipment; Dir-Gen. BELKACEM BERRABAH.

Entreprise Nationale des Jus et Conserves Alimentaires (ENAJUC): BP 108, zone industrielle-Ben-Boulaid Blida; tel. (3) 41-78-90; telex 72849; fax (3) 41-74-91; f. 1983; manufacture of food products; Dir-Gen. TEMER DAHMANE.

Entreprise Nationale de la Pêche Hauturière et Oceanique: Quai d'Aigues Mortes, Port d'Alger; tel. (2) 71-52-68; telex 61346; fax (2) 71-52-67; f. 1979, as Entreprise Nationale des Pêches, to replace (with ECOREP, which is responsible for fishing equipment) former Office Algérien des Pêches; production, marketing, importing and exporting of fish; Man. Dir HACHANI MADANI.

Entreprise Nationale de Sidérurgie (SIDER): BP 342, Chaiba, el-Hadjar, 23000 Annaba; tel. (8) 83-19-99; telex 81661; fax (8) 83-89-57; f. 1964 as Société Nationale de Sidérurgie, restructured 1983; steel, cast iron, zinc and products; Man. Dir MESSAOUD CHETTIH.

Entreprise Nationale de Transformation de Produits Longs (ENTPL): BP 1005, 19 ave Mekki Khelifa, El Manouar; tel. (6) 34-52-40; telex 22953; fax (6) 34-19-50; f. 1983; production and distribution of girders; Dir-Gen. MUHAMMAD BOUTCHACHA.

Entreprise Nationale de Tubes et de Transformation de Produits Plats (ENTTPP): BP 131, route de la Gare, Reghaia, Algiers; tel. (2) 80-91-86; telex 68116; f. 1983; manufacture and distribution of tubing; Dir-Gen. RACHID BELHOUS.

Entreprise Nationale des Véhicules Industriels (SNVI): BP 153, 5 route nationale, 35300 Rouiba; tel. (2) 85-19-70; telex 68134; fax (2) 85-13-45; f. 1981; manufacture of industrial vehicles; Dir-Gen. ALI BEKKOUCHE.

Entreprise Nationale du Fer et du Phosphate (Ferphos): BP 122, Zhun 2, Tebessa; tel. (8) 47-49-10; telex 95004; fax (8) 47-43-38; f. 1983; production, import and export of iron and phosphate products; Dir-Gen. AHMAD BENSLIMANE.

Entreprise Publique Economique Asmidal, SpA: BP 326, route des Salines, 23000 Annaba; tel. (8) 83-20-22; telex 81922; fax (8) 84-47-20; f. 1985; production of ammonia, fertilizers, pesticides and sodium tripolyphosphate.

Entreprise Publique Economique des Manufactures de Chaussures et Maroquinerie (EMAC): BP 150, route de Sidi Bel-Abbès, Sig 29300; tel. (5) 83-82-15; telex 13935; fax (6) 83-84-51; f. 1983; manufacture of shoes and leather goods; Dir-Gen. DJELLOUL BENDJEDID.

Office Régional du Centre des Produits Oléicoles (ORECPO): route de Ain Bessem Bouira, 10000 Algiers; tel. (3) 92-92-11; telex 77098; fax (3) 92-00-88; f. 1982; production and marketing of olives and olive oil; Dir-Gen. CHABOUR MUSTAPHA.

Secrétariat d'Etat aux Forêts et au Reboisement: Direction Generale des Forêts, rue des quatre Canons, Algiers; tel. (2) 74-80-03; telex 52854; fax (2) 74-80-14; f. 1971; production of timber, care of forests; Man. Dir ABJELLAH GHEBALOU.

Société Nationale de Constructions Mécaniques (SONACOME): Algiers; tel. (2) 65-93-92; telex 52800; f. 1967; to be reorganized into 11 smaller companies, most of which will specialize in manufacture or distribution of one of SONACOME's products; Dir DAOUD AKROUF.

Société Nationale de Constructions Métalliques (SN METAL): Algiers; tel. (2) 63-29-30; telex 52889; f. 1968; produc-

tion of metal goods; Chair. HACHEM MALIK; Man. Dir ABD AL-KADER MAIZA.

Société Nationale de Fabrication et de Montage du Matériel Electrique (SONELEC): 4 & 6 blvd Muhammad V, Algiers; tel. (2) 63-70-82; telex 52867; electrical equipment.

Société Nationale des Industries Chimiques (SNIC): BP 641, 4–6 blvd Muhammad V, Algiers; tel. (2) 64-07-73; telex 52802; production and distribution of chemical products; Dir-Gen. RACHID BEN IDDIR.

Société Nationale des Industries des Lièges et du Bois (SNLB): BP 61, 1 rue Kaddour Rahim, Hussein Dey, Algiers; tel. (2) 77-99-99; telex 52726; f. 1973; production of cork and wooden goods; Chair. MALEK BELLANI.

Société Nationale des Industries des Peaux et Cuirs (SONIPEC): BP 113, 100 rue de Tripoli, Hussein Dey, Algiers; tel. (2) 77-21-22; telex 52832; fax (2) 77-76-13; f. 1967; hides and skins; Chair. MUHAMMAD CHERIF AZI; Man. Dir NACERI ABDENOUR.

Société Nationale des Matériaux de Construction (SNMC): Algiers; tel. (2) 64-35-13; telex 52204; f. 1968; production and import monopoly of building materials; Man. Dir ABD AL-KADER MAIZI.

Société Nationale de Recherches et d'Exploitations Minières (SONAREM): 127 blvd Salah Bouakouiz, Algiers; tel. (2) 63-15-55; telex 52910; f. 1967; mining and prospecting; Dir-Gen. OUBRAHAM FERHAT.

Société Nationale des Tabacs et Allumettes (SNTA): 40 rue Hocine-Nourredine, Algiers; tel. (2) 66-18-68; telex 52780; monopoly of manufacture and trade in tobacco, cigarettes and matches; Dir-Gen. MUHAMMAD TAHAB BOUZEGHOUB.

TRADE UNIONS

Union Générale des Travailleurs Algériens (UGTA): Maison du Peuple, place du 1er mai, Algiers; tel. (2) 66-89-47; telex 65051; f. 1956; 800,000 mems; Sec.-Gen. ABDELMADJID SIDI SAID .

There are 10 national 'professional sectors' affiliated to UGTA. These are:

Secteur Alimentation, Commerce et Tourisme (Food, Commerce and Tourist Industry Workers): Gen. Sec. ABD AL-KADER GHRIBLI.

Secteur Bois, Bâtiments et Travaux Publics (Building Trades Workers): Gen. Sec. LAIFA LATRECHE.

Secteur Education et Formation Professionnelle (Teachers): Gen. Sec. SAÏDI BEN GANA.

Secteur Energie et Pétrochimie (Energy and Petrochemical Workers): Gen. Sec. ALI BELHOUCHET.

Secteur Finances (Financial Workers): Gen. Sec. MUHAMMAD ZAAF.

Secteur Information, Formation et Culture (Information, Training and Culture).

Secteur Industries Légères (Light Industry): Gen. Sec. ABD AL-KADER MALKI.

Secteur Industries Lourdes (Heavy Industry).

Secteur Santé et Sécurité Sociale (Health and Social Security Workers): Gen. Sec. ABD AL-AZIZ DJEFFAL.

Secteur Transports et Télécommunications (Transport and Telecommunications Workers): Gen. Sec. EL-HACHEMI BEN MOUHOUB.

Al-Haraka al-Islamiyah lil-Ummal al-Jazarivia (Islamic Movement for Algerian Workers): Tlemcen; f. 1990; based on teachings of Islamic faith and affiliated to the FIS.

Union Nationale des Paysans Algériens (UNPA): f. 1973; 700,000 mems; Sec.-Gen. AÏSSA NEDJEM.

Transport

RAILWAYS

A new authority, Infrafer (Entreprise Publique Economique de Réalisation des Infrastructures Ferroviaires), was established in 1987 to take responsibility for the construction of new track. In the following year a project to build an underground railway network in Algiers was revived in a modified form. Work on the first 12.5-km section of the 26-km line of the network, which was to be constructed by local companies with foreign assistance, began in 1990. It was projected that the line would take 10 years to complete.

Infrafer (Entreprise Publique Economique de Réalisation des Infrastructures Ferroviaires): BP 208, 35300 Rouiba; tel. (2) 85-27-47; telex 68152; fax (2) 85-17-55; f. 1987; Pres. and Dir-Gen. K. BENMAMI.

Société Nationale des Transports Ferroviaires (SNTF): 21–23 blvd Muhammad V, Algiers; tel. (2) 71-15-10; telex 66333; fax (2) 74-81-90; f. 1976 to replace Société Nationale des Chemins de Fer Algériens; 4,290 km of track, of which 301 km are electrified and 1,055 km are narrow gauge; daily passenger services from Algiers to the principal provincial cities and services to Tunisia and Morocco; Dir-Gen. ABDELADIM BENALLEGUE.

ROADS

In 1996 there were an estimated 104,000 km of roads and tracks, of which 640 km were motorways, 25,200 km were main roads and 23,900 km were secondary roads. The French administration built a good road system (partly for military purposes), which, since independence, has been allowed to deteriorate in parts. New roads have been built linking the Sahara oil fields with the coast, and the Trans-Sahara highway is a major project. In 1996 it was estimated that the cost of renovating the national road system would total US $4,124m.

Société Nationale des Transports Routiers (SNTR): 27 rue des Trois Frères Bouadou, Bir Mourad Rais, Algiers; tel. (2) 54-06-00; telex 62120; fax (2) 56-53-73; f. 1967; holds a monopoly of goods transport by road; Chair. El-Hadj HAOUSSINE; Dir-Gen. ESSAID BENDAKIR.

Société Nationale des Transports des Voyageurs (SNTV): Algiers; tel. (2) 66-00-52; telex 52603; f. 1967; holds monopoly of long-distance passenger transport by road; Man. Dir M. DIB.

SHIPPING

Algiers is the main port, with anchorage of between 23 m and 29 m in the Bay of Algiers, and anchorage for the largest vessels in Agha Bay. The port has a total quay length of 8,380 m. There are also important ports at Annaba, Arzew, Béjaia, Djidjelli, Ghazaouet, Mostaganem, Oran, Skikda and Ténès. Petroleum and liquefied gas are exported through Arzew, Béjaia and Skikda. Algerian crude petroleum is also exported through the Tunisian port of La Skhirra. In December 1996 Algeria's merchant fleet totalled 151 vessels, amounting to 982,528 grt.

Compagnie Algéro-Libyenne de Transports Maritimes (CALTRAM): 19 rue des Trois Frères Bouadou, Bir Mourad Rais, Algiers; tel. (2) 57-17-00; telex 62150; fax (2) 54-21-04; Dir-Gen. M. ZITOUNI.

Entreprise Nationale de Réparations Navales (ERENAV): quai no. 12, Ex d'Aurey, Algiers; tel. (2) 63-71-48; telex 66650; fax (2) 64-60-93; f. 1987; ship repairs; Dir-Gen. MOHAMED MOSLI.

Entreprise Nationale de Transport Maritime de Voyageurs—Algérie Ferries (ENTMV): BP 467, 5,6 Jawharlal Nehru, Algiers; tel. (2) 74-04-85; telex 55100; fax (2) 64-88-76; f. 1987 as part of restructuring of SNTM-CNAN; responsible for passenger transport; operates car ferry services between Algiers, Annaba, Skikda, Alicante, Marseilles and Oran; Dir-Gen. A. CHERIET.

Entreprise Portuaire d'Alger (EPAL): BP 259, 2 rue d'Angkor, Alger-Gare, Algiers; tel. (2) 71-54-39; telex 61275; fax (2) 71-54-52; e-mail ferrah@ist.cerist.dz; f. 1982; responsible for management and growth of port facilities and sea pilotage; Dir-Gen. ALI FERRAH.

Entreprise Portuaire d'Annaba (EPAN): BP 1232, Môle de la Cigogne-Quai nord, Annaba; tel. (8) 86-31-31; telex 81652; fax (8) 86-54-15; Man. Dir D. SALHI.

Entreprise Portuaire d'Arzew (EPA): BP 46, 7 rue Larbi Tebessi, Arzew; tel. (6) 37-24-91; telex 12919; fax (6) 47-49-90; Man. Dir CHAIB OUMER.

Entreprise Portuaire de Béjaia (EPB): BP 94, Môle de la Casbah, Béjaia; tel. (5) 21-18-07; telex 83055; fax (5) 22-25-79; Man. Dir M. BOUMSILA.

Entreprise Portuaire de Djen-Djen (EPDJ): BP 87, El Achouat, Djen-Djen, Djidjelli; tel. (5) 45-94-63; telex 84060; fax (5) 45-90-72; f. 1984; Man. Dir MOHAMED ATMANE.

Entreprise Portuaire de Ghazaouet (EPG): BP 217, Enceinte Portuaire Môle de Batna, Ghazaouet; tel. (7) 32-13-45; telex 18836; fax (7) 32-12-55; Man. Dir B. ABDELMALEK.

Entreprise Portuaire de Mostaganem (EPM): BP 131, quai du Port, Mostaganem; tel. (6) 21-14-11; telex 14097; fax (6) 21-78-05; Dir M. CHERIF.

Entreprise Portuaire d'Oran (EPO): BP 106, 6 blvd Mimouni Lahcène, Oran; tel. (6) 39-26-25; telex 22422; fax (6) 39-53-52; Man. Dir M. S. LOUHIBI.

Entreprise Portuaire de Skikda (EPS): BP 65, 46 ave Rezki Rahal, Skikda; tel. (8) 75-68-27; telex 87840; fax (8) 75-20-15; Man. Dir M. LEMRABET.

Entreprise Portuaire de Ténès (EPT): BP 18, 02200 Ténès; tel. (3) 76-72-76; telex 78090; fax (3) 76-61-77; Man. Dir K. EL-HAMRI.

NAFTAL Direction Aviation Maritime: BP 70, Aéroport Houari Boumedienne, Dar-el-Beïda, Algiers; tel. (2) 50-86-23; telex 64579; fax (2) 50-74-81; Dir ZERROUK BEN MERABET.

Société Générale Maritime (GEMA): 2 rue J. Nehru, Algiers; tel. (2) 74-73-00; telex 56079; fax (2) 74-76-73; f. 1987 as part of restructuring of SNTM-CNAN; responsible for merchant traffic; Dir-Gen. ABDULLAH SERIAI.

Société Nationale de Transport Maritime et Compagnie Nationale Algérienne de Navigation (SNTM-CNAN): BP 280, 2 quai no. 9, Nouvelle Gare Maritime, Algiers; tel. (2) 71-14-78; telex 66581; fax (2) 61-59-64; f. 1963; state-owned co which owns and operates fleet of freight ships; rep. office in Marseilles and rep. agencies in Antwerp, Valencia and the principal ports in many other countries; Gen. Man. GHAZI REGAÏNIA.

Société Nationale de Transports Maritimes des Hydrocarbures et des Produits Chimiques (SNTM-HYPROC): BP 60, Arzew, 31200 Oran; tel. (6) 37-30-99; telex 12097; fax (6) 37-28-30; f. 1982; Dir-Gen. CHAÏB OUMEUR.

CIVIL AVIATION

Algeria's main airport, Houari Boumedienne, 20 km from Algiers, is a class A airport of international standing. At Constantine, Annaba, Tlemcen and Oran there are also airports that meet international requirements. There are, in addition, 65 aerodromes, of which 20 are public, and a further 135 airstrips connected with the petroleum industry.

Air Algérie (Entreprise Nationale d'Exploitation des Services Aériens): BP 858, 1 place Maurice Audin, Immeuble el-Djazair, Algiers; tel. (2) 74-24-28; telex 67145; fax (2) 74-44-25; f. 1953 by merger; state-owned from 1972; internal services and extensive services to Europe, North and West Africa, and the Middle East; Sec.-Gen. ALI DJERABA; Dir-Gen. FAYSAL KHALIL.

Air Maghreb: planned consortium of the national airlines of Algeria, Libya, Mauritania, Morocco and Tunisia; the merger of the airlines has been delayed indefinitely.

Tourism

Algeria's tourist attractions include the Mediterranean coast, the Atlas mountains and the desert. In 1996 a total of 93,491 tourists visited Algeria, compared with 722,682 in 1991. Receipts from tourism totalled about US $64m. in 1990. In 1996 there were 737 hotels, with a total of 64,937 beds.

Entreprise de Gestion Touristique du Centre (EGT CENTRE): 70 rue Hassiba Ben-Bouali, Algiers; tel. (2) 67-03-05; telex 66165; fax (2) 67-49-00; Dir-Gen. SALAH EDDINE SENNI.

Office National du Tourisme (ONT): 2 rue Ismail Kerrar, Algiers; tel. (2) 71-29-82; telex 55362; fax (2) 71-29-85; f. 1990; state institution; oversees tourism promotion policy; Dir-Gen. SADDEK ZERROUK.

ONAT-TOUR (Opérateur National Algérien de Tourism): 25–27 rue Khélifa-Boukhalfa, 16000 Algiers; tel. (2) 74-33-76; telex 66383; fax (2) 74-32-14; f. 1962; Dir-Gen. ABID KERAMANE.

Société de Développement de l'Industrie Touristique en Algérie (SODITAL): 72 rue Asselah Hocine, Algiers; f. 1989; Dir-Gen. NOUREDDINE SALHI.

Defence

Commander-in-Chief of the Armed Forces: Maj.-Gen. KHALED NEZZAR.

Inspector-General of the Armed Forces: Maj.-Gen. TAYEB DERRADJI.

Chief of Staff of the Army: Lt-Gen. MUHAMMAD LAMARI.

Commander of the Land Force: Maj.-Gen. AHMED GAÏD.

Commander of the Air Force: Gen. MUHAMMAD BENSLIMANE.

Commander of the Naval Forces: Gen. CHAABANE GHODBANE.

Defence Budget (1997): AD 94,000m.

Military Service: 18 months national service (army only).

Total Armed Forces (August 1997): 124,000: army 107,000 (75,000 conscripts); navy 7,000; air force 10,000.

Paramilitary Forces: 146,200 (including a gendarmerie of 25,000).

Education

As a result of reforms that the government initiated in 1973, education in the national language (Arabic) is now officially compulsory for a period of nine years, for children between six and 15 years of age. Primary education begins at the age of six and lasts for six years, comprising two cycles of three years each. Secondary education begins at 12 years of age and lasts for a maximum of six years, comprising two cycles of three years each. In 1995 the total enrolment at primary and secondary schools was equivalent to 85% of the school-age population (males 90%; females 80%). Primary enrolment in that year included 95% of children in the relevant age-group (males 99%; females 91%). The comparable ratio for secondary enrolment was 56% (males 59%; females 53%). The 1995 budget allocated education and training AD 86,800m., representing 11.8% of total government expenditure.

There were some 4,617,000 pupils at primary schools in 1995/96, compared with about 800,000 in 1962. Facilities for middle and secondary education are still very limited, although they have greatly improved since independence, accommodating 1,691,561 pupils at middle schools, and 853,303 pupils at secondary schools in 1995/96, compared with 48,500 at middle and secondary schools in 1962. Whereas before independence most teachers were French, in 1975/76 more than 95% of primary teachers were Algerian, as were about

65% of middle and secondary teachers. Most education at primary level is in Arabic, but at higher levels French is still widely used. The majority of foreign teachers in Algeria come from Egypt, Syria, Tunisia and other Arab countries.

In 1994/95 the number of students receiving higher education was 298,767. In addition to the 10 main universities there are seven other *centres universitaires* and a number of technical colleges. Several thousand students go abroad to study. Adult illiteracy, which, according to UNESCO estimates, averaged 38.4% (males 26.1%; females 51.0%) in 1995, has been combated by a large-scale campaign, in which instruction is sometimes given by young people who have only recently left school, and in which the broadcasting services are widely used.

Bibliography

Ageron, Charles-Robert. *Modern Algeria: A History from 1830 to the present.* London, Hurst, 1992.

Al-Ahnaf, M., Botiveau, B., and Frégosi, F. *L'Algérie par ses islamistes.* Paris, Karthala, 1992.

Alazard, J., and others. *Invitation à l'Algérie.* Paris, 1957.

Allais, M. *Les Accords d'Evian, le référendum et la résistance algérienne.* Paris, 1962.

Amin, Samir. *The Maghreb in the Modern World: Algeria, Tunisia, Morocco.* Harmondsworth, Penguin, 1970.

Amrane-Minne, Danièle Djamila. *Des Jemmes dans la Guerre d'Algérie.* Paris, Editions Karthala, 1996.

Aron, Raymond. *La Tragédie Algérienne.* Paris, 1957.

Baduel, Pierre R. *L'Algérie incertaine.* Aix-en-Provence, Edisud, 1993.

Barakat, H. *Contemporary North Africa. Issues of development and integration.* London, Croom Helm, 1985.

Bennoune, M. *The Making of Contemporary Algeria (1830–1987).* Cambridge, Cambridge University Press, 1988.

Boudiaf, Muhammad. *Où va l'Algérie?* Algeria, Rahma, 1992.

Boukhobza, M'Hammed. *Ruptures et transformations sociales en Algérie.* Algiers, OPU 1989.

Bourdieu, Pierre. *The Algerians.* Boston, 1962.

    Sociologie de l'Algérie. Paris, Que Sais-je, 1958.

Brace, R. and J. *Ordeal in Algeria.* New York, 1960.

Burgat, F., and Dowell, W. *The Islamic Movement in North Africa.* Austin, Texas, University of Texas Press, 1993.

Chaliand, G. *L'Algérie, est-elle Socialiste?* Paris, Maspéro, 1964.

De Gaulle, Charles. *Mémoires d'espoir: Le Renouveau 1958–1962.* Paris, Plon, 1970.

Encyclopaedia of Islam. *Algeria.* New edition, Vol. I. London and Leiden, 1960.

Eveno, P., and Planchais, J. *La Guerre d'Algérie.* Paris, La Découverte, 1989.

Favrod, Ch.-H. *Le FLN et l'Algérie.* Paris, 1962.

First, Ruth. *The Barrel of a Gun: Political Power in Africa and the Coup d'Etat.* London, Allen Lane, The Penguin Press, 1970.

Francos, Avia, and Séréri, J.-P. *Un Algérien nommé Boumedienne.* Paris, 1976.

Garon, Lise. *L'obsession unitaire et la Nation trompée: la fin de l'Algérie socialiste.* Montreal, University of Laval Press, 1993.

Gillespie, Joan. *Algeria.* London, Benn, 1960.

Gordon, David. *North Africa's French Legacy, 1954–1963.* London, 1963.

    The Passing of French Algeria. Oxford, 1966.

Goytisolo, Juan. *Argelia en el vendaval.* Madrid, El País-Aguilar, 1994.

Harbi, Muhammad. *L'Algérie et son destin.* Paris, Arcantère, 1992.

Hassan. *Algérie, histoire d'un naufrage.* Paris, Seuil, 1995.

Henissart, Paul. *Wolves in the City: The Death of French Algeria.* London, Hart-Davis, 1971.

Horne, Alistair. *A Savage War of Peace: Algeria 1954–1962.* London, Macmillan, 1977.

Humbaraci, Arslan. *Algeria—A Revolution that Failed.* London, Pall Mall, 1966.

Ibrahimi, A. Taleb. *De la Décolonisation à la Révolution Culturelle (1962–72).* Algiers, SNED, 1973.

Jeanson, F. *La Révolution Algérienne; Problèmes et Perspectives.* Milan, 1962.

Joesten, Joachim. *The New Algeria.* New York, 1964.

Julien, Charles-André. *Histoire de l'Algérie contemporaine, conquête et colonisation, 1827–1871.* Paris, Presses Universitaires de France, 1964.

Kettle, Michael. *De Gaulle and Algeria.* London, Quartet, 1993.

Khelladi, A. *Les islamistes algériens face au pouvoir.* Algiers, Alfa, 1992.

Lacheraf, Mostepha. *L'Algérie, Nation et Société.* Paris, Maspéro, 1965.

Laffont, Pierre. *L'Expiation: De l'Algérie de papa à l'Algérie de Ben Bella.* Paris, Plon, 1968.

Lakehal, M. *Algérie: De l'indépendance à l'Etat d'urgence.* Paris, L'Harmattan, 1992.

Lambotte, R. *Algérie, naissance d'une société nouvelle.* Paris, Editions Sociales, 1976.

Lebjaoui, Mohamed. *Vérités sur la Révolution Algérienne.* Paris, Gallimard, 1970.

Leca, Jean, and Vatin, Jean-Claude. *L'Algérie politique, institutions et régime.* Paris, Fondation nationale des sciences politiques, 1974.

López, B., Martín Muñoz, G., Larramendi, M. *Elecciones, participación y transiciones políticas en el norte dé Africa.* Madrid, ICMA, 1992.

Lyotard, Jean-François. *La Guerre des Algériens Ecrits 1956–1963.* Paris, Galilée, 1989.

Mallarde, Etienne. *L'Algérie depuis.* Paris, La Table Ronde, 1977.

Mandouze, André. *La Révolution Algérienne par les Textes.* Paris, 1961.

Martens, Jean-Claude. *Le modèle algérien de développement (1962–1972).* Algiers, SNED, 1973.

Martin, Claude. *Histoire de l'Algérie Française 1830–1962.* Paris, 1962.

Martín Muñoz, G. *Democracia y derechos humanos en el mundo árabe.* Madrid, ICMA, 1994.

Mouilleseaux, Louiz. *Histoire de l'Algérie.* Paris, 1962.

Nyssen, Hubert. *L'Algérie en 1970.* 1970.

Ottaway, David and Marina. *Algeria. The Politics of a Socialist Revolution.* Berkeley, University of California Press, 1970.

Ouzegane, Amar. *Le Meilleur Combat.* Paris, Julliard, 1962.

Pierre, Andrew J., and Quandt, William B. *The Algerian Crisis, Policy Options for the West.* Washington, DC, The Brookings Institution, 1997.

Quandt, William B. *Revolution and Political Leadership: Algeria, 1954–1968.* MIT Press, 1970.

Redjala, R. *L'opposition en Algérie depuis 1962.* Paris, L'Harmattan, 1988.

Reudy, John D. *Land Policy in Colonial Algeria: The Origins of the Rural Public Domain.* Berkeley, University of California Press, 1967.

Robson, P., and Lury, D. *The Economics of Africa.* London, Allen & Unwin, 1969.

Ruedy, J. *Modern Algeria: The origins and development of a nation.* Bloomington, Indiana University Press, 1992.

Sa'dallah, A. Q. *Studies on Modern Algerian Literature.* Beirut, Al Adab, 1966.

Sanderson, H. *Laïcité islamique en Algérie.* Paris, CNRS, 1983.

Segura i Mas, Antoni. *El Magreb, del colonialismo al islamismo.* Barcelona, Universidad de Barcelona, 1994.

Sivan, Emmanuel. *Communisme et Nationalisme en Algérie (1920–1962).* Paris, 1976.

Smith, Tony. *The French Stake in Algeria 1945–1962.* Cornell University Press, 1978.

Stone, Martin. *The Agony of Algeria.* London, C. Hurst & Co Ltd, 1998.

Sulzberger, C. L. *The Test, de Gaulle and Algeria.* London and New York, 1962.

Talbott, John. *France in Algeria, 1954–1962.* New York, Knopf, 1980.

Vatin, Jean-Claude. *L'Algérie politique, histoire et société.* Paris, Fondation nationale des sciences politiques, 1974.

Vidal-Naquet, Pierre. *L'Affaire Audin.* Paris, Les éditions de Minuit, 1989.

Face à la Raison d'Etat: Un Historien dans la Guerre d'Algérie. Paris, La Découverte, 1989.

BAHRAIN

Geography

The State of Bahrain consists of a group of about 35 islands, situated midway along the Persian (Arabian) Gulf, about 24 km (15 miles) from the east coast of Saudi Arabia, and 28 km (17 miles) from the west coast of Qatar.

The total area of the Bahrain archipelago is 707.3 sq km (273.1 sq miles). Bahrain itself, the principal island, is about 50 km (30 miles) long and between 13 km and 25 km (8 miles and 15 miles) wide. To the north-east of Bahrain, and linked to it by causeway and road, lies Muharraq island, which is approximately 6 km (4 miles) long. A causeway also links Bahrain to Sitra island. Some of the other islands in the state are Nabih Salih, Jeddah, Hawar, Umm Nassan and Umm Suban. A causeway linking Bahrain and Saudi Arabia was opened in November 1986.

The total population of Bahrain increased from 216,078 in April 1971 to 508,037 at the census of November 1991. Of the 1991 total, 323,305 were Bahraini citizens. According to official estimates, in mid-1996 the total population was 598,625. About 80% of the population are thought to be of Arab ethnic origin, and 20% Iranian. In 1991 the port of Manama, the capital and seat of government, had a population of 136,999. Bahrain's Muslim population (82% of the total in 1991) is estimated to consist of between 40% and 45% of the Sunni sect and between 55% and 60% of the Shi'ite sect. The Bahraini labour force, 60% of whom were estimated to be of non-Bahraini origin in 1993, was expected to double between 1989 and the end of the century. The ruling family are Sunnis.

History

After several centuries of independence, Bahrain passed first under the rule of the Portuguese (1521–1602) and then under periodic Persian rule (1602–1782). The Persians were expelled in 1783 by the Utub tribe from Arabia, whose leading family, the al-Khalifas, became the independent sheikhs of Bahrain and have ruled Bahrain ever since, except for a brief period before 1810. Nevertheless, claims, based on the Persian occupation of the islands in the 17th and 18th centuries, were renewed intermittently.

In the 19th century European powers began to take an interest in the Gulf area. Britain was principally concerned with preventing French, Russian and German penetration towards India, and suppressing the trade in slaves and weapons. In 1861 the Sheikh of Bahrain undertook to abstain from the prosecution of war, piracy and slavery by sea in return for British support in case of aggression. In 1880 and 1892 the Sheikh further undertook not to cede, mortgage or otherwise dispose of parts of his territories to anyone except the British Government, nor to enter into a relationship with any other government without British consent. A convention acknowledging Bahrain's inde-pendence was signed by the British and Ottoman Governments in 1913, although the islands remained under British administration.

Under Sheikh Sulman bin Hamad al-Khalifa (who became ruler of Bahrain in 1942), social services and public works were considerably extended. Sheikh Sulman died in November 1961 and was succeeded by his eldest son, Sheikh Isa bin Sulman al-Khalifa. In February 1956 elections were held for members of an Education and Health Council (the first election in Bahrain had been held in 1919 for the Municipal Council). Shortly after the 1956 elections, there was a strike in the petroleum refinery, alleged to be partly a protest against the paternalism of the British adviser to the Sheikh. There were further disturbances at the time of the Suez crisis. Other symbols of Bahrain's growing independence included the establishment of Bahraini, as opposed to British, legal jurisdiction over a wide range of nationalities (1957), the issue of Bahrain's own postage stamps (1960) and the introduction of a separate currency (1965). Bahrain also pioneered free education and health services in the Gulf region. In 1967 Britain transferred its principal Arabian military base from Aden to Bahrain, but by 1968 the British Government had decided to withdraw all forces 'East of Suez' before the end of 1971. In October 1973, at the time of the

Arab–Israeli war, the Bahrain Government gave one year's notice to quit to the US Navy, whose ships had docking facilities in Bahrain. The evacuation did not, in fact, take place, but negotiations continued and Bahrain finally took over the base in July 1977.

Extensive administrative and political reforms came into effect in January 1970, when a 12-member Council of State was established. The formation of this new body, which became the state's supreme executive authority, represented the first formal derogation of the ruler's powers. Sheikh Khalifa bin Sulman al-Khalifa, the ruler's eldest brother, became President of the Council. Only four of the initial 12 'Directors' were members of the royal family, but all were Bahrainis, and the British advisers were reduced to the status of civil servants. Equal numbers of Sunni and Shi'ite Muslims were included (the royal family apart) to reflect Bahrain's religious balance. When Bahrain became fully independent, in August 1971, the Council of State became the Cabinet of the State of Bahrain (with Sheikh Khalifa as Prime Minister), with authority to direct the country's internal and external affairs.

After 1968 Bahrain was officially committed to membership of the embryonic Federation of Arab Emirates. The Bahraini Government, however, failed to negotiate an agreement on the terms of the federal constitution with the richer, but less developed, sheikhdoms in the region. Bahrain's position was strengthened in May 1970, when Iran accepted the findings of a UN report on Bahrain's future. The UN representatives had visited the archipelago in April and found that popular opinion overwhelmingly favoured complete independence rather than union with Iran.

On 15 August 1971 Bahrain's full independence was proclaimed, a new treaty of friendship was signed with the United Kingdom, and Sheikh Isa took the title of Amir. Bahrain became a member of the Arab League and of the UN. In December 1972 elections were held for a Constituent Assembly. This body drafted a new Constitution, which came into force on 6 December 1973. Elections to a 44-member National Assembly were held on the following day. Of the members, 30 were chosen by the all-male electorate, and the remaining 14 were members of the Government. A delay in the establishment of trade unions, for which the Constitution made provision, and a sharp rise in the cost of living provoked industrial unrest in 1974. In August 1975 the Prime Minister submitted his resignation, complaining that the National Assembly was preventing the Government from carrying out its functions. The Amir invited him to form a new government, and, two days later, dissolved the National Assembly and suspended the Constitution. Despite the arrest of 'leftists' in December 1975, sporadic unrest continued. The traditional administrative system of *majlis* (assembly), where citizens and non-citizens present petitions to the Amir, remains.

Bahrain joined other Arab states in condemning the Egyptian-Israeli peace treaty in March 1979, and suspended diplomatic relations with Egypt. In September 1979 Iranian Shi'ite elements exhorted Bahraini Shi'ites, who are in the majority and many of whom are of Iranian descent, to demonstrate against the Sunni Amir. Calm was restored but it was apparent that the new regime in Iran was interested in reviving the Iranian claim to Bahrain, which the Shah of Iran had not renounced until 1975. In December 1981 between 50 and 60 people, mainly Bahrainis, were arrested in Bahrain on charges of conspiring to overthrow the Government. Bahrain's Minister of the Interior alleged that the plot was the work of Hojatoleslam Hadi al-Mudarasi, an Iranian clergyman, who was operating in the name of the Islamic Front for the Liberation of Bahrain (IFLB). In 1984 the discovery of a cache of weapons in a Bahraini village renewed fears of Iranian attempts to disrupt the island's stability, and in June 1985 there was increased concern over Bahrain's security when a further plot to overthrow the Government was discovered. Despite subsequent assurances from President Rafsanjani of Iran, and cordial relations with his successor, President Khatami, Bahrain has continued to monitor carefully both the political situation in Teheran and domestic stability. Strict censorship is imposed, and political parties and trade unions are banned. The Government has been severely criticized by human rights organizations for its alleged use of torture and detention without trial.

Concern over regional security was one of the reasons why Bahrain joined five other Gulf states in forming the Gulf Co-operation Council (GCC, see p. 246) in March 1981. In January 1987 the USA agreed to sell 12 F-16 fighter aircraft to Bahrain as part of a contract, valued at $400m., to provide military equipment. In mid-1990 Bahrain became the first Gulf nation to receive such aircraft. Bahrain's intention to maintain its security through collective defence has also been emphasized by the country's participation in joint military manoeuvres with Qatar and other Gulf states, and in the GCC's 'Peninsula Shield' military exercises. Bahrain provides onshore facilities for US forces, and there is a large US navy presence.

In April 1986 a long-standing territorial dispute between Bahrain and Qatar erupted into a military confrontation. Qatari military forces raided the island of Fasht ad-Dibal, a coral reef situated midway between Bahrain and Qatar, over which both claim sovereignty. During the raid Qatar seized 29 foreign workers (all of whom were subsequently released), who were constructing a Bahraini coastguard station on the island. Officials of the GCC met representatives from both states in an attempt to reconcile them and avoid a split within the Council. Fasht ad-Dibal was the third area of dispute between the two countries, the others being Zubara, on mainland Qatar, and the Hawar islands. In July 1991 Qatar instituted proceedings at the International Court of Justice (ICJ) in The Hague in an attempt to resolve the dispute over the potentially oil-rich Hawar islands, the shoals of Dibal and Quitat Jaradah and the delineation of the maritime boundary. In mid-1992 Qatar rejected Bahrain's attempt to broaden the issue to include its claim to part of the Qatari mainland, around Zubara, which had been Bahraini territory until the early 20th century. In February 1995, following deliberations, the ICJ declared that it would have authority to adjudicate in the dispute, even though Qatar had applied unilaterally to the Court. Bahrain continued to insist that a bilateral solution be sought, rejected the jurisdiction of the ICJ in the matter and welcomed a Saudi Arabian offer to mediate in the dispute. In September relations between Bahrain and Qatar deteriorated further, following the Bahraini Government's decision to construct a tourist resort on the disputed Hawar islands.

In 1990 Bahrain upgraded its relations with Iran to ambassadorial level. Subsequently, in early 1992, Bahrain signed an important protocol for industrial co-operation with Iran. The first official Israeli delegation to visit Bahrain arrived in late September 1994, and in the following month the Israeli Minister of the Environment, Yossi Sarid, attended multilateral Middle East talks in Manama on environmental issues. During his visit Sarid met with Bahrain's Minister of Foreign Affairs, marking the first contact at ministerial level between Bahrain and Israel.

In August 1990 Bahrain's position assumed new strategic importance as a result of Iraq's occupation and annexation of Kuwait. Following the annexation, Bahrain firmly supported the implementation of UN economic sanctions against Iraq, and permitted the stationing of US combat aircraft in Bahrain. British armed forces participating in the multinational force for the defence of Saudi Arabia and the liberation of Kuwait were also stationed in Bahrain in 1990–91. In May 1991 representatives of the Bahraini Government met defence officials from the USA, the United Kingdom and Germany to discuss post-war security arrangements, and the role that the USA should play in the implementation of any regional security plan. In June the Amir visited Kuwait for talks on regional security, and it was announced that Bahrain would remain a regional support base for the USA, but would not become the headquarters of a Gulf-based US military command and control centre. At the end of October Bahrain and the USA signed a defence co-operation agreement allowing for joint military exercises, the storage of equipment and the use of Bahraini port facilities by US forces. In January 1994 memoranda of military co-operation were signed with the USA and the United Kingdom.

In July 1992 Bahrain's Prime Minister expressed the hope that the country's relations with Iraq would improve and that, eventually, both Iraq and Iran would be incorporated into the GCC. This was the first time that a government of a GCC state had openly recommended the restoration of contacts with Iraq. At the GCC summit in Riyadh, however, in December 1993, there was criticism of both Iraq and Iran. In the final communiqué the Heads of State of the six GCC member countries demanded that international pressure on Iraq to observe all of the UN resolutions pertaining to it should be maintained, and that the sovereignty of Kuwait should be respected. It was also decided to double the size of the Saudi-based 'Peninsula Shield' joint defence force. In October 1994, when Iraqi troops were again positioned in the Iraq-Kuwait border area, Bahrain deployed combat aircraft and naval units to join GCC and US forces in the defence of Kuwait. In a statement issued in mid-October Bahrain, together with the other GCC member states and Egypt and Syria, condemned Iraqi threats against Kuwait and reaffirmed its full support for Kuwait's sovereignty.

In November 1992 the Amir announced the formation of a new, 30-member Consultative Council. The Council had little scope to question or alter government policy and power remained with the Amir and the ruling al-Khalifa family. The establishment of the Council met with little popular enthusiasm.

Fears of renewed unrest among Bahrain's Shi'ite majority have continued to preoccupy the ruling regime and to prompt an uncompromising response to popular disaffection. In December 1993 a human rights organization, Amnesty International, published a report that was highly critical of the Bahraini Government, claiming that Bahraini Shi'ites had been deprived of their nationality and forcibly exiled by their own Government. In response to the criticism, the Amir issued a decree in March 1994 pardoning 64 Bahrainis exiled since the 1980s and permitting them to return to Bahrain. Unrest continued in the following months as young men demonstrated against rising unemployment among Bahraini nationals, particularly the Shi'ite population. In November 1994 12 Shi'ite villagers were reported to have been arrested in Jidd Hafs, to the west of Manama, following the violent disruption of a charity running event in which a group of expatriate men and women was participating. In early December the police arrested a young Shi'ite cleric, Sheikh Ali Salman, imam of the main Shi'ite mosque in Manama, who had demanded the release of those arrested at Jidd Hafs and had also condemned the participation of women in the race. Moreover, he had appealed for the restoration of the National Assembly (suspended in 1975) and criticized the ruling family, the large number of foreign workers employed on the island, and the decline of moral standards. Cassettes of his speeches had been widely circulated throughout Bahrain. Widespread rioting followed across the island, especially in Shi'ite areas; in the Shi'ite quarter of Manama demonstrators appealed for the release of Sheikh Salman. In an attempt to defuse the crisis, the Amir, in an address on 16 December, promised 'to encourage consultation' and to ensure that the Consultative Council, established in 1992, became 'a sincere expression of the feelings and aspirations of all citizens'. The rioting continued and several people died in clashes with armed police. The crisis was particularly embarrassing for the Government as it occurred as Bahrain was about to host the fifteenth summit of the GCC, an event which had attracted numerous foreign journalists to the island. Later in the month the authorities acknowledged the existence of political unrest and blamed Sheikh Salman and certain 'foreign interests', a coded reference to Iran. The police proceeded to make a large number of arrests; according to the opposition some 2,500 Bahrainis, mainly Shi'-ites, had been arrested by mid-January 1995. While some observers pointed to the role of Shi'ite clerics in instigating the unrest—many of whom received their religious training in the Iranian city of Qom—others have emphasized that these disturbances were very different from the events of 1981 when the new Islamic Republic urged Bahraini Shi'ites to overthrow the Amir. By late 1994 Iran, accused by Israel and the USA of having nuclear ambitions, had been trying to improve its relations with its Gulf neighbours, and the Iranian press was cautious in reporting the troubles. Indeed the political slogans employed during these demonstrations were not urging the establishment of an Islamic republic in Bahrain but, rather, the restoration of parliamentary life by re-establishing the National Assembly. Sheikh Salman had been active in supporting a petition which had been circulating since October 1994 appealing for the restoration of the National Assembly, the involvement of women in the democratic process and free elections. According to opposition sources some 21,000–25,000 signatures had been obtained, including those of Sunnis and Shi'ites from the professional classes, despite the vigilance of the security services. The thwarted aspirations of the Shi'ite majority, primarily a result of socio-economic factors, especially rising unemployment, also contributed to the crisis. Shi'ite workers felt particularly threatened by the recruitment of cheap and well-qualified Asian labour, a practice encouraged by several members of the royal family who benefited financially from immigration. Resentment had also grown owing to the presence of a large number of highly-paid expatriates employed especially in the financial sector.

In mid-January 1995 Sheikh Salman, together with two associates, was deported from Bahrain. When Sheikh Salman arrived in the United Kingdom seeking political asylum, the Bahraini Minister of Foreign Affairs, Sheikh Muhammad bin Mubarak al-Khalifa, was dispatched to London to demand that Salman's request be denied. The Crown Prince of Bahrain, Sheikh Hamad bin Isa al-Khalifa, accused Britain of sheltering 'terrorists and saboteurs'. The Government confirmed that the demonstrators arrested during the unrest in December would stand trial but denied foreign press reports of renewed civil disturbances.

Throughout the crisis the Amir was able to depend on the full support of Saudi Arabia which, according to Bahraini opposition sources, had rapidly dispatched two brigades of its National Guard (around 4,000 men) across the causeway to Bahrain to assist the local police in quelling the rioting. During a visit to Manama in late December the Saudi Minister of the Interior, Prince Nayef ibn Abd al-Aziz as-Sa'ud, reiterated his country's support for the Bahraini Government's firm stance against the demonstrators, as Saudi Arabia was particularly concerned that any unrest among the Shi'ites of Bahrain should not spread to its own Shi'ite population, mainly concentrated in the oil-rich Eastern Province. Shortly afterwards, Egypt expressed its support for the Amir.

In early March 1995 the Amir ordered the release of 100 detainees, including some of those arrested during the disturbances in December 1994—300 of whom reportedly remained in prison. Meanwhile, as part of its efforts to confront anti-government protests, Bahrain convened a meeting of GCC Ministers of the Interior in Manama in April. In a statement issued following the meeting the GCC states fully supported the measures taken by Bahrain to maintain security and stability and declared their determination to fight 'the phenomenon of extremism which is alien to Islam'. Further violence had erupted at the end of March, in which at least two people died, and there

were reports of almost daily protests during the first week in April. The Prime Minister claimed that 'the acts of sabotage' were linked to 'foreign groups' and were premeditated. Reports suggested that business life had been largely unaffected by the disturbances, but the US embassy in Manama nevertheless advised US nationals not to leave their homes at night or at the weekend. According to Amnesty International at least 700 people had been arrested since December 1994. In May and July 1995 several Bahrainis were sentenced to prison terms ranging from one year to life imprisonment for their role in the disturbances, and one Bahraini was sentenced to death for his part in the murder of a policeman in March. In mid-August the Amir issued a decree pardoning 150 people detained since the disturbances. In the same month the Government initiated talks with Shi'ite opposition leaders in an apparent attempt at reconciliation, although in mid-September it was announced that the talks had failed. Nevertheless, in late September an influential Shi'ite clergyman, Sheikh Abd al-Amir al-Jamri (imprisoned in April), was released from detention; more than 40 other Shi'ite detainees were released shortly afterwards.

At the end of June 1995 the Prime Minister, Sheikh Khalifa bin Sulman al-Khalifa, announced the first major cabinet reshuffle in nearly 20 years. Cabinet changes had been expected since the outbreak of political unrest in December 1994 but the regime stressed that the reshuffle was not a result of the pro-democracy demonstrations but had been planned for some time. There were no changes, however, at the key Defence, Foreign Affairs, Finance and National Economy and Interior portfolios. Within the new 16-man Cabinet seven posts were retained by members of the ruling family and five by Shi'ites. Reducing unemployment by creating new job opportunities, and improving the standard of living were identified as the Government's major priorities but education, public services and development were also to receive greater attention. It was announced that the Bahrain Defence Force would be expanded 'to protect the nation'. The opposition denounced the reshuffle as purely cosmetic and accused the Government of ignoring new political developments. While Bahraini official sources claimed that stability had been completely restored, the opposition stated that, in the absence of meaningful dialogue, and given the Government's refusal to consider demands for political representation, rioting could erupt again.

Meanwhile, the opposition maintained that, during the reconciliation talks which they had initiated during the summer, the authorities had agreed to release all detainees and to allow the return of political exiles. In return, the opposition pledged to exert their influence in an attempt to end the violence. By early October some 400 political prisoners had been released but others remained in detention. Accusing the Government of having failed to fulfil its promise to release all detainees, in October 1995 seven opposition leaders led by Sheikh al-Jamri staged a hunger strike. They demanded the release of all political prisoners, permission for those dissidents who had been deported to return to Bahrain, and an agreement by the authorities to resume open talks with the opposition regarding the restoration of the 1973 Constitution; the Government had denied that earlier meetings with the opposition had actually taken place. However, Sheikh al-Jamri and the other protesters ended their hunger strike at the beginning of November without achieving their objectives.

Disturbances erupted again in November 1995 (especially among students) and, according to opposition sources, the police made hundreds of arrests. The authorities sought assistance from Saudi Arabia, and it was reported that Saudi security officers were again dispatched to reinforce the Bahraini police. In January and February 1996 the conflict escalated when a number of bombs exploded in Manama's business district. The IFLB claimed responsibility for a bomb attack on the Diplomat Hotel in February in which a number of people were wounded. The security forces had closed mosques where prominent leaders had continued to urge the authorities to restore democracy, and in late January eight opposition leaders, including Sheikh al-Jamri, had been rearrested. They were expected to stand trial on charges of inciting unrest. For the first time in the recent disturbances the authorities also detained a prominent Sunni member of the Committee for Popular Petition; Ahmad ash-Shamlan (a lawyer) was arrested after he distributed a statement criticizing the Government's authoritarian action. Ash-Shamlan was released in May following strong representation by international organizations. The closure of mosques provoked renewed violence, as protesters clashed with police. Mass arrests were reported, and at the beginning of February the Ministry of the Interior admitted that some 600 people had been detained, although the opposition estimated the number of arrests at 2,000. Reports suggested that most of those detained were held without charge or trial and that they included women and children. A report published in September 1995 by Amnesty International had underlined the systematic use of torture by the security services when interrogating political prisoners. Previously, civil disturbances had been dealt with by the Ministry of the Interior, but in a statement issued at the end of January 1996 the Ministry of Defence announced that it was prepared to introduce martial law and to deploy the Bahrain Defence Force to restore effective order in the future.

In March 1996 as unrest continued, seven Bangladeshi workers were killed in a fire-bomb attack on a restaurant in Sitra, representing the worst arson attack since the disturbances began. Within days the Ministry of the Interior announced that it had arrested a number of individuals who had confessed to the attack, but many Bahrainis suspected that the attack was carried out by government agents. The opposition condemned the attack, while the Bangladeshi Government was critical of the Bahrain security forces' handling of the case. On 20 March the Amir issued a decree transferring jurisdiction for a range of offences from ordinary courts to the Higher Court of Appeal, sitting as the State Security Court. This effectively introduced a 'fast track' system where the accused has no right of appeal and the role of the defence is greatly limited. On 26 March, Isa Ahmad Hassan Qambar was executed by firing squad after being sentenced to death for killing a policeman during clashes with security forces in March 1995. It was the first execution in Bahrain for almost 20 years. Qambar's trial was condemned by Amnesty International for ignoring 'internationally accepted human rights standards', while the Bahraini opposition described it as a 'political murder' intended to prompt popular compliance. There were allegations that the case against Qambar had been based on confessions made in detention and under torture. The execution provoked mass protests, with police using tear-gas to disperse young Shi'ite protesters. Thousands of people observed a week of mourning declared by the opposition to mark Qambar's execution. In April the Government announced the creation of a Higher Council of Islamic Affairs, appointed by the Prime Minister and headed by the Minister of Justice and Islamic Affairs, to supervise religious activities in the country, including those of the Shi'ite population. Leading figures in the Shi'ite community immediately condemned the move as an attempt to interfere in their affairs. At the end of April the Government announced that the State Security Court had imprisoned 11 people on charges connected with the disturbances, including arson, sabotage and membership of illegal organizations. It was reported that large numbers of defendants had been tried in groups and sentenced to long terms of imprisonment by the Court. At the beginning of May, after the death of a demonstrator as a result of the security forces opening fire on a crowd of protestors, a number of bombs exploded throughout the country, killing several people including two policemen. Although the IFLB maintains a 'relations office' in Teheran, most observers are convinced that the pro-democracy movement is locally-rooted, unifying various trends and sections of Bahraini society with no outside support, despite the insistence of the authorities that the dissidents have foreign backers.

At the beginning of June 1996 the Government organized a press conference in Manama at which it announced that some 10 prisoners had confessed to belonging to the military branch of Hezbollah Bahrain, a previously unknown organization. The authorities stated that the prisoners had admitted that this terrorist group had been created on the instruction of Iran's Revolutionary Guards and had received financial support from them. They alleged that young Bahraini Shi'ites had received military training in the Iranian holy city of Qom and in guerrilla bases in the Beka'a valley in Lebanon. They also claimed that the previous 18 months of unrest had been the culmination of a 'terrorist programme of sabotage' perpetrated by this group

in order to overthrow the regime and replace it with a pro-Iranian government. However, the authorities were satisfied that they had arrested the movement's leaders. The day after the press conference, as the prisoners made their confessions before television cameras, one of them claimed that Sheikh al-Jamri had 'sanctioned' two bomb attacks carried out in July 1995. The country's two leading daily newspapers praised the Minister of the Interior and the security services for their vigilance and published messages of loyalty and support for the Amir and Prime Minister. However, an opposition spokesman in London rejected claims that a Hezbollah group sponsored by Iran was active in Bahrain, and claimed that the regime was merely using Iran as a scapegoat. Independent sources cast doubt on the validity of the confessions, claiming that the prisoners had been denied legal representation during their detention, and referred to Amnesty International's report in September 1995 which alleged that political detainees were systematically tortured. They also pointed out that recent acts of sabotage were not professionally executed and therefore not consistent with the presence of a well-trained and well-armed movement such as Hezbollah. This was the first time that the Bahrain Government had directly accused Iran of supporting the unrest, allegations which Iran continued to deny. Bahrain recalled its ambassador to Teheran and downgraded its diplomatic representation there.

In July 1996, the State Security Court imposed the death sentence on three of the eight young Bahrainis convicted of the arson attack in Sitra. Another four men were sentenced to life imprisment. The death sentences provoked widespread protests and, after international criticism, the Government agreed to allow an appeal against the ruling. In October the Court of Cassation ruled that it had no jurisdiction to overturn the verdict, and the fate of the three men seemed likely to be decided by the Amir. There were more anti-government demonstrations in July and August, and a campaign of civil disobedience organized by the exiled Bahrain Freedom Movement (BFM) was reported to have been well supported, notably among the Shi'a population. Towards the end of the year, Government plans to close a number of Shi'a mosques resulted in further unrest. Demonstrators gathered at the Ras Roman mosque in central Manama became involved in a violent confrontation with the security forces during which police fired tear-gas at worshippers. Civil unrest continued in December, prompting rumours that the ruling family was divided over how to respond to the crisis.

In September 1996, in what was interpreted as a move to counter opposition demands, the Amir expanded the membership of the government-appointed Consultative Council from 30 to 40 and to allowed up to one-half of the members to be elected indirectly through professional and cultural organizations. The new Council was comprised of 22 members of the previous council and 18 new members nominatd by the Amir. Appointed for a four-year term, the new Council will comment on most areas of government policy (the previous Council had been restricted to consideration of Cabinet-proposed legislation) but will still enjoy very limited powers since its recommendations will continue to be non-binding on the Government. A new decree, issued by the Amir in June, divided Bahrain into four new administrative regions known as *Mohafadat*, with the aim of improving services and making officials more accountable. However, opponents argued that the new system would enable the interior ministry to intensify security measures, particularly following reports that the ministry was to be reorganized and the intelligence service expanded. In January 1997 the Amir issued a decree establishing a National Guard to provide support for the National Defence Force and the security forces of the interior ministry. The Amir's son Hamad, Commander-in-Chief of the Defence Force, was also appointed to command the new force, and there was speculation that its primary duty would be to protect the ruling family.

Unrest continued during 1997, and in March a week of anti-Government protests marked the first anniversary of the execution of Isa Ahmad Hassan Qambar. Although stricter security measures had resulted in fewer public demonstrations, arson attacks increased substantially, especially against commercial premises in Manama. During 1994–97 more than 30 people were killed in arson attacks and small-scale bombings. Two car bomb explosions in the capital, in June and October 1997, were considered by some observers to signal the beginning of a heightened campaign of violence on the part of the opposition. A pronounced increase in the number of Asian workers targeted by arsonists between 1996 and early 1998 was attributed, in part, to mounting frustration among less privileged sections of Bahraini society at rising unemployment.

In April 1997 the US military command in Bahrain placed its forces on alert after reports of possible terrorist operations against US navy personnel by Hezbollah Bahrain. In January the security forces had successfully contained large-scale anti-Government demonstrations organized by opponents of the regime on the occasion of the second anniversary of the arrest of Sheikh Abd al-Amir al-Jamri. The deteriorating health of the prominent Shi'ite cleric lent a sense of urgency to the occasion, particularly as Amnesty International had already raised concerns about his well-being. In July, following the death in custody of another senior Shi'ite dissident cleric, Human Rights Watch, an independent organization based in New York, published a report which condemned the security practices of the Government. The report urged the US Government to take active steps to review its involvement in Bahrain and to put pressure on the ruling family to restore civil liberties. A UN sub-commission and the European Parliament were also critical of Bahrain's human rights record. The European Parliament in particular urged the Bahraini Government to release political prisoners and to grant access to human rights organizations. Growing concern for human rights in Bahrain resulted in unprecedented scrutiny of Bahraini internal affairs by the international community, and recent sentences against political opponents have been noticeably lenient. In mid-April 1997 the trial of 81 Bahrainis accused of membership of the terrorist organization Hezbollah Bahrain ended unexpectedly with relatively light sentences; no death sentences were passed and the maximum terms of imprisonment imposed were 15 years, for the alleged leaders. A lawsuit filed by the Government in October against eight Shi'ite members of the opposition residing abroad followed a similar course. Despite the severity of the charges, which included inciting violence, establishing Hezbollah Bahrain, and attempting to overthrow the regime, the dissidents, who were tried *in absentia*, received prison sentences of between five and 15 years. During 1997 the authorities released a substantial number of political detainees (approximately 3,000 according to unofficial sources).

In January 1998 the Amir announced a further enlargement of the Consultative Council. Media coverage of Council proceedings, meanwhile, have increased substantially and access to meetings has been granted to the press and to the state-controlled television. In addition, during 1997 the Ministry of Information relaxed publishing restrictions considerably. Administrative reorganization of the country is continuing, and two members of the ruling family were appointed to the governorships of Manama and Muharraq island in 1997 and 1998; they were to be directly responsible to the Ministry of the Interior. These new developments were interpreted as further evidence of an ongoing power struggle between the Prime Minister and the Crown Prince. In late February Ian Henderson, the long-serving, British-born head of the State Security Investigation Directorate, was replaced by Khalid bin Muhammad al-Khalifa, a close associate of the Crown Prince. The dismissal of Henderson, considered to be central to the apparatus of state repression, was welcomed by opponents of the Government, who stated that a pre-condition for dialogue with the Government was the 'Bahrainization' of the security forces; in 1997 opposition sources estimated that as many as 50,000 non-Bahrainis were employed in the country's security.

The Bahrain Government has received support from Pakistan, Egypt, Syria and Jordan, but Saudi Arabia has remained its most steadfast ally, and is believed to have pledged increased financial support to enable the al-Khalifa regime to suppress the recent unrest. Early in 1996 Saudi Arabia announced that it was allocating its share of output from the Abu Saafa oilfield to Bahrain (see Economy). A number of GCC countries have offered their support for maintaining the status quo in Bahrain, but it is unclear whether they accept Bahrain's argument that if the dissidents succeed there, unrest will spread to other states in the region. However, regional tensions have continued to

arise. An appeal made by a number of leading Kuwaiti personalities to the Amir to renew dialogue with the opposition resulted in an official Bahraini protest to the Kuwaiti Government and the UAE's request for an end to UN sanctions against Iraq was similarly rejected by Bahrain, which supports Saudi Arabia's uncompromising stance on this issue. Relations with Qatar, traditionally tense as a result of the longstanding dispute over the Hawar islands (see above), deteriorated sharply at the end of 1995. During a meeting between the countries' rulers at the GCC annual summit meeting in Muscat they failed to reach any agreement on the territorial dispute. Qatar criticized Bahrain's decision to build a tourist resort on the disputed islands and urged co-operation with the ICJ on the resolution of the dispute. Bahrain, however, defended its decision, maintaining that the islands were 'sovereign territory' and again refused to accept the jurisdiction of the ICJ on this issue. Relations between Qatar and Bahrain deteriorated at the end of 1996, following an announcement, made by the Bahrain Government in early December, that two Qatari nationals had been arrested in Bahrain and charged with spying. (The two men were subsequently acquitted.) Qatar retaliated with public accusations of Bahraini involvement in the failed February coup attempt. Bahrain boycotted the GCC annual summit convened in Doha in December, at which it was decided to establish a quadripartite committee (comprising those GCC countries not involved in the dispute) to facilitate a solution. Attempts by the committee to foster improved relations between Bahrain and Qatar achieved a degree of success, and meetings between prominent government ministers from both countries in London (United Kingdom) and Manama (Bahrain) in February and March 1997 resulted in the announcement that diplomatic relations at ambassadorial level were to be established between the two countries by mid-1997. However, while the Qatari Government appointed its diplomatic representative soon after the exchange of ambassadors was agreed, by mid-1998 the Bahraini authorities had yet to name their representative to Doha. There were renewed tensions between the two countries in mid-1997, when the Bahraini authorities opened a new hotel on the Hawar islands; plans to build a housing complex there were also announced at that time, and in February 1998 the Amir made a widely publicized visit to the islands. There have been repeated regional attempts to find a solution to the dispute, particularly by Saudi Arabia and the UAE, whose opposition to Qatar's stance has encouraged Bahrain to emphasize its belief in its territorial rights there by increasing its occupancy of the islands. Bahrain has repeatedly stated that it will disregard any final decision made by the ICJ, and has dismissed as forgeries a series of documents submitted by the Qatari Government in support of its own claim.

Relations with Jordan, which had been strained since the Gulf crisis in 1990, improved during 1995, and Bahrain nominated a new ambassador to Amman in September. Jordan's new Prime Minister, Abd al-Karim al-Kabariti, indicated that the Jordanian Government would consider sending troops to Bahrain to assist the authorities if they were to request its help. In early June, a meeting of GCC foreign ministers warned Iran against acts of destabilization in the region. Bahrain attended the Arab League summit meeting in Cairo at the end of June 1996, where the final communiqué criticized Iran for its 'interference in the internal affairs of Bahrain'. In October the Bahraini Minister of Foreign Affairs announced an improvement in relations with Iran. Following mediation by the Syrian foreign minister in July, it was reported that the Iranian authorities had agreed to halt media coverage of disturbances in Bahrain as well as interviews with exiled opposition leaders. Relations have improved steadily since the election of Sayed Muhammad Khatami as President of Iran in May 1997. The new Iranian foreign minister, Kamal Kharraz, visited Bahrain in November and discussed the expansion of diplomatic, cultural and economic relations between the two countries with his Bahraini counterpart. In March 1998 the former Iranian President, Hashemi Rafsanjani, held talks with the Amir during a two-day visit to Manama. In early 1997, in co-operation with the Bahrain intelligence service, the Kuwaiti authorities arrested 11 Bahrainis in Kuwait accused of membership of a new dissident group, Hezbollah-Gulf, allegedly committed to the overthrow of all Gulf regimes. However, the arrests were criticized by Shi'a members of the Kuwaiti National Assembly and, as a result, the authorities refused to extradite the men to Bahrain. However, relations between the two Governments have remained cordial and in July 1998 the Amir received the Kuwaiti Minister of the Interior to discuss joint security measures to counter seditious activities in the two countries.

The Bahrain Government continued to receive support from its traditional Western allies, the USA and the United Kingdom in its efforts to suppress recent domestic instability. The United Kingdom, under pressure from Saudi Arabia, had made it clear that dissidents from the Gulf region, including Bahrain, were no longer welcome there. In December 1995, with some reluctance, Bahrain agreed to a US request to allow the temporary stationing of American military aircraft in Bahrain. In March 1996 an agreement was reached with the USA to supply Bahrain with an advanced frigate and air-defence system. The USA condemned Iran for interfering in Bahrain's internal affairs, and in June 1996, after the Bahraini authorities announced the discovery of an alleged Iranian-backed plot to destabilize the archipelago, the Government made public US President Clinton's assurances to the Amir that the USA pledged its 'total support to his Government, his sovereignty and the security of Bahraini territories'. In late 1997 the USA supported Bahrain's candidature to the UN Security Council. However, relations between the two countries deteriorated subsequently; in early 1998 a US Department of State review of human rights was extremely critical of Bahrain's record, and relations deteriorated further in February when Bahrain opposed any military intervention in Iraq, and advocated a diplomatic solution to the impasse between UN weapons inspectors and the Iraqi's authorities (see chapter on Iraq). (During a visit to France in mid-February, the Bahraini Minister of Foreign Affairs expressed his hope that France would take the lead in the ongoing diplomatic negotiations between Iraq and the UN.) In March the Bahraini Government agreed to accommodate a continued US military presence, and in April US forces replaced their combat and air support units using Bahrain as a base, in order to strengthen US attack capabilities; Bahraini forces also participated in naval exercises

with both US and British units. However, following a visit by the Amir to the USA in June—the first such visit by a Gulf leader for more than five years—it seemed that the US Government was intending to reduce its military presence in the region. The Amir's second visit to France in late May was followed by talks with President Clinton and UN Secretary-General Kofi Annan in Washington in early June, and underlined Bahrain's support for the implementation of Middle East peace accords in line with the policy of the League of Arab States (Arab League, of which Bahrain is a member). Relations with the United Kingdom have been strained by the election there, in May 1997, of a Labour Government which has placed greater importance on human rights issues in its foreign policy dealings. In January 1997 Muhammad Ibrahim al-Mutawa, the Minister of Cabinet Affairs and Information, held talks with the French in Paris in a move to develop both diplomatic and economic relations. In the past, France has enjoyed closer links with Qatar but is reportedly keen to improve relations with Bahrain.

Bahrain declined to make official comment when Israeli television stated in November 1995 that Bahrain, together with Qatar and Oman, was preparing to open consular offices in Israel. While contacts at ministerial level have taken place between Bahrain and Israel (see above) it is thought that Bahrain will follow the example of Saudi Arabia and refuse a move towards diplomatic relations until there is a comprehensive Middle East peace settlement and the status of Jerusalem, in particular, is resolved. Bahrain, unlike Qatar and Oman, declined to send a representative to the funeral of assassinated Israeli Prime Minister Rabin in November and denied that there had been any contact between the Bahraini Minister of Commerce and his Israeli counterpart at the Middle East and North Africa Economic Summit conducted in Jordan during the previous month. In March 1997, in protest at Israel's decision to construct a Jewish settlement in a disputed area of East Jerusalem, the League of Arab States voted to suspend negotiations to establish diplomatic links with Israel, close Israeli missions, restore the economic boycott and withdraw from multilateral peace talks.

Economy

ALAN J. DAY

Based on an earlier article by Dr. P. T. H. Unwin, with subsequent revision by Richard I. Lawless
Revised for this edition by the Editor

INTRODUCTION

During the 1970s and 1980s the exploitation of Bahrain's hydro-carbon resources was the basis for considerable economic diversification, particularly in the construction, industry and banking sectors. After the Gulf crisis of 1990–91 Bahrain encountered some difficulty in regaining the momentum for economic growth. The unemployment rate in 1996 was unofficiallly estimated to be as high as 18%, the population growth rate (currently around 3.3% per year) having for some years exceeded the rate of real GDP growth (which in 1996 was 3.1%). The creation of new jobs was, therefore, a government priority.

In 1991 the Government established the Bahrain Development Bank to provide long-term loans and venture capital to attract investors, and the Bahrain Marketing and Promotions Office to encourage companies to establish a base in the region. Incentives to new investors introduced in the 1993 Government Incentive Programme included major tax concessions, rebates on rent and power charges to small and medium-sized companies, and a subsidy for every Bahraini national employed. Official procedures were simplified and full foreign ownership of companies was allowed provided that they were engaged in industrial activities or were establishing a base for the sale of manufactured goods and services in the Gulf region. According to the Government, this constituted the best foreign investment incentive package in the region. There was also duty-free access to the wider GCC market for Bahrain-based industries whose products met GCC eligibility criteria.

Having encouraged new private industrial investment, Bahrain was forced to consider the crucial future expansion of infrastructure, including water and electricity supply systems in imminent need of additional capacity to meet rising demand. The Government, however, was reluctant to embark on a major capital spending programme as long as it continued to experience problems in containing the existing budget deficit. Approval for several major development projects was postponed during 1994 and 1995, when it was widely predicted that the Government would eventually seek foreign private investment for key infrastructure developments. During 1996, however, the Government's financial situation (already benefiting from higher oil export prices) was greatly strengthened by Saudi Arabia's decision to allocate its share of the 1996 annual output of petroleum from the jointly-owned Abu Saafa oilfield to Bahrain. By early 1997 the Government had approved a medium-term investment programme totalling more than US $3,000m., including a new port and industrial area and additional water and power plants, giving rise to expectations of a period of strong growth after the relative stagnation of recent years.

AGRICULTURE AND FISHING

Agriculture has declined rapidly since the 1960s, and in 1996 contributed less than 1% of gross domestic product (GDP). The Bahrain islands are largely barren and have never been able to support farming on more than a limited scale. About three-quarters of the agricultural land in traditional farming areas in the north had been abandoned by the end of the 1970s. This reduction in agriculture was caused both by the increasing salinity of traditional supplies of water, and by the attractions of other sectors of the economy. The Government was nevertheless keen to develop the archipelago's agricultural potential. By 1988 milk production had risen sufficiently to satisfy 50% of local demand, and vegetable production had increased to meet 75% of requirements. Self-sufficiency in egg production had also been achieved. In order to increase the national agricultural area, the Government initiated a two-stage irrigation project, costing an estimated BD 12m., that entailed ozonizing and storing treated sewage at the Tubli sewage works for distribution and application to fields. In 1996 there were an estimated 17,000 cattle, 29,000 sheep and 18,000 goats in the country.

In 1979 the Bahrain Fishing Company was forced to cease its operations because of the virtual disappearance of shrimps from the Gulf, owing to pollution. In 1981 the Government initiated a five-year plan to revive the industry by acquiring more sophisticated equipment and establishing training schemes. In 1985 the Government announced an investment of BD 20,000 ($54,000) to revive the pearling industry. In December 1988 a fisheries development programme, with a projected cost of BD 19m., was initiated, but in mid-1989 about 75% of the country's fish resources remained unexploited, and one-third of local fish requirements were being supplied by imports. In June 1993 the Ministry of Agriculture and Fisheries sold a government fishing project at Mina Salman to the private sector, the local Banz Group. There are plans to modernize the fishing fleet and processing facilities at Mina Salman, which could eventually supply 25% of the local market for fish products.

PETROLEUM AND GAS

Bahrain's average production of crude petroleum from the onshore Awali field peaked at 76,639 b/d in 1970 and subsequently decreased steadily as reserves were depleted. Since the 1980s output has generally been kept below a 42,000 b/d ceiling in order to regulate the rate of depletion. In 1996 production averaged 39,638 b/d. The field is operated by the state-owned Bahrain National Oil Company. At 1 January 1997 Bahrain's proven published reserves of petroleum were estimated at 200m. barrels; in 1996 total national production averaged 104,000 b/d. Between 1981 and 1984 the Government spent $20m. on exploration and drilling, but no significant discoveries were made. Offshore exploration between 1991 and 1995 was similarly unproductive. However, Bahrain does have a long-standing entitlement to a 50% share in revenues from the Abu Saafa field, situated between Bahrain and Saudi Arabia and operated by Saudi Aramco. In the mid-1990s the field was producing an average 140,000 b/d. At the beginning of 1993 Saudi Arabia increased Bahrain's allocation to 100,000 b/d for two years and in early 1996 agreed to allocate the entire Abu Saafa revenue to Bahrain, this decision apparently being unconditional and open-ended.

A 250,000 b/d refinery at Sitra processes all Bahrain's onshore output and supplies Bahrain's domestic product requirements of around 10,000 b/d. However, the bulk of its crude supply is imported via pipeline from Saudi Arabia and the bulk of its product output is exported. The refinery is operated by the Bahrain Petroleum Company (BAPCO), which from 1981 was owned by the Bahrain Government (60%) and Caltex (40%) until in April 1997 the Government acquired the Caltex shareholding to become sole owner. The Government thus assumed complete control of Bahrain's oil exports and became the sole decision-maker on the question of implementing a major refinery modernization programme which had been repeatedly deferred throughout the 1990s. During the first half of the 1990s the Sitra refinery normally operated at close to its nominal capacity (which was sometimes exceeded). In 1996 it processed an averaged 250,975 b/d of crude oil. It has storage facilities for 14m. barrels and operates a six-berth export terminal.

Bahrain's proven reserves of natural gas totalled 150,000m. cu m at the end of 1996, sufficient to sustain production at current rates for more than 20 years. Marketed gas output in 1996 (excluding gas flared or reinjected into oil wells) was 7,200m. cu m. Nearly one-third of Bahrain's gas output is reinjected, with the remainder used by power stations, by the ALBA aluminium smelter, by the Sitra oil refinery and (as feedstock) by the local petrochemicals industry. The 75% state-owned Bahrain National Gas Company (BANAGAS) has the capacity to process 4.8m. cu m of gas per day to produce liquefied products (propane, butane and naphtha) for export, and dry gases (mainly methane and ethane) for local use as industrial fuels.

INDUSTRY

Manufacturing accounted for about 22% of GDP in 1995 and for a similar proportion of exports in 1996. In the mid-1990s government efforts were concentrated on encouraging private foreign investment in the industrial sector to achieve greater diversification and to promote more export-oriented industries. Investment is being sought in downstream industries related to aluminium and pharmaceuticals, as well as in new activities. The Government's Incentive Programme, introduced in 1993, offers a wide range of concessions and incentives to attract foreign investment, and official procedures have been greatly simplified. There were seven designated industrial areas in Bahrain in 1996 offering competitively priced leases on manufacturing units with infrastructrual support services in place.

The aluminium industry remains central to the Government's strategy to expand the country's export-oriented industries. In 1994 some 23 downstream aluminium projects were being promoted by the state and private sectors. The development of Bahrain's aluminium industry began in 1969 when the Government formed a consortium with British, Swedish, French and US companies to construct and operate an aluminium smelter with a capacity of 120,000 metric tons per year. Production at the new smelter of Aluminium Bahrain (ALBA) began in 1972 using alumina imported from Australia. The Bahrain Government now owns 77% of ALBA together with the Public Investment Fund of Saudi Arabia (20%) and Breton Investments of Germany (3%). A $1,500m.-expansion programme to increase the annual capacity of the smelter to 460,000 tons was completed in November 1992, making it one of the largest in the world. In 1996 ALBA increased its output by 10,500 tons to 461,245 tons, this being the first year in which the smelter operated above its nominal design capacity. At the start of 1997 a third potline came on stream, increasing annual capacity to 496,500 tons from the middle of the year. During 1996 ALBA readjusted its production mix to raise annual output of extrusion billets to 200,000 tons and output of rolling slabs to 100,000 tons per year, in response to the changing demands of local secondary processors. The remainder of ALBA's output consists of aluminium ingots for remelt. Infrastructural facilities within the ALBA production complex include two desalination plants with a combined capacity of 3,000 cu m per day, a 800-MW main power plant and an additional 164-MW gas turbine (added in 1997). Aluminium accounts for about one-half of Bahrain's non-oil exports. ALBA's output is marketed abroad by the Bahrain-Saudi Aluminium Marketing Company (BALCO). About one-third of 1996 production was sold within Bahrain and other GCC countries.

Seven major secondary enterprises, related to aluminium, now exist in Bahrain. The first downstream venture was the International Bahrain Aluminium Atomizer Company, established in 1973 with 51% government ownership in association with Eckart Werke of Germany. It produces 7,000 tons of atomized aluminium powder a year which is marketed in Japan, Germany, the United Kingdom and the USA.

The Bahrain Aluminium Extrusion Company (BALEXCO, established in state ownership in 1977 and transferred to the private sector in 1995) produces aluminium profiles and sections for domestic and foreign markets. In 1997 it completed a third extrusion line which brought its total capacity up to 21,000 tons per year. During 1996 BALEXCO added a 12,000 tons-per-year scrap recycling plant and a powder coating facility to its operations.

Midal Cables, established under private ownership in 1978, was producing around 50,000 tons per year of aluminium rods and coils (including overhead transmission conductors) in 1997 and planned to add more capacity in the future. Its subsidiary, Metal Form, was set up in 1994 to produce products from Midal's own aluminium rods. Another subsidiary, Aluwheel, established in 1991, produces semi-finished aluminium wheel hubs for European car manufacturers; its 1996 output was around 600,000 units.

Gulf Aluminium Rolling Mill Company (GARMCO, established in 1986 under the auspices of the Gulf Organization for Industrial Consulting—see p. 272) had a total production capacity of 120,000 tons per year of aluminium plate and sheet products in 1997, following a major expansion of its plant.

Bahrain Alloys Manufacturing Company, established by overseas investors in 1994, produces alloys for the automotive and aerospace industries.

The Gulf Petrochemical Industries Corpn (GPIC) built a petrochemicals plant at Sitra in 1985 with a capacity of 1,200 tons a day each of ammonia and methanol. The complex is a joint venture between the Bahrain National Oil Company, the Saudi Basic Industries Corpn and Kuwait's Petrochemical Industries Corpn. Output of ammonia and methanol totalled 777,000 tons in 1996, when GPIC recorded an operating profit of $52m. A new plant under construction in 1997 was designed to produce urea using ammonia feedstock from the existing GPIC facility.

In June 1993 the National Chemical Industries Corpn (NACIC) signed a $13.1m.-contract with United Engineers International of the USA to build a sulphur derivatives plant near the refinery at Sitra. The plant was to produce 18,000 tons of sodium sulphite and sodium metabisulphite each year. NACIC is owned by the Bahraini United Gulf Industries Corpn (55%), together with the Qatar Industrial Manufacturing Company (15%), the Saudi Arabian Industry Development Company (10%), and the United Group for the Development of Riyadh (5%).

The Arab Shipbuilding and Repair Yard (ASRY) Company's dry dock, financed by the members of the Organization of Arab Petroleum Exporting Countries (OAPEC—see p. 259), was opened in 1977. It first recorded a full year's profitable trading in 1987. In 1992 ASRY invested $61m. in two floating docks, giving the yard increased flexibility. The yard originally had a single 500,000-ton graving dock. In response to increased demand, in June 1995 the company announced plans to expand the shipyard over the next two–three years at a cost of $87m. Plans include dredging a new 1,000-m channel, constructing a 1,000-m quay wall, purchasing another crane and constructing workshops, and land installations. ASRY reported operating profits of $8.5m. in 1995, 16% more than in 1994. Net ship-repair revenues rose to $72.6m., representing an increase of 10.8% compared with 1994, and the number of vessels repaired during the year rose from 104 to 113. The Bahrain Ship Repairing and Maintenance Company specializes in smaller-scale ship repairs.

In 1981 the Bahrain Government attempted further to diversify the economy by forming the Arab Iron and Steel Company (AISCO), with shareholders from Bahrain, Kuwait, Jordan and the United Arab Emirates (UAE). The company opened the Gulf's first iron-pelletizing plant in December 1984, with a capacity of 4m. tons per year. After operating at a heavy financial loss, AISCO was sold in 1988 to Gulf Industrial Investment Company (a subsidiary of the Kuwait Petroleum Corpn).

In 1995 W. S. Atkins completed a feasibility study for a 1.2m. tons-per-year sponge iron plant to be built by the Bahrain Ispat Company (BIC), established by India's Ispat Group. The $290m.-plant will produce briquettes of compressed iron pellets to be used in steel making, for export to India, Asia, the Middle East and Europe. The US company Midrex is to provide the direct reduction technology for the plant. In April 1996 the Gulf Investment Corpn, financial advisor to the project, announced that both local and international banks had expressed interest in raising some $210m. for the project; a further $80m. would be provided in the form of equity by the Mittal family of India who control the Ispat Group. The project is due to be commissioned in mid-1989.

In 1985 the Gulf Acid Industries Company began production of sulphuric acid and distilled water. Light industry, including the production of supplementary gas supplies, asphalt, prefabricated buildings, plastics, soft drinks, air-conditioning equipment and paper products, also continued to develop during 1986. In 1987 the Government imposed a 20% tariff on competing imported goods for a trial period of 12 months, as part of a programme to support the expansion of light industry. In 1987 Wires International became the first Bahraini company to export an industrial product, aluminium fly mesh, to the Far East. In 1988 the Government announced plans to increase import substitution to a level of 30%, with guaranteed state protection of markets. In 1989 Bahrain Berger Paints, in a joint venture with United Breweries of India, announced a new $3,000m.-project for a pharmaceuticals plant, the first of its kind in Bahrain. Following the introduction of the Government's Incentive Programme in 1993, two joint ventures were agreed: a tissue paper mill—a joint venture between Olayan of Saudi Arabia and Kimberly-Clark of the USA—and a factory producing prefabricated pipeline systems, a joint venture between Shaw Industries of the USA and the local Ahmad Nass Industrial Services. The tissue paper mill started production in March 1995. Output is marketed in the Gulf states, mainly in Saudi Arabia. A factory to manufacture construction chemicals is being set up in the North Sitra industrial area by Sika Gulf, a group of investors led by the Swiss chemical firm Sika and including Saudi Arabian interests. Output will be marketed mainly in Saudi Arabia and the UAE.

In January 1995 the Government launched a programme to encourage investment in medium-scale industrial projects in order to strengthen economic diversification. Some 13 industrial projects have been identified in food, engineering, textiles and healthcare, pre-feasibility studies have been completed and technology partners, mostly European companies, have been identified. As the new projects are of a modest scale, the Government hopes to attract investment from Bahraini entrepreneurs and provide more employment and training for Bahraini nationals. In early 1994 Bahrain became the first Gulf state to secure access to the EU equity investment funds for small and medium-sized industrial joint ventures. Up to 20% of the equity for joint ventures between local and European partners can be provided by the EU as well as concessional funding for feasibility studies and human resource development.

POWER AND WATER

Industrial expansion and rapid population growth have put increasing pressure on electricity and water supplies. Bahrain has four power stations, a gas-fired 126-MW station at Manama, a steam-fired 120-MW station at Sitra, a 38-MW station on Muharraq and the largest station, an open-cycle gas turbine plant, at Rifa'a with capacity of 700 MW. In 1991 plans for an increase in electricity supplies were activated. The Sitra power station was refurbished, and in 1994 the ALBA aluminium complex's 800-MW power plant was linked to the national grid, giving the Ministry of Power and Water access to an additional 250 MW of generating capacity for a period of 10 years. However, peak electricity demand in the summer of 1996 was, at 1,050 MW, only 150 MW short of the national grid's maximum supply capability at that time. In October 1996 the Government approved the construction on reclaimed land at Hidd of a new 260-MW power station and an associated desalination plant with a capacity of 30m. gallons (136,380 cu m) per day. The $458m. contract for the Hidd project was signed in January 1997, with a scheduled completion date in 1999, and in March 1997 the Government approved an associated causeway development to link the Hidd site to Mina Salman. The National Bank of Bahrain was to arrange and underwrite a loan facility for the power and desalination project. In 1993 $21.2m. was spent on upgrading the distribution network. While the existing network can absorb the new capacity from Hidd, any further expansion of capacity would require a major reinforcement of the transmission network. The Government was forecasting an electricity demand of 1,280 MW in 2000, rising to 1,600 MW by 2005.

In early 1994 the Bahrain Centre for Studies and Research warned that the island's primary water resources could be exhausted by 2010 unless measures were taken to limit the rate of extraction from the underground aquifer. Extraction rates had in past decades been so far in excess of the natural replenishment rate of about 67.5m. gallons (306,820 cu m) per day that it was estimated that full regeneration of the aquifer could take centuries. Water pumped from underground had become increasingly saline, affecting crop yields in agriculture and necessitating an increasing admixture of desalinated water for domestic use. In 1994 the Ministry of Power imposed a ceiling on total water use which had the effect of reducing the groundwater extraction rate to about 29.2m. gallons (132,500 cu m) per day. Tariffs were introduced for agricultural water use in 1997.

Bahrain had three desalination plants in 1996: a multi-stage flash plant near Sitra power station with a capacity of 25m. gallons (113,650 cu m) per day; a reverse osmosis plant at Abu Jajour with a capacity of 10m. gallons (45,460 cu m) per day; and another 10m. gallons-per-day reverse osmosis plant at Ad-Dur. However, both the Sitra and Ad-Dur plants were in need of extensive renovation work to bring them up to full capacity utilization. This work was scheduled to start in 1997. At a later date it was intended to increase the capacity of the Abu Jajour plant by up to 30%.

BANKING, FINANCE AND TRADE

The Bahrain Monetary Agency (BMA), established in 1973 to replace the Bahrain Currency Board, has exercised all the powers of a central bank since 1975. The BMA oversees the issuing of currency, regulates exchange control and credit policy, and licenses and controls the banking and financial system. The Bahrain dinar is formally linked to the SDR, with the US dollar as intervention currency. Since 1975 a licensing status of 'offshore banking unit' (OBU) has been available to banks using Bahrain as a base from which to conduct exclusively offshore business (such companies being exempt from the shareholder nationality requirements applicable to banks providing services within Bahrain). There was a rapid expansion of offshore banking activities in the late 1970s and early 1980s, with Bahrain well placed to serve as a centre for the boom in international bank lending to Saudi Arabia and other major petroleum exporters in the Gulf.

The number of OBUs licensed in Bahrian peaked at 74 in 1985, when—in addition to the 20 locally-incorporated commercial banks within Bahrain's domestic banking system—there were also 60 representative offices, more than 12 licensed investment banks, six money brokers and 43 money changers. In subsequent years the number of OBUs declined as financial institutions adjusted to changing regional economic conditions at a time of declining oil prices. Moreover, new opportunities were becoming available to international banks to operate from financial centres outside the region or to establish offices within Gulf countries hitherto served from off shore. However, forecasts of a major decline in Bahrain's offshore financial services sector proved to be unfounded, with the combined assets of the remaining OBUs (numbering 65 in 1988) reaching a new record level of $68,100m. in 1988. The annual contribution of OBUs to Bahrain's economy was officially estimated to exceed $500m. in 1988.

The second half of the 1980s was also a period of readjustment for Bahrain's domestic commercial banks, some of which recorded reduced profits or net losses in 1986 and 1987 after making large provisions for loan defaults by recession-hit borrowers. By 1989 banking profits were generally much improved. The Gulf crisis of 1990–91 had a strong impact on Bahrain's banking sector as funds were withdrawn on a large scale. However, the BMA ensured that dinar liquidity was maintained, and by October 1990 the outflow of capital had been stemmed.

Between 1992 and 1997 the number of financial institutions in Bahrain increased from 155 to 183, the latter total comprising 19 commercial banks serving the domestic market, 47 OBUs, 30 investment banks, 12 Islamic banks, 41 representative offices and 27 money changers. In 1996 Bahrain-based banks had approval to market a total of 281 collective investment schemes (mutual funds) in or from Bahrain.

The aggregate assets of OBUs at the end of 1997 were $72,053m. At the end of September 1996 the aggregate assets of Bahrain's commercial banks were BD 3,800m. ($10,000m.) and their aggregate credit outstanding within Bahrain amounted to BD 941.2m. ($2,490m.), of which 32% was personal lending, 21% was for the trade sector, 13% for manufacturing and 16.7% for construction. Bahrain's five main conventional commercial banks in 1996 (with end-1996 assets) were National Bank of Bahrain ($2,272m.), Bank of Bahrain and Kuwait ($2,010m.), Al-Ahli Commercial Bank ($628m.), Bahraini Saudi Bank ($358m.) and Grindlays Bahrain Bank ($203m.). Bahrain's two largest Islamic banks in 1996 were Bahrain Islamic Bank ($392m.) and Faysal Islamic Bank ($356m.). There were 16 Islamic financial institutions in Bahrain in 1996—the highest

concentration for any country having both conventional and Islamic banking—following the efforts of the Bahrain Monetary Authority to promote Bahrain as a centre of Islamic-banking. Important investment banks in Bahrain—owned by shareholders in the Gulf but having most of their earning assets outside the region—included in 1996 Investcorp (end-1996 assets $1,741m.), Bahrain Middle East Bank ($646m.) and Bahrain International Bank ($640.8m.). Foreign life insurance companies, whose entry into Bahrain had been restricted to representative offices since 1987 were to be permitted to set up branch offices from 1997.

In 1982, when oil provided 80% of Bahrain's budgetary revenues, there was a budget surplus of BD 46.4m.—the latest in a succession of such surpluses. In 1983 budget deficit of a similar margin was recorded, mainly because of a 17% decline in oil revenue. Thereafter, budget deficits have recurred, despite the Government's efforts to moderate its spending programmes and despite the receipt of annual grant aid from Kuwait and Saudi Arabia (each providing about $50m.). Moreover, from January 1993 Saudi Arabia waived part (and from April 1996 waived all) of its entitlement to 50% of the revenue from oil produced in the shared Abu Saafa field.

Bahrain's two-year budget for 1995–96 provided for deficits of BD 65.2m. in 1995 and BD 114.0m. in 1996. In 1995 there was provision for total revenue of BD 560.8m. (57% from petroleum) and total expenditure of BD 626m. (83% recurrent and 17% capital). In 1996 there was provision for total revenue of BD 530m. (48% from oil) and total expenditure of BD 644m. (81% recurrent and 19% capital). In view of advantageous developments subsequent to publication of the 1996 budget (increased Abu Saafa revenues and relatively strong world oil prices in 1996), actual revenue in 1996 was BD 615.5m., with expenditure of BD 581.3m., resulting in a surplus of BD 34.2m. The two-year budget for 1997–98, drawn up at the end of 1996, provided for a deficit of BD 75m. in each year (1997 revenue BD 615m., expenditure BD 690m.; 1998 revenue BD 630m., expenditure BD 705m.). In March 1996 the Government approved a public expenditure management strategy for the period 1997–2006, outlining a wide range of actions to eliminate the budget deficit within 10 years. The strategy document did not consider the introduction of a direct income tax, the absence of which was regarded as an important factor in Bahrain's appeal to foreign investors.

Provisional trade figures for 1997 indicated a deficit of US $880.1m., in 1996 they had indicated a surplus of $508m. (exports $4,437m., imports $3,929m.). Bahrain's imports of Saudi Arabian crude petroleum in 1996 were valued at $1,710m., while exports of petroleum products were valued at $3,180m. Manufactured goods accounted for 21.4% of 1996 exports, while re-exports were responsible for just 1% of the total. In 1995 there had been a trade surplus of $466.1m., based on export earnings of $4,080.6m. (60% from petroleum products) and import spending of $3,614.5m. (including 36.7% on crude petroleum). In 1994 there had been a trade deficit of $130.9m., based on export earnings of $3,607.1m. (61.5% from petroleum products) and import spending of $3,738m. (including 31.8% on crude petroleum). Apart from Saudi Arabia, significant suppliers of imports in the mid-1990s included the United States, the United Kingdom, Germany and Japan. Important export markets in the mid-1990s included India, Japan, the Republic of Korea, Saudi Arabia, Canada and the United Arab Emirates.

Tourism, which has been systematically promoted by the Government since 1985, generated estimated spending of $870m. by visitors in 1995, of which $450m. was classed as 'direct income to Bahrain's economy'. Spanning both the recreational and conference markets, tourism contributed 9.2% of GDP and employed 16.7% of the workforce in 1995. Events at the Bahrain International Exhibition Centre attracted nearly 250,000 visitors in 1996. Inaugurated in 1991, the purpose-built centre was scheduled to undergo a major expansion programme to be completed in 1999. A new International Convention Centre was opened at Bahrain's Gulf Hotel in 1997.

The Bahrain Stock Exchange opened in June 1989 with an initial market capitalization of BD 1,121m. In 1995 32 companies were listed and market capitalization was BD 2,120m. Since the end of 1994 the stock exchanges of Bahrain and Oman have listed each other's shares under a reciprocal agreement.

Bahrain and Jordan made similar reciprocal listing arrangements in March 1996. Under liberalized rules introduced in 1997 non-GCC investors may hold up to 24% of shares in any listed company provided that they have resided in Bahrain for at least one year or are resident outside Bahrain.

TRANSPORT AND COMMUNICATIONS

Bahrain's role as a major financial centre has been associated with an expansion of the country's air and telephone services. The Bahrain International Airport was opened in 1971 on Muharraq island and it has also become the headquarters of Gulf Air, which is owned jointly by the Governments of Bahrain, Oman, Qatar and the UAE. In 1996 the airport (currently in the fourth phase of an expansion programme) handled nearly 56,600 flights and abut 3.4m. passengers (about 55% of them transit passengers). In 1995 the airport handled around 100,000 tons of cargo, about 30% of which was transhipment cargo.

In 1995 Gulf Air (with regional competitors including the recently established Qatar Airways and Oman Airline Services) recorded an annual loss of BD 61.9m. ($164m.), prompting a programme of aircraft disposals and route cuts designed to eliminate some of the 60 destinations previously served. In 1995 Gulf Air carried over 5m. passengers and 170,000 tons of cargo. Its finances had been depleted by a large loan-servicing burden in respect of aircraft purchased in the late 1980s. During 1996 measures were adopted which reduced operating costs by 5% and increased operating revenue by 5%, but the airline nevertheless reported an annual loss of BD 25.2m. ($66.8m.). Recommendations to increase the airline's capital from BD 150m. to BD 250m. were discussed by the shareholder Governments in January 1997. An offer by Abu Dhabi to inject more capital in return for an increased shareholding was rejected by Oman and Qatar, and it was instead agreed that the shareholder Governments should provide 'discretionary loans' totalling $200m. to Gulf Air. The shareholders' respective contributions were not specified. By early 1997 Gulf Air had sold seven Boeing 767s and reduced its total number of destinations to 50. In that year the company recorded an operating profit of $8m.

The Bahrain Telecommunications Company (BATELCO) was formed in July 1981, with capital of BD 60m. (60% government-owned). At the beginning of 1986 Bahrain became the 45th member of the London-based International Maritime (now Mobile) Satellite Organization (INMARSAT), and during 1986 BATELCO also introduced a cellular telephone system. In 1992 the digitalization of Bahrain's 120,000-line domestic network was completed. There is a digital international exchange. The capacity of the mobile telephone system was expanded to 25,000 lines in 1997. BATELCO's profits rose by 7% in 1995 to BD 25.8m. In March 1996 it was announced that BD 100m. was to be invested in the network over the next five years. Projects contained in the BD 27m.-investment budget for 1996 included work on a regional fibre-optic link between Bahrain, Qatar, Kuwait and the UAE. An International Services Digital Network (ISDN) capability was in place in Bahrain in 1997.

A container terminal was opened at the port of Mina Salman in 1979, with a 400-m quay allowing simultaneous handling of two 180-m vessels. In total, Mina Salman has 14 conventional berths, two container terminals and a roll-on/roll-off berth. Plans to build a new port and industrial zone at Hidd were approved by the Cabinet in March 1997. At an estimated total cost of $330m., the proposed port would have an annual handling capacity of 234,000 TEUs and would include a general cargo berth and two container berths with roll-on/roll-off facilities. The project was expected to be put out to tender in 1998. The same cabinet meeting approved the construction of a new $80m.-causeway linking Hidd and Mina Salman. Completion of the first section was required by the end of 1997 in order to carry cabling for a new power and water plant being built at Hidd, with completion of the whole causeway scheduled for 2001. A second 2.5-km Manama to Muharraq causeway was opened at the start of 1997.

The inauguration, in February 1987, of a causeway between Bahrain and Saudi Arabia led to increased motor traffic in Bahrain, in the light of which the road network has been upgraded and traffic management studies have been undertaken. The causeway was used by 1.3m. vehicles in its first year of operation. There were nearly 144,000 cars and more than 30,500 goods vehicles and buses registered in Bahrain at the end of 1996.

EDUCATION AND HEALTH

The high level of petroleum revenues during the 1970s enabled the Government to embark on an ambitious programme to expand education and health services. By 1991 there were some 3,052 classes in government educational institutions, with 100,658 students enrolled. Included within the state sector are commercial schools in which pupils aged 15 to 18 study work-related subjects and have access to work experience opportunities approved by the Higher Council for Vocational Training. The University of Bahrain has faculties of education, engineering, science, medicine, computing, commerce and arts; 6,760 students were enrolled in 1995. The Bahrain Government allocated BD 80.5m. (13.8% of total expenditure) for education in 1996. The partly-completed Arabian Gulf University had fewer than 400 students in 1993, disbursements of funds for its further development having been delayed by the seven sponsoring Arab Governments. Despite such investments in education and technical training, Bahrain continues to rely heavily on expatriate labour.

Health services and housing have received considerable support. In 1985 there were 518 physicians, 19 dentists and 1,148 nursing personnel working in Bahrain. By 1988 there were seven hospitals, 19 government health centres and seven government maternity centres. In 1996 the Ministry of Health was responsible for 89% of out-patient services, 72% of hospital bed places and 90% of nursing employment in Bahrain. In the same year the health minister employed 63% of physicians and 60% of dentists. (The Bahrain Defence Force provide the remaining medical facilities.) A comprehensive primary health-care system was developed during the 1980s. The Government provides primary, secondary and tertiary health care free of charge to all Bahrainis and charges nominal fees to non-Bahraini residents. In 1994 some 4.3% of Bahrain's GNP was devoted to health expenditure. Overall health spending per caput was $350, of which $220 was Ministry of Health spending. The Government is a significant provider of low- and middle-cost housing, particularly in the new towns. In the first half of 1997 the Goverment received a $49.7m. loan from the Arab Fund for Economic and Social Development (see p. 243), and a $27m. funding pledge from the Abu Dhabi Development fund to finance new housing projects. Several previous public housing projects were aided by Gulf donors, including Saudi Arabia.

Statistical Survey

Source (unless otherwise stated): Central Statistics Organization, POB 5835, Manama; tel. 725725; telex 8853; fax 728989.

AREA AND POPULATION

Area (1995): 707.3 sq km (273.1 sq miles).

Population: 350,798 (males 204,793, females 146,005) at census of 5 April 1981; 508,037 (males 294,346, females 213,691), comprising 323,305 Bahrainis (males 163,453, females 159,852) and 184,732 non-Bahraini nationals (males 130,893, females 53,839), at census of 16 November 1991; 598,625 (official estimate) at mid-1996.

Density (mid-1996): 846.4 per sq km.

Principal Towns (population in 1991): Manama (capital) 136,999; Muharraq Town 74,245. *Mid-1992:* Manama 140,401.

Births, Marriages and Deaths (1995): Registered live births 13,481 (birth rate 23.3 per 1,000); Registered marriages 3,321 (marriage rate 5.7 per 1,000); Registered deaths 1,910 (death rate 3.3 per 1,000).

Expectation of Life (UN estimates, years at birth, 1990–95): 71.6 (males 69.8; females 74.1). Source: UN, *World Population Prospects: The 1994 Revision.*

Economically Active Population (persons aged 15 years and over, 1991 census): Agriculture, hunting, forestry and fishing 5,108; Mining and quarrying 3,638; Manufacturing 26,618; Electricity, gas and water 2,898; Construction 26,738; Trade, restaurants and hotels 29,961; Transport, storage and communications 13,789; Financing, insurance, real estate and business services 17,256; Community, social and personal services 83,944; Activities not adequately defined 2,120; *Total employed* 212,070 (males 177,154; females 34,916); Unemployed 14,378 (males 9,703; females 4,675); *Total labour force* 226,448 (males 186,857; females 39,591), comprising 90,662 Bahrainis (males 73,118, females 17,544) and 135,786 non-Bahraini nationals (males 113,739, females 22,047). **Mid-1996** (estimates): Agriculture, etc. 4,000; Total 251,000 (Source: FAO, *Production Yearbook*).

AGRICULTURE, ETC.

Principal Crops (FAO estimates, '000 metric tons, 1996): Tomatoes 9; Other vegetables 7; Dates 20; other fruits 5. Source: FAO, *Production Yearbook.*

Livestock (FAO estimates, '000 head, year ending September 1996): Cattle 17; Camels 1; Sheep 29; Goats 18. Source: FAO, *Production Yearbook.*

Livestock Products (FAO estimates, '000 metric tons, 1996): Mutton and lamb 6; Goat meat 2; Poultry meat 5; Milk 20; Poultry eggs 4. Source: FAO, *Production Yearbook.*

Fishing ('000 metric tons, live weight): Total catch 9.0 in 1993; 7.6 in 1994; 9.4 in 1995. Source: FAO, *Yearbook of Fishery Statistics.*

MINING

Production (1995): Crude petroleum 14,459,000 barrels; Natural gas 7,701.7 million cubic metres.

INDUSTRY

Production ('000 barrels, unless otherwise indicated, 1995): Liquefied petroleum gas 365; Naphtha 12,772; Motor spirit (Gasoline) 7,766; Kerosene 11,327; Jet fuel 6,219; Fuel oil 20,807; Diesel oil and Gas oil 31,024; Petroleum bitumen (asphalt) 1,399; Electric energy 4,611.9 million kWh; Aluminium (unwrought) 461,245 metric tons (1996).

FINANCE

Currency and Exchange Rates: 1,000 fils = 1 Bahraini dinar (BD). *Sterling and Dollar Equivalents* (31 May 1998): £1 sterling = 613.1 fils; US $1 = 376.0 fils; 100 Bahraini dinars = £163.09 = $265.96. *Exchange Rate:* Fixed at US $1 = 376.0 fils (BD 1 = $2.6596) since November 1980.

Budget (BD million, 1996): *Revenue:* Taxation 180.1 (Taxes on income and profits 31.2, Social security contributions 64.4, Domestic taxes on goods and services 26.3, Import duties 47.5); Entrepreneurial and property income 402.2; Other current revenue 32.9; Capital revenue 0.3; Total 615.5, excl. grants from abroad (18.8). *Expenditure:* General public services 106.5; Defence 108.5; Public order and safety 85.5; Education 80.5; Health 57.1; Social security and welfare 22.6; Housing and community amenities 7.7; Recreational, cultural and religious affairs and services 3.7; Economic affairs and services 88.5 (Fuel and energy 60.3, Transport and communications 21.3); Other purposes 20.7 (Interest payments 19.9); Total 581.3 (Current 486.9, Capital 94.4), excl. lending minus repayments (108.0). Source: IMF, *Government Finance Statistics Yearbook.* **1997** (estimates, BD million): Revenue 615; Expenditure 690; **1998** (estimates, BD million): Revenue 630; Expenditure 705.

International Reserves (US $ million at 31 December 1997): Gold (valued at cost of acquisition) 6.6; IMF special drawing rights 16.1; Reserve position in IMF 63.0; Foreign exchange 1,211.2; Total 1,296.9. Source: IMF, *International Financial Statistics.*

Money Supply (BD million at 31 December 1997): Currency outside banks 104.66; Demand deposits at commercial banks 201.49; Total money 306.14. Source: IMF, *International Financial Statistics.*

Cost of Living (Consumer Price Index for Bahraini nationals; base: 1990 = 100): 104.0 in 1994; 106.8 in 1995; 106.6 in 1996. Source: IMF, *International Financial Statistics.*

Expenditure on the Gross Domestic Product (BD million, 1996): Government final consumption expenditure 427.8; Private final consumption expenditure 494.4; Increase in stocks –56.3; Gross fixed capital formation 447.7; *Total domestic expenditure* 1,313.6; Exports of goods and services 2,436.8; *Less* Imports of goods and services 1,734.6; *GDP in purchasers' values* 2,015.8. Source: IMF, *International Financial Statistics.*

Gross Domestic Product by Economic Activity (BD million at current prices, 1995): Agriculture, hunting, forestry and fishing 20.5; Mining and quarrying 316.6; Manufacturing 412.1; Electricity, gas and water 58.4; Construction 97.9; Trade, restaurants and hotels 151.0; Transport, storage and communications 158.2; Finance, insurance, real estate and business services 328.0; Government services 369.5; Other community, social and personal services 97.2; *Sub-total* 2,009.4; *Less* Imputed bank service charge 170.7; *GDP at factor cost* 1,838.7; Indirect taxes (net) 61.6; *GDP in purchasers' values* 1,900.2.

Balance of Payments (US $ million, 1995): Exports of goods f.o.b. 4,112.8; Imports of goods f.o.b. –3,344.1; *Trade balance* 768.6; Exports of services 1,325.5; Imports of services –861.4; *Balance on goods and services* 1,232.8; Other income received 343.1; Other income paid –796.5; *Balance on goods, services and income* 779.4; Current transfers received 156.6; Current transfers paid –379.0; *Current balance* 557.0; Direct investment from abroad –27.1; Portfolio investment assets –18.4; Other investment assets 278.5; Other investment liabilities –316.0; Net errors and omissions –375.9; *Overall balance* 98.2. Source: IMF, *International Financial Statistics.*

EXTERNAL TRADE

Total Trade (BD million): *Imports c.i.f.:* 1,397.1 in 1995; 1,538.8 in 1996; 1,454.2 in 1997. *Exports:* 1,546.4 in 1995; 1,730.5 in 1996; 1,624.6 in 1997. Source: IMF, *International Financial Statistics.*

Principal Commodities (US $ million, 1995): *Imports c.i.f.:* Food and live animals 320.0; Mineral fuels, lubricants, etc. 1,382.2 (Crude petroleum 1,330.1); Chemicals and related products 316.2; Basic manufactures 557.5; Machinery and transport equipment 588.3; Miscellaneous manufactured articles 279.8; Total (incl. others) 3,624.8. *Exports f.o.b.:* Mineral fuels, lubricants, etc. 2,455.6 (Crude petroleum 2,454.5); Chemicals and related products 206.4; Basic manufactures 1,153.7; Miscellaneous manufactured articles 125.5; Total (incl. others) 4,092.1. Source: UN, *International Trade Statistics Yearbook.*

Principal Trading Partners (US $ million, 1995): *Imports c.i.f.:* Australia 172.6; Brazil 72.9; People's Republic of China 51.5; France 84.7; Germany 145.2; India 89.3; Italy 79.2; Japan 147.9; Republic of Korea 39.9; Malaysia 41.1; Netherlands 52.4; Saudi Arabia 178.9; Switzerland 45.1; United Arab Emirates 96.1; United Kingdom 212.6; USA 298.2; Total (incl. others) 3,624.8. *Exports f.o.b.:* India 103.6; Iran 46.6; Japan 142.2; Jordan 41.4; Republic of Korea 157.5; Kuwait 58.3; Malaysia 42.3; Netherlands 46.9; Saudi Arabia 250.7; Singapore 79.0; United Arab Emirates 74.1; USA 130.7; Total (incl. others) 4,092.1. Note: Except for totals, figures exclude trade in petroleum (US $ million): Imports 1,330.1; Exports 2,454.5. Source: UN, *International Trade Statistics Yearbook.*

TRANSPORT

Road Traffic (registered motor vehicles, 31 December 1996): Passenger cars 143,878; Buses and coaches 4,189; Lorries and vans 26,358; Motorcycles 1,739. Source: IRF, *World Road Statistics.*

Shipping (international sea-borne freight traffic, '000 metric tons, 1990): *Goods loaded:* Dry cargo 1,145; Petroleum products 12,140. *Goods unloaded:* Dry cargo 3,380; Petroleum products 132. Source:

UN, *Monthly Bulletin of Statistics. Merchant Fleet* (31 December 1996): Registered vessels 83; Total displacement 164,258 grt. Source: Lloyd's Register of Shipping, *World Fleet Statistics*.

Civil Aviation (1995): Kilometres flown (million) 21; Passengers carried ('000) 1,073; Passenger-km (million) 2,766; Total ton-km (million) 395. Figures include an apportionment (equivalent to one-quarter) of the traffic of Gulf Air, a multinational airline with its headquarters in Bahrain. Source: UN, *Statistical Yearbook*.

TOURISM

Tourist Arrivals (1995): 2,483,000.

Tourist Receipts (1995): US $288 million.

COMMUNICATIONS MEDIA

Radio Receivers (1995): 320,000 in use.

Television Receivers (1995): 260,000 in use.

Telephones (1995): 141,000 main lines in use.

Telefax Stations (telephone subscriptions, 1995): 5,730.

Mobile Cellular Telephones (subscribers, 1995): 27,600.

Book Production (1989, estimate): 150 titles.

Daily Newspapers (1995): 3 (estimated circulation 70,000 copies).

Non-daily Newspapers (1993): 5 (circulation 17,000 copies).

Other Periodicals (1993): 26 (circulation 73,000 copies).

Sources: UNESCO, *Statistical Yearbook*; UN, *Statistical Yearbook*.

EDUCATION

Government Institutions (1994/95): *Primary:* 59,378 pupils. *Intermediate:* 26,851 pupils. *Secondary* (general): 15,210 pupils; (commercial): 3,194 pupils; (industrial): 3,560 pupils. *Total:* 108,606 pupils; 6,661 teachers; 174 schools; 4,116 classes. *Higher:* 2 universities and 5 institutes.

Directory

The Constitution

A 108-article Constitution was ratified in June 1973. It states that 'all citizens shall be equal before the law' and guarantees freedom of speech, of the press, of conscience and religious beliefs. Other provisions include the outlawing of the compulsory repatriation of political refugees. The Constitution also states that the country's financial comptroller should be responsible to the legislature and not to the Government, and allows for national trade unions 'for legally justified causes and on peaceful lines'. Compulsory free primary education and free medical care are also laid down in the Constitution. The Constitution, which came into force on 6 December 1973, also provided for a National Assembly, composed of 14 members of the Cabinet and 30 members elected by popular vote, although this was dissolved in August 1975.

The Government

HEAD OF STATE

Amir: Sheikh ISA BIN SULMAN AL-KHALIFA (succeeded to the throne on 2 November 1961; took the title of Amir on 16 August 1971).

Crown Prince and Commander-in-Chief of Bahraini Defence Force and National Guard: Sheikh HAMAD BIN ISA AL-KHALIFA.

CABINET
(September 1998)

Prime Minister: Sheikh KHALIFA BIN SULMAN AL-KHALIFA.

Minister of Justice and Islamic Affairs: Sheikh ABDULLAH BIN KHALIFA AL-KHALIFA.

Minister of Foreign Affairs: Sheikh MUHAMMAD BIN MUBARAK BIN HAMAD AL-KHALIFA.

Minister of the Interior: Sheikh MUHAMMAD BIN KHALIFA BIN HAMAD AL-KHALIFA.

Minister of Transport and Civil Aviation: Sheikh ALI BIN KHALIFA BIN SALMAN AL-KHALIFA.

Minister of State: JAWAD SALIM AL-ARRAYEDH.

Minister of Housing, Municipalities and Environment: Sheikh KHALID BIN ABDULLAH BIN KHALID AL-KHALIFA.

Minister of Public Works and Agriculture: MAJID JAWAD AL-JISHI.

Minister of Finance and National Economy: IBRAHIM ABD AL-KARIM MUHAMMAD.

Minister of Defence: Maj.-Gen. Sheikh KHALIFA BIN AHMAD AL-KHALIFA.

Minister of Cabinet Affairs and Information: MUHAMMAD IBRAHIM AL-MUTAWA.

Minister of Oil and Industry: Sheikh ISA BIN ALI AL-KHALIFA.

Minister of Commerce: ALI SALEH ABDULLAH AS-SALEH.

Minister of Education: Brig.-Gen. ABD AL-AZIZ BIN MUHAMMAD AL-FADHIL.

Minister of Health: Dr FAISAL RADHI AL-MOUSAWI.

Minister of Power and Water: ABDULLAH MUHAMMAD JUMA.

Minister of Labour and Social Affairs: ABD AN-NABI ASH-SHULA.

Minister of Amiri Court Affairs: Sheikh ALI BIN ISA BIN SULMAN AL-KHALIFA.

MINISTRIES

Amiri Court: POB 555, Riffa Palace, Manama; tel. 666666; telex 8666.

Office of the Prime Minister: POB 1000, Government House, Government Rd, Manama; tel. 225522; telex 9336; fax 229022.

Ministry of Cabinet Affairs and Information: POB 26613, Government House, Government Rd, Manama; tel. 223366; telex 7424; fax 225202.

Ministry of Commerce: POB 5479, Diplomatic Area, Manama; tel. 531531; fax 530455.

Ministry of Defence: POB 245, West Rifa'a; tel. 665599; telex 8429; fax 662854.

Ministry of Education: POB 43, Isa Town; tel. 685558; telex 9094; fax 680161.

Ministry of Finance and National Economy: POB 333, Diplomatic Area, Manama; tel. 530800; telex 8933; fax 532853.

Ministry of Foreign Affairs: POB 547, Government House, Government Rd, Manama; tel. 227555; fax 212603.

Ministry of Health: POB 12, Sheikh Sulman Rd, Manama; tel. 255555; fax 254459.

Ministry of Housing, Municipalities and Environment: POB 11802, Diplomatic Area, Manama; tel. 533000; fax 534115.

Ministry of the Interior: POB 13, Police Fort Compound, Manama; tel. 272111; telex 9572; fax 262169.

Ministry of Justice and Islamic Affairs: POB 450, Diplomatic Area, Manama; tel. 531333; fax 532984.

Ministry of Labour and Social Affairs: POB 32333, Isa Town; tel. 687800; fax 686954.

Ministry of Oil and Industry: POB 1435, Manama; tel. 291511; telex 8344; fax 290302.

Ministry of Power and Water: POB 2, Manama; tel. 533133; telex 8515; fax 537151.

Ministry of Public Works and Agriculture: POB 5, Muharraq Causeway Rd, Manama; tel. 535222; telex 8515; fax 533095.

Ministry of Transport and Civil Aviation: POB 10325, Diplomatic Area, Manama; tel. 534534; telex 8989; fax 537537.

CONSULTATIVE COUNCIL

The Consultative Council is an advisory body of 40 members appointed by the ruling authorities for a four-year term, which is empowered to advise the Government but has no legislative powers. The Council held its inaugural session on 16 January 1993.

President: IBRAHIM MUHAMMAD HUMAIDAN.

Legislature

NATIONAL ASSEMBLY

In accordance with the 1973 Constitution, elections to a National Assembly took place in December 1973. About 30,000 electors elected

30 members for a four-year term. Since political parties are not allowed, all 114 candidates stood as independents but, in practice, the National Assembly was divided almost equally between conservative, moderate and more radical members. In addition to the 30 elected members, the National Assembly contained 14 members of the Cabinet. In August 1975 the Prime Minister resigned because, he complained, the National Assembly was preventing the Government from carrying out its functions. The Amir invited the Prime Minister to form a new Cabinet, and two days later the National Assembly was dissolved by Amiri decree. It has not been revived.

Diplomatic Representation

EMBASSIES IN BAHRAIN

Algeria: POB 2604, Villa 579, Rd 3622, Adliya, Manama; tel. 713669; telex 7775; fax 713662; Ambassador: LAHSSAN BOUFARES.

Bangladesh: POB 26718, House 159, Rd 2004, Area 320, Hoora; tel. 293373; telex 7029; fax 291272; Chargé d'affaires: MUHAMMAD ABD AL-HYE.

China, People's Republic: POB 3150, Bldg 158, Road 382, Juffair Ave, Block 341, Manama; tel. 723800; fax 727304; Ambassador: WANG XIAOZHUANG.

Egypt: POB 818, Adliya; tel. 720005; telex 8248; fax 721518; Ambassador: MAHMOUD SAMI ESMAT.

Finland: POB 5794, Manama; tel. 530995; telex 8211; fax 536631.

France: POB 11134, Road 1901, Building 51, Block 319, Diplomatic Area, Manama; tel. 291734; telex 8323; fax 293655; Ambassador: GEORGES DUQUIN.

Germany: POB 10306, Al-Hasan Bldg, Sheikh Hamad Causeway, Manama; tel. 530210; telex 7128; fax 536282; Ambassador: NORBERT HEINZE.

India: POB 26106, Bldg 182, Rd 2608, Area 326, Adliya, Manama; tel. 712785; telex 9047; fax 715527; e-mail indemb@batelco.com.bh; internet http://www.indianembassy-bh.com; Ambassador: S. S. GILL.

Iran: POB 26365, Entrance 1034, Rd 3221, Area 332, Mahooz, Manama; tel. 722400; telex 8238; fax 722101; Chargé d'affaires: SAYEED MUHAMMAD AHMADI.

Iraq: POB 26477, Ar-Raqib Bldg, No 17, Rd 2001, Comp 320, King Faysal Ave, Manama; tel. 786929; telex 8325; fax 786220; Chargé d'affaires: AHMAD TAYES ABDULLAH.

Japan: 55 Salmaniya Ave, Manama Tower 327, Manama; tel. 716565; telex 7002; fax 712950; Ambassador: TOSHIAKI TANABE.

Jordan: POB 5242, Villa 43, Rd 915, Area 309, Hoora; tel. 291109; telex 7650; fax 291280; Dr SHAKER ARABIAT.

Korea, Republic: POB 11700, Bldg 69, Rd 1901, Block 319, Hoora; tel. 291629; fax 291628; Ambassador: LEE SOO-WHAN.

Kuwait: POB 786, Rd 1703, Diplomatic Area, Rd 1703, Manama; tel. 534040; telex 8830; fax 533579; Ambassador: ABD AL-MUHSIN SALIM AL-HARUN.

Lebanon: POB 2102, Manama; tel. 531385; fax 536489.

Morocco: POB 26229, Manama; tel. 740566; telex 8018; fax 740178.

Oman: POB 26414, Diplomatic Area, Bldg 37, Rd 1901, Manama; tel. 293663; telex 9332; fax 293540; Ambassador: RASHID BIN OBAID AL-GHARAIBI.

Pakistan: POB 563, Bldg 261, Rd 2807, Block 328, Segeiya, Manama; tel. 244113; fax 255960; Ambassador: MUHAMMAD NASSER MIAN.

Philippines: POB 26681, Bldg 81, Rd 3902, Block 339, Umm Al-Hassan; tel. 710200; fax 710300; Ambassador: AKMAD ATLAH SAKKAM.

Russia: POB 26612, House 877, Rd 3119, Block 331, Zinj, Manama; tel. 725222; telex 7006; fax 725921; Ambassador: ALEKSANDR NOVOZHILOV.

Saudi Arabia: POB 1085, Bldg 1450, Rd 4043, Area 340, Juffair, Manama; tel. 537722; telex 8061; fax 533261; Ambassador: ABDULLAH BIN ABD AR-RAHMAN ASH-SHEIKH.

South Africa: POB 15574, Manama; tel. 786699; fax 786429.

Tunisia: POB 26911, House 54, Rd 3601, Area 336, Manama; tel. 714149; telex 7136; fax 715702; Ambassador: MOHSEN FRINI.

Turkey: POB 10821, Flat 10, Bldg 81, Rd 1702, Area 317, Manama; tel. 533448; telex 7049; fax 536557; e-mail tcbahrbe@batelco.com.bh; Ambassador: ENGIN TÜRKER.

United Arab Emirates: POB 26505, Manama; tel. 723737; fax 727343.

United Kingdom: POB 114, 21 Government Ave, Area 306, Manama; tel. 534404; telex 8213; fax 531273; e-mail britemb@batelco.com.bh; Ambassador: DAVID IAN LEWTY.

USA: POB 26431, Bldg 979, Rd 3119, Block 331, Zinj, Manama; tel. 273300; fax 272594; Ambassador: JOHNY YOUNG.

Yemen: POB 26193, House 1048, Rd 1730, Area 517, Saar; tel. 277072; telex 8370; fax 262358; Ambassador: NASSER M. Y. ALGAADANI.

Judicial System

Since the termination of British legal jurisdiction in 1971, intensive work has been undertaken on the legislative requirements of Bahrain. The Criminal Law is at present contained in various Codes, Ordinances and Regulations. All nationalities are subject to the jurisdiction of the Bahraini courts which guarantee equality before the law irrespective of nationality or creed.

Directorate of Courts: POB 450, Government House, Government Rd, Manama; tel. 531333.

Religion

At the November 1991 census the population was 508,037, distributed as follows: Muslims 415,427; Christians 43,237; Others 49,373.

ISLAM

Muslims are divided between the Sunni and Shi'ite sects. The ruling family is Sunni, although the majority of the Muslim population (estimated at almost 60%) are Shi'ite.

CHRISTIANITY

The Anglican Communion

Within the Episcopal Church in Jerusalem and the Middle East, Bahrain forms part of the diocese of Cyprus and the Gulf. There are two Anglican churches in Bahrain, St Christopher's Cathedral in Manama and the Community Church in Awali, and the congregations are entirely expatriate. The Bishop and Archdeacon in Cyprus and the Gulf are both resident in Cyprus.

Provost: Very Rev. KEITH W. T. W. JOHNSON, St Christopher's Cathedral, POB 36, Al-Mutanabi Ave, Manama; tel. 253866; fax 246436; e-mail provost@batelco.com.bh.

Roman Catholic Church

A small number of adherents, mainly expatriates, form part of the Apostolic Vicariate of Arabia. The Vicar Apostolic is resident in the United Arab Emirates.

The Press

DAILIES

Akhbar al-Khalij (Gulf News): POB 5300, Manama; tel. 620111; telex 8565; fax 621566; f. 1976; Arabic; Chair. IBRAHIM AL-MOAYED; Man. Dir and Editor-in-Chief Dr HILAL ASH-SHAIJI; circ. 17,000.

Al-Ayam (The Days): POB 3232, Manama; tel. 727111; fax 729009; f. 1989; publ. by Al-Ayam Establishment for Press and Publications; Chair. and Editor-in-Chief NABIL YAQUB AL-HAMER; circ. 37,000.

Gulf Daily News: POB 5300, Manama; tel. 620222; telex 8565; fax 622141; e-mail gdn1@batelco.com.bh; internet http://www.gulf-daily-news.com; f. 1978; English; Editor-in-Chief GEORGE WILLIAMS; Deputy Editor LES HORTON; circ. 50,000.

Khaleej Times: POB 26707, City Centre Bldg, Suite 403, 4th Floor, Government Ave, Manama; tel. 213911; telex 8973; fax 211819; f. 1978; English; circ. 79,000.

WEEKLIES

Al-Adhwaa' (Lights): POB 250, Old Exhibition Rd, Manama; tel. 291226; telex 8564; fax 293166; f. 1965; Arabic; publ. by Arab Printing and Publishing House; Chair. RAID MAHMOUD AL-MARDI; Editor-in-Chief MUHAMMAD QASSIM SHIRAWI; circ. 7,000.

Akhbar BAPCO (BAPCO News): Bahrain Petroleum Co BSC, POB 25149, Awali; tel. 755055; telex 8214; fax 755047; e-mail khalid_fahad_mehmas@bapco.net; f. 1981; formerly known as *an-Najma al-Usbou'* (The Weekly Star); Arabic; house journal; Editor KHALID F. MEHMAS; circ. 3,000.

Al-Bahrain ath-Thaqafya: POB 26613, Manama; tel. 290210; fax 292678; Arabic; publ. by the Ministry of Cabinet Affairs and Information; Editor ABDULLAH YATIM.

BAPCO Weekly News: Refinery, Bahrain; tel. 755049; telex 8214; fax 755047; English; publ. by the Bahrain Petroleum Co BSC; Editor KATHLEEN CROES; circ. 600.

Huna al-Bahrain: POB 26005, Isa Town; tel. 731888; fax 681292; Arabic; publ. by the Ministry of Cabinet Affairs and Information; Editor HAMAD AL-MANNAI.

Al-Mawakif (Attitudes): POB 1083, Manama; tel. 231231; fax 271720; f. 1973; Arabic; general interest; Editor-in-Chief MANSOOR M. RADHI; circ. 6,000.

Oil and Gas News: POB 224, Bldg 149, Exhibition Ave, Manama; tel. 293131; telex 8981; fax 293400; English; publ. by Al-Hilal Publishing and Marketing Co; Editor GURDIP SINGH.

Sada al-Usbou' (Weekly Echo): POB 549, Bahrain; tel. 291234; telex 8880; fax 290507; f. 1969; Arabic; Owner and Editor-in-Chief ALI SAYYAR; circ. 40,000 (in various Gulf states).

OTHER PERIODICALS

Arab Agriculture: POB 10131, Manama; tel. 213900; fax 211765; annually; English and Arabic; publ. by Fanar Publishing WLL; Editor-in-Chief ABDUL WAHED AL-ALWANI; Gen. Man. FAYEK ALARAYED.

Arab World Agribusiness: POB 10131, Manama; tel. 213900; fax 211765; nine per year; English and Arabic; publ. by Fanar Publishing WLL; Editor-in-Chief ABDUL WAHED AL-ALWANI; Gen. Man. FAYEK ALARAYED.

Discover Bahrain: POB 10704, Manama; f. 1988; publ. by G. and B. Media Ltd; Publr and Editor ROBERT GRAHAM.

Gulf Construction: POB 224, Exhibition Ave, Manama; tel. 293131; telex 8981; fax 293400; e-mail hilalpmg@batelco.com.bh; monthly; English; publ. by Al-Hilal Publishing and Marketing Group; Editor BINA PRABHU GOVEAS; circ. 10,200.

Gulf Economic Monitor: POB 224, Exhibition Ave, Manama; tel. 293131; fax 293400; e-mail hilalpmg@batelco.com.bh; weekly; English; published by Al-Hilal Publishing and Marketing Group; Man. Dir RONNIE MIDDLETON.

The Gulf Tourism Directory: POB 33770, Manama; tel. 244613; fax 731067; f. 1990; English; Publr RASHID BIN MUHAMMAD AL-KHALIFA.

Al-Hayat at-Tijariya (Commerce Review): POB 248, Manama; tel. 229555; telex 8691; fax 224985/212937; e-mail bahcci@batelco.com.bh; monthly; English and Arabic; publ. by Bahrain Chamber of Commerce and Industry; Editor KHALIL YOUSUF; circ. 7,500.

Al-Hidayah (Guidance): POB 450, Manama; tel. 522384; fax 534626; f. 1978; monthly; Arabic; publ. by Ministry of Justice and Islamic Affairs; Editor-in-Chief ABD AR-RAHMAN BIN MUHAMMAD RASHID AL-KHALIFA; circ. 5,000.

Al-Mohandis (The Engineer): POB 835, Manama; e-mail mohandis @batelco.com.bh; internet http://www.mohandis.org; f. 1972; quarterly; Arabic and English; publ. by Bahrain Society of Engineers; Editor MUHAMMAD K. AS-SAYED.

Al-Murshid (The Guide): POB 553, Manama; fax 293145; monthly; English and Arabic; includes 'What's on in Bahrain'; publ. by Arab Printing and Publishing House; Editor M. SOLIMAN.

Al-Musafir al-Arabi (Arab Traveller): POB 10131, Manama; tel. 213900; fax 211765; f. 1984; six per year; Arabic; publ. by Fanar Publishing WLL; Editor-in-Chief ABDUL WAHED AL-ALWANI; Gen. Man. FAYEK ALARAYED.

Panorama: POB 3232, Manama; tel. 727111; fax 729009; monthly; Editor IBRAHIM BASHMI; circ. 15,000.

Profile: POB 10243, Manama; tel. 291110; fax 294655; f. 1992; monthly; English; publ. by Bahrain Market Promotions; Editor ISA KHALIFA AL-KHALIFA.

Al-Quwwa (The Force): POB 245, Manama; tel. 291331; fax 659596; f. 1977; monthly; Arabic; publ. by Bahrain Defence Force; Editor-in-Chief Maj. AHMAD MAHMOUD AS-SUWAIDI.

Shipping and Transport News International: POB 224, Exhibition Ave, Manama; tel. 293131; telex 8981; fax 293400; six per year; English; publ. by Al-Hilal Publishing and Marketing Group; Editor FREDERICK ROCQUE; circ. 5,500.

Travel and Tourism News Middle East: POB 224, Exhibition Ave, Manama; tel. 293131; telex 8981; fax 293400; e-mail hilalpmg@batelco.com.bh; f. 1983; monthly; English; travel trade; publ. by Al-Hilal Publishing and Marketing Group; Editorial Research MARIA D'SOUZA; circ. 6,050.

NEWS AGENCIES

Agence France-Presse (AFP): POB 5890, Kanoo Tower, Phase 3, Tijaar Ave, Manama; tel. 259115; telex 8987; fax 277438; Dir JEAN-PIERRE PERRIN.

Associated Press (AP) (USA): POB 26940, Mannai Bldg, Manama; tel. 273238; telex 9470; fax 530249.

Deutsche Presse-Agentur (dpa) (Germany): POB 26995, Rd 2772, Villa 2788, Adliya 327, Manama; tel. 716655; telex 9542; fax 714119; Correspondent UTE MEINEL.

Gulf News Agency: POB 301, Manama; tel. 687272; telex 9030; fax 687008; Editor-in-Chief KHALID ZAYANI.

Inter Press Service (IPS) (Italy): c/o Gulf News Agency, POB 301, Manama; tel. 532235; fax 687008.

Press Trust of India: POB 2546, Manama; tel. 713431; telex 8482; Chief of Bureau SHAKIL AHMAD.

Reuters (United Kingdom): POB 1030, UGB Bldg, 6th Floor, Diplomatic Area, Manama; tel. 536111; telex 8301; fax 536192; Bureau Man. KENNETH WEST.

Publishers

Arab Communicators: POB 551, Manama; tel. 534664; telex 8263; fax 531837; publrs of annual Bahrain Business Directory; Dirs AHMAD A. FAKHRI, HAMAD A. ABUL.

Falcon Publishing WLL: POB 5028, Manama; tel. 253162; telex 8917; fax 259695; business magazines and directories; Chair. ABD AL-NABI ASH-SHOALA.

Gulf Advertising: POB 5518, Manama; tel. 226262; telex 8494; fax 228660; e-mail gulfad@batelco.com.bh; f. 1974; advertising and marketing communications.

Al-Hilal Publishing and Marketing Group: POB 224, Exhibition Ave, Manama; tel. 293131; fax 293400; e-mail hilalpmg@batelco.com.bh; f. 1977; specialist magazines and newspapers of commercial interest; Chair. A. M. ABD AR-RAHMAN; Man. Dir R. MIDDLETON.

Manama Publishing Co WLL: POB 1013, Manama; tel. 213223; telex 9246; fax 211548.

Al-Masirah Journalism, Printing and Publishing House: POB 5981, Manama; tel. 258882; telex 7421; fax 276178.

Tele-Gulf Directory Publications, WLL: POB 2738, 3rd Floor, Bahrain Tower, Manama; tel. 213301; fax 210503; e-mail telegulf@batelco.com.bh; publrs of annual *Gulf Directory* and *Arab Banking and Finance*; Chair. ABD AN-NABI ASH-SHO'ALA.

Government Publishing House

Directorate of Publications: POB 26005, Manama; tel. 689077; Dir MUHAMMAD AL-KHOZAI.

Broadcasting and Communications

TELECOMMUNICATIONS

AT & T Communications Middle East: POB 2603, Manama; tel. 233233; telex 7999; fax 230222; telecommunications systems.

Bahrain Telecommunications Co BSC (BATELCO): POB 14, Manama; tel. 881881; telex 8201; fax 883451; f. 1981; operates all telecommunications services; cap. BD 100m.; 80% owned by Government of Bahrain, financial institutions and public of Bahrain, 20% by Cable and Wireless PLC (United Kingdom); Chair. Sheikh ALI BIN KHALIFA BIN SALMAN AL-KHALIFA; CEO ANDREW HEARN.

Cabletron Systems: POB 3282, Manama; tel. 214642; fax 214645; telecommunications systems.

Intercol Telecom Systems: POB 584, Manama; tel. 727177; fax 727228; e-mail intersid@batelco.com.bh.

Manama Telecom: POB 20211, Manama; tel. 404242; fax 404088; telecommunications.

Satlink WLL: POB 3300, Manama; tel. 213333; telex 8172; fax 536666; satellite and telecommunications services.

Société Internationale de Télécom: POB 45, Manama; tel. 254081; telex 8252; fax 246093; telecommunications services.

Telecommunications Directorate: POB 11170, Manama; tel. 534534; telex 7184; fax 533544; regulatory body; Dir Dr RASHID JASSIM ASHOOR.

BROADCASTING

Radio

English language radio programmes, broadcast from Saudi Arabia by the US Air Force in Dhahran and by the Arabian-American Oil Co (Aramco), can be received in Bahrain.

Bahrain Radio and Television Corpn: POB 702, Manama; tel. 781888; telex 9259; f. 1955; state-owned and -operated enterprise; two 10-kW transmitters; programmes are in Arabic and English, and include news, plays and talks; Dir of Broadcasting ABD AR-RAHMAN ABDULLAH.

Radio Bahrain: POB 702, Manama; tel. 781888; telex 8311; fax 780911; e-mail brtcnews@batelco.com.bh; f. 1977; commercial radio station in English language; Head of Station AHMAD M. SULAIMAN.

Television

English language television programmes, broadcast by the Arabian-American Oil Co (Aramco), can be received in Bahrain.

Bahrain Radio and Television Corpn: POB 1075, Manama; tel. 781888; telex 8311; fax 681544; commenced colour broadcasting in 1973; broadcasts on five channels, of which the main Arabic and the main English channel accept advertising; covers Bahrain, eastern Saudi Arabia, Qatar and the UAE; an Amiri decree in early 1993 established the independence of the Corpn, which was to be controlled by a committee; Dir H. AL-UMRAN.

Finance

(cap. = capital; p.u. = paid up; res = reserves; dep. = deposits; m. = millions; brs = branches; amounts in Bahraini dinars unless otherwise stated)

BANKING

Central Bank

Bahrain Monetary Agency (BMA): POB 27, Manama; tel. 535535; telex 8295; fax 534170; e-mail bmalbr@batelco.com.br; internet http://www.bma.gov.bh; f. 1973, in operation from January 1975; controls issue of currency, regulates exchange control and credit policy, organization and control of banking system and bank credit; cap. 200m., res 47.3m., dep. 91.2m., total assets 455.7m. (Dec. 1996); Governor ABDULLAH HASSAN SAIF; Chair. Sheikh KHALIFA BIN SULMAN AL-KHALIFA.

Locally-incorporated Commercial Banks

Al-Ahli Commercial Bank BSC: POB 5941, Bahrain Car Park Bldg, Government Rd, Manama; tel. 224333; telex 9130; fax 224322; f. 1977; full commercial bank; cap. 13.2m., res 28.8m., dep. 208.4m. (Dec. 1997); Chair. MUHAMMAD Y. JALAL; CEO MICHAEL J. FULLER; 9 brs.

Bahrain Islamic Bank BSC: POB 5240, Government Rd, Manama; tel. 223402; telex 9388; fax 223956; f. 1979; cap. 11.5m., res 2.5m., dep. 130.2m. (May 1997); Chair. Sheikh ABD AR-RAHMAN AL-KHALIFA; Gen. Man. ABD AL-LATIF ABD AR-RAHIM JANAHI; 4 brs.

Bahrain Middle East Bank EC: POB 797, Manama; tel. 532345; telex 9706; fax 530987; f. 1982; owned by Burgan Bank (28%) and GCC nationals (72%); cap. US $84.0m., res US $22.8m., dep. US $531.0m. (Dec. 1996); Chair. ABD AR-RAHMAN SALEM AL-ATEEQI; CEO ALBERT I. KITTANEH; 1 br overseas and 1 rep. office.

Bahraini Saudi Bank BSC (BSB): POB 1159, Government Rd, Manama; tel. 211010; telex 7232; fax 210989; f. 1983; commenced operations in early 1985; licensed as a full commercial bank; cap. 20.0m., res 5.5m., dep. 104.2m. (Dec. 1996); Chair. Sheikh IBRAHIM BIN HAMAD AL-KHALIFA; Gen. Man. MANSOOR AS-SAYED ALI; 4 brs.

Bank of Bahrain and Kuwait BSC (BBK): POB 597, Manama; tel. 223388; telex 8919; fax 229822; f. 1971; cap. 56.9m., res 35.0m., dep. 737.0m. (Dec. 1997); Chair. RASHID ABD AR-RAHMAN AZ-ZAYANI; Gen. Man. and CEO MURAD ALI MURAD; 22 local brs, 2 brs overseas.

Faysal Islamic Bank of Bahrain EC: Chamber of Commerce Bldg, POB 2820, King Faysal Rd, Manama; tel. 211373; telex 9995; fax 210717; f. 1982 as Massraf Faysal Al-Islami of Bahrain EC; renamed as above in 1987; cap. US $100.00m., res US $16.3m., dep. US $70.7m. (Dec. 1996); Pres. and CEO NABIL ABD AL-ILLAH NASEER; 2 brs.

Grindlays Bahrain Bank BSC: POB 793, Manama; tel. 225999; telex 8335; fax 224482; f. 1984; commercial bank owned by Bahraini shareholders (60%) and ANZ Grindlays Bank PLC, London (40%); cap. 6.0m., res 4.0m., dep. 64.6m. (Dec. 1996); Chair. MUHAMMAD ABDULLAH AZ-ZAMIL; Gen. Man. PETER TOMKINS; 6 brs.

Gulf International Bank BSC (GIB): POB 1017, Al-Dowali Bldg, 3 Palace Ave, Manama; tel. 534000; telex 8802; fax 522633; e-mail gibmktg@batelco.com.bh; internet http://www.gibonline.com; f. 1975; owned by the Gulf Investment Corpn; cap. US $450.0m., res US $243.9m., dep. US $887.8m. (Dec. 1997); Gen. Man. Dr ABDULLAH I. AL-KUWAIZ; 2 brs.

National Bank of Bahrain BSC (NBB): POB 106, Government Ave, Manama; tel. 228800; telex 8242; fax 263876; f. 1957; 49% govt-owned; cap. 40.0m., res 48.0m., dep. 842.1m. (Dec. 1997); Gen. Man. ABD AR-RAZAK A. HASSAN; CEO HUSSAN ALI JUMA; 25 brs.

Foreign Commercial Banks

ABN AMRO Bank NV (Netherlands): POB 350, Manama; tel. 255420; telex 8356; fax 262241; internet http://www.abnamro.com; Man. C. A. A. VAN DER HAM; 1 br.

Arab Bank PLC (Jordan): POB 395, Government Rd, Manama; tel. 212255; telex 8232; fax 210443; internet http://www.arabbank.com; Chair. ABD AL-MAJEED SHOMAN; 4 brs.

Bank Melli Iran: POB 785, Government Rd, Manama; tel. 259910; telex 8266; fax 270768; Gen. Man. ALI ASGHAR KAMALI ROUSTA; 2 br.

Bank Saderat Iran: POB 825, Government Rd, Manama; tel. 210003; telex 8363; fax 210398; Man. MUHAMMAD JAVAD NASSIRI; 2 brs.

Banque du Caire (Egypt): POB 815, Manama; tel. 227454; telex 8298; fax 213704; Man. ES-SAYED MOUSTAFA EL-DOKMAWEY.

Banque Paribas FCB (France): POB 5241, Manama; tel. 225275; telex 8458; fax 224697; Gen. Man. M. APTHORPE.

British Bank of the Middle East (BBME): POB 57, Al-Khalifa Rd, Manama; tel. 242555; telex 8230; fax 256822; CEO ROGER J. JORDAN; 4 brs.

Citibank NA (USA): POB 548, Government Rd, Manama; tel. 223344; telex 8225; fax 211323; Gen. Man. MUHAMMAD ASH-SHROOGI; 1 br.

Habib Bank Ltd (Pakistan): POB 566, Manama Centre, Manama; tel. 227118; telex 9448; fax 213421; f. 1941; Exec. Vice-Pres. and Gen. Man. ASHRAF BIDIWALA; 5 brs.

Rafidain Bank (Iraq): POB 607, Manama; tel. 275796; telex 8332; fax 255656; f. 1969; Man. IBTISAM NAJEM ABOUD; 1 br.

Standard Chartered Bank (United Kingdom): POB 29, Government Rd, Manama; tel. 255946; telex 8229; fax 230503; f. in Bahrain 1920; Man. PETER RAWLINGS; 5 brs.

United Bank Ltd (Pakistan): POB 546, Government Rd, Manama; tel. 224032; telex 8247; fax 224099; Gen. Man. ZAFAR AL-HAQ MEMON; 3 brs.

Specialized Financial Institutions

Bahrain Development Bank (BDB): POB 20501, Manama; tel. 537007; telex 7022; fax 534005; f. 1992; invests in manufacturing, agribusiness and services; cap. 10.0m., res 0.1m., dep. 0.1m. (Dec. 1996); Chair. Sheikh EBRAHIM BIN KHALIFA AL-KHALIFA.

The Housing Bank: POB 5370, Diplomatic Area, Manama; tel. 534443; telex 8599; fax 533437; f. 1979; provides housing loans for Bahraini citizens and finances construction of commercial properties. Chair. Sheikh KHALID BIN ABDULLAH BIN KHALID AL-KHALIFA; Gen. Man. ISA SULTAN ADH-DHAWADI.

'Offshore' Banking Units

Bahrain has been encouraging the establishment of 'offshore' banking units (OBUs) since 1975. An OBU is not permitted to provide local banking services, but is allowed to accept deposits from governments and large financial organizations in the area and make medium-term loans for local and regional capital projects. Prior to the Iraqi invasion of Kuwait in August 1990, there were 56 OBUs in operation in Bahrain. By 1997, however, the number of OBUs had declined to 47.

Representative Offices

In 1997 there were 41 representative offices in Bahrain.

Investment Banks

Al-Baraka Islamic Investment Bank BSC (EC): POB 1882, 1 Al-Hedaya Bldg, Government Rd, Manama; tel. 274488; telex 8220; fax 274499; f. 1984; cap. and res US $54.5m., dep. US $91.2m., total assets US $155.6m. (Dec. 1996); Chair. Sheikh SALEH ABDULLAH KAMEL; 17 brs.

INVESTCORP Bank EC: POB 5340, Diplomatic Area, Manama; tel. 532000; telex 9664; fax 530816; f. 1982 as Arabian Investment Banking Corpn (INVESTCORP) EC, current name adopted in 1990; cap. US $100.0m., res US $79.1m., dep. US $549.5m. (Dec. 1997); Pres. and CEO NEMIR A. KIRDAR.

Nomura Investment Banking (Middle East) EC: POB 26893, 10th and 11th floor, BMB Centre, Diplomatic Area, Manama; tel. 530531; telex 9070; fax 530365; f. 1982; cap. US $25m., res US $100.9m., dep. US $75.6m. (Dec. 1996); Chair. TAKASHI TSUTSUI.

TAIB Bank EC: POB 20485, Sehl Centre, Diplomatic Area, Manama; tel. 533334; telex 8598; fax 533174; f. 1979 as Trans-Arabian Investment Bank EC; current name adopted in 1994; cap. US $84.4m., res US $15.6m., dep. US $204.8m. (Dec. 1996); Chair. ABD AR-RAHMAN AL-JERAISY; Vice-Chair. and CEO IQBAL G. MAMDANI.

United Gulf Bank (BSC) EC: POB 5964, UGB Tower, Diplomatic Area, Manama; tel. 533233; telex 9556; fax 533137; f. 1980; cap. US $200.0m., res US $14.9m., dep. US $147.3m. (Dec. 1997); Chair. FAISAL H. ALAYYAR; Gen. Man. MUHAMMAD HAROUN.

Other investment banks operating in Bahrain include the following: ABC Islamic Bank EC, Amex (Middle East) EC, Arab Financial Services Co EC, Arab Islamic Bank EC, Bahrain Investment Bank BSC, Bahrain Islamic Investment Co BSC, Capital Union EC, Daiwa Middle East EC, Faysal Investment Bank of Bahrain EC, First Islamic Investment Bank EC, Islamic Investment Company of the Gulf (Bahrain) EC, Man-Ahli Investment Bank EC, Merrill Lynch Int. Bank Ltd, Nikko Europe Plc, Okasan Int. (Middle East) EC, Sumitomo Finance (Middle East) EC, Turk-Gulf Merchant Bank EC, Yamaichi Int. (Middle East) EC.

STOCK EXCHANGE

Bahrain Stock Exchange: POB 3203, Manama; tel. 259690; telex 7937; fax 276181; f. 1989; nine mems; linked to Muscat Securities Market (Oman) in March 1995, and to Amman Financial Market

(Jordan) in March 1996; Dir-Gen. Sheikh AHMAD BIN MUHAMMAD AL-KHALIFA.

INSURANCE

Abdullah Yousuf Fakhro Corpn: POB 39, Government Ave, Manama; tel. 275000; telex 8867; fax 256999; general.

Al-Ahlia Insurance Co BSC: POB 5282, Manama; tel. 225860; telex 8761; fax 224870; internet http://www.alahlia.com; f. 1976; Chair. TAQI MUHAMMAD AL-BAHARNA.

Arab Insurance Group BSC (ARIG): POB 26992, Arig House, Diplomatic Area, Manama; tel. 544444; telex 9395; fax 531155; e-mail info@arig.com.bh; internet http://www.arig.com.bh; f. 1980; owned by Governments of Kuwait, Libya and the UAE (49.5%), and other shareholders; reinsurance and insurance; Chair. and CEO ABD AL-WAHAB A. AT-TAMMAR.

Arab International Insurance Co EC (AIIC): POB 10135, Manama; tel. 530087; telex 9226; fax 530122; f. 1981; non-life reinsurance; Chair. and Man. Dir Sheikh KHALID J. AS-SABAH.

Bahrain Insurance Co BSC (BIC): POB 843, Suite 310, City Centre, Government Ave, Manama; tel. 227800; telex 8463; fax 224385; internet http://www.bahins.com; f. 1969; all classes including life insurance; 80% Bahraini-owned, 19% Iraqi-owned; merger with National Insurance Co pending in 1998; Gen. Man. PATRICK N. V. IRWIN; 3 brs.

Bahrain Kuwait Insurance Co BSC: POB 10166, Diplomatic Area, Manama; tel. 532323; telex 8672; fax 530799; e-mail bkicbah@batelco.com.bh; internet http://www.bkic.com; f. 1975; Gen. Man. HAMEED AL-NASSER.

Gulf Union Insurance and Reinsurance Co: POB 10949, Ground Floor, Manama Centre, Manama; tel. 215622; fax 215421; e-mail guirco@batelco.com.bh; internet http://www.gulfunion-bah.com; Chair. IBRAHIM BIN HAMAD AL-KHALIFA.

Moustafa bin Abd al-Latif: POB 18, Bab al-Bahrain Rd, Manama; tel. 253417; telex 8558; fax 291423; Dir Sheikh MUHAMMAD YOUSUF NAJEEBI.

National Insurance Co BSC (NIC): POB 1818, Unitag House, Government Rd, Manama; tel. 228877; telex 8908; fax 228870; f. 1982; all classes of general insurance; merger with Bahrain Insurance Co pending in 1998; Chair. J. A. WAFA; Gen. Man. SAMIR AL-WAZZAN.

Trade and Industry

CHAMBER OF COMMERCE

Bahrain Chamber of Commerce and Industry: POB 248, New Chamber of Commerce Bldgs, King Faysal Rd, Manama; tel. 229555; telex 8691; fax 224985; e-mail bahcci@batelco.com.bh; internet http://www.bahchamber.com; f. 1939; 7,300 mems (1996); Pres. ALI BIN YOUSEF FAKHROO; Sec.-Gen. JASSIM MUHAMMAD ASH-SHATTI.

STATE HYDROCARBONS COMPANIES

Bahrain National Gas Co BSC (BANAGAS): POB 29099, Rifa'a; tel. 756222; telex 9317; fax 756991; f. 1979; responsible for extraction, processing and sale of hydrocarbon liquids from associated gas derived from onshore Bahraini fields; ownership is 75% Government of Bahrain, 12.5% Caltex and 12.5% Arab Petroleum Investments Corpn (APICORP); produced 202,955 metric tons of LPG and 189,803 tons of naphtha in 1996; Chair. Sheikh HAMAD BIN IBRAHIM AL-KHALIFA; Gen. Man. Dr. Sheikh MUHAMMAD BIN KHALIFA AL-KHALIFA.

Bahrain National Oil Co (BANOCO): POB 25504, Awali; tel. 754666; telex 8670; fax 753203; f. 1976; responsible for exploration, production, processing, transportation and storage of petroleum and petroleum products; distribution and sales of petroleum products (including natural gas), international marketing of crude petroleum and petroleum products, supply and sales of aviation fuels; produced an average of 40,000 barrels per day in 1994; Man. Dir MUHAMMAD SALEH SHEIKH ALI; Gen. Man. Dr FAYEZ HASHIM AS-SADAH.

Bahrain Petroleum Co BSC (BAPCO): POB 25504, Manama; tel. 754444; telex 8214; fax 752924; e-mail kathleen.croes@bapco.net; f. 1980; a refining company wholly owned by the Government of Bahrain; refined 92m. barrels of crude petroleum in 1997; Chair. Minister of Oil and Industry; Chief Exec. JOHANN F. LUBBE.

Gulf Petrochemical Industries Co BSC (GPIC): POB 26730, Sitra; tel. 731777; telex 9897; fax 731047; f. 1979 as a joint venture between the Governments of Bahrain, Kuwait and Saudi Arabia, each with one-third equity participation; a petrochemical complex at Sitra, inaugurated in 1981; produces 1,200 tons of both methanol and ammonia per day (1990); Chair. Sheikh ISA BIN ALI AL-KHALIFA; Gen. Man. MUSTAFA AS-SAYED.

UTILITIES

Ministry of Power and Water: (see Ministries, above); provides electricity and water throughout Bahrain.

MAJOR COMPANIES

Al-Khajah Establishment and Factories: POB 5042, Sitra Industrial Area; tel. 730611; telex 8619; fax 731340; e-mail alkhajah@batelco.com.bh; f. 1972; sales BD 12m. (1992); cap. and res BD 2.3m.; contracting, trading and manufacture of switchgear and light fittings; numerous subsidiaries within the Gulf; Chair. and Man. Dir JASSIM AL-KHAJAH; approx. 450 employees.

Aluminium Bahrain BSC (ALBA): POB 570, Manama; tel. 830000; telex 8253; fax 830083; f. 1971; operates a smelter owned by the Government of Bahrain (77%) and the Saudi Public Investment Fund (20%), the remainder being held by Breton Investments; capacity now stands at 500,000 metric tons per year; Chair. Sheikh ISA BIN ALI AL KHALIFA; acting CEO A. KARIM SALIMI.

Az-Zamil Group of Cos: POB 285, Manama; tel. 253445; telex 8381; fax 231803; f. 1930; manufacture of prefabricated metal buildings, aluminium doors, windows and frames, plastic industrial and household products, marble fascias, stairways, floors, etc., nails and screws; services include a travel agency, ship repair, maintenance, camp accommodation and catering, high technology services to petroleum sector, processing of refrigerated and frozen foods, civil, mechanical and electrical engineering; a Commercial Division handles trading, representation and sponsorship activities and all dealings in real estate, land development and property leasing; Chair. MUHAMMAD AZ-ZAMIL; approx. 7,500 employees.

Bahrain Aluminium Extrusion Co BSC (BALEXCO): POB 1053, Manama; tel. 730073; fax 736924; f. 1977; supplies aluminium profiles in mill finish, powder coated and anodized; capacity 20,000 metric tons per year; cap. BD 10m.; Chair. MURAD ALI MURAD; Gen. Man. MAHMOUD AS-SOUFI.

Bahrain Atomizers International: POB 5328, Manama; tel. 830880; fax 830025; f. 1973; produces 7,000 metric tons of atomized aluminium powder per year; owned by the Government of Bahrain (51%) and Breton Investments (49%); Chair. Y. SHIRAWI.

Bahrain Danish Dairy Co WLL: POB 601, Manama; tel. 591591; telex 8590; fax 591150; f. 1963; sales BD 7.0m.; cap. and res BD 1.5m.: processing, packaging and distribution of milk, ice-cream and fruit juice; Gen. Man. PAUL MIKKELSEN; 200 employees.

Bahrain Light Industries Co BSC: POB 26700, Manama; tel. 830222; telex 8538; fax 830399; e-mail blico@batelco.com.bh; cap. and res BD 5m.; manufacture of solid wood and veneered furniture, internal partitions and doors; Gen. Man. N. NATARAJAN; 180 employees.

Bahrain-Saudi Aluminium Marketing Co (BALCO): POB 20079, Manama; tel. 532626; telex 9110; fax 532727; f. 1976; to market ALBA products; owned by the Government of Bahrain (74.33%) and Saudi Basic Industries Corpn (25.67%); Gen. Man. HASSAN ALI FALAH.

Gulf Acid Industries Co: POB 2770, Manama; tel. 730686; fax 731991; f. 1983; cap. BD 2m.; manufacture and sale of distilled water engine coolant, engine flush and sulphuric acid using double catalysis and double absorption; Man. Dir MUHAMMAD AHMAD NASS.

Gulf Aluminium Rolling Mill Co (GARMCO): POB 20725, Manama; tel. 731000; telex 9786; fax 730542; f. 1980 as a joint venture between the Governments of Bahrain, Saudi Arabia, Kuwait, Iraq, Oman and Qatar; produced 120,000 tons of rolled aluminium in 1997; Chair. and Man. Dir Sheikh IBRAHIM BIN KHALIFA AL-KHALIFA; Gen. Man. ANTHONY LEWIS.

Maskati Brothers and Co: POB 24, Manama; tel. 729911; telex 8621; fax 725454; f. 1957; sales BD 9.0m. (1995); cap. and res BD 9m.; paper converters, polyethylene manufacture, injection moulders; Man. Dir KHALID H. MASKATI; 400 employees.

Midal Cables Ltd: POB 5939, Manama; tel. 830111; telex 9127; fax 830168; f. 1978; cap. US $4.08m.; sales US $100m. (1995); manufacture of aluminium and aluminium alloy electrical rods and conductors for overhead transmission and distribution lines; Man. Dir HAMID R. AL-ZAYANI; CEO SALMAN ASH-SHEIKH; 220 employees.

TRADE UNIONS

There are no trade unions in Bahrain.

Transport

RAILWAYS

There are no railways in Bahrain.

ROADS

At 31 December 1996 Bahrain had 2,938 km of roads, of which 75% were hard-surfaced. Most inhabited areas of Bahrain are linked by bitumen-surfaced roads. A modern network of dual highways is being developed, and a 25-km causeway link with Saudi Arabia was opened in 1986. A three-lane dual carriageway links the causeway to Manama. Other causeways link Bahrain with Muharraq island and with Sitra island. In March 1997 the Government approved the construction of a US $80m.-causeway linking Hidd on Muharraq island with the port of Mina Salman; the new causeway was scheduled to be completed in 2001. A second 2.5-km Manama-to-Muharraq causeway was opened in early 1997.

Directorate of Roads: POB 5, Sheikh Hamad Causeway, Manama; tel. 535222; telex 7129; fax 532565; responsible for traffic engineering, safety, planning, road maintenance and construction; Dir ISAM A. KHALAF.

SHIPPING

Numerous shipping services link Bahrain and the Gulf with Europe, the USA, Pakistan, India, the Far East and Australia. In 1988 a total of 14,316 vessels called at Bahraini ports.

The deep-water harbour of Mina Salman was opened in 1962; it has 13 conventional berths, two container terminals and a roll-on/roll-off berth. Two nearby slipways can accommodate vessels of up to 1,016 tons and 73m in length, and services are available for ship repairs afloat. The second container terminal, which has a 400-m quay (permitting two 180-m container ships to be handled simultaneously), was opened in 1979. Further development of Mina Salman, to allow handling of larger quantities of container cargo, was completed in 1985. During 1992 Mina Salman handled about 90,000 TEUs (20-ft equivalent units).

Plans to build a new port and industrial zone at Hidd, on Muharraq island, were approved by the Cabinet in March 1997. At an estimated total cost of US $330m., the proposed port would have an annual handling capacity of 234,000 TEUs and would include a general cargo berth and two container berths with roll-on/roll-off facilities. The project was expected to be put out to tender in 1998.

Directorate of Customs and Ports: POB 15, Manama; tel. 725555; telex 8642; fax 725534; responsible for customs activities and acts as port authority; Pres. of Customs and Ports EID ABDULLAH YOUSUF; Dir-Gen. of Ports Capt. MAHMOOD Y. AL-MAHMOOD; Dir-Gen. of Customs JASSIM JAMSHEER.

Arab Shipbuilding and Repair Yard Co (ASRY): POB 50110, Hidd; tel. 671111; telex 8455; fax 670236; e-mail Asryco@batelco.com.bh; f. 1974 by OAPEC members; 500,000-ton dry dock opened 1977; two floating dry docks in operation since 1992; repaired 116 ships in 1997; Chair. Sheikh DAIJ BIN KHALIFA AL-KHALIFA; CEO MUHAMMAD M. AL-KHATEEB.

Principal Shipping Agents

Gray Mackenzie & Co Ltd: POB 210, Manama; tel. 712750; telex 7068; fax 712749; Dir A. A. MACASKILL.

The Gulf Agency Co (Bahrain) Ltd: POB 412, Manama; tel. 254228; telex 8211; fax 530063; Man. Dir SKJALM BANG.

International Agencies Co Ltd: POB 584, Manama; tel. 727114; telex 8273, fax 727509; Dir SADIQ M. AL-BAHARNA.

Al-Jazeera Shipping Co WLL: POB 302, Manama; tel. 728837; telex 7891; fax 728217.

Al-Sharif Shipping Agency: POB 1322, Manama; tel. 530535; telex 8341; fax 537637; e-mail alsharif@batelco.com.bh; Dir ABD AL-HUSSAIN AL-SHARIF.

Yusuf bin Ahmad Kanoo: POB 45, Al-Khalifa Rd, Manama; tel. 254081; telex 8215; fax 246093; air and shipping cargo services; Dir AHMAD KANOO.

CIVIL AVIATION

Bahrain International Airport has a first-class runway, capable of taking the largest aircraft in use. In 1996 there were 56,751 flights to and from the airport, carrying a total of 3.4m. passengers. Extension work to the airport's main terminal building was completed in mid-1992. Further extension work was due to be carried out in 1995, in order to increase the airport's cargo-handling facilities.

Department of Civil Aviation Affairs: POB 586, Bahrain International Airport, Muharraq; tel. 321095; telex 9186; fax 321139; e-mail bahintapt@bahrainairport.co;internet http://www.bahrainairport.com; Under-Sec. IBRAHIM ABDULLAH AL-HAMER.

Gulf Air Co GSC (Gulf Air): POB 138, Gulf Air Tower, Muharraq; tel. 322200; telex 8255; fax 338033; f. 1950; jointly owned by Govts of Bahrain, Oman, Qatar and Abu Dhabi (part of the United Arab Emirates) since 1974; services to the Middle East, South-East Asia, Africa and Europe; Chair. Sheikh AHMAD BIN NASSER BIN FALEH ATH-THANI (Qatar); Pres. and Chief Exec. Sheikh AHMAD BIN SAIF AN-NAHYAN (Abu Dhabi).

Tourism

There are several archaeological sites of importance. Bahrain is the site of the ancient trading civilization of Dilmun. There is a wide selection of hotels and restaurants, and a new national museum opened in 1989. In 1995 some 2.5m. tourists visited Bahrain, and income from tourism totalled more than US $280m.

Bahrain Tourism Co (BTC): POB 5831, Manama; tel. 530530; telex 8929; fax 530867; e-mail bahtours@batelco.com.bh; Chair. MUHAMMAD YOUSUF JALAL.

Directorate of Tourism and Archaeology: POB 26613, Manama; tel. 201200; telex 8311; fax 210969; Dir Dr KADHIM RAJAB.

Defence

Commander-in-Chief of Bahraini Defence Force and National Guard: Sheikh HAMAD BIN ISA AL-KHALIFA.

Estimated Defence Budget (1997): BD 109m.

Military Service: voluntary.

Total Armed Forces (August 1997): 11,000 (army 8,500; navy 1,000; air force 1,500).

Paramilitary Forces: estimated 9,850 (police 9,000; national guard 600; coast guard 250).

Education

In 1995 enrolment at primary level included 100% of children in the relevant age-group (males 99%; females 100%). In that year, enrolment at secondary level was equivalent to 97% (males 95%; females 99%) of children in the relevant age-group. Education is compulsory between the ages of six and 17, and is available free of charge. In 1994/95, 108,606 pupils were receiving education in 174 government-operated schools. Private and religious education are also available.

Education begins at six years of age. From the ages of six to 11, children attend primary school. Secondary education, beginning at the age of 12, lasts for six years and is divided into two stages, each lasting three years. (An alternative structure for secondary education provides for eight years divided into two four-year stages.) In early 1988, according to the Ministry of Education, more than 65% of teachers were native Bahrainis. The University of Bahrain, established by Amiri decree in 1986, comprises five colleges: the College of Engineering, the College of Arts, the College of Science, the College of Education and the College of Business and Management. About 6,760 students were enrolled at the University in 1995. Higher education is also provided by the College of Health Sciences (528 students) and the Hotel and Catering Training Centre.

The first phase of the Arabian Gulf University (AGU), funded by seven Arab Governments, was completed in 1988. The University campus is due to be completed at the end of 2006, and will accommodate 5,000 students. In 1993 368 students were enrolled at the AGU.

In 1981 the average rate of adult illiteracy among the indigenous Bahraini population was 31.3% (males 21.2%; females 41.4%). In 1991, according to census results, the illiteracy rate among all adults resident in Bahrain was 15.9% (males 11.4%; females 23.0%). According to UNESCO estimates, in 1995 the rate of adult illiteracy was 14.8% (males 10.9%; females 20.6%). Expenditure on education by the central Government in 1996 was BD 80.5m. (13.8% of total expenditure).

Bibliography

Adamiyat, Fereydoun. *Bahrain Islands: A Legal and Diplomatic Study of the British-Iranian Controversy.* New York, Praeger, 1955.

Dabrowska, Karen. *Bahrain Briefing: The Struggle for Democracy.* London, Colourmast, 1997.

Faroughby, Abbas. *The Bahrain Islands.* New York, 1951.

Hakima, A. M. *The Rise and Development of Bahrain and Kuwait.* Beirut, 1965.

Hay, Sir Rupert. *The Persian Gulf States.* Washington, DC, Middle East Institute, 1959.

Khuri, F. I. *Tribe and State in Bahrain.* Chicago University Press, 1981.

Lawson, Fred H. *The Modernization of Autocracy.* Boulder, Colorado, Westview Press, 1989.

Marlowe, John. *The Persian Gulf in the 20th Century.* London, Cresset Press, 1962.

Matveev, Konstantin. *Bahrain: The Drive for Democracy.* London, Prittle, 1997.

Miles, S. B. *The Countries and Tribes of the Persian Gulf.* 3rd edition, London, Cass, 1970.

Nakhleh, Emile A. *Bahrain: Political Development in a Modernizing Society.* Lexington, Massachusetts, Lexington Books, 1976.

Nugent, Jeffrey, and Thomas, Theodore. *Bahrain and the Gulf: Prospects for the Future.* London, Croom Helm, 1985.

Routine Abuse, Routine Denial: Civil Rights and the Political Crisis in Bahrain. New York, Human Rights Watch, 1997.

Rumaihi, Mohammed al-. *Bahrain: Social and Political Change since the First World War.* Durham Univ., Bowker, in association with the Centre for Middle Eastern and Islamic Studies, 1977.

Ward, Philip. *Bahrain—A Travel Guide.* Cambridge, The Oleander Press, 1993.

Wilson, Sir A. T. *The Persian Gulf.* Oxford University Press, 1928.

CYPRUS

Physical and Social Geography

W. B. FISHER

The island of Cyprus, with an area of 9,251 sq km (3,572 sq miles), is situated in the north-eastern corner of the Mediterranean Sea, closest to Turkey (which is easily visible from its northern coast), but also less than 160 km (100 miles) from the Syrian coast. Its greatest length (including the long, narrow peninsula of Cape Andreas) is 225 km (140 miles). The census of 1 October 1982, which was held in Greek Cypriot areas only, recorded a total population (including an estimate for the Turkish-occupied region) of 642,731. According to an official estimate, the population was 735,900 (including 90,600 in the Turkish-occupied region) at 31 December 1995. However, these figures exclude settlers from Turkey in the 'Turkish Republic of Northern Cyprus' ('TRNC'), who are regarded as illegal residents by the Greek Cypriot authorities. This group was believed to total more than 90,000 in 1995. The authorities in the 'TRNC' estimated the population of the region to be 179,208 in 1994, rising to 183,290 by 1995, and to 200,587 according to a census conducted in the 'TRNC' on 15 December 1996. Thus the total number of inhabitants of Cyprus exceeded 800,000 by the mid-1990s.

PHYSICAL FEATURES

Cyprus owes its peculiar shape to the occurrence of two ridges that were once part of two much greater arcs running from the mainland of Asia westwards towards Crete. The greater part of these arcs has disappeared, but remnants are found in Cyprus and on the eastern mainland, where they form the Amanus range of Turkey. In Cyprus the arcs are visible as two mountain systems—the Kyrenia range of the north, and the much larger and imposing Troödos massif in the centre. Between the two mountain systems lies a flat lowland, open to the sea in the east and west and spoken of as the Mesaoria. Here also lies the chief town, Nicosia (Lefkoşa in Turkish).

The mountain ranges are actually very different in structure and appearance. The Kyrenia range is a single narrow fold of limestone, with occasional deposits of marble, and its maximum height is 900 m (3,000 ft). As it is mainly porous rock, rainfall soon seeps below ground; and so its appearance is rather arid, but very picturesque, with white crags and isolated pinnacles. The soil cover is thin. The Troödos, on the other hand, has been affected by folding in two separate directions, so that the whole area has been fragmented, and large quantities of molten igneous rock have forced their way to the surface from the interior of the earth, giving rise to a great dome that reaches 1,800 m (6,000 ft) above sea-level. As it is impervious to water, there are some surface streams, rounder outlines, a thicker soil, especially on the lower slopes, and a covering of pine forest.

CLIMATE

The climate in Cyprus is strongly 'Mediterranean' in character, with the usual hot dry summers and warm, wet winters. As an island with high mountains, Cyprus receives a fair amount of moisture, and up to 1,000 mm (40 ins) of rain falls in the mountains, with the minimum of 300 mm–380 mm (12 ins–15 ins) in the Mesaoria. Frost does not occur on the coast, but may be sharp in the higher districts, and snow can fall fairly heavily in regions over 900 m (3,000 ft) in altitude. In summer, despite the nearness of the sea, temperatures are surprisingly high, and the Mesaoria, in particular, can experience over 38°C (100°F). A feature of minor importance is the tendency for small depressions to form over the island in winter, giving a slightly greater degree of changeability in weather than is experienced elsewhere in the Middle East.

Cyprus is noteworthy in that between 50% and 60% of the total area is under cultivation—a figure higher than that for most Middle Eastern countries. This is partly to be explained by the relatively abundant rainfall; the expanses of impervious rock that retain water near the surface; and the presence of rich soils derived from volcanic rocks which occur around the Troödos massif. The potential of the tourist trade and the export markets in wine and early vegetables add to the incentives to development. In the southern (Greek) part of the island economic recovery after partition has been considerable: far less so in the north.

History

Revised for this edition by ALAN J. DAY

EARLY HISTORY

Cyprus first became important in recorded history when the island fell under Egyptian control in the second millennium BC. After a long period during which the Phoenicians and the people of Mycenae founded colonies there, Cyprus, in the eighth century BC, became an Assyrian protectorate, at a time when the Greeks of the mainland were extending their settlements in the island. From the sixth century BC it was a province of the Persian empire and took part in the unsuccessful Ionian revolt against Persian rule in 502 BC. Despite the Greek triumph over Xerxes in 480 BC, subsequent efforts by the Greek city states of the mainland to free Cyprus from Persian control met with little success, largely because of dissension among the Greek cities of Cyprus itself. For more than two centuries after 295 BC the Ptolemies of Egypt ruled in Cyprus until it became part of the Roman Empire.

Cyprus prospered under the enlightened Roman rule of Augustus, for trade flourished while the Romans kept the seas free of piracy. When Jerusalem fell to the Emperor Titus in AD 70, many Jews found refuge in Cyprus where they became numerous enough to undertake a serious revolt in AD 115. Christianity, apparently introduced into the island in the reign of the Emperor Claudius (AD 41–54), grew steadily in the next three centuries, during which Cyprus, isolated from a continent frequently ravaged by barbarian inroads, continued to enjoy a relative degree of prosperity. From the time of Constantine the Great, Cyprus was a province governed by officials appointed from Antioch and formed part of the diocese of the East. In the reign of Theodosius I (379–395) the Greek Orthodox Church was firmly established there and in the fifth century proved strong enough to resist the attempts of the Patriarchs of Antioch to control the religious life of the island.

The Arab attack of 649 began a new period in the history of Cyprus which now became, for more than 300 years, the object of dispute between the Byzantines and the Muslims. Whenever the Byzantine fleet was weak, Cyprus remained a doubtful possession of the Empire. After the decisive Byzantine reconquest of 964–65, Cyprus enjoyed, for more than two centuries, a period of relative calm.

WESTERN RULE

In 1192 King Richard I of England, having taken the island from the Greek usurper Comnenus, sold it to the Knights Templar, who, in turn, sold it to Guy de Lusignan, formerly King of Jerusalem. Thus began almost 400 years of Western rule, which saw the introduction of Western feudalism and of the Latin Church into a land which hitherto had been Greek in its institutions and Orthodox in its religious beliefs.

In the period from 1192 to 1267 (when the direct line of the Lusignan house became extinct) the new regime was gradually elaborated. The Lusignan monarchy was limited in character, for the royal power was effective only in the military sphere, all other important business of state being decided in a high court which consisted of the nobles, the fief-holders, and the great officers of state. This court applied to the island a highly developed code of feudal law derived from the Assizes of Jerusalem, the Cypriots being allowed to retain their own laws and customs in so far as these did not conflict with the feudal law. The period was also marked by the determined efforts of the Latin clergy, supported by the Papacy, to establish complete control over the Orthodox Church, a policy carried out with much harshness, which the Crown and the feudal nobility often sought to mitigate in order to keep the loyalty of the subject population. The dominance of the Latin Church was finally assured by the Bulla Cypria of Pope Alexander IV (1260).

During the second half of the 13th century the kingdom of Cyprus (now ruled by the house of Antioch-Lusignan) played an important role in the last struggle to maintain the Latin states in Syria against the Mamluk offensive. The influence of the monarchy was further strengthened in this period, and when, in 1324, Hugues IV became king, the great age of feudal Cyprus had begun. Cyprus was now of great importance in the commerce which the Italian republics maintained with the East, and Famagusta became a flourishing port. The Papacy, however, always anxious to weaken the power of Mamluk Egypt, placed severe limitations on the trade of the Italian republics with that state and charged Cyprus and Rhodes with their enforcement. Thus began a conflict between the kings of Cyprus and the great republics of Venice and Genoa, which did not endanger Cyprus provided that the Papacy could mobilize sentiment in the West to support the crusading state of the Lusignans. When, as the 14th century advanced, the Papacy lost its power to command such support in the West, Cyprus was left to face unaided the ambitions of Genoa and Venice, which she was powerless to withstand.

Before this decline began, Cyprus enjoyed a brief period of great brilliance under her crusading king, Peter I (1359–69). In 1361 he occupied the port of Adalia on the south coast of Asia Minor, then held by the Turkish emirate of Tekke, and in the years 1362–65 he toured Europe in an effort to win adequate support for a new crusade. His most memorable exploit came in 1365, when he captured Alexandria in Egypt, sacking it so completely that even as late as the 16th century it had not recovered its former splendour. With his assassination in 1369 the great period of the Lusignan house was ended.

The reign of King Janus I (1398–1432) was a long struggle to drive out the Genoese, who had seized Famagusta during the war with Cyprus in 1372–74, and to repel the attacks of Mamluk Egypt, which had become weary of the repeated sea-raids undertaken from the ports of Cyprus. After plundering Larnaca and Limassol in 1425, the Mamluks crushed the army of Cyprus in a battle at Khoirakoitia in 1426, King Janus himself being captured, and his capital, Nicosia, sacked. The king was released in 1427, when he had promised the payment of a large ransom and of an annual tribute. The last years of Lusignan power were marked by dissension in the ruling house and by the increasing domination of Venice which, with the consent of Caterina Cornaro, the Venetian widow of the last Lusignan king, annexed Cyprus in 1489.

TURKISH RULE

Venice held Cyprus until 1570 when the Ottoman Turks began a campaign of conquest which led to the fall of Nicosia in September 1570 and of Famagusta in August 1571. The Turks now restored to the Greek Orthodox Church its independence and ended the former feudal status of the peasantry. The Cypriots paid a tax for the freedom to follow their own religion and were allowed to cultivate their land as their own and to hand it to their descendants on payment of a portion of the produce. About 30,000 Turkish soldiers were also given land on the island, thus forming a Turkish element in the population which was later reinforced by immigration from Asia Minor.

The 17th and 18th centuries were a melancholy period in the history of Cyprus. Repeated droughts and ravages of locusts preceded a famine in 1640 and an outbreak of plague in 1641. In 1660 the Ottoman Government, in order to limit the extortions of its officials and of the tax-farmers, recognized the Orthodox Archbishop and his three suffragans as guardians of the Christian peasantry, but this step did not prevent revolts in 1665 and 1690. A great famine in 1757–58 and a severe attack of plague in 1760 reduced the numbers of the peasantry very considerably, causing a widespread distress which culminated in the revolt of 1764–66. From 1702 Cyprus had been a fief of the Grand Vizier who normally sold the governorship to the highest bidder, usually for a period of one year. This practice created great opportunities for financial oppression. Perhaps the most striking development of the period was the continued rise in the power of the Orthodox bishops, whose influence was so great in the late 18th century that the Turkish administration depended on their support for the collection of revenues. The Turkish elements in Cyprus, resenting the dominance of the Orthodox bishops, accused them in 1821 of having a secret understanding with the Greeks of the Morea (who had revolted against Turkish rule) and carried out a massacre of the Christians at Nicosia and elsewhere, which brought the supremacy of the bishops to an end.

In 1833 the Sultan granted Cyprus to Muhammad Ali, Pasha of Egypt, who was forced, however, to renounce possession of it in 1840 at the demand of the Great Powers. During the period of reforms initiated by Sultan Mahmud II (1808–39) and continued by his immediate successors, efforts were made to improve the administration of the island. The practice of farming out taxes was abolished (although later partially re-introduced) and the Governor became a salaried official, ruling through a divan that was half-Turkish and half-Christian in composition.

BRITISH RULE

At the Congress of Berlin of 1878 the Great Powers endorsed an agreement between the United Kingdom and the Sultan of Turkey, whereby Cyprus was put under British control, to be used as a base from which to protect the Ottoman Empire against the ambitions of Russia. Control of Cyprus was now regarded as vital, since the opening of the Suez Canal (1869) had made the eastern Mediterranean an area of great strategic importance. Under the agreement of 1878, Cyprus remained legally a part of the Ottoman Empire, to which a tribute was paid, consisting of the surplus revenues of the island, calculated at less than £93,000 per annum.

From 1882 until 1931 the island had a legislative council that was partly nominated and partly elected. Various reforms were carried out in this first period of British rule: the introduction of an efficient judicial system and of an effective police force, and considerable improvements in agriculture, roads, education and other public services.

When Turkey joined the Central Powers in World War I, Britain immediately annexed Cyprus (1914) and then offered it to Greece (1915), provided the latter joined the Allies: this offer was refused, however, and was not repeated when Greece eventually joined the hostilities in 1917. Under the terms of the Treaty of Lausanne of 1923, both Greece and Turkey recognized British sovereignty over Cyprus, which became a Crown Colony in 1925. Thereafter, discontent among the Greek Cypriots began to assume serious proportions, culminating in anti-British riots in 1931 and the suspension of constitutional rule.

In the period after 1931 the desire to achieve self-government within the British Commonwealth grew stronger, but the movement for Enosis (union with Greece) became the dominant influence in the political life of the island. Cypriot troops performed valuable services in the war of 1939–45, for example in Libya, under Lord Wavell, and in the Greek campaign of 1941. Later, Cyprus was used as a place of detention for illegal Jewish immigrants into Palestine, the last of such detention camps being closed in 1949. Following his election as head of the Orthodox Church of Cyprus in 1950, Archbishop Makarios III assumed the leadership of the Enosis movement. An unofficial plebiscite, conducted by the Church in that year, demonstrated overwhelming support for Enosis among Greek Cypriots.

CONSTITUTIONAL PROPOSALS

In July 1954 the United Kingdom made known its intention to prepare a restricted form of constitution for Cyprus, with a legislature containing official, nominated and elected members. The Greek Cypriots, insisting that their ultimate goal was Enosis, viewed the proposed constitution with disfavour, whereas the Turkish Cypriots declared their readiness to accept it. The Greek Government at Athens now brought the problem of Cyprus before the United Nations (UN). The United Kingdom, however, argued that the question was one with which it alone was competent to deal. The result was that, in December 1954, the UN resolved to take no immediate action in the matter.

The more extreme advocates of Enosis, grouped together in EOKA (National Organization of Cypriot Combatants) under the leadership of Gen. George Grivas (Dhigenis), now began a campaign of terrorist activities against the British administration. A conference including representatives from the United Kingdom, Greece and the Turkish Republic met in London in August 1955. The British offer of substantial autonomy for Cyprus failed to win the approval of Greece, since it held out no clear prospect of self-determination for the island, and the conference therefore ended in frustration.

A new and more violent wave of terrorism swept Cyprus in November 1955. A state of emergency was declared on 27 November whereby the death penalty was imposed for the bearing of arms, life imprisonment for sabotage and lesser sentences for looting and the harbouring of terrorists. All public assemblies of a political nature were forbidden; the British troops in Cyprus (about 10,000 in all) assumed the status of active service in war time. The Governor now ruled the island through an executive council consisting of four officials from the administration, two Greek Cypriots and one Turkish Cypriot.

At the beginning of 1956 the Governor, Sir John Harding, discussed the situation with Archbishop Makarios. Since the United Kingdom was now willing to accept the principle of ultimate independence for Cyprus, agreement seemed to be within reach. In March 1956, however, the discussions were suspended, and Archbishop Makarios, implicated in the activities of EOKA, was deported to the Seychelles Islands.

RELEASE OF MAKARIOS

In March 1957 Archbishop Makarios was released from detention in the Seychelles and, since he was not allowed to return to Cyprus, went to Athens. The British authorities also relaxed some of the emergency laws, such as the censorship of the press and the mandatory death penalty for the bearing of arms. These measures facilitated the holding of further discussions but little progress was made by the end of the year.

The tide of violence ran high in Cyprus during the first half of 1958. EOKA carried out an intensive campaign of sabotage, especially at Nicosia and Famagusta. At the same time strife between the Greek Cypriots and the Turkish Cypriots was becoming more frequent and severe, the outbreaks in June 1958 being particularly serious. There was increased tension, too, between the governments at Athens and at Ankara.

It was amid this situation that in June 1958 the United Kingdom made public a new scheme for Cyprus, which came into force in October. The island was to remain under British control for seven years; full autonomy in communal affairs would be granted, under separate arrangements, to the Greek Cypriots and the Turkish Cypriots; internal administration was to be reserved for the Governor's Council, which would include representatives of the Greek Cypriot and Turkish Cypriot communities and also of the Greek and Turkish Governments in Athens and Ankara.

ACHIEVEMENT OF INDEPENDENCE

As a result of a conference held in Zürich, it was announced in February 1959 that Greece and Turkey had devised a compro-

mise settlement concerning Cyprus. A further conference in London decided that Cyprus was to become an independent republic with a Greek Cypriot president and a Turkish Cypriot vice-president. There would be a Council of Ministers (seven Greeks, three Turks) and a House of Representatives (70% Greek, 30% Turkish) elected by universal suffrage for a term of five years. Communal Chambers, one Greek, one Turkish, were to exercise control in matters of religion, culture and education. The Turkish inhabitants in five of the main towns would be allowed to establish separate municipalities for a period of four years.

Cyprus was not to be united with another state, nor was it to be subject to partition. The United Kingdom, Greece and Turkey guaranteed the independence, the territorial integrity and the Constitution of Cyprus. Greece received the right to station a force of 950 men on the island, and Turkey a force of 650 men. The United Kingdom retained under its direct sovereignty two base areas in Cyprus—at Akrotiri and at Dhekelia.

In November 1959 agreement was attained in regard to the delimitation of the executive powers to be vested in the President and Vice-President of Cyprus. A further agreement defined the composition of the Supreme Constitutional Court. In December the state of emergency came to an end and Archbishop Makarios was elected to be the first President of Cyprus. The post of Vice-President was awarded, unopposed, to the Turkish Cypriot leader, Dr Fazil Küçük. After long negotiations, concluded in July 1960, the United Kingdom and Cyprus reached agreement over the precise size and character of the two military bases to be assigned to British sovereignty.

Cyprus formally became an independent republic on 16 August 1960, and, in September, a member of the UN. The Conference of Commonwealth Prime Ministers, meeting in London, resolved in March 1961 to admit Cyprus as a member of the Commonwealth.

CONSTITUTIONAL PROBLEMS

As Cyprus entered into its independence, serious problems began to arise over the interpretation and working of the Constitution. There was divergence of opinion between Greek and Turkish Cypriots over the formation of a national army, in accordance with provisions of the Zürich agreement of 1959 (2,000 men; 60% Greek, 40% Turkish); the main point of dispute being the degree of integration to be established between the two components. In October 1961 the Turkish Vice-President, Dr Küçük, used his power of veto to ban full integration, which President Makarios favoured at all levels of the armed forces.

Difficulties also arose over the implementation of the 70:30 ratio of Greek Cypriot to Turkish Cypriot personnel in the public services. There was friction too in the House of Representatives, about financial affairs, such as customs duties and income tax laws.

The year 1962 saw the development of a serious crisis over the system of separate Greek and Turkish municipalities in the five main towns of Cyprus—Nicosia, Famagusta, Limassol, Larnaca and Paphos. In December the Turkish Communal Chamber passed a law maintaining the Turkish municipalities in the five towns from 1 January 1963, and also establishing a similar municipality in the predominantly Turkish town of Lefka. President Makarios now issued a decree stating that, from 1 January 1963, government-appointed bodies would control municipal organizations throughout the island—a decree which the Turkish Cypriots denounced as an infringement of the Constitution.

The Constitutional Court of Cyprus, sitting in judgement on the financial disputes, ruled in February 1963 that, in view of the veto exercised by the Turkish members of the House of Representatives since 1961, taxes could be imposed on the people of the island, but that no legal machinery existed for the collection of such taxes. In April the court declared that the Government had no power to control the municipalities through bodies of its own choosing and that the decision of the Turkish Communal Chamber to maintain the separate Turkish municipalities in defiance of the Cyprus Government was likewise invalid.

Negotiations between President Makarios and Vice-President Küçük to resolve the deadlock broke down in May. Accordingly, in November, Archbishop Makarios put forward proposals for a number of reforms. However, these proved to be unacceptable to the Turkish Cypriots.

CIVIL WAR

Meanwhile, underground organizations, prepared for violence, had been formed among both the Greek and the Turkish communities. In December 1963 serious conflict broke out. The United Kingdom suggested that a joint force composed of British, Greek and Turkish troops based in Cyprus should be established to restore order. The governments at Nicosia, Athens and Ankara gave their assent to this scheme. At this time the forces of Turkey serving in the island occupied a strong position, north of Nicosia, which gave them control of the important road to Kyrenia on the northern coast of Cyprus—a road which was to become the scene of much conflict in the future. As a result of the December crisis, co-operation between the Greek Cypriots and the Turkish Cypriots in government and in other sectors of public life came almost to an end, most notably in the Turkish Cypriot boycott of the House of Representatives.

There was renewed violence in February 1964, especially at Limassol. Arms in considerable quantities were being brought secretly into the island for both sides, and the number of armed 'irregulars' was increasing rapidly. These developments also gave rise to friction between Athens and Ankara.

ESTABLISHMENT OF UN PEACE-KEEPING FORCE

In January 1964, following a request by the Cyprus Government, the UN nominated Lt-Gen. Prem Gyani of India to act as its representative to the island. Later in the same month the Cyprus Government informed U Thant, the Secretary-General of the UN, that it would be glad to see a UN force established in the island. The UN Security Council debated the Cyprus question in February, finally adopting, on 4 March, a resolution to establish the UN Peace-keeping Force in Cyprus (UNFICYP). Advance units of the Canadian contingent reached the island in March, and by 22 May the UN headquarters at Nicosia controlled 6,931 men.

There was more fighting between Greek and Turkish Cypriots in March and April 1964. On 1 June the Cyprus House of Representatives approved legislation establishing a National Guard and rendering all male Cypriots between the ages of 18 and 59 liable to six months of service. Only members of the National Guard, of the regular police and of the armed forces would now have the right to bear arms. One purpose of the legislation was to suppress the irregular bands which increasingly tended to escape the control of the established regime.

Under the agreements concluded for the independence of Cyprus in 1959–60, Turkey maintained a contingent of troops on the island, the personnel of this force being renewed from time to time on a system of regular rotation. A new crisis arose in August–September 1964 when the Government at Nicosia refused to allow such a rotation of personnel. After much negotiation through the UN officials on the island, the Cyprus Government agreed to raise its existing blockade of the Turkish Cypriots entrenched in the Kokkina district and to allow the normal rotation of troops for the Turkish force stationed at Cyprus. The Government at Ankara now consented that this force should come under UN command in Cyprus.

GENERAL GRIVAS

There was further tension in Cyprus during March 1966 over the position of Gen. Grivas, the former head of EOKA. Grivas had returned to the island in June 1964 at a time when it was felt that he might be able, with his high personal prestige, to bring to order the small 'private armies' and 'irregular bands' which had emerged among the Greek Cypriots and which were violently defying the Cyprus Government.

In March 1966 President Makarios attempted to limit the functions of Gen. Grivas in Cyprus and so to end a situation which saw political control vested in himself, while command of the armed forces (both the Greek Cypriot National Guard and also the 'volunteer' Greek troops stationed in Cyprus), rested with the General, who took his orders from Athens. The President suggested that the National Guard should be transferred to the control of the Cyprus Minister of Defence—a proposal which found favour neither with Gen. Grivas nor in

Athens, where it provoked a serious political crisis. The whole affair underlined the distrust separating President Makarios and Gen. Grivas and the doubts existing in Athens regarding the ultimate intentions of the President.

The military coup in Greece in April 1967 was followed by a brief improvement in Greco–Turkish relations. The Prime Ministers and Foreign Ministers of Greece and Turkey met in Thrace in September, but failed to reach an agreement on Cyprus, Greece rejecting any form of partition, which was implicit in the Turkish proposal to accept Enosis in return for military bases and 10% of the island's territory.

TURKISH CYPRIOT ADMINISTRATION

On 29 December 1967 the Turkish Cypriot community announced the establishment of a 'Transitional Administration' to administer their affairs until the provisions of the 1960 Constitution were implemented. Measures were approved to establish separate executive, legislative and judicial authorities, and Dr Küçük, who remained the official Vice-President of Cyprus, was appointed President of the Transitional Administration, with Rauf Denktaş as Vice-President. A legislative body was established, consisting of the Turkish Cypriot members of the House of Representatives elected in 1960 and the members of the Turkish Communal Chamber. The Executive Council's nine members functioned as the administration. President Makarios described the Transitional Administration as 'totally illegal', but it continued to function as the *de facto* Government of the Turkish community in Cyprus.

INTERCOMMUNAL TALKS, 1968–74

Between January and April 1968 the Cypriot Government gradually relaxed the measures it had adopted against the Turkish community. With the exception of the Turkish area in Nicosia, freedom of movement for Turkish Cypriots was restored, checkpoints were removed and unrestricted supplies to Turkish areas were permitted. In April Rauf Denktaş, the Vice-President of the Turkish Cypriot Administration, was permitted to return from exile, and in May he began talks with Glavkos Klerides, the President of the House of Representatives. These negotiations were intended to form the basis of a settlement of the constitutional differences between the Greek and Turkish communities, but very little progress was made. After years of intermittent discussion, there was still an impasse, the Turks demanding local autonomy, the Greeks rejecting any proposals tending towards a federal solution, fearing that it might lead to partition. In June 1972 Dr Kurt Waldheim, the UN Secretary-General, attended the talks, stressing the need for a peaceful settlement and expressing a hope that UNFICYP might be withdrawn in the near future. By the end of 1973 the Greek Cypriot representative seemed to have accepted the principle of local autonomy, but the talks still dragged on, with no acceptable compromise having been found on the scope of local autonomy or the degree of control to be exercised by the central government over local authorities. A statement by Bülent Ecevit, Prime Minister of Turkey, calling for a federal settlement of the constitutional problem, caused the talks to break down in April 1974. The Greek and Cypriot Governments claimed that the negotiations had been conducted on the understanding that any solution would be in terms of a unitary state; Denktaş declared that federation would not necessarily mean partition. Denktaş also feared that the Greek Government was giving support to the Enosis movement. Each side accused the other of trying to sabotage the talks.

TERRORISM AND ELECTIONS

While the talks between the Greek and Turkish communities continued, there was a marked reduction in intercommunal violence, but the Greek population of the island was divided between supporters of Makarios, and his aim of an independent unitary state, and those who demanded union with Greece. In 1969 the National Front, an organization advocating immediate Enosis, embarked on a campaign of terrorism, raiding police stations to steal arms, bombing British military buildings and vehicles, shooting and wounding the chief of police and making several unsuccessful bomb attacks on government ministers. Georgios Papadopoulos, the Greek Prime Minister, denounced terrorism in Cyprus and the National Front in particular.

On 8 March 1970 there was an attempt to assassinate President Makarios, attributed to the National Front. A week later Polykarpos Georghadjis, a former Minister of the Interior, was found shot dead. At the trial of the President's would-be assassins, Georghadjis was named as a party to the conspiracy.

Despite the activities of the National Front, the Government decided to hold a general election on 5 July 1970. The dissolved House of Representatives had been in existence since 1960, and the elections which should have been held in 1965, according to the Constitution, had been postponed from year to year, owing to the continuing crisis. The continued absence of the 15 Turkish members, who met as part of the Turkish Legislative Assembly, meant that the Greek Cypriot House of Representatives contained only 35 members. Fifteen of the Greek Cypriot seats were won by the Unified Party, led by Glavkos Klerides, with a policy of support for President Makarios and a united independent Cyprus. The communist Anorthotiko Komma Ergazomenou Laou (Progressive Party of the Working People—AKEL) won nine seats, to become the second largest in the House. None of the candidates of the Demokratikon Ethnikon Komma (Democratic National Party—DEK—which advocated Enosis), won a seat. The elections held at the same time by the Turkish Cypriots resulted in a victory for the National Solidarity Party, led by Rauf Denktaş.

RETURN OF GRIVAS AND EOKA-B

The ideal of Enosis was still attractive to many Greek Cypriots, despite the lack of success for pro-Enosis candidates in the election. Greek Cypriot students condemned President Makarios's support for the creation of an independent unitary state, and called for an end to the intercommunal talks. Gen. Grivas attacked the President in an article in an Athens newspaper, calling for his resignation on the grounds that, by abandoning Enosis, the President had betrayed EOKA's struggle for freedom.

At the beginning of September 1971 Gen. Grivas returned secretly to Cyprus and began to hold meetings with the leaders of the National Front and his followers in the EOKA movement of the 1950s. President Makarios threatened to arrest the General for setting up armed bands, and declared his opposition to the achievement of Enosis by violent means. His opponents, pro-Enosis Greek Cypriots, condemned the intercommunal talks and rejected the idea of a negotiated compromise with the Turkish community. The Cyprus Government imported a considerable quantity of arms from Czechoslovakia as a precautionary measure, but after protests from the Greek and Turkish foreign ministries that the distribution of these arms would serve only to aggravate an already tense situation, the consignment was placed under the custody of UNFICYP.

The President had been under pressure for some time from the Greek Government to dismiss ministers considered hostile to Athens. In February 1972 it was suggested in Athens that a Cypriot government of national unity should be formed, including moderate representatives of Gen. Grivas. For some months the President resisted this pressure, and it seemed that the Greek Government, in alliance with dissident bishops and Gen. Grivas, was intent on forcing his resignation. In May Spyros Kyprianou, the Foreign Minister, who had been the main target of Greek hostility and one of the President's closest collaborators, resigned, and in June the President capitulated and carried out an extensive reorganization of his Cabinet.

Gen. Grivas organized a new guerrilla force, which became known as EOKA-B, and launched a series of attacks on the Makarios Government, similar to those against British rule in the 1950s. While the Committee for the Co-ordination of the Enosis Struggle, Grivas's political front organization, demanded a plebiscite on Enosis and rejected intercommunal agreement as a means of settling the future of Cyprus, EOKA-B raided police stations, quarries and warehouses, stealing arms, ammunition, dynamite and radio transmitters.

1973 PRESIDENTIAL ELECTION

The demand for a plebiscite from supporters of Gen. Grivas was put forward as an alternative to the election for the presidency, called by President Makarios as a test of strength. The President's speech of 8 February 1973 explained his position; while believing in Enosis, he considered that talks with the Turkish community on the basis of an independent Cyprus were the only practical possibility. He condemned terrorism and violence as counter-productive, likely to lead to Turkish intervention and unsupported by the Greek and Cypriot authorities. The Greek Government also repudiated terrorism and expressed its support for a constitutional solution.

On 8 February 1973 Makarios was returned unopposed for a third five-year term as President, and in the Turkish quarter of Nicosia Rauf Denktaş was declared elected Vice-President, following the withdrawal of Ahmet Berberoğlu.

EOKA-B continued its terrorist activities throughout 1973, concentrating on bombings and raids on police stations. In July the Minister of Justice, Christos Vakis, was kidnapped, prompting an escalation in violence. The President refused to submit to violence or to blackmail, rejecting the terms put forward by Grivas for the release of Vakis. Numerous police and National Guard officers, suspected of being Grivas sympathizers, were dismissed, and Vakis was released in August. Action by security forces against secret EOKA bases resulted in many arrests, the seizure of quantities of munitions and the discovery of plans to assassinate the President. President Papadopoulos of Greece publicly condemned the activities of 'the illegal organization of Gen. Grivas', which undermined the Greek policy of 'support for the finding of a solution to the Cyprus problem through the enlarged local talks aimed at ensuring an independent, sovereign and unitary state'.

ABORTIVE 1974 MILITARY COUP

The deposition of the three bishops of the Orthodox Church of Cyprus for attempting to remove Archbishop Makarios from the Church, and the resultant demonstrations of popular support for the President enabled the Cypriot Government to take strong measures against other supporters of Gen. Grivas. Forces loyal to the President waged guerrilla war against EOKA-B, and carried out a purge of the armed forces and police, some of whose members had collaborated with EOKA and helped in their raids on police stations in search of arms. The Grivas campaign of terrorism seemed to have been checked by the beginning of 1974, and when Gen. Grivas died as a result of a heart attack in January the President granted an amnesty to 100 of his imprisoned supporters, hoping to restore normality in Cyprus.

In June 1974 President Makarios ordered a purge of EOKA supporters in the police, civil service, schools and National Guard, and on 2 July he wrote to President Ghizikis of Greece, accusing the Greek military regime of giving arms and subsidies to EOKA and of using the Greek army officers attached to the Cyprus National Guard for subversion. The President demanded that the Greek officers who had collaborated with EOKA should be withdrawn, and began to take steps to ensure that the Guard were loyal to Cyprus, rather than to Greece and Enosis. The National Guard, apparently with Greek support, then staged a coup. On 15 July a former EOKA gunman, Nikos Sampson, was appointed President. Makarios fled to Britain, the resistance of his supporters was crushed, and Greece sent more officers to reinforce the National Guard.

Rauf Denktaş, the Turkish Cypriot leader, called for military action by the United Kingdom and Turkey, as guarantors of Cypriot independence, to prevent Greece imposing Enosis. Having failed to induce the United Kingdom to intervene, Turkey acted unilaterally. Turkish troops landed in Cyprus on 20 July, and seized the port of Kyrenia and a corridor connecting it to the Turkish sector in Nicosia. A cease-fire on 22 July did not prevent further Turkish advances, and the UN peacekeeping force had little success in its efforts to interpose itself between the two Cypriot communities. Massacres and other atrocities were reported from many bi-communal villages, reinforcing the hostility between the Greeks and Turks.

TURKEY OCCUPIES NORTHERN CYPRUS

The successful Turkish invasion had foiled Greek plans to take over Cyprus using the National Guard, and when the military Government of Greece resigned on 23 July 1974, Sampson did likewise. Glavkos Klerides, the moderate Speaker of the House of Representatives who had led the Greek Cypriot delegation to the intercommunal talks, was appointed President, and began negotiations with Rauf Denktaş. In Geneva, the United

Kingdom, Greece and Turkey also held talks, seeking a settlement, but negotiations broke down following Turkish demands for the establishment of a cantonal federation giving almost a third of the area of Cyprus to the Turkish Cypriots.

On 14 August, the day after the Geneva talks ended, the war was renewed. Turkish forces seized the whole of Cyprus north of what became the 'Attila line', running from Morphou through Nicosia to Famagusta, and the new civilian Government in Greece announced its inability to intervene. Turkey proclaimed that, by this *fait accompli*, the boundaries of an autonomous Turkish Cypriot administration had been established, while Denktaş spoke of establishing a completely independent Turkish Cypriot state north of the 'Attila line' and of encouraging the immigration of Turkish Cypriots from areas still under Greek Cypriot control, to produce a permanent ethnic and political partition of the island. The UN Secretary-General, Dr Kurt Waldheim, succeeded in arranging talks between Klerides and Denktaş, but was unable to bring about any constructive results from these negotiations. An important round of peace talks on the Cyprus problem began in Vienna between Klerides and Denktaş in January 1975, under the aegis of Dr Waldheim. The success of the negotiations depended on whether the two sides could reach agreement on the political future of the island: the Turkish Cypriots wanting a Greek-Turkish bi-regional federation with strong regional governments, whereas the Greeks, whilst not ruling out a bi-zonal solution, favoured a multiregional or cantonal federation with strong central government. Both parties stressed the need for an independent, non-aligned, demilitarized Cyprus.

On 13 February 1975 a 'Turkish Federated State of Cyprus' ('TFSC') was proclaimed in the part of the island under Turkish occupation. The new State was not proclaimed as an independent republic, but as a restructuring of the Autonomous Turkish Cypriot Administration, a body established after the invasion, 'on the basis of a secular and federated state until such time as the 1960 Constitution of the Republic . . . is amended in a similar manner to become the Constitution of the Federal Republic of Cyprus'. Rauf Denktaş was appointed President of the new 'state'. Greece denounced this move as a threat to peace and declared that the issue would be taken to the UN Security Council, which, in March, adopted a resolution regretting the unilateral decision to establish a Federated Turkish State. Talks were resumed in April, and the foundation was laid for intercommunal reconciliation and co-operation, when the Cypriot leaders agreed to form an expert committee, under the auspices of Dr Luis Weckmann-Muñoz, Special Representative of the UN Secretary-General, to consider the powers and functions of a central government for Cyprus and present their findings in June to the Cypriot negotiators in Vienna.

The flight of Turkish Cypriots to British bases after the National Guard coup and the withdrawal of Greek Cypriot civilians before the advancing Turkish army had created a major problem in Cyprus. In August 1974 the UN estimated that there were some 225,600 refugees in Cyprus, of whom 183,800 were Greek Cypriots. In the southern part of Cyprus, under Greek Cypriot control, were 198,800 of these refugees, of whom 35,000 were Turkish Cypriots, including prisoners of war. This problem remained unsolved in 1976, with an estimated 200,000 refugees on the island. However, 9,000 Turkish Cypriots were given the opportunity to move to the northern sector in August 1975. In return the Turkish Cypriot authorities allowed 800 relatives of Greeks who remained in the north to join them in the Turkish sector. The concern over the treatment of Greeks in the Turkish-occupied area gave rise in August 1975 to an investigation by the European Commission of Human Rights which, in a report published in January 1977, found Turkey guilty of committing atrocities in Cyprus.

In December 1974 Archbishop Makarios returned to Cyprus, and resumed the presidency. In January 1975 Britain decided to permit the resettlement of over 9,000 Turkish Cypriot refugees from the British Sovereign Base at Akrotiri. In retaliation for the alleged ill-treatment of Turkish Cypriots still living in Greek areas, and in order to force a decision on the release of the refugees and their resettlement, the Turks threatened to expel all remaining Greek Cypriots in northern Cyprus and launched a massive scheme to colonize the area, bringing thousands of farmers and peasants from mainland Turkey and settling them in Greek-owned property. Before the Turkish invasion of July 1974, the population of Cyprus numbered 639,000 of whom 18% were Turkish Cypriots and 78% Greek Cypriots.

ELECTIONS AND INTERCOMMUNAL TALKS 1975–76

In September 1975 talks between the two sides were resumed in New York. However, these and further discussions in February 1976 were completely unproductive. In April 1976 the divergence in the policies of Archbishop Makarios and Glavkos Klerides, the Greek Cypriot negotiator, eventually led to the resignation of the latter and his replacement by Tassos Papadopoulos. At the same time Umit Süleyman Onan replaced Rauf Denktaş as the Turkish Cypriot negotiator.

During 1976 general elections were held on both sides of the 'Attila line'. In June Rauf Denktaş was elected President of the 'TFSC'. His election placed him constitutionally above party politics but in fact his position depended upon the support of the Ulusal Bırlık Partisi (National Unity Party—UBP). Under the terms of the Constitution promulgated by the Turkish Cypriot authorities, 40 deputies were elected to a legislative assembly, with the UBP gaining a majority. Nejat Konuk, the Secretary-General of the UBP, was appointed Prime Minister. In September general elections were held in the government-controlled area. A new party under Spyros Kyprianou, the Democratic Front (supporting the policies of Archbishop Makarios), won a decisive victory, gaining 21 of the 35 seats. The party of Glavkos Klerides, the Dimokratikos Synagermos (Democratic Rally—DISY), did not win any seats.

In January 1977 Denktaş initiated a meeting with Archbishop Makarios to establish preliminaries for resuming intercommunal talks (suspended since February 1976); Archbishop Makarios made it clear that he was prepared to accept a bi-zonal federation provided the Turkish authorities made territorial concessions, and only if there was provision for a central government with adequate powers. A sixth round of talks, which opened in Vienna in March, broke down, was resumed in Nicosia in May but was suspended until after the general elections in Turkey in June.

DEATH OF MAKARIOS, ACCESSION OF KYPRIANOU

The death of Archbishop Makarios on 3 August 1977, put an end to hopes for an immediate continuation of negotiations and gave rise to fears about the stability of the Greek Cypriot regime in his absence, especially since there was no obvious successor. Spyros Kyprianou, the President of the House of Representatives, was elected on 31 August to serve the remainder of Makarios's term of office. In the elections of January 1978 he was re-elected unopposed and formed a new Cabinet with an increased membership of 13. Shortly afterwards the EOKA-B announced its dissolution, but in April, after the discovery of a plot, 22 of its members were arrested. In the same month, following criticism in the Turkish Cypriot press about rising prices, Nejat Konuk resigned as Prime Minister of the 'TFSC' and was replaced by Osman Orek, former President of the National Assembly, who formed a new Cabinet.

In April and July 1978 President Kyprianou was subjected to criticism from within his own Government, both from the powerful left wing and from the followers of Makarios. This resulted in the dismissal of his chief negotiator with the Turkish Cypriots, Tassos Papadopoulos. In December there was a crisis in the 'TFSC' as a result of factional disputes within the UBP. Amid widespread rumours about the establishment of a multinational company to which the Turkish Cypriot unions were opposed, all nine cabinet ministers resigned, followed by the Prime Minister, Osman Orek. A new Cabinet was formed under Mustafa Çağatay, formerly Minister of Labour, Social Affairs and Health. In April 1979 a new party, the Democratic Party, was formed by Nejat Konuk, the former Prime Minister, as the UBP lost support in the legislature.

On 19 May 1979 Kyprianou and Denktaş drew up a 10-point agenda, based on the Makarios/Denktaş agreement. However, intercommunal talks in June were adjourned after a week, over differences in the interpretation of the agreement, which Turkish Cypriots saw as providing for bi-zonality on the island. In November Süleyman Demirel became Prime Minister of Turkey, and in March 1980 Turkey signed a new defence agree-

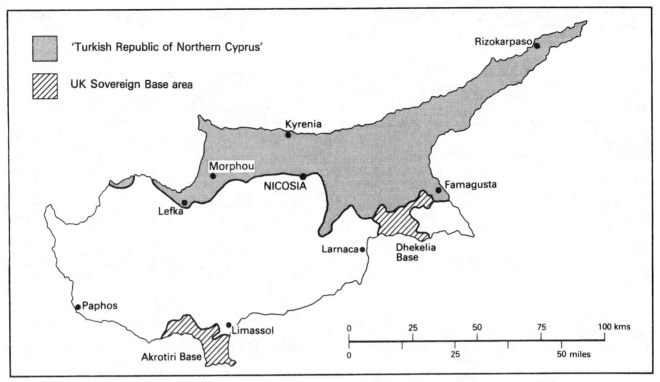

Cyprus, showing the 'Turkish Republic of Northern Cyprus'

ment with the USA. Meanwhile, the mandate of the UN Peace-keeping Force (UNFICYP) continued to be extended at six-monthly intervals.

On 9 September 1980 the Greek Cypriot Government's reshuffle led to the appointment of seven new ministers. As a result, President Kyprianou was again attacked by AKEL and by the right-wing opposition under Klerides, thus losing his overall majority in the House of Representatives. During the next three months, three new 'centrist' political parties were established: the Pankyprio Ananeotiko Metopo (Pancyprian Renewal Front—PAME), the Dimokratiko Komma (Democratic Party—DIKO) and the Enosi Kentrou (Centre Union).

ELECTIONS AND FURTHER TALKS 1980–81

On 16 September 1980, in the shadow of the military coup in Turkey, the intercommunal peace-talks were resumed after an interval of 15 months. These were to be held within the frame-work of a procedural formula proposed by Hugo Gobbi, the UN Special Representative for Cyprus. The negotiators for the Greek and Turkish sides were, respectively, George Ioannides and Umit Süleyman Onan. There were to be four main areas of discussion: the re-settlement of Varosha (the Greek area of Famagusta); constitutional aspects; territorial aspects; and 'ini-tial practical measures by both sides to promote goodwill, mutual confidence and the return to normal conditions'. The talks continued intermittently, but by the spring of 1981 no concrete results had been achieved.

In March 1981 there was a resumption of negotiations with Britain about outstanding development payments to Cyprus, which, according to the Cypriots, amounted to £150m. since 1960. In the same month the Foreign Minister, Nikos Rolandis, expressed his opposition to the possible use of the British airbases at Akrotiri and Dhekelia by the USA's proposed Rapid Deployment Force.

Growing criticism of Kyprianou's Government for its failure to avert an economic crisis or to make any real progress in the intercommunal talks led the House of Representatives to vote almost unanimously on 16 April for the dissolution of the Gov-ernment. In the subsequent parliamentary elections, held on 24 May 1981, under a system of proportional representation, the communist AKEL party and the DISY party of Glavkos Klerides each won 12 of the 35 Greek Cypriot seats in the House of Representatives, while President Kyprianou's DIKO party

achieved only eight seats. In the elections held in the 'TFSC' in June, President Rauf Denktaş was returned to office, but with only 52% of the vote. His right-wing UBP won 18 out of 40 seats, compared with 23 at the previous elections.

The intercommunal talks continued throughout 1981, but little progress was made. In August there were signs of hope when fresh proposals were put forward by the Turkish Cypriots. These envisaged handing back 3% to 4% of the 35.8% of land now controlled by them, as well as the buffer zone between the two communities, and allowing some 40,000 of the 200,000 Greek Cypriot refugees to return to the Famagusta area. The constitutional issue remained the main problem: the Greek Cypriots wanted a federation with a strong central government and freedom of movement throughout the island; the Turkish Cypriots favoured something similar to a partition within a confederation, equal representation in government and strong links with the mother country. The Greek Cypriots, although they agreed to the principle of an alternating presidency, objected to disproportionate representation of the Turkish com-munity, who form less than 20% of the population. The Turkish proposals were rejected by the Greek Cypriots, but it was agreed that the talks should continue.

NEW UN PEACE PROPOSAL

In November 1981 the UN put forward a new peace plan, or 'evaluation', for a federal, independent and non-aligned Cypriot state. Although more favourable to the Greek side than the Turkish Cypriot proposals had been, this was only accepted reluctantly as a basis for negotiation by the Greek Cypriots, in the face of opposition from the Church and some political groups. The Turkish Cypriots accepted the plan.

The socialist Government of Greece, elected in October 1981, pledged more active support for the Greek Cypriots than their predecessors. Andreas Papandreou, the Greek Prime Minister, who visited Cyprus early in 1982, wanted to see the withdrawal of all Greek and Turkish troops from the island, and favoured an international conference on Cyprus rather than the continu-ation of the intercommunal talks.

With presidential elections in view, President Kyprianou and his DIKO party formed an alliance with the communist AKEL party in April 1982, based on a 'minimum programme' of continu-ance of the non-aligned *status quo*, defence of the mixed economy and support for the intercommunal talks. This put a strain on relations with the Greek Government since it was contrary to the policy which had recently been laid down by Athens and Nicosia. The alliance with AKEL involved a cabinet reshuffle in which all but three ministers were replaced.

In the 'TFSC' the Çağatay Government resigned in December 1981. A three-month crisis followed until March 1982, when a coalition government was formed by Çağatay between his own UBP, the Democratic People's Party and the Turkish Unity Party.

In February 1983 President Kyprianou was re-elected for a five-year term by a comfortable 56.5% majority. Glavkos Klerides's DISY party polled 34%, and Vassos Lyssarides's Socialistiko Komma Kyprou EDEK (EDEK Socialist Party of Cyprus—EDEK) 9.5%. President Kyprianou reiterated that communist policies would not be introduced and that no communists would be given cabinet rank.

In May the UN General Assembly voted overwhelmingly in favour of the withdrawal of Turkish troops from Cyprus, although the USA and the United Kingdom abstained in protest against the partisan wording of the resolution. In retaliation, Rauf Denktaş threatened to boycott any further intercommunal talks and to call a referendum in the 'TFSC' to decide whether to make a unilateral declaration of independence and seek international recognition. The Cyprus pound was replaced by the Turkish lira as legal tender in the 'TFSC'.

Informal talks, under the auspices of the UN, continued in August 1983 but no agreement was reached, and in September the Greek Cypriot Minister of Foreign Affairs resigned because of policy differences with President Kyprianou over the proposed resumption of the intercommunal talks.

DECLARATION OF 'TURKISH REPUBLIC OF NORTHERN CYPRUS'

UN proposals for a summit meeting between Denktaş and Kyprianou in late 1983 were unsuccessful. On 15 November the 'TFSC' made a unilateral declaration of independence as the 'Turkish Republic of Northern Cyprus' ('TRNC'), with Denktaş as President. Later that month, Mustafa Çağatay resigned as Turkish Cypriot Prime Minister and as leader of the UBP. On 2 December the Legislative Assembly of the 'TRNC' adopted legislation for the establishment of a 70-member constituent assembly (comprising the 40 elected members of the Legislative Assembly and 30 others appointed from representative groups within the community), which met for the first time on 6 December. On the following day President Denktaş appointed Nejat Konuk (who had been Prime Minister of the 'TFSC' in 1976–78 and was then President of the 'TRNC' Legislative Assembly) to be Prime Minister in an interim Cabinet, pending elections in 1984. Like the 'TFSC', the 'TRNC' was recognized only by Turkey, and the declaration of independence was condemned by the UN Security Council in November. The EC resolved not to apply trade sanctions against the 'TRNC', and the mandate of UNFICYP continued to be extended at six-monthly intervals. Conciliatory proposals that were made by the 'TRNC', including the resettlement of 40,000 Greek Cypriot refugees, were rejected by the Cyprus Government in January 1984, while the 'TRNC', in turn, refused to accept President Kyprianou's proposal that the Turkish Cypriots should be allowed to administer 25% of the island (despite the fact that they comprised only 18% of the population) on condition that the declaration of independence be withdrawn before talks were reopened.

In April 1984 Turkey and the 'TRNC' exchanged ambassadors, and plans were made for a referendum on 19 August to approve a new constitution, to be followed by a general election on 4 November to elect members for the Constituent Assembly. (These elections were subsequently postponed.) The establishment of diplomatic links with Turkey was followed by a formal rejection of UN proposals for a 'freezing' of independence as a pre-condition of peace talks, along with a continued refusal to return the Varosha (Greek Cypriot) area of Famagusta.

ABORTIVE 1985 KYPRIANOU-DENKTAŞ SUMMIT

In August and September 1984 the Greek and Turkish Cypriots conferred separately with the UN Secretary-General, Javier Pérez de Cuéllar, whose aim was to bring the two sides together for direct negotiations. The Turkish Cypriots reiterated that they would accept the proposed creation of a bi-zonal federation only if power were to be shared equally between the north and the south. The third round of negotiations, begun in November, were seen as being crucial to any long-term solution of the problem but, despite some concessions on the part of the Turkish Cypriots, an impasse was reached. In December 1984, after the third round of talks had ended, the leaders of the two communities, Spyros Kyprianou and Rauf Denktaş, agreed to hold a summit meeting in January 1985. No agreement was reached at the meeting, however, and Denktaş subsequently declared that a further summit meeting could not be arranged until after the elections which were due to be held in the 'TRNC' in June. The new Constitution of the 'TRNC' was approved by a referendum in May, and this was followed by a presidential election on 9 June, at which Rauf Denktaş was returned to power with over 70% of the vote. A general election followed on 23 June, with the UBP, led by Dr Derviş Eroğlu, winning more seats than any other party (24) but failing to win an overall majority in the 50-seat Legislative Assembly.

In July 1985 the UN Secretary-General drew up further proposals, which the Greek Cypriots accepted. The new UN proposals were for a bi-zonal federal Cyprus (with the Turkish Cypriots occupying 29% of the land) in which the government would be led by a Greek Cypriot president and a Turkish Cypriot vice-president, both having limited power of veto over federal legislation. Ministers would be appointed in a ratio of seven Greek Cypriots to three Turkish Cypriots. One 'major' ministry would always be held by a Turkish Cypriot, and a special working party would consider demands that the Minister of Foreign Affairs should always be a Turkish Cypriot. There would be two assemblies: an upper house, with a 50:50 community representation, and a lower house, weighted 70:30 in favour of the Greek Cypriots. Legislation on important issues would require 'separate majorities in both chambers'. A tripartite body, including one non-Cypriot voting member, would have the final say in constitutional clashes concerning the extent of federal power. However, serious problems remained over the crucial questions of a timetable for the withdrawal of Turkey's troops and the nature of international guarantees for a newly united Republic of Cyprus. This plan was underwritten by foreign governments (in effect the USA), which were to subsidize two funds: one to help the poorer Turkish Cypriot community, and the other to aid both Greek and Turkish Cypriots who had been displaced as a result of the events of 1974. However, the Turkish Cypriots did not accept the revised plan, as they wanted Turkish troops to remain on the island indefinitely, to protect their interests, and they felt that any peace settlement must include Turkey as a guarantor. They had also revised their opinion on allowing Greek Cypriot refugees to return to the 'TRNC'.

1985 GREEK CYPRIOT ELECTIONS

President Kyprianou had come under severe criticism, from within the House of Representatives, over the failure of the summit in January 1985. He reshuffled the Council of Ministers and terminated his alliance with the communist party, AKEL. This alliance had become increasingly strained, mainly because of Kyprianou's unyielding attitude to the intercommunal talks. In November, following an acrimonious debate over Kyprianou's leadership, the House of Representatives was dissolved. A general election was not due to be held until May 1986, but the two largest parties, AKEL and the conservative DISY, had formed an alliance with the intention of achieving a two-thirds majority in the House, which would enable them, under Article 44, to amend the Constitution and so force an early presidential election. However, they were one vote short of the required majority.

A general election was held on 8 December 1985 for an enlarged House of 56 Greek Cypriot seats (compared with 35 previously), while the nominal allocation of seats to the Turkish Cypriot community was increased from 15 to 24. Significant gains were made by Kyprianou's DIKO party, although it remained a minority party. It won 16 seats and increased its share of the vote to 27.6% (compared with 19.5% in the 1981 election). The AKEL party suffered a set-back, gaining only 15 seats, while its share of the vote fell to 27.4% from 32.8% in 1981. This ended a communist ascendancy in Greek Cypriot politics which dated back to the independence of Cyprus from

Britain in 1960 (although AKEL partially recovered its position in the local elections in May 1986). The DISY party replaced AKEL as the largest party in the House by winning 19 seats, with 33.6% of the vote, compared with 31.9% in 1981. The socialist party, EDEK, which supported Kyprianou's stand on peace negotiations, won six seats with 11.1% of the vote, compared with 8.2% in 1981. Campaigning was dominated by two issues: the proposed peace plan and Kyprianou's argument that, constitutionally, the President was not bound by the decisions of the House. The result of the election was interpreted as evidence of widespread support for President Kyprianou's policies.

Further meetings to discuss the UN peace plan were conducted in March 1986. On this occasion the Turkish Cypriots accepted the draft peace plan (which was still based on the idea of establishing a bi-zonal federal republic, with specified posts and ratios for the Greek and Turkish Cypriot participants in the federal government) while the Greek Cypriots stated that it was the same as that put forward in January 1985 (which they had rejected). The Greek Cypriots' principal objections were that the plan failed to envisage the withdrawal of the Turkish troops prior to implementation of the plan; the removal from Cyprus of settlers from the Turkish mainland; the provision of suitable international guarantors for the settlement, with the exclusion of Turkey; and the assurance of the 'three basic freedoms', namely the right to live, move and work anywhere in Cyprus. Kyprianou and other Greek Cypriot leaders, as well as Prime Minister Papandreou of Greece, were all opposed to the plan but were careful not to reject it absolutely. They wanted a summit meeting between the two leaders (Kyprianou and Denktaş) or an international conference to discuss the matter. The latter suggestion was first put forward by the USSR, which also proposed a complete withdrawal of all foreign troops from the island, including UNFICYP. President Denktaş, however, later stated that he would not accept an international conference which treated the Greek Cypriots as the official government of Cyprus and the Turkish Cypriots as a minority population. He said that, should such a conference be arranged, he would seek international recognition of the 'TRNC'.

In July 1986 Turgut Özal, the Prime Minister of Turkey, made his first visit to the 'TRNC' and urged the adoption of an economic model similar to that in Turkey. The Toplumcu Kurtuluş Partisi (Communal Liberation Party) disagreed with this policy, and in August it withdrew from the coalition Government of the 'TRNC'. In September the Prime Minister, Dr Derviş Eroğlu, formed a new administration in coalition with the Yeni Doğuş Partisi (New Dawn Party—YDP).

In July 1987 it was reported that the Cyprus Government had proposed to the UN Secretary-General that the Cypriot National Guard be dissolved, and orders for military equipment cancelled, in exchange for the withdrawal of Turkish forces from the island. In an address to the UN General Assembly in October, President Kyprianou proposed an international peacekeeping force to replace the armed forces of both the Greek and Turkish Cypriots. President Denktaş, however, maintained that negotiations on the establishment of a federal bi-zonal republic should precede any demilitarization.

ELECTION OF VASSILIOU AS PRESIDENT

The first round of voting in presidential elections took place in the Greek Cypriot zone on 14 February 1988. There were four main candidates, including the incumbent President Kyprianou, who was seeking his third consecutive five-year term. The three other main candidates were: Georghios Vassiliou, who presented himself as an independent, but who was unofficially backed by the communist party, AKEL (although he, himself, was not a communist); Glavkos Klerides, the leader of the conservative DISY; and Dr Vassos Lyssarides, leader of the socialist EDEK. Since no candidate received more than 50% of the total vote, a second round was held a week later, to decide between the two candidates who had received the most votes—Glavkos Klerides, with 33.3% of the total vote, and Georghios Vassiliou, with 30.1% of the total vote. Kyprianou was third, with 27.3% of the total vote. This surprising defeat was widely interpreted as a result of the failure of Kyprianou's uncompromising policies for the reunification of Cyprus. The outgoing President decided not to support either of the remaining presidential candidates. In the second round

of voting, Georghios Vassiliou, with the backing of EDEK and a significant number of Kyprianou supporters, was elected as the new President by a narrow margin, with 167,834 votes (51.6% of the total), whilst Glavkos Klerides gained 157,228 votes (48.4%).

Although it was predicted that President Vassiliou would promote his predecessor's policies regarding a settlement for the divided island, he, unlike Kyprianou, quickly expressed his willingness to enter into direct informal dialogue with the Turkish Cypriot leader. Vassiliou also promised to re-establish the National Council, which was to include representatives from all the main Greek Cypriot political parties, to negotiate plans for the settlement of the Cyprus problem. On 28 February 1988 Vassiliou was officially sworn in as the new President and named his new nine-member Council of Ministers. On the same day President Vassiliou proposed a meeting with the Turkish Prime Minister, Turgut Özal, to discuss the withdrawal of Turkish troops from Cyprus. Özal responded by claiming that Vassiliou's priority, as regards the Cyprus problem, should be to talk with President Denktaş of the 'TRNC'. In March Denktaş submitted a series of goodwill proposals to President Vassiliou, via the new Special Representative of the UN Secretary-General, Oscar Camilión. Vassiliou immediately rejected the proposals, which included a plan to form committees to study the possibilities of intercommunal co-operation. In the same month President Vassiliou held talks with the Greek Prime Minister, Andreas Papandreou, in Athens, to examine the prospects for a Cyprus settlement. Papandreou said that, despite the recent breakthrough in Greco–Turkish relations, there could be no overall improvement unless progress was made towards solving the Cyprus problem.

RESUMPTION OF INTERCOMMUNAL TALKS

After a meeting with the newly-revived National Council in June 1988, President Vassiliou agreed to a proposal by the UN Secretary-General to resume intercommunal talks, without preconditions, with President Denktaş of the 'TRNC', in the capacity of the leaders of two communities. Following a meeting with the Turkish Government in July, Denktaş also approved the proposal. Consequently, the impasse between the two sides was ended and a Cyprus summit meeting took place in Geneva on 24 August, under the auspices of the UN. At this summit, which was the first such meeting between Greek and Turkish Cypriot leaders since January 1985, President Vassiliou and President Denktaş resumed direct talks on a settlement of all aspects of the Cyprus problem. As a result of this meeting, the two leaders began the first formal round of substantive direct negotiations, under UN auspices, in Nicosia on 15 September. A target date of 1 June 1989 was, rather optimistically, set for the conclusion of a comprehensive political settlement. Despite several rounds of intensive direct talks, under the supervision of the UN, in Nicosia and New York, however, it became apparent, by the end of June 1989, that no progress had been achieved as a result of the discussions. The general consensus seemed to be that, although the two leaders expressed their willingness that Cyprus should be reunited as a bi-zonal federation, they disagreed on what form government should take. In addition, attitudes regarding three issues due to which former talks had broken down (i.e. the withdrawal of Turkish troops, the right of Turkey to intervene as a guarantor, and the assurance of the 'three basic freedoms'—see above) appeared irreconcilable. Vassiliou and Denktaş agreed to hold another meeting with the UN Secretary-General to review the intercommunal talks in New York in September 1989.

In mid-May 1989, under the supervision of the UNFICYP, a deconfrontation agreement (reached at the end of March) was implemented, which involved the withdrawal of Greek Cypriot and Turkish Cypriot troops from 24 military posts along the central Nicosia sector of the 'Attila line'. It was hoped that this limited withdrawal would reduce the tension (there were five fatal shootings reported during the period May 1988–December 1988), which persisted in this troubled area. In July, however, crowds of Greek Cypriot women held angry demonstrations at the buffer zone to protest against the continuing partition of Cyprus. There was a dramatic escalation in tension when more than 100 protesters were arrested by the Turkish Cypriot forces during the demonstration and were detained for several days.

ABORTIVE 1990 VASSILIOU-DENKTAŞ SUMMIT

Despite a relaxation, in November 1989, of entry restrictions for Greek Cypriots with compelling reasons to travel to the 'TRNC', no significant progress was made towards a political settlement in the first half of 1990. A new round of UN-sponsored talks, which began in late February 1990 in New York, came to a premature end in early March, following disagreement arising from demands by Rauf Denktaş that the right to self-determination of the Turkish Cypriots be recognized by the Greek Cypriot community. President Vassiliou accused Denktaş of deliberately frustrating hopes of a settlement by introducing new conditions to the negotiations and implicitly advocating some form of partition or secession. Denktaş, in turn, accused Vassiliou of refusing to consider any form of compromise. A resolution approved by the UN Security Council later in March rejected Denktaş's stance and reaffirmed the UN's commitment to a resolution based on a bicommunal federal republic.

Later in March 1990 Denktaş resigned the presidency in order to call early presidential elections on 22 April. Denktaş, standing as an independent, received 66.7% of the votes cast, while İsmail Bozkurt, who also stood as an independent, received about 32%, and Alpay Durduran of the Yeni Kıbrıs Partisi (New Cyprus Party—YKP) slightly more than 1%. Denktaş's victory was widely interpreted as a sign of public approval of the President's stance throughout the recent negotiations with President Vassiliou, although opposition parties advocating a more conciliatory approach commanded significant support in the 'TRNC'.

The UBP retained its majority in the 'TRNC' Legislative Assembly at a general election on 6 May 1990, when it received 55% of the votes cast, thereby securing 34 of the 50 available seats. In June Denktaş approved the appointment of several newcomers to the Council of Ministers, which Derviş Eroğlu continued to head as Prime Minister. In local elections on 24 June the UBP consolidated its position when its candidates were elected to 14 out of a total of 22 mayoral positions.

Rumours in the Greek Cypriot zone of widespread disaffection within the communist party, AKEL, were substantiated in early 1990, when resignations and dismissals from the party's central committee and politburo followed calls for democratic reform of the party structure. At least five of the party's 15 parliamentary representatives were thought to belong to the dissident faction. A new political party, the Ananeotiko Demokratiko Sosialistiko Kinima (Democratic Socialist Reform Movement—ADISOK), was formed in April 1990, and was expected to attract many dissatisfied supporters of AKEL.

In July 1990 Cyprus formally applied for full membership of the European Community. International observers regarded the political division within the island as a major obstacle to Cyprus's achieving member status, while President Denktaş declared that the 'unilateral' application by the Greek Cypriots on behalf of the whole island would further complicate the search for a political settlement for Cyprus.

In July and October 1990, in retaliation for the EC application, the 'TRNC' Government and Turkey signed an agreement envisaging the creation of a customs union, the abolition of passport controls and the introduction of a 'TRNC' currency backed by the Turkish central bank. These 'unilateral' steps were condemned by the Greek Cypriot Government, which claimed that the 'TRNC' was also actively planning to settle sensitive northern areas, such as Varosha, with Palestinians and Bulgarian Turkish immigrants. (In June 1989 President Denktaş had advocated the transfer of Bulgarian Turkish refugees from Turkey to the 'TRNC' but the Turkish Government had declined the offer.)

UN-sponsored efforts to revive intercommunal talks on the Cyprus question were hindered by international preoccupation with the conflict in the Persian (Arabian) Gulf after August 1990. As a supporter of the multinational coalition against Iraq, the Vassiliou Government drew parallels between the Iraqi invasion of Kuwait and the Turkish occupation of northern Cyprus in 1974. The 'TRNC' and Turkish authorities, however, maintained that any similarities lay rather with the attempted Greek military takeover of Cyprus in 1974, which had precipitated the Turkish action. Of the obstacles to an outline agreement as proposed by the UN, the most intractable remained the demands of the Turkish Cypriots for recognition as a 'people'

with the right to self-determination in UN terms, a demand which was interpreted by the Greek Cypriots as a desire for distinct sovereignty. Another major point of contention remained each side's rejection of the other's preferred negotiating framework: whereas the Greek Cypriots, with support from Greece, advocated a UN-chaired conference to be attended by the five permanent members of the UN Security Council, the Turkish Cypriots, with Turkish support, favoured a conference at which participation would be limited to representatives of the Turkish and Greek Cypriot sectors as well as Turkey and Greece.

While efforts to resume the negotiating process revolved mainly around the UN and the US Government, the Greek Cypriots also attached importance to the potential role of the EC and the newly-institutionalized Conference on Security and Co-operation in Europe (CSCE). In November 1990 President Vassiliou urged the CSCE to consider the plight of Cyprus in the context of its situation as 'the only European country facing foreign occupation'. In April 1991 the EC ministers of foreign affairs authorized Luxembourg (the presiding member nation at that time) to organize an independent diplomatic initiative for Cyprus, to be co-ordinated with that of the UN.

1991 GREEK CYPRIOT ELECTIONS

In general elections for the 56 Greek Cypriot seats in the House of Representatives, which took place on 19 May 1991, campaigning focused on economic and social issues, there being only marginal policy differences between the parties regarding the Cyprus issue. The conservative DISY party, in alliance with the Komma ton Phileleftheron (Liberal Party), received 35.8% of the votes cast (2.2% more than in 1985) and secured 20 seats, representing a gain of one seat. The AKEL communists, despite competition from ADISOK, unexpectedly achieved the biggest advance, with 30.6% of the vote and 18 seats, representing a gain of three seats. The EDEK socialists also gained ground by securing seven seats in the House, while support for the 'centrist' DIKO party decreased from 27.6% of votes cast and 16 seats in 1985 to 19.5% of the vote and just 11 seats in 1991. Both ADISOK and the Pankyprio Komma Prosfygon ke Pligenton (Pancyprian Party of Refugees and Stricken Persons—PAKOP) failed to win a seat in the House.

On 30 May 1991, at the inaugural meeting of the newly-constituted House of Representatives, Alexis Ghalanos (the former parliamentary spokesman for DIKO) was elected President of the House in succession to the EDEK leader, Dr Vassos Lyssarides.

RESUMPTION OF UN-SPONSORED TALKS, 1991–92

US diplomatic efforts resulted in an announcement, made by President George Bush in August 1991, that the Greek and Turkish Prime Ministers had confirmed their willingness to attend a UN-sponsored conference in New York with the aim of finding a solution to the Cyprus question. However, although Presidents Vassiliou and Denktaş declared their support for this initiative, hopes of a breakthrough receded when the UN Secretary-General made it clear that the conference would not be convened unless progress had been made on resolving outstanding differences. No such progress being immediately apparent, the Bush schedule for a conference in September was not met. In a report to the UN Security Council in October, Pérez de Cuéllar stated that in the latest discussions Denktaş had asserted 'that each side possessed a sovereignty which it would retain after the establishment of a federation, including the right of secession', and had sought 'extensive changes in the text of the ideas that were discussed'. Recalling that the UN Security Council had 'posited a solution based on the existence of one state of Cyprus comprising two communities', he concluded that the introduction of the Denktaş concept would 'fundamentally alter the nature of the solution' as envisaged previously.

On taking office on 1 January 1992, the new UN Secretary-General, Dr Boutros Boutros-Ghali, initiated another attempt to establish the basis for a high-level conference on Cyprus. To this end, UN envoys visited Cyprus, Turkey and Greece in February, and Dr Boutros-Ghali had meetings in New York with Presidents Vassiliou and Denktaş in January and March. However, in a report to the Security Council in April, the UN Secretary-General advised that no progress had been made towards resolving basic disagreements and that 'there has even been regression'. Although there was a measure of agreement on the shape of a federal government structure, the issues of 'territorial adjustment' and the return of displaced persons remained serious problems. In a resolution adopted on 10 April, the Security Council reaffirmed that a settlement 'must be based on a state of Cyprus with a single sovereignty and international personality and a single citizenship, with its independence and territorial integrity safeguarded, and comprising two politically equal communities'.

In accordance with Security Council instructions, Dr Boutros-Ghali had further separate talks with Presidents Vassiliou and Denktaş in New York in June 1992, when deliberations centred on UN proposals for the demarcation of Greek Cypriot and Turkish Cypriot areas of administration under a federal structure. In view of the reluctance of the parties to discuss lines on a map, the cartographic ideas put forward by Dr Boutros-Ghali were described as a 'non-map'. Although both sides undertook to observe a news blackout on the talks, pending a further round in mid-July, the Boutros-Ghali 'non-map' was published by the Turkish Cypriot press on 30 June. It showed that the area of Turkish administration would be about 25% smaller than the 'TRNC', from whose present territory the Greek Cypriots would recover the towns of Morphou and Varosha (although not old Famagusta) and a total of 34 villages. According to the published details, the new division would, among other things, create a Turkish enclave to the east of Nicosia and a Greek enclave in the north-east tip of the island. It was estimated that under the UN plan some 60,000 displaced Greek Cypriots would be able to return to their pre-1974 homes and remain under Greek Cypriot administration.

While denying that he had leaked details of the 'non-map' (which were eventually released by the UN in August), Denktaş seized the opportunity presented by its publication to assert that its proposals were totally unacceptable to the 'TRNC' Government. On the Greek Cypriot side, government spokesmen took the view that the disclosure of the UN plan was a ploy by which the Turkish Cypriots hoped to gain negotiating leverage. As regards the content of the 'non-map' and related ideas for a settlement, Greek Cypriot opinion was divided: whereas AKEL and DISY continued to express broad support for President Vassiliou's conduct of the negotiations, DIKO and EDEK spokesmen declared that the UN plan would entrench an unacceptable partition of the island. Greek Cypriot critics of the emerging proposals also complained that there appeared to be no provision for the removal of post-1974 Turkish settlers from Cyprus. Among prominent opponents of the UN plan was Archbishop Chrysostomos, who stated that the Church of Cyprus could not accept any permanent surrender of Greek land to the Turks.

Following further unsuccessful UN-sponsored talks, conducted in New York during October and November 1992, the Secretary-General took the unusual step of publishing a tabulation of the respective responses to his settlement ideas. This revealed that, whereas the Greek Cypriot side accepted the proposals and the UN map as the basis for a negotiated settlement, the Turkish Cypriot side had reservations with regard to nine of the 100 articles, all of which dealt with crucial matters. The tabulation demonstrated that, apart from the basic issues of sovereignty and territorial division, the Turkish Cypriots were continuing to insist that the posts of federal President and Vice-President should rotate between the two communities and that the federal Government should contain an equal number of Greek Cypriot and Turkish Cypriot ministers. The Greek Cypriots proposed that the two premier positions should be decided by 'federation-wide and weighted universal suffrage', and also endorsed the UN proposal that there should be a 7:3 ratio of Greek Cypriot and Turkish Cypriot ministers, although they accepted that a Turkish Cypriot should normally hold one of the three main portfolios of foreign affairs, finance and defence. Moreover, while both sides accepted the 'security and guarantees' section of the UN proposition (including provisions for the withdrawal of all non-Cypriot forces), considerable disagreement persisted as to whether or not the 1959 treaty of guarantee afforded Turkey a unilateral right of intervention in Cyprus.

Reporting to the UN Security Council on the failure of the latest round of negotiations, Dr Boutros-Ghali noted that a 'lack of political will ... continues to block the conclusion of an agreement', adding that 'it is essential that the Turkish Cypriot side adjust its position'. This assessment was reflected in the resultant Security Council Resolution 789, adopted in late November 1992, which also incorporated a set of proposed confidence-building measures. These included a reduction in the level of armed forces on both sides, the extension of the UN security zone to include the disputed Varosha suburb of Famagusta, the easing of restrictions on 'people to people' contacts and the reopening of Nicosia international airport.

GREEK CYPRIOT AND TURKISH CYPRIOT ELECTIONS, 1993

The veteran DISY leader, Glavkos Klerides, was the unexpected victor in Greek Cypriot presidential elections conducted in two rounds on 7 and 14 February 1993, narrowly defeating Vassiliou's bid for a second term. Standing, once again, as an independent with AKEL support, Vassiliou headed the first-round voting with 44.2%, compared with 36.7% for Klerides and 18.6% for a joint DIKO-EDEK candidate, Paschalis Paschalides. Although DISY had previously declared its support for the Government's conduct of the settlement negotiations, in the election campaign Klerides distanced himself from Vassiliou's stance. This enabled DIKO and EDEK, both strongly opposed to the UN plan, to transfer their support to Klerides, who won 50.3% of the second-round vote compared with 49.7% for Vassiliou. The new Government, appointed by the President-elect on 25 February, contained six DISY ministers and five from DIKO.

Despite his long-standing personal relationship with Denktaş, Klerides failed to obtain any significant compromise in the Turkish Cypriots' declared objections to the confidence-building measures at reconvened talks in New York during May and June 1993. Denktaş submitted counter-proposals urging international recognition of certain other parts of Turkish-controlled northern Cyprus, but these were interpreted by Klerides as an attempt to obtain a degree of international acceptance of the division of Cyprus, in opposition to the Greek Cypriot (and UN) insistence that the island should remain a single state.

Despite the recommendation of the new Turkish President, Süleyman Demirel, that Denktaş should adopt a more conciliatory approach to the negotiations, Denktaş failed to meet the Secretary-General's proposed deadline of mid-June for acceptance of the confidence-building measures. A mission to Athens, Cyprus and Ankara, undertaken by the UN Secretary-General's new Special Representative in Cyprus, Joe Clark, failed to foster any significant new initiative for peace.

An early general election in the 'TRNC' on 12 December 1993 partially resolved a long power-struggle between Denktaş and the Prime Minister, Derviş Eroğlu, in the former's favour. The UBP, once led by Denktaş but now advocating Eroğlu's openly pro-partition stance, remained the largest party in the Legislative Assembly, but failed to win an overall majority. The pro-Denktaş Demokrat Parti (Democrat Party—DP) and the left-wing Cumhuriyetçi Türk Partisi (Republican Turkish Party—CTP) thereupon agreed to form a coalition under the premiership of Hakki Atun, the DP leader (hitherto the Speaker of the Assembly). The new coalition supported the Denktaş policy that talks should continue, while at the same time confirming policy positions likely to ensure continued deadlock.

DEADLOCK ON CONFIDENCE-BUILDING MEASURES

Negotiations in the first half of 1994 on the UN-sponsored confidence-building measures centred on the proposed transfer to UN administration of the Turkish-held Varosha suburb of Famagusta (so that its former Greek Cypriot inhabitants might then return) and the reopening of Nicosia airport for use by both sides. Despite a further visit by Clark in May, no agreement could be reached, in particular because Denktaş claimed that the proposals envisaged greater concessions by the Turkish Cypriots than by the Greek Cypriots. In a report submitted to the Security Council in May, the UN Secretary-General again censured the Turkish Cypriot side for failing to show the political will needed to produce a settlement. In the following month, however, he amended this verdict by stating that there was 'a very substantial measure of agreement' and that the only obstacle to implementation of the confidence-building measures was disputed methodology. The Greek Cypriots reacted angrily that this assessment did not give 'the true picture' of the persisting differences between the two sides.

In a concurrent deterioration, Denktaş warned, on 30 May 1994, that, if Greek Cyprus was admitted to the European Community (now European Union—EU) without reference to the Turkish Cypriots, the 'TRNC' would opt for integration with Turkey. However, this warning did not deter Greek Cypriot spokesmen from welcoming an EU decision, in June, to include Cyprus in the next phase of enlargement. The Greek Cypriot Government was also gratified by a ruling of the European Court of Justice on 5 July, banning EU members from importing goods from the 'TRNC' (see Economy section). This ruling was condemned by the 'TRNC' authorities, who proceeded to organize large-scale public celebrations to commemorate the 20th anniversary of the 1974 Turkish invasion of the island. In late August the 'TRNC' Legislative Assembly sought co-ordination with Turkey on defence and foreign policy, and rejected a federal solution, urging instead 'political equality and sovereignty' for the Turkish Cypriots.

In Resolution 939, adopted on 29 July 1994, the UN Security Council effectively conceded that confidence-building measures were not a realistic possibility in the absence of agreement on fundamental issues. Yet another round of UN-sponsored talks then reached familiar deadlock by September, whereupon President Klerides demanded coercive UN measures to achieve a settlement and appealed for the support of the UN General Assembly. Pursuant to a November 1993 agreement placing Cyprus within 'the Greek defence area', joint Greek/Greek Cypriot military exercises were held for the first time in October 1994, matching similar military co-operation between the 'TRNC' and Turkey.

TURKISH CYPRIOT PRESIDENTIAL ELECTION, 1995

In the approach to the 1995 Turkish Cypriot presidential election, Atun resigned as 'TRNC' Prime Minister on 24 February, after the CTP had opposed President Denktaş's pre-election offer to distribute to 'TRNC' citizens the title deeds to property in the north owned by Greek Cypriots; however, after Eroğlu of the UBP had rejected an invitation to form a government, the DP leader was reappointed in the following month. At the presidential election, on 15 and 22 April, Denktaş for the first time failed to win an outright majority in the first round (receiving only 40.4% of the votes), although he achieved a comfortable 62.5% to 37.5% victory over arch-rival Eroğlu in the second round of voting. Protracted inter-party negotiations were then needed to produce a new government, which was a further DP-CTP coalition under the premiership of Atun.

In a forceful statement on 2 May 1995, Denktaş opined that war might result from unilateral Greek Cypriot accession to the EU, because it would constitute a form of Enosis with Greece (already an EU member) and would be in breach of international treaty stipulations that Cyprus was barred from joining any supranational grouping which did not include both Greece and Turkey. Nevertheless, President Klerides on 4 May headed a visit to Athens by the Greek Cypriot National Council (consisting of the main party leaders) for a 'unity' meeting with Greek government leaders, at which he expressed gratitude for Greek support for his Government's EU application.

1996 GREEK CYPRIOT ELECTIONS — NEW 'TRNC' GOVERNMENT

In the wake of its success in achieving a Bosnian peace accord in November 1995, the US Government gave renewed attention to the Cyprus issue, regarding it as the remaining major source of instability in the eastern Mediterranean region to affect the allied countries; but political instability in Turkey and the impending Greek Cypriot legislative elections precluded any progress being made in the early months of 1996.

The elections to the Greek Cypriot House of Representatives were held on 26 May 1996 and the DISY-DIKO government coalition retained a comfortable majority. DISY remained the largest single party, with 20 seats (34.5% of the vote), slightly ahead of the opposition AKEL, which achieved 19 seats (33.0%).

DIKO lost one of its 11 seats (16.4%), while the EDEK Socialists retained only five seats (8.1%) and the new Free Democrats, led by ex-President Vassiliou, took the remaining two seats (3.7%).

US diplomatic efforts on Cyprus gathered pace in June 1996, partly owing to President Clinton's desire to make substantive progress towards a settlement before the US presidential election in November. UN and EU endeavours to bring the sides together continued in parallel to the US initiative, while in May the British Government appointed Sir David Hannay, the United Kingdom's former ambassador to the UN, to be its own special representative for Cyprus. President Klerides had talks with President Clinton in Washington in mid-June, and at the end of the month the UN Security Council unanimously urged both sides to respond 'urgently and positively' to the Secretary-General's efforts to break the deadlock.

Following policy disagreements, the DP-CTP coalition Government of the 'TRNC' resigned in July 1996; the UBP authorized Eroğlu to begin talks with the DP, now headed by Serdar Denktaş (the President's son, who had been elected in May), on forming a new government. After a successful conclusion to the negotiations, the protocol of the new DP-UBP coalition Government was signed in mid-August; ministers assumed their duties shortly thereafter, with Eroğlu replacing Atun as Prime Minister and Serdar Denktaş becoming Deputy Prime Minister.

1996 VIOLENCE IN THE UN BUFFER ZONE — CRISIS OVER GREEK CYPRIOT PURCHASE OF RUSSIAN MISSILES

From mid-1996 intercommunal relations descended to some of their most hostile levels since 1974, as the result of a series of violent incidents in the UN buffer zone. In early June Turkish Cypriot forces shot and killed an unarmed Greek Cypriot soldier in the Nicosia sector, and on 11 August a Greek Cypriot anti-partition demonstrator was beaten to death by Turkish nationalist extremists during a protest rally, at which an estimated 50 people were injured. The victim's funeral on 14 August was followed by further violence, in which a Greek Cypriot was shot dead by Turkish Cypriot guards (as he attempted to remove a Turkish flag at a fortified post in the buffer zone), and a further 11 people, including two UN officials, were injured. Greek Cypriot outrage at the killings intensified when the Turkish Minister of Foreign Affairs, Tansu Çiller, visited the 'TRNC' on 15 August and warned that Turkey would continue to retaliate with force against those who insulted the Turkish flag. Tensions were further exacerbated in September when a Turkish Cypriot soldier was shot and killed, and another wounded, across the buffer zone, in the south-eastern sector, and on 13 October another Greek Cypriot was shot dead by Turkish Cypriot forces near the British army's military base at Dhekelia.

Renewed international attempts at mediation prompted by the intercommunal crisis in Cyprus, resulted in meetings between Sir David Hannay and the two Cypriot leaders in October, as a result of which the British special representative announced that sufficient progress had been made to enable direct negotiations to resume in 1997, under UN auspices. At the same time, senior military commanders from both sides began UN-sponsored talks which aimed to defuse tension along the demarcation line. In December Malcolm Rifkind became the first British Foreign Secretary to undertake an official visit to Cyprus since 1960. Rifkind met both leaders and unveiled a 10-point document promoting a peaceful settlement.

In a landmark judgment delivered on 18 December 1996, the European Court of Human Rights ruled that Turkey, as the effective power in the 'TRNC', had breached the European Convention on Human Rights by denying a Greek Cypriot woman access to her property in Kyrenia since the 1974 invasion. Applauded by the Greek Cypriot Government, the ruling opened the way for compensation claims against Turkey by other displaced persons.

Another severe crisis developed in January 1997, when it was confirmed that the Greek Cypriot Government had signed an agreement to purchase a Russian surface-to-air missile (SAM) system. Amid international criticism of the purchase, particularly by the USA, the 'TRNC' authorities described the agreement as an 'act of aggression', while the Turkish Government warned that it would be prepared to use military force to prevent deployment of the system. Mediation by the USA and other foreign governments succeeded in defusing the immediate crisis on the basis of an assurance by the Greek Cypriot Government that the missiles would not be deployed for at least 13 months. However, indications of continuing tension included a 'TRNC'-Turkish commitment to a joint defence strategy, whereby an attack on the 'TRNC' would be regarded as an attack on Turkey itself.

1997 KLERIDES–DENKTAŞ TALKS – EU ACCESSION NEGOTIATIONS SCHEDULED

In April 1997 major changes to the Greek Cypriot Government included the appointment of Yiannakis Kasoulides as Minister of Foreign Affairs. Two months later, Kasoulides welcomed President Clinton's appointment of Richard Holbrooke as US mediator on Cyprus, in the hope that Holbrooke would be able to repeat his success as the chief broker of the Dayton peace agreement on Bosnia. Following proximity talks which had begun in March, Klerides and Denktaş attended their first direct discussions for three years on 9–12 July at Troutbeck, New York State (USA). The meetings were chaired by UN Special Representative Diego Córdovez and were attended by the UN Secretary-General, Kofi Annan, and other Security Council representatives. Sufficient progress was made for further direct talks to be held by the two leaders in late July, in Nicosia, where agreement was reached regarding the implementation of measures to establish the fate of persons missing since the hostilities which took place both prior to and during 1974.

Meanwhile, the Greek Cypriot Government's objective of EU membership became a critical source of dissension in July 1997, when an EU summit in Amsterdam (the Netherlands) formally agreed that Cyprus would be included in the next phase of EU enlargement, on which negotiations were to begin in 1998. The decision was to apply to Cyprus as a whole and was regarded by the EU as a possible device for bringing about a settlement which would preserve Cyprus as a single sovereignty. However, the Turkish Cypriot authorities categorically rejected any EU negotiations which were not based on Turkish Cypriot sovereignty, while the Turkish Government also opposed any accession by Cyprus to the EU which did not accommodate Turkish Cypriot demands or which preceded the admittance of Turkey itself. On 20 July, at celebrations to mark the 23rd anniversary of Turkish military intervention on the island, President Denktaş and the Turkish Deputy Prime Minister, Bülent Ecevit, signed a joint declaration threatening to integrate the 'TRNC' into Turkey, if EU negotiations with the Greek Cypriot administration commenced as planned.

Further formal intercommunal talks, which took place in Montreux (Switzerland) on 11–15 August 1997, demonstrated that the conceptual gulf between the two sides remained as wide as ever, notably in that Denktaş continued to insist upon recognition of separate Turkish Cypriot sovereignty, while accusing both Klerides and the EU of having disregarded the rights of the Turkish Cypriot community. Talks broke down on 15 August with Denktaş claiming that the Cypriot application for EU membership was illegal, since it had not been made on behalf of the population of the whole island. Further meetings between Klerides and Denktaş were conducted in Nicosia on 26 September and 11 November—the latter hosted by Holbrooke during his first visit to Cyprus as official US mediator—but failed to break the deadlock. Relations worsened in December when an EU summit in Luxembourg issued a formal invitation to Cyprus to begin accession negotiations in 1998; the 'TRNC' responded by suspending its participation in intercommunal talks.

RE-ELECTION OF KLERIDES, 1998—MILITARY TENSIONS

The five DIKO ministers resigned from the coalition Greek Cypriot Government in early November 1997 (and were replaced by non-partisan technocrats), following an announcement by Klerides that he intended to seek a second presidential term with the endorsement of DISY. In the first round of the presidential election, conducted on 8 February 1998, Georghios Iacovou (who had secured the support of AKEL and DIKO) obtained a narrow victory over Klerides, while the five other candidates were eliminated. However, in the second round of voting, conducted on 15 February, Klerides gained 50.8% of the votes, narrowly defeating Iacovou. The decision of EDEK, whose candidate had gained 10.6% of the votes in the first round of the election, to support Klerides in the second round had been crucial to his success. A new Government of national unity was sworn in on 28 February and included ministers from DISY, DIKO, EDEK, the Liberal Party and Enomeni Dimokrates (United Democrats—EDE). Former President Vassiliou was appointed chief negotiator for Cyprus at the EU accession talks, which were formally inaugurated on 31 March.

Meanwhile, there had been renewed tensions in January 1998 following the completion of a new Greek Cypriot military airfield at Paphos. In the absence of a Cypriot air force, the new airfield was intended to be an emergency base for Greek war planes, and was to be protected by the controversial Russian-made SAM missiles. This development provoked vociferous opposition from Denktaş, prompting the Greek Government to emphasize that the new site had the status of a Greek military base, and any attack on the site would be regarded as an attack on a mainland base. In May and June there was some speculation that the missiles had already been delivered; however, the Greek Cypriot authorities stressed that the missiles would be deployed later in the year, following the necessary staff-training, and again insisted that they were being deployed in a purely defensive capacity.

Two further visits to Cyprus were undertaken by Richard Holbrooke, in April and early May 1998, but failed to produce a resumption of direct talks. Following the May visit, Holbrooke asserted that any meaningful exchange between the two sides seemed impossible, identifying the two main obstacles as the Turkish Cypriots' demand that EU accession talks be suspended, and their insistence that any future intercommunal negotiations be on a 'state-to-state' basis. There was further tension in mid-June when six Turkish war planes landed at a 'TRNC' airfield, in response to the landing of Greek military aircraft at the new Paphos airfield the previous week. While Greek Cypriot and Greek spokesmen described the Turkish action as 'completely illegal', the US Department of State condemned both deployments as unhelpful to the peace process and urged an end to such actions. A new UN Security Council resolution adopted on 26 June described the *status quo* as 'unacceptable' and instructed the Secretary-General to resume a sustained process of direct negotiations to achieve a settlement based on federal arrangement which preserved the island's single sovereignty and territorial integrity.

At the end of June 1998, President Konstantinos Stefanopoulos of Greece paid an official visit to Cyprus (the first such visit by a Greek head of state since independence in 1960), during which he publicly envisaged 'a free and truly independent Cyprus', with equality for all its citizens; he also appealed to the Turkish Cypriots to seize the opportunity offered by the prospective accession to the EU. In July Klerides began a four-day visit to Russia, prior to which he had reiterated his willingness to postpone, and even cancel, the deployment of the SAM missiles in return for a resumption of intercommunal negotiations and real progress on UN proposals for the demilitarization of the island. However, Denktaş again rejected the Greek Cypriot offer, and warned of retaliatory action if the missiles were installed.

Economy

Revised for this edition by ALAN J. DAY

Geographically, Cyprus may be divided into four regions, distinguished by their natural and climatic features. These are the northern coastal belt, including the narrow Kyrenia mountain chain; the central plain, known as the Mesaoria, from Famagusta and Larnaca to Morphou Bay; the mountainous area of the south-centre, dominated by the Troödos massif, with the summit of Mt Olympus (1,951 m or 6,403 ft above sea-level) as its highest point; and the coastal plain of the south, running from a point west of Larnaca to Limassol and Paphos.

Since the middle of 1974, however, the most important division in Cyprus has been that between the areas to the north and south of the 'Attila line' which divides the island (see map, p. 361). The northern two-fifths of the country, under Turkish Cypriot control, are closely linked to the economy of Turkey, and have almost no economic contact with the south of the island. The unilateral declaration of independence by the 'Turkish Republic of Northern Cyprus' ('TRNC') in November 1983 reinforced the economic embargo, which has caused serious problems for the northern sector. Both areas suffered severe disruption as a result of the events of 1974. As well as the physical damage caused by the fighting, more than one-third of the total population of around 640,000 became refugees, some 180,000 Greek Cypriots fleeing to the south and about 45,000 Turkish Cypriots moving to the north. The collapse of essential services in many places reduced economic activity to a low level. Crops were not harvested, tourism ceased, and industrial buildings and plants were destroyed or lost their workforce.

THE SOUTHERN ECONOMY

Since 1974 the economies to the north and the south of the 'Attila line' have diverged. The economy of the south made a remarkable recovery, despite having lost 38% of the island's territory, 70% of its productive resources, 30% of its factories, 60% of the tourist installations, the main port (Famagusta), 66% of the grain-producing land and 80% of the citrus fruit groves, all of which were on the northern side of the line. In 1975 the gross domestic product (GDP) was only two-thirds of the 1973 level, but during 1976 and 1977 production rose at an average of 18% per year. Even with the growth rate falling to an average 7% annually during 1978 and 1979, at the end of that period, production in the southern part of the island was 12% higher than for the whole of Cyprus in 1973. Unemployment was reduced from almost 25% of the labour force in late 1974 to 1.8% in 1979, partly by the emigration of workers but largely through the promotion of labour-intensive industry and massive expansion of the construction sector, both for private housing and development projects.

By 1980, however, it was clear that the post-1976 boom in the Cypriot economy would not continue at the same level. This was partly the result of the disappearance of short-term factors which had favoured growth: in 1977 market conditions in the Middle East and Europe were advantageous to Cypriot exports, and petroleum prices were temporarily stable, whereas by 1979 it was becoming difficult for agricultural products from Cyprus to penetrate the European market, while petroleum prices were once more rising sharply. However, there was also a deeper instability in the economy. Recovery was based on labour-intensive production by a low-wage workforce—wages in 1976 were lower than in 1973—but, with full employment from 1977, wage rises escalated. Between 1976 and 1979 real wages increased by an average 10% annually, and in 1980 average wages rose by 20%, not allowing for inflation, or by 6.5% in real terms. Rising wages and the increasing cost of imported petroleum, among other factors, helped to increase inflation, from an annual average of 4% in 1976–77, to 9.8% in 1979 and 13.4% in 1980. The Cyprus Government was also faced with a growing balance-of-payments deficit and a budgetary deficit. Economic growth had been stimulated by tax incentives and direct government investment in development projects. Consequently, revenue failed to keep pace with expenditure. Despite loans from international agencies and foreign governments, and

extensive borrowing abroad, Cyprus's reserves in 1980 were perilously low. The Government adopted a stabilization programme which was designed to reduce imports, to cut the budget deficit and to limit inflation. As a result, inflation declined from 10.8% in 1981 to 5% in 1985. The trade deficit continued to widen, however, despite a reduction in visible imports in 1985. It rose from C£345.2m. in 1983 to C£413.2m. in 1984, and to C£431.8m. in 1985. The deficit on the current account of the balance of payments, however, returned to 1983 levels, owing to an increase in earnings from tourism, which reduced the deficit to C£98.7m. in 1985, compared with C£116.7m. in 1984 and C£93.4m. in 1983.

Real GDP increased by an annual average of 5.6% in 1980–1985, and in 1985–90 GDP at constant 1985 prices increased by an annual average of 6.8%. The rate of growth was only 0.9% in 1991, but rose sharply to 9.9% in 1992 (partly a consequence of the introduction of value-added tax—VAT, see below). The Government's Five-Year Economic Plan for the period 1989–93, adopted in June 1989, envisaged annual growth of 5%. However, in 1993 the growth rate was only 1.8%, owing to the effects on the Cyprus economy of the European recession, before approaching the Government's 5% target in 1994 and 1995. The annual growth rate then decreased to 1.9% in 1996, before recovering to about 3% in 1997 on the strength of a vigorous economic performance in the second half of the year. In 1993, according to estimates by the World Bank, Cyprus's gross national product (GNP), measured at average 1991–93 prices, was US $7,539m., equivalent to $10,380 per head, significantly greater than that of Greece. On the basis of 'purchasing power parity' (valuing domestic production in terms of international prices), the World Bank estimated the island's GNP per head in 1993 as $15,470. However, these levels of GNP per head were calculated on the basis of a mid-1993 population of 726,000, i.e. excluding Turkish immigrants in the 'TRNC' (numbering more than 80,000 in 1993 and accounting for nearly one-half of the region's inhabitants), who are regarded as illegal residents by the Greek Cypriot authorities. According to independent estimates, Greek Cyprus's GNP per head rose to $12,500 in 1994 and to $13,300 in 1995 (compared with $4,000 in the 'TRNC'). In August 1991, in view of the government-controlled area's encouraging economic performance, the World Bank removed Cyprus from its official list of developing countries, thereby ending Cyprus's qualification for development loans at preferential rates. The average level of unemployment decreased steadily from 3.6% of the registered labour force in 1986 to 1.8% in 1990; it fluctuated during the early 1990s and stood at 2.7% in 1995, before rising to 3.1% by December 1996 and to 3.3% (10,424 persons) by December 1997. After a reduction in the average annual rate of inflation to 1.2% in 1986 (its lowest level for 20 years), an increase in economic activity caused the rate to rise again, reaching an annual average of 4.7% during 1990–95. The rate fell to 2.6% in 1995, before rising marginally to 3.0% in 1996 and then falling to 2.5% in 1997.

The 1991 budget, adopted by the House of Representatives in December 1990, provided for total expenditure of C£835.7m. (including C£181.7m. for a supplementary defence budget) and aimed to reduce the budget deficit to 1.9% of GDP (from 2.6% in 1989). Among the provisions of the new budget were measures designed to encourage investment in industry, while the maximum rate of income tax was reduced to 40%. In fact, the 1991 budget deficit amounted to C£135m. (4.8% of GDP). The 1992 budget, in its final form, contained provision for total government expenditure of C£965.2m. and revenues of C£848.5m., thus envisaging a deficit of C£116.7m. (3.9% of GDP). The anticipated revenue total included receipts from VAT, which was introduced on 1 July 1992 at a rate of 5% on consumer goods and services (food and other basic items being zero-rated). Under the terms of an austerity programme, introduced by the Government in May 1993 (see below), the rate of VAT was increased to 8%.

A persistent substantial trade deficit (with imports regularly being three or four times as great as exports in terms of value) has been offset by an increasingly healthy invisible balance, arising mainly from earnings from tourism. The effect has been a manageable current-account deficit, which increased from C£54.2m. in 1988 to C£298.0m. in 1992 (compared with trade deficits in those years of C£528.4m. and C£1,092.2m. respectively). In 1993 there was a current-account surplus (officially stated to be the first since 1967) of C£49.8m. (and an overall balance-of-payments surplus of C£50.8m.), owing mainly to a much-reduced trade deficit of C£794m. and an invisible surplus of C£843.8m. In 1995, however, the current-account balance returned to a deficit of C£99.4m. (while there was an overall balance-of-payments deficit of C£111m.), with a net invisible surplus of C£889.8m. being exceeded by a trade deficit of C£989.2m. (from exports of C£510.2m. and imports of C£1,499.4m.). In 1996 the current-account balance worsened to produce a deficit of C£228.2m. (with the overall balance-of-payments deficit amounting to C£219.7m.), as the result of a crude trade deficit of C£1,070.3m. (from exports of C£597.1m. and imports of C£1,667.4m.) and a reduced surplus on the invisible account of C£842.1m. Nevertheless, at the end of 1996 foreign exchange reserves totalled C£2,249.7m. (compared with C£1,861.4m. at the end of 1995), mainly as the result of a large increase in non-resident deposits. In 1997 both the current-account deficit and the overall balance-of-payments deficit decreased, to C£183.7m. and C£119.3m. respectively. A small rise in the trade deficit to C£1,099.0m. (from exports of C£605.7m. and imports of C£1,704.7m.) was offset by a surplus on invisibles of C£915.3m. and a net capital movement surplus of C£110.7m. By December 1997 foreign-exchange reserves had risen to C£2,607.8m.

The 1980s saw a diversification of the Greek Cypriot economy, with less reliance being placed on the agricultural sector, and increased emphasis on the development of more broadly-based services and industrial sectors, particularly tourism, shipping and financial services. One of the main problems facing the economy, however, is the continuing high level of foreign debt. Total outstanding external debt (government, semi-government and private) increased from C£736m. in 1988 to C£1,042.2m. in 1993, then decreased to an estimated C£1,029.5m. in 1994.

The Greek Cypriot economy was adversely affected by the crisis in the Persian (Arabian) Gulf region in 1990 and 1991 and the consequent embargo on trade with Iraq, which had supplied 70% of the island's oil imports. Disruption to the eastern Mediterranean significantly weakened the tourist, shipping and manufacturing sectors. Following the resolution of the crisis in February 1991, however, the economy recovered its forward impetus. A feature of economic policy in 1992 was the gradual adaptation of economic practices and procedures to prepare for full membership of the European Community (EC, now the European Union—EU), for which the Cyprus Government had applied in July 1990 (having achieved customs union with the EC from 1 January 1988). In addition to the introduction of VAT (see above), in June 1992 the Government linked the Cyprus pound to the narrow band of the EC's exchange rate mechanism (ERM).

The departure of the United Kingdom (the island's principal trading partner) from the ERM in September 1992, and the subsequent devaluation of sterling, had an adverse effect on trade with the United Kingdom, and also contributed to a decline in tourist arrivals from the United Kingdom during 1993. Nevertheless, both the Vassiliou administration and its successor expressed support for a policy of economic harmonization with EC guidelines, including those detailed in the Treaty on European Union (which had been agreed by EC heads of government at Maastricht, the Netherlands, in December 1991) for eventual economic and monetary union. Full achievement of the Maastricht 'convergence' criteria was identified as a central objective of the Government's Strategic Development Plan for the period 1994–98, the three 'axes' of which were the preparation for Cyprus's accession to the EU; the technological upgrading, restructuring and modernization of the economy, with the general aim of creating the necessary conditions for a satisfactory growth rate within a climate of external and internal stability; and the improvement of the quality of life in Cyprus, with particular emphasis on the environment and on

cultural development. Specific targets of the Plan included an average annual growth rate over the five-year period of 4% and, by 1998, a fiscal deficit of no more than 3% of GDP and public debt of 53.3% of GDP. Within the framework of the Plan, in October 1995 the Government announced a US $2,000m. programme of infrastructural projects.

A feature of the campaign for the February 1993 elections was the contrast in assessment of the state of the economy expounded by Vassiliou and by the opposition. While the former stressed the high rate of growth and low rate of unemployment, the latter focused on the burgeoning budget deficit, claiming that Cyprus was heading for economic crisis. In May 1993 the new Klerides Government announced a programme of austerity measures designed to reduce the budget deficit and the public debt (which totalled C£2,400m.). An increase in the rate of VAT from 5% to 8% was to take effect from October 1993, while new, higher taxes were to be imposed on petrol and cigarettes. A proposed end to the index-linking of wages to inflation encountered considerable opposition from trade unions. However, the economic stance of the new Government received endorsement from an IMF report, published in July, which warned that wage increases were surpassing productivity gains and eroding competitiveness, and from the Governor of the Central Bank of Cyprus, who, later in the month, urged broader deregulation of capital markets and speedier progress towards trade liberalization.

The budget for 1994 envisaged expenditure and net lending of C£1,221.6m., against revenue and grants of C£1,108.9m. The main items of development expenditure under the 1994 budget were the road network (C£43.5m.), water development (C£19.4m.), education (C£17.5m.), public construction (C£13.6m.) and airports (C£10.2m.). The fiscal deficit fell to 1.4% of GDP in 1994 (from 2.4% in 1993). The 1995 budget provided for expenditure of C£1,306m. and revenue of C£1,267m. (a deficit equivalent to 1.0% of GDP), while the 1996 budget (designed to encourage 'stability and modernization') set expenditure at C£1,349m. and anticipated revenue of C£1,321m., resulting in a deficit estimated to be equivalent to 0.6% of GDP for that year. A reduction in the performance of the economy in 1996 was attributable mainly to a decline in tourism and in investment and private consumption expenditure. The 1997 budget, adopted in February, forecast net expenditure of C£1,689m. against revenue of C£1,106m. and was accompanied by a series of measures designed to boost tourism, manufacturing, exports, investment and agriculture. In May 1997 the government approved a plan of action for 'the harmonization, adjustment and convergence of the Cyprus economy with the EU *acquis*', the aim being to prepare the ground for formal accession negotiations in 1998. The 1998 budget, approved in January, provided for total net expenditure of C£1,603m. and revenues of C£1,080m., the projected growth and average unemployment rates for the year being 4.5% and 3.0% respectively. In May the House of Representatives rejected a Government-proposed package of increased VAT and other taxes, designed to reduce the fiscal deficit. Following an IMF warning in June that the fiscal deficit was on the verge of becoming unsustainable, the Government drafted further proposals designed to reduce government spending and to increase revenues.

The regional financial importance of Cyprus was signalled by the opening of the Official Stock Exchange in Nicosia in March 1996. In February 1997 the Government approved a number of relaxations to the rules governing foreign investment in Cyprus and investment by Cypriots overseas, the aim being to create an environment of minimum intervention, in accordance with EU legislation. Allowing foreign investment in Cyprus provided that it 'does not pose a national risk, has no negative environmental impact and is not a burden on the economy,' the new rules permitted foreigners to own 100% of share capital in companies in the clothing, footwear, furniture, wholesale and retail sectors, and up to 49% of share capital in those in the primary sector (agriculture, fisheries and forestry) and in the tourism and leisure sectors. Foreign ownership of banks, finance and insurance companies, newspapers and new airlines would, in future, be permitted according to individual merit, although sectors which continued to exclude foreign investment included real estate, utilities such as electricity and water, and tertiary education. The recovery of the tourist industry in 1997, combined with optimistic economic projections for 1998, produced a significant increase in investment activity on the Cyprus Stock Exchange from December 1997. The average daily trading volume increased to C£1.9m. in March 1998, from C£0.9m. in February and C£0.7m. in January. Trading activity in banking shares increased following the announcement, in January, that the Bank of Cyprus would have a listing on the London Stock Exchange (the first such foreign listing of a Cypriot concern).

THE NORTHERN ECONOMY

Since 1974 the economy of the area north of the 'Attila line' has not made nearly as much progress as the Greek Cypriot area, despite an extensive programme of development, based on aid from Turkey (estimated to amount to some 20% of projected budget expenditure in recent years). Initial development priorities of the 'TRNC' authorities were the improvement of communications, irrigation, and the restoration of damaged citrus groves, in the pursuit of which the methods of central planning were used for some years. Beginning in 1978, successive development plans aimed, according to official statements, 'to secure the achievement of the highest rate of growth compatible with the maintenance of economic stability'. Other goals included increased capital investment, particularly in tourism and industry, balance-of-payments improvement, 'the more equitable distribution of economic burdens and national income', and 'the further expansion and improvement of the financial sector and social services'. From 1987, however, the emphasis switched to the encouragement of free-market economic activity, with priority being given to the development of trade, tourism, banking, education, transportation and the industrial sector.

Assessment of the real performance of the 'TRNC' economy has been notoriously difficult, because of the lack of objective data. Much of the statistical material issued by the northern authorities is not regarded as accurate by the Greek Cypriot side (or by many independent observers). According to official 'TRNC' figures, northern GNP increased by 87% in the period 1977–92, measured at constant 1977 prices. However, the annual growth target of 7.5% during the first Five-Year Plan (1978–82) was not thought to have been achieved: in 1981, for example, the 'TRNC' economy contracted by 7.5%. By the final year of the second Five-Year Plan (1983–87) GNP had officially risen to TL5,684m. (at 1977 prices), compared with TL3,810.5m. in 1977. The targets of the third Five-Year Plan (1988–92) included an annual growth rate of 7%, but the out-turn was officially assessed at 4.6%, in part because of an actual 5.3% decline in 1991. Measured at 1977 prices, total GNP reached TL7,125m. in 1992, according to official figures, which also claimed that GNP per head had increased by 66.4% over the period of the plan, to stand at US $3,343 in 1992 (compared with $2,009 in 1987). Independent observers, however, estimated annual GNP per head to be no higher than $1,650 in both 1992 and 1993. The sectors which were reported to have contributed most to economic growth in 1988–92 were manufacturing, construction, tourism and services, which yielded average annual growth rates of 9.2%, 7.7%, 9.6% and 7.2% respectively. After a 7.8% increase in 1992, GNP expanded by 5.9% in 1993 (well above the original projection), but contracted by 3.7% in 1994, to US $554m., yielding a GNP per head of $3,093. According to official statistics, aggregate GNP rose to $755.7m. in 1995 and to $773.9m. in 1996, the latter figure resulting in annual GNP per capita of $4,222—a figure not greatly in excess of independent estimates. In 1996 trade and tourism contributed 15.6% of GDP, industry 14.1%, agriculture 10.4% and transport and communications 11.2%.

Total local revenues, according to official reports, showed 'an ascending tendency' during the period 1987–92, with an average annual growth rate of 5.9%. During the same period total budgetary expenditures increased by 3% annually, whereas as a proportion of GNP they declined from 36.7% to 33.9%. As a result, the ratio of budget deficit to GNP was reduced from 16.3% to 12.2%, and to total budget from 44.3% to 36%. On 1 July 1992, in partial parallel to Greek Cypriot policy, the 'TRNC' Government introduced VAT on consumer goods, at a rate of 10% (compared with the introductory rate of 5% in the south). The 1993 budget envisaged a 9.9% increase in total local revenues, while expenditure and the budget deficit were projected

to increase by 7.6% and 3.5% respectively; these targets implied a ratio of revenue, expenditure and deficit to GNP of 23.5%, 35.9% and 12.4% respectively. In the 1994 Annual Programme total local revenues were projected to increase by 5.4% at 1993 prices, the growth targets for expenditure and budget deficit being 4.6% and 3% respectively. Actual 1994 local revenues were officially reported as the equivalent of US $137.7m. and budgeted expenditure as $198.6m., the shortfall being covered by foreign aid loans of $60.8m. The 1995 budget provided for expenditure of TL14,450,000m. against local revenue of TL8,000,000m., with the shortfall to be covered by foreign aid and loans of TL6,450,000. The 1996 budget envisaged expenditure of TL24,380,624.4m. against local revenue of TL15,528,392.7m., with the shortfall to be met by foreign aid and loans of TL8,852,231.7m.

The 'TRNC' has experienced a persistently high level of inflation, much of it 'imported' from Turkey, in that the Turkish lira is the currency in use and the local authorities have no control over the money supply. Having reached 93% in 1980, the annual inflation rate fell to 33% in 1982, but then rose again to an estimated 69% in 1990, before dipping to 61% in 1993. A further inflationary surge in 1994, to 215%, was reversed in 1995 to 72.2%, although the rate rose again in 1996 to 87.5%. Agreements that Turkey and the 'TRNC' signed in 1990 envisaged the eventual replacement of the Turkish lira in the 'TRNC' by a local currency, backed by the Turkish central bank (as well as the creation of a full customs union between the two entities), but no substantive progress had been made on these goals by mid-1998. The official unemployment rate remained low in the 'TRNC', despite an increase of 11.8% in the working population in the period 1987–92, to a total of 74,037 (increasing to 76,454 in 1995). According to official figures, the unemployment rate declined from 1.8% of the labour force in 1987 to 0.9% (or 704 persons) in 1994 and to 0.7% (567 persons) in 1995. The official unemployment rate for 1996 was 1.2% of a total labour force of some 79,400 people.

The liberal trade policies adopted by the 'TRNC' since 1987 have resulted in the establishment of trading relations with over 60 countries. Its volume of trade was officially said to have increased from US $276.1m. in 1987 to $426m. in 1992, with imports increasing by 68% from $221m. to $371.4m. and exports decreasing from $55.1m. to $54.6m., with the result that the trade deficit grew from $165.9m. in 1987 to $316.8m. in 1992. Net tourism revenues rose from $103.5m. in 1987 to $175.1m. in 1992 (i.e. by an annual average of 11%), while other invisible earnings increased by 15% per annum, so that the current-account deficit in 1992 was only $23.4m. Moreover, a positive capital movements balance, of $41.7m. in 1992, produced an overall balance-of-payments surplus of $18.3m. in 1992, compared with $23.1m. in 1987. After falling to $275m. in 1993, the trade deficit showed a further official contraction to $233.2m. in 1994, when net receipts from tourism were $172.9m. and from other invisibles $56.1m., so that the current-account deficit was only $4.2m. In 1995 both exports and imports increased, and the deficit widened to $266.7m.; net receipts from tourism were $187.3m. and other invisibles yielded $62.8m., resulting in a current-account deficit of only $16.6m. In 1996 imports of $318.4m. and exports of $70.5m. resulted in a crude trade deficit of $247.9m., although net receipts from tourism of $175.6m. and other invisibles reduced the current-account deficit to $2m. End-1996 foreign-exchange reserves totalled $510.9m.

From August 1990 the northern economy encountered major difficulties as a result of the collapse, with debts of some £1,300m., of Polly Peck International, a fruit-packaging, tourism and publishing conglomerate based in the United Kingdom but with substantial interests in the 'TRNC'. In December 1990 charges of theft and fraud were preferred against the Turkish Cypriot chairman of the conglomerate, Asil Nadir, whose various companies were estimated to have provided more than one-third of the GDP in the 'TRNC', accounting for 60% of total exports. Pending Nadir's trial, British administrators of the collapsed concern attempted to locate the conglomerate's assets in the 'TRNC', but encountered legal and political obstacles. Further complications arose when Greek Cypriot authorities claimed that several of Polly Peck's major properties in the 'TRNC' had been expropriated from Greek Cypriots after 1974. In May 1993 Nadir fled to the 'TRNC', claiming that he could not expect a fair trial from the British authorities. It was reported that he intended to revive the remnants of the Polly Peck empire in northern Cyprus. Whether or not he had the official support of the 'TRNC' authorities in this endeavour remained unclear. At mid-1998 legal and other efforts by British administrators to recover Polly Peck assets in the 'TRNC' were still in progress.

Further prospective damage was done to the 'TRNC' economy by a European Court of Justice ruling on 6 July 1994, banning EU member states from importing goods originating from the 'TRNC'. Under an earlier decision, the Council of Ministers of the then EC had enjoined in 1983 that exports from the Turkish-controlled area of Cyprus would be allowed to enter EC countries only if accompanied by documents from the Greek Cypriot Government, and that such goods also had to pass through ports controlled by that administration. However, this restriction had been evaded by the 'TRNC' by use of Turkey as an export channel, and the United Kingdom, in particular, had been prepared to import goods from northern Cyprus as long as the export documents did not bear the stamp of the 'TRNC'. The Court ruling said, *inter alia*, that 'co-operation is excluded with the authorities of an entity such as that established in the northern part of Cyprus, which is recognized neither by the Community nor by the member states'. It was subsequently reported that the United Kingdom and other EU Governments were taking measures to ensure compliance with the ruling, one consequence of which was that hundreds of 'TRNC' textile workers were made redundant.

AGRICULTURE

Until quite recently agriculture was the most important single economic activity in Cyprus, but in recent years, in the Greek Cypriot sector, agriculture has been superseded in importance by tourism, manufacturing and financial services. In 1974 agriculture employed 33% of the island's labour force. In 1995 some 23% of the northern sector's working population were engaged in agriculture, compared with 10.7% of the employed labour force in the south. In that year the agricultural sector contributed about 10.9% of GDP in the north and 5.5% in the south. The chief crops are citrus fruits, potatoes, carrots, grapes, carobs, tobacco, wheat and barley.

After the division of the island in 1974, the Government of the Republic of Cyprus initiated a series of emergency development plans in which agriculture and irrigation featured prominently. Loans were given to farmers, and agricultural production responded rapidly. Most of the island's citrus trees were in the north, so they were replaced as the main agricultural product in the south by potatoes and other vegetables. Total exports of agricultural products (mainly citrus fruits and potatoes) accounted for more than one-third of the value of all domestic exports from the government-controlled area in 1977. Following a disappointing year in 1978, exports of fruit and vegetables recovered in 1979, owing largely to an increase in the production and export of citrus fruits, grapes and wine. Although potatoes remained the single most important crop, the importance of fruits and wine continued to grow throughout the 1980s. Record agricultural exports were achieved in 1984, owing principally to an outstanding potato crop, and agriculture's contribution to GDP increased by 9.3%. This was followed by a severe overall decline in 1985, owing to adverse climatic conditions which affected potato production in particular and reduced agriculture's share of GDP by 1%. Having declined again in 1986, the sector's contribution to GDP increased by 5.3%, in real terms, in 1987, although a significant increase in the volume of manufactured exports reduced the sector's share of the total value of domestic exports (excluding re-exports and stores for ships and aircraft) to 22%, compared with 26% in 1986. This share decreased again in 1988 to less than 20% but revived to 21% in 1989, when agricultural exports were valued at C£55.3m. In 1990 drought conditions restricted production to 1989 levels, but significantly higher export prices for potatoes and citrus fruit resulted in an increase in the value of agricultural exports to C£67.9m., representing 26% of the value of total domestic exports. Potato exports increased in value to C£29m. in 1990 (from C£16m. in 1988 and C£21m. in 1989), while the value of exports of citrus fruit increased to C£22m. (from C£14m. in 1988 and C£17m. in 1989). In 1991 total agricultural exports

fell to C£62.6m. (although still representing 26% of total exports), with potatoes accounting for C£28.1m., citrus fruit C£19.7m. and vegetables C£3.1m.

A damaging frost in the early months of 1992 and a noticeable deterioration in quality resulted in a sharp fall in the value of agricultural exports to C£39.1m. in that year (18% of total exports), with citrus fruit overtaking potatoes (C£11.4m.) as the most valuable export category. During the period 1989–92 agricultural production increased by an average of 1.5% annually. Failure to attain the planning target of 2.5% was due mainly to the effects of periodic drought conditions. In 1993 agricultural exports recovered to C£43.3m. (21.6% of the total), with potatoes (C£20.1m.) regaining the lead over citrus fruit (C£13.5m.) and fresh vegetables (C£2.5m.) combined. In 1994, however, a disastrous blight destroyed 25% of the spring potato crop, obliging Greek Cyprus to become a net importer of potatoes; overall agricultural production fell by 8.5%. Agricultural GDP increased, in real terms, by an annual average of 3.0% in 1985–93.

During 1995 agricultural production expanded by 12.9%, mainly owing to a 25% increase in output of potatoes, vegetables and fruit, while a small overall increase of 2.7% was recorded in livestock production. Exports of potatoes reached 187,903 tons in 1995 (worth C£43m.), compared with 95,303 tons in 1994 (C£23.7m.), when production was severely affected by an insect-induced disease. Exports of citrus fruit expanded by a substantial 26% in 1995, reaching 99,032 tons, compared with 78,515 tons in 1994. Large increases were also recorded for exports of oranges (56%), mandarins (36%) and grapefruit (28%), although there was an 11% decrease in the export of lemons. Production of cereals declined from 162,000 tons in 1994 to 145,000 tons in 1995. The total value of raw agricultural products in 1995 was provisionally estimated at C£67.7m., compared with C£45m. in 1994. In 1996 agricultural production fell by 3.3%, as a result of a decrease of 7% in the output of crops such as potatoes and fruit, although livestock and meat production increased by 3%. Production of cereals and grapes declined to 141,200 and 113,000 tons respectively. Exports of potatoes fell to 178,532 tons in 1996, while the prices secured in foreign markets were some 30% lower than in 1995, as a result of competition from other suppliers. Exports of citrus fruit fell to 83,934 tons, owing principally to a 23% decrease in the export of grapefruit. The total value of raw agricultural products fell by approximately 20% in 1996, to some C£53.3m. Agricultural production during 1997 was seriously affected by adverse weather conditions and was estimated to have declined by some 20% compared with 1996. Severe drought caused production of cereals to decrease to about 47,000 tons, while the potato crop was badly hit by frost, with the result that exports fell dramatically to 35,218 tons. Exports of citrus fruits, at 60,409 tons, were slightly below 1996 levels. The total value of raw agricultural exports fell by 32.6% in 1997 to C£35.9m., although meat production expanded by 4.5%, the largest increases being recorded in the production of beef and poultry.

The Paphos project, completed in 1983 at a cost of C£24m., involved the irrigation of some 5,000 ha along the south-western coast, to facilitate the production of tropical fruits such as mango, avocado and papaya, as well as grapes and early vegetables. The Government is currently working on the Southern Conveyor Project, the completed first phase of which carries water from the mountainous region of western Cyprus to the main potato-growing area in the south-east of the island. The second phase of the project, completed in 1994, increased water supplies to Nicosia, Larnaca and Limassol. The project is the largest water treatment and irrigation programme ever undertaken on the island, and total costs are expected to amount to C£175m. Another major investment is the Pitsilia Integrated Rural Development Project, which aims to stem the tide of rural depopulation by doubling the irrigated area in the mountainous central regions of the island. In early 1992 the Greek Cypriot Government approved initial plans for the construction of a number of desalination plants, intended to compensate for the shortfall in water resources resulting from inconsistent rainfall. The first such plant, at Dhekelia on the southern coast, became operational in 1997, providing 20,000 cu m of water a day. A second desalination plant, at Tersephanou, was inaugurated in May 1998, initially providing 6,000 cu m of water a day to

Nicosia and having a total capacity of 90,000 cu m a day when fully operational (scheduled for 1999). By mid-1998 one of the most protracted droughts of the 20th century had reduced reservoirs to their lowest-ever levels, obliging the authorities to institute stringent rationing and conservation measures. Government backing was also given to promising new research by the Cyprus Higher Technical Institute into the use of applied solar energy in reducing the high energy costs of the desalination process.

The Turkish Cypriot north inherited about 80% of the island's citrus groves, all the tobacco fields, 40% of the carobs, 80% of carrots and 10%–15% of potatoes. Nevertheless, agriculture in the north has lagged behind that of the south. In the chaos which followed the fighting, many citrus trees were neglected and died, or contracted diseases. Production resumed gradually, with exports of citrus fruit rising from 66,174 tons in 1976/77 to 96,637 tons in 1980 and 115,163 tons in 1982. The growing importance of citrus fruit in the Turkish Cypriot economy was reflected in the fact that the value of citrus fruit exports in 1986 totalled US $28.5m. (54.8% of total export revenue), although in 1987 the value of citrus fruit exports declined to $22.5m. and the proportion of total export revenue derived from citrus fruit decreased to 40.9%. In 1990–91 the collapse of Polly Peck International (see above) seriously disrupted the northern citrus fruit industry, resulting in the closure of some processing plants and severely reducing export volumes. Agricultural exports from the 'TRNC' were valued at $24.3m. in 1993, representing 44.6% of total exports, and increased to $25.7m. and 48.1%, respectively, in 1994. However, the European Court of Justice ruling in July 1994, effectively barring the import of 'TRNC' goods and produce by EU countries unless certificated by the recognized Cypriot authorities, had damaging consequences. In 1995, figures showed that agricultural exports had decreased to 40% of the total, valued at $27m., although in 1996 there was a partial recovery to $31m., representing 44% of total export value.

INDUSTRY

Industry, also, was severely affected by the war of 1974. It was estimated that the Greek Cypriots lost 70% of gross domestic manufacturing output, yet the growth of this sector since 1975 has been spectacular. Government incentives for investment, combined with a decline in real wages, stimulated a rapid expansion of manufacturing industry, especially in small-scale labour-intensive plants which produce goods for export. The share of manufactured products in total exports increased from around 40% in 1975 to more than 62% in 1981, although it declined to 58% in 1982. During 1983 exports of manufactured goods were valued at C£134.3m., compared with a record of almost C£142m. in 1981. Largely owing to competition from south-east Asia, however, the revenue from manufactured exports (nearly 80% of which go to the Middle East) fell by almost 30%, from C£140m. in 1985 to C£98.4m. in 1986. The most striking success in manufacturing has been clothing and footwear, with exports rising from C£3.2m. in 1974 to C£82m. in 1991, representing some 30% of total domestic export earnings. A greater emphasis was placed on the sector in the late 1980s and, although manufacturing has gradually declined as a proportion of GDP, the sector continues to grow in real terms, and exports have recovered. Manufacturing, construction and utilities, combined, employed about 26% of the labour force in 1991 and accounted for 27% of GDP in 1990, when manufactured exports were valued at C£186m. and accounted for 72% of total domestic exports (compared with 60% in 1987). In 1991 exports of manufactured goods were valued at C£178.2m. The value of the output of manufactured goods increased from C£132.2m. in 1980 to C£366.7m. in 1990, representing 14.4% of GDP. Cement production increased from 338,000 metric tons in 1974 to 1,233,000 tons in 1980. It declined to 659,000 tons in 1985, but had recovered to 1,132,000 tons by 1992. In the late 1980s one of the main areas of growth was the cigarette industry. Production of cigarettes increased from 3,718m. in 1987 to 6,177m. in 1992. Export earnings from cement and cigarettes were valued at C£16.5m. in 1990 (compared with C£13.6m. in 1988). In 1992 manufacturing output (excluding construction and utilities) was valued at C£416.9m. (equivalent to 14.1% of GDP), of which C£172.1m. was exported (representing 80% of total exports). In 1993 output fell to C£407.1m. (13.3% of GDP),

of which C£154.3m. was exported (representing 77% of total exports). Employment in the industrial sector as a whole (manufacturing, construction and utilities) declined gradually as a proportion of the total, from 26.6% in 1988 to an estimated 24.4% in 1994, in which year there was a modest 3% recovery in manufacturing output. In 1995 25.3% of the employed labour force were engaged in the sector, when industry contributed 24.7% of GDP totalling C£3,976m. Total GDP in 1996 was C£4,125.5m., of which the industrial sector accounted for about 25%.

By 1992 the availability of footwear produced in Asia (utilizing cheaper labour) had begun to pose a serious threat to the Cypriot shoe-manufacturing industry. In August 1992, therefore, the Government imposed a ban on the import of inexpensive shoes from non-EC countries, and placed restrictions on the import of more expensive footwear. In April 1993, moreover, the new Klerides administration agreed to extend 'substantial assistance' to the industrial sector, with the aim of increasing its competitiveness. Clothing has remained the largest manufacturing category, albeit declining in value, yielding exports of C£51.0m. in 1993 (compared with C£74.6m. in 1988), representing 25% of total domestic exports by value. By 1997 the value of clothing exports had fallen to C£29.9m., representing 17% of total domestic exports by value.

The construction sector grew rapidly after the 1974 Turkish invasion, with an average annual growth of 40% in 1975–79. The most important growth area was the housing sector, which provided accommodation for refugees. A record 9,449 units of housing were constructed in 1979. The manufacturing and construction sectors were hampered, in the early 1980s, by the adverse effects of the Government's measures to deflate the economy and by the accumulated results of wage inflation over several years. However, the construction sector enjoyed a period of rapid growth in the late 1980s, contributing C£240m. (10%) to GDP in 1990, in which year authorized building permits increased by 47% in value and by 22% in volume, in comparison with 1989. The number of building permits authorized decreased from 7,259 in 1995, to 7,156 in 1996 and to 6,614 in 1997. Construction activity showed a sharp decline in 1997, as indicated by the quantity index of the main construction materials for local use, which during 1997 fell by 6% (compared with a marginal decline of 0.2% in 1996). However, the volume of building permits authorized showed a 10.7% increase in the fourth quarter of 1997 compared with the same period in 1996, indicating a recovery in the construction sector after several years of deceleration.

In the period 1989–92 the output of the manufacturing sector increased at an average rate of 3% per year, compared with the planning target of 5% annually. Failure to attain the projected growth rate was attributed to adverse conditions in major markets, such as the United Kingdom and the Arab states. From the mid- to late 1980s the service industries, such as banking, insurance and consultancy, grew at a remarkable rate and emerged as an important part of the Greek Cypriot economy. By the end of 1994 more than 17,000 foreign companies were registered in the Greek Cypriot sector, although only about 10% maintained offices on the island. In the period 1989–92 the services sector expanded at an average annual rate of 8% in real terms, exceeding the original planning target of 5.7%. In this period all service areas, both those directly connected with tourism (e.g. hotels, restaurants and transport) and other activities (e.g. commerce, communications, banking and professional services), expanded at substantially higher rates than had been projected. By 1995 the services sector was providing 69.8% of GDP and engaging 64.0% of the employed labour force. The 'offshore' sector produced revenue of C£147m. in 1994.

In 1995 mining and quarrying production declined by 8% compared with the previous year, mainly owing to large decreases in output of building stone, marble and umber, while production of sand, gravel and road aggregate (the bulk of this sector's output) increased from 6,000 tons in 1994 to 6,200 tons in 1995. Domestic exports of manufactured products continued on a downward trend, decreasing by some 1.6% compared with 1994. The decline was attributed principally to an erosion of competitiveness (including high production costs and low quality output) and an increase in the value of the Cyprus pound relative to the pound sterling and other currencies. Mining and quarrying production rose by 10.2% in 1996, compared with 1995, although the manufacturing sector continued its downward trend. During the second half of 1996 domestic exports of manufactured products showed a partial recovery, increasing by some 12% compared with the same period in 1995. The manufacturing sector demonstrated a partial recovery in 1997, fostered by a revival in foreign and domestic demand. The volume index of manufacturing production fell by 0.9% compared with a 5.1% decline in 1996, the biggest decreases being recorded in the non-metallic mineral products industry (cement, bricks and tiles), which declined by 9.7% owing to the decrease in construction activity, in the paper products and printing industry (down 6.7%) and in textiles, clothing and leather (down 4.2%). The food, beverages and tobacco industry showed a 0.7% increase, retaining its leading position in the manufacturing sector by contributing 31% to manufacturing value added. Increases in production were also recorded in the sub-groups 'other manufacturing industries' (mainly goldsmiths and silversmiths), which increased by 8.3%, chemical, petroleum and plastic products (4.2%), and metal products and machinery (2.7%). Domestic exports of manufactured goods began to recover from the second quarter of 1997, increasing by 5.5% over the year to a value of C£176.3m. Large decreases were recorded in exports of clothing, fruit juices and wine; these were more than offset by increases in exports of other products, the largest increases being recorded in cathodes of refined copper (248.3%) and cigarettes (70.1%). The price index of manufacturing production rose by 2.3% in 1997 (compared with 2.7% in 1996), as a result of an increase of 5.8% in export prices and of 1.6% in local market prices. Mining and quarrying production, at 6,500 tons in 1997, decreased by 0.3% compared with 1996, mainly because of a 5.1% decline in output of sand, gravel and road aggregate, although significant increases were recorded in the production of havara, gypsum, bentonite and marble.

Although the labour market loosened somewhat in the early 1980s, an increase in economic activity, beginning in 1986, resulted in a shortage of skilled labour. In conditions of effective full employment in 1990, the Government authorized the recruitment of 1,600 additional foreign workers (mainly from Bulgaria and Poland) to fill vacancies in the construction and manufacturing sectors. In the early years after 1974, the Government encouraged the temporary emigration of workers as a solution to unemployment. Now the emphasis is more on encouraging workers to return, although their remittances are still important to Cyprus's foreign reserves. By mid-1992 renewed labour shortages had induced the Greek Cypriot Government to authorize the recruitment of another 8,000 foreign workers (some 2%–3% of the labour force). Owing to Government fears that permanent immigration might engender social problems, the maximum contract period was restricted to two years.

The Turkish-occupied area has few industrial resources. The share of industrial exports in total 'TRNC' exports, however, increased from 28.3% (US $14.7m.) in 1986 to 55.0% ($30.0m.) in 1993, before falling slightly to 51.3% ($27.4m.) in 1994. The textile and clothing industry has grown rapidly since the early 1980s (although most of the raw material has to be imported), overtaking citrus fruit as the largest source of export revenue, with earnings of $18m. (33.7% of the total) in 1994.

It is estimated that 90% of Cyprus's mining operations are in the Greek zone, while the Turkish zone has no petroleum refinery. Hitherto also lacking electricity-generating capacity, the 'TRNC' was reported, in July 1994, to be about to open its first power plant, located near Kyrenia and financed by Turkey; however, an explosion at the site rendered the start-up date uncertain. Meanwhile, the Cyprus Electricity Authority was continuing to supply electricity to both zones and the Turkish north's debt for unbilled consumption had reached some $270m. by the end of 1993. A successful energy conservation programme is under way in the Greek Cypriot sector, involving the exploitation of solar and wind energy and the development of hydroelectricity potential.

TRADE, TOURISM AND COMMUNICATIONS

Cyprus has experienced a trade deficit for many years. In 1979 both exports and imports exceeded the growth target of the Emergency Action Plan for 1979–81 but the deficit increased from C£154.3m. in 1978 to C£195.7m. Imports of fuel and raw materials increased, due to demands made by the restructuring of the industrial sector, but the value of imports of capital goods fell, as a result of a slackening in investment. In 1981 a continuing increase in the value of petroleum imports (up 34.8% to C£102.6m.) helped to produce a visible deficit of C£254.8m. Despite government efforts to stimulate exports, the trade deficit continued to widen, and by 1985 it had reached a record C£471.7m. In 1986, however, the trade deficit declined by 15%, to C£398.9m., owing to a 13.5% fall in the cost of imports (including a 39% reduction in the value of petroleum imports, due to the decrease in international petroleum prices). Despite the improved growth in exports of manufactured goods (following depressed figures in 1986), the trade deficit increased, reaching C£1,092.2m. in 1992, before falling to C£795.9m. in 1993. The trade deficit increased to C£1,114.8m. in 1995, when imports were valued at C£1,670.4m. and exports at C£555.6m. Total imports increased by 11.2% in 1996, to a value of C£1,857.6m., while total exports expanded by 17.6%, to a value of C£653.5m. Large increases were recorded in imports of fuels and lubricants, consumer goods and capital items, while a decline in domestic exports (notably of agricultural products) was offset by a sharp increase in re-exports.

In 1997, due to restrained domestic demand, total imports (excluding imports of military equipment) recorded a small increase of less than 3%, to C£1,704.7m., with increases in imports of consumer goods and of fuels and lubricants of 14.9% and 3%, respectively, being offset in particular by a 7.6% decrease in imports of transport equipment. During 1997 EU countries supplied 47.6% of total imports (including 11.4% from the UK), other European countries 8.1%, the USA 19% and Asian countries 16%. Total exports declined to C£605.7m., so that the crude trade deficit (excluding military imports) widened to C£1,099m.

There was a significant alteration in the Greek Cypriot trading pattern in the mid-1980s, with EC countries taking over the dominant role from Arab countries (chiefly Lebanon, Egypt, the states of the Arabian peninsula, and Libya), although exports to the latter rose again in the early 1990s. The Arab countries' share of total Greek Cypriot exports was reduced from 48% in 1985 to 28% in 1990, largely as a result of the conflict in the Persian (Arabian) Gulf region; thereafter they recovered to some 40% in 1991–93, with the economic revival of Lebanon, in particular, providing an expanding market. Greek Cypriot exports to EC countries, on the other hand, increased from 32.4% of total domestic export revenue in 1985 to 53.2% in 1990, although they declined in the succeeding years, to 41.7% in 1993. In 1987 the Greek Cypriot Government established a Council for the Promotion of Exports (COPE), one of the main aims of which was to promote exports to Europe. EC countries were also the main suppliers of goods to the Greek Cypriot sector, their share of the region's total imports, by value, increasing to 60.8% in 1986, before decreasing slightly, to 57% in 1987 and 54% in 1990, only to increase again to 58% in 1992. Imports from Arab countries, in turn, declined after 1985, when they accounted for 10.1% of total import costs, to 6.1% in 1987 and to 5% in 1993. In 1994 the United Kingdom remained the largest individual trading partner of Cyprus, supplying 11.4% of its imports and taking 27.1% of total Cypriot exports. A feature of Cypriot trade in 1995 was the rapid growth in imports from and exports to the USA, although the EU countries (particularly the United Kingdom) remained the dominant trading partners.

In November 1985 the EC Council of Ministers approved the admission of Cyprus to a customs union with the EC. The terms of this union were agreed by both sides and a protocol with the EC was signed in October 1987, which came into effect on 1 January 1988. The protocol defined an initial 10-year phase (1988-98), during which time tariffs on imports to Cyprus were to be reduced by 10% annually, leading to their complete removal by 1998. For some products, which are important to the island's economy (e.g. clothing and footwear), tariffs were to fall by only 4% annually in the first phase. The EC agreed to waive quantitative restrictions on exports to the EC of Cypriot garments and to make concessions to Cypriot agricultural exports, particularly potatoes, grapes, wine and citrus fruit. Cyprus, in turn, agreed to dismantle its quantitative restrictions on imports of industrial products from EC countries, yet, was to be allowed to retain a 20% tariff on up to 15% of imports that competed with local products. A second phase, lasting four to five years, which was to be introduced after a review of the first phase, was to lift all remaining restrictions and trade barriers on products covered by the agreement. Cyprus was, then, expected to adopt the EC's common customs tariff, in accordance with its third-country provisions, freeing it of restrictions within the EC. The President of the 'TRNC', Rauf Denktaş, strongly attacked the customs union, claiming that the EC was not entitled to negotiate the agreement without consulting representatives of the Turkish sector of the island. The EC, however, made it clear that the union would apply to the whole island: an assertion that was reiterated in an EC report, published by the Commission in June 1993, which confirmed Cyprus's eligibility for EC membership. Under the fourth EU-Cyprus financial protocol, signed in June 1995 in the framework of the existing association agreement, the island was to receive ECU 74m. in loans and grants over five years, in support of efforts to promote economic integration and to prepare for EU membership.

Tourism was one of the areas of the Greek Cypriot economy which was most adversely affected by the 1974 war, as 90% of the island's hotels came under Turkish Cypriot control. Following the introduction of a government loan plan, however, the number of hotel beds increased from a low point of 3,880 in 1975 to 18,197 in 1985. Tourist receipts rose to C£71m. in 1980, with 353,375 visitors. The sector continued to expand rapidly in the 1980s, and in 1986 the number of tourist arrivals rose to 900,727; the tourist industry became the Republic of Cyprus's largest source of income, with receipts totalling C£257m. By 1990 the annual total of tourist arrivals had increased to 1,561,479 (of whom 44% were from the United Kingdom). Receipts from tourism in that year totalled C£573m., representing an increase of 13% over 1989's total (compared with a 27% increase between 1988 and 1989). There were an estimated 47,500 tourist beds (many of them in self-catering accommodation) in 1988, with projects to provide a further 15,500 already in progress. Employment in the hotel and restaurant sector increased to 24,000 in 1990, accounting for almost 10% of the employed labour force. In 1991 the number of tourist arrivals decreased to 1,385,129, owing to the negative impact of the political crisis in the Persian (Arabian) Gulf region, and net receipts fell to C£387.2m. A recovery of the sector in 1992, to 1,991,000 arrivals and net receipts of C£593.3m., was followed, in 1993, by a reduction to 1,841,000 visitors (with net receipts of C£698.0m.), as a result of depreciation in the value of the pound sterling, and a general economic recession in Europe. In 1994, however, tourism again expanded, with 2,069,000 arrivals and net receipts of C£812m., following which further expansion was achieved in 1995 (2,100,000 arrivals and net receipts of C£813m.). In promoting the industry, the Greek Cypriot authorities laid emphasis on the desirability of developing 'high-value' tourism (as opposed to the 'package' holiday trade) and on sustainable tourist development. In 1996 efforts were mounted to attract more tourists from the USA, although the UK, Scandinavia and Germany continued to provide the majority of visitors to the island. Tourism revived in 1997, largely owing to the strength of sterling against the Cyprus pound, the economic upswing in most EU countries and the restrained pricing policy followed by Cypriot hoteliers. Total tourist arrivals increased by 5.3% on the 1996 figure, to 2,646,363, of which 32.9% came from the United Kingdom, and large increases were recorded in arrivals from Russia, Switzerland and Israel. Foreign-exchange earnings from tourism in 1997 totalled C£830m., with the sector accounting for 20% of GDP and 12% of employment.

Tourism in the north has also expanded, giving rise to a shortage of hotel beds. The best hotels still exist in the Turkish sector, but most remained unused and derelict after the invasion, although some have been taken over, much against the will of the Greek Cypriot owners. The number of non-Turkish visitors rose steadily from 8,172 in 1978 to 36,372 in 1987.

Turkish visits from the mainland remained fairly steady between 1978 (when they totalled 104,738) and 1986, increasing to 147,965 in 1987, when net income from tourism totalled US $103.5m. By 1990 tourism receipts had increased to $224.8m. (from 243,269 Turkish visitors and 57,541 others), then declined appreciably in the following two years, before recovering to $224.6m. in 1993 (281,370 Turkish visitors and 77,943 others). In 1994 net tourism revenue again decreased, to $172.9m. (from 256,549 Turkish visitors and 95,079 others); although 1995 revenue increased to $218.9m. (from 298,026 Turkish visitors and 87,733 others), a further downturn in 1996 resulted in net revenue of $175.6m. (from 289,131 Turkish visitors and 75,985 others).

As part of a programme of economic diversification, the Greek Cypriot sector has become a major maritime trading centre. Shipping heads the 'offshore' sector in terms of turnover, providing some 30% of revenue receipts from 'offshore' activities. From 1989 to mid-1992 the number of shipping companies registered in Cyprus doubled to more than 700, making the Cyprus registry the fastest-growing in the world. By the end of 1996 Cyprus had climbed to fifth position in terms of displacement, which totalled more than 23m. grt.

Famagusta formerly handled 83% of Cyprus's freight traffic but, now that it is in Turkish hands, it has been largely superseded by Larnaca and Limassol. In 1996 a total of 5,109 vessels visited Greek Cypriot ports, of which 3,747 visited Limassol. Port development schemes for Larnaca and Limassol are expected to cost US $65m., and a new port is also planned for Paphos. There has been a suggestion that Cyprus should be used as an entrepôt for distributing food supplies to Saudi Arabia and the Gulf states. Cyprus has, to some extent, benefited from the paralysis of Beirut, although none of its ports has the capacity of Beirut.

PROSPECTS

The economy and its future are inextricably linked with the political deadlock in the island, which seems unlikely to be resolved by diplomacy in the near future. The Turkish Cypriot opposition to accession negotiations with the EU aggravates the problem. Meanwhile, both sides are proceeding with their own plans for development on either side of the 'Attila line'.

Trade between the EU and the Greek Cypriots will retain its predominant share of both exports and imports, providing new opportunities for local industries, but, at the same time, presenting them with the challenge of competing with EU exports to Cyprus. The 1990–91 crisis in the Persian (Arabian) Gulf region was a set-back for the expanding Greek Cypriot economy, which had benefited from reconstruction activity in the Gulf region; it has quickly recovered its forward momentum, however, and seems likely to receive increasing economic benefit from its geographical location as a staging-post between Europe and the Middle East and from its long-standing connections in Eastern Europe and the former Soviet republics. For the Greek Cypriot Government, entry into the EU remains a cardinal goal, in which context it welcomed the formal opening of accession negotiations in March 1998. Also considered to be significant was the EU's assertion that the division of the island, if it persisted, should not delay the negotiations.

A serious restraint on future economic growth is likely to be a shortage of labour. Rather than incur the social problems assumed to be associated with unrestricted immigration of foreign workers, the Greek Cypriot authorities prefer to maintain severe entry restrictions, despite the probable inhibition of economic expansion. A political solution to the island's division would release the labour potential of the stagnant north for the thriving south; meanwhile, the economic division of the two sectors of the island seems likely to worsen.

Statistical Survey

Source (unless otherwise indicated): Department of Statistics and Research, Ministry of Finance, Nicosia; tel. (2) 309301; telex 3399; fax (2) 374830.

Note: Since July 1974 the northern part of Cyprus has been under Turkish occupation. As a result, some of the statistics relating to subsequent periods do not cover the whole island. Some separate figures for the 'TRNC' are given on pp. 376–377.

AREA AND POPULATION

Area: 9,251 sq km (3,572 sq miles), incl. Turkish-occupied region.

Population: 735,900 (males 367,000; females 368,900), incl. 90,600 in Turkish-occupied region, at 31 December 1995 (official estimate). Note: Figures for the Turkish-occupied region exclude settlers from Turkey, estimated at more than 90,000 in 1995.

Ethnic Groups (estimates, 31 December 1995): Greeks 623,200 (84.7%), Turks 90,600 (12.3%), others 22,100 (3.0%); Total 735,900.

Principal Towns (population at 1 October 1992): Nicosia (capital) 181,234 (excl. Turkish-occupied portion); Limassol 139,424; Larnaca 62,178; Famagusta (Gazi Mağusa) 39,500 (mid-1974); Paphos 33,246; (estimated population at 31 December 1995): Nicosia 191,000 (excl. Turkish-occupied portion); Limassol 148,700; Larnaca 66,400; Paphos 36,300.

Births and Deaths (government-controlled area, 1995): Registered live births 9,869 (birth rate 15.4 per 1,000); Registered deaths 4,935 (death rate 7.7 per 1,000).

Expectation of Life (government-controlled area, years at birth, 1992–93): males 74.6; females 79.1. Source: UN, *Demographic Yearbook*.

Employment (government-controlled area, provisional figures, '000 persons aged 15 years and over, excl. armed forces, 1995): Agriculture, hunting, forestry and fishing 30.5; Mining and quarrying 0.8; Manufacturing 44.0; Electricity, gas and water 1.5; Construction 25.7; Trade, restaurants and hotels 74.6; Transport, storage and communications 18.5; Financing, insurance, real estate and business services 22.6; Community, social and personal services 63.8; employment on British sovereign bases 3.1; Total 285.1 (males 173.0, females 112.1).

AGRICULTURE, ETC.

Principal Crops (government-controlled area, '000 metric tons, 1996): Wheat 13; Barley 131; Potatoes 220; Olives 10; Tomatoes 40; Watermelons 29*; Melons 9*; Grapes 122; Apples 9; Oranges 50; Tangerines, mandarins, etc. 20; Grapefruit 58; Lemons and limes 25. *FAO estimate. Source: FAO, *Production Yearbook*.

Livestock (government-controlled area, '000 head, 1995): Cattle 69; Sheep 250; Goats 220; Pigs 374; Chickens 3,400.

Livestock Products (government-controlled area, '000 metric tons, 1996): Beef and veal 5; Mutton and lamb 4; Goat meat 4; Pig meat 46; Poultry meat 31; Cows' milk 138; Sheep's milk 19; Goats' milk 24; Cheese 5; Hen eggs 10. Source: FAO, *Production Yearbook*.

Forestry (government-controlled area, '000 cubic metres, 1995): Roundwood removals (excl. bark) 39; Sawnwood production (incl. railway sleepers) 20.

Fishing (metric tons, live weight, government-controlled area): Total catch 3,022 in 1995.

MINING AND QUARRYING

Selected Products (metric tons, government-controlled area, 1995): Sand and gravel 6,200,000; Marble 30,000; Gypsum 148,275; Bentonite 51,234.

INDUSTRY

Selected Products (government-controlled area, 1995): Cement 1,021,703 metric tons; Bricks 54.6 million; Mosaic tiles 1.6 million sq metres; Cigarettes 2,528 million; Footwear (excluding plastic and semi-finished shoes) 3.4 million pairs; Beer 34.9 million litres; Wines 59.1 million litres; Carbonated soft drinks 58.9 million litres.

FINANCE

Currency and Exchange Rates: 100 cents = 1 Cyprus pound (Cyprus £). *Sterling and Dollar Equivalents* (31 May 1998): £1 sterling = 85.69 Cyprus cents; US $1 = 52.55 Cyprus cents; Cyprus £100 = £116.70 sterling = $190.30. *Average exchange rate* (US $ per Cyprus £): 2.2113 in 1995; 2.1446 in 1996; 1.9476 in 1997.

Budget (estimates, Cyprus £ million, government-controlled area, 1996): *Revenue:* Taxation 1,058.26 (Taxes on income 254.91, Social security contributions 197.51, Taxes on payroll 21.41, Taxes on property 24.27, Excises 117.49, Value-added tax 198.00, Other domestic taxes on goods and services 50.24, Import duties 95.54,

Other taxes 98.89); Entrepreneurial and property income 155.08; Administrative fees and charges, non-industrial and incidental sales 78.64; Other current revenue 28.53; Capital revenue 0.78; Total 1,321.29, excl. grants from abroad (2.41). *Expenditure:* General public services 93.95; Defence 53.53; Public order and safety 80.61; Education 161.41; Health 88.50; Social security and welfare 358.83; Housing and community amenities 58.43; Recreational, cultural and religious affairs and services 23.06; Economic affairs and services 199.58 (Agriculture, forestry, fishing and hunting 96.40, Mining 0.12, Road transport 40.87, Other transport and communication 28.64, Other economic affairs 33.55); Other purposes 231.53; Sub-total 1,349.43 (Current 1,204.86, Capital 144.57); Adjustment 113.33; Total 1,462.76, excl. lending minus repayments (2.99).

International Reserves (US $ million at 31 December 1997): Gold (national valuation) 133.9; IMF special drawing rights 0.3; Reserve position in IMF 34.3; Foreign exchange 1,356.9; Total 1,525.5. Source: IMF, *International Financial Statistics*.

Money Supply (Cyprus £ million at 31 December 1997, government-controlled area): Currency outside banks 276.3, Demand deposits at deposit money banks 427.2; Total money (incl. others) 704.5.

Cost of Living (Retail Price Index, government-controlled area; base: 1992 = 100): 109.78 in 1994; 112.65 in 1995; 116.01 in 1996.

Gross Domestic Product in Purchasers' Values (Cyprus £ million at current prices, government-controlled area): 3,250.5 in 1993; 3,599.6 in 1994; 3,905.1 in 1995.

Gross Domestic Product by Economic Activity (provisional, Cyprus £ million at current prices, government-controlled area, 1995): Agriculture, hunting, forestry and fishing 199.5; Mining and quarrying 11.4; Manufacturing 465.6; Electricity, gas and water 84.0; Construction 338.8; Wholesale and retail trade, restaurants and hotels 759.6; Transport, storage and communications 299.7; Finance, insurance, real estate and business services 644.9; Government services 507.1; Other community, social and personal services 296.9; Other services 31.9; *Sub-total* 3,639.4; Import duties 185.6; Value-added Tax 191.6; *Less* Imputed bank service charges 111.5; *Total* 3,905.1.

Balance of Payments (US $ million, government-controlled area, 1995): Exports of goods f.o.b. 1,228.7, Imports of goods f.o.b. –3,314.2, *Trade balance* –2,085.5; Exports of services 2,960.1, Imports of services –1,102.7, *Balance on goods and services* –228.1; Other income received 142.3, Other income paid –244.0, *Balance on goods, services and income* –329.8; Current transfers received 134.8; Current transfers paid –17.7, *Current balance* –212.6; Direct investment abroad –6.6, Direct investment from abroad 119.1; Portfolio investment assets –23.7, Portfolio investment liabilities –29.4, Other investment assets –1,060.7, Other investment liabilities 945.8, Net errors and omissions –94.9, *Overall balance* –363.1. Source: IMF, *International Financial Statistics*.

EXTERNAL TRADE

Principal Commodities (Cyprus £ '000, government-controlled area, 1995): *Imports c.i.f.:* Textiles and textile articles 122,798 (Clothing and clothing accessories 29,594); Road vehicles, parts and accessories 166,864; Mineral products 132,882 (Crude oil 45,286); Base metals and articles of base metal 109,303; Products of chemical or allied industries 116,527; Prepared foodstuffs, beverages, spirits and vinegar, tobacco and manufactured tobacco substitutes 241,878 (Tobacco and manufactured tobacco substitutes 165,573); Plastics and articles thereof 52,280; Paper, paperboard and articles thereof 47,374; Live animals and animal products 29,788; Total (incl. others) 1,670,408. *Exports f.o.b.:* Clothing 44,303; Footwear 4,937; Potatoes 43,072; Citrus fruit 16,797; Cement 7,801; Pharmaceutical products 17,841; Alcoholic beverages 9,647 (Wines 9,105); Fruit and vegetable juices 7,690; Total (incl. others) 238,675. Figures for exports exclude re-exports (Cyprus £'000): 316,932.

Total Trade (Cyprus £ '000, government-controlled area): *Imports c.i.f.* (incl. military equipment): 1,316,078 in 1993; 1,482,222 in 1994; 1,670,408 in 1995. *Exports f.o.b.* (incl. re-exports): 431,462 in 1993; 475,978 in 1994; 555,607 in 1995.

Principal Trading Partners (Cyprus £ '000, government-controlled area, 1995): *Imports c.i.f.:* France 68,674; Germany 136,264; Greece 120,058; Italy 163,589; Japan 111,658; Russia 66,417; United Kingdom 196,718; USA 217,433; Total (incl. others) 1,670,408. *Exports f.o.b.* (excl. re-exports): Belgium-Luxembourg 7,024; France

6,878; Germany 23,820; Greece 11,469; Israel 6,093; Lebanon 12,568; Russia 12,183; United Kingdom 67,337; Total (incl. others) 238,675.

TRANSPORT

Road Traffic (licensed motor vehicles, government-controlled area, 31 December 1995): Private passenger cars 212,152; Taxis and self-drive cars 7,597; Buses and coaches 2,670; Lorries and vans 101,182; Motorcycles 50,393; Total (incl. others) 387,559.

Shipping (freight traffic, '000 metric tons, government-controlled area, 1995): Goods loaded 2,255, Goods unloaded 5,023. At 31 December 1996 a total of 1,652 merchant vessels (combined displacement 23.8 m. grt) were registered in Cyprus. (Source: Lloyd's Register of Shipping, *World Fleet Statistics*).

Civil Aviation (government-controlled area, 1995): Overall passenger traffic 4,665,276; Total freight transported 39,701 metric tons.

TOURISM

Foreign Visitors by Country of Origin (excluding one-day visitors and visitors to the Turkish-occupied zone, 1995): Germany 235,000, Greece 65,000, Middle East and Gulf countries 105,000, Russia 95,000, Scandinavian countries 230,000, Switzerland 110,000, United Kingdom 850,000; Total (incl. others) 2,100,000.

Tourist Arrivals (government-controlled area): 2,100,000 in 1995; 2,194,800 in 1996; 2,646,363 in 1997.

Tourist Receipts (Cyprus £ million, government-controlled area): 698 in 1993; 812 in 1994; 813 in 1995.

COMMUNICATIONS MEDIA

Radio Receivers (government-controlled area): 215,000 in 1993; 220,000 in 1994; 230,000 in 1995. Source: UNESCO, *Statistical Yearbook*.

Television Receivers (government-controlled area): 235,000 in 1994; 240,000 in 1995. Source: UNESCO, *Statistical Yearbook*.

Telephones (main lines in use): 311,000 in 1993; 330,000 in 1994; 347,000 in 1995.

Telefax Stations (number in use): 6,000 in 1992; 7,000 in 1993. Source: UN, *Statistical Yearbook*.

Mobile Telephones (subscribers): 15,288 in 1993; 22,938 in 1994; 44,453 in 1995. Source: UN, *Statistical Yearbook*.

Book Production (government-controlled area): 1,040 titles and 1,551,700 copies in 1994; 1,128 titles and 1,723,400 copies in 1995.

Newspapers (1995): 10 daily (circulation 84,000 copies); 27 non-daily (circulation 165,000 copies).

EDUCATION

1995/96 (government-controlled area): Kindergarten: 647 institutions, 1,323 teachers, 26,254 pupils; Primary schools: 381 institutions, 3,411 teachers, 64,660 pupils; Secondary schools (Gymnasia and Lyceums): 112 institutions, 4,258 teachers, 55,435 pupils; Technical colleges: 11 institutions, 574 teachers, 4,410 pupils; University of Cyprus: 201 teachers, 1,962 students; Other post-secondary: 32 institutions, 527 teachers, 6,912 students.

'Turkish Republic of Northern Cyprus'*

Source: Office of the London Representative of the 'Turkish Republic of Northern Cyprus', 29 Bedford Sq., London WC1B 3EG
(tel. (171) 631-1920; telex 8955363; fax (171) 631-1948).

AREA AND POPULATION

Area: 3,355 sq km (1,295 sq miles).

Population (census, 15 December 1996): 200,587 (males 105,978; females 94,609).

Ethnic Groups (census, 15 December 1996): Turks 197,264, English 627, Greeks 384, Maronites 173, Russians 130, Germans 106, Others 1,903; Total 200,587.

Principal Towns (estimated population within the municipal boundary, 1996): Lefkoşa (Nicosia) 42,767 (Turkish-occupied area only); Gazi Mağusa (Famagusta) 22,216; Girne (Kyrenia) 7,893.

Births, Marriages and Deaths (registered, 1996): Birth rate 18.0 per 1,000; Marriage rate 6.1 per 1,000; Death rate 8.0 per 1,000.

Employment (1995): Agriculture, forestry and fishing 17,383; Industry 8,348; Construction 9,584; Trade and tourism 8,367; Transport and communications 6,510; Financial institutions 2,397; Business and personal services 7,276; Public Services 16,589; *Total employed* 76,454. Total unemployed 567; *Total labour force* 77,021.

AGRICULTURE, ETC.

Principal Crops ('000 metric tons, 1996): Wheat 18.6; Barley 74.8; Potatoes 14.3; Legumes 2.2; Tomatoes 1.7; Onions 2.0; Artichokes 0.9; Watermelons 3.1; Melons 1.0; Cucumbers 0.7; Carobs 3.4; Olives 2.1; Lemons 10.8; Grapefruit 40.6; Oranges 92.4; Tangerines 1.0.

Livestock ('000 head, 1996): Cattle 24.2; Sheep 222.2; Goats 61.5; Chickens 3,741.2.

Livestock Products ('000 metric tons, unless otherwise indicated, 1996): Sheep's and goats' milk 11.5; Cows' milk 37.9; Mutton and lamb 3.1; Goat meat 0.9; Beef 1.6; Poultry meat 5.6; Wool 0.3; Eggs (million) 22.7.

Fishing (metric tons, 1994); Total catch 400.

FINANCE

Currency and Exchange Rates: Turkish currency: 100 kuruş = 1 Turkish lira (TL) or pound. *Sterling and Dollar Equivalents* (31 May 1998): £1 sterling = 418,364 liras; US $1 = 256,555 liras; 1,000,000 Turkish liras = £2.390 = $3.898. *Average Exchange Rate* (liras per US dollar): 45,845 in 1995; 81,405 in 1996; 151,865 in 1997.

Budget (million Turkish liras, 1996): *Revenue:* Internal revenue 15,528,392.7 (Direct taxes 6,158,720.4, Indirect taxes 4,847,867.6, Non-tax revenue 3,138,274.4; Aid from Turkey 6,119,642.4; Aid from other countries 106,795.4; Loans 2,625,793.9; Total 24,380,624.4. *Expenditure:* Personnel 9,275,954.3; Other goods and services 1,395,649.7; Transfers 9,867,171.5; Investments 2,594,348.9; Defence 1,247,500.0; Total 24,380,624.4

Cost of Living (Retail Price Index at December; base: December of previous year = 100): 315.0 in 1994; 172.1 in 1995; 187.5 in 1996.

Expenditure on the Gross Domestic Product ('000 million Turkish liras at current prices, 1996): Government final consumption expenditure 14,228.8; Private final consumption expenditure 39,612.5; Increase in stocks 1,057.1; Gross fixed capital formation 8,842.8; *Total domestic expenditure* 63,741.2; Exports of goods and services, *less* Imports of goods and services 52,616.9; *GDP in purchasers' values* 116,359.1; *GDP at constant 1977 prices* (million liras) 7,637.7.

Gross Domestic Product (GDP) by Economic Activity (million Turkish liras, 1996): Agriculture, forestry and fishing 6,129,290.1; Industry 8,283,677.9 (Mining and quarrying 427,409.8; Manufacturing 4,952,157.2; Electricity and water 2,903,615.9); Construction 1,880,364.5; Wholesale and retail trade 6,400,410.6; Restaurants and hotels 2,746,901.1; Transport and communications 6,557,584.6; Finance 6,878,817.2; Ownership of dwellings 1,340,915.2; Business and personal services 6,212,406.1; Government services 12,323,927.4; *Sub-total* 58,754,294.7; Import duties 4,526,903.8; *GDP in purchasers' values* 63,281,198.5.

Balance of Payments (US $ million, 1996): Merchandise exports f.o.b. 70.5; Merchandise imports c.i.f. –318.4; *Trade balance* –247.9; Services and unrequited transfers (net) 245.9; *Current balance* –2.0; Capital movements (net) 99.4; Net errors and omissions 1.5; *Total* (net monetary movements) 95.9.

EXTERNAL TRADE

Principal Commodities (US $ million, 1996): *Imports c.i.f.:* Food and live animals 53.1; Beverages and tobacco 19.2; Mineral fuels, lubricants, etc. 32.8; Chemicals 29.2; Basic manufactures 77.4; Machinery and transport equipment 73.5; Miscellaneous manufactured articles 24.6; Total (incl. others) 318.4. *Exports f.o.b.:* Food and live animals 35.5 (Citrus fruit 22.6, Potatoes 0.9, Concentrated citrus 1.7); Beverages and tobacco 5.9; Crude materials (inedible) except fuels 2.6; Chemicals 1.2; Basic manufactures 3.2; Clothing 21.7; Total (incl. others) 70.5.

Principal Trading Partners (US $ million, 1996): *Imports c.i.f:* Belgium 3.1; France 5.1; Germany 9.0; Hong Kong 12.4; Italy 11.2; Japan 5.5; Lebanon 3.1; Netherlands 3.7; Romania 6.5; Sri Lanka 11.8; Turkey 176.1; United Kingdom 44.0; USA 4.3; Total (incl. others) 318.4. *Exports f.o.b.:* Germany 5.9; Israel 3.4; Kuwait 1.3; Netherlands 3.5; Norway 0.8; Russia 2.3; Saudi Arabia 0.8; Turkey 34.0; United Kingdom 15.0; USA 0.7; Total (incl. others) 70.5.

TRANSPORT

Road Traffic (registered motor vehicles, 1996): Saloon cars 52,895; Estate cars 7,076; Pick-ups 2,855; Vans 6,489; Buses 1,585; Trucks 772; Lorries 4,760; Motor cycles 13,773; Agricultural tractors 5,896; Total (incl. others) 97,713.

Shipping (1996): Freight traffic ('000 metric tons): Goods loaded 508.0, Goods unloaded 646.0; Vessels entered 3,416.

Civil Aviation: Kilometres flown (Turkish Cypriot Airlines) 1,126,848 (1985); Passenger arrivals and departures 624,189 (1994); Freight landed and cleared (metric tons) 3,303 (1994).

TOURISM

Visitors (1996): 365,116 (including 289,131 Turkish); **Accommodation** (1996): Hotels 41, Tourist beds (in all tourist accommodation, including pensions and hotel-apartments) 8,267; **Net Receipts** (US $ million, 1996): 175.6.

COMMUNICATIONS MEDIA

Radio Receivers (1994, provisional): 56,450 in use.

Television Receivers (1994, provisional): 52,300 in use.

Telephones (31 December 1996): 70,845 subscribers.

EDUCATION

1996/97: *Primary and pre-primary education:* 124 institutions, 1,555 teachers, 24,546 pupils; *High schools:* 14 institutions, 639 teachers, 5,512 students; *Vocational schools:* 13 institutions, 341 teachers, 2,627 students; *Higher education:* 7 institutions, 18,388 students.

* Note: Following a unilateral declaration of independence in November 1983, the 'Turkish Federated State of Cyprus' became known as the 'Turkish Republic of Northern Cyprus'.

Directory

The Constitution

The Constitution, summarized below, entered into force on 16 August 1960, when Cyprus became an independent republic.

THE STATE OF CYPRUS

The State of Cyprus is an independent and sovereign Republic with a presidential regime.

The Greek Community comprises all citizens of the Republic who are of Greek origin and whose mother tongue is Greek or who share the Greek cultural traditions or who are members of the Greek Orthodox Church.

The Turkish Community comprises all citizens of the Republic who are of Turkish origin and whose mother tongue is Turkish or who share the Turkish cultural traditions or who are Muslims.

The official languages of the Republic are Greek and Turkish.

The Republic shall have its own flag of neutral design and colour, chosen jointly by the President and the Vice-President of the Republic.

The Greek and the Turkish Communities shall have the right to celebrate respectively the Greek and the Turkish national holidays.

THE PRESIDENT AND VICE-PRESIDENT

Executive power is vested in the President and the Vice-President, who are members of the Greek and Turkish Communities respectively, and are elected by their respective communities to hold office for five years.

The President of the Republic as Head of the State represents the Republic in all its official functions; signs the credentials of diplomatic envoys and receives the credentials of foreign diplomatic envoys; signs the credentials of delegates for the negotiation of international treaties, conventions or other agreements; signs the letter relating to the transmission of the instruments of ratification of any international treaties, conventions or agreements; confers the honours of the Republic.

The Vice-President of the Republic, as Vice-Head of the State, has the right to be present at all official functions; at the presentation of the credentials of foreign diplomatic envoys; to recommend to the President the conferment of honours on members of the Turkish Community, which recommendation the President shall accept unless there are grave reasons to the contrary.

The election of the President and the Vice-President of the Republic shall be direct, by universal suffrage and secret ballot, and shall, except in the case of a by-election, take place on the same day but separately.

The office of the President and of the Vice-President shall be incompatible with that of a Minister or of a Representative or of a member of a Communal Chamber or of a member of any municipal council including a Mayor or of a member of the armed or security forces of the Republic or with a public or municipal office.

The President and Vice-President of the Republic are invested by the House of Representatives.

The President and the Vice-President of the Republic in order to ensure the executive power shall have a Council of Ministers composed of seven Greek Ministers and three Turkish Ministers. The Ministers shall be designated respectively by the President and the Vice-President of the Republic who shall appoint them by an instrument signed by them both. The President convenes and presides over the meetings of the Council of Ministers, while the Vice-President may ask the President to convene the Council and may take part in the discussions.

The decisions of the Council of Ministers shall be taken by an absolute majority and shall, unless the right of final veto or return is exercised by the President or the Vice-President of the Republic or both, be promulgated immediately by them.

The executive power exercised by the President and the Vice-President of the Republic conjointly consists of:

Determining the design and colour of the flag.

Creation or establishment of honours.

Appointment of the members of the Council of Ministers.

Promulgation by publication of the decisions of the Council of Ministers.

Promulgation by publication of any law or decision passed by the House of Representatives.

Appointments and termination of appointments as in Articles provided.

Institution of compulsory military service.

Reduction or increase of the security forces.

Exercise of the prerogative of mercy in capital cases.

Remission, suspension and commutation of sentences.

Right of references to the Supreme Constitutional Court and publication of Court decisions.

Address of messages to the House of Representatives.

The executive powers which may be exercised separately by the President and Vice-President include: designation and termination of appointment of Greek and Turkish Ministers respectively; the right of final veto on Council decisions and on laws concerning foreign affairs, defence or security; the publication of the communal laws and decisions of the Greek and Turkish Communal Chambers respectively; the right of recourse to the Supreme Constitutional Court; the prerogative of mercy in capital cases; and addressing messages to the House of Representatives.

THE COUNCIL OF MINISTERS

The Council of Ministers shall exercise executive power in all matters, other than those which are within the competence of a Communal Chamber, including the following:

General direction and control of the government of the Republic and the direction of general policy.

Foreign affairs, defence and security.

Co-ordination and supervision of all public services.

Supervision and disposition of property belonging to the Republic.

Consideration of Bills to be introduced to the House of Representatives by a Minister.

Making of any order or regulation for the carrying into effect of any law as provided by such law.

Consideration of the Budget of the Republic to be introduced to the House of Representatives.

THE HOUSE OF REPRESENTATIVES

The legislative power of the Republic shall be exercised by the House of Representatives in all matters except those expressly reserved to the Communal Chambers.

The number of Representatives shall be 50, subject to alteration by a resolution of the House of Representatives carried by a majority comprising two-thirds of the Representatives elected by the Greek

Community and two-thirds of the Representatives elected by the Turkish Community.

Out of the number of Representatives 70% shall be elected by the Greek Community and 30% by the Turkish Community separately from amongst their members respectively, and, in the case of a contested election, by universal suffrage and by direct and secret ballot held on the same day.

The term of office of the House of Representatives shall be for a period of five years.

The President of the House of Representatives shall be a Greek, and shall be elected by the Representatives elected by the Greek Community, and the Vice-President shall be a Turk and shall be elected by the Representatives elected by the Turkish Community.

THE COMMUNAL CHAMBERS

The Greek and the Turkish Communities respectively shall elect from amongst their own members a Communal Chamber.

The Communal Chambers shall, in relation to their respective Community, have competence to exercise legislative power solely with regard to the following:

All religious, educational, cultural and teaching matters.

Personal status; composition and instances of courts dealing with civil disputes relating to personal status and to religious matters.

Imposition of personal taxes and fees on members of their respective Community in order to provide for their respective needs.

THE PUBLIC SERVICE AND THE ARMED FORCES

The public service shall be composed as to 70% of Greeks and as to 30% of Turks.

The Republic shall have an army of 2,000 men, of whom 60% shall be Greeks and 40% shall be Turks.

The security forces of the Republic shall consist of the police and gendarmerie and shall have a contingent of 2,000 men. The forces shall be composed as to 70% of Greeks and as to 30% of Turks.

OTHER PROVISIONS

The following measures have been passed by the House of Representatives since January 1964, when the Turkish members withdrew:

The amalgamation of the High Court and the Supreme Constitutional Court (see Judicial System section).

The abolition of the Greek Communal Chamber and the creation of a Ministry of Education.

The unification of the Municipalities.

The unification of the Police and the Gendarmerie.

The creation of a military force by providing that persons between the ages of 18 and 50 years can be called upon to serve in the National Guard.

The extension of the term of office of the President and the House of Representatives by one year intervals from July 1965 until elections in February 1968 and July 1970 respectively.

New electoral provisions; abolition of separate Greek and Turkish rolls; abolition of post of Vice-President, which was re-established in 1973.

The Government*

HEAD OF STATE

President: GLAVKOS KLERIDES (took office 28 February 1993; re-elected 15 February 1998).

COUNCIL OF MINISTERS

A Government of national unity, comprising DISY, EDEK, EDE (United Democrats) and Independents.

(September 1998)

Minister of Foreign Affairs: YIANNAKIS KASOULIDES (DISY).

Minister of Defence: YIANNAKIS OMIROU (EDEK).

Minister of the Interior: DINOS MICHAELIDES (Independent).

Minister of Finance: CHRISTODOULOS CHRISTODOULOU (DISY).

Minister of Justice and Public Order: NIKOS KOSHIS (DISY).

Minister of Commerce, Industry and Tourism: NICQS ROLANDIS (DISY).

Minister of Education and Culture: LYKOURGOS KAPPAS (Independent).

Minister of Health: CHRISTOS SOLOMIS (DISY).

Minister of Labour and Social Insurance: ANDREAS MOUSHATTAS (Independent).

Minister of Communications and Works: LEONTIOS IERODIAKONOU (DISY).

Minister of Agriculture, Natural Resources and the Environment: KOSTAS THEMISTOKLEOUS (EDE).

* Under the Constitution of 1960, the vice-presidency and three posts in the Council of Ministers are reserved for Turkish Cypriots. However, there has been no Turkish participation in the Government since December 1963. In 1968 President Makarios announced that he considered the office of Vice-President in abeyance until Turkish participation in the Government is resumed, but the Turkish community elected Rauf Denktaş Vice-President in February 1973.

MINISTRIES

Ministry of Agriculture, Natural Resources and the Environment: Loukis Akritas Ave, Nicosia; tel. (2) 300807; fax (2) 781156.

Ministry of Commerce, Industry and Tourism: 2 Andreas Araouzos St, Nicosia; tel. (2) 867100; fax (2) 375120.

Ministry of Communications and Works: Dem. Severis Ave, 1424 Nicosia; tel. (2) 302830; fax (2) 465462.

Ministry of Defence: 4 Emmanuel Roides St, Nicosia; tel. (2) 303187; fax (2) 366225.

Ministry of Education and Culture: Greg. Afxentiou St, 1434 Nicosia; tel. (2) 800600; fax (2) 427559; e-mail roc1@cytanet.com.cy.

Ministry of Finance: Ex Secretariat Compound, 1439 Nicosia; tel. (2) 302164; fax (2) 366080.

Ministry of Foreign Affairs: 18–19 Dem. Severis Ave, Nicosia; tel. (2) 300600; fax (2) 451881.

Ministry of Health: 10 Markou Drakou St, Nicosia; tel. (2) 309526; fax (2) 305803.

Ministry of the Interior: Dem. Severis Ave, Ex Secretariat Compound, Nicosia; tel. (2) 302238; fax (2) 453465.

Ministry of Justice and Public Order: 12 Helioupoleos, Nicosia; tel. (2) 303855; fax (2) 781427.

Ministry of Labour and Social Insurance: Byron Ave, Nicosia; tel. (2) 303481; telex 6011; fax (2) 450993.

President and Legislature

PRESIDENT

Election, 8 and 15 February 1998*

Candidates	Votes	%
GLAVKOS KLERIDES (Democratic Rally)	206,879 (158,763)	50.8 (40.1)
GEORGHIOS IACOVOU (Independent, with AKEL/DIKO support)	200,222 (160,918)	49.2 (40.6)
VASSOS LYSSARIDES (EDEK—Socialist Party)	— (41,978)	— (10.6)
ALEXIS GALANOS (Independent)	— (16,003)	— (4.0)
GEORGHIOS VASSILIOU (United Democrats)	— (11,908)	— (3.0)
NIKOS KOUTSOU (New Horizons)	— (3,625)	— (0.9)
NIKOS ROLANDIS (Liberal Party)	— (3,104)	— (0.8)
Total	407,101 (396,299)	100.0 (100.0)

* Figures from the first round of voting appear in brackets.

HOUSE OF REPRESENTATIVES

The House of Representatives originally consisted of 50 members, 35 from the Greek community and 15 from the Turkish community, elected for a term of five years. In January 1964 the Turkish members withdrew and set up the 'Turkish Legislative Assembly of the Turkish Cypriot Administration' (see p. 380). At the 1985 elections the membership of the House was expanded to 80 members, of whom 56 were to be from the Greek community and 24 from the Turkish community (according to the ratio of representation specified in the Constitution).

President: SPYROS KYPRIANOU.

Elections for the Greek Representatives, 26 May 1996

Party	Votes	% of Votes	Seats
DISY (Democratic Rally)/Liberal Party	127,380	34.5	20
AKEL (Communist Party) . .	121,958	33.0	19
DIKO (Democratic Party) . .	60,726	16.4	10
EDEK (Socialist Party) . . .	30,033	8.1	5
KED (Free Democrats)* .	13,623	3.7	2
New Horizons	6,317	1.7	—
ADISOK*	5,311	1.4	—
Ecologists	3,710	1.0	—
Independents	463	0.1	—
Total	369,521	100.0	56

* Merged in December 1996 to form Enomeni Dimokrates (United Democrats—EDE).

Political Organizations

Anorthotiko Komma Ergazomenou Laou (AKEL) (Progressive Party of the Working People): POB 1827, 4 Akamantos St, 1513 Nicosia; tel. (2) 761121; fax (2) 761574; e-mail k.e.akel@cytanet.com.cy; f. 1941; successor to the Communist Party of Cyprus (f. 1926); Marxist-Leninist; supports demilitarized, non-aligned and independent Cyprus; over 14,000 mems; Sec.-Gen. DEMETRIS CHRISTO-FIAS.

Dimokratiko Komma (DIKO) (Democratic Party): POB 3979, 50 Grivas Dhigenis Ave, Nicosia; tel. (2) 472002; fax (2) 366488; f. 1976; absorbed Enosi Kentrou (Centre Union, f. 1981) in 1989; supports settlement of the Cyprus problem based on UN resolutions; Pres. SPYROS KYPRIANOU; Vice-Pres. DINOS MICHAELIDES; Sec.-Gen. STATHIS KITTIS.

Dimokratikos Synagermos (DISY) (Democratic Rally): POB 5305, 23 Pindarou St, 1061 Nicosia; tel. (2) 759791; fax (2) 752751; e-mail disy@org.cy; internet http://www.disy.org.cy; f. 1976; absorbed Democratic National Party (DEK) in 1977 and New Democratic Front (NEDIPA) in 1988; advocates entry of Cyprus into the European Union and greater active involvement by the EU in the settlement of the Cyprus problem; 26,000 mems; Pres. NIKOS ANASTA-SIADES; Gen. Sec. ELENI VRAHIMI.

Enomeni Dimokrates (EDE) (United Democrats): POB 3494, 8 Iassonos St, Nicosia; tel. (2) 663030; fax (2) 664747; f. Dec. 1996 by merger of Ananeotiko Dimokratiko Socialistiko Kinema (ADISOK—Democratic Socialist Reform Movement) and Kinema ton Eleftheron Dimokraton (KED—Movement of Free Democrats); Pres. GEORGHIOS VASSILIOU; Gen. Sec. KOSTAS THEMISTOKLEOUS.

Komma ton Phileleftheron (Liberal Party): POB 7282, 19 Gregoriou Xenopoulou St, 1st Floor, Nicosia; tel. (2) 452117; telex 2483; fax (2) 368900; f. 1986; supports settlement of the Cyprus problem based on UN resolutions; Pres. NIKOS A. ROLANDIS; Gen. Sec. PHIVOS MAVROVOUNIOTIS.

Neyi Orizontes (NEO) (New Horizons): POB 2064, 9 Byzantiou St, Strovolos, Nicosia; tel. (2) 475333; fax (2) 476044; e-mail neo@logos.cy.net; f. 1996; supports settlement of the Cyprus problem through political means and the establishment of a non-federal unitary state with single sovereignty throughout the whole territory of the island; Pres. NIKOS KOUTSOU; Gen. Sec. STELIOS AMERIKANOS.

Pankyprio Komma Prosfygon ke Pligenton (PAKOP) (Pancyprian Party of Refugees and Stricken Persons): POB 1216, 7 Androkleous St, Nicosia; tel. (2) 458764; fax (2) 367053; f. 1991; Pres. YIANNAKIS EROTOKRITOU; Gen. Sec. CHRISTOS IOANNOU.

Socialistiko Komma Kyprou EDEK (EDEK Socialist Party of Cyprus): POB 1064, 40 Byron Ave, Nicosia; tel. (2) 458617; telex 3182; fax (2) 458894; f. 1969 as Ethniki Dimokratiki Enosi Kyprou (EDEK) (Cyprus National Democratic Union); supports independent, non-aligned, unitary, demilitarized Cyprus; advocates the establishment of a socialist structure; Pres. Dr VASSOS LYSSARIDES; First Vice-Pres. YIANNAKIS OMIROU.

Diplomatic Representation

EMBASSIES AND HIGH COMMISSIONS IN CYPRUS

Australia: 4 Annis Komninis St, 2nd Floor, Nicosia; tel. (2) 473001; fax (2) 366486; High Commissioner: J. W. SULLIVAN.

Bulgaria: POB 4029, 13 Konst. Paleologos St, 2406 Engomi, Nicosia; tel. (2) 472486; fax (2) 456598; Ambassador: ALEXEI IVANOV.

China, People's Republic: POB 4531, 28 Archimedes St, 2411 Engomi, Nicosia; tel. (2) 352182; telex 6376; fax (2) 353530; Ambassador: YIN ZUOJIN.

Cuba: 7 Yiannis Taliotis St, Strovolos 147, Nicosia; tel. (2) 512332; fax (2) 512331; Ambassador: MANUEL PARDIÑAS AJENO.

Czech Republic: POB 5202, 48 Arsinois St, 1307 Nicosia; tel. (2) 421118; fax (2) 421059; Chargé d'affaires: JIŘÍ MICHOVSKY.

Egypt: POB 1752, 3 Egypt Ave, 1097 Nicosia; tel. (2) 465144; telex 2102; fax (2) 462287; Ambassador: FADEL EL-KADI.

France: POB 1671, 6 Ploutarchou St, Engomi, Nicosia; tel. (2) 465258; telex 2389; fax (2) 452289; Ambassador: JEAN BERNARD DE VAIVRE.

Germany: POB 1795, 10 Nikitaras St, Ay. Omoloyitae, 1513 Nicosia; tel. (2) 664362; fax (2) 665694; Ambassador: Dr GABRIELE VON MALSEN-TILBORCH.

Greece: POB 1799, 8/10 Byron Ave, Nicosia; tel. (2) 441880; telex 2397; fax (2) 511290; Ambassador: KYRIAKOS RODOUSSAKIS.

Holy See: POB 1964, Holy Cross Catholic Church, Paphos Gate, 1515 Nicosia (Apostolic Nunciature); tel. (2) 462132; fax (2) 466767; Apostolic Pro-Nuncio: Most Rev. PIETRO SAMBI, Titular Archbishop of Belcastro (with residence in Jerusalem).

Hungary: POB 4067, 13/A Princess Anne St, 1700 Nicosia; tel. (2) 779074; fax (2) 779243; e-mail hungcomm@spidernet.com.cy; Ambassador: JÁNOS HERMAN.

India: POB 5544, 3 Indira Gandhi St, Engomi, Nicosia; tel. (2) 351741; telex 4146; fax (2) 350402; e-mail india@spidernet.com.cy; High Commissioner: SHYAMALA B. COWSIK.

Iran: POB 8145, 42 Armenias St, Akropolis, Nicosia; tel. (2) 314459; telex 6416; fax (2) 315446; Chargé d'affaires: ALI AKBAR FARAZI.

Israel: POB 1049, 4 I. Gryparis St, Nicosia; tel. (2) 445195; fax (2) 453486; Ambassador: SHEMI TZUR.

Italy: 11 25th March St, Engomi 2408, Nicosia; tel. (2) 357635; telex 3847; fax (2) 357616; Ambassador: FRANCESCO BASCONE.

Lebanon: POB 1924, 1 Vasilisis Olgas St, Nicosia; tel. (2) 442216; telex 3056; fax (2) 267662; Ambassador: ZEIDAN ZEIDAN.

Libya: POB 3669, 14 Estias St, 1041 Nicosia; tel. (2) 317366; telex 3277; fax (2) 316152; Chargé d'affaires: MUFTAH FITOURI.

Poland: 11 Acharnon St, Strovolos, Nicosia; tel. (2) 427077; fax (2) 510611.

Romania: 83 Kennedy Ave, Nicosia; tel. (2) 379303; fax (2) 379121; Chargé d'affaires: FLORIAN UNCHIASU.

Russia: Ay. Prokopias St and Archbishop Makarios III Ave, Engomi, Nicosia; tel. (2) 772141; telex 5808; fax (2) 774854; Ambassador: GEORGII MURATOV.

Slovakia: POB 1165, 4 Kalamatas St, 2002 Strovolos Nicosia; tel. (2) 311683; fax (2) 311715; Chargé d'affaires a.i.: DUŠAN ROZBORA.

Switzerland: POB 729, MEDCON Bldg, 6th Floor, 46 Themistoklis Dervis St, Nicosia; tel. (2) 766261; fax (2) 766008; Chargé d'affaires a.i.: MARGRITH BIERI.

Syria: POB 1891, Cnr Androkleous and Thoukidides Sts, Nicosia; tel. (2) 474481; telex 2030; fax (2) 446963; Chargé d'affaires a.i.: Dr AHMAD HAJ-IBRAHIM.

United Kingdom: POB 1978, Alexander Pallis St, Nicosia; tel. (2) 861100; fax (2) 861125; High Commissioner: DAVID MADDEN.

USA: 7 Ploutarchou, 2406 Engomi, Nicosia; tel. (2) 476100; fax (2) 465944; Ambassador: KENNETH BRILL.

Yugoslavia: 2 Vasilissis Olgas St, Nicosia; tel. (2) 445511; fax (2) 445910; Chargé d'affaires a.i.: IVAN MRKIĆ.

Judicial System

Supreme Council of Judicature: Nicosia. The Supreme Council of Judicature is composed of the President and Judges of the Supreme Court. It is responsible for the appointment, promotion, transfer, etc., of the judges exercising civil and criminal jurisdiction in the District Courts, the Assize Courts, the Family Courts, the Military Court and the Industrial Dispute Court.

SUPREME COURT

Supreme Court: Char. Mouskos St, Nicosia; tel. (2) 302237; fax (2) 304500. The Constitution of 1960 provided for a separate Supreme Constitutional Court and High Court but in 1964, in view of the resignation of their neutral presidents, these were amalgamated to form a single Supreme Court.

The Supreme Court is the final appellate court in the Republic and the final adjudicator in matters of constitutional and administrative law, including recourses on conflict of competence between state organs on questions of the constitutionality of laws, etc. It deals with appeals from Assize Courts and District Courts as well as from the decisions of its own judges when exercising original jurisdiction in certain matters such as prerogative orders of *habeas corpus*, *mandamus*, *certiorari*, etc., and in admiralty cases.

President: GEORGHIOS M. PIKIS.

Judges: I. C. Constantinides, T. Eliades, Chr. C. Artemides, G. Niko-laou, P. Kallis, Fr. G. Nikolaides, Y. Chr. Chrysostomis, S. Nikitas, P. Ch. Artemis, M. Kronides, A. Kramvis, R. Gavrielides.

Attorney-General: Alekos Markides.

OTHER COURTS

As required by the Constitution a law was passed in 1960 providing for the establishment, jurisdiction and powers of courts of civil and criminal jurisdiction, i.e. of six District Courts and six Assize Courts. In accordance with the provisions of new legislation, approved in 1991, a permanent Assize Court, with powers of jurisdiction in all districts, was established.

In addition to a single Military Court, there are specialized Courts concerned with cases relating to industrial disputes, rent control and family law.

'Turkish Republic of Northern Cyprus'

The Turkish intervention in Cyprus in July 1974 resulted in the establishment of a separate area in northern Cyprus under the control of the Autonomous Turkish Cypriot Administration, with a Council of Ministers and separate judicial, financial, police, military and educational machinery serving the Turkish community.

On 13 February 1975 the Turkish-occupied zone of Cyprus was declared the 'Turkish Federated State of Cyprus', and Rauf Denktaş declared President. At the second joint meeting held by the Executive Council and Legislative Assembly of the Autonomous Turkish Cypriot Administration, it was decided to set up a Constituent Assembly which would prepare a constitution for the 'Turkish Federated State of Cyprus' within 45 days. This Constitution, which was approved by the Turkish Cypriot population in a referendum held on 8 June 1975, was regarded by the Turkish Cypriots as a first step towards a federal republic of Cyprus. The main provisions of the Constitution are summarized below:

The 'Turkish Federated State of Cyprus' is a democratic, secular republic based on the principles of social justice and the rule of law. It shall exercise only those functions which fall outside the powers and functions expressly given to the (proposed) Federal Republic of Cyprus. Necessary amendments shall be made to the Constitution of the 'Turkish Federated State of Cyprus' when the Constitution of the Federal Republic comes into force. The official language is Turkish.

Legislative power is vested in a Legislative Assembly, composed of 40 deputies, elected by universal suffrage for a period of five years. The President is Head of State and is elected by universal suffrage for a period of five years. No person may be elected President for more than two consecutive terms. The Council of Ministers shall be composed of a prime minister and 10 ministers. Judicial power is exercised through independent courts.

Other provisions cover such matters as the rehabilitation of refugees, property rights outside the 'Turkish Federated State', protection of coasts, social insurance, the rights and duties of citizens, etc.

On 15 November 1983 a unilateral declaration of independence brought into being the 'Turkish Republic of Northern Cyprus', which, like the 'Turkish Federated State of Cyprus', was not granted international recognition.

The Constituent Assembly, established after the declaration of independence, prepared a new constitution, which was approved by the Turkish Cypriot electorate on 5 May 1985. The new Constitution is very similar to the old one, but the number of deputies in the Legislative Assembly was increased to 50.

HEAD OF STATE

President of the 'Turkish Republic of Northern Cyprus': Rauf R. Denktaş (assumed office as President of the 'Turkish Federated State of Cyprus' 13 February 1975; became President of the 'TRNC' 15 November 1983; re-elected for five-year terms on 9 June 1985, on 22 April 1990 and on 22 April 1995).

COUNCIL OF MINISTERS
(September 1998)

A coalition of the Demokrat Parti (DP) and the Ulusal Bırlık Partisi (UBP).

Prime Minister: Dr Derviş Eroğlu (UBP).

Minister of State and Deputy Prime Minister: Serdar Denktaş (DP).

Minister of Foreign Affairs and Defence: Taner Etkin (DP).

Minister of the Interior and Rural Affairs: İlkay Kamil (UBP).

Minister of Finance: Salih Coşar (DP).

Minister of the Economy: Erdal Onurhan (UBP).

Minister of Education, Culture, Youth and Sports: Günay Caymaz (UBP).

Minister of Agriculture and Forestry: Kenan Akın (DP).

Minister of Communications, Works and Tourism: Mehmet Bayram (UBP).

Minister of Social Welfare and Rehabilitation: Onur Borman.

Minister of Health and the Environment: Dr Ertuğrul Hasi-poğlu (UBP).

MINISTRIES

All ministries are in Lefkoşa (Nicosia). Address: Lefkoşa (Nicosia), Mersin 10, Turkey.

Prime Minister's Office: tel. (22) 83141; fax (22) 87280; e-mail talsin@cc.emu.edu.tr.

Ministry of State and Deputy Prime Minister's Office: tel. (22) 77283; telex 5744; fax (22) 73976.

Ministry of Agriculture and Forestry: tel. (22) 83735; telex 57419; fax (22) 86945.

Ministry of Communications, Works and Tourism: tel. (22) 83666; telex 57169; fax (22) 81891.

Ministry of the Economy and Finance: tel. (22) 83116; telex 57268; fax (22) 73049.

Ministry of Education, Culture, Youth and Sports: tel. (22) 83136; fax (22) 82334.

Ministry of Foreign Affairs and Defence: tel. (22) 83241; telex 57612; fax (22) 84290.

Ministry of Health and the Environment: tel. (22) 83173; fax (22) 83893.

Ministry of the Interior and Rural Affairs: tel. (22) 85453; fax (22) 83043.

Ministry of Social Welfare and Rehabilitation: tel. (22) 78765; fax (22) 76349.

PRESIDENT

Election, 15 April 1995* and 22 April 1995

Candidates	Votes		%	
Rauf R. Denktaş (Independent)	53,235	(37,541)	62.48	(40.40)
Dr Derviş Eroğlu (UBP) .	31,972	(22,476)	37.52	(24.19)
Özker Özgür (CTP) . .	—	(17,639)	—	(18.98)
Mustafa Akıncı (TKP) . .	—	(13,179)	—	(14.18)
Alpay Durduran (YKP) .	—	(1,619)	—	(1.74)
Ayhan Kaymak (Independent) .	—	(345)	—	(0.37)
Sami Güdenoğlu (Independent)	—	(133)	—	(0.14)
Total	85,207†(92,932)‡		100.00	(100.00)

* Figures from the first round of voting appear in brackets.

† Excluding 5,684 invalid votes.

‡ Excluding 3,560 invalid votes.

LEGISLATIVE ASSEMBLY

Speaker: Hakki Atun (DP).

Deputy Speaker: Olgun Paşalar (UBP).

General Election, 12 December 1993

Party	% of votes	Seats
Ulusal Bırlık Partisi	29.9	16
Demokrat Parti	29.2	16
Cumhuriyetçi Türk Partisi	24.2	13
Toplumcu Kurtuluş Partisi	13.3	5
Others*	3.5	—
Total	100.0	50

* The other parties that contested the election were the National Struggle Party, which won 2% of the votes; the Yeni Kıbrıs Partisi, which obtained 1.2%; and the Unity and Sovereignty Party, which won 0.3%.

POLITICAL ORGANIZATIONS

Cumhuriyetçi Türk Partisi (CTP) (Republican Turkish Party): 99A Şehit Salahi, Şevket Sok., Lefkoşa (Nicosia), Mersin 10, Turkey; tel. (22) 73300; fax (22) 81914; e-mail ctp@cypronet.net; f. 1970 by members of the Turkish community in Cyprus; socialist principles with anti-imperialist stand; district organizations at Gazi Mağusa (Famagusta), Girne (Kyrenia), Güzelyurt (Morphou) and Lefkoşa (Nicosia); Leader Mehmet Ali Talat; Gen. Sec. Mustafa Ferdi Soyer.

Demokrat Parti (DP) (Democrat Party): Lefkoşa (Nicosia), Mersin 10, Turkey; tel. (22) 83795; fax (22) 87130; f. 1992 by disaffected UBP representatives; merged with the Yeni Doğuş Partisi (New Dawn Party; f. 1984) and Sosyal Demokrat Partisi (Social Democrat Party) in May 1993; Leader SERDAR DENKTAŞ; Sec.-Gen. (vacant).

Hür Demokrat Parti (Free Democrat Party): Lefkoşa (Nicosia), Mersin 10, Turkey; f. 1991. Leader ÖZEL TAHSIN.

Toplumcu Kurtuluş Partisi (TKP) (Communal Liberation Party): 44 İkinci Selim Sok., Lefkoşa (Nicosia), Mersin 10, Turkey; tel. (22) 72555; f. 1976; merged with the Atılımcı Halk Partisi (Progressive People's Party, f. 1979) in 1989; democratic left party; wants a solution of Cyprus problem as an independent, non-aligned, bi-zonal and bi-communal federal state; Leader MUSTAFA AKINCI; Gen. Sec. HÜSEYİN ANGOLEMLİ.

Ulusal Bırlık Partisi (UBP) (National Unity Party): 9 Atatürk Meydanı, Lefkoşa (Nicosia), Mersin 10, Turkey; tel. (22) 73972; f. 1975; right of centre; based on Atatürk's reforms, social justice, political equality and peaceful co-existence in an independent, bi-zonal, bi-communal, federal state of Cyprus; Leader Dr DERVIŞ EROĞLU; Sec.-Gen. Dr VEHBI ZEKI SERTER.

Ulusal Dirilis Partisi (UDP) (National Revival Party): Lefkoşa (Nicosia), Mersin 10, Turkey; f. 1997; Leader ENVER EMIN.

Unity and Sovereignty Party (BEP): Lefkoşa (Nicosia), Mersin 10, Turkey; Leader ARIF SALIH KIRDAĞ.

Yeni Doğuş Partisi (New Dawn Party): Lefkoşa (Nicosia); f. 1984; merged with DP in May 1993, revived 1997.

Yeni Kıbrıs Partisi (YKP) (New Cyprus Party): Lefkoşa (Nicosia), Mersin 10, Turkey; tel. (22) 74917; fax (22) 71476; e-mail YKP@cc.emu.edu.tr; f. 1989; Leader ALPAY DURDURAN.

DIPLOMATIC REPRESENTATION
Embassy in the 'TRNC'

Turkey: Bedrettin Demirel Cad., Lefkoşa Büyükelçisi, Lefkoşa (Nicosia), Mersin 10, Turkey; tel. (22) 72314; fax (22) 82289; Ambassador: ERTUĞRUL APAKAN.

Turkey is the only country officially to have recognized the 'Turkish Republic of Northern Cyprus'.

JUDICIAL SYSTEM

Supreme Court: The highest court in the 'TRNC' is the Supreme Court. The Supreme Court functions as the Constitutional Court, the Court of Appeal and the High Administrative Court. The Supreme Court, sitting as the Constitutional Court, has exclusive jurisdiction to adjudicate finally on all matters prescribed by the Constitution. The Supreme Court, sitting as the Court of Appeal, is the highest appellate court in the 'TRNC'. It also has original jurisdiction in certain matters of judicial review. The Supreme Court, sitting as the High Administrative Court, has exclusive jurisdiction on matters relating to administrative law.

The Supreme Court is composed of a president and seven judges.

President: SALİH S. DAYIOĞLU.

Judges: GÖNÜL ERÖNEN, NEVVAR NOLAN, CELÂL KARABACAK, TANER ERGİNEL, METİN A. HAKKI, MUSTAFA ÖZKÖK, SEYİT A. BENSEN.

Subordinate Courts: Judicial power other than that exercised by the Supreme Court is exercised by the Assize Courts, District Courts and Family Courts.

Supreme Council of Judicature: The Supreme Council of Judicature, composed of the president and judges of the Supreme Court, a member appointed by the President of the 'TRNC', a member appointed by the Legislative Assembly, the Attorney-General and a member elected by the Bar Association, is responsible for the appointment, promotion, transfer and matters relating to the discipline of all judges. The appointments of the president and judges of the Supreme Court are subject to the approval of the President of the 'TRNC'.

Attorney-General: SAİT AKIN.

Religion

Greeks form 77% of the population and most of them belong to the Orthodox Church, although there are also adherents of the Armenian Apostolic Church, the Anglican Communion and the Roman Catholic Church (including Maronites). Most Turks (about 18% of the population) are Muslims.

CHRISTIANITY
The Orthodox Church of Cyprus

The Autocephalous Orthodox Church of Cyprus, founded in AD 45, is part of the Eastern Orthodox Church; the Church is independent, and the Archbishop, who is also the Ethnarch (national leader of the Greek community), is elected by representatives of the towns and villages of Cyprus. The Church comprises six dioceses, and in 1995 had an estimated 600,000 members.

Archbishop of Nova Justiniana and all Cyprus: Archbishop CHRYSOSTOMOS, POB 1130, Arch. Kyprianos St, Nicosia; tel. (2) 430696; fax (2) 432470.

Metropolitan of Paphos: Bishop CHRYSOSTOMOS.

Metropolitan of Kitium: Bishop CHRYSOSTOMOS, Dem. Lipertis St, Larnaca; fax (41) 55588.

Metropolitan of Kyrenia: Bishop PAULUS.

Metropolitan of Limassol: Bishop CHRYSANTHOS.

Metropolitan of Morphou: (vacant).

The Roman Catholic Church
Latin Rite

The Patriarchate of Jerusalem covers Israel, Jordan and Cyprus. The Patriarch is resident in Jerusalem (see the chapter on Israel).

Vicar Patriarchal for Cyprus: Father UMBERTO BARATO.

Maronite Rite

Most of the Roman Catholics in Cyprus are adherents of the Maronite rite. Prior to June 1988 the Archdiocese of Cyprus included part of Lebanon. At December 1996 the archdiocese contained an estimated 10,000 Maronite Catholics.

Archbishop of Cyprus: Most Rev. BOUTROS GEMAYEL, POB 2249, Maronite Archbishop's House, 8 Ayios Maronas St, Nicosia; tel. (2) 458877; fax (2) 368260.

The Anglican Communion

Anglicans in Cyprus are adherents of the Episcopal Church in Jerusalem and the Middle East, officially inaugurated in January 1976. The Church has four dioceses. The diocese of Cyprus and the Gulf includes Cyprus, Iraq and the countries of the Arabian peninsula.

Bishop in Cyprus and the Gulf: Rt Rev. CLIVE HANDFORD, c/o POB 2075, Diocesan Office, 2 Grigoris Afxentiou St, 1517 Nicosia; tel. (2) 451220; fax (2) 466553.

Other Christian Churches

Among other denominations active in Cyprus are the Armenian Apostolic Church and the Greek Evangelical Church.

ISLAM

Most adherents of Islam in Cyprus are Sunni Muslims of the Hanafi sect. The religious head of the Muslim community is the Mufti.

Mufti of Cyprus: AHMET CEMAL İLKTAÇ (acting), PK 142, Lefkoşa (Nicosia), Mersin 10, Turkey.

The Press
GREEK CYPRIOT DAILIES

Alithia (Truth): POB 1695, 26A Pindaros and Androklis St, 1060 Nicosia; tel. (2) 463040; fax (2) 463945; f. 1952 as a weekly, 1982 as a daily; morning; Greek; right-wing; Dir SOCRATIS HASIKOS; Chief Editor ALEKOS KONSTANTINIDES; circ. 11,000.

Apogevmatini (Afternoon): POB 5603, 5 Aegaleo St, Strovolos, Nicosia; tel. (2) 353603; fax (2) 353223; f. 1972; afternoon; Greek; independent; Dirs EFTHYMIOS HADJIEFTHIMIOU, ANTONIS STAVRIDES; Chief Editor ALKIS ANDREOU; circ. 8,000.

Cyprus Mail: POB 1144, 24 Vassilios Voulgaroktonos St, Nicosia; tel. (2) 462074; fax (2) 366385; e-mail cyprus.mail@cytanet.com.cy; internet http://www.cynews.com; f. 1945; morning; English; independent; Dir. KYRIACOS IAKOVIDES; Editor STEVEN MYLES; circ. 4,000.

Fileleftheros (Liberal): POB 1094, Commercial Centre, 1 Diogenous St, 3rd, 6th–7th Floor, Engomi, 1501 Nicosia; tel. (2) 590000; fax (2) 590122; e-mail artemiou@phileleftheros.com; f. 1955; morning; Greek; independent, moderate; Dir N. PATTICHIS; Editorial Dir A. LYKAVGIS; Chief Editor T. KOUNNAFIS; circ. 26,000.

Haravghi (Dawn): POB 1556, ETAK Bldg, 6 Akamantos St, Nicosia; tel. (2) 476356; fax (2) 365154; f. 1956; morning; Greek; organ of AKEL (Communist Party); Dir NIKOS KATSOURIDES; Chief Editor ANDREAS ROUSOS: circ. 9,000.

Machi (Battle): POB 7628, 4A Danaes, Engomi, Nicosia; tel. (2) 356676; fax (2) 356701; f. 1961; morning; Greek; right-wing; Dir SOTIRIS SAMSON; Chief Editor DEMETRIS SAVVIDES; circ. 3,000.

Simerini (Today): POB 1836, 31 Archangelos Ave, Strovolos, Nicosia; tel. (2) 353532; fax (2) 352298; f. 1976; morning; Greek; right-wing; supports DISY party; Dir KOSTAS HADJIKOSTIS; Chief Editor SAVVAS IAKOVIDES; circ. 9,000.

TURKISH CYPRIOT DAILIES

Bırlık (Unity): 43 Yediler Sok., PK 841, Lefkoşa (Nicosia), Mersin 10, Turkey; tel. (22) 72959; fax (22) 83959; f. 1980; Turkish; organ of UBP; Editor LÜTFI ÖZTER.

Halkın Sesi (Voice of the People): 172 Kyrenia Sok., Lefkoşa (Nicosia), Mersin 10, Turkey; tel. (22) 73141; telex 57173; f. 1942; morning; Turkish; independent Turkish nationalist; Editor AKAY CEMAL; circ. 6,000.

Kıbrıs: Dr Fazil Küçük Bul., Lefkoşa (Nicosia), Mersin 10, Turkey; tel. (22) 81922; telex 57177; fax 81934; Editor MEHMET ALI AKPINAR; circ. 13,000.

Ortam (Political Conditions): 158A Girne Cad., Lefkoşa (Nicosia), Mersin 10, Turkey; tel. (22) 74872; Turkish; organ of the TKP; Editor ÖZAL ZIYA; circ. 1,250.

Vatan (Homeland): Lefkoşa (Nicosia), Mersin 10, Turkey; Editor ERTEN KASIMOĞLU.

Yeni Demokrat (New Democrat): 1 Cengiz Han Cad., Kösklüçiftlik, Lefkoşa (Nicosia), Mersin 10, Turkey; tel. (22) 81485; fax (22) 72558; Turkish; organ of the DP; Editor MUSTAFA OKAN; circ. 450.

Yeni Düzen (New System): Yeni Sanayi Sok., Lefkoşa (Nicosia), Mersin 10, Turkey; tel. (22) 56658; fax (22) 53240; e-mail yeniduze @north-cyprus.net; Turkish; organ of the CTP; Editor ÖZKAN YORGAN-CIOĞLU; circ. 1,000.

GREEK CYPRIOT WEEKLIES

Athlitiki tis Kyriakis: 5 Epias, Engomi, Nicosia; tel. (2) 352966; fax (2) 348835; f. 1996; Greek; athletic; Dir PANAYIOTIS FELLOUKAS; Chief Editor SAWAS KOSHARIS; circ. 4,000.

Cyprus Financial Mirror: POB 4280, 80B Thermopylon St, 2007 Nicosia; tel. (2) 495790; fax (2) 495907; e-mail finmir@logos.cy.net; internet http://www.cfm.com.cy; f. 1993; English (with Greek-language supplement, Russian edition); independent; Dirs MASIS DER PARTHOGH, SHAVASB BOHDJALIAN; circ. 3,500.

Cyprus Weekly: POB 4977, Suite 102, Trust House, Gryparis St Nicosia; tel. (2) 666047; fax (2) 668665; f. 1979; English; independent; Dirs GEORGES DER PARTHOGH, ALEX EFTHYVOULOS, A. HADJIPAPAS; Chief Editor MARTYN HENRY; circ. 15,000.

Epilogi: 19 Nikitara St, Ay. Omologiles, Nicosia; tel. (2) 367345; fax (2) 367511; f. 1997; Greek; Chief Editor COSTAS ZACHARIADES.

Ergatiki Phoni (Workers' Voice): POB 5018, SEK Bldg, 23 Alkeou St, Engomi, Nicosia; tel. (2) 441142; fax (2) 476360; f. 1947; Greek; organ of SEK trade union; Dir MICHALAKIS IOANNOU; Chief Editor XENIS XENOFONTOS; circ. 10,000.

Ergatiko Vima (Workers' Tribune): POB 1185, 31-35 Archemos St, Nicosia; tel. (2) 349400; fax (2) 349382; f. 1956; Greek; organ of the PEO trade union; Editor-in-Chief KOSTAS GREKOS; circ. 14,000.

Official Gazette: Printing Office of the Republic of Cyprus, Nicosia; tel. (2) 302202; fax (2) 303175; f. 1960; Greek; published by the Government of the Republic of Cyprus.

Paraskinio (Behind the Scenes): 39 Kennedy Ave, Nicosia; tel. (2) 313334; fax (2) 314193; f. 1987; Greek; Dir and Chief Editor D. MICHAEL; cir. 3,000.

Selides (Pages): POB 1094, 1501 Nicosia; tel. (2) 590000; fax (2) 590122; f. 1991; Greek; Dir N. PATTICHIS; Chief Editor A. MICHAELIDES; circ. 16,500.

Ta Nea (News): POB 4349, 40 Vyronos Ave, Nicosia; tel. (2) 476575; fax (2) 476512; f. 1968; Greek; organ of EDEK (Socialist Party); Chief Editor PHYTOS SOCRATOUS; circ. 3,000.

Tharros (Courage): POB 7628, 4A Danaes, Engomi, Nicosia; tel. (2) 356676; fax (2) 356701; f. 1961; Greek; right-wing; Dir SOTIRIS SAMSON; Chief Editor DIMITRIS SAVVIDES; circ. 3,500.

To Periodiko: POB 1836, Dias Bldg, 31 Archangelos Ave, Strovolos, Nicosia; tel. (2) 353646; fax (2) 352268; f. 1986; Greek; Dir KOSTAS HADJIKOSTIS; Chief Editor PHILIPPOS STYLIANOU; circ. 16,000.

TURKISH CYPRIOT WEEKLIES

Cyprus Today: A. N. Graphics Ltd, Dr Fazil Küçük Bul., PK 831, Lefkoşa (Nicosia), Mersin 10, Turkey; tel. (22) 81922; fax (22) 81934; f. 1991; English; political, social, cultural and economic; Editor GILL FRASER; circ. 5,000.

Ekonomi (The Economy): Bedrettin Demirel Cad. No.90, Lefkoşa (Nicosia), Mersin 10, Turkey; tel. (22) 83760; telex 57511; fax (22) 83089; f. 1958; Turkish; published by the Turkish Cypriot Chamber of Commerce; Editor-in-Chief SAMI TAŞARKAN; circ. 3,000.

Şafak: PK 228, Lefkoşa (Nicosia), Mersin 10, Turkey; tel. (22) 71472; fax (22) 87910; f. 1992; Turkish; circ. 1,000.

Yeni Çağ: 28 Ramadan Cad., Lefkoşa (Nicosia), Mersin 10, Turkey; tel. (22) 74917; fax (22) 71476; f. 1990; Turkish; publ. of the YKP; circ. 500.

OTHER WEEKLIES

Lion: 55 AEC Episkopi, British Forces Post Office 53; tel. (5) 263263; fax (5) 263181; e-mail carl@dial.cylink.com.cy; distributed to British Sovereign Base Areas, United Nations Forces and principal Cypriot towns; weekly; includes British Forces Broadcasting Services programme guide; Editor CARL BEAUMONT; circ. 5,000.

Middle East Economic Survey: Middle East Petroleum and Economic Publications (Cyprus), POB 4940, 1355 Nicosia; tel. (2) 445431; telex 2198; fax (2) 474988; e-mail mees@spidernet.com.cy; f. 1957 (in Beirut); weekly review and analysis of petroleum, finance and banking, and political developments; Publr BASIM W. ITAYIM; Editor IAN SEYMOUR.

GREEK CYPRIOT PERIODICALS

Cool: POB 8205, 86 Iphigenias St, 2091 Nicosia; tel. (2) 378900; fax (2) 378916; f. 1994; Greek; youth magazine; Chief Editor: PROMETHEAS CHRISTOPHIDES; circ. 4,000.

Cypria (Cypriot Woman): POB 8506, 56 Kennedy Ave, 11th Floor, 1076 Nicosia; tel. (2) 494907; fax (2) 427051; f. 1983; every 2 months; Greek; Owner MARO KARAYIANNI; circ. 7,000.

Cyprus Bulletin: 1465 Nicosia; tel. (2) 801102; fax (2) 366123; e-mail pioxx@cytanet.com.cy; internet http://www.pio.gov.cy; f. 1964; fortnightly; Arabic, English, Greek, Spanish; published by the Cyprus Press and Information Office; Principal Officers M. CHARALAMPIDES, A. LYRITSAS, A. STYLIANOU; circ. 20,000.

Cyprus P.C.: POB 4989, Diogenous 1, Block C, Engomi, 1306 Nicosia; tel. (2) 343044; fax (2) 349867; e-mail mariao@infomedia .cy.net; internet http://www.infomedia.cy.net; f. 1990; monthly; Greek; computing magazine; Dir LAKIS VARNAVA; circ. 5,000.

Cyprus Time Out: POB 3697, 4 Pygmalionos St, 1010 Nicosia; tel. (2) 472949; fax (2) 360668; f. 1978; monthly; English; Dir ELLADA SOPHOCLEOUS; Chief Editor LYN HAVILAND; circ. 8,000.

Cyprus Today: c/o Ministry of Education and Culture, Nicosia; tel. (2) 303337; fax (2) 443565; f. 1963; quarterly; English; cultural and information review; published and distributed by Press and Information Office; Principal Officer NIKOS PANAYIOTOU; circ. 15,000.

Dimosios Ypallilos (Civil Servant): 3 Dem. Severis Ave, 1066 Nicosia; tel. (2) 442278; fax (2) 465189; fortnightly; published by the Cyprus Civil Servants' Association (PASYDY); circ. 14,000.

Eso-Etimos (Ever Ready): POB 4544, Nicosia; tel. (2) 443587; f. 1913; quarterly; Greek; publ. by Cyprus Scouts' Asscn; Editor TAKIS NEOPHYTOU; circ. 2,500.

Eva: 39 Kennedy, Nicosia; tel. (2) 493510; fax (2) 314193; f. 1996; Greek; Dir DINOS MICHAEL; Chief Editors CHARIS PONTIKIS, KATIA SAVVIDOU; circ. 4,000.

Hermes International: POB 4706, Nicosia; tel. (2) 581880; fax (2) 581884; f. 1992; quarterly; English; lifestyle, business, finance, management; Chief Editor ALAN GATHERGOOD; circ. 8,500.

Nicosia This Month: POB 1015, Nikoklis Publishing House, Ledras and Pygmalionos St, Nicosia; tel. (2) 473124; telex 5374; fax (2) 463363; f. 1984; monthly; English; Chief Editor ELLADA SOPHOCLEOUS; circ. 4,000.

Omicron: POB 5211, 1 Commercial Centre Diogenous, 2nd Floor, 1307 Nicosia; tel. (2) 590110; fax (2) 590410; f. 1996; Greek; Dir NIKOS CHR. PATTICHIS; Chief Editor STAVROS CHRISTODOULOU; circ. 8,000.

Paediki Chara (Children's Joy): POB 136, 18 Archbishop Makarios III Ave, 1065 Nicosia; tel. (2) 442638; fax (2) 360410; e-mail poed@ logos.cy.net; f. 1962; monthly; for pupils; publ. by the Pancyprian Union of Greek Teachers; Editor SOFOCLES CHARALAMBIDES; circ. 15,000.

Super Flash: POB 9246, 11 Kolokotronis St, Kaimakli, Nicosia; tel. (2) 437887; fax (2) 434197; f. 1979; fortnightly; Greek; Dir ANTHI VATI; circ. 4,000.

Synergatiko Vima (The Co-operative Tribune): Kosti Palama 5, 1095 Nicosia; tel. (2) 458757; fax (2) 446833; f. 1983; monthly; Greek; official organ of the Pancyprian Co-operative Confederation Ltd; circ. 5,000.

Synthesis (Composition): 39 Kennedy Ave, Nicosia; tel. (2) 429589; fax (2) 314193; f. 1988; every 2 months; Greek; interior decorating; Dir DINOS MICHAEL; circ. 6,000.

Tele Ores: POB 8205, 2nd Floor, 86 Iphigenias St, 2091 Nicosia; tel. (2) 378900; fax (2) 378916; f. 1993; Greek; fortnightly; television guide; Chief Editor PROMETHEAS CHRISTOPHIDES; circ. 17,000.

TV Kanali (TV Channel): POB 5603, 5 Aegaleo St, Strovolos, Nicosia; tel. (2) 353603; fax (2) 353223; f. 1993; Greek; Dirs A. STAVRIDES, E. HADJIEFTHYMIOU; Chief Editor CHARIS TOMAZOS; circ. 13,000.

TV Radio Programme: POB 1397, Cyprus Broadcasting Corpn, 1397 Nicosia; tel. (2) 422231; telex 2333; fax (2) 492867; e-mail rik@cybc.com.cy; fortnightly; Greek and English; published by the CyBC; radio and TV programme news; circ. 23,000.

TURKISH CYPRIOT PERIODICALS

Güvenlik Kuvvetleri Magazine: Lefkoşa (Nicosia), Mersin 10, Turkey; tel. (22) 75880; publ. by the Security Forces of the 'TRNC'.

Halkbilimi: Has-Der, PK 199, Lefkoşa (Nicosia), Mersin 10, Turkey; tel. (22) 83146; fax (22) 84125; f. 1986; 2 a year; publ. of Folk Arts Assoc.; academic; Turkish; Editors ENGIN ANIL, ÖCAL ERTEN; circ. 750.

Kıbrıs—Northern Cyprus Monthly: Ministry of Foreign Affairs and Defence, Lefkoşa (Nicosia), Mersin 10, Turkey; tel. (22) 83241; telex 57612; fax (22) 84290; f. 1963; Editor GÖNÜL ATANER.

Kültür Sanat Dergisi: Girne Cad. 92, Lefkoşa (Nicosia), Mersin 10, Turkey; tel. (22) 83313; telex 82432; publ. of Türk Bankası; circ. 1,000.

Kuzey Kıbrıs Kültür Dergisi (North Cyprus Cultural Journal): PK 157, Lefkoşa (Nicosia), Mersin 10, Turkey; tel. (22) 31298; f. 1987; monthly; Turkish; Chief Editor GÜNSEL DOĞASAL.

New Cyprus: PK 327, Lefkoşa (Nicosia), Mersin 10, Turkey; tel. (22) 78914; telex 2585; fax (22) 72592; English; publ. by the North Cyprus Research and Publishing Centre; also Turkish edition *Yeni Kıbrıs*; Editor AHMET C. GAZIOĞLU.

Pan Magazine: Atü Apt 4, Sht. İbrahim Yusuf Sok., Lefkoşa (Nicosia), Mersin 10, Turkey; tel. (22) 77813; f. 1980; Dir ARMAN RATIP.

OTHER PERIODICALS

The Blue Beret: POB 1642, HQ UNFICYP, 1590 Nicosia; tel. (2) 359550; fax (2) 359752; monthly; English; circ. 1,000.

International Crude Oil and Product Prices: Middle East Petroleum and Economic Publications (Cyprus), POB 4940, 1355 Nicosia; tel. (2) 445431; telex 2198; fax (2) 474988; e-mail mees@spidernet.com.cy; f. 1971 (in Beirut); 2 a year; review and analysis of petroleum price trends in world markets; Publisher BASIM W. ITAYIM.

NEWS AGENCIES

Cyprus News Agency: POB 3947, 7 Kastorias St, 2002 Strovolos, 1685 Nicosia; tel. (2) 319009; telex 4787; fax (2) 319006; e-mail cna@cytanet.com.cy; f. 1976; English and Greek; Dir (vacant).

Kuzey Kıbrıs Haber Ajansı (Northern Cyprus News Agency): Alirizin Efendi Cad., Vakiflar Işhani, Kat 2, No. 3, Ortaköy, Lefkoşa (Nicosia), Mersin 10, Turkey; tel. (22) 81922; telex 57536; fax (22) 81934; f. 1977; Dir-Gen. M. ALI AKPINAR.

Papyrus General Press Distribution Agency: POB 12669, 5 Arch. Kyprianou, Latsia, Nicosia; tel. (2) 488855; fax (2) 488883.

TürkAjansı-Kıbrıs (TAK) (Turkish News Agency of Cyprus): POB 355, 30 Mehmet Akif Cad., Lefkoşa (Nicosia), Mersin 10, Turkey; tel. (22) 71818; telex 57448; fax (22) 71213; e-mail tak@cc.emu.edu.tr; internet http://www.emu.edu.tr/ruTak; f. 1973; Dir EMIR HÜSEYIN ERSOY.

Foreign Bureaux

Agence France-Presse (AFP) (France): POB 7242, Loizides Centre, 7th Floor, 36 Kypranoros St, Nicosia; tel. (2) 754050; telex 2824; fax (2) 765125; e-mail nicosie.redaction@afp.com; Bureau Chief MICHEL GARIN.

Agencia EFE (Spain): 64 Metochiou St, Office 401, Nicosia; tel. (2) 775725; fax (2) 781662; Correspondent DOMINGO DEL PINO.

Agenzia Nazionale Stampa Associata (ANSA) (Italy): Middle East Office, 10 Katsonis St, Ayii Omoloyites, Nicosia; tel. (2) 491699; telex 4139; fax (2) 492702; Rep. VITTORIO FRENQUELLUCCI.

Associated Press (AP) (USA): POB 4853, Neoelen Marina, 10 Katsonis St, Nicosia; tel. (2) 492599; telex 2459; fax (2) 491617; Correspondent ALEX EFTY.

Athinaikon Praktorion Eidiseon (Greece): Flat 64, Tryfonos Bldg, Eleftherias Sq., 1011 Nicosia; tel. (2) 441110; fax (2) 457418; Rep. GEORGE LEONIDAS.

Bulgarian News Agency: 1 Konstantinou Kavafi St, Limassol; tel. (5) 332187.

Informatsionnoye Telegrafnoye Agentstvo Rossii—Telegrafnoye Agentstvo Suverennykh Stran (ITAR—TASS) (Russia): POB 2235, 5–6 Evangelias St, Archangelos, Nicosia; tel. (2) 382486; telex 2368; Rep. ALEXEI YEROVTCHENKOV.

Iraqi News Agency: POB 1098, Flat 201, 11 Ippocratous St, Nicosia; tel. (2) 472095; telex 2197; fax (2) 472096; Correspondent AHMAD SULEYMAN.

Jamahiriya News Agency (JANA) (Libya): Flat 203, 12 Kypranoros, Nicosia; tel. (2) 361129; Rep. MOHAMED ALI ESHOWEIHIDI.

Polska Agencja Prasowa (PAP) (Poland): POB 2373, Prodromos St 24, Nicosia; Rep. MICHALAKIS PANTELIDES.

Prensa Latina (Cuba): 12 Demophon St, 5th Floor, Apt 501, Nicosia; tel. (2) 464131; telex 4505; Rep. LEONEL NODAL.

Reuters: POB 5725, 5th Floor, George and Thelma Paraskevaides Foundation Bldg, 36 Grivas Dhigenis Ave, Nicosia; tel. (2) 365087; telex 4922; fax (2) 475487; Correspondent MICHELE KAMBAS.

Sofia-Press Agency (Bulgaria): 9 Roumeli St, Droshia, Larnaca; tel. (4) 494484; Rep. IONKA VERESIE.

United Press International (UPI) (USA): 24A Heroes Ave, Nicosia 171; tel. (2) 456643; telex 2260; fax (2) 455998; Rep. GEORGES DER PARTHOGH.

Xinhua (New China) News Agency (People's Republic of China): 12 Byzantiou St, Flat 201, Ayios Dhometios, Nicosia; tel. (2) 590133; telex 5265; fax (2) 590146; Rep. HUANG JIANMING.

Publishers

GREEK CYPRIOT PUBLISHERS

Action Publications: POB 4676, 35 Ayiou Nicolaou St, Engomi, 1302 Nicosia; tel. (2) 590555; fax (2) 590048; e-mail actionpr@spidernet.com.cy; f. 1971; travel; Pres. TONY CHRISTODOULOU.

Alithia (Truth): POB 1695, 5 Pindaros and Adroklis St, Nicosia; tel. (2) 463040; fax (2) 463945.

Andreou Chr. Publications: POB 2298, 67a Regenis St, Nicosia; tel. (2) 466813; fax (2) 466649; f. 1979.

James Bendon Ltd: POB 6484, 3307 Limasol; tel. (5) 5311235; fax (5) 5311228; e-mail bendon@dial.cylink.com.cy; Pres. JAMES BENDON: Vice-Pres. RIDA BENDON.

Chrysopolitissa: 27 Al. Papadiamantis St, 2400 Nicosia; tel. (2) 353929; e-mail rina@spidernet.com.cy.

KY KE M: POB 4108, Nicosia; tel. (2) 450302; fax (2) 463624; Pres. NIKOS KOUTSOU.

Leventis Foundation: c/o Cyprus Museum, 28 Soufoulis St, Nicosia; tel. (2) 461706; fax (2) 459090.

MAM (The House of Cyprus Publications): POB 1722, Phaneromeni Library Building, 46 Phaneromeni St, Nicosia; tel. (2) 472744; fax (2) 465411; e-mail mam@logos.cy.net; f. 1965.

Nikoklis Publishing House: POB 3697, Nicosia; tel. (2) 456544; fax (2) 360668; Man. ELLADA SOPHOCLEOUS.

Omilos Pnevmatikis Ananeoseos: 29 Ionon St, Nicosia; tel. (2) 477654; fax (2) 311931

Pierides Foundation: Larnaca; tel. (2) 442483; fax (2) 466412.

POLTE (Pancyprian Organization of Tertiary Education): c/o Higher Technical Institute, Nicosia; tel. (2) 305030; fax (2) 494953; Pres. KOSTAS NEOKLEOUS.

Romantic Cyprus: POB 2375, Nicosia; fax (2) 445155.

TURKISH CYPRIOT PUBLISHERS

Birlik Gazetesi: Yediler Sok., Lefkoşa (Nicosia), Mersin 10, Turkey; tel. (22) 72959; f. 1980; Dir MEHMET AKAR.

Bolan Matbaası: 35 Pençizade Sok., Lefkoşa (Nicosia), Mersin 10, Turkey; tel. (22) 74802.

Devlet Basımevi (Turkish Cypriot Government Printing House): Şerif Arzik Sok., Lefkoşa (Nicosia), Mersin 10, Turkey; tel. (22) 72010; Dir S. KÜRŞAD.

Halkın Sesi Ltd: 172 Girne Cad., Lefkoşa (Nicosia), Mersin 10, Turkey; tel. (22) 73141.

Kema Matbaası: 1 Tabak Hilmi Sok., Lefkoşa (Nicosia), Mersin 10, Turkey; tel. (22) 72785.

K. Rüstem & Bro.: 22–24 Girne Cad., Lefkoşa (Nicosia), Mersin 10, Turkey; tel. (22) 71418.

Sebil International Press: 59 Atatürk Ave, Gönyeli, PK 7, Lefkoşa (Nicosia), Mersin 10, Turkey; tel. (22) 46805; fax (22) 31080; f. 1985; technical and scientific; Principal Officer E. BAŞARAN.

Tezel Matbaası: 35 Şinasi Sok., Lefkoşa (Nicosia), Mersin 10, Turkey; tel. (22) 71022.

Broadcasting and Communications

TELECOMMUNICATIONS

Cyprus Telecommunications Authority (CYTA): POB 4929, Nicosia; tel. (2) 313111; fax (2) 494940; internet http://www.cytanet.com.cy; provides national, international and cellular services in Cyprus.

BROADCASTING

Radio

Cyprus Broadcasting Corporation (CyBC): POB 4824, Broadcasting House, 1397 Nicosia; tel. (2) 422231; telex 2333; fax (2) 314050; e-mail rik@cybc.com.cy; internet http://www.cybc.com.cy; radio f. 1952; Programme I in Greek, Programme II in Greek, Turkish, English and Armenian, Programme III in Greek; two medium wave transmitters of 100 kW in Nicosia with relay stations at Paphos and Limassol; three 30 kW ERP VHF FM stereo transmitters on Mount Olympus; and three relay stations; Chair. ANTONIS DRAKOS; Dir-Gen. PAVLOS SOTERIADES; Head of Radio (vacant).

Logos: Church of Cyprus, POB 7400, 1644 Nicosia; tel. (2) 355444; fax (2) 355737; e-mail director@logos.cy.net; Chair. ANDREAS PHIL-IPPOU; Dir Gen. CHRISTODOULOS PROTOPAPAS.

Radio Astra: POB 8892, 145 Athalassas Ave, Strovolos, 2045 Nicosia; tel. (2) 313200; fax (2) 319261; Chair. ANDREAS ALONEFTIS; Dir TAKIS HADJIGEORGIOU.

Radio Proto: POB 3477, 31 Archangelos St, Parissinos, 2054 Nicosia; tel. (2) 353545; fax (2) 352266; Chair. KOSTAS HADJIKOSTIS; Gen. Man. PAVLOS PAPACHRISTODOULOU.

Services Sound and Vision Corpn, Cyprus: Akrotiri, British Forces Post Office 57; tel. (5) 252009; fax (5) 268580; e-mail patrick e@bfbs.com; f. 1948; incorporates the British Forces Broadcasting Service, Cyprus; broadcasts a two-channel 24-hour radio service in English on VHF; Station Man. PATRICK EADE; Engineering Man. DAVE RAMSAY.

Bayrak Radio and TV Corpn (BRTK): Atatürk Sq., Lefkoşa (Nicosia), Mersin 10, Turkey; tel. (22) 85555; telex 57264; fax (22) 81991; e-mail brt@cc.emu.edu.tr; internet http://www.cc.emu.edu.tr; in July 1983 it became an independent Turkish Cypriot corpn, partly financed by the Govt; Radio Bayrak f. 1963; home service in Turkish, overseas service in Turkish, Greek, English, Arabic and German; broadcasts 52.5 hours per day; Chair. GÜNAY YORGANCIOĞLU; Dir. ISMET KOTAK; Head of Radio ŞIFA NESIM.

Türkiye Radyo Televizyon (TRT): 3 channels of radio programmes in Turkish, transmitted to the Turkish sector of Cyprus.

First FM and Interfirst FM: Lefkoşa (Nicosia), Mersin 10, Turkey; f. 1996.

Kıbrıs FM: Dr Fazil Küçük Blvd, Yeni Sanayi Bolgesi, Lefkoşa (Nicosia), Mersin 10, Turkey; tel. (22) 81922; fax (22) 81934; Dir MEHMET ALI AKPINAR.

Radio Emu: Gazi Mağusa (Famagusta), Mersin 10, Turkey; e-mail radioemu@cc.emu.edu.tr; internet http://www.emu.edu.tr/~radioemu.

Television

In 1991, under an agreement between Cyprus and Greece, Cypriot viewers were to be given access to Greek television channels for several hours daily via satellite.

Antenna T.V.: POB 923, 1655 Nicosia: tel. (2) 311111; fax (2) 314959; Chair. LOUCIS PAPAPHILIPPOU; Gen. Man. IOANNIS PAPOUTS-ANIS (acting).

Cyprus Broadcasting Corporation (CyBC): POB 4824, Broadcasting House, 1397 Nicosia; tel. (2) 422231; telex 2333; fax (2) 314050; e-mail rik@cybc.com.cy; television f. 1957; **Channel 1:** one Band III 100/10 kW transmitter on Mount Olympus. **Channel 2:** one Band IV 100/10 kW ERP transmitter on Mount Olympus. **ET 1:** one Band IV 100/10 kW ERP transmitter on Mount Olympus for transmission of the ETI Programme received, via satellite, from Greece. The above three TV channels are also transmitted from 77 transposer stations; Chair. ANTONIS DRAKOS; Dir-Gen. PAVLOS SOTERIADES.

Lumier T.V. Ltd.: POB 6556, 1 Diogenous, Block A, 1st and 2nd Floors, 2122 Nicosia; tel. (2) 357272; fax (2) 354638; encoded signal; Chair. CHRIS ECONOMIDES; Gen. Man. AKIS AVRAAMIDES.

O Logos: POB 7400, 1644 Nicosia; tel. (2) 355444; fax (2) 355737; e-mail director@logos.cy.net; Chair. ANDREAS PHILIPPOU; Dir CHRISTO-DOULOS PROTOPAPAS.

Services Sound and Vision Corpn, Cyprus: Akrotiri, British Forces Post Office 57; tel. (5) 252009; fax (5) 268580; e-mail patrick@bfbs.com; f. 1948; incorporates the British Forces Broadcasting Service, Cyprus; broadcasts a daily TV service; Station Man. PATRICK EADE; Engineering Man. DAVE RAMSAY.

Sigma: POB 1836, 1513 Nicosia; tel. (2) 357070; fax (2) 352237; island-wide coverage; Chair. and Dir KOSTAS HADJIKOSTIS; Man. DINOS MENELAOU; New Business Devt Dir VIVIEN LADOMATOS.

Bayrak Radio and TV Corpn (BRTK): Atatürk Sq., Lefkoşa (Nicosia), Mersin 10, Turkey; tel. (22) 85555; telex 57264; fax (22) 81991; e-mail brt@cc.emu.edu.tr; internet http://www.cc.emu.edu.tr/press/brt/brt.htm; in July 1983 it became an independent Turkish Cypriot corpn, partly financed by the Govt; Bayrak TV f. 1976; transmits programmes in Turkish, Greek, English and Arabic on nine channels; Chair. GÜNAY YORGANCIOĞLU; Dir. ISMET KOTAK; Head of Television TÜLIN URAL.

Türkiye Radyo Televizyon (TRT): 2 channels of television programmes in Turkish, transmitted to the Turkish sector of Cyprus.

Finance

(brs = branches; cap. = capital; p.u. = paid up; auth. = authorized; dep. = deposits; res = reserves; m. = million; amounts in Cyprus pounds)

BANKING
Central Bank

Central Bank of Cyprus: POB 5529, 80 Kennedy Ave, 1395 Nicosia; tel. (2) 379800; telex 2424; fax (2) 378153; e-mail cbcinfo@centralbank.gov.cy; f. 1963; cap. p.u. 15m., res 15m., dep. 828m. (Dec. 1997); Gov. A. C. AFXENTIOU.

Greek Cypriot Banks

Bank of Cyprus Group: POB 1472, 51 Stassinos St, Ayia Paraskevi, Strovolos 140, 1599 Nicosia; tel. (2) 378000; telex 2451; fax (2) 378111; e-mail tsolakis@logos.cy.net; f. 1899, reconstituted 1943 by the amalgamation of Bank of Cyprus, Larnaca Bank Ltd and Famagusta Bank Ltd; cap. 74.0m., res 46.8m. (Dec. 1996); Chair. SOLON A. TRIANTAFYLLIDES; Group Chief Exec. CHR. PANTZARIS; 253 brs.

Co-operative Central Bank Ltd: POB 4537, 8 Gregoris Afxentiou St, 1389 Nicosia; tel. (2) 442921; telex 2313; fax (2) 360261; f. 1937 under the Co-operative Societies Law; banking and credit facilities to member societies, importer and distributor of agricultural requisites, insurance agent; cap. 0.1m., res 4.9m., dep. 491m. (Dec 1997); Chair. A. SOTERIADES; Sec.-Gen. D. PITSILLIDES; 4 brs.

The Cyprus Popular Bank Ltd: POB 2032, Popular Bank Bldg, 154 Limassol Ave, 1598 Nicosia; tel. (2) 752000; telex 2494; fax (2) 811491; f. 1901; full commercial banking; cap. 75.1m., res 85.7m. dep. 2,172.9m. (Dec. 1996); Chair. and Group Chief Exec. KIKIS N. LAZARIDES; 143 local brs.

Hellenic Bank Ltd: POB 4747, 1394 Nicosia; tel. (2) 360000; telex 3311; fax (2) 454074; e-mail hellenic@hellenicbank.com; f. 1974; financial services group; cap. p.u. 21.3m., res 25.7m., dep. 850.5m. (1996); Chair. and Chief Exec. PANOS CHR. GHALANOS; 115 brs.

Housing Finance Corpn: POB 3898, 41 Themistoklis Dervis St, Hawaii Tower, Nicosia; tel. (2) 761777; fax (2) 762870; f. 1980; provides long-term loans for home-buying; cap. 8.8m., res 134.2m. (Dec. 1997); Chair. I. TYPOGRAPHOS; Gen. Man. CH. SHAMBARTAS; 5 brs.

Lombard NatWest Bank Ltd: POB 1661, Cnr of Chilon and Gladstone St, Stylianos Lenas Square, Nicosia; tel. (2) 474333; telex 2262; fax (2) 457870; f. 1960; locally incorporated although foreign-controlled; cap. 6.0m., res 3.5m., dep. 294.6m. (Sept. 1997); Chair. M. G. KOLOKASSIDES; Man. Dir E. IOANNOU; 22 brs.

National Bank of Greece (Cyprus) Ltd: POB 1191, Galaxias Centre, 2nd Floor, 36 Ayias Elenis St, 1597 Nicosia; tel. (2) 362262; telex 2445; fax (2) 362090; f. 1994 by incorporating all local business of the National Bank of Greece SA; full commercial banking; cap. p.u. 15m. (Jan. 1997); Chair. TH. KARATZAS; Man. Dir M. TAGAROULIAS; 29 brs.

Turkish Cypriot Banks
(amounts in Turkish liras)

Akdeniz Garanti Bankası Ltd: PK 149, 2–4 Celaliye Sok. Inönu Meydan, Lefkoşa (Nicosia), Mersin 10, Turkey; tel. (22) 86742; telex 57572; fax (22) 86741; f. 1989 as Mediterranean Guarantee Bank; cap. 49,337.0m., res 116,556.2m., dep. 3,434,030.4m. (Dec. 1997); Chair. GÜLTEKIN BOĞAÇHAN.

Asbank Ltd: 8 Mecidiye Sok., PK 448, Lefkoşa (Nicosia), Mersin 10, Turkey; tel. (22) 83023; telex 57305; fax (22) 81244; f. 1986; cap. and res 620,716m., dep. 7,204,395m. (Dec. 1997); Chair. MUSTAFA ALTUNER; Exec. Dir M. ERGUN OLGUN; 6 brs.

Cyprus Altinbaş Bank Ltd: PK 843, 2 Müftü Ziyai Efendi Sok., Lefkoşa (Nicosia), Mersin 10, Turkey; tel. (22) 82222; telex 57347; fax (22) 83603; f. 1993; cap. 50,000m., res 8,050m., dep. 901,051m. (Dec. 1996); Chair. VAKKAS ALTINBAŞ; Gen. Man. OLGUN BEYOĞLU.

Everest Bank Ltd: Sarayönü 23A, Lefkoşa (Nicosia), Mersin 10, Turkey; tel. (22) 88281; telex 57624; fax (22) 89787; f. 1993; cap. 50,000m., res 28,366m., dep. 680,344m. (Dec. 1995); Pres. and Chair. ELMAS GÜZELYURTLU; 6 brs.

First Merchant Bank OSH Ltd.: 25 Serif Arzik Sok., Lefkoşa (Nicosia), Mersin 10, Turkey; tel. (22) 75373; telex 57376; fax (22) 75377; f. 1993; also provides offshore services; cap. US $10m., res US $2.9m., dep. US $1,667.2m. (March 1998); Chair. and Gen. Man. Dr H. YAMAN.

Kıbrıs Endüstri Bankası Ltd: (Industrial Bank of Cyprus Ltd): Bedrettin Demirel Cad., Başbakanlık Kavşağı, Lefkoşa (Nicosia), Mersin 10, Turkey; tel. (22) 83770; telex 57397; fax (22) 71830.

Kıbrıs Eurobank Ltd: PK 35, 18 Mecidiye Sok., Lefkoşa (Nicosia), Mersin 10, Turkey; tel. (22) 87382; telex 57629; fax (22) 87670; f. 1993; cap. 25,000m., dep. 36,835m. (Dec. 1994); Pres. and Chair. KEMAL AKKAYA; Gen. Man. YALÇIN POYRAZ.

Kıbrıs Finansbank Ltd: 13 İplik Pazari St, Lefkoşa (Nicosia), Mersin 10, Turkey; tel. (22) 75141; telex 57440; fax (22) 72298; f. 1997; cap. 55,000m., res 280m., dep. 949,246m. (Dec. 1997); Pres. and Chair. FEHIM KÜÇÜK.

Kıbrıs Hürbank Ltd (Cyprus Liberal Bank Ltd): Sht. Tekin Yurdabak Cad., POB 887, Göçmenköy, Lefkoşa (Nicosia), Mersin 10, Turkey; tel. (22) 36612; telex 57631; fax (22) 36707; f. 1993; Chair. Dr ERDOĞAN MIRATA; Gen. Man. MAHMUT SEZINLER; 6 brs.

Kıbrıs İktisat Bankası Ltd: 151 Bedrettin Demirel Cad., Lefkoşa (Nicosia), Mersin 10, Turkey; tel. (22) 85300; fax (22) 86860; f. 1990; cap. 50,000m., res 41,219m., dep. 775,869m. (Dec. 1995); Chair. METİN MENTESH; Gen. Man. METE OZMERTER; 5 brs.

Kıbrıs Kredi Bankası Ltd (Cyprus Credit Bank Ltd): 5–7 İplik Pazarı Sok., Lefkoşa (Nicosia), Mersin 10, Turkey; tel. (22) 75026; telex 57336; fax (22) 76999; f. 1978; cap. p.u. 30,930m., res 164,131m., dep. 2,628,193m. (Dec. 1994); Chair. SALIH BOYACI; Gen. Man. YÜKSEL YAZGIN; 12 local brs.

Kıbrıs Ticaret Bankası Ltd (Cyprus Commercial Bank Ltd): 111 Bedrettin Demirel Ave, Lefkoşa (Nicosia), Mersin 10, Turkey; tel. (22) 83180; telex 57395; fax (22) 82278; f. 1982; cap. p.u. 89,860m., res 436,084m., dep. 6,582,073m. (Dec. 1997); Chair. YÜKSEL AHMET RAŞİT; Gen. Man. PEKER M. TURGUD; 9 brs.

Kıbrıs Türk Kooperatif Merkez Bankası Ltd (Cyprus Turkish Co-operative Central Bank): 49–55 Mahmut Paşa Sok., PK 823, Lefkoşa (Nicosia), Mersin 10, Turkey; tel. (22) 73398; telex 57558; fax (22) 76787; e-mail ataman@coopcb.com; f. 1959; cap. and res 914,817m., dep. 12,236,327m. (Dec. 1996); banking and credit facilities to member societies and individuals; Chair. EREN RIFAT ERTANIN; Gen. Man. TAŞKENT ATASAYAN; 10 brs.

Kıbrıs Vakiflar Bankası Ltd: 58 Yediler Sok., PK 212, Lefkoşa (Nicosia), Mersin 10, Turkey; tel. (22) 75109; telex 57122; fax (22) 75169; f. 1982; cap. and res 32,220m., dep. 922,750m. (Dec. 1994); Chair. Dr TUNCER ARIFOĞLU; 6 brs.

Limassol Turkish Co-operative Bank Ltd: 10 Orhaneli Sok., Kyrenia, PK 27, Mersin 10, Turkey; tel. (2) 8156786; telex 57607; fax (2) 8156959; f. 1939; cap. 5,890m., res 121,102m, dep. 3,982,849m. (Dec. 1996); Chair. GÜZEL HALIM; Gen. Man. TANER EKDAL.

Türk Bankası Ltd (Turkish Bank Ltd): 92 Girne Cad., PK 242, Lefkoşa (Nicosia), Mersin 10, Turkey; tel. (22) 83313; telex 2585; fax (22) 82432; f. 1901; cap. p.u. 1,000,019m., res 2,039,895m., dep. 33,477,487m. (Dec. 1996); Chair. M. TANJU ÖZYOL; Gen. Man. C. YENAL MUSANNIF; 12 brs.

Turkish Cypriot Bankers' Association

Northern Cyprus Bankers' Association: Lefkoşa (Nicosia), Mersin 10, Turkey; f. 1987; tel. (22) 83180; fax (22) 82278; 31 mems (1998).

Investment Organization

Cyprus Investment and Securities Corpn: POB 597, Ghinis Bldg, 4th Floor, 58–60 Dhigenis Akritas Ave, Nicosia; tel. (2) 451535; fax (2) 445481; f. 1982 to promote development of capital market; member of Bank of Cyprus Group; issued cap. 1m. (1990); Chair. J. CL. CHRISTOPHIDES; Gen. Man. SOKRATES R. SOLOMIDES.

Development Bank

The Cyprus Development Bank Ltd: POB 1415, Alpha House, 50 Archbishop Makarios III Ave, 1508 Nicosia; tel. (2) 457575; telex 2797; fax (2) 464322; f. 1963; cap. 12.0m., res 5.2m., dep. 75.5m. (Dec. 1996); aims to accelerate the economic development of Cyprus by providing medium- and long-term loans for productive projects, developing the capital market, encouraging joint ventures and providing technical and managerial advice to productive private enterprises; Chair. J. CHR. STRONGYLOS; Gen. Man. JOHN G. JOANNIDES; 1 br.

Savings Bank

Universal Savings Bank Ltd (Designated Financial Institution): POB 8510, Kennedy Ave 6A, 2080 Nicosia; tel. (2) 764111; telex 2720; fax (2) 767175; e-mail offshore@universalbank.com.cy; internet http://www.universalbank.com.cy; f. 1908 (closed 1974, reopened 1990); provides loan facilities and other banking services; cap. p.u. 5.0m., res 0.1m. (Dec. 1997); Chair. GEORGE SYRIMIS; Gen. Man. GEORGE MAKARIOU; 3 brs.

Foreign Banks

Arab Bank PLC: POB 5700, 28 Santaroza St, 1393 Nicosia; tel. (2) 457111; telex 5717; fax (2) 457890; f. 1984; commercial; Area Exec. T. DAJANI; 18 brs.

Commercial Bank of Greece SA: POB 5151, 4 Ionos St, 2015 Nicosia; tel. (2) 363646; telex 4055; fax (2) 473923; f. 1992; Country Man. G. KANTIANIS; 2 brs.

Türkiye Cumhuriyeti Ziraat Bankası: Girnekapi Cad., Ibrahimpaşa Sok. 105, Lefkoşa (Nicosia), Mersin 10, Turkey; tel. (22) 83050; telex 57499; fax (22) 82041.

Türkiye Halk Bankası AŞ: Osman Paşa Cad., Ümit Office, Lefkoşa (Nicosia), Mersin 10, Turkey; tel. (22) 72145; telex 57241; fax (22) 72146.

Türkiye İş Bankası AŞ: Girne Cad. 9, Lefkoşa (Nicosia), Mersin 10, Turkey; tel. (22) 83133; telex 57569; fax (22) 78315; f. 1924; Man. KEMAL AĞANOĞLU.

Offshore Banking Units

Cyprus-based Offshore Banking Units (OBUs) are fully-staffed units which conduct all forms of banking business from within Cyprus with other offshore or foreign entities and non-resident persons. (OBUs are not permitted to accept deposits from persons of Cypriot origin who have emigrated to the United Kingdom and taken up permanent residence there.) Although exempt from most of the restrictions and regulatory measures applicable to onshore banks, OBUs are subject to supervision and inspection by the Central Bank of Cyprus. OBUs may conduct business with onshore and domestic banks in all banking matters which the latter are allowed to undertake with banks abroad. OBUs are permitted to grant loans or guarantees in foreign currencies to residents of Cyprus (conditional on obtaining an exchange control permit from the Central Bank of Cyprus). Interest and other income earned from transactions with residents is subject to the full rate of income tax (20%), but the Minister of Finance is empowered by law to exempt an OBU from the above tax liability if satisfied that a specific transaction substantially contributes towards the economic development of the Republic. In 1997 there were 32 OBUs operating in Cyprus.

Agropromstroybank (Cyprus Offshore Banking Unit): POB 5297, Maximos Court B, 17 Leontiou St, Limassol; tel. (5) 384747; telex 5065; fax (5) 384858; Man. ALEXANDRE MOKHONKO.

Allied Business Bank SAL: POB 4232, 3rd Floor, Flat 31, Lara Court, 276 Archbishop Makarios III Ave, Limassol; tel. (5) 363759; telex 6040; fax (5) 372711; Local Man. NAJIBA HAWILLA.

Arab Bank PLC: POB 5700, 28 Santaroza Ave, 1393 Nicosia; tel. (2) 7671111; fax (2) 760890; OBU licence granted 1997; Area Exec. TOUFIC J. DAJAN.

Arab Jordan Investment Bank SA (Cyprus Offshore Banking Unit): POB 4384, Libra Tower, 23 Olympion St, Limassol; tel. (5) 351351; telex 3809; fax (5) 360151; f. 1978; cap. and dep. US $216m., total assets US$315m. (Dec. 1996); Man. ABED ABU-DAYEH.

AVTOVAZBANK: 5 Promitheos St, Flat No. 2, POB 2025, 1516 Nicosia; tel. (2) 361561; fax. (2) 361525; Local Man. A. TSELOUNOV.

Banca Română de Comerţ Exterior (Bancorex) SA: Margarita House, 5th Floor, 15 Them. Dervis St, POB 2538, 1309 Nicosia; tel. (2) 367992; telex 4815; fax (2) 367945; Local Man. GRIGORE IOAN BUDISAN.

Bank Menatep: 1 Lambousas St, 4th Floor, 1095 Nicosia; tel. (2) 442444; fax (2) 442464; CEO VLADIMIR I. PEREVERZIN.

Bank of Beirut and the Arab Countries SAL: POB 6201, Emelle Bldg, 1st Floor, 135 Archbishop Makarios III Ave, Limassol; tel. (5) 381290; telex 5444; fax (5) 381584; Man. O. S. SAAB.

Banque du Liban et d'Outre-Mer SAL: POB 3243, P. Lordos Centre Roundabout, Byron St, Limassol; tel. (5) 376433; telex 4424; fax (5) 376292; Local Man. S. FARAH.

Banque Nationale de Paris Intercontinentale SA: POB 58, Hanseatic House, 111 Spyrou Araouzou Ave, Limassol; tel. (5) 360166; telex 5519; fax (5) 376519; Local Man. M. PIANO.

Banque SBA (Cyprus Offshore Banking Unit): POB 4405, Iris House, Kanika Enaerios Complex, 8c Kennedy St, Limassol; tel. (5) 588650; telex 3569; fax (5) 581643; branch of Banque SBA (fmrly Société Bancaire Arabe), Paris; Local Man. N. DAGISTANI.

Barclays Bank PLC, Cyprus Offshore Banking Unit: POB 7320, 88 Dhigenis Akritas Ave, Nicosia; tel. (2) 764777; telex 5200; fax (2) 754233; Senior Man. CLIVE BRITTON.

BEMO—Banque Européenne pour le Moyen-Orient SAL: POB 6232, Doma Court, 1st-2nd Floors, 227 Archbishop Makarios III Ave, Limassol; tel. (5) 368668; telex 5575; fax (5) 368611; Local Man. N. A. HCHAIME.

Beogradska Banka: POB 530, 34 Kennedy Ave, Nicosia; tel. (2) 453493; telex 6413; fax (2) 453207; Man. Dir B. VUČIĆ.

Byblos Bank SAL: POB 218, Loucaides Bldg, 1 Archbishop Kyprianou St/St Andrew St, Limassol; tel. (5) 341433; telex 5203; fax (5) 367139; Man. ANTOINE SMEIRA.

Commercial Bank of Greece SA: 1 Iona Nicolaou, POB 7587, Engomi, 2431 Nicosia, tel. (2) 363686; fax (2) 363688; Man. G. KANTIANIS.

Crédit Libanais SAL (Cyprus Offshore Banking Unit): POB 3492, Chrysalia Court, 1st Floor, 206 Archbishop Makarios III Ave, 3030 Limassol; tel. (5) 376444; telex 4702; fax (5) 376807; e-mail credub@inco.com.lb; Local Man. HAYAT HARFOUCHE.

Crédit Suisse First Boston (Cyprus) Ltd: POB 7530, 199 Christodolou Hadsipavlou Ave, 3316 Limassol; tel. (5) 341244; fax (5)

817424; f. 1996, OBU status granted 1997; cap. US $2.0m., dep. US $171.3m., total assets US $180.5m. (Dec. 1996); Gen. Man. ANTONIS ROUVAS.

Federal Bank of the Middle East Ltd: POB 5566, Megaron Lavinia, Santa Rosa Ave and Mykinon St, Nicosia; tel. (2) 761716; telex 4700; fax (2) 761751; f. 1983; cap. and res US $35.4m., dep. $188.01m. (Dec. 1997); Chair. A. F. M. SAAB; Chief Exec. JAMES V. HOEY.

First Investment Bank Ltd: POB 16023, corner of Kennedy Ave & 39 Demoforitos St, 4th Floor, Flat 401, 2085 Nicosia; tel. (2) 760150; telex 4264; fax (2) 376560; Gen. Man. ENU NEDELE.

HSBC Investment Bank Cyprus Ltd: POB 5718, 1311 Nicosia; tel. (2) 376116; telex 4980; fax (2) 376121; f. 1984, as Wardley Cyprus Ltd; Man. Dir T. TAOUSHANIS.

Inkombank: 67 Spyros Araouzos St, Karmozi House, POB 3349, 3302 Limassol; tel. (5) 745949; telex 5817; fax (5) 747067; Gen. Man. ALEXEI KROKHIN.

Jordan National Bank PLC, Cyprus Offshore Banking Unit: POB 3587, 1 Anexartissias St, Pecora Tower, 2nd Floor, 3303 Limassol; tel. (5) 356669; telex 5471; fax (5) 356673; e-mail jnb@cytanet.com.cy; f. 1984; Reg. Man. KHALIL NASR.

Karić Banka, COBU: Flat 22, Cronos Court, 66 Archbishop Makarios III Ave, Nicosia; tel. (2) 374977; telex 6510; fax (2) 374151; Man. Dir BILJANA CAMILOVIĆ.

Lebanon and Gulf Bank SAL: POB 337, Akamia Court, 3rd Floor, corner of G. Afxentiou and Archbishop Makarios III Ave, Larnaca; tel. (4) 620500; telex 5779; fax (4) 620708; Local Man. M. HAMMOUD.

Permcombank (Permanent Joint-Stock Commercial Bank): POB 6037, 66 Archbishop Makarios III Ave, Of. 43, Nicosia; tel. (2) 361566; telex 4572; fax (2) 361466; Man. V. NOVIKOV.

Russian Commercial Bank (Cyprus) Ltd: POB 6868, 2 Amathuntos St, 3310 Limassol; tel. (5) 342190; telex 4561; fax (5) 342192; cap. US $10.8m., res US $3.6m., dep. US $101.7m. (Dec. 1996); Gen. Man. YURI V. BABKIN.

Société Générale Cyprus Ltd: POB 8560, 7–9 Grivas Dhigenis Ave, Nicosia; tel. (2) 764885; telex 5342; fax (2) 764471; Gen. Man. GÉRARD MALHAME.

Vojvodjanska Bank AD: POB 872, Xenios Commercial Centre, 5th floor, Suite 502, Archbishop Makarios III Ave, 1664 Nicosia; tel. (2) 374918; fax (2) 374937; OBU status granted 1997; Local CEO MILAN BORKOVIĆ.

STOCK EXCHANGE

Cyprus Stock Exchange: POB 5427, 54 Grivas Dhigenis Ave, 1309 Nicosia; tel. (2) 668782; telex 2077; fax (2) 668790; e-mail cyse@zenon.logos.cy.net; internet http://www.cse.com.cy; official trading commenced in March 1996; 41 companies listed in 1997; Chair. DINOS PAPADOPOULOS; Gen. Man. N. METAXAS.

INSURANCE

Office of the Superintendent of Insurance: Treasury Department, Ministry of Finance, Nicosia; tel. (2) 303256; telex 3399; fax (2) 302938; f. 1969 to control insurance companies, insurance agents, brokers and agents for brokers in Cyprus.

Greek Cypriot Insurance Companies

Aegis Insurance Co Ltd: POB 3450, 7 Klimentos St, Ayios Antonios, 1061 Nicosia; tel. (2) 343644; fax (2) 369359; Chair. ARISTOS KAISIDES; Principal Officer PANTELAKIS SOUGLIDES.

Aetna Insurance Co Ltd: POB 8909, 19 Stavrou St, 2035 Strovolos; tel. (2) 510933; fax (2) 510934; f. 1966; Chair. KONSTANTINOS L. PRODROMOU; Principal Officer KONSTANTINOS TSANGARIS.

Agrostroy Insurance Co Ltd: POB 6624, 89 Kennedy Ave, Office 201, 1077 Nicosia; tel. (2) 379210; fax (2) 379212; f. 1996; offshore captive company operating outside Cyprus; Chair. VALERIE V. USHAKOV; Principal Officer IOANNIS ELIA.

Allied Assurance & Reinsurance Co Ltd: POB 5509, 66 Grivas Dhigenis Ave, 1310 Nicosia; tel. (2) 457131; fax (2) 441975; f. 1982; offshore company operating outside Cyprus; Chair. HENRI J. G. CHALHOUB; Principal Officer DEMETRIOS DEMETRIOU.

Akelius Insurance Ltd: POB 3415, 59–61 Strovolos Ave, 2018 Strovolos; tel. (2) 318883; fax (2) 318925; f. 1989; offshore company operating outside Cyprus; Chair. ROGER AKELIOUS; Principal Officer IOANNIS LOIZOU.

AMI Alpha Marine Insurance Cyprus Co. Ltd: POB 3250, 8 Alasias St, 3095 Limassol; tel. (5) 373279; fax (5) 355869; f. 1995; offshore captive company operating outside Cyprus; Principal Officer CHRIS GEORGHIADES.

Antarctic Insurance Co Ltd: POB 613, 199 Archbishop Makarios III Ave, Neokleou Bldg, 3030 Limassol; tel. (5) 362818; fax (5) 359262; offshore captive company operating outside Cyprus; Principal Officer ANDREAS NEOKLEOUS.

Apac Ltd: POB 5403, 5 Mourouzi St, Apt 1, 1055 Nicosia; tel. (2) 455186; telex 2766; fax (2) 343146; f. 1983; captive offshore company operating outside Cyprus; Chair. KYPROS CHRYSOSTOMIDES; Principal Officer GEORGHIOS POYATZIS.

APOL Insurance Ltd: 24 Perea St, Mocassino Centre, 3rd Floor, 2023 Strovolos, Nicosia; tel. (2) 425550; fax (2) 425147; offshore company operating outside Cyprus; Chair. M. ARBOUZOV; Principal Officer STELIOS MICHAEL.

Asfalistiki Eteria I 'Kentriki' Ltd: POB 5131, Greg Tower, 3rd Floor, 7 Florinis St, Nicosia 136; tel. (2) 473931; telex 4987; fax (2) 366276; f. 1985; Chair. ARISTOS CHRYSOSTOMOU; Principal Officer GEORGHIOS GEORGALLIDES.

Aspis Pronia Insurance Co Ltd: POB 5183, 101 Acropolis Ave, 2012 Strovolos; tel. (2) 510333; fax (2) 492402; f. 1996; Chair. P. PSOMIADES; Principal Officer CHRISTAKIS ELEFTHERIOU.

Atlantic Insurance Co Ltd: POB 4579, 37 Prodromou St, 2nd Floor, 1090 Strovolos; tel. (2) 444052; telex 6446; fax (2) 474800; f. 1983; Chair. and Man. Dir ZENIOS PYRISHIS; Principal Officer EMILIOS PYRISHIS.

Axioma Insurance (Cyprus) Ltd: POB 4881, 2 Ionni Klerides St, Demokritos No. 2 Bldg, Flat 83, 1070 Nicosia; tel. (2) 374197; fax (2) 374972; offshore company operating outside Cyprus; Principal Officer KONSTANTINOS KYAMIDES.

B & B Marine Insurance Ltd: POB 2545, 46 Gladstonos St, 1095 Nicosia; tel. (2) 466456; fax (2) 446476; f. 1996; offshore company operating outside Cyprus; Chair. DMITGRI MOLTCHANOV; Principal Officer GEORGHIOS YIANGOU.

Berytus Marine Insurance Ltd: POB 132, 284 Arch. Makarios III Ave, 3105 Limassol; tel. (5) 362424; fax (5) 370055; f. 1997; offshore company operating outside Cyprus; Principal Officer CHRIS GEORGHIADES.

Cathay General Insurance Ltd: POB 4708, Ayias Zonis & Gladstonos, Roussos Centre, 6th floor, Office 6A, Limassol; f. 1997; offshore captive company operating outside Cyprus; Principal Officer ARETI CHARIDEMOU.

Commercial Union Assurance (Cyprus) Ltd: POB 1312, Commercial Union House, 101 Archbishop Makarios III Ave, 1071 Nicosia; tel. (2) 377373; telex 2547; fax (2) 459011; e-mail mailbox@commercial-union.com.cy; f. 1974; Chair. J. CHRISTOPHIDES; Gen. Man. KONSTANTINOS P. DEKATRIS.

Cosmos (Cyprus) Insurance Co Ltd: POB 1770, 1st Floor, Flat 12, 6 Ayia Eleni St, 1060 Nicosia; tel. (2) 441235; fax (2) 457925; f. 1982; Chair. and Gen. Man. ANDREAS K. TYLLIS.

Crown Insurance Co Ltd: POB 4690, Royal Crown House, 20 Mnasiadou St, Nicosia 136; tel. (2) 455333; fax (2) 455757; f. 1992; Chair. W. R. ROWLAND; Principal Officer PHILIOS ZACHARIADES.

Cygnet Insurance Ltd: POB 8482, 56 Grivas Dhigenis Ave, Anna Tower, 4th floor, Office 42, 3101 Limassol; tel. (5) 353253; fax (5) 354514; f. 1997; offshore captive company operating outside Cyprus; Principal Officer MARIOS LOUKAIDES.

Cyprialife Ltd: POB 2535, 2 Amphipoleos St, Strovolos, 1522 Nicosia; tel. (2) 360030; fax (2) 510990; f. 1995; Chair. KIKIS LAZARIDES; Principal Officer ANDREAS ALONEFTIS.

E.F.U. General Insurance Ltd: POB 1612, 3 Themistoklis Dervis St, Julia House, Nicosia; tel. (2) 453053; fax (2) 475194; offshore company; Chair. ROSHEN ALI BHIMJEE; Principal Officer CHARALAMBOS ZAVALLIS.

Emergency Market Insurance Ltd: POB 613, 199 Arch. Makarios Ave, Neokleous Bldg, 3030 Limassol; tel. (5) 362818; fax (5) 359262; f. 1997; offshore captive company operating outside Cyprus; Principal Officer ANDREAS NEOKLEOUS.

Eurolife Ltd: POB 1655, 40 Them. Dervis St, Eurolife House, 1066 Nicosia; tel. (2) 442044; telex 3313; fax (2) 451040; Chair. ANDREAS PATSALIDES; Principal Officer ANDREAS KRITOTIS.

Eurosure Insurance Co Ltd: POB 1961, 8 Michalaki Karaoli St, Anemomylos Office Bldg, 3rd Floor, 1095 Nicosia; tel. (2) 463439; telex 2302; fax (2) 459084; Chair. STELIOS IOANNOU.

Excelsior General Insurance Co Ltd: POB 6106, 339 Ayiou Andreou St, Andrea Chambers, Of. 303, Limassol; tel. (5) 427021; fax (5) 312446; f. 1995; Chair. CLIVE E. K. LEWIS; Principal Officer MARIA HADJIANTONIOU.

FAM Financial and Mercantile Insurance Co Ltd: POB 132, 284 Archbishop Makarios III Ave, Fortuna Bldg, Block 'B', 2nd Floor, 4007 Limassol; tel. (5) 362424; telex 2566; fax (5) 370055; f. 1993; offshore captive company operating outside Cyprus; Chair. VLADIMIR MOISSEEV; Principal Officer CHR. GEORGHIADES.

General Insurance Co of Cyprus Ltd: POB 1668, 2–4 Themistoklis Dervis St, 1066 Nicosia; tel. (2) 450444; telex 2311; fax (2) 446682; f. 1951; Chair. A. PATSALIDES; Gen. Man. A. STYLIANOU.

Geopolis Insurance Ltd: POB 8530, 6 Neoptolemou St, 2045 Strovolos; tel. (2) 490094; fax (2) 490494; f. 1993; Chair. MARIOS PROIOS; Principal Officer NIKOS DRYMIOTIS.

Granite Insurance Co Ltd: POB 613, 199 Archbishop Makarios III Ave, Neokleou Bldg, 3030 Limassol; tel. (5) 362818; telex 2948; fax (5) 359262; captive offshore company operating outside Cyprus; Chair. and Gen. Man. KOSTAS KOUTSOKOUMNIS; Principal Officer ANDREAS NEOKLEOUS.

Greene Insurances Ltd: POB 132, 4th Floor, Vereggaria Bldg, 25 Spyrou Araouzou St, 3036 Limassol; tel. (5) 362424; telex 2566; fax (5) 363842; f. 1987; Chair. GEORGHIOS CHRISTODOULOU; Principal Officer JOSIF CHRISTOU.

Hermes Insurance Co Ltd: POB 4828, 1st Floor, Office 101–103, Anemomylos Bldg, 8 Michalakis Karaolis St, 1095 Nicosia; tel. (2) 448130; telex 3466; fax (2) 461888; f. 1980; Chair. and Man. Dir P. VOGAZIANOS.

I.G.R. Co Ltd: POB 1343, 20 Vasilissias Friderikis St, El Greco House, Office 104, 1066 Nicosia; tel. (2) 473688; fax (2) 455259; f. 1996; offshore company operating outside Cyprus; Principal Officer CHRISTODOULOS VASSILIADES.

Interamerican Insurance Co Ltd: POB 819, 64 Archbishop Makarios III Ave and I Karpenisiou, 1077 Nicosia; tel. (2) 374100; fax (2) 374030; f. 1992; Principal Officer MICHALIS MICHAELIDES.

Iris Insurance Co Ltd: POB 4841, Flat A5–A6, 1st Floor, 'Aspelia' Bldg, 34 Costis Palamas St, 1096 Nicosia; tel. (2) 448302; telex 3675; fax (2) 449579; e-mail iris@cytanet.com.cy; Chair. and Gen. Man. PAVLOS CL. GEORGHIOU.

Laiki Insurance Co Ltd: POB 2069, 6 Evgenias & Antoniou Theodotou St, 1517 Nicosia; tel. (2) 752000; fax (2) 466890; f. 1981; Chair. K. N. LAZARIDES; Man. A. PISSIRIS.

LCF Reinsurance Co Ltd: POB 3589, 3 Themistoklis Dervis St, Julia House, Nicosia; tel. (2) 453053; telex 2046; fax (2) 475194; f. 1984; Chair. LELLOS DEMETRIADES; Principal Officer SOPHIA XINARI.

Ledra Insurance Ltd: POB 3942, 93 Kennedy Ave, 1077 Nicosia; tel. (2) 378200; fax (2) 378330; f. 1994; Chair. KONSTANTINOS KITTIS; Principal Officer ALEKOS PULCHERIOS.

Liberty Life Insurance Ltd: POB 6070, 75 Limassol Ave, 5th Floor, Nicosia; tel. (2) 319300; fax (2) 429134; f. 1994; Chair. KONSTANTINOS KITTIS; Principal Officer EURIPIDES NEOKLEOUS.

Medlife Insurance Ltd: POB 1675, Themistoklis Dervis St and Florinis St, Nicosia; tel. (2) 475181; fax (2) 473909; e-mail office@medlife.net; f. 1995; Chair. Dr WOLFGANG GOSHNIK.

Metropolitan Insurance Ltd: POB 6516, 2 Kretes St, Pelekanos Court, Of. 1, 1060 Nicosia; tel. (2) 751444; fax (2) 752444; e-mail metropolitan@cytanet.com.cy; f. 1993; Chair. MICHALAKIS ZIVANARIS; Principal Officer PANOS IOANNOU.

Minerva Insurance Co Ltd: POB 866, 8 Epaminondas St, 1684 Nicosia 137; tel. (2) 445134; telex 2608; fax (2) 455528; f. 1970; Chair. and Gen. Man. K. KOUTSOKOUMNIS.

Pancyprian Insurance Ltd: POB 1352, Mepa Tower, 66 Grivas Dhigenis Ave, 1095 Nicosia; tel. (2) 442235; telex 3015; fax (2) 477656; f. 1993; Chair. HENRI CHALHOUB; Principal Officer VASSOS STYLIANIDES.

Paneuropean Insurance Co Ltd: POB 553, 88 Arch. Makarios III Ave, 1660 Nicosia; tel. (2) 377960; fax (2) 377396; f. 1980; Chair. N. K. SHACOLAS; Gen. Man. POLIS MICHAELIDES.

Philiki Insurance Co Ltd: POB 2274, 45 Byzantium St, 2064 Strovolos, Nicosia; tel. (2) 444444; telex 2353; fax (2) 442026; f. 1982; Chair. NIKOS SHAKOLAS; Principal Officer DOROS ORPHANIDES.

Progressive Insurance Co Ltd: POB 2111, 44 Kallipoleos St, 1071 Nicosia; tel. (2) 758585; fax (2) 754747; Chair. ANDREAS HADJIANDREOU; Principal Officer TAKIS HADJIANDREOU.

Saviour Insurance Co Ltd: POB 3957, 8 Michalakis Karaolis St, Anemomylos Bldg, Flat 204, 1687 Nicosia; tel. (2) 365085; fax (2) 446097; f. 1987; Chair. ROBERT SINCLAIR; Principal Officer KONSTANTINOS KITTIS.

Sunlink Insurance Co Ltd: POB 3585, 3 Themistoklis Dervis St, Julia House, 1066 Nicosia, tel. (2) 453053; telex 4857; fax (2) 475194; f. 1995; offshore captive company operating outside Cyprus; Chair. ANDREAS STYLIANOU; Principal Officer MARIA LAMBROU.

Technolink Insurance Services Ltd: POB 7007, 70 Kennedy Ave, Papavasiliou House, 1076 Nicosia; tel. (2) 496000; fax (2) 493000; f. 1996; offshore captive company operating outside Cyprus; Principal Officer GEORGHIOS YIALLOURIDES.

Tercet Insurance Ltd: POB 2545, 46 Gladstones St, 1095 Nicosia; tel. (2) 466456; telex 2046; fax (2) 466476; f. 1994; Chair. ANDREAS STYLIANOU; Principal Officer MARIA PIPINGA.

Triada Insurance Ltd: POB 1675, corner Themistoklis Dervis & Florinis St, Stadyl Bldg, 6th Floor, 1512 Nicosia; tel. (2) 475182; fax (2) 461926; f. 1996; offshore captive company operating outside Cyprus; Principal Officer PANOS PAPADOPOULOS.

Trust International Insurance Co (Cyprus) Ltd: POB 4857, 284 Archbishop Makarios III Ave, Fortuna Bldg, 2nd Floor, 4007 Limassol; tel. (5) 369404; telex 5054; fax (5) 377871; f. 1992; Chair. GHAZI K. ABU NAHL; Principal Officer CHR. GEORGHIADES.

Universal Life Insurance Company Ltd: POB 1270, Universal Tower, 85 Dhigenis Akritas Ave, 1505 Nicosia; tel. (2) 761222; fax (2) 761343; f. 1970; Chair. J. CHRISTOPHIDES; Principal Officer ANDREAS GEORGHIOU.

UPIC Ltd: POB 7237, Nicolaou Pentadromos Centre, 10th Floor, Ayias Zonis St, 3314 Limassol; tel. (5) 347664; fax (5) 347081; f. 1992; Principal Officer POLAKIS SARRIS.

Veritima Insurance Ltd: POB 956, 2B Orpheus St, Office 104, 1070 Nicosia; tel. (2) 375646; fax (2) 375620; f. 1996; offshore captive company operating outside Cyprus; Principal Officer SANDROS DIKEOS.

VTI Insurance Co Ltd: POB 613, 199 Archbishop Makarios III Ave, Neokleou Bldg, 4004 Limassol; tel. (5) 362818; telex 2948; fax (5) 359262; f. 1994; Chair. SOTERIS PITTAS; Principal Officer ANDREAS NEOKLEOUS.

WOB Insurances Ltd: POB 613, 199 Archbishop Makarios III Ave, Neokleou Bldg, 4004 Limassol; tel. (5) 362818; telex 2948; fax (5) 359262; captive offshore company operating outside Cyprus; Principal Officer ANDREAS NEOKLEOUS.

Zako Insurance Ltd: POB 2274, 45 Vyzantium St, 2064 Nicosia; tel. (2) 444433; telex 2250; fax (2) 442026; Chair. STAVROS DAVERONAS.

Turkish Cypriot Insurance Companies

Akfinans Sigorta Insurance AŞ: 16 Osman Paşa Cad., Lefkoşa (Nicosia), Mersin 10, Turkey; tel. (22) 84506; fax (22) 85713.

Ankara Sigorta: 50–58 Muzaffer Paşa Cad., Lefkoşa (Nicosia), Mersin 10, Turkey; tel. (22) 85815; fax (22) 83099.

Cyprus Insurance Co Ltd: Osman Paşa Cad., Yağcıoğlu Işhanı 4, Lefkoşa (Nicosia), Mersin 10, Turkey; tel. (22) 83022; fax (22) 79277.

Gold Insurance Ltd: Mehmet Akif Cad., Okay 7 Apt 1, Kumsal, Lefkoşa (Nicosia), Mersin 10, Turkey; tel. (22) 86479.

Güven Sigorta (Kıbrıs) Sirketi AŞ: Mecidiye Sok. 8, Lefkoşa (Nicosia), Mersin 10, Turkey; tel. (22) 81431; fax (22) 81244.

Işlek Sigorta: Bahçelievler Bul., Güzelyurt (Morphou), Mersin 10, Turkey; tel. (71) 42473; fax (71) 45507.

Liberty Sigorta: 25 Şehit Azrık Sok. Köşklüçiftlik, Lefkoşa (Nicosia), Mersin 10, Turkey; tel. (22) 81848; fax (22) 81844.

Saray Sigorta: 182 Girne Cad., Lefkoşa (Nicosia), Mersin 10, Turkey; tel. (22) 72976; fax (22) 79001.

Şeker Sigorta (Kıbrıs) Ltd: 27–29 Mecidiye Sok., PK 664, Lefkoşa (Nicosia), Mersin 10, Turkey; tel. (22) 85883; fax (22) 74074.

Sigma Reasürans AŞ: 25 Şehit Arzık Sok., Köşklüçiftlik, Lefkoşa (Nicosia), Mersin 10, Turkey; tel. (22) 88511; fax (22) 88122.

Trade and Industry

GREEK CYPRIOT CHAMBERS OF COMMERCE AND INDUSTRY

Cyprus Chamber of Commerce and Industry: POB 1455, 38 Grivas Dhigenis Ave, 1509 Nicosia; tel. (2) 669500; telex 2077; fax (2) 669048; e-mail chamber@ccci.org.cy; f. 1927; Pres. VASSILIS ROLOGIS; Sec.-Gen. PANAYIOTIS LOIZIDES; 7,000 mems, 86 affiliated trade asscns.

Famagusta Chamber of Commerce and Industry: POB 3124, 339 Ayiou Andreou St, Andrea Chambers Bldg, 2nd Floor, Office No 201–202, 3300 Limassol; tel. (5) 370165; fax (5) 370291; e-mail chamberf@cytanet.com.cy; f. 1952; Pres. PHOTIS PAPATHOMAS; Sec. IACOVOS HADJIVARNAVAS; 450 mems.

Larnaca Chamber of Commerce and Industry: POB 287, 12 Gregoriou Afxentiou St, Skouros Bldg, Apt 43, 4th Floor, 6302 Larnaca; tel. (4) 655051; telex 3187; fax (4) 628281; Pres. IACOVOS DEMETRIOU; Sec. OTHON THEODOULOU; 450 mems.

Limassol Chamber of Commerce and Industry: POB 347, 25 Spyrou Araouzou St, Veregaria Bldg, 3rd Floor, 3603 Limassol; tel. (5) 362556; fax (5) 371655; e-mail chamberl@dial.cylink.com.cy; f. 1962; Pres. MICHALIS POLYDORIDES; Sec. CHRISTOS NICOLAOU; 750 mems.

Nicosia Chamber of Commerce and Industry: POB 1455, 38 Grivas Dhigenis Ave, Chamber Bldg, 1509 Nicosia; tel. (2) 669500; telex 2077; fax (2) 667433; f. 1962; Pres. GEORGE ARGYROPOULOS; Sec. PANIKOS MICHAELIDES; 1,200 mems.

Paphos Chamber of Commerce and Industry: POB 82, Athinon Ave & corner Alexandrou Papayou Ave, 8100 Paphos; tel. (6) 235115; telex 2888; fax (6) 244602; Pres. THEODOROS ARISTODEMOU; Sec. KENDEAS ZAMPIRINIS; 450 mems.

TURKISH CYPRIOT CHAMBERS OF COMMERCE AND INDUSTRY

Turkish Cypriot Chamber of Industry: 14 Osman Paşa Cad., PK 563, Köşklüçiftlik, Lefkoşa (Nicosia), Mersin 10, Turkey; tel. (22) 84596; fax (22) 84595; Pres. EREN ERTANIN.

Turkish Cypriot Chamber of Commerce: Bedrettin Demirel Cad., PK 718, Lefkoşa (Nicosia), Mersin 10, Turkey; tel. (22) 83645; telex 57511; fax (22) 83089; f. 1958; more than 6,000 regd mems; Chair. SALİH BOYACI; Sec.-Gen. JANEL BURCAN.

GREEK CYPRIOT EMPLOYERS' ORGANIZATION

Cyprus Employers' & Industrialists' Federation: POB 1657, 30 Grivas Dhigenis Ave, 1511 Nicosia; tel. (2) 445102; fax (2) 459459; e-mail oeb@dial.cylink.com.cy; f. 1960; 40 member trade associations, 400 direct and 2,500 indirect members; Dir-Gen. ANTONIS PIERIDES; Chair. ANDREAS PITTAS. The largest of the trade association members are: Cyprus Building Contractors' Association; Cyprus Hotel Keepers' Association; Clothing Manufacturers' Association; Cyprus Shipping Association; Shoe Makers' Association; Cyprus Metal Industries Association; Cyprus Bankers Employers' Association; Motor Vehicles Importers' Association.

TURKISH CYPRIOT EMPLOYERS' ORGANIZATION

Kıbrıs Türk İşverenler Sendikası (Turkish Cypriot Employers' Association): PK 674, Lefkoşa (Nicosia), Mersin 10, Turkey; tel. (22) 76173; Chair. ALPAY ALİ RIZA GÖRGÜNER.

UTILITIES
Electricity

Electricity Authority of Cyprus (EAC): POB 4506, Nicosia; tel. (2) 367477; fax (2) 360034; e-mail sepaik@spidernet.com.cy; internet http://www.sepaik.org.cy; generation, transmission and distribution of electric energy in government-controlled area; total capacity 690 MW at power stations.

Water

Water Development Department: Ministry of Agriculture, Natural Resources and the Environment, Loukis Akritis Ave, Nicosia; tel. (2) 302171; fax (2) 445156; dam storage capacity 300m. cu m.

MAJOR COMPANIES
Greek Cypriot Companies

Covotsos Textiles Ltd: POB 1090, Limassol; tel. (5) 391344; telex 2672; fax (5) 390754.

Cyprus Canning Co Ltd: POB 21, Limassol; tel. (5) 392078; telex 3928; fax (5) 392083.

Cyprus Cement Co Ltd: POB 378, Limassol; telex 2684.

Cyprus Forest Industries Ltd: POB 4043, Nicosia; tel. (2) 832121; telex 2177; fax (2) 833564.

Cyprus Phassouri Plantations Ltd: POB 180, Limassol; tel. (5) 252211; telex 2396; fax (5) 252225.

Cyprus Pipes Industries Ltd: 172 St Andrew St, Limassol; telex 2496.

Cyprus Trading Corporation Ltd: POB 1744, Nicosia; tel. (2) 482800; telex 2415; fax (2) 485385.

Keo Ltd: POB 209, 1 Franklin Roosevelt Ave, Limassol; tel. (5) 362053; telex 2449; fax (5) 373429; f. 1927; cap. C£5m; manufacturers of wine, beer and spirits, fruit juices, canned vegetables and mineral water; Exec. Chair. E. PANTELIDES; Man. Dir A. M. ZAMBARTAS; 500 employees.

Vassiliko Cement Works Ltd: POB 2281, 1519 Nicosia; tel. (4) 333001; telex 5000; fax (4) 332651; f. 1963; cap. C£10.7m; cement manufacturers; Exec. Chair. PANOS CHR. GHALANOS; Gen. Man. GEORGE A. SIDERIS; 35 employees.

Turkish Cypriot Companies

Cypfruvex Ltd: Güzelyurt, PK 433, Lefkoşa (Nicosia), Mersin 10, Turkey; tel. (22) 43495; telex 57131; state-owned; fruit exporters; Gen. Man. MUSTAFA REFIK.

Eti Ltd: Abdi İpekci Cad., PK 452, Lefkoşa (Nicosia), Mersin 10, Turkey; tel. (22) 71222; state-owned; import and distribution of foodstuffs.

Hilmi Toros Industries Ltd: Mehmet Akif Ave, PK 526, Lefkoşa (Nicosia), Mersin 10, Turkey; tel. (22) 72412; textile and clothing manufacturers.

Kıbrıs Türk Petrolleri Ltd, Şti (Turkish Cypriot Petroleum Co Ltd): Gazi Mağusa, (Famagusta). PK 117, Mersin 10, Turkey; tel. (36) 63260; telex 57582; fax (36) 65230; import, storage and distribution of petroleum and petroleum derivatives.

Kıbrıs Türk Sanayi İşletmeleri Holding Ltd, Şti (Turkish Cypriot Industrial Enterprises Holding Ltd): PK 445, Lefkoşa (Nicosia), Mersin 10, Turkey; tel. (22) 83231; telex 57575; fax (22) 82441; state-owned; manufacturers and exporters of water pumps, paints, plastics, detergents, cosmetics, textiles, foodstuffs, polypropylene and polyethylene sacks, cables, polystyrene and polyurethane foam; Dir HÜSNÜ SAYGINSOY.

Kıbrıs Türk Tütün Endüstri Ltd (Turkish Cypriot Tobacco Industry Ltd): 27 Atatürk Cad., Lefkoşa (Nicosia), Mersin 10, Turkey; tel. (22) 73403; state-owned; cigarette manufacturers.

Learned Ltd: Lefkoşa (Nicosia), Mersin 10, Turkey; hotels, packaging, fruit processing; Dir. SIDIKA ATALAY.

TAŞEL (Turkish Spirits and Wine Enterprises Ltd): Gazi Mağusa (Famagusta), PK 48, Mersin 10, Turkey; tel. (36) 65440; fax (36) 66330; f. 1961; state-owned; manufacturers of alcoholic beverages; Gen. Man. HASAN YUMUK.

Toprak Ürünleri Kurumu: 11 Şehit Mustafa Hacı Sok., Yenişehir, Lefkoşa (Nicosia), Mersin 10, Turkey; tel. (22) 71211; state-owned; potato exporters.

TRADE UNIONS
Greek Cypriot Trade Unions

Cyprus Civil Servants' Trade Union: 3 Dem. Severis Ave, Nicosia; tel. (2) 442278; fax (2) 465199; f. 1949, registered 1966; restricted to persons in the civil employment of the Government and public authorities; 6 brs with a total membership of 15,383; Pres. N. PANAYIOTOU; Gen. Sec. A. POLYVIOU.

Dimokratiki Ergatiki Omospondia Kyprou (Democratic Labour Federation of Cyprus): POB 1625, 40 Byron Ave, Nicosia; tel. (2) 456506; fax (2) 449494; f. 1962; 4 unions with a total membership of 6,329; Gen. Sec. RENOS PRENTZAS.

Pankypria Ergatiki Omospondia—PEO (Pancyprian Federation of Labour): POB 1885, 31–35 Archermos St, Nicosia; tel. (2) 349400; fax (2) 349382; e-mail peo@cytanet.com.cy; f. 1946, registered 1947; previously the Pancyprian Trade Union Committee f. 1941, dissolved 1946; 10 unions and 176 brs with a total membership of 75,000; affiliated to the WFTU; Gen. Sec. AVRAAM ANTONIOU.

Pankyprios Omospondia Anexartition Syntechnion (Pancyprian Federation of Independent Trade Unions): 4B Dayaes St, 2369 Ay. Dhometios; POB 7521, 2430 Nicosia; tel. (2) 356414; fax (2) 354216; f. 1956, registered 1957; has no political orientations; 8 unions with a total membership of 798; Gen. Sec. KYRIACOS NATHANAEL.

Synomospondia Ergaton Kyprou (Cyprus Workers' Confederation): POB 5018, 23 Alkaiou St, Engomi, Nicosia; tel. (2) 441142; telex 6180; fax (2) 476360; f. 1944, registered 1950; 7 federations, 5 labour centres, 47 unions, 12 brs with a total membership of 56,935; affiliated to the ICFTU and the ETUC; Gen. Sec. MICHAEL IOANNOU; Deputy Gen. Sec. DEMETRIS KITTENIS.

Union of Cyprus Journalists: POB 3495, 2 Kratinos St, Strovolos, Nicosia; tel. (2) 454680; fax (2) 464598; f. 1959; Chair. ANDREAS KANNAOUROS.

Turkish Cypriot Trade Unions

In 1996 trade union membership totalled 22,390.

Devrimci İşçi Sendikaları Federasyonu (Dev-İş) (Revolutionary Trade Unions' Federation): 8 Serabioğlu Sok., Lefkoşa (Nicosia), Mersin 10, Turkey; tel. (22) 72640; f. 1976; two unions with a total membership of 1,016 (1996); affiliated to WFTU; Pres. (acting) and Gen.-Sec. BAYRAM ÇELİK.

Kıbrıs Türk İşçi Sendikaları Federasyonu (TÜRK-SEN) (Turkish Cypriot Trade Union Federation): POB 829, 7–7A Şehit Mehmet R. Hüseyin Sok., Lefkoşa (Nicosia), Mersin 10, Turkey; tel. (22) 72444; fax (22) 87831; f. 1954, regd 1955; 12 unions with a total membership of 4,196 (1996); affiliated to ICFTU, ETUC, CTUC and the Confederation of Trade Unions of Turkey (Türk-İş); Pres. ÖNDER KONULOĞLU; Gen. Sec. ASLAN BIÇAKLI.

Transport
RAILWAYS

There are no railways in Cyprus.

ROADS

In December 1995 there were 25,378 km of roads in the government-controlled areas, of which 5,942 km were paved and the remainder were earth or gravel roads. The Nicosia–Limassol four-lane dual carriageway, which was completed in 1985, was subsequently extended with the completion of the Limassol and Larnaca bypasses. New highways between Nicosia and Larnaca, and Larnaca and Kophinou have been completed, as well as the Aradippo–Dhekelia and Larnaca Airport bypasses. The Nicosia–Anthoupolis–Kokkinotrimithia highway was completed in 1994. At December 1995 the total extent of the highway network was 178.4 km., which was expected to be increased further with the construction of a Limassol–Paphos highway (the first section of which opened in January 1997; work was scheduled to be completed in 2000). In October 1997 work began on a Dhekelia–Ammochostos (Famagusta) highway. The north and south are now served by separate transport systems, and there are no services linking the two sectors.

SHIPPING

Until 1974 Famagusta, a natural port, was the island's most important harbour, handling about 83% of the country's cargo. Since its capture by the Turkish army in August 1974 the port has been officially declared closed to international traffic. However, it continues to serve the Turkish-occupied region.

The main ports which serve the island's maritime trade at present are Larnaca and Limassol, which were constructed in 1973 and 1974 respectively. Both ports have since been expanded and improved. There is also an industrial port at Vassiliko and there are three specialized petroleum terminals, at Larnaca, Dhekelia and Moni. A second container terminal became operational at Limassol in 1995.

In 1996, 5,109 vessels, with a total net registered tonnage of 17,767,000, visited Cyprus, carrying 9,500,000 metric tons of cargo to and from Cyprus. In addition to serving local traffic, Limassol and Larnaca ports act as transhipment load centres for the Eastern Mediterranean, North Adriatic and Black Sea markets and as regional warehouse and assembly bases for the Middle East, North Africa and the Persian (Arabian) Gulf. Containerized cargo handled at Cypriot ports amounted to 3,428,000 metric tons in 1996.

Both Kyrenia and Karavostassi are under Turkish occupation and have been declared closed to international traffic. Karavostassi used to be the country's major mineral port, dealing with 76% of the total mineral exports. However, since the war minerals have been passed through Vassiliko which is a specified industrial port. A hydrofoil service operates between Kyrenia and Mersin on the Turkish mainland. Car ferries sail from Kyrenia to Taşucu and Mersin, in Turkey.

The total number of merchant vessels registered in Cyprus on 30 June 1997 was 2,787, amounting to a total displacement of 25.7m. grt.

Department of Merchant Shipping: POB 6193, Kyllinis St, Mesk Geitonia, 4405 Limassol; tel. (5) 848100; fax (5) 848200; e-mail dms@cytanet.com.cy; Dir. SERGHIOS SERGHIOU.

Cyprus Ports Authority: POB 2007, 23 Crete St, 1516 Nicosia; tel. (2) 756100; telex 2833; fax (2) 765420; e-mail cpa@cytanet.com.cy; internet http://www.cpa.gov.cy; f. 1973; Chair. KOSTAS EROTOKRITOU; Gen. Man. MICHAEL VASSILIADES.

Cyprus Shipping Council: POB 6607, 3309 Limassol; tel. (5) 360717; fax (5) 358642; e-mail csc@dial.cylink.com.cy; internet http://www.swaypage.com/csc; Gen. Sec. THOMAS A. KAZAKOS.

Greek Cypriot Shipping Companies

Amer Shipping Ltd: 6th Floor, Ghinis Bldg, 58–60 Dhigenis Akritas Ave, Nicosia; tel. (2) 751707; telex 6513; fax (2) 751460; Reps SHASHI K. MEHROTRA, DEMETRI ANGELOU.

C. F. Ahrenkiel Shipmanagement (Cyprus) Ltd: 4th Floor, O & A Tower, 25 Olympion St, 3035 Limassol; tel. (5) 359731; telex 6309; fax (5) 359714; Reps PETER DE JONGH, JOHN KONSTANTINOU.

Columbia Shipmanagement Ltd: POB 1624, Columbia House, Dodekanissou and Kolonakiou Corner, Limassol; tel. (5) 320900; telex 3206; fax (5) 320325; f. 1978; Chair H. SCHOELLER, Man. Dir D. FRY.

Hanseatic Shipping Co Ltd: POB 127, 111 Spyrou Araouzou St, Limassol; tel. (5) 345111; telex 3282; fax (5) 342879; f. 1972; Man. Dirs A. J. DROUSSIOTIS, R. GROOL.

Interorient Navigation Co Ltd: POB 1309, 3 Thalia St, 3504 Limassol; tel. (5) 341616; telex 2629; fax (5) 345895; e-mail management@interorient.com.cy; Man. Dir JAN LISSOW.

Louis Cruise Lines: POB 1301, 54-58 Evagoras I Ave, Nicosia; tel. (2) 442114; telex 2341; fax (2) 459800; Reps KOSTAKIS LOIZOU, STELIOS KILIARIS.

Marlow Navigation Co Ltd: POB 4077, Marlow Bldg, cnr 28th October St and Sotiris Michaelides St, Limassol; tel. (5) 348888; telex 2019; fax (5) 748222; Gen. Man. ANDREAS NEOPHYTOU.

Oldendorff Ltd, Reederei Nord Klaus E: POB 6345, Libra Tower, 23 Olympion St, 3306 Limassol; tel. (5) 370262; telex 5938; fax (5) 345077; e-mail a14cy288@gncomtext.com; Chair. and Man. Dir KLAUS E. OLDENDORFF.

Seatankers Management Co Ltd: POB 3562, Flat 411, Deana Beach Apartments, Promachon Eleftherias St, 4103 Limassol; tel. (5) 326111; telex 5606; fax (5) 323770; Man. Dir DANIEL IONNIDES; Gen. Man. DEMETRIS HANNAS.

Turkish Cypriot Shipping Companies

Armen Shipping Ltd: Altun Tabya Yolu No. 10–11, Gazi Mağusa (Famagusta), Mersin 10, Turkey; tel. (36) 64086; fax (36) 65860; e-mail armen@birimnet.com; Dir AYHEN VARER.

Compass Shipping Ltd: Seagate Court, Gazi Mağusa (Famagusta), Mersin 10, Turkey; tel. (36) 66393; fax (36) 66394.

Denko Koop Marine Cargo Department: PK 4, Gazi Mağusa (Famagusta), Mersin 10, Turkey; tel. (36) 65419; telex 57608; fax (36) 62773; Dir MEHMET EFE.

Ertürk Ltd: Kyrenia (Girne), Mersin 10, Turkey; tel. (81) 55834; fax (81) 51808; Dir KEMAL ERTÜRK.

Fergun Maritime Co: Kyrenia (Girne), Mersin 10, Turkey; tel. (81) 54993; ferries to Turkish ports; Owner FEHIM KÜÇÜK.

Kıbrıs Türk Denizcilik Ltd, Şti (Turkish Cypriot Maritime Co Ltd): 3 Bülent Ecevit Bul., Gazi Mağusa (Famagusta), Mersin 10, Turkey; tel. (36) 65995; telex 57547; fax (36) 67840.

Medusa Marine Shipping Ltd: Aycan Apt, Gazi Mağusa (Famagusta), Mersin 10, Turkey; tel. (36) 63945; fax (36) 67800; Dir ERGÜN TOLAY.

Orion Navigation Ltd: Seagate Court, Gazi Mağusa (Famagusta), Mersin 10, Turkey; tel. (36) 62643; telex 57583; fax (36) 64773; f. 1976; shipping agents; Dir O. LAMA; Shipping Man. L. LAMA.

Özari Shipping Ltd: Seagate Court, Gazi Mağusa (Famagusta), Mersin 10, Turkey; tel. (36) 66555; fax (36) 67098; Dir YALÇIN RUHI.

Tahsin Transtürk ve Oğlu Ltd: 11 Kizilkule Yolu, Gazi Mağusa (Famagusta), Mersin 10, Turkey; tel. (36) 65409.

CIVIL AVIATION

There is an international airport at Nicosia, which can accommodate all types of aircraft, including jets. It has been closed since July 1974 following the Turkish invasion. A new international airport was constructed at Larnaca, from which flights operate to Europe, the USA, the Middle East and the Gulf. Another international airport at Paphos began operations in November 1983.

Avistar: POB 5532, Nicosia; tel. (2) 459533; fax (2) 477367; f. 1990; freight; Chief Exec. Dr WALDEMAR HAAS.

Cyprus Airways: 21 Alkeou St, Engomi 2404, POB 1903, 1514, Nicosia; tel. (2) 663054; telex 2225; fax (2) 663167; internet http://www.cyprusair.com; f. 1947; jointly owned by Cyprus Government and local interests; wholly-owned charter subsidiaries Cyprair Tours Ltd, Eurocypria Airlines Ltd and Duty Free Shops Ltd; Chair. TAKIS KYRIAKIDES; CEO DEMETRIS PANTAZIS; Gen. Man. CHRISTOS KYRIAKIDES; services throughout Europe and the Middle East.

Eurocypria Airlines (ECA): POB 970, 97 Artemidos Ave, Artemis Bldg, Larnaca; tel. (4) 658000; fax (4) 658000; services to European destinations from Larnaca and Paphos; Chair. VASSILIS ROLOGIS; Gen. Man. CHARALAMBOS HADJIPANAYIOTOU.

In 1975 the Turkish authorities opened Ercan (formerly Tymbou) airport, and a second airport was opened at Geçitkale (Lefkoniko) in 1986.

Kıbrıs Türk Hava Yolları (Turkish Cypriot Airlines): Bedrettin Demirel Cad., PK 793, Lefkoşa (Nicosia), Mersin 10, Turkey; tel. (22) 83901; telex 57350; fax (22) 81468; internet http://www.cyp-net.com/cta/cta.html; f. 1974; jointly owned by the Turkish Cypriot Community Assembly Consolidated Improvement Fund and Turkish Airlines Inc; services to Turkey and five European countries; Gen. Man. Dr FERDA ÖNEŞ.

Tourism

In 1997 a total of 2,646,363 foreign tourists visited the Greek Cypriot area, and receipts from tourism amounted to C£830m. In 1996 an estimated 365,116 tourists visited the Turkish Cypriot area, and in 1995 revenue from tourism reached US $218.9m.

Cyprus Tourism Organization (CTO): POB 4535, 19 Limassol Ave, 2112 Nicosia; tel. (2) 337715; fax (2) 331644; e-mail cto@cyta.com.cy; Chair. A. EROTOCRITOU; Dir-Gen. FRYNI MICHAEL.

Turkish Cypriot Tourism Enterprises Ltd: Kyrenia (Girne), Mersin 10, Turkey; tel. (81) 52165; telex 57128; fax (81) 52073; f. 1974; Chair. YALÇIN VEHIT.

Defence

The National Guard was set up by the House of Representatives in 1964, after the withdrawal of the Turkish members. Men between the ages of 18 and 50 are liable to 26 months' conscription. In August 1997 it comprised an army of 10,000 regulars, mainly composed of Cypriot conscripts, but with some seconded Greek Army officers and NCOs, and 88,000 reserves. There is also a Greek Cypriot paramilitary force comprising 570 armed police and 320 maritime police. In August 1997 the 'TRNC' had an army of about 4,000 regulars and 26,000 reserves. Men between the ages of 18 and 50 are liable to 24 months' conscription. In 1997 it was estimated that the 'TRNC' forces were being supported by about 30,000 Turkish troops. Cyprus also contains the UN Peace-keeping Force and the British military bases at Akrotiri and Dhekelia.

Commander of the Greek Cypriot National Guard: Lt-Gen. NIKOLAOS VORVOLAKOS.

Commander of 'TRNC' Security Forces: Brig.-Gen. HASAN PEKER GUNAL.

UNITED NATIONS PEACE-KEEPING FORCE IN CYPRUS (UNFICYP)

Headquarters at POB 1642, Nicosia; tel. (2) 464000; telex 2329.

Set up for a three-month period in March 1964 by Security Council resolution (subsequently extended at intervals of three or six months by successive resolutions) to keep the peace between the Greek and Turkish communities and help to solve outstanding issues between them. In mid-1993, following an announcement by troop-providing countries that they were to withdraw a substantial number of troops, the Security Council introduced a system of financing UNFICYP by voluntary and assessed contributions. At 1 August 1997 the Force comprised 1,270 military and police personnel, drawn from six countries (compared with 2,078 at November 1992).

Commander: Maj.-Gen. EVERGISTO DE VERGARA (Argentina).

Special Adviser to the UN Secretary-General: Dr DIEGO CÓRDOVEZ (Ecuador).

See p. 224.

BRITISH SOVEREIGN BASE AREAS
Akrotiri and Dhekelia

Headquarters British Forces Cyprus, British Forces Post Office 53; tel. (5) 263395; fax (5) 211593.

Under the Cyprus Act 1960, the United Kingdom retained sovereignty in two sovereign base areas and this was recognized in the Treaty of Establishment signed between the United Kingdom, Greece, Turkey and the Republic of Cyprus in August 1960. The base areas cover 99 square miles. The Treaty also conferred on Britain certain rights within the Republic, including rights of movement and the use of specified training areas. In August 1997 an estimated 3,700 military personnel were resident in the sovereign base areas.

Administrator: Maj.-Gen. ANGUS RAMSAY.

Chief Officer of Administration: PATRICK ROTHERAM.

Senior Judge of Senior Judge's Court: (vacant).

Resident Judge of Judge's Court: GORDON WARD.

Education

Until 1965 each community in Cyprus managed its own schooling through a Communal Chamber. On 31 March, however, the Greek Communal Chamber was dissolved and a Ministry of Education was established to take its place. Intercommunal education has been placed under this Ministry.

GREEK CYPRIOT EDUCATION

Primary education is compulsory and is provided free in six grades to children between 5½ and 12 years of age. In some towns and large villages there are separate junior schools consisting of the first three grades. Apart from schools for the deaf and blind, there are also seven schools for handicapped children. In 1995/96 there were 647 Kindergartens (including privately run pre-primary schools) for children aged 3–5½ years of age. There were 381 primary schools, with 3,411 teachers and 64,660 pupils in 1995/96. In 1995 enrolment in primary education included 96% of children in the relevant age-group (males 96%; females 96%).

Secondary education is also free for all years of study and lasts six years, three years at the Gymnasium being followed by three years at technical school or the Lyceum. Attendance for the first cycle of secondary education is compulsory. Pupils at the Lyceums may choose one of five main fields of specialization: humanities, science, economics, commercial/secretarial and foreign languages. At technical schools students may undertake one of several specializations offered within two categories of courses—technician and craft; the school-leaving certificate awarded at the end of the course is equivalent to that of the Lyceum. In 1995/96 there were 123 secondary schools (gymnasia, lyceums and technical schools) with 4,832 teachers and 59,845 pupils. In addition, there were numerous privately-operated secondary schools, where instruction is in English. In 1995 enrolment in secondary education included 93% of children in the relevant age-group (males 91%; females 94%).

Post-Secondary education is offered at the University of Cyprus, which was inaugurated in September 1992 with 440 undergraduates. There are currently schools in the humanities and social sciences, pure and applied sciences, and economics and management. The University is expected to reach its full operational level of 4,000 students by 2000. In addition, there are five other public third-level institutions. The Higher Technical Institute offers sub-degree courses, leading to a diploma, in civil, electrical, mechanical and marine engineering and in computer studies. Other specialized training is provided at the Forestry College, the Higher Hotel Institute, the Mediterranean Institute of Management and the School of Nursing. There are also a number of private third-level institutions, registered with the Ministry of Education and Culture, offering courses in various fields.

In 1994/95, 9,188 students were studying at universities abroad, mainly in Greece, the USA, and the United Kingdom.

TURKISH CYPRIOT EDUCATION

With the exception of private kindergartens, a vocational school of agriculture attached to the Ministry of Agriculture, a training school for nursing and midwifery attached to the Ministry of Health and Social Welfare, and a school for hotel catering attached to the Ministry of Communications, Public Works and Tourism, all schools and educational institutes are administered by the Ministry of National Education and Culture.

Education in the Turkish Cypriot zone is divided into two sections, formal and adult education. Formal education covers nursery, primary, secondary and higher education. Adult (informal) education caters for special training outside the school system.

Formal education is organized into four categories: pre-primary, primary, secondary and higher education. Pre-primary education is provided by kindergartens for children between the ages of 5 and 6. In 1996/97 there were 6 public kindergartens with 41 teachers catering for 798 children. Primary education is provided at two stages. The first stage (elementary) lasts five years and caters for children aged 7–11. The second stage (junior), lasting three years, is intended for pupils aged 12–14. Both stages of primary education are free and compulsory. In 1996/97 there were 92 elementary primary schools with 1,088 teachers and 15,261 pupils. In that year there were 26 junior primary schools with 426 teachers and 8,487 pupils. Secondary education consists of a three-year programme of instruction for pupils aged 15–17. Pupils elect either to prepare for higher education, to prepare for higher education with vocational training, or to prepare for vocational training only. Secondary education is free, but not compulsory. In 1996/97 there were 14 schools and lycées, with 639 teachers and 5,512 pupils. There were also 13 lycées and technical secondary schools, with 341 teachers and 2,627 pupils.

In 1982 an Institute of Islamic Banking and Economics was opened to provide postgraduate training. Cyprus's first university, The Eastern Mediterranean University, which is located near Gazi Mağusa (Famagusta), was opened in October 1986. The university has four main faculties: Engineering, Arts and Sciences, Tourism and Hotel Management, and Economics and Business Administration. A total of 9,030 students attended the university in 1996/97. There are a further six institutions which provide higher education in the Turkish Cypriot zone: the Teachers' Training College in Lefkoşa (Nicosia), which trains teachers for the elementary school stage, attended by 142 students in 1996/97; the Near East University College in Lefkoşa (Nicosia), with 4,188 students; the International American University, with 758; the Girne (Kyrenia) American University, with 861; the Anadolu Open University, with 2,574; and Lefke (Levka) University, with 853.

In 1996/97 3,411 students were pursuing higher education studies abroad, mainly in Turkey, the USA and the United Kingdom.

Bibliography

Alastos, D. *Cyprus in History*. London, 1955.

Arnold, Percy. *Cyprus Challenge*. London, Hogarth Press, 1956.

Barker, Dudley. *Grivas*. London, Cresset Press, 1960.

Byford-Jones, W. *Grivas and the Story of EOKA*. London, Robert Hale, 1960.

Casson, S. *Ancient Cyprus*. London, 1937.

Crawshaw, Nancy. *The Cyprus Revolt: An Account of the Struggle for Union with Greece*. London, Allen and Unwin, 1978.

Denktaş, Rauf R. *The Cyprus Triangle*. London, K. Rüstem and Bros, 1988.

Emilianides, Achille. *Histoire de Chypre*. Paris, 1963.

Esin, Emel. *Aspects of Turkish Civilization in Cyprus*. Ankara, Ankara University Press, 1965.

Foley, Charles. *Island in Revolt*. London, Longmans Green, 1962.

   Legacy of Strife. London, Penguin, 1964.

Foot, Sylvia. *Emergency Exit*. London, Chatto and Windus, 1960.

Foot, Sir Hugh. *A Start in Freedom*. London, 1964.

Grivas (Dhigenis), George. *Guerrilla Warfare and EOKA's Struggle*. London, Longman, 1964.

   Memoirs of General Grivas. London, Longman, 1964.

Harbottle, Michael. *The Impartial Soldier*. Oxford University Press, 1970.

Hill, Sir George. *A History of Cyprus*. 4 vols, London, 1940–1952.

Hitchens, Christopher. *Cyprus*. London, Quartet, 1984.

House, William J. *Cypriot Women in the Labour Market: An Exploration of Myths and Reality*. London, International Labour Office, 1985.

Kyle, Keith. *Cyprus*. London, Minority Rights Group, 1984.

Kyriakides, S. *Cyprus – Constitutionalism and Crisis Government*. Philadelphia, University of Pennsylvania Press, 1968.

Lavender, D. S. *The Story of Cyprus Mines Corporation*. San Marino, Calif., 1962.

Luke, Sir H. C. *Cyprus under the Turks 1571–1878*. Oxford, 1921.

   Cyprus: A Portrait and an Appreciation. London, Harrap, 1965.

Meyer, A. J. (with S. Vassiliou). *The Economy of Cyprus*. Harvard University Press, 1962.

Newman, Philip. *A Short History of Cyprus*. 1940.

Panteli, Stavros. *The Making of Modern Cyprus*. Interworld, 1990.

Papadopoullos, T. *The Population of Cyprus (1570–1881)*. Nicosia, 1965.

Purcell, H. D. *Cyprus*. London, Benn, 1969.

Richard, J. *Chypre Sous les Lusignan*. Paris, 1962.

Sonyel, Salahi R. *Cyprus: The Destruction of a Republic. British Documents 1960–65*. London, Eothen Press, 1997.

Spyridakis, Dr C. *A Brief History of Cyprus*. Nicosia, 1964.

Storrs, Sir Ronald. *A Chronology of Cyprus*. Nicosia, 1930.

Stylianou, A. and J. *Byzantine Cyprus*. Nicosia, 1948.

Xydis, S. G. *Cyprus – Conflict and Conciliation 1945–58*. Columbus, Ohio, Ohio State University Press, 1967.

Official Books of Reference:

Cyprus: Documents relating to Independence of Cyprus and the Establishment of British Sovereign Base Areas. London, Cmnd 1093, HMSO, July 1960.

Cyprus: Treaty of Guarantee, Nicosia, 16 August 1960.

EGYPT

Physical and Social Geography

W. B. FISHER

SITUATION

The Arab Republic of Egypt occupies the north-eastern corner of the African continent, with an extension across the Gulf of Suez into the Sinai region which is usually, but not always, regarded as lying in Asia. The area of Egypt is 1,002,000 sq km (386,874 sq miles) but only 5.5% can be said to be permanently settled or cultivated, the remainder being desert or marsh. Egypt lies between Lat. 22° and 32°N; and the greatest distance from north to south is about 1,024 km (674 miles), and from east to west 1,240 km (770 miles), giving the country a roughly square shape, with the Mediterranean and Red seas forming respectively the northern and eastern boundaries. Egypt has political frontiers on the east with Israel, on the south with the Republic of Sudan, and on the west with the Great Socialist People's Libyan Arab Jamahiriya. The actual frontiers run, in general, as straight lines drawn directly between defined points, and do not normally conform to geographical features. Between June 1967 and October 1973 the *de facto* frontier with Israel was the Suez Canal. As a result of the 1979 Peace Treaty, the frontier reverted to a line much further to the east (see p. 121).

Egypt occupies a significant place in the world as one of the regions where, in all probability, the earliest developments of civilization and organized government took place. Though many archaeologists would not wholly subscribe to the view of Egypt as actually the first civilized country, there can be no doubt that from very early times the lower Nile Valley has been prominent as possessing strongly marked unity, with a highly specialized and characteristic way of life.

PHYSICAL FEATURES

The remarkable persistence of cultural cohesion amongst the Egyptian people may largely be explained by the geography of the country. Egypt consists essentially of a narrow, trough-like valley, some 3 km to 15 km wide, cut by the River Nile in the plateau of north-east Africa. At an earlier geological period a gulf of the Mediterranean Sea probably extended as far south as Cairo, but deposition of silt by the Nile has entirely filled up this gulf, producing the fan-shaped Delta region (22,000 sq km in area), through which flow two main distributary branches of the Nile—the eastern, or Damietta branch (240 km long), and the western, or Rosetta branch (235 km), together with many other minor channels. As deposition of silt takes place, large stretches of water are gradually impounded to form shallow lakes, which later become firm ground. At present there are four such stretches of water in the north of the Delta: from east to west, and, in order of size, lakes Menzaleh, Brullos, Idku and Mariut.

Upstream from Cairo the Nile Valley is at first 10 km to 15 km in width, and, as the river tends to lie close to the eastern side, much of the cultivated land, and also most of the big towns and cities, lie on the western bank. Towards the south the river valley gradually narrows until, at about 400 km from the frontier of Sudan, it is no more than 3 km wide. Near Aswan there is an outcrop of resistant rock, chiefly granite, which the river has not been able to erode as quickly as the rest of the valley. This gives rise to a region of cascades and rapids which is known as the First Cataract. Four other similar regions occur on the Nile, but only the First Cataract lies within Egypt. The cataracts form a barrier to human movement upstream and serve to isolate the Egyptian Nile from territories farther south. In Ancient Egypt, when river communications were of paramount importance, there was a traditional division of the Nile Valley into Lower Egypt (the Delta), Middle Egypt (the broader valley above the Delta), and Upper Egypt (the narrower valley as far as the cataracts). Nowadays, it is usual to speak merely of Upper and Lower Egypt, with the division occurring at Cairo.

The fertile strip of the Nile Valley is isolated to the south by the cataracts and by the deserts and swamps of Sudan; to the north by the Mediterranean Sea; and to east and west by desert plateaux, about which a little more must be said. The land immediately to the east of the Nile Valley, spoken of as the Eastern Highlands, is a complex region with peaks that rise 1,800 m to 2,100 m but also much broken up by deep valleys which make travel difficult. Owing to aridity the whole region is sparsely populated, with a few partly nomadic shepherds, one or two monasteries and a number of small towns associated chiefly with the exploitation of minerals—petroleum, iron, manganese and granite—that occur in this region. Difficult landward communications mean that contact is mostly by sea, except in the case of the ironfields. The Sinai, separated from the Eastern Highlands by the Gulf of Suez, is structurally very similar, but the general plateau level is tilted, giving the highest land (again nearly 2,100 m in elevation) in the extreme south, where it rises in bold scarps from sea-level. Towards the north the land gradually slopes down, ultimately forming the low-lying sandy plain of the Sinai desert which fringes the Mediterranean Sea. Because of its low altitude and accessibility, the Sinai, in spite of its desert nature, has been for many centuries an important corridor linking Egypt with Asia. It is now crossed only by a motor road, the railway having been destroyed in 1968 by occupying Israeli forces. Since its return to Egypt, efforts at development have been made by the Egyptian Government.

West of the Nile occur the vast expanses known as the Western Desert. Though by no means uniform in height, the land surface is much lower than that east of the Nile, and within Egypt rarely exceeds 300 m above sea-level. Parts are covered by extensive masses of light, shifting sand that often form dunes; but in addition there are a number of large depressions, some with the lowest parts actually below sea-level. These depressions seem to have been hollowed out by wind action, breaking up rock strata that were weakened by the presence of underground water, and most hollows still contain supplies of artesian water. In some instances (as, for example, the Qattara depression, and the Wadi Natrun, respectively south-west and south-east of Alexandria) the subterranean water is highly saline and consequently useless for agriculture; but in others—notably the oases of the Fayum, Siwa, Dakhlia, Behariya and Farafra—the water is sufficiently good to allow use for irrigation, and settlements have grown up within the desert.

CLIMATE

The main feature of Egyptian climate is the almost uniform aridity. Alexandria, the wettest part, receives only 200 mm of rain annually, and most of the south has 80 mm or less. In many districts rain may fall in quantity only once in two or three years, and it is apposite to recall that throughout most of Egypt, and even in Cairo itself, the majority of the people live in houses of unbaked, sun-dried brick. During the summer, temperatures are extremely high, reaching 38°C–43°C at times and even 49°C in the southern and western deserts. The Mediterranean coast has cooler conditions, with 32°C as a maximum; as a result the wealthier classes tend to move to Alexandria for the three months of summer. Winters are generally warm, with very occasional rain; but cold spells occur from time to time, and light snow is not unknown. Owing to the large extent of desert, hot dry sand-winds (called *khamsin*) are fairly frequent particularly in spring, and much damage can be caused to crops; it has been known for the temperature to rise by 20°C in two hours, and the wind to reach 150 km per hour. Another unusual condition is the occurrence of early morning fog in Lower Egypt during spring and early summer. This, on the other hand, has a beneficial effect on plant growth in that it supplies moisture and is a partial substitute for rainfall.

IRRIGATION

With a deficient rainfall over the entire country, human existence in Egypt is heavily dependent on irrigation from the Nile; in consequence it is now necessary to consider the regime of the river in some detail. It may be stated, in summary, that the river rises in the highlands of East Africa, with its main stream issuing from lakes Victoria and Albert. In southern Sudan it wanders sluggishly across a flat, open plain, where the fall in level is only 1:100,000. Here the shallow waters become a vast swamp, full of dense masses of papyrus vegetation, and this section of the Nile is called the Sudd (Arabic for 'blockage'). Finally, in the north of Sudan, the Nile flows in a well-defined channel and enters Egypt. In Upper Egypt the river is in the process of cutting its bed deeper into the rock floor; but in the lower part of its course silt is deposited, and the level of the land is rising—in some places by as much as 10 cm per century.

The salient feature of the Nile is, of course, its regular, annual flood, which is caused by the onset of summer rains in East Africa and Ethiopia. The flood travels northward, reaching Egypt during August, and within Egypt the normal rise in river level was at first 6.4 m, declining to 4.6 m as irrigation works developed. This cycle of flood had been maintained for several thousand years until, in 1969, construction of the Aswan High Dam made it a feature of the past (see below) so far as Egypt is concerned.

Originally, the flood waters were simply retained in specially prepared basins with earthen banks, and the water could then be used for three to four months after the flood. Within the last century, the building of large barrages, holding water all the year round, has allowed cultivation at any season. The old (basin) system allowed one or two crops per holding per year; the newer (perennial) system, allows three or even four. In the past, barley and wheat were the main crops; under perennial irrigation maize and cotton, which can tolerate the great summer heat, provided they are watered, have assumed equal importance.

The change-over from basin to perennial irrigation allowed a considerable population increase in Egypt, from about 2.5m. in 1800 to over 50m. in the 1990s, giving rural densities of over 2,500 per sq km in some areas; and, as 99% of all Egyptians live within the Nile valley (only 4% of the country's area), there is considerable pressure on the land.

With most Egyptians entirely dependent upon Nile water, almost all the water entering Egypt is fully utilized. However, there are enormous losses by evaporation which at present amount to some 70% of the total flow. Difficulties and opportunities over use of Nile water were exemplified by the High Dam scheme at Aswan, which created a lake 500 km (350 miles) in length and 10 km (6 miles) wide that extends southwards across the Sudanese frontier. The scheme necessitated the inundation of the Sudanese town of Wadi Halfa, whose 55,000–60,000 inhabitants were resettled at Kashm el-Girba, a district lying south-east of Khartoum, whilst displaced Egyptians were settled in 33 villages around Kom Ombo. Considerable Soviet financial assistance was secured for the scheme, and in May 1964 the first phase of the High Dam was inaugurated by President Nasser and Soviet leader Khrushchev. The High Dam is 3,600 m across, with a girth of 980 m at the river bed and 40 m at the top. It holds back one of the largest artificial lakes in the world (Lake Nasser), and makes possible large-scale storing of water from year to year, and a regular planned use of all Nile water independently of the precise amount of annual flood. Its irrigation potential is 2m. feddans for Lower Egypt alone, and the provision for the Nile valley (including Upper Egypt) was expected to add 30% to the total cultivable area of Egypt. Twelve generator units incorporated in the dam give considerable quantities of low-cost electric power. This power has been a most important aid to industrialization, especially for the new metal industries. The Dam was completed in July 1970 and officially inaugurated in January 1971.

However, adverse effects were soon noticed: scouring of the Nile bed below the dam; increased salinity in the lower stretches; reduced sedimentation below the dam and heavy deposition within the basin, resulting in the need for increasing use of artificial fertilizers, which must be imported; and, perhaps more seriously, the disappearance of fish (particularly sardines) off the Mediterranean coast of Egypt. Possibly the most serious effect of all was a notable rise in the water-table in some areas, owing to hydrostatic pressures, and the year-round presence of water. Besides disturbing irrigation systems (which are adapted to pre-existing conditions), salinity and gleying of a more permanent nature began to appear; reports of bilharzia and other parasitic diseases increased; and the appearance of the plant water hyacinth threatened to choke irrigation systems.

LANGUAGE

Arabic is the language of almost all Egyptians, though there are very small numbers of Berber-speaking villages in the western oases. Most educated Egyptians also speak either French or English, often with a preference for the former. This is a reflection of the traditional French interest in Egypt, which is reciprocated: governmental decrees are sometimes published in French, as well as Arabic, and newspapers in French have an important circulation in Cairo and Alexandria. Small colonies of Greeks and Armenians are also a feature of the larger Egyptian towns. It should perhaps be noted that the Arabic name for Egypt, Misr, is always used within the country itself.

History

Updated for this edition by SIMON CHAPMAN

PRE-ARAB EGYPT

Egypt's relative isolation, with the majority of the population living in the Nile Valley and the Nile Delta, with desert on either side, has produced a high degree of cultural individuality. Pharaonic Egypt lasted from the end of the fourth millennium BC until conquest by the Assyrians in 671 BC. The building of the pyramids and other works in the third millennium BC indicate a powerful monarchy commanding great resources. After the rule of Rameses II (c.1300–1234 BC), Egypt passed into a decline but, after the Assyrian conquest in 671, native rule was soon restored until 525, when Persia conquered Egypt.

The Persian kings patronized the religion of their subjects and were officially regarded as pharaohs. Another change occurred in 332 when the Persian satrap surrendered to Alexander the Great, who was recognized as a pharaoh and founded the city of Alexandria. After Alexander's death Egypt fell to his General, Ptolemy, and his dynasty was Greek in origin and outlook.

On the death of Cleopatra in 30 BC Egypt passed under Roman rule and became a province of a great Mediterranean empire. Christianity was introduced, and the Coptic church of Egypt clung to its monophysite beliefs in the face of Byzantine opposition.

THE COMING OF THE ARABS

Except for a brief Sasanian (Persian) invasion in 616, Egypt remained under Byzantine rule until, with the birth and advance of Islam in the seventh century AD, the Arab army under 'Amr ibn al-As invaded Egypt from Syria. The conquest was virtually complete by 641, but for some centuries Egypt remained an occupied rather than a Muslim country. The Copts, who disliked Byzantine rule, had not opposed the conquest. In the course of time, however, Egypt became an Arabic-speaking country with a Muslim majority, but there remained a Coptic Christian minority. For over two centuries Egypt was administered as part of the Abbasid caliphate of Baghdad, but the Tulunid and Ikshidid dynasties functioned in virtual independence of the caliph between 868 and 969. Ikshidid rule was ended in 969 by a Fatimid invasion from Tunisia. The Fatimids were Shi'a Muslims and Egypt was to remain under Shi'ite (as opposed to orthodox Sunni) rule until 1171.

Under the early Fatimids, Egypt enjoyed a golden age. The country was a well-administered absolute monarchy and it formed the central portion of an empire which, at its height, included North Africa, Sicily and western Arabia. The city of Cairo was developed and the mosque of al-Azhar founded. But, by the long reign of al-Mustansir (1035–94) decay had set in, and when the Kurdish Salah ad-Din ibn Ayyub, known to Europe as Saladin, rose to prominence as he opposed the Syrian Crusader states in the 12th century, he was able to become sultan over Egypt and almost the whole of the former Crusader territory.

When Saladin died in 1193, his Empire was divided amongst his heirs, one branch of which, the Egyptian Ayyubids, reigned in Cairo. Louis IX of France led an attack on Egypt in 1249, but was stopped at the battle of al-Mansura in 1250. Thereafter Egypt was ruled by Mamluk sultans until the Ottoman advance at the beginning of the 16th century.

OTTOMAN EGYPT: 1517–1798

By the beginning of the 16th century the Ottoman Turks had made dramatic advances. Constantinople was captured by them in 1453, and early in the 16th century the Turks were threatening Vienna. In their expansion southwards the Turks defeated the Mamluks at the battle of Marj Dabiq, north of Aleppo, in 1516, and overthrew the last Mamluk sultan at a second battle, outside Cairo, in 1517. Egypt became a province of the Ottoman Empire, but the Turks usually interfered little with the Egyptian administration. From time to time Mamluk grandees were virtually sovereign in Egypt.

At the end of the 18th century Egypt became a pawn in the war between France and Britain. Napoleon wanted to disrupt British commerce and eventually overthrow British rule in India. He landed at Alexandria in 1798, but in 1801 the French were forced to capitulate by a British and Ottoman force. French interest in Egyptian affairs and Egyptian culture continued, however.

INCREASED EUROPEAN INFLUENCE

The expulsion of the French was followed by a struggle for power in which the victor was an Albanian officer in the Ottoman forces, Muhammad Ali. In 1807 he defeated a British force which had occupied Alexandria, and between 1820 and 1822 his army conquered most of northern Sudan.

In 1824 Muhammad Ali sent his son Ibrahim with an Egyptian force to help the Sultan suppress the Greek struggle for independence, but European intervention in 1827 led to the destruction of the Turkish and Egyptian fleets at Navarino. On the rejection by the Sultan of Muhammad Ali's demand that he should be given Syria in recompense, Ibrahim invaded Syria in 1831. Ibrahim was eventually defeated and Muhammad Ali's dominion was restricted to Egypt and the Sudan, but his governorship was made hereditary. He died in 1849, having been predeceased by Ibrahim. Muhammad Ali introduced many features of Western intellectual life into Egypt, and a Western-educated class began to emerge. Muhammad Ali was succeeded by his grandson, Abbas I (1849–54), under whom Westernization was reduced, and he by Said (1854–64), Muhammad Ali's surviving son.

In 1854 Said granted a concession to a French engineer, Ferdinand de Lesseps, to build the Suez Canal, but work did not begin until 1859 and the canal was opened in 1869. By this time Said had been succeeded by Ibrahim's son, Ismail. Ismail extended his Sudanese dominions, built railways and constructed telegraph lines. Moreover, his personal expenses were high, and between 1863 and 1876 Egyptian indebtedness rose from £7m. to nearly £100m. In 1875 Ismail averted a financial crisis by selling his Suez Canal shares to the British Government. As part of the Ottoman Empire, Egypt was bound by the Capitulations—treaties with European powers giving European communities in Ottoman territories a considerable degree of autonomy under the jurisdiction of their consuls, and, under conditions of indebtedness and the necessity of loans from the European powers, financial control by outsiders increased.

Ismail was succeeded by his son Tawfiq, who ostensibly governed through a responsible Egyptian ministry, but strict financial control was exercised by a French and a British controller. Meanwhile a nationalist outlook was developing among those Egyptians who had been touched by Western influences, many of whom regarded the Khedive, Tawfiq, as a puppet maintained by France and Britain. In 1881 a group of army officers, led by Arabi Pasha, forced Tawfiq to form a new ministry and to summon the Chamber of Notables, a consultative body originally set up by Ismail. France opposed any concessions to placate Egyptian opinion, and Britain concurred in this. Feelings in Egypt hardened, and in 1882 the Khedive had to appoint a nationalist ministry with Arabi as Minister for War. France and Britain sent naval squadrons, but France subsequently withdrew support and a British expeditionary force landed at Ismailia and routed the Egyptian army at Tel el-Kebir. Cairo was occupied and Tawfiq's prerogatives were restored, to be subsequently exercised under British control.

INCREASED BRITISH INFLUENCE

Britain hoped to set Egyptian affairs in order and then withdraw, but Egypt's financial difficulties contributed towards Britain prolonging its stay. From 1883 to 1907 the Egyptian Government was dominated by the British Agent and Consul-General, Sir Evelyn Baring, who in 1891 became Lord Cromer. Tawfiq was succeeded by his son Abbas II in 1892. He resented Cromer's authority and a new nationalist movement developed under Mustafa Kamil, a young lawyer. A series of puppet governments preserved a façade of constitutionalism, but educated youth turned increasingly to opposition. British officials increased from about 100 in 1885 to over 1,000 in 1905, and were out of touch with the growing strength of nationalist feeling.

Cromer was succeeded in 1907 by Sir Eldon Gorst, who established better relations with the Khedive, and Gorst was in turn followed by Lord Kitchener in 1911. When Turkey entered the First World War in November 1914 on the side of Germany, Egypt was still nominally a province of the Ottoman Empire. Egypt was declared a British protectorate, with a British High Commissioner, and Britain assumed responsibility for the defence of the Suez Canal. In December Abbas II was deposed and the British Government offered the title of Sultan to Hussain Kamil, the brother of Tawfiq. When Hussain died in 1917 he was succeeded by his brother Fouad. The nationalist movement flourished under wartime conditions, and in November 1918 the nationalist leader Saad Zaghloul presented the High Commissioner, Sir Reginald Wingate, with a demand for autonomy, which Britain refused. The nationalists became known as the *Wafd* (Delegation), but a negotiated settlement was not forthcoming and on 28 February 1922 Britain unilaterally abolished the protectorate and recognized Egypt as an independent sovereign state. Britain, however, reserved to itself the security of the Suez Canal and the defence of Egypt. In March 1922 Fouad took the title of King of Egypt.

INDEPENDENCE

The years between independence and the Second World War brought a triangular struggle between the King, the Wafd and the British Government. The Wafd wanted a revolution, but the King owed his throne to the British. Elections usually gave the Wafd a majority, but a Wafd ministry was unacceptable to King Fouad, who normally had the concurrence of the British Government. In 1935 Fouad was succeeded by his son Farouk, and in 1936 an Anglo-Egyptian treaty of 20 years' duration was signed which terminated British occupation but empowered Britain to station forces in the Suez Canal Zone until the Egyptian army was in a position to ensure the security of the canal.

During the Second World War Egypt was a vital strategic factor as the British base in the Middle East. Egyptian support for the Allied cause was by no means total. The Wafd favoured co-operation with the British, and Britain forced Farouk's acquiescence in the formation of a Wafdist Government under Nahas Pasha in 1942. Nahas became increasingly enthusiastic about Arab unity and was instrumental in establishing the League of Arab States (Arab League). In 1944 his Government fell.

Egypt joined Iraq, Syria and Jordan in military action following the declaration of the State of Israel in May 1948. Military failure resulted. The King's early popularity had vanished; the Muslim Brotherhood, a puritanical religious body, had become a threat, and communism had gained new adherents. The discredited regime made a last bid for royal and popular support when Nahas, again in power, abrogated the 1936 Treaty with Britain. Terrorism and economic sanctions were then employed in an attempt to compel the British forces to withdraw from the Canal Zone.

THE REVOLUTION: 1952–56

On 23 July 1952 a group of young army officers, the 'Free Officers', who had long been planning a *coup d'état*, seized power in Cairo. They invited the veteran politician, Ali Maher, to form a government under their control, and secured the abdication of King Farouk in favour of his infant son, Ahmad Fuad II, on 26 July. Farouk sailed into exile.

Gen. Muhammad Neguib, an associate of the Free Officers who had incurred the enmity of King Farouk and who had earlier made himself popular by his condemnation of the British action in 1942, was made Commander-in-Chief of the Armed Forces and head of the military junta. A Council of Regency was formed in August. On 7 September, after an attempt by the Wafd and other parties to resume the political battle on their own terms, a new Cabinet, with Gen. Neguib as Prime Minister, was substituted for that of Ali Maher. Real power, however, lay with the nine officers who formed the Revolutionary Command Council (RCC).

The Revolution soon gained momentum. In September 1952 land ownership was limited to 300 acres in any one family and the power of the feudal class, which had for so long dominated Egyptian political life, was destroyed. Land owned by the royal family was confiscated. On 10 December the Constitution was abolished, and on 16 January 1953 all political parties were dissolved. It was announced that there would be a three-year transition period before representative government was restored. On 18 June the monarchy was abolished and Egypt declared a republic, with Neguib as President and Prime Minister as well as Chairman of the RCC. Col Gamal Abd an-Nasser, who, although leader of the Free Officers, had hitherto remained in the background, became Deputy Prime Minister and Minister of the Interior, and Abd al-Hakim Amer was appointed Commander-in-Chief of the Armed Forces.

A struggle for power soon developed between Gen. Neguib, whose personal tendencies were Islamic and conservative, and Col Nasser. On 25 February 1954 Neguib was relieved of his posts as President, Prime Minister and Chairman of the RCC and accused of having attempted to concentrate power in his own hands. Nasser became Prime Minister and Chairman of the RCC in his place for a few days but Neguib was restored as President and reassumed both the other posts, only to be ousted again as Prime Minister by Nasser in April. Neguib had suffered a defeat and his liberal measures were rescinded. When in October a member of the Muslim Brotherhood attempted to assassinate Nasser, its leaders and several thousand alleged supporters were arrested and in subsequent trials a number of death sentences were passed. On 14 November 1954 Neguib was relieved of the office of President and accused of being involved in a Muslim Brotherhood conspiracy against the regime. He was placed under house arrest and Nasser became acting Head of State.

A settlement of the Sudan and Suez problems had been facilitated by the expulsion of King Farouk. The claim to the joint monarchy of Egypt and Sudan was dropped and negotiations with Sudanese leaders were facilitated because Neguib himself was half-Sudanese and popular in Sudan. An Anglo-Egyptian agreement, signed on 12 February 1953, ended the Condominium and offered the Sudanese the choice of independence or union with Egypt. Egyptian expectation that they would choose the latter was disappointed; the overthrow of Neguib

and the suppression of the Muslim Brotherhood fed the century-old suspicion of Egyptian motives.

An Anglo-Egyptian agreement on Suez was signed on 19 October 1954; this provided for the withdrawal of British troops from the Canal Zone within 20 months. The agreement recognized the international importance of the Suez Canal (which was described as 'an integral part of Egypt') and expressed the determination of both parties to uphold the 1888 Constantinople Convention.

Under Nasser Egypt began to assert its importance in world affairs. He sought influence in three circles: the Islamic, the African and the Arab, and his visit to the Bandung conference in 1955 added a fourth: the 'non-aligned'. Egypt led the opposition among certain Arab states to the Baghdad Pact (later to become the Central Treaty Organization). In October 1955 Egypt concluded defence agreements with Syria and with Saudi Arabia and in April 1956 a military pact was signed between Egypt, Saudi Arabia and Yemen. Tension with Israel remained high, and raids and counter-raids across the border of the Gaza Strip called for unceasing vigilance on the part of the UN observers stationed on the frontier. In September 1955 Nasser announced an arms deal with Czechoslovakia which was to supply large quantities of military equipment, including Soviet tanks and aircraft, in return for cotton and rice.

In 1956 a constitutional basis for Col Nasser's authority was established. A new Constitution providing for a strong presidency was proclaimed in January and on 23 June approved in a plebiscite in which the citizens of the Egyptian Republic also elected Nasser as President.

THE SUEZ CRISIS AND ITS CONSEQUENCES: 1956–57

President Nasser's policy of non-alignment, which implied willingness to deal with both power blocs, was followed by the Egyptian attempt to obtain funds for the ambitious High Dam project at Aswan. By this project the Egyptian Government aimed to increase cultivable land and generate electricity for industrialization, which was seen as the main solution to Egypt's increasing population problem. Following offers of assistance from the USA and Britain and, separately, from the USSR, the International Bank for Reconstruction and Development (IBRD) offered a loan of $200m. in February 1956, on condition that the USA and Britain lent a total of $70m. and that the agreement of the riparian states to the scheme was obtained; Egypt was to provide local services and material.

The last British troops were withdrawn from Egypt in June 1956, in accordance with the 1954 agreement. Relations with the West were impeded, however, by Egyptian opposition to the Baghdad Pact and strong propaganda attacks on Britain, France and the USA. On 20 July the USA and Britain withdrew their offers of finance for the High Dam, noting that agreement between the riparian states had not been achieved and that Egypt's ability to devote adequate resources to the scheme was doubtful. The USSR made no compensating move. On 26 July President Nasser announced that the Suez Canal Company had been nationalized and that revenue from the Canal would be used to finance the High Dam.

Britain, France and the USA protested strongly at this action, and, after an international conference had met in London in August, a committee, under the chairmanship of the Prime Minister of Australia, went to Cairo to submit proposals for the operation of the Canal under an international system. These were rejected by the Egyptian Government. At a second London conference, in September, a Suez Canal Users' Association was formed and was later joined by 16 states. On 13 October the UN Security Council voted on an Anglo-French resolution embodying basic principles for a settlement agreed earlier between the British, French and Egyptian Ministers of Foreign Affairs in the presence of the UN Secretary-General. The first part of this, outlining the agreed principles, was adopted unanimously; the second, endorsing the proposals of the first London conference and inviting Egypt to make prompt proposals providing no less effective guarantees to users, was vetoed by the USSR.

Britain and France, thus frustrated in their attempts to retain some measure of control over the Suez Canal, at this stage reached a secret understanding with Israel involving military action. Following the disclosure on 24 October that a unified military command had been formed by Egypt, Jordan and Syria, Israeli forces crossed into Sinai on 29 October, ostensibly to attack Egyptian *fedayin* bases, and advanced towards the Suez Canal. On 30 October France and Britain called on Israel and Egypt to cease warlike action and withdraw their forces from either side of the Canal; Egypt was requested to agree to an Anglo-French force moving temporarily into key positions at Port Said, Ismailia and Suez; Israel agreed but Egypt refused. The same day, at a meeting of the UN Security Council, Britain and France vetoed US and Soviet resolutions calling for an immediate Israeli withdrawal and calling on all UN members to refrain from the use of force or the threat of force.

Anglo-French air operations against Egypt began on 31 October but paratroops and seaborne forces landed in the Port Said area only on 5 November. Meanwhile, on 2 November, the UN General Assembly called for a cease-fire and two days later adopted a Canadian proposal to create a UN Emergency Force to supervise the ending of the hostilities. On 6 November, following considerable US pressure, the British Prime Minister, Sir Anthony Eden, announced that, subject to confirmation that Egypt and Israel had accepted an unconditional cease-fire, the armed conflict would end at midnight.

The organization of the UN force was rapidly undertaken and the first units reached Egypt on 15 November. The withdrawal of the Anglo-French forces was completed the following month. Israeli forces, which had occupied the entire Sinai peninsula, withdrew from all areas except the Gaza Strip, which they wished to prevent becoming a base for more raids, and Sharm esh-Sheikh at the entrance to the Gulf of Aqaba, which commanded the seaway to the port of Eilat. These areas were returned to Egyptian control in March 1957 after pressure on Israel by the USA.

The Suez Canal, which had been blocked by the Egyptians, was cleared by a UN salvage fleet and reopened at the end of March 1957. The terms under which the Canal reopened were full control by the Egyptian Canal Authority and respect for the Constantinople Convention of 1888, which provided that the Suez Canal should be open to vessels of all nationalities, in war and peace. Disputes would be settled in accordance with the UN Charter or referred to the International Court of Justice.

UNION OF EGYPT AND SYRIA

Elections to the Egyptian National Assembly, provided for in the 1956 Constitution, were held in July 1957. Only candidates approved by President Nasser and his colleagues were permitted to stand and it was clear that the 350 members elected (who included women) were not expected to exert much influence on the Government.

Following the defence agreement in 1955, discussions had been held in the following two years on union between Egypt and Syria. Both countries were aligned against the West and looked to the USSR and other communist states for support, and in Syria pro-Egyptian elements were in the ascendant. On 1 February 1958 the union of Egypt and Syria, under the title of the United Arab Republic (UAR), was announced, but it was not until 21 July 1960 that the first National Assembly of the UAR, consisting of deputies from both Egypt and Syria, was opened in Cairo by President Nasser.

EXTERNAL RELATIONS: 1958–61

During this period President Nasser was actively concerned with changes in the rest of the Arab world.

An invitation was extended to other Arab states to join the new union and in March 1958 the UAR and Yemen entered into a loose association referred to as the United Arab States. This association did not prosper, however, and was terminated by the UAR in December 1961.

The military revolution in Iraq in July, in which the royal family and the Prime Minister, Nuri as-Said, were murdered, destroyed the only Arab regime in the Middle East to have identified itself explicitly with the West. The immediate dispatch of American troops to Lebanon and of British forces to Jordan drew strong protests from the UAR which were echoed by the USSR. The USA and Britain gave warning of the grave consequences of any conflict between their forces and those under the control of Egypt and Syria. President Nasser visited Moscow and on his return received in Damascus a delegation

from the new republican regime in Baghdad. A joint communiqué on 19 July declared that the UAR and Iraq would assist each other to repel any foreign aggression.

President Nasser's hostility to the West found favour with the USSR, with which the UAR established closer ties during these years. Soviet military and industrial aid was granted and in December 1958 an agreement was concluded which ensured Soviet assistance for the building of the Aswan High Dam. Work on the first stage of the High Dam began in January 1960.

Relations with the West improved during 1959 and 1960. Through the mediation of the IBRD an agreement with Britain was signed on 1 March 1959 providing for the payment by the UAR of £27.5m. as compensation for British private property taken over at the time of the Suez crisis in 1956. Diplomatic relations with Britain were resumed at chargé d'affaires level in December 1959 and raised to ambassadorial level early in 1961. A $56.5m. loan to improve the Suez Canal was obtained from the World Bank in 1959, and other aid came from the USA in 1960.

SYRIAN WITHDRAWAL FROM UAR

President Nasser replaced the two Regional Executive Councils and the Central Cabinet of the UAR with a single central government in August 1961. Syria had by now become dissatisfied with the union and on 28 September the Syrian army seized control in Damascus and Syria withdrew from the UAR. President Nasser at first called for resistance to the Syrian *coup d'état* but, when the rebels were seen to be in firm control, said on 5 October that he would not oppose recognition of Syria's independence. The loss of Syria was a bitter blow to President Nasser and his Egyptian colleagues who now set about a re-examination of their policies which resulted in a renewal of revolutionary fervour.

The UAR Government (Egypt retained the full title) was reformed on 18 October and a National Congress of Popular Forces, consisting of 1,750 delegates, representing economic and professional interests and other social groups, rather than geographical areas, met in Cairo on 21 May 1962. President Nasser presented the National Congress with a draft National Charter outlining his programme for developing the UAR according to Arab socialist principles. A new democratic system of government was introduced, based on the Arab Socialist Union (ASU) (replacing the National Union) and including popular councils of which at least one-half of the members would be workers or *fellahin*.

MORE ATTEMPTS AT UNION

The Syrian *coup d'état* had been preceded by the overthrow in February 1963 of the regime of Gen. Kassem in Iraq. These changes in power brought Syria and Iraq into closer alignment with Egypt and it was announced on 17 April that agreement had been reached on the formation of a federation of the three countries under the name of the United Arab Republic. Rivalries, however, arose in both Baghdad and Damascus between supporters of the Baath Party and 'Nasserists', and by August President Nasser had withdrawn from the agreement, claiming that the Baathists had established one-party dictatorships in Syria and Iraq and ignored his insistence on wider nationalist representation.

A month later President Aref of Iraq called for a Baathist union of the three countries but, after the expulsion of Baath leaders from Iraq in November 1963 and the consolidation of power in Aref's hands, the unity movement between Iraq and Syria fell apart and Iraq and Egypt again moved closer together. A Unified Political Command between Iraq and Egypt began work in early 1965, but progress towards unity was slow.

During 1964 President Nasser took an important initiative in Arab League affairs by calling two Arab summit meetings in Egypt, which determined Arab policy on the use of water from the River Jordan and also strengthened the armies of Syria, Lebanon and Jordan. A further £E1m. was set aside for the formation of the Palestine Liberation Organization (PLO).

The Arab reconciliation and presentation of a united front lasted until the spring of 1965. Iraq, Kuwait, Yemen (Arab Republic), Algeria and Lebanon continued to follow President Nasser's lead, only Syrian critics complaining that UAR policy was not sufficiently anti-Israeli. Relations between the UAR and Jordan improved strikingly and, after a conference of heads of Arab governments in Cairo in January 1965 to discuss co-ordination of Arab policies, King Hussein, previously the object of UAR attacks and derision, himself paid a visit to Cairo.

In Yemen, despite Egyptian support, the republican regime seemed no closer to victory over the royalists, who held the mountainous regions of the north-east and were assisted by Saudi Arabian finance and supplies of arms. This military stalemate and the financial burden of maintaining some 50,000 troops in Yemen moved President Nasser to attempt to disengage, but negotiations ended in deadlock and Egyptian troops remained in Yemen. On 22 February 1966, the day the British Government announced that British forces would leave Aden and South Arabia when that territory became independent in 1968, President Nasser stated that Egyptian troops would not be withdrawn until the Revolution in Yemen could 'defend itself against the conspiracies of imperialism and reactionaries'.

CHANGES OF INTERNATIONAL ALIGNMENT

The years 1964 and 1965 saw a deterioration of UAR relations with the West and increasing dependence on the Soviet Union.

Relations with the USA were adversely affected by UAR support for the Stanleyville rebels in the Congo during the winter of 1964–65. Diplomatic relations with Britain, already worsened by Egyptian encouragement of dissident elements in South Arabia, were severed by the UAR in December 1965 over the Rhodesia issue, in common with eight other members of the Organization of African Unity (OAU).

Relations with the USSR had been strengthened in May 1964 when the Soviet Premier, Nikita Khrushchev, made a 16-day visit to Egypt to attend the ceremony marking the completion of the first stage of the Aswan High Dam, being built with Soviet aid. President Nasser paid his third visit to the USSR in August 1965 and (Khrushchev having been overthrown) the new Soviet Premier, Alexei Kosygin, visited the UAR in May 1966, expressing support for UAR policies and again demonstrating Soviet interest in the Middle East.

DOMESTIC TROUBLES

Although President Nasser obtained over 99% of the votes cast in the presidential referendum in March 1965, there were subsequently more signs of discontent in the UAR than at any time since he had come to power. In a speech to Arab students during his visit to Moscow in August 1965, he disclosed that a plot against his life had been discovered, in which the prohibited Muslim Brotherhood was thought to have been involved.

In September 1965 a new Government headed by Zakaria Mohi ed-Din replaced that of Ali Sabri, who became Secretary-General of the ASU. Thereafter, administrative changes were made and the security system was improved. Taxation was increased and measures of retrenchment were introduced because of increasing economic difficulties, particularly the acute shortage of foreign exchange. US wheat supplies were continued, credits from France, Japan and Italy and a loan from Kuwait were obtained and there were increased drawings from the International Monetary Fund (IMF). Nevertheless the level of imports, particularly food to feed the growing population, and the debt-service burden resulting from the first Five-Year Plan caused a continuing drain on foreign exchange reserves and the UAR faced a balance of payments crisis. The second Five-Year Plan was revised and extended over seven years and President Nasser gave public warnings that sacrifices were necessary in every field as Egypt lacked the foreign currency to pay for imports. He refused, however, to abandon the expensive commitment in Yemen. Zakaria Mohi ed-Din's replacement in September 1966 by Sidki Sulaiman (a technocrat who retained his post as Minister of the High Dam) was seen as the outcome of disagreement over retrenchment measures. When the UAR defaulted on repayments due to the IMF in December 1966, the country was on the verge of bankruptcy.

WIDENING RIFT WITH SAUDI ARABIA

The rift between the UAR and Saudi Arabia widened. President Nasser in February 1966 expressed opposition to an Islamic grouping which King Faisal was promoting, and in the succeeding months propaganda warfare between the two countries was intensified. In the middle of the year the President stated that he would not attend an Arab summit conference with Saudi Arabia and Jordan, both of which he criticized for obtaining British and US military aid, and advocated for the indefinite postponement of the conference planned for September. A majority of Arab states agreed, but in October Tunisia severed relations with the UAR over continued differences on Arab League policies.

In Yemen, Egyptian forces had been withdrawn from northern and eastern areas and concentrated in the triangle between San'a, Hodeida and Taiz. Egyptian control over the republican armed forces and administration was increased and when, in September 1966, after President Sallal had returned to Yemen from a year's absence in Cairo, the republican Prime Minister, Hassan al-Amri, and seven senior members of his Cabinet visited Egypt to make a plea for greater independence, they were arrested and detained there. The following month, about 100 senior Yemen officials were dismissed and arrests and executions were carried out.

WAR WITH ISRAEL

The events of May 1967 were to transform the Middle East. There had been an increase in Syrian guerrilla activities in Israel during the previous six months and in April the tension led to fighting in the Tiberias area, during which six Syrian aircraft were shot down. Israeli warnings to the Syrian Government, culminating on 12 May in the threat by Prime Minister Eshkol of severe reprisals if terrorist activities were not controlled, prompted Syrian allegations that Israel was about to mount a large-scale attack on Syria. President Nasser, who had been reproached for not aiding Syria in the April fighting in accordance with the mutual defence agreement, responded immediately, moving large numbers of troops to the Israeli border. He secured the dissolution of the UN Emergency Force, which depended on Egyptian permission for its presence on the Egyptian side of the frontier, and reoccupied the gun emplacement at Sharm esh-Sheikh on the Straits of Tiran. He later justified these steps by claiming that he had received Syrian and Soviet warnings that Israeli troops were concentrated on the Syrian border (an allegation subsequently disproved by reports of UN truce observers) and an invasion of Syria was imminent.

When on 23 May President Nasser closed the Straits of Tiran to Israeli shipping, thereby effectively blockading the Israeli port of Eilat, his prestige in the Arab world increased considerably. Britain and the USA protested that the Gulf of Aqaba was an international waterway; Israel regarded the blockade of the Straits as an unambiguous act of war. As tension increased, King Hussein of Jordan concluded a mutual defence pact with the UAR and was immediately joined by Iraq.

On 5 June Israel launched large-scale air attacks on Egyptian, Jordanian, Syrian and Iraqi airfields, and Israeli ground forces made rapid advances into the Gaza Strip, Sinai and western Jordan; there was also fighting on the Israeli-Syrian border. The outcome was decided within hours by the air strikes, which destroyed the bulk of the Arab air forces, and the Israeli ground forces were everywhere successful. By 10 June, when all participants had accepted the UN Security Council's demand for a cease-fire, Israeli troops were in control of the Sinai peninsula as far as the Suez Canal (including Sharm esh-Sheikh), the West Bank of the Jordan (including the Old City of Jerusalem), the Gaza Strip and Syrian territory extending 12 miles from the Israeli border. The Suez Canal was blocked by Egypt in the course of the fighting. President Nasser offered to resign, but popular support led him to withdraw his resignation. He dismissed a number of senior army officers and took over himself the duties of Prime Minister and Secretary-General of the ASU.

The implications of the catastrophe were only gradually realized. It was estimated that the loss of revenue from the Suez Canal, from oil produced in Sinai and from tourism amounted to some £E12.5m. per month, or almost half Egypt's foreign currency earnings. Also, the withdrawal of a large part of the Egyptian force in Yemen reduced Nasser's ability to influence affairs both in that country and in Aden and South Arabia (which became independent as the Republic of Southern Yemen on 30 November 1967, after the withdrawal of British troops).

The USSR, which had given the Arab cause strong verbal support throughout the crisis, continued to take a strong pro-Arab stand at the UN and President Podgorny paid a lengthy visit to Cairo to discuss future Egyptian policy. The USSR replaced about half the lost Egyptian aircraft and provided other military supplies and instructors.

Israel demanded direct negotiations with the Arab states for a peace settlement but the fourth conference of Arab Heads of State, held in Khartoum at the end of August 1967, decided neither to recognize nor negotiate with Israel. At this conference, in which Syria did not participate, it was agreed that the embargo on oil supplies to Western countries (applied the previous June) should be ended, that the Suez Canal should remain closed until Israeli forces were withdrawn, and that Saudi Arabia, Kuwait and Libya should give special aid of £95m. a year to the UAR (and also £40m. a year to Jordan) until the 'effects of the aggression' were eliminated. King Faisal and President Nasser announced their agreement on a peace plan for Yemen under which Egyptian troops were to be withdrawn within three months and Saudi Arabia was to stop supplying the royalists; the withdrawal was subsequently completed by December (President Sallal being deposed by republican leaders in November).

After repeated violations of the cease-fire by both sides, the UN Security Council, on 22 November 1967, adopted a British resolution laying down the principles for a just and lasting peace in the Middle East and authorizing the appointment of a UN special representative to assist in achieving a settlement. This was Resolution 242 (see Documents on Palestine, p. 115), which has subsequently formed the basis of most attempts to restore peace to the Middle East. Dr Gunnar Jarring was appointed UN Special Representative to the region and quickly began discussions with Arab and Israeli leaders which continued for a number of years.

THE UAR AFTER THE JUNE WAR

Meanwhile President Nasser faced daunting economic difficulties and a disturbed political situation in Egypt. An austerity budget had been framed in July 1967. The cost of re-equipping the armed forces required reductions in investment, in spite of Soviet aid and assistance from other Arab governments. Socialist policies were still pursued, as demonstrated by the decision, announced in October, to nationalize the whole-sale trade. The continuing shortage of foreign exchange made it desirable to improve the UAR's relations with the West and in December diplomatic relations with Britain were resumed. A bridging loan from British, West German and Italian banks, obtained in February 1968, enabled the UAR to make the repayments to the IMF which had been outstanding since the end of 1966, and in March the IMF approved further drawings.

Widespread demonstrations by students and workers took place in Cairo, Helwan and other centres, towards the end of February 1968. Initially organized to protest against the leniency of court sentences passed against senior air force officers for their failure to prevent the destruction of the UAR air force on 5 June, they revealed widespread discontent. Several people were killed in clashes with police, and the universities were closed; nevertheless President Nasser realized the need for immediate conciliatory action. Retrials were ordered and comprehensive changes to the Cabinet were announced, including the introduction of a number of civilian experts. Ali Sabri, who had been reinstated as Secretary-General of the ASU in January, was also included but Zakaria Mohi ed-Din left the Government. President Nasser retained the premiership.

In March President Nasser announced a new plan to build a modern state in Egypt based on democracy, science and technology. The single party system would remain but there would be free elections throughout the ASU. In a plebiscite on 2 May the 'Declaration of 30 March' was overwhelmingly approved. The first of a number of ASU elections were held in June; these proceedings, however, attracted little public interest.

Deprived of foreign exchange by the continued closure of the Canal and the reduction in the tourist trade, the UAR remained dependent on the regular aid payments from Saudi Arabia, Kuwait and Libya and on Soviet assistance. There were signs that the civilian economy ministers favoured some relaxation of over-rigid state control in industry and more encouragement

of private enterprise and foreign investment. Meanwhile, military expenditure in 1968 and 1969 remained high; Soviet arms deliveries continued, as did the presence in Egypt of some 3,000 Soviet military advisers and instructors.

The efforts of Dr Jarring, the Special Representative of the UN Secretary-General, to reconcile Israel, the UAR and Jordan had, by the end of 1968, yielded little success. In April 1969, following initiatives by the USSR and France, those two countries, together with Britain and the USA, as permanent members of the UN Security Council, embarked on a series of discussions in an unsuccessful attempt to promote a settlement.

A pattern of sporadic action, involving artillery duels across the Suez Canal, commando raids and air combat developed throughout 1969 and into 1970, with growing Soviet involvement in Egypt's defence. In the summer of 1970 the US Secretary of State, William Rogers, presented a set of proposals for solving the continuing Middle East crisis. An uneasy cease-fire, but no permanent solution, resulted.

EGYPT AFTER NASSER

Although President Nasser had clear differences with the Palestinian guerrillas over their rejection of the US peace proposals and the hijacking of western airliners at the beginning of September 1970, one of his final acts was to secure agreement in Cairo between King Hussein of Jordan and the Palestinian leader, Yasser Arafat, for an end to the fighting between the Jordanian army and the guerrillas.

Nasser's sudden death on 28 September 1970 came as a profound shock, precipitating fears that peace prospects for the Middle East would now be jeopardized. A close associate of Nasser, and Vice-President at the time of his death, Col Anwar Sadat, was immediately appointed provisional President by the Cabinet and the ASU, being later elected President in a national referendum, and by mid-1971 he was firmly in control of the government of Egypt.

In November 1970 President Sadat had agreed to the creation of a federation with Sudan and Libya. Sudan, however, later postponed its membership of the union. In April 1971 Syria agreed to become the third member of the federation. The federation proposals, together with Sadat's plan for the reopening of the Canal, precipitated a crisis in the leadership, which led to a comprehensive purge by Sadat of opponents at all levels of the Government, including Ali Sabri, one of the two Vice-Presidents. In July new elections were held, not only for all levels of the ASU, but also for trade unions and professional bodies. The first permanent Constitution since the 1952 revolution was approved in September. It contained important clauses governing personal freedoms and replaced the name of United Arab Republic with that of the Arab Republic of Egypt.

During 1971 Egypt made repeated declarations of its intention to wage war against Israel—at an opportune time—and Egyptian officials mounted an extensive diplomatic campaign to summon support from the West. In September 1971 the first large-scale military operations on the Canal since the August 1970 cease-fire were mounted and in December the UN passed a resolution advocating the resumption of the Jarring peace mission.

Egypt was becoming increasingly dependent on the USSR, both militarily and economically. Student riots at the beginning of 1972 prompted assurances from President Sadat that an armed confrontation with Israel was definitely intended. Against this background of increasing internal unease Egypt intensified efforts to diversify sources of development aid and armaments. The Suez–Alexandria (Sumed) pipeline received promises of Western backing and in May 1972 a five-year preferential trade agreement was concluded with the EC.

CRISIS IN EGYPTIAN–SOVIET RELATIONS

The most striking event of 1972 was the dismissal of Soviet military advisers from Egypt in July. This did not lead to a rupture in Egyptian–Soviet relations but neither did it result in any significant *rapprochement* with the West; anti-American feeling persisted. A new round of diplomatic visits to state Egypt's case, particularly in the West and the Far East, ensued and arms supplies were requested from France and Britain. With the announcement on 2 August 1972 of Egypt's plan to merge with Libya, France stated that supplies of *Mirage* fighters to Libya would continue, Libya not being in direct conflict with Israel.

Contacts with the USSR continued and economic relations appeared unaffected by the events of July but it was clear that the USSR was looking elsewhere to maintain its presence in the Mediterranean. It was unclear to what extent Sadat's hand had been forced in ordering the Soviet withdrawal.

INTERNAL UNREST

A law enacted in August 1972 provided for penalties as severe as life imprisonment for offences endangering national unity, including opposing the Government by force and inciting violence between Muslims and the Coptic minority. Clashes between these two communities were becoming more frequent and, along with increasing student unrest, were seen as an expression of dissatisfaction with the state of 'no-peace-no-war'. The Government resorted to repeated assurances of military preparations. Indeed, in December 1972 Sadat ordered preparations for war, after strong criticism in the People's Assembly (the new legislative body comprising 350 elected members and 10 presidential nominees–instituted by the new Constitution, and elected in October and November 1971) of the Government's policies. Another cause of uneasiness was the proposed merger with Libya, which many felt might give Col Muammar al-Qaddafi, the Libyan leader, excessive control over Egypt's destiny.

In January 1973 there were violent clashes between police and students. In February a number of left-wing elements, including several journalists, were expelled from the ASU; student unrest continued and in March President Sadat took over from Aziz Sidqi (who was appointed in January 1972 in succession to Dr Mahmoud Fawzi, 1970–72) as Prime Minister. The new administration's policies were approved by the People's Assembly but the Government was criticized for failing to follow a clear-cut economic policy, particularly with regard to the latest Five-Year Plan.

RELATIONS WITH LIBYA

Egypt and Libya had agreed a programme providing for full union by stages at a meeting between the two Heads of State in Benghazi, Libya, in August 1972, and a merger of the two countries was planned to take place on 1 September 1973. The Libyan leader, Col Qaddafi, demonstrated greater enthusiasm than President Sadat for total union, and in July 1973 Qaddafi organized a 40,000-strong Libyan march on Cairo, in order to bring pressure to bear on Egypt. The march was turned back about 200 miles from Cairo, however, and Sadat, although still supportive of eventual union, stated that 'enthusiasm and emotional impulses are not a sufficient basis for unity'. An agreement in principle was nevertheless signed on 29 August, but few practical steps were taken to ensure its prompt implementation.

Throughout 1974 and early 1975 relations between the two countries deteriorated to such an extent that President Sadat asserted in a press interview in April 1975 that Qaddafi was '100% sick'. At the time Libya had been threatening to take action against Egyptians working in Libya. Relations worsened when a large Soviet-Libyan arms agreement was revealed later in the month. President Sadat hastily accused Libya and the USSR of conducting an international campaign against him and his Middle East policy. Libya was among the Arab countries severely critical of the Second Interim Disengagement Agreement between Egypt and Israel in September 1975. In July 1977 open warfare took place on the border between Egypt and Libya, and when Sadat visited Israel in November 1977 (see below), relations deteriorated even further, with Egypt severing diplomatic relations with Libya in December. Libya joined the rest of the Arab world in condemning the Egypt-Israel peace treaty in March 1979, and it was reported that renewed outbreaks of fighting on the Egypt-Libya border were prevented only by the intervention of the USA. In March 1980 Libya constructed airfields and fortifications on the border with Egypt, and in June 1980 Egypt declared martial law in the border area with Libya for a period of one year.

THE OCTOBER WAR AND ITS AFTERMATH

Between the June 1967 war and October 1973 Egyptian leaders frequently stated that the war against Israel would be resumed, but when Egyptian forces crossed the Suez Canal on 6 October 1973, it came as a surprise to Israel and to the rest of the world. For President Sadat the war was a considerable triumph; it appeared to end the years of stalemate with Israel, and his personal reputation was greatly enhanced. As a result of the Disengagement Agreement which Israel and Egypt signed on 18 January 1974, Egyptian forces regained a strip of territory to the east of the Suez Canal (see map on p. 118).

After the war extensive and far-reaching changes took place in Egypt. An amnesty was granted to many important political prisoners in January 1974, and in April was further extended to more than 2,000 persons who had been imprisoned for political or criminal offences. Press censorship was lifted in February, and in May, at a national referendum, some 8.5m. voters gave a 99.95% endorsement to a programme of economic and social reform which concentrated on reconstruction, attracting foreign investment, limiting police interference in everyday life, and the introduction of a private enterprise sector in the economy while still maintaining the public sector.

One result of the October War was Egypt's improved relations with the USA. Diplomatic relations between Egypt and the USA were restored in November 1973 and the US Secretary of State, Dr Henry Kissinger, maintained a cordial relationship with President Sadat during the disengagement talks. American initiatives in peacemaking were generally welcomed by Egypt, while the Americans became more conscious of the extent of their dependence on Arab oil. It was, therefore, in an atmosphere of *rapprochement* that President Nixon visited Cairo in June 1974.

RETURN TO STALEMATE

The euphoria which the crossing of the Suez Canal engendered began to dissipate during 1974. Increases in the cost of living, and the slow rate of progress of the promised economic reform provoked riots in Cairo on 1 January 1975, and further disturbances among textile workers in March 1975, when the textile complex at el-Mahalla el-Koubra was closed for several days after violent clashes over pay demands.

As a result of these disturbances Dr Abd al-Aziz Higazi, who had succeeded President Sadat as Prime Minister in September 1974, resigned the premiership and was replaced in April 1975 by Gen. Mamdouh Muhammad Salem, the former Minister of the Interior and Deputy Prime Minister. On 1 May 1975 President Sadat announced that all lower-paid public-sector employees would receive additional cost-of-living allowances equal to 30% of their pay, and later in May, in a speech to the People's Assembly, the Prime Minister, Salem, promised that steps would be taken to ensure that the economic programme of 1974 would be implemented and that foreign investors, whether from Western countries or from the Eastern bloc, would be given every facility.

During the first eight months of 1975 Dr Kissinger engaged in considerable 'shuttle diplomacy' and in September Egypt and Israel signed the Second Interim Disengagement Agreement. In brief, Israel withdrew from the Giddi and Mitla passes and Egypt recovered the Abu Rudeis oilfield in Sinai, while Article I of the Agreement stated that Egypt and Israel agreed that 'the conflict between them and in the Middle East shall not be resolved by military force but by peaceful means'. This agreement brought upon President Sadat the strong disapproval of other Arab interests, particularly Syria, Jordan, Iraq and the PLO, as it appeared to them that Egypt was seeking to commit the whole Arab world to a policy of peace with Israel. The position had also been complicated by the fact that, at the Arab summit at Rabat in October 1974, the PLO had achieved the status of the sole legitimate representative of the Palestinian people. In May 1976 Egypt attempted to consolidate an improvement in relations with the PLO by asking the Arab League to admit the PLO as a full member. Relations with Syria, at a particularly low ebb during the Lebanese civil war, improved after the Riyadh and Cairo summits in October 1976.

The rest of the Arab world was also aware that Egypt was establishing closer links with the USA; certainly, Sadat was becoming disillusioned with the USSR. In March 1976 he abrogated the Treaty of Friendship with the USSR, which Egypt had signed in 1971. In a speech to the Egyptian People's Assembly, Sadat accused the USSR of exerting political, economic and military pressure on Egypt by criticizing his Middle East policies, refusing to reschedule Egypt's debts, and declining to provide supplies of weapons and spares. Egypt decided to expel about 40 Soviet diplomats in protest against the Soviet invasion of Afghanistan in December 1979.

POLITICAL ADVANCE AND DOMESTIC DIFFICULTIES

During 1976 and for most of 1977, President Sadat was forced to involve himself increasingly in domestic issues. In March 1976 three political 'platforms' were allowed to form within the ASU, and in the November 1976 elections to the People's Assembly the 'platforms' entered the contest as full-scale political parties. The Arab Socialists (a party of the centre, supporting Sadat) won 280 seats, while the Liberal Socialists (supporting political and economic liberalization) won 12 seats. The left-wing National Progressive Unionist Party (NPUP) won two seats. After the elections President Sadat announced that the ASU would take a less active political role in the future, acting more as a supervisory body for the three parties' activities.

During 1976 Egypt's economy was experiencing severe difficulty (see Economy), and when in January 1977 Sadat announced a budget which, because of the withdrawal of subsidies, outlined significant price increases, severe riots erupted in Cairo and other centres. Consequently Sadat revoked the price increases and in February he introduced a law which made a wide range of new offences (including some relating to industrial action) punishable by hard labour for life. The legislation was subsequently endorsed by a national referendum.

By June 1977 Sadat considered the internal situation in Egypt to be sufficiently under control to address the introduction of regulations to permit the creation of new political parties. A law was adopted by the People's Assembly stipulating that each prospective new party must include at least 20 members of the People's Assembly (existing parties excepted, and must have no history of political activity during the time of the monarchy). This effectively excluded the Communist Party, the Muslim Brotherhood and the New Wafd Party.

PROGRESS TOWARDS A PEACE TREATY WITH ISRAEL

In November 1977, however, domestic issues were completely overshadowed by Sadat's visit to Israel and his address to the Knesset, the Israeli legislature. It was by no means certain whether any definite peace proposals would result from Sadat's talks with Menachem Begin, the newly-elected Likud Premier of Israel, whose hitherto aggressive attitude did not seem to augur well for the cause of peace, but who might use his newly acquired power to promote a daring initiative. In the event, no significant breakthrough was made immediately. The status of any future Palestinian state presented the main obstacle. Talks continued in 1978, in spite of the opposition of much of the Arab world, which regarded Egypt's unilateral bid for peace with Israel as detrimental to Arab unity. Egypt had pre-empted action being considered by Syria, Libya, Algeria, Iraq and the People's Democratic Republic of Yemen, by severing diplomatic relations with these countries in December 1977. In September 1978 an unexpected breakthrough was achieved when, after talks at Camp David in the USA under the guidance of US President Carter, Sadat and Begin signed two agreements. The first was a 'framework for peace in the Middle East' (see p. 119) and the second was a 'framework for the conclusion of a peace treaty between Egypt and Israel'. The first agreement provided for a five-year transitional period during which the inhabitants of the Israeli-occupied West Bank of the Jordan and the Gaza Strip would obtain full autonomy and self-government, and the second agreement provided for the signing of a peace treaty within three months. In the event the signing of the peace treaty was delayed because of the question of whether there should be any linkage between the conclusion of the peace treaty and progress towards autonomy in the Israeli-occupied areas, but on 26 March 1979, after another intervention by President

Carter, the signing took place. The treaty (see p. 121) provided for a phased Israeli withdrawal from Sinai over a period of three years. This withdrawal went according to plan, and for the first time, diplomatic relations between Egypt and Israel were established on 26 February 1980 and the two countries exchanged ambassadors.

Proposals for Palestinian autonomy were contained in a separate letter published with the treaty, and provided for both sides to attempt to complete negotiations within 12 months. There would then be elections of Palestinian local councils and a five-year transitional period would follow during which the final status of the West Bank and Gaza would be negotiated. The autonomy negotiations began in May 1979, but the deadline of 26 May 1980 passed without agreement being reached. The main obstructions were the presence and growth of Israeli settlements on the West Bank, Israel's increasing insistence that Jerusalem was its eternal indivisible capital, and a fundamental difference between Egyptian ideas of Palestinian autonomy, which were tantamount to an independent state, and those of Israel, which envisaged a limited form of self-government.

The Camp David agreements and the subsequent peace treaty resulted in Egypt's isolation in the Arab world. Syria, Algeria, Libya and the PLO had met in Damascus in September 1978 and strongly condemned the Camp David agreements, and in March 1979, after the signing of the peace treaty, the Arab League Council met in Baghdad, Iraq, and passed a series of resolutions (see p. 122) comprising the withdrawal of Arab ambassadors to Egypt, the severing of economic and political links with Egypt, the withdrawal of Arab aid and the removal of the headquarters of the Arab League from Cairo to Tunis. Egypt had already been threatened with these sanctions at an earlier Arab summit in Baghdad in November 1978. Some Arab states were reluctant to honour these decisions, but when Saudi Arabia severed diplomatic relations with Egypt in late April, Egypt's isolation became potentially serious, although private Arab investment continued. (In the event, only Oman, Sudan and Somalia maintained diplomatic relations with Egypt.) As a result, Egypt became increasingly dependent on financial and military aid from the USA. During 1980 it became evident that Egypt's isolation was having little practical effect. The damage inflicted by the economic measures imposed against Egypt were offset by the growing strength of Egypt's own economy. The exchange of ambassadors between Egypt and Sudan and Egypt's sale of arms worth US $25m. to Iraq in the same month were indicative of its reduced isolation.

INTERNAL POLITICAL CHANGE

Since 1976 President Sadat had been trying to allow the formation of political parties while at the same time ensuring that dangerous opposition did not achieve too much influence. In a law of June 1977 political parties were legalized. Disturbed by the revival of the Wafd Party (as the New Wafd Party) and the criticisms of the NPUP, Sadat won approval in a referendum for new regulations on political parties which resulted in the disbanding of the New Wafd Party and the suspension of the NPUP. In July Sadat announced the creation of a new political party, the National Democratic Party (NDP), with himself as leader, which in practice replaced the Arab Socialist Party. In September 1978 an official opposition party, the Socialist Labour Party (SLP), was formed.

The signing of the Camp David agreements in September 1978, although causing the resignation of the Egyptian Minister of Foreign Affairs, Muhammad Ibrahim Kamel, was popular in Egypt and in October Sadat appointed a new Government, designed to further the peace process, with Mustafa Khalil as Prime Minister. Khalil also became Minister of Foreign Affairs in February 1979. The signing of the peace treaty in March was followed by a referendum in April at which 99.95% of the voters approved the document. A simultaneous referendum gave Sadat a mandate for fresh general elections and for future constitutional changes. The elections, held in June, resulted in a convincing win for Sadat's NDP, which obtained 302 seats in the expanded 392-seat People's Assembly. On 30 April 1980 the People's Assembly approved a number of amendments to the Constitution (see p. 442), the most important of which provided Sadat with the opportunity to seek further terms as President and recognized that Islamic jurisprudence was the basis of Egyptian law.

On 12 May 1980 the Prime Minister, Mustafa Khalil, offered his resignation because Egypt was 'on the threshold of a new stage of national construction', which required a new government. Two days later, Sadat appointed a government in which he himself became Prime Minister. The constitutional amendments then received the approval of more than 98% of the voters at yet another referendum. One of these amendments provided for the election of a 210-member Majlis ash-Shura (Advisory Council) to replace the former Central Committee of the ASU. Elections took place in September 1980 and the NDP won all 140 elective seats. The remaining 70 members were appointed by the President. The NDP also gained more seats in the People's Assembly in 1980 and early 1981, as at least 13 members of the official opposition SLP defected to the NDP or became independents.

MUBARAK SUCCEEDS SADAT

Although political parties had been allowed by Sadat, power had remained with his own NDP, yet opposition was never far beneath the surface. In the summer of 1981 there had been clashes between Copts and Islamic fundamentalists, resulting in numerous arrests and the closure of various newspapers. Sadat was trying to stifle the opposition, of whatever religious or political persuasion.

On 6 October, however, Sadat was assassinated at a military parade by a group of Islamic fundamentalists led by Lt Khaled Islambouli, who was executed with four associates on 15 April 1982. An Islamic rebellion, which began in Asyut immediately after the assassination, was quickly suppressed, and Vice-President Muhammad Hosni Mubarak was confirmed as President at a referendum on 13 October.

Following his sudden rise to power, Mubarak demonstrated that he was not the nonentity which many believed him to be while he was Vice-President. Although many of Sadat's religious and political detainees were released, Mubarak continued to arrest Muslim fundamentalists, several hundred of whom were tried on charges of belonging to the al-Jihad organization which plotted to overthrow the Government in 1981. In September 1984, 174 of the 302 people arrested in connection with Sadat's murder were acquitted of plotting to overthrow the Government; 16 were sentenced to hard labour for life; and the remainder received prison sentences ranging from two to 15 years. The state of emergency that had been declared after the assassination of President Sadat was subsequently extended at regular intervals.

In his first government reshuffle, in January 1982, Mubarak replaced Dr Ali Abd ar-Razzaq Abd al-Majid (the architect of Egypt's 'open door policy') as Deputy Prime Minister for Finance and Economy, signalling a concern to correct the great inequalities of wealth in Egypt. A second reshuffle in August, including the dismissal of three Deputy Prime Ministers, was intended to secure an improved economic performance. Nevertheless, opposition parties felt that the pace of economic and political reform was too slow, and their criticisms found an outlet in a press that was less fettered than during the last days of Sadat. Mubarak gained approval for his anti-corruption drive, a policy leading to the dismissal, in March 1983, of the Minister of Industry (Fouad Ibrahim Abu Zaglah) and the Minister of Supply (Ahmad Ahmad Nuh), who were implicated in the trial for fraud of Sadat's half-brother, Esmat.

In foreign affairs, the early months of Mubarak's presidency were preoccupied with the question of the return of Sinai by Israel under the 'Camp David process'. After many last-minute snags, the last section was returned to Egypt on 25 April 1982—although a dispute persisted until 1989 concerning the 1 sq km of the Taba enclave on the Egypt-Israel border, north of the Gulf of Aqaba, which was still occupied by Israel. Relations between the two countries were subsequently soured, most significantly, by Israel's invasion of Lebanon in June 1982, in protest at which Egypt withdrew its ambassador from Tel-Aviv; and by Israel's suppression of the Palestinian uprising in the Occupied Territories (see below). Of the formulae to secure the withdrawal of foreign forces from Lebanese territory, Mubarak urged Arab states to support the agreement between Israel and Lebanon which was sponsored by the US Secretary of State,

George Shultz. Although, in so doing, Egypt was at variance with most of the Arab world, there were signs during 1983—such as the readiness of Iraq and the PLO to restore normal diplomatic links, the resumption of trade with Jordan, after four years, and with Iraq, and the increased flow of Arab money into Egyptian banks—that the period of the country's ostracism by other Arab states (with the exception of those with the most severe regimes, such as Algeria, Libya and Syria) was drawing to a close. President Mubarak had openly supported Yasser Arafat when a Syrian-inspired revolt against his leadership of the PLO erupted out in 1983, in the Beka'a Valley, in Lebanon. In recognition of Egypt's support, Arafat visited Mubarak for talks in Cairo in December 1983, his first visit to Egypt for six years, marking the end of the rift between Egypt and the PLO. Substantial proof of Egypt's rehabilitation was provided by its readmission to the OIC in March 1984, although several countries, notably Libya and Syria, opposed the move.

RELATIONS WITH SUDAN: 1982–87

A joint Egypt-Sudan Nile Valley Parliament, a Higher Integration Council and a Joint Fund, based on the two countries' common interests in the River Nile, were established by charter in October 1982. The Parliament, comprising 60 Egyptian and 60 Sudanese members, was inaugurated in May 1983. Relatively powerless in itself, it was designed to be the first step towards economic integration and an ultimate federation of the two states. The Higher Integration Council was to meet regularly to organize and review joint economic projects and to plan all aspects of the transition to the hoped-for federation. It was also to be used as a forum to co-ordinate policy on Pan-Arab questions and on matters of mutual concern such as the Iran–Iraq War, Lebanon, Palestinian autonomy, etc.

In October 1984 Egypt unilaterally withdrew from the confederation agreement for a 'Union of Arab Republics', which it had entered into with Syria and Libya in 1971, saying it was no longer relevant. In April 1985 President Nimeri of Sudan was deposed by Lt-Gen. Abd ar-Rahman Swar ad-Dahab in a bloodless coup, which was endorsed by Col Qaddafi of Libya, who urged Arabs to overthrow other 'reactionary' regimes, implicitly including Egypt. Lt-Gen. Swar ad-Dahab reaffirmed Sudan's commitment to the integration agreement of 1982 during a visit to Egypt in October, but the Sudanese Government, led by Sadiq al-Mahdi (who became Prime Minister in May 1986), sought to improve its relations with Libya. It was also feared that relations between Egypt and the new Sudanese regime would be embittered by the presence of ex-President Nimeri in Egypt, where he had been granted political asylum. (In July 1986 lawyers representing the Sudanese Government in Cairo requested Nimeri's extradition.) Bilateral links were placed on a more secure footing in February 1987, when Sadiq al-Mahdi and his Egyptian counterpart, Atif Sidqi (appointed in November 1986, see below), signed a 'Brotherhood Charter' in Cairo. This was understood to supersede the integration charter of October 1982 and to form the basis for future relations between the two countries. It was agreed in July 1987 that the issue of Nimeri's political asylum in Egypt should not be permitted to jeopardize bilateral links.

THE RE-EMERGENCE OF THE NEW WAFD PARTY

The right-wing New Wafd, as the Wafd Party, had led the Egyptian nationalist movement against Britain between 1919 and 1952. In the slightly more liberal atmosphere developing under Mubarak, the New Wafd reformed in August 1983, and Fuad Serag ed-Din emerged from political retirement to lead the party. Alarmed, as Sadat had been in 1978, at the New Wafd's potential for popular support, Mubarak's Government refused to recognize the party, but its legality was finally established by the courts in January 1984. In its modern guise, the New Wafd was more heterogeneous than before, comprising Copts, Nasserites, Muslim fundamentalists, former army officers (both pro- and anti-Nasser) and socialist and liberal businessmen.

THE GENERAL ELECTION OF 1984

In April 1984, in the hope that he could consolidate his authority and also (by restoring a measure of real democracy) establish himself as a popular leader, tolerant, within limits, of opposition, Mubarak promised the first 'free, honest and sincere' elections in Egypt for more than 30 years. Safe passage in these elections for his ruling National Democratic Party (NDP) had effectively been assured by an electoral law passed in July 1983, requiring parties to gain a minimum 8% of the total vote in order to be represented in the People's Assembly, which was to be increased from 392 elected seats to 448 from 48 constituencies. Elections to the People's Assembly took place on 27 May, and the NDP accordingly took 72.9% of the total vote (the turn-out was officially only 43.14% of those eligible to vote), entitling it to 389 seats. Of the four other participating parties, only the New Wafd, with 15.1% of the vote, crossed the 8% threshold, winning 59 seats in the Assembly. The opposition parties claimed that the elections had been undemocratic, accusing the Government of widespread fraud and intimidation of voters. The electoral alliance of the New Wafd and the fundamentalist Muslim Brotherhood was thought to have alienated many of Egypt's 6m. Copts, potentially a major constituency for the New Wafd.

The Assembly elections left Mubarak firmly in power, with a viable, yet politically brittle, opposition in the New Wafd, and the subversive Muslim Brotherhood in a relatively open political role, in which their activities could more easily be monitored. The Prime Minister, Fuad Mohi ed-Din, died on 5 June, and on 16 July Mubarak reshuffled his Cabinet.

DIPLOMATIC DEVELOPMENTS

As if to signal its progress back into the Arab fold, Egypt severed diplomatic relations with El Salvador and Costa Rica in May 1984, in response to a call from the Jerusalem Committee of the OIC, after both countries had transferred their embassies in Israel from Tel-Aviv to Jerusalem (see The Jerusalem Issue, p. 98). Egypt and Morocco agreed, in principle, to resume diplomatic relations, while President Mubarak and King Hassan discussed moves to end Egypt's suspension from the Arab League, the last major obstacle to Egypt's reintegration into the Arab community of states.

The full resumption of diplomatic relations with the USSR was also achieved during 1984, following the visit to Cairo in May of Vladimir Polyakov, the last Soviet Ambassador to Egypt, who had been expelled with 1,000 or more experts by President Sadat in 1981. Mubarak had previously allowed the experts to return, and had signed trade and cultural agreements with the USSR. Whilst it sought improved relations with the USSR, Egypt stood second only to Israel in the amount of economic and military aid which it received from the USA.

Relations with Israel became strained after the latter's invasion of Lebanon, but Egypt's renewed commitment to issues affecting the entire Arab community (in particular, as concerning its relations with Israel, the Palestinian question) gave it the confidence to use its influence with both sides in the Arab–Israeli conflict to try to achieve a general peace in the Middle East. Israel repeatedly accused Egypt of contraventions of the military provisions of the 1979 peace treaty, and the question of ownership of the disputed Taba region was a further obstacle to any improvement in bilateral relations. In January 1986 Israel agreed to submit the dispute to international arbitration, provided that this was preceded by a period of conciliation during which arbitrators would try to secure a compromise solution before delivering a binding decision. After the appointment of arbitrators (three independent and one each from Egypt and Israel) and the demarcation of the Taba enclave had been agreed, the arbitration document was finally approved by both countries on 10 September 1986. The process of arbitration began in December. In May 1987 each side presented its case for sovereignty to the arbitration panel, and, in September, a three-member 'conciliation chamber' was established. This failed to formulate a compromise solution in the 60 days allotted to it. In January 1988 Israel rejected a US plan, whereby Egypt would be granted sovereignty over Taba, while Israel was given access to the area, and in July Egypt rejected further attempts at compromise which failed to establish Egyptian sovereignty. The arbitration panel effectively awarded sovereignty to Egypt on 29 September, but left a key border undefined. Discussions on the final arrangements for the Taba enclave were held in January 1989, and Egypt assumed control over the area in March.

EGYPT'S REHABILITATION AND MIDDLE EAST PEACE INITIATIVES

In September 1984 Jordan decided to resume diplomatic relations with Egypt. The gradual rehabilitation of Egypt as a political force in the Middle East was deeply frustrating to Libya and Syria, as it was progressing without Egypt's being required to renounce the Camp David agreements or the 1979 treaty with Israel, which had been the cause of its ostracism. Furthermore, Egypt's rehabilitation suggested the emergence of a moderate alignment in Arab politics which could bring its influence to bear on the seemingly intractable problems facing the region, in opposition to the particular aims of Syria. Egypt's confidence in its role in international affairs was demonstrated by Mubarak's active involvement in attempts to find a diplomatic solution to the Iran–Iraq War. (He made an unexpected visit to Baghdad in March 1985, despite the fact that diplomatic relations between Egypt and Iraq had been severed in 1979.) The division of loyalties in this conflict reflected the wider split in the Arab world, with Egypt, Jordan, Saudi Arabia and, less vocally, the remaining Gulf states supporting Iraq, while Libya and Syria, hoping to usurp Egypt's traditional role as leader of the Arab community, backed Iran. Egypt accused Iran and Libya of laying mines in the Red Sea and the Gulf of Suez in order to disrupt traffic through the Suez Canal, after explosions damaged 19 merchant vessels in the area between July and September 1984. Relations with Libya continued to deteriorate. In July 1985 Col Qaddafi barred Egyptian workers (of whom there were some 100,000 in the country at the time) from Libya, in retaliation against a similar Egyptian measure preventing Libyans from working in Egypt.

Consolidating the contacts first made between them after Yasser Arafat's expulsion from Lebanon at the end of 1983, following the revolt against his leadership of Fatah, the PLO leader, King Hussein of Jordan and President Mubarak continued their discussions on the Palestinian issue during 1984 and 1985, in Cairo and Amman. In February 1985 King Hussein and Yasser Arafat agreed, in principle, that a joint Jordanian-Palestinian delegation could take part in a Middle East peace conference that would include the members of the UN Security Council, though the questions of the composition of such a delegation and the basis on which peace talks would proceed were not resolved. The PLO rejected UN Resolution 242 as a basis for negotiation and it was not clear whether the Palestinian representation in the joint delegation would comprise members of the PLO. So that progress should not be brought to a complete halt, Mubarak suggested that, prior to direct negotiations with Israel, a joint Jordanian-Palestinian delegation (including PLO members, Mubarak finally conceded) should hold talks with the USA in Washington, after which Israel and other Arab parties would join the negotiations and make preparations for a full peace conference. The Reagan Administration in the USA, for its part, maintained that it would not negotiate with the PLO unless it accepted Resolution 242 and therefore, implicitly, Israel's right to exist; King Hussein, for his, voiced equivocal approval only, standing by the agreement he had made with Arafat. Mubarak's proposals were not adopted but he persisted in trying to facilitate ultimate negotiations between the Arabs and Israel.

A series of terrorist incidents during the second half of 1985, in which factions of the PLO loyal to Yasser Arafat were implicated, damaged the PLO's credibility as a participant in peace negotiations and virtually assured the failure of the Jordanian-PLO peace initiative. On 7 October, in the first of two incidents directly involving Egypt, an Italian cruise liner, the *Achille Lauro*, was hijacked in the eastern Mediterranean by four Palestinians belonging to the Palestine Liberation Front (PLF— one of two factions of that name—led by Muhammad (Abu) Abbas, an Arafat loyalist). They murdered a Jewish American passenger before surrendering to the Egyptian authorities in Port Said. Rather than put the terrorists on trial in Egypt, President Mubarak placed them into the custody of Muhammad Abbas (who, as well as being leader of the PLF, was a member of the PLO Executive Committee) to be tried, as he thought, by the PLO. The USA accused Muhammad Abbas of planning the *Achille Lauro* operation and criticized Mubarak for allowing him to go free. On 10 October US fighter aircraft intercepted the Egyptian aircraft that was taking Muhammad Abbas and the four Palestinians to Tunis, forcing it to land at a US air force base in Sicily. This action aroused considerable anti-American feeling in Egypt. Then, in November, in the second incident involving Egypt, an EgyptAir airliner carrying 98 passengers was hijacked to Malta by Palestinians, whom Egypt immediately linked with the renegade PLO leader, Abu Nidal, and his Libyan backers, though the only clear claim of responsibility came from a group calling itself 'Egypt's Revolution'. Egyptian special forces were sent to Malta to release the hostages, but their assault on the aircraft resulted in the deaths of 61 passengers and strong criticism of Egypt's handling of the affair. Earlier in November, in Cairo, Yasser Arafat, responding to pressure from King Hussein and President Mubarak for the PLO to renounce violence, had reiterated a PLO decision of 1974 to confine military operations to Israel and the Occupied Territories; this was hardly the unequivocal statement that the two leaders had sought and was immediately repudiated by Arafat's aides.

In September 1986 President Mubarak of Egypt and Prime Minister Peres of Israel met in Alexandria, Egypt, to discuss ways of reviving the Middle East peace process. After the summit meeting (the first between Egypt and Israel since August 1981), and following the signing of the Taba arbitration agreement, President Mubarak appointed Muhammad Bassiouni, Egypt's former chargé d'affaires in Tel-Aviv, as ambassador to Israel. The previous Egyptian Ambassador had been recalled from Israel in 1982, following the Israeli invasion of Lebanon.

It was largely as a result of its links with Israel that a new rift occurred between Egypt and the PLO in 1987. The crisis in relations was precipitated by the reunification of the Palestinian movement that took place at a session of the Palestine National Council (PNC) in Algiers in April 1987. One of the conditions that dissident PLO factions exacted as the price for their return to the mainstream of the movement, under Yasser Arafat's leadership, was the reduction of Arafat's links with Egypt. The Popular Front for the Liberation of Palestine (PFLP) initially demanded the immediate severance of relations but the PNC finally adopted a compromise resolution, urging the reappraisal of PLO links with Egypt, and making future contacts dependent on Egypt's abrogation of the Camp David accord and the 1979 peace treaty with Israel. President Mubarak responded by closing all the PLO's offices in Egypt at the end of April 1987.

INTERNAL DISSENSION

At home, President Mubarak had to tread warily to avoid confrontation with sections of the Egyptian population. While conscious of the need to relieve the country's finances of the crippling burden of state subsidies, he was also aware of the dangers to social stability inherent in increasing the prices of basic commodities. These dangers were demonstrated by riots in the town of Kafr ad-Dawar in September 1984, which were prompted by modest price increases in staple foodstuffs. The Government, nevertheless, continued gradually to reduce subsidies on food, electricity and oil.

The campaign by Muslim fundamentalists for the legal system fully to adopt the principles of the *Shari'a* (Islamic holy law) intensified and became part of a wider resurgence of Islamic consciousness in Egypt. An amendment to the Constitution, endorsed by the People's Assembly in 1980, made Islamic law the basis of national law, and this was largely, but not fully, implemented. As well as taking account of the views of a potentially volatile puritan Islamic section of the community, Mubarak had to take care not to alienate the country's Coptic Christians (many of whom occupied important positions in commerce, industry and the professions). In May 1985 the People's Assembly rejected immediate changes in the legal system and advocated thorough study of the 2% of Egyptian law which did not conform to Islamic precepts before proceeding further. Mubarak did make concessions to purist doctrine by imposing tighter censorship on books and films and by restricting the progress of female emancipation. However, Mubarak continued to take measures to prevent agitation by fundamentalists from destabilizing the country: banning Islamic rallies, arresting militant Islamic leaders and, in July 1985, placing all mosques under the control of the Ministry of Awqaf (Islamic Endowments).

A further threat to public order arose from Egypt's poor economic state, which exaggerated the already wide discrepancy in living standards between the vast and growing numbers of people who lived in great poverty, and a rich minority. Seeking to prioritize this issue, President Mubarak appointed Dr Ali Lutfi, a former Minister of Finance under President Sadat, as Prime Minister on 4 September 1985, following the resignation of Gen. Kamal Hassan Ali and his Council of Ministers. Ali Lutfi presided over a Council of Ministers containing nine new appointments and three members who, while retaining their portfolios, were elevated to the rank of Deputy Prime Minister, making four in all.

On 25 February 1986, reacting to speculation that their period of service was to be extended by one year, to four years, some 17,000 poorly-paid conscripts to the Central Security Force (CSF) staged violent protests in and around Cairo, destroying two luxury hotels and damaging other buildings used by tourists in the Pyramids area of the city. The disturbances lasted for three days and there were clashes between the conscripts and the Army, which was trying to regain control of the city. According to government figures, 107 people died as a result of the mutiny, and 1,324 members of the CSF were arrested. There were reports of violence in other cities, including Asyut, Ismailia and Suhag. The Minister of the Interior, Ahmad Rushdi, who was held responsible for the failure of the intelligence services to detect signs of unrest in the CSF, was dismissed and replaced by Maj.-Gen. Zaki Badr.

In November 1986 President Mubarak accepted the resignation of the Prime Minister, Ali Lutfi. A new Council of Ministers, containing, among 11 changes, a new Minister of Finance and three other new ministers in positions related to the management of the economy, was appointed under a new Prime Minister, Dr Atif Sidqi. President Mubarak was believed to have been critical of Ali Lutfi's apparent readiness to accede to demands from the IMF for the introduction of far-reaching economic reforms, in return for financial aid, and yet dissatisfied with the pace of reform to combat the continuing deterioration of the economy.

THE 1987 GENERAL ELECTION

Agitation by Islamic fundamentalists led to student riots in Asyut in October 1986 (in protest against the university authorities' refusal to allow women to veil their faces on university premises) and in February 1987. In December 1986 it was revealed that, three or four months earlier, four reserve army officers and 29 civilians, allegedly linked with the Islamic Jihad organization, had been arrested in Cairo, accused of plotting to overthrow the Government. This was the first known case of fundamentalist infiltration of the armed forces. Another, communist-inspired, coup plot was reportedly foiled in December.

A referendum was held on 12 February 1987, to decide whether the People's Assembly should be dissolved, prior to the holding of a general election on the basis of a new electoral law, providing for a total of 48 seats for independent candidates in the 458-seat assembly. The new law had been quickly adopted in December 1986 to pre-empt a ruling by the Supreme Constitutional Court that the general election of 1984 had been unconstitutional, as independent candidates had not been allowed to stand. An overwhelming vote in the referendum in favour of the dissolution of the People's Assembly facilitated the holding of a general election on 6 April. Mubarak hoped that the election would establish his Government on a firm constitutional basis and effectively secure him a second term as President. The SLP, the Liberal Socialist Party (LSP) and the Muslim Brotherhood (which was legally barred from forming its own political party) decided to form an electoral alliance, principally in order to overcome the requirement for political parties to win at least 8% of the total vote before they qualified for seats in the People's Assembly, a requirement that effectively prevented a single opposition party from gaining significant representation. The influence of the Muslim Brotherhood was evident in the fact that the doctrine of wholesale application of Islamic law, the Brotherhood's principal tenet, was a prominent element in the alliance's campaign.

The election campaign was marred by sectarian clashes between Muslims and Christians in several towns, including

Suhag and Beni Suef, in February and March 1987, and the opposition parties accused the Government of electoral fraud, the intimidation of opposition candidates and other forms of corruption. On the eve of the election, hundreds of opposition party workers were arrested. They were understood to be mostly members of the Muslim Brotherhood, who, according to the authorities, were campaigning, illegally, on their own behalf.

The election resulted in a large, though reduced, majority for the ruling NDP in the People's Assembly. The NDP won 346 seats (compared with 389 at the previous election in 1984), the opposition parties won a total of 95, and independents seven. The SLP/LSP/Muslim Brotherhood alliance won a combined total of 60 seats, of which the Brotherhood took 37, making it the largest single opposition group in the new Assembly. The New Wafd Party, which, with 58 seats, had been the only opposition party to be represented in the previous Assembly, won only 35 seats.

In July 1987 Mubarak was nominated by the necessary two-thirds majority of the members of the People's Assembly to seek a second six-year term as President. The only candidate, Mubarak was duly confirmed in office by national referendum on 5 October, polling 97.1% of the votes cast. Prime Minister Atif Sidqi submitted the resignation of the Egyptian Government on 12 October and formed a new Council of Ministers, with only minor changes in personnel.

The principal threat to Mubarak's position remained the activities of Muslim militants. More than 500 Islamic fundamentalists, mostly members of Islamic Jihad and Jama'at al-Islamiyah, were reportedly arrested after the attempted assassination of the former Minister of the Interior, Maj.-Gen. Hassan Abou Basha, and two US diplomats in May 1987, and of a left-wing magazine editor in June. Egypt severed its remaining diplomatic ties with Iran in May, closing the Iranian interests section at the Swiss embassy, which, it was alleged, maintained contacts with Muslim extremists.

RELATIONS RESTORED WITH ARAB LEAGUE

President Mubarak and Yasser Arafat held two sessions of discussions in Addis Ababa, Ethiopia, in July 1987, beginning to heal the rift that led to the closure of the PLO's offices in Egypt in April. (They were reopened, unofficially, at the end of July and, formally, at the end of November.) Both leaders endorsed proposals (which were already supported by Egypt and Jordan) for the convening of an international peace conference on the Middle East, under UN auspices, involving the five permanent members of the UN Security Council and all parties to the conflict, including the PLO. President Mubarak and the Israeli Minister of Foreign Affairs, Shimon Peres, had agreed in principle on the need for an international conference when the latter visited Egypt in February, though the issue of PLO representation remained an obstacle to further progress. The Israeli Prime Minister, Itzhak Shamir, was opposed to a peace conference in any form, and suggested direct talks between Israel, Egypt, a Jordanian-Palestinian delegation, and the USA. President Mubarak urged the PLO to devise a formula for its inclusion in an international peace conference, and, during a visit to Israel in July (the first by a high-ranking Egyptian since 1982), the Egyptian Minister of Foreign Affairs, Dr Esmat Abd al-Meguid, appealed to the Israeli Government to participate in an international conference.

In November 1987, at a summit conference in Amman, Jordan, which was attended by the majority of Arab leaders (excluding Col Qaddafi of Libya), the Syrian President, Hafiz Assad, obstructed proposals to readmit Egypt to membership of the League of Arab States. However, recognizing Egypt's support for Iraq in its war against Iran and acknowledging the influence that Egypt (as the most populous and, militarily, the most powerful Arab nation) could bring to bear on the problems of the region, the conference approved a resolution putting the establishment of diplomatic links with Egypt at the discretion of member governments. One week after the end of the conference, nine Arab states (the United Arab Emirates, Iraq, Kuwait, Morocco, the Yemen Arab Republic, Bahrain, Saudi Arabia, Mauritania and Qatar) had re-established full diplomatic relations with Egypt. Of the remaining 12 members of the League, three (Sudan, Somalia and Oman) had maintained diplomatic links with Egypt throughout the period of the boycott, Jordan

and Djibouti had re-established them in 1985 and 1986, respectively, and the PLO (to which the League accorded nation status) had recently begun to settle its differences with Egypt. In February 1988 the People's Democratic Republic of Yemen restored full diplomatic relations with Egypt, leaving Algeria, Lebanon, Libya and Syria as the only Arab League members not to have done so. Libya was the most outspoken critic of the change in the League's policy towards Egypt, complaining that the 1979 peace treaty with Israel, the original reason for Egypt's ostracism, remained in force. In November Algeria announced that it would re-establish diplomatic relations with Egypt, and in June 1989 full diplomatic relations with Lebanon were restored.

Following Jordan's decision, in July 1988, to sever its legal and administrative links with the West Bank region (annexed by Jordan in 1950 but, like the Gaza Strip, under Israeli occupation since 1967), President Mubarak urged the PLO to exercise caution in its plans to declare an independent Palestinian state and to form a government-in-exile. In September, however, during a tour of Western Europe, he sought support for proposals to convene an international conference on the Middle East. In November Egypt granted full recognition to the newly-declared Palestinian state.

The visit of King Fahd of Saudi Arabia to Cairo in March 1989 was a further sign of the rehabilitation of Egypt's standing in the Arab world. In May President Mubarak represented Egypt at an emergency summit meeting of the League of Arab States in Casablanca, Morocco. The meeting, convened to rally support for the diplomatic initiatives of Yasser Arafat following the Palestinian declaration of independence, was preceded by a meeting of foreign ministers of the majority of the members of the League, which endorsed Egypt's formal readmission to the Arab League after an absence of 10 years. Despite Libya's opposition to Egypt's readmission to the League, Col Qaddafi attended the meeting, and held separate talks with President Mubarak. In June 1989 it was announced that Egypt was preparing to reopen its border with Libya, and in October Col Qaddafi visited Egypt, the first such visit for 16 years, for further discussions with President Mubarak.

MIDDLE EAST PEACE MOVES

Egypt was hopeful that its improved standing in the Arab world would enhance its role as a mediator in the Middle East peace process. In February 1989, during a tour of five Middle Eastern countries, Eduard Shevardnadze made the first visit to Egypt by a Soviet Minister of Foreign Affairs for 15 years, and held talks with both President Mubarak and Moshe Arens, the Israeli Minister of Foreign Affairs. In the wake of the Israeli peace initiative announced in April 1989 (see Documents on Palestine, p. 128), Egypt directed its diplomatic efforts towards activating preliminary negotiations between Palestinian and Israeli delegations. In September President Mubarak sought to persuade the Israeli Government to accept 10 points clarifying its peace initiative (the 'Mubarak plan') so that direct Palestinian-Israeli negotiations could begin. The 10 points in question were: a commitment by Israel to accept the results of the elections proposed under its initiative; the supervision of the elections by international observers; the granting of immunity to elected representatives; the withdrawal of the Israeli Defence Force from the balloting area; a commitment by Israel to begin negotiations within three to five years after the proposed elections; the ending of Israeli settlement of the West Bank; complete freedom as regards election propaganda; a ban on entry of all Israelis to the Occupied Territories on the day of the proposed elections; the participation of residents of East Jerusalem in the elections; a commitment by Israel to the principle of exchanging land for peace. An offer by President Mubarak to host talks between Palestinian and Israeli delegations was approved by the USA, but rejected by Israel's 'inner Cabinet' in early October. In early December, following two months of US diplomatic support for (and development of) the 'Mubarak plan', Egypt accepted a five-point US framework for the holding of elections in the Occupied Territories. It was reported that the US Secretary of State would meet the Egyptian and Israeli Ministers of Foreign Affairs in January 1990, with the aim of facilitating direct discussions between an Israeli and a Palestinian delegation. By early 1990, however, there had been no appreciable progress in the peace process, which had been further complicated by Israel's apparent intention to settle in the Occupied Territories some of the Soviet Jewish immigrants who had arrived in the country in large numbers throughout 1989 and continued to do so in 1990.

Egypt's increasing frustration at the lack of progress in the peace process and its concern about the escalation of the Palestinian *intifada* (especially after the murder of seven Palestinians by an Israeli civilian at Rishon Le Ziyyon in May 1990) led it to assume a more critical stance towards the Israeli Government in the first half of 1990. In May President Mubarak warned that the increased immigration of Soviet Jews into Israel threatened to destroy the whole peace process and could lead to a new war in the Middle East. In June, after the formation of a new Israeli Government by Itzhak Shamir, the Egyptian Government condemned Israel in even harsher terms, suggesting that it was preparing for war in the region. Following the suspension by the US Government of its dialogue with the PLO in June 1990, Egypt again attributed the disintegration of the peace process to 'Israeli intransigence' and urged the resumption of the US–PLO dialogue.

President Mubarak undertook a tour of the six states of the Gulf Co-operation Council (GCC) in January 1988 but denied reports that Egypt had agreed to send troops to the Gulf as part of an Arab task-force to defend GCC states against Iranian attack, in return for payment of Egypt's military debt to the USA. However, military co-operation and financial assistance were discussed during President Mubarak's visit, and it was known that several hundred Egyptian military advisers had already been sent to Iraq and Kuwait.

In March 1988 Egypt signed an arms co-operation agreement with the USA, replacing the memorandum of understanding signed in 1979. The new five-year agreement placed Egypt on the same footing with the USA as Israel and the members of NATO, giving it access to US defence contracts and to the latest weaponry, as well as exempting Egyptian military exports from US import duties. In April the US Government notified the Congress that it intended to proceed with controversial plans to sell 555 battle tanks to Egypt, at a cost of $2,000m. Three months later, similar intentions were announced regarding the sale of 144 US *Maverick* air-to-ground missiles, costing $27m. The arrest, in July, of an Egyptian with American citizenship, who was charged with stealing US missile parts and attempting to smuggle them to Egypt, placed these and further sales of US arms to Egypt in doubt. Egypt's embarrassment at this arrest was cited as the main reason for President Mubarak's decision, in April 1989, to transfer the influential Minister of Defence, Field Marshal Ghazalah, to the newly-created position of Presidential Assistant, which was widely regarded as a sinecure.

SOCIAL REPERCUSSIONS OF ECONOMIC CRISIS

The extreme caution with which Egypt implemented economic reforms was largely due to fears that they would provoke further social unrest and increase the threat to social stability posed by Islamist activists. In December 1988 it was reported that more than 500 militant Muslim students in Cairo and Asyut had been arrested on suspicion of involvement in 'anti-state activities'; and in April and May 1989, facing mounting popular discontent over price increases and food shortages, the Government acted to pre-empt disturbances during the month of Ramadan by detaining more than 2,000 Islamist extremists. In June elections to the 210-member Advisory Council were contested by opposition parties (the 'Islamic Alliance', consisting of the Muslim Brotherhood, the LSP and the SLP) for the first time since the establishment of the Council in 1980. Other political parties, however, boycotted the elections in protest at the prevailing state of emergency. None of the candidates from the 'Islamic Alliance' was elected, and it was subsequently alleged that the NDP had achieved its victory by fraudulent means.

In July and August 1989, in a further attempt by the Government to suppress political opposition, members of the proscribed Egyptian Communist Workers' Party and Shi'ite Muslims, including prominent members of the Muslim Brotherhood, were arrested on charges of subversion. By early September, following international protests, it was reported that most of the detainees had been released. In December there was speculation that Muslim fundamentalists had been responsible for the attempted assassination of the Minister of the Interior, Maj.-Gen. Zaki Badr, who had conducted the Government's campaign against political dissent. The ruthlessness of the campaign had not only alienated those targeted by it, but had also caused embarrassment within the Government itself. In January 1990 Badr was dismissed from his post and replaced by Muhammad Abd al-Halim Moussa. In the same month the Egyptian Organization for Human Rights (EOHR) condemned the violence which, it alleged, was routinely inflicted on political detainees by the Egyptian security forces.

In April three new political parties, the Green Party, the Democratic Unionist Party (DUP) and the Young Egypt Party (YEP), were legalized, bringing the total number of officially recognized political parties in Egypt to nine.

THE 1990 GENERAL ELECTION

In May a constitutional crisis arose after Egypt's Supreme Constitutional Court ruled that elections to the People's Assembly in 1987 had been unconstitutional because the electoral law promulgated in 1986 unfairly discriminated against independent candidates. Legislation which had subsequently been passed by the Assembly was deemed to be valid, but the Court declared that any new laws approved after 2 June 1990 could not be endorsed. In September President Mubarak announced that a popular referendum would be held on 11 October in order to decide whether the People's Assembly should be dissolved; and that the electoral law would be amended with regard to the limited number of independent candidates previously permitted to participate in elections. (The People's Assembly, in recess since 4 June, had granted the President permission to legislate by decree in its absence.) Some 58.6% of the electorate subsequently participated in the referendum, and, of these, 94.34% voted for the dissolution of the Assembly. The People's Assembly was duly dissolved on 12 October.

Campaigning for the elections to a new Assembly took place amid tensions resulting from the crisis in the Gulf (see below) and from the threat to Egypt's security posed by Islamic extremists hostile to the Government's pro-Western stance over Iraq's invasion of Kuwait. The assassination of Dr Rifa'at el-Mahgoub, the Speaker of the People's Assembly, on 12 October in Cairo, increased tensions and led to the most comprehensive security operation since the murder of President Sadat in 1981. Hundreds of Muslim fundamentalists were arrested and detained in the known centres of Muslim extremism in the suburbs of Cairo and the cities of Asyut and Beni Suef. The Ministry of the Interior claimed that eight members of an extreme Islamist group, Al-Jihad (arrested at the end of October), had been responsible for the assassination.

At the legislative elections held on 29 November and 6 December 1990, the former requirement for political parties to win a minimum of 8% of the total vote in order to gain representation in the Assembly was abolished, and restrictions on independent candidates were removed. However, the Government refused to concede the opposition parties' demands that the elections be removed from the supervision of the Ministry of the Interior, and that the emergency regulations (in force since 1981) be repealed. The elections resulted in a clear victory for the ruling NDP: of the 444 elective seats in the new Assembly, the NDP won 348 (compared with 346 at the 1987 general election), the NPUP won six, and independent candidates (of whom 56 were affiliated to the NDP, 14 to the New Wafd Party, eight to the SLP and one to the LSP) won 83. Voting in the remaining seven seats was suspended. President Mubarak exercised his right to appoint 10 additional deputies, including five Copts.

In a poll that was characterized by a low turn-out of voters (estimated at no greater than 20%–30% of the electorate), four of the main opposition groups, the New Wafd Party, the SLP, the LSP and the prohibited—but officially tolerated—Muslim Brotherhood, boycotted the elections after the Government refused their demands concerning the conduct of the elections (see above). Several opposition members who ignored the boycott were subsequently dismissed by their party organizations, leaving the NPUP, with its six representatives, as leader of the official opposition. The new People's Assembly convened on 13 December and elected Dr Ahmad Fathi Surur, formerly Minister of Education, as its Speaker.

THE CRISIS IN THE GULF IN 1990–91

In December 1989 Egypt and Syria restored full diplomatic relations after a break lasting 12 years. In May 1990 President Mubarak visited Damascus for talks with President Assad of Syria, and in July President Assad visited Egypt. The *rapprochement* between Egypt and Syria was widely regarded as signalling a shift away from the balance of power which had prevailed in the Arab world throughout the 1980s.

In November 1989 reports of widespread acts of violent discrimination against Egyptian expatriate workers in Iraq threatened the special relationship which had developed between Egypt and Iraq during the Iran–Iraq War, when Egypt provided Iraq with military equipment and advisers. Prior to the crisis in the Gulf precipitated by Iraq's invasion and annexation of Kuwait in August 1990, Egypt sought to mediate between Iraq and Kuwait, appealing for dialogue between the two sides in the interests of Arab solidarity. Following the invasion of Kuwait, Egypt sought initially to maintain its role as a mediator, immediately proposing the convening of—and subsequently hosting—a summit meeting of Arab leaders. At the summit meeting, held on 10 August, Egypt firmly demanded the withdrawal of Iraqi forces from Kuwait, and 12 of the 20 Arab League member states participating in the meeting voted to send an Arab deterrent force to the Gulf in support of the USA's effort to deter an Iraqi invasion of Saudi Arabia. By late August about 5,000 Egyptian troops were reported to be in Saudi Arabia.

Egypt's quick success in mobilizing the support of 'moderate' Arab states for the economic sanctions imposed on Iraq by the UN, and for the defence of Saudi Arabia, emphasized the extent of the improvement in relations with Syria. While Iraq called on the Egyptian people to overthrow the Egyptian Government, there was no evidence of widespread popular support in Egypt for President Saddam Hussein of Iraq, and the Government's action was judged to have bolstered its domestic popularity. While it condemned Iraq's invasion of Kuwait, however, the Muslim Brotherhood, demanded the immediate withdrawal of US forces from the Gulf and opposed the dispatch of Egyptian troops to Saudi Arabia as part of an Arab deterrent force. It was feared, too, that Egyptian expatriate workers (totalling some 800,000 in Iraq and some 100,000 in Kuwait before the Iraqi invasion), returning in large numbers from Iraq and Kuwait to almost certain unemployment in Egypt, might have a destabilizing effect. Some 85,000 were reported to have returned to Egypt by the end of August 1990, the total rising to more than 600,000, following the outbreak of hostilities between Iraq and the UN multinational force in January 1991.

On 28 August 1990 President Mubarak and President Assad of Syria met in Alexandria to discuss Arab efforts to avert war in the Gulf. An extraordinary meeting of Ministers of Foreign Affairs of Arab League member states took place in Cairo on 30 August, but it was attended by representatives of only 12 member states (those which had supported the proposal to send an Arab deterrent force to Saudi Arabia), reflecting the divisions which had arisen in the Arab world as a result of Iraq's invasion of Kuwait.

Following the outbreak of hostilities between Iraq and a UN multinational force in January 1991, the Egyptian Government continued to support the anti-Iraq coalition. Egypt's contingent within the multinational force, eventually boosted to 35,000 troops, sustained only light casualties in the fighting. On the domestic front, there were few disturbances during the war, and the opposition's predictions of popular unrest proved unfounded. In fact, Egypt emerged from the conflict in the Gulf with its international reputation enhanced, largely as a result of President Mubarak's firm leadership of 'moderate' Arab opinion. Moreover, the economy benefited from the waiving of almost US $14,000m. of Egypt's debts to the USA and other Western and Gulf states at an early stage in the crisis, and by the signing of an agreement with the IMF in mid-May 1991, which, later in the same month, led to the rescheduling of $10,000m. of Egypt's debt to the 'Paris Club' of Western creditors, and the cancellation of the remaining $10,000m. over a three-year period.

Following the conclusion of the war in February 1991, Egypt took part in a meeting of the eight Arab nations (the six GCC member states, Egypt and Syria) that had participated in the UN multinational force, held on 5–6 March in Damascus. The statement issued after the meeting, known as the 'Damascus Declaration', called for 'a new Arab order to bolster joint Arab action'. It proposed, *inter alia*, that Egyptian and Syrian troops already deployed in Saudi Arabia and the Gulf states should constitute the nucleus of an Arab regional security force. However, in early May Egypt unexpectedly announced that its forces in Saudi Arabia and Kuwait were to be withdrawn. No Arab regional security force has since been formed.

Representatives from all the Arab League member states met in Cairo on 30 March 1991 for the first regular meeting of the Arab League since the outbreak of the crisis in the Gulf. The meeting was conciliatory in tone and attempted to establish an Arab consensus. A further meeting took place on 15 May, at which Dr Ahmad Abd al-Meguid, hitherto Egypt's Minister of Foreign Affairs, was endorsed as the League's new Secretary-General, in succession to Chedli Klibi who had resigned in September 1990.

EGYPT AND THE MIDDLE EAST PEACE PROCESS

Since the end of the crisis in the Gulf in 1990–91, the Government's foreign policy has continued to focus on the twin themes of Arab reconciliation and a settlement of the Arab–Israeli dispute, with particular emphasis being given to the Palestinian dimension. Egypt participated in the inaugural meeting of the Middle East peace conference in Madrid in October 1991. In later stages it attended bilateral sessions as an observer and multilateral sessions as a participant. Despite the procedural delays and the slow progress of the negotiations, Egypt felt that the conference represented the best hope for a durable peace in the region and that it had an important role to play in co-ordinating Arab strategy and providing diplomatic expertise. The choice of Egypt's former deputy Prime Minister, Dr Boutros Boutros-Ghali, as the new Secretary-General of the UN was regarded by Egypt as recognition of its moderating regional influence. President Mubarak welcomed the change of government in Israel in June 1992, and in July the Israeli Prime Minister, Itzhak Rabin, visited Cairo for talks with President Mubarak, who reportedly emphasized to him his opinion that progress in the peace process was dependent on a halt to Jewish settlements in the Occupied Territories.

Egyptian mediators played an active role during the secret negotiations which led to the Gaza-Jericho interim peace agreement between Israel and the PLO on 13 September 1993. The agreement made provision for limited Palestinian self-rule in the Gaza Strip and the town of Jericho on the West Bank. Once the agreement was announced, Egypt was the first Arab state that the PLO looked to for support. In October, PLO and Israeli negotiating teams began meeting regularly in Cairo, or at Taba on the Red Sea, to discuss the detailed implementation of the agreement. On the whole, the agreement was welcomed by the Egyptian press, although it was denounced by the Nasserites and the Muslim Brotherhood as a betrayal of the struggle for the Palestinians' homeland. In November King Hussein of Jordan visited Cairo for talks on the Middle East peace process, his first visit since the Gulf crisis of 1990–91 which had strained relations between the two countries. In December, when talks between the PLO and Israel became deadlocked, President Mubarak convened an emergency summit meeting in Cairo between the Israeli Prime Minister and the PLO leader, Yasser Arafat. However, the meeting failed to achieve an agreement on the withdrawal of Israeli armed forces from Gaza and Jericho which had been scheduled to start on 13 December.

The massacre of more than 40 Palestinians in Hebron on the West Bank by an Israeli settler on 25 February 1994 provoked several days of angry demonstrations in Cairo. Egypt withdrew its ambassador from Israel for consultations, but Egyptian diplomats tried to persuade both the PLO and Israel to resume their negotiations. Talks between Israel and the PLO recommenced in Cairo on 29 March. On 4 April President Assad of Syria visited Cairo for talks with President Mubarak, reportedly about Syria's dissatisfaction with Egypt's support for the Israeli-PLO agreement. On 4 May, after months of negotiations, an agreement on Palestinian self-rule in Gaza and Jericho was signed in Cairo by the Israeli Prime Minister and the PLO Chairman at a ceremony presided over by President Mubarak and attended by the US Secretary of State and the Russian Minister of Foreign Affairs. Under the terms of the agreement

Israeli forces withdrew from Gaza on 13 May and from Jericho on 17 May.

Although the Middle East peace process continued to dominate Egyptian foreign policy, Egypt was also involved in mediation efforts involving Libya, Yemen and Somalia. Egypt's relations with Libya have been dominated by the repercussions of the 'Lockerbie affair' (see chapter on Libya). With an estimated 1m. Egyptians working in Libya, Egypt has used its diplomacy to try to avert a confrontation between Libya and the West which could not only threaten the jobs of its workers, but also undermine a steadily growing market for its exports. Egypt also regards the Qaddafi regime as a useful ally in its struggle against Islamist militancy in the region. At the beginning of November 1993, as the UN Security Council was being urged by the USA, the United Kingdom and France to impose tougher economic sanctions on Libya, President Mubarak met Col Qaddafi, but Egyptian mediation efforts failed to engineer a compromise. Egypt was deeply embarrassed when a leading opponent of the Libyan regime, Mansour al-Kikhia, disappeared in Cairo in December 1993 during a human rights conference. There was speculation that al-Kikhia, who was living in exile in the USA, had been kidnapped by Libyan agents, despite assurances regarding his safety from senior Egyptian officials. (In 1997 the US Central Intelligence Agency claimed that it had evidence that Egyptian agents had been involved in al-Kikhia's abduction and that he had subsequently been executed by the Libyan regime.) In March 1994 Egypt attempted to mediate between rival Yemeni leaders, and hosted peace talks in Cairo between rival Somali factions. However, UN-sponsored talks in Cairo in June failed to achieve a cease-fire in the Yemeni civil war and Egypt was accused by the northerners of favouring the breakaway south. In May the 11th ministerial conference of the Non-Aligned Movement took place in Cairo and provided an opportunity for the Egyptian Minister of Foreign Affairs to meet his Iranian counterpart, Ali Akbar Velayati, who was the first senior Iranian minister to visit Egypt since the Iranian Revolution. However, there was no improvement in relations between the two countries; Egypt maintained that Iran was assisting Egypt's Islamist militants. Following an increase in commercial and economic exchanges during 1993, Egypt resumed diplomatic relations with South Africa in May 1994, one month before President Mubarak stood down as Chairman of the OAU. Egypt's relations with its southern neighbour, Sudan, deteriorated following the visit to Khartoum, in December 1991, of a large Iranian delegation led by President Rafsanjani. Acutely aware of the dangers posed by its own Islamist militants, Egypt was alarmed by Iran's support for Sudan's military regime, which is dominated by the National Islamic Front, and by the dangerous escalation of Islamist violence in Algeria, which virtually plunged that country into civil war. In June 1993 President Mubarak held private talks with the Sudanese President, Lt-Col al-Bashir, who was visiting Cairo for the annual meeting of the OAU, in an attempt to reduce tensions between Egypt and Sudan.

THE UPSURGE IN ISLAMIST VIOLENCE

Since the early part of 1992 militant Islamist groups have intensified their campaign to overthrow the Government and establish an Islamic state. Militant Islamists have been particularly active in Asyut Governorate in Upper Egypt, the traditional stronghold of Islamic militancy, and also in the poorer districts of Cairo, such as Imbaba. At the beginning of June 1992 some 5,000 members of the security forces were deployed in Asyut Governorate in the most extensive military operation against militant Islamists for many years, and at the end of July the People's Assembly adopted a new law to combat terrorism which imposed the death sentence for some crimes. In October it was reported that terrorists would be tried by military courts. In December an Egyptian military court sentenced to death eight militant Islamists, after finding them guilty of conspiring to overthrow the Government. It was reported that over the previous 12 months some 70 people had been killed as a result of Islamist violence. Foreign tourists were targeted by militant Islamists for the first time in 1992 and several were killed. The leader of the Jama'at al-Islamiyah, one of the two main Egyptian Islamist groups, publicly attacked the very concept of foreign tourism in Egypt and threatened to destroy the

country's major tourist attractions, the Pharaonic sites. Tourist numbers were reported to have fallen by 40% by the end of 1992, with a loss of foreign currency earnings of $1,500m. Among those killed during 1992 was the writer Farag Fouda, one of Egypt's most outspoken critics of militant Islam. He was murdered on 9 June by members of Islamic Jihad, the group believed to have been responsible for the assassinations of President Sadat and the Speaker of the People's Assembly, Rifa'at el-Mahgoub. A year later, at the trial of those charged with Fouda's murder, Sheikh Muhammad el-Ghazali, a leading Islamist scholar, claimed that it was legitimate to kill any Muslim who opposed the application of Islamic law.

The problem of Islamist violence became more acute in 1993 and attempts to control it came to dominate the domestic political agenda. After several car-bomb explosions in Cairo at the beginning of the year, a wave of attacks by militant Islamists ensued. More than one-third of the attacks were directed against police and security forces. Cinemas, videotape shops and Coptic churches were also targeted, and several attacks were carried out against leading politicians and senior members of the security forces. In April 1993, Safwat Muhammad ash-Sharif, the Minister of Information, narrowly escaped death when his car was ambushed. Ironically, the Minister had been criticized by liberals for filling the television schedules with religious programmes, which was regarded as a crude and unconvincing attempt to appease Islamist opinion. The Minister of the Interior, Hassan Muhammad al-Alfi, was seriously wounded in an assassination attempt outside his office in the centre of Cairo in August. Officials stated that the attack had been carried out by the Vanguards of Conquest, a faction of Islamic Jihad. In November the Prime Minister, Atif Sidqi, escaped unharmed when a car-bomb exploded near his residence, killing a schoolgirl and injuring 18 other people. The police stated that the attack was once again the work of the Vanguards of Conquest, although Islamic Jihad claimed responsibility. Attacks on foreign tourists occurred regularly during the year, damaging the country's vital tourist industry. The number of tourist nights fell by 30% during the first eight months of 1993 as a result of the Islamists' campaign of violence and many international tour operators withdrew from Egypt. Revenues from tourism fell by about $800m. in 1993, to $1,300m.

Harsh measures were employed by the security forces to counter the escalation in Islamist violence, and those arrested were increasingly tried by military courts which were seen as more effective than the civil courts in securing quick convictions. During 1993 military courts sentenced 38 militant Islamists to death and 29 were hanged. This was the largest number of political executions in Egypt's recent history.

In April 1993 President Mubarak had dismissed the Minister of the Interior, Muhammad Abd al-Halim Moussa, because he had indicated that he was willing to start a dialogue with imprisoned leaders of Islamic Jihad and Jama'at al-Islamiyah. He was replaced by Gen. Hassan Muhammad al-Alfi (see above) who immediately reaffirmed the Government's uncompromising commitment to suppressing militant Islamist groups. However, the new Minister won approval in some quarters for favouring a more subtle approach to the security question. He pledged to stop the security forces carrying out indiscriminate mass arrests—a policy strongly criticized by human rights organizations—and stressed the need for greater efforts to improve social conditions. The crude methods employed by the police were revealed in August when a panel of eight judges found the 24 defendants on trial for the assassination of Rifa'at el-Mahgoub not guilty of murder. The court strongly criticized police practices and revealed that medical reports had shown that 16 of the defendants had been tortured. Safwat Abd al-Ghani, the political leader of Jama'at al-Islamiyah, one of 10 defendants convicted of lesser offences, stated that the Mahgoub case highlighted the injustice of the military courts which accepted police evidence unchallenged. In December a civil court acquitted Abd al-Ghani on the charge of ordering the assassination of Farag Fouda from his prison cell. On his reappointment as Minister of the Interior in October 1993, al-Alfi stated that the new Government would confront terrorism 'with extreme force, resolution and firmness'. However, he denied that torture was used to extract confessions from Islamist suspects. Mass arrests began again—for example, around 30 suspected militant Islamists were arrested every day during a single week in mid-October—and the Government continued to use the so-called 'fast track' military courts for the trials of militant Islamists.

Policing methods and the use of military courts in the campaign against Islamist violence provoked widespread international criticism. In late May 1993 a human rights organization, Amnesty International, published a report in which it strongly condemned the 'frightening brutality' of the Egyptian security forces and alleged that, in response to the increased killings of police officers and others, the security forces appeared to have been given 'a licence to kill with impunity'. It labelled the military courts 'a travesty of justice'. In November the UN Committee against Torture accused the Egyptian security forces of carrying out systematic torture against suspects in security cases and in ordinary criminal cases. The EOHR issued a statement endorsing the UN's accusations and claimed that 13 people had died under torture in jails, police stations or state security headquarters during 1993. The EOHR also drew attention to the 221 cases of torture it had documented since July 1986 when Egypt ratified the UN convention on torture. Nevertheless, in January 1994 the EOHR admitted that the major responsibility for all acts of violence in the country lay with militant Islamist groups, and it produced figures which showed that Islamist groups were responsible for the death of 137 people in 1993. The EOHR also accused the Government of acceding to Islamist pressure to ban books and of permitting the state-controlled media and education system to promote Islamist ideas. In November the Advisory Council also warned that Islamist influence was increasing in the mass media and in the universities. Earlier in the year the leftist NPUP (Tagammu), the only opposition party represented in the People's Assembly, accused the Government of allowing the message of Islamic intolerance to be widely disseminated in the media. The Government moved to take some action in these areas. Already in February 1993 a trade union election law had been passed requiring the participation of at least 50% of the members for an election to be valid. Earlier, the Muslim Brotherhood had gained control of the Lawyers', Engineers' and Doctors' Syndicates. Press censorship was increased and a number of high-profile corruption cases were prosecuted. In order to demonstrate the Government's determination to expedite social spending programmes in low income areas, President Mubarak announced in December that governors would now be made accountable for progress in slum improvements in their governorates.

Following the bombing of the International Trade Centre in New York in February 1993, FBI investigations led to the dismantling of some of the Islamist networks in the USA and the arrest of the influential militant Islamist, Sheikh Omar Abd ar-Rahman. At the beginning of July the Government requested the extradition of Sheikh Abd ar-Rahman so that he could face charges of inciting violence in Egypt. Meanwhile, leaders of the Islamist militant groups continued to operate in some European countries. For example, it was reported that Tala'at Muhammad Tala'at, one of the leaders of the Vanguards of Conquest, was living in Denmark and that Egyptian requests for his extradition had been rejected. Ayman az-Zawari, the leader of Islamic Jihad, sentenced to death *in absentia* for his part in the assassination of President Sadat, was reported to be living in Switzerland and to have applied for political asylum. Az-Zawari was believed to be linked to Muhammad Mekawi, considered to be the field officer of the Vanguards of Conquest in Afghanistan, and responsible for the training of several hundred Egyptian militants there.

In November 1993 it was reported that a preliminary agreement had been reached between the leaderships of Islamic Jihad and Jama'at al-Islamiyah, urging joint action and greater co-ordination between the two groups in confronting the security forces. It was also agreed that Sheikh Abd ar-Rahman should be the leader of the clandestine Islamic movement as a whole, including Islamic Jihad and Jama'at al-Islamiyah, and that a committee composed of members of the advisory councils of both groups should be formed to overcome differences and strengthen co-operation.

MUBARAK'S THIRD TERM

President Mubarak was formally nominated for a third six-year term of office in July 1993. Although his nomination was supported by 439 of 448 votes cast in the People's Assembly, none of the opposition parties, nor the prohibited but officially tolerated Muslim Brotherhood, endorsed his candidature for a third term of office, arguing that the people should be allowed to choose the President from a list of candidates and not just approve the decision of the Assembly. Mubarak's nomination was approved by nationwide referendum on 4 October. According to official figures, he gained 96.3% of the valid votes cast in an 84% turn-out. However, despite an intensive publicity campaign by the ruling NDP, the general mood appeared to be one of apathy and independent observers commented on the small numbers of people voting. Mubarak immediately promoted the Minister of Defence, Gen. Muhammad Hussain Tantawi, to the rank of Field Marshal, an honour accorded to only four other generals since the revolution. Senior Air Force and air defence officers were also promoted. Some observers saw this as a move to placate the Army, the ultimate power behind the regime, after Mubarak's refusal to appoint a Vice-President, a post that the military had traditionally regarded as its own. In a newspaper interview in October, Tantawi stated that he would deploy the Army against Islamist extremists if they threatened the security of the state. This was the first time that the Army had publicly declared its readiness to involve itself in the battle against militant Islamist groups. Hitherto the campaign against Islamist extremists had been carried out by forces under the command of the Ministry of the Interior.

There was considerable internal and external pressure for fundamental changes to the Government in order to meet the challenge of economic reform and to counter the Islamist threat. However, when the new Council of Ministers was sworn in on 14 October 1993, Dr Atif Sidqi—first appointed in 1986—was retained as Prime Minister and the key portfolios of foreign affairs, defence, the interior and information remained unchanged. Muhammad Salah ed-Din Hassab-Allah, the former general manager of Arab Contractors, Egypt's largest construction company, was appointed to the new post of Minister of Housing and Utilities, while Ministers of State were appointed with responsiblity for housing affairs and the family and for new communities, including the unprofitable new industrial cities built around Cairo during the previous 15 years. The President announced that the priorities of his third term would be security and stability, economic reform, social justice, educational reform, combating unemployment, dealing with the problem of high population growth and improving Egypt's unwieldy bureaucracy. He made no reference to political reform.

However, Mubarak did propose a 'broad national dialogue' involving all parties which rejected violence and terrorism and supported democracy. The idea was first broached by the President at the end of September 1993 and at the beginning of December Egypt's 10 principal legal political parties, together with the Muslim Brotherhood and the Communists, issued a statement welcoming dialogue but insisting that the discussions should be comprehensive and focus on the question of political reform. Officials of the ruling NDP, headed by the Deputy Prime Minister, Yousuf Wali, eventually indicated that they would be willing to hold wide-ranging discussions covering political, social and economic reforms, but that the dialogue would be confined to the principal political parties in the first instance. There seemed little doubt that the decision not to include professional and trade unions was taken because several of them were controlled by the Muslim Brotherhood. The national dialogue meetings were scheduled to start in February 1994, but were postponed until April and then again until late May. In April President Mubarak stated that he would nominate a 25-member preparatory committee composed of party and trade union leaders to prepare a report on the terms of reference for dialogue. The Minister of Information indicated that the President had established three main guidelines for the proposed dialogue. These were that the discussions should include all legal political parties and forces, including the trade unions; that the NDP would not try to impose its views on other participants; and that the discussions would be wide-ranging and include political as well as economic and social issues. The reference to legal political parties indicated that the Muslim Brotherhood would remain excluded from direct participation in the deliberations. However, it was assumed that its views would be expressed through its electoral ally, the SLP, and by union delegates. Serious doubts remained, however, over whether the NDP was genuinely willing to share power.

When the President inaugurated the first session of the 40-member preparatory committee of the National Dialogue Conference it was heavily dominated by the NDP. The Communist Party, the Muslim Brotherhood and various Coptic groups were not allocated seats on the committee and the opposition parties claimed that the Government had no intention of seriously discussing political change, but was merely using the conference to isolate the main Islamist political movement. The New Wafd Party and the Nasserist Arab Democratic Party announced that they were withdrawing from the conference and the Chairman of the New Wafd Party, Fouad Serag ed-Din, accused the Government of monopolizing all aspects of the planning of the conference and of deliberately excluding important topics for discussion, such as constitutional reform.

Despite these criticisms the first session of the National Dialogue Conference took place on 25 June 1994. President Mubarak told the 276 participants—including delegates from 10 political parties, deputies in the People's Assembly, trade union leaders, journalists, academics, businessmen, economists and, predominantly, NDP members—that dialogue was necessary not only to forge a united front against terrorism, but also to make the opposition feel that it was part of the system of government and that its views would be taken into account. The conference's political, economic and social and cultural committees completed their deliberations on 7 July and recommended only limited changes, reflecting the Government's success in controlling the agenda. The recommendations of the political committee closely followed NDP policy in proposing that no amendments to the Constitution should be made at this time and that the Advisory Council should play a more important role in revising draft laws and the state budget. It also recommended that the individual list system used in the 1990 parliamentary elections should be abandoned in favour of the former party list system in the elections planned for November 1995. The party list system, whereby candidates of each party were required to campaign collectively in each constituency, with seats being allocated among the parties according to the proportion of the vote they received, had been used in the 1984 and 1987 elections to the People's Assembly, but after the Supreme Constitutional Court found that it discriminated against independent candidates, it was replaced by the individual list system. The economic committee, while favouring the move to a market economy, recommended that the state should retain control over certain key sectors of the economy, such as infrastructure and monetary and credit policies, and that it should ensure social justice through the distribution of wealth. The social and cultural committee recommended the extension of compulsory education to include the preparatory and secondary stages and emphasized the importance of eradicating illiteracy. The recommendations of the three committees were communicated to President Mubarak, but he was under no obligation to act on them. The majority of Egyptians greeted the dialogue process with indifference and few believed that it would lead to any significant political changes.

In January 1995 the NDP announced that the parliamentary elections planned for November of that year would not be contested on the party list system as recommended by the National Dialogue Conference, but that the individual list system would be retained. Most opposition parties, including the banned Muslim Brotherhood, indicated that they would not boycott the elections as in 1990. Pope Shenouda III urged all Copts to vote in the forthcoming elections to the People's Assembly and to become more involved in the country's political life. In the approach to the elections, there was a government crackdown on the activities of the Muslim Brotherhood including the arrest of a number of prominent Brotherhood officials (see below). The Government also acted to reduce the Brotherhood's influence within key professional organizations. In his 1995 May Day speech, President Mubarak appeared to confirm his opposition to any further democratization of the political system.

At the beginning of November 1993 the US newspaper, the *Wall Street Journal*, alleged that over the previous two years two

former Egyptian generals had received substantial commissions from major US corporations in connection with military sales to Egypt. One of the generals was described as a former colleague of Mubarak when they were both in the air force. *Ash-Shaab*, the newspaper of the pro-Islamist SLP, called for an investigation into the allegations. Over the previous two months, several journalists from *Ash-Shaab*, together with Helmi Murad, the Vice-President of the SLP, had been detained for alleging that the Mubarak regime was corrupt. *Ash-Shaab* later claimed that senior figures in the regime had received favours from property magnate Fawzi es-Sayyid which had enabled him to build several apartment blocks in Nasr City in violation of building codes. Following these allegations, the Prime Minister, Atif Sidqi, Omar Abd al-Akhter, the Governor of Cairo, and Zakaria Azmi, the head of the presidential office, filed libel suits against the SLP leader, Ibrahim Shukri, and the editor of *Ash-Shaab*, Magdi Hussein. In February 1994 the public prosecutor referred Shukri and Hussein to the criminal court to face charges of libel and slander. There were further reports in the US press at the end of 1994 alleging corruption in high places (see below), and the Egyptian opposition press continued to publish regular articles about the business activities of the 'sons of high officials'. The introduction of stringent amendments to the penal code, increasing the penalties for libel and aimed specifically at the media, was regarded by many observers as an attempt by the Government to protect senior officials from journalists investigating their private business affairs as well as to improve the Government's image in the approach to the November elections. The new measures were immediately condemned by the EOHR while the Press Syndicate launched a campaign against the new law and the regime, threatening to take strike action. At first President Mubarak insisted that the law would remain unchanged, but as opposition to it increased he agreed to refer the new law to the Supreme Constitutional Court. In addition, a committee, including representatives of the press, was set up to draft a replacement law for submission to the next session of the People's Assembly.

At the beginning of June 1995 the NDP won all but two of the 90 vacant seats in elections for the 210-member Advisory Council, which had failed to excite much public interest. The SLP and the LSP offered only 29 candidates and most of the remaining opposition parties decided not to contest the elections. Independent candidates won the two seats that did not go to the NDP.

THE CAMPAIGN AGAINST MILITANT ISLAMISTS INTENSIFIES

In February 1994 militant Islamist groups intensified their attacks on tourists and also targeted foreign investors. Jama'at al-Islamiyah sent a series of warnings by fax to international news agencies warning that tourists and foreign investors should leave Egypt, and that anyone helping a regime that opposed Islam would receive 'the same punishment as the oppressors'. This policy, however, was condemned by the Vanguards of Conquest which, in a statement from Islamabad in Pakistan, declared that targeting foreigners and foreign investors was harmful to Muslim interests because it would increase the hardships of the Muslim people. Earlier there had been reports of differences between the two extremist groups and of their failure to establish a joint advisory council as agreed in November 1993. In February and March 1994 there were several attacks on tourist trains in Upper Egypt, injuring a number of foreigners, and in early March a German tourist was killed when shots were fired at Nile cruise ships. Jama'at al-Islamiyah also carried out a series of bomb attacks on banks in Cairo and towns in Upper Egypt. Jama'at al-Islamiyah had issued a warning to Egyptians to close their accounts at banks practising *riba* (usury) by 22 February. On 9 April Maj.-Gen. Raouf Khairat, the head of the state security Department for Combating Religious Activity and a key figure in the campaign against Islamist violence, was assassinated. Jama'at al-Islamiyah claimed responsibility for the attack. In February suspected militant Islamists had shot dead the chief prosecution witness in the trial against those arrested for the attempted assassination of the Prime Minister, Atif Sidqi.

The crackdown by the security forces was unrelenting. Figures released by the Ministry of the Interior showed that 29,000

Islamist militants had been jailed following mass arrests. The security forces claimed to have arrested 900 Islamist suspects in a single week in February 1994. The EOHR criticized police action during a raid on an apartment in Zawiya al-Hamra on 1 February after witnessess claimed that seven militants had been killed in cold blood. The police, however, stated that the men had been killed during a gun battle. The security forces claimed to have inflicted a serious blow against their opponents when they killed the military commanders of both Jama'at al-Islamiyah and Islamic Jihad in April. Adil Awad Siyam, the military commander of Islamic Jihad, was killed during a security operation in Giza, while Talaat Yasin Himam, believed to be the military commander of Jama'at al-Islamiyah, was killed in a shoot-out in Asyut along with four of his comrades. In March two army officers were executed for their part in a plot to assassinate President Mubarak when he arrived at Sidi Barrani airport, near the Libyan border, on his way to visit Col Qaddafi.

On 10 April 1994 a new law was passed abolishing local elections and granting the Ministry of the Interior powers to appoint village *omdas* or mayors. In response to criticism from opposition deputies, the Government claimed that many *omdas* had refused to co-operate in security matters and were corrupt. The following day the emergency laws, which gave the security forces wide powers to arrest and detain suspects, were renewed for a further three years. The authorities also redoubled their efforts to curb the activities of leaders of extremist groups living abroad. In early April an extradition treaty was signed with Pakistan and there were reports that the authorities in Yemen and Saudi Arabia were co-operating with Egypt in security matters. Local and Western journalists were warned to ensure that their articles on the Islamist challenge conformed with official guidelines or they would face arrest or expulsion. A propaganda offensive against the Islamists was launched in the state-controlled media and included television broadcasts of confessions by former members of underground Islamist groups. Allegations that several senior police officers were being investigated for supplying arms to Islamist militants were strongly denied by the Minister of the Interior in March.

The major battle between the security forces and the armed Islamist movement continued unabated in the southern province of Asyut, one of the poorest in the country. The political violence there was believed to have intensified because of the widespread tradition of *thaar*, or blood feud, strongly rooted in local culture. Asyut became the scene of almost daily clashes between security forces and armed Islamists. The police claimed that 54 people had been killed in these clashes between January and March 1994—30 policemen, 13 civilians and 11 Islamists—and 67 wounded. In March an Islamist gunman fired into a crowd of Coptic Christians outside the Muharraq monastery near Asyut, killing five people and wounding three others in the most serious incident to date involving a Christian place of worship. In April the Minister of the Interior announced that the province was to be divided into four zones, each headed by a senior officer, in order to assist the security forces in controlling the area. At the same time, it was reported that several development projects were under way to improve basic services there. In mid-June the Minister of the Interior announced that the security forces had successfully infiltrated militant Islamist groups operating inside the country and abroad and that they were now under control. (His statement followed the police raids in April which resulted in the deaths of Talaat Yasin Himam (see above) and Adil Awad Siyam.) Further raids in May led to the arrest of almost 100 Islamist cadres and the seizure of caches of arms. The police had also arrested Abd el-Harith Madani, a lawyer acting for the Islamist militants, and raided his offices. After Madani's death in police custody the Ministry of the Interior claimed that he was a 'terrorist' who had acted as an intermediary between imprisoned Islamist militants and those still at liberty, and as a channel for transferring funds raised abroad to Jama'at groups inside the country. Madani's death provoked widespread protests and demands for a public inquiry and, following the threat of a general strike by several professional unions, the Government reluctantly agreed to investigate claims of torture.

Claiming to have won the battle against the armed movements, the Government moved to isolate the more moderate Muslim Brotherhood and to weaken its political influence in the approach to the parliamentary elections planned for November 1995. Several leading members of the Brotherhood were arrested in late January and both President Mubarak and the Minister of the Interior claimed that there was evidence of links between it and more extreme groups. At the end of March five members of the Doctors' Syndicate, which is controlled by the Muslim Brotherhood, were detained on charges of using medical relief operations as a cover for military training abroad. The Government acted to exert more control over other professional organizations, in order to counter Islamist influence within them. In February the People's Assembly passed an amendment to legislation governing professional organizations, giving the judiciary wide powers to intervene in trade union elections and to prevent Muslim Brotherhood members from standing.

However, Government claims that the security forces had suppressed the Islamist groups responsible for the violence proved premature. Towards the end of the year the Jama'at al-Islamiyah appeared to have regrouped and to have renewed its attacks, but, owing to tight police control over its traditional stronghold in Asyut province, the conflict moved to the neighbouring provinces, in particular the areas around the towns of Mallawi and Samalut in Menia province, much of which was under curfew. In October 1994, after Egypt's internationally renowned novelist and Nobel Prize winner, Naguib Mahfouz, had been stabbed in Cairo, the Ministry of the Interior announced that the attack had been ordered by the leadership in exile of the Jama'at al-Islamiyah. The 82-year-old Mahfouz, who had been denounced as an 'infidel' by the extremists, survived the attack which was condemned by intellectuals of all political tendencies. Clashes between militant Islamists and the security forces in Upper Egypt claimed 87 lives in January 1995, the highest figure for any month in three years. Security officials announced that 123 people had been killed in Menia province alone in the first three months of 1995, compared to 77 in the whole of the previous year. In August 1994 the Jama'at al-Islamiyah resumed its attacks on foreign tourists, striking for the first time at the country's Red Sea resorts. A massive security campaign was mounted in early September when Cairo hosted the controversial UN International Conference on Population and Development which was attended by more than 10,000 delegates from 156 countries and the world's press corps. The conference's draft resolution incensed many Muslims in Egypt and beyond; Islamist extremists warned delegates against attending a 'conference on licentiousness' and the Muslim Brotherhood condemned the conference as unislamic for condoning abortion and encouraging sexual promiscuity. Egypt's most celebrated cleric, Sheikh Muhammad Metoualli Charaoui, stated that he was 'scandalized' by the draft resolution and declared that the meeting was 'hostile to Islam'. President Mubarak criticized those Muslim countries that refused to participate—they included Saudi Arabia—and argued that it was in the interests of the Islamic nation that Muslim representatives attended in order to oppose any interpretation contrary to religion and Islamic law. The conference proceeded without incident and the Egyptian Government even won praise from the Muslim Brotherhood for its 'commendable role' in ensuring that the final declaration did not offend Muslim values.

RENEWED CRITICISM OF THE SECURITY FORCES' METHODS

Harsh security measures remained in force and the continued use of special military courts to try suspected Islamists was criticized by human rights groups. Some 62 Islamists had been sentenced to death by military courts since 1992. Mass arrests continued. Among those arrested in December 1994 was the Secretary-General of the pro-Islamist SLP, Adel Hussein, a former Marxist turned Islamist, who was accused of having links with militant extremist groups and of supporting the Jama'at al-Islamiyah in its efforts to overthrow the Government. A prominent journalist, Hussein had written several articles vigorously denouncing official corruption. He was detained for one month and only released after strong protests from journalists, intellectuals and opposition party leaders. In the early months of 1995 some 20 members of the SLP were arrested in Menia and charged with distributing anti-government leaflets and of supporting the Jama'at al-Islamiyah. In September 1994

Amnesty International stated that Egypt's record on human rights was at an all-time low, and in December the EOHR warned that harsh security measures would not solve the problem of violence; only freedom of opinion and organization and democratic access to power would prevent the same kind of conflict developing in Egypt as in Algeria. The security forces were accused of torture and summary executions, and of intimidating the relatives of suspected Islamists. According to the US-based Middle East Watch, more than 8,000 political prisoners were being held in detention, most of them accused of being Islamist militants. In February 1995 the US Department of State published a highly critical report on the methods employed by the Egyptian security forces and concluded that, faced with the regime's strict control over the country's political life, Egyptians despaired of seeing greater democracy. The pro-government press was quick to interpret US attacks on Egypt's human rights record as an attempt to persuade the Government to abandon its stand on the Nuclear Non-Proliferation Treaty (NPT, see below).

On 26 June 1995 President Mubarak escaped an assassination attempt in Ethiopia while he was travelling from the airport in Addis Ababa to attend the opening session of the OAU summit meeting. Mubarak, who was being driven in his own bullet-proof car, was unharmed and returned immediately to Cairo. On 29 June, before a meeting of workers in Cairo, the President claimed that Sudan was responsible for the attempt on his life and denounced the Sudanese regime. Sudan strenuously denied the allegation. In early July Jama'at al-Islamiyah claimed responsibility for the assassination attempt. Two of the President's assailants who were killed during the attack, and a further three who were killed in subsequent raids by Ethiopian security forces, were believed to be Egyptians. In September the Ethiopian authorities stated that nine members of Jama'at al-Islamiyah formed the team which had planned to kill the President and a further two members had controlled the operation from Sudan. Ethiopia accused the Sudanese security forces of complicity in the attack, claiming that the assailants had safe houses in Sudan and that they had received training in special camps near Khartoum. The Ethiopian authorities also alleged that some of the equipment used in the attack had been traced to purchases made by the Sudanese security services. Egypt has long claimed that Egyptian Islamist militants are being armed and trained in Sudan. Mounting evidence of Sudan's complicity in the assassination attempt against the Egyptian President was one of the factors which led the UN to impose sanctions against Sudan in 1996 (see below). The attempt on the President's life raised the sensitive issue of who would succeed him. Mubarak has deliberately avoided appointing a Vice-President and there is no obvious successor, although the names of Muhammad Safwat ash-Sharif, the Minister of Information, Field Marshal Muhammad Hussain Tantawi, the Minister of Defence, and Amr Moussa, the Minister of Foreign Affairs, have been suggested as potential presidential candidates.

By the end of 1995 the militants appeared to be under strong pressure from the security forces. In August it had been reported that the Jama'at al-Islamiyah was planning to revive its terrorist campaign in Cairo, which had been largely unaffected by Islamist militancy for more than a year, and in the following months several groups of militants were arrested, allegedly for planning to assassinate leading politicians. It was repeatedly claimed that Jama'at militants were receiving weapons and training in Sudan. At the end of November security forces arrested a large group of alleged militants belonging to Islamic Jihad who were accused of planning to explode a car bomb in the Khan al-Khalili, Cairo's main tourist bazaar, and to assassinate leading public figures. There were further arrests of alleged Jihad militants in December, and the Ministry of the Interior claimed that they were being organized, funded and supplied with weapons by exiled Islamic Jihad leaders in the United Kingdom and Sudan. In November, during a visit to Paris, France, President Mubarak deplored the fact that certain European countries, including the United Kingdom and Germany, had offered political asylum to Islamist 'criminals', stating that in the future they would be punished for their action. The Egyptian Government accused the United Kingdom of harbouring two of the main leaders of Islamic Jihad. In January 1996, after a US court sentenced Sheikh Omar Abd

ar-Rahman, the spiritual leader of the Jama'at al-Islamiyah, to life imprisonment for conspiracy to blow up the UN and FBI buildings in New York, the Jama'at threatened revenge attacks on US interests.

In February 1996 violence erupted once again in Asyut province, which had been relatively quiet for some two years, when the Jama'at al-Islamiyah launched a violent campaign in revenge for the killing of two of its members by the police in the neighbouring province of Menia. Observers remarked that some four years of political violence had intensified local feuds and that, as a result, the periodic upsurge of violence was virtually impossible to control. By the end of February some 24 people had died in the province in clashes between the police, Jama'at militants and rival families supporting either the security forces or the militant Islamists. In contrast, in mid-March the Government felt sufficiently confident that the security situation in and around Mallawi in Menia province was under control to lift a 20-month curfew imposed on the town. Mass arrests by the security forces across the country were reported in March and April, including the detention of some 245 men alleged to be members of the extremist Takfir wal-Higara group which had not been active since the 1970s, but which the Ministry of the Interior claimed to be regrouping and planning a campaign of violence. In September 1995 the EOHR issued a report condemning the harsh conditions under which Islamists were being detained in certain desert prisons, claiming that almost 20 had died in two prisons in less than a year. The allegations were dismissed by the Ministry of the Interior. In an interview in Paris, France, in November, President Mubarak denied allegations by Amnesty International of human rights abuses in Egypt and the growing number of deaths in detention, accusing the organization of making propaganda to destabilize the country. He claimed that all those in prison had been arrested according to the law and that his Government did not interfere in the judicial system. However, the Government continued to prefer using military courts to try Islamist militants rather than civilian courts.

Beginning with the attempt on President Mubarak's life in Addis Ababa in June 1995 (see above), Islamist militants have carried their struggle abroad. In October the Jama'at al-Islamiyah claimed responsibility for a car bomb explosion in the Croatian port of Rijeka, while just before the legislative elections in Egypt in November an Egyptian diplomat was assassinated in Geneva. A few days later a suicide bomber killed 16 people, including five Egyptians, and wounded 60 in an attack on the Egyptian embassy in Islamabad, Pakistan. The Group for International Justice (GIJ), believed to be part of the Jama'at al-Islamiyah, claimed responsibility for the murder of the Egyptian diplomat, while the GIJ, Jama'at al-Islamiyah and Islamic Jihad all claimed responsibility for the bombing of the Egyptian embassy.

In November 1995, as Egypt's peak winter tourism season began, militants from Jama'at al-Islamiyah advised all foreign tourists to leave the country and resumed their attacks on trains carrying tourists to sites in the south. In April 1996 four gunmen perpetrated the first major attack on tourists in the Cairo region since 1993 after they opened fire on a group of Greek tourists outside the Europa Hotel in Cairo, killing 17 of them and one Egyptian, and wounding another 15. Jama'at al-Islamiyah claimed responsibility for the attack, stating that it had planned to strike at a group of Israeli tourists in revenge for Israeli attacks on Hezbollah bases in Lebanon. In the aftermath of the attack, the security forces conducted raids on Islamist hide-outs in and around Cairo, arresting many alleged militants. In March three Egyptians had hijacked an EgyptAir aircraft carrying tourists from Luxor to Cairo and forced it to fly to Libya. None of the passengers was hurt and the hijackers were extradited at the end of March, but the breach in security was an embarrassment for the authorities.

In mid-1996 the Ministry of the Interior claimed that militant Islamist activities had been considerably reduced and were now largely confined to parts of Menia, Asyut and Suhag Governorates in Upper Egypt where tight security measures remained in place. The security services reported that despite a series of violent robberies carried out by activists of the Jama'at al-Islamiyah, a sharp decline in high-profile attacks on foreign tourists and senior government officials indicated that the group had been effectively isolated from its overseas leadership and funds. In early May the offer of a cease-fire by the Jama'at was rejected by the Minister of the Interior, who insisted that there would be no dialogue with 'killers and assassins'. Later that month his ministry announced that the security forces had killed one of the Jama'at's leaders and arrested 33 of the group's activists. It was also announced that the security forces had killed a prominent member of Ash-Shawqiyun (a branch of the Jama'at) and had arrested 13 of his supporters. Further arrests of Islamist militants were announced in June, and in September and October the police launched major operations in Asyut and Suhag Governorates to trace militants who had taken refuge there. The Government claimed to have made many arrests, but other sources reported that most of the militants had eluded capture. In September official sources announced the arrest of 16 leading members of the military wing of Islamic Jihad, and in October the detention of more than 50 members of a clandestine Shi'a group was reported. Earlier that month President Mubarak had accused Iran of both providing support for Egyptian Islamist militants and of involvement in his attempted assassination in June 1995. Iranian officials rejected the President's allegations and claimed that he was attempting to transfer responsibility for Egypt's internal problems. As the Government continued its campaign to subdue Islamist militancy, the large number of political prisoners held in Egyptian jails provoked criticism from human rights groups. The Arab Organization for Human Rights claimed that 17,000 political prisoners, most of them Islamist, had been detained since 1991. By January 1997, 83 Islamist militants had been sentenced to death by military courts since 1992, of whom 54 had been executed.

In September 1996 Egypt urged the British Government to prohibit the organization of a large international conference of militant Islamist groups, due to have been held in London that month, claiming that the United Kingdom was indirectly supporting international terrorism. The Egyptian media also criticized the United Kingdom for harbouring Islamist extremists, including Yasser Tawfiq as-Sirrim, alleged to be a leading strategist of Islamic Jihad.

At the end of February 1997 the People's Assembly approved a presidential decree whereby emergency law provisions were extended for a further three years. According to the Prime Minister, such an extension was necessary in order to prevent terrorists from disrupting the country's economic reform programme and discouraging urgently needed foreign investment. Human rights groups, however, insisted that the law was being used not only to counter Islamist militancy but also to undermine support for political groups opposed to the regime. In the early months of 1997 there were a number of reports of attacks by militant Islamist groups against Coptic Christians in Upper Egypt. In February guerrillas attacked a church in the village of Al-Fikriya, in Menia Governorate, killing several Christian worshippers. Copts were also murdered in a nearby village. Although Jama'at al-Islamiyah denied responsibility for the attack, the group's leader stated that the Christian inhabitants of the village were no longer 'protected non-Muslims', prompting speculation that they had been attacked for failing to pay protection money to the Islamist militants. Indeed, militant groups were believed to be targeting the Christian minority in Upper Egypt as a source of funds in order to maintain their armed struggle against the Government. In another attack, in March, Islamist militants killed eight Christians and four Muslims in the village of Izbat Dawud, and shortly afterwards guerrillas fired on the Aswan–Cairo train in the same area. Jama'at al-Islamiyah was suspected of both incidents but again denied responsibility. In the same month Islamic Jihad and the Vanguards of Conquest announced that they had merged and proclaimed their commitment to continuing a campaign of violence. In April Mustafa Mashhour, a leader of the Muslim Brotherhood, stated that Copts, as non-Muslims, should pay a special tax and should not be allowed to serve in the armed forces, as their loyalty could not be depended upon. His comments provoked public outrage and were later withdrawn.

ATTACKS ON FOREIGN TOURISTS IN CAIRO AND LUXOR

Despite the extension of Egypt's emergency law provisions for a further three years in February 1997, a number of people were killed by Islamist militants in Upper Egypt in the following month and, again, in August. In mid-September a military court in Haekstep, north of Cairo, held Egypt's largest trial to date of suspected Islamist militants; 98 people were convicted on charges of subversion, four of whom were sentenced to death and eight to life imprisonment. A few days later, in the first such attack for almost 18 months, suspected Islamist militants opened fire on and launched petrol bombs at a tourist bus in Cairo, killing nine German tourists and injuring 11 others. Although the perpetrators of the attack were widely believed to be members of Jama'at al-Islamiyah, the Government, in an apparent attempt to protect the country's vital tourist industry, claimed that the attack was an isolated incident perpetrated by 'mentally deranged' individuals with no terrorist connections. The reports of eye-witnesses to the attack, which differed from the Government's account in some respects, were dismissed, and military prosecutors subsequently prohibited the publication of articles which challenged the official version of events. At the end of October two men were convicted of conducting the attack and were sentenced to death by the Higher Military Court.

In November 1997 the Government's campaign against the armed Islamist movement suffered a devastating reversal when 70 people, including 58 foreign tourists, were massacred by members of Jama'at al-Islamiyah near the tomb of Queen Hatshepsut in the ancient city of Luxor. The damage to the Egyptian tourist industry was apparent in the immediate aftermath of the attack as foreign tour operators cancelled bookings and foreign governments advised their citizens to leave the country. It was generally agreed that the armed Islamist movement in Egypt was profiting from the deadlock in the Arab–Israeli peace process; from frustrations felt in Egypt at the lack of legitimate means to express political opposition; economic hardship which had resulted from the country's programme of fiscal reform; and the corruption which had resulted from that programme. A spokesman of the Egyptian Muslim Brotherhood condemned the attack at Luxor but emphasized the need for the Government to engage in dialogue with those among its political opponents who rejected violence, as part of a wider process of political, economic and social reform.

Following the attack at Luxor, President Mubarak criticized the security forces for failing to protect tourists and publicly accused the Minister of the Interior, Hassan Muhammad al-Alfi, who had conceived the Government's hardline strategy to eradicate Islamist militancy, of failure. Al-Alfi was forced to resign immediately and was replaced by Habib Ibrahim el-Adli, hitherto the head of the state security services. President Mubarak ordered a heightened security presence at all tourist sites and placed the Prime Minister at the head of a special committee, which was to devise a plan to safeguard the lucrative tourist industry. Later in November 1997 the Government published a list of wanted exiled Islamist militants and accused the countries that permitted them residency rights (particularly the United Kingdom) of condoning terrorist acts of violence.

Prior to the attack at Luxor, evidence had emerged of a willingness among the jailed leadership of both Jama'at al-Islamiyah and Islamic Jihad to cease the movements' armed operations. In early December 1997 a statement that had apparently been approved by an exiled leader of Jama'at al-Islamiyah condemned the attack at Luxor, thereby fuelling speculation that a rift had developed between the exiled leadership and those in command of armed units within Egypt. It also undermined the Government's claim that exiles had been responsible for planning the attack at Luxor. It was not, therefore, clear whether an order to cease all attacks on foreign tourists, reportedly issued in early December by the exiled leadership, would be observed by all Jama'at armed units.

ELECTIONS TO THE PEOPLE'S ASSEMBLY

As elections to the People's Assembly in November 1995 approached, the opposition remained weak and divided. After many months of negotiations the different parties were unable to agree on terms for a united front against the ruling NDP, failing to draw up an 'opposition charter' that was to have demanded the right for political parties to organize and campaign without hindrance, that elections be placed under judicial scrutiny, and that legal controls placed on the media be ended. The main disagreement appeared to be between the secular and pro-Islamist opposition parties. The Muslim Brotherhood spokesman, Maamoun al-Hodaiby, for example, had insisted that his party would only support a common agenda that explicitly demanded the application of *Shari'a* law by the government in power.

Despite the opposition's outspoken lack of confidence in the electoral process, on 20 August 1995 the New Wafd Party formally announced that it would participate in the elections and the other parties quickly followed its example. Following the attempted assassination of President Mubarak in June, the pre-election security operation against the Muslim Brotherhood intensified. In the months preceding the election 19 members of the Brotherhood's consultative council were arrested and accused of colluding with Sudan to promote terrorism. In a separate raid a further 200 members were arrested in several cities, representing the largest single operation against the movement since the assassination of President Sadat in 1981. At the end of August 1995, President Mubarak's decision to refer 49 leading members of the Brotherhood for trial by military courts attracted widespread criticism, even from the movement's political opponents. Tagammu, the Nasserist Party and the New Wafd Party, among others, endorsed a statement of protest against the military trials, observing that the Muslim Brotherhood was committed to dialogue. Some commentators argued that the government crackdown had not targeted the Brotherhood's Supreme Guidance Council for fear that the arrest of the leadership might result in younger, more uncompromising activists taking their place; instead it had targeted the movement's most effective principal organizers, including many professional people, in order to destroy the party's structure. Just days before the election, some 54 of the Brotherhood's members, including many parliamentary candidates, received prison sentences of three to five years for 'unconstitutional activities' from a military court which also closed down the movement's headquarters in central Cairo. In November the Minister of the Interior repeated his claim to have evidence of close links between the Brotherhood and the Islamist militants, and accused the Brotherhood, Jama'at al-Islamiyah and Islamic Jihad of being, ultimately, part of one single organization. Earlier in the month, in an interview in Paris, France, President Mubarak had referred to the Muslim Brotherhood's assassination of two Egyptian Prime Ministers and a Minister of Finance before the revolution, its attempt to assassinate Nasser and the killing of Sadat. He also claimed that there was no difference between the Muslim Brotherhood and the Islamist extremists and insisted that their behaviour was contrary to the fundamental principles of Islam. Over 1,000 Brotherhood members, including several hundred due to monitor the polls and witness the counting of votes, were arrested on the eve of the elections. The SLP also complained that the police had arrested some of its members in the approach to the elections and accused the regime of intimidation.

An unprecedented number of candidates—more than 4,000, approximately 10 for each seat—contested seats in the first round of voting, with more than two-thirds of them standing as independents. Only the ruling NDP was able to present candidates for all 444 seats, while the New Wafd Party contested 182 seats, the Muslim Brotherhood 150, the SLP 120 and Tagammu a mere 40. The combined results of the first and second rounds of voting, held on 29 November and 6 December respectively, were announced by the Minister of the Interior on 7 December. The ruling NDP won 316 of the total 444 seats, independent candidates 115 and the opposition parties only 13—the New Wafd Party six, Tagammu five, and the LSP and the Nasserist Party one each. For the first time, the NDP pitted powerful government ministers against prominent Islamist candidates, most of whom were defeated in the first round. After the vote 99 independent deputies were reported to have joined the NDP, giving the ruling party an overwhelming victory with 93% of all parliamentary seats. Five women won seats, all of them candidates of the NDP. The Independent Commission for Electoral Review (ICER) noted that 56 Coptic candidates contested the elections, but that no Copts were included on NDP nomination lists. No Copts were elected, but of the 10 deputies appointed by the President six were Copts. Voter attendance was officially registered at 50% in the first round of voting—out of 21m. registered voters—and 49.73% in the second round; the ICER claimed that fear of violence and lack of faith in the fairness of the elections after criticism in the opposition press, had resulted in a considerable increase in voter abstention in the second round. Despite government assurances that the elections would be fair, and official press releases during the elections confirming the Government's neutrality and the efficiency of the police in securing and regulating the electoral process, they were widely denounced as the most fraudulent in Egypt's recent history. Furthermore, the ICER claimed that they had been characterized by unprecedented violence and bloodshed. This was confirmed by other sources. Figures for casualties varied, but the Egyptian Centre for Human Rights and Legal Aid recorded that 51 people were killed and 878 injured during the electoral campaign. The ICER attributed the violence to popular feeling that the Government had been indifferent towards irregularities committed, while other reports stated that some of the violent incidents were armed exchanges between supporters of rival candidates. Prior to the first round of the elections, the ICER, which employed some 600 volunteers to monitor 88 electoral districts, received numerous complaints about faulty voting lists—many included names repeated up to 20 times, and the names of deceased people—and about the illegal, but widespread practice of mass registration. Some opposition candidates complained that they had been assigned negative symbols, such as a sword or a pistol, so that voters would think that they supported the Islamists. On the first day of voting the ICER received 1,240 complaints of irregularities from candidates, election agents and voters, more than one-half of them from Muslim Brotherhood and SLP members. They reported ballot-box stuffing, refusal to admit election agents into polling areas and, in some cases, physical abuse. Particularly disturbing were complaints by Coptic candidates citing examples of the NDP urging people not to vote for Christians. The revival of old traditions of tribalism among the supporters of various candidates and their re-emergence in the country's major cities was identified as perhaps the most dangerous outcome of the elections.

The ICER, which had been formed in October 1995 in a pre-election initiative by a group of prominent Egyptians and organizations active in civil society, was vigorously attacked by the Prime Minister. Its Chairman and Secretary-General were pressured to disband the organization by the security services, and its members were subjected to state harassment. Other observers, however, believed that the Commission reflected the vitality of Egypt's civil society and saw its creation as possibly the most exciting development of the 1995 campaign.

AL-GANZOURI APPOINTED PRIME MINISTER

At the beginning of January 1996 President Mubarak replaced Dr Atif Sidqi, the long-serving Prime Minister, and appointed the Deputy Prime Minister and Minister of Planning, Dr Kamal al-Ganzouri, to head a new administration. After the parliamentary elections Mubarak had been under some pressure to improve the Government's image by creating a more efficient administration with less ministerial conflict. With the President maintaining firm personal control over the portfolios of defence, the interior and foreign affairs, the Prime Minister's role was to take charge of economic affairs, hasten economic reform, especially privatization, and to raise living standards. Although regarded as an economic conservative, international institutions expressed the hope that with strong support from the President, the new Prime Minister would prove more decisive than Sidqi in implementing reforms. Al-Ganzouri, who retained the planning portfolio, stated that he would give priority to job creation, to accelerating economic development and to encouraging foreign investment. In the reshuffle of the Council of Ministers that followed his appointment, the main changes were to the economic portfolios. As expected there were no changes at the key ministries of defence, foreign affairs, the interior and information, and long-serving technocrats retained the portfolios of oil, energy and electricity and social affairs. However, new appointments were made to the new Ministry of Health and Population, and to the Ministry of Awqaf (Religious Endowments). In January the President also replaced 17 of the country's 26 provincial governors, appointing new governors to Asyut and Menia, the strongholds of Islamist militancy, while retaining the governors of key provinces, such as Cairo, Giza and Alexandria.

After several cases in which Islamist lawyers had instituted legal proceedings against prominent Egyptians for contravening what they claimed to be Islamic morality, in January 1996 the People's Assembly passed a new *jesba* law to limit such claims of unislamic conduct. In March a new draft of the controversial proposed law governing the media was agreed which went some way towards reducing the harsh penalties for slander and libel proposed in the original draft; however, journalists expressed concern that the new version did not remove the threat of state intimidation of the press. In June, the decision of the Advisory Council to reintroduce the harsh penalties from the original press law into the new draft, encountered strong opposition from the Press Syndicate, prompting President Mubarak to intervene and annul most of the amendments by presidential decree. His decision was approved by the People's Assembly, which endorsed the revised press law on 17 June. With a few exceptions, including criticism of the President and his family, journalists no longer faced long prison sentences for libel and slander, although they continued to risk heavy fines. In September 1997 an Egyptian journalist at the Saudi Arabian-owned daily newspaper, *Asharq al-Awsat*, was sentenced to six months' imprisonment after having been convicted of libelling the President's two sons, and in October, following the attack on German tourists in Cairo (see above), strict controls were imposed on the reporting of attacks on tourists by both foreign and local journalists. In February 1998 Magdi Hussein, the chief editor of the Islamist newspaper, *Ash-Shaab*, and a journalist employed by the paper, were each sentenced to one year in prison, with hard labour, after having been found guilty on charges of libel, slander and defamation against two sons of the former Minister of the Interior, Hassan al-Alfi. In March the Government banned more than 30 foreign-registered companies from printing in industrial 'free zones' around Cairo. The prohibition was subsequently overruled by the Prime Minister, although restrictions remained on the printing of the *Cairo Times* and the *Middle East Times*. In March the Government ordered the closure of *Ad-Dustur* for publishing comments by a Jama'at al-Islamiyah sympathizer. In July Magdi Hussein and his colleague were released from prison after their sentences were overturned.

At the end of March 1996, after the death of Jad al-Haq, the Grand Sheikh of al-Azhar, who had been accused of being sympathetic to militant Islamist groups, President Mubarak appointed Muhammad Sayed Tantawi, formerly the Grand Mufti, to the post. In contrast to Jad al-Haq, Tantawi was widely considered to take a more liberal approach to religious issues. In November, Nasr Wassel, also regarded as a liberal, was appointed to succeed Tantawi as Grand Mufti.

The Government's intimidation of the Muslim Brotherhood continued after the parliamentary elections. In April 1996 12 leading members of the Brotherhood were arrested and charged with trying to re-establish the movement's clandestine activities and its links with extremist groups. For the first time, the authorities arrested a member of the movement's Supreme Guidance Council. Three of those arrested were founder members of a new political grouping, the Al-Wasat (Centre) Party, and included Abu-Ela Mada, a former Deputy Secretary-General of the Engineers' Syndicate, who had campaigned to obtain official recognition of the new party. Mada was accused of trying to use Al-Wasat as a cover for Brotherhood activities, but the founders of the new party, including young Islamist, Christian, leftist and Nasserist activists, claimed that they were trying to create a political movement occupying the middle ground between the state and the Islamist militants. In April the Government moved once again to reduce Islamist control over professional associations. The Bar Association, which had been dominated by members of the Muslim Brotherhood, was placed under the control of court-appointed custodians following allegations of financial mismanagement, leaving the Doctors' Syndicate as the only major professional union controlled by Islamists. In May the Supreme Constitutional Court upheld a decree, issued by the Minister of Education in July 1994, prohibiting

girls from wearing the *niqab* (veil) in schools. In the same month the Advisory Council's Political Parties' Committee rejected Al-Wasat's application for a political licence, but in August Mada and the two other founder members of Al-Wasat were acquitted after trial by a military court. In contrast, seven members of the Muslim Brotherhood were sentenced to up to three years' imprisonment for supporting the new party. Some observers argued that the authorities were trying to exacerbate existing divisions within the Muslim Brotherhood between the young reformers of Al-Wasat and the older, more conservative, leadership. In October the three founder members of Al-Wasat were among 13 members who resigned from the Brotherhood. In December the People's Assembly made it an offence to preach in a mosque that had not been licensed by the Ministry of Awqaf. The Government thereby intended to extend its control over the country's many private mosques which it claimed were used by militant Islamist groups, such as the Brotherhood, for their political activities. There were further arrests of Brotherhood supporters in December, including members of the SLP who were accused of using the party's headquarters in Helwan for subversive activities. This latest round of arrests was regarded as a government attempt to weaken the Brotherhood before local elections took place in April 1997. In March 1997 the Brotherhood announced that it would not contest the forthcoming elections because it did not expect them to be free or fair. The other main opposition party, the New Wafd, also indicated that it would boycott the elections.

Predictably, at the local elections held on 7 April the ruling NDP won the vast majority of seats. In fact, official sources indicated that the NDP gained 44.4% of the 47,382 seats unopposed. The Minister of Information expressed the opinion that, as a result of the violence surrounding the 1995 parliamentary elections, potential opponents had declined to come forward, while local human rights organizations suggested that the electorate had simply lost faith in the electoral process. The elections attracted little interest among voters. Although the Government declared that attendance was 40% in urban areas and 75% in the countryside, independent sources maintained that it was much lower: between 5% and 20%. Although the ruling NDP faced little or no opposition, there were widespread claims of electoral fraud. Two days before the elections, the State Security Prosecutor ordered the arrest of 27 members of the Muslim Brotherhood which claimed that hundreds of its followers had been detained to prevent them from participating. No comprehensive monitoring of the voting took place, but human rights groups and opposition sources claimed that electoral malpractice had once again been widespread.

A reshuffle of the Council of Ministers took place on 8 July 1997. Three new full ministerial appointments were made: Mahmoud Abu Zeid as Minister of Public Works and Resources, Mervat Talawi as Minister of Social Insurance and Social Affairs, and Mufid Shehab as Minister of Higher Education. Other changes were limited, the most significant being Yousuf Boutros-Ghali's reappointment to ministerial office.

In June 1998 the NDP secured 85 of the 88 contested seats at mid-term elections to the Advisory Council. The remaining three seats were won by independent candidates. Most opposition parties had decided not to contest the election.

EGYPT STRIVES TO REASSERT ITS REGIONAL STATUS

While the Middle East peace process continued to dominate Egypt's foreign policy, there was growing concern that as more Arab states established relations with Israel, Egypt's dominant regional role might be threatened. As the contours of a Middle East at peace were unclear, it was suggested that Egypt and Israel, allies in the Middle East peace negotiations, could become rivals, as both competed for the leading role in the region.

Egypt's diplomatic efforts to promote the Arab–Israeli peace process continued. In July 1994 President Mubarak travelled to Damascus in an effort to break the deadlock in the negotiations between Syria and Israel, and before returning to Cairo he met the Israeli Prime Minister, Itzhak Rabin, at Taba. Mubarak reportedly urged Rabin to effect a full Israeli withdrawal from the occupied Golan Heights. In August the Syrian Minister of Foreign Affairs, Farouk ash-Shara', held talks with President Mubarak in Alexandria, while the Egyptian Minister of Foreign

Affairs, Amr Moussa, made his first official visit to Israel. In October the US Secretary of State, Warren Christopher, took part in talks with the Chairman of the Palestine National Authority (PNA), Yasser Arafat, and President Mubarak in Alexandria. Despite the first official visit to Egypt by the Israeli President, Ezer Weizman, in December relations between Egypt and Israel began to deteriorate. Egypt was concerned that the peace process might collapse unless Israel showed more flexibility in the negotiations and the Palestinians secured some real benefits from the peace agreement as quickly as possible.

In December 1994 and February 1995 Egypt hosted two mini-summit meetings which some observers regarded as an attempt by the Government to demonstrate its continuing role as the key intermediary in the region and to counter the view, expressed by some members of the new Republican majority in the US Congress, that Egypt no longer deserved substantial US aid. A meeting between President Assad of Syria, King Fahd of Saudi Arabia and President Mubarak took place on 28–29 December 1994 in Alexandria and, according to some reports, was convened in response to Syrian anxiety about the number of Arab states seeking to normalize their relations with Israel before significant progress had been made in peace negotiations between Syria and Israel. The final communiqué of the meeting expressed support for a comprehensive settlement based on the exchange of land for peace. The Israeli Government interpreted the summit as a move hostile to Israel and as a negative response to President Weizman's invitation to Mubarak to make a reciprocal visit to Israel. Moreover, Shimon Peres, the Israeli Minister of Foreign Affairs, expressed his fear of the re-emergence of an Arab alliance hostile to Israel. During a visit to Cairo in January 1995 Peres was informed that Egypt had no desire to obstruct the normalization of relations between Israel and the Arab states. However, tension between the two states remained as Mubarak reiterated his threat that Egypt would not sign the NPT, which was due for renewal in April, unless Israel also agreed to sign it; and urged other Arab states to do likewise. Egypt refused to accept Israeli claims to 'special status' and viewed Israel's nuclear capability as a threat to its own regional position.

President Mubarak met King Hussein of Jordan at Aqaba in January 1995, his first visit to Jordan since the Gulf crisis of 1990–91. The visit was regarded as a sign of an improvement in relations between the two countries now that Jordan had signed a peace treaty with Israel. King Hussein, together with Yasser Arafat and Itzhak Rabin, attended a hastily convened meeting in Cairo in early February 1995 after another suicide bomb attack on an Israeli civilian target threatened to halt the peace process. Although US officials described the summit meeting as 'historic', little was achieved beyond the participants' agreement to take part in a further meeting. Tensions between Egypt and Israel over the NPT continued, with Israel accusing Egypt of attempting to use the issue to disrupt its efforts to normalize relations with other Arab states. In March Israel offered to sign the NPT once it had concluded peace treaties with all the Arab states and Iran; and to allow Egypt to inspect its research nuclear reactor at Nahal Shorek, but not the nuclear facility at Dimona. Egypt rejected both offers, but adopted a more conciliatory line on the issue. Both states appeared anxious to avoid a major crisis in their relations. At the end of March Egypt failed to obtain agreement on a common approach to the issue among Arab League member states. It was reported that the USA had brought strong pressure to bear on the Gulf states to ensure that no united Arab stance should emerge.

Egypt's position regarding the NPT antagonized the USA, which insisted that the continuation of US aid depended on Egypt signing it. This was just one of the issues which had strained US–Egyptian relations. In late 1994 a number of US newspapers and journals published articles criticizing Mubarak's links with Col Qaddafi of Libya, pointing to corruption in high office, including the presidential family, and the lack of genuine political reform. They questioned whether Egypt should continue to receive substantial US economic aid. There was an angry response in the Egyptian press, which accused the USA of betraying a loyal ally which had supported it throughout the Gulf crisis. The US Administration assured Egypt that the press campaign had not been mounted with official approval, praised Egypt's role in the Middle East peace process and insisted that

relations with Egypt were excellent. However, Egypt remained concerned about its relations with the USA and feared that, weakened as he was after the Republican victory in the US Congress, President Clinton might become even more dependent on the support of the pro-Israel lobby. It was also reported that Egypt suspected that President Clinton had been advised to establish contact with the Islamist opposition in order to avoid making the same mistakes that the USA had made in Iran. When President Mubarak visited Washington in April 1995 Egypt's relations with the USA had reached their lowest level for many years. The dispute with Israel over the NPT dominated discussions during the visit, at the end of which President Mubarak pledged that Egypt would not withdraw from the Treaty nor persuade other states to suspend their membership. However, the possibility of a reduction in US aid to Egypt continued to be openly discussed.

As the dispute over the NPT came to a head at the UN in New York in May 1995, Egypt led the Arab states in demanding a resolution requiring Israel to sign the Treaty. However, under pressure from the USA, the Arab states agreed to a resolution which did not mention Israel by name, but instead urged all states in the Middle East without exception to sign the NPT and accept inspection by the International Atomic Energy Agency (IAEA) of their nuclear facilities. Egypt also led the Arab states in condemning Israel's plan to confiscate Palestinian land in occupied East Jerusalem and demanded the convening of an emergency Arab League summit meeting on the question. However, at the end of May the Israeli Government decided to suspend the confiscation, and at the beginning of June, after a meeting in Cairo between President Mubarak, Itzhak Rabin and Warren Christopher, the US Secretary of State claimed that relations between Egypt and Israel had been 'rejuvenated'. However, relations deteriorated again in August when it was revealed that Israeli soldiers had killed large numbers of Egyptian prisoners of war during the Suez crisis in 1956 and the Six-Day War in 1967. After the discovery of mass graves in Sinai, President Mubarak demanded that the Israeli Government investigate these crimes. At first Israel refused, offering instead to pay compensation to the families of the victims. In spite of this dispute, Egypt continued its intermediary role in the complex negotiations which eventually led to signing of the Israeli-Palestinian Interim Agreement on the West Bank and the Gaza Strip in Washington, DC, in September 1995. On 6 November Mubarak made his first visit to Israel as President of Egypt to attend the funeral of Itzhak Rabin. Egypt also participated in meetings which led to the start of more substantive talks between Israel and Syria at the end of 1995. However, disputes over Israel's nuclear capability and the execution of Egyptian prisoners of war continued, with the Egyptian Minister of Foreign Affairs, Amr Moussa, taking a tough line on both issues when Israel's new Prime Minister, Shimon Peres, visited Cairo in December 1995. After the visit Peres reversed a decision by his predecessor and announced the appointment of an investigatory commission into past war crimes. He subsequently stated that Israel would be prepared to relinquish its nuclear capability if a comprehensive Middle East peace settlement were achieved. In April 1996, following reports of a possible leak of nuclear waste from Israel's Dimona reactor, Amr Moussa urged that the reactor should be dismantled and rejected any co-operation on security with Israel while it retained a nuclear capability. On 11 April the African Nuclear Weapon Free Zone Treaty was signed in Cairo. At the signing ceremony, President Mubarak urged all Middle Eastern countries to make the region a nuclear-free zone by signing the NPT.

After a number of devastating suicide bomb attacks in Israel, Egypt, together with the USA, co-hosted a one day 'Summit of Peacemakers' in March 1996 at the Red Sea resort of Sharm esh-Sheikh which was attended by 29 world leaders. Little of substance was achieved at the hastily organized meeting. Israel and the USA wished to address ways of combating terrorism involving greater regional and international co-operation, but President Mubarak, together with other Arab leaders, preferred to concentrate on preventing the collapse of the Middle East peace process. Many regarded the meeting as simply a move to reassure Israel and to lend support to Prime Minister Peres during the approach to the Israeli legislative elections in May. Egypt's relations with Israel quickly deteriorated again in April when Israeli forces began air and artillery attacks on Hezbollah bases in Lebanon, inflicting heavy casualties on Lebanese civilians. In mid-April the Lebanese Prime Minister, Rafik Hariri, visited Cairo to seek assistance against Israeli aggression. Diplomatic efforts by the Egyptian Minister of Foreign Affairs to achieve a cease-fire were unsuccessful and in exasperation he complained that Israel's actions threatened the credibility of the entire peace process. Relations did not improve when it was announced, in April, that Israel and Turkey had concluded a military agreement in February allowing Israeli aircraft to fly from Turkish airbases and Israeli warships to use Turkish ports during joint naval manoeuvres. The Egyptian Minister of Foreign Affairs denounced the agreement, arguing that it did not serve the interests of peace or stability in the region. Military strategists in Egypt regarded it as the creation of 'a second front against the Arabs', while other observers maintained that a new strategic partnership was emerging in the region between Israel, the USA, Jordan and Turkey that could only serve to increase Egypt's marginalization. Egypt remains distrustful of military co-operation between Israel and Turkey, in spite of an assurance, made by President Demirel of Turkey during a visit to Egypt in September 1997, that such co-operation poses no threat to Egypt.

THE PEACE PROCESS STAGNATES

During the approach to the Israeli elections at the end of May 1996, President Mubarak did not disguise his preference for a Labour victory, while the semi-official *Al-Ahram* newspaper warned that the Arabs should prepare for tough negotiations in case Likud won. After the victory of Likud leader Binyamin Netanyahu was confirmed on 30 May, it was reported that President Mubarak had telephoned the new Israeli Prime Minister and invited him to visit Cairo. On 1 June the President stated that the new Israeli administration had to be given time 'to clarify its viewpoints and intentions towards the peace process'. The Minister of Foreign Affairs took a harder line, however, declaring that peace required a complete Israeli withdrawal from occupied territory and insisting that he would only be satisfied by the creation of a Palestinian state and a solution to the issues of Jerusalem, refugees, settlements and water. At the end of June, however, after Netanyahu had repeated his rejection of the principle of 'land for peace', President Mubarak convened an emergency summit meeting of the Arab League in Cairo—the first full-scale summit meeting for six years. (Iraq was not invited because of what President Mubarak referred to as 'continuing sensitivities'.) The summit reaffirmed Egypt's central role in the Arab world. Egyptian efforts at reconciliation created a semblance of unity in the Arab ranks, with President Mubarak attempting to mediate in disputes between some Arab leaders. However, a veteran Egyptian political commentator, Muhammad Heikal, described the meeting as 'little more than a smoke-screen', although he acknowledged that the symbolism of Arab unity remained important. The summit's final communiqué reaffirmed the Arabs' commitment to peace, but warned that peace and any further *rapprochement* between the Arabs and Israel depended on Israel's returning all of the Arab land occupied in 1967. Israel immediately rejected all of the resolutions adopted at the summit meeting, and Netanyahu declared that unilateral demands had to cease if the peace process was to continue successfully.

Although Netanyahu was invited for talks with President Mubarak in Cairo in July 1996, relations with Israel became increasingly strained. The Egyptian Government argued that it had worked hard to restrain some of the more militant Arab states, but that the Israeli Prime Minister had not responded: he had neither moderated his uncompromising stance nor fulfilled Israel's commitments to the Palestinians under the Oslo accords. In August President Mubarak threatened to cancel the third Middle East and North Africa economic conference, due to take place in Cairo in November, unless Israel agreed to move forward on the Palestinian peace track. However, in September, in response to pressure from the USA and from the Egyptian business community, the President indicated that the summit would proceed as planned. Relations between Egypt and Israel deteriorated further when Egypt carried out large-scale military manoeuvres near the Suez Canal in early September. Later that month there were popular demonstrations in Egypt after the Israeli Government opened an ancient tunnel in East Jeru-

salem, close to Muslim religious sites. Violent clashes erupted between Israeli troops and Palestinians and public anger prevented Egypt from acting as mediator in the crisis. Although Prime Minister Netanyahu, King Hussein of Jordan and the Palestinian leader, Yasser Arafat, attended a summit meeting in Washington, DC, to try to defuse the crisis, President Mubarak resisted US pressure to participate, stating that an immediate resolution was unlikely to be achieved. Despite a goodwill visit to Cairo by the President of Israel, Ezer Weizman, in October, his reassurances about Israel's peace commitments failed to ease tensions between the two countries. In December a new dispute arose when the Israeli Minister of Foreign Affairs accused Egypt of interfering in talks between Israel and the Palestinians on the partial withdrawal of Israeli troops from the town of Hebron on the West Bank. President Mubarak insisted that Prime Minister Netanyahu had invited Egypt to act as mediator in the talks, but David Levy, the Israeli Minister of Foreign Affairs, stated that Egypt's involvement would only complicate the negotiations. Nevertheless, in early January 1997 a series of meetings on Hebron took place in Egypt between Yasser Arafat, Dennis Ross—the US Middle East peace co-ordinator—and Abdul Karim Kabariti, the Jordanian Prime Minister. President Mubarak also sent a team of legal experts to assist the Palestinian negotiating team. However, it was the intervention of King Hussein of Jordan that eventually secured an agreement on the redeployment of Israeli forces in Hebron and other areas of the West Bank.

Despite the collapse of the peace process in late February 1997, after Israel announced its determination to proceed with the construction of a new Jewish settlement at Har Homa on the outskirts of Arab East Jerusalem, Prime Minister Netanyahu made a second visit to Cairo at the beginning of March. Little was achieved in his talks with President Mubarak, and it was suggested that the Egyptian President had only allowed the visit to proceed in order not to alienate the USA, where he was due to meet President Clinton a few days later. When Netanyahu addressed a meeting of Egyptian businessmen and intellectuals he received a hostile reception. As unrest erupted in the West Bank and Gaza Strip, President Mubarak held talks about the crisis in late March with Rafik Hariri, the Lebanese Prime Minister, Farouk ash-Shara', the Syrian Minister of Foreign Affairs, Yasser Arafat and Dore Gold, the Israeli premier's foreign policy adviser. When the Ministers of Foreign Affairs of the Arab League member states met in Cairo at the end of March, it was decided to reintroduce the economic boycott of Israel and to halt the normalization of relations. Egypt was exempt from the boycott, however, because of its peace treaty with Israel. In early April President Mubarak insisted that relations with Israel would remain secure. Indeed, Egypt wished to maintain its intermediary role and its economic links with the country. Nevertheless, there were many signs of popular dissatisfaction with the normalization of relations with Israel. On 24 April a large political rally in Cairo was attended by representatives from across Egypt's political spectrum in protest against Israeli policies in Jerusalem.

At the end of May 1997 President Mubarak met the Israeli Prime Minister at Sharm esh-Sheikh in order to try to reactivate the peace process. President Mubarak agreed to contact the Palestinian leader, Yasser Arafat, who had refused to meet with Netanyahu after Israel announced its decision to proceed with the new settlement in East Jerusalem. On 8 June Osama el-Baz, President Mubarak's senior adviser, conferred with Israeli and Palestinian negotiators in Cairo. Despite el-Baz's claims of a positive atmosphere during the talks, Israel's continued building of settlements in East Jerusalem seemed likely to prolong the deadlock. For the remainder of the year the Egyptian Government, in its role as principal mediator, attempted unsuccessfully to revive the peace process. Increasingly, official announcements on the stalled negotiations were made in a tone of desperation, not least because Israel's intransigence, to which the Government frequently referred, strengthened the position of the armed militant Islamist opposition in Egypt.

In September 1997, in a personal message to the Israeli Prime Minister, President Mubarak warned of the possibility of strategic changes in the Middle East, with negative consequences for all moderate forces, if there was no movement towards peace in the coming months. In the same month Egypt's relations with Israel were further impaired when an Egyptian state security court sentenced an Israeli Arab, Azam Azam, to 15 years' imprisonment, with hard labour, having convicted him of spying for the Israeli intelligence services. The Israeli Government denied that Azam had been involved in espionage and described the sentence as an 'outrage'. In October Egypt announced a prohibition of imports of Israeli goods produced in the Occupied Territories. In the same month President Mubarak stated that the peace process had never before 'reached such an impasse'. In November Egypt, together with several other Arab countries, boycotted the fourth Middle East and North Africa economic conference in Doha, Qatar, in protest at Israel's failure to honour its commitments to the Palestinians under the terms of the 1993 Oslo peace agreements. (It was not clear to what extent Egypt's abstention was responsible for a subsequent deterioration in relations with Qatar. In November Qatar accused Egypt of involvement in an attempted *coup d'état* against the Qatari Government in 1996. After Saudi Arabia had apparently mediated a reconciliation between the two countries in December 1997, it was reported in February 1998 that Qatar had dismissed all Egyptians employed in the Qatari Ministry of the Interior and planned to expel them from the country.)

In April 1998, in their first meeting for 11 months, President Mubarak and Prime Minister Netanyahu of Israel held talks in Cairo. The focus of their discussions was reportedly a US initiative to restart the peace process, which proposed that Israel should withdraw from a further 13.1% of West Bank territory. Prior to his meeting with President Mubarak, Netanyahu had rejected the US proposal. In an attempt to elicit a more positive response from the Israeli Prime Minister, Mubarak described the US initiative as 'the minimum of what is necessary to revive the peace process, especially in the light of the positive reaction of the Palestinian side'. In his view, Israel's acceptance of the proposal would facilitate the resumption of permanent status negotiations between Israel and the Palestinians, and of Israel's negotiations with Syria and Lebanon.

Relations with the USA remained strained, with Egypt convinced that the Clinton Administration had forfeited its role as impartial mediator in the region because of its close alliance with Israel. The US Secretary of Defense, William Perry, visited Cairo in April 1996 and denied rumours that the USA had signed a secret defence agreement with Israel. He was reported to have shown President Mubarak firm evidence that Libya was building a huge chemical weapons factory at Tarhuna. However, the President remained unconvinced by the US claims and, while offering to mediate with Col Qaddafi on this issue, warned against any new US military action against Libya. Perry did, however, announce that the USA would supply advanced military equipment to Egypt, including 21 F-16 fighter aircraft, in acknowledgement of its key role in the peace process. In September 1996 US missile attacks against military targets in southern Iraq provoked criticism from the Egyptian authorities. Egypt indicated that it strongly opposed moves to partition Iraq and condemned Turkish attempts to establish a security zone inside the northern region. In December, the US veto of a second term of office for Boutros Boutros-Ghali, the UN Secretary-General, provoked widespread outrage in the Egyptian media. The USA was accused of removing Boutros-Ghali, formerly a senior Egyptian minister, because he had tried to maintain the UN's independence in the face of US pressure.

Egypt has sought to mediate in disputes between Iraq and the UN since 1991. In September 1997, in a joint declaration with Russia, Egypt urged the restoration of Iraq's status as a full member of the international community, while insisting that it should comply with relevant UN resolutions. In February 1998, following consultations with other Arab leaders, President Mubarak presented the US Secretary of State, Madeleine Albright, with an 'integrated' Arab plan to resolve Iraq's latest conflict with the UN over weapons inspections. Mubarak subsequently warned the US Secretary of State that further military action against Iraq might provoke Islamist militancy against secular Arab governments and thus destroy the Arab–Israeli peace process.

Egypt's relations with Jordan, strained since the 1990–91 Gulf crisis, deteriorated in August 1995 when King Hussein changed policy on Iraq, granted asylum to Saddam Hussain's two defecting sons-in-law and their wives, and broke decisively

with the Iraqi leader. King Hussein's appeal for political change in Iraq was strongly criticized by the Egyptian regime, which expressed its opposition to any kind of outside intervention to depose Saddam Hussain. In reply, Jordan claimed that Egypt resented the more active role that Jordan was now playing in the Middle East region. Addressing an economic summit meeting in Amman in October, the Egyptian Minister of Foreign Affairs criticized Jordan for proceeding too quickly towards a peace treaty with Israel.

There was surprise in some quarters when it was announced in November 1994 that Egypt had applied for permanent observer status and possible membership of the Union of the Arab Maghreb (UAM), a regional economic and security grouping of Mauritania, Morocco, Algeria, Tunisia and Libya. Egypt had collaborated for some time with Algeria and Tunisia in the struggle against Islamist militancy, but the reasons behind the application appeared to be linked to its desire to reassert its central role in the Middle East as Israel successfully normalized its relations with a growing number of Arab states; and, by emphasizing its Mediterranean role, to give a higher priority to diplomatic relations with Europe in the hope of securing economic benefits from the EU.

Relations with neighbouring Sudan, always uneasy, deteriorated in August 1994, when each side accused the other of mistreating its nationals. In the following month Sudan alleged that Egyptian troops had entered the disputed border area of Halaib and, in response, impounded the ferry from Aswan to Wadi Halfa, claiming that it was carrying troops. Relations worsened sharply in June 1995, after the unsuccessful attempt to assassinate President Mubarak in Addis Ababa (see above). The Egyptian Government accused Sudan of complicity in the attack, and Egypt immediately strengthened its control of the Halaib triangle. In July, in contravention of an agreement concluded with Sudan in 1978, Egypt imposed visa and permit requirements on Sudanese nationals visiting or resident in Egypt. Relations deteriorated further in September 1995, when the OAU accused Sudan of direct involvement in the attempted assassination, and in December, when it demanded that Sudan should immediately extradite three individuals who were sought in connection with the attack. In February 1996 Sudan introduced permit requirements for Egyptian nationals resident in Sudan. Presidents Mubarak and al-Bashir met at the Arab League summit meeting in Cairo in May. In July, however, Egypt accused Sudan of harbouring Egyptian terrorists, contrary to an agreement concluded at the summit meeting. None the less, Egypt opposed the imposition of more stringent economic sanctions against Sudan by the UN (in addition to diplomatic sanctions and an embargo on international flights operated by Sudan Airways), on the grounds that they would harm the Sudanese people more than the Sudanese regime.

In January 1997 Egypt refused to provide the Sudanese government with military support in its struggle against rebel advances in southern Sudan. In June Sudan accused Egypt of providing the opposition with military training, and in October the Sudanese press reported that Egypt was obstructing the import of medical supplies to Halaib. Despite such accusations, there was evidence, from mid-1997, of attempts to improve bilateral relations. In August security talks between the two countries resumed after a year-long suspension, and in October the Sudanese First Vice-President, Maj.-Gen. Zubair Muhammad Salih, visited Egypt to discuss the normalization of relations. Egypt has stated its opposition to the potential partition of Sudan that it fears might result from an eventual conclusion of the conflict in southern Sudan, and in November John Garang, the leader of the Sudan People's Liberation Movement, the principal rebel faction opposing the Sudanese Government, made a visit to Cairo for talks with President Mubarak. In January 1998 elements of the Sudanese opposition expressed their concern at the ongoing improvement in Egyptian–Sudanese relations, claiming that the Sudanese regime continued to lend support to the armed Islamist movement in Egypt. In February, as part of the process of normalization, river transport resumed between the Egyptian port of Aswan and the Sudanese port of Wadi Halfa. In April an agreement to form a joint ministerial committee, comprising each country's Ministers of Higher Education, Defence and Irrigation, was announced.

There were signs, from late 1997, of a possible improvement in Egypt's relations with Iran. In December the Egyptian Minister of Foreign Affairs attended an OIC meeting in Teheran and met Iranian President Khatami. It was reported that Egypt had stipulated no conditions for the restoration of diplomatic relations with Iran, which had been severed in 1979. However, this process of normalization appeared to suffer a set-back in early 1998 when Egypt described Iranian criticism of the Algerian regime as 'blatant interference in the affairs of a fraternal Arab country'.

Economy

Updated for this edition by the Editor

INTRODUCTION

Over the last few decades, Egypt's economy has been fundamentally influenced by various political vicissitudes. In particular, relations with Israel have had major repercussions on the nature of expenditure and foreign aid, while in recent years the Government has moved away from state socialism and towards a market economy. Underneath these changes of direction, however, lie the important physical constraints of a large and rapidly growing population, and the dearth of land available for agriculture and water for irrigation.

The total area of Egypt is 1,002,000 sq km, but more than 90% of the country is desert. With no forested land, and hardly any permanent meadows or pastures, the arable land available is greatly overcrowded. Relating the population, numbering 38.2m. at the 1976 census, to the inhabited area (about 35,200 sq km), a density of 1,085 persons per sq km gave 5.7 persons per acre of arable land, representing one of the highest man/land ratios in the world. Since then, the root of Egypt's poverty has remained the rapid rise in the population, of 2.8% per annum between 1976 and 1986, which added about 1.3m. people per year. According to the results of the 1986 census, the population had risen to 48.2m., and only 4% of the land area was occupied. The average annual rise in population in the 1980s was 2.4%, compared with 2.1% in 1965–80, but this was projected to fall to 1.8% in the decade to 2000. World Bank figures estimated an average annual rate of increase in population of 2.0% during 1990–96. The census of December 1996 recorded a permanently-resident Egyptian population of 59,272,382. Family planning has been heavily promoted by the Government since the establishment of a National Population Council in 1985. An estimated 48% of families were practising contraception in 1992, when the average number of births per mother fell below four for the first time since records have been kept. The Government's long-term aim is to extend the practice of contraception to 70% of Egyptian families by 2010.

Lack of employment opportunities drove people from the country into already overcrowded cities, which grew at a rate of 3.4% per annum in the late 1970s (the population of Greater Cairo increased from 7m. in 1976 to more than 10m. in 1985), and hastened the emigration of qualified personnel the country could ill afford to lose. In 1983 3.28m. Egyptians were working abroad. Many originally went to much better-paid jobs in the rich Gulf states and Libya, although a considerable number were forced to return from the former in the 1980s, owing to a downturn in the oil industry, and from the latter because of a government order of 1985, prohibiting the employment of Egyptian workers. Poor job prospects were not improved by the return of thousands of expatriate workers (including about 5,000 from Libya in 1985, and about 250,000 who left Iraq in the first half of 1986, when new restrictions were imposed on the amount of money they were allowed to send home). This trend also helped swell the bureaucracy, since the Government had been committed to giving a post to every Egyptian graduate who could not find other employment. By the time of the census in late 1996 the number of Egyptians living abroad had fallen to an estimated 2.18m. In February 1998 the Egyptian Mobilization and Statistics Agency estimated that there were 3.0m. Egyptians living abroad, 720,000 of whom were permanent immigrants. In mid-1991 government officials estimated that the number of unemployed was in the range of 20%–22% of the total labour force. The urban population was believed to have peaked in 1990 at 47%. According to the 1996 census, 43% of the population was estimated to be urban, compared with the 44% comprising the urban population at the 1976 census and 41% in 1965. In 1990, according to estimates by the World Bank, Egypt's gross national product (GNP) per head was $600, having increased at an average rate of 4.1% per year, in real terms, since 1965. The average annual growth of overall gross domestic product (GDP), measured in constant prices, was 7.3% in 1965–80, slowing to 5.0% in 1980–90. The World Bank estimated Egypt's GNP per head in 1992 as $650 on a conventional exchange-rate basis, or as $3,670 using an 'international dollar' calculation based on a current Egyptian rating of 15.9 in the World Bank's international 'purchasing power parity' (PPP) index (USA = 100). The Bank's estimates for 1996, at average 1994–96 prices, gave GNP per head as $1,080 on the standard calculation and as $2,860 on the PPP basis. During 1990–96, it was estimated, GNP per head increased, in real terms, by an annual average of 2.2%.

In 1990/91 the crisis in the Gulf had a damaging short-term effect on the Egyptian economy, due in particular to a decline in tourism and the return of hundreds of thousands of Egyptian nationals from Iraq and Kuwait, which was only partially offset by higher revenues from oil exports. However, the Government's political and military alignment with the anti-Iraq coalition brought important post-war benefits in the form of generous debt relief and increased aid from major donors (see below). Tourism recovered strongly in 1991/92, but underwent a new decline in 1992/93 when foreign tourists were among the targets of a terrorist campaign by militant Islamist elements. At the end of 1993 the level of unemployment in Egypt was officially estimated to be between 1.4m. and 1.5m. (about 10% of the labour force), significantly below the lowest estimates of most independent analysts. Up to 3m. Egyptians were estimated to be working abroad in mid-1995, including about 1.2m. in Saudi Arabia, 70,000 in Kuwait, 50,000 in Iraq and up to 500,000 in Libya. In late 1997 the official unemployment rate was 9.4% of the labour force. In early 1998 the Government was requested to review its policy on child labour, after a report, compiled by the National Centre for Social Research, claimed that children comprised 70% of the rural work-force. Although it is illegal to employ children under the age of 14, the report found that many employers were exploiting a rule allowing children to be trained from the age of 12 years.

Population growth averaged 2.1% per annum between 1986 and 1996, according to the 1996 census. The population of Cairo (excluding Giza) rose from 6,068,695 in 1986 to 6,789,479 in 1996. The number of Egyptians resident in new industrial cities rose from 200,214 (in nine cities) in 1986 to 618,665 (in 19 cities) in 1996. One of the objectives of a long-term development strategy proposed by the Government in 1997 was to reduce the undeveloped proportion of Egypt's land area (used neither for habitation, agriculture nor industry) to 75% by 2017, compared with more than 95% in 1997. According to Egyptian government estimates, GDP per head at current prices in 1997 was US $1,256. An increasingly effective programme of structural economic reform had by 1996/97 improved Egypt's annual rate of real economic growth to around 5.9%, according to the IMF (compared with 2.9% in 1992/93), providing a sound basis for a government initiative to generate higher levels of private investment in future years.

During the 1960s Egypt, under Nasser, followed an economic policy which was based on socialist planning. However, the wars with Israel in 1967 and 1973, and Nasser's death in 1970, heralded a major period of change in Egypt's economic relations, both with its Arab neighbours and with the superpowers. Since

1973 great efforts have been made to repair the war damage, and Sadat's Law No. 43 of 1974 led to the replacement of Nasser's socialist planning by an 'open door policy' (*infitah*), encouraging foreign investment. The economic implications of Sadat's assassination in October 1981 were slight at first, but his successor, Hosni Mubarak, gradually encouraged the private sector. Basic tax on company profits was reduced from 40% to 32% in early 1982, while the enactment in 1990 of Law No. 230, a revised and refined version of the 1974 Law, was regarded as a sign of the Government's commitment to the growth of private enterprise and deregulation. This shift from an essentially centrally controlled economy to one that is much more open to private enterprise and foreign investment has itself caused considerable strain on, and problems in, the economy. Private investment increased sharply following the institution of the 'open door policy': it totalled £E1,025m. in 1983, compared with £E443m. in 1982, and by 1990 it had reached £E10,700m., of which 64% was Egyptian, 19% Arab and 17% from other sources. The 1970s also saw a great increase in aid from the oil-rich Arab states. In 1967–73 Arab aid to Egypt was estimated at an annual average of US $310m. In 1973 this increased to $720m., and in 1974 it rose to $1,260m., while by 1977 it had risen to between $1,700m. and $2,000m. Much of this aid came from the Gulf Organization for the Development of Egypt (GODE), set up by Saudi Arabia, Kuwait, the United Arab Emirates and Qatar in 1977. Saudi sources, in fact, claimed in May 1979 that Egypt had received more than US $13,000m. from the four GODE countries in the preceding six years.

By signing the peace treaty with Israel in March 1979, however, Sadat undertook the risk of losing this Arab aid. The Arab League Council which met in Baghdad immediately after the signing of the peace treaty, agreed on a policy of economic and political isolation of Egypt. At first it seemed unlikely that the economic sanctions would be stringently carried out by some of the Arab countries, but, when, in late April, Saudi Arabia severed diplomatic relations with Egypt, some of the more 'moderate' Arab states implemented the boycott. The Arab Fund for Economic and Social Development suspended all future aid and credit relations with Egypt, although honouring transactions already in progress, and in May Saudi Arabia, Qatar and the United Arab Emirates withdrew from the Arab Organization for Industrialization (AOI), which was an Egypt-based Arab arms enterprise, causing its collapse. Egypt, however, responded by planning to establish its own arms industry with Western capital (see Manufacturing Industry, below). During 1980 Egypt and Israel signed agricultural, trade, aviation and health agreements, and their common border was opened to commercial and tourist traffic towards the end of the year. While the loss of Saudi military aid, estimated at an annual rate of just under $2,000m., was undoubtedly significant, the fact that only about 7% of Egypt's total trade was with Arab countries implied that the Arab trade boycott would probably not be of major importance. The loss of Arab aid from the GODE was significant, however, although Egypt ceased to pay interest due on sums already loaned in 1979. By 1987 the resulting arrears in interest on GODE loans totalled almost $2,000m. Sadat hoped that Egypt's economic difficulties would be alleviated by the 'Carter Plan', which he saw in the same light as the 'Marshall Plan', by which Egypt would receive US $12,250m. over a period of five years, mainly from the USA, Western Europe and Japan. The USA promised that it would be no less generous to Egypt after the peace treaty with Israel than it was to Israel itself in terms of economic aid; as a result, Egypt became the second largest recipient of US aid, after Israel. The return of multinationals such as Coca-Cola and Cadbury Schweppes, associated with the normalization of relations with Israel, clearly demonstrated the increased readiness of foreign capital to invest in Egypt. Between 1975 and 1985, according to USAID, US economic assistance to Egypt totalled $10,897.8m. In June 1988, in order to comply with a congressional mandate which required the suspension of aid to countries failing to meet terms imposed by the IMF as conditions for a debt-rescheduling agreement, the USA halted the disbursement of $230m. of financial aid allocated to Egypt in 1988/89. Egypt's total debt to the USA was by then estimated at $10,000m., of which $4,500m. was military debt. In April 1989, following the Government's decision to raise energy prices to industry by 30%–40%, the US Administration

agreed to release the $230m. and several other categories of aid. In 1990 Egypt received a total of $5,604m. (or 15.9% of its GNP) in official development aid from OECD members, Arab countries and multilateral organizations, compared with $1,568m. in 1989, $1,537m. in 1988, $1,774m. in 1987 and $1,716m. in 1986. The principal OECD donors, apart from the USA, were the Federal Republic of Germany and Japan. In the 1989/90 US fiscal year USAID allocations to Egypt amounted to $815m.

In February 1989 Egypt was a founder member of the Arab Co-operation Council (ACC), together with Jordan, Iraq and the Yemen Arab Republic (YAR), and in May, Egypt was formally readmitted to the Arab League and its various economic committees. However, hopes that the ACC would provide a framework for increased economic co-operation were dissipated, at least temporarily, by the impact of the Gulf crisis of 1990–91.

ECONOMIC POLICY AND PLANNING

Between 1918 and 1939, when the Egyptian pound was tied to sterling and a fairly free trade policy was being pursued, manufacturing industry had little chance of developing and agricultural production, though expanding, could not sustain the rapidly rising population. A gradual deterioration of living standards ensued. This trend did not change direction until the immediate post-war period, when cotton prices improved. These reached their greatest heights during the Korean boom of 1951–52, when 'soft-currency cotton', including Egyptian cotton, enjoyed high premia over dollar-cotton. But the collapse of the boom, the easing of the world dollar scarcity and the beginning of American subsidization of cotton exports in the mid-1950s, marked a turning point in raw cotton terms of trade which, until quite recently, showed a declining trend.

The regime which assumed power in 1952 and ended the monarchy gave urgent attention to Egypt's economic problems. Its policies included measures of agrarian reform, land reclamation, the High Dam scheme, and a programme of industrialization which was accelerated in 1960 by the formation of a comprehensive social and economic development plan.

According to the Permanent Constitution of 1971 the economy of Egypt was to be based on socialism with the people controlling all means of production. In practice this meant that the Government took ownership or control of practically every unit in the economy worth controlling. Although the doctrine of socialism was invoked from the first land reform in 1952, the economy remained largely in private hands until 1961, except for the nationalization of the Suez Canal Company in 1956 and that of British and French property during the Suez attack. During 1961 all cotton exporting firms were nationalized, and the Alexandria futures market was closed. Other nationalization measures followed, so that the only sectors of the economy remaining outside complete government ownership were agriculture and urban real estate, but even these were overwhelmingly regulated by laws and decrees. In June 1991 the Government introduced new legislation to reform public-sector companies, with the aim of reducing state intervention in such companies to a minimum. The reforms envisaged the establishment of state-owned holding companies to replace the general bodies hitherto in control of groups of state-owned companies. By May 1993 a total of 16 state-owned holding companies controlled a total of 317 subsidiary companies, grouped together in such a way as to minimize functional duplication and maximize adminstrative efficiency within the public sector.

Egypt's first Five-Year Development Plan aimed to increase real national income by 40% between 1960 and 1965. The five-year growth target was virtually fulfilled, so that the second Plan was replaced by a more ambitious Seven-Year Plan (1965–72), which aimed to double real income by its end. Lack of finance, however, frustrated this new plan and after two years of uncertainty, a three-year 'accomplishment' plan, beginning July 1967, was proclaimed. This plan was abandoned as a result of the 1967 war and was substituted by annual development appropriations. Apart from a few select new projects, the whole emphasis of Egyptian planning was turned towards rationalizing the existing industries, and introducing incentives to improve their performance.

After 1967 the Government introduced yet more restrictive measures aimed at curbing consumer demand, including a variety of taxes, forced savings and compulsory contributions out of wages and salaries. Following Nasser's death in 1970, however, President Sadat embarked on a gradual retreat from old-style socialist economic policies. Under what was termed 'denasserization', the sequestrations of the 1960s were ruled illegal, new laws were passed to allow private-sector participation in former state preserves such as exporting and importing and transport, and foreign investment was seen as the key to development.

In 1971 President Sadat proclaimed a decennial plan which aimed to double the national economy by 1982. This, however, was never fully implemented, and it was soon replaced by a transitional 18-month plan, to be followed by a more thorough five-year plan to cover the years 1976–80. Owing to the financial problems of 1976, this new plan was then postponed to cover 1978–82. It foresaw total expenditure at some £E12,000m. ($17,000m. at the parallel rate), and its main objective was to achieve annual economic growth rates of 8%. However, this was, in its turn, replaced by the 1980–84 five-year Peace Plan with planned investment of £E25,185m.; according to figures provided by the World Bank, the average annual growth of GDP in 1965–80 was 6.8%.

Under Mubarak, economic policy sought to increase exports and employment through meticulous planning for the public, private and co-operative sectors. Particular attention was to be paid to social problems. Investment resources were to be increased through new channels for private investment, increasing the contribution of the banking sector, improving the efficiency of the tax system, increasing indigenous financial resources, reducing government expenditure, and limiting the consumption of imported goods. The Government's aim was to use the public sector as the main prop of production, regarding manpower as the real wealth of the country. The negative effects of subsidies (mainly on food, but also on oil, petrol, gas and electricity) were acknowledged, but the Government regarded the sole remedy to be increased rates of development and the promotion of productivity. It committed itself to strenuous efforts to reduce the level of imports, and all import operations in the future were to be undertaken through the banks without the transfer of currency. The Government planned to increase its export earnings, particularly through sales of petroleum, and the expansion of the war production sector. In agriculture, it envisaged reclamation as continuing to play an important role. Transport, communications, housing, tourism, health and education were also all to be boosted.

At the end of 1982 proposals were put forward for the next Five-Year Plan (1982–87), with a target for GDP growth in real terms of 7.9% per annum. The strategy behind the Plan was to reduce the proportion of private consumption and of imports in total expenditure, so as to mobilize domestic resources for investment and to reduce the growing trade deficit, which had developed as a result of the policy of *infitah*. Planned investment was to be £E27,216m. ($32,790m.) in the public sector and £E8,271m. ($8,965m.) in the private sector. The Plan's objectives could be achieved, however, only if there was an improvement in Egypt's balance of payments. In this regard, the progressive decline in world oil demand (oil being Egypt's principal export commodity) undermined the viability of the Plan's targets. These doubts were confirmed by the collapse in the price of oil in 1986, when Egypt's net revenues from oil sales declined to less than $1,000m. The annual rate of growth of GDP during the Plan reached only about 5%, well short of its target of 7.9%. It was reported that only 15% of projects outlined in the Plan had actually been carried out when it ended in June 1987, owing to inadequate funding.

The next Five-Year Plan, which began in July 1987, provided for investment of £E46,500m. The Plan was designed to encourage public-sector production, to increase the manufacturing of commodities and to raise the level of exports. It also devoted more resources to the development of the private sector, which was to receive 39% of total investment (£E18,000m.), compared with 23% under the 1982–87 Plan. It was hoped to achieve annual growth in GDP of 5.8% during the Plan. Another important feature of the new Plan was the improvement of agricultural output, so as to minimize food imports, which accounted for 60% of Egypt's requirements. To this end, it was intended to bring an extra 100,000 feddans of land into

production during each year of the Plan. However, even before the onset of the Gulf crisis in 1990, the Plan's targets had been placed in serious doubt by the lack of funds available to finance development projects. According to one Egyptian newspaper, the shortage of foreign currency reserves forced the Government to order the National Investment Bank to halt financing of the Plan in March 1988 and to cancel imports of a number of foodstuffs.

Despite the non-fulfilment of the 1987–92 Plan and the general move to a market economy, a further Five-Year Plan was drawn up for the period beginning 1 July 1992. This document envisaged a 4% growth in GDP in the 1992/93 financial year, to £E131,000m., and thereafter by 5.1% per annum, to £E161,000m. in 1996/97 (at constant 1991/92 prices). Total investment of £E154,000m. was projected for the Plan period, of which 58% would come from the private sector, and it was envisaged that 2.5m. new jobs would be created (the current work-force numbering 14m., of whom 5.3m. were in the state sector).

Draft planning proposals for the 1997–2002 period, outlined in a cabinet document published in April 1997, envisaged total investment of around £E400,000m. over five years, including £E58,000m. (60% from the private sector) during the fiscal year beginning July 1997. The target rate of economic growth for the 1997–2000 period was an average 6.8% per annum. At the same time the Government outlined targets for the 20 years up to 2017. These envisaged a doubling of GDP between 1997 and 2007 and the same rate of increase between 2007 and 2017, eventually totalling £E1,100,000m. The target for GDP per head in 2017 was 'at least £E13,750'. It was hoped that economic growth would average 7.6% per annum after 2002, while the rate of price inflation was to be kept below 5% from 1997 to 2017. The budget deficit was to be eliminated and, if possible, replaced by a surplus before the end of the 20-year period, while the target rate for the creation of new jobs was 550,000 per year throughout this period.

ECONOMIC REFORM 1986–90

In June 1986 the Egyptian Government made renewed efforts to deal with the burden of subsidies. The new Prime Minister, Dr Ali Lutfi, proposed a system of cash benefits for those most affected by a 15% reduction in food subsidies under the 1986/87 budget, which set total expenditure for subsidies at £E1,746m. ($802m.) for the year, 12% less than the previous year. However, Dr Lutfi resigned as Prime Minister in November 1986, owing to President Mubarak's opposition to his apparent willingness to accede to proposals by the IMF for the introduction of economic reforms, in return for a stand-by credit arrangement. The IMF's demands included the adoption of a unified exchange rate (meaning an effective substantial devaluation), the progressive elimination of state subsidies, increases in real interest rates, tax reforms, and increases in customs duties as a means of reducing the level of imports.

The new Prime Minister, Dr Atif Sidqi, rejected the IMF's demands as too extreme, particularly those referring to the unification of the exchange rate system and a 75% reduction in subsidies. By May 1987, however, Dr Sidqi was himself beginning to yield to IMF pressure. Domestic energy prices rose by 60%–85% on 1 May, thereby reducing the 'hidden' energy subsidy. The exchange rate was allowed, partially, to 'float' in mid-May, with a daily rate, competitive with the 'black'-market rate, being fixed by a panel of commercial banks in order to attract remittances. Plans were also announced to reduce the budget deficit to 13% of GDP in 1987/88, compared with 15% in 1986/87, and to cut expenditure on subsidies to £E1,650m. In mid-May, following the IMF's approval of the Egyptian Government's programme of economic reform, the IMF indicated its support for the programme's aims by according Egypt a stand-by credit of $325m., of which $150m. was made available immediately. At the end of May an agreement was reached with the 'Paris Club' of Western creditor nations to reschedule, over 10 years, payments of $12,000m. in civilian and military debt from Egypt's estimated $44,000m. of foreign debt. One month earlier, the USSR had agreed to reschedule, over 25 years, without interest, more than $3,000m. in military debt outstanding since 1977. Military debt totalled an estimated $13,500m. in February 1988, including $4,500m. owed to the USA. In November 1987 Egypt signed an agreement rescheduling the payment of $1,600m. in military and civil debt to the USA. Similar agreements, covering debt repayments of $8,000m. up to the end of June 1988, had been concluded with the remaining 17 'Paris Club' members by the end of July 1988.

By mid-1988, however, the Egyptian Government was concerned that the pace of economic reform required by the IMF was such as to risk a repetition of earlier riots over increases in the price of food, and it urged the introduction of a new reform programme, which would be implemented at a more gradual rate and supported by financial assistance for the balance of payments. The Government opposed further reductions in state subsidies which, it claimed, would fuel an inflation rate that was already as high as 30%; it was resolved to maintain the artificially high fixed Central Bank exchange rate of US$1 = £E0.70 (used for imports of basic commodities), which acted as an indirect subsidy on food prices and which the IMF wished to be abolished. The Prime Minister, Dr Atif Sidqi, said that increases in energy prices of between 30% and 40% required by the IMF, were too great; that the Government refused to raise interest rates to 20%–25%; and that the budget deficit would not fall to the IMF's target of 10% of GDP in 1988/89 (in which year, budgeted expenditure on subsidies rose to £E1,813m.). The IMF conceded that a shortfall of about $1,400m. in the aid allocations needed to support a reform programme was a hindrance to its implementation. However, Egypt's request for further balance-of-payments support for the duration of a long-term programme of economic reform did not meet with a favourable response. The IMF's stand-by credit of $325m. was, accordingly, frozen after only one disbursement of $150m. in May 1987, owing to IMF dissatisfaction with the pace of reform in Egypt.

By June 1988 the Government's wages bill was estimated to have increased by 25%, and to have contributed greatly to a budget deficit equivalent to 16%–17% of GDP in 1987/88, compared with the IMF's target of 13%. The Government's public sector salary commitments were expected to rise by a further 42% in 1988/89. Negotiations between the Government and senior IMF officials, regarding the elaboration of a new economic reform programme, recommenced in mid-1988 and continued intermittently for the remainder of the year without success. While the Government argued that it had made significant achievements in its reform of the exchange rate and prices, the IMF pressed for faster, more wide-ranging reform, including an increase of 30%–40% in energy prices to industry.

Further negotiations between the Government and the Fund in January 1989 remained deadlocked over the timing of the economic reform programme. While the Government argued that it should be allowed four years to implement the Fund's demands, the Fund refused to concede any more than two years for their implementation. In mid-April, however, despite further economic pressure in the form of a depreciation of 20% in the value of the Egyptian pound against foreign currencies since mid-March, the Government was reported to have undertaken to raise energy prices to industry by 30%–40%, and to be ready to begin a programme of public sector reform. The 1989/90 budget, announced in June, granted greater autonomy to public companies, and in September the Central Bank rate of US $1 = £E0.70 was raised to US $1 = £E1.10. Moreover, although budget expenditure on subsidies rose to £E2,061m., the overall budget deficit was set at 8% (in fact, a deficit of 7% was recorded). However, no further progress towards an agreement with the Fund was achieved during the remainder of 1989.

Technical discussions, as distinct from negotiations proper, between the IMF and the Government resumed in June 1990. In the first half of the year the Government had taken some steps towards fulfilling the conditions stated by the Fund; in particular, subsidies applicable to a wide range of basic commodities had been reduced, causing sharp price increases. Despite these steps, and provision for a budget deficit again within 10% of the country's GDP for 1990/91, the IMF remained dissatisfied with the level of interest rates, the size of the budget deficit provision and the slow speed at which energy prices were being raised. Further discussions were overtaken, however, by the onset of the Gulf crisis, precipitated by Iraq's invasion of Kuwait in August 1990.

THE GULF CRISIS AND THE 1991 IMF AGREEMENT

Egypt's economic reform programme was disrupted by the 1990/91 Gulf crisis, which reduced foreign exchange earnings from tourism and remittances from Egyptian nationals working in Iraq and Kuwait. Losses in these two areas were officially estimated by the Government at, respectively, $1,500m. in the 1990/91 tourist season (see 'Transport and Tourism', below) and $2,400m. in the 1990 calendar year. After a decline in the mid-1980s, a new boom in the oil-producing Gulf states had resulted in total remittances increasing to $4,235m. in 1989, a large proportion of which derived from the estimated 1.5m. Egyptians then working in Iraq and Kuwait. By late 1990 about 400,000 workers had returned to Egypt (the total rising to more than 600,000 following the outbreak of hostilities between Iraq and the US-led multinational force in January 1991); their return caused serious social problems for the Egyptian authorities and led to an increase in the existing level of unemployment of around 20%. On the other hand, an anticipated fall in Suez Canal revenues in 1990, due to the UN embargo on trade with Iraq, failed to materialize; instead, earnings increased by 14% over 1989 (see 'Suez Canal', below). Moreover, increased world oil prices in the third quarter of 1990 almost doubled Egypt's revenues from oil exports to $210m. per month (compared with average monthly receipts of $138m. in 1989/90), thereby offsetting losses from suspended trade with Iraq and Kuwait. One further consequence of the crisis was an increase in the budget deficit, to 17% of GDP in 1990/91.

The Iraqi invasion of Kuwait did, however, result in a sharp increase in aid to Egypt, in addition to the waiver or rescheduling of certain Egyptian debts to other countries. Emergency aid was allocated through the Gulf Financial Crisis Co-ordinating Group (GFCCG), which by March 1991 had arranged funding amounting to $11,741m. for Egypt, Turkey and Jordan. Saudi Arabia, Japan and Kuwait were the largest donors, while Saudi Arabia, which in 1990 made its first development loans to Egypt since the resumption of bilateral relations in 1988, also announced that it had written off outstanding Egyptian debts of $4,000m. Moreover, in November 1990 the US Congress finally consented to waive some $7,000m. in Egyptian debts for arms purchases in the 1970s (comprising $4,500m. in principal and $2,500m. in interest and penalties). With smaller amounts being written off by other Western and Gulf states, Egypt's debt was reduced from some $50,000m. before the Gulf crisis to around $36,000m. by early 1991.

The agreement of Western nations to reschedule Egypt's remaining debts depended on a new accord being concluded with the IMF. Negotiations resumed after the end of the Gulf war, and were conducted in a more sympathetic climate in view of Egypt's active participation in the anti-Iraq coalition. Progress was also expedited by the following factors: the introduction in February 1991 of new market-related currency exchange arrangements, as a prelude to a single unified rate and full convertibility no later than February 1992; trade liberalization measures, under which most existing tariff and other barriers were to be phased out over three years; publication in April of a further list of 60 state-owned enterprises which the Government sought to privatize; price increases in April, ranging from 14% to 66% on petroleum products, gas and electricity; the introduction in May of new sales taxes of between 5% and 30% on most goods and services (although certain basic items such as bread, meat, fish, petrol and gas were exempted); and the adoption of a budget for 1991/92 providing for a deficit of 9.3% of GDP, falling to 6.5% in 1992/93 and to 3.5% in 1993/94 (see National Budget, below). The new exchange rate arrangements resulted in an effective devaluation of some 38% by May 1991, while interest rates underwent a consequential significant rise (see 'Banking', below).

Against this background, a new stand-by facility was formally approved by the IMF in mid-May 1991, under which some $372m. would be made available to Egypt over a period of 18 months to provide balance-of-payments assistance for its economic reform programme. This was rapidly followed by a decision of the 'Paris Club' of Western creditors to write off, over a three-year period, $10,000m. of the $20,000m. owed by Egypt to creditor nations and to reschedule repayment of the remaining $10,000m. on favourable terms. Defending the IMF agreement in a speech to the Egyptian people on 1 May, President Mubarak said that it provided the opportunity to put the country's economy in order and stressed that the required restructuring would be fully under Egyptian control.

In accordance with the IMF agreement, the commercial and Central Bank exchange rates for the Egyptian pound were unified on 8 October 1991 (several months ahead of schedule) at the prevailing market rate of $1 = £E3.31. This made the pound almost fully convertible, in that for the first time most state-owned enterprises could freely maintain foreign exchange accounts to finance their hard currency requirements. The only exceptions were state exporters of cotton and rice, and the state oil and gas sector (which was required to deposit any surplus revenue beyond what it needed to cover foreign currency requirements).

In early 1992 the World Bank concluded that the Egyptian economic reform programme was broadly on course. Their report noted: that real GDP had risen by 2% in 1990/91; that the current account was set to record a surplus in 1991/92; that inflation and the budget deficit were within the prescribed parameters; and that trade liberalization and subsidy reductions were on target. Remaining obstacles were the slow pace of privatization, investment authorization and deregulation. In March the General Authority for Investments, in response to the World Bank criticism, introduced five new measures to facilitate investment. An initial 15% of Egypt's $20,000m. 'Paris Club' debt was cancelled shortly after the formal announcement of the 1991 IMF stand-by arrangement, with cancellation of a further 15% scheduled to take effect at such time as the IMF formally approved the terms of a follow-up arrangement. (The remainder of the promised write-off, amounting to 20% of the original debt, was scheduled to take effect half-way through the duration of such a follow-up arrangement, provided that the IMF was broadly satisified with government economic policy at that point.)

Notwithstanding Egypt's announcement that it did not intend to draw on the final $180m.-tranche of the 1991 stand-by facility because of strong growth in the country's foreign-exchange reserves during 1992, formal expiry of the facility (originally set for the end of November 1992) was postponed by the IMF for two successive periods of three months.

The World Bank, for its part, delayed from June 1992 to March 1993 the release of the second half of a $300m.-structural–adjustment loan, eventually announcing the release of the funds shortly after the Government had announced the start of the active phase of its long-awaited privatization programme. The 20 firms whose shares were offered to local and foreign private investors in this initial privatization exercise included hotels, a cement company, beverage producers and vineyards. Other liberalization measures announced in the first quarter of 1993 included a cut from 100% to 80% in Egypt's top rate of import tariffs.

On 19 March 1993 (one week after the World Bank's release of funds) the IMF's executive board formally declared that Egypt had fulfilled its commitments under the 1991 stand-by arrangement. This opened the way for negotiations on the terms of a follow-up arrangement. In July the Government announced that it would undertake to achieve a further reduction in the budget deficit, to maintain exchange-rate stability and to keep the annual rate of inflation below 8%. It would aim eventually to privatize public-sector assets with an estimated market value totalling £E40,000m., and it hoped to be able to complete around 25% of the privatization programme within three years. On trade liberalization (reportedly the most contentious issue in negotiations with the IMF), the Government's declared aim was to reduce Egypt's maximum import tariff from 80% to 50% over a four-year period. As an apparent gesture to IMF negotiators who had sought a much swifter cut in the top rate, the Government acted in mid-July to lift certain import restrictions (on timber, paints and household appliances) and to abolish preferential tariffs for public-sector industries. In September the IMF's executive board approved an extended fund facility of $560m., to be drawn down in six-monthly tranches over a period of three years. Earlier in September, the Egyptian Government had reached 'substantial agreement' with the World Bank on the monitoring of the process of structural economic reform over the same period. In view of the recent strengthening of the country's balance-of-payments position (attributed mainly to

the attractive rates of return on local currency deposits), no new World Bank loan was associated with this agreement.

Having secured implementation of the second phase of the 'Paris Club' debt waiver in September 1993, the Egyptian Government was in mid-1994 seeking formal IMF/World Bank approval for the current economic position and outlook in order to activate the final phase of the promised debt write-off. The only perceived obstacle to the early achievement of this goal was a difference of opinion between the Government and the IMF on the currency exchange rate (which stood at $1 = £E3.38 in May 1994). In the Fund's economic judgement, some devaluation was desirable, whereas the Government regarded exchange-rate stability as an important factor in maintaining investor confidence in the economy.

In other respects, the Government's monetary and fiscal policies were broadly on course to satisfy IMF targets, while the World Bank-monitored restructuring programme was gathering momentum, with up to £E3,200m. of public-sector assets scheduled for sale during the second half of 1994. Privatization deals approved by mid-1994 involved the sale of two bottling companies and a boiler-making company (in each case to consortia of foreign and local interests and on terms which included guarantees to maintain employment levels for agreed periods), while negotiations for the sale of a large state-owned hotel were well advanced.

Many of the businesses offered for sale in the initial privatization exercise had, however, failed to attract adequate bids from single buyers, prompting the Government to modify its privatization strategy to include sales of shares in state enterprises through the local securities market. It was also decided that 10% of the shares in about 100 public-sector companies should be earmarked for sale to employee shareholders' associations over a period of years. The Government's overall target for sales of shares in the 1994/95 fiscal year was £E9,000m. The state shareholding in the Commercial International Bank (Egypt) was reduced from 70% to 43% in September 1993 as a result of a heavily-oversubscribed issue of new shares. State-owned banks were recommended to reduce their shareholdings in joint-venture banks (i.e. those with mixed public and private ownership) to 25% by the end of 1995.

The maximum import tariff was cut to 70% in February 1994 as part of a wide-ranging reform package which included substantial tariff reductions for many raw materials, coupled with various fiscal incentives to exporters. Further trade liberalization measures, including cuts in import tariffs on capital goods, were due to come into effect in December 1994. By mid-1994 price subsidies had been eliminated or substantially reduced throughout the public sector, and timetables existed to remove the remaining subsidies.

In 1991 the Government established a Social Development Fund (SDF) in order to alleviate the impact of the economic reforms. The initial phase of the project, from 1992–96, received funding of some $746m., which was channelled into community development, enterprise development and vocational training schemes. Over this period the SDF has created 250,000 permanent jobs and 110,000 temporary jobs. Donors have pledged some $710m. for the 1997–2000 second stage of the SDF's operations.

The pace of the Government's privatization programme remained very slow throughout the 1994/95 fiscal year, when investors were able to purchase minority stakes in a small number of companies whose shares were offered through the local securities market. It was unusual for more than 10% of a company's shares to be placed on the market at one time, and none of the companies concerned disposed of more than 20% of their total shares during the course of 1994/95. Six of the 17 holding companies within the public sector—those responsible for metallurgy; engineering; mining and refractories; chemicals; public works and land reclamation; and housing, tourism and cinema—had privatization units in place in 1994, and four more holding companies were due to establish their own units before the end of 1995. By mid-1995 share offers were being brought to the market at the rate of about two per month, the Government's aim being to achieve a total of 50 such disposals during the course of the year. The Government strongly defended its gradualist approach to the privatization process, which had attracted public criticism from representatives of the World Bank and other interested organizations at a Cairo conference on private-sector development in October 1994. With the Government also maintaining its resistance to IMF pressure for a currency devaluation of around 30%, Egypt did not secure a formal IMF/World Bank endorsement of its economic policy in the 1994/95 fiscal year, with the result that the final phase of the Paris Club debt write-off remained in abeyance in July 1995. The World Bank estimated Egypt's total external indebtedness in 1994 as $33,358m. and its 1994 debt-service burden as $2,279m. (a debt-service to export ratio of 14.6%).

In October 1995 the IMF withdrew its objections to the Government's exchange-rate policy following the release of trade statistics showing strong export growth in the first nine months of the 1994/95 fiscal year. A senior IMF official stated that 'there is nothing in the Egyptian economy now that indicates the need for a change in the exchange rate'. No formal IMF review of the economy was undertaken at this point, however, nor was any such review completed in the remainder of the 1995/96 fiscal year. (Egypt, for its part, had by mid-1996 made no drawings under its 1993 extended fund facility agreement with the IMF.) The new Egyptian Government appointed in January 1996 undertook to accelerate the process of structural economic reform by introducing measures to stimulate private investment in new projects (including major industrial developments) while setting revised targets for the sale of shares in state enterprises. The new Government aimed to generate up to £E27,000m. of privatization revenues in 1996, £E20,000m. of this to come from asset sales by state holding companies (mainly through the stock market) and the balance from sales of public-sector shares in joint-venture banks. Cumulative receipts from earlier privatizations amounted to an estimated £E5,500m. at the end of 1995. Of the 314 companies within the public sector at the end of 1995, 224 were trading profitably in the 1994/95 fiscal year, when the combined operations of all 314 companies showed an overall net profit of £E1,500m. However, the aggregate liabilities of public-sector companies at the end of 1995 amounted to £E70,000m., settlement of which was a high priority in the Government's spending plans for projected privatization receipts. As part of its drive to stimulate industrial investment, the Government cut import tariffs on capital goods (hitherto between 20% and 40%) to 10% in January 1996. In the same month the Investment Authority approved 131 mainstream projects involving total investment of $7,790m. and 13 free-zone projects involving total investment of $2,025m.

In October 1996 the IMF approved a $391m. two-year, stand-by arrangement for Egypt (although in view of the strength of the country's reserves position the Government had no plans to make any drawings on it). This arrangement prompted renewed discussion on activating the final stage of the 'Paris Club' debt write-off. Egypt, meanwhile, repaid $300m. to 'Paris Club' creditors in January 1997, in accordance with existing arrangements. A total of $2,500m. ($1,500m. in grants and $1,000m. in long-term development loans) was pledged to Egypt for 1997/98 by major aid donors at a World Bank-sponsored meeting in May 1997. An IMF review in late January 1997 concluded that most aspects of Egypt's current economic performance were satisfactory, while some were 'more than satisfactory'. As regards privatization, the IMF noted that the Government had disposed of majority holdings in 22 companies and minority holdings in a further eight companies in the second half of 1996. Together, these transactions (representing about one-sixth of the total net worth of state-owned enterprises) had generated proceeds of around $1,300m. The maximum tariff applicable to the bulk of Egyptian imports was cut from 70% to 55% in October 1996 and to 50% in July 1997. A new investment law passed in May 1997 reaffirmed basic guarantees to investors and unified and rationalized the framework for investment incentives. Its provisions included 10-year tax exemptions for projects in designated 'new industrial areas' and 'remote areas' and 20-year tax exemptions for projects in the proposed New Valley development area (see 'The High Dam' below).

In May 1988 the IMF expressed concern that inefficient bureaucracy and inadequate industry and export facilities could result in a minimal rate of increase in GDP over the next five years. According to the IMF, an 8% increase in investment in these fields would yield a 6.9% increase in GDP by 2003. Following a subsequent review, in July 1998, the IMF urged

the Government to increase exports, to attract further foreign investment, and to complete its structural reform. In early 1998 the Government announced that it was to facilitate the establishment of new companies: new legislation would allow new ventures to be automatically approved within 10 days of the founders' submitting an application, subject to the approval of the regulatory body.

Despite the Government's gradualist approach, the stock exchange has increased its trading volume from 200,000 investors in 1995 to 1.1m. in 1997. In late 1997 the Government announced that it was to invest its £E77,000m. state pension fund surplus on the stock market as part of a move to boost domestic sources of investment capital. The Government also launched reforms to computerize the stock exchange in order to create a real-time trading system, so as to accelerate trading. By July 1998 the Government had sold shares in 105 state-owned companies since the beginning of its privatization programme, thereby gaining £E8,400m. in proceeds.

THE NATIONAL BUDGET

The price increases and the new sales tax introduced in April–May 1991 (see above) were incorporated in the Government's budget for fiscal year 1991/92 (beginning 1 July), which provided for a gross deficit equivalent to 9.3% of GDP. In the event, the deficit was trimmed to 7.1% of GDP, compared with 17% of GDP in 1990/91. Budgeted expenditure in 1991/92 showed a notional increase of more than one-third compared with the previous year, but much of this rise reflected a 38% depreciation of the Egyptian pound since the move to market-determined exchange rates in February 1991 (a rate of US $1 = £E3.24 being used for the budget). The 1992/93 budget provided for total expenditure of £E62,533m. and total revenue of £E53,389m., the resulting deficit of £E9,144m. representing under 5% of GDP. This was to be achieved by measures affecting both revenue and expenditure sections of the budget, although ministers promised there would be no tax or customs increases. Calculated at an exchange rate of $1 = £E3.33 (virtually unchanged from 1992/93), the 1993/94 budget provided for expenditure totalling £E65,313m. and revenue totalling £E56,330m., leaving a gross deficit of £E8,983m. (3.5% of GDP). After financing, there remained a net deficit (to be covered by treasury bills) of £E1,338m., compared with £E2,298m. in 1992/93. Categories of expenditure in 1993/94 included public sector wages (£E11,300m.), defence (£E5,417m.), foreign debt servicing (£E4,850m.) and subsidies (£E3,600m.). Sources of budgeted revenue included general taxes (£E14,937m.), sales tax (£E8,000m.) and customs duties (£E6,070m.). By mid-1993 the annual inflation rate was around 9%, compared with an annual average of 11.8% in the decade to 1990 and a recent peak of over 20% in 1991. The Government's stated economic growth target for 1993/94 was 4%.

The 1994/95 budget (calculated at an exchange rate of $1 = £E3.38) provided for an 8.4% increase in total expenditure to £E70,790m. (broadly in line with the rate of inflation), coupled with a 4.3% reduction in the gross deficit (to £E8,600m.) and a 63.5% reduction (to £E488m.) in the net budget deficit after financing. The Government's target for GDP growth in 1994/95 was 4.3%. Real GDP growth in 1993/94 was provisionally estimated as 2%, compared with 0.5% growth in 1992/93. As at February 1994, the year-on-year rise in consumer prices was 7.3%, while the average inflation rate over the previous 12 months was 11.3%. The 1995/96 budget provided for total expenditure of £E71,492m. (9.9% higher than actual expenditure in 1994/95) and a gross deficit of £E5,297m. (5.3% higher than the actual gross deficit in 1994/95). The net budget deficit after financing was expected to amount to £E407m. in 1995/96. The budget included social spending totalling £E24,997m. (with particular emphasis on education and health). Total public-sector wages were set to reach £E15,720m. in 1995/96, while just over £E2,000m. was budgeted for subsidies on basic goods. Revenue targets included £E18,262m. from general taxation, £E10,043m. from sales taxes and £E8,110m. from customs duties, the Government's objective being to achieve a current-account surplus of around £E4,000m. within the overall budget for 1995/96. The target for real GDP growth in 1995/96 was 5.4%. The overall investment target for 1995/96 was £E42,000m. (53% of this from the private sector), while the target for the creation of new jobs was stated as 498,000 (which would increase the officially estimated labour force to 16.9m.). The 1996/97 budget provided for total expenditure of £E77,400m. and total revenue of £E71,100m., leaving a gross deficit of £E6,300m., most of which was to be financed by domestic savings instruments and foreign loans. The 1997/98 budget provided for total expenditure of £E83,792m. and total revenue of £E76,398m. The gross deficit of £E7,394m. was stated to be equivalent to about 1.2% of GDP. The 1998/99 budget provided for a 9.9% increase in total expenditure to £E91,800m., whilst revenues were anticipated to increase by 8.9% to £E83,200m., leaving a gross domestic deficit of £E8,600m., equivalent to about 1% of GDP. The Government's forecast for GDP growth for the financial year 1998/99 was 6.2%. The budget included social spending totalling some £E34,500m. (with health and education being of central importance). Total public-sector wages were set to reach £E22,532m., whilst £E4,906m. was to be allocated for subsidies on basic goods. Revenue of some £E56,000m. was expected to be accrued through a 12% increase in total tax and customs.

AGRICULTURE

Egyptian agriculture is dominated by the river Nile and the necessity for irrigation. The main summer crops are cotton, rice, maize and sorghum, and in winter the chief crops are wheat, beans, berseem (Egyptian clover, used for animal feed) and vegetables. While there is self-sufficiency in fruit and vegetables (some of which are exported to the EU), it is with the basic grains that shortages are encountered. During the 1970s agriculture's contribution to GDP remained fairly constant at just less than 30%, but fell steadily in the 1980s, to reach 17% by 1990. In 1978 the agricultural sector accounted for approximately 60% of total export earnings, but by 1979 this had fallen to 50%, and by 1990 to around 10%. During the 1970s the increase in agricultural production was clearly outstripped by population growth, and this reflected a diminishing emphasis on agriculture in government plans. Between 1970 and 1976 food imports, in terms of weight, more than doubled, and exports of rice declined to one-third of their former weight. Agricultural production averaged an annual increase of 2.6% in 1980–88 and this has meant a continued dependence on substantial imports of foodstuffs. From a position of self-sufficiency in food during the early 1970s, Egypt now has to import more than one-half of its food. The difficulties in the agricultural sector are well illustrated by the riots against the increases in the prices of basic foodstuffs in Kafr ed-Dawar in September 1984, and by the heavy subsidies on bread and flour. Although the riots were not as serious as those in Cairo in January 1977, they emphasized the critical problem which the Government faced in attempting to reduce basic subsidies (see 'Economic Policy and Planning', above).

The increase in the rate of wheat consumption exemplifies the problems faced by the agricultural sector. The annual consumption of wheat by Egyptians rose from 80 kg per head in 1960, to 197 kg in 1970 and 300 kg in 1986/87, making Egyptians the world's biggest consumers of wheat per head of population. National consumption rates are also amongst the highest in the world: Egypt consumed 8,850,000 tons of wheat in 1986/87, compared with 4,154,000 tons in 1970, an annual rate of increase of 7%. On several occasions during the 1980s Egypt bought wheat and wheat flour from the USA on preferential terms, although it also buys subsidized grain from the EU. Other grain suppliers have included Australia and Canada. Egyptian wheat production totalled 4.62m. tons in 1992 (the third successive record harvest), and was forecast to approach 5m. tons in 1993. The total wheat import requirement in 1992 was 5.9m. tons while the forecast requirement for 1993 was 5.5m. tons. In 1994 the Egyptian wheat harvest of 4.6m. tons supplied about 46% of consumption. Farmers were encouraged to expand the area under wheat to 2.45m. feddans in 1995 (an increase of about one-fifth compared with the previous year) as part of a drive to attain 60% self-sufficiency in wheat production. A harvest of around 6m. tons was achieved in 1995, when the yield per feddan stood at twice its 1980 level. A wheat import requirement of up to 6m. tons was forecast for 1996. In 1997/98 it was hoped to increase wheat production to 6.5m. tons through the wider use of high-yielding strains.

In July 1997 the Ministry of Health, in response to concerns about food safety, issued a decree which prohibited imports of genetically altered grain, soya beans and pulses, and stipulated that all other non-gene altered consignments must carry proof of their status. The decree was relaxed the following month, however, after exporters forecast widespread disruption to grain exports and the prospect of a wheat shortage. The modified legislation permits imports of genetically engineered crops which have been safely introduced into their country of origin, and non gene-altered products without certification. Consignments may, however, be subjected to inspection.

The overall value of Egyptian farm output was estimated by the US Department of Agriculture to amount to $9,526m. in 1992, of which $6,309m. was contributed by crops, and the balance by livestock. The 1992 total represented an annual increase of 4%, compared with a 2.2% increase in 1991 and a 7.2% increase in 1990. Strong growth in crop production from 1990 onwards was attributed to changes in producer price policy, greater use of multiple cropping and a shift in land use from berseem to vegetables, while the relative stagnation of livestock output over the same period was linked to problems in introducing new supply and pricing arrangements for animal feedstuffs. The Egyptian Ministry of Agriculture estimated the value of farm output in the 1994/95 fiscal year at £E32,500m. ($9,587m.). The value of agricultural exports in that year was $615.5m. (representing about 14% of Egypt's total export earnings).

The arable area is about 5% of the total land area, and not much more than two-fifths of this is serviced by main and secondary drains. This deficiency is significant because an unforeseen effect of the High Dam (see below) has been to make the water-table rise (because of more abundant water and more intensive cropping) and led to widespread waterlogging and high soil salinity. Insufficient attention to drainage has therefore been a serious problem with agricultural planning.

The extension of the cultivable area through reclamation has been slow, difficult and costly, but remains at the forefront of government policy. The increasing pressure of people on the land has led to an intensification of cultivation almost without parallel anywhere. Dams, barrages, pumps and an intricate network of canals and drains bring perennial irrigation to almost the whole area. The strict pursuit of crop rotation, lavish use of commercial fertilizer and pesticides, and the patient application of manual labour not only make multiple cropping possible, but also raise land yields to high levels. Despite the difficulties concerning reclamation, early in 1981 the Government announced plans to reclaim 1.2m. ha of land at a rate of 63,000 ha per year over the next 20 years. The largest planned development was at West Nuberiya near Alexandria where, in the first phase, 10,100 ha of land were to be irrigated and drained. A second major agricultural reclamation project has been in progress in the northern Tahrir region; a third project was intended for the region south of Port Said, and further long-term plans included the New Valley project from Aswan to the Qattara Depression. While these developments look promising on paper, there is nevertheless much scepticism over official figures relating to the amount of land which has so far been reclaimed. Moreover, the reclamation programme is counterbalanced by the fact that about 20,000 ha of agricultural land are being lost every year owing to urban growth and the depredations of the red clay brick manufacturing industry which pays farmers large sums for the rich, red topsoil from their fields, to be used as raw material. A ban on the manufacture of red bricks was introduced in August 1985. In June 1989 the Government announced plans, within the framework of the socio-economic development plan for 1989/90, to reclaim a further 175,000 feddans of land for agriculture. A record cereal harvest in 1991 was officially attributed, in part, to the reclamation of some 125,000 feddans of land in Sinai and the Alexandria region. In 1995 the total area under cultivation was 7.6m. feddans (3.2m. ha), including 1.4m. feddans (588,100 ha) of reclaimed desert land.

The bulk of agricultural production from reclamation is intended for the market place and not for subsistence. Nearly three-quarters of agricultural income comes from field crops, the remainder deriving from fruit, vegetables, livestock and dairy products.

Long-staple cotton is the most important field crop but the area under cultivation has declined since the late 1960s. Egypt produces about one-third of the world crop of long-staple cotton (1.125 in and longer) and is the world's largest exporter of the premium grades that have been least affected by competition from man-made fibres. Cotton provides 15% of all agricultural employment and helps to support a substantial textile industry. Many factors combine to give the high yields and excellent quality of Egyptian cotton. Among these are climatic, soil and labour conditions, and a long experience of careful planting, watering and picking. Government assistance and supervision have always been important. Fertilizers and pesticides are distributed through the government-sponsored agricultural credit banks and agricultural co-operatives. However, investment in cotton has been inadequate to develop the full potential of the industry. Plans were announced at the beginning of 1993 to liberalize Egypt's internal trade in cotton and to end the public-sector monopoly of cotton exports which had been in force for over 30 years. Forming part of a deregulation programme agreed with the World Bank, the cotton industry reforms were designed to improve the crop's financial appeal to farmers and to encourage wider use of high-yield cultivation techniques. Total production in 1992 amounted to 348,000 tons. During recent years the Egyptian textile industry has absorbed about 80% of the country's cotton crop, and the volumes available for export have often fallen some way short of the prevailing levels of world demand.

Production of cotton in the 1993/94 marketing season (ending in August) was expected to be more than 25% higher than in the previous year, while the volume of cotton contracted for export was by early May 1994 over five times higher than the export volume for the entire 1992/93 season. The relevant export contracts—accounting for almost one-third of the season's forecast production—were worth an estimated £E700m. Draft legislation was introduced in mid-1994 to revive the Alexandria Cotton Exchange, which had been closed down in 1961. The 1994/95 cotton season saw year-on-year reductions of about 18% in the area planted, about 40% in the tonnage produced and about 43% in the tonnage exported. Adverse weather and pest infestation coincided with the application of market reforms, the impact of which was not clear in these circumstances. Following allegations that raw cotton prices (initially driven up by the production shortfall) were being further inflated by speculative hoarding of stocks, the Government in October 1995 imposed a price ceiling on ginned cotton supplied to local textile mills. At the same time it banned the export of cotton until domestic demand had been met. This temporary export ban was lifted in February 1996, while in the following month the cotton export trade was opened up to the private sector. At the same time Egypt's cotton import trade (hitherto limited to US supplies from California and Arizona, where strict fumigation procedures were observed) was opened up to all countries, with all shipments to be fumigated and sterilized at the point of entry into Egypt. Egyptian textile mills were expected to turn increasingly to competitively priced imports of short-staple cotton from such suppliers as Turkey and Syria, leaving the bulk of Egypt's long-staple crop available for export to Japan, Switzerland, Italy and other markets with a strong demand for premium-grade cotton. Production of at least 7m. kantars (350,000 metric tons) of cotton from a planted area of more than 1m. feddans (420,000 ha) was forecast for the 1996/97 season, compared with production of around 4.8m. kantars from 700,000 feddans planted in 1995/96. Production of cotton lint in the 1996 calendar year totalled 5.7m. kantars (an increase of 42% over 1995). The cotton crop for the 1997/98 season was forecast to reach 8m. kantars.

Rice is another important crop and is now, after cotton, almost as important as fruit in the agricultural sector as a foreign currency earner. Production of rice in 1992 was a record 3.91m. tons, compared with the wheat harvest of 4.62m. tons and a maize harvest of 4.5m. tons. The total area planted with cereals in 1992 was approximately 3m. feddans. Rice output in 1993 amounted to 4m. tons, compared with local consumption of 2.2m. tons. Rice exporters were among the main beneficiaries of a lifting of export licensing regulations for farm produce in late 1993. In 1996 rice exports generated US $177.7m.

Another high yielding crop is sugar cane. In 1992 the state-owned sugar refining company (which currently supplies two-thirds of Egypt's annual consumption of 1.5m. tons) was 90% reliant on cane as a raw material, the balance of its input being

beet and corn. Although the company's plans for the future expansion of sugar production were mainly based on beet rather than cane, it was also planning to add new value to its cane-based operations by developing a plant to manufacture newsprint from *bagasse* (cane waste). Total production of sugar cane in 1995 was 1.1m. tons, including 400,000 tons for export. Other crops include lucerne (alfalfa), a nitrogen-fixing fodder, beans, potatoes and onion and garlic. A pilot project to produce palm oil in the Western Desert (currently imported from Malaysia and Indonesia) began in 1993.

The many kinds of fruit, vegetables and horticultural products grown are capable of some expansion and are increasingly important as exports. Particular efforts are being made to promote the production of these items, especially citrus fruit, and special areas are being allocated along the Mediterranean coast for their cultivation. Output of fruit totalled 3.5m. tons (including a record 2.2m. tons of citrus) in 1992, while tomato production totalled 4.3m. tons and other vegetable production 4.45m. tons. There was particularly rapid growth in production of high-value items for which there was strong export demand, such as peaches (over 35,000 tons) and strawberries (around 50,000 tons). The value of fruit exports totalled $23m. in 1996.

Recent attention has been given to animal husbandry in an attempt to raise dairy and meat production, but there has so far been little increase in either number of livestock or productivity. Egypt is a net importer of meats to supplement its own output of around 800,000 tons per year. Increases in animal feed prices to world levels were partly responsible for some well-publicized problems in 1992/93, including a fall in poultry production to as little as 55% of capacity as the industry adjusted to a new cost structure. In early 1996 the Social Fund for Development allocated £E100m. for livestock development projects designed to boost annual output of red meat and dairy products by more than 20m. tons. In August 1997 the Government ended a 10-year prohibition on poultry imports but placed an 80% tariff on a minimum price of $1,600 per ton of the produce, to be reduced at a rate of 2.4% per year. Importers will be charged duties totalling some $1,200 per ton of poultry.

In May 1988 measures were announced to conserve water supplies owing to the fall in the level of the Nile. These included a reduction in the area planted with rice to 900,000 feddans; a moratorium on the allocation of land for the cultivation of sugar cane; and a ban on the extension of the area planted to crops requiring large amounts of water. Major irrigation and drainage projects in preparation in 1992 included the 'Suez Siphon', which was intended to convey Nile water under the Suez Canal into the Sinai desert, and a scheme to update the drainage of about 720,000 feddans of existing cultivated land (about 10% of the country's total cultivable area). The Siphon project, which was expected to be completed in late 1996, involved the construction of a system whereby water (mostly recycled from agricultural drainage) would be pumped into North Sinai at a rate of 160 cu m per second over a distance of 150 km. In August 1997 the Government announced plans to convert 265,000 ha of orchards to drip irrigation from flood irrigation in an attempt to save 1,000m. cu m of water per year. Farmers making the conversions, costing £E1,500–£E4,000 per feddan, will be assisted by subsidized loans from the Government.

AGRARIAN REFORM

Immediately after the Egyptian Revolution of 1952 an experiment in land reform was initiated. This project achieved a degree of success, though only the very large estates were dismembered while medium-sized estates remained untouched. Among other measures, a limit of 200 feddans was imposed on individual ownership of land. This limit was lowered to 100 feddans in 1961 and again to 50 feddans in 1969. The primary aim of this reform was the destruction of the feudal power of the old politicians, an aim which was easily realized. In 1952, 5.7% of all landowners held 64.6% of the total area, but only a quarter of the country's cultivable land (i.e. some 1.25m. feddans of a total of about 5m. feddans) was in plots of over 100 acres each. By 1961, however, this area had dwindled to about 1m. feddans, nearly all of which had been appropriated by the Ministry of Agrarian Reform and redistributed to landless peasants. The 1969 land reform affected a further 1.13m. feddans owned by 16,000 land-owners.

Other measures of agrarian reform included rent control; the regulation of land tenure; consolidation of fragmented holdings for production purposes; and the drive to build co-operatives. In 1986 there were 5,150 agricultural co-operatives (compared with 1,727 in 1952 and 5,384 in 1984). However, in the process of dispossessing the large landowners and promoting co-operatives, the authorities unwittingly helped to eliminate many highly efficient medium-sized farmers. On balance, however, the redistribution of land was accompanied by improved land productivity and not the reverse.

By 1984 only 13.9% of the total cultivated area was held by owners with 50 feddans or more. However, since land reform affected only about one-sixth of the total land, the main structure of land-ownership remained unaffected; in 1984, 4.7% of the owners (i.e. those with more than 5 feddans) still held 47% of the land while 95.3% of the owners shared the remaining 53%. The fundamental land tenure problem is not so much one of distribution but of an overall scarcity.

Given the land shortage, special attention has naturally been paid to increasing the arable area. In view of the fact that the land to be reclaimed is often arid desert, reclamation is a costly process requiring substantial capital outlays, and the question has to be asked whether new investment should not be directed to the development of manufacturing industry instead, where returns to the scarce capital may well be higher. Between 1952 and 1976, 912,000 feddans were reported to have been reclaimed, 536,000 feddans being reclaimed during the 1960–65 Plan period. By 1985/86, 1,221,500 feddans were stated to have been reclaimed (though only one-half of this land is actually in production), and 1,072,000 feddans to have been redistributed to 440,000 families as a result of agrarian reform measures. Under the Five-Year Plan for 1982–87, only 325,000 feddans were reclaimed, compared with a target of 636,000 feddans. The 1987–92 Plan envisaged reclamation at a rate of not less than 150,000 feddans per year. At the end of 1996 Egypt's cultivated area was estimated to total 7.6m. feddans, including 2.4m. feddans of reclaimed land.

In November 1993 the Government rescheduled some £E200m. of debts owed to agricultural credit institutions as part of an initiative to deal with growing arrears in the farm sector. In March 1994 the World Bank approved $121m. of financing (including $67m. in International Development Association credits) for a $269m. project designed to provide 250,000 farming families with improved access to agricultural credit facilities. It was announced in early 1997 that the Principal Bank for Agricultural Development was to provide seven-year concessionary loans to tenants wishing to purchase land from owners under a new land tenure law implemented in October of that year. The introduction of the new law, which has abolished both fixed rents and security of inherited tenure, has proved unpopular with many farmers, and a number of deaths and hundreds of arrests have resulted from clashes between farmers, landowners and police.

THE HIGH DAM

The decision to invest more than £E400m. in the Aswan High Dam project (including Soviet credits of £E194m.) was partly informed by the possibility of developing cheap hydroelectric energy for industry. The project was started in January 1960, completed in July 1970, and officially inaugurated in January 1971, with a generating capacity of 10,000m. kWh, compared with the 6,012m. kWh produced in all Egypt in 1967. By 1974 revenue from the dam had exceeded the cost of its construction. Transmission lines carry the current from the dam site to Cairo and further north, and a scheme aimed at the complete electrification of Egypt's villages is in progress. The Aswan II hydroelectric power station started up in early 1986, adding 270 MW of capacity to the national grid. In August 1991 a $140m.-contract was signed with a west European consortium for the renovation of the High Dam's older generating turbines and related installations.

The dam's primary purpose was to store the annual Nile flood which reaches its peak in August, allowing yearly control of the downstream flow, and, therefore, the possibility of perrenial irrigation and further land reclamation. Between 1964 and 1978 Lake Nasser (maximum capacity 169,000m. cu m) behind the dam gradually filled and ensured that Egypt did not suffer the worst effects of the drought experienced in much of north-east Africa. Under the terms of an agreement signed with Sudan in 1959, Egypt is allocated 55,500m. cu m of Nile water a year out of an estimated 84,000m. cu m annual average flow as measured at Aswan. Sudan receives 18,500m. cu m and the remainder is calculated to be the annual evaporation loss from Lake Nasser. By June 1988, more than 10 years of drought at the source of the Blue Nile in Ethiopia (which provides approximately 70% of the flow at Aswan), had reduced the water level in Lake Nasser to 153 m, just above the 150 m point at which the High Dam's hydroelectricity turbines would be affected, drastically reducing their generating capacity, and approaching the 147 m level at which they would have to be shut down completely. However, an exceptionally high flood after torrential rainfall on the Ethiopian plateau in August 1988 raised the water beyond the danger level. In September 1990 the water level in Lake Nasser was 167 m and live storage was calculated to be 83,700m. cu m. In October 1993, following inflows from an above-average flood, the water level reached 174 m, while storage behind the dam amounted to 116,110m. cu m of water. In September 1994 the water level reached 176.2m, and the stored volume 127,580m. cu m, when a very high Nile flood occurred in the aftermath of a reduction of 5m. cu m per day in farmers' irrigation requirements (a result of early planting in the previous growing season). The 500 km-long Lake Nasser is expected to become a major fisheries resource, the development of which would replace the sardine catch in the Mediterranean, lost as a result of the building of the dam.

During the 1996 Nile flood the water level behind the dam reached an unprecedented 178m, increasing storage in Lake Nasser to 137,000m. cu m by the start of October, at which point water from the lake began to overflow into the Toshka reservoir to the west. Early rains in Ethiopia in 1997 gave rise to expectations of a similarly high Nile flood in 1997. In January 1997 the Government inaugurated a 'New Valley' project to build a 30-m wide canal from Lake Nasser to the oasis regions in the central Western Desert. In March 1998 a contract was signed to build a new pumping station to extract water from Lake Nasser, just north of the Toshka outfall, in order to fill the canal, which is to be the central feature of a scheme to irrigate up to 500,000 feddans (210,000 ha) of land and to open up adjacent areas for development. Overall, the Southern Egypt Development Project was designed to resettle 3m. Egyptians around the oases over the next 20 years at a cost of up to £E300,000m. A total of £E5,800m. in government funding was allocated to the project for 1997–2002.

THE SUEZ CANAL

After the October 1973 war, the most pressing need was to restore and reopen the Suez Canal and, at Sadat's initiative, the Canal was reopened on 5 June 1975, the eighth anniversary of the outbreak of war which led to its closure in 1967. Expansion was made even more urgent because of the vast increase in oil-tanker sizes after June 1967 which the closure of the Canal helped to provoke. The Canal Authority set the dues for ships using the Canal 90%–100% higher than in 1967, and revenue in the first year of operation was $230m. In December 1980 the first phase of work to widen and deepen the southern end of the Canal was completed at an estimated cost of $1,275m. Income reached $888m. in 1981, compared with $676m. in 1980. In 1982 Suez Canal revenue was reported to have reached $1,000m. for the first time, with $956m. being derived from transit tolls and $44m. coming from services to ships in transit. Earnings from Suez Canal tolls were reported to have been $974m. in fiscal 1983/84 (July–June) (other services raised the overall revenue to more than $1,000m.) but fell to $897m. in 1984/85. Despite an increase in transit rates in January 1984, revenue in 1984 totalled only $960m., $100m. less than had been projected, owing to reduced tanker traffic and the planting of mines in the Red Sea approaches to the Canal, which deterred shipping from using it in the summer of 1984. Transit rates were raised by an average of 5% in 1985 and 3.4% in 1986. In 1986 revenue totalled $1,107m., compared with $929m. in 1985. Transit rates were raised again on 1 January 1987, by 7.4% for the first 5,000 tons and by 3.8% for the next 15,000 tons and during the year total revenue from tolls and other services was a record $1,222m. (for fiscal 1988/89 the total was $1,340m., compared with

$1,289m. in 1987/88). The chairman of the Suez Canal Authority attributed the increase to the Authority's success in attracting large oil tankers and container vessels by offering them a 17% reduction in transit fees. A $400m.-development scheme, which was nearing completion in mid-1993, was designed to allow passage of vessels of 56 ft draught, or up to 170,000 deadweight tons (dwt), compared with 130,000 dwt previously. A further scheme to deepen the canal to 72 ft (to accommodate vessels of up to 300,000 dwt) remained in abeyance in 1993 after feasibility studies had shown it to be uneconomic at current levels of world trade.

Reconstruction of the canal cities, some of them up to 80% destroyed, was also put in hand and by 1979 more than 1m. Egyptians had returned to Port Said, Ismailia and Suez. In November 1979 construction of the Salem canal, to take water from the East Nile to Sinai, was started and in October 1980 the 1.64-km Ahmad Hamdi tunnel was opened, thus providing the first road link under the Suez Canal.

Transit rates were increased by an average of 5% from 1 January 1990. Despite initial forecasts that the Gulf crisis of 1990/91 would adversely affect the Canal, revenue in 1990/91 increased by 14% compared with 1989/90, to reach $1,664m. From 1 January 1991 transit tolls were increased by 6% (4% for dry bulk carriers), while an average 3% increase in 1992 was below the rate of inflation of the Suez Canal Authority's operating costs. A carefully structured programme of selective discounts—e.g. for southbound tankers in ballast—kept the Canal keenly competitive with rival shipping routes in the first half of 1993, when a total of 8,670 ships generated revenue totalling $981m., compared with the January–June 1992 figures of 8,353 ships generating revenue of $927m. The Suez Canal Authority's 1994 tariff schedule incorporated average toll increases of about 4%, coupled with further refinements of the structure of selective discounts. In addition to the commercially determined discounts for different categories of cargo vessel, a 35% discount was introduced for passenger cruise ships in support of the Government's campaign to bolster the tourism industry. The number of vessels using the Canal fell from 17,312 (including 3,185 tankers) in 1993 to 16,370 (including 2,722 tankers) in 1994. Transit tolls were frozen, and some new discounts offered, in 1995. In 1995 the Canal handled 15,051 vessels and generated total revenue of $1,942m. At the start of 1996 the Canal Authority responded to a decline in tanker traffic by introducing substantial discounts for northbound oil tankers which discharged part of their cargo at the Ain Sukhna terminal of the Sumed pipeline, later reloading it at the northern end of the pipeline. These vessels would benefit from a new charging system based on the tonnage of their residual cargo. Operators of tanker fleets were offered volume discounts linked to the total annual tonnage which they routed via the Canal. In mid-1996 the Canal Authority was finalizing a new discount scheme to attract iron-ore and coal carriers away from the Cape route. During 1996 the Canal was used by 14,731 vessels (a total of 355m. net tons). Revenue for the first 10 months of 1996 was 7.8% lower than in the corresponding period of 1995, and in November 1996 the Canal authority announced new discounts for oil tankers, LNG carriers and container vessels. Basic transit fees remained unchanged in 1997. The number of vessels using the Canal during 1997 was 14,430 (with net displacement totalling 369m. tons), generating a revenue of $1,822m. In 1998 the Government placed the Suez Canal Authority under the auspices of the Prime Minister as part of an initiative, the Government claimed, to improve the efficiency of the Canal.

MANUFACTURING INDUSTRY

During the 1970s manufacturing industry suffered from a lack of foreign exchange, and some excess capacity resulting from shortages of spare parts and raw materials. Food processing and textiles have traditionally dominated the industrial sector, contributing 55%–60% of the total value of industrial output in the mid-1970s. With the growing importance of oil, though, this situation has changed. Provisional employment data for 1995 indicated a work-force of 2,224,200 in manufacturing and mining, 967,600 in construction, and 166,800 in electricity, gas and water, totalling 21.9% of employed labour. In the year ending June 1995 the manufacturing sector accounted for 26.6%

of GDP, while industry as a whole accounted for 33.4% of GDP (compared with 45% in 1990 and 27% in 1965).

The manufacturing sector has suffered from considerable inefficiency. A World Bank report, published in 1987, showed that returns on investment were low and that, despite considerable investment, the industrial sector was neither diversified nor efficient, and, therefore, was unable to compete in the international market-place. Among the problems identified by the report were overstaffing and excessive government protection from foreign competition. The Egyptian authorities have admitted that productivity is low, as is plant utilization (only 30% of capacity in some cases), but have blamed the international recession and the lack of foreign exchange, in addition to problems of poor incentives and low salary levels among the work-force. In addition, private sector investment has been attracted to service industries rather than manufacturing industry. Nevertheless, private firms were responsible for about 50% of Egypt's $2,000m.-worth of manufactured exports in 1992.

In the manufacturing industry textiles, having once accounted for about one-third of total output, contributed only 16% in 1989. However, exports of textile fibres and products contributed about 27% of total export revenue in 1990, compared with 26% in 1984. The Government has embarked on a three-stage rehabilitation of the cotton-ginning industry costing $40.4m. and assisted by an $18.5m. loan from the IDA. The Arab Fund for Economic and Social Development (AFESD) was to lend Egypt $40m. to finance a spinning and weaving project at Kafr ed-Dawar and Bayda. In 1994 finished garments accounted for nearly 30% of Egypt's total textile exports as the industry shifted increasingly towards value-added products. Private-sector manufacturers predominated in the dyeing, knitting and finished clothing industries in mid-1997, whereas the public sector was responsible for about 90% of the spinning industry and 60% of weaving activity (state textile enterprises having so far been a low priority for privatization because of widespread financial problems in this sector). Textile exports increased by 64% during 1995/96–1996/97, amounting to some £E900m. in the latter year. Recent developments in the food processing industry have included a major expansion of sugar refining, undertaken to reduce an import requirement of 600,000 tons per year, costing an estimated $60m. Annual consumption per head has more than doubled since the mid-1960s to 28 kg.

Within heavy industry the development of projects established in the 1970s has continued. The Egyptian Iron and Steel Co complex at Helwan, developed around a Soviet-built plant first opened in 1973, was by late 1993 producing at its design capacity of 1.2m. tons per year for the first time, following a 10-year upgrading programme financed by the World Bank and Germany. The Alexandria Iron and Steel Co complex at Dikheila—a Japanese-built plant, in production since the end of 1986—produced 1.1m. tonnes of high-quality steel reinforcing bars and wire rods in 1993, when the company made a net profit of £E112m. on sales of £E1,300m. (including exports worth $70m.). Plans were announced in early 1994 for an expansion scheme to add 400,000 tons of additional production capacity at Dikheila, one element in the proposed financial arrangements for the scheme being a fresh injection of private capital which would reduce the public-sector shareholding in the company from 87.4% to about 60%. Completion of the $350m. expansion scheme was scheduled for 1997. In 1995 the Alexandria complex recorded a net profit of £E120.5m. on sales of £E1,530m. (including exports worth $71m.). Its output in 1995 was just over 1.2m. tons of steel bars. New steel industry projects under consideration in 1994 included a special products mill with a capacity of 140,000 tons per year, to be built at Sadat City, north of Cairo. Egypt's total manufacturing capacity in steel products in 1994 was around 3m. tons, compared with a total annual demand of about 4m. tons which was expected to rise sharply in coming years. A long-term growth strategy for the industry was under discussion by public- and private-sector experts in mid-1994. In October 1997 a contract was signed for the construction of a giant steel plant in Suez, to produce some 1m. tons of flat steel sheets annually, 40% of which will be exported. Investment in the plant is expected to total some £E2,000m. In June 1998 the Aswan Development and Mining Company (Adamco) signed an agreement to mine iron ore and construct an integrated iron and steel plant south of Aswan to produce 1.42m. tons per year of steel billets. In April 1998 the Government announced plans to establish a £E500m. company to develop iron ore deposits south of Aswan.

The Aluminium Co of Egypt, whose complex at Naga Hammadi opened in 1975 (having been developed to take advantage of power supplied from the Aswan High Dam), was in 1993 in the process of upgrading its annual production capacity from 180,000 tons to 250,000 tons with no extra power use. Egypt exported £E405.4m. worth of aluminium rods and sections and £E94.4m. worth of unwrought aluminium in the 1994/95 fiscal year. The new 60,000 tons-per-year rolling mill began production in 1995.

Egypt's cement industry underwent rapid expansion in the 1980s. Annual consumption of cement rose from 4.1m. tons in 1977 to about 16m. tons in 1986. Four cement works began production in 1985, adding 5.2m. tons per year and reaching an installed capacity of 7.7m. tons by 1987. Egypt produced 7.6m. tons of cement in 1985 but imported 9.1m. tons. The conversion of a Soviet-built cement works at Asyut created the largest production line in Africa, with a nominal output capacity of 5,000 tons per day. Under the 1987–92 Five-Year Plan, five new works were to be built, adding 5m. tons to Egypt's annual capacity, and steps have also been taken to expand output at existing plants. By the early 1990s local supply had been brought more closely into balance with demand, and, in mid-1993, an announcement of plans to triple the capacity of a Suez cement plant was coupled with plans to export part of the additional output. In early 1996 Egypt had an installed cement production capacity of 16.6m. tons per year and an import requirement of 2m. tons per year. By mid-1997 cement production had increased to 18m. tons per year, while imports remained the same. According to the Minister of Industry, Sulayman Reda, output was equivalent to 19.7m. tons per year by mid-1998. The construction of three new ventures was forecast to increase production by a further 4.2m. tons per year by 1999. The proliferation of new projects has been prompted by prospects of increased demand over the next few years, owing to construction projects such as the Toshka irrigation scheme and new tourist developments. In June 1998 Reda predicted that production would expand to 40m. tons per year by 2007. Financial analysts have been more cautious, however, and expressed concern that a surplus in capacity could appear in five to 10 years. A contract was awarded in 1995 for the construction in 10 Ramadan City of a float glass factory with an annual capacity of 100,000 tons of clear and coloured plate glass. The factory was scheduled for completion in 1998.

Partly due to surprisingly buoyant foreign exchange earnings in the early 1980s and the freer availability of raw materials, there were signs that the construction industry was beginning to expand rapidly. Indeed, housing dominated construction during the 1982–87 Plan, with investment set at £E4,600m., 13.3% of the total. The private sector had been expected to provide 94% of investment in housing construction, itself 54% of total projected private-sector investment under the Plan. The housing programme constituted only about 25% of all construction activity, which has been dominated by the building of public utilities (mainly water and sewerage projects). The Plan provided for £E2,900m. to be invested in public utilities' construction but the projects involved, such as the Greater Cairo sewerage and the Alexandria waste-water schemes, are so vast that they are being funded outside the Plan and their duration will extend far beyond the Plan period.

Evidence of increased foreign investment in Egyptian industry was provided by the World Bank's loan of $69m. towards the $109.3m. cost of the National Weaving and Spinning Co's building programme at Alexandria, the Japanese interest in the ed-Dikheila steel plant, and the World Bank's $50m. loan towards the cost of expanding the National Paper Co.

Within the field of the motor industry, Egypt has been assembling and manufacturing parts of Italian Fiat passenger cars since the early 1960s. The El-Nasr Automotive Manufacturing Co (NASCO) produces these cars at a rate of 12,000 per year, as well as buses, trucks and other vehicles. General Motors Egypt (GME, owned 31% by General Motors of the USA, 20% by Isuzu of Japan and 49% by private Egyptian and Saudi investors), was established in 1985 to build light commercial vehicles at 6 October City, south-west of Cairo. By 1993 GME

was producing 10,000 such vehicles per year, 10% of which were exported to Syria, Jordan and the Gulf region, and was due to start assembling a passenger car (the Opel Vectra) later in the year. Other companies were meanwhile developing local assembly plants for various other makes of car, including Hyundai, Suzuki, Peugeot and Citroen, while Daimler-Benz was studying the feasibility of setting up a truck factory in Egypt.

In 1994 GME's output of Opel Vectras was running at the rate of 1,000 a month, while Suzuki Egypt (51% owned by the local Suzuki dealer) was producing Suzuki Swifts at the rate of about 850 per month and Centre for Trade and Development (51% owned by Peugeot) was producing about 100 Peugeot 405s per month. Production of Hyundai Excels (licensed to the locally-owned bus and coach assembler, Ghabbour Brothers) was due to start in the last quarter of 1994 at an annual rate of 17,000 cars, some of them for export to neighbouring countries. Production of Citroen cars and vans (licensed to the locally-owned JAC Car Makers) was due to start at the end of 1994 at an initial annual rate of 4,000 AX models, to be increased to 24,000 vehicles (including other models) at the end of 1995. The local assembly of Nissan cars and vans was scheduled to begin at the end of 1995 at an annual rate of 10,000 vehicles. A plant to manufacture Pirelli radial tyres under licence was due to open in Alexandria at the end of 1994 with a workforce of 800 and a capacity of 350,000 tyres per year.

The local assembly of Mercedes trucks and utility vehicles was due to begin in 1996 and to build up to a level of 7,000 vehicles per year in 1998. A separate plant to produce E-class Mercedes cars began production in November 1997 at an initial rate of 2,500 cars per year; local component content would be 40% (the minimum local-content requirement under current Egyptian law). A plant to assemble Skoda cars was scheduled to begin production by 1997. In mid-1996 Egypt had about 100 motor component plants supplying a total of 12 vehicle assembly projects. The German-based Volkswagen Group announced in June 1996 that it was to open a purchasing office in Egypt with the aim of obtaining about 10 types of component from Egyptian suppliers. Plans to assemble Daewoo cars and pick-up trucks and BMW cars in Egypt were approved by the Investment Authority in September 1996.

In early 1997 Egypt had seven car assembly plants in operation with a total capacity of 85,000 units per year, although current output was only about one-third of capacity. In June 1997 BMW opened an assembly plant on the same site as a Nissan factory, as part of an unprecedented agreement in which both companies would share the paint shop in order to minimize costs. BMW predicted annual production of 2,000 units. In 1996 the Egyptian market for cars was around 65,000 units, of which about half were assembled locally. The export of locally-assembled cars was not permitted under licensing agreements between foreign parent manufacturers and Egyptian assembly plants, whose financial viability depended on substantial tariff protection in the Egyptian domestic market. Egyptian tariffs on vehicle imports—specifically excluded from the general reductions in tariffs in 1996 and 1997—ranged in mid-1997 from 40% on the smallest cars to 135% on cars with engine capacities of 1.6 litres or more. According to some industry estimates in 1996, a further 15 years of tariff protection would be needed for Egyptian vehicle plants to develop internationally-competitive cost structures.

Early in 1983 the Egyptian Chief of Staff of the Armed Forces stated that Egypt was interested in the joint manufacture of weapons with other countries, and in November 1987 Egypt began to press its former partners in the Arab Organization for Industrialization (AOI) (Saudi Arabia, Qatar and the UAE) to revive their involvement in a regional Arab defence industry. The AOI was funded in 1974 to provide an Arab challenge to Israel's advanced defence industry but Egypt's three co-founders withdrew from the organization in 1979, after Egypt signed a peace treaty with Israel. The armaments industry is being seen in Egypt as a possible source of revenue to offset the decline in receipts from the traditional revenue earners, and the decision of its former partners to re-establish diplomatic relations with Egypt after the Arab League summit meeting in Amman, in November 1987, gave rise to hopes that new Arab investment in the AOI might be forthcoming. Sales of armaments earned a reported $1,000m. in 1982, when Iraq, at a critical stage in its war with Iran, turned to Egypt for spare parts and ammunition for its mainly Soviet-built equipment, and bought battle tanks from Egypt's strategic reserves. Egypt has acquired licences to rebuild and modify old Soviet tanks and its most ambitious project involves the assembly, under licence, of the US General Dynamics Land System's M1A1 Abrams battle tank. Some 75 of the latter had been produced by the beginning of 1994, when production was proceeding at the rate of 10 tanks per month towards a cumulative target of 540 tanks (all intended for use by the Egyptian armed forces).

According to a report by the General Organization for Industrialization, private investment in new industrial ventures totalled £E1,889m. in 1993, creating 30,000 new jobs in 799 projects.

The needs of heavy industry, and the plan to extend electric power to all Egypt's rural communities underlined the need for more power generation than that supplied by the Aswan High Dam. The dam represented some 2,000 MW of total installed capacity of 3,700 MW at the start of the 1982–87 Five-Year Plan. The Plan provided for the expansion of installed capacity by 3,430 MW, of which 270 MW was to be obtained through the Aswan II scheme, and the remainder from thermal power stations and eight nuclear plants, which were to be completed by 2005, at a cost of $36,000m. Total net installed capacity rose to 5,850 MW in 1985. However, the nuclear programme came under government reappraisal in the aftermath of the disaster at the Chernobyl plant in the USSR in April 1986, and the collapse of oil prices; while some of the thermal units, which were intended to be oil- and gas-fired, were redesigned to burn coal from Australia. It was proposed that a 2,600-MW plant, costing $1,800m. to construct, and ultimately using 15m. tons of Australian coal per year, would be built at Zaafarana on the Gulf of Suez during the 1987–92 Five-Year Plan, with an associated port, capable of handling 7m.–8m. tons of coal per year initially, rising to 12m.–15m. tons. Annual consumption of electricity was given at 34,000m. kWh in 1985 and was expected to increase threefold by the end of the century. Hence, plans to implement the Qattara Depression scheme to generate energy by flooding the depression with waters from the Mediterranean were given the final go-ahead late in 1980, at an estimated cost of at least $2,600m. In August 1980 the USA agreed to provide a $102m. loan to modernize the electricity grid, and plans for the implementation of complete rural electrification are in an advanced stage. In May 1985 USAID also agreed to provide $55m. of an estimated $156m. required for the fourth 315-MW power unit at Shoubra el-Kheima power station in Cairo. The station, whose first three units, costing $604m., became operational in early 1986, provides up to 75% of Cairo's electricity. The fourth unit was completed in the late 1980s, bringing total capacity to more than 1,000 MW. Since 1981, Egypt's total installed capacity increased by 7,000 MW to reach 10,938 MW in 1991. It is planned to add a further 6,000 MW by 2000, including the commissioning of a 400 MW combined cycle plant at Damietta, east of Alexandria, and the rehabilitation of an old Soviet plant at Suez which will boost capacity by 185 MW. Annual output of electricity totalled 84,870m. kWh in 1997 and was expected to reach 100,000m. kWh in 1998. Power supplies were priced at about 90% of cost in mid-1994, a level of subsidy which the Government was pledged to eliminate by the end of 1996 as part of its economic reform programme. A further aim of the sector is to reduce oil consumption. In 1990 the sector accounted for 8.3m. tons of oil, equivalent to 16% of total production. Where possible, power stations were being converted to use natural gas in the early 1990s, the Government's target being to increase the contribution of gas to thermal power generation from 60% in 1992 to 80% by 1997 (thus minimizing domestic use of petroleum that could be used to generate valuable export revenue). (In 1997 thermal power stations accounted for 79% of electicity output.) Plans were being drawn up in 1993 to link the Egyptian and Jordanian electricity grids as part of a regional inter-connection project to be financed by the Arab Fund for Economic and Social Development.

In June 1981 the USA signed an agreement for nuclear co-operation with Egypt, which was to lead to the construction of two nuclear power stations. More recently, Egypt turned to France for additional assistance with its nuclear projects, and also to Italy, with whom a nuclear co-operation agreement was

signed in March 1984. A Franco-Italian consortium was to build Egypt's first nuclear plant at ed-Daba, 160 km west of Alexandria but the French withdrew in early 1987, owing to export-credit problems. The Government initially planned to build eight nuclear power units at a cost of $36,000m., with a total capacity of 8,000 MW, to meet 40% of Egypt's energy needs by the year 2005, buying uranium from Niger. However, in April 1986, the Government announced that only three nuclear power units would be built up to the year 2005, the first of which, at ed-Daba, was under review in early 1991.

To guard against severe power shortages arising from low water levels at the Aswan High Dam (see above), the Government announced, in January 1988, that 20 thermal power plants, with a combined capacity of 5,500 MW, would be built by the end of 1992. Four 300-MW plants were to be built at Abu Qir (No. 5), Asyut, Suez (No. 4) and Damanhûr; a 270-MW hydroelectric plant is under construction at Esmat, on the upper Nile; and a gas-fired plant, with a capacity of 700 MW, was planned for Damietta. It was subsequently announced that four plants, at Ayoun Mousa, Zaafarana, Sidi Krier and Kurimat, each of 1,200 MW generating capacity and originally designed to be coal-fired, would be oil- and gas-fired. In May 1989 the USSR granted Egypt a 'soft' loan (repayable over 12 years) for the construction of a 600-MW power station in the Sinai desert. In February 1991 it was confirmed that USAID funds of $200m. would be allocated to the Kurimat project, the total cost of which was estimated at $1,000m., and an initial consultancy contract was signed with a US firm, Ebasco Overseas, in October 1991. In mid-1995 Egypt's total installed electricity generating capacity of 13,068 MW comprised 7,246 MW of steam plant, 2,805 MW of hydroelectric plant, 1,574 MW of combined-cycle plant and 1,443 MW of gas plant. Power stations consumed 2.17m. tons of fuel oil and 7.788m. cu m of natural gas in the 1994/95 fiscal year. In March 1998 a contract was signed for the construction of five new power transformer stations with a total capacity of 250,000 kW. The £E56m. project will provide electricity in rural areas of Abu el-Matamir, Motobus, Tel el-Kebîr, Dekernes, and Samalût.

Major urban redevelopment schemes are also under way. The first stage of an urban mass-transit railway system was completed in Cairo in August 1987 by a French consortium (see 'Transport and Tourism'). At the end of 1982 the first contract, worth $55m., was awarded for the Greater Cairo sewerage renewal scheme. The $3,000m. scheme involves the digging of a 10-mile tunnel which will connect Cairo's drains to the largest sewage-pumping station in the world in the northern suburb of al-Ameriya. Elsewhere, there are plans to build new towns to accommodate 5m. people by 2000 and relieve the pressures on existing urban centres of a rapidly increasing population, though even these provisions are in danger of becoming obsolete in the face of an ever accelerating birth rate. The Egyptian telephone network, controlled by the National Telecommunications Organization (Arento), had a total installed capacity of about 2.8m. lines at the end of 1994. In 1995 Arento was finalizing an expansion programme to add a further 500,000 lines over five years with the support of $200m. in grant aid from the US Agency for International Development. At the beginning of 1984 a 20-year Master Plan for Alexandria was announced. It envisaged growth of the city's population to 4.75m. by 2005. The urban development schemes which have so far been undertaken have not, however, been as successful as was anticipated. An example of this is the new town of 10 Ramadan, 30 km from Cairo, begun in 1978, which was estimated to have as few as 100,000 residents (a quarter of its intended residential population) by 1993. To provide for the large number of Egyptians returning from the Gulf in 1990–91, the Government announced the creation of eight project zones, some of them free zones for tariff purposes, designed to provide factory employment for displaced workers. By March 1994, the total population of new industrial cities around Cairo was officially given as 265,000, and plans were announced to encourage their further growth by providing incentives for workers to take up residence in them.

The Government's awareness that Egypt's urban slum areas were fertile breeding grounds for social unrest prompted a 1993/94 budget allocation of £E250m. to improve the housing conditions and basic amenities in such areas, the Government's eventual aim being to invest over £E3,000m. in a long-term development programme covering 404 districts in 10 provinces. New incentives for investment in the economically-deprived Upper Egypt region were announced in January 1995. Industrial zones in Beni Suef (120 km south of Cairo) and five population centres further to the south (Menia, Asyut, Suhag, Luxor and Aswan) became subject to accelerated planning procedures and other measures to attract new investors. In December 1997 the International Development Association pledged credits worth $15m. to settle 26,000 low-income families on reclaimed land east of the Delta. The Government's co-operative housing authority aims to attract new residents by subsidizing approximately 50% of the cost of a house with a loan to be repaid over a period of 30–40 years. The Government expects its investment in new towns to reach £E142,000m. by 2017.

Egypt's mineral resources are now being reappraised. Iron ore has traditionally been mined from the Aswan area, but new and better quality reserves have recently been discovered in the Bahariya Oasis region. Phosphate production from mines at Isna, Hamrawein and Safaga exceeded 600,000 tons per annum in the 1980s, and exports reached around 300,000 tons in 1992/93. A new phosphate mine at Abu Tartur in the Western Desert was due to be brought into production at a rate of 2.2m. tons per year at the end of 1994, rising to twice that rate by 1996, when 600,000 tons of its output would be earmarked for export. However, production had still not begun in 1997, when the Government announced that private-sector investment would be sought to complete the project. Manganese is being mined in the Eastern Desert and Sinai, there are chromium deposits in the Eastern Desert, and uranium has been discovered in Sinai. In 1985 a British company, Minex Minerals Egypt, was awarded concessions to prospect for gold in two areas at Barramiya and es-Sid. In 1997 an Australian company, Pharoah Gold Mines, was preparing to open a mine in the Eastern Desert, while a new gold discovery was announced in the far south-west of Egypt at Jabal Kamel, where Egyptian geologists had been prospecting for iron ore. There are extensive coal deposits in Sinai, including an estimated 21m. tons at Maghâra, where a deep mine (disused since 1967), was reopened in the mid-1990s. The company responsible, Sinai Coal Company, was under parliamentary investigation in 1997 following allegations of 'financial, operational and environmental shortcomings'.

In 1998 the Government announced plans to establish a 3,000-acre zone for technological production called the Sinai Technology Valley (STV). Immediate projects are to be established on a 250-acre site and are due for completion in late 1999. The Government expects the zone to increase technology exports from $200m. per year in 1998 to $2,000m. per year by 2002. Companies establishing in the STV will be entitled to tax incentives for a 10-year period.

PETROLEUM AND GAS

The development of Egypt's hydrocarbon sector has had a major impact on the economy, although petroleum production in Egypt remains relatively small by Middle Eastern standards. Production of crude petroleum at the end of 1980 averaged approximately 600,000 barrels per day (b/d), compared with 420,000 b/d in 1977, and continued to rise thereafter. Petroleum revenue rose to $3,431m. in 1981/82 (representing about 60% of total export earnings), compared with $960m. in 1979. In 1982/83 gross revenue from petroleum sales fell to $2,977m. It rose to $3,127m. in 1983/84 and to $3,340m. in 1984/85. Overall production averaged 785,000 b/d in 1983/84, rising to almost 900,000 b/d in 1985/86, compared with capacity of 1m. b/d. Of average daily output, about 50% is used locally and between 25%–30% is taken by foreign oil companies, which leaves only about one-quarter of output or less available for export. In 1986 the effect of the collapse in oil prices, coupled with Egypt's decision voluntarily to reduce production, was to limit average output to about 770,000 b/d, while exports fell to a rate of only 150,000 b/d.

Domestic consumption of hydrocarbons, was, until 1984, rising at a rate of 12%–15% each year, while oil production was rising by only 7% annually. Subsidies on petroleum placed a considerable strain on the nation's finances: the estimated $3,600m. spent on them in 1983 kept oil products at less than one-fifth of their price on the world market. Substitution of natural gas for fuel oil helped to slow the rate of increase in

domestic oil consumption during the latter part of the 1980s, while sharp reductions in price subsidies in 1991 helped to stabilize domestic hydrocarbon consumption at just under 27m. tons in both the 1990/91 and 1991/92 fiscal years. In the calendar year 1995 total hydrocarbon consumption was 29.3m. tons, comprising 19.4m. tons of petroleum products and 9.9m. tons of natural gas. The most significant factors in explaining the great increases in oil production so far are the return by Israel of the Alma Oilfield, renamed the Sha'b Ali field, in the Gulf of Suez, in November 1979 and, in 1982, the Sinai oilfields (notably the Abu Rudeis area), and the increase in concessions and finds particularly in the Gulf of Suez and the Western Desert. At the end of 1996 Egypt's proven oil reserves totalled 3,700m. barrels, equivalent to 11.4 years' production at 1996 output levels.

Egypt, not being a member of OPEC, is able to maintain a flexible pricing policy. In 1983 and 1984, by maintaining a higher price for its oil (as much as $28.50 per barrel for the premium Suez 33° API oil blend, which accounts for about 60% of all oil exports), Egypt's policy was consistent with its support for OPEC's programme to prevent a collapse in world oil prices. In February 1985, however, Egypt dissociated itself from OPEC's policies, steadily reducing the price of its oil, as demand remained slack. A decline in the value of the US dollar and a reduction in Iranian oil exports led to increases in all blends (including the 26° API Belayim blend and Râs Ghârib, the heaviest Egyptian crude) during the last third of 1985. During 1986, however, the oil price, already weakened by the glut of oil on world markets, fell sharply after OPEC decided to increase production, in order to secure a 'fair' share of the reduced market. In order to remain competitive, Egypt was forced to cut production and make a series of reductions in the price of its oil. For the second half of July the Suez blend was valued at only $7.35 per barrel, compared with $11.30 in June and $26.70 in December 1985. Egypt's average output was cut by some 300,000 b/d in early 1986, and in April exports were reduced to about 50,000 b/d, compared with more than 250,000 b/d at the end of 1985. After OPEC decided in August 1986 to reintroduce a production ceiling, the price of petroleum on world markets began to increase again. Following several increases, the Suez and Ras al-Bihar blends were priced at $17.60 per barrel in the second half of January 1987. In February the price of Suez and Ras al-Bihar was reduced to $17.25 but there were no further alterations until July, when the prices rose to $17.75 per barrel. Egypt's production rose after August 1986, reaching 940,000 b/d in December, but it agreed to restrict its output to 870,000 b/d for the first half of 1987, in support of OPEC's new production and prices strategy. However, according to the Egyptian General Petroleum Corporation (EGPC), average output exceeded 900,000 b/d during this period, and reached 904,000 b/d in the year as a whole. By mid-July 1988, with the world market once more oversupplied with petroleum, the price of the Suez and Ras al-Bihar blends had been reduced to $12.75 per barrel. Net petroleum revenues, which totalled $2,630m. in 1985, declined to $704m. in 1986 and rose to $1,446m. in 1987, following an improvement in world oil prices; in the 1988/89 fiscal year they amounted to $1,451m., while in 1989/90 they rose to $1,651m. In 1990/91 oil exports totalled $2,539m. and oil imports $978m., making a surplus of $1,561m. In the calendar year 1992 Egypt's oil trade surplus totalled $1,258m., falling to $1,170m. in 1993 (when oil export earnings totalled $2,147m. and oil import costs totalled $977m.). In 1994 oil exports were valued at $2,148m. and oil imports at $819m., making a surplus of $1,329m. In 1995 Egypt had an oil trade surplus of $1,470m. (exports $2,430m., imports $960m.). In 1997 oil exports totalled $2,483m. and imports $1,606m., resulting in a surplus of $877m.

The plan for the hydrocarbon sector in 1982/83–1986/87 envisaged an increase in oil and gas production by 85% from 34m. tons in 1981 to 63m. tons by 1987. However, these plans had to be revised owing to the crisis in the world oil market. Actual production totalled 48m. tons in 1985 (oil 44.3m. tons; gas 3.7m. tons), fell to 44.6m. tons in 1986 (oil 40.3m. tons; gas 4.3m. tons) but rose to 50m. tons in 1987 (oil 45.2m. tons; gas 4.8m. tons). Production amounted to 49.6m. tons in 1988 and rose to 50.4m. tons in 1989, 50m. tons in 1990 and 51.6m. tons in 1991. In 1992 total hydrocarbon production of 53.6m. tons comprised 44.2m. tons of crude oil, 7.6m. tons of natural gas, 1.1m. tons of condensates and 0.7m. tons of butane. Total output was

56.4m. tons in 1993 (oil 45.5m. tons, gas 8.8m. tons, condensates 1.3m. tons, butane 0.8m. tons); and 56.2m tons in 1994 (oil 44.8m. tons, gas 9.3m. tons, condensates 1.3m. tons and butane 0.8m. tons). The 1995 production total was 56.65m. tons (oil 44.6m. tons, gas 9.9m. tons, condensates 1.3m. tons and butane 0.85m. tons). Preliminary data for 1996 indicated a decline of 3% in oil production and an increase of 5.6% in oil consumption, while natural gas production rose by 4.7% and gas consumption increased by 4.1%. In 1997 oil production was recorded at 43.9m. tons and consumption at 25.9m. tons. Natural gas production totalled 10.5m. tons and consumption was 10.4m. tons. The Government reduced oil production levels from 850,000 b/d to 820,000 b/d in July 1998 in an attempt to stabilize oil prices.

Egypt has made numerous oil concession and exploration agreements with foreign companies. The US company, Amoco, was responsible for nearly 50% of all Egyptian crude output in the early 1990s. Exploration was greatly stimulated by the oil price rises of the early 1970s, leading to new oil finds in the Gulf of Suez, on the Red Sea coast and in the Eastern and Western Deserts. Western Desert oilfields contributed 6.5% of national output in 1987 (compared with more than 90% for the Gulf of Suez), when 41 of Egypt's oilfields were situated in the Gulf of Suez and 26 in the Western Desert. Twelve new finds were reported in the Gulf of Suez in 1980, leading to a doubling of Egypt's known oil reserves. These rates of discovery continued in 1981, when 12 main new oil discoveries, 10 of which were in the Gulf of Suez, were made.

Exploration continued in 1982, and early in 1983 four new major production sharing agreements were signed by the EGPC with Shell Winning, Getty Oil, Deminex, and a partnership of BP, Elf Aquitaine, Occidental Petroleum and IEOC. Expansion continued during 1984, with petroleum flowing ashore from the first of the Deminex Egyptian Oil Company's platforms in the Ras Fanar field, in the Gulf of Suez, in January. Further concessions were also signed with Deminex in the Zeit area; with Marathon, Aminoil and IEOC in the southern part of the Gulf of Suez; and with Shell Winning in the East Gamsa area of the Gulf of Suez and in the Qaraouan area of the Western Desert. The Zeit Bay oilfield came 'on stream' in 1984, with an initial output of 10,000 b/d, which had risen to 65,000 b/d by April 1985. The third oilfield in the Gulf of Suez to begin production during 1984 was Ras al-Bihar, the largest field yet struck by EGPC. With an initial output of 12,000 b/d, it helped to push overall production up to the target of 1m. b/d in 1985. A consortium of Western oil companies, including Total-CFP and BP, discovered oil in Egyptian waters off the coast of North Sinai in early 1986; an exploration well yielded 5,000 b/d–10,000 b/d. Texas International Inc and Conoco made two discoveries of oil in a 200,000-ha concession 325 km west of Alexandria in mid-1985, one of which is of commercial quality. More than 350 exploratory wells have been drilled in the Gulf of Suez, and some 40 fields discovered. During 1986, new discoveries were reported in the Western Desert by Khalda Petroleum (a joint venture of EGPC, Texas International and Conoco). New exploration agreements were signed with BP, Shell, Amoco and Agip in mid-1987 for concessions in the Gulf of Suez and the Sinai desert, reflecting more advantageous production sharing terms being offered by EGPC to encourage foreign participation. In September 1987 the EGPC announced that 78 oil deposits had been discovered since 1982, of which 41 were in production and 31 were to begin production during the next five years. According to the EGPC, a record 49 exploration agreements with foreign oil companies were approved by the Egyptian Government in 1989.

The results of exploration in the late 1980s were generally disappointing, especially in the Western Desert, and a new round of invitations to bid for concessions, issued by the EGPC in 1990, elicited only a limited response. Partly as a result, BP announced in November 1991 that it would sell its 16.6% stake in the Suez Petroleum Company (SUCO), while other Western companies scaled down their activities in Egypt. Nevertheless, several new oil and gas finds were announced in 1990/92, one by British Gas in December 1990, in its offshore North Zaafarana concession in the Gulf of Suez, being described as 'the most significant in the area for nearly a decade'. Other finds announced in early 1992 included strikes of both oil and gas in the Western Desert, the Gulf of Suez and the Nile delta, close to existing fields. According to government sources, there was

known potential for the proving of a further 2,000m. barrels of oil reserves in Egypt, although it was conceded that they were in relatively small pockets which would be difficult to exploit.

In June 1989 Egypt was readmitted to the Organization of Arab Petroleum Exporting Countries (OAPEC), and it has since sought to increase co-operation with Libya, Syria, Jordan, Oman, Yemen and the other Gulf States. Companies from Kuwait and the UAE have invested in exploration concessions in Egypt.

In 1993 the EGPC made strenuous efforts to revitalize oil exploration activity, concluding seven new agreements in February for blocks in the Western Desert and the Gulf of Suez; the companies involved included British Gas, Amoco, Mobil and Agip. Bids for a further five blocks (two of them in the Delta region) were being evaluated in mid-1993, while bidding for 15 more blocks (five of them in the Mediterranean region) was to close near the end of the year. Reported improvements in terms included increased block sizes, improved cost-recovery formulae and flexible withdrawal options. Production-sharing terms (which were negotiable on a case-by-case basis) reportedly envisaged a reduction in the EGPC's share of output to between 70% and 80%, compared with its entitlements of between 80% and 89% under existing production-sharing agreements.

Egypt's Minister of Petroleum and Mineral Wealth said that in order to attract exploration dollars it was essential to adopt a flexible negotiating stance in an environment of 'intense international competition'. In a further demonstration of its pragmatic approach to oil development, the Government agreed in 1993 to allow Agip's local affiliate to merge a total of 14 separate agreements, of widely differing terms and lengths, into one unified agreement with an extended expiry date, thereby improving the viability of the company's capital investment programme. (The Agip-affiliated International Egyptian Oil Company was Egypt's second largest oil producer and largest gas producer in 1992.) Nine exploration blocks (including the last available blocks in the Gulf of Suez) were opened to bids in 1995, after which only 40% of Egyptian territory (including the 15% without any sedimentary rocks) would remain unallocated for exploration. The Government's intention was to have exploration agreements in place in every geologically appropriate area by 1998. Having concluded concession agreements in respect of eight of the nine blocks offered in 1995, the Government opened a further nine blocks to bids in 1996. In 1997 the EGPC offered 12 exploration blocks, 11 of which were awarded in mid-1998. Participating companies envisage drilling 63 wells in total, with total investment of $208m. Nine exploration blocks were opened to bids in early 1998, and bids for a further nine blocks were to be opened later in the year.

A 320-km Suez-Mediterranean (Sumed) crude pipeline, operated by the Arab Petroleum Pipeline Co (owned 50% by Egypt and 50% by Saudi Arabia, Kuwait, Qatar and Abu Dhabi, mostly through state oil companies), opened in 1977 with a throughput capacity of 1.6m. b/d. An expansion of capacity to 2.3m. b/d was due to be completed in March 1994. Terminals at Ain Sukhna (near Suez) and Sidi Krier (near Alexandria) can accommodate tankers otherwise too large to navigate the Suez Canal. Oil storage capacity at these terminals in 1993 totalled 2.4m. barrels, which many users considered to be insufficient to ensure efficient utilization of the forthcoming increase in the throughput capacity of the pipeline. Proposals to build as much as 4.5m. barrels of additional storage capacity were under consideration in mid-1993. As well as providing an oil transit service, the Sumed company does some trading on its own account (buying crude at the Red Sea terminal for resale at the Mediterranean terminal).

Egypt has oil refineries at Suez (two), Mosturud (near Cairo), Ameriya and Mex (near Alexandria), Tanta and Wadi Feirân. Annual output of refined products totalled 23.3m. tons in 1992, 24.6m. tons in 1993, 25.4m. tons in 1994 and 26.3m. tons in 1995. The main population centres are served by an extensive network of product pipelines. Downstream development initiatives for the mid-1990s are expected to include refinery modernization to bring the local industry's product mix more closely into line with the pattern of domestic demand (e.g. by adding the capability to produce diesel fuel, one of several categories of oil product that were still being imported in 1993). Plans were also well advanced in 1995 to construct a largely export-oriented 100,000 b/d refinery next to the Sumed pipeline terminal at Sidi Krier. Scheduled for completion in 1999 at an estimated cost of more than $1,000m., the proposed plant would be 80% owned by Israeli/Swiss and Egyptian private citizens and 20% by EGPC.

Having brought its first natural gas field on-stream in 1974 at a rate of 3.5m. cubic metres per day (cu m/d), Egypt was producing around 6m. cu m/d by the early 1980s, when the country's proven gas reserves totalled around 85,000m. cu m. Substantial new discoveries in succeeding years helped to boost proven reserves to 400,000m. cu m by the end of 1992, during which year Egyptian gas output averaged 31.15m. cu m/d (having increased by nearly 25% since 1990 and by nearly 50% since 1987). Until the late 1980s gas pipelines were developed primarily to serve industrial plants (including the Helwan iron and steel complex). Thereafter, power stations became the largest consumers of Egyptian gas, most of the steep rise in gas consumption in the early 1990s being attributable to a national strategy to substitute gas for oil wherever possible.

Almost 40% of Egypt's gas output in 1992 came from the Abu Madi and El Qara fields in the Nile Delta (foreign participant Agip), while about 25% came from the Badr ed-Din field in the Western Desert (foreign participant Shell). The most important new gas discovery of 1992 was made by Shell Egypt in the coastal region of the Western Desert, involving the Obaiyed field, which was expected to add between 40,000m. cu m and 250,000m. cu m to the country's proven reserves when fully appraised. Other companies with major Egyptian gas interests include Amoco and Phillips Petroleum. Having significantly improved its financial terms for gas development and production in 1988, the Government further enhanced the return to producing companies in 1993, when it raised its main reference price by 12.5%, bringing it roughly into line with European gas prices. Egypt's gas production averaged 36.83m. cu m/d in 1994. At the end of 1994 EGPC, Amoco and the Agip-affiliated International Egyptian Oil Co signed an agreement to establish an Egypt Trans-Gas Co to take charge of a project to build a 500-km gas pipeline from Port Said to Gaza and Israel, to handle proposed exports of gas to these markets, and to assess the potential for the eventual development of further markets in Lebanon and Turkey. An exportable surplus of gas was expected to become available from 1997/98 when new offshore fields north of the Nile Delta were brought into production. In 1995 Egypt's gas production averaged 39.19m. cu m/d, while its year-end gas reserves (including recent discoveries in the Nile Delta and eastern Mediterranean) were estimated to exceed 630,000m. cu m. At the end of 1997 Egypt's proven gas reserves totalled 780,000 cu m.

There are five main fertilizer plants using Egypt's hydrocarbon feedstocks: Talkha I in Lower Egypt, which began in 1976 and produces 380,000 tons per year of nitrogenous fertilizers; Talkha II opened in 1979 and produces 396,000 tons per year of ammonia, which is then used for making urea (both plants use gas from the Abu Madi field); Suez, producing 250,000 tons per year of nitrogenous fertilizer, using gas from Abu Gharadeq; the plant at Dikheila, using Abu Qir gas, which has a capacity of 500,000 tons per year of urea and 100,000 tons per year of ammonium nitrate; and the Abu Qir fertilizer works, in Alexandria, which produces 450,000 tons per year of ammonia/urea. An extension to the Abu Qir plant, which is being built by a German company, Uhde, will have a daily production capacity of 1,000 tons of ammonia, 1,800 tons of nitric acid, and 2,300 tons of ammonium nitrate. In January 1998 a contract was signed for the construction of a fertilizer complex in Suez, to produce 1,200 tons per day of urea and 1,925 tons per day of ammonia. A project to develop a major ethylene-based integrated petrochemicals complex on the Gulf of Suez was under discussion in 1996. In April 1998 a contract was signed for the 120,000-tons-per-year polypropylene plant at Alexandria to produce feedstock for the local manufacture of synthetic textiles. In 1997 bids were invited for the development of Egypt's first polyethylene complex, to produce 200,000 tons per year, using feedstock from an ethylene plant already under construction.

BANKING

In late 1971, reorganization of the banking system resulted in the merger of three of the banks into others, with each of the rest being entrusted with specialized functions. The National Bank of Egypt was entrusted with foreign trade, the Bank of Port Said merged into Misr Bank which was to deal with home trade, including agricultural finance, the Industrial Bank merged into the Bank of Alexandria which was to deal with manufacturing, the Mortgage Credit Bank merged with the Crédit Foncier Egyptien and was to deal with construction and housing and the Bank of Cairo was left to deal with operations of the public sector. In 1975, in line with the liberalization of the banking system, these restrictions on the sectoral operations of the major banks were removed. A new bank, the Nasser Social Bank, was created to deal with pensions and other forms of social security. The Egyptian International Bank for Foreign Trade and Development was also created in 1971 to promote foreign trade and attract foreign investment but was later transformed into the Arab International Bank for Foreign Trade and Development with Egypt, Libya and other Arab investors holding shares. These banks are additional to the Central Bank of Egypt, which was created from the issue department of the National Bank of Egypt in 1960, and the Public Organization for Agricultural Credit and Co-operatives, which the Crédit Agricole became in 1964.

Foreign banks have been welcome in Egypt since it began liberalizing its economy in earnest in 1974, and about 50 of them now operate in the country. The biggest impact on the Egyptian banking system from foreign banks, however, has come from the joint ventures established with Egyptian banks. These include Misr International Bank, which partners Misr Bank with First National Bank of Chicago, Banco di Roma and UBAF Bank (London); Egyptian-American Bank, which pairs American Express and Bank of Alexandria; Cairo Barclays International Bank, a venture between Banque du Caire and Barclays Bank International; Misr-America International Bank, part-owned by Bank of America, the Kuwait Real Estate Bank and the First Arabian Corporation on the foreign partners' side, and by the Development Industrial Bank and Misr Insurance Company on the Egyptian side; and Banque du Caire et de Paris, a pairing of Banque Nationale de Paris and Banque du Caire. All these, with the exception of Cairo Barclays, were established as 51/49 ventures in favour of the Egyptian side. Cairo Barclays, being a 50/50 venture, was not permitted domestic banking activity under the banking regulations in force at the time of its establishment. Other developments included the opening in Cairo in July 1979 of the Faisal-Islamic bank, with 49% Saudi and Gulf equity participation. This was the first Egyptian bank to do business according to the *Shari'a* (Islamic Law). By 1987, however, the major public-sector banks (National Bank of Egypt, Banque Misr, Banque du Caire, and Bank of Alexandria) all had Islamic banking facilities. Some Islamic investment companies also appeared, although they encountered problems owing to excessive dividend payments. As a result, the Central Bank tightened its control over the banking sector in early 1987.

During 1980 a number of changes took place in the banking structure. In December Egypt's first international bank, the Egyptian International Bank, was opened with a capital of $100m. Of this capital 50% was subscribed by the country's four main banks: the National Bank of Egypt, Bank of Alexandria, Banque de Caire, and Banque Misr, with the other half being provided by the Central Bank of Egypt. In addition a National Investment Bank was established earlier in the year to monitor public investment, and there were also plans to establish an import-export bank. The fiscal year was also changed in 1980 to begin in July and not January.

An incentive exchange rate was introduced in December 1984 in an effort to check a slide in the value of the Egyptian pound against the US dollar and to undercut the 'black' market in currency, which had grown following a major devaluation of the Egyptian pound, by one-half, against the US dollar in 1979. (Egypt maintained different exchange rates for specific purposes, e.g. for basic commodity transactions, for workers' remittances, for public sector purchases etc.) A series of measures by successive finance ministers, including the authorization of preferential exchange rates at Egypt's four public sector banks, failed to attract remittances from Egyptians working abroad who preferred to deal on the 'black' market, where the rate of exchange on the US dollar remained above the official level.

Only about 40% of the estimated $4,000m. which is generated annually in remittances reaches Egyptian banks. In January 1985 the Minister of Finance, Dr Mustafa as-Said, established a 'floating' exchange rate to reflect more accurately the value of the Egyptian pound against the US dollar, to restrain rising imports, and to counter 'black' market transactions by attracting remittances to the banks. The official rate of exchange remained some 10% below the free market level and failed to divert remittances. Meanwhile, measures restraining imports, including the obligation to purchase letters of credit in Egyptian pounds, proved too restrictive, causing long delays for importers, particularly in the private sector, who were competing for short supplies of currency in the banks. Dr as-Said resigned at the end of March 1985 after a banking scandal, which was the direct result of his 1983 decree banning banks from dealing with certain 'black' market operators. His replacement, Dr Sultan Abu Ali, immediately withdrew the currency regulations of his predecessor: importers were once again able to fund imports by securing hard currency from the 'black' market without having to declare the source; and in June 112 items were removed from the list of restricted imports.

By 1987, Egypt was under considerable pressure, particularly from the IMF, to unify its multiple exchange rates. The IMF wanted the change to be effected within one year but the Government required 18 months. In May 1987, however, the Government acted to curb the 'black' market in currency and announced the partial 'flotation' of its currency, with a daily ('free pool') exchange rate being set by a panel consisting of representatives of eight banks, in order to attract foreign currency. The unofficial market rate persisted but the new 'floating' rate was much closer to it and made the federal banking system more accessible to foreign exchange. The fixed Central Bank rate was adjusted from US $1 = £E0.70 to US $1 = £E1.10 in September 1989. However, the old rate was still applied to revenues from the Suez Canal and the EGPC. The commercial bank exchange rate ($1 = £E1.35 in May 1987), which was used to finance public sector imports and customs duties, was phased out by the end of March 1988, having been allowed to depreciate in order to merge with the 'free pool' rate, which was set every day by a committee of Central Bank and commercial bank officials ($1 = £E2.708 at 30 June 1990). Before the doubts expressed by the Egyptian Government over the reforms required of it, the IMF expected the unification of the remaining exchange rates (the Central Bank rate; the bank 'free pool' rate; the $1 = £E0.40 rate, used for barter deals with the Communist bloc; and a new rate of $1 = £E1.89, introduced in April 1988, for customs duties) to have been achieved by the end of 1988.

In May 1989, as part of a comprehensive adjustment of the interest rate structure, the Central Bank raised interest rates by three percentage points. The measure was designed to encourage savings in the local currency and facilitate a renewed agreement with the IMF. Under reforms agreed with the IMF, which became operative in late February 1991, a new currency exchange system was introduced. It provided for the determination by the commercial banks of a free-market rate of exchange, although an 'official' Central Bank rate continued to be set at not more than 5% less (in terms of the Egyptian pound's free-market value) than the commercial bank rate. This two-tier system resulted in an effective devaluation of nearly 40% compared with the official rate in the previous year, and was officially stated to be a prelude to a unified exchange rate and full currency convertibility commencing in February 1992. By May 1991 the exchange rate was US $1 = £E3.24. Moreover, the new exchange system also resulted in an increase in the Central Bank's interest rates, which rose from 16.2% to more than 20% by May 1991.

For some years the Government has been concerned about the growth of Islamic investment companies, which have been attracting a significant proportion of private savings, including remittances from Egyptians working abroad, and channelling domestic funds and vital foreign exchange away from the official banking system. According to the Islamic precepts under which these investment companies operate, they are not permitted to charge or pay interest. Instead, they pay depositors out of profits, at a high rate of return (up to 24%, compared with the 13% interest available from banks), from their speculations and investments at home and abroad. There are four or five major

companies and more than 100 smaller ones, with 2m.–3m. customers (mostly small investors), which effectively constitute a large, unregulated financial sector in competition with the official banking institutions. The largest Islamic investment house, Ar-Rayan, holds deposits of $2,000m.–$3,500m. (more than all but the largest banks), and estimates of the combined deposits of all the Islamic companies are in the range of $12,000m.–$20,000m., compared with total commercial bank deposits of $15,000m. at the end of 1987.

In 1987 the Government announced plans to regularize the activities of Islamic investment companies, and in June 1988 the Majlis passed a law requiring them to become regular shareholding companies (issuing share certificates in exchange for deposits, rather than simple receipts) and placing a limit of £E50m. on their authorized capital. All companies were forbidden to take new deposits for three months, while they decided whether to comply with the new regulations or to go into liquidation. The measures provoked strong resistance among the Islamic investment companies, and many leading executives protested that they would not be able to continue in business if they complied with them (see 'Islamic Banking and Finance', p. 180).

It was feared that the collapse of several of Egypt's Islamic investment companies in late 1988 would lead to the loss of several thousand depositors' funds. There was also evidence, by mid-1989, that the resulting loss of confidence in the economy had led to a sharp decline in Egyptian workers' remittances from abroad, which was exacerbated by Iraq's invasion of Kuwait in August 1990. The Government estimated, too, that Egyptian deposits worth $14,000m. in Kuwaiti banks, and $540m. in Iraqi banks, had been lost as a result of the invasion. A new banking law, presented to parliament in November 1991, tightened the financial regulations relating to banks and strengthened the supervisory powers of the Central Bank. Under the measure (which attracted some criticism in financial circles), Egyptian banks were required to have paid-up capital of at least £E50m. (as against £E500,000 previously), while foreign banks had to have at least $10m.

An amendment was introduced in March 1993 to allow branches of foreign banks to take deposits and give loans in Egyptian pounds, regardless of whether they were locally incorporated or had local shareholders. A total of 22 foreign banks had branches in Egypt at this time, and several of them were expected to develop a full range of services, placing particular emphasis on the introduction of new products and the creation of modern capital market structures in Egypt.

Total deposits in the Egyptian banking system stood at £E159,000m. (nearly two-thirds of this in local currency) at the beginning of February 1993, an increase of almost 50% over the previous six months as depositors took advantage of the first opportunity for decades to earn a positive return on their money (Egypt's inflation rate having fallen to around 10% while bank deposit rates stood at 15%). The attractiveness of the local currency (which had maintained a stable exchange rate for over a year in conditions of virtually free convertibility) was such that the Central Bank was buying about $1,000m. of 'surplus' foreign exchange each month—a development which helped to boost Egypt's foreign exchange reserves to a record $14,300m. during the first quarter of 1993. By mid-1994 the country's foreign-exchange reserves had reached $16,600m., and were forecast by the Government to rise to around $20,000m. by the end of 1995. The amount of surplus liquidity in the Egyptian banking system was estimated at around £E4,400m. in the first half of 1994. Surplus liquidity in the banking system was substantially reduced in April 1995 when a £E3,000m. issue of five-year treasury bonds was fully subscribed. A 49% ceiling on foreign banks' shareholdings in some local joint-venture and private banks was abolished in June 1995. The same amending legislation increased the maximum amount that any bank could lend to a single creditor (hitherto defined as a sum equal to 25% of the bank's capital) to a sum equal to 30% of its capital.

At the end of 1996 Egypt's official reserves exceeded $18,000m., representing nearly 15 months' import cover. By the start of 1997 sales of state shares had reduced the number of joint-venture banks in majority state ownership from nine to four. A committee was formed in January 1997 to plan the establishment of a new bank to provide unsecured loans to families on very low incomes. The new bank (inspired by similar institutions pioneered in Bangladesh) was to be covered by a special law. In January 1998 the Government introduced a new law to prevent banks and businesses from securing a double tax exemption by taking out loans carrying tax relief to invest in treasury bills (t-bills) on which earnings are tax-free. The legislation, stipulating that banks and businesses can only purchase t-bills with their own funds, immediately prompted concern that profits would drop, owing to a significant increase in their tax burdens; share prices subsequently dropped as investors speculated on a decrease in earnings. Clarification of the law, issued in June, demonstrated that the effects of the new system were less severe than anticipated, and that banks which did not depend heavily on t-bills and corporate bonds would not be liable to large tax increases.

In May 1998 the Egyptian legislature adopted a law allowing the Egyptian or international private sector to invest in Egypt's four most prestigious wholly state-owned commercial banks. A similar law to privatize the four largest public insurance companies was also approved. In June 1998 the People's Assembly approved a draft law restricting private-sector shares in the state-owned banks to just 10%, in response to concerns that conflicts between multinational and Egyptian interests might arise. Total deposits in the Egyptian banking sector were recorded at £E206,000m. in 1997.

FOREIGN TRADE AND PAYMENTS

Despite careful government examination of all external payments, the pressure of population on resources is the crucial factor responsible for keeping the balance of payments in a precarious state. Although the development of the petroleum sector has alleviated the difficulties to some extent, food imports have continued to be substantial, accounting for 31% of the value of total imports in 1990 (compared with 26% in 1965), while imports of machinery and transport equipment increased from 23% in 1965 to 29% in 1988, before falling back to 23% in 1990. Exports have traditionally been agricultural goods, with raw cotton accounting for almost one-third of the value in 1977. However, by 1979 a change was apparent, with crude petroleum accounting for 30% of the exports against raw cotton's 21%. By 1982 crude petroleum accounted for 55% of exports, but this proportion had fallen to 40% by 1990, as domestic requirements outstripped production.

The external trade deficit has persisted almost without interruption since before the Second World War. In 1991/92 there was a sharp rise in Egypt's current-account surplus to about $3,737m., with income rising to some $18,779m. (including $1,727m. from tourism) while a $1,370m. fall in the value of imports (to $10,054m) helped to contain total expenditure. In 1992/93 the current-account surplus reached $4,774m. Visible export earnings totalled $3,417m. (53% of this from crude oil), while import spending totalled $10,732m. (one-fifth of this for foodstuffs), leaving a visible trade deficit of $7,315m. Income from services amounted to $9,173m. (21% of this from Suez Canal charges and 14% from tourism), while outgoings totalled $5,701m. (25% of this being interest payments and 18% repayments of principal under loan agreements). Inward private transfers, including both remittances from workers abroad and deposits attracted by high interest rates, totalled $7,260m. (almost enough to offset the visible trade deficit), while inward official transfers amounted to $1,357m.

In 1993/94 the value of visible imports totalled $10,647.1m., while the value of visible exports totalled $3,337.3m. (40.8% of this from crude oil and petroleum products), leaving a visible trade deficit of $7,309.8m. Income from services in 1993/94 was $9,004m. (22% of this from Suez Canal charges and an estimated 20% from tourism), while outgoings totalled $5,489m. (25.2% of this being interest payments), leaving a surplus of $3,515m. on services. The remaining elements in the 1993/94 payments balance were inward private transfers of $6,164m. and inward official transfers of $829m., placing the current account in overall surplus by $3,198.2m, according to the Central Bank's established calculating methods. In 1996 the Central Bank recalculated the 1993/94 payments data using revised accounting procedures (notably for private transfers) which had the effect of reducing the recorded current-account surplus for 1993/94 to $191.4m.

The 1994/95 payments statistics (calculated on the new basis) showed a visible trade deficit of $7,853.5m. (exports $4,957m., imports $12,810.5m.), a surplus of $4,286.4m. on services (payments $5,519.5m., receipts $9,805.9m.), and net inward transfers totalling $4,197.6m. (of which private transfers accounted for $3,279m.). The overall current-account surplus for 1994/95 totalled $630.5m. The value of non-oil exports showed a 68.5% rise in 1994/95, compared with a 19.6% rise in exports of crude oil and petroleum products, giving the non-oil sector a two-thirds share of Egypt's visible export earnings for 1994/95. Major export categories included textiles and garments ($1,077m.), agricultural commodities ($615.5m.) and products of the metallurgical and heavy industrial sector ($498m.). Suez Canal charges contributed 21% and tourism 23.4% of income from services in 1994/95. Interest payments accounted for 22.4% of expenditure on services, while foreign travel by Egyptians (not separately categorized in previous payments statistics) accounted for 20.5% of expenditure on services. Egypt's estimated net surplus on travel and tourism in 1994/95 was $1,169.9m. (income $2,298.9m., expenditure $1,129m.).

In 1995/96 there was a visible trade deficit of $9,233m. (exports $4,593m., imports $13,826m.), a surplus of $5,376m. on services (payments $5,023m., receipts $10,399m.), and net inward transfers totalling $3,732m. (of which private transfers accounted for $2,799m.). There was an overall current-account deficit of $125m. Suez Canal charges contributed 18.1%, and tourism 28.9%, of income from services in 1995/96. Interest payments accounted for 23.8%, and foreign travel by Egyptians for 24.9%, of expenditure on services in 1995/96. Significant trends in 1995/96 included a decline in non-oil exports (attributable mainly to problems in the textile industry), strong growth in tourism receipts resulting in a 30% rise in the net surplus on travel and tourism, and increased spending on imports of machinery and transport equipment, attributable to a rise in investment in productive sectors of the economy. The 1996/97 payments statistics showed a visible trade deficit of $9,788m. (exports $4,930m., imports $14,718m.), a surplus of $6,193m. on services (payments $5,048m., receipts $11,241m.), and net inward transfers totalling $4,145m. (of which private transfers accounted for $3,256m.). The overall current account surplus totalled $550m. Non-oil exports were valued at $2,800m. in 1997.

Negotiations were in progress between Egypt and the European Union (EU) in early 1997 for a partnership agreement within the framework of the EU's Euro-Mediterranean initiative to phase out most trade barriers between the EU and Mediterranean countries, which would be eligible for EU grants and 'soft' loans during the transition period. The EU's reluctance to move towards completely free trade in agricultural produce as well as manufactures was strongly challenged by Egypt, which emphasized that it was currently the world's twelfth largest importer of European farm produce and had in 1995 recorded a deficit of $685m. in agricultural trade with the EU (out of a deficit of $2,900m. in its overall trade with the EU). In March 1997 Egypt's negotiating demands included annual duty-free quotas of 750,000 tons of potatoes, 300,000 tons of oranges, 475,000 tons of rice and 30,000 tons of cut flowers, whereas the EU was understood to be offering import quotas of 220,000 tons of potatoes, 73,000 tons of oranges, 32,000 tons of rice and 2,000 tons of cut flowers.

TRANSPORT AND TOURISM

Egypt's principal ports are at Alexandria, Port Said and Suez. The Government is aiming to expand both the Mediterranean and Red Sea port capacities to cope with traffic passing through the Suez Canal. Alexandria port is being expanded, aided by a $95m. loan from the World Bank, and a completely new port is planned, west of Alexandria, at Dikheila, with a capacity of 20m. tons per year, compared with Alexandria's present capacity of 13m. tons. Safaga on the Red Sea is also being developed but mainly to handle mineral imports and exports. The first stage of a port situated 10 miles west of the Nile's Damietta tributary, and capable of handling up to 16m. tons of cargo per year, was opened in July 1986. A second stage will increase the port's capacity to 25m. tons per year. In 1998 the Government announced the formation of a new body, the Egyptian Company for Port Said Area Ports, to develop a huge hub port on the east bank of the bypass channel of the Suez Canal. The company will also be responsible for the construction of an industrial and storage zone in the area. Plans for the construction of a port at Sharq et-Tafrea to provide transhipments to the eastern Mediterranean, and the construction of a port to cater primarily for industrial and distribution interests in the Suez zone, were also under discussion.

River transport is being expanded to relieve the load on roads and railways for internal distribution. Navigable waterways total about 3,100 km, of which about one-half is the Nile and the rest canals. Canals such as the Nubariya canal in the delta and the Bahr Yousuf, between El-Fayoum and Asyut, make it possible to link Alexandria with Upper Egypt through Cairo.

Egypt has over 5,000 km of railway and modernization is urgently needed. A project using loans from various sources is being undertaken to modernize the railway system and expand its carrying capacity, as well as to draw up a comprehensive national transport survey. This includes modernization of the line from Cairo to Upper Egypt, for which funding of $300m. was sought from the World Bank in 1990. Earlier modernization plans have not been carried out. Plans are in hand to repair 300 km of the railway network in the south of the country and to replace all locomotives in the country with modern rolling stock. Under active consideration in late 1991 was a plan to upgrade the 160-km railway link between the Tabbia industrial zone to the south of Cairo and areas of mineral deposits in the Western Desert. Work began in mid-1995 on a project to create a rail link from Ismailia across Sinai to the town of Rafah in the Palestinian-administered Gaza Strip. Construction of the first stage of the French-designed Cairo metro system, consisting of a 42.5-km line, which runs from el-Marg in the north to Helwan in the south, began in 1982. Incorporating 33 stations, including six underground, on a 4.2-km line tunnelled beneath the centre of Cairo (the first underground transport system in the Middle East and North Africa), this section connected with an existing line to Helwan; it was completed in July 1987 (18 months later than originally planned) and was opened in September. Traffic on the metro reached a record 988,000 passengers per day in March 1993. Construction work began in 1992 on Cairo's second metro line (which will run north to the suburb of Shoubra el-Kheima, and, eventually, south to within a few hundred metres of the Greater Cairo ring road, south of Giza railway station). The second line will serve a total of 21 stations. Completion of the first section of the second metro line was scheduled for August 1996, with a further section due to open a year later and the final section provisionally scheduled to open at the start of 2000. Plans for a third line to run from Old Cairo to Imbaba were being discussed in 1998. Tender documents for the initial phase of construction of a new metro project in Alexandria were expected to be issued in late 1998. The 45-km Alexandria Metro line is to be constructed in three phases; the first stage will be a 22-km line from Abu Qir in the east to Misr Station in the west, with a capacity to carry up to 60,000 passengers an hour. The second section, an 8-km tunnel connecting Misr Station to El-Mex, is due for completion in 2010. The final section, expected to be completed in 2015, will continue west from El-Mex for a further 15km.

Good roads connect Cairo with Alexandria, the canal towns and Upper Egypt. In 1997 international companies were invited to submit proposals for the design, construction and maintenance of six major new highways running from Alexandria to Aswan and serving oases in the Western Desert. The routes concerned were Alexandria to Fayum (199 km), Fayum to Dayrout (21) km), Dayrout to Aswan (433 km), Dayrout to Al-Farafra (263 km), Al-Khârga to East Oweinat (520 km) and As-Sallum to Wadi en-Nâtrun (508 km). There were an estimated 2.2m. vehicles in Egypt in 1996, including 1,354,000 cars and 397,000 goods vehicles.

In 1998 construction work began on a 2.4-km suspension bridge over the Suez Canal, designed to relieve congestion and to improve infrastructure for repopulation and industrial purposes. The bridge is expected to be operational by 2002. The Government has also approved proposals to build two 2.6-km road tunnels beneath Old Cairo, again to facilitate the flow of traffic and to preserve the architecture in the city; the £E400m. project is expected to be completed in 2000.

EgyptAir, the state airline, operates a network of domestic and international routes. It made a profit of £E82.7m. in 1991/92, following a loss of £E257.3m. in 1990/91 because of severe problems caused by the regional security crisis. The company made a net loss of £E30.5m. in 1992/93 after experiencing a 50% fall in its Western tourist traffic which contributed to a decision in March 1993 to suspend its current five-year expansion plans. EgyptAir's existing debt in respect of past aircraft purchases amounted to $545m. in early 1993. Following a loss of £E197m. in 1993/94, EgyptAir made profits of £E10.6m. in 1994/95, £E50.9m. in 1995/96 and £E253.6m. in 1996/97. In 1997 it announced plans to increase its capital from £E800m. to £E1,500m. by transferring funds from reserves. Cairo airport handled over 7m. of the 11m. passengers who travelled through Egyptian airports in 1995. Plans were announced in 1996 to build a third passenger terminal at Cairo to increase the airport's annual handling capacity from 9m. to 20m. passengers. In November 1997 the Government announced several measures to open up the aviation sector as part of an initiative to make the transport system more effective and improve services for exporters. The Government will abolish its 10% sales tax on imported aircraft and spare parts, no longer apply customs duties on imported aircraft, permit the private sector to utilize airports for ground services, and reduce its 45% customs duty on refrigerated airfreight to 5%. The number of tourists visiting Egypt reached 1.3m. in 1986 and rose to 2.5m. in 1990, slightly above the 1989 level, but below the original target of 2.9m. because of the impact of the Gulf crisis. Revenue from tourism was about $800m. in 1984/85, and rose to about $2,500m. by 1989/90, making tourism one of the most dynamic sectors of the Egyptian economy. The management of several public-sector hotels has been transferred to international groups, legislation to reduce land speculation enacted, and the aviation industry liberalized. However, the industry is one of the most immediately vulnerable to instability in the region. An increase in terrorist activity in the Middle East during the second half of 1985 and the anti-American reaction in the region, following the bombing of Libyan cities by US forces in April 1986, combined to deter tourists, particularly Americans, from visiting Egypt. The prospect of renewed and protracted instability in the region, following the Iraqi invasion of Kuwait in August 1990 and the subsequent international response, accordingly posed a serious threat to the sector's vital contribution to Egypt's limited supplies of foreign exchange. In February 1991 tourist arrivals slumped to 57,000, compared with 208,000 in February 1990. By April 1991, however, the resolution of the Gulf crisis had led to a recovery in the number of tourist arrivals, which increased to 276,000 in August 1991 and reached the record figure of some 3m. in the 12 months to June 1992, over which period tourism's total contribution to the economy (including indirect benefits not quantified in simple balance-of-payments analyses) was officially estimated at $3,500m.

Having planned for a 1m. rise in visitor numbers in 1992/93, the tourism industry instead experienced a sharp downturn when an Islamist terrorist campaign included foreign tourists as targets. The number of tourists visiting Egypt fell by about 22% in 1993, while revenue fell by 38% because the length of the average stay was shorter. Having failed to eliminate the problem of terrorism through its campaign against militant Islamists, the Government allocated $25m. for a venture to promote tourism in 1994, with the aim of restoring revenue from this sector to its 1992 level. However, the number of visitors in the first three months of 1994 was 15% on the 1993 level, while the average length of stay was rather shorter than in 1993. Upper Egypt (hardest hit by the terrorist campaign) reported little sign of a recovery, whereas Cairo hotels had a 60% occupancy rate and most Red Sea and Sinai resorts reported some upturn in tourist business. A similar pattern was evident in the first-half of 1995, when many Upper Egypt hotels were operating at one-third of capacity, as against a two-thirds occupancy rate in Cairo and virtually full utilization of the increasingly popular Sinai resorts. Total tourist arrivals in Egypt were around 2.5m. in both 1993 and 1994, compared with an estimated 3.3m. in the peak year of 1992. In 1995 there was a 24% increase in tourist arrivals to 3.205m. (with the sharpest upturn in the last quarter of the year), followed by further growth in the first quarter of 1996. The total number of nights visitors spent in the country rose by one-third, from 15.431m. in 1994 to 20.517m. in 1995. In 1996 Egypt's tourism industry recorded very strong growth, with some 3.9m. visitors spending a total of 23.8m. nights in the country and generating revenue of around $3,000m.

In January 1993 the World Bank approved a $130m.-loan for the development of new tourism infrastructure within the framework of a $805m.-programme involving also $330m. of private-sector equity financing, $300m. of commercial bank lending, $40m. of Egyptian government funding and $5m. from the World Bank's global environment facility. The main focus of the programme was the development of new resorts on Egypt's Red Sea coast as part of a policy of diversification into the seaside holiday market. By mid-1995 work had begun on a major resort development in the Abu Soma area, while plans were well advanced for another development further up the Red Sea coast at Sahl Hashish. The Tourism Development Authority had meanwhile approved 27 new projects at locations on the south Sinai coast, where it was also inviting proposals for the development of a yacht harbour. A total of 89 tourism projects received government approval in January 1996.

Growth in the tourism industry suffered a dramatic reversal in late 1997. Fears for the safety of travellers after a terrorist attack on a German tour bus in Cairo in September, which resulted in the deaths of nine Germans and an Egyptian, were exacerbated the following month by the massacre of 58 tourists and four Egyptians in Luxor (see Recent History). Many travel companies cancelled operations to the region, while other travellers were advised to leave immediately. In response to the attacks, in December the Government inaugurated a '100-day plan' to encourage internal tourism in the region. EgyptAir, which lost 85,000 passengers owing to cancellations in the aftermath of the attack, reduced its domestic fares by 50%; the airline anticipated a loss of up to £E600m. between December 1997 and June 1998. The Government also announced a three-month moratorium on debt-service repayments by tourist ventures. In January 1998 68,000 tourists visited Egypt, 55% fewer than in January 1997. Tourism companies are presently offering discounted holidays in order to entice visitors back to the region.

Statistical Survey

Sources (unless otherwise stated): Central Agency for Public Mobilization and Statistics, POB 2086, Cairo (Nasr City); tel. (2) 604632; telex 92395; Research Department, National Bank of Egypt, Cairo.

Area and Population

AREA, POPULATION AND DENSITY

Area (sq km)	1,002,000*
Population (census results)	
17–18 November 1986†	48,254,238
31 December 1996‡	
Males	30,330,804
Females	28,941,578
Total	59,272,382
Density (per sq km) at 31 December 1996	59.2

* 386,874 sq miles. Inhabited and cultivated territory accounts for 55,039 sq km (21,251 sq miles).
† Excluding Egyptian nationals abroad, totalling an estimated 2,250,000.
‡ Preliminary results, excluding Egyptian nationals abroad, totalling an estimated 2,180,000.

GOVERNORATES (population at 1996 census*)

Governorate	Area (sq km)†	Population ('000)	Capital
Cairo	457	6,789.5	Cairo
Alexandria . . .	2,879	3,328.2	Alexandria
Port Said . . .	1,351	469.5	Port Said
Ismailia . . .	4,483	715.0	Ismailia
Suez . . .	2,500	417.6	Suez
Damietta . . .	1,029	914.6	Damietta
Dakahlia . . .	3,459	4,223.7	Mansoura
Sharkia . . .	4,190	4,287.8	Zagazig
Kalyubia . . .	1,001	3,302.9	Benha
Kafr esh-Sheikh .	3,748	2,222.9	Kafr esh-Sheikh
Gharbia . . .	1,943	3,404.8	Tanta
Menufia . . .	2,158	2,758.5	Shibin el-Kom
Behera . . .	9,504	3,981.2	Damanhur
Giza . . .	4,840	4,779.9	Giza
Beni Suef . . .	9,576	1,860.2	Beni Suef
Fayum . . .	4,949	1,989.9	Fayum
Menia . . .	2,263	3,308.9	Menia
Asyut . . .	1,558	2,802.2	Asyut
Suhag . . .	1,574	3,123.0	Suhag
Qena . . .	12,743	2,441.4	Qena
Aswan . . .	34,608	973.7	Aswan
Luxor City . .	55	360.5	Luxor
Red Sea . . .	130,000	155.7	Hurghada
El-Wadi el-Jadid .	376,505	141.7	El-Kharijah
Matruh . . .	212,000	211.9	Matruh
North Sinai . .	31,000	252.8	El-Arish
South Sinai . .	28,438	54.5	Et-Toor

* Preliminary results.
† The sum of these figures is 888,811 sq km, compared with the official national total of 1,002,000 sq km.

PRINCIPAL TOWNS (estimated population at 1 July 1992)

El-Qahira (Cairo, the capital)* . .	6,789,479	Asyut	321,000
		Zagazig	287,000
El-Iskandariyah (Alexandria)* . .	3,328,196	Ismailia	255,000
		El-Fayoum (Fayum) .	250,000
El-Giza* . . .	4,779,865	Kafr ed-Dawar . .	226,000
Shoubra el-Kheima .	834,000	Damanhur . . .	222,000
Bur Sa'id (Port Said)*	469,533	Aswan	220,000
El-Mahalla el-Koubra	408,000	El-Minya (Menia) .	208,000
Es-Suweis (Suez)* .	417,610	Beni Suef . . .	179,000
Tanta . . .	380,000	Shebin el-Kom . .	158,000
El-Mansoura . . .	371,000	Suhag	156,000

* At census of December 1996.

Source: mainly UN, *Demographic Yearbook*.

BIRTHS, MARRIAGES AND DEATHS

	Registered live births		Registered marriages		Registered deaths	
	Number	Rate (per 1,000)	Number	Rate (per 1,000)	Number	Rate (per 1,000)
1989	1,743,000	32.1	392,000	7.5	417,000	7.7
1990	1,717,000	30.9	405,000	7.6	395,000	7.1
1991	1,662,000	29.9	400,000	7.3	393,000	6.9
1992	1,521,000	26.2	397,000	7.1	385,000	6.6
1993	1,623,000	27.4	432,000	7.6	382,000	6.5
1994*	1,748,000	28.9	452,000	7.8	408,000	6.7
1995*	1,714,000	27.7	519,000	8.7	432,000	7.0
1996*	1,746,000	27.6	489,000	8.0	396,000	6.2

* Provisional figures.

Expectation of life (years at birth, 1991): males 62.86; females 66.39.

ECONOMICALLY ACTIVE POPULATION*

(sample surveys, '000 persons aged 12 to 64 years)

	1993	1994	1995
Agriculture, hunting, forestry and fishing	5,188.4	5,360.5	5,215.6
Mining and quarrying	45.4	47.3	40.7
Manufacturing	2,045.2	2,055.1	2,183.5
Electricity, gas and water	147.6	154.1	166.8
Construction	949.5	1,019.4	967.6
Trade, restaurants and hotels	1,437.0	1,561.1	1,587.7
Transport, storage and communications	806.5	843.3	907.6
Finance, insurance, real estate and business services	276.4	295.3	282.7
Community, social and personal services	3,805.4	3,903.1	3,990.8
Activities not adequately defined	1.9	2.1	1.2
Total employed	14,703.4	15,241.4	15,344.2
Unemployed	1,800.6	1,877.4	1,917.0
Total labour force	16,504.0	17,118.8	17,261.2
Males	12,718.6	13,107.3	13,393.2
Females	3,785.4	4,011.5	3,868.0

* Figures for each year represent the average of two surveys, conducted in May and November.

Agriculture

PRINCIPAL CROPS ('000 metric tons)

	1994	1995	1996
Wheat	4,437	5,722	5,735
Rice (paddy)	4,583	4,888	4,895
Barley	129	368	120
Maize	5,112	5,115	5,165
Sorghum	731	769	604
Potatoes	1,325	2,599	1,133
Sweet potatoes	152	165	114
Taro (Coco yam)*	115	120	125
Dry broad beans	357	392	442
Other pulses	65	69	64
Soybeans (Soya beans)	67	64	40
Groundnuts (in shell)	117	131	125
Sunflower seed	51	68	69*
Cottonseed	411	380	540†
Cotton (lint)†	255	237	350
Olives	130	208	210*
Cabbages	496	477	354
Tomatoes	5,011	5,034	5,038
Cauliflowers*	76	78	80
Pumpkins, squash and gourds*	305	310	315
Cucumbers and gherkins*	248	250	253
Aubergines*	345	350	355
Green chillies and peppers*	192	198	200
Onions (dry)	481	574	448
Garlic	105†	119†	120*
Green beans*	107	108	109
Green peas*	105	106	107

— continued	1994	1995	1996
Carrots	118	131	101
Other vegetables	681	691	697
Watermelons*	716	720	730
Melons*	450	460	470
Grapes	707	739	740*
Dates	646	678	680*
Sugar cane	13,822	13,827	14,105
Sugar beets	825	920	842
Apples	313	438	455*
Pears*	90	93	95
Peaches and nectarines*	58	58	60
Oranges	1,513	1,555	1,608†
Tangerines, mandarins, clementines and satsumas	250	471	475*
Lemons and limes	296	308	330*
Mangoes	180	232	240*
Bananas	459	499	500*
Other fruits and berries	559	564	570

* FAO estimate(s).   † Unofficial figure(s).

Source: FAO, *Production Yearbook*.

LIVESTOCK ('000 head, year ending September)

	1994	1995	1996
Cattle	2,750*	2,700†	2,700†
Buffaloes	2,850*	2,800†	2,800†
Sheep*	4,000	3,648	3,491
Goats	3,100*	3,210†	3,250†
Pigs	27	27†	27†
Horses†	10	11	11
Asses†	1,650	1,680	1,690
Camels	133	133†	135†

Chickens (million): 38 in 1994; 40† in 1995; 42† in 1996.
Ducks (FAO estimates, million): 8 in 1994; 8 in 1995; 9 in 1996.

* Unofficial figure(s).   † FAO estimate(s).

Source: FAO, *Production Yearbook*.

LIVESTOCK PRODUCTS ('000 metric tons)

	1994	1995	1996
Beef and veal*	170	168	163
Buffalo meat*	160	153	150
Mutton and lamb*	63	58	55
Goat meat*	42	43	44
Pig meat*	3	3	3
Poultry meat	383	409	429
Other meat*	89	90	92
Cows' milk	999	1,000	1,000*
Buffaloes' milk*	1,580	1,590	1,600
Sheep's milk*	16	16	16
Goats' milk*	43	43	44
Butter and ghee*	82	82	82
Cheese*	341	349	349
Hen eggs	154†	158†	160*
Honey*	10	10	11
Wool: greasy*	2	2	2
Cattle and buffalo hides*	38	37	37
Sheepskins*	8	7	7
Goatskins*	6	6	6

* FAO estimate(s).   † Unofficial figure.

Source: FAO, mainly *Production Yearbook*.

Forestry

ROUNDWOOD REMOVALS

('000 cubic metres, excluding bark)

	1993	1994	1995
Industrial wood	120	123	125
Fuel wood	2,467	2,520	2,573
Total	2,587	2,643	2,698

Source: FAO, *Yearbook of Forest Products*.

Fishing

('000 metric tons, live weight)

	1993	1994	1995
Common carp	22.4	20.1	30.9
Nile tilapia	117.5	121.0	122.2
Mudfish	23.9	21.1	19.6
Other freshwater fishes	18.1	32.3	20.7
Flathead grey mullet	14.0	14.1	24.5
Jacks and crevalles	14.4	11.8	1.8
Sardinellas	14.4	11.1	11.9
Other marine fishes	68.8	63.0	66.4
Total fish	293.5	294.7	298.0
Crustaceans and molluscs	9.3	11.1	11.6
Total catch	302.8	305.7	309.6
Inland waters	207.5	220.3	226.2
Mediterranean and Black Sea	44.6	41.5	44.5
Indian Ocean	50.7	43.9	38.9

Source: FAO, *Yearbook of Fishery Statistics*.

Mining

('000 metric tons, year ending 30 June)

	1993/94	1994/95	1995/96
Crude petroleum	45,000	44,000	44,000
Iron ore*	2,703	2,433	2,098
Salt (unrefined)	1,116	1,193	1,632
Phosphate rock	864	1,044	1,238
Gypsum (crude)	1,481	2,361	2,092
Kaolin	195	233	293

* Figures refer to gross weight. The estimated iron content is 50%.

Natural gas (estimates, petajoules): 376 in 1993; 411 in 1994; 530 in 1995 (Source: UN, *Industrial Commodity Statistics Yearbook*).

Industry

SELECTED PRODUCTS ('000 metric tons, unless otherwise indicated)

	1993	1994	1995
Wheat flour	3,352	3,662	3,767
Raw sugar*	1,093	1,190	1,132
Cottonseed oil (refined)	329	318	305
Beer ('000 hectolitres)	350	360	360
Cigarettes (million)	38,844	39,145	42,469
Cotton yarn (pure)†	253.9	251.0	250.3
Jute yarn	21.6	20.8	19.8
Jute fabrics	18.2	16.6	19.3
Wool yarn	19.2	15.2	14.1
Paper and paperboard*	220	219	221
Rubber tyres and tubes ('000)‡	3,368	3,858	3,690
Sulphuric acid (100%)	122	112	113
Caustic soda (Sodium hydroxide)	59	49	48
Nitrogenous fertilizers§	5,588	5,918	6,136
Phosphate fertilizers‖	689	765	913
Motor spirit (petrol)	4,073	4,356	4,520
Kerosene	1,930	1,405	1,169
Distillate fuel oils	4,747	5,246	5,792
Residual fuel oil (Mazout)	11,735	12,071	12,044
Petroleum bitumen (asphalt)	617	683	740
Cement	12,576	13,554	14,237
Pig-iron	92	109	69
Radio receivers ('000)	13	52	n.a.
Television receivers ('000)	269	234	243
Passenger motor cars—assembly (number)	4,000	6,000	9,000
Electric energy (million kWh)	47,470	47,920	48,864

* Data from the FAO.

† Figures refer to the year ending 30 June.

‡ Tyres and inner tubes for road motor vehicles (including motorcycles) and bicycles.

§ Production in terms of nitrogen.

‖ Production in terms of phosphoric acid.

Source: mainly UN, *Industrial Commodity Statistics Yearbook*.

Finance

CURRENCY AND EXCHANGE RATES

Monetary Units

1,000 millièmes = 100 piastres = 5 tallaris = 1 Egyptian pound (£E).

Sterling and Dollar Equivalents (31 May 1998)

£1 sterling = £E5.525;

US $1 = £E3.388;

£E100 = £18.10 sterling = $29.52.

Note: From February 1991 foreign exchange transactions were conducted through only two markets, the primary market and the free market. With effect from 8 October 1991, the primary market was eliminated, and all foreign exchange transactions are effected through the free market. For external trade purposes, the average value of the Egyptian pound was 29.53 US cents in 1994, 29.48 US cents in 1995 and 29.49 US cents in 1996.

STATE PUBLIC BUDGET (£E million, year ending 30 June)

Revenue	1993/94	1994/95	1995/96*
Current revenue	49,418	52,925	57,708
Central Government	46,384	49,889	54,486
Tax revenue	31,373	34,279	38,249
Taxes on income and profits	12,003	12,134	13,707
Domestic taxes on goods and services	8,080	9,333	10,450
Customs duties	6,120	7,017	7,911
Stamp duties	2,657	2,874	3,074
Other current revenue	15,011	15,610	16,237
Profit transfers	9,070	10,542	11,133
Petroleum Authority	4,610	4,443	4,717
Suez Canal Authority	2,610	3,132	3,015
Central Bank of Egypt	1,200	2,072	2,318
Local government	1,984	1,951	2,125
Service authorities	1,050	1,085	1,097
Capital revenue	3,149	2,794	3,185
Total	52,567	55,719	60,893

Expenditure	1993/94	1994/95	1995/96*
Current expenditure	46,097	47,632	51,967
Wages	11,096	12,519	14,045
Pensions	3,914	4,146	4,256
Goods and services	2,857	2,986	3,214
Defence	5,873	6,410	6,954
Public debt interest	16,498	14,790	16,027
Local	11,816	11,177	12,231
Foreign	4,682	3,613	3,796
Subsidies	3,265	3,818	4,331
Capital expenditure (net)	10,167	10,624	11,922
Total	56,264	58,256	63,889

* Figures are provisional.

1996/97 (estimates, £E million, year ending 30 June): Revenue 65,300 (current 61,700, capital 3,600); Expenditure 68,100 (current 54,700, capital 13,400).

1997/98 (projections, £E million, year ending 30 June): Revenue 76,398 (current 70,107, capital 6,290); Expenditure 83,236 (current 64,993, capital 18,243).

INTERNATIONAL RESERVES (US $ million at 31 December)

	1995	1996	1997
Gold*	704	695	609
IMF special drawing rights	103	123	113
Reserve position in IMF	80	77	73
Foreign exchange	15,998	17,198	18,479
Total	16,885	18,093	19,274

* Valued at market-related prices.

Source: IMF, *International Financial Statistics*.

MONEY SUPPLY (£E million at 31 December)

	1995	1996	1997
Currency outside banks . . .	22,750	24,954	28,215
Demand deposits at deposit money banks	17,282	18,026	18,920
Total money (incl. others) . .	41,540	44,521	48,708

Source: IMF, *International Financial Statistics.*

COST OF LIVING (Consumer Price Index; base: 1990 = 100)

	1994	1995	1996
Food*	148.7	164.0	176.5
Clothing	188.2	194.4	208.4
Rent, fuel and light . . .	146.2	157.8	162.1
All items (incl. others) . .	165.0	178.7	191.6

* Including tobacco.

Source: ILO, *Yearbook of Labour Statistics.*

1997: All items 200.4 (Source: UN, *Monthly Bulletin of Statistics*).

NATIONAL ACCOUNTS
(£E million, year ending 30 June)

Expenditure on the Gross Domestic Product (at current prices)

	1994/95	1995/96	1996/97
Government final consumption expenditure	21,500	23,600	26,100
Private final consumption expenditure	148,900	171,700	189,400
Increase in stocks . . .	700	1,550	1,200
Gross fixed capital formation .	38,600	42,100	50,200
Total domestic expenditure	209,700	238,950	266,900
Exports of goods and services .	45,100	48,450	52,700
Less Imports of goods and services	49,800	59,100	63,800
GDP in purchasers' values .	205,000	228,300	255,800

Source: IMF, *International Financial Statistics.*

Gross Domestic Product by Economic Activity
(at constant 1991/92 factor cost)

	1993/94	1994/95	1995/96
Agriculture, hunting, forestry and fishing	23,072	23,741	24,470
Mining and quarrying . . } Manufacturing . . . . }	37,640	39,452	41,335
Electricity	2,382	2,525	2,658
Construction	7,079	7,485	7,898
Trade, restaurants and hotels .	25,315	26,929	28,545
Transport and communications .	15,112	15,422	16,116
Finance, insurance and real estate	7,733	8,239	8,832
Government services . . .	10,120	10,565	11,039
Other services	11,169	11,791	12,476
Total	139,622	146,149	153,369

BALANCE OF PAYMENTS (US $ million)

	1994	1995	1996
Exports of goods f.o.b. . . .	4,044	4,670	4,779
Imports of goods f.o.b. . . .	−9,997	−12,267	−13,169
Trade balance	−5,953	−7,597	−8,390
Exports of services . . .	8,070	8,590	9,271
Imports of services . . .	−5,645	−4,873	−5,084
Balance on goods and services	−3,528	−3,880	−4,023
Other income received . .	1,330	1,578	1,901
Other income paid . . .	−2,114	−1,983	−1,556
Balance on goods, services and income	−4,312	−4,285	−3,858
Current transfers received . .	4,622	4,284	3,888
Current transfers paid . .	−279	−253	−222
Current balance . . .	31	−254	−192
Direct investment abroad . .	−43	−93	−5
Direct investment from abroad .	1,256	598	636
Portfolio investment liabilities .	3	20	545
Other investment assets . .	−905	−396	−565
Other investment liabilities . .	−1,761	−1,974	−2,070
Net errors and omissions . .	255	272	−74
Overall balance	−1,164	−1,827	−1,725

Source: IMF, *International Financial Statistics.*

External Trade

Note: Figures exclude trade in military goods.

PRINCIPAL COMMODITIES (distribution by SITC, US $ million)

Imports c.i.f.	1994	1995	1996
Food and live animals . . .	2,263.3	2,611.7	3,056.6
Cereals and cereal preparations .	1,126.6	1,299.2	1,705.1
Wheat and meslin (unmilled) .	766.6	875.7	1,231.3
Maize (unmilled) . . .	263.8	349.3	435.2
Crude materials (inedible) except fuels	716.3	1,059.3	1,142.4
Cork and wood	377.4	551.0	501.9
Simply worked wood and railway sleepers	344.8	522.3	452.3
Simply worked coniferous wood	256.2	445.6	346.5
Sawn coniferous wood . .	256.1	445.6	346.5
Animal and vegetable oils, fats and waxes	193.4	510.3	512.8
Fixed vegetable oils and fats . .	172.4	466.7	481.7
Chemicals and related products	1,154.5	1,550.8	1,617.0
Organic chemicals	190.7	289.1	277.1
Artificial resins, plastic materials, etc.	358.3	448.4	496.2
Products of polymerization, etc.	288.3	72.4	33.0
Basic manufactures . . .	1,821.4	2,360.3	2,580.6
Paper, paperboard and manufactures	282.6	530.1	406.6
Paper and paperboard (not cut to size or shape) . . .	261.8	504.3	367.5
Textile yarn, fabrics, etc. . .	242.3	279.7	288.8
Iron and steel	546.1	777.5	1,007.5
Machinery and transport equipment	2,784.3	2,967.8	3,313.1
Machinery specialized for particular industries . .	439.1	481.4	613.4
General industrial machinery, equipment and parts . . .	657.5	790.6	846.0
Telecommunications and sound equipment	201.4	212.0	237.8
Other electrical machinery, apparatus, etc. . . .	444.7	96.3	97.4
Road vehicles and parts* . .	667.3	623.2	598.2
Passenger motor cars (excl. buses)	213.5	216.7	201.1
Parts and accessories for cars, buses, lorries, etc.* . . .	228.1	228.4	201.5
Miscellaneous manufactured articles	370.6	392.1	427.7
Total (incl. others) . . .	9,592.1	11,738.8	13,012.1

* Excluding tyres, engines and electrical parts.

Exports f.o.b.	1994	1995	1996
Food and live animals . . .	266.3	324.2	359.2
Cereals and cereal preparations .	86.0	60.3	122.7
Rice	79.2	56.7	117.7
Vegetables and fruit . . .	121.0	206.8	169.9
Fresh or simply preserved vegetables . . .	75.5	152.7	120.6
Crude materials (inedible) except fuels	305.2	241.3	180.0
Textile fibres (excl. wool tops) and waste	250.4	169.4	102.4
Cotton	237.6	157.8	92.3
Raw cotton (excl. linters) . .	233.8	152.2	91.8
Mineral fuels, lubricants, etc.	1,360.9	1,282.9	1,681.1
Petroleum, petroleum products, etc.	1,321.2	1,231.7	1,633.9
Crude petroleum oils, etc. .	793.4	719.2	861.1
Refined petroleum products .	503.8	496.3	809.6
Residual fuel oils . .	486.7	16.3	8.1
Chemicals and related products	159.3	201.4	176.5
Basic manufactures . .	1,047.4	1,033.2	785.4
Textile yarn, fabrics, etc. . .	619.2	570.1	425.3
Textile yarn . . .	387.1	322.2	204.0
Cotton yarn . . .	378.1	304.8	192.5
Woven cotton fabrics (excl. narrow or special fabrics) .	121.3	109.2	88.7
Unbleached fabrics (not mercerized) . . .	111.7	105.9	83.8
Iron and steel . . .	134.8	159.8	68.8
Non-ferrous metals . . .	168.3	199.8	157.4
Aluminium and aluminium alloys	167.3	149.7	164.7
Worked aluminium and alloys	139.4	47.8	20.3
Aluminium bars, wire, etc.	125.6	9.2	6.7
Other metal manufactures .	70.7	47.5	44.0
Miscellaneous manufactured articles	305.4	331.4	325.9
Clothing and accessories (excl. footwear) . . .	230.7	252.5	239.2
Men's and boys' outer garments of non-knitted textile fabrics .	25.8	94.2	91.1
Knitted or crocheted undergarments (incl. foundation garments of non-knitted fabrics) . . .	73.0	4.9	8.2
Cotton undergarments, non-elastic	72.9	n.a.	n.a.
Total (incl. others) . . .	3,474.5	3,444.1	3,532.5

PRINCIPAL TRADING PARTNERS
(countries of consignment, US $ million)

Imports c.i.f.	1994	1995	1996
Argentina	93.5	115.1	237.5
Australia	403.3	82.4	386.0
Belgium-Luxembourg . .	214.6	236.8	211.8
Brazil	158.2	189.9	265.5
China, People's Repub. . .	194.5	295.9	283.4
Denmark	96.3	95.0	94.1
Finland	135.7	183.0	166.3
France (incl. Monaco) . .	592.6	685.2	576.6
Germany	913.9	1,044.6	1,088.6
India	123.9	170.6	184.3
Ireland	200.3	217.9	131.7
Italy	614.0	731.1	870.4
Japan	401.2	314.0	344.7
Korea, Republic . . .	107.1	2.0	0.2
Malaysia	93.7	220.4	240.9
Netherlands	285.7	381.4	363.3
Romania	121.5	160.4	197.0
Russia	273.9	405.3	370.5
Saudi Arabia . . .	194.2	249.0	290.4
Spain	143.1	184.4	210.7
Sweden	157.6	259.6	306.5
Switzerland-Liechtenstein .	211.6	311.9	333.9
Turkey	143.4	179.6	352.7
United Kingdom . . .	349.8	379.8	441.1
USA	1,616.9	2,211.0	2,607.2
Total (incl. others) . . .	9,592.0	11,738.8	13,012.1

Exports f.o.b.	1994	1995	1996
Belgium-Luxembourg . . .	71.3	110.4	50.5
France (incl. Monaco) . . .	138.3	144.2	144.0
Germany	209.8	207.0	162.8
Greece	117.2	137.3	142.3
India	66.1	53.0	14.1
Israel	188.3	173.6	343.4
Italy	426.7	458.8	438.1
Japan	49.8	43.7	41.3
Jordan	21.0	30.9	44.6
Korea, Republic . . .	106.3	0.0	0.2
Lebanon	35.1	43.4	33.0
Libya	44.1	52.9	51.7
Netherlands	207.2	166.7	364.6
Romania	43.4	41.3	36.9
Russia	41.0	31.9	37.7
Saudi Arabia . . .	155.1	113.1	122.7
Singapore	146.7	92.8	90.0
Spain	149.1	157.1	98.2
Syria	57.5	56.1	55.0
Turkey	71.5	82.7	115.2
United Arab Emirates . .	40.8	41.0	44.4
United Kingdom . . .	144.0	142.4	165.3
USA	364.6	521.8	459.7
Total (incl. others) . . .	3,474.5	3,444.1	3,532.5

Source: UN, *International Trade Statistics Yearbook.*

Transport

RAILWAYS (traffic, year ending 30 June)

	1993/94	1994/95	1995/96
Passenger-km (million) . . .	46,721	48,243	50,665

1993/94: Freight ton-km (million): 3,621 (Source: UN, *Statistical Yearbook*).

ROAD TRAFFIC (motor vehicles in use at 31 December)

	1994	1995*	1996*
Passenger cars	1,228,606	1,280,000	1,354,000
Buses and coaches . . .	37,231	36,630	37,620
Lorries and vans	408,691	387,000	397,000
Motorcycles and mopeds . .	383,592	397,000	418,000

* Estimates.

Source: IRF, *World Road Statistics*.

SHIPPING
Merchant Fleet (registered at 31 December)

	1994	1995	1996
Number of vessels . . .	393	385	375
Displacement ('000 grt) . . .	1,262	1,269	1,230

Source: Lloyd's Register of Shipping, *World Fleet Statistics*.

Suez Canal Traffic

	1995	1996	1997
Transits (number)	15,051	14,731	14,430
Displacement ('000 net tons) .	360,372	354,974	368,720
Northbound goods traffic ('000 metric tons)	144,024	136,092	144,448
Southbound goods traffic ('000 metric tons)	149,100	145,923	151,456
Net tonnage of tankers ('000) .	96,930	80,895	78,012

Source: Suez Canal Authority.

CIVIL AVIATION (traffic on scheduled services)

	1993	1994	1995
Kilometres flown (million) . .	44	54	55
Passengers carried ('000) . . .	2,881	3,538	3,897
Passenger-km (million) . . .	5,277	6,324	7,678
Total ton-km (million) . .	606	763	864

Source: UN, *Statistical Yearbook*.

Tourism

	1993	1994	1995
Tourist arrivals ('000) . . .	2,291	2,356	2,872
Tourist receipts (US $ million) .	1,332	1,384	2,700

UN, *Statistical Yearbook*.

Communications Media

	1993	1994	1995
Radio receivers ('000 in use) . .	18,500	18,950	19,400
Television receivers ('000 in use) .	n.a.	6,700	6,850
Daily newspapers:			
Number	n.a.	17	14
Average circulation ('000 copies)	n.a.	3,949	2,600*
Telephones ('000 main lines in use)†	2,235	2,456	2,716
Telefax stations (number in use) .	17,608	21,591	n.a.
Mobile cellular telephones			
(subscribers)	6,877	7,371	7,368

* Estimate.
† Year ending 30 June.
Sources: UNESCO, *Statistical Yearbook*; UN, *Statistical Yearbook*.

Education

(1995/96, unless otherwise indicated)

	Schools	Teachers	Students
Pre-primary	2,060	10,913	266,502
Primary*	16,188	302,916	7,470,437
Secondary:			
General*	205,519†	235,313	4,242,245
Vocational	n.a.	133,794	1,900,406

* Excluding Al-Azhar education.   † 1994/95.

Higher Education (excl. private institutions): *Universities and equivalent* (excl. Al-Azhar University): Teachers 38,828 in 1993/94; Students 620,145 in 1993/94, 696,988 in 1994/95. *Other institutions:* Students 107,737 in 1990/91.

Source: mainly UNESCO, *Statistical Yearbook*.

Directory

The Constitution

A new Constitution for the Arab Republic of Egypt was approved by referendum on 11 September 1971.

THE STATE

Egypt is an Arab Republic with a democratic, socialist system based on the alliance of the working people and derived from the country's historical heritage and the spirit of Islam.

The Egyptian people are part of the Arab nation, who work towards total Arab unity.

Islam is the religion of the State; Arabic is its official language and the Islamic code is a principal source of legislation. The State safeguards the freedom of worship and of performing rites for all religions.

Sovereignty is of the people alone which is the source of all powers.

The protection, consolidation and preservation of the socialist gains is a national duty: the sovereignty of law is the basis of the country's rule, and the independence of immunity of the judiciary are basic guarantees for the protection of rights and liberties.

THE FUNDAMENTAL ELEMENTS OF SOCIETY

Social solidarity is the basis of Egyptian society, and the family is its nucleus.

The State ensures the equality of men and women in both political and social rights in line with the provisions of Muslim legislation.

Work is a right, an honour and a duty which the State guarantees together with the services of social and health insurance, pensions for incapacity and unemployment.

The economic basis of the Republic is a socialist democratic system based on sufficiency and justice in a manner preventing exploitation.

Ownership is of three kinds: public, co-operative and private. The public sector assumes the main responsibility for the regulation and growth of the national economy under the development plan.

Property is subject to the people's control.

Private ownership is safeguarded and may not be sequestrated except in cases specified in law nor expropriated except for the general good against fair legal compensation. The right of inheritance is guaranteed in it.

Nationalization shall only be allowed for considerations of public interest in accordance with the law and against compensation.

Agricultural holding may be limited by law.

The State follows a comprehensive central planning and compulsory planning approach based on quinquennial socio-economic and cultural development plans whereby the society's resources are mobilized and put to the best use.

The public sector assumes the leading role in the development of the national economy. The State provides absolute protection of this sector as well as the property of co-operative societies and trade unions against all attempts to tamper with them.

PUBLIC LIBERTIES, RIGHTS AND DUTIES

All citizens are equal before the law. Personal liberty is a natural right and no one may be arrested, searched, imprisoned or restricted in any way without a court order.

Houses have sanctity, and shall not be placed under surveillance or searched without a court order with reasons given for such action.

The law safeguards the sanctities of the private lives of all citizens; so have all postal, telegraphic, telephonic and other means of communication which may not therefore be confiscated, or perused except by a court order giving the reasons, and only for a specified period.

Public rights and freedoms are also inviolate and all calls for atheism and anything that reflects adversely on divine religions are prohibited.

The freedom of opinion, the Press, printing and publications and all information media are safeguarded.

Press censorship is forbidden, so are warnings, suspensions or cancellations through administrative channels. Under exceptional circumstances, as in cases of emergency or in war time, censorship may be imposed on information media for a definite period.

Egyptians have the right to permanent or provisional emigration and no Egyptian may be deported or prevented from returning to the country.

Citizens have the right to private meetings in peace provided they bear no arms. Egyptians also have the right to form societies which have no secret activities. Public meetings are also allowed within the limits of the law.

SOVEREIGNTY OF THE LAW

All acts of crime should be specified together with the penalties for the acts.

Recourse to justice is a right of all citizens. Those who are financially unable will be assured of means to defend their rights.

Except in cases of *flagrante delicto*, no person may be arrested or their freedom restricted unless an order authorizing arrest has been given by the competent judge or the public prosecution in accordance with the provisions of law.

SYSTEM OF GOVERNMENT

The President, who must be of Egyptian parentage and at least 40 years old, is nominated by at least one-third of the members of the People's Assembly, approved by at least two-thirds, and elected by popular referendum. His term is for six years and he 'may be re-elected for another subsequent term'. He may take emergency measures in the interests of the State but these measures must be approved by referendum within 60 days.

The People's Assembly, elected for five years, is the legislative body and approves general policy, the budget and the development plan. It shall have 'not less than 350' elected members, at least half of whom shall be workers or farmers, and the President may appoint up to 10 additional members. In exceptional circumstances the Assembly, by a two-thirds vote, may authorize the President to rule by decree for a specified period but these decrees must be approved by the Assembly at its next meeting. The law governing the composition of the People's Assembly was amended in May 1979 (see People's Assembly, below).

The Assembly may pass a vote of no confidence in a Deputy Prime Minister, a Minister or a Deputy Minister, provided three days' notice of the vote is given, and the Minister must then resign. In the case of the Prime Minister, the Assembly may 'prescribe' his responsibility and submit a report to the President: if the President disagrees with the report but the Assembly persists, then the matter is put to a referendum: if the people support the President the Assembly is dissolved; if they support the Assembly the President must accept the resignation of the Government. The President may dissolve the Assembly prematurely, but his action must be approved by a referendum and elections must be held within 60 days.

Executive Authority is vested in the President, who may appoint one or more Vice-Presidents and appoints all Ministers. He may also dismiss the Vice-Presidents and Ministers. The President has 'the right to refer to the people in connection with important matters related to the country's higher interests.' The Government is described as 'the supreme executive and administrative organ of the state'. Its members, whether full Ministers or Deputy Ministers, must be at least 35 years old. Further sections define the roles of Local Government, Specialized National Councils, the Judiciary, the Higher Constitutional Court, the Socialist Prosecutor General, the Armed Forces and National Defence Council and the Police.

POLITICAL PARTIES

In June 1977 the People's Assembly adopted a new law on political parties, which, subject to certain conditions, permitted the formation of political parties for the first time since 1953. The law was passed in accordance with Article Five of the Constitution which describes the political system as 'a multi-party one' with four main parties: 'the ruling National Democratic Party, the Socialist Workers (the official opposition), the Liberal Socialists and the Unionist Progressive'. (The legality of the re-formed New Wafd Party was established by the courts in January 1984.)

1980 AMENDMENTS

On 30 April 1980 the People's Assembly passed a number of amendments, which were subsequently massively approved at a referendum the following month. A summary of the amendments follows:

(i) the regime in Egypt is socialist-democratic, based on the alliance of working people's forces.

(ii) the political system depends on multiple political parties; the Arab Socialist Union is therefore abolished.

(iii) the President is elected for a six-year term and can be elected for 'other terms'.

(iv) the President shall appoint a Consultative Council to preserve the principles of the revolutions of 23 July 1952 and 15 May 1971.

(v) a Supreme Press Council shall safeguard the freedom of the press, check government censorship and look after the interests of journalists.

(vi) Egypt's adherence to Islamic jurisprudence is affirmed. Christians and Jews are subject to their own jurisdiction in personal status affairs.

(vii) there will be no distinction of race or religion.

The Government

THE PRESIDENCY

President: MUHAMMAD HOSNI MUBARAK (confirmed as President by referendum, 13 October 1981, after assassination of President Sadat; re-elected and confirmed by referendum, 5 October 1987 and 4 October 1993).

COUNCIL OF MINISTERS

(September 1998)

Prime Minister and Minister for Planning and International Co-operation: Dr KAMAL AHMAD AL-GANZOURI.

Deputy Prime Minister and Minister of Agriculture and Land Reclamation: Dr YOUSUF AMIN WALI.

Minister of Transport and Communications: Eng. SULAYMAN MUTAWALLI SULAYMAN.

Minister of Defence: Field Marshal MUHAMMAD HUSSAIN TANTAWI.

Minister of Electricity and Energy: Eng. MUHAMMAD MAHER ABAZAH.

Minister of Information: MUHAMMAD SAFWAT MUHAMMAD YOUSUF ASH-SHARIF.

Minister of Foreign Affairs: AMR MUHAMMAD MOUSSA.

Minister of Supply and Trade: AHMAD GUEILY.

Minister of Finance: MOHIEDDIN EL-GHARIB.

Minister of Awqaf (Islamic Endowments): MAHMOUD HAMDI ZAK-ZOUK.

Minister of Justice: FAROUK MAHMOUD SAYF AN-NASR.

Minister of Culture: FAROUK ABD AL-AZIZ HOSNI.

Minister of Cabinet Affairs and Monitoring: TALAAT SAID AHMAD HAMMAD.

Minister of Rural Development: MAHMOUD SAYED AHMAD SHARIF.

Minister of Education: HUSSAIN KAMAL BAHAEDDIN.

Minister of Petroleum: Dr Eng. HAMDY AL-BANBI.

Minister of the Interior: HABIB IBRAHIM EL-ADLI.

Minister of Housing, Utilities and New Communities: Dr Eng. MUHAMMAD IBRAHIM SULAYMAN.

Minister of Tourism: Dr MAMDOUH EL-BELTAGI.

Minister of Economy: YOUSUF BOUTROS-GHALI.

Minister of Public Works and Water Resources: Dr MAHMOUD ABD AL-HALIM ABU ZEID.

Minister of Health and Population: ISMAIL AWADALLAH SALAM.

Minister of Higher Education and Minister of State for Scientific Research: Dr MUFID MAHMOUD SHEHAB.

Minister of Industry and Mineral Resources: SULAYMAN REDA.

Minister of Labour and Migration: AHMAD AHMAD EL-AMAWI.

Minister of Insurance and Social Affairs: MERVAT MIHANNA TALAWI.

Minister of the Public Enterprise Sector: Dr ATIF MUHAMMAD OBEID.

Minister of State for Parliamentary Affairs: KAMAL SHAZLI.

Minister of State for Administrative Development: MAHMOUD ABU AMER.

Minister of State for Military Production: Dr Eng. MUHAMMAD EL-GHAMRAWI DAWOUD.

Minister of State for Environment: NADIA MAKRAM OBEID.

Minister of State for Planning and International Co-operation: ZAFER SALIM EL-BESHRY.

MINISTRIES

Ministry of Agriculture and Land Reclamation: Sharia Wizaret az-Ziraa, Dokki, Giza; tel. (2) 702677; telex 93006.

Ministry of Awqaf (Islamic Endowments): Sharia Sabri Abu Alam, Ean el-Luk, Cairo; tel. (2) 3929402; fax 3900362; e-mail mawkaf@idsc1.gov.eg.

Ministry of Cabinet Affairs and Monitoring: Sharia Majlis ash-Sha'ab, Cairo; tel. (2) 3558037; fax (2) 3542612; e-mail cabinet1@idsc.gov.eg.

Ministry of Civil Aviation: Sharia Matar, Cairo (Heliopolis); tel. (2) 969555.

Ministry of Culture: Sharia Shagaret ed-Dor, Cairo (Zamalek); tel. (2) 3402195; fax (2) 3406449; e-mail mculture@idsc.gov.eg.

Ministry of Defence: 5 Sharia Ismail Abaza, Qasr el-Eini, Cairo; tel. (2) 2602556; telex 92167; fax (2) 2916227; e-mail mod@idsc1.gov.eg.

Ministry of Economy: 8 Sharia Adly, Cairo; tel. (2) 3935147; fax (2) 3908159; e-mail mineco@idsc.gov.eg.

Ministry of Education: 4 Sharia Ibrahim Nagiv, Cairo (Garden City); tel. (2) 5787643; fax (2) 3562952; e-mail moe@idsc.gov.eg.

Ministry of Electricity and Energy: Sharia Ramses, Cairo (Nasr City); tel. (2) 2616317; fax (2) 2616302; e-mail mee@idsc.gov.eg.

Ministry of Finance: Sharia Majlis ash-Sha'ab, Lazoughli Sq., Cairo; tel. (2) 3541055; telex 22386; fax (2) 3563899; e-mail mofinance@idsc1.gov.eg.

Ministry of Foreign Affairs: Corniche en-Nil, Cairo (Maspiro); tel. (2) 5749816; telex 92220; fax (2) 5749533; e-mail minexter@idsc1.gov.eg.

Ministry of Health and Population: Sharia Majlis ash-Sha'ab, Lazoughli Sq., Cairo; tel. (2) 3541507; telex 94107; fax (2) 3553966; e-mail moh@idsc.gov.eg.

Ministry of Higher Education and Scientific Research: Sharia Qasr el-Eini, Cairo; tel. (2) 3557952; fax (2) 3558609; e-mail mheducat@idsc.gov.eg.

Ministry of Housing, Utilities and New Communities: 1 Ismail Abaza, Qasr el-Eini, Cairo; tel. (2) 3553468; fax (2) 3557836; e-mail mhuuc@idsc1.gov.eg.

Ministry of Industry and Mineral Resources: 2 Sharia Latin America, Cairo (Garden City); tel. (2) 3557034; telex 93112; fax (2) 3553966; e-mail moimw@idsc1.gov.eg.

Ministry of Information: Radio and TV Bldg, Corniche en-Nil, Cairo (Maspiro); tel. (2) 5748984; fax (2) 5748981; e-mail rtu@idsc.gov.eg.

Ministry of Insurance and Social Affairs: Sharia Sheikh Rihan, Cairo; tel. (2) 3370039; fax (2) 3375390; e-mail msi@idsc.gov.eg.

Ministry of the Interior: Sharia Sheikh Rihan, Cairo; tel. (2) 3557500; fax (2) 5792031; e-mail moi2@idsc.gov.eg.

Ministry of Justice: Justice Bldg, Lazoughli Sq., Cairo; tel. (2) 3551176; fax (2) 3555700; e-mail mojeb@idsc1.gov.eg.

Ministry of Labour and Migration: 3 Sharia Yousuf Abbas, Abbassia, Cairo (Nasr City); tel. (2) 2606018; fax (2) 2609891; e-mail mwlabor@idsc1.gov.eg.

Ministry of Maritime Transport: 4 Sharia Ptolemy, Alexandria; tel. (3) 4842119; telex 54142; fax (3) 4842096.

Ministry of Petroleum: Sharia el-Mokhayem ed-Dayem, Cairo (Nasr City); tel. (2) 2631000; telex 92197; fax (2) 2636060; e-mail mopm@idsc1.gov.eg.

Ministry of Planning: Sharia Salah Salem, Cairo (Nasr City); tel. (2) 604489.

Ministry of Public Enterprise Sector: Sharia Majlis ash-Sha'ab, Lazoughli Sq., Cairo; tel. (2) 3558026; fax (2) 3555882; e-mail mops@idsc.gov.eg.

Ministry of Public Works and Water Resources: Sharia Corniche en-Nil, Imbaba, Cairo; tel. (2) 3497470; fax (2) 3497788; e-mail mpwwr@idsc.gov.eg.

Ministry of Supply and Trade: 99 Sharia Qasr el-Eini, Cairo; tel. (2) 3557598; telex 93497; fax (2) 3544973; e-mail msit@idsc.gov.eg.

Ministry of Tourism: Misr Travel Tower, Abbassia Sq., Cairo; tel. (2) 2828439; telex 94040; fax (2) 2829551; e-mail mol@idsc.gov.eg.

Ministry of Transport and Communications: Sharia Qasr el-Eini, Cairo; tel. (2) 3555566; telex 92802; fax (2) 3555564; e-mail garb@idsc.gov.eg.

Legislature

MAJLIS ASH-SHA'AB
(People's Assembly)

There are 222 constituencies, which each elect two deputies to the Assembly. Ten deputies are appointed by the President, giving a total of 454 seats.

Speaker: Dr AHMAD FATHI SURUR.

Deputy Speakers: Dr ABD AL-AHAD GAMAL AD-DIN, AHMAD ABU ZEID.

Elections, 29 November and 6 December 1995

	Seats
National Democratic Party*	316
New Wafd Party	6
National Progressive Unionist Party	5
Liberal Socialist Party	1
Nasserist Party	1
Independents	115
Total†	444

* Official candidates of the National Democratic Party (NDP) gained 316 seats in the two rounds of voting. However, after the elections it was reported that 99 of the 115 candidates who had successfully contested the elections as independents had either joined or rejoined the NDP.

† There are, in addition, 10 deputies appointed by the President.

MAJLIS ASH-SHURA
(Advisory Council)

In September 1980 elections were held for a 210-member **Shura (Advisory) Council**, which replaced the former Central Committee of the Arab Socialist Union. Of the total number of members, 140 are elected and the remaining 70 are appointed by the President. The opposition parties boycotted elections to the Council in October 1983, and again in October 1986, in protest against the 8% electoral threshold. In June 1989 elections to 153 of the Council's 210 seats were contested by opposition parties (the 'Islamic Alliance', consisting of the Muslim Brotherhood, the LSP and the SLP). However, all of the seats in which voting produced a result (143) were won by the NDP. NDP candidates won 88 of the 90 seats on the Council to which mid-term elections were held in June 1995. The remaining two elective seats were gained by independent candidates. The SLP and the LSP offered only 29 candidates for election and most of the remaining opposition parties did not participate. On 21 June new appointments were made to 47 vacant, non-elective seats.

Speaker: Dr MUSTAFA KAMAL HELMI.

Deputy Speakers: THARWAT ABAZAH, AHMAD AL-IMADI.

Political Organizations

Democratic People's Party: f. 1992; Chair. ANWAR AFIFI.

Democratic Unionist Party: f. 1990; Pres. MUHAMMAD ABD AL-MONEIM TURK.

Et-Takaful: f. 1995; Chair. Dr USAMA MUHAMMAD SHALTOUT.

Green Party: f. 1990; Chair. ABD AL-MONEIM EL-AASAR.

Ikhwan (Brotherhood): f. 1928; officially illegal, the (Muslim) Brotherhood advocates the adoption of the *Shari'a*, or Islamic law, as the sole basis of the Egyptian legal system; Sec.-Gen. MAAMOUN AL-HODAIBY.

Liberal Socialist Party (LSP): Cairo; f. 1976; advocates expansion of 'open door' economic policy and greater freedom for private enterprise; Leader (vacant).

Nasserist Party: Cairo; f. 1991; Chair. DIAA ED-DIN DAOUD.

National Democratic Party (NDP): Cairo; f. 1978; government party established by Anwar Sadat; has absorbed Arab Socialist Party; Leader MUHAMMAD HOSNI MUBARAK; Sec.-Gen. Dr YOUSUF AMIN WALI; Political Bureau: Chair. MUHAMMAD HOSNI MUBARAK; mems: KAMAL HASSAN ALI, Dr MUSTAFA KHALIL, Dr RIFA'AT EL-MAHGOUB, Dr SUBHI ABD AL-HAKIM, Dr MUSTAFA KAMAL HILMI, FIKRI MAKRAM OBEID, Dr ISMAT ABD AL-MEGUID, Dr AMAL OSMAN, SAFWAT ASH-SHARIF, Dr YOUSUF AMIN WALI, HASSAN ABU BASHA, KAMAL HENRY BADIR, Dr AHMAD HEIKAL.

National Progressive Unionist Party (Tagammu): 1 Sharia Karim ed-Dawlah, Cairo; f. 1976; left-wing; Leader KHALED MOHI ED-DIN; Sec. Dr RIFA'AT ES-SAID; 160,000 mems.

New Wafd Party: Cairo; original Wafd Party f. 1919; banned 1952; re-formed as New Wafd Party Feb. 1978; disbanded June 1978; re-formed 1983; Leader FOUAD SERAG ED-DIN; Sec.-Gen. IBRAHIM FARAG.

Social Justice Party: f. 1993; Chair. MUHAMMAD ABD AL-AAL.

Socialist Labour Party (SLP): 12 Sharia Awali el-Ahd, Cairo; f. 1978; official opposition party; Leader IBRAHIM SHUKRI.

Umma (National) Party: Islamic religious party, based in Khartoum, Sudan; Leader SADIQ AL-MAHDI (fmr Prime Minister of Sudan).

Young Egypt Party: f. 1990; Chair. ALI ALDIN SALIH.

Diplomatic Representation

EMBASSIES IN EGYPT

Afghanistan: 59 Sharia el-Orouba, Heliopolis, Cairo; tel. and fax (2) 417728; Ambassador: SAYED FAZLULLAH FAZIL.

Albania: 29 Sharia Ismail Muhammad, Cairo (Zamalek); tel. (2) 3415651; Ambassador: ARBEN PANDI CICI.

Algeria: 14 Sharia Bresil, Cairo (Zamalek); tel. (2) 3418527; Ambassador: MUHAMMAD ABRAHIMI EL-MILY.

Angola: 12 Foud Mohi ed-Din Sq., Mohandessin, Cairo; tel. (2) 3498259; fax (2) 3378683; Ambassador: HERMINO JOAQUIM ESCORCIO.

Argentina: 8 Sharia as-Saleh Ayoub, Cairo (Zamalek); tel. (2) 3401501; telex 92260; fax (2) 3414355; e-mail argemb@idsc.gov.eg; Ambassador: DOMINGO CULLEN.

Armenia: 20 Sharia Muhammad Mazhar, Cairo (Zamalek); tel. (2) 3414157; fax (2) 3424158; e-mail armenemb@idsc.gov.eg; Ambassador: EDWARD NALBANDIAN.

Australia: Cairo Plaza South, Corniche en-Nil, Cairo; tel. (2) 5750444; telex 92257; fax (2) 5780638; e-mail austremb@idsc.gov.eg; Ambassador: MICHAEL SMITH.

Austria: Sharia en-Nil, Cnr of Sharia Wissa Wassef, Cairo (Giza); tel. (2) 5702975; telex 92258; fax (2) 5702979; e-mail austemb @idsc.gov.eg; Ambassador: HEINRICH QUERNER.

Bahrain: 8 Sharia Gamiet an-Nisr, Dokki, Giza; tel. (2) 3407996; Ambassador: EBRAHIM AL-MAJED.

Bangladesh: 47 Sharia Ahmad Heshmat, Cairo (Zamalek); tel. (2) 3412642; fax (2) 3412642; e-mail bdoot@wnet1.worldnet.com.eg; Ambassador: RUHUL AMIN.

Belarus: 12–49 Misakha Sq., Cairo (Dokki); tel. and fax (2) 3493743; Chargé d'affaires: IGOR LESCHENYA.

Belgium: 20 Sharia Kamal esh-Shennawi, Cairo (Garden City); tel. (2) 3547494; telex 92264; Ambassador: ALAIN RENS.

Bolivia: Cairo; tel. and fax (2) 3546390; Ambassador: HERNANDO VELASCO.

Bosnia and Herzegovina: 26 July Square, (Sphinx) Agouza, Cairo; tel. (2) 3456091; fax (2) 3456029; Chargé d'affaires a.i.: AVDIJA HADROVIĆ.

Brazil: 1125 Corniche en-Nil, Cairo 11561 (Maspiro); tel. (2) 5756938; telex 92044; fax (2) 761040; e-mail brazemb@idsc.gov.eg; Ambassador: VIRGILIO MORETZSOHN DE ANDRADE.

Brunei: 24 Sharia Hassan Assem, Cairo (Dokki); tel. (2) 3406656; Ambassador: (vacant).

Bulgaria: 6 Sharia el-Malek el-Ajdal, Cairo (Dokki); tel. (2) 3413025; fax (2) 3413826; Ambassador: PETKO DIMITROV.

Burkina Faso: POB 306, Ramses Centre, 9 Sharia el-Fawakeh, Mohandessin, Cairo; tel. (2) 3379098; telex 93871; fax (2) 3495310; Ambassador: AMADÉ OUÉDRAOGO.

Burundi: 22 Sharia en-Nakhil, Madinet ed-Dobbat, Cairo (Dokki); tel. (2) 3373078; telex 20091; Ambassador: GERVAIS NDIKUMAGNEGE.

Cambodia: 2 Sharia Tahawia, Cairo (Giza); tel. (2) 3489966; Ambassador: IN SOPHEAP.

Cameroon: POB 2061, 15 Sharia Israa, Madinet el-Mohandessin, Cairo; tel. (2) 3441101; telex 92088; fax (2) 3459208; Ambassador: MOUCHILI NJI MFOUAYO.

Canada: POB 1667, 5 Midan es-Saraya el-Kobra, Cairo (Garden City); tel. (2) 3543110; fax (2) 3563548; e-mail cairo@ cairo01.x400.gc.ca; Ambassador: MARIE-ANDRÉE BEAUCHEMIN.

Central African Republic: 41 Sharia Mahmoud Azmy, Mohandessin, Cairo (Dokki); tel. (2) 3446873; Ambassador: HENRY KOBA.

Chad: POB 1869, 12 Midan ar-Refaï, Cairo 11511 (Dokki); tel. (2) 3373379; telex 92285; fax (2) 3373232; Ambassador: ADOUM ATTIMER.

Chile: 5 Sharia Chagaret ed-Dorr, Cairo (Zamalek); tel. (2) 3408711; telex 92519; fax (2) 3403716; e-mail chilemb@idsc.gov.eg; Ambassador: NELSON HADAD HERESI.

China, People's Republic: 14 Sharia Bahgat Aly, Cairo (Zamalek); tel. (2) 3417691; e-mail chinaemb@idsc.gov.eg; Ambassador: YANG FUCHANG.

Colombia: 6 Sharia Gueriza, Cairo (Zamalek); tel. (2) 3414203; fax (2) 3407429; e-mail colombemb@idsc.gov.eg; Ambassador: JAIME GIRÓN DUARTE.

Congo, Democratic Republic: 5 Sharia Mansour Muhammad, Cairo (Zamalek); tel. (2) 3403662; telex 92294; Ambassador: KAMIMBAYA WA DJONDO.

Côte d'Ivoire: 39 Sharia el-Kods esh-Sherif, Madinet el-Mohandessin, Cairo (Dokki); tel. (2) 699009; telex 2334; Ambassador: Gen. FÉLIX ORY.

Croatia: 13 Sharia Adel Hussain Nessim, Dokki, Giza; tel. (2) 3405812; Ambassador: DANIEL BUCAN.

Cuba: 6 Sharia el-Fawakeh, Madinet el-Mohandessin, Cairo (Dokki); tel. (2) 3350564; telex 93966; fax (2) 3612739; e-mail cubaemb@ idsc.gov.eg; Ambassador: ORLANDO MARINO LANCIS SUÁREZ.

Cyprus: 23A Sharia Ismail Muhammad, Cairo (Zamalek); tel. (2) 3411288; fax (2) 3415299; Ambassador: STAVROS ORPHANOU.

Czech Republic: 4 Sharia Dokki, Cairo 12511 (Giza); tel. (2) 3485531; fax (2) 3485892; Ambassador: BŘETISLAV VACHALA.

Denmark: 12 Sharia Hassan Sabri, Cairo (Zamalek); tel. (2) 3407411; telex 92254; fax (2) 3411780; e-mail rdemb@idsc.gov.eg; Ambassador: ERLING HARILD NIELSEN.

Djibouti: 11 Sharia el-Gazaer, Aswan Sq., Cairo (Agouza); tel. (2) 709787; telex 93143; Ambassador: ADEN Sheikh HASSEN.

Ecuador: Suez Canal Bldg, 4 Sharia Ibn Kasir, Cairo (Giza); tel. (2) 3496782; fax (2) 3609327; e-mail ecuademb@idsc.gov.eg; Ambassador: MANUEL ROMERO.

Ethiopia: 6 Sharia Abd ar-Rahman Hussein, Midan Gomhuria, Cairo (Dokki); tel. (2) 3353696; fax (2) 3353699; Ambassador: KONGIT SINEGIORGIS.

Finland: 3 Sharia Abu el-Feda, Cairo (Zamalek); tel. (2) 3411487; fax (2) 3405170; Ambassador: GARTH CASTRÉN.

France: POB 1777, 29 Sharia Charles de Gaulle, Giza, Cairo; tel. (2) 5703916; fax (2) 5710276; Ambassador: JEAN-MARC DE LA SABLIÈRE.

Gabon: 15 Sharia Mossadek, Cairo (Dokki); tel. (2) 702963; telex 92323; Ambassador: MAMBO JACQUES.

Germany: 8B Sharia Hassan Sabri, Cairo (Zamalek); tel. (2) 3399600; telex 92023; fax (2) 4310530; e-mail germemb@idsc.gov.eg; Ambassador: Dr PETER MICHAEL DINGENS.

Ghana: 1 Sharia 26 July, Cairo (Zamalek); tel. (2) 3444000; Ambassador: BON OHANE KWAPONG.

Greece: 18 Sharia Aicha at-Taimouria, Cairo (Garden City); tel. (2) 3555915; fax (2) 3563903; Ambassador: GEORGE ASIMAKOPOULOS.

Guatemala: POB 8062, 8 Sharia Muhammad Fahmi el-Mohdar, Primer Zone, Madinet Nasr, Cairo; tel. (2) 2611813; fax (2) 2611814; Ambassador: JUAN ALFREDO RENDÓN.

Guinea: 46 Sharia Muhammad Mazhar, Cairo (Zamalek); tel. (2) 3408109; fax (2) 3411446; Ambassador: MOHAMED TSSIOGA KOUROUMA.

Guinea-Bissau: 37 Sharia Lebanon, Madinet el-Mohandessin, Cairo (Dokki).

Holy See: Apostolic Nunciature, Safarat al-Vatican, 5 Sharia Muhammad Mazhar, Cairo (Zamalek); tel. (2) 3402250; fax (2) 3406152; e-mail nunteg@rite.com; Apostolic Nuncio: Most Rev. PAOLO GIGLIO, Titular Archbishop of Tindari.

Hungary: 29 Sharia Muhammad Mazhar, Cairo (Zamalek); tel. (2) 3400659; fax (2) 3408648; Ambassador: ERNŐ JUHÁSZ.

India: 5 Sharia Aziz Abaza, Cairo (Zamalek); tel. (2) 3413051; telex 92081; fax (2) 3414038; e-mail indiaemb@idsc.gov.eg; Ambassador: KENWAL GIBAL; also looks after Iraqi interests at 5 Aziz Abaza St, Cairo (Zamalek) (tel. (2) 3409815).

Indonesia: POB 1661, 13 Sharia Aicha at-Taimouria, Cairo (Garden City); tel. (2) 3547200; telex 92555; fax (2) 3562495; Ambassador: Dr BOER MAUNA.

Iraq: *Interests served by India.*

Ireland: POB 2681, 3 Sharia Abu el-Feda, Cairo (Zamalek); tel. (2) 3408264; telex 92778; fax (2) 3412863; Ambassador: HUGH SWIFT.

Israel: 6 Sharia ibn el-Malek, Cairo (Giza); tel. (2) 3610545; fax (2) 3610414; Ambassador: ZVI MAZEL.

Italy: 1079 Corniche en-Nil, Cairo (Garden City); tel. (2) 3543194; telex 942229; Ambassador: FRANCESCO ALOISI DE LARDEREL.

Japan: Cairo Centre Bldg, 2nd and 3rd Floors, 2 Sharia Abd al-Kader Hamza or 106 Sharia Qasr el-Eini, Cairo (Garden City); tel. (2) 3553962; fax (2) 3563540; e-mail japanemb@idsc.gov.eg; Ambassador: KUNIO KATAKURA.

Jordan: 6 Sharia Juhaini, Cairo; tel. (2) 3487543; Ambassador: NABIH AN-NIMR.

Kazakhstan: 4 Road 256 New Maadi, Cairo; tel. (2) 3508471; fax (2) 3521900; Ambassador: BOLATKHAN K. TAIZHANOV.

Kenya: POB 362, 7 Sharia el-Mohandes Galal, Cairo (Dokki); tel. (2) 3453628; telex 92021; fax (2) 3443400; Ambassador: MUHAMMAD A. MAHMOUD.

Korea, Democratic People's Republic: 6 Sharia as-Saleh Ayoub, Cairo (Zamalek); tel. (2) 650970; Ambassador: PAK YONG-HO.

Kuwait: 12 Sharia Nabil el-Wakkad, Cairo (Dokki); tel. (2) 701611; ABD AR-RAZAK ABD AL-KADER AL-KANDRI.

Lebanon: 5 Sharia Ahmad Nessim, Cairo (Giza); tel. (2) 3610474; telex 92227; fax (2) 3610463; Ambassador: HISHAM DIMASHKIEH.

Liberia: 3 Midan Amman, Cairo (Dokki); tel. (2) 3367046; telex 22474; fax (2) 3365701; Ambassador: Dr BRAHIMA D. KABA.

Libya: 7 Sharia as-Saleh Ayoub, Cairo (Zamalek); tel. (2) 3401864; Secretary of People's Bureau: AHMAD GADDAF'ADDAM.

Malaysia: 29 Sharia Taha Hussein, Cairo (Zamalek); tel. (2) 3410863; Ambassador: Dato RAJA MANSUR RAZMAN.

Mali: 3 Sharia al-Kawsar, Cairo (Dokki); tel. (2) 3371641; telex 94319; fax (2) 3371841; Ambassador: ALLAYE ALPHADY CISSÉ.

Malta: 25 Sharia 12, Ma'adi, Cairo; tel. (2) 3754451; fax (2) 3754452; e-mail maltaemb@idsc.gov.eg; Ambassador: (vacant).

Mauritania: 114 Mohi ed-Din, Abu-el Ezz, Mohandessin, Cairo; tel. (2) 3490671; MUHAMMAD LEMINE OULD.

Mauritius: 5 Sharia 26 July, Lebanon Sq., Mohandessin, Cairo; tel. (2) 3470929; telex 93631; fax (2) 3452425; Ambassador: Dr SAHID MAUDARBOCUS.

Mexico: 6 Sharia Ahmed Shawki, 11111 Cairo (Giza); tel. (2) 5716155; fax (2) 623404; e-mail mexemb@idsc.gov.eg; Ambassador: HÉCTOR CÁRDENAS RODRÍGUEZ.

Mongolia: 3 Midan en-Nasr, Cairo (Dokki); tel. (2) 3460670; Ambassador: SONOMDORJIN DAMBADARJAA.

Morocco: 10 Sharia Salah Eddine, Cairo (Zamalek); tel. (2) 3409849; fax (2) 3411937; e-mail morocemb@idsc.gov.eg; Ambassador: ABD AL-LATIF MOULINE.

Myanmar: 24 Sharia Muhammad Mazhar, Cairo (Zamalek); tel. (2) 3404176; telex 20957; fax (2) 3416793; Ambassador: U Aung Gyi.

Nepal: 9 Sharia Tiba, Cairo (Dokki); tel. (2) 3603426; fax (2) 704447; Ambassador: Jitendra Raj Sharma.

Netherlands: 18 Sharia Hassan Sabri, Cairo (Zamalek); tel. (2) 3406434; telex 92028; fax (2) 3415249; e-mail nlgovkai@rite.com.eg; Ambassador: Ronald H. Loudon.

Niger: 101 Sharia Pyramids, Cairo (Giza); tel. (2) 3865607; telex 2880; Ambassador: Mamane Oumarou.

Nigeria: 13 Sharia Gabalaya, Cairo (Zamalek); tel. (2) 3406042; telex 92038; Chargé d'affaires a.i.: P. S. O. Eromobor.

Norway: 8 Sharia el-Gezireh, Cairo (Zamalek); tel. (2) 3403340; telex 92259; fax (2) 3420709; Ambassador: Mette Ravn.

Oman: 52 Sharia el-Higaz, Mohandessin, Cairo; tel. (2) 3035942; telex 92272; Ambassador: Abdulla bin Hamed al-Busaidi.

Pakistan: 8 Sharia es-Salouli, Cairo (Dokki); tel. (2) 3487677; fax (2) 3480310; Ambassador: Gul Haneef.

Panama: POB 62, 4a Sharia Ibn Zanki, 11211 Cairo (Zamalek); tel. (2) 3411093; telex 92776; fax (2) 3411092; Chargé d'affaires a.i.: Roy Francisco Luna González.

Peru: 8 Sharia Kamel esh-Shenawi, Cairo (Garden City); tel. (2) 3562973; telex 93663; fax (2) 3557985; Ambassador: Manuel Veramendi I. Serra.

Philippines: 5 Sharia Ibn el-Walid, Cairo (Dokki); tel. (2) 3480396; fax (2) 3480393; Ambassador: Menandro P. Galenzoga.

Poland: 5 Sharia el-Aziz Osman, Cairo (Zamalek); tel. (2) 3417456; Ambassador: Roman Czyzycki.

Portugal: 57 Sharia el-Giza, Cairo (Giza); tel. (2) 3363950; telex 20325; fax (2) 3363952; Ambassador: Francisco do Valle.

Qatar: 10 Sharia ath-Thamar, Midan an-Nasr, Madinet al-Mohandessin, Cairo; tel. (2) 704537; telex 92287; Ambassador: Badir ad-Dafa.

Romania: 4 Sharia Aziz Abaza, Cairo (Zamalek); tel. (2) 3410107; telex 93807; fax (2) 3410851; Ambassador: Radu Onofrei.

Russia: 95 Sharia Giza, Cairo (Giza); tel. (2) 3489353; fax (2) 3609074; Ambassador: Vladimir Goudev.

Rwanda: 23 Sharia Babel, Mohandessin, Dokki, Giza; tel. (2) 3461126; telex 92552; fax (2) 3461079; Ambassador: Célestin Kabanda.

Saudi Arabia: 2 Sharia Ahmad Nessim, Cairo (Giza); tel. (2) 3490775; Ambassador: Assad Abd al-Karem Abou an-Nasr.

Senegal: 46 Sharia Abd al-Moneim Riad, Mohandessin, Cairo (Dokki); tel. (2) 3458479; telex 92047; Ambassador: Shams ed-Dine Ndoye.

Sierra Leone: *Interests served by Saudi Arabia.*

Singapore: POB 356, 40 Sharia Babel, Cairo (Dokki); tel. (2) 704744; telex 21353; fax (2) 3481682; Ambassador: V. K. Rajan.

Slovakia: 3 Sharia Adel Hussein Rostom, 12511 Cairo (Giza); tel. (2) 718240; telex 22029; fax (2) 715810; Ambassador: Ján Bóry.

Slovenia: 5 es-Saraya el-Kobra Sq., Cairo (Garden City); tel. (2) 3555798; Ambassador: Andrej Žlebnik.

Somalia: 27 Sharia es-Somal, Dokki, Giza; tel. (2) 704038; Ambassador: Abdalla Hassan Mahmoud.

South Africa: 18th Floor, Nile Tower Bldg, 21–23 Sharia Giza, Cairo; tel. (2) 5717238; fax (2) 5717241; Ambassador: Justus de Goede.

Spain: 41 Sharia Ismail Muhammad, Cairo (Zamalek); tel. (2) 3406397; telex 92255; fax (2) 3405829; e-mail spainemb@idsc.gov.eg; Ambassador: Juan Alfonso Ortiz.

Sri Lanka: POB 1157, 8 Sharia Sri Lanka, Cairo (Zamalek); tel. (2) 3400047; fax (2) 3417138; e-mail srilanka@idsc.gov.eg; Ambassador: H. K. J. R. Bandara.

Sudan: 4 Sharia el-Ibrahimi, Cairo (Garden City); tel. (2) 3549661; Ambassador: Izz ad-Din Hamid.

Sweden: POB 131, 13 Sharia Muhammad Mazhar, Cairo (Zamalek); tel. (2) 3414132; telex 92256; fax 3404357; e-mail sveamcai@link.com.eg; Ambassador: Christer Sylvén.

Switzerland: POB 633, 10 Sharia Abd al-Khalek Saroit, Cairo; tel. (2) 5758133; fax (2) 5745236; Ambassador: Blaise Godet.

Syria: 14 Sharia Ahmad Hechmar, Cairo (Zamalek); Ambassador: Dr Issa Darwish.

Tanzania: 9 Sharia Abd al-Hamid Lotfi, Cairo (Dokki); tel. (2) 704155; telex 23537; Ambassador: Muhammad A. Foum.

Thailand: 2 Sharia al-Malek el-Afdal, Cairo (Zamalek); tel. (2) 3410094; fax (2) 3400340; e-mail thaiemb@idsc.gov.eg; Ambassador: Buntham Bairaj-Vinichai.

Tunisia: 26 Sharia el-Jazirah, Cairo (Zamalek); tel. (2) 3404940; Ambassador: Abd al-Hamid Ammar.

Turkey: 25 Sharia Felaki, Cairo (Bab el-Louk); tel. and fax (2) 3548885; telex 21236; Ambassador: Yaşar Yakiş.

Uganda: 9 Midan el-Messaha, Cairo (Dokki); tel. (2) 3485544; telex 92087; fax (2) 3485980; Ambassador: Ibrahim Mukiibi.

United Arab Emirates: 4 Sharia Ibn Sina, Cairo (Giza); tel. (2) 729955; Ambassador: Hamed Hilal Sabit el-Kuwaiti.

United Kingdom: 7 Sharia Ahmad Raghab, Cairo (Garden City); tel. (2) 3540852; fax (2) 3540859; Ambassador: Sir David Blatherwick.

USA: 8 Sharia Kamal ed-Din, Cairo (Garden City); tel. (2) 3557371; telex 93773; fax (2) 3573200; Ambassador: Charles Kurtzer.

Uruguay: 6 Sharia Lotfallah, Cairo (Zamalek); tel. (2) 3415137; telex 92435; fax (2) 3418123; Ambassador: Julio César Franzini.

Venezuela: 15a Sharia Mansour Muhammad, Cairo (Zamalek); tel. (2) 3413517; fax (2) 3417373; Ambassador: Dario Bauder.

Viet Nam: 39 Sharia Kambiz, Cairo (Dokki); tel. (2) 3371494; fax (2) 3496597; Ambassador: Nguyen Le Bach.

Yemen: 28 Sharia Amean ar-Rafai, Cairo (Dokki); tel. (2) 3604806; Ambassador: Abd al-Ghalil Ghilan Ahmad.

Yugoslavia: 33 Sharia Mansour Muhammad, Cairo (Zamalek); tel. (2) 3404061; telex 21046; Ambassador: Dr Ivan Iveković.

Zambia: POB 253, Dokki; 6 Abd ar-Rahman Hussein, Mohandessin, Cairo 12311; tel. (2) 3610282; telex 92262; fax (2) 3610833; Ambassador: Dr Angel Alfred Mwenda.

Zimbabwe: 36 Sharia Wadi en-Nil, Mohandessin, Cairo; tel. (2) 3471217; telex 21876; fax (2) 3474872; Ambassador: Dr Henry Moyana.

Judicial System

The Courts of Law in Egypt are principally divided into two juridical court systems: Courts of General Jurisdiction and Administrative Courts. Since 1969 the Supreme Constitutional Court has been at the top of the Egyptian judicial structure.

THE SUPREME CONSTITUTIONAL COURT

The Supreme Constitutional Court is the highest court in Egypt. It has specific jurisdiction over: (i) judicial review of the constitutionality of laws and regulations; (ii) resolution of positive and negative jurisdictional conflicts and determination of the competent court between the different juridical court systems, e.g. Courts of General Jurisdiction and Administrative Courts, as well as other bodies exercising judicial competence; (iii) determination of disputes over the enforcement of two final but contradictory judgments rendered by two courts each belonging to a different juridical court system; (iv) rendering binding interpretation of laws or decree laws in the event of a dispute in the application of said laws or decree laws, always provided that such a dispute is of a gravity requiring conformity of interpretation under the Constitution.

COURTS OF GENERAL JURISDICTION

The Courts of General Jurisdiction in Egypt are basically divided into four categories, as follows: (i) The Court of Cassation; (ii) The Courts of Appeal; (iii) The Tribunals of First Instance; (iv) The District Tribunals; each of the above courts is divided into Civil and Criminal Chambers.

(i) Court of Cassation: Is the highest court of general jurisdiction in Egypt. Its sessions are held in Cairo. Final judgments rendered by Courts of Appeal in criminal and civil litigation may be petitioned to the Court of Cassation by the Defendant or the Public Prosecutor in criminal litigation and by any of the parties in interest in civil litigation on grounds of defective application or interpretation of the law as stated in the challenged judgment, on grounds of irregularity of form or procedure, or violation of due process, and on grounds of defective reasoning of judgment rendered. The Court of Cassation is composed of the President, 41 Vice-Presidents and 92 Justices.

President: Hon. Abd al-Borhan Noor.

(ii) The Courts of Appeal: Each has geographical jurisdiction over one or more of the governorates of Egypt. Each Court of Appeal is divided into Criminal and Civil Chambers. The Criminal Chambers try felonies, and the Civil Chambers hear appeals filed against such judgment rendered by the Tribunals of First Instance where the law so stipulates. Each Chamber is composed of three Superior Judges. Each Court of Appeal is composed of President, and sufficient numbers of Vice-Presidents and Superior Judges.

(iii) The Tribunals of First Instance: In each governorate there are one or more Tribunals of First Instance, each of which is divided into several Chambers for criminal and civil litigations. Each Chamber is composed of: (a) a presiding judge, and (b) two sitting judges. A Tribunal of First Instance hears, as an Appellate Court, certain litigations as provided under the law.

(iv) District Tribunals: Each is a one-judge ancillary Chamber of a Tribunal of First Instance, having jurisdiction over minor civil and criminal litigations in smaller districts within the jurisdiction of such Tribunal of First Instance.

PUBLIC PROSECUTION

Public prosecution is headed by the Attorney General, assisted by a number of Senior Deputy and Deputy Attorneys General, and a sufficient number of chief prosecutors, prosecutors and assistant prosecutors. Public prosecution is represented at all levels of the Courts of General Jurisdiction in all criminal litigations and also in certain civil litigations as required by the law. Public prosecution controls and supervises enforcement of criminal law judgments.

Attorney General: GAMAL SHOMAN.

Prosecutor-General: MUHAMMAD ABD AL-AZIZ EL-GINDI.

ADMINISTRATIVE COURTS SYSTEM
(CONSEIL D'ETAT)

The Administrative Courts have jurisdiction over litigations involving the state or any of its governmental agencies. The Administrative Courts system is divided into two courts: the Administrative Courts and the Judicial Administrative Courts, at the top of which is the High Administrative Court. The Administrative Prosecutor investigates administrative crimes committed by government officials and civil servants.

President of Conseil d'Etat: Hon. MUHAMMAD HILAL QASIM.

Administrative Prosecutor: Hon. RIFA'AT KHAFAGI.

THE STATE COUNCIL

The State Council is an independent judicial body which has the authority to make decisions in administrative disputes and disciplinary cases within the judicial system.

THE SUPREME JUDICIAL COUNCIL

The Supreme Judicial Council was reinstituted in 1984, having been abolished in 1969. It exists to guarantee the independence of the judicial system from outside interference and is consulted with regard to draft laws organizing the affairs of the judicial bodies.

Religion

According to the 1986 census, some 94% of Egyptians are Muslims (and almost all of these follow Sunni tenets). According to government figures published in the same year, there are about 2m. Copts (a figure contested by Coptic sources, whose estimates range between 6m. and 7m.), forming the largest religious minority, and about 1m. members of other Christian groups. There is also a small Jewish minority.

ISLAM

There is a Higher Council for the Isamic Call, on which sit: the Grand Sheikh of al-Azhar (Chair); the Minister of Awqaf (Islamic Endowments); the President and Vice-President of Al-Azhar University; the Grand Mufti of Egypt; and the Secretary-General of the Higher Council for Islamic Affairs.

Grand Sheikh of al-Azhar: Sheikh MUHAMMAD SAYED ATTIYAH TANTAWI.

Grand Mufti of Egypt: NASR WASSEL.

CHRISTIANITY
Orthodox Churches

Coptic Orthodox Church: St Mark Cathedral, POB 9035, Anba Ruess, 222 Sharia Ramses, Abbassia, Cairo; telex 23281; fax (2) 2825983; f. AD 61; Leader Pope SHENOUDA III; c. 10m. followers in Egypt, Sudan, other African countries, the USA, Canada, Australia, Europe and the Middle East.

Greek Orthodox Patriarchate: POB 2006, Alexandria; tel. (3) 4835839; fax (3) 4835684; e-mail goptalex@tecmina.com; internet http://www.greece.org/goptalex; f. AD 64; Pope and Patriarch of Alexandria and All Africa His Beatitude PETROS VII; 350,000 mems.

The Roman Catholic Church

Armenian Rite

The Armenian Catholic diocese of Alexandria, with an estimated 1,580 adherents at 31 December 1996, is suffragan to the Patriarchate of Cilicia. The Patriarch is resident in Beirut, Lebanon.

Bishop of Alexandria: BOUTROS TAZA, Patriarcat Arménien Catholique, 36 Sharia Muhammad Sabri Abou Alam, Cairo; tel. (2) 3938429; fax (2) 3932025.

Chaldean Rite

The Chaldean Catholic diocese of Cairo had an estimated 2,080 adherents at 31 December 1996.

Bishop of Cairo: YOUSUF IBRAHIM SARRAF, Evêché Chaldéen, Basilique-Sanctuaire Notre Dame de Fatima, 141 Sharia Nouzha, 11361 Heliopolis, Cairo; tel. and fax (2) 2455718.

Coptic Rite

Egypt comprises the Coptic Catholic Patriarchate of Alexandria and five dioceses. At 31 December 1996 there were an estimated 194,250 adherents in the country.

Patriarch of Alexandria: His Beatitude STEPHANOS II (ANDREAS GHATTAS), Patriarcat Copte Catholique, POB 69, 34 Sharia Ibn Sandar, Koubbeh Bridge, Cairo; tel. (2) 2571740; fax (2) 4545766.

Latin Rite

Egypt comprises the Apostolic Vicariate of Alexandria (incorporating Heliopolis and Port Said), containing an estimated 6,900 adherents at 31 December 1996.

Vicar Apostolic: Fr EGIDIO SAMPIERI (Titular Bishop of Ida in Mauretania), 10 Sharia Sidi el-Metwalli, Alexandria; tel. (3) 4836065; also at 2 Sharia Banque Misr, Cairo; tel. (2) 41280.

Maronite Rite

The Maronite diocese of Cairo had an estimated 5,000 adherents at 31 December 1996.

Bishop of Cairo: JOSEPH DERGHAM, Evêché Maronite, 15 Sharia Hamdi, Daher, Cairo; tel. (2) 5939610.

Melkite Rite

His Beatitude MAXIMOS V HAKIM (resident in Damascus, Syria) is the Greek-Melkite Patriarch of Antioch, of Alexandria and of Jerusalem.

Patriarchal Exarchate of Egypt and Sudan: Patriarcat Grec-Melkite Catholique, 16 Sharia Daher, Cairo; tel. (2) 5905790; 6,500 adherents (31 December 1996); Exarch Patriarchal Mgr PAUL ANTAKI, Titular Archbishop of Nubia.

Syrian Rite

The Syrian Catholic diocese of Cairo had an estimated 1,776 adherents at 31 December 1996.

Bishop of Cairo: JOSEPH HANNOUCHE, Evêché Syrien Catholique, 46 Sharia Daher, Cairo; tel. (2) 5923932.

The Anglican Communion

The Anglican diocese of Egypt, suspended in 1958, was revived in 1974 and became part of the Episcopal Church in Jerusalem and the Middle East, formally inaugurated in January 1976. The Province has four dioceses: Jerusalem, Egypt, Cyprus and the Gulf, and Iran, and its President is the Bishop in Egypt. The Bishop in Egypt has jurisdiction also over the Anglican chaplaincies in Algeria, Djibouti, Eritrea, Ethiopia, Libya, Somalia and Tunisia.

Bishop in Egypt: Most Rev. GHAIS ABD AL-MALIK, Diocesan Office, POB 87, 5 Sharia Michel Lutfalla, Cairo (Zamalek); tel. (2) 3320313; fax (2) 3408941; e-mail diocese@intouch.com.

Other Christian Churches

Armenian Apostolic Church: 179 Sharia Ramses, Cairo, POB 48-Faggalah; tel. (2) 5901385; fax (2) 906671; Archbishop ZAVEN CHINCHINIAN; 7,000 mems.

Protestant Churches of Egypt: POB 1304, Cairo 11511; tel. (2) 5903925; f. 1902, independent since 1926; 200,000 mems (1985); Gen. Sec. (vacant).

Other denominations active in Egypt include the Coptic Evangelical Church (Synod of the Nile) and the Union of the Armenian Evangelical Churches in the Near East.

JUDAISM

The 1986 census recorded 794 Jews in Egypt.

Jewish Community: Office of the Community, President ESTHER WEINSTEIN, 13 Sharia Sebil el-Khazindar, Abbassia, Cairo; tel. (2) 4824613; fax (2) 4824885; internet http://www.geocities.com/rainforest/vines/5855.

The Press

Despite a fairly high illiteracy rate in Egypt, the country's press is well developed. Cairo is one of the largest publishing centres in the Middle East and Africa.

All newspapers and magazines are supervised, according to law, by of the Supreme Press Council. The four major publishing houses of al-Ahram, Dar al-Hilal, Dar Akhbar al-Yawm and Dar at-Tahrir, operate as separate entities and compete with each other commercially.

The most authoritative daily newspaper is the very long-established *Al-Ahram*.

DAILIES

Alexandria

Bareed ach-Charikat (Companies' Post): POB 813, Alexandria; f. 1952; Arabic; evening; commerce, finance, insurance and marine affairs, etc.; Editor S. BENEDUCCI; circ. 15,000.

Al-Ittihad al-Misri (Egyptian Unity): 13 Sharia Sidi Abd ar-Razzak, Alexandria; f. 1871; Arabic; evening; Propr ANWAR MAHER FARAG; Dir HASSAN MAHER FARAG.

Le Journal d'Alexandrie: 1 Sharia Rolo, Alexandria; French; evening; Editor CHARLES ARCACHE.

As-Safeer (The Ambassador): 4 Sharia as-Sahafa, Alexandria; f. 1924; Arabic; evening; Editor MUSTAFA SHARAF.

Tachydromos-Egyptos: 4 Sharia Zangarol, Alexandria; tel. (3) 35650; f. 1879; Greek; morning; liberal; Publr PENNY KOUTSOUMIS; Editor DINOS KOUTSOUMIS; circ. 2,000.

Cairo

Al-Ahram (The Pyramids): Sharia al-Galaa, Cairo 11511; tel. (2) 5747011; telex 92002; fax (2) 5747089; f. 1875; Arabic; morning, incl. Sundays (international edition published in London, England; North American edition published in New York, USA); Editor and Chair. IBRAHIM NAFEH; circ. 900,000; 1.1m. (Friday).

Al-Ahrar: 58 Manshyet al-Sadr, Kobry al-Kobba, Cairo; tel. (2) 4823046; fax (2) 4823027; f. 1977; organ of Liberal Socialist Party; Editor-in-Chief SALAH QABADAYA.

Al-Akhbar (The News): Dar Akhbar al-Yawm, Sharia as-Sahafa, Cairo; tel. (2) 5782600; telex 20321; fax (2) 5782520; f. 1952; Arabic; Chair. IBRAHIM ABU SADAH; Man. Editor GALAL DEWIDAR; circ. 980,000.

Arev: 3 Sharia Sulayman Halabi, Cairo; tel. (2) 754703; f. 1915; Armenian; evening; official organ of the Armenian Liberal Democratic Party; Editor AVEDIS YAPOUDJIAN.

Egyptian Gazette: 24–26 Sharia Zakaria Ahmad, Cairo; tel. (2) 5783333; telex 92475; fax (2) 5781717; f. 1880; English; morning; Editor-in-Chief MUHAMMAD ALI IBRAHIM; circ. 35,000.

Al-Gomhouriya (The Republic): 24 Sharia Zakaria Ahmad, Cairo; tel. (2) 5783333; telex 92475; fax (2) 5781717; f. 1953; Arabic; morning; Chair. SAMIR RAGAB; Editor MAHFOUZ AL-ANSARI; circ. 900,000.

Le Journal d'Egypte: 1 Sharia Borsa Guédida, Cairo; f. 1936; French; morning; Gen. Man. LITA GALLAD; Editor-in-Chief MUHAMMAD RACHAD; circ. 72,000.

Al-Misaa' (The Evening): 24 Sharia Zakaria Ahmad, Cairo; telex 92475; f. 1956; Arabic; evening; Editor-in-Chief SAMIR RAGAB; circ. 105,000.

Phos: 14 Sharia Zakaria Ahmad, Cairo; f. 1896; Greek; morning; Editor S. PATERAS; Man. BASILE A. PATERAS; circ. 20,000.

Le Progrès Egyptien: 24 Sharia Zakaria Ahmad, Cairo; tel. (2) (2) 5783333; telex 92475; fax (2) 5781717; f. 1890; French; morning including Sundays; Editor-in-Chief KHALED ANWAR BAKIR; circ. 21,000.

PERIODICALS

Alexandria

Al-Ahad al-Gedid (New Sunday): 88 Sharia Said M. Koraim, Alexandria; tel. (3) 807874; f. 1936; Editor-in-Chief and Publr GALAL M. KORAITEM; circ. 60,000.

Alexandria Medical Journal: 4 G. Carducci, Alexandria; f. 1922; English, French and Arabic; quarterly; publ. by Alexandria Medical Asscn; Editor AMIN RIDA; circ. 1,500.

Amitié Internationale: 59 ave el-Hourriya, Alexandria; tel. (3) 23639; f. 1957; publ. by Asscn Egyptienne d'Amitié Internationale; Arabic and French; quarterly; Editor Dr ZAKI BADAOUI.

L'Annuaire des Sociétés Egyptiennes par Actions: 23 Midan Tahrir, Alexandria; f. 1930; annually in Dec.; French; Propr ELIE I. POLITI; Editor OMAR ES-SAYED MOURSI.

L'Echo Sportif: 7 Sharia de l'Archevêché, Alexandria; French; weekly; Propr MICHEL BITTAR.

Egyptian Cotton Gazette: POB 433, 12 Sharia Talaat Nooman, Alexandria; tel. (3) 4806971; fax (3) 4833002; e-mail alcotexa@idsc.gov.eg; organ of the Alexandria Cotton Exporters' Association; English; 2 a year; Chief Editor GALAL REFAI.

Informateur des Assurances: 1 Sharia Sinan, Alexandria; f. 1936; French; monthly; Propr ELIE I. POLITI; Editor SIMON A. BARANIS.

Sina 'at en-Nassig (L'Industrie Textile): 5 rue de l'Archevêché, Alexandria; Arabic and French; monthly; Editor PHILIPPE COLAS.

Voce d'Italia: 90 Sharia Farahde, Alexandria; Italian; fortnightly; Editor R. AVELLINO.

Cairo

Al-Ahali (The People): 23 Sharia Abd al-Khalek, Tharwat, Cairo; tel. (2) 3923306; fax (2) 3900412; f. 1978; weekly; published by the National Progressive Unionist Party; Chair. LOTFI WAKID; Editor-in-Chief ABD EL-BAKOURY.

Al-Ahram al-Arabi: Sharia al-Galaa, Cairo 11511; f. 1997; Arabic; weekly; political, social and economic affairs; Editor-in-Chief IBRAHIM NAFIE.

Al-Ahram Hebdo: Sharia al-Galaa, Cairo 11511; tel. (2) 4180034; fax (2) 4182663; f. 1993; French; weekly; Editor-in-Chief MUHAMMAD SALMAWI.

Al-Ahram al-Iqtisadi (The Economic *Al-Ahram*): Sharia al-Galaa, Cairo 11511; telex 20185; fax (2) 5786833; Arabic; weekly; economic and political affairs; owned by Al-Ahram publrs; Chief Editor ISSAM RIFA'AT; circ. 74,000.

Al-Ahram Weekly (The Pyramids): Al-Ahram Bldg, Sharia al-Galaa, Cairo; tel. (2) 5786064; telex 20185; fax (2) 5786833; f. 1989; English; weekly; published by Al-Ahram publications; Editor-in-Chief HOSNI GUINDY; circ. 150,000.

Akhbar al-Hawadith: 6 Sharia as-Sahafa, Cairo; tel. (2) 5782600; fax (2) 5782510; f. 1993; weekly; crime reports; Editor-in-Chief SAMIR TAWFIK.

Akhbar al-Nogoome: 6 Sharia as-Sahafa, Cairo; tel. (2) 5782600; fax (2) 5782510; f. 1991; weekly; theatre and film news; Editor-in-Chief MUHAMMAD TABARAK.

Akhbar ar-Riadah: 6 Sharia as-Sahafa, Cairo; tel. (2) 5782600; fax (2) 5782510; f. 1990; weekly; sport; Editor-in-Chief FATHI SANAD.

Akhbar al-Yaum (Daily News): 6 Sharia as-Sahafa, Cairo; tel. (2) 5782600; fax (2) 5782510; f. 1944; Arabic; weekly (Saturday); Chair. and Editor-in-Chief IBRAHIM ABU SEDAH; circ. 1,158,000.

Akher Sa'a (Last Hour): Dar Akhbar al-Yawm, Sharia as-Sahafa, Cairo; telex 92215; f. 1934; Arabic; weekly (Wed.); independent; Editor-in-Chief MUHAMMAD WAJDI KANDIL; circ. 150,000.

Aqidaty My Faith): 24–26 Sharia Zakaria Ahmad, Cairo; tel. (2) 5781010; fax (2) 5784747; weekly; Muslim religious newspaper; circ. 300,000.

Al-Azhar: Idarat al-Azhar, Sharia al-Azhar, Cairo; f. 1931; Arabic; Islamic monthly; supervised by the Egyptian Council for Islamic Research of Al-Azhar University; Dir MUHAMMAD FARID WAGDI.

Al-Bitrul (Petroleum): Cairo; monthly; published by the Egyptian General Petroleum Corporation.

Computerworld Middle East: World Publishing Ltd (Egypt), 41A Masaken al-Fursan Bldg, Sharia Kamal Hassan Ali, Cairo 11361; tel. (2) 3460601; fax (2) 3470118; English; monthly; specialist computer information.

Contemporary Thought: University of Cairo, Cairo; quarterly; Editor Dr Z. N. MAHMOUD.

Ad-Da'wa (The Call): Cairo; Arabic; monthly; organ of the Muslim Brotherhood.

Ad-Doctor: 8 Sharia Hoda Shaarawy, Cairo; f. 1947; Arabic; monthly; Editor Dr AHMAD M. KAMAL; circ. 30,000.

Echos: 1–5 Sharia Mahmoud Bassiouni, Cairo; f. 1947; French; weekly; Dir and Propr GEORGES QRFALI.

The Egyptian Mail: 24–26 Sharia Zakaria Ahmad; telex 92475; weekly; Sat. edn of *The Egyptian Gazette*; English; circ. 35,000.

Al-Fusoul (The Seasons): 17 Sharia Sherif Pasha, Cairo; Arabic; monthly; Propr and Chief Editor SAMIR MUHAMMAD ZAKI ABD AL-KADER.

Al-Garidat at-Tigariyat al-Misriya (The Egyptian Business Paper): 25 Sharia Nubar Pasha, Cairo; f. 1921; Arabic; weekly; circ. 7,000.

Hawa'a (Eve): Dar al-Hilal, 16 Sharia Muhammad Ezz el-Arab, Cairo; tel. (2) 3625450; fax (2) 3625469; women's magazine; Arabic; weekly (Sat.); Chief Editor EKBAL BARAKA; circ. 160,837.

Al-Hilal Magazine: Dar al-Hilal, 16 Sharia Muhammad Ezz el-Arab, Cairo; telex 92703; f. 1895; Arabic; literary monthly; Editor MOUSTAFA NABIL.

Huwa wa Hiya (He and She): POB 525, Cairo 11511; tel. (2) 3506752; fax (2) 3508604; f. 1977; monthly; news, leisure, sport, health, religion, women's issues; Dir GEORGE TAWFIK.

Industrial Egypt: POB 251, 26A Sharia Sherif Pasha, Cairo; tel. (2) 3928317; telex 92624; fax (2) 3928075; f. 1924; quarterly bulletin and year book of the Federation of Egyptian Industries in English and Arabic; Editor ALI FAHMY.

Informateur Financier et Commercial: 24 Sharia Sulayman Pasha, Cairo; f. 1929; weekly; Dir HENRI POLITI; circ. 15,000.

Al-Iza'a wat-Television (Radio and Television): 13 Sharia Muhammad Ezz el-Arab, Cairo; f. 1935; Arabic; weekly; Editor and Chair. SAKEENA FOUAD; circ. 80,000.

Al-Kerazeh (The Sermon): Cairo; Arabic; weekly newspaper of the Coptic Orthodox Church.

Al-Kawakeb (The Stars): Dar al-Hilal, 16 Sharia Muhammad Ezz el-Arab, Cairo; tel. (2) 3625450; fax (2) 3625469; f. 1952; Arabic; weekly; film magazine; Editor-in-Chief RAGAA AL-NAKKASH; circ. 86,381.

Kitab al-Hilal: Dar al-Hilal, 16 Sharia Muhammad Ezz el-Arab, Cairo; monthly; Founders EMILE and SHOUKRI ZEIDAN; Editor MOUSTAFA NABIL.

Al-Liwa' al-Islami (Islamic Standard): 11 Sharia Sherif Pasha, Cairo; f. 1982; Arabic; weekly; govt paper to promote official view of Islamic revivalism; Propr AHMAD HAMZA; Editor MUHAMMAD ALI SHETA; circ. 30,000.

Lotus Magazine: 104 Sharia Qasr el-Eini, Cairo; f. 1992; English, French and Arabic; quarterly; computer software magazine; Editor BEREND HARMENS.

Magallat al-Mohandeseen (The Engineer's Magazine): 28 Sharia Ramses, Cairo; f. 1945; publ. by The Engineers' Syndicate; Arabic and English; 10 a year; Editor and Sec. MAHMOUD SAMI ABD AL-KAWI.

Al-Magallat az-Zira'ia (The Agricultural Magazine): Cairo; monthly; agriculture; circ. 30,000.

Mayo (May): Sharia al-Galaa, Cairo; organ of National Democratic Party; Supervisor MUHAMMAD SAFWAT ASH-SHARIF; Chair. ABDULLAH ABD AL-BARY; Chief Editor SAMIR RAGAB; circ. 500,000.

Medical Journal of Cairo University: Manyal University Hospital, Sharia Qasr el-Eini, Cairo; f. 1933; Kasr el-Eini Clinical Society; English; quarterly.

The Middle East Observer: 41 Sharia Sherif, Cairo; tel. (2) 3926919; fax (2) 3939732; e-mail fouda@soficom.com.eg; f. 1954; English; weekly; specializing in economics of Middle East and African markets; also publishes supplements on law, foreign trade and tenders; agent for IMF, UN and IDRC publications, distributor of World Bank publications; Man. Owner AHMAD FODA; Chief Editor MUHAMMAD ABDULLAH HESHAM A. RAOUF; circ. 20,000.

Al-Musawar: Dar al-Hilal, 16 Sharia Muhammad Ezz el-Arab, Cairo; tel. (2) 3625450; telex 92703; fax (2) 3625469; f. 1924; Arabic; weekly; Editor-in-Chief MAKRAM MUHAMMAD AHMAD; circ. 130,423.

Nesf ad-Donia: Sharia al-Galaa, Cairo 11511; tel. (2) 5786100; f. 1990; weekly; women's magazine; Editor-in-Chief SANAA AL-BESI.

October: 1119 Sharia Corniche en-Nil, Cairo; tel. (2) 777077; fax (2) 5744999; monthly; Chair. and Editor-in-Chief RAGAB AL-BANA; circ. 140,500.

Al-Omal (The Workers): 90 Sharia Galal, Cairo; telex 93255; publ. by the Egyptian Trade Union Federation: Arabic; weekly; Chief Editor AHMAD HARAK.

Progrès Dimanche: 24 Sharia Galal, Cairo; tel. 741611; telex 92475; French; weekly; Sunday edition of *Le Progrès Egyptien*; Editor-in-Chief KHALED ANWAR BAKIR.

Radio and TV Magazine: At-Tahrir Printing and Publishing House, 24 Sharia Zakaria Ahmad, Cairo; tel. (2) 3643314; fax (2) 3543030; Arabic; weekly; Editor-in-Chief MAHMOUD ALI.

Rose al-Yousuf: 89A Sharia Qasr el-Eini, Cairo; tel. (2) 3540888; fax (2) 3556413; f. 1925; Arabic; weekly; political; circulates throughout all Arab countries; Chair. of Board and Editor MAHMOUD TUHAMI; circ. 35,000.

As-Sabah (The Morning): 4 Sharia Muhammad Said Pasha, Cairo; f. 1922; Arabic; weekly (Thurs.); Editor RAOUF TAWFIK.

Sabah al-Kheir (Good Morning): 18 Sharia Muhammad Said Pasha, Cairo; Arabic; weekly; light entertainment; Chief Editor MOFEED FAWZI; circ. 70,000.

Ash-Shaab (The People): 313 Sharia Port Said, Cairo; organ of Socialist Labour Party; weekly; Editor-in-Chief ADEL HUSSEIN; circ. 130,000.

At-Tahrir (Liberation): 5 Sharia Naguib, Rihani, Cairo; Arabic; weekly; Editor ABD AL-AZIZ SADEK.

At-Taqaddum (Progress): c/o 1 Sharia Jarim ed-Dawlah, Cairo; f. 1978; organ of National Progressive Unionist Party.

Tchehreh Nema: 14 Sharia Hassan el-Akbar (Abdine), Cairo; f. 1904; Iranian; monthly; political, literary and general; Editor MANUCHEHR TCHEHREH NEMA MOADEB ZADEH.

Up-to-Date International Industry: 10 Sharia Galal, Cairo; Arabic and English; monthly; foreign trade journal.

Al-Wafd: 1 Sharia Boulos Hanna, Cairo (Dokki); tel. (2) 3482079; fax (2) 3602007; f. 1984; weekly; organ of the New Wafd Party; Editor-in-Chief GAMAL BADAWI; circ. 360,000.

Watani (My Country): 27 Sharia Abdel Khalek Sarwat, Cairo; tel. (2) 3927201; fax (2) 3935946; f. 1958; Arabic; independent Sun. newspaper addressing Egyptians in general and the Christian Copts in particular; Chief Officers Y. SIDHOM, S. AZIZ, F. A. SAYED; circ. 50,000.

Yulio (July): July Press and Publishing House, Cairo; f. 1986; weekly; Nasserist; Editor ABDULLAH IMAM; and a monthly cultural magazine, Editor MAHMOUD AL-MARAGHI.

NEWS AGENCIES

Middle East News Agency: 17 Sharia Hoda Sharawi, Cairo; tel. (2) 3933000; telex 92252; fax (2) 3935055; e-mail newsroom@ mena.org.eg; f. 1955; regular service in Arabic, English and French; Chair. and Editor-in-Chief MOUSTAFA NAGUIB.

Foreign Bureaux

Agence France-Presse (AFP): POB 1437-15511, 2nd Floor, 10 Misaha Sq, Cairo; tel. (2) 3481236; telex 92225; fax (2) 3603282; Chief SAMMY KETZ.

Agencia EFE (Spain): 35A Sharia Abu el-Feda, 4th Floor, Apt 14, Cairo (Zamalek); Correspondent DOMINGO DEL PIÑO.

Agenzia Nazionale Stampa Associata (ANSA) (Italy): 19 Sharia Abd al-Khalek Sarwat, Cairo; tel. (2) 3929821; telex 93365; fax (2) 3938642; Chief ANTONELLA TARQUINI.

Allgemeiner Deutscher Nachrichtendienst (ADN) (Germany): 17 Sharia el-Brazil, Apt 59, Cairo (Zamalek); tel. (2) 3404006; telex 92339; Correspondent RALF SCHULTZE.

Associated Press (AP) (USA): POB 1077, 1117 Sharia Corniche en-Nil, (Maspiro), Cairo 11221; tel. (2) 5784091; telex 92211; fax (2) 5784094; Chief of Middle East Services EARLEEN FISHER.

Deutsche Presse-Agentur (dpa) (Germany): 14th Floor, 1125 Corniche en-Nil, Cairo; tel. (2) 5780351; fax (2) 5780354; e-mail 101234,46@compuserve.com; Chief HANS DAHNE.

Informatsionnoye Telegrafnoye Agentstvo Rossii—Telegrafnoye Agentstvo Suverennykh Stran (ITAR—TASS) (Russia): 30 Sharia Muhammad Mazhar, Cairo (Zamalek); tel. (2) 3419784; telex 93008; fax (2) 3417268; Dir MIKHAIL I. KROUTIKHIN.

Jiji Press (Japan): 9 Sharia el-Kamel Muhammad, Cairo (Zamalek); tel. (2) 3411411; telex 20940; fax (2) 3405244; Chief FUMIHIKO SUGIYAMA.

Kyodo News Service (Japan): Flat 301, 15 Sharia Hassan Sabri, Cairo 11211 (Zamalek); tel. (2) 3411756; telex 20435; fax (2) 3406105; Chief JITSURO KIHARA.

Magyar Távirati Iroda (MTI) (Hungary): 6A Sharia el-Malek el-Afdal, Cairo (Zamalek); tel. (2) 3402892; fax (2) 3402898; Correspondent IMRE KERESZTES.

Reuters (United Kingdom): POB 2040, 21st Floor, Bank Misr Tower, 153 Sharia Muhammad Farid, Cairo; tel. (2) 777150; telex 92210; fax (2) 771133; Chief Correspondent JONATHAN WRIGHT.

United Press International (UPI) (USA): POB 872, 4 Sharia Eloui, Cairo; tel. (2) 3928106.

Xinhua (New China) News Agency (People's Republic of China): 2 Moussa Galal Sq., Mohandessin, Cairo; tel. (2) 3448950; telex 93812.

The Iraqi News Agency (INA) reopened its office in Cairo in 1985.

PRESS ASSOCIATION

Foreign Press Association: Room 2037, Mariot Hotel, Cairo; tel. (2) 3419957.

Publishers

General Egyptian Book Organization: 117 Sharia Corniche en-Nil, Boulac, Cairo; tel. (2) 775000; fax (2) 5754213; e-mail ssarhan@ idsc.gov.eg; f. 1961; affiliated to the Ministry of Culture; Chair. Dr SAMIR SARHAN.

Alexandria

Alexandria University Press: Shatby, Alexandria.

Egyptian Printing and Publishing House: Ahmad es-Sayed Marouf, 59 Safia Zaghoul, Alexandria; f. 1947.

Maison Egyptienne d'Editions: Ahmad es-Sayed Marouf, Sharia Adib, Alexandria; f. 1950.

Maktab al-Misri al-Hadith li-t-Tiba wan-Nashr: 7 Sharia Noubar, Alexandria; also at 2 Sharia Sherif, Cairo; Man. AHMAD YEHIA.

Cairo

Al-Ahram Establishment: 6 Sharia al-Galaa, Cairo; tel. (2) 576069; telex 92001; fax 5786023; f. 1875; publ. newspapers, magazines and books, incl. *Al-Ahram*; Chief Ed. IBRAHIM NAFEI.

Akhbar al-Yawm Publishing Group: 6 Sharia as-Sahafa, Cairo; tel. (2) 5748100; telex 20321; fax (2) 5748895; f. 1944; publ. *Al-Akhbar* (daily), *Akhbar al-Yawm* (weekly), and colour magazine *Akher Sa'a* (weekly); Pres. IBRAHIM SAAD.

Argus Press: 10 Sharia Zakaria Ahmad, Cairo; Owners KARNIG HAGOPIAN and ABD AL-MEGUID MUHAMMAD.

Boustany Publishing House: 29 Sharia Faggalah, Cairo 11271; tel. (2) 5915315; fax 4177915; e-mail bph@ritsec3.com.eg; internet http://www.boustanys.com; f. 1900; fiction, poetry, history, biography, philosophy, Arabic language, literature, politics, religion, archaeology, Egyptology; Chief Exec. Dr FADWA BOUSTANY.

Dar al-Gomhouriya: 24 Sharia Zakaria Ahmad, Cairo; tel. (2) 5781010; fax (2) 5784747; affiliate of At-Tahrir Printing and Publishing House; publications include the dailies, *Al-Gomhouriya, Al-Misaa', Egyptian Gazette* and *Le Progrès Egyptien*; Pres. SAMIK RAGAB.

Dar al-Hilal Publishing Institution: 16 Sharia Muhammad Ezz el-Arab, Cairo; tel. (2) 20610; telex 92703; f. 1892; publ. *Al-Hilal, Riwayat al-Hilal, Kitab al-Hilal, Tabibak al-Khass* (monthlies); *Al-Mussawar, Al-Kawakeb, Hawaa, Samir, Mickey* (weeklies); Chair. MAKRAN MUHAMMAD AHMAD.

Dar al-Kitab al-Arabi: Misr Printing House, Sharia Noubar, Cairo (Bab el-Louk); f. 1968; Man. Dir Dr SAHAIR AL-KALAMAWI.

Dar al-Kitab al-Masri: POB 156, 33 Sharia Qasr en-Nil, Cairo; tel. (2) 3922168; telex 23081; fax (2) 3924614; f. 1929; religion, history, books for children, general interest, etc.; Man. Dir HASSAN EZ-ZEIN.

Dar al-Maaref: 1119 Sharia Corniche en-Nil, Cairo; tel. (2) 777077; fax (2) 5744999; f. 1890; publishing, printing and distribution of all kinds of books in Arabic and other languages; publishers of *October* magazine; Chair. and Man. Dir RAGAB AL-BANA.

Dar an-Nashr (formerly Les Editions Universitaires d'Egypte): POB 1347, 41 Sharia Sherif, Cairo 11511; tel. (2) 3934606; fax (2) 3921997; f. 1947; university textbooks, academic works, encyclopaedia.

Dar ash-Shorouk: 16 Sharia Gawad Hosni, Cairo; tel. (2) 3929333; telex 93091; fax (2) 3934814; f. 1968; publishing, printing and distribution; publishers of books on modern Islamic politics, philosophy and art, and books for children; Chair. ABRAHIM EL-MOALLIM ADEL.

Editions Horus: 1 Midan Soliman Pasha, Cairo.

Editions le Progrès: 6 Sharia Sherif Pasha, Cairo; Propr WADI SHOUKRI.

Egyptian Co for Printing and Publishing: 40 Sharia Noubar, Cairo; tel. (2) 21310; Chair. MUHAMMAD MAHMOUD HAMED.

Higher University Council for Arts, Letters and Sciences: University of Cairo, Cairo.

Lagnat at-Taalif wat-Targama wan-Nashr (Committee for Writing, Translating and Publishing Books): 9 Sharia el-Kerdassi (Abdine), Cairo.

Librairie La Renaissance d'Egypte (Hassan Muhammad & Sons): POB 2172, 9 Sharia Adly, Cairo; f. 1930; religion, history, geography, medicine, architecture, economics, politics, law, philosophy, psychology, children's books, atlases, dictionaries; Man. HASSAN MUHAMMAD.

Maktabet Misr: POB 16, 3 Sharia Kamal Sidki, Cairo; tel. (2) 5898553; fax (2) 5907593; f. 1932; publs wide variety of fiction, biographies and textbooks for schools and universities; Man. AMIR SAID GOUDA ES-SAHHAR.

National Centre for Educational Research and Development: 12 Sharia Waked, el-Borg el-Faddy, POB 836, Cairo; tel. (2) 3930981; f. 1956; formerly Documentation and Research Centre for Education (Ministry of Education); bibliographies, directories, information and education bulletins; Dir Prof. ABD EL-FATTAH GALAL.

National Library Press (Dar al-Kutub): Midan Ahmad Maher, Cairo; bibliographic works.

Senouhy Publishers: 54 Sharia Abd al-Khalek Sarwat, Cairo; f. 1956; Dir LEILA A. FADEL.

Ash-Shaab: 313 Sharia Port Said, Sayeda Zeinab, Cairo; tel. (2) 3909716; fax (2) 3900283; e-mail elshaab@idsc.gov.eg; f. 1979; bi-weekly (Tuesday and Friday); Editor-in-Chief MAGDI AHMED HUSSEIN.

As-Syassa ad-Dawliah: Sharia al-Galaa, Cairo 11511; tel. (2) 5786022; fax (2) 5786023; f. 1965; political quarterly; Editor-in-Chief Dr OSAMA AL-GHAZALI HARB.

At-Tahrir Printing and Publishing House: 24 Sharia Zakaria Ahmad, Cairo; tel. (2) 5781010; telex 92475; fax (2) 5784747; f. 1953; affil. to Shura (Advisory) Council; Chair. and Man. Dir SAMIR RAGAB.

Watani: Sharia Talaat Harb, Cairo; tel. (2) 3927201; fax (2) 3935946; weekly; Editor-in-Chief Dr SAMI AZIZ.

Broadcasting and Communications

TELECOMMUNICATIONS

Egypt Telecommunications Co: Sharia Ramses, Cairo 11511; tel. (2) 7676244; telex 92100; fax (2) 771306; Chair. Eng. ABD AL-FATTAH ABU SEREE.

BROADCASTING

Radio

Egyptian Radio and Television Union (ERTU): POB 11511, Cairo 1186; tel. (2) 5787120; telex 92152; fax (2) 746989; internet http://www.sis.gov.eg/vidaudio/html/audiofm.htm; f. 1928; 450 hours daily. Home Service radio programmes in Arabic, English and French; foreign services in Arabic, English, French, Swahili, Hausa, Bengali, Urdu, German, Spanish, Armenian, Greek, Hebrew, Indonesian, Malay, Thai, Hindi, Pushtu, Persian, Turkish, Somali, Portuguese, Fulani, Italian, Zulu, Shona, Sindebele, Lingala, Afar, Amharic, Yoruba, Wolof, Bambara; Pres. AMIN BASSIOUNI.

Middle East Radio: Société Egyptienne de Publicité, 24-26 Sharia Zakaria Ahmad, Cairo; tel. (2) 5781010; fax 5784747; e-mail www.tahriv.net.

Television

Egyptian Radio and Television Union (ERTU): (see Radio).

Finance

(cap. = capital; p.u. = paid up;
dep. = deposits; res = reserves; m. = million; brs = branches;
amounts in Egyptian pounds unless otherwise stated)

BANKING

The whole banking system was nationalized in 1961. Since 1974 foreign and private-sector banks have been allowed to play a role in the economy, and in mid-1995 there were 84 banks operating in Egypt.

Central Bank

Central Bank of Egypt: 31 Sharia Qasr en-Nil, Cairo; tel. (2) 3931514; telex 22386; fax (2) 3926361; f. 1961; state-owned; cap. 100m., dep. 81,285m., res 3,447m., total assets 129,811m. (June 1997); Gov. and Chair. ESMAIEL HASSAN MUHAMMAD; 3 brs.

Commercial and Specialized Banks

Alexandria Commercial and Maritime Bank: POB 2376, 85 ave el-Hourriya, Alexandria 21519; tel. (3) 4921556; telex 54553; fax (3) 4913706; f. 1981; the Almar Co has a 19.2% shareholding, the National Investment Bank has a 12.7% interest and the Egyptian Co for Maritime Transport has an 8% interest. Other interests 60.1%; cap. 60.1m., dep. 830.5m., total assets 1,090.1m. (Dec. 1996); Chair. MUHAMMAD ADEL EL-BARKOUKI; Gen. Man. KAMAL E. A. ZAYED; 6 brs.

Bank of Alexandria, SAE: 6 Sharia Salah Salem, Alexandria; and 49 Sharia Qasr en-Nil, Cairo; tel. (3) 4830159 (Alexandria), (2) 3913822 (Cairo); telex 54107 (Alexandria), 22218 (Cairo); fax (3) 4839968 (Alexandria), (2) 3919805 (Cairo); f. 1957; state-owned; cap. 700m., dep. 15,686m., res 744m., total assets 20,320m. (June 1997); Chair. ABD AL-KARIM MUHAMMAD HAMID; 184 brs.

Bank of Commerce and Development: POB 1373, 13 Sharia 26 July, Sphinx Sq., Mohandessin, Cairo; tel. (2) 3472063; telex 21607; fax (2) 3450581; f. 1980; cap. 205.9m., dep. 559.9m., total assets 900.2m. (Dec. 1997); Chair. and Man. Dir SAMIR MUHAMMAD FOUAD EL-QASRI; 6 brs.

Banque du Caire, SAE: POB 1495, 30 Sharia Rushdi, Cairo; tel. (2) 3904554; telex 92022; f. 1952; state-owned; cap. 750.0m., res 167.3m., dep. 22,358.8m., total assets 26,897m. (June 1996); Chair. MUHAMMAD ABD EL-FATHI; 233 brs.

Banque Misr: 151 Sharia Muhammad Farid, Cairo; tel. (2) 3912711; telex 92242; fax (2) 3919779; f. 1920; state-owned since 1960; cap. p.u. 1,000m., res 264.2m., dep. 41,792.6m., total assets 47,680m. (June 1996); Chair. ESSAM ED-DIN EL-AHMADY; 400 brs.

Commercial International Bank (Egypt), SAE: POB 2430, Nile Tower Bldg, 21-23 Sharia Giza, Giza; tel. (2) 5701949; telex 20202; fax (2) 5703172; f. 1975 as Chase National Bank (Egypt) SAE; adopted present name 1987; National Bank of Egypt has 19.5% interest, International Finance Corpn 5%; cap. 650m., dep. 8,560m., total assets 13,470m. (Dec. 1997); Exec. Chair. MAHMOUD ABD AL-AZIZ; 28 brs.

Crédit Foncier Egyptien: 11 Sharia el-Mashadi, POB 141, Cairo; tel. (2) 3911977; telex 93863; fax (2) 3907363; f. 1880; state-owned; cap. p.u. 100m., total assets 1,173.5m. (June 1993); Chair. ADEL MAHMOUD ABD AL-BAKI; Gen. Man. ABD AL-WAHAB EL-ILADYDY; 9 brs.

Egyptian British Bank SAE: POB 126 D, Abu el-Feda Bldg, 3 Sharia Abu el-Feda, Cairo (Zamalek); tel. (2) 3409186; telex 20505; fax (2) 3414010; f. 1982; the Hongkong and Shanghai Banking Corporation has a 40% shareholding, Egyptian interests 51%, other Arab interests 9%; cap. 100.8m., res 8.5m., dep. 1,384.7m., total assets 1,682.2m. (Dec. 1996); Chair. Dr IBRAHIM ABU EL-EYOUN A. KAMAL; 6 brs.

Export Development Bank of Egypt: Evergreen Bldg, 10 Sharia Talaat Harb, Cairo; f. 1983 to replace National Import-Export Bank; tel. (2) 777003; telex 20850; fax (2) 774553; cap. p.u. 69m., res 119.7m., dep. 1,395.6m., total assets 1,942m. (June 1996); Chair. MAHMOUD MUHAMMAD MAHMOUD; 4 brs.

Industrial Development Bank of Egypt: 110 Sharia al-Galaa, Faggalah, Cairo; tel. (2) 779087; telex 23377; fax (2) 777324; f. 1975; cap. p.u. 146.2m.; total assets 1,865m. (June 1993); Chair. MUHAMMAD A. BASSAL; 14 brs.

National Bank for Development: POB 647, 5 Sharia el-Borsa el-Gedida, Cairo; tel. (2) 3563505; telex 20878; f. 1980; cap. p.u. 150.7m., res 92.0m., dep. 4,460m., total assets 5,363m. (Dec. 1996); Pres. MUHAMMAD ZAKI EL-ORABI; 66 brs; there are affiliated National Banks for Development in 16 governorates.

National Bank of Egypt: POB 11611, 1187 Corniche en-Nil, Cairo; tel. (2) 5749101; telex 20069; fax (2) 762672; f. 1898; nationalized 1960; handles all commercial banking operations; cap. 1,000m., dep. 39,193m., total assets 53,224m. (June 1996); Chair. MAHMOUD ABD AL-AZIZ MUHAMMAD; 343 brs.

Principal Bank for Development and Agricultural Credit: POB 11669, 110 Sharia Qasr el-Eini, Cairo; tel. (2) 3551204; fax (2) 3548337; f. 1976 to succeed former credit organizations; state-owned; cap. p.u. 1,105m., res 245m., dep. 5,244m., total assets 10,257m. (June 1997); Chair. HASSAN KHIDR; 8 brs.

Société Arabe Internationale de Banque: POB 54, 56 Sharia Gamet ed-Dowal al-Arabia, Mohandessin, Cairo (Giza); tel. (2) 3499463; telex 22087; fax (2) 3603497; f. 1976; the Arab International Bank has a 39.3% share, other interests 60.7%; cap. p.u. US $28m., res US $21m., dep. US $263.8m., total assets US $333m. (Dec. 1996); Chair. Dr HASSAN ABBAS ZAKI; 4 brs.

Social Bank

Nasser Social Bank: POB 2552, 35 Sharia Qasr en-Nil, Cairo; tel. (2) 744377; telex 92754; f. 1971; state-owned; interest-free savings and investment bank for social and economic activities, participating in social insurance, specializing in financing co-operatives, craftsmen and social institutions; cap. p.u. 20m.; Chair. NASSIF TAHOON.

Multinational Banks

Arab African International Bank: POB 60, 5 Midan es-Saray el-Koubra, Majlis ash-Sha'ab, Cairo 11516 (Garden City); tel. (2) 3545094; telex 93531; fax (2) 3558493; f. 1964; cap. p.u. US $100.0m., res US $21.6m., dep. US $921.8m., total assets US $1,151.0m (Dec. 1996); commercial investment bank; shareholders are Govts of Kuwait, Egypt, Algeria, Jordan and Qatar, Bank Al-Jazira (Saudi Arabia), Rafidain Bank (Iraq), individuals and Arab institutions; Chair. Dr FAHED MUHAMMAD AR-RASHED; 6 brs in Egypt, 6 abroad.

Arab International Bank: POB 1563, 35 Sharia Abd al-Khalek Sarwat, Cairo; tel. (2) 3918794; telex 92098; fax (2) 3916233; f. 1971 as Egyptian International Bank, renamed 1974; cap. p.u. US $200m., res US $104.6m., dep. US $1,824.8m., total assets US $2,189.3m. (June 1997); offshore bank; aims to promote trade and investment in shareholders' countries and other Arab countries; owned by Egypt, Libya, UAE, Oman, Qatar and private Arab shareholders; Chair. Dr MUSTAFA KHALIL; 6 brs in Egypt, 1 in Bahrain.

Commercial Foreign Venture Banks

Alwatany Bank of Egypt: POB 63, 13 Sharia Semar, Dr Fouad Mohi ed-Din Sq., Gameat ed-Dewal al-Arabia, Mohandessin, Cairo; tel. (2) 3379134; telex 93268; fax (2) 3379302; f. 1980; cap. p.u. 82.6m., res 62.2m., dep. 1,642m., total assets 2,002.3m. (Dec. 1996); Chair. ADEL HUSSEIN EZZI; 10 brs.

Banque du Caire Barclays International, SAE: POB 110, 12 Midan esh-Sheikh Yousuf, Cairo (Garden City); tel. (2) 3542195; telex 93734; fax (2) 3552746; f. 1975 as Cairo Barclays Int. Bank; name changed 1983; Banque du Caire has 51%, Barclays Bank 49%; cap. 50m., dep. 1,661m., total assets 2,033m. (Dec. 1996); Chair. MUHAMMAD ABO EL-FATH; 4 brs.

Banque du Caire et de Paris: POB 2441, 3 Sharia Latin America, Cairo (Garden City); tel. (2) 3548323; telex 93722; fax (2) 3540619; e-mail bcpegypt@bcpegypt.com; f. 1977; Banque Nationale de Paris has 76% interest and Banque du Caire 22%; cap. p.u. 50.5m., res 19.8m., dep. 716.1m., total assets 857.8m. (Dec. 1995); Chair. SAMIR MANSOUR; 6 brs.

Cairo Far East Bank SAE: POB 757, 104 Corniche en-Nil, Cairo (Dokki); tel. (2) 3362516; telex 93977; fax (2) 3483818; f. 1978; cap. p.u. 51.0m., dep. 180.9m., total assets 372.6m. (Dec. 1996); Chair. Dr HASSAN FAG EN-NOUR; 3 brs.

Crédit International d'Egypte: 46 Sharia el-Batal Ahmad Abd al-Aziz, Mohandessin, Cairo; tel. (2) 3361897; telex 21217; fax (2) 3608673; f. 1977; Crédit Commercial de France has 51% interest, National Bank of Egypt 20% and Berliner Handels und Frankfurter Bank 10%; cap. 50.2m., res 28.7m., dep. 435.3m., total assets 919.3m. (Dec. 1996); Gen. Man. MOUSTAFA KIWAN; 3 brs.

Delta International Bank: POB 1159, 1113 Corniche en-Nil, Cairo; tel. (2) 5753492; telex 93833; fax (2) 5743403; f. 1978; cap. p.u. 300m., dep. 1,214m. (Dec. 1997); Chair. and Man. Dir ALI MUHAMMAD NEGM; 16 brs.

Egyptian American Bank: POB 1825, 4 Sharia Hassan Sabri, Cairo (Zamalek); tel. (2) 3416150; telex 92683; fax (2) 3409430; f. 1976; Amex Holdings Inc. has 40.8% interest, Bank of Alexandria 35.3% and Public 23.8%; cap. p.u. 120m., res 228.5m., dep. 3,365.2m., total assets 4,076.5m. (Dec. 1997); Chair. ABD AL-KARIM MUHAMMAD ABD AL-HAMID; Man. Dir JAMES D. VAUGHN; 29 brs.

Egyptian Commercial Bank: POB 92, 4th Floor, Evergreen Bldg, 10 Sharia Talaat Harb, Majlis ash-Sha'ab, Cairo; tel. (2) 779766; telex 21394; fax (2) 764844; f. 1978 as Alexandria-Kuwait International Bank, name changed as above in 1997; Bank of Alexandria 71.68%, Kuwaiti Egyptian Real Estate Investment Co 1.8%, Principal Bank for Development and Agric. Credit 1.62%, Kato Aromatic 1.07%, other interests 23.83%; cap. 50m., res 11.5m., dep. 615m., total assets 855.4m. (Dec. 1993); Chair. MUHAMMAD ABD AL-WAHAD; 7 brs.

Egyptian Gulf Bank: POB 56, El-Orman Bldg, 8–10 Sharia Ahmad Nessim, Cairo (Giza); tel. (2) 3606640; telex 20214; fax (2) 3606512; f. 1981; Misr Insurance Co has 24.4% interest; cap. 85.0m., res 14.8m., dep. 1,229.8m., total assets 1,486.3m. (Dec. 1996); Chair. SALAH ED-DIN MUHAMMAD MAHMOUD; 5 brs.

Egyptian-Saudi Finance Bank: Es-Sabbah Tower, 8 Sharia Ibrahim Naguib, Cairo (Garden City); tel. (2) 3546208; telex 21086; fax (2) 3542911; f. 1980 as Pyramids Bank; cap. 63.2m., res 7.7m., dep. 692.2m., total assets 1,072.1m. (Dec. 1996); Chair. Sheikh SALEH ABDULLAH KAMAL; Man. Dir ABD AL-LATIF YOUSUF ABD AL-LATIF; 7 brs.

Faisal Islamic Bank of Egypt: POB 2446, 1113 Corniche en-Nil, Cairo; tel. (2) 5753109; telex 93877; fax (2) 777301; f. 1979; all banking operations conducted according to Islamic principles; cap. p.u. US $155.0m., res US $33.9m., dep. US $5,475.8m., total assets US $6,248.2m. (May 1997); Chair. Prince MUHAMMAD AL-FAISAL AS-SA'UD; Gen. Man. YOUSUF AL-BAGKIR MUDAWI; 14 brs.

Misr Exterior Bank, SAE: POB 272, Cairo Plaza Bldg, Corniche en-Nil, Ataba, Cairo; tel. (2) 778701; telex 94061; fax (2) 762806; e-mail meb2@rite.com; internet http://www.misrext.com; f. 1981; Misr International Bank has 30% interest, Banque Misr 19.5%, Domestic and International Funds 14%, Egyptian/Arab private investors 25%; cap. p.u. 51.1m., res 124.9m., dep. 3,345.2m., total assets 3,746.0m. (Dec. 1996); Chair. MUHAMMAD NABIL IBRAHIM; 9 brs.

Misr International Bank, SAE: POB 218, 54 Sharia al-Batal Ahmad Abd al-Aziz, Mohandessin, Cairo 12411; tel. (2) 3497091; telex 20840; fax (2) 3498072; f. 1975; the Banque Misr has 24.4% interest, Banco di Roma 10%, UBAF London 8.5%, Europartners 7.9%; cap. p.u. 112.5m., res 441.9m., dep. 7,658.3m., total assets 8,970.8m. (Dec. 1997); Chair. ESSAM ED-DIN MUHAMMAD EL-AHMADY; Vice-Chair. MUHAMMAD MONIEB; 14 brs.

Misr-America International Bank: POB 1003, 12 Sharia Nadi es-Seid, Dokki, Giza; tel. (2) 3616623; telex 21505; fax (2) 3616610; f. 1977; Banque du Caire has 33% interest, Misr Insurance Co 33%, Industrial Development Bank of Egypt 17%, S.A. for Investments, Luxembourg 17%; cap. p.u. 56m., res 10.8m., dep. 873.9m., total assets 984.9m. (Dec. 1995); Chair. and Man. Dir Dr YOUSRY ALI MOUSTAFA; 6 brs.

Misr-Romanian Bank, SAE: 54 Sharia Lebanon, Mohandessin, Cairo; tel. (2) 3039825; telex 92099; fax (2) 3039804; f. 1977; Banque Misr has 33% interest, Romanian Bank for Foreign Trade (Bucharest) 19%, Bank of Agriculture (Bucharest) 15%, and Romanian Bank for Development (Bucharest) 15%; cap. p.u. 58.0m., res 159.8., dep. 1,129.3m, total assets 1,486.9m. (Dec. 1997); Chair. Dr BAHAA ED-DIN HELMY ISMAIL; 5 brs in Egypt, 3 in Romania.

Mohandes Bank: POB 170, 3-5 Sharia Mossadek, Cairo (Dokki); tel. (2) 3373110; telex 20762; fax (2) 3362741; f. 1979; Engineers' Syndicate has 32.1% interest, National Investment Bank 12.5%, Becorb Holding Co 10%, Suez Canal Bank 9%, Suez Canal Authority 10%, other interests 36.4%; cap. p.u. 100,000m., res 0.1m., dep. 2,191m., total assets 2,910m. (Dec. 1996); Chair. Eng. HUSSEIN FAYEK SABBOUR; 10 brs.

Nile Bank, SAE: POB 2741, 35 Sharia Ramses, Cairo; tel. (2) 5741417; telex 20825; fax (2) 5756296; f. 1978; total assets 1,426.4m. (Dec. 1997); Chair. and Man. Dir ISSA EL-AYOUTY; 17 brs.

Suez Canal Bank, SAE: POB 2620, 11 Sharia Muhammad Sabry Abu Alam, Cairo; tel. (2) 3931033; telex 93852; fax (2) 3913522; f. 1978; cap. p.u. 50m., res 170.8m., dep. 5,056.6m., total assets 5,589.1m. (Dec. 1996); Chair. and Man. Dir MOUSTAFA FAYEZ HABLAS; 16 brs.

Non-Commercial Banks

Arab Investment Bank: POB 826, Cairo Sky Center Bldg, 8 Sharia Abd el-Khalik Tharwat, Cairo; tel. (2) 5759267; telex 20191; fax (2) 770329; f. 1978 as Union Arab Bank for Development and Investment; Egyptian/Syrian/Libyan joint venture; cap. p.u. 18.5m., res 31.8m., dep. 625m., total assets 977m. (Dec. 1990); Chair. Prof. Dr MUHAMMAD AHMAD ER-RAZAZ; 13 brs.

Egypt Arab African Bank: POB 61, Majlis ash-Sha'ab, 5 Midan es-Saray, el-Koubra, Cairo (Garden City); tel. (2) 3550948; telex 21600; fax (2) 3556239; e-mail eaab01@eaab.com.eg; internet http:// www.EAAB.com.eg; f. 1982; Arab African International Bank has 49% interest, Egyptian businessmen have 11.3%, Al-Mansour and Al-Maghraby Investment Co has 7.0%, Arab African International Bank's Pension Fund has 7%, other interests 25.7%; cap. p.u. 75m., res 60.8m., dep. 1,021.2m., total assets 1,364m. (Dec. 1997); merchant and investment bank services; Chair. Dr AHMAD ABD EL-WAHAB EL-GHANDOUR; 6 brs.

Housing and Development Bank, SAE: POB 234, 12 Sharia Syria, Mohandessin, Cairo; tel. (2) 3492013; telex 20175; fax (2) 3600712; e-mail hdbank@ie-eg.com; f. 1979; cap. p.u. 54m., res 149.8m., dep. 1,503.5m., (Dec. 1997); Chair. and Man. Dir Eng. MUHAMMAD HOSNI IBRAHIM ABUL ENEEN; 24 brs.

Islamic International Bank for Investment and Development: POB 180, 4 Sharia Ali Ismail, Mesaha Sq., Cairo (Dokki); tel. (2) 3489983; telex 20442; fax (2) 3600771; f. 1980; cap. p.u. 133.8m., res 1.7m., dep. 2,158.4m., total assets 2,360.6m. (Dec. 1996); Chair. MUHAMMAD ABD AL-WAKIL GABER; 8 brs.

Misr Iran Development Bank: POB 219, The Nile Tower, 21–23 Charles de Gaulle Ave, Cairo, Giza; tel. (2) 5727311; telex 21407; fax (2) 5701185; f. 1975; the Bank of Alexandria has 39.73% interest, Misr Insurance Co 39.73%, Bank Melli, Iran, 10.27%, Bank of Industry and Mines 10.27%; cap. p.u. 211.4m., res 94.1m., dep. 691.7m., total assets 1,267.8m. (Dec. 1996); Chair. Dr MAHMOUD SALAH ED-DIN HAMED; Man. Dir Dr AL-MOTAZ MANSOUR; 6 brs.

National Investment Bank: POB 3726, 37 Kwame Nkrumah Ave, Cairo; tel. (2) 669301; telex 2481; fax (2) 669307; f. 1980; state-owned; responsible for government projects; Chair. ZAFER EL-BESHRY.

National Société Générale Bank, SAE: POB 2664, 10 Sharia Talaat Harb, Cairo; tel. (2) 5749376; telex 22307; fax (2) 776249; f. 1978; the National Bank of Egypt has 18% interest, Société Générale de Paris 51%, other interests 31%; cap. p.u. 120m., res 129.8m., dep. 3,428.2m., total assets 3,935.9m. (Dec. 1997); Chair. MUHAMMAD MADBOULY; 8 brs.

STOCK EXCHANGES

Capital Market Authority: 20 Sharia Emad ed-Din, Cairo; tel. (2) 762626; fax (2) 5794176; f. 1979; Chair. ABD AL-HAMID IBRAHIM.

Cairo Stock Exchange: 4 Sharia esh-Sherifein, Cairo; tel. (2) 3921447; fax (2) 3928526; f. 1904; Chair. Dr MUHAMMAD HAMED.

Alexandria Stock Exchange: 11 Sharia Talaat Harb, Menshia, Alexandria; tel. (3) 4835432; fax (3) 4823039; f. 1861; Chair. EDWARD ANIS GEBRAYIL.

INSURANCE

Arab International Insurance Co: POB 2704, 28 Sharia Talaat Harb, Cairo; tel. (2) 5746322; telex 92599; fax (2) 760053; f. 1976; a joint-stock free zone company established by Egyptian and foreign insurance companies; Chair. and Man. Dir HASSAN MUHAMMAD HAFEZ.

Ach-Chark Insurance Co, SAE: 15 Sharia Qasr en-Nil, Cairo; tel. (2) 5753265; telex 92276; fax (2) 766963; f. 1931; Chair. Dr BORHAM ATALLAH; general and life.

Egyptian Reinsurance Co, SAE: POB 950, 7 Sharia Abd al-Latif Boltia, Cairo (Garden City); tel. (2) 3543354; telex 92245; fax (2) 3557483; f. 1957; Chair. MUHAMMAD MUHAMMAD AHMAD ET-TEIR.

L'Epargne, SAE: POB 548, Immeuble Chemla, Sharia 26 July, Cairo; all types of insurance.

Al-Iktisad esh-Shabee, SAE: 11 Sharia Emad ed-Din, Cairo; f. 1948; Man. Dir and Gen. Man. W. KHAYAT.

Misr Insurance Co: POB 261, 44A Sharia Dokki, Giza; tel. (2) 3355350; telex 22080; fax (2) 3370428; f. 1934; all classes of insurance and reinsurance; Chair. Dr MUHAMMAD ELTEIR.

Mohandes Insurance Co: POB 62, 3 El-Mesaha Sq., Dokki, Giza; tel. (2) 3352162; telex 93392; fax (2) 3352697.

Al-Mottahida: POB 804, 9 Sharia Sulayman Pasha, Cairo; f. 1957.

National Insurance Co of Egypt, SAE: 41 Sharia Qasr en-Nil, Cairo; tel. (2) 3910731; telex 92372; fax (2) 3909133; f. 1900; cap. 100m.; Chair. MUHAMMAD ESH-SHAZLY.

Provident Association of Egypt, SAE: POB 390, 9 Sharia Sherif Pasha, Alexandria; f. 1936; Man. Dir G. C. VORLOOU.

Trade and Industry

GOVERNMENT AGENCY

Egyptian Geological Survey and Mining Authority (EGSMA): 3 Sharia Salah Salem, Abbassia, Cairo; tel. (2) 4829935; telex 22695; fax (2) 4820128; f. 1896; state supervisory authority concerned with geological mapping, mineral exploration and other mining activities; Chair. GABER M. NAIM.

DEVELOPMENT ORGANIZATION

General Authority for Investment and Free Zones: POB 1007, 8 Sharia Adly, Cairo; tel. (2) 3906163; telex 92235; fax (2) 3907315; Exec. Pres. Dr IBRAKUM FAWZY.

CHAMBERS OF COMMERCE

Federation of Chambers of Commerce: 4 el-Falaki Sq., Cairo; tel. (2) 3551164; telex 92645; fax (2) 3557940; Pres. MAHMOUD EL-ARABY.

Alexandria

Alexandria Chamber of Commerce: 31 Sharia el-Ghorfa Altoga-riya, Alexandria; tel. (3) 809339; telex 4180; fax (2) 808993; Pres. MOSTAFA EL-NAGGAR.

Cairo

Cairo Chamber of Commerce: 4 el-Falaki Sq., Cairo; tel. (2) 3558261; telex 927753; fax (2) 3563603; f. 1913; Pres. MAHMOUD EL-ARABY; Sec.-Gen. MOSTAFA ZAKI TAHA.

In addition, there are 20 local chambers of commerce.

EMPLOYERS' ORGANIZATION

Federation of Egyptian Industries: POB 251, 26A Sharia Sherif Pasha, Cairo, and 65 Gamal Abd an-Nasser Ave, Alexandria; tel. (2) 3928317 (Cairo), (3) 4928622 (Alexandria); fax (2) 3928075; f. 1922; Pres. MUHAMMAD FARID KHAMIS; represents the industrial community in Egypt.

PETROLEUM

Arab Petroleum Pipelines Co (SUMED): POB 158 es-Saray, 431 El-Geish Ave, Louran, Alexandria; tel. (3) 5864138; telex 55446; fax (3) 5871295; f. 1974; Suez-Mediterranean crude petroleum transportation pipeline (capacity: 117m. tons per year) and petroleum terminal operators; Chair. and Man. Dir Eng. HAZEM AMIN HAMMAD.

Belayim Petroleum Co (PETROBEL): POB 7074, Sharia el-Mokhayam Cairo (Nasr City); tel. (2) 2621738; fax (2) 2609792; f. 1978; capital equally shared between EGPC and International Egyptian Oil Co, which is a subsidiary of ENI of Italy; petroleum and gas exploration, drilling and production.

Egyptian General Petroleum Corporation (EGPC): POB 2130, 4th Sector, Sharia Palestine, New Maadi, Cairo; tel. (2) 3531340; telex 92049; state supervisory authority generally concerned with the planning of policies relating to petroleum activities in Egypt with the object of securing the development of the petroleum industry and ensuring its effective administration; Chair. MUSTAFA SHAARAWI.

General Petroleum Co (GPC): 8 Sharia Dr Moustafa Abou Zahra, Cairo (Nasr City); f. 1957; wholly-owned subsidiary of EGPC; operates mainly in Eastern Desert.

Gulf of Suez Petroleum Co (GUPCO): POB 2400, 4th Sector, Sharia Palestine, New Maadi, Cairo; tel. (2) 3520985; telex 92248; fax (2) 3521286; f. 1965; partnership between EGPC and Amoco-Egypt Oil Co, which is a subsidiary of Amoco Corpn, USA; developed the el-Morgan oilfield in the Gulf of Suez, also holds other exploration concessions in the Gulf of Suez and the Western Desert; Chair. AHMAD SHAWKY ABDINE.

Western Desert Petroleum Co (WEPCO): POB 412, Alexandria; tel. (3) 4928710; telex 54075; f. 1967 as partnership between EGPC (50% interest) and Phillips Petroleum (35%) and later Hispanoil (15%); developed Alamein, Yidma and Umbarka fields in the Western Desert and later Abu Qir offshore gas field in 1978 followed by NAF gas field in 1987; Chair. Eng. MUHAMMAD MOHI ED-DIN BAHGAT.

Numerous foreign petroleum companies are prospecting for petroleum in Egypt under agreements with EGPC.

TRADE UNIONS

Egyptian Trade Union Federation (ETUF): 90 Sharia al-Galaa, Cairo; tel. (2) 5740362; fax (2) 5753427; f. 1957; 23 affiliated unions; 5m. mems; affiliated to the International Confederation of Arab Trade Unions and to the Organization of African Trade Union Unity; Pres. MUHAMMAD ES-SAYED RACHID; Gen. Sec. MUHAMMAD ES-SAYED MORSI.

General Trade Union of Air Transport: 5 Sharia Ahmad Sannan, St Fatima, Heliopolis; 11,000 mems; Pres. ABD AL-MONEM FARAG EISA; Gen. Sec. SHEKATA ABD AL-HAMID.

General Trade Union of Banks and Insurance: 2 Sharia el-Kady el-Fadel, Cairo; 56,000 mems; Pres. MAHMOUD MUHAMMAD DAB-BOUR; Gen. Sec. ABDOU HASSAN MUHAMMAD ALI.

General Trade Union of Building Workers: 9 Sharia Emad ed-Din, Cairo; 150,000 mems; Pres. HAMID HASSAN BARAKAT; Gen. Sec. SALEM ABD AR-RAZEK.

General Trade Union of Chemical Workers: 90 Sharia al-Galaa, Cairo; fax (2) 5750490; 120,000 mems; Pres. IBRAHIM EL-AZHARY; Gen. Sec. GAAFER ABD EL-MONEM.

General Trade Union of Commerce: 70 Sharia el-Gomhouriya, Cairo; tel. (2) 914124; f. 1903; more than 100,000 mems; Pres. ABD AR-RAZEK ESH-SHERBEENI; Gen. Sec. KAMAL HUSSEIN A. AWAD.

General Trade Union of Food Industries: 3 Sharia Housni, Hadaek el-Koba, Cairo; 111,000 mems; Pres. SAAD M. AHMAD; Gen. Sec. ADLY TANOUS IBRAHIM.

General Trade Union of Health Services: 22 Sharia esh-Sheikh Qamar, es-Sakakiny, Cairo; 56,000 mems; Pres. IBRAHIM ABOU EL-MUTI IBRAHIM; Gen. Sec. AHMAD ABD AL-LATIF SALEM.

General Trade Union of Hotels and Tourism Workers: POB 606, 90 Sharia al-Galaa, Cairo; tel. and fax (2) 773901; 70,000 mems; Pres. MUHAMMAD HILAL ES-SHARKAWI.

General Trade Union of Maritime Transport: 36 Sharia Sharif, Cairo; 46,000 mems; Pres. THABET MUHAMMAD ES-SEFARI; Gen. Sec. MUHAMMAD RAMADAN ABOU TOR.

General Trade Union of Military Production: 90 Sharia al-Galaa, Cairo; telex 93255; 64,000 mems; Pres. MOUSTAFA MUHAMMAD MOUNGI; Gen. Sec. FEKRY IMAM.

General Trade Union of Mine Workers: 5 Sharia Ali Sharawi, Hadaek el-Koba, Cairo; 14,000 mems; Pres. ABBAS MAHMOUD IBRAHIM; Gen. Sec. AMIN HASSAN AMER.

General Trade Union of Petroleum Workers: 5 Sharia Ali Sharawi, Hadaek el-Koba, Cairo; tel. (2) 820091; telex 93255; fax (2) 834551; 60,000 mems; Pres. MUHAMMAD ZAD ED-DIN; Gen. Sec. ABD AL-KADER HASSAN ABD AL-KADER.

General Trade Union of Postal Workers: 90 Sharia al-Galaa, Cairo; telex 93255; 80,000 mems; Pres. HASSAN MUHAMMAD EID; Gen. Sec. SALEM MAHMOUD SALEM.

General Trade Union of Press, Printing and Information: 90 Sharia al-Galaa, Cairo; tel. (2) 740324; telex 93255; 55,000 mems; Pres. MUHAMMAD ALI EL-FIKKI; Gen. Sec. AHMAD ED-DESSOUKI.

General Trade Union of Public and Administrative Workers: 2 Sharia Muhammad Haggag, Midan et-Tahrir, Cairo; tel. (2) 742134; telex 93255; 210,000 mems; Pres. ABD AR-RAHMAN KHEDR; Gen. Sec. MAHMOUD MUHAMMAD ABD EL-KHALEK.

General Trade Union of Public Utilities Workers: 30 Sharia Sharif, Cairo; tel. and fax (2) 3938293; telex 93255; 290,000 mems; Pres. MUHAMMAD ES-SAYED MORSI; Gen. Sec. MUHAMMAD TALAAT HASSAN.

General Trade Union of Railway Workers: POB 84 (el-Faggalah), 15 Sharia Emad ed-Din, Cairo; tel. (2) 5930305; fax (2) 5917776; 90,000 mems; Pres. SABER AHMAD HUSSAIN; Gen. Sec. YASIN SOLUMAN.

General Trade Union of Road Transport: 90 Sharia al-Galaa, Cairo; tel. (2) 5740413; telex 93255; fax (2) 5752955; 245,000 mems; Pres. MOUNIR BADR CHETA; Gen. Sec. SALINI GUNIDI.

General Trade Union of Telecommunications Workers: POB 651, Cairo; telex 93255; 60,000 mems; Pres. KHAIRI HACHEM; Sec.-Gen. IBRAHIM SALEH.

General Trade Union of Textile Workers: 327 Sharia Shoubra, Cairo; 244,000 mems; Pres. ALI MUHAMMAD DOUFDAA; Gen. Sec. HASSAN TOULBA MARZOUK.

General Trade Union of Workers in Agriculture and Irrigation: 31 Sharia Mansour, Cairo (Bab el-Louk); tel. (2) 3541419; 150,000 mems; Pres. MUKHTAR ABD AL-HAMID; Gen. Sec. FATHI A. KURTAM.

General Trade Union of Workers in Engineering, Metal and Electrical Industries: 90 Sharia al-Galaa, Cairo; tel. (2) 742519; telex 93255; 160,000 mems; Pres. SAID GOMAA; Gen. Sec. MUHAMMAD FARES.

Transport

RAILWAYS

The area of the Nile Delta is well served by railways. Lines also run from Cairo southward along the Nile to Aswan, and westward along the coast to Salloum.

Egyptian Railways: Station Bldg, Midan Ramses, Cairo; tel. (2) 5751000; telex 92616; fax (2) 5740000; f. 1852; length 8,600 km; 42 km electrified; a 346-km line to carry phosphate and iron ore from the Bahariya mines, in the Western Desert, to the Helwan iron and steel works in south Cairo, was opened in 1973, and the Quena–Safaga line (length 223 km) came into operation in 1989; Chair. M. M. MAREI.

Alexandria Passenger Transport Authority: POB 466, 3 Sharia Aflatone, esh-Shatby, Alexandria; tel. (3) 5975223; telex 54637; fax (3) 5971187; f. 1860; controls City Tramways (28 km), Ramleh Electric Railway (16 km), suburban buses (450 km); 126 tram cars, 42 light railway three-car sets; construction of the Alexandria Metro (55 km) began in 1997; Chair. Eng. ESSAM HASBY; Tech. Dir Eng. MEDHAT HAFEZ.

Cairo Metro: National Authority for Tunnels, Ministry of Transport, POB 466, Ramses Bldg, Midan Ramses, Cairo 11794; construction of the first underground transport system in Africa and the Middle East began in Cairo in 1982; connects electrified Helwan line of Egyptian railways with the diesel el-Marg line, via a 4.2-km tunnel with five stations beneath central Cairo, making a 42.5-km regional line with a total of 33 stations; gauge 1,435 mm, electrified; work on the first stage of the system was completed in July 1987, and it was opened in September; the second stage was completed in 1989; work on a second line linking Shubra el-Khaima with central Cairo and Giza commenced in 1992. This new line will have a total length of 19.5 km. (13 km in tunnel) and 18 stations, two of which will interconnect with the first line. The first stage started operating between Shubra el-Khaima and Ramses Square in 1996, the service extending to Tahrir Square in 1997. The rest of the line, extending to Cairo University, is under construction and is due to be completed in 1999; Chair. Eng. H. ABD ES-SALAM.

Cairo Transport Authority: POB 254, Madinet Nasr, Cairo; tel. (2) 830533; length 78 km (electrified); gauge 1,000 mm; operates 16 tram routes and 24 km of light railway; 720 cars.

Lower Egypt Railway: Mansura; f. 1898; length 160 km; gauge 1,000 mm; 20 diesel railcars.

ROADS

There are good metalled main roads as follows: Cairo–Alexandria (desert road); Cairo–Benna–Tanta–Damanhur–Alexandria; Cairo–Suez (desert road); Cairo–Ismailia–Port Said or Suez; Cairo–Fayum (desert road); in 1997 there were some 41,300 km of roads, including 22,000 km of highways. The Ahmad Hamdi road tunnel (1.64 km) beneath the Suez Canal was opened in 1980. A 320-km macadamized road linking Mersa Matruh, on the Mediterranean coast, with the oasis town of Siwa was completed in 1986.

General Authority for Roads and Bridges, Ministry of Transport: 105 Sharia Qasr el-Eini, Cairo; tel. (2) 3557429; fax (2) 3550591; e-mail garb@idsc.gov.eg; Chair. MUHAMMAD NABIL ELKOUSY.

SHIPPING

Egypt's principal ports are Alexandria, Port Said and Suez. A port constructed at a cost of £E315m. and designed to handle up to 16m. tons of grain, fruit and other merchandise per year (22% of the country's projected imports by the year 2000) in its first stage of development, was opened at Damietta in 1986. The second stage will increase handling capacity to 25m. tons per year. A ferry link between Nuweibeh and the Jordanian port of Aqaba was opened in 1985.

Alexandria Port Authority: 66 ave Gamal Abd an-Nasser, Alexandria; Head Office: 106 Sharia el-Hourriya, Alexandria; tel. (3) 4834321; fax (3) 4829714; f. 1966; Chair. Adm. SALAH MOKHTAR.

Major Shipping Companies

Alexandria Shipping and Navigation Co: POB 812, 557 ave el-Hourriya, Alexandria; tel. (3) 62923; telex 54029; services between Egypt, N. and W. Europe, USA, Red Sea and Mediterranean; 5 vessels; Chair. and Man. Dir Eng. MAHMOUD ISMAIL; Man. Dir ABD AL-AZIZ QADRI.

Egyptian Navigation Co: POB 82, 2 Sharia en-Nasr, Alexandria; tel. (3) 4800050; telex 54131; fax (3) 4831345; f. 1930; owners and operators of Egypt's mercantile marine; services Alexandria/Europe, USA, Black Sea, Adriatic Sea, Mediterranean Sea, Indian Ocean and Red Sea; 30 vessels; Chair. FATHI SOROUR.

Pan-Arab Shipping Co: POB 39, 404 ave el-Hourriya, Rouchdy, Alexandria; tel. (3) 5468835; telex 54123; fax (3) 5469533; f. 1974; Arab League Co; 5 vessels; Chair. Adm. SHERIF ES-SADEK; Gen. Man. Capt. MAMDOUH EL-GUINDY.

THE SUEZ CANAL

In 1997 a total of 14,430 vessels, with a net displacement of 369m. tons, used the Suez Canal, linking the Mediterranean and Red Seas.

Length of Canal 190 km; maximum permissible draught: 17.68 m (58 ft); breadth of canal at water level and breadth between buoys defining the navigable channel 365 m and 225 m respectively in the northern section and 365 m and 205 m in the southern section.

Suez Canal Authority (Hay'at Canal as-Suweis): Irshad Bldg, Ismailia; tel. (64) 330000; telex 63238; fax (64) 320784; Cairo Office: 6 Sharia Lazoughli, Cairo (Garden City); f. 1956; Chair. Adm. AHMAD ALI FADEL.

CIVIL AVIATION

The main international airports are at Heliopolis (23 km from the centre of Cairo) and Alexandria (7 km from the city centre). An international airport was opened at Nuzhah in 1983.

EgyptAir: Cairo International Airport, Heliopolis, Cairo; tel. (2) 2454400; fax (2) 2449727; f. 1932 as Misr Airwork; known as United

Arab Airlines 1960–1971; operates internal services in Egypt and external services throughout the Middle East, Far East, Africa, Europe and the USA; Chair. Eng. MUHAMMAD FAHIM RAYAN.

Egyptian Civil Aviation Authority: Sharia Airport, Cairo; tel. (2) 2678544; fax (2) 2678542; Chair. ALI OSMAN ZIKO.

Tourism

Tourism is currently Egypt's second-largest source of revenue, generating around US $3,000m. annually. Traditionally the industry has attracted tourists to its pyramids and monuments. Recently the industry has diversified; the Red Sea coastline boasts 1,000 km of beaches along which developments, including two international airports at Taba and Suba Bay, are under construction.

Ministry of Tourism: Misr Travel Tower, Abbassia Sq., Cairo; tel. (2) 2828430; telex 94040; fax (2) 2829771; f. 1965; brs at Alexandria, Port Said, Suez, Luxor and Aswan; Minister of Tourism Dr MAMDOUH EL-BELTAGI.

Egyptian General Authority for the Promotion of Tourism: Misr Travel Tower, Abbassia Sq., Cairo; tel. (2) 2853576; fax (2) 2854363; Chair. ADEL ABD AL-AZIZ.

Egyptian General Co for Tourism and Hotels: 4 Sharia Latin America, Cairo (Garden City); tel. (2) 3026470; telex 92363; fax (2) 3024456; f. 1961; affiliated to the holding co for Housing, Tourism and Cinema.

Defence

Supreme Commander of the Armed Forces: President MUHAMMAD HOSNI MUBARAK.

Commander-in-Chief of the Armed Forces: Field Marshal MUHAMMAD ABD AL-HALIM ABU GHAZALAH.

Chief of Staff of the Armed Forces: Lt-Gen. SAFIY AD-DIN ABU SHINAF.

Commander of the Air Force: Air Marshal MUHAMMAD ABD AL-HAMID HELMI.

Commander of Air Defence: Maj.-Gen. MUSTAFA AHMAD ASH-SHADHILI.

Commander of the Navy: Admiral MUHAMMAD SHARIF AS-SADIQ.

Budgeted Defence Expenditure (1997): £E8,700m. (US $2,600m.).

Military service: Three years, selective.

Total armed forces (August 1997): 450,000; army 320,000; air defence command 80,000; navy 20,000; air force 30,000. Reserves 254,000. Paramilitary forces: 230,000 (Central Security Forces 150,000, National Guard 60,000, etc.).

Education

Education is compulsory for five years between six and 11 years of age. Secondary education, beginning at 12 years of age, lasts for a further six years, comprising two equal cycles of three years each. Enrolment at primary and secondary schools in 1995 was equivalent to 87% of children in the relevant age-groups (boys 93%; girls 80%). In that year primary enrolment was equivalent to 100% of children in the relevant age-group (males 107%; females 93%), while the comparable ratio for secondary enrolment was 74% (males 80%; females 68%). More than 13.8m. people were receiving state education in 1993. There are 13 universities. Education is free at all levels. The 1996 census recorded the rate of adult illiteracy as 38.6%, compared with 49.6% in the 1986 census. During 1986–96 the number of university graduates increased by 3%, to 7.3% of the population.

Bibliography

GENERAL

Abdel-Malek, Anwar. *Egypte, société militaire.* Paris, 1962.

Idéologie et renaissance nationale / L'Egypte moderne. Paris, 1969.

Ahmed, J. M. *The Intellectual Origins of Egyptian Nationalism.* London, Royal Institute of International Affairs, 1960.

Aldridge, James. *Cairo: Biography of a City.* London, Macmillan, 1970.

Armbrust Walter. *Mass Culture and Modernism in Egypt.* Cambridge University Press, 1996.

Ayrout, H. H. *The Egyptian Peasant.* Boston, 1963.

Baddour, Abd. *Sudanese-Egyptian Relations. A Chronological and Analytical Study.* The Hague, Nijhoff, 1960.

Badeau, J. S. *The Emergence of Modern Egypt.* New York, 1953.

Baer, Gabriel. *A History of Landownership in Modern Egypt 1800–1950.* London, Oxford University Press, 1962.

The Evolution of Landownership in Egypt and the Fertile Crescent, the Economic History of the Middle East 1800–1914. Chicago and London, University of Chicago Press, 1966.

Studies in the Social History of Modern Egypt. Chicago and London, University of Chicago Press, 1969.

Baker, Raymond William. *Egypt's Uncertain Revolution under Nasser and Sadat.* Harvard University Press, 1979.

Berger, Morroe. *Bureaucracy and Society in Modern Egypt: a Study of the Higher Civil Service.* Princeton University Press, 1957.

Islam in Egypt Today: Social and Political Aspects of Popular Religion. Cambridge University Press, 1970.

Berque, Jacques. *Egypt: Imperialism and Revolution.* London, Faber, 1972.

Boktor, Amin. *The Development and Expansion of Education in the UAR.* Cairo, The American University, 1963.

Cannuyer, Christian. *Les Copres.* Turnhout, Editions Brepol 1991.

Chevillat, Alain and Evelyne. *Moines du désert d'Egypte.* Lyons, Editions Terres du Ciel, 1991.

Coult, Lyman H. *An Annotated Bibliography of the Egyptian Fellah.* University of Miami Press, 1958.

Cromer, Earl of. *Modern Egypt.* 2 vols, London, 1908.

Dawisha, A. I. *Egypt in the Arab World.* London, Macmillan, 1976.

Dodwell, H. *The Founder of Modern Egypt.* Cambridge, 1931, reprinted 1967.

Driault, E. *L'Egypte et l'Europe.* 5 vols, Cairo, 1935.

Garzouzi, Eva. *Old Ills and New Remedies in Egypt.* Cairo, Dar al-Maaref, 1958.

Harris, C. P. *Nationalism and Revolution in Egypt: the Role of the Muslim Brotherhood.* The Hague, Mouton and Co, 1964.

Harris, J. R. (Ed.). *The Legacy of Egypt.* 2nd edn Oxford University Press, 1972.

Holt, P. M. *Egypt and the Fertile Crescent.* London, Longman, 1966.

Hopkins, Harry. *Egypt, The Crucible.* London, Secker and Warburg, 1969.

Hurst, H. E. *The Nile.* London, 1952.

The Major Nile Projects. Cairo, 1966.

Kepel, Gilles. *The Prophet and the Pharaoh: Muslim Extremism in Egypt.* London, Al Saqi Books, 1985.

King, Joan Wucher (Ed.). *An Historical Dictionary of Egypt.* Metuchen, NJ, Scarecrow Press, 1984.

Lacouture, Jean and Simonne. *Egypt in Transition.* London, Methuen, 1958.

Lauterpacht, E. (Editor). *The Suez Canal Settlement.* London, Stevens and Sons, 1960, under the auspices of the British Institute of International and Comparative Law.

Lengye, Emil. *Egypt's Role in World Affairs.* Washington, DC, Public Affairs Press, 1957.

Little, Tom. *Modern Egypt.* London, Ernest Benn, 1967, New York, Praeger, 1967.

Lloyd, Lord. *Egypt since Cromer.* 2 vols, London, 1933–34.

Marlowe, J. *Anglo-Egyptian Relations.* London, 1954.

Nasser, Gamal Abdel. *Egypt's Liberation: The Philosophy of the Revolution.* Washington, 1955.

Neguib, Mohammed. *Egypt's Destiny: A Personal Statement.* New York, 1955.

Owen, Robert, and Blunsum, Terence. *Egypt, United Arab Republic, The Country and its People.* London, Queen Anne Press, 1966.

Pick, Christopher. *Egypt: A Traveller's Anthology.* London, John Murray, 1991.

Riad, Hassan. *L'Egypte Nassérienne.* Paris, Editions de Minuit, 1964.

Robin, Barry. *Islamic Fundamentalism in Egyptian Politics.* London, Macmillan, 1990.

Stewart, Desmond. *Cairo*. London, Phoenix House, 1965.

Vaucher, G. *Gamal Abdel Nasser et son Equipe*. 2 vols, Leiden, Brill, 1950.

Viollet, Roger, and Doresse, Jean. *Egypt*. New York, Cromwell, 1955.

Waterfield, Gordon. *Egypt*. London, Thames and Hudson, 1966.

Watt, D. C. *Britain and the Suez Canal*. London, Royal Institute of International Affairs, 1956.

Wavell, W. H. *A Short Account of the Copts*. London, 1945.

Weaver, Mary Ann. *A Portrait of Egypt: A Journey Through the World of Militant Islam*. New York, Fawar, Straus and Giroux, 1998.

Wilbur, D. N. *The United Arab Republic*. New York, 1969.

Wilson, John A. *The Burden of Egypt*. Chicago, 1951.

Wynn, Wilton. *Nasser of Egypt: The Search for Dignity*. Cambridge, Mass., 1959.

ANCIENT EGYPT

Aldred, Cyril. *Egypt to the End of the Old Kingdom*. London, Thames and Hudson, 1965.

Bernard, Jean-Louis. *Aux origines de l'Egypte*. Paris, Laffont, 1976.

Breasted, James Henry. *A History of Egypt from the Earliest Times to the Persian Conquest*. New York, Harper and Row, 1959.

De Lubicz, A. S. *The Temples of Karnak*. 2 vols, London, 1961.

Fischel, Walter J. *Ibn Khaldun in Egypt*. University of California Press, 1967.

Forster, E. M. *Alexandria: a History and a Guide*. New York, Doubleday, 1961.

Gardiner, Sir Alan Henderson. *Egypt of the Pharaohs*. Oxford, Clarendon Press, 1961.

Glanville, S. R. K. (Ed.). *The Legacy of Egypt*. Oxford, 1942.

Greener, L. *The Discovery of Egypt*. London, Cassell, 1966, New York, Viking Press, 1967.

James, T. G. H. *Howard Carter—The Path to Tutankhamun*. London, Kegan Paul International, 1993.

A Short History of Ancient Egypt from Pre-dynastic to Roman Times. London, Cassell, 1996.

Johnson, Allan C. *Egypt and the Roman Empire*. Ann Arbor, 1951.

Meyer-Ranke, Peter. *Der Rote Pharao*. Hamburg, Christian Wegner Verlag, 1964.

Montet, Pierre. *Das Leben der Pharaonen*. Frankfurt/Berlin/Vienna, 1970.

Murnane, William J. *The Penguin Guide to Ancient Egypt*. London, Penguin, 1984.

Pirenne, Jacques. *Histoire de la Civilization de l'Egypte antique*. Neuchâtel, 1966.

La Religion et la Morale de l'Egypte antique. Neuchâtel, La Baconnière, 1966.

Posener, G. (Ed.). *A Dictionary of Egyptian Civilization*. London, Methuen, 1962.

Rice, Michael. *Egypt's Making: the origins of Ancient Egypt 5000–2000BC*. London, Routledge, 1990.

Egypt's Legacy: The archetypes of Western civilization 3000–30 BC. London, Routledge, 1997.

MODERN HISTORY

Avram, Benno. *The Evolution of the Suez Canal State 1869–1956. A Historico-Juridical Study*. Geneva, Paris, Librairie E. Droz, Librairie Minard, 1958.

Baker, Raymond William. *Sadat and After: struggles for Egypt's political soul*. London, I. B. Tauris, 1990.

Baraway, Rashed El-. *The Military Coup in Egypt*. Cairo, Renaissance Bookshop, 1952.

Barraclough, Geoffrey (Ed.). *Suez in History*. London, 1962.

Blunt, Wilfred Scawen. *Secret History of the English Occupation of Egypt*. London, Martin Secker, 1907.

Brown, Nathan J. *Peasant Politics in Modern Egypt: the struggle against the state*. New Haven and London, Yale University Press, 1990.

Carter, B. L. *The Copts in Egyptian Politics*. London, Croom Helm, 1986.

Cohen, Raymond. *Culture and Conflict in Egyptian-Israeli Relations: A Dialogue of the Deaf*. Indiana University Press, 1994.

Connell, John. *The Most Important Country. The Story of the Suez Crisis and the Events leading up to It*. London, Cassell, 1957.

Cooper, Mark N. *The Transformation of Egypt*. London, Croom Helm, 1982.

Efendi, Husein. *Ottoman Egypt in the Age of the French Revolution* (trans. and with introduction by Stanford J. Shaw). Cambridge, Mass., Harvard Univ. Press, 1964.

Farnie, D. A. *East and West of Suez. The Suez Canal in history, 1854–1956*. Oxford, Clarendon Press, 1969.

Fawzi, Mahmoud. *Suez 1956*. London, Shorouk International, 1986.

Finklestone, Joseph. *Anwar Sadat: Visionary Who Dared*. London, Frank Cass, 1998.

Heikal, Muhammad. *The Road to Ramadan*. London, Collins, 1975.

Sphinx and Commissar: The Rise and Fall of Soviet Influence in the Arab World. London, Collins, 1978.

Autumn of Fury: The Assassination of Sadat. London, André Deutsch, 1983.

Cutting the Lion's Tail: Suez through Egyptian eyes. London, André Deutsch, 1986.

Hirst, David, and Beeson, Irene. *Sadat*. London, Faber, 1981.

Holt, P. M. *Political and Social Change in Modern Egypt*. Oxford University Press, 1967.

Hussein, Mahmoud. *La Lutte de Classes en Egypte de 1945 à 1968*. Paris, Maspero, 1969.

Ismael, Tareq Y., and El-Said, Rifa'at. *The Communist Movement in Egypt 1920–1988*. Syracuse University Press, 1990.

Issawi, Charles. *Egypt in Revolution*. Oxford, 1963.

Joesten, Joachim. *Nasser: The Rise to Power*. London, Odhams, 1960.

Kamel, Muhammad Ibrahim. *The Camp David Accords: A Testimony by Sadat's Foreign Minister*. London, Routledge and Kegan Paul, 1986.

Kinross, Lord. *Between Two Seas: The Creation of the Suez Canal*. London, John Murray, 1968.

Kyle, Keith. *Suez*. London, Weidenfeld, 1991.

Lacouture, Jean. *Nasser: A Biography*. London, Secker and Warburg, 1973.

Lane-Poole, S. *History of Egypt in the Middle Ages*. 4th edn, reprinted, London, Frank Cass, 1967.

Love, K. *Suez: the Twice-fought War*. Longman, 1970.

Mansfield, Peter. *Nasser's Egypt*. London, Penguin Books, 1965.

Nasser. London, Methuen, 1969.

The British in Egypt. London, Weidenfeld and Nicolson, 1971.

Marlowe, John. *Cromer in Egypt*. London, Elek Books, 1970.

Marsot, Afaf Lutfi as-Sayyed. *A Short History of Modern Egypt*. Cambridge University Press, 1985.

Nutting, Anthony. *No End of a Lesson; the Story of Suez*. London, Constable, 1967.

Nasser. London, Constable, 1972.

O'Ballance, E. *The Sinai Campaign 1956*. London, Faber, 1959.

Quandt, William B. *Camp David: Peacemaking and Politics*. Washington, DC, Brookings Institution, 1986.

Raymond, André. *Artisans et commerçants au Caire au XVIIIe siècle*. 2 vols Paris, Librairie Adrien-Maisonneuve 1973–74.

Richmond, J. C. B. *Egypt, 1798–1952: Her Advance towards a Modern Identity*. London, Methuen, 1977.

Sadat, Anwar Al-. *Revolt on the Nile*. London, Allen Wingate, 1957.

Safran, Nadav. *Egypt in Search of Political Community. An analysis of the intellectual and political evolution of Egypt, 1804–1952*. Cambridge, Mass., Harvard University Press, London, Oxford University Press, 1961.

Sayyid, Afaf Lutfi Al-. *Egypt and Cromer: A Study in Anglo-Egyptian Relations*. London, John Murray, New York, Praeger, 1968.

Schonfield, Hugh A. *The Suez Canal in Peace and War, 1869–1969*. London, Vallentine, Mitchell, 2nd revised edn, 1969.

Shaw, Tony. *Eden, Suez and the Mass Media: Propaganda and Persuasion During the Suez Crisis*. London, I. B. Tauris, 1995.

Shazly, Gen. Saad El-. *The Crossing of Suez: The October War (1973)*. London, Third World Centre for Research and Publishing, 1980.

Stephens, R. *Nasser*. London, Allen Lane, The Penguin Press, 1971.

Tignor, R. L. *Modernization and British Colonial Rule in Egypt 1882–1914*. Princeton, 1966.

Vatikiotis, P. J. *A Modern History of Egypt*. New York, Praeger, 1966; London, Weidenfeld and Nicolson, 1969, revised edn, 1980.

The Egyptian Army in Politics. Bloomington, Indiana University Press, 1961.

Waterbury, John. *The Egypt of Nasser and Sadat: The Political Economy of Two Regimes*. Princeton University Press, 1983.

Zaki, Abdel Rahman. *Histoire Militaire de l'Epoque de Mohammed Ali El-Kebir*. Cairo, 1950.

ECONOMY

El Ghonemy, M. Riad. *Economic and Industrial Organization of Egyptian Agriculture since 1952, Egypt since the Revolution*. London, Allen and Unwin, 1968.

Hvidt, Martin. *Water, Technology and Development: Upgrading Egypt's Irrigation System*. London, Tauris Academic Studies, 1997.

El Kammash, M. M. *Economic Development and Planning in Egypt*. London, 1967.

Kardouche, G. S. *The UAR in Development*. New York, Praeger, 1967.

Mabro, Robert. *The Egyptian Economy 1952–1972*. London, Oxford University Press, 1974.

Mead, Donald C. *Growth and Structural Change in the Egyptian Economy*. Homwood, Ill., Irwin, 1967.

O'Brien, Patrick. *The Revolution in Egypt's Economic System 1952–65*. Oxford, 1966.

Saab, Gabriel S. *The Egyptian Agrarian Reform 1952–1962*. London and New York, Oxford University Press, 1967.

Warriner, Doreen. *Land Reform and Economic Development*. Cairo, 1955.

Land Reform and Development in the Middle East—A Study of Egypt, Syria and Iraq. 2nd edn London, Oxford University Press, 1962.

IRAN

Physical and Social Geography

W. B. FISHER

SITUATION

The Islamic Republic of Iran is bounded on the north by the Caspian Sea, Azerbaijan and Turkmenistan, on the east by Afghanistan and Pakistan, on the south by the Persian Gulf and Gulf of Oman, and on the west by Iraq and Turkey.

PHYSICAL FEATURES

Structurally, Iran is an extremely complex area and, owing partly to political difficulties and partly to the difficult nature of the country itself, complete exploration and investigation have not so far been achieved. In general, Iran consists of an interior plateau, 1,000 m to 1,500 m (3,000 ft to 5,000 ft) above sea-level, ringed on almost all sides by mountain zones of varying height and extent. The largest mountain massif is that of the Zagros, which runs from the north-west of Iran, where the frontiers of Iran, Azerbaijan, Turkmenistan, Turkey and Iraq meet, first south-westwards to the eastern shores of the Persian Gulf, and then eastwards, fronting the Arabian Sea, and continuing into Baluchistan (Pakistan). Joining the Zagros in the north-west, and running along the southern edge of the Caspian Sea, is the narrower but equally high Elburz range; whilst along the eastern frontier of Iran are several scattered mountain chains, less continuous and imposing than either the Zagros or the Elburz, but sufficiently high to act as a barrier.

The Zagros range begins in north-west Iran as an alternation of high tablelands and lowland basins, the latter containing lakes, the largest of which is Lake Urmia. This lake, having no outlet, is saline. Further to the south-east the Zagros becomes much more imposing, consisting of a series of parallel hog's-back ridges, some of which reach over 4,000 m in height. In its southern and eastern portions the Zagros becomes distinctly narrower, and its peaks much lower, though a few exceed 3,000 m. The Elburz range is very much narrower than the Zagros, but equally, if not more abrupt, and one of its peaks, the volcanic cone of Mt Damavand, at 5,604 m (18,386 ft), is the highest in the country. There is a sudden drop on the northern side to the flat plain occupied by the Caspian Sea, which lies about 27 m below sea-level, and is shrinking rapidly in size. The eastern highlands of Iran consist of isolated massifs separated by lowland zones, some of which contain lakes from which there is no outlet, the largest being the Hirmand Basin, on the borders of Iran and Afghanistan.

The interior plateau of Iran is partly covered by a remarkable salt swamp (termed *kavir*) and partly by loose sand or stones (*dasht*), with stretches of better land mostly round the perimeter, near the foothills of the surrounding mountains. In these latter areas much of the cultivation of the country is practised, but the lower-lying desert and swamp areas, towards the centre of the plateau, are largely uninhabited. The Kavir is an extremely forbidding region, consisting of a surface formed by thick plates of crystallized salt, which have sharp, upstanding edges. Below the salt lie patches of mud, with, here and there, deep drainage channels—all of which are very dangerous to travellers, and are hence unexplored. Because of the presence of an unusually intractable 'dead heart', it has proved difficult to find a good central site for the capital of Iran—many towns, all peripheral to a greater or lesser degree, have in turn fulfilled this function, but none has proved completely satisfactory. The choice of the present capital, Teheran, dates only from the end of the 18th century.

Iran suffers from occasional earthquakes, which can cause severe loss of life, damage to property and disruption of communications. A particularly bad example occurred around Tabas in the north-eastern Khurasan province in September 1978, when an estimated 20,000 lives were lost; severe damage was inflicted, extending over 2,000 sq km. Even more devastating was the major earthquake which struck north-western Iran (principally the provinces of Gilan and Zanjan) in June 1990. Estimates put the number of those killed during the first quake and a series of severe tremors and aftershocks at between 35,000 and 40,000, while more than 60,000 were reported to have been injured in the disaster.

The climate of Iran is one of great extremes. Owing to its southerly position, adjacent to Arabia and near the Thar Desert, the summer is extremely hot, with temperatures in the interior rising possibly higher than anywhere else in the world—certainly a temperature exceeding 55°C has been recorded. In winter, however, the great altitude of much of the country and its continental situation result in far lower temperatures than one would expect to find for a country in such low latitudes. Temperatures of –30°C have been recorded in the north-west Zagros, and –20°C is common in many places.

Another unfortunate feature is the prevalence of strong winds, which intensify the temperature contrasts. Eastern Iran is subject to the so-called 'Wind of 120 Days', which blows regularly throughout summer, occasionally reaching a velocity of more than 160 km per hour and often raising sand to such an extent that the stone walls of buildings are sometimes scoured away and turn to ruins.

Most of Iran is arid; but in contrast, parts of the north-west and north receive considerable rainfall—up to 2,000 mm along parts of the Caspian coast, producing very special climatic conditions in this small region, recalling conditions in the lower Himalayas. The Caspian coast has a hot, humid climate and this region is by far the most densely populated of the whole country. Next in order of population density comes the north-west Zagros area—the province of Azerbaijan, with its capital, Tabriz, the fourth city of Iran. Then, reflecting the diminished rainfall, next in order come the central Zagros area, and adjacent parts of the interior plateau, round Isfahan, Hamadan, Shiraz and Kermanshah, with an extension as far as Teheran. The extreme east and south, where rainfall is very scarce, were historically extremely lightly populated, except in the few parts where water is available, by nomadic groups. Over the past few years, however, a development programme has been initiated, and the effects are seen in the expansion of the towns, some of which have grown by 30%–40% since 1972.

ECONOMIC LIFE

Owing to the difficulties of climate and topography, there are few districts, apart from the Caspian plain, that are continuously cultivated over a wide area. Settlement tends to occur in small clusters, close to water supplies, or where there are especially favourable conditions—a good soil, shelter from winds, or easy communications. Away from these cultivated areas, which stand out like oases among the barren expanses of desert or mountain, most of the population live as nomads, by the herding of animals. The nomadic tribesmen have had great influence on the life of Iran. Their principal territory is the central Zagros, where the tribal system is strongly developed; but nomads are found in all the mountain zones, though their numbers are very few in the south and east. Reza Shah (see History) made considerable efforts to break the power of the nomadic tribes and to force them to settle as agriculturalists. Now, with the development of the economy, many nomads have moved into towns (though some still remain).

Economic activity has suffered from the handicaps of topography and climate, prolonged political and social insecurity (with constant pressure by foreign powers), and widespread devastation in the later Middle Ages by Mongol invaders. Agricultural methods in particular are primitive, so that yields are low; but the drawbacks to efficient production—archaic systems of land tenure, absentee landlords, lack of education, and shortage of capital—are gradually being overcome. In the north and west, which are by far the most productive regions, a wide variety of cereals (including wheat, barley and rice) and much fruit are grown, but in the south and east the date is the principal source of food.

Iran has a number of mineral resources, some of which are exploited on a commercial scale. Copper deposits at Sar Cheshmeh are among the largest in the world. Iran also has very significant oil and natural gas resources; and there are large deposits of good-quality coal and iron ore near Kerman. Iranians have always had a good reputation as craftsmen—particularly in metal-work and in carpet making. Although Reza Shah attempted to develop modern mechanized industry by placing state-owned factories in most large towns—some of which proved successful, others not—bazaar manufactures have retained their importance. Teheran is now a major manufacturing centre, with a considerable spread of activities from the processing of foodstuffs to the manufacture of consumer and construction goods and an increasing range of more complex items: electronics, motor manufacturing and high-grade chemicals.

The adverse nature of geographical conditions has greatly restricted the growth of communications in Iran. The country is very large in relation to its size of population—it is 2,250 km from north-west to south-west—and, because of the interior deserts, many routes must follow a circuitous path instead of attempting a direct crossing. Then, too, the interior is isolated by ranges that are in parts as high as the Alps of Europe, but far less broken up by river valleys. Road construction is generally difficult, but since the mid-1960s increasing effort has been devoted to providing all-weather trunk routes between major cities for which special allocations have been made in the five-year plans. An important link is the railway constructed with great effort before the Second World War between the Caspian coast, Teheran and the Persian Gulf. Other rail links with bordering countries already exist or are under construction. Although there are mountain streams, many flowing in deep, inaccessible gorges, only one, the Karun river, is at all navigable. The Caspian ports are subject to silting, while most of the harbours in the south are either poorly sheltered or difficult of access from the interior. However, there has been a deliberate focusing of development on the Gulf, in response to the enhanced economic and political status of the region, now one of the wealthiest parts of the world. Development was undertaken in the region of the Shatt al-Arab in the last years of the Shah's regime. However, the war between Iran and Iraq, beginning in September 1980, greatly impeded economic prospects, both there and in the Persian Gulf. Overall, the effect of the Revolution of 1979 was to reduce, though not entirely to terminate, the sophisticated industrial developments that were initiated under the Shah, and to shift external trading more towards imports of basic raw materials and food, balanced (often by direct exchange approaching barter) by exports of petroleum which, though reduced (in part because of war in the Gulf), are still considerable.

RACE AND LANGUAGE

Iran has numerous ethnic groups of widely differing origin. In the central plateau there occurs a distinctive sub-race, termed by some anthropologists Iranian or Irano-Afghan. In the mountain districts there are many other smaller groups of separate racial composition. A number of nomads, including the Bakhtiari tribes, would seem to be of Kurdish stock; whilst Turki (Mongoloid) strains are apparent in others, such as the Qashqai tribes. Smaller groups from the Caucasus (Georgians and Circassians) are represented in Azerbaijan and the Caspian provinces, whilst Turki influence is again apparent in the racial composition of the eastern districts of Iran, especially round Meshed. The southern Zagros near the Arabian Sea has a small population that tends to be of mixed Iranian, Afghan, and Hindu stock. Some observers have suggested that in this region there may also be representatives of a primitive negrito race, related to the hill-tribes of India and of south-east Asia.

With so many differing ethnic groups, it is not surprising to find that several languages are current in Iran. Persian (Farsi), an Indo-Aryan language related to the languages of western Europe, is spoken in the north and centre of the country, and is the one official language of the state. As the north is by far the most densely peopled region of Iran, the Persian language has an importance somewhat greater than its territorial extent would suggest. Various dialects of Kurdish are current in the north and central Zagros mountains, and alongside these are found several Turki-speaking tribes. Baluchi is spoken in the extreme south-east. English and French are spoken by most of the educated classes.

History

Updated for this edition by SIMON CHAPMAN

EARLY HISTORY

The Achaemenid empire, the first Persian empire, was founded by Cyrus who revolted against the Median empire in 533 BC. After the defeat of the Median empire, Babylon was taken in 529 BC, and in 525 BC under Cambyses, the successor of Cyrus, Egypt was conquered. The period of conquest was rounded off by Darius who reduced the tribes of the Pontic and Armenian mountains and extended Persian dominion to the Caucasus. The main work of Darius, however, lay not in the conquest but in the organization which he gave to the empire. During his reign wars with Greece broke out and in 490 BC the Persian army suffered a major defeat at Marathon; an expedition under Xerxes, the successor of Darius, which set out to avenge this defeat was, after initial successes, defeated at Salamis in 480 BC. The empire was finally overthrown by Alexander who defeated the Persian army at Arbela in 331 BC and then burnt Persepolis, the Achaemenid capital; the last Darius fled and was killed in 330 BC. Alexander thereafter regarded himself as the head of the Persian empire. The death of Alexander was followed by a struggle between his generals, one of whom, Seleucus, took the whole of Persia, apart from northern Media and founded the Seleucid empire. About the year 250 BC a reaction against Hellenism began with the rise of the Parthian empire of the Arsacids. Although by origin nomads from the Turanian steppe, the Arsacids became the wardens of the northeast marches and were largely preoccupied in defending themselves in the east against the Scythians who, with the Tocharians and Sacae, repeatedly attacked the Parthian empire, while in the west they were engaged in fending off attacks by the Romans.

The Arsacids were succeeded by the Sasanians, who, like the Achaemenids, came from Fars and, like them, were Zoroastrians. Ardashir b. Babak, after subduing the neighbouring states (c. AD 212), made war on the Arsacid, Artabanus V, whom he eventually defeated. The empire which he founded largely continued the traditions of the Achaemenids, although it never equalled the Achaemenid empire in extent. The monarchy of the Sasanian period was a religious and civil institution. The monarch, who ruled by divine right, was absolute but his autocracy was limited by the powers of the Zoroastrian hierarchy and the feudal aristocracy. In the reign of Qubad (AD 488–531) a movement of revolt, partly social and partly religious, led by Mazdak, gained ground. Under Qubad's successor Anushiravan (531–79) orthodoxy was restored, but at the cost of the imposition of a military despotism. Like the Arsacids before them the Sasanians were occupied in the west with wars with Rome and in the east with repelling the advances of nomads from Central Asia.

MUSLIM PERSIA

By the beginning of the seventh century AD Persia had been greatly weakened by these wars, and when the Muslim Arabs attacked, little effective resistance was offered. The decisive battles were fought at Qadisiyya (AD 637) and Nihavand (*c.* AD 641). Persia did not re-emerge as a political entity until the 16th century AD, although with the decline of the Abbasid empire semi-independent and independent dynasties arose in different parts of Persia and at times even incorporated under their rule an area extending beyond the confines of present-day Iran. As a result of the Arab conquest Persia became part of the Muslim world. Local administration remained largely in the hands of the indigenous population and many local customs continued to be observed. In due course a new civilization developed in Persia, the unifying force of which was Islam.

With the transfer of the capital of the Islamic empire from Damascus to Baghdad (*c.* AD 750) Persian influence began to be strongly felt in the life of the empire. Islam had already replaced Zoroastrianism and by the 10th century modern Persian, written in the Arabic script and including a large number of Arabic words in its vocabulary, had established itself. Its emergence was of immense importance; the literary tradition for which it became the vehicle has perhaps more than any other factor kept alive a national consciousness among the Iranians and preserved the memory of the great Persian empires of the past.

By the eighth century AD the Abbasid caliphate had begun to disintegrate and when in the 11th century control of the north-eastern frontiers broke down, the Ghuzz Turks invaded Persia. This movement, of which the Seljuqs became the leaders, was ethnologically important since it altered the balance of population, the Turkish element from then on being second only to the Persian in numbers and influence. Secondly, it was in the Seljuq empire that the main lines of the politico-economic structure, which was to last in Persia in a modified form down to the 20th century AD, were worked out. The basis of this structure was the land assignment, the holder of which was often virtually a petty territorial ruler, who was required, when called upon to do so, to provide the ruler with a military contingent.

The Seljuq empire itself broke up in the 12th century into a number of succession states; the 13th century saw the Mongol invasion and in 1258 Hulagu, the grandson of Chinghiz (Jenghiz) Khan, sacked Baghdad and destroyed the caliphate. For some years the Ilkhan dynasty, founded by Hulagu, ruled Persia as vassals of the Great Khan in Qaraqorum, but from the reign of Abaqa (1265–81) onwards they became virtually a Persian dynasty. Their empire, like that of the Seljuqs before them—and for very much the same reason—broke up at the beginning of the 14th century into a number of succession states. Towards the end of the century Persia again fell under the dominion of a military conqueror, when Timur, who had started his career as the warden of the marches in the Oxus-Jaxartes basin against the nomads of Central Asia, undertook a series of military campaigns against Persia between 1381 and 1387. The kingdom founded by him was shortlived and rapidly disintegrated on the death of his son Shahrukh, the western part falling first to the Turkomans of the Black Sheep and then to the Turkomans of the White Sheep, while Transoxania passed into the hands of the Uzbegs.

THE PERSIAN MONARCHY

The 16th century saw the foundation of the Safavid empire, which was accompanied by an eastward movement of the Turkomans from Asia Minor back into Persia. For the first time since the Muslim conquest Persia re-emerged as a political unit. The foundations of the Safavid empire were laid by Isma'il Safavi (1502–24). He deliberately fostered a sense of separateness and of national unity *vis-à-vis* the Ottoman Turks with whom the Safavids were engaged in a struggle for supremacy in the west, and the main weapon he used to accomplish his purpose was Shi'ism. Not only the Turks but the majority of his own subjects were at the time Sunni Muslims—nevertheless he imposed Shi'ism upon them by force and created among the population of his dominions, many of whom, especially among his immediate followers, were Turks, a sense of national unity as Persians. Apart from a brief interlude under Nadir Shah, Shi'ism has since then remained the majority rite in Persia and is the official rite of the country at the present day. Under Shah Abbas (1587–1629) the Safavid empire reached its zenith and Persia enjoyed a power and prosperity which it has not achieved since.

GREAT POWER RIVALRY

During the Safavid period, contact with Europe increased. Various foreign embassies interested mainly in the silk trade reached the Safavid court via Russia and via the Persian Gulf. In the latter area in the early years of the 16th century a struggle for supremacy developed between the British and the Dutch. 'Factories' were established by the East India Company in the Gulf from the early 16th century.

Under the later Safavids internal decline set in and from 1722–30 Persia was subject to Afghan invasion and occupation while in the west and north it was threatened by Turkey and Russia. After the death of Peter the Great there was a temporary slackening of Russian pressure, but the Turks continued to advance and took Tabriz in 1725, peace being eventually made at Hamadan in 1727. The Afghans were finally evicted by Nadir Shah Afshar whose reign (1736–47) was remarkable chiefly for his military exploits. The Afsharids were succeeded by Karim Khan Zand (1750–79) whose relatively peaceful reign was followed by the rise of the Qajars who continued to reign until 1925. Under them the capital was transferred from Isfahan to Teheran. During the Qajar period events in Persia became increasingly affected by Great Power rivalry until not only Persia's foreign policy was dominated by this question, but its internal politics also.

With the growth of British influence in India in the late 18th and early 19th centuries the main emphasis in Anglo-Persian relations, which during the 16th and 17th centuries had been on commerce, began to shift to strategy. The region of Persia and the Persian Gulf came to be regarded as one of the main bastions protecting British India, and the existence of an independent Persia as a major British interest. In the early 19th century fear of a French invasion of India through Persia exercised the minds of the British in India and Whitehall. French envoys were active in Persia and Mesopotamia from 1796 to 1809, and to counter possible French activities Captain (afterwards Sir) John Malcolm was sent to Persia in 1800 by the Governor-General of India. He concluded a political and commercial treaty with Fath Ali Shah, the main purpose of which was to ensure that the Shah should not receive French agents and would do his utmost to prevent French forces entering Persia. With the defeat of Napoleon in Egypt the matter was no longer regarded as urgent and the agreement was not ratified. Subsequently the French made proposals to Persia for an alliance against Russia and in 1807 Persia concluded the Treaty of Finkenstein with France after which a military mission under General Gardanne came to Persia. In 1808 another British mission was sent under Malcolm. Its object was 'first, to detach the Court of Persia from the French alliance and to prevail on that Court to refuse the passage of French troops through the territories subject to Persia, or the admission of French troops into the country. If that cannot be obtained, to admit English troops with a view of opposing the French army in its progress to India, to prevent the creation of any maritime post, and the establishment of French factories on the coast of Persia'. Malcolm's task was complicated by the almost simultaneous arrival of a similar mission from Whitehall. In 1809 after the Treaty of Tilsit, which debarred the French from aiding the Shah against Russia, Gardanne was dismissed.

WARS WITH RUSSIA AND TURKEY

Meanwhile the formal annexation of Georgia by Russia in 1801 had been followed by a campaign against Russia. This proved disastrous to Persia and was temporarily brought to an end by the Treaty of Gulistan (1813) by which Persia ceded Georgia, Qara Bagh and seven other provinces. British policy continued to be concerned with the possibility of an invasion of India via Persia and in 1814 the Treaty of Teheran was concluded with Persia by which Great Britain undertook to provide troops or a subsidy in the event of unprovoked aggression against Persia. Although the treaty provided for defence against any European power it was primarily intended to counteract the designs of Russia. In fact it proved ineffective and when the Perso–Russian war recommenced in 1825 Great Britain did not interfere except as a peacemaker and discontinued the subsidy to Persia, which was technically the aggressor. The war was concluded in 1828 by the Treaty of Turkomanchai, under the terms of which Persia ceded Erivan and Nakhjivan and agreed to pay an indemnity;

in addition, it was prohibited from having armed vessels on the Caspian.

During this period Persia was also engaged in hostilities with Turkey. Frontier disputes in 1821 culminated in the outbreak of war, which was concluded by the Treaty of Erzerum (1823).

By the 19th century the Persian Government had ceased to exercise effective control over the greater part of Khurasan. Russian policy, which became conciliatory towards Persia during the 25 years or so after the Treaty of Turkomanchai, encouraged the Shah to reimpose Persian rule on the eastern provinces. British policy, on the other hand, having come to regard Afghanistan as an important link in the defence of India, urged moderation upon the Persian Government. After the accession of Muhammad Shah in 1834, an expedition was sent against Herat. The siege of Herat began in 1837 but was raised when the Shah was threatened with British intervention. Subsequently local intrigues enabled the Persians to enter Herat. The seizure of the city by Persia led to the outbreak of the Anglo–Persian war in 1856, which was terminated by the Treaty of Paris (1857) after a British force had occupied the island of Kharg in the Persian Gulf.

In the second half of the century the subjection of the Turkoman tribes by Russia, its capture of Marv in 1854, and the occupation of the Panjeh, meant that Russian influence became dominant in Khurasan in the same way as the advance of Russia to the Araxes after the Persian wars in the early part of the 19th century had made Russian influence dominant in Azerbaijan.

INCREASED FOREIGN INTERVENTION

Internally the second half of the 19th century was remarkable chiefly for the beginnings of the modernist movement, which was stimulated on the one hand by internal misgovernment and on the other by increased intervention in the internal affairs of the country by Russia and Britain. Towards the end of the century numerous concessions were granted to foreigners largely in order to pay for the extravagances of the court. The most fantastic of these was the Reuter concession. In 1872 a naturalized British subject, Baron de Reuter, was given by the Shah a monopoly for 70 years of railways and tramways in Persia, all the minerals except gold, silver and precious stones, irrigation, road, factory and telegraph enterprises, and the farm of customs dues for 25 years. Eventually this concession was cancelled and permission instead given for the foundation of a Persian state bank with British capital, which was to have the exclusive right to issue banknotes; and accordingly in September 1889 the Imperial Bank of Persia began business. In the same year Dolgoruki obtained for Russia the first option of a railway concession for five years. In November of the following year the railway agreement with Russia was changed into one interdicting all railways whatsoever in Persia. By the turn of the century there had been 'a pronounced sharpening of Anglo–Russian hostility as a consequence of a whole series of Russian actions, not only in northern Persia, where Russian ascendancy to a large extent had to be admitted, but as well in southern and eastern Persia which had hitherto been predominantly British preserves'. In 1900 a Russian loan was given. Subsequently various short-term advances and subsidies from the Russian treasury including advances to the heir apparent, Muhammad Ali, were made so that by 1906 some £7.5m. was owing to the Russians. Under the 1891 Russo-Persian tariff treaty, trade between the two countries had increased, and when, under the 1901 Russo-Persian commercial treaty, a new customs tariff was announced in 1903, Russian exports to Persia were considerably aided, and, up to 1914, Russian commerce with Persia continued to grow.

The grant of these various concessions to foreigners and the raising of foreign loans gave rise to growing anxiety on the part of the Persian public. Further, large numbers of Persians had fled the country and were living in exile. When a tobacco monopoly was granted to a British subject in 1890, various elements of the population, including the intellectuals and the religious classes, combined to oppose it. Strikes and riots threatened and the monopoly was rescinded. No effective steps, however, were taken to allay popular discontent. In 1901 protests were made against the loans and mortgages from Russia which were being contracted to pay for Muzaffar ud-Din Shah's jour-

neys to Europe. By 1905–6 the demand for reform had grown in strength and finally on 5 August 1906, after 12,000 persons had taken sanctuary in the British legation, a constitution was granted. A long struggle then began between the constitutionalists and the Shah. The Cossack Brigade, formed during the reign of Nasir ud-Din Shah, which was under Russian officers and was the most effective military force in the country, played a major part in this struggle and was used by Muhammad Ali Shah to suppress the National Assembly in 1908. Civil war ensued and Muhammad Ali Shah's abdication was forced in 1909.

Meanwhile in 1907 the Anglo-Russian convention had been signed. The convention, which included a mutual undertaking to respect the integrity and independence of Persia, divided the country into three areas, that lying to the north of a line passing from Qasr-e-Shirin to Kakh, where the Russian, Persian and Afghan frontiers met in the east, that lying to the south of a line running from Qazik on the Perso-Afghan frontier through Birjand and Kerman to Bandar Abbas on the Persian Gulf, and that lying outside these two areas. Great Britain gave an undertaking not to seek or support others seeking political or economic concessions in the northern area; Russia gave a similar undertaking with reference to the southern area. In the central area the freedom of action of the two parties was not limited and their existing concessions (which included the oil concession granted to D'Arcy in 1901) were maintained. The conclusion of this convention—which had taken place partly because of a change in the relative strength of the Great Powers and partly because the British Government hoped thereby to terminate Anglo–Russian rivalry in Persia and to prevent further Russian encroachments—came as a shock to Persian opinion which had hoped for much from the support which the British Government had given to the constitutional movement. It was felt that Persian interests had been bartered away by Great Britain for a promise of Russian support in the event of a European war. In fact, the convention failed in its object. Russian pressure continued to be exercised on Persia directly and indirectly. In 1911, as a result of Russian pressure, the National Assembly was suspended, and the resignation forced of the American Administrator-General of the Finances, Shuster, who had been appointed in the hope of bringing order to the finances of Persia.

THE FIRST WORLD WAR

During the First World War Persia was nominally neutral but, in fact, pro-Turkish. By the end of the war the internal condition of Persia was chaotic. To the British Government the restoration of order was desirable and with this end in view the Agreement of 1919 was drawn up whereby a number of men were to be lent to reorganize the Persian army and to reform the Ministry of Finance and a loan of £2m. was to be given. There was opposition to this agreement in the USA and France and in Persia, and the treaty was not ratified. A *coup d'état* took place in 1921, Reza Khan (later Reza Shah) becoming Minister of War. In February 1921 the Soviet-Persian Treaty was signed whereby the USSR declared all treaties and conventions concluded with Persia by the Tsarist Government null and void. Under Article VI the USSR was permitted 'to advance her troops into the Persian interior for the purpose of carrying out the military operations necessary for its defence' in the event of a third party attempting 'to carry out a policy of usurpation by means of armed intervention in Persia, or if such a Power should desire to use Persian territory as a base of operations against Russia. . .'

REZA SHAH, 1925–41, AND AFTER

In 1923 Reza Khan became Prime Minister and finally in 1925 the crown of Persia was conferred upon him. His first task was to restore the authority of the central Government throughout the country, and the second to place Persia's relations with foreign countries on a basis of equality. All extra-territorial agreements were terminated from 1928. Lighterage and quarantine duties on the Persian littoral of the Persian Gulf, hitherto performed by Great Britain, were transferred to the Persian Government in 1930. The Indo-European Telegraphy Company, which had been in operation since 1872, had almost entirely been withdrawn by 1931 and the British coaling stations were transferred from Basidu and Henjam to Bahrain in 1935.

In 1932 the cancellation of the Anglo-Persian Oil Co's concession was announced by Persia. The original concession obtained by D'Arcy in 1901 had been taken over by the Anglo-Persian Oil Co (later the Anglo-Iranian Oil Co) in 1909 and the British Government had acquired a controlling interest in the company in 1914. The Persian Government's action in cancelling the concession was referred to the League of Nations. Eventually an agreement was concluded in 1933 for a new concession whereby the concession area was materially reduced and the royalty to be paid to the Persian Government increased. The concession was to run to 1993.

Internally Reza Shah's policy aimed at modernization and autarchy. In the later years of his reign the Government became increasingly totalitarian in nature. Compulsory military service was introduced and the army much increased in size. Communications were greatly improved; the construction of a trans-Persian railway was begun. Education was remodelled on western lines. Women were no longer obliged to wear the veil after 1936. Foreign trade was made a state monopoly, and currency and clearing restrictions were established. These arrangements were compatible with the economy of Germany and, by the outbreak of the Second World War, Germany had acquired considerable commercial and political influence in Persia.

On the outbreak of war Persia declared its neutrality. In 1941 the Allies demanded a reduction in the number of Germans in the country, and when no satisfaction was obtained sent another communication demanding the expulsion of all German nationals, except such as were essential to the Persian economy and harmless to the Allies. This demand was not complied with and on 26 August 1941, Persia was invaded. Hostilities lasted some two days. On 16 September Reza Shah abdicated in favour of his son Muhammad Reza. In January 1942 a Tripartite Treaty of Alliance was concluded with Great Britain and the USSR whereby Great Britain and the USSR undertook jointly and severally 'to respect the territorial integrity, sovereignty and political independence of Persia' and 'to defend Persia by all means in their command from aggression'. The Persian Government undertook to give the Allies, for certain military purposes, the unrestricted right to use, maintain and guard, and in the case of military necessity, to control, all means of communications in Persia. Allied forces were to be withdrawn not later than six months after the conclusion of hostilities between the Allied Powers and Germany and its associates. In so far as the establishment of communications with the USSR was concerned the Treaty was effective; its operation in other respects was less satisfactory. In the Russian zone of occupation the Persian authorities were denied freedom of movement and effective administration made impossible. American advisers were appointed by the Persian Government in 1942 and 1943 in the hope of reorganizing certain aspects of the administration, but little success was achieved.

In 1943 a British company applied for an oil concession in south-east Persia and in 1944 the Socony Vacuum and Sinclair Oil Cos made various proposals to the Persian Government. In September the Persian Cabinet issued a decree deferring the granting of oil concessions until after the war. The USSR meanwhile asked for an oil concession in the north and brought heavy, though unavailing, pressure to bear on the Persian Government to accede to this demand. Persian security forces were prevented by Soviet forces from entering Azerbaijan or the Caspian provinces, and an autonomous government was set up in Azerbaijan, with Soviet support, in December 1945. In January 1946 the Persian Government had recourse to the UN Security Council. In March the Tripartite Treaty expired and British and US forces evacuated Persia, Soviet forces remaining. The Persian Government again presented a note to the Security Council. In April an understanding was reached, whereby a joint Soviet-Persian company to exploit the oil in the northern provinces was to be formed. In May Soviet forces evacuated the country. Soviet pressure, however, continued to be exerted through the communist Tudeh party, the Democrat movement in Azerbaijan, and the Kurdish autonomy movement, and the Persian Government was unable to re-enter Azerbaijan until December. In the following October, the Soviet Oil Agreement was presented to the National Assembly but was not ratified. In October 1947 an agreement was signed with the USA, providing for a US military mission in Persia to co-operate with the Persian Ministry of War in 'enhancing the efficiency of the Persian army'.

NATIONALIZING THE OIL INDUSTRY

Meanwhile unrest and discontent at internal misgovernment increased, culminating in the nationalist movement of 1950–51. In July 1949 a Supplemental Oil Agreement with the Anglo-Iranian Oil Co was initialled. Opposition to this agreement (whereby Persia was offered considerable financial gains) was strong. In November 1950 the oil commission of the National Assembly recommended its rejection. Meanwhile Persia had received a loan of $25m. from the Export & Import Bank of Washington and a grant of $500,000 under the Point IV allocation. Subsequently in 1952 the Point IV aid programme was expanded. In April 1951 the National Assembly passed a Bill for the nationalization of the oil industry, and in May Dr Muhammad Musaddiq, who had led the campaign for nationalization of oil, became Prime Minister. In spite of efforts to involve the International Court of Justice (ICJ), the *status quo* could not be maintained in Persia and the Anglo-Iranian Oil Co evacuated the country, being unable to continue operations.

On 22 July 1952, the ICJ found that it had no jurisdiction in the oil dispute. This decision, however, was not a decision on the merits of the case. The Company accordingly maintained its claim to be entitled to all crude oil and oil products derived from the area covered by its concession agreement, and stated its intention to take such action as was necessary to protect its interests. US policy showed an increasing interest in Persian affairs. During the period August to October 1952, considerable correspondence passed between the British, US and Persian Governments in the oil dispute, culminating in a joint offer by Sir Winston Churchill and President Truman, concerning proposals to assess the compensation to be paid to the Anglo-Iranian Oil Co and 'to permit the resumption of the flow of oil to world markets. The Persian Government rejected these proposals and put forward counter proposals which were unacceptable. On 22 October the Persian Government broke off diplomatic relations with Great Britain. Further Anglo-American proposals for an oil settlement were put forward in February 1953, which the Persian Government rejected. Meanwhile dissension between Musaddiq and some of his supporters broke out, and a rift also developed between him and the Shah. The economic situation of the country began to deteriorate rapidly, culminating in the overthrow of Musaddiq by General Zahedi in August 1953. Musaddiq was tried and sentenced to three years solitary confinement for allegedly trying to overthrow the regime and illegally dissolving the Majlis-e-Shura (Consultative Assembly).

The new Government resumed diplomatic relations with Great Britain in December 1953, and negotiations with British and American oil interests began for the solution of the oil problem. In September 1954 an agreement was signed, and ratified by the Majlis and Senate in October, granting a concession to a consortium of eight companies (subsequently increased to 17) on a percentage basis.

It was also agreed that the claims of the Anglo-Iranian Oil Co and the Persian Government against each other were to be settled by the payment of a lump sum to the Company, which was also to receive compensation from the other members of the consortium. The profits arising within Persia from the oil operations were to be equally shared between the Persian Government and the consortium. The agreement was for a period of 25 years with provision for three five-year extensions, conditional upon a progressive reduction of the original area. The National Iranian Oil Co (NIOC) was to operate the Naft-i Shahr oilfield and the Kermanshah refinery to meet part of Persia's own needs and to handle the distribution of oil products in Persia and to be responsible for all facilities and services not directly part of the producing, refining, and transport operations of the two operating companies set up under the agreement. The greater part of the cost of these facilities and services, which would include industrial training, public transport, road maintenance, housing, medical care, and social welfare, would be recovered by the NIOC from the operating companies.

GROWING POWER OF THE SHAH

Internally, order was restored. The communist Tudeh Party was proscribed, but continued to exist underground. The failure of the Government to push forward actively with reform, however, led, in due course, to a reappearance of unrest and discontent. In April 1955 Zahedi resigned and was succeeded by Hussein Ala, the Shah henceforward taking a more active part in the administration. In October, Persia joined the Baghdad Pact. In November an attempt was made on the Prime Minister's life. The country had not recovered from the financial difficulties brought on by the Musaddiq regime, in spite of considerable financial aid granted by the USA to enable the country to carry on until oil revenues were received. More than US $800m. were poured into Iran between the end of the Second World War and September 1960. On 5 March 1959 a bilateral defence agreement was signed in Ankara between the USA and Iran. Under the agreement, the Government of the USA would 'in case of aggression, take such appropriate action, including the use of armed force, as may be mutually agreed, and as envisaged in the Joint Resolution to promote peace and security in the Middle East'. (The Joint Resolution refers to the 'Eisenhower Doctrine'.)

Relations with the USSR in the years following the fall of Musaddiq were not cordial, but in December 1954 an agreement providing for the repayment by the USSR of its war debts to Persia for goods supplied and services rendered, and mapping of the revised frontiers, was signed.

On 3 April 1957, Hussein Ala resigned and was succeeded as Prime Minister by Dr Manoutchehr Egbal, who formed a new Government. Immediately after taking office Dr Egbal issued a decree ending martial law and declared his intention of forming a democratic two-party system, in accordance with the wishes of the Shah. In February 1958 a pro-government Nation Party was formed. An opposition People's Party had been formed in 1957. Elections contested by both these political parties disclosed electoral irregularities, and in August 1960 Jaafar Sharif-Emami replaced Dr Egbal as Prime Minister.

In May 1961, however, Dr Emami resigned as a result of criticism of his handling of a teachers' strike, and the Shah called upon Dr Ali Amini, the leader of the opposition, to form a new government.

Dr Amini quickly took stern measures to halt the political and economic chaos in Iran. A drive against corruption in the government and civil service was coupled with policies of land reform, decentralization of administration, control of government expenditure and limitation of luxury imports. Both houses of Parliament were dissolved pending the passing of a new electoral law which would make free and fair elections possible. Postponement of elections, in July 1962, led to disorder in Teheran, and the added difficulty of producing a reasonably balanced budget led Dr Amini to tender his resignation.

A new Government was quickly formed by Assadollah Alam, the leader of the Mardom (People's) Party. Alam, one of Iran's largest landowners and administrator of the Pahlavi Foundation, had previously distributed much of his land voluntarily amongst the peasants. He stated that Iran would remain closely linked to the West, and that he would continue the land reform programme and the struggle against internal political corruption.

REFORMS OF THE SHAH

In 1950 the Shah had begun distributing his estate amongst the peasants. By the end of 1963 he had disposed of all his Crown Properties. The Pahlavi Foundation was established in 1958 and received considerable gifts from the Shah for the purpose of improving standards of education, health and social welfare amongst the poorer classes. In October 1961 the Shah created the £40m. Pahlavi Dynasty Trust, the income of which was used for social, educational and health services for the Iranian people.

In January 1963 a referendum was held, as a result of which overwhelming approval was given to the Shah's six-point plan for the distribution of lands among the peasants, the promotion of literacy, the emancipation of women, etc. The break-up of great estates began almost immediately, and the programme was finally completed in September 1971. Another important measure was the formation of the Literacy Corps (and later of

the Health Corps), in which students could serve their period of national service as teachers, working in the villages.

Elections in September 1963 resulted in an overwhelming victory for Alam's National Union. The elections, at which, for the first time, women were allowed to vote, were held in the face of strong opposition from the left-wing parties of Iran, notably the National Front and the Tudeh Party, which campaigned unsuccessfully for a boycott. The Shah called on the new Parliament to inaugurate a 20-year programme of economic and social reform and political development and he also announced a second phase of the land reform programme, whereby it was hoped that another 20,000 villages would be added to the 10,000 already handed over to the tenants. The Alam Government continued until March 1964, when, without offering any reason, Alam resigned. The new leader was Hassan Ali Mansur, a former minister and founder of the Progressive Centre, which had played a prominent part in Alam's coalition the previous year. In December 1963 he had formed the New Iran Party, which by now had the support of some 150 members of the Majlis. The second stage of the land reform plan was placed before the Majlis in May and this aimed to break down the great estates more thoroughly; the maximum permissible size was to range from 120 ha in arid regions to 30 ha in more fertile areas.

On 21 January 1965 Mansur was assassinated by members of the right-wing religious sect Fedayin Islam. The assassins were reportedly followers of the Ayatollah Ruhollah Khomeini, a Shi'ite Muslim religious leader who had been exiled in 1964 for his opposition to the Shah's reforms.

Amir Abbas Hoveida, the Minister of Finance, was immediately appointed acting premier, and became Prime Minister on the day following Mansur's death, retaining his post at the Ministry of Finance. He pledged himself to the continuation of his predecessor's policies, and was given the massive support of the Majlis. Elections took place in 1967, 1971 and 1975. Hoveida continued as Prime Minister until August 1977, when he was succeeded by Dr Jamshid Amouzegar.

FOREIGN RELATIONS

Iran began a period of good relations with the USSR in 1964–65 when various mutually beneficial trading and technical agreements were signed, and a regular air service between Teheran and Moscow was inaugurated. It had been an avowed part of Mansur's policy that Iran should be as much interested in maintaining links with the USSR as with the West. In June 1965 the Shah visited Moscow, and in October an agreement was signed for the construction by Soviet engineers of a steel mill. Relations with Iraq in early 1966 became strained when the long-standing disagreement over the Shatt al-Arab waterway erupted into a series of border incidents.

The coronation of the Shah in October 1967 seemed to augur forthcoming prosperity and the apparent stability of Iran was emphasized, not only by economic development and by the organization of international gatherings, but also by the formal ending in November of US economic aid under the Point IV allocation. Iran, which had been the first country to accept this aid in 1951, was now the second (after the Taiwan Province of China) able to dispense with it. Military aid, however, was to continue. At the same time economic co-operation with the USSR was developed, and an agreement was made for the purchase of £40m. of munitions, the first occasion on which the USSR had concluded an arms transaction with a member of the Western bloc.

In January 1968 the British Government announced its decision to withdraw all its forces from the Gulf by the end of 1971. Since these forces had apparently helped to preserve the local *status quo*, a revival of the ancient rivalry between Arabs and Persians over supremacy in the Gulf then seemed a likely prospect following their removal. The Iranian Government's reiteration of its claim to Bahrain in February 1968 did not facilitate relations with the Arab world, but Iran cautiously welcomed the proposed Federation of Arab Emirates (which it was thought would incorporate Bahrain).

A UN Mission visiting Bahrain in early 1970 found that the large Arab majority overwhelmingly preferred full independence to joining Iran or remaining a British protectorate. Iran had previously agreed to accept the mission's findings, and it did so without complaint, though expressing concern for the future of Iranians in the Gulf states. In June 1970 a dispute with other Gulf states also arose over Iran's claim to the islands of Abu Musa and the Tunbs belonging to Sharjah and Ras al-Khaimah respectively. The dispute was only settled at the beginning of December 1971. The Sheikh of Sharjah agreed to share his island of Abu Musa with Iran. The Sheikh of Ras al-Khaimah was less accommodating, so Iran invaded his possessions of the Greater and Lesser Tunbs and took them by force. After occupying Abu Musa and the Tunbs, Iran developed them as military bases to command the Strait of Hormuz at the neck of the Gulf. Iran regarded the maintenance of freedom of passage through the Strait of Hormuz as vital to its strategic and economic interests.

Iran's relations with the more radical Arab states were less friendly under the Shah. These states had long been suspicious of Iran's close ties with the West, and especially of the generous US military aid to the powerful Iranian armed forces. Moreover, the Arab states distrusted Iran's attitude to Israel. Although no formal diplomatic links existed, trade, particularly in oil, was conducted with Israel. One of the first actions of the Khomeini regime in early 1979 was to end any ties with Israel and to align Iran firmly behind the Arab cause, by allowing, for example, the opening of a PLO office in Teheran.

Iran's only frontier with an Arab state is with Iraq. Near the Gulf the border is delineated by the 185-km Shatt al-Arab waterway, the estuary of the Tigris and Euphrates, which flows into the Gulf, and, by the terms of the 1937 treaty, the frontier followed the eastern, i.e. Iranian, bank; thus, Iraq legally had sovereignty over the whole waterway. For many years, Iran resented this provision, and in April 1969 it decided to abrogate the treaty by sending Iranian vessels, flying the national flag, through the waterway, while heavy naval forces stood ready to intervene. The aim was apparently to force a renegotiation of the treaty. In September 1969 there were further armed clashes on the border. In January 1970 Iraq accused the Iranian Government of supporting an abortive coup in Iraq, and diplomatic relations between the two countries were severed.

Diplomatic relations between Iran and Iraq were restored soon after the outbreak of the Arab–Israeli War in October 1973, but border incidents continued. In March 1975, however, it was announced at an OPEC meeting in Algiers that the Shah and Saddam Hussain (then Vice-President of the Iraqi Revolutionary Command Council) had signed an agreement which 'completely eliminated the conflict between the two brotherly countries'. Not only did this agreement settle the outstanding border differences, but it also deprived the Kurds in Iraq of the help which they had been receiving from Iran in their struggle against the Iraqi Government, thus causing a Kurdish collapse and a virtual end to the Kurdish War.

The border agreement provided that Iran and Iraq would define their frontiers on the basis of the Protocol of Constantinople of 1913 (which allowed the Ottoman Empire to retain control over the Shatt al-Arab but granted sovereignty over the east bank to Persia) and the verbal agreement on frontiers of 1914, and that the Shatt al-Arab frontier would be defined according to the Thalweg Line (i.e. the middle of the deepest shipping channel). The treaty giving effect to this agreement was signed on 15 June 1975 and later became one of the key issues of the war with Iraq which broke out in September 1980 (see below).

INTERNAL PROBLEMS

Internally, signs of opposition to the Shah's regime, never far from the surface of Iranian life, became more and more evident as the celebrations for the 2,500th anniversary of the Persian monarchy were in preparation for October 1971. The combination of the very unequal distribution of the enormous earnings from oil and the suppression of any sign of dissent was made more politically explosive as the lavishness of the celebrations and the huge extent of the accompanying security precautions became apparent. From then, until the final fall of the Shah in early 1979, there were countless stories of the stifling of opposition by the ruthless activities of SAVAK, the government security agency.

In March 1975 the Shah, dissatisfied with the current structure of party politics in Iran and wanting to weld together all those who supported the principles of his 'White Revolution' policy (later known as the 'Revolution of the Shah and People'), announced the formation of a single party system, the Iran National Resurgence Party (Rastakhiz), with the Prime Minister, Amir Abbas Hoveida, as Secretary-General. By 1978 it became clear that the single-party Rastakhiz system was not solving the problem of internal opposition in Iran, but few people in early 1978 would have forecast that, within a year, a completely new political system would take its place.

FALL OF THE SHAH

During 1977 and 1978 demonstrations centred around the universities and acts of political violence increased. Attempts by the Shah to control the situation, first by greater liberalization and then through firmer suppression, proved ineffective. In August 1977 Dr Jamshid Amouzegar, who had become Secretary-General of Rastakhiz, replaced the long-serving Amir Abbas Hoveida as Prime Minister but he resigned a year later. In August 1978 Jaafar Sharif-Emami was appointed Prime Minister (an office he had previously held in 1960–61) and, in response to the emerging mood of the country, promised that his Government would observe Islamic tenets. Unrest continued, however. Martial law was introduced in September, and in November the Shah established a military Government headed by the army Chief of Staff, Gen. Gholamreza Azhari. Censorship was imposed, but industrial action undertaken by workers in the oil industry and public services left the Shah in a desperate situation, and in early January 1979 he charged Dr Shapour Bakhtiar, a former deputy leader of the National Front, with forming a 'last-chance' government. Dr Bakhtiar undertook to dissolve SAVAK (the security police), halt the export of oil to South Africa and Israel and support the Palestinians. However, opposition to the Shah continued to such an extent that he left the country on 15 January, never to return.

The opposition within Iran had stemmed from two main sources, with little in common except their desire to overthrow the Shah. By the time the Shah left Iran, opposition from the left and the more liberal National Front had been overshadowed by the success of the opposition movement surrounding the exiled religious leader Ayatollah Khomeini. He conducted his campaign from France where he had arrived in early October after 14 years of exile in Iraq for opposing the Shah's 'White Revolution' (1963) because it conflicted with traditional Islamic values.

In January Khomeini formed an Islamic Revolutionary Council from his base near Paris and pressure in Iran grew for his return. The Bakhtiar Government tried to delay his return for as long as possible, but on 1 February Khomeini arrived in Teheran from Paris to a tumultuous welcome from the Iranian people. Bakhtiar refused to recognize Khomeini but, after several demonstrations and outbreaks of violence, the army withdrew its support from Dr Bakhtiar and he resigned on 11 February. Dr Mehdi Bazargan, who had been named 'Provisional Prime Minister' by Khomeini on 6 February, formed a provisional government later in the month but it soon became clear that real power rested with Khomeini's 15-man Islamic Revolutionary Council.

IRAN UNDER AYATOLLAH KHOMEINI

Although Khomeini became the *de facto* leader of Iran, riding on a wave of public euphoria, the difficulties of putting into practice the ideals of the Islamic Revolution severely tested the Revolutionary Government. From the very outset conflict arose between the Islamic Revolutionary Council, which gave effect to its policies through a network of *Komitehs*, and the Prime Minister, Dr Bazargan.

Tension over Iran's ethnic minorities, either not in evidence or stifled under the Shah, became a problem after the Revolution. Most serious was the demand for autonomy from the Kurds in the north-west, which often led to open warfare in that area. Other minorities also demanded autonomy. These included the Baluchis in the south-east, the Turkomans in the north-east and the Azerbaijanis in the north-west. Conflict with the Arabs in the south-west also interacted with hostile relations with Iraq, which later developed into the Iran–Iraq War in September 1980 (see below). The position was complicated by the fact that these minorities were Sunni Muslims, while the Khomeini regime and the majority of Iranians were Shi'ite.

Another major difficulty was Iran's relations with the USA and, as an extension of that, with the Western world. Khomeini's regime from the outset had condemned previous US interference in Iranian affairs, and when, on 4 November 1979, Iranian students seized 53 hostages in the US Embassy in Teheran, Khomeini was quite ready to offer his support to the students who demanded the return of the Shah (then in the USA) to Iran to face trial. This problem dominated relations with the USA for the next 14 months, and was not resolved by the death of the Shah in Egypt on 27 July 1980. The USA launched an airborne military operation to free the hostages, landing a commando force in eastern Iran. The operation was cancelled at an early stage, however, owing to equipment failure, and eight men died when a helicopter collided with a transport aircraft as the force prepared to abandon the mission. Internal disagreements meant that the first Islamic Majlis, elected in March and May 1980, was slow to grapple with the problem of the hostages, who were not released until 20 January 1981.

Another problem was the intensity of Islamic fervour in Iran. Ayatollah Khalkhali, at one time Chief Justice of the Islamic Revolutionary Courts, set about his task with extraordinary zeal and by May 1980 claimed to have ordered more than 300 executions. Moreover, in May 1980 he destroyed the tomb of Reza Shah, an action which was later condemned by President Bani-Sadr, who pointed out that such actions were counter-productive to the Revolution. Not all Iranians approved of the ardour with which the 'Bureau to Stop Bad Acts' set about cleaning up the moral lapses in Iranian society.

CONSTITUTIONAL DEVELOPMENT

At the end of March 1979 Khomeini held a referendum to ascertain the level of popular support for the creation of an Islamic republic. The result was almost unanimously in favour, and on 1 April the Islamic Republic of Iran was declared. A draft constitution proposed that Iran be governed by a president, prime minister and a single-chamber Islamic Consultative Assembly (Majlis-e-Shura) of 270 deputies. Although there was pressure in Iran to submit the draft constitution to a newly-elected Constituent Assembly, Khomeini submitted it for revision to a 'Council of Experts' consisting of 75 members who were elected on 3 August. After prolonged deliberations the revised Constitution was submitted to a referendum at the beginning of December 1979. The most important change from the draft Constitution was provision for a *wali faqih* (religious leader), whose extensive powers (see The Constitution) secured for him the most important executive influence in Iran. Votes against the Constitution were negligible.

Presidential elections followed on 25 January 1980, and resulted in a convincing win for Abolhasan Bani-Sadr, who polled about 75% of the votes. All this time the Islamic Revolutionary Council had effectively been administering the country, although there was a Government headed by Dr Mehdi Bazargan until his resignation in mid-November 1979 over Khomeini's support for the retention of the US hostages. Thereafter the Islamic Revolutionary Council, with President Bani-Sadr becoming its Chairman in February 1980, ruled more openly, and appointed ministers to run the country until elections to the Majlis in the spring of 1980.

The elections took place in two rounds, on 14 March and 9 May 1980. A total of 3,300 candidates contested 270 seats, 30 of which were in Teheran. Disturbances in Kurdish areas and various allegations of fraud resulted in the fact that, when the Majlis began its first session on 28 May 1980, only 234 deputies had been decided, and, of those, only 213 had received their credentials. It was clear, however, that the Islamic Republican Party (IRP), the party identified with the policies of Ayatollah Khomeini and led by Ayatollah Beheshti, was in a majority, claiming 130 seats. Ayatollah Beheshti presented a threat to the leadership of President Bani-Sadr. On 7 May Khomeini had given Bani-Sadr authority to appoint a prime minister until the Majlis convened, but Beheshti successfully prevented this, insisting that this appointment be the responsibility of the Majlis.

The Islamic Revolutionary Council was dissolved on 18 July 1980, but there followed a delay in forming a government. Many

of the candidates for ministerial office who were proposed by the Majlis and supported by the IRP were unacceptable to President Bani-Sadr. The President agreed to the appointment of Muhammad Ali Rajai as Prime Minister only with reluctance, doubting his competence. The ministries of finance and economic affairs, commerce and foreign affairs were left without ministers for some months, and a feud developed between President Bani-Sadr, on the one hand, and Rajai and the IRP, on the other. An abortive three-man commission tried to resolve these differences in March 1981, but on 10 June Khomeini dismissed Bani-Sadr as Commander-in-Chief of the Armed Forces. A few days later, Bani-Sadr was deprived of the presidency, and he later fled to France, where he formed a 'National Council of Resistance' in alliance with Massoud Rajavi, the former leader in Iran of the opposition guerrilla group, the Mujahidin-e-Khalq. (Bani-Sadr left the council in 1984 because of his objection to Rajavi's increasing co-operation with the Iraqi Government—see Political Organizations, p. 519.) A three-man Presidential Council replaced Bani-Sadr after his dismissal, until new presidential elections could be held on 24 July. On 28 June, however, a bomb exploded at the headquarters of the IRP, killing Ayatollah Beheshti (the Chief Justice and Head of the IRP), four cabinet ministers, six deputy ministers and 20 parliamentary deputies.

On 24 July 1981 the presidential election took place and resulted in a win for the Prime Minister, Muhammad Ali Rajai. Muhammad Javad Bahonar then became Prime Minister of a Government introduced to the Majlis on 13 August. A further bomb outrage occurred on 29 August, this time killing both the President (Rajai) and the Prime Minister (Bahonar). Ayatollah Muhammad Reza Mahdavi Kani became Prime Minister in September, and another round of presidential elections was held on 2 October. Hojatoleslam Ali Khamenei, a leading figure of the IRP, was elected President, winning more than 16m. of the 16.8m. votes cast. At the end of October, after the resignation of Ayatollah Muhammad Reza Mahdavi Kani, Mir Hossein Moussavi was appointed Prime Minister.

THE IRAN–IRAQ WAR

It was generally thought by outsiders at this time that the whole Iranian Islamic Revolution was about to crumble. In addition to internal troubles, Iran had been at war with Iraq for over a year. Fighting between the two countries had begun after Iran ignored Iraqi demands for the withdrawal of Iranian forces from Zain ul-Qos, in Diali province on the border between the two countries. Iraq maintained that this territory should have been returned to it under the 1975 agreement with Iran. Iraq therefore abrogated the 1975 Shatt al-Arab agreement and invaded Iran on 22 September 1980. Most observers now believe that this was no more than a pretext on Iraq's part, the real objective of its President, Saddam Hussain, being to topple what he regarded as the threatening but vulnerable Iranian regime.

Iranian resistance was spirited, and a position of stalemate was soon reached along a 480-km front. Various international peace missions all proved of no avail, and in the spring of 1982 the Iranian forces broke the stalemate by launching two offensives, the first in the Shush-Dezful area in March, and the second on a 60-mile front south of Susangerd to the port of Khorramshahr at the end of April. Both offensives achieved considerable success, with Iran recapturing Khorramshahr in the middle of May. It then carried the war into Iraqi territory, but a speedy conclusion to the war, for which Iran had hoped, did not materialize. In February 1983 Iran began a major offensive in the area of Iraq's Misan province, but the impetus was soon lost, and a fresh Iranian offensive in April similarly proved indecisive. A further Iranian offensive in July (combined with operations to suppress renewed activity by Kurdish guerrillas in the area) saw its forces entrenched 15 km within northern Iraq. The attack seemed to be consistent with Iran's policy of waging a war of attrition, keeping Iraq on a war footing and thereby exerting pressure on the weakening Iraqi economy which might topple the regime of Saddam Hussain. Action by Iran prevented Iraq from exporting oil through the Gulf and a pipeline through Syria was cut off. Iraq was able to continue the war only with financial aid from Saudi Arabia and Kuwait.

During the second half of 1983 Iraq stepped up missile and aircraft raids against Iranian towns and petroleum installations and, in the autumn, took delivery of five French-built *Super*

Etendard fighter aircraft. With these, and with the *Exocet* missiles already in its possession, Iraq threatened to destroy Iran's oil export industry, centred on Kharg Island in the Gulf, which financed the Iranian war effort. Iran countered by promising to make the Gulf impassable to all shipping (one-sixth of the Western world's petroleum requirement passed through the Gulf) if Iraqi military action rendered it unable to export oil from the Gulf via the Strait of Hormuz. In retaliation for the sale of *Super Etendard* aircraft to Iraq, Iran severed most of its economic ties with France.

In March 1984 a further Iranian offensive succeeded in taking part of the marshlands around the southern Iraqi island of Majnoun, the site of rich oilfields, though only at a great cost in lives. Iraq subsequently retook some of the territory which it had lost, but seemed more intent on consolidating its defences than making further ground. A team of UN observers, sent in at the request of the Iranian Government, found that Iraq had used mustard gas to counter the offensive. A long-awaited Iranian offensive against Basra failed to materialize. While Iran delayed, Iraq developed a formidable network of defensive fortifications along its southern border.

Although it had earlier declared a maritime exclusion zone at the north-east end of the Gulf around Kharg Island and made spasmodic attacks against shipping (not only oil tankers), which in some cases was well outside the zone, Iraq refrained from attacking tankers using the Kharg Island oil terminal until May 1984. Iran retaliated with attacks against Saudi and Kuwaiti tankers in the Gulf.

INTERNAL DEVELOPMENTS

At the time of the bomb outrages in mid-1981 the Iranian regime appeared to the rest of the world to be on the point of collapse. Subsequent events, however, demonstrated that it possessed greater resilience than was at one time thought possible. An extended campaign against the main anti-government guerrilla group, the Mujahidin-e-Khalq, waged sometimes with savage ferocity, eventually achieved some success, and in February 1982 the Mujahidin leader in Iran, Musa Khiabani, was killed.

In April 1982 an anti-government plot was uncovered in which Ayatollah Shariatmadari, one of Iran's leading mullahs, was accused of being involved. He subsequently denied this, but admitted knowledge of the plot, in which the former Minister of Foreign Affairs, Sadeq Ghotbzadeh, was deeply implicated. Ghotbzadeh was subsequently tried and executed in September. Ayatollah Shariatmadari died in April 1986, having been under house arrest in Qom for two years.

In 1983 the Iranian Government turned its attention to the Iranian communist party, the Tudeh Party. The party had been banned under the Shah, but had come into the open after the 1979 Revolution. In February the party's Secretary-General, Nour ed-Din Kianuri, was arrested on charges of spying for the USSR. Kianuri was subsequently the first of a number of Tudeh members publicly to confess on TV to this and other crimes against the state. Further arrests of Tudeh Party members followed, bringing the total of arrests to about 1,000, and 18 Soviet diplomats were expelled. The party was officially banned again in April.

An intense rivalry within the Government, reflecting a wider divergence of views in the country, became increasingly apparent after the Revolution. The two rival groups were the right-wing Hojjatieh, identified with the traditionalist clerical and merchant ('bazaari') communities, and the radical technocrats. The Hojjatieh were opposed on grounds of religion and self-interest to radical economic reforms such as the nationalization programme and the reform of the laws governing land ownership (the clergy are extensive land owners), which were advocated by the technocrats, who were motivated by more secular, socialist concerns. The Hojjatieh had extensive representation in the first Majlis.

Elections to the second Majlis took place on 15 April and 17 May 1984, significantly altering the distribution of influence in the assembly. Slightly more than one-half of the outgoing first Majlis were clerical men and that majority had given them the power to determine policy according to largely religious considerations. A high proportion of the 1,230 or more candidates who contested the elections were of a more secular cast; doctors, scientists, engineers; people with a practical economic background. The elections were boycotted by former Prime Minister Dr Mehdi Bazargan's Liberation Movement opposition party (the only party recognized by the ruling IRP), in protest against what he considered to be the undemocratic conditions prevailing in Iran. It was estimated that more than 50% of the seats in the new assembly were filled by new members giving rise to speculation that a more sympathetic Majlis might allow Moussavi greater success in implementing his economic programme. However, the Council of Guardians, which exists to determine whether Majlis legislation is both constitutional and Islamic, was of a conservative, clerical character and proved to be a major obstacle to economic reform.

Islamic codes of correction were introduced in 1983, including the dismembering of a hand for theft; flogging for more than 50 offences including forgery, consumption of alcohol, fornication and violations of the strict code of dress for women; and stoning to death for adultery. These began to be more rigidly enforced in 1985, in response to demonstrations in April by young Muslim fundamentalists demanding stricter adherence to Islamic law. There were clashes between opponents of the regime and fanatical *hezbollahi* (members of the Party of God) who supported the continuation of the Iran–Iraq War and the rigid observance of Islamic codes of behaviour. Widespread active popular opposition to the Teheran regime was not conspicuous until 1985. Dissatisfaction with the conduct of the war with Iraq and with austere economic conditions sparked demonstrations and rioting in several Iranian cities, including Teheran. Government supporters staged numerous counter-demonstrations.

Active suppression of opposition to the Government continued. In 1985, according to Amnesty International, 399 people were executed in Iran in the period to the end of October, bringing the total to 6,426 since the Revolution. A UN Human Rights Commission report, published in February 1987, estimated the number of executions at a minimum of 7,000 between 1979 and 1985.

President Ali Khamenei was due to complete his four-year term of office in September 1985, and a presidential election was held on 16 August, with only three candidates, including Ali Khamenei, taking part. The Council of Guardians rejected the candidature of nearly 50 people who had applied to stand in the election, including Dr Mehdi Bazargan. Ali Khamenei was re-elected President, gaining 85.7% of the 14,244,630 votes cast.

Although 99 deputies either voted against him or abstained, Hossein Moussavi was confirmed as Prime Minister by the Majlis on 13 October 1985. A dispute over the composition of the new Council of Ministers, which President Khamenei considered to be too radical, initially withholding his approval from half of Moussavi's appointees, was not resolved until the intervention of Ayatollah Khomeini on Moussavi's behalf, so that the list submitted to the Majlis contained only two changes. All but seven of the new Council of Ministers had served in the previous Government.

DEVELOPMENTS IN THE IRAN–IRAQ WAR IN 1985–86

A resumption of Iraqi attacks on shipping in the Gulf in December 1984 had the effect of reducing Iranian oil exports to an estimated 1.1m. barrels per day (b/d) and causing the Teheran Government to suspend imports temporarily. Although Iraqi raids on Iranian petroleum installations and oil tankers in the Gulf undeniably affected the level of oil exports, they failed to halt them altogether: the Kharg Island oil terminal remained in operation, largely undamaged, and Iran's economy appeared to be capable of sustaining the cost of continuing the war, albeit under severe pressure. Iraq had an estimated 580 combat aircraft and 130 armed helicopters at the beginning of 1985, compared with Iran's 110 combat aircraft, of which only 50–60 were thought to be operational, but it failed fully to exploit its superiority. The People's Republic of China became the leading supplier of military equipment to Iran during the war, and it was estimated that businesses or governments in 44 countries, including both the USA and the USSR, had sold armaments to Iran during the war. Other major suppliers included the Democratic People's Republic of Korea and Israel.

Iran mounted an assault in the region of the al-Hawizah marshes in southern Iraq, east of the Tigris, in March 1985. This did not appear to be the long-awaited decisive thrust, as it involved, at the most, only 50,000 troops. The Iranian forces crossed the Tigris and succeeded, for a time, in closing the main road between Baghdad and Basra. The Iraqis launched a counter-offensive, repulsing the Iranians, with heavy casualties sustained by both sides. Iraq was again accused of using chemical weapons during this battle.

The UN had painstakingly engineered an agreement between Iran and Iraq in June 1984, suspending attacks on civilian targets, but, after the failure of the Iranian offensive in March 1985, and with the war on the ground once more at stalemate, Iraq resumed its air attacks on Iranian cities from the ground and from the air. The first Iraqi air raid on Teheran in four years took place in March. Iran retaliated, shelling Basra and other Iraqi towns, and hit Baghdad with ground-launched missiles, but Iraq, in this instance making full use of its air superiority, hit more than 30 Iranian population centres in the first half of 1985, killing hundreds of civilians. President Saddam Hussain's stated intention was to carry the war to every part of Iran until Khomeini decided to come to the negotiating table.

In April 1985 the UN Secretary-General, Javier Pérez de Cuéllar, visited both Teheran and Baghdad, in an attempt to establish a basis for peace negotiations, but Iran's terms remained the same. The Iranian claim for Iraqi war reparations was US $350,000m., and, though there was less official insistence on the removal of Hussain and his Baathist regime from power as a condition of peace, it was accepted by the Iranian Government that, if all the other conditions (the payment of reparations, an Iraqi admission of responsibility for starting the war, and the withdrawal of Iraqi troops from all Iranian territory) were met, he would fall anyway.

Also in April 1985, Saddam Hussain ordered the suspension of air raids on Iranian towns in order to give Iran the opportunity to declare a cease-fire and begin negotiations. Iran did not respond. After six weeks, Iraqi air raids resumed with greater intensity at the end of May, with Iran retaliating in kind. A 16-day moratorium in June achieved the same result.

Until mid-1985 Iraq had failed to launch attacks against the main Iranian oil export terminal on Kharg Island of sufficient frequency or intensity seriously to threaten the continuation of oil exports. In August, however, Iraq made the first of a concentrated series of raids upon Kharg, causing a reduction in Iranian oil exports from 1.2m.–1.5m. b/d, in the months leading up to the raids, to less than 1m. b/d in September. Exports from Kharg were temporarily halted altogether during the latter half of September. By the end of 1985 exports from Kharg had reportedly been reduced to a trickle compared with its 6.5m. b/d capacity. In February 1986 Iraq announced an expansion of the area from which it would try to exclude Iranian shipping. Previously confined to the waters around Iran's Gulf ports, the area was broadened to include the coast of Kuwait. Attacks on tankers and other commercial vessels in the Gulf were increased by both sides during 1986, and Iran intensified its practice of intercepting merchant shipping and confiscating goods which it believed to be destined for Iraq.

The next important engagement, in terms of land gained, did not occur until 1986. On 9 February Iran launched the Wal-Fajr (Dawn) 8 offensive, so called to commemorate the month of Ayatollah Khomeini's return to Iran in 1979 from exile in France. Iranian forces (some 85,000 troops were thought to be involved in the operation) crossed the Shatt al-Arab waterway and, on 11 February, occupied the disused Iraqi port of Faw, on the Persian Gulf, and, according to Iran, about 800 sq km of the Faw peninsula. From this position, within sight of the Kuwaiti island of Bubiyan, commanding the Khor Abdullah channel between the Faw peninsula and the island, Iran threatened Iraq's only access to the Gulf and, if it could extend the offensive to the west, Iraq's Umm Qasr naval base. However, the marsh and then desert terrain to the west was not conducive to further Iranian gains, and the position on the Faw peninsula was defensible only with difficulty, given the problem of maintaining supply lines across the Shatt al-Arab. At the same time as the attack upon Faw, Iran began a complementary operation along the Faw–Basra road to divert Iraqi forces. When Iraq launched a counter-offensive on Faw in mid-February, Iran opened up a second front in Iraqi Kurdistan, hundreds of miles to the north, with the Wal-Fajr 9 offensive.

At the end of February 1986 the UN Security Council, while urging a cease-fire, blamed Iraq for starting the war for the first time. Despite heavy fighting, Iraq's counter-offensive made little progress and failed to dislodge an estimated 30,000 Iranian troops, now firmly entrenched in and around Faw.

In May 1986 Iraq adopted different tactics by making its first armed incursions into Iran since withdrawing its forces from Iranian territory in 1982. About 150 sq km of land, including the deserted town of Mehran (about 160 km east of Baghdad), were occupied. (Iran recaptured Mehran in July.) Also in May, in the first Iraqi air raid on Teheran since June 1985, Iran's second largest oil refinery was bombed, signalling a renewal of reciprocal attacks on urban and economic targets, which continued for the remainder of 1986 and into 1987. According to the *Washington Post* in December 1986, for the previous two years Iraq had received US intelligence assistance in targeting attacks on Iranian oil terminals and power plants. However, in the following month, US intelligence sources were reported as saying that both Iran and Iraq had been supplied with deliberately distorted or misleading information to assist the policies of the Reagan administration.

On 24 December 1986 Iran mounted an offensive (named Karbala-4 after the holy Shi'ite city in Iraq) in the region of Basra but failed to penetrate Iraqi defences on four islands in the Shatt al-Arab waterway. On 8 January 1987 a two-pronged attack (Karbala-5) was launched towards Basra. Iranian forces, attacking from the east, established a bridgehead inside Iraq, between the Shatt al-Arab, to the west, and the artificial Fish Lake to the east, and advanced gradually towards Basra, sustaining heavy casualties, while an assault from the south-east secured a group of islands in the Shatt al-Arab. Iran opened a second front, 400 km to the north, with the Karbala-6 offensive, on 13 January. By mid-February, Iranian forces from the east had advanced to within about 10 km of Basra, but no further gains were made and the Karbala-5 offensive was officially terminated at the end of the month.

In November 1986 it emerged that the USA, despite its official discouragement of arms sales to Iran by other countries, had been conducting secret negotiations with the Islamic Republic since July 1985, and had made three shipments of weapons and spare parts (valued at an estimated $100m.) to Iran, through Israeli and Saudi intermediaries, in September 1985, and July and October 1986. The shipments were allegedly in exchange for Iranian assistance in securing the release of US hostages who had been kidnapped by Shi'ite extremists in Lebanon, and an Iranian undertaking to abstain from involvement in international terrorism. The talks were reportedly conducted on the Iranian side by the Speaker of the Majlis, Hojatoleslam Hashemi Rafsanjani, with Ayatollah Khomeini's consent but without the knowledge of other senior government figures, including the Prime Minister and the President.

THE IRAN–IRAQ WAR: 1987

Iran rejected the offer of a cease-fire and peace talks, which was made by President Hussain of Iraq in January 1987, and in the following months demonstrated its ability to launch attacks from one end to the other of its 1,200-km frontier with Iraq. The Karbala-7 offensive, in March, penetrated north-eastern Iraqi territory to a depth of about 20 km in the Gerdmand mountains, near Rawanduz, itself only some 100 km from Iraq's largest oilfields, at Kirkuk. On the southern front, in April, Iran launched the Karbala-8 offensive from the salient 10 km east of Basra, which had been secured in Karbala-5. The Iranians claimed that the attack established a new front line about 1 km towards Basra, west of the artificial Twin Canals water barrier, though Iraq claimed that it had been repulsed. An almost simultaneous offensive, Karbala-9, was mounted in the central sector of the Iran-Iraq border, from near the Iranian town of Qasr-e-Shirin.

The Iran–Iraq War entered a potentially explosive new phase in 1987. Once more, the danger of an escalation of the conflict was focused on the shipping lanes of the Persian Gulf. During 1986 there were about 100 attacks by Iran and Iraq on shipping in the Gulf. Iran had begun to use squads of high-speed patrol boats, crewed by Islamic Revolutionary Guards (*Pasdaran Inqilab*), stationed on islands in the Gulf, in attacks on commercial ships. Reflecting its anger at Kuwait's support for Iraq, Iranian attacks were concentrated on Kuwaiti shipping and on neutral vessels and tankers carrying oil or other cargoes to and from Iraq, via Kuwait. Between October 1986 and April 1987 15 ships bound to or from Kuwait were attacked by Iran in the Gulf, and several Kuwaiti cargoes were seized. Alarmed by the repeated attacks on its merchant ships and by the apparent indifference of the outside world to the war, Kuwait sought the protection of the leading powers for its shipping in the Gulf, and, by involving them more closely, hoped to persuade them of the urgent need for international co-operation in achieving a peaceful end to the conflict. The USSR and, subsequently, the USA were asked to re-register Kuwaiti ships under their flags, which they would then be obliged to defend if they came under attack. On 24 March, the day after the USA had made its navy available to escort Kuwaiti tankers, Iran threatened to halt the traffic in oil through the Gulf. In April the USSR allowed Kuwait to charter three Soviet tankers and proposed international talks on the protection of commercial shipping in the Gulf. The USA rejected the Soviet proposal but in May agreed to re-register 11 Kuwaiti tankers under the US flag and to increase its naval presence in the Gulf in order to protect them. This decision followed the apparently accidental attack in the Gulf by an Iraqi *Mirage* F-1 fighter plane on the USS *Stark* on 17 May, only hours after one of the Soviet tankers chartered by Kuwait had struck a mine while approaching a Kuwaiti port. Iraq desisted from attacks on tankers for the next five weeks.

At the end of June 1987, following a hiatus of five weeks, and one week after Iraq, Iran resumed its attacks on Gulf shipping using high speed launches based on the islands of Minou, Farsi and Abu Musa. Iran made it clear that it considered the US naval presence in the Gulf to be provocative, and fears of a military confrontation grew.

The escalation of tension in the Gulf resulted in a rare display of unanimity in the UN Security Council, which adopted a 10-point resolution (No. 598) on 20 July 1987, urging an immediate cease-fire in the Iran–Iraq War; the withdrawal of all forces to internationally recognized boundaries; and the co-operation of Iran and Iraq in mediation efforts to achieve a peace settlement. Iraq said that it would abide by the resolution if Iran did so (Iraqi attacks on tanker traffic had been halted in mid-July). Iran criticized the resolution for failing to identify Iraq as the original aggressor in the war, and claimed that the belligerent US naval presence in the Gulf (which rose to a peak of 48 vessels in 1987) rendered it null and void, but failed to deliver an official, unequivocal response.

The USS *Bridgeton* and the USS *Gas Prince*, the first Kuwaiti tankers to be re-registered under the US flag, passed unharmed through the Strait of Hormuz with a US naval escort on 22 July 1987. However, on 24 July the *Bridgeton* struck a mine (probably Iranian) near the Iranian island of Farsi, and struggled to port in Kuwait. The US naval force in the Gulf was ill-equipped to deal with mines and US Government requests for minesweeping assistance were initially refused by its main NATO allies, who were anxious to avoid a confrontation with Iran. In August, however, the United Kingdom and France announced that they were to send minesweepers to the Gulf region and, in September, these were followed by minesweeping vessels from Belgium, the Netherlands and Italy. Iran was believed to have laid mines on the shipping routes to Kuwait, including the al-Ahmadi channel, the approach to Kuwait's main oil ports.

POLITICAL AND DIPLOMATIC DEVELOPMENTS IN 1987–88

During 1987 the conviction grew among the international community that Iran was attempting to spread the Islamic Revolution through a network of agents operating in its diplomatic missions abroad, and controlled by the Iranian Ministry of Intelligence and Internal Security. In March Tunisia broke off diplomatic relations with Iran, accusing it of fomenting Islamic fundamentalist opposition to the Government, and of recruiting Tunisians for terrorist operations abroad through its embassy in Tunis. Eight suspected terrorists (six of whom held Tunisian passports) were arrested in Paris in March. They were believed to be members of a network of 'sleeper' terrorist cells co-ordinated by Iran and established several years before. In June the French authorities sought to interview Wahid Gordji, who was officially listed as a translator at the Iranian embassy in Paris, in connection with a bombing campaign in the city in 1986. Although Gordji did not have diplomatic status the Iranians

refused to give him up, and armed French police surrounded the embassy. The Iranian Government retaliated by throwing a cordon of armed Revolutionary Guards around the French embassy in Teheran. On 17 July France severed its diplomatic relations with Iran. The embassy siege was lifted at the end of November, when Gordji was permitted to leave France. Two days after his release, two French hostages, held by Iranian-backed groups in Lebanon, were set free. The French Prime Minister, Jacques Chirac, denied that a ransom had been paid to the hostages' captors but admitted that negotiations were continuing between France and Iran over the repayment of the $670m. balance on the $1,000m. loaned by the Shah to France in 1978. It was also rumoured that France had agreed to supply arms to Iran in order to secure the hostages' release. France and Iran resumed diplomatic relations and exchanged ambassadors in June 1988.

In June 1987 Ayatollah Khomeini approved a proposal by Hashemi Rafsanjani, the Speaker of the Majlis, which was reluctantly supported by President Khamenei, to disband the IRP. In a letter to Khomeini, the two leaders said that, the institutions of the Islamic Republic having been established, contrary to the IRP's intended function, 'party polarization under the present conditions may provide an excuse for discord and factionalism'.

On 31 July 1987 attention was diverted from the Gulf by the deaths in riots in Mecca of 402 people, including 275 Iranian pilgrims (the majority of them women) engaged on the *Hajj* (pilgrimage) to the city's Muslim shrines. The Saudi authorities maintained that most of the victims had been trampled to death when some 150,000 Iranians (who, in contravention of Saudi laws governing the *Hajj*, had been demonstrating in support of Ayatollah Khomeini) went on the rampage, attacking Saudi security forces. The Iranians, on the other hand, alleged that the Saudi police had opened fire on the pilgrims, and accused Saudi Arabia and the USA of planning the incident. A 'day of hatred' was proclaimed by the Government on 2 August, and Hashemi Rafsanjani (the Speaker of the Majlis) promised vengeance.

In August 1987 Hojatoleslam Mehdi Hashemi, a close associate of Ayatollah Montazeri (Ayatollah Khomeini's designated successor), was tried by a specially-appointed Islamic court and convicted of murder, the kidnapping of a Syrian diplomat in Teheran, of forming a private army (with the aim of overthrowing the Government and installing a more rigorous Islamic regime), and of planning explosions in Mecca during the *Hajj*. It was Hashemi who, in an attempt to disrupt the planned sale of US arms to Iran, had revealed to a Lebanese magazine, *Ash-Shira'*, details of the secret visits of the then US National Security Adviser, Robert McFarlane, and Col Oliver North to Teheran in May 1986. Hashemi was executed on 28 September 1987.

In April 1988, following further Iranian attacks on Saudi and other neutral shipping in the Gulf, Saudi Arabia severed its diplomatic relations with Iran. Iran had been insisting on sending up to 150,000 pilgrims on the *Hajj* to the holy places in Saudi Arabia in 1988 (the same number as in 1987), despite the events of July 1987 and the subsequent deterioration in bilateral relations. A meeting of the OIC, in Amman, had agreed a formula for 1988, whereby each Muslim nation would be permitted to send 1,000 pilgrims per 1m. citizens, giving Iran a quota of 45,000. Finally, Iran decided that it would send no pilgrims on the *Hajj* at all.

THE UN FAILS TO ENFORCE RESOLUTION 598

Frustrated by Iran's temporizing over a definitive response to UN Security Council Resolution 598, on 29 August 1987 Iraq, contrary to advice from Western governments, resumed attacks on Iranian oil installations and industrial targets, and on tankers in the Gulf transporting Iranian oil. Iran had exploited the 45-day lull in Iraqi attacks by raising the level of oil production and exports. Resolution 598 made provision for unspecified sanctions in the event of the failure of either or both sides to comply with its terms for a cease-fire. However, the resumption of Iraqi attacks weakened the UN's position in its attempts to secure a cease-fire through diplomacy, and made it less likely that the USSR, if it would accept the principle at all, could be persuaded that the arms embargo proposed by the USA and the United Kingdom should apply only to Iran.

Iranian threats of reprisals against Saudi Arabia and Kuwait for their support of Iraq ceased to be purely rhetorical when Iran fired three *Silkworm* missiles into Kuwaiti territory at the beginning of September 1987 (and a further three before the end of the year). Kuwait expelled five Iranian diplomats on 5 September. The visit of the UN Secretary-General, Pérez de Cuéllar, to Iran and Iraq between 11 and 15 September, was preceded by an intensification of Iraqi attacks on Iranian economic targets. In Teheran Iranian leaders told Pérez de Cuéllar that they supported the provision in Resolution 598 for the setting up of an 'impartial body' to apportion responsibility for starting the war, but that Iraq's guilt in this matter had to be established before Iran would observe a cease-fire. For its part, Iraq was prepared to accept the ruling of a judicial body in determining responsibility for the war but stated that a formal cease-fire, according to the terms of Resolution 598, should precede the setting up of such a body.

Signs of an apparent willingness on Iran's part to modify its stand on Resolution 598 forestalled attempts by the USA, the United Kingdom and France to promote their proposal of an arms embargo against Iran, and also pre-empted the adoption of diplomatic or other sanctions by the Arab League, at its meeting in Tunis on 20 September 1987.

On 25 September 1987 Iran presented a plan to the UN Security Council, according to which it would observe a *de facto* cease-fire while a UN-appointed commission of inquiry determined which side was responsible for starting the war. An official cease-fire would take effect when the commission had identified the aggressor (by implication, Iraq). Iraq rejected these proposals as being a deviation from the terms of Resolution 598.

By mid-October 1987 the number of tankers being employed by Iran to shuttle oil from Kharg Island to Sirri and Larak Islands had declined to an estimated 20 vessels, owing to damage sustained during Iraq's intensified campaign of attacks in the Gulf. On 19 October four US naval vessels destroyed Iran's Rostam and Rakhsh oil platforms, about 100 km east of Qatar, which were, the USA alleged, being used to launch military operations against shipping.

On 22 December 1987 the USSR proposed discussions within the UN Security Council to consider a mandatory ban on the sale of arms to Iran. According to the Soviet proposal, these talks would take place at the same time as discussions on the introduction of an international naval force in the Gulf, under the control of the UN, which would replace the various national forces patrolling the region. Although all the five permanent members of the Security Council subsequently agreed on the need for further measures to be taken to ensure the compliance of both combatants with Resolution 598, the USSR's insistence on the withdrawal of foreign navies and the deployment of a UN naval force in the Gulf as a complementary measure, and the USA's growing military involvement in the area during 1988 (see below), prevented the adoption of an arms embargo.

CEASE-FIRE AND NEGOTIATIONS: 1988–89

During the first half of 1988 Iran suffered a series of military set-backs in the war with Iraq, which offset the gains that it had made during the previous few years. Meanwhile, divisions within the Government over the conduct of the war became more apparent, as Ayatollah Khomeini grew more frail and the political struggle for the succession intensified. However, the world was taken by surprise in July 1988 when, after 12 months of prevarication, Iran agreed, unconditionally, to accept Resolution 598 in all its parts.

In January 1988 Ayatollah Khomeini had intervened in a debate over the role of the government in an Islamic Republic to reject a narrow interpretation of its competence by President Khamenei, who had said that the government operated 'within the limits of Islamic law and Islamic principles'. Khomeini had replied that, on the contrary, the government was the primary instrument of Islamic rule and was competent to override certain aspects of Islam, even such practices as prayer (*salat*), fasting and the *Hajj* (three of the five 'pillars' of Islam), if it was in the interests of the state. In asserting the primacy of the government, Khomeini was believed to have strengthened the position

of reformers, identified with Hashemi Rafsanjani, the Speaker of the Majlis, and Prime Minister Moussavi, who were attempting to enact legislation hitherto obstructed by the conservative clerics on the Council of Guardians.

The elections to the third Majlis in April and May 1988 provided a further boost for the reformers. The elections were the first not to be contested by the IRP, which had been dissolved in June 1987. Instead, all 1,600 candidates for the 270 seats in the Majlis were examined for eligibility by local committees and sought election as individuals. A record 16,988,799 people (68% of the electorate) voted in the first round of the elections on 8 April (when the majority of seats were contested), compared with 15.8m. in 1984 and 10.8m. in 1980. In June Hashemi Rafsanjani was re-elected as Speaker of the Majlis and Hossein Moussavi was overwhelmingly endorsed as Prime Minister. He presented a new Council of Ministers to the Majlis in July.

In January 1988 Iraq resumed the so-called 'tanker war'. During 1987, according to Lloyd's of London, Iran and Iraq had damaged 178 vessels in the Gulf (34 in December alone), compared with 80 during 1986. Although the US Navy continued safely to escort reflagged Kuwaiti vessels, traffic not under its protection, including Kuwaiti shipping, remained a target for Iranian attack. (When a cease-fire was proclaimed in July, a total of 546 vessels had been attacked since 1981, when the 'tanker war' began in earnest.)

At the end of February 1988 Iraq resumed the so-called 'war of the cities' (which, apart from sporadic attacks, had not been pursued in earnest since early 1987), by bombing a petroleum refinery on the outskirts of Teheran. Iran retaliated by bombing a petrochemicals plant in Basra. This was the beginning of a series of reciprocal attacks on civil and economic targets in the two countries which lasted for several months.

During 1987/88, for the first time in six years, owing to poor mobilization, disorganization and a shortage of volunteers, Iran was unable to launch a major winter offensive and began to lose ground to Iraqi advances along the length of the war front. In mid-April 1988 Iraqi forces regained control of the Faw peninsula, where the Iranians, who had been unable to strike out to make further gains since capturing the area in 1986, had scaled down their presence. Iran accused Kuwait of allowing Iraqi forces to use Bubiyan Island during the offensive. In March the Mujahidin Iranian National Liberation Army (NLA), supported by Iraq, undertook a major offensive for the first time since its creation in 1987, attacking Iranian units in Iran's south-western province of Khuzestan. In May Iraq recaptured the Shalamcheh area, south-east of Basra, driving Iranian forces across the Shatt al-Arab into Iran.

Identifying military inefficiency as the principal cause of these reverses, Ayatollah Khomeini appointed Hashemi Rafsanjani as acting Commander-in-Chief of the Armed Forces on 2 June 1988 and gave him the task of unifying the command structure and improving co-ordination between the regular armed forces, the Revolutionary Guards Corps (*Pasdaran*) (with its own land, naval and air forces) and the Mobilization (*Basij*) Volunteers Corps. At the beginning of July Rafsanjani announced the creation of a general command headquarters to rationalize the disjointed military command structure, but a merger of the army and the Revolutionary Guards was ruled out.

The changes came too late to prevent further Iranian defeats. Having won back more territory from the Iranian army in the north of Iraq near Sulaimaniya, in mid-June 1988, at the end of the month Iraq recaptured Majnoun Island and the surrounding area (the site of one of the world's biggest oilfields) in the al-Hawizah marshes, on the southern front.

In the Gulf, fears of a serious military confrontation between Iran and the USA were realized on 18 April 1988, when the US navy destroyed two Iranian oil platforms (Sassan and Nasr) in the southern Gulf, and six Iranian warships (a guided-missile boat, three speedboats and two frigates) were either sunk or badly damaged, in retaliation for damage allegedly inflicted on a US frigate by an Iranian mine on 14 April. On 3 July the USS *Vincennes*, the US navy's most sophisticated guided-missile destroyer, which had only recently been deployed in the Gulf to counter the threat to shipping of Iran's *Silkworm* missiles (which, the USA believed, were soon to become operational from a permanent site near the Strait of Hormuz), mistakenly shot down an Iran Air Airbus A300B over the Strait of Hormuz, having assumed it to be an attacking F-14 fighter-bomber. All 290 passengers and crew on board the scheduled flight to Dubai were killed.

Iranian forces were expelled from more Iraqi territory in Kurdistan during June and July 1988. Iraqi troops forced Iranian units back over the international border in the central sector of the war front, crossing into Iranian territory on 13 July for the first time since 1986, and capturing the Iranian border town of Dehloran. In mid-July the last pockets of Iranian occupation in southern Iraq were cleared by Iraqi troops. On 18 July Iran officially announced its unconditional acceptance of Resolution 598. The first clause of the Resolution required the combatants to withdraw to international borders and to observe a cease-fire. Iraqi troops advanced further into Iran before retiring behind the border on 24 July. On the other hand, the NLA, over which Iraq claimed to have no control, launched a three-day offensive on 25 July, penetrating as far as 150 km into Iranian territory, before being forced to withdraw. Iraq professed to have no designs on Iranian territory, but was possibly using the NLA as a proxy to prevent the Iranian forces from regrouping during a cease-fire which might prove to be only temporary. The implementation of a cease-fire was delayed by Iran's refusal to accede to an Iraqi demand for direct peace talks, under UN auspices, to commence prior to a cessation of hostilities. Iran protested that Resolution 598 did not require this. However, Iraq withdrew its demand and a cease-fire finally came into force on 20 August, monitored by a specially-created UN observer force of 350 officers, the UN Iran-Iraq Military Observer Group (UNIIMOG).

Negotiations between Iran and Iraq for a comprehensive peace settlement began at foreign ministerial level in Geneva on 25 August 1988, under the aegis of the UN. One of the most contentious issues to be decided at these talks was the status of the Algiers Agreement of 1975 between Iran and Iraq, which Iran insisted should be the basis for negotiations, but which Iraq rejected. According to the terms of the Algiers Agreement, which defined the southern border between Iran and Iraq as running along the deepest channel of the Shatt al-Arab waterway (the Thalweg line), the two countries exercise joint sovereignty over the waterway. However, President Saddam Hussain of Iraq publicly tore up the agreement (to which he had been a signatory) immediately prior to the Iraqi invasion of Iran in 1980, demanding full Iraqi sovereignty over the waterway, which Iraq held under previous agreements in 1847, 1913 and 1937. The matter of determining responsibility for starting the war was another potential obstacle to the negotiation of a lasting peace. It was generally accepted that Iraq initiated the conflict by invading Iran on 22 September 1980. Iraq, however, maintained that the war began on 4 September with Iranian shelling of Iraqi border posts. Resolution 598 provided for the establishment of an impartial body to apportion responsibility for the war. Finally, Iraq rejected Iranian demands for the payment of reparations, for which Resolution 598 did not provide.

The peace negotiations soon became deadlocked in disputes concerning sovereignty over the Shatt al-Arab, and the right of navigation in the waterway and the Gulf, the exchange of prisoners of war, and the withdrawal of troops to within international borders. By August 1989 progress in the negotiations, at least as far as the border issue was concerned, had been insignificant, although some exchanges of prisoners of war had taken place. In November, in an attempt to unblock the negotiations, Iran proposed an immediate exchange of prisoners of war, accompanied by the withdrawal of troops to within international borders. By the end of the year, however, the cease-fire remained the only element of Resolution 598 to have been successfully implemented.

THE RUSHDIE AFFAIR

On 14 February 1989 Ayatollah Khomeini issued a religious edict, pronouncing a sentence of death on the British author Salman Rushdie and his publishers, and exhorting all Muslims to carry out the sentence. Khomeini's edict followed demonstrations in India and Pakistan in protest at the imminent publication in the USA of Rushdie's novel, *The Satanic Verses*, the content of which was considered to be blasphemous by some Muslims. (Rushdie, born a Muslim himself, was therefore guilty of apostasy, an offence punishable by death under *Shari'a* law.)

The novel had first been published in the United Kingdom in September 1988. Khomeini's edict, which, despite an apology by Rushdie for any offence his novel had given to Muslims, was reiterated on 19 February, led to a sharp deterioration in relations between Iran and the United Kingdom and other Western countries. On 20 February Khomeini's sentence on Rushdie was condemned at a meeting of the Ministers of Foreign Affairs of the 12 EC member states. Senior-level diplomatic contacts between the member states and Iran were suspended, while the United Kingdom announced the withdrawal of its diplomatic representatives and personnel in Teheran. Iran, in turn, announced the withdrawal of all diplomatic representatives and staff in EC member countries on 21 February, and on 7 March severed diplomatic relations with the United Kingdom.

While the significance of the Rushdie affair was initially defined in terms of its effect on Iran's foreign relations, it soon became apparent that the issue was being used tactically by vying factions within the Iranian leadership. In a speech on 22 February 1989 Khomeini referred explicitly to a division in the Iranian leadership (between 'liberals' who sought Western participation in Iran's post-war reconstruction, and 'conservatives' who opposed Western involvement) in terms which implied that *The Satanic Verses* was the culmination of a Western conspiracy against Islam, and declared that he would never allow the 'liberal' faction within the leadership to prevail.

By late March 1989 it was clear that Khomeini's intervention had decisively strengthened the hand of the 'conservatives'. In early April the 'liberal' Ayatollah Montazeri, who had been elected as successor to Ayatollah Khomeini by the Council of Experts in 1985, resigned. It was reported that, in the absence of any individual with sufficient authority to assume the role, the Council of Experts had established a five-member leadership council to replace Montazeri as Khomeini's successor. On 24 April a 20-member council was appointed by Ayatollah Khomeini to draft amendments to the Iranian Constitution.

IRAN AFTER KHOMEINI

The death of Ayatollah Khomeini, long anticipated by manoeuvres within the Iranian leadership, occurred on 3 June 1989. In an emergency session on 4 June the Council of Experts elected President Khamenei to succeed Ayatollah Khomeini as Iran's spiritual leader, and on 5 June the Iranian Prime Minister, Hossein Moussavi, declared his support, and that of all government institutions, for Khamenei. On 8 June Hashemi Rafsanjani reiterated his intention to stand as a candidate at the forthcoming presidential election, and on 12 June he was re-elected for a further one-year term as Speaker of the Majlis.

Despite the apparent intensification in the struggle for power within the Iranian leadership in the months preceding Ayatollah Khomeini's death, both 'conservatives' and 'liberals' gave their support to the candidacy of Hashemi Rafsanjani for the Presidency. The presidential election, held on 28 July, was contested by only Rafsanjani and Abbas Sheibani, a former minister who was widely regarded as a 'token' candidate. According to official figures, Rafsanjani received some 15.5m. (95.9%) of a total 16.2m. votes cast. Abbas Sheibani received 632,247 (3.9%) of the total votes cast. At the same time, 95% of those who voted approved the 45 proposed amendments to the Constitution, the most important of which were the elevation of the President to the Government's Chief Executive and the abolition of the post of Prime Minister. Rafsanjani was sworn in as President on 17 August. The new Council of Ministers was regarded as a balanced coalition of 'conservatives', 'liberals' and technocrats, and its endorsement by the Majlis was viewed as a mandate for Rafsanjani to conduct a more conciliatory foreign policy towards the West, in particular with regard to the Western hostages held captive by pro-Iranian Shi'ite groups in Lebanon; and to introduce reforms designed to stimulate economic reconstruction.

While the amendments to the Constitution increased the power of the Presidency, it was anticipated that Rafsanjani's leadership would be challenged by several factions, including Ahmad Khomeini, son of the late Ayatollah Khomeini, and by the Minister of the Interior, Ali Akbar Mohtashami, and the Minister of Intelligence, Muhammad Muhammadi Reyshahri, both of whom were known to be advocates of a doctrine of 'permanent revolution' and to approve of international terrorism to achieve this aim. Both Mohtashami and Reyshahri were excluded from the Council of Ministers that the Majlis endorsed in August 1989.

While Western support was regarded as vital to Iran's economic reconstruction by Rafsanjani and his supporters within the Iranian leadership, it was regarded as anathema by his opponents, who feared that it would lead to the erosion of Islamic values and the betrayal of the Revolution. Rafsanjani's fundamental problem on assuming the presidency was to find a way of gaining Western support without alienating the 'conservative' faction within the leadership, which remained too powerful to be directly confronted. The urgency of the need for economic reform was demonstrated by increased incidents of popular protest against food shortages and high prices in early 1990. In May 1990 an 'open letter' was addressed to Rafsanjani by 90 prominent clerics, professionals and retired soldiers associated with the Liberation Movement of Iran, which was legal but did not enjoy official approval. The 'open letter' criticized government policies, complained of massive corruption and regretted Iran's international isolation. It led to widespread arrests, which appeared to indicate that Rafsanjani was unable to control his 'conservative' opponents. Divisions within ruling circles were exemplified by the dispute between Rafsanjani and his opponents over whether to accept Western aid following an earthquake in Gilan and Zanjan provinces in June 1990, in which more than 40,000 people died. After some initial hesitations, Western aid was accepted in what was regarded as an important victory for Rafsanjani.

FOREIGN RELATIONS

Although the death sentence on the British author Salman Rushdie remained in force, the tension created by its initial pronouncement in February 1989 lessened somewhat in the ensuing months. In March EC Ministers of Foreign Affairs agreed that member states should be allowed to reinstall their ambassadors in Teheran. There was evidence, too, of an improvement in relations between Iran and the communist countries. In late June Rafsanjani visited the USSR, where he and the Soviet leader, Mikhail Gorbachev, signed a 'declaration on the principles of relations' between Iran and the USSR. These relations were strained in January 1990, however, when Iranian politicians voiced support for the Muslim Azerbaijani revolt against the Soviet central Government in the Nukhichevan enclave on the Iranian border.

In mid-July 1989 the USA unexpectedly offered to pay compensation directly to the families of the 290 passengers and crew of the Iran Air Airbus A300B mistakenly shot down by the USS *Vincennes* in July 1988. However, the Iranian Government insisted that the compensation should be distributed through its agencies, rather than privately, and took the dispute to the ICJ. The fragility of Iran's relations with the USA was underlined in early August when, in response to the abduction by Israeli forces of the Lebanese Shi'a Muslim leader, Sheikh Abdul Karim Obeid, a US hostage in Lebanon, Lt-Col William Higgins, was executed by his captors, who threatened the execution of more hostages if Sheikh Obeid was not released. While Iran denied any involvement in the killing of Lt-Col Higgins, it was widely suspected of complicity. Whatever its role, the USA immediately engaged in urgent negotiations with Iranian leaders in order to prevent further killings. In November 1989 the USA agreed to release US $567m. of the total of $810m. of Iranian assets that had been seized 10 years previously, at the time of the siege of the US embassy in Teheran, in order to secure US bank claims on Iran.

In April 1990, following the release of two US citizens who had been held hostage by pro-Iranian groups in Lebanon, the USA thanked both the Syrian and the Iranian Governments for the part that they had played in securing the hostages' release. In March 1990 a report in an Iranian newspaper had assured the USA that Iran would do what it could to secure the release of hostages, while elsewhere it had been reported that indirect contacts between the USA and Iran were taking place with regard to their release. Two Iranian diplomats were reported to be acting as liaison officers between Teheran and the pro-Iranian Hezbollah. In May 1990 the USA and Iran concluded a 'small claims agreement', whereby US claimants were to be repaid for losses that they had incurred during the Iranian

Revolution in 1979; and in June 1990 Iran agreed to pay the US company Amoco $600m. in compensation for US oil operations which had been expropriated during the Revolution.

Relations between Iran and the United Kingdom fluctuated during the first half of 1990. In February the United Kingdom expelled nine Iranian diplomats for reasons of national security, and, as a retaliatory gesture, Iran closed the BBC office in Teheran. In the same month, however, President Rafsanjani described the *fatwa* (religious edict) that had been pronounced against Rushdie as an exclusively Islamic issue (implying that it ought not to interfere with the re-establishment of normal relations between Iran and the United Kingdom), while trade between the United Kingdom and Iran was reported to be increasing. In May 1990 it was reported that the United Kingdom was involved in indirect contacts with Iran concerning four UK nationals held hostage by pro-Iranian groups in Lebanon, and the United Kingdom announced that it was prepared to resume direct talks with the Iranian Government. In June, however, Ayatollah Khamenei declared that the *fatwa* could never be repealed.

Iran's position of strict neutrality during the Kuwait conflict (see below) brought rapid dividends. On 27 September 1990 Iran and the United Kingdom resumed diplomatic relations after, in an exchange of letters, Iran had assured the United Kingdom of its respect for international law and of its commitment to achieving the release of Western hostages held in Lebanon. The United Kingdom assured Iran of its respect for Islam and stated that it understood the offence which Salman Rushdie's novel, *The Satanic Verses*, had caused to Muslims. In October 1990 the EC revoked its ban on senior-level diplomatic contacts with Iran.

In May 1990 an Iranian delegation met EC officials in Dublin (Ireland). During the meeting Iran reiterated its pledge to work towards securing the release of Western hostages in Lebanon. A diplomatic initiative by the Irish Government was believed to have brought about the release, in August 1990, of an Irish citizen held hostage for four years by a pro-Iranian group in Lebanon. In July 1990, having boycotted the *Hajj* for the third successive year, Iran accused Saudi Arabia of being unfit to administer Islam's shrines, following an incident in which more than 1,400 pilgrims were trampled to death in a stampede in a tunnel near Mecca.

IRAQ CONCEDES IRAN'S PEACE TERMS

In early 1990 Iran and Iraq agreed to resume negotiations in the USSR, at the invitation of the Soviet Ministry of Foreign Affairs. In July the Iraqi and Iranian Ministers of Foreign Affairs conferred at the UN's European headquarters in Geneva. It was the first such direct meeting between them since the cease-fire in the war had taken effect. It had been facilitated by an exchange of letters between Presidents Saddam Hussain and Rafsanjani in May. This breakthrough in the peace process was quickly overtaken by the consequences of Iraq's invasion and annexation of Kuwait in August 1990.

On 16 August 1990 Saddam Hussain abruptly sought an immediate, formal peace with Iran by accepting all the claims that Iran had pursued since the declaration of a cease-fire, including the reinstatement of the Algiers Agreement of 1975, dividing the Shatt al-Arab. While these concessions were transparently dictated by expediency (on 17 August Iraq began to redeploy in Kuwait troops hitherto positioned on its border with Iran) and thus left the conflicts underlying the Iran–Iraq War unresolved, they were welcomed by Iran, although it insisted that the issue of peace with Iraq was separate from that of Iraq's occupation of Kuwait. Exchanges of an estimated 80,000 prisoners of war commenced on 17 August, and on 18 August Iraq began to withdraw troops from the central border areas of Ilam, Meymak, Mehran and Naft Shahr. On 11 September Iran and Iraq re-established diplomatic relations.

The withdrawal of all armed forces to the internationally recognized boundaries was verified and confirmed as complete on 20 February 1991 by the UNIIMOG, whose mandate was terminated on 28 February 1991 by the UN Security Council. Iran and Iraq subsequently initiated a 'confidence-building' process of reducing the levels of troops and military equipment in the border areas. Exchanges of prisoners of war continued until 16 January 1991, when the multinational force commenced military operations to expel Iraqi armed forces from Kuwait. At this time Iran still held 30,000 Iraqi prisoners of war. Preliminary negotiations on the full implementation of Resolution 598 were also curtailed. Relations between Iran and Iraq again deteriorated after March 1991, when Iraqi Shi'ite Muslims participated in a rebellion against the Baath regime in the aftermath of Iraq's decisive military defeat by the multinational force.

The publication in August 1991 of the report of a UN delegation sent to Iran—in accordance with the terms of Resolution 598—to assess the level of human and material damage caused by the war with Iraq seemed to indicate that the UN was once again considering the need for a comprehensive peace settlement. The Iranian Government released its own assessment of the damage caused by the war with Iraq. It estimated that during the war Iran experienced direct damage amounting to 30,811,000m. Iranian rials; that 50 towns and 4,000 villages were destroyed or badly damaged; and that 14,000 civilians were killed and 1.25m. people displaced.

IRAN AND THE CONFLICT OVER KUWAIT

Iran condemned Iraq's invasion of Kuwait in August 1990 and offered to defend other Gulf states from Iraqi aggression, but it welcomed Iraq's offer of a formal settlement of the Iran–Iraq War on Iran's terms (see above). While Iran stated that it would observe the economic sanctions imposed on Iraq by the UN, Iraq was believed to have tried to persuade Iran to trade oil for food. However, the Iranian Government adhered to its pledge to implement economic sanctions for the duration of the conflict over Kuwait, sending only supplies of food and medicine to Iraq on a humanitarian basis.

As the deployment of a multinational force (assembled in accordance with Article 51 of the UN Charter) for the defence of Saudi Arabia gathered pace, Iran urged the simultaneous and unconditional withdrawal of Western—above all of US—armed forces from the Gulf region, and of Iraqi armed forces from Kuwait. In September 1990 Ayatollah Khamenei almost endorsed the demands of 'conservatives', such as Hojatoleslam Ali Akbar Mohtashemi, for Iran to ally itself with Iraq in a *jihad* against Western forces in the Gulf. President Rafsanjani's position was that the presence of these forces was tolerable on condition that they withdrew as soon as the conflict in Kuwait had been resolved.

Following the outbreak of military hostilities between Iraq and the multinational force in January 1991, Iran attempted, unsuccessfully, to intercede. After having consulted with Algeria, Yemen, France, the USSR and the Non-Aligned Movement (NAM), Iran urged an 'Islamic solution' to the conflict. On 4 February 1991 President Rafsanjani announced that the terms of an Iranian peace proposal had been conveyed to President Saddam Hussein of Iraq during the visit to Teheran, on 1–3 February, of Iraq's Deputy Prime Minister, Dr Sa'adoun Hammadi; and claimed that the terms of the proposal were consistent with resolutions adopted by the UN Security Council. An immediate cease-fire was to be followed by the simultaneous and complete withdrawal of Iraqi armed forces from Kuwait, and of all foreign forces from the Gulf region. In deference to Iraq's insistence on the 'linkage' of the conflict in Kuwait with other conflicts in the Middle East (in particular the continuing Israeli occupation of the West Bank and the Gaza Strip), Iran also urged the immediate cessation of new Israeli settlements in the Occupied Territories.

While the Iranian peace proposal was welcomed by the USSR, it was rejected by the USA, and on 8 February 1991, in a letter to President Rafsanjani, Saddam Hussein dismissed it, stating that Iraq had no intention of withdrawing from Kuwait, and accusing the USA of seeking to dominate the Middle East by destroying Iraq. There was no clear expression of support for the Iranian peace proposal at a closed session of the NAM, held in Belgrade, Yugoslavia, on 11–12 February, and thereafter Soviet diplomacy came to the fore in attempting to find peace terms which might avert a ground war. Iran claimed some of the credit for the concessions offered in an Iraqi peace proposal on 15 February, and urged the multinational force not to initiate hostilities on the ground until the limits of Iraq's flexibility had been determined. However, the countries contributing to the multinational force were unwilling, by this stage, to allow Iraq the opportunity to procrastinate.

As the air bombardment of Iraq and occupied Kuwait continued, Iran accused the multinational force of exceeding the terms of resolutions adopted by the UN Security Council by seeking to destroy Iraq's military and industrial facilities. However, when, in late January 1991, more than 100 Iraqi fighter aircraft landed in Iran without having sought permission to do so, Iran lodged a protest with Iraq and impounded both the aircraft and their pilots for the duration of the conflict.

Relations between Iran and Iraq deteriorated after the conclusion of hostilities between Iraq and the multinational force on 28 February 1991. In response to the suppression, by Iraqi armed forces loyal to President Saddam Hussein, of a Shi'a-led rebellion against the Baath regime in southern and central Iraq, Iran declared its commitment to the territorial integrity of Iraq, but demanded the resignation of Saddam Hussein and protested at the damage inflicted by Iraqi armed forces on Shi'a shrines at Najaf, Karbala and Samarra. Iraq accused Iran of providing material and human support for the southern and central rebellions, citing the involvement of the Teheran-based Supreme Council of the Islamic Revolution in Iraq. In a clear indication of deteriorating relations, Iraq later resumed support for the military activities of the largest Iranian dissident groups, the Mujahidin-e-Khalq and the Kurdish Democratic Party (KDP). Iraq's suppression of the internal rebellions led to a mass flight of Iraqi Kurds and Shi'a Muslims across the Iranian border. By May 1991 more than 1m. Iraqi Kurds had fled to Iran, while the number of Shi'a refugees in Iran was estimated at 65,000.

Iran supported the Western initiative to establish 'safe havens' for Iraqi Kurds in northern Iraq, and urged, unsuccessfully, similar support for Iraqi refugees in Iran. Throughout June and July 1991 Iran accused the Iraqi armed forces of harassing Iraqi Shi'a Muslims who had fled into the marshes of southern Iraq after the defeat of the southern rebellion in March. There were conflicting reports regarding the accuracy of these allegations and of the number—estimated by Iran at 600,000—of Shi'a Muslims who had sought refuge in the marshes.

DOMESTIC REFORM UNDER RAFSANJANI

While the onset of the crisis in the Gulf in August 1990 led to further friction between the rival factions in the Iranian leadership, President Rafsanjani gradually asserted his authority and began the long process of seeking to reduce the power of the 'conservatives'. At times his relationship with Ayatollah Khamenei became tense, especially with regard to foreign policy issues. However, in October 1990 they formed an alliance to prevent the election of many powerful 'conservatives' to the 83-seat Council of Experts, which chooses Iran's supreme leader and interprets the Constitution. Hojatoleslam Ali Akbar Mohtashemi and Ayatollah Khalkhali were among those rejected as candidates by Khamenei, on the grounds that their expertise in the Koran was inadequate. In December 1990 the Majlis enacted legislation which allowed defendants legal representation. The new legislation was thought to signal a move towards the less rigorous application of Islamic law.

In April 1991 it was announced that Iran's internal security services—the police, the gendarmerie and the Islamic *Komitehs*—were to be merged. The *Komitehs* had hitherto acted as the chief enforcers of 'Islamic behaviour' within post-revolutionary Iranian society. In the same month the release of a British businessman, Roger Cooper, who had been imprisoned without trial since 1985 for alleged espionage, was regarded as a further sign of Rafsanjani's ascendancy. In May 1991 the human rights organization, Amnesty International, was allowed access to Iran for the first time since the Revolution.

Disturbances and demonstrations in Teheran and other parts of the country in August 1991 indicated significant levels of popular discontent. In April and May 1992 further demonstrations occured, most notably in Teheran and Mashad. Eight protestors were executed by the authorities. An important factor in the unrest was municipal action in many cities against squatter settlements.

Elections to the fourth Majlis in April and May 1992 seemed to provide Rafsanjani with the opportunity further to shift the balance of power against the 'conservatives'. It was estimated that about 70% of the deputies elected to the new Majlis were supporters of Rafsanjani. The new deputies appeared to be more highly educated, younger and more technocratic in orientation than their predecessors. Rafsanjani installed a new Speaker of the Majlis, Ali Akbar Nateq Nouri, who replaced the 'conservative', Mahdi Karrubi. However, it subsequently became clear that assessments predicting the support of the majority of the new deputies for Rafsanjani's policies were incorrect.

The new Government indicated that it wished to proceed rapidly with measures to end all subsidies and the system of multiple foreign exchange rates; and to allow full foreign ownership of companies. In fact, the pace of economic reform in the months following the election to the fourth Majlis remained cautious. Rafsanjani remained constrained by tensions within his own policies, not least by the fact that economic reform was lowering the standard of living of the traditional constituency of the Islamic regime, the urban lower classes. The middle classes, supposedly one of the engines of reform, remained deeply distrustful of the regime. Rafsanjani quickly discovered, too, that the deputies in the new Majlis who were expected to be in favour of reform were far from uncritical in their support for his policies.

The extent to which Rafsanjani had lost popular support became clear when he stood for re-election to the presidency on 11 June 1993. Competing against three ostensibly 'token' candidates, Rafsanjani received 63.2% of the vote in a low electoral turn-out of 56%. His nearest rival, former Minister of Labour, Ahmed Tavakkoli, received 24% of the vote, a performance widely attributed to his stringent criticisms of state corruption, social injustice and economic mismanagement. Rafsanjani's re-election was regarded as a popular comment on the lack of any realistic alternative to him rather than as a positive endorsement of his record in office.

During 1994 there were numerous signals that the problems encountered by Rafsanjani in carrying through his reform programme were emboldening 'conservative' forces, encouraged by Ayatollah Khamenei, to challenge the President more directly. In February there was an attempt on his life during a speech he made at Khomeini's tomb. Responsibility for the attack was later claimed by the self-styled 'Free Officers of the Revolutionary Guards'. Later in the month the President was obliged to replace the Minister of Culture and Islamic Guidance in the Council of Ministers after Ayatollah Khamenei had approved the appointment of the incumbent minister, Ali Larijani, to replace the President's brother, Muhammad Hashemi, as director-general of the national broadcasting authority. Prior to his dismissal Muhammad Hashemi Rafsanjani had, for several months, been criticized by 'conservatives' within the Majlis for mismanagement and for encouraging immoral broadcasts. Mostafa Mirsalim became the new Minister for Culture and Islamic Guidance. While President Rafsanjani denied that the dismissal of his brother reflected on him, it was perhaps significant that, shortly afterwards, he announced that he would not seek a constitutional amendment which would allow him to serve a third term as President. Opponents of the President in the Majlis also sought to modify economic reforms proposed by the Government. In May the Government indicated that it would proceed more cautiously with a plan to reduce economic subsidies applied to basic commodities.

The atmosphere of political malaise was further deepened in June 1994 by the bombing of the Imam Reza shrine in Mashad which left at least 24 dead. The Government blamed the Mujahidin-e-Khalq; others speculated that it might be the work of militant members of the Sunni minority in Iran, angered by the destruction of a Sunni mosque earlier in the year. The atmosphere of malaise turned to one of near crisis in the following month when, in the space of a few days, two Iranian Christian leaders were assassinated in Teheran and bombs wrought havoc against Jewish targets in London, United Kingdom, and Buenos Aires, Argentina.

In August 1994 riots were reported to have occurred in the cities of Qazvin and Tabriz. In Qazvin they were caused by the defeat in the Majlis of a government proposal to separate the city from the province of Zanzan and to establish it as the capital of a new province. In response to the riots the Government announced that Qazvin would immediately be incorporated into

Teheran province, a decision which was formally approved in September.

In April 1995 riots in Islamshahr, a suburb of Teheran, were interpreted as a protest against the Government's programme of economic reforms, which had led to shortages of some consumer goods during the previous 12 months, and had caused the price of petrol to double in the previous month. In August members of the special commission for monitoring political parties were reported to have stated that political parties, associations and groups were free to conduct political activities in Iran on condition that they honoured the country's constitution. At the same time, however, it was reported that Nehzat-Azadi (Liberation Movement of Iran) had been refused permission formally to register as a political party, despite its hitherto quasi-legal status. Earlier in the month representatives of Nehzat-Azadi had criticized new electoral legislation which granted the 12-member Council of Guardians the power to approve election candidates.

Elections to the fifth Majlis in March and April 1996 provided another important gauge of the shifting balance of power between 'liberals' and 'conservatives' in Iranian politics. The 'liberals' were grouped around a political faction named the Servants of Iran's Construction, which enjoyed the tacit support of President Rafsanjani. Its 'conservative' counterpart was the Society of Combatant Clergy, of which the unofficial patron was Ayatolloh Khamenei. While a total of 10 political groups were acknowledged to have presented candidates for election, official disapproval of such groups was reflected in the authorities' refusal to publish the political affiliations of successful candidates. However, according to unofficial sources the Society of Combatant Clergy was expected to enjoy the support of 110–120 deputies in the new Majlis, and the Servants of Iran's Construction that of 90–100.

The response of the 'conservatives' to this electoral setback—the Society of Combatant Clergy had held the allegiance of 150–160 deputies in the outgoing Majlis—was to revive extra-parliamentary methods of harassing the advocates of political liberalization, which had been the principal issue of contention during the election campaign. The cause of the 'conservatives' was given initial impetus by the Israeli attacks on and partial invasion of Lebanon in April 1996 (see chapter on Lebanon).

FOREIGN RELATIONS UNDER RAFSANJANI

Efforts at domestic reform under Rafsanjani were accompanied by periodic diplomatic initiatives by Iran, aimed at securing its reintegration into the international community. The greatest single obstacle to improved relations with Western countries was initially Iran's perceived complicity in the holding of Western hostages in Lebanon by groups linked to the pro-Iranian Hezbollah. Between August and December 1991, with Iran, Syria, Israel and the UN diplomatically active, all remaining UK and US hostages were released. While the aim of the captors was to trade the release of the UK and US hostages for the release of Shi'a hostages held by Israel, it was decided ultimately to release the UK and US hostages unconditionally. The last remaining Western hostages were released in June 1992.

The release of US hostages and some progress at the US-Iran Claims Tribunal in The Hague, Netherlands, temporarily removed some of the tension between the USA and Iran. In September 1990 the USA paid Iran $200m. for armaments not delivered after the Revolution of 1979. In December 1991 a further $278m. was paid by the USA. In March 1992 the USA was ordered to compensate Iran for property frozen in the USA after 1979.

Relations between the USA and Iran deteriorated after President Clinton took office in January 1993. Throughout the year the USA pressed initially reluctant Western allies to reduce levels of economic assistance to Iran and sought to block Iranian efforts to reschedule its international debts. In May 1994 US pressure was evident when it emerged that no new loans would be made to Iran by the World Bank in the foreseeable future. In June President Rafsanjani stated at a press conference that Iran sought a gesture of goodwill, such as the release of frozen assets, from the USA as a prelude to improved relations. In July bomb attacks against Jewish targets in London, United Kingdom, and Buenos Aires, Argentina, prompted the USA to accuse Iran—which it alleged was responsible for the attacks—of seeking to disrupt the Middle East peace process. In August, however, the Argentinian authorities decided that there was insufficient evidence to pursue charges against four Iranians for whose arrest international warrants had earlier been issued.

In early 1995 the USA, the United Kingdom and Israel were reported to be alarmed at the possibility that Iran might be able to manufacture nuclear weapons within a few years. This was at the time of a final preparatory UN session before a conference on the extension of the Nuclear Non-Proliferation Treaty (NPT) took place, and Iran was reported to be seeking a more effective effort from the five principal nuclear powers to disarm further, and insisting that Israel should also sign the NPT. (Israel had previously refused to do so because it perceived itself to be potentially at risk of nuclear attack by Syria, Iraq and Iran.) According to some observers, Iran's aim was to pressurize Western governments into offering it assistance with its civilian nuclear programme. The head of the Atomic Energy Organization of Iran (AEOI) subsequently suggested that Iran would remain party to the NPT whether Israel signed it or not. The International Atomic Energy Agency (IAEA) stated that it had found no evidence to suggest that Iran was seeking to develop nuclear weapons. In late February 1995 Russia was reported to be determined to sell at least one 1,000-MW nuclear reactor to Iran in accordance with an agreement concluded in early January 1995, despite the objections of the USA, where members of the Republican opposition in the US Congress had raised the possibility of discontinuing aid to Russia in retaliation for the sale. Japan's decision, in February, to postpone the extension of a $450m.-loan to Iran to finance the Godar-e-Landar dam was reported to be the result of US diplomacy, in particular the disclosure to the Japanese authorities of US intelligence reports about unspecified Iranian activities. In March the US company Conoco withdrew from a contract to develop Iranian oil fields after the USA announced that President Clinton would shortly issue an executive order prohibiting US companies from such activities.

On 30 April 1995 US efforts to isolate Iran internationally culminated in the announcement of a complete ban on trade with Iran within 30 days: all US companies and their foreign subsidiaries would be prevented from investing in Iran, and from undertaking any trade with it. There was no international support for such an embargo, and without the support of Iran's European trading partners and of Japan it was far from clear how the embargo would damage Iran's long-term economic interests. In the immediate aftermath of its announcement, however, the value of the Iranian rial declined by about one-third. In an interview in a US cable television broadcast in early July President Rafsanjani denied US allegations that Iran sponsored terrorism and was seeking to develop nuclear weapons; and that Iran was offering any practical assistance to Palestinian groups opposed to the Middle East peace process.

In late 1995, in response to the lack of international support—except that of Israel—for the ban on trade with Iran, the US Congress drafted legislation which aimed to pressurize other countries into observing it. The US Administration, however, opposed initial attempts by the US Congress to force the USA's trading partners to impose trade sanctions on Iran; and Japan and the EU threatened to refer the issue to the World Trade Organization if such legislation were to be adopted. In March 1996 the USA and Israel accused Iran of being an active supporter of the Palestinian group, Hamas, which had claimed responsibility for a wave of suicide bombings in Israel. Iran denied any involvement in the bombing campaign. US suspicions of Iranian involvement in state terrorism continued during 1996, and the US Government publicly stated that it was investigating allegations of Iranian involvement in the June 1996 bomb attack on US military personnel at al-Khobar, near Dhahran, in Saudi Arabia.

In June 1996 the US House of Representatives approved legislation which would penalize companies operating in US markets which were investing $40m. or more in Iran's oil and gas industry. The sanctions received presidential assent despite sustained protests from Japan and the EU. In April 1997 the EU and the USA reached a compromise to protect European companies from penalities under the act.

The continuing dispute over the British author Salman Rushdie (see above) remained a major obstacle to any improvement in Iran's relations with the United Kingdom and the other EU member states. At a summit meeting held in Edinburgh, in the United Kingdom, on 13 December 1992, leaders of the EC criticized alleged abuses of human rights in Iran and stated 'that Iran's arms procurement should not pose a threat to regional stability'. In August 1993 talks took place between the United Kingdom and Iran, with the aim of raising diplomatic links between the two countries to ambassadorial level.

In April 1994, however, Iran's relations with the United Kingdom again deteriorated after the United Kingdom accused Iran of involvement with the illegal Irish Republican Army (IRA). In May Iran alleged that the UK intelligence services had installed listening devices at its embassy in London, and at the end of the month and in early June mutual expulsions of diplomatic personnel took place. In late September talks between the UK and Iranian Ministers of Foreign Affairs in New York, USA, failed to achieve any progress towards an improvement in relations. In April 1995 the Ministers of Foreign Affairs of the EU member states agreed that they would seek from Iran a guarantee of Salman Rushdie's safety from attack, in the EU and anywhere else, and confirmation that Iran's foreign relations were conducted in accordance with international law. In June there was speculation that the EU member states might offer Iran better trading terms and increased political co-operation in return for the formal lifting of the *fatwa*, while in July Norway announced the withdrawal of its ambassador from Iran because the death sentence on Rushdie remained unrevoked. In September UK officials were reported to be dissatisfied at the result of a meeting with Iranian counterparts on the Rushdie affair. Iranian officials were reported to have given verbal assurances that Iran did not intend to enforce the *fatwa* against Rushdie, but had refused to confirm this in writing when asked to do so.

Despite US pressure (see above), the EU persisted with a policy of 'critical dialogue' with Iran. However, in March 1996 it threatened to reconsider this policy following alleged remarks by President Rafsanjani welcoming the assassination of the Israeli Prime Minister, Itzhak Rabin. In the same month the German Government announced that a warrant had been issued for the arrest of the Iranian Minister of Information, Ali Falahian, in connection with the murders of four prominent members of the dissident Democratic Party of Iranian Kurdistan Berlin in 1992. 'Critical dialogue' was suspended in April 1997, after a German court ruled that the Iranian authorities had ordered the dissidents' assassination: testimonies at the trial directly implicated senior members of the Iranian political and religious establishment in the murders, and, moreover, alleged that Iran's former Minister of Information, Ali Falahian, had attempted to influence the outcome of the case. (The court found two defendants—an Iranian and a Lebanese national—guilty of the murders, sentencing them to life imprisonment, and two others—both Lebanese nationals—of having been accessories to the killings.) Germany announced the withdrawal of its ambassador to Teheran and expelled four Iranian diplomats, and other EU members similarly withdrew their representatives. Iran retaliated by threatening to bring lawsuits against 24 German companies allegedly involved in supplying chemical weapons to Iraq during the Iran–Iraq War.

During the conflict over Kuwait in 1990/91 Iran sought to normalize its relations with Egypt, Tunisia, Jordan and the Gulf states. In March 1991 it re-established diplomatic relations with Saudi Arabia, and about 115,000 Iranian pilgrims were subsequently able to participate in the 1991 *Hajj*. Thereafter, however, relations were characterized by mistrust. In August 1991 Iran and Iraq met directly for talks on a comprehensive settlement to the 1980–88 war. A UN Commission had formally blamed Iraq for starting the Iran–Iraq War and Iran expected a proposed UN conference to award it $100,000m. in reparations. In April 1992 Iran launched airstrikes against Mujahidin-e-Khalq camps in Iraq. Iraq protested to the UN Security Council. The treatment by the Iraqi Government of its southern Shi'a population continued to obstruct relations between Iran and Iraq. In February 1995 and in May Iran denied Iraqi allegations that armed groups under Iranian control had been responsible for attacks, inside Iraqi territory, on Iraqi armed forces and on a base of the Mujahidin-e-Khalq. In May there was evidence, in the form of preparations for a visit to Baghdad of the Iranian Minister of Foreign Affairs, that Iran was seeking an improvement in its relations with Iraq, possibly so that the two countries could co-operate to counter US hostility. In August, however, on the anniversary of the end of the Iran–Iraq War, the Iraqi President made an uncompromising speech, in which he criticized Iran for continuing to detain Iraqi prisoners of war, refusing to release Iraqi aircraft impounded in January 1991 and for rejecting Iraqi efforts to secure peace.

In the aftermath of the Kuwait conflict, Iran sought to assert itself as a regional power. It reacted negatively to efforts based on the Damascus Declaration of March 1991 to create a regional security structure in the Gulf from which it was itself excluded. While opposing the defence agreements which the Gulf states subsequently negotiated with the USA, Iran focused its diplomatic efforts on improving its relations with them. Significant progress in that sphere was thwarted by a dispute between Iran and the United Arab Emirates (UAE) over the islands of Abu Musa after March 1992, when Iran occupied those parts of the Abu Musa islands and the Greater and Lesser Tunbs that had remained under the control of Sharjah, in the UAE, since the original occupation in 1971. In September 1992 the Arab League expressed its support for the UAE in the dispute over the islands, and at the end of the month negotiations between Iran and the UAE on this issue collapsed. In September 1993 Iran refused to accept any pre-conditions for discussions with the UAE on the dispute. In December 1994 the UAE announced its intention to refer the dispute to the ICJ. In November 1995 Iran and the UAE held direct talks on the issue for the first time in three years, but again no progress was made.

A further source of tension between Iran and the GCC member states arose in June 1996, when the GCC accused Iran of plotting to overthrow the Government of Bahrain. Iran rejected the allegation.

The dramatic developments in the USSR after August 1991 opened up a new arena for Iranian diplomacy in Central Asia. Iran, Saudi Arabia and Turkey are vying for influence in the newly-independent states of Central Asia. While well-placed geopolitically, Iran lacks the money to pursue its ambitions and is further disadvantaged by the fact that Central Asia is Sunni Muslim, with the exception of Azerbaijan, and speaks languages belonging to the Turkic family, with the exception of Tajikistan. Iran is seeking to strengthen its position in Central Asia through bilateral agreements and institutions such as the revived Economic Co-operation Organization (ECO), comprising the states of Central Asia, Iran, Turkey and Pakistan. Iran recognized the independence of most of the former Soviet republics in late 1991, and proceeded to establish full diplomatic relations with them. At a summit meeting held in Teheran in mid-February 1992 it was agreed to expand the membership of the ECO to include Azerbaijan, Turkmenistan, Uzbekistan, Tajikistan and Kyrgyzstan. At the same time, the formation of a Caspian Sea co-operation zone, grouping Iran, Russia, Azerbaijan, Turkmenistan and Kazakhstan as members; and the formation of a cultural association, grouping together Tajikistan, Afghan guerrillas and Iran, was announced. These new alliances gave rise to renewed concern in the West at the extent of Iranian political and religious influence. In June 1994, under the auspices of the UN, Iran attempted to mediate a cease-fire in the civil war which had erupted in Tajikistan in 1992. In September 1994 the Tajikistan Government and its opponents signed a cease-fire agreement in Teheran. In July 1995 Iran sponsored further talks between the Tajikistan Government and its opponents, which resulted in an extension of the cease-fire agreement.

During 1996 Iran became increasingly interested in events in Afghanistan, owing to the military advance of the Sunni fundamentalist Taliban guerrilla fighters in that country. Following the Taliban capture of the Afghan capital, Kabul, in September 1996, Iran accused the group of being a proxy for US, Saudi and Pakistani interests in the country. The Iranian Government refused to recognize the Taliban-sponsored authorities in Kabul, and continued to express support for ousted President Rabbani. In early June 1997, amidst accusations of espionage activities, the new authorities in the Afghan capital closed the Iranian embassy and requested the departure from Afghanistan of all Iranian diplomats. In retaliation, Iran ordered the halt of all trade (including goods in transit) across its land border to Afghanistan, prompting Taliban accusations that Iran had perpetrated 'a violation of international protocols'.

In April–May 1991 President Rafsanjani made an official visit to Turkey—the first such visit by an Iranian Head of State since 1975—where he publicly stated his agreement with Turkey's President Özal that a Kurdish state should not be established in northern Iraq. In early 1992 Turkey alleged that Iran was lending support to guerrillas of the Kurdish Workers' Party (PKK) engaged in hostilities with Turkish armed forces in northeast Turkey. Further deteriorations in Iran's relations with Turkey were reported to have occurred in June and September. In October the Turkish Prime Minister, Süleyman Demirel, made a visit to Teheran. As a result of the visit, Iran and Turkey agreed to increase economic and political co-operation. In December 1993 Iran's First Vice-President, Hassan Habibi, visited Turkey, where he signed an agreement, first drawn up in November, on security co-operation between Turkey and Iran. In March 1995 Iran criticized a military operation undertaken by the Turkish armed forces against PKK fighters in northern Iraq, fearing that the hostilities might spread to Iran. In July Iran was reported to have organized a month-long extension of a cease-fire between rival Kurdish groups in Iraqi Kurdistan, prompting Iraq to denounce Iranian interference in Iraqi internal affairs. In April 1996 new tensions arose in relations with Turkey after four Iranian diplomats were arrested in Turkey for alleged espionage. Retaliatory expulsions of Turkish diplomats by Iran ensued. Iran was reported to be increasingly anxious at growing military co-operation between Turkey and Israel. In June 1996 the rise to power of a governing coalition in Turkey led by the Islamist Welfare Party facilitated closer relations between Turkey and Iran. However, Iranian influence was cited as one of the main reasons for the sustained political offensive by the Turkish military to bring down the coalition, which duly collapsed in June 1997. In the same month Iran became a founder member of the Istanbul-based Developing Eight (D-8, see p. 269) group of Islamic countries. Meanwhile, in February 1998 the Iranian ambassador to Turkey provoked a diplomatic crisis by advocating the introduction of Islamic (Shari'a) law in Turkey. Criticism of the actions of the Turkish military by an Iranian consul-general later in that month resulted in both men being asked to leave the country. Iran responded by expelling two Turkish diplomats. However, both countries immediately undertook initiatives to restore relations, and in March it was agreed, during a visit to Turkey by Iran's Minister of Foreign Affairs, that all bilateral agreements were to be pursued.

Iran has expressed support for Azerbaijan in its conflict with Armenia, and in September 1993 agreed to establish refugee camps inside Azerbaijan for an estimated 100,000 civilians who had fled fighting between Armenian and Azerbaijani forces. It was feared that an influx of refugees into Iran might increase the pressure from the large Azerbaijani community there for Iranian military intervention in the conflict.

In August 1992 the Iranian Government was reported to be seeking ways of lending support to Bosnian Muslims engaged in hostilities with mainly Serb forces in Bosnia and Herzegovina. In April 1995 the USA claimed that the Iranian Government had supplied large quantities of small weapons and ammunition to the Bosnian Government. In July the Iranian Ministry of Foreign Affairs declared that the UN embargo on the supply of weapons to the Bosnian Government was invalid, and the Iranian Minister of Foreign Affairs travelled to Bosnia in order to discuss ways of delivering military support to the Government. In April 1996 the USA admitted that it had approved covert shipments of Iranian military equipment to Bosnia between early 1994 and January 1996. Following the end of the civil war in Bosnia the USA exerted pressure on Bosnia to sever all links with Iran.

In September 1996 Iran appealed for international assistance to provide emergency aid to as many as 500,000 Kurdish refugees, who had fled towards the Iranian border in response to inter-Kurdish hostilities around the towns of Arbil and As-Sulaimaniya in the Kurdish 'safe haven' in northern Iraq. Supporting the Patriotic Union of Kurdistan (PUK) in these hostilities, Iran aimed to defeat US allies in Iraqi Kurdistan and assert its own influence.

ELECTION OF KHATAMI

The months following the 1996 Majlis elections were something of an 'interregnum' as 'liberals' and 'conservatives' manoeuvred in anticipation of the presidential elections scheduled for May 1997. Renewed calls within the 'liberal' camp for the amendment of the Constitution in order to allow Rafsanjani to seek re-election for a third term were rejected. In March 1997 Rafsanjani was appointed Chairman of the Committee to Determine the Expediency of the Islamic Order (which arbitrates in disputes between the Majlis and the Council of Guardians) for a further five-year term, indicating that he would continue to play an influential role in political life upon the expiry of his presidential mandate. In May the Council of Guardians approved four candidatures for the presidential election (a further 234 were rejected). The selected candidates were Ali Akbar Nateq Nouri (Speaker of the Majlis); Sayed Muhammad Khatami (a presidential adviser and former Minister of Culture and Islamic Guidance); Muhammad Muhammadi Reyshahri (a former Minister of Intelligence and Internal Security, Prosecutor-General and, of late, Khamenei's representative in *Hajj* and pilgrimage affairs); and Sayed Reza Zavarei (hitherto vice-president of the judiciary and a member of the Council of Guardians). Despite early expectations that Nateq Nouri would secure an easy victory, Khatami emerged as a strong contender in the days prior to the election, which took place on 23 May. Regarded as a 'liberal' candidate, Khatami—supported by the Servants of Iran's Construction, as well as by intellectuals, by women's and youth groups, and by the business classes—gained some 69.1% of the total votes cast, ahead of Nateq Nouri, who gained 24.9%. The rate of participation by voters was in excess of 88%. (Nateq Nouri was re-elected Speaker of the Majlis at the beginning of June.)

Khatami was sworn in by Khamenei on 3 August 1997, and took the presidential oath of office before the Majlis on the following day. The new President stated that it would be the responsibility of his administration to create a safe forum for free speech, within the framework of regulations defined by Islam and the Constitution, and to promote 'easy and transparent' relations between the people and the organs of state. Khatami emphasized his commitment to fostering sustained and balanced growth in the political, economic, cultural and educational spheres, and to the freedom of the individual and respect for the rights of the nation, in the context of the rule of law. In foreign affairs, the President undertook to promote the principle of mutual respect, but pledged that Iran would resist any power seeking to subjugate Iranian sovereignty. Despite some concern that 'conservatives' in the Majlis might oppose some of the more liberal members of Khatami's first Council of Ministers, which was presented for approval in mid-August, all of the nominees were endorsed by the assembly after several days' debate. Notable among the 'moderate' appointees were Ata'ollah Mohajerani (a former Vice-President) as Minister of Culture and Islamic Guidance, and Abdollah Nuri as Minister of the Interior (a post he had previously held in 1989–1993). Kamal Kharrazi (hitherto Iran's ambassador to the UN) replaced Ali Akbar Velayati as Minister of Foreign Affairs, while Qorbanali Dorri Najafabadi became Minister of Information. Upon taking office, Khatami had reappointed Hassan Habibi as First Vice-President. Six further Vice-Presidents were named later in the month, among them Muhammad Hashemi Rafsanjani, who retained the post of Vice-President in charge of Executive Affairs; Ma'sumeh Ebtekar, as Vice-President and Head of the Organization for the Protection of the Environment, was the first woman to be appointed to a government post of such seniority since the Islamic Revolution. In mid-October Khatami named former Prime Minister Moussavi as his senior adviser.

Although Khatami pledged his allegiance to Khamenei as Iran's spiritual leader, the new President's assumption of office revived long-standing rivalries among the senior clergy. The focus of opposition to Khamenei was seemingly Ayatollah Montazeri (Khomeini's designated successor prior to March 1989), who began openly to question Khamenei's authority and to demand that Khatami be allowed to govern without interference. In mid-November 1997 police used tear-gas to disperse a violent demonstration in Qom by supporters of Khamenei, who had gathered to denounce Montazeri and one of his allies, Ayatollah Azari Qumi. Demonstrations in support of Khamenei

persisted in Qom, Teheran and elsewhere for several days, until Khamenei urged an end to the protests; none the less, he demanded that Montazeri be tried for treason, and that all others who questioned his authority be prosecuted in accordance with the law. In mid-December the General Secretary of Nehzat-Azadi, Ibrahim Yazdi, who had reportedly met with Montazeri shortly before the latter had publicly criticized Khamenei, was detained for almost two weeks, on charges of desecrating religious sanctities, after he had signed an open letter to Khatami urging that Montazeri's rights be respected. Meanwhile, in late November the President appointed a new Committee for Ensuring and Supervising the Implementation of the Constitution.

During the first months of his presidency, in spite of his relative lack of experience in government, Khatami was judged to have strengthened his position, and that of his supporters, mainly through the successful conduct of foreign policy (see below); and in January 1998 the Iranian Union of Journalists was sufficiently emboldened to express rare public criticism of the head of the judiciary, Muhammad Yazdi, whom it accused of seeking to obstruct the freedom of the press. In April the Mayor of Teheran, Gholamhossein Karbaschi, became the focus of political rivalry when he was arrested on charges of fraud and mismanagement. Karbaschi was a popular national figure and a prominent supporter of President Khatami, and on the day of his arrest the Council of Ministers issued a public statement criticizing the decision to detain him. Later in the month students demonstrating in support of Karbaschi were involved in violent clashes with the police. The political nature of the case was further underlined in May, when it was announced that the Servants of Iran's Construction had obtained official permission to form a political party of the same name and that Karbaschi would be the party's Secretary-General.

Karbaschi's trial, broadcast in full on Iranian television, commenced in early June 1998 and achieved unprecedented publicity. Any concerns that an unwarranted level of attention was being directed at a simple case of corruption in local government were dispelled on 21 June by the impeachment, by 'conservative' deputies in the Majlis, of the Minister of the Interior, Abdollah Nuri, who had expressed his personal support for Karbaschi in April. Nuri was duly dismissed from the interior portfolio, the Majlis having upheld a motion expressing 'no confidence' in him. However, Khatami promptly demonstrated his full support for Nuri by appointing him Vice-President in charge of Development and Social Affairs, an appointment which allowed him to retain a position in the Council of Ministers, beyond the scrutiny of the Majlis. In July the Majlis approved the appointment of Khatami's former Vice-President in charge of Legal and Parliamentary Affairs, Sayed Abdolvahed Musavi-Lari, as Minister of the Interior. Later in the month Karbaschi was sentenced to five years' imprisonment and 60 lashes. He was also fined and banned from holding public office for 20 years.

FOREIGN RELATIONS UNDER KHATAMI

The success of President Khatami's reformist project depends on ending Iran's isolation—both political and economic—by seeking an improvement in relations with the West. Any such improvement will be determined by the course of Iran's relations with the USA. This key area of foreign policy is also most likely to provoke conflict between opposed factions within the Iranian leadership. In August 1997, in an address to the Majlis, President Khatami identified Iran's need for 'an active and fresh presence' in the sphere of foreign relations. Towards the end of the first year of his presidency some important successes were already apparent.

The initial response of the US Administration to the election of the new Iranian President did not appear to augur well for an improvement in relations. The US Department of State greeted the announcement of a new Iranian Council of Ministers in August 1997 with a statement of its willingness to engage in dialogue, provided that Iran would discuss the issues of nuclear weapons, 'terrorism' and the Middle East peace process. This was tantamount to setting impossible conditions for dialogue: Iran's definition of 'terrorism', for instance, was substantially different to that of the USA; and Iran had long regarded the Middle East peace process as dead. In mid-1997 official US attitudes towards Iran continued to be dominated by concern about the country's weapons programmes. In June, during a tour of the Gulf states, the US Secretary of Defense, William Cohen, repeatedly claimed that such programmes posed a threat to Iran's weaker neighbours. Later in the month, the commander of US forces in the Gulf warned that Iran was still seeking to develop nuclear weapons and that it might be closer to achieving this goal than had previously been thought. In July the announcement that Russia was to assist Iran to complete the nuclear power plant at Bushehr prompted the USA to reiterate its concern that Iran might seek to exploit civilian nuclear technology for the development of nuclear weapons. In September the US Vice-President announced that US and Russian investigators had concluded that Iran was engaged in a 'vigorous effort' to obtain technology for the manufacture of nuclear weapons and ballistic missiles capable of transporting them. (Earlier in September the Russian authorities had stated that they would be willing to allow the USA to monitor the Bushehr nuclear plant.) In the same month it was reported that Israel was attempting to persuade the Clinton administration to impose sanctions on Russian organizations and companies involved in supplying missile technology to Iran. In October China announced an end to the sale of nuclear technology, as well as of conventional weaponry, to Iran. In November Iran became a signatory to the International Chemical Weapons Convention; under its terms, which prohibit the production and possession of chemical weapons, Iran became subject to mandatory international inspections. Earlier in the month it was reported that the USA had purchased fighter aircraft from Moldova, in order to prevent their sale to Iran.

Khatami's election had inevitably aroused widespread speculation in Western media regarding the prospects for an improvement in relations with the USA and with other Western countries. However the US Administration might feel disposed towards a new Iranian President with exemplary democratic credentials, who had clearly revealed his reformist instincts, the secondary sanctions act, sponsored by US Senators D'Amato and Kennedy, and approved by the US Congress in June 1996 (also known as the Iran-Libya sanctions act) remained an obstacle to any *rapprochement*; but the sanctions act was being increasingly undermined by commercial and geopolitical realities: European companies, and their governments, were simply not prepared to forgo opportunities in the development of the energy resources of the newly-independent states of Central Asia for the sake of US foreign policy aims. In July 1997 the Clinton administration raised no formal objection to a project to construct a 2,000-mile pipeline to carry gas from Central Asia to Turkey and, thence, to Europe, despite the fact that the pipeline would cross some 788 miles of Iranian territory. The dilemma of the USA regarding sanctions was to become more acute as the year progressed. At the end of July 1997 it became clear that the French energy company, Total, was determined, in partnership with Gazprom of Russia and Petronas of Malaysia, to proceed with a \$2,000m.-investment in Iran's South Pars gas field. US Senator Alfonse D'Amato, who had been instrumental in the conception of the sanctions act, immediately urged the US Administration to impose sanctions on Total. However, such a move would risk provoking a 'trade war' with the EU, damaging relations with Russia, and thus further complicating other areas of US foreign policy—the question of Iraq's compliance with UN Security Council resolutions, for instance—where European and Russian co-operation was essential. US commercial interests were also at stake. At the same time, the US Administration was conscious that ending objections to investments in the Iranian gas industry could precipitate the collapse of its aim, in the longer term, to direct the flow of energy from the Caspian Basin via Turkey rather than Iran. In October the USA was reported to be seeking an agreement with the EU under which it would suspend the implementation of sanctions in return for increased European pressure on Iran to curb its alleged involvement in terrorism.

Any failure by the USA to impose sanctions could be claimed as a 'victory' by the Iranian authorities. In combination with other factors, the 'Iran-Libya sanctions act' began to have the perverse effect of isolating the USA rather than Iran. This was nowhere more apparent than at the eighth summit meeting of the ILC, held in Teheran in early December 1997: the attendance of the leaders of many of the USA's erstwhile Arab allies

appeared to undermine the USA's credibility in the region, primarily owing to its failure to promote any progress in the Middle East peace process. The presence of so many Arab leaders at the meeting was in stark contrast to the US-sponsored Middle East and North Africa economic conference in Doha, Qatar, the previous month. Both the Wali Faqih, Ayatollah Khamenei, and President Khatami addressed the inaugural session of the OIC summit meeting, in dramatically differing tones. While Khamenei lambasted the pernicious, corrupting influence of the West, on which he fixed the blame for the 'calamitous condition' of the Islamic world, Khatami spoke of the accomplishments of Western civilization and their potential role in the development of the Islamic world. Later in December 1997, at a press conference in Teheran, President Khatami expressed his hope for a 'thoughtful dialogue' with the 'great American people'. Such a gesture, unprecedented in the recent history of US–Iranian relations, appeared to perturb the US authorities, triggering in some official quarters the stock reaction that Iran remained a sponsor of terrorism, a manufacturer of weapons of mass destruction and a potential saboteur of the Middle East peace process. However, the response of the US President was unexpectedly warm, expressing a cautious willingness to discuss relevant issues.

In late April 1998 the US Department of State identified Iran as the most active state sponsor of terrorism, alleging that during the past year Iranian agents had perpetrated at least 13 assassinations and noting the continued support of the Iranian Government for 'extremist' groups, such as Hezbollah and Hamas. On 19 June, however, the USA demonstrated readiness to improve relations with Iran, when, in a speech in New York, the US Secretary of State, Madeleine Albright, indicated US willingness to grant Iran a role in regional security provided that it abided by 'international standards of behaviour'.

The election of President Khatami and the appointment, in August 1997, of a new Minister of Foreign Affairs apparently led to a relaxation of tensions in EU–Iranian relations (see above), and in November a compromise arrangement was finally reached allowing the return to Iran of all ambassadors from EU countries. The EU's policy of 'critical dialogue' remained in suspension, however, and the new Iranian regime was initially apparently either unwilling or unable to make the compromises which might facilitate a resolution of the Rushdie affair. In late September 1998, however, following intensive negotiations between the British Secretary of State for Foreign and Commonwealth Affairs, Robin Cook, and the Iranian Minister of Foreign Affairs, Kamal Kharrazi, it was announced that the British Government had secured oral assurances from the Iranian Government that it would not support the bounty on Rushdie's head, although the 1989 *fatwa* could not be formally revoked. In January 1998 Germany's troubled relations with Iran were further complicated when an Iranian court sentenced to death a German businessman whom it had found guilty of illicit sexual relations with a Muslim woman. In late February the EU lifted a ban it had imposed on high-level ministerial contacts between member states and Iran, stating that it wished to encourage moderate political forces in the Islamic Republic. Shortly afterwards, in March, the Italian Minister of Foreign Affairs, Lamberto Dini, visited Teheran, where he asserted that Iran was not engaged in terrorist activities and that its weapons programmes posed no threat. Commentators in the Italian media suggested that, in addition to wishing to support moderate political forces, Dini's remarks might also have been aimed at furthering Italy's commercial interests. The Rushdie affair and the Iran-Libya sanctions act notwithstanding, European companies were actively pursuing opportunities in the energy industries of the Caspian Basin and in Iran.

The 'active and fresh presence' in the sphere of foreign relations to which President Khatami referred in August 1997 had, by mid-1998, yielded results in the field of Iranian–Arab relations. To the declared openness of the new Iranian regime, there now corresponded a growing perception, even among the most 'conservative', US-aligned Arab states, that the (perhaps irremediably) obstructed Middle East peace process was nurturing a popular backlash which improved relations with the Islamic Republic might help to forestall. Syria was reported to have played an important background role in effecting this *rapprochement*, exploiting a shared suspicion in the Arab world of closer relations between Turkey and Israel.

The OIC summit meeting held in Teheran in December 1997 illustrated how far the Arab position had shifted towards Iran. Saudi Arabia, long the target of Iranian criticism for the style of its guardianship of the holy cities of Mecca and Medina and its dependence on the USA for its security, was represented at the OIC summit meeting by Crown Prince Abdullah ibn Abd al-Aziz as-Sa'ud and by its Minister of Foreign Affairs. Their attendance was considered to represent a significant further stage in the process of reconciliation, which had begun with the visit of a Saudi Arabian ministerial delegation to Iran in July, and culminated, in February 1998, in an official visit by former Iranian President Hashemi Rafsanjani to Saudi Arabia. This was the first visit by an Iranian leader of such seniority since the Revolution in 1979, and its aims transcended the largely symbolic nature of earlier contacts to address pressing economic issues. Iran was reported to be seeking Saudi Arabian support for a reallocation of OPEC production quotas; it also sought to persuade Saudi Arabia to take fuller advantage of Iranian infrastructure to transport its exports to Central Asia; and to make greater use of surplus Iranian labour. It was also reported that Iran would raise the issue of a regional security alliance incorporating all of the states bordering the Persian (Arabian) Gulf. In May 1998 Iran and Saudi Arabia concluded a comprehensive co-operation agreement, the scope of which extended from key economic areas to culture and sports.

Since the election of President Khatami there have also been signs of an improvement in relations with Iraq. In September 1997 Iraq opened its border with Iran in order to allow Iranian pilgrims access to its Shi'ite shrines for the first time in 17 years. At the end of the month, however, Iranian aircraft violated the air exclusion zone over southern Iraq in order to bomb two bases of the Mujahidin-e-Khalq in that country (prompting Iraqi aircraft also to enter the zone, in pursuit of the Iranian bombers). The Iraqi Vice-President, Taha Yassin Ramadan, attending the eighth summit meeting of the OIC in December, was the most senior Iraqi official to visit Iran since 1979. Following the summit, President Khatami expressed the hope that problems between the two countries could be resolved 'through negotiation and understanding'. In April 1998 Iran was reported to have released more than 5,000 Iraqi prisoners of war in recent weeks, while Iraq had released 319 Iranian prisoners of war.

Iran's relations with the UAE (see above) deteriorated further in 1996, after Iran opened an airport on Abu Musa in March and a power-station on Greater Tunb in April. In January and February 1997 the UAE protested that Iran was repeatedly violating the UAE's territorial waters. Talks held in March were inconclusive, and in June the UAE protested to Iran and the UN about Iran's construction of a pier on Greater Tunb. Following a meeting with the UAE's Minister of Foreign Affairs at the time of the December 1997 OIC summit, President Khatami emphasized his willingness to discuss bilateral issues directly with President Zayed bin Sultan an-Nahyan of the UAE. Although the latter was reported to be cautious about Iran's attempts at *rapprochement*, in the following month authorities in the UAE and Iran stated that the UAE was willing to enter into negotiations. None the less, both countries continued to assert their sovereignty over the three disputed islands (see

above). In March 1998 Iran pre-empted an expected demand by the GCC member states that it should resolve its dispute with the UAE as a condition for a general improvement in relations by organizing a conference in Teheran for its own diplomatic representatives to those countries. At the conference, the Iranian Minister of Foreign Affairs was reported to have emphasized the importance that Iran attached to its relations with the GCC states, while making no mention of the dispute with the UAE. The Minister's address was also reported to contain implicit criticism of the GCC's support for the US military presence in the Gulf region. Observers noted the relative isolation of the UAE in its dispute with Iran. Oman and Qatar had maintained good relations with Iran, while Iran's relations with Saudi Arabia, Kuwait and Bahrain continued to improve.

A major priority of Iran's economic policy under President Khatami is the increased development of its reserves of natural gas, and it is also seeking to exploit its potential as a principal transit point for the export of hydrocarbons from the Central Asian republics of the former USSR. These two factors have, moreover, hindered US-led attempts to isolate Iran by means of economic sanctions (see above). In December 1997 a pipeline was inaugurated to transport natural gas from Turkmenistan to northern Iran and it was anticipated that the project would subsequently be extended to Turkey and, ultimately, to western Europe. (For Turkmenistan the project was of equal significance because Russia had hitherto controlled all export outlets for energy from Turkmenistan, Kazakhstan and Azerbaijan.) In May 1998 Iran issued an international tender for the construction of a pipeline to carry oil from the Caspian Basin to Teheran; the first stage of a project which aims, eventually, to transport oil to Iran's Kharg terminal in the Gulf.

In September 1997 the Taliban leadership in Afghanistan accused Iran of providing military assistance to its opponents and threatened retaliatory action. In late 1997 it was reported that, since the election of President Khatami, Iran had begun to participate in meetings at the UN with (among others) US officials in an attempt to identify ways of ending the Afghan civil war. Iran's principal concerns with regard to Afghanistan are to contain any instability resulting from the conflict there, and to remove the strain placed on its domestic resources by the presence of large numbers of Afghan refugees. Eleven Iranian diplomats and more than 30 other Iranian nationals were among those allegedly captured by Taliban forces during a renewed offensive in Afghanistan during August 1998. This development prompted warnings from the Iranian leadership that retaliatory action would be undertaken if the hostages were not released unharmed. In early September, following Taliban denials that they were holding the diplomats hostage, the Iranian Government organized large-scale military exercises (involving some 70,000 troops) near the border with Afghanistan. Tensions continued to escalate in mid-September, following the discovery, in Afghanistan, of the bodies of several of the missing diplomats, and the situation was exacerbated by further territorial gains made by Taliban forces and reports that thousands of Afghanistan's Shi'a Muslim population were being slaughtered as a result. Relations remained tense in late September, as the number of Iranian troops in the border region was increased to some 250,000 and Ayatollah Khamenei announced that the country's armed forces should be placed on full alert.

Economy

Revised for this edition by ALAN J. DAY

Traditionally an agricultural country, Iran has benefited in the twentieth century from the exploitation of its large oil and gas reserves, exports of which have been its major source of revenue since the Second World War. Under successive five-year plans since 1947, oil revenues have been used to finance balanced economic development, including non-oil industrialization and the maintenance of a substantial agricultural sector. The Islamic Revolution of 1979 represented a major watershed, not only politically but also economically. The new regime declared its determination to end Iran's large degree of dependence on the West, the resultant dislocation being compounded by the 1980–88 war with Iraq. Since that conflict, efforts to resume broad economic development and diversification have been hindered by volatile world oil prices, by internal structural weaknesses and rampant inflation, and by persistent political tensions with the West, especially with the USA. Although the oil sector has accounted for a diminishing share of gross domestic product (GDP) in recent years, the Government remains heavily dependent on oil revenues in its quest to improve the living standards of Iran's large population

At the census of November 1966 the population of Iran was recorded as 25,788,722. Of this total, about 9.8m. were urban residents. The November 1976 census enumerated a total population of 33,708,744, and the October 1986 census recorded 49,445,010 inhabitants (including 2.6m. refugees), of whom 26,844,561 resided in urban areas, an increase of 70% since 1976. In early 1992 the Statistical Centre of Iran reported that the population had increased by almost 40% since 1979, to more than 58m. The rate of growth in urban areas was twice that recorded in rural areas. The population of Teheran was reported to have more than doubled since the late 1970s, exceeding 10m. According to the 1996 census, the population of Iran (in October of that year) was 60,055,488, of whom 61.3% were urban dwellers. Iran's average annual population growth rate has decreased from 2.5% during 1986–92, to 1.5% during 1992–97. It was estimated that by 2025 some three-quarters of Iran's population would be living in cities. Much of the Iranian population is concentrated in the fertile northern areas of the country, while the central desert lands are sparsely populated.

Major refugee influxes in the 1980s included the arrival of up to 3m. Afghans and over 1m. Iraqi Kurds and Shi'as. By mid-1990 a large proportion of the Afghan refugees had returned home, whereas Iran continued to be a haven for many oppressed Iraqi groups as well as a number of Azerbaijani refugees.

Government officials have cited Iran's expanding population as a major constraint on economic development. In July 1992 the head of the Population and Family Planning Department of the Ministry of Health stated that if the population continued to grow at a rapid rate, 600,000 new jobs would have to be created each year, and 40,000 classrooms and 500,000 houses constructed. The country's farmers would not be able to meet the demand for food and half the population would face starvation. Unemployment in 1991 was officially estimated at about 11% of the labour force, although other sources had suggested as recently as the previous year that the rate of unemployment might in fact be as high as 20%. Only 2.2m. new jobs were created between 1980 and 1990: an inadequate total, in view of the rising demand for employment. According to official sources, unemployment at the end of the 1996/97 Iranian year (running from 21 March to 20 March) had fallen to 9.1%, compared with 11.1% a year earlier. The size of the nomadic population, estimated at 248,463 in October 1986, has declined dramatically since the 1940s (it was estimated to be 641,937 at the 1966 census), as a result of government settlement programmes.

In 1978, the last year of the Shah's reign, per caput income was calculated at about US $2,500, up from about $200 in 1963. During the period of the Fourth Development Plan (1968–73), Iran's gross national product (GNP) rose at an annual average of 11.2% in real terms. Over the period of the 1973–78 Plan, GNP rose in real terms from $17,000m. to $55,300m. The growth

rate of GNP, which was as much as 41% in 1974/75, slowed to about 17% in the following year, owing to declining revenues from petroleum (which provided about 40% of the total GNP). In real terms, GDP was estimated to have grown by as little as 2.6% in 1975/76. In 1976/77 GDP grew at over 14% in real terms, but during 1977 the economy showed signs of further deceleration. Total GDP for 1977/78 was estimated at $56,500m., representing growth in real terms of about 10% over the previous year.

The revolutionary Government that followed the Shah's downfall reassessed nearly all of Iran's economic and social strategies. The new leaders announced that priority would be given to low growth rates, a concentration on small-scale projects in industry, emphasis on traditional agriculture and stringent control of petroleum exports. Three years after the Revolution, however, Iran's economy was in deep crisis. The war with Iraq, loss of forecast petroleum revenues in mid-1980 as the world went into economic recession, and the failure of public utilities (mainly electricity) were among the problems advanced to account for a deteriorating economic situation. The war had indeed taken its toll of physical damage to infrastructure in the south. However, political conflicts and confusion over the management of the economy aggravated these problems and resulted in contradictions in policy and economic mismanagement.

In early 1981 the then President, Bani-Sadr, reported that agricultural output remained static, industrial production had declined dramatically and even the minimum petroleum output that Iran required for national survival was not being attained. The disappointing performance of the major economic sectors had resulted in declines in real GDP of 13% in 1979/80 and 10% in 1980/81, and in a further fall in 1981/82. At the same time, Ayatollah Khomeini warned Iranians that there would be 10 years of austerity ahead before the country became productive enough to fulfil its needs from domestic sources.

Some real growth in the economy did take place as a result of developments in the construction sector and some expansion in industrial output. However, as both were at low base levels, real gains were small. In reality it was the petroleum sector which was responsible for the improvement in the country's economic prospects in 1982 and 1983. An increase in sales of crude petroleum during 1982, by means of discounts and special incentives to purchasers, resulted in rising revenues, which, in turn, stimulated economic activity. The Iranian economy remained petroleum-based, and the pattern of growth reflected the performance of that sector. The oil sector fared badly in 1984, with production down by 13% in a deteriorating market oversupplied with oil and subject to falling world prices. Production costs have always been higher for Iran than for its regional competitors, and the situation was aggravated by the escalation of the conflict with Iraq, with the consequent rise in the costs of insurance, storage and transport. As a result of the continuing decline in international prices for crude petroleum, government income was seriously reduced during 1986, and income from oil exports totalled $6,600m. in 1986/87, according to OPEC. This downward trend was halted in early 1987, when the volume of exports of oil increased and prices rose. In 1987/88 the value of oil exports was estimated at $8,000m.–$9,000m., with a further $1,100m. in earnings from rising non-oil exports.

From September 1980 until the August 1988 cease-fire, the war with Iraq dominated all economic and political life in Iran. War needs dictated planning priorities, distorting the economy and forcing long-term objectives to be sacrificed to expediency. It has been estimated that annual expenditure of foreign exchange on the war was $5,000m.–$9,000m. After the announcement of the cease-fire, attempts were made to assess the extent of the damage inflicted on the Iranian economy during the war and widely diverging figures were quoted for the cost of reconstruction. The cost of repairing industrial plant alone was estimated at $40,000m. Positive leadership often appeared to be lacking, resulting in the inability or unwillingness to resolve fundamental issues of principle. One crucial issue affecting the economy after the Revolution was disagreement over the degree of government involvement in business. After 1981 the Government appeared to favour an increase in state control, particularly the nationalization of foreign trade. However, conservative religious leaders, businessmen, the Council of Guardians (which ensures that legislation conforms with Islamic precepts) and many members of the Majlis maintained that the Government should play a minimal role. Although new appointments to the Council of Ministers and the changing character of the Majlis strengthened those elements in government favouring more control of the economy by the state (in particular more land reform, nationalization of trade and the spread of collective organization among the industrial work-force), the conservative elements in government (in particular, the Council of Guardians) succeeded in delaying radical reform. In a vigorous press campaign at the end of 1985 the radicals alleged that the courts were overturning revolutionary measures and allowing expropriated industries to be returned to their former owners. In January 1988 Ayatollah Khomeini decreed that government policies could overrule Islamic law where this was in the interest of the state. In the following month a 13-member assembly was appointed to settle disputes by majority vote whenever the Majlis and the Council of Guardians could not agree on the direction of policy. However, despite the strength of the radicals in the third Majlis, the assembly proceeded cautiously, seeking to maintain a consensus between conservatives and radicals.

In the agricultural sector, the problem of rights of ownership has affected about 1.2m. ha, or one-quarter of Iran's prime cultivable land, since the Revolution, and government plans for land reform were consistently obstructed by the Council of Guardians, making long-term planning difficult. As a result, the technocrats in government have concentrated on industry and other areas of the economy where quick results were easier to obtain. In February 1989 the Minister of Oil, Gholamreza Aqazadeh, announced the end of a six-month debate concerning the future structure of the Iranian economy. The Council of Ministers had decided, he reported, to approve a limited number of foreign loans for infrastructural schemes, and to encourage private enterprise. In May 1989 the Minister of Planning and Budget, Massoud Roghani Zanjani, outlined the Government's plans for the economy over the next five years. He confirmed that they included 'privatization' of non-strategic state-owned industries. It was also revealed that Imam Khomeini had approved foreign borrowing to finance major projects if it did not result in political dependence. Foreign-financed projects should lead to savings in convertible currency or generate new revenue in convertible currency.

On his election to the Presidency on 28 July 1989, Ali Akbar Hashemi Rafsanjani announced that his immediate economic aims would be to combat inflation and unemployment by increasing industrial output. Existing factories would receive more foreign exchange to raise production, which was running at only 40% of capacity; and, in an attempt to generate more productive investment, the private sector was to be given a bigger role in the economy. In the long term, Rafsanjani indicated, his Government would concentrate on developing energy, transport and basic industrial and educational resources. Some experts suggested that, in order to achieve a rapid economic recovery, Rafsanjani would have to resort to large-scale foreign financing. However, this would have exposed the President to accusations of compromising Iran's revolutionary ideology and independence. In August 1989 it was announced that the Government had allocated $4,800m. for imports of food and consumer goods during the following year, to improve standards in the short term. Other short-term measures to revive the economy included the privatization of state enterprises, the reopening of the Teheran stock exchange and the liberalization of regulations controlling the availability of foreign exchange. The introduction of a new Five-Year Development Plan, in January 1990, was expected to help to revive the economy. The new Plan, together with the announcement of the annual budget in March 1990, strengthened economic activity, resulting in increased imports of raw materials, equipment and spares.

As a consequence of Iraq's invasion of Kuwait in August 1990, Iran's economic prospects improved briefly. According to official sources, earnings from exports of petroleum rose to $18,400m. in 1990–91 as a result of an increase in volume and price

triggered by the conflict over Kuwait. With his leadership strengthened, President Rafsanjani took advantage of extra oil revenues to accelerate the implementation of economic reforms which resulted in the rapid dismantling of the state-controlled economy created during the years of war with Iraq. The private sector expanded and came to play a significant role in trade and investment. Imports by the private sector rose, non-petroleum exports doubled and considerable investment occurred in housing construction and industry after the deregulation of price and trade controls. However, his reforms to revive the economy caused widespread hardship and contributed to the riots and urban unrest in mid-1992. Moreover, the economy remained excessively dependent on oil, while bureaucratic inefficiency and a serious shortage of skilled workers and managers continued to obstruct the realization of optimistic aims.

At the start of his second term of office in August 1993, President Rafsanjani vowed to proceed with economic reforms so that Iran would no longer be dependent on other countries for their markets and products. He stated that during his first term of office the old state economy had been transformed, production had increased and unemployment had fallen from 16% to 10%–11%. Outlining his policies for the next four years to the Majlis on 4 August, Rafsanjani declared that his Government would not embark on adventures abroad but would concentrate on reforming and rebuilding the economy. He stressed that costly state subsidies had to be reduced but promised that this would be done gradually so as not to disrupt peoples' lives. In the Majlis and the press, however, there was strong criticism of the Government for mishandling the economy and allowing the country to accumulate some $20,000m. in external debts. On 16 August the Majlis refused to approve the reappointment of Mohsen Nourbakhsh as Minister of the Economy. *Jomhuri Eslami,* the Persian language daily, accused the Government's economic team of being 'deceived by liberal Western economic theories', argued that the reforms had been introduced too rapidly and urged the reintroduction of some state controls. Since mid-1992 Iran had faced problems in paying its external debts as low oil prices resulted in falling oil revenues. Much of the short-term debt resulted from high levels of imports in the early 1990s. Oil revenues for 1993/94 were projected at around $18,000m., but in August 1993 the Minister of Oil informed the Majlis that they would probably reach only $16,500m. By January 1994 officals estimated that revenues would not exceed $12,000m. Oil revenues were projected at only $10,150m. for 1994/95. By the end of 1993 at least $7,000m. of debt payments were in arrears. Acute shortages of some essential imports occurred as foreign companies held back deliveries when Iranian banks fell behind with their payments. It was reported that some factories had been forced to close and others to cut production and lay off workers. Prices and unemployment rose rapidly. During the final quarter of 1993 the rial's free market value fell by about one-third owing to reduced supplies of foreign exchange to importers. Growth in GDP, which had been projected at 6%–7% in 1993/94, was estimated to have slowed to 4%–5%.

In response to these criticisms, in August the Bank Markazi relaxed some import restrictions to ease pressures on industry and consumers. However, Rafsanjani rejected calls in the Majlis to postpone the second Five-Year Plan until 1996 because of the economic crisis. The President presented the plan document to the Majlis on 21 December and sought approval for higher spending based on increased domestic revenues. The day before, Ayatollah Khamenei had announced new guidelines for economic and social planning, urging a reduction in the country's dependence on foreign finance and special efforts to settle outstanding obligations. He also urged caution in privatizing state enterprises and emphasized that privatization should promote economic development and conform with the Constitution of the Islamic Republic. He stressed that social equity should be central to the Government's development policy. Deprived regions should receive more attention and development policies should benefit those who had worked hard for the Revolution. Priority should be given to promoting domestic production, particularly agriculture, in order to satisfy the basic needs of the people. Imports of consumer goods should be reduced and non-oil exports increased. Corruption should be eliminated and waste and extravagance discouraged. At the same time Khamenei gave his support to the President and attempted to underplay the scale of the country's economic problems.

In early January 1994 Rafsanjani declared that the Iranian economy was no longer totally dependent on oil revenues and could survive even if oil exports were completely cut off; falling oil prices would not hurt Iran so much as other oil exporters. He pointed to Iran's success in increasing its non-oil exports, which he estimated would earn $5,000m. in 1993/94, nearly one-third of total hard currency revenues. In contrast, Mohammad Reza Bahonar, a member of the Majlis economy and finance committee, argued that Iran must free itself from its dependence on oil revenues during the next few years because low oil prices and a rapidly growing population had resulted in a fall in per caput oil income to about $15 a month. Rafsanjani also repeated accusations made by other Iranian officials that the 30% fall in oil prices during 1993 had been orchestrated by hostile countries, principally the USA, because they were alarmed by Iran's economic recovery. Later in the year Khamenei accused Saudi Arabia of helping 'international thieves' to keep oil prices low. In March 1994 the Majlis reduced projected revenue and expenditure before approving the Government's 1994/95 budget because of concern over low oil prices and the high level of foreign debt. Announcing the decision, Ali Akbar Nateq Nouri, the Speaker of the Majlis, stated that economic reforms, including the reduction of subsidies, should be slowed down to protect the vulnerable strata of society. Yet despite opposition from within the Majlis, in April Rafsanjani renewed his attack on some state subsidies which he stated cost the country $15,000m. every year. He declared that energy subsidies alone cost $11,000m. a year, more than projected oil revenues for 1994/95. He argued that subsidies for agriculture and for assisting the families of those killed during the Revolution and the war with Iraq were justified, whereas bread subsidies for the general population and energy subsidies were unjust and should be eliminated. This programme was a matter of urgency because subsidies were preventing the country's economic recovery. After the failure of an attempt within the Majlis in May to remove control over price-setting from the Government, Rafsanjani appeared to compromise and promised that subsidy reforms would be introduced gradually. Nothing would be done until the new Five-Year Development Plan was ready because subsidy cuts directly affected the people's standard of living and could cause resentment against the Government. The President stated that 'It needs at least 10 years for us to remove the iniquities that exist in fuel and bread consumption'. By the end of 1994 the Bank Markazi had successfully rescheduled almost $10,000m. in short-term foreign debts into medium-term obligations. By the early months of 1995 official and private reschedulings were reported to have reached $14,000m., marking the end of the immediate debt crisis which had destroyed the country's creditworthiness. Most of the rescheduling agreements provided Iran with a two-year grace period, with repayments deferred until 1996. Nevertheless, the country faced an annual foreign debt-servicing burden of between $4,000m. and $5,000m. until the end of the century, which could only aggravate the side-effects of the Government's reform programme. Despite opposition from the USA, Switzerland and Germany began once again to offer insurance cover for exports to Iran in the early part of 1995. However, poor relations with the West continued to accentuate Iran's economic difficulties. In May 1995 the USA imposed a near total trade embargo on Iran with the aim of crippling the country's economy and urged other Western nations to follow its example. The embargo affected primarily the oil industry. US oil companies had purchased nearly a quarter of Iran's crude oil output in 1994. However, in June 1995 oil traders reported that Iran appeared to have experienced no difficulty finding alternative markets for the oil previously sold to US companies.

At the sectoral level, agriculture finally appeared to have experienced a revival by the mid-1990s after decades of decline, achieving higher farm output and greater efficiency. The Ministry of Agriculture even predicted that Iran would become a net exporter of foodstuffs by the turn of the century. Moreover, the gap between farmers' income and that of average city-dwellers closed considerably. Industry has proved more difficult to reform, with low rates of capacity utilization persisting in some branches, especially the state-owned heavy industries.

The restructuring of ailing industries has experienced problems, but the Government remains committed to removing most state subsidies by 2000. Privatization plans were delayed in mid-1994, when the Majlis passed legislation giving certain groups privileged access to shares in companies being sold off. Officials admitted that the new legislation would slow down the privatization process, which was expected to resume in mid-1995 when the necessary bylaws had been completed. Nevertheless, in early 1995 the Minister of Industries declared that by 2000 only 10% of Iranian industry would be state-owned, compared with 45% in 1990, and that, ultimately, only very large industries would remain under state control. Plans to attract foreign investment in Iranian industry met with little success despite amendments to the foreign investment law. In his new year message on 21 March 1995, President Rafsanjani promised that Iran would become self-sufficient by the turn of the century and would not have to depend on foreign assistance to run the economy. He stated that reconstruction would be accelerated under the second Five-Year Plan, ending in March 2000, because the country was now less reliant on imported materials.

For ordinary Iranians rapid price rises resulting, in part, from cuts in state subsidies have been the main concern. As the Government attempts to restructure the economy, life for the average Iranian has become harder, provoking widespread dissatisfaction. At the beginning of April 1995 the first mass protests against the Government's economic policies erupted as rioting took place in the working-class suburb of Islamshahr, close to Teheran. Demands for better water supplies turned into a wider protest against the doubling of fuel prices introduced in March as part of the new Five-Year Plan. Less than a year before, President Rafsanjani had promised that cuts in fuel subsidies would be introduced gradually. The police quickly restored order, but the demonstrations were seen by some observers as a warning to the Government that there could be further trouble if economic conditions continued to deteriorate.

In December 1995 the World Bank released an economic memorandum on Iran in which it concluded that substantial progress had been made in macroeconomic stabilization and in implementing structural reforms over the past six years and pointed to a dramatic improvement in social indicators since the mid-1980s. However, both the World Bank and the IMF advised the Government that it would achieve a higher rate of economic growth and more success in reducing inflation if it adopted more ambitious stabilization and structural reform policies, given the extent of macroeconomic imbalances, distortions in resource allocation, and the external environment. They urged the Government to speed up the programme of economic reforms, and to improve resource mobilization and the quality of management. In discussions with the IMF, Bank Markazi officials emphasized that they were giving top priority to repaying the country's foreign debts on time, reducing inflation and strengthening the bank's external reserves. However, they insisted that the objectives of the second Five-Year Plan could be achieved by following a gradualist approach to stabilization and structural reform.

In January 1996 during the approach to legislative elections a group of senior officials, including the Governor of the Bank Markazi, Mohsen Nourbakhsh, and the Mayor of Teheran, Gholamhossein Karbaschi, all close allies of President Rafsanjani, issued a statement urging voters to support the President's tough economic policies. They argued that the main threat facing the country was not from external pressures, but from internal economic problems. Iranians should direct their efforts towards strengthening the country's economic policies and social structures. Economic issues dominated campaigning during the week before the first round of voting on 8 March, with the pro-Rafsanjani modernizers of the newly-formed Servants of Iran's Construction challenging the conservative Society of Combatant Clergy, which had used its predominance in the previous Majlis (Consultative Assembly) to slow down the President's economic reform programme. At the end of the first round of voting both groups claimed victory although some Iranian newspapers proclaimed that candidates of the Servants of Iran's Construction would dominate the new Majlis. Following the second round of voting in April it emerged that the Society of Combatant Clergy had lost overall control in the new Majlis but remained the largest single group.

On the eve of the second round of voting in the legislative elections, the Bank Markazi declared that the economy had improved significantly as a result of the Government's successful strategy to restore financial credibility. A senior bank official stated that 'We are now relaying a message of confidence to the world and the Iranian public'. The Government's budget proposals for 1996/97 foresaw high expenditure of hard currency, but central bank officials stressed that the country would still meet all of its debt repayments.

At the beginning of August 1996 the US Administration ceded to pressure from the Republican-dominated US Congress and the President signed a bill imposing penalties on non-US companies investing in oil and gas projects in Iran (see Petroleum, below). He described Iran as one of the most dangerous supporters of terrorism in the world. The US trade embargo imposed in June 1995 had had little effect on Iranian oil exports, and most observers maintained that the new sanctions were unlikely to damage the country's export capacity. Despite US pressure and the threat of legislation imposing a secondary boycott on Iran, several European oil companies continued with their investment programmes in the oil and gas sectors during the first half of 1996 and agreements on a number of important new finance lines were reached with European and Japanese banks. However, some analysts argued that the effect of the new sanctions would be indirect and psychological and might undermine business confidence and make it more difficult for the Government to carry out its economic reforms. In April 1997, moreover, all EU governments except Greece suspended 'critical dialogue' with Iran after a German court implicated the Iranian leadership in the assassination of Iranian Kurdish dissidents in Berlin in 1992.

Between the Majlis elections in early 1996 and the presidential elections in mid-1997 there were few new economic policy initiatives and the Government concentrated on restoring economic confidence in Iran and ensuring repayments of the country's foreign debt. Higher oil prices during most of 1996 and the early months of 1997 enabled the Bank Markazi to meet annual foreign debt repayments of some $5,000m., and allowed a modest increase in the value of imports which had been reduced since 1994.

The trade surplus increased from $5,586m. in 1995/96 to $7,402m. in 1996/97, while the current-account surplus increased from $3,358m. to $5,232m. over the same period. Preliminary figures for 1997/98, however, estimated that the trade surplus had decreased to $3,511m., and the current-account surplus had been reduced to $1,235m. The IMF acknowledged Iran's achievements in curbing inflation (by nearly 50% in 1996/97), reducing the external debt and meeting foreign debt payments, and registering GDP growth of 4.5% in 1996/97 (against an annual average of 3.8% over the previous four years), with growth in the non-oil sector increasing to over 5%. Nevertheless the Fund warned that the reimposition of strict foreign exchange controls in 1995, while reducing inflation, had damaged non-oil exports. It also warned that the slow pace of economic restructuring meant that large sectors of the economy continued to be dependent on state subsidies, with subsequent market distortion and inefficiency.

The victory of the pro-reform Sayed Muhammad Khatami in the May 1997 presidential election heralded a more determined pursuit of economic restructuring, deregulation, and liberalization. Improved relations with the EU persuaded the latter's Ministers of Foreign Affairs in February 1998 to rescind the ban on ministerial contacts with Iran, although there was no resumption of the previous 'critical dialogue' between the two sides. The following month, the Iranian Government announced that almost all aspects of oil and gas development would be made available to foreign investors, including onshore projects, which had been excluded from the previous opening to foreign investors in 1988. In the same month Khatami advocated a fundamental reform of Iran's economy, citing major income disparities, a preference for speculation over production, and over-dependence on oil exports as the key weaknesses. However, options for reform were reduced by a sharp fall in world oil prices from late 1997, which necessitated at least two revisions of the 1998/99 budget, as originally presented, to account for expectations of much lower oil revenue (see Finance, below).

The further opening of the oil and gas industry to foreign investment was expedited by a US decision in mid-May 1998 not to seek to apply the 1996 Iran–Libya sanctions act against the EU and some other states in respect of investment in Iran. A list of 42 projects for which foreign tenders were invited was officially published at a London conference in early July; it was forecast that total investment of some $8,000m. would be attracted from European and other sources (although not from US companies, which remained prohibited from investing in Iran under the sanctions act).

FIVE-YEAR DEVELOPMENT PLANS

The five-year development planning concept was introduced in 1947 by the Shah's regime, whose fifth and last plan ended in March 1978. A projected sixth plan remained unpublished at the time of the 1979 Revolution. What became known as the first Five-Year Development Plan (FFYDP) of the new Islamic Republic, drafted in 1981–82 was scheduled to begin in March 1983 but was deferred owing to the demands of the 1980–88 war with Iraq. The FFYDP was eventually effected in March 1989, its primary objective being 'to remove the legacy of the economic burdens brought about by the Iraqi invasion of Iran.' It envisaged an annual growth rate of 8%, the creation of some 2m. new jobs, the rehabilitation and expansion of the industry, and greater decentralization and private-sector participation.

Despite various inhibiting factors, including rapid population increase and endemic inflation, the FFYDP was hailed as a success by the Government. In a review of the plan published in September 1994, Bank Markazi recorded that $110,000m., mostly generated from oil revenues, had been disbursed among the various development sectors, compared with $128,000m., originally envisaged. The FFYDP's major achievements reportedly included the transfer of a number of public-sector industries to the private sector; average annual GDP growth of 7.3%; an increase of per caput GDP from IR197,000 to IR246,000; rises in private and public consumption of 7.7% and 5.5% per annum respectively; and annual growth of 5.6% in agriculture, 15% in the industrial sector, 18.9% in water, gas and electricity, and 11.9% in the transport sector. However, following rapid expansion in the five plan years, buoyed by an increase in world oil prices and the temporary lifting of OPEC quotas (resulting from Iraq's invasion of Kuwait), decreasing oil prices in 1992 and a consequent decline in imports by the Government resulted in a deceleration of economic growth. Additionally, macroeconomic imbalances emerged, including a deteriorating balance of payments and an increase in external debt arrears, while government investment continued to outpace private investment, at 14.1% and 8% respectively.

The Second Five-Year Development Plan (SFYDP) was drafted, taking into account the achievements and failures of the FFYDP with a specific objective to complete unfinished infrastructure and development projects. Covering the period March 1995 to 2000, the SFYDP envisages an annual average GDP growth rate of 5.1% over the five years (including 1.6% for the oil sector, 4.3% for agriculture, 5.9% for industry and mining, and 3.1% for the services sector), an average annual inflation rate of 12.4% and the creation of a further 2m. new jobs. Imports are projected to increase at an average annual rate of 4.3%, oil exports at 3.4% per annum and non-oil exports at 8.4% per annum. Development and administrative expenditure was projected to total $135,500m. over the plan period, deriving principally from anticipated oil revenues of $86,500m. and tax revenues of $40,400m. The key SFYDP objectives and policies in the external sphere are that the foreign-exchange system should be based on a managed unified floating exchange rate consistent with maintaining convertibility of the rial for current international payments; and that the level of customs tariffs should take account of the need to protect domestic producers and consumers and to maintain comparative advantage for Iranian goods in international markets. In the fiscal sector, plan objectives include increasing the share of direct taxes (excluding wage taxes) in total tax revenue; channelling oil revenue to development expenditure; and undertaking a tax system reform. In the agricultural sector, the maintenance of sustained growth is combined with the aim of reducing subsidies and making them more transparent in the budget. In the social sphere, the SFYDP pays special attention to the role of mothers 'in the

AGRICULTURE

Of a total surface area of 165m. ha, the 1988 agricultural census reported, there were 56m. ha of cultivable farm land, of which 16.8m. ha were actually being cultivated. Cultivable land has since risen to 18.5m. ha., of which about one-half is dry-farmed, while rain-fed agriculture is important in the western provinces of Kermanshah, Kurdistan and Azerbaijan. Irrigated areas are fed from modern water-storage systems or from the ancient system of *qanat* (underground water channels), although these have fallen into disrepair in recent years. In 1986 Iran had 17 operational dams which provided irrigation for 871,200 ha of land. Irrigated land currently accounts for nearly 80% of food output excluding livestock. By 1996 a further 49 dams were under construction, the aim being to increase utilization of water resources from 70,000m. cu m to 110,000m. cu m by 2000.

The traditional dominance of agriculture was eroded by post-1945 oil and gas exploitation, which became the country's major source of export revenues as population growth obliged Iran to become a net importer of foodstuffs. The agricultural sector has nevertheless usually been the largest contributor to GDP, its share falling only slightly in the 1990s, from 23.9% in 1992/93 to 20.9% in 1996/97, when it was narrowly overtaken by the industrial sector. An objective of the SFYDP was to encourage food self-sufficiency and transform Iran into a net exporter of agricultural produce. However, the latter aim remained unfulfilled half-way through the plan period, the value of agricultural exports decreasing to just $5m. in 1995/96, after increasing dramatically to $90m. in 1994/95. The chief factors limiting the size of agricultural production are: inadequate communications, which limits access to markets; poor seeds, implements and techniques of cultivation; scarcity of water and under-capitalization, chiefly the result of the low incomes of peasant households. About four-fifths of all farms have an area of less than 11 ha. Iran was self-sufficient in foodstuffs until the late 1960s but then began importing vast quantities, owing to the failure of agricultural output to keep pace with increasing domestic consumption and the failure of the Government to produce a sound agricultural policy. Natural disasters have also taken their toll. Early in 1992 nearly 5% of cultivated land, mostly in the north of the country, was damaged by floods.

A large variety of crops are cultivated in the diverse climatic regions of Iran. Grains are the chief crops, including wheat (the major staple), barley and rice. According to the 1988 agricultural census, the area sown to wheat rose to 5.3m. ha during the previous six years, while the average yield per hectare reached 1,082 kg. Under the Five-Year Development Plan (introduced in January 1990), it was aimed to increase wheat production to 11m. metric tons per year by 1995. In 1991 Iran's Deputy Minister of Agriculture declared that wheat yields would rise significantly, from 1.96 tons per hectare to 3.2 tons per hectare, through the expansion of irrigation; and that by 1993 wheat production would reach 12.5m. tons, making self-sufficiency possible. However, the use of scarce water resources for the cultivation of cereals rather than of crops that would give higher yields has been questioned. Moreover, given the current trend away from wheat cultivation to more profitable cash crops, expectations regarding the achievement of self-sufficiency appear to be misplaced. According to the FAO, Iranian production rose from a low of 5.79m. tons in the drought year 1989 to 7m. tons in 1990. Production was estimated at 8.9m. tons in 1991. The 1992 wheat harvest totalled 10.2m. tons, 17% more than forecast in the Five-Year Plan. The Ministry of Agriculture stated that production would meet 80% of domestic requirements and that 2.5m. tons only would be imported. Under the new Five-Year Plan which began in March 1995, annual wheat production is projected to rise by 40% to 14m. tons. According to official sources, wheat production in 1996/97 decreased to 10m. tons from an area of 6.3m. ha. Barley production reached 2.6m. tons in 1989, while the yield per hectare was 1,040 kg; production was estimated at 3.6m. tons in 1991, but fell to 3.1m. tons in the three succeeding years and to 2.7m. tons in 1996 from an area of 1.7m. ha. In 1988 rice production rose to more than 1.5m. tons, although the yield per hectare improved only

slightly, to 2,700 kg. After falling to 1.2m. tons in 1989, rice production rose to 1.7m. tons in 1990, declining, however, to 1.4m. tons in 1991. Production rose again, to 2.4m. tons, in 1992, falling to 2.3m. tons in 1993 but thereafter rising steadily to 2.7m. tons in 1996, from an area of 600,000 ha. Some farmers are reported to have shifted from grain cultivation to more profitable poultry farming and in the early 1990s, as milk prices rose, to dairy farming and commercial milk production. Between 1982 and 1988 the area sown with sugar beet declined by 65,000 ha, to 131,890 ha, but annual production remained steady at 3.4m. tons. Production was estimated at 3.4m. tons again in 1989. In 1991/92 sugar beet production rose to 5m. tons, 1.4m. tons more than in the previous year, according to the Ministry of Agriculture. Sugar beet provides 50% of Iran's sugar requirements. Production of sugar beet reached 5.5m. tons in 1995, but fell sharply in 1996 to 3.7m. tons from a much reduced area of 149,000 ha. Output of cotton was 523,000 tons in 1994 and increased to 600,000 tons in 1996, from an area of 320,000 ha. Output of potatoes declined from 2.3m. tons in 1987 to an estimated 1.4m. tons in 1989, while the planted area remained almost the same, at 77,000 ha but increased sharply, reaching 3.1m. tons in 1996, from an area of 143,000 ha. Tea, almonds, pistachios and dates are of commercial importance, while olives and a variety of fruits and vegetables, as well as tobacco, are also cultivated. Sugar cane is cultivated at Haft Teppeh, in the southern province of Khuzestan (production reached an estimated 2m. tons in 1991), and a paper plant has been established in association with the plantation. Also of commercial importance is production of green tea (277,000 tons in 1996/97), oil seeds (210,000 tons), tobacco (17,000 tons), onions (1.2m. tons), dates (850,000 tons), pistachio nuts (260,000 tons) and caviare (140 tons). Iran's status as the world's largest producer and exporter of pistachio nuts was jeopardized in September 1997 by an EU prohibition of imports from Iran after toxic substances had been found in some consignments. However, the ban was lifted in December after the Iranian industry (employing some 300,000 people) had given quality assurances. Iranian exports of pistachio nuts to EU countries declined to 40,000 tons in 1997 (from 84,000 tons in 1996).

Despite the early social and political benefits of land reform, which the Shah had vigorously pursued in the 1960s and 1970s, agriculture in general suffered under the Shah, to the point where it became one of the principal issues raised against him by his opponents. Typical of the Shah's grandiose projects were four joint ventures set up with foreign companies in 1970 on over 60,000 ha of land in Khuzestan, in the south-west, involving the removal of some 6,500 peasant families. Despite massive infusions of funds, the projects began to collapse within a few years owing to inadequate planning, a lack of skilled manpower and delays in irrigation schemes. By the time that the Revolution ousted the Shah the projects were in the process of being wound up.

Having made such an issue of agriculture in the political battle against the Shah, the victorious revolutionaries made its revival one of their priorities. Self-sufficiency in foodstuffs, above all else, became central to their economic philosophy, but the authorities have acknowledged that, unlike the former regime, they do not have the money to extend the cultivated area through building dams and irrigation schemes. Instead of spending capital, the Government has emphasized the intensification of agriculture, i.e. the improvement of farming on existing lands. To this end, the Government increased support prices for grains and other crops. The biggest subsidies have gone to wheat, the country's most important crop. The Government increased its support to IR53 ($0.74) per kg, compared with the pre-Revolution price of IR18 ($0.20). Since March 1983 the Government has been providing further subsidies in kind as well as giving tax exemption for 10 years to all farmers who follow official guidelines. For each ton of wheat produced, the Government offers 100 kg of fertilizer, four kg of cube sugar, and one kg of tea. Farmers have also been told that they can pay for a tractor at cost price in wheat delivered to the local grains and cereals organization. Subsidies, though less generous, have been introduced for rice and other grains. However, many farmers can sell their wheat on the unofficial market for as much as IR60–IR70 ($0.65–$0.75). It has been estimated that the government agencies purchase less than 15% of Iran's total wheat production. Towards the end of 1991 the Government announced that it had purchased 1.82m. tons of wheat in the current farming year, and announced its intention to purchase 20% more wheat from farmers the following season in order to encourage the cultivation of the crop after the high production and modest prices of the previous season. In early 1994 President Rafsanjani stated that the $350m. spent on subsidizing the agricultural sector were justified and should be maintained. Rural projects, such as the building of schools, mosques, public baths, silos, roads and irrigation networks and the extension of electricity to villages, have been undertaken by the Ministry of Construction Jihad, which combines the roles of three agencies of the Shah's 'White Revolution', the Literacy, Health and Agricultural Extension corps. It was constituted as a Ministry at the end of 1983, and in July 1984 announced a plan to commit 1m. ha to dry farming. Delays in implementing these projects have added to rural insecurity and are an additional cause of rural-to-urban migration.

The Ministry of Construction Jihad and the Ministry of Agriculture are known to hold conflicting views on almost every aspect of policy, with the Ministry of Construction Jihad strongly in favour of more extensive land reform. Proposals for the merger of the two Ministries in 1987 encountered resistance inside both organizations. While the Ministry of Agriculture favours an essentially advisory and technical role in the agricultural sector, the Jihad promotes the creation of collective farming organizations and a reduction in the role of the private land-owner. Although the Jihad has achieved spectacular success in some villages, fears have been expressed that an extension of its authority could impede production, with ideological factors taking precedence over sound farm management.

Short-term credit to farmers has been greatly increased. In the last year of the old regime the Agricultural Bank lent some $600m.; in 1982/83 it lent $11,900m., and in 1983/84 $2,300m. In spite of expanded credit facilities, farmers have been reluctant to start long-term, high-value cultivation of perennial crops. Instead, they have put their effort into annual crops that yield a quick return, particularly wheat. Moreover, the impact has been uneven, with big changes in the centre of the country, around Teheran, but in other areas, those disrupted by the war and those where tribe-state relations are bad, the villages have hardly been touched by the new policies. More than a decade after the Revolution, Iran was no more self-sufficient than it was in the latter days of the Shah's rule. In spite of successes claimed in increasing agricultural output, US Department of Agriculture estimates revealed that Iranian imports of foodstuffs reached $3,670m. in 1984 and were only modestly reduced in 1985. Agricultural imports reached $1,900m. in 1987/88, according to the Minister of Agriculture. The allocation for agricultural imports in 1988/89 was $2,000m. In the Iranian year 1990/91 the value of food imports through government agencies was $5,300m. Imports by the private sector are not officially recorded. Imports of wheat were estimated at 4.5m. tons, those of rice at 800,000 tons and those of coarse grains at 1.3m. tons. In May 1997 the International Grains Council stated that wheat imports during 1995/96 reached 5m. tons, the highest on record, and predicted that 6.6m. tons would be imported in 1996/97.

Problems of land ownership and uncertainty about the Government's land reform policies have added to the difficulties affecting the agricultural sector. After the fall of the Shah, when the authority of the central Government was weak, land seizures began in many villages. The most dramatic examples occurred in Turkoman and Kurdish areas, where concentrations of large absentee land-holdings were especially pronounced, but other areas were also affected. In some cases the Government did not intervene but, where it did, it tended to oppose land seizures. The events were accompanied by mass migration from the countryside to the cities—nearly 1.5m. rural dwellers migrated to Teheran alone during the first year of the Revolution. The regime recognized the economic disaster that this migration threatened. Nearly one-quarter of the most fertile farm land awaits settlement of ownership claims between big landlords and the farmers who have taken over their lands. The redistribution of these lands is decreed by the Revolution but, according to the rules of Islam, property is sacred and the right to it absolute. The issue has been complicated by the radical element

in the Government which advocates the appropriation of more land by the state. A land reform programme, prepared by the Ministry of Agriculture, was submitted to the Revolutionary Council at the end of 1979. The programme planned to limit the size of holdings to three times the average in an area. The large landowners were accused of influencing the clergy to oppose the new measures, but the necessary legislation was eventually introduced. It was approved by the Majlis in 1981, but was later rejected by the Council of Guardians as un-Islamic. The form of the land reform bill was then altered considerably. Land was to be confiscated only from former enemies of the Revolution and only if it was barren or uncultivated. After many months before the Majlis and deep controversy over the acceptability of the law in the light of Islamic principles, the bill was again rejected by the Council of Guardians. A compromise law, giving farmers, peasants and squatters rights to land (amounting to some 800,000 ha) settled by them after the Revolution, but allowing big landlords who avoided the redistribution of land to retain their estates, was approved by the Majlis in May 1985, though it was not ratified by the Council of Guardians. The law would affect about 630,000 ha of farmland belonging to some 5,300 landlords who fled the country or whose lands were appropriated. Some 800,000 ha of land, confiscated from officers and others linked with the Shah's regime, have been redistributed since the Revolution. (More than 50% of this land is uncultivable or grazing land, but 200,000 ha of cultivable land have been given to poor or landless peasants.) For more than a decade the authorities have been trying to reconcile Islamic principles with revolutionary goals and expectations, while a comprehensive settlement of the land ownership reform question is still awaited.

In early 1990 changes in government policy on the utilization of agricultural land were announced. Instead of granting confiscated and unused land to small farmers, henceforth official teams (consisting of seven members) were to grant land in blocks to groups of investors, in order to ensure its rapid development. Consequently, some 200,000 ha of land have been leased to farmers for temporary cultivation, and it is aimed to lease a further 250,000 ha under the new terms.

Agriculture has been described as the weakest spot in the Iranian economy and the biggest impediment to progress. Although it was given high priority in the 1983/84–1987/88 Five-Year Development Plan (see Development Plans, p. 480), the Government was unable to make it fulfil its designated role. The Five-Year Development Plan, introduced in January 1990, envisaged investment of $64,000m. in agriculture. Of this sum, one-third was to be invested by the Government and the remainder by the private sector. Some $340m. were to be spent on increasing the output of cotton, sugar cane and maize, on animal husbandry and on schemes to mechanize the farming of wheat on 2m. ha of irrigated land. Plans also included the development of major agro-industrial complexes in Mazandaran and Khuzestan.

The war with Iraq imposed numerous constraints. Between 1980 and 1982 10% of agricultural land fell under Iraqi occupation; a disproportionate number of volunteers for the war effort were drawn from the villages; and the heavy financial burden of the war imposed limits on spending. Since the end of the war, despite drought in the western rain-fed areas and the earthquake of 1990, which destroyed irrigation works, orchards and farms in the fertile north-western provinces of Gilan and Zanjan, the Ministry of Agriculture claims to have succeeded in reviving the agricultural sector after three decades of decline. The Ministry reported that an annual growth in farm output of 6% had been achieved under the 1990–94 Five-Year Development Plan, wheat output had doubled to 11m. tons, sugar plants were now working at full capacity, agriculture had been made more viable by reducing subsidies to farmers on products such as fertilizers and pesticides, and water reservoirs had been expanded. Under the new Plan which began in March 1995, the Ministry of Agriculture projects annual growth of 5%. It is planned to build some 20 dams during the term of the Plan and to increase water utilization by cutting losses in irrigation canals. Subsidies on pesticides are to be phased out within three years and those on fertilizers within five years. Increased mechanization is a key priority, especially in rice farming. As the average Iranian farm is small, only 5.3 ha, farmers must pool their land for successful mechanization. The Minister of Agriculture stated that the Majlis has approved the necessary legislation. Co-operatives are being encouraged and will be supplied with machinery and a guarantee that the Government will buy 70% of their production. The new Plan aims for the expansion of food processing industries with investment mainly from the private sector, which has shown particular interest in processing plants for vegetables and fruits and dairy products. The Minister of Agriculture stated that he welcomed foreign investment in agriculture and expected that most of it would be directed towards food processing industries. A $47m.-baby food factory was set up in 1994 by Nestlé of Switzerland as a joint venture with a local firm. The Minister of Agriculture stated that Iran was currently producing 84% of its food requirements, compared with 75% in 1990, and predicted that by the end of 1999 the country would be exporting more food than it imported. However, wheat imports reached a record level of 5m. tons in 1997/98, although they were projected to fall to 3m. tons in 1998/99, representing about a third of domestic consumption. Special efforts were being made to improve the processing and packaging of fruit for export to markets in the Gulf and Europe and this sector was scheduled for rapid growth. The Minister forecast self-sufficiency in sugar, fodder crops, tea, meat and dairy products by 2000. Some imports would be necessary, especially of vegetable oil, of which about 85% of requirements is imported; however, a major effort is to be made to expand olive cultivation. The Minister of Agriculture also maintained that the gap between rural and urban incomes had narrowed and that within the next five years no village would be without proper roads, electricity or health facilities.

The principal products of the nomad sector of Iranian agriculture are livestock products—dairy produce, wool, hair and hides. According to the 1988 agricultural census, nomads' herds included 40.7m. sheep and lambs, of which more than one-third were in the provinces of Khorassan and east and west Azerbaijan. About 40% of sheep and goats are raised by semi-nomadic tribal herdsmen. Production is limited by the prevalence of animal pests and the apparently inevitable poor productivity of pastoral stock breeding compared with its domestic counterpart. However, account must be taken of the fact that most of the land grazed by the nomads' herds is land which could not be made economically viable in any other way. During the reign of Reza Shah (1925–41) the Iranian Government tried to enforce settlement on the nomads but the tribes rebelled. Since the early 1960s, government 'encouragement' and economic pressures have resulted in significant settlement. By contrast, the Revolutionary Government accepts the tribes as part of the social structure and is providing the nomads with support to expand meat production. Local output of red meat increased from 560,000 tons in 1989/90 to 680,000 tons in 1994/95.

About 11.5% of Iran is under forest or woodland, including the Caspian area—the main source of commercial timber—and the Zagros mountains. Forestry in an economic sense is a recent activity and it is only since the nationalization of forest land in 1963 that effective attempts have been made, under the Forestry Commission, at protection, conservation and reafforestation. Total roundwood output in 1990 was estimated at 6.7m. cu m.

Although Iran has direct access to both the Caspian Sea and the Gulf, fishing remains poorly developed in both areas. The total Iranian catch amounted to an estimated 368,300 tons in 1995. With the assistance of new investment, the Government hopes to increase the annual catch to 730,000 tons per year. The Caspian fisheries are chiefly noted for the production of caviare, mostly for export. Caviare exports in recent years have been estimated at around 100 tons; output in 1995 rose to 120 tons. During the 1990s prices have fallen by about one-third due to an increase in smuggling through Russia. In August 1993 Iran, Russia, Azerbaijan, Kazakhstan and Turkmenistan agreed to establish a cartel to regulate international prices of caviare, to co-ordinate exports and to protect stocks of sturgeon. Pollution and the steadily falling water-level of the Caspian Sea are two serious problems being tackled under a Soviet-Iranian agreement signed in 1973. One survey estimated that, if fully developed, Iran's southern fisheries could earn as much as $200m. annually, chiefly from high-grade shrimps and prawns. At the end of 1982 a $1,300m. five-year plan for the development of the fishing industry was announced. The first phase of a giant fishing port at Javad al-A'emeh, in Hormozgan province, was completed in June 1986, at a cost of $3m. Under a $20m.-protocol signed in August 1987, Iran agreed to buy 36 trawlers from the People's Republic of China, 18 of which were to be assembled in Iran from Chinese parts. China was also to assist in the construction of factories producing canned fish at three Iranian ports. Government expenditure of $4,520m. on the sector was planned over the period 1990–95; projects included the construction of 13 new fishing ports along the Gulf and the Sea of Oman, and the purchase or charter of fishing vessels. In May 1993 a new fishing port, which was to be equipped with cold storage facilities, opened on Hormuz Island. At the end of November 1993 a $1.4m.-fish canning plant was opened in the Qeshm Island free zone, with a daily capacity of 40,000 cans. As a result of pollution caused by the war in the Gulf in 1991, Iran's shrimp catch was reported to have fallen by almost two-thirds to 4,000 tons in the Iranian year 1991/92.

PETROLEUM

The major economic activity in Iran is the petroleum industry. According to official figures, Iran's proven oil reserves at the end of 1997 were 93,000m. barrels, representing 9% of Middle East reserves, and were expected to last about 70 years at current production rates.

The history of commercial exploitation dates back to 1901, when W. K. D'Arcy was granted a 60-year monopoly of the right to explore for and exploit petroleum in Iran, with the exception of the five northern provinces, which fell within the sphere of Russian influence. Petroleum was eventually discovered in commercial quantities at Masjid-i-Sulaiman in 1908 and the Anglo-Persian Oil Co was formed in 1909. The Company was renamed Anglo-Iranian in 1935. A long series of disputes between the Iranian Government and Anglo-Iranian ended with the nationalization of the petroleum industry by Iran in 1951 and the replacement in 1954 of Anglo-Iranian by what became known as the Consortium until it was dissolved in March 1979. The Consortium was an amalgam of interests (British Petroleum 40%; Royal Dutch Shell 14%; Gulf Oil, Socony, Mobil, Exxon, Standard Oil of California and Texaco each with 7%; Compagnie Française des Pétroles 6%; a group of independents under the umbrella of the Iricon Agency 5%) which was formed to extract petroleum in the area of the old Anglo-Iranian concession as redefined in 1933. The Consortium's concession was to have lasted until 1979, with the possibility of a series of extensions under modified conditions for a further 15 years. Ownership of petroleum deposits throughout Iran and the right to exploit them, or to make arrangements for their exploitation, was vested in the National Iranian Oil Co (NIOC), an Iranian state enterprise.

Until 1973 Iran had a leasing agreement with the Consortium, but the Iranian Government then insisted that the companies should either continue under existing arrangements until 1979 and then become ordinary 'arm's-length buyers', or else negotiate an entirely new 'agency' agreement immediately. The Consortium opted for the latter plan, and on 31 July 1973 a contract was signed in Teheran under which NIOC formally took over ownership and control of the petroleum industry in the Consortium area, while the Consortium was to set up a new operating company, Oil Service Co of Iran, which would act as production contractor for NIOC. In return, the western companies were granted a 20-year supply of crude petroleum as privileged buyers, which they would take in proportion to their shareholding in the Consortium.

Strikes at the petroleum installations, halting petroleum exports, constituted one of the difficulties which forced the Shah to leave Iran in January 1979. The strikers announced that exports would not resume until the Shah left the country; Iran did not restore supplies to the rest of the world until 5 March 1979. The first shipments were sold on the spot market, fetching prices as high as $20 per barrel, but NIOC announced that this was a temporary measure. Within a matter of weeks, three dozen long-term contracts were signed with international companies for the supply of Iranian petroleum.

NIOC cancelled the 1973 agreement to market Iranian petroleum through the Consortium, and since 5 March 1979 has sold petroleum directly to individual companies and countries. After initial resistance, the former members of the Consortium accepted the new arrangement and signed new nine-month supply agreements effective from 1 April. The role of the Consortium effectively came to an end on 1 July 1981, when Kala Ltd, a subsidiary of NIOC which had been established to undertake purchasing and service functions for Iran's petroleum industry, replaced the Iranian Oil Service Co (IROS), one of the subsidiaries of the Consortium.

Iran's greatest difficulty after November 1979, however, was finding customers willing to pay the high prices that it demanded. Supplies of about 900,000 barrels per day (b/d) to the USA were stopped in November, and by May 1980 deliveries of about 800,000 b/d to Japan and British Petroleum and Royal Dutch Shell were also halted. The USA stopped taking delivery for political reasons in order to put pressure on Iran for the release of its hostages in the US Embassy in Teheran, taken over by Iranian students in November 1979; BP and Shell, themselves under pressure from the USA, refused to buy Iranian petroleum from 21 April, when the Ministry of Oil raised the price of its lightest crude to $35 per barrel, retroactive from 1 April. Including surcharges and other conditions Iran's oil was costing its customers closer to $37.50 per barrel, perhaps the highest for any OPEC country (this price compared with $17.17 per barrel less than a year earlier). With the (at least temporary) loss of its major Western customers, Iran began to investigate the Eastern bloc and developing countries for its principal markets.

The Government targeted average exports of crude petroleum for the Iranian year 1360 (March 1981–March 1982) at 2.5m. b/d: within the 3m. b/d ceiling which had been set after the Revolution as the optimum production level. Before the Revolution, Iran was producing 5m.–6m. b/d, of which around 800,000 b/d were required for domestic consumption. Political action in late 1978 brought production almost to a standstill but it recovered to around 3m. b/d during the following 18 months. Average production in 1979 was just over 3m. b/d, and in 1980 declined to 1.5m. b/d, 49.5% less than the 1979 level, owing to price disputes and the crisis in relations with the West.

After the Prime Minister, Muhammad Ali Rajai, presented his April 1981 budget, with expenditure set at an ambitious US $44,000m., NIOC was apparently instructed to raise production to 2.5m. b/d to generate foreign exchange for the budget requirements. A special effort was made by NIOC to improve performance in petroleum exports by seeking contract customers as quickly as possible. By mid-1981 contracts for sales totalling 1m. b/d had been signed (207,000 b/d to Eastern bloc countries). Not all of these contracts, however, yielded foreign exchange. Crude contracts with CMEA countries (including the USSR) during the 1980s, and subsequently with other countries, including Turkey and India, were normally on a barter basis, with only the balance being made up in hard currency. In return for petroleum, these countries exported industrial goods and services, plus some food.

In October 1981, as a result of growing internal political violence and the war damage caused by Iraq, the main purchasers of Iranian petroleum announced that they would cease to lift Iranian crude. The contracts held by BP for 65,000 b/d, Mitsubishi for 40,000 b/d, Daikyo Oil for 10,000 b/d and Showa Oil for 18,000 b/d lapsed as from the end of September 1981. A group of nine Japanese firms also stopped purchases from Iran; only Shell retained its contract. In September 1981 the Government announced that all agreements and contracts signed under the Shah's regime had been abrogated. At the beginning of 1982 Japanese buyers re-entered the Iranian market.

The pricing of Iranian crude petroleum also had an adverse effect on exports, as both Iranian Light and Iranian Heavy have been priced towards the upper end of the market for similar API crudes. In April 1980 the price for Light was raised from $32.5 to $35 per barrel, with an additional premium of $2.5 per barrel. The Japanese, who had been taking 520,000 b/d, suspended purchases, while Shell and BP refused to buy until the price was below $35 per barrel. In July 1980 differentials between Iranian and similar Gulf crudes narrowed as Iraq and Kuwait raised prices up to the $32 benchmark agreed at the OPEC meeting in Algiers. In January 1981 prices were raised by $1.63 to $37 for Light and $36 for Heavy, with an additional premium of $1.8 per barrel. However, against this pricing policy,

Iran was reported in early 1981 to have offered discounts of up to 20% to offset the very high insurance rates of loading in the war zone of Kharg Island and to have offered 60 days' credit instead of 30 days'.

In July and August 1981 Iran refused requests by its main customers for negotiations on prices of crude petroleum despite a difference of $5.50 per barrel between the Saudi reference price and the $37.50 per barrel charged by Iran. After the OPEC meeting in Abu Dhabi in December 1981, Iran reduced its prices to $34.20, just 20 cents above the reference price charged by Saudi Arabia, and in February 1982, as part of its drive to increase petroleum exports, NIOC announced two price cuts, each of $1. Taking into account 30 days' credit, the NIOC prices were $32.20 for 34° API crude and $30.30 for 31° API crude. These reductions made Iran's petroleum the cheapest in the Middle East.

The period April 1980 to June 1981 was, in almost every way, very poor for the Iranian petroleum industry. Apart from the factors already mentioned, the country was in a continuous state of political turmoil, which spilled over into the hydrocarbon industry. Stoppages, strikes, go-slows and sabotage seriously hindered production. The loss of foreign personnel for oilfield maintenance on the onshore fields was compounded by the May 1980 EC sanctions, imposed in support of the USA over the American hostages in Iran. The EC's action prevented Iran from purchasing some of the sophisticated spares and components required for repairs and maintenance. Iran's response, however, deprived the country of some petroleum customers, since it suspended supplies to any country supporting the sanctions.

The Iraqi attack on Iran across the Shatt al-Arab in September 1980 and the consequent expanded and prolonged hostilities further weakened the industry. Iraqi shelling of the 628,000 b/d Abadan refinery put the plant out of action. Spasmodic attacks on shipping in the Gulf caused some disruption, but the movement of ultra-large cargo carriers and other vessels was virtually uninterrupted until May 1984, when Iraq began to concentrate its attacks on ships using Iran's main terminal for crude oil exports, at Kharg Island, and on the terminal itself. Only part of the terminal's export capacity was damaged, and, with an installed capacity of 6.5m. b/d, the loss of an estimated 2.5m. b/d capacity still enabled the terminal to deal effectively with Iran's levels of export in early 1983, which remained well below pre-Revolution figures. During periods of concerted Iraqi action in the Gulf, there were massive increases in insurance charges for tankers, followed by sharp falls during periods of relative military inactivity. Iraqi raids disrupted the product lines extending from Bandar Mahshahr along the length of the country, and delayed construction of the giant petrochemical complex at Bandar Khomeini, a joint Iranian-Japanese project expected to cost $4,000m.

From the depressed levels of early 1982, Iran's output of petroleum rose significantly during the first half of 1983. In January 1983 oil rationing for domestic consumers was ended. Domestic consumption in mid-1982 was believed to be between 600,000 b/d and 700,000 b/d, of which some 300,000 b/d was being refined outside Iran, leaving exports at between 1.6m. b/d and 1.7m. b/d. In the second half of 1983, output dropped to 2.6m. b/d, compared with an OPEC production quota of 2.4m. b/d, under which exports of 1.7m. b/d were possible, after domestic consumption. Petroleum exports in June 1984 rose to 1.4m. b/d after falling below 1m. b/d in May, following Iraqi attacks on tankers in the Gulf. Japanese companies, the principal customers for Iranian crude oil, lifted more than 400,000 b/d in early 1984. Between May and July 1984 Japan banned its tankers from Kharg Island, and Iran offered lower prices to certain customers to bolster sales in the absence of its largest customer.

In 1982/83, with its oil priced at $34 per barrel, export earnings reached $23,000m.; in 1983/84, when Iran's oil was priced at $28 per barrel, earnings totalled $21,500m., about $4,000m. more than the OPEC quota (which was reduced by 100,000 b/d, to 2.3m. b/d, in October 1984) would have allowed. Iran responded to the need to increase earnings by breaking OPEC production limits (Iran repeatedly pressed for an increase in its OPEC production quota, until the crisis of 1985–86, when prices fell precipitously in a glutted market (see below)) and by energetic price-cutting policies, actions which offended its OPEC partners. It was reliably reported that Iran priced its crude petroleum in 1984 considerably below the official market level of $29 per barrel, as it was known to have done with the previous official price of $34. Some liftings were reportedly offered at approximately $26.50 per barrel in September and October 1984. Special insurance rates were made available to offset Iraqi threats to tanker traffic in the Gulf, and extended credit was also reportedly used as an incentive. Some customers, in particular Japan, began to turn to Saudi Arabia and Kuwait for their oil, as the risk of attacks on tankers and, commensurately, the rate of insurance were lower. Barter trading continued, but there was some evidence of Iran's dissatisfaction with such arrangements, owing to the failure of partners to deliver materials which had been promised, and to supply goods according to specification. In 1985, despite its stated wish to abide by OPEC's official pricing structure, Iran continued to offer discounts on its oil, below official OPEC prices, to attract customers otherwise deterred by risks to shipping in the Gulf from Iraqi air attacks, and by the increased rates of insurance charged on vessels using the Kharg Island oil terminal. In January Iran brought its prices into line with those of OPEC by raising the price of its light crude oil by $1.11 to $29.10 per barrel. In February, when OPEC prices were reduced, Iran cut the price of its light crude by $1.05 to $28.05 per barrel. By mid-1985, however, Iran was again offering discounts on its oil. Despite efforts to remain competitive (which included rebate incentives, discounts and the shuttling of oil from Kharg Island by tanker to a safer lifting point, see below), Iran's revenue from oil exports (of 1.68m. b/d) fell to $17,000m. in 1984/85, 15% less than had been predicted. The Government blamed the war with Iraq and the OPEC decision to reduce its prices by $1.00 per barrel.

During 1985 Iran achieved an output of some 2.3m. b/d, in spite of heavy Iraqi bombing of the Kharg Island terminal in the last third of the year, with exports running at some 1.5m. b/d–1.7m. b/d. Falling oil prices severely affected Iran, and in January 1986 the Minister of Oil offered to halve Iranian exports, in an attempt to curb the fall in the price of crude, if other OPEC states would do the same. The Ministry of Oil argued publicly against the use of barter deals to stimulate oil exports while the Ministry of Foreign Affairs adopted barter and bilateral agreements as one of the main features of Iran's foreign policy. New barter deals were agreed in 1985 but their profitability was low and often fell short of the country's real needs; bartering returned to favour, however, with the appointment of a new Council of Ministers in January 1986.

A suggested long-term solution to the threat to oil exports, posed by Iraqi attacks on Kharg Island, was the construction of a new oil terminal, either at the end of a pipeline outside the Gulf area, or at Sirri Island, close to the mouth of the Gulf, 450 km south-east of Kharg Island, safer from Iraqi attack. An immediate and cheaper alternative, more a short-term solution to the problem of Iraqi air raids on Kharg, involved the establishment of a tanker shuttle service between Kharg and a makeshift floating oil terminal at Sirri Island, using tankers anchored off shore, where the oil was stored and reloaded. The Sirri facility began operating in March 1985 and proved its worth between August 1985 and January 1986, when Iraq launched a series of some 60 attacks against the Kharg Island terminal (which was still responsible for more than 80% of Iran's oil exports). The frequency and effectiveness of these attacks diminished during October, but at the beginning of the month exports were reported to be only 750,000 b/d–800,000 b/d, compared with an average of 1.5m. b/d in August and 1m. b/d in September. However, by dint of rapid repairs, employing the ample spare capacity on Kharg and exploiting alternative means of export, such as the shuttle to Sirri, Iran could claim that exports in October finally averaged 1.7m. b/d. However, further Iraqi raids were said to have reduced exports from Kharg to a trickle by January 1986. In June 1986, as a precaution against possible Iraqi attacks on the Sirri facility, a new floating terminal, called Wal-Fajr 2 (Dawn 2), was established at Larak Island, 210 km east of Sirri, using at least three of the supertankers formerly based at Sirri.

Average oil production in Iran at the end of 1985 was between 2.2m. b/d and 2.5m. b/d, while exports averaged about 1.6m. b/d. The rate of export fell from about 1.5m. b/d in January 1986 to 1.2m. b/d in February. At the end of January Iran

offered to halve its oil production, and in February pressed OPEC to suspend oil exports for two weeks in an attempt to force prices up again. It was perhaps no coincidence that Iran's most vehement advocacy of production discipline within OPEC occurred at a time when the depredations of war prevented it from producing and exporting sufficient oil in excess of its OPEC quota to obviate the effects of falling prices. In fact, it could barely meet its quota in early 1986. In July prices fell below $10 per barrel (following six months of unrestrained production by OPEC in pursuit of a 'fair' market share), and in August OPEC members, at Iran's suggestion, agreed to cut output for two months from 1 September, effectively reverting to the production quotas imposed in October 1984, giving Iran a quota of 2.3m. b/d. Although Iraq refused to participate in the agreement, considering its quota of less than 1.5m. b/d to be too low, and demanding one commensurate with its production capacity or, at least, the equal of Iran's, Iran averred that military action in the Gulf would effectively restrain Iraqi oil production.

In October 1986, when the price of oil had risen to about $15 per barrel, OPEC members agreed to increase collective production by some 200,000 b/d. In December all OPEC members (with the exception of Iraq, which, once more, since it was not expected to comply, received a notional quota) accepted a 7.25% reduction in their output, effective for the first half of 1987. It was hoped that this measure would enable the organization to support a fixed price of $18 per barrel, effective from 1 February, replacing the policy of pricing according to spot market rates, which prevailed in 1986. The reduction gave Iran a production quota of 2.26m. b/d, compared with 2.32m. b/d in November 1986–January 1987. Iran's average output of crude oil was estimated by OPEC to be 2.04m. b/d in 1986, compared with 2.19m. b/d in 1985, well below its OPEC quota. Production fluctuated during the first half of 1987 between 1.7m. b/d in February and 2.6m. b/d in June.

The OPEC production programme succeeded in sustaining the price of its oil at $18 per barrel during the first half of 1987, and during the month of July prices on the spot market rose above $20 per barrel, in response to alarm over the growing threat to oil supplies posed by developments in the Iran–Iraq War. In June OPEC members agreed to retain the $18 per barrel benchmark, but to increase their collective production by 800,000 b/d during the second half of the year to 16.6m. b/d (including a notional quota for Iraq). Iran's quota was raised to 2.37m. b/d, an increase of 111,000 b/d. In August, however, output averaged 2.8m. b/d, according to oil industry sources, despite having counselled restraint at the June meeting. Iran had, since 1985, urged a return to a price of $28 per barrel, as OPEC's ultimate goal, in tandem with lower production—obviously with regard to its own difficulties in sustaining production levels.

In June 1987 Iraqi aircraft attacked the Kharg Island terminal for the first time since January. It was reported that, in the interim, three oil-loading berths at Kharg had been made operational again. Exports averaged 2.2m. b/d in August and 1.6m. b/d in September, according to oil industry sources, compared with an OPEC quota of 1.7m. b/d. By mid-October Iraqi attacks had reduced the number of tankers shuttling oil from Kharg to 20.

At the OPEC meeting which was held in December 1987, Iran demanded an increase in the central reference price of at least $2 per barrel and output reductions by members, and refused to participate in a new agreement which awarded Iraq the same quota as that given to Iran. It was finally agreed to retain the $18 per barrel reference price and the ceiling of 16.6m. b/d (15.06m. b/d excluding Iraq) on collective production for a further six months from 1 January 1988. Prices remained well below the OPEC reference level during the first half of 1988, owing to member states' flouting of their quotas, but in May OPEC decided to retain the 16.6m. b/d ceiling and the $18 reference price for a further six months. In August, when the cease-fire in the Iran–Iraq War took effect, Iran was producing at its quota level of about 2.37m. b/d, though, owing to Iraqi attacks on oil installations (including the first on Larak Island for five months in May), it had rarely been able to produce so much during the preceding six months. While Iranian representatives at OPEC meetings strongly urged reductions in output, to defend the $18 benchmark, Iran was allegedly so desperate for oil revenue that it was selling oil at less than $10 per barrel.

At a meeting of OPEC's Long-Term Strategy Committee in November 1988 (at which Iran reluctantly adopted a more flexible approach to Iraq's demand for quota parity), member states agreed a production ceiling of 18.5m. b/d for the first half of 1989. By December it was apparent that world demand for oil had surged, and prices strengthened to a level close to the $18 per barrel reference price which remained in force. According to oil industry sources, Iranian production averaged 2.27m. b/d in 1988, while OPEC's provisional estimate of Iranian petroleum revenues in 1988 was $8,170m.

In early 1989 the agreement that had been signed in November 1988 was undermined when Kuwait rejected the quota assigned to it within the 18.5m. b/d ceiling. By the time that the next full OPEC meeting was held, at the beginning of June 1989, prices had weakened considerably. To take account of the increased volume of Kuwaiti production, which OPEC member states regarded as inevitable, the production ceiling was raised by only 1m. b/d, to 19.5m. b/d, thus reducing the extra volume to which other members were entitled.

At the meeting of OPEC's Long-Term Strategy Committee (subsequently redesignated a full-scale quota and pricing meeting) in June 1989, Iran demanded a redistribution of quotas, to favour Kuwait, the UAE, Ecuador and Gabon, within a ceiling of 21.5m. b/d. In the event, a ceiling of 20.5m. b/d was set; Kuwait duly rejected its quota of 1.149m. b/d for the final quarter of 1989, and overproduction continued to such an extent that by the end of 1989 total OPEC output had reached almost 24m. b/d. According to oil industry sources, Iranian production averaged 2.87m. b/d during 1989, while Iran's petroleum revenues were estimated at $13,600m. At the next full OPEC meeting, held in November 1989, the production ceiling was raised to 22m. b/d, although most members regarded this as inadequate, since the *de facto* level of production was already 24m. b/d.

In early 1989 the Ministry of Oil issued a number of contracts for the construction and repair of offshore oil platforms destroyed during the Iran–Iraq War as part of a major $2,000m.-expansion programme. Offshore production had totalled some 500,000 b/d before the war but by 1986 it was estimated that production had fallen to 250,000 b/d. Offshore production may have fallen to 50,000 b/d by the end of the war. In April 1988 US warships severely damaged Salman, one of three rigs 150 km west of Sirri Island, feeding the Lavan Island terminals, and installations in the Nasr oilfield off Sirri. Rigs in the Reshadat and Risala'at oilfields, and the Raksh and Rostan platforms, had been destroyed by US attacks in April and October 1987.

By January 1990, prompted by optimistic demand estimates issued by OPEC and by members' closer adherence to their quotas, the price of crude petroleum had risen to its highest level for two years. Between January and May 1990, however, prices fell steadily, as quotas were largely ignored. In May 1990, at a meeting of OPEC's Monitoring Committee, it was agreed to reduce production by 1.445m. b/d, bringing it just within the previously agreed ceiling. A report issued by the International Energy Agency (IEA) in July, however, showed that this reduction had not been implemented.

In June 1990 it was reported that Iran had agreed to pay the US oil company Amoco $600m. in compensation for operations which had been expropriated during the Revolution. This was the first major settlement of US corporate oil claims totalling $1,800m., and was regarded as a step towards the re-establishment of oil trade between Iran and the USA. In December it was announced that a US company, Atlantic Richfield, had secured compensation of $9m. from Iran for its share in the former international oil Consortium; this represented the last in a series of settlements (totalling $320m.) made by Iran to US members of the former Iranian international oil Consortium. At the end of 1990 the USA eased the three-year ban on purchases of Iranian crude, but Iran objected to the US Administration's stipulation that all payments had to be made into a security account in The Hague, Netherlands, for use by the special US–Iran Claims Tribunal. However, in early 1991 Iran approved two sales to US companies, Coastal Corpn and Mobil Corpn. Coastal Corpn, Chevron and Amerada Hess purchased

shipments of Iranian oil for the US market in 1991. Mobil and other US oil firms have also purchased Iranian crude petroleum, but for delivery outside of the USA. In August 1992 Atlantic Richfield and Sun Oil agreed to accept $130m. each in compensation for their share in the joint venture, Lavan Petroleum Company, nationalized after the Revolution. Two other US shareholders, Murphy and Union, settled in 1986. Payment was to be made from the special security account created by Iran at The Hague under the 1981 Algiers agreement. This compensation payment settled the last of the US oil company claims.

By mid-July 1990 prices had fallen as low as $14.40 per barrel, and both Iran and Iraq were demanding that a minimum reference price of $25 per barrel be fixed at the full OPEC meeting scheduled for the end of July. At the meeting, however, a minimum reference price of $21 per barrel was set, within a 22.5m. b/d ceiling. Nevertheless, the agreement apparently indicated a new political alliance between Iran, Iraq and Saudi Arabia, and its immediate effect was to raise prices.

Iraq's invasion and annexation of Kuwait in August 1990 gave rise to a further, dramatic rise in the price of crude petroleum. It also created serious divisions within OPEC. Iran criticized those member states, principally Saudi Arabia, which, in the aftermath of the Iraqi invasion, sought to raise OPEC production in order to compensate for the loss of Iraqi and Kuwaiti supplies, due to the economic sanctions imposed by the UN. At an emergency OPEC meeting convened in late August and attended by the oil ministers of all member states except Iraq and Libya, a draft agreement was signed which effectively allowed for a suspension of the production quotas agreed in July. Iran refused to support the agreement, however, and proposed that oil companies and industrialized countries release petroleum stocks in order to relieve pressure on prices, which had risen above $30 per barrel during August. However, it appeared likely in late August that production quotas would be ignored until a resolution of the Gulf conflict made it possible to convene an OPEC meeting in which all 13 members could participate.

In October 1990 the Iranian Ministry of Oil announced that, since August, output of crude oil had been averaging 3.2m. b/d, slightly above the OPEC quota of 3.14m. b/d. It was further reported that exports of crude oil to Japan had trebled and that exports to the Republic of Korea and the Philippines had also increased. Sales to Asian countries accounted for nearly 60% of total oil exports. For the first time, contracts in convertible currency were signed with several eastern European countries that had previously bought oil from Iran through clearing accounts linked to reciprocal purchases of goods. In addition, in late 1990 and early 1991 revenue from oil exports increased by between $700m. and $800m. per month, as a result of the rise in prices for oil (precipitated by the crisis in the Gulf region).

Sustainable output of crude oil from both onshore and offshore fields was estimated at 3.5m. b/d in mid-1991. Domestic consumption has risen rapidly, and in mid-1991 it was reported to exceed 1m. b/d. In January 1991 the Ministry of Oil announced a revision of long-term investment plans for the sector, including additional investment of $2,000m. over two years, aimed at increasing output from the southern fields on the mainland. Under the Five-Year Development Plan (introduced in January 1990), projected onshore output was set at 3.5m. b/d–3.7m. b/d, but was later revised to between 4.1m. b/d and 4.6m. b/d. The Ministry projected a combined onshore and offshore capacity of some 5m. b/d by the end of the Plan's term. However, some Western experts believed that such a significant increase in capacity was not technically feasible. NIOC has emphasized that its ambitious development plans can only be achieved through major inputs of technology, funding and personnel from abroad, and has stressed the scope it offers for joint ventures and foreign technical co-operation. In August 1992 the head of the Southern oil fields stated that the crude output expansion programme required the drilling of nearly 300 new wells. Most of the wells had been drilled during the previous 12 months and when the programme was completed there would be a total of 600 wells in 47 fields. He estimated onshore production capacity at 3.4m. b/d, compared with 2.4m. b/d at the end of the Iran–Iraq War, with a further 250,000 b/d in offshore capacity, to be raised to more than 500,000 b/d in 1993. Most of Iran's crude oil exports go through Kharg Island. Loading capacity was reduced to 2.5m. b/d as a result of Iraqi air attacks, but in August 1992 it was reported that capacity would be restored to 5m. b/d within two years. It was also reported that storage capacity at the terminal had been restored to nearly 50% of its pre-war level of 22m. barrels and further reconstruction would raise capacity to 16m. barrels. Reconstruction of the main oil export terminal at Kharg Island was being undertaken by French, Italian and South Korean companies.

Iran's production of crude petroleum in 1991 is reported to have averaged 3,238,000 b/d, with exports averaging 2.41m. b/d, of which 2.35m. b/d were from onshore fields and 65,000 b/d from offshore fields. Iran's production capacity was estimated to have increased from 3.5m. b/d in 1991 to almost 4m. b/d in 1992. On 20 January 1992 the Ministry of Oil announced that it was reducing petroleum production by 50,000 b/d in an attempt to increase the international price of crude petroleum. In March the Ministry stated that, as of 1 March, oil production had been reduced to 3.184m. b/d in line with new OPEC quota allocations. However, the Minister of Oil reaffirmed Iran's intention to expand production capacity to 4.5m. b/d by March 1993—including an increase of 500,000 b/d in the course of 1992. Many observers doubt whether export capacity can be raised significantly above the level of 2.4m. b/d. To increase onshore capacity involves drilling new wells and injecting gas into depleting reservoirs, notably at the Gachsaran, Karanj, Pars, Marun and Ahwaz fields.

When NIOC began to negotiate prepaid sales in order to raise short-term finance, a ceiling of $2,000m. was placed on these sales, but in 1991 the Minister of Oil announced that this limit had been removed. This appeared to indicate a return to significant prepaid sales of crude petroleum which, in the past, have involved payment up to 18 months in advance of delivery. It has been argued that prepaid, or usance, sales are inefficient and that they can undermine future sales prospects; but for Iran they are more acceptable, ideologically, than raising direct foreign loans. Four Japanese trading houses arranged prepaid packages worth $600m. in 1991 and in November 1991 it was announced that a group of more than 25 banks, led by Banque Nationale de Paris and Crédit Lyonnais, had concluded a similar package involving several supply contracts between NIOC and international oil companies, worth $1,000m.

Early in 1992 repairs to the offshore Nasr platform were completed and initial production of 35,000 b/d was due to rise to 85,000 b/d after the installation of new pumps. The rebuilt Salman platform was due to commence production at an initial rate of 180,000 b/d in mid-1992. Offshore production was scheduled to rise to 500,000 b/d by early 1993, although some sources considered this projection to be over-optimistic. It was reported that in 1993, the Lavan Island facilities, with a capacity of 220,000 b/d, became fully operational and would export crude oil piped from the Salman offshore field. In October 1992 the head of the Iran Offshore Oil Co announced that agreements were being negotiated with several international oil companies for the development of a number of offshore fields, Balal, and Sirri E and A fields, and for new installations at the Abuzar field, which would together add about 300,000 b/d to national production. Bids were also to be invited for the exploration and development of the Hormuz reservoir at the mouth of the Gulf, following the withdrawal of the Japanese consortium, Japex. However, little progress was made, largely due to financial and political problems.

According to Gholamreza Aqazadeh, the Minister of Oil, oil production was officially raised to 3.5m. b/d–3.6m. b/d from 23 September 1992 following divisions within OPEC over production policy. In mid-October oil production was temporarily raised to 4m. b/d to demonstrate Iran's improved capacity and to establish Iran's position as OPEC's biggest producer after Saudi Arabia, and to support its claims for a larger share of OPEC's market. The well-publicized increase in output, 3.6m. b/d from onshore fields and 400,000 b/d from offshore fields, was maintained for a week. Normal production in previous months had averaged about 3.5m. b/d with about 1m. b/d designated for domestic consumption. Officials stated that production capacity would be raised to 4.5m. b/d in March 1993—equivalent to about 50% of Saudi Arabia's capacity—though actual production would be in line with OPEC quotas. Observers argued that export capacity would be limited to about 2.5m. b/d until work on the

reconstruction of the Kharg Island terminal was completed in 1994. In December 1992 the Minister of Oil announced that crude oil production would average 3.5m. b/d from 1 December 1992 to 31 March 1993, representing a cutback of 400,000 b/d from the November level of 3.9m. b/d. Oil exports during the Iranian year beginning March 1993 were forecast at 2.7m. b/d, about 10% higher than in the previous year. In March 1993 the Minister of Oil announced that output had been cut to 3.34m. b/d on 1 March in line with OPEC's new quota, but explained that the reduction would be compensated for by higher prices. About 2.4m. b/d would be available for export. A Plan and Budget Organization report released in April 1993 revealed that oil exports during the first nine months of 1992/93 averaged 2.386m. b/d, 448,000 b/d less than the budget level and 265,000 b/d less than the Ministry of Oil's export timetable. Observers estimated oil revenues for the Iranian year ending 20 March 1993 at $14,500m., $2,000m. below the budget projection. At a conference in April 1993, Mehdi Hossaini, an adviser to the Minister of Oil, presented figures which cited maximum 1993 capacity as 4.2m. b/d, 300,000 b/d below the 4.5m. b/d target. He indicated that capacity would be raised to 4.6m. b/d in 1994, 5m. b/d in 1995, rising to above 5.5m. b/d in 2000. Some Western experts doubted that the 4.2m. b/d capacity could be sustained because of the poor condition of the Southern oil fields and argue that Iran could only achieve higher targets with the involvement of the international oil companies in field maintenance and secondary recovery programmes

Following the OPEC meeting at Geneva in September 1993 the Minister of Oil, Aqazadeh, announced that from 1 October Iran's quota would be 3.6m.b/d, 240,000 b/d more than the previous level, allowing exports to rise to 2.6m. b/d. However, international traders stated that actual exports had averaged 2.7m. tons in 1993, with production estimated at some 200,000 b/d more than Iran's earlier OPEC quota of 3.34m. b/d. Aqazadeh reiterated previous claims that output was scheduled to rise to 4.6m. b/d in 1994, with a further rise to 5.5m.–6m. b/d by 2000. It is interesting to note that this was the level of production before the Revolution. He also stated that Iran planned to produce an average of 4.5m. b/d during the second Five-Year Plan due to begin in March 1994. Early in 1994 reports suggested that Iran was having difficulty producing crude to the level of its OPEC quota of 3.6m. b/d, but these were denied by the Minister of Oil. In January 1994 Mostafa Khoee, managing director of the Iranian Offshore Oil Co, stated that crude capacity was 4.2m. b/d; 3.8m. b/d on shore and 400,000 b/d off shore. He did not indicate whether these figures were sustainable. Actual output during 1993 averaged 3.6m. b/d. Defending his record as Minister of Oil before the Majlis in August 1993, Aqazadeh stated that during the first 52 months of the Five-Year Plan ending in March 1994, oil revenues totalled $61,720m., slightly higher than the Plan's target. He predicted that high sales would raise total annual revenues for 1993/94 to about $16,500m., about 10% below the target of $18,000m. By January 1994 these figures had been revised downwards because of low oil prices and ministry officials estimated that revenues would not exceed $12,000m. The budget for 1994/95 projected oil revenues at only $10,150m.

Early in 1994 the Minister of Oil, Aqazadeh, announced that 9,530m. barrels of oil, worth $45,000m. had been discovered during the term of the Five-Year Plan ending in March 1994. In January 1994 it was reported that production of 5,000 b/d had begun at the Qal-e Nar oilfield near Andimeshk and was scheduled to increase to 15,000 b/d. During the debate in the Majlis on the draft of the new Five-Year Plan to begin in 1994, the Minister of Oil, Aqazadeh, stated that oil revenues during the plan period were projected at $64,000m. This figure was $13,600m. lower than that given in mid-November 1993, when the Council of Ministers reviewed the draft plan. The projections, based on oil prices of between $14 and $16 a barrel over the plan period, were criticised in the Majlis as too optimistic. Aqazadeh also stated that domestic fuel subsidies would be reduced over the following five years because an increase in fuel prices was needed to help finance the ministry's development projects. However, in May 1994 it appeared that Rafsanjani, faced with opposition in the Majlis to his plans to cut subsidies, had been forced to compromise and to promise that the phasing out of energy subsidies would now take place over a much longer period. During the new Five-Year Plan the Ministry of Oil has declared that it hopes to invest $16,600m. of government funds and $9,000m. in foreign credits in the country's oil industry, together with an additional $3,800m. in government funds in gas, in order to increase production. However, officials admitted that the programme might be delayed because of low oil prices.

Rebuilding of oil-loading jetties and storage tanks at Kharg Island was completed in December 1994. The repairs were carried out by local contractors, ETPM Entrepose of France and Sasangyong of South Korea. The terminal's export capacity is estimated at 5m. b/d. In September 1994 it was reported that an official of the NIOC had stated that the company's work on gas re-injection schemes at the Bibi Hakimeh, Kupal and Ramsahir oilfields would not be completed until 1999. In early 1995 NIOC announced the discovery of a new oilfield named Shur, south of Gachsaran in Khuzistan province, with recoverable reserves estimated at 100m. barrels. Production was 10,000 b/d and output was due to rise to 30,000 b/d when two more wells came on stream.

Independent observers state that Iran has been producing crude at or near 3.6m. b/d since early 1993 and that at the end of 1994 sustained production capacity was at least 3.8m. b/d and perhaps 3.9m. b/d compared with the official claim of 4.2m. b/d. In May 1995 the NIOC ordered a 500,000 b/d increase in oil production for one week. NIOC officials stated that by boosting production to 4.1m. b/d Iran was demonstrating its potential following the US embargo on direct oil purchases (see below) and proving that it could produce well above its OPEC quota of 3.6m. b/d. Onshore fields contributed 3.6m. b/d with offshore fields making up the rest. The Minister of Oil claimed that onshore production could easily have been raised to 3.7m. b/d. Offshore output is to be increased to 600,000 b/d by March 1996 and will eventually rise to 1m. b/d. By 2000 total capacity is planned to reach nearly 5.5m..b/d, close to its pre-revolution level. Nevertheless, speculation remained that, owing to shortages of equipment and technical problems, Iran would not be able to maintain production at that level. It was reported that considerable drilling of new wells and recovery work on its existing fields was necessary to achieve its crude capacity expansion plans. In January 1996 the Ministry of Oil denied Western press reports that output of crude petroleum had fallen sharply at the end of 1995 and stated that output was 3.6m. b/d, Iran's agreed OPEC quota. In early 1996 a Western press report accused Iran of exceeding its OPEC quota in January 1996, an allegation also denied by the NIOC. At a meeting in June 1996 OPEC ministers agreed that production quotas would remain unchanged until the end of the year. Iran criticized countries which regularly exceeded their quotas and the Iranian Oil Minister, Gholamreza Aqazadeh, was appointed to chair a ministerial monitoring committee on quota observance. Aqazadeh warned members that if they persisted in violating their quotas, Iran would respond by setting its own production levels. Existing OPEC quotas were renewed in November for a further six months. Average Iranian production in 1996 was 3.66m. b/d, compared with 3.57m. b/d in 1995, slightly above its OPEC quota of 3.6m. b/d. The dramatic decrease in world oil prices from late 1997, to below early 1973 levels in real terms, prompted OPEC to decree that its members should reduce production from 1 April 1998 in an effort to boost prices. Iran's allotted cut was 140,000 b/d, so that its quota became 3.942m. b/d. This action having failed to produce the desired effect, OPEC implemented further cuts on 1 July, Iran's additional reduction being 165,000 b/d for a new quota of 3.777m. b/d. In light of the OPEC decision, Iran instituted a 10% cut in its oil production from 1 July, even though its current output was reported to be already at the level of the new OPEC quota.

In early 1994 a number of international oil companies showed renewed interest in Iran's offshore fields in the Gulf. In March 1994 the Minister of Oil confirmed that talks were being held with several US companies and that Conoco of Houston had submitted a proposal to develop the offshore Sirri E crude oilfield. An agreement between Conoco and NIOC to develop the Sirri A and E offshore fields, which have combined reserves estimated at nearly 500m. barrels and are expected to produce 120,000 b/d of crude, was finally concluded at the beginning of March 1995. The $600m.-scheme was to have been financed through a buy-back agreement. However, on 14 March the US Administration announced that President Clinton would shortly issue an executive order banning US companies from developing Iran's oil. Conoco subsequently announced that it was withdrawing from the agreement, the first oilfield development scheme awarded to a foreign company since 1979. The intervention by the US Administration was part of an intensive campaign aimed at isolating and crippling Iran economically. President Clinton's executive order of 8 May 1995 formally imposing an economic embargo against Iran (see below) prevents US oil companies from work in developing Iran's oil and gas resources for the foreseeable future. Some observers argued that by granting the contract to Conoco, rather than to French companies, Iran was making a political gesture to the USA. President Rafsanjani confirmed this in a US television interview on 15 May. However, Conoco also had advantages over other companies in that it was already operating in the region and would have been able to take associated gas from Sirri for use in its operations in Dubai. In May the Ministry of Oil announced that it was negotiating with Total of France and the Royal Dutch Shell Group to develop the Sirri oilfields. In July 1995 NIOC announced that the contract had been awarded to Total, which had been involved in three years of negotiations for work in Iran. Earlier, on 16 March, the Ministry of Oil had announced that a Dutch-German consortium, John Brown Engineers and Constructors and Ingenieurbetrieb Anlagenbau Leipzig, had agreed to renovate the offshore Abuzar oilfield and to finance and develop the South Pars gas field. The announcement came the day after President Clinton had issued an executive order banning US companies from participation in the development of Iran's hydrocarbon recources. The Minister of Oil declared that Iran did not need US companies and that Europe welcomed oil co-operation with Iran. The Abuzar project involves the reconstruction of the war-damaged platform in the northern Gulf and expansion of capacity to 150,000 b/d–200,000 b/d. Overall responsibility for the project was awarded to a local firm, the Iranian Offshore Engineering and Construction Co, a NIOC subsidiary, after a US/French/Japanese consortium failed to raise the necessary finance, which was estimated at $270m.

In January 1996 the Minister of Oil announced that a $68m.-drilling rig, built at a facility set up on the Caspian Sea, with assistance from Rauma-Repola of Finland, was being transferred to a drilling site at the Meysam-1 oilfield, 30 km off shore. If oil and gas were found there in commercial quantities a refinery would be built in the north. In May 1996 the local Iran Sadra Marine Industries Co reported that it had completed more than one-third of reconstruction work on the Abuzar oil platform which is expected to be back in operation by March 1997. The Iran Sadra Marine Industries Co also began repair work in early 1996 on the Salman platform, west of Lavan Island, which had been destroyed during the Iran–Iraq War. In March 1996 it was reported that the offshore Now Ruz oilfield, which was also damaged during the Iran–Iraq War, had been partially repaired and was producing at a rate of 5,500 b/d. It is intended to raise production to 60,000 b/d by 2000. At a press conference held at the end of January 1996 the Chairman of Total, Thierry Desmarest, stated that the company was having no problems finding partners to share the work and cost of developing the Sirri A and E fields, in spite of the USA's plans to extend the sanctions in force against Iran's oil and gas industries. Total awarded a drilling contract for the Sirri field to Dublin-based Momentum Engineering in early 1996, and in April National Petroleum Construction of Abu Dhabi, Technip, ETPM Entrepose and Bouygues of France were among the firms which submitted bids for a $300m.-contract for engineering, construction and procurement for platforms in the two offshore fields. Several other French firms were reported to be involved in negotiations to develop other oil and gas resources. In February 1996, when the French Minister of Transport visited Teheran, President Rafsanjani told him that Iran appreciated France's principled stand against a trade and investment ban on Iran. In late December 1995 Russia had signed a provisional agreement with Iran to establish joint venture companies in oil exploration, production and sales. In December 1995 the US Senate had approved legislation for a secondary economic boycott of Iran, which apparently aimed to paralyse the Iranian oil industry, and in early August 1996, under pressure from the Republican-dominated Congress, US President Clinton finally endorsed legislation which would penalize non-US companies which invested $40m. or more a year in oil and gas projects in Iran and Libya. Contracts already signed were exempt from the new legislation. The USA's attempt to extend its domestic legislation abroad was strongly criticized by the EU and Russia. Iran stated that it did not believe that European companies would be deterred by the new legislation and pointed out that existing US sanctions had harmed US companies, which had lost business to their European competitors. Independent observers argued that the US trade embargo imposed in June 1995 had not damaged Iran's oil exports, and that even a total freeze on foreign investment in the Iranian oil industry would not reduce Iran's export capacity until beyond the year 2000. They predicted that Iran's main trading partners were unlikely to take any action that would make it more difficult for Iran to repay its substantial foreign debts.

In August 1996 Total announced that Petronas of Malaysia had agreed to purchase a 30% state in its development of the Sirri A and E offshore fields and that the partnership deal had been approved by the Iranian authorities. It was also reported that deliniation drilling in the Sirri E field had begun and that by November two wells had been almost completed. Work is believed to be on schedule with production expected to begin at 20,000 b/d in early 1998, rising to 120,000 b/d once the drilling programme has been completed. Onshore work for the projects is being executed by Entrepose International of France. NIOC plans to increase total offshore output to 1m. b/d by 2000 and is seeking foreign partners to develop the Balal, Doroud and Soroush fields on similar terms to the agreement with Total. The state-owned Iranian Offshore Engineering Company was reported to be bidding to repair and renovate the Soroush field which was seriously damaged during the Iran–Iraq War and subsequently ceased production. At the end of May 1997 it was announced that NIOC was about to award the contract for the development of the offshore Balal field. Bow Valley of Canada and Pell Frischmann of the UK were considered to be the most likely concessionaires. The field is estimated to contain 135m. barrels of crude petroleum, and a production capacity of 40,000 b/d is envisaged. This was intended to be the first major oil contract to be awarded since the US imposed sanctions on non-US companies investing in Iran's hydrocarbons industry. The contract was delayed, however, when the UK/Canadian group failed to secure finance; Pell Frischmann subsequently withdrew from the project. The Balal field was re-tendered in August, with Bow Valley maintaining interest. Additional offshore projects under consideration by NIOC also involve foreign partners, and include five fields in the Strait of Hormuz and two close to Kharg and Lavan Islands. US sanctions do not appear to have prevented NIOC from proceeding with its programme to expand offshore production, but production at some of its fields may have been affected due to problems in obtaining spare parts for equipment already supplied by US companies.

In early August 1994 the Majlis approved the outline of the second Five-Year Development Plan which included cuts in fuel and energy subsidies which cost the country $11,000m. a year. In mid-August the Minister of Oil recommended that domestic petrol prices be raised by 400% in 1995 and pointed out that if Iran adopted prices for oil products similar to those in other Gulf countries, domestic consumption of 1m. b/d–1.3m. b/d could be reduced by 200,000 b/d–300,000 b/d. Oil ministry officials warned that, at present rates of consumption, Iran would be unable to export any crude by the year 2010. In November 1994 the Majlis approved a doubling of fuel prices, beginning in March 1995, and further, smaller annual increases until the end of the decade. Under the new Five-Year Plan, the Government is required to reduce the annual growth in consumption of oil products from 6% to 3% in order to conserve resources. During a debate in the Majlis on this issue, the Minister of Oil stressed that, in addition to the need to conserve resources, his ministry needed extra funds for major development projects in the hydro-carbons sector. In December President Rafsanjani welcomed the Majlis' decision as 'a good beginning', but stated that it was not enough to curb rising domestic fuel consumption, which was 167m. litres a day, an increase of more than 6% compared with 1993. In April 1996 a significant increase was applied to domestic fuel prices. The price of premium gasoline went up by 20%, that of regular gasoline by 30%, and that of kerosene and

diesel fuel by 50%. The price of motor oil rose more than threefold. Price increases effected in 1995 had contributed to riots in southern Teheran, but this time there were no reports of any disturbances. Despite these increases, Iranian fuel prices remain among the lowest in the world, and the Government maintains that this encourages waste and smuggling to neigh-bouring countries. The Ministry of Oil has stated that price rises effected since 1995 have helped to reduce domestic con-sumption by some 10% but a further reduction was still neces-sary. The Minister of Oil claimed that domestic fuel consumption had fallen by 100,000 b/d in 1995/96 and that it was expected to fall by a further 70,000 b/d in 1996/97. In 1996 domestic fuel consumption was 1.1m. b/d leading to speculation by some officials that government attempts to reduce domestic use had been unsuccessful and that new measures were needed to address the problem. In April 1997 domestic fuel prices were increased again: supergasoline rose from IR130/litre to IR160/litre, premium gasoline from IR180/litre to IR220/litre, gas oil and kerosene from IR20/litre to IR40/litre and fuel oil from IR15/litre to IR20/litre. In April 1995 it was reported that Iran's exports of liquefied petroleum gas (LPG) would rise by about 10% in 1995 to 850,000 tons, and to 1m. tons in 1997; thereafter exports would rise only slightly because of a 20% annual increase in domestic demand. In 1994 Finland purchased 250,000 tons of LPG and South Korea 100,000–200,000 tons.

In October 1994 the Minister of Oil announced that oil rev-enues during the first half of 1994/95 had exceeded the official budget projection by 20% and that this trend was expected to continue for the remainder of the year. No figures were released, but analysts predicted that oil revenues should reach $12,000m. and possibly rise to $14,000m. following the recovery in the international market in May 1994. Presenting the draft budget for 1995/96 to the Majlis in December 1994, President Rafsan-jani stated that oil exports would contribute 61% of the Gov-ernment's total revenue of $23,000m., implying a rise in oil revenues to $14,300m. Rafsanjani confirmed that oil production capacity had risen to 4.2m. b/d and would remain at that level until March 1996. Crude production was 3.6m. b/d, the ceiling set by OPEC. He pointed out that oil exports were falling and that whereas they averaged 2.34m. b/d in the first-half of 1994, the average would fall to 2.23m. b/d in 1995. In March 1995, when the Majlis finally approved the 1995/96 budget, oil rev-enues were projected at $13,500m., based on a crude oil price of $15 a barrel. In late June 1995 the Minister of Oil stated that oil revenues during the first quarter of the Iranian year beginning 21 March 1995 had been $500m. higher than forecast in the state budget. During that period the price of Iranian oil averaged $17 a barrel. He predicted total oil revenues of $16,000m. in 1995/96. According to the head of the Majlis' plan and budget committee, $1,230m. in hard currency was to be spent on developing the oil and gas industry in 1995/96. During 1996 the price of Iranian oil averaged nearly $19 a barrel. The hydrocarbons sector accounted for 15.5% of GDP in 1996/97 (against 18.9% in 1994/95). Crude oil production averaged about 3.6m. b/d in 1996/97, during which a modest increase in domestic consumption, combined with a decline in exports of refined products, served to maintain crude oil exports at an annual average level of 2.44m. b/d. The average price of exported Iranian crude oil in 1996/97 was approximately $20 (some $4 higher than the average over the previous three years), yielding a 27% increase in oil export earnings, reaching $19,300m.

The executive order issued by US President Clinton in early May 1995, imposing a near total economic embargo against Iran, affected primarily the oil industry. US oil companies and their foreign subsidiaries were banned from buying Iranian oil. US companies have been prohibited from importing Iranian oil into the USA since the late 1980s, but in 1994 they purchased 610,000 b/d for third countries, worth an estimated $3,000m.–$4,000m., nearly one-quarter of the total value of Iran's exports of crude. Japanese companies purchased 440,000 b/d in 1994, 17% of total production. US companies were allowed one month to terminate their business affairs in Iran, and it was reported that most US oil companies had ended their activities by 6 June 1995. There was little disruption to the country's oil exports, however, and NIOC increased the volumes of crude purchased by Asian and European companies. Average crude oil exports increased to 2.56m. b/d in 1996 compared with

2.51m. in 1995. Oil purchases by Asian companies grew from 791,000 b/d in 1995 to 1m. b/d in 1996, while liftings by European companies grew from 380,000 b/d to 495,000 b/d. Since the departure of US companies, Japanese oil companies have become the largest overseas purchasers of Iranian crude.

In November 1994 Iran took a 5% share in an international consortium formed to develop three oilfields in the Republic of Azerbaijan. The consortium is led by British Petroleum and includes Norwegian, US, Saudi Arabian, Turkish and Russian companies. Iran was brought into the $7,000m.-scheme by the Azeri state oil company, which was unable to contribute its portion of the financing and agreed to give Iran a quarter of its 20% share in return for some $350m. to help Azerbaijan finance energy projects. Iran has encouraged states in the Caspian Sea basin to export their oil through its territory and in September the consortium had indicated that it hoped to use Iranian facilities to export some of its initial output from the offshore oilfields in the Caspian Sea. Iran offered to help the consortium export up to 260,000 b/d of Azeri oil through oil-swap deals. Azeri oil would be delivered to Iran for use in its northern refineries and an equivalent amount of Iranian crude would be delivered to the consortium's customers from the Gulf. Iran also sought to promote the use of an Iranian route for an export pipeline, connecting, eventually, with a Turkish terminal on the Mediterranean coast. However, the Azeri decision to bring Iran into the consortium was strongly opposed by the USA and in March 1995 the consortium vetoed Iranian participation. In April it was disclosed that, under US pressure, Azerbaijan had withdrawn its offer to Iran, whose 5% share had been transferred to the Exxon Corpn of the USA. In response, Iran questioned the legality of the consortium agreement. For some years Iran has been discussing a treaty with Russia, Azerbaijan, Kazakhstan and Turkmenistan that would make any development of energy resources in the Caspian Sea basin subject to approval from other member states. In May the President of Azerbaijan stated that he wished to avoid any further deterioration in relations with Iran and that the construction of an export pipeline through Turkey, via Iran, had not been ruled out. When imposing an oil and trade embargo on Iran in early May, US President Clinton exempted from the embargo US companies wishing to conclude swap deals of the kind described above with Iran, in order to supply crude oil from their operations in Azerbaijan, Kazakhstan and Turkmenistan to outside markets. However, Iran warned that it might reject such deals involving US companies in Azerbaijan unless the USA abandoned its opposition to Iranian participation in the consortium developing the Azeri oilfields. Iranian officials stated that it was unfair of the consortium to reject Iran's participation and, at the same time, expect Iranian help in exporting Azeri oil. An official at the Ministry of Oil was reported to have stated that Iran still considered its agreement with Azerbaijan to be valid and argued that the consortium was dependent on Iran to export its oil, the first shipments of which were due in 1995. Alternative export routes through Georgia, Armenia and Russia present serious political and economic problems. Nevertheless, in June the chairman of US McDermott International stated that the consortium was not considering proposals for pipelines through Iran, but that agreement was close to build two pipelines, one through Russia and the other through Georgia. In January 1996 it was reported that the National Iranian Drilling Co and SOCAR, the Azeri state oil company, had agreed in principle to establish a joint-venture drilling company to explore for oil in the Iranian sector of the Caspian Sea. In May 1996 Oil Industries Engineering & Construction, partly owned by NIOC, agreed to take a 10% stake in Azerbaijan's Shakh-Deniz oilfield in the Caspian Sea, which is being developed by a consortium comprising SOCAR, British Petroleum, Statoil of Norway and TPAO of Turkey. The field is estimated to contain some 1,800m. barrels of oil, light oil condensates and gas, and the total cost of development is estimated at about $4,000m. Azerbaijan was reported to have offered Iran a share in the Shakh-Deniz field after withdrawing its earlier offer of a share in Azerbaijan International Operating Consortium (see above). After some seven months of negotiations, Iran and Kazakhstan signed an oil swap agreement in May 1996. The agreement was regarded as a breakthrough for Iran's economic and political ambitions in the Central Asian region. Swap deals with Iran involving US

oil companies operating in the area of the former USSR were exempted from the US trade and investment embargo imposed on Iran in June 1995. However the agreement with Kazakhstan was not implemented until January 1997, partly because both countries wished to circumvent possible difficulties caused by US sanctions. The contract lasts ten years with average deliveries scheduled to rise from 40,000 b/d during the first two years to 120,000 b/d by the sixth year. Crude from Kazakhstan's Tengiz oil field will be delivered to the Iranian port of Neka on the Caspian Sea and an equivalent amount of Iranian crude will be lifted at Iran's Gulf terminal at Kharg Island. The Kazakh crude involved in the swap deal will come from supplies owned by the Kazakh Government and not from the US companies Mobil and Chevron which are partners in the development of the Tengiz oilfield. The first deliveries of Kazakh crude to northern Iran took place in January 1997 but problems arose because of the oil's inferior quality and it was not until May that the first lifting of Iranian crude from the Gulf began. In December 1996 Iran and Russia announced that they had formed a joint company to explore for oil under the Caspian Sea. In May 1997 it was reported that Oil Industries Engineering and Construction had obtained a 10% stake in the Lenkoran-Talyush Deniz offshore oilfield in Azerbaijan being developed by Elf-Aquitaine and Total of France, Deminex of Germany, Agip of Italy and SOCAR, the Azeri state oil company.

The loss of the Abadan refinery, destroyed in the early stages of the war with Iraq, with a production capacity which had reached 628,000 b/d, affected the already difficult situation in Iran for oil products. Iran has traditionally imported some refined products, such as kerosene in winter, and has had shortages in the middle distillates range (diesel oil, kerosene and heating oil). The loss of Abadan denied Iran the flexibility of changing product volumes to meet market or seasonal variations of demand. Abadan was a highly sophisticated and flexible refinery, capable of substantial product conversion. It was also one of the main sources of aviation fuel and gasoline. With the Abadan refinery destroyed, Iran's refining capacity stood at 555,000 b/d in 1980; this had risen to 574,000 b/d by mid-1985, produced at Isfahan (200,000 b/d), Teheran (254,000 b/d), Tabriz (80,000 b/d) and Shiraz (40,000 b/d). However, Iran succeeded in raising its refinery output to levels far above rated capacity. Refinery output was 642,000 b/d in 1983/84 and 685,310 b/d in 1984/85, and at the end of 1985 it was reported that the refineries were operating at 31% above design capacity, giving a total output of 728,000 b/d. The refineries at Isfahan (its capacity increased to 380,000 b/d by 1986) and Shiraz were said to be producing at 50% and 35% above their respective capacities. However, Iraqi air attacks were believed to have reduced capacity to about 500,000 b/d by 1988, resulting in the re-imposition of petrol rationing and the need to import some petroleum products. Further attacks in 1988 resulted in damage to the Isfahan, Shiraz and Tabriz refineries.

Following the cease-fire, the Government started to rebuild its oil facilities. The Abadan oil refinery is symbolic of this reconstruction, and the first phase was completed in April 1989, allowing production of 130,000 b/d. The second phase was completed in April 1991, bringing the plant's capacity to 250,000 b/d. In early 1996 the refinery was reported to be operating at 300,000 b/d, about one-half of its pre-war capacity. In March 1996 the refinery began producing jet fuel, with a daily output of 1.33m. litres, saving Iran an estimated $200,000 a day in hard currency previously spent on imports. The reconstruction of the Abadan refinery brought the total output of domestic refineries to about 800,000 b/d.

In April 1993 President Rafsanjani stated that imports of petroleum products amounting to 300,000 b/d were a wasteful expenditure, costing up to $1,800m. a year. He predicted that the newly installed refinery capacity would allow the country to stop importing refined products by early 1994. The Minister of Oil told a press conference held in April 1993 that Iran's refining capacity would reach 1,285m. b/d in early 1994, and could be raised to 1.6m. b/d in emergencies. He stated that 1993 was the last year that refined products would have to be imported. In May 1995, however, the Ministry of Oil projected that oil product imports would amount to 70,000 b/d during 1995/96 and that they had been as high as 100,000 b/d during the winter months.

In September 1989 it was announced that the reconstruction of the Tabriz and Isfahan oil refineries was complete and that they were supplying almost 50% of Iran's domestic oil requirements. Expansion work at the Teheran and Kermanshah refineries was also reported to have begun. Bids for a continuous catalytic reforming unit for the Teheran refinery commenced in April 1992. In September 1994 a new furnace was commissioned at the Shiraz oil refinery which, together with other work, raised capacity there from 45,000 b/d to 55,000 b/d. In early 1995 it was reported that the Tabriz and Teheran refineries together could process more than 300,000 b/d and the Isfahan refinery 300,000 b/d. The construction of new refineries at Bandar Abbas, Bandar Taheri and Arak, and the expansion of the Isfahan refinery, were designated priority projects by the NIOC, but the programme has experienced considerable delays. The contract for the 150,000 b/d-Arak refinery was awarded to an Italian-Japanese consortium in May 1989. The $1,100m.-refinery was inaugurated by President Rafsanjani in September 1993, and in April 1994 it was reported to be producing 165,000 b/d, 10% more than its nominal capacity. Construction of the export refinery at Bandar Abbas should have been completed in 1993, but financial problems delayed work on the project. The contract had originally been awarded to Snamprogetti of Italy and Chiyoda Corpn of Japan, but when the partnership had financing problems the NIOC handed over the project to local contractors working under the supervision of Snamprogetti and Chiyoda. Three-quarters of the work on the $1,600m.-refinery had been completed by January 1996, according to the project director, but the plant was not due to become operational until mid-1997. It will have a crude refining capacity of 232,000 b/d and will process 12,000 b/d of condensates from the nearby Sarkhun fields. In March 1994 the Director-General of the National Iranian Tanker Co announced that six 80,000-ton tankers would be purchased in order to supply the Bandar Abbas refinery. A $10m.-jetty, near Bandar Abbas port, for handling tankers bringing crude oil from the Kharg Island terminal to the Bandar Abbas refinery, was due to open in March 1996. The Bandar Abbas refinery received its first cargo of crude oil in May 1997 and was officially opened on 26 July 1997. In March 1995 the Minister of Oil stated that Iran plans to increase refinery capacity from 1.1m. b/d to 1.7m. b/d by 2000. In October 1996 the oil ministry announced that the country's current refinery capacity had reached 1.24m. b/d: Abadan (400,000 b/d), Isfahan (265,000 b/d), Teheran (225,000 b/d), Arak (150,000 b/d), Tabriz (112,000 b/d), Shiraz (40,000 b/d), Kermanshah (30,000 b/d), Lavan (20,000 b/d). A new condensate refinery was planned at Bandar Taheri, but in 1994 it was decided to locate the facility at the port of Asaluyeh. However, in April 1995 the Ministry of Oil announced that the project had been cancelled and that the facility would instead become part of the Bandar Abbas refinery now under construction and would be built by local contractors to reduce the cost of the scheme. In early 1994 several international companies had expressed interest in bidding for the work. The refinery will still be supplied with condensates from the Nar-Kangan gasfields, as originally planned, and will start production in mid-1998. In June 1995 it was reported that the Daewoo Corpn of South Korea was to build five 300,000-dwt oil tankers for the National Iranian Tanker Co, to be delivered in 1996. A $490m.-loan had been arranged from a banking consortium led by South Korean institutions. With the increase in domestic refinery capacity, petrol rationing was ended in February 1991. Three years after the end of the war with Iraq the NIOC's inability to meet growing domestic demand for petroleum products provoked strong criticism. Iran continues to experience fuel shortages during the winter months of most years because of insufficient refinery capacity and transportation problems. In January 1994 the Minister of Oil stated that there was a stockpile of some 1,700m. litres of fuel so that no serious shortages were envisaged that year. It was also reported that Iran expected to resume oil supplies to the Sasolburg refinery in South Africa, in which the NIOC has had a 17.5% share since 1970. Until 1979, when oil supplies were suspended, Iran was supplying 70% of the refinery's crude oil under a 20 year-agreement. The NIOC has retained its shareholding despite the suspension in oil supplies. Negotiations between Iran and South Africa began early in 1994 for South African refineries to resume purchases of Iranian crude after the multi-racial elections in

April. Iran was South Africa's major supplier of crude until 1979. In early January 1995 it was reported that the NIOC was negotiating to lease part of the 45m. barrels of crude oil storage space at Saldanha Bay near Cape Town to improve its access to African and possibly transatlantic markets. In September 1994 NIOC stated that purchases of Iranian crude by South Africa had risen to 180,000 b/d. During a visit to Teheran in April 1996, South Africa's Minister of Foreign Affairs, stated that the agreement negotiated in 1995 for storage facilities for Iranian crude at Saldanha Bay (see above) was pending resolution of technical problems unrelated to politics. He reaffirmed that, in spite of US pressure, South Africa would continue to co-operate with Iran in oil, gas and mining. Since the end of apartheid, Iran has supplied almost three-quarters of South Africa's crude oil imports. When President Rafsanjani visited South Africa in September 1996 he advocated greater co-operation between the two countries' oil industries but indicated that Iran would not be making use of the Saldanha Bay facility immediately because it had insufficient supplies of crude petroleum available.

The country's internal pipeline network currently handles 1.2m. b/d of crude and oil products for domestic use. A 14-in pipeline is being constructed between the Teheran refinery and Tabriz and another line is to be built from the new Bandar Abbas refinery to cities such as Rafsanjan, Kerman and Yazd. In early 1988 the Government revived the Moharram pipeline project, which had been abandoned in mid-1986. However, only one of two planned 320-km export pipelines, running from the Gurreh pumping station on the mainland, just north of the main Kharg Island export terminal, to export facilities at Taheri, near the central Gulf, was to be built. The project was intended to provide a safer alternative to the Kharg terminal. The pipeline was expected to have a capacity of 600,000 b/d, just over one-third of Iran's total exports (1.7m. b/d), as stipulated by OPEC. Tank farms and single-buoy moorings off the coast, as terminals for tankers, are being built at Taheri. Plans have also been approved to extend the line a further 700 km to Jask, outside the Gulf, construction of which would take about two years. Since the disintegration of the Soviet Union, Iran has been keen to promote itself as the best route for the export of oil from the newly-independent Central Asian republics (see above). In early December 1994 the NIOC announced that it had started transferring the first shipment of 3,600 tons of crude oil from Kazakhstan to the Gulf for export as part of an agreement to help Kazakhstan export a total of 200,000 tons. However, in June 1995 the international consortium developing the Azeri oilfields indicated that it did not propose to export its oil through Iran, but was near to an agreement to build pipelines through Georgia and Russia. In April 1997 Kazakhstan signed an agreement with Russia and several foreign companies to build a pipeline from Kazakhstan's Tengiz oilfield to the Russian port of Novorossiisk on the Black Sea, bypassing Iran. Nevertheless, European oil companies continued to evince interest in Central Asian hydrocarbons being exported via pipelines through Iran, on the basis that such connections might be less expensive and more secure than those through former Soviet republics. In late 1997 Royal Dutch Shell was engaged in negotiations with Iran and Turkmenistan on the construction of a 3,200-km pipeline for the export of Turkmen gas via Iran.

NATURAL GAS

With proven reserves of 21,000,000m. cu m, Iran is the world's second richest country in gas resources after Russia, with 12.6% of the global total and 15% of the Middle East regional total. According to a statement by the Minister of Oil in February 1994, 3,200,000m. barrels of gas, worth $200,000m, were discovered during the term of the Five-Year Plan ending in March 1994. In August 1988 it was announced that a large reservoir of natural gas had been discovered near Asaluyeh on the Gulf coast, 70 km south-east of Kangan. The NIOC has announced a $1,000m.-scheme to develop the Aghar Dalan fields, 120 km north-east of Kangan, and plans have been announced to construct a gas refinery there at a cost of $900m. Gas discoveries have also been made in the Caspian Sea area. The first phase of the $1,000m.-Nar-Kangan gas treatment plant, 260 km east of Bushehr, began operating in June 1989. It will produce 34m. cu m per day, and the second phase, which began production in

May 1990, was expected to increase output to 80m. cu m per day by exploiting the nearby Kangan field, whose reserves are estimated at 820,000m. cu. m. Gas from the Nar-Kangan field will be piped north to Teheran via the IGAT-2 trunkline. Plans to quadruple gas-refining capacity, and to lay 3,000 km of gas pipeline by 1994, were announced in order to reduce consumption of petroleum products and make more crude petroleum available for export. It was planned to raise gas-refining capacity from just over 10,000m. cu m in 1990 to 46,000m. cu m by 1994 and, eventually, to 80,000m. cu m. In March 1995 the Minister of Oil stated that annual natural gas production was projected to increase from 56,000m. cu m to 82,000m. cu m by 2000. In March 1996 President Rafsanjani opened the Sarkhun-2 gas refinery near Bandar Abbas, built by the National Iranian Gas Co and local contractors. The refinery was reported to be treating about 11m. cu m per a day of natural gas from the Sarkhun field and the plant will eventually process about 14m. cu m per day. The processed gas will supply the Bandar Abbas power station, the new steel plant at Hormuzgan, a power plant at Sarcheshmeh and also residential and industrial users. In early May 1996 the first phase of the Aghar Dalan gas treatment plant was opened. The plant will produce 17m. cu m per day, eventually rising to 40m. cu m per day. The gas is carried by a 330-km pipeline to the Marun oilfield, where it is used to maintain sustainable output at 600,000 b/d. According to the Ministry of Oil, the project will permit the recovery of an extra, 3,000m. barrels of crude from the field, valued at $50,000m.

The main gas pipeline projects concern the extension of the IGAT-2 trunkline from Nar-Kangan to Teheran and the west; the extension of the third trunkline from Khangiran to the west along the Caspian coast; and the laying of a pipeline from Sarkhun northwards to Rafsanjan.

In 1980 Iran suspended daily deliveries of some 30m. cu m of natural gas to the USSR, from the Nar and Kangan fields, via the IGAT-1 gas trunkline, which had been carrying natural gas from the southern oilfields to northern Iran and the USSR, a total distance of 1,130 km. In 1983 Iran's Ministry of Oil announced that it was no longer interested in gas export projects, in spite of the country's huge resources, and indicated that the gas industry would seek to satisfy the rapidly growing energy requirements of the industrial, commercial and residential markets within Iran. In August 1986 the Ministry announced that gas exports to the USSR would resume before the end of the year but, in November, the date for their resumption was postponed to mid-1987. Plans to convert IGAT-1 to carry 700,000 b/d of oil appear also to have been abandoned, and the pipeline is used to satisfy domestic demand only. Only the southern section of the 56-in diameter IGAT-2 natural gas pipeline, which was started before the Revolution, also to supply gas to the USSR, has been completed, and extends only as far as Isfahan. The 632-km pipeline from Kangan to Isfahan, costing $200m., was completed at the end of 1985 by the Italian contractors Saipem, who have also been involved in the construction of a $1,000m.-gas-gathering complex at Kangan and the smaller neighbouring gasfield of Nar (with combined reserves of 720,000m. cu m), which will supply IGAT-2. In November 1989 an agreement was concluded to resume natural gas exports to the USSR, and the first supplies were piped in April 1990. Some 3,000m. cu m per year were to be supplied via the IGAT-1 trunkline, rising eventually to the pre-Revolution level of 10,000m. cu m. The agreement also permitted Iranian gas to be exported to eastern Europe via the Soviet pipeline system. Revenues from these exports, estimated at about $300m. annually, were to be used to pay for nine Soviet-assisted projects in the Iranian power, gas, mining and metallurgy sectors. In October 1990 a further agreement was reached with the USSR to export natural gas to eastern Europe, starting in 1991. Under the scheme, the capacity of IGAT-1 was to be increased and the possible completion of the IGAT-2 trunkline was also envisaged. In return for the supply of Iranian gas to the southern Soviet republics, the USSR was to deliver an equivalent quantity of gas to eastern European countries, using its own pipeline system. In October 1991 the Minister of Oil stated that exports of gas would be restricted to the USSR, which was purchasing some $200m.-worth annually; and that gas exports would not become a significant source of foreign currency until the second half of the 1990s. He announced that by 2000 Iran expected to be

exporting some 50,000m. cu m of gas annually if pipeline projects currently envisaged were realized. More than half of the exports would be to Europe and the remainder to Pakistan. Exports of liquefied natural gas (LNG) have been resumed and reports suggest that some 400,000 tons were exported in 1991/92. Since the disintegration of the USSR, Iran has established economic agreements with the newly-independent former Soviet republics. In February 1992 the Iranian Minister of Oil announced details of an agreement, signed in January, to supply gas to the Ukraine via Azerbaijan. Some 3,000m. cu m of gas were to be supplied during 1992 through the existing IGAT-1 pipeline. Over the four years covered by the agreement gas exports are to total 75,000m. cu m. It is planned to construct three new gas pipelines by 1996. In February 1993 Iran and Ukraine agreed to build a gas pipeline from Iran to Ukraine through Azerbaijan and Russia, with a capacity of 25,000m. cu m a year. In March 1993 it was reported that the gas project had failed to gain formal consent from Russia. In November 1992 an agreement was signed with Azerbaijan for Iran to supply 300m. cu m of gas a year in exchange for 100,000 tons of gas-oil. Gas is to be supplied through the IGAT-1 trunkline. Gas-oil from Azerbaijan will supply Iran's northwestern provinces to make up for shortages in domestic distribution. In August 1994 an agreement was announced on the supply of Iranian gas to the Azeri Republic of Nakhichevan and to Georgia. It was reported that the gas exports will be taken from the IGAT-1 trunkline during off-peak months as most of the throughput now supplies Iranian domestic users. Georgia will be supplied with 5m. cu m a day, starting in 1994, using an existing pipeline through the Republic of Azerbaijan; and an 80-km pipeline will be built to Nakhichevan to carry 1m. cu m of gas starting in 1996. Also in August 1994 Iran and Turkmenistan agreed to co-operate in the construction of a gas pipeline to Europe, a project that would take six years to complete and cost an estimated $7,000m. The pipeline would be 4,000 km long, with some 1,450 km passing through Iran. The cost of the Iranian section was estimated at $3,500m., but no details were given about how the scheme would be financed. Iran would earn transit fees for Turkmen gas passing through the pipeline. According to the Ministry of Oil the pipeline would carry up to 15,000m. cu m of gas a year in the first phase, with throughput eventually almost doubling to 28,000m. cu m. The proposed pipeline provoked opposition from the USA, which urged Turkmenistan to seek alternative routes. In September 1995 it was reported that Iran and Turkmenistan had agreed on a $190m.-project to build a gas pipeline across their common border. However, in February 1996 Turkmenistan signed a memorandum of understanding with Turkey for the supply of natural gas which appeared to replace plans for a pipeline via Iran to Europe.

In January 1994 officials of the Iranian Institute for Political and International Studies announced that they had proposed a major gas pipeline loop system around Iran from which spurs could be constructed to India, the Central Asian republics, Turkey and, eventually, Europe through Turkey. They had named it PEACE: 'Pipeline extending from Asian Countries to Europe'. More than half of the loop was already in existence. One of the officials commented that liquefied natural gas schemes were not economical while oil prices remained below $20 a barrel. In spite of the resumption of gas exports, the use of gas is still being encouraged for domestic purposes, in order to save oil and to reduce pollution. More than 13,000 km of gas distribution lines have been built in cities since 1979, but implementation of the residential gas programme has been delayed by a shortage of regulators. The Five-Year Plan which began in March 1995 proposes greater domestic use of gas resources in order to allow more oil to be exported.

In October 1990 NIOC announced a joint study with Gaz de France to assess the cost of transporting natural gas to France and other European countries. In April 1993 it was reported that Ruhrgas of Germany, Austria's ONV and Enagas of Spain would take part in the consortium with Gaz de France. If the plans go ahead central and eastern European countries could be supplied first by pipeline, but for western Europe it remained unclear whether transport by pipeline or ship would be preferred. In November 1993 Iran and India signed a memorandum of understanding regarding a gas pipeline from Bandar Abbas to the Indian state of Gujerat. During a visit to New Delhi in April 1995 by President Rafsanjani, India and Iran agreed on wide-ranging co-operation in the oil and gas sectors, which included the completion, in 1995, of the feasibility study for a 2,200-km gas pipeline from southern Iran to the west coast of India, a project estimated to cost $5,000m. Iran was reported to favour a route through Pakistan, but India preferred an underwater route off the Pakistan coast. The pipeline would have a capacity of 50m. cu m a day and could be commissioned by the turn of the century. In September 1994 Iran agreed to participate in a $3,200m.-project, initiated by the UAE-based Crescent Petroleum Co, to build a 1,600-km pipeline to carry gas from Qatar to Pakistan. Under the agreement Iran will allow the pipeline to go through Iranian coastal waters and has the option of using the line for its own gas exports, but will have no financial involvement. The pipeline is to have a capacity of 45m. cu m a day by 1999 and its capacity could be doubled by increasing the number of compressors in the line. Discussions have been taking place between Iran and Pakistan for some time about a possible overland gas pipeline linking the two countries and in January 1995 it was reported that Iran and Pakistan had reached an agreement to set up a consortium to build a gas pipeline from Bandar Asaluyeh to Karachi. As a number of US companies are involved in the Qatar gas line, the future of Iranian participation may be questioned as a result of the US trade embargo on Iran introduced in May 1995. In February 1996 the National Iranian Gas Co announced that construction work would begin in July on a joint natural gas pipeline with Pakistan, following completion of a feasibility study. The pipeline, which will take four years to construct, will have a capacity of about 45m. cu m per day and will cost $2,000m. Talks were reported to have begun with foreign companies about their participation in the project.

In mid-November 1994 a team from Ente Nazionale Idrocarburi (ENI) of Italy had visited Teheran for talks on participation in gas, pipeline and energy projects in Iran, Central Asia and the Caucasus. ENI stated that it wished to participate in the proposed $7,000m.-gas pipeline project from Turkmenistan to Europe via Iran and Turkey and had discussed Iran's own gas export pipeline scheme to Europe.

In August 1996 Iran signed an agreement worth $20,000m. to supply gas to Turkey over a 22-year period. The contract was worded so that the Turkish state oil company, Botas, would not incur US sanctions for its involvement in the project. Nevertheless several members of the US Congress condemned the accord and demanded sanctions against Botas. US officials visited Ankara but failed to persuade the Turkish Government to withdraw from the project: they insisted that the agreement was a necessary element of their plans to diversify the country's energy sources. The project involves the construction of a 42-in. pipeline, 1,420-km long, from Tabriz in Iran to Erzurum in Turkey. An extension of the Turkish section of the pipeline from Erzurum to the capital, Ankara, is planned at a later stage. Under the original schedule the pipeline was to have been completed by 1999, with initial deliveries of gas rising from 3,000m. cu m/d to 10,000m. cu m/d in 2005. However, after a visit to Turkey by the Iranian Minister of Oil in November 1996 the timetable was revised to allow deliveries to begin a year early. Each country is responsible for financing the section of the pipeline in its own territory. Botas invited tenders for the Turkish section of the pipeline in December and work was due to begin in May 1997. At the end of December 1996 Minister of Oil, Aqazadeh, signed a memorandum of understanding with the Turkish oil minister and the Deputy Prime Minister of Turkmenistan for the delivery of Turkmen gas to Turkey via the Iranian pipeline system after the completion of the Turkish-Iranian gas pipeline. At the end of July 1997 the US Administration announced that it would not oppose the construction of a $1,600m. pipeline to carry natural gas from land-locked Turkmenistan to Turkey across a 788-km stretch of northern Iran because the project did not technically violate the 1996 sanctions law. It was reported that Iran had agreed to finance and build the section of the pipeline passing through its territory. Turkey signed an agreement in May 1997 to purchase Turkmen gas, and US officials maintained that agreement would ensure Turkey's reliance on Turkmen rather than Iranian gas. However an oil industry source stated that under the agreement Turkmen gas

would be pumped into the Iranian pipeline system and that Iran would send an equivalent amount of gas to Turkey.

The First Five-Year Development Plan (introduced in 1989) sought some $3,400m. in foreign funding to be allocated to the development of the Pars and South Pars fields for export to Japan or Europe. In 1992 the NIOC awarded the $17,000m.-contract to develop the gas reserves of the offshore South Pars field to a consortium led by TPL of Italy and including Saipam of Italy, Machinoimport of Russia and Mitsubishi Corpn of Japan. This was the largest offshore gas project awarded since the Revolution. The South Pars field is an extension into Iranian waters of Qatar's North field, the largest gas field in the world. By the end of 1993, when the consortium had completed nearly all the basic engineering and had drilled two wells in the field, the NIOC announced that it was suspending the project because of cash shortages. Payment arrears on Iran's external debt appear to have made foreign banks reluctant to finance the project. In late 1994 the development of the South Pars gas field was awarded to the newly-created NIOC subsidiary, Petroleum Development and Engineering Co (Petco), in an attempt to reduce the hard currency costs of the project. Petco has estimated that the work will cost $900m., of which half will be in hard currency. The contract originally awarded to the consortium led by TPL would have cost Iran $1,700m. Petco and NIOC were considering bids by European and Japanese firms for design and management contracts. In March 1995 the Ministry of Oil announced that a Dutch-German consortium, John Brown Engineers and Constructors and Ingenieurbetrieb Anlagenbau (IAB) Leipzig, had agreed to help finance and develop the South Pars gas field. The consortium's involvement was reported to be for the project's initial phase. It was reported that separate negotiations, which had begun in 1994, were continuing with Royal Dutch Shell on developing the field. In March 1996 Petco reported that first-phase design work on the South Pars field was on schedule and would be completed by the end of 1996. In early 1996, despite US legislation imposing penalties on non-US firms investing in the development of Iran's oil and gas reserves (see above), the Royal Dutch Shell Group was reported to be continuing talks concerning the second phase of the South Pars gas field development scheme. However, in early April 1996 US Senator Alfonse D'Amato, a leading supporter of additional sanctions against Iran, claimed that he had received assurances from JGC Corpn of Japan and Australia's BHP Petroleum that they would not participate in either gas field or gas pipeline projects in Iran. Senator D'Amato had warned both companies that the proposed new sanctions against Iran might be made retroactive. JGC had been among 50 foreign firms that attended a NIOC briefing in November 1995 about an international tender for 10 onshore and offshore energy projects, and had indicated its interest in investing some $380m. in three onshore gas projects known as Amak, NGL 1200 and NGL 1300. In late February 1996 JGC's manager in Teheran told the press that the company was still interested in participating in the three projects and indicated that talks would begin soon. However, in March JGC's Chairman told Senator D'Amato that the company's participation in the projects would not be possible because of lack of finance and the 'current economic and political situation surrounding Iran'. At the beginning of 1997 the first phase of the development of the South Pars field was being implemented by Petco and negotiations had been taking place since mid-1996 between Total and NIOC for the second stage of the project which is expected to cost $850m. Studies also indicated that the South Pars field in Iran could be even bigger than the Qatari section of the field. The first phase of the project is scheduled for completion in September 1997, with a production of 1,000m. cu ft per day of gas together with condensate and sulphur. The project will include a refinery at Assaluyeh, 270 km from Bushehr, together with a terminal connecting with the IGAT 3 gas pipeline. In May 1997 NIOC and Total had allegedly signed an agreement for the second and third phases of the South Pars project worth an estimated $3,500m., although Total insisted that negotiations were still continuing.

In April 1993 preliminary discussions began between the National Iranian Gas Co and a number of foreign companies on the development of the offshore Pars field, often referred to as North Pars, as distinct from South Pars. Plans to develop the field, based on exports of liquefied natural gas, were first discussed in the 1970s, but were abandoned after the Revolution. Under the revised scheme gas would be treated for domestic use only. In January 1994 it was reported that negotiations were under way with Royal Dutch Shell for an agreement on engineering studies for the North Pars field. Shell appeared to be insisting on equity participation in the project, but foreign ownership of national hydrocarbon resources is not permitted under the Iranian constitution. However, in March it was reported that the Majlis had authorized the NIOC to raise up to $3,500m. in foreign finance on a buy-back basis in order to develop oil and gas fields together with two refineries. There was speculation that this decision might lead to a compromise with Shell over financing arrangements for the North Pars field. In November 1994 the Minister of Oil stated that negotiations between the NIOC and Royal Dutch Shell about developing the North Pars gas field were continuing, but that there were differences between the rate of return requested by Shell and that which Iran had agreed to give. The Minister said that Shell was considering exporting gas from the field to Pakistan. Shell officials confirmed that differences over the level of remuneration remained, but that negotiations were continuing because both sides were keen to reach an agreement. In early 1994 the Minister of Oil announced the discovery of a new offshore gas field 50 km west of the South Pars field and 180 km south-east of Bushehr, estimated to contain 566,000m. cu m of gas and 1,000m. barrels of condensate. In February 1995 it was reported that Iran and Oman had agreed on the joint development of the Hengam-Khasib gas field near the Iranian island of Hengam in the Strait of Hormuz. The field has reserves of 28,300m. cu m and could be brought into production within three years according to the NIOC. Negotiations between the two countries were concluded in January 1997 and Iran was expected to tender the development of the field under a 'buyback deal' at a later date.

Production of natural gas increased by 8% in 1996/97 to a level of 64,200,000m. cu m, the bulk of which was consumed domestically in line with the Government's policy of substituting gas for petroleum production for the purposes of home consumption.

OTHER MINERALS

According to the Minister of Mines and Metals, in June 1988 there were 780 producing mines in Iran, employing 73,500 people. Some 870 exploration permits were awarded during 1990/91. Deposits of lead-zinc ore are mined at Bafq near Yazd, at Khomeini, west of Isfahan, and at Ravanj near Qom, with a combined potential of 600 tons of concentrates daily, though current plans for development are limited to Bafq. In June 1992 a German/Canadian consortium won a $250m.-contract to build a zinc plant in Zanjan province. However, the facility was eventually built by local firms and opened in April 1997. The plant has a capacity of 7,000 tons of zinc sheets a year and there are plans to double output. Another zinc plant is to be built at Bafq, with an annual output capacity rising to 24,000 tons. Iran's largest lead mine is at Nakhlak, near Isfahan. Chromium from the Elburz mountains and near Bandar Abbas, red oxide from Hormuz in the Persian Gulf and turquoise from Nishapur are all produced for export. Sulphur and salt are produced on the coast of the Gulf, near Bandar Abbas, and Iran exported 105,000 tons in the year 1985/86 (21 March–20 March). Iran is also the second largest exporter of strontium, after Mexico, and during the second half of 1985/86 and the first half of 1986/87 exported 25,000 tons, valued at $2.9m. Strontium reserves are estimated at 1.1m. tons. In 1986 Iran's phosphate resources were calculated at 220m. tons. Annual imports of phosphate fertilizers total 1m. tons, worth $300m., so a major portion of domestic demand would be met by developing the country's phosphate reserves. In July 1992 it was announced that the country's largest phosphate deposit, with reserves of 400m. tons, had been discovered in Charam in the southern province of Yasuj.

The major iron ore deposits are in Kerman province in southeast Iran, in particular at Bafq, where proven reserves total 911m. tons of ore, and at Chadormelo mine, in Yazd province, which has proven reserves of 500m. tons. In February 1992 it was reported that Bafq was producing 4m. tons a year. In December 1991 a Japanese consortium signed a contract to build an ore concentrator at Chadormelo, with a projected annual production rate of 5m. tons. The concentrator will supply the Mobarakeh steel complex. In late 1991 the Ministry of Mines and Metals invited bids to expand the existing Chogart iron ore complex near Yazd. After lengthy negotiations the $100m.-contract was eventually offered to a European consortium led by Voest Alpine of Austria in October 1994. The consortium will supply two concentrators, each with an annual capacity of 1.6m. tons and will also carry out engineering work, supervision of erection and the commissioning of the facility, which is due to be completed in 33 months. Output at the mine is scheduled to rise from 3m. tons to 6m. tons a year. The ore from Bafq will be carried 540 km by a specially developed railway to the $4,700m. Mobarakeh steel plant at Isfahan. In July 1986 the Government claimed that the mine at Sangan, in Khorassan province, with reserves of 127m. tons, would supply Isfahan with iron ore for the next 200 years. The Gol-e-Gohar iron ore mining complex in Kerman province, originally planned before the Revolution, was officially opened in March 1994 by President Rafsanjani. Production at the $114m.-complex began in December 1993. Output of 2.5m. tons of concentrate will be used to supply the Mobarakeh steel plant at Isfahan. Production will eventually be expanded to 5m. tons per year.

Coal reserves are estimated at 6,000m. tons, of which about one-third are capable of exploitation. The main mines are around Kerman and in Mazandaran, Semnan and Tabas, where output is to be expanded. An 85-km railway is being built from Kerman, the major mining area, to supply coal shale to the Zarand refinery. At the Shahroud mines in Semnan output of 232,000 tons per year was to be increased to a projected 360,000 tons per year by 1989. The mines supply 15% of the requirements of the Isfahan steel mill. In 1987/88 Iran produced 95,706 tons of melted cast iron and 1,471,699 tons of steel. Coal production in 1985 recovered to the pre-Revolutionary level of 900,000 tons per year, but remains insufficient for domestic consumption, and imports of around 400,000 tons per year are required. Production declined to 722,000 tons in 1986, and was 791,000 tons in 1987.

Deposits of copper ore have been found in Azerbaijan, Kerman and in the Yazd and Anarak areas. A number of very important deposits have been discovered since 1967 in the Kerman area, the most important being at Sar Cheshmeh. However, of the 330 copper mines in Iran, with combined reserves of an estimated 1,600m. tons, only those at Sar Cheshmeh and Birjand are currently being exploited. The reserves at Sar Cheshmeh are estimated at 1,200m. tons (the second largest deposit in the world), including perhaps 600m. tons of 1.12% copper content, with another 600m. tons of lower grade beneath. The giant project includes the construction of road and rail links to connect the mine with Bandar Abbas 400 km away on the Gulf, a training school, and a new town for the families of the 3,000-man work-force. The construction of a large smelter/refinery and associated rolling mill and two continuous casting mills was halted during the Revolution. The mine was officially opened in May 1982. Initially the plant operated at substantially below its capacity of 158,000 tons of refined copper per year but, since production began in mid-1984, output has risen to 40,000 tons in 1985/86, and to 50,000 tons in 1986/87. Following the opening of new units in February 1989, output rose to 100,000 tons a year by mid-1992. Techpro Mining and Metallurgy of the United Kingdom has been appointed as general consultant by the National Iranian Copper Industries Co to advise on expanding production at Sar Cheshmeh. By 1994 Sar Cheshmeh had a capacity of 120,000 tons a year and there were plans eventually to expand it to 200,000 tons. A molybdenum production unit started operating at the Sar Cheshmeh copper refinery in June 1983. A copper extrusion plant was installed at the Shahid Bahonar copper complex, in Kerman, in 1987. Output of copper and copper alloy semi-finished products—tube, sheet, bar and rods from the plant, which opened in 1989, has risen from less than 10,000 tons a year to 18,000 tons a year. The plant is expected to reach full capacity of 55,000 tons in 1996. One-third of the output is exported, mainly to Japan and other countries in the Far East, earning some $10m. a year. There are plans to export half of the plant's production in the future. In 1986/87 28,000 tons of copper and molybdenum from Sar Cheshmeh were exported in the form of copper wire and molybdenite, and a further 6,000 tons of blister copper. A much smaller copper mine at Minakhan, developed in association with Japanese interests, has been brought under complete Iranian ownership. In September 1994 work began on a $106m.-copper smelter at Khatounabad, about 40 km west of the main Sar Cheshmeh mine and complex. The smelter, which will have a capacity of 80,000 tons, will use ore from the undeveloped Meidouk mines nearby, and ore from Sungun in East Azerbaijan and Ahar mines will also be used. Output will supply the Sar Cheshmeh complex and nearby downstream facilities. The project is a joint venture between the National Copper Industries Co and National Non-Ferrous Metals Co of China. Originally it had been projected to cost $300m., but in order to save hard currency about 40% of the work will be done with domestic resources. According to the Minister of Mines and Metals, national copper production increased from 74,000 tons to 100,000 tons in the Iranian year ending 21 March 1995. In 1996 the managing director of the state copper company (NICICO) projected that copper production in 1996/97 would reach 150,000 tons, with capacity increasing to 250,000 tons within a few years. Some 30,000 tons of copper would be exported in 1996/97. To augment production capacity NICICO purchased an 80,000 tons-a-year smelter from the People's Republic of China which is expected to start production by 2000. Some parts of NICICO's operations have already been privatized and the company was preparing to be floated on the Teheran stock market during 1997.

In March 1976 it was announced that important uranium deposits had been found in Iran's northern and western regions, and in 1978 agreements were signed with West German and French companies to carry out surveys. The scope and pace of exploration were reduced after the Revolution, but deposits of more than 5,000 tons of uranium ore were discovered in the Saghand region of Yazd in central Iran in 1984 and there were plans to develop the site. Long-term plans, proposed during the reign of the Shah, for a network of 20 nuclear power stations were abandoned because the project was too expensive, too dependent on Western technology and unnecessary in view of the availability of cheap natural gas.

In mid-1988 construction work began on a gold-processing plant at Muteh, near Isfahan. The plant, Iran's second, was scheduled to start producing in 1991, using ore from an estimated 1.2m.-ton deposit, which, it is hoped, will yield 5 tons of gold.

Two rich mineral deposits were discovered in the northern provinces of Gilan and Mazandaran in the first half of 1985: one consisted of an estimated 51,000 tons of mica and the other of 20m. tons of silica. Further discoveries of reserves of silica, limestone, granite and iron, totalling an estimated 194m. tons, were made in Gilan during the last quarter of 1985. Proven reserves of bauxite at Jafarm are estimated at 22m. tons, with an average purity of 48%, and annual production of 280,000 tons of alumina is planned to commence in 1994. In November 1994 a memorandum of understanding was signed with the Czech Republic in order to settle outstanding debts and to allow Czech companies to build a $200m.-alumina plant in Khorassan province. In June 1995 President Rafsanjani inaugurated work on a 20,000 ton-per-year pilot alumina extraction plant being constructed at Azarshahr, in eastern Ajerbaijan province. The plant is due to be completed in two years and will extract alumina from the nepheline-syenite mines of Kolebar and Sarab which have estimated deposits of 30,000m. tons.

Iran's exports of non-hydrocarbon minerals in 1985/86, mainly copper, coal, chromite and metal concentrates, were valued at $70m., and the total was increased to $85m. in 1986/87, when, of the 50m. tons of minerals extracted, 230,000 tons were exported. Mineral exports reached 486,413 tons in 1987/88, worth $90.2m., although total mineral extraction from Iran's 780 active mines declined to 45m. tons. During the five years to March 1993 it was planned to spend some $5,000m. in order to increase the mining sector's share of GDP from 1% to 5%. This represented the fulfilment of one of the Iranian Government's stated aims: the development of the country's non-hydrocarbon raw materials to supply the demands of the country's expanding metal manufacturing facilities. In April 1994 Hossein Mahloodji, the Minister of Mines and Metals, announced that exports of metal concentrates and minerals had earned $1,400m. during the three years to March 1994. At the beginning of 1995 the Minister of Mines and Metals stated that more than 1,000 mines had been privatized in recent years and that the ministry retained control over only three to four big mines which required heavy investment. The non-oil mining sector's share of GDP remained consistently at 0.5% during 1992–97. The value of exports of minerals and metals increased by nearly 50% by 1997/98, to $374m., and was projected to rise to $460m. in 1998/99.

INDUSTRY

After the Revolution, no clear policy was formulated for the industrial sector. Of the modern manufacturing plants that were established under the Shah's regime, those which remained in production (estimated at only 20% of the total by value of output) have encountered serious difficulties. Raw materials have been in short supply, as have spare parts and other inputs. In March 1981 the then President, Bani-Sadr, estimated that in the period March 1979–March 1980 industrial and related output declined by 34% and was still falling, possibly at an even faster rate. In 1982 some reports indicated that increased reserves of foreign exchange and larger imports of raw materials had allowed production in many factories to be expanded. They also noted that factories producing goods for the war effort were working overtime, with Iranian engineers and technicians learning to repair, adapt and make items that had formerly been imported. Nevertheless, officials admitted that only a small number of factories were properly operational. Many factories were operating at only 30% capacity in the late 1980s, although considerable improvement has been reported in state-owned industrial producers since 1990.

Official thinking about the future of this sector appears confused. The stated policies of the new revolutionary Government favoured small-scale, traditional or bazaar-related enterprises. It is estimated that private industry is responsible for 20%–30% of Iran's industrial output. Yet, in sharp contrast, financial allocations to industry have tended to follow the pattern which was formulated by the previous regime. In late 1982 Khomeini lectured ministers and post-revolutionary technocrats on their preoccupation with modern industry.

Reports on industrial production have provided confusing conclusions. The National Iranian Industries Organization (NIIO) claimed that output rose by 23% during 1983/84. Other sources indicate that 1985/86 was a poor year for industry. Investment declined in most sectors because of limited access to credits and to imported raw materials and capital goods. In May 1985 the Majlis approved legislation granting permanent status to the Ministry of Heavy Industry. The Ministry was to take over all aspects of heavy industry (formerly the responsibility of the Ministry of Industry), including iron and steel, foundry, engine, motor vehicle, machine-building and general engine plants. In September 1994 the Majlis approved legislation merging the Ministry of Heavy Industries with the Ministry of Industry, but rejected a proposal to include the Ministry of Metals and Minerals in the merger on the grounds that a special ministry was necessary to develop minerals as a major export item. The plan to merge the three ministries had been proposed in the Majlis three years previously, but was opposed by the Government.

After the end of the war with Iraq the 1989–94 Five-Year Plan placed emphasis on the development of heavy industry and this sector was given priority access to reserves of foreign exchange. In spite of debate about the privatization of Iranian industry, until 1991 almost all industrial projects were state-sponsored. However, in February 1991 the Minister of Economic Affairs and Finance announced that 400 state-controlled light industrial companies would be sold during the next three years as part of the Government's plans for privatization. It was also announced that heavy industry, previously monopolized by the state, would be opened to private investment. In May 1991 the Minister of Industries announced that the NIIO was to offer shares to the value of IR100,000m. in its companies for acquisition by the public during 1991–92. In April the Ministry of Oil invited the private sector to invest in petrochemical projects and gave an assurance that other sectors of the oil industry would be made accessible to private investors. In addition, foreign companies are now able to invest in heavy industries. On 5 May 1992 the Supreme Council for Investment approved new regulations which removed the 49% share ceiling held by foreign partners in joint ventures, removed nearly all restrictions on the repatriation of profits and provided guarantees against nationalization. There was speculation that the Government would face criticism—on purely political grounds—for opening the door to foreign capital even though the Constitution does not forbid foreign investment or ownership. In July 1992 it was reported that the International Finance Corporation (IFC) was entering the private-sector market in Iran with possible equity participation or finance for two large industrial projects. The IFC's involvement followed the return to Iran of the World Bank. Privatization of state industries appears to have made only slow progress. In March 1994 Massoud Roghani Zanjani of the Plan and Budget Organization stated that privatization through the Teheran stock exchange had not proved satisfactory. The Government planned to sell factories by auction or negotiation in order to speed up the privatization process. In August 1993 shares were offered on the Teheran stock exchange in Iran Khodrow, the country's largest car assembly plant. The plant was nationalized after the Revolution. Some 33% of the shares were reserved for workers, with employees at the plant offered preferential terms. Despite legal changes introduced in the 1990s allowing foreign shareholdings, only a few joint ventures with foreign investors have been agreed. One example is that between Elin Anwendung of Austria and the local company, Joyain, who propose to build a $63m.-plant at Sabezevar to make electromotors and generators. Financial arrangements were expected to be completed in 1994. Another joint venture is the al-Mahdi Aluminium Company's smelter at Bandar Abbas, the first phase of which opened in June 1997. The company is a joint venture between the International Development Corporation of Dubai and local state firms, Iran Copper, Miduk Copper and Mineral Exports. There are plans to expand production capacity to 330,000 tons a year. In 1994 Nestlé of Switzerland agreed to set up a 50-50 joint venture with the local Mimas to build a $47m.-baby food factory near Teheran.

Privatization plans received a set-back in mid-1994 when the Majlis passed legislation which gave selected groups, such as former prisoners of war, the war disabled, the families of those killed in the Iran–Iraq War and members of the paramilitary *bassij*, privileged access to shares. The priority goal of the privatization process is to achieve a more equitable distribution of wealth and the new legislation requires proceeds from share sales to be devoted to the country's underdeveloped regions. The aims conflict with those of the Industrial Development and Renovation Organization (IDRO) and the NIIO, the two state organizations involved in the privatization programme, which hoped to use the sales to raise revenues, to develop the capital market and to raise the standard of industrial management. IDRO officials admitted that the new legislation had made privatization more difficult and had slowed down the process. However, they expressed the hope that the involvement of new, less affluent groups of shareholders would inject new vigour into the privatization process. In the three years to March 1994, out of a total of 130 companies scheduled for privatization, IDRO had sold 50 factories through the Teheran stock exchange and in bilateral deals, raising IR240,000m. ($140m.). Of the 80 remaining companies, which have an aggregate turnover of $1,000m., 10 car makers account for over one-half of the annual turnover. The IDRO expects that they will be difficult to sell because of their large size. By mid-1997 the privatization process had resumed and more than 200 companies were quoted on the Teheran stock exchange. In early 1995 the Minister of Industries forecast that only 10% of Iranian industry would be state-owned by 2000, compared with 45% in 1990. Only very large industries would ultimately remain under state control. Early in 1997 it was reported that the Government was still committed to the sale of 57% of all IDRO's assets by 2000. The privatization programme had been relatively slow between 1992 and 1996 raising only $200m., but sales rose sharply in 1996/97 when IDRO raised an estimated $260m. State-owned vehicle companies, which have undergone considerable restructuring, are likely to be targeted for privatization in 1997/98 when IDRO hopes to raise $260m. from sales of its assets. Nevertheless it will be many years before Iranian industry shifts from predominantly state to largely private ownership. More than one-half

of the country's annual budget expenditure is devoted to supporting loss-making state industries and banks.

The Government's aim of restructuring ailing industries has also encountered difficulties. Much of the restructuring has been imposed by the phased currency devaluation which began in 1991, and more recent cuts in state subsidies. In early 1995 the Minister of Industries declared that his ministry was now letting market forces operate to bring about economic restructuring. He claimed that state subsidies were only applied in parts of the food manufacturing sector, to paper manufacture, to medicines and to some washing powders. He maintained that even the food and pharmaceuticals industries could survive without subsidies, but the Government retained them for social reasons. He stated that only food industries would be subsidized by 2000.

Both the Ministry of Industries and the Ministry of Mines and Metals have emphasized the need to encourage training in modern management and the establishment of research and development departments. Co-operation is also being encouraged between industry and the country's universities. The Minister of Industries has claimed that Iran can design in many fields and has an inward engineering capability. In addition to the private companies that have grown up around the Isfahan Steel complex (see below), innovation has been notable in the car industry. An affiliate of IDRO, Sazeh Gostar Co, has redesigned, and re-engineered the Renault 5 car, which used to be assembled from imported kits, and the first completely Iranian-made model is expected to be manufactured by early 1996 and on sale at half the price of its nearest equivalent. Some predict a transformation of the Iranian car industry in the coming years as more local design, engineering and manufacture develops. The country's own design and engineering capacity is being utilized increasingly through the greater involvement of local contractors in building industrial plants, reducing costs and leading to savings in hard currency.

Plans to attract foreign investment in Iranian industry have met with little success. The Majlis is being asked to make certain amendments to existing legislation, especially the lifting of the 49% ceiling on foreign shareholding. The Majlis was not expected to complete its debate on this issue until late 1995. The head of the Majlis plan and budget committee, Dori Najafabadi, stated in early 1995 that he did not expect any problem with the amendments proposed and saw no opposition on ideological grounds to wholly-owned foreign companies operating in Iran. However, the Minister of Industries predicted that foreign involvement above 49% would probably be restricted to high technology industries.

It has been suggested that average industrial output may have risen to 60% in 1994 after falling below 50% in 1993. In early 1995 the Minister of Industries claimed that average capacity utilization was 70% in his sector. The best performance is believed to be in food, chemical and cement industries operating at 100% capacity compared with only 25% capacity utilization in state-owned heavy industries. The performance of the vast Mobarakeh steel complex and the Sar Cheshmeh copper complex have been singled out for criticism. A new strategic plan for industry has been incorporated into the second Five-Year Plan which began in March 1995; the emphasis is on the themes of restructuring, good administration, privatization, mobilizing domestic expertise and manufacturing capacity, selective foreign investment, and developing exports. It is hoped that industrial exports will eventually earn between $2,000m. and $4,000m. annually with food manufacturing industries registering the greatest expansion in export earnings. At present it is steel, copper and aluminium which earn the major share of export earnings. In July 1996 the Minister of Industries reported that industrial output was expanding rapidly and was estimated to be 65% higher than in 1995/96. He stated that the Government was ensuring that the industrial sector received allocations of foreign exchange to pay for vital inputs and that some $640m. had been allocated to fund imports for the industrial sector during 1996/97. The minister also proposed new legislation to establish a clearer framework to encourage greater private investment in the industrial sector. In November 1996 in his budget speech to the Majlis, President Rafsanjani commented on the success of the industrial sector in recent years and claimed that the value of industrial exports had increased from $150m. in 1989/90 to a projected $1,500m. in 1996/97.

Steel, petrochemicals and copper remain the country's three basic industries. Other important branches are automobile manufacture (many assembled from kits, under licence from Western and Japanese manufactures, such as Nissan), which has expanded rapidly in recent years, machine tools, construction materials, pharmaceuticals, textiles and food processing. With the exception of one major petrochemical plant and a number of textile and construction materials ventures, all these industries were nationalized after the Revolution. Annual cement production doubled between 1976 and 1986, reaching 13m. tons in the latter year. Output declined to 12.5m. tons in 1988. In early 1989 a $40m.-foreign exchange allocation was announced to equip a cement works. Two plants have been built in Kurdistan and Hormuzgan, and a 2,300 tons-per-day plant at Orumiyah commenced operations in 1989. In 1990 the Ministry of Industries announced plans to increase the total national output of cement to 33m. tons per year by the late 1990s. Some 27 new cement works were to be built, at a cost of $800m., in the five years to 1995. In 1990 the annual capacity of the existing 15 cement plants was 17m. tons, but only 12m. tons per year was being produced, owing to shortages of foreign exchange and electricity. Production in the Iranian year ending 20 March 1993 was estimated at 16m. tons and annual domestic demand at 20m. tons. In November 1992 the Ministry of Industries stated that 19 cement plants, costing $555m., were under construction and another 31 'in-principle' agreements had been signed. During 1993 the IFC was involved in negotiations concerning investment in or lending to at least four cement schemes and was negotiating with several European equipment suppliers as potential investors. In January 1995 it was reported that 20 new cement plants would start production within two years, raising national output to 25m. tons and allowing substantial exports. Officials stated that some 40 cement companies were producing 13.7m. tons a year. In August 1994 the Minister of Industries had stated that cement plants with a combined capacity of more than 9m. tons a year would be built during the second Five-Year Plan period, raising national capacity to 26m. tons. He also stated that the cement industry was the only sector that did not require state subsidies, but was paying the equivalent of $130m. a year to the Organization for the Protection of Consumers and Producers. In early 1995 the Chamber of Commerce and Industry reported that Iran's textile mills were operating at an average of 56% of capacity owing to shortages of foreign exchange and raw material. In the Iranian year ending 20 March 1995 just over 24m. sq m of textiles were produced. At the beginning of 1996 the Ministry of Industries announced that output from local sugar plants had reached just under 1m. tons per year and would be sufficient to meet domestic demand within 10 years. Annual consumption of sugar was projected to rise to 2m. tons by 1998. In March 1996 the Minister of Industries stated that 80,000 passenger cars had been manufactured locally in the year 1995/96 and that the industry had been allowed additional hard currency for imports in order to expand production capacity to 135,000 in 1996/97.

Electricity generation was severely restricted by Iraqi attacks on power stations during the Iran–Iraq War, reducing viable capacity from 8,000 MW to 5,000 MW, according to one estimate. In December 1988 the Minister of Energy stated that the generating capacity of the national grid was deficient by 2,500 MW, owing to war damage, lack of fuel and inadequate rainfall. It was reported that electricity demand increased from 2,876 MW to 7,850 MW between 1979 and 1989. The Government planned to increase generation by 1,000 MW annually during the period 1989–94, and allocated $7,500m. to this end. In 1989 $1,200m. in foreign exchange was set aside for the reactivation of dormant contracts and for the completion of repairs to damaged power stations. Installed capacity was reported to be 14,630 MW in 1990. In September 1992 the head of the state power generation and transmission company, Tavanir, stated that the national grid needed to be expanded by more than 1,000 MW a year for the foreseeable future in order to meet increasing demand, particularly at peak times in winter and summer when there are frequent power cuts. In September 1994 the Minister of Energy stated that the national electricity network generated 73,400m. kWh of electricity in the Iranian year ending 20 March

1994, 11% more than in the previous year. Some 86.5% of electricity was produced by thermal power plants and the rest by hydroelectric stations. He reported that power generation in the first four months of the Iranian year beginning 21 March 1994 rose by 10.3%, compared with the same period in the previous year; and claimed that since 1993 2,000 MW of new power generating capacity had been added to the network. It is forecast that consumption will have reached 109,000m. kWh in 1998. Residential consumption currently accounts for about 40% of total consumption and industry for about one-quarter. However, industrial demand is forecast to rise dramatically and to account for almost one-half of total consumption by 1998. Two-thirds of total capacity in 1998 will be provided by steam power and about one-fifth by hydroelectricity. By 1998 it is planned to build more than 20,000 km of transmission lines to supply electricity to 5m. new customers and 16,000 new villages. Only one-half of Iran's villages currently have electricity, but supplies are expected to reach more than two-thirds by 1998. In June 1991 Kraftwerk Union AG of Germany was awarded a $1,450m.-contract to construct a 2,080 MW-combined-cycle plant south of Teheran, the largest single power contract to be awarded since the Revolution. The company had earlier won a $700m.-contract to construct a smaller plant in Guilan. In January 1992 a Canadian-European consortium won a $770m.-contract to build a 1,100-MW gas/oil-fired-power station at Arak, to be completed in 1996. Work was due to start in late 1992, but more than a year after the contract was awarded implementation of the project was still being delayed because of financing problems. In early 1992 it was also reported that repairs to the country's biggest power plant at Neka on the Caspian Sea, damaged during the war with Iraq, had been completed. In November 1992 it was reported that Bharat Heavy Electricals of India had been selected to build a 1,000-MW thermal power station in Kerman. Some of the major hydroelectric power schemes require large amounts of foreign exchange and it is unclear whether the development programme will remain on schedule. The programme may also be affected by the disintegration of the USSR which formerly participated in several major dam projects. In May 1992 a consortium led by Asea Brown Boveri was awarded a $1,250m.-contract to build a 3,000-MW hydroelectric dam on the Karun river, designated as Karun-3, but in June 1994 the Ministry of Energy cancelled the contract and awarded it to a local company, Sabir, a subsidiary of the Ministry of Energy, claiming that this would halve the cost of the project. Asea Brown Boveri had encountered difficulties arranging finance for the project. Construction work, to be carried out in two stages, began in early 1995. In May 1993 Japan's Overseas Economic Co-operation Fund disbursed the first tranche ($458m.) of a $1,450m.-untied concessionary loan for the Godar-e-Landar hydroelectric dam on the Karun river, 160km north of Ahwaz, in Khuzistan, previously known as Karun 4. The dam, which is to be operational by 2001, will have a capacity of 1,000 MW and a further 1,000 MW will be added in the second phase. Preconstruction work started in 1992 and the contract for the main construction work was expected to be awarded towards the end of 1994. However, in early 1995 several international consortia were still awaiting invitations to talks following bids in early 1994 for the first phase of the 164 m high dam. Work on the first stage eventually began in November 1994. Japan was originally due to have disbursed the second tranche of $602m. in May 1994, but came under pressure from the USA not to make the loan. In April 1995 a $463m.-contract for civil works at the dam was awarded to Daelim Industrial Co of South Korea, which has taken charge of the project. In January 1996 there was an unconfirmed report that the Japanese Government had decided to continue its freeze on loans to Iran, in particular the second tranche of the loan package for the Godar-e-Landar dam, until March 1997 in order to avoid antagonizing the USA. In March 1993 the World Bank approved a loan of $165m. to upgrade the country's power plants and distribution network, including the conversion of the Qom power station to combined cycle. The conversion will double the plant's capacity to 600 MW. In April 1994 the contract for the conversion work was awarded to Asea Brown Boveri. The plant is expected to go into operation in late 1996. The World Bank loan also covers the cost of constructing 400-kV substations and transmission lines to strengthen the country's north–south connection. Subsidiaries of Asea Brown Boveri received three equipment supply orders in mid-1995 worth nearly $40m., and in early 1996 the company's Swedish subsidiary was awarded a $60m.-contract to supply instrument transformers and to help set up local support facilities for the state-owned Iran Electric Organization. In April 1996 Tavanir invited prequalification bids for the construction of a 650-MW steam power plant in East Azerbaijan province, the first big power project for some years. Most other power generation work is linked to hydroelectricity projects and the Bushehr nuclear facility. In April 1996 the official Iranian news agency stated that a $46m.-power plant had been built on the disputed Gulf island of Greater Tunb. In March 1995 the Ministry of Energy awarded a contract to Monenco AGRA of Canada to prepare a masterplan for the development of the electricity sector. The plan will assist the Ministry in preparing a comprehensive strategy, including the evaluation of energy resources, pricing strategies, environmental impact assessments and recommendations for training, research and development. The project is also included in the World Bank loan.

In October 1994 the Ministry of Energy awarded a $700m.-contract to build a dam on the Karkheh river in Khuzistan to the Islamic Revolutionary Guards, in line with the Government's new policy of involving more local organizations and companies in construction to reduce costs. The Karkheh dam will generate 400 MW of electricity and irrigate 220,000 ha in Khuzistan province. As part of an agreement signed in May 1995 China is to co-operate in the building of the combined cycle power plant at Arak, and to take part in the construction of the Karun 3 and Karkheh dams. The Ministry of Energy stated in April 1995 that Godar-e-Landar and Karun were among 30 large dams under construction. Two of these dams, Shahid Abbaspur and Barun, were due to be completed by March 1996 while a number of others, including Tanguyeh in Kerman, Alavian and Nahand in Khorassan, Raysar-Delvari in Bushehr and Salman Farsi, Kavar and Hanna in Fars, were to be completed later. The ministry also reported that two large tunnels, Kuhrang and Gavmishan were being completed to take water from the Karun river in Khuzistan to the Zayandehrud river in Isfahan. In May 1996 the Iran Water and Power Resources Development Co, an affiliate of the Ministry of Energy, invited international power generation companies to submit prequalification bids for the construction of four hydro-electric power plants: a 1-GW plant in Gotvand and a 750-MW plant on the Karun dam (Karun-4) both in Khuzestan, a 320-MW plant in Hini and a 250-MW plant in Sazbon, both in Ilam province. Companies submitting bids would also be required to arrange financing for the projects. In September 1992 it was announced that the Government planned to extend the privatization programme to electricity generation plants. Most power stations will be run as independent companies, and 51% of shares in power plants are to be transferred to the staff.

In May 1987 Iran and Argentina signed a nuclear power co-operation agreement, the details of which were not disclosed, but were thought to include an Argentine letter of intent to supply a $5.5m.-reactor core and enriched uranium for a nuclear research centre to be established in Teheran University. Kraftwerk Union AG of the Federal Republic of Germany (FRG) began building a 2,400-MW twin reactor nuclear plant at Bushehr before the Revolution; most of the work on the plant had been completed by the time of the outbreak of the Iran–Iraq War. After several Iraqi air attacks on the plant, however, the company withdrew its staff in 1987. The FRG Government refused to issue export licences for machinery and equipment until a peace agreement had been signed between Iran and Iraq. More than $3,700m. has already been spent on the plant. Iran wishes to complete at least one of the 1,200-MW reactors and has estimated the cost of this at about $1,000m. Independent sources, however, have argued that the true cost is more likely to be $3,000m. and have advised against proceeding. The Ministry of Energy does not have responsibility for the Bushehr nuclear facility, and a decision to complete what could be one of Iran's largest power plants could divert scarce financial resources from other parts of the country's ambitious energy programme. Iran is believed to have received technical advice and training for its atomic engineers from Pakistan. In November 1989 the head of the Atomic Energy Organization of Iran

(AEOI) announced that work on the Bushehr nuclear power plant had recommenced, and it is thought that vital equipment, placed in storage during the Iran–Iraq War, has been reinstalled. In January 1992 it was reported that Brazil had offered to resell to Iran equipment purchased from the FRG for the construction of its third nuclear plant, which had been delayed as a result of financial problems. Such equipment could be used in the construction of the Bushehr plant. On 15 February 1993, during a tour of the facility, President Rafsanjani stated that the Bushehr plant would be completed, whatever the cost. In August 1992 the AEOI announced that it had filed international suits against Siemens of Germany (Kraftwerk Union AG's parent company), for breaking the contract to complete the Bushehr reactor. Kraftwerk Union maintained that it was unable to do so because of a German government ban on the export of sensitive equipment. For some years negotiations with Indian, Russian and other suppliers ended in failure because of opposition from the USA which suspects that Iran is trying to develop a nuclear weapon. However, in December 1993 the Russian ambassador to Iran stated that Russia had agreed in principle, to complete the Bushehr plant and to build a conventional power plant at Bushehr. A spokesman for Siemens stated that the main building at Bushehr would not be suitable for a Russian-designed reactor and there was speculation that Iran may be planning to use some of the facilities at Bushehr to reduce the cost of the Russian reactor. In 1993 Iran signed an agreement with the People's Republic of China for at least one 300-MW nuclear reactor and despite pressure from the USA, China has indicated that it plans to proceed with the agreement. Teams from the International Atomic Energy Agency (IAEA) visited nuclear sites in Iran in February 1992 and November 1993 and reported that they had found no evidence that Iran was developing nuclear weapons. In January 1995 Russia signed a $800m.-contract to build a 1,000-MW pressurized light water-cooled VVER-100 reactor at Bushehr on the base of the reactor left unfinished by Siemens. Russia was also believed to have options on building three other reactors. The USA reiterated its opposition to any nuclear co-operation with Iran by Russia, asserting that the deal would help Iran accelerate a secret programme to develop nuclear weapons. However, Russian officials expressed their determination to proceed with the deal and to sell nuclear reactors to Iran and denied that work on the Bushehr project was in any way connected with the development of nuclear weapons. In March the head of the AEOI stated that some 200 Russian and 500 Iranian experts and technicians were co-operating on the construction of the Bushehr reactor. In June 1996 the Russian Government indicated that it would invest $60m. in the Bushehr project during 1996. A Russian intelligence agency issued a report in early 1995 supporting the IAEA's assertion that there was no evidence of a military nuclear programme in Iran. In April 1995 China also rejected US appeals not to sell nuclear reactors to Iran, and Chinese officials maintained that negotiations with Iran to supply two 300-MW nuclear reactors did not pose a threat to the Nuclear Non-Proliferation Treaty. The USA stated that nuclear co-operation and the transfer of technology to Iran was dangerous as it was open to abuse. Iran appears to be aiming at a nuclear programme of 3,000 MW–5,000 MW, compared with the Shah's ambitious programme of 24,000 MW. The AEOI argues that it needs to familiarize itself with nuclear technology in order to carry out medical and other civilian research and to place greater reliance on renewable sources of energy so that its hydrocarbon resources are available for export. At a nuclear safety summit meeting held in Moscow in April 1996 the Russian Minister of Nuclear Energy refused to discuss the Bushehr reactor, but insisted that the facility would use too little nuclear material to allow Iran to develop nuclear weapons. He added that IAEA officials had visited the plant and that Russia was adhering to the Nuclear Non-Proliferation Treaty. The USA continued to oppose the involvement of Russian companies in the project. In July 1997 the announcement that Russia was to assist Iran to complete the nuclear power plant at Bushehr prompted the USA to reiterate its concern that Iran might seek to exploit civilian nuclear technology for the development of nuclear weapons. In September the US Vice-President announced that US and Russian investigators had concluded that Iran was engaged in a 'vigorous effort' to obtain technology for the manufacture of nuclear weapons and ballistic missiles capable of transporting them. (Earlier in September the Russian authorities had stated that they would be willing to allow the USA to monitor the Bushehr nuclear plant.) In the same month it was reported that Israel was attempting to persuade the Clinton administration to impose sanctions on Russian organizations and companies involved in supplying missile technology to Iran. In October China announced an end to the sale of nuclear technology, as well as of conventional weaponry, to Iran. After allegations by both the USA and Israel that Iran had a top secret nuclear plant at Neka on the Caspian Sea coast, the IAEA stated in April 1996 that it had inspected all suspected nuclear sites in Iran and it had not discovered any nuclear facilities at Neka. In June 1995 President Rafsanjani opened the first section of a nuclear research centre in East Azerbaijan province which will enable experiments with preserving fresh fruit and vegetables by irradiation. A 5-kV solar power plant, built by the Atomic Energy Organization, opened in Ardakan, near Teheran, in November 1993. It was reported in October 1993 that new funds would be allocated to research into solar energy during the second Five-Year Plan. In May 1994 President Rafsanjani stated that there should be greater investment in new sources of energy in order to reduce dependence on oil. Iran's first wind-powered electricity plant is being constructed at Manjil in the north-west of the country. In January 1996 President Rafsanjani, on a visit to a facility run by the AEOI to carry out nuclear, solar, tidal, geothermal and wind energy research, stated that Iran would continue with research on fusion and other alternative energy sources despite opposition from the USA. Iranian radio reported that the AEOI had set up four solar and wind-powered power plants. In February 1996 it was announced that Iran, together with Russia, China and India, had agreed to establish the Asiatic Fund for Thermonuclear Research to explore the possibility of harnessing thermonuclear power for commercial purposes. It is planned to construct an experimental reactor by 1998.

In 1996/97 the industrial sector continued to be dominated by relatively few state enterprises accounting for 70% of manufacturing value added. Real growth in 1996/97 reached 6.3% while the share of industry in total value added increased to 21.0% (from 19.7% in 1995/96 and 18.6% in 1994/95). The most dynamic industrial sub-sector in 1996/97 was construction, which expanded by 10.6% (compared with 4.5% the previous year).

Steel

Government policies, like those of the Shah, are directed towards achieving self-sufficiency in steel production and ending dependence on imports. In 1980 steel accounted for almost one-sixth of total imports. Consumption was estimated at 6m. metric tons per year in mid-1981 and was expected to rise to 10m. tons by 1983. Domestic production and development plans were severely affected by the Revolution and the war with Iraq. By early 1983, output had been raised to 58,000 tons per month, equivalent to about 700,000 tons per year, produced by an old-fashioned coal-fired steel mill which was built by the USSR in Isfahan (formerly known as the Aryamehr Steel Mill), where installed capacity before the Revolution was claimed to be 1.1m. tons per year. Built under a $286m. credit arrangement which had been concluded with the USSR in 1965, the mill came into operation in March 1973. Subsequently, however, the mill has been beset by technical and production problems. For some time output was running at about 50% of its design capacity of 1.9m. tons a year. Agreements with the former USSR to expand the obsolete facility appear to have been abandoned and in January 1992 Danieli of Italy won a $600m.-contract to expand steel-making and rolling capacity at the plant. In October 1994 it was reported that the plant was producing at 2m. tons a year, slightly above design capacity, and was no longer receiving state subsidies. A $470m.-expansion plan is under way to raise output to 2.4m. tons a year in 1997. In December 1994 Danieli was reported to have renegotiated its contract at the plant and is to expand capacity at the existing Isfahan Steel Co complex to 3.2m. tons a year by adding a line for nearly 800,000 tons of flat products. Negotiations were also reported with a number of European firms for a complete change of instrumentation at the complex. Management of the plant is reported to have improved greatly,

although it still suffers from overmanning despite a reduction of the work-force by one-third to 19,000. Further cuts are to be made to reduce the work-force to 12,000 by 1998. The Isfahan steel mill has become a centre for new technological developments in steel. At the end of 1994 Isfahan Steel Co's managing director, Ahmad Sadeqi, claimed to have developed a commercially viable new direct-reduction process in steel manufacture at a pilot plant in Isfahan which is being patented under the name of Tahre Qaem. Sadeqi has stated that he plans to convert the Isfahan steel mill from the coke-burning technology introduced by the former Soviet Union to direct reduction, using natural gas. The cost of the new technology is projected at one-half of that of the Midrex direct-reduction modules installed at Mobarakeh. A private firm, one of 30 companies set up by former managers and employees at the Isfahan Steel Co to provide services ranging from transport to engineering, has commissioned a ferrosilicon pilot plant with a capacity of 3,000 tons a year, which is now supplying about one-third of the steel plant's requirements for ferrosilicon. A 30,000-tons-a-year ferro-manganese plant at the Isfahan industrial estate was due to be completed in 1995. The plant will supply both the Isfahan and Mobarakeh steel complexes. Hylsa of Mexico has a contract at Iran's second largest production facility, the Ahwaz steel plant, to expand the unit's capacity to 1.1m. tons a year and, eventually, to 1.7m. tons a year. The National Iranian Steel Co (NISCO) reported that the plant produced 805,000 tons of steel in the Iranian year ending 20 March 1993, an increase of 54% over the previous year. In December 1993 it was reported that production at the plant had improved and that it was now producing quality steel for export. In December 1994 it was reported that Danieli had been contracted to carry out work worth $100m. to improve flexibility in semi-finished products at Ahwaz, but some uncertainty was expressed over whether the project would go ahead. In June Kudremukh Iron Ore Co of India signed an agreement with the NISCO to provide technical services for the Ahwaz steel plant. By 1996 the Ahwaz complex was producing 1.5m. tons a year. Furnace capacity was being increased by 3.2m. tons a year and there were plans for a new sheet mill with a capacity of 3.8m. tons a year. Another direct-reduction plant with a capacity of 700,000 tons a year using the new Iranian technology developed at Isfahan should begin production in 1998. In September 1991 President Rafsanjani opened the first stage of the Mobarakeh steel mill in Isfahan, one of the most modern steel mills in the world. However, the plant was reported to have encountered problems achieving the target annual production capacity of 2.4m. tons and in 1995 production capacity was only 1.6m. tons a year. NISCO plans to expand capacity to 3.2m. tons a year by March 1998. A reheating furnace is to be built at the complex and NISCO has indicated that it may extend the hot and cold rolling mills to raise capacity to almost 5m. tons a year. In June 1989 the construction of a $192m. steel-rolling complex at Miyaneh, in East Azerbaijan province, was announced. In February 1992 a Japanese-Italian consortium won a $550m.-contract to build a steel plant near Yazd, which was inaugurated by President Rafsanjani in June 1997. In March 1993 it was announced that Italy's Simimpianti had won a $112m.-contract to supply equipment, supervision, expertise and training for a specialized steel mill near Mashad which will have an annual capacity of 250,000 tons. In late 1994 Danieli of Italy was awarded a contract to build the steel-rolling mill at Miyaneh and a second new mill at Neishabur in Khorassan province. The Miyaneh mill will have a capacity of 350,000 tons and will process slabs imported from the CIS republics on the western side of the Caspian Sea. The $160m.-Neishabur complex will have an initial capacity of 600,000 tons a year but production is due to rise to 1.8m. tons. In February 1996 a syndicate of European and Japanese banks granted a $561m.-loan to finance a steel mill project for Danieli of Italy. The loan is underwritten by the Italian state export credit guarantee agency, Sace. The NISCO was also reported to be engaged in negotiations with foreign companies for the construction of a 1m.-ton-a-year integrated steel mill in Hormuzgan, near the Strait of Hormuz, and a 1.2m.-ton mill in Kerman. Financial difficulties may delay these projects until state insurance agencies resume cover for Iran. Hormuzgan is also the site of a ferro-alloy plant built with Chinese assistance. The $39m.-plant became operational in early 1995 producing 15,000 tons a year of ferro-chrome and 20,000 tons a year of ferro-manganese. Some 5,000 tons were exported to Japan in April 1995 and the plant is expected to earn some $10m. a year in export sales. In mid-1996 it was reported that NISCO had secured a $561m.-loan from Japanese and European banks to finance the renovation and upgrading of steel plants at Ahwaz, Khorassan and Miyaneh to be carried out by Danieli of Italy. Between 1981 and 1986 Iranian steel production officially totalled 5.3m. tons, of which 1.2m. tons were produced in 1986. According to the Ministry of Mines and Metals, Iran's steel production in the year ending March 1989 totalled 1.4m. tons and rose to 3.8m. tons in 1992/93. Output for 1993/94 was projected at 4.5m. tons and the Minister of Mines and Metals stated in August 1993 that a target of 12m. tons had been set for 1999. The Ministry of Mines and Metals had earlier forecast an expansion in output to 5.5m. tons a year by March 1994 when the first Five-Year Plan ended. Actual output was well below target even according to the Ministry's own figures. Somewhat lower output figures have been given by the NISCO and the target figures for 1999 appear wildly optimistic. According to the Ministry of Mines and Metals, steel output rose by 20% to 4.6m. tons in the Iranian year ending 20 March 1995. According to the NISCO, steel output will reach 6m. tons in the Iranian year beginning March 1996. In 1996 NISCO announced a development plan to expand steel production capacity by 1m. tons a year until 2006 when total capacity is projected to reach 17.5m. tons a year. The deputy minister for mines and metals is reported to have indicated that NISCO could be privatized within the next five years. In October 1992 it was reported that the International Institute of Iron and Steel had accepted Iran as a full member, as its raw steel production exceeded 2m. tons a year. For many years Iran has been a major purchaser of steel on the world market, and imports, principally from Spain and Japan, have averaged 2m.–5m. tons a year. Domestic consumption of steel was estimated at 3.5m. tons a year in early 1989 and was projected to rise to 7m. tons annually as post-war reconstruction got under way. In January 1994 the Ministry of Mines and Metals announced that 1.35m. tons of steel had been exported during the first nine months of the Iranian year beginning March 1993. Steel exports during the first six months of the Iranian year beginning 21 March 1994 were 71,000 tons, according to the Ministry of Mines and Metals, and total exports for 1994 were estimated at 1.5m. tons. Despite its emergence as a steel exporter, Iran is still a net importer of steel. As part of its plan to increase production, Japan's Nippon Steel Co was awarded a $1.8m.-contract in May 1993 to improve the management of the NISCO. Total steel production in 1998 was expected to be 6.7m. tons, of which 1.5m. tons would be exported.

Petrochemicals

The Shah had planned a huge petrochemical sector that would not only meet local demand, but also provide $2,000m.-worth of exports by 1983. Development of the industry was paralysed after the Revolution. However, in 1983 the Ministry of Oil announced that it would place greater emphasis on further development and expansion of the petrochemicals industry. Several new plants were to be built with the aim of making Iran not only self-sufficient, but also an exporter of surplus nitrogenous fertilizer, plastics and other products; indeed, Iran intends to become a leading world producer of petrochemicals during the 1990s. At present the sector comprises the following major ventures: the Iran Fertilizer Co, the Razi Chemical Co (formerly Shahpour), the Abadan Petrochemical Co, the Kharg Chemical Co, the Iran Carbon Co, the Iran Nippon Chemical Co, Aliaf Co and Polyacryl Corpn. All these companies were nationalized in 1979 and are administered by the National Petrochemical Co (NPC) under the Ministry of Oil.

Under the Shah the cornerstone of the petrochemical industry, was the Iran-Japan petrochemical complex at Bandar Khomeini, which had a planned capacity of 300,000 tons per year of olefins and aromatics. This began in 1973 as a joint venture shared equally between the NIOC and a Mitsui-led consortium, the Iran Chemical Development Co (ICDC). It was originally projected to cost $300m., but this estimate had increased to $3,000m. by 1979. The immense 13-unit complex was 85% finished at the time of the Revolution. Work was resumed briefly in the summer

of 1980, but was halted again after Iraqi bombers attacked the plant several times in late September and early October. Disputes between the NPC and its Japanese partners were numerous. In mid-1984 Iran suspended a $10.8m.-interest payment on a loan because the Japanese consortium, concerned with safety in the war zone, had withdrawn its technicians from the site. After renewed Iraqi bombings in September 1984, the ICDC again withdrew all of its technicians. In February 1986 Iran decided to end all repayments on credits and loans received from Japan. In the late 1980s Mitsui estimated that it would cost at least $2,000m. to complete the scheme, taking into account extensive war damage and the fact that some of the original units were obsolete. Iran disputed these estimates. The Japanese consortium expressed its desire to withdraw from the scheme, but Iran stated that it wished to complete the project and claimed that the Japanese estimates were pessimistic and that the cost would be about $1,000m. In November 1989, after prolonged negotiations, the Japanese consortium agreed to dissolve the $4,500m.-partnership for the complex, and in February 1990, as part of the agreement, it paid the Iranian Government $910m. Dutch and German companies are helping the NPC to reconstruct some of the complex's 13 units. In November 1990 the Daelim Industrial Co, a South Korean venture, secured a $150m.-contract to reconstruct the olefins plant. In April 1994 the head of the NPC stated that test production would start that month on the second phase of the complex which would treble annual production capacity to 3m. tons. Three-quarters of the plant's output had been sold in advance to German, French and Finnish companies to help finance its construction. The complex is the country's biggest petrochemical plant. Its second phase opened in August 1994 and in September the head of the NPC stated that 500,000 tons of liquefied petroleum gas would be exported to South Korea in 1995. This represented part of the $900m. of the plant's production which has been sold in advance in order to finance construction. Under the second Five-Year Plan, which began in March 1995, the annual capacity of the olefin unit of the complex is to be doubled. In November 1994 it was announced that the port of Bandar Khomeini and the nearby petrochemical complexes, the Bandar Khomeini complex and the Razi fertilizer complex, would be declared a protected industrial zone in early 1995. Freezone regulations would apply to the region in order to promote joint ventures and attract foreign investment in petrochemicals. The NPC was trying to interest private investors in the construction of a methyl tertiary butyl ether plant at the Bandar Khomeini complex. In March 1995 the official news agency reported that the polyvinyl chloride unit at the complex had started production with an annual capacity of 175,000 tons. The aromatics unit was due to open later in 1995. In May 1996 the NPC announced plans to build a paraxylene plant with an annual capacity of 150,000 tons at the Bandar Khomeini petrochemical plant.

The expanded Shiraz petrochemical complex, located next to a smaller 20-year-old unit at Marvdasht, 50 km from the city, was opened in February 1986. The plant's daily output has been increased nearly tenfold to produce 1,200 tons of ammonia, 1,500 tons of urea, 100 tons of nitric acid and 750 tons of ammonium nitrate. The initial capacity of the Shiraz plant was 500,000 tons per year, rising to 850,000 tons in 1987. A chloro-alkali unit with a capacity of 60,000 tons per year was completed in February 1989 at Shiraz, and the Shiraz methanol plant commenced production in May 1990. Contracts worth $33m. have been awarded to expand a dense soda ash plant and the ammonia plant. In September 1993 NPC officials reported that the Razi fertilizer complex near Bandar Khomeini was operating at only three-quarters of its planned capacity of 2m. tons a year. In October 1994 it was announced that the war-damaged sulphuric acid unit at the Razi complex had resumed production at 1,320 tons a day. As part of the NPC's ambitious petrochemicals expansion programme a $2,200m.-complex has been constructed at Arak using feedstocks from the Isfahan refinery and the new Arak refinery. The first phase of the complex was opened in July 1993 and planned output is 550,000 tons of products a year. Another project was the petrochemicals complex at Isfahan to produce benzene and toluene as well as polyethylene, polystyrene and polyols. In April 1994 it was reported that the Ministry of Heavy Industry had taken over responsibility for a $1,900m.-olefins petrochemical complex at Isfahan from the NPC. The project will be financed by a buy-back arrangement. In October 1993 it was reported that the benzene plant would start production in March 1994 with an annual capacity of 50,000 tons. Japan's Kawasaki Corpn and MW Kellog Co of the USA are building a petrochemical complex in Khorassan in the north-east of the country. Work on the plant, which will produce 330,000-tons a year of ammonia and 495,000-tons a year of urea, began in 1988 and production was scheduled to start in March 1995. A $1,000m.-petrochemical complex is also being built at Tabriz, near to the Tabriz refinery, and was due to become operational in March 1995. A $80m.-private sector petrochemical plant is also to be built at Tabriz, producing 50,000 tons of polypropylene, half of which will be exported. In October 1993 two German companies, Lurgi and BASF, were awarded the contract to set up and equip the plant for Polynar, a subsidiary of Narhan, a private consulting firm involved in local petrochemical and oil industries. The financial package was to be concluded in 1994 and construction is due to be completed in three years. Polynar was given the concession in 1992 by the NPC as part of its programme to encourage more private sector investment in petrochemicals. The Tabriz plant is reported to be one of nine petrochemical projects handed over to the private sector, including a 660,000-ton-a-year methanol plant and a 500,000-ton-a-year methyl tertiary butyl ether facility. In September 1994 the head of the NPC stated that as part of the state company's privatization programme, production units were being leased to the newly-established Petrochemical Investment Co as an intermediate step towards their flotation on the stock market. No further details were given. In October 1994 the NPC approached Lurgi of Germany to carry out basic engineering for a major new methanol plant on Kharg Island with construction, carried out by local firms, beginning in 1995. The complex will use gases from a petrochemical plant on the island and when operational will produce 660,000 tons a year of methanol and 50,000 tons a year of acetic acid. Some two-thirds of the methanol output is destined for export, with the balance fed to the new methyl tertiary butyl ether plant to be built at Bandar Khomeini (see above). In February 1996 it was reported that Belleli of Italy had been awarded a $7.5m.-contract to supply two 250-ton petrochemical reactors early in 1997 for use in the methanol plant on Kharg Island. This plant is one of five petrochemical projects to be given priority during the second Five-Year Plan which began in March 1995. The other projects include the expansion of the olefins unit at Bandar Khomeini, a methyl tertiary butyl ether plant in the south to manufacture additives for 500,000 tons of unleaded gasoline a year, and two plastics plants. The five projects are estimated to require government investment of $1,800m.

The total import bill for petrochemicals was $1,500m. in 1987. During the 1990s, if its plans are completed, Iran hopes to be able to satisfy internal demands and have a surplus output to export a range of products. Output has risen steadily since the end of the war with Iraq, reaching 2.1m. tons in 1989/90 and more than 3.5m. tons in 1990/91. Output in 1991/92 totalled 4.3m. tons, according to the NPC, and 970,000 tons of petrochemicals were exported, worth $100m. About 5.4m. tons of petrochemicals were produced in 1992/93. In February 1994 the head of the NPC stated that annual production had reached 5.5m. tons, well below the target figure of 9m. tons planned for March 1994. However, in January 1995 he claimed that petrochemical output had increased by almost 40% in 1994, to 7.5m. tons, and would rise to 9m. tons in 1995 and to 14.5m. tons by 2000. There were conflicting figures from other sources. In March the Minister of Oil claimed that Iran's annual output of petrochemical products was 9m. and would rise to 15.5m. by 2000. In late September 1994 the Minister of Economy and Finance claimed that annual production of petrochemicals had increased twentyfold since 1989, to about 8m. tons a year. NPC reported that output in 1995/96 rose by 1.2m. tons to 8.6m. tons, and that 2.4m. tons were exported. Other sources claimed that production at the end of 1996 was around 10m. tons a year and that annual capacity would be increased to 15.5m. tons by 2000, with a higher proportion of output destined for export. In August 1993 the head of the NPC urged the Majlis to approve new incentives to encourage private and foreign investment in petrochemical projects during the term of the second Five-Year Plan. He

reported that 14 projects which commenced under the Five-Year Plan which ended in March 1994 had been delayed because of the shortage of funds. Foreign finance and expertise were urgently needed if the petrochemical sector was to be developed successfully over the next five years. The NPC was seeking approval from the Majlis to guarantee foreign loans and secure concessionary domestic credit for private projects from March 1994. In October 1994 the head of the NPC stated that no private local or foreign investors had expressed interest in petrochemical ventures. He is reported to have asked to Majlis to allow foreign investors to take 100% ownership in projects instead of the 49% currently permitted. In 1996 officials reported increased interest in the petrochemicals sector from private investors. In 1992 around 1.5m. tons of petrochemicals were exported, earning $150m. Nevertheless, the head of the NPC stated in September 1993 that Iran was still spending $3,000m. a year on petrochemical imports. The NPC stated that annual production in 1993/94 was worth $1,000m. and was expected to rise to $1,800m. in 1994/95. Petrochemical exports were estimated to have earned $200m. in 1993/94, and according to NPC earned $408m. in 1995/96. Exports in 1996/97 were $506m., and increased to $560m. in 1997/98. Exports in 1998/99 were projected at $600m. According to the NPC, more than 650,000 tons of sulphur, from total production of 880,000 tons, was exported in the Iranian year ending 20 March 1994, making Iran the sixth biggest sulphur exporter in that period. The NPC stated in January 1995 that Iran was meeting 85% of its petrochemical needs from domestic production.

TRADE AND COMMUNICATIONS

Iran's exports of crude petroleum or petroleum products account for the major part of the country's export revenue. Non-oil exports rose from $283.7m. in 1982/83 to $1,002m. in 1986/87, and $1,158m. in 1987/88 (a record $485m. of which accrued from sales of carpets), but fell to $1,021m. in 1988/89. In 1984/85 (the Iranian year runs from 21 March to 20 March) oil exports of 1.68m. b/d were worth $17,000m. However, the value of oil exports declined to $13,100m. in 1985/86, and to $6,600m. in 1986/87. The value of oil exports in 1987/88 rose to $8,600m. and total earnings of foreign exchange were $9,600m. The Government's utilization, from early 1989, of pre-financed oil sales has increased oil exports and has raised vital foreign exchange for post-war reconstruction. Pre-financing involves the delivery of crude oil 12–18 months after payment and thus amounts, in effect, to the raising of short-term foreign credit. The value of non-military imports fell sharply, to $5,600m., in 1986/87, reflecting the decline in revenue from oil. As a result of the sharp decline in income from oil exports in 1986, the Government decided to place greater emphasis on increasing non-oil exports and thereby reduce dependence on oil. In 1986/87, according to the Governor of the Bank Markazi (Central Bank), 24% of state revenue was provided by sales of petroleum, compared with 74% in 1975/76 and 63% in 1983/84. During the same period, the proportion of revenue deriving from non-oil exports rose from 2% to 8.5%. The Government is committed to increasing the value of non-oil exports. In 1991/92 the value of non-oil exports nearly doubled to $2,500m. Earnings from carpet exports totalled $1,000m., with most of the balance provided by pistachios, caviare and other traditional items. In the budget for the Iranian year beginning 21 March 1992 the Government set a target of $4,248m. for the value of non-oil export revenues. The value of industrial exports was projected at $2,043m., that of carpets at $1,152m. and that of agricultural exports at $660m. Figures released in December 1992 for the first eight months of the Iranian year, showed that although the value of non-oil exports rose to $1,771m. during that period, it was well below the Government's target. Carpets accounted for 40.7% of earnings. According to official sources, the value of non-oil exports in 1993/94 rose to $3,500m. Carpets and handicrafts accounted for 39% of the value of non-oil exports, industrial products for 26%, farm products for 24% and minerals and other goods for 11%. Oil revenues fell sharply in 1993 due to low oil prices and in the year 1993/94 it was estimated that they would not exceed $12,000m. Oil revenues for 1994/95 were projected at only $10,150m., but in October 1994 the Minister of Oil announced that revenues had exceeded the official budget projections by 20% and that this trend would continue until the end of the year. Observers predicted total revenues in 1994/95 of $12,000m.–$14,000m. In May 1995 the Majlis approved the 1995/96 budget, which estimated oil revenues at $13,500m., based on a crude oil price of $15 a barrel. In June 1995 the Minister of Oil forecast oil revenues of $16,000m. in 1995/96 on the basis of higher oil prices. In April 1996 the Minister of Oil confirmed that oil revenues in 1995/96 were almost $16,000m., $1,600m. above the budgeted figure. The 1996/97 budget forecast oil revenues of just under $16,000m., based on a crude oil price of $15.5 per barrel. However, in April 1996 the Minister of Oil reported that to date oil revenues were above the targeted level owing to high oil prices. Iranian heavy crude export grade was priced at slightly more than $20 per barrel in early April. Despite the enactment of US legislation in August 1996 which would penalize non-US firms investing in Iran's oil and gas industry, independent analysts argued that the country's oil export capacity was unlikely to be affected (see above). Non-oil exports earned $4,825m. in 1994/95, but their value fell sharply, to $3,200m., in 1995/96 after strict foreign exchange restrictions were imposed in May 1995, requiring exporters to repatriate all their earnings at the official exchange rate of $1 = IR3,000 (see Finance). However, a senior official of the central bank claimed that exporters had tended to under-report their earnings since the introduction of the new restrictions and argued that the main reason why earnings had fallen was the Government's ban on exports of manufactured goods, such as steel and petro-chemicals, and of certain agricultural products in short supply. The ban on industrial exports may have cost the Government $500m. in foreign exchange earnings, but it was claimed that the restrictions had helped to control inflation. As a result of higher oil prices, the value of Iranian exports during the first six months of 1996/97 rose to $10,700m., compared with $9,500m. during the equivalent period for 1995/96. Oil and gas revenues rose from $7,700m. in the first half of 1995/96 to $9,300m. in the first half of 1996/97, suggesting that oil and gas exports for the whole of 1996/97 would total some $18,500m. In contrast, non-oil exports for 1996/97 decreased to about $2,800m., owing mainly to government-imposed currency restrictions.

After the Revolution, the Government declared that it would pursue an increase in trade with Islamic and developing countries. New trading patterns have emerged, but Iran remains heavily dependent on the advanced industrial economies.

Iran's imports in 1980/81 were valued at IR776,841m. ($10,844m.), an increase of 13.5% over the 1979/80 level, despite the imposition of sanctions by the USA, the EC and Japan, and the outbreak of war with Iraq in September 1980. This compares with a total of $14,100m. in 1978/79, the year immediately before the Revolution began to affect trade levels. Despite efforts to reduce the import bill, the value of imports rose from $11,845m. in 1982/83 to $24,200m. in 1983/84. With the tight-ening of import controls, the value of imports declined to $17,500m. in 1984/85 and to an estimated $15,000m. in 1985/86. Further controls, introduced in 1987, permitted the import of basic commodities only. As a result, the value of imports was reported to have fallen to $10,000m. in 1986/87. However, it rose in 1987/88 to $12,760m., considerably more than the budgeted maximum of $9,000m.

Following the seizure of the US hostages and the almost complete embargo on US sales to Iran, the value of imports from the USA plunged dramatically in 1980/81, falling to almost nothing, compared with $2,200m. in 1977/78. As a result of the suspension of US imports and the imposition of sanctions by the EC and Japan, Iran began to find new sources of supply in the Third World and among non-aligned countries in Western Europe. There was also a considerable increase in imports from East European countries such as the USSR, Romania and Bulgaria. A protocol which envisaged the development of econ-omic relations between Iran and the USSR was signed in Moscow in September 1985. Under an economic co-operation agreement signed in October 1987, Iran was to supply 5m. tons of crude oil to the USSR annually, 2m. tons of which were to be returned as refined products. Major imports are foodstuffs, equipment and raw materials for industry, power transmission and generating equipment, and purchases of armaments and refined oil products.

During 1981/82 the USA re-emerged as a significant trading partner. The value of direct US sales rose to $300m. in 1981,

making the USA the eighth highest OECD exporter to Iran in that year. However, the value of US exports to Iran in 1986 fell to $34m., compared with US purchases of Iranian goods worth $600m. In 1987 the USA became the largest purchaser of Iranian oil (with the value of exports reaching $1,592m., 14.6% of the total value of Iranian exports), closely followed by Japan (with exports worth $1,426m., 13% of market share). In October 1987 the USA placed a ban on all imports of Iranian goods, and in November imposed tighter restrictions on US exports to Iran. It had earlier been revealed that, in July, Iran had become the second largest supplier of petroleum to the USA, and that, by October, Iranian exports to the USA (valued at some $1,000m.) were already at a higher level than in any year since the Islamic Revolution, except 1983. These measures were taken by the USA as a 'direct result' of Iranian policy in the Iran–Iraq War. In support of the US measures, Japanese companies agreed not to increase their purchases of Iranian oil during the first quarter of 1988.

The sanctions that the EC imposed in 1989, as a result of the Rushdie affair (see History), were repealed in October 1990, and in early November the USA eased its three-year ban on imports of Iranian oil. The increase in oil revenues that followed Iraq's invasion of Kuwait in August 1990 precipitated a sharp rise in imports, the value of which was reported to have exceeded $20,000m. in 1990. Exports by Iran's leading suppliers increased by 50% during 1991 compared to 1990, with Germany, Italy and the USA registering the biggest increases. Germany, which remains Iran's major supplier, increased its share of the market in 1991, with the value of its exports totalling $4,000m., an increase of some 60%. Japan, the second biggest supplier, reported exports worth more than $2,500m., an increase of some 56%. The value of Italian exports increased by 64% to $1,800m. That of US sales rose from a mere $166m. in 1990 to $546m. in 1991. The value of imports and import commitments in the Iranian year ending 20 March 1991 was almost at a record high of $22,000m. Despite the Government's stated intention to set a ceiling of about $16,000m. on the value of imports in the year beginning 21 March 1991, according to the Bank Markazi, the value of imports in the Iranian year ending 20 March 1992 rose dramatically, to $28,000m. According to the Iranian Customs Office, the value of imports in the year to the end of March 1993 fell to $17,000m. though it was reported that there was still a glut of foreign products on the market, such as textiles and rice. The Bank Markazi, however, which uses a different method in its calculations, recorded the value of imports at the higher level of $23,300m. In 1993/94, as oil revenues declined sharply and Iran experienced problems servicing its external debt, the value of imports fell to $19,287m. and it was predicted that Iran would have to keep its imports at around this level for another two years in order to clear payment arrears. Early in 1994 the Majlis voted to reduce hard currency spending on essential imports during the year beginning March 1994 and in May 1994 an advisor to the Bank Markazi stated that imports during 1994/95 would be kept at the same level as the previous year. He stated that this was necessary in order to release extra funds to repay foreign debts at a time when oil revenues were low. Imports from Iran's leading suppliers declined by about one-half in 1993. Sales by Japan experienced the greatest fall, their value falling by more than 50% to about $1,500m. The value of Iran's exports to Japan declined by 18% to $2,500m. Germany reported that the value of its exports fell by slightly less than 50% in the first 10 months of 1993 to $2,000m. The value of Iran's exports to Germany, however, rose by more than 20% to about $1,000m. The value of Italian exports to Iran declined by 20% during the first nine months of 1993 to $960m., but that of Italian imports from Iran remained at about the same level of $1,000m. The value of the United Kingdom's exports to Iran fell by only 12% to $742m., while that of its imports from Iran doubled to $365m. France was the only major supplier to record an increase in the value of its exports to Iran, which totalled $725m., an increase of 4.5%. Iranian exports to France rose by 41% in value, to $1,430m. The value of US exports to Iran fell by 18% to $616m. and that of its imports from Iran was only $200,000.

Imports were reduced severely in 1994. Germany, for example, Iran's main supplier, reported exports worth $1,600m. to Iran in 1994, down by more than one-third compared with 1993. The value of German imports from Iran fell by 2%, to $600m. during the first three-quarters of 1994. Japan, Iran's second largest supplier, reported a 41% fall in the value of exports to Iran, to $1,000m., in 1994, with that of imports from Iran falling by 5% to $1,980m. during the first three-quarters of the year. The United Kingdom recorded a decline of nearly 42% (to $443m.) in the value of its exports to Iran in 1994, while that of imports fell by almost 46%, to $203m. Direct US exports to Iran in 1994 fell by 47%, to $329m., while the value of imports from Iran was less than $1m. However, US commodities worth an estimated $500m.–$1,000m. are believed to have reached Iran via third countries such as the UAE. The value of Italian exports was sustained at $1,160m. in January–November 1994, suggesting that the total for the whole year would be around the 1993 level of $1,250m. The value of exports from Iran to Italy, however, was down by more than 40% to $675m. France was the only leading supplier to increase the value of its exports to Iran in 1994. This rose by 8.5% to $816m., with industrial products and capital equipment marking the biggest gains. There was a decline in French exports of semi-finished goods, consumer goods and foodstuffs. The value of exports from Iran to France fell by nearly 30%, to $1,030m. French purchases of Iranian oil and foodstuffs declined, but imports of industrial and consumer goods increased. During the first three-quarters of 1994 Iran's six leading suppliers—Germany, Japan, Italy, France, the United Kingdom and the USA—exported goods with a total value of $3,300m., while their imports from Iran, mainly oil, were valued at $4,000m, the first time a trade surplus in Iran's favour had been recorded. Iran registered a trade surplus of nearly $2,000m. with the EU member states in 1994. US President Clinton imposed a near total trade embargo on Iran in early May 1995, and by early June most US oil companies and exporters had terminated their business links with Iran. The trade embargo mainly affected US oil companies, which in recent years have purchased an estimated $3,500m.-worth of Iranian crude for sale to non-US clients. Observers predicted that indirect exports to Iran, especially through ports such as Dubai in the UAE, would continue at a substantial level. Since early 1994 the Government has sharply reduced imports, imposing strict controls on purchases of non-essential goods. The value of imports in 1994 was $12,700m. Most of Iran's leading suppliers reported an average fall in the value of exports of nearly one-third in 1995, and it was estimated that the value of imports in 1995 might not exceed the figure for 1994. The value of Italian exports to Iran during the first three-quarters of 1995 showed the biggest decline, falling by 38% to $358m. However, the value of Italian imports from Iran increased by 55% to $1,180m. France reported that the value of its exports to Iran in 1995 fell by 37%, to $570m., while that of its imports from Iran rose by some 20% to $1,388m. The value of Japanese exports to Iran in 1995 fell by 35% to $628m., the lowest figure on record. The value of Japan's imports from Iran fell slightly, by about 6%, to $2,678m. The value of imports from Dubai, which had reached $1,139m. in 1994, fell to $880m. in 1995 owing to restrictions imposed on allocations of foreign exchange and a crackdown on smuggling. The value of Iranian exports to Dubai during the first half of 1995 was $118m. Germany, which remains Iran's biggest supplier, reported that the value of its exports to Iran fell by only 9% in 1995, to $1,658m., while the value of exports from Iran to Germany fell by nearly 13%, to $822m. The United Kingdom was the only leading supplier to record an increase in the value of its exports to Iran during 1995. This rose by 15%, to $520m., while Iranian imports from the United Kingdom fell by 5%, to $196m. Following the imposition of trade sanctions in June 1995, the value of US exports to Iran remained at the mid-year figure of $223m. In April 1996 the Bank Markazi stated that the Government had allocated $19,000m. to finance imports of basic goods and machinery and to service debts in 1996, indicating an easing of the reduction on imports. A trade surplus of $6,818m. was recorded in 1994/95 (after deficits in the two previous years) on the strength of exports valued at $19,435m. (of which $14,604m. was from oil and gas) and imports down to $12,617m. In 1995/96 the surplus was somewhat lower at $5,586m., from exports of $18,360m. ($15,103m. from oil and gas) and imports of $12,774m. In 1996/97 the surplus recovered to a record $7,402m. from exports of $22,391m. ($19,271m. from oil and gas) and

imports of $14,989m. In 1997/98, according to preliminary figures, a reduced trade surplus, of $3,511m., was recorded as a result of exports valued at $18,506m. ($15,464m. from oil and gas) and imports of $14,995m. In 1995/96 Japan remained substantially Iran's largest customer, taking 15.1% of exports by value, followed by Italy (8.6%), the United Kingdom (7.8%) and South Korea (6.0%). In the same year, Germany remained Iran's most important source of imports with 14.4% of the total, followed by Japan (7.2%), Belgium (5.4%), Argentina (4.4%), Italy (4.3%), Switzerland (4.1%) and the United Kingdom (4.1%).

Increased trade led to the revival, in October 1984, of the Regional Co-operation for Development pact with Pakistan and Turkey, which had been inaugurated at the instigation of the late Shah in 1964. Under a new name, the Economic Co-operation Organization (ECO), the pact was ratified in January 1985. In February 1992 the ECO was expanded to include five Muslim republics of the former USSR: Azerbaijan, Turkmenistan, Uzbekistan, Tajikistan and Kyrgyzstan, all of which need new communication links with the outside world, access to new markets and sources of investment and expertise. A 10% cut in trade tariffs was agreed and it was planned eventually to remove all tariff and non-tariff barriers. At a summit in Teheran on 16–17 February 1992, the importance of developing transport and communications links and co-operation in the fields of energy, industry and agriculture within the ECO was stressed. Talks are in progress for new rail links and ambitious gas and oil pipeline projects. In April 1992 the ECO announced the establishment of a new trade and development bank, jointly owned by Iran, Turkey and Pakistan, with capital of $320m. Under the auspices of ECO, Iran has established strong trading links with the Central Asian states. By 1996 Iran had become Azerbaijan's major trading partner and early in 1997 an oil-swap agreement with Kazakhstan was inaugurated (see above).

In December 1995 Iran signed a trade agreement with Kuwait, replacing an agreement which had been concluded in 1968. The annual value of trade between the two countries is believed to be around $100m. and consists mainly of imports from Iran. However, official figures released for Kuwait's exports to Iran probably do not include large amounts of refined oil products. In January 1996 Iran and five other Asian Clearing Union countries (India, Pakistan, Sri Lanka, Bangladesh and Myanmar) agreed to settle their trade in dollars rather than local currencies, an arrangement that was predicted to lead to an increase in trade between them.

For several years following the Revolution, government policy concerning foreign trade favoured forms of trade other than cash payments. Straight barter—a direct exchange of goods for oil—was rare; much more common were the counter-trade triangle and the clearing account. During the early part of 1985, though, the Government urged foreign suppliers to take payment for goods in crude oil in order to maintain oil exports at a time of weak demand, and to conserve reserves of foreign exchange. The shift in policy caused argument within the establishment. The Ministry of Oil would have preferred to sell petroleum for cash, as it foresaw an improvement in the market. In the second half of April, partly owing to barter deals, oil exports reached a post-revolutionary peak of more than 2.3m. b/d and the practice of barter trading lost some of its appeal. From May, customers for bartered oil were required to refine it in their own countries and to supply it to their domestic markets alone. By 1991 existing barter arrangements, mainly with east European countries, were being progressively terminated, in favour of cash transactions.

After the Revolution, the new Government declared itself in favour of the nationalization of foreign trade, and progress has been made towards its achievement. Nearly all foreign trade was channelled through government-controlled purchasing and distribution companies (PDCs), of which 13 were established during the 1980s for chemicals, electrical appliances, electronic and surgical instruments, food processing, a variety of light industrial products, machinery and spare parts, metals, plastics materials, textiles, tools and hardware, and wood and paper. Their main aim was to exercise strict controls over prices and import levels. In spite of the nationalization measures, the Government found it difficult, in practice, to exercise proper control over all aspects of imports and distribution. Consequently, by 1991 the PDCs were being progressively dissolved, and efforts were under way to simplify regulations and to eliminate bureaucratic obstacles to international trade. The PDCs were officially abolished in August 1991. Part of the responsibility for foreign trade lay with the Ministry of Commerce and part with the Bank Markazi, which exerted considerable control over foreign trade through constraints on letters of credit and the issue of regulations. However, in April 1995 President Rafsanjani confirmed that the Ministry of Commerce now had sole responsibility for trade policy.

In September 1981 the central bank suspended the issue of all letters of credit and imposed more stringent controls on the activities of the new import centres. In January 1982 the Government, faced with a poor rate of foreign exchange earnings from petroleum exports and a deteriorating foreign reserves position, announced that restrictions on imports, other than vital commodities, would remain in force. Foodstuffs, medicines, agricultural goods and industrial supplies were permitted but all other items were classified as luxury goods and excluded. A dramatic improvement in external accounts, as a result of the aggressive petroleum pricing policy, transformed a $2,000m.-trade deficit in 1981 into a $5,000m.-surplus in 1982. It was thought that import restrictions on certain goods might be lifted but controls were tightened towards the end of 1985/86 in response to the decline in oil revenues, and further controls were introduced in 1987, which permitted the import of only basic commodities. In spite of these efforts, estimates of the trade deficit varied from $1,500m. to $4,000m. In December 1988 the Government eased restrictions on private-sector imports of several pharmaceutical products and foodstuffs. In December 1991 it was announced that some import regulations would be simplified so that a number of goods, including electrical and electronic equipment, tools and construction items and other tools for industrial use, could be imported without a foreign exchange licence. In January 1991 some of the restrictions on foreign currency transactions were removed, as a result of which convertible currency could be legally exchanged by foreign visitors at the 'floating' free-market rate. Iran's non-oil exports were also expected to benefit from the ending of restrictions. After January 1991 the 12 exchange rates were reduced to three: the official rate of $1 = IR70 for food, defence and other strategic imports; the competitive rate of $1 = IR600 for imports of raw materials and spares; and the free floating rate of about $1 = IR1,350 for other imports and exports and for travellers. According to official sources, private importers were no longer required to obtain hard currency from government sources, or special permits for their imports, but instead simply paid 10% of the value of the goods to the Government as trading profit. In October 1991 the Governor of the Bank Markazi announced that the official exchange rate was being phased out and that only the competitive and free-floating rates would apply to all transactions until the final unification of the two exchange rates. On 13 April 1993 the central bank declared the rial fully convertible. The Governor of the Bank Markazi, Muhammad Hossain Adeli, announced that all those who needed foreign currency should refer to the banking system for their various needs. Importers of authorized goods and services could open letters of credit and buy foreign exchange without limitations from state banks. Some 32 bank branches in Teheran would sell up to $5,000 to anyone who asked, without requiring any documents. These measures were reversed in November 1993 when the Government imposed limits on hard currency sales by state banks in order to stabilize the rial and conserve foreign exchange. Under these new regulations state banks could only sell hard currency to importers, travellers, students and government personnel on missions abroad. Before their goods could be released from customs, importers had to prove that they had obtained hard currency from banks and not on the open market. Further restrictions on the availability of hard currency for imports were announced by Bank Markazi in February 1994 (see Finance).

In July 1993 Bank Markazi relaxed restrictions on imports of primary raw materials and spare parts and at the same time restrictions were tightened on cheap consumer imports through the country's free zones. These measures were designed to assist local industry, following complaints from industrialists. However, the Governor of the Bank urged industrialists to restrict their cash imports to the most urgent commodities and

to use medium-term rather than short-term credit facilities. The new measures were welcomed by industrialists, but they also increased the demand for foreign exchange resulting in a fall in the rial's free-market value. In October 1993 it was reported that the Majlis had authorized the Government to increase customs tariffs to help protect local industry from cheap imports. The devaluation of the rial by 95% in March 1993 effectively cut import duties. The import tax on primary raw materials for industry, together with machinery and spare parts that could not be manufactured locally, was not to be raised. It was expected to take some months to prepare the necessary export-import legislation. In March 1994 the Government made the Ministry of Commerce responsible for the administration of export-import regulations. In October 1994 the Ministry of Commerce imposed restrictions on exports of raw materials in order to counteract shortages in supplies to domestic factories and shops. The new policy began with a temporary ban on food exports, but also affected a wide range of raw materials including petrochemicals and steel and was predicted to slow down the high rate of growth of non-oil export earnings. Under the new regulations the internal market must be saturated with a particular raw material before an export licence is issued for it. The restrictions were extended to cover the Iranian year beginning 21 March 1995. In May strict foreign exchange restrictions were imposed, requiring exporters to repatriate all their earnings at the official exchange rate of $1 = IR3,000 (see Finance). In June the Minister of Economy and Finance stated that the Government would probably decide to apply for membership of the General Agreement on Tariffs and Trade (GATT) as the country's imports and exports were becoming more balanced. In 1996 Iran applied to join the World Trade Organization but the application was blocked by the USA. There were also differences within the Iranian leadership over the application. President Rafsanjani and his supporters were keen to promote the liberalization of trade and therefore favoured membership, but they were opposed by conservative clergy and traditional merchants who feared that their control over the country's trade would be weakened.

Since the late 1980s Qeshm and Kish Islands in the Gulf have been developed as free-trade and industrial zones. Kish Island was designated a free zone before the Revolution. The port of Chahbahar has also been designated a free zone and is being promoted as the gateway to the newly independent states of Central Asia. In addition there are three special trade zones for transit trade in Sirjan, Sarakhs and Bandar Enzeli. After a prolonged debate and amendments demanded by the Council of Constitutional Guardians, the legislation confirming the special status of the free zones was ratified in September 1993, but it was another year before basic regulations governing investment in the free zones was completed. The free zones are intended to act as centres of production, export and tourism attracting foreign investment and promoting non-oil exports. They are exempt from most restrictions in force on the mainland. All foreign investments in these zones are guaranteed, profits can be repatriated and disputes taken to international arbitration. Foreign ownership is allowed up to 100%. Foreign banks and foreign credit institutions are also allowed to set up branches in the free zones where the exchange rate will be determined by the free market. In 1993, however, there was criticism that the free zones were using their special status to import some $1,500m. of finished consumer products into Iran every year. In July 1993 business people and government agencies were banned from purchasing individual travellers' rights to bring in goods from the free zones to form large-scale commercial import operations. In November 1993 the amount of goods travellers can bring into Iran from the free zones was reduced from $700 to $200 from Kish and $80 from Qeshm. In December 1993 it was reported that President Rafsanjani had sacked the heads of the country's free zones and there was speculation that this action was taken because of their opposition to these new restrictions. According to the General Secretary of the High Council of Free-Trade Zones, Morteza Alviri, in a statement at the beginning of 1995, Qeshm had attracted most attention from potential investors because it offers discounted natural gas to energy-intensive industries. Negotiations were under way with the Ministry of Oil so that the free zone could offer gas at prices competitive with other Gulf free zones. In early

February 1995 the High Council approved a proposal by the Daewoo Corpn of South Korea to build a petrochemical plant on Qeshm, and Sun-Lin of Singapore has signed a memorandum of understanding for a 180,000 b/d oil refinery there. Kobe Steel of Japan was still negotiating to set up a hot-briquetted iron plant, and INDCONS of India has proposed building a $350m.-fertilizer plant to produce urea and ammonia. Alviri admitted that infrastructure was still inadequate at Qeshm, but stated that an international airport would be opened later in 1995. In March 1996 the head of the Qeshm Free Zone Authority reported that the free zone had attracted $4,000m. from 541 investors and that many projects had been carried out, including the construction of a ferro-manganese plant and an aluminium smelter. The island's population was reported to have increased by 40%, to 75,000, in recent years and was expected to exceed 400,000 within 10 years. The aluminium smelter on Qeshm is a joint venture between Prime International, a UK-registered Iranian company, and the Qeshm Free Zone Authority. A 33,000-ton-a-year potline has been purchased from ZSNP of Slovakia and will be refurbished before being recommissioned in Iran. Production at the $30m.-plant, known as Qeshm Alum, is scheduled to begin in early 1997. Most of the raw materials will come from domestic sources, but production will be mainly for export. There are plans to expand the smelter's capacity to 150,000 tons a year by 1998, with a possible further expansion to 200,000 tons a year. Qeshm Alum is Iran's first privately-owned aluminium smelter. There is a state-owned smelter at Arak, which produces some 120,000 tons a year, and another, with a capacity of 110,000 tons a year, is being built near Bandar Abbas and is due to start production from 1997 (see above). In April 1996 the Majlis approved legislation to relax foreign exchange rules in the free-trade zones. Under the new rules, exchange dealings are allowed at a free market rate and branches of foreign banks in the zone are placed under international regulations. The new legislation also permits the free transfer of hard currency from the free trade zones abroad and into Iran. Transfers into the zones from the rest of the country remain strictly controlled by the state. Later in the year the Majlis amended the legislation at the insistence of the Council of Guardians so that the established IR3,000 = $1 export rate will now apply to the free zones.

The threat of a US naval embargo in the Gulf at the time of the hostage crisis in 1980 focused attention on land supply lines through the USSR and Turkey and air routes from Pakistan. A protocol with the USSR, including arrangements for land supply lines across the border, was approved by the Islamic Revolutionary Council in May 1980. However, after the Revolution, there was little investment in the transport and communication sector, and in many areas the low level of maintenance of roads and railways led to the reduction in the efficiency of existing routes. Conflicts of interest over resource allocation affected the planning of new roads, and there was pressure to give priority to improving transport in rural areas. The Ministry of Roads and Transport and the Ministry of Construction Jihad built thousands of kilometres of primary roads and about 20,000 km of secondary roads in the provinces. In contrast, plans to improve road access to the ports suffered. Ministry officials criticized the annual allocation of $150m. for road construction as inadequate. They argued that two-thirds of the $30,000m. spent on transporting goods within the country is wasted because of inadequate transport facilities and poor co-ordination. This situation appears to be changing, however, and in 1990 the Ministry of Roads and Transport announced that expenditure on the transport system during the 1990–1994 Development Plan's term would total some $16,000m., including $4,300m. in convertible currency. In August 1993 it was reported that the Government planned to denationalize a wide range of transport activities and that a detailed plan would be completed by the Ministry of Roads and Transport early in 1994. The involvement of the private sector in the country's transportation system has been encouraged by the Government since 1991 and a number of projects have already been offered to the private sector. These include the new Teheran international airport, the proposed motorway from Teheran to the Caspian Sea and a railway line from Mashad to Bafq. The Supreme Administrative Council wants to reduce state expenditure on transport in the future by involving the private and co-operative sectors in developing and

maintaining all parts of the transport network. In December 1992 the Ministry of Roads and Transport stated that more than 1,400 km of roads had been repaired since March and that another 11,000 km were under construction. In November 1993 it was reported that the Ministry of Roads and Transport had approved the $800m.-motorway from Teheran to Chalus on the Caspian Sea and that the private sector had been invited to participate in its construction.

The State Railways Organization is extending and upgrading the country's 6,000-km rail network with the assistance of several international firms. The major improvement since the Revolution has been the opening of the final section of electrified track on the 146-km link between Tabriz and Djulfa, used to bring imports from the former USSR. Priority was given to completing a 730-km line connecting Bandar Abbas to Bafq and the national network, and to constructing a 560-km line from Kerman to Zahedan, providing a link with Pakistan. In August 1992 Iran and Pakistan agreed to establish a joint venture to lay track between Bafq and Bandar Abbas. In September 1992 Pakistan Railways engineers were due to visit Teheran in order to discuss the rehabilitation of the 540-km Kerman–Zahedan and the 500-km Kerman–Bandar Abbas lines. The 112-km line from Bandar Khomeini to Ahwaz is to be double-tracked, in order to reduce congestion at the port, and long-term projects include double-tracking the line from Teheran to Ahwaz and the construction of new lines. The first phase of construction of a 175-km line from Mashad to Sarakhs by the Engineering Corps of the Islamic Revolutionary Guards Corps began in May 1992. Since the disintegration of the USSR the line now forms part of a plan to link the rail systems of the newly independent Central Asian republics to the Iranian national network and the Gulf, thus establishing Iran as the gateway to Central Asia. In March 1995 President Rafsanjani opened the 730-km Bafq–Bandar Abbas railway at a ceremony attended by the Presidents of Turkmenistan, Kyrgyzstan, Armenia and Afghanistan. The new rail link, which cost nearly $900m. and took 13 years to build, links Iran's main port, Bandar Abbas, with the national network, which in turn connects with the Turkish railway system. In the north west, the national network runs to the Azerbaijan border and in the north east local contractors are completing a 140-km link to the Turkmen border at Sarakhs. At the opening ceremony President Rafsanjani stated that the new rail link was important for the newly-independent states of Central Asia and the Caucasus, providing them with the option of another link to the world, removing the monopoly of only one route. He invited Arab Gulf states to use the line for access to areas north of Iran. In April 1995 it was reported that the Indian Railway Construction Co (Ircon) might participate in building a 700-km rail link between Mashad and Bafq. The scheme would cost $400m. and would provide direct access from Bandar Abbas to the Turkmen border at Sarakhs. Ircon has also been asked to submit offers for track and signalling work for sections of the Kerman–Zahedan railway link and has been awarded a $25m.-contract to install signalling equipment on the Ahvaz–Bandar Khomeini line. The 110-km line from Ahwaz to Khorramshahr reopened in July 1989. The State Railways Organization has proposed a high-speed rail line between Teheran and Isfahan, involving a possible investment of $2,500m., and proposals from German, French and Japanese firms are also being considered. The highest speed rail service at present is on the Teheran–Qazvin line. The electrification of the Teheran–Tabriz line is expected to go ahead soon and it has been proposed to shorten and improve the Tabriz line to the Turkish border. Under the first Five-Year Development Plan $6,800m. was allocated to the State Railways Organization. It was aimed to increase annual transport capacity to 10m. passengers and 25m. tons of freight. About 1,000 km of new track were to be completed by 1995 and 1,750 km of existing track were to be renovated during the same period. In February 1994 the deputy director of the State Railways Organization stated that the railways carried 9m. passengers a year and 19m. tons of freight. During preliminary discussions about the second Five-Year Plan the Minister of Roads and Transport stated that the allocation to railways should be doubled to $17,700m. An underground railway project for Teheran began in the late 1970s, but work stopped for some 10 years after the Revolution. Construction began again in the late 1980s, but negotiations with foreign suppliers were not completed because of financing problems. Only a few contracts were awarded, including a $52m.-deal for a maintenance workshop with HMT International of India. However, in May 1995 the Teheran Urban and Suburban Railway Co signed the last of three contracts with Chinese companies to supply equipment for two underground railway lines, including rolling stock, locomotives, and signalling equipment, and for a rapid transit line west of the capital. Together the contracts are worth $573m. Some 80% of the civil engineering work on the two underground lines had already been completed. One 32-km line will link north and south Teheran, and a second 20-km line will run east-west across the city. The original plan envisaged five lines, but officials indicated that a decision on the remaining three lines would only be taken if the first phase of the project proved successful. The third contract is for a 43-km electrified railway from Teheran to the western suburb of Karaj. There was some criticism that Chinese companies had been awarded the work. According to some experts, the People's Republic of China is inexperienced in such projects and has awarded its own underground railway schemes to European companies. Financial reasons appear to have determined the choice of Chinese companies as Teheran encountered financial difficulties in its discussions with European contractors. In March 1996 it was reported that the Teheran Urban and Suburban Railway Co had arranged for two letters of credit, worth $230m., to be opened in favour of the Chinese companies providing equipment for the Teheran underground railway system, with a third, worth $4,270m., to be opened in the Iranian year beginning 21 March 1996. The three Chinese companies involved in the project are China North Industries Corpn, China National Technology Import and Export and China International Trust and Investment Corp. The first underground line is due to start operating in February 1997. In May 1996 a 300-km railway line was opened linking the Iranian national network with that of the former Soviet Union and allowing Turkmenistan access to Iran's Gulf ports. As part of an accord signed in February 1996, France is to assist in the construction of an express rail link between Teheran and Isfahan.

In the ports sector a decision was taken in September 1981 to complete work on a major extension of Bandar Abbas, a project designed before the Revolution but scaled down after the fall of the Shah. Because of war damage at the traditional seaports of Bandar Khomeini and Khorramshahr, Iran became heavily dependent on Bandar Abbas for its sea-borne imports. A new port, Bandar Shahid Rajai, was inaugurated in 1983, handling 9m. tons of the total of 12m. tons of cargo passing through Iran's Persian Gulf ports every year. Work on the port development at Bandar Abbas began in February 1985. However, only two of the original three phases of the project have been completed. There are plans to build a new jetty at the port for mineral exports, at a cost of $770m. The jetty will have a handling capacity of 10m. tons per year. Two new ports at Chah Bahar (the first called Shahid Beheshti, costing $37m.) were opened in February 1984 and September 1988, respectively, while Bushehr port is being expanded. The Ganaveh oil export port, with an export capacity of 2m. b/d, was opened in August 1988. Before the cease-fire in the Iran–Iraq War was announced, in preparation for a possible international economic embargo and closure of the Gulf to shipping, Iran made arrangements to use ports and oil refineries in neighbouring countries. Agreements were signed with Pakistan, Turkey and the USSR. Pakistan agreed in October 1987 to permit Iran's use of Karachi and Qasim ports to import up to 2m. tons of goods. In August 1992 it was announced that the port of Khorramshahr, destroyed in the Iran–Iraq War, had been reopened to freight traffic. In November 1994 it was reported that four new jetties were to be built at Bandar Anzali port on the Caspian Sea as part of a $2.2m.-expansion project. The tonnage of goods handled by the port increased by almost one-third in 1994 compared with the previous year. In January 1996 it was reported that Iran was building a harbour on the disputed Gulf island of Abu Musa and that the first of two port jetties would be operational in March.

One of Iran's major transport projects is the construction of the Imam Khomeini international airport south-west of Teheran. When the first phase is completed in 1997 the airport will be capable of handling 12m. passengers a year, according to the head of the Civil Aviation Organization, and it will eventually have a capacity of 30m. passengers a year. It was hoped that the new airport would replace Mehrabad Airport for all international flights by 1997 and would be linked to Teheran by a special underground railway system. In July 1992 it was announced that some $800m. in foreign credits had been allocated towards the cost of completing Imam Khomeini International Airport, and another $350m. to other airports. Some IR30,000m. was spent on airport modernization during 1991/92. Abadan airport reopened in 1991 and started handling international traffic in January 1994. The Civil Aviation Organization announced in early 1995 that 56 airports would be built under the second Five-Year Plan and another 43 airport projects undertaken in subsequent years. In December 1995 Aéroport de Paris won the design contract for the terminal at Imam Khomeini international airport, and in February 1996 an agreement was signed under the terms of which France will assist in establishing repair facilities and other services at the new international airport. In March 1996 it was reported that in order to improve the country's air transport the Supreme Economic Council had allocated $164m. for 10 radar units, $17m. for compass units and additional sums for new equipment for the control towers of Teheran and Shiraz airports and to pay for the leasing of 10 passenger aircraft. In recent years the national carrier, Iran Air, which uses Boeing and Airbus aircraft, has experienced problems obtaining more aircraft from the USA and Europe owing to economic sanctions. Although Iran took delivery of two Airbus passenger jets in 1994/95, restrictions on further purchases from the West prompted it to charter Russian aircraft to meet the shortfall in capacity. Iran also entered into a joint venture with the Ukrainian aircraft manufacturer Antonov for the construction at Isfahan of up to 10 An-140 passenger jets per year, with production scheduled to begin in 1999.

FINANCE

The first post-revolutionary budget, for the Iranian year 1979/80, was set at $34,000m., a little more than one-half of the target that was set during the previous year by the Shah's regime. The following year's budget (1980/81) was set at $40,000m., including provisions for a deficit of $6,500m. In fact, the deficit amounted to almost $12,000m., mainly because of the fall in the Government's petroleum revenues from an estimated $23,000m. to $11,900m. For 1981/82 the budget was set at $44,000m. and it was forecast that there would be no deficit, the entire expenditure plan being financed through petroleum revenues and taxes, and petroleum production being boosted to the point where sufficient revenue was earned. However, the Governor of the Bank Markazi criticized the use of non-replenishable resources to finance excessive current expenditures, as a matter of principle, and also stressed that, with the world glut of oil, it would be practically impossible to raise enough money from petroleum. Many members of the Majlis also attacked the budget strongly. In July 1981 the Majlis reduced total allocations to $37,000m. Some $2,500m. was subtracted from defence expenditure, and $3,100m. from the Development Plan. An overall reduction of 5% in expenditure by government departments was also demanded. Even so, a deficit of $8,500m. was forecast.

For the year March 1982 to March 1983 the Government presented a budget of $39,050m. for approval by the Majlis. Revenues were estimated at $31,902m., leaving a deficit of $7,150m. Priority for expenditure was given to the reconstruction of war-damaged areas in the south, and great emphasis was placed on restoring the existing agricultural and industrial base in order to create employment, to reduce dependency on petroleum and to limit imports. A supplementary budget of $4,856m. was approved on 13 October 1982, the principal increases being allocated to the war effort and reconstruction projects ($1,820m.), current government expenditure ($1,200m.), and the remainder mostly to power, road and port construction, government building and other infrastructural projects.

According to the then Prime Minister, Hossein Moussavi, some 30% of the 1983/84 budget, totalling an estimated IR3,600,000m. ($42,400m.), was spent on the war effort. A budget of $48,300m. for the fiscal year beginning in March 1984 was presented to the Majlis. Budgeted expenditure was about 14% higher than in 1983/84, and allowed for a deficit of $3,600m. The Prime Minister stated that government revenues were projected at $44,600m., of which more than one-half ($23,400m.) would come from sales of petroleum. The war effort was given a direct budget of $4,000m., but war-related allocations accounted for some 31% of total budgeted expenditure. Planned current expenditure by the Government accounted for $30,000m. of the total. Education was the largest single item of expenditure. Development expenditure was set at $15,200m. The Ministry of Construction Jihad was allocated more than $2,500m. However, before it was approved by the Majlis, which traditionally considers government spending to be excessive and inflationary, proposed expenditure had to be reduced by 15%.

A budget of $42,000m. for the year 1985/86 was presented to the Majlis. It envisaged a 25% reduction in the deficit, compared with the level ($10,000m.) projected for 1984/85. Of total projected expenditure, 30.6% was devoted to the war effort and war-related costs, with education receiving the second largest sectoral allocation. The Plan and Budget Committee of the Majlis cut the budget to $38,300m., almost the entire reduction being made in current expenditure, to bring it in line with the expected decline in revenue from oil sales. The Majlis approved the revised budget at the end of February 1985.

The budget for 1986/87 was presented to the Majlis in December 1985. With total expenditure set at IR4,049,700m. ($50,600m.), it provided for an increase of 12.5% in defence spending, while allocations to all other sectors were set at lower levels than in 1985/86. In a debate in February 1986 the Government was criticized for not taking full account of the rapid decline in oil prices, and for overestimating oil revenues in its preparation of the budget. An additional problem was the accumulated deficit on foreign exchange receipts and payments from 1985/86, when oil revenues, budgeted at $19,700m., actually amounted to only $13,000m.–$15,000m. Contrary to expectations, however, in March 1986 the Majlis increased planned expenditure under the 1986/87 budget to IR4,249,700m. ($53,100m.). Projected oil revenues were revised downwards to IR1,500,000m. ($18,600m.), but even this proved to be an appreciable overestimate, with actual revenue failing to reach one-half of that figure.

In March 1987 the Majlis approved a budget of IR4,000,000m. ($55,555m.) for 1987/88 (an increase of 15% compared with 1986/87), of which IR3,000,000m. ($41,670m.) were allocated to current expenditure and IR704,700m. ($9,788m.) to development. The rise in current expenditure reflected the demands of the war effort and was at the expense of domestic development. War-related expenditure was budgeted to absorb IR700,000m. ($9,722m.), or 24% of current expenditure. The Government had originally allocated IR430,000m. ($5,972m.) to the war effort, but the Majlis Plan and Budget Committee increased the figure to IR660,000m. ($9,167m.), and a further IR118,000m. ($1,639m.) was allocated from the development budget. In the late 1980s actual expenditure on the war effort was much greater than forecast. For 1987/88 a budget deficit of some $13,820m. was predicted, mainly as a result of the low level of foreign exchange earnings, with oil revenues projected at only $11,740m. It was reported in early 1989 that the deficit had been as high as $18,200m. in 1987/88. Expenditure of $57,000m. for the year 1988/89 was approved in March 1988, and proposals for expenditure of $55,000m. in 1989/90 were presented to the Majlis in December 1988. After a long debate and much criticism of the Government for its lack of direction in economic affairs, the Assembly approved a budget of $70,000m., including $9,814m. in foreign exchange for export earnings. A detailed analysis of planned expenditure was not disclosed, but there appeared to be provision for a high level of domestic borrowing to finance a deficit of as much as $20,000m. Approval for foreign credit of as much as $2,500m. was given. Allocations for annual defence spending were not revealed, but it was reported informally in Teheran that they had been almost halved, from $10,000m. to $5,850m.

The budget for 1990/91, approved by the Majlis in March 1990, projected overall expenditure of $79,900m. and revenue of $57,300m., leaving a deficit of $22,600m. An additional $21,000m. was to be invested by state enterprises. Major pro-

jects were allocated $5,400m. in foreign credits. In July 1990 the Majlis authorized an amendment to the annual budget, whereby the allocations for disaster relief and post-war reconstruction were doubled; in addition, it approved a $300m.-emergency fund for provinces devastated by the earthquake of 21 June 1990; the cost of damage to the provinces of Gilan and Zanjan was believed to exceed $7,000m. In March 1991 the World Bank approved an emergency loan of $250m. for reconstruction projects to repair damage caused by the earthquake. A supplementary budget was introduced in November 1990 to cover the remaining five months of the year; the revised estimates assumed higher revenues than had previously been forecast. Total government revenue in the period March–September 1990 was reported to have amounted to $37,700m., and expenditure to $46,400m., leaving a deficit of $8,700m. Oil and gas revenues over the same period were estimated at $8,000m. With oil and gas revenues expected to rise (owing to increases in both prices and output), the 1991/92 budget forecast total government revenue of IR7,300,000m. and expenditure of IR8,640,000m. (an increase of 54% compared with 1990/91), leaving a deficit of IR1,340,000m. A further budget of IR11,440,000m. was agreed for state-owned companies, bringing overall planned expenditure in the general budget for 1991/92 to IR20,080,000m. The budget in convertible currency, set at $24,000m., was the highest ever introduced. On 30 January 1992 the Majlis approved the budget law for 1992/93 despite criticism by deputies of its inflationary aspects. The general budget remained at the level requested by the Government, IR28,800,000m., but within it, the Government budget was increased from around IR10,000,000m. to IR12,400,000m. Deficit financing remained unchanged at IR623,000m. The Majlis increased the proportion of revenues from taxation in order to reduce dependence on oil revenues. In addition it reduced the proportion of current spending (i.e. that on education, health and social security) and increased that of development expenditure to one-third of the total. In October 1992 the Minister of Economy and Finance forecast that the budget deficit for 1992/93 would amount to $10,570m. The Government's budget proposals for 1993/94 finally received approval by the Majlis on 2 February 1993. The general budget was set at IR54,400,000m. and the Government's budget at IR25,400,000m. Efforts by the Majlis to reduce expenditure by 10% appeared to have been unsuccessful. The Government set aside $3,800m. at the existing official exchange rate of about $1 = IR70 in order to subsidize essential imports and prices. Subsidies included $1,200m. for oil product imports, the same amount for basic food items, $452m. for medicine and baby food, $80m. for Iranian students abroad and $850m. for defence. The Majlis authorized the NIOC to use up to $2,600m. in foreign finance in order to build and expand the Bandar Abbas oil refinery and its lubricants unit, and for five offshore oil fields in the Gulf.

The Majlis, concerned about low oil prices and debt repayment problems, secured cuts in both projected expenditure and revenue before the Government's budget for the year beginning March 1994 was approved. Projected revenue was reduced by 10% and expenditure by 7%–13% in various sectors. Revenue was projected at IR30,700,000m. ($17,700m.), including oil revenues of $10,150m. The overall budget was set at IR69,800,000m. ($36,900m.), of which government expenditure accounted for IR32,300,000m. ($18,500m.), with the balance to state banks and companies. Despite the reductions secured by the Majlis, the overall budget was still substantially higher than the level approved for the year 1993/94. The Government's proposal to reduce subsidies on fuel prices in order to raise revenues was rejected by the Majlis.

In December 1994 President Rafsanjani presented the draft budget for the year commencing 21 March 1995 to the Majlis. On the basis of higher oil revenues the President requested approval for spending of IR95,300,000m. ($54,500m.), 37% higher than the 1994/95 level. In March 1995 the Majlis approved a nominally balanced budget which was slightly higher than the draft proposal, at IR96,100,000m. ($54,900m.). However, it imposed new controls on the Government instead of granting its request to be allowed greater flexibility. Oil revenues for 1995/96 were projected at $13,500m., based on a crude oil price of $17 a barrel. Some IR2,180,000m. ($1,240m.) was allocated for defence, and $1,750m. for essential imports, including medicine and powdered milk for babies. A further $1,100m. in foreign exchange was allocated to the Ministry of Oil, but with the requirement that spending must be justified on a monthly basis. No new state firms could be established and existing ones were required to make their accounts available at the request of the Majlis. State enterprises were also forbidden to purchase goods abroad if equivalents were available locally.

In January 1996 the Majlis approved the budget for the year beginning 21 March 1996 after making only minor amendments. The budget proposed total expenditure of IR55,780,000m. ($31,870m.), of which $16,000m. was to be provided by oil revenues, based on an oil price of $15.5 per barrel. The contribution of earnings from oil to total revenue was forecast to fall by 9% compared with the year beginning 21 March 1995—one of the lowest contributions since the Revolution. The budget made no reference to non-oil exports, which declined sharply in 1995/96. Total expenditure was forecast at IR137,120,000m. ($78,370m. at the official exchange rate), about $400m. less than the original draft had requested. It was reported that about 60% of total expenditure would be allocated to subsidize loss-making state industries and banks. State subsidies for basic food items were increased by $212m. to $1,460m. in hard currency allocations. A further $388m. was allocated for subsidies for medicine and powdered milk. The Government is also required, under the new budget legislation, to reduce the country's debt by $1,640m. in 1996/97. The allocation to the Ministry of Defence was increased slightly, from $1,250m. to $1,260m., although it was reported that the total defence budget had been increased by almost one-third to $3,310m. The Majlis also approved a special fund of some $20m. to counter a proposal before the US Congress to establish a covert action fund to destabilize the Iranian Government. Iran had threatened to begin proceedings against the USA at the ICJ if the US Congress approved the proposal. In April 1996 the Government announced that it was committed to higher expenditure of hard currency in 1996/97 and that it had allocated $19,000m. to finance imports of basic goods and machinery and to service debts. Non-oil revenues were projected at a conservative $3,000m. Officials of the Bank Markazi insisted that higher targeted expenditure would not affect the country's ability to service its external debts.

In November 1996 President Rafsanjani presented the draft budget for the year beginning 21 March 1997 to the Majlis. He emphasized that his Government remained committed to strict controls over spending but would maintain its efforts to protect low-income groups. Overall budget expenditure was set at IR188,149,000m. which analysts believed to be about 10% higher, in real terms, than the level set in 1996/97. Some IR117,960,000m. was allocated for state-owned industries and IR81,287,000m. for the general government budget. IR29,100,000m. of the general government budget was allocated to development projects including the oil sector, water and electricity. Of the general budget revenue projected at IR75,909,000m., IR30,713,000m. was to come from oil revenues and IR18,727,000m. from taxation. Oil revenues were projected on the basis of an average export price for Iranian oil of $17.5 per barrel.

As tabled in late November 1997, the first version of the 1998/99 budget was based on the Government's assumption of an average oil price of $17.50 per barrel and provided for a balance between expenditure and income at IR233,700,000m. However, sharply falling world prices from late 1997 necessitated two successive revisions of the budget, the first in 1998 based on a $16 per barrel price assumption and the second in April on $12 per barrel. It was officially stated that the latest version was a 'temporary' budget that would be amended again if oil prices increased later in the year. However, a further decrease in the Gulf crude price to under $10 per barrel by mid-1988 again undermined the feasibility of the final 1998/99 budget.

Inflation has become a persistent problem for the economy. Import controls have tended to increase inflation in a situation of growing shortages and especially in view of a policy favouring wage increases for the lower paid without increases in productivity. The annual rate of inflation officially fell from 32.5% in 1980/81 to 17% in 1983/84, and in May 1985 the central bank reported that wholesale prices had risen by only 7.6% in 1984/

85 (year to 20 March). IMF figures suggest that inflation for the year ended September 1984 was approximately 13%–14%. In October 1985 the Government continued to maintain that inflation was falling, and that the annual rate was a mere 5.5%. In the first half of 1987, when the annual rate of inflation was unofficially estimated at 30%–50%, the Government appeared tacitly to admit the seriousness of the problem by announcing that, henceforth, the prices of 22 basic commodities would be controlled in order to check inflation. In an interview in November 1991 the Governor of the Bank Markazi stated that inflation was running at 15%. Given the reconstruction and development programmes and the adjustment of a war-stricken economy that were taking place, he regarded the level of inflation as a matter of minor concern. According to the central bank, the rate of inflation rose to 22% in 1993/94 when the rial was devalued and oil prices fell sharply. A year of 'monetary discipline' was declared in 1994/95 and it was predicted that a tight monetary policy would reduce inflation to less than 20%. The Majlis was reported to have imposed a 15% ceiling on the growth of liquidity in 1994/95 in order to control inflation, while the rates charged by state banks on loans to various sectors were to remain unchanged. In October 1994 President Rafsanjani announced an anti-profiteering campaign after a surge in inflation to about 40%. In its first phase price controls were applied to government-controlled goods, such as sugar, flour, primary dairy products, red meat, washing powder, domestically-produced paper and tyres, fodder, chemical fertilizers and ironware. There were temporary shortages as traders withheld goods, but the Government subsequently saturated the market with emergency imports sold through co-operatives and state stores in order to undermine the merchants. The Government also announced that in 1995 it was opening a chain of 1,000 publicly-owned stores selling goods at low prices, a move aimed at breaking the hold of the bazaar merchants. The campaign against inflation was reinforced in January 1995 when the list of goods subject to price controls was extended. Since the beginning of 1995 price controls have been applied to hundreds of items, including cars, household appliances, medicines, cigarettes, foodstuffs, construction materials and beverages. Some 1,000 centres were set up across the country in order to investigate public complaints and to prosecute offenders. There were official raids on some warehouses where merchants were hoarding goods. According to the central bank, the annual rate of inflation rose to a record 58.8% in April/May 1995 following a substantial decline in the value of the rial which forced the Government to fix the exchange rate at $1 = IR3,000 and to impose strict hard currency controls in May. Prices of many goods were reported to have fallen in the second half of June. At the beginning of 1996 the Ministry of Justice announced that some 280,000 rulings had been issued by the special courts to enforce state prices since they were established in October 1994; and that fines totalling IR32,000m. ($11m.) had been imposed. Potatoes were added to the list of goods subject to price controls after their price doubled at the end of 1995. The special courts were criticized in the media, however: it was claimed that they were not effective and that the anti-inflation measures had merely created a thriving black market. After rising to 49.4% in the 1995/96 Iranian year, the annual inflation rate was halved to 23.3% in 1996/97 and then further reduced to 17.3% in 1997/98, although renewed inflationary pressures in the first half of 1998 were expected to increase the 1998/99 level to 20%.

The state offers a wide range of subsidies on basic foodstuffs. In an interview in November 1991 the Minister of Economic Affairs and Finance stated that the Government would continue to subsidize essential goods, notably foodstuffs, such as bread, rice, cooking oil and sugar, and medicines, until 1994. Other subsidies would gradually be reduced. Figures produced by the Consumer and Producer Protection Organization indicated that prices of local goods were rising much faster than claimed by the central bank. Rising prices in the extensive 'black market' in goods are not taken into account in official price indices, while rents in the housing market have increased substantially in urban areas throughout the country. At the beginning of his second term of office in August 1993, President Rafsanjani warned the country to expect a gradual reduction of some state subsidies and the elimination of others, particularly those on fuel and electricity. He stated that subsidies were wasting public funds, distorting the economy and preventing the growth of a healthy private sector. Furthermore, he believed that the system of subsidies was unjust. The rich were the main beneficiaries because of their high level of consumption. The result was that the majority of Iranians were in effect subsidizing the living standards of the richest 10% of the population. Some subsidies had been removed during 1992/93, but a comprehensive programme to phase them out was incorporated into the draft second Five-Year Plan. These proposals met with strong opposition in the Majlis, largely because of the political risks involved. In February 1994 the Majlis rejected proposed price increases for petroleum products and domestic gas supplies. Nevertheless, the President renewed his attack on subsidies in April 1994, stating that energy subsidies alone cost the Government $11,000m. a year, which was more than projected oil revenues for 1994/95. He estimated that the total cost of subsidies was $15,000m. a year. He acknowledged that some subsidies were justified; these included the $360m. for agriculture, and $230m. for assistance to families of those killed in the Revolution and the Iran–Iraq War. However, he condemned bread and energy subsidies as unjust because the rich benefited most from them. In April some deputies proposed legislation to cancel all price rises announced since 21 March and to transfer price-setting powers from the Supreme Economic Council, which is headed by the President, to the Majlis. Since February 1994 the Supreme Economic Council had authorized increases in telephone charges, postal rates and domestic air fares, while there were also increases in inter-city bus and train fares. The motion was postponed indefinitely as other deputies supported the Government, but at the end of May Rafsanjani announced that the Government would act cautiously on subsidies and indicated that those on bread and fuel would not be removed during the next five years. However, in November 1994, under pressure from the Government, the Majlis approved the doubling of fuel prices from March 1995 and annual increases of 20% until the end of the decade. However, in April 1996 domestic fuel prices were increased by more than 20% (see Petroleum). In December 1995 the IMF had recommended that domestic fuel prices should be increased in stages to international levels by 2000. In April 1997 domestic fuel prices were again substantially increased, but again the overall impact was negligible because of the effect of inflation. In April 1998 the IMF estimated that the 'implicit subsidies' arising from the underpricing of domestic petroleum products were equivalent to nearly 10% of GDP, the largest share being attributed to gas-oil, the domestic price of which was about one-fourteenth of the prevailing world price. Hard currency allocations for state subsidies on basic food items were increased by $212m. to $1,460m. in the 1996/97 budget, but were reduced slightly to $1,420m. in the 1997/98 budget. Subsidies to cover the cost of medicines and other goods rose from $338m. in 1996/97 to a projected $500m. in 1997/98.

In June 1990, under pressure to reduce inflation, the Government enacted major reforms of the foreign exchange market and import-export regulations. Foreign currency dealings outside authorized money-changing houses became illegal and restrictions on importers and exporters were relaxed. A new rate for the rial against the US dollar was intended to encourage exports by giving industrialists access to hard currency for raw materials and machinery. In February 1993 the Minister of Economy and Finance announced that the Government would use a variety of financial instruments, including forward selling, to keep the rial stable after the planned currency devaluation on 21 March. Public sector demand for hard currency would be controlled in order to create a hard currency surplus to support the rial in the free market. The rial was declared fully convertible by the central bank on 13 April 1993. After devaluing the rial by more than 96% in April 1993, the central bank responded to downward market pressure by further devaluing its floating rate. The value of the rial fell to record lows from late 1993. After April 1994, when new restrictions were introduced requiring nearly all importers to use limited official supplies of hard currency earned from non-oil exports, the rial's value on the open market plunged dramatically. On 7 May 1994 the central bank introduced a new currency exchange rate, known as the import-against-export rate, which was applied to most imports. The rate announced on 7 May was $1=IR2,585, compared with a floating rate of $1=IR1,748. The central bank stated that the

new rate would be IR50 below the open market rate which had fluctuated between IR2,500–IR2,800. The new rate effectively devalued the rial by 32%. A bank official stated that very limited funds had been allocated by the Government to some ministries for essential imports, such as machinery and medicine, but that most goods would have to be imported at the new rate.

Following his appointment as Governor of the Bank Markazi in September 1994, Mohsen Nourbakhsh stated that he would work to introduce a single foreign exchange rate and moved quickly to tighten supervision of hard currency transactions. At the beginning of October police arrested at least 30 money dealers operating in Teheran, but by January 1995 many were back in action using motorcycles to deliver foreign currency directly to their customers. By late January the free market value of the rial had fallen to an all-time low of $1 =IR4,000. However, the rial recovered somewhat when the central bank announced that it was easing some import restrictions so that exporters would be able to use half of their hard currency earnings to purchase goods from abroad; and increasing the supply of gold coins sought by investors. The Governor of the Bank Markazi informed the Majlis that the fall in the value of the rial was due to a lack of investment opportunities which encouraged the public to engage in speculative activities. New export-import regulations became effective from 4 February 1995. Exporters were once again permitted to sell up to half of their hard currency earnings to importers, on condition that they repatriated the other half of their earnings from abroad. There had been speculation that much of Iran's hard currency earnings from non-oil exports in 1993/94 had been kept abroad. In April 1995, in a move aimed at encouraging exporters to repatriate their hard currency earnings, the central bank effectively devalued the rial by 43%. The export exchange rate was changed from $1 = IR2,340 to $1 = IR4,123 in late April. The official floating rate of $1 = IR1,750 continued to apply for essential imports. The value of the rial against the US dollar fell sharply in April and May, with the biggest losses occurring after President Clinton announced a trade embargo on Iran. The rial fell to $1 = IR6,300 in early May, losing about one-third of its value in only two weeks. President Rafsanjani blamed 'speculators and profiteers' for the sharp fall in the rial and threatened resolute action against them. There was further criticism of the central bank which was accused in the local press of having lost control over the foreign exchange market. On 17 May the Government revalued the rial and imposed strict foreign exchange controls. The new regulations, which took effect on 21 May, set a fixed rate of $1 = IR 3,000. This was initially valid until March 1996, but was subsequently extended. All other rates were eliminated except the official rate of $1 = IR1,750, used for imports of essential commodities. All hard currency transactions had to be carried out through state banks—an allocation system was to be introduced giving priority to imports of raw materials and spare parts for industry—and exporters had to repatriate all their hard currency earnings from abroad. A new government crackdown on illegal exchange dealers was reported to have begun. However, there was speculation that the Government would not be able to maintain the new fixed rate for more than two months. Some observers argued that the new regulations requiring exporters to repatriate all their hard currency earnings within six months could damage non-oil exports, but central bank officials claimed that non-oil exports would become more competitive. In late 1995 the IMF, as part of its economic programme for Iran, recommended that the unification of exchange rates should take place by 21 March 1996, with market-related management of rates to continue after unification. However, the central bank indicated that it preferred to continue with a more gradualist approach, with currency reforms proceeding in sequence and the stringent foreign exchange restrictions imposed in May 1995 to be dismantled last of all. The central bank's Deputy Governor stated that the Government would continue its campaign against the currency black market and smuggling for the foreseeable future; and insisted that the Government's intervention in the foreign currency market in May 1995 and the stabilization of the rial had had a positive effect on inflation. Early in 1997 the Governor of the Bank Markazi indicated that the exchange rate system was unlikely to be unified until mid-1999. He also acknowledged that reimposing strict exchange controls had resulted in some negative effects, notably the reappearance of an active parallel currency market. By the end of the 1996/97 financial year, according to the IMF, the rial had appreciated by about 80% in real terms against the official 'export' rate of $1 = IR3,000, although this appreciation was partly offset by the effective depreciation of the weighted average exchange rate resulting from the shifting of transaction from the more appreciated 'floating' rate to the 'export' rate. Accordingly, on a weighted average basis, the real effective appreciation amounted to only about 16% in 1996/97 (for current account transactions).

Following the June 1979 nationalization of banking and insurance, in 1980 the Government announced the establishment of an Islamic banking system, which officially came into force on 21 March 1984. Interest on loans (*riba,* which is prohibited under Islamic law) was replaced by a commission—4% per year, compared with the traditional 14%—and interest on deposits was replaced with profits—estimated at a minimum 7%–8.5% per year. The banks would become temporary shareholders in major industrial enterprises to which they lent money. On 21 March 1985 all bank loans and advances were Islamized.

In March 1980 the 22 small commercial banks were merged into two major new institutions, Bank Tejarat and Bank Mellat. Today the Iranian commercial banking system is composed of 10 institutions: Bank Keshavarzi, Bank Mellat, Bank Melli Iran, Bank Refah Kargaran, Bank Saderat Iran, Bank Sepah, Bank Tejarat, the Islamic Economy Organization, Bank Sanat va Madan and the Export Development Bank of Iran.

In 1992 rumours that state banks might be privatized were strongly denied by the central bank. Nevertheless, in recent years the state banks have been encouraged to operate on more commercial lines and competition between them for customers is now intense. In May 1994 the Council of Ministers authorized the establishment of private savings and loan associations which were described by the Governor of the Bank Markazi as 'non-banking credit associations' which would be allowed to take deposits and make loans, but would not be permitted to offer current accounts. He stated that the aim of these associations was to encourage savings by providing a range of institutions able to take deposits. It was not clear whether the interest-free Islamic banking law would be applied to the new associations. For some years there has been pressure, mainly from business and industry, for the reintroduction of a private commercial banking system along international lines. The existing system is regarded as an impediment to developing business and industry. Some officials are believed to acknowledge that the banking system needs to be changed, but this would pose serious constitutional and religious obstacles.

No official information regarding Iran's reserves of foreign exchange was released between 1982 and 1994. In 1982 reserves were recorded at $5,700m. (excluding gold), representing less than 50% of the level prevailing before the Revolution. In March 1984 the Majlis approved legislation preventing the Government from spending more than it earned. As a result, drawings on foreign reserves were believed to have been limited in 1984 and 1985. About $3,000m. were withdrawn by the Government during 1986, when the price of oil collapsed, but there followed a steady improvement in reserve holdings. In mid-1988 Iran's foreign exchange reserves were estimated at $6,000m.–$7,000m. (including gold holdings) compared with $3,000m.–$4,000m. in mid-1986. In June 1991 the Bank for International Settlements (BIS) reported that the value of Iranian assets had fallen by 25% during the previous 12 months to $5,019m., while, during the same period, the extent of Iran's liabilities had risen to $3,784m. The BIS reported that liabilities to OECD commercial banks were at an all-time high of $9,105m. in March 1993, when Iranian deposits with the same banks were estimated at $5,935m. By the final quarter of 1993 the BIS reported that liabilities to foreign banks and other financial institutions were $8,553m., with Iran's assets standing at $5,561m. In the second half of 1994 the BIS reported that Iranian deposits in commercial banks in OECD countries rose by about $1,000m. to $6,492m. and in December 1994 they had returned to the same level as in early 1991. Sources in Teheran reported that the central bank intended to add another $1,000m.–$2,000m. to reserves in 1995, raising the total to about $8,000m., the highest level since the mid-1980s. This increase in reserves was being achieved by reducing expenditure and imports and was an attempt by Iran to improve its international creditworthiness and to guarantee the repayment of foreign debts due in 1996. According to the BIS, Iran's liabilities to commercial banks in OECD countries rose by $1,700m. to $9,910m. in the third quarter of 1994. In the third quarter of 1995 Iranian deposits in commercial banks in OECD countries rose by $458m. to the record level of $8,398m., according to the BIS. Iran's liabilities to these banks rose by $290m. to $11,660m. According to Bank Markazi, net repayment of foreign debt resulted in a $2,115m. decrease in exchange reserves in the first half of the 1997/98 financial year; no figure for the remaining reserves was given, but Western estimates put them at $5,000m.–$6,000m. at the end of the year. The Bank's Governor stressed that reserves were not allowed to drop below six months' import cover and that all foreign obligations would continue to be met on time. According to the BIS, Iran's deposits in commercial banks in OECD countries had fallen to $7,457m. by September 1997, against total liabilities of $8,613m.

According to the World Bank, reporting for the first time since 1979, Iran's total external debt had risen to just over $9,000m. by December 1990, of which one-fifth consisted of long-term commitments. Figures from the BIS and the OECD indicated that Iran's external debt rose from $5,560m. in December 1989 to $6,469m. in June 1990, and to $10,000m. by the end of that year. According to the BIS, external debts rose rapidly in 1991, reaching an estimated $13,653m. by December. By June 1992 they had increased to about $15,000m. A lower figure of $11,500m. was reported by the World Bank for December 1991. The World Bank estimate showed a $2,500m.-increase compared to December 1990, and a $5,000m.-increase compared to December 1989. According to the World Bank, $8,775m. of the total external debt consisted of short-term debts and $2,775m. of long-term debts. However, in February 1993 the Chairman of the Majlis Plan and Budget Committee declared that Iran had accumulated about $30,000m. in short-term external debts by March 1992—the first official acknowledgement of the country's high external indebtedness. He reported that $18,000m. had been added to the external debt since 1989. The World Bank reported a lower estimate of $14,166m. in December 1992, of which $11,102m. consisted of short-term debts. The Bank estimated that the total cost of debt servicing was $810m. The BIS estimated Iran's total external debt at $16,107m. in mid-1993, consisting of $8,826m. in external bank claims and $7,281m. of non-bank credits.

By the end of the 1993/94 Iranian year, Iran's total external debt had reached $23,000m., of which $17,600m. was in the form of short-term credits accumulated during the early years of President Rafsanjani's first term of office, when government spending was at a high level. From mid-1992 Iran experienced problems paying its external debts as oil revenues declined. During 1993 Western creditors became increasingly concerned about arrears on repayments, which are believed to have risen as high as $10,000m. until the massive reschedulings of 1994 (see below). In early 1993 a series of rescheduling agreements were concluded regarding letters of credit payments not covered by export guarantee organizations. In April 1993 German, French and Japanese banks holding more than $2,000m. in Iranian letters of credit agreed to defer payment for one year to allow Iran time to bring its short-term debt repayments back on schedule. Belgian creditors followed and by the end of the year agreement had been reached to reschedule debts totalling $3,000m. In November 1993 Iran's total payment arrears were estimated to have reached at least $7,000m. Early in 1994 it was rumoured that Iran was exploring the possibility of bilateral government-to-government deals with Germany and France in order to avoid a 'Paris Club' rescheduling, the implications of which would be politically unacceptable to the Iranian Government. Despite opposition from the USA, agreements of bilateral rescheduling were concluded with several European creditors and with Japan during the first half of 1994. In February Germany agreed to restructure about $2,400m. of short-term debts into medium-term ones. Similar agreements followed with Japan, Austria, Switzerland, Denmark, Spain, Belgium, Italy and France. The package included a two-year grace period, with payments spread over four years starting in 1996. The agreements reached with Italy and France in June 1994 brought the amount of debt rescheduled to about $8,000m. A central bank official stated in May that the refinancing deals had been arranged so that annual repayments beginning in 1996 would not exceed 25% of projected government revenue. In September 1994 the Bank Markazi reported that it had signed 75 agreements with various creditors to reschedule arrears. It estimated Iran's total foreign debt at $18,000m.–$20,000m. and described the 21% ratio of foreign debt to GDP as relatively low when compared with similar economies. In the second half of 1994 rescheduling agreements were signed with Finland, and with German creditors without state insurance cover, raising German debt reschedulings to more than $3,000m.; and with Swiss creditors without state insurance cover. After some technical and political problems with the rescheduling of debts to Italian creditors, for which an in-principle agreement had been reached in July 1994, a rescheduling package for $1,000m. owed to official creditors was finalized in early 1995 and another agreement for $400m. for private Italian creditors was due to be signed in March 1995. In February it was reported that Crédit Suisse had been instructed to organize and administer the repayment of Iranian debts to UK creditors without official insurance cover. A five-year rescheduling package of up to $500m. was expected to be finalized in March. The agreements with private creditors included the immediate settlement of some small claims, or a percentage payment with the balance to be paid in instalments. In January 1995 a central bank official stated that official and private reschedulings totalled about $12,000m. and would cover $14,000m. by March. The Bank Markazi was reported to be determined to ensure that all new payment commitments were honoured. All letters of credit opened by the Bank since March 1994 were being paid on time, together with interest payments and small claims related to the debt reschedulings. In April 1995 the central bank reported that foreign loans and letters of credit due in the Iranian year ending 20 March 1995 had been paid on time and although no figures were released, experts suggested that they totalled at least $10,000m., with about $3,500m. devoted to the repayment of rescheduled debts. In January 1995 the Swiss export credit guarantee agency, ERG, became the first Western agency to resume insurance cover for exports to Iran following the rescheduling of most of Iran's foreign debts. Germany, which had initiated the process of rescheduling Iran's foreign debts, began to offer limited insurance cover in February, despite opposition from the USA.

At the end of December 1995 creditor nations which had rescheduled some $14,000m. of Iran's foreign debt since 1993 received their first payment of principal. In February 1996 the central bank reported that the total principal foreign debt stood at $23,412m. on 22 September 1995. Of this, $20,145m. was classified as long- and medium-term debt and $3,267m. as short-term debt. The Bank Markazi's, figures indicated that total debt stocks, including principal and interest obligations, were $30,600m. In April 1996 the Bank Markazi reported that repayments of rescheduled short-term debt and medium-term obligations had totalled $5,660m. in the year ending 20 March 1996, a substantially higher amount than the central bank's earlier projection of $4,300m. and than an independent estimate of $4,800m. Announcing a rise in hard currency spending in April 1996, the central bank insisted that the country's ability to service its external debts would not be affected, and independent observers appeared confident that Iran would repay its debts on time in order to try to regain its international creditworthiness. The Government is obliged by law to reduce its foreign debt by $1,640m. each year and new borrowing is illegal. Debt repayments were expected to account for more than one-quarter of the country's oil revenues in 1996/97. In January 1996 Iran's ambassador to Russia stated that a $700m.-agreement with

Russia for the supply of aircraft would increase Iran's debts to Russia to $1,200m. This was to be repaid in annual installments of $250m. until 1999. In mid-February 1996 the Russian Ministry of Foreign Economic Relations reported that Iran had agreed to settle debts to Russia in $230m.-worth of oil and $150m. in cash in order to improve trade relations between the two countries. In October 1995 Berliner Handels und Frankfurter (BHF), a German bank, agreed to provide medium- and long-term financing facilities totalling DM 1,000m. ($676m.) for five Iranian banks (Bank Melli, Bank Mellat, Bank Tejarat, Bank Saderat and Bank Sepah). The agreement, which came into force in December, provides for financing over 5–12 years, depending on the projects for which it is requested, and on approval by the German state insurance agency, Hermes. In May it was reported that AKA Ausfuhrkredit-Gesellschaft, set up by 42 German banks to provide export credits, had reached an agreement with 10 Iranian banks under which it would provide unlimited amounts of long-term loans for projects approved under the second Five-Year Plan. The financing is for a maximum of 10 years. This agreement was regarded as a significant breakthrough for Iran in its efforts to secure international finance. Despite the opposition of the USA, Iran has succeeded in securing long-term finance facilities from other foreign banks. In February 1996 a syndicate of 10 European and Japanese banks granted a $560m.-loan to finance a contract awarded to Danieli and Co of Italy by the NISCO (see Steel). In the same month there was speculation that the French state insurance agency, Coface, would restore cover following French government support for rail and airport projects in Iran. In 1996 the Governor of the Bank Markazi stated that Iran had repaid $15,400m. of debt between March 1992 and March 1996 ($6,800m. of rescheduled debt and $8,600m. of non-rescheduled debt) and that the remaining debt would be paid off in five years. Further progress was achieved in 1996/97 in reducing the outstanding stock of external debt and improving its maturity structure. Total outstanding external debt declined from $21,900m. in March 1996 to $16,800m. by March 1997, of which about $12,000m. was medium- and long-term debt (down from $16,000m. at the end of 1994/95.) Concurrently, the outstanding short-term debt dropped substantially to $4,800m. by March 1997 and external arrears were virtually eliminated. By March 1998 total external debt had been further reduced to $11,700m., of which $5,300m. consisted of rescheduled debts. Rescheduled debt repayments in 1998/99 were expected to total less than $4,000m. and to fall sharply in 1999/2000.

Early in 1994 the USA succeeded in its campaign to stop further World Bank loans to Iran, and in April the Bank's lending programme was frozen at $850m. A $150m.-loan proposal to develop livestock and arable land and a $125m.-proposal to develop basic education were shelved indefinitely. Earlier, in September 1993, Iran had been told to seek alternative sources of funding for two proposals for gas flaring reduction and rail and ports rehabilitation because the Bank considered them to be controversial. However, in December 1996 the Bank agreed to extend a 25-year credit facility worth $600m. to Iran to fund infrastructure and health projects. Moreover, a resumption of full participation in the World Bank appeared more feasible as US–Iranian relations began to thaw in the first half of 1998. In April the Bank Markazi Governor led an Iranian delegation to the spring meeting of the Bank and the IMF in Washington, reportedly with the aim of securing support to rescind the 1994 ban. In 1996 Iran stated that it would take legal action to secure the release of Iranian assets which remain 'frozen' in the USA. The Iranian Government claimed that these assets total $12,000m. but independent sources suggest that they are probably between $3,500m. and $5,000m. As of mid-1998, the Iranian assets remained 'frozen'.

Statistical Survey

The Iranian year runs from 21 March to 20 March.

Source (except where otherwise stated): Statistical Centre of Iran, Dr Fatemi Ave, Cnr Rahiye Moayeri,
Opposite Sazeman-e-Ab, Teheran 14144; tel. (21) 655061; telex 213233; fax (21) 653451.

Area and Population

AREA, POPULATION AND DENSITY

Area (sq km)	1,648,000*
Population (census results)†	
1 October 1991	55,837,163
25 October 1996	
Males	30,515,159
Females	29,540,329
Total	60,055,488
Density (per sq km) at October 1996	36.4

* 636,296 sq miles.
† Excluding adjustment for underenumeration.

PROVINCES (1996 census)*

Province (Ostan)	Population	Provincial capital
Tehran (Teheran)	11,176,139	Tehran (Teheran)
Markazi (Central)	1,228,812	Arak
Gilan	2,241,896	Rasht
Mazandaran	4,028,296	Sari
East Azarbayejan . . .	3,325,540	Tabriz
West Azarbayejan . . .	2,496,320	Orumiyeh
Bakhtaran (Kermanshah) . .	1,778,596	Bakhtaran
Khuzestan	3,746,772	Ahwaz
Fars	3,817,036	Shiraz
Kerman	2,004,328	Kerman
Khorasan	6,047,661	Mashad
Esfahan	3,923,355	Esfahan
Sistan and Baluchestan . .	1,722,579	Zahedan
Kordestan	1,346,383	Sanandaj
Hamadan	1,677,957	Hamadan
Chaharmahal and Bakhtiari . .	761,168	Shahr-e-Kord
Lorestan	1,584,434	Khorramabad
Ilam	487,886	Ilam
Kohgiluyeh and Boyerahmad . .	544,356	Yasuj
Bushehr	743,675	Bushehr
Zanjan	1,036,873	Zanjan
Semnan	501,447	Semnan
Yazd	750,769	Yazd
Hormozgan	1,062,155	Bandar-e-Abbas
Ardabil	1,168,011	Ardabil
Qom	853,044	Qom
Total	60,055,488	—

* On 1 January 1997 the legislature approved a law creating a new province, Qazvin (with its capital in the city of Qazvin). In June 1997 the Council of Ministers approved draft legislation to establish another new province, Gorgan (with its capital in the city of Gorgan), by dividing the existing province of Mazandaran.

PRINCIPAL TOWNS (population at 1996 census)

Tehran (Teheran,		Rasht . . .	417,748
the capital) . .	6,758,845	Mehrshahr . . .	413,299*
Mashad (Meshed) .	1,887,405	Hamadan . . .	401,281
Esfahan (Isfahan) .	1,266,072	Kerman	384,991
Tabriz . . .	1,191,043	Arak	380,755
Shiraz . . .	1,053,025	Ardabil (Ardebil). .	340,386
Karaj . . .	940,968	Yazd . . .	326,776
Ahwaz . . .	804,980	Qazvin . . .	291,117
Qom . . .	777,677	Zanjan . . .	286,295
Bakhtaran		Sanandaj . . .	277,808
(Kermanshah) . .	692,986	Bandar-e-Abbas . .	273,578
Orumiyeh . . .	435,200	Khorramabad . .	272,815
Zahedan. . . .	419,518	Eslamshahr	
		(Islam Shahr) .	265,450

* Estimated population at 1 October 1994 (Source: UN, *Demographic Year-book*).

BIRTHS AND DEATHS (UN estimates, annual averages)

	1980–85	1985–90	1990–95
Birth rate (per 1,000) . .	46.1	41.4	35.5
Death rate (per 1,000) . .	10.4	8.1	6.7

Expectation of life (UN estimates, years at birth, 1990–95): 67.5 (males 67.0; females 68.0).

Source: UN, *World Population Prospects: The 1994 Revision*.

1991: Registered live births 1,885,649 (birth rate 33.8 per 1,000); Registered deaths 461,443 (death rate 8.3 per 1,000).

1994: Registered live births 1,304,255 (birth rate 21.9 per 1,000); Registered deaths 175,438 (death rate 2.9 per 1,000).

Note: Registration is incomplete.

ECONOMICALLY ACTIVE POPULATION
(persons aged 6 years and over, 1996 census)

	Males	Females	Total
Agriculture, hunting and forestry .	3,024,380	294,156	3,318,536
Fishing	38,418	309	38,727
Mining and quarrying . . .	115,185	4,699	119,884
Manufacturing	1,968,806	583,156	2,551,962
Electricity, gas and water supply .	145,239	5,392	150,631
Construction.	1,634,682	15,799	1,650,481
Wholesale and retail trade; repair of motor vehicles, motorcycles and personal and household goods .	1,804,143	38,146	1,842,289
Hotels and restaurants . .	82,293	2,485	84,778
Transport, storage and communications .	955,271	17,541	972,792
Financial intermediation . .	139,286	13,586	152,872
Real estate, renting and business activities	137,039	12,051	149,090
Public administration and defence; compulsory social security	1,519,449	98,651	1,618,100
Education	581,597	459,459	1,041,056
Health and social work . .	184,242	118,897	303,139
Other community, social and personal service activities . .	183,246	41,159	224,405
Private households with employed persons .	57,037	4,933	61,970
Extra-territorial organizations and bodies.	660	220	880
Central departments and offices .	30,389	2,563	32,952
Activities not adequately defined .	204,808	52,220	257,028
Total employed	12,806,170	1,765,402	14,571,572

Unemployed ('000 persons, 1996 census): 1,455 (males 1,183; females 272).

Agriculture

PRINCIPAL CROPS ('000 metric tons)

	1994	1995	1996
Wheat	10,870	11,228	11,200*
Rice (paddy)	2,259	2,301	2,300*
Barley	3,045	2,952	3,000†
Maize	512	545	600†
Potatoes	3,185	2,974	3,200*
Dry beans	110	129	140†
Chick-peas	299	355	360†
Lentils	160*	110†	110†
Soybeans	147	134†	134†
Cottonseed	232	314	307*
Cotton (lint)* . . .	118	165	156
Tomatoes	2,088	2,403	2,150*
Pumpkins, squash and gourds† .	215	220	220
Cucumber and gherkins . .	1,227	1,286	1,250†
Onions (dry) . . .	1,112	1,130	1,200*
Other vegetables† . .	1,185	1,216	1,215
Watermelons† . . .	2,580	2,650	2,650
Melons†	1,185	1,215	1,215
Grapes	1,893	1,846	1,900*
Dates	774	780	795*
Apples	2,008	1,824	2,000*
Pears†	179	184	184
Peaches and nectarines† . .	123	126	126
Plums†	133	137	137
Oranges	1,584	1,556	1,600
Tangerines, mandarins, clementines and satsumas .	629	599	630
Lemons and limes . .	649	726	655
Other citrus fruits† . .	125	150	130
Apricots†	118	121	121
Other fruits and berries . .	1,456	1,495†	1,496†
Sugar cane . . .	1,857	1,859	1,900†
Sugar beets . . .	5,295	5,521	4,000†
Almonds†	67	69	69
Pistachios	195	239	282*
Walnuts†	66	68	68
Tea (made)	56	54	56*
Tobacco (leaves)	10	14	17†

* Unofficial figure(s).   † FAO estimate(s).

Source: FAO, *Production Yearbook*.

LIVESTOCK ('000 head, year ending September)

	1994	1995	1996
Horses*	250	250	250
Mules†	137	137	137
Asses†	1,400	1,400	1,400
Cattle	8,202	8,347	8,492
Buffaloes	438	447	456
Camels	143	143	143
Sheep	50,285	50,889	51,499
Goats	25,757	25,757	25,757

Chickens (million): 186* in 1994; 186* in 1995; 202 in 1996.

* FAO estimate(s).   † Unofficial figures.

Source: FAO, *Production Yearbook*.

LIVESTOCK PRODUCTS ('000 metric tons)

	1994	1995	1996
Beef and veal	276*	276*	277
Buffalo meat*	10	10	10
Mutton and lamb . . .	254*	256*	280
Goat meat	101*	101*	100
Poultry meat	635	659	672
Other meat*	16	16	17
Cows' milk	3,126†	3,400*	3,809
Buffaloes' milk . . .	121†	121*	160
Sheep's milk	541†	540*	438
Goats' milk	662†	668*	412
Cheese*	207	216	196
Butter*	104	112	119
Hen eggs	516	466	520
Honey*	8	8	8
Wool:			
greasy	50†	51†	51
clean	28*	28*	28
Cattle and buffalo hides* . .	40	40	40
Sheepskins*	48	48	53
Goatskins*	18	18	18

* FAO estimate(s).   † Unofficial figure.

Source: FAO, *Production Yearbook*.

Forestry

ROUNDWOOD REMOVALS ('000 cubic metres, excl. bark)

	1993	1994	1995
Sawlogs, veneer logs and logs for sleepers	412	396	386
Pulpwood	523	580	509
Other industrial wood* . .	4,007	4,007	4,007
Fuel wood	2,531	2,549	2,561
Total	7,473	7,532	7,463

* Annual output assumed to be unchanged since 1974.

Source: FAO, *Yearbook of Forest Products*.

SAWNWOOD PRODUCTION
('000 cubic metres, incl. railway sleepers)

	1993	1994	1995
Total (all broadleaved) . . .	170	178	159

Source: FAO, *Yearbook of Forest Products*.

Fishing

('000 metric tons, live weight)

	1993	1994	1995
Freshwater fishes . . .	46.2	47.8	58.9
Diadromous fishes . . .	45.6	64.4	53.4
Marine fishes . . .	216.8	211.8	246.3
Marine crustaceans and molluscs .	9.5	8.5	9.7
Total catch	318.1	332.4	368.3
Inland waters	96.9	115.0	117.3
Indian Ocean	221.2	217.4	251.0

Source: FAO, *Yearbook of Fishery Statistics*.

Production of caviar (metric tons, year ending 20 March): 281 in1988/89; 310 in 1989/90; 233 in 1990/91.

Mining

CRUDE PETROLEUM
(net production, '000 barrels per day, year ending 20 March)

	1988/89	1989/90	1990/91
Southern oilfields . . .	2,454	2,716	2,987
Offshore oilfields. . . .	103	231	244
Doroud–Forouzan–Abouzar–			
Soroush.	58	162	166
Salman–Rostam–Resalat .	23	40	46
Sirri–Hendijan–Bahregan .	22	29	32
Total	**2,557**	**2,947**	**3,231**

1991/92 ('000 barrels per day): Total production 3,366.
1992/93 ('000 barrels per day): Total production 3,484.
1993/94 ('000 barrels per day): Total production 3,609.
1994/95 ('000 barrels per day): Total production 3,603.
1995/96 ('000 barrels per day): Total production 3,600.
1996/97 ('000 barrels per day): Total production 3,595.

Source: Ministry of Oil.

NATURAL GAS (million cu metres, year ending 20 March)

	1994/95	1995/96	1996/97
Consumption (domestic)* . .	35,500	39,000	42,400
Flared	11,600	11,800	13,200
Exports	100	0	0
Regional uses and wastes. .	7,700	8,600	8,600
Total production . . .	**54,900**	**59,400**	**64,200**

* Includes gas for household, commercial, industrial, generator and refinery consumption.

OTHER MINERALS ('000 metric tons, year ending 20 March)

	1993/94	1994/95	1995/96
Hard coal	970	980†	1,000†
Iron ore*	2,137	4,300‡	4,500‡
Copper ore*§	86.6	117.9	102.2
Lead ore*§	14.7	18.3	15.9
Zinc ore*§	70.0	72.9	145.1
Manganese ore* . . .	18.7	13.0‡	n.a.
Chromium ore*	48	37‡	37‡
Magnesite‡	49.4	40.0	40.0
Fluorspar (Fluorite)‡ . . .	10.0	10.0	10.0
Barytes‡	226	139	150
Salt (unrefined)‡ . . .	720	1,050	936
Gypsum (crude)‡	8,800	8,430	8,230

* Figures refer to the metal content of ores.
† Estimated production.
‡ Figure(s) from the US Bureau of Mines.
§ Data from *World Metal Statistics* (London).

Source: UN, *Industrial Commodity Statistics Yearbook*.

Industry

PETROLEUM PRODUCTS
(estimates, '000 metric tons, year ending 20 March)

	1993/94	1994/95	1995/96
Liquefied petroleum gas . . .	2,800	3,100	3,710
Naphtha	400	300	400
Motor spirit (petrol) . . .	6,291	6,200	6,300
Aviation gasoline	90	100	100
Kerosene	4,400	4,500	4,600
White spirit	300	300	300
Jet fuel	1,100	1,200	1,250
Gas-diesel (distillate fuel) oil .	14,200	14,400	14,500
Residual fuel oils	14,300	14,100	14,100
Lubricating oils	600	610	610
Petroleum bitumen (asphalt) .	2,200	2,100	2,200

Source: UN, *Industrial Commodity Statistics Yearbook*.

OTHER PRODUCTS (year ending 20 March)*

	1993/94	1994/95	1995/96
Refined sugar ('000 metric tons) .	1,060	1,052	1,151
Cigarettes (million)	7,835	7,939	9,787
Paints ('000 metric tons) . .	46	36	32
Cement ('000 metric tons) . .	16,321	16,250	16,861
Refrigerators ('000) . . .	789	629	636
Gas stoves ('000)	191	215	243
Telephone sets ('000) . . .	288	218	161
Radios and recorders ('000) . .	174	138	33
Television receivers ('000) . .	502	360	250
Motor vehicles (assembled) ('000) .	66	69	92
Footwear (million pairs) . . .	23	19	17
Machine-made carpets ('000 sq m) .	14,480	16,560	13,823

* Figures refer to production in large-scale manufacturing establishments with 50 workers or more.

Production of Electricity (million kWh, year ending 20 March): *Ministry of Energy:* 71,335 in 1993/94; 77,086 in 1994/95; 80,044 in 1995/96; 85,825 in 1996/97; 92,310 in 1997/98. *Private Sector:* 4,679 in 1993/94; 4,933 in 1994/95; 4,925 in 1995/96; 5,026 in 1996/97.

Finance

CURRENCY AND EXCHANGE RATES
Monetary Units
100 dinars = 1 Iranian rial (IR).

Sterling and Dollar Equivalents (31 May 1998)
£1 sterling = 2,872.9 rials;
US $1 = 1,761.8 rials;
10,000 Iranian rials = £3.481 = $5.676.

Average Exchange Rate (rials per US $)
1995   1,747.93
1996   1,750.76
1997   1,752.92

Note: In March 1993 the multiple exchange rate system was unified, and since then the exchange rate of the rial has been market-determined. The foregoing information refers to the base rate, applicable to receipts from exports of petroleum and gas, payments for imports of essential goods and services, debt-servicing costs and imports related to large national projects. There is also an export rate, set at a mid-point of US $ = 3,007.5 rials in May 1995, which applies to receipts from non-petroleum exports and to all other official current account transactions not effected at the base rate.

BUDGET ('000 million rials, year ending 20 March)*

Revenue	1995/96	1996/97†	1997/98‡
Oil and gas revenues	29,431	38,153	39,633
Non-oil revenues	15,577	24,222	38,090
Taxation	7,313	12,560	19,020
Income and wealth taxes . .	5,649	8,971	8,109
Corporate taxes . . .	3,296	5,378	5,261
Public corporations . .	1,065	2,328	2,143
Private corporations . .	2,231	3,050	3,118
Taxes on wages and salaries .	902	1,586	609
Taxes on other income . .	967	1,408	1,642
Import taxes.	1,250	2,934	5,368
Customs duties . . .	793	1,536	2,880
Order registration fees . .	405	1,358	2,400
Taxes on consumpton and sales	414	655	5,543
Excise tax on special goods	n.a.	n.a.	1,600
Goods and services price			
differential . . .	n.a.	n.a.	3,100
Non-tax revenues	4,683	6,409	12,672
Services and sales of goods .	1,346	2,139	3,246
Other revenues§	3,337	4,270	9,426
Excises on petroleum			
products	788	1,514	2,743
Special revenues	3,581	5,253	6,398
Total	**45,008**	**62,375**	**77,723**

Expenditure‖					1995/96	1996/97‡	1997/98‡
General services	.	.	.	.	3,149	3,957	6,111
National defence	.	.	.	.	2,774	3,532	5,812
Social services	.	.	.	.	14,556	17,137	25,757
Education	.	.	.	.	7,153	7,999	12,493
Health and nutrition	.	.	.	2,280	2,397	3,619
Social security and welfare	.	.	2,663 ⎫	6,741 ⎧	5,088
Other social services	.	.	.	2,460 ⎭		4,557
Economic services	.	.	.	.	15,350	14,752	16,803
Agriculture	.	.	.	.	1,647	1,101	1,671
Water resources	.	.	.	1,514	2,021	2,559
Petroleum, fuel and power	.	.	5,245	7,532	7,064
Transport and communication	.	1,929	3,067	4,269
Commerce	.	.	.	.	4,493 ⎫	1,031 ⎧	327
Other economic services	.	.	522 ⎭		913
Other expenditure§	.	.	.	.	2,774	13,736	17,828
Foreign exchange obligations	.	.	9,298	2,757	5,837
Special expenditures	.	.	.	3,581	5,253	6,397
Total	.	.	.	.	51,482	61,124	84,545
Current	.	.	.	.	38,599	40,395	56,010
Capital	.	.	.	.	12,883	20,729	28,535

* Figures refer to the consolidated accounts of the central Government, comprising the General Budget, the operations of the Social Security Organization and special (extrabudgetary) revenue and expenditure.
† Provisional figures.
‡ Forecasts. The provisional total (in '000 million rials) for expenditure in 1996/97 is 67,571 (current 49,317; capital 18,254), excluding net lending (–67).
§ Including operations of the Organization for Protection of Consumers and Producers, a central government unit with its own budget.
‖ Excluding lending minus repayments ('000 million rials): –14 in 1995/96; –25 (forecast) in 1996/97; –712 (forecast) in 1997/98.

Source: IMF, *Islamic Republic of Iran – Statistical Appendix* (October 1996) and *Islamic Republic of Iran: Recent Economic Developments* (April 1998).

INTERNATIONAL RESERVES (US $ million at 31 December)*

	1993	1994	1995
Gold (national valuation) . .	229	242	252
IMF special drawing rights . .	144	143	134
Total	373	385	386

* Excluding reserves of foreign exchange, for which no figures are available since 1982 (when the value of reserves was US $5,287m.).

1996 (US $ million at 31 December): IMF special drawing rights 345.

Source: IMF, *International Financial Statistics*.

MONEY SUPPLY ('000 million rials at 20 December)

	1995	1996	1997
Currency outside banks . .	7,949	9,598	11,271
Non-financial public enterprises' deposits at Central Bank . .	2,020	2,639	2,642
Demand deposits at commercial banks . .	24,373	33,628	41,064
Total money	34,342	45,865	54,977

Source: IMF, *International Financial Statistics*.

COST OF LIVING (Consumer Price Index in urban areas, year ending 20 March; base: 1990/91 = 100)

	1994/95	1995/96	1996/97
Food, beverages and tobacco . .	270.7	434.0	499.2
Clothing	198.2	320.0	431.0
Housing, fuel and light . .	215.6	278.0	375.4
All items (incl. others) . .	249.3	372.4	458.8

1997/98 (base: 1996/97 = 100): All items 117.3.

Source: Bank Markazi Jomhouri Islami Iran.

NATIONAL ACCOUNTS
('000 million rials at current prices, year ending 20 March)
National Income and Product

	1994/95	1995/96	1996/97*
Domestic factor incomes† . .	110,383.4	152,726.3	195,624.5
Consumption of fixed capital .	18,967.4	28,073.8	38,026.1
Gross domestic product (GDP) at factor cost . . .	129,350.8	180,800.1	233,650.6
Indirect taxes . . . ⎫ *Less* Subsidies . . . ⎭	–968.9	–1,925.1	–908.9
GDP in purchasers' values .	128,381.9	178,875.0	232,741.7
Factor income from abroad ⎫ *Less* Factor income paid abroad ⎭	–3,015.3	–1,809.4	–2,819.3
Gross national product (GNP) .	125,366.6	177,065.6	229,922.4
Less Consumption of fixed capital .	18,967.4	28,073.8	38,026.1
National income in market prices	106,399.2	148,991.9	191,896.3

* Provisional figures.
† Compensation of employees and the operating surplus of enterprises.

Expenditure on the Gross Domestic Product

	1994/95	1995/96	1996/97*
Government final consumption expenditure . . .	16,176.7	23,053.5	31,283.2
Private final consumption expenditure . . .	71,962.9	108,921.5	143,664.1
Increase in stocks† . . .	1,265.3	–6,507.2	–13,202.9
Gross fixed capital formation . .	29,853.1	41,511.0	59,473.7
Total domestic expenditure .	119,258.0	166,978.5	221,218.1
Exports of goods and services . .	31,909.1	36,747.3	43,828.4
Less Imports of goods services .	22,785.2	24,850.8	32,304.8
GDP in purchasers' values . .	128,381.9	178,875.0	232,741.7
GDP at constant 1982/83 prices‡	13,180.9	13,740.5	14,549.7

* Provisional figures.
† Including statistical discrepancy.
‡ Including adjustment for changes in terms of trade ('000 million rials): –1,704.2 in 1994/95; –1,574.4 in 1995/96; –1,543.3 (provisional) in 1996/97.

Gross Domestic Product by Economic Activity (at factor cost)

	1994/95	1995/96	1996/97*
Agriculture, hunting, forestry and fishing	27,272.8	40,091.0	48,911.0
Mining and quarrying† . . .	25,069.3	29,952.2	37,541.1
Manufacturing†	17,725.5	25,877.2	33,882.4
Electricity, gas and water . .	1,321.6	2,430.4	3,465.8
Construction	4,428.8	6,386.3	10,345.8
Trade, restaurants and hotels . .	19,978.4	28,988.7	36,902.6
Transport, storage and communications . .	8,166.8	11,368.2	13,721.4
Finance, insurance, real estate and business services . . .	12,273.0	17,053.5	23,872.3
Government services	11,689.1	15,686.8	20,910.5
Other services	2,420.9	3,706.4	4,729.4
Sub-total	130,346.2	181,540.7	234,282.3
Less Imputed bank service charge .	995.4	740.6	631.7
Total	129,350.8	180,800.1	233,650.6

* Provisional figures.
† Refining of petroleum is included in mining and excluded from manufacturing.

BALANCE OF PAYMENTS (US $ million, year ending 20 March)

	1995/96	1996/97	1997/98*
Exports of goods f.o.b. . . .	18,360	22,391	18,506
Petroleum and gas . . .	15,103	19,271	15,464
Non-petroleum and gas exports .	3,257	3,120	3,042
Imports of goods f.o.b. . .	−12,774	−14,989	−14,995
Trade balance . . .	5,586	7,402	3,511
Exports of services . . .	593	860 ⎫	
Imports of services . .	−2,339	−3,083 ⎪	−2,535
Other income received . .	316	488 ⎬	
Other income paid . . .	−794	−898 ⎭	
Balance on goods, services and income	3,362	4,769	976
Unrequited transfers (net) . .	−4	463	259
Current balance . . .	3,358	5,232	1,235
Long-term capital (net) . .	1,457	−5,246	−3,549
Short-term capital (net) . .	−2,231	−262	−1,268
Net errors and omissions . .	284	2,622	−123
Overall balance . . .	2,868	2,346	−3,705

* Estimates.

Sources: Bank Markazi Jomhouri Islami Iran; IMF, *International Financial Statistics*.

External Trade

PRINCIPAL COMMODITIES (US $ million, year ending 20 March)

Imports c.i.f.*	1993/94	1994/95	1995/96
Food and live animals . . .	2,446	1,369	2,404
Cereals and cereal preparations .	1,376	693	1,444
Sugar, sugar preparations and honey	167	251	376
Crude materials (inedible) except fuels	551	649	660
Mineral fuels, lubricants, etc. . .	83	324	228
Animal and vegetable oils and fats	431	392	490
Vegetable oils and fats . . .	414	376	455
Chemicals	2,023	1,376	1,733
Chemical elements and compounds	405	306	430
Plastic materials, etc. . . .	516	237	259
Basic manufactures . . .	3,344	1,654	2,533
Paper, paperboard, etc. . .	249	256	527
Iron and steel	1,667	686	820
Machinery and transport equipment	10,036	5,525	3,656
Non-electric machinery . . .	6,957	4,054	2,285
Electrical machinery, apparatus, etc.	1,780	834	892
Transport equipment . . .	1,299	637	479
Miscellaneous manufactured articles	760	403	306
Scientific instruments, watches, etc.	564	316	222
Total (incl. others) . . .	20,037	11,795	12,313

* Including registration fee, but excluding defence-related imports.

Source: IMF, *Islamic Republic of Iran: Recent Economic Developments* (April 1998).

1996/97 US $ million): Total imports c.i.f. 16,806 (Source: Bank Markazi Jomhouri Islami Iran).

Exports f.o.b.*	1994/95	1995/96	1996/97
Agricultural and traditional goods	3,258.6	1,901.0	1,645.8
Carpets	2,132.9	981.1	642.5
Fruit and nuts (fresh and dried)	628.3	580.0	639.2
Pistachios	389.8	424.7	477.5
Animal skins and hides, and leather	134.6	115.0	98.4
Metal ores	55.9	73.4	46.8
Industrial manufactures . . .	1,510.0	1,276.3	1,413.1
Chemical products . . .	35.3	71.4	76.7
Textile manufactures . .	96.1	75.0	75.3
Copper bars, sheets and wire .	106.8	64.2	40.6
Domestic appliances and sanitary ware . . .	137.6	41.6	59.1
Iron and steel	340.5	168.9	69.9
Hydrocarbons (gas) . . .	74.4	96.8	112.8
Total	4,824.5	3,250.7	3,105.7

* Excluding exports of petroleum (US $ million): 14,603 in 1994/95; 15,103 in 1995/96; 19,271 in 1996/97.

Source: Bank Markazi Jomhouri Islami Iran.

PRINCIPAL TRADING PARTNERS
(US $ million, year ending 20 March)

Imports c.i.f.	1993/94	1994/95	1995/96
Argentina	363	287	544
Australia	402	260	412
Austria	394	228	189
Azerbaijan	239	392	210
Belgium	537	649	663
Brazil	342	176	227
Canada	273	293	458
China, People's Republic . .	326	147	232
France	663	479	498
Germany	3,997	2,209	1,777
India	224	214	222
Indonesia	34	58	205
Italy	1,939	1,008	535
Japan	2,341	894	886
Korea, Republic . . .	469	320	342
Netherlands	374	263	281
Pakistan	40	53	165
Russia	187	268	370
Spain	155	136	154
Switzerland	525	212	509
Thailand	541	69	225
Turkey	408	274	240
United Arab Emirates . .	1,120	647	441
United Kingdom . . .	1,007	544	505
USA	824	347	476
Total (incl. others) . . .	20,037	11,795	12,313

Exports f.o.b.	1993/94	1994/95	1995/96
Azerbaijan	66	204	170
Bahamas	485	—	—
Belgium	473	466	524
Bermuda	559	—	—
Brazil	102	374	277
China, People's Republic . .	329	223	216
France	450	398	848
Germany	939	1,203	783
Greece	615	704	839
India	364	493	555
Italy	397	758	1,587
Japan	2,476	2,941	2,775
Korea, Republic . . .	780	927	1,108
Poland	258	158	109
Singapore	542	702	392
Spain	50	403	781
Sweden	174	199	243
Switzerland	927	552	140
Taiwan	240	280	302
Turkey	908	865	761
United Arab Emirates . .	352	780	809
United Kingdom . . .	1,975	1,790	1,439
USA	1,409	2,707	762
Total (incl. others) . . .	18,080	19,434	18,360

Source: Bank Markazi Jonhouri Islami Iran.

Transport

RAILWAYS (traffic)

	1994	1995	1996
Passenger-km (million) . . .	6,479	7,294	7,044
Freight ton-km (million) . . .	10,700	11,865	13,638

ROAD TRAFFIC (estimates, '000 motor vehicles in use)

	1994	1995	1996
Passenger cars	1,636	1,714	1,793
Lorries and vans	626	657	692

Source: International Road Federation, *World Road Statistics*.

SHIPPING

Merchant Fleet (registered at 31 December)

	1994	1995	1996
Number of vessels . . .	429	424	414
Displacement ('000 grt) . . .	3,803.3	2,902.4	3,566.8

Source: Lloyd's Register of Shipping, *World Fleet Statistics*.

International Sea-borne Freight Traffic
('000 metric tons)

	1994	1995	1996
Goods loaded	128,026	132,677	140,581
Crude petroleum and petroleum products	123,457	127,143	134,615
Goods unloaded	20,692	22,604	27,816
Petroleum products . . .	6,949	7,240	7,855

CIVIL AVIATION (traffic on scheduled services)*

	1994	1995	1996
Passengers carried ('000) . .	5,441	5,809	5,889
Passenger-km (million) . . .	5,055	5,384	5,840
Cargo ton-km (million) . . .	515	547	643

* Figures refer only to traffic of Iran Air.

Tourism

	1993	1994	1995
Tourist arrivals ('000) . . .	304.1	362.0	443.2
Tourist receipts (US $ million) .	131	153	160

Source: UN, *Statistical Yearbook*.

Communications Media

	1993	1994	1995
Radio receivers ('000 in use) . .	14,730	15,550	15,580
Television receivers ('000 in use) .	4,050	4,076	4,300
Telephones ('000 main lines in use)*	3,642	4,320	5,090
Telefax stations (number in use)*	25,000	30,000	n.a.
Mobile cellular telephones (subscribers)*	n.a.	9,200	26,300
Book production†:			
Titles	8,183	10,753	9,716
Copies ('000)	n.a.	n.a.	61,652
Daily newspapers	26	28	29
Non-daily newspapers . . .	50‡	n.a.	n.a.
Other periodicals	411	403	623

* Twelve months ending March following the year stated.
† Including pamphlets (140 titles in 1994).
‡ Figure refers to 1990.

Sources: partly UNESCO, *Statistical Yearbook*; UN, *Statistical Yearbook*.

Education

(1994/95)

	Institutions	Teachers	Students
Pre-primary	2,715	6,151	141,728
Primary	61,889	305,380*	9,745,600
Secondary:			
General	n.a.	228,889	7,284,611
Teacher-training . . .	n.a.	538	21,210
Vocational	n.a.	19,880	347,008
Higher:			
Universities, etc. . . .	n.a.	n.a.	758,150
Distance-learning . . .	n.a.	3,177	104,631
Others	n.a.	5,208	46,695

* Teachers in public education only.

1995/96: Higher education: Universities, etc. 42,782 teachers, 869,748 students; Distance-learning 3,635 teachers, 118,496 students; Others 6,395 teachers, 58,849 students.

Source: UNESCO, *Statistical Yearbook*.

Directory

The Constitution

A draft constitution for the Islamic Republic of Iran was published on 18 June 1979. It was submitted to a 'Council of Experts', elected by popular vote on 3 August 1979, to debate the various clauses and to propose amendments. The amended Constitution was approved by a referendum on 2–3 December 1979. A further 45 amendments to the Constitution were approved by a referendum on 28 July 1989.

The Constitution states that the form of government of Iran is that of an Islamic Republic, and that the spirituality and ethics of Islam are to be the basis for political, social and economic relations. Persians, Turks, Kurds, Arabs, Balochis, Turkomans and others will enjoy completely equal rights.

The Constitution provides for a President to act as chief executive. The President is elected by universal adult suffrage for a term of four years. Legislative power is held by the Majlis (Islamic Consultative Assembly), with 270 members who are similarly elected for a four-year term. Provision is made for the representation of Zoroastrians, Jews and Christians.

All legislation passed by the Islamic Consultative Assembly must be sent to the Council for the Protection of the Constitution (Article 94), which will ensure that it is in accordance with the Constitution and Islamic legislation. The Council for the Protection of the Constitution consists of six religious lawyers appointed by the Faqih (see below) and six lawyers appointed by the High Council of the Judiciary and approved by the Islamic Consultative Assembly. Articles 19–42 deal with the basic rights of individuals, and provide for equality of men and women before the law and for equal human, political, economic, social and cultural rights for both sexes.

The press is free, except in matters that are contrary to public morality or insult religious belief. The formation of religious, political and professional parties, associations and societies is free, provided they do not negate the principles of independence, freedom, sovereignty and national unity, or the basis of Islam.

The Constitution provides for a Wali Faqih (religious leader) who, in the absence of the Imam Mehdi (the hidden Twelfth Imam), carries the burden of leadership. The amendments to the Constitution that were approved in July 1989 increased the powers of the Presidency by abolishing the post of Prime Minister, formerly the Chief Executive of the Government.

The Government

WALI FAQIH (RELIGIOUS LEADER)

Ayatollah SAYED ALI KHAMENEI.

HEAD OF STATE

President: Hojatoleslam Dr SAYED MUHAMMAD KHATAMI (assumed office 3 August 1997).

Vice-President in charge of Executive Affairs: MUHAMMAD HASHEMI RAFSANJANI.

Vice-President in charge of Legal and Parliamentary Affairs: Hojatoleslam MUHAMMAD ALI SADUQI.

Vice-President in charge of Development and Social Affairs: ABDOLLAH NURI.

Vice-President and Head of the Organization for the Protection of the Environment: MA'SUMEH EBTEKAR.

Vice-President and Head of the Plan and Budget Organization: MUHAMMAD ALI NAJAFI.

Vice-President and Head of the Physical Education Organization: SAYED MOSTAFA HASHEMI-TABA.

Vice-President and Secretary General of the Organization for Administrative and Employment Affairs: MUHAMMAD BAQERIAN.

COUNCIL OF MINISTERS
(September 1998)

Minister of Foreign Affairs: KAMAL KHARRAZI.
Minister of Education: HOSSEIN MOZAFAR.
Minister of Culture and Islamic Guidance: ATA'OLLAH MOHAJERANI.
Minister of Information: QORBANALI DORRI NAJAFABADI.
Minister of Commerce: MUHAMMAD SHARI'ATMADARI.
Minister of Health: MUHAMMAD FARHADI.
Minister of Posts, Telegraphs and Telephones: MUHAMMAD REZA AREF.

Minister of Justice: MUHAMMAD ISMAÏL SHOUSHTARI.
Minister of Defence and Logistics: ALI SHAMKHANI.
Minister of Roads and Transport: MAHMUD HOJJATI.
Minister of Industries: GHOLAMREZA SHAFE'I.
Minister of Higher Education: MOSTAFA MO'IN.
Minister of Mines and Metals: ESHAQ JAHANGIRI.
Minister of Labour and Social Affairs: HOSSEIN KAMALI.
Minister of the Interior: SAYED ABDOLVAHED MUSAVI-LARI. ABDOLLAH NURI.
Minister of Agriculture: ISA KALANTARI.
Minister of Housing and Urban Development: ALI ABD AL-ALIZADEH.
Minister of Energy: HABIBOLLAH BITARAF.
Minister of Oil: BIZAM NAMDAR-ZANGENEH.
Minister of Economic Affairs and Finance: HOSSEIN NAMAZI.
Minister of Construction Jihad: MUHAMMAD SA'IDI-KIA.
Minister of Co-operatives: MORTEZA HAJI.

MINISTRIES

All ministries are in Teheran.

Ministry of Mines and Metals: 248 Somayeh Ave, Teheran; tel. (21) 836051; telex 212718.

Ministry of Roads and Transport: 49 Taleghani Ave, Teheran; tel. (21) 661034; telex 213381.

President and Legislature

PRESIDENT

Election, 23 May 1997

Candidates	Votes	%
SAYED MUHAMMAD KHATAMI	20,088,338	69.1
ALI AKBAR NATEQ NOURI	7,233,568	24.9
SAYED REZA ZAVAREI	771,463	2.7
MUHAMMAD MUHAMMADI REYSHAHRI	742,599	2.6
Spoilt votes	240,994	0.8
Total	**29,076,962**	**100.0**

MAJLIS-E-SHURA E ISLAMI—ISLAMIC CONSULTATIVE ASSEMBLY

Voting in the first round of elections to the fifth Majlis took place on 8 March 1996. It was reported that 145 candidates had gained a sufficiently large proportion (at least one-third in single-member constituencies, or selection by at least one-third of voters in multi-member constituencies where electors cast multiple votes) of the total votes cast in their constituencies to take up seats in the 270-member Majlis. About 77% of the approximately 32m. eligible voters were reported to have participated in the first round of the election. A second round of voting to the 125 seats which remained unfilled took place on 19 April. In May the Council of Constitutional Guardians, charged with monitoring the elections, declared the results of polling in 19 constituencies to be null and void. By-elections to the 19 vacant seats were held in April 1997.

Speaker: ALI AKBAR NATEQ NOURI.

Deputy Speakers: Hojatoleslam HOSSEIN HASHEMIAN, ASADOLLAH BAYAT.

SHURA-YE ALI-YE AMNIYYAT-E MELLI—SUPREME COUNCIL FOR NATIONAL SECURITY

Formed in July 1989 to co-ordinate defence and national security policies, the political programme and intelligence reports, and social, cultural and economic activities related to defence and security. The Council is chaired by the President and includes two representatives of the Wali Faqih, the Head of the Judiciary, the Speaker of the Majlis, the Chief of Staff, the General Command of the Armed Forces, the Minister of Foreign Affairs, the Minister of the Interior, the Minister of Information and the Head of the Plan and Budget Organization.

MAJLIS-E KHOBREGAN—COUNCIL OF EXPERTS

Elections were held on 10 December 1982 to appoint a Council of Experts which was to choose an eventual successor to the Wali Faqih, then Ayatollah Khomeini, after his death. The Constitution provides for a three- or five-man body to assume the leadership of the country if there is no recognized successor on the death of the Wali Faqih. The Council comprises 83 clerics. Elections to a second term of the Council were held on 8 October 1990.

Speaker: Ayatollah ALI MESHKINI.

First Deputy Speaker: Hojatoleslam ALI AKBAR HASHEMI RAFSAN-JANI.

Secretaries: Hojatoleslam HASSAN TAHERI-KHORRAMABADI, Ayatollah MUHAMMAD MOMEN-QOMI, Ayatollah IBRAHIM AMINI.

SHURA-E-NIGAHBAN—COUNCIL OF GUARDIANS

The Council of Guardians, composed of six qualified Muslim jurists appointed by Ayatollah Khomeini and six lay Muslim lawyers, appointed by the Majlis from among candidates nominated by the Head of the Judiciary, was established in 1980 to supervise elections and to examine legislation adopted by the Majlis, ensuring that it accords with the Constitution and with Islamic precepts.

Chairman: Ayatollah MUHAMMAD MUHAMMADI GUILANI.

SHURA-YE TASHKHIS-E MASLAHAT-E NEZAM— COMMITTEE TO DETERMINE THE EXPEDIENCY OF THE ISLAMIC ORDER

Formed in February 1988, by order of Ayatollah Khomeini, to arbitrate on legal and theological questions in legislation passed by the Majlis, in the event of a dispute between the latter and the supervisory Council of Guardians. Its permanent members, defined in March 1997, are Heads of the Legislative, Judiciary and Executive Powers, the jurist members of the Council of Guardians and the Minister or head of organization concerned with the pertinent arbitration.

Chairman: Hojatoleslam ALI AKBAR HASHEMI RAFSANJANI.

HEY'AT-E PEYGIRI-YE QANUN ASASI VA NEZARAT BAR AN—COMMITTEE FOR ENSURING AND SUPERVISING THE IMPLEMENTATION OF THE CONSTITUTION

Formed by President Khatami in November 1997; members are appointed for a four-year term.

Members: Dr GUDARZ EFTEKHAR-JAHROMI; MUHAMMAD ISMAÏL SHOUSHTARI; SAYED ABDOLVAHED MUSAVI-LARI; Dr HOSSEIN MEHRPUR; Dr MUHAMMAD HOSSEIN HASHEMI.

Political Organizations

The Islamic Republican Party (IRP) was founded in 1978 to bring about the Islamic Revolution under the leadership of AYATOLLAH KHOMEINI. After the Revolution the IRP became the ruling party in what was effectively a one-party state. In June 1987 AYATOLLAH KHOMEINI officially disbanded the IRP at the request of party leaders, who said that it had achieved its purpose and might only 'provide an excuse for discord and factionalism' if it were not dissolved. Of the parties listed below, only the Nehzat-Azadi (Liberation Movement of Iran) has been afforded a degree of official recognition and been allowed to participate in elections.

Ansar-e Hezbollah: f. 1995; seeks to gain access to the political process for religious militants.

Democratic Party of Iranian Kurdistan: f. 1945; seeks autonomy for Kurdish area; mem. of the National Council of Resistance; 54,000 mems; Sec.-Gen. MUSTAPHA HASSANZADEH.

Fedayin-e-Khalq (Warriors of the People): urban Marxist guerrillas; Spokesman FARRAKH NEGAHDAR.

Fraksion-e Hezbollah: f. 1996 by deputies in the Majlis who had contested the 1996 legislative elections as a loose coalition known as the Society of Combatant Clergy; Leader ALI AKBAR HOSSAINI.

Hezb-e-Komunist Iran (Communist Party of Iran): f. 1979 on grounds that Tudeh Party was Moscow-controlled; Sec.-Gen. 'AZARYUN'.

Komala: f. 1969; Kurdish wing of the Communist Party of Iran; Marxist-Leninist; Leader IBRAHIM ALIZADEH.

Majma-e Hezbollah: f. 1996 by deputies in the Majlis who supported President Rafsanjani and who had contested the 1996 legislative elections as a loose coalition known as the **Servants of Iran's Construction** (f. as a political organization of this name in 1998; Sec.-Gen. GHOLAMHOSSEIN KARBASCHI); Leader ABDOLLAH NURI.

Mujahidin-e-Khalq (Holy Warriors of the People): Islamic guerrilla group; since June 1987 comprising the National Liberation Army; mem. of the National Council of Resistance; Leaders MASSOUD RAJAVI and MARYAM RAJAVI (in Baghdad, 1986–).

National Democratic Front: f. March 1979; Leader HEDAYATOLLAH MATINE-DAFTARI (in Paris, January 1982–).

National Front (Union of National Front Forces): comprises Iran Nationalist Party, Iranian Party, and Society of Iranian Students; Leader Dr KARIM SANJABI (in Paris, August 1978–).

Nehzat-Azadi (Liberation Movement of Iran): f. 1961; emphasis on basic human rights as defined by Islam; Gen. Sec. Dr IBRAHIM YAZDI; Principal Officers Prof. SAHABI, S. SADR, Dr SADR, Eng. SABAGHIAN, Eng. TAVASSOLI.

Pan-Iranist Party: extreme right-wing; calls for a Greater Persia; Leader Dr MOHSEN PEZESHKPOUR.

Sazmane Peykar dar Rahe Azadieh Tabaqe Kargar (Organization Struggling for the Freedom of the Working Class): Marxist-Leninist.

Tudeh Party (Communist): f. 1941; declared illegal 1949; came into open 1979, banned again April 1983; First Sec. Cen. Cttee ALI KHAVARI.

The National Council of Resistance (NCR) was formed in Paris in October 1981 by former President ABOLHASAN BANI-SADR and the Council's current leader, MASSOUD RAJAVI, the leader of the Mujahidin-e-Khalq in Iran. In 1984 the Council comprised 15 opposition groups, operating either clandestinely in Iran or from exile abroad. BANI-SADR left the Council in 1984 because of his objection to RAJAVI'S growing links with the Iraqi Government. The French Government asked RAJAVI to leave Paris in June 1986 and he is now based in Baghdad, Iraq. On 20 June 1987 RAJAVI, Secretary of the NCR, announced the formation of a National Liberation Army (10,000–15,000-strong) as the military wing of the Mujahidin-e-Khalq. There is also a National Movement of Iranian Resistance, based in Paris. Dissident members of the Tudeh Party founded the Democratic Party of the Iranian People in Paris in February 1988.

Diplomatic Representation

EMBASSIES IN IRAN

Afghanistan: Dr Beheshi Ave, Pompe Benzine, Corner of 4th St, Teheran; tel. (21) 627531; Ambassador: MOHAMMAD KHEIRKHAH.

Albania: Teheran; Ambassador: GILANI SHEHU.

Angola: Teheran; Ambassador: MANUEL BERNARDO DE SOUSA.

Argentina: 3rd Floor, 7 Argentina Sq., Teheran; tel. (21) 8718294; fax (21) 8712583; Chargé d'affaires: EDUARDO LIONEL DE'AUP.

Armenia: 1 Ostad Shahriar St, Corner of Razi, Jomhouri Islami Ave, Teheran 11337; tel. (21) 674833; fax (21) 670657; Ambassador: YAHAN BAIBOURDIAN.

Australia: POB 15875-4334, 13 23rd St, Khaled al-Islambuli Ave, Teheran 15138; tel. (21) 8724456; fax (21) 8720484; Ambassador: STUART HUME.

Austria: 3rd Floor, 78 Argentine Sq., Teheran; tel. (21) 8710753; fax (21) 8710778; Ambassador: Dr HELMUTH WERNER EHRLICH.

Azerbaijan: Teheran; Ambassador: ALIYAR FARLI.

Bahrain: 31 Khaled al-Islambuli Ave, Teheran; tel. (21) 682079; Chargé d'affaires: RAMSEY JALAL.

Bangladesh: POB 11365-3711, Gandhi Ave, 5th St, Building No. 14, Teheran; tel. (21) 8772979; fax (21) 8778295; Ambassador: MUAZZEM ALI.

Belgium: POB 11365-115, Fayazi Ave, Shabdiz Lane, 3 Babak St, Teheran 19659; tel. (21) 2009507; telex 2009554; Ambassador: CHRISTIAAN COURTOIS.

Brazil: Vanak Sq., Vanak Ave No. 58, Teheran 19964; tel. (21) 2265175; telex 212392; fax (21) 8883348; Ambassador: SERGIO TUTIKIAN.

Bulgaria: POB 11365-7451, Vali Asr Ave, Tavanir St, Nezami Ganjavi St, No. 82, Teheran; tel. (21) 685662; telex 212789; Ambassador: STEFAN POLENDAKOV.

Canada: POB 11365-4647, 57 Shahid Sarafraz St; tel. (21) 8732623; fax 8733202; Ambassador: MICHEL DE SALABERRY.

China, People's Republic: Pasdaran Ave, Golestan Ave 1, No. 53, Teheran; tel. (21) 245131; Ambassador: WANG SHIJIE.

Colombia: Teheran; Ambassador: RAFAEL CANAL SANDOVAL.

Congo, Democratic Republic: Teheran; tel. (21) 222199; Chargé d'affaires a.i.: N'DJATE ESELE SASA.

Cuba: Teheran; tel. (21) 685030; Ambassador: ENRIQUE TRUJILLO RAPALLO.

Czech Republic: POB 11365-4457, Mirza-ye Shirazi Ave, Ali Mirza Hassani St, No. 15, Teheran; tel. (21) 8716720; fax (21) 8717858; Chargé d'affaires: Eng. JIŘÍ DOLEŽAL.

Denmark: POB 19395-5358, 18 Dashti Ave, Teheran 19148; tel. (21) 261363; telex 212784; fax (21) 2030007; Ambassador: HUGO ØESTERGAARD-ANDERSEN.

Ethiopia: Teheran; Ambassador: MOHAMMED HASAN KAHIM.

Finland: POB 15115-619, Vali Asr Ave, Vanak Sq., Nilou St, Teheran; tel. (21) 8889151; telex 212930; fax (21) 8889107; Ambassador: A. KOISTINEN.

France: 85 ave Neauphle-le-Château, Teheran; tel. (21) 676005; Ambassador: PHILIPPE DE SUREMAIN.

Gabon: Teheran; tel. (21) 823828; telex 215038; Ambassador: J. B. ESSONGUE.

Gambia: Teheran; Ambassador: OMAR JAH.

Georgia: POB 19575-379, Farmaniye, Teheran; tel. (21) 2295135; fax (21) 2295136; Ambassador: JEMSHID GIUNASHVILI.

Germany: POB 11365-179, 324 Ferdowsi Ave, Teheran; tel. (21) 3114111; telex 212488; fax (21) 398474; Ambassador: Dr HORST BÄCHMANN.

Ghana: Teheran; Ambassador: Mr AL-HASSAN.

Greece: POB 11365-8151, Africa Expressway (Ex. Jordan Ave), Esfandiar St No. 43, Teheran 19686; tel. (21) 2050533; Ambassador: DIMITRI TSIKOURIS.

Guinea: POB 11365-4716, Teheran; tel. (21) 7535744; fax (21) 7535743; Ambassador: MAMDGU SOALIOU SYLLA.

Holy See: Apostolic Nunciature, POB 11365-178, Razi Ave, No. 97, ave Neauphle-le-Château, Teheran; tel. (21) 6403574; fax (21) 6419442; Apostolic-Nuncio: Most Rev. ROMEO PANCIROLI, Titular Archbishop of Noba.

Hungary: POB 19395-6363, Africa Ave, 16 Arash Blvd, Teheran; tel. (21) 2057939; Ambassador: Dr ISTVAN TOLLI.

India: POB 11365-6573, Saba-e-Shomali Ave, No. 166, Teheran; tel. (21) 894554; telex 212858; Ambassador: S. K. ARORA.

Indonesia: POB 11365-4564, Ghaem Magham Farahani Ave, No. 210, Teheran; tel. (21) 626865; telex 212049; Ambassador: BAMBANG SUDARSONO.

Iraq: Vali Asr Ave, No. 494, Teheran.

Ireland: Mirdamad Blvd, 10 North Razan St, Teheran 19116; tel. (21) 2227672; telex 213865; fax (21) 2222731; Ambassador: THOMAS D. LYONS.

Italy: POB 11365-7863, 81 ave Neauphle-le-Château, Teheran; tel. (21) 6496955; telex 214171; fax (21) 6496961; Ambassador: LUDOVICO ORTONA.

Japan: POB 11365-814, Bucharest Ave, N.W. Corner of 5th St, Teheran; tel. (21) 623396; telex 212757; Ambassador: TSUNEO OYAKE.

Jordan: POB 19395-4666, No. 6, 2nd Alley, Shadavar St, Mahmoodieh Ave, Teheran; tel. (21) 291432; telex 226899; fax (21) 2007160; Ambassador YASIN ISTANBULI.

Kazakhstan: Darrus, Hedayat St, Masjed, No. 4, Teheran; tel (21) 2565933; telex 216877; fax (21) 2546400; Ambassador: MURZATAY ZHOLDASBEKOV.

Kenya: 60 Hormoz Satari St, Africa Ave, Teheran; tel. (21) 2270795; telex 213652; fax (21) 2270160; Ambassador: SALIM JUMA.

Korea, Democratic People's Republic: Fereshteh Ave, Sarvestan Ave, No. 11, Teheran; tel. (21) 298610; Ambassador: CHOE YONG RO.

Korea, Republic: 37 Bucharest Ave, Teheran; tel. (21) 8751125; telex 212693; fax (21) 8737917; Ambassador: JAE KYU KIM.

Kuwait: Dehkadeh Ave, 3–38 Sazman-Ab St, Teheran; tel. (21) 636712; Ambassador: ABDULLAH ABD AL-AZIZ AD-DUWAYKH.

Kyrgyzstan: Teheran.

Laos: Teheran; Ambassador: CHANPHENG SIHAPHOM.

Lebanon: Teheran; Ambassador: MOUNIR TALHOUK

Libya: Ostad Motahhari Ave, No. 163, Teheran; tel. (21) 859191; Sec.-Gen. Committee of People's Bureau: MAHDI AL-MABIRASH.

Malaysia: 72 Fereshteh Ave, Teheran; tel. (21) 2009275; fax (21) 2009143; Ambassador: MUHAMMAD KHALIS.

Mauritania: Teheran.

Mexico: POB 15875-4636, No. 24, Shabnam Alley, Africa Expressway, Teheran; tel. (21) 2225374; telex 216557; fax (21) 2225375; Ambassador: ANTONIO DUEÑAS PULIDO.

Mongolia: Teheran; Ambassador: L. KHASHOAT.

Morocco: Teheran; tel. (21) 2059707; fax (21) 2051872; Ambassador: MOHAMMAD AZAROUAL.

Mozambique: Teheran; Ambassador: MURADE ISAC MIGUIGY MURARGY.

Myanmar: Teheran; Ambassador: U SAW HLAING.

Namibia: Teheran; Ambassador: MWAILEPENI T. P. SHITILIFA.

Nepal: Teheran; Ambassador: Gen. ARJUN NARSING RONA.

Netherlands: POB 11365-138, Vali Asr Ave, Ostad Motahhari Ave, Sarbederan St, Jahansouz Alley, No. 36, Teheran; tel. (21) 896011; telex 212788; fax (21) 8892087; Ambassador: M. DAMME.

New Zealand: POB 15875-4313, 57 Javad Sarafarez St, Ostad Motahhari Ave, Teheran; tel. (21) 8757052; fax (21) 8757056; Ambassador: WARWICK ALEXANDER HAWKER.

Nigeria: POB 11365-7148, Khaled Islamboli Ave, 31st St, No. 9, Teheran; tel. (21) 8774935; telex 213151; fax (21) 8774921; Ambassador: ADO SANUSI.

Norway: POB 19395-5398, Pasdaran Ave, Kouhestan 8, Ekhtiarieh Shomali 412, Teheran; tel. (21) 2291333; telex 213009; fax (21) 2292776; Chargé d'affaires: CARL S. WIBYE.

Oman: POB 41-1586, Pasdaran Ave, Golestan 9, No. 5 and 7, Teheran; tel. (21) 286021; telex 212835; Chargé d'affaires a.i.: RASHID BIN MUBARAK BIN RASHID AL-ODWALI.

Pakistan: Dr Fatemi Ave, Jamshidabad Shomali, Mashal St, No. 1, Teheran; tel. (21) 934332; KHALID MAHMUD.

Panama: Teheran; Ambassador: G. MOVAGA.

Philippines: POB 19395-4797, 24 Golazin Blvd., Africa Ave, Zafaranieh, Teheran; tel. (21) 2055134; fax (21) 2057260; Ambassador HARON P. ALONTO.

Poland: Africa Expressway, Piruz St, No. 1/3, Teheran; tel. (21) 227262; Ambassador: STEFAN SZYMCZYKIEWICZ.

Portugal: Vali Asr Ave, Tavanir Ave, Nezami Ghanjavi Ave, No. 30, Teheran; tel. (21) 8772132; telex 212588; fax (21) 8777834; Ambassador: Dr MANUEL MARCELO CURTO.

Qatar: Africa Expressway, Golazin Ave, Parke Davar, No. 4, Teheran; tel. (21) 221255; telex 212375; Ambassador: ALI ABDULLAH ZAID AL-MAHMOOOD.

Romania: Fakhrabad Ave 12, Darvaze Shemiran, Teheran; tel. (21) 7509309; telex 212791; fax (21) 7509841; Ambassador: CRISTIAN TEODORESCU.

Russia: 39 ave Neauphle-le-Château, Teheran; tel. (21) 671163; Ambassador: KONSTANTIN SHUVALOV.

Saudi Arabia: 10 Saba Blvd, Africa Ave, Teheran; tel. (21) 2050081; fax (21) 2050083; Ambassador: ABD AL-LATIF ABDULLAH AL-MEIMANI.

Slovakia: POB 11365-4451, No. 24, Babak Markazi St, Africa Ave, Teheran; tel. (21) 2271058; fax (21) 2271057; Chargé d'affaires a.i.: ALEXANDER BAJKAI.

Somalia: Shariati Ave, Soheyl Ave, No. 20, Teheran; tel. (21) 272034; Ambassador: ABDI SHIRE WARSAME.

South Africa: POB 11365-7476, Yetha St 5, Vali-Asr Ave, Teheran; tel. (21) 2702866; fax (21) 2719516; Ambassador: MOOSA MOOLLA.

Spain: Vali-Asr Ave, 76 Sarv St, Teheran; tel. (21) 8714575; telex 212980; fax (21) 8724581. Ambassador: GABRIEL BUSQUETS.

Sri Lanka: 6 Arash St, Africa Expressway, Teheran; tel. (21) 2053902; telex 216776; fax (21) 2052688; Ambassador: Y. L. M. ZAWAHIR.

Sudan: Khaled Islambouli Ave, 23rd St, No. 10, Teheran; tel. (21) 628476; telex 213372; Ambassador: Dr ABDEL RAHANA MOHAMMED SAID.

Sweden: POB 19575-458, 2 Nastaran St, Teheran; tel. (21) 2296802; telex 212822; fax (21) 2286021; Ambassador: HANS ANDERSSON.

Switzerland: POB 19395-4683, 13/1 Boustan Ave, 19649 Teheran; tel. (21) 268227; fax 269448; Ambassador: RUDOLF WEIERSMÜLLER.

Syria: Africa Ave, 19 Iraj St, Teheran; tel. (21) 229032; Ambassador: AHMAD AL-HASSAN.

Tajikistan: Teheran.

Thailand: POB 11495-111, Baharestan Ave, Parc Amin ed-Doleh, No. 4, Teheran; tel. (21) 7531433; telex 214040; fax (21) 7532022; Ambassador: MAHADI WIMANA.

Tunisia: Teheran; Ambassador: Dr NOUREDDINE AL-HAMDANI.

Turkey: Ferdowsi Ave, No. 314, Teheran; tel. (21) 3115299; telex 213670; fax (21) 3117928; Ambassador: SENCAR ÖZSOY.

Turkmenistan: Teheran.

Ukraine: Hefez Avenue, Teheran 487; tel. (21) 675148; telex 112574; Chargé d'affaires: IVAN G. MAYDAN.

United Arab Emirates: Zafar Ave, No. 355–7, Teheran; tel. (21) 221333; telex 212697; Ambassador: AHMAD MUHAMMAD BORHEIMAH.

United Kingdom: POB 11365-4474, 143 Ferdowsi Ave, Teheran 11344; tel. (21) 675011; fax (21) 678021; e-mail britemb@neda.net; Chargé d'affaires: N. W. BROWNE.

Uruguay: 45 Shabnam Alley, Atefi Shargi St, Jordan Ave, Teheran; tel. (21) 2052030; Ambassador: MARCIAL BIRRIEL IGLESIAS.

Uzbekistan: Teheran.

Venezuela: POB 15875-4354, Bucharest Ave, 9th St, No. 31, Teheran; tel. (21) 625185; telex 213790; fax (21) 622840; Ambassador: Dr HERNÁN CALCURIAN.

Viet Nam: Teheran; Ambassador: VUXNAN ANG.

Yemen: Bucharest Ave, No. 26, Teheran; Chargé d'affaires a.i.: Dr AHMAD MUHAMMAD ALI ABDULLAH.

Yugoslavia: POB 11365-118, Vali Asr Ave, Fereshteh Ave, Amir Teymour Alley, No. 12, 19659 Teheran; tel. (21) 2044126; telex 214235; fax (21) 2044978; Chargé d'affaires: STOJAN GLIGORIĆ.

Judicial System

In August 1982 the Supreme Court revoked all laws dating from the previous regime which did not conform with Islam. In October 1982 all courts set up prior to the Islamic Revolution were abolished. In June 1987 Ayatollah Khomeini ordered the creation of clerical courts to try members of the clergy opposed to government policy. A new system of *qisas* (retribution) was established, placing the emphasis on speedy justice. Islamic codes of correction were introduced in 1983, including the dismembering of a hand for theft, flogging for fornication and violations of the strict code of dress for women, and stoning for adultery. In 1984 there was a total of 2,200 judges. The Supreme Court has 16 branches.

Head of the Judiciary: Ayatollah MUHAMMAD YAZDI.

SUPREME COURT

Chief Justice: Hojatoleslam MUHAMMAD MUHAMMADI GUILANI.

Prosecutor-General: Hojatoleslam MORTEZA MOQTADAI.

Religion

According to the 1979 constitution, the official religion is Islam of the Ja'fari sect (Shi'ite), but other Islamic sects, including Zeydi, Hanafi, Maleki, Shafe'i and Hanbali, are valid and will be respected. Zoroastrians, Jews and Christians will be recognized as official religious minorities. According to the 1976 census, there were then 310,000 Christians (mainly Armenian), 80,000 Jews and 30,000 Zoroastrians.

ISLAM

The great majority of the Iranian people are Shi'a Muslims, but there is a minority of Sunni Muslims. Persians and Azerbaijanis are mainly Shi'i, while the other ethnic groups are mainly Sunni.

CHRISTIANITY

The Roman Catholic Church

At 31 December 1996 there were an estimated 12,700 adherents in Iran, comprising 6,100 of the Chaldean Rite, 2,600 of the Armenian Rite and 4,000 of the Latin Rite.

Armenian Rite

Bishop of Isfahan: Dr VARTAN TEKEYAN, Armenian Catholic Bishopric, Khiaban Ghazzali 22, Teheran; tel. (21) 677204; fax (21) 8715191.

Chaldean Rite

Archbishop of Ahwaz: HANNA ZORA, Archbishop's House, POB 61956, Naderi St, Ahwaz; tel. (61) 24890.

Archbishop of Teheran: YOUHANNAN SEMAAN ISSAYI, Archevêché, Forsat Ave 91, Teheran 15819; tel. (21) 8823549.

Archbishop of Urmia (Rezayeh) and Bishop of Salmas (Shahpour): THOMAS MERAM, Khalifagari Kaldani Katholiq, POB 338, Orumiyeh 57135; tel. (441) 22739.

Latin Rite

Archbishop of Isfahan: IGNAZIO BEDINI, Consolata Church, POB 11365-445, 75 Neauphle-le-Château Ave, Teheran; tel. (21) 673210; fax (21) 6494749.

The Anglican Communion

Anglicans in Iran are adherents of the Episcopal Church in Jerusalem and the Middle East, formally inaugurated in January 1976. The Rt Rev. HASSAN DEHQANI-TAFTI, the Bishop in Iran from 1961 to 1990, was President-Bishop of the Church from 1976 to 1986. He was succeeded by the Bishop of Jerusalem during 1986–96 and the Bishop of Egypt from 1996 onwards.

Bishop in Iran: Rt Rev. IRAJ KALIMI MOTTAHEDEH, St Luke's Church, Abbas-abad, POB 81465-135, Isfahan; tel. (31) 231435; diocese founded 1912.

Presbyterian Church

Synod of the Evangelical (Presbyterian) Church in Iran: Assyrian Evangelical Church, Khiaban-i Hanifnejad, Khiaban-i Aramanch, Teheran; Moderator Rev. ADEL NAKHOSTEEN.

ZOROASTRIANS

There are about 30,000 Zoroastrians, a remnant of a once widespread sect. Their religious leader is MOUBAD.

OTHER COMMUNITIES

Communities of Armenians, and somewhat smaller numbers of Jews (an estimated 30,000 in 1986), Assyrians, Greek Orthodox Christians, Uniates and Latin Christians are also found as officially recognized faiths. The Bahá'í faith, which originated in Iran, has about 300,000 Iranian adherents, although at least 10,000 are believed to have fled since 1979 in order to escape persecution. The Government banned all Bahá'í institutions in August 1983.

The Press

Teheran dominates the media, as many of the daily papers are published there, and the bi-weekly, weekly and less frequent publications in the provinces generally depend on the major metropolitan dailies as a source of news. A press law announced in August 1979 required all newspapers and magazines to be licensed and imposed penalties of imprisonment for insulting senior religious figures. Offences against the Act will be tried in the criminal courts. Under the Constitution the press is free, except in matters that are contrary to public morality, insult religious belief or slander the honour and reputation of individuals.

PRINCIPAL DAILIES

Abrar (Rightly Guided): 26 Shahid Denesh Kian Alley, Below Zartasht St, Valiassr Ave, Teheran; tel. (21) 8848270; fax (21) 8849200; f. 1985 after closure of *Azadegan* by order of the Prosecutor-General; morning; Farsi; circ. 75,000.

Alik: POB 11365-953, Jomhoori Islami Ave, Alik Alley, Teheran 11357; tel. (21) 676671; f. 1931; afternoon; political and literary; Armenian; Propr A. AJEMIAN; circ. 3,400.

Bahari Iran: Khayaban Khayham, Shiraz; tel. (71) 33738.

Ettela'at (Information): Mirdamad Ave, South Naft St, Teheran; tel. (21) 29999; telex 212336; fax (21) 2258022; f. 1925; evening; Farsi; political and literary; owned and managed by Mostazafin Foundation from October 1979 until 1 January 1987, when it was placed under the direct supervision of Wilayat-e-Faqih (religious jurisprudence); Editor S. M. DOAEI; circ. 500,000.

Iran News: 41 Lida St, Valiassr Ave, North Vanak Sq, tel. (21) 8880231; telex 216966; fax (21) 8786475; Teheran; English.

Kayhan (Universe): Ferdowsi Ave, Teheran; tel. (21) 310251; telex 212467; f. 1941; evening; Farsi; political; also publishes *Kayhan International* (f. 1959; daily and weekly; English; Editor HOSSEIN RAGHFAR), *Kayhan Arabic* (f. 1980; daily and weekly; Arabic), *Kayhan Persian* (f. 1942; daily; Persian), *Kayhan Turkish* (f. 1984; monthly; Turkish), *Kayhan Havaie* (f. 1950; weekly for Iranians abroad; Farsi), *Kayhan Andishe* (World of Religion; f. 1985; 6 a year; Farsi), *Zan-e-Ruz* (Woman Today; f. 1964; weekly; Farsi), *Kayhan Varzeshi* (World of Sport; f. 1955; weekly; Farsi), *Kayhan Bacheha* (Children's World; f. 1956; weekly; Farsi), *Kayhan Farhangi* (World of Culture; f. 1984; monthly; Farsi); *Kayhan Yearbook* (yearly; Farsi); *Period of 40 Years, Kayhan* (series of books; Farsi); owned and managed by Mostazafin Foundation from October 1979 until 1 January 1987, when it was placed under the direct supervision of Wilayat-e-Faqih (religious jurisprudence); Chief Editor HOSSEIN SHARIATMADARI; circ. 350,000.

Khorassan: Meshed; Head Office: Khorassan Daily Newspapers, 14 Zohre St, Mobarezan Ave, Teheran; f. 1948; Propr MUHAMMAD SADEGH TEHERANIAN; circ. 40,000.

Rahnejat: Darvazeh Dowlat, Isfahan; political and social; Propr N. RAHNEJAT.

Ressallat (The Message): Teheran; tel. (21) 8902642; fax (21) 8900587; organ of right-wing group of the same name; political, economic, social; Propr Ressallat Foundation; circ. 100,000.

Salam: 2 Reza Shahid Nayebi Alley, South Felestin St, Teheran; tel. (21) 6495831; telex 222959; fax (21) 6495835; f. 1991; Farsi; political, economic, social; Editor MUHAMMAD MUSAVI KHOIENI.

Teheran Times: 32 Bimeh Alley, Nejatullahi Ave, Teheran 15998; tel. (21) 8810293; telex 8809470; fax (21) 8808214; f. 1979; independent; English.

PRINCIPAL PERIODICALS

Acta Medica Iranica: Faculty of Medicine, Poursina St, Teheran Medical Sciences Univ., Teheran 14-174; tel. (21) 6112743; fax (21) 6404377; f. 1960; quarterly; English; under the supervision of the Research Vice-Associate (A. JAWADIAN) and the Editorial Board; Editor-in-Chief PARVIZ JABAL-AMELI (Dean, Faculty of Medicine); circ. 2,000.

Akhbar-e-Pezeshki: 86 Ghaem Magham Farahani Ave, Teheran; weekly; medical; Propr Dr T. FORUZIN.

Ashur: Ostad Motahhari Ave, 11-21 Kuhe Nour Ave, Teheran; tel. (21) 622117; f. 1969; Assyrian; monthly; Founder and Editor Dr W. BET-MANSOUR; circ. 8,000.

Auditor: 77 Ferdowsi Ave North, Teheran; quarterly; financial and managerial studies.

Ayandeh: POB 19575-583, Niyavaran, Teheran; tel. (21) 283254; fax (21) 6406426; monthly; Iranian literary, historical and book review journal; Editor Prof. IRAJ AFSHAR.

Bulletin of the National Film Archive of Iran: POB 5158, Baharestan Sq., Teheran 11365; tel. 311242; telex 214283; f. 1989; English periodical; Editor M. H. KHOSHNEVIS.

Daneshmand: POB 15875-3649, Teheran; tel. (21) 8741323; f. 1963; monthly; scientific and technical magazine; Editor-in-Chief A. R. KARAMI.

Daneshkadeh Pezeshki: Faculty of Medicine, Teheran Medical Sciences University; tel. (21) 6112743; fax (21) 6404377; f. 1947; 10 a year; medical magazine; Propr Dr HASSAN AREFI; circ. 1,500.

Donaye Varzesh: Khayyam Ave, Ettela'at Bldg, Teheran; tel. (21) 3281; telex 212336; fax (21) 3115530; weekly; sport; Editor G. H. SHABANI; circ. 200,000.

Echo of Islam: POB 14155-3987, Teheran; monthly; English; published by the Foundation of Islamic Thought.

Ettela'at Elmi: 11 Khayyam Ave, Teheran; tel. (21) 3281; telex 212336; fax (21) 3115530; f. 1985; fortnightly; sciences; Editor Mrs GHASEMI; circ. 75,000.

Ettela'at Haftegi: 11 Khayyam Ave, Teheran; tel. (21) 3281; telex 212336; fax (21) 3115530; f. 1941; general weekly; Editor F. JAVADI; circ. 150,000.

Ettela'at Javanan: POB 11335-9365, 11144 Khayyam Ave, Teheran; tel. (21) 3281; telex 212336; fax (21) 3115530; f. 1966; weekly; youth; Editor M. J. RAFIZADEH; circ. 120,000.

Farhang-e-Iran Zamin: POB 19575-583, Niyavaran, Teheran; tel. (21) 283254; annual; Iranian studies; Editor Prof. IRAJ AFSHAR.

Film International: POB 11365-5875, Teheran; tel. (21) 6457480; fax (21) 6459971; e-mail filmmag@apadana.com; f. 1993; quarterly in English; Editor HOUSHANG GOLMAKANI; circ 20,000.

Iran Press Digest (Economic): POB 11365-5551, Hafiz Ave, 4 Kucheh Hurtab, Teheran; tel. (21) 668114; telex 212300; weekly; Editor J. BEHROUZ.

Iran Press Digest (Political): POB 11365-5551, Hafiz Ave, 4 Kucheh Hurtab, Teheran; tel. (21) 668114; telex 212300; weekly.

Iranian Cinema: POB 5158, Baharestan Sq., Teheran 11365; tel. 311242; f. 1985; annually; English; Editor B. REYPOUR.

Javaneh: POB 15875-1163, Motahhari Ave, Cnr Mofatteh St, Teheran; tel. (21) 839051; published by Soroush Press; quarterly.

Kayhan Bacheha (Children's World): Shahid Shahsheragi Ave, Teheran; tel. (21) 310251; telex 212467; f. 1956; weekly; Editor AMIR HOSSEIN FARDI; circ. 150,000.

Kayhan Varzeshi (World of Sport): Ferdowsi Ave, Teheran; tel. (21) 310251; telex 212467; f. 1955; weekly; Dir MAHMAD MONSETI; circ. 125,000.

Mahjubah: POB 14155-3897, Teheran; tel. (21) 890226; fax (21) 8758296; Islamic women's magazine; published by the Islamic Thought Foundation.

Majda: POB 14155-3695, 94 West Pirouzi St, Kooye Nasr, Teheran; tel. (21) 639591; telex 212918; fax (21) 639592; f. 1963; four a year; medical; journal of the Iranian Dental Association; Pres. Dr ALI YAZDANI.

Music Iran: 1029 Amiriye Ave, Teheran; f. 1951; monthly; Editor BAHMAN HIRBOD; circ. 7,000.

Negin: Vali Asr Ave, Adl St 52, Teheran; monthly; scientific and literary; Propr and Dir M. ENAYAT.

Pars: Alley Dezhban, Shiraz; f. 1941; irregular; Propr and Dir F. SHARGHI; circ. 10,000.

Salamate Fekr: M.20, Kharg St, Teheran; tel. (21) 223034; f. 1958; monthly; organ of the Mental Health Soc.; Editors Prof. E. TCHEHRAZI, ALI REZA SHAFAI.

Soroush: POB 15875-1163, Motahhari Ave, Corner Mofatteh St, Teheran; tel. (21) 830771; f. 1972; two monthly magazines in Farsi, one for children and one for adolescents; Editor MEHDI FIROOZAN.

Zan-e-Ruz (Woman Today): Ferdowsi Ave, Teheran; tel. (21) 301570; telex 216186; fax (21) 301569; f. 1964; weekly; women's; circ. over 60,000.

NEWS AGENCIES

Islamic Republic News Agency (IRNA): POB 764, 873 Vali Asr Ave, Teheran; tel. (21) 892050; telex 212827; fax (21) 895068; e-mail irna.com; internet http://www.irna.com; f. 1936; Man. Dir FEREYDOUN VERDINEZHAD.

Foreign Bureaux

Agence France-Presse (AFP): POB 15115-513, Office 207, 8 Vanak Ave, Vanak Sq., Teheran 19919; tel. (21) 8777509; fax (21) 8886289; Correspondent CHRISTOPHE DE ROQUEFEUIL.

Agenzia Nazionale Stampa Associata (ANSA) (Italy): Khiabane Shahid Bahonar (Niavaran) Kuche Mina No. 16, Teheran 19367; tel. (21) 276930; telex 213629; Chief of Bureau LUCIANO CAUSA.

Anatolian News Agency (Turkey): Teheran.

Informatsionnoye Telegrafnoye Agentstvo Rossii–Telegrafnoye Agentstvo Suverennykh Stran (ITAR–TASS) (Russia): Kehyaban Hamid, Kouche Masoud 73, Teheran.

Kyodo Tsushin (Japan): No. 23, First Floor, Couche Kargozar, Couche Sharsaz Ave, Zafar, Teheran; tel. (21) 220448; telex 214058; Correspondent MASARU IMAI.

Novinska Agencija Tanjug (Yugoslavia): Teheran.

Reuters (UK): POB 15875-1193, Teheran; tel. (21) 847700; telex 212634.

Xinhua (New China) News Agency (People's Republic of China): 75 Golestan 2nd St, Pasdaran Ave, Teheran; tel. (21) 241852; telex 212399; Correspondent CHEN MING.

Publishers

Amir Kabir: POB 11365-4191; Esteghlal Sq, Teheran; f. 1950; historical, social, literary and children's books; Dir A. H. MALEKIT-ABAR.

Ebn-e-Sina: Meydane 25 Shahrivar, Teheran; f. 1957; educational publishers and booksellers; Dir EBRAHIM RAMAZANI.

Eghbal Printing & Publishing Organization: 15 Booshehr St, Dr Shariati Ave, Teheran; tel. (21) 768113; f. 1903; Man. Dir DJAVAD EGHBAL.

Iran Chap Co: Khayyam Ave, Teheran; tel. (21) 3281; telex 212336; fax (21) 3115530; f. 1966; newspapers, books, magazines, book binding, colour printing and engraving; Man. Dir M. DOAEI.

Iran Exports Publication Co Ltd: POB 14335-746, 27 Eftekhar St, Vali Asr Ave, Teheran 15956; tel. (21) 8801800; fax (21) 8900547; f. 1987; business and trade.

Ketab Sara: Teheran; Chair. SADEGH SAMII.

Khayyam: Jomhoori Islami Ave, Teheran; Dir MUHAMMAD ALI TARAGHI.

Majlis Press: Ketab-Khane Majlis-e-Showray-e Eslami No. 1, Baharestan Sq., Teheran 11564; tel. (21) 3124339; f. 1924; Ketab Khane Majlis-e-Showray-e Eslami No. 2, Imam Khomeini Ave, Teheran 13174; tel. (21) 6462906; fax (21) 3124339; f. 1950; Dir GHOLAMREZA FADAI ARAGHI.

Sahab Geographic and Drafting Institute: POB 11365-617, 30 Somayeh St, Hoquqi Crossroad, Dr Ali Shariati Ave, Teheran 16517; tel. (21) 7535670; telex 222584; fax (21) 7535876; maps, atlases, and books on geography, science, history and Islamic art; Founder and Pres. ABBAS A. SAHAB.

Scientific and Cultural Publications Co: Ministry of Culture and Higher Education, 64th St, Sayyed Jamal-ed-Din Asad Abadi Ave; tel. (21) 8048037; f. 1974; Iranian and Islamic studies and scientific and cultural books; Pres. SAYED JAVAD AZHARS.

Teheran University Press: 16 Kargar Shomali Ave, Teheran; tel. (21) 632062; fax (21) 632063; f. 1944; university textbooks; Man. Dir ABBAS RASTGOU.

Broadcasting and Communications

TELECOMMUNICATIONS

Telecommunication Company of Iran (TCI): Dr Shariati Ave, Teheran; tel. (21) 864796; telex 212444; fax (21) 866023; Chair. and Man. Dir Dr SAYED ABDOLLAH MIRTAHERI.

BROADCASTING

Islamic Republic of Iran Broadcasting (IRIB): POB 19395-3333, Vali Asr Ave, Jame Jam St, Teheran; tel. (21) 21961; telex 2045056; fax (21) 213910; semi-autonomous government authority; non-commercial; operates five national television and three national radio channels, as well as local provincial radio stations throughout the country; Dir-Gen. ALI LARIJANI.

Radio

Radio Network 1 (Voice of the Islamic Republic of Iran): there are three national radio channels: Radio Networks 1 and 2 and Radio Quran, which broadcasts recitals of the Quran (Koran) and other programmes related to it; covers whole of Iran and reaches whole of Europe, the Central Asian republics of the CIS, whole of Asia, Africa and part of USA; medium-wave regional broadcasts in local languages; Arabic, Armenian, Assyrian, Azerbaijani, Balochi, Bandari, Dari, Farsi, Kurdish, Mazandarani, Pashtu, Turkoman, Turkish and Urdu; external broadcasts in English, French, German, Spanish, Turkish, Arabic, Kurdish, Urdu, Pashtu, Armenian, Bengali, Russian and special overseas programme in Farsi; 53 transmitters.

Television

Television (Vision of the Islamic Republic of Iran): 625-line, System B; Secam colour; two production centres in Teheran producing for two networks and 28 local TV stations.

Finance

(cap. = capital; res = reserves; dep. = deposits; brs = branches; m. = million; amounts in rials)

BANKING

Banks were nationalized in June 1979 and a revised commercial banking system was introduced consisting of nine banks (subsequently expanded to 10). Three banks were reorganized, two (Bank Tejarat and Bank Mellat) resulted from mergers of 22 existing small banks, three specialize in industry and agriculture and one, the Islamic Bank (now Islamic Economy Organization), set up in May 1979, was exempt from nationalization. The tenth bank, the Export Development Bank, specializes in the promotion of exports. A change-over to an Islamic banking system, with interest (forbidden under Islamic law) being replaced by a 4% commission on loans, began on 21 March 1984. All short- and medium-term private deposits and all bank loans and advances are subject to Islamic rules.

Although the number of foreign banks operating in Iran has fallen dramatically since the Revolution, some 30 are still represented.

Central Bank

Bank Markazi Jomhouri Islami Iran (Central Bank): POB 11365-8551, Ferdowsi Ave, Teheran; tel. (21) 3110231; telex 212359; fax (21) 390323; f. 1960; Bank Markazi Iran until Dec. 1983; central note-issuing bank of Iran, government banking; cap. 200,000m., res 220,690m., dep. 53,473,238m., total assets 82,598,349m. (March 1996); Gov. Dr MOHSEN NOURBAKHSH.

Commercial Banks

Bank Keshavarzi (Agricultural Bank): POB 14155-6395, 129 Patrice Lumumba Ave, Jalal al-Ahmad Expressway, Teheran; tel. and fax (21) 8252246; telex 212058; f. 1979 as merger of the Agricultural Development Bank of Iran and the Agricultural Co-operative Bank of Iran; state-owned; cap. 408,322m., dep. 1,751,733m. (March 1996); 1,565 brs; Man. Dir SAYED ALI MILANI HOSSEINI.

Bank Mellat (Nation's Bank): Shahid Fayazbakhsh Ave, Keshavarzi St, Teheran; tel. (21) 32491; telex 212619; fax (21) 673396; f. 1980 as merger of the following: International Bank of Iran, Bank Bimeh Iran, Bank Dariush, Distributors' Co-operative Credit Bank, Iran Arab Bank, Bank Omran, Bank Pars, Bank of Teheran, Foreign Trade Bank of Iran, Bank Farhangian; state-owned; cap. 605,000m., dep. 8,693,000m., total assets 11,436,000m. (March 1995); 1,081 brs throughout Iran and 5 brs abroad; Chair. and Man. Dir S. MANOUCHEHRI.

Bank Melli Iran (The National Bank of Iran): POB 11365-171, Ferdowsi Ave, Teheran; tel. (21) 3231; telex 212890; fax (21) 302813; f. 1928; state-owned; cap. 1,145,000m., res 18,475m., dep. 21,724,454m., total assets 33,700,185m. (March 1996); 2,510 brs throughout Iran, 22 brs abroad; Chair. and Man. Dir ASSADOLLAH AMIRASLANI.

Bank Refah Kargaran: POB 15714, 40 Shirazi St, Mollasadra Ave, Teheran; tel. (21) 8042926; fax (21) 8042926; f. 1960; state-owned; cap. 55,000m., dep. 1,278,224m. (March 1996); 461 brs throughout Iran; Man. Dir J. SABER KHIABANI.

Bank Saderat Iran (The Export Bank of Iran): POB 15745-631, Bank Saderat Tower, 43 Somayyeh Ave, Teheran; tel. (21) 832699; telex 212352; fax (21) 8839539; f. 1952, reorganized 1979; state-owned; cap. 948,000m., res. 8,784.5m., dep. 9,498,354m., total assets 13,613,573.5m. (March 1996); 3,345 brs in Iran, 23 foreign brs; Chair. and Man. Dir MUHAMMAD REZA MOGHADASSI.

Bank Sepah (Army Bank): POB 9569, Imam Khomeini Sq, Teheran; tel. (21) 3111091; telex 212462; fax (21) 3112138; f. 1925, reorganized 1979; state-owned; cap. 400,000m., res 3,481,779m., dep. 11,286,255.3m., total assets 13,654,350.4m. (March 1997); 1,269 brs throughout Iran and 5 brs abroad; Chair. and Man. Dir VALIOLLAH SAIF.

Bank Tejarat (Commercial Bank): POB 11365-5416, 130 Taleghani Ave, Nejatoullahie, Teheran 15994; tel. (21) 81041; telex 212077; fax (21) 8828215; f. 1979 as merger of the following: Irano-British Bank, Bank Etebarate Iran, The Bank of Iran and the Middle East, Mercantile Bank of Iran and Holland, Bank Barzagani Iran, Bank Iranshahr, Bank Sanaye Iran, Bank Shahriar, Iranians' Bank, Bank Kar, International Bank of Iran and Japan, Bank Russo-Iran; state-owned; cap. 571,120m., res 14,883m., dep. 12,211,491m., total assets 14,951,980m. (March 1996); 1,489 brs in Iran and 3 abroad; Man. Dir and Chair. A. R. KHATIB.

Islamic Economy Organization (formerly Islamic Bank of Iran): Ferdowsi Ave, Teheran; f. February 1980; cap. 2,000m.; provides interest-free loans and investment in small industry.

Development Banks

Bank Sanat va Madan (Bank of Industry and Mines): POB 15875-4456, 593 Hafiz Ave, Teheran; tel. (21) 893271; telex 212816; fax (21) 895052; f. 1979 as merger of the following: Industrial Credit Bank (ICB), Industrial and Mining Development Bank of Iran (IMDBI), Development and Investment Bank of Iran (DIBI), Iranian Bankers Investment Company (IBICO); cap. 1,280,000m., res 36,257m., total assets 2,447,396m. (1996); Man. Dir MOJTABA HARATI NIK.

Export Development Bank of Iran: POB 15875-5964, 129 Khaled Eslambouli St, Teheran 15139; tel. (21) 8716607; telex 226895; fax (21) 8716979; e-mail edbi@dci.iran.com; cap. 100,000m., res. 971m., dep. 223,611m., total assets 331,419m. (1995); 17 brs; Chair and Man. Dir Dr NOWROUZ KOHZADI.

Housing Bank

Bank Maskan (Housing Bank): Ferdowsi Ave, Teheran; tel. (21) 675021; telex 226871; f. 1980; state-owned; cap. 42,663.8m., dep. 221,153.4m., total assets 3,594,364m. (June 1985); provides mortgage and housing finance; 187 brs; Chair. and Man. Dir AHMAD FARSHCHIAN.

STOCK EXCHANGE

Teheran Stock Exchange: 228 Hafez Ave, Teheran 11389; tel. (21) 670155; telex 223282; fax (21) 672524; f. 1966; Sec.-Gen. AHMAD MIRMOTAHARI.

INSURANCE

The nationalization of insurance companies was announced in June 1979.

Bimeh Alborz (Alborz Insurance Co): POB 4489-15875, Alborz Bldg, 234 Sepahboad Garani Ave, Teheran; tel. (21) 8803773; fax (21) 8803771; f. 1959; state-owned insurance company; all types of insurance; Man. Dir ALI FATHALI.

Bimeh Asia (Asia Insurance Co): POB 1365-5366, Asia Insurance Bldg, 297-299 Taleghani Ave, Teheran; tel. (21) 836040; telex 213664; fax (21) 827196; all types of insurance; Man. Dir MASOUM ZAMIRI.

Bimeh Dana (Dana Insurance Co): 25 Fifteenth Ave, Gandi St, Teheran; tel. (21) 8770971; fax 8770812; life, personal accident and health insurance; Chair. and Man. Dir. ALI FARHANDI.

Bimeh Iran (Iran Insurance Co): POB 11365-9153, Saadi Ave, Teheran; tel. (21) 304026; telex 212782; fax (21) 313510; all types of insurance; Man. Dir ALI MOSAREZA.

Bimeh Markazi Iran (Central Insurance of Iran): POB 15875-4345, 149 Ayatollah Taleghani Ave, Teheran 15914; tel. (21) 6409912; telex 212888; fax (21) 6405729; supervises the insurance market and tariffs for new types of insurance cover; the sole state reinsurer for domestic insurance companies, which are obliged to reinsure 50% of their direct business in life insurance and 25% of business in non-life insurance with Bimeh Markazi Iran; Pres. ABDOL NASSER HEMMATI.

Trade and Industry

CHAMBER OF COMMERCE

Iran Chamber of Commerce, Industries and Mines: 254 Taleghani Ave, Teheran; tel. (21) 8846031; fax (21) 8825111; supervises the affiliated 32 Chambers in the provinces; Pres. ALINAQI KHAMOUSHI.

INDUSTRIAL AND TRADE ASSOCIATIONS

National Iranian Industries Organization (NIIO): POB 14155-3579, 133 Dr Fatemi Ave, Teheran; tel. (21) 656031-40; telex 214176; fax (21) 658070; f. 1979; owns 400 factories in Iran.

National Iranian Industries Organization Export Co (NECO): POB 14335-589, No. 8, 2nd St, Ahmad Ghasir Ave, Teheran 15944; tel. (21) 8733564; telex 212429; fax (21) 8732586.

STATE HYDROCARBONS COMPANIES

Iranian Offshore Oil Co (IOOC): POB 15875-4546, 339 Dr Beheshti Ave, Teheran; tel. (21) 8714102; telex 212707; fax (21) 8717420; wholly owned subsidiary of NIOC; f. 1980; development, exploitation and production of crude petroleum, natural gas and other hydrocarbons in all offshore areas of Iran in the Persian Gulf and the Caspian Sea; Chair. M. AGAZADEH; Dir S. A. JALILIAN.

National Iranian Gas Co (NIGC): Man. Dir MUHAMMAD ISMAIL KARACHIAN.

National Iranian Oil Co (NIOC): POB 1863, Taleghani Ave, Teheran; tel. (21) 6151; telex 212514; a state organization controlling all 'upstream' activities in the petroleum and natural gas industries; incorporated April 1951 on nationalization of petroleum industry to engage in all phases of petroleum operations; in February 1979 it was announced that, in future, Iran would sell petroleum direct to the petroleum companies, and in September 1979 the Ministry of Oil assumed control of the National Iranian Oil Company, and the Minister of Oil took over as Chairman and Managing Director; Chair. of Board and Gen. Man. Dir BIZAM NAMDAR-ZANGENEH (Minister of Oil).

National Refining and Distribution Co (NRDC): f. 1992 to assume responsibility for refining, pipeline distribution, engineering, construction and research in the petroleum industry from the NIOC; Chair. and Man. Dir GHOLAMREZA AQAZADEH.

CO-OPERATIVES

Central Organization for Co-operatives of Iran: Teheran; in October 1985 there were 4,598 labour co-operatives, with a total membership of 703,814 and capital of 2,184.5m. rials, and 9,159 urban non-labour co-operatives, with a total membership of 262,118 and capital of 4,187.5m. rials.

Central Organization for Rural Co-operatives of Iran (CORC): Teheran; Man. Dir SAYED HASSAN MOTEVALLI-ZADEH.

The CORC was founded in 1963, and the Islamic Government of Iran has pledged that it will continue its educational, technical, commercial and credit assistance to rural co-operative societies and unions. At the end of the Iranian year 1363 (1984/85) there were 3,104 Rural Co-operative Societies with a total membership of 3,925,000 and share capital of 25,900m. rials. There were 181 Rural Co-operative Unions with 3,097 members and capital of 7,890m. rials.

Transport

RAILWAYS

Iranian Islamic Republic Railways: Shahid Kalantary Bldg, Railway Sq., Teheran 13185; tel. (21) 5641600; fax (21) 5650532; f. 1934; Man. Dir Eng. SADEGH AFSHAR; Vice-Pres. Sheikh ALIREZA MAHFOUZI (Admin. and Finance), Vice-Pres. FARROKH MOADELI (Technical and Infrastructure), Vice-Pres. HORMOZ GHOTBI (Operation and Traffic), Vice-Pres. Eng. MOHSAN POUR SEYED AGHAIE (Fleet Affairs).

The total length of main lines in the Iranian railway system, which is generally single-tracked, is 5,433 km (5,337 km of 1,435 mm electrified gauge and 96 km of 1,676 mm gauge). The system includes the following main routes:

Trans-Iranian Railway runs 1,392 km from Bandar Turkman on the Caspian Sea in the north, through Teheran, and south to Bandar Imam Khomeini on the Persian Gulf.

Southern Line links Teheran to Khorramshahr via Qom, Arak, Dorood, Andimeshk and Ahwaz; 937 km.

Northern Line links Teheran to Gorgan via Garmsar, Firooz Kooh and Sari; 499 km.

Teheran–Kerman Line via Kashan, Yazd and Zarand; 1,106 km.

Teheran–Tabriz Line linking with the Azerbaijan Railway; 736 km.

Tabriz–Djulfa Electric Line: 146 km.

Garmsar–Meshed Line connects Teheran with Meshed via Semnan, Damghan, Shahrud and Nishabur; 812 km. A line is under construction to link Meshed with Sarakhs on the Turkmen border. A 768-km line linking Meshed with Bafq is also under construction.

Qom–Zahedan Line when completed will be an intercontinental line linking Europe and Turkey, through Iran, with India. Zahedan is situated 91.7 km west of the Baluchistan frontier, and is the end of the Pakistani broad gauge railway. The section at present links Qom to Kerman via Kashan, Sistan, Yazd, Bafq and Zarand; 1,005 km. A branch line from Sistan was opened in 1971 via Isfahan to the steel mill at Zarrin Shahr; 112 km. A broad-gauge (1,976-mm) track connects Zahedan and Mirjaveh, on the border with Pakistan; 94 km.

Zahedan–Quetta (Pakistan) Line: 685km; not linked to national network.

Ahwaz–Bandar Khomeini Line connects Bandar Khomeini with the Trans-Iranian railway at Ahwaz; this line is due to be double-tracked; 112 km.

Azerbaijan Railway extends from Tabriz to Djulfa (146.5 km), meeting the Caucasian railways at the Azerbaijani frontier. Electrification works for this section have been completed and the electrified line was opened in April 1982. A standard gauge railway line (139 km) extends from Tabriz (via Sharaf–Khaneh) to the Turkish frontier at Razi.

Bandar Abbas–Bafq: construction of a 730-km double-track line to link Bandar Abbas and Bafq commenced in 1982. The first phase, linking Bafq to Sirjan (260 km), was opened in May 1990, and the second phase was opened in March 1995. The line provides access

to the copper mines at Sarcheshmeh and the iron ore mines at Gole-Gohar.

Bafq–Chadormalou: a 130-km line connecting Bafq to the Chadormalou iron-ore mines is under construction.

Chadormalou–Tabas: a 220-km line is under construction.

Underground Railway

Teheran Urban and Suburban Railway Co: POB 4661, 37 Mir Emad St, Teheran 15875; tel. (21) 8740144; telex 215676; fax (21) 8740114; Chair. and Man. Dir MOHSEN HASHEMI: in May 1995 the Teheran Urban and Suburban Railway Co concluded agreements with three Chinese companies for the completion of the Teheran underground railway, on which work had originally commenced in 1978. It was reported that about 85% of the work on two regular lines (one, 34 km in length, running north to south, and a second, 20 km in length, running east to west) and the express line (42 km in length—running west to the satellite city of Karaj) had been completed.

ROADS

In 1996 there were an estimated 162,000 km of roads, including 470 km of motorways, 22,900 km of highways, main or national roads and 43,500 km of secondary or regional roads; about 50% of the road network was paved. There is a paved highway (A1, 2,089 km) from Bazargan on the Turkish border to the Afghanistan border. The A2 highway runs 2,473 km from the Iraqi border to Mir Javeh on the Pakistan border.

Ministry of Roads and Transport: 49 Taleghani Ave, Teheran; tel. (21) 661034; telex 213381.

INLAND WATERWAYS

Principal waterways:

Lake Rezaiyeh (Lake Urmia): 80 km west of Tabriz in North-West Iran; and River Karun flowing south through the oilfields into the River Shatt al-Arab, thence to the head of the Persian Gulf near Abadan.

Lake Rezaiyeh: From Sharafkhaneh to Golmankhaneh there is a twice-weekly service of tugs and barges for transport of passengers and goods.

River Karun: Regular cargo service is operated by the Mesopotamia-Iran Corpn Ltd. Iranian firms also operate daily motor-boat services for passengers and goods.

SHIPPING

Persian Gulf: The main oil terminal is at Kharg Island. The principal commercial non-oil ports are Bandar Shahid Rajai (which was officially inaugurated in 1983 and handles 9m. of the 12m. tons of cargo passing annually through Iran's Persian Gulf ports), Bandar Khomeini, Bushehr, Bandar Abbas and Chah Bahar. A project to develop Bandar Abbas port, which predates the Islamic Revolution and was originally to cost IR 1,900,000m., is now in progress. Khorramshahr, Iran's biggest port, was disabled in the war with Iraq, and Bushehr and Bandar Khomeini also sustained war damage, which has restricted their use. In August 1988 the Iranian news agency (IRNA) announced that Iran was to spend $200m. on the construction of six 'multi-purpose' ports on the Arabian and Caspian Seas, while ports which had been damaged in the war were to be repaired.

Caspian Sea: Principal ports Bandar Anzali (formerly Bandar Pahlavi) and Bandar Nowshahr.

Ports and Shipping Organization: 751 Enghelab Ave, Teheran; tel. (21) 8809280; telex 212271; fax (21) 8804100; Man. Dir Eng. MUHAMMAD MADAD.

Principal Shipping Companies

Irano–Hind Shipping Co: POB 15875-4647, Sedaghat St, Vali Asr Ave, Teheran; tel. (21) 2058095; telex 215233; fax (21) 2057739; joint venture between the Islamic Republic of Iran and the Shipping Corpn of India; Chair. Capt. P. P. RADHAKRISHNAN.

Islamic Republic of Iran Shipping Lines (IRISL): POB 15875-4646, 675 North East Corner of Vali Asr Sq., Teheran; tel. (21) 833061; telex 213240; fax (21) 889413; f. 1967; affiliated to the Ministry of Commerce Jan. 1980; liner services between the Persian (Arabian) Gulf and Europe, the Far East and South America and the Caspian Sea and Central Asia; Chair. and Man. Dir MAHMOUD F. TARJOMAN.

National Iranian Tanker Co: POB 16765-947, 67–8 Atefis St, Africa Ave, Teheran; tel. (21) 2229093; telex 213543; fax (21) 2223011; Chair. and Man. Dir MUHAMMAD SOURI.

CIVIL AVIATION

The two main international airports are Mehrabad (Teheran) and Abadan. An international airport was opened at Isfahan in July

1984 and the first international flight took place in March 1986. Work on a new international airport, 40 km south of Teheran, abandoned in 1979, resumed in the mid-1980s, and work on three others, at Tabas, Ardebil and Ilam was under way in mid-1990. The airports at Urumiyeh, Ahwaz, Bakhtaran, Sanandaz, Abadan, Hamadan and Shiraz were to be modernized and smaller ones constructed at Lar, Lamard, Rajsanjan, Barm, Kashan, Maragheh, Khoy, Sirjan and Abadeh. In early 1995 the Economic Co-operation Organization (ECO) agreed to establish a regional airline (Eco Air), based in Teheran. Construction of Imam Khomeini airport in Teheran, anticipated to be one of the largest airports in the world, is due to begin in 1998.

Iran Air (Airline of the Islamic Republic of Iran): POB 13185-755, Iran Air Bldg, Mehrabad Airport, Teheran; tel. (21) 979111; telex 212795; fax (21) 6003248; f. 1962; serves the Middle East and Persian Gulf area, Europe, Asia and the Far East; Man. Dir AHMAD REZA KAZEMI.

Iran Air Tours: 191 Motahari Ave, Dr Moffateh Rd, Teheran 15879; tel. (21) 8708390; fax (21) 8555884; f. 1992; serves Middle East; Chair. A. M. KHALILI.

Iran Asseman Airlines: POB 141748, Mehrabad Airport, Teheran 13145-1476; tel. (21) 6484198; telex 212575; fax (21) 6404318; f. after Islamic Revolution as result of merger of Air Taxi Co (f. 1958), Pars Air (f. 1969), Air Service Co (f. 1962) and Hoor Asseman; Man. Dir ALI ABEDZADEH; domestic routes and charter services.

Kish Air: POB 19395-4639, 215 Africa Highway, Teheran 19697; tel. (21) 8778547; telex 226124; fax (21) 8776630; f. 1991 under the auspices of the Kish Development Organization; serves Persian Gulf area, Frankfurt, London and Paris; Pres. Capt. Y. KHALILI.

Saha Airline: POB 13445-965, Teheran 13873; tel. (21) 6696200; fax (21) 6698016; f. 1990; weekly cargo service between Teheran and Singapore.

Tourism

Tourism has been adversely affected by political upheaval since the Revolution. Iran's chief attraction for tourists is its wealth of historical sites, notably Isfahan, Rasht, Tabriz, Susa and Persepolis. Some 362,000 international tourist arrivals were recorded in 1994, compared with 153,615 in 1990. Receipts from tourism in 1994 totalled US $153m. Tourism centres are currently administered by the State, through the Ministry of Culture and Islamic Guidance, although in late 1997 the ministry indicated its intention to transfer all tourism affairs to the private sector.

Defence

Budgeted defence expenditure (1997): 8,200,000m. rials (US $4,700m.).

Chairman of the Supreme Defence Council: Ayatollah SAYED ALI KHAMENEI.

Chief of Staff of the Armed Forces and Commander of the Gendarmerie: Brig.-Gen. ALI SHAHBAZI.

Commander of the Army: Brig.-Gen. ALI SHAHBAZI.

Commander of the Air Force: Gen. SHAHRAM ROSTAMI (acting)

Commander of the Navy: Cdre MUHAMMAD HOSSEIN MALEK-ZADEGAN.

Chief of Staff of the Revolutionary Guards Corps (Pasdaran): ALI-REZA AFSHAR.

Commander of the Islamic Revolutionary Guards Corps: Maj.-Gen. MOHSEN REZAI.

Commander of Basij (Mobilization) War Volunteers Corps: MUHAMMAD ALI RAHMANI.

Military service: 24 months.

Total armed forces: At the beginning of the Iran–Iraq War in September 1980 Iran's army was estimated to total between 120,000 and 150,000 men, and the navy to total 30,000. In August 1997 it was estimated that the armed forces totalled 518,000 men: army 350,000 men; navy 18,000; air force 30,000; reserves 350,000; revolutionary guard corps (*Pasdaran*, which has its own army, navy and marines units) 120,000.

Education

PRIMARY AND SECONDARY EDUCATION

Primary education, beginning at age six and lasting for five years, is compulsory for all children and is provided free of charge. In 1996/97 some 9,238,000 pupils were enrolled in primary education. Secondary education may last for a further seven years, divided into two cycles; one of three, and another of four, years. In 1996/97 between 8m. and 9m. pupils were receiving secondary education. In 1994 the total enrolment at primary and secondary schools was equivalent to 84% of the school-age population (89% of boys; 78% of girls). In 1991 primary enrolment included 97% of children in the relevant age-group (100% of boys; 93% of girls).

According to the Government, 24,000 schools were built between the Revolution in 1979 and 1984.

HIGHER EDUCATION

Iran has 36 universities of various types, including 15 in Teheran. Universities were closed by the government in 1980 but have been reopened gradually since 1983. According to official sources, 579,070 students were enrolled at Iran's colleges and universities in the 1996/97 academic year. Apart from Teheran, there are universities in Bakhtaran, Isfahan, Hamadan, Tabriz, Ahwaz, Babolsar, Meshed, Kermanshah, Rasht, Shiraz, Zahedan, Kerman, Shahrekord, Urmia and Yazd. There are c. 50 colleges of higher education, c. 40 technological institutes, c. 20 teacher training colleges, several colleges of advanced technology, and colleges of agriculture in Hamadan, Zanjan, Sari and Abadan. Vocational training schools also exist in Teheran, Ahwaz, Meshed, Shiraz and other cities.

In 1994/95, according to official figures, the rate of illiteracy among the population aged six years and over was 22%. Expenditure on education by the central Government in the financial year 1996/97 was budgeted at IR 7,999,000m. (13.1% of total spending).

In recent years much emphasis has been put on agriculture and vocational programmes in higher education.

Bibliography

GENERAL

Abdalian, S. *Damavand (Iran)*. Teheran, 1943.

Amirahmadi, Hooshang, and Entessar, Nader. *Iran and the Arab World*. Basingstoke, The Macmillan Press Ltd, 1993.

Barth, F. *Nomads of South Persia*. London, 1961.

Cambridge History of Iran.
  Volume I: *The Land of Iran*.
  Volume V: *The Seljuq and Mongol Periods*.
  Both Cambridge University Press, 1968.

Cottam, Richard W. *Iran and the United States: A Cold War Case Study*. Pittsburgh, Pa, University of Pittsburgh Press, 1990.

Curzon, Lord. *Persia and the Persian Question*. 2 vols, London, 1892.

De Planhol, X. *Recherches sur la Géographie humaine de l'Iran Septentrional*. Paris, 1964.

Ehteshami, A. and Hinnebusch, R. *Syria and Iran: Middle Powers in a Penetrated Regional System*. London/New York, Routledge, 1997.

Elwell-Sutton, L. P. *Modern Iran*. London, 1941.

A Guide to Iranian Area Study. Ann Arbor, 1952.

Persian Oil: A Study in Power Politics. London, 1955.

Eskelund, Karl. *Behind the Peacock Throne*. New York, Alvin Redman, 1965.

Frye, Richard N. *Persia*. London, Allen and Unwin, 3rd ed. 1969.

Furon, Raymond. *L'Iran*. Paris, 1952.

  Géologie du Plateau iranien. Paris, 1941.

  La Perse. Paris, 1938.

Haeri, Shahla. *Law of Desire: temporary marriage in Iran*. London, I. B. Tauris, 1990.

Huot, Jean Louis. *Persia*, Vol. I. London, Muller, 1966.

Iqbal, Muhammad. *Iran*. London, 1946.

Iran Almanac. Teheran, Echo of Iran, annually.

Iran: A Selected and Annotated Bibliography. Washington, 1951.

Iran Research Group (Ed.). *Who's Who in Iran*. Wisbech, Menas Associates, 1990.

Keddie, Nikki R. *Historical Obstacles to Agrarian Change in Iran*. Claremont, 1960.

Iran. Religion, Politics and Society. London, Frank Cass, 1980.

(Ed. with Gasiorowski, Mark). *Neither East nor West: Iran, the Soviet Union and the United States.* New Haven, Conn., Yale University Press, 1990.

Kemp, N. *Abadan.* London, 1954.

Khomeini, Ayatollah Ruhollah. *A Clarification of Questions.* Boulder, Westview Press, 1985.

Lambton, A. K. S. *Landlord and Peasant in Persia.* New York, 1953.

Islamic Society in Persia. London, 1954.

A Persian Vocabulary. Cambridge, 1961.

The Persian Land Reform 1962–66. Oxford, Clarendon Press, 1969.

Marlowe, John. *Iran, a Short Political Guide.* London and New York, Pall Mall Press, 1963.

Mehdevi, A. S. *Persian Adventure.* New York, 1954.

Persia Revisited. London, 1965.

Millspaugh, A. C. *Americans in Persia.* Washington, 1946.

Motter, T. H. Vail. *The Persian Corridor and Aid to Russia.* Washington, 1952.

Ramazani, Rouhollah K. *The Persian Gulf: Iran's Role.* Charlottesville, University Press of Virginia, 1972.

Sabahi, Hushang. *British Policy in Persia 1918–1925.* London, Frank Cass, 1990.

Sanghvi, Ramesh. *Aryamehr: The Shah of Iran.* London, Macmillan, 1968.

Savory, Roger. *Iran under the Safavids.* Cambridge University Press, 1980.

Shah of Iran. *Mission for My Country.* London, Hutchinson, 1961.

Shearman, I. *Land and People of Iran.* London, 1962.

Sirdar, Ikbal Ali Shah. *Persia of the Persians.* London, 1929.

Stark, Freya. *The Valleys of the Assassins.* London, 1934.

East is West. London, 1945.

al-Suwaidi, J. *Iran and the Gulf.* Abu Dhabi, Emirates Centre for Strategic Studies and Research, 1996. (Distrib. I. B. Tauris, London).

Tharaud, Jérôme. *Vieille Perse et Jeune Iran.* Paris, 1947.

Wickens, G. M., and Savory, R. M. *Persia in Islamic Times, a practical bibliography of its history, culture and language.* Montreal, Institute of Islamic Studies, McGill University, 1964.

Wilber, Donald N. *Iran: Past and Present.* Princeton University Press, 1955, 8th edn 1977.

Iran: Oasis of Stability in the Middle East. New York, Foreign Political Association, Inc., 1959.

Zabih, Sepehr. *The Communist Movement in Iran.* University of California Press, 1967.

CIVILIZATION AND LITERATURE

Arberry, A. J. (Ed.). *The Legacy of Persia.* London and New York, 1953.

Shiraz: The Persian City of Saints and Poets. Univ. of Oklahoma Press, 1960.

Tales from the Masnavi. London, 1961.

More Tales from the Masnavi. London, 1963.

(Ed.). *The Cambridge History of Iran.* Cambridge University Press, 1969.

Bausani, A. *Der Perser: von den Anfängen bis zur Gegenwart.* Stuttgart, Kohlhammer, 1965.

Bell, Gertrude L. *Persian Pictures.* London, 1928.

Browne, E. G. *A Literary History of Persia.* 4 vols, Cambridge, 1928.

Colledge, M. A. R. *The Parthians.* London, Thames and Hudson, 1968.

Culican, William. *The Medes and the Persians.* 1965.

Duchesne-Guillemin, Jacques. *The Hymns of Zarathustra* (trans. with commentary). Beacon, L. R., Boston, Mass., 1963.

Ferrier, R. W. *A Journey to Persia: Jean Chardin's portrait of a seventeenth-century empire.* London, I. B. Tauris, 1996.

Ghirshman, R. *L'Iran: des Origines à Islam.* Paris, 1951.

Iran from the Earliest Times to the Islamic Conquest. London, 1954.

Arts of Ancient Persia from the Origins to Alexander the Great. London, 1963.

Iran. New York, 1964.

Herzfeld, E. *Iran in the Ancient East.* Oxford, 1941.

Levy, Reuben. *The Persian Language.* New York, 1952.

Persian Literature. 1928.

Lockhart, L. *Famous Cities of Iran.* London, 1939.

The Fall of the Safavi Dynasty and the Afghan Occupation of Persia. Cambridge University Press, 1958.

Melville, Charles (Ed.). *Safavid Persia.* 1996.

Milani, Farzaneh. *Veils and Words: The Emerging Voices of Iranian Women Writers.* London, I. B. Tauris, 1990.

Monteil, V. *Les Tribus du Fars et la sédentarisation des nomades.* Paris and The Hague, Mouton, 1966.

Olmstead, A. T. *History of the Persian Empire, Achaemenid Period.* Chicago, 1948.

Pope, Arthur. *Survey of Persian Art from Prehistoric Times to the Present.* Vols 1–6. Oxford University Press, 1938–58.

Rice, Cyprian. *The Persian Sufis.* London, Allen and Unwin, 1964.

Ross, Sir Denison. *Eastern Art and Literature.* London, 1928.

The Persians. London, 1931.

Storey, C. A. *Persian Literature.* London, 1927.

Sykes, Sir Percy. *Persia.* Oxford, 1922.

A History of Persia (2 vols; 3rd edition, with supplementary essays). London, 1930.

Teague-Jones, Reginald. *Adventures in Persia.* London, Gollancz, 1990.

Widengren. *Die Religionen Irans.* Stuttgart, Kohlhammer, 1965.

Wulfe, H. E. *The Traditional Crafts of Persia.* Cambridge, Mass., M.I.T. Press, 1966.

RECENT HISTORY

Akhavi, Shahrough. *Religion and Politics in Contemporary Iran.* State University of New York Press, 1980.

Amirahmadi, Hooshang, and Entessar, Nader. *Reconstruction and Regional Diplomacy in the Persian Gulf.* London, Routledge, 1992.

Amirsadeghi, Hossein. *Twentieth Century Iran.* London, Heinemann, 1977.

Assadollah, Alam. *The Shah and I: The Confidential Diaries of Iran's Royal Court, 1969–77.* London, I. B. Tauris, 1991.

Azimi, Fakhreddin. *Iran: The Crisis of Democracy 1941–1953.* London, I. B. Tauris, 1990.

Bakhash, Shaul. *The Reign of the Ayatollahs.* London, I. B. Tauris, 1984.

Balta, Paul. *Iran–Irak: une guerre de 5,000 ans.* Paris, Editions Anthropos, 1987.

Banani, Amin. *The Modernization of Iran, 1921–1924.* Stanford, 1961.

Bani-Sadr, Abol-Hassan. *My Turn to Speak: Iran, the revolution and secret deals with the US.* New York, Brassey's, 1991.

Benard, Cheryl, and Zalmay Khalilzad. *The Government of God: Iran's Islamic Republic.* New York, Columbia University Press, 1984.

Bill, James A. *The Lion and the Eagle: the Tragedy of American-Iranian Relations.* New Haven, Conn., Yale University Press, 1988.

Bullard, Render. *Letters from Tehran: a British ambassador in World War II Persia.* London, I. B. Tauris, 1991.

Bunya, Ali Akbar. *A Political and Diplomatic History of Persia.* Teheran, 1955.

Chubin, Shahram, and Tripp, Charles. *Iran and Iraq at War.* London, I.B. Tauris, 1988.

Chubin, Shahram, and Zabih, Sepehr. *The Foreign Relations of Iran: A Developing State in the Zone of a Great-Power Conflict.* University of California Press, 1975.

Cordesman, Anthony H. *The Iran–Iraq War and Western Security 1984–87.* London, Jane's Publishing Company, 1987.

Cottam, R. W. *Nationalism in Iran.* Pittsburgh University Press, 1964.

Iran and the United States: a cold war case study. Pittsburgh, University of Pittsburgh Press, 1988.

Delannoy, Christian. *Savak.* Paris, Editions Stock, 1991.

Ehteshami, A. *After Khomeini: The Iranian Second Republic.* London/New York, Routledge, 1995.

Farsoon, Samih K., and Mashayekhi, Mehrdad. *Iran: Political Culture in the Islamic Republic.* London, Routledge, 1993.

Fischer, M. J. *Iran: From Religious Dispute to Revolution.* Harvard University Press, 1980.

Goode, James F. *The United States and Iran, 1946–51: The Diplomacy of Neglect.* New York, St. Martin's Press, 1989.

Halliday, Fred. *Iran: Dictatorship and Development.* London, 1978.

Hamzavi. A. H. K. *Persia and the Powers: An Account of Diplomatic Relations, 1941–46.* London, 1946.

Heikal, Muhammad. *The Return of the Ayatollah*. London, André Deutsch, 1981.

Herzig, Edmund. *Iran and the Former Soviet South*. London, Chatham House, 1996.

Hiro, Dilip. *Iran under the Ayatollahs*. London, Routledge and Kegan Paul, 1984.

Hoveyda, Ferydoun. *The Fall of the Shah*. London, Weidenfeld and Nicolson, 1979.

Humphreys, Eileen. *The Royal Road: a popular history of Iran*. London, Scorpion, 1991.

Huyser, General Robert E. *Mission to Tehran*. London, André Deutsch, 1986.

Ismael, Tareq Y. *Iran and Iraq: Roots of Conflict*. Syracuse, N.Y., Syracuse University Press, 1983.

Issawi, Charles. *The Economic History of Iran, 1800–1919*. University of Chicago Press, 1972.

Kapuscinski, Ryszard. *Shah of Shahs*. San Diego, Harcourt Brace Jovanovich, 1985.

Katzman, Kenneth. *The Warriors of Islam: Iran's Revolutionary Guard*. Boulder, Co, and Oxford, United Kingdom, Westview Press, 1994.

Keddie, Nikki. *Roots of Revolution*. Yale University Press, 1982.

Khomeini, Ayatollah Ruhollah. *Islam and Revolution: Writings and Declarations of Imam Khomeini, trans. and ed. by Hamid Algar*. Berkeley, Calif., Mizan Press, 1982.

Laing, Margaret. *The Shah*. London, Sidgwick and Jackson, 1977.

Lenczowski, George. *Russia and the West in Iran*. Cornell University Press, 1949.

Lenczowsci, G. (Ed.). *Iran under the Pahlavis*. Stanford, Hoover Institution Press, 1978.

Mottahedeh, Roy. *The Mantle of the Prophet: Religion and Politics in Iran*. London, Chatto and Windus, 1985.

Nakhai, M. *L'Evolution Politique de l'Iran*. Brussels, 1938.

Naraghi, Ehsan. *Des Palais du Chah aux prisons de la révolution*. Paris, Editions Balland, 1993.

Omid, Homa. *Islam and the Post-Revolutionary State in Iran*. London, Macmillan, 1993.

Paidar, Parvin. *Women and the Political Process in Twentieth-Century Iran*. Cambridge, Cambridge University Press, 1995.

Parsa, Misagh. *Social Origins of the Iranian Revolution*. New Brunswick, New Jersey and London, Rutgers University Press, 1989.

Parsons, Sir Anthony. *The Pride and the Fall: Iran 1974–79*. London, Jonathan Cape, 1984.

Pelletiere, Stephen. *The Iran–Iraq War: chaos in a vacuum*. London and New York, Praeger Publishers, Inc., 1992.

Rahnema, Ali, and Nomani, Farhad. *The Sewlar Miracle: religion, politics and economic policy in Iran*. London, Zed Books, 1990.

Rahnema, Saeed, and Bedad, Sohrab (Eds). *Iran After the Revolution: Crisis of an Islamic State*. London, I. B. Tauris, 1995.

Rajaee, Farhang (Ed.). *The Iran–Iraq War: The Politics of Aggression*. Gainsville, University Press of Florida, 1994.

Ramazani, Rouhollah K. *The Foreign Policy of Iran 1500–1941*. University Press of Virginia, 1966.

Rezun, Miron (Ed.). *Iran at the Crossroads: global relations in a turbulent decade*. Oxford, Westview Press, 1990.

Roosevelt, Kermit. *Countercoup: the Struggle for the Control of Iran*. McGraw-Hill, 1980.

Sick, Gary. *All Fall Down: America's Tragic Encounter with Iran*. New York, Random House, 1985.

   October Surprise. New York, Random House, 1991.

Stempel, John D. *Inside the Iranian Revolution*. Indiana University Press, 1982.

Steppat, Fritz. *Iran zwischen den Grossmächten, 1941–48*. Oberursel, 1948.

Taheri, Amir. *The Spirit of Allah: Khomeini and the Iranian Revolution*. London, Hutchinson, 1985.

Upton, Joseph M. *The History of Modern Iran: An Interpretation*. Harvard University Press, 1960.

Villiers, Gerard de. *The Imperial Shah: An Informal Biography*. London, Weidenfeld and Nicolson, 1977.

Wroe, Ann. *Lives, Lies and the Iran-Contra Affair*. London, I. B. Tauris, 1991.

Zonis, Marrin. *Majestic Failure: The Fall of the Shah*. University of Chicago Press, 1991.

ECONOMY AND PETROLEUM

Amid, Mohammad Javad. *Poverty, Agriculture and Reform in Iran*. London, Routledge, 1990.

Amuzegar, Jahangir. *An Economic Profile*. Middle East Institute, 1977.

   The Dynamics of the Iranian Revolution. SUNY Press, 1991

   Iran's Economy under the Islamic Republic. London, I. B. Tauris, 1993.

Baldwin, George B. *Planning and Development in Iran*. Baltimore, Johns Hopkins Press, 1967.

Bharier, Julian. *Economic Development in Iran 1900–1970*. London, Oxford University Press, 1971.

Elm, Mostafa. *Oil, Power and Principle: Iran's oil nationalization and its aftermath*. Syracuse, Syracuse University Press, 1992.

Ghosh, Sunil Kanti. *The Anglo–Iranian Oil Dispute*. Calcutta, 1960.

Gupta, Raj Narain. *Iran: An Economic Study*. New Delhi, 1947.

Mason, F. C. *Iran: Economic and Commercial Conditions in Iran*. London, HMSO, 1957.

Mofid, Kamran. *The Economic Consequences of the Gulf War*. London, Routledge, 1990.

Nahai, L., and Kibell, C. L. *The Petroleum Industry of Iran*. Washington, US Department of the Interior, Bureau of Mines, 1963.

Nirumand, Bahman. *Persien, Modell eines Entwicklungslande, oder Die Diktatur der freien Welt*. Reinbek-bei-Hamburg, Rowohlt-Verlag, 1967.

Sotoudeh, H. *L'Evolution Economique de l'Iran et ses Problèmes*. Paris, 1957.

IRAQ

Physical and Social Geography

W. B. FISHER

Iraq is bounded on the north by Turkey, on the east by Iran, on the south by Kuwait and the Persian Gulf, on the south-west by Saudi Arabia and Jordan, and on the north-west by Syria. The actual frontier lines present one or two unusual features. In the first place, there exists between Iraq, Kuwait, and Saudi Arabia a 'neutral zone', rhomboidal in shape, which was devised to facilitate the migrations of pastoral nomads, who cover great distances each year in search of pasture for their animals and who move regularly between several countries. Hence the stabilization or closing of a frontier could be for them a matter of life and death. Secondly, the frontier with Iran in its extreme southern portion, below Basra, follows the course of the Shatt al-Arab channel (the confluence of the Tigris and Euphrates), which flows into the Persian Gulf, but from 1936 until March 1975 the frontier was at the left (east) bank, placing the whole of the river within Iraq. This situation had become increasingly unacceptable to Iran, and under the Algiers Agreement of March 1975 the border was restored to the Thalweg Line in the middle of the deepest shipping channel in the Shatt al-Arab estuary. The dispute over the precise position of this border was one of the causes of the war with Iran which began in 1980. Thirdly, the inclusion of the northern province of Mosul within Iraq was agreed only in 1926. Because of its petroleum deposits, this territory was in dispute between Turkey, Syria and Iraq. Again, the presence of large numbers of migratory nomads, journeying each season between Iran, Turkey, Syria and Iraq, was a further complicating factor. In March 1984 a treaty was signed by Jordan and Iraq which finally demarcated the border between the two countries and under which Iraq ceded some 50 sq km to Jordan.

PHYSICAL FEATURES

The old name of Iraq (Mesopotamia = land between the rivers) indicates the main physical aspect of the country—the presence of the two river valleys of the Tigris and Euphrates, which merge in their lower courses. On the eastern side of this double valley the Zagros Mountains appear as an abrupt wall, over-hanging the riverine lowlands, particularly in the south, below Baghdad. North of the latitude of Baghdad the rise to the mountains is more gradual, with several intervening hill ranges, such as the Jebel Hamrin. These ranges are fairly low and narrow at first, with separating lowlands, but towards the main Zagros topography becomes more imposing, and summits over 3,000 m in height occur. This region, lying north and east of Baghdad, is the ancient land of Assyria; nowadays the higher hill ranges lying in the extreme east are known as Iraqi Kurdistan, since many Kurdish tribes inhabit them.

On the western side of the river valley the land rises gradually to form the plateau which continues into Syria, Jordan, and Saudi Arabia, and its maximum height in Iraq is about 1,000 m. In places it is possible to trace a cliff formation, where a more resistant bed of rock stands out prominently, and from this the name of the country is said to be derived (Iraq = cliff). There is no sharp geographical break between Iraq and its western neighbours comparable with that between Iraq and Iran; the frontier lines are artificial.

THE RIVERS

The Tigris, 1,850 km (1,150 miles) in length, rises in Turkey, and is joined by numerous and often large tributaries both in Turkey and Iraq. The Euphrates, 2,350 km (1,460 miles) in length, also rises in Turkey and flows first through Syria and then Iraq, joining the Tigris in its lower course at Qurna, to form the stream known as the Shatt al-Arab (or Arvand river, as it is called by the Iranians), which is 185 km (115 miles) in length. Unlike the Tigris, the Euphrates receives no tributaries during its passage of Iraq. Above the region of Baghdad both rivers flow in well-defined channels, with retaining valley walls. Below Baghdad, however, the vestiges of a retaining valley disappear, and the rivers meander over a vast open plain with only a slight drop in level—in places merely 1.5 m or 2 m in 100 km. Here the rivers are raised on great levees, or banks of silt and mud (which they themselves have laid down), and now lie several feet above the level of the surrounding plain. One remarkable feature is the change in relative level of the two river beds—water can be led from one to the other according to the actual district, and this possibility, utilized by irrigation engineers for many centuries, still remains the basic principle of present-day development. Old river channels, fully or partially abandoned by the river, are also a feature of the Mesopotamian lowland, associated with wide areas of swamp, lakes, and sand-bars. The Tigris, though narrower than the Euphrates, is swifter, and carries far more water.

As the sources of both rivers lie in the mountains of Turkey, the current is very fast, and upstream navigation is difficult in the middle and upper reaches. In spring, following the melting of snows in Asia Minor, both rivers begin to rise, reaching a maximum in April (Tigris) and May (Euphrates). During the season floods of 3.6 m to 6.0 m occur, and 10 m is known—this in a region where the land may fall only 4 m or less in level over 100 km. Immense areas are regularly inundated, levees often collapse, and villages and roads, where these exist, must be built on high embankments. The Tigris is particularly liable to sudden flooding, and can rise at the rate of one foot per hour. In lower Iraq wide expanses are inundated every year. Construction of the Wadi Tharthar control scheme has, however, greatly reduced the incidence of severe flooding, particularly along the Tigris, and continued expansion of irrigation schemes (which has been a feature of Iraq since the late 1960s) is having a further effect.

Roads were formerly difficult to maintain because of floods, and the rail system was of different gauges. New standard-gauge rail links have now been constructed: north-south from Mosul to Basra via Baghdad; various cross-country lines; and an extension along the Euphrates valley towards north-eastern Syria.

Because of the former difficulties in communication, many communities of differing cultures and ways of life have persisted. Minority groups have thus been a feature in Iraq.

CLIMATE AND ECONOMIC ACTIVITY

The summers are overwhelmingly hot, with shade temperatures of over 43°C. Winters may be surprisingly cold: frost, though very rare in the south, can be severe in the north. Sudden hot spells during winter are another feature in the centre and south of Iraq. Rainfall is scanty over all of the country, except for the north-east (Assyria), where annual falls of 400 mm–600 mm occur—enough to grow crops without irrigation. Elsewhere farming is entirely dependent upon irrigation from river water. The great extent of standing water in many parts of Iraq leads to an unduly high air humidity, which explains the notorious reputation of the Mesopotamian summer.

The unusual physical conditions outlined present a number of obstacles to human activity. The flood waters are rather less 'manageable' than in Egypt, for example, and there is less of the regular deposition of thick, rich silt that is such a feature of the Nile. The effects of this are strikingly visible in the relatively small extent of land actually cultivated—at most, only one-sixth of the potentially cultivable territory and 3% of the total area of the country. Because of the easy availability of agricultural land, wasteful, 'extensive' farming methods are often followed, giving a low yield. On the whole, Iraq is under-populated, and could support larger numbers of inhabitants.

A feature of recent years has been the use of petroleum royalties for development schemes, particularly in irrigation. Various early plans allocated up to £30m. annually, but this was not always used. Now, with much higher oil revenues, the figure has been revised upward, and far more extensive development is planned.

The unusual physical conditions have greatly restricted movement and the development of communications of all kinds. In the upper reaches of the rivers, boat journeys can only be made downstream, whilst nearer the sea the rivers are wider and slower but often very shallow. Roads and railways are difficult to maintain because of the floods.

THE PEOPLE

In the marshes of the extreme south there are a number of boat-and-raft-based Arab communities. Other important minorities live in, or close to, the hill country of the north: the Kurds, who number an estimated 3.5m. and migrate extensively into Syria, Turkey and Iran (see History); the Yazidis of the Jebel Sinjar; the Assyrian Christians (the name refers to their geographical location, and has no historical connection); and various communities of Uniate and Orthodox Christians. In addition, there were important groups of Jews—more than in most other Muslim countries—though, since the establishment of the State of Israel, much emigration has taken place. It should be noted that, while the majority of the Muslims follow Shi'a rites, the wealthier Muslims have tended to be of Sunni adherence.

Ethnically, the position is very complicated. The northern and eastern hill districts contain many racial elements—Turki, Persian, and proto-Nordic, with Armenoid strains predominating. The pastoral nomads of western Iraq are, as might be expected, of fairly unmixed Mediterranean ancestry, like the nomads of Syria, Jordan, and Saudi Arabia; but the population of the riverine districts of Iraq displays a mixture of Armenoid and Mediterranean elements. North of the Baghdad district the Armenoid strain is dominant, but to the south, it is less important, though still present.

Arabic is the official and most widely used language, Kurdish and dialects of Turkish are current in the north, whilst variants of Persian are spoken by tribes in the east. An estimate, probably over-generous to the Arabic speakers, puts the relative proportions at: Arabic 79%, Kurdish 16%, Persian 3%, and Turkish 2% of the total population.

History

Revised for this edition by RICHARD I. LAWLESS

EARLY HISTORY

By the advent of Islam in the seventh century AD Iraq had already experienced more than 3,500 years of civilization. The Sumerians were, in turn, succeeded by the Elamites, the Amorites, the Mittani, the Hittites, and the Assyrians, until in 612 BC the subject peoples rose and sacked Nineveh. Iraq then became the centre of a neo-Babylonian state, which, under Nebuchadnezzar (604–538 BC), included much of the Fertile Crescent (from the Euphrates to the Nile Valley), but soon fell to the Persians, who seized Babylon in 539–538 BC.

Iraq then became a province of the Achaemenid Empire until the military successes of Alexander the Great in 334–327 BC. After about 100 years of Seleucid rule Iraq became a frontier province of the Parthian Empire against the might of Rome. Between AD 113 and 117 Trajan conquered much of Iraq but his successor Hadrian withdrew. Roman reoccupation later took place. Parthian rule eventually gave way before the emergence of the Sasanid regime in the second century AD. Frontier wars with Rome broke out from time to time, but by the seventh century both Persia and Byzantium were exhausted, and the way was open to conquest from the south.

THE RISE OF ISLAM

The spectacular birth and growth of Islam in the first quarter of the seventh century set the Arabs on the path of conquest outside Arabia. In 637, at the battle of Jalula, the Arabs virtually ended Sasanid power in Iraq. There immediately followed a period of struggle between Ali, the son-in-law of the Prophet, and Mu'awiya, who had been governor of Syria. Ali fell in battle, however, in 661, making way for the Umaiyad dynasty, under Syrian hegemony, until 750. A movement arose known as the Shi'atu Ali (i.e. the party of Ali) and most new converts gave their allegiance to the Shi'a, partly as an expression of their social and political grievance against the established order. In 750 Umaiyad rule was replaced by that of the Abbasid dynasty, with Iraq becoming the dominant and most prosperous part of the empire. The second Abbasid, al-Mansour (754–775), quickly abandoned the Shi'ite extremists who had brought the Abbasids to power. Abbasid power waned, and Baghdad fell under the rule of the Shi'ite Buwaihids from the middle of the 10th to the middle of the 11th century, when effective power passed to the Seljuq Turks, although the Abbasid Caliph was, in name, the head of state.

MONGOL INVASIONS

In 1253 Hulagu, a grandson of Chinghiz (Jenghiz) Khan, moved westward in force, captured Baghdad in 1258 and thus made an end of the Abbasid Caliphate. Now subordinate to the Mongol Khan of Persia, Iraq became a mere frontier province. After the death of the Mongol Khan Abu Sa'id in 1335, Iraq passed to the Jala'irids who ruled until the early years of the 15th century. Iraq then passed successively under the power of two rival Turcoman confederations (the Black Sheep and the White Sheep) until, in the years 1499–1508, the White Sheep regime was destroyed by the Safavid Ismail, who made himself Shah of Persia. The Sunni Ottoman Turks considered the Shi'ite Ismail to be a threat, and the Sultan Suleyman, in the course of his campaign against Persia, conquered Baghdad in 1534–35.

OTTOMAN IRAQ

Although Persian control was restored for a brief period between 1623 and 1638, Iraq was to remain, at least nominally, under Turkish control until the First World War. A series of Mamluk pashas in the 18th century engaged in wars with Persia, and, towards the end of the century, had to contend with Kurdish insurrection in the north and raids by Wahhabi tribesmen from the south. In the early 19th century the Ottoman Sultan decided to regain direct possession of Iraq and end the Mamluk system. Sultan Mahmoud II sent Ali Ridha Pasha to perform this task in 1831. A severe outbreak of plague hampered the Mamluks, Da'ud Pasha was deposed, and the Mamluk regiments were exterminated.

WESTERN INFLUENCE

Although some of the European nations had long been in contact with Iraq through their commercial interests in the Persian Gulf, Western influences were slow to penetrate into the province. By 1800 there was a British Resident at Basra and two years later a British Consulate at Baghdad. France also maintained agents in these cities. French and Italian religious orders had settlements in the land. It was not, however, until after 1831 that signs of more rapid European penetration became visible, such as steamboats on the rivers of Iraq in 1836, telegraph lines from 1861 and a number of proposals for railways, none of which was to materialize for a long time to come. The Ottoman Government did much in the period between 1831 and 1850 to impose direct control over Kurdistan and the mountainous areas close to the Persian border, but the introduction of reforms was not, in fact, begun until 1869, when Midhat Pasha arrived at Baghdad. Although much of his work, performed in the brief space of three years, proved to be superficial and ill-considered, achievements, however imperfect, such as a newspaper, military factories, a hospital, an alms-house, schools, conscription for the army, municipal and administrative councils, comparative security on the main routes and a reasoned policy of settling tribes on the land did bear solid witness to the vigour of his rule. After his departure in 1872, reform and European influence continued to advance, although slowly. Postal services were much developed, a railway from Baghdad to Samarra was completed in 1914 (part of the projected *Baghdad-bahn* which betokened the rapid growth of German interest in the Ottoman Empire) and the important Hindiya Barrage on the Euphrates was rebuilt between 1910 and 1913. The measures of reform and improvement introduced between 1831 and 1914 must indeed be judged as belated and inadequate—the Iraq of 1900 differed little from that of 1500— yet a process of fundamental change had begun.

In November 1914 Britain and the Ottoman Empire were at war. British troops occupied the Shatt al-Arab region and, through the necessity of war, transformed Basra into an efficient and well-equipped port. A premature advance on Baghdad in 1915 ended in the retreat of the British forces to Kut, their prolonged defence of that town and, when all attempts to relieve it had failed, the capitulation to the Ottomans in April 1916. A new offensive launched from Basra in the autumn of that year brought about the capture of Baghdad in March 1917. Kirkuk was taken in 1918, but, before the Allies could seize Mosul, the Ottoman Government sought and obtained an armistice in October. For two years, until the winter of 1920, the Commander-in-Chief of the British Forces, acting through a civil commissioner, continued to be responsible for the administration of Iraq from Basra to Mosul, all the apparatus of a modern system of rule being created at Baghdad—e.g. departments of land, posts and telegraphs, agriculture, irrigation, police, customs, finance, etc. The new regime was Christian, foreign and strange; resented by reason of its very efficiency, feared and distrusted no less by those whose loyalties were Muslim and Ottoman than by important elements who desired self-determination for Iraq.

The last phase of Ottoman domination in Iraq, especially during the years after the Young Turk Revolution in 1908, had witnessed a marked growth of Arab nationalist sentiment. Local circles in Iraq now made contact with the Ottoman Decentralization Party at Cairo, founded in 1912, and with the Young Arab Society, which moved from Paris to Beirut in 1913. Basra, in particular, became a centre of Arab aspirations and took the lead in demanding from Istanbul a measure of autonomy for Iraq. A secret organization, al-'Ahd (the Covenant), included a number of Iraqi officers serving in the Ottoman armies. The prospect of independence which the Allies held out to the Arabs in the course of the war strengthened and extended the nationalist movement. In April 1920 Britain received from the conference at San Remo a mandate for Iraq. This news was soon followed by a serious insurrection amongst the tribesmen of the south. The revolt, caused partly by instinctive dislike of foreign rule but also by vigorous nationalist propaganda, was not wholly suppressed until early in the next year. In October 1920 military rule was formally terminated in Iraq. An Arab Council of State, advised by British officials and responsible for the administration, now came into being and in March 1921 the Amir Faisal ibn Hussain agreed to rule as King at Baghdad. His ceremonial accession took place on 23 August 1921.

The Najdi (Saudi Arabian) frontier with Iraq was defined in the Treaty of Mohammara in May 1922. Saudi concern over loss of traditional grazing rights resulted in further talks between Ibn Saud and the British Civil Commissioner in Iraq, and a Neutral Zone of 7,000 sq km was established adjacent to the western tip of the Kuwait frontier. No military or permanent buildings were to be erected in the zone and the nomads of both

countries were to have unimpeded access to its pastures and wells. A further agreement concerning the administration of this zone was signed between Iraq and Saudi Arabia in May 1938.

MODERN IRAQ

Despite the opposition of the more extreme nationalists, an Anglo-Iraqi Treaty was signed on 10 October 1922. It embodied the provisions of the mandate, safeguarded the judicial rights of foreigners and guaranteed the special interests of Britain in Iraq. An electoral law facilitated the choice of a constituent assembly, which met in March 1924 and, despite strong opposition by the nationalists, ratified the treaty with Britain. It accepted, too, an organic law declaring Iraq to be a sovereign state with a constitutional hereditary monarchy and a representative system of government. In 1925 the League of Nations recommended that the *wilaya* (administrative district) of Mosul, to which the Turks had laid claim, be incorporated into the new kingdom, a decision finally implemented in the treaty of July 1926 between the interested parties: Britain, Turkey and Iraq. By 1926 a fully constituted parliament was in session at Baghdad and all the ministries, as well as most of the larger departments of the administration, were in effective control. In 1930 a new treaty was signed with Britain, which established between the two countries a close alliance for a period of 25 years and granted Britain the use of airbases at Shuaiba and Habbaniya. On 3 October 1932 Iraq entered the League of Nations as an independent power, the mandate being now terminated.

Numerous difficulties confronted the Kingdom in the period after 1932: e.g. the animosities between the Sunni Muslims and the powerful Shi'ite tribes on the Euphrates, which tended to divide and embitter political life; the problem of relations with the Kurds, some of whom wanted a separate Kurdish state, and with other minorities like the Assyrians; the complicated task of reform in land tenure and of improvement in agriculture, irrigation, flood control, public services and communications. During these years the Government was little more than a façade of democratic forms concealing faction and intrigue. The realities of the political scene were an often ill-informed and xenophobic press; 'parties' better described as cliques gathered around prominent personalities; a small ruling class of tribal sheikhs; landowners; and the intelligentsia—lawyers, students, journalists, doctors, ex-officers—frequently torn by sharp rivalries. It is not surprising, therefore, that the first years of full independence made rather halting progress towards efficient rule. The dangerous nature of domestic tensions was demonstrated by the Assyrian massacre of 1933 perpetrated by troops of the Iraqi army. Political intrigue from Baghdad was partly responsible for the outbreak of tribal revolt along the Euphrates in 1935–36. The army crushed the insurrection without much difficulty and then, under the leadership of General Bakr Sidqi, and in alliance with disappointed politicians and reformist elements, brought about a *coup d'état* in October 1936. The new regime failed to fulfil its assurances of reform; its policies alienated the tribal chieftains and gave rise to serious tensions even within the armed forces, tensions which led to the assassination of Bakr Sidqi in August 1937.

Of vast importance for Iraq was the rapid development of the petroleum industry during these years. Concessions were granted in 1925, 1932 and 1938 to the Iraq, Mosul and Basra Petroleum Cos. Oil had been discovered in the Kirkuk area in 1927 and by the end of 1934 the Iraq Petroleum Co (IPC) was exporting crude oil through two 30-cm (12-inch) pipelines, one leading to Tripoli and the other to Haifa. Exploitation of the Mosul and Basra fields did not begin on a commercial scale until after the Second World War.

In 1937 Iraq joined Turkey, Persia and Afghanistan in the Sa'dabad Pact, which arranged for consultation in all disputes that might affect the common interests of the four states. A treaty signed with Persia in July 1937 and ratified in the following year provided for the specific acceptance of the boundary between the two countries as it had been defined in 1914. Relations with Britain deteriorated in the period after 1937, mainly because of the growth of anti-Zionist feeling and of resentment at British policy in Palestine. German influence increased very much at this time in Iraq, especially among those political and military circles associated with the army group later to be known as the Golden Square. Iraq severed its diplomatic connections with Germany at the beginning of the Second World War, but in 1941 the army commanders carried out a new *coup d'état*, establishing, under the nominal leadership of Rashid 'Ali al-Gaylani, a regime which announced its non-belligerent intentions. A disagreement over the passage of British troops through Iraq left no doubt of the pro-German sympathies of the Gaylani Government and led to hostilities that ended with the allied occupation of Basra and Baghdad in May 1941. Thereafter, Iraq co-operated with the Allies and declared war on the Axis powers in 1943.

Iraq, during the years after the Second World War, was to experience much internal tension and unrest. Negotiations with Britain led to the signing, at Portsmouth in January 1948, of a new Anglo-Iraqi agreement designed to replace that of 1930 and incorporating substantial concessions, amongst them the British evacuation of the airbases at Shuaiba and Habbaniya and the creation of a joint board for the co-ordination of all matters relating to mutual defence. The animosities arising from the situation in Palestine provoked riots at Baghdad directed against the new agreement with Britain, which were sufficiently disturbing to oblige the Iraqi Government to repudiate the Portsmouth settlement.

ARAB–ISRAELI WAR, 1948

With anti-Jewish and anti-Western feeling so intense, it was inevitable that troops should be sent from Iraq to the Arab–Israeli war which began on 15 May 1948. The Iraqi troops shared in the hostilities for a period of just over two months, their participation terminating in a truce operative from 18 July. Their final withdrawal from Palestine did not commence, however, until April 1949. Subsequently, there was a considerable emigration of Jews from Iraq to Israel, especially in the years 1951–52.

The expense of the war against Israel, together with bad harvests and the general indigence of the people created serious tensions resulting in rioting at Baghdad in November 1952 and the imposition of martial law until October 1953. None the less, there were some favourable prospects for the future—notably a large expansion of the oil industry. New pipelines were built to Tripoli in 1949 and to Banias in Syria in 1952; the oilfields of Mosul and Basra were producing significant amounts of crude petroleum by 1951/52. A National Development Board was created in 1950 and became later, in 1953, a national ministry. An agreement of February 1952 allowed the Iraqi Government 50% of the oil companies' profits before deductions for foreign taxes. Abundant resources were thus available for development projects of national benefit (e.g. the flood control and irrigation works opened in April 1956 on the Tigris at Samarra and on the Euphrates at Ramadi).

THE BAGHDAD PACT

Iraq, in the field of foreign relations, was confronted during these years with a choice between the Western powers, eager to establish in the Middle East an organized pattern of defence, and the USSR, entering at this time into a diplomatic propaganda and economic drive to increase its influence in the Arab lands. In February 1955 Iraq made an alliance with Turkey for mutual co-operation and defence. Britain acceded to this pact in the following April, agreeing also to end the Anglo-Iraqi agreement of 1930 and to surrender its air bases at Shuaiba and Habbaniya. With the adherence of Pakistan in September and of Iran in October 1955, the so-called Baghdad Pact was completed: a defensive cordon now existed along the southern fringe of the USSR.

CONSEQUENCES OF THE SUEZ CRISIS

The outbreak of hostilities between Israel and Egypt on 29 October 1956, and the armed intervention of British and French forces against Egypt (31 October–6 November) led to a delicate situation in Iraq, where strong elements were still opposed to all connections with the Western Powers. Iraq, indeed, broke off diplomatic relations with France on 9 November and announced that, for the immediate future at least, it could give no assurance of taking part in further sessions of the Council of the Baghdad Pact, if delegates from Britain were present.

The equivocal attitude of the Baghdad Government during the Suez crisis had provoked unrest in Iraq. Disturbances at Najaf and Mosul resulted in some loss of life. Student demonstrations against the Anglo-French intervention in Egypt and the Israeli campaign in Sinai led the Iraqi Government to close colleges and schools. Martial law, imposed on 31 October 1956, was not raised until 27 May 1957.

The tension born of the Suez crisis persisted for some time to come. President Eisenhower of the USA, concerned over the flow of Soviet arms to Syria and Egypt, sought permission from Congress to deploy US armed forces to defend nations exposed to danger from countries under the influence of international communism. He also secured authorization to disburse economic and military aid to the Middle East states prepared to co-operate with the West. This programme became known as the 'Eisenhower Doctrine'.

RELATIONS WITH SYRIA AND JORDAN

At the time of the Suez crisis there had been sharp tension between Iraq and Syria. Pumping-stations located inside Syria and belonging to the Iraq Petroleum Co were sabotaged in November 1956. Iraq consequently suffered a large financial loss through the interruption in the flow of oil to the Mediterranean coast. Not until March 1957 did Syria allow the Iraq Petroleum Co to begin the repair of the pipelines.

Since the Suez crisis of 1956 troops of Iraq and Syria had been stationed in Jordan as a precaution against an Israeli advance to the east. Iraq, in December 1956, announced that its troops would be withdrawn; the Syrian forces, however, still remained in Jordan. The fear that Syria might intervene in favour of the elements in Jordan opposed to King Hussein brought about further recriminations between Baghdad and Damascus. The danger of an acute crisis receded in April 1957, when the USA declared that the independence of Jordan was a matter of vital concern and underlined this statement by sending its Sixth Fleet to the eastern Mediterranean. In February 1958 King Faisal of Iraq and King Hussein of Jordan joined together in an abortive Arab Federation.

OVERTHROW OF THE MONARCHY

King Faisal II, together with the Crown Prince of Iraq and Gen. Nouri as-Said, lost their lives in the course of a *coup d'état* begun on 14 July 1958 by units of the Iraqi army. Iraq was now to become a republic. Power was placed in the hands of a Council of Sovereignty exercising presidential authority, and of a Cabinet led by Brig. Abd al-Karim Kassem, with the rank of Prime Minister.

A power struggle developed between the two main architects of the July *coup d'état*—Brig. (later Gen.) Kassem, the Prime Minister, and Col (later Field-Marshal) Abd as-Salam Muhammad Aref, the Deputy Prime Minister and Minister of the Interior. Col Aref was associated with the influential Baath Party and had shown himself to be a supporter of union between Iraq and the United Arab Republic (UAR—the union of Egypt and Syria). In September 1958 he was dismissed from his offices and, in November, was tried on a charge of plotting against the interests of Iraq. As reconstituted in February 1959 the new regime was more hostile to the UAR and inclined to favour a form of independent nationalism with left-wing tendencies.

Gen. Kassem announced the withdrawal of Iraq from the Baghdad Pact on 24 March 1959. Since the revolution of July 1958 Iraq's adherence to the Pact had been little more than nominal. One result of this withdrawal was the termination of the special agreement existing between Britain and Iraq since 1955 under the first article of the Baghdad Pact. On 31 March it was made known that the British Royal Air Force contingent at Habbaniya would be recalled.

PROBLEMS OF THE KASSEM REGIME

Earlier in 1959 the communist elements in Iraq had been refused representation in the Government. The communists operated through a number of professional organizations and also through the so-called People's Resistance Force. Communist elements had infiltrated into the armed forces of Iraq and into the civil service. Gen. Kassem now began to introduce measures which would limit communist influence inside the Government and the administration of the country. In July 1959 fighting occurred at Kirkuk between the Kurds (supported by the People's Resistance Force) and the Turcomans, with the result that Kassem disbanded the People's Resistance Force. More important for the Government at Baghdad was the fact that, in March 1961, a considerable section of the Kurdish population in northern Iraq rose in rebellion under Mustafa Barzani, the President of the Democratic Party of Kurdistan (DPK)—a party established in 1958 after the return of Barzani from an exile occasioned by an earlier unsuccessful revolt in 1946. The refusal of the central regime at Baghdad to grant the reiterated Kurdish demands for autonomous status had contributed greatly to bringing about the new insurrection. Mustafa Barzani in March 1961 proclaimed an independent Kurdish state. By September 1961 the rebels controlled some 250 miles of mountainous territory along the Iraqi-Turkish and Iraqi-Persian frontiers, from Zakho in the west to Sulaimaniya in the east. The Kurds were able to consolidate their hold over much of northern Iraq during the course of 1962. The Kurds used guerrilla tactics with much success to isolate and deprive the government garrisons in the north of supplies. By December 1963 Kurdish forces had advanced south towards the Khanaqin area and the main road linking Iraq with Iran. The government troops found themselves in fact confined to the larger towns such as Kirkuk, Sulaimaniya and Khanaqin. Negotiations for peace began near Sulaimaniya in January 1964 and led to a cease-fire on 10 February. The national claims of the Kurds were to be recognized in a new provisional constitution for Iraq. Moreover, a general amnesty would be granted by the Iraqi Government. The Kurdish tribes, however, refused to lay aside their arms until their political demands had been given practical effect. Despite the negotiation of this settlement it soon emerged that no final solution of the Kurdish problem was apparent.

FALL OF KASSEM

A military coup, carried out in Baghdad on 8 February 1963, overthrew the regime of Gen. Kassem, the General himself being captured and shot. The coup arose out of an alliance between nationalist army officers and the Baath Party. Col Aref was now raised to the office of President and a new Cabinet was created under Brig. Ahmad al-Bakr. The Baath Party, founded in 1941 (in Syria) and dedicated to the ideas of Arab unity, socialism and freedom, drew its main support from military elements, intellectuals and the middle classes. It was, however, divided in Iraq into a pro-Egyptian wing advocating union with the UAR and a more independent wing disinclined to accept authoritarian control from Egypt. The coup of February 1963 was followed by the arrest of pro-Kassem and communist elements, by mass trials and a number of executions, by confiscations of property and by a purge of the officer corps and of the civil service.

A number of efforts were made, during the years 1963–65, to further the cause of Arab unification, but agreements made between Syria and Iraq, and between Egypt, Syria and Iraq, had little practical effect.

MANOEUVRES OF THE BAATH PARTY

These same years saw in Iraq itself a conflict for control between the extremist and the more moderate Baath elements. At the end of September 1963 the extremists dominated the Baath Regional Council in Iraq. An international Baath conference held at Damascus in October 1963 strengthened the position of the extremists through its support of a federal union between Syria and Iraq and its approval of more radical social and economic policies. A further Baathist conference at Baghdad in November 1963 enabled the moderates to elect a new Baath Regional Council in Iraq with their own adherents in control. At this juncture the extremists attempted a *coup d'état*, in the course of which air force elements attacked the Presidential Palace and the Ministry of Defence.

On 18 November 1963 President Aref assumed full powers in Iraq, with the support of the armed forces, and a new Revolutionary Command was established at Baghdad. Sporadic fighting occurred between government troops and the pro-Baathist National Guard. A main factor in the sudden fall of the Baathists was the attitude of the professional officer class. Officers with communist, Kassemite or pro-Nasser sympathies,

or with no strong political views, or of Kurdish origin, had all been removed from important commands and offices. The privileged position of the National Guard caused further resentment in the army. The long drawn-out operations against the Kurds, the known dissensions within the Baathist ranks in Iraq and the intervention of Baath politicians from abroad in Iraqi affairs also contributed to discredit the extreme elements amongst the Baathists. On 20 November 1963 a new Cabinet was formed at Baghdad, consisting of officers, moderate Baathists, independents and non-party experts.

THE ARAB SOCIALIST UNION

On 14 July 1964 President Aref announced that all political parties would be merged in a new organization known as the 'Iraqi Arab Socialist Union'. At the same time it was revealed that all banks and insurance companies, together with 32 important industrial concerns, would undergo nationalization.

In July 1965 a number of pro-Nasser ministers resigned. At the beginning of September a new administration was installed with Brig. Aref Abd ar-Razzaq as Prime Minister. The Brigadier, reputed to be pro-Nasser in his sympathies, attempted to seize full power in Iraq, but his attempted *coup d'état* failed and, on 16 September he himself, together with some of his supporters, found refuge in Cairo. On 13 April 1966 President Abd as-Salam Aref was killed in a helicopter crash. His brother Maj.-Gen. Abd ar-Rahman Aref succeeded him as President with the approval of the Cabinet and of the National Defence Council. In late June Abd ar-Razzaq led a second abortive coup, which was foiled by the prompt action of President Aref.

KURDISH NATIONALISM

The war against the Kurds, halted only for a short while by the cease-fire of February 1964, dragged out its inconclusive course during 1964–66. Some of the fighting in December 1965 occurred close to the Iraq-Iran border, leading to a number of frontier violations which exacerbated tensions between the two states during the first half of 1966. In June 1966 Dr Abd ar-Rahman al-Bazzaz, Prime Minister of Iraq since September 1965, formulated new proposals for a settlement of the conflict with the Kurds. Kurdish nationalism and language would receive legal recognition; the administration was to be decentralized, allowing the Kurds to run educational, health and municipal affairs in their own districts; the Kurds would have proportional representation in parliament and in the Cabinet and the various state services; the Kurdish armed forces (some 15,000 strong) were to be dissolved. Mustafa Barzani, the Kurdish leader, declared himself to be well disposed towards these proposals.

This entente was implemented only to a limited extent. The Cabinet formed in May 1967 contained Kurdish elements, and President Aref, after a visit to the north in late 1967, reaffirmed his intention to make available to the Kurds appointments of ministerial rank, to help with the rehabilitation of the war-affected areas in Kurdistan, and to work towards effective co-operation with the Kurds in the government of Iraq. This state of quiescence was, however, broken in the first half of 1968 by reports of dissension amongst the Kurds themselves, with open violence between the adherents of Mustafa Barzani and the supporters of Jalal Talabani, who had co-operated with the Government.

OIL DISPUTES AND THE JUNE WAR

Although the winter of 1966–67 brought an improvement in relations with Iran, it also witnessed a dispute between Syria and the Iraq Petroleum Co over alleged losses of revenue on oil from Iraq passing through Syria by pipeline. The flow of oil was halted for a time and settlement was not reached until well into 1967.

When the Arab–Israeli war was renewed in June 1967, the movement of Iraqi oil was again affected. Problems connected with its production and export constituted a major preoccupation of the Baghdad Government during the period immediately following the war. Iraq had at the outset severed diplomatic relations with the USA and Britain after Arab charges that the two states had aided Israel in the war and it also banned the export of oil to them. When, at the end of June, supplies of Iraqi oil began to be moved once more from the pipeline terminals on the Mediterranean, this embargo remained. In August Iraq, Syria and Lebanon resolved to allow the export of Iraqi oil to most of the countries of Europe, the United Kingdom being still subject, however, to the embargo.

Relations with the West improved slightly during the autumn and winter of 1967. The remaining oil embargoes were gradually removed, and in December Gen. Sabri led a military delegation to Paris. This was followed by President Aref's official visit to France in February 1968, and in April France agreed to supply Iraq with 54 *Mirage* aircraft over the period 1969–73. In May diplomatic relations with the United Kingdom were resumed.

THE 1968 COUP AND ITS AFTERMATH

Throughout the first half of 1968 the regime conspicuously lacked popular support, being commonly thought to be both corrupt and inefficient, and the sudden bloodless *coup d'état* of 17 July did not surprise many observers. Gen. Ahmad Hassan al-Bakr, a former Prime Minister, became President; the deposed President Aref went into exile and his Prime Minister, Taher Yahya, was imprisoned on corruption charges. A new Government was soon dismissed by the President, who accused it of 'reactionary tendencies'. He then appointed himself Prime Minister and Commander-in-Chief of the Armed Forces.

During the second half of 1968 the internal political situation deteriorated steadily. By November there were frequent reports of a purge directed against opponents of the new regime, and freedom of verbal political comment seemed to have disappeared. A former Minister of Foreign Affairs, Dr Nasser al-Hani, was found murdered, and a distinguished former Prime Minister, Dr al-Bazzaz, and other members of former governments were arrested as 'counter-revolutionary leaders'; most were later sentenced to long terms of imprisonment. Open hostilities with the Kurds erupted in October 1968 for the first time since the June 1966 cease-fire, and continued on an extensive scale throughout the winter. Iraqi army and air force attempts to enforce the writ of the Baghdad Government had little success; the regime claimed that the rebels were receiving aid from Iran and Israel. Fighting continued unabated through 1969, the Kurds demanding autonomy within the state and asking for UN mediation.

SETTLEMENT WITH THE KURDS

The most important event of 1970 was the settlement with the Kurds when, in March, a 15-article peace plan was announced by the Revolutionary Command Council (RCC) and the Kurdish leaders. The plan conceded that the Kurds should participate fully in government; that Kurdish officials should be appointed in areas inhabited by a Kurdish majority; that Kurdish should be the official language, along with Arabic, in Kurdish areas; that development of Kurdish areas should be implemented; and that the Provisional Constitution should be amended to incorporate the rights of the Kurds.

The agreement was generally accepted by the Kurdish community and fighting ceased immediately. The war had been very expensive for Iraq and it had seriously delayed the national development programme. The Kurdish settlement, although not entirely satisfactory, did introduce an element of stability into life in Iraq and allowed a number of reforms to be initiated. In October 1970 the state of emergency, in operation almost continuously since July 1958, was lifted. Many political detainees, including former ministers, were released. Censorship of mail was abolished at the end of the year, having lasted for over 13 years, and a month later the censorship of foreign correspondents' cables was brought to an end after a similar period.

Kurdish unity was boosted in February 1971 by the decision of the Kurdish Revolutionary Party (KRP) to merge with the DPK, led by Masoud Barzani, and in July 1971 a new Provisional Constitution was announced, which embodied many of the points contained in the 1970 settlement. The Kurds were directed by the Supreme Committee for Kurdish Affairs to surrender their arms by August 1971.

Evidence of unrest, however, was growing both in Kurdistan and in the Government itself. In July 1971 an attempted coup by army and air force officers was put down by the Government but dissatisfaction continued to be reported. The Kurds were beginning to show discontent with the delays in implementing

the 1970 agreement. Their demand for participation in the RCC was refused and in September 1971 an attempt was made on Barzani's life.

THE CONTINUING KURDISH PROBLEM

During 1972, possibly because of increasing preoccupation with foreign affairs, dissension within the Government was less evident. Clashes with the Kurds, however, became more frequent and there was another plot to assassinate Barzani in July. The Baath Party's deteriorating relations with the Kurds brought a threat from the DPK to renew the civil war. One of the main Kurdish grievances was that the census agreed upon in 1970 had still not taken place. The two sides met to discuss their differences, the Kurdish side pointing to the unfulfilled provisions of the 1970 agreement and the Baath reiterating the various development projects carried out in Kurdish areas. In December 1972 divisions arose in the Kurdish ranks when it was reported that a breakaway party was to be established in opposition to Barzani's party.

FOREIGN RELATIONS 1968–71

The more radical section of the Arab world had initially viewed the July 1968 coup with disfavour and the new regime was at pains to prove itself as militant an exponent of Arab nationalism as its predecessor. The regime gradually became an accepted member of the nationalist group, but there was some Arab criticism of its policies, notably the public hangings and their effect on world opinion.

Iraq adopted an uncompromising attitude to the Palestinian problem. All peace proposals—US, Egyptian and Jordanian—were rejected. In theory, total support was given to the Palestine liberation movement. However, despite a threat to the Jordanian Government at the beginning of September 1970 to intervene in Jordan on behalf of the Palestinian guerrillas, the Iraqi forces stationed there did not take part in the fighting. In January 1971 most of Iraq's 20,000 troops withdrew from both Jordan and Syria. In March it was reported in Cairo that Iraq's monthly contribution to the Palestine Liberation Army (PLA) had ceased. Iraq's attitude to Middle East peace proposals provoked a rift with Egypt even before President Nasser's death, and Iraq's contempt for the proposed Egypt-Libya-Syria federation, as well as for any negotiated settlement with Israel, preserved its isolation from Egypt and almost all the other Arab states. In July 1971 there were signs that Iraq wished to effect a degree of reconciliation, offering to co-operate again with the Arab states if they abandoned attempts to negotiate with Israel, but the renewal of hostilities between the Jordanian Government and the guerrillas prompted a deterioration in relations with Jordan. Iraq closed the border, demanded Jordan's expulsion from the League of Arab States (Arab League) and proscribed its participation in the Eighth International Baghdad Fair.

Meanwhile, relations with Iran remained hostile. Iraq frequently accused the Iranian Government of assisting the Kurdish rebellion and in April 1969 the Shatt al-Arab waterway again caused a minor confrontation. Iraq had benefited by a 1937 treaty which gave it control of the waterway. Iran attempted to force a renegotiation of the treaty by illegally sending through vessels flying the Iranian flag. Being unwilling (or politically unable) to yield any of its sovereignty, and unable to challenge Iran militarily, Iraq was obliged to accept this situation. Iraq proposed referring the dispute to the International Court of Justice (ICJ) in The Hague, but Iran rejected the suggestion. Minor border clashes between the two sides' forces continued to occur sporadically and both Iran and Iraq accused each other of attempting to foment coups. Not surprisingly, the two countries were also divided on policy towards the Gulf states. Iraq severed diplomatic relations with Iran (and Britain) after Iran's seizure of the Tunb Islands in the Persian (Arabian) Gulf in November 1971.

Relations with the Western world, and the USA in particular, remained poor, and several people were arrested or expelled in late 1968, after having been accused of spying for the USA. Meanwhile, cordial relations with the Soviet Union remained the major factor influencing Iraq's foreign policy, particularly since the USSR was supplying the major portion of Iraq's military equipment.

THE PROBLEM OF OIL

In June 1972 Iraq nationalized the IPC's interests and agreement on outstanding points of dispute was finally reached on 28 February 1973. The company agreed to settle Iraqi claims for retrospective royalties by paying £141m., and to waive its objections to Law No. 80 under which the North Rumaila fields were seized in 1961. The Government agreed to deliver a total of 15m. tons of crude petroleum from Kirkuk, to be loaded at Eastern Mediterranean ports, to the companies as compensation. The Mosul Petroleum Co agreed to relinquish all its assets without compensation and the Basrah Petroleum Co, the only one of the group to remain operational in Iraq, undertook to increase output from 32m. tons in 1972 to 80m. tons in 1976. This agreement was regarded on the whole as a victory for the Iraqi Government, although the companies were by no means financially disadvantaged by it.

With the IPC dispute settled, Iraq showed its unwillingness to continue indefinitely with exporting oil on a barter basis to the Eastern bloc countries. The Government emphasized that it would press for a cash basis to future agreements.

FOREIGN RELATIONS 1972–73

The nationalization of the IPC brought expressions of approval from a number of countries, including Arab states and the USSR. The 15-year friendship treaty with the USSR, signed in March 1972, was ratified in July, and Iraq's relations with the Eastern bloc remained cordial. Despite this, the Government was well aware of the dangers of too close and too exclusive a relationship with the Soviet bloc. France was specifically identified as the Western country most favoured by the Arabs, and the President's fourth anniversary speech in July revealed that Iraq would not be unwilling to initiate friendly relations with Western countries. Although diplomatic relations with the USA remained severed, the USA established an 'interests section' in Baghdad.

CONSTITUTIONAL CHANGE

In July 1973 an abortive coup took place, led by the security chief, Nazim Kazzar, in which the Minister of Defence, Gen. Hammad Shehab, was killed. There was some speculation that the coup had been attempted by a civilian faction within the Baath Party in an attempt to eliminate President Bakr and the military faction. Consequences of the attempted coup included an amendment to the Constitution giving more power to the President, and the formation of a National Front between the Baath Party and the Iraqi Communist Party (ICP).

CLIMAX AND END OF KURDISH WAR

According to the agreement made between the Iraqi Government and the Kurds in March 1970 the deadline for implementation of the agreement was 11 March 1974. An uneasy peace between the Kurds and the Iraqis existed between those two dates. On expiry of the deadline, Saddam Hussain Takriti, the Vice-President of the RCC and the 'strong man' of the regime, announced the granting of autonomy to the Kurds. Barzani and his DPK felt that the Iraqi offer did not fulfil their demands for full government representation, which included membership of the RCC. A minority of Kurds, who belonged to Abd as-Satter Sharif's KRP welcomed the proposals, however. Barzani and his militia, the *peshmerga* (literally, 'those who confront death'), began armed resistance in north Iraq. In April 1974 the Iraqi Government replaced five Kurdish ministers known to support Barzani by five other Kurds who supported the government plan for giving the Kurds a measure of autonomy. Later in April the Iraqi Government appointed a Kurd, Taha Mohi ed-Din Marouf, as Vice-President of Iraq, but since he had long been a supporter of the Baghdad Government, it seemed unlikely that this would mollify the Kurds of the DPK.

By August 1974 the Kurdish war had reached a new level of intensity. The Baghdad Government was directing large military resources against the *peshmerga*, and was deploying tanks, field guns and bombers. About 130,000 Kurds, mainly women, children and old men, took refuge in Iran. The *peshmerga* were able to continue their resistance in Iraq only with the help of arms and other supplies from Iran. When, therefore, an agreement to end their border dispute was signed by Iraq and Iran

at the OPEC meeting in Algiers on 6 March 1975, both countries also agreed to end 'infiltrations of a subversive character' and the Kurdish rebellion collapsed. Barzani felt that he could not continue his struggle without Iran's aid, and fled to Teheran. A cease-fire was arranged on 13 March and a series of amnesties granted to Kurds who had fled to Iran encouraged most of them to return to Iraq. By February 1976, however, it was reported that the DPK was secretly reorganizing inside Iraqi Kurdistan and preparing to resume its struggle. In March there were reports of clashes between Kurds and Iraqi security forces in the Rawanduz area, after Iraqi attempts to clear the frontier area with Iran and resettle Kurds in less sensitive areas of Iraq. A new political organization, the National Union of Kurdistan (NUK), was also established in Damascus quite separately from the DPK, which, in the opinion of the NUK, had become discredited. Renewed Kurdish activity occurred in 1976 but was not serious enough to weaken the Iraqi claim that the Kurdish problem had been solved. Reconstruction and school-building was certainly undertaken in Kurdish areas in 1977, and in April 1977 the Iraqi authorities allowed 40,000 Kurds who had been compulsorily settled in the south in 1975 to return to their homes in the north. It was also decided in April 1977, by the Executive Council of the Kurdish Autonomous Region, that Kurdish should become the official language to be used in all communications and by all government departments in the Kurdish Autonomous Region which had no connection with the central Government.

FOREIGN AFFAIRS 1973–76

At the outbreak of the October 1973 war between the Arabs and Israel, Iraq sent considerable land forces to the Syrian front and took advantage of Iran's offer to resume diplomatic relations. The Iraqi Government, however, had taken offence at President Sadat's failure to consult Iraq prior to the offensive, and, therefore, Iraqi forces were withdrawn from Syria as soon as the cease-fire went into effect, and Iraq boycotted the Arab summit meeting in Algiers in November.

Relations deteriorated with Iran in the early months of 1974, when frontier fighting broke out, and it was only after the appointment of a UN mediator in March that 'normal' relations on the frontier were restored, and they worsened again in August in spite of talks in Istanbul between Iraqi and Iranian diplomats. Further border clashes took place in December 1974, and secret talks in Istanbul between the Iraqi and Iranian Ministers of Foreign Affairs in January 1975 failed to prevent the outbreak of fresh clashes in February. It was therefore something of a surprise when, at the OPEC meeting at Algiers in March 1975, it was announced that Saddam Hussain Takriti, Vice-President of the RCC, and the Shah of Iran had signed an agreement which 'completely eliminated the conflict between the two brotherly countries'. This agreement also ended the Kurdish war (see above), and was embodied in a treaty signed between the two countries in June 1975. The frontiers were defined on the basis of the Protocol of Constantinople of 1913 and the verbal agreement on frontiers of 1914. The Shatt al-Arab frontier was defined according to the Thalweg Line, which runs down the middle of the deepest shipping channel.

THE BAATH PARTY AND RELATIONS WITH SYRIA

Iraq was one of the many Arab states which were severely critical of the second interim disengagement agreement signed between Egypt and Israel in September 1975. Iraqi reaction to the agreement was similar to that of Syria, but this condemnation was perhaps the only thing upon which the two countries agreed between 1975 and 1978. Rivalry between the two wings of the Baath party in Baghdad and Damascus, and a dispute over the sharing of the water from the Euphrates were just two areas of contention. In February 1976 Iraq was reported to be diverting much of its oil from pipelines to the Mediterranean to terminals near Basra, thus depriving Syria of valuable pipeline revenues. Iraq was also very critical of Syria's intervention in Lebanon. In addition, Syrian agents were blamed for violence which took place in the Shi'a holy cities of Najaf and Karbala in February 1977. Relations with Syria deteriorated even further in late 1977, and Iraq became somewhat isolated after President Sadat of Egypt's peace initiative in visiting Jerusalem in November 1977. At the Tripoli Conference, summoned by the states which opposed President Sadat's approach, Iraq advocated a specific rejection of UN Security Council Resolution 242 (see Documents on Palestine, p. 000). The stand taken by the other participants (Syria, Libya, the People's Democratic Republic of Yemen (PDRY), Algeria and the Palestine Liberation Organization (PLO)) were considered too moderate by Iraq, which abandoned the conference. Iraq subsequently boycotted the Algiers conference of 'rejectionist' states in February 1978, hoping, unsuccessfully, to form its own 'steadfastness and liberation front' at a Baghdad conference.

NEW ALIGNMENTS

Iraq opposed the Camp David agreements made between Egypt and Israel in September 1978, but, continuing its policy of boycott, it did not attend the Damascus Arab summit which immediately followed the Camp David agreements. In October, however, President Assad of Syria visited Baghdad and, as a result, Iraq and Syria signed a charter outlining plans for political and economic union between the two countries. Old rivalries and animosities were set aside in an effort to form a political and military power which would constitute a sizeable counterweight to Egypt in Middle Eastern affairs. In November Iraq successfully convened a Pan-Arab summit which threatened sanctions against Egypt if a peace treaty with Israel should be signed, and in March 1979, when the peace treaty became a fact, Baghdad was the venue for the meeting of the Arab ministers of foreign and economic affairs which resolved to put into practice the threats made to Egypt in the previous November.

The plans for complete political and economic union of Iraq and Syria were pursued with enthusiasm but little real practical application by both countries until July 1979. On 16 July 1979 Saddam Hussain replaced Bakr as President of Iraq and Chairman of the RCC. A few days later, an attempted coup was reported, and several members of the RCC were sentenced to death for their alleged part in the plot. Saddam Hussain believed Syria to be implicated, in spite of Syrian denials, and the newly-formed alliance foundered. Another aspect of this political unrest in Iraq was the dissolution of the alliance between the Baath Party and the ICP. In the summer of 1978 21 army personnel were executed for conducting political activity in the armed forces. Relations with the communists continued to deteriorate; they withdrew from the National Progressive Front in March 1979, and in early 1980 President Hussain referred to them in a speech as 'a rotten, atheistic, yellow storm which has plagued Iraq'. This led to a decrease in dependence on the USSR and to tentative moves to improve relations with the West. Hussain joined in the general Arab condemnation of the Soviet invasion of Afghanistan at the end of 1979.

In February 1980 President Hussain announced his 'National Charter', which reaffirmed the principles of non-alignment, rejecting 'the existence of foreign armies, military forces, troops and bases in the Arab Homeland', and made a plea for Arab solidarity. With President Sadat of Egypt compromised by his *rapprochement* with Israel, Hussain saw himself in a position of virtual pre-eminence in the Arab world and, with the Non-Aligned Summit due to take place in Baghdad in 1982, he would be in a position to present himself as the responsible leader of the non-aligned world.

Domestically, Hussain was engaged in restoring parliamentary government to Iraq. The intention had been announced some years earlier, but on 16 March 1980 laws were adopted for the election of an Iraqi National Assembly of 250 deputies for a four-year session, and also for a Legislative Council for the Autonomous Region of Kurdistan, consisting of 50 members elected for a three-year session. Elections took place on 20 June 1980, and deputies were elected by a direct, free and secret ballot. The first session of the National Assembly opened on 30 June, and one of the deputy premiers, Naim Haddad, was elected Chairman and Speaker. Elections to a 50-member Kurdish Legislative Council took place in September 1980.

WAR WITH IRAN

Although the 1975 peace agreement with Iran virtually ended the Kurdish rebellion, Iraq was dissatisfied and wanted a return to the Shatt al-Arab boundary whereby it controlled the whole waterway, and also the withdrawal of Iranian forces from Abu

Musa and Tunb Islands, which Iran occupied in 1971. Conflict also became evident after the Iranian Revolution over Arab demands for autonomy in Iran's Khuzestan (termed 'Arabistan' by Arabs), which Iran accused Iraq of encouraging. In addition, Iraq's Sunni leadership was suspicious of Shi'ite Iran and fearful that the Islamic Revolution in Iran might spread to its own Shi'ites, who are in the majority in Iraq. Border fighting between Iran and Iraq frequently occurred as 1980 progressed, and open warfare began on 22 September when Iraqi forces advanced into Iran along a 300-mile front. Iran had ignored Iraqi diplomatic efforts demanding the withdrawal of Iranian forces from Zain ul-Qos on the border. Iraq maintained that this territory should have been returned by Iran under the 1975 agreement. Iraq therefore abrogated the Shatt al-Arab agreement on 16 September.

Most commentators agree that Saddam Hussain's real intention when he invaded Iran was to topple the Islamic revolutionary regime. Resistance was fiercer than he expected, however, and stalemate was soon reached along a 300-mile front, while various international peace missions sought in vain for a solution. In the spring of 1982 Iranian forces launched successful counter-offensives, one in the region of Dezful in March, and another in April which resulted in the recapture of Khorramshahr by the Iranians in May.

By late June 1982 Saddam Hussain had to acknowledge that the invasion of Iran had been a failure, and he arranged for the complete withdrawal of Iraqi troops from Iranian territory. In July the Iranian army crossed into Iraq, giving rise to the heaviest fighting of the war, thus far.

INTERNAL OPPOSITION TO SADDAM HUSSAIN

As well as the deteriorating military situation, Saddam Hussain faced a number of other threats to his position from within Iraq. The 'Iraqi Front of Revolutionary, Islamic and National Forces', consisting of Kurds, exiled Shi'ites and disaffected Baath party members, had been formed in 1981 with the backing of Syria, whose President Assad was as anxious as Ayatollah Khomeini to see the downfall of Saddam Hussain, his Baathist rival. In northern Iraq, Kurdish rebels were becoming active again and there existed the possibility that Iraq's majority Shi'ite community (55% of the population) would turn against the Sunnis (the sect of the Iraqi leadership). However, the bulk of Iraq's Shi'ites seemed to distrust the harsh fundamentalism of Khomeini's Iran. Against this background, Hussain was re-elected Chairman of the RCC and regional secretary of the Arab Baath Socialist Party, and in July 1982, having purged his administration, was apparently more firmly in control than ever.

In November 1982 new opposition arose from the Supreme Council of Iraqi Opposition Groups, under the leadership of an exiled Shi'ite leader, Hojatoleslam Muhammad Baqir Hakim, in Teheran. However, as the war with Iran degenerated into a conflict of attrition after the first Iranian advance into Iraq, the severe burden which it placed upon the country's economy emerged as the most critical concern for Hussain in 1983. Petroleum revenues had been slashed by almost 75%, following the destruction of Iraq's Gulf terminals, the closure of the pipeline across hostile Syria and the decline in oil prices. Iraq was searching for ways to avoid defaulting on payments for foreign construction contracts and was already borrowing money from friendly Gulf states.

In October 1983 there were rumours of an attempted coup in Baghdad, led by the recently dismissed head of intelligence, Barzan at-Takriti (the President's half-brother), and a number of senior army officers, who were later reported to have been executed.

An abiding problem for Iraqi governments has been the question of Kurdish autonomy within Iraq. The drain on military and financial resources, resulting from efforts to contain Kurdish secessionist forces, was of particular significance at this time, since costly equipment and manpower was being diverted from critical areas in the war with Iran. Unable to fight wars on two fronts, Hussain sought an accommodation with the Kurds. A series of talks with Jalal Talibani, leader of the Patriotic Union of Kurdistan (PUK) and of an estimated 40,000 Kurdish soldiers, began in December 1983, after a cease-fire was agreed. The PUK demanded the release of 49 Kurdish political prisoners, the return of 8,000 Kurdish families, moved from Kurdistan to southern Iraq, and the extension of the Kurdish autonomous area to include the oil town of Kirkuk. The talks could have provided only a partial solution, as they did not include the DPK, which sought to further the cause of Kurdish autonomy by siding with Iran (and which was antipathetic towards the PUK). Thoughts of a government of national unity, including the PUK and the ICP, were short-lived. Hussain's attitude changed, possibly prompted by the greater international support for Iraq which was forthcoming in the first half of 1984, and the talks broke down in May. The dialogue between the two sides was resumed and continued on a sporadic basis, with Hussain trying to persuade the PUK to join the National Progressive Front. To win its support, Hussain would have had to make major concessions to the PUK, such as granting Kurdish control of Kirkuk province, where Iraq's main oilfields are situated, and giving the Kurds a fixed share of national oil revenues (perhaps 20%–30%), and this he was unlikely to do. Negotiations on Kurdish autonomy collapsed again in January 1985 and fighting broke out in Kurdistan between PUK guerrillas and government troops after a 14-month cease-fire. The PUK blamed the Government's continued persecution and execution of Kurds; its refusal to include consideration of the one-third of Kurdistan containing the Kirkuk oilfields in autonomy talks; and an agreement with Turkey to act jointly to quell Kurdish resistance, which had been made in October 1984. The PUK then rejected the offer of an amnesty for President Hussain's political opponents at home and abroad in February, and fighting has continued.

THE IRAN–IRAQ WAR, OCTOBER 1983–DECEMBER 1984

Beginning in October 1983, Iran launched a series of attacks across its northern border with Iraq. About 700 sq km (270 square miles) of Iraqi territory were gained, threatening the last outlet for Iraqi exports of petroleum through the Kirkuk pipeline. Iraq intensified its missile attacks and bombing raids against Iranian towns and petroleum installations. During the autumn of 1983 Iraq took delivery of five French-built *Super Etendard* fighter aircraft. With these, and with the *Exocet* missiles already in its possession, Iraq threatened to destroy Iran's petroleum export industry, centred on the Kharg Island oil terminal in the Gulf. (In fact, Iraq did not use the *Super Etendards* and *Exocet* missiles in tandem until the end of March 1984 in the Gulf.) Iran responded by promising to make the Gulf impassable to all traffic (including exports of one-sixth of the West's petroleum requirements) by blocking the Strait of Hormuz, if Iraqi military action made it impossible for Iran to export its own petroleum by that route.

Despite approaches from the UN and various governments (Egypt, Saudi Arabia and Syria among them), Iran refused to negotiate with Iraq and was adamant that nothing less than the removal of the regime of Saddam Hussain, the withdrawal of Iraqi troops from Iranian territory and the agreement to pay reparations for war damages could bring hostilities to an end.

In August 1982 Iraq declared a maritime exclusion zone in the Gulf, extending from the Khor Abdullah channel, at the mouth of the Shatt al-Arab waterway, to a point south of the Iranian port of Bushehr. This zone included the Kharg Island oil terminal. Iraq carried out sporadic attacks on shipping (not only tankers) making for Kharg or returning from it, or fired indiscriminately on ships well outside the zone. The aim was to make the export of petroleum from Iran as difficult and expensive as possible and, by the threat of military action, to deter shipping from using Iranian ports, thus starving Iran of vital oil revenues. These tactics succeeded to a limited extent. Rates of insurance for shipping using the Gulf rose dramatically, and Japan, the largest customer for Iranian oil, briefly ordered its tankers not to use Iranian ports in mid-1984. Iraq refrained, however, from implementing its threat to attack Kharg Island itself and tankers loading there until May 1984. When the attack came, it was not immediately followed up, and the sequence of isolated attacks of limited effectiveness seemed to be continuing. The dangers of the war's spreading to other Gulf states were shown when Iran retaliated by attacking Saudi Arabian and Kuwaiti tankers, and tankers using oil terminals belonging to those countries. During 1984 the conviction grew

that neither Iran nor Iraq possessed the capability to give effect to its worst threats.

Iraq certainly had no shortage of financial and military supporters. Egypt is estimated to have supplied military equipment and spare parts worth more than US $2,000m.; according to *The Washington Post*, the People's Republic of China sold arms to Iraq worth $3,100m. between 1981 and 1985 (compared with sales to Iran, over the same period, worth $575m.); Brazil and Chile sold weapons to Iraq; the USSR (previously officially neutral in the war) increased its aid, following a *rapprochement* with Iraq in March 1984, and had already sold SS-12 missiles to Iraq; and the USA supplied helicopters and other heavy military equipment, though it remained officially neutral. (Both the USA and the USSR also sold arms to Iran.) Saudi Arabia and Kuwait supported Iraq with loans and the revenue from sales of up to 310,000 barrels per day (b/d) of petroleum (250,000 b/d from the neutral zone and the remainder from Saudi Arabia), sold on Iraq's behalf.

In February 1984 Iran launched an offensive in the marshlands around Majnoon Island, the site of rich oilfields in southern Iraq, near the confluence of the rivers Tigris and Euphrates. Iraq failed to regain control of this territory and was condemned for using mustard gas in the fighting. Iraq subsequently established extensive and formidable defences, including a system of dams and embankments, along the southern front, near Basra, in anticipation of a possibly decisive offensive by Iran, which massed some 500,000 men there.

In 1984 the balance of military power moved in Iraq's favour, and the USA and the USSR, both officially neutral in the war with Iran, provided aid. The USSR increased its military aid following a *rapprochement* in March between the two Governments, precipitated by Iran's anti-Soviet stance, and was responsible for supplying an estimated two-thirds of Iraq's total armaments and much of its ammunition. At the end of 1987 it was estimated that the USSR had supplied Iraq with military aid worth $10,000m. since lifting a ban on arms sales in 1982. The USA assisted Iraq with the financing of crucial oil export pipeline projects and with an increasing allocation of commodity credits. Iraq and the USA re-established full diplomatic relations on 26 November 1984, more than 17 years after they had been broken off by Iraq following the Arab–Israeli war of 1967.

Iraq had a substantial advantage in the strength of its air force. At the end of 1984 Iraq had 580 combat aircraft and 130 armed helicopters, while Iran had 110 combat aircraft, only 50 to 60 of which were thought to be operational. On the ground, Iraq's tank force was superior in numbers and sophistication.

THE IRAN–IRAQ WAR, 1985–86

A resumption in December 1984 of Iraqi attacks on shipping in the Gulf, in particular on oil tankers using the terminal at Kharg Island caused a sharp increase in hull insurance rates. Iran's oil exports fell to a record low level in January 1985 as a result of Iraqi action but, after another lull in military activity, in a pattern which became familiar during the next four years, insurance rates were reduced and custom returned. Attacks on shipping continued but Iraq failed decisively to exploit its superiority in the air. The Kharg Island oil terminal remained operational and largely undamaged for much of 1985 and Iran was quite successful in circumventing Iraqi attempts to debilitate its oil export industry. It consistently offered oil at discount and rebate deals to attract customers deterred by the high cost of war insurance, and in February established a makeshift floating export terminal at Sirri Island, militarily a much less exposed location (journeys to which commanded lower rates of insurance), 800 km (500 miles) south-east of Kharg, from where it received its oil by tanker shuttle.

In March Iran committed an estimated 50,000 troops to an offensive on the southern front in the region of the Hawizah marshes, east of the Tigris. Iranian forces succeeded in crossing the Tigris and for a time closed the main road connecting Baghdad and Basra before being repulsed. Iraq was again accused of using chemical weapons during this engagement.

In June 1984 the UN engineered the suspension by Iran and Iraq of attacks on civilian targets. However, in March 1985, with the war on the ground at a stalemate, Iraq resorted to air raids on Iranian towns and declared Iranian airspace a war zone. Saddam Hussain's stated intention was to carry the war to every part of Iran until Ayatollah Khomeini should decide to come to the negotiating table. The first Iraqi air raid on Teheran in four years took place in March. Although Iraq initially identified its targets as industrial, government and military installations only, thousands of civilians inevitably were killed as Iraqi aircraft attacked more than 30 Iranian towns with bombs, missiles and shellfire. Iran retaliated with shelling and air raids of its own on Iraqi economic, industrial and civilian targets, and with ground-based missile attacks on Baghdad itself. In this instance, Iraq was taking full advantage of its military superiority. In March King Hussein of Jordan and President Mubarak of Egypt unexpectedly visited Baghdad to show their support for Saddam Hussain, despite the fact that full diplomatic relations had not existed between Egypt and Iraq since Egypt's signing of the peace treaty with Israel in 1979.

The UN Secretary-General, Javier Pérez de Cuéllar, visited both Teheran and Baghdad in April to try to establish a basis for peace negotiations. Iraq made it clear that it was interested only in a permanent cease-fire and immediate peace negotiations; while Iran, though placing less official emphasis on the removal of Saddam Hussain's regime as a pre-condition of peace, accepted that, if he acquiesced in the other conditions, including the payment of reparations calculated by Iran at $350,000m. in March 1985, he would fall anyway.

Twice during 1985 (in April and June) President Saddam Hussain ordered a suspension of air raids on Iranian cities, as an inducement to Iran to begin peace negotiations. On both occasions Iran ignored the gesture and Iraqi air raids were resumed.

In response to a joint Irano-Libyan strategic alliance which was becoming more open in character, Iraq withdrew its diplomatic mission from Tripoli in June 1985 and asked the Libyans to withdraw theirs from Baghdad. Iraq had severed its diplomatic links with Libya in late 1980, accusing Col Qaddafi of assisting Iran in the war, but limited diplomatic contact was restored and Libya was said to have had diplomatic representatives in Baghdad since 1984.

Until mid-1985 Iraq had failed to launch attacks against the main Iranian oil export terminal on Kharg Island of sufficient frequency or intensity seriously to threaten the continuation of oil exports. In August, however, Iraq made the first of a concentrated series of raids on Kharg, causing a reduction in Iranian oil exports from 1.2m. b/d–1.5m. b/d, in the months leading up to the raids, to less than 1m. b/d in September. Exports from Kharg were temporarily halted altogether during the latter half of September. During October–December the raids became progressively less frequent and less damaging in their effect, and, by dint of rapid repairs and the taking up of Kharg's ample spare capacity, the Iranian Ministry of Oil was able to claim in October, with little exaggeration, that exports of oil had risen to 1.7m. b/d. Between August and the end of 1985 some 60 attacks on Kharg Island were reported. Despite Iran's earlier success in minimizing the effect of Iraqi raids and in developing alternative means of exporting oil (such as the floating terminal at Sirri Island), by the end of 1985 exports from Kharg had reportedly been reduced to a trickle compared with its 6.5m. b/d capacity, and Iraq had turned its attention to the tankers shuttling oil to Sirri Island for transhipment.

In February 1986 Iraq announced an expansion of the area of the Gulf from which it would try to exclude Iranian shipping. Previously confined to the waters around Iran's Gulf ports, the area was broadened to include the coast of Kuwait. Attacks on tankers and other commercial vessels in the Gulf were intensified by both sides during 1986, and they totalled 105 during the year. In the first half of 1986 Iraq continued to attack Kharg Island and tankers shuttling oil to Sirri Island, and in August an Iraqi raid demonstrated that the Sirri export facility itself was vulnerable to attack, bringing about an immediate doubling of insurance rates for vessels travelling there. Iran was forced to transfer more of its oil export operations to the remoter floating terminal at Larak Island, at the mouth of the Gulf, but this, too, proved accessible to Iraqi aircraft, employing mid-air refuelling facilities, and was itself attacked in November. Loading berths, refining facilities, and several tankers docked at Iran's Lavan Island oil terminal, were destroyed or badly damaged by an Iraqi raid in September 1986.

In the land war, the next important engagements, in terms of land gained, occurred in 1986, when, on 9 February, Iran launched the Wal-Fajr (Dawn) 8 offensive. Some 85,000 Iranian troops (leaving about 400,000 uncommitted on the southern front) crossed the Shatt al-Arab waterway and, on 11 February, occupied the disused Iraqi oil port of Faw, on the Persian Gulf, and, according to Iran, about 800 sq km of the Faw peninsula. From this position, within sight of the Kuwaiti island of Bubiyan, commanding the Khor Abdullah channel between the Faw peninsula and the island, Iran threatened Iraq's only access to the Gulf and, if it could extend the offensive to the north-west, Iraq's Umm Qasr naval base. However, the marsh and then desert terrain to the west was not conducive to further Iranian gains, and the position on the Faw peninsula was defensible only with difficulty, given the problem of maintaining supply lines across the Shatt al-Arab. At the same time as the attack upon Faw, Iran began a complementary operation along the Faw–Basra road to divert Iraqi forces. When Iraq launched a counter-offensive on Faw in mid-February, Iran opened up a second front in Iraqi Kurdistan, hundreds of miles to the north, with the Wal-Fajr 9 offensive. Iranian forces drove Iraqi and counter-revolutionary Iranian Kurds out of some 40 villages in the area of Sulaimaniya.

At the end of February the UN Security Council, while urging for a cease-fire, effectively accused Iraq of starting the war. Despite heavy fighting, Iraq failed to dislodge an estimated 30,000 Iranian troops from in and around Faw. The proximity of Kuwaiti territory to the hostilities notwithstanding, Iran promised not to involve Kuwait in the war, provided that it did not allow Iraq the use of its territory (part of which, Bubiyan Island, is claimed by Iraq) for military purposes.

The Faw offensive prompted a change in tactics by Iraq. In May 1986 Iraq made its first armed incursions into Iran since withdrawing its forces from Iranian territory in 1982. An area of about 150 sq km of Iranian land was occupied, including the deserted town of Mehran (about 160 km east of Baghdad), but Iran recaptured the town in July and forced the Iraqis back across the border. Also in May, Iraqi aircraft raided Teheran for the first time since June 1985, signalling a new wave of reciprocal attacks on urban and industrial targets in Iran and Iraq that continued for the remainder of 1986. For perhaps the first time during the war, Iraq took full advantage of its aerial superiority to damage Iran's industry and to limit its oil production, with numerous attacks on oil installations and tankers shuttling oil to floating terminals near the mouth of the Gulf.

In July the ruling Arab Baath Socialist Party held an extraordinary regional conference, the first since June 1982. Three new members were elected to the party's Regional Command, increasing its number to 17. Naim Haddad, who had been a member of the Regional Command and of the ruling RCC since their formation in 1968, was not re-elected to the Regional Command and was subsequently removed from the RCC, on which he was replaced by Sa'adoun Hammadi, the Chairman, or Speaker, of the National Assembly. These changes effectively strengthened Saddam Hussain's position as leader of the party.

A meeting between the Ministers of Foreign Affairs of Iraq and Syria, scheduled for June 1986, which was heralded as the beginning of a reconciliation between the two countries, was cancelled at the last minute by President Assad of Syria. However, rumours of a *rapprochement* were revived by reports that President Hussain and President Assad had met in secret in Jordan in April 1987. Ministers from both countries met on several occasions in the ensuing weeks, and the reopening of the oil pipeline from Haditha, in Iraq, to the Syrian port of Banias, was discussed. There were, however, no public statements from either side to confirm the improvement in relations.

THE IRAN–IRAQ WAR, 1987

From mid-1986 onwards, Iran was reported to be reinforcing its army at numerous points along the Iraqi border. When an Iranian offensive (Karbala-4: after the holy Shi'ite city in Iraq) was launched on 24 December, it came, as anticipated, in the region of Basra, but failed to penetrate Iraqi defences on four islands in the Shatt al-Arab waterway. On 8 January 1987 a two-pronged attack (Karbala-5) was launched towards Basra. Iranian forces, attacking from the east, established a bridgehead inside Iraq, between the Shatt al-Arab, to the west, and the artificial water barrier, Fish Lake, to the east, and slowly advanced towards Basra, sustaining heavy casualties; while an assault from the south-east secured a group of islands in the Shatt al-Arab. (On 13 January Iran mounted the Karbala-6 offensive in north-east Iraq.) By mid-February Iranian forces from the east had advanced to within about 10 km of Basra but no further gains were made and the Karbala-5 offensive was officially terminated at the end of the month.

In January 1987, at the height of the Karbala-5 offensive, President Hussain of Iraq offered Iran a cease-fire and peace negotiations. Iran rejected the offer, and in the following months demonstrated its ability to launch attacks at several points from one end to the other of the 1,200-km war front. The Karbala-7 offensive, in March, penetrated north-eastern Iraqi territory to a depth of about 20 km in the Gerdmand heights, near Rawanduz, only some 100 km from Iraq's largest oilfields, at Kirkuk. In April, on the southern front, Iran launched the Karbala-8 offensive from the salient, 10 km east of Basra, which had been secured in Karbala-5. The Iranians claimed that the attack established a new front line about 1 km nearer Basra, west of the artificial Twin Canals water barrier, though Iraq claimed that it had been repulsed. At the same time, another offensive, Karbala-9, was mounted in the central sector of the war front, from near the Iranian border town of Qasr-e-Shirin.

Iraq announced a two-week moratorium on its bombing of Iranian towns and cities on 18 February, which Iran agreed to observe in respect of its artillery and missile bombardment of Iraqi cities. In April, following new Iranian attacks east of Basra, and well after the initially stipulated two-week period had expired, Iraq said that it was no longer bound by the unofficial agreement. However, Iraqi air raids did not resume in earnest until May.

Iraq continued to attack tankers shuttling Iranian oil from Kharg Island to the floating terminals at Sirri and Larak islands during the first half of 1986. However, an apparently accidental attack in the Gulf by an Iraqi *Mirage* F-1 fighter plane on the frigate USS *Stark*, part of the US naval force, which had been deployed in the Gulf to protect shipping, created a crisis in Iraqi–US relations. The fighter fired two *Exocet* missiles at the *Stark*, only one of which exploded, killing 37 US sailors. Iraq apologized for the 'error' and desisted from attacks on tankers for the next five weeks. Although it is plausible that the attack was the result of error and inexperience on the part of the Iraqi pilot, Iraq had recently had occasion to record its displeasure at US policy regarding the war. In November 1986 it had emerged that the USA, contrary to its official policy of neutrality, and of discouraging sales of arms to Iran by other countries, had made three shipments of weapons and military spare parts to the Islamic Republic since September 1985. Then, in December, it was reported in *The Washington Post* that the USA had been supplying Iraq with detailed intelligence information for at least two years, to assist it in the war with Iran. In particular, the USA's Central Intelligence Agency (CIA) was said to have provided satellite reconnaissance data, to assist Iraq in its raids on Iranian oil installations and power plants. One month later, US intelligence sources revealed that the USA had, in fact, provided both Iran and Iraq with deliberately misleading or inaccurate information. The explanation of the apparent contradictions in US policy seemed to be that the USA had been trying to engineer a stalemate in the Iran–Iraq War, to prevent either side from gaining a decisive advantage. Iraq subsequently attributed the loss of the disused oil port of Faw in February 1986 to false intelligence reports supplied by the USA.

Tension in the Gulf escalated in May 1987 after the USA's decision to accede to a request from Kuwait for 11 Kuwaiti tankers to be re-registered under the US flag, entitling them to US naval protection. Apart from the financial aid it gave Iraq, Kuwait was a transit point for goods (including military equipment) destined for Iraq, and for exports of oil sold on Iraq's behalf. Iran warned Kuwait on several occasions of the dire consequences of its continued support for Iraq, and between October 1986 and April 1987 15 ships bound to or from Kuwait were attacked in the Gulf by Iran, and several Kuwaiti cargoes were seized. After the USA made its navy available to escort reregistered Kuwaiti tankers through the Gulf, Iran announced that it would not hesitate to sink US warships if provoked.

The possibility of a confrontation between the USA and Iran resulted in a rare display of unanimity in the UN Security Council, which, on 20 July, adopted a resolution (No. 598) urging an immediate cease-fire in the Iran–Iraq War; the withdrawal of all forces to internationally recognized boundaries; and the co-operation of Iran and Iraq in mediation efforts to achieve a peace settlement. Iraq agreed to abide by the terms of the resolution if Iran did so. Iran said that the Resolution was 'unjust', and criticized it for failing to identify Iraq as the original aggressor in the war. Moreover, it maintained that the belligerent US naval presence in the Gulf, effectively in support of Iraq, rendered the Resolution null and void. However, by mid-September Iran had still not delivered an unequivocal response to the Resolution. Iraq, meanwhile, had halted its attacks on tankers in the Gulf in mid-July and Iran had exploited the lull by raising the level of its oil production and exports.

THE UN FAILS TO ENFORCE RESOLUTION 598

Contrary to advice from Western governments, Iraq resumed attacks on Iranian oil installations and industrial targets, and on tankers in the Gulf transporting Iranian oil, on 29 August. Resolution 598 made provision for unspecified sanctions in the event of the failure of either or both sides to comply with its terms. However, the resumption of Iraqi attacks weakened the UN's position in its attempts to secure a cease-fire through diplomacy, and made it less likely that the USSR could be persuaded to agree to the imposition of an arms embargo, whether against Iran alone or against both protagonists.

During the remainder of the year the UN Secretary-General, Javier Pérez de Cuéllar, sought a cease-fire formula which would be acceptable to Iran. His visit to the Gulf region, for talks in Iran and Iraq, between 11 and 15 September, was preceded by an intensification of Iraqi attacks on Iranian economic targets. In Teheran, Iranian leaders told Pérez de Cuéllar that they supported the provision in Resolution 598 for the establishment of an 'impartial body' to apportion responsibility for starting the war, but that Iraq's guilt in this matter had to be established before Iran would observe a cease-fire. For its part, Iraq was prepared to accept the ruling of a judicial body in determining responsibility for the war but refused to countenance any deviation from the original terms of Resolution 598, which stated that a formal cease-fire should precede the establishment of such a body.

Signs of an apparent willingness on Iran's part to modify its stand on Resolution 598 forestalled attempts by the USA, the United Kingdom and France to promote their proposal of an arms embargo against Iran, and also pre-empted the adoption of diplomatic or other sanctions by the Arab League, at its meeting in Tunis on 20 September 1987. An extraordinary session of the Arab League in Amman, Jordan, from 8–11 November, produced a final communiqué which unanimously condemned Iran for prolonging the war with Iraq and for its occupation of Arab (i.e. Iraqi) territory, and urged Iran to implement Resolution 598 without pre-conditions.

Following the summit meeting in Amman, the Iraqi Government, in common with a number of other Arab countries, re-established diplomatic relations with Egypt. During the summit, a meeting had taken place between President Hussain and President Assad, reviving speculation of a *rapprochement* between Iraq and Syria, which had supported Iran in war. President Assad, however, obstructed the League's adoption of an Iraqi proposal that member states should sever their diplomatic links with Iran, and Syria subsequently averred that its good relations with Iran were unimpaired.

On 3 November 1987 the Iranian Deputy Minister of Foreign Affairs, Muhammad Javad Larijani, stated that Iran would observe a cease-fire if the UN Security Council were to identify Iraq as the aggressor in the Iran–Iraq War. The USA and the United Kingdom interpreted this announcement as a device to forestall a change in Soviet policy on the question of an arms embargo. The USSR had persistently refused to consider an embargo, and argued that Iran should be allowed more time in which to accept Resolution 598. At the beginning of December, during further discussions with Pérez de Cuéllar in New York, Larijani made the additional condition that Iraq should agree to pay war reparations prior to the introduction of a cease-fire, and cited Iraqi intransigence and the presence of US ships in the Gulf as the principal obstacles to peace.

On 22 December the USSR itself proposed discussions within the Security Council to consider a mandatory prohibition on the sale of arms to Iran, which would take place at the same time as discussions on the introduction of an international naval force in the Gulf, under the control of the UN, to replace the various national forces patrolling the region. Although all the five permanent members of the Security Council subsequently agreed on the need for further measures to be taken to ensure the compliance of both combatants with Resolution 598, the USSR's insistence on the withdrawal of foreign navies followed by the deployment of a UN naval force in the Gulf, and the USA's growing military involvement in the area during 1988, prevented the adoption of an arms embargo.

CEASE-FIRE IN THE IRAN–IRAQ WAR

During the first half of 1988 Iraq regained much of the territory which it had lost to Iran in previous years, taking advantage of Iranian military inefficiency and the confused aims of a divided Iranian leadership. However, the world was taken by surprise in July 1988 when, after 12 months of prevarication, Iran agreed, unconditionally, to accept Resolution 598.

In January 1988 Iran and Iraq rebuffed a Syrian initiative to engineer a diplomatic end to the war by opening a dialogue between Iran and the Gulf states. After a lull of 10 days, Iraq resumed the so-called 'tanker war', accusing Syria of violating Arab solidarity against Iran. During 1987, according to Lloyd's of London, Iranian and Iraqi attacks had damaged 178 vessels in the Gulf (including 34 in December alone), compared with 80 during 1986. (When a cease-fire was proclaimed in July, a total of 546 vessels had been hit since 1981, when the 'tanker war' began in earnest.)

At the end of February 1988 Iraq resumed the 'war of the cities' (which, apart from sporadic attacks, had been halted in early 1987), signalling the beginning of a series of reciprocal raids on civil and economic targets in the two countries which lasted for several months.

During 1987/88, for the first time in six years, owing to poor mobilization, disorganization and a shortage of volunteers, Iran was unable to launch a major winter offensive and began to lose ground to Iraqi advances along the length of the war front. However, this was not before Kurdish guerrillas, in February 1988, had advanced into government-controlled territory in Iraqi Kurdistan, where Iranian forces, with Kurdish assistance, had established bridgeheads, particularly in the Mawat region, along the Iranian border. The Kurdish part in these operations represented the largest Kurdish offensive since 1974/75, uniting forces from the DPK and the PUK, which, in November 1986, had agreed to co-ordinate their military and political activities and were in the process of forming a coalition of Kurdish nationalist groups (see below). In March 1988, in a retaliatory attack against the captured town of Halabja, Iraq is believed to have used chemical weapons, killing 4,000 Kurdish civilians. (In July Iraq admitted its use of chemical weapons during the war. A UN report compiled in April had concluded that there were victims of chemical weapons on both sides; a team of UN experts reported in August that Iraq had used mustard gas against Iranian civilians.)

After the success of the Iranian-Kurdish offensive, the following months witnessed a catalogue of Iraqi victories over Iranian forces. In March the National Liberation Army (NLA), the military wing of the Iranian resistance group, Mujahidin-e-Khalq, supported by Iraq, undertook a major offensive for the first time since its creation in 1987, attacking Iranian units in Iran's south-western province of Khuzestan. In mid-April Iraqi forces regained control of the Faw peninsula, where the Iranians, who had been unable to strike out to make further territorial gains since capturing the area in 1986, had scaled down their presence. (Iran accused Kuwait of allowing Iraqi forces to use the nearby Bubiyan Island during the Faw offensive.) Then, in May, Iraq recaptured the Shalamcheh area, south-east of Basra, driving the Iranians back across the Shatt al-Arab.

A radical military reorganization by Iran, undertaken in June and July, failed to reverse the tide of defeat. Having won back more territory in the north of Iraq, near Sulaimaniya, in mid-

June, Iraq recaptured Majnoon Island and the surrounding area in the al-Hawizah marshes (the site of one of the world's biggest oilfields), on the southern front, at the end of the month. Also at the end of June, and in July, Iraq expelled Iranian forces from Iraqi territory in Kurdistan, recapturing the border town of Mawat and key mountain areas to the north-east of Halabja. On 13 July, in the central sector of the front, Iraqi forces crossed into Iranian territory for the first time since 1986, and captured the Iranian border town of Dehloran. The last pockets of Iranian occupation in southern Iraq were cleared by Iraqi troops in mid-July and, on 18 July, Iran officially announced its unconditional acceptance of Resolution 598. Iraqi troops in the central sector advanced further into Iran before retiring behind the border on 24 July. However, the NLA, over which Iraq claimed to have no control, launched a three-day offensive on 25 July, penetrating as far as 150 km into Iranian territory, before being forced to withdraw. Iraq professed to have no designs on Iranian territory but it was suggested that the NLA was being used as a proxy by Iraq to prevent Iranian forces from reorganizing during a cease-fire which might prove to be only temporary. At the beginning of August, owing to uncertainty over the war, Iraq's general elections, which had been scheduled to take place at the end of the month, were postponed for six months.

The implementation of a cease-fire was delayed by an Iraqi demand for the initiation of direct peace talks with Iran, under UN auspices, prior to a cessation of hostilities. Iran protested that Resolution 598 did not require this. However, on 6 August Iraq withdrew its insistence on the necessity for direct talks to take place before a cease-fire and, on the following day, Iran agreed to direct talks following the end of hostilities. Accordingly, a cease-fire finally came into force on 20 August, monitored by a specially-created UN observer force of 350 officers, the UN Iran-Iraq Military Observer Group (UNIIMOG).

PEACE TALKS

Negotiations between Iran and Iraq for a comprehensive peace settlement, based on the full implementation of Resolution 598, began at foreign ministerial level in Geneva on 25 August 1988, under the aegis of the UN. With the question of the location of frontiers a matter of dispute, the requirement in Clause One of Resolution 598 for military forces to retire behind internationally recognized borders was causing problems before the talks began, and, once started, they soon reached stalemate. Iran insisted that the Algiers Agreement of 1975 between the two countries should be the basis for negotiations. According to the terms of the Algiers Agreement, which defined the southern border between Iran and Iraq as running along the deepest channel of the Shatt al-Arab waterway (the Thalweg Line), the two countries exercise joint sovereignty over the waterway. However, President Hussain of Iraq, who had been a signatory to the agreement, publicly rejected it immediately prior to the Iraqi invasion of Iran in 1980, claiming that it had been made under duress, and demanded full Iraqi sovereignty over the Shatt al-Arab, which Iraq held under previous agreements in 1847, 1913 and 1937. Iraq also claimed the right of navigation through the Shatt al-Arab and the Gulf during the cease-fire, unhindered by Iranian vessels. When Iran claimed to have stopped and searched an Iraqi cargo vessel which was making its way through the Strait of Hormuz into the Gulf on 20 August, Iraq (though it denied the Iranian claim) threatened to resume hostilities if Iraqi vessels were harassed in this way. It also insisted that an agreement for the dredging of the Shatt al-Arab and the removal of sunken ships be finalized before the discussion of final (mainly Iraqi) troop withdrawals and the exchange of prisoners of war could proceed. Iran claimed that it was, technically, still at war with Iraq and was, therefore, entitled, under international law, to search Iraqi and other vessels for war supplies, for as long as Iraqi troops were in occupation of Iranian territory (an estimated 1,500 sq km, according to Iran).

These disputes, largely concerning issues for which there was no provision in Resolution 598, delayed the implementation of the Resolution beyond the introduction of a cease-fire. Clause Three, for example, urged the repatriation of prisoners of war. By mid-1988 the Red Cross had registered 50,182 Iraqi prisoners of war held in Iran, and 19,284 Iranians held in Iraq, although the actual figures were thought to be higher, as the Red Cross had not been allowed access to all prisoners. In November Iran and Iraq agreed to exchange all sick and wounded prisoners of war. The first exchanges took place in the same month, but the arrangements collapsed shortly afterwards, following a dispute over the number of prisoners involved. Resolution 598 also provided for the creation of an impartial judicial body to determine where the responsibility for starting the war lay. It was generally accepted that Iraq had initiated the conflict by invading Iran on 22 September 1980. Iraq, however, maintained that the war began on 4 September with Iranian shelling of Iraqi border posts. The negotiations for a comprehensive peace settlement remained deadlocked for two years.

On 16 August 1990 President Hussain of Iraq abruptly sought an immediate, formal peace with Iran (for full details, see chapter on Iran, History, p. 469) by accepting almost all of the claims that Iran had pursued since the declaration of a cease-fire in the war in August 1988. On 10 September 1990 Iran and Iraq formally agreed to resume diplomatic relations.

IRAQI SUPPRESSION OF THE KURDS

Since 1987, when the Iranian military threat began to wane, Iraq had concentrated more resources in the north of the country to deal with the Kurdish separatist movement, which claimed to control a 'liberated zone' of 10,000 sq km. It had intensified its 'scorched earth' policy, which is believed first to have been employed in Kurdistan in 1975 when, following the suppression of a Kurdish guerrilla campaign, 800 Kurdish villages along the border with Iran were razed to create a 'security belt', and Kurds were resettled inside Kurdistan or deported to the south of Iraq. The systematic depopulation of Kurdish areas, achieved by the destruction of Kurdish villages and the resettlement elsewhere in the country of those inhabitants who were not driven into more remote mountain areas, or into neighbouring Iran, was intensified in early 1988, in response to Kurdish support for new Iranian offensives in Iraqi Kurdistan. It was estimated at this time that, with the destruction of some 1,000 villages during the previous year, only about 1,000 of the 4,000 Kurdish villages which had existed before were still standing, and more than one-third of the area of Iraqi Kurdistan was completely depopulated.

In May 1988 the two principal Kurdish dissident groups, the DPK and the PUK, announced the formation of a coalition of six organizations, which would continue the struggle for Kurdish self-determination and co-operate militarily with Iran. Apart from the DPK and the PUK, the new front consisted of the Socialist Party of Kurdistan (SPK), the People's Democratic Party of Kurdistan (PDPK), the United Socialist Party of Kurdistan (USPK), and the predominantly Kurdish ICP.

The introduction of a cease-fire in the Iran–Iraq War in August 1988 allowed Iraq to divert more troops and equipment to Kurdistan, apparently in an attempt to effect a final military solution to the problem of the Kurdish separatist movement. At the end of August an estimated 60,000–70,000 Iraqi troops launched a new offensive to conquer guerrilla bases near the borders with Iran and Turkey, bombarding villages, allegedly using chemical weapons, and forcing thousands of Kurdish civilians and fighters (*peshmerga*) to escape into Iran and Turkey. By mid-September more than 100,000 Kurdish refugees were believed to have fled across the border into Turkey, while Iraqi Kurds seeking refuge in Iran joined an estimated 100,000 others from their country, some 40,000 of whom had escaped from Halabja, after the chemical attack on the city in March. The death toll from the new offensive was estimated at 15,000 in early September.

On 26 August 1988 the UN Security Council adopted a resolution (No. 620) unanimously condemning the use of chemical weapons in the Iran–Iraq War. However, Iraq was not censured by name and continued to deny that it was using chemical weapons against the Kurds, despite what the USA, in September, called 'compelling evidence' to the contrary. On 9 September the US Senate voted to impose economic sanctions against Iraq, which, if they were legally adopted, would halt US credits and exports of US goods worth $800m., prohibit US imports of Iraqi oil, and require US representatives on international financial bodies to vote against all loans and aid to Iraq. Reacting to the vote of the US Senate, an estimated

150,000 Iraqis took part, in Baghdad, in a massive anti-US demonstration.

On 6 September 1988, with its army effectively in control of the border with Turkey, the Iraqi Government offered a full amnesty to all Iraqi Kurds inside and outside the country (excluding only Jalal Talibani, the leader of the PUK), inviting those Kurds abroad to return within 30 days and promising to release all Kurds held on political grounds. The offer was generally dismissed by Kurds as a propaganda ploy, although the Government subsequently claimed that more than 60,000 Kurdish refugees had taken advantage of the amnesty to return to Iraq.

On 17 September 1988 the Government began to evacuate inhabitants of the Kurdish Autonomous Region to the interior of Iraq, as the first step towards the creation of a 30 km-wide uninhabited 'security zone' along the whole of Iraq's border with Iran and Turkey. In June 1989 Kurdish opposition groups appealed for international assistance to halt the evacuations, claiming that they were, in fact, forcible deportations of Kurds to areas more susceptible to government control, and that many of the evacuees (reported to number 300,000 by August 1989) did not reside in the border strip which was to be incorporated into the 'security zone', but in other areas of the Kurdish Autonomous Region. However, the Iraqi Government apparently remained impervious to international criticism of the 'evacuation' programme.

PROPOSED POLITICAL REFORMS

While the cease-fire in the Iran–Iraq War in August 1988, which was precipitated by Iraqi military successes, strengthened Saddam Hussain's position, it also allowed domestic conflicts to find expression again. Hussain's regime is widely regarded as one of the most autocratic in the Arab world, and in February 1989 there were reports of a further attempt by senior army officers to stage a coup. In November 1988 Hussain announced a programme of political reforms, including the introduction of a multi-party political system, and in January 1989 he declared that a committee was to be established to draft a new constitution. These developments were regarded as attempts to retain the loyalty of Iraq's Shi'ite community, which sought the liberalization of Iraqi society as a reward for its role in the war against Iran.

In April 1989 elections were held to the 250-member National Assembly for the third time since its creation in 1980. The 250 seats were reportedly contested by 911 candidates, one-quarter of whom were members of the Baath Party. The remaining candidates were reported to be either independent or members of the National Progressive Front. It was estimated that 75% of Iraq's electorate (totalling about 8m.) voted in the elections, and that more than 50% of the newly-elected deputies were members of the Baath Party. A new, draft Constitution was completed in January 1990, and approved by the National Assembly in July, when its provisions were published in the Iraqi press. It allowed for a multi-party political system, and there was speculation that defunct political parties, such as the National Democratic Party (NDP), would be permitted to re-form and participate in future elections. Under the terms of the draft Constitution, a Consultative Assembly was to be established. This, together with the National Assembly, was to assume the duties of the RCC, which was to be abolished after a presidential election (to be held within two months of the draft Constitution's approval by the National Assembly) had taken place. Following its approval by the National Assembly, the draft Constitution was to be subjected to a popular referendum before ratification by the President.

FOREIGN RELATIONS

From late 1989 there was increased concern in Western countries about the scale of a military expansion programme apparently under way in Iraq; about the involvement of Western companies in the programme; and about covert attempts by Iraq to obtain advanced military technology from the West. International attention focused on Iraq in September 1989, following an explosion at an Iraqi defence industry complex which was thought to be a major installation in a missile development programme.

In March 1990 Iraq's conviction for espionage, and subsequent execution, of an Iranian-born UK journalist, Farzad Bazoft, provoked international outrage and damaged relations with the United Kingdom. The incident emphasized the sensitivity of the Iraqi Government to the question of its military capabilities: in his defence, Bazoft claimed that, as a *bona fide* journalist, he had been investigating the explosion at the Iraqi defence industry complex in September 1989. At the end of March 1990 the British Government claimed to have thwarted attempts by Iraq to import prohibited military devices from the United Kingdom, and in April it alleged that steel tubes which Iraq had ordered from a British company were to be used to construct a 'supergun'.

In April 1990 the US President, George Bush, also urged Iraq to abandon production of chemical weapons, and in June the US media alleged that France had helped to extend the range, and improve the accuracy, of Iraqi missiles. At the end of July the US Congress voted to impose sanctions on Iraq, which formally prohibited sales of weapons and military technology to Iraq.

As its relations with the West deteriorated, Iraq's reputation in the Arab world improved. The outrage that was provoked by Iraq's execution of Farzad Bazoft, together with more general criticisms in Western media of its human rights record, elicited expressions of support for Iraq from the Arab League and from individual Arab states. In April 1990, after Saddam Hussain had referred to Iraq's chemical weapons as a deterrent against a nuclear attack by Israel, there were further expressions of support, even from Iraq's staunchest Arab rival, Syria, for Iraq's right to defend itself.

IRAQ'S INVASION OF KUWAIT

Prior to a meeting of the OPEC ministerial council in Geneva on 25 July 1990, Iraq had implied that it might take military action against countries which continued to flout their oil production quotas. It had also accused Kuwait of violating the Iraqi border in order to steal Iraqi oil resources worth $2,400m., and suggested that Iraq's debt to Kuwait, accumulated largely during the Iran–Iraq War, should be waived. On the eve of the OPEC meeting in Geneva, Iraq stationed two armoured divisions (about 30,000 troops) on its border with Kuwait.

The Iraqi threat and military mobilization led to a sharp increase in regional tension. Before the OPEC meeting in Geneva on 25 July 1990, President Mubarak of Egypt and Chedli Klibi, the Secretary-General of the Arab League, travelled to Baghdad in an attempt to calm the situation. The USA, meanwhile, placed on alert its naval forces stationed in Bahrain. At the conclusion of the OPEC meeting, however, the threat of Iraqi military action appeared to recede: both Kuwait and the United Arab Emirates (UAE) agreed to reduce their petroleum production, while OPEC agreed to raise its 'benchmark' price of crude petroleum from $18 to $21 per barrel.

Direct negotiations between Iraq and Kuwait commenced in Saudi Arabia at the end of July 1990, with the aim of resolving disputes over territory, oil pricing and Iraq's debt to Kuwait. Kuwait was expected to accede to Iraqi demands for early negotiations to draft a border demarcation treaty, and Iraq was expected to emphasize a claim to the strategic islands of Bubiyan and Warbah, situated at the mouth of the Shatt al-Arab. (After Kuwait obtained independence in 1961—it had formerly been under the protection of the United Kingdom—Iraq claimed sovereignty over the country. Kuwait was placed under the protection of British troops, who were later withdrawn and replaced by Arab League forces. On 4 October 1963 the Iraqi Government formally recognized Kuwait's complete independence and sovereignty within its present borders.) On 1 August, however, the talks collapsed, and on 2 August Iraq invaded Kuwait, taking control of the country and establishing a (short-lived) Provisional Free Government.

There was no evidence at all to support Iraq's claim that its forces had entered Kuwait at the invitation of insurgents who had overthrown the Kuwaiti Government. The invasion appeared more likely to have been motivated by Iraq's financial difficulties in the aftermath of the Iran–Iraq War; by strategic interests—Iraq had long sought the direct access to the Persian Gulf which it gained by occupying Kuwait; and by Iraq's pursuit of regional hegemony.

The immediate response, on 2 August 1990, of the UN Security Council to the invasion of Kuwait was to convene and to adopt unanimously a resolution (No. 660), which condemned the Iraqi invasion of Kuwait; demanded the immediate and unconditional withdrawal of Iraqi forces from Kuwait; and appealed for a negotiated settlement of the conflict. On 6 August the UN Security Council convened again and adopted a further resolution (No. 661), which imposed mandatory economic sanctions on Iraq and on occupied Kuwait, affecting all commodities with the exception of medical supplies and foodstuffs 'in humanitarian circumstances'.

As early as 3 August 1990 it was feared that the economic sanctions being imposed on Iraq and Kuwait would be superseded by international military conflict. On 3 August Iraqi troops began to deploy along Kuwait's border with Saudi Arabia, and the USA and the United Kingdom announced that they were sending naval vessels to the Gulf. On 7 August, at the request of King Fahd of Saudi Arabia, the USA dispatched combat troops and aircraft to Saudi Arabia, in order to secure the country's border with Kuwait against a possible attack by Iraq. US troops began to occupy positions in Saudi Arabia on 9 August, one day after Iraq announced its formal annexation of Kuwait. On the same day, the UN Security Council convened and adopted a unanimous resolution (No. 662), which declared the annexation of Kuwait to be null and void, and urged all states and institutions not to recognize it.

The dispatch of US troops signified the beginning of 'Operation Desert Shield' for the defence of Saudi Arabia, in accordance with Article 51 of the UN Charter. By the end of January 1991 some 30 countries had contributed ground troops, aircraft and warships to the multinational force in Saudi Arabia and the Gulf region. By far the biggest contributor was the USA, which, it was estimated, had deployed some 500,000 military personnel. Arab countries participating in the multinational force were Egypt, Syria, Morocco and the members of the Co-operation Council for the Arab States of the Gulf (Gulf Co-operation Council—GCC)—Bahrain, Kuwait, Oman, Qatar, Saudi Arabia and the UAE. It was estimated that Iraq had deployed some 555,000 troops in Kuwait and southern Iraq by the end of January 1991.

Iraq's invasion and annexation of Kuwait altered the pattern of relations prevailing in the Arab world. In the immediate aftermath of the invasion, individual Arab states condemned Iraq's action, and on 3 August 1990 a hastily-convened meeting of the Arab League in Cairo agreed a resolution (endorsed by 14 of the 21 member states and opposed by Iraq, Jordan, Mauritania, Sudan, Yemen and the PLO) which condemned the invasion of Kuwait and demanded the immediate and unconditional withdrawal of Iraqi forces. At a summit meeting of Arab League Heads of State, held in Cairo on 10 August, the demand for Iraq to withdraw from Kuwait was reiterated, and 12 of the 20 members participating in the meeting voted to send an Arab deterrent force to the Gulf in support of the US-led effort to deter potential aggression against Saudi Arabia.

As the crisis in the Gulf developed, Western diplomacy strove to maintain Iraq's isolation. The invasion of Kuwait had provoked widespread popular support for Iraq, notably in Jordan, where there was a huge Palestinian population, and also in the Maghreb states. Although conducted with the approval of the UN, in pursuit of aims formulated in specific UN resolutions, and with the active support of Egypt, Syria, Morocco and the Gulf states, both 'Operation Desert Shield' and its successor, 'Operation Desert Storm', were widely perceived, in parts of the Arab world, to be US-led campaigns to secure US interests in the Gulf region.

On 12 August 1990 Saddam Hussain proposed an initiative for the resolution of the conflict in the Gulf, linking Iraq's occupation of Kuwait with other conflicts in the Middle East, in particular the continuing Israeli occupation of the West Bank of Jordan and the Gaza Strip, and the Palestinian question. This was the first explicit example of so-called 'linkage' in diplomatic efforts to resolve the crisis in the Gulf. Practically, 'linkage' would have amounted to the trading of an Iraqi withdrawal from Kuwait for, at least, the convening of an international conference on the Palestinian issue, and it was repeatedly rejected by the USA, which considered that 'linkage' would reward Iraq's aggression and enhance the country's reputation in the Arab world.

The authority for the deployment of a multinational force for the defence of Saudi Arabia was contained in Article 51 of the UN Charter, which affirms 'the inherent right of individual or collective self-defence if an armed attack occurs against a member of the United Nations, until the Security Council has taken measures necessary to maintain international peace and security'. The UN Security Council warned, however, that its authorization would be necessary for the use of force to implement the economic sanctions imposed on Iraq and Kuwait. Article 42 of the UN Charter provided for the taking of 'such action by air, sea or land forces as may be necessary to maintain international peace and security', including the use of a blockade. In order to clarify the Charter's provisions, the USA drafted a resolution which would allow the UN to use legitimately the force necessary to maintain a blockade against Iraq. On 25 August 1990 the UN Security Council adopted a resolution (No. 665) which requested, with immediate effect, member states deploying maritime forces in the area to use 'such measures commensurate to the specific circumstances as may be necessary under the authority of the Security Council to halt all inward and outward maritime shipping in order to inspect and verify the cargoes and destinations' and ensure the implementation of the mandatory economic sanctions against Iraq and Kuwait. The resolution also invited all states to co-operate, by political and diplomatic means, to ensure compliance with sanctions.

Successive diplomatic efforts to achieve a peaceful solution to the crisis in the Gulf—undertaken, at different times, by the UN and by numerous individual countries—between August 1990 and mid-January 1991 foundered, virtually without exception, on Iraq's steadfast refusal to withdraw its forces from Kuwait. Diplomacy was initially complicated by the treatment of Western citizens residing in Iraq and Kuwait. On 9 August 1990 Iraq closed its borders to foreigners, and on 13 August all US and UK nationals in Kuwait were ordered to assemble at hotels prior to their removal to Iraq. Iraq subsequently announced that Westerners would be housed near military locations in order to deter an attack on Iraq by the multinational force in Saudi Arabia. On 28 August, however, Iraq announced that all foreign women and children were free to leave Iraq and Kuwait, extending this permission to all foreigners on 6 December.

On 29 November 1990 the UN Security Council convened and adopted a resolution (No. 678), drafted by the USA, which, with reference to its previous resolutions regarding Iraq's occupation of Kuwait, authorized 'all member states co-operating with the Government of Kuwait, unless Iraq on or before 15 January 1991, fully implements . . . the foregoing resolutions, to use all necessary means to uphold and implement Security Council Resolution 660 and all subsequent relevant resolutions and to restore international peace and security in the area'. Iraq denounced Resolution 678, the first UN resolution since 1950 which authorized the use of force, as a threat, and reiterated its demand for the UN Security Council to address equally all the problems of the Middle East.

'Operation Desert Storm'—in effect, war with Iraq—in pursuance of the liberation of Kuwait, as demanded by UN Resolution 660, commenced on the night of 16–17 January 1991. It was preceded by intense diplomatic activity to achieve a peaceful solution to the crisis in the Gulf, in particular a visit, on 10 January, by the UN Secretary-General, Javier Pérez de Cuéllar, to Baghdad for talks with Saddam Hussain. The failure of this mission was widely regarded as signalling the inevitability of military conflict. On 14 January Iraq's National Assembly approved a resolution which afforded the President all constitutional powers to respond to any 'US-led' attack.

The declared aim of the multinational force in Saudi Arabia, in the initial phase of 'Operation Desert Storm', was to gain air superiority, and then air supremacy, over Iraqi forces, in order to facilitate air attacks on Iraqi military and industrial installations. Hostilities commenced with air raids on Baghdad, and by late February 1991 a total of 91,000 attacking air missions were reported to have been flown over Iraq and Kuwait by the multinational air forces.

The multinational force claimed air supremacy over Iraq and Kuwait on 30 January 1991, and air attacks were refocused on the fortified positions of Iraqi ground troops in Kuwait, in preparation for a ground offensive. During the initial phase of the air campaign, the Iraqi air force appeared to have offered surprisingly little resistance. Indeed, by 8 February it was reported that more than 100 Iraqi fighter aircraft had sought refuge in Iran, and the apparent good faith of Iran's reaffirmation of its neutrality in the conflict prompted speculation that they had been directed there deliberately in an attempt to prevent the total destruction of the Iraqi air force.

Iraq's most serious response to the military campaign waged against it was attacks with *Scud* missiles on Israel. While these were of little military significance, they threatened to provoke Israeli retaliation against Iraq and the consequent disintegration of the multinational force, since it would have been politically impossible for any Arab state to fight alongside Israel against Iraq. US diplomacy, together with the installation in Israel of advanced US air defence systems, averted the threat of Israeli retaliation for the attacks by the missiles, 37 of which had been launched by late February 1991. In addition, Iraq launched 35 *Scud* missiles against Saudi Arabia.

On 6 February 1991 Iraq formally severed diplomatic relations with the USA, the United Kingdom, France, Italy, Egypt and Saudi Arabia. Between August 1990 and January 1991 many foreign embassies in Baghdad had closed, and most countries had withdrawn their diplomatic staff before the outbreak of hostilities in the Gulf.

On 15 February 1991 the Iraqi Government abruptly expressed its willingness to 'deal with' the UN Security Council resolutions pertaining to its occupation of Kuwait. However, its offer to do so was conditional upon the fulfilment of a long list of requirements (including an assurance that the as-Sabah family would not be restored to power in Kuwait) and was accordingly unacceptable to the countries contributing to the multinational force. The offer to 'deal with' the UN resolutions was nevertheless thought to indicate a new flexibility on the part of the Iraqi leadership.

Soviet diplomacy came to the fore in seeking to persuade Iraq to alter its offer to withdraw from Kuwait into one which the multinational force could accept. On 21 February 1991 Iraq agreed to an eight-point Soviet peace plan which stipulated that: Iraq should make a full and unconditional withdrawal from Kuwait; the withdrawal was to begin on the second day of a cease-fire; the withdrawal should take place within a fixed time-frame; after two-thirds of Iraq's forces had withdrawn from Kuwait, the UN-sponsored economic sanctions were to be repealed; the relevant UN Security Council resolutions should be waived following Iraq's withdrawal; all prisoners of war were to be released following a cease-fire; the withdrawal was to be monitored by observers from neutral countries following a cease-fire; other details were to be discussed at a later stage.

The eight-point Soviet peace plan remained unacceptable to the multinational force, not least because it stipulated that a cease-fire should take effect before Iraq began to withdraw from Kuwait. On 22 February 1991, in response, the USA, representing the multinational force, demanded that Iraq commence a large-scale withdrawal of its forces from Kuwait by noon (US Eastern Standard Time) on 23 February, and that the withdrawal should be completed within one week. In response to this ultimatum, the USSR proposed a further plan for peace, this time containing six points—subsequently formally approved by Iraq—in a final attempt to avert a ground war in Kuwait and Iraq. However, once again the plan was rejected by the multinational force because it did not amount to the unconditional withdrawal of Iraqi forces from Kuwait which UN Security Council Resolution 660 demanded.

During the night of 23–24 February 1991 the multinational force launched a ground offensive for the liberation of Kuwait. Iraqi troops defending Kuwait's border with Saudi Arabia were quickly defeated, offering little resistance to the multinational force. A flanking movement, far to the west, by French units and elements of the 101st US Airborne Division succeeded in severing the main road west from Basra, while the road leading north from Basra was breached by repeated bombing. Divisions of Iraq's élite Republican Guards in the Kuwait area were thus isolated to the south of the Tigris and Euphrates rivers and prevented from retreating towards Baghdad. On 28 February 1991 President Bush announced that the war to liberate Kuwait had been won, and he declared a cease-fire. Iraq had agreed to renounce its claim to Kuwait, and to release all prisoners of war. It also indicated that it would comply with the remaining relevant UN Security Council resolutions. On 3 March Iraq accepted the cease-fire terms that had been dictated, at a meeting with Iraqi military commanders, by the commander of the multinational force, Gen. Norman Schwarzkopf of the US army.

On 3 April 1991 the UN Security Council adopted a resolution (No. 687) which stipulated the terms for a full cease-fire in the Gulf. These terms were accepted on 5 April by Iraq's RCC, and on the following day by the National Assembly. A separate UN Security Council resolution (No. 689), adopted on 9 April, created a demilitarized zone between Iraq and Kuwait, to be monitored by military personnel from the five permanent members of the UN Security Council.

INTERNAL REVOLT

Following the rout of the Iraqi army by the UN-sponsored multinational force in February 1991, armed rebellion broke out among the largely Shi'ite population of southern Iraq and among the Iraqi Kurds in the Kurdish northern provinces of the country. In the south the town of Basra was the centre of the rebellion. On 4 March it was reported that supppporters of the Teheran-based Supreme Council for the Islamic Revolution in Iraq (SCIRI) had gained control of the towns of Basra, Amarah, Samawah and Nasiriyah. At a conference of Iraqi groups opposed to the Government of Saddam Hussain, in Beirut on 11–13 March, it was claimed that, despite the prominent role of the SCIRI, the uprising in the south was secular and was not an attempt to establish an Iranian-style Islamic republic in Iraq. Already, on 5 March, the assessment of US intelligence sources, that the southern rebellion lacked sufficient organization to succeed, appeared to be corroborated: armed forces loyal to the Government were reported to be regaining control of the cities which had fallen to the rebels. On the same day it was announced that Ali Hassan al-Majid had been appointed Minister of the Interior, with express instructions to suppress the southern rebellion; and on the following day the Government announced financial bonuses for certain elements of the armed forces, in order to stem disaffection. Crucially, there was no military intervention by the multinational force in support of the rebellion. In this respect there appeared to have been a fundamental shift in the policy of the US Government: claiming that actively to support the southern rebellion would constitute unjustified interference in Iraq's internal affairs, its principal aim now seemed to be to prevent the disintegration of Iraq, rather than to oust Saddam Hussain from power. By contrast, at the conference of Iraqi opposition groups held in Beirut in mid-March, it was agreed to seek the overthrow of Saddam Hussain; the abolition of the Arab Baath Socialist Party; and the establishment of a democratic system of government in Iraq.

By mid-March 1991 armed forces loyal to the Government had effectively crushed the rebellion in the south, but their deployment there had allowed a simultaneous revolt by Kurdish guerrilla groups in the Kurdish northern provinces of Iraq to gather momentum. In late March it was reported that Kurdish rebels had gained control of Kirkuk and of important oil installations to the west of the city, and in early April Kurdish leaders claimed that as many as 100,000 guerrillas were involved in hostilities against government forces. The various Kurdish factions appeared to have achieved greater unity of purpose through their alliance, in May 1988, in the Kurdistan Iraqi Front (KIF). Rather than seeking the creation of an independent Kurdish state (which would not be tolerated by the Turkish and Iranian Governments), the KIF claimed that the objective of the northern insurrection was the full implementation of the 15-article peace plan which had been concluded between Kurdish leaders and the Iraqi Government in 1970. At the same time, however, the KIF invited the leaders of other Iraqi groups opposed to the Government to join it in the newly captured areas of northern Iraq in order to establish a unified anti-government movement.

Lacking military support from the multinational force—which was denied to them for the same reasons that it had been denied

to the southern insurgents—the Kurdish guerrillas were unable to resist the onslaught of the Iraqi armed forces, which were redeployed northwards as soon as they had crushed the uprising in southern Iraq. By early April 1991 government forces had recaptured Kirkuk, Arbil, Dohok and Zakho. Some 50,000 Kurds were reported to have been killed in the hostilities, and, fearing genocide, an estimated 1m.–2m. Kurds fled before the Iraqi army across the northern mountains into Turkey and Iran. On 5 April, as Saddam Hussain offered an amnesty to all Kurds with the exception of 'criminal elements', the UN Security Council adopted a resolution (No. 688) which condemned 'the repression of the Iraqi civilian population in many parts of Iraq' and demanded that the Iraqi Government permit the immediate access of international humanitarian organizations to persons in need of assistance. As relief operations were subsequently mounted, the means were sought whereby the Kurdish refugees could return to Iraq without fear of a renewed onslaught by the Iraqi armed forces.

As the 'Kurdish crisis' had developed, France, the United Kingdom and the USA had all committed troops to maintain a 'safe haven' for the Kurds in northern Iraq. On 8 April 1991 a proposal by the British Prime Minister, John Major, that a UN-supervised enclave should be created in northern Iraq, for the protection of the Kurdish population, was approved by the leaders of the member states of the EC (European Community, now European Union—EU). The US Government withheld its formal approval of the proposal, but on 10 April it warned Iraq that any interference in relief operations north of latitude 36°N would prompt military retaliation. The UN response to the proposal to create Kurdish 'safe havens' under its auspices also remained cautious. On 17 April the UN Secretary-General, Javier Pérez de Cuéllar, warned that the Iraqi Government's permission would have to be obtained before foreign troops were deployed in northern Iraq, and that the UN Security Council would need to approve the policing of the Kurdish enclave by a UN-backed force. Nevertheless, in late April UN relief agencies reported that Kurdish refugees were returning to Iraq in large numbers.

In mid-May 1991 the UN reported that progress had been achieved in the implementation of Security Council Resolution 688, and the Secretary-General announced that the UN was negotiating with the Iraqi Government over the deployment of a 'UN police force' to safeguard the Kurdish enclave. By mid-June UN agencies and other non-governmental organizations were reported to have assumed responsibility for the provision of essential services in the Kurdish enclave, and the transition from military to UN-backed security was under way.

As international diplomacy sought to create secure conditions for Iraqi Kurds within Iraq, the leaders of Kurdish groups began negotiations with the Iraqi Government on the future status of Iraqi Kurds. In late April 1991 the leader of the PUK, Jalal Talibani, announced that President Saddam Hussain had agreed in principle to implement the provisions of the Kurdish peace plan of 1970. By mid-June, however, negotiations with the Iraqi Government were reported to be in deadlock over the question of the frontiers of the Kurdish Autonomous Area, and at the end of August leaders of Kurdish groups announced their decision to suspend further negotiations with the Iraqi Government until various issues relating to an autonomy agreement had been clarified. Renewed clashes between government forces and Kurdish guerrillas in northern Iraq in September were succeeded, in late October, by the Iraqi Government's withdrawal of all services from Iraqi Kurdistan, effectively subjecting it to an economic blockade.

In the absence of a negotiated autonomy agreement with the Iraqi Government, the KIF organized elections to a 105-member Kurdish National Assembly, and for a paramount Kurdish leader. The result of the elections to the Assembly, held on 19 May 1992 and in which virtually the whole of the estimated 1.1m.-strong electorate participated, was that the DPK and the PUK were entitled to an almost equal number of seats. None of the smaller Kurdish parties achieved representation and the DPK and the PUK subsequently agreed to share equally the seats in the new Assembly. The election for an overall Kurdish leader was inconclusive, Masoud Barzani, the leader of the DPK, receiving 47.5% of the votes cast; and Jalal Talibani, the leader of the PUK, 44.9%. A run-off election was to be held at a future date. In December a member of the Kurdish Cabinet, elected by the Kurdish National Assembly in July 1992, appealed for increased Western aid for the Kurdish-controlled area of northern Iraq, and criticized the UN for its use of Saddam Hussain's regime as an intermediary in the provision of humanitarian relief. At the end of the year it was announced that relief supplies entering the Kurdish-controlled north from Turkey or central Iraq would be protected by UN forces in order to prevent the recurrence of acts of sabotage allegedly perpetrated by agents of Saddam Hussain's regime. The Iraqi Government was reported to have agreed, in principle, to allow UN forces to escort food convoys into Kurdish-controlled areas.

DEVELOPMENTS IN THE KURDISH ENCLAVE

In March 1993 the Kurdish Cabinet elected in July 1992 was dismissed by the Kurdish National Assembly for its failure to deal effectively with the crisis in the region. A new Cabinet was appointed at the end of April. In late December armed conflict was reported to have taken place between fighters of the PUK and the Islamic League of Kurdistan (ILK, also known as the Islamic Movement of Iraqi Kurdistan (IMIK)). The two parties were reported to have signed a peace agreement in February 1994 following mediation by the Iraqi National Congress (INC). More serious armed conflict, between fighters belonging to the PUK and the DPK, was reported in May to have led to the division of the northern Kurdish-controlled enclave into two zones. The two parties were reported to have concluded a peace agreement in early June, but fighting broke out again in August. In late November the PUK and the DPK were reported to have concluded another peace agreement, which provided for a census of the region and for the holding of elections in May 1995. In November 1994 it was also reported that the Kurdish Prime Minister had tendered the resignation of the Kurdish Cabinet to the Kurdish National Assembly but had been urged to continue in office in an interim capacity. A further outbreak of fighting in late December was succeeded by another short-lived peace agreement. In early January 1995 fighting erupted again, prompting Saddam Hussain to offer, on 16 January, to mediate in the dispute, and the United Kingdom to warn that the conflict might provide Iraq with a pretext to reassert control over the north. Both sides denied responsibility for a car bomb which exploded in Zakho in late February, resulting in 80 deaths. In March Turkey mounted a major operation to destroy Kurdish Workers' Party (PKK) bases in the Kurdish enclave, deploying some 35,000 troops across the border. By early May, after appeals from the USA and the EU, Turkey had withdrawn its troops, but 30,000 Turkish troops were again briefly deployed across the border in July. In June the IMIK withdrew from the INC, accusing its leadership of incompetence and corruption. There was renewed fighting between PUK and DPK forces in July, prompting attempts at mediation by the USA and Iran. In the opinion of the USA, inter-Kurdish hostilities strengthened the Iraqi regime, but it was strongly opposed to Iranian mediation, fearing that this would allow Iran to exert greater influence in the Kurdish enclave. As a result of the resumption of fighting between Kurdish factions, elections to the Kurdish National Assembly were abandoned and the existing council extended its mandate for another year.

After delegations from Amnesty International had visited the Kurdish enclave during the first half of 1995, the organization reported widespread human rights abuses and urged the Kurdish leadership to end arbitrary arrests, torture and deliberate and arbitrary killings. According to information received by UNHCR staff, conditions in the enclave were worsening owing to the continuing insecurity, with serious shortages of medicine and inadequate relief supplies to the poorest families.

US-sponsored peace negotiations near Dublin, Ireland, in September 1995 made little progress. The PUK and DPK failed to agree on a common approach to the PKK, whose forces had clashed with the DPK in the Kurdish enclave; to the demilitarization of the enclave's capital, Arbil; or to the sharing of income from customs duties levied on traffic crossing the border from Turkey. Another cease-fire was, however, agreed and despite some clashes between PUK and DPK forces there was no resumption of widespread fighting. The PKK was reported to have taken advantage of the instability in the enclave to strengthen its bases there. In September, Kusrat

Rasoul Ali, the Kurdish Prime Minister, survived a bomb attack in Arbil. The PUK accused the DPK of being responsible for the attack, but the DPK denied any involvement in it. In November an official from the US Department of State visited the enclave and held talks with leaders of the two principal Kurdish factions in an attempt to broker a peace agreement and to counter Iranian efforts to mediate between the warring factions. Both the USA and Turkey expressed concern at reports that the 5,000-strong Badr brigade, part of the armed wing of the pro-Iranian Supreme Council for the Islamic Revolution in Iraq (SCIRI), had begun to deploy inside the Kurdish enclave in November. Turkey continued to support the DPK in its efforts to expel PKK fighters from the enclave, and there were reports of fierce clashes between DPK and PKK forces. Turkish support for the DPK was believed to have encouraged the PUK to turn to Iran for support.

In February 1996 Turkey and NATO agreed to continue 'Operation Provide Comfort' under which US, British and French aircraft based in Turkey enforce the Iraqi air exclusion zone north of latitude 36°N in order to protect the Kurdish enclave. However, the operation became increasingly controversial in Turkey because of the existence of PKK bases in the enclave from which attacks were launched into Turkish territory, and the Turkish Prime Minister promised the Turkish National Assembly that the arrangement would not continue beyond June 1996. In that month the Turkish parliament extended the operation's mandate for one month and at the end of July the National Assembly agreed to a further prolongation until the end of 1996. Early in 1996 Jalal Talibani, the leader of the PUK, offered to take part in direct or indirect talks with the DPK about a peace settlement, and to participate in new elections to the Kurdish National Assembly. However, he criticized the DPK for controlling some 70% of the region's revenue and for not spending these funds fairly. Control over customs duties has been a major source of discord between the two rival groups. The DPK controls the lucrative customs duties levied on vehicles crossing the Turkish border, and while it claims to use these revenues to finance its organization and military forces, it has been alleged that some of the money is embezzled by party officials. Although the PUK levies similar duties on cross-border trade with Iran, this route is much less profitable. In February there were signs that the DPK and the PKK might settle their differences after Abdullah Ocalan, the PKK leader, met a delegation from the DPK and agreed to participate in further negotiations in the near future.

At the end of April Masoud Barzani and a DPK delegation visited Damascus for talks with the Syrian leadership concerning the situation in the enclave and in Iraq as a whole. There were reports of renewed shelling of villages in the enclave by Baghdad and by Turkey. In May the PUK and DPK held separate talks with Robert Deutsch of the US Department of State but failed to reach an agreement. Nevertheless at the end of the month the PUK announced that it had agreed with the DPK to extend the mandate of the Kurdish National Assembly for another year and that the Assembly, in which each party holds 50 seats, should seek to resolve the differences between the rival groups. Both parties agreed to examine ways of enlarging the Assembly to include members from other political groups, and independent deputies.

In the early months of 1996 a series of clandestine meetings were reported to have been held between the DPK and representatives of Saddam Hussain's administration following a visit to the enclave by Mukarem Talibani, a Kurdish official in the Baghdad Government, whose attempts to mediate between the DPK and PUK were intended to increase Baghdad's influence in the Kurdish-controlled area. Following further discussions between DPK representatives and Saddam Hussain's son, Qusai, Iraqi government experts were permitted to enter DPK-controlled areas to examine the oil pipeline from Iraq to Turkey to be used for oil exports under the oil-for-food accord (see below). In late July Iranian troops were reported to have entered the enclave in pursuit of Kurdish Democratic Party of Iran (KDPI) guerrillas who had retreated to an area held by the DPK. There was some speculation that, following the DPK's refusal to grant permission to Iranian agents to continue the pursuit, the Iranian authorities had colluded in the organization of a PUK attack against DPK positions in the region. US officials, who had persisted with efforts to reconcile the two rival Kurdish factions, held private talks in London with representatives of the PUK and DPK at the end of August to discuss a new cease-fire and the creation of an observer system to monitor it. However, the talks were abandoned after Iraqi security forces invaded the enclave on 31 August, seized the administrative centre, Arbil, and advanced towards Sulaimaniya. Deputy Prime Minister Tareq Aziz announced that military action to curb Iranian activity in the enclave—in support of the PUK—had been authorized only after a formal request for military assistance had been made by the DPK. The Iraqi assault, involving some 40,000 troops with tanks and artillery, amounted to Baghdad's largest offensive since 1991. PUK spokesmen claimed the Iraqi air force had also attacked their forces, close to Arbil, thereby flouting observance of the air exclusion zone. Jalal Talibani warned that the PUK would seek Iranian support if Iraqi forces threatened Sulaimaniya and the Western allies did not intervene. (US military forces in the region were ordered to adopt an increased state of alert.) The Turkish foreign minister warned Iraq to withdraw its forces immediately from the Kurdish enclave and also insisted that any military co-operation between Iran and the PUK must end. On 2 September there were unconfirmed reports that Iraqi forces were withdrawing from Arbil, entrusting the city to DPK control. In early September, having failed to secure the support of other Gulf War coalition partners for allied military intervention to force an Iraqi withdrawal from the enclave (largely as a result of international uncertainty regarding the extent to which such an undertaking could be justified by the terms of those UN resolutions which had prescribed the end of the Gulf War), US forces launched a series of air missile attacks (operation 'Desert Strike') against Iraqi military installations in southern Iraq. However, despite both sides' use of powerful rhetoric, and a unilateral US declaration of an expansion of the air exclusion zone north to the 33rd parallel, continuing lack of international support for the US initiative (only the United Kingdom fully endorsed the action) discouraged the US Government from engaging in more direct military confrontation. Domestic media coverage of the DPK's Government-backed capture (from the PUK) of Sulaimaniya, some days later (see below), suggested that the Iraqi Government had inflicted a severe diplomatic humiliation on the USA.

Renewed fighting was reported between PUK and DPK forces around Arbil and on 9 September 1996 the PUK-controlled city of Sulaimaniya fell to DPK forces resulting in the flight to the Iranian border of thousands of refugees. Within days some 20,000 Kurds had crossed the border into Iran, and Iranian officials expressed concern that tens of thousands more were waiting to enter the country. Following the fall of Sulaimaniya Saddam Hussain announced that amnesty was to be extended to all Kurdish opponents who had occupied the northern 'safe havens', while declaring the restoration of trade links with the northern regions and the reassertion of Iraqi sovereignty over the Kurdish Autonomous Regions. Suggestions that Kurds who had co-operated with humanitarian agencies and non-governmental organizations would be exempt from the amnesty prompted fears for the safety of such individuals, and US and EU missions prepared to evacuate some 8,000 Kurdish employees from the region. Such a large-scale evacuation would inevitably result in the collapse of the assistance programmes established in the region over the previous five years. After the public execution of nearly one hundred members of of the INC (see p. 578) by the Iraqi army during their assault on Arbil, most of the Iraqi opposition groups based in Iraqi Kurdistan fled the region. Many observers were convinced that a major objective of Iraqi intervention in the north was the elimination of the INC.

After the capture of Sulaimaniya, the PUK leader, Jalal Talibani, pledged to continue fighting, declaring that the struggle was no longer between Kurdish factions but between the Kurds and those who had sided with the enemy of the Kurdish people. Talibani also condemned the USA and its allies for failing to honour their stated commitment to protect the Kurdish population. In late September the DPK announced that it was to lead a 16-member coalition government for the Kurdish Autonomous Regions, also comprising members of other regional ethnic groupings (but excluding the PUK). In mid-October,

however, the PUK regained much of the territory they had lost in September, including Sulaimaniya. Their forces also advanced on Arbil but did not attack the city for fear of provoking renewed intervention by Baghdad. However, PUK forces took control of the Dukan dam and power station which supplies both Arbil and Sulaimaniya with water and electricity. At the end of October the US Assistant Secretary of State, Robert Pelletreau, announced that a truce had been negotiated between the two rival factions, following US mediation of a meeting in Ankara, Turkey. Both the PUK and the DPK agreed to work towards a permanent cease-fire, to avoid enlisting the help of external forces, and to accept the organization and deployment of a peace monitoring body. The agreement also proposed that all customs duties and other taxes collected should be accounted for and shared in order to benefit all the people of the region. The US brokered a new round of peace talks in November at which both factions agreed to attempt to resolve their political differences and to co-operate in re-establishing a regional administration. Nevertheless, as a technical delegation attempted to delineate the cease-fire line, each side accused the other of violating the peace. At the same time the DPK was reportedly attempting to improve its relations with Iran while the PUK was believed to be communicating privately with Baghdad. In December the Iranian authorities reported that many of the 70,000 Iraqi Kurds who had fled to Iran during fighting in August and September had started to return to their homes. In the same month the US began to evacuate 5,000 Iraqi Kurds employed by American relief organizations in the enclave who were to be granted political asylum in the USA. It was feared that their departure would impede food distribution procedures established under the terms of UN Resolution 968 (see below). Other aid agencies reported that many of their Kurdish staff were also demanding to be evacuated, fearing reprisals by Baghdad. Early in 1997 relief agencies still operating in the enclave claimed that more than 70,000 Iraqi Kurds, including women and children, had been forcibly displaced since the cease-fire; both the PUK and the DPK were accused of intimidating and persecuting rival supporters living in their territory, although both factions rejected such allegations. Relief agencies also stated that tens of thousands of refugees remained destitute, while uncertainty about future Western funding of aid programmes continued.

In April 1997 David Welch, the acting US Assistant Secretary of State for Near Eastern Affairs, held talks with Barzani and Talibani, both of whom reaffirmed their commitment to the reconciliation process begun in November 1996. President Clinton later announced that further talks between the rival factions had been arranged to consolidate the cease-fire and to encourage the DPK and PUK to resolve their political differences. Also in April a Peace Monitoring Force (PMF), with US political, financial and logistical support, began deployment in the region to demarcate the cease-fire boundary and to monitor the truce between the DPK and the PUK. In May President Clinton reported that the PMF had already resolved several violations of the terms of the cease-fire, but that security in the enclave remained tenuous. Nevertheless, he stated that progress had been made, especially in securing the release of prisoners held by both factions, and that both the DPK and the PUK were participating in a joint Higher Co-ordination Committee in an attempt to improve the provision of basic services such as electricity and health care.

At the end of December 1996 'Operation Provide Comfort' was terminated at Turkey's request and was replaced by a new surveillance system whereby air cover alone was to be provided by Turkey, the USA and Britain. France refused to participate in this new operation, which was inaugurated on 1 January 1997, since it did not include the provision of humanitarian aid. At the end of 1996 Turkish forces resumed artillery and air attacks on PKK bases in northern Iraq, which were immediately denounced by the Iraqi Government. In mid-May 1997 an estimated 25,000–50,000 Turkish troops, with support from tanks and fighter aircraft, crossed into northern Iraq to launch another attack on PKK bases there. Turkish sources claimed that more than 900 rebels were killed, a figure rejected as a gross exaggeration by pro-PKK sources. Fighting was also reported between DPK and PKK forces in Arbil. A DPK spokesman claimed that PKK activities threatened peace and security in the city and hampered relief work by the UN and other aid agencies. During the fighting between the DPK and the PUK in August and September 1996 the PKK was reported to have increased its influence in the mountainous region along the Turkish border. Turkey claimed that its latest incursion into northern Iraq was undertaken in order to help the DPK regain control of the border areas.

As a result of the Turkish incursion, which was fiercely condemned by the Iraqi Government, the Baghdad authorities postponed a planned military campaign against the PUK which aimed to recapture the Dukan dam. The Iraqi Government had accused the PUK of cutting off the water supply to the provinces of Kirkuk and Ba'qubah and of depriving large areas of agricultural land in the Tigris basin of water for irrigation. A new round of peace talks between the PUK and the DPK, sponsored by the USA, the UK and Turkey, which began in Ankara on the same day as the Turkish incursion, promptly collapsed. Further talks between the two factions in July failed to produce an agreement. Although Turkey had withdrawn most of its troops from northern Iraq, it launched a new military campaign against the PKK at the end of September 1997, and there were reports that Turkish forces—8,000–15,000 troops with armoured vehicles and air support—had penetrated Iraqi territory. It appeared that the Turkish strategy of using a client militia in a war against the PKK had failed, forcing Ankara to provide direct support to the DPK. The PUK, on the other hand, lent military support to the PKK in its battle with the DPK, increasing instability in the enclave. Fighting erupted between DPK and PUK forces in October in violation of the cease-fire agreement concluded in 1996. The PUK reportedly achieved some success in its attempt to secure control over the lucrative north-south supply route, but in November the DPK, supported by Turkish forces, launched a successful counter-attack, thereby regaining control of the route. In January 1998 the PUK leader Jalal Talibani, proposed peace and reconciliation and the establishment of a transitional government, in which both the PUK and the DPK would be represented, to assume sole responsibility for customs duties on cross-border trade. Following its recent military success against the PUK, however, the DPK leadership did not respond. Iran continued to offer some support to the PUK but appeared unwilling to become more directly involved in the Kurdish enclave. There were reports that delegations from both Kurdish factions had been invited for talks in Baghdad in November 1997. However, Saddam Hussain's aim of eventually re-establishing Baghdad's control over the northern region could only be encouraged by continued in-fighting between the Kurdish factions. By mid-1998 the fragile cease-fire between the PUK and the DPK appeared to be holding and, after a number of meetings between representatives of the two factions, agreement was reached on an exchange of prisoners and on the establishment of a joint committee to promote co-operation in public health, education and energy. However, the issue of DPK control over customs duties on cross-border trade from Turkey, which has thwarted previous attempts to reconcile the rival factions, remained unresolved.

OTHER POST-WAR DEVELOPMENTS

By mid-August 1991, despite the failure of his Kuwaiti adventure and the outbreak of internal revolts in its aftermath, the overthrow of President Saddam Hussain, which had been widely predicted during the crisis in the Gulf, seemed unlikely in the short term. Indeed, it was arguable that his position was more secure than it had been at the time of the invasion of Kuwait: opponents of the Government in the south of the country had been ruthlessly suppressed; a negotiated settlement of the Kurdish question was under discussion; and, in the wake of several alleged attempts to mount a military *coup d'état*, the Government appeared to have strengthened its control of the army, which remained the key to its survival in power. A reshuffle of the Council of Ministers in March 1991 had placed the President's closest supporters and members of his family in the most important positions of government and additional governmental adjustments later in the year, and in February and August 1992, furthered this process. Above all, it emerged that the US Government was not willing actively to seek Saddam Hussain's overthrow at the expense of the integrity of Iraq.

The survival of the Iraqi Government in the long term depended on three factors: its continued control of the armed forces; the length of time and the stringency with which economic sanctions would continue to be applied against Iraq; and the degree to which popular disaffection, created by the economic sanctions, could be appeased by the granting of limited political reform.

In September 1991 the Government introduced legislation providing for the establishment of a multi-party political system, in accordance with the draft of the new permanent Constitution. New political parties were to be subject to stringent controls, however, and later in the month the President stated that the Baath Party would retain its leading role in Iraqi political life. In early September the Baath Party held its 10th Congress—the first such Congress since 1982—at which Saddam Hussain was re-elected Secretary-General of the party's powerful regional command.

Iraq's post-war relations with the international community have been dominated by conflicts over the way in which the Iraqi regime has apparently sought to circumvent demands by the UN—as stipulated by UN Security Council Resolution 687—that it should disclose the full extent of its programmes to develop chemical weapons, nuclear weapons and missiles, and should eliminate its weapons of mass destruction. One consequence of the conflicts over Iraqi compliance with Resolution 687 was that there was no easing of the economic sanctions that were first imposed on Iraq on 6 August 1990, under the terms of UN Security Council Resolution 661.

In May 1991 the UN Security Council decided to establish a compensation fund for victims of Iraqi aggression (both governments and individuals), to be financed by a levy (subsequently fixed at 30%) on Iraqi petroleum revenues. In August the UN Security Council adopted a resolution (No. 706, subsequently approved in Resolution 712 in September) proposing that Iraq should be allowed to sell petroleum worth up to $1,600m. over a six-month period, the revenue from which would be paid into an escrow account controlled by the UN. Part of the sum thus realized was to be made available to Iraq for the purchase of food, medicines and supplies for essential civilian needs.

Iraq rejected the terms proposed by the UN for the resumption of exports of petroleum, and in February 1992 withdrew from further negotiations on the issue. In April the UN reiterated its demand that Iraq should comply with the terms of Security Council Resolutions 706 and 712 before resuming petroleum exports. In late June a further session of negotiations between Iraq and the UN on the resumption of petroleum exports ended indecisively. On 2 October the UN Security Council adopted a resolution (No. 778) permitting it to confiscate up to $500m.-worth of oil-related Iraqi assets in order to place further pressure on Iraq to accept the UN's terms for renewed exports of petroleum. In late October the UN commission responsible for the supervision of the destruction of Iraqi weapons proposed a relaxation of the embargo on sales of Iraqi oil in return for increased co-operation by Iraq with the UN. However, this suggestion did not gain the support of Western governments or of Iraqi opposition movements, and in late November the UN Security Council refused a request by an Iraqi delegation to repeal the economic sanctions in force against Iraq.

In January 1993 a 52-member team of UN weapons inspectors arrived in Iraq, the Government having revoked a prohibition on all UN flights into the country, in response to renewed air attacks by Western forces (see below). In early July, however, another team of UN weapons inspectors departed abruptly from Baghdad after the Government had refused to allow them to station surveillance equipment at missile-testing locations. Iraq continued to refuse the terms of UN Security Council Resolution 715, which governed the long-term monitoring of its weapons programmes. In early July a further session of negotiations between Iraq and the UN on the resumption of petroleum exports ended inconclusively, and later in the month the UN Security Council renewed the economic sanctions in force against Iraq. At the beginning of September Iraq's Deputy Prime Minister, Tareq Aziz, met the UN Secretary-General to discuss the resumption of Iraqi petroleum sales and the lifting of the economic sanctions. The UN was reportedly anxious to raise funds from such sales in order to finance its own operations in Iraq. The talks were inconclusive, however, and at the end of September the economic sanctions in force against Iraq were renewed. In early October the Government agreed to UN demands that it should release details of its weapons suppliers. In the absence of any progress on the issue of UN Security Council Resolution 715, however, economic sanctions were extended for a further 60 days in late November. Shortly after their renewal, the Iraqi Government was reported to have agreed to the provisions for weapons-monitoring contained in Resolution 715, and the UN to have begun plans for their implementation. However, it was clear by the end of December that neither the UN Security Council nor the US Government would be willing to allow even a partial easing of sanctions until Iraq had demonstrated its commitment to the dismantling of its weapons systems for a period of at least six months. Moreover, the US Government insisted that Iraq must first also comply with all other relevant UN resolutions, recognize the newly-demarcated border with Kuwait and cease the repression of its Kurdish and southern Shi'ite communities. In September hundreds of inhabitants of Iraq's southern marshlands were reported to have been killed by government forces using chemical weapons; and in November the UN accused the Government of indiscriminate attacks on civilians in that area.

From March 1994 the Iraqi Government engaged in a campaign of diplomacy to obtain the lifting of economic sanctions, and in mid-July evidence emerged of a division within the UN Security Council regarding their continuation. Russia, France and China were all reported to be in favour of acknowledging Iraq's increased co-operation with UN agencies. In September, however, the Security Council extended the sanctions for a further period of 60 days. Russia and France had proposed that the Security Council should draw up a timetable for the ending of sanctions, but had not obtained the agreement of other permanent members of the Council.

On 6 October 1994 the leader of the UN's Special Commission on Iraq (UNSCOM—responsible for inspecting the country's weapons) announced that a system for monitoring Iraqi defence industries was ready to begin operating. On the same day, however, there was a large movement of Iraqi forces towards the border with Kuwait, apparently to draw attention to Iraq's demands for swift action to ease the sanctions. In response, Kuwait deployed most of its army to protect its side of the border on 9 October, and the USA sent reinforcements to Kuwait and other parts of the Gulf region to support the 12,000 US troops already stationed there. On 10 October Iraq announced that it would withdraw its troops northward from their positions near the Kuwaiti border. On 15 October the Security Council adopted a resolution (No. 949) demanding that the withdrawal of all Iraqi forces recently transferred to southern Iraq be completed immediately; and stipulating that Iraq must not 'utilize its military or any other forces in a hostile or provocative manner to threaten its neighbours or the UN operations in Iraq'.

On 10 November 1994 the Iraqi National Assembly voted to recognize Kuwait within the borders defined by the UN in April 1992 and May 1993. Nevertheless, on 14 November the UN Security Council renewed the economic sanctions in force against Iraq for a further 60 days. Russia, China and France were all reportedly in favour of responding to Iraq's recognition of Kuwait with an easing of the sanctions. In a statement issued on 16 November, however, the Security Council welcomed Iraq's recognition of Kuwait, but emphasized that it must comply with all the relevant UN resolutions before any such relaxation could occur.

In mid-December 1994 the Iraqi Deputy Prime Minister visited Moscow, Russia, for talks with the Russian Minister of Foreign Affairs, Andrei Kozyrev. Following the talks, Kozyrev stated that the UN Security Council should adopt a more flexible attitude towards Iraq in respect of economic sanctions. On 20 December the Security Council met to study a report by the head of UNSCOM, in which he expressed his confidence that Iraq no longer had any nuclear, chemical or ballistic weapons. Russia, France, China and Spain were all reported to have urged the Security Council to acknowledge Iraq's co-operation with the UN's weapons inspectorate. The USA and the United Kingdom, however, expressed concern at Iraq's past failures to co-operate.

On 7 January 1995 the UN Secretary-General offered to resume dialogue with Iraq on a partial lifting of the economic sanctions. On 12 January the UN Security Council renewed the sanctions in force against Iraq for a further 60 days. Both the US and the UK Governments had again reportedly insisted that Iraq should comply with all the relevant UN resolutions before sanctions were eased, prompting Iraq to accuse them of unfairness and illegality. France and Russia were reported to have argued within the Security Council for a partial lifting of sanctions, provided that Iraq co-operated fully with the UN weapons-monitoring programme. The division between the members of the Security Council regarding the easing of sanctions had intensified as a result of France's announcement, on 6 January, that it was to establish an interests section at the Romanian embassy in Baghdad.

UN sanctions against Iraq were again renewed for 60 days on 13 March 1995. In April the Iraqi Government rejected as a violation of its sovereignty a revised UN proposal (Resolution 986) for the partial resumption of exports of Iraqi petroleum (see Economy, p. 565). Iraqi attempts to secure an end to the sanctions had suffered a serious reversal in February when, following a visit to Baghdad in the same month, the head of UNSCOM announced that the Iraqi authorities had failed satisfactorily to account for a substantial amount of material used in the manufacture of biological weapons, known to have been imported by Iraq in 1988. Further concerns regarding the use of these stockpiles were expressed by the Commission in April, May and June. However, expectations of a prompt easing of sanctions were renewed in early July, following the Iraqi Government's acknowledgement of the past existence of a biological weapons development programme for offensive as well as research purposes. Notwithstanding this admission, on 11 July the UN Security Council voted to extend sanctions against Iraq for a further 60 days, prompting the Iraqi Minister of Foreign Affairs, Muhammad Saeed as-Sahaf, to insist that the Special Commission should complete its report and promote an end to the sanctions by the end of August if it wished to avoid the complete cessation of co-operation from the Iraqi authorities. By mid-August, however, the Iraqi Government had adopted a more conciliatory stance towards the Commission, and it was reported that crucial new information regarding Iraq's military programme had been made available to its officers. This change in attitude and the sudden appearance of new information appeared to be related to the defection of Hussain Kamel al-Majid (see below), a former Iraqi Minister of Industry and Military Production, and consequent Iraqi fears that he might divulge information to the UN and hamper efforts to obtain the lifting of sanctions. Rolf Ekeus, the head of UNSCOM, stated that preliminary work on the new data appeared to show that Iraq had developed a more extensive weapons programme than had so far been discovered, and that it had been concealing a significant biological weapons programme. In September it was reported that illegal shipments of oil from Iraq were continuing, even though the US Navy had increased its efforts to enforce the UN blockade. (Since October 1994 14 cargoes had been confiscated by the US Navy.) In October 1995 UNSCOM reported that its work was far from over and that Iraq had concealed evidence of biological weapons development, chemical missile flight tests and work on missiles with nuclear capability. As a result, areas of investigation that had been closed would have to be reopened. At the end of November the head of the Commission told a press conference that Iraq had not been co-operating fully in its investigations and that it was still trying to mislead UN inspection teams. In December Jordan intercepted missile parts and toxic chemicals destined for Iraq.

Meanwhile, on 26 August 1992 the Governments of the USA, the United Kingdom, France and Russia had announced their decision to establish a zone in southern Iraq, south of latitude 32°N, from which all flights by Iraqi fixed-wing and rotary-wing aircraft were to be excluded. Although the air exclusion zone was not formally established by a UN Security Council resolution, the UN Secretary-General subsequently indicated his own support for the measure and stated that it enjoyed that of the Security Council. The exclusion zone was established in response to renewed attacks by Iraqi government forces on southern Iraqi Shi'ite communities and on the inhabitants of the marshlands of southern Iraq. In April 1992 Saddam Hussain had ordered the evacuation of the marshlands and the resettlement of their inhabitants; and in June Iraqi armed forces were reported to have encircled the areas and to have intensified their attacks on the communities there. The Iraqi Government reacted with predictable anger to the establishment of the air exclusion zone, but it was reported in early September to have withdrawn all flights over the area. However, large numbers of troops remained there and continued to attack the civilian population. Other Arab governments, notably those of Algeria, Jordan, Sudan, Syria and Yemen, also condemned the establishment of the air exclusion zone as a step towards the disintegration of Iraq, which, as a result of the other, UN-authorized exclusion zone north of latitude 36°N (see above), was now effectively divided into three parts.

In late December 1992 a US combat aircraft shot down an Iraqi fighter aircraft which had allegedly entered the southern air exclusion zone; and on 6 January 1993 the USA, with the support of the British and French Governments, demanded that Iraq should withdraw anti-aircraft missile batteries from within the zone. Iraq was reported to have complied with this demand, but subsequent Iraqi military operations inside Kuwaiti territory, to recover military equipment, provoked air attacks by Western forces on targets in southern Iraq on 13 January. A ban which the Iraqi Government had imposed on UN flights into the country was cited as a further justification for the attacks. Further air raids by Western forces on targets in northern and southern Iraq took place in late January. In late May, in response to the deployment of Iraqi armed forces close to the UN-authorized exclusion zone north of latitude 36°N, the USA warned Iraq that it might suffer military reprisals in the event of any incursion into the Kurdish-held north. In late June the USA launched an attack against intelligence headquarters in Baghdad, in retaliation for Iraq's role in an alleged conspiracy to assassinate former US President Bush in Kuwait in April 1993. Iraq made a formal protest to the UN Security Council over the attack, which provoked widespread international condemnation, not least because it was regarded by many observers as an attempt by the Clinton administration to increase its domestic popularity. In early July Iraqi armed forces were reported to have renewed the Government's offensive against the inhabitants of the marshlands of southern Iraq, and the London-based INC urged the UN Security Council to send emergency supplies of food and medicine to the communities there. In late July the Food and Agriculture Organization (FAO) of the UN warned that pre-famine conditions existed in much of Iraq and appealed for the economic sanctions in force against the country to be either alleviated or lifted. In late August it was reported that the Government had drained some 70% of the southern marshlands and that some 3,000 of their inhabitants had fled to Iran. In December 1995 the SCIRI reported that Iraqi armed forces were continuing their offensive against the civilian population in the southern marshlands, but claimed that its own forces were carrying out regular attacks against Iraqi military positions in the south. In January 1996 it was reported that the exodus of refugees from the southern marshlands was continuing, with an estimated 60,000–70,000 people living in camps in south-western Iran and many more in other parts of the country. In addition it was estimated that some 200,000 people in southern Iraq had been internally displaced, having fled to other parts of the country.

ECONOMIC CRISIS, MILITARY INSTABILITY AND CONFLICTS WITHIN HUSSAIN'S REGIME

By October 1994 the living standards of large sections of the Iraqi population had reportedly been reduced to subsistence level. The Iraqi Government appeared increasingly desperate to maintain order in the face of this economic crisis. In May 1994 Saddam Hussain himself had assumed the post of Prime Minister in a reshuffle of the Council of Ministers in which the Ministers of Finance and Agriculture were dismissed. In June, and again in September, harsh new punishments for those convicted of theft were announced by the RCC. Also in September a substantial reduction in the daily ration of some staple food items was announced. In December another Minister of Agriculture was dismissed, and subsequent reports claimed that he had been imprisoned on charges relating to the neglect of

his duties. (The agriculture portfolio was allocated to Khalid Abd al-Munim Rashid in April 1995.)

Dissatisfaction within the armed forces resurfaced in early 1995. An unsuccessful coup attempt in January prompted a comprehensive reorganization of military ranks, including the (unconfirmed) dismissal of 68 air force officers. In March another coup attempt, organized by the former head of Iraqi military intelligence during the 1990–91 hostilities in the Gulf, and supported by Kurdish insurgents in the north and Shi'ite rebels in the south, was also thwarted. Further reorganization of military personnel resulted in the appointment of a new Chief of the General Staff in April 1995. The scale of disruption within the armed forces provoked widespread anxiety among the civilian population, and civil disturbances began to escalate (particularly in Anbar province), leading to the replacement of the Minister of the Interior in May. Regional reports of a substantial insurrection by the armed forces at the Abu Ghraid army base, near Baghdad, in mid-June were strenuously denied by the Iraqi Government. However, there was mounting evidence to suggest that an uprising had been organized by members of the Sunni Dulaimi clan (many of whom had been killed in continuing disturbances in Ramadi, the capital of Anbar province), with the support of the élite 14 July battalion of the Iraqi army. While unconfirmed reports suggested that those responsible for the rebellion had been immediately and severely punished (many by execution), the loss of the support of the previously loyal Dulaimi clan was widely interpreted as the beginning of the disintegration of Saddam Hussain's traditional support base of powerful Sunni Muslim clans.

A minor reorganization of portfolios in the Council of Ministers was effected in late June 1995, and in July a new Minister of Defence and a new Chief of the General Staff were appointed in an attempt to consolidate support for the President. However, in early August further significant divisions within Saddam Hussain's power base became apparent following the defection to Jordan of two sons-in-law of the President, Lt-Gen. Hussain Kamel al-Majid and his brother Col Saddam Kamel, together with their wives. Both were senior figures in the regime. Hussain Kamel had been Minister of Industry and Military Production, responsible for Iraq's weapons development programme, and Saddam Kamel the head of the Presidential Guard, responsible for presidential security. It was rumoured that they had become alarmed at the increasing concentration of power in the hands of Saddam Hussain's two sons, Uday and Qusai, and that they feared for their lives. The two men were immediately granted political asylum by King Hussein of Jordan. From Amman, Hussain Kamel urged the Iraqi army to overthrow Saddam Hussain's regime, and Iraqi opposition groups to unite and form a government-in-exile. There was speculation that he himself was regarded as a possible successor to Saddam Hussain. Hussain Kamel also met Rolf Ekeus, the head of UNSCOM, and was believed to have provided further information on Iraq's weapons development programmes. Iraq condemned both men as traitors and a wave of arrests and executions followed their defection as Saddam Hussain ordered a purge of senior army officers and government officials who had been close to the two brothers.

In a move widely interpreted as an attempt to re-establish domestic and international recognition of Saddam Hussain's mandate, a meeting of the RCC was convened on 7 September 1995 and an interim amendment to the Constitution was approved whereby the elected Chairman of the RCC would automatically assume the Presidency of the Republic, subject to the approval of the National Assembly and endorsement by national plebiscite. Saddam Hussain's candidature was duly approved by the National Assembly on 10 September. The meticulously organized referendum took place on 15 October and a 99.96%-endorsement of the President's continuance in office for a seven-year renewable term was recorded. An official turnout of 99.47% of the estimated 8.4m. electorate was reported to have voted. This unprecedented level of support provoked widespread incredulity throughout the international community. At the end of October Hussain promised further elections and 'more democratization' and emphasized the leading role of Baath Party in achieving political pluralism. Some observers argued that as a result of the conflict within his immediate family and the defections of Hussain and Saddam Kamel,

Saddam Hussain might use the Baath Party structures, his original power base, to bolster his position. The Iraqi leader appeared to have curbed the power of his son Uday at least temporarily. The Deputy Prime Minister Tareq Aziz implied in October that Uday had no official political role. There were further changes in the Council of Ministers at the end of the year, with new appointments made to to the portfolios of education, agriculture, irrigation and finance.

In February 1996 the two defectors, Hussain and Saddam Kamel, returned to Baghdad, having been granted a pardon by Saddam Hussain. Immediately after their return to Iraq the two men (who were promptly divorced from their wives) were assassinated. Unconfirmed reports suggested that their father, Kamel Hassan al-Majid, and a number of their children were also killed in the attack, allegedly perpetrated by men under the command of Saddam Hussain's son, Uday. Their assassination led to international condemnation and was followed by reports of armed clashes among rival clans in Baghdad, and in the Ajwa region of Tikrit. In December Uday sustained serious injuries after surviving an attempted assassination in Baghdad. Both the Dulaimi tribe and the Shi'a group, Ad-Da'wa al-Islamiya, claimed responsibility for the attack, but there was considerable speculation that the attack had been perpetrated in retaliation for the murders of Hussain and Saddam Kamel. At the end of March another high-level defection had occurred when Lt-Gen. Nizar Kharaji, Chief of Staff of the Iraqi Army during the Gulf War, fled to Amman, Jordan, where he joined the Iraqi National Accord (INA), (see below). In June reports emerged of a new coup plot involving senior officers of the Republican Guard and close associates of Saddam Hussain from Tikrit. More than one hundred officers, including two army commanders, were arrested and subsequently executed. Mounting opposition to the President from within the armed forces was widely considered to have prompted his decision to transfer responsibility for the national military intelligence department from the Ministry of Defence, and to create new paramilitary units entrusted with the protection of his own family.

Elections to 220 of the 250 seats in the National Assembly were held in March 1996. Predictably, all 160 candidates from the ruling Baath Party gained seats, with the remaining 60 seats being won by so-called independent candidates. According to official sources, 93.5% of the approximately 8m.-strong electorate participated in the poll. Iraqi opposition groups derided the regime's claim to have introduced greater democracy and denounced the elections as a farce. Elections to local councils were conducted in May. The new councils were to be responsible not only for municipal services, but also for food rationing. In December Latif Jasim was relieved of the Labour and Social Affairs portfolio in order to devote himself to Baath Party activities; he was succeeded by Abd al-Hamid Aziz Muhammad Salih as-Sayigh.

In May 1996 government forces were reported to have launched a major offensive against the Shi'a opposition and tribes in the Basra Governorate and further fighting in the southern marshlands was reported in September. At the end of the year there were armed clashes between the security forces and the Shi'a opposition throughout the southern regions as the Government attempted to eliminate popular unrest in that part of the country. Early in 1997, the US-based Human Rights Watch condemned the fiercely repressive activities of Iraqi Government forces in the southern marshlands during 1996 and also claimed that Saddam Hussain's regime was continuing to engage in severe abuses of human rights against the Iraqi people. Saddam Hussain's absence from celebrations organized to mark his 60th birthday, at the end of April 1997, prompted speculation that security concerns surrounding the President had intensified severely since the assassination attempt on his son, Uday. In June it was reported that a senior air force commander, Maj.-Gen. Izz ad-Dulaimi, had been assassinated in Baghdad. In mid-1997 a number of changes were made to senior military posts, including, most notably, the reported replacement of Qusai Hussain by one of the President's nephews, Kemal Mustafa at-Tikriti, as Commander of the Republican Guard, in August. (Qusai's removal was somewhat unexpected since his political profile appeared to have been enhanced since the attempt on his brother's life, and some commentators had

described his recent status as being akin to 'heir apparent'.) New appointments were also made to head the national intelligence directorate (where a new anti-corruption campaign for the ranks of the Baath Party and the armed forces was to be formulated) and to a number of provincial governorships in the central and southern regions. Ali Hassan al-Majid, a former member of the RCC and a cousin of the President, was appointed Military Governor of the southern provinces of Basra and Nasiriya. Al-Majid had gained a reputation for his uncompromising response to insurrection during the Kurdish uprisings of the late 1980s, and reports soon emerged of a fresh campaign of subjugation in the southern marshlands.

In August 1997 Vice-President and Deputy Prime Minister, Taha Yassin Ramadan, replaced Izzat Ibrahim (who was reported to be suffering from ill health) as Vice-Chairman of the RCC. In the same month a reorganization of the Council of Ministers was effected: Abd al-Jabbar Tawfiq Muhammad was transferred from the Ministry of Education to the Ministry of Higher Education and Scientific Research where he replaced Humam Abd al-Khaliq Abd al-Ghafur, who moved to the Ministry of Culture and Information; Fahd Salim ash-Shakrah was appointed new Minister of Education.

Towards the end of 1997 reports began to emerge of renewed efforts by Saddam Hussain to impose his authority on the nation. A number of senior military officers and Baath Party members (several of them relatives or known associates of Maj.-Gen. Wafiq as-Samarrai, a former head of military intelligence who had fled Iraq some three years previously to join the opposition INC, and had successfully sought political asylum in the United Kingdom) were executed, as were an estimated 800 prisoners suspected of belonging to opposition organizations. Many mid-level and senior Baath Party officials were also replaced in a political purge that was thought to have been organized in order to dilute the influence of increasingly powerful provincial party groups.

Iraqi opposition groups, however, remained weak and divided. One of the founding members of the INA, Gen. Tawfiq al-Yasiri, resigned in February 1998, accusing the organization's leadership of misappropriating funds. In early 1998 one of the leaders of the rival, London-based INC, Ahmad Chalabi, visited Washington, DC (USA) to lobby support from the US Congress. Chalabi claimed that Iraq was ripe for a broad-based revolt and urged the US Government to transform the existing air exclusion zones in the north and south of the country into total exclusion zones for the Baghdad authorities, from which an INC provisional government could operate, protected from Saddam Hussain's military forces. Although certain Republican politicians in Washington were sympathetic to Chalabi's request, the US Administration remained cautious about encouraging civil war in Iraq and questioned the INC's ability to topple the Iraqi leader.

The annual report of the UN special rapporteur on Iraq, Max Van der Stoel, presented to the UN Human Rights Commission in Geneva in April 1998, was once again highly critical of the Iraqi regime's record on human rights. The report stated that at least 1,500 people had been executed during 1997, mainly for political reasons, and that most of that number were killed as part of the 'prison cleansing' operation conducted in November and December 1997. Iraqi officials dismissed the report as 'a mere repetition of the same allegations and false accusations'. (A separate report published in March claimed that some 16,000 instances of forced disappearance had been registered in Iraq during the previous 10 years—the highest number in the world.) Also in April the Iran-based SCIRI opposition group claimed that a renewed offensive against the Shi'a opposition in the southern regions had resulted in the execution of some 60 Shi'ites during March. Van der Stoel later denounced the assassination of two senior Shi'a religious leaders, Ayatollah Murtada al-Burujirdi and Grand Ayatollah Mirza Ali al-Gharawi, killed in April and June respectively. Van der Stoel reported that both men had been harassed and warned by the Iraqi authorities to cease organizing prayer meetings, and expressed fears that the murders were part of a systematic attack on the independent leadership of Iraq's Shi'a Muslims. Although Ayatollah al-Gharawi had never been involved in political activity, there had been reports that the Iraqi Government wished to replace him as *Marja* (a senior spiritual leader of Shi'a Muslims) by another candidate whom many leading Shi'a religious scholars believed was unqualified for the position. Van der Stoel stated that in both cases the Iraqi authorities failed to investigate the murder thoroughly. The Iraqi Government, however, denied any involvement in the murders, attributing them instead to 'malicious foreign-based elements'.

In May 1998 the Minister of Labour and Social Affairs, Abd al-Hamid Aziz Muhammad Salih as-Sayigh, was dismissed after stating that Iraq's prisons were grossly over-populated. He was replaced in July with Saadi Tuma-Abbas. In June Jordanian newspapers reported that Saddam Hussain's daughter, Rana, was seeking to gain control of a bank account in Amman, which had been opened by her late husband, Saddam Kamel, after his defection. The report provided the first firm evidence that the Iraqi authorities were trying to recover some of the tens of millions of dollars believed to have been taken out of the country by Saddam and Hussain Kamel (see above).

CONCLUSION OF AGREEMENT ON PETROLEUM SALES

In January 1996 Iraq indicated that it was willing to 'enter into a dialogue' on an oil-for-food agreement with the UN, provided that no conditions were attached to it. Iraq had originally rejected UN Security Council Resolution 986 of April 1995 (see above), arguing that the terms were a violation of its sovereignty. Under the conditions of the resolution, Iraq had to accept UN monitoring of the distribution of humanitarian supplies and to agree to the supply of specified amounts of food and medicine to the Kurdish-controlled enclave in the north. On several occasions the Iraqi Government had indicated that it wished to renegotiate the terms of the Resolution, but the UN Security Council had refused and insisted that Iraq must accept the conditions as set out in the original offer. The Security Council agreed that the UN Secretary-General should begin new talks with Iraq on the implementation of Resolution 986, and a first round commenced in early February 1996. By the end of April UN and Iraqi negotiators had held three rounds of talks, but no agreement had been reached on a draft memorandum of understanding. It was reported that agreement could have been reached, but that the USA and the United Kingdom had insisted on certain changes to the original terms of Resolution 986, including a demand that Iraq should play no part in the supply and distribution of supplies to the Kurdish governorates. Despite these problems, Iraq proceeded in early March to sign a protocol with Turkey on resuming oil exports through the two pipelines from the Kirkuk oilfields to the Turkish ports of Ceyhan and Yumurtalık on the Mediterranean. A fourth round of talks between the UN and Iraq began in early May, but in the middle of the month the two sides remained divided over the conditions which should govern limited sales of Iraqi petroleum. On 20 May, however, Iraq accepted the UN terms. The memorandum of agreement, which must be renewed every six months, detailed stringent conditions for the sale of up to $4,000m.-worth of Iraqi oil a year in order to purchase food and medicine, and to finance UN operations in Iraq. The agreement stipulated that 30% of the revenues obtained would be used to pay war reparations, and that a further 13%–15% would be spent on aid to the Kurdish provinces. Independent inspection agents would be appointed by the UN to verify the arrival of humanitarian supplies in Iraq and their equitable distribution. The UN would take direct charge of the distribution of supplies in the Kurdish-held areas. Dr al-Anbari, Iraq's chief negotiator at the UN, hoped that the agreement would be the first step leading to the gradual lifting of the embargo, but this appeared unlikely. There was, however, general acknowledgement that the agreement represented the biggest change in Iraq's relations with the international community since the war with the multinational force in 1991.

In March 1996 UN sanctions against Iraq were renewed for a further 60 days. The head of UNSCOM, Rolf Ekeus, reported to the Security Council that Iraq had not yet surrendered certain proscribed weapons or related materials and he expressed concern that Iraq might still be engaged in the development of prohibited weapons systems. He feared that Iraq was concealing as many as 16 surface-to-surface missiles armed with biological warheads from UN inspectors. On 27 March, in response to these fears, the Security Council unanimously approved Resolution 1051 which provided for the establishment of an elaborate system to monitor the export of any material and equipment to Iraq that could be used in the production of weapons of mass destruction, to come into force as soon as trade sanctions were lifted.

Confrontations between UN inspectors and Iraqi officials continued. In March 1996, for example, inspectors were prevented from entering and searching sites on five occasions. In June, during a visit to Baghdad, Ekeus signed an agreement with Tareq Aziz, according to which Iraq promised to grant UN inspectors immediate access to sites provided they fully respected Iraq's concerns over sovereignty when visiting those sites deemed to be 'sensitive'. Yet, despite this, in late July a team of UN inspectors was barred from entering a 'sensitive site' and was forced to suspend its operations.

In late July 1996 Iraq's chief negotiator at the UN stated that Iraq's amended food distribution plan had been approved by the UN Secretary-General and that Iraq hoped that the agreement would now be swiftly implemented. On 31 July, however, it was announced that the USA, at a meeting of the UN Security Council sanctions committee, had withheld its approval of the amended food distribution plan as it required further details of monitoring procedures. Final approval of the sanctions committee (including that of the USA) for the implementation of Resolution 986 was granted on 8 August, and it was announced that the means of monitoring exports of Iraqi petroleum and the purchase and distribution of humanitarian goods inside Iraq were in the process of being established. In mid-September, however, the implementation of Resolution 986 was postponed indefinitely, following the deployment of Iraqi armed forces (in alliance with the forces of the DPK) inside the Kurdish 'safe haven' in northern Iraq. In response the USA launched missile attacks on targets in southern Iraq. The threat of further retaliatory US attacks on Iraqi targets receded on 13 September when Iraq announced that it would cease targeting allied aircraft enforcing the air exclusion zones. There was, in any case, little support among the international community for the escalation of retaliatory action which the USA appeared, initially, to wish to pursue. The US Government, nevertheless, continued to reinforce its military capabilities in the Gulf region. At the end of October Italy followed France in opening an interests section in a diplomatic mission in Baghdad, and in December Spain announced that it was sending a permanent diplomatic representative to its Baghdad embassy. Other Western countries were expected to begin to re-establish diplomatic relations with Iraq (suspended in 1991) following the implementation of the oil-for-food agreement.

At the beginning of December 1996 the UN Secretary-General issued a memorandum of understanding finally implementing Resolution 986, Iraq having accepted all the conditions stipulated by the United Nations. Petroleum began to flow through the pipeline to Turkey on 10 December. Revenues from the sale of Iraqi oil are to be deposited in a special account at the Banque Nationale de Paris in New York which will issue letters of credit for all supplies of food and medicine ordered by the Iraqi authorities, and funds will only be released when the goods have been inspected and verified by UN monitors on the Iraqi border. UN teams have the right to visit all humanitarian supply centres in Iraq without prior warning, and 151 UN monitors will supervise the actual distribution of humanitarian supplies. However, international agencies have expressed doubts that the funds made available for humanitarian relief under the terms of the agreement will be sufficient to alleviate the high levels of malnutrition and disease among the Iraqi population. Part of Iraq's oil revenue will be allocated to the UN Compensation Commission (UNCC), which has been unable to settle the majority of Gulf War compensation claims due to inadequate funds. The first shipments of food and humanitarian supplies purchased under the new agreement reached Iraq in late March 1997.

Following approval of the 'oil-for-food' agreement, a new dispute arose between UNSCOM and the Iraqi authorities. Ekeus reported that Iraqi officials had refused UN inspectors permission to remove *Scud* missile components for examination abroad. At the end of December all UN sanctions against Iraq were renewed for a further 60 days. At the beginning of April 1997 Iraq violated the southern air exclusion zone in order to fly pilgrims to Jeddah in Saudi Arabia, and at the end of the month, ignoring US warnings Iraqi helicopters collected returning pilgrims from the Saudi border. Both President Clinton and the US Secretary of Defense, William Cohen, issued renewed warnings to the Iraqi Government that it should not challenge international restrictions on the use of its airspace, but no retaliatory measures were undertaken. In its six-monthly report, presented to the UN Security Council on 18 April, UNSCOM stated that it was still not satisfied that Iraq had disclosed full details of its past nuclear, biological and chemical weapons programme and warned that there could be 'political consequences' if Baghdad continued to undermine the Commission's activities. These claims were rejected by the Iraqi Deputy Prime Minster, Tareq Aziz, in a letter to the Chairman of the Security Council published on 23 April. In May Iraq again accused the USA of disrupting the delivery of food and medicine purchased under UN Resolution 986 by delaying its approval of contracts without satisfactory reason.

Reporting to the US Congress in May 1997 on efforts to secure Iraq's compliance with UN resolutions, President Clinton reaffirmed that Saddam Hussain remained a serious threat to the Iraqi people and to regional peace and stability. He declared that the USA would not relax its sanctions until the Iraqi authorities complied with all their obligations under UN resolutions. The President stated that the northern and southern air exclusion zones would be maintained and emphasized the scale of US forces in the region. He criticized the Iraqi leadership for refusing to co-operate fully with UN weapons inspectors and condemned Iraqi efforts to impose new restrictions on UN officials responsible for monitoring the distribution of humanitarian supplies to the Iraqi people. He stated that his administration would continue to support the various Iraqi opposition groups and non-governmental organizations that are monitoring the human rights situation in Iraq. At the beginning of June the UN Security Council unanimously approved the extension of the 'oil-for-food' agreement for a further six months, despite complaints from both Washington and Baghdad. The Security Council indicated that it would consider extending the programme for a third six-month period if there were no major problems during the second stage, but rejected Iraq's request to increase the amount of oil that it is permitted to sell under the agreement. In response to demands from the USA and the United Kingdom for more information on the distribution of humanitarian supplies, the UN Secretary-General, Kofi Annan, dispatched his Under-Secretary-General for Humanitarian Affairs, Yasushi Akashi, to Iraq to investigate these concerns. Akashi confirmed that almost all of the UN World Food Programme observers were in place and had been given access to all parts of the country, but had discovered no evidence of discrimination in the distribution of supplies. Akashi's report also drew attention to certain administrative and financial deficiencies in the UN's implementation of the 'oil-for-food' agreement which continued to result in serious delays in the processing and distribution of humanitarian supplies. However, later in June Iraq suspended oil exports under the agreement and on 18 June the Minister of Oil, Amir Muhammad Rashid, stated that exports would resume following UN approval of a new distribution plan proposed by the Iraqi authorities.

The Iraqi authorities continued to complain about the large number of contracts, especially for medical and water-treatment equipment, that had either been rejected or delayed by the UN Security Council sanctions committee, and to accuse the USA of obstructing humanitarian efforts. The Iraqi authorities drew attention to the contrast between the slow pace of progress of the work of the sanctions committee and the speed at which the UN Compensations Committee (UNCC) had moved to deal with claims for compensation arising from Iraq's invasion of Kuwait. US officials, however, insisted that the Iraqi Government was deliberately abusing its humanitarian imports facility to obtain goods that could be used for other purposes. Iraq and the UN agreed a new distribution plan in early August 1997, incorporating improvements designed to accelerate the approval process, and Iraqi oil exports resumed on 14 August. In order to enable Iraq to meet its revenue target for the first three months of the second phase of the 'oil-for-food' agreement, in September the UN Security Council extended the deadline to the beginning of October. By the end of August, 672 contracts had been approved

by the sanctions committee, 20 rejected and 83 withheld. The UN renewed the agreement for a third six-month period on 4 December and agreed to consider changes to the procedures and value of oil exports during that period. This move failed to satisfy Iraq and oil exports were immediately suspended. In early January 1998 revisions proposed by Iraq to a new plan for the distribution of food and medicine during the third phase were approved by the UN Secretary-General, and by mid-January Iraqi oil exports had resumed.

Following a visit to Iraq in January 1998, the UN Secretary-General, Kofi Annan, recommended an increase in the value of oil exports allocated to Iraq under the 'oil-for-food' agreement, and on 20 February the UN Security Council agreed Resolution 1153, which more than doubled, to $5,200m., the level of six-monthly revenue permitted to the Iraqi Government. Iraq was to be entitled to spend up to $3,550m. every six months on humanitarian imports, the definition of which was broadened to include investment in infrastructure projects such as repairs to oil production facilities and power generators. The remaining $1,650m. was to be used to pay war reparations and the cost of UN operations in Iraq. Some aspects of the new arrangement provoked criticism from Baghdad. The Iraqi authorities were particularly insistent that all additional revenues should be allocated to humanitarian imports. They also stated that they would not recognize any agreements concluded between the UN and the Kurds without consultation with Baghdad, and would refuse to be dictated to by the UN on decisions relating to infrastructure projects. Despite its acceptance of the original 'oil-for-food' agreement, the Iraqi Government had always been concerned that the deal would delay the full lifting of sanctions. The Iraqi authorities complained that the new arrangement implied a permanence to the agreement, and that it further violated Iraq's sovereignty. In addition, Iraq's ambassador to the UN, Nizar Hamdoon, stated that until vital rehabilitation of the oil sector was completed, Iraq could export no more than $4,000m. of oil every six months. A UN technical team visited Iraq in mid-March and reported that six-monthly exports worth only $3,000m. were currently possible and that this level of production could only be maintained if Iraq was permitted to import essential spare parts. As a result the UN Secretary-General asked the Security Council to allocate $300m. for repairs to oil production facilities and requested that the value of Iraqi oil exports under the revised agreement be reduced to $4,000m. every six months. Iraq was required to submit a new aid distribution programme before the revised agreement could take effect. The new plan was submitted in early May and approved by the UN Secretary-General at the end of the month. It provided for oil sales of $4,500m. over the following six months, of which $3,100m. was to be allocated for humanitarian supplies and emergency infrastructure repairs, while the remainder would finance war reparations.

In March 1998 the US Department of State welcomed efforts by Iraq's neighbours, particularly Iran, to curtail the illegal export of crude oil and petroleum products by Saddam Hussain's regime. The scale of the smuggling, mainly through Iran, Turkey and the Gulf, was difficult to quantify but US officials estimated that during February Iraq had been illegally transporting 100,000 b/d, providing the regime with annual revenues of some $700m. which, it was believed, would be devoted to the security services and to the purchase of luxury goods for the political élite.

Following a number of incidents during June 1997 in which UNSCOM inspectors were further obstructed by Iraqi officials, on 21 June the UN Security Council unanimously adopted Resolution 1115, condemning the Iraqi authorities for repeatedly refusing to allow inspection teams access to sites and indicating that further sanctions might be imposed on Iraq if the authorities failed to co-operate with UNSCOM. A decision on the imposition of further sanctions was postponed until October. In July Rolf Ekeus, who had headed UNSCOM for six years, resigned and was replaced by an Australian diplomat, Richard Butler. During a visit to Baghdad, undertaken soon after his appointment, Butler noted a new spirit of co-operation with the Iraqi authorities, but in the weeks that followed UN operations were systematically frustrated by Iraqi officials. In October Butler presented his report of UNSCOM's operations during the previous five months to the UN Security Council. Despite noting significant progress in determining the scale of

Iraq's chemical weapons programme, the report was essentially highly critical of the authorities in Baghdad, emphasizing a persistent lack of co-operation from the Iraqi Government. Subsequently, within the UN Security Council, the USA and the UK proposed a resolution to prohibit Iraqi officials considered to be responsible for obstructing weapons inspectors from leaving the country. France and Russia objected to the draft resolution but approved a revised version to impose a travel ban on Iraqi officials in April 1998 should non-co-operation with UNSCOM continue. At the same time sanctions against Iraq were renewed for a further 60 days.

In late October 1997 the RCC criticized the high proportion of UNSCOM personnel supplied by the USA, claiming that they were opposed to the lifting of sanctions. Iraq demanded that all such personnel should leave the country by 5 November. This deadline was extended by one week, however, in order to allow a UN mission to travel to Baghdad in an attempt to resolve the dispute. Negotiations proved unsuccessful and therefore the UN Security Council unanimously adopted a resolution (No. 1137) which immediately activated the travel ban proposed earlier. The resolution also stipulated that Iraq should retract its decision to expel US personnel and stated that further Iraqi intransigence regarding weapons inspections would result in the suspension of the 60-day sanctions review until April 1998 and, furthermore, possibly provoke military action. Nevertheless, Iraq refused to rescind its decision and US weapons inspectors were forced to leave the country on 13 November. In response to the escalating crisis, both the USA and the UK ordered military reinforcements into the region, with both Kuwait and Bahrain reluctantly allowing warplanes to be deployed on their territory. Tensions appeared to ease on 19 November after the Iraqi Deputy Prime Minister, Tareq Aziz, met the Russian Minister of Foreign Affairs, Yevgenii Primakov, who affirmed that Russia would continue to urge the lifting of economic sanctions, provided that Iraq complied with Resolution 1137. Following this assurance, UNSCOM weapons inspectors were permitted to return to Iraq on 21 November. Renewed Iraqi co-operation with UNSCOM was short-lived, however: shortly after the inspectors' return, Iraqi officials refused to allow UNSCOM the unconditional access to areas designated as presidential palaces which it sought. In mid-December Richard Butler, accompanied by commissioners from the UK, France and Russia, held talks in Baghdad with Tareq Aziz. Although Aziz expressed satisfaction at the presence of representatives of countries other than the USA, no progress was achieved. In response to the impasse, the US Secretary of Defense, William Cohen, reiterated the threat of military action in order to force Saddam Hussain to capitulate to UN demands, a move which was condemned by Russia. On 12 January 1998 Iraq prohibited inspections by a former US marine officer, Scott Ritter, claiming that he was spying for the CIA. On 19 January Richard Butler returned to Iraq, where he agreed to Russian requests to introduce outside experts into technical talks regarding the weapons inspections, scheduled to commence in February, thereby diluting the presence of US personnel. In spite of this concession, Iraq maintained a policy of non-co-operation with UNSCOM. In response, the US Secretary of State, Madeleine Albright, warned that the time for diplomacy was fast expiring and embarked on an intensive diplomatic mission in Europe and the Middle East in order to gain support for possible military action against Iraq. The US Secretary of State subsequently announced that Egypt, Jordan, Kuwait, Bahrain, Saudi Arabia and Israel were prepared for a military response. France, the People's Republic of China and Russia opposed the use of force. The apparently increased likelihood of air strikes against Iraq prompted Russia's Deputy Minister of Foreign Affairs, Viktor Posuvalyuk, to hold extensive talks with Iraqi officials in Baghdad in late January and early February. The USA did not consider that Russia had achieved a breakthrough and began to make preparations to evacuate 450 UN staff to secure hotels. However, the Russian President, Boris Yeltsin, maintained that progress was indeed being made and threatened that Russia would veto any Security Council resolutions authorizing military attacks on Iraq. The extent of Russian opposition to military force became evident on 4 February, after Yeltsin warned that US military strikes could have serious international repercussions. Indeed, and despite Albright's earlier claims, it became apparent that

there was little support among the Gulf states for military action. Only Kuwait announced its approval of force if diplomatic efforts should fail, while Saudi Arabia and Bahrain refused to authorize military attacks from their territories. Meanwhile, senior representatives from the Arab League, Russia, Turkey and France met on 3 February, in Baghdad, in an attempt to defuse the crisis. In mid-February the five permanent members of the UN Security Council approved a compromise formula, which proposed that a special group of diplomats, appointed by the UN Secretary-General in consultation with experts from UNSCOM and the International Atomic Energy Agency (IAEA), would be allowed unconditional and unrestricted access to presidential palaces. A visit to Baghdad by Kofi Annan on 22 February resulted in agreement on a memorandum of understanding between the UN and Iraq, which narrowly averted the immediate threat of military action. Under the terms of the memorandum, signed on 23 February, the Iraqi Government (which reiterated its acceptance of all relevant UN resolutions) agreed to grant UNSCOM immediate, unconditional and unrestricted access to all sites, while UNSCOM agreed to respect the legitimate concerns of Iraq relating to national security, sovereignty and dignity. A Special Group to inspect the eight presidential sites was to be created, comprising senior diplomats and experts from UNSCOM, and headed by a Commissioner appointed by the UN Secretary-General. The Special Group was to operate under the established procedures of UNSCOM, and specific detailed procedures which were to be developed given the special nature of the presidential sites. Noting the progress already achieved by UNSCOM and the need to intensify efforts to complete its mandate, the UN and the Iraqi Government agreed to improve co-operation, and efficiency, effectiveness and transparency of work. Finally the memorandum noted that the lifting of sanctions was of paramount importance to the people and Government of Iraq, and the Secretary-General undertook to bring this matter to the full attention of members of the UN Security Council. Iraq's Deputy Prime Minister, Tareq Aziz, who signed the memorandum on behalf of the Iraqi Government, claimed on 24 February that Iraq had achieved 'excellent political gains for the present and for the future and practical gains related to the lifting of sanctions'. Kofi Annan was careful to highlight the role played by the USA in securing the agreement, stating that 'diplomacy backed up by force' had facilitated the negotiating process. There was general agreement that Saddam Hussain had improved his position at home and in the Arab world by confronting the USA. Iraq also viewed the personal involvement of the UN Secretary-General as an important achievement, hoping that he would use his influence to effect an early end to the regime's international isolation. On the other hand, Iraq had been forced to make some concessions, notably to allow UNSCOM access to all suspect areas, including presidential sites. However, it was clear that the establishment of the Special Group to inspect the presidential sites would complicate the work of UNSCOM and the organization of surprise visits to these sites. The Secretary-General had also declined to place a six-month time limit on UNSCOM's work, as requested by Iraq, insisting that sanctions would only be lifted when UNSCOM confirmed that all of Iraq's alleged nuclear, chemical and biological weapons and facilities had been destroyed. According to some observers, Saddam Hussain's decision to accept the compromise agreement brokered by Kofi Annan was strongly influenced by his reluctance to see the key pillars of his regime, the Republican Guard and the Presidential Guard, become the target of US and UK air strikes. Despite the apparent breakthrough, both the USA and the UK remained cautious and urged the UN Security Council to adopt a resolution advocating the use of force should Iraq breach the agreement. On 2 March the UN Security Council unanimously approved a resolution warning of extreme consequences, but not immediate use of force, if the agreement was reneged upon by Iraq. UNSCOM inspection teams returned to Iraq on 5 March and, after a meeting with Tareq Aziz on 23 March, Richard Butler reported that his teams had been allowed access to many 'sensitive' sites. In early March Kofi Annan appointed the Indian diplomat Prakash Shah to be the UN Secretary-General's special representative to Iraq. The Special Group, led by Jayantha Dhanapala, who had been appointed chief UN disarmament officer in February, completed a first round of inspections of presidential sites in late March and early April, finding most of the buildings virtually empty. On 3 April Dhanapala stated that the Group had been 'able to fulfil their mandated task'. In contrast, Charles Duelfer, the deputy head of UNSCOM, reported that Iraqi officials had informed him that inspections of presidential sites would not be permitted indefinitely and concluded that the fundamental problem of continuing access had been postponed rather than solved. The US press accused some top UN officials close to the Secretary-General of supporting Iraqi complaints against UNSCOM inspectors and advocated an end to sanctions and weapons inspections. In his six-monthly report to the UN Security Council in April, Richard Butler stated that virtually no progress in verifying disarmament had been made since October 1997 because of the recent crisis, for which he held Baghdad responsible, and he insisted that the destruction of Iraq's chemical and biological weapons was far from complete. Butler criticized Iraq's policy of 'disarmament by declaration' and stated that verification was essential to establish the credibility of these claims. The Iraqi authorities continued to maintain that they had destroyed all weapons of mass destruction and requested the complete and comprehensive ending of sanctions. On 27 April the Security Council, having reviewed Butler's latest report, voted not to review the sanctions regime against Iraq. Russia, however, did prepare a draft resolution urging an end to UN inspections into Iraq's nuclear weapons programme. The IAEA had recently reported that it had no evidence of a covert Iraqi nuclear weapons programme and that the authorities in Baghdad had answered all relevant questions on the subject satisfactorily. Despite French and Chinese support for the resolution, opposition from the UK and the USA forestalled further discussion of the draft document. Meanwhile, Iraqi officials continued to complain that, despite the increased involvement of some Russian and French diplomats in UNSCOM, the weapons inspectorate was still dominated by specialists from the UK and the USA.

In late June 1998 Richard Butler reported to the UN Security Council that traces of a lethal chemical agent known as VX had been discovered following US laboratory tests on remnants of missile warheads recovered from an Iraqi weapons destruction pit. Despite claims by a former head of Iraqi military intelligence (currently resident in the United Kingdom—see above) that VX had been employed in Iraq's war with Iran, the Iraqi Government stressed that the chemical had never been used as a weapon. In response to Iraqi demands that the tests should be repeated at more neutral locations, in early July the UN agreed to re-examine fragments of the warheads at laboratories in France and Switzerland. On 2 August Butler visited Baghdad for talks with Iraqi officials which it was hoped would expedite completion of the arms inspection programme. Negotiations collapsed two days later, however, after Tareq Aziz rejected Butler's proposal for further inspections. Furthermore, Aziz urged the UNSCOM Chairman to report to the UN Security Council that Iraq had eliminated its weapons of mass destruction, a request which Butler claimed he could not fulfil, owing to lack of evidence. Consequently, the Iraqi Council of Ministers suspended arms inspections on 5 August and Saddam Hussain presented new terms and conditions for the inspections to resume, including the establishment of a new executive bureau to oversee UNSCOM's operations and the transfer of UNSCOM headquarters from New York to Vienna. Resumption of arms inspections was authorized by the UN on 18 August, but the Iraqi authorities continued to insist that co-operation with the inspection teams would be withheld. On 14 September the Iraqi Government announced that it was suspending all co-operation with UNSCOM indefinitely, unless the UN Security Council revoked a decision, taken on 9 August, to suspend the periodic review of the maintenance of sanctions against Iraq.

RELATIONS WITH NEIGHBOURING STATES

Since the end of the conflict in the Gulf in 1990–91 Jordan had continued to distance itself from Saddam Hussain's regime and on a number of occasions King Hussein spoke publicly of the need for political change in Iraq. However, the defections of Saddam Hussain's sons-in-law in August 1995 marked a sharp deterioration in relations between the two countries. Jordan immediately granted the two men political asylum and shortly after their defection King Hussein praised Hussain Kamel as a

great patriot and strongly criticized the Iraqi leader, accusing him of planning a new invasion of Kuwait and of Saudi Arabia's oil-rich eastern province. The King also referred at length to the period when Iraq was under Hashemite rule and to the brief union between Jordan and Iraq, although he denied that he was seeking to revive a Hashemite claim to Iraq. Iraq's response to King Hussein's remarks was muted and despite their political differences economic co-operation between the two countries continued. Iraq remained Jordan's principal supplier of oil, and Jordan remained Iraq's most important link with the international community. King Hussein acknowledged that it would be difficult to sever all economic links with Iraq and refused a request by the USA to increase the pressure on Saddam Hussain by closing Jordan's border with Iraq, although border controls were tightened. In October King Hussein renewed his criticism of the Iraqi regime, denouncing the presidential elections there as a farce. He also made contact with Iraqi opposition groups based in London, United Kingdom, and promoted the idea of a congress in Amman to bring the different factions together in order to discuss political change in Iraq. However, the Iraqi opposition groups vociferously objected to the King's suggestion of a federal approach to Iraq's political future on the grounds that it might lead to the fragmentation of the country. In April 1996 Jordan gave permission for the stationing of US fighter aircraft at an air force base at Azraq to assist in the enforcement of the air exclusion zone in southern Iraq. Diplomatic sources in Washington, DC, reiterated that the USA had promised military support for Jordan in the event of an attack by Iraq. However, the Jordanian Government insisted that it would not permit the country to be used as a base for attacks against Iraq. Nevertheless, King Hussein had met with Iraqi opposition leaders in London in March and allowed the INA to open an office in Amman. At the end of June it was reported that US, British, Saudi Arabian and Jordanian intelligence officers had met in Saudi Arabia in January and that they had agreed that Amman would become the centre of operations for the Iraqi opposition. They agreed to support the INA, which had been established in 1990 with funding from Saudi Arabia. The INA claims to have contacts with high-ranking officers in the Iraqi armed forces and favours a decisive *coup d'etat* that would depose Saddam Hussain but leave the country intact. It was also reported that US President Clinton had authorized a grant of some £6m. to finance the INA's operations in Amman, which include radio broadcasts to most parts of Iraq. Additional funds were to be provided by Saudi Arabia, Kuwait and several other Arab countries. Speaking in Washington, DC, in June, the Jordanian Minister of Information stated that Jordan preferred to support the INA because its rival, the INC, had no credibility in either Iraq or Jordan. (The INC, an umbrella organization of some 30 groups, which is based in Kurdish-controlled northern Iraq, has been paralysed by internal dissent.) In May 1996 relations with Iraq deteriorated further after the murder of a Jordanian student in Baghdad, the fifth Jordanian student to have been killed in Iraq since the beginning of the year. With growing concern for Jordanian nationals living in Iraq, the Jordanian Prime Minister informed the Iraqi authorities that he held them responsible for the safety of all Jordanians living in Iraq and recalled Jordan's ambassador from Baghdad for consultations.

Some observers regarded Jordan's dramatic break with Saddam Hussain and its *rapprochement* with Saudi Arabia and the Gulf states as part of a plan carefully orchestrated by the USA to redraw the political map of the region with the aim of further isolating Iraq, politically and economically. In April 1996, when it was revealed that Turkey had signed a secret military agreement with Israel earlier in the year, some analysts argued that a new strategic partnership was emerging in the region, bringing together the USA, Israel, Turkey and Jordan in a military union designed essentially to protect Israeli and US interests and to isolate those states opposed to them. Both the Egyptian and Syrian Governments expressed disquiet at Jordan's new policy towards Iraq, fearing that they were being excluded from plans for Iraq's future after the proposed fall of Saddam Hussain. Syria condemned the defector, Hussain Kamel, and stated its commitment to preserving Iraq's territorial integrity, and its opposition to foreign interference in the country's internal affairs. These sentiments were appreciated in Iraq and the Iraqi Minister of Foreign Affairs stated that Iraq was willing to build new relations with any Arab country. However, in view of the long-standing differences between the two regimes, any significant improvement in relations appeared unlikely. Indeed, in April Syria hosted a congress of Iraqi opposition groups, including the SCIRI, the PUK and the newly formed Hizb al-Watan, or Homeland Party. Nevertheless it was alleged that Saddam Hussain had conducted a clandestine meeting with the Syrian President, Hafiz al-Assad, on the Syrian-Iraqi border in early May to discuss common issues including Turkey's military agreement with Israel, although some sources maintained that the meeting was only attended by their representatives.

In October 1995 Sheikh Zayed, the President of the UAE, appealed for the lifting of the UN-imposed sanctions on Iraq and for reconciliation between Iraq and the Gulf states. His remarks were criticized by Saudi Arabia and Kuwait, which, together with Bahrain, continued to express extreme disapproval of Saddam Hussain's regime. Oman and Qatar, however, like the UAE, have pursued more conciliatory policies towards Iraq. In March 1995 the Iraqi Minister of Foreign Affairs had visited Doha for talks with his Qatari counterpart, after which the Qatari Government expressed surprise that economic sanctions on Iraq had not been lifted. The Kuwait National Committee for Missing People and Prisoners of War claimed in 1994 that 625 Kuwaiti nationals were still in detention, or missing, in Iraq, and the fate of missing persons remains a major obstacle to any future normalization of relations between the two countries. Since mid-1996 Iraqi and Kuwaiti officials have held meetings in the mutual border area to discuss the fate of those not accounted for. The meetings have been conducted in closed sessions under the auspices of the International Committee of the Red Cross (ICRC), and have been attended by international observers. Although the Iraqi Government stated that it was holding no Kuwaiti prisoners of war, in late 1997 Kuwait claimed to be in possession of documentation, given to the ICRC by Iraq, relating to 126 Kuwaiti prisoners of war. In July 1998 delegations from both countries met in Geneva, Switzerland, for 'highly confidential' discussions on this issue. Iraq was the only state not invited to the emergency summit meeting of Arab League member states in Cairo, Egypt, at the end of June, because of what President Mubarak of Egypt referred to as 'continuing sensitivities'. However, the final communiqué of the meeting urged all Arabs to oppose any policy that affected the territorial integrity of Iraq. In September US missile attacks against targets in southern Iraq were condemned by several Arab states, including Jordan and Saudi Arabia, both of which refused to allow their airbases to be used for new US air strikes against Iraq. Kuwait, however, reluctantly endorsed the US attacks and allowed the reinforcement of US military forces stationed in the emirate. At the GCC's annual summit in Qatar in December, the UAE again requested reconciliation with Iraq, but this initiative was rejected by the other member states. The summit also condemned Iraq's failure to implement all UN resolutions pertaining to the Gulf War, indicating that any normalization of relations between Iraq and the Gulf states would be dependent on Baghdad fulfilling the terms of those resolutions. The UAE, meanwhile, continued to send food and medical supplies to Iraq.

At the end of 1996 Jordan attempted to improve relations with Iraq by sending a ministerial delegation to Baghdad, the first high-level meeting between officials of the two countries since August 1995. King Hussein reportedly had been opposed to any relaxation of sanctions against Saddam Hussain's regime until Baghdad's acceptance of Resolution 986. The Iraqi foreign and trade ministers held talks with the Jordanian Prime Minister in Amman in December at which Jordanian industrialists were informed that they would be given preference when Iraq began placing orders for the supply of basic goods. Nevertheless, the INA was permitted to maintain its office in Amman, despite reports that it had been infiltrated by Iraqi agents. The Jordanian Government repeatedly asserted that Jordan would not be used as a base for armed operations against the Iraqi regime. Suggestions of improved relations between Syria and Iraq emerged in May 1997 when an economic delegation from Syria which included the Chairman of the Federation of Syrian Chambers of Commerce, and six other Syrian businessmen met the Iraqi Minister of Trade, Muhammad Mahdi Salih, in Baghdad to discuss possible Syrian exports to Iraq following the implementation of the 'oil-for-food' agreement. On 2 June, as discussions on bilateral trade agreements proceeded, border crossings between the two countries, which had remained closed for 18 years, were reopened. Contracts worth $20m. (for Syrian exports of food and medicines to Iraq) were signed during the visit. An Iraqi delegation led by the head of the Baghdad Chamber of Commerce and Industry visited Damascus in June. The import of goods to Iraq through Syrian ports and the reopening of the oil pipeline from Iraq to the Mediterranean through Syria, which has been closed since 1982, were discussed and agreement was reached to open three border posts. The Iraqi Minister of Foreign Affairs, Muhammad Saeed as-Sahaf, was keen to portray these contacts as a major diplomatic breakthrough, whereas Syrian officials were more cautious and emphasized the fact that the economic links proposed were in accordance with UN resolutions. Syria's willingness to improve its relations with Iraq appeared to be strongly influenced by its concerns about Turkey's military co-operation with Israel, and Ankara's recent military operations in northern Iraq. In June Iraq closed down Voice of Arab Syria, a radio station established in the late 1970s in Baghdad, which had been broadcasting attacks on the Assad regime, and the following month the Syrian Government curtailed the operations of Radio Voice of Iraq, a radio station which had been broadcasting anti-Iraqi propaganda since 1980. In August the Syrian Chamber of Commerce obtained a contract for exports to Iraq worth $13m., and further economic co-operation between the two countries was encouraged by UN approval of a new border crossing at al-Walid. Despite considerable progress in re-establishing economic links, at the end of September Muhammad Saeed as-Sahaf voiced frustration at the slow pace of *rapprochement* with Syria. However, at the end of the year, as tension between Iraq and the USA mounted, the Iraqi Deputy Prime Minister, Tareq Aziz, was received in Damascus by the Syrian Minister of Foreign Affairs, Farouk ash-Shara, the first public meeting between senior ministers of the two countries for 17 years. After the meeting there were reports that ash-Shara travelled to Riyadh with a communication from President Assad to King Fahd, detailing proposals for reintegrating Iraq into the Arab 'fold'. It was also claimed that Iraq was prepared to make a goodwill concession to Kuwait by providing information on alleged Kuwaiti prisoners of war held in Iraq. Tareq Aziz was also offficially received in Cairo, and, although he did not meet President Mubarak, his visits to Syria and Egypt were viewed in some quarters as a significant diplomatic victory for Saddam Hussain's regime. In early February 1998, when the USA sought renewed regional support for air strikes against Iraq, Syria strongly opposed such action. President Assad received as-Sahaf in Damascus on 10 February, the first time that he had met publicly with a senior Iraqi official since the early 1980s. In March Iyad ash-Shatti, the Syrian Minister of Health, became the first Syrian minister to visit Baghdad for almost 20 years. Kuwait, however, remained firmly opposed to any rehabilitation of Iraq under Saddam Hussain, and a meeting of the GCC in Kuwait in late December 1997 demanded that Iraq comply with all UN Security Council resolutions 'without selection' and blamed the Iraqi leader for the continued suffering of the Iraqi people. Earlier in the year pressure from the Kuwaiti Government had frustrated efforts by Baghdad to re-establish links with Lebanon. In February 1998 Kuwait was the only Arab state which publicly supported US demands for new air strikes against Iraq. In March Kuwait's First Deputy Prime Minister and Minister of Foreign Affairs, Sheikh Sabah al-Ahmad al-Jaber as-Sabah, stated that normalization of relations with Iraq would be possible only when Baghdad had formally apologized for the invasion of Kuwait, implemented all relevant UN resolutions and released all Kuwaiti prisoners of war. Saudi Arabia did not publicly support US recommendations for the use of force against Iraq in February 1998 but some analysts speculated that the USA would have been permitted to launch military strikes from Saudi bases if diplomatic efforts had failed to defuse the crisis. Although anxious to see Iraq's territorial integrity maintained, Saudi Arabia has continued to resist Baghdad's reintegration into the Arab world.

In Jordan, meanwhile, Abdul-Karim Kabariti, a vociferous critic of Iraq, was replaced as Prime Minister in March 1997 by Abd as-Salam al-Majali, who attempted to improve relations with Baghdad, ordering the closure, in July, of an INC-controlled radio station established in 1996. In December the execution, in Baghdad, of four young Jordanians convicted, by Iraqi courts, of smuggling activities, was denounced by King Hussein as a 'heinous crime', and prompted widespread popular outrage in Jordan. The Jordanian Government expelled almost one-half of the total number of Iraqi diplomatic staff in Amman and recalled its chargé d'affaires from Baghdad. In an attempt to defuse the situation, Iraq commuted the death sentence passed against a fifth Jordanian convicted of a similar charge and promised the release of other Jordanians in Iraqi prisons. Iraq's deputy ambassador to Jordan, Hikmat al-Hajou, his wife and a prominent Iraqi businessman were among the casualties of a multiple murder in Amman in January 1998, prompting speculation that Iraqi Government agents had been involved in the incident; the murders threatened to exacerbate tensions between the two countries. However, following the arrests of several Jordanians on charges connected to the murders, the Jordanian Minister of the Interior, Nadhir Rashid, insisted that the attack had not been politically motivated and had no connection with neighbouring countries. During the crisis between the USA and Iraq in February, the Jordanian authorities urged Iraq to comply with UN resolutions regarding weapons inspections but also stated that they would not allow Jordanian territory or airspace to be used in an attack on Iraq. Widespread popular support for Iraq prevailed throughout the crisis, although the Jordanian Government prohibited pro-Iraqi demonstrations.

Iraq's relations with Turkey deteriorated in early 1995. In March Turkish armed forces mounted a major operation to destroy PKK bases in the Kurdish enclave in northern Iraq (see above), and although the troops were withdrawn in May a smaller force crossed the border again in July. These actions, and statements by the Turkish President, Süleyman Demirel, revived fears of a Turkish claim to the former Ottoman province of Mosul. In a number of interviews with the Turkish media in May, Demirel stated that the alignment of the border with Iraq was wrong and that certain adjustments were needed to improve Turkey's security. He also pointed out that that the province of Mosul was still Ottoman territory when the Turkish Republic was founded in 1923 and had not become part of Iraq until 1929. Although Turkish officials emphasized that only minor border changes were being suggested, the President's comments were denounced by Iraq. However, the appointment of a new Turkish Government under Prime Minister Necmettin Erbakan was followed by an improvement in relations between Iraq and Turkey, and in mid-August 1996 the two countries signed a 'mutual understanding' memorandum which provided for improved political and economic links, increased trade and the construction of a gas pipeline. Under the agreement Turkey indicated that it hoped to supply all of Iraq's food imports and to receive payment in Iraqi oil. Turkey insisted that the 'oil-for-food' agreement had been signed within the framework of UN Resolution 986. However, some analysts observed that the memorandum was politically inspired and unlikely to have any tangible results. At the end of August, Ankara condemned Baghdad's invasion of the Kurdish enclave but did not endorse US missile attacks against Iraq in early September. Nevertheless, at the same time Turkey announced that it was establishing a security zone in northern Iraq (just south of the border) which would be patrolled by Turkish army units, and launched new attacks against PKK bases in the Kurdish enclave. Iran, Egypt, Jordan and Syria demanded that Turkey cease actions which threatened the territorial integrity of Iraq. In May 1997 a major new Turkish assault on PKK bases in northern Iraq was condemned by Baghdad and by several Arab countries, notably Syria. Before the invasion, Turkey had accused both Syria and Iran of mobilizing troops along the border with northern Iraq and providing support for the PKK. Tentative moves by Syria to improve relations with Iraq (see above) were attributed, in part, to growing concern in Damascus over Turkish actions

in northern Iraq and by Ankara's 1996 military co-operation agreement with Israel. The UN Secretary-General, Kofi Annan, demanded that Turkish troops withdraw from the area and declared that UN relief operations, as well as food supplies to the Kurdish enclave, could be jeopardized by the invasion. The USA, however, anxious to 'disengage' from northern Iraq, appeared to support the Turkish intervention. Despite Turkey's military operations in northern Iraq, economic links between the two countries showed some improvement. In July Turkey lifted its ban on border trade with Iraq and in September an under-secretary of state at the Turkish Ministry of Foreign Affairs visited Baghdad to discuss economic co-operation. During the visit agreement was reached on increasing the number of Turkish diplomats in Baghdad and on the transfer of Turkish prisoners held in Iraq to prisons in Turkey. At the end of September, however, Turkish forces again invaded northern Iraq, and although the campaign was smaller in scale than that of May, Turkish troops were reported to have penetrated much deeper into Iraqi territory. Iraq protested to the UN and portrayed the Turkish invasion as part of a US-Zionist campaign aimed at 'the Arab nations'. Although Turkey's aims in northern Iraq appeared to be limited to the removal of PKK bases there, Syria and the Kurdish groups insisted that Ankara still had designs on Mosul and Kirkuk. In May 1998 the Iraqi Minister of Foreign Affairs repeated claims that Turkey was violating international law by building several dams on the Euphrates and Tigris rivers without consultation with other riparian nations.

Iraq has expressed disquiet at Iran's growing involvement in the conflict between Kurdish factions in the Kurdish enclave (see above). Disputes over the question of prisoners of war from the 1980–88 Iran–Iraq War, and each country's support for the other's opponents, have prevented any significant improvement in relations. Early in 1996 Iraq urged Iran to adopt an 'objective and serious approach' to their relations, based on respect for each country's sovereignty and non-interference in each other's internal affairs. Later in 1996 there were unconfirmed reports of Iranian military intervention in northern Iraq, where the Iranian Government had developed a range of activities, including the supply of humanitarian relief. One of the reasons given by Iraqi officials for Baghdad's intervention in the Kurdish enclave in August was the need to address Iran's growing influence there. In November Saddam Hussain sent an envoy to Teheran to inform the Iranian leadership that he wished to achieve good relations with Iran and to engage in discussions concerning regional issues, as well as the release of prisoners of war. After the visit, Iran released more than 700 Iraqi prisoners of war and indicated that it was willing to discuss the release of other prisoners in order to foster improved relations. According to Iraqi sources, more than 18,000 Iraqi prisoners of the 1980–88 Iran–Iraq War are still being held in Iran. Several visits were undertaken at ministerial level during 1997, and in August Saddam Hussain offered to allow Iranian pilgrims to visit Shi'a holy shrines in Iraq. The Ministers of Foreign Affairs of the two countries held talks at the UN in New York in late September but as-Sahaf stated that further gestures of reconciliation from Teheran, in particular the return of Iraqi fighter aircraft that had taken refuge in Iran at the beginning of the 1990–91 Gulf War, were necessary if relations were to improve. A few days later Iranian military aircraft attacked bases of an Iranian opposition group, Mujahidin-e-Khalq, near Baghdad. In December Iraqi Vice-President Taha Yassin Ramadan held talks with the new Iranian President, Sayed Muhammad Khatami, at a meeting of the Organization of the Islamic Conference in Teheran. Iran was opposed to US demands for renewed air strikes against Iraq in February 1998, but in March US officials welcomed Iranian efforts to curtail the illegal export of Iraqi oil through Iranian territorial waters. In early April it was reported that some 1,500 Iraqi and 89 Iranian prisoners of the 1980–88 war had been exchanged by the two sides as part of an arrangement to release 5,592 Iraqi and 250 Iranian prisoners of war. In May the two countries embarked on an unprecedented joint operation to locate the remains of soldiers killed in the 1980–88 war.

Economy

Revised for this edition by the Editor

INTRODUCTION

Having begun to recover from the effects of the 1980–88 war with Iran, the Iraqi economy entered a new period of trauma in August 1990, as a result of the UN sanctions that were imposed because of Iraq's invasion of Kuwait. It then suffered substantial material damage in the war with the US-led multi-national force in early 1991; a UN report suggested that aerial bombardment had reduced Iraq to a 'pre-industrial' state in the immediate aftermath of the 1991 hostilities. Although the authorities succeeded in restoring a measure of basic infrastructural viability by early 1992, having given priority to the rapid rebuilding of key installations and facilities, there was no prospect of a full normalization of economic life while Iraq remained subject to UN trade sanctions. Having relied on petroleum for 98% of export earnings over the previous decade, the country suffered a massive loss of revenue when it was excluded from the world oil market in 1990. In September 1993 Iraq's Minister of Trade estimated that three years of sanctions had cost the country US $60,000m. in lost oil revenues. By 1994 the living standards of large sections of the Iraqi population had been reduced to subsistence level by the prolongation of conditions of acute economic hardship. According to unofficial Western estimates, the annual rate of decline in Iraq's gross domestic product (GDP) was about 10% in 1994 and 1995 and 15% in 1996, suggesting a GDP of $11,500m. at the end of that year. In March 1996 the Chairman of the UN Special Commission on Iraq (UNSCOM) estimated that the country was losing about $15,000m. of revenue per year as as result of trade sanctions. In the previous month Iraq had opened negotiations with the UN with a view to agreeing terms for the export of a limited volume of oil to finance a UN-supervised humanitarian programme (centred on the import and distribution of medical and food supplies). UN trade sanctions would be subject to temporary modification while the proposed scheme was operating. No date for the full lifting of sanctions could be foreseen in mid-1998 in view of the slow progress of UN weapons inspection work, which continued to be hampered by Iraqi delaying tactics.

The earlier war with Iran had itself severely affected Iraq's economic development, which had been steadily gaining momentum since 1977, forcing expenditure on former priority areas, such as water and electricity, to be reduced, with funds being transferred to defence. Towards the end of that conflict, the Government initiated, in March 1987, an economic reform programme which was supposed to reduce the extent of state control over industry, this having previously been an article of faith of the Baath Socialist Party regime which came to power in 1968. Many state organizations were abolished, and others sold to the private sector, the emphasis being placed on securing greater efficiency in the industrial and agricultural sectors and on the performance of workers and management, rather than on the state bureaucracy. More liberal import regulations—including the use of 'offshore' foreign currency funds—were introduced to enable private companies to become more involved in foreign trade.

As it emerged from the 1980–88 war, Iraq was generally considered to have strong development prospects, despite its continuing allocation of huge sums to military expenditure. Unlike other Arab states in the region, Iraq had the advantage of a relatively large population (16,335,199 at the census of October 1987), giving it the labour force necessary for industrial development. It also placed considerable emphasis on education and the creation of a skilled work-force. Moreover, Iraq continued to have an extensive and productive agricultural sector, assisted by substantial investment funds, ample supplies of irrigation water and availability of fertile land. However, by the late 1980s agriculture had become overshadowed by large-scale production of petroleum and natural gas. Both the 1970–75 and the 1976–80 development plans had given priority to the petroleum and industrial sectors, the aim being not only to maximize earnings from exports of oil and gas, but also to

diversify into other industrial exports. These objectives were maintained in the 1981–85 development plan, but this was abandoned amid the exigencies of the 1980–88 war with Iran, after which planning was conducted on an annual basis. The country's increasing industrialization was reflected in the population distribution: according to World Bank estimates, 71% of the population were classed as urban at mid-1990, compared with 51% in 1965 and 64% in 1977, when only 30% of the labour force were employed in agriculture, compared with 53% in 1960. Nevertheless, the industrial sector remained totally dominated by oil and gas production, which accounted for more than 99% of export earnings in 1989.

Lack of reliable official data has prevented the World Bank from publishing recent statistics for Iraq's overall national output and income. According to the Statistical Office of Iraq, GDP at factor cost increased from ID 1,139m. in 1970 to ID 15,647m. in 1980, while GDP per caput rose from ID 120 to ID 1,181 over the same period. The Iran–Iraq War resulted in a decline in GDP to ID 11,215m. in 1981, and in GDP per caput to ID 820, but thereafter GDP rose steadily, to ID 15,551m. in 1987 and to ID 20,811m. in 1989, while GDP per caput recovered to ID 1,186 by 1989, just above the pre-war level. The effect of the 1980–88 war was particularly apparent in the decline in oil export revenues, from ID 7,718.4m. in 1980 to ID 5,982.4m. in 1982, although by 1988 revenue from this source had recovered to ID 7,223.9m. National income increased from ID 10,589m. (ID 826 per caput) in 1979 to ID 17,290m. (ID 986 per caput) in 1989. According to Iraqi officials, overall GDP in dinar terms rose by 16% in 1989, compared with 1988 (and per caput GDP by 20%) and by 78% during 1979–89 (in which period national income grew by 63%), despite the adverse effects of the Iran–Iraq War. According to Western estimates, the real growth in GDP in 1989 was 6.5%, following zero growth in 1988, an increase of 7.7% in 1987, an actual decline of 2.9% in 1986, an increase of 3.2% in 1985 and an increase of 15.7% in 1984.

Iraq's development plans were, however, seriously compromised by a continuing shortage of foreign exchange (reserves were estimated at between zero and $2,000m. in 1987) and the accumulation of massive foreign debts during the 1980–88 war. Estimated at more than $50,000m. at the end of 1986, Iraq's total foreign debt was thought to have increased to about $65,000m. by mid-1990, including some $30,000m. in the form of loans from neighbouring Gulf states, about $13,000m. in civil debt guaranteed by export credit agencies and a further $6,000m. owed to Western companies and not covered by export credit guarantees; some $3,000m. per year was required to service the Western portion of the debt. In the late 1980s Iraq successfully negotiated a number of debt-rescheduling agreements, enabling it to proceed with major development projects in the petroleum, industrial and water-management sectors, with foreign contractors accepting deferred payment terms or using credit lines to finance contracts. Nevertheless, Iraq's international financial standing continued to be eroded by the decline in international petroleum prices in 1989 and early 1990, which, in turn, explained the country's fierce criticism of Kuwait and other Gulf states for exceeding OPEC production quotas (see Petroleum and Natural Gas, below). Against this background, Iraq's invasion of Kuwait in August 1990 had a powerful economic motivation, although in the event it was to lead to economic catastrophe.

CONSEQUENCES OF THE 1990–91 GULF CRISIS

The mandatory economic sanctions that were imposed on Iraq (and Iraqi-controlled Kuwait) by the UN Security Council on 6 August 1990 included bans on the purchase or transhipment of Iraqi oil and other commodities and on the sale or supply of all goods and products to Iraq (with possible humanitarian exceptions for medical supplies and foodstuffs). Also prescribed were an interdiction of new investment in Iraq and Kuwait and the 'freezing' of Iraqi and Kuwaiti assets abroad. Adopted unanimously and applied by virtually the whole international community, these sanctions were tightened on 25 September to cover interdiction of air traffic and obligatory detention of Iraqi-registered ships violating the trade embargo. Their effect was to place the Iraqi economy in almost total isolation, except that the land route from Jordan remained open for certain supplies. Particularly damaging for Iraq was the abrupt cessation of its oil and gas exports, including those via pipelines through Saudi Arabia and Turkey, which were closed. With its prime source of revenue thus interrupted, the Government responded by introducing rationing for basic food items and by taking various emergency measures to promote economic self-sufficiency. It also sought to counter the damaging effects of the flight from Iraq and Kuwait of hundreds of thousands of foreign workers, mostly from other Arab countries and the Indian sub-continent. Moreover, under Law 57 of 1990, announced on 18 September but backdated to 8 August, the Government declared Iraq's non-recognition of all seizures of Iraqi assets and decreed the seizure of the assets of all countries and organizations which 'issued arbitrary decisions' against Iraq. As part of this strategy, Iraq suspended debt repayments to the USA and other members of the anti-Iraq coalition.

Western reports indicated that, despite some shortages and steeply rising prices, the Iraqi economy continued to function on an emergency basis in the latter months of 1990. The situation changed dramatically, however, during the active hostilities of January–February 1991, particularly as a result of the massive allied bombing campaign against both military and strategic economic targets. According to an official UN report compiled in mid-March 1991, the conflict 'wrought near-apocalyptic results on the economic infrastructure', destroying or damaging most modern means of life support and relegating Iraq for some time to come to a 'pre-industrial age but with all the disabilities of post-industrial dependency on an intensive use of energy and technology'. The report detailed the effects of the war in the various economic sectors (see separate sections, below) and warned, in particular, of the danger of famine and epidemics spreading because of the collapse of water-distribution and sewerage systems. Of various forecasts made of the potential cost of repairing the war damage, US officials estimated in April that some $30,000m. would be required for the reconstruction of roads, power plants and oil installations. Other Western estimates assessed the total cost of the conflict to Iraq at some $50,000m. as at mid-May 1991, including the loss of 50% of GDP since August 1990 as well as war damage. The Iraqi Government, in April 1991, estimated the cost of reconstruction at $25,800m., excluding repairs in the private sector and damage to the military and nuclear industries.

The maintenance of most UN sanctions after the cease-fire agreement of 3 March 1991 (except those on food and medical supplies), meant that the Iraqi Government was obliged to begin its reconstruction efforts within those constraints, involving the continued non-availability of crucial oil revenues. An emergency six-month reconstruction budget, announced on 2 May, incorporated a reduction of state expenditure in 1991 to the equivalent of $44,760m. (from the original total of $47,080m.) but still assumed a partial resumption of oil revenues in the second half of the year. As a result of the consequential Iraqi campaigning for the removal of the UN embargo, the sanctions committee agreed on 9 May to a partial 'unfreezing' of Iraqi assets abroad, officially estimated at $4,000m., so that Iraq could pay for essential civilian items. However, Iraqi requests for the repeal of the oil export embargo were complicated by the UN Security Council's decision, on 20 May, to establish a Geneva-based Compensation Commission (UNCC) to administer a fund for victims of Iraq's aggression (governments, corporations and individuals), to be financed by a percentage levy on Iraqi oil revenues. With Western estimates valuing the possible extent of claims for damages at between $50,000m. and $100,000m., Iraq appealed for a five-year moratorium on payments from the fund and also urged that the country be permitted to export at least $1,000m.-worth of oil in 1991 to pay for urgently-needed imports. It also opposed, as unrealistic, the level of 'up to 30%' which the Security Council eventually set for the UNCC's fund level, on the proposal of the UN Secretary-General.

In support of its requests to the UN for more lenient treatment, the Iraqi Government, on 29 April 1991, took the unprecedented step of submitting a report on its external debt position.

This showed that at the end of 1990 outstanding debts totalled $43,320m., excluding interest already due (of some $32,350m.) and what Iraq termed 'grants' from other Gulf states (estimated at between $30,000m. and $40,000m.). The report calculated that a total of $75,450m. would be required to service the debt in the 1991–95 period (during which 97% of the outstanding amount fell due) and that the foreign currency requirement for imports, development and reconstruction would total $140,000m. Export earnings over this period were forecast at $65,455m., on the assumption of progress to approaching pre-war oil export levels by 1993, so that an overall external deficit of $150,000m. was expected to accumulate by 1995. Western analysts noted that these calculations were based on the conservative assumption of a constant nominal price for crude petroleum of $16 per barrel. They nevertheless agreed that, if any substantial proportion of Iraqi oil revenues was diverted to war reparations in this period, an even greater deficit would accumulate and that the other commitment categories would not be fulfilled as specified.

In the event, Iraqi resistance to full observance of the UN cease-fire resolution terms meant that the UN embargo was still in force in late 1998. Moreover, UN Security Council Resolutions 706 and 712 of 16 August and 19 September 1991 respectively, authorizing Iraq to export oil to the value of $1,600m. to pay for emergency food and medical imports, were not immediately utilized by Iraq, which claimed that the stringent terms attached thereto amounted to an infringement of the country's sovereignty. The Security Council's decision was prompted by an FAO study of Iraq, warning that a 'widespread and acute food supply crisis' threatened 'massive starvation throughout the country', and describing the effects of the economic blockade as 'alarming'. Iraq's rejection of Resolutions 706 and 712 was reaffirmed in February 1994 by a government spokesman, who said that no oil would be sold on terms which constituted 'a flagrant violation of Iraq's sovereignty'. UN Security Council Resolution 986 of 14 April 1995 extended a revised offer to Iraq to permit the supervised export of petroleum to the value of $2,000m. over a period of 180 days, with the possibility of further 180-day renewals thereafter. Revised monitoring arrangements would allow limited use of Iraq's Gulf export facilities (rather than requiring all the petroleum to be piped via Turkey), while the UN would be more flexible than previously proposed in its monitoring of the distribution of the humanitarian supplies to be purchased with 50% of the permitted petroleum export income. Some 30% of the revenue would be allocated to war reparations, and most of the remaining 20% to UN relief work in northern Iraq. Initially Iraq rejected the scheme, objecting in particular to the use of petroleum income to fund relief work in the predominantly Kurdish north, a proposal which the Government interpreted as 'part of a UN plan to dissect Iraqi sovereignty and establish secession in the north'.

Countries which 'unfroze' part of the Iraqi assets under their jurisdiction included the United Kingdom (in November 1991) and Italy (in January 1992). Such relaxations enabled Iraq to import some urgently-needed items, although the country relied mainly on overland supplies, in breach of UN sanctions. According to a US report of January 1992, substantial 'seepage' through the sanctions net had resulted in Iraq being able to import goods worth some $2,000m. since the end of the war, representing about 25% of the pre-crisis level.

During the first half of 1993 it was clear that Iraq's economic position was rapidly deteriorating; hyperinflation in the market prices of most goods, including basic foodstuffs, was accompanied by a collapse in the value of the currency and sharp rises in unemployment and destitution. Even in the central regions, where the Government was most concerned to underpin minimum living standards, growing numbers of people lacked the means to supplement the official ration of subsidized staple foods. Increases in this ration entitlement in early 1993 raised its estimated calorific value to about two-thirds of the minimum subsistence level defined by UN humanitarian agencies. The Government claimed in March 1993 that nearly 234,000 people, including 83,000 children under the age of five, had died 'as a result of sanctions' between August 1990 and January 1993, over which period the provision of basic health care had been compromised by an 85% shortfall in medical supplies. A UNICEF report estimated that Iraq's infant mortality rate had tripled over this period. Subsequent reports from UN agencies re-emphasized the human costs of the situation. The FAO and the World Food Programme issued a statement on 26 May 1994 describing present-day Iraq as a country crippled by 'massive deprivation, chronic hunger, endemic under-nutrition for the vast majority of the population, collapse of personal incomes and rapidly increasing numbers of destitute people'. In September the World Food Programme announced a six-month emergency programme to supply over 100,000 tons of food aid to 1.3m. people in Iraq at a cost of $33.6m. In May 1995 the UN agencies monitoring Iraq's economic crisis estimated that about 4m. Iraqis currently depended on the basic state food ration, that at least 1m. of these experienced chronic hunger, and that about 23% of children under the age of five were suffering from malnutrition. A $183.3m. UN aid programme for Iraqi civilians was proposed for the 12 months to March 1996 to alleviate hunger, to support health, water, sanitation and educational projects and to resettle displaced families. By October 1995, however, less than $40m. had been pledged to this relief programme by donors.

By the end of May 1994 (two months before its scheduled closing date for claims) the UNCC had received claims totalling $81,000m. (including $15,000m. claimed by the Kuwait Government). The UNCC's resources at this time totalled about $43m., derived from frozen Iraqi assets and voluntary contributions by Saudi Arabia and the USA. These resources were expected to be significantly depleted by payments to priority claimants, namely individuals who had been severely injured and families of those who had been killed. The first awards in this category (to 670 persons from 16 countries) were approved on 26 May and totalled $2.7m.

It was estimated that funds held in the escrow account established under Security Council Resolution 778 (see 'Finance and Banking' section below) might be sufficient to meet an estimated $150m. in claims by workers forced to leave Kuwait as a result of the invasion, and might also cover the slightly lower estimate for aggregate claims by individuals who had suffered personal losses of up to $100,000, including loss of earnings or assets held in Kuwait. However, the claims which made up the greater part of the total—those submitted by governments and businesses and by individuals with losses exceeding $100,000—stood no chance of even partial settlement while the intended funding mechanism remained inoperable for want of any Iraqi oil revenues to appropriate.

In early April 1996 the World Food Programme made an urgent appeal to donor countries for $162m. of emergency food supplies for Iraq. On 20 May, at the conclusion of four rounds of talks over a period of four months, the Iraqi Government signed a memorandum of understanding accepting the terms of UN Security Council Resolution 986 of April 1995. Having taken this step, Iraq was required to agree a detailed implementation plan with the UN sanctions committee. The UN subsequently came under pressure from the USA to establish strong supervisory mechanisms at every stage of the proposed export, import and distribution activities. The USA was particularly concerned to ensure that the UN applied a very narrow definition of humanitarian supplies in order to prevent the import of items that could be diverted to other uses.

An implementation plan was eventually approved by the UN sanctions committee in early August 1996, and it was expected that all the required procedures and personnel would be established by mid-September. However, the new crisis in US–Iraqi relations at the start of September 1996 (see History) caused a temporary suspension of UN preparatory work within Iraq, and it was not until late November that arrangements to monitor oil sales under the terms of Resolution 986 were completed. Production of oil for export under UN supervision began on 10 December 1996. The export of some $2,000m.-worth of oil was to be permitted over a period of 180 days, and all proceeds were to be paid into a special UN escrow account in New York. Of the $2,000m., $20m. was allocated for the operation of the escrow account, $44.32m. for UN operational and administrative costs, $15m. for UNSCOM (tasked with verifying compliance with cease-fire conditions) and $600m. for the UNCC's fund for war reparations. This left $1,320.68m. available for spending on humanitarian supplies, of which $260m. was assigned for UN co-ordinated relief programme in Kurdish-controlled areas

of Iraq and $1,060.68m.—for supplies to the remainder of Iraq. Some 61% of total humanitarian spending was allocated for imports of foodstuffs, 16% for medicines and 8% for soaps and detergents. Priority imports for the electricity, agricultural and educational sectors accounted for 11% of authorized humanitarian spending, compared with 3% for water and sanitation services and 1% for health infrastructure and nutrition. By mid-March 1997, the UN had approved a total of 39 oil export contracts and had received $719m. of deposits in the relevant escrow account, of which $473m. had been allocated to humanitarian supplies. The UNCC used its first allowance of oil export revenues to pay a total of $144m. to 57,636 claimants from 63 countries on 1 March 1997. The first shipment of humanitarian goods arrived in Iraq on 25 March, by which time more than 100 international inspectors had been appointed to monitor the distribution process. In May 1997 the Iraqi Government accused the USA of seeking to 'delay and disrupt' deliveries of humanitarian supplies, including medicines and ambulances, by challenging the validity of many of the import contracts submitted by Iraq for UN approval. It was subsequently stated that more than 40 'medical contracts' (including an order for agricultural pesticides) were being delayed by the UN sanctions committee in response to US insistence.

By the end of May 1997, shortly before the expiry of the first 180-day 'oil-for-food' arrangement, the UN had processed approximately $2,110m.-worth of oil export contracts, had received nearly $1,750m. in oil sales revenues and had issued a total of $466m. of bank credits to pay for humanitarian supplies. The renewal of the arrangement for a further 180 days was unanimously approved by the UN Security Council on 5 June. However, Iraq suspended its UN-supervised oil exports at the start of the renewal period in protest at the slow rate of delivery of humanitarian supplies under existing arrangements. The Government intended to maintain the suspension until a more satisfactory distribution plan was implemented. Cumulative food deliveries to Iraq under Resolution 986 amounted to around 1m. tons by early July. In that month Iraq submitted a new distribution plan, and, following UN approval, it recommenced exports of petroleum in mid-August.

The 'oil-for-food' arrangement was renewed in December 1997, and revised in February 1998, after the UN Security Council approved a plan to increase Iraq's export entitlement to $5,200m., of which $3,550m. was to be spent on humanitarian goods and $1,650m. was to finance reparations and UN operations. Exports were expected to increase following agreement on a new distribution programme between Iraq and the UN, which was duly approved at the end of May. The programme did not cover Iraq's full export entitlement, owing to Iraqi claims that it could not fulfil the quota unless essential repairs to oil installations were made. The distribution plan provided for oil exports of up to $4,500m. over six months, if oil production facilities were upgraded; of this amount, $3,100m. would be used to purchase humanitarian goods. In mid-June the UN Security Council unanimously approved a resolution allowing Iraq to purchase $300m.-worth of equipment for its oil industry. In early July the Iraqi Minister of Oil announced that 40 contracts for oil equipment worth $50m. had been awarded.

The UNCC had received about $400m. of oil export revenues by late April 1997, enabling it to settle many of the individual and small claims and to make plans for substantial payments in the second half of the year (although the disbursement schedule had to be modified because of Iraq's suspension of oil exports in June 1997). Meanwhile, the UNCC was beginning its evaluation of the corporate claims (numbering more than 6,000) which accounted for the bulk of the reparations being sought from Iraq. About one-half of the claims were by bodies in Kuwait, including the Kuwait Oil Company, whose entitlement in respect of the cost of extinguishing oilfield fires started by Iraqi troops was provisionally assessed by the UNCC at $613m. (plus interest). The home countries of non-Kuwaiti corporate claimants included the United Kingdom (451 claimants), Egypt (450), Germany (314) and the USA (152).

A survey carried out in April 1997 by the World Food Programme, UNICEF and the Iraqi Ministry of Health found that 27% of Iraq's child population of five years of age and less were affected by chronic malnutrition. In September the Minister of Health, Umeed Madhat Mubarak, claimed that sanctions had dramatically increased the mortality rate of Iraqi citizens: the rate for children under five years of age had increased from an annual average of 506 per month in the pre-war years to an annual average of 6,500 per month following the imposition of sanctions. Likewise, the death rate of those over five years of age had increased from a yearly average of 1,600 per month before the sanctions to 8,000 per month in the period after their implementation.

AGRICULTURE AND FOOD

Despite the increasing dominance of oil and gas production, the Government continued, through the 1980s, to allocate substantial resources to the development of agriculture, with the aim of achieving food self-sufficiency and even surpluses for export. At the same time, state control of the agricultural sector was steadily relaxed in favour of allowing a greater role for private initiative and for private-sector investment from both Iraqi and other Arab sources. The total area under cultivation rose from 3.2m. ha in 1984 to about 3.7m. in 1989, it being estimated that a further 20% increase was required to achieve self-sufficiency. Like the rest of the economy, however, agriculture suffered major disruption in the Gulf crisis and hostilities of 1990–91, one consequence of which was a return to state control and direction.

Until the 1958 revolution, agricultural improvement was often inhibited by the need for adequate land reform. In October 1958 the incoming Government announced a new and more radical land reform project. This provided for the break-up of large estates whose owners were to be compelled to forfeit their 'excess' land to the Government, which would redistribute the land to new peasant owners. Landowners losing land were to be compensated in state bonds (in 1969 all the state's liabilities to recompense land-owners were cancelled). It was hoped that the reform would take only five years to complete but the application of the law was initially mismanaged: expropriation of land was administered much faster than its redistribution. By the end of 1972 some 4.73m. dunums (1 dunum = 0.25 ha approx.) had been requisitioned from landlords and allocated to 100,646 families. By 1988, more than 300,000 families had received 10.8m. dunums. The Government has been promoting the growth of co-operatives and collective farms since 1967. By the end of 1987 there were 857 agricultural co-operatives, with a total of 376,329 members. In 1984 there were 23 state farms, covering 188,000 ha. By 1996 the percentage of the labour force engaged in agriculture had decreased to 10.7%, compared with 50% in 1965 and 53% in 1960.

Government awareness that the rate of progress in the agricultural sector had been disappointing encouraged measures to be taken to allow greater private involvement in agriculture. By 1986, the land area occupied by state farms had fallen to only 52,925 ha, and by 1988 more than 220,000 ha had been leased—a total investment estimated at ID 72m.—as a result of the 1983 law enabling local and other Arab companies or individuals to lease land at nominal rates. Other incentives included encouragement for agriculturists and graduates working for the Ministry of Agriculture and Agrarian Reform to take up farming, and there was a more liberal attitude towards profit-making. Farmers could now bypass the state marketing system and sell direct, either to public wholesale markets or to private shops which were licensed for wholesale trade. Higher procurement prices were now paid by the state. These concessions were intended to ease supply difficulties, and to encourage local farmers.

In May 1987 came belated recognition of criticism voiced in 1982, at the Baath Party regional congress, that state intervention had often proved more of a hindrance than a help to small farms, and that state and collective farms were frequently unprofitable. It was announced that all state farms (including six dairy farms) were for sale or lease to local or Arab investors or companies, providing that the land continues to be used for agriculture. In July 1987 the Ministry of Agriculture and Agrarian Reform was reorganized, and in September the ministry was merged with the Ministry of Irrigation to become the Ministry of Agriculture and Irrigation.

A wide variety of crops is grown but the most important are barley and wheat. Production estimates vary considerably. In the case of wheat, annual output fluctuated around 950,000 metric tons in the 1980s, although drought severely affected

the 1984 crop, which slumped to 471,000 tons. A good crop is dependent on favourable rains, and 1996 saw an estimated 1.0m. tons of wheat produced, while barley production was estimated at 500,000 tons, compared with 743,000 tons in 1987.

Other crops are rice, vegetables, maize and millet, sugar cane and beet, oil seeds, pulses, dates and other fruits (the main fruit being melon), fodder, tobacco and cotton. Drought caused production to fall in 1984, but output recovered after 1986. In 1996 Iraq produced an estimated 270,000 metric tons of paddy rice and 85,000 tons of maize, compared with 196,000 tons and 61,000 tons respectively in 1987. Total vegetable output (including cabbages, spinach, carrots, tomatoes, okra, beans, cauliflowers and potatoes), which had been about 3m. tons per year in 1982 and 1983, fell to an estimated 1.8m. tons in 1984. In 1996 production of vegetables was estimated at 2.3m. tons.

Production of dates, the country's main export after petroleum, was also affected by drought. During 1983–88 production of dates averaged 350,000 tons per year. Iraq had about 29m. date palms in 1987, compared with 25m. in 1985. In 1986/87 some 150,000 metric tons were exported to Japan, France, Canada, India and to Arab and Asian countries. Exports rose to 163,000 tons in 1988/89, and to 373,000 tons (worth $75m.) in 1989/90. Dates are not only a lucrative export, but are also being put to industrial use. Several years ago, the former Ministry of Industry and Minerals started a major programme to produce sugar, dry sugar alcohol, vinegar and concentrated protein from dates. Such factories together with the private sector, will use up to 100,000 tons of dates per year when operating at full capacity. As part of the Government's programme for economic reform, a new mixed-sector company, the Iraqi Date Processing and Marketing Company (IDPMC), was established to replace the Iraqi Dates Commission, which was formerly responsible for production and marketing. Deliveries to the IDPMC in the 1990/91 season were estimated at 350,000 tons. Production of dates was estimated at 550,000 tons in 1996.

The livestock and poultry sector was developed in the 1980s with the assistance of Dutch, British, West German and Hungarian companies. Iraq's annual output of eggs was 1,274m. in 1988, almost enough to meet local demand which is estimated at about 1,350m. eggs per year. White meat production amounted to 199,000 tons in 1988. A significant decline in livestock products was witnessed in the mid-1990s, owing to reduced production of animal feed. A report compiled by UN and US sources stated that domestic production of meat, milk and eggs during 1993–96 was less than 50% of levels of output recorded in 1990.

Provision has also been made to develop a fishing industry and the private sector has been encouraged to establish fish farms on many of the lakes and reservoirs which have been created by the construction of new dams. In 1995 catches of freshwater fish were estimated at 19,000 tons, while the marine fish catch was estimated at 4,000 tons.

Aid to farmers is channelled through the Agricultural Co-operative Bank, which loaned ID 570m. over the period 1980–87 and increased its lending after the cease-fire in the Iran–Iraq War. To encourage farmers to use its services, the bank offers a low interest rate and has raised its maximum credit limit.

The country's food import bill, which reached $3,100m. in 1984, declined to $2,712m. in 1986, and remains at about $2,500m. per year. The USA was formerly a major agricultural supplier, retaining a large share of the market under a credit programme. The EC (European Community, now European Union—EU) supplied some $345m. worth of farm products in 1986, equivalent to a 12.7% market share, compared with 16% in 1984. Canada and Australia were long-term wheat suppliers. Cuba is a long-standing sugar supplier and Thailand supplies rice.

Following the implementation of UN economic sanctions against Iraq in August 1990, the Government announced the introduction, from 1 September, of rationing for flour, tea, sugar and rice; other items, such as cooking oil, children's milk and salt, were later added to the list. The Government also steadily raised the official purchase prices for important crops, with the aim of encouraging greater production, and initiated an urgent programme to increase the cultivated area, especially in northern Iraq. From October it became compulsory for cereal farmers to deliver their output to state collection centres within two weeks of harvesting. The Government also took emergency powers to confiscate land from farmers who failed to fulfil production quotas, and from November it introduced the death penalty for hoarding of cereals. According to Iraqi officials, the 1990 cereal harvest was the best for several years, including nearly 1.2m. tons of wheat (an increase of 75% compared with 1989), more than 1.8m. tons of barley and 500,000 tons of rice. These figures were, however, questioned by US government officials, who estimated that Iraq would need to import some 1.75m. tons of grain in 1991 to feed its population.

The combined effect of rationing, increased local production, use of reserves and imports through Jordan was to prevent the development of serious food shortages in Iraq until the outbreak of actual hostilities in January 1991, although prices rose steeply. Thereafter, the devastation resulting from allied bombing seriously disrupted not only agricultural production but also food distribution, and food stocks declined to a record low in the war's immediate aftermath. On 23 March the UN Security Council's sanctions committee eased restrictions on food exports to Iraq, following which several countries agreed in principle to resume supplies. However, the continuing UN embargo on Iraqi petroleum exports rendered payment for imported food problematical, even though the UN committee decided, on 9 May, to 'unfreeze' sufficient Iraqi assets to pay for emergency food and medical supplies (see Consequences of the 1990–91 Gulf Crisis, above).

As part of its post-war reconstruction plans, the Government launched a national agricultural campaign on 12 April 1991, involving new incentives for farmers, priority allocation of fuel and machinery, and the creation of a special ministerial committee to supervise the 1991 harvest and to maintain the state's monopoly of food sales. The emergency six-month reconstruction budget, announced on 2 May, included provision for substantial state subsidies on cereal production in order to reduce consumer prices.

An FAO report of August 1991 found that Iraq would have to spend about $500m. to restore the country's agricultural output. The FAO estimated the 1991 grain harvest at only 1.25m. tons, about a third of the 1990 yield, while other crops, as well as the livestock and poultry sectors, had been devastated by the war. Prospects of speedy recovery were regarded as bleak, in that seed stocks were deficient and much of the sector's machinery and irrigation system were out of commission. The Iraqi Minister of Agriculture, speaking in May 1992, estimated that 50% of the country's cereal and seed stocks had been destroyed during the 1991 war, as had 95% of the breeding stock of the poultry and livestock industry. Efforts by the Government to import food supplies included the signing of agreements with Thailand (for rice), Malaysia (for palm oil), Sri Lanka (for tea), France and Australia (for wheat) and Morocco (various items).

In July 1993 the FAO estimated that Iraq's food import requirement for the coming year would amount to 5.4m. tons, valued at $2,500m. FAO experts said that the threat of famine was exacerbated by the prolonged deadlock over utilization of the emergency petroleum export quota authorized by the UN Security Council on humanitarian grounds in summer 1991. Western observers had earlier reported that the Government had started using gold reserves to fund essential food imports in the latter part of 1992, having virtually exhausted its hard-currency resources.

The execution in July 1992 of 42 merchants accused of 'profiteering' served only to intensify the problem of persistent food price inflation, as a consequent drop in the volume of trade with Jordan added further scarcity value to items in short supply. The market prices of such staple items as wheat flour reached up to 500 times their mid-1990 levels at some points during the first half of 1993, while the estimated ratio between the average urban wage and the average market price of a typical family's food requirements widened from about 1:3 to 1:9 between April and July 1993.

Following increases in January and April 1993, the monthly ration of state-subsidized foodstuffs comprised 9 kg of flour, 2.25 kg of rice, 1.75 kg of cooking-oil and 1.5 kg of sugar. The Government implicitly acknowledged the seriousness of the food supply situation when it distributed an extra month's rations (in September 1992), brought forward a scheduled distribution date (in February 1993) and announced a supplementary Ram-

adan distribution of one chicken per family (in March 1993). So-called 'economic crime squads' were established in March 1993 to enforce harsh laws against overcharging for price-controlled basic foods.

Efficient administration of the rationing system was reported throughout most of Iraq, with the main exceptions in government-controlled Kurdish areas to the south of the Kurdish-controlled 'safe havens'. The availability of subsidized supplies in these areas was assessed to represent no more than 10% of the ration entitlement. There were also reports of some supply shortfalls in southern cities, attributed by Shi'a spokesmen to a government policy of moving food-processing operations and storage facilities out of the southern air exclusion zone.

The prices of a wide range of food items outside the rationing system, including meat, eggs and dairy produce, exceeded the budget of the average Iraqi worker in mid-1993. Government efforts to stimulate domestic food production included price incentives for farmers to sell staple crops through state marketing channels, coupled with penalties for such offences as failing to harvest crops.

There were reports in May 1993 that Kurdish farmers were being harassed by troops based in Iraqi-controlled cities south of the Kurds' northern 'safe haven', but it was not clear whether there was any systematic government campaign to commandeer local agricultural production. Within the Kurdish-controlled 'safe haven', there was a heavy dependence on international relief supplies in mid-1993, when early efforts to rebuild local agriculture were being hampered by shortages of fertilizer and other inputs. Agricultural rehabilitation projects and the provision of food supplements remained high on the UN's list of aid priorities for the 'safe haven' in 1994.

Against a background of worsening hyperinflation, the Iraqi Government ordered the official rations of rice, cooking-oil and tea (but not flour or sugar) to be increased by up to one-third from February 1994. However, supplies of food to supplement the still-meagre ration were priced even further beyond the reach of most wage-earners as the depreciation of the Iraqi dinar accelerated in subsequent months. By mid-May the average monthly salary of a schoolteacher would buy about 800 g of meat, or 21 eggs or 70 centilitres of cooking oil, at current market prices. It was not unusual for middle-class households to sell or barter valuable possessions in order to buy food, while Iraq's crime rate (once very low by regional standards) increased dramatically as theft became a major problem.

In early May 1994 the Government announced that the theft of goods worth more than ID 5,000 (about $12 at the prevailing unofficial exchange rate) would henceforth be punishable by the amputation of a hand, while in early June branches of the Baath Party were empowered to incarcerate shopkeepers or traders who violated official price guidelines. The Minister of Agriculture was dismissed on 25 May for having 'failed to check the rise in food prices', and on 22 June the Government banned the import of many foodstuffs, including canned meat, fish, eggs, potatoes, spaghetti and chicken, in order to conserve foreign exchange. Traders who failed to clear their shelves of banned goods within two months would be subject to 'stringent penalties'. The Iraqi business community was urged to make voluntary financial contributions to the Government (repayable after the lifting of UN sanctions) to finance government food imports. Public-sector wages, pensions and allowances were increased from July, bringing little real benefit against a background of spiralling price inflation. In September the Government reduced the monthly ration of basic foodstuffs to 6 kg of flour, 1.25 kg of rice, 750 g of sugar and 625 g of cooking-oil, prompting a wave of panic buying which caused the market prices of many commodities to double in a matter of days. Public-sector incomes were again increased by amounts which barely kept pace with inflation. By early November rice was selling for ID 350 per kg and flour for ID 450 per kg in the shops, while the average civil service salary was ID 2,500 per month. By the end of January 1995, when the average civil service salary was ID 3,000 per month, meat was selling for around ID 1,150 per kg, while the price of a litre of imported vegetable oil had reached a similar level. Six months later an average civil service salary of ID 3,500 per month was sufficient to buy 38 eggs at prevailing market prices. Subsequent pay rises of 70% for military personnel and 50% for civil servants were expected to fuel a further round of price inflation. According to UN estimates, average shop prices of essential commodities stood at 850 times their July 1990 level in July 1995.

In October 1995 the Government announced increases in the monthly rations of flour (from 6 kg to 7 kg) and vegetable oil (from 625 g to 750 g), giving no explanation for the availability of additional supplies at this time. Estimates published by the FAO in April 1996 gave Iraq's 1994/95 cereal production as 2.2m. tons (20% less than in 1993/94 and 25% below the average for the previous five years). The cost of Iraq's basic food import requirements in 1995/96 was estimated by the FAO at $2,700m. Iraq's estimated wheat imports totalled 933,000 tons in 1993/94 and around 1m. tons in 1994/95, compared with an annual average of 3.1m. tons in the four years preceding the imposition of UN trade sanctions. The severity of Iraq's food supply crisis was believed to be the main motivating factor behind the Government's January 1996 decision to seek an early agreement on limited oil exports. Food prices within Iraq (which could be expected to stabilize after implementation of such an agreement) became subject to violent fluctuation during the first half of 1996 as traders responded to every reported development in the negotiations taking place at UN headquarters in New York.

The arrival in March 1997 of Iraq's first food imports under the long-delayed 'oil-for-food' scheme had a dramatic effect on local market prices, causing immediate reductions of up to 45% for eggs and 33% for flour and meat. In April the Government increased the monthly flour ration to 9 kg, while in May the rice ration was raised to 2 kg and the cooking-oil ration to 1 kg. In July the monthly rice ration was further increased to 2.5 kg and the ration of pulses was doubled from 500 g to 1 kg. Other ration entitlements in July included 2 kg of sugar, 150 g of tea, 250 g of soap, 350 g of detergent and 150 g of table salt. It was reported in mid-1997 that Iraqi cereal growers had been guaranteed 'above-market' crop prices by the Government in order to protect them from the impact of resumed food imports.

In May 1998 the Government reduced the monthly ration of basic foodstuffs, citing slow distribution of aid under the 'oil-for-food' agreement as the reason for the cuts. The new rations included 100 g of tea, 625 g of cooking-oil and 150 g of pulses.

A survey of Iraqi agricultural output over the period 1990–96 (based on US and UN estimates) indicated a decrease in yields of poultry and livestock products to less than one-half of the 1990 level, from 1993 onwards. This was due to a lack of local and imported animal feed, coupled with reductions in local output of animal feed as greater priority was given to crops for human consumption. Recent poor cereal crops (see above) were attributed in part to a lack of pesticides which had caused yields to decline at a rate faster than that by which farmers had increased the areas planted. However, total grain production in 1996 was estimated to have recovered to 3.3m. tons (95% of the 1990 level) following a good harvest. Within the Kurdish-controlled areas of Iraq, grain production exceeded local consumption by an estimated 100,000 tons per year from 1994 onwards, and in 1996 the Baghdad authorities agreed to supply electricity, fuel and rice to these areas in exchange for Kurdish farmers' surplus grain. In 1995 Iraq produced an estimated 870,000 tons of tomatoes (up from 722,000 tons in 1990) following a policy decision to devote irrigated land primarily to vegetable production. Production of potatoes reached 420,000 tons in 1995 (compared with 167,000 tons in 1991), while date production was 600,000 tons in 1995 (more than 50% higher than in the 1980s). Barley, previously regarded as an animal feed, was used as a supplementary ingredient in bread-making as supplies of wheat-flour diminished during the first half of the 1990s. In 1996 the average daily calorific intake of Iraqis was thought to be about 30% below its 1990 level. According to international aid organizations, at least 2.15m. Iraqis were receiving less than 50% of their calorific requirement in 1996.

RIVER CONTROL AND IRRIGATION

River control policy in Iraq has three main objectives: the provision of water for irrigation, the prevention of devastating floods, and the creation of hydroelectric power. An extensive dam-building programme has been instituted on the River Tigris and its tributaries in northern Iraq, with the aim of using stored water to irrigate land which has traditionally been rain-fed.

However, such installations were among those which suffered serious damage and dislocation in the 1991 Gulf hostilities.

When operational, the main systems providing flow irrigation are based in the Euphrates (serving nearly 3m. dunums), the Tigris (1.7m. dunums), the Diyalah river and the Lesser Zab river. Pumps are used extensively along both the Euphrates and the Tigris. A series of dams, barrages or reservoirs (at Samarra, Dokan, Derbendi Khan, and Habbaniya) provide security against flood dangers. When the waters of the Euphrates and Tigris are fully utilized through dams and reservoirs, the area of cultivated land in Iraq will be almost doubled.

After delays during the Iran–Iraq War, the Government evinced renewed determination to proceed with its programme of water control and storage. In the summer of 1984 the Government was able to release stored water to farmers, to offset the low levels of the Euphrates. It was hoped that the completion of the Mosul (on the Tigris) and Haditha (on the Euphrates) dams (renamed the Saddam and Qadisiya dams) would ease concern over Syrian and Turkish dam-building plans for the upper reaches of the Tigris and Euphrates, which were expected to reduce the flow of water significantly. The Qadisiya dam and its associated 600-MW hydroelectric power plant were opened in 1986. By 1990, however, the distribution of these water resources had become a fundamental issue in Iraq's relations with Syria and Turkey, following Turkey's diversion of the Euphrates in order to fill the reservoir of its new Atatürk dam. Discussions between Iraq, Syria and Turkey, held in June 1990, failed to resolve the issue, and Iraq subsequently announced that future water shortages might create the need for water rationing. In early 1993 Turkey appointed a German-led consortium to implement a major hydroelectric project at Birecik on the Euphrates. Iraq, which had condemned this project as an infringement of its water rights under international law, announced its intention to take legal action against the contractors.

In September 1986 a $1,485m.-contract to build the Bekme dam, in the north-east, 40 km from the Iranian border, on the Greater Zab, a tributary of the Tigris, was awarded to a joint venture of Turkey's Enka and Yugoslavia's Hidrogradnja companies. Work on the dam commenced in 1987, and the first phase of the diversion of the Greater Zab had been completed by June 1990. In November 1990 the Bekme dam was renamed 'Al-Faris' (Knight), an appellation which the Iraqi media often used for Saddam Hussain. Another Yugoslav company, Energoprojekt, was chosen to design dams at Badush, also on the Tigris, and at Mandawa, on the Greater Zab. There are also plans to construct dams at Taqtaq, Dujala and Farha. River control projects are also under way at Hindiya, Kifl-Shinafiya and Baghdadi.

In December 1983 the 87,500-ha first stage of the massive Kirkuk irrigation project (now renamed Saddam) was opened. More than 300,000 ha will eventually be irrigated at a cost of more than ID 1,000m. Contracts have been awarded to Chinese and South Korean companies to work on the North Jazira irrigation project, which will be fed with water stored by the Saddam dam; and to local and international companies for work on the East Jazira irrigation project, involving the installation of irrigation networks on more than 70,000 ha of rain-fed land near Mosul. These projects are part of an ID 820m.-scheme to irrigate 250,000 ha of the Jazira plain. South of Baghdad, completed land reclamation schemes include Lower Khalis, Diwaniya-Dalmaj, Ishaqi, Dujaila and much of Abu Ghraib. The massive Dujaila project is intended to produce about 22% of Iraq's output of crop and animal products. Consultants have designed irrigation schemes for Kifl-Shinafiya, East Gharraf, Saba Nissan, New Rumaitha, Zubair, Bastora, Greater Musayyib and Makhmour. The project's main outfall canal, completed in December 1992, is known as the 'third river'. It runs for 565 km from Mahmudiya, south of Baghdad, to Qurna, north of Basra, and carries saline water (flushed away from 1.5m. ha of reclaimed land) to an outlet on the Gulf.

A 120-km 'fourth river', designed to irrigate an area of 250,000 ha, and the 140-km Qadisiyah canal, branching off from the Euphrates and designed to irrigate an area of 125,000 ha, were under construction in early 1993. Political opponents of the Iraqi Government claimed that this major programme of irrigation works, together with a number of drainage schemes in the southern marshes in 1992/93, was partly aimed at Shi'ite dissidents living in the area. However, the Government was able to provide numerous economic justifications for its policy (including, on the issue of marsh drainage, the fact that the area contained large untapped petroleum reserves).

Since 60% of Iraq's land area has no access to the major river irrigation schemes, a programme of well-drilling has been initiated under the direction of the State Co for Water Wells Drilling (SCWWD). In November 1990 the SCWWD announced that it had drilled 1,615 wells and supplied 1,159 pumps since its creation in 1987.

In the war with the multinational force in 1991, several dams were hit in the bombing campaign, but the wholesale dislocation of the country's river control and irrigation systems was mainly attributable to the multinational force's destruction of Iraq's power supply network. Restoration of such installations to proper functioning became a major priority of the Government's post-war reconstruction programme, as did restoration of drinking water supplies and sewerage systems in Baghdad and other major cities. Many of the failures of urban sewerage systems in 1992/93 were attributed to shortages of imported spare parts for pump motors. The UN Development Programme (UNDP), which had a $4m.-budget for projects in Iraq, said in June 1994 that $1m. had been allocated for the rehabilitation of two major sewage plants in Baghdad and $1m. for the repair of water treatment plants in southern population centres. Serious sewerage breakdowns and contamination of water supplies continued to be reported in Iraqi towns and cities in 1998. In mid-1998 the UK Department for International Development announced that it was financing a $3.2m. project to improve water and sanitation.

PETROLEUM AND NATURAL GAS

Following the nationalization of the hydrocarbons sector in the early 1970s, Iraq rapidly increased its output of crude petroleum, becoming, by 1979, the world's second largest exporter, after Saudi Arabia. Production in 1979 totalled 170.6m. metric tons (compared with 83.5m. tons in 1971, the last full year before nationalization, and 47.5m. tons in 1960). Exports in 1979 and 1980 averaged 3.3m. barrels per day (b/d), producing revenues of $21,300m. and $26,300m. respectively. However, because of the outbreak of the Iran–Iraq War in September 1980, output sharply declined in 1981 and exports fell to 800,000 b/d by 1982 (worth $10,000m.), before rising to 1.4m. b/d in 1986, although lower world petroleum prices reduced revenues in that year to $7,000m. The end of the war with Iran in 1988 facilitated further recovery in production, from 127.4m. tons (2.6m. b/d) in 1988 to 138.6m. tons (2.8m. b/d) in 1989, earning export revenues of some $13,000m. and $12,000m. respectively. In the first half of 1990 production was averaging about 3.1m. b/d (almost back to the pre-1980 level) and 1990 export earnings from this source were expected to total $15,400m. However, Iraq's petroleum exports were then brought to a virtual halt by the UN embargo, imposed as a consequence of its invasion of Kuwait, and in the Gulf hostilities of early 1991 the massive damage sustained by Iraqi oil installations brought production to a standstill. Independent analysts estimated Iraq's end-1996 petroleum reserves at 112,000m. barrels (equivalent to 10.8% of total world petroleum reserves).

Iraq's petroleum industry has been highly dependent on pipelines carrying Iraqi oil through neighbouring territories or to the Gulf coast. In 1980 these were the 'strategic' reversible-flow pipeline (with a capacity of 1m. b/d) from Rumaila to Haditha and Kirkuk which links oilfields in the north and south of Iraq; a pipeline running for 980 km (609 miles) from Kirkuk, through Turkey, to Dörtyol, on the Mediterranean coast in the Gulf of İskenderun; another from Haditha, via Syria, to Tripoli, in Lebanon and Banias, in Syria; and lines running from the southern oilfields near Basra to the offshore Gulf export terminals of Mina al-Bakr and Khor al-Amaya, with capacities of 2.7m. b/d and 1.8m. b/d, respectively, which were exporting up to 2.9m. b/d before the Iran–Iraq War.

Following Iranian air raids on key installations in the early stages of the war, however, exports soon ceased from Iraq's offshore oil terminals in the Gulf, and production declined to 900,000 b/d in 1981. Refineries, pipelines, pumping stations and petrochemical plants were all damaged. Exports of petroleum

were, at first, diverted to Mediterranean ports via Iraq's reversible pipeline pumping network, but these were then brought to a halt by an explosion on the line through Turkey, reportedly the work of Kurdish guerrillas, and by Iranian bombing of the K-1 pumping station at the Kirkuk oilfield in the north.

By December 1980 petroleum exports through the Mediterranean ports had resumed but total exports consisted only of petroleum being pumped through the pipeline across Turkey at a rate of around 650,000 b/d, supplemented by 60,000 b/d–80,000 b/d transported by road to Jordan. Not all of this was for worldwide exports, however, since Turkey was taking 250,000 b/d as its entitlement under the pipeline transit agreement. Preference for sales was given to countries which were major customers for Iraqi petroleum before the war and which had suffered most from the cessation of petroleum exports in the fourth quarter of 1980. These included Japan and France.

Pumping through the Banias pipeline resumed in early December 1981, despite tense political relations between Iraq and Syria and the Iraqi decision of April 1976 to suspend deliveries through the pipeline because of a dispute over transit fees and other political issues. The long period of disuse limited the throughput to 350,000 b/d, compared with the full capacity of 1.4m. b/d, and pumping soon halted, not to be resumed until the end of February 1982. On 10 April 1982, however, Syria closed the pipeline, depriving Iraq of a possible $17m. per day in revenues and leaving the Turkish pipeline as Iraq's only outlet for petroleum exports. The loss of the Gulf terminals and the vulnerability of the Turkish and Syrian pipelines forced Iraq to consider alternative pipelines.

To complement the pipeline through Turkey, which was pumping about 1m. b/d by mid-1987, the Government decided to build new export pipelines across Turkey (to run parallel to the existing line), Saudi Arabia and Jordan. In September 1984 a $507m.-order to build the first (640 km) phase of the Saudi Arabian project (IPSA-1)—to link Iraq's southern oilfields with Saudi Arabia's east-west Petroline to the terminal at Yanbu—was awarded to an Italian consortium, led by Saipem and including France's Spie-Capag. The French and Italian Governments provided credit to support the project, and the contractors agreed to accept Iraqi petroleum in part-payment. The spur line began pumping in September 1985. Although Japanese and Indian customers were secured, throughput was limited to 350,000 b/d–400,000 b/d by the Saudi Arabian Government. In March 1987, however, Saudi Arabia agreed to allow Iraq to export petroleum through its terminal at Yanbu at the spur line's full capacity of 500,000 b/d, on condition that it charged OPEC's official prices for crude. The second phase (IPSA-2), for which a contract was awarded in September 1987 to a consortium led by Italian and Japanese companies, envisaged an independent 970-km Iraqi pipeline (with a capacity of 1.15m. b/d) across Saudi Arabia, parallel to the Saudi line, to a new export terminal on the Red Sea coast, near Yanbu, providing a total throughput via Saudi Arabia of 1.65m. b/d.

A consortium of Italian and Turkish companies began work in February 1986 on the second 980-km trans-Turkey line, parallel to the existing line from Kirkuk to the Mediterranean port of Yumurtalık in Turkey. With a capacity of 500,000 b/d, this boosted total possible exports through Turkey to 1.5m. b/d, when it became operational at the end of July 1987, and there were plans to double the capacity of this line. Plans for an oil pipeline to Aqaba, in Jordan, were suspended in 1984, as Iraq could secure no guarantee of compensation from the US Bechtel Corpn, the project's managing contractor, for loss of earnings in the event of Israeli sabotage of the pipeline, which would have terminated near the Israeli border. In April 1987 Turkey and Iraq agreed plans to construct a third trans-Turkish pipeline, with a capacity of 70,000 b/d, from oilfields at Ain Zalah, near Mosul, to the Batman oil refinery in Turkey, a distance of 240 km. With its promised new export capacity, Iraq now had less need for the reopening of the pipeline across Syria, despite speculation in 1987 of a possible reconciliation with Damascus. When the new lines across Turkey and the two phases of the trans-Saudi Arabia development are in full operation, Iraq's export capacity will be about 3.2m. b/d. The facilities in the south, which were put out of action by the war with Iran, could provide another 3m. b/d in exports. Repair work started in March 1989, and by July tankers were lifting 200,000 b/d from the Mina al-Bakr terminal. Iraq has also exported between 100,000 b/d and 250,000 b/d of refined petroleum products by road through Jordan and Turkey. In 1986 Saudi Arabia and Kuwait, through the Arabian Oil Co which operates in the Neutral Zone, renewed an agreement whereby they sold as much as 310,000 b/d (250,000 b/d from the Zone and the remainder from Saudi Arabia), with the proceeds going to Iraq to compensate it for lost export capacity. This agreement was terminated at the end of 1988.

When war broke out with Iran in September 1980, many major oil and gas development projects were in progress. War damage was not as extensive as was originally believed, although the Basra petroleum refinery, with a capacity of 140,000 b/d, was bombed early in the war. Repair work began in 1988, and by mid-1989 the refinery was again producing oil products for export. Iraq was already short of refining capacity, so the damage to the Basra refinery had a severe impact on the domestic supply of petroleum products. The country was left with the 70,000 b/d Dawra refining facility, near Baghdad, which also came under attack, and some 100,000 b/d topping capacity at a number of other locations. At 1 January 1981 refinery capacity stood at 118,000 b/d. The 150,000 b/d north Baiji refinery (Baiji II), built by Chiyoda of Japan, was opened in 1983, complementing the 71,000 b/d Czechoslovak-built refinery (Baiji I) already in operation. In the first quarter of 1987 the Baiji lubricating oil refinery, built by Technip of France, began operations. During its first year of operations, about 70,000 tons were expected to be available for export, rising subsequently to 200,000 tons per year. Plans were also announced to quadruple refining capacity. In mid-1988 international companies submitted offers to construct a 140,000 b/d refinery south of Baghdad.

Before the outbreak of war in 1980, the West German-US consortium of Thyssen Rheinstahl Technik and C.E. Lummus completed a petrochemicals complex at Khor az-Zubair, near Basra. The plant sustained minor damage during the war, but recommissioning began in 1988, and by 1989 some units had resumed operations. The complex was intended to produce 150,000 tons per year of low- and high-density polyethylene and PVC, and 40,000 tons per year of caustic soda, using 90m. cu ft per day of natural gas as feedstock. The Government also approved plans for a second petrochemicals complex about 60 km south of Baghdad, near the planned new refinery.

Other projects in the Basra area include a gas liquefaction and treatment plant at Zubair, which was constructed by a French company, Technip, under a $239m.-'turnkey' contract, awarded in March 1980. The recommissioning of this plant began in 1989, with the intention that it would use as feedstock 6,000m. cu m of associated gas from the Rumaila oilfields to produce 4m. tons of propane and butane and 1.5m. tons per year of condensate. The plant is part of the southern gas project, which entails gathering and compression facilities that will be capable of handling 16,000m. cu m of gas per year from the Rumaila oilfields. Part of the project, a southern gas-gathering complex with the capacity to process and export as much as 4m. tons of associated gas annually, commenced operations in July 1990. A similar scheme exists in the north. Both are part of a government programme to increase its use of gas as an energy resource.

Total gas reserves, three-quarters of which are associated with oil, were estimated at 3,100,000m. cu m at 1 January 1992. Gas production rose from 5,900m. cu m in 1966 to 20,160m. cu m in 1979, but declined, owing to the war with Iran, to 5,290m. cu m in 1984. By 1986 output had recovered to 8,270m. cu m, and in 1989 it totalled 10,680m. cu m. Whereas 80% of gas production was flared in 1979, projects to make wider use of gas, particularly in industry, resulted in a decline in this proportion to 40% by 1989. Gas exports also increased, from 8.3% of production in 1986 to some 30% in 1989. Shortly before the onset of the August 1990 Gulf crisis, Petrobrás of Brazil shipped Iraq's first export cargo of liquefied petroleum gas (LPG).

In 1986 a Soviet contractor, Tsvetmetpromexport (TSMPE), was awarded a $154m.-contract to construct the first section, 345 km in length, of the trans-Iraq dry gas pipeline. This section runs from Nasiriya, in the south, to Baghdad, and will initially carry 4.2m. cu m of gas per day. TSMPE was also expected to

win the contract for the second stage of the trans-Iraq gas pipeline project, which will extend the line to the border with Turkey. After being linked to the northern gas-gathering network, the pipeline will supply a national gas grid. Eventually, power stations and industrial plants will be connected to the gas grid. At the end of 1996 Iraq's proven gas reserves totalled 3,340,000m. cu m.

In the late 1970s and early 1980s the Iraq National Oil Co (INOC), then the supreme state body exercising control over the hydrocarbons sector, pursued a programme of further exploration for oil and gas reserves. Five major fields were identified in 1981 for future development—Majnoon, Nahr-Umr, Halfaya, East Baghdad and West Qurnah. These fields are likely to increase production capacity by some 2m. b/d. Exploitation of the East Baghdad field (with estimated reserves of 5,000m. barrels) began at the end of 1984, with the award of a $60m.-contract to establish a plant to process and degas an initial 30,000 b/d to Italy's Snamprogetti and its British affiliate. Production began in April 1989, and capacity was to be eventually increased to 150,000 b/d. The main contractor at West Qurnah was Technoexport of the USSR, with TPL of Italy. The Soviet company also undertook development work at the North Rumaila field, which was producing at a rate of 500,000 b/d in 1987, compared with potential capacity of 800,000 b/d. Development of Halfaya and Nahr-Umr was delayed by the war with Iran. In the north, exploitation of the Sfaya oilfield is under way. In 1988 experimental production started at Nasiriya, Gharraf, Subba, Balad and West Tikrit. Contracts were awarded in 1988 to Technip, of France, and Mannesmann, of West Germany, to develop the Khabbaz and Saddam oilfields to produce 30,000 b/d and 45,000 b/d respectively; both came into production in 1990. The recapture from Iran of Majnoon Island and the surrounding area of the al-Hawizah marshes, in June 1988, restored to Iraq oilfields containing reserves estimated at 30,000m. barrels. Plans for a second reversible-flow pipeline, parallel to the first, 670 km in length, linking new oilfields in the south with northern petroleum installations, and capable of pumping 900,000 b/d, were announced in April 1988. Plans for a $500m.-oil-products storage complex at Khor az-Zubair have also been announced.

INOC's activities extended beyond exploration for, and production of, crude petroleum. In 1972 it established an autonomous company to be responsible for the operation and management of a tanker fleet. In May 1987, however, INOC and the Ministry of Oil were merged as part of a programme to reorganize the oil industry and make it more efficient. At the same time, a number of state organizations, hitherto responsible for, among other functions, oil-refining, distribution and industrial training, under the auspices of INOC, were removed from INOC control and converted into separate national companies, responsible to the ministry.

Iraq is one of the founder members of the Organization of the Petroleum Exporting Countries (OPEC, see p. 264). It was not required to make a reduction in its output in October 1984, when OPEC cut production by 1.5m. b/d in order to prevent a further decrease in prices on the world market, which was oversupplied with oil. With new export outlets becoming available, Iraq frequently lobbied for an increase in its OPEC production quota, while consistently exceeding its allocation. During 1986 oil prices continued to decline, falling below $10 per barrel in July. When, in August, OPEC decided to reduce production to a maximum 16.7m. b/d for two months from 1 September, effectively reverting to the quota restrictions imposed in October 1984, in order to raise petroleum prices, Iraq declined to be a party to the decision, demanding at least parity with Iran, and continued to produce as much as it could to finance its war effort. The proposal for a reduction in output was made by Iran, whose Minister of Oil said that Iran would 'act in a way to prevent Iraq getting its desired quota'. Iraq then opted out of a succession of OPEC production agreements, between October 1986 and May 1988 (though it was allocated notional quotas in each), and stated that it would continue to do so while its quota allocations were lower than those allotted to Iran, and failed to take account of Iraq's increased export capacity. For the second half of 1987 a ceiling of 16.6m. b/d was placed on OPEC production, including a notional quota for Iraq of 1.54m. b/d, compared with actual export capacity of about 2.7m. b/d in August, and the 2.37m. b/d allocated to Iran. A reference price for OPEC petroleum of $18 per barrel had been in force since February 1987. At OPEC's meeting in December 1987 Iraq declined to participate in the agreement covering production in the first half of 1988, whereby the ceiling on collective output and Iraq's notional quota were unchanged.

The cease-fire in the Iran–Iraq War prompted preliminary efforts by OPEC to accommodate Iraq in future production agreements by raising its quota to take account of increased export capacity, even though Iran had clearly stated that it would not participate in an agreement which awarded Iraq quota parity with itself. In late 1988 OPEC granted Iraq parity with Iran and set its production quota at 2.64m. b/d. Iraqi production had reached 2.8m. b/d in November 1987, and was subject to government reviews during 1988, when output was maintained at about 2.6m. b/d. By the end of 1988 production had risen to about 2.7m. b/d, and exports were running at about 2.3m. b/d. On 1 January 1989 Iraq temporarily reduced production to match its quota, halting the bulk of its crude petroleum exports by road to Jordan and Turkey. In mid-1989 Iraq's quota was raised to 2.783m. b/d, still maintaining parity with Iran, and average output in 1989 amounted to some 2.8m. b/d.

In view of its need to reconstruct its economy, Iraq sought, following the cease-fire in the Iran–Iraq War, to maximize its oil revenues and to raise the OPEC minimum reference price. At the OPEC meeting held in June 1989, Kuwait claimed a quota of 1.35m. b/d, rather than the 1.12m. b/d which would have been allocated to it under a simple pro-rata distribution of the 20m. b/d ceiling which the majority of members judged to be reasonable in order to stabilize prices. Since Kuwaiti overproduction was now regarded as inevitable (it had already been overproducing by some 800,000 b/d–900,000 b/d in May and June), the new production ceiling was raised by only 1m. b/d, to 19.5m. b/d. In September a new ceiling of 20.5m. b/d was fixed, but Kuwait rejected its quota of 1.149m. b/d for the final quarter of 1989. Overproduction continued, and by the end of 1989 total OPEC output had reached almost 24m. b/d, with a consequential depressive effect on world petroleum prices.

At the next OPEC meeting, held in November 1989, the production ceiling was raised to 22m. b/d, although the *de facto* level of production was already 24m. b/d. Quotas were redistributed, with Kuwait being allocated 6.82% of total output, compared with 5.61% previously. Owing to optimistic estimates of demand, and closer adherence to quotas by member states, prices rose following the November meeting, reaching their highest level for two years in January 1990. By May, however, quotas were again largely being ignored, and prices had slumped. Iraq's crude petroleum production at this time was estimated at about 3.14m. b/d—approximately its quota level.

By May 1990 overproduction had continued to such an extent that increasing numbers of tankers were being chartered for floating storage. At a meeting of OPEC's ministerial monitoring committee, held on 2 May, it was agreed to reduce production by 1.445m. b/d from an average level of 23.5m. b/d. However, the effect of this on prices was negligible. In June 1990 an Iraqi Deputy Prime Minister, Dr Sa'adoun Hammadi, condemned Kuwait and the UAE for producing above their quota levels, and stated that there should be no further review of quotas until a 'fair' price for crude petroleum—$25 per barrel—had been achieved. Kuwaiti overproduction was regarded as an attempt to wreck efforts within OPEC to raise the minimum reference price above $18 per barrel, and Iraq claimed to be losing $1,000m. annually for every reduction of $1 per barrel in the price of petroleum. In July President Saddam Hussain blamed overproduction for low petroleum prices, and warned of action against those states—Kuwait and the UAE—which persistently flouted their quotas. He claimed that the decline in the price of petroleum in the first half of 1990 had cost Iraq $14,000m. Iraq subsequently accused Kuwait of violating the Iraqi border in order to acquire resources worth more than $2,400m. from Iraq's section of the Rumaila oilfields.

At the full OPEC meeting held in Geneva in late July 1990, Iraq sought to raise the minimum reference price for crude petroleum to $25 per barrel. Although the agreement that was achieved at the meeting raised the reference price to only $21 per barrel until the end of 1990, and fixed the production ceiling

at 22.5m. b/d, it was regarded as OPEC's most serious attempt to address the problem of overproduction for many years. However, the markets were thrown into turmoil by Iraq's invasion and annexation of Kuwait at the beginning of August 1990 and by the consequential imposition of mandatory UN sanctions on all trade with Iraq and Iraqi-controlled territory. By late August, prices had risen as high as $30 per barrel, and an emergency OPEC meeting was held in an attempt to restore stability to the market. At the meeting, which was attended by the oil ministers of all OPEC member states except Libya and Iraq, draft agreement to suspend the production quotas that had been agreed in July (and thus compensate for the loss of Iraqi and Kuwaiti production) was endorsed by all member states attending except Iran.

In the context of the UN embargo and the closure of its pipeline outlets through Saudi Arabia and Turkey, Iraq reduced its production to less than 400,000 b/d in the latter months of 1990, sufficient to supply its domestic refining capacity. Although consumer prices increased sharply, a move by the Minister of Oil to introduce petrol rationing on 19 October was countermanded by the Revolutionary Command Council 10 days later (and the Minister was dismissed). The situation deteriorated rapidly with the onset of hostilities in January 1991, when the allied bombing campaign resulted in the destruction of most of Iraq's oil and gas installations, both upstream and downstream. By mid-February petrol was officially rationed (but virtually unobtainable), as were heating-oil and gas. A UN report, compiled in March, estimated that restoration of 25% of pre-war refinery capacity—the minimum needed for survival—would take from four to 13 months. Some refineries resumed limited production in April–May, enabling the Government to end petrol rationing on 28 April and to reduce consumer prices, but government claims that oil exports of 1.5m. b/d could be resumed in July 1991 (if UN sanctions were repealed), rising to 2m. b/d in 1992, were not put to the test, because the UN embargo remained in place. In its emergency six-month reconstruction budget, announced on 2 May, the Government identified the restoration of oil production, refining and pipeline facilities as a central priority. The appointment of a new Minister of Oil on 27 May confirmed the dominance over the hydrocarbons sector of the Ministry of Industry, Minerals and Military Industrialization.

By mid-1992 Iraq appeared to have made substantial progress in restoring its production, refining and storage capacity, in accordance with the priorities laid down in the reconstruction plan. Annual average oil production (including natural gas liquids) rose from 235,000 b/d in 1991 to 480,000 b/d in 1992 (compared with average production of 2.01m. b/d in 1990 and a production level of over 3m. b/d before the August 1990 invasion of Kuwait). Output averaged 495,500 b/d in 1993 and 601,700 b/d in 1994. In the first half of 1992, Iraq claimed that it had restored its output capacity to 3m. b/d, although the non-availability of export markets (and Iraq's refusal to utilize the UN concession of limited, authorized exports to pay for emergency imports) precluded an early attempt to bring the bulk of this capacity back on stream. Iraq's oil-refining capacity, which has averaged 3,200 b/d since the mid-1980s, increased to 585,000 b/d in 1992 and averaged 530,000 b/d from 1993 to 1996.

In April 1993 the head of oil operations in the south of the country announced that available productive capacity in this region amounted to 1.8m. b/d (compared with production of 2.25m. b/d from the southern fields in August 1990), and that facilities were in place to export up to 800,000 b/d via the Mina al-Bakr terminal and 1m. b/d via the strategic pipeline to the north. Mina al-Bakr was Iraq's preferred export point for UN-authorized petroleum exports, whereas the sanctions administrators proposed that any shipments should be made via Turkey to facilitate strict monitoring. The Turkish authorities also declared their anxiety about possible corrosion problems associated with a prolonged pipeline shut-down. Technical arrangements for repairing and flushing Iraq's Turkish pipeline were agreed in principle between the two Governments in the first half of 1994, with Turkey proposing to use the resulting outflow of trapped petroleum on its domestic market and to arrange for 30% of the payment due to Iraq to be deposited in the UNCC's fund for victims of Iraq's aggression, while the remaining 70% would be used to finance Iraqi imports of essential foodstuffs and medical supplies. It was estimated that 12m. barrels of petroleum (of which 3.8m. barrels were already owned by Turkey) would be discharged in the course of the proposed maintenance operation. Iraq made it clear that the scheme (for which Turkey was hoping to obtain early UN clearance) could not proceed if the UN sought to attach the same conditions that had caused Iraq to reject Security Council Resolutions 706 and 712.

In March 1995 Iraq's Minister of Oil stated that the country was currently producing petroleum at the rate of 700,000 b/d but could raise output to 2m. b/d 'within a few weeks' of the lifting of UN trade sanctions. He estimated that it would take 14 months to achieve an output level of 3.5m. b/d and four to five years to bring capacity up to 4.5m. b/d. A full-scale resumption of Iraq's oil development programme (including the opening of hitherto undeveloped oilfields) would, he said, require investment totalling around $30,000m. over a period of five to eight years. French and Russian oil companies were widely reported to have reached preliminary agreements with Iraq in 1993/94 to develop key oilfields after the lifting of UN sanctions, while companies from several other countries (including Italy and Brazil) had held discussions on aspects of Iraq's oil development plans. Delegates from 29 countries attended a two-day seminar on future oil and gas markets, held in Baghdad in March 1995. Many of the claims made by Iraqi officials during the Baghdad seminar were challenged in the following month at the annual conference of the London-based Centre for Global Energy Studies (CGES), whose executive director estimated that it could take Iraq up to three years after the lifting of the export embargo to increase its production capacity to 3.2m b/d, and rather longer to bring export capacity fully into line with production capacity. The CGES estimated that Iraq would need to spend up to $6,000m. on essential repairs and reconstruction in the oil sector. The CGES conference was attended by a representative of the London-based opposition Iraqi National Congress, who stated that foreign oil companies currently negotiating with Iraq should not expect any 'post-Saddam democratic government' to honour oil agreements drawn up in the present circumstances.

Although the resumption of its own petroleum exports remained in abeyance, Iraq continued to attend OPEC meetings to express formal opposition to pricing and production decisions adopted by the other member countries from 1991 to mid-1993. At the end of 1992 the Iraqi Minister of Oil accused OPEC of failing to uphold 'the interests of producing countries'. In June 1993 the Deputy Prime Minister, Tareq Aziz, indicated that Iraq's eventual return to the oil export market would be geared to the country's revenue needs, and that the Government would be prepared to see prices fall to $5 per barrel if necessary, 'since now we get nothing'. He pointed out that the UN had defined the proposed emergency export quota in cash terms, setting no limit on the volume of petroleum that could be exported to generate income of $1,600m. By early 1994 Iraqi ministers and officials had moderated their criticism of OPEC, and appeared to be laying the foundations for a reasoned claim for a high OPEC quota allocation at such time as Iraq was able to rejoin the export market. At the end of 1994 Iraq's formal claim within OPEC was for quota parity with Iran when exports resumed.

In March 1996 Iraq and Turkey held technical talks on the reopening of pipelines to handle part of the limited oil exports for which Iraq was currently seeking UN approval. A Turkish company was mandated to repair any pipeline damage, although this work would not start until all negotiations with the UN had been satisfactorily concluded. The effective capacity of the Kirkuk to Yumurtalık pipeline was expected to be in the range of 300,000 b/d to 500,000 b/d in the initial stages because of the settling of trapped oil and the loss of an important pumping station in northern Iraq (destroyed by bombing during the Gulf War). In the south, Iraq claimed to have an initial 1.2m. b/d of export capacity available at its Gulf terminal of Mina al-Bakr, which was said to be ready to handle tankers of up to 350,000 dwt. Both the safety of the port approaches and the adequacy of the loading facilities were, however, called into question by Western oil analysts. Iraq's estimated oil output in the first half of 1996 was between 550,000 b/d and 700,000 b/d, of which up to 80,000 b/d was exported to Jordan and the balance consumed within Iraq. At current prices, Iraq expected to have to increase

its production by between 700,000 b/d and 800,000 b/d to take full advantage of the formula set out in UN Security Council Resolution 986 (which provided for export revenue of up to $2,000m. over a period of 180 days). In June 1996 an OPEC ministerial meeting agreed that Iraq's OPEC production quota (currently a nominal 400,000 b/d) should be raised to 1.2m. b/d in the second half of 1996 in anticipation of an early agreement between Iraq and the UN on implementation of Resolution 986. The subsequent delay in implementation of Resolution 986 until December meant that Iraq's average 1996 oil output was, at an estimated 590,000 b/d, only 50,000 b/d higher than the average for 1995. The greater part of the oil exported under UN supervision in the first half of 1997 was pumped via Yumurtalık, with the balance shipped from Mina al-Bakr. The largest single export contract concluded at the end of 1996 was for the supply of 75,000 b/d to the Turkish refiner Tupras throughout the 180 days of the initial export period authorized by the UN Security Council. It later emerged that Iraq was seeking to divide its export allocation among a large number of different buyers requiring delivery of limited volumes over short periods. In addition to contract sales, the UN authorized some spot-market transactions in February 1997 to maintain oil earnings at target levels. In June 1998 production resumed at three southern oilfields after a suspension of some 20 years.

In 1997 Iraqi oil production averaged some 1.3m. b/d (compared with 630,000 b/d in 1996). Following the February 1998 revision of the terms of the UN 'oil-for-food' arrangement, whereby the value of Iraqi oil exports permitted by the UN was to be increased from $2,000m. to $5,200m. in a six-month period, production increased significantly, and exports were officially estimated to be averaging 1.6m.–1.7m. b/d by mid-June, although UN officials calculated that exports peaked at 2.4m. b/d in the final two weeks of June. It was expected that exports would approach a sustainable 2.6m. b/d by early 1999, following UN approval, announced in June, of an Iraqi request to spend $300m. on the purchase of vital new equipment to upgrade and overhaul oil–production facilities. Without the necessary renovation, it was estimated, Iraq would be able to fulfil only $4,000m. of its new six-monthly export quota.

In March 1997 Iraq signed an agreement with Russia (ratified by the Iraqi National Assembly in the following month) for the future development of the West Qurnah oilfield in southern Iraq. A consortium of Russian companies was to take a 75% interest (Lukoil 52.5%, RVO Zarubezhneft 11.25% and VO Mashinoimport 11.25%) and Iraq a 25% interest in a 23-year contract to develop 600,000 b/d of production capacity and associated infrastructure after the lifting of UN sanctions against Iraq. In June the Chinese National Petroleum Corporation signed an agreement to develop 90,000 b/d of capacity in the Adhab oilfield after the lifting of sanctions. A consortium of Turkish companies reached a preliminary agreement with Iraq in May, envisaging the development of a major gas export project after the ending of sanctions. In March 1998 the French petroleum company, Total, announced that it was negotiating an agreement to develop the Bin Umar oilfield (with an estimated production capacity of 450,000 b/d), whilst Ranger Oil, the Canadian group, confirmed that it was in the process of securing a $250m.-field-development contract and exploration block in the Western Desert. In June an Indian joint venture between the Oil and Natural Gas Corporation and Reliance Petroleum secured a deal to develop the Tuba oilfield.

In July 1998 Iraq and Syria signed an agreement to reopen the Kirkuk–Banias oil pipeline which had been inactive since 1982. An initial capacity of 300,000 b/d was expected. An agreement was also reached to construct a second pipeline to the Mediterranean with a 1.4m. b/d capacity.

INDUSTRY

Until the 1970s Iraq had few large industries apart from petroleum. In greater Baghdad the larger enterprises were concerned with electricity and water supply and the building materials industry. In addition, there was a large number of smaller-unit industries concerned with food and drink processing (date-packing, breweries, etc.), cigarette-making, textiles, chemicals, furniture, shoe-making, jewellery and various metal manufactures.

In recent years greater priority has been given to industrial developments, as the Government has sought to reduce Iraq's dependence on the petroleum industry. Between 1970 and 1986 more than ID 14,000m. was invested in the industrial sector. Iraq now has some major industrial plants, with others under construction. An iron and steel works at Khor az-Zubair, built by Creusot-Loire of France, began operations in 1978 and should eventually have a maximum annual output of 1.2m. tons of sponge iron and 400,000 tons of steel. Plans for a second iron and steel works were announced at the beginning of 1988. Khor az-Zubair is also the site of a major petrochemicals complex (see Petroleum and Natural Gas, above).

Iraq's mineral resources, apart from hydrocarbons, include sulphur and phosphate rock. Sulphur has been mined at Mishraq, near Mosul, since 1972. The mining complex, which includes a sulphuric acid plant, has a design capacity of 1.25m. tons per year. However, a record 1.4m. tons were produced in 1989, of which 1.2m. tons were for export, compared with 950,000 tons and 750,000 tons, respectively, in 1988. A new sulphur recovery and sulphuric acid plant, built by Japanese contractors, uses Mishraq sulphur. Production began in 1988 and has raised exports of sulphur by more than 50%, from their former level of 500,000 tons per year. Some 500,000 tons of sulphur are sent for sulphuric acid production at the phosphate processing plant at al-Qaim, but Iraq hopes to maintain sulphur exports by increasing the rate of sulphur recovery (currently 90%) during hydrocarbon processing. A new recovery unit is being built at Kirkuk. In 1988 proven reserves of sulphur stood at 515m. tons, the largest in the world according to the Iraqi Government.

Phosphate rock reserves, mostly in the Akashat area, and in the Marbat region, north-west of Baghdad, were estimated at 10,000m. tons in 1988. The phosphate fertilizer plant at al-Qaim was built by Sybetra of Belgium, which also installed the phosphate mine in Akashat. The mine, which has reserves estimated at 3,500m. tons, opened in 1981 and was intended to produce 3.4m. metric tons per year of phosphate rock for the al-Qaim plant, which received the first loads from the mine by rail in 1982. Iraq is now self-sufficient in fertilizers, producing slightly more than 1.2m. tons in 1989. Of this, some 766,000 tons were exported. The al-Qaim plant started production in 1984, and is scheduled to export 75% of its output. A $400m.-programme to double production at al-Qaim began in 1989. Daily production of 1,000 tons of ammonia and 1,700 tons of urea also commenced at a fourth nitrogenous fertilizer factory at Baiji. One of the contractors, the M. W. Kellogg Co, was appointed in 1988 to double capacity at the Baiji plant. There are also plans to build a new ammonia/urea factory at al-Qaim, and work to expand capacity at the Basra fertilizer plant commenced in early 1990.

Major state factories also include a textile factory at Mosul, producing calico from local cotton; three sugar refineries, at Karbala, Sulaimaniya and Mosul, with another four planned; a tractor assembly plant which produced 2,500 tractors in 1975; a paperboard factory at Basra, a synthetic fibres complex, at Hindiya; and a number of flour mills. Shoe and cigarette factories serve the domestic market. Other developments in the manufacturing sector have included factories to produce pharmaceuticals, electrical goods, telephone cables and plastics, together with additional food-processing plants. In 1984 Iraq's annual capacity for cement production was 11m. tons; this is expected to reach 20m. tons when the country's newest cement works operate at full capacity. Two cement works, a plant at al-Qaim with a capacity of 1m. tons per year, and another at Sinjar, in Nineveh Governorate, with a capacity of 2m. tons, were built by Uzinexportimport of Romania. Exports of 1m. tons of cement to Egypt began in 1986. Production of cement reached 13m. tons in 1989, when 5.4m. tons were exported, mainly to other Arab countries. Brick production in 1984 reached 1,607m. units, rising to 1,773m. in 1986. Much of the output was used to build homes. Up to 4m. homes are expected to be built in the years 1981–2000. According to official plans, the local construction industry would also be supplied by three new factories—a steel foundry, a central moulds factory and a steel formworks—built on at-Taji industrial estate. Trucks and buses designed by the Swedish firm Saab-Scania have been assembled under licence in Iskandariya since 1973.

The latest developments in the manufacturing sector have been in the production of pharmaceuticals, electrical goods, telephone cables and plastics, and in the establishment of more food processing plants.

The USSR assisted with the construction of 11 factories, including a steel mill and an electrical equipment factory at Baghdad, a drug factory at Samarra and a tractor plant at Musayib. A large share of industrial development took place in co-operation with Eastern bloc countries and several agreements were signed, including one at the end of 1984 with Bulgaria's Bulgartabac to extend the northern tobacco industry. Other projects include the establishment of an electronics industry, by Thomson CSF of France.

Local industry came under increasing scrutiny during 1987 and 1988 and a wide improvement was sought both in the quantity and the quality of production, while particular emphasis was placed on import substitution by local production and on producing surpluses for export. Priority continued to be given to meeting local demands for raw materials, spare parts, new machinery and equipment. There has also been official recognition of private and mixed-sector companies' ability to meet vital consumer needs more effectively than the state.

In July 1988, following a number of earlier attempts to reorganize the government departments responsible for industry in Iraq, responsibility for all civilian and military industry was placed under the control of a single Ministry of Industry, Minerals and Military Industrialization. This was to run large-scale and strategic industries such as power generation, minerals and petrochemicals, and military industrial production, through the Military Industries Commission which was attached to it. Some state factories producing light industrial goods were auctioned off to private companies, or to newly established mixed-sector firms. In August 1988 the new ministry announced that it was to sell 47 factories to the private sector by the end of the year. Iraq allocated the equivalent of $11,500m. to investment in development projects in fiscal 1988, some 42% of which was to be devoted to industrial and agricultural schemes. Some 229 light industrial schemes (involving investment of ID 234m.) were listed in the Five-Year (1986–90) Industrial Development Plan and were also open to private and Arab investment. In April 1988, the Arab Investment Law No. 46 was passed, offering Arab investors tax exemptions and profit remittances.

Industrial production was valued at a record $8,500m. in 1987, owing, said government sources, to optimum use of production facilities and greater use of local, rather than imported, raw materials, which was estimated to have saved $130m. By 1987 the proportion of the labour force employed in industry was just over 21%. The foreign labour force was reduced by one-third during 1987, saving an additional $50m., according to government announcements. Some 218 development projects worth a total of ID 2,496m. ($8,051m.) were completed in 1987, according to the Ministry of Planning, including 50 agricultural schemes (worth $2,319m.) and 33 industrial schemes ($1,574m.). During 1989 the Ministry of Industry, Minerals and Military Industrialization emerged as the leading client for new business. Danieli of Italy was awarded a contract to construct a special steel factory at Taji, and a rolling mill for flat steel products at Khor az-Zubair. Contracts for new pipe factories were awarded to companies from Italy and the Federal Republic of Germany. The Ministry's Technical Corpn for Special Projects also assumed responsibility for the new petrochemicals complex and for the new central oil refinery in mid-1989. The Ministry also announced plans in 1989 to manufacture cars, tractors, trucks and buses. A licensing agreement for the production of cars has been signed with General Motors of the USA, and an agreement for the production of trucks and buses has been signed with Mercedes-Benz of Germany.

Investment in the power generation sector, which was severely disrupted during the early years of the Iran–Iraq War, has been given a high priority by the Government. In 1981 a large number of contracts—worth more than $2,000m.—were awarded for additional generation and transmission facilities (including a 600-MW power station at Haditha), as well as for the expansion and renovation of local and national networks, and the supply of emergency back-up systems. Since 1982, contracts for 400-kV 'supergrid' and 132-kV transmission lines and substations have been awarded to South Korean, French, Italian, Yugoslav and Japanese companies. The first of three 1,200-MW thermal power stations planned during the early 1980s was to be built at al-Musayyib, under a $730m.-contract awarded to the Hyundai Engineering and Construction Co of South Korea. The second, at Yousufia, on the Euphrates, comprising six 200-MW units, was to be built by the USSR's Techno-promexport under the terms of a Soviet-Iraq agreement covering the period 1986–90, which also provided for co-operation on an 800-MW power plant in Mosul; and a 300–400-MW hydroelectric plant and dam, costing $200m., in Baghdadi, on the Euphrates. The USSR also helped to build an 840-MW thermal power plant in Nasiriya; a 400-MW hydroelectric plant in Dukan; and a 200-MW thermal power plant in Najibiya. A West German consultant, Fichtner, was chosen to design the third 1,200-MW power station, the al-Anbar plant, which was to be built near Ramadi, on the Euphrates. Italy's GIE has completed expansion of Baghdad's Dawra power station, and was appointed in 1989 to add two 350-MW units to al-Musayyib power station. Another new plant, the 1,400-MW oil-fired power station at ash-Shamal, on the Tigris, was being designed by Energoprojekt of Yugoslavia, and four 350-MW turbine generators were to be supplied by Northern Engineering Industries of the United Kingdom.

In 1987 six new hydroelectric plants, one power station and 18 transformer units began operating, raising Iraq's generating capacity by 6% to 8,538 MW. By mid-1990 capacity had reached 9,000 MW and was expected to double by the end of the century. However, it was estimated that demand for power would increase four-fold by 2000. By 1990 about 95% of the population had access to electricity, with millions connected to the network since the rural supply scheme began in 1975. Consumption was 1,450 kWh per head in 1987, compared with 1,344 kWh per head in 1986. The connection with the Turkish grid has been completed, and wider inter-Arab power connections have also been discussed. Supplies for Turkey were scheduled to flow in December 1988, making Iraq the first exporter of electricity in the Middle East.

Iraq's experimental 70-MW Osirak nuclear reactor was destroyed by an Israeli air force bombing attack in June 1981. In 1990, according to official sources, Iraq had only one nuclear reactor: the 5-MW reactor at Temmuz, supplied by the USSR in the 1960s. Nevertheless, the USA and allied governments remained convinced that Iraq was pursuing a large-scale nuclear development programme with the aim of producing nuclear weapons. During the 1991 hostilities, it was reported that Iraqi nuclear installations had been bombed to destruction. However, the issue resurfaced in the post-war period, when it became apparent that Iraq's nuclear potential had partially survived, although the Government continued to insist that only civilian nuclear research was being conducted.

The UN embargo that was imposed on Iraq in August 1990 resulted in the suspension of most industrial development projects involving foreign co-operation. The industrial sector was also adversely affected by the loss of technicians from Western countries. The outbreak of actual hostilities in January 1991 led to massive destruction of Iraq's heavy industrial capacity and infrastructure, including as much as 90% of its electricity generating and transmission facilities as well as oil refineries, oil export terminals, petrochemical plants, iron and steel foundries, engineering factories, and phosphate and cement plants. The light industrial sector, which normally supplied the domestic market, was also badly disrupted by the general infrastructural collapse, chronic shortages of fuel and power, and destruction of communications. By early 1992 the Government claimed that 75% of the national power grid had been restored.

The director-general of one of Iraq's main power stations stated in early June 1997 that the national electricity-generating system was currently operating at less than 50% of capacity because of a lack of spare parts. He added that the $36m. allocated (but not yet disbursed) for the purchase of parts under the current 180-day oil export agreement with the UN would meet 'only 4% of the needs of the power grid'. In 1998 it was announced that Baghdad had been suffering power cuts for five–six hours daily, whilst rural areas had been known to lack electricity for 14–16 hours daily.

A major priority in the Government's six-month emergency reconstruction budget, announced on 2 May 1991, was the restoration of sufficient industrial production to ensure self-sufficiency in certain basic areas. Sectors that were identified for special attention included drug manufacturing, geological surveys and mining, phosphate, fertilizer and sulphur production, and electricity generation and transmission. Priority repairs were also to be undertaken to factories making electrical fittings, bricks, cigarettes and textiles. According to the minister responsible, the rebuilding of civilian industry would have priority over military production (which had traditionally absorbed a large, albeit undisclosed, proportion of resources); however, Western reports of urgent Iraqi moves to re-establish its armaments production capacity (to as much as 87% of the pre-war level by September 1992) cast doubt on this stated policy. Also in May 1991, the Government approved the replacement of Arab Investment Law No. 46 of 1988 by new rules that were designed to encourage greater Arab investment in the private and mixed industrial sectors by granting Arab nationals the right to implement industrial projects and offering them tax and other incentives. Moreover, in August 1991 Law 115 of 1982 was replaced by Law 25 of 1991, which aimed to accelerate industrial development in the private and mixed sectors through the provision of state assistance to selected projects. Strategic and export-oriented industries using local raw materials were to be targeted under the new policy, which specified that a project must involve the use of plant worth at least ID 100,000.

In April 1993 the Iraqi Minister of Labour stated that the prolonged UN embargo was causing many factories to close or to shed labour, with the result that 'for the first time in Iraqi's modern history we have registered a large number of unemployed people'. In September the Ministry of Industry and Minerals (which had reverted to its former name in 1991), which was responsible for thousands of state enterprises in areas other than oil production and arms manufacture, was authorized to incorporate these enterprises as limited companies and to offer up to 75% of their shares for sale on the Baghdad stock exchange. Companies which passed into majority private ownership would enjoy tax exemptions for 10 years. About 150m. shares in four of the largest companies—producing textiles, bricks and cement—were offered for sale later in the year, but the level of public indifference to this exercise was such that less than 1m. shares were bought. In the case of a major cement company, the reported take-up was 40,000 shares, each priced at ID 125, out of 75m. shares offered. By mid-1995, however, the Baghdad stock exchange was reported to be trading as many as 6m. shares per week, mainly in companies still under formation. Within the state-controlled armaments industry, import-substitution achievements announced in 1995 included the local manufacture of electrical production-line equipment for use in a 'major steel project'.

COMMUNICATIONS

The communications sector was considered to be of major importance under the provisions of the 1981–85 Plan, and there was considerable activity in this sector during 1981. In May a consortium of British consultants was awarded a $129m.-contract to design an extensive underground public transport system for Baghdad. It was believed to be the largest design contract ever awarded in Iraq, and the full cost of constructing the system was estimated to be up to $10,000m. The consortium, known as the British Metro Consultants Group, was to act as project designer. Contracts for detailed designs for the various sections have so far been awarded to a German consortium of JV Dorsch, to the US company DeLeuw Cather International, to a Brazilian consortium, led by Promon Engenharia, and to Belgium's Transurb Consult; and the contract for soil investigation has been tendered. However, the project had already been reduced in priority before the 1991 hostilities rendered its future even more uncertain.

Another major project is the construction of the new Baghdad international airport. In April 1979 a $900m.-contract was awarded to two French companies—Spie Batignolles and Fourgerolle Construction—to build the airport for the State Organization for Roads and Bridges. The first stage has been completed and is used by Western European airlines and Iraqi Airways. In preparation for the substantial increase in traffic that the opening of the new airport is expected to bring, Iraqi Airways began expanding its fleet and network, acquiring two Boeing

747s and three 727s from the USA in 1981 at a cost of $183.6m. Passenger traffic was expected to rise by 10% per year, but was limited by regulations which permitted only night flights in and out of Baghdad airport. In 1989 Iraqi Airways carried 1,171,600 passengers, compared with 695,538 in 1988 and 525,948 in 1987. The airline normally flies to about 42 cities in Iraq and abroad.

A new international airport was built at Basra during the Iran–Iraq War by West German contractors and was opened in August 1988, after the cease-fire. The airport has a 4,000-m runway, capable of taking the biggest wide-bodied aircraft now available. Consultants have designed the country's third international airport, at Mosul, and a local airport at Arbil. The latter is intended to form part of a domestic network which will also include Amara, Kirkuk and Najaf. It was reported in mid-1990 that Airbus Industries had concluded the sale of five Airbus A310-300 aircraft to Iraq, but discussions concerning the financing of the sale were cancelled following the imposition of UN economic sanctions against Iraq. The two aircraft scheduled for delivery to Iraq in 1992 were allocated to other customers and no work was undertaken on the remainder of the contract.

Total freight carried by Iraqi Airways amounted to 31,539 tons in 1989, compared with 24,752 tons in 1988 and 16,833 tons in 1987. In 1990 plans were announced to establish a separate freight airline, Iraqi Airways Cargo.

Iraq's main port is at Basra but it was not able to operate during the Iran–Iraq War, and its future depends on there being a lasting political decision over the ownership and use of the Shatt al-Arab waterway. Before the war, two new ports were developed, at Umm Qasr and Khor az-Zubair. The latter is linked with Umm Qasr and the Gulf by a 40-km ship canal. Clandestine operations to clear this canal began before the end of the war with Iran, and after August 1988 extensive dredging operations were begun in order to clear navigation channels to both ports. Deep-water channels were certified free from hazards in early 1990, and the ports now have the capacity to handle general cargo, sulphur, petrochemicals, iron ore, grain, sugar and fertilizers. A further 13 berths are to be constructed at Umm Qasr, at a projected cost of more than $500m. Just before the Iraqi invasion of Kuwait in August 1990, work commenced on the construction of two floating docks at Khor az-Zubair. The first cargo to be unloaded at Umm Qasr since 1990 was a food shipment in November 1993. In March 1994 the UAE announced its intention to apply to the UN sanctions committee for permission to set up a direct shipping link with Umm Qasr to ferry in approved supplies from the UAE port of Jebel Ali.

River transport has been given increasing prominence. Dredging of several stretches of the Tigris between Baghdad and Basra has been completed, and navigation channels are being laid out. A French consultant, Sogreah, was appointed to study the navigation possibilities on the Euphrates between Haditha and Qurnah, and Iraq has invited consultants to bid for a navigation development study of the Tigris as a whole—from Mosul to Basra. The artificial 'third river', completed in December 1992, is navigable by 5,000-ton cargo barges.

The Government sought to proceed with plans to build some 2,400 km of railways between 1981 and 1985. The two major existing lines (between Baghdad and Basra, and from Baghdad north to Mosul and Tel Kotchek) will eventually be superseded by more modern, high-speed tracks. The cost of the Baghdad–Basra line, for which companies were reported in August 1990 to be preparing bids, has been estimated at $6,000m. The contract for the building of the first stage of the new Baghdad–Umm Qasr line has been delayed. Designs for the new line north from the capital to the Turkish border, via Mosul, Arbil and Kirkuk, have been completed by French consultants. A 273-km (170-mile) line between Kirkuk, Baiji and Haditha, built by South Korean firms, and the 550-km (342-mile) line from Baghdad to Husaibah, on the Syrian border, built by Construction Mendes of Brazil, were both opened in 1986. An Indian company has built the third and fourth stages of the Musayyib–Samarra line. All lines entering Baghdad will eventually be connected to the 112-km (70-mile) Baghdad loop line. Designs have been completed for the project, which involves the expansion of the capital's two main passenger stations, the development of a new freight terminal, and the building of three new bridges. The Indian Railways Enterprise and the Iraq

Rail Establishment signed a memorandum of understanding in March 1996 'to execute new railways projects in Iraq' at an unspecified future date. A Czech company which had supplied 100 diesel locomotives to Iraq at the end of the 1970s announced plans in 1996 to bid to supply a further 70 locomotives as soon as UN trade sanctions were lifted.

Negotiations with Kuwait and Saudi Arabia over the establishment of rail links have taken place over a number of years. A working link and joint operation with Turkey may be developed first. The Government hopes eventually to link its rail system with Kuwait, Saudi Arabia and Turkey as part of a European-Gulf network.

Considerable emphasis is also being put on road construction. A 137-km section, from Tulaiha to Rutba, of the six-lane 1,200-km international Expressway Number One, was opened in August 1987. It is the main section in a project designed to create a road link between the Gulf states and the Mediterranean. The bulk of the project had been completed by 1989. In Baghdad, a South Korean company is working on the Abu Ghraib expressway, which will connect the capital with Expressway Number One.

A second expressway is intended to link Baghdad with the Turkish border via Samarra, Kirkuk, Arbil, Mosul, Dohuk and Zakho. Cowiconsult of Denmark has completed designs for the project, which will cost an estimated $6,000m. A six-lane highway, running from Safwan, on the Kuwaiti border, to Baghdad, via Zubair and Nasiriya, was completed in 1987. Several urban expressways and bridges have been built in Baghdad, though further work on the capital's planned motorway network is expected to be delayed for some years. A three-stage programme to build 10,000 km of rural roads is also being implemented.

Iraq has been modernizing its telecommunications system for some years and has introduced crossbar telephone switching, a telex system, a microwave link between major cities and an earth satellite connection for international communications. By 1985 more than 1m. lines had been added to the network. Iraq is also investigating the potential of fibre optics, and awarded a contract to a Japanese firm at the end of 1982. At the end of 1985 bids were invited for a 1,000-km cable to link Baghdad and Basra. Prior to the 1991 hostilities the Government's aim was to increase the total number of telephone lines to 2m. by 1995.

Iraq's communications infrastructure was a prime target of the multinational force's bombing campaign during the 1991 hostilities and suffered massive damage as a result. According to an official UN report compiled in March 1991, all modern communications systems were destroyed, including the internal and external telephone networks, and heavy damage was inflicted on roads, railways and ports. Of 123 bridges hit by allied bombs, about one-third were totally destroyed, and in the war's immediate aftermath the only viable surface transport link to the outside world was through Amman (Jordan) to the port of Aqaba. In June the Government estimated the cost of repairing bridges and other installations that had been built by the Ministry of Housing and Construction at $1,450m. Repair of roads and bridges was given priority in the post-war reconstruction programme, it being claimed that 35 bridges had been repaired by the end of June 1991. By January 1992 the Government claimed that 99 bridges had been repaired, while the colossal damage to the telephone system (including the destruction of nearly half of the country's 900,000 telephone lines) was also being remedied. Completion of a new 190-m telecommunications tower in Baghdad, to replace the tower destroyed in the 1991 war, was scheduled for November 1993. However, at the end of 1994 Iraq's international telecommunications services remained severely restricted, while the domestic telephone network was officially estimated to be operating at 30% of its pre-1991 capacity. Despite continued progress in the reconstruction of bridges, roads and other elements of the transport infrastructure, the quality of Iraq's public transport services underwent a marked deterioration in 1994 because of lack of access to spare parts for vehicles and essential equipment. In January 1992 Iraqi Airways resumed regular commercial flights between Baghdad and Basra. However, around 37 Iraqi Airways aircraft, which were flown out of the country during the 1990–91 Gulf crisis, remained abroad in mid-1998, their return to Iraq being prohibited by UN sanctions administrators. The airline stated in early 1995 that it was maintaining intensive training programmes for pilots, engineers and technicians whose normal duties had been disrupted by the UN embargo.

FINANCE AND BANKING

Owing to Iraq's inability to export large quantities of petroleum during the early years of the Iran–Iraq War, the reduction of petroleum prices, the heavy cost of the conflict (estimated at $600m.–$1,000m. per month at the beginning of 1986) and the additional burden of funding economic development, the country's official reserves of foreign exchange had declined to below $5,000m. by mid-1983. This was to be compared with the pre-war estimate of $35,000m. Little new information has become available since, and 1989 estimates were between zero and $2,000m. To minimize the continuing annual deficits on the current account of the balance of payments (an estimated $1,571m. in 1986), the Iraqi Government imposed stringent controls on foreign currency payments and imports. In the absence of Iraqi statistics, Western sources estimated, before the 1990–91 Gulf crisis, that the current account deficit would be about $1,500m. in 1990, declining to $200m. per year by 1992 and then going into increasing surplus in the mid-1990s. However, the combined effects of the UN embargo, the 'freezing' of Iraqi assets abroad, the physical destruction of the 1991 war and the post-war requirement on Iraq to pay reparations served to reduce Iraq's national finances to a state of total disarray (see Consequences of the 1990–91 Gulf Crisis, above).

In comparison with other Arab countries, Iraq has few banks and all are state-controlled, although in May 1991 the Government adopted an amendment to the banking laws, enabling the creation of private banks, provided that they undertook to operate under the supervision of the Central Bank. The Central Bank of Iraq, founded in 1947 as a successor to the National Bank of Iraq, was one of the first Arab monetary authorities.

For many years, the only commercial bank was Rafidain Bank, which was founded in 1941. Rafidain was long considered the biggest Arab commercial bank in terms of deposits and gross assets. In 1986 its total assets reached ID 12,800m., up from ID 10,379m. in 1985; profits rose for the third successive year, to ID 348.3m. Rafidain has 152 local branches and nine branches abroad. Rafidain is also permitted to take part in the Arab and international markets for syndicated loans and bonds. It is a shareholder in several European-Arab consortia banks, such as the Paris-based Union de Banques Arabes et Françaises, and development agencies. It is also one of the seven shareholders in Gulf International Bank, established in Bahrain in 1977 as a regional commercial bank. At the end of 1981, Rafidain established a joint venture bank with Banco do Brasil. Its capital was set at $17.5m.; each bank has an equal share. In 1987 Rafidain's capital was doubled to ID 100m. in the first stage of a programme to upgrade and expand the banking system. In May 1988 the Government announced that a second commercial bank, Rashid Bank, would be established, with capital of ID 100m., to compete with Rafidain Bank. Competition was also to be encouraged in the insurance sector. The three companies in this sector have all been absorbed into the Ministry of Finance, as have the country's three specialist banks. The ministry is encouraging them to expand, and the banks are being given administrative and financial autonomy, bound only by the Government's fiscal policy.

The oldest specialized bank is the Agricultural Co-operative Bank, established in 1936, which provides medium- and long-term credits to farmers and agricultural development organizations. After 1981, when a record ID 186m. was loaned, lending levels fell as a consequence of the war. In 1987 the bank loaned a total of ID 25.4m., compared with ID 43.2m. in 1986. Total lending by the bank over the period 1980–87 amounted to ID 570m. There are two other specialized banks. The Industrial Bank, established in 1940, provides short-, medium- and long-term loans to public and private industrial companies. Between 1980 and 1987 the bank extended ID 52m. in loans and credits. During 1987 total loans amounted to ID 1.5m., compared with ID 14.9m. in 1982. The bank holds shares worth $62.9m. in 14 mixed-sector joint-stock companies and has been instructed to become more involved in offering finance to both local and

Arab investors, as private and mixed-sector companies are encouraged to play a wider role in the development of the economy. The bank is also administering a $28m.-loan for the Kuwait-based Arab Fund for Economic and Social Development (AFESD) to assist in the development of light industry. The Real Estate Bank, founded in 1949, provides credits for housing, construction and tourism. Because of the high demand for housing, the bank has expanded rapidly in recent years. Lending over the period 1980–87 totalled ID 2,770m., although annual levels have declined since the 1982 peak of ID 750.5m. In mid-1988 the bank's capital was raised by ID 50m., to ID 800m. to enable it to play a wider role in encouraging people to build their own houses. A government decree of June 1991 established a new state-owned Socialist Bank, with an initial capital of ID 500m., its principal stated role being to make interest-free loans to civil servants and decorated veterans of the war with Iran.

Iraq was also a major aid donor before the Iran–Iraq War, being the third biggest among Arab states, after Saudi Arabia and Kuwait. In 1979, according to OECD figures, its disbursements totalled $861.5m., representing about 3% of gross national product (GNP). Most of this was channelled through the Iraqi Fund for External Development which had a capital of $677m. In mid-1979 Iraq decided to compensate poorer customers for its petroleum for any future petroleum price increases by granting them long-term interest-free loans. Under this system, 12 developing countries (Bangladesh, India, Madagascar, Morocco, Mozambique, Pakistan, the Philippines, Senegal, Somalia, Sri Lanka, Tanzania and Viet Nam) received over $200m. in the second half of 1979.

Donations of aid had resumed by 1990, and in June Iraq announced that it would grant Jordan $50m. (for 1990) and the PLO $25m. In September 1990 the Iraqi Government offered to supply free petroleum to developing countries, but this was widely seen as a public relations exercise, intended to undermine international support for the UN embargo that had been imposed on Iraq in the previous month because of its invasion of Kuwait.

An amendment to Law 64 of 1976, introduced in May 1991, authorized the operation of private banks and thus ended the state monopoly of banking dating from 1964. Applications were subsequently lodged by four prospective new banks, namely the Alitimad Bank, the Baghdad Bank, the Iraqi Commercial Bank and the Private Bank. The step was intended to encourage a wider private-sector role in the economy, in accordance with the Government's post-1989 liberalization policy. However, observers commented that the authorization of private banks was unlikely to affect the banking system substantially until the Central Bank relaxed its tight control of monetary policy. A stock exchange was established in Baghdad in March 1992.

Having acted as the Iraqi Government's main means of paying external debts before the country was isolated from the international financial system, Rafidain Bank was exposed to numerous claims from overseas creditors after 1990. However, a creditors' meeting held in London in April 1993 was informed by British liquidation experts that liquidation of Rafidain's international operations would yield only a minimal recovery, as these operations currently showed a net deficiency of funds totalling £5,560m. ($8,800m.).

UN Security Council Resolution 778 of 2 October 1992 authorized the impounding of oil-related Iraqi assets ('frozen' in overseas accounts since August 1990) for the purpose of funding UN programmes connected with the Gulf crisis and its aftermath, including humanitarian relief operations, administration of war victims' compensation claims and inspection and destruction of Iraqi weapons. Assets so impounded were to be transferred to a UN escrow account in New York, disbursements from which would be refundable to Iraq if the Iraqi Government agreed to sell petroleum under UN supervision.

Notwithstanding an Iraqi Government threat to take legal action against foreign banks transferring funds to the escrow account, a total of $101.5m. had been so transferred by 30 April 1993. In response to a UN appeal for further transfers to meet ongoing programme costs, the US Government said that it was prepared to authorize the transfer of $200m. of the $637.4m. of impounded Iraqi assets within its jurisdiction, provided that transfers of US-based funds never exceeded 50% of total transfers. Among other overseas fund holders, the Bank of Tokyo said that assets totalling $44.88m. could not be transferred in view of third-party rights over them, while Tunisia indicated that $15.8m. in locally-held assets had been used to offset outstanding Iraqi debts to Tunisia.

Total Iraqi assets held in UK banks fell from about $1,100m. at the time of the invasion of Kuwait to $748m. at the beginning of 1995, as a result of the release of funds to pay debts owed to British companies and to finance exports of food and medicines to Iraq. In March 1995 the Iraqi Ministry of Finance claimed that seven Arab countries owed Iraq a total of $1,282m. in loans, payments for oil, profits withheld by Arab companies and assets belonging to Iraqi banks. Saudi Arabia was said to owe 35% of the total, Syria 28%, Bahrain 20%, Kuwait 10% and Somalia 5%, with the UAE and Egypt responsible for the remainder.

The black-market value of the Iraqi dinar, already worth only a fraction of the official exchange rate of $1 = ID 0.31, was further depressed by the UN Security Council's October 1992 decision on external asset transfers. Punctuated by occasional extreme fluctuations (e.g. from $1 = ID 23 in February 1993 to $1 = ID 95 in April 1993), the underlying decline of the currency continued during the first half of 1993, taking the average market rate to around $1 = ID 65 during July.

In early May 1993 the Iraqi Government announced a six-day deadline for the exchange of old-style Swiss-printed 25-dinar notes for locally-printed equivalents, introduced after the 1990–91 Gulf crisis. The old-style notes were not exchangeable outside the country, and the border with Jordan, where speculators and currency traders held notes with an estimated market value of $200m., was closed during the exchange period. Within Iraq, this exercise highlighted the problematical status of the Kurdish-controlled area in the north, which was effectively deprived of the exchange facility yet unable to relinquish its formal currency link with Baghdad. It led to a marked rise in Kurdish use of the Turkish lira as a preferred medium of exchange within the 'safe haven', this arrangement being presented as a strictly practical (i.e. politically neutral) matter.

Western observers had difficulty in discerning a clear-cut economic motive for the May 1993 currency initiative. It was readily accepted in Iraqi government circles that the post-war reconstruction drive had been accompanied by rapid growth in the money supply, making price inflation and currency depreciation inevitable while the external position continued to deteriorate. Moreover, the Government had virtually institutionalized the unofficial currency trade by itself relying on the black market to supply part of its hard currency requirement (estimated at $90m. per month in the first half of 1993) to maintain the food rationing system.

The unofficial exchange rate fell below $1 = ID 100 for the first time on 26 October 1993. The Government responded to this development by halting its own purchases of dollars on the black market. At the beginning of December, when the unofficial rate had fallen below $1 = ID 150, the Government authorized its ministries to deal in hard currency with the private sector. At the beginning of January 1994 Iraqis were permitted to deal legally in foreign exchange and to open foreign cash accounts in domestic banks, while 28 firms were licensed by the Central Bank to buy and sell foreign currency at rates determined by 'daily supply and demand'. On 5 February, after the unofficial exchange rate had fallen below $1 = ID 200, state banks were authorized to buy and sell hard currency outside the official rate of $1 = ID 0.31. As Iraq's chronic economic crisis intensified, the rate of currency depreciation accelerated, taking the unofficial rate per dollar to around 250 dinars in March, 300 dinars in April, 400 dinars in mid-May and 500 dinars by the beginning of June. The Central Bank, which had previously issued no currency notes above 25 dinars, announced the launch of a 50-dinar note in March and a 100-dinar note in May. During January 1995, when the Central Bank issued a 250-dinar note for the first time, the unofficial exchange rate declined from $1 = ID 665 to $1 = ID 750, while the authorized dealing rate was devalued from $1 = ID 550 to $1 = ID 600. The unofficial exchange rate reached 1,000 dinars to the dollar for the first time in March, after which the value of the currency depreciated further to 1,300 dinars per dollar by late June and 1,450 dinars per dollar by mid-July. In May the Government announced an

issue of five-year bonds paying interest of 20% per year (more than the prevailing bank deposit rates but far less than the rate of inflation). The annual interest rate for two-year deposits at state-owned commercial banks was raised from 15% to 18% in June.

The unofficial exchange rate slumped from 2,000 dinars per dollar in September 1995 to 2,600 dinars per dollar in October 1995. The Government had in September lifted an import ban on 232 types of foreign goods (imposed in 1993 for exchange-control reasons). In mid-December, when the unofficial rate was around 2,550 dinars per dollar, the Government devalued its authorised dealing rate from $1 = ID 600 to $1 = ID 1,000, stating that it was determined 'not to allow the exchange rate to suffer any further setbacks'. In January 1996 the Government halted the printing of new banknotes; raised petrol prices by 600%; and doubled the fees for official building permits; and further relaxed the exchange-control and currency trading regulations. Having depreciated below the level of $1 = ID 3,000 for the first time in early January the unofficial exchange rate recovered to $1 = ID 1,500 towards the end of the month following Iraq's decision to open talks on UN Security Council Resolution 986. As the talks proceeded the dinar's free-market value moved above the authorised dealing rate of 1,000 dinars per dollar. In mid-June the unofficial exchange rate stood at 900 dinars to the dollar, having touched a high point of 580 dinars per dollar in February. During the second half of 1996 the rate decreased to a low point of 1,780 dinars per dollar in November before recovering to 600 dinars per dollar in mid-December after the delayed implementation of Resolution 986. From October 1996 state banks were authorized to exchange dinars for hard currency needed for any legitimate purpose, whereas previously they had sold hard currency only to licensed importers, students studying abroad and Iraqis receiving medical treatment abroad. In January 1997 it was reported that the Central Bank was applying 'strict monetary policies' in order to support the exchange rate of the dinar. The unofficial exchange rate fluctuated mainly within the range 1,000 to 1,200 dinars per dollar during the first half of 1997.

FOREIGN TRADE

Exports of petroleum have been, by far, Iraq's most important source of revenue, providing more than 95% of the country's earnings of foreign exchange. Receipts from these exports rose sharply in the mid- and late 1970s, partly because of higher production, but mainly because of the rise in prices. By 1979, Iraq's petroleum exports were earning three times as much as in 1974, and by 1980 these exports were worth $26,278m. However, owing to Iraq's inability to export sufficient petroleum, because of the war with Iran, and to the drop in prices, exports fell to $9,198m. in 1981. Revenues from oil exports were in the range $9,000m.–$11,000m. per year in 1982–85, and declined to an estimated $6,813m. in 1986. The higher oil prices recorded in the first half of 1987 were believed to have brought about a revival in the value of petroleum sales to more than $11,000m. in 1987, to about $13,000m. in 1988 and to about $12,000m. in 1989. While earnings declined in 1981 and 1982, Iraq continued to spend, importing goods worth more than $18,000m. in 1981 and $19,000m. in 1982, before imposing a sharp decrease in the level of imports, to about $12,000m. per year in 1983, 1984 and 1985. Imports were reduced to between $8,000m. and $9,000m. per year in 1986 and 1987 (though Western analysts estimate that they reached $9,700m. in 1987), and to $7,146m. in 1988. In 1989, according to Western calculations, total exports were worth $12,080m., while imports rose to $10,290m.

Most trade is normally with Western Europe, the USA and Japan, but Iraq also exports significant amounts of petroleum to Brazil, Yugoslavia, eastern Europe and Turkey. Trade with the USSR consisted mainly of Soviet military supplies. Among Western countries, France has been one of Iraq's most important trading partners. It is estimated that, after the outbreak of war with Iran, Iraq bought more than $5,500m. worth of French armaments in the 1980s, while French contractors won orders worth more than $4,500m.

Although several countries experienced a decline in exports to Iraq during the second half of the 1980s, imports from Western countries generally rose during 1988 and 1989. The value of Japanese exports rose to $406m. in 1988 and to $490m.

in 1989, compared with \$391m. in 1987. French exports were worth \$445m. in 1988 and \$478m. in 1989, compared with \$391m. in 1987, while the value of the United Kingdom's exports rose from \$445m. in 1987 to \$720m. per year in both 1988 and 1989. The value of West German exports rose from \$457m. in 1987 to \$884m. in 1988 and to \$1,168m. in 1989. The value of imports from Italy declined to \$174m. in 1988, compared with \$225m. in 1987, but rose to \$372m. in 1989, while that of imports from Brazil fell to \$228m. in 1988, compared with \$305m. in 1987. The value of imports from the USSR declined from \$511m. in 1987 to \$509m. in 1988 and to \$405m. in 1989. In 1988 the USA supplanted Turkey as Iraq's leading trading partner, exporting \$1,156m. worth of goods (mainly agricultural products), compared with \$683m. in 1987. US exports to Iraq were valued at \$1,173m. in 1989. Like the United Kingdom, the USA extended a credit line to Iraq in 1988 in order to guarantee the volume of its exports. The value of Turkish exports to Iraq increased from \$945m. in 1987 to \$986m. in 1988, but fell to \$445m. in 1989.

The value of Iraq's exports to the USA, at \$2,408m., more than quadrupled in 1989, compared with 1987, as a result of Iraq's decision to market its crude petroleum more attractively in the USA. Another leading importer of Iraqi petroleum was the USSR, the value of whose total imports from Iraq rose from \$1,243m. in 1987 to \$1,585m. in 1988, but declined to \$1,549m. in 1989. The value of Turkish imports from Iraq was \$1,650m. in 1989, compared with \$1,154m. in 1987, while the value of Italian imports declined from \$1,214m. in 1987 to \$996m. in 1988 and to \$674m. in 1989.

In the first half of 1990 there were increased efforts by Iraq's trading partners to prevent exports of industrial goods which might possibly serve as components for missiles and atomic weapons. In March the United Kingdom and the USA claimed to have frustrated Iraqi attempts to import nuclear detonators, and in April two UK companies were prevented from exporting to Iraq steel cylinders which were later proved to be components for a planned 'supergun'. The USA has also claimed that Iraq planned to use loans made improperly by the Atlanta (USA) branch of Italy's Banca Nazionale del Lavoro to acquire military technology. In February 1995 a US company which had illegally supplied artillery fuses to Iraq in 1990 was fined \$500,000 by a US court and was ordered to dissolve itself.

The imposition of the UN trade embargo on Iraq in August 1990 and the subsequent Gulf hostilities brought about the total disruption of Iraq's external trade, subsequently prolonged by disagreements between the Iraqi Government and UN sanctions administrators (see Consequences of the 1990–91 Gulf Crisis, above). The IMF estimated the value of Iraq's total imports in 1992 as ID 78.2m., compared with ID 118.9m. in 1991 and ID 2,042.4m. in 1990. The estimated 1992 total was equivalent to about \$250m. at the official exchange rate, but only a fraction of this at prevailing black-market rates. Unofficial estimates of Iraq's external trade in 1994 suggested that import spending had totalled \$2,000m., while exports had earned \$500m. The volume of basic commodities imported via the Jordanian port of Aqaba in the first quarter of 1995 totalled 233,800 tons (of which nearly two-thirds was wheat). The embargo on Iraqi oil exports from the Gulf was closely monitored by naval patrols acting on behalf of the UN, which occasionally reported instances of vessels attempting to use false Iranian documentation as a cover for shipments of Iraqi oil. By the end of April 1996 the UN's naval patrols had boarded about 10,000 vessels in all, of which 76 had come under suspicion of breaking the trade embargo. Amid growing speculation about an early relaxation of UN sanctions, Western and other foreign business representatives visited Baghdad in substantial numbers in 1994/95 to assess the prospects for a resumption of trading relations with Iraq. In the first half of 1996 foreign business interest was centred on the trading opportunities that could be expected to open up when UN Security Council Resolution 986 was implemented.

DEVELOPMENT AND PLANNING

At the beginning of the 1980s Iraq did not need to seek external loans, economic development having been funded mainly from the State's petroleum revenues. The sustained rise in petroleum prices gave Iraq a major opportunity to increase its development spending. Despite the high costs incurred by the war with Iran, the 1982 expenditure programme allocated an estimated ID 7,000m. to the ordinary budget and ID 7,000m. to investment spending. The import programme was allocated ID 5,000m. Iraq was unable to maintain the early momentum of its development programme, however, because of falling petroleum revenues and the high cost of the Iran–Iraq War. No detailed budget figures were disclosed from 1982 to 1989, and the 1981–85 Development Plan had to be abandoned, although longer-term plans were published for specific sectors.

In the Government's published budget for 1990, expenditure was forecast at ID 24,400m. The new 'consolidated general budget' reportedly projected a deficit of ID 6,600m., compared with a deficit of ID 7,200m. in 1989. The budget proposals also incorporated a total investment allocation of ID 5,600m., of which industry was to receive ID 2,965m. Because of the Gulf crisis, no details were disclosed of the 1991 budget until it was substantially revised to take account of damage sustained in the hostilities. A six-month emergency reconstruction budget, announced on 2 May 1991, reduced planned expenditure in the general consolidated budget to ID 13,876m. (from the original total of ID 14,596m.) and cut the investment budget to ID 1,660m. (from ID 2,340m.). It was stated that non-essential development projects had been postponed until 1992, and available resources diverted to the reconstruction effort. Nevertheless, over the five-year period 1991–95, it was envisaged that ID 28,700m. (\$92,580m.) would be spent on development projects, of which the foreign currency component would be some \$56,000m.

In the 1980s Iraq attracted substantial foreign investment for its development projects, notably from West European countries, Japan and the USSR. In 1984 the USSR pledged \$2,000m. in long-term credits for Iraq, which also obtained lines of credit or other credit facilities from the United Kingdom, the USA and the Federal Republic of Germany (the latter two agreeing in 1987–88 to restore export credit guarantees which had earlier been withdrawn when Iraq defaulted on debt repayments). Nevertheless, as a result of persistent repayment problems, much of the credit—and the goodwill—had again ceased by the end of the decade, despite the conclusion of various intergovernmental refinancing agreements. By mid-1990 the claims on Iraq of banks reporting to the Bank for International Settlements were calculated as totalling \$7,690m. worldwide, while national credit guarantee agencies with major exposure to outstanding Iraqi debts were headed by Coface of France (some \$3,200m.) and included those of Japan and Italy (each some \$3,000m.) and of Germany (\$2,000m.).

On a multilateral basis, loans worth more than \$250m. were agreed with the Islamic Development Bank to fund imports and hospital work. The Arab Monetary Fund also loaned money (\$523m. between 1983 and mid-1989) to support Iraq's balance of payments. Loans to support a coldstore project, telecommunications, an earthquake warning system, agricultural and industrial development and the upgrading and extension of power generation units were made by the AFESD. Iraq secured two Euroloans of \$500m., in 1983 and 1985, to finance foreign trade and development projects, but was forced to reschedule payments due on them, owing to a shortage of foreign exchange.

Against this background, there was considerable doubt regarding continued foreign investment in Iraqi development projects even before the onset of the Gulf crisis in August 1990 brought about the suspension of virtually all such co-operation and of Iraqi repayments on outstanding debts. In September 1990 Iraq's total foreign debt was estimated at \$65,000m., a total which the Iraqi Government itself appeared to revise upwards in a post-war submission to the UN in April 1991 (see Consequences of the 1990–91 Gulf Crisis, above).

Statistical Survey

Source (unless otherwise indicated): Central Statistical Organization, Ministry of Planning, Karradat Mariam, ash-Shawaf Sq., Baghdad; tel. (1) 537-0071; telex 212218.

Area and Population

AREA, POPULATION AND DENSITY*

Area (sq km)	438,317†
Population (census results)	
17 October 1987	16,335,199
17 October 1997	
Males	10,940,764
Females	11,077,219
Total	22,017,983
Density (per sq km) in October 1997	50.2

* No account has been taken of the reduction in the area of Iraq as a result of the adjustment to the border with Kuwait that came into force on 15 January 1993.

† 169,235 sq miles. This figure includes 924 sq km (357 sq miles) of territorial waters but excludes the Neutral Zone, of which Iraq's share is 3,522 sq km (1,360 sq miles). The Zone lies between Iraq and Saudi Arabia, and is administered jointly by the two countries. Nomads move freely through it but there are no permanent inhabitants.

GOVERNORATES (population at 1987 census)

	Area* (sq km)	Popu- lation	Density (per sq km)
Nineveh	37,698	1,479,430	39.2
Salah ad-Din	29,004	726,138	25.0
At-Ta'meem	10,391	601,219	57.9
Diala	19,292	961,073	49.8
Baghdad	5,159	3,841,268	744.6
Al-Anbar	137,723	820,690	6.0
Babylon	5,258	1,109,574	211.0
Karbala	5,034	469,282	93.2
An-Najaf	27,844	590,078	21.2
Al-Qadisiya	8,507	559,805	65.8
Al-Muthanna	51,029	315,816	6.2
Thi-Qar	13,626	921,066	67.6
Wasit	17,308	564,670	32.6
Maysan	14,103	487,448	34.6
Al-Basrah (Basra) . . .	19,070	872,176	45.7
Autonomous Regions:			
D'hok	6,120	293,304	47.9
Irbil (Arbil)	14,471	770,439	53.2
As-Sulaimaniya . . .	15,756	951,723	60.4
Total	437,393	16,335,199	37.3

* Excluding territorial waters (924 sq km).

PRINCIPAL TOWNS (estimated population, 1970)

Baghdad (capital) .	1,984,142	An-Najaf . . .	147,855
Al-Basrah (Basra) .	333,684	Al-Hillah (Hilla) .	103,544
Al-Mawsil (Mosul) .	310,313	As-Sulaimaniya .	103,091
Kirkuk . . .	191,294	Irbil (Arbil) .	101,779

BIRTHS AND DEATHS (UN estimates, annual averages)

	1980–85	1985–90	1990–95
Birth rate (per 1,000) . . .	41.0	40.3	38.1
Death rate (per 1,000) . . .	8.4	7.2	6.7

Source: UN, *World Population Prospects: The 1994 Revision.*

Registered live births (1992) 502,415 (birth rate 26.4 per 1,000); Registered deaths (1990) 76,683 (death rate 4.4 per 1,000). Note: Registration is incomplete.

Expectation of life (official estimates, years at birth, 1990): males 77.43; females 78.22.

ECONOMICALLY ACTIVE POPULATION*
(persons aged 7 years and over, 1987 census)

	Males	Females	Total
Agriculture, forestry and fishing .	422,265	70,741	493,006
Mining and quarrying . .	40,439	4,698	45,137
Manufacturing . . .	228,242	38,719	266,961
Electricity, gas and water. . .	31,786	4,450	36,236
Construction. . . .	332,645	8,541	341,186
Trade, restaurants and hotels. .	191,116	24,489	215,605
Transport, storage and communications . . .	212,116	12,155	224,271
Financing, insurance, real estate and business services . . .	16,204	10,811	27,015
Community, social and personal services	1,721,748	233,068	1,954,816
Activities not adequately defined .	146,616	18,232	167,848
Total labour force	3,346,177	425,904	3,772,081

* Figures exclude persons seeking work for the first time, totalling 184,264 (males 149,938, females 34,326), but include other unemployed persons.

Source: ILO, *Yearbook of Labour Statistics.*

Agriculture

PRINCIPAL CROPS ('000 metric tons)

	1994	1995	1996
Wheat	1,342	1,050	1,000
Rice (paddy)	383	403*	270*
Barley	971	700†	500†
Maize	128	90*	85†
Potatoes	418	420†	380†
Dry broad beans† . . .	19	18	18
Sunflower seed . . .	56	63*	55†
Sesame seed*	14	14	13
Olives†	14	13	12
Cabbages†	22	23	21
Tomatoes	863	870†	800†
Cauliflower†	36	36	34
Pumpkins, etc.† . . .	61	62	60
Cucumbers†	340	345	340
Aubergines†	155	160	150
Green peppers† . . .	31	32	30
Onions (dry)	70	75†	70†
Carrots†	10	11	10
Other vegetables . . .	738	758†	747
Watermelons†	460	450	450
Melons†	220	220	225
Grapes†	282	280†	300†
Dates	576	600†	550†
Sugar cane†	63	60	58
Apples	86	90†	80†
Peaches and nectarines† . .	25	26	25
Plums†	31	32	30
Oranges	315	318†	310†
Tangerines, etc. . . .	45	45†	40†
Lemons and limes† . .	16	17	16
Apricots†	31	32	30
Other fruits and berries . .	93	95†	93†
Tobacco (leaves)† . . .	2	3	2
Cottonseed†	19	18	18
Cotton (lint)†	10	9	9

* Unofficial figure(s).   † FAO estimate(s).

Source: FAO, *Production Yearbook.*

LIVESTOCK (FAO estimates, '000 head, year ending September)

	1994	1995	1996
Horses	20	20	20
Mules	12	12	12
Asses	148	146	145
Cattle	1,050	1,030	1,000
Buffaloes	85	80	75
Camels	13	13	13
Sheep	5,150	5,100	5,000
Goats	600	500	350

Poultry (FAO estimates, million): 42 in 1994; 42 in 1995; 42 in 1996.

Source: FAO, *Production Yearbook*.

LIVESTOCK PRODUCTS (FAO estimates, '000 metric tons)

	1994	1995	1996
Beef and veal	29	28	28
Buffalo meat	10	10	10
Mutton and lamb . . .	15	15	14
Goat meat	3	3	3
Poultry meat	110	110	110
Cows' milk	210	205	200
Buffalo milk	20	20	19
Sheep's milk	110	105	100
Goats' milk	32	25	18
Cheese	20	19	17
Butter	5	5	5
Hen eggs	41	40	40
Wool:			
greasy	17	16	15
clean	9	8	8
Cattle and buffalo hides . .	4	4	4
Sheepskins	3	3	3
Goatskins	1	1	n.a.

Source: FAO, *Production Yearbook*.

Forestry

ROUNDWOOD REMOVALS ('000 cubic metres, excl. bark)

	1993	1994	1995
Sawlogs, veneer logs and logs for			
sleepers*	20	20	20
Other industrial wood* . .	30	30	30
Fuel wood	105	105	111
Total	155	155	161

* Annual output assumed to be unchanged since 1980.

Sawnwood production ('000 cubic metres, incl. railway sleepers): 8 per year in 1980–95.

Source: FAO, *Yearbook of Forest Products*.

Fishing

(FAO estimates, '000 metric tons, live weight)

	1993	1994	1995
Inland waters	19.0	18.0	18.6
Indian Ocean	4.5	4.0	4.0
Total catch	23.5	22.0	22.6

Source: FAO, *Yearbook of Fishery Statistics*.

Mining

('000 metric tons, unless otherwise indicated)

	1993	1994	1995
Crude petroleum	32,298	36,666	36,089
Natural gas (petajoules) . .	99	124	123†
Native sulphur*	250	250	250
Natural phosphates* . . .	800	1,000	1,000
Salt (unrefined)* . . .	300	300	250
Gypsum (crude)* . . .	450	450	450

* Estimates by the US Bureau of Mines. Data on natural phosphates refer to gross weight. The estimated phosphoric acid content was 30%.
† Provisional.

Source: UN, *Industrial Commodity Statistics Yearbook*.

Industry

SELECTED PRODUCTS
('000 metric tons, unless otherwise indicated)

	1993	1994	1995
Naphtha*	500	500	520
Motor spirit (petrol)* . .	2,960	2,970	2,990
Kerosene*	1,100	1,120	1,130
Jet fuel*	910	1,110	1,120
Gas-diesel (distillate fuel) oil* .	6,800	6,880	6,900
Residual fuel oils* . . .	8,880	9,000	9,000
Lubricating oils* . . .	200	200	200
Paraffin wax* . . .	80	100	100
Petroleum bitumen (asphalt)* .	410	420	420
Liquefied petroleum gas:			
from natural gas plants* .	486	700	1,560
from petroleum refineries* .	600	600	600
Cement† . . .	12,000	15,000	18,000
Electric energy (million kWh)* .	26,300	28,000	29,000

* Estimated production.
† Estimates by the US Bureau of Mines.

Cigarettes: 5,794 million in 1992.
Footwear (excluding rubber): 4,087,000 pairs in 1992.

Source: UN, *Industrial Commodity Statistics Yearbook*.

Finance

CURRENCY AND EXCHANGE RATES

Monetary Units
  1,000 fils = 20 dirhams = 1 Iraqi dinar (ID).

Sterling and Dollar Equivalents (31 May 1998)
  £1 sterling = 506.91 fils;
  US $1 = 310.86 fils;
  100 Iraqi dinars = £197.27 = $321.69.

Exchange Rate
  From February 1973 to October 1982 the Iraqi dinar was valued at US $3.3862. Since October 1982 it has been valued at $3.2169. The dinar's average value in 1982 was $3.3513. The aforementioned data refer to the official exchange rate. There is, in addition, a special rate for exports and also a free-market rate. The unofficial exchange rate was $1 = 1,600 dinars in March 1998.

BUDGET ESTIMATES (ID million)

Revenue	1981	1982
Ordinary	5,025.0	8,740.0
Economic development plan	6,742.8	7,700.0
Autonomous government agencies . . .	7,667.8	n.a.
Total	19,434.9	n.a.

Petroleum revenues (estimates, US $ million): 9,198 in 1981; 10,250 in 1982; 9,650 in 1983; 10,000 in 1984; 11,900 in 1985; 6,813 in 1986; 11,300 in 1987.

Expenditure					1981	1982
Ordinary	.	.	.	.	5,025.0	8,740.0
Economic development plan	.	.	.	.	6,742.0	7,700.0
Autonomous government agencies.	.	.	.	7,982.4	n.a.
Total	.	.	.	.	19,750.2	n.a.

1991 (ID million): General consolidated state budget expenditure 13,876; Investment budget expenditure 1,660.

CENTRAL BANK RESERVES (US $ million at 31 December)

			1975	1976	1977
Gold	.	.	168.0	166.7	176.1
IMF special drawing rights	.	.	26.9	32.5	41.5
Reserve position in IMF .	.	.	31.9	31.7	33.4
Foreign exchange .	.	.	2,500.5	4,369.8	6,744.7
Total	.	.	2,727.3	4,600.7	6,995.7

IMF special drawing rights (US $ million at 31 December): 132.3 in 1981; 81.9 in 1982; 9.0 in 1983; 0.1 in 1984; 7.2 in 1987.

Reserve position in IMF (US $ million at 31 December): 130.3 in 1981; 123.5 in 1982.

Note: No figures for gold or foreign exchange have been available since 1977.

Source: IMF, *International Financial Statistics*.

COST OF LIVING (Consumer Price Index; base: 1990 = 100)

									1991*
Food. . . .	.	.	.	.	.	.	.	.	363.9
Fuel and light .	.	.	.	.	.	.	.	.	135.4
Clothing . .	.	.	.	.	.	.	.	.	251.1
Rent. . .	.	.	.	.	.	.	.	.	107.0
All items (incl. others)	.	.	.	.	.	.	286.5

* May to December only.

Source: ILO, *Yearbook of Labour Statistics*.

NATIONAL ACCOUNTS (ID million at current prices)
National Income and Product

			1989	1990	1991
Compensation of employees	.	.	6,705.2	7,855.4	8,989.9
Operating surplus .	.	.	11,866.0	12,936.6	10,405.2
Domestic factor incomes	.	.	18,571.2	20,792.0	19,395.1
Consumption of fixed capital .	.	1,836.7	2,056.3	1,918.2
Gross domestic product (GDP) **at factor cost**. . . .			20,407.9	22,848.3	21,313.3
Indirect taxes .	.	.	1,035.0	1,024.8	485.6
Less Subsidies .	.	.	417.1	576.3	1,859.2
GDP in purchasers' values.	.	21,025.8	23,296.8	19,939.7
Net factor income from the rest of the world . . .	.		−704.3	−773.9	−650.5
Gross national product .	.	20,321.5	22,522.9	19,289.2
Less Consumption of fixed capital .		1,836.7	2,056.3	1,918.2
National income in market **prices**	.		18,484.8	20,466.6	17,371.0
Net current transfers from abroad	.	−149.3	−49.3	122.8
National disposable income	.	18,335.5	20,417.3	17,493.8

Source: UN, *National Accounts Statistics*.

Expenditure on the Gross Domestic Product

			1989	1990	1991
Government final consumption expenditure . .	.	.	5,990.1	6,142.0	7,033.3
Private final consumption expenditure . .	.	.	11,232.4	11,760.5	9,611.1
Increase in stocks .	.	.	−2,317.5	−976.9	−520.0
Gross fixed capital formation .	.	6,305.5	6,220.0	3,289.1
Total domestic expenditure	.	21,210.5	23,145.6	20,453.5
Exports of goods and services .	.	4,482.6	4,305.4	547.8
Less Imports of goods and services		4,667.3	4,154.2	1,061.6
GDP in purchasers' values.	.	21,025.8	23,296.8	19,939.7

Source: UN, *National Accounts Statistics*.

Gross Domestic Product by Economic Activity (at factor cost)

			1989	1990	1991
Agriculture, hunting, forestry and fishing . . .	.	.	3,346.1	4,613.3	6,047.0
Mining and quarrying .	.	.	3,894.8	3,330.6	149.4
Manufacturing . .	.	.	2,694.2	2,058.7	1,273.9
Electricity, gas and water* .	.	269.0	247.5	162.4
Construction. .	.	.	1,417.8	1,693.2	812.4
Trade, restaurants and hotels*	.	2,376.4	3,454.7	3,608.2
Transport, storage and communications .	.	.	1,533.3	2,103.9	2,645.9
Finance, insurance and real estate†		2,384.8	2,781.2	3,150.4
Government services .	.	.	3,599.1	3,823.5	4,845.7
Other services .	.	.	305.0	292.2	489.8
Sub-total	.	21,820.5	24,398.8	23,185.1
Less Imputed bank service charge		1,412.6	1,550.5	1,871.8
Total	.	20,407.9	22,848.3	21,313.3
GDP at constant 1975 prices .		6,491.8	6,492.9	2,199.8

* Gas distribution is included in trade.
† Including imputed rents of owner-occupied dwellings.

Source: UN, *National Accounts Statistics*.

External Trade

PRINCIPAL COMMODITIES (ID million)

Imports c.i.f.			1976	1977*	1978
Food and live animals .	.	.	159.6	154.0	134.5
Cereals and cereal preparations . .	.	.	70.0	79.9	74.9
Sugar, sugar preparations and honey. . . .	.	.	37.2	24.1	10.2
Crude materials (inedible) **except fuels** . .	.	.	33.7	20.5	25.1
Chemicals . . .	.	.	58.5	47.4	58.7
Basic manufactures .	.	.	293.3	236.7	285.2
Textile yarn, fabrics, etc. .	.		44.3	69.4	72.7
Iron and steel .	.	.	127.5	44.3	73.2
Machinery and transport **equipment** . .	.	.	557.4	625.8	667.4
Non-electric machinery .	.		285.4	352.5	368.1
Electrical machinery, apparatus, etc.	.	.	106.9	120.2	160.5
Transport equipment. .	.		165.2	153.1	138.8
Miscellaneous manufactured **articles** . . .	.	.	33.2	49.4	51.7
Total (incl. others) .	.	.	1,150.9	1,151.3	1,244.1

* Figures are provisional. Revised total is ID 1,323.2 million.

Total imports (official estimates, ID million): 1,738.9 in 1979; 2,208.1 in 1980; 2,333.8 in 1981.

Total imports (IMF estimates, ID million): 6,013.0 in 1981; 6,309.0 in 1982; 3,086.2 in 1983; 3,032.4 in 1984; 3,285.7 in 1985; 2,773.0 in 1986; 2,268.7 in 1987; 2,888.8 in 1988; 3,077.1 in 1989; 2,028.5 in 1990; 131.5 in 1991; 187.3 in 1992; 165.6 in 1993; 154.9 in 1994; 191.4 in 1995; 152.8 in 1996; 208.1 in 1997 (Source: IMF, *International Financial Statistics*).

Total exports (ID million): 5,614.6 (crude petroleum 5,571.9) in 1977; 6,422.7 (crude petroleum 6,360.5) in 1978; 12,522.0 (crude petroleum 12,480.0) in 1979.

Exports of crude petroleum (estimates, ID million): 15,321.3 in 1980; 6,089.6 in 1981; 5,982.4 in 1982; 5,954.8 in 1983; 6,937.0 in 1984; 8,142.5 in 1985; 5,126.2 in 1986; 6,988.9 in 1987; 7,245.8 in 1988.

Source: IMF, *International Financial Statistics*.

PRINCIPAL TRADING PARTNERS (US $ million)

Imports c.i.f.	1988	1989	1990
Australia	153.4	196.2	108.7
Austria	n.a.	1.1	50.9
Belgium and Luxembourg	57.6	68.2	68.3
Brazil	346.0	416.4	139.5
Canada	169.9	225.1	150.4
China, People's Republic	99.2	148.0	157.9
France	278.0	410.4	278.3
Germany	322.3	459.6	389.4
India	32.3	65.2	57.5
Indonesia	38.9	122.7	104.9
Ireland	150.4	144.9	31.6
Italy	129.6	285.1	194.0
Japan	533.0	621.1	397.2
Jordan	164.3	210.0	220.3
Korea, Republic	98.5	123.9	149.4
Netherlands	111.6	102.6	93.8
Romania	113.3	91.1	30.1
Saudi Arabia	37.2	96.5	62.5
Spain	43.4	129.0	40.5
Sri Lanka	50.1	33.5	52.3
Sweden	63.0	40.6	64.8
Switzerland	65.7	94.4	126.6
Thailand	22.3	59.2	68.9
Turkey	874.7	408.9	196.0
USSR	70.7	75.7	77.9
United Kingdom	394.6	448.5	322.1
USA	979.3	1,001.7	658.4
Yugoslavia	154.5	182.0	123.1
Total (incl. others)	5,960.0	6,956.2	4,833.9

Exports f.o.b.	1988	1989	1990*
Belgium and Luxembourg	147.5	249.6	n.a.
Brazil	1,002.8	1,197.2	n.a.
France	517.4	623.9	0.8
Germany	122.0	76.9	1.7
Greece	192.5	189.4	0.3
India	293.0	438.8	14.7
Italy	687.1	549.7	10.6
Japan	712.1	117.1	0.1
Jordan	28.4	25.2	101.6
Netherlands	152.9	532.3	0.2
Portugal	120.8	125.8	n.a.
Spain	370.0	575.7	0.7
Turkey	1,052.6	1,331.0	83.5
USSR	835.7	1,331.7	8.9
United Kingdom	293.1	167.0	4.4
USA	1,458.9	2,290.8	0.2
Yugoslavia	425.4	342.0	10.4
Total (incl. others)	10,268.3	12,333.7	392.0

* Excluding exports of most petroleum products.
Source: UN, *International Trade Statistics Yearbook*.

Transport

RAILWAYS (traffic)

	1994*	1995*	1996†
Passenger-km (million)	2,334	2,198	1,169
Freight ton-km (million)	1,901	1,120	931

* Source: UN, *Statistical Yearbook*.
† Source: Railway Gazette International, *Railway Directory*.

ROAD TRAFFIC ('000 motor vehicles in use)

	1993	1994	1995
Passenger cars	672.4	678.5	680.1
Commercial vehicles	309.3	317.2	319.9

Source: UN, *Statistical Yearbook*.

SHIPPING
Merchant Fleet (registered at 31 December)

	1994	1995	1996
Number of vessels	117	114	113
Total displacement ('000 grt)	884.7	857.8	856.9

Source: Lloyd's Register of Shipping, *World Fleet Statistics*.

CIVIL AVIATION (revenue traffic on scheduled services)

	1991	1992	1994*
Kilometres flown (million)	0	0	0
Passengers carried ('000)	28	53	31
Passenger-km (million)	17	35	20
Freight ton-km (million)	0	3	2

* Figures for 1993 unavailable.
Source: UN, *Statistical Yearbook*.

Tourism

	1993	1994	1995
Tourist arrivals ('000)*	400	330	340
Tourist receipts (US $ million)	15	12	13

* Including same-day visitors.
Source: UN, *Statistical Yearbook*.

Communications Media

	1993	1994	1995
Radio receivers ('000 in use) . .	4,225	4,335	4,500
Television receivers ('000 in use) .	1,450	1,500	1,600
Daily newspapers	n.a.	4*	4†

* Combined average circulation 532,000 copies per issue.

† Estimate.

Non-daily newspapers: 12 in 1988.

Source: UNESCO, *Statistical Yearbook*.

Telephones ('000 main lines in use): 674 in 1987; 678 in 1988; 675 (estimate) in 1989 (Source: UN, *Statistical Yearbook*).

Education

	Teachers		Pupils/Students	
	1990	1992*	1990	1992*
Pre-primary . .	4,908	4,778	86,508	90,836
Primary . .	134,081	131,271	3,328,212	2,857,467
Secondary:				
General . .	44,772	48,496	1,023,710	992,617
Teacher				
training . .	n.a.	1,303	n.a.	22,018
Vocational . .	n.a.	9,318	n.a.	130,303

* Figures for 1991 are unavailable.

Schools: Pre-primary: 646 in 1990; 578 in 1992. Primary: 8,917 in 1990; 8,003 in 1992.

Higher education (1988): Teachers 11,072; Students 209,818.

1994: Pre-primary: 576 schools; 4,972 teachers; 93,028 pupils.

Source: UNESCO, *Statistical Yearbook*.

Directory

The Constitution

The following are the principal features of the Provisional Constitution, issued on 22 September 1968:

The Iraqi Republic is a popular democratic and sovereign state. Islam is the state religion.

The political economy of the State is founded on socialism.

The State will protect liberty of religion, freedom of speech and opinion. Public meetings are permitted under the law. All discrimination based on race, religion or language is forbidden. There shall be freedom of the Press, and the right to form societies and trade unions in conformity with the law is guaranteed.

The Iraqi people is composed of two main nationalities: Arabs and Kurds. The Constitution confirms the nationalistic rights of the Kurdish people and the legitimate rights of all other minorities within the framework of Iraqi unity.

The highest authority in the country is the Council of Command of the Revolution (or Revolutionary Command Council—RCC), which will promulgate laws until the election of a National Assembly. The Council exercises its prerogatives and powers by a two-thirds majority.

Two amendments to the Constitution were announced in November 1969. The President, already Chief of State and Head of the Government, also became the official Supreme Commander of the Armed Forces and President of the RCC. Membership of the latter body was to increase from five to a larger number at the President's discretion.

Earlier, a Presidential decree replaced the 14 local government districts by 16 governorates, each headed by a governor with wide powers. In April 1976 Tikrit (Salah ad-Din) and Karbala became separate governorates, bringing the number of governorates to 18, although three of these are designated Autonomous Regions.

The 15-article statement which aimed to end the Kurdish war was issued on 11 March 1970. In accordance with this statement, a form of autonomy was offered to the Kurds in March 1974, but some of the Kurds rejected the offer and fresh fighting broke out. The new Provisional Constitution was announced in July 1970. Two amendments were introduced in 1973 and 1974, the 1974 amendment stating that 'the area whose majority of population is Kurdish shall enjoy autonomy in accordance with what is defined by the Law'.

The President and Vice-President are elected by a two-thirds majority of the Council. The President, Vice-President and members of the Council will be responsible to the Council. Vice-Presidents and Ministers will be responsible to the President.

Details of a new, permanent Constitution were announced in March 1989. The principal innovations proposed in the permanent Constitution, which was approved by the National Assembly in July 1990, were the abolition of the RCC, following a presidential election, and the assumption of its duties by a 50-member Consultative Assembly and the existing National Assembly; and the incorporation of the freedom to form political parties. The new, permanent Constitution is to be submitted to a popular referendum for approval.

In September 1995 an interim constitutional amendment was endorsed by the RCC whereby the elected Chairman of the RCC will assume the Presidency of the Republic subject to the approval of the National Assembly and endorsement by national referendum.

In July 1973 President Bakr announced a National Charter as a first step towards establishing the Progressive National Front. A National Assembly and People's Councils are features of the Charter. A law to create a 250-member National Assembly and a 50-member Kurdish Legislative Council was adopted on 16 March 1980, and the two Assemblies were elected in June and September 1980 respectively.

The Government

HEAD OF STATE

President: SADDAM HUSSAIN (assumed power 16 July 1979; according to official results, at a national referendum conducted on 15 October 1995, 99.96% of Iraq's 8.4m. electorate recorded its endorsement of President Saddam Hussain's continuance in office for a further seven years).

Vice-Presidents: TAHA YASSIN RAMADAN, TAHA MOHI ED-DIN MARUF.

REVOLUTIONARY COMMAND COUNCIL

Chairman: SADDAM HUSSAIN.

Vice-Chairman: TAHA YASSIN RAMADAN.

Other Members:

IZZAT IBRAHIM	MUHAMMAD HAMZAH AZ-ZUBAYDI
TAREQ AZIZ	TAHA MOHI ED-DIN MARUF
Gen. SULTAN HASHIM AHMAD	SA'ADOUN HAMMADI MAZBAN KHADR HADI

COUNCIL OF MINISTERS
(September 1998)

Prime Minister: SADDAM HUSSAIN.

Deputy Prime Ministers: TAREQ AZIZ, TAHA YASSIN RAMADAN, MUHAMMAD HAMZAH AZ-ZUBAYDI.

Minister of the Interior: MUHAMMAD ZIMAN ABD AR-RAZZAQ.

Minister of Defence: Gen. SULTAN HASHIM AHMAD.

Minister of Foreign Affairs: MUHAMMAD SAEED AS-SAHAF.

Minister of Finance: HIKMAT MIZBAN IBRAHIM.

Minister of Agriculture: ABDULLAH HAMEED MAHMOUD SALEH.

Minister of Culture and Information: HUMAM ABD AL-KHALIQ ABD AL-GHAFUR.

Minister of Justice: SHABIB AL-MALKI.

Minister of Irrigation: MAHMOUD DIYAB AL-AHMAD.

Minister of Industry and Minerals: ADNAN ABD AL-MAJID JASSIM.

Minister of Oil: Gen. AMIR MUHAMMAD RASHID.

Minister of Education: FAHD SALIM ASH-SHAKRAH.

Minister of Health: UMEED MADHAT MUBARAK.

Minister of Labour and Social Affairs: Gen. SAADI TUMA ABBAS.

Minister of Planning: SAMAL MAJID FARAJ.

Minister of Higher Education and Scientific Research: ABD AL-JABBAR TAWFIQ MUHAMMAD.

Minister of Housing and Construction: MAAN ABDULLAH SARSAM.

Minister of Transport and Communications: Dr AHMAD MURTADA AHMAD KHALIL.

Minister of Awqaf (Religious Endowments) and Religious Affairs: Dr ABD AL-MUNIM AHMAD SALIH.

Minister of Trade: MUHAMMAD MAHDI SALIH.

Minister of State for Military Affairs: Gen. ABD AL-JABBAR KHALIL ASH-SHANSHAL.

Ministers of State: ARSHAD MUHAMMAD AHMAD MUHAMMAD AZ-ZIBARI, ABD AL-WAHHAB UMAR MIRZA AL-ATRUSHI.

Presidential Advisers: WATBAN IBRAHIM AL-HASSAN, SAFA HADI JAWAD, ABD AS-SATTAR AHMAD AL-MAINI, ABD AL-WAHHAB ABDULLAH AS-SABBAGH, ABDULLAH FADEL-ABBAS, AMER HAMMADI AS-SAADI HATIM AL-AZAWI, NIZAR JUMAH ALI AL-QASIR.

MINISTRIES

Office of the President: Presidential Palace, Karradat Mariam, Baghdad.

Ministry of Agriculture and Irrigation: Khulafa St, Khullani Sq., Baghdad; tel. (1) 887-3251; telex 212222.

Ministry of Awqaf (Religious Endowments) and Religious Affairs: North Gate, St opposite College of Engineering, Baghdad; tel. (1) 888-9561; telex 212785.

Ministry of Culture and Information: Nr an-Nusoor Sq., fmrly Qasr as-Salaam Bldg, Baghdad; tel. (1) 551-4333; telex 212800.

Ministry of Defence: North Gate, Baghdad; tel. (1) 888-9071; telex 212202.

Ministry of Education: POB 258, Baghdad; tel. (1) 886-0000; telex 2259.

Ministry of Finance: Khulafa St, Nr ar-Russafi Sq., Baghdad; tel. (1) 887-4871; telex 212459.

Ministry of Foreign Affairs: Opposite State Org. for Roads and Bridges, Karradat Mariam, Baghdad; tel. (1) 537-0091; telex 212201.

Ministry of Health, Labour and Social Affairs: Khulafa St, Khullani Sq., Baghdad; tel. (1) 887-1881; telex 212621.

Ministry of Industry and Minerals: Nidhal St, Nr Sa'adoun Petrol Station, Baghdad; tel. (1) 887-2006; telex 212205.

Ministry of Local Government: Karradat Mariam, Baghdad; tel. (1) 537-0031; telex 212568.

Ministry of Oil: POB 6178, al-Mansour, Baghdad; tel. (1) 443-0749; telex 212216.

Ministry of Planning: Karradat Mariam, ash-Shawaf Sq., Baghdad; tel. (1) 537-0071; telex 212218.

Ministry of Trade: Khulafa St, Khullani Sq., Baghdad; tel. (1) 887-2682; telex 212206.

Ministry of Transport and Communications: Nr Martyr's Monument, Karradat Dakhil, Baghdad; tel. (1) 776-6041; telex 212020.

KURDISH AUTONOMOUS REGION

Executive Council: Chair. MUHAMMAD AMIN MUHAMMAD (acting).

Legislative Council: Chair. AHMAD ABD AL-QADIR AN-NAQSHABANDI.

In May 1992, in the absence of a negotiated autonomy agreement with the Iraqi Government, the KIF (see below) organized elections to a 105-member Kurdish National Assembly. The DPK and the PUK were the only parties to achieve representation in the new Assembly and subsequently agreed to share seats equally between them. Elections held at the same time as those to the National Assembly, to choose an overall Kurdish leader, were inconclusive and were to be held again at a later date.

Legislature

NATIONAL ASSEMBLY

No form of National Assembly existed in Iraq between the 1958 revolution, which overthrew the monarchy, and June 1980. (The existing provisional Constitution, introduced in 1968, contains provisions for the election of an assembly at a date to be determined by the Government. The members of the Assembly are to be elected from all political, social and economic sectors of the Iraqi people.) In December 1979 the RCC invited political, trade union and popular organizations to debate a draft law providing for the creation of a 250-member National Assembly (elected from 56 constituencies) and a 50-member Kurdish Legislative Council, both to be elected by direct, free and secret ballot. Elections for the first National Assembly took place on 20 June 1980, and for the Kurdish Legislative Council on 11 September 1980, 13 August 1986 and 9 September 1989. The Assembly was dominated by members of the ruling Baath Party.

Elections for the fourth National Assembly were held on 24 March 1996. Some 689 candidates contested 220 of the Assembly's 250 seats, while the remaining 30 seats (reserved for representatives of the Autonomous Regions of Arbil, D'hok and As-Sulaimaniya) were filled by presidential decree. According to official sources, 93.5% of Iraq's 8m.-strong electorate participated in the elections.

Chairman: Dr SA'ADOUN HAMMADI.

Chairman of the Kurdish Legislative Council: AHMAD ABD AL-QADIR AN-NAQSHABANDI.

Political Organizations

National Progressive Front: Baghdad; f. July 1973, when Arab Baath Socialist Party and Iraqi Communist Party signed a joint manifesto agreeing to establish a comprehensive progressive national and nationalistic front. In 1975 representatives of Kurdish parties and organizations and other national and independent forces joined the Front; the Iraqi Communist Party left the National Progressive Front in mid-March 1979; Sec.-Gen. NAIM HADDAD (Baath).

Arab Baath Socialist Party: POB 6012, al-Mansour, Baghdad; revolutionary Arab socialist movement founded in Damascus in 1947; has ruled Iraq since July 1968, and between July 1973 and March 1979 in alliance with the Iraqi Communist Party in the National Progressive Front; founder MICHEL AFLAQ; Regional Command Sec.-Gen. SADDAM HUSSAIN; Deputy Regional Command Sec.-Gen. IZZAT IBRAHIM; mems of Regional Command: TAHA YASSIN RAMADAN, TAREQ AZIZ, MUHAMMAD HAMZAH AZ-ZUBAYDI, ABD AL-GHANI ABD AL-GHAFUR, SA'ADOUN HAMMADI MAZBAN KHADR HADI, ALI HASSAN AL-MAJID, KAMIL YASSIN RASHID, MUHAMMAD ZIMAM ABD AR-RAZZAQ, MUHAMMAD YOUNIS AL-AHMAD, KHADER ABD AL-AZIZ HUSSAIN, ABD AR-RAHMAN AHMAD ABD AR-RAHMAN, NOURI FAISAL SHAHIR, MIZHER MATNI AL-AWWAD, FAWZI KHALAF, LATIF NUSAYYIF JASIM, ADEL ADBULLAH MEHDI; approx. 100,000 mems.

Kurdistan Revolutionary Party: f. 1972; succeeded Democratic Kurdistan Party; admitted to National Progressive Front 1974; Sec.-Gen. ABD AS-SATTAR TAHER SHAREF.

There are several illegal opposition groups, including:

Ad-Da'wa al-Islamiya (Voice of Islam): f. 1968; based in Teheran; mem. of the Supreme Council of the Islamic Revolution in Iraq (see below); guerrilla group; Leader Sheikh AL-ASSEFIE.

Iraqi Communist Party: Baghdad; f. 1934; became legally recognized in July 1973 on formation of National Progressive Front; left National Progressive Front March 1979; proscribed as a result of its support for Iran during the Iran–Iraq War; First Sec. AZIZ MUHAMMAD.

Umma (Nation) Party: f. 1982; opposes Saddam Hussain's regime; Leader SAAD SALEH JABR.

There is also a breakaway element of the Arab Baath Socialist Party represented on the Iraqi National Joint Action Cttee (see below); the Democratic Gathering (Leader SALEH DOUBLAH); the Iraqi Socialist Party (ISP; Leader Gen. HASSAN AN-NAQUIB); the Democratic Party of Kurdistan (DPK; f. 1946; Leader MASOUD BARZANI); the Patriotic Union of Kurdistan (PUK; f. 1975; Leader JALAL TALIBANI); the Socialist Party of Kurdistan (SPK; f. 1975; Leader RASSOUL MARMAND); the United Socialist Party of Kurdistan (USPK; Leader MAHMOUD OSMAN), a breakaway group from the PUK; the Kurdistan People's Democratic Party (KPDP; Leader SAMI ABD AR-RAHMAN); the Kurdish Workers' Party (PKK); the Islamic League of Kurdistan (ILK, also known as the Islamic Movement of Iraqi Kurdistan (IMIK)); the Kurdish Hezbollah (Party of God; f. 1985; Leader Sheikh MUHAMMAD KALED), a breakaway group from the DPK and a member of the Supreme Council of the Islamic Revolution in Iraq (SCIRI), which is based in Teheran under the leadership of the exiled Iraqi Shi'ite leader, Hojatoleslam MUHAMMAD BAQIR AL-HAKIM, and has a military wing, the Badr Brigade; the Iraqi National Accord (INA); and Hizb al-Watan or Homeland Party (Leader MISHAAN AL-JUBOURI.

Various alliances of political and religious groups have been formed to oppose the regime of Saddam Hussain in recent years. They include the Kurdistan Iraqi Front (KIF; f. 1988), an alliance of the DPK, the PUK, the SPK, the KPDP and other, smaller Kurdish groups; the Iraqi National Joint Action Cttee, formed in Damascus in 1990 and grouping together the SCIRI, the four principal Kurdish parties belonging to the KIF, Ad-Da'wa al-Islamiya, the Movement of the Iraqi Mujahidin (based in Teheran; Leaders Hojatoleslam MUHAMMAD BAQIR AL-HAKIM and SAID MUHAMMAD AL-HAIDARI), the Islamic Movement in Iraq (Shi'ite group based in Teheran; Leader Sheikh MUHAMMAD MAHDI AL-KALISI), Jund al-Imam (Imam Soldiers; Shi'ite; Leader ABU ZAID), the Islamic Action Organization (based in Teheran; Leader Sheikh TAQI MODARESSI), the Islamic Alliance (based in Saudi Arabia; Sunni; Leader ABU YASSER AL-

ALOUSI), the Independent Group, the Iraqi Socialist Party, the Arab Socialist Movement, the Nasserite Unionist Gathering and the National Reconciliation Group. There is also the London-based Iraqi National Congress (INC; Presidential Council: MASOUD BARZANI, Gen. HASSAN AN-NAQUIB, MUHAMMAD BAHR AL-OLOUM), which has sought to unite the various factions of the opposition and in November 1992 organized a conference in Iraqi Kurdistan, at which a 25-member executive committee and a three-member presidential council were elected. In September 1992 the KPDP, the SPK and the Kurdish Democratic Independence Party were reported to have merged to form the Kurdistan Unity Party (KUP).

Diplomatic Representation

EMBASSIES IN IRAQ

Albania: Baghdad; Ambassador: GYLANI SHEHU.

Algeria: ash-Shawaf Sq., Karradat Mariam, Baghdad; tel. (1) 537-2181; Ambassador: AL-ARABI SI AL-HASSAN.

Argentina: POB 2443, Hay al-Jamia District 915, St 24, No. 142, Baghdad; tel. (1) 776-8140; telex 213500; Ambassador: GERÓNIMO CORTES-FUNES.

Australia: POB 661, Masba 39B/35, Baghdad; tel. (1) 719-3434; telex 212148; Ambassador: P. LLOYD.

Bahrain: POB 27117, al-Mansour, Hay al-Watanabi, Mahalla 605, Zuqaq 7, House 4/1/44, Baghdad; tel. (1) 542-3656; telex 213364; Ambassador: ABD AR-RAHMAN AL-FADHIL.

Bangladesh: 75/17/929 Hay Babel, Baghdad; tel. (1) 719-6367; telex 2370; Ambassador: MUFLEH R. OSMARRY.

Belgium: Hay Babel 929/27/25, Baghdad; tel. (1) 719-8297; telex 212450; Ambassador: MARC VAN RYSSELBERGHE.

Brazil: 609/16 al-Mansour, Houses 62/62–1, Baghdad; tel. (1) 541-1365; telex 2240; Ambassador: MAURO SERGIO CONTO.

Bulgaria: POB 28022, Ameriya, New Diplomatic Quarter, Baghdad; tel. (1) 556-8197; Ambassador: ASSEN ZLATANOV.

Canada: 47/1/7 al-Mansour, Baghdad; tel. (1) 542-1459; telex 212486; Ambassador: DAVID KARSGAARD.

Central African Republic: 208/406 az-Zawra, Harthiya, Baghdad; tel. (1) 551-6520; Chargé d'affaires: RENÉ BISSAYO.

Chad: POB 8037, 97/4/4 Karradat Mariam, Baghdad; tel. (1) 537-6160; Ambassador: MAHAMAT DJIBER AHNOUR.

China, People's Republic: New Embassy Area, International Airport Rd, Baghdad; tel. (1) 556-2741; telex 2195; fax (1) 541-7628; Ambassador: SUN BIGAN.

Cuba: St 7, District 929 Hay Babel, al-Masba Arrasat al-Hindi; tel. 776-5324; telex 212389; Ambassador: LUIS MARISY FIGUEREDO.

Czech Republic: Dijlaschool St, No. 37, Mansour, Baghdad; tel. (1) 541-7136; telex 213543; fax (1) 543-0275; Chargé d'affaires: MIROSLAV BELICA.

Denmark: POB 2001, Zuqaq No. 34, Mahalla 902, Hay al-Wahda, House No. 18/1, Alwiyah, Baghdad; tel. (1) 719-3058; telex 212490; Ambassador: TORBEN G. DITHMER.

Djibouti: POB 6223, al-Mansour, Baghdad; tel. (1) 551-3805; Ambassador: ABSEIA BOOH ABDULLA.

Finland: POB 2041, Alwiyah, Baghdad; tel. (1) 776-6271; telex 212454; Ambassador: (vacant).

Greece: 63/3/913 Hay al-Jamia, al-Jadiriya, Baghdad; tel. (1) 776-6572; telex 212479; Ambassador: EPAMINONDAS PEYOS.

Holy See: POB 2090, as-Sa'adoun St 904/2/46, Baghdad (Apostolic Nunciature); tel. (1) 719-5183; fax (1) 719-6520; Apostolic Nuncio: Most Rev. GIUSEPPE LAZZAROTTO, Titular Archbishop of Numana.

Hungary: POB 2065, Abu Nuwas St, az-Zuwiya, Baghdad; tel. (1) 776-5000; telex 212293; Ambassador: TAMÁS VARGA; also represents Italian interests.

India: POB 4114, Zuqaq 25, Mahalla 306, Baghdad; tel. (1) 422-5438; telex 212248; Ambassador: ARIF QAMARAIN.

Indonesia: 906/2/77 Hay al-Wahda, Baghdad; tel. (1) 719-8677; telex 2517; Ambassador: A. A. MURTADHO.

Iran: Karradat Mariam, Baghdad; Ambassador: (vacant).

Ireland: 913/28/101 Hay al-Jamia, Baghdad; tel. (1) 776-8661; Ambassador: PATRICK MCCABE.

Japan: 929/17/70 Hay Babel, Masba, Baghdad; tel. (1) 719-5156; telex 212241; fax (1) 719-6186; Ambassador: TAIZO NAKAMARA.

Jordan: POB 6314, House No. 1, St 12, District 609, al-Mansour, Baghdad; tel. (1) 541-2892; telex 2805; Ambassador: HILMI LOZI.

Korea, Republic: 915/22/278 Hay al-Jamia, Baghdad; tel. (1) 776-5496; Ambassador: BONG RHUEM CHEI.

Libya: Baghdad; Head of the Libyan People's Bureau: ABBAS AHMAD AL-MASSRATI (acting).

Malaysia: 6/14/929 Hay Babel, Baghdad; tel. (1) 776-2622; telex 2452; Ambassador: K. N. NADARAJAH.

Malta: 2/1 Zuqaq 49, Mahalla 503, Hay an-Nil, Baghdad; tel. (1) 772-5032; Chargé d'affaires a.i.: NADER SALEM RIZZO.

Mauritania: al-Mansour, Baghdad; tel. (1) 551-8261; Ambassador: MUHAMMAD YEHYA WALAD AHMAD AL-HADI.

Mexico: 601/11/45 al-Mansour, Baghdad; tel. (1) 719-8039; telex 2582; Chargé d'affaires: VÍCTOR M. DELGADO.

Morocco: POB 6039, Hay al-Mansour, Baghdad; tel. (1) 552-1779; Ambassador: ABOLESLAM ZENINED.

Netherlands: POB 2064, 29/35/915 Jadiriya, Baghdad; tel. (1) 776-7616; telex 212276; Ambassador: Dr N. VAN DAM.

New Zealand: POB 2350, 2D/19 az-Zuwiya, Jadiriya, Baghdad; tel. (1) 776-8177; telex 212433; Ambassador: (vacant).

Nigeria: POB 5933, 2/3/603 Mutanabi, al-Mansour, Baghdad; tel. (1) 542-1750; telex 212474; Ambassador: A. G. ABDULLAHI.

Oman: POB 6180, 213/36/15 al-Harthiya, Baghdad; tel. (1) 551-8198; telex 212480; Ambassador: KHALIFA BIN ABDULLA BIN SALIM AL-HOMAIDI.

Pakistan: 14/7/609 al-Mansour, Baghdad; tel. (1) 541-5120; Ambassador: KHALID MAHMOUD.

Philippines: Hay Babel, Baghdad; tel. (1) 719-3228; telex 3463; Ambassador: AKMAD A. SAKKAN.

Poland: POB 2051, 30 Zuqaq 13, Mahalla 931, Hay Babel, Baghdad; tel. (1) 719-0296; Ambassador: KRZYSZTOF SLOMINSKI.

Portugal: POB 2123, 66/11 al-Karada ash-Sharqiya, Hay Babel, Sector 925, St 25, No. 79, Alwiya, Baghdad; tel. (1) 718-7524; telex 212716; Ambassador: (vacant).

Qatar: 152/406 Harthiya, Hay al-Kindi, Baghdad; tel. (1) 551-2186; telex 2391; Ambassador: MUHAMMAD RASHID KHALIFA AL-KHALIFA.

Romania: Arassat al-Hindia, Hay Babel, Zuqaq 31, Mahalla 929, No 452/A, Baghdad; tel. (1) 776-2860; telex 2268; Chargé d'affaires: GHEORGHE TSARLESCU.

Russia: 4/5/605 al-Mutanabi, Baghdad; tel. (1) 541-4749; Ambassador: VIKTOR J. MININ.

Senegal: 569/5/10, Hay al-Mansour Baghdad; tel. (1) 542-0806; Ambassador: DOUDOU DIOP.

Slovakia: POB 238, Jamiyah St, No. 94, Jadiriyah, Baghdad; tel. (1) 776-7367; telex 214068.

Somalia: 603/1/5 al-Mansour, Baghdad; tel. (1) 551-0088; Ambassador: ISSA ALI MOHAMMED.

Spain: POB 2072, ar-Riyad Quarter, District 908, Street No. 1, No. 21, Alwiya, Baghdad; tel. (1) 719-2852; telex 212239; Ambassador: JUAN LÓPEZ DE CHICHERI.

Sri Lanka: POB 1094, 07/80/904 Hay al-Wahda, Baghdad; tel. (1) 719-3040; Ambassador: N. NAVARATNARAJAH.

Sudan: 38/15/601 al-Imarat, Baghdad; tel. (1) 542-4889; Ambassador: ALI ADAM MUHAMMAD AHMAD.

Sweden: 15/41/103 Hay an-Nidhal, Baghdad; tel. (1) 719-5361; telex 212352; Ambassador: HENRIK AMNEUS.

Switzerland: POB 2107, Hay Babel, House No. 41/5/929, Baghdad; tel. (1) 719-3091.

Thailand: POB 6062, 1/4/609, al-Mansour, Baghdad; tel. (1) 541-8798; telex 213345; Ambassador: CHEUY SUETRONG.

Tunisia: POB 6057, Mansour 34/2/4, Baghdad; tel. (1) 551-7786; Ambassador: LARBI HANTOUS.

Turkey: POB 14001, 2/8 Waziriya, Baghdad; tel. (1) 422-2768; telex 214145; Ambassador: SÖNMEZ KÖKSAL.

Uganda: 41/1/609 al-Mansour, Baghdad; tel. (1) 551-3594; Ambassador: SWAIB M. MUSOKE.

United Arab Emirates: al-Mansour, 50 al-Mansour Main St, Baghdad; tel. (1) 551-7026; telex 2285; Ambassador: HILAL SA'ID HILAL AZ-ZU'ABI.

Venezuela: al-Mansour, House No. 12/79/601, Baghdad; tel. (1) 552-0965; telex 2173; Ambassador: FREDDY RAFAEL ALVAREZ YANES.

Viet Nam: 29/611 Hay al-Andalus, Baghdad; tel. (1) 551-1388; Ambassador: TRAN KY LONG.

Yemen: Jadiriya 923/28/29, Baghdad; tel. (1) 776-0647; Ambassador: MUHAMMAD ABDULLAH ASH-SHAMI.

Yugoslavia: POB 2061, 16/35/923 Hay Babel, Jadiriya, Baghdad; tel. (1) 776-7887; telex 213521; fax (1) 217-1069; Chargé d'affaires a.i.: JOVAN KOSTIĆ.

Judicial System

Courts in Iraq consist of the following: The Court of Cassation, Courts of Appeal, First Instance Courts, Peace Courts, Courts of Sessions, *Shari'a* Courts and Penal Courts.

The Court of Cassation: This is the highest judicial bench of all the Civil Courts; it sits in Baghdad, and consists of the President and a number of vice-presidents and not fewer than 15 permanent judges, delegated judges and reporters as necessity requires. There are four bodies in the Court of Cassation, these are: (*a*) the General body, (*b*) Civil and Commercial body, (*c*) Personal Status body, (*d*) the Penal body.

Courts of Appeal: The country is divided into five Districts of Appeal: Baghdad, Mosul, Basra, Hilla, and Kirkuk, each with its Court of Appeal consisting of a president, vice-presidents and not fewer than three members, who consider the objections against the decisions issued by the First Instance Courts of first grade.

Courts of First Instance: These courts are of two kinds: Limited and Unlimited in jurisdiction.

Limited Courts deal with Civil and Commercial suits, the value of which is 500 Iraqi dinars and less; and suits, the value of which cannot be defined, and which are subject to fixed fees. Limited Courts consider these suits in the final stage and they are subject to Cassation.

Unlimited Courts consider the Civil and Commercial suits irrespective of their value, and suits the value of which exceeds 500 Iraqi dinars with first grade subject to appeal.

First Instance Courts consist of one judge in the centre of each *Liwa*, some *Qadhas* and *Nahiyas*, as the Minister of Justice judges necessary.

Courts of Sessions: There is in every District of Appeal a Court of Sessions which consists of three judges under the presidency of the President of the Court of Appeal or one of his vice-presidents. It considers the penal suits prescribed by Penal Proceedings Law and other laws. More than one Court of Sessions may be established in one District of Appeal by notification issued by the Minister of Justice mentioning therein its headquarters, jurisdiction and the manner of its establishment.

Shari'a Courts: A *Shari'a* Court is established wherever there is a First Instance Court; the Muslim judge of the First Instance Court may be a *Qadhi* to the *Shari'a* Court if a special *Qadhi* has not been appointed thereto. The *Shari'a* Court considers matters of personal status and religious matters in accordance with the provisions of the law supplement to the Civil and Commercial Proceedings Law.

Penal Courts: A Penal Court of first grade is established in every First Instance Court. The judge of the First Instance Court is considered as penal judge unless a special judge is appointed thereto. More than one Penal Court may be established to consider the suits prescribed by the Penal Proceedings Law and other laws.

One or more Investigation Court may be established in the centre of each *Liwa* and a judge is appointed thereto. They may be established in the centres of *Qadhas* and *Nahiyas* by order of the Minister of Justice. The judge carries out the investigation in accordance with the provisions of Penal Proceedings Law and the other laws.

There is in every First Instance Court a department for the execution of judgments presided over by the Judge of First Instance if a special president is not appointed thereto. It carries out its duties in accordance with the provisions of Execution Law.

Religion

ISLAM

About 95% of the population are Muslims, more than 50% of whom are Shi'ite. The Arabs of northern Iraq, the Bedouins, the Kurds, the Turkomans and some of the inhabitants of Baghdad and Basra are mainly of the Sunni sect, while the remaining Arabs south of the Diyali belong to the Shi'i sect.

CHRISTIANITY

There are Christian communities in all the principal towns of Iraq, but their principal villages lie mostly in the Mosul district. The Christians of Iraq comprise three groups: (*a*) the free Churches, including the Nestorian, Gregorian and Syrian Orthodox; (*b*) the churches known as Uniate, since they are in union with the Roman Catholic Church, including the Armenian Uniates, Syrian Uniates and Chaldeans; (*c*) mixed bodies of Protestant converts, New Chaldeans and Orthodox Armenians.

The Assyrian Church

Assyrian Christians, an ancient sect having sympathies with Nestorian beliefs, were forced to leave their mountainous homeland in northern Kurdistan in the early part of the 20th century. The estimated 550,000 members of the Apostolic Catholic Assyrian Church of the East are now exiles, mainly in Iraq, Syria, Lebanon and the USA. Their leader is the Catholicos Patriarch, His Holiness MAR DINKHA IV.

The Orthodox Churches

Armenian Apostolic Church: Bishop AVAK ASADOURIAN, Primate of the Armenian Diocese of Iraq, POB 2280, Younis as-Saba'awi Sq.,

Baghdad; tel. (1) 885-1853; fax (1) 885-1857; nine churches (four in Baghdad); 18,000 adherents, mainly in Baghdad.

Syrian Orthodox Church: about 12,000 adherents in Iraq.

The Greek Orthodox Church is also represented in Iraq.

The Roman Catholic Church

Armenian Rite

At 31 December 1996 the archdiocese of Baghdad contained an estimated 2,200 adherents.

Archbishop of Baghdad: Most Rev. PAUL COUSSA, Archevêché Arménien Catholique, Karrada Sharkiya, POB 2344, Baghdad; tel. (1) 719-1827.

Chaldean Rite

Iraq comprises the patriarchate of Babylon, five archdioceses (including the patriarchal see of Baghdad) and five dioceses (all of which are suffragan to the patriarchate). Altogether, the Patriarch has jurisdiction over 21 archdioceses and dioceses in Iraq, Egypt, Iran, Lebanon, Syria, Turkey and the USA, and the Patriarchal Vicariate of Jerusalem. At 31 December 1996 there were an estimated 202,998 Chaldean Catholics in Iraq (including 150,000 in the archdiocese of Baghdad).

Patriarch of Babylon of the Chaldeans: His Beatitude RAPHAËL I BIDAWID, POB 6112, Patriarcat Chaldéen Catholique, Baghdad; tel. (1) 887-9604; fax (1) 884-9967.

Archbishop of Arbil: Most Rev. JACQUES ISHAQ, Archevêché Catholique Chaldéen, Ainkawa, Arbil; tel. (665) 24701.

Archbishop of Baghdad: the Patriarch of Babylon (see above).

Archbishop of Basra: Most Rev. DJIBRAIL KASSAB, Archevêché Chaldéen, POB 217, Ahsar-Basra; tel. (40) 210323.

Archbishop of Kirkuk: Most Rev. ANDRÉ SANA, Archevêché Chaldéen, Kirkuk; tel. (50) 213978.

Archbishop of Mosul: Most Rev. GEORGES GARMO, Archevêché Chaldéen, Mayassa, Mosul; tel. (60) 762022; fax (60) 772460.

Latin Rite

The archdiocese of Baghdad, directly responsible to the Holy See, contained an estimated 3,000 adherents at 31 December 1996.

Archbishop of Baghdad: Most Rev. PAUL DAHDAH, Archevêché Latin, Hay al-Wahda—Mahalla 904, rue 8, Imm. 44, POB 35130, Baghdad; tel. (1) 719-9537; fax (1) 717-2471.

Melkite Rite

The Greek-Melkite Patriarch of Antioch (MAXIMOS V HAKIM) is resident in Damascus, Syria.

Patriarchal Exarchate of Iraq: Rue Asfar, Karrada Sharkiya, Baghdad; tel. (1) 719-1082; 600 adherents (31 December 1995); Exarch Patriarchal: Archimandrite NICOLAS DAGHER.

Syrian Rite

Iraq comprises two archdioceses, containing an estimated 52,450 adherents at 31 December 1996.

Archbishop of Baghdad: Most Rev. ATHANASE MATTI SHABA MATOKA, Archevêché Syrien Catholique, Baghdad; tel. (1) 719-1850; fax (1) 719-0168.

Archbishop of Mosul: Most Rev. CYRILLE EMMANUEL BENNI, Archevêché Syrien Catholique, Mosul; tel. (60) 762160.

The Anglican Communion

Within the Episcopal Church in Jerusalem and the Middle East, Iraq forms part of the diocese of Cyprus and the Gulf. Expatriate congregations in Iraq meet at St George's Church, Baghdad (Hon. Sec. GRAHAM SPURGEON). The Bishop in Cyprus and the Gulf is resident in Cyprus.

JUDAISM

Unofficial estimates assess the present size of the Jewish community at 2,500, almost all residing in Baghdad.

OTHERS

About 30,000 Yazidis and a smaller number of Turkomans, Sabeans and Shebeks reside in Iraq.

Sabean Community: 20,000 adherents; Head Sheikh DAKHIL, Nasiriyah; Mandeans, mostly in Nasiriyah.

Yazidis: 30,000 adherents; Leader TASHIN BAIK, Ainsifni.

The Press

DAILIES

Al-Baath ar-Riyadhi: Baghdad; sports; Propr and Editor UDAY SADDAM HUSSEIN.

Babil (Babylon): Baghdad; f. 1991; Propr and Editor UDAY SADDAM HUSSAIN.

Baghdad Observer: POB 624, Karantina, Baghdad; f. 1967; tel. (1) 416-9341; telex 212984; English; state-sponsored; Editor-in-Chief NAJI AL-HADITHI; circ. 22,000.

Al-Iraq: POB 5717, Baghdad; f. 1976; Kurdish; formerly *Al-Ta'akhi*; organ of the National Progressive Front; Editor-in-Chief SALAHUDIN SAEED; circ. 30,000.

Al-Jumhuriya (The Republic): POB 491, Waziriya, Baghdad; f. 1963, refounded 1967; Arabic; Editor-in-Chief SAMI MAHDI; circ. 150,000.

Al-Qadisiya: Baghdad; organ of the army.

Ar-Riyadhi (Sportsman): POB 58, Jadid Hassan Pasha, Baghdad; f. 1971; Arabic; published by Ministry of Youth; circ. 30,000.

Tariq ash-Sha'ab (People's Path): as-Sa'adoun St, Baghdad; Arabic; organ of the Iraqi Communist Party; Editor ABD AR-RAZZAK AS-SAFI.

Ath-Thawra (Revolution): POB 2009, Aqaba bin Nafi's Square, Baghdad; tel. (1) 719-6161; f. 1968; Arabic; organ of Baath Party; Editor-in-Chief HAMEED SAEED; circ. 250,000.

WEEKLIES

Alif Baa (Alphabet): POB 491, Karantina, Baghdad; tel. (1) 416-9341; telex 212984; fax (1) 416-1875; Arabic; Editor-in-Chief KAMIL HAMDI ASH-SHARQI; circ. 150,000.

Al-Idaa'a wal-Television (Radio and Television): Iraqi Broadcasting and Television Establishment, Karradat Mariam, Baghdad; tel. (1) 537-1161; telex 212246; radio and television programmes and articles; Arabic; Editor-in-Chief KAMIL HAMDI ASH-SHARQI; circ. 40,000.

Majallati: Children's Culture House, POB 8041, Baghdad; telex 212228; Arabic; children's newspaper; Editor-in-Chief RAAD BENDER; circ. 35,000.

Ar-Rased (The Observer): Baghdad; Arabic; general.

Sabaa Nisan: Baghdad; f. 1976; Arabic; organ of the General Union of the Youth of Iraq.

Sawt al-Fallah (Voice of the Peasant): Karradat Mariam, Baghdad; f. 1968; Arabic; organ of the General Union of Farmers Societies; circ. 40,000.

Waee ul-Ummal (The Workers' Consciousness): Headquarters of General Federation of Trade Unions in Iraq, POB 2307, Gialani St, Senak, Baghdad; Arabic; Iraq Trades Union organ; Chief Editor KHALID MAHMOUD HUSSEIN; circ. 25,000.

PERIODICALS

Afaq Arabiya (Arab Horizons): POB 2009, Aqaba bin Nafi's Sq., Baghdad; monthly; Arabic; literary and political; Editor-in-Chief Dr MOHSIN J. AL-MUSAWI.

Al-Aqlam (Pens): POB 4032, Adamiya, Baghdad; tel. (1) 443-3644; telex 214135; f. 1964; publ. by the Ministry of Culture and Information; monthly; Arabic; literary; Editor-in-Chief Dr ALI J. AL-ALLAQ; circ. 7,000.

Bagdad: Dar al-Ma'mun for Translation and Publishing, POB 24015, Karradat Mariam, Baghdad; tel. (1) 538-3171; telex 212984; fortnightly; French; cultural and political.

Al-Funoon al-Ida'iya (Fields of Broadcasting): Cultural Affairs House, Karradat Mariam, Baghdad; quarterly; Arabic; supervised by Broadcasting and TV Training Institute; engineering and technical; Chief Editor MUHAMMAD AL-JAZA'RI.

Gilgamesh: Dar al-Ma'mun for Translation and Publishing, POB 24015, Karradat Mariam, Baghdad; tel. (1) 538-3171; telex 212984; quarterly; English; cultural.

Hurras al-Watan: Baghdad; Arabic.

L'Iraq Aujourd'hui: POB 2009, Aqaba bin Nafi's Sq., Baghdad; f. 1976; bi-monthly; French; cultural and political; Editor NADJI AL-HADITHI; circ. 12,000.

Iraq Oil News: POB 6178, al-Mansour, Baghdad; tel. (1) 541-0031; telex 2216; f. 1973; monthly; English; publ. by the Information and Public Relations Div. of the Ministry of Oil.

The Journal of the Faculty of Medicine: College of Medicine, University of Baghdad, Jadiriya, Baghdad; tel. (1) 93091; f. 1935; quarterly; Arabic and English; medical and technical; Editor Prof. YOUSUF D. AN-NAAMAN.

Majallat al-Majma' al-'Ilmi al-'Iraqi (Iraqi Academy Journal): POB 4023, Waziriya, Baghdad; tel. (1) 422-1733; fax (1) 425-4523; f. 1950; quarterly; Arabic; scholarly magazine on Arabic Islamic culture; Editor-in-Chief MUSTAFA T. AL-MUKHTAR.

Majallat ath-Thawra az-Ziraia (Magazine of Iraq Agriculture): Baghdad; quarterly; Arabic; agricultural; published by the Ministry of Agriculture and Irrigation.

Al-Maskukat (Coins): State Organization of Antiquities and Heritage, Karkh, Salihiya St, Baghdad; tel. (1) 537-6121; f. 1969; annually; the journal of numismatics in Iraq; Chair. of Ed. Board Dr MUAYAD SA'ID DAMERJI.

Al-Masrah wal-Cinema: Iraqi Broadcasting, Television and Cinema Establishment, Salihiya, Baghdad; monthly; Arabic; artistic, theatrical and cinema.

Al-Mawrid: POB 2009, Aqaba bin Nafi's Sq., Baghdad; f. 1971; monthly; Arabic; cultural.

Al-Mu'allem al-Jadid: Ministry of Education, al-Imam al-A'dham St, A'dhamaiya, Nr Antar Sq., Baghdad; tel. (1) 422-2594; telex 212259; f. 1935; quarterly; Arabic; educational, social, and general; Editor-in-Chief KHALIL I. HAMASH; circ. 190,000.

An-Naft wal-Aalam (Oil and the World): Ministry of Oil, POB 6178, Baghdad; f. 1973; monthly; Arabic; Editor-in-Chief Gen. AMIR MUHAMMAD RASHID.

Sawt at-Talaba (The Voice of Students): al-Maghreb St, Waziriya, Baghdad; f. 1968; monthly; Arabic; organ of National Union of Iraqi Students; circ. 25,000.

As-Sina'a (Industry): POB 5665, Baghdad; every 2 months; Arabic and English; publ. by Ministry of Industry and Minerals; Editor-in-Chief ABD AL-QADER ABD AL-LATIF; circ. 16,000.

Sumer: State Organization of Antiquities and Heritage, Karkh, Salihiya St, Baghdad; tel. (1) 537-6121; f. 1945; annually; archaeological, historical journal; Chair. of Ed. Board Dr MUAYAD SA'ID DAMERJI.

Ath-Thaquafa (Culture): Place at-Tahrir, Baghdad; f. 1970; monthly; Arabic; cultural; Editor-in-Chief SALAH KHALIS; circ. 5,000.

Ath-Thaquafa al-Jadida (The New Culture): Baghdad; f. 1969; monthly; pro-Communist; Editor-in-Chief SAFA AL-HAFIZ; circ. 3,000.

At-Turath ash-Sha'abi (Popular Heritage): POB 2009, Aqaba bin Nafi's Sq., Baghdad; monthly; Arabic; specializes in Iraqi and Arabic folklore; Editor-in-Chief LUTFI AL-KHOURI; circ. 15,000.

Al-Waqai al-Iraqiya (Official Gazette of Republic of Iraq): Ministry of Justice, Baghdad; f. 1922; Arabic and English weekly editions; circ. Arabic 4,000, English 400; Dir HASHIM N. JAAFER.

PRESS ORGANIZATIONS

The General Federation of Journalists: POB 6017, Baghdad; tel. (1) 541-3993.

Iraqi Journalists' Union: POB 14101, Baghdad; tel. (1) 537-0762.

NEWS AGENCIES

Iraqi News Agency (INA): POB 3084, 28 Nissan Complex—Baghdad, Sadoun; tel. (1) 8863024; telex 212267; f. 1959; Dir-Gen. UDAI EL-TAIE.

Foreign Bureaux

Agence France-Presse (AFP): POB 190, Apt 761-91-97, Baghdad; tel. (1) 551-4333; Correspondent FAROUQ CHOUKRI.

Agenzia Nazionale Stampa Associata (ANSA) (Italy): POB 5602, Baghdad; tel. (1) 776-2558; Correspondent SALAH H. NASRAWI.

Associated Press (AP) (USA): Hay al-Khadra 629, Zuqaq No. 23, Baghdad; tel. (1) 555-9041; telex 213324; Correspondent SALAH H. NASRAWI.

Deutsche Presse-Agentur (dpa) (Germany): POB 5699, Baghdad; Correspondent NAJHAT KOTANI.

Informatsionnoye Telegrafnoye Agentstvo Rossii—Telegrafnoye Agentstvo Suverennykh Stran (ITAR—TASS) (Russia): 67 Street 52, Alwiya, Baghdad; Correspondent ANDREI OSTALSKY.

Reuters (UK): House No. 8, Zuqaq 75, Mahalla 903, Hay al-Karada, Baghdad; tel. (1) 719-1843; telex 213777; Correspondent SUBHY HADDAD.

Xinhua (New China) News Agency (People's Republic of China): al-Mansour, Adrus District, 611 Small District, 5 Lane No. 8, Baghdad; tel. (1) 541-8904; telex 213253; Correspondent ZHU SHAOHUA.

Publishers

National House for Publishing, Distribution and Advertising: Ministry of Culture and Information, POB 624, al-Jumhuriya St, Baghdad; tel. (1) 425-1846; telex 2392; f. 1972; publishes books on politics, economics, education, agriculture, sociology, commerce and science in Arabic and other Middle Eastern languages; sole importer and distributor of newspapers, magazines, periodicals and books; controls all advertising activities, inside Iraq as well as outside; Dir-Gen. M. A. ASKAR.

Afaq Arabiya Publishing House: POB 4032, Adamiya, Baghdad; tel. (1) 443-6044; telex 214135; fax (1) 444-8760; publisher of literary monthlies, *Al-Aqlam* and *Afaq Arabiya*, periodicals, *Foreign Culture, Art, Folklore*, and cultural books; Chair. Dr MOHSIN AL-MUSAWI.

Dar al-Ma'mun for Translation and Publishing: POB 24015, Karradat Mariam, Baghdad; tel. (1) 538-3171; telex 212984; publisher of newspapers and magazines including: the *Baghdad Observer* (daily newspaper), *Bagdad* (monthly magazine), *Gilgamesh* (quarterly magazine).

Al-Hurriyah Printing Establishment: Karantina, Sarrafia, Baghdad; tel. (1) 69721; telex 212228; f. 1970; largest printing and publishing establishment in Iraq; state-owned; controls *Al-Jumhuriyah* (see below).

Al-Jamaheer Press House: POB 491, Sarrafia, Baghdad; tel. (1) 416-9341; telex 212363; fax (1) 416-1875; f. 1963; publisher of a number of newspapers and magazines, *Al-Jumhuriyah, Baghdad Observer, Alif Baa, Yord Weekly*; Pres. SAAD QASSEM HAMMOUDI.

Al-Ma'arif Ltd: Mutanabi St, Baghdad; f. 1929; publishes periodicals and books in Arabic, Kurdish, Turkish, French and English.

Al-Muthanna Library: Mutanabi St, Baghdad; f. 1936; booksellers and publishers of books in Arabic and oriental languages; Man. ANAS K. AR-RAJAB.

An-Nahdah: Mutanabi St, Baghdad; politics, Arab affairs.

Kurdish Culture Publishing House: Baghdad; f. 1976; attached to the Ministry of Culture and Information.

Ath-Thawra Printing and Publishing House: POB 2009, Aqaba bin Nafi's Sq., Baghdad; tel. (1) 719-6161; telex 212215; f. 1970; state-owned; Chair. TAREQ AZIZ.

Thnayan Printing House: Baghdad.

Broadcasting and Communications

TELECOMMUNICATIONS

Iraqi Telecommunications and Posts: POB 2450, Karrada Dakhil, Baghdad; tel. (1) 718-0400; telex 212002; fax (1) 718-2125; Dir-Gen. Eng. MEZHER M. HASAN.

BROADCASTING

State Enterprise for Communications and Post: f. 1987 from State Org. for Post, Telegraph and Telephones, and its subsidiaries.

State Organization for Broadcasting and Television: Broadcasting and Television Bldg, Salihiya, Karkh, Baghdad; tel. (1) 537-1161; telex 212246.

Iraqi Broadcasting and Television Establishment: Salihiya, Baghdad; tel. (1) 884-4412; telex 212246; fax (1) 541-0480; f. 1936; radio broadcasts began 1936; home service broadcasts in Arabic, Kurdish, Syriac and Turkoman; foreign service in French, German, English, Russian, Azeri, Hebrew and Spanish; there are 16 mediumwave and 30 short-wave transmitters; Dir-Gen. SABAH YASEEN.

Radio

Idaa'a Baghdad (Radio Baghdad): f.1936; 22 hours daily.

Idaa'a Sawt al-Jamahir: f. 1970; 24 hours.

Other stations include **Idaa'a al-Kurdia, Idaa'a al-Farisiya** (Persian).

Radio Iraq International: POB 8145, Baghdad.

Television

Baghdad Television: Ministry of Culture and Information, Iraqi Broadcasting and Television Establishment, Salihiya, Karkh, Baghdad; tel. (1) 537-1151; telex 212446; f. 1956; government station operating daily on two channels for 9 hours and 8 hours respectively; Dir-Gen. Dr MAJID AHMAD AS-SAMARRIE.

Kirkuk Television: f. 1967; government station; 6 hours daily.

Mosul Television: f. 1968; government station; 6 hours daily.

Basra Television: f. 1968; government station; 6 hours daily.

Missan Television: f. 1974; government station; 6 hours daily.

Kurdish Television: f. 1974; government station; 8 hours daily.

There are 18 other TV stations operating in the Iraqi provinces.

Finance

(cap. = capital; p.u. = paid up; dep. = deposits; res = reserves; brs = branches; m. = million; amounts in Iraqi dinars)

All banks and insurance companies, including all foreign companies, were nationalized in July 1964. The assets of foreign companies were taken over by the State. In May 1991 the Government announced its decision to end the State's monopoly in banking, and by mid-1992 three private banks had commenced operations.

BANKING

Central Bank

Central Bank of Iraq: POB 64, Rashid St, Baghdad; tel. (1) 886-5171; telex 212558; f. 1947 as National Bank of Iraq; name changed as above 1956; has the sole right of note issue; cap. and res 125m. (Sept. 1988); Gov. SUBHI N. FRANKOOL; brs in Mosul and Basra.

Nationalized Commercial Banks

Rafidain Bank: New Banks St, Baghdad; tel. (1) 415-8001; telex 2211; f. 1941; state-owned; cap. 500m., res 1,379.7m., dep. 213,284.4m., total assets 234,444.2m. (Dec. 1995); Pres. DHIA HABIB AL-KHAYYOON; 152 brs in Iraq, 9 brs abroad.

Rashid Bank: 7177 Haifa St, Baghdad; tel. (1) 523-9123; telex 214357; f. 1988; state-owned; cap. 200m., res 209.1m., dep. 53,377.1m., total assets 61,005.9m. (Dec. 1994); Chair. and Gen. Man. SAMI SALEH ADH-DHAMIN; 133 brs.

Private Commercial Banks

Baghdad Bank: POB 64, Rashid St, Baghdad; tel. (1) 717-5007; fax (1) 717-3487; f. 1992; cap. 100m.; Chair. HASSAN AN-NAJAFI.

Iraqi Commercial Bank SA: POB 5639, 902/14/13 Al-Wahda St, Baghdad; tel. (1) 707-0049, telex 213305; fax (1) 718-4312; f. 1992; cap. 500m.; Chair. ABD AL-MUHSAN SHANSHAL.

Specialized Banks

Al-Ahli Bank for Agricultural Investment and Financing: Al-Huria Sq., Al-Ahh, Baghdad.

Agricultural Co-operative Bank of Iraq: POB 2421, Rashid St, Baghdad; tel. (1) 886-4768; fax (1) 886-5047; f. 1936; state-owned; cap. p.u. 295.7m., res 14m., dep. 10.5m., total assets 351.6m. (Dec. 1988); Dir-Gen. HDIYA H. AL-KHAYOUN; 32 brs.

Industrial Bank of Iraq: POB 5825, as-Sinak, Baghdad; tel. (1) 887-2181; telex 2224; fax (1) 888-3047; f. 1940; state-owned; cap. p.u. 59.7m., dep. 77.9m. (Dec. 1988); Dir-Gen. BASSIMA ABD AL-HADDI ADH-DHAHIR; 5 brs.

Iraqi Bank for Investment SA: POB 3724, 102/91/24 Hay as-Sadoon, Alwiya, Baghdad; tel. (1) 718-4624; fax (1) 719-8505; f. 1993; cap. 200m., res 35.9m. (July 1998); Man. Dir MOWAFAQ HASAN MAHMOOD.

Iraqi Islamic Bank SA: POB 940, Al-Kahiay, Bab Al-Muathem, Baghdad; tel. (1) 414-0694; telex 213890.

Iraqi Middle East Bank for Investment: POB 10379, Bldg 65 Hay Babel, 929 Arasat al-Hindiay, Baghdad; tel. (1) 717-3745.

Real Estate Bank of Iraq: POB 8118, 29/222 Haifa St, Baghdad; tel. (1) 885-3212; telex 5880; fax (1) 884-0980; f. 1949; state-owned; gives loans to assist the building industry; cap. p.u. 800m., res 11m., total assets 2,593.6m. (Dec. 1988); acquired the Co-operative Bank in 1970; Dir-Gen. ABD AR-RAZZAQ AZIZ; 18 brs.

INSURANCE

Iraqi Life Insurance Co: POB 989, Aqaba bin Nafi's Sq., Khalid bin al-Waleed St, Baghdad; tel. (1) 719-2184; telex 213818; f. 1959; state-owned; Chair. and Gen. Man. ABD AL-KHALIQ RAUF KHALIL.

Iraq Reinsurance Co: POB 297, Aqaba bin Nafi's Sq., Khalid bin al-Waleed St, Baghdad; tel. (1) 719-5131; telex 214407; fax (1) 791497; f. 1960; state-owned; transacts reinsurance business on the international market; total assets 93.2m. (1985); Chair. and Gen. Man. K. M. AL-MUDARIES.

National Insurance Co: POB 248, Al-Khullani St, Baghdad; tel. (1) 886-0730; telex 2397; f. 1950; cap. p.u. 20m.; state monopoly for general business and life insurance; Chair. and Gen. Man. MOWAFAQ H. RIDHA.

STOCK EXCHANGE

Capital Market Authority: Baghdad; Chair. MUHAMMAD HASSAN FAG EN-NOUR.

Trade and Industry

CHAMBERS OF COMMERCE

Federation of Iraqi Chambers of Commerce: Mustansir St, Baghdad; tel. (1) 886-1811; fax (1) 886-0283; f. 1969; all Iraqi Chambers of Commerce are affiliated to the Federation; Chair. ZUHAIR A. AL-YOUNIS; Sec.-Gen. FALIH A. AS-SALEH.

INDUSTRIAL AND TRADE ASSOCIATIONS

In 1987 and 1988, as part of a programme of economic and administrative reform, to increase efficiency and productivity in industry and agriculture, many of the state organizations previously responsible for various industries were abolished or merged, and new state enterprises or mixed-sector national companies were established to replace them.

Military Industries Commission (MIC): Baghdad; attached to the Ministry of Defence; Chair. ABD AT-TAWAB ABDULLAH MULLAH HAWAISH.

State enterprises include the following:

Iraqi State Enterprise for Cement: f. 1987 by merger of central and southern state cement enterprises.

National Co for Chemical and Plastics Industries: Dir-Gen. RAJA BAYYATI.

The Rafidain Co for Building Dams: f. 1987 to replace the State Org. for Dams.

State Enterprise for Battery Manufacture: f. 1987; Dir-Gen. ADEL ABBOUD.

State Enterprise for Construction Industries: f. 1987 by merger of state orgs for gypsum, asbestos, and the plastic and concrete industries.

State Enterprise for Cotton Industries: f. 1988 by merger of State Org. for Cotton Textiles and Knitting, and the Mosul State Org. for Textiles.

State Enterprise for Drinks and Mineral Water: f. 1987 by merger of enterprises responsible for soft and alcoholic drinks.

State Enterprise for the Fertilizer Industries: f. by merger of Basra-based and central fertilizer enterprises.

State Enterprise for Import and Export: f. 1987 to replace the five state organizations responsible to the Ministry of Trade for productive commodities, consumer commodities, grain and food products, exports and imports.

State Enterprise for Leather Industries: f. 1987; Dir-Gen. MUHAMMAD ABD AL-MAJID.

State Enterprise for Sugar Beet: f. 1987 by merger of sugar enterprises in Mosul and Sulaimaniya.

State Enterprise for Textiles: f. 1987 to replace the enterprise for textiles in Baghdad, and the enterprise for plastic sacks in Tikrit.

State Enterprise for Tobacco and Cigarettes.

State Enterprise for Woollen Industries: f. by merger of state orgs for textiles and woollen textiles and Arbil-based enterprise for woollen textiles and women's clothing.

AGRICULTURAL ORGANIZATIONS

The following bodies are responsible to the Ministry of Agriculture and Irrigation:

State Agricultural Enterprise in Dujaila.

State Enterprise for Agricultural Supplies: Dir-Gen. MUHAMMAD KHAIRI.

State Enterprise for Developing Animal Wealth.

State Enterprise for Fodder.

State Enterprise for Grain Trading and Processing: Dir-Gen. ZUHAIR ABD AR-RAHMAN.

State Enterprise for Poultry (Central and Southern Areas).

State Enterprise for Poultry (Northern Area).

State Enterprise for Sea Fisheries: POB 260, Basra; telex 7011; Baghdad office: POB 3296, Baghdad; tel. (1) 92023; telex 212223; fleet of 3 fish factory ships, 2 fish carriers, 1 fishing boat.

PEASANT SOCIETIES

General Federation of Peasant Societies: Baghdad; f. 1959; has 734 affiliated Peasant Societies.

EMPLOYERS' ORGANIZATION

Iraqi Federation of Industries: Iraqi Federation of Industries Bldg, al-Khullani Sq., Baghdad; f. 1956; 6,000 mems; Pres. HATAM ABD AR-RASHID.

UTILITIES
Electricity

State Enterprise for Generation and Transmission of Electricity: f. 1987 from State Org. for Major Electrical Projects.

PETROLEUM AND GAS

Ministry of Oil: POB 6178, al-Mansour City, Baghdad; tel. (1) 551-0031; telex 212216; solely responsible until mid-1989 for petroleum sector and activities relevant to it; since mid-1989 these responsibilities have been shared with the Technical Corpn for Special Projects of the Ministry of Industry and Military Industrialization (Ministry of Industry and Minerals from July 1991); the Ministry was merged with INOC in 1987; the state organizations responsible to the ministry for petroleum refining and gas processing, for the distribu-

tion of petroleum products, for training personnel in the petroleum industry, and for gas were simultaneously abolished, and those for northern and southern petroleum, for petroleum equipment, for petroleum and gas exploration, for petroleum tankers, and for petroleum projects were converted into companies, as part of a plan to reorganize the petroleum industry and make it more efficient; Minister of Oil Gen. AMIR MUHAMMAD RASHID.

Iraq National Oil Co (INOC): POB 476, al-Khullani Sq., Baghdad; tel. (1) 887-1115; telex 212204; f. in 1964 to operate the petroleum industry at home and abroad; when Iraq nationalized its petroleum industry, structural changes took place in INOC, and it became solely responsible for exploration, production, transportation and marketing of Iraqi crude petroleum and petroleum products. INOC was merged with the Ministry of Oil in 1987, and the functions of some of the organizations under its control were transferred to newly-created ministerial departments or to companies responsible to the ministry.

Iraqi Oil Drilling Co: f. 1990.

Iraqi Oil Tankers Co: POB 37, Basra; tel. (40) 319990; telex 207007; fmrly the State Establishment for Oil Tankers; re-formed as a company in 1987; responsible to the Ministry of Oil for operating a fleet of 17 oil tankers; Chair. MUHAMMAD A. MUHAMMAD.

National Co for Distribution of Oil Products and Gas: POB 3, Rashid St, South Gate, Baghdad; tel. (1) 888-9911; telex 212247; fmrly a state organization; re-formed as a company in 1987; fleet of 6 tankers; Dir-Gen. ALI H. IJAM.

National Co for Manufacturing Oil Equipment: fmrly a state organization; re-formed as a company in 1987.

National Co for Oil and Gas Exploration: INOC Building, POB 476, al-Khullani Sq., Baghdad; fmrly the State Establishment for Oil and Gas Exploration; re-formed as a company in 1987; responsible for exploration and operations in difficult terrain such as marshes, swamps, deserts, valleys and in mountainous regions; Dir-Gen. RADHWAN AS-SAADI.

Northern Petroleum Co (NPC): POB 1, at-Ta'meem Governorate; f. 1987 by the merger of the fmr Northern and Central petroleum organizations to carry out petroleum operations in northern Iraq; Dir-Gen. GHAZI SABIR ALI.

Southern Petroleum Co (SPC): POB 240, Basra; fmrly the Southern Petroleum Organization; re-formed as the SPC in 1987 to undertake petroleum operations in southern Iraq; Dir-Gen. ASRI SALIH (acting).

State Co for Oil Marketing (SCOM): Man.-Dir ZEIN SADDAM AT-TIKRITI.

State Co for Oil Projects (SCOP): POB 198, Oil Compound, Baghdad; tel. (1) 774-1310; telex 212230; fmrly the State Org. for Oil Projects; re-formed as a company in 1987; responsible for construction of petroleum projects, mostly inside Iraq through direct execution, and also for design supervision of the projects and contracting with foreign enterprises, etc.; Dir-Gen. FALIH AL-KHAYYAT.

State Enterprise for Oil and Gas Industrialization in the South: f. 1988 by merger of enterprises responsible for the gas industry and petroleum refining in the south.

State Enterprise for Petrochemical Industries.

State Establishment for Oil Refining in the Central Area: Dir-Gen. KAMIL AL-FATLI.

State Establishment for Oil Refining in the North: Dir-Gen. TAHA HAMOUD.

State Establishment for Pipelines: Dir-Gen. SABAH ALI JOUMAH.

TRADE UNIONS

General Federation of Trade Unions of Iraq (GFTU): POB 3049, Tahrir Sq., Rashid St, Baghdad; tel. (1) 887-0810; telex 212457; f. 1959; incorporates six vocational trade unions and 18 local trade union federations in the governorates of Iraq; the number of workers in industry is 536,245, in agriculture 150,967 (excluding peasants) and in other services 476,621 (1986); GFTU is a member of the International Confederation of Arab Trade Unions and of the World Federation of Trade Unions; Pres. FADHIL MAHMOUD GHAREB.

Union of Teachers: Al-Mansour, Baghdad; Pres. Dr ISSA SALMAN HAMID.

Union of Palestinian Workers in Iraq: Baghdad; Sec.-Gen. SAMI ASH-SHAWISH.

There are also unions of doctors, pharmacologists, jurists, artists, and a General Federation of Iraqi Women (Chair. MANAL YOUNIS).

Transport
RAILWAYS

The metre-gauge line runs from Baghdad, through Khanaqin and Kirkuk, to Arbil. The standard gauge line covers the length of the country, from Rabia, on the Syrian border, via Mosul, to Baghdad (534 km), and from Baghdad to Basra and Umm Qasr (608 km), on the Arabian Gulf. A 404-km standard-gauge line linking Baghdad to Husaibah, near the Iraqi-Syrian frontier, was completed in 1983. The 638-km line from Baghdad, via al-Qaim (on the Syrian border), to Akashat, and the 252-km Kirkuk–Baiji–Haditha line, which was designed to serve industrial projects along its route, were opened in 1986. The 150-km line linking the Akashat phosphate mines and the fertilizer complex at al-Qaim was formally opened in January 1986 but had already been in use for two years. Lines totalling some 2,400 km were planned at the beginning of the 1980s, but by 1988 only 800 km had been constructed. All standard-gauge trains are now hauled by diesel-electric locomotives, and all narrow-gauge (one-metre) line has been replaced by standard gauge (1,435 mm). As well as the internal service, there is a regular international service between Baghdad and Istanbul. A rapid transit transport system is to be established in Baghdad, with work to be undertaken as part of the 1987–2001 development plan for the city.

Responsibility for all railways, other than the former Iraq Republic Railways (see below), and for the design and construction of new railways, which was formerly the province of the New Railways Implementation Authority, was transferred to the newly created State Enterprise for Implementation of Transport and Communications Projects.

State Enterprise for Iraqi Railways: Baghdad Central Station Bldg, Damascus Sq., Baghdad; tel. (1) 543-4404; telex 212272; fax (1) 884-0480; fmrly the Iraqi Republic Railways, under the supervision of State Org. for Iraqi Railways; re-formed as a State Enterprise in 1987, under the Ministry of Transport and Communications; total length of track (1996): 2,029 km, consisting of 1,496 km of standard gauge, 533 km of one-metre gauge; Dir-Gen. Dr YOUSUF ABD AL-WAHID JASSIM.

New Railways Implementation Authority: POB 17040, al-Hurriya, Baghdad; tel. (1) 537-0021; telex 2906; f. to design and construct railways to augment the standard-gauge network and to replace the metre-gauge network; Sec.-Gen. R. A. AL-UMARI.

ROADS

At the end of 1996, according to the International Road Federation, there was an estimated total road network of 47,400 km, of which approximately 40,760 km were paved.

The most important roads are: Baghdad–Mosul–Tel Kotchuk (Syrian border), 521 km; Baghdad–Kirkuk–Arbil–Mosul-Zakho (border with Turkey), 544 km; Kirkuk–Sulaimaniya, 160 km; Baghdad–Hilla–Diwaniya–Nasiriya–Basra, 586 km; Baghdad–Kut-Nasirya, 186 km; Baghdad–Ramadi–Rurba (border with Syria), 555 km; Baghdad–Kut–Umara–Basra–Safwan (border with Kuwait), 660 km; Baghdad–Baqaba–Kanikien (border with Iran). Most sections of the six-lane 1,264-km international Express Highway, linking Safwan (on the Kuwaiti border) with the Jordanian and Syrian borders, had been completed by June 1990. Studies have been completed for a second, 525-km Express Highway, linking Baghdad and Zakho on the Turkish border. The estimated cost of the project is more than US $4,500m. and is likely to preclude its implementation in the immediate future. An elaborate network of roads was constructed behind the war front with Iran in order to facilitate the movement of troops and supplies during the 1980–88 conflict.

Iraqi Land Transport Co: Baghdad; f. 1988 to replace State Organization for Land Transport; fleet of more than 1,000 large trucks; Dir Gen. AYSAR AS-SAFI.

Joint Land Transport Co: Baghdad; joint venture between Iraq and Jordan; operates a fleet of some 750 trucks.

State Enterprise for Implementation of Expressways: f. 1987; Dir-Gen. FAIZ MUHAMMAD SAID.

State Enterprise for Roads and Bridges: POB 917, Karradat Mariam, Karkh, Baghdad; tel. (1) 32141; telex 212282; responsible for road and bridge construction projects to the Ministry of Housing and Construction.

SHIPPING

The ports of Basra and Umm Qasr are usually the commercial gateway of Iraq. They are connected by various ocean routes with all parts of the world, and constitute the natural distributing centre for overseas supplies. The Iraqi State Enterprise for Maritime Transport maintains a regular service between Basra, the Gulf and north European ports. There is also a port at Khor az-Zubair, which came into use during 1979.

At Basra there is accommodation for 12 vessels at the Maqal Wharves and accommodation for seven vessels at the buoys. There is one silo berth and two berths for petroleum products at Muftia and one berth for fertilizer products at Abu Flus. There is room for eight vessels at Umm Qasr. There are deep-water tanker terminals at Khor al-Amaya and Faw for three and four vessels respectively.

The latter port, however, was abandoned during the early part of the Iran–Iraq War.

For the inland waterways, which are now under the control of the General Establishment for Iraqi Ports, there are 1,036 registered river craft, 48 motor vessels and 105 motor boats.

General Establishment for Iraqi Ports: Maqal, Basra; tel. (40) 413211; telex 207008; f. 1987, when State Org. for Iraqi Ports was abolished; Dir-Gen. ABD AR-RAZZAQ ABD AL-WAHAB.

State Enterprise for Iraqi Water Transport: POB 23016, Airport St, al-Furat Quarter, Baghdad; telex 212565; f. 1987 when State Org. for Iraqi Water Transport was abolished; responsible for the planning, supervision and control of six nat. water transportation enterprises, incl.:

    State Enterprise for Maritime Transport (Iraqi Line): POB 13038, al-Jadiriya al-Hurriya Ave, Baghdad; tel. (1) 776-3201; telex 212565; Basra office: 14 July St, POB 766, Basra; tel. 210206; telex 207052; f. 1952; Dir-Gen. JABER Q. HASSAN; Operations Man. M. A. ALI.

Shipping Company

Arab Bridge Maritime Navigation Co: Aqaba, Jordan; tel. (03) 316307; telex 62354; fax (03) 316313; f. 1987; joint venture by Egypt, Iraq and Jordan to improve economic co-operation; an expansion of the company that established a ferry link between the ports of Aqaba, Jordan, and Nuweibeh, Egypt, in 1985; cap. US $6m.; Chair. NABEEH AL-ABWAH.

CIVIL AVIATION

There are international airports near Baghdad, at Bamerni, and at Basra. A new airport, Saddam International, is under construction at Baghdad. Internal flights connect Baghdad to Basra and Mosul. Civilian, as well as military, airports sustained heavy damage during the war with the multinational force in 1991. Basra airport reopened in May 1991.

National Co for Civil Aviation Services: al-Mansour, Baghdad; tel. (1) 551-9443; telex 212662; f. 1987 following the abolition of the State Organization for Civil Aviation; responsible for the provision of aircraft, and for airport and passenger services.

    Iraqi Airways Co: Saddam International Airport, Baghdad; tel. (1) 887-2400; telex 213453; fax (1) 887-5808; f. 1948; Dir-Gen. NOUR ED-DIN AS-SAFI HAMMADI; formerly Iraqi Airways, prior to privatization in September 1988; operates limited domestic services.

Tourism

The Directorate-General for Tourism was abolished in 1988 and the various bodies under it and the services that it administered were offered for sale or lease to the private sector. The directorate was responsible for 21 summer resorts in the north, and for hotels and tourist villages throughout the country. These were to be offered on renewable leases of 25 years or sold outright. In 1995 an estimated 340,000 tourists visited Iraq. Tourist receipts in that year were estimated at US $13m.

Defence

Defence Expenditure (1996): an estimated $1,300m.

Military service: 18 months–2 years.

Total armed forces (August 1997): 387,500 (mostly conscripted): army 350,000; air force 35,000; navy 2,500; army reserves 650,000.

Commander-in-Chief of the Armed Forces: SADDAM HUSSAIN.

Chief of the General Staff: Gen. ABD AL-WAHHAB CHANNAN AR-RABBAT.

Commander of the Popular Army: TAHA YASSIN RAMADAN.

Commander of the Air Force: Lt-Gen. MUZAHIM SA'AB HASSAN.

Commander of the Republican Guard: Maj.-Gen. KEMAL MUSTAFA AT-TIKRITI.

Education

Since the establishment of the Republic in 1958, there has been a marked expansion in education at all levels. Spending on education increased substantially after that time, reaching ID 211m. in the 1980 budget. During the mid-1970s free education was established at all stages from pre-primary to higher and private education was abolished; all existing private schools were transformed into state schools. Pre-school education is expanding, although as yet it reaches only a small proportion of children in this age-group. Primary education, lasting six years, is now officially compulsory, and there are plans to extend full-time education to nine years as soon as possible. Primary enrolment of children aged six to 11 reached 99% in 1980, but by 1992 enrolment included just 79% of students in the relevant age-group. At present, secondary education, which is expanding rapidly, is available for six years (two three-year cycles). In 1992 enrolment at secondary schools included 37% of students in the relevant age-group. A US $22m. anti-illiteracy campaign began during the 1978/79 academic year. There are seven teacher training institutes in Iraq. Teacher training schools were abolished at the end of the 1985/86 academic year.

Science, medical and engineering faculties of the universities have undergone considerable expansion, although technical training is less developed. Two branches of Baghdad University at Basra and

Mosul became independent universities in 1967. There are eight universities—the universities of Baghdad, Basra, Mosul, Salah ad-Din (in Arbil), al-Mustansiriya (in Baghdad), Tikrit and a university of engineering and science and another of technology (both in Baghdad). Preliminary designs of two new universities at Salah ad-Din and ar-Rashid have been completed, and in February 1988 plans were announced for a further four to be established in Tikrit, al-Kufa, Ramadi (in al-Anbar governorate) and Diwaniya (in al-Qadisiya governorate). The Foundation for Technical Institutes incorporates 18 institutes of technology throughout the country. The number of students enrolled in higher education increased from 86,111 in 1975 to 209,818 in 1988.

Bibliography

GENERAL

Al-Khalil, Samir. *The Monument: Art, Vulgarity and Responsibility in Iraq.* London, André Deutsch, 1991.

Bell, Lady Florence (Ed.). *The Letters of Gertrude Lowthian Bell.* 2 vols, London, 1927.

Burgoyne, Elizabeth (Ed.). *Gertrude Bell, from her personal papers, 1914–26.* London, 1961.

Korn, David A. *Human Rights in Iraq.* New Haven, CT, Yale University Press, 1990.

Lloyd, Seton, F. H. *Iraq: Oxford Pamphlet.* Bombay, 1943.

Twin Rivers: A Brief History of Iraq from the Earliest Times to the Present Day. Oxford, 1943.

Foundations in the Dust. Oxford, 1949.

Longrigg, S. H., and Stoakes, F. *Iraq.* London, Ernest Benn, 1958.

Nakash, Yitzhak. *The Shi'is of Iraq.* Princeton, Princeton University Press, 1995.

Salter, Lord, assisted by Payton, S. W. *The Development of Iraq: A Plan of Action.* Baghdad, 1955.

Stark, Freya. *Baghdad Sketches.* London, John Murray, 1937.

Stewart, Desmond, and Haylock, John. *New Babylon: a Portrait of Iraq.* London, Collins, 1956.

ANCIENT HISTORY

Braidwood, R. J., and Howe, B. *Prehistoric Investigation in Iraqi Kurdistan.* Chicago, 1961.

Cambridge Ancient History. Vols I and II, New Ed., Cambridge, 1962.

Chaterji, S. *Ancient History of Iraq.* Calcutta, M. C. Sarkar Ltd, 1961.

Frankfort, H. *Archaeology and the Sumerian Problem.* Chicago, 1932.

The Birth of Civilization in the Near East. New York, Anchor, 1951.

Lloyd, Seton F. H. *The Art of the Ancient Near East.* London, 1961.

Ruined Cities of Iraq. Oxford, 1945.

Mesopotamia. London, 1936.

Mounds of the Near East. Edinburgh, 1964.

Mallowan, M. E. L. *Early Mesopotamia and Iran.* London, Thames and Hudson, 1965.

Oates, E. E. D. M. *Studies in the Ancient History of Northern Iraq.* London, British Academy, 1967.

Oppenheim, A. Leo. *Ancient Mesopotamia.* Chicago U.P., 1964.

Letters from Mesopotamia. Chicago U.P., 1967.

Parrot, A. *Nineveh and Babylon.* London, 1961.

Sumer. London, 1961.

Piggott, S. (Ed.). *The Dawn of Civilization.* London, 1962.

Roux, Georges. *Ancient Iraq.* London, 1964.

Saggs, H. W. F. *The Greatness that was Babylon.* London, Sidgwick and Jackson, 1962.

Stark, Freya. *Rome on the Euphrates.* London, John Murray, 1966.

Woolley, Sir C. L. *Abraham.* London, 1936.

Mesopotamia and the Middle East. London, 1961.

The Sumerians. Oxford, 1928.

Ur of the Chaldees. London, 1950.

Ur Excavations. 8 vols. Oxford, 1928–.

ISLAMIC PERIOD

Creswell, K. A. C. *Early Muslim Architecture.* 3 vols, Oxford, 1932–50.

Hitti, P. K. *A History of the Arabs.* 2nd edn, London, 1940.

Le Strange, Guy. *The Lands of the Eastern Caliphate.* Cambridge, 1905.

RECENT HISTORY

Al-Khalil, Samir. *Republic of Fear: Saddam's Iraq.* London, Hutchinson Radius, 1989.

Al-Marayati, Abid A. *A Diplomatic History of Modern Iraq.* New York, Speller, 1961.

Ali, Omar. *Crisis in The Arab Gulf: an independent Iraqi view.* London, The European Group, 1994.

Anderson, Ewan W., and Rashidian, Khalil. *Iraq and the Continuing Middle East Crisis.* London, Printer Publishers, 1991.

Baram, Amatzia. *Culture, History and Ideology in the Formation of Baathist Iraq, 1968–89.* Basingstoke, Macmillan, 1991.

Batatu, Hanna. *The Old Social Classes and the Revolutionary Movements of Iraq.* Princeton University Press, 1978.

Bennis, Phyllis, and Moushabeck, Michael (Eds). *Beyond the Storm: A Gulf Crisis Reader.* Edinburgh, Canongate Press, 1992.

Chubin, Shahram, and Tripp, Charles. *Iran and Iraq at War.* London, I. B. Tauris, 1988.

Cordesman, Anthony H. *The Iran-Iraq War and Western Security 1984–87.* London, Jane's Publishing Company, 1987.

Dann, Uriel. *Iraq under Qassem: A Political History 1958–63.* New York, Praeger, 1969.

Darwish, Adel, and Alexander, Gregory. *Unholy Babylon: the secret history of Saddam's war.* London, Gollancz, 1991.

Dauphin, Jacques. *Incertain Irak: Tableau d'on royaume avant la tempête.* Paris, Geuthner, 1993.

Editions du Monde Arabe. *The Iraq-Iran Conflict.* Trans. from French, Paris, 1981.

Farouk-Slugett, Marion, and Slugett, Peter. *Iraq since 1958: from Revolution to Dictatorship.* London, KPI Limited, 1988.

Foster, H. A. *The Making of Modern Iraq.* London, 1936.

Gallman, W. J. *Iraq under General Nuri.* Johns Hopkins Press, 1964.

Gittings, John (Ed.). *Beyond the Gulf War: The Middle East and the New World Order.* London, Catholic Institute for International Relations, 1991.

Haj, Samira. *The Making of Iraq, 1900–1963: Capital, Power and Ideology.* State University of New York Press, 1997.

Heikal, Mohammed. *Illusions of Triumph: An Arab View of the Gulf War.* London, HarperCollins, 1992.

Henderson, Simon. *Instant Empire: Saddam's Ambition for Iraq.* San Francisco, Mercury House, 1991.

Hiro, Dilip. *Desert Shield to Desert Storm.* London, HarperCollins, 1992.

Ismael, Tareq Y. *Iran and Iraq: Roots of Conflict.* Syracuse, New York, Syracuse University Press, 1983.

Karsh, Efraim, and Ravtsi, Inari. *Saddam Hussein: A Political Biography.* London, Brasseys (UK), 1992.

Kent, Marian. *Oil and Empire: British Policy and Mesopotamian Oil, 1900–1920.* London, Macmillan, 1976.

Khadduri, Majid. *Independent Iraq 1932–58, A Study of Iraqi Politics.* 2nd edition, Oxford University Press, 1960.

Republican Iraq: A study in Iraqi Politics since the Revolution of 1958. Oxford University Press, 1970.

Socialist Iraq: A Study in Iraqi Politics since 1968. Washington, The Middle East Institute, 1978.

Kienle, Eberhard. *Ba'th versus Ba'th: The Conflict between Iraq and Syria.* London, I. B. Tauris, 1990.

Leigh, David. *Betrayed.* London, Bloomsbury, 1993.

Longrigg, S. H. *Four Centuries of Modern Iraq.* Oxford, 1925.

Iraq 1900–1950: A Political, Social and Economic History. London, 1953.

Lowther, William. *Arms and the Man: Dr Gerald Bull, Iraq and the Supergun.* London, Macmillan, 1991.

MacArthur, Brian (Ed.). *Despatches from the Gulf War.* London, Bloomsbury, 1991.

Mark, Phoebe. *The History of Modern Iraq.* London, Longman, 1983.

Millar, Ronald. *Kut: The Death of an Army.* London, 1969.

Moberly, F. J. *The Campaign in Mesopotamia, 1914–1918.* 4 vols, London, 1923–27.

Mosallam, Mosallam Ali. *The Iraqi Invasion of Kuwait: Saddam Hussein, his State and International Politics.* London, I. B. Tauris, 1996.

PAIFORCE: the official story of the Persia and Iraq Command, 1941–1946. London, 1948.

Penrose, Edith and E. F. *Iraq: International Relations and National Development.* Benn, Tonbridge, 1978.

Salih, Khalid. *State-Making, Nation-Building and the Military: Iraq 1941–1958.* Göteborg University Press, 1996.

Schofield, R. *Kuwait and Iraq: Historical Claims and Territorial Disputes.* 2nd edition, London, Royal Institute of International Affairs, 1993.

Simpson, John. *From the House of War.* London, Hutchinson, 1991.

Sweeney, John. *Trading with the Enemy.* London, Pan Macmillan, 1993.

Timmerman, Kenneth R. *The Death Lobby.* London, Fourth Estate, 1992.

Weller, Marc. *The Control and Monitoring of Iraqi Weaponry.* Cambridge University Press, 1995.

Wilson, Sir A. T. *Loyalties: Mesopotamia, 1914–17.* London, 1930.

Mesopotamia, 1917–20: a Clash of Loyalties. London, University Press, 1931.

Zaki, Salih. *Origins of British Influence in Mesopotamia.* New York, 1941.

ECONOMY

Ainsrawy, Abbas. *Finance and Economic Development in Iraq.* New York, Praeger, 1966.

Gabbay, R. *Communism and Agrarian Reform in Iraq.* London, Croom Helm, 1978.

Jalal, Ferhang. *The Role of Government in the Industrialization of Iraq 1950–1965.* London, Frank Cass, 1972.

Longrigg, S. H. *Oil in the Middle East.* London, 1954.

MINORITIES

Arfa, Hassan. *The Kurds.* Oxford, Oxford University Press, 1966.

Badger, G. P. *The Nestorians and their Rituals.* 2 vols, London, 1888.

Blunt, A. T. N. *Bedouin Tribes of the Euphrates.* 2 vols, London, 1879.

Cook, Helena. *The Safe Haven in Northern Iraq: International Responsibility for Iraqi Kurdistan.* Kurdistan Human Rights Project, 1995.

Damluji, S. *The Yezidis.* Baghdad, 1948 (in Arabic).

Drower, E. S. *Peacock Angel (Being some account of Votaries of a Secret Cult and their Sanctuaries).* London, 1941.

The Mandeans of Iraq and Iran. Oxford, 1937.

Field, H. *Arabs of Central Iraq: Their History, Ethnology, and Physical Characters.* Chicago, 1935.

The Anthropology of Iraq. 4 vols, 1940, 1949, 1951, 1952, Chicago (first 2 vols), Cambridge, Mass. (last 2 vols).

Kinnane, Dirk. *The Kurdish Problem.* Oxford, 1964.

The Kurds and Kurdistan. Oxford, 1965.

Luke, Sir H. C. *Mosul and its Minorities.* London, 1925.

McDowall, David. *A Modern History of the Kurds.* London, I. B. Tauris, 1995.

O'Ballance, Edgar. *The Kurdish Revolt 1961–1970.* London, Faber and Faber, 1974.

Randall, Johnathan. *After Such Knowledge What Forgiveness?* New York, Farrar, Straus and Giroux Inc, 1997.

Salim, S. M. *Marsh Dwellers of the Euphrates Delta.* New York, 1961.

Short, Martin, and McDermott, Anthony. *The Kurds.* London, Minority Rights Group, 1975.

Thesiger, Wilfred. *The Marsh Arabs.* London, 1964.

Van Bruinessen, Martin. *Agha, Sheikh and State. The Social and Political Structures of Kurdistan.* London, Zed Books, 1992.

ISRAEL

Physical and Social Geography

W. B. FISHER

The pre-1967 frontiers of Israel are defined by armistice agreements signed with neighbouring Arab states, and represent the stabilization of a military front as it existed in late 1948 and early 1949. These boundaries are thus, in many respects, fortuitous, and have little geographical basis. It may be pertinent to recall that, prior to 1918, the whole area which is now partitioned between Syria, Israel, the emerging Palestinian entity and the Kingdom of Jordan formed part of the Ottoman Empire, and was spoken of as 'Syria'. Then, after 1918, came the establishment of the territories of Lebanon, Syria, Palestine and Transjordan—with the frontier between the last two lying, for the most part, along the Jordan river.

The present state of Israel is bounded on the north by Lebanon, on the north-east by Syria, on the east by the Hashemite Kingdom of Jordan and the emerging Palestinian Autonomous Area in the West Bank, and on the south and south-west by the Gulf of Aqaba and the Sinai Desert, occupied in 1967 and returned in April 1982 to Egyptian sovereignty. The so-called 'Gaza Strip', a small piece of territory some 40 km long, formed part of Palestine but was, under the Armistice Agreement of February 1949, then left in Egyptian control. (Since May 1994 the 'Gaza Strip' has been under the limited jurisdiction of the Palestine National Authority and will eventually—it is envisaged—form part of a single Palestinian entity, together with the emerging Palestinian Autonomous Area in the West Bank.) The territories which were occupied after the war of June 1967 are not recognized as forming part of the State of Israel, although it seems unlikely that Israel will reverse its annexation of the Old City of Jerusalem. The geographical descriptions of these territories are, therefore, given in the supplementary section at the end of the chapter.

Because of the nature of the frontiers, which partition natural geographical units, it is more convenient to discuss the geography of Israel partly in association with that of its neighbour, Jordan. The Jordan Valley itself is dealt with in the chapter on Jordan, but the uplands of Samaria-Judaea, from Jenin to Hebron, and including Jerusalem, which form a single unit, will be discussed below, though parts of this territory lie outside the frontiers of Israel.

PHYSICAL FEATURES

The physical geography of Israel is surprisingly complex and, though the area of the state is small, a considerable number of regions are easily distinguished. In the extreme north the hills of the Lebanon range continue without break, though of lower altitude, to form the uplands of Galilee, where the maximum height is just over 1,200 m. The Galilee hills fall away steeply on three sides: on the east to the well-defined Jordan Valley (see Jordan), on the west to a narrow coastal plain, and to the south at the Vale of Esdraelon or 'Emek Yezreel'. This latter is a rather irregular trough formed by subsidence along faults, with a flat floor and steep sides, and it runs inland from the Mediterranean south-eastwards to reach the Jordan Valley. At its western end the vale opens into the wide Bay of Acre, 25 km–30 km in breadth, but it narrows inland to only a few km before opening out once again where it joins the Jordan Valley. This lowland area has a very fertile soil and an annual rainfall of 400 mm, which is sufficient, with limited irrigation, for agriculture. Formerly highly malarial and largely uncultivated, the vale is now very productive. For centuries it has been a corridor of major importance linking the Mediterranean coast and Egypt with the interior of south-west Asia, and has thus been a passage-way for ethnic, cultural and military invasions.

South of Esdraelon there is an upland plateau extending for about 150 km. This is a broad upfold of rock, consisting mainly of limestone and reaching 900 m in altitude. In the north, where there is a moderate rainfall, the plateau has been eroded into valleys, some of which are fertile, though less so than those of Esdraelon or Galilee. This district, centred on Jenin and Nablus, is the ancient country of Samaria, until 1967 part of Jordan. Further south rainfall is reduced and erosion is far less prominent; hence this second region, Judaea proper, stands out as a more strongly defined ridge, with far fewer streams and a barer open landscape of a more arid and dusty character. Jerusalem, Bethlehem and Hebron are the main towns. Towards the southeast rainfall becomes scanty and the Wilderness of Judaea, an area of semi-desert, unfolds. In the extreme south the height of the plateau begins to decline, passing finally into a second plateau only 300 m–450 m above sea-level, but broader, and broken by occasional ranges of hills that reach 900 m in height. This is the Negev, a territory comprising nearly one-half of the total area of Israel, and bounded on the east by the lower Jordan Valley and on the west by the Sinai Desert. Agriculture, entirely dependent on irrigation, is carried on in a few places in the north, but for the most part the Negev consists of steppe or semi-desert. Irrigation schemes have been developed in those areas where soils are productive.

Between the uplands of Samaria-Judaea and the Mediterranean Sea there occurs a low-lying coastal plain that stretches southwards from Haifa as far as the Egyptian frontier at Gaza. In the north the plain is closely hemmed in by the spur of Mount Carmel (550 m), which almost reaches the sea; but the plain soon opens out to form a fertile lowland—the Plain of Sharon. Still further south the plain becomes broader again, but with a more arid climate and a sandier soil—this is the ancient Philistia. Ultimately the plain becomes quite arid, with loose sand dunes, and it merges into the Sinai Desert.

One other area remains to be mentioned—the Shephelah, which is a shallow upland basin lying in the foothills of the Judaean plateau, just east of the Plain of Sharon. This region, distinguished by a fertile soil and moister climate, is heavily cultivated, chiefly in cereals.

CLIMATE

Climatically Israel has the typical 'Mediterranean' cycle of hot, dry summers, when the temperature reaches 32°C–38°C, and mild, rainy winters. Altitude has a considerable effect, in that although snow may fall on the hills, it is not frequent on the lowlands. Several inches of snow may fall in Jerusalem in winter, whereas Upper Galilee may receive several feet. The valleys, especially Esdraelon and adjacent parts of the upper Jordan, lying below sea-level, can become extremely hot (more than 40°C) and very humid.

Rainfall varies greatly from one part of Israel to another. Parts of Galilee receive over 1,000 mm annually, but the amount decreases rapidly southwards, until in the Negev and Plain of Gaza, it is 250 mm or less. This is because the prevailing southwesterly winds blow off the sea to reach the north of Israel, but further south they come from Egypt, with only a short sea track, and therefore lack moisture.

RACE AND LANGUAGE

Discussion of the racial affinities of the Jewish people has continued for many years, but there has been little agreement on the subject. One view is that the Jewish people, whatever their origin, have now taken on many of the characteristics of the peoples among whom they have lived since the Dispersal—e.g. the Jews of Germany were often quite similar in anthropological character to the Germans; the Jews of Iraq resembled the Arabs; and the Jews of Ethiopia had black skin. Upholders of such a view would largely deny the separateness of ethnic qualities amongst the Jews. On the other hand, it has been suggested that the Jews are really a particular and somewhat individual intermixture of racial strains that are found over wider areas of the Middle East: a special genetic 'mix' with ingredients by no means restricted to the Jews themselves. The correctness of either viewpoint is largely a matter of personal interpretation.

Under British mandatory rule there were three official languages in Palestine—Arabic, spoken by a majority of the inhabitants (all Arabs and a few Jews); Hebrew, the ancient language of the Jews; and English. This last was considered to be standard if doubt arose as to the meaning of translation from the other two.

Since the establishment of the State of Israel the relative importance of the languages has changed. Hebrew is now dominant, Arabic has greatly declined following the flight of Arab refugees, and English is also less important, though it remains the first foreign language of many Israelis.

Hebrew, widely current in biblical days, was largely eclipsed after the dispersal of Jewish people by the Romans, and until fairly recently its use was largely restricted to scholarship, serious literature and religious observance. Most Jews of Eastern and Southern Europe did not employ Hebrew as their everyday speech, but spoke either Yiddish or Ladino, the former being a Jewish-German dialect current in East and Central Europe, and the latter a form of Spanish. Immigrants into Israel since 1890, however, have been encouraged to use Hebrew in normal everyday speech, and Hebrew is now the living tongue of most Israeli Jews. The revival has been a potent agent in the unification of the Israeli Jewish people since, in addition to the two widely different forms of speech, Yiddish and Ladino, most Jewish immigrants spoke yet another language according to their country of origin, and the census of 1931 recorded more than 60 such languages in habitual use within Palestine. Now, as the proportion of native-born Israelis increases, Hebrew is dominant, and the use of other languages is diminishing.

It is only by a revival of Hebrew that the Jewish community has found a reasonable *modus vivendi*—yet this step was not easy, for some devout Jews opposed the use of Hebrew for secular speech. Furthermore, there was controversy as to the way Hebrew should be pronounced, but the Sephardic pronunciation was finally adopted.

History

TOM LITTLE

Revised for this edition by PAUL COSSALI

For most Jews, the creation of the State of Israel in 1948 was the fulfilment of Biblical prophecy; to some, in this more secular age, it is a country justifiably won by political skill and force of arms in a world that denied them one for nearly 2,000 years; but, however regarded, it is seen as the fulfilment of Jewish history.

Although clearly a more ancient people from east of the Euphrates, the Jews trace their descent from Abraham, the first of the Patriarchs, who departed from Ur, the centre of the ancient Chaldean civilization, about 2,000 years BC. Oral tradition, as recorded in the Old Testament, states that he was instructed by God to leave Chaldea with his family and proceed to Canaan (Phoenicia), or Palestine, the land of the Philistines, where he would father a great nation which would play an important part in human history. The authors of the Old Testament were primarily concerned to establish the descent of the Jewish people from Abraham under the guidance of God but, in so doing, they preserved the ancient history of the Jews which archaeology has tended to confirm within a debatable chronology.

Abraham's nomad family eventually reached Canaan and grazed their flocks there for a time before crossing Sinai to the richer pastures of Egypt. They remained in Egypt for probably about 400 years and multiplied greatly, but their separateness in race, religion and customs at last excited the fears of the pharaohs, who enslaved them. Moses, who had escaped this slavery because he was brought up as an Egyptian, fled with the Jews from the country (c. 1200 BC) and gave them his law (the Torah), proclaiming the absolute oneness of God and establishing the disciplines for worship. They wandered for some decades in the wilderness before reaching the River Jordan. Moses' successor, Joshua, led some of the families (or tribes) across the Jordan and conquered Canaan. It was a stormy occupation of constant conflict with the indigenous peoples until the warrior Saul triumphed and became the first 'king'. His successor, David, completed the subjugation of the Israelites' enemies and briefly united all the tribes. King Solomon, his son, raised the country to its peak and built the Temple of Jerusalem which came to be recognized as the temple of all the Jews and the focal point of worship. His magnificence burdened the people, and this and his tolerance of the worship of idols provoked a successful revolt of the 10 northern tribes under Jereboam who established Israel as his own kingdom. This division into two

parts, Israel and Judah (which contained Jerusalem), was disastrous, for Israel was soon overcome by the Assyrians and its people were taken into captivity and lost to history. About 100 years later Judah fell victim to the Babylonians and its people were also taken captive, but their community endured to become an important element in the future of Judaism. The Babylonians destroyed Solomon's temple.

When the Persian leader Cyrus conquered Babylon he gave the Jews permission to return to Jerusalem, and some did so. There they set about rebuilding the Temple which was completed about 500 BC, and in 200 years of relative tranquillity their religion was consolidated by a series of great teachers. Palestine, in turn, was conquered by Alexander the Great, becoming (together with the Jews) part of his empire; but Alexander was tolerant, as were his successors in Egypt, the Ptolemies, and consequently Alexandria became the centre of a learned school of Hellenic Judaism.

This tolerant policy was reversed under the Roman Empire, which succeeded the Ptolemies. The Jews rebelled against the oppressive Roman rule and Nero sent his greatest general, Vespasian, and his son, Titus, to suppress them. The conquest was completed by Titus; Jerusalem and the second temple were destroyed (c. AD 70), and the Diaspora which began with the Assyrian conquest of Israel was complete. A small community of Jews remained in Jerusalem and the surrounding countryside, and devoted themselves to their religion, producing their version of the Talmud, the repository of Judaic history, learning and interpretation which, with the Torah and the Old Testament became the essence of the faith. However, it was the version of the Talmud produced by the Babylonian scholars which became the accepted document.

Scattered across the world, throughout Arabia, Asia as far as China, North Africa and Europe as far as Poland and Russia, Jewish communities continued to exist, sometimes powerful, often persecuted, but united by religion and certain central themes: their belief in the oneness of God, His promise to Abraham, the promise of the 'return', and the Temple as the temple of all Jews. The duration of Jewish occupation of Palestine was relatively short and for even less of that time did they hold or rule it all, but the scattered communities continued to look towards Jerusalem.

THE ZIONIST MOVEMENT

In the late 19th century there were affluent and even powerful groups of Jews in Europe but the people as a whole were usually treated as second-class citizens in the countries where they lived. The large, pious and orthodox groups in Eastern Europe, in particular, were subject intermittently to persecution, and in 1881 there was a series of pogroms in Russia which stirred the conscience of world Jewry into forming plans for their escape. For the Eastern Jews there could be only one destination: Palestine. The pogroms led directly to the formation in Russia of a movement called the Lovers of Zion (Hovevei Zion), and within that movement another was formed, called the Bilu, by a large community of young Jews in the Kharkov region. In 1882 a Bilu group in Constantinople issued a manifesto demanding a home in Palestine. They proposed that they should beg it from the Sultan of Turkey, in whose empire Palestine lay.

The word Zionism was coined by a Russian about a decade later as a spiritual-humanitarian concept but Theodor Herzl, who became the leader of the movement, defined its aim specifically at the Basle Congress of 1897 (see Documents on Palestine, p. 108): 'Zionism', he said, 'strives to create for the Jewish people a home in Palestine secured by public law.' He wrote in his journal after the congress: 'At Basle I founded the Jewish State . . . perhaps in five years, and certainly fifty, everyone will know it.' Herzl is recognized as the founder of political Zionism.

Herzl was concerned essentially with the creation of a safe refuge for the suffering communities of Eastern Europe and thought that their migration and settlement could and should be financed by prosperous Jews. When he failed to get help from the Sultan he considered other possible 'homes' as far apart as Uganda and Latin America, but even safe places could never have the same appeal to orthodox Jews as Palestine, sanctioned in their scriptures and 'promised' to them by God. Some of the Jews of Russia and Poland escaped persecution to make their own way to Palestine and became the earliest immigrant communities there.

When the Turkish Empire was destroyed by Allied forces in the 1914–18 war new possibilities of securing a 'home' or state in Palestine opened up before the Zionists. In the years 1915–16 Sir Mark Sykes for Britain and M. Charles Georges-Picot for France had, in fact, drafted an agreement (see Documents on Palestine, p. 108) in which, while undertaking 'to recognize and protect an independent Arab State or Confederation of Arab States', the two powers in effect carved the Middle East into their respective spheres of influence and authority pending the time of its liberation from Turkey. Influential Zionists, notably Dr Chaim Weizmann, saw their opportunity to press Britain for a commitment to provide a home for the Jews in Palestine and secured the help of Judge Louis Brandeis, a leading US Zionist and principal adviser to President Woodrow Wilson, in bringing the USA into the war on the side of the Allies in April 1917. The outcome was the Balfour Declaration (see Documents on Palestine, p. 109) which was contained in a letter from Arthur James Balfour to Lord Rothschild on behalf of the Zionist Federation, dated 2 November 1917. It stated:

'His Majesty's Government view with favour the establishment in Palestine of a national home for the Jewish people, and will use their best endeavours to facilitate the achievement of this object, it being clearly understood that nothing shall be done which may prejudice the existing civil and religious rights of existing non-Jewish communities in Palestine, or the rights and political status of Jews in other countries.'

The San Remo Conference decided on 24 April 1920 to give the Mandate under the newly formed League of Nations to Britain (the terms of which were approved by the USA, which was not a member of the League, before they were finally agreed by the League Council on 24 July 1922). The terms (see Documents on Palestine, p. 111) included a restatement of the Balfour Declaration and provided that 'an appropriate Jewish agency' should be established to advise and co-operate with the Palestine Administration in matters affecting the Jewish national home and to take part in the development of the country. This gave the Zionist Organization a special position because the Mandate stipulated that it should be recognized as such an agency if the mandatory authority thought it appropriate. Britain took over the Mandate in September 1923.

THE MANDATE

Herzl's first aim had thereby been achieved: the national home of the Jewish people had been 'secured by public law'; but major obstacles were still to be overcome before the home, or state, became a reality. When the Mandate was granted, the Arabs constituted 92% of the population and owned 98% of the land in Palestine, and it could clearly not be a home unless the demography and land ownership were changed in favour of the Jews. It was to these ends that the Zionist movement now directed itself, but Britain had different views concerning what was meant by 'favouring' the establishment of the home, both in the matter of boundaries and immigration, even while it remained sympathetic to the enterprise. This was important, for although nominally under the supervision of the Mandates Commission of the League, Britain was able to run Palestine very much as a Crown Colony and administered it through the Colonial Office.

The World Zionist Organization had presented a memorandum to the Paris Peace Conference in 1919 setting forth its territorial concept of the home, as follows:

The whole of Palestine, southern Lebanon, including the towns of Tyre and Sidon, the headwaters of the Jordan river on Mount Hermon and the southern portion of the Litani river; the Golan Heights in Syria, including the town of Quneitra, the Yarmuk river and Al-Himmeh hot springs; the whole of the Jordan valley, the Dead Sea, and the eastern highlands up to the outskirts of Amman, thence in a southerly direction along the Hedjaz railway to the Gulf of Aqaba; in Egypt, from El-Arish, on the Mediterranean coast, in a straight line in a southerly direction to Sharm esh-Sheikh on the Gulf of Aqaba.

The League of Nations and the Peace Settlement did not accept these boundaries but the Mandate given to Britain included Transjordan, the territory east of the river and beyond Amman. Britain allotted Transjordan as an Emirate to Emir Abdullah in 1921 and with the grant of full independence in 1946 it became a kingdom.

The Arabs bitterly opposed the Balfour Declaration and Jewish immigration and advocated the prohibition of land sales to Jews. Britain would neither accede to their demands nor to Jewish claims to a majority in Palestine. There were intermittent outbreaks of Arab violence, notably in 1922 and 1929, which brought the Arabs into conflict with the mandatory government and there were four British Commissions of Inquiry and two White Papers were issued (see Documents on Palestine, p. 112) on the situation before 1936, none of which envisaged a Jewish majority. In 1936 there was an effective six-month general strike of the Arab population followed by a large-scale rebellion which lasted until the outbreak of the Second World War, and in 1939 another Commission issued the third White Paper (see Documents on Palestine, p. 113) which stated that Britain would not continue to develop the Jewish national home beyond the point already reached and proposed that 75,000 more Jews should be admitted over five years after which time Jewish immigration would cease. Finally, it proposed that self-governing institutions should be established at the end of the five years. This would have preserved the Arab majority in the country and its legislature.

THE BILTMORE PROGRAMME AND AFTER

International opinion at that time was conditioned by the horrifying Nazi policy of exterminating Jews—a practice which was to reach even more frightful proportions after the outbreak of war. Zionists and Jews generally regarded the White Paper as a betrayal of the terms of the Mandate. During a visit to New York in 1942 by David Ben-Gurion, Chairman of the Jewish Agency Executive, an Extraordinary Zionist Conference was held at the Biltmore Hotel, which utterly rejected the White Paper and reformulated Zionist policy. The declaration of the conference (see Documents on Palestine, p. 114), issued on 11 May 1942, concluded as follows:

The conference urges that the gates of Palestine be opened; that the Jewish Agency be vested with control of immigration into Palestine and with the necessary authority for upbuilding the country, including the development of its unoccupied and uncultivated lands; and that Palestine be established as a Jewish Commonwealth integrated into the new structure of the democratic world.

This policy brought the Jews into direct conflict with the Palestine Government before the war was over. Those in Europe who escaped the Nazi holocaust were herded into refugee camps and some, with organized Zionist help, tried to reach Palestine, but the British authorities, in accordance with the 1939 policy, attempted to prevent their entry.

The British failed. The Jewish population which had been 56,000 at the time of the Mandate was 608,000 in 1946 and was estimated to be 650,000 on the eve of the creation of Israel, or about two-fifths of the entire population. Furthermore, the Jewish Agency had formed its own military organizations, the Haganah, and its units of shock troops, the Palmach, which were strengthened by those Jews who had fought on the side of the British during the war, and supported by two smaller extremist groups, the Irgun Zvaei Leumi and the Stern Gang. Towards the end of the war they embarked on a policy of violence designed to impose the Biltmore programme. They successfully made the Mandate unworkable and Britain referred it to the United Nations (which had replaced the League) on 2 April 1947.

The UN General Assembly sent a Special Commission (UNSCOP) to Palestine to report on the situation, and its report, issued on 31 August 1947, proposed two plans: a majority plan for the partition of Palestine into two states, one Jewish and one Arab, with economic union; and a minority plan for a federal state. The Assembly adopted the majority plan (see Documents on Palestine, p. 114) on 29 November by 33 votes for and 13 against, with 10 abstentions. The plan divided Palestine into six principal parts, three of which, comprising 56% of the total area, were reserved for the Jewish state, and three (with the enclave of Jaffa), comprising 43% of the area, for the Arab state. It provided that Jerusalem would be an international zone administered by the UN as the holy city for Jews, Muslims and Christians. The Arabs refused to accept this decision and, in the subsequent disorders, about 1,700 people were killed. In April 1948 the Jewish forces launched a full-scale attack and, by the time the Mandate was terminated on 14 May, 400,000 Arabs had evacuated their homes to become refugees in neighbouring Arab countries.

THE STATE ESTABLISHED

The Mandate was relinquished by Britain at 6 p.m. Washington time; at 6.01 p.m. the State of Israel was officially declared by the Jewish authorities in Palestine; at 6.11 p.m. the USA accorded it recognition and immediately afterwards the USSR did likewise. Thus Israel came into existence only one year later than Herzl's 50-year diary prophecy. The Arab states belatedly came to the help of the Palestinian Arabs but their attempt to overthrow the new state failed and Israel was left in possession of more territory than had been allotted to it under the UN partition plan, including new (non-Arab) Jerusalem. Israel rejected the proposed internationalization of the city, for the Jews considered the return to Jerusalem to be central to their divine legacy.

A provisional government was formed in Tel-Aviv the day before the Mandate ended, with Ben-Gurion as Prime Minister and other members of the Jewish Agency Executive in leading ministerial posts. The Constitution and electoral laws had already been prepared and the first general elections were held in January 1949 for a single-chamber Knesset (or Parliament) elected by proportional representation. This enabled several parties to gain representation, with Ben-Gurion's Labour Party (Mapai) usually in the majority but never predominant. As a result, government has usually been conducted by uneasy coalitions.

After the war another 400,000 Arabs fled from the additional territory conquered by Israel and in the course of another year about 300,000 more left the impoverished Arab West Bank for Transjordan. (In 1950 Abdullah held a referendum in which the West Bank Arabs agreed to be part of his kingdom which then became known as Jordan.) The Israeli Government maintained the mandatory military control, established in the earlier disorders, over those Arab populations which remained within its territory but allowed 'co-operative' Arabs to be elected to the Knesset; four were elected to the first Parliament.

A gigantic programme of immigration was launched immediately after the Provisional Government took over and within three years the Jewish population was doubled. This result, unparalleled in history, was assisted by Iraq which expelled the larger part of its age-old Jewish communities. The 1961 census recorded Israel's population at 2,260,700, of whom 230,000 were Arabs. The two-millionth Jew arrived in May 1962 and the three-millionth early in 1972. A massive plan for land development to provide for the new people was executed concomitantly with the early immigration programme; the Jewish National Fund took over 3m. dunums of former Arab land and used heavy mechanical equipment to bring it rapidly back into production. This was made possible by the stupendous support from abroad which came in the form of private gifts from world Jewry, state loans and aid, and private Jewish investments. The USA was both privately and publicly the major contributor, but following negotiations conducted between the Conference on Jewish Material Claims and the Israeli and West German authorities at The Hague (the Netherlands) in 1952, the Federal Republic of Germany agreed to pay reparations for Nazi crimes. These payments amounted to £216m. in Deutsche Marks before they were concluded in 1966. One effect of this influx of unearned money from all sources was to cause serious inflation which was still a problem in the 1990s (see Economy).

Israel was admitted to the UN, albeit on conditions concerning Jerusalem and refugees which were contrary to its overall policy and were never fulfilled. Its relations with the Arab states were governed by a series of armistice agreements reached in Rhodes in 1949 which, in effect, established an uneasy truce without an Arab commitment to permanent peace. The Arabs continued to insist that the creation of Israel was a usurpation of Arab territory and rights and a denial of UN principles. Defence policy therefore dominated Israel's political thinking and firmly established the principle that it would remain militarily superior to any combination of Arab states. In the early 1950s, however, it was the Palestinian refugees who caused intermittent frontier trouble, mainly from Syria and Jordan, but to some extent from the Gaza Strip which, since the 1948 war, had been administered by Egypt.

Whenever one of the frontiers became too troublesome, Israel mounted a retaliatory raid *pour décourager les autres*. Acting on the principle that Nasser's Egypt was the only serious danger, Ben-Gurion ordered a raid which, on 28 February 1955, annihilated the small Egyptian garrison at Gaza and the reinforcements travelling by road to its support. The result was contrary to Ben-Gurion's intention; Nasser determined to secure adequate military strength and to that end entered into the 'Czech' arms agreement in August 1955, by which he bartered cotton and took credits from the USSR for substantial quantities of arms and aircraft which began to arrive promptly. The threat to Israel was therefore increased.

SUEZ

On 26 July 1956 Nasser nationalized the Suez Canal Co of which Britain and France were the principal shareholders (see Egypt) and the two European powers prepared to retake control of it. Neither could expect any support from the two superpowers, or from world opinion in general, for open invasion, but in October Ben-Gurion entered into a secret pact with them by which Israel would invade Sinai and thus justify Britain and France intervening to keep the combatants apart. Israel invaded on 29 October, with powerful armoured columns, and rapidly advanced towards the Canal. The following day Britain and France issued their ultimatum that both sides should withdraw to 20 miles from the Canal. Israel, which had by this time taken almost all of the Sinai, including the Gaza Strip and Sharm esh-Sheikh at the entrance to the Gulf of Aqaba, readily agreed to comply with the ultimatum, but Egypt refused on the grounds that it was being asked to withdraw from its own territory.

The Anglo-French force thereupon invaded the Port Said area and advanced some miles along the Suez Canal. There it was halted by Sir Anthony Eden, the British Prime Minister, in face of the forthright condemnation of the UN and financial sanctions threatened by the USA; a decision which the French Prime Minister, M. Guy Mollet, reluctantly accepted. Both countries withdrew their troops before the end of the year. This was a severe blow to Ben-Gurion who had counted on holding at least a security buffer zone on a line from el-Arish, on the Mediterranean coast, to Sharm esh-Sheikh (the Zionist 1919 frontier proposal). Therefore Israel delayed its final withdrawal from Egypt until January, and from the Gaza Strip until March 1957 when a UN Emergency Force was safely established on the Sinai frontier and at Sharm esh-Sheikh.

A development of great consequence to Israel at this time was the increasing involvement of the Soviet Union in the Middle East, especially in Egypt. The USSR took no less than 50% of Egyptian exports in 1957, and in 1958 agreed to finance and direct the building of the mammoth High Dam at Aswan. In keeping with this policy, the Soviet Union adopted a strongly pro-Arab and anti-Israeli line and steadily rearmed Nasser's forces.

Ben-Gurion resigned 'for personal reasons' in June 1963 and was succeeded by Levi Eshkol, the Minister of Finance, who had been a minister continuously since joining the Provisional Government from the Jewish Agency in 1948. He was politically inclined to a more conciliatory policy which he hoped would in time erode Arab enmity. This was opposed by many in the ruling hierarchy, notably the veteran Ben-Gurion and Gen. Moshe Dayan, who had commanded the Israeli forces in their brilliant victory in 1956.

There was a notable increase in Arab guerrilla activity across the frontiers with Egypt, Jordan and Syria in the mid-1960s. The Palestinians formed a guerrilla organization called al-Fatah, for which the Syrian Prime Minister publicly declared his support in 1966. Mutual accusations of frontier violations followed, and President Nasser warned that he would have to activate the Egypt-Syrian Joint Defence Agreement if Israel's 'aggression' did not cease. In May 1967 King Hussein brought Jordan into the agreement and in that same month Nasser received information, which later proved to be unfounded, that Israeli troops were massing on the Syrian frontier. In response Nasser ordered the withdrawal of the UN Emergency Force from the Gaza Strip, the Sinai Desert and Sharm esh-Sheikh. U Thant, the Secretary-General of the UN, immediately complied, and Nasser then imposed a total blockade on Israeli shipping in the Straits of Tiran, although Israel had always made it plain that this would be considered a *casus belli*.

U Thant flew to Cairo on 22 May 1967 but, by that time, Nasser had already strengthened his forces in the Sinai and summoned his reserves. Israel, Jordan and Syria had also mobilized. Israel formed a national government, introducing to the Cabinet one representative of each of the three opposition parties. Gen. Moshe Dayan, the leader of the 1956 Sinai campaign was appointed Minister of Defence.

THE JUNE WAR

Israel made its pre-emptive strike in the early hours of 5 June when its armoured forces moved into Sinai. At 0600 hours GMT Israeli planes attacked 25 airfields in Egypt, Jordan, Syria and Iraq, destroying large numbers of aircraft on the ground and disabling the runways, thus effectively depriving the Egyptian and Jordanian ground forces of air cover. There were some fierce armoured battles in the Sinai but Israeli forces were in position along the Suez Canal on 8 June: they took Sharm esh-Sheikh without armed opposition. On the eastern front, they reached the Jordan river on 7 June and entered and conquered Old (Arab) Jerusalem on the same day. Their main forces destroyed, President Nasser and King Hussein accepted a cease-fire on 8 June. Israel then turned its attention to the Syrian fortifications on the Golan Heights from which Israeli settlements were being shelled. In a brilliant but costly action, armour and infantry captured the heights. Syria accepted a cease-fire on 9 June but Israel ignored it until 10 June, by which time its troops were in possession of Quneitra, on the road to Damascus. The 'Six-Day War', as it became known, was over; Israel had achieved a victory more sweeping even than that of 1956.

Israel had recovered Jerusalem and access to the Western Wall of the Temples of Solomon and Herod, which were the most sacred places of worship for all Jews but to which they had been denied access since the partition of the city between the Arabs and Israel in 1948. Israel immediately tore down the barriers, reunited the city, put the administration of Arab

Jerusalem under its existing city administration, and effectively annexed it. The UN General Assembly passed a resolution on 4 July (which Israel disregarded), urging the Israeli authorities to rescind all the measures taken and to desist from any further action that would change the status of the holy city. Israel asserted from the outset that it would not countenance the return of Old Jerusalem to Arab possession in any peace settlement.

The UN and the world powers busied themselves with the peace process. On 29 August the heads of the Arab states began a summit conference in Khartoum at which they decided to seek a political settlement but not to make peace with or recognize Israel, nor to negotiate directly with it, and meanwhile 'to adopt necessary measures to strengthen military preparation to face all eventualities'. On 22 November, after many attempts, the UN Security Council agreed to Resolution 242, which stated that the establishment of a just and lasting peace in the Middle East should include the application of the following principles:

(i) withdrawal of Israeli armed forces from territories occupied in the recent conflict; and (ii) termination of all claims or states of belligerency and respect for and acknowledgement of the sovereignty, territorial integrity, and political independence of every State in the area, and their right to live in peace within secure and recognized boundaries free from threats or acts of force. The Council affirmed also the necessity for (*a*) guaranteeing freedom of navigation through international waterways in the area, and (*b*) achieving a just settlement of the refugee problem.

The UN Secretary-General designated Ambassador Gunnar Jarring of Sweden as Special Representative to assist the process of finding a peaceful settlement on this basis.

The essential ambiguity of the Resolution was contained in the phrase 'withdrawal ... from territories occupied ...' (which in the French translation became 'les territoires'), and the Israeli Government contended that it meant an agreed withdrawal from some occupied territories 'to secure and recognized boundaries'. This was, in Israel's view, precluded by the Arab states' Khartoum Resolution and their insistence that Resolution 242 meant total withdrawal from the territories occupied in 1967. Furthermore, Israel insisted that it would only negotiate withdrawal directly with Egypt and the Arab states as part of a peace settlement and that the function of Jarring was to bring this about and not to initiate proposals of his own for a settlement.

UNEASY SECURITY

Meanwhile Israel based its policy on retention of the Occupied Territories as warranty for its security. The 1967 defeat had severely damaged the USSR's prestige in the Arab world, and to repair its position it began immediately to restore the Egyptian armed forces, including the air force. Meanwhile in 1967 President de Gaulle imposed an arms embargo on Israel and refused to deliver 50 supersonic *Mirage* IV fighters which Israel had ordered and paid for. Israel therefore turned to the USA arguing that the balance of military power must, for its security, be maintained in its favour. This point was conceded by the USA in 1968 with a contract to deliver 50 *Phantom* jet fighter-bombers, which brought Cairo within range and were more powerful than any MiG aircraft in Egypt.

Using powerful artillery installed by the USSR west of the Canal, Nasser began in 1968 a 'war of attrition' in order to force Israel to accept his terms. Relatively heavy casualties were inflicted on the Israeli troops, notably in July and October, and throughout the period Israel retaliated with air and artillery attacks which forced Egypt to evacuate the Canal zone towns. Suez and its oil refineries were destroyed. The zone remained unsettled until 1970.

Israel's Prime Minister, Levi Eshkol, died on 26 February 1969, and was succeeded in the following month by Mrs Golda Meir, who had been Minister for Foreign Affairs from 1956 to 1966.

President Nixon, who had taken office in the USA, supported an initiative by his Secretary of State, William Rogers, 'to encourage the parties to stop shooting and start talking'. This was announced on 25 June 1970, and was unfavourably received in the Arab world. Nasser flew to Moscow with a proposal to accept it on condition that Russia supplied SAM-III missiles capable of destroying low-flying aircraft. He returned to Cairo and stunned Egypt and the Arab world with an unconditional acceptance of the Rogers plan and its related Canal zone 90-day cease-fire. King Hussein immediately associated Jordan with Nasser's acceptance. Israel accepted the Rogers plan on 7 August but immediately complained that Egypt had broken the cease-fire agreement by moving SAM-III missile sites into the 30-mile wide standstill area along the canal.

President Nasser died suddenly on 28 September 1970, but President Sadat, who succeeded him, sustained his policy. Although he only agreed to extend the cease-fire for another 90 days, it continued indefinitely. The US effort was directed towards securing an interim agreement by which Israel would withdraw from the Suez Canal and allow it to be reopened, but Israel, again on the basic principle of its security, would only consider a limited withdrawal and would not agree that Egyptian troops should cross the Canal, terms which Egypt would not accept. US–Israeli relations, vital to Israel, were uneasy during most of 1971 while the Department of State pressed the Israeli Government to concede unacceptable terms of withdrawal from the Canal. President Sadat gave the end of the year as a deadline for 'peace or war', but before the year was over Mrs Golda Meir secured a commitment to Israeli security from President Nixon firmer than any obtained in the past; the Rogers plan was thereby abandoned, and 1972 began without the threatened outbreak of war with Egypt. Instead, there was a series of terrorist acts by various Palestinian groups, which in turn provoked punitive raids by Israeli forces.

The stated objective of Israeli raids on Syria and Lebanon was to compel both countries to prevent the Palestinian resistance groups from mounting raids from within their borders, whether against Israel or in other countries. This objective seemed most successfully achieved in Lebanon on 10 April 1973 by a daring commando raid into the heart of Beirut, where the raiders killed three resistance leaders, while other commando units attacked two refugee camps outside the city and destroyed the headquarters of the Popular Democratic Front for the Liberation of Palestine, killing one of its leaders. The Israeli authorities were able to make a number of arrests in the Occupied Territories from information gained in this raid.

THE OCCUPIED TERRITORIES

About 380,000 Arabs fled from the West Bank to Jordan, but nearly one million remained under Israeli occupation; of these, the 70,000 in East (Arab) Jerusalem, which was annexed, were treated as Israeli citizens and the remainder brought under military administration. This was of necessity strict for the first three years because of help given to Palestinian guerrillas by the Arabs in the Occupied Territories and, in some instances, in Israel proper. The Gaza Strip was by far the most troublesome and it was not until the end of 1971 that Israeli security operations, including the clearance of one large refugee camp which had proved particularly difficult, brought the area under control. It was announced in March 1973 that the strip would be incorporated into Israel, that Jewish settlement in the strip would continue and that Arab inhabitants could circulate freely in Israel during the day. Higher living standards enjoyed by the Arabs under the occupation, 60,000 of whom found work in Israel itself, the inevitable growth of collaboration with the Israeli authorities and, finally, the disarray in which the Palestinian movement found itself by late 1970, rendered the security problem inside the country minimal during 1971. In March of the following year the Israeli military authorities successfully held elections for the mayors and municipalities in the main Arab towns, despite guerrilla threats of reprisals against any Arabs taking part.

Government policy was officially that in a peace settlement there would be substantial territories returned to the Arabs but there was no clear consensus in the Government or the country as to what they would amount to, except to the extent that Israel should have 'secure frontiers'. However, statements by ministers emphasized that in addition to East Jerusalem and the Gaza Strip, which had been effectively annexed, the Golan Heights of occupied Syria and parts of the Jordanian West Bank would not be returned. There was also increasing evidence on the ground. An extensive building programme to house immigrants was rapidly being executed in and around Jerusalem; 42 settlements had been established by January 1973 although, according to Israeli figures, only 3,150 Israeli civilians had been allowed to take up permanent residence in the areas.

Israel radio announced on 18 August 1973 that another 35 settlements would be built in the Occupied Territories, bringing the total to 77. The Jewish National Fund and the Israeli Lands Administration had between them acquired 15,000 acres (6,070 ha) of Arab land and the army was in occupation of another 20,000 acres (8,100 ha). A plan advanced by Deputy Prime Minister Yigal Allon, although not publicly approved by the Government, seemed to be in process of *de facto* execution. He proposed that a chain of Israeli settlements should be established along the Jordan river (which was effectively being done) a second chain along the Samarian hills on the West Bank, and a third along the road from Jerusalem to Jericho, in order to establish Israel's security. The rest of the West Bank and the main towns, excepting Jericho, would then be returned to Jordan.

The virtue of the Allon plan for most Israelis was that it would absorb few Arabs, for the core of the dispute within Israel remained the question of demographic balance between Arabs and Jews which would be changed in the Arabs' favour by the absorption of territory in which there were many of them resident. For that reason, the Government refused the request, submitted by the newly-elected mayors of the Arab towns on the West Bank, that those Arabs who had fled the area after the 1967 war should be allowed to return. To restore the population balance the Jewish Agency, which was responsible for organizing immigration, concentrated upon Jews in the USSR, who were the largest reservoir of would-be immigrants. The USSR began to relax its stringent opposition to Jewish emigration in 1971, with the result that thousands of Soviet Jews began to arrive in Israel.

THE YOM KIPPUR WAR

Although the Arab world had been urging Sadat to attack Israel, it was firmly believed that Egypt was afraid to go to war again and that the Bar-Lev defences along the eastern bank of the Suez Canal could not be overcome. In fact Sadat was working steadily towards war, against the advice of his Soviet ally. He secured the financial support of King Faisal of Saudi Arabia to buy arms for hard currency, the agreement of Syria's President Hafiz al-Assad to a limited war for the recovery of territories lost in 1967, made his peace with King Hussein of Jordan and finally secured the arms required from the USSR.

At 2 p.m. on 6 October 1973—the most important religious festival in Israel, Yom Kippur—the Egyptians launched their attack, demolishing the supposedly impregnable sand banks of the Bar-Lev line with powerful water-jets, throwing pontoon bridges across the Suez Canal and breaking into Sinai. By midnight that day, the Egyptians had 500 tanks and missiles across the Canal and destroyed 100 Israeli tanks. Almost simultaneously the Syrian armed forces had broken through the Israeli lines on the Golan Heights.

Israel began the rapid mobilization of its reserve forces, the highly trained and numerically most important part of its defensive system, but before they could play an effective part Egyptian armed forces had occupied the east bank of the Canal to a depth of several miles and by the third day were advancing to the strategic Mitla pass in Sinai. The Syrian forces had by that time reached a point five miles from the Israeli frontier in Golan.

While fierce tank battles, said to be bigger than any in the Second World War, raged in Sinai, Israel halted the Syrian forces on its vulnerable northern frontier and counter-attacked successfully, driving them in a fighting retreat back over the 1967 cease-fire lines to within 20 miles of Damascus, where its forces were halted on the Syrian second line of defence. The Egyptian forces held their positions in Sinai but did not reach the Mitla pass.

The Egyptian High Command blundered on the twelfth day when it allowed a small Israeli commando force to cross to the west bank of the Suez Canal near Deversoir at the northern end of the Great Bitter Lake. The Israeli force was able to reinforce the bridgehead with a force strong enough to swing southwards to Suez and endanger the Egyptian Third Army on the east bank. Losses were very heavy on both sides.

After three UN Security Council resolutions, a precarious cease-fire came into effect on 25 October, but even this was honoured more in the breach than the observance until the end of the year. The US Secretary of State, Dr Henry Kissinger, did much to maintain a peace-making momentum by touring the Arab countries to secure negotiations for a permanent settlement in Geneva on 18 December, and in November Israel had accepted 'in principle' the terms of an agreement Dr Kissinger had reached with President Sadat for the 'scrupulous' observance of the cease-fire.

Talks were soon adjourned to an unspecified date in order to allow time for the Israeli general elections, which had been postponed from 30 October to 31 December 1973 because of the war. Kissinger returned to the Middle East in January and after days of intensive diplomatic activity, shuttling back and forth between Israel and Egypt, he secured the agreement of both countries to a disengagement of their forces which was announced on 17 January 1974 (see Documents on Palestine, p. 117). Israel agreed to withdraw its troops in Sinai to a line approximately 20 miles from the Suez Canal and Egypt to reduce its forces on the east bank. There was to be a neutral buffer zone between the two armies manned by troops of the UN Emergency Force.

Agreement for the disengagement of forces on the northern front was not signed until 31 May (see Documents on Palestine, p. 117) and then only after further shuttle diplomacy by Dr Kissinger. Israel and Syria agreed to withdraw their troops to lines on each side of the 1967 cease-fire line, and the ruined town of Quneitra, capital of the Golan Heights, was handed back to Syria.

Two important factors weakened Israel's position. In the last days of the war the Arab oil-producing states banned the supply of oil to the USA and the Netherlands, and reduced supplies to Western Europe. (Britain and France were exempted but, in fact, were unable to obtain their full supplies.) This, combined with steep increases in oil prices which caused serious balance-of-payments problems for the European countries—although this had nothing to do with the war—led the EC to issue a joint declaration in the Arab favour. Even more damaging to Israel was the confrontation which almost developed between the USSR and the USA when they both began delivering heavy supplies of war equipment to the Arabs and Israel respectively. Dr Kissinger emphasized to Israel that the USA would continue to support Israel, but only within the limits imposed by *détente* with the USSR. It was unquestionably a form of pressure on Israel, although this was denied. President Nixon went on a peace-making mission to the Middle East in June, and shortly afterwards Israel's Minister of Finance, Shimon Peres, visited Washington. The outcome was the conversion of a $500m. loan into a gift and an undertaking to supply a powerful fleet of fighter aircraft to ensure Israel's security.

THE AFTERMATH

The war had a profoundly disturbing effect on Israeli public opinion. The country had never suffered such losses before; nearly 3,000 dead and missing. The ease with which the Egyptian forces had crossed the Canal and overrun the Bar-Lev line and the firmness with which the Syrian forces held the second line of defence 20 miles from Damascus were not offset in Israeli eyes by the fact that Israeli troops had broken through and recrossed the Canal and had made territorial gains in Syria; the Arab forces had fought with hitherto unknown determination and had used their sophisticated Soviet weaponry with great skill. The public's confidence in the overwhelming superiority of their own army and air force was severely shaken, with the result that a sharp division of opinion occurred between those who thought the war emphasized the need to keep defensible frontiers at all costs and those, less numerous, who viewed it as an argument for a more diligent search for a permanent peace. There was widespread dissatisfaction with the Government and a public debate ensued over the failure to anticipate the outbreak of war and the breakdown of military intelligence. There were mutual recriminations among the generals and the Minister of Defence Moshe Dayan's popularity in the country slumped. General Ariel Sharon, whose forces had made the

breakthrough and Canal crossing in Egypt, resigned from the army to join the right-wing Likud party.

The elections of December 1973 reflected this confusion. The Labour Alignment, led by the United Workers' Party (Mapam), emerged as the strongest party, with 51 seats. Likud, the main opposition, made substantial gains and won 39 seats. Mrs Golda Meir reformed her coalition but resigned in April 1974, when the report on the 1973 war was published. She was succeeded in June by Gen. Itzhak Rabin, whose Cabinet contained neither Moshe Dayan nor Abba Eban, who had been Minister of Foreign Affairs since 1966. General Rabin and his Minister of Foreign Affairs, Yigal Allon, were both willing to make territorial sacrifices to achieve a settlement with the Arabs, and in September 1975 Israel and Egypt signed a second disengagement agreement, whereby Israeli forces withdrew from some territory in the Sinai peninsula.

Meanwhile, the Palestine Liberation Organization (PLO) had achieved recognition by the Arabs as 'sole representative of the Palestinian people' at the Rabat summit of November 1974, but Rabin asserted Israeli policy, which he was to maintain throughout his premiership, of refusing to recognize a PLO delegation at any renewed Geneva peace talks.

Rabin was never able to command the support that he needed as Prime Minister. Moreover, Israel's economic difficulties cost Rabin considerable popularity, and it seemed that the austerity measures that he was forced to introduce to combat inflation were hugely unpopular, discouraged immigration, and made little visible progress towards a sounder economy.

In December 1976 the National Religious Party (NRP) abstained in a 'confidence' vote in the Knesset arising from charges that the Sabbath had been desecrated at a ceremony marking the arrival of three US aircraft. Rabin subsequently dismissed two NRP ministers from the Cabinet, and the consequent withdrawal of NRP support left the Government in a minority in the Knesset, thus precipitating Rabin's resignation.

Rabin continued in a caretaker capacity until the election of May 1977, but in April 1977 he resigned as leader of the Labour Party. On 10 April the Labour Party selected Shimon Peres as its new leader. Peres had earlier been narrowly defeated by Rabin in the February poll for the leadership of the Labour Party.

ISRAEL UNDER BEGIN

When the elections for the ninth Knesset took place on 17 May 1977, the result was a surprise victory for the Likud, under Menachem Begin, who won 43 of the 120 seats—the largest single total. The Likud victory removed the Labour Party from the predominant position it had held in Israel since 1949. With the support of the NRP, the Union of Israel (Agudat Israel) and Ariel Sharon's Realization of Zion (Shlomzion), Begin was able to form a government on 19 June, and his position was strengthened in October 1977 when the Democratic Movement for Change (DMC) joined the Likud coalition. In September 1978, however, the DMC split into two factions, with seven Knesset members leaving Begin's coalition because they felt that his policy of announcing plans for further Israeli settlements on the West Bank was endangering prospects for peace.

A permanent peace settlement suddenly seemed possible when President Sadat of Egypt visited Jerusalem in November 1977 and addressed the Knesset. Talks between Sadat and Begin continued, and after various delays an unexpected breakthrough occurred in September 1978 after talks at Camp David in the USA under the guidance of President Carter, when Begin and Sadat signed two agreements. The first was a 'framework for peace in the Middle East' (see p. 119) and the second was a 'framework for the conclusion of a peace treaty between Egypt and Israel'. The first agreement provided for a five-year transitional period during which the inhabitants of the Israeli-occupied West Bank and Gaza would obtain full autonomy and self-government, and the second agreement provided for the signing of a peace treaty between Egypt and Israel, which was finally signed on 27 March 1979. The treaty provided for a phased withdrawal from Sinai which was successfully completed on 25 April 1982. Diplomatic relations between Israel and Egypt were opened on 26 January 1980.

Proposals for Palestinian autonomy provided for negotiations to be completed by 26 May 1980. However, that date passed with no agreement concluded. It became clear during the negotiations that Egypt and the Palestinians were considering 'autonomy' in terms of an independent Palestinian state, whereas Israel envisaged only some form of administrative self-government for the Palestinian Arabs in the West Bank. The announcement of fresh Israeli settlements in the West Bank, and a Knesset bill making East Jerusalem an integral part of the Jewish capital, gave Arabs little ground for hope that their concept of Palestinian autonomy would ever emerge from the negotiations, though both Israel and Egypt maintained their adherence to the 'Camp David process'.

BEGIN'S PROBLEMS

After becoming Prime Minister, Begin had to contend with two opposed factions in his Cabinet. Ariel Sharon, then Minister of Agriculture and the Minister responsible for Settlements, followed the policy of the Gush Emunim movement, which endeavoured to push the maximum number of Israeli settlements into the West Bank as quickly as possible. Sometimes voices requesting moderation prevailed, but more often settlements went ahead unopposed. As the deadline for the autonomy talks (26 May) approached, plans for more settlements were announced. Begin prevaricated on the subject of the settlements, but more often than not he supported them. The uncertainty of his exact position on many policy matters led to tensions in the Cabinet. Begin's health was also a cause for concern at times. In October 1979 Moshe Dayan resigned as Minister of Foreign Affairs, because he considered the Israeli Government stand on Palestinian autonomy to be too intransigent, and at the end of May 1980 Ezer Weizman resigned as Minister of Defence, ostensibly because of reductions in planned expenditure on defence, but his dissatisfaction with the settlements position and with the autonomy talks was well-known. Begin encountered difficulty when trying to arrange the consequent Cabinet reshuffle. He was hoping to appoint the Minister of Foreign Affairs, Itzhak Shamir, to the post of Minister of Defence but, when this proposal encountered opposition, Begin assumed the defence portfolio himself.

Begin's biggest problem, however, was the state of the Israeli economy (see Economy). Rampant inflation demanded austerity measures, and the Minister of Finance, Yigael Hurwitz, resigned in early January 1981 when the Knesset voted to award pay increases to teachers. Hurwitz withdrew his Rafi Party, with three Knesset members, from the Likud coalition and the Government could no longer command a majority. General elections were then planned for 30 June. It was thought in early 1981 that Begin was certain to be defeated in the forthcoming elections, but his position grew stronger as they approached. The tax-cutting policies of the new Minister of Finance, Yoram Aridor, proved popular. Begin's support for the Christians in Lebanon, in their struggle with the Syrians, who had stationed SAM missiles on Lebanese soil, also proved electorally popular.

A SECOND TERM FOR BEGIN

Although the election results were close, Begin was able to present a new coalition to the Knesset in early August. This was possible only by making an agreement with the religious parties, in particular Agudat Israel, by which numerous undertakings on religious observance, affecting most aspects of everyday life, were guaranteed. Although these measures were welcomed by zealots, more secular elements in Israeli society found them unpalatable.

Begin's majority was precarious, and it is remarkable that his Government survived as long as it did. In December he formally annexed the strategically important Golan Heights, a step which pleased right-wing political elements in Israel, but which angered the USA enough to cause it to suspend the strategic co-operation agreement which it had signed with Israel less than a month before.

As the time for withdrawal from Sinai drew nearer, there was increasing pressure from settlers in Sinai (particularly Yamit) to remain there. Squatters from the extreme right-wing Tehiya party adopted a belligerent stance, but they were eventually removed and the withdrawal took place as planned on 25 April 1982.

ADVANCE INTO LEBANON

During 1982 and the first half of 1983, Arab disturbances on the West Bank became more severe, and there were even Jewish demonstrations against Israel's settlement of the area. The number of Jewish settlements in the West Bank increased to more than 100 in 1983, and more land was expropriated. The event which provoked another major Middle East crisis, however, was Israel's 'Operation Peace for Galilee', an armed incursion into Lebanon which was launched on 6 June 1982 and intended as a brief and limited campaign. By the end of June, however, Israeli forces had advanced across Lebanon and surrounded West Beirut, where 6,000 PLO fighters had become trapped. Israel's action met with disapproval from most of the world, and the support of the USA became questionable after Secretary of State Haig's resignation at the end of June, and his replacement by George Shultz. Israel declared a cease-fire and demanded that the Palestinians lay down their heavy arms and leave Lebanon.

Intensive diplomatic efforts, hampered by repeated outbreaks of fighting, were made between June and August to find an acceptable basis for the supervised withdrawal of the trapped Palestinian and Syrian forces. With the help of a US envoy, Philip Habib, their evacuation began on 21 August and was completed by 1 September (estimates put the number of evacuees at 14,500–15,000).

Israeli forces remained in effective control of Beirut, although, under the terms of the evacuation agreement, an international peace-keeping force (predominantly comprising US, French and Italian troops) was stationed in various parts of the city until early September. Despite US protests, Israeli forces moved into West Beirut again on 15 September, taking up positions around Palestine refugee camps located in the Muslim sectors. On 17 September reports began to emerge of a massacre committed in the Sabra and Chatila camps by armed men who were ostensibly seeking PLO guerrillas. The identity of the killers was uncertain but evidence suggested their being Christian Phalangist militiamen, whose entry into the camps had been facilitated by Israeli troops. Israel rejected the Arab world's charge of responsibility for the massacre, but on 28 September the Government initiated a full judicial inquiry, led by the Chief Justice of the Supreme Court, Itzhak Kahan. Published on 8 February 1983, the report of the inquiry placed actual responsibility for the massacre on Lebanese Phalangists, but concluded that Israel's political and military leaders bore indirect responsibility for the tragic events by failing properly to supervise the militiamen in the area. Begin was censured merely for showing indifference to reports reaching him of Phalangists entering the camps. As recommended by the inquiry, Ariel Sharon resigned as Minister of Defence (though he remained in the Government as Minister without Portfolio), to be replaced by the Ambassador to the USA, Moshe Arens.

Direct talks between Israel and Lebanon for the withdrawal of foreign forces began on 28 December. Progress was slow but a 12-article agreement, formulated by US Secretary of State Shultz and declaring the end of hostilities, was finally signed on 17 May 1983. Syria rejected the agreement and its forces held their positions in the Beka'a valley, raising the possibility of open war with Israel, which, in turn, refused to withdraw while the Syrians remained. On the same day that Israel signed its agreement with Lebanon, it concluded another secret one with the USA which recognized Israel's right, despite the accord with Lebanon, to retaliate against terrorist attacks in Lebanon and to delay its withdrawal, beyond the date (three months from the date of signing) which had been agreed in that accord, if Syrian and PLO forces remained there.

In July, Israel, with its casualties from guerrilla attacks increasing, decided to redeploy its forces south of Beirut along the Awali river.

BEGIN'S RESIGNATION

Support for Begin's Government had been sustained throughout the early weeks of 'Operation Peace for Galilee' but, as the planned, limited incursion developed into a costly occupation, opposition to government policy increased, not only among the Israeli public but also in the army.

By the summer of 1983, Israel was sliding into an economic crisis and the involvement in Lebanon had become an expensive stalemate. The Government's prestige had been badly damaged by the Beirut massacres and by a capitulation to wage demands by the country's doctors, whose four-month strike for higher pay had taken medical services to the brink of collapse. Begin, already depressed by the death of his wife in November and by the events in Lebanon, announced his resignation as Prime Minister and leader of the Likud bloc on 30 August 1983. Itzhak Shamir, the Minister of Foreign Affairs since 1980, was elected leader of Likud on 2 September. Begin withheld his formal resignation until 15 September, while a period of political wrangling ensued to find a viable coalition government. Although Labour was the largest single party in the Knesset, Shamir was asked to form a government on 21 September, his Likud grouping having a theoretical majority of seven seats with the support of minority religious parties. Shamir pronounced himself committed to the Israeli presence in Lebanon, to the continuation of the West Bank settlement programme and to tackling the country's economic problems.

During the second half of 1983 the monetary crisis (see Economy) emerged as the main cause of the Government's declining popularity. The lack of a single-minded approach to the crisis led to the resignation in October of the Minister of Finance, Yoram Aridor, whose policies, diluted by the Cabinet, failed to prevent inflation from soaring. The more thoroughly pursued austerity measures of Aridor's successor, Yigal Cohen-Orgad, only threatened to alienate elements of Shamir's shaky coalition (in particular the Tami party), concerned over the effects of cuts in social services and increases in the price of food, and caused growing labour unrest. Further uproar greeted a plan virtually to 'freeze' the programme of creating Jewish settlements on Israeli-occupied territory in the West Bank and the Gaza Strip, in order to save money, at the beginning of 1984. Although the rate of settlement had slowed down (owing to Israel's economic recession and the shortage of government funds with which to finance new communities), the number of settlements established since 1967 had risen to 129 (114 in the West Bank) by March 1985, and the number of Israeli settlers to 46,000 (42,500 in the West Bank). By March 1985, Israel had direct control of more than 50% of the 490,000 ha of land in the West Bank. The depth of feeling on the issue was illustrated by the exposure in April 1984 of a Jewish anti-Palestinian terrorist organization operating in the West Bank, some of whose members were active in Gush Emunim, the main West Bank settlement organization.

THE 1984 GENERAL ELECTION

Inflation continued to rise sharply in 1984 and in January the Government narrowly survived a vote of 'no confidence' in the Knesset. Its position was further weakened by the resignation from the Cabinet (and the loss of the guaranteed vote) of the Minister without Portfolio, Mordechai Ben-Porat, one week later. Finally, in March, the Government failed by 61 votes to 58 to prevent the passage of a bill, sponsored by the Labour Party, proposing the dissolution of the Knesset prior to a general election. In this vote the Tami party supported the opposition. The general election was set for 23 July.

The election campaign was conducted against a background of strikes as the state of the economy continued to deteriorate. The overall rate of inflation passed 400% in July and it was apparent that the main issue determining voters' likely preference in the election was the economy. Bans which had been imposed by the parliamentary election committee on the ultra-right-wing Kach and the left-wing Progressive List for Peace parties, preventing them from contesting the election, were overturned by the Supreme Court so that 27 parties (including 16 new groupings, mostly splinter groups from existing parties) were expected to compete for seats on 23 July.

Although an opinion poll conducted three weeks before the election indicated a clear Labour lead, the election produced no conclusive result. The Labour Alignment won 44 seats in the Knesset (an insufficient number to enable it to form Israel's first single-party government), while Likud gained 41. The balance of power lay, once again, with the minority parties which won the remaining 35 seats in the 120-seat assembly. When what was required was the swift establishment of a new government to deal with the deteriorating economy, both Labour and Likud were embroiled in negotiations to win the support of

the minority parties for a viable coalition administration. These talks provided no clear majority in the Knesset for either side, and it became increasingly likely that a government of national unity, comprising both Labour and Likud, presented the only resolution to the political impasse, short of calling a second election. President Herzog nominated the Labour leader, Shimon Peres, as Prime Minister-designate on 5 August and invited him to form a government of national unity. The 11th Knesset was inaugurated on 13 August in an atmosphere of great uncertainty as to whether Labour and Likud could bridge the political gap between them and could agree on the formation of a national government.

THE ISRAELI OCCUPATION OF SOUTHERN LEBANON

The withdrawal in September 1983 of Israeli forces in Lebanon to the Awali river, south of Beirut, produced a *de facto* partition of the country. Israeli troops (reduced to some 10,000 by the end of 1983) faced about 50,000 Syrian troops and 2,000–4,000 Palestinian guerrillas entrenched in the Beka'a valley to the north. The 2,500 men of Maj. Sa'ad Haddad's Israeli-controlled southern Lebanese militia, the so-called 'South Lebanon Army' (SLA), were employed to police the occupied area, with the Israeli troops, and to combat guerrilla attacks on the occupying forces. Israel also armed other, independent, militias (including Shi'ite Muslim groups) so that they could control their own areas of influence. Despite these measures and, perhaps, partly because of them, Israeli soldiers continued to be the target of guerrilla attacks (the Israeli death toll in the 'Peace for Galilee' operation approached 600 by July 1984). Although, after the withdrawal to the Awali river, the Israeli air force and navy were involved in attacks on Syrian targets in north Lebanon and against the PLO in the port of Tripoli (in November and December 1983), there were no serious land-based exchanges between Israeli and Syrian forces in Lebanon during the first half of 1984. Some isolated Israeli shelling of Palestinian positions in the Beka'a took place in retaliation against the activities of Palestinian guerrilla squads which infiltrated the Israeli-occupied areas to make their attacks.

Major Sa'ad Haddad died in December 1983 and Maj.-Gen. Antoine Lahad replaced him as leader of the SLA in March 1984. In the same month, under the influence of Syria, President Gemayel abrogated the 17 May agreement with Israel. Although the agreement had effectively been a 'dead-letter' for some time, the rising cost of involvement in Lebanon and the unpopularity of that policy at home disposed Israel at least to consider withdrawing. It was clear, however, that, much as Israel would prefer to spare the expense of occupation and the lives of its people by leaving the policing of southern Lebanon to Maj.-Gen. Lahad's and other militias, it would not withdraw either until it felt secure within its existing boundaries against terrorist attacks launched from Lebanese territory, or until it was politically impossible for it to remain. The official policy of the Shamir Government was that Syrian withdrawal from Lebanon was a pre-condition of Israeli withdrawal. Shimon Peres, the Labour Party leader, had pledged to adopt a more flexible pragmatic approach to negotiations on an Israeli withdrawal if he came to power. However, Labour's failure to win an overall majority in the election, and the likely formation of a government of national unity with Likud, meant that Labour might have to make compromises, over controversial issues, in the very policies which distinguished it from Likud.

THE GOVERNMENT OF NATIONAL UNITY

Six weeks of negotiation were required before Peres and Itzhak Shamir could agree on the composition and policy of a coalition government. The new Government, whose component parties accounted for 97 of the 120 Knesset seats, was formed on 13 September. It contained representatives of the two major party groupings (Labour and Likud), four religious parties (the NRP, Shas, Agudat Israel and Morasha) and the Shinui, Yahad and Ometz parties. Under the terms of the coalition agreement, Shimon Peres was to hold the premiership for the first two years and one month of the government, while Itzhak Shamir served as Deputy Prime Minister and Minister of Foreign Affairs, after which time they were to exchange their respective posts for a further period of two years and one month. Within the Cabinet of 25 ministers, an inner Cabinet of 10 (including five members each from Labour and Likud) was formed.

ISRAEL'S WITHDRAWAL FROM LEBANON

The Government of national unity pledged itself to withdrawing the Israel Defence Force (IDF) from Lebanon, and to tackling the problems of the economy. Any withdrawal agreement with Lebanon was not to be without conditions. To ensure the security of its northern border, ideally, Israel sought Syrian commitments not to redeploy its forces in areas evacuated by the IDF; to prevent the infiltration of PLO terrorists into the south of Lebanon; to grant freedom of operation to the SLA; and to allow the UN Interim Force in Lebanon (UNIFIL) to deploy north of the SLA area up to Syrian lines in the Beka'a valley. Lebanon, for its part, demanded $10,000m. in reparations, and the unconditional withdrawal of the IDF. More realistically, Israel dropped its demand for simultaneous Syrian withdrawal, provided satisfactory military arrangements could be made, and Syria approved a series of talks, under UN auspices, between Lebanese and Israeli army representatives, to agree the terms of withdrawal. The talks began in Naqoura (Lebanon) in November but repeatedly foundered on the question of which forces should take the place of the IDF, to prevent intercommunal fighting. The Lebanese, influenced by Syria, wanted UNIFIL to police the Israel-Lebanon border (as it had been mandated to do in 1978), and the Lebanese army to deploy north of the Litani river, between UNIFIL and the Syrian forces. Israel was not convinced of the competence of the Lebanese army, and wanted UNIFIL to be deployed north of the Litani while the SLA patrolled the southern Lebanese border. In the absence of any agreement, Israel withdrew from talks, and on 14 January 1985 the Israeli Cabinet voted to take unilateral steps towards withdrawal, arousing fears of civil war in southern Lebanon when they departed. The Cabinet agreed a three-phase withdrawal plan whose final aim was the return of the IDF to the international border. The first phase took place in February 1985 and involved the evacuation of the IDF from the western occupied sector, around Sidon, to the Litani river area, around Nabatiyah. The UN force was asked to police the vacated area with the Lebanese army. In the second phase, the IDF was to leave the occupied central and eastern sector (including the southern Beka'a valley), and redeploy around Hasbayyah. The third and final phase, taking the IDF behind Israel's northern border and leaving an apparatus of control inside southern Lebanon (based on the SLA, with IDF backing), was to be completed some nine months after the first.

The cost of the withdrawal was estimated at $100m., and that of the entire 'Operation Peace for Galilee' at some $3,500m. The second stage of the withdrawal began on 3 March 1985, with no fixed duration. The Shi'ites of southern Lebanon, antipathetic towards the PLO, had initially welcomed the IDF, but now they attacked it in retreat. Guerrilla attacks increased the Israeli death toll in Lebanon during the invasion and occupation to more than 650 by April, with about 50 of these deaths having occurred during the withdrawal. In retaliation, Israel pursued an 'Iron Fist' policy, purging Shi'ite villages of suspected guerrillas or attacking them indiscriminately, killing innocent inhabitants. Instead of decreasing, the number of attacks on Israeli forces, orchestrated by the Shi'ite National Resistance Movement, Amal and Hezbollah (the Party of God), multiplied, and during March Israel accelerated the process of withdrawal. The second stage was completed with the evacuation of Tyre on 29 April.

On 4 April 1985 Israel released 750 Shi'ite prisoners, detained as part of the 'Iron Fist' policy, from Ansar camp, prior to withdrawing from that part of western Lebanon. At the same time, contrary to international conventions (as they were not prisoners of war), 1,200 Lebanese and Palestinian detainees were transferred to prisons in Israel. Then, on 20 May, 1,150 Lebanese and Palestinian prisoners were exchanged for three Israeli prisoners of war. The release of 766 Shi'ite prisoners, transferred from Lebanon to Atlit prison in Israel, became the central demand of Amal guerrillas who hijacked a TWA airliner and held it and its predominantly US crew and passengers at Beirut airport in June. Israel refused to release the prisoners unless requested to do so by the USA. Some 450 of them were freed at the end of June and in early July, though Israel denied

that their release was related to the hostage crisis, and the rest by 10 September.

Israel announced the completion of the third and final stage of the withdrawal of the IDF, ahead of the original schedule, at the beginning of June, though it was common knowledge that about 500 Israeli troops and advisers remained in Lebanon to support the SLA in patrolling the defensive buffer zone which formed a strip, 11 km–20 km wide, inside the border. The SLA had been depleted by desertion and defections to the Shi'ite resistance during the withdrawal. Syria, the Lebanese Government and leaders of the Shi'ite and Druze communities in Lebanon did not recognize the SLA's role in policing the border with Israel. Despite a continued Israeli presence in Lebanon, Syria withdrew 10,000 of its troops from the Beka'a valley at the end of June and the beginning of July, leaving fewer than 25,000 men in the country. Attacks on the security zone, and on the SLA policing it, were frequent, but the zone remained intact.

After the initial euphoria of the Israeli withdrawal from Sidon in February, fighting erupted between the Christian Phalange (allegedly incited by Israel), the Lebanese army, Amal, and other Shi'ite groups, and Palestinians in the refugee camps. From the Israeli point of view, the return of some 2,000 PLO fighters to the Palestinian refugee camps around Sidon was a serious development. However, the Shi'ites of southern Lebanon and the Syrians had no desire to see a pro-Arafat PLO re-establish itself militarily in the region, and tried to prevent it from doing so.

Israel was confronted by a more firmly entrenched enemy in the Shi'ite community just across its northern border. After the final stage of the Israeli evacuation was completed, Shi'ite guerrilla attacks on the SLA continued and the PLO steadily re-established itself in southern Lebanon. Israeli forces repeatedly pursued PLO fighters across the border and raided PLO positions in Lebanon by land and air in retaliation for attacks on Israeli territory made by PLO guerrillas. According to Israel the 'frequency' of attempts by guerrillas to infiltrate northern Israel increased significantly after December 1987, when the Palestinian uprising (*intifada*) in the Occupied Territories began (see below).

DOMESTIC AND DIPLOMATIC ISSUES

The state of the economy presented the main domestic problem to the Government of National Unity and was the cause of considerable argument within the Cabinet between those convinced of the necessity for strict budgetary control and those concerned at the consequences such control might have for Israel's defensive capability and for civil order (see Economy).

On the question of Jewish settlement of the occupied West Bank and Gaza Strip, the document establishing the Government of National Unity effectively allowed Shimon Peres and his fellow Labour ministers in the Cabinet to obstruct plans for new settlements. The coalition agreement provided for the establishment of five or six new settlements in each of the Government's four years in office. However, between October 1984 and October 1986 only two new settlements were opened in the West Bank, though the population of the 114 existing settlements increased from 42,500 in October 1984 to about 60,000 in mid-1986. Before his two-year period of office as Prime Minister terminated in October 1986, Shimon Peres said that no new settlements would be established in 1986/87, and that the budget for investments would be used to consolidate existing settlements. However, on assuming the premiership, Itzhak Shamir stated that the settlement programme would be carried out in accordance with the coalition agreement. By the end of 1987, the number of settlements in the Occupied Territories had risen to 139 (118 in the West Bank) and the number of Jewish settlers to 70,023 (67,648 in the West Bank). Of the total land area of the West Bank, 52% had been expropriated.

After 1974 and the fall of Emperor Haile Selassie, Israel had smuggled Falashas (Ethiopian Jews) out of Ethiopia. Between 1980 and 1982 some 2,000 were brought to Israel. In 1984 and 1985 respectively, with the co-operation of international Jewish organizations, 7,800 and 2,035 Falashas were airlifted via Europe to resettlement camps in Israel from Sudan, to which they travelled from famine-stricken Ethiopia. Owing to international publicity, criticism of the operation from Ethiopia's Marxist regime and the possibility of Arab opposition to it, the

Sudanese Government suspended the airlift in January 1985, leaving 1,000 Falashas awaiting transportation in Sudan and a further 12,000 stranded in Ethiopia. The USA secretly completed the airlift of Falashas from Sudan at the end of March.

In January 1985 Israel and Egypt embarked on a series of talks, the first for two years, to determine the sovereignty of the minute Taba coastal strip on the Red Sea, which Israel had not vacated when it left Sinai in 1982. The Taba issue threatened the survival of the fragile coalition on several occasions. Negotiations were not finally concluded until February 1989, when Israel agreed to return Taba to Egyptian control by 15 March. Israel was to continue providing Taba with water, electricity and telephone lines, and Israeli citizens with valid passports were to be granted free access.

THE FAILURE OF THE JORDANIAN-PALESTINIAN PEACE INITIATIVE

In 1984 Israel rejected a request by King Hussein of Jordan for a peace conference involving all the concerned parties in the Arab-Israeli conflict. The formal establishment by King Hussein and Yasser Arafat of a combined Jordanian-Palestinian position on future peace talks, on 23 February 1985 in Amman, providing for a joint Jordanian-Palestinian delegation to such talks, gave new impetus to the search for a diplomatic solution to the Palestinian question. Although Israel supported the involvement of the five permanent members of the UN Security Council in the peace process, it rejected the call for an international peace conference, which was reiterated in 1985 by King Hussein and President Mubarak of Egypt, and also their suggestion of preliminary talks between the USA, Egypt and a joint Jordanian-Palestinian delegation, if it contained PLO members. Israel was interested only in direct talks once an acceptable Palestinian delegation was agreed on. In July Israel rejected a list of seven Palestinians, all members or supporters of Yasser Arafat's Fatah, nominated by the PLO as members of a joint delegation with Jordan to hold talks with the USA prior to direct negotiations with Israel. Israel refused to talk to any members of the PLO or the Palestine National Council (PNC) and considered US participation in talks with them as a violation of their commitment not to deal with the PLO until it recognized Israel's right to exist. Peres subsequently accepted two men on the list who satisfied his requirement for 'authentic Palestinian representatives' from the Occupied Territories. The other major obstacle to progress at this time was the PLO's position regarding UN Security Council Resolution 242. The PLO consistently refused to accept this resolution as a basis for negotiations as it referred only to a Palestinian refugee problem and not to the right of Palestinians to self-determination and a state of Palestine. The PLO Executive Committee repudiated Resolution 242 again after the Amman agreement with Jordan, although it was King Hussein's contention that Arafat had privately acknowledged (and would, in time, publicly accept) the resolution. However, despite persistent cajoling by King Hussein, Arafat made no public declaration.

The peace process was further hampered by a series of terrorist incidents in which the PLO was implicated. Firstly, in September 1985, three Israelis were murdered by terrorists in Larnaca, Cyprus. Israel held the PLO's élite Force 17 responsible, and, at the beginning of October, bombed the organization's headquarters in Tunis. Then, in October, an Italian cruise ship, the *Achille Lauro*, was 'hijacked' in the eastern Mediterranean by members of the Palestine Liberation Front (PLF; one of two groups of that name, this being the pro-Arafat PLF, led by Muhammad Abbas—'Abu Abbas'). They killed a Jewish American passenger before surrendering to the Egyptian authorities in Port Said.

These incidents gave Israel further cause to reject the PLO as a prospective partner in peace negotiations, and raised doubts as to Arafat's desire for a peaceful settlement. Meanwhile, Jewish settlers in the Occupied Territories had asserted that any attempt to negotiate Israeli sovereignty over the disputed areas would provoke a campaign of civil disobedience.

In November, in Cairo, Yasser Arafat, under pressure from King Hussein of Jordan and President Mubarak of Egypt to renounce the use of violence, reiterated a PLO decision of 1974 to confine military operations to the Occupied Territories and Israel, though his aides immediately repudiated the statement.

In December 17 people were killed when terrorists, believed to belong to Abu Nidal's anti-Arafat Fatah Revolutionary Council, attacked passengers at the desks of the Israeli state airline, El Al, in Rome and Vienna airports.

King Hussein, who had already prepared the ground for an alternative approach to the Palestinian question by initiating a *rapprochement* with Syria, formally severed political links with the PLO on 19 February 1986, 'until such time as their word becomes their bond, characterized by commitment, credibility and constancy'. It emerged that, in January, the USA (without Israel's knowledge) had undertaken to invite the PLO to an international peace conference, on condition that the PLO publicly accepted UN Security Council Resolutions 242 and 338 as the basis for negotiation. Arafat refused to make such a commitment without a similar US acceptance of the Palestinians' right to self-determination.

After the collapse of the Jordanian-Palestinian peace initiative, Jordan resisted Israeli requests for direct talks excluding the PLO, and there was little prospect of a speedy revival of the peace process.

CABINET DISCONTENT

The coalition Government continued its precarious existence in 1986, beset by a number of contentious issues which divided Labour and Likud, its largest constituents. In February, after the success of the first seven months of the Government's economic stabilization programme, Prime Minister Peres drew criticism from the Minister of Finance, Itzhak Modai of Likud, when he expressed support for various reflationary measures (see Economy). Their difference of opinion culminated in April, when Modai accused Peres of being a 'flying Prime Minister' with no understanding of economics. Peres demanded Modai's resignation as Minister of Finance (although he agreed to Modai's remaining in the Government), and the Likud members of the Cabinet threatened to resign *en masse* if Modai was dismissed or replaced. Modai offered to resign, rather than endanger the existence of the Government, but Likud refused to countenance this. The crisis lasted for 10 days until a compromise was agreed, whereby Modai exchanged cabinet portfolios with Moshe Nissim, the Minister of Justice. Itzhak Shamir, the leader of Likud, asserted that the exchange of cabinet posts would remain valid only until he took over the premiership from Peres in October.

SHAMIR ASSUMES THE PREMIERSHIP

In accordance with the terms of the agreement under which the coalition Government of National Unity was formed in September 1984, Shimon Peres, the leader of the Labour Party, resigned as Prime Minister on 10 October 1986, to allow Itzhak Shamir, the Minister of Foreign Affairs, to assume the premiership on 14 October. The transfer of power was delayed while the coalition parties negotiated the composition of the new Cabinet, which was approved by the Knesset on 20 October. The Labour group had objected to the reinstatement of Itzhak Modai, but his name was finally included in the Cabinet, in which he was one of five ministers without portfolio. The only unscheduled changes in the Cabinet were the replacement of Dr Josef Burg, who resigned as Minister of Religious Affairs, by Zvulun Hammer, and the naming of Shoshana Arbeli-Almoslino as Minister of Health, instead of Mordechai Gur, who refused to serve under Itzhak Shamir. (Mordechai Gur returned to the Cabinet in April 1988.) The composition of the inner Cabinet was unchanged. Peres and Shamir duly exchanged posts on 20 October.

THE SHIN BET CONTROVERSY

The activities of Shin Bet, the Israeli internal military intelligence agency, came under scrutiny in 1986, when it was suggested that the deaths, under interrogation, of two Palestinians in April 1984 had been deliberately concealed. The official Shin Bet version of events was that all four Palestinians involved in the 'hijacking' of an Israeli bus had been killed at the time of the incident. Photographs revealed that two terrorists were captured alive. Two subsequent official inquiries, between April 1984 and August 1985, confirmed that the two terrorists had 'died at a later stage', and identified Brig.-Gen. Itzhak Mordechai as the prime suspect in their murders. Mordechai was acquitted by a military court in August 1985, and the Attorney-General, Itzhak Zamir, initiated investigations into the affair. He was told by leading Shin Bet officials that Avraham Shalom, the director of the agency, had ordered the prisoners' execution and had falsified evidence and suborned witnesses at the two official inquiries. Zamir insisted on a police investigation into the affair. In May 1986 the Cabinet refused to suspend Shalom, the Shin Bet director, and (though the Labour group, with the exception of Shimon Peres, supported some form of investigation) continued to resist the suggestion of a police inquiry. Likud, in particular, feared that such an investigation would reveal too much about the operations of Shin Bet, thus preventing the organization from functioning effectively and so endangering national security. On 1 June Itzhak Zamir, who had wanted to resign in February, was replaced as Attorney-General by Josef Harish. At the end of June Avraham Shalom resigned as director of Shin Bet, he and three of his deputies having been assured of a pardon and immunity from prosecution by the President of Israel, Chaim Herzog. In a letter to President Herzog, Shalom stated that his actions had been taken 'on authority and with permission', presumably from Itzhak Shamir, to whom, as Prime Minister at the time of the killings and the cover-up, he was responsible. In August a further seven Shin Bet agents were granted a presidential pardon for their alleged involvement in the killings or the subsequent subterfuge. In July the Supreme Court challenged the Government to explain why it had not instituted a police investigation into the affair. The Cabinet then voted, by a narrow margin, for a police inquiry (which was supported by Likud and the small religious parties), rather than a full judicial inquiry (supported by Labour). Later that month, after criticizing Shimon Peres for his handling of the Shin Bet affair, Itzhak Modai resigned from the Cabinet. In December a secret report, compiled by the Ministry of Justice and based on a three-month-long police investigation into the affair, absolved Itzhak Shamir from any blame for the deaths of the two Palestinians or for the subsequent attempts by Shin Bet to conceal the truth of the incidents in question; it also exonerated Shimon Peres and Moshe Arens, respectively the Prime Minister during one of the official inquiries, and the Minister of Defence when the killings occurred. Following further revelations of illegal Shin Bet practices in 1987, the Government established a commission of inquiry in June, under Moshe Landau, the former Supreme Court President, to investigate the agency.

In October 1986, using information supplied by Mordechai Vanunu, a former technician at Israel's nuclear research establishment at Dimona, *The Sunday Times* of London claimed that Israel had succeeded in developing thermonuclear weapons and was stockpiling them at Dimona. Vanunu subsequently disappeared from London, and at the end of October Israeli authorities admitted that he was in their custody and would be tried for breaching national security. It was alleged that Vanunu had been lured to Rome, by a female agent of Mossad (the Israeli external security agency), where he was kidnapped and smuggled to Israel. His trial began in September 1987.

Following the revelation in a Lebanese magazine, in November 1986, that the USA had made three deliveries of military equipment to Iran since September 1985, it emerged that the sale of weapons and spare parts had been effected through Israeli intermediaries, with the knowledge, and even partly at the instigation, of Prime Minister Peres. According to some reports, Israel had itself been supplying armaments to Iran since the outbreak of the Iran–Iraq War in 1980.

ATTEMPTS TO REVIVE THE MIDDLE EAST PEACE PROCESS

On 11 September 1986 President Mubarak of Egypt and Prime Minister Peres of Israel met in Alexandria, Egypt, to discuss ways of reviving the Middle East peace process. They agreed to form a committee to prepare for an international peace conference (though Peres did not have cabinet endorsement for this initiative), but failed to agree on the nature of the Palestinian representation at such a conference. Following the summit meeting (the first between Egypt and Israel since August 1981) and the signing of the Taba arbitration agreement, President Mubarak appointed Muhammad Bassiouni as Egyptian ambas-

sador to Israel. The previous ambassador had been recalled from Israel in 1982, following the Israeli invasion of Lebanon.

Under the premiership of Itzhak Shamir, however, official Israeli policy regarding a Middle East peace settlement remained divided. Shamir opposed the concept of an international peace conference, involving the five permanent members of the Security Council, and instead proposed direct negotiations between Israel, Egypt, the USA and a joint Jordanian-Palestinian delegation, excluding the PLO. Although King Hussein resisted Shamir's advances, Jordan and Israel appeared to have a common interest in fostering a Palestinian constituency in the West Bank, which was independent of the PLO and with which they could deal, and, to this extent, their policy in the region coincided after the demise of the joint Jordanian-PLO peace initiative. In 1986, under the premiership of Shimon Peres (who said that the 'freeze' in the building of new Jewish settlements in the West Bank would continue), Israel revived a programme of limited Palestinian autonomy, with the appointment of Palestinians to replace Israeli officials in municipal government, though this resulted in civil protests by pro-PLO Palestinians and the intimidation or assassination of Israeli appointees. In August Jordan announced a major five-year investment programme in the Occupied Territories and gave its approval to an Israeli proposal for the establishment of branches of the Amman-based Cairo-Amman Bank in Nablus, under dual Jordanian/Israeli authority, to provide financial services to the Palestinian community. However, support for Yasser Arafat and the PLO remained strong in the West Bank.

In the less influential role of Minister of Foreign Affairs, Shimon Peres continued to pursue his own diplomatic initiative to secure international agreement on the terms for a peace conference.

In February 1987, although Prime Minister Shamir warned him that he had no authority to enter into agreements with a foreign power on Israel's behalf, Shimon Peres revisited President Mubarak in Egypt, and, at the conclusion of their discussions, Peres and the Egyptian Minister of Foreign Affairs issued a joint statement urging 'the convening in 1987 of an international conference leading to direct negotiations' between the main protagonists in the Middle East conflict. The outstanding issues to be resolved remained those of Palestinian representation and the participation of the USSR. On the Israeli side, the main obstacle to any negotiated settlement remained the refusal of any Israeli leader to accept the participation of the PLO in peace negotiations. In May Peres claimed to have made significant progress on the issue of Palestinian representation with King Hussein of Jordan, and to have the consent of Egypt, Jordan and the USA for convening an international peace conference, including a delegation of Palestinians (presumably not PLO members) who rejected terrorism and violence and accepted UN Security Council Resolutions 242 and 338 as the basis for negotiations. King Hussein continued publicly to insist on the need for the PLO to be represented, but he appeared to have accepted (contrary to his long-standing view) that the conference would have no decision-making powers and be only a preliminary to direct negotiations.

However, Peres failed to gain the approval of the 10-member inner Israeli Cabinet for his plan, and his Labour bloc did not have the necessary support in the Knesset to force an early general election on the issue, or to be sure of being able to form a coalition government, thereafter, which excluded Shamir's Likud bloc. Likud and other right-wing Israeli groups remained implacably opposed to the principle of an Israeli offer to exchange territory taken in 1967 for peace with its Arab opponents, which Peres would have sought to apply at a peace conference.

In July 1987 Egypt's Minister of Foreign Affairs, Dr Esmat Abd al-Meguid, on the first visit to Israel by a leading member of the Egyptian Government since the Israeli invasion of Lebanon in 1982, appealed to the Israeli Government to participate in an international peace conference, which must, he said, inevitably include a PLO delegation. He rejected Prime Minister Shamir's alternative proposal of direct peace negotiations between Israel, Egypt, Jordan, the USA and Palestinian representatives.

PALESTINIAN UPRISING

The frequency of anti-Israeli demonstrations and violent incidents in the Occupied Territories increased during 1987, in
particular following the reunification of the PLO and its abrogation of the 1985 Jordanian-PLO accord in Algiers in April.
However, the authorities were not prepared for the wave of
violent demonstrations against Israeli rule (the worst since
Israel occupied the Territories in 1967) which began in
December. The rioting was apparently precipitated by the
deaths of four Palestinians on 8 December 1987, when the two
vehicles in which they were travelling were in collision with an
Israeli army truck at a military checkpoint in the Gaza Strip.
Rioting in the Gaza Strip soon spread to the other Occupied
Territories, and the number of Palestinians shot dead by the
heavily reinforced Israeli army and security forces rose to 38
by mid-January 1988. There was widespread international condemnation of the 'iron fist' tactics that Israeli forces employed
to control rioters who hurled bricks, stones and petrol bombs.
A series of strikes was widely observed in the Occupied Territories, and many of the estimated 120,000 Palestinians who
commuted to work in Israel stayed at home. The uprising
(*intifada*), which had probably begun more as a spontaneous
expression of accumulated frustration at 20 years of occupation,
degrading living conditions, overcrowding and declining opportunities in education and employment, than as a politically co-
ordinated demonstration, was soon being exploited and orchestrated by an underground leadership, the Unified National
Leadership of the Uprising (UNLU), comprising elements from
across the Palestinian political spectrum (the PLO, the Communist Party and Islamic Jihad). The UNLU organized strikes,
the closure of shops and businesses, and other forms of civil
disobedience, including the non-payment of taxes. It also distributed regular bulletins, exhorting Palestinians to continue the
struggle and instructing them in means of revolt.

On 22 December 1987 the USA abstained from a UN Security
Council Resolution (No. 605) deploring Israel's violent methods
of suppressing Palestinian demonstrations. On 5 January 1988,
however, the USA voted in support of Resolution 607, which
urged Israel to comply with the International Red Cross's fourth
Geneva Convention of 1949, concerning the treatment of civilians in wartime, and to abandon its plans to deport nine Palestinian political activists from the Occupied Territories. (This was
the first time since 1981 that the USA had supported a UN
resolution which was critical of Israel.) However, on 13 January
during a fact-finding mission to the Occupied Territories by a
UN Under-Secretary-General, Marrack Goulding, four of the
Palestinians were deported to Lebanon. By mid-January up to
1,000 Palestinians had been arrested, and 24-hour curfews were
in force around 12 or more refugee camps in the Gaza Strip and
the West Bank, preventing the entry of food and supplies. The
Israeli Cabinet repeatedly endorsed the security forces' 'iron
fist' policy but was divided over the long-term solution to the
Palestinian question. Shimon Peres, in contrast to Itzhak
Shamir's Likud bloc (which considered the Occupied Territories
to be a non-negotiable part of 'Greater Israel'), believed that
only a political solution could end the uprising, and favoured
a demilitarization of those areas and the removal of Jewish
settlements prior to a negotiated agreement.

At the end of January 1988, by order of Itzhak Rabin, the
Minister of Defence, Israeli security forces adopted a policy of
indiscriminate, pre-emptive beatings of Palestinians, allegedly
to avoid shootings, which was internationally condemned. The
new policy, combined with the periodic imposition of curfews on
refugee camps, towns and villages, far from quelling unrest,
appeared to provoke it and encouraged greater self-reliance and
organization among the Palestinians, who established committees to oversee the collection and distribution of food and other
supplies, and to co-ordinate resistance. In addition, the Israeli
economy began to feel the effects of an absence of labour,
as Palestinian workers from the Occupied Territories either
boycotted their jobs in Israel or were prevented from travelling
to them by curfew, so that production at industrial plants
and fruit plantations declined. Equally worrying for the Israeli
authorities was the prominent role which was adopted by
Islamic fundamentalists in organizing demonstrations and
appealing for a *jihad* (holy war) against Israel. The most powerful of the militant Islamic groups was the Islamic Resistance

Movement, founded as a radical reincarnation of the Muslim
Brotherhood, and known by its Arab acronym, Hamas (Harakat
al-Muqawama al-Islamiyya). Meanwhile, Israeli Arabs (and
some Jews) demonstrated in Nazareth and Tel-Aviv in opposition to the Government's treatment of the Palestinians in the
Occupied Territories.

THE SHULTZ PLAN

At the end of February 1988 the US Secretary of State, George
Shultz, embarked on a tour of Middle Eastern capitals, in an
attempt to elicit support for a new peace initiative. The Shultz
Plan, as the initiative came to be known, proposed the convening
of an international peace conference, involving all parties to the
Arab–Israeli conflict and the five permanent members of the
UN Security Council, with the Palestinians represented in a
joint Jordanian/Palestinian delegation, excluding the PLO.
However, this conference would have no power to impose a
peace settlement and would act only as a consultative forum
prior to and during subsequent direct talks between Israel and
each of its Arab neighbours, and between Israel and a joint
Jordanian/Palestinian delegation. The latter talks would determine the details of a three-year transitional period of autonomy
for the 1.5m. Palestinians in the Occupied Territories, leading
(before the transitional period began) to negotiations to determine the final status of government in the Territories.

When Shultz returned to the USA at the beginning of March,
his plan appeared to be, already, a hopeless cause. The plan's
failure to provide for the participation of the PLO immediately
made it impossible for the Arab nations to accept, while the
divisions within the Israeli Government precluded a coherent
response from that quarter. Having expressed initial reservations over the Shultz proposals, Shimon Peres had generally
endorsed them. For Itzhak Shamir, however, they had 'no
prospect of implementation'.

THE INTIFADA CONTINUES

Meanwhile, the demonstrations against Israeli occupation of
the West Bank and the Gaza Strip continued, apparently
unabated. The uprising had demonstrated a surprising resilience and, at the end of March, Israel redoubled its efforts to
extinguish the Palestinian revolt by economic as well as military
means. The flow of money into the Occupied Territories was
restricted to prevent PLO funds from reaching the Palestinian
resistance movement; a partial ban was imposed on the export
of goods from the Occupied Territories to Jordan and Israel;
telephone links between the Territories and the outside world
were cut; access to the Territories for the media and the press
was strictly curtailed; restrictions were placed on the freedom
of movement between areas within the Territories; a 24-hour
curfew was imposed on the entire Gaza Strip for three successive
days; and the Occupied Territories were sealed off from each
other and from Israel, for the first time since 1967, and declared
'closed military areas'. The restrictions on movement within,
and on access to and from the West Bank and the Gaza Strip
were primarily introduced as a temporary measure to prevent
Palestinians in the Territories and Arabs in Israel joining forces
in a massive demonstration which the UNLU had planned for
Land Day on 30 March (commemorating the killing of six Israeli
Arabs in 1976, who had been demonstrating against Israeli land
seizures) and were lifted on 1 April. However, they could be
reintroduced at any time and used in combination with the
other economic and administrative sanctions as part of Israel's
long-term strategy to starve the *intifada* of publicity and to
force it into submission by depriving Palestinians of the funds
and supplies they required to compensate for losses incurred by
them in a campaign of strikes, shop and business closures,
and civil disobedience. By the end of March more than 100
Palestinians had been killed during the uprising and an estimated 4,000 had been arrested and detained without trial for
six months, under martial law. Once more, however, the result
of these measures seemed to be to steel the Palestinians' resolve
to continue the uprising.

George Shultz returned to the Middle East in mid-April but,
in talks with Israeli leaders, with President Assad of Syria and
with King Hussein of Jordan, he made no further progress
towards the acceptance of his peace plan. His lack of success in
Israel was partly due to the obstinacy of Israeli Prime Minister

Shamir and partly to the unwillingness of Shultz to exert persuasive pressure on him.

THE ASSASSINATION OF 'ABU JIHAD'

On 16 April 1988, in Tunis, an Israeli assassination squad murdered Khalil al-Wazir (alias 'Abu Jihad'), PLO leader Yasser Arafat's deputy, and the military commander of the Palestine Liberation Army (PLA). Although there was satisfaction in Israeli political circles at the success of the operation, the incident provoked the most violent demonstrations in the Occupied Territories since the uprising began, and 16 Palestinians were reportedly killed in a single day. New curfews were introduced in 17 towns and villages in the Occupied Territories for one week after the disturbances.

At the beginning of June 1988 an extraordinary summit of the League of Arab States was held in Algiers to discuss the *intifada* and the prospects for peace in the Middle East. The communiqué issued at the end of the summit effectively rejected the Shultz Plan by demanding the participation of the PLO in any future international peace conference and insisting on the Palestinians' right to self-determination and the establishment of an independent Palestinian state in the Occupied Territories. The summit hailed the 'heroic' *intifada* and pledged all necessary assistance (including an unspecified amount of financial aid) to ensure its continuance.

JORDAN SEVERS ITS LINKS WITH THE WEST BANK

During the Algiers summit, Bassam Abu Sharif, a close adviser of the PLO leader, Yasser Arafat, distributed a paper entitled *PLO View: Prospects of a Palestinian-Israeli Settlement*, which clearly stated that the PLO was seeking peace with Israel through direct negotiations within the context of a UN-sponsored international conference, on the basis of all relevant UN Security Council resolutions, including Resolutions 242 and 338. Although Arafat did not publicly endorse the document and it provoked fierce arguments within the PLO, it did give rise to speculation that a PLO peace initiative might be forthcoming. The suggestion that the PLO might be ready to take political responsibility for its own future and that of the Palestinian people, reflected the new confidence it had acquired since the *intifada* began and was substantiated by subsequent developments which affected the status of the West Bank.

The *intifada* increased Palestinian aspirations to statehood and reinforced support in the Occupied Territories for the PLO. The endorsement of the uprising that was expressed at the Arab summit in Algiers finally persuaded King Hussein of Jordan to end the speculation as to his intentions regarding the West Bank and to grant the PLO the larger role in determining the future of Palestine that it had sought. On 28 July 1988 Jordan cancelled its Five-Year Development Plan for the West Bank and, on 31 July, King Hussein officially severed Jordan's legal and administrative links with the West Bank. The House of Representatives, in which deputies representing the West Bank held 30 of the 60 seats, was dissolved (for further details, see chapter on Jordan).

King Hussein's action appeared finally to end hopes that the Shultz Plan could be implemented and to damage the prospects of a victory for Shimon Peres' Labour Alignment in the Israeli general election, which was scheduled to take place in November 1988. The peace plans of both Shultz and Peres had relied on the Palestinians being represented at negotiations in a joint Jordanian-Palestinian delegation (the so-called 'Jordanian option'). Without the participation of Jordan, which had voluntarily withdrawn from the West Bank and renounced any pretension to represent the Palestinians, the PLO could make a stronger claim to be, in the eyes of the world, as well as the Arab nations, the sole legitimate representative of the Palestinian people. The Israeli Government, however, was united in refusing to negotiate with the PLO. The possibility did exist, though, that the PLO might make the sort of concessions which would persuade Israel to reconsider its position. The severance of Jordanian links with the West Bank stimulated a heated debate within the PLO on the issues of recognizing Israel's right to exist, declaring an independent Palestinian state in the West Bank and proclaiming a Palestinian government-in-exile. To have done so would, by implication, have been to place the emphasis of the Palestinian independence

movement on a diplomatic and political search for a solution, rather than on armed struggle. Israel's Prime Minister Shamir, however, immediately announced that he would use an 'iron fist' to prevent the creation of such a government or state. The Labour Party of Shimon Peres, on the other hand, bereft of the 'Jordanian option', offered to talk to 'any Palestinians' who renounced the use of violence and recognized the Jewish state.

NEW INITIATIVES BY THE PLO

In continuation of the spirit expressed at the June 1988 Arab summit, the Palestine National Council met in Algiers in November and the PLO declared an independent Palestinian state (notionally on the West Bank) and endorsed UN Security Council Resolution 242, thereby implicitly granting recognition to Israel. A month later, Yasser Arafat stated explicitly in Stockholm that 'the Palestine National Council accepted two states, a Palestinian state and a Jewish state, Israel'. Later in December, Arafat presented a three-point peace initiative to the UN General Assembly in Geneva. He proposed the convening of an international conference under UN auspices, the creation of a UN force to supervise Israeli withdrawal from the Occupied Territories, and the implementation of a comprehensive settlement based on UN Security Council Resolutions 242 and 338. Although the USA refused to accept the PLO proposals (alleging ambiguities), the PLO's explicit rejection of violence encouraged the US Government to open a dialogue with the PLO, implying a change in the direction of US-Israeli policy over Palestine. The United Kingdom and the USSR, among other countries, urged Israel to make a positive response to the change in the PLO's position.

ISRAELI PEACE PLANS

External initiatives appeared to have little impact on the daily operations of the *intifada* and by the time of the Israeli general election on 1 November 1988, it had claimed the lives of an estimated 300 Palestinians and six Israelis. The election once again produced a result whereby neither Likud (which won 40 of the 120 seats in the Knesset) nor Labour (with 39 seats) secured enough seats to be able to form a coalition with groups of smaller parties. The religious parties won 18 seats, gaining potential significance in the formation of a government either by Likud or Labour. After two changes of direction, Peres and the Labour Party eventually agreed to the formation in December of another government of national unity under the Likud leader, Itzhak Shamir, with Peres as Deputy Prime Minister and Minister of Finance. The protracted wrangling over forming a coalition had diverted attention from the PLO's peace initiative, and in the coalition accord no mention was made of an international peace settlement, nor were any new proposals advanced for solving the Arab–Israeli problem.

When municipal elections took place at the end of February 1989, Likud made sweeping gains, obtaining control of six of the 10 largest cities and also of many middle-sized towns. Likud regarded these election results as a vindication of their bitter opposition to the PLO. Shamir continued to maintain that the PLO remained a terrorist organization and presented his own four-point proposals for peace when he visited Washington in April. The proposals comprised: (i) reaffirmation by Egypt, Israel and the USA of their dedication to the 1978 Camp David accords; (ii) abandonment by Arab states of their hostility towards Israel; (iii) efforts to solve the Arab refugee problem; (iv) free democratic elections in the West Bank and Gaza to elect delegates who could negotiate self-rule under Israeli authority, but only if the violence ceased. A 20-point programme, developed from these proposals, was endorsed by both the Cabinet and the Knesset in May.

Although Palestinian activists dismissed these proposals as unacceptable (because direct negotiations with the PLO were excluded), many observers felt that they offered a chance for negotiations to begin.

After a meeting of the Likud Central Committee on 5 July 1989, however, Shamir agreed to attach stringent conditions to the Government's peace initiative. He stated that Israel would never allow the establishment of a Palestinian state on the West Bank nor negotiate peace with the PLO, nor would it end Jewish settlements in the territories. This tougher approach threatened to cause the dissolution of the coalition, as Labour considered that it destroyed any chance of the plan's success. This threat was averted, however, when the Cabinet reaffirmed the original peace initiative on 23 July.

The USA was, by now, exerting pressure on the PLO to consider the Israeli plan for elections in the West Bank and Gaza, but in August 1989 Yassir Abed Rabbo, a senior PLO spokesman, declared that 'the PLO does not consider, in any way, that elections can establish the basis for a political settlement'. In mid-September 1989 President Mubarak of Egypt invited Israeli clarification on 10 points connected with Shamir's election plans and at the same time offered to convene an Israeli-Palestinian meeting to discuss election details. Mubarak's 10-point plan was accepted by the Labour Party members of the inner Cabinet, but was vetoed in early October by the Likud ministers on the grounds that they did not want any direct contact with a Palestinian delegation. In early November the inner Cabinet provisionally accepted a five-point initiative proposed by the US Secretary of State, James Baker, regarding a preliminary Israeli-Palestinian meeting to discuss the holding of elections in the West Bank and Gaza Strip, on condition that Israel would not be required to negotiate directly with a Palestinian delegation, and that the talks would be concerned only with Israel's election proposals. However, the PLO continued to demand a direct role in talks with Israel.

At the end of July 1989, Israeli agents abducted Sheikh Obeid, a leading Shi'a Muslim, from a village in southern Lebanon, with the aim of securing the release of three Israeli soldiers held by Hezbollah (see chapter on Lebanon). Col William Higgins, a US hostage held by Hezbollah, was murdered in retaliation. World attention was then focused on the position of all Middle East hostages, and it seemed at first that some agreement leading to their release was imminent. However, no final solution to the problem was immediately forthcoming.

In January 1990 the dismissal from the Government of Ezer Weizman, the Labour Minister of Science and Technology, for unauthorized contact with the PLO, endangered the fragile Likud-Labour coalition. The Labour Party claimed that, under the coalition agreement, Prime Minister Shamir was not allowed to dismiss Labour ministers. A compromise was eventually reached, whereby Weizman resigned from the inner Cabinet (recently expanded to 12 members), but retained the Science and Technology portfolio. The coalition was further undermined on 28 January when five disaffected members of the Knesset, led by Itzhak Modai, the Minister of Economic Affairs, split from the Likud to form an independent party, the Movement for the Advancement of the Zionist Idea (MAZI).

In February 1990 Ariel Sharon launched a campaign for the premiership after resigning the post of Minister of Trade and Industry in protest at Shamir's peace policy and the Government's failure to suppress the *intifada*. One obstacle to the progress of the peace negotiations was the question of whether residents of East Jerusalem should be allowed to participate in proposed elections in the Occupied Territories. On 28 February the USA suggested a compromise solution, which would allow East Jerusalem residents with second homes in the West Bank and some deported activists to stand in the elections. The USA attempted to apply further pressure to Israel to accelerate the pace of the peace process at the beginning of March, when President Bush opposed the grant to Israel of a $400m. loan for the housing of Soviet immigrants, since Israel would give no assurances that the housing in question would not be in the Occupied Territories, including East Jerusalem.

LIKUD-LABOUR COALITION COLLAPSES

On 11 March 1990 Shimon Peres and five Labour colleagues withdrew from a cabinet meeting in protest at further delays to a proposed vote on US plans for talks between an Israeli and a Palestinian delegation. Two days later Prime Minister Shamir dismissed Peres, the Labour leader and Minister of Finance, from the Government, prompting the resignation of all the Labour ministers. On 15 March a vote of 'no confidence' was upheld against Prime Minister Shamir, the first such vote against an Israeli Government to have succeeded. Shamir was left in charge of a transitional administration, since he had managed to ensure he would retain the premiership by preventing the vote of 'no confidence' from being brought forward

to when the Labour ministers remained in office (all resignations and dismissals take 48 hours to come into effect). On 20 March President Herzog invited Peres to form a new coalition government after he had received assurances of the support of five members of the Knesset belonging to Agudat Israel. A two-month period of political wrangling ensued, however, during which both Likud and the Labour Party tried to establish a viable coalition government by soliciting the support of the minor religious parties represented in the Knesset.

The concessions extracted by the minor religious parties during the period of political manoeuvring aroused growing public resentment that became manifest in a demonstration in Jerusalem on 8 April 1990. The demands of the estimated 100,000 people present for electoral reform subsequently led to a ruling by the Supreme Court requiring all political parties to make public the details of coalition agreements before a government could be formed. By the end of April Peres acknowledged failure in his own attempts to form a new government. President Herzog accordingly invited Shamir to form a new administration. Although initially given 21 days to accomplish this task, this period was later extended by Herzog as it emerged that the announcement of a new Likud-led coalition was being delayed by arguments with potential coalition partners over cabinet posts. The political wrangling in Israel took place against a backdrop of ongoing unrest and violence. In mid-April riots engulfed parts of the Christian quarter of Jerusalem's Old City when 150 Orthodox Jewish settlers occupied the St John's Hospice, a Greek patriarchate building. Palestinian anger was fuelled by revelations that Israel's Ministry of Housing had financed the occupation. Tensions were exacerbated on 19 May when seven Palestinian workers were murdered in Rishon le Zion by an Israeli civilian gunman. Reports that the killer was mentally unstable and politically unaffiliated failed to prevent three days of sustained demonstrations in the Occupied Territories resulting in the deaths of 21 Palestinians. At the end of the month, gunmen of the Palestine Liberation Front (PLF) were intercepted by Israeli forces as they attempted a sea-borne raid south of Tel-Aviv. The aim of the abortive raid was unclear, but the US Government immediately urged Yasser Arafat to issue a condemnation of the group. When he failed to do so in terms satisfactory to Washington, the US Department of State declared that it was suspending dialogue with the PLO. On 31 May the USA also vetoed a UN Security Council resolution urging the dispatch of international observers to the Occupied Territories.

THE RIGHT RETURNS TO POWER

On 8 June 1990 Itzhak Shamir announced the formation of a new Government, following the signing of a coalition agreement which gave him the support of 62 of the 120 members of the Knesset. A policy document underlined the uncompromising character of the new partnership. In it Shamir emphasized the right of Jews to settle in all parts of Greater Israel; his opposition to the creation of an independent Palestinian state; and his refusal to negotiate with the PLO, indeed with any Palestinians other than those resident in the Occupied Territories (excluding East Jerusalem). On 11 June in the Knesset the new Government won a vote of confidence by 62 votes to 57 with one abstention. The Government thus empowered was a narrow, right-wing coalition of Likud and five small parties (the MAZI, the NRP, Shas and the Tzomet and Tehiya parties), together with three independent members of the Knesset. Ariel Sharon was appointed Minister of Housing in the new Government; Moshe Arens Minister of Defence; and David Levy Minister of Foreign Affairs.

On 18 June Prime Minister Shamir invited President Assad of Syria to visit Israel for the purpose of peace negotiations, and on 22 June Jean-Claude Aimé, a special envoy of the UN Secretary-General, visited Israel to discuss issues related to the Occupied Territories. Shamir was believed to be seeking to appease the USA after US Secretary of State, James Baker, had expressed impatience at the lack of progress in the peace process. However, on 27 June Shamir wrote to US President Bush rejecting the principal elements of US proposals for direct talks between Israeli and Palestinian delegations.

Controversy surrounding the settlement of Soviet Jewish immigrants in the Occupied Territories intensified in June 1990 when Moshe Arens, the Minister of Defence, ordered the creation of a civil guard in the West Bank in order to protect Jewish settlers. The huge influx of immigrants from the USSR (250,000 were expected to arrive in 1990 and 1m. by 1992, increasing Israel's population by one-fifth) gave rise to fears of the further erosion of Arab rights. On 16 June the EC criticized Israel for failing to respect the human rights of the Palestinian community in the Occupied Territories. Israel rejected the criticism, however, and on 18 July refused to sanction the establishment of an EC consulate in East Jerusalem. By the beginning of August 1990 it was estimated that 683 Palestinians had been killed by Israeli forces and 42 Israelis had died since the onset of the *intifada*.

Israel's relations with African countries, the USSR and other eastern European countries improved significantly in late 1989 and 1990. In September 1989 Hungary became the first 'eastern bloc' country to restore diplomatic relations (severed in 1967) with Israel. In January 1990 the USSR upgraded its diplomatic links with both Israel and the PLO, while Israeli and East German officials held secret talks on establishing diplomatic relations. In February Israel restored diplomatic relations with Poland and Czechoslovakia, and with Bulgaria in May. The Greek Government also formally recognized Israel in May 1990, the last member state of the EC to do so, following an Israeli High Court ruling that the settlers who had occupied the St John's Hospice in Jerusalem should evacuate the building (see above).

ISRAEL AND THE CONFLICT OVER KUWAIT

Iraq's invasion of Kuwait on 2 August 1990 led to improved relations between Israel and the USA, because it was vital, if a broad coalition of Western and Arab powers opposed to Iraq were to be maintained, that Israel did not become actively involved in the new conflict. On 12 August President Saddam Hussein of Iraq offered to withdraw his forces from Kuwait if Israel would withdraw from the Occupied Territories. Israel firmly rejected any analogy between the occupation of Kuwait and its presence in the Occupied Territories. As a crisis developed in the Gulf region, as a result of Iraq's invasion and annexation of Kuwait, there was support for Iraq from both Palestinians resident in the Occupied Territories and from the PLO. The PLO's support for Iraq led left-wing Israeli groups to cancel scheduled meetings with PLO representatives and other Palestinian leaders.

The improvement taking place in US–Israeli relations was seriously jeopardized in October 1990, when Israeli police shot and killed some 17 Palestinians on the Temple Mount in Jerusalem, after they had clashed with Jewish worshippers there. The killings provoked international outrage and sustained the arguments of those who sought to link Iraq's occupation of Kuwait with the Israeli presence in the Occupied Territories in any solution to the crisis in the Gulf region. There was intense pressure on the UN to respond to this outrage, since it was with UN authority that a multinational force had been deployed in Saudi Arabia for the protection of the Kingdom. To many Arabs, the disparity between the vigour with which the UN was seeking to implement successive resolutions pertaining to the occupation of Kuwait and its long-standing impotence with regard to successive resolutions pertaining to the Occupied Territories was now more conspicuous than before.

The UN Security Council voted to send a mission to the Occupied Territories to investigate the Temple Mount killings, but the Israeli Cabinet announced that it would not co-operate with any such UN delegation and rejected the UN's criticism of its decision. In early November 1990 the UN Secretary-General asked the Security Council to request the convening of an unprecedented international conference, with the aim of forcing Israel to accept that Palestinians in the Occupied Territories were protected by the provisions of the Fourth Geneva Convention (concerning the protection of civilians during wartime). On 13 November the Israeli Government announced that it would permit a UN emissary to visit Israel to discuss the situation in the Occupied Territories.

In late November 1990 there was increased concern in Israel about the security of its borders with Lebanon and Jordan, and about improvements in relations between the USA and Syria, which, it was feared, might damage Israel's interests.

In mid-December 1990 the USA resisted attempts by the UN Security Council to draft a resolution advocating the convening of a Middle East peace conference and an increase in the UN presence in the Occupied Territories. The USA feared that the holding of a peace conference, at this time, could be construed as a concession to Saddam Hussain's concept of 'linkage'.

In mid-December 1990 Shamir visited the USA to confer with President Bush. He was reported to have sought, and received, assurances from President Bush that any diplomatic solution of the crisis in the Gulf region would protect Israeli interests. Nevertheless, only days later, the USA proposed a UN Security Council resolution condemning Israel's reinstatement of a policy of deporting Palestinians, in response to violence in the Occupied Territories, as a violation of the Fourth Geneva Convention. The USA also supported further criticism by the UN of Israel's treatment of the Palestinian population in the Occupied Territories and supported a separate UN appeal for an 'active negotiating process' in the Middle East 'at an appropriate time'. However, in view of the crisis in the Gulf, the USA did not believe that such a time had arrived.

Attacks on Israel by Iraqi *Scud* missiles, beginning on 18 January 1991, created the most serious threat to the integrity of the multinational force which had commenced hostilities against Iraq on 16–17 January. It was widely expected that Israel would retaliate immediately, so risking the withdrawal of Arab countries from the multinational force. While Egypt implied that it would accept a measured degree of retaliation, Syria stated bluntly that it would change sides in response to any Israeli attacks on Iraq which violated Jordanian airspace. Graver still was the possibility of Iranian involvement on the side of Iraq in response to Israeli military action. US diplomacy, supported by the installation in Israel of advanced US air defence systems, succeeded in averting an immediate Israeli military response, although Israel vowed that it would, ultimately, retaliate for the attacks. By late February Iraq had launched 39 *Scud* missiles against Israel, killing two people and injuring more than 200.

Wider strategic considerations apart, a policy of restraint appeared to be in Israel's best interest. The Iraqi missile attacks, together with fears that similar attacks using chemical warheads might be launched, provoked a rare, open outburst of international sympathy for Israel. They also strengthened the Israeli case for rejecting any 'linkage' between the occupation of Kuwait and the Occupied Territories, and undermined the PLO's claim to be the only credible interlocutor in a future dialogue with the Israeli Government. In response to the widespread support, expressed by ordinary Palestinians and in the official policy of the PLO, for Saddam Hussain, the attitude of the Israeli Government hardened. Its new mood was symbolized by the appointment by Shamir, in February 1991, of Gen. Rechavam Ze'evi, the leader of the Moledet (Homeland) party, as Minister without Portfolio and a member of the policy-making inner Cabinet. The appointment was strongly opposed by some cabinet members, as Ze'evi was known to advocate a policy of 'transfer' (i.e. the forcible, mass deportation of Palestinians) as a solution to the Arab–Israeli conflict. In early February, in a speech to the Knesset, Shamir again rejected, with more authority than he had been able to muster for many months, proposals for convening an international conference on the Palestinian issue, and promoted his own peace plan, formulated in 1989 (see above), as the only starting-point for any peace dialogue involving the Israeli Government.

RENEWED ATTEMPTS TO CONVENE A PEACE CONFERENCE

For Israel the defeat of Iraq by the multinational force in February 1991 had ambiguous implications, since it left President Saddam Hussain in power—Israel had openly urged his removal—as a potential threat to Israel's security. Israel's greatest gain from the conflict over Kuwait had been the renewed goodwill of the USA: in late February the US Secretary of State, James Baker, signed a guarantee for a loan to Israel—previously approved by the US Congress—of $400m. for the housing of immigrants. (Baker had previously refused to sign the guarantee, owing to his concern that the funds would be used to establish communities of immigrants in the Occupied Territories.) However, it was clear that the USA would seek to use its increased influence in the Middle East to achieve a resolution of the Arab–Israeli conflict, and that the USA's continued extension of goodwill and financial aid would require concessions by the Shamir Government.

At the beginning of March 1991 President Bush of the USA stated that a settlement of the Arab–Israeli conflict was one of the principal aims of US foreign policy in the post-war period, and in mid-March James Baker made his first visit, as US Secretary of State, to Israel, where he sought to initiate a 'confidence-building' process between Israelis and Arabs, as a preparatory step towards peace negotiations. The visit to Israel was followed by one to Syria, where Baker held talks with President Assad.

The USA's diplomatic efforts to initiate peace negotiations intensified in April 1991. In the first half of the month the US Secretary of State returned to the Middle East, visiting Israel, Egypt and Syria, in order to promote the idea of a regional peace conference. The proposal gained only limited support. While the Israeli Government tentatively endorsed the idea of a regional conference—comprising an initial, symbolic session, to be followed by direct negotiations with Arab states and a joint Jordanian-Palestinian delegation—its continued refusal to negotiate with any Palestinian delegation which comprised either residents of East Jerusalem or members of the PLO appeared to present an insurmountable obstacle to any further progress towards a settlement of the Arab–Israeli conflict. Syria, Egypt and the PLO, meanwhile, rejected the proposed regional conference outright, favouring instead an international conference fully supported by the UN and with the full participation of the PLO.

After the US Secretary of State had again failed, following further talks with Shamir in mid-April 1991, to extract any flexibility from the Israeli Government, the question of a settlement to the Arab–Israeli conflict appeared as intractable as it had before Iraq's invasion of Kuwait in August 1990. It was generally accepted that Shamir would seek to prevaricate to a degree which would allow him to continue to enjoy both the goodwill—and financial aid—of the USA and the support of the extreme right-wing elements of his coalition Government, which remained firmly opposed to peace negotiations. The continued settlement of Soviet Jewish immigrants to Israel in the Occupied Territories became increasingly controversial. Visiting the USA in late April 1991, the Israeli Minister of Housing and Construction, Ariel Sharon (with whom the settlement policy was most closely identified), was rebuffed when he sought meetings with senior members of the US Government. The US Secretary of State described the settlement of the immigrants in the Occupied Territories as the biggest obstacle to the convening of a Middle East peace conference.

On 18 July 1991, in a remarkable volte-face, President Assad of Syria agreed for the first time, following a meeting with the US Secretary of State, to participate in direct negotiations with Israel at a regional conference, for which the terms of reference would be a comprehensive peace settlement based on UN Security Council Resolutions 242 (see Documents on Palestine, p. 115) and 338 (ibid, p. 117). By agreeing to participate in a peace conference on the terms proposed by the USA, Syria decisively increased the intense diplomatic pressure on Israel to do likewise: the US initiative already enjoyed the express support of the 'G7' group of industrialized countries, the USSR, the UN Security Council and the EC; and, following Syria's concession, Egypt and Jordan indicated that they would also be willing to participate in direct negotiations with Israel.

On closer examination, however, substantive progress towards a resolution of the Arab–Israeli conflict appeared illusory. The publicly-stated positions of the Israeli and Syrian Governments remained as far apart as ever. Each claimed, towards the end of July 1991, to have received confidential (and incompatible) assurances from the USA: Israel with regard to the composition of a Jordanian-Palestinian delegation to the peace conference; and Syria with regard to the return of the Israeli-occupied Golan Heights. For its part, the US Government insisted that there were no pre-conditions for attending the peace conference, and that, with regard to the composition of the Jordanian-Palestinian delegation, only members of the PLO were excluded.

On 31 July 1991, at the conclusion of a summit meeting between Presidents Bush and Gorbachev, the USA and the USSR announced their intention to act as joint chairmen of a Middle East peace conference which they had scheduled—without having received the prior, formal consent of the Israeli Government—to take place in October 1991, and which representatives of the UN and the EC would attend in the capacity of observers. On 4 August 1991 the Israeli Cabinet formally agreed to attend a peace conference on the terms proposed by the USA and the USSR.

OTHER POST-WAR DEVELOPMENTS

The signing, in May 1991, by Syria and Lebanon of a treaty of 'fraternity, co-operation and co-ordination' was immediately denounced by Israel as a further step towards the formal transformation of Lebanon into a Syrian protectorate. The signing of the treaty appeared to reduce the likelihood that, in response to the deployment of the Lebanese army in southern Lebanon, Israel would comply with UN Security Council Resolution 425 (adopted in March 1978) and withdraw its forces from its self-declared security zone in southern Lebanon. As the Lebanese army began to deploy east of the coastal town of Sidon in July 1991, Israel continued to launch attacks on Palestinian and Hezbollah militia units which, it claimed, the Lebanese army (which it regarded as little more than a Syrian proxy force) was unable to suppress. A serious escalation of the conflict endemic to southern Lebanon occurred in February 1992, when Israeli armed forces advanced beyond Israel's self-declared security zone to attack the alleged positions of Hezbollah; and again in May, when the Israeli air force attacked Hezbollah villages to the north and west of Israel's self-declared security zone, in response to attacks by Hezbollah units on positions occupied by the South Lebanon Army.

In August 1991 Israel claimed that one of a number of conditions to which the USA had agreed in return for Israel's participation in the regional peace conference scheduled for October was the re-establishment of full diplomatic relations with the USSR. Soviet promotion of the USA's proposed regional peace conference had already led to closer contacts between Israel and the USSR. In April 1991 Shamir met the Soviet Prime Minister, Valentin Pavlov, in London, United Kingdom; and in May the Soviet Minister of Foreign Affairs, Aleksandr Bessmertnykh, made a visit to Israel, where he met the Israeli Prime Minister and the Minister of Foreign Affairs, David Levy. Full diplomatic relations with the USSR—superseded by the establishment of relations with some of the newly-independent, former Soviet republics—were formally re-established, after an interval of 24 years, in November; and in January 1992 Israel established diplomatic relations with the People's Republic of China for the first time.

DEADLOCKED NEGOTIATIONS

By March 1992, following an initial, 'symbolic' session of the conference, held in Madrid, Spain, in October 1991, four sessions of negotiations between Israeli, Syrian, Lebanese and Palestinian-Jordanian delegations had been held, but little progress had been achieved with regard to the substantive issues which the conference was intended to address, in particular the question of transitional Palestinian autonomy in the West Bank and Gaza Strip, pending negotiations on the 'permanent status' of those territories. Rather, these bilateral talks had become deadlocked over procedural issues. Israeli delegations, wary of making any gesture which might be construed as recognition of Palestinian independence, consistently questioned the status of the Palestinian-Jordanian delegation and the right of the Palestinian component to participate separately in negotiations; while Israel's refusal to halt the construction of new settlements in the Occupied Territories posed a constant threat to the faltering peace process. Israel's continued refusal to concede over the settlement issue further damaged its relations with the USA. As early as May 1991 the US Secretary of State, James Baker, had identified this issue as the main obstacle to US efforts to achieve a Middle Eastern peace settlement. In February 1992, immediately prior to the fourth session of the peace negotiations, Baker demanded a complete halt to Israeli settlement in the Occupied Territories as a condition for the granting of US $10,000m. in US-guaranteed loans for the housing of Jewish immigrants from the former USSR.

While the Israeli Government's refusal to halt the construction of new settlements was regarded as provocative by all the other parties to the peace conference, and by the US Government, the right-wing minority members of Israel's governing coalition, which opposed any Israeli participation in the peace conference at all, threatened to withdraw from the coalition if funds were not made available for the settlement programme. In December 1991 the Government's majority in the 120-seat Knesset was reduced when the Minister of Agriculture, Rafael Eitan (a member of the right-wing, nationalist Tzomet Party), resigned his portfolio in protest at the Prime Minister's opposition to electoral reform; and in mid-January 1992 the majority was lost entirely when two other right-wing, nationalist political parties, Moledet and Tehiya (which together held five seats in the Knesset) withdrew from the coalition. Their withdrawal was a deliberate attempt to obstruct the third session of the Middle East peace conference in Moscow, Russia, where delegates had begun to address the granting of transitional autonomy to Palestinians in the West Bank and Gaza Strip. A general election was subsequently scheduled to be held in June 1992, and Itzhak Shamir remained the head of a transitional, minority government.

In late February 1992 Shamir retained the leadership of the Likud, receiving 46.4% of the votes cast at a party convention. At the same time, Itzhak Rabin, a former Israeli Prime Minister, was elected Chairman of the Labour Party, replacing Shimon Peres. Rabin's election was regarded as having significantly improved the Labour Party's prospects at the forthcoming general election, since, while he favoured the continuation of peace negotiations, he also enjoyed more popular confidence than Peres with regard to issues affecting Israel's security. A future Likud-Labour government of national unity, with Rabin as head of the Labour component, was thus viewed as more capable of conducting peace negotiations—and more likely to receive international, especially US, support—than another coalition composed of the Likud and minority, right-wing, nationalist and religious parties.

A fifth round of bilateral negotiations, between Israeli, Syrian, Lebanese and Palestinian-Jordanian delegations, was held in Washington, USA, at the end of April 1992. In this latest session of the peace conference procedural issues were reported to have been resolved, and, in its talks with the Palestinian component of the Palestinian-Jordanian delegation, the Israeli delegation presented proposals for the holding of municipal elections in the West Bank and Gaza Strip; and for the transfer of control of health amenities there to Palestinian authorities. The Palestinian delegation, for its part, did not reject the proposals outright, although they fell far short of Palestinians' ambition for full legislative control of the Occupied Territories. No progress was made in the meetings between Israeli and Syrian delegations to discuss the principal dispute between Israel and Syria—Israel's continued occupation of the Golan Heights.

In May 1992 the first multilateral negotiations between the parties to the Middle East peace conference commenced, as had been arranged at the third session of bilateral talks in Moscow in January. However, these negotiations were boycotted by Syria and Lebanon, which argued that they were futile until progress had been made in the bilateral negotiations. Various combinations of delegations attended meetings convened to discuss regional economic co-operation; regional arms control; the question of Palestinian refugees; water resources; and environmental issues. A Jordanian delegation, for instance, attended all five meetings, and the Palestinian component all except the one on regional arms control. Israel boycotted the meetings on Palestinian refugees and regional economic development after the USA approved Palestinian proposals to allow exiles (i.e. non-residents of the Occupied Territories) to be included in the Palestinian delegations to these two meetings. The session of talks on Palestinian refugees became especially controversial after both the Palestinian and the Jordanian components of the Palestinian-Jordanian delegation asserted the right of Palestinian refugees to return to the Occupied Territories, in accordance with UN General Assembly Resolution 194 of 1948. However, the US Government subsequently indicated that the terms of reference for the peace conference were UN Security Council Resolutions 242 and 338 only.

A NEW LABOUR COALITION

In the general election, held on 23 June 1992, the Labour Party won 44 seats in the Knesset and Likud 32. Meretz—an alliance of Ratz (Civil Rights and Peace Movement), Shinui and the United Workers' Party which had won 12 seats in the Knesset—formally confirmed its willingness to form a coalition government with the Labour Party on 24 June. However, even with the support of the two Arab parties—the Arab Democratic Party and Hadash—which together had won five seats in the Knesset, such a coalition would have enjoyed a majority of only two votes over the so-called 'right bloc' (Likud, Tzomet, Moledet and Tehiya) and the religious parties which had allied themselves with Likud in the previous Knesset. Formally invited to form a government on 28 June, the Labour leader, Itzhak Rabin, was accordingly obliged to solicit support among those religious parties which, he had indicated on 24 June, he was willing to incorporate into a coalition led by Labour in return for their support of Labour's policies. On 13 July Rabin was able to present a new government for approval by the Knesset. The new coalition, an alliance of Labour, Meretz and the ultra-orthodox Jewish party, Shas, had a total of 62 seats in the 120-seat Knesset; and also enjoyed the unspoken support of five deputies from the two Arab parties.

Immediately after the election the Labour Party had re-affirmed its commitment to granting Palestinian autonomy within nine months, while maintaining Israel's control of defence and security measures in the Occupied Territories, and its responsibility for existing settlements there. It also expressed its desire for improved relations with the USA. However, it remained unclear precisely what the Party's policy would be with regard to the occupied Golan Heights and occupied areas of southern Lebanon. As it strove to form a coalition that included right-wing religious parties, the Labour Party became of necessity less outspoken in its commitment to some of its stated aims, giving rise to fears that improved relations with the USA might ultimately force Palestinians to accept limited autonomy entirely on Israel's terms.

A sixth round of bilateral negotiations between Israeli, Syrian, Lebanese and Palestinian-Jordanian delegations, the first since the new Israeli Government had taken office, commenced in Washington in late August 1992. Again, little progress was achieved on substantive issues. The Israeli delegation and the Palestinian component of the Palestinian-Jordanian delegation, for instance, were unable to agree terms for negotiating an initial, five-year period of Palestinian autonomy in the West Bank and Gaza Strip prior to a permanent settlement. Talks between the Israeli and the Syrian delegations remained deadlocked over the issue of the Golan Heights, and in private delegates were reported to have admitted that they were likely to remain so without the eventual diplomatic intervention of the USA.

In early October 1992, in a clear gesture of support for the new Israeli Government, the USA granted Israel the US $10,000m. in US-guaranteed loans for the housing of immigrants that it had previously withheld, owing to Israel's housing construction programme in the Occupied Territories. In late October a seventh round of bilateral negotiations between the parties to the Middle East peace conference commenced in Washington, USA. The negotiations were adjourned, pending the conclusion of the US presidential election, but multilateral negotiations on regional economic co-operation, in which an Israeli delegation participated, took place in Paris, France, at the end of October. The seventh round of bilateral negotiations resumed in early November, but, again, no tangible progress was achieved. Multilateral negotiations on the issue of refugees took place in Ottawa, Canada, on 11–12 November. In spite of the hopes that had been expressed for the prospects of the peace process since the election of the Labour-led Israeli Government, the months of October and November were marked by violent clashes between Palestinians and members of the Israeli security forces in the Occupied Territories. At the end of November it was reported that, since 1987, 959 Palestinians, 543 alleged Palestinian 'collaborators' and 103 Israelis had died in the Palestinian *intifada*.

DEPORTATIONS STALL TALKS

In early December 1992 an eighth round of bilateral negotiations between Israeli and Arab delegations commenced in Washington. However, the talks were quickly overtaken by events in the Occupied Territories, which led to the withdrawal of the Arab delegations. On 16 December, in response to the deaths in the Occupied Territories of five members of the Israeli security forces, and to the abduction and murder by the Islamic Resistance Movement (Hamas) of an Israeli border policeman, the Israeli Cabinet ordered the deportation to Lebanon of more than 400 alleged Palestinian supporters of Hamas. Owing to the Lebanese Government's refusal to co-operate in this action, the deportees were stranded in the territory between Israel's self-declared southern Lebanese security zone and Lebanon proper.

The deportations caused international outrage, and intense diplomatic pressure was placed on Israel to revoke the expulsion order. On 18 December the UN Security Council unanimously approved a resolution (No. 799) condemning the deportations and demanding the return of the deportees to Israel. At the end of December, however, the Israeli Government announced that only 10 of the deportees had been unjustifiably expelled and could return to Israel. The remainder would continue in exile. The future of the Middle East peace process, meanwhile, remained in doubt. The Palestinian delegation to the eighth round of bilateral negotiations had indicated that it would not resume negotiations until all of the deportees had been allowed to return to Israel, and the PLO formally expressed the same position in mid-January 1993. At the beginning of February the Israeli Government was reported to have indicated its willingness to allow some 100 of the deportees to return to Israel, but insisted that the remainder should serve a period of exile lasting at least until the end of 1993. On 5 February the ninth round of bilateral negotiations was formally suspended, but later in the month the UN Security Council was reported to have welcomed the Israeli Government's decision to permit 100 of the deportees to return to Israel, and to be ready to take no further action over the issue. Palestinians party to the peace negotiations, however, insisted that UN Security Council Resolution 799 should be implemented in full before a Palestinian delegation would resume negotiations. In late February the US Secretary of State, Warren Christopher, made a tour of the Middle East, visiting Syria, Saudi Arabia, Kuwait, Lebanon and Israel, in an attempt to revive the peace negotiations.

During March 1993 the number of violent confrontations between Palestinians and the Israeli security forces in the Occupied Territories—especially in the Gaza Strip—increased to such an extent that, at the end of the month, the Israeli Cabinet responded by sealing off the West Bank and the Gaza Strip indefinitely. Also, in late March the Knesset elected Ezer Weizman, leader of the Yahad political party, to replace Chaim Herzog as President of Israel in May 1993; and Binyamin Netanyahu was elected leader of the opposition Likud in place of Itzhak Shamir.

On 27 April 1993 the ninth round of bilateral negotiations in the Middle East peace process, which had been formally suspended in February, resumed in Washington. It was reported that the Palestinian delegation had only agreed to attend the ninth round of talks under pressure to do so from Arab governments, and after Israel had agreed to allow Faisal Husseini, the nominal leader of the Palestinian delegation, to participate in the talks. Israel had previously refused to grant this concession because Husseini was a resident of East Jerusalem, the status of which Israel regards as distinct from that of the West Bank, the Gaza Strip and the Golan Heights. Israel was also reported to have agreed that it would not, in future, resort to deportations as a punitive measure, and to have restated, together with the USA, its commitment to UN Security Council Resolutions 242 and 338 as the terms of reference for the peace process. However, as previously, the ninth round of bilateral talks achieved no progress on substantive issues. In particular, Israel and the Palestinian delegation were reported to have failed to agree on a statement of principles regarding Palestinian self-rule in the Occupied Territories.

In mid-May 1993 Ezer Weizman formally assumed the presidency of Israel. At the end of the month a minor reshuffle of the Cabinet averted the defection of the ultra-orthodox Jewish party, Shas, from the governing coalition.

A tenth round of bilateral negotiations, held in Washington on 15 June–1 July, concluded in deadlock, having achieved no progress on a statement of principles concerning Palestinian self-rule in the Occupied Territories, which was now regarded as the key element in the Middle East peace process. However, it was reported that a committee had been established in an attempt to facilitate progress on this issue. By the same token, there was no progress on the issues of contention between the Israeli delegation and its Syrian, Lebanese and Jordanian counterparts.

UNEXPECTED BREAKTHROUGH IN THE PEACE PROCESS

In late July 1993 Israeli armed forces mounted the most intensive air and artillery attacks on targets in Lebanon since 'Operation Peace for Galilee' in 1982. The attacks were mounted in retaliation for attacks by Hezbollah fighters on settlements in northern Israel, and provoked widespread international criticism for the high number of civilian casualties that they caused and for the perceived threat they posed to the Middle East peace process. At the eleventh round of bilateral negotiation, however, which commenced in Washington on 31 August, a major, unexpected breakthrough was achieved between Israel and the Palestinian delegation, which culminated in the signing, on 13 September, by Israel and the PLO, of a declaration of principles on Palestinian self-rule in the Occupied Territories. The agreement, which entailed mutual recognition by Israel and the PLO, had been elaborated during a series of secret negotiations mediated by Norwegian diplomacy. The Declaration of Principles established a detailed timetable for Israel's disengagement from the Occupied Territories and stipulated that a permanent settlement of the Palestinian question should be in place by December 1998. From 13 October 1993 Palestinian authorities were to assume responsibility for education and culture, health, social welfare, direct taxation and tourism in the Gaza Strip and the Jericho area of the West Bank, and a transitional period of Palestinian self-rule was to begin on 13 December 1993. (For full details of the Declaration of Principles on Palestinian Self-Rule, see Documents on Palestine, p. 128.)

REACTION TO THE DECLARATION OF PRINCIPLES

While it was welcomed as a major breakthrough in the Middle East peace process, the Declaration of Principles was nevertheless regarded as only a tentative first step towards the resolution of the region's conflicts that could be threatened from many directions. Although the Israeli Prime Minister was able to obtain the ratification of the Declaration of Principles, and of Israel's recognition of the PLO, by the Knesset on 23 September 1993, there was widespread opposition to it from right-wing Israeli political groups. By the same token, the conclusion of the agreement aggravated divisions within the PLO and the wider Palestinian liberation movement. Within the PLO some senior officials, hitherto loyal to Yasser Arafat's leadership, now declared their opposition to him, while dissident groups, such as the Democratic Front for the Liberation of Palestine, Hamas and Islamic Jihad denounced the Declaration of Principles as treason. Most observers regarded the future success of the agreement between Israel and the PLO as dependent on the ability of the mainstream PLO to gain popular support for it from Palestinians residing in the West Bank and the Gaza Strip. Reaction to the Declaration of Principles by other Arab governments engaged in peace negotiations with Israel was mixed. King Hussein welcomed the agreement and Jordan immediately agreed an agenda for direct negotiations with Israel, which was also ratified by the Knesset on 23 September. Lebanon, however, feared that the divisions that the Declaration of Principles had provoked within the Palestinian movement might in future lead to renewed conflict in Lebanese territory. It remained unclear, too, whether Syria—which neither condemned nor welcomed the Declaration of Principles—would continue to support those Palestinian groups opposed to the PLO's position.

In mid-September 1993 the resignation of Arye Deri as Minister of the Interior, following allegations of corruption, provoked the resignation of other members of Shas from the Cabinet and meant that the governing coalition was now effectively reduced to an alliance between the Labour Party and Meretz; and the

Government's majority in the Knesset to only two. It followed that it might prove more difficult to obtain the Knesset's approval for any controversial measures associated with the Middle East peace negotiations. In mid-March 1994, however, the Labour Party and Shas were reported to have concluded a new coalition agreement. In early February 1994 the Minister of Health, Haim Ramon, resigned after the Government refused to endorse a health insurance bill that he had drawn up. Ephraim Sneh was appointed as his replacement in early June.

BEGINNING OF PALESTINIAN SELF-RULE

In early October 1993 Itzhak Rabin and Yasser Arafat held their first meeting in the context of the Declaration of Principles in Cairo, Egypt, where they agreed to begin talks on the implementation of the Declaration of Principles on 13 October, and to establish general liaison, technical, economic and regional co-operation committees.

On 13 October 1993 the PLO-Israeli joint liaison committee met for the first time, the delegations to it headed, respectively, by Mahmoud Abbas and by Shimon Peres, the Israeli Minister of Foreign Affairs. It was agreed that the committee should meet at regular, short intervals to monitor the implementation of the Declaration of Principles. The technical committee also held three meetings during October in the Egyptian coastal resort of Taba. Its task was to establish the precise details of Israel's military withdrawal from the Gaza Strip and Jericho, which, under the terms of the Declaration of Principles, was scheduled to take place between 13 December 1993 and 13 April 1994. At the meetings that took place in October progress was reported to have been made on the creation of a Palestinian police force, although the issue of security measures to protect Israeli settlers in the Gaza Strip remained unresolved. Israel was also reported to have agreed to the gradual release of some of the Palestinian prisoners that it held. Also in early October the Central Council of the PLO formally approved the Declaration of Principles by a large majority.

The joint PLO-Israel technical committee met on several occasions during November 1993, but by the end of the month it appeared unlikely that it would have made sufficient progress for Israel's military withdrawal from the Gaza Strip and from Jericho to begin by 13 December. In particular, it was proving difficult to reach agreement on three issues: arrangements for border security; the delineation of the Jericho area; and the release of Palestinian prisoners.

At the beginning of October 1993 talks had taken place in Washington between Crown Prince Hassan of Jordan and Shimon Peres. Despite reports of subsequent secret negotiations, King Hussein of Jordan insisted, during visits to Egypt and Syria in November, that Jordan would not conclude a separate peace agreement with Israel.

As had been feared, it proved impossible satisfactorily to negotiate the details of Israel's military withdrawal from the Gaza Strip and Jericho by 13 December 1993. This failure cast doubt on the whole of the September agreement between Israel and the PLO. The main cause of the failure remained the issue of security arrangements for border crossings between the Gaza Strip and Jericho and Jordan and Egypt. The PLO continued to insist that the border crossings should come under full, exclusive Palestinian control. Israel opposed this claim since to grant it would imply at least a partial recognition of something like Palestinian sovereignty.

Following meetings between the US Secretary of State, Warren Christopher, and President Assad of Syria and the Syrian Minister of Foreign Affairs in Damascus in early December 1993, Syria announced its willingness to resume bilateral negotiations with Israel in early 1994. Syrian Jews wishing to leave Syria were also to be granted exit visas. In early January 1994, before a meeting between US President Clinton and Syria's President Assad took place, Israel appeared to indicate, tentatively, that it might be prepared to execute a full withdrawal from the Golan Heights in return for a comprehensive peace agreement with Syria. On 17 January it was reported that the Government would put the issue to a referendum before making such a withdrawal. This was interpreted as an attempt by the Government to deflect in advance any pressure for a swift move towards a peace agreement with Syria which might emerge at the forthcoming summit meeting

between the US and Syrian Presidents. There was likely to be far less support in the Knesset for a peace agreement with Syria—in particular, for concessions regarding the Golan Heights—than there had been for an agreement with the PLO. Bilateral negotiations between Israeli and Syrian delegations resumed in Washington on 24 January after a four-month hiatus.

On 9 February 1994 Israel and the PLO appeared to achieve a breakthrough in their stalled negotiations when they signed an agreement to share control of the two future international border crossings. It was reported that security arrangements for Jewish settlers in the Gaza Strip had also been decided: three access routes to Jewish settlements there were to remain under Israeli control. However, the boundaries of the Jericho enclave remained undefined. Further talks began on 14 February to address the issues of the implementation of the first stage of Palestinian autonomy in the Gaza Strip and the Jericho area; the size, structure and jurisdiction of a future Palestinian police force; control of sea and air space; and the delineation of the Jericho enclave.

In late February 1994 the PLO, together with the other Arab parties, withdrew from the peace process with Israel, following the murder, by a right-wing Jewish extremist, of some 30 Muslim worshippers in a mosque in Hebron on the West Bank. Negotiations between the PLO and Israel resumed at the end of March, when the two sides signed an agreement on security in Hebron and the whole of the Occupied Territories. Israel agreed, among other things, to allow a team of international observers to travel to Hebron, where they were to monitor efforts to restore stability. Earlier in the month the UN Security Council had adopted a resolution (No. 904) condemning the killings in Hebron, prompting Syria, Jordan and Lebanon to agree to resume negotiations with Israel in April.

In late April 1994 Israel and the PLO signed an agreement concerning economic relations between Israel and the autonomous Palestinian entity during the five-year period leading to self-rule. At the end of the month it was reported that the US Secretary of State, Warren Christopher, had submitted to President Assad of Syria Israel's proposals regarding a withdrawal from the occupied Golan Heights in exchange for a full peace agreement with Syria.

On 4 May 1994 in Cairo (Egypt), Israel and the PLO signed an agreement which set forth detailed arrangements for Palestinian self-rule in Gaza and Jericho. The agreement provided for Israel's military withdrawal from Gaza and Jericho and the deployment there of a 9,000-strong Palestinian police force. A nominated Palestine National Authority (PNA) was to assume the responsibilities of the Israeli military administration in Gaza and Jericho, although Israeli authorities were to retain control in matters of external security and foreign affairs. It was also announced that elections for a Palestinian Council, which, under the terms of the Declaration of Principles, were to have taken place in Gaza and the West Bank in July 1994, had been postponed until October. Israel's military withdrawal from Gaza and Jericho was reported to have been completed on 13 May, and on 17 May the PLO formally assumed control of the Israeli civil administration's departments in Gaza and Jericho. On 18 May Yasser Arafat held talks with Israel's Minister of Foreign Affairs, Shimon Peres, regarding future negotiations on the extension of Palestinian self-rule in the West Bank. On 26–28 May an incomplete PNA held its inaugural meeting in Tunis, Tunisia, setting out a political programme and distributing ministerial portfolios. It had originally been Arafat's intention to appoint 24 members to the PNA (12 from within the Occupied Territories and 12 from the Palestinian diaspora). In the event, some of his chosen appointees refused to serve on the PNA—reflecting the extent of divisions within the mainstream Palestinian movement regarding the terms of the peace with Israel—and only 20 members assembled in Tunis. The PNA held its first meeting in Gaza in late June.

On 1 July 1994 Yasser Arafat returned to Gaza City, a homecoming that had far more symbolic than practical significance. Negotiations with Israel continued on the extension of Palestinian authority, the redeployment of Israeli armed forces in the West Bank and on the holding of Palestinian elections. In late July Israel and Jordan signed a joint declaration that formally ended the state of war between them and further defined the arrangements for future negotiations between the two sides. In late August Israel and the PLO signed an agreement which extended the authority of the PNA to include education, health, tourism, social welfare and taxation. In September the PNA was reported to have approved plans in preparation for elections in Gaza and the West Bank within three months. However, the size of the future Palestinian legislature remained unclear. The PLO was reported to wish to elect a 100-member council, while Israel insisted that its size should be restricted to no more than 25 members.

IMPROVED RELATIONS WITH THE ARAB WORLD

At the beginning of September 1994 Morocco became the second Arab state to establish diplomatic relations with Israel, albeit at a low level. Tunisia established diplomatic relations with Israel the following day. On 8 September Itzhak Rabin announced the details of a plan for a partial withdrawal of Israeli armed forces from the occupied Golan Heights, after which a three-year trial period of Israeli-Syrian 'normalization' would ensue. The proposals were rejected by President Assad of Syria; however, he did state his willingness, in an address to the Syrian People's Assembly on 10 September, to work towards peace with Israel. Israel also continued to enjoy rapidly improving relations with Jordan. King Hussein met with Itzhak Rabin in Aqaba at the end of September to draft a timetable to draw up a full Israeli–Jordanian peace treaty. This was achieved in late October when the two countries signed a formal peace agreement, fixing their borders and providing for normal relations. The treaty was criticized by the Syrian Government, which had long opposed such bilateral initiatives. Despite the belief in the Arab world that Jordan's move to normalize relations with Israel had been overly hasty, there were continuing signs of a less antagonistic attitude towards the Jewish State. On 29 September the six member states of the Co-operation Council for the Arab States of the Gulf (GCC) announced their decision to lift the subsidiary elements of the Arab economic boycott of Israel. At the end of October President Clinton visited Damascus in an attempt to break the deadlock in negotiations between Israel and Syria. In December it was reported that high-level military contacts had been made between the two countries. In February 1995 Israel completed its withdrawal from a small area of Jordanian territory it had occupied since the war of June 1967.

NEW CRISIS IN NEGOTIATIONS

A conference of international donors, sponsored by the World Bank, in Paris, France, on 8-9 September 1994, collapsed almost immediately owing to an Israeli–Palestinian dispute over Palestinian investment plans to fund projects in East Jerusalem. According to Israel, such plans would have compromised negotiations on the final status of Jerusalem which, under the terms of the Declaration of Principles, were not due to begin before May 1996. On 13 September Yasser Arafat and the Israeli Minister of Foreign Affairs met in Oslo, Norway, and negotiated a 15-point agreement whose aim was to accelerate economic aid to the PNA. The issue of economic aid was to assume increasing importance during the remaining months of 1994 and early 1995, as Arafat's leadership of the PNA and, indeed, the authority of the entire so-called moderate Palestinian movement that had negotiated the Declaration of Principles became ever more crisis-stricken as a result of what its opponents regarded as its increasingly conspicuous injustices. Within the mainstream Palestinian movement it would be argued that it was impossible for the newly-formed Palestinian police force to keep the peace in the volatile Gaza Strip without increased economic aid; while opponents of the Declaration of Principles would argue that economic conditions were merely a side issue, and that Arafat and the mainstream Palestinian movement had been ensnared by the Declaration of Principles. The failure of the Palestinian authorities to guarantee security in the areas over which they now had partial control provided Israel with an excuse not to allow them to extend their jurisdiction in the West Bank, even though Israeli armed forces had never been able to guarantee secure conditions in the Gaza Strip either. On 25 September Arafat and Rabin met at the Erez crossing point between Gaza and Israel to discuss the future Palestinian elections in the Gaza Strip and the West Bank. It was agreed to meet again in

October to negotiate a compromise on the size of the Palestinian Council, Israel having rejected Arafat's proposal to hold the elections on 1 November 1994 as unrealistic. At the same time, Arafat agreed to 'take all measures' to prevent attacks on Israeli targets by opponents of the Declaration of Principles.

One of the reasons for the growing crisis in the negotiations between Israel and the Palestinians was the revival of the controversial issue of Jewish settlements in the West Bank. On 26 September Rabin approved a plan to construct some 1,000 new housing units at a Jewish settlement some 3 km inside the West Bank in an apparent reversal of the 'freeze' he had imposed on new constructions in 1992 in return for US loan guarantees. The PLO claimed that this decision contravened both the letter and the spirit of the Declaration of Principles; and it simply reinforced the objections of those who opposed the Declaration of Principles from the outset. (By the end of the year it was reported that there had been a 10% increase in the number of Jewish settlers in the West Bank during 1994.)

ISLAMIST ATTACKS THREATEN PEACE PROCESS

The Islamist organizations remained the most militant opponents of the Oslo process and in the autumn of 1994 both Hamas and Islamic Jihad escalated their campaigns of violence. On 9 October Hamas claimed responsibility for an attack in Jerusalem, in which an Israeli soldier and a Palestinian died. On the same day another Israeli soldier was kidnapped by Hamas fighters near Tel-Aviv; they subsequently demanded the release from Israeli jails of their leader, Sheikh Ahmad Yassin, and other Palestinian prisoners in exchange for his life. Despite Palestinian action to detain some 300 Hamas members in the Gaza Strip, the kidnapped soldier was killed in the West Bank on 14 October during an abortive rescue attempt by the IDF. On 19 October an attack by a Hamas suicide bomber in Tel-Aviv, in which 22 people died, prompted Israel to close its borders with the West Bank and the Gaza Strip for an indefinite period.

On 2 November 1994 a member of Islamic Jihad was killed in a car bomb attack in Gaza. The attack was blamed on the Israeli security forces by many Palestinians. On 11 November three Israeli soldiers were killed in a suicide bomb attack near a Jewish settlement in the Gaza Strip. Islamic Jihad claimed responsibility for the attack, which it said had been to avenge the death of its member on 2 November. Inevitably the arrest by the PNA of Hamas and Islamic Jihad cadres increased tensions between the opposing factions. These tensions erupted into violence on 18 November when Palestinian security forces opened fire on Islamist demonstrators in the centre of Gaza. Twelve Palestinians were reportedly killed in the incident and the subsequent violence that broke out throughout the Gaza Strip. The shootings appeared to confirm the perception of opponents of the peace process that the PNA and its security forces were fast becoming a proxy of the State of Israel. The EU responded to the crisis by stating that it would expedite $125m. in loans and guarantees promised earlier in the month. For its part, the Palestinian opposition denied that the clashes had arisen as a result of economic factors, attributing the disturbances instead to the perceived intrinsic deficiencies of the Declaration of Principles. Further violence in the Gaza Strip on 19 November resulted in the deaths of two Palestinians and an Israeli soldier, prompting a UN official to claim that aid programmes to the PNA were failing and that the situation in Gaza was more explosive than it had been before the start of the Oslo process.

It became clear in December 1994 that Israel's concern about security would inevitably continue to delay the redeployment of its armed forces in the West Bank and the holding of Palestinian elections. In the middle of the month Rabin stated that the elections would either have to take place in the continued presence of Israeli armed forces, or be postponed for a year.

Perhaps the most serious blow yet to the peace negotiations between Israel and the PLO was the suicide bomb attack at Beit Lid in Israel on 22 January 1995, in which 21 people—mostly Israeli soldiers–died and more than 60 were injured. Islamic Jihad claimed responsibility for the attack, in response to which the Israeli Cabinet again closed Israel's borders with the Gaza Strip and the West Bank and postponed the planned release of some 5,500 Palestinian prisoners. The gravity of the situation was reflected in the opinion of the Israeli President, Ezer Weizman: 'I believe we should suspend the talks–not stop them but suspend them.' Opinion polls published in Israel on 27 January revealed that the majority of Israeli citizens now opposed the peace process; while the majority of Palestinians were shown to be in favour of increased suicide attacks against Israeli targets. The polls also revealed a drastic decline in support for the Israeli Labour Party. The leader of Likud, Binyamin Netanyahu, responding to the popular mood, made an electoral promise to end the peace negotiations, take tougher measures against suspected terrorists and abandon the promised return of more land occupied in 1967.

At the beginning of February 1995 an emergency meeting of the leaders of Egypt, Israel, Jordan and the PLO was held in Cairo with the aim of lending support to the troubled peace process. A communiqué issued at the conclusion of the summit meeting condemned acts of terror and violence; and expressed support for the Declaration of Principles and the wider peace process. On 12 February 1995 US President Clinton held a meeting with the Israeli and the Egyptian Ministers of Foreign Affairs and the Palestinian (PNA) Minister of Planning and Economic Co-operation, Nabil Shaath, in Washington, DC. Shimon Peres, the Israeli Minister of Foreign Affairs, was reported to have stated after the meeting that any further expansion of Palestinian self-rule in the West Bank was conditional upon real progress by the PNA in suppressing terrorism. Elsewhere, fears were expressed in early February that the lack of democratic accountability of the PNA posed a significant threat to the peace process. In early March Yasser Arafat and the Israeli Minister of Foreign Affairs met in Gaza for talks. At the conclusion of the meeting it was announced that 1 July 1995 had been adopted as the date by which an agreement on the expansion of Palestinian self-rule in the West Bank should be concluded.

CABINET RESHUFFLES

On 21 February 1995 Rabin appointed ministers, in an acting capacity, to two portfolios which had been reserved for the Shas religious party. (Shas had announced at the beginning of the month that, owing to its fears regarding Jewish security and the peace process, it would not rejoin the coalition Government.) Uzi Baram became acting Minister of the Interior, while the Minister of the Economy and of Science and Technology, Shimon Sheetrit, assumed responsibility for religious affairs. In early June the Minister of Justice, David Libai, was appointed acting Minister of the Interior in place of Uzi Baram, who retained the tourism portfolio. The Likud party appeared to suffer a serious division in the same month, when one of its most prominent members, the former Minister of Foreign Affairs, David Levy, announced that he was forming a new party to contest the legislative elections scheduled for 1996. The division was reportedly the result of Levy's opposition to new selection procedures for general election candidates which Likud had formally adopted on 5 June. Levy's new, anonymous political movement was formally inaugurated on 18 June, although Levy himself remained a member of Likud.

ISRAEL–SYRIA TALKS RESUME

In mid-March 1995 it was announced that Israel and Syria had agreed to resume peace negotiations, talks between the two countries having been suspended since February 1994. The resumption of negotiations would initially involve the Israeli and Syrian ambassadors to the USA, meeting, at Syria's insistence, in the presence of US officials. At a later stage it was planned to introduce to the negotiations military technicians and, ultimately, the Syrian and Israeli Chiefs of Staff. Speculation that a breakthrough in the talks between Israel and Syria might shortly be achieved was subdued, however, in late April, when the Syrian Vice-President made it clear that Syria had no intention of renouncing its demand that Israel should withdraw from the Golan Heights to the border pertaining before the June 1967 war. Nevertheless, on 24 May Syria and Israel were reported to have concluded a 'framework understanding on security arrangements' which would facilitate negotiations on security issues. At the end of the month Shimon Peres made public the Government's position with regard to the talks with Syria. Israel, he stated, had proposed that its forces should

withdraw from the Golan Heights over a four-year period. Syria, however, had insisted that the withdrawal should be effected over 18 months. Peace negotiations between Israel and Syria resumed in late December 1995 in Maryland, USA, and a second round of US-mediated talks took place there in early January 1996.

VIOLENCE PRECEDES AGREEMENT

In early April 1995 two suicide bomb attacks in the Gaza Strip killed seven Israeli soldiers and wounded more than 50 people. Hamas and Islamic Jihad subsequently claimed responsibility for the attacks, in the aftermath of which the Palestinian police force was reported to have arrested as many as 300 members of the two groups. The following day the Minister of Justice in the PNA announced that the Palestinian police force would disarm all members of 'rejectionist' groups opposed to the peace process. On 18 April PNA officials met representatives of Islamic Jihad and Hamas and demanded that the two groups should terminate all of their armed operations against Israeli targets in and from the autonomous areas. The Islamic Jihad and Hamas representatives were reported to be willing to agree to a limited cease-fire, provided that the PNA released members of the two organizations held in detention, did not disarm the groups, and undertook not to allow Israeli armed forces to carry out operations against them. Attention once again shifted to the issue of settlements, when in late April it was announced that the Israeli Government had approved a plan to take possession of some 54 ha of mainly Arab-owned land in two sections of East Jerusalem. The land was to be used by the Ministry of Housing for the construction of Jewish neighbourhoods and facilities. An emergency meeting of the Arab League condemned the Israeli Government's decision to expropriate the land. The UN Security Council subsequently convened and prepared a resolution which demanded that Israel rescind its decision. However, in spite of the support of all of the other 14 members of the Security Council for the resolution, the USA exercised its veto to prevent its adoption. On 22 May 1995, however, the Israeli Government announced that the plan had been suspended after Hadash and the Democratic Arab Party drafted a 'no-confidence' motion in response, which Likud was likely to have supported. (The Arab Democratic Party subsequently forced a confidence vote in the Knesset which the Government won.)

Despite intensive efforts to achieve a breakthrough, it proved impossible to conclude an agreement on expansion of Palestinian self-rule in the West Bank by the target date of 1 July 1995. The principal obstacles to an agreement were the question of to where, exactly, Israeli troops in the West Bank would redeploy; and the precise nature of security arrangements to be made for the approximately 130,000 Jewish settlers who were to remain in the West Bank.

On 21 August 1995 a suicide bomb attack on a bus in Jerusalem killed six people. Hamas claimed responsibility for the attack, which raised the number of deaths in bombings over the previous 16 months to 77 and inevitably provoked further demands from those Israeli elements opposed to the Declaration of Principles that the talks should be suspended. Some opponents of the peace process argued that there was now little point in proceeding with interim agreements, and that final status negotiations between Israel and the Palestinians should begin immediately. This was the general consensus of the nationalist Right and derived from a belief that the less land that was under Palestinian control at the time of final status talks, the weaker the PNA's bargaining position would be over such crucial issues as settlement and Jerusalem.

It was not until 28 September 1995 that the Israeli-Palestinian Interim Agreement on the West Bank and the Gaza Strip was finally signed by Israel and the PLO (see Documents on Palestine, p. 136). Its main provisions were the withdrawal of Israeli armed forces from a further six West Bank towns (Nablus, Ramallah, Jenin, Tulkaram, Kakilya and Bethlehem) and a partial redeployment away from the town of Hebron; national Palestinian legislative elections to an 82-member Palestinian Council, and for a Palestinian Executive President; and the release, in three phases, of Palestinian prisoners detained by Israel. There were many criticisms of the new agreement, many of which focused on the sheer complexity–and corresponding vagueness–of the 400-page document. It was inevitable, too, that the agreement would raise further, serious doubts about precisely what kind of entity the PNA might be at the conclusion of final status negotiations, given Israel's clear desire to maintain jurisdiction over the West Bank settlements. Opposition Palestinian groups condemned the agreement as inadequate, whilst Israeli hard-liners denounced the agreement because they believed that too much had been conceded to the Palestinians. In mid-October, meanwhile, Israeli armed forces launched an intensive military operation in southern Lebanon after a bomb attack by Hezbollah had caused the deaths of six Israeli soldiers on 16 October 1995.

RABIN'S ASSASSINATION AND ITS AFTERMATH

The peace process was once again jeopardized on 4 November 1995 when the Israeli Prime Minister was assassinated while leaving a peace rally in Tel-Aviv. His assassin, Yigal Amir, was a young religious nationalist who opposed the peace process, and in particular Israeli withdrawal from the West Bank. While it was apparently an independent act, the assassination seemed certain further to marginalize those on the extreme right wing of Israeli politics who had advocated violence as a means of halting the implementation of the Declaration of Principles on Palestinian self-rule. The assassination also provoked criticism of Likud which, it was widely felt, had not sufficiently distanced itself from such extremist elements. Following the assassination, Shimon Peres, hitherto the Minister of Foreign Affairs, became acting Prime Minister. On 15 November, with the agreement of the opposition Likud, Peres was invited to form a new government. On 21 November the leaders of the outgoing coalition parties—Labour, Meretz and Yi'ud—signed a new coalition agreement, and Peres announced a new Cabinet, which was formally approved by the Knesset on the following day. An opinion poll conducted on the eve of Peres' appointment showed the Labour leader enjoying a lead of more than 30% over Binyamin Netanyahu, his Likud rival.

In spite of Rabin's assassination, Israeli armed forces completed their withdrawal from the town of Jenin, in the West Bank, on 13 November 1995, and during December they withdrew from Tulkaram, Nablus, Kakilya, Bethlehem and Ramallah. With regard to Hebron, Israel and the PNA signed an agreement transferring jurisdiction in some 17 areas of civilian affairs from Israel to the PNA. In early December Shimon Peres and Yasser Arafat held talks at the Erez border point between Israel and the Gaza Strip for the first time since the assassination of Rabin. Peres confirmed at the talks that Israel would release some 1,000 Palestinian prisoners before the Palestinian legislative and presidential elections scheduled for January 1996. In February 1996 Peres announced that elections to the Knesset and—for the first time—the direct election of the Prime Minister, would take place as soon as electoral legislation allowed—in late May 1996.

RELATIONS WITH JORDAN

On 10 January 1996 King Hussein of Jordan began a public visit to Tel-Aviv, during the course of which Israel and Jordan signed a number of agreements relating to the normalization of economic and cultural relations. These included a transport agreement dealing with road links between Israel, Jordan and the Palestinian Autonomous Areas and providing for an air link between Israel and Jordan. However, the attempted assassination of Hamas leader Khalid Meshaal by Israeli Mossad agents in Amman, Jordan, in late September 1997 provoked a flurry of diplomatic activity to preserve cordial relations between Israel and Jordan (see below).

SUICIDE BOMB ATTACKS RESUME

Palestinian legislative and presidential elections were held in late January 1996 and, in the normal course of events, Palestinian and Israeli negotiators would, on their completion, have initiated the final stage of the peace process, addressing such issues as Jerusalem, the rights of Palestinian refugees, the status of Jewish settlements in the Palestinian Autonomous Areas and the extent of that autonomy. In late February and early March, however, suicide bomb attacks in Jerusalem, Ashkelon and Tel-Aviv caused the death of more than 50 Israelis

and led to a further suspension of the peace process. Following the attacks in Jerusalem and Ashkelon, Israel ordered the indefinite closure of the West Bank and the Gaza Strip and demanded that the Palestinian authorities should suppress the activities of Hamas and Islamic Jihad in the areas under their control. It was unclear, however, whether either of these groups was responsible for the bomb attacks. A hitherto unknown group, the 'Yahya Ayyash Units', claimed responsibility for the first attacks on 25 February, which were apparently carried out to avenge the assassination—allegedly by Israeli agents—of a leading member (Yahya Ayyash) of Hamas in January 1996. Yasser Arafat, now the elected Palestinian President, condemned the bombings and in late February more than 200 members of Hamas were reported to have been detained by the Palestinian security forces.

The two suicide bomb attacks carried out at the beginning of March 1996 (for which the 'Yahya Ayyash Units' again claimed responsibility) led Israel to impose even more stringent security measures and Israel asserted the right of its armed forces to enter the areas under Palestinian jurisdiction when its security was at stake. The Palestinian authorities were reported to have held emergency talks with the leadership of Hamas and Islamic Jihad and to have outlawed their armed wings and other, unspecified Palestinian paramilitary groups.

The suicide bomb attacks also affected the talks taking place between Israeli and Syrian negotiating teams in the USA. Following the second attacks in March 1996 the Israeli team returned to Israel. On 18 March Peres revealed that peace negotiations with Syria had effectively been suspended because Syria had refused to condemn the bombings in precisely the way the USA had indicated that it should; and to give an assurance that it would not sponsor terrorist activities. Syria claimed that it did condemn terrorism in all forms, but drew a distinction between terrorism and legitimate resistance against occupation.

OPERATION 'GRAPES OF WRATH'

Syria and Lebanon both declined an invitation to attend a summit meeting, held in the Egyptian town of Sharm esh-Sheikh on 13 March 1996, at which representatives of 27 countries expressed their support for the Middle East peace process and pledged to redouble their efforts to combat terrorism. On 10 April Israel launched a 16-day bombing operation ('Grapes of Wrath') to destroy Hezbollah bases in southern Lebanon, resulting in the displacement of some 400,000 civilians (see chapter on Lebanon). The military campaign ended suddenly after Israeli shells hit a UN base at Qana and killed more than 100 Lebanese civilians sheltering there. On 27 April a partial cease-fire was agreed between the two sides, stipulating that neither side should target civilians. An international monitoring committee, consisting of French, Israeli, Syrian, Lebanese and US officials, was established in order to oversee adherence to the terms of the cease-fire. The Israeli authorities insisted that the Qana shelling had been an accident, and on 14 June 1997 Israel rejected a UN resolution proposing that it should pay a total of $1.7m. in compensation for the victims of the incident.

In early April 1996 Israel and Turkey signed a number of military co-operation agreements, one of which provided for the establishment of a joint organization for research and strategy. Syria condemned the agreement as a threat to its own security and to that of all Arab and Islamic countries. A visit by Peres to Oman and Qatar at the beginning of the month resulted in an agreement between Israel and Qatar to increase co-operation in trade.

Israel welcomed the decision of the Palestine National Council in late April 1996 to amend the Palestinian Covenant (the constitution of the Palestinian resistance movement), thereby removing all of its clauses which demanded the destruction of Israel. Indeed, the Israeli Government had demanded that the Covenant be amended by 7 May 1996 as a pre-condition for its participation in the final stage of peace negotiations with the PLO.

LIKUD RETURNS TO POWER

In the months following the assassination of Itzhak Rabin the victory of the Labour Party and the Labour leader, Shimon Peres, in the legislative and prime ministerial elections held on

29 May 1996 was widely regarded as a foregone conclusion. Most significantly the US Administration appeared to exclude the possibility of any other outcome, even after the suicide bomb attacks during February and March 1996 led to increased support—expressed in opinion polls—for Likud and other right-wing political groups. No party gained an outright majority of the 120 seats in the new Knesset, but the Likud leader, Binyamin Netanyahu, gained a marginal and unexpected victory over Shimon Peres in the direct election of the Prime Minister in which they were the only candidates. Prior to the legislative election a formal alliance between Likud, the Tzomet party and Gesher (a new party, headed by David Levy) had been announced. The success of the religious parties, Shas and the NRP—even though they probably gained seats at the expense of the Likud-led alliance—was the key factor in determining that the new Government would be formed by Likud. Some 79.7% of the 3.9m.-strong Israeli electorate were reported to have participated in the elections.

The election of a new, Likud-led Israeli Government appeared to have grave implications for the future of the peace negotiations between Israel and the Palestinian authorities since, during the election campaign, the Likud alliance had explicitly stated that it would never agree to the establishment of a Palestinian state and even, at times, seemed to indicate that it was prepared to renege on some aspects of agreements which Israel had already concluded with the Palestinians. On 31 May 1996 the Palestinian Council of Ministers (formed after the Palestinian legislative elections in January 1996) and the Executive Committee of the PLO held a joint meeting in Gaza and urged any new Israeli Government to implement all agreements which had already been concluded and to commence the final stage of the peace negotiations.

Prime Minister Netanyahu commenced negotiations to form a cabinet on 2 June 1996, and on 16 and 17 June signed a series of agreements between the Likud alliance and Shas, the NRP, Israel B'Aliyah, United Torah Judaism and the Third Way to incorporate their representatives into a coalition which would command the support of 66 deputies in the 120-member Knesset. In addition, Moledet agreed to support the Government, but did not formally enter the coalition. On 18 June the new Government received the approval of the Knesset and presented a summary of the policies it would pursue in office. This excluded the possibility of granting Palestinian statehood or, with regard to Syria, of relinquishing *de facto* sovereignty of the occupied Golan Heights.

On 21–23 June 1996, in response to Likud's electoral victory, a summit meeting of the leaders of all Arab countries with the exception of Iraq was convened in Cairo. The meeting issued a final communiqué in which the participants reiterated Israel's withdrawal from all occupied territories (including East Jerusalem) as a basic requirement for a comprehensive Middle East peace settlement. In July the intransigent character of the new Israeli Government was enhanced by the incorporation into the Cabinet of Ariel Sharon—who had played a leading role in the creation and expansion of controversial Jewish settlements in the West Bank—although his appointment as Minister of Infrastructure was made only after the Minister of Foreign Affairs had forced it by threatening to resign, thus endangering Likud's alliance with Gesher.

IDF–PNA CLASHES THREATEN PEACE PROCESS

By late August 1996 Palestinian frustration at what were regarded as deliberate attempts by the new Israeli Government to slow down the peace process was increasingly evident. In June it was reported that Prime Minister Netanyahu had postponed further discussion of the withdrawal of Israeli armed forces from the West Bank town of Hebron—where they remained in order to provide security for a community of some 400 Jewish settlers. An agreement for their withdrawal by 20 March 1996 had been concluded with the Palestinian authorities, but had been suspended by Shimon Peres following the suicide bomb attacks in February and March. Furthermore, Netanyahu had refused to meet Yasser Arafat and had stated he would never do so. As a sign of their growing dissatisfaction with the new Likud-led Government, the PNA organized a short general strike at the end of the month. The strike was held in particular protest at the refusal of the Israeli authorities to allow Palesti-

nian Muslims to participate in Friday prayers at the al-Aqsa mosque in Jerusalem and also at a government decision to construct more housing units at existing Jewish settlements in the West Bank. In response to US pressure Netanyahu and Arafat met, for the first time, at the Erez crossing point between Israel and Gaza, on 4 September. At a press conference, following the meeting, they confirmed their commitment to the interim agreement and their determination to implement it. Reports persisted, however, that Israel was seeking to modify some of the agreements concluded within its framework.

In mid-September 1996, at a meeting of the Arab League member states, the Syrian Minister of Foreign Affairs stated that the Arab states represented there had agreed in future to link relations with Israel to progress made in the peace process. Shortly afterwards it was announced that the Israeli Ministry of Defence had approved plans to construct some 1,800 new housing units at existing Jewish settlements in the West Bank.

On 25 September 1996 violent confrontations began between members of the Palestinian security forces, Palestinian civilians and members of the Israeli armed forces in which at least 50 Palestinians and 18 Israelis were killed and hundreds wounded. The West Bank town of Ramallah was the initial point of confrontation and the cause of the disturbances was attributed to the decision of the Israeli Government to open the north end of the Hasmonean tunnel which ran beneath the al-Aqsa mosque in East Jerusalem. Most observers, however, viewed the violent confrontations as the inevitable culmination of Palestinian anger at the Israeli Government's apparent determination not to abide by some of the agreements it had signed with the Palestinian authorities. There was speculation that the violence, the most serious in the West Bank and Gaza since 1967, marked the beginning of a new Palestinian *intifada* and signalled the end of the peace process. The Israeli military authorities declared a state of emergency in the Gaza Strip and the West Bank and threatened military intervention to suppress the disturbances. A special session of the UN Security Council was convened and intense international diplomacy led to the holding of a crisis summit meeting in Washington, DC, hosted by US President Clinton and attended by Binyamin Netanyahu, Yasser Arafat and King Hussein of Jordan. The meeting reportedly achieved nothing, but on 6 October it was announced that, following further US mediation, Israel had agreed to resume negotiations on the partial withdrawal of its armed forces from Hebron. On 7 October, at the opening of the winter session of the Knesset, Netanyahu stated that once the question of the redeployment from Hebron had been settled Israel would reopen its borders with the West Bank and the Gaza Strip—which had remained closed since February 1996—and move quickly towards seeking a final settlement with the Palestinians.

HEBRON AGREEMENTS

In mid-January 1997 Israel and the PNA finally concluded an agreement on the withdrawal of Israeli armed forces from Hebron. The principal terms of the agreement, which had been negotiated with the help of US diplomacy, were that Israeli armed forces should withdraw from 80% of the town of Hebron within ten days, and that the first of three subsequent withdrawals from the West Bank should take place six weeks after the signing of the agreement, and the remaining two by August 1998. With regard to security arrangements for Jewish settlers in central Hebron, Palestinian police patrols would be armed only with pistols in areas close to the Jewish enclaves, while joint Israeli-Palestinian patrols would secure the heights above the enclaves. The 'final status' negotiations on borders, the Jerusalem issue, Jewish settlements and Palestinian refugees— arguably the most intractable elements of the entire Arab–Israeli dispute—were to commence within two months of the signing of the agreement on Hebron. As guarantor of the agreements, the USA undertook to obtain the release of some Palestinian prisoners, and to ensure that Israel continued to engage in negotiations for the establishment of a Palestinian airport on the Gaza Strip and for safe passage between the West Bank and the Gaza Strip for Palestinians. The USA also undertook to ensure that the Palestinians would continue to combat terrorism, complete the revision of the Palestinian Covenant and consider Israeli requests to extradite Palestinians suspected of involvement in attacks in Israel.

HAR HOMA

The conclusion of the agreement on the withdrawal of Israeli armed forces from Hebron marked the first significant progress in the peace process since Netanyahu's election as Prime Minister. However, renewed hopes for the future of the process appeared to be short-lived. The Israeli decision of February 1997 to proceed with the construction of 6,500 housing units at Har Homa in East Jerusalem attracted international criticism, but two UN Security Council resolutions, submitted during March, urging Israel to reconsider its construction plans were vetoed by the USA. The first veto was issued at a time of increasing tension between Israel and the PNA after a unilateral decision was made by Israel to redeploy its troops from only 9% of the West Bank. The Israeli decision angered not only Yasser Arafat, who rejected the proposal, but also King Hussein of Jordan who sent a personal letter to Netanyahu, accusing him of being 'intent on destroying' efforts made to restore the peace process. Anti-Israeli sentiments intensified throughout the Arab world, but the Arab cause continued to be undermined by violent atrocities, including the massacre by a Jordanian soldier of seven Israeli schoolgirls in Nayarayim, an enclave between Israel and Jordan, on 13 March. On 14 March King Hussein visited the families of the deceased to express his condolences. Continuing Israeli intransigence over Har Homa prompted the Palestinians to abandon the 'final status' talks, scheduled to begin on 17 March, and on the following day construction at the site began. Riots erupted immediately, reaching a climax on 21 March when a bomb, planted by Hamas, exploded in a north Tel-Aviv café, killing four and wounding more than 60 people. Netanyahu accused Arafat of extending an invitation to Islamist activists to resume terrorist attacks, and the Israeli Cabinet immediately ordered a general closure of the West Bank and Gaza Strip. At the end of the month the League of Arab States voted to resume their economic boycott of Israel, suspend moves to establish diplomatic relations with that country, and withdraw from multilateral peace talks. (Jordan, the PNA and Egypt were excluded from the legislation owing to their binding bilateral agreements with Israel.) On 1 April it was reported that two suicide bombers had succeeded only in killing themselves in an attempted attack on two busloads of schoolchildren travelling from Jewish settlements in the Gaza Strip. Despite the claims of an anonymous caller that the bombers were members of Hamas, both Hamas and Islamic Jihad denied responsibility for the attack, and the PNA claimed that one of the alleged bombers had been, in fact, the victim of an Israeli grenade attack. Meanwhile, in New York, Arab states continued to petition the UN General Assembly to appeal for a halt to the Har Homa development. On 7 April Netanyahu met President Clinton in Washington and insisted that he would not 'freeze' construction. Riots erupted in Hebron the following day after an Arab man was allegedly murdered by Jewish settlers. Three people died and more than one hundred were wounded in the clashes. Demonstrations continued during the rest of the month but eventually subsided, and at the end of April the Gaza Strip and the West Bank were reopened.

The intensity of Palestinian opposition to the construction of Jewish settlements became increasingly apparent when, despite the opposition of human rights groups, at the beginning of May 1997 the Palestinian Minister of Justice, Furayh Abu Middayn, announced that the PNA would sentence to death any Palestinian who was found to have sold land to Jews. This proclamation provoked a spate of unlawful killings: within one month three Arab land dealers were reportedly executed by a newly established vigilante group called 'The Guardians of the Holy Land'. The extent of renewed Israeli–Palestinian hostility was made evident also during May when the USA's chief peace process negotiator, Dennis Ross, returned to the USA following a nine-day mediation initiative in the region, having failed to secure any hope of a resumption of peace talks.

Both the Har Homa construction and the limited redeployment of the West Bank supported by the Israeli Government were regarded by many as a vitiation of the 1993 Declaration of Principles. The agreement was further undermined in May 1997 when the Minister of National Infrastructure, Ariel Sharon, proposed to deny Palestinians the right to drill for water and suggested that Israel should assume authority for one-half of the water resources on the West Bank. Hopes for the future resumption of the Oslo peace process were further frustrated when the Israeli daily newspaper, *Ha'aretz* reported the results of a US study which claimed that more than 25% of the Jewish settlers' homes in the Gaza Strip and West Bank were uninhabited (a claim which was rejected by the Israeli Central Board of Statistics which argued that only 12% of the settlements were unoccupied). The same newspaper later reported that Netanyahu's original plan, evolved within the framework of the Oslo accords, to relinquish an eventual 90% of the West Bank had been revised in a new proposal—the so-called 'Allon plus' plan—to a 40% redeployment.

In mid-June 1997 the US House of Representatives voted in favour of recognizing Jerusalem as the undivided capital of Israel and of transferring the US embassy there, from Tel-Aviv. President Clinton was reported to have strongly disapproved of the vote and of its possible implications for the peace process. The decision coincided with violent clashes between Palestinian civilians and Israeli troops in both Gaza and Hebron: within one week more than 150 Palestinians were reportedly shot and wounded. Fighting continued, reaching a climax in Hebron at the end of the month when anti-Islamic posters displayed in the town caused popular outrage. Meanwhile Yasser Arafat, fearing Israeli reoccupation of the town, assigned 200 police officers to patrol the streets in order to address the security crisis. Although the police presence appeared to have a largely positive effect in Hebron, four police officers were arrested by Israeli police outside Nablus on suspicion of conspiring to attack Israeli targets. At the same time the Palestinian police force announced the discovery of large stocks of ammunition in Beit Sahur on the West Bank, alleged to belong to Hamas.

JERUSALEM BOMBS THWART HOPES FOR RENEWED TALKS

At the beginning of July 1997 a series of meetings were held between the US Under-Secretary of State for Political Affairs, Thomas Pickering, and Israeli and Palestinian officials with the aim of resuming negotiations between the PNA and the Israeli Government. On 28 July both sides announced that peace talks were to be resumed in early August. However on 30 July, the eve of Dennis Ross' visit to reactivate the negotiations, two Hamas suicide bombers killed 14 civilians and wounded more than 150 others at an outdoor Jewish market in Jerusalem. The event effectively paralysed the peace process: Ross cancelled his visit and Israel immediately halted payment of tax revenues to the PNA and closed the Gaza Strip and the West Bank. The sanctions provoked furious protest from the Palestinians as well as widespread international condemnation. Nevertheless Binyamin Netanyahu insisted that restrictions would remain until increased efforts to combat the activities of such terrorist groups became evident. On 18 August 30% of some $50m. in tax revenue owed to the Palestinians was released by the Israeli Government. Rather than condemning Palestinian political organizations, Arafat convened a two-day forum in August during which he publicly embraced Hamas leaders and urged them, together with Islamic Jihad to unite with the Palestinian people against Israeli policies. On 26 August Hamas rejected a request from Palestinian leaders to suspend their attacks. Nevertheless, Israel relaxed its closure of the West Bank and the Gaza Strip on 1 September. Sanctions were reinforced on 4 September, however, after a triple suicide bombing took place in West Jerusalem, killing eight people (five Israelis and the bombers), and wounding more than 150 others. The bombing, followed one day later by the death of 12 Israeli commandos in Lebanon (see below), prompted warnings from the Israeli Security Cabinet that possible military attacks on Palestinian and Arab territories might be launched. The security forces' statement cast doubt on the viability of a planned visit by Madeleine Albright, US Secretary of State, to the Middle East in mid-September, when it was hoped that substantive political issues would be discussed. However, Albright's tour of the region, undertaken during 10–15 September, was positively received, and renewed diplomatic activity resulted, in early October, in the first direct discussions between the Israeli Prime Minister and the Palestinian leader for eight months.

ISRAELI CASUALTIES IN LEBANON

The deterioration in relations between Israel and the PNA coincided with renewed hostilities in the north of the country, after Hezbollah launched their first major rocket attack for 16 months on civilians in the Israeli town of Kiryat Shmona in early August 1997. The barrage, in retaliation for attacks by Israeli commandos in which five Hezbollah members were killed, prompted further air-strikes against targets in southern Lebanon. Violence escalated and on 18 August the Israeli military proxy, the South Lebanon Army (SLA) shelled the Lebanese port of Sidon, killing at least six and wounding more than 30 civilians. Israeli denials of responsibility, claiming that the attack was the sole initiative of the SLA, were rejected by Hezbollah. The international monitoring committee convened in mid-August in response to the escalating violence but failed to achieve a reconciliation. Indeed, any hopes for an immediate restoration of peace were shattered when, on 5 September, 12 Israeli marines, who were alleged to be planning to assassinate Shi'ite leaders, were killed in the village of Insariyeh, south of Sidon. The Israeli commandos were reportedly killed by the joint forces of Hezbollah, Amal, and Lebanese soldiers. The death toll, the highest since 1985 when troops receded to the buffer zone, was expected to have grave implications for regional security.

NETANYAHU'S DOMESTIC PROBLEMS

In addition to the escalating security crisis in the region (see above), Netanyahu also faced increasing domestic difficulty in April 1997, after police recommended that he be charged with fraud and breach of trust following his appointment in January 1997 of an undistinguished lawyer, Roni Bar-On, as Attorney-General. Bar-On resigned within 12 hours of his appointment after it was alleged that his promotion had been made in order to facilitate a plea bargain for Aryeh Der'i, leader of the orthodox Shas party, who was facing separate corruption charges. There were suggestions that in return for Bar-On's appointment, Der'i had pledged Shas party support for the Cabinet's decision regarding the withdrawal from Hebron. In early May Aryeh Der'i was indicted for obstruction of justice but Elyaqim Rubenstein, Bar-On's successor, ruled that, owing to lack of evidence, charges would not be brought against Netanyahu. Despite Netanyahu's acquittal, there were strong demands for his resignation, and his credibility was further undermined by the resignations of the Finance Minister, Dan Meridor, and the Minister of Communications, Limor Livnat, who, although retaining her ministerial position, resigned from her post as Cabinet Spokeswoman. (On 9 July Michael Eitan was approved as Minister of Science, following the resignation of Binyamin Begin, and Yaacov Ne'eman was appointed Minister of Finance.) The extent of Netanyahu's declining popularity was made apparent on 21 July, when the Government was defeated by five votes in a motion of 'no confidence'. The Government survived, however, since legislation demands that an absolute majority of 61, which was not achieved, is required before change can be implemented.

In June Ehud Barak, a former cabinet minister and chief of staff of the army, won the Labour Party leadership election (to replace Shimon Peres), with 51% of the votes.

FLUCTUATING RELATIONS WITH JORDAN

On 25 September 1997 two Israeli Mossad agents, travelling on forged Canadian passports, were detained in the Jordanian capital, Amman, in connection with the attempted assassination, by poisoning, of the local Hamas chief, Khalid Meshaal. The two agents were apprehended by bodyguards at the scene of the incident, immediately after the attack. In response to the incident, which caused severe embarrassment to the Israeli Government, Canada withdrew its ambassador to Tel-Aviv, while King Hussein of Jordan threatened to try the arrested men for murder and to sever diplomatic relations with Israel unless the Israeli authorities promptly supplied an antidote for the potentially lethal chemical agent used in the attack. The antidote was duly dispatched by Israel, and in late September diplomats and senior government officials engaged in frantic efforts to preserve cordial relations between the two countries. In early October the release from Israeli prisons of dozens of

Arab detainees, including Sheikh Ahmad Yassin, one of the founders of Hamas, was thought to have been negotiated with the Jordanian authorities in exchange for the return of the Mossad agents apprehended at the scene of the attack. Yassin's return to Gaza on 6 October prompted scenes of popular jubilation, and proved a further embarrassment for Netanyahu, who had persistently exhorted the PNA to distance itself from the Hamas leadership. The bungled Mossad attempt and its aftermath reportedly created tensions within Netanyahu's Cabinet; it was alleged that the Minister of Foreign Affairs, David Levy, and the Minister of Defence, Itzhak Mordechai, were furious with Netanyahu for not having consulted them over the decision to attempt Meshaal's assassination. However, the Minister of Infrastructure, Ariel Sharon, defended the Prime Minister, praising him for his 'leadership and control' during the crisis. Although Sharon's sympathetic intervention may have appeared surprising (his personal antipathy towards Netanyahu had been widely reported), some observers regarded his timely support for the beleaguered Netanyahu as a bid to advance the fortunes of cabinet hard-liners (and his stewardship of the faction) at the expense of the pragmatists led by Levy and Mordechai. The report of a commission of investigation into the incident, appointed by the Government, was published in February 1998 and was highly critical of the planning and execution of the 'mission', though not of the wider strategy. The head of Mossad, Maj.-Gen. Danny Yatou, resigned as a result of the report, and was replaced, in March, by Ephraim Halevy, a former diplomat. A series of high-level ministerial meetings between Jordanian and Israeli delegations (including direct contacts between Netanyahu and Crown Prince Hassan) were conducted in early March, resulting in renewed commitments to co-operate in the fields of bilateral trade, water and electricity resources and tourism. Netanyahu described the thaw in relations between the two sides as 'a new beginning'.

INTERNAL PROBLEMS

An attempt by Netanyahu to consolidate his leadership of Likud at a party conference convened in November 1997 prompted a crisis within the party and within the governing coalition, after the conference endorsed a proposal to reform the electoral system. According to the proposed reform, Likud candidates standing for election to the Knesset would henceforth be selected by the party's 2,700-strong Central Committee (dominated by Netanyahu's supporters) rather than the 200,000 registered members of the party. However, following numerous press reports that Likud party opponents and coalition party members alike were considering the creation of new parties in an attempt to arrest this consolidation of Netanyahu's support at the expense of the democratic process, Netanyahu retracted the plan, stating that the reform issue would be the subject of a future referendum. Meanwhile, also in November, a number of speakers, including the Labour Party leader, Ehud Barak, addressed a crowd of some 200,000 Israelis who had gathered to commemorate the second anniversary of the assassination of Itzhak Rabin. Barak pledged to continue Rabin's pursuit of a Middle East peace.

REDEPLOYMENT PROPOSALS

Bilateral negotiations between Israel and Palestinian negotiators resumed in early November 1997. Israel offered to decelerate its construction of Jewish settlements in return for Palestinian approval of a plan to delay further redeployments of Israeli troops from the West Bank. At the same time, the Israeli Government announced plans to build 900 new housing units in the area, frustrating both the USA and PNA. The virtual stalemate in the peace process prompted several Arab states to boycott the Middle East and North Africa economic conference, held in Doha, Qatar, on 16–18 November. Separate peace talks, held between Madeleine Albright, Netanyahu and Arafat in mid-November, were inconclusive. Albright urged Israel to present plans for a significant withdrawal from the West Bank in the near future. On 30 November the Israeli Cabinet agreed in principle to a partial withdrawal from the West Bank, but specified neither its timing nor its scale; implementation would be dependent on the PNA meeting its security commitments. The withdrawal proposals also affirmed Israel's right to continue 'reinforcement of settlements in Judaea and Samaria'. In addition to the agreement, the Cabinet undertook to create a team of ministers to decide which areas of the West Bank would be permanently retained by Israel, before the implementation of the second redeployment. Such a unilateralist initiative directly contravened the Oslo Agreement, which stated that the final settlement agreement was to be negotiated with the PNA. A subsequent statement issued by Likud mayors in the West Bank settlements expressed support for the principle of 'separation' in Judaea, Samaria and Gaza. The statement not only bolstered Netanyahu's argument with nationalist hard-liners in the Knesset (Likud municipal chiefs represented some 80% of Jewish settlers in the West Bank) but also marked a significant departure for Likud, which had previously adhered very firmly to the belief that all of historic Palestine was an indivisible part of the Jewish State. However, the Palestinians and much of the international community deemed the proposal to be an unacceptable departure from the Oslo and Hebron protocols. The Labour leader, Ehud Barak, dismissed the Government's proposals as 'irrelevant' and the Clinton administration in the USA also signalled that the latest initiative was inadequate.

INDUSTRIAL UNREST, 1997

Meanwhile, the stringent fiscal and economic policies being pursued by the Minister of Finance, Yaacov Ne'emen, were increasingly bringing the Government into confrontation with the Histadrut (Israel's General Federation of Labour). Since his appointment, Ne'emen had enthusiastically promoted a campaign of privatization and public-spending cuts, measures which were welcomed by the business community but mistrusted by the Histadrut, which drew attention to rising unemployment figures and the threat of deteriorating social services. Of particular concern to the unions was speculation that Ne'emen was planning to revise the terms of new pensions legislation, endorsed by the previous administration, which he considered to be 'excessively generous'. Tensions were exacerbated in early December 1997 following Ne'emen's comparison of the critics who were seeking to undermine his monetary policy to the Palestinian suicide bombers who had frustrated recent peace initiatives. Despite issuing an apology for the ill-advised comparison, Ne'emen's confrontational style appeared to provide the final provocation for the organization, by union officials, of a general strike on 3 December. (A half-day general strike organized on 29 September, also in protest at the Government's economic policies, had been observed by an estimated 500,000 workers.) The industrial action, which was thought to involve some 700,000 mainly public sector employees, resulted in the closure of government offices, banks, schools and the Tel-Aviv stock exchange, and the suspension of many public transport facilities. Employees returned to work on 7 December following assurances from Ne'emen that the fundamental principles of the pensions reform proposal would be adhered to by the Likud-led coalition.

THE COALITION WEAKENED

Evidence of further divisions within the coalition emerged at the end of December 1997, owing to the forthcoming 1998 budget vote, effectively a demonstration of confidence in the Prime Minister. In order to muster the necessary support, Netanyahu granted concessions to various parties, in particular to right-wing members of the coalition. These included such financial rewards as increased funding for construction on the West Bank and for Orthodox schools. Opposition parties claimed that the Prime Minister had bribed coalition members in order to remain in power. David Levy, the leader of Gesher, also denounced the budget, claiming it to be an infringement of social principles; and on 4 January 1998 Levy resigned and Gesher withdrew from the Government, attributing the departure to dissatisfaction with the budget and with the slow rate of progress in the peace talks. The withdrawal of Gesher left Netanyahu with a majority of 61–59, and prompted speculation about the Government's imminent collapse. However, on the following day the budget was approved by a 58–52 majority. Later in the same month the Deputy Prime Minister and Minister of Education, Culture and Sport, Zevulun Hammer (the leader of the NRP), died. His cabinet responsibilities were assumed by Itzhak Levi, the NRP Minister of Transport and Energy. Levi was confirmed as Minister of Education and Culture, and of Religious Affairs

(as well as new leader of the NRP) in February. Levi was replaced as Minister of Transport and Energy by Shaul Yahalom, also of the NRP. Plans to form a government of national unity for a period of six months, proposed by Shimon Peres, were rejected after the former Labour leader failed to secure enough support from party members. In October Ariel Sharon was appointed Minister of Foreign Affairs. Sharon was to retain his duties as Minister of National Infrastructure for a further three months.

REJECTION OF US REDEPLOYMENT PROPOSALS

The departure of David Levy from the Cabinet reinforced a perceived shift to the right in the balance of power in the Israeli Government, and did little to ease mounting US concerns over the future of the peace process. A visit to Israel and the Occupied Territories undertaken by Dennis Ross on 6–9 January 1998 failed to ease relations between the Israelis and the Palestinians sufficiently to prepare for negotiations on further Israeli redeployment. Indeed, ignoring the exhortations of the US Secretary of State to suspend all construction activities in the Occupied Territories, the Israeli Government announced expansion plans for two West Bank settlements during Ross's visit. Netanyahu responded to criticism of these decisions by asserting that the Israeli Government was not bound to cease settlement activity by the terms of the Oslo Agreement. In January 1998 President Clinton invited Netanyahu and Arafat to attend separate meetings in Washington, DC, on 20 and 22 of the month respectively. Prior to discussions with the President and the Secretary of State, Netanyahu attended a series of high-profile meetings with pro-Israeli opponents of the Clinton administration, including the Speaker of the House of Representatives, Newt Gingrich, other senior Republicans and representatives of the evangelical Christian movement. During the discussions with President Clinton, Netanyahu was reported to have rejected a US proposal for a phased second redeployment from the West Bank involving 10%–15% of the territory (a proposal which Arafat was reported to have reluctantly agreed to, despite initial indications that the PNA would not contemplate acceptance of redeployment from less than 30% of the land) in return for the Palestinians' further revision of the Palestinian National Charter and fulfilment of Israeli security requirements.

Netanyahu was insistent that any second stage of redeployment would have to involve less than 10% of the territory. The Israeli Prime Minister's departure from the USA coincided with the announcement in Israel of the finalization of a $1,400m. loan agreement with the US Government and the delivery, from the USA, of two highly advanced combat aircraft, purchased under favourable terms. By late January it was reported that direct contacts between the Palestinian delegation and the Israeli Prime Minister had been broken off. In late March the Israeli Cabinet rejected a new US proposal, delivered in Jerusalem by Dennis Ross, for an Israeli withdrawal from slightly more than 13% of West Bank territory, prompting US Secretary of State Albright to state that the peace process was on the verge of collapse, indicating that the USA was considering ending its involvement as a mediator. It had become increasingly evident that even if agreement could be reached between the Palestinians and the Israelis on the scale of a proposed second redeployment from the West Bank, the issue of whether the withdrawal should take place prior to the commencement of 'final status' talks remained far more contentious.

WEIZMAN RE-ELECTED PRESIDENT

On 4 March 1998 the Knesset re-elected Ezer Weizman as President for a further five-year term, by 63 votes to 49. Weizman defeated Shaul Amor, a Likud member of the Knesset whose candidacy had been sponsored by Prime Minister Netanyahu.

PROPOSED WITHDRAWAL FROM LEBANON

In late 1997 and early 1998 Israel's Minister of Defence, Itzhak Mordechai, indicated that Israel would be prepared to withdraw, in accordance with UN Security Council Resolution 425 (of March 1978), but with the stipulation that Lebanon provide guarantees of the security of Israel's northern border. On 1 April 1998 the Israeli 'inner' Security Cabinet voted to adopt

Resolution 425, on this condition. However, Lebanon emphasized that Resolution 425 demanded an unconditional withdrawal, and stated that neither would it be able to guarantee Israel's immunity from attack, nor would it be prepared to deploy the Lebanese army in southern Lebanon for this purpose; furthermore, Lebanon could not support the continued presence there of the SLA (whose integration with the Lebanese army was sought by the Israelis). Concern was also expressed that a unilateral withdrawal from Lebanon in the absence of a comprehensive Middle East peace settlement might foment regional instability. Israel's demand that Hezbollah be disarmed prior to any Israeli withdrawal was, moreover, unacceptable not only to Lebanon but also to Syria, which regarded its support for the resistance in southern Lebanon as essential leverage in its efforts to secure a parallel Israeli withdrawal from the Golan Heights.

INCREASED EU INVOLVEMENT

In early 1998 the European Commission published a detailed report on EU policies towards the Middle East, urging the adoption of a higher profile in the peace process. The report was highly critical of Israeli policies towards the PNA, and made particular reference to 'obstacles to trade and economic activity' being responsible for economic deterioration in Palestinian areas. In February the President of the European Commission, Jacques Santer, visited the Middle East and questioned Israel's obstructionism towards economic development in the West Bank and Gaza, and, in particular, its blocking of a free-trade agreement between the EU and the PNA. Although Santer ruled out the imposition of any form of EU sanctions against Israel, this concession did little to allay Likud's traditional suspicions of Europe. In March the British Secretary of State for Foreign and Commonwealth Affairs, Robin Cook, visited Israel and the Occupied Territories, representing the UK presidency of the EU. A proposed visit by Cook to the site of the Har Homa settlement in the company of Faisal Husseini, the PNA Minister with Responsibility for Jerusalem Affairs was declared 'unacceptable' by Netanyahu. Cook eventually agreed to be escorted to Har Homa by Israel's Cabinet Secretary, David Naveh, a compromise that satisfied neither the Israelis nor the Palestinians. In the event, Cook's visit to Har Homa degenerated into an undignified spectacle as the British politician was jostled by a crowd of right-wing settlers. Cook subsequently travelled to East Jerusalem where he met Husseini and laid a wreath to commemorate the Palestinian victims of the 1948 massacre at Deir Yassin. Netanyahu responded by cancelling a planned dinner engagement with Cook, cutting short another scheduled meeting to a symbolic 15 minutes. Relations between Europe and Israel deteriorated further in June 1998 after the Commission instructed Israel not to award 'made in Israel' certificates to goods originating from Israeli settlements in the Occupied Territories, as these were not entitled to receive the tax exemptions intended for goods produced in the State of Israel. The Commission also instructed Israeli exporters to desist from claiming that goods made by Palestinians in the West Bank and Gaza originated in Israel. A Commission official insisted that its warning to Israel was motivated primarily by concerns that its trade agreements were correctly implemented, but conceded that Israeli violations had first been noted some time ago. In late June EU foreign ministers met in Luxembourg and urged Israel to provide 'clarification' of its application of the EU's 'rules of origin' regulations. The British Prime Minister, Tony Blair, visited Israel and the Occupied Territories as part of a tour of the Middle East undertaken in April. Blair invited Netanyahu and Arafat to attend talks in London, scheduled for the following month, in an attempt to break the deadlock over redeployment.

LIMITED POPULARITY SUSTAINED AND REDEPLOYMENT TALKS REACTIVATED

Netanyahu's rejectionist position with regard to redeployment was unpopular with centrists within the governing coalition as well as with broad sections of the Israeli public. (In April 1998 the Council for Peace and Security, an influential grouping of retired senior officers from the army, police and security services, placed a full page advertisement in the Israeli press supporting a withdrawal from 10%–13% of the West Bank.)

However, threats made by Itzhak Mordechai to resign as Minister of Defence over the lack of movement on the redeployment issue were not carried out as Netanyahu maintained his lead in the opinion polls. The Israeli Premier's buoyancy was aided by ongoing disarray within the Labour Party. Barak's decision to court the ring-wing vote had caused dismay and disaffection among many party members and support for the party consequently declined. In May he made a highly controversial visit to two ultra-nationalist settlements, once considered hostile territory for Labour officials, where he pledged strong support for the settlement movement. Following the tour his chief aide, Tsali Reshef, resigned stating that there was currently little ideological disparity between the Likud and Labour leaders.

At the beginning of May 1998 Israeli and Palestinian leaders met US Secretary of State, Madeleine Albright, for separate talks, held in London, aimed at reactivating negotiations concerning redeployment. The discussions ended inconclusively but with a further invitation for Israeli and Palestinian delegations to visit Washington in mid-May for another round of talks with President Clinton and the US Department of State. Once again, these talks concluded with no obvious sign of progress but not before Netanyahu had again demonstrated to the Clinton administration the depth of support in the US Congress for his own Government and its uncompromising security agenda. Newt Gingrich was especially responsive to Netanyahu and reportedly advised the Israeli Prime Minister to defy US pressure over the redeployment issue. Moreover, Gingrich described Madeleine Albright as 'an agent for the Palestinians'. His comments were strongly rebuked by the US Department of State.

RENEWED FRICTION IN JERUSALEM

Developments in Jerusalem also served to sustain frictions between the US and Israeli Governments: at the end of May 1998, a Jewish settler organization began constructing a new religious complex on disputed land in the Muslim quarter of East Jerusalem's Old City. (The site had previously been occupied by a Palestinian charitable organization but dwellings were demolished by the Jerusalem municipality on the grounds that they had been built without a licence.) According to press reports, the head of the group had met with Netanyahu, Ariel Sharon and Israel's police chief, Yehuda Wilk, prior to commencement of the building work, prompting speculation that there had been high-level government collusion with the settler operation. Peace groups promptly condemned the settler activity and a protest march to the site by Palestinian parliamentarians erupted into violence, with several of the politicians sustaining injuries. Building work was suspended in June after a restraining order was obtained from the Antiquities Authority on the grounds that the Old City walls were being damaged. The settlers agreed to abandon the construction on condition that they would be able to submit a tender to build a religious school and 12 apartments after the Antiquities Authority had surveyed the site. In the mean time it was agreed that the settlers would guard the site during excavation work. James Rubin, spokesman for Madeleine Albright, denounced the Israeli settlers and their supporters for undermining the creation of an environment necessary for any Israeli-Palestinian reconciliation. In mid-June Jerusalem once again became a focus of international concern after Netanyahu won cabinet approval for a draft plan to widen the municipal boundaries of Jerusalem to encompass suburbs lying to the west of the city and also part of the territory of the West Bank. The Prime Minister attempted to avert criticism of the proposals by describing them as being aimed principally at rationalizing service provision and tax efficiency; nevertheless, he conceded that his strategic goal was to guarantee 'an absolute Jewish majority of at least 70%' in the city. The PNA complained that the proposals would alter the demography of the city by increasing the Jewish population by 30,000 and also expressed fears that the plan was the precursor to the eventual extension of city boundaries to incorporate such large urban settlements as Ma'aleh Edomin, an eventuality which would effectively split the West Bank in two. A decision by the Jerusalem and Ma'aleh Edomin municipalities to create a joint industrial zone in a strategic location between the borders of their jurisdictions had already heightened suspicions of Israel's long-term intentions.

BREAKTHROUGH ON REDEPLOYMENT?

By mid-1998 US exasperation with Israeli procrastination and intransigence had become increasingly apparent. Speaking at a news conference with the Egyptian Minister of Foreign Affairs on 10 July, Madeleine Albright stated that the existing stalemate 'couldn't go on indefinitely'. Three days later James Rubin expressed the view that Israel was responsible for sustaining the impasse and urged the Israeli Government to work with the Palestinians, who according to Rubin were willing to reactivate negotiations. On 19 July Israeli negotiators met their Palestinian counterparts directly for the first substantive talks in many months. After three days, however, Arafat withdrew his team from the negotiations, accusing the Israeli side of creating 'obscure formulations' on the US initiative. According to Israeli press reports the Palestinians had been angered by an Israeli proposition that 3% of the 13.1% of the West Bank territory subject to discussion under the US proposals should be transformed into a 'nature reserve' on which both Palestinian and Israeli construction would be prohibited. In late July a prominent Likud Knesset member and former intelligence chief, Gideon Ezra, exacerbated existing tensions by stating on Israeli television that Netanyahu wanted the 'final status' negotiations to continue for a minimum of 15 years in order to test Palestinian goodwill. Speculation that an unexpected breakthrough had been achieved on the issue of redeployment emerged in late September following renewed contacts between the Israeli and Palestinian leaders at a US mediated meeting in Washington, DC. The adoption of a more conciliatory stance by both sides in early October encouraged hopes for significant progress at a new round of talks convened in mid-October near Washington, DC.

NO PROGRESS ON THE SYRIA TRACK

The possibility of a resumption of negotiations on peace between Israel and Syria emerged after it was reported that the two countries had agreed to a French initiative to resume dialogue, based on an Israeli acceptance of the 'land-for-peace' formula and Syrian acceptance of Israel's security needs. However, prior to a visit to Paris by the Syrian President, Hafiz al-Assad, in mid-July 1998, it was reported that Netanyahu had retracted his decision to accept the French initiative, reportedly owing to opposition from coalition partners. On 23 July the Knesset gave preliminary approval to a bill which would require a majority vote in the Knesset and a referendum to be held prior to allowing an Israeli withdrawal from either the Golan Heights or Jerusalem. The Knesset vote was fiercely denounced in Syria.

Syria, Iran, Iraq and Egypt were among a number of Middle Eastern states to react angrily to joint military exercises, codenamed 'Reliant Mermaid', conducted by Israeli, Turkish and US forces in the Mediterranean in January 1998.

Economy

Revised for this edition by Simon Chapman and the Editor

INTRODUCTION

In 1995 Israel's gross domestic product (GDP), measured at constant prices, increased by 7.1%, compared with average annual growth of about 6% during the previous five years. The business sector recorded real growth of 8.3% in 1995, compared with an average annual rate of growth of 7% in 1990–94.

In 1995 private consumption increased by 7.2% in real terms. Relatively high growth was recorded in the consumption of durable goods. Consumption per head, which reflects the standard of living, increased by 4.6% in 1995, compared with an increase of 6.3% in 1994. The decline in per-caput growth in private consumption was accompanied by an upturn in the rate of private savings, following a continued fall in private savings during 1992–94. As the economy grew at an accelerated rate, the number of persons in employment increased by some 5.4%. Some 80% of this increase was accounted for by the business sector. The rate of unemployment continued to decline for the third consecutive year, falling to 6.9% of the labour force at the end of 1995.

In 1995 consumer prices increased at an average annual rate of 10.0%, compared with an increase of 12.3% in 1994. Price increases in 1995 were not uniform, however. Ignoring seasonal factors, there was a significant deceleration in the pace of inflation during the first third of the year, but inflation rose during the remainder of the year. The reasons for the decline in prices in the first part of the year were, primarily, significant falls in the prices of fruit and vegetables; and, to a lesser extent, a slower rate of increase in house prices. These increased by an overall rate of 13.6%. The wholesale price index of industrial output rose by some 10% during 1995, a rate of increase similar to that recorded in 1994.

During 1995 the expansion of almost all economic sectors continued. The output of the construction sector increased by some 12% in real terms, mainly because of expanded public residential construction. The output of the industrial sectors—which accounts for approximately one-third of total business production—grew, in real terms, by 8%. Industrial exports, however, increased at a lower rate of about 6% in real terms, and this erosion of profitability was attributed to the continued appreciation in the value of Israel's currency, the shekel, in 1995. Output in the trade and services sectors increased, in real terms, by some 8%, while output in the public and community services sectors grew by some 4%, in real terms, in 1995.

In 1995 the country's central bank, the Bank of Israel, reduced the rate of interest on monetary tenders from an annual rate of 17% (an effective rate of 18.5%) at the beginning of the year to an annual nominal rate of 13.2% (an effective rate of 14.1%) in August. In October-November the Bank of Israel raised interest rates on monetary tenders by a cumulative rate of 1% to an annual nominal rate of 14.2%.

In 1995 the capital market was characterized by extreme volatility in share prices, together with a sharp decline in the volume of trading. For the year as a whole, the general index of share prices recorded a slight increase.

In 1996 Israel's GDP growth, in real terms, slowed to 4.5%, equivalent to a rise of 1.7% per head (compared with an increase of 4.2% per head in 1995). Business sector production increased by 5.2% in 1996, compared with 8.9% growth in the previous year. In the first half of 1996 the consumer price index increased by 15.4% (in annual, seasonally-adjusted terms) but slowed in the last six months resulting in an average annual increase of 11.3%. In 1996 the inflationary trend was accordingly uneven; its rapid acceleration in the first six months caused the Bank of Israel to adopt a restrictive monetary policy and to raise its interest rates on sources. Consequently, inflation decreased in the second half of 1996 to an annual average of 6.2%. In 1996 high rates of interest, compared with overseas rates, contributed to an inflow of foreign capital. In relation to a 'basket' of five major foreign currencies, the shekel depreciated by a mere 1.6% in 1996—in contrast to the rate of increase of consumer prices.

While the deceleration of economic growth in 1996 was largely the result of significant reduction in the rate of growth of both exports and investment, private consumption expanded by 6.1% in 1996—equivalent to an increase of 3.4% per head.

The unemployment rate continued to decline from its record level of 11.2% in 1992 to 6.6% in June 1996. The reduction of unemployment concurrent with the process of immigrant absorption was regarded as a highly impressive achievement. Despite the apparent reduction in unemployment, the number of job-seekers actually increased in 1996, owing mainly to the large influx of immigrants into Israel. In the final quarter of 1996 the unemployment level began to increase, rising to 7% at the end of the year. Real wages per labour hour increased by 1.4% in 1996, while wages in the business sector rose by 2.1%: a significant contrast to the annual average decrease of 1.7% in

1991–95. Labour productivity in the business sector also grew by 1.4% during 1996.

In 1996, as in previous years, there was a substantial deficit in the operations of the state budget. Total revenue (including borrowings from the National Insurance Institute) in 1996 was 116,648m. shekels. This amount excludes grants received from abroad (12,985m. shekels) and proceeds from the sale of government assets (349m. shekels). Total expenditure (including repayments to the National Insurance Institute) in the same year was 141,099m. shekels. This excludes net lending operations of the Government (807m. shekels).

In the first four months of 1996 the Bank of Israel's reduced interest rates on monetary tenders stabilized to a nominal annual average of 13.9% (an effective rate of 14.9%). Between May and July, however, the central bank raised its lending rate to 17% (an effective rate of 18.5%) on an annual basis. In the last months of 1996 this was reduced by a cumulative 1.8%, and in March 1997 the rate returned to 13.9%. In mid-June, after the resignation of the Minister of Finance, Dan Meridor, an additional reduction of 1% in the interest rate was announced. However, in August 1997 the central bank announced that the rate would be increased to 13.4% in order to curb rising inflation. After various adjustments, the rate was reduced in May 1998 to 11.6%, its lowest level for four years.

During 1996 the stock market remained relatively stable and experienced a reduction in the volume of activity. High interest rates in local currency, large withdrawals from provident funds, and increased activity from non-resident investors made a significant impact on the capital market. Issues of capital on the Tel-Aviv Stock Exchange during 1996 totalled more than 758m. shekels. During 1996 the general share index decreased in real terms. The multi-sided index declined by 8.5%. In terms of December 1996 prices, average daily trade in that year was 108m. shekels, having decreased by 16.9% from the 130m. shekels recorded in 1995. At the end of 1996 the current market value of shares and negotiable securities was 117,000m. shekels at current prices. In the first quarter of 1997 the capital market recovered, however: the indexes of the *Mishtarim* (top 100 Tel-Aviv Stock Exchange shares) and the *Maof* (top 25 shares) registered yields of 16.4% and 15.9% respectively. Daily trading volumes also increased during this period, totalling an average of 140m. shekels.

In 1996 the means of payments expanded by 12%, matching the nominal GDP growth rate. In order to counteract the effects of the 66,000m. shekels allocated to finance the budget deficit, the Bank of Israel was authorized to increase the quota of its short-term debt certificates to 25% more (in nominal terms) than the 1995 limit. In addition, the central bank cancelled its monetary tenders. In 1996 the volume of unrestricted credit increased by 21%, in nominal terms, while the foreign currency component rose by 38%, its expansion having been encouraged by high interest in the local currency segment.

In 1997 Israel's GDP increased, in real terms, by only 1.9%. As the country's population increased by more than 2%, there was a decline in real GDP per head during the year. The average rate of unemployment in 1997 reached 7.7% of the labour force, compared with 6.7% in 1996. The rate stood at 7.1% in the first two quarters of 1997, 8.7% in the third quarter and 7.9% in the fourth quarter. Unemployment was 8.1% in the first quarter of 1998. Consumer prices increased at an average rate of 9.0% in 1997, and inflation slowed to 4.4% in the year to March 1998. According to provisional figures, state budget revenue in 1997 totalled 133,946m. shekels (with foreign grants providing a further 10,390m. shekels), while total expenditure was 153,801m. shekels.

AREA AND POPULATION

The total area of the State of Israel, within its 1949 armistice frontiers, amounts to 20,700 sq km. This compares with the area of Palestine under the British mandate, which totalled 27,090 sq km. At the census of 4 June 1983 the population of Israel (including East Jerusalem and the Golan Heights) was 4,037,620, of whom 3,349,997 (83%) were Jews. In addition, there were about 1m. persons in other areas which were brought under Israeli administration as a result of the 1967 war, and after the Sinai peninsula was evacuated at the end of April 1982. According to official estimates, the population (*de jure*) of

Israel at 31 December 1996 was 5,759,400, of whom 4,637,400 (80.5%) were Jews. At 31 December 1997 the population was estimated to have increased to 5,896,400, of whom 4,703,700 (79.8%) were Jews.

The population density of Israel was 184 per sq km at the June 1983 census and 262.4 per sq km at the end of 1996. The population is heavily concentrated in the coastal strip, with about three-quarters of the Jewish inhabitants and nearly two-thirds of the non-Jewish population located between Ashkelon and Naharia. According to official estimates at the end of 1996, the Tel-Aviv District had a population of 1,139,700, accounting for 19.8% of the total population. A further 1,257,500 (21.8%) lived in the Central District, 758,200 (13.2%) in the Haifa District, 798,700 (13.9%) in the Southern District (comprising almost two-thirds of Israel's land area, but including the Negev Desert, which is largely uninhabited except for nomads), 977,900 (17%) in the Northern District (including 32,600 in the Golan Heights) and 677,200 (11.8%) in the Jerusalem District. The remaining 150,200 were Israelis residing at Jewish localities in the West Bank and the Gaza Strip. Of the 1996 population, 5,246,900 (comprising 4,204,100 Jews and 1,042,900 non-Jews), or 91.1% of the total, were defined as urban, i.e. resident in localities with 2,000 or more inhabitants. The remaining 433,300 Jews and 79,200 non-Jews were rural residents. Within this total there were 47,300 persons (7,000 Jews and 40,300 non-Jews), including Bedouin tribes, who were living outside localities.

The main reason for the growth of the Jewish population has been immigration, accounting for 58% of the yearly increase between 1948 and 1977. On 31 December 1996, 38.4% of the Jewish population had been born abroad. These included 1,202,200 born in Europe and America, 327,100 in Africa and 249,900 in Asia. Of the 2,858,200 Israeli-born Jews, 1,198,400 were second-generation Israelis. Immigration up to 1948 totalled 482,857 persons, of whom nearly 90% came from Europe and America. The biggest wave of immigrants arrived within six years of the founding of the new state. These were refugees from war-torn Europe, followed by Jews emigrating from the Arab states. Large numbers have come from North Africa as a result of political developments there, and during 1955–64 more than 200,000 emigrated from Africa into Israel. Since 1956 immigration from Eastern Europe has resumed. In the mid-1960s immigration declined, falling from 55,036 in 1964 to 14,469 in 1967, but the level of immigration rose considerably after the 1967 war, bringing the total numbers of immigrants between 1965 and 1974 to more than 300,000. Almost 70% of these came from Europe and America. After the Yom Kippur war, immigration declined again, falling from 54,886 in 1973 to 31,981 in 1974, and to 19,754 in 1976. Immigrants totalled 12,599 in 1981, rising to 19,981 in 1984, including 7,800 Ethiopian Jews (Falashas). In 1988 the number of people who emigrated from Israel totalled 18,900 (including Israelis who had spent more than one year abroad), while 13,034 people settled in Israel. In 1989 the number of immigrants, mainly from the USSR, rose sharply, to 24,050 people; a further increase, to 199,516 people, was reported in 1990; in 1996 the number totalled 70,919.

In 1996 the Israeli civilian labour force averaged 2,156,700, or 53.7% of the population aged 15 years and over, and comprised 43.5% women and 56.5% men. The growth in the labour force from 735,800 in 1960 was due chiefly to the rise in total population, since the participation rate declined slightly. On average, unemployment affected 6.7% of the labour force in 1996, and totalled 144,100 individuals. In 1997 unemployment averaged 169,800 persons (7.7% of the labour force).

During 1996, of 2,012,700 employees, some 51,000 were employed in agriculture, forestry and fishing; 405,100 in mining and manufacturing; 18,500 in electricity and water; 150,000 in construction; 331,200 in trade, maintenance, restaurants and hotels; 124,300 in transport, storage and communications; 261,200 were engaged in financing and business services; 660,600 in other services; and 10,800 in activities not adequately defined.

AGRICULTURE

The agricultural sector is relatively small, accounting for about 4.5% of domestic product in 1995 and employing 2.5% of the employed labour force in 1996. In spite of this, Israeli agriculture has attracted a great deal of international attention and more than any other sector of the economy, has been the focus of ideological pressure. For centuries, Jews in the Diaspora were barred from owning land and the Zionist movement therefore saw land settlement as one of the chief objectives of Jewish colonization. Since the establishment of the state, government agricultural policy has centred chiefly on the attainment of self-sufficiency in foodstuffs, in view of military considerations and Israel's possible isolation from its chief foreign food supplies; on the saving of foreign exchange through import substitution and the promotion of agricultural exports; and on the absorption of the large numbers of immigrants in the agricultural sector. In line with these objectives, the promotion of mixed farming and of co-operative farming settlements has also been an important element in government policy. Although the increase in agricultural production (which rose by an annual average of 0.05% during 1985–96) has resulted in Israel becoming largely self-sufficient in foodstuffs—it is seriously deficient only in grains, oils and fats—and important savings have been made in foreign exchange, government intervention in the agricultural sector has been criticized as having resulted in a misallocation of resources and in the impairment of the economic efficiency of agriculture.

Cultivation has undergone a profound transformation and from an extensive, primitive and mainly dry-farming structure it has developed into a modern intensive irrigated husbandry. A special feature of Israel's agriculture is its co-operative settlements which have been developed to meet the special needs and challenges encountered by a farming community new both to its surroundings and its profession. While there are a number of different forms of co-operative settlements, all are derived from two basic types: the *moshav* and the *kibbutz*. The *moshav* is a co-operative smallholders' village. Individual farms in any one village are of equal size and every farmer works his own land to the best of his ability. He is responsible for his own farm, but his economic and social security is ensured by the co-operative structure of the village, which handles the marketing of his produce, purchases his farm and household equipment, and provides him with credit and many other services. On 31 December 1996 a total of 179,900 people inhabited 455 *moshavim* and collective *moshavim*.

The *kibbutz* is a collective settlement of a unique form developed in Israel. It is based on common ownership of resources and on the pooling of labour, income and expenditure. Every member is expected to work to the best of his ability; he is paid no wages but is supplied by the *kibbutz* with all the goods and services he needs. The *kibbutz* is based on voluntary action and mutual liability, equal rights for all members, and assumes for them full material responsibility. On 31 December 1996 a total of 268 *kibbutzim* were inhabited by 122,500 people (2.1% of the total population).

During the years following the establishment of the State of Israel, a large-scale expansion of the area under cultivation took place. This was caused by the heavy influx of immigrants and the recultivation and rehabilitation of land from which Arabs had been forced to flee. The cultivated area increased from 1,650,000 dunums (1 dunum = 1,000 sq m) in the 1948/49 agricultural year to 4,110,000 dunums in 1958/59 and to 4,402,000 dunums in 1978/79. The cultivated area in 1995 totalled 4,366,000 dunums, including 1,993,000 dunums of irrigated crops. Production of water in 1996 reached 2,198m. cu m, of which 2,031 cu m was consumed domestically.

Without taking into consideration the cost or availability of irrigation water, it is estimated that the land potential ultimately available for farming under irrigation is 5.3m. dunums, while an estimated 4.1m. dunums are potentially available for dry farming. There are also 8.5m. dunums available for natural pasture and 0.9m. dunums for afforestation.

The main factor limiting agricultural development is not land, but the availability of water. Since, on average, 800 cu m of water are needed per annum to irrigate one dunum of cultivated area, it is obvious that Israel must harness all water resources. For this reason, the Government established a special Water Administration, headed by a Water Commissioner who has statutory powers to control and regulate both the supply and the consumption of water.

The Water Administration has been charged, among other tasks, with the implementation of the national water project. The purpose of this project is to convey a substantial part of the waters of the River Jordan and of other water sources from the north to southern Judaea and to the Negev, to store excess supplies of water from winter to summer and from periods of heavy rainfall to periods of drought, and to serve as a regulator between the various regional water supply systems. Essential to the national water project is the main conduit from Lake Tiberias to Rosh Haayin (near Tel-Aviv), known as the National Water Carrier, which has an annual capacity of 320m. cu m. Two other large schemes, also in operation, are the Western Galilee-Kishon and the Yarkon-Negev projects.

In 1996 agricultural production generated revenue of 8,828m. new shekels. In that year wheat production reached 147,959 metric tons, a decrease of 18% in comparison with 1995, while potato crops rose by 20% to 303,730 tons. Tomato production fell by 8% in 1996, to 450,697 tons. Cucumber production rose to 88,728 tons, and the output of carrots totalled 69,141 tons. Avocado production rose by 30% in 1995/96, to 75,069 tons, while banana production declined by 12% in the same crop year, to 85,959 tons.

In 1996 apple production declined by 32%, to 86,738 tons. Production of table grapes totalled 45,163 tons, and that of wine grapes 32,000 tons, in the same year.

Cultivation of citrus fruit is one of the oldest and most important agricultural activities, and produces the main export crop. In 1996 Israel exported 341,535 tons of citrus fruit, valued at $170m., a decline in value of 4% in comparison with 1995. Total area under cultivation in 1995 was 305,439 dunums. The Citrus Marketing and Control Board supervises all aspects of the growing and marketing of the fruit, particularly exports. The principal markets for citrus exports are the United Kingdom, Germany and France.

Increasing emphasis is being laid on the cultivation of floral plants. About 90% of production is usually exported to the European Union (EU, formerly European Community (EC)). In 1996 Israel exported 1,262m. flowers and ornamental branches (mainly roses, carnations and gypsophilia), earning $196.6m., an increase of 2% compared with the previous year. The state-owned Flower Marketing Board is increasing the number of its packing-houses, and is investing heavily in modern equipment. In 1995, 11,298 dunums were under glasshouse cultivation.

In 1996 production of cotton lint and seed cotton rose by 18%, to 132,000 tons. Some 16,095 tons of cotton fibres were exported in that year, earning $47m. In 1996 Israel exported an estimated $15m.-worth of potatoes.

In 1996 production of cows' milk reached 1,100m. litres.

In the poultry sector, egg production reached 1,547m. in 1996. In the same year Israel's output of poultry meat totalled 279,249 tons (296,819 tons in 1995). Beef production (live weight) totalled 24,411 tons in 1996 (22,457 tons in 1995). Fish production reached 13,696 tons in 1996 (13,262 tons in 1995).

CONSTRUCTION AND INDUSTRY

As a unit, construction is the leading sector in Israel since, with affiliated industries (cement, wood, glass and ceramics), it accounts for about 20% of GNP. During 1996 there were 9,390,000 sq m of building area completed, of which 2,045,000 sq m were public buildings and 7,345,000 sq m private constructions.

In 1996 there were 18,993 establishments, which engaged employees whose number totalled 374,800. Of these establishments, 450 engaged between 100 and 300 persons, and 138 more than 300 persons. In the latter category 112,400 were employed. On the other hand, 9,083 establishments engaged four or fewer persons, and 4,091 between five and nine persons; 18,603 establishments belonged in 1996 to the private sector, 363 to the Histadrut (the National Labour Federation) and 27 to the public sector (mainly government companies). The main branches of these establishments were: metal products; wood and its products; clothing and made-up textiles; food, beverages and tobacco.

Israel's industry was originally developed to supply such basic commodities as soap, vegetable oil and margarine, bread, ice, printing and electricity. It used raw materials available locally to produce citrus juices and other citrus by-products, canned fruit and vegetables, cement, glass and bricks. In order to save foreign exchange, imports of manufactured goods were curtailed, thus giving local industry the opportunity of adding local labour value to semi-manufactures imported from abroad.

Although most of Israel's industrial production is still for domestic consumption, industrial exports (excluding diamonds) constituted 91% of total exports in 1996. In this area also, there has been a very rapid expansion as a result of tax and investment incentives from the government. The value of Israeli industrial exports, only US $18m. in 1950, had risen to $780m. by 1971, and by 1996 had reached $12,986m. (excluding diamonds).

Israel's most important industrial export product is cut and polished diamonds, most of the expertise for the finishing of which was supplied by immigrants from the Low Countries. In 1996 Israel exported $5,260.5m.-worth of cut diamonds, compared with $4,921.6m.-worth supplied in 1995, and was one of the world's largest traders, second only to Belgium in processing diamonds, with approximately three-quarters of the international market in medium-sized stones, Israel's speciality. Israel obtains about 50% of its rough diamonds directly from the Central Selling Organization (the marketing arm of De Beers).

Excluding diamonds (which accounted for almost 26% of industrial exports in 1996), industrial exports consisted of 3.3% foodstuffs; 5.5% textiles, clothing and leather; 1.6% mining and quarrying products; 13.2% chemical and chemical products; 27.7% metal products, machinery and electrical and electronic equipment. The value of all exports rose by 277% between 1980 and 1996.

The food, beverage and tobacco industries accounted for 12% of manufactures in 1995. About 90% of output was sold on the local market; the rest, such as juices, wines, chocolate and coffee, was sold abroad. The value of manufactured food exports totalled $608.5m. in 1996, compared with $616.5m. in 1995.

The textiles and clothing industry, which was developed chiefly because of its low capital-labour ratio, accounted for some 9% of industrial production in 1996, when it exported goods worth some $999.3m.

Israel also has a rapidly expanding electronics industry, specializing in equipment for military and communications purposes. The value of exports from this sector and of metal products and machinery rose from $12.8m. in 1970 to $5,026.5m. in 1996.

In view of the heavy power needs of irrigation and the water installations, agriculture as well as industry is a large-scale consumer of electricity. Total installed generating capacity at the end of 1996 was 7,736 MW. Generation during 1996 totalled 32,497m. kWh. Out of 29,633m. kWh total sales of electricity, industry used about 26%. Total water production during 1996 reached 2,198m. cu m.

MINERALS

The Petroleum Law of 1952 regulates the conditions for the granting of licences for petroleum prospecting, divides the country into petroleum districts and fixes a basic royalty of 12.5%. Petroleum was discovered in 1955 at the Heletz-Bror field on the coastal plain and later at Kokhav, Brur and Negba. Signs of petroleum were also discovered near Ashdod. From the time of the 1967 war to the 1975 disengagement agreement, Israel was able to exploit the petroleum resources of the Sinai and, during 1978–79, those of the Suez Gulf (Alma fields). In July 1988 the Israeli Government awarded an offshore oil-prospecting concession of 7,000 sq km, about 16 km from Israel's southern Mediterranean coast, to a consortium of local and foreign companies headed by the late Dr Armand Hammer, chairman of Occidental Petroleum Inc. The consortium, Negev Joint Venture, invested $25.5m. in test drilling over a three-year period from autumn 1988.

Output of natural gas from Rosh-Zohar in the Dead Sea area, Kidod, Hakanaim and Barbur is transported through a 29-km pipeline (diameter 15 cm) to the Dead Sea potash works at Sodom and through a 49-km line (diameter 10 cm or 15 cm) to towns in the Negev and to the Oron phosphate plant. Production totalled 21.3m. cu m in 1994.

Lacking large scale resources of fuel and power, Israel is forced to import more than 90% of its energy requirements. Imports of petroleum and petroleum products, which rose in value from $210.6m. in 1973 to $597m. in the following year and to $775m. in 1978, reached about $2,000m. in 1980 and

cost $2,141.2m., at current prices, in 1996. In the same year petroleum constituted 7% of all goods imports (or 21% of the trade deficit). The large increases in the petroleum import bill since 1979 are directly attributable to the peace agreement with Egypt. In 1978 Israel produced one-quarter of its oil requirements from the Alma oilfields which it discovered in Sinai. The Alma fields were handed over to Egypt in 1979, in accordance with the terms of the peace treaty. Israel now imports most of its crude oil requirements of about 48m. barrels per year under long-term contracts with Egypt (which provides about 25% of the total), Mexico (35%) and Norway (10%), and buys the remainder on the 'spot' market. Most imported crude oil is refined at the Haifa oil refinery, which has a capacity of more than 6m. tons per year.

The Dead Sea, which contains potash, bromides, magnesium and other salts in high concentration, is the country's chief source of mineral wealth. The potash works on the southern shore of the Dead Sea are owned by Dead Sea Works Ltd. The works are linked by road to Beersheba, from where a railway runs northward. Phosphates are mined at Oron in the Negev, and in the Arava. A total of 2.45m. metric tons of phosphate rock was produced in 1996. In the same year Israel produced 12,243 tons of sodium hydrochlorate, 40,892 tons of caustic soda, 34,630 tons of chlorine, 8,324 tons of paraffin, and 2,939 tons of potassium carbonate.

Gold in potentially commercial quantities was discovered near the Negev copper mines in 1988, and further exploration is under way.

BALANCE OF PAYMENTS AND TRADE

Israel's balance-of-payments deficit on trade in goods and services stood at US $10,185m. in 1996, declining to $8,490m. in 1997. The value of exports of goods and services in 1997 amounted to $30,320m., compared with $28,800m. in 1996, while the value of imports amounted to $38,810m., compared with $38,984m. in 1996.

Israel's deficit on merchandise trade, which relates to goods only, amounted to $5,848m. in 1997, compared with the record deficit of $7,646m. incurred in 1996.

In 1997 net transfer payments, most of which consisted of US aid, were worth $6,267m., compared with $6,370m. in 1996. They covered 73.8% of the deficit on goods and services in 1997, compared with 62.5% in 1996. Israel recorded a deficit on the current account of the balance of payments (goods, services, income and transfers) in each of the years 1990–97. The deficit increased from $6,205m. in 1995 to a record $6,646m. in 1996, but was reduced to $5,014m. in 1997.

The value of Israel's merchandise exports increased from $20,758m. in 1996 to $21,894m. in 1997. Meanwhile, imports of goods (valued f.o.b.) declined from $28,404m. in 1996 to $27,742m. in 1997. The focus of Israel's foreign trade is mainly the EU and North America. An Israeli-EC Chamber of Commerce was founded in June 1986. Duties on goods imported from the EC and the USA were reduced by an average of 60% on 1 January 1987, under the terms of separate bilateral trade agreements. Spain refused to sign the draft agricultural goods access agreement between the EC and Israel in December 1986, demanding the reduction by Israel of tariffs on Spanish industrial exports in line with the reductions on EC goods implemented on 1 January 1987. In October 1988 the European Parliament approved three trade protocols, giving Israel privileged access to EC markets, having withheld its approval in March and July and delayed further votes, in protest against Israel's treatment of Palestinians during the *intifada* in the Occupied Territories. The Israeli Government, in an attempt to placate the EC, had undertaken to allow Palestinian farmers in the West Bank to export their produce directly to the EC, unimpeded by the occupation authorities.

BANKING, TRANSPORT AND COMMUNICATIONS

Israel possesses a highly developed banking system, consisting of a central bank (Bank of Israel), 14 commercial banks, five mortgage banks, and other financial institutions. Nevertheless, three bank-groups—namely Bank Leumi group, Bank Hapoalim and Bank Discount—hold 92% of the total assets of the banking system. Their subsidiaries are represented all over the world and enjoy a growing reputation; due to devaluation their share in the consolidated balance sheet is increasing markedly. Long-term credits are granted by mortgage banks, the Israel Agricultural Bank, the Industrial Development Bank and the Maritime Bank. At the end of 1996 the amount of outstanding credit allocated by the banks to the public stood at 146,248m. shekels in Israeli currency and 54,190m. shekels in foreign currency.

The function of the central bank is to issue currency (and commemorative coins), to accept deposits from banking institutions and extend temporary advances to the government, to act as the government's sole fiscal and banking agent and to manage the public debt. Its Governor supervises the liquidity position of the commercial banks and regulates the volume of bank advances.

The significant changes that have characterized the financial world and international capital markets in recent years have also affected the Israeli banking system. The banks are gradually losing their traditional monopoly as financial intermediaries, as other financial entities assume this role. One consequence of this development has been to encourage the banks to enter other fields of financial activity, hitherto closed to them.

Since 1949 Israel has operated its own international air carrier—El Al Israel National Airlines Ltd. Regular scheduled services to Europe, the USA, Canada, Cyprus, and parts of Africa and Asia are maintained. In June 1997 the Government announced plans to privatize the airline by the end of 1998. It was proposed that 10% of El Al's shares would be offered to employees and the remainder would be sold to the public. In 1976 a new private company—CAL, which specializes in cargo air transportation to Europe—was constituted. In addition, 14 international airlines call at Ben-Gurion Airport, near Tel-Aviv. The number of passengers carried in 1996 reached 7.36m. Israel's merchant navy has been undergoing expansion, while the passenger fleet has been practically abolished. The number of ships under the Israeli flag at 31 December 1997 totalled 55. Their combined displacement was 793,890m. gross tons. Israel Shipyards Ltd, at Haifa, can build ships with a capacity of as much as 10,000 dwt. In the north, the port of Haifa and its Kishon harbour extension provide Israel's main port facilities. The south is served by the port at the head of the Gulf of Aqaba, and mainly by the deep-water port at Ashdod, some 50 km south of Tel-Aviv. The amount of cargo loaded at seaports in 1996 totalled 10.68m. metric tons, while the amount unloaded was 25.9m. tons (including coal).

Israeli railways operate some 610 km of main lines and 355 km of branch lines. The service extends from Nahariya, north of Haifa to Jerusalem and Tel-Aviv and then southwards through Beersheba. In 1965 it reached Dimona and in 1970 the phosphate works at Oron. Traction is wholly by diesel locomotives. In 1995 traffic consisted of 4.8m. passengers and 9.38m. tons of freight.

Roads are the chief means of transport. At the beginning of 1996 there were 14,700 km of paved roads, of which 4,845 km were inter-urban, out of which 300 km were motorways with four or more lanes. Travelling them at the end of 1996 were 1,184,765 private vehicles, 11,214 buses and coaches and 277,880 lorries and vans.

TOURISM

The decline in the number of tourists entering Israel which began in 1973 (a slowdown had already been recorded in the second half of 1972), continued in 1975; 1976 witnessed a recovery, and the number of tourists rose, reaching 1,175,800 in 1980. Then, in 1981, a slight drop, to 1,137,055, was recorded, and in 1982 the industry slumped by 12%, with only 997,510 tourists entering Israel. The war in Lebanon, labour disputes at El Al and less favourable exchange rates for tourists were responsible for the situation. These reasons also contributed to the number of Israeli tourists leaving the country; in 1982 they totalled about 600,000, spending some US $600m. abroad. Nevertheless, 1984 witnessed a recovery, when 1,260,000 tourists visited the country, and income from tourism doubled in the six years up to 1984, reaching $1,000m. per year. In 1985 a total of 1,264,367 tourists visited Israel. In 1986 the total declined by 13%, to 1,101,481, and revenue from tourism fell by $107m. In 1987 the number of tourists rose by 25%, to 1,378,742, and revenue increased to a record $1,635m. In 1988, however, the number of tourists declined to 1,169,582, mainly as a result of continued unrest in the Occupied Territories. In 1989 the number of tourists rose slightly, to reach 1,176,500, with revenue totalling $1,467.7m. This increase continued throughout the first half of 1990. However, following Iraq's invasion of Kuwait in August 1990 and the ensuing crisis in the Persian (Arabian) Gulf region, the number of tourist arrivals declined sharply. The total for the year was 1,131,700. Revenue amounted to $1,381.7m. Tourism revived again in 1992, when some 1,502,092 tourist arrivals were recorded, and revenue from tourism amounted to $1,891m. In 1995 tourist arrivals totalled 2,214,646, an increase of 20% on the previous year's figure. Total revenue from tourism amounted to $2,784m. in that year. In 1996 tourism declined once again, however, by 9.5%, with 2,100,051 tourist arrivals generating revenues of $2,711m. This trend continued the following year: by August 1997 activity had reportedly decreased by 10% from the 1996 level and revenue was projected to fall to approximately $2,200m. by the end of the year.

Overall administration of Israeli tourism is sponsored by the Ministry of Tourism which maintains 20 offices abroad. It is also in charge of regulating tourist services in Israel, including arrangement of 'package' tours and the provision of multilingual guides. In 1976 the Ministry promoted the inauguration of charter flights from the USA and Europe to Israel. During 1995 a total of 4,803 charter flights landed in Israel, bringing some 1,259,466 passengers into the country.

Statistical Survey

Source: Central Bureau of Statistics, POB 13015, Hakirya, Romema, Jerusalem 91130; tel. 2-553553; fax 2-553325.

Area and Population

AREA, POPULATION AND DENSITY

Area (sq km)	
Land	21,501
Inland water	445
Total	21,946*
Population (*de jure*; census results)†	
20 May 1972	3,147,683
4 June 1983	
Males	2,011,590
Females	2,026,030
Total	4,037,620
Population (*de jure*; official estimates at 31 December)†	
1994	5,471,500
1995	5,609,100
1996	5,759,400
Density (per sq km) at 31 December 1996 . . .	262.4

* 8,473.4 sq miles. Area includes East Jerusalem, annexed by Israel in June 1967, and the Golan sub-district (1,176 sq km), annexed by Israel in December 1981.

† Including the population of East Jerusalem and Israeli residents in certain other areas under Israeli military occupation since June 1967. Beginning in 1981, figures also include non-Jews in the Golan sub-district, an Israeli-occupied area of Syrian territory. Census results exclude adjustment for underenumeration.

ADMINISTERED TERRITORIES*

	Area (sq km)	Estimated population (31 December 1993)
Golan	1,176	29,000
Judaea and Samaria . . .	5,879	1,084,400‡
Gaza Area†	378	748,900‡
Total	7,433	1,862,300

The area figures in this table refer to 1 October 1973. No later figures are available.

* The area and population of the Administered Territories have changed as a result of the October 1973 war.

† Not including El-Arish and Sinai, which, as of April 1979 and April 1982 respectively, were returned to Egypt.

‡ Excluding Israelis in Jewish localities. The population in this category at 31 December 1993 totalled 111,600 in Judaea and Samaria, and 4,800 in the Gaza Area.

POPULATION BY RELIGION (estimates, 31 December 1994)

	Number	%
Jews	4,441,100	81.17
Muslims	781,500	14.28
Christians	157,300	2.87
Druze and others	91,700	1.68
Total	5,471,500	100.00

PRINCIPAL TOWNS (estimated population at 31 December 1994)

Jerusalem (capital) .	578,800*	Beersheba	147,900
Tel-Aviv—Jaffa .	355,200	Netanya . . .	144,900
Haifa . . .	246,700	Bat Yam . . .	142,300
Holon . . .	163,700	Bene Beraq . .	127,100
Rishon LeZiyyon .	160,200	Ramat Gan . .	122,200
Petach-Tikva . .	152,000		

* Including East Jerusalem, annexed in June 1967.

BIRTHS, MARRIAGES AND DEATHS*

	Registered live births		Registered marriages		Registered deaths	
	Number	Rate (per 1,000)	Number	Rate (per 1,000)	Number	Rate (per 1,000)
1989 . .	100,757	22.3	32,303	7.1	28,600	6.3
1990 . .	103,349	22.2	31,746	6.8	28,734	6.2
1991 . .	105,725	21.4	32,291	6.5	31,266	6.3
1992 . .	110,062	21.5	32,769	6.4	33,327	6.5
1993 . .	112,330	21.3	34,344	6.5	33,000	6.3
1994 . .	114,543	21.2	n.a.	n.a.	33,535	6.2
1995 . .	116,461	21.0	34,051	6.1	35,117	6.3
1996 . .	120,749	21.2	34,561	6.1	34,420	6.0

* Including East Jerusalem.

Expectation of life (years at birth, 1993): Males 75.3; Females 79.1 (Source: UN, *Demographic Yearbook*).

IMMIGRATION*

	1992	1993	1994
Immigrants:			
on immigrant visas. . . .	70,580	68,624	69,226
on tourist visas† . . .	5,825	7,650	9,930
Potential immigrants:			
on potential immigrant visas	103	91	36
on tourist visas†	522	440	652
Total	77,057	76,805	79,844

* Excluding immigrating citizens (2,868 in 1992; 3,467 in 1993; 3,315 in 1994) and Israeli residents returning from abroad.

† Figures refer to tourists who changed their status to immigrants or potential immigrants.

ECONOMICALLY ACTIVE POPULATION (annual averages, '000 persons aged 15 years and over, excluding armed forces)*

	1994	1995	1996
Agriculture, forestry and fishing	62.3	57.2	51.0
Mining and quarrying . . .	5.7 }	404.6	405.1
Manufacturing	390.4 }		
Electricity and water . . .	20.3	19.1	18.5
Construction.	118.0	140.9	150.0
Trade, restaurants and hotels. .	280.8	n.a.	331.2
Transport, storage and communications . . .	109.0	115.0	124.3
Financing and business services	206.4	224.3	261.2
Public and community services .}	667.3 {	515.5 }	660.6
Personal and other services . .}		125.3 }	
Activities not adequately defined	11.2	n.a.	10.8
Total employed . . .	1,871.4	1,967.9	2,012.7
Unemployed	158.3	133.0	144.1
Total civilian labour force .	2,029.7	2,100.9	2,156.7
Males	1,162.0	n.a.	1,217.7
Females	867.7	n.a.	939.0

* Figures are estimated independently, so the totals may not be the sum of the component parts.

Agriculture

PRINCIPAL CROPS ('000 metric tons)

	1994	1995	1996
Wheat	103	180	150
Barley	1	7	7*
Potatoes.	272	281	280*
Groundnuts (in shell). . .	24	24	24*
Cottonseed	55	70	70*
Olives	27	37	37*
Cabbages	76	69	69*
Tomatoes	430	504	504*
Pumpkins, squash and gourds* .	34	34	34
Cucumbers*	85	85	85
Peppers (green)*	55	55	55
Onions (dry).	67	100	100*
Carrots	88	71	71*
Watermelons*	125	125	125
Melons*	90	90	90
Grapes	80	86	86*
Apples	86	134	134*
Peaches*	59	59	59
Oranges	357	381	381*
Tangerines, mandarins, clementines and satsumas . .	100	130	130*
Lemons and limes . . .	26	27	27*
Grapefruit	338	404	404*
Avocados*	50	50	50
Bananas	90	105	105*
Strawberries*	13	13	13
Cotton (lint)	31	43	43*

* FAO estimate(s).

Source: FAO, *Production Yearbook*.

LIVESTOCK ('000 head, year ending September)

	1994	1995	1996*
Cattle	368	379	379
Pigs.	113*	109*	105
Sheep	339	352	352
Goats	96	91	90
Poultry	27,000*	27,000*	27,000

* FAO estimate(s).

Source: FAO, *Production Yearbook*.

LIVESTOCK PRODUCTS ('000 metric tons)

	1994	1995	1996
Beef and veal	37	37*	37*
Mutton and lamb* . . .	5	5	5
Pig meat*	8	8	8
Poultry meat	227	227*	227*
Cows' milk	1,073	1,136	1,136*
Sheep's milk.	17	17	17*
Goats' milk	13	12	12*
Cheese*	86	86	86
Butter	5	4	4*
Hen eggs	117	102†	98†
Honey	2	2	2*

* FAO estimate(s).   † Unofficial figure.

Source: FAO, *Production Yearbook*.

Forestry

ROUNDWOOD REMOVALS
('000 cubic metres, excl. bark)

	1993	1994	1995
Sawlogs, veneer logs and logs for sleepers	36	36	36
Pulpwood	32	32	32
Other industrial wood . . .	32	32	32
Fuel wood	13	13	13
Total	113	113	113

Source: FAO, *Yearbook of Forest Products*.

Fishing

(metric tons, live weight)

	1993	1994	1995
Inland waters	15,579	17,159	17,410
Mediterranean and Black Sea .	3,387	3,295	3,154
Indian Ocean	80	—	—
Total catch	19,046	20,454	20,564

Source: FAO, *Yearbook of Fishery Statistics*.

Mining

	1993	1994	1995
Crude petroleum (million litres)	5.9	4.5	n.a.
Natural gas (million cu m) . .	24	21.3	n.a.
Phosphate rock ('000 metric tons)	2,662	2,779	2,642
Potash salts ('000 metric tons)* .	2,139	2,073	2,214

* Figures refer to K_2O content.

Industry

SELECTED PRODUCTS
('000 metric tons, unless otherwise indicated)

	1992	1993	1994
Refined vegetable oils (metric tons)	56,463	57,558	45,447
Margarine	35.1	33.8	24.7
Wine ('000 litres). . . .	12,373	12,733	n.a.
Beer ('000 litres). . . .	51,078	58,681	50,750
Cigarettes (metric tons) . .	5,742	5,525	5,638
Newsprint (metric tons) . .	0	247	0
Writing and printing paper (metric tons)	66,334	65,426	65,790
Other paper (metric tons). .	32,368	30,446	28,985
Cardboard (metric tons) . .	92,072	95,108	103,142
Rubber tyres ('000) . . .	892	854	966
Ammonia (metric tons) . .	41,072	n.a.	n.a.
Ammonium sulphate (metric tons)	12,444	n.a.	n.a.
Sulphuric acid	138	n.a.	n.a.
Chlorine (metric tons) . .	33,912	35,241	37,555
Caustic soda (metric tons) .	29,459	29,851	32,765
Polyethylene (metric tons) .	128,739	144,147	126,979
Paints (metric tons) . . .	58,963	57,429	53,260
Cement	3,960	4,536	4,800
Commercial vehicles (number) .	852	836	1,260
Electricity (million kWh) . .	24,731	26,042	28,327

1995 ('000 metric tons, unless otherwise indicated): Margarine 36; Cigarettes (metric tons) 4,933; Rubber tyres ('000) 918; Chlorine 38; Caustic soda 45; Paints 57.7; Cement 6,204; Commercial vehicles (number) 1,217; Electricity (provisional, million kWh) 29,100 (Source: UN, *Industrial Commodity Statistics Yearbook*).

1996: Commercial vehicles (number) 1,199 (Source: International Road Federation, *World Road Statistics*).

Finance

CURRENCY AND EXCHANGE RATES

Monetary Units

100 agorot (singular: agora) = 1 new sheqel (plural: sheqalim) or shekel.

Sterling and Dollar Equivalents (31 May 1998)

£1 sterling = 5.959 new shekels;
US $1 = 3.654 new shekels;
100 new shekels = £16.78 = $27.36.

Average Exchange Rate (new shekels per US $)

1995   3.0113
1996   3.1917
1997   3.4494

Note: The new shekel, worth 1,000 of the former units, was introduced on 1 January 1986.

STATE BUDGET (million new shekels)

Revenue*	1996	1997†	1998†
Tax revenue‡	93,941	111,365	121,100
Taxes on income and profits .	42,421	51,290	58,070
Companies	9,597	12,030	n.a.
Individuals	32,824	39,260	n.a.
Taxes on property . . .	3,634	3,860	3,440
Taxes on goods and services .	46,885	54,715	58,030
Value-added tax . . .	32,506	37,725	40,440
Excises	5,647	6,990	7,430
Fuel	4,159	5,280	5,620
Purchase tax . . .	7,672	8,820	8,850
Non-tax revenue	22,707	27,998	27,488
Interest	2,465	2,840	3,180
Loans from National Insurance Institute	5,370	6,872	6,600
Fees, royalties, pension provisions, etc. . . .	5,618	6,064	8,570
Revenue for revenue-dependent expenditure	7,539	10,712	7,923
Total	116,648	139,363	148,588

Expenditure§	1996	1997†	1998†
General administration . .	8,242	9,514	10,722
Defence	30,852	32,297	34,793
Public order	3,521	3,912	4,260
Education	20,211	23,339	25,508
Health	8,802	15,204	13,097
Labour and welfare . . .	21,891	18,709	19,905
Other social services . .	11,769	13,539	13,063
Housing	9,226	10,646	9,895
Economic services . . .	9,792	11,157	11,522
Manufacturing . . .	3,290	3,738	3,948
Unallocable and other functions .	26,679	32,218	35,089
Interest	20,403	22,476	23,800
General transfers . . .	4,142	3,812	4,732
Reserves‖	—	3,781	4,220
Sub-total	141,758	159,889	167,957
Adjustment	−659	−88	893
Total	141,099	159,801	168,850
Current‖	133,622	151,114	160,114
Capital	7,477	8,687	8,736

* Excluding proceeds from sale of assets (million new shekels): 349 in 1996; 4,300 (forecast) in 1997; 4,300 (forecast) in 1998. Also excluded are grants received from abroad (million new shekels): 12,985 in 1996; 10,695 (forecast) in 1997; 11,070 (forecast) in 1998.

† Figures are forecasts. Provisional totals (in million new shekels) for 1997 are: Revenue 133,946 (tax 107,120; non-tax 26,826), excluding grants from abroad (10,390); Expenditure 153,801, excluding net lending.

‡ Excluding fees, classified as non-tax revenue. The figure for 1996 includes an adjustment (−264 million new shekels).

§ Expenditure includes repayments to the National Insurance Institute (million new shekels): 3,230 in 1996; 3,882 (forecast) in 1997; 4,480 (forecast) in 1998. It excludes the central Government's lending minus repayments (million new shekels): 807 in 1996; 629 (forecast) in 1997; −809 (forecast) in 1998.

‖ Net transfers to reserves are included in current expenditure.

Source: IMF, *Israel: Background Studies, Information Notes, and Statistical Appendix* (April 1998).

CENTRAL BANK RESERVES (US $ million at 31 December)

	1995	1996	1997
Gold*	0.5	0.4	0.4
IMF special drawing rights . .	0.6	1.4	0.0
Foreign exchange . . .	8,118.7	11,413.2	20,332.0
Total	8,119.8	11,415.0	20,332.5

* Valued at SDR 35 per troy ounce.

Source: IMF, *International Financial Statistics*.

MONEY SUPPLY (million new shekels at 31 December)

	1995	1996	1997
Currency outside banks . . .	6,731	7,772	8,767
Demand deposits at deposit money banks . .	9,870	12,227	13,502
Total money (incl. others) . .	16,716	n.a.	n.a.

Source: IMF, *International Financial Statistics*.

COST OF LIVING

(Consumer Price Index, annual averages; base: 1990 = 100)

	1994	1995	1996
Food (incl. beverages) . . .	150.3	161.1	176.6
Fuel and light . . .	157.9	176.7	189.6
Clothing (incl. footwear) . . .	131.3	140.7	150.1
Rent	232.6	265.7	308.1
All items (incl. others) . . .	166.0	182.7	203.4

Source: ILO, *Yearbook of Labour Statistics*.

1997: Food 193.1; All items 221.7 (Source: UN, *Monthly Bulletin of Statistics*).

NATIONAL ACCOUNTS (million new shekels at current prices)

National Income and Product (provisional)

	1992	1993	1994
Compensation of employees . .	84,038	97,959	120,490
Operating surplus . . .	35,501	39,277	43,683
Domestic factor incomes . .	119,539	137,236	164,173
Consumption of fixed capital . .	22,407	26,908	32,698
Gross domestic product at factor cost	141,946	164,144	196,871
Indirect taxes	34,897	38,451	44,531
Less Subsidies	4,934	4,801	5,213
GDP in purchasers' values .	171,909	197,794	236,189
Factor income received from abroad	3,994	3,589	3,695
Less Factor income paid abroad .	8,937	8,958	10,363
Gross national product . .	166,966	192,425	229,521
Less Consumption of fixed capital .	22,407	26,908	32,698
National income in market prices	144,559	165,517	196,823
Other current transfers received from abroad . . .	17,178	19,425	21,039
Less Other current transfers paid abroad	719	1,002	904
National disposable income .	161,018	183,940	216,958

Source: UN, *National Accounts Statistics*.

Expenditure on the Gross Domestic Product

	1995	1996	1997
Government final consumption expenditure	77,695	90,774	100,646
Private final consumption expenditure	161,831	187,831	209,611
Increase in stocks	3,408	2,547	2,013
Gross fixed capital formation .	61,393	70,634	71,000
Total domestic expenditure .	304,328	351,786	383,270
Exports of goods and services .	82,919	93,660	105,381
Less Imports of goods and services	126,074	141,634	150,850
GDP in purchasers' values .	261,173	303,812	337,800
GDP at constant 1990 prices .	141,328	147,628	150,488

Source: IMF, *International Financial Statistics*.

Net Domestic Product by Economic Activity (at factor cost)

	1992	1993	1994
Agriculture, hunting, forestry and fishing	3,375	3,304	4,021
Manufacturing, mining and quarrying	24,698	29,007	31,206
Electricity, gas and water . .	1,943	2,266	2,750
Construction	9,997	10,418	12,877
Wholesale and retail trade, restaurants and hotels . .	13,217	15,779	18,635
Transport, storage and communications . . .	9,131	10,264	11,642
Finance, insurance, real estate and business services . .	29,755	36,003	42,497
Government services . . .	27,042	31,068	39,946
Other community, social and personal services	5,045	6,003	7,249
Statistical discrepancy . .	−157	−992	420
Sub-total	124,046	143,120	171,243
Less Imputed bank service charge	5,835	6,064	6,602
Other adjustments (incl. errors and omissions)	1,331	181	−468
Total	119,542	137,236	164,173

Source: UN, *National Accounts Statistics*.

BALANCE OF PAYMENTS (US $ million)

	1995	1996	1997
Exports of goods f.o.b. . . .	19,237	20,758	21,894
Imports of goods f.o.b. . . .	−26,834	−28,404	−27,742
Trade balance	−7,597	−7,646	−5,848
Exports of services . . .	7,733	8,042	8,426
Imports of services . . .	−9,842	−10,580	−11,068
Balance on goods and services	−9,706	−10,185	−8,490
Other income received . .	1,690	1,809	2,067
Other income paid . . .	−4,061	−4,641	−4,858
Balance on goods, services and income	−12,077	−13,016	−11,281
Current transfers received .	6,123	6,650	6,539
Current transfers paid . .	−251	−279	−273
Current balance . . .	−6,205	−6,646	−5,014
Capital account (net) . . .	1,408	1,538	1,778
Direct investment abroad .	−606	−670	−665
Direct investment from abroad .	1,548	2,091	2,706
Portfolio investment assets .	135	231	−125
Portfolio investment liabilities .	1,412	2,135	2,522
Other investment assets . .	−1,104	839	2,151
Other investment liabilities .	2,856	1,910	3,739
Net errors and omissions . .	1,639	1,958	2,255
Overall balance . . .	1,082	3,388	9,345

Source: IMF, *International Financial Statistics*.

External Trade

PRINCIPAL COMMODITIES (US $ million)

Imports c.i.f.*	1992	1993	1994
Food and live animals . . .	1,041.1	1,086.0	1,299.2
Crude materials (inedible) except fuels	567.2	552.9	599.3
Mineral fuels, lubricants, etc. .	1,464.5	1,521.5	1,439.1
Petroleum, petroleum products, etc.	1,460.9	1,517.5	1,434.5
Crude petroleum oils, etc. . .	1,327.1	1,349.3	1,242.0
Chemicals and related products	1,753.0	1,848.6	2,056.4
Organic chemicals . . .	394.8	442.9	496.3
Plastic materials, etc. . . .	446.1	442.7	477.7
Basic manufactures . . .	6,010.8	6,555.7	7,544.7
Textile yarn, fabrics, etc. . . .	632.5	692.2	744.2
Non-metallic mineral manufactures	3,502.3	3,952.4	4,602.7
Pearls, precious and semi-precious stone, unworked or worked	3,124.2	3,578.2	4,152.4
Diamonds (excl. sorted industrial diamonds), unmounted	3,078.1	3,541.6	4,124.7
Diamonds, rough, sorted and simply worked .	2,586.9	2,997.4	3,485.1
Diamonds, cut, etc., unmounted	491.2	544.2	639.7
Iron and steel	551.2	580.8	607.4
Machinery and transport equipment	5,981.1	6,706.9	8,228.3
Machinery specialized for particular industries . .	660.7	779.9	893.8
General industrial machinery, equipment and parts . .	773.5	838.0	994.3
Office machines and automatic data-processing equipment . .	556.2	620.9	743.7
Telecommunications and sound equipment	421.8	531.7	680.8
Other electrical machinery, apparatus, etc. . . .	1,179.8	1,406.1	1,762.6
Switchgear, parts, etc. . . .	312.6	395.2	513.7
Transistors, valves, etc. . .	292.8	392.4	502.0
Road vehicles and parts† . .	1,673.0	1,753.2	2,177.1
Passenger cars, excl. buses . .	1,049.2	1,003.9	1,257.8
Motor vehicles for goods transport and special purposes	351.5	454.0	588.4
Goods vehicles	329.9	432.0	532.3
Other transport equipment and parts†	323.5	370.1	532.7
Aircraft, associated equipment and parts†	151.0	296.9	503.8
Miscellaneous manufactured articles	1,406.5	1,661.6	1,948.2
Total (incl. others) . . .	18,813.6	20,517.7	23,778.9

Exports f.o.b.	1992	1993	1994
Food and live animals . . .	788.4	792.2	809.9
Vegetables and fruit	560.9	516.6	516.2
Crude materials (inedible) **except fuels**	423.3	403.1	469.3
Chemicals and related products	1,759.0	2,079.3	2,316.9
Organic chemicals . . .	495.0	566.8	625.7
Inorganic chemicals . . .	269.3	290.4	281.7
Manufactured fertilizers . .	296.3	238.1	288.1
Basic manufactures . .	4,664.0	5,036.7	6,046.4
Textile yarn, fabrics, etc. . . .	334.0	326.7	350.4
Non-metallic mineral manufactures	3,756.6	4,142.7	5,019.0
Pearls, precious and semi-precious stones, unworked or worked . . .	3,730.0	4,113.8	4,967.6
Diamonds (excl. sorted industrial diamonds), unmounted . . .	3,655.3	4,040.1	4,892.2
Diamonds, rough, sorted and simply worked .	445.0	398.2	524.6
Diamonds, cut, etc., unmounted . . .	3,210.3	3,642.0	4,367.2
Machinery and transport **equipment** . . .	3,589.6	4,603.4	5,182.7
Machinery specialized for particular industries . .	769.3	1,305.7	1,382.3
Printing and bookbinding machinery and parts . .	304.3	376.3	411.3
Machinery, apparatus and accessories for type-setting, etc.	253.5	319.4	260.1
General industrial machinery, equipment and parts . .	460.2	461.0	549.8
Office machines and automatic data-processing equipment . .	436.0	590.7	525.2
Telecommunications and sound equipment. . . .	694.2	906.3	1,197.9
Other electrical machinery, apparatus, etc. . . .	743.8	807.6	965.3
Transistors, valves, etc. . .	335.3	385.5	407.3
Electronic microcircuits . .	318.7	366.5	397.6
Road vehicles and other transport equipment and parts† . .	350.6	382.5	422.8
Aircraft, associated equipment and parts†	294.1	340.9	355.9
Miscellaneous manufactured **articles** . . .	1,742.1	1,772.5	1,961.4
Clothing (excl. footwear) . .	593.6	571.0	627.4
Professional, scientific and controlling instruments, etc. .	270.7	278.3	321.9
Jewellery, goldsmiths' and silversmiths' wares, etc. .	390.7	419.3	413.2
Jewellery of gold, silver or platinum-group metals (excl. watches and watch cases) and goldsmiths' or silversmiths' wares, incl. set gems . .	388.9	417.2	408.2
Articles of jewellery and parts, of precious metal or rolled precious metal . .	387.1	400.0	379.7
Total (incl. others)	13,082.3	14,825.3	16,934.0

* Figures exclude military goods. After deducting net returned imports, the value of total imports (in US $ million) was: 20,261.5 in 1992; 22,623.4 in 1993; 25,237.3 in 1994.

† Data on parts exclude tyres, engines and electrical parts.

Source: UN, *International Trade Statistics Yearbook*.

Total trade (US $ million, net of returned goods): Imports c.i.f. 29,579 in 1995, 31,686 in 1996, 30,783 in 1997; Exports f.o.b. 19,046 in 1995, 20,610 in 1996, 22,502 in 1997 (Source: UN, *Monthly Bulletin of Statitics*).

PRINCIPAL TRADING PARTNERS (US $ million)

Imports (excl. military goods)	1992	1993	1994
Belgium-Luxembourg . . .	2,391.0	2,503.2	3,038.4
France	844.7	857.6	1,058.0
Germany	2,246.9	2,132.2	2,467.5
Hong Kong	183.5	248.8	281.1
Italy	1,307.9	1,495.7	1,848.1
Japan	998.2	1,047.1	963.6
Korea, Republic . .	102.6	137.9	282.4
Netherlands	615.7	700.5	789.2
Southern African Customs Union .	261.5	244.0	234.9
Spain	203.8	208.5	398.0
Sweden	206.4	286.2	326.7
Switzerland-Liechtenstein .	1,265.6	1,432.0	1,447.8
United Kingdom	1,459.0	1,730.4	2,004.7
USA	3,229.5	3,634.5	4,256.3

Exports	1992	1993	1994
Australia	115.6	134.7	180.4
Belgium-Luxembourg . . .	650.4	797.5	910.4
France	620.5	576.1	584.0
Germany	762.7	786.6	850.3
Hong Kong	666.4	722.5	843.8
India	127.5	228.3	361.9
Italy	459.6	437.3	505.2
Japan	689.1	769.0	989.4
Netherlands	553.8	554.0	633.1
Philippines	109.9	187.1	207.9
Russia	67.2	118.5	192.5
Spain	242.8	199.2	236.3
Switzerland-Liechtenstein .	231.1	271.9	346.9
Thailand	91.1	146.7	248.9
United Kingdom	1,004.9	815.9	848.9
USA	3,995.8	4,621.7	5,262.4

Transport

RAILWAYS (traffic)

	1994	1995	1996
Freight ton-km (million) . . .	1,079	1,176	1,251
Passenger-km (million) . . .	238	267	294

ROAD TRAFFIC (vehicles in use)

	1994	1995	1996
Passenger cars	1,057,522	1,121,730	1,184,765
Buses and coaches . . .	10,429	10,794	11,214
Lorries and vans	246,824	261,799	277,880
Motorcycles and mopeds . .	58,323	64,695	69,011

Source: International Road Federation, *World Road Statistics*.

SHIPPING
Merchant Fleet (registered at 31 December)

	1995	1996	1997
Number of vessels	55	54	55
Displacement ('000 grt) . . .	598.7	678.9	793.9

Source: Lloyd's Register of Shipping, *World Fleet Statistics*.

International Sea-borne Freight Traffic ('000 metric tons)*

	1994	1995	1996
Goods loaded	11,675	10,880	10,680
Goods unloaded	22,929	27,370	25,900

* Excluding petroleum.

CIVIL AVIATION (traffic on scheduled services)

	1993	1994	1995
Kilometres flown (million) . .	59	64	70
Passengers carried ('000) . .	2,569	2,980	3,453
Passenger-km (million) . .	8,747	9,662	11,412
Total ton-km (million) . . .	1,654	1,832	2,103

Source: UN, *Statistical Yearbook*.

Tourism

	1994	1995	1996
Tourist arrivals	1,838,700	2,214,646	2,100,051
Tourist receipts (US $ million) .	2,266	2,784	2,771

Communications Media

	1993	1994	1995
Radio receivers ('000 in use) . .	2,510	2,610	2,700
Television receivers ('000 in use).	1,430	1,500	1,600
Telephones ('000 main lines in use)	1,958	2,138	2,343
Telefax stations (number in use)	80,000	110,000	140,000
Mobile cellular telephones (subscribers) . . .	64,484	140,000	300,000*
Daily newspapers . . .	n.a.	34	34*

* Estimate.

Book production (1992): 4,608 titles; 9,368,000 copies.

Non-daily newspapers (1988): 80.

Other periodicals (1985): 807.

Sources: UNESCO, *Statistical Yearbook*, and UN, *Statistical Yearbook*.

Education

(1994/95)

	Schools	Pupils	Teachers
Jewish			
Kindergarten	n.a.	287,500	n.a.
Primary schools	1,323	539,270	45,132
Intermediate schools . . .	354	142,664	17,829
Secondary schools . . .	603	242,363	32,041
Vocational schools . . .	304	105,226	n.a.
Agricultural schools . .	23	6,840	n.a.
Teacher training colleges . .	n.a.	18,830	n.a.
Others (handicapped) . .	209	12,946	4,028
Arab			
Kindergarten	n.a.	25,500	n.a.
Primary schools	324	146,557	8,639
Intermediate schools . . .	95	39,653	2,840
Secondary schools . . .	98	42,032	3,468
Vocational schools . . .	51	9,835	n.a.
Agricultural schools . .	2	161	n.a.
Teacher training colleges . .	n.a.	1,193	n.a.
Others (handicapped) . .	40	2,228	484

Directory

The Constitution

There is no written constitution. In June 1950 the Knesset voted to adopt a state constitution by evolution over an unspecified period. A number of laws, including the Law of Return (1950), the Nationality Law (1952), the State President (Tenure) Law (1952), the Education Law (1953) and the 'Yad-va-Shem' Memorial Law (1953), are considered as incorporated into the state Constitution. Other constitutional laws are: The Law and Administration Ordinance (1948), the Knesset Election Law (1951), the Law of Equal Rights for Women (1951), the Judges Act (1953), the National Service and National Insurance Acts (1953), and the Basic Law (The Knesset) (1958). The provisions of constitutional legislation that affect the main organs of government are summarized below:

THE PRESIDENT

The President is elected by the Knesset for a maximum of two five-year terms.

Ten or more Knesset members may propose a candidate for the Presidency.

Voting will be by secret ballot.

The President may not leave the country without the consent of the Government.

The President may resign by submitting his resignation in writing to the Speaker.

The President may be relieved of his duties by the Knesset for misdemeanour.

The Knesset is entitled to decide by a two-thirds majority that the President is too incapacitated owing to ill health to fulfil his duties permanently.

The Speaker of the Knesset will act for the President when the President leaves the country, or when he cannot perform his duties owing to ill health.

THE KNESSET

The Knesset is the parliament of the state. There are 120 members.

It is elected by general, national, direct, equal, secret and proportional elections.

Every Israeli national of 18 years or over shall have the right to vote in elections to the Knesset unless a court has deprived him of that right by virtue of any law.

Every Israeli national of 21 and over shall have the right to be elected to the Knesset unless a court has deprived him of that right by virtue of any law.

The following shall not be candidates: the President of the State; the two Chief Rabbis; a judge (shofet) in office; a judge (dayan) of a religious court; the State Comptroller; the Chief of the General Staff of the Defence Army of Israel; rabbis and ministers of other religions in office; senior state employees and senior army officers of such ranks and in such functions as shall be determined by law.

The term of office of the Knesset shall be four years.

The elections to the Knesset shall take place on the third Tuesday of the month of Marcheshvan in the year in which the tenure of the outgoing Knesset ends.

Election day shall be a day of rest, but transport and other public services shall function normally.

Results of the elections shall be published within 14 days.

The Knesset shall elect from among its members a Chairman and Vice-Chairman.

The Knesset shall elect from among its members permanent committees, and may elect committees for specific matters.

The Knesset may appoint commissions of inquiry to investigate matters designated by the Knesset.

The Knesset shall hold two sessions a year; one of them shall open within four weeks after the Feast of the Tabernacles, the other within four weeks after Independence Day; the aggregate duration of the two sessions shall not be less than eight months.

The outgoing Knesset shall continue to hold office until the convening of the incoming Knesset.

The members of the Knesset shall receive a remuneration as provided by law.

THE GOVERNMENT

The Government shall tender its resignation to the President immediately after its election, but shall continue with its duties until the formation of a new government. After consultation with representatives of the parties in the Knesset, the President shall charge one of the members with the formation of a government. The Government shall be composed of a Prime Minister (directly elected from May 1996) and a number of ministers from among the Knesset members or from outside the Knesset. After it has been chosen, the Government shall appear before the Knesset and shall be considered as formed after having received a vote of confidence. Within seven days of receiving a vote of confidence, the Prime Minister and the other ministers shall swear allegiance to the State of Israel and its Laws and undertake to carry out the decisions of the Knesset.

The Government

HEAD OF STATE

President: EZER WEIZMAN (took office 13 May 1993; re-elected 4 March 1998).

THE CABINET
(October 1998)

Prime Minister and Minister of Housing and Construction: BINYAMIN NETANYAHU (elected 29 May 1996) (Likud).

Deputy Prime Minister, Minister of Agriculture and Rural Development and Minister of the Environment: RAFAEL EITAN (Tzomet).

Deputy Prime Minister and Minister of Tourism: MOSHE KATZAV (Likud).

Minister of Foreign Affairs and National Infrastructure: ARIEL SHARON (Likud).

Minister of the Interior: ELIAHU SUISSA (Shas).

Minister of Trade and Industry: NATAN SHARANSKY (Israel B'Aliyah).

Minister of Finance: YAACOV NE'EMAN (Likud).

Minister of Defence: ITZHAK MORDECHAI (Likud).

Minister of Communications: LIMOR LIVNAT (Likud).

Minister of Transport and Energy: SHAUL YAHALOM (NRP).

Minister of Education and Culture, and of Religious Affairs: ITZHAK LEVI (NRP).

Minister of Justice: TZACHI HANEGBI (Likud).

Minister of Health: YEHOSHUA MATZA (Likud).

Minister of Science and Technology: SILVAN SHALOM (Likud).

Minister of Immigrant Absorption: YULI EDELSTEIN (Israel B'Aliyah).

Minister of Labour and Social Welfare: ELIYAHU YISHAI (Shas).

Minister of Internal Security: AVIGDOR KAHALANI (Third Way).

MINISTRIES

Office of the Prime Minister: POB 187, 3 Rehov Kaplan, Kiryat Ben-Gurion, Jerusalem 91919; tel. 2-6705555; fax 2-6512631.

Ministry of Agriculture: POB 7011, 8 Arania St, Hakirya, Tel-Aviv 61070; tel. 3-6971444; fax 3-6968899.

Ministry of Communications: 23 Jaffa St, Jerusalem 91999; tel. 2-6706320; fax 2-6706372.

Ministry of Defence: Kaplan St, Hakirya, Tel-Aviv 67659; tel. 3-5692010; telex 32147; fax 3-6916940.

Ministry of Education, Culture and Sport: POB 292, 34 Shivtei Israel St, Jerusalem 91911; tel. 2-5603700; fax 2-5603706; e-mail yairlevin@netvision.net.il.

Ministry of Energy and Infrastructure: POB 13106, 234 Jaffa St, Jerusalem 91130; tel. 2-316111; fax 2-381444.

Ministry of the Environment: POB 34033, 5 Kanfei Nesharim St, Givat Shaul, Jerusalem 95464; tel. 2-6553777; telex 25629; fax 2-6535934; e-mail is–enviv@netvision.net.il.

Ministry of Finance: POB 13191, 1 Rehov Kaplan, Kiryat Ben-Gurion, Jerusalem 91008; tel. 2-5317111; telex 25216; fax 2-5637891.

Ministry of Foreign Affairs: Hakirya, Romema, Jerusalem 91950; tel. 2-5303111; fax 2-5303506.

Ministry of Health: POB 1176, 2 Ben-Tabai St, Jerusalem 91010; tel. 2-6705705; telex 26138; fax 2-6796491.

Ministry of Housing and Construction: POB 18110, Kiryat Hamemshala (East), Jerusalem 91180; tel. 2-5825501; fax 2-5811904.

Ministry of Immigrant Absorption: POB 13061, 13 Rehov Kaplan, Kiryat Ben-Gurion, Jerusalem 91006; tel. 2-6752696; fax 2-5618138.

Ministry of the Interior: POB 6158, 2 Rehov Kaplan, Kiryat Ben-Gurion, Jerusalem 91061; tel. 2-6701411; fax 2-6701628.

Ministry of Internal Security: POB 18182, Kiryat Hamemshala, Jerusalem 91181; tel. 2-5308003; fax 2-5847872.

Ministry of Justice: 29 Rehov Salahadin, Jerusalem 91010; tel. 2-6708511; fax 2-6708714.

Ministry of Labour and Social Welfare: POB 915, 2 Rehov Kaplan, Kiryat Ben-Gurion, Jerusalem 91008; tel. 2-6752311; fax 2-6752803.

Ministry of National Infrastructure: POB 13106, 234 Jaffa St, Jerusalem 91130; tel. 2-5316111; fax 2-5380855; also responsible for **Israel Lands Administration:** 6 Shamai St, Jerusalem 94631; tel. 2-5208422; fax 2-5234960.

Ministry of Police: POB 18182, Bldg No. 3, Sheikh Jarrah, Kiryat Hamemshala (East), Jerusalem 91181; tel. 2-308088; fax 2-826770.

Ministry of Religious Affairs: POB 13059, 236 Jaffa St, Jerusalem 91130; tel. 2-5311175; fax 2-5311183.

Ministry of Science and Technology: POB 18195, Kiryat Hamemshala, Hamizrachit, Government Offices, Bldg 3, Jerusalem 91181; tel. 2-5825222; fax 2-5825725; e-mail nps@most.gov.il.

Ministry of Tourism: POB 1018, 24 Rehov King George, Jerusalem 91009; tel. 2-6754811; fax 2-6253407.

Ministry of Trade and Industry: POB 299, 30 Rehov Agron, Jerusalem 91002; tel. 2-6220339; fax 2-6259274.

Ministry of Transport: Klal Bldg, 97 Jaffa St, Jerusalem 91000; tel. 2-5319211; fax 2-5319693.

Legislature

KNESSET

Speaker: DAN TICHON.

General Election, 29 May 1996

Party	Seats
Labour	34
Likud-Tzomet-Gesher	32
Shas	10
National Religious Party	9
Meretz (an alliance of Ratz, Shinui and the United Workers' Party)	9
Israel B'Aliyah	7
Hadash	5
United Torah Judaism	4
The Third Way	4
United Arab List	4
Moledet	2
Total	**120**

According to Israel's General Election Committee, 79.7% of the 3.9m.-strong electorate participated in the legislative elections which were held on 29 May 1996. Likud, the Tzomet Party and Gesher announced a formal electoral alliance prior to voting. In 1996, for the first time, the position of Prime Minister became elective and voting to select the leader of the government took place at the same time as that to return deputies to the Knesset. In the election of the Prime Minister the leader of Likud, Binyamin

Netanyahu, received 50.5% (1,501,023) of the total number of valid votes cast while Shimon Peres, the leader of the Labour Party, received 49.5% (1,471,566). Almost 5% of the votes cast in the election of the Prime Minister were reported to have been spoiled.

Political Organizations

Agudat Israel: POB 513, Jerusalem; tel. 2-385251; fax 2-385145; orthodox Jewish party; stands for strict observance of Jewish religious law; Leaders AVRAHAM SHAPIRO, MENACHEM PORUSH.

Agudat Israel World Organization (AIWO): POB 326, Hacherut Sq., Jerusalem 91002; tel. 2-5384357; f. 1912 at Congress of Orthodox Jewry, Kattowitz, Germany (now Katowice, Poland), to help solve the problems facing Jewish people all over the world; more than 500,000 mems in 25 countries; Chairs. Rabbi J. M. ABRAMOWITZ (Jerusalem), Rabbi M. SHERER (New York); Gen. Secs Rabbi MOSHE GEWIRTZ, Rabbi CHAIM WEINSTOCK.

Council for Peace and Security: f. 1988 by four retd Israeli generals: Maj.-Gen. AHARON YARIV, Maj.-Gen. ORI ORR, Brig.-Gen. YORAM AGMON and Brig.-Gen. EPHRAIM SNEH; MOSHE AMIRAV of Centre Party a founder mem.; aims: an Israeli withdrawal from the Occupied Territories in return for a peace treaty with the Arab nations.

Degel Hatora: 103 Rehov Beit Vegan, Jerusalem; tel. 2-418167; fax 2-438105; f. 1988 as breakaway from Agudat Israel; orthodox Western Jews; Chair. AVRAHAM RAVITZ.

Democratic Arab Party (DAP): Nazareth; tel. 6-560937; f. 1988; aims: to unify Arab political forces so as to influence Palestinian and Israeli policy; international recognition of the Palestinian people's right to self-determination; the withdrawal of Israel from all territories occupied in 1967, including East Jerusalem; the DAP also aims to achieve full civil equality between Arab and Jewish citizens of Israel, to eliminate discrimination and improve the social, economic and political conditions of the Arab minority in Israel; Chair. ABD AL-WAHAB DARAWSHAH.

Gesher (Bridge): f. 1996; Leader DAVID LEVY.

Gush Emunim (Bloc of the Faithful): f. 1967; engaged in unauthorized establishment of Jewish settlements in the Occupied Territories; Leader Rabbi MOSHE LEVINGER.

Hadash (Democratic Front for Peace and Equality): POB 26205, 3 Rehov Hashikma, Tel-Aviv; tel. 3-827492; descended from the Socialist Workers' Party of Palestine (f. 1919); renamed Communist Party of Palestine 1921, Communist Party of Israel (Maki) 1948; pro-Soviet anti-Zionist group formed New Communist Party of Israel (Rakah) 1965; Jewish Arab membership; aims for a socialist system in Israel, a lasting peace between Israel and the Arab countries and the Palestinian Arab people, favours full implementation of UN Security Council Resolutions 242 and 338, Israeli withdrawal from all Arab territories occupied since 1967, formation of a Palestinian Arab state in the West Bank and Gaza Strip, recognition of national rights of state of Israel and Palestine people, democratic rights and defence of working class interests, and demands an end to discrimination against Arab minority in Israel and against oriental Jewish communities; Sec.-Gen. MEIR VILNER.

Israel B'Aliyah: f. 1995; campaigns for immigrants' rights; Leader NATAN SHARANSKY.

Israel Labour Party: 110 Ha'yarkon St, Tel-Aviv 61032; tel. 3-5209222; fax 3-5271744; f. 1968 as a merger of the three Labour groups, Mapai, Rafi and Achdut Ha'avoda; a Zionist democratic socialist party; Chair. EHUD BARAK.

Kahane Chai (Kahane Lives): POB 5379, 111 Agripas St, Jerusalem; tel. 2-231081; f. 1977 as 'Kach' (Thus); right-wing religious nationalist party; advocates creation of a Torah state and expulsion of all Arabs from Israel and the annexation of the Occupied Territories; Leader Rabbi BINYAMIN ZEEV KAHANE.

Likud (Consolidation): 38 Rehov King George, Tel-Aviv 61231; tel. 3-5630666; fax 3-5282901; f. September 1973; is a parliamentary bloc of Herut (Freedom; f. 1948; Leader ITZHAK SHAMIR; Sec.-Gen. MOSHE ARENS), the Liberal Party of Israel (f. 1961; Chair. AVRAHAM SHARIR), Laam (For the Nation) (f. 1976; fmrly led by YIGAEL HURWITZ, who left the coalition to form his own party, Ometz, before the 1984 general election), Ahdut (a one-man faction, HILLEL SEIDEL), Tami (f. 1981; represents the interests of Sephardic Jews; Leader AHARON UZAN), which joined Likud in June 1987, and an independent faction (f. 1990; Leader ITZHAK MODAI), which formed the nucleus of a new Party for the Advancement of the Zionist Idea; Herut and the Liberal Party formally merged in August 1988 to form the Likud-National Liberal Movement; aims: territorial integrity (advocates retention of all the territory of post-1922 mandatory Palestine); absorption of newcomers; a social order based on freedom and justice, elimination of poverty and want; development of an economy that will ensure a decent standard of living; improvement of the environment and the quality of life; Leader of Likud BINYAMIN NETANYAHU.

Meretz (Vitality): an alliance of Ratz, Shinui and the United Workers' Party; stands for civil rights, electoral reform, welfarism, Pales-

tinian self-determination, separation of religion from the state and a halt to settlement in the Occupied Territories; Leader YOSSI SARID.

Moledet (Homeland): 14 Rehov Yehuda Halevi, Tel-Aviv; tel. 3-654580; f. 1988; right-wing nationalist party; aims: the expulsion ('transfer') of the 1.5m. Palestinians living in the West Bank and Gaza Strip; united with Tehiya—Zionist Revival Movement (see below) in June 1994 as the Moledet—the Eretz Israel Faithful and the Tehiya; Leader Gen. RECHAVAM ZE'EVI.

Movement for the Advancement of the Zionist Idea (MAZI): f. 1990 as breakaway group of Likud; Leader ITZHAK MODAI.

National Religious Party (NRP): 12 Sarei Israel St, Jerusalem; tel. 2-377277; fax 2-377757; f. 1902; as the Mizrachi Organization within the Zionist Movement; present name adopted in 1956; stands for strict adherence to Jewish religion and tradition, and strives to achieve the application of religious precepts of Judaism in everyday life; it is also endeavouring to establish a Constitution for Israel based on Jewish religious law (the Torah); 126,000 mems; Leader ITZHAK LEVI; Sec.-Gen. ZEVULUN ORLEV.

New Liberal Party: Tel-Aviv; f. 1987 as a merger of three groups: Shinui-Movement for Change (f. 1974 and restored 1978, when Democratic Movement for Change split into two parties; centrist; Leader AMNON RUBINSTEIN), the Centre Liberal Party (f. 1986 by members of the Liberal Party of Israel; Leader ITZHAK BERMAN), and the Independent Liberal Party (f. 1965 by seven Liberal Party of Israel Knesset mems, after the formation of the Herut Movement and Liberal Party of Israel bloc; 20,000 mems; Chair. MOSHE KOL; Gen. Sec. NISSIM ELIAD); Leaders AMNON RUBINSTEIN, ITZHAK BERMAN and MOSHE KOL.

Poale Agudat Israel: f. 1924; working-class Orthodox Judaist party; Leader Dr KALMAN KAHANE.

Political Zionist Opposition (Ometz): f. 1982; one-man party, YIGAEL HURWITZ.

Progressive List for Peace: 5 Simtat Lane, Nes Tziona, Tel-Aviv; tel. 3-662457; fax 3-659474; f. 1984; Jewish-Arab; advocates recognition of the PLO and the establishment of a Palestinian state in the West Bank and the Gaza Strip; Leader MUHAMMAD MI'ARI.

Ratz (Civil Rights and Peace Movement): 21 Tchernihovsky St, Tel-Aviv 63291; tel. 3-5254847; fax 3-5255008; f. 1973; concerned with human and civil rights, opposes discrimination on basis of religion, gender or ethnic identification and advocates a peace settlement with the Arab countries and the Palestinians; Leader Mrs SHULAMIT ALONI.

Religious Zionism Party (Matzad): Tel-Aviv; f. 1983; breakaway group from the National Religious Party; also known as Morasha (Heritage); Leader Rabbi HAIM DRUCKMAN.

Shas (Sephardic Torah Guardians): Beit Abodi, Rehov Hahida, Bene Beraq; tel. 3-579776; f. 1984 by splinter groups from Agudat Israel; ultra-orthodox Jewish party; Spiritual Leader Rabbi ELIEZER SHACH.

Shinui (Centre Party): 10 Ha-Arbaa St, Tel-Aviv 64739; tel. 3-5620118; fax 3-5620139; f. 1974 as a new liberal party; combines a moderate foreign policy with a free-market economic philosophy. Leader AVRAHAM PORAZ.

Tehiya—Zionist Revival Movement: POB 355, 34 Rehov Hahaluts, Jerusalem; tel. 2-259385; f. 1979; aims: Israeli sovereignty over Judaea, Samaria, Gaza; extensive settlement programme; economic independence; uniting of religious and non-religious camps; opposes Camp David accords; united with Moledet in June 1994 (see above); Leaders GERSHON SHAFAT, GEULA COHEN, ELYAQIM HAEZNI, DAMI DAYAN.

Third Way: f. 1995; Leader AVIGDOR KAHALANI.

Tzomet Party: 22 Rehov Huberman, Tel-Aviv; tel. 3-204444; f. 1988; right-wing nationalist party; breakaway group from Tehiya party; Leader RAFAEL EITAN.

United Arab List: Arab party affiliated to Labour Party.

United Torah Judaism: electoral list of four minor ultra-orthodox parties (Moria, Degel Hatora, Poale Agudat Israel, Agudat Israel) formed, prior to 1992 election, to overcome the increase in election threshold from 1% to 1.5% and help to counter the rising influence of the secular Russian vote; Spiritual Leader Rabbi ELIEZER SHACH.

United Workers' Party (Mapam): POB 1777, 4 Rehov Itamar Ben-Avi, Tel-Aviv 61016; tel. 3-6972111; fax 3-6910504; f. 1948; left-wing socialist-Zionist Jewish-Arab party; grouped in Labour-Mapam Alignment with Israel Labour Party from January 1969 until Sept. 1984 when it withdrew in protest over Labour's formation of a Government with Likud; member of the Socialist International; 77,000 mems; Chair. CHANAN EREZ; Sec.-Gen. VICTOR BLIT.

Yahad (Together): f. 1984; advocates a peace settlement with the Arab peoples and the Palestinians; joined the Labour Party parliamentary bloc in January 1987.

Yi'ud: f. 1994; breakaway group from the Tzomet Party.

Diplomatic Representation

EMBASSIES IN ISRAEL

Argentina: 22nd Floor, Diamond Tower, 3A Jabolinsky Rd, Ramat Gan, Tel-Aviv 63571; tel. 3-5759173; fax 3-5759178; Ambassador: JOSÉ MARÍA V. OTEGUI.

Australia: Beit Europa, 4th Floor, 37 Shaul Hamelech Blvd, Tel-Aviv 64928; tel. 3-6950451; telex 33777; fax 3-6968404; Ambassador: IAN WILCOCK.

Austria: POB 11095, 11 Rehov Herman Cohen, Tel-Aviv 61110; tel. 3-5246186; telex 33435; fax 3-5244039; Ambassador: Dr HERBERT KRÖLL.

Belarus: 2 Rehov Kaufman, Tel-Aviv 68012; tel. 3-5102236; fax 3-5102235; Ambassador: MIKHAIL FARFEL.

Belgium: 266 Rehov Hayarkon, Tel-Aviv 63504; tel. 3-6054164; telex 342211; fax 3-5465345; Ambassador: MARK GELEYN.

Bolivia: 7A Rehov Hashalom, Mevasseret Zion 90805; tel. 2-5335195; fax 2-5335196; e-mail totova@netvision.net.il; Ambassador: Dr VÍCTOR TORRES ACHA.

Brazil: 2 Rehov Kaplan, Beit Yachin, 8th Floor, Tel-Aviv 64734; tel. 3-6919292; telex 33752; fax 3-6916060; Ambassador: (vacant).

Bulgaria: 9th Floor, 124 Ibn Gvirol, Tel-Aviv 62038; tel. 3-5241751; fax 3-5241798; Ambassador: SVETLOMIR BAEV.

Cameroon: POB 50252, Dan Panorama Hotel, 10 Rehov Kaufman, Tel-Aviv 61500; tel. and fax 3-5190011; Chargé d'affaires a.i.: ETONNDI ESSOMBA.

Canada: 220 Rehov Hayarkon, Tel-Aviv 63405; tel. 3-5272929; fax 3-5272333; Ambassador: (vacant).

Chile: 7 Havakook St, Tel-Aviv 63505; tel. 3-6020130; telex 342189; fax 3-6020133; e-mail echileil@inter.net.il; Ambassador: JOSÉ RODRÍGUEZ ELIZONDO.

China, People's Republic: Tel-Aviv: Ambassador: LIN ZHEN.

Colombia: 52 Rehov Pinkas, Apt 26, Tel-Aviv 62261; tel. 3-5461717; telex 342165; fax 3-5461404; e-mail emcolis@netvision.net.il; Chargé d'affaires a.i.: Dr EUFRACIO MORALES.

Congo, Democratic Republic: Apt 5, 60 Hei Be'Iyar, Kikar Hamedina, Tel-Aviv 62198; tel. 3-452681; telex 371239; Ambassador: Gen. ELUKI MONGA AUNDU.

Costa Rica: 13 Rehov Diskin, Apt 1, Kiryat Wolfson, Jerusalem 92473; tel. 2-5666197; telex 33533; fax 2-5632591; e-mail emcri@netmedia.net.il; Ambassador: MANUEL ENRIQUE LÓPEZ-TRIGO.

Côte d'Ivoire: POB 14371, Kikar Hamédina, 14 Hei Be'Iyar, Tel-Aviv 62093; tel. 3-6963727; telex 341143; fax 3-6968888; Ambassador: LÉON HOUADJA KACOU.

Czech Republic: POB 16361, 23 Rehov Zeitlin, Tel-Aviv 61664; tel. 3-6918282; fax 3-6918286; Ambassador: JIŘÍ SCHNEIDER.

Denmark: POB 21080, 23 Rehov Bnei Moshe, Tel-Aviv 61210; tel. 3-5442144; telex 33514; fax 3-5465502; Ambassador: CARSTEN STAUR.

Dominican Republic: 4 Sderot Shaul Hamelech, Apt 81, Tel-Aviv 64733; tel. 3-6957580; fax 3-6962032; Ambassador: JOSÉ BATLLE-NICOLÁS.

Ecuador: POB 30, Room 211, 'Asia House', 4 Rehov Weizman, Tel-Aviv 64239; tel. 3-258764; telex 342179; fax 3-269437; Ambassador: PAULINA GARCÍA DE LARREA.

Egypt: 54 Rehov Bazel, Tel-Aviv 62744; tel. 3-5464151; telex 361289; fax 3-5441615; Ambassador: MUHAMMAD ABD AL-AZIZ BASSIOUNI.

El Salvador: POB 4005, Jerusalem 91039; tel. 2-6728411; fax 2-6733641; e-mail embasal@inter.net.il; internet http://www.el-salvador.org.il; Ambassador: RAFAEL A. ALFARO-PINEDA.

Ethiopia: Dan Panorama Hotel, 10 Rehov Kaufman, Tel-Aviv 61500; tel. 3-519019; Chargé d'affaires a.i.: Dr TESHOME TEKLU.

Finland: POB 20013, 8th Floor, Beit Eliahu, 2 Rehov Ibn Gvirol, Tel-Aviv 64077; tel. 3-6950527; fax 3-6966311; e-mail sanomat.tel@formi.fi; Ambassador: PASI PATOKALLIO.

France: 112 Tayeleth Herbert Samuel, Tel-Aviv 63572; tel. 3-5245371; telex 33662; fax 3-5249294; e-mail ambafran@actcom.co.il; Ambassador: JEAN-NOËL DE BOUILLANE DE LACOSTE.

Germany: POB 16038, 19th Floor, 3 Rehov Daniel Frisch, Tel-Aviv 61160; tel 03-6931313; telex 33621; fax 3-6950608; Ambassador: THEODOR WALLAU.

Greece: 47 Bodenheimer St, Tel-Aviv 62008; tel. 3-6055461; telex 341227; fax 3-6054374; Ambassador: Dr SOTIRIOS VAROUXAKIS.

Guatemala: 74 Rehov Hei Be'Iyar, Apt 6, Tel-Aviv 62198; tel. 3-5467372; Ambassador: JULIO ROBERTO PALOMO SILVA.

Haiti: 16 Rehov Bar Giora, Tel-Aviv 64336; tel. 3-280285; Ambassador: FRANCK M. JOSEPH.

Holy See: POB 150, 1 Netiv Hamazalot, Old Jaffa 68037; tel. 3-6835658; fax 3-6835659; Apostolic Nuncio: Mgr PIETRO SAMBI, Titular Archbishop of Belcastro.

Honduras: 46 Rehov Hei Be'Iyar, Apt 3, Kikar Hamedina, Tel-Aviv 62093; tel. 3-5469506; fax 3-5469505; e-mail Honduras@netvision.net.il; Ambassador: FRANCISCO LÓPEZ REYES.

Hungary: 18 Rehov Pinkas, Tel-Aviv 62661; tel. 3-5466860; fax 3-5468968; Ambassador: Dr ISTVÁN CSEJTEI.

India: 4 Rehov Koifman, Tel-Aviv; tel. 3-5101431; telex 371583; fax 3-5101434; Ambassador: SHIVSHANKAR MENON.

Italy: 'Asia House', 4 Rehov Weizman, Tel-Aviv 64239; tel. 3-6948428; telex 342664; fax 3-6964223; Ambassador: PIER LUIGI RACHELE.

Japan: 'Asia House', 4 Rehov Weizman, Tel-Aviv 64239; tel. 3-6957292; telex 242202; fax 3-6910516; Ambassador: YUKATA KAWASHIMA.

Jordan: 12 Rehov Abba Hillel, Ramat-Gan, Tel-Aviv 52506; tel. 3-7517722; fax 3-7517713; Ambassador: MARWAN MUASHER.

Latvia: 52 Pinkas St, Apt 51, Tel-Aviv 62261; tel. 3-5462438; fax 3-5444372; e-mail latvembi@netvision.net.il; Ambassador: IVARS SILĀRS.

Liberia: 6 Shimon Frug, Ramat-Gan, Tel-Aviv 524282; tel. 3-728525; telex 361637; Ambassador: Maj. SAMUEL B. PEARSON, Jr.

Lithuania: POB 23920, 14th Floor, Top Tower, Dizengoff Centre, Tel-Aviv 61231; tel. 3-5288514; fax 3-5257265; Ambassador: ROMAS JONAS MISIUNAS.

Mexico: 3 Rehov Bograshov, Tel-Aviv 63808; tel. 3-5230367; telex 32352; fax 3-5237399; e-mail embamex@netvision.net.il; Ambassador: JORGE ALBERTO LOZOYA.

Myanmar: 26 Rehov Hayarkon, Tel-Aviv 68011; tel. 3-5170760; telex 371504; fax 3-5171440; Ambassador: U KYAW MYINT.

Netherlands: 'Asia House', 4 Rehov Weizman, Tel-Aviv 64239; tel. 3-6957377; telex 342180; fax 3-6957370; Ambassador: CHRISTIAAN M. J. KRÖNER.

Nigeria: POB 3339, 34 Gordon St, Tel-Aviv 61030; tel. 3-5222144; fax 3-5237886; Ambassador: I. C. OLISEMEKA.

Norway: 40 Rehov Hei Be'Iyar, Tel-Aviv 63506; tel. 3-5442030; telex 33417; fax 3-5442034; Ambassador: SVEN ERIK SVEDMAN.

Panama: 10 Rehov Hei Be'Iyar, Kikar Hamedina, Tel-Aviv 62998; tel. 3-6960849; fax 3-6910045; Ambassador: Prof. PAULINO C. ROMERO.

Peru: 37 Rehov Hamarganit, Shikun Vatikin, Ramat-Gan, Tel-Aviv 52584; tel. 3-6135591; telex 371351; fax 3-5465532; e-mail emperu@metrovision.net.il; Ambassador: JORGE TORRES.

Philippines: POB 50085, 13th Floor, Textile Centre Bldg, 2 Rehov Kaufmann, Tel-Aviv 68012; tel. 3-5175263; telex 32104; fax 3-5102229; Ambassador: ROSALINDA DE PERIO-SANTOS.

Poland: 16 Rehov Soutine, Tel-Aviv; tel. 3-5240186; telex 371765; fax 3-5237806; Ambassador: Chargé d'affaires a.i.: ZBIGNIEW ŻELAZOWSKI.

Portugal: 4 Rehov Weizman, Tel-Aviv; tel. 3-6956373; Ambassador: PAULO COUTO BARBOSA.

Romania: 24 Rehov Adam Hacohen, Tel-Aviv 64585; tel. 3-5230066; Ambassador: Dr RADU HOMESCU.

Russia: 120 Rehov Hayarkon, Tel-Aviv 63573; tel. 3-5226733; fax 3-5226713; Ambassador: MIKHAIL BOGDANOV.

Slovakia: POB 6459, Jabotinsky 37, Tel-Aviv 61064; tel. 3-5440066; fax 3-5440069; Ambassador Dr FRANTIŠEK DLHOPOLČEK.

South Africa: POB 7138, 16th Floor, Top Tower, 50 Dizengoff St, Tel-Aviv 61071; tel. 3-5252566; fax 3-5253230; Ambassador: FRANK LAND.

Spain: Dubnov Tower, 3 Rehov Daniel Frisch, 16th Floor, Tel-Aviv 64731; tel. 3-6965218; fax 3-6965217; Ambassador: FERMÍN ZELADA JURADO.

Sweden: 'Asia House', 4 Rehov Weizman, Tel-Aviv 64239; tel. 3-6958111; telex 33650; fax 3-6958116; Ambassador: JOHN H. M. HAGARD.

Switzerland: 228 Rehov Hayarkon, Tel-Aviv 63405; tel. 3-5464455; fax 3-5464408; e-mail vertretung@tel.rep.admin.ch; Ambassador: PIERRE MONOD.

Togo: POB 50222, Beit Hatassianim, 29 Rehov Hamered, Tel-Aviv 68125; tel. 3-652206; Ambassador: KOFFI-MAWUENAM KOWOUVI.

Turkey: 202 Rehov Hayarkon, Tel-Aviv 63405; tel. 3-35241101; fax 3-35240499; Ambassador: BARLAS ÖZENER.

Ukraine: 12 Stricker St, Tel-Aviv 62006; tel. 3-6040242; fax 3-6042512; Ambassador: DMYTRO MARKOV.

United Kingdom: 192 Rehov Hayarkon, Tel-Aviv 63405; tel. 3-5249171; fax 3-5243313; Ambassador: FRANCIS CORNISH (designate).

USA: 71 Rehov Hayarkon, Tel-Aviv 63903; tel. 3-5197575; telex 33376; fax 3-5173227; Ambassador: EDWARD WALKER.

Uruguay: 52 Rehov Pinkas, Apt. 10, 2nd Floor, Tel-Aviv 62261; tel. 3-440411; telex 342669; Ambassador: ANÍBAL DÍAZ MONDINO.

Venezuela: Textile Center, 2 Rehov Kaufmann, 16th Floor, Tel-Aviv 61500; tel. 3-5176287; telex 342172; fax 3-5176210; Ambassador: FREDDY ALVAREZ.

Yugoslavia: Iderot Shaul Hamelech 8, Tel-Aviv 64733; tel. 3-6938412; fax 3-6938411; Charge d'affaires a.i.: MIRKO STEFANOVIĆ.

The Jewish Agency for Israel

POB 92, Jerusalem 91000; tel. 2-202222; fax 2-202303.

Organization: The governing bodies are the Assembly which determines basic policy, the Board of Governors which sets policy for the Agency between Assembly meetings and the Executive responsible for the day-to-day running of the Agency.

Chairman of Executive: AVRAHAM BURG.

Chairman of Board of Governors: CHARLES H. GOODMAN.

Director-General: MOSHE NATIV.

Secretary-General: HOWARD WEISBAND.

Functions: According to the Agreement of 1971, the Jewish Agency undertakes the immigration and absorption of immigrants in Israel, including absorption in agricultural settlement and immigrant housing; social welfare and health services in connection with immigrants; education, youth care and training; neighbourhood rehabilitation through project renewal.

Budget (1993): US $500m.

Judicial System

The law of Israel is composed of the enactments of the Knesset and, to a lesser extent, of the acts, orders-in-council and ordinances that remain from the period of the British Mandate in Palestine (1922–48). The pre-1948 law has largely been replaced, amended or reorganized, in the interests of codification, by Israeli legislation. This legislation generally follows a pattern which is very similar to that operating in England and the USA.

Attorney-General: ELYAQIM RUBENSTEIN.

CIVIL COURTS

The Supreme Court: Sha'arei Mishpat St, Kiryat David Ben-Gurion, Jerusalem 91950; tel. 2-6759666; fax 2-6759648. This is the highest judicial authority in the state. It has jurisdiction as an Appellate Court over appeals from the District Courts in all matters, both civil and criminal (sitting as a Court of Civil Appeal or as a Court of Criminal Appeal). In addition it is a Court of First Instance (sitting as the High Court of Justice) in actions against governmental authorities, and in matters in which it considers it necessary to grant relief in the interests of justice and which are not within the jurisdiction of any other court or tribunal. The High Court's exclusive power to issue orders in the nature of *habeas corpus, mandamus,* prohibition and *certiorari* enables the court to review the legality of and redress grievances against acts of administrative authorities of all kinds and religious tribunals.

President of the Supreme Court: AHARON BARAK.

Deputy-President of the Supreme Court: SH. LEVIN.

Justices of the Supreme Court: Y. KEDMI, Mrs D. BEINISCH, Y. TURKEL, M. CHESHIN, E. GOLDBERG, Mrs T. STRASBERG-COHEN, T. OR, E. MAZZA, Y. ENGLARD, Mrs D. DORNER, Y. ZAMIR, Y. GOLDBERG.

Registrars: Judge ORIT EPHAL-GABAI, Judge MICHAL AGMON.

The District Courts: There are five District Courts (Jerusalem, Tel-Aviv, Haifa, Beersheba, Nazareth). They have residual jurisdiction as Courts of First Instance over all civil and criminal matters not within the jurisdiction of a Magistrates' Court, all matters not within the exclusive jurisdiction of any other tribunal, and matters within the concurrent jurisdiction of any other tribunal so long as such tribunal does not deal with them. In addition, the District Courts have appellate jurisdiction over appeals from judgments and decisions of Magistrates' Courts and judgments of Municipal Courts and various administrative tribunals.

Magistrates' Courts: There are 29 Magistrates' Courts, having criminal jurisdiction to try contraventions, misdemeanours and certain felonies, and civil jurisdiction to try actions concerning possession or use of immovable property, or the partition thereof whatever may be the value of the subject matter of the action, and other civil claims not exceeding one million shekels.

Labour Courts: Established in 1969. Regional Labour Courts in Jerusalem, Tel-Aviv, Haifa, Beersheba and Nazareth, composed of judges and representatives of the public. A National Labour Court in Jerusalem. The Courts have jurisdiction over all matters arising out of the relationship between employer and employee or parties to a collective labour agreement, and matters concerning the National Insurance Law and the Labour Law and Rules.

RELIGIOUS COURTS

The Religious Courts are the courts of the recognized religious communities. They have jurisdiction over certain defined matters of personal status concerning members of their respective communities. Where any action of personal status involves persons of different religious communities the President of the Supreme Court decides which Court will decide the matter. Whenever a question arises as to whether or not a case is one of personal status within the exclusive jurisdiction of a Religious Court, the matter must be referred to a Special Tribunal composed of two Justices of the Supreme Court and the President of the highest court of the religious community concerned in Israel. The judgments of the Religious Courts are executed by the process and offices of the Civil Courts. Neither these Courts nor the Civil Courts have jurisdiction to dissolve the marriage of a foreign subject.

Jewish Rabbinical Courts: These Courts have exclusive jurisdiction over matters of marriage and divorce of Jews in Israel who are Israeli citizens or residents. In all other matters of personal status they have concurrent jurisdiction with the District Courts.

Muslim Religious Courts: These Courts have exclusive jurisdiction over matters of marriage and divorce of Muslims who are not foreigners, or who are foreigners subject by their national law to the jurisdiction of Muslim Religious Courts in such matters. In all other matters of personal status they have concurrent jurisdiction with the District Courts.

Christian Religious Courts: The Courts of the recognized Christian communities have exclusive jurisdiction over matters of marriage and divorce of members of their communities who are not foreigners. In all other matters of personal status they have concurrent jurisdiction with the District Courts.

Druze Courts: These Courts, established in 1963, have exclusive jurisdiction over matters of marriage and divorce of Druze in Israel, who are Israeli citizens or residents, and concurrent jurisdiction with the District Courts over all other matters of personal status of Druze.

Religion

JUDAISM

Judaism, the religion of the Jews, is the faith of the majority of Israel's inhabitants. On 31 December 1994 Judaism's adherents totalled 4,441,100, equivalent to 81.17% of the country's population. Its basis is a belief in an ethical monotheism.

There are two main Jewish communities: the Ashkenazim and the Sephardim. The former are the Jews from Eastern, Central, or Northern Europe, while the latter originate from the Balkan countries, North Africa and the Middle East.

There is also a community of about 10,000 Falashas (Ethiopian Jews) who have been airlifted to Israel at various times since the fall of Emperor Haile Selassie in 1974.

The supreme religious authority is vested in the Chief Rabbinate, which consists of the Ashkenazi and Sephardi Chief Rabbis and the Supreme Rabbinical Council. It makes decisions on interpretation of the Jewish law, and supervises the Rabbinical Courts. There are 8 regional Rabbinical Courts, and a Rabbinical Court of Appeal presided over by the two Chief Rabbis.

According to the Rabbinical Courts Jurisdiction Law of 1953, marriage and divorce among Jews in Israel are exclusively within the jurisdiction of the Rabbinical Courts. Provided that all the parties concerned agree, other matters of personal status can also be decided by the Rabbinical Courts.

There are 195 Religious Councils, which maintain religious services and supply religious needs, and about 405 religious committees with similar functions in smaller settlements. Their expenses are borne jointly by the State and the local authorities. The Religious Councils are under the administrative control of the Ministry of Religious Affairs. In all matters of religion, the Religious Councils are subject to the authority of the Chief Rabbinate. There are 365 officially appointed rabbis. The total number of synagogues is about 7,000, most of which are organized within the framework of the Union of Israel Synagogues.

Head of the Ashkenazi Community: The Chief Rabbi ISRAEL MEIR LAU.

Head of the Sephardic Community: Jerusalem; tel. 2-244785; The Chief Rabbi ELIAHU BAKSHI-DORON.

Two Jewish sects still loyal to their distinctive customs are:

The Karaites, a sect which recognizes only the Jewish written law and not the oral law of the Mishna and Talmud. The community of about 12,000, many of whom live in or near Ramla, has been augmented by immigration from Egypt.

The Samaritans, an ancient sect mentioned in 2 Kings xvii, 24. They recognize only the Torah. The community in Israel numbers about 500; about one-half of this number live in Holon, where a

Samaritan synagogue has been built, and the remainder, including the High Priest, live in Nablus, near Mt Gerazim, which is sacred to the Samaritans.

ISLAM

The Muslims in Israel are mainly Sunnis, and are divided among the four rites of the Sunni sect of Islam: the Shafe'i, the Hanbali, the Hanafi and the Maliki. Before June 1967 they numbered approx. 175,000; in 1971, approx. 343,900. On 31 December 1994 the total Muslim population of Israel was 781,500.

Mufti of Jerusalem: POB 19859, Jerusalem; tel. 2-283528; Sheikh ABD AL-QADIR ABIDIN (also Chair. Supreme Muslim Council for Jerusalem). The Palestine National Authority also claims the right to appoint the Mufti of Jerusalem and has named Sheikh AKRAM SA'ID SABRI as its choice.

There was also a total of 91,700 Druzes in Israel at 31 December 1994.

CHRISTIANITY

The total Christian population of Israel (including East Jerusalem) at 31 December 1994 was 161,000.

United Christian Council in Israel: POB 116, Jerusalem 91000; tel. 2-6714351; fax 2-6721349; f. 1956; 26 mems (churches and other bodies); Chair. CHARLES KOPP; Gen. Sec. TREVOR MARZETTI.

The Roman Catholic Church

Armenian Rite

The Armenian Catholic Patriarch of Cilicia is resident in Beirut, Lebanon.

Patriarchal Exarchate of Jerusalem: POB 19546, Via Dolorosa 41, Third and Fourth Stations of the Cross, Jerusalem; tel. 2-284262; fax 2-272123; f. 1885; Exarch Patriarchal ANTREAS BEDOGHOLIAN.

Chaldean Rite

The Chaldean Patriarch of Babylon is resident in Baghdad, Iraq.

Patriarchal Exarchate of Jerusalem: Chaldean Patriarchal Vicariate, Saad and Said Quarter, Nablus Rd, Jerusalem; Exarch Patriarchal Mgr PAUL COLLIN.

Latin Rite

The Patriarchate of Jerusalem covers Palestine, Jordan and Cyprus. At 31 December 1996 there were an estimated 70,000 adherents.

Bishops' Conference: Conférence des Evêques Latins dans les Régions Arabes, Patriarcat Latin, POB 14152, Jerusalem; tel. 2-292323; f. 1967; Pres. His Beatitude MICHEL SABBAH; Patriarch of Jerusalem.

Patriarchate of Jerusalem: Patriarcat Latin, POB 14152, Jerusalem; tel. 2-6282323; fax 2-6271652; e-mail latinpatr@isdn.co.il; Patriarch: His Beatitude MICHEL SABBAH; Vicar-General for Israel: BOULOS GIACCINTO (Titular Bishop of Emmaus), Vicariat Patriarcal Latin, Nazareth; tel. 6-6554075; fax 6-6452416.

Maronite Rite

The Maronite community, under the jurisdiction of the Maronite Patriarch of Antioch (resident in Lebanon), has about 7,000 members.

Patriarchal Exarchate of Jerusalem: Vicariat Maronite, 25 Maronite St, Jerusalem; tel. 2-6282158; fax 2-6272821; Exarch Patriarchal Mgr PAUL NABIL SAYAH (also the Archbishop of Haifa and the Holy Land).

Melkite Rite

The Greek-Melkite Patriarch of Antioch (MAXIMOS V HAKIM) is resident in Damascus, Syria.

Patriarchal Vicariate of Jerusalem: Vicariat Patriarcal Grec-Melkite Catholique, POB 14130, Porte de Jaffa, Jerusalem 91141; tel. 2-6282023; fax 2-6286652; about 3,300 adherents (1996); Vicars Patriarchal Mgr HILARION CAPUCCI (Titular Archbishop of Caesarea in Palestine), Mgr LUTFI LAHAM (Titular Archbishop of Tarsus).

Archbishop of Akka (Acre): Most Rev. MAXIMOS SALLOUM, Archevêché Grec-Catholique, POB 279, 33 Hagefen St, Haifa; tel. 04-8523114; 47,000 adherents at 31 December 1996.

Syrian Rite

The Syrian Catholic Patriarch of Antioch is resident in Beirut, Lebanon.

Patriarchal Exarchate of Jerusalem: Vicariat Patriarcal Syrien Catholique, POB 19787, Chaldean St No. 6, Nablus Road, Jerusalem 91190; tel. 2-282657; fax 2-284217; 3,197 adherents (Dec. 1996); Exarch Patriarchal Mgr PIERRE ABD AL-AHAD.

The Armenian Apostolic (Orthodox) Church

Patriarch of Jerusalem: TORKOM MANOOGIAN, St James's Cathedral, Jerusalem; tel. 2-6264853; fax 2-6264862 .

The Greek Orthodox Church

The Patriarchate of Jerusalem contains an estimated 260,000 adherents in Israel, the Israeli-occupied territories, Jordan, Kuwait, the United Arab Emirates and Saudi Arabia.

Patriarch of Jerusalem: DIODOROS I, POB 19632-633, Greek Orthodox Patriarchate St, Old City, Jerusalem; tel. and fax 2-6282048.

The Anglican Communion

Episcopal Church in Jerusalem and the Middle East: POB 1248, St George's Close, Jerusalem; tel. 2-6271670; fax (2) 6273847; e-mail ediosces@netvision.net.il; President-Bishop The Rt. Rev. RIAH ABU AL-ASSAL.

Other Christian Churches

Other denominations include the Coptic Orthodox Church (700 members), the Russian Orthodox Church, the Ethiopian Orthodox Church, the Romanian Orthodox Church, the Lutheran Church and the Church of Scotland.

The Press

Tel-Aviv is the main publishing centre. Largely for economic reasons, there has developed no local press away from the main cities; hence all papers regard themselves as national. Friday editions, issued on Sabbath eve, are increased to as much as twice the normal size by special weekend supplements, and experience a considerable rise in circulation. No newspapers appear on Saturday.

Most of the daily papers are in Hebrew, and others appear in Arabic, English, French, Polish, Yiddish, Hungarian and German. The total daily circulation is 500,000–600,000 copies, or 21 papers per hundred people, although most citizens read more than one daily paper.

Most Hebrew morning dailies have strong political or religious affiliations. *Al-Hamishmar* is affiliated to Mapam, *Hatzofeh* to the National Religious Party—World Mizrachi. *Davar* is the long-established organ of the Histadrut. Most newspapers depend on subsidies from political parties, religious organizations or public funds. The limiting effect on freedom of commentary entailed by this party press system has provoked repeated criticism. There are around 400 other newspapers and magazines including some 50 weekly and 150 fortnightly; over 250 of them are in Hebrew, the remainder in 11 other languages.

The most influential and respected dailies, for both quality of news coverage and commentary, are *Ha'aretz* and the trade union paper, *Davar*, which frequently has articles by government figures. These are the most widely read of the morning papers, exceeded only by the popular afternoon press, *Ma'ariv* and *Yedioth Aharonoth*. The *Jerusalem Post* gives detailed and sound news coverage in English.

The Israeli Press Council (Chair. ITZHAK ZAMIR), established in 1963, deals with matters of common interest to the Press such as drafting the code of professional ethics which is binding on all journalists.

The Daily Newspaper Publishers' Association represents publishers in negotiations with official and public bodies, negotiates contracts with employees and purchases and distributes newsprint.

DAILIES

Al Anba (The News): POB 428, 37 Hillel St, Jerusalem; f. 1968 circ. 10,000.

Davar Rishon: POB 199, 45 Sheinkin St, Tel-Aviv; tel. 3-5286141; telex 33807; fax 3-6294783; f. 1925; morning; official organ of the General Federation of Labour (Histadrut); Editor RON BEN YSHAI; circ. 39,000; there are also weekly magazine editions.

Globes: 127 Igal Alon St, Tel-Aviv 67443; tel. 3-6979797; fax 3-6917573; e-mail shimoni@globes.co.il; f. 1983; evening; business, economics; Editor H. GOLAN; circ. 36,000.

Ha'aretz (The Land): POB 233, 21 Salman Schocken St, Tel-Aviv 61001; tel. 3-5121212; fax 3-6810012; f. 1918; morning; Hebrew; liberal, independent; Editor HANOCH MARMARI; circ. 65,000 (weekdays), 75,000 (weekends).

Hadashot (The News): 108 Yigal Alon St, Tel-Aviv; 3-5120555; fax 3-5623084; late morning; Hebrew.

Hamodia (The Informer): POB 1306, Yehuda Hamackabbi 3, Jerusalem; fax 2-539108; morning; Hebrew; organ of Agudat Israel; Editors M. A. DRUCK, H. M. KNOPF; circ. 15,000.

Hatzofeh (The Watchman): 66 Hamasger St, Tel-Aviv; tel. 3-5622951; fax 3-5621502; f. 1938; morning; Hebrew; organ of the National Religious Party; Editor M. ISHON; circ. 16,000.

Israel Nachrichten (News of Israel): 49 Tschlenow St, Tel-Aviv 66048; tel. 3-5372059; fax 3-6877142; f. 1974; morning; German; Editor ALICE SCHWARZ-GARDOS; circ. 20,000.

Israelski Far Tribuna: 113 Givat Herzl St, Tel-Aviv; tel. 3-3700; f. 1952; Bulgarian; circ. 6,000.

Al-Ittihad (Unity): POB 104, Haifa; tel. 4-511296; fax 4-511297; f. 1944; Arabic; organ of the Israeli Communist Party (Maki); Chief Editor NAZIR MJALLI ZUBIEDAT.

The Jerusalem Post: POB 81, Romema, 91000, Jerusalem; tel. 2-531566; fax 2-5387408; e-mail jpedt@jpost.co.il; f. 1932; morning; English; independent; Pres. and Pblr NORMAN SPECTOR; Editor JEFF BORAK; circ. 30,000 (weekdays), 50,000 (weekend edition); there is also a weekly international edition, circ. 70,000, and a weekly French-language edition, circ. 7,500.

Le Journal d'Israel: POB 28330, 26 Agra St, Tel-Aviv; f. 1971; French; independent; Chief Editor J. RABIN; circ. 10,000; also overseas weekly selection; circ. 15,000.

Letzte Nyess (Late News): POB 28034, 52 Harakevet St, Tel-Aviv; f. 1949; morning; Yiddish; Editor S. HIMMELFARB; circ. 23,000.

Ma'ariv (Evening Prayer): 2 Carlebach St, Tel-Aviv 61200; tel. 3-5632111; telex 33735; fax 3-5610614; f. 1948; mid-morning; Hebrew; independent; published by Modiin Publishing House; Editor OFFER NIMRODI; circ. 160,000 (weekdays), 270,000 (weekends).

Mabat: 8 Toshia St, Tel-Aviv 67218; tel. 3-5627711; fax 3-5627719; f. 1971; morning; economic and social; Editor S. YARKONI; circ. 7,000.

Nasha Strana (Our Country): 52 Harakeret St, Tel-Aviv 67770; tel. 3-370011; fax 3-5371921; f. 1970; morning; Russian; Editor S. HIMMELFARB; circ. 35,000.

Al-Quds (Jerusalem) POB 19788, Jerusalem; tel. 2-6272663; fax 2-5855003; e-mail alquds@p-ol.com; internet http://www.alquds.com; f. 1968; circ. 60,000.

Uj Kelet: 49 Tchlenor St, Tel-Aviv; tel. 3-5371395; fax 3-377142; f. 1918; morning; Hungarian; independent; Editor D. DRORY; circ. 20,000.

Viata Noastra: 49 Tchlenor St, Tel-Aviv 61351; tel. 3-5372059; fax 3-6877142; e-mail erancourt@shani.co.il; f. 1950; morning; Romanian; Editor GEORGE EDRI; circ. 30,000.

Yated Ne'eman: POB 328, Bnei Brak; tel. 3-5709171; fax 3-5709181; f. 1986; morning; religious; Editors Y. ROTH and N.GROSSMAN; circ. 25,000.

Yedioth Aharonoth (The Latest News): 2 Yehuda and Noah Mozes St, Tel-Aviv 61000; tel. 3-6972222; telex 33847; fax 3-6953950; f. 1939; evening; independent; Editor-in-Chief MOSHE VARDI; circ. 300,000, Friday 600,000.

WEEKLIES AND FORTNIGHTLIES

Bama'alah: 120 Kibbutz Gabuyot St, Tel-Aviv; tel. 3-6814488; fax 3-6816852; Hebrew; journal of the young Histadrut Movement; Editor ODED BAR-MEIR.

Bamahane (In the Camp): Military POB 1013, Tel-Aviv; f. 1948; military, illustrated weekly of the Israel Armed Forces; Hebrew; Editor-in-Chief YOSSEF ESHKOL; circ. 70,000.

Davar Hashavua (The Weekly Word): 45 Shenkin St, Tel-Aviv; tel. 2-286141; f. 1946; weekly; Hebrew; popular illustrated; published by Histadrut, General Federation of Labour; Editor TUVIA MENDELSON; circ. 43,000.

Ethgar (The Challenge): 75 Einstein St, Tel-Aviv; twice weekly; Hebrew; Editor NATHAN YALIN-MOR.

Gesher (The Bridge): Jerusalem; fortnightly; Hebrew; Editor ZIAD ABU ZAYAD.

Glasul Populurui: Tel-Aviv; weekly of the Communist Party of Israel; Romanian; Editor MEÏR SEMO.

Haolam Hazeh (This World): POB 136, 3 Gordon St, Tel-Aviv 61001; tel. 3-5376804; fax 3-5376811; f. 1937; weekly; independent; illustrated news magazine; Editor-in-Chief RAFFI GINAT.

Harefuah (Medicine): Twin Towers No. 2, 35 Jabotinsky St, Ramat-Gan, Tel-Aviv; tel. 3-6100444; fax 3-5751616; f. 1920; fortnightly journal of the Israeli Medical Association; Hebrew with English summaries; Editor Y. ROTEM; circ. 12,000.

Hotam: Al-Hamishmar House, Choma U'Migdal St, Tel-Aviv; Hebrew.

Al-Hurriya (Freedom): 38 King George St, Tel-Aviv; Arabic weekly of the Herut Party.

Illustrirte Weltwoch: Tel-Aviv; f. 1956; weekly; Yiddish; Editor M. KARPINOVITZ.

Jerusalem Post International Edition: POB 81, Romema, Jerusalem 91000; tel. 2-5315666; fax 2-5389527; e-mail jpedt@jpost.co.il; f. 1959; weekly; overseas edition of the *Jerusalem Post* (q.v.); circ. 70,000 to 106 countries.

The Jerusalem Times: POB 20185, Jerusalem; tel. 2-6264883; fax 2-6264975; e-mail tjt@palnet.com; f. 1994; weekly; English; Editor HANNA SINIORA.

Kol Ha'am (Voice of the People): Tel-Aviv; f. 1947; Hebrew; organ of the Communist Party of Israel; Editor B. BALTI.

Laisha (For Women): POB 28122, 35 Bnei Brak St, Tel-Aviv 67132; tel. 3-638-6969; fax 3-638-6922; f. 1946; Hebrew; women's magazine; Editor ZVI ELGAT.

Ma'ariv Lanoar: 2 Carlebach St, Tel-Aviv 67132; tel. 3-5632111; fax 3-5632030; f. 1957; weekly for youth; Hebrew; Editor AVI MORGENSTERN; circ. 100,000.

MB (Mitteilungsblatt): POB 1480, Tel-Aviv 61014; tel. 3-5164461; fax 3-5164435; f. 1932; German monthly journal of the Irgun Olei Merkas Europa (The Association of Immigrants from Central Europe); Editor Prof. PAUL ALSBERG.

Otiot: Beit Orot, Hordes Post, Jerusalem 95908; tel. 2-895097; fax 2-895196; f. 1987; weekly for children; English; Editor URI AUERBACH.

People and Computers Weekly: POB 11616, 64 Pinsker St, Tel-Aviv 11616; tel. 3-295145; telex 341667; fax 3-295144; weekly; Hebrew; information technology; circ. 6,000.

Reshumot: Ministry of Justice, Jerusalem; f. 1948; Hebrew, Arabic and English; official government gazette.

Sada at-Tarbia (The Echo of Education): published by the Histadrut and Teachers' Association, POB 2306, Rehovot; f. 1952; fortnightly; Arabic; educational; Editor TUVIA SHAMOSH.

OTHER PERIODICALS

Ariel: the Israel Review of Arts and Letters: Cultural and Scientific Relations Division, Ministry for Foreign Affairs, Jerusalem; Distributor: Youval Tal Ltd, POB 2160, Jerusalem 91021; tel. 2-6248897; fax 2-6245434; e-mail ariel-mail@usa.net; Editorial Office: 214 Jaffa Road, Jerusalem 91130; tel. 2-5381515; fax 2-538062; f. 1962; quarterly review of all aspects of culture in Israel; regular edns in English, Spanish, French, German, Arabic and Russian; occasional edns in other languages; Editor ASHER WEILL; Asst Editor ALOMA HALTER; circ. 35,000.

Asakim Vekalkala (Business and Economics): POB 20027, 84 Hashmonaim St, Tel-Aviv 61200; tel. 3-5631010; telex 33484; fax 3-5619025; monthly; Hebrew; Editor ZVI AMIT.

Avoda Urevacha Ubituach Leumi: POB 915, Jerusalem; f. 1949; monthly review of the Ministry of Labour and Social Welfare, and the National Insurance Institute, Jerusalem; Hebrew; Chief Editor AVNER MICHAELI; Editor MICHAEL KLODOVSKY; circ. 2,500.

Bitaon Heyl Ha'avir (Israel Air Force Magazine): Military POB 01560, Zahal; tel. 3-5693886; fax 3-5695806; e-mail iaf@inter.net.il; f. 1948; bi-monthly; Hebrew; Dep. Editor U. ETSION; Editor-in-Chief MERAV HALPERIN; circ. 30,000.

Al-Bushra (Good News): POB 6088, Haifa; f. 1935; monthly; Arabic; organ of the Ahmadiyya movement; Editor FALAHUD DIN O'DEH.

Business Diary: 37 Hanamal St, Haifa; f. 1947; weekly; English, Hebrew; shipping movements, import licences, stock exchange listings, business failures, etc.; Editor G. ALON.

Challenge: POB 41199, Jaffa 61411; tel. and fax 2-6792270; internet http://members.aol.com/challng/index.html; f. 1989; magazine on the Israeli–Palestinian conflict, published by Hanitzotz Publishing House; bi-monthly in English; circ. 1,000; Editor RONI BEN EFRAT.

Christian News from Israel: 30 Jaffa Rd, Jerusalem; f. 1949; half-yearly; English, French, Spanish; issued by the Ministry of Religious Affairs; Editor SHALOM BEN-ZAKKAI; circ. 10,000.

Di Goldene Keyt: 30 Weizmann St, Tel-Aviv; f. 1949; literary quarterly; Yiddish; published by the Histadrut; Man. Editor MOSHE MILLIS; Editor A. SUTZKEVER.

Divrei Haknesset: c/o The Knesset, Jerusalem; f. 1949; Hebrew; records of the proceedings of the Knesset; published by the Government Printer, Jerusalem; Editor DVORA AVIVI (acting); circ. 350.

The Easy Way to do Business with Israel: POB 20027, Tel-Aviv; published by Federation of Israeli Chambers of Commerce; Editor Y. SHOSTAK.

Eitanim (Popular Medicine): POB 16250, Merkez Kupat Holim, Tel-Aviv 62098; f. 1948; Hebrew; monthly; circ. 20,000.

Family Physician: POB 16250, 101 Arlosoroff St, Tel-Aviv 62098; tel. 3-433388; fax 3-433474; f. 1970; published three times per year in Hebrew and English; scientific articles on family medicine, community medicine, health care and general practice; Editor Prof. MAX POLLIACK.

Folk un Zion: POB 7053, Tel-Aviv 61070; tel. 3-5423317; f. 1950; bi-monthly; current events relating to Israel and World Jewry; circ. 3,000; Editor MOSHE KALCHHEIM.

Frei Israel: POB 8512, Tel-Aviv; progressive monthly; published by Asscn for Popular Culture; Yiddish.

Gazit: POB 4190, 8 Zvi Brook St, Tel-Aviv; f. 1932; monthly; Hebrew and English; art, literature; Publisher G. TALPHIR.

Hameshek Hahaklai: 21 Melchett St, Tel-Aviv; f. 1929; Hebrew; agricultural; Editor ISRAEL INBARI.

Hamizrah Hehadash (The New East): Israel Oriental Society, The Hebrew University, Mount Scopus, Jerusalem 91905; f. 1949; annual of the Israel Oriental Society; Middle Eastern, Asian and African Affairs; Hebrew with English summary; Editor HAIM GERBER; circ. 1,500–2,000.

Hamionai (The Hotelier): POB 11586, Tel-Aviv; f. 1962; monthly of the Israel Hotel Asscn; Hebrew and English; Editor Z. PELTZ.

Hapraklit: POB 14152, 8 Wilson St, Tel-Aviv 61141; tel. 3-5614695; fax 3-561476; f. 1943; quarterly; Hebrew; published by the Israel Bar Asscn; Editor-in-Chief A. POLONSKI; Editor ARNAN GAVRIELI; circ. 9,000.

Hassadeh: POB 40044, 8 Shaul Hamelech Blvd, Tel-Aviv 61400; tel. 3-6929018; fax 3-6929979; f. 1920; monthly; review of Israeli agriculture; English; Publr GUY KLUG; circ. 10,000.

Hed Hagan: 8 Ben Saruk St, Tel-Aviv 62969; tel. 3-6922958; f. 1935; Hebrew; educational; Editor Mrs ZIVA PEDAHZUR; circ. 8,400.

Hed Hahinukh: 8 Ben Saruk St, Tel-Aviv 62969; tel. 3-5432911; fax 3-5432928; f. 1926; monthly; Hebrew; educational; published by the Israeli Teachers' Union; Editor DALIA LACHMAN; circ. 40,000.

Israel Economist: POB 7052, 6 Hazanowitz St, Jerusalem 91070; tel. 2-234131; fax 2-246569; f. 1945; monthly; English; independent; political and economic; Editor BEN MOLLOV; Publisher ISRAEL KELMAN; also publishes *Keeping Posted* (diplomatic magazine), *Mazel and Brucha* (jewellers' magazine); annuals: *Travel Agents' Manual, Electronics, International Conventions in Israel, Arkia, In Flight,* various hotel magazines.

Israel Environment Bulletin: Ministry of the Environment, POB 34033, Jerusalem 95464; tel. 2-6553777; telex 25629; fax 2-6535934; f. 1973; Editor SHOSHANA GABBAY; circ. 3,000.

Israel Export and Trade Journal: POB 11586, Tel-Aviv; f. 1949; monthly; English; commercial and economic; published by Israel Periodicals Co Ltd; Man. Dir ZALMAN PELTZ.

Israel Journal of Chemistry: POB 35409, Merkaz Sapir 6/37, Givat Shaul, Jerusalem 91352; tel. 2-6522226; fax 2-6522277; e-mail laserpages@netmedia.net.il; f. 1951; quarterly; Editor Prof. H. LEVANON.

Israel Journal of Mathematics: POB 7695, Jerusalem 91076; tel. 2-6586656; fax 2-5633370; f. 1951; monthly, four vols of three issues per year; published by Magnes Press; Editor Prof. G. KALAI.

Israel Journal of Medical Sciences: 2 Etzel St, French Hill, 97853 Jerusalem; tel. 2-5817727; fax 2-5815722; f. 1965; monthly; Editor-in-Chief Dr M. PRYWES; circ. 5,500.

Israel Journal of Psychiatry and Related Sciences: Gefen Publishing House Ltd, POB 36004, Jerusalem 91360; tel. 2-5380247; fax 2-5388423; e-mail isragefen@netmedia.net.il; f. 1963; quarterly; Editor-in-Chief Dr DAVID GREENBERG.

Israel Journal of Veterinary Medicine: POB 3076, Rishon Le-Zion 75130; tel. 9-7419929; fax 9-7431778; f. 1943; quarterly of the Israel Veterinary Medical Asscn; formerly *Refuah Veterinarith*; Editors G. SIMON, I. GLAS.

Israel Scene: World Zionist Org., POB 92, Jerusalem 91920; tel. 2-527156; telex 26436; fax 2-533542; f. 1980; monthly; English; Zionist; cir. 50,000.

Israel-South Africa Trade Journal: POB 11587, Tel-Aviv; f. 1973; bi-monthly; English; commercial and economic; published by Israel Publications Corpn Ltd; Man. Dir Z. PELTZ.

Israels Aussenhandel: POB 11586, Tel-Aviv 61114; tel. 3-5280215; telex 341118; f. 1967; monthly; German; commercial; published by Israel Periodicals Co Ltd; Editor PELTZ NOEMI; Man. Dir ZALMAN PELTZ.

Al-Jadid (The New): POB 104, Haifa; f. 1951; literary monthly; Arabic; Editor SALEM JUBRAN; circ. 5,000.

Journal d'Analyse Mathématique: f. 1955; 2 vols per year; published by Magnes Press; Editor Prof. L. ZALCMAN.

Kalkalan: POB 7052, 8 Akiva St, Jerusalem; f. 1952; monthly; independent; Hebrew commercial and economic; Editor J. KOLLEK.

Kibbutz Trends: Yad Tabenkin, Ramat Efal 52960; tel. 3-5301217; fax 3-5346376; e-mail yadtab@actcom.co.il; quarterly; English language journal on kibbutz; Editors RUTH LACEY, IDIT PAZ, NEIL HARRIS; circ. 1,500.

Labour in Israel: 93 Arlosorof St, Tel-Aviv 62098; tel. 3-6921111; telex 342488; fax 3-6969906; quarterly; English, French, German and Spanish; bulletin of the Histadrut (General Federation of Labour in Israel); circ. 28,000.

Leshonenu: Academy of the Hebrew Language, POB 3449, Jerusalem 91034; tel. 2-5632242; fax 2-5617065; f. 1929; 4 a year; for the study of the Hebrew language and cognate subjects; Editor J. BLAU.

Leshonenu La'am: Academy of the Hebrew Language, POB 3449, Jerusalem 91034; tel. 2-5632242; fax 2-5617065; f. 1945; 4 a year; popular Hebrew philology; Editors C. E. COHEN, D. TALSHIR, Y. OFER.

Ma'arachot (Campaigns): POB 7026, Hakirya, 3 Mendler St, Tel-Aviv 61070; tel. 3-5694345; fax 3-5694345; f. 1939; military and political bi-monthly; Hebrew; periodical of Israel Defence Force; Editors HAGGAI GOLAN, EFI MELZER.

Ma'ariv Lanoar: POB 20020, 2 Carlebach St, Tel-Aviv; tel. 3-5632111; fax 3-5610614; f. 1957; children's weekly; circ. 100,000.

Magallati (My Magazine): POB 28049, Tel-Aviv; tel. 3-371438; f. 1960; bi-monthly children's magazine; circ. 3,000.

Melaha Vetaassiya (Trade and Industry): POB 11587, Tel-Aviv; f. 1969; bi-monthly review of the Union of Artisans and Small Manufacturers of Israel; Hebrew; Man. Dir Z. PELTZ; circ. 8,500.

M'Lakha V'ta Asiya (Israel Industry): POB 11587, 40 Rembrandt St, Tel-Aviv; monthly; circ. 8,500.

Molad: POB 1165, Jerusalem 91010; f. 1948; annual; Hebrew; independent political and literary periodical; published by Miph'ale Molad Ltd; Editor EPHRAIM BROIDO.

Monthly Bulletin of Statistics: Israel Central Bureau of Statistics, POB 13015, Jerusalem 91130; tel. 2-6521340; fax 2-6553400; f. 1949.

> **Foreign Trade Statistics:** f. 1950; Hebrew and English; appears annually, 2 vols; imports/exports.

> **Foreign Trade Statistics Quarterly:** f. 1950; Hebrew and English.

> **Tourism and Hotel Services Statistics Quarterly:** f. 1973; Hebrew and English.

> **Price Statistics Monthly:** f. 1959; Hebrew.

> **Transport Statistics Quarterly:** f. 1974; Hebrew and English.

> **Agricultural Statistics Quarterly:** f. 1970; Hebrew and English.

> **New Statistical Projects and Publications in Israel:** f. 1970; quarterly; Hebrew and English.

> **Selected Economic Indicators:** e-mail neumann@cbs.gov.il; f. 1996; monthly; Hebrew.

Moznaim (Balance): POB 7098, Tel-Aviv; tel. 3-6953256; fax 3-6919681; f. 1929; monthly; Hebrew; literature and culture; Editor ASHER REICH; circ. 2,500.

Nekuda: Hebrew; organ of the Jewish settlers of the West Bank and Gaza Strip.

New Outlook: 9 Gordon St, Tel-Aviv 63458; tel. 3-5236496; fax 3-5232252; f. 1957; bi-monthly; Israeli and Middle Eastern Affairs; dedicated to the quest for Arab-Israeli peace; Editor-in-Chief CHAIM SHUR; Senior Editor DAN LEON; circ. 10,000.

People and Computers Israel: POB 11616, 13 Yad Harutzim St, Tel-Aviv 11616; tel. 3-295145; telex 341667; fax 3-295144; monthly; Hebrew; information technology; cir. 9,500.

Proche-Orient Chrétien: POB 19079, Jerusalem 91190; tel. 2-6283285; fax 2-6280764; e-mail mafrproc@jrol.com; f. 1951; quarterly on churches and religion in the Middle East; circ. 1,000.

Quarterly Review of the Israel Medical Asscn (Mif'al Haverut Hutz—World Fellowship of the Israel Medical Asscn): POB 33289, 39 Shaul Hamelech Blvd, Tel-Aviv 61332; tel. (3) 6955521; fax 3-6956103; quarterly; English; Editor-in-Chief YEHUDA SHOENFELD.

The Sea: POB 33706, Hane'emanim 8, Haifa; tel. 04-529818; every six months; published by Israel Maritime League; review of marine problems; Pres. M. POMROCK; Chief Editor M. LITOVSKI; circ. 5,000.

Shituf (Co-operation): POB 7151, 24 Ha'arba St, Tel-Aviv; f. 1948; bi-monthly; Hebrew; economic, social and co-operative problems in Israel; published by the Central Union of Industrial, Transport and Service Co-operative Societies; Editor L. LOSH; circ. 12,000.

Shivuk (Marketing): POB 20027, Tel-Aviv 61200; tel. 3-5612444; fax 3-5612614; monthly; Hebrew; publ. by Federation of Israeli Chambers of Commerce; Editor SARA LIPKIN.

Sinai: POB 642, Jerusalem; tel. 2-526231; f. 1937; Hebrew; Torah science and literature; Editor Dr YITZCHAK RAPHAEL.

Sindibad: POB 28049, Tel-Aviv; f. 1970; children's monthly; Arabic; Man. JOSEPH ELIAHOU; Editor WALID HUSSEIN; circ. 8,000.

At-Ta'awun (Co-operation): POB 303, 93 Arlosoroff St, Tel-Aviv 62098; tel. 3-431813; telex 342488; fax 3-267368; f. 1961; Arabic; published by the Arab Workers' Dept of the Histadrut; co-operatives irregular; Editor ZVI HAIK.

Terra Santa: POB 14038, Jaffa Gate, Jerusalem 91140; tel. 2-6272692; fax 2-6286417; e-mail cicbarat@netmedia.net.il; f. 1921; every two months; published by the Custody of the Holy Land (the official custodians of the Holy Shrines); Italian, Spanish, French, English and Arabic editions published in Jerusalem, by the Franciscan Printing Press, German edition in Munich, Maltese edition in Valletta.

Tmuroth: POB 23076, 48 Hamelech George St, Tel-Aviv; f. 1960; monthly; Hebrew; organ of the Liberal Labour Movement; Editor S. MEIRI.

WIZO Review: Women's International Zionist Organization, 38 Sderot David Hamelech Blvd, Tel-Aviv 64237; tel. 3-6923805; fax 3-6958267; f. 1947; English edition (quarterly), Spanish and German editions (two a year); Editor HILLEL SCHENKER; circ. 20,000.

The Youth Times: POB 54065; tel. 2-6273293; fax 2-6287893; e-mail youthtimes@jerusalem_times.com; f. 1998; monthly; Arabic and English; Editor-in-Chief HANIA BITAR.

Zion: POB 4179, Jerusalem 91041; tel. 2-5637171; fax 2-5662135; f. 1935; quarterly; published by the Historical Society of Israel; Hebrew, with English summaries; research in Jewish history; Editors R. I. COHEN, A. OPPENHEIMER, Y. KAPLAN; circ. 1,000.

Zraim: POB 40027, 7 Dubnov St, Tel-Aviv; tel. 3-691745; fax 3-6953199; f. 1953; Hebrew; journal of the Bnei Akiva (Youth of Tora Va-avoda) Movement; Editor URI AUERBACH.

Zrakor: Haifa; f. 1947; monthly; Hebrew; news digest, trade, finance, economics, shipping; Editor G. ALON.

The following are all published by Laser Pages Publishing Ltd of Israel, POB 50257, 40/18 Levi Eshkol Blvd, Jerusalem 97665; tel. 2-829770; fax 2-818782.

Israel Journal of Earth Sciences: f. 1951; quarterly; Editors Dr Y. BARTOV, Y. KOLODNY.

Israel Journal of Plant Sciences: f. 1994; quarterly; Editor Prof. A. M. MAYER.

Israel Journal of Zoology: f. 1951; quarterly; Editor Prof. D. GRAUER.

Lada'at (Science for Youth): f. 1971; Hebrew; ten issues per vol.; Editor Dr M. ALMAGOR.

Mada (Science): POB 801, 8A Horkanya St, Jerusalem 91007; tel. 2-783203; fax 2-783784; f. 1955; popular scientific bi-monthly in Hebrew; Editor-in-Chief Dr YACHIN UNNA; circ. 10,000.

PRESS ASSOCIATIONS

Daily Newspaper Publishers' Asscn of Israel: POB 51202, 74 Petach Tikva Rd, Tel-Aviv 61200; fax 3-5617938; safeguards professional interests and maintains standards, supplies newsprint to dailies; negotiates with trade unions, etc.; mems all daily papers; affiliated to International Federation of Newspaper Publishers; Pres. SHABTAI HIMMELFARB; Gen. Sec. BETZALEL EYAL.

Foreign Press Asscn: Govt. Press Office Bldg, 9 Rehov Itamar Ben Avi, Tel-Aviv; tel. 3-6916143; fax 3-6961548; Chair. NICOLAS B. TATRO.

Israel Press Asscn: Sokolov House, 4 Kaplan St, Tel-Aviv.

NEWS AGENCIES

Jewish Telegraphic Agency (JTA): Israel Bureau, Jerusalem Post Bldg, Romema, Jerusalem; Dir DAVID LANDAU.

ITIM, News Agency of the Associated Israel Press: 10 Tiomkin St, Tel-Aviv; f. 1950; co-operative news agency; Dir and Editor ALTER WELNER.

Palestine Press Service: Salah ad-Din St, East Jerusalem; Proprs IBRAHIM QARA'EEN, Mrs RAYMONDA TAWIL; only Arab news agency in the Occupied Territories.

Foreign Bureaux

Agence France-Presse: POB 1507, 206 Jaffa Rd, Jerusalem 91014; tel. 2-5373243; telex 26401; fax 2-5373873; e-mail afpjer@netvision .net.il; Correspondent LUC DE BAROCHEZ.

Agencia EFE (Spain): POB 37190, 18 Hilel St, Jerusalem 91371; tel. 2-6242038; fax 2-6242056; Correspondent ELÍAS-SAMUEL SCHERBA-COVSKY.

Agenzia Nazionale Stampa Associata (ANSA) (Italy): 30 Dizengoff St, Tel-Aviv 64332; tel. 3-6299319; fax 3-5250302; Bureau Chief FURIO MORRONI; c/o Associated Press, Jerusalem 92233 (see below); tel. 2-250571; fax 2-258656; Correspondent GIORGIO RACCAH.

Associated Press (AP) (USA): POB 20220, 30 Ibn Gavirol St, Tel-Aviv 61201; tel. 3-262283; telex 341411; POB 1625, 18 Shlomzion Hamalcha, Jerusalem; tel. 2-224632; telex 25258; Chief of Bureau NICHOLAS TATRO.

Deutsche Presse-Agentur (dpa) (Germany): 30 Ibn Gvirol St, Tel-Aviv 64078; tel. 3-6959007; fax 3-6969594; e-mail dpatlv@trend line.co.il; Correspondents Dr HEINZ-RUDOLF OTHMERDING, JEFF ABRA-MOVITZ.

Jiji Tsushin-Sha (Japan): 9 Schmuel Hanagld, Jerusalem 94592; tel. 2-232553; fax 2-232402; Correspondent HIROKAZU OIKAWA.

Kyodo News Service (Japan): 19 Lessin St, Tel-Aviv 62997; tel. 3-6958185; telex 361568; fax 3-6917478; Correspondent HAJIME OZAKI.

Reuters (UK): 38 Hamasger St, Tel-Aviv 67211; tel. 3-5372211; telex 361567; fax 3-5372045; Jerusalem Capital Studios (JCS) 206 Jaffa Rd, Jerusalem 91131; tel. 2-5370502; fax 2-5374241; Chief of Bureau PAUL HOLMES.

United Press International (UPI) (USA): 138 Petah Tikva Rd, Tel-Aviv; Bureau Man. BROOKE W. KROEGER; Bureau Man. in Jerusalem LOUIS TOSCANO.

Informatsionnoye Telegrafnoye Agentstvo Rossii—Telegrafnoye Agentstvo Suverennykh Stran (ITAR—TASS) (Russia) is also represented.

Publishers

Achiasaf Ltd: POB 4810, 13 Yosef Hanassi St, Tel-Aviv 65236; tel. 3-5283339; fax 3-5286705; f. 1933; general; Man. Dir MATAN ACHI-ASAF.

Am Hassefer Ltd: 9 Bialik St, Tel-Aviv; tel. 3-53040; f. 1955; Man. Dir DOV LIPETZ.

'Am Oved' Ltd: POB 470, 22 Mazah St, POB 470, Tel-Aviv; tel. 3-6291526; fax 3-6298911; f. 1942; fiction, non-fiction, reference books, school and university textbooks, children's books, poetry, classics, science fiction; Man. Dir AHARON KRAUS.

Amichai Publishing House Ltd: 5 Yosef Hanassi St, Tel-Aviv 65236; tel. 3-284990; f. 1948; fiction, general science, linguistics, languages, arts; Dir YITZHAK ORON.

Arabic Publishing House: POB 28049, 17A Hagra St, Tel-Aviv; tel. 3-371438; f. 1960; established by the Histadrut; periodicals and books; Dir JOSEPH ELIAHOU.

Ariel Publishing House: POB 3328, 28 Nayadot St, Pisgat Ze'ev, Jerusalem 91033; tel. 2-524414; fax 2-436164; f. 1976; history, geology, religion, geography; CEO ELY SCHILLER.

Bitan Publishers Ltd: 50 Yeshayahu St, Tel-Aviv 62494; tel. 3-5189033; fax 3-5189037; f. 1965; aeronautics, aviation, biography, child development, fiction, educational, literature and literary criticism, mysteries, leisure, travel, women's studies; Man. A. BITAN.

Boostan Publishing House: 36 Moshav, Ben Shemen 73115; tel. 3-221821; fax 3-221299; f. 1969; education, fiction, poetry, biography, history, medicine, psychology, psychiatry; Man. Dir MORDECHAI BOOSTAN.

Carta, The Israel Map and Publishing Co Ltd: POB 2500, 18 Ha'uman St, Industrial Area Talpiot, Jerusalem 91024; tel. 2-6783355; fax 2-6782373; e-mail cartaben@netvision.net.il; f. 1958; the principal cartographic publisher; Pres. and CEO SHAY HAUSMAN.

Dvir Publishing Co Ltd: POB 22383, 32 Schocken St, Tel-Aviv; tel. 3-6812244; fax 3-6826138; f. 1924; literature, science, art, education; Publrs O. ZMORA, A. BITAN.

Encyclopedia Publishing Co: 29 Jabotinski St, Jerusalem 92141; tel. 2-5664568; f. 1947; Hebrew Encyclopedia and other encyclopedias; Chair. ALEXANDER PELI.

Rodney Franklin Agency: POB 37727, 53 Mazeh St, Tel-Aviv 65789; tel. 3-5600724; fax 3-5600479; e-mail rodney@actcom.co.il; exclusive representative of various British and US publishers; Dir RODNEY FRANKLIN.

Gazit: POB 4190, 8 Zvi Brook St, Tel-Aviv; tel. 3-53730; art publishers; Editor GABRIEL TALPHIR.

Gefen Publishing House Ltd: POB 36004, Jerusalem 91360; tel. 2-5380247; fax 2-5388423; e-mail isragefen@netmedia.net.il; f. 1981; art, religion, archaeology, English as a second language, fiction, history, arts, linguistics, law, medicine, military, science, poetry, psychology, psychiatry, theology, food and drink; CEO MURRAY S. GREENFIELD.

Gvanim Publishing House: POB 11138, 29 Bar-Kochba St, Tel-Aviv; tel. 3-5283648; fax 3-5283648; f. 1992; poetry, belles lettres, fiction; Man. Dir MARITZA ROSMAN.

Hakibbutz Hameuchad Publishing House Ltd: POB 1542, 23 Hayarkon, Bnei Brak, Tel-Aviv; tel. 3-5785810; fax 3-5785811; f. 1940; general; Dir UZI SHAVIT.

Hanitzotz A-Sharara Publishing House: POB 41199, Jaffa 61411; tel. 3-6839145; fax 3-6839148; e-mail odaa@p-ol.com; 'progressive' booklets and publications in Arabic, Hebrew and English.

Hod-Ami: POB 6108, Herzliya 46160; tel. 9-9564716; fax 9-9571582; e-mail info@hod-ami.co.il; f. 1984; computer science; CEO ITZHAK AMIHUD.

Intermedia Audio, Video and Book Publishing Ltd: 20 Hashmal St, Tel-Aviv 61367; tel. 3-5608501; fax 3-5608513; business, education, English as a second language, journalism, health, nutrition, mathematics, medicine, nursing, dentistry, self-help; Man. Dir ARIE FRIED.

Israeli Music Publications Ltd: POB 7681, 25 Keren Hayesod St, Jerusalem 91076; tel. 2-6251370; fax 2-6241378; f. 1949; books on music and musical works; Dir of Music Publications SERGEI KHANUKAEV.

Izre'el Publishing House Ltd: 76 Dizengoff St, Tel-Aviv; tel. 3-285350; f. 1933; Man. ALEXANDER IZRE'EL.

The Jerusalem Publishing House Ltd: POB 7147, 39 Tchernechovski St, Jerusalem 91071; tel. 2-5636511; fax 2-5634266; f. 1967; biblical research, history, encyclopaedias, archaeology, arts of the Holy Land, cookbooks, guidebooks, economics, politics; Dir SHLOMO S. GAFNI; Man. Editor RACHEL GILON.

Jewish History Publications (Israel 1961) Ltd: POB 1232, 29 Jabotinski St, Jerusalem; tel. 2-5632310; f. 1961; encyclopaedias, World History of the Jewish People series; Chair. ALEXANDER PELI.

Karni Publishers Ltd: POB 22383, 32 Schocken St, Tel-Aviv 61223; tel. 3-6812244; fax 3-6826138; f. 1951; children's and educational books; Publrs O. ZMORA.

Keter Publishing House Ltd: POB 7145, Givat Shaul B, Jerusalem 91071; tel. 2-6557822; fax 2-6536811; e-mail heter01@netvision .net.il; f. 1959; original and translated works of fiction, encyclopedias, non-fiction, guidebooks and children's books; publishing imprints: Israel Program for Scientific Translations, Keter Books, Encyclopedia Judaica; Man. Dir YIPTACH DEKEL.

Kinneret Publishing House: 14 Habanai St, Holon 58850; tel. 3-5582252; fax 3-5582255; f. 1980; child development and care, cookery, dance, educational, humour, non-fiction, music, home-care, psychology, psychiatry, travel; Man. Dir YORAM ROS.

Kiryat Sefer: 15 Arlosoroff St, Jerusalem; tel. 2-521141; f. 1933; concordances, dictionaries, textbooks, maps, scientific books; Dir AVRAHAM SIVAN.

Ma'ariv Book Guild Ltd: 3 Rehov Hilazon, Ramat Gan 52522; tel. 3-5752020; fax 3-7525906; f. 1954 as Sifriat-Ma'ariv Ltd; Man. Dir IZCHAK KFIR; Editor-in-Chief ARYEH NIR.

Magnes Press: The Hebrew University, POB 7695, Jerusalem 91076; tel. 2-5660341; telex 25391; fax 2-5633370; f. 1929; biblical studies, Judaica, and all academic fields; Dir DAN BENOVICI.

Rubin Mass Ltd: POB 990, 7 Ha-Ayin- Het St, Jerusalem 91000; tel. 2-6277863; fax 2-6277864; e-mail rmass@inter.net.il; internet http://www.age.co.il/mas/index/htm; f. 1927; Hebraica, Judaica, export of all Israeli books and periodicals; Dir OREN MASS.

Massada Press Ltd: Jabotinsky 29, Jerusalem 92141; tel. 2-5632310; f. 1932; biography, history, education, cookery, psychology, psychiatry, philosophy, religion, science, social sciences, sociology; Chair. and CEO ALEXANDER PELI.

Ministry of Defence Publishing House: 107 Ha' Hashmonaim St, Tel-Aviv 67133; tel. 3-5655900; fax 3-5655994; f. 1939; military literature, Judaism, history and geography of Israel; Dir JOSEPH PERLOVITZ.

M. Mizrachi Publishing House: 106 Allenby Rd, Tel-Aviv; tel. 3-621492; fax 3-5660274; f. 1960; children's books, novels; Dir MEIR MIZRACHI.

Mosad Harav Kook: POB 642, Jerusalem; tel. 2-526231; f. 1937; editions of classical works, Torah and Jewish studies; Dir Rabbi M. KATZENELENBOGEN.

Otsar Hamoreh: POB 303, 8 Ben Saruk, Tel-Aviv; tel. 3-260211; f. 1951; educational.

Alexander Peli Jerusalem Publishing Co Ltd: POB 1232, 29 Jabotinsky St, Jerusalem; tel. 2-5632310; f. 1977; encyclopedias, Judaica, history, the arts, educational material; Chair. ALEXANDER PELI.

Schocken Publishing House Ltd: POB 2316, 24 Nathan Yelin Mor St, Tel-Aviv 67015; tel. 3-5610130; fax 3-5622668; f. 1938; general; Dir Mrs RACHELI EDELMAN.

Shikmona Publishing Co Ltd: POB 7145, Givat Shaul B, Jerusalem 91071; tel. 2-6557822; fax 2-536811; e-mail ketera@netvision .net.il; f. 1965; Zionism, archaeology, art, guidebooks, fiction and non-fiction; Man. Dir YIPTACH DEKEL.

Sifriat Poalim Ltd: Gate 3, 24 Kibbutz Galuiot St, Tel-Aviv 68166; tel. 3-5183143; fax 3-5183191; f. 1939; general literature; Gen. Man. NATHAN SHAHAM.

Sinai Publishing Co: 72 Allenby St, Tel-Aviv 65172; tel. 3-663672; f. 1853; Hebrew books and religious articles; Dir MOSHE SCHLESINGER.

Steinhart-Katzir: POB 16540, Tel-Aviv 61164; tel. 3-6997561; fax 3-6997562; e-mail skp@netvision.net.il; f. 1991; travel.

Tcehrikover Publishers Ltd: 12 Hasharon St, Tel-Aviv 66185; tel. 3-370621; fax 3-374729; education, psychology, economics, psychiatry, literature, literary criticism, essays, history geography, criminology, art, languages, management; Man. Editor S. TCHERIKOVER.

MAP-Mapping and Publishing: MAP House, 18 Tchernikhovski St, Tel-Aviv 61560; tel. 3-6203252; fax 3-5257725; e-mail info@ mapa.co.il; f. 1985; history; specializes in maps, guides and scholastic books; Man. Dir DANI TRACZ; Editor-in-Chief MOULI MELTZER.

World Zionist Organization Torah Education Dept: POB 10615, Jerusalem 91104; tel. 2-6759232; fax 2-6759230; f. 1945; education, Jewish philosophy, studies in the Bible, children's books published in Hebrew, English, French, Spanish, German, Swedish and Portuguese.

Yachdav United Publishers Co Ltd: POB 20123, 29 Carlebach St, Tel-Aviv; tel. 3-5614121; fax 3-5611996; e-mail tbpai@theclub .ipc.co.il; f. 1960; educational; Chair. EPHRAIM BEN-DOR; Exec. Dir AMNON BEN-SHMUEL.

Yavneh Publishing House Ltd: 4 Mazeh St, Tel-Aviv 65213; tel. 3-6297856; telex 35770; fax 3-6293638; f. 1932; general; Dir NIRA PREISKEL.

Yeda Lakol Publications Ltd: POB 1232, 29 Jabotinsky St, Jerusalem; tel. 2-5632310; f. 1961; encyclopaedias, Judaica, the arts, educational material, children's books; Chairs. ALEXANDER PELI, RUTH PELI.

Yedioth Ahronoth Books: POB 37744, 5 Mikunis St, Tel-Aviv 61376; tel. 3-374889; telex 33847; fax 3-5377820; f. 1952; non-fiction, Jewish religion, health, music, dance, fiction, education; Man. Dir ISRAEL SHALEV; Editor-in-Chief JON FEDER.

S. Zack and Co: 2 King George St, Jerusalem 94229; tel. 2-6257819; fax 2-6252493; f. c. 1930; fiction, science, philosophy, Judaism, children's books, educational and reference books, dictionaries; Dir MICHAEL ZACK.

PUBLISHERS' ASSOCIATION

Israel Book Publishers' Association: POB 20123, 29 Carlebach St, Tel-Aviv 67132; tel. 3-5614121; fax 3-5611996; e-mail tbpai@ theclub.ipc.co.il; f. 1939; mems: 84 publishing firms; Chair. SHAI HAUSMAN; Man. Dir AMNON BEN-SHMUEL.

Broadcasting and Communications

TELECOMMUNICATIONS

Barak I.T.C.: Sival Industrial Park, 15 Harnelacha St, Rosh Hnáyin 48091; fax 3-9001023.

Bezeq, The Israel Telecommunication Corpn Ltd: POB 1088, 15 Hazvi St, Jerusalem 91010; tel. 2-5395333; telex 25225; fax 2-5378184; 73.6% state-owned; total assets US $4,869m. (Dec. 1996); Pres. ISAAC KAUL.

BROADCASTING

Radio

Israel Broadcasting Authority (IBA) (Radio): POB 28080, Jerusalem; tel. 2-240124; telex 26488; fax 2-257034; f. 1948; station in Jerusalem with additional studios in Tel-Aviv and Haifa. IBA broadcasts six programmes for local and overseas listeners on medium, shortwave and VHF/FM in 16 languages; Hebrew, Arabic, English, Yiddish, Ladino, Romanian, Hungarian, Moghrabi, Persian, French, Russian, Bucharian, Georgian, Portuguese, Spanish and Amharic; Chair. MICHA YINON; Dir-Gen. URI PORAT; Dir of Radio (vacant); Dir External Services VICTOR GRAJEWSKY.

Galei Zahal: MPOB 01005, Zahal; tel. 3-814888; fax 3-814697; f. 1950; Israeli Defence Force broadcasting station, Tel-Aviv, with studios in Jerusalem; broadcasts music, news and other programmes on medium-wave and FM stereo, 24-hour in Hebrew; Dir MOSHE SHLENSKY; Dir of Engineering G. KERNER.

Kol Israel (The Voice of Israel): POB 1082, 21 Heleni Hamalka, Jerusalem 91010; tel. 2-248715; telex 25263; fax 2-253282; internet http://www.artificia.com/html/news.cgi; broadcasts music, news, and multilingual programmes for immigrants in Hebrew, Arabic, French and English on medium wave and FM stereo; Dir and Prog. Dir AMNON NADAV.

Television

Israel Broadcasting Authority (IBA): POB 7139, Jerusalem 91071; tel. 2-5301333; fax 2-292944; broadcasts began in 1968; station in Jerusalem with additional studios in Tel-Aviv; one colour network (VHF with UHF available in all areas); one satellite channel; broadcasts in Hebrew, Arabic and English; Dir-Gen URI PORAT; Dir of Television YAIR STERN; Dir of Engineering RAFI YEOSHUA.

Israel Educational Television: Ministry of Education and Culture, 14 Klausner St, Tel-Aviv; tel. 3-6415270; fax 3-6427091; f. 1966 by Hanadiv (Rothschild Memorial Group) as Instructional Television Trust; began transmission in 1966; school programmes form an integral part of the syllabus in a wide range of subjects; also adult education; Gen. Man. AHUVA FAINMESSE; Dir of Engineering S. KASIF.

In 1986 the Government approved the establishment of a commercial radio and television network to be run in competition with the state system.

Finance

(cap. = capital; p.u. = paid up; dep. = deposits; m. = million;
res = reserves; brs = branches; amounts in shekels)

BANKING

During 1991–97 the Government raised some US $3,640m. through privatization and the issuance of shares and convertible securities in the banking sector.

Central Bank

Bank of Israel: POB 780, Bank of Israel Bldg, Kiryat Ben-Gurion, Jerusalem 91007; tel. 2-6552211; telex 25214; fax 2-6528805; e-mail webmaster@bankisrael.gov.il; f. 1954 as the Central Bank of the State of Israel; cap. and res 320m., dep. 75,991m. (Dec. 1997); Gov. Prof. Jacob A. Frenkel; 2 brs.

Principal Israeli Banks

American Israel Bank Ltd: 28A Rothschild Blvd, Tel-Aviv 61013; tel. 3-5647070; telex 341217; fax 3-5647114; f. 1933; subsidiary of Bank Hapoalim BM; total assets 3,765m., dep. 3,477m. (Dec. 1997); Chair. Y. Elinav; 18 brs.

Bank Hapoalim BM: POB 27, 50 Rothschild Blvd, Tel-Aviv 66883; tel. 3-5673333; telex 342342; fax 3-5607028; e-mail international@bnhp.co.il; f. 1921 as the Workers' Bank, name changed as above 1961; 12.3% state-owned; total assets 160,221m., dep. 147,897m. (Dec. 1997); Chair. Bd of Man. and CEO Amiram Sivan; 346 brs in Israel and abroad.

Bank Leumi le-Israel BM: POB 2, 24–32 Yehuda Halevi St, Tel-Aviv 65546; tel. 3-5148111; telex 33586; fax 3-5661872; f. 1902 as Anglo-Palestine Co; renamed Anglo-Palestine Bank 1930; reincorporated as above 1951; 63.5% state-owned total assets 145,080m., dep. 132,171m. (Dec. 1997); Chair. Eitan Raff; Pres. and CEO Galia Maor; 228 brs.

Euro-Trade Bank Ltd: POB 37318, 41 Rothschild Blvd, Tel-Aviv 66883; tel. 3-5643838; telex 371530; fax 3-5602483; f. 1953; total assets 166,650m., dep. 127,357m. (Dec. 1996); Chair. Reuven Kokolevitz; Man. Dir Menahem Weber.

First International Bank of Israel Ltd: POB 29036, Shalom Mayer Tower, 9 Ahad Ha'am St, Tel-Aviv 65251; tel. 3-5196111; telex 341252; fax 3-5100316; f. 1972 as a result of a merger between The Foreign Trade Bank Ltd and Export Bank Ltd; total assets 39,528m., cap. 25,438m., dep. 32,699m. (Dec. 1997); Chair. Yigal Arnon; Man. Dir Shlomo Piotrkowsky; 77 brs.

Industrial Development Bank of Israel Ltd: POB 33580, 2 Dafna St, Tel-Aviv 61334; tel. 3-6972727; telex 033646; fax 3-6972893; f. 1957; total assets 9,718.4m. (Dec. 1996); Chair. Shlomo Borochev; Gen. Man. Yehoshua Ichilov.

Israel Continental Bank Ltd: POB 37406, 65 Rothschild Blvd, Tel-Aviv 61373; tel. 3-5641616; telex 341447; fax 3-200399; f. 1974; capital held jointly by Bank Hapoalim BM (63%) and Bank für Gemeinwirtschaft AG (37%); cap. and res 148.3m., dep. 821.9m. (Dec. 1996); Chair. A. Sivan; Man. Dir P. Horev; 3 brs.

Israel Discount Bank Ltd: 27-31 Yehuda Halevi St, Tel-Aviv 65136; tel. 3-5145555; telex 35611; fax 3-5145346; e-mail intidb@netvision.net.il; internet http://www.israel-discount-bank.co.il; f. 1935; 51.5% state-owned; cap p.u. 93m., dep. 77,105m. (March 1998); Chair. Arie Mientkavich; Pres. and CEO Avraham Asheri; some 165 brs in Israel and abroad.

Israel General Bank Ltd: POB 677, 38 Rothschild Blvd, Tel-Aviv 61006; tel. 3-5645645; telex 33515; fax 3-5645210; f. 1934 as Palestine Credit Utility Bank Ltd, name changed as above 1964; total assets 2,883.2m., dep. 2,620.4m. (Dec. 1996); Chair. Baron Edmond de Rothschild; Man. Dir Eliezer Yones; 3 brs.

Leumi Industrial Development Bank Ltd: POB 2, 35 Yehuda Halevi St, Tel-Aviv 65136; tel. 3-5149945; telex 33586; fax 3-5149897; f. 1944; subsidiary of Bank Leumi le-Israel BM; cap. and res 81m. (Dec. 1997); Chair. B. Naveh; Gen. Man. M. Ziv.

Maritime Bank of Israel Ltd: POB 29373, 35 Ahad Ha'am St, Tel-Aviv 65202; tel. 3-5642222; telex 33507; fax 3-5642323; f. 1962; total assets 874.3m., dep. 614.3m. (Dec. 1997); Chair. Shimon Topor.

Mercantile Bank of Israel Ltd: POB 512, 24 Rothschild Blvd, Tel-Aviv; tel. 3-5607541; telex 341344; fax 3-5607949; f. as Barclays Discount Bank Ltd in 1971 by Barclays Bank International Ltd and Israel Discount Bank Ltd to incorporate Israel brs of Barclays; Israel Discount Bank Ltd became the sole owner in February 1993; total assets 334.3m., dep. 297.8m. (Dec. 1995); Gen. Man. Leon Gershon.

Union Bank of Israel Ltd: POB 2428, 6–8 Ahuzat Bayit St, Tel-Aviv 65143; tel. 3-5191276; telex 033493; fax 3-5191606; f. 1951; 23% state-owned; total assets 12,150m., dep. 10,953m. (Dec. 1997); Chair. D. Friedmann; 27 brs.

United Mizrahi Bank Ltd: POB 309, 13 Rothschild Blvd, Tel-Aviv 61002; tel. 3-5679211; telex 03-33625; fax 3-5604780; e-mail info@mizrahi.co.il; internet http://www.mizrahi.co.il; f. 1923 as Mizrahi Bank Ltd; 1969 absorbed Hapoel Hamizrahi Bank Ltd and name changed as above; 46.0% state-owned; total assets 42,899.1m., dep. 38,879.9m. (Dec. 1997); Pres. and CEO Victor Medina; 93 brs.

Mortgage Banks

Discount Mortgage Bank Ltd: 16–18 Simtat Beit Hashoeva, Tel-Aviv 65814; tel. 3-7107333; fax 3-5661704; f. 1959; subsidiary of Israel Discount Bank Ltd; cap. p.u. 1.3m., res 463.6m. (Dec. 1997); Chair. A. Mientkavich; Man. M. Eldar.

First International Mortgage Bank Ltd.: 39 Montefiore St, Tel-Aviv 65201; tel. 3-5643311; fax 3-5643321; f. 1922 as the Mortgage and Savings Bank, name changed as above 1996; subsidiary of First International Bank of Israel Ltd; cap. and res 334m. (Dec. 1996); Chair. S. Piotrkowsky; Man. Dir P. Hamo; 50 brs.

Leumi Mortgage Bank Ltd: POB 69, 31–37 Montefiore St, Tel-Aviv 65201; tel. 3-5648444; fax 3-5648334; f. 1921; subsidiary of Bank Leumi le-Israel BM; total assets 18,234.2m. (Dec. 1996); Chair. A. Zeldman; Gen. Man. R. Zabag.

Mishkan-Hapoalim Mortgage Bank Ltd: POB 1610, 2 Ibn Gvirol St, Tel-Aviv 64077; tel. 3-6970505; fax 3-6959662; f. 1950; subsidiary of Bank Hapoalim BM; total assets 8,289m., dep. 10,268.3m. (Dec. 1993); Chair. M. Olenik; Man. Dir A. Kroizer; 131 brs.

Tefahot, Israel Mortgage Bank Ltd: POB 93, 9 Heleni Hamalka St, Jerusalem 91902; tel. 2-6755222; fax 2-6755344; f. 1945; subsidiary of United Mizrahi Bank Ltd; cap. and res 1,181m., total assets 18,973m. (Dec. 1994); Chair. David Brodet; Man. Dir Uri Würzburger; 60 brs.

STOCK EXCHANGE

Tel-Aviv Stock Exchange: POB 29060, 54 Ahad Ha'am St, Tel-Aviv 65202; tel. 3-5677411; fax 3-5105379; e-mail spokesperson@tase.co.il; internet http://www.tase.co.il; f. 1953; Chair. Prof. Yair E. Orgler; Gen. Man. Saul Bronfeld.

INSURANCE

The Israel Insurance Assen lists 35 companies, a selection of which are listed below; not all companies are members of the association.

Ararat Insurance Co Ltd: Ararat House, 13 Montefiore St, Tel-Aviv 65164; tel. 3-640888; telex 341484; f. 1949; Co-Chair. Aharon Dovrat, Philip Zuckerman; Gen. Man. Pinchas Cohen.

Aryeh Insurance Co of Israel Ltd: 9 Ahad Ha'am St, Tel-Aviv 65251; tel. 3-5141777; fax 3-5179337; e-mail aryeh@isdn.net.il; f. 1948; Chair. Eliezer Kaplan.

Clal Insurance Co Ltd: POB 326, 42 Rothschild Blvd, Tel-Aviv 61002; tel. 3-627711; telex 341701; fax 3-622666; f. 1962; Man. Dir Rimon Ben-Shaoul.

Hassneh Insurance Co of Israel Ltd: POB 805, 115 Allenby St, Tel-Aviv 61007; tel. 3-5649111; telex 341105; f. 1924; Man. Dir M. Michael Miller.

Israel Phoenix Assurance Co Ltd: 30 Levontin St, Tel-Aviv 65116; tel. 3-5670111; telex 341199; fax 3-5601242; f. 1949; Chair. of Bd Joseph D. Hackmey; Man. Dir Dr Itamar Borowitz.

Maoz Insurance Co Ltd: Tel-Aviv; f. 1945; formerly Binyan Insurance Co Ltd; Chair. B. Yekutieli.

Menorah Insurance Co Ltd: Menorah House, 73 Rothschild Blvd, Tel-Aviv 65786; tel. 3-5260771; telex 341433; fax 3-5618288; f. 1935; Gen. Man. Shabtai Engel.

Migdal Insurance Co Ltd: POB 37633, 26 Sa'adiya Ga'on St, Tel-Aviv 61375; tel. 3-5637637; telex 32361; part of Bank Leumi Group; f. 1934; Chair. S. Grofman; CEO U. Levy.

Palglass Palestine Plate Glass Insurance Co Ltd: Tel-Aviv 65541; f. 1934; Gen. Man. Akiva Zalzman.

Sahar Israel Insurance Co Ltd: POB 26222, Sahar House, 23 Ben-Yehuda St, Tel-Aviv 63806; tel. 3-5140311; telex 33759; f. 1949; Chair. G. Hamburger.

Samson Insurance Co Ltd: POB 33678, Avgad Bldg, 5 Jabotinski Rd, Ramat-Gan 52520, Tel-Aviv; tel. 3-7521616; fax 3-7516644; f. 1933; Chair. E. Ben-Amram; Gen. Man. Giora Sagi.

Sela Insurance Co Ltd: 53 Rothschild Blvd, Tel-Aviv 65124; tel. 3-61028; telex 35744; f. 1938; Man. Dir E. Shani.

Shiloah Co Ltd: 2 Pinsker St, Tel-Aviv 63322; f. 1933; Gen. Man. Dr S. Bamirah; Man. Mme Bamirah.

Yardenia Insurance Co Ltd: 22 Maze St, Tel-Aviv 65213; f. 1948; Man. Dir H. Lebanon.

Zion Insurance Co Ltd: POB 1425, 41–45 Rothschild Blvd, Tel-Aviv 61013; f. 1935; Chair. A. R. Taiber.

Trade and Industry

CHAMBERS OF COMMERCE

Federation of Bi-National Chambers of Commerce and Industry with and in Israel: POB 50196, 76 Ibn Gvirol St, Tel-Aviv 61500; tel. 3-5173261; telex 342315; fax 3-5173283; federates: Israel-British Chamber of Commerce; Australia-Israel Chamber of Commerce; Chamber of Commerce and Industry Israel-Asia; Chamber of Commerce Israel-Belgique-Luxembourg; Canada-Israel Chamber of Commerce and Industry; Israel-Denmark Chamber of Commerce; Chambre de Commerce Israel-France; Chamber of Commerce and Industry Israel-Germany; Camera di Commercio Israeli-Italia; Israel-Japan Chamber of Commerce; Israel-Latin America, Spain and Portugal Chamber of Commerce; Netherlands-Israel Chamber of Commerce; Israel-Yugoslavia Chamber of Commerce; Israel-Greece Chamber of Commerce; Israel-Bulgaria Chamber of Commerce; Israel-Ireland Chamber of Commerce; Handelskammer Israel-Schweiz; Israel-South Africa Chamber of Commerce; Israel-Sweden Chamber of Commerce; Israel-Hungary Chamber of Commerce; Israel-Romania Chamber of Commerce; Israel-Russia Chamber of Commerce; Israel-Poland Chamber of Commerce; Israel-Austria Chamber of Commerce; Israel-Ukraine Chamber of Commerce; Israel-Africa Chamber of Commerce; Israel-Jordan Chamber of Commerce; Israel-Egypt Chamber of Commerce; Israel-Morocco Chamber of Commerce; Israel-Moldova Chamber of Commerce; Israel-Norway Chamber of Commerce; Israel-Slovakia Chamber of Commerce; Israel-Portugal Chamber of Commerce; Israel-Finland Chamber of Commerce; Israel-Kazakhstan Chamber of Commerce; Israel-Turkey Chamber of Commerce; Israel-Thailand Chamber of Commerce; Chair. G. PROPPER.

Federation of Israeli Chambers of Commerce: POB 20027, 84 Hahashmonaim St, Tel-Aviv 67011; tel. 3-5631010; telex 33484; fax 3-5619025; co-ordinates the Tel-Aviv, Jerusalem, Haifa and Beer-sheba Chambers of Commerce; Pres. DAN GILLERMAN.

Haifa Chamber of Commerce and Industry (Haifa and District): POB 33176, 53 Haatzmaut Rd, Haifa 31331; tel. 4-8626364; fax 4-8645428; f. 1921; 700 mems; Pres. S. GANTZ; Man. Dir C. WINNYKAMIN.

Israel-British Chamber of Commerce: POB 4610, 65 Allenby Road, Tel-Aviv 61046; tel. 3-5252232; telex 342315; fax 3-6203032; e-mail isbrit@netvision.net.il; f. 1951; 350 mems; Chair. AMNON DOTAN; Exec. Dir FELIX KIPPER.

Jerusalem Chamber of Commerce: POB 2083, 10 Hillel St, Jerusalem 91020; tel. 2-6254333; fax 2-6254335; f. 1908; c. 300 mems; Pres. JOSEPH PERLMAN.

Tel-Aviv-Jaffa Chamber of Commerce: POB 20027, 84 Hahashmonaim St, Tel-Aviv 61200; tel. 3-5631010 telex 33484; fax 3-5619025; f. 1919; 1,800 mems; Pres. DAN GILLERMAN.

INDUSTRIAL AND TRADE ASSOCIATIONS

Agricultural Export Co (AGREXCO): Tel-Aviv; state-owned agricultural marketing organization; Dir-Gen. AMOTZ AMIAD.

The Agricultural Union: Tchlenov 20, Tel-Aviv; consists of more than 50 agricultural settlements and is connected with marketing and supplying organizations, and Bahan Ltd, controllers and auditors.

Central Union of Artisans and Small Manufacturers: POB 4041, Tel-Aviv 61040; f. 1907; has a membership of more than 40,000 divided into 70 groups according to trade; the union is led by a 17-man Presidium; Chair. JACOB FRANK; Sec. ITZHAK HASSON; 30 brs.

Citrus Marketing Board: POB 80, Beit Dagan 50250; tel. 3-9683811; fax 3-9683838; f. 1942; the central co-ordinating body of citrus growers and exporters in Israel; represents the citrus industry in international organizations; licenses private exporters; controls the quality of fruit; has responsibility for Jaffa trademarks; mounts advertising and promotion campaigns for Jaffa citrus fruit worldwide; carries out, research into and development of new varieties of citrus fruit, and 'environmentally friendly' fruit; Chair. D. KRITCHMAN; Gen. Man. M. DAVIDSON.

Farmers' Union of Israel: POB 209, 8 Kaplan St, Tel-Aviv; tel. 3-69502227; fax 3-6918228; f. 1913; membership of 7,000 independent farmers, citrus and winegrape growers; Pres. PESACH GRUPPER; Dir-Gen. SHLOMO REISMAN.

Fruit Board of Israel: POB 20117, 119 Rehov Hahashmonaim, Tel-Aviv 61200; tel. 3-5612929; fax 3-5614672; Dir-Gen. SHALOM BLAYER.

General Assen of Merchants in Israel: 6 Rothschild Blvd, Tel-Aviv; the organization of retail traders; has a membership of 30,000 in 60 brs.

Israel Cotton Production and Marketing Board Ltd: POB 384, Herzlia B'46103; tel. 3-9509491; fax 3-9509159.

Israel Diamond Exchange Ltd: POB 3222, Ramat-Gan, Tel-Aviv; tel. 3-5760211; fax 3-5750652; f. 1937; production, export, import and finance facilities; net exports (1997) US $4,101m.; Pres. ITZHAK FOREM.

Israel Export Institute: POB 50084, 29 Rehov Hamered, Tel-Aviv 68125; tel. 3-5142830; fax 3-5142902; Dir-Gen. AMIR HAYEK.

Israel Journalists' Assen Ltd: 4 Kaplan St, Tel-Aviv; tel. 3-256141; Sec. YONA SHIMSHI.

Kibbutz Industries' Assen: 8 Rehov Shaul Hamelech, Tel-Aviv 64733; tel. 3-6955413; fax 3-6951464; e-mail luz@netvision.net.il; liaison office for marketing and export of the goods produced by Israel's kibbutzim; Pres. MICHA HERTZ.

Manufacturers' Assen of Israel: POB 50022, Industry House, 29 Hamered St, Tel-Aviv 61500; tel. 3-5198787; fax 3-5162026; 1,700 mem.-enterprises employing nearly 85% of industrial workers in Israel; Pres. DAN PROPPER.

UTILITIES

The Israel Electric Corporation and the **Mekorot—Water Corporation** are two of Israel's largest state-owned companies, with total assets valued at US $10,390m. and US $2,018m., respectively, at the end of 1996.

MAJOR COMPANIES

Elbit Ltd: POB 539, Haifa 31053; tel. 4-315315; telex 46586; fax 4-550002; producers of computers and defence electronics; subsidiary of ELRON Electronic Industries; sales US $176m., profits US $16m. (1986/87); Pres. and CEO EMMANUEL GILL.

Elscint Ltd: Haifa; tel. 4-8310310; telex 46656; fax 4-525608; f. 1969; designers and mfrs of electronic medical diagnostic equipment (body and brain scanners), nuclear medicine cameras and processors, whole body computerized tomographers, magnetic resonance imagers (MRI) and ultrasound scanners; Pres. JONATHAN ADERETH; 1,970 employees.

Israel Aircraft Industries Ltd (IAI): Ben-Gurion International Airport; tel. 3-9353111; telex 38014; fax 3-9353131; f. 1953; 100% state-owned; total assets US $1,635m. (Dec. 1996); designers and mfrs of military and civil aerospace; Pres. and CEO MOSHE KERET; 13,100 employees.

Israel Chemicals: Tel-Aviv; 49% state-owned; total assets US $3,056m. (Dec. 1996).

Koor Industries Ltd: Tel-Aviv; telex 33758; Israel's largest industrial company; subsidiary of Hevrat Haovdim, the Histadrut's (the National Labour Federation) industrial arm; Man. Dir JONATHAN KOLBER; 31,000 employees (June 1988).

Polgat Industries: mfrs of textiles; Chair. ISRAEL POLLACK.

Scitex Ltd: Herzliya; telex 341939; f. 1968; mfr of computerized imaging equipment for the publishing industry; Chair. and CEO ARIE ROSENFELD.

Soltam: mfr of artillery; Man. Dir ELAZAR BARAK.

Tadiran Israel Electronics Industries Ltd: Givat Shmuel; telex 341692; Israel's leading mfr of civil and military electronics; subsidiary of Koor Industries Ltd.

The Histadrut

Hahistadrut Haklalit shel Haovdim Beeretz Israel (General Federation of Labour in Israel): 93 Arlosoroff St, Tel-Aviv 62098; tel. 3-6921111; telex 342488; fax 3-6969906; f. 1920; publs *Labour in Israel* (quarterly) in English, French, Spanish and German.

The General Federation of Labour in Israel, usually known as the Histadrut, is the largest voluntary organization in Israel, and the most important economic body in the state. It is open to all workers, including the self-employed, members of co-operatives and of the liberal professions, as well as housewives, students, pensioners and the unemployed. Members of two small religious labour organizations, Histadrut Hapoel Hamizrahi and Histadrut Poale Agudat Israel, also belong to the trade union section and social services of the Histadrut, which thus extend to c. 85% of all workers. Dues—between 3.6% and 5.8% of wages—cover all its trade union, health insurance and social service activities. The Histadrut engages in four main fields of activity: trade union organization (with some 50 affiliated trade unions and 65 local labour councils operating throughout the country); social services (including a comprehensive health insurance scheme 'Kupat Holim', pension and welfare funds, etc.); educational and cultural activities (vocational schools, workers' colleges, theatre and dance groups, sports clubs, youth movement); and economic development (undertaken by Hevrat Haovdim (Labour Economy), which includes industrial enterprises partially or wholly owned by the Histadrut, agricultural and transport co-operatives, workers' bank, insurance company, publishing house etc.). A women's organization, Na'amat, which also belongs to the Histadrut, operates nursery homes and kindergartens, provides vocational education and promotes legislation for the protection and benefit of working women. The Histadrut publishes its own daily newspaper, *Davar*, in Hebrew. The Histadrut is a member of the ICFTU and its affiliated trade secretariats, APRO, ICA and various international professional organizations.

Secretary-General: HAIM RAMON.

ORGANIZATION

In 1989 the Histadrut had a membership of 1,630,000. In addition some 110,000 young people under 18 years of age belong to the Organization of Working and Student Youth, a direct affiliate of the Histadrut.

All members take part in elections to the Histadrut Convention (Veida), which elects the General Council (Moetsa) and the Executive Committee (Vaad Hapoel). The latter elects the 41-member Executive Bureau (Vaada Merakezet), which is responsible for day-to-day implementation of policy. The Executive Committee also elects the Secretary-General, who acts as its chairman as well as head of the organization as a whole and chairman of the Executive Bureau. Nearly all political parties are represented on the Histadrut Executive Committee.

The Executive Committee has the following departments: Trade Union, Organization and Labour Councils, Education and Culture, Social Security, Industrial Democracy, Students, Youth and Sports, Consumer Protection, Administration, Finance and International.

TRADE UNION ACTIVITIES

Collective agreements with employers fix wage scales, which are linked with the retail price index; provide for social benefits, including paid sick leave and employers' contributions to sick and pension and provident funds; and regulate dismissals. Dismissal compensation is regulated by law. The Histadrut actively promotes productivity through labour management boards and the National Productivity Institute, and supports incentive pay schemes.

There are unions for the following groups: clerical workers, building workers, teachers, engineers, agricultural workers, technicians, textile workers, printing workers, diamond workers, metal workers, food and bakery workers, wood workers, government employees, seamen, nurses, civilian employees of the armed forces, actors, musicians and variety artists, social workers, watchmen, cinema technicians, institutional and school staffs, pharmacy employees, medical laboratory workers, X-ray technicians, physiotherapists, social scientists, microbiologists, psychologists, salaried lawyers, pharmacists, physicians, occupational therapists, truck and taxi drivers, hotel and restaurant workers, workers in Histadrut-owned industry, garment, shoe and leather workers, plastic and rubber workers, editors of periodicals, painters and sculptors and industrial workers.

Histadrut Trade Union Department: Dir HAIM HABERFELD.

ECONOMIC ACTIVITIES AND SOCIAL SERVICES

These include Hevrat Haovdim (employing 260,000 workers in 1983), Kupat Holim (the Sick Fund, covering almost 77% of Israel's population), seven pension funds, and Na'amat (see above).

Other Trade Unions

General Federation of West Bank Trade Unions: Sec.-Gen. SHAHER SAAD.

Histadrut Haovdim Haleumit (National Labour Federation): 23 Sprintzak St, Tel-Aviv 64738; tel. 3-6958351; fax 3-6961753; f. 1934; 170,000 mems; Chair. HIRSHZON ABRAHAM.

Histadrut Hapoel Hamizrahi (National Religious Workers' Party): 166 Even Gavirol St, Tel-Aviv 62023; tel. 3-5442151; fax 3-5468942; 150,000 mems in 85 settlements and 15 kibbutzim; Sec.-Gen. ELIEZER ABTABI.

Histadrut Poale Agudat Israel (Agudat Israel Workers' Organization): POB 11044, 64 Frishman St, Tel-Aviv; tel. 3-5242126; fax 3-5230689; has 33,000 members in 16 settlements and 8 educational insts.

Transport

RAILWAYS

Freight traffic consists mainly of grain, phosphates, potash, containers, petroleum and building materials. Rail service serves Haifa and Ashdod ports on the Mediterranean Sea, while a combined railroad service extends to Eilat port on the Red Sea. Passenger services operate between the main towns: Nahariya, Haifa, Tel-Aviv and Jerusalem. In 1988 the National Ports Authority assumed responsibility for the rail system.

Israel Railways: POB 18085, Central Station, Tel-Aviv 61180; tel. 3-6937401; telex 46570; fax 3-6937480; the total length of main line is 530 km and there are 170 km of branch line; gauge 1,435 mm; Gen. Man. EHUD HADAR.

Underground Railway

Haifa Underground Funicular Railway: 122 Hanassi Ave, Haifa 34633; tel. 04-376861; fax 04-376875; opened 1959; 2 km in operation; Man. AVI TELLEM.

ROADS

In 1996 there were 15,065 km of paved roads, of which 56 km were motorways, 4,745 km highways, main or national roads and 10,064 km other roads.

Ministry of National Infrastructure: POB 13198, Public Works Dept, Jerusalem; tel. 2-584711; fax 2-823532.

SHIPPING

At 31 December 1997 Israel's merchant fleet consisted of 55 vessels amounting to 793,990 grt.

Haifa and Ashdod are the main ports in Israel. The former is a natural harbour, enclosed by two main breakwaters and dredged to 45 ft below mean sea-level. In 1965 the deep water port was completed at Ashdod which had a capacity of about 8.6m. tons in 1988.

The port of Eilat is Israel's gateway to the Red Sea. It is a natural harbour, operated from a wharf. Another port, to the south of the original one, started operating in 1965.

The Israel Ports and Railways Authority: POB 20121, Maya Building, 74 Petach Tikva St, Tel-Aviv 61201; tel. 3-5657000; fax 3-5121048; f. 1961; to plan, build, develop, administer, maintain and operate the ports and railways. In 1988/89 investment plans amounted to US $68m. for the development budget in Haifa, Ashdod and Eilat ports. Cargo traffic April 1989–March 1990 amounted to 16.2m. tons (oil excluded); Chair. ARTHUR ISRAELOVICHI; Dir-Gen. SHORESH LEVER.

ZIM Israel Navigation Co Ltd: POB 1723, 7–9 Pal-Yam Ave, Haifa 31000; tel. 4-8652111; telex 46501; fax 4-8652956; e-mail zimpress@zim.co.il; internet http://www.zim.co.il; f. 1945; runs cargo and container services in the Mediterranean and to northern Europe, North, South and Central America, the Far East, Africa and Australia; operates 80 ships (including 6 general cargo ships, 23 container ships, 7 multipurpose ships, 1 bulk carrier and 1 pure car carrier); total cargo carried: more than 973,000 TEUs in 1997; Chair. A. MAR-HAIM; Pres. and CEO Dr Y. SEBBA.

CIVIL AVIATION

Israel Airports Authority: Ben-Gurion International Airport, Tel-Aviv; tel. 3-9710576; telex 381050; fax 3-9721722; Dir-Gen. AVI KOSTELITZ.

El Al Israel Airlines Ltd: POB 41, Ben-Gurion International Airport, Tel-Aviv 70100; tel. 3-9716111; telex 381007; fax 3-9716040; f. 1948; 100% state-owned; total assets US $305m. (Dec. 1996); daily services to most capitals of Europe; over 20 flights weekly to New York; services to the USA, Canada, China, Egypt, India, Kenya, South Africa, Thailand and Turkey; Pres. JOEL FELDSCHUH.

Arkia Israeli Airlines Ltd: POB 39301, Sde-Dov Airport, Tel-Aviv 61392; tel. 3-6902222; telex 341749; fax 3-6991390; f. 1980 through merger of Kanaf-Arkia Airlines and Aviation Services; scheduled passenger services linking Tel-Aviv, Jerusalem, Haifa, Eilat, Rosh Pina and Masada; charter services to European destinations; Chair. Y. ARNON; Pres. and CEO Prof. ISRAEL BOROVICH.

Tourism

In 1996 some 2,100,051 tourists visited Israel. Tourist receipts in that year totalled US $2,771m.

Ministry of Tourism: POB 1018, 24 King George St, Jerusalem 91000; tel. 2-6754811; fax 2-6250890; Minister of Tourism MOSHE KATZAV; Dir-Gen. DAVID LITVAK.

Defence

The General Staff: This consists of the Chiefs of the General Staff, Manpower, Logistics and Intelligence Branches of the Defence Forces, the Commanders of the Air Force and the Navy, and the officers commanding the three Regional Commands (Northern, Central and Southern). It is headed by the Chief of Staff of the Armed Forces.

Chief of Staff of the Armed Forces: Lt-Gen. AMNON LIPKIN-SHAHAK.

Head of Ground Forces Command: Maj.-Gen. ISRAEL TAL.

Commander of the Air Force: Maj.-Gen. AVIHU BIN-NUN.

Commander of the Navy: Rear-Admiral AVRAHAM BEN SHOSHAN.

Defence Budget (1997): 22,000m. shekels.

Military Service (Jewish and Druze population only; Christians and Arabs may volunteer): Officers are conscripted for regular service of 48 months, men 36 months, women 21 months. Annual training as reservists thereafter, to age 42 for men (54 for some specialists), 24 (or marriage) for women.

Total Armed Forces (August 1997): 175,000: including 138,500 conscripts; this can be raised to 605,000 by mobilizing the 430,000 reservists within 48–72 hours; army 134,000 (114,700 conscripts; navy 9,000 (2,000–3,000 conscripts); air force 32,000 (21,800 conscripts).

Paramilitary Forces (August 1997): 6,050.

Education

The present-day school system is based on the Compulsory Education Law (1949), the State Education Law (1953), the School Inspection Law (1969) and on certain provisions of the 1933 Education Ordinance dating back to the British Mandatory Administration. The first of these introduced free compulsory primary education for all children aged between the ages of five and 13 (one year kindergarten, eight years' elementary schooling). This law was extended, with the school reform of 1968, to include the ninth and tenth grades. In the 1979/80 school year free, but not compulsory, education was extended up to and including the 12th grade.

The State Education Law abolished the old complicated Trend Education System, and vested the responsibility for education in the Government, thus providing a unified state-controlled elementary school system. The law does, however, recognize two main forms of Primary Education—(*a*) State Education; (*b*) Recognized Non-State Education. State Education may be sub-divided into two distinct categories of schools—State Schools and State Religious Schools where the language of instruction is Hebrew, and State Schools where the language of instruction is Arabic. Schools and kindergartens of the state system are in the joint ownership of the state and the local authorities, while the recognized non-state institutions are essentially privately-owned and mainly religious, although they are subsidized, and supervised by the state and the local authorities.

The largest 'recognized' school system is the Agudat Israel Schools (ultra-orthodox religious). The others are mainly Christian denominational schools.

State Primary Education is financed by a partnership of the central government and the local authorities. Since 1953 the salaries of all teachers of State Schools have been paid by the central government, while the cost of maintenance and of maintenance services, and the provision of new buildings and equipment have been the responsibility of the local authorities. The state does not impose an education tax but local authorities may, with the Ministry's approval, levy a rate on parents for special services.

The State provides schools in which the language of instruction is either Hebrew or Arabic according to the language spoken by the majority of the local population. Nevertheless, some Arab children attend Jewish secondary, vocational, agricultural and teacher-training colleges. In the Jewish sector there is a distinct line of division between the secular State Schools and the religious State Schools, which are established on the demand of parents in any locality, provided that a certain minimum number of pupils have first been enrolled. In the Arab Schools all instruction is in Arabic, and there is a special Department for Arabic Education in the Ministry of Education and Culture. The administration of Arab education is in the process of being decentralized. Some 90% of the Arab children attend school regularly.

The Compulsory Education Law and the institutions it established for absorbing weak students have cancelled the need for special systems for working youth. The law provides special education for emotionally or physically handicapped children. In addition, special attention is given to those children who are culturally deprived and a great variety of methods are being devised to bring them up to the level of the other children.

Post-Primary Education is free, lasts six years, four of which are compulsory, and is divided into an intermediate and a higher level.

The intermediate level provides general education and the higher level is roughly divided into academic; technical and vocational; and agricultural. The last two categories also have pre-academic streams lasting from one to two years and receive all the benefits of the regular post-primary schools. The pupils graduating from academic high school receive either a school leaving certificate or *bagrut* (matriculation). The *bagrut* certificate entitles the pupil to enter university, although the university is not obliged to accept him or her.

The frameworks offered by vocational and technical schools can be divided into three types: practical-technical; general-technical; and secondary-technical. All three types are of three or four years' duration, depending on whether they are run under the Reform or under the old system. Very few of the practical-technical schools still offer a two-year course, i.e. a total of 11 years' schooling. The practical-technical schools train their pupils mainly for a profession and the ratio between general studies and vocational-technical studies is 40:60. The general-technical schools award a school leaving certificate to those pupils who complete the course successfully. This entitles them to continue their studies in the third level of education after some complementary examinations, either for one additional year to obtain a technician's certificate (Techna'i), or for two additional years to obtain the certificate of a practical engineer (Handessa'i). The ratio between general studies and vocational studies in these schools is 50:50. All graduates of the secondary-technical schools may sit for the *bagrut* examinations. Even without achieving the *bagrut* certificate the pupils may continue their studies in the short-cycle post-secondary schools, described above, without further examination and obtain the technician or practical engineer certificate. The ratio between general studies and technical-vocational studies in these schools is 60:40. Those who graduate and complete their matriculation (*bagrut*) examinations are eligible for admission to any Israeli university.

Agricultural post-primary courses are of either three or four years' duration (again depending on the Reform) and some schools offer an additional year or year-and-a-half (13th and 14th grade) leading to a practical engineer certificate. The holders of this certificate are eligible, without further examinations, for study in agricultural engineering or general agricultural higher studies in the Technion (the Israel Institute of Technology) at Haifa or the Faculty of Agriculture at the Hebrew University of Jerusalem. Unlike pupils at vocational-technical post-primary schools, all those completing agricultural courses may sit for the *bagrut* examinations. By and large, agricultural post-primary schools are boarding schools although some, mainly those of the kibbutz and the moshav movements, are regional day schools.

Adult Education. There is an extensive adult education programme. Programmes extend from literacy courses through primary and secondary level studies up to second-chance university facilities. There are post-army preparatory courses for entry into the university. High school courses may be completed in the army and in 1976 the Everyman's University began, based on the British model of Open University.

Teacher Training. Almost all kindergarten and primary school teachers are trained in three to three-and-a-half year courses at post-secondary teacher training institutions (Mossadot Le-Hakhsharat Morim Ve Gananot). The Ministry's policy is to have only three-year teacher training colleges and to extend the training period to four years for a B.Ed. degree. Government regulations require that teachers for grades seven to 10 have a BA and a university teaching certificate, while for grades 11 and 12 they are required to have a master's degree and a university teaching certificate. The *bagrut* certificate and a passing grade in the psychometric examination are required for admittance to the above teacher training institutions. In some of the teacher training schools there are special courses for instruction in Arabic education, in addition to separate Arab teacher training schools.

Occupied Territories

THE GOLAN HEIGHTS

Location, Climate

The Golan Heights, a mountainous plateau which formed most of Syria's Quneitra Province (1,710 sq km) and parts of Dera'a Province, was occupied by Israel after the 1967 Arab–Israeli War. Following the Disengagement Agreement of 1974, Israel continued to occupy some 70% of the territory (1,176 sq km), valued for its strategic position and abundant water resources (the headwaters of the River Jordan have their source on the slopes of Mount Hermon). The average height of the Golan is approximately 1,200 m above sea-level in the northern region and about 300 m above sea-level in the southern region, near Lake Tiberias (the Sea of Galilee). Rainfall ranges from about 1,000 mm per year in the north to less than 600 mm per year in the southern region.

Administration

Prior to the Israeli occupation, the Golan Heights were incorporated by Syria into a provincial administration of which the city of Quneitra, with a population at the time of 27,378, was capital. The disengagement agreement that was mediated in 1974 by the US Secretary of State, Henry Kissinger, after the 1973 Arab–Israeli War, provided for the withdrawal of Israeli forces from Quneitra. Before they withdrew, however, Israeli army engineers destroyed the city. In December 1981 the Israeli Knesset enacted the Golan Annexation Law, whereby Israeli civilian legislation was extended to the territory of Golan, now under the administrative jurisdiction of the Commissioner for the Northern District of Israel. The Arab-Druze community of the Golan immediately responded by declaring a three-day strike and appealed to the UN Secretary-General to force Israel to rescind the annexation decision. At the seventh round of multilateral talks between Israeli and Arab delegations in Washington in August 1992, the Israeli Government of Itzhak Rabin for the first time accepted that UN Security Council Resolution 242, adopted in 1967, applied to the Golan Heights. The withdrawal of Israel from the Golan Heights is one of President Assad of Syria's primary objectives in any future peace agreement with Israel.

Demography and Economic Affairs

As a consequence of the Israeli occupation, an estimated 93% of the ethnically diverse Syrian population of 147,613, distributed across 163 villages and towns and 108 individual farms, was expelled. The majority were Arab Sunni Muslims, but the population also included Alawite and Druze minorities and also some Circassians, Turcomen, Armenians and Kurds. Approximately 9,000 Palestinian refugees from the 1948 Arab–Israeli War also inhabited the area. At the time of the occupation, the Golan was a predominantly agricultural province, 64% of the labour force of which was employed in agriculture. Only one-fifth of the population resided in the administrative centres. By 1991 the Golan Heights had a Jewish population of approximately 12,000 living in 21 Jewish settlements (four new settlements had been created by the end of 1992), and a predominantly Druze population of approximately 16,000 living in the only six remaining villages, of which Majd ash-Shams is by far the largest. The Golan Heights have remained predominantly an agricultural area, and, although large numbers of the Druze population now work in Israeli industry in Eilat, Tel-Aviv and Jerusalem, the indigenous economy relies almost solely on the cultivation of apples, for which the area is famous. The apple orchards benefit from a unique combination of fertile soils, abundance of water and a conducive climate.

EAST JERUSALEM

Location, Climate

Greater Jerusalem includes Israeli West Jerusalem (99% Jewish), the Old City and Mount of Olives, East Jerusalem (the Palestinian residential and commercial centre), Arab villages declared to be part of Jerusalem by Israel in 1967 and Jewish neighbourhoods constructed since 1967, either on land expropriated from Arab villages or in areas requisitioned as 'government land'. Although the area of the Greater Jerusalem district is 627 sq km, the Old City of Jerusalem covers just 1 sq km.

Administration

Until the 1967 Arab–Israeli War, Jerusalem had been divided into the new city of West Jerusalem—captured by Jewish forces in 1948—and the old city, East Jerusalem, which was part of Jordan. Israel's victory in 1967, however, reunited the city under Israeli control. Two weeks after the fighting had stopped, on 28 June, Israeli law was applied to East Jerusalem and the municipal boundaries were extended by 45 km (28 miles). Jerusalem had been, in effect, annexed. Israeli officials, however, still refer to the 'reunification' of Jerusalem.

Demography and Economic Affairs

In June 1993 the Deputy Mayor of Jerusalem, Avraham Kahila, declared that the city now 'had a majority of Jews', based on population projections which estimated the Jewish population at 158,000 and the Arab population at 155,000. This was a significant moment for the Israeli administration, as this had been a long-term objective. Immediately prior to the June 1967 Arab–Israeli War, East Jerusalem and its Arab environs had an Arab population of approximately 70,000, and a small Jewish population in the old Jewish quarter of the city. By contrast, Israeli West Jerusalem had a Jewish population of 196,000. As a result of this population imbalance, in the Greater Jerusalem district as a whole the Jewish population was in the majority even prior to the occupation of the whole city in 1967. Israeli policy following the occupation of East Jerusalem and the West Bank consisted of encircling the eastern sector of the city with Jewish settlements. In contrast to the more politically sensitive siting of Jewish settlements in the old Arab quarter of Jerusalem, the Government of Itzhak Rabin concentrated on the outer circle of settlement building. Greater Jerusalem has been reported to have a Jewish majority of 73%.

The Old City, within the walls of which are found the ancient quarters of the Jews, Christians, Muslims and Armenians, has a population of approximately 25,500 Arabs and 2,600 Jews. In addition, there are some 600 recent Jewish settlers in the Arab quarter.

Many imaginative plans have been submitted with the aim of finding a solution to the problem of sharing Jerusalem between Arabs and Jews, including the proposal that the city be placed under international trusteeship, under the auspices of the UN. However, to make the implementation of such plans an administrative as well as a political quagmire, the Israeli administration, after occupying the whole city in June 1967, began creating 'facts on the ground'. Immediately following the occupation, all electricity, water and telephone grids in West Jerusalem were extended to the east. Roads were widened and cleared, and the Arab population immediately in front of the 'Wailing Wall' was forcibly evicted. Arabs living in East Jerusalem became 'permanent residents' and could apply for Israeli citizenship if they wished (in contrast to Arabs in the West Bank and Gaza Strip). However, few chose to do so. None the less, issued with identity cards (excluding the estimated 25,000 Arabs from the West Bank and Gaza Strip living illegally in the city), the Arab residents were taxed by the Israeli authorities, and their businesses and banks became subject to Israeli laws and business regulations. Now controlling approximately one-half of all land in East Jerusalem and the surrounding Palestinian villages (previously communally, or privately, owned by Palestinians), the Israeli authorities allowed Arabs to construct buildings on only 10%–15% of the land in the city; and East Jerusalem's commercial district has been limited to three streets. The Palestinian economy was quite seriously affected by the drop in tourism during the *intifada* and by curfews, enforced tax collections and confiscations of property exercised by the Israeli authorities.

Since the 1993 signing of the Declaration of Principles on Palestinian Self-Rule, the future status of Jerusalem and the continuing expansion of Jewish settlements in East Jerusalem have emerged as two of the most crucial issues affecting the peace process (see section on History, and The Jerusalem Issue, p. 98).

Bibliography

GENERAL

Arian, Asher. *Security Threatened: Surveying Israeli Opinion on Peace and War*. Cambridge University Press, 1996.

Avnery, Uri. *Israel without Zionists*. London, Collier-Macmillan, 1969.

Black, Ian, and Morris, Benny. *Israel's Secret Wars: History of Israel's Intelligence Services*. New York, Grove Weidenfeld, 1992.

Burr, Gerald. *Behind the Star: inside Israel today*. London, Constable, 1990.

Cohen, Mark R., and Udovitch, Abraham L. *Jews among Arabs: Contacts and Boundaries*. Princeton, The Darwin Press, 1994.

Eban, Abba. *Personal Witness: Israel through my eyes*. London, Jonathan Cape, 1993.

Ellis, Mark H. *Beyond Innocence and Redemption: Confronting the Holocaust and Israeli Power*. San Francisco, Harper and Row, 1990.

Ezrahi, Yaron. *Rubber Bullets: Power and Conscience in Modern Israel*. New York, Farrar Strauss Giroux, 1997.

Glueck, Nelson. *The River Jordan*. Philadelphia, 1946. *Rivers in the Desert*. London, 1959.

Hersh, Seymour. *The Samson Option: Israel, America and the Bomb*. London, Faber and Faber, 1991.

Koestler, Arthur. *The Thirteenth Tribe*. London, Random House, 1976.

Kohn, Hans. *Nationalism and Imperialism in the Hither East*. London, 1932.

Kollek, Teddy, and Pearlman, Moshe. *Jerusalem, Sacred City of Mankind*. London, Weidenfeld and Nicolson, 1968.

Landau, David (Ed.). *Battling for Peace*. London, Weidenfeld and Nicolson, 1995.

Marmorstein, Emile. *Heaven at Bay: The Jewish Kulturkampf in the Holy Land*. Oxford University Press, 1969.

Orni, E., and Efrat, E. *The Geography of Israel*. New York, Darey, 1965.

Parkes, J. W. *The Emergence of the Jewish Problem, 1878–1939*. Oxford, 1946.

   A History of Palestine from AD *135 to Modern Times*. London, Gollancz, 1949.

   End of Exile. New York, 1954.

   Whose Land? A History of the Peoples of Palestine. Harmondsworth, Pelican, 1970.

Patai, R. *Israel Between East and West*. Philadelphia, 1953.

   Culture and Conflict. New York, 1962.

Raviv, Dan, and Melman, Yossi. *Every Spy a Prince: the complete history of Israel's intelligence community*. Boston, Houghton Mifffin, 1990.

Shapiro, Harry L. *The Jewish People: a biological history*. UNESCO, 1960.

Tuchman, Barbara W. *Bible and Sword*. London, Redman, 1957; New York, Minerva, 1968.

Weingrod, Alex. *Reluctant Pioneers, Village Development in Israel*. New York, Cornell University Press, 1966.

Zander, Walter. *Israel and the Holy Places of Christendom*. Weidenfeld and Nicolson, 1972.

ANCIENT HISTORY

De Vaux, R. *Ancient Israel: Its Life and Institutions*. New York, 1961.

Orlinsky, H. M. *Ancient Israel*. Cornell University Press.

Smith, Sir G. A. *Historical Geography of the Holy Land*. 24th edn, London, 1931.

Yadin, Yigael. *Message of the Scrolls*. New York, Grosset and Dunlap.

   Masada. London, Weidenfeld and Nicolson, 1966.

RECENT HISTORY

Allon, Yigal. *The Making of Israel's Army*. London, Vallentine, Mitchell, 1970.

Aruri, Naseer. *The Obstruction of Peace: the US, Israel and the Palestinians*. Monroe, Maine, Common Courage Press, 1995.

Barbour, Nevill. *Nisi Dominus: a survey of the Palestine Controversy*. London, Harrap, 1946, reprinted by the Institute for Palestine Studies, Beirut, 1969.

Ben-Zvi, Abraham. *The United States and Israel: the limits of the special relationship*. New York, Columbia University Press, 1993.

Bentwich, Norman and Helen. *Mandate Memories, 1918–1948*. London, Hogarth Press, 1965.

Bermant, Chaim. *Israel*. London, Thames and Hudson, 1967.

Berger, Earl. *The Covenant and the Sword, Arab-Israel Relations 1948–56*. Toronto, University of Toronto Press, 1965.

Bethell, Nicholas. *The Palestine Triangle: the Struggle Between the British, the Jews and the Arabs, 1935–48*. London, André Deutsch, 1979.

Cattan, Henry. *Palestine, the Arabs and Israel*. London, Longmans Green, 1969.

   The Palestine Question. London, Croom Helm; New York, Methuen, 1987.

Cohen, Michael J. *Palestine, Retreat from the Mandate: The Making of British Policy*. London, Elek, 1978.

Crossman, R. H. S. *Palestine Mission*. London, 1947.

Draper, T. *Israel and World Politics: Roots of the Third Arab-Israeli War*. London, Secker and Warburg, 1968.

Esco Foundation for Palestine. *Palestine: A Study of Jewish, Arab and British Policies*. 2 vols, New Haven, 1947.

Farsoun, Samir K., and Zacharia, Christina E. *Palestine and the Palestinians*. London, Harper Collins, 1997.

Finkelstein, Norman G. *Image and Reality of the Israel-Palestine Conflict*. London and New York, Verso, 1995.

Frankel, Glenn. *Beyond the Promised Land: Jews and Arabs on a hard road to a new Israel*. New York, Simon and Schuster, 1995.

Fraser, T. G. *The Arab-Israeli Conflict*. London, Macmillan, 1995.

Gabbay, Rony E. *A Political Study of the Arab-Jewish Conflict, the Arab Refugee Problem*. Geneva and Paris, 1959.

Green, Stephen. *Taking Sides: America and Israel in the Middle East, 1948–1967*. London, Faber and Faber, 1984.

   Living by the Sword: America and Israel in the Middle East, 1968–1987. London, Faber and Faber, 1988.

Grossman, David. *The Yellow Wind*. London, Jonathan Cape, 1988.

Heller, Joseph. *The Stern Gang: ideology, politics and terror 1940–49*. London, Frank Cass, 1995.

Howard, M., and Hunter, R. *Israel and the Arab World*. Beirut, Institute for Palestine Studies.

Jansen, Michael. *The Battle of Beirut*. London, Zed Press, 1982.

Jiryis, Sabri. *The Arabs in Israel*. Beirut, Institute for Palestine Studies, 1968.

Kader, Razzak Abdel. *The Arab-Jewish Conflict*. 1961.

Karsh, Efraim. *Peace in the Middle East: the challenge for Israel*. London, Frank Cass, 1994.

Katz, Samuel M. *Guards without Frontiers: Israel's war against terrorism*. London, Arms and Armour Press, 1990.

Khalidi, Walid. *From Haven to Conquest: Readings in Zionism and the Palestine Problem until 1948*. Beirut, Institute for Palestine Studies, 1971.

Kimche, Jon. *Palestine or Israel*. London, Secker & Warburg, 1973.

Kimche, Jon and David. *Both Sides of the Hill: Britain and the Palestine War*. London, Secker and Warburg, 1960.

Koestler, Arthur. *Promise and Fulfilment: Palestine, 1917–1949*. London, 1949.

   Thieves in the Night. New York and London, 1946.

Landau, Jacob M. *The Arabs in Israel*. London, Oxford University Press, 1969.

Laqueur, Walter. *The Road to War 1967*. London, Weidenfeld and Nicolson, 1968.

   The Israel-Arab Reader. London, Weidenfeld and Nicolson, 1969.

Lazin, A., and Mahler, G. S. *Israel in the Nineties: Development and Conflict*. University Press of Florida, 1996.

Levran, Aharon. *Israeli Strategy after Desert Storm: lessons of the second Gulf war*. London, Frank Cass, 1997.

Lilienthal, Alfred M. *The Other Side of the Coin: An American Perspective of the Arab-Israeli Conflict*. New York, 1965.

Lorch, N. *The Edge of the Sword: Israel's War of Independence 1947–49*. New York, Putnam, 1961.

Lucas, Noah. *The Modern History of Israel*. London, Weidenfeld and Nicolson, 1974–75.

McDowall, David. *Palestine and Israel: the uprising and beyond.* London, I.B. Tauris, 1989.

Marlowe, John. *The Seat of Pilate, An Account of the Palestine Mandate.* London, Cresset, 1959; Philadelphia, Dufour, 1958.

O'Ballance, E. *The Arab-Israeli War.* New York, Praeger, 1957.

　The Third Arab-Israeli War. London, Faber & Faber, 1972.

Oz, Amos. *In the Land of Israel.* London, Chatto and Windus, 1983.

Peretz, Don. *Israel and the Palestine Arabs.* Washington, The Middle East Institute, 1958.

　Intifada. Oxford, Westview Press, 1990.

Perlmutter, Amos. *Military and Politics in Israel, 1948–1967.* 2nd edn. London, Frank Cass, 1977.

　Politics and the Military in Israel, 1967–1976. London, Frank Cass, 1977.

Rabin, Yitzhak. *The Rabin Memoirs.* London, Weidenfeld and Nicolson, 1979.

Rizk, Edward. *The Palestine Question, Seminar of Arab Jurists on Palestine, Algiers, 1967.* Beirut, Institute for Palestine Studies, 1968.

Rodinson, Maxime. *Israel and the Arabs.* Harmondsworth, Penguin Books, 1968; New York, Pantheon, 1969.

Rouleau, Eric, and Held, Jean-Francis. *Israël et les Arabes.* Paris, Editions du Seuil, 1967.

Royal Institute of International Affairs. *Great Britain and Palestine 1915–45.* London, 1946.

Sachar, Howard M. *A History of Israel:* Vol. I: *From the Rise of Zionism to Our Time;* Vol. II: *From the Aftermath of the Yom Kippur War.* Corby, Oxford University Press, 1987.

Savir, Uri. *The Process: 1,100 Days that Changed the Middle East.* London, Random House, 1998.

Schiff, Ze'ev, and Ehud Ya'ari. *Israel's Lebanon War.* New York, Simon and Schuster, 1984.

　Intifada: the Palestinian uprising—Israel's third front. London, Simon and Shuster, 1990.

Schindler, Colin. *Ploughshares into Swords?: Israelis and Jews in the Shadow of the Intifada.* London, I. B. Tauris, 1992.

　Israel, Likud and the Zionist Dream: Power, Politics, and Ideology from Begin to Netanyahu. London, I. B. Tauris, 1995.

Shahak, Israel. *Open Secrets: Israeli Foreign and Nuclear Policies.* London, Pluto Press, 1997.

Sharabi, Hisham B. *Palestine and Israel: The Lethal Dilemma.* New York, Van Nostrand Reinhold, 1969.

Shipler, David K. *Arab and Jew: Wounded Spirits in a Promised Land.* London, Bloomsbury, 1987.

Stendel, Ori. *The Arabs in Israel.* Sussex Academic, 1996.

Sykes, Christopher. *Crossroads to Israel.* London, Collins, 1965.

Timerman, Jacob. *The Longest War.* London, Chatto and Windus, 1982.

Weizman, Ezer. *The Battle for Peace.* New York, Bantam Books, 1981.

Wolf, Aaron T. *Hydropolitics Along the Jordan River: Scarce Water and its Impact on the Arab-Israeli Conflict.* Tokyo, United Nations Press, 1996.

Yaniv, Avner. *Dilemmas of Security—Politics, Strategy and the Israeli Experience in Lebanon.* Oxford, Oxford University Press, 1987.

THE STATE

Al-Haj, Majid, and Rosenfeld, Henry. *Arab Local Government in Israel.* Boulder, San Francisco and London, Westview Press, 1990.

Avi-hai, Avraham. *Ben Gurion, State Builder.* Israel Universities Press, 1974.

Badi, Joseph. *Fundamental Laws of the State of Israel.* New York, 1961.

Bar-Zohar, Michael. *Ben-Gurion: A Biography.* London, Weidenfeld and Nicolson, 1978.

Baruth, K. H. *The Physical Planning of Israel.* London, 1949.

Ben Gurion, D. *Rebirth and Destiny of Israel.* New York, 1954.

　Israel: A Personal History. London, New English Library, 1972.

Bentwich, Norman. *Fulfilment in the Promised Land 1917–37.* London, 1938.

　Judaea Lives Again. London, 1944.

　Israel Resurgent. Ernest Benn, 1960.

　The New-old Land of Israel. Allen and Unwin, 1960.

　Israel, Two Fateful Years 1967–69. London, Elek, 1970.

Brecher, Michael. *The Foreign Policy System of Israel.* London, Oxford University Press, 1972.

Comay, Joan, and Pearlman, Moshe. *Israel.* New York, 1965.

Crossman, R. H. S. *A Nation Reborn.* London, Hamish Hamilton, 1960.

Davis, Moshe (Ed.). *Israel: Its Role in Civilisation* New York, 1956.

Davis, Uri. *Israel: An Apartheid State.* London, Zed Press, 1987.

Dayan, Shmuel. *The Promised Land.* London, 1961.

De Gaury, Gerald. *The New State of Israel.* New York, 1952.

Eban, Abba. *The Voice of Israel.* New York, Horizon Press, 1957.

　The Story of Modern Israel. London, Weidenfeld and Nicolson, 1973.

Edelman, Maurice. *Ben Gurion, a Political Biography.* London, Hodder and Stoughton, 1964.

Frankel, William. *Israel Observed: An Anatomy of the State.* London, Thames and Hudson, 1980.

Hollis, Rosemary. *Israel on the Brink of Decision: division, unity and cross-currents in the Israeli body politic.* London, Research Institute for the Study of Conflict and Terrorism, 1990.

Janowsky, Oscar I. *Foundations of Israel: Emergence of a Welfare State.* Princeton, Anvil Nostrand Co, 1959.

Kraines, O. *Government and Politics in Israel.* London, Allen and Unwin, 1961.

Likhovski, Eliahu S. *Israel's Parliament: The Law of the Knesset.* Oxford, Clarendon Press, 1971.

Medding, Peter. *Mapai in Israel: Political Organisation and Government in a New Society.* London, Cambridge University Press, 1972.

Meir, Golda. *This is our Strength.* New York, 1963.

Merhav, Peretz. *The Israeli Left: History, Problems, Documents.* Tantivy Press, 1981.

Nusseibeh, Sari, and Heller, Mark A. *No Trumpets, No Drums: A Two-State Settlement of the Israeli-Palestinian Conflict.* London, I. B. Tauris, 1992.

Perlmutter, Amos. *The Times and Life of Menachem Begin.* New York, Doubleday, 1987.

Preuss, W. *Co-operation in Israel and the World.* Jerusalem, 1960.

Sachar, Howard M. *The Peoples of Israel.* New York, 1962.

Safran, Nadav. *The United States and Israel.* Harvard University Press, 1963.

Samuel, The Hon. Edwin. *Problems of Government in the State of Israel.* Jerusalem, 1956.

Segre, V. D. *Israel: A Society in Transition.* London, Oxford University Press, 1971.

Shatil, J. *L'Économie Collective du Kibboutz Israëlien.* Paris, Les Editions de Minuit, 1960.

Teveth, Shabtai. *Ben-Gurion.* Boston, Houghton Mifflin, 1987.

ZIONISM

Avishai, Bernard. *The Tragedy of Zionism.* Farrar Strauss Giroux, 1986.

Bein, Alex. *Theodor Herzl.* London, East and West Library, 1957.

Cohen, Israel. *A Short History of Zionism.* London, Frederick Muller, 1951.

Dieckhoff, Alain. *Les Espaces d'Israël.* Paris, Fondation pour les études de la défense nationale, 1987.

Engle, Anita. *The Nili Spies.* London, Frank Cass, 1997.

Fisch, Harold. *The Zionist Revolution: A New Perspective.* London, Weidenfeld and Nicolson, 1978.

Frankl, Oscar Benjamin. *Theodor Herzl: The Jew and Man.* New York, 1949.

Laqueur, Walter. *A History of Zionism.* London, Weidenfeld and Nicolson, 1972.

Lowenthal, Marvin (Ed. and trans.). *Diaries of Theodor Herzl.* New York, Grosset and Dunlap, 1965.

O'Brien, Conor Cruise. *The Siege: The Saga of Israel and Zionism.* London, Weidenfeld and Nicolson, 1986.

Rose, Norman. *Chaim Weizmann.* London, Weidenfeld and Nicolson, 1987.

Schama, Simon. *Two Rothschilds and the Land of Israel.* London, Collins, 1978.

Schechtman, J. *Rebel and Statesman: the Jabotinsky Story.* New York, Thomas Yoseloff, 1956.

Sober, Moshe. *Beyond the Jewish State: confessions of a former Zionist.* Toronto, Summerhill Press, 1990.

Sokolow, Nahum. *History of Zionism.* 2 vols, London, Longmans, 1919; New York, Ktav, 1969.

Stein, Leonard and Yogev, Gedilia (Editors). *The Letters and Papers of Chaim Weizmann; Volume I 1885–1902.* Oxford University Press, 1968.

Vital, David. *The Origins of Zionism.* Oxford University Press, 1975, re-issued 1980.

Zionism: The Formative Years. Oxford University Press, 1981.

Weisgal, Meyer, and Carmichael, Joel. *Chaim Weizmann — a Biography by Several Hands.* London, Weidenfeld and Nicolson, 1962.

Weizmann, Dr Chaim. *The Jewish People and Palestine.* London, 1939.

Trial and Error: the Autobiography of Chaim Weizmann. London, Hamish Hamilton, 1949; New York, Schocken, 1966.

ECONOMY

Aharoni, Yair. *The Israeli Economy: Dreams and Realities.* London, Routledge, 1991.

Haidar, Aziz. *On The Margins: The Arab Population in the Israeli Economy.* Hurst and Co, 1997.

OFFICIAL PUBLICATIONS

Report of the Palestine Royal Commission, 1937. Cmd 5479, London.

Report of the Palestine Partition Commission, 1938. Cmd 5854, London.

Statement of Policy by His Majesty's Government in the United Kingdom. Cmd 3692, London, 1930; Cmd 5893, London, 1938; Cmd 6019, London, 1939; Cmd 6180, London, 1940.

Government Survey of Palestine. 2 vols, 1945–46, Jerusalem. Supplement, July 1947, Jerusalem.

Report of the Anglo-American Committee of Enquiry. Lausanne, 1946.

Report to the United Nations General Assembly by the UN Special Committee on Palestine. Geneva, 1947.

Report of the UN Economic Survey Mission for the Middle East. December 1949, United Nations, Lake Success, NY; HM Stationery Office.

Annual Yearbook of the Government of Israel.

Jewish Agency for Palestine. Documents Submitted to General Assembly of UN, relating to the National Home, 1947.

The Jewish Plan for Palestine. Jerusalem, 1947.

Statistical Survey of the Middle East. 1944.

Statistical Abstract of Israel. Central Bureau of Statistics, annual.

OCCUPIED TERRITORIES

Friedland, Roger, and Hecht, Richard. *To Rule Jerusalem.* Cambridge University Press, 1997.

Humphries, Hugh. *In the beginning — Jerusalem: Israeli or Palestinian owned? How to occupy and dominate a city: a lay guide.* Glasgow, Scottish Friends of Palestine, 1997.

Emerging Palestinian Autonomous Areas
Physical and Social Geography

The territory in which an independent State of Palestine may be declared in May 1999 includes, at present, an undetermined area of the West Bank and the Gaza Strip. The West Bank (Judaea and Samaria) covers an area of 5,879 sq km (2,270 sq miles) and can be divided into three major sub-regions: the Mount Hebron massif, approximately 45 km long by 20 km wide, the peaks of which rise to between 700 m and 1,000 m above sea-level; the Jerusalem mountains, which extend to the northernmost point of the Hebron-Bethlehem massif; and the Mount Samaria hills, the central section of which—the Nablus mountains—reaches heights of up to 800 m before descending to the northern, Jenin hills, of between 300 m and 400 m. The eastern border of the West Bank is bounded by the valley of the River Jordan, leading to the Dead Sea (part of the Syrian–African rift valley), into which the River Jordan drains. The latter is 400 m below sea-level. Annual rainfall ranges between 600 mm and 800 mm on the massif and averages 200 mm in the Jordan valley; 36% of the area is classified as cultivable land, 32% grazing land, 27% desert or rocky ground and 5% natural forest. Apart from the urban centres of Bethlehem and Hebron to the south, the majority of the Palestinian population is concentrated in the northern districts around Ramallah, Nablus, Jenin and Tulkaram. In November 1988 the Palestine National Council proclaimed Jerusalem as the capital of a newly-declared independent State of Palestine. In fact, West Jerusalem has been the capital of the State of Israel since 1950. In 1967 East Jerusalem was formally annexed by Israel and is regarded as part of Israel by the Israeli authorities, although the annexation has never been recognized by the United Nations (UN). Under the terms of the Declaration of Principles on Palestinian Self-Rule, concluded by Israel and the Palestinian component of the Jordanian–Palestinian delegation to the Middle

East peace conference in September 1993, negotiations on the final status of the city were scheduled to begin not later than the beginning of the third year of the five-year transitional period following the completion of Israel's withdrawal from the Gaza Strip and the Jericho area. By mid-1998, however, final status negotiations had still not commenced (see below). Greater Jerusalem includes Israeli West Jerusalem (whose population is 99% Jewish), the Old City and Mount of Olives, East Jerusalem (the Palestinian residential and commercial centre), Arab villages declared to be part of Jerusalem by Israel in 1967 and Jewish neighbourhoods constructed since 1967, either on land expropriated from Arab villages or in areas requisitioned as 'government land'. Although the area of the Greater Jerusalem district is 627 sq km, the Old City of Jerusalem covers just 1 sq km. The future of Jerusalem is probably the most bitterly contentious of all the issues subject to final status talks, and, in the opinion of some observers, may elude agreement by negotiation. Palestinians have responded with outrage to Israel's extension of Jerusalem's municipal boundaries to include areas of land extending southwards almost to the Bethlehem-Bet Sahur area, and northwards almost as far as Ramallah. According to some sources, confiscations of Arab land have proceeded at a higher rate than ever before since the signing of the Oslo Agreement in September 1993. Furthermore, a process appears to have been initiated by the Israeli authorities whereby the residency rights of Palestinian East Jerusalemites are being cancelled.

The Gaza Strip, lying beside the Mediterranean Sea and the border with Egypt, is approximately 45 km long by 8 km wide at its widest point. Crossed only by two shallow valleys, the 378 sq km area is otherwise almost entirely flat, and has no surface water. Annual average rainfall is 300 mm. Gaza City is the main population centre.

Recent History

Until the end of the 1948 Arab–Israeli War, the West Bank formed part of the British Mandate of Palestine, before becoming part of the Hashemite Kingdom of Jordan under the Armistice Agreement of 1949. It remained under Jordanian sovereignty, despite Israeli occupation in 1967, until King Hussein of Jordan formally relinquished legal and administrative control on 31 July 1988. Under Israeli military occupation, the West Bank was administered by a military government, which divided the territory into seven sub-districts. The Civil Administration, as it later became known, did not extend its jurisdiction to the many Israeli settlements that were established under the Israeli occupation; settlements remained subject to the Israeli legal and administrative system. By 1998 approximately 24% of the West Bank was under Israeli military control, with responsibility for civil administration transferred to the Palestinian authorities; 3% was under full Palestinian control; and the remainder under complete Israeli control.

An administrative province under the British Mandate of Palestine, Gaza was transferred to Egypt after the 1949 armistice and remained under Egyptian administration until June 1967, when it was invaded and occupied by Israel. Following Israeli occupation, the Gaza Strip, like the West Bank, became an 'administered territory'. Until the provisions of the Declaration of Principles on Palestinian Self-Rule began to take effect, the management of day-to-day affairs was the responsibility of the area's Israeli military commander. Neither Israeli laws nor governmental and public bodies—including the Supreme Court—could review or alter the orders of the military command to any great extent. In 1993 it was estimated that approximately 50% of the land area was under Israeli control, either through the establishment of Jewish settlements or through the closure of areas by the military authorities.

TOWARDS AN INDEPENDENT PALESTINE

In accordance with the Declaration of Principles on Palestinian Self-Rule of September 1993, and the Cairo Agreement on the Gaza Strip and Jericho, the Palestine Liberation Organization (PLO) assumed control of the Jericho area, in the West Bank, and the Gaza Strip on 17 May 1994. In November and December 1995, under the terms of the Israeli–Palestinian Interim Agreement on the West Bank and the Gaza Strip (the 'Oslo Agreement', signed by Israel and the PLO on 28 September 1995), Israeli armed forces

withdrew from the West Bank towns of Nablus, Ramallah, Jenin, Tulkaram, Kalkilya and Bethlehem. In late December the PLO assumed responsibility in some 17 areas of civil administration in the town of Hebron. In all of these localities the PLO's jurisdiction was exercised through the Palestinian Legislative Council (PLC), elected in January 1996. (Under the terms of the Israeli–Palestinian Interim Agreement, the PLO was eventually to assume full responsibility for civil affairs in the 400 surrounding villages, but the Israeli armed forces were to retain freedom of movement to act against potential hostilities there.) In Hebron Israel effected a partial withdrawal of its armed forces in January 1997, but retained responsibility for the security of some 400 Jewish settlers occupying some 15% of the town. Responsibility for security in the rest of Hebron passed to the Palestinian police force, but Israel retained responsibility for security on access roads. Under the terms of the Israeli–Palestinian Interim Agreement, Israel was to retain control over a large area of the West Bank (including Jewish settlements, rural areas, military installations and the majority of junctions between Palestinian roads and roads used by Israeli troops and settlers until July 1997. Following the first phase of the redeployment and the holding, on its completion, of elections to the PLC and for a Palestinian executive president, Israel was to effect a second phase of redeployment from rural areas, to be completed by July 1997. The Israeli occupation was to be maintained in Jewish settlements, military installations, East Jerusalem and the Jewish settlements around Jerusalem until a final settlement of the Palestinian question, scheduled for May 1999. Subsequent postponements, and negotiations within the context of the Oslo peace process, resulted in a new timetable for redeployment, which envisaged two phases, subsequent to the Hebron withdrawal, to be completed by October 1997 and August 1998. Final status negotiations on borders, the Jerusalem issue, Jewish settlements and Palestinian refugees were to commence within two months of the signing of the agreement on Hebron. As guarantor of the agreements, the USA undertook to obtain the release of some Palestinian prisoners, and to ensure that Israel continued to engage in negotiations for the establishment of a Palestinian airport in the Gaza Strip and for safe passage for Palestinians between the West Bank and the Gaza Strip. The USA also undertook to ensure that the Palestinian authorities would continue to combat terrorism, complete the revision of the Palestinian National Charter (or Covenant), adopted in 1964 and amended in 1968, and consider Israeli requests to extradite Palestinians suspected of involvement in attacks in Israel. By July 1998, however, conflicting interpretations of the extent of both the phased and total final redeployment (90% of the West Bank, according to the Palestinians; less than 50%, according to the Israelis) had resulted in a seemingly intractable impasse in the Oslo peace process. Those within the wider Palestinian movement who had never accepted the Oslo peace process argued, with some justification, that an essential weakness of the Israeli–Palestinian Interim Agreement had made such a situation inevitable: while it, and subsequent revisions, detailed timetables for the withdrawals of Israeli armed forces, the Agreement did not stipulate the precise area of the territory over which the Palestinian authorities should thereby assume control. The implementation of the Agreement was further complicated by the election, in May 1996, of Binyamin Netanyahu as Israeli Prime Minister. Netanyahu formed a new coalition Government, in which his party, Likud, was the dominant force. Likud had never sought to conceal its opposition to the Oslo Agreement negotiated by its Labour predecessor, and in mid-1998 it appeared determined to ensure that a final settlement with the Palestinians would not be negotiated in accordance with the terms of the Agreement.

By July 1998 progress on the redeployment of Israeli armed forces had been impeded for some 15 months. This paralysis emerged from the decision of the Israeli Government, announced in February 1997, to begin the construction of a new Jewish settlement on Jabal Abu Ghunaym (Har Homa in Hebrew), near Bet Sahur. Construction in this area was particularly controversial because, if completed, the new settlement would make it impossible to reach East Jerusalem from the West Bank without crossing Israeli territory, thereby prejudicing final status negotiations concerning Jerusalem. In response, the Palestinians withdrew from final status talks which had been scheduled to commence on 17 March. The beginning of construction work at Jabal Abu Ghunaym on 18 March provoked rioting among the Palestinian population and a resumption of attacks by the military wing of the Islamic Resistance Movement (Hamas) on Israeli civilian targets. The Israeli Cabinet responded by ordering a general closure of the West Bank and the Gaza Strip.

The intensity of Palestinian opposition to the construction of Jewish settlements was evident when, at the beginning of May 1997, the Palestinian Minister of Justice, Furayh Abu Middayn, announced that the Palestine National Authority (PNA) would sentence to death any Palestinian who was found to have sold land to Jews. The extent of renewed Israeli–Palestinian hostility was also apparent during May, when the USA's special envoy to the Middle East, Dennis Ross, returned to the USA following a nine-day mediation initiative in the region, having failed to secure any hope of resuming peace talks.

Both the Jabal Abu Ghunaym (Har Homa) construction and Israel's unilateral decision to redeploy its armed forces from only 9% of West Bank territory (announced in March 1997) were regarded by many observers as a vitiation of both the Oslo and the subsequent post-Hebron agreements. These were further undermined by the publication, in the Israeli daily newspaper *Ha'aretz*, of the results of a US study which claimed that more than 25% of Jewish settlers' homes in the Gaza Strip and the West Bank were uninhabited (a claim rejected by the Israeli Central Bureau of Statistics, which argued that only 12% of the settlements were unoccupied). The same newspaper later reported that Netanyahu's original plan, evolved within the framework of the Oslo Agreement, eventually to relinquish 90% of the West Bank, had been revised in a new proposal—the so-called 'Allon plus' plan—to a 40% redeployment.

In mid-June 1997 the US House of Representatives voted in favour of recognizing Jerusalem as the undivided capital of Israel and to transfer the US embassy to the city from Tel-Aviv. President Bill Clinton was reported to have strongly disapproved of the vote, owing to its possible implications for the peace process. The decision coincided with violent clashes between Palestinian civilians and Israeli troops in both Gaza and Hebron, which reached a climax in Hebron at the end of the month, when anti-Islamic posters, displayed in the town, caused popular outrage.

At the beginning of July 1997 a series of meetings took place between the US Under-Secretary of State for Political Affairs, Thomas Pickering, and Israeli and Palestinian officials, with the aim of resuming negotiations between the PNA and the Israeli Government. On 28 July both sides announced that peace talks were to be resumed in early August. However, on 30 July, on the eve of Dennis Ross's visit to reactivate the negotiations, Hamas carried out a 'suicide bomb' attack at an outdoor Jewish market in Jerusalem, in which 14 civilians were killed and more than 150 others injured. Ross cancelled his visit, and the Israeli Government immediately halted payment of tax revenues to the PNA (see Economy) and closed the Gaza Strip and the West Bank. These sanctions provoked furious protest from the Palestinians, as well as widespread international condemnation. Nevertheless, the Israeli Prime Minister insisted that such measures would remain in force

until increased efforts by the Palestinian authorities to combat the activities of Hamas became evident.

In the aftermath of the July 1997 'suicide bomb' attack in Jerusalem, the Palestinian authorities commenced a campaign to detain members of Hamas and Islamic Jihad, another militant group. In late August, however, President Yasser Arafat convened a Palestinian national dialogue conference in Gaza, in response to the imposition of sanctions by the Israeli authorities. On this occasion, representatives of Hamas, who had boycotted a similar conference held in the previous year, agreed to take part in the dialogue, on the condition that the Palestinian authorities would address the issue of the Hamas members whom they were holding in detention. During the conference Arafat publicly embraced Hamas leaders and urged them, and representatives of Islamic Jihad, to unite with the Palestinian people against Israeli policies. On 26 August Hamas rejected a request from Palestinian leaders to suspend their attacks on Israeli targets.

At the beginning of September 1997, in anticipation of a visit to the Middle East in mid-September by the US Secretary of State, Madeleine Albright, the Israeli authorities relaxed the closure that they had imposed on the Gaza Strip and the West Bank on 30 July. On 4 September, however, a further 'suicide bomb' attack in Jerusalem, in which eight people died (including the bombers themselves), led to the reimposition of Israeli sanctions. Hamas claimed responsibility for the attack, and the Israeli Prime Minister immediately renewed his demand that the Palestinian authorities should take effective action against the 'terrorist infrastructure', referring critically to Arafat's willingness to embrace representatives of Hamas in the previous month. In the international media the latest 'suicide bomb' attack provoked outrage, but was widely viewed in the context of Palestinians' disenchantment with the peace process and their fears for the future of Jerusalem. The attack also prompted speculation that Hamas might be susceptible to manipulation by foreign powers, such as Syria and Iran, so as to wage a proxy war in Israel, similar to that conducted by Hezbollah guerrillas in southern Lebanon.

The visit to the Middle East in September 1997 by the US Secretary of State, Madeleine Albright, failed to reactivate the peace process. Indeed, the Secretary of State acknowledged such a conclusion herself, declaring publicly that she had no intention of returning to the region until Israeli and Palestinian leaders had made the 'hard decisions' necessary to break the deadlock. During her visit, Albright was reported to have stated that Israel should halt the construction of Jewish settlements on Arab lands, cease confiscations of land and the demolition of Arab dwellings, and end its policy of confiscating Palestinian identity documents. At the same time, she endorsed Netanyahu's demand that the Palestinian authorities should take more effective measures to suppress the military wing of Hamas. (In late September the Israeli authorities claimed to have traced the origin of four of the five Hamas members responsible for the 'suicide bomb' attack in Jerusalem earlier in the month to the West Bank village of Azira Shamaliya.) One outcome of the US Secretary of State's visits was a re-examination of the role of the USA in the Middle East peace process since Netanyahu's election in May 1996. Attention was focused on the long period of inactivity at the highest levels of US diplomacy which had preceded Albright's visit: it was suggested that, having all but openly supported the re-election of a Labour government at the Israeli general election of May 1996, the US Administration had simply not known what approach to adopt in its dealings with Netanyahu, who had subsequently exerted himself to weaken the development of a Palestinian state. US bewilderment had been compounded by a movement to the political right of powerful Jewish lobbying organizations with influence within the Republican-dominated US House of Representatives; and by the failure of the Palestinian authorities to conduct an effective campaign against Netanyahu, which had strengthened organizations such as Hamas. Impatience within the US Administration at the Israeli Government's apparently provocative acts was demonstrated by the US Secretary of State's criticism of Netanyahu's decision, announced in late September 1997, to permit the construction of 300 new homes for Jewish settlers in Efrat on the West Bank. According to some observers, the decision reduced US–Israeli relations to their lowest point since Netanyahu's election.

On 28 September 1997 it was announced that, as a result of US diplomatic efforts, Israeli and Palestinian officials had agreed to recommence negotiations in early October. The first round of talks, scheduled to commence on 6 October, would reportedly focus on the outstanding issues of the Israeli-Palestinian Interim Agreement of 1995, in particular the opening of an airport and seaport facilities in the Gaza Strip, the establishment of a safe corridor linking the Gaza Strip with the West Bank and the release of Palestinian prisoners being detained by the Israeli authorities. A second round of talks was to commence on 13 October, at which the participants were to address the issues of security co-operation between the Palestinian and the Israeli authorities; the long-delayed redeployment of Israeli armed forces from the West Bank; Israeli expansion and construction of settlements; and questions pertaining to 'final status' negotiations.

In late September 1997 it was reported that the Palestinian authorities had closed some 16 institutions—mainly providers of social welfare services—with links to Hamas, and arrested 'scores' of its officials since the bomb attack in Jerusalem earlier in the month. Hamas officials who remained at liberty, however, insisted that the organization's campaign against Israeli civilian targets would continue. In particular, the attempted assassination in the Jordanian capital, Amman, in late September of Khalid Meshaal, the head of the Hamas political bureau in Jordan, provoked warnings of retaliation both before and after official confirmation that agents of the Israeli security service, Mossad, had been responsible for the attack. In order to secure the release of its agents by the Jordanian authorities, Israel was obliged, on 1 October, to free (together with other Arab political prisoners) Sheikh Ahmad Yassin, the founder and spiritual leader of Hamas, who had been sentenced to life imprisonment in Israel in 1989 for complicity in attacks on Israeli soldiers. As had been widely predicted, Israel's release of Sheikh Yassin into Jordanian custody was swiftly followed by his return, on 6 October, to Gaza, where his presence further complicated co-operation between the Israeli and the Palestinian authorities on security issues.

The return of Sheikh Yassin to Gaza, where he received an enthusiastic welcome from the local population, also prompted speculation concerning the possible benefits which President Arafat and the Palestinian authorities might derive from increased political co-operation with Hamas. In the view of most observers, the suspension of the peace process with Israel, together with widespread allegations of corruption within the PNA and strong criticism of the methods employed by the security forces under its control (see below), seriously undermined the credibility of the Palestinian authorities, while support for Hamas had grown. However, it appeared in late October 1997 that Yassin, while prepared to promote Palestinian unity, would not approve the acceptance of even the original terms of the Oslo Agreement. It was reported in mid-November that potential successors to Arafat had initiated political manoeuvres amid enduring rumours that the President was in poor health. Among those cited as possible candidates to replace him were Djibril Rajoub, the head of the Palestinian preventive security services in the West Bank and Muhammad Dahlan, his counterpart in the Gaza Strip. It was claimed that Mahmoud Abbas, the chief Palestinian negotiator, was the officially sanctioned candidate to replace Arafat in the event of his death or incapacity through illness.

On 7 October 1997 talks resumed between Palestinian and Israeli negotiators on the outstanding issues of the Oslo Agreement, and on the following day the Palestinian President and the Israeli Prime Minister held their first meeting for eight months at the Erez crossing-point between Israel and the Gaza Strip. In mid-November, however, the talks remained deadlocked, to the evident frustration of the US Secretary of State. On 16 November, speaking at the Middle East and North Africa economic conference in Doha, Qatar, which many Arab states had boycotted because of the attendance of an Israeli delegation, Albright publicly accused Israel of creating the calamitous economic conditions in the West Bank and the Gaza Strip.

In early December 1997, following further US pressure, it was reported that the Israeli Cabinet had agreed in principle to withdraw troops from an unspecified area of West Bank territory. Some two weeks later, however, it remained uncertain whether Netanyahu would persuade intransigent elements within his Government to endorse this decision. In early January 1998 the US special envoy to the Middle East, Dennis Ross, visited Israel in a further attempt to break the deadlock regarding the redeployment of Israeli armed forces from the West Bank. However, in the second week of January the Israeli Government declared that it would not conduct such a redeployment until the Palestinian authorities had fulfilled a series of conditions. Among these were requirements that the Palestinian leadership should make a 'systematic and effective' effort to counter terrorism; that it should reduce the strength of its security forces from 40,000 to 24,000; and that the Palestinian Covenant should be revised to recognize explicitly Israel's right to exist. Palestinian officials maintained that these conditions had already been met when the agreement regarding the withdrawal of Israeli armed forces from Hebron was concluded one year earlier. There was further evidence of a hardening of the Israeli position during the approach to a summit meeting, scheduled to take place in Washington, DC, in the third week of January. The Israeli Cabinet issued a communiqué detailing 'vital and national interests' in the West Bank which it was not prepared to relinquish. The document asserted that Israel would, among other areas, retain control of the territory surrounding the Jerusalem region. In total, areas listed as 'vital and national interests' to Israel amounted to some 60% of the entire West Bank territory.

On 20 January 1998 President Clinton held discussions with the Israeli Prime Minister in Washington, DC. During the course of the talks it was reported that the USA was seeking to persuade Israel

to effect a second withdrawal of its armed forces from some 12% of the West Bank over a period of 80 days, in exchange for increased co-operation on security issues by the Palestinian authorities. On 25 January, however, Mahmoud Abbas reported that direct contacts between the Palestinian delegation and the Israeli Prime Minister had collapsed. President Arafat was reported to be seeking to convene an Arab summit meeting to discuss the deadlocked Middle East peace process.

In early March 1998 it was reported that Israeli armed forces had seized a consignment of weapons that was being smuggled from Jordan across the Dead Sea, prompting speculation that the PNA had begun to store arms in preparation for armed conflict with Israel in the event of the irrevocable collapse of the peace process. On 11 March widespread rioting erupted among the Palestinian population of the West Bank, following the shooting, by Israeli soldiers, of three Palestinian workers at a military checkpoint, apparently as the result of a misunderstanding. Observers noted that many of the mourners attending the men's funerals displayed their allegiance to Hamas.

In late March 1998 details emerged of a US plan to present new proposals regarding the withdrawal of Israeli armed forces at separate meetings between the US Secretary of State and Arafat and Netanyahu in Europe. On 26 March Dennis Ross arrived in Jerusalem in order to present details of the latest US initiative. Although no details had officially been made public, it was widely reported that the US proposals would involve an Israeli withdrawal from slightly more than 13% of West Bank territory, and a suspension of settlement construction in return for further efforts by the PNA to combat organizations, such as Hamas, engaged in campaigns of violence against Israeli targets. President Arafat was reported to be seeking an Israeli withdrawal from a further 30% of West Bank territory, but there were indications that he might accept an initial withdrawal from some 13% of the West Bank. However, it was evident that, even if agreement could be reached between the two sides, the issue of whether a subsequent withdrawal should take place prior to the commencement of final status negotiations remained far more contentious. In any case, the Israeli Cabinet rejected the reported details of the new US initiative. At the end of March the US Seceretary of State, Madeleine Albright, stated that the peace process was on the verge of collapse, and indicated that the USA was considering ending its involvement as a mediator.

In late April 1998 it emerged that the EU was seeking to play a greater role in the deadlocked Middle East peace process. On 20 April it was reported that, during a visit to Gaza City, the British Prime Minister, Tony Blair, had obtained the agreement of President Arafat to attend a conference in London, based on the most recent US initiative for restarting the peace process. A summit meeting, hosted by Blair and attended by Netanyahu, Arafat and the US Secretary of State, took place in early May. At its conclusion the US Secretary of State invited Netanyahu and Arafat to attend a summit meeting with President Clinton in Washington, DC, on 12 May. The USA had reportedly proposed that the parties could proceed to final status negotiations as soon as the scope of the next Israeli withdrawal from the West Bank had been agreed. However, the Israeli Government subsequently rejected the US initiative in advance of Clinton's direct participation. Further discussions in mid-May, involving the US Secretary of State, achieved no progress.

In early June 1998 the details of the US initiative were unofficially disclosed in the Israeli press. Israel would have to agree to 'no significant expansion' of Jewish settlements and relinquish slightly more than 13% of West Bank territory over a period of 12 weeks in exchange for increased Palestinian co-operation. The adoption, by the Israeli Cabinet in late June 1998, of a plan to extend the boundaries of Jerusalem and construct homes there for a further 1m. people prompted incredulity at the US Department of State, and accusations by Palestinian representatives that the proposal amounted to a *de facto* annexation of territories that were officially subject to final status negotiations. The Israeli Prime Minister claimed that the plan was purely administrative, 'with no political implications'. It was subsequently reported that the Israeli Government was considering holding a popular referendum on a further withdrawal of Israeli armed forces from West Bank territory.

On 7 July 1998 the United Nations General Assembly, in defiance of objections from the USA and Israel, approved a resolution, by a vote of 124–4, to upgrade the status of the PLO at the UN. The new provision allows the PLO to participate in debates, to co-sponsor resolutions, and to raise points of order during discussions of Middle Eastern affairs.

INTERNAL AFFAIRS

In late April 1997 President Arafat's audit office reported the misappropriation of US $326m. of public funds by PNA ministers. Khalid al-Quidram, the General Prosecutor of the PNA (who promptly resigned following the accusations), was reportedly placed under house arrest in early June. At the end of July a parliamentary committee, appointed by Arafat to conduct an inquiry into the affair, concluded that the Cabinet should be dissolved and some members of the Government put on trial: half of the ministers were allegedly implicated. In early August the Cabinet submitted its resignation to Yasser Arafat, which was duly accepted in December. However, the Cabinet was to remain in a provisional capacity until a new Government was formed in early 1998. However, there was further disruption to the Cabinet in March and April 1998, following the deaths of the Minister of Tourism, Elias Furayz, and the Minister of Awqaf (Religious Endowments), Hassan Tahboob, respectively. (Some reports suggested that Furayz had withdrawn from the PNA as early as May 1997, owing to ill health.) Arafat's long-awaited new Cabinet was announced on 5 August and was promptly denounced by all sides. Only one prominent minister had been completely removed from the Cabinet, many others assuming alternative responsibilities or becoming ministers of state without portfolios. (The size of the Cabinet was increased significantly by the appointment of a number of PLC members to minister-of-state status.) Despite the immediate resignations of the newly-appointed Ministers of Higher Education (Hanan Ashrawi) and Agriculture (Abd al-Jawad Saleh), the new Cabinet was approved by 55 votes to 28 in the PLC on 10 August. In mid-September the Minister of State for the Environment, Yousuf Abu Safia, was reported to have tendered his resignation.

In addition to persistent allegations of corruption within the PNA, President Arafat himself has been the target of criticism from within the Palestinian leadership, which has accused him of autocracy. In October 1997 Haider Abd ash-Shafi, who had played a prominent role in the peace negotiations with Israel and who was reportedly held in high popular esteem, resigned in protest at the style of Arafat's leadership and at the way in which peace negotiations with Israel were being conducted. In March 1998 the PLC threatened to organize a vote of 'no confidence' in President Arafat's leadership, in protest at alleged corruption within the PNA, the long delay in approval of the 1998 budget and the failure to hold local government elections. There was speculation that the PNA had postponed these elections because it feared that voting would reveal widespread dissatisfaction at the lack of progress in the peace process with Israel. The PLC renewed its threat in mid-1998, when it issued an ultimatum to the Palestinian President and the Cabinet, demanding that they respond to allegations of corruption and mismanagement and that they approve a budget for 1998 within two weeks.

In February 1998 President Arafat took firm action to suppress popular demonstrations in support of Iraq, which had exposed itself to threats of military action by the USA in a dispute over UN-conducted weapons inspections. It was reported that many members of Arafat's own party, Fatah, had been arrested for disregarding a ban on such demonstrations, and that the publication and broadcasting of reports expressing support for President Saddam Hussain of Iraq had been forbidden.

In March 1998 US officials confirmed that the US Central Intelligence Agency (CIA) was assisting the Palestinian security forces in the spheres of espionage, information-gathering and interrogation, in an attempt to increase the confidence of the Israeli Government in their ability to wage an effective campaign against groups involved in attacks on Israeli targets. Later in the month the discovery in Ramallah, in mysterious circumstances, of the body of Muhi ad-Din Sharif, the second-highest ranking member of the military wing of Hamas, the Izz ad-Din Qassim Brigades, prompted accusations of PNA collusion with Israeli security forces in his murder, and fears that a new wave of retributive bomb attacks would be unleashed against Israeli targets. However, a succession of conflicting accusations and confessions surrounding the murder (including a number which alleged that Sharif's murder was the result of an internal dispute among the organization's leadership) appeared to defuse the immediate tensions in the region. In mid-1998 a prominent human rights organization, Human Rights Watch, published a report in which it criticized the Palestinian security forces for their alleged use of intimidation and torture during the previous three years.

In August 1998 the Palestinian Ministry of the Interior dissolved the Palestinian Ahd Party, the Palestinian Labour Party, the Ahrar Party, and the Popular Forces party, claiming that, as small individual entities which were unsuccessful in the previous legislative elections, the groups were not financially viable. According to a spokesman at the Ministry of the Interior, plans to merge small parties with similar ideologies were announced, in order to increase activity.

Economy

INTRODUCTION

Economic conditions in the Gaza Strip, the West Bank and East Jerusalem have significantly deteriorated since the signing of the Israeli–Palestinian Interim Agreement on the West Bank and the Gaza Strip (the 'Oslo Agreement') in September 1993. As illustrated below, the dominant characteristic of these economies has been their dependence on Israeli markets and their consequent vulnerability to the closures imposed at various times during 1993–98 by the Israeli authorities, mainly in response to attacks on Israeli civilians by members of Palestinian organizations which reject the Oslo Agreement. Measures to reduce the dependency of the Palestinian economy, such as the opening of an airport and seaport facilities in the Gaza Strip, and of a safe corridor between the Strip and the West Bank, had not materialized by mid-1998 owing to the prolonged delay in implementing the Oslo Agreement. In the third quarter of 1997 the Palestinian Central Bureau of Statistics (PCBS) estimated that 18.2% of the labour force in the West Bank and 31.6% of the labour force in the Gaza Strip were unemployed. Corresponding figures for underemployment were, respectively, 11.4% and 2.7%. Other sources indicated that in March 1997 Israeli border closures had cost the Palestinian economy some US $5m.–$6m. per day, amounting, on an annual basis, to more than the sum of funds pledged—but not necessarily disbursed—to the Palestine National Authority (PNA) by international donors.

Perhaps the strongest link with the Israeli economy, and the one which proved the most difficult to break, was the employment that Palestinians found within the 'Green Line', which provided many families with their livelihoods. In 1992 some 35% of the West Bank's and 45% of the Gazan labour force was employed in Israel, mainly in unskilled and semi-skilled occupations—especially in the construction industry. In 1993, following a series of attacks on Jews within Israel, the Israeli Prime Minister, Itzhak Rabin, ordered the closure of Israel's borders with the West Bank and the Gaza Strip, preventing an estimated 70,000 West Bank and some 50,000 Gazan Palestinians from travelling to work. Significantly, controls on cross-border movement were relaxed only after considerable pressure from Israeli employers; the 'reserve labour force' of some 100,000 unemployed Israelis had been reluctant to do the Palestinians' work, which was often of a low-paid, menial nature.

Since February 1996 Israel and East Jerusalem have been closed to most Palestinian residents of the West Bank and the Gaza Strip. As the closures affect movement in both directions, the economy of East Jerusalem, deprived of West Bank markets for its goods and services, has all but collapsed. Closures have had a similarly disruptive effect within the West Bank, since they restrict communications between Palestinian towns via Israeli-controlled Jewish areas of the West Bank. Such areas comprise most of the territory of the West Bank outside Palestinian population centres.

POPULATION

According to the preliminary results of the first census conducted by the PCBS, the Palestinian population numbered 2.89m. (males 1.46m.; females 1.42m.) at 31 December 1997. Of the total population, 1.6m. were resident in the West Bank (excluding East Jerusalem), 1m. in the Gaza Strip and an estimated 210,000 in East Jerusalem. According to the census, 54% of the population (excluding the 16% of the population resident in refugee camps) were located in urban areas, and 30% in rural areas.

LABOUR FORCE

In the third quarter of 1997, according to the PCBS, the strength of the Palestinian labour force was estimated at almost 500,000. Of this total, it was estimated that some 390,000 were employed and 107,000 unemployed. A total of 63,000 Palestinians were recorded as working in Israel, in Israeli settlements or the industrial zones of the West Bank and the Gaza Strip (see below). The rate of unemployment was estimated at 18% in the West Bank and at 32% in the Gaza Strip. The labour survey conducted in the third quarter of 1997 indicated that there were more Palestinians working in Israel than the number of work permits issued by the Israeli authorities, and that the importance of Israel as a source of employment had declined in recent years. In July 1997 the Israeli authorities issued 60,000 work permits to Palestinians, the highest number for the year to July. All permits were cancelled in the month of August, and for most of the month of September. After 21 September 33,000 work permits were issued to Palestinians by the Israeli authorities.

NATIONAL ACCOUNTS

In 1996, according to preliminary estimates by the PCBS, Palestinian gross national product (GNP) totalled US $4,509m. Net factor income from abroad comprised $525m. in wage income, mainly from Palestinian workers in Israel; and $87m. in net property income from abroad. Gross domestic product (GDP) in market prices amounted to $3,897m. GDP at factor cost totalled 10,602m. new Israeli shekels in 1996. Of this total, private services (including trade, rental services and transport) contributed 38%, public services (including central and local government) 23%, industry (manufacturing, quarrying and the supply of utilities) 16%, agriculture and fishing 14%, and construction 9%. On the basis of these estimates and surveys by the PCBS of the population in 1996, average GNP per head in the West Bank and the Gaza Strip amounted to $1,700 in that year, while average GDP per head was $1,470. On the basis of these figures and conjectural price deflators, the World Bank has calculated that Palestinian GDP increased by 10% in real terms in 1994, but declined by 6% in 1995 and remained static in 1996. Real GNP rose by an estimated 8% in 1994, declining by 5% in 1995 and by 1% in 1996. On the same basis, the World Bank estimates that real GDP per head increased by 4% in 1994, but fell by 12% in 1995 and by 6% in 1996. Real GNP per head increased by 2% in 1994, but declined by 10% in 1995 and by 7% in 1996. Over the period 1994–96 real GDP per head fell by 14%, and real GNP per head by 16%.

CONSUMER PRICES

In 1997, according to the PCBS, annual consumer price inflation in the Palestinian economy averaged 7.6%. In the Gaza Strip an annual average inflation rate of 8.6% was recorded, while inflation averaged 7.6% in the West Bank and 7.3% in East Jerusalem. The highest price increases recorded were those for clothing (12.8%), furniture (10.8%), medical care (10.4%) and beverages (9.6%). Price increases averaged 4.9% for education, 5.5% for housing, 6.2% for food, and 6.6% for transport.

AGRICULTURE

According to the PCBS, agriculture and fishing contributed 14% of Palestinian GDP in 1996. In the third quarter of 1997 agriculture, fishing and forestry employed 14.9% of the labour force in the West Bank and 6.4% of the labour force in the Gaza Strip. Olives, citrus fruits, vegetables and potatoes are all important crops, and the livestock sector is also significant. Agro-industrial production is focused on the dairy and olive oil sectors. Although about one-half of Palestinian exports are derived from agricultural production, the sector remains orientated towards supplying local needs. Like other sectors of the economy, agricultural production and export trade are characterized by a high degree of dependence on Israel, and consequent vulnerability to Israeli border policy: some 60% of the Gaza Strip's agricultural production is exported via Israel as originating in Israel. One example is the lucrative, export-orientated production of carnations in Gaza. In 1994, of total production of 120m. flowers, only 2m. were exported directly to European markets, the remainder being distributed through Israel. Border closures and delays in the issue of transport permits have a devastating effect on the sector. Carnation production is also heavily reliant on water resources controlled by the Israeli authorities.

Expansion of agricultural production in the West Bank and Gaza Strip is severely limited by problems with irrigation. Traditionally, wells and cisterns have accounted for some 66% of all water consumed, highland springs for some 27% and surface run-off water and water purchased from the Israeli water utilities for the remainder. Some 75% of annual rainfall is lost to evaporation. Agriculture uses about 70% of water consumed in the West Bank, but only 4% of the total land area in the West Bank is irrigated, compared with 45% within Israel. In the mid-1990s Palestinian agricultural production consumed some 152m. cu m of water annually, compared with consumption (for the same purpose) of 56m. cu m by the approximately 120,000 Jewish settlers in the West Bank. In the Gaza Strip irrigation of the important citrus crop has been affected by rising salinity in the ground-water supply. In central Gaza ground-water salinity levels are three times as high as the World Health Organization's recommended safety level. The area also suffers from a water deficit. Estimated annually at approximately 50m. cu m, the water deficit could reach 150m. cu m by 2000.

The fishing industry, formerly one of the Gaza Strip's most profitable activities, has been severely constricted by Israeli military control over the area in which Palestinian boats may fish, including the prohibition of any fishing beyond a 30-km radius, established by the Israeli authorities.

INDUSTRY

According to Palestinian sources, industrial activity has contributed, on average, about 10% of Palestinian GDP since the 1970s, employing some 9% of the West Bank labour force and 14% of the Gazan labour force over the same period. The IMF and the Palestinian Economic Council for Development and Reconstruction (PECDAR) estimated the contribution of industry (excluding construction) to Palestinian GDP at 8.2% in 1994. According to the PCBS, industry (manufacturing, quarrying and the supply of utilities) contributed 16% of Palestinian GDP in 1996. In the third

quarter of 1997, according to the same source, mining, quarrying and manufacturing employed 16.6% of the labour force in the West Bank and 13.6% of the labour force in the Gaza Strip.

A World Bank study, conducted in 1993, indicated the potential competitiveness, at free-market prices, of a sample of Palestinian enterprises. Food-processing and the production of textiles, footwear, cosmetics, cigarettes, household detergents and construction materials have all been identified as suitable for expansion through import-substitution. According to the PCBS, manufacturing enterprises in the West Bank and Gaza Strip totalled 11,559 in 1994, including 39 foreign-owned companies. According to the IMF and PECDAR, the contribution of the construction sector to Palestinian GDP in 1994 was 16.8%, compared with 16.2% in 1993 and 13.0% in 1992. The PCBS estimated the contribution of the construction sector to GDP at 9% in 1996. According to the PCBS, the construction sector employed 19.5% of the labour force in the West Bank and 14.3% of the labour force in the Gaza Strip in the third quarter of 1997.

The frequent closure of the West Bank and the Gaza Strip by the Israeli authorities in 1993–98 has prompted the development of free-trade industrial zones on the Palestinian side of the boundaries separating Israel from the West Bank and the Gaza Strip. Israeli and Palestinian enterprises can continue to take advantage of low-cost Palestinian labour at times of closure, and the zones also benefit from tax exemptions and export incentives. Small and medium-sized enterprises dominate production in the three Gazan and six West Bank industrial zones. At the Erez zone, adjacent to the crossing between Israel and the Gaza Strip, textile production has emerged as a significant industry. In January 1998 the World bank announced a loan of US $10m. to the PNA for the development of the Gaza Industrial Estate project. The estate, which required total financing of $84.5m., was scheduled to open in mid-1998 and was expected to create as many as 50,000 jobs in the Gaza Strip. Other donors included the International Finance Corporation and the European Investment Bank.

SERVICES

In 1996, according to the PCBS, private services (including trade, rental services and transport) contributed 38% of Palestinian GDP, and public services (including central and local government) 23%. In the third quarter of 1997, according to the PCBS, 20% of the labour force in the West Bank and 19.4% of the labour force in the Gaza Strip were employed in commerce (including restaurants and hotels). In the same period 5% of the labour force in the West Bank and 4.6% of the labour force in the Gaza Strip were employed in transport, storage and communications; while 24% of the labour force in the West Bank and 41.7% of the labour force in the Gaza Strip were employed in the provision of other services.

In 1991 the official financial services sector, comprising mainly banks and insurance companies, was estimated to employ slightly more than 1% of the Palestinian labour force. In February 1997 a stock exchange, the Palestinian Securities Exchange (PSE), was inaugurated. With an initial listing of 23 companies, the aim is to develop the PSE as the foundation of a Palestinian capital market and to facilitate the investment of expatriate funds.

EXTERNAL TRADE

Israel remains by far the largest market for goods and services from the West Bank. Trade with Israel represents some 75% of exports from, and 87% of imports to, the Territories. Prior to the *intifada*, in 1987, the West Bank recorded a trade deficit with Israel of US $420.2m.; the value of exports to Israel amounted to $160.5m., compared with imports worth $580.7m. During 1988–90 exports of goods and services from the West Bank decreased at an average annual rate of 16%, and the overall trade deficit was aggravated by the 1990–91 crisis in the Persian (Arabian) Gulf region, when the closure of borders and reduced demand affected the export of agricultural goods and manufactures to Arab markets. In 1992 the Gaza Strip recorded a trade deficit with Israel of $264.7m. (exports $63.8m., imports $328.5m.). In its trade with all countries the Gaza Strip recorded a deficit of $286.9m. (exports $79.3m., imports $366.2m.) in 1992. The value of Gazan exports to Jordan in 1992 amounted to $11.9m., while that of imports from Jordan was negligible. In its trade with all other countries, the Gaza Strip recorded a deficit of $34.1m. (exports $3.6m., imports $37.7m.) in 1992. In 1997 the West Bank and the Gaza Strip recorded a trade deficit of an estimated $1,593m., and a deficit of $917m. on the current account of the balance of payments. During that year the value of exports (f.o.b.) to Israel was estimated at $212m., while the value of imports (c.i.f.) amounted to an estimated $1,463m.

In January 1998 Israel opened its borders (in accordance with the 1994 economic agreement signed with the PLO), allowing Palestinians to export various items of agricultural produce to Israel. According to the UN Special Co-ordinator in the Occupied Territories, the volume of exports from the West Bank and the Gaza

Strip rose by 37.3% in the first six months of 1998, while that of imports increased by 32.4%.

PUBLIC FINANCES

In January 1998 the PNA drafted a budget for the period 1998–2000, envisaging projected expenditure totalling US $3,600m. The budget, expected to be completely financed by donor countries, was to allocate $1,690m. to infrastructure projects, $856m. to the public sector, $604m. to manufacturing and $304m. to private institutions. According to data released by the Israeli Ministry of Foreign Affairs in July 1997, more than 60% of the PNA's revenues are derived from tax transfers by the Israeli authorities. In 1997 total revenues of US $814.2m. comprised $301.1m. in local revenues and $513.1m. in revenues transferred from Israel. In 1996 the Gaza Strip's and West Bank's budget deficit was estimated at $112m. (equivalent to 3.5% of GDP).

Sanctions imposed on the West Bank and the Gaza Strip by the Israeli authorities in August 1997 included the partial suspension of transfers of tax revenues. One month after the closures, according to the World bank, losses in the West Bank and Gaza Strip were reported to total $4m.–$5m. per day, and tax and customs transfers suspended by the Israeli authorities amounted to $65m. The PNA was reported to have been obliged to borrow heavily from local banks in order to pay the salaries of its 81,000 employees. Some funds were, in fact, released in August and September 1997, and Israel announced in October that it would release the balance of suspended transfers.

ENERGY

The Palestinian Energy Authority (PEA) has been established to develop the energy and power sectors. Apart from the Jerusalem District Electric Company (which supplies the cities of Jerusalem, Jericho, Bethlehem, Ramallah and El Bireh), there is no utility supplying electric power, although it was agreed to establish the Palestine Electricity Company in August 1997. In Gaza the distribution of electric power supply is the responsibility of 16 municipalities and village councils, which purchase electricity from the Israel Electric Corporation (IEC). In the West Bank, distribution is the responsibility of 252 municipalities and village councils, of which 110 purchase electricity from the IEC, 67 receive partial supplies from village generator systems, and 75 have no formal supplies.

AID AND ECONOMIC DEVELOPMENT

Following the signing of the Declaration of Principles on Palestinian Self-Rule in the Occupied Territories in September 1993, hopes were raised in the West Bank that future economic reconstruction would be financed from abroad. A World Bank report on the Occupied Territories estimated that a 10-year programme to construct essential infrastructure and social facilities would cost US $3,000m. The Palestine Liberation Organization, with a more ambitious Palestine Development Programme, estimated that the reconstruction of the Palestinian economy during 1994–2000 would cost $11,600m. The planners expected to generate $2,000m. from domestic savings, and the remainder from external donors; however, it was unclear how much of the total would be allocated to the West Bank if the plan were to be implemented. Following the signing of the Declaration of Principles in 1993, international donors pledged to invest some $2,900m. in the Gaza Strip and the West Bank. However, only $1,348m. of the $2,490m. pledged between 1994 and 1996 actually reached the Palestinian authorities, owing to the vicissitudes of the peace process and to donors' concerns about the accountability of the Palestinian institutions involved. In December 1997, following a meeting of the Consultative Group of donors (to the Palestinian authorities), held under the auspices of the World Bank, a three-year economic development plan, involving projected expenditure of some $2,600m., was approved. The scheme aimed to rehabilitate the national economy and to reduce Palestinian dependence on Israel. The most substantial investments that the plan envisaged were to be made in infrastructure projects, including improvement of irrigation, road construction, and waste disposal. Private-sector projects, including agriculture and tourism, would also receive funds. The donor countries committed some $750m.-worth of aid for 1998, which would help to finance projects during the initial year of the development plan.

In January 1998 the European Commission reported that member states and institutions of the European Union had pledged 1,700m. European currency units to the Palestinian authorities since the signing of the Oslo Agreement in September 1993. Total international donor commitments since September 1993 amounted to US $2,800m.

According to a study by the World Bank, programmes operated by the United Nations Relief and Works Agency for Palestine Refugees in the Near East (UNRWA, see p. 225) form the basis of the social welfare system in the West Bank and the Gaza Strip, since about 50% of the population there are registered refugees. A number of these programmes are directed at particularly vulnerable groups, such as the aged and the physically disabled. Palestinians working for Israeli employers are required to participate in Israel's national social security scheme. However, taxes deducted from Palestinian workers finance only very limited benefits to Palestinians because residency in Israel is a prerequisite for most Israeli schemes.

Health services in the West Bank (excluding those areas where jurisdiction has been transferred to the PNA) are provided by the Israeli Civil Administration, UNRWA, private voluntary organizations and private, profit-making organizations. Institutions operated by the Israeli Civil Administration in the West Bank derive from Jordanian systems. Until 1974, when a government health insurance scheme was introduced, residents of the West Bank were entitled to free health care from these facilities. Now only members of the government health insurance scheme may receive comprehensive care at government facilities without charge. Pre-natal care and preventive services are provided by the Civil Administration free of charge to all children under the age of three years. UNRWA has traditionally provided basic health care free of charge to some 940,000 registered refugees in the West Bank and the Gaza Strip. It has also reimbursed refugees for 60% of the cost of hospital treatment obtained outside the UNRWA system. In 1991 UNRWA spent about US $8m. on health programmes in the West Bank, and $12m. on those in the Gaza Strip. UNRWA provides its services through a network of 33 health centres in the West Bank, where some 61 physicians care for about 400,000 refugees. UNRWA also operates feeding centres, dental clinics, maternity centres and a 34-bed hospital. Nine health centres in the Gaza Strip provide UNRWA services. There are 82 physicians serving more than 500,000 refugees. Two government hospitals in the Gaza Strip are used to provide secondary care. In the West Bank and the Gaza Strip more than 700 physicians (about one-third of all physicians practising there) work at clinics in the voluntary and private sectors.

In August 1997 UNRWA was confronted by a financial crisis (a budget deficit of some $70m. in 1997), which obliged the agency to give notice of its intention to abolish free education services, cancel 218 teaching jobs, suspend job vacancies, combine school classes, introduce charges for books and medicine, and cancel treatment allowances and special financial support. In October 1997 the Commissioner-General of UNWRA disclosed that the organization was close to bankruptcy, and urged international donors to address a crisis in morale in the Gaza Strip, brought about by severe economic and social hardship.

Directory

Administration

PALESTINE NATIONAL AUTHORITY*
(August 1998)

Appointed in May 1994, the Palestine National Authority (PNA) has assumed some of the civil responsibilities formerly exercised by the Israeli Civil Administration in the Gaza Strip and the Jericho Area of the West Bank.

CABINET
(September 1998)

Minister of Civil Affairs: JAMIL AT-TARIFI (Fatah).

Minister of the Interior: AHMAD TAMIMI (Fatah).

Minister of Planning and International Co-operation: NABIL SHAATH (Fatah).

Minister of Finance: MUHAMMAD ZOHDI AN-NASHASHIBI (Independent).

Minister of Justice: FURAYH ABU MIDDAYN (Fatah).

Minister of Sports and Youth: (vacant).

Minister of Culture, Arts and Information: YASSER ABD AR-RABBUH (Democratic Party).

Minister of Awqaf (Religious Endowments): (vacant)

Minister of Local Authorities: Dr SAEB URAYQAT (Fatah).

Minister of Social Affairs: INTISAR AL-WASIR (Fatah).

Minister of Housing: ABD AR-RAHMAN HAMAD (Fatah).

Minister of Telecommunications: IMAD AL-FALLOULI (Islamist).

Minister of Public Works: AZZAM AL-AHMAD (Fatah).

Minister of Supply: ABD AL-AZIZ SHAHEEN (Fatah).

Minister of Health: RIYAD AZ-ZAANOUN (Fatah).

Minister of Education: (vacant).

Minister of Higher Education: MUNZER SALAH.

Minister of Transport: ALI AL-KAWASMEH (Fatah).

Minister of Economy and Commerce: MAHER AL-MASRI (Fatah).

Minister of Industry: SAADI AL-KARNAZ.

Minister of Labour: RAFIK AN-NATSHA.

Minister of Tourism: METRI ABU ATTIA.

Minister of Agriculture: HEKMAT ZAID.

Minister of Bethlehem 2000 Affairs: NABIL QAIS.

Minister of Parliament: NABIL AMR.

Ministers of State: HISHAM ABD AR-RAZZAK (Prisoners' Affairs), ZIAD ABU ZIAD, HASSAN ASFOUR, TALAL SADR.

MINISTRIES

Ministry of Civil Affairs: Ramallah; tel. (2) 9987336; fax (2) 9987334.

Ministry of Planning and International Co-operation: Ramallah; tel. (2) 5747045; fax (2) 5747046; Gaza; tel. (7) 829260; fax (7) 824090.

Ministry of Finance: Ramallah; tel. (2) 9985881; fax (2) 9985880; Gaza; tel. (7) 863994; fax (7) 820696.

Ministry of the Interior: Gaza; tel. (7) 824670; fax (7) 862500.

Ministry of Justice: Gaza; tel. (7) 822231; fax (7) 867109.

Ministry of Sports and Youth: Ramallah; tel. (2) 9985981; fax (2) 9985991.

Ministry of Culture, Arts and Information: Ramallah; tel. (2) 9986205; fax (2) 9986204.

Ministry of Awqaf (Religious Endowments): Ramallah; tel. and fax (2) 9986410.

Ministry of Local Government: Jericho; tel. (2) 9922619; fax (2) 9921240.

Ministry of Social Affairs: Ramallah; tel. (2) 9986181; fax (2) 9955723.

Ministry of Housing: Gaza; tel. (2) 822233; fax (2) 822235.

Ministry of Telecommunications: Ramallah; tel. (2) 9986555; fax (2) 9986556.

Ministry of Public Works: Gaza; tel. (7) 845707; fax (7) 822310; e-mail mopgaza@palnet.com.

Ministry of Supply: Gaza; tel. (7) 824324; fax (7) 868475.

Ministry of Health: Nablus; tel. (9) 829173; fax (9) 869809; e-mail pnamoh@palnet.com.

Ministry of Education: Ramallah; tel. (2) 9983222; fax (2) 9983200.

Ministry of Higher Education: Gaza; tel. (7) 829211.

Ministry of Transport: Ramallah; tel. (2) 9986947; fax (2) 9986943.

Ministry of Economy and Commerce: Gaza; tel. (7) 9982370; fax (7) 5449032.

Ministry of Industry: Gaza; tel. and fax (7) 5749032.

Ministry of Labour: Ramallah; tel. (2) 9985607; fax (2) 9986496.

Ministry of Tourism and Antiquities: POB 534, Bethlehem; tel. (2) 741581; fax (2) 743753.

Ministry of Agriculture: Ramallah; tel. (2) 9986502; fax (2) 9987422.

President

President: YASSER ARAFAT (took office 12 February 1996).

The first election for a Palestinian Executive President was contested on 20 January 1996 by two candidates: Yasser Arafat and Samiha Khalil. Arafat received 88.1% of the votes cast and Samiha Khalil 9.3%. The remaining 2.6% of the votes cast were spoilt.

Legislature

PALESTINIAN LEGISLATIVE COUNCIL

General Election, 20 January 1996

Party	Seats
Fatah	55
Independent Fatah	7
Independent Islamic	4
Independent Christian	3
Independent	15
Samaritan	1
Other	1
Total	**86***

* The total number of seats in the Palestinian Legislative Council—including one which is automatically reserved for the Palestinian President—is 89. Two seats were not filled at the general election and remained vacant in mid-1998.

The first Palestinian legislative elections took place in 16 multi-member constituencies—including East Jerusalem—on 20 January 1996. Some 75% of the estimated 1m. eligible Palestinian voters were reported to have participated in the elections. During the approach to the elections European Union observers criticized the election commission appointed by Yasser Arafat—and, indeed, Arafat himself—for late alterations to electoral procedure, which, it was felt, might prejudice the prospects of some candidates at the forthcoming polls. Some irregularities were reported to have occurred while voting took place, but these were not regarded as sufficiently serious to compromise the final outcome. The elections were officially boycotted by all sections of the so-called Palestinian rejectionist opposition, including Hamas and Islamic Jihad, although Hamas did endorse a list of 'approved' candidates for those voters who chose not to boycott the elections. All deputies elected to the Legislative Council automatically became members of the Palestine National Council, the existing 483 members of which were subsequently permitted to return from exile by the Israeli authorities, in order, among other things, to consider amendments to the Palestinian National Charter, which has in many ways been superseded by the agreements concluded between Israel and the PLO since September 1993.

Speaker: AHMAD QURAY.

Political Organizations

Palestine Liberation Organization (PLO): Hammam ash-Shaat, Tunis, Tunisia; since the conclusion of the Cairo Agreement on the Gaza Strip and Jericho, signed by the PLO and Israel on 4 May 1994, the PLO has been in the process of transferring its administrative infrastructure and its officers from Tunis to the Gaza Strip, where its headquarters are in Gaza City; f. 1964; the supreme organ of the PLO is the Palestine National Council (PNC), while the Palestine Executive Committee deals with day-to-day business. Fatah (the Palestine National Liberation Movement) joined the PNC in 1968, and all the guerrilla organizations joined the Council in 1969; Chair. YASSER ARAFAT.

The most important guerrilla organizations are:

Fatah (The Palestine National Liberation Movement): f. 1957; the largest single Palestinian movement, embraces a coalition of varying views from conservative to radical; leader YASSER ARAFAT; Sec.-Gen. FAROUK KADDOUMI; Central Cttee (elected by Fatah's 530-member Congress, 31 May 1980): YASSER ARAFAT, SALAH KHALAF, FAROUK KADDOUMI, MAHMOUD ABBAS, KHALID AL-HASSAN, HAYIL ABD AL-HAMID, MUHAMMAD GHUNAIM, SALIM AZ-ZA'NUN, RAFIQ AN-NATSHAH, HANI AL-HASAN.

Popular Front for the Liberation of Palestine (PFLP): Box 12144, Damascus, Syria; f. 1967; Marxist-Leninist; publ. *Democratic Palestine* (monthly, in English); Leader: GEORGE HABASH; in 1994 the PFLP announced the formation of the Democratic National Action Front (DNAF), which it described as an open political, popular forum, an extension of the PFLP.

Democratic Front for the Liberation of Palestine (DFLP): Damascus, Syria; Marxist; split from the PFLP in 1969; Leader: NAIF HAWATMEH.

Arab Liberation Front (ALF): f. 1969; Iraqi-backed; Leader: MAHMOUD ISMAIL.

Palestine Popular Struggle Front (PPSF): f. 1967; Sec.-Gen. SAMIR GHOUSHA.

Palestine People's Party: formerly Palestine Communist Party, admitted to the PNC at its 18th session in 1987; Sec.-Gen. SULEIMAN NAJJAB.

Palestine Liberation Front (PLF): split from PFLP-GC in April 1977; the PLF split into two factions at the end of 1983, both of which retained the name PLF; one faction (leader 'ABU ABBAS') based in Tunis and Baghdad and remaining nominally loyal to Yasser Arafat; the other faction belonging to the anti-Arafat National Salvation Front and having offices in Damascus, Syria, and Libya. A third group derived from the PLF was reported to have been formed by its Central Cttee Secretary, Abd al-Fattah Ghanim, in June 1986. At the 18th session of the PNC, a programme for the unification of the PLF was announced, with Talaat Yaqoub (died November 1988) named as Secretary-General and 'Abu Abbas' appointed to the PLO Executive Committee, while unification talks were held. The merging of the two factions was announced in June 1987, with 'Abu Abbas' becoming Deputy Secretary-General.

The anti-Arafat **National Salvation Front** includes the following organizations:

Popular Front for the Liberation of Palestine-General Command (PFLP-GC): Damascus, Syria; split from the PFLP; pro-Syrian; Leader: AHMAD JIBRIL.

Saiqa (Vanguard of the Popular Liberation War): f. 1967; Syrian-backed; Leader: ISSAM AL-QADI.

Palestine Revolutionary Communist Party: Damascus; Sec.-Gen.: ARBI AWAD.

Alliance of Palestinian Forces: f. 1994; 10 members representing the PFLP, the DFLP, the PLF, the PPSF, the Palestine Revolutionary Communist Party and the PFLP-GC; opposes the Declaration of Principles on Palestinian Self-Rule signed by Israel and the PLO in September 1993, and subsequent agreements concluded within its framework. The **Fatah Revolutionary Council**, headed by Sabri Khalil al-Banna, alias 'Abu Nidal', split from Fatah in 1973. Its headquarters were formerly in Baghdad, Iraq, but the office was closed down and its staff expelled from the country by the Iraqi authorities in November 1983 and a new base was established in Damascus, Syria, in December. Al-Banna was readmitted to Iraq in 1984, having fled Syria. With 'Abu Musa' (whose rebel Fatah group is called **Al-Intifada**, or 'Uprising'), 'Abu Nidal' formed a joint rebel Fatah command in February 1985, and both had offices in Damascus until June 1987, when those of 'Abu Nidal' were closed by the Syrian Government. In 1989 the Fatah Revolutionary Council was reported to have disintegrated, and in June 1990 forces loyal to Abu Nidal surrendered to Fatah forces at the Rashidiyeh Palestinian refugee camp near Tyre, northern Lebanon.

The Islamic fundamentalist organizations, Islamic Jihad (Gen. Sec. RAMADAN ABDALLAH SHALLAH) and the Islamic Resistance Movement (Hamas; Spiritual Leader Sheikh AHMAD YASSIN) are also active in the Gaza Strip and the West Bank, where they began to play an increasingly prominent role in the *intifada* during 1989. Like the organizations represented in the Alliance of Palestinian Forces, they are strongly opposed to the Declaration of Principles on Palestinian Self-Rule. The formation of the Right Movement for Championing the Palestinian People's Sons by former members of Hamas was announced in April 1995. The Movement, based in Gaza City, was reported to support the PNA.

Diplomatic Representation

Countries with which the PLO maintains diplomatic relations include:

Afghanistan, Albania, Algeria, Angola, Austria, Bahrain, Bangladesh, Benin, Bhutan, Botswana, Brunei, Bulgaria, Burkina Faso, Burundi, Cambodia, Cameroon, Cape Verde, Central African Republic, Chad, China (People's Rep.), Comoros, Congo (Dem. Rep.), Congo (Rep.), Cuba, Cyprus, Czechoslovakia (former), Djibouti, Egypt, Equatorial Guinea, Ethiopia, Gabon, Gambia, Ghana, Guinea, Guinea-Bissau, Hungary, India, Indonesia, Iran, Iraq, Jordan, Korea (Dem. People's Rep.), Kuwait, Laos, Lebanon, Libya, Madagascar, Malaysia, Maldives, Mali, Malta, Mauritania, Mauritius, Mongolia, Morocco, Mozambique, Nepal, Nicaragua, Niger, Nigeria, Norway, Oman, Pakistan, Philippines, Poland, Qatar, Romania, Russia, Rwanda, São Tomé and Príncipe, Saudi Arabia, Senegal, Seychelles, Sierra Leone, Somalia, Sri Lanka, Sudan, Swaziland, Sweden, Tanzania, Togo, Tunisia, Turkey, Uganda, United Arab Emirates, Vanuatu, the Vatican City, Viet Nam, Yemen, Yugoslavia, Zambia, Zimbabwe.

The following states, while they do not recognize the State of Palestine, allow the PLO to maintain a regional office: Belgium, Brazil, France, Germany, Greece, Italy, Japan, the Netherlands, Portugal, Spain, Switzerland, and the United Kingdom.

A Palestinian passport has been available for residents of the Gaza Strip and the Jericho area only since April 1995. In September 1995 the passport was recognized by 29 states, including: Algeria, Bahrain, Bulgaria, China (People's Rep.), Cyprus, Egypt, France, Germany, Greece, India, Israel, Jordan, Malta, Morocco, the Netherlands, Pakistan, Qatar, Romania, Saudi Arabia, South Africa, Spain, Sweden, Switzerland, Tunisia, Turkey, the United Arab Emirates, the United Kingdom and the USA.

Judicial System

In the Gaza Strip and the West Bank towns of Jericho, Nablus, Ramallah, Jenin, Tulkaram, Kalkilya, Bethlehem and Hebron, the PNA has assumed limited jurisdiction with regard to civil affairs. However, the situation is confused owing to the various, sometimes conflicting legal systems which have operated in the territories occupied by Israel in 1967: Israeli military and civilian law; Jordanian law; and acts, orders-in-council and ordinances that remain from the period of the British Mandate in Palestine. Religious and military courts have been established under the auspices of the PNA. In February 1995 the PNA established a Higher State Security Court in Gaza to decide on security crimes both inside and outside the PNA's area of jurisdiction; and to implement all valid Palestinian laws, regulations, rules and orders in accordance with Article 69 of the Constitutional Law of the Gaza Strip of 5 March 1962.

General Prosecutor of the PNA: FAYIZ ABU RAHMA.

The Press

NEWSPAPERS

Filastin ath-Thawra (Palestine Revolution): normally published in Beirut, but resumed publication from Cyprus in November 1982; weekly newspaper of the PLO.

Al-Hadaf: organ of the PFLP; weekly.

Al-Haria (Liberation): organ of the DFLP.

Al-Hayat al-Jadidah: West Bank; f. 1994; weekly; Editor NADIL AMR.

Al-Istiqal: Gaza City; organ of the Islamic Jihad; weekly.

Al-Watan: Gaza City; supports Hamas; weekly.

PERIODICALS

Filastin (Palestine): Gaza City; f. 1994; weekly.

Shu'un Filastiniya (Palestine Affairs): POB 5614, 92 Gr. Afxentiou St, Nicosia, Cyprus; tel. 461140; telex 4706; monthly.

NEWS AGENCY

Wikalat Anbaa' Filastiniya (WAFA, Palestine News Agency): formerly in Beirut, but resumed activities in Cyprus and Tunis, November 1982; official PLO news agency; Editor ZIAD ABD AL-FATTAH.

Broadcasting and Communications

Palestinian Broadcasting Corpn: Dir-Gen. RADWAN ABU AYYASH.

Sawt Filastin (Voice of Palestine): c/o Police HQ, Jericho; tel. (2) 921220; official radio station of the PLO; broadcasts in Arabic from Jericho; Dir. RADWAN ABU AYYASH.

Finance

(cap. = capital; dep. = deposits; brs = branches; m. = million)

BANKING
Palestine Monetary Authority

It is intended to develop the Palestine Monetary Authority (PMA) into the Central Bank of Palestine. In July 1995 the PMA began to license, inspect and supervise the Palestinian and foreign commercial banks operating in the Gaza Strip and the Jericho enclave in the West Bank at that time. In December 1995 the PMA assumed responsibility for 13 banks in the Palestinian autonomous areas over which the Central Bank of Israel had hitherto exercised control. Three currencies circulate in the Palestinian economy—the Jordanian dinar, the Israeli shekel and the US dollar. The PMA, which is seeking a reserve base of US $10m. from donors, currently has no right of issue. According to the PMA, in mid-1998 there were eight national banks with a total of 35 branches. In the 12-month period to mid-1998 total credit facilities increased from $520m. to $718m. Deposits increased from $1,787m. to $2,237m. over the same period. Two new banks, the Islamic Al-Aqsa Bank and the Palestinian Housing and Development Bank (with initial capital of $50m.) were to be established in late 1998; Gov. FOUAD BESEISO; fax (7) 86414.

National Banks

Bank of Palestine Ltd: brs in Gaza, Rafah, Ar-Rimal, Khan Younis and Jericho.

Commercial Bank of Palestine: Ramallah; tel. (2) 9954141.

Palestine International Bank: Al-Bireh/Ramallah; tel. (2) 9983300; fax (2) 9983333.

Investment Banks

Arab Palestine Investment Bank: f. 1996; Arab Bank of Jordan has a 51% share; cap. p.u. US $15m.

Jerusalem Bank for Development and Investment: Ramallah.

Palestine Investment Bank: POB 4045, Omar al-Mukhtar St, Gaza City; tel. (7) 822105; fax (7) 822107; f. 1995 by the PNA; some shareholders based in Jordan and the Gulf states; cap. p.u. US $20m.; provides full commercial and investment banking services throughout the Gaza Strip and the West Bank; 3 brs.

Islamic Banks

Arab Islamic Bank: Ramallah.

Palestinian Islamic Bank: Ramallah.

Foreign Banks

Arab Bank plc (Jordan): Regional Management: POB 1476, Ramallah; tel. (2) 9954816; fax (2) 9954815; dep. of some US $800m. held by 12 brs in the West Bank and the Gaza Strip at Sep. 1996; Regional Man. SHUKRI BISHARA.

Other foreign banks include ANZ Grindlays Bank Ltd, the Arab Real Estate Bank (Egypt), the Bank of Jordan, the British Bank of the Middle East, the Cairo-Amman Bank (Jordan), the Development and Agricultural Credit Bank (Egypt), the Jordan Gulf Bank, the Jordan-Kuwait Bank, the Jordanian Housing Bank, the Jordanian National Bank and the Union Savings and Investment Bank (Jordan).

INSURANCE

A very small insurance industry exists in the West Bank.

Arab Insurance Establishment Co (AIEC): Nablus; Man. Dir IBRAHIM ABD AL-HADI.

DEVELOPMENT FINANCE ORGANIZATION

Palestinian Council for Economic Development and Reconstruction: Gov. NABIL SHAATH.

Trade and Industry

CHAMBERS OF COMMERCE

Bethlehem Chamber of Commerce: Bethlehem; tel. (2) 742742; fax (2) 741327.

Hebron Chamber of Commerce and Industry: Hebron; tel. (2) 928218; fax (2) 927490.

Jenin Chamber of Commerce: Jenin; tel. (6) 503388.

Jericho Chamber of Commerce: Jericho; tel. and fax (2) 922394.

Jerusalem Chamber of Commerce: Jerusalem; tel. (2) 282351; fax (2) 272615.

Kalkilya Chamber of Commerce: Kalkilya; tel. (6) 940164.

Nablus Chamber of Commerce: Nablus; tel. (9) 379615; fax (9) 377605.

Palestinian Chamber of Commerce (Gaza): Gaza; tel. (7) 866919; fax (7) 821172.

Palestinian-European Chamber of Commerce: tel. (2) 894883.

Ramallah Chamber of Commerce: Ramallah; tel. (2) 9956043.

Tulkaram Chamber of Commerce: POB 51, Tulkaram; tel. (9) 671010; fax (9) 675623; e-mail tulkarem@netvision.net.il; f. 1945.

TRADE AND INDUSTRIAL ORGANIZATIONS

Union of Industrialists: Gaza.

Transport

CIVIL AVIATION

Palestinian Civil Aviation Authority (PCAA): Gaza International Airport, Gaza; intends to operate services between Gaza and Egypt, Jordan, Cyprus, Turkey, Saudi Arabia, the Gulf States and the United Kingdom through its subsidiary, Palestinian Airlines; Palestinian Airlines currently operates a limited service from Port Said, Egypt, pending the conclusion of an agreement with the Israeli authorities which would allow it to use Gaza International Airport; Chair. and Dir-Gen. FAYEZ ZAIDAN.

Defence

Dir-Gen. of the Palestinian National Security Forces: Maj-Gen. Nasser Youssef.

Estimated Security Budget (1997): US $250m.

Paramilitary Forces (August 1997): an estimated 35,000: including Public Security Force 14,000; Civil Police Force 10,000; General Intelligence Force 3,000; Preventive Security Force 3,000; Military Intelligence 500; Presidential Security 3,000. In addition there are small forces belonging to Coastal Police, Civil Defence, Air Force, Customs and Excise Police Force and the University Security Service.

Education

According to the World Bank, Palestinians are among the most highly educated of any Arab group. However, basic and secondary education facilities in the West Bank and the Gaza Strip are described as poor. In the West Bank the Jordanian education system is in operation. Services are provided by the Israeli Civil Administration, the UNRWA and private, mainly charitable, organizations. In the West Bank and the Gaza Strip schools operated by the Civil Administration enrol some 62% of all primary and secondary school students. The UNRWA provides education to about 31%. In 1991 enrolment in primary schools was equivalent to about 102% of the estimated population aged 6–12 years (due to either underestimation of that population or the enrolment of over-age students). Education has been severely disrupted since 1987. Vocational education is offered by both the Civil Administration and the UNWRA. All university and most community college education is provided by private, voluntary organizations. There are 20 community and teachers' training colleges in the West Bank, and six universities, including an open university. In the 1991/92 academic year 16,368 students attended courses at Palestinian universities. Some 40% of university students in the West Bank are women. Some 170 literacy centres are operated by voluntary organizations in the West Bank and the Gaza Strip during the 1991/92 school year. Two-thirds of these worked for the Civil Administration and about 22% were employed by the UNRWA.

Educational facilities in the Gaza Strip are broadly the same as those described in the West Bank. The Egyptian system of education operates in the Gaza Strip. There are two universities and one teacher training college in the Gaza Strip. Palestinian universities have played a major role in the political activities of the West Bank and the Gaza Strip and were closed by the Israeli Civil Administration between 1987 and 1992. There are some 27 literacy centres in the Gaza Strip. In 1991 the UNRWA budgeted about $35m. for spending on education in the Gaza Strip. Per student expenditure was about $334.

Since May 1994 the PNA has assumed responsibility for education in the Gaza Strip and parts of the West Bank.

Bibliography

A very large literature on the Palestinian question exists and many works belonging to it are included in the bibliography which concludes the chapter on Israel. The following are mainly volumes which have appeared since the signing of the Declaration of Principles on Palestinian Self-Rule by Israel and the PLO in September 1993.

Abu-Amr, Ziad. *Islamic Fundamentalism in the West Bank and Gaza: Muslim Brotherhood and Islamic Jihad.* Bloomington, Indiana University Press, 1995.

Ahmed, Hisham. *Hamas: from religious salvation to political transformation — the rise of Hamas in Palestinian society.* Jerusalem, The Palestinian Academic Society for the Study of International Affairs, 1994.

Artz, Donna E. *Refugees into Citizens: Palestinians and the End of the Arab–Israeli Conflict.* New York, Council on Foreign Relations, 1997.

Aruri, Naseer. *The Obstruction of Peace: the US, Israel and the Palestinians.* Monroe, Common Courage Press, 1995.

Ashrawi, Hanan. *This Side of Peace.* London, Simon and Schuster, 1995.

Butt, Gerald. *Life at the Crossroads: a history of Gaza.* London, Rimal-Scorpion Cavendish, 1995.

Cubert, Harold M. *The PFLP's Changing Role in the Middle East.* London, Frank Cass, 1997.

Darweish, Marwan, and Rigby, Andrew. *Palestinians in Israel: nationality and citizenship.* University of Bradford, 1995.

Khalidi, Rashid. *Palestinian Identity: the construction of modern national consciousness.* New York, Columbia University Press, 1997.

Levenberg, Haim. *The Military Preparations of the Arab Community in Palestine 1945–48.* London, Frank Cass, 1993.

Masalha, Nur (Ed.). *The Palestinians in Israel: is Israel the state of all its citizens and 'absentees'?* Haifa, Galilee Centre for Social Research, 1993.

A Land Without a People: Israel, Transfer and the Palestinians 1949–96. London, Faber and Faber, 1997.

Mazzawi, Musa. *Palestine and the Law.* Reading, Ithaca Press, 1997.

McDowall, David. *The Palestinians — the road to nationhood.* London, Minority Rights Publications, 1995.

Milton-Edwards, Beverley. *Islamic Politics in Palestine.* London, I. B. Tauris, 1996.

Neff, Donald. *Fallen Pillars: US Policy towards Palestine and Israel, 1947–1994.* Institute for Palestine Studies, 1995.

Peleg, Ilan. *Human Rights in the West Bank and Gaza: legacy and politics.* Syracuse, NY, Syracuse University Press, 1995.

Robinson, Glenn E. *Building a Palestinian State: The Incomplete Revolution.* Indiana University Press, 1997.

Roy, Sara. *The Gaza Strip: The Political Economy of De-Development.* Institute for Palestine Studies, 1995.

Rubinstein, Danny. *The Mystery of Arafat.* Vermont, Steerforth Press, 1995.

Said, Edward W. *The Politics of Dispossession: the struggle for Palestinian self-determination 1969–1994.* London, Chatto and Windus, 1994.

Peace and its Discontents. London, Vintage, 1995.

Schiff, Benjamin N. *Refugees unto the Third Generation — UN aid to Palestinians.* Syracuse, NY, Syracuse University Press, 1995.

Sherman, A. J. *Mandate Days: British Lives in Palestine, 1918–1948.* London, Thames and Hudson, 1997.

Usher, Graham. *The Oslo Agreement: Palestine and the Struggle for Peace.* London, Pluto Press, 1995.

Victor, Barbara. *Hanan Ashrawi: A Passion for Peace.* London, Fourth Estate, 1995.

JORDAN

Physical and Social Geography

W. B. FISHER

The Hashemite Kingdom of Jordan (previously Transjordan) came officially into existence under its present name in 1947 and was enlarged in 1950 to include the districts of Samaria and part of Judaea that had previously formed part of Arab Palestine. The country is bounded on the north by Syria, on the north-east by Iraq, on the east and south by Saudi Arabia, and on the west by Israel. The total area of Jordan is 97,740 sq km (37,738 sq miles). The territory west of the Jordan river (the West Bank)—some 5,600 sq km (2,160 sq miles)—has been occupied by Israel since June 1967, but since May 1994 the Palestine National Authority (PNA) has assumed jurisdiction for civil affairs in some areas. The population of the East and West Banks at mid-1995 was estimated by the UN to be 5,439,000. According to a census in December 1994, the population of the East Bank (area 89,206 sq km—34,443 sq miles) was 4,095,579, compared with 2,100,019 at the census of November 1979. In June 1995 there were 1,288,197 Palestinian refugees registered with the United Nations Relief and Works Agency (UNRWA) in Jordan, and a further 517,412 in the West Bank.

PHYSICAL FEATURES

The greater part of the State of Jordan consists of a plateau lying some 700 m–1,000 m above sea-level, which forms the north-western corner of the great plateau of Arabia (see Saudi Arabia). There are no natural topographical frontiers between Jordan and its neighbours Syria, Iraq, and Saudi Arabia, and the plateau continues unbroken into all three countries, with the artificial frontier boundaries drawn as straight lines between defined points. Along its western edge, facing the Jordan Valley, the plateau is uptilted to give a line of hills that rise 300 m–700 m above plateau-level. An old river course, the Wadi Sirhan, now almost dry with only occasional wells, fractures the plateau surface on the south-east and continues into Saudi Arabia.

The Jordanian plateau consists of a core or table of ancient rocks, covered by layers of newer rock (chiefly limestone) lying almost horizontally. In a few places (e.g. on the southern edge of the Jordan Valley) these old rocks are exposed at the surface. On its western side the plateau has been fractured and dislocated by the development of strongly marked tear faults that run from the Red Sea via the Gulf of Aqaba northwards to Lebanon and Syria. The narrow zone between the faults has sunk, to give the well-known Jordan rift valley, which is bordered both on the east and west by steep-sided walls, especially in the south near the Dead Sea, where the drop is often precipitous. The valley has a maximum width of 22 km (14 miles) and is now thought to have been produced by lateral shearing of two continental plates that on the east have been displaced by about 80 km (50 miles).

The floor of the Jordan Valley varies considerably in level. At its northern end it is just above sea-level; the surface of Lake Tiberias (the Sea of Galilee) is 209 m below sea-level, with the deepest part of the lake over 200 m lower still. Greatest depth of the valley is at the Dead Sea (surface 400 m below sea-level, maximum depth 396 m).

Dislocation of the rock strata in the region of the Jordan Valley has had two further effects: firstly, earth tremors are still frequent along the valley (Jerusalem has minor earthquakes from time to time); and secondly, considerable quantities of lava have welled up, forming enormous sheets that cover wide expanses of territory in the state of Jordan and southern Syria, and produce a desolate, forbidding landscape. One small lava flow, by forming a natural dam across the Jordan Valley, has impounded the waters to form Lake Tiberias.

The River Jordan rises just inside the frontiers of Syria and Lebanon—a recurrent source of dispute between the two countries and Israel. The river is 251 km (156 miles) long, and after first flowing for 96 km (60 miles) in Israel it lies within Jordanian territory for the remaining 152 km (94 miles). Its main tributary, the Yarmouk, is 40 km (25 miles) long, and close to its junction with the Jordan forms the boundary between the state of Jordan, Israel and Syria. A few kilometres from its source, the River Jordan used to open into Lake Huleh, a shallow, marsh-fringed expanse of water which was for long a breeding ground of malaria, but which has now been drained. Lake Tiberias, also, like the former Huleh, in Israel, covers an area of 316 sq km (122 sq miles) and measures 22 km (14 miles) from north to south, and 26 km (16 miles) from east to west. River water outflowing from the lake is used for the generation of hydroelectricity.

The river then flows through the barren, inhospitable country of its middle and lower valley, very little of which is actually, or potentially, cultivable, and finally enters the Dead Sea. This lake is 65 km (40 miles) long and 16 km (10 miles) wide. Owing to the very high air temperatures at most seasons of the year evaporation from the lake is intense, and has been estimated as equivalent to 8.5m. tons of water per day. At the surface the Dead Sea water contains about 250g of dissolved salts per litre, and at a depth of 110 m the water is chemically saturated (i.e. holds its maximum possible content). Magnesium chloride is the most abundant mineral, with sodium chloride next in importance; but commercial interest centres on the less abundant potash and bromide salts.

Climatically, Jordan shows close affinity to its neighbours. Summers are hot, especially on the plateau and in the Jordan Valley, where temperatures up to 49°C have been recorded. Winters are fairly cold, and on the plateau frost and some snow are usual, though not in the lower Jordan Valley. The significant element of the climate of Jordan is rainfall. In the higher parts (i.e. the uplands of Samaria and Judaea and the hills overlooking the eastern Jordan Valley) 380 mm–630 mm of rainfall occur, enough for agriculture; but elsewhere as little as 200 mm or less may fall, and pastoral nomadism is the only possible way of life. Only about 25% of the total area of Jordan is sufficiently humid for cultivation.

Hence the main features of economic life in Jordan are subsistence agriculture of a marginal kind, carried on in Judaea-Samaria and on the north-eastern edge of the plateau, close to Amman, with migratory herding of animals—sheep, goats, cattle and camels—over the remaining and by far the larger portion of the country. As a result, the natural wealth of Jordan is small and tribal ways of life exist in parts. Before the June 1967 war, tourism (with which must be included religious pilgrimage, mainly to the holy Christian places of Jerusalem) had developed into a very important industry but was then seriously jeopardized by the Israeli occupation of the West Bank territory and annexation of Jerusalem. However, the civil war in Lebanon and the reopening of the Suez Canal (which greatly affects the Jordanian port of Aqaba) were very favourable factors. The war between Iran and Iraq also had a very beneficial effect at first, since Aqaba, with the denial of Gulf ports to Iraq, became a major supply base. Iraq was Jordan's most important export market between 1980 and 1983 but the cost of continuing the war later severely curtailed the purchase by Iraq of goods from Jordan. By August 1990, when Iraq temporarily occupied Kuwait, Iraq had again become Jordan's principal trading partner; and the economic sanctions imposed on Iraq as a consequence of its invasion of Kuwait had a disastrous effect on the Jordanian economy (see Economy).

The shift of trade from Lebanon, a very much better economic and political relationship with Egypt and Iraq, continuing (though cool) relations with Syria, the inflow of remittances from Jordanians working abroad, and subventions from Arab funds together greatly improved the Jordanian economy. However, the growth of the economy slowed in the 1980s. Foreign aid of various kinds continues to account for more than 40% of budgetary revenues, and workers in the service sector greatly outnumber those in directly productive activities. With so many Jordanians working abroad, local activities are hampered by lack of managerial and technical skills.

RACE, LANGUAGE AND RELIGION

A division must be drawn between the Jordanians living east of the River Jordan who, in the main, are ethnically similar to the desert populations of Syria and Saudi Arabia, and the Arabs of the Jordan Valley and Samaria-Judaea. These latter are slightly taller, more heavily built, and have a broader head-form. Some authorities suggest that they are descendants of the Canaanites, who may have originated far to the north-east, in the Zagros area. An Iranian racial affinity is thus implied— but this must be of very ancient date, as the Arabs west of the Jordan Valley have been settled in their present home for many thousands of years. Besides the two groups of Arabs, there are also small colonies of Circassians from the Caucasus of Russia, who settled in Jordan as refugees during the 19th and 20th centuries AD.

Arabic is spoken everywhere, except in a few Circassian villages, and, through contacts with Britain, some English is understood in the towns.

Over 80% of the population are Sunni Muslims, and King Hussein can trace unbroken descent from the Prophet Muhammad. There is a Christian minority, and there are smaller numbers of Shi'a Muslims.

History

Revised for this edition by RICHARD I. LAWLESS

Jordan, as an independent state, is a 20th-century development. Before then it was seldom more than a rugged and backward appendage to more powerful kingdoms and empires, and indeed never had any separate existence. In biblical times the area was covered roughly by Gilead, Ammon, Moab and Edom, and the western portions formed for a time part of the Kingdom of Israel. During the sixth century BC the Arabian tribe of the Nabateans established their capital at Petra in the south and continued to preserve their independence when, during the fourth and third centuries, the northern half was incorporated into the Seleucid province of Syria. It was under Seleucid rule that cities such as Philadelphia (the Biblical Rabbath Ammon and the modern Amman) and Gerasa (now Jerash) rose to prominence. During the first century BC the Nabateans extended their rule over the greater part of present-day Jordan and Syria; they then began to recede before the advance of Rome, and in AD 105–6 Petra was incorporated into the Roman Empire. The lands east of the Jordan shared in a brief blaze of glory under the Palmyrene sovereigns Odenathus (Udaynath) and Zenobia (az-Zabba') in the middle of the third century AD, and during the fifth and sixth centuries formed part of the dominions of the Christian Ghassanid dynasty, vassals of the Byzantine Empire. Finally, after 50 years of anarchy in which Byzantine, Persian and local rulers intervened, Transjordania was conquered by the Arabs and absorbed into the Islamic Empire.

For centuries nothing more is heard of the country; it formed normally a part of Syria, and as such was generally governed from Egypt. From the beginning of the 16th century it was included in the Ottoman *vilayet* (administrative district) of Damascus, and remained in a condition of stagnation until the outbreak of the First World War in 1914. European travellers and explorers of the 19th century rediscovered the beauties of Petra and Gerasa, but otherwise the desert tribes were left undisturbed. Even the course of the war in its early stages gave little hint of the upheaval that was to take place in Jordan's fortunes. The area was included in the zone of influence allocated to Britain under the Sykes-Picot Treaty of May 1916 (see Documents on Palestine, p. 108), and Zionists held that it also came within the area designated as a Jewish National Home in the promise contained in the Balfour Declaration of November 1917. Apart from these somewhat remote political events the tide of war did not reach Jordanian territory until the capture of Aqaba by the Arab armies under Faisal, the third son of King Hussein of the Hedjaz, in July 1917. A year later, in September 1918, they shared in the final push north by capturing Amman and Deraa.

The end of the war thus found a large area, which included almost the whole of present-day Jordan, in Arab hands under the leadership of Faisal. To begin with, the territory to the east of the River Jordan was not looked on as a separate unit. Faisal, with the assistance of British officers and Iraqi nationalists, established an autonomous government in Damascus, a step encouraged by the Anglo-French Declaration of 7 November 1918, favouring the establishment of indigenous governments in Syria and Iraq. Arab demands, however, as expressed by Faisal at the Paris Peace Conference in January 1919, went a good deal further in claiming independence throughout the Arab world. This brought them sharply up against both French and Zionist claims in the Near East, and when, in March 1920, the General Syrian Congress in Damascus declared the independence of Syria and Iraq, with Faisal and Abdullah, Hussein's second son, as kings, the decisions were denounced by France and Britain. In the following month the San Remo Conference awarded the Palestine Mandate to Britain, and thus separated it effectively from Syria proper, which fell within the French share. Faisal was forced out of Damascus by the French in July and left the country.

THE KINGDOM OF TRANSJORDAN

The position of Transjordania was not altogether clear under the new dispensation. After the withdrawal of Faisal the British High Commissioner informed a meeting of notables at es-Salt that the British Government favoured self-government for the territory with British advisers. In December 1920 the provisional frontiers of the Mandates were extended eastwards by Anglo-French agreement so as to include Transjordania within the Palestine Mandate, and therefore presumably within the provisions regarding the establishment of a Jewish National Home. Yet another twist of policy came as the result of a conference in Cairo in March 1921 attended by Winston Churchill, the new British Colonial Secretary, Abdullah, T. E. Lawrence and Sir Herbert Samuel, High Commissioner for Palestine. At this meeting it was recommended that Faisal should be proclaimed King of Iraq, while Abdullah was persuaded to stand down in his favour by the promise of an Arab administration in Transjordania. He had in fact been in effective control in Amman since his arrival the previous winter to organize a rising against the French in Syria. This project he now abandoned, and in April 1921 was officially recognized as *de facto* ruler of Transjordan. The final draft of the Palestine Mandate confirmed by the Council of the League of Nations in July 1922 contained a clause giving the Mandatory Power considerable latitude in the administration of the territory east of the Jordan (see Documents on Palestine, p. 111). On the basis of this clause, a memorandum was approved in the following September, expressly excluding Transjordan from the clauses relating to the establishment of the Jewish National Home, and, although many Zionists continued to press for the reversal of this policy, the country thenceforth remained in practice separate from Palestine proper.

Like much of the post-war boundary delineation, the borders of the new state were somewhat arbitrary. Although they lay mainly in desert areas, they frequently cut across tribal areas and grazing grounds, with small respect for tradition. Of the 300,000–400,000 inhabitants, only about one-fifth were town-dwellers, and these confined to four small cities ranging in population from 10,000 to 30,000. Nevertheless, Transjordan's early years were destined to be comparatively peaceful. On 15 May 1923 Britain formally recognized Transjordan as an independent constitutional state under the rule of the Amir Abdullah with British tutelage, and with the aid of a British subsidy it was possible to make some slow progress towards development and modernization. A small but efficient armed force, the Arab Legion, was built up under the guidance of Peake Pasha and later Glubb Pasha; this force distinguished itself particularly during the Iraqi rebellion of May 1941. It also played a significant role in the fighting with Israel during 1948. Other British advisers assisted in the development of health services and schools.

The Amir Abdullah very nearly became involved in the fall of his father, King Hussein, in 1924. It was in Amman on 5 March 1924, that the latter was proclaimed Caliph, and during the subsequent fighting with Ibn Sa'ud Wahhabi troops penetrated into Transjordanian territory. They subsequently withdrew to the south, and in June 1925, after the abdication of Hussein's eldest son, Ali, Abdullah formally incorporated Ma'an and Aqaba within his dominions. The move was not disputed by the new ruler of the Hedjaz and Najd, and thereafter the southern frontier of Transjordan remained unaltered.

INDEPENDENCE

In February 1928 a treaty was signed with Great Britain granting a still larger measure of independence, though reserving for the advice of a British Resident such matters as financial policy and foreign relations. The same treaty provided for a constitution, and this was duly promulgated in April 1928, the first Legislative Council meeting a year later. In January 1934 a supplementary agreement was added permitting Transjordan to appoint consular representatives in Arab countries, and in May 1939 Britain agreed to the conversion of the Legislative Council into a regular Cabinet with ministers in charge of specified departments. The outbreak of war delayed further advances towards independence, but this was finally achieved in name at least by the Treaty of London of 22 March 1946. On 25 May 1946 Abdullah was proclaimed king and a new constitution replaced the now obsolete one of 1928.

Transjordan was not slow in taking its place in the community of nations. In 1947 King Abdullah signed treaties with Turkey and Iraq and applied for membership of the United Nations (UN); this last, however, was thwarted by the Soviet veto and by lack of US recognition of Transjordan's status as an independent nation. In March 1948 Britain agreed to the signing of a new treaty in which virtually the only restrictive clauses related to military and defence matters. Britain was to have certain peacetime military privileges, including the maintenance of airfields and communications, transit facilities and co-ordination of training methods. It was also to provide economic and social aid.

Transjordan had, however, not waited for independence before making its weight felt in Arab affairs in the Middle East. It had not been very active before the war, and, in fact its first appearance on the international scene was in May 1939, when Transjordanian delegates were invited to the Round Table Conference on Palestine in London. Transjordan took part in the preliminary discussions during 1943 and 1944 that finally led to the formation of the Arab League in March 1945, and was one of the original members of that League. During the immediately following years it seemed possible that political and dynastic differences would be forgotten in this common effort for unity. Under the stresses and strains of 1948, however, the old contradictions began to reappear. Abdullah had long favoured the project of a 'Greater Syria', that is, the union of Transjordan, Syria and Palestine, as a step towards the final unification of the Fertile Crescent by the inclusion of Iraq. This was favoured on dynastic grounds by various parties in Iraq, and also by some elements in Syria and Palestine. On the other hand it met with violent opposition from many Syrian nationalists, from the rulers of Egypt and Saudi Arabia—neither of whom were disposed to favour any strengthening of the Hashemite house—and of course from the Zionists and the French. It is in the light of these conflicts of interest that developments subsequent to the establishment of the State of Israel must be seen.

FORMATION OF ISRAEL

On 14–15 May 1948 British troops were withdrawn into the port of Haifa as a preliminary to the final evacuation of Palestine territory, the State of Israel was proclaimed, and Arab armies entered the former Palestinian territory from all sides. Only those from Transjordan played any significant part in the fighting, and by the time that major hostilities ceased in July they had succeeded in occupying a considerable area. The suspicion now inevitably arose that Abdullah was prepared to accept a *fait accompli* and to negotiate with the Israeli authorities for a formal recognition of the existing military boundaries. Moreover, whereas the other Arab countries refused to accept any other move that implied a tacit recognition of the status quo—such as the resettlement of refugees—Transjordan seemed to be following a different line. In September 1948 an Arab government was formed at Gaza under Egyptian tutelage, and this was answered from the Transjordanian side by the proclamation in December at Jericho of Abdullah as King of All Palestine. In the following April the country's name was changed to Jordan and three Palestinians were included in the Cabinet. In the mean time, armistices were being signed by all the Arab countries, including Jordan, and on 31 January 1949 Jordan was at last recognized by the USA.

On the three major problems confronting the Arab states in their dispute with Israel, Jordan continued to differ more or less openly with its colleagues. It refused to agree to the internationalization of Jerusalem, it initiated plans for the resettlement of the Arab refugees, and it showed a disposition to accept as permanent the armistice frontiers. In April 1950, after rumours of negotiations between Jordan and Israel, the Arab League Council in Cairo succeeded in getting Jordan's adherence to resolutions forbidding negotiations with Israel or annexation of Palestinian territory. Nevertheless, in the same month elections were held in Jordan and Arab Palestine, the results of which encouraged Abdullah formally to annex the latter territory on 24 April 1950. This step was immediately recognized by Britain.

At the meeting of the Arab League that followed, Egypt led the opposition to Jordan, who found support, however, from Iraq. The decisions reached by the Council were inconclusive, but thereafter Jordan began to drift away from Arab League policy. Jordan supported the UN policy over Korea, in contradistinction to the other Arab states, and signed a four-point agreement with the USA in March 1951. Although there was at the same time constant friction between Jordan and Israel, the unified opposition of the Arab states to the new Jewish state seemed to have ended, and inter-Arab differences were gaining the upper hand.

ABDULLAH ASSASSINATED

On 20 July 1951 King Abdullah was assassinated in Jerusalem. Evidence brought out at the trial of those implicated in the plot showed that the murder was as much as anything a protest against his Greater Syria policy and it was significant that Egypt refused to extradite some of those convicted. Nevertheless, the stability of the young Jordanian state revealed itself in the calm in which the King's eldest son Talal succeeded to the throne, and the peaceful elections held shortly afterwards. In January 1952 a new constitution was promulgated. Even more significant, perhaps, was the dignity with which, only a year after his accession, King Talal, whose mental condition had long been giving cause for anxiety, abdicated in favour of his son, Hussein, still a minor. In foreign policy Talal had shown some signs of a reaction against his father's ideas in favour of a *rapprochement* with Syria and Egypt, one step being Jordan's signature of the Arab Collective Security Pact which it had failed to join in the summer of 1950.

This policy was continued during the reign of his son, King Hussein, notably by the conclusion of an economic and financial agreement with Syria in February 1953, and a joint scheme for the construction of a dam across the Yarmouk River to supply irrigation and hydroelectric power. One problem which became pressing in 1954 was the elaborate scheme sponsored by the USA for the sharing of the Jordan waters between Jordan, Iraq, Syria and Israel, which could make no progress in the absence of political agreement.

During December 1954 a financial aid agreement was signed in London with the United Kingdom, and the opportunity was taken to discuss the revision of the Anglo-Jordanian Treaty of 1946. Agreement over this was not possible owing to British insistence that any new pact should fit into a general Middle East defence system. In May 1955 Premier Abu'l-Huda was replaced by Sa'id al-Mufti, while an exchange of state visits with King Sa'ud hinted at a *rapprochement* with Saudi Arabia. Nevertheless, in November Jordan declared its unwillingness to adhere either to the Egyptian-Syrian-Saudi Arabian bloc or to the Baghdad Pact.

DISMISSAL OF GLUBB PASHA

On 15 December 1955, following a visit to General Sir G. Templer, Chief of the Imperial General Staff, Sa'id al-Mufti resigned and was replaced by Hazza al-Majali, known to be in favour of the Baghdad Pact. The following day there were violent demonstrations in Amman, and on 20 December Ibrahim Hashim became Prime Minister, to be succeeded on 9 January 1956 by Samir Rifai. In February the new Prime Minister visited Syria, Lebanon, Iraq, Egypt and Saudi Arabia, and shortly after his return, on 2 March, King Hussein announced the dismissal of Glubb Pasha, Commander-in-Chief of the Jordanian armed forces, and replaced him with Maj.-Gen. Radi Annab. The Egyptian-Syrian-Saudi Arabian bloc at this juncture offered to replace the British financial subsidy to Jordan; but the latter was not in fact withdrawn, and King Hussein and the Jordanian Government evidently felt that they had moved far enough in one direction, and committed themselves to a policy of strict neutrality. In April, however, the King and the Prime Minister paid a visit to the Syrian President in Damascus, and in May Maj.-Gen. Annab was replaced by his deputy, Lt-Col Ali Abu Nuwar, generally regarded as the leader of the movement to eliminate foreign influence from the Jordanian army and government. This coincided with the reappointment of Sa'id al-Mufti as Prime Minister. During the same period discussions culminated in agreements for military co-operation between Jordan and Syria, Lebanon and Egypt, and in July Jordan and Syria formed an economic union. At the beginning of the same month al-Mufti was replaced by Ibrahim Hashim.

RELATIONS WITH ISRAEL AND WITH THE OTHER ARAB STATES

Meanwhile, relations with Israel, including the problem of the Arab refugees, the use of Jordan waters, the definition of the frontier, and the status of Jerusalem, continued to provide a standing cause for anxiety. Tension between Jordan and Israel was further increased after the Israeli, British and French military action in Egypt. A new Cabinet, headed by Suleiman Nabulsi, had taken office in October, and new elections were followed by the opening of negotiations for the abrogation of the Anglo-Jordan Treaty of 1948, and the substitution of financial aid from the Arab countries, notably Saudi Arabia, Egypt and Syria. Owing to subsequent political developments, however, the shares due from Egypt and Syria were not paid. On 13 March 1957 an Anglo-Jordanian agreement was signed abrogating the 1948 treaty, and by 2 July the last British troops had left. In the mean time, Nabulsi's evident leanings towards the Soviet connection, clashing with the recently enunciated Eisenhower doctrine, led to his breach with King Hussein and his resignation on 10 April, to be succeeded by Ibrahim Hashim. All political parties were suppressed, and plans to establish diplomatic relations with the USSR were dropped. Gen. Ali Abu Nuwar was removed from the post of Commander-in-Chief, and the USA announced its determination to preserve Jordan's independence—a policy underlined by a major air-lift of arms to Amman in September in response to Syria's alignment with the USSR. In May Syrian troops serving under the joint Syro-Egypto-Jordanian command were withdrawn from Jordanian territory at Jordan's request, and in June there was a partial rupture of diplomatic relations with Egypt.

On 14 February 1958 the merger of the kingdoms of Iraq and Jordan in a federal union to be called the Arab Federation was proclaimed in Amman by King Faisal of Iraq and King Hussein. This new federation proved abortive. Samir Rifai became Prime Minister of Jordan in May, on the resignation of Ibrahim Hashim who took up the appointment of vice-premier in the short-lived Arab Federation.

British troops were flown to Amman from Cyprus on 17 July 1958, in response to an appeal by King Hussein. They had all been withdrawn by the beginning of November—under UN auspices—and in the two years that followed Jordan settled down to a period of comparative peace. Hazza al-Majali succeeded Rifai as Prime Minister on 6 May 1959. Firm measures were taken against communism and subversive activities and collaboration with the West was, if anything, encouraged by the country's isolation between Iraq, Israel and the two halves of the United Arab Republic (UAR). American loans continued to arrive at the rate of about $50m. per year, and there was also technical aid of various kinds from Britain, West Germany and other countries. An important development was the official opening of the port of Aqaba on the Red Sea, virtually Jordan's only outlet.

Relations with Jordan's Arab neighbours continued to be uneasy, though diplomatic relations with the UAR, broken off in July 1958, were resumed in August 1959. Incidents on the Syrian border were almost as frequent as on the Israeli, and there were no signs of a *rapprochement* with Iraq. In January 1960 both the King and the Prime Minister condemned the Arab leaders' approach to the Palestine problem, and in February Jordanian citizenship was offered to all Arab refugees who applied for it. On the other side of the balance sheet, King Hussein paid a flying visit to King Sa'ud in February 1960, and in March strongly anti-Zionist statements appeared in the Jordanian press. Nevertheless, there seemed to be no change in the general position that Jordan wished for formal recognition of its absorption of the Palestinian territory west of the Jordan, while the UAR and other Arab countries favoured the establishment of an independent Palestine Arab government.

On 29 August 1960 the Jordanian Prime Minister, Hazza al-Majali, was assassinated. He was followed by a succession of prime ministers during the next five years. In April 1965 a constitutional uncertainty was resolved, with the nomination of the King's brother Hassan as Crown Prince; the King's own children were thus excluded from the succession to the throne.

Meanwhile, in September 1963 the creation of a unified 'Palestinian entity' was approved by the Council of the Arab League, despite opposition from the Jordanian Government, which regarded the proposal as a threat to Jordan's sovereignty over the West Bank. The first congress of Palestinian Arab groups was held in the Jordanian sector of Jerusalem in May–June 1964, when the participants unanimously agreed to form the Palestine Liberation Organization (PLO) as 'the only legitimate spokesman for all matters concerning the Palestinian people'. The PLO was to be financed by the Arab League and was to recruit military units, from among refugees, to constitute a Palestine Liberation Army (PLA). From the outset, King Hussein refused to allow the PLA to train forces in Jordan or the PLO to levy taxes from Palestinian refugees in his country.

WAR WITH ISRAEL

During the latter part of 1966 Jordan's foreign relations were increasingly worsened by the widening breach with Syria. Charges and counter-charges were made of plots to subvert each other's governments, and while the UAR and the USSR supported Syria, Jordan looked for backing to Saudi Arabia and the USA. This situation made it increasingly difficult for Jordan's relations with Israel to be regularized. In July 1966 Jordan suspended support for the PLO, accusing its secretary, Ahmad Shukairi, of pro-communist activity. In November an Israeli reprisal raid aroused bitter feeling in Jordan and elsewhere. While Jordan introduced conscription and Saudi Arabia promised military aid, Syria and the PLO appealed to Jordanians to revolt against King Hussein. Negotiations to implement the resolution of the Supreme Council for Arab Defence that Iraqi and Saudi troops should be sent to Jordan, to assist in its defence, collapsed in December. This was followed by clashes on the Jordanian–Syrian frontier, by PLO-sponsored bomb outrages in Jordan (resulting in the closure of the PLO headquarters in Jerusalem), and by worsening relations between

Jordan and the UAR and a ban by the latter on aircraft carrying British and American armaments to Jordan. In retaliation, Jordan withdrew recognition of the Sallal regime in Yemen, and boycotted the next meeting of the Arab Defence Council. On 5 March Wasfi at-Tal resigned and was succeeded by Hussein bin Nasser at the head of an interim government.

As the prospect of war with Israel drew nearer, King Hussein composed his differences with Egypt, and personally flew to Cairo to sign a defence agreement. Jordanian troops, together with those of the UAR, Iraq and Saudi Arabia, went into action immediately on the outbreak of hostilities in June 1967. By the end of the Six-Day War, however, all Jordanian territory west of the River Jordan had been occupied by Israeli troops, and a steady stream of West Bank Jordanians began to cross the River Jordan to the East Bank. Estimated at between 150,000 and 250,000 persons, they swelled Jordan's refugee population and presented the Government with intractable social and economic problems.

In August 1967 King Hussein formed a nine-man Consultative Council, composed of former premiers and politicians of varying sympathies, to meet weekly and to participate in the 'responsibility of power'. Later a Senate was formed, consisting of 15 representatives from the inhabitants of the West Bank area and 15 from eastern Jordan. Several changes of government took place and the King took over personal command of the country's armed forces.

Meanwhile, the uneasy situation along the frontier with Israel persisted, aggravated by the deteriorating economic situation in Jordan. Reprisal actions by Israel, after numerous commando raids directed against its authority in Jerusalem and the West Bank and operating from Jordanian territory, provoked Jordan to appeal for UN intervention. In June 1969 Israeli commandos blew up the diversion system of the Ghor Canal, Jordan's principal irrigation project.

THE GUERRILLA CHALLENGE

The instability in Amman after the June war was reflected in the short life of Jordanian Cabinets—it became rare for one to remain unchanged for more than three months. A careful balance had to be struck between the Palestinians and the King's traditional supporters. Thus, in the new Cabinet announced after the June 1970 crisis, Palestinians were given more of the key ministries, including the interior portfolio. Abd al-Munem Rifai, Jordan's senior diplomat, became Prime Minister for the second time.

The main factor in Jordan's internal politics between June 1967 and 1971 was the rivalry between the Government and Palestinian guerrilla organizations, principally the Palestine National Liberation Movement, known as al-Fatah ('Conquest'), which was led by Yasser Arafat, the Chairman of the PLO. These organizations gradually assumed effective control of the refugee camps and commanded widespread support amongst the Palestinian majority of Jordan's present population. They also received armaments and training assistance from other Arab countries, particularly Syria, and finance from the oil-rich states bordering the Persian (Arabian) Gulf. Some camps became commando training centres, the younger occupants of these, almost all unemployed, welcoming the sense of purpose and relief from idleness and boredom that recruitment into a guerrilla group offered. The *fedayeen* ('martyrs') movement virtually became a state within a state. Its leaders stated that they 'have no wish to interfere in the internal affairs of Jordan provided it does not place any obstacles in the way of our struggle to liberate Palestine'. In practice, however, its popularity and influence represented a challenge to the Government, whilst its actions attracted Israeli reprisals that did serious damage to the East Bank, now the only fertile part of Jordan, and generally reduced the possibilities of a peace settlement on which Jordan's long-term future depended.

A major confrontation between the two forces occurred in November 1968, after massive demonstrations in Amman on the anniversary of the Balfour Declaration. Extensive street fighting broke out between guerrillas and the army, and for a short period a civil war seemed possible, but both sides soon backed down. Similar confrontations followed in February and June 1970, and on both occasions the Government was forced to yield to Palestinian pressures. King Hussein and Arafat

(whose own position was threatened by the rise of small extremist groups in Jordan) concluded an agreement redefining their respective spheres of influence. The guerrillas appeared to have granted little or nothing, but Hussein was forced to dismiss his Commander-in-Chief and a cabinet minister, both relatives. These were regarded as the leaders of the anti-*fedayeen* faction, which remained strong amongst the Bedouin sheikhs. Despite the agreement, the tension between the Government and the guerrillas continued, aggravated by opposition to the Government's concessions from intransigent army officers.

A new and dangerous stage in the relations between the two sides in Jordan was reached in July 1970 with the acceptance by the Government of the US peace proposals for the Middle East. The guerrilla groups, with few exceptions, rejected these, and, as the cease-fire between the UAR and Israel came into operation on 7 August, it was clear that the Jordanian Government was preparing for a full-scale confrontation with them.

CIVIL WAR

Bitter fighting between government and guerrilla forces broke out at the end of August 1970. This escalated into full civil war in the latter half of September, with thousands of deaths and injuries. On 16 September a military Cabinet was formed under Brig. Muhammad Daoud—in any case martial law had been in force since the end of the June 1967 war—and immediately Field Marshal Habis Majali replaced as Commander-in-Chief Lt-Gen. Mashour Haditha, who had been sympathetic to the commandos and had tried to restrain their severest opponents in the army.

In the fighting that followed, the guerrillas claimed full control in the north, aided by Syrian forces and, it was later revealed, three battalions of the PLA sent back by President Nasser from the Suez front. The Arab states generally appealed for an end to the fighting. Libya threatened to intervene and later broke off diplomatic relations, while Kuwait stopped its aid to the Government; however, the Iraqi troops stationed on the eastern front against Israel notably failed to intervene. On the government side talks were held with the USA about direct military assistance. In the event such a dangerous widening of the Palestinian confrontation was avoided by the scale of the casualties in Jordan and by the diplomacy of Arab Heads of State (reinforced by President Nasser's reported threat to intervene on the guerrillas' behalf) who prevailed upon King Hussein and Yasser Arafat to sign an agreement in Cairo on 27 September 1970, ending the war. The previous day a civilian Cabinet had been restored under Ahmad Toukan. Five military members were retained.

A definitive agreement, very favourable to the liberation organizations, was signed by Hussein and Arafat on 13 October 1970 in Amman, but this proved to be simply the beginning of a phase of sporadic warfare between the two parties, punctuated by new agreements, during which the commandos were gradually forced out of Amman and driven from their positions in the north back towards the Syrian frontier. At the end of October a new Government, still containing three army officers, was formed under Wasfi at-Tal. By January 1971 army moves against the Palestine guerrillas had become much more blatant, and the UAR, Syria and Algeria all issued strong protests at the Jordanian Government's attempt to 'liquidate' the liberation movements. All but two brigades of Iraqi troops were, however, withdrawn from Jordan.

By April 1971 the Jordanian Government seemed strong enough to set a deadline for the guerrillas' withdrawal of their remaining men and heavy armaments from the capital. On 13 July a major government attack began on the guerrillas entrenched in the Jerash-Ajloun area. Four days later it was all over. The Government claimed that all the bases had been destroyed and that 2,300 of 2,500 guerrillas in them had been captured. Most of the Palestinians taken prisoner by the Jordanian Government were released a few days later, either to leave for other Arab states or to return to normal life in Jordan.

The 'solution' (in King Hussein's word) of the guerrilla 'problem' provoked strong reaction from other Arab governments. Iraq and Syria closed their borders with Jordan; Algeria suspended diplomatic relations; and Egypt, Libya, Sudan and both Yemens voiced public criticism. Relations with Syria deteriorated fastest of all, but normal trading and diplomatic relations were restored by February 1972.

In the mean time, Saudi Arabia had been attempting to bring together guerrilla leaders and Jordanian Government representatives to work out a new version of the Cairo and Amman agreements. Meetings did take place in Jeddah but were fruitless, and the Palestinians responded in their own way to the events of July. Three unsuccessful attempts were made in September to hijack Jordanian airliners. Then, on 28 September 1971, Wasfi at-Tal, the Prime Minister and Minister of Defence, was assassinated by members of a Palestinian guerrilla group, the Black September Organization, and other assassination attempts were made.

HUSSEIN'S ANSWER

Throughout the period since the liquidation of the guerrillas in July 1971 Hussein had been seeking to strengthen his political position. In August he announced the creation of a tribal council—a body of sheikhs or other notables, appointed by him and chaired by the Crown Prince—which was to deal with the affairs of tribal areas. A month later the formation of the Jordanian National Union was announced. This (renamed the Arab National Union in March 1972) was to be Jordan's only legal political organization. It was not a party in the usual sense; proponents of 'imported ideologies' were debarred from membership; the King became president, and the Crown Prince vice-president, and appointed the 36 members of the Supreme Executive Committee.

However, the King's boldest political move, and an obvious attempt to regain his standing in the eyes of Palestinians, was his unfolding of plans for a United Arab Kingdom in March 1972. This Kingdom was to federate a Jordanian region, with Amman as its capital and also federal capital, and a Palestinian region, with Jerusalem as its capital. Each region was to be virtually autonomous, though the King would rule both and there would be a federal Council of Ministers.

Outside Jordan there was almost universal criticism of this plan from interested parties—Israel, the Palestinian organizations and Egypt, which in the following month broke off diplomatic relations. Jordan's isolation in the Arab world had never been more complete.

Throughout the rest of 1972 and the first half of 1973 Hussein continued to adhere to his original plans for a United Arab Kingdom, but at the same time he insisted that peace with Israel could be arrived at only within the framework of UN Security Council Resolution 242 (see Documents on Palestine, p. 115) and strongly denied suggestions from other Arab states that he was considering signing a separate peace treaty with Israel.

The internal security of Jordan was threatened in November 1972 when an attempted military coup in Amman by Major Rafeh Hindawi was thwarted. In February 1973 Abu Daoud, one of the leaders of al-Fatah, and 16 other guerrillas were arrested on charges of infiltrating into Jordan for the purpose of subversive activities.

The latter affair took place while King Hussein was on a visit to the USA requesting defence and financial aid. On his return he commuted the death sentences passed on the guerrillas by a Jordanian military court and previously confirmed by himself, to life imprisonment. In May 1973 Hussein's Prime Minister, Ahmad Lauzi, resigned for health reasons and a new government under Zaid ar-Rifai, who was known as an opponent of the Palestinian guerrillas, was formed.

In September 1973 Hussein attended a 'reconciliation summit' with Presidents Sadat of Egypt and Assad of Syria. This was Jordan's first official contact with the two states since they had broken diplomatic relations, and they were restored after the summit. The meeting was condemned by al-Fatah, Libya and Iraq, but Jordan regained some stature in the Arab world after Hussein's general amnesty for all political prisoners; among those released was Abu Daoud.

During the Middle East War in October 1973 Jordan sent troops to support Syria on the Golan Heights but was otherwise not actively involved, and did not open a third front against Israel as in the 1967 war. Jordan was represented at the Geneva talks in December 1973. During February 1974 there was considerable unrest among sections of the army, although this was

settled by increases in pay, ordered by Hussein, who was out of the country when the disturbances started. In April Hussein announced that the Arab National Union, which was then the sole political organization in Jordan, was to be reorganized with an executive and council of reduced numbers.

During most of 1974 the main characteristic of Hussein's policy towards the PLO and the status of the West Bank was extreme ambiguity. He continued to try to preserve the West Bank as part of his Kingdom despite strong pressure from other Arab states and the increasing influence of the PLO. In September 1974 after a meeting between Egypt, Syria and the PLO expressing support for the PLO as the 'only legitimate representative of the Palestinian people', Jordan refused to participate in further Middle East peace talks. However, in October 1974 at the Arab Summit Conference at Rabat (see Documents on Palestine, p. 118), representatives of 20 Arab Heads of State unanimously recognized the PLO as the sole legitimate representative of the Palestinians, and its right to establish a national authority over any liberated Palestinian territory. Effectively ceding Jordan's claim to represent the Palestinians and reincorporate the West Bank, when recaptured, into the Hashemite Kingdom, Hussein reluctantly assented to the resolution. He said that Jordan would continue to strive for the liberation of the West Bank and recognize the full rights of citizenship of Palestinians in Jordan. The prospect of a separate, independently-ruled Palestinian state was strongly condemned by Israel.

JORDAN AFTER THE RABAT SUMMIT

Following the Rabat Conference Hussein was given more extensive powers in revisions to the Jordanian Constitution approved by the National Assembly in November 1974. He was allowed to rule without the National Assembly for a year, and to reorganize his Kingdom in order to lessen the numbers of Palestinians in the executive and legislative branches of government, his 1972 plan for a United Arab Kingdom now being wholly defunct. The National Assembly was dissolved and a new Government formed in November, with Zaid ar-Rifai remaining Prime Minister. Palestinian representation was decreased, and the question of citizenship of the estimated 800,000 Palestinians on the East Bank became contentious. Elections in Jordan were postponed in March 1975 and when the National Assembly was briefly reconvened in February 1976 a constitutional amendment was enacted to suspend elections indefinitely.

The success of the PLO at the Rabat Conference had, despite internal feuds, considerably strengthened its position. This was further the case when the UN acknowledged the PLO as the sole legitimate representative of the Palestinians by an overwhelming majority in November. The PLO was also granted observer status at the UN.

One of the most notable results of the Rabat Summit Conference, and of Hussein's virtual abandonment of his claim to the West Bank, was an improvement in relations with the Arab world in general, and with Syria in particular. During 1975 various links with Syria were forged and strengthened. Early in the year Hussein visited Damascus and President Assad visited Jordan in June. A supreme joint committee was set up to co-ordinate military and political planning, with the two countries' Prime Ministers as chairmen. In August a Supreme Command Council, headed by the King and President Assad, was formed to direct military and political action against Israel, and in December 1976 it was announced that a form of political union between the two countries was to be elaborated.

This close relationship, however, was jeopardized by President Sadat's visit to Israel in November 1977, and subsequently threatened by Syria's proposed *rapprochement* with Iraq. Jordan, unlike Syria, was anxious not to condemn Sadat's peace initiative, but did not want to destroy its growing relationship with Syria. King Hussein, therefore, remained uncommitted and tried to act as a conciliator between Egypt on the one hand and the 'rejectionist' states (Algeria, Libya, Iraq, Syria and the People's Democratic Republic of Yemen) on the other. Jordan, however, emphatically rejected Israel's peace proposals which were put forward by Prime Minister Begin in December 1977, and maintained its policy of demanding an Israeli withdrawal from Gaza and the West Bank, including East Jerusalem, leaving no Jewish settlements. Jordan also wanted the creation of a Palestinian homeland, the nature of whose link with Jordan should be decided by a referendum.

It was these factors which helped to determine Jordan's attitude to the Camp David agreements (see Documents on Palestine, p. 119) in September 1978 and the subsequent peace treaty between Egypt and Israel (see Documents on Palestine, p. 121) in March 1979. Jordan refused to be drawn into the Camp David talks by the USA, and joined the other Arab states at the Baghdad Arab summit in drawing up a list of sanctions against Egypt.

Immediately prior to the signing of the peace treaty, Jordan showed its commitment to the PLO by welcoming Yasser Arafat on an official visit, and after the treaty was signed Jordan was the first Arab country still having diplomatic relations with Egypt to break them off. In the months that followed the signing of the peace treaty, however, Jordan's hostility to Egypt subsided, and was replaced by the souring of relations with Syria. In spite of Jordanian denials, Syria was convinced that the Muslim Brotherhood (allowed limited freedom in Jordan) was fostering treachery inside Syria. Syria also disapproved of Jordan's support for Iraq in the Iran–Iraq War. These factors led to a build-up of Syrian and Jordanian troops on the frontier in December 1980, and to mediation between the two sides by Saudi Arabia. Relations did not improve in February 1981 when the Jordanian Chargé d'affaires in Beirut was abducted (allegedly by Syrians), and Jordan responded by abrogating a six-year economic and customs agreement with Syria.

Throughout 1981 Jordan continued with its policy of supporting Iraq, and in January 1982 Hussein announced that he was prepared to take charge of a special 'Yarmouk Force' of Jordanians to give military help to Iraq. In April, however, as Iraq's position in the war with Iran grew weaker, Hussein tried, unsuccessfully, to encourage a negotiated settlement between Iran and Iraq (by 1984, however, Hussein was, once more, offering troops and other military assistance to Iraq). He also supported a revival of Saudi Arabia's Fahd plan for a resolution of the Arab–Israeli question. After the Israeli invasion of Lebanon in June 1982, Hussein found himself a key part of President Reagan's peace plan, involving the creation of an autonomous Palestinian authority on the West Bank in association with Jordan (see Documents on Palestine, p. 124). Hussein discussed the matter in Washington in December, and in January 1983 held talks with the PLO leader, Yasser Arafat, in Amman.

Opinion within Jordan was very sceptical of the supposed advantages that would accrue to Jordan if Hussein associated himself too deeply with President Reagan's peace plan. As well as a military threat from Syria, there was the possibility of the withdrawal of aid from other Arab countries. Talks between Hussein and Arafat again took place in early April 1983, however, when Arafat stressed his commitment to the Fez plan which had been agreed at the Arab summit in September 1982 (see Documents on Palestine, p. 124). By the middle of April the Reagan peace plan seemed dead, when Arafat rejected the draft agreement which Hussein had prepared. In the weeks that followed, Hussein still claimed to support the Reagan plan. Much of his time, however, was spent in taking steps to control emigration of Palestinians from the West Bank in Jordan.

In domestic affairs, Hussein had dissolved the House of Representatives in 1974, but in April 1978 he formed a 60-member National Consultative Council (NCC) appointed by Royal Decree. The third term of the NCC began on 20 April 1982. In December 1979 Sharif Abd al-Hamid Sharaf replaced Mudar Badran as Prime Minister. Sharaf, however, died of a heart attack on 3 July 1980, and was replaced as Prime Minister by the former Minister of Agriculture, Qassim ar-Rimawi. In August, however, a new government under former Prime Minister Mudar Badran was introduced, although little change of policy resulted.

THE RECALL OF THE NATIONAL ASSEMBLY

Despite the failure to agree a formula for the creation of a Palestinian state on the West Bank with Yasser Arafat, Jordan gave diplomatic support to Arafat when a Syrian-backed revolt against his leadership of al-Fatah, the major guerrilla group within the PLO, erupted in Lebanon in May 1983. During the last three months of 1983, Jordanian diplomats in several

European countries, and targets in Amman, came under attack from terrorists who were thought to be members of a radical Arab group, based in Syria, which was angered by Jordan's call for Egypt to be readmitted to the community of Arab states, by its backing for Arafat and by the prospect of a revival of President Reagan's peace plan which their improved relations raised.

With a view to recovering something from the West Bank before Jewish settlement there produced a *de facto* extension of Israel, King Hussein dissolved the National Consultative Council on 5 January 1984 and reconvened the National Assembly, which had been suspended in 1974, for its first session since 1967. At the same time, he embarked upon a series of talks with Yasser Arafat, dealing with the Palestinian question, which sought to consolidate their good relations and to establish a moderate core of opinion as a counter-weight to the intransigent Syrian, Libyan and extremist PLO position, that a solution could only be achieved by armed struggle. Hussein, moreover, could not forget that some 60% of his subjects were Palestinians. By recalling the National Assembly, Hussein seemed, effectively, to be creating the kind of Palestinian forum which was called for in the Reagan plan. This was not, as it turned out, a prelude to a concerted move by Hussein and Arafat towards establishing a Palestinian state on the West Bank. The National Assembly provided a focus for a debate which revealed strong opposition among Jordanian Palestinians to the Reagan plan. As the talks between Hussein and Arafat progressed, they were at pains to stress that they stood by the resolution of the Rabat Summit Conference in 1974, which recognized the PLO as the sole legitimate representative of the Palestinian people.

Israel allowed the surviving West Bank deputies to attend the reconvened House of Representatives (the Lower House), which unanimously approved constitutional amendments enabling elections to the House to be held in the East Bank alone but giving itself the right to elect deputies from the West Bank, without whom the House would have been inquorate. The first elections in Jordan for 17 years, and the first in which women were allowed to vote, took place on 12 March 1984 (although political parties were still banned). The House of Representatives had already, in January, elected seven deputies from the West Bank by majority vote to fill the places of members who had died since 1974, increasing the membership of the House to 52. The 12 March elections filled the remaining 8 seats from the East Bank. Any thought that Hussein, in reviving the National Assembly, might, in the absence of agreement with the PLO on the Reagan plan, seek a mandate from the West Bank deputies to begin talks with Israel on Palestinian autonomy, was set further aside by the election of three Muslim fundamentalists and an Arab nationalist in the eight East Bank by-elections. The extent of the opposition to a solution based on the Reagan plan was apparent.

The nucleus of a moderate body of Arab opinion on the Palestinian question did, none the less, give the impression of being formed around Jordan and Yasser Arafat, with likely support to come from Saudi Arabia, Egypt and the Gulf states. The opposition to these developments of other Arab groups was reaffirmed when the Jordanian embassy in Tripoli, Libya, was burnt down in February 1984. Jordan responded by severing diplomatic relations with Libya. Sporadic attacks on Jordanian diplomats, principally in European countries, continued throughout 1984 and 1985, for which responsibility was claimed by various extremist Arab groups including the Islamic Jihad and the re-emergent Black September organization, which was formed after the expulsion of the PLO from Jordan in September 1970. Jordan suspected Syria and Libya of being behind these attacks.

In January 1984 the Jordanian Cabinet resigned, and a new one, containing a higher proportion of Palestinians and led by Ahmad Ubeidat, as Prime Minister, took office.

RELATIONS WITH THE SUPERPOWERS

At the beginning of 1984 the US Government tried to renew its efforts to gain congressional approval for a $220m.-plan to supply Jordan with arms and equipment for an 8,000-strong Jordanian strike force. King Hussein tried to distance Jordan from any interest or involvement in the creation of such a force.

Plans for a Jordanian strike force were abandoned by the Reagan Administration in June.

Hussein, frustrated by the unwillingness of the USA to use its influence with Israel to 'freeze' Jewish settlement of the West Bank and unable to buy arms from the USA, began to look to the USSR for diplomatic backing in solving the problem of Palestinian autonomy and for armaments with which to defend his country. In January 1985 Jordan purchased an air defence system from the USSR, having already made an agreement to buy French anti-aircraft missiles in September 1984. The need to re-equip the Jordanian air force was acute: in 1984 the Jordanians possessed only about 100 effective fighter aircraft, compared with the 630 and 600 aircraft respectively of Israel and Syria, according to 1982/83 figures.

Although US President Reagan was advocating the sale of arms worth $500m.–$750m. to Jordan in 1985, there was still considerable opposition to the proposal, and he was advised not to put it before Congress and risk a Senate veto. Instead, on 12 June, King Hussein was offered extra economic aid of $250m., to be spread over 1985 and 1986, by Secretary of State Shultz, as a token of US support for his efforts to achieve a peace settlement between the Arabs and Israel. Jordan received US aid of $136m. in 1984, and the level of aid in 1985 and 1986 had originally been set at $111.7m. and $117m. respectively. The Senate authorized the aid but spread it over 27 months, not 15, as the Reagan Administration had requested.

JOINT JORDANIAN-PALESTINIAN PEACE PROPOSALS

In September 1984, to the anger of radical Arab states, Jordan decided to re-establish diplomatic relations with Egypt, five years after breaking them off in protest at the Egypt-Israel peace treaty of 1979. Hussein rejected the Israeli offer of direct negotiations, excluding the PLO, in October, calling instead for a conference of all the concerned parties in the Middle East, including, on an equal footing with nation states in the region, the PLO. He required Israel to accept the principle of 'land for peace'—this is, talks leading to the restoration of occupied territories (including East Jerusalem) to Jordan, in return for a comprehensive Arab–Israeli peace treaty. Negotiations, according to Hussein, should proceed on the basis of UN Security Council Resolution 242 of November 1967. This last point was the impediment to Jordanian and PLO agreement to a programme for peace talks. Resolution 242 had not been acceptable to the PLO as it referred to the Palestinian Arabs as refugees, implicitly denying the existence of a Palestinian nation and Palestinians' right to self-determination, and recognized Israel's right to exist. The Palestine National Council (PNC), which finally convened in Amman in November 1984, replied non-committally to King Hussein's offer of a joint Jordanian-Palestinian peace initiative, without explicit rejection or acceptance of the principles embodied in Resolution 242, and referred the proposal to the PLO Executive Committee for examination.

On 23 February 1985, in Amman, King Hussein and Yasser Arafat announced the terms of a joint Jordanian-Palestinian agreement on the framework for a peace settlement in the Middle East, which the two leaders had finalized on 11 February. It held that peace talks should take the form of an international conference including the five permanent members of the UN Security Council and all parties to the conflict, including the PLO, representing the Palestinian people in a joint Jordanian-Palestinian delegation. The Palestinian people would in future exercise their right to self-determination in the context of a proposed confederated state of Jordan and Palestine. The Jordanian Government claimed that the agreement was based on a number of UN resolutions and not solely UN Security Council Resolution 242, though the published text of the accord (see Documents on Palestine, p. 125) gave land in exchange for peace, a central tenet of that resolution, as its first principle. The PLO Executive Committee, in approving the terms of the accord (providing that they received full Arab support) on 20 February, complicated the position by stressing that the joint position stemmed, in fact, from a rejection of Camp David, the Reagan plan and Resolution 242 as well. According to King Hussein, Arafat subsequently accepted Resolution 242 as the basis for future peace negotiations, but made no public declaration of acceptance. Argument over the implications of the agree-

ment persisted, and the PLO adopted a new position on the status of the Palestinian representation at future peace negotiations, which, it said, should be within a united Arab, not merely a Jordanian-Palestinian, delegation. Syria and Libya and the rebel PLO factions predictably rejected the Amman agreement.

In March 1985 President Mubarak of Egypt called for talks between Egypt, the USA and a joint Jordanian-Palestinian delegation. The PLO Executive Committee rejected the proposal as it deviated from the accord with Jordan. Israel rejected the idea of preliminary talks and any suggestion that the USA might negotiate with the PLO, as it had always refused to do unless the PLO renounced terrorism and accepted Israel's right to exist. In May King Hussein, still averring that the PLO accepted UN Security Council Resolutions 242 and 338 as the basis for negotiations, put foward a four-stage plan in Washington. Under the terms of the plan, the USA would first meet a Jordanian-Palestinian delegation, not including PLO representatives. Arafat would then be prepared to make a formal declaration of the PLO's readiness to recognize and negotiate with Israel if the USA publicly stated its support for Palestinian self-determination within the context of a Jordanian-Palestinian confederation, as proposed in the 11 February agreement between King Hussein and Arafat. The USA would then hold a second meeting with a Jordanian-Palestinian delegation, including PLO representatives, at which the terms of the third and fourth stages of the plan, an international conference under the auspices of the five permanent members of the UN Security Council, leading to direct negotiations between Israel and a Jordanian-Palestinian delegation, would be discussed. Israel rejected the plan and the call for an international peace conference, and instead proposed enlisting the support of the permanent members of the Security Council for direct talks between Israel and a joint Jordanian-Palestinian delegation including 'authentic Palestinian representatives' from the Occupied Territories who were not members of the PLO or the PNC. In July Israel rejected a list of seven Palestinians, five of whom were members of the PLO loyal to Yasser Arafat or had links with the PNC, whom King Hussein had presented to the USA as candidates for inclusion in a joint Jordanian-Palestinian delegation to hold preliminary talks with the USA. The Israeli Prime Minister, Shimon Peres, later conceded that two of the seven fulfilled his requirements.

The Prime Minister, Ahmad Ubeidat, resigned in April 1985. On 5 April a new Cabinet, only four of whose 23 members was retained from the previous Government, was sworn in under the premiership of Zaid ar-Rifai, who had served as Prime Minister during the 1970s.

THE COLLAPSE OF THE JORDANIAN-PALESTINIAN PEACE INITIATIVE

King Hussein and Yasser Arafat continued to seek Arab support for their peace initiative, but an extraordinary meeting of the Arab states in Casablanca, in August 1985 (which was boycotted by Syria, Libya, Lebanon, the People's Democratic Republic of Yemen—PDRY— and Algeria), merely noted the existence of the Jordanian-Palestinian agreement and reaffirmed Arab allegiance to the Fez plan of September 1982.

Further progress was then hampered by a series of terrorist attacks, carried out by Palestinian organizations. In September three Israelis were murdered by terrorists in Larnaca, Cyprus. Israel blamed the PLO's élite Force 17 and retaliated by bombing the PLO's headquarters in Tunis on 1 October. Later in October an Italian cruise ship, the *Achille Lauro,* was 'hijacked' in the eastern Mediterranean by members of the Palestine Liberation Front (the faction of that name led by 'Abu' Abbas, nominally loyal to Arafat), who killed an elderly American Jewish passenger.

King Hussein was under increasing pressure to advance the peace process, if necessary without the participation of the PLO. In September President Reagan revived a plan to sell US arms worth $1,900m. to Jordan. The proposal was approved by Congress on the condition that Jordan entered into direct talks with Israel before 1 March 1986. However, a *rapprochement* developed between Jordan and Syria, which made such a development even more unlikely. In February 1986 the administration of President Reagan in the USA indefinitely postponed its proposed arms sale to Jordan (worth $1,500m., with the withdrawal of *Hawk* missiles from the package) when it became clear that it would not be approved by the Senate. King Hussein said that he would look instead to European countries and the USSR for arms supplies.

Relations between Jordan and Syria had been poor since 1979, when Syria had accused Jordan of harbouring anti-Syrian groups. Their policies also diverged in respect of the Iran–Iraq War, in which Syria supported Iran, and Jordan Iraq. In November 1985 King Hussein admitted that Jordan had, unwittingly, been a base for the Sunni fundamentalist Muslim Brotherhood in its attempts to overthrow Syria's President Assad, but stated that members of the group would no longer receive shelter there. The Prime Ministers of the two countries met in Damascus in November and agreed on the need for 'joint Arab action' to achieve peace in the Middle East. At previous talks in Saudi Arabia in October, Jordan and Syria had rejected 'partial and unilateral' solutions and affirmed their adherence to the Fez plan, omitting all mention of the Jordanian-Palestinian peace initiative. President Assad and King Hussein confirmed the improved state of Syrian-Jordanian relations when they met in Damascus in December.

By pursuing a reconciliation with Syria, which was opposed to Yasser Arafat's leadership of the PLO, King Hussein may have hoped to exert pressure on Arafat to take the initiative in the peace process and finally signal PLO acceptance of Resolution 242. Arafat was also under pressure from King Hussein and President Mubarak of Egypt to promote the PLO's credibility as a prospective partner in peace talks by renouncing terrorism. He responded to their appeals in November 1985, in Cairo, by effectively reiterating a PLO decision of 1974 to confine military operations to the Occupied Territories and Israel. Any credence that this declaration may have won was immediately dispelled by Arafat's aides, who repudiated it. Then, in December, the PLO Executive Committee reiterated its opposition to Resolution 242.

Shimon Peres, the Israeli Prime Minister, although he remained opposed to the idea of preliminary negotiations excluding Israel, intimated in a speech at the UN in October 1985 that he would not rule out the possibility of an international conference on the Palestinian question. Rumours of a secret meeting between King Hussein and Peres were followed at the end of October by the disclosure to the Israeli press of a document, drawn up by the Israeli Prime Minister's office, which purported to summarize the state of negotiations between Israel and Jordan. The document suggested the establishment of an interim Israeli-Jordanian condominium of the West Bank, granting a form of Palestinian autonomy, and recorded mutual agreement on the need for an international forum for peace talks. Israel would consent to the participation of the USSR in such a forum (on the condition that it re-established diplomatic relations with Israel), and of Syria, but not of the PLO, on whose involvement King Hussein still insisted.

Given Yasser Arafat's persistent refusal to accept UN Security Council Resolutions 242 and 338 as the basis for peace talks, the demise of the Jordanian-Palestinian peace initiative had been forecast for some time. On 19 February 1986 King Hussein publicly severed political links with the PLO 'until such time as their word becomes their bond, characterized by commitment, credibility and constancy'. Arafat was ordered to close his main PLO offices in Jordan by 1 April. The activities of PLO members in the country were henceforth to be restricted to an even greater extent than before, and a number of officers of al-Fatah, loyal to Arafat, were expelled. King Hussein made efforts to strengthen Jordanian influence and create a Palestinian constituency in the Occupied Territories, independent of Arafat's PLO, including: the passing of a draft law by the House of Representatives in March 1986, increasing the number of seats in the House from 60 to 142 (71 seats each for the East and West Bank), thereby providing for greater West Bank Palestinian representation in the House; and the introduction, in August 1986, with Israeli support, of a $1,300m. five-year development plan for the West Bank and the Gaza strip.

This last measure provoked strong criticism from Yasser Arafat and from West Bank Palestinians, who claimed that it represented a normalization of relations between Jordan and Israel. There was considerable support for Arafat among Palestinians in Jordan and in the West Bank, and this was consolidated

after he re-established himself at the head of a reunified PLO at the PNC session in Algiers in April 1987 (when the Jordan-PLO accord of 1985 was formally abrogated). As criticism of King Hussein mounted in Jordan and in the West Bank, the authorities responded by imposing new security measures, arresting dissidents (in particular members of the fundamentalist Muslim Brotherhood and the banned Jordanian Communist Party), tightening press censorship and 'blacklisting' journalists deemed too critical of the government.

After the termination of political co-ordination with the PLO, Jordan continued to reject Israeli requests for direct peace talks which excluded a form of PLO representation. However, Jordan's subsequent efforts to strengthen its influence in Israeli-occupied territories and to foster a Palestinian constituency there which was independent of the PLO, complemented Israeli measures to grant limited autonomy to the Palestinian community in the West Bank, by appointing Arab mayors instead of Israeli military administrators in four towns. In May 1987, after a number of secret meetings with King Hussein, Peres (who was now the Israeli Minister of Foreign Affairs) claimed to have made significant progress on the critical issue of Palestinian representation at a peace conference, and to have the consent of Egypt, Jordan and the USA for convening an international conference, including the five members of the UN Security Council and a delegation of Palestinians (presumably not PLO members) who 'reject terrorism and violence' and accept UN Security Council resolutions 242 and 338 as the basis for negotiations. King Hussein continued publicly to insist on the need for the PLO to be represented, but he appeared to have accepted (contrary to his long-standing official policy) that the conference would have no power to impose a peace settlement, and would be only a preliminary to direct talks between the main protagonists in the Middle East conflict. However, the prospect of an international peace conference remained academic for as long as there was no majority in the Israeli Cabinet in favour of Peres' plan and, therefore, for as long as the Israeli coalition Government of National Unity remained in power. The Prime Minister, Itzhak Shamir, was opposed in principle to an international conference, which would negotiate on the basis of an Israeli offer of the return of occupied territory in exchange for peace. He reiterated his alternative proposal to Peres' plan, namely, direct regional talks involving Israel, Egypt, Jordan, Palestinian representatives and the USA.

ARAB LEAGUE SUMMIT IN AMMAN

During 1987 King Hussein pursued his efforts, begun in 1986, to reconcile Syria and Iraq, with the wider aim of securing Arab unity. He was instrumental in arranging the first full summit meeting of the Arab League (excluding Egyptian representation) for eight years, which took place in Amman in November, principally to discuss the Iran–Iraq War. In September Jordan had restored diplomatic relations with Libya, which had modified its support for Iran and now urged a cease-fire. The Arab summit meeting unanimously adopted a resolution of solidarity with Iraq, which condemned Iran for its occupation of Arab territory and for prolonging the war (although Syria obstructed the adoption of diplomatic or other sanctions). King Hussein's appeal for Egypt to be restored to membership of the League was successfully resisted by Syria and Libya, but nine Arab states re-established diplomatic relations with Egypt soon after the summit, and these were followed by Tunisia in January 1988 and by the PDRY in February. President Saddam Hussain of Iraq and President Assad of Syria held two sessions of talks at the summit, and the resumption of co-operation between Jordan and the PLO was announced.

THE INTIFADA AND THE SHULTZ PLAN

In December 1987 a violent Palestinian uprising (*intifada*), against Israeli occupation of the West Bank and Gaza Strip, erupted in the Occupied Territories. Despite intensive and often brutal security measures, Israel was unable to suppress the revolt. Public demonstrations in Jordan (60% of whose population were of Palestinian origin) in support of the *intifada* were muted, owing mainly to security precautions taken by the authorities to prevent unrest. In April the Palestinian extremist group, Black September, claimed responsibility for a series of bomb attacks in Amman, which, it said, were directed against the 'client Zionist regime in Jordan'.

The intensity of the *intifada* and the world-wide condemnation of Israeli security tactics, and revulsion at the degrading conditions in which many Palestinians were forced to live in the Occupied Territories, alerted the international community to the need for a revival of the efforts to secure an Arab-Israeli peace agreement. At the end of February 1988 the US Secretary of State, George Shultz, embarked on a tour of Middle East capitals, in an attempt to elicit support for a new peace initiative. The Shultz plan, as the initiative came to be known, proposed the convening of an international peace conference, involving all parties to the Arab–Israeli conflict and the five members of the UN Security Council, with the Palestinians represented in a joint Jordanian-Palestinian delegation, excluding the PLO. This conference would have no power to impose a settlement and would act only as a consultative forum prior to and during subsequent direct talks between Israel and each of its Arab neighbours, and between Israel and a joint Jordanian-Palestinian delegation. The latter talks would determine the details of a three-year transitional period of autonomy for the 1.5m. Palestinians in the Occupied Territories, leading (before the start of the transitional period) to negotiations to determine the final status of government in the Territories. (For full details of the Shultz plan, see Documents on Palestine, p. 125.)

The plan's refusal to contemplate the participation of the PLO, the Palestinians' right to self-determination, and the establishment of an independent Palestinian state in the West Bank (i.e. the principles of the plan formulated at the Arab summit in Fez in 1982), made it impossible for the Arab nations to accept. Jordan, which had initially welcomed a renewal of the USA's commitment to peace in the Middle East, became disillusioned by its failure to apply persuasive pressure on Israel's Prime Minister, Itzhak Shamir, to modify his opposition to the Shultz plan. King Hussein pronounced himself sceptical that Israel would withdraw militarily from the West Bank prior to the transitional autonomy period, as the plan would require it to do, and reiterated his opposition, in accordance with Arab summit resolutions, to 'partial or interim solutions'. He welcomed the USA's acceptance, on 1 March 1988, of the concept of the Palestinians' 'legitimate rights', although he asked the USA to clarify its definition of those 'rights'. However, given the resumption of Jordanian political co-operation with the PLO, the enhanced status conferred on the organization by the *intifada,* and the potentially threatening reaction of Palestinians in Jordan, King Hussein was effectively constrained from supporting the Shultz plan.

An extraordinary summit meeting of the Arab League was held in Algiers in June 1988 to discuss the continuing *intifada* and the Arab-Israeli conflict in general. Addressing the summit, King Hussein gave his unconditional support to the *intifada* and disclaimed any ambition to restore Jordanian rule in the West Bank. He insisted that the PLO must represent the Palestinians at any future peace conference, and repeatedly stressed the PLO's status as 'the sole legitimate representative of the Palestinian people'. The Shultz plan, he claimed, had been launched only because the *intifada* had taken on the appearance of a Palestinian war against Israel.

The summit hailed the 'heroic' Palestinian uprising and its final communiqué effectively rejected the Shultz plan by endorsing the Palestinians' right to self-determination and the establishment of an independent Palestinian state in the West Bank, and insisting on the participation of the PLO in future peace talks.

JORDAN SEVERS ITS LINKS WITH THE WEST BANK

The effect of the *intifada* had been to increase international support for Palestinian national rights, to heighten Palestinian aspirations to statehood and to reinforce support for the PLO (which was helping to organize the uprising) as the Palestinians' representative in achieving it. From King Hussein's point of view, the *intifada* had created a new set of conditions in which Jordan could no longer realistically present itself as an alternative to the PLO. The King's subsequent actions were entirely consistent with his acknowledgement of the new realities, as expressed at the Algiers summit, yet they were still greeted with surprise.

On 28 July 1988 Jordan cancelled its $1,300m. Development Plan for the West Bank, which had been opposed by the PLO since its launch in 1986 and had remained substantially underfunded. Then, two days later, King Hussein severed Jordan's legal and administrative links with the West Bank, dissolving the lower house of the Jordanian Parliament (the House of Representatives), where Palestinian representatives for the West Bank occupied 30 of the 60 seats. The King explained that his actions were taken in accordance with the wishes of the PLO and with the resolutions of the Rabat and Fez Arab summits in 1974 and 1982, and the positions adopted at the recent Algiers summit, which recognized the PLO as 'the sole legitimate representative of the Palestinian people'.

The extent to which Jordan was actually disengaging from the West Bank was uncertain and it appeared that King Hussein was leaving the way open for the resumption of political co-ordination between Jordan and the PLO in the future. For example, King Hussein stopped short of formally and irrevocably repealing the 'union agreement' of 1950 (Jordan's annexation of the West Bank) uniting the East and West Banks of the River Jordan, while the notion that, by dissolving the House of Representatives and dismantling Jordanian civil institutions, the King was actually transferring administrative responsibility for the West Bank to the PLO was difficult to take seriously: the Jordanian legislature had exercised little or no practical influence over the affairs of the West Bank since the Israeli occupation began in 1967, and Israel soon introduced measures to restrict the activities of Palestinian institutions, in order to prevent the PLO from filling the administrative vacuum left by the dismissal of about 20,000 Jordanian teachers and civil servants who had continued to run public services in the West Bank after the Israeli occupation. It was suggested that, in placing responsibility for the Palestinians in the West Bank and for furthering the peace process in the hands of the PLO, King Hussein foresaw the inevitable failure of the PLO to finance and administer public services, and a political and diplomatic impasse that would demonstrate to Palestinians the necessity of Jordanian involvement if their hopes for self-government were to be realized. For its part, the PLO leadership complained that King Hussein had not consulted it prior to announcing the removal of Jordanian links, but the move was generally welcomed by the 850,000 Palestinians in the West Bank. According to the Jordanian Government, Palestinians residing in the West Bank were no longer considered to be Jordanian citizens. They were still entitled to hold a Jordanian passport, but this would, in future, only have the status of a 'travel document'.

Jordan's withdrawal from the West Bank appeared finally to make the Shultz plan redundant and to damage the prospects of a victory for Shimon Peres' Labour Party in the Israeli general election, which was scheduled to take place in November 1988. The peace plans of both Shultz and Peres had relied on the Palestinians' being represented at negotiations by a joint Jordanian-Palestinian delegation. Deprived of the so-called 'Jordanian option', the Israeli Labour Party signalled its willingness to negotiate with 'any Palestinians' who renounced the use of violence and recognized Israel's right to exist.

On 15 November 1988 the PNC proclaimed the establishment of an independent State of Palestine and, for the first time, endorsed UN Security Council Resolution 242 as a basis for a Middle East peace settlement, thus implicitly recognizing Israel. Jordan and 60 other countries recognized the new state. In December Yasser Arafat addressed a special session of the UN General Assembly in Geneva, where he renounced violence on behalf of the PLO. Subsequently, the USA opened a dialogue with the PLO, and (although the Israeli Prime Minister, Itzhak Shamir, denounced Arafat's renunciation of terrorism as deceitful) it appeared that Israel would have to negotiate directly with the PLO if it wished to seek a solution to the Palestinian question.

In December 1988 Marwan al-Qassim was appointed Minister of Foreign Affairs, replacing Taher al-Masri, who had been the principal opponent of King Hussein's decision to withdraw from the West Bank and also of the severe economic measures which the Prime Minister, Zaid ar-Rifai, had introduced. In April 1989 riots erupted in several cities in southern Jordan, spreading rapidly to areas near the capital, Amman, after the Government had imposed price rises of between 15% and 50% on basic goods and services. The gravity of the situation was emphasized by reports that only Bedouin and native Jordanians, from whom the Government traditionally drew most of its support, had participated in the riots, while the Palestinians, who formed an estimated 60% of the country's population, were uninvolved; and by the early return to Jordan of King Hussein, who had been making an official visit to the USA when the riots began. The riots led to the resignation of the Prime Minister and his Cabinet. On 24 April Field Marshal Sharif Zaid ibn Shaker, who had been Commander-in-Chief of the Jordanian armed forces between 1976 and 1988, was appointed Prime Minister, at the head of a new 24-member Cabinet. While King Hussein refused to make any concessions regarding the price increases which had provoked the disturbances (and which had been implemented in accordance with an agreement with the IMF), he had announced, immediately prior to the appointment of the new Prime Minister, that a general election would be held for the first time since 1967.

TOWARDS DEMOCRACY

A general election to the 80-seat House of Representatives took place on 8 November 1989 and was contested by 647 candidates, most of whom were independent, as the ban on political parties (in force since 1963) had not been withdrawn. However, it was possible for the Muslim Brotherhood (MB) to present candidates for election, owing to its legal status as a charity rather than a political party. At the election, in which 63% of the total electorate of 877,475 voted, the MB won 20 seats, while independent Islamic candidates, who supported the MB, won a further 14 seats. It was estimated that Palestinian or Arab nationalist candidates won seven seats and that candidates who were supporters of 'leftist' political groupings won four seats. The remaining seats were won by candidates who were broadly considered to be supporters of the Government. The strength of support for the opposition candidates was regarded as surprising, both in Jordan and abroad, especially since a disproportionately large number of seats had been assigned to rural areas, from which the Government had traditionally drawn most support.

On 4 December 1989 Mudar Badran was appointed Prime Minister by King Hussein. Badran had served as Prime Minister twice previously, during 1976–79 and 1980–84. The new Government did not include any members of the MB who had been elected to the House of Representatives, the MB having declined participation after its demand for the education portfolio had been rejected. Included in the new Cabinet, however, were three independent Muslim deputies and three 'leftists', all of whom were regarded as members of the opposition. The Government received a vote of confidence from the House of Representatives on 1 January 1990. The Prime Minister affirmed continuing support for prevailing austerity measures, and at the end of January announced the abolition of the 1954 anti-communism law.

The discovery of fraud and embezzlement at Petra Bank, Jordan's second largest commercial bank, had led to the seizure of its assets in August 1989 and the subsequent arrest of 22 former employees and business associates of the bank. The scandal spread to the national airline, Alia, and some 37 other companies. Following the 1989 election, King Hussein, under increasing pressure to initiate constitutional reform, promised to allow political parties more freedom and to tighten controls on corruption. In April 1990 he appointed a 60-member Royal Commission to draft a National Charter to regulate political life in Jordan. A former Prime Minister, Ahmad Ubeidat, was appointed Chairman of the commission, whose members included figures from the country's various political and religious groupings, including left-wingers and religious fundamentalists, and whose influence in all areas of public life became increasingly evident during the course of the year. In October 1990 a National Islamic Bloc was formed by more than one-half of the deputies in the House of Representatives. In a cabinet reshuffle in January 1991 Taher al-Masri, a leading Palestinian who was to be a strong supporter of Iraq's position in the Gulf crisis (see below), was appointed Minister of Foreign Affairs (a post that he had held between 1984 and 1988), in succession to

Marwan al-Qassim. Four members of the MB were given portfolios in the new Cabinet.

On 9 June 1991 the National Charter to regulate political life was endorsed by the King and leading political figures. Among other things, the Charter revoked the ban on Jordanian political parties (which had been imposed since 1963) in return for their allegiance to the monarchy. On 19 June the King accepted the resignation of the Government headed by Mudar Badran and appointed a new Cabinet, with Taher al-Masri, the erstwhile Minister of Foreign Affairs, as Prime Minister. Taher al-Masri was Jordan's first Palestinian-born Prime Minister and, in spite of his support for Saddam Hussain during the 1990–91 Gulf crisis, was known for his liberal, pro-Western views. Badran's resignation was attributed to the King's disapproval of his sympathy for the MB, which had urged that *Shari'a* (Islamic) law should govern the new National Charter and whose members were again excluded from the Cabinet. The new Government obtained a vote of confidence in the House of Representatives on 18 July.

On 7 July 1991 the King issued a decree repealing the provisions of martial law which had been in force since 1967, reportedly at the request of the new Prime Minister, who sought to continue the progress towards greater political freedom and democracy.

ARAB LEAGUE SUMMIT IN BAGHDAD

An emergency summit meeting of the Arab League was held in Baghdad on 28–30 May 1990. Convened under pressure from Jordan and the Palestinians to discuss the 'threat to pan-Arab security' that was presented by the mass emigration of Soviet Jews to Israel, the meeting was boycotted by President Assad of Syria, a long-term adversary of Iraq's President Saddam Hussain, and by four other Arab Heads of State. In October 1989 King Hussein had warned against further Jewish colonization of the Occupied Territories, claiming that Israel was seeking to settle the Soviet immigrants there, thus causing more Palestinians (who already comprised 60% of the population of his country) to flee to Jordan and effectively transform it into a surrogate Palestinian state. The *intifada* had already resulted in a net movement of Palestinians into Jordan. King Hussein urged other Arab nations to provide economic and military assistance to Jordan, declaring that mass Jewish immigration into Israel and the Occupied Territories posed a threat to Jordan which it could not afford to confront alone. Israel had selected Jordan as 'the point through which to penetrate . . . . the Arab Nation', he declared. The PLO leader, Yasser Arafat, urged other Arab states, in vain, to impose economic sanctions on countries involved in the transfer of Jews to Arab lands. President Saddam Hussain of Iraq, supported by King Hussein (who rejected the more moderate stance of both Egypt and Saudi Arabia), vehemently denounced Israel and threatened to use weapons of mass destruction against it. In a final statement, issued at the end of the summit, Arab leaders criticized US economic and military assistance to Israel and reaffirmed their commitment to the defence of Jordanian sovereignty and national security. The question of financial aid for Jordan would be a matter for bilateral negotiations. An Iraqi promise of US $50m. on 1 June was followed by further promises of aid from Saudi Arabia ($100m.) and from Kuwait and the UAE ($200m.).

The issue of Soviet-Jewish emigration to Israel figured prominently in discussions between the British Secretary of State for Foreign and Commonwealth Affairs, Douglas Hurd, and Prime Minister Badran during the former's visit to Jordan on 30–31 May 1990. In May 1991 the then Soviet Minister of Foreign Affairs, Aleksandr Bessmertnykh (visiting Amman for talks with King Hussein), emphasized that Israel's policy of building Jewish settlements in the Occupied Territories was obstructing progress towards peace in the Middle East. Later that month King Hussein declared that the Arab–Israeli conflict had reached its most critical point since the formation of Israel in 1948, and he urged the world to act decisively to prevent a drift towards extremism.

JORDAN'S POSITION IN THE GULF CRISIS

Even before Iraq's invasion of Kuwait on 2 August 1990, Jordan's economy was in severe difficulties; the country's foreign debt of $800m. was equivalent to one-quarter of annual GDP. Of all the Arab states affected, Jordan was probably the nation which was most likely to suffer from the effects of the conflict and the imposition of economic sanctions against Iraq, as stipulated by UN Security Council Resolution 661 of 6 August 1990. The loss of remittances from thousands of Jordanian workers who returned, destitute, from Iraq and Kuwait; the increased cost of importing petroleum products (almost all of Jordan's oil had been imported from Iraq); the threatened loss of as much as one-quarter of the country's exports and its transit trade with Iraq and Kuwait; the sudden decline in activity at the Red Sea port of Aqaba, as a result of the naval blockade and increases in insurance rates for shipping in the war zone; the enormous cost of humanitarian aid to refugees fleeing the conflict through its territory: all these were potentially disastrous for Jordan, which was embroiled in events beyond its control.

Following Iraq's invasion of Kuwait, the Palestinians and the PLO supported Saddam Hussain. Officially Jordan, in its own interests, remained neutral in the conflict. King Hussein 'regretted', but did not condemn, the action of Saddam Hussain in invading Kuwait, and Jordanian public opinion was solidly pro-Iraq for the duration of the crisis. Arab League ministers, attending a meeting of the Organization of the Islamic Conference in Cairo on 3 August 1990, issued a statement, opposed by Jordan, condemning the invasion and demanding Iraq's immediate and unconditional withdrawal. At the emergency summit meeting of the Arab League, held in Cairo on 10 August, Jordan abstained in a vote to denounce the annexation of Kuwait and to advocate the deployment of a pan-Arab force to defend Saudi Arabia and neighbouring states from invasion by the forces of Saddam Hussain. King Hussein welcomed Saddam Hussain's proposal, on 12 August, to link Iraq's occupation of Kuwait with the continued Israeli occupations, and he held talks with the Iraqi leader in Baghdad on the following day. Another Arab League meeting in Cairo (30–31 August) was boycotted by Jordan and other Arab nations which supported Iraq. King Hussein persistently argued in favour of an Arab solution to the crisis and opposed the deployment of a multinational armed force in the Gulf region.

In the West, which had always regarded King Hussein as one of its chief allies in the region, there was much criticism of the King's pro-Iraq stance, though this was tempered with acknowledgement of the extremely difficult position in which he found himself. Talks in the USA between the King and President Bush, at Kennebunkport on 16 August, resulted in promises of US financial assistance in return for Jordanian observance of the economic embargo imposed on Iraq. A report by a UN envoy in October 1990 estimated that the crisis would cost Jordan some 30% of its GDP in 1990 and as much as 50% in 1991.

Following the Iraqi invasion of Kuwait, Jordan was overwhelmed by an influx of refugees, who included thousands of migrant workers from Egypt and the Indian sub-continent, fleeing the conflict. The congestion was such that Jordan was forced temporarily to close its border with Iraq in late August 1990, in an attempt to cope with the accumulation of refugees who could not immediately be transported to the Red Sea port of Aqaba or airlifted to their countries of origin. On 3 September Jordan issued an urgent appeal for international aid, partially to offset the costs of caring for the refugees. By October some 800,000 refugees had passed through the country, at a cost of some $40m. to the Jordanian authorities. About 700 still awaited repatriation.

In mid-September 1990 two of King Hussein's former Palestinian opponents, George Habbash of the Popular Front for the Liberation of Palestine (PFLP) and Nayef Hawatmeh of the Democratic Front for the Liberation of Palestine (DFLP), who had been expelled during the civil war in 1970, were allowed to return to Amman for a pro-Iraqi conference of 'Arab Popular Forces'. The two Damascus-based leaders were received by the King in a display of unity and reconciliation fostered by the Gulf crisis. The conference, which was opened by the Speaker of the Jordanian House of Representatives (although not attended by the King), heard severe criticisms of governments opposed to Saddam Hussain and ended with pledges to wage a *jihad* against foreign forces in the Gulf region if Iraq were attacked. This led to a denunciation of King Hussein by the Saudi Arabian Ambassador in Washington, and Saudi Arabia

subsequently expelled Jordanian diplomats and many Jordanian immigrant workers. It also halted oil supplies to the Kingdom, claiming that Jordan had not paid for earlier deliveries.

King Hussein invested considerable personal effort in the search for a peaceful solution to the crisis, visiting London, Paris and Washington. In late August 1990 he arrived in Libya at the start of a peace mission among Arab leaders. He continued to advocate an Arab solution to the crisis and, in a televised message to the US Congress and people on 23 September, he urged the immediate withdrawal of the multinational force from the Gulf region. Speaking at the World Climate Conference in Geneva on 6 November, the King warned of the potentially disastrous environmental consequences of war in the Gulf region (a fear which was subsequently realized when Iraq released oil into the waters of the Gulf and ignited Kuwait's oil installations).

Following talks in Baghdad with Saddam Hussain on 4 December 1990, the King proposed a peace plan linking the Iraqi–Kuwait dispute and the Arab–Israeli conflict. He urged the convening of a peace conference on the Middle East, and that all Arab leaders should take part in a dialogue on the crisis, to take place simultaneously with the talks between the USA and Iraq, which had been proposed by President Bush at the end of November.

THE 1991 GULF WAR

The King's diplomatic efforts continued into 1991, when he embarked, in January, on a fresh tour of European capitals in a final attempt to avert war in the Gulf region. Diplomatic ties with Iran, severed in 1981 after the start of the Iran–Iraq War, were resumed in mid-January 1991, and Jordan was later reported to be supporting Iranian proposals to end the crisis. On 10 January Jordan had closed its ar-Ruweishid border post, on the frontier with Iraq, to all except Jordanian refugees. As war became imminent, Jordan feared a further influx of refugees from Iraq and Kuwait, and claimed that it had still not received UN aid promised for the August 1990 exodus. However, after receiving assurances of UN assistance with the cost of caring for the refugees, the border was reopened on 18 January.

Following the outbreak of hostilities between Iraq and a multinational force on 16 January 1991, the Jordanian Government condemned the bombardment of Iraq as a 'brutal onslaught against an Arab and Muslim nation'. Large-scale anti-Western and anti-Israeli demonstrations occurred throughout the country, and overwhelming popular support for Iraq was expressed in all sections of society. Sentiments were further aroused when air attacks on goods vehicles (including tanker-trucks carrying oil) on the Baghdad–Ruweishid highway in late January killed at least six Jordanian civilians. Jordan had been entirely dependant on Iraqi oil since Saudi Arabian supplies were suspended in September 1990. Now these consignments were halted, and Jordan, which introduced petrol-rationing in February, was obliged to obtain more expensive supplies from Syria and Yemen. Oil imports from Iraq were eventually resumed in April 1991.

In a televised address in February 1991, King Hussein paid tribute to the people and armed forces of Iraq, describing them as victims of this 'savage and large-scale war' and claiming that the war was directed against all Arabs and Muslims. The speech was condemned by the US Administration, which accused Jordan of abandoning its neutrality and threatened to review its economic aid. In March the US Congress approved legislation cancelling a $57m. aid programme. The law was signed by President Bush in April. However, the effects were offset, to some extent, by the announcement of a $450m. Japanese concessionary loan. As the multinational force launched a ground offensive to liberate Kuwait on 24 February, Prime Minister Badran announced that the conflict had at that point cost Jordan some $8,000m.

Fears that Iraq would provoke Israel into entering the conflict, thus making Jordan part of the combat zone, were not realized, owing to the Israeli decision not to retaliate in response to the *Scud* missile attacks launched by Iraq against its territory. At the end of December 1990, Jordan had deployed 80,000 troops in defensive positions facing Israel. King Hussein declared, in mid-January 1991, that Jordan would defend its territory and air space against any incursions. In early February a Jordanian air force officer and a truck-driver were executed, having been convicted by a military court of spying for Israel.

On 1 March 1991, following the liberation of Kuwait and the end of hostilities between Iraq and the multinational force, King Hussein, in a televised address to the nation, advocated regional reconciliation. In late March he travelled to Damascus, for the first time for one year, for talks with President Assad, and subsequently sought to improve relations with the West, visiting President Mitterrand in Paris later that month.

MIDDLE EAST PEACE PROCESS 1991–94

US Secretary of State James Baker visited Jordan on 20–21 July 1991, when King Hussein announced his intention to accept an invitation to Jordan to attend a Middle East peace conference sponsored by the USA and the USSR. It was hoped that the conference would be attended by delegations from Israel, Egypt, Syria and Lebanon, and by a joint Jordanian-Palestinian delegation; and that it would thus become the first occasion when Israel, the Palestinians and the Arab nations would participate in direct negotiations. The Jordanian House of Representatives opposed the plan, however, demanding Israeli withdrawal from the Occupied Territories and East Jerusalem as a precondition for Jordan's attendance, and rejecting Israel's insistence that neither Palestinians from East Jerusalem nor overt supporters of the PLO should be allowed to attend. James Baker visited Amman again in September and October—he had visited the region eight times since the end of the Gulf War—for further rounds of pre-conference diplomacy, and on 12 October King Hussein announced that a Jordanian delegation would attend the conference, in spite of intense opposition from the MB and leftist political groupings. He stated that he had received assurances from the USA that it would do its utmost to ensure that a transitional period of Palestinian 'autonomy' in the Occupied Territories would be negotiated within one year of the opening of the conference; and that he had considered abdicating over the Arab–Israeli confrontation, but believed that attending the conference would increase international pressure on Israel to withdraw from the Occupied Territories. The Central Council of the PLO, meeting in Tunis on 16–17 October, approved the formation of a joint Jordanian-Palestinian delegation, a decision strongly criticized by the leader of the PFLP, George Habbash.

The opening session of the historic Middle East peace conference, convened within the framework of UN Security Council Resolutions 242 and 338, and chaired by President Bush of the USA and the Soviet President, Mikhail Gorbachev, was held in Madrid, Spain, during 30 October–1 November 1991. The joint Jordanian-Palestinian delegation was led by Kamel Abu Jaber, a US-educated professor of political science, who had been appointed Jordan's Minister of Foreign Affairs following the resignation, on 3 October, of Abdullah Nusur and two other ministers opposed to Jordan's participation. The delegation included diplomats, civil servants and academics. In his speech, calling for the withdrawal of Israeli forces from all occupied lands, Abu Jaber stated that King Hussein would have preferred a separate Palestinian delegation but 'we have no objection to providing an umbrella for our Palestinian brethren ... the Palestinian people must be allowed to exercise their right of self-determination in their ancestral homeland'. 'Let me speak plainly', he added, 'Jordan has never been Palestine and will not be so.'

Subsequent negotiations in Washington and Moscow between the Israeli and the joint Jordanian-Palestinian delegations remained deadlocked, with regard to substantive issues. However, secret talks between the PLO and the Israeli Government in Norway, which had begun early in 1993, led to an agreement on a Declaration of Principles on 19 August 1993 which involved a degree of Palestinian self-government in the Occupied Territories. The Declaration of Principles (see p. 128) was signed in Washington on 13 September 1993. News of the agreement apparently came as a surprise to King Hussein who had not been informed that negotiations were taking place in Oslo and the agreement is reported to have caused grave embarrassment to the Palestinian negotiators in Washington. Despite the King's initial irritation at the Israeli-PLO accord, which presented a socio-economic as well as a political challenge for Jordan, he quickly accepted the Declaration of Principles. On 14 September, the day after the Washington signature of the accord, Jordan

and Israel concluded a 'common agenda' for subsequent negotiations between the two countries. The agenda aimed to achieve 'a just, lasting and comprehensive peace' between the Arab States, the Palestinians and Israel. Jordan and Israel agreed to respect each other's security and to discuss future co-operation on territorial and economic issues. The signing of the agenda was publicized as being the first agreement between an Arab state and Israel since the peace agreement between Egypt and Israel in 1979. King Hussein, however, stressed that the agenda was not a peace agreement but an outline of topics to be discussed at future talks. Much of the agenda had already been agreed in 1992 but an official signing was delayed because of objections by the Palestinians.

Within Jordan, news of the Israeli-PLO accord was greeted with considerable cynicism. Opposition to the accord appeared to be strongest in the vast Palestinian refugee camp at Baqaa. Most Islamist and leftist politicians condemned the accord. (Following the Hebron massacre on 25 February 1994, it was reported that any support for the peace process among Palestinians in Jordan had almost entirely disappeared and that in their frustration many were turning to the Islamist movements.) The agreement between the PLO and Israel in September 1993 initiated a sometimes acrimonious debate on the vexed question of Palestinian identity and the future of Palestinians in Jordan. Since October 1993 Jordan had become increasingly frustrated with the PLO over its failure to implement agreements on closer co-operation. In particular Jordan was concerned that the PLO Chairman, Yasser Arafat, appeared to be unwilling to sign a draft economic agreement that had been drawn up earlier in the year. At the beginning of 1994 King Hussein publicly criticized Arafat because Jordan had not been continuously advised about the progress of talks between the PLO and Israel concerning the implementation of Palestinian self-rule in Gaza and Jericho and economic co-operation. He requested that Arafat stop making references to a future Jordanian-Palestinian confederation because this was an issue on which no decision had yet been made. In the past King Hussein had appeared to favour such an arrangement, but more recently Jordan had decided not to discuss the final relationship with the Occupied Territories. Following the King's criticisms, a PLO delegation led by Farouq Qaddoumi, the head of the PLO's political department, visited Amman and an agreement on economic co-operation, covering tourism, agriculture, infrastructure, investment promotion, and private sector co-operation, was signed on 7 January 1994. Just over a week later, Jordan and the PLO drew up a draft accord on security and the exchange of intelligence information. Jordan was particularly concerned about who would control the bridges across the river Jordan after the establishment of Palestinian autonomy. At a meeting of the Higher Jordanian-Palestinian Committee in February it was agreed that a number of joint committees, originally set up in 1993 to discuss relations between Jordan and the Occupied Territories during the period of transitional Palestinian self-rule, would be reconvened. Jordanian experts were reported to be present as observers at talks between the PLO and Israel in Paris on economic and monetary questions. Yet in spite of a personal visit to Amman by Arafat to brief King Hussein on the Cairo talks with Israel, relations between Jordan and the PLO remained strained. At the end of March King Hussein blamed the PLO for mishandling the negotiations leading up to Security Council Resolution 904 which had allowed the USA to abstain on the paragraph in the preamble concerning Jerusalem. The King argued that the American vote could have been avoided if the PLO had consulted Jordan. There was a relatively low-key reaction from the Jordanian Government to the Cairo accord between Israel and the PLO (see p. 132) signed on 4 May. Arafat visited Amman on 5 May to brief King Hussein on the Cairo agreement but the King remained disillusioned by Arafat's failure to liaise with Jordan in the peace process.

Following a secret meeting in November 1993 between King Hussein and Shimon Peres, the Israeli Minister of Foreign Affairs, there was optimism in Israeli government circles that Jordan would soon sign a formal peace agreement with Israel. These hopes were dashed in late January 1994 when King Hussein insisted that the key issues which lay behind the Arab-Israeli conflict must be discussed before any accord could be signed and that it was unacceptable to leave negotiations until after the signing. Jordan, together with Syria and Lebanon, withdrew temporarily from the current round of bilateral talks with Israel in Washington immediately after the Hebron massacre in February, although the gesture appeared to be largely symbolic and aimed at appeasing public anger at the incident. The King firmly rejected calls made by Islamist deputies for Jordan to withdraw permanently from the peace talks.

The National Assembly requested that the Government link Jordan's resumption of peace negotiations with new arrangements for inspecting ships with cargo bound for Iraq through Aqaba port. There had been growing criticism of the policy of intercepting and searching ships bound for Aqaba in the Tiran Straits by a multinational inspection force led by the US navy. The system of inspection, introduced in August 1991 in order to verify compliance with international sanctions against Iraq, resulted in long delays and loss of revenue to the Jordanian authorities. When the USA failed to respond to Jordanian requests for new arrangements, this was interpreted in Amman as a means of putting pressure on Jordan to finalize a peace agreement with Israel. In late March 1994 King Hussein announced that Jordan would not resume peace negotiations with Israel unless the naval blockade of Aqaba was lifted. However, it was not until the end of April that the USA accepted a Jordanian proposal for a new land-based system of inspection. Prime Minister Majali told the press on 25 April that his Government was now willing to sign agreements on all individual items on the Jordan-Israel agenda and to participate in all multilateral talks in the hope that the negotiations would lead eventually to a peace treaty. He emphasized that a peace treaty could only be achieved in this way.

THE PEACE TREATY WITH ISRAEL

In May–June 1994 the peace process received a new impetus, after King Hussein unexpectedly decided to proceed unilaterally with talks with Israel. After secret talks between the King and the Israeli Prime Minister, Itzhak Rabin, in London, United Kingdom, at the end of May, negotiations resumed at a meeting of the Jordanian-Israeli-US Trilateral Commission, held on 6–7 June in Washington, DC. At the meeting Jordan and Israel agreed to hold future bilateral talks in Israel and Jordan, and to establish joint sub-commissions on boundary demarcation, security, and water and environmental issues. These sub-commissions began work on 18–19 July, at a meeting on the Jordanian–Israeli border.

At a ceremony at the White House on 25 July 1994 King Hussein and the Prime Minister of Israel, Itzhak Rabin, signed the 'Washington Declaration' ending the state of war which had existed between the two countries since 1948. After years of secret meetings, it was the first time that King Hussein had publicly met an Israeli Prime Minister. The declaration stopped short of a full peace treaty, but US Secretary of State, Warren Christopher, stated that he expected it to speed the process for formal peace agreement 'within a matter of months'.

In Jordan opposition to the Declaration was limited, and there were no large-scale protests. Islamists declared 'a day of sadness and mourning' and at a modest protest meeting at the central mosque in Amman, Bahjat Abu-Gharbiah, head of the Arab-Jordanian Popular Committee Against Normalization, told the demonstrators that the peace was 'an attempt to consolidate the hegemony of the Zionist entity through normalization that allows its cancerous spread until the shores of the Arabian Gulf'. From Gaza, PLO Chairman Arafat sent his congratulations to the Israeli and Jordanian leaders on the declaration and expressed the hope that Syria and Lebanon would also make peace with Israel. However, Palestinian leaders were angered by a statement in the Declaration endorsing the special role of King Hussein as guardian of the Muslim holy places in Jerusalem. They argued that it undermined the Palestinian claim to sovereignty over Jerusalem, and that it contradicted the Israeli-PLO Declaration of Principles, which stated that the final status of Jerusalem would be determined by negotiation between Israel and the PLO. The Syrian press criticized the Washington Declaration, arguing that separate peace deals weakened the Arab cause. Nevertheless, President Assad appeared to be privately reconciled to the negotiations.

Bilateral talks between Jordanian and Israeli delegations continued in August and September 1994. In mid-October, des-

pite reports that problems remained over border demarcation and water resource allocation, the Israeli Prime Minister, Itzhak Rabin, visited Amman, and agreement was reached on a final peace treaty between the two countries. On 26 October the Treaty was formally signed at a ceremony held on the Jordanian–Israeli border, Jordan thus becoming only the second Arab state (after Egypt) to conclude a peace treaty with Israel. The Peace Treaty included agreements on border demarcation, security, water allocation and the restoration of economic relations between the two states. King Hussein's role as guardian of the Muslim shrines in Jerusalem was also reaffirmed. The Treaty was adopted by both houses of the Jordanian National Assembly, and ratified by King Hussein on 9 November. As agreed in the Treaty, full diplomatic relations between Jordan and Israel were established in late November. (However, ambassadors were not exchanged until April 1995, apparently owing to disagreement in the Israeli Government over the ambassadorial appointment.) Also in November the Jordanian–Israeli border was opened to citizens of the two countries, and Israeli troops began withdrawing from some 340 sq km of land occupied since the 1967 war.

Within Jordan little effort had been made to prepare public opinion for the peace agreement. Following a demonstration against the treaty in Amman by some 5,000 people, organized by Islamic groups, the Government banned all public meetings. The IAF and its allies continued to oppose the treaty and began a campaign in the National Assembly against the normalization of relations with Israel. They attempted to prevent the repeal of legislation limiting relations with Israel, including a law (adopted in 1973) prohibiting land sales to Israelis, a 1958 law imposing a total economic boycott of Israel, and legislation from 1953 outlawing trade between the two states. Rumours that Israeli citizens had already bought land in certain parts of Jordan were strongly denied by the Minister of Justice.

Initially, the Peace Treaty did little to improve relations with the Palestinian leadership. The reaffirmation of King Hussein's special role as guardian of the Muslim holy places in East Jerusalem was criticized by the PLO leadership. In September 1994 the Palestine National Authority (PNA) had claimed responsibility for all Islamic institutions in East Jerusalem, the West Bank and Gaza. In response, Jordan had agreed to relinquish its rights over sites in the West Bank and Gaza, but it refused to renounce its guardianship over the holy shrines of East Jerusalem. A compromise was reached on the issue in late January 1995, when an accord was signed by the two sides. The Palestinians agreed to recognize the Jordanian-Israeli Peace Treaty, thus implying *de facto* recognition of Jordanian rights over the Jerusalem shrines, at least until the city came under Palestinian sovereignty. In return, Jordan reaffirmed its support for Palestinian autonomy and for the future creation of a Palestinian state with East Jerusalem as its capital. The accord also covered economic, cultural and administrative affairs, and included an agreement to use the Jordanian currency in Palestinian territories. The timing of the agreement prompted observers to argue that Arafat was seeking better relations with Jordan, because of Israel's increasingly unco-operative approach on the Palestinian question, and as a response to growing pressure from Islamic groups violently opposed to the PLO-Israel accords.

POLITICAL REFORM AND MULTI-PARTY ELECTIONS

On 6 October 1991 an alliance of 49 deputies in the House of Representatives, from the MB, the 'constitutional bloc', the 'Democratic Alliance', and some independent Islamic deputies, signed a petition in protest at the terms of Jordan's participation in the Middle East peace conference. They urged the resignation of the Government, and on 16 November Taher al-Masri resigned as Prime Minister, having lost the confidence of the House. The King appointed his cousin, Field Marshal Sharif Zaid ibn Shaker, who had led a transitional government in 1989, as Prime Minister, and a new, broader-based government received a vote of confidence on 16 December. Kamel Abu Jaber retained his position as Minister of Foreign Affairs. The MB was again excluded from the Cabinet and 18 of its members voted against the new Government in the confidence motion.

In June 1992 an extraordinary session of the House of Representatives was convened in order to debate new laws regarding political parties and the press. In early July the House adopted new legislation whereby, subject to certain conditions, political parties were formally legalized, in preparation for the country's first multi-party elections since 1956, which were to be held before November 1993. The new legislation was approved by royal decree at the end of August, and by March 1993 nine political parties had received the Government's formal approval of their activities.

In May King Hussein appointed a new cabinet, in which Abd as-Salam al-Majali, the leader of the Jordanian delegation to the Middle East peace conference, replaced Field Marshal Sharif Zaid ibn Shaker as Prime Minister. The new Government was regarded as a transitional administration, pending the country's first multi-party election.

At the beginning of August 1993 King Hussein unexpectedly dissolved the House of Representatives, provoking criticism from some politicians who had expected the House to debate proposed changes to the country's electoral law. Changes in voting procedures at the general election, which was scheduled to be held on 8 November, were subsequently announced by the King in mid-August. Voters were to be allowed to cast one vote only, rather than a number equal to that of the number of candidates contesting a given constituency, as before.

After the announcement of the Israeli-PLO accord in September 1993 King Hussein appeared to be unsure whether or not to proceed with the elections, fearing that they might be dominated by the debate about the peace process. Eventually the King decided to hold the elections as planned on 8 November 1993. The election campaign went smoothly and peacefully. Some 820,000 Jordanians (52% of elegible voters and 68% of registered voters) cast ballots at one of the 2,906 polling stations in the 20 electoral districts. However, the independent New Jordan Research Centre estimated that 70% of Jordanians of Palestinian origin abstained. This low level of participation was attributed to the fact that Jordanians of Palestinian origin did not feel part of the Jordanian political system and also that the current system of electoral districts favoured areas dominated by East Bankers. For example, the predominantly Palestinian second electoral district of Amman, which has some 220,000 elegible voters, elects three deputies, whereas the southern district of Tufeila, with only c. 24,000 eligible voters (few of whom are of Palestinian origin), also elects three deputies.

In all some 534 candidates contested the election and half of the 20 registered political parties fielded candidates. The majority of candidates, however, stood as independents. The political parties, which had been legal for less than a year, had little time to organize and amass public support. With the exception of the Islamic Action Front (IAF), most political parties had a low profile in the elections. Abdul Hadi al-Majali of the Pledge Party admitted that the political parties were not rooted in the political system and that successful candidates won because of their own qualities, personalities and relationships rather than the support of political parties. Domestic issues, such as unemployment, were the main issues in the electoral campaign, with traditionalist candidates focusing on local issues and promising to improve the provision of public services in their constituencies. Of the 80 deputies returned, 45 were independents. With the traditions of tribalism deeply rooted in the customs of the country, they won largely because of their tribal affiliations and personal influence. Talal ar-Ramhi, the Secretary-General of the Popular Unity Party, described the new parliament as a *majlis 'ashairi*—a tribal council.

The IAF, an alliance between the MB and other Islamist groups, won 16 seats, the largest number of any political party, but six fewer than in the 1989 elections. This reversal was largely thought to result from the new electoral law which embodied the one-man one-vote principle. Indeed, the new law was widely interpreted as an attempt to weaken the IAF. Others felt that the Islamists had misjudged the mood of the country and had not devoted enough attention in their campaign to basic issues related to the impact of the economic recession on the lives of ordinary Jordanians. The IAF's Secretary-General, Dr Ishaq Farhan, however, stated that his party did not consider the election a setback. It has been calculated that successful Islamist candidates won almost one-third of all votes cast for the 80 elected deputies. Of the other political parties, leftists and Arab nationalists won eight seats while five conservative and right-of-centre parties claimed a total of 14 seats. Only 14 of the 80 new deputies were of Palestinian origin. Among the new deputies was the first woman to be elected to the Assembly, Toujan al-Faisal, who won one of the seats reserved for the Circassian minority.

Soon after the election a number of political groupings were formed in addition to the IAF. The Progressive Democratic Coalition, consisting of liberal deputies and leftist and Arab nationalists, claimed the support of 22 deputies; the National Action Front (NAF) and the Jordan Action Front (JAF), both groupings of conservative parties and their allies, claimed 18 and 9 seats respectively. The IAF remained the largest single political organization in the country. Some deputies saw the emergence of parliamentary blocs as the first step in a move towards the formation of larger political parties.

Taher al-Masri, widely regarded as the most influential Palestinian in Jordanian politics and a former Prime Minister, was elected Speaker of the National Assembly on 23 November 1993. Al-Masri won an overwhelming victory against his rival, an IAF deputy. An IAF deputy had held the post of Speaker in the outgoing National Assembly. Dr Abd as-Salam al-Majali remained Prime Minister and although he made few significant changes to his Cabinet, there was some surprise that for the first time it did not include any parliamentary deputies. His new Government won a vote of 'confidence' on 8 December after a prolonged debate during which the Prime Minister was criticized for changes to the country's electoral law and for not making an independent statement of government policy but simply adopting the King's speech from the throne at the opening of Parliament.

In January 1994 there were bomb attacks on cinemas in Amman and Zarqa which were attributed to Islamist extremists. Several arrests were made and the Ministry of the Interior claimed that it had successfully thwarted further outrages. It was reported that some of those arrested were men who had fought with the *mujahidin* in Afghanistan and the Government implied that the cinema bombings were the work of the Prophet Muhammad's Army, an organization set up by militant Islamists who had defected from the MB. The attacks were embarrassing for the moderate IAF which condemned political violence but at the same time demanded better treatment for the 72 detainees which it claimed were still in custody in April.

In another cautious move towards democratization, in March 1994 the National Assembly approved legislation to allow municipal elections in Greater Amman, where some two-fifths of the country's population live. The Government, no doubt concerned about the strength of Palestinian and Islamist opposition in the capital, had originally proposed that only half of the municipal council should be elected but this was increased to two-thirds by the National Assembly. The remaining one third of the council together with the mayor were to continue to be appointed by the Government.

In early June 1994 Prime Minister al-Majali announced a major cabinet reshuffle. There were no changes in the important portfolios of finance, the interior and information, but 18 new appointments were made to the 31-member Cabinet. Among the new ministers were deputies from the three main political groupings in the lower house, the NAF, the Jordanian National Alliance and the Progressive Democratic Coalition, but none were selected from the biggest parliamentary faction, the IAF. However, one well-known Islamic activist, Abdel-Baki Jammu, was included in the new Government.

In early January 1995 there was a further extensive reorganization of the Government, following the dismissal of al-Majali as Prime Minister. He was replaced by Sharif Zaid ibn Shaker, who had served as Prime Minister in 1989 and 1991–93, and was a close ally and a cousin of the King. Only seven ministers from the previous administration retained their portfolios in the new Government. Among the new ministers were Basel Jardaneh, as Minister of Finance, and Abdul-Karim Kabariti, as Minister of Foreign Affairs. At the same time, Taher al-Masri resigned as Speaker of the House of Representatives, and was replaced by Saed Hayel as-Srour, who represented one of the northern Bedouin constituencies. He defeated Abdel-Razzaq Tubeishat, an independent Islamic candidate, who was supported by the IAF. The new Government easily won a vote of 'confidence' in January 1995, with 54 votes in favour and only 23 against.

Two new political blocs emerged in the National Assembly in early 1995. The Independent National Action Front (INAF), with 17 deputies, was formed by a merger of the NAF and the bloc of independent deputies in the Assembly. The former Speaker of the National Assembly, Taher al-Masri, formed a second new grouping of some 15 liberal and independent Islamist deputies. In early June the authorities arrested six members of an illegal Islamist organization, the Islamic Renewal Group, believed to be active among Jordanians who had returned from Kuwait after the Iraqi invasion of 1990, and claimed to have found weapons and explosives that were to be used in attacks against US interests in Jordan. Early in 1996 the Prime Minister admitted that there had been 36 attempted terrorist attacks in the previous six months aimed at destabilizing the country. In municipal elections held nationwide for the first time in July 1995 Islamic and left-wing groups failed to gain significant popular support, most elected candidates being largely pro-government or independent. The IAF alleged that its poor performance was due to a low level of voter participation, and to government harassment of its members during the campaign. In November King Hussein warned that the country's professional organizations, several of which strongly opposed the normalization of relations with Israel, were becoming too involved in national politics and that this was against the interest of their members. In December Leith Shbeilat, the head of the Jordan Engineers' Association and an outspoken Islamist, was arrested and later jailed for three years, a move regarded by some observers as an attempt to intimidate supporters of the movement against the normalization of relations with Israel.

KABARITI APPOINTED PRIME MINISTER

At the beginning of February 1996 King Hussein appointed the Minister of Foreign Affairs, Abdul-Karim Kabariti as Prime Minister. King Hussein was believed to have clashed with his predecessor, Sharif Zaid ibn Shaker, on the pace of normalization with Israel and the severing of ties with Iraq. Kabariti's appointment was followed by the most radical reshuffle of the Government for many years. He appointed a new Cabinet in which the majority of ministers took office for the first time. Twenty-two of the 31 members, including the Minister of the Interior, were deputies in the House of Representatives, strengthening the new administration's democratic credentials. Negotiations between the new Prime Minister and the IAF leadership failed to achieve agreement, and there was some criticism among Islamist deputies who argued that their leaders should have adopted a more positive line about entering government. The King hoped that the new Government would 'go with all its energy and capability towards full and comprehensive change'. In early March Kabariti's new administration easily won a vote of 'confidence', in the House of Representatives, gaining the approval of deputies for its domestic policy. The Prime Minister emphasized the need to promote pluralism and democracy, safeguard public freedoms, and respect human rights. Kabariti announced his commitment to the independence of the judiciary and the media, to increasing public access to information and, eventually, to the abolition of the Ministry of Information. He also outlined plans to reform the Ministry of the Interior and the system of government appointments in order to combat nepotism and corruption, which had become an important political issue in recent years. Kabariti retained the foreign affairs portfolio and was known to be a strong supporter of the King's new policy on Iraq and of strengthening ties with Israel, policies that were likely to prove more controversial than his domestic programme.

The popularity of Kabariti's Government in the House of Representatives and, indeed, in the country as a whole was short-lived. In mid-August 1996 fierce rioting erupted in the south of the country after the Government more than doubled the price of bread. The price rise was part of an economic plan supervised by the IMF to remove the agricultural subsidies that stabilized food prices and thus help reduce the budget deficit in order to meet IMF fiscal targets. About one-third of Jordan's population are believed to live below the poverty line, and many people feared that the rise in the price of bread, the country's

staple food, would lead to increases in the prices of all foodstuffs. The rioting quickly spread to other parts of the country, including the poor suburbs of Amman. The King vowed to employ stern measures to suppress the demonstrations and told the Western media that he believed that the ringleaders had been 'educated in Iraq'. He suspended the legislature and deployed élite units of the army to re-establish control in Karak, the scene of the most severe rioting, where several banks, the local offices of the Ministry of Education and a school were set on fire. The army quickly regained control over the town, which was placed under curfew, before any fatalities occurred, and it was reported that some 190 people had been arrested. After peace was restored, King Hussein visited different parts of the country to meet with civil and tribal leaders in a reconciliation attempt. The curfews were soon lifted, and by November 1996 all those arrested during the demonstrations had been released and charges against them dropped. Price increases, however, were not revoked. The IAF (which had earlier protested vigorously at the price increases), together with a number of smaller opposition parties, urged Kabariti to resign, blaming his Government for the rioting. Several observers argued that, although the demonstrations had been triggered primarily by the Government's austerity programme, the deeply unpopular peace treaty with Israel and the King's dramatic break with Iraq had also contributed to growing discontent in the country. In an attempt to calm political tensions, the IAF had cancelled a mass demonstration against the economic austerity measures, scheduled for 23 August, and withdrew its demand for the Prime Minister's resignation. In response, King Hussein emphasized that the rioters were not members of the IAF. In November the King ordered the release of Leith Shbeilat, a leading Islamist, who had served only six months of his three-year sentence. In January 1997 the Shura Council of the MB, the dominant group within the IAF, voted against the party's joining a future Government because this would imply recognition of Israel. However, moderates in the IAF opposed the Shura Council's decision, maintaining that it condemned the party to a relatively ineffective role in politics and could lose them electoral support.

King Hussein did not hold his Prime Minister responsible for the August riots, and Kabariti quickly attempted to restore his reputation. The resignation of the Telecommunications Minister, Jamal Sarayrah, in December and his public criticism of the Prime Minister's style of government did not appear to damage Kabariti's position, and he was expected to remain in office until the parliamentary elections, due in November 1997. It therefore came as a surprise when the King dismissed Kabariti on 19 March 1997 and appointed Abd as-Salam al-Majali to the premiership. There were reports that the King and Kabariti had disagreed over issues relating to the peace process and relations with Israel, as well as rumours of enmity between Kabariti and Crown Prince Hassan. King Hussein's public criticism of the outgoing Prime Minister suggested that he was unlikely to appoint Kabariti to head a future government. The new Prime Minister, a veteran and trusted politician who had been head of government when Jordan signed the peace treaty with Israel in October 1994, appointed a 23-member Cabinet consisting mainly of technocrats; he retained five ministers from the previous administration, including Dr Abdullah an-Nusur, an East Banker, promoted to Deputy Prime Minister, and Dr Jawad al-Anani, a Palestinian with experience as Minister of Labour and Industry in a previous administration, also became a Deputy Prime Minister, with special responsibility for development matters. In his letter of appointment to al-Majali, King Hussein gave priority to internal affairs. The new Government's primary task was to be supervision of the forthcoming legislative elections. In preparation for the elections, the National Assembly voted to continue the 'one man one vote' system adopted for the 1993 elections, rather than return to the previous multi-vote system. The King also urged the new Government to eliminate corruption in public office, to alleviate unemployment and to modify the education system to the needs of society. In May 1997, following increasing media criticism of a number of government policies, a number of amendments were made to legislation governing the press, prompting strong protests from editors, journalists, professional associations and opposition groups. The amendments included a considerable increase in the minimum capital that weekly journals were required to raise as a precondition for publishing, an extension of the range of prohibited subjects to include the armed forces and the security services, and a substantial rise in the fines that could be levied for contravening the press legislation. Opposition activists feared that these measures represented the return of closer state control over the press. Also in May 1997 nine centre parties, including Pledge and the Jordan National Party, announced that they had united to form the National Constitutional Party (NCP), which became the country's largest political grouping. The formation of the NCP, together with the establishment in 1996 of the Unionist Arab Democratic Party (a coalition of three leftist parties), reduced the total number of political parties from 24 to 14. A further political grouping subsequently emerged; the progressive alliance included a number of eminent political figures (among them two former prime ministers, Ahmad Ubeidat and Taher al-Masri, and a former parliamentary speaker, Suleiman Arar). In June King Hussein appointed his close associate and adviser, Zaid ar-Rifai, as Speaker of the Senate.

THE 1997 ELECTIONS AND 1998 GOVERNMENT

In July 1997 the MB declared that it would boycott the forthcoming parliamentary elections, which, King Hussein had announced, were to proceed in November, as scheduled. This decision, which was opposed by some prominent members of the movement, appeared to reflect growing disillusionment with the role of the National Assembly, which was perceived to have little or no influence over important political and economic decisions in the country. After intensive discussions, the IAF endorsed the MB's decision by a large majority, but opponents included prominent members of the party, notably Ishaq Farhan, the party spokesman, Hamzeh Mansur, and a former minister. (Some political commentators had predicted that, as a result of popular dissatisfaction with the peace process and the country's increasing economic problems, the IAF would certainly have increased its representation in the Assembly and might have won as many as 30 of the 80 seats.) In the two months prior to the elections, discussions between the government and the opposition parties failed to achieve any progress. The IAF, together with nine smaller leftist and nationalist parties, had, in particular, demanded changes in the electoral legislation, arguing that the existing 'one man, one vote' system favoured candidates with strong tribal affiliations over those representing 'ideological' parties; however, King Hussein and al-Majali refused to make any concessions. In September the Government suspended some 13 weekly newspapers for three months (effectively during the electoral period) for failing to comply with the amendments to the press regulations that had been introduced in May.

The elections on 4 November 1997, which were boycotted by many parties, professional associations and respected political figures, attracted little popular enthusiasm. According to official figures, only 44% of the registered electorate participated, with a voter turn-out of only 26% in parts of Amman. There were widespread allegations of electoral malpractice, and in a number of regions the security forces were obliged to intervene to suppress clashes between rival candidates and their supporters. Deputies with tribal affiliations dominated the new parliament. Only 26 deputies who served in the outgoing parliament were re-elected, and many leading political figures, such as Taher al-Masri and Abdul-Karim Kabariti, were absent from the new legislature. The NCP, which some sections of the press referred to as the 'party of the regime', presented 11 candidates but won only two seats. A series of resignations from the party followed, including that of the deputy leader, Abdel-Roauf al-Rawabdeh. Although some opponents of the Government were represented in the new Assembly, including Islamist politicians Abdullah Akaileh and Muhammad Azaydeh (who contested the election in defiance of the IAF boycott), government claims of a significant opposition presence appeared to be greatly exaggerated. Saed Hayel as-Srour was re-elected Speaker of the House of Representatives. Among the new members appointed by King Hussein to the 40-member Senate was Kabariti (a move which was viewed as marking his political rehabilitation). Zaid ar-Rifai was retained as Speaker of the Senate. Political figures critical of the Government were completely absent from the upper

house. King Hussein also confirmed the appointment of al-Majali to the office of Prime Minister.

Elections to the IAF's ruling body, the 120-member Shura Council, took place in December 1997. Despite the victory of the hard-liners who ensured that the party boycotted the parliamentary elections in November, moderates and centrists succeeded in maintaining their dominant position on the Council, indicating that the party would avoid outright confrontation with the Government. In January 1998 the High Court ruled that the amendments to the press regulations introduced in May 1997 were unconstitutional and that actions taken by the Government under the amendments consequently had no validity. The authorities reluctantly agreed to accept the ruling, and a number of newspapers that had been banned resumed publishing in March. The country's Chief Justice, Farouq al-Kailani, claimed that, owing to his role in the High Court ruling on the press legislation, the Government had forced him to resign.

During the increase in tension between the USA and Iraq in early 1998 (see below) there was widespread support among Jordanians for Iraq and, to a certain extent, for the Iraqi leader, Saddam Hussain. The authorities, however, decided to ban all pro-Iraqi demonstrations and put heavy pressure on the press to adopt the official government policy on the situation. When a grouping of Islamists, leftists and nationalists opposed to US policy in the Middle East attempted to hold a large rally in Amman in February, the police quickly dispersed the meeting, and a number of leading government opponents were assaulted during the disturbances. Later in February there were violent clashes in the southern town of Maan when members of the security forces intervened to prevent a pro-Iraqi demonstration; the security forces subsequently denied responsibility for the death of one of the demonstrators. The Minister of the Interior, Nadhir Rashid, claimed that the riots in Maan had been instigated by Leith Shbeilat, an outspoken Islamist critic of the regime, who had addressed a meeting in the town that day, and stated that he would be put on trial for his involvement in the disturbances. Supporters of Shbeilat, however, insisted that he had left Maan before the violence erupted and was arrested on his return to Amman. Shbeilat was later sentenced to nine months' imprisonment, but King Hussein ordered his release in May. The situation in Maan remained tense for some days after the disturbances, although order was quickly restored. The authorities imposed a curfew on the town for almost a week, during which schools were closed, telephone links suspended and food supplies disrupted. Many arrests were made and some of those detained were not released until the beginning of April.

In early 1998 al-Majali announced a cabinet reorganization, in which five new ministers were appointed, notably Dr Bassam al-Umush, a member of the MB who had been suspended from the movement in 1997. The other new ministers had served with al-Majali when he was premier in the early 1990s. Rashid, who had been criticized for the suppression of the pro-Iraqi demonstrations by the security forces, retained his portfolio, but Samir Mutawi was replaced as Minister of State for Information and his responsibilities assigned to one of the two Deputy Prime Ministers, Abdullah an-Nusuf. Dr Fayez at-Tarawneh, hitherto the Minister of Foreign Affairs, became Chief of the Royal Court, traditionally a move towards the premiership, with Jawad al-Anani assuming the foreign affairs portfolio.

In July 1998 severe water shortages and a deterioration in the quality of existing water supplies in Amman caused public discontent, prompting the resignation of the Minister of Water and Irrigation, Mundhir Haddadin. In August King Hussein (who was undergoing medical treatment in the USA) appointed at-Tarawneh to the office of Prime Minister, replacing al-Majali. Al-Majali's removal was largely attributed to the criticism that the Government had attracted over the continuing water crisis in Amman. Later in August a new Cabinet, which included 10 new ministers, was installed; al-Anani replaced at-Tarawneh as Chief of the Royal Court.

RELATIONS WITH THE USA

On 20 June 1991 the US House of Representatives voted to withhold US $27m. in military aid, pending assurances that 'the Government of Jordan has taken steps to advance the peace process in the Middle East'. However, the US Department of State indicated that the Bush administration opposed legislation to prohibit the sending of US aid to Jordan. In October, following Jordan's acceptance of an invitation to attend the opening session of the Middle East peace conference in Madrid (see above), President Bush announced the USA's intention to resume military aid to Jordan.

In June 1992 the USA postponed a joint military exercise with Jordan in order to express its disapproval of the assistance that Jordan was allegedly providing to Iraq to enable it to circumvent the UN trade embargo. The USA subsequently proposed that UN observers should be dispatched to Jordan in order to suppress the smuggling of goods to Iraq. Jordan rejected the proposal outright as an infringement of its sovereignty. In late August both the Jordanian Government and the House of Representatives condemned Western plans to establish an air exclusion zone in southern Iraq. In January 1993 King Hussein strongly criticized renewed air attacks on targets in Iraq by Western air forces, but did not express support for the Iraqi President, Saddam Hussain. At the same time he emphasized that Jordan would remain on friendly terms with the USA under the newly-elected Clinton administration. In June King Hussein visited the USA, where he held talks, for the first time, with President Clinton. Although relations between the USA and Jordan were described as good, the USA was reported to be continuing to withhold financial aid in retaliation for Jordan's alleged assistance to Iraq during the 1991 Gulf War. Prior to his visit to the USA, King Hussein had stated publicly that he did not support the Iraqi leadership or its policies. At the end of July the USA was reported to have informed Jordan that it must make payments to the UN's Compensation Fund for Kuwait if it continued to receive deliveries of petroleum from Iraq. In mid-September, however, US President Clinton announced that some $30m. in economic and military aid to Jordan was to be released, in recognition of the country's enforcement of sanctions against Iraq and of its role in the Middle East peace process.

As part of his plans to improve relations with the USA, King Hussein visited Washington in late January 1994 where he met President Clinton and the Secretary of State, Warren Christopher. Their talks included discussions about the Arab-Israeli peace process and future US arms sales to Jordan. During the visit the King stated publicly that he would be willing to meet Itzhak Rabin, the Israeli Prime Minister. For the first time openly, he also met with a group of leading Jewish Americans through Project Nishma, a Jewish organization that promotes peace between the Arab states and Israel. In March, however, new tensions emerged with the USA over Jerusalem and over the US-led naval blockade of Jordan's only port at Aqaba. After the adoption of Resolution 904 by the UN Security Council on 18 March 1994, Jordan protested strongly about the US position on the status of Jerusalem. The USA had abstained on two paragraphs in the preamble, in which East Jerusalem was referred to as part of the Occupied Territories. Jordan was worried about the legal and political implications of what appeared to be an important change in US policy towards Jerusalem. However, most of King Hussein's fury over this reversal was directed towards PLO Chairman Yasser Arafat who was accused of mishandling the negotiations which preceded the adoption of the Resolution by failing to consult with Jordan on its wording.

At the end of March 1994 the Jordanian Government told the USA that the interception of ships bound for Aqaba by the US-led multilateral inspection force as part of UN sanctions against Iraq was seriously damaging the Jordanian economy. Jordan pointed out that since August 1991, when the inspection started, not one violation of sanctions had been discovered although some 1,700 ships had been stopped and searched. Jordan warned that unless this problem was resolved, it would not return to the peace negotiations. After months of deliberations, the US Administration announced on 25 April that it had accepted a Jordanian proposal for a new system of monitoring cargo bound for Aqaba. The announcement followed a meeting in London between King Hussein and US Secretary of State, Warren Christopher.

In an address to the Jordanian National Assembly on 26 October 1994, US President Clinton pledged to cancel Jordan's official debts to the USA, totalling $702m., apparently as a reward for signing the peace treaty with Israel. Although some

$220m. of debt was written off during the fiscal year 1994, the new Republican-dominated US Congress was inclined to be less generous in 1995. President Clinton had requested the cancellation of $270m.-worth of debt in the fiscal year 1995, but the US House of Representatives only agreed to write off $50m. During a visit to Jordan in March 1995, US Vice-President Al Gore pledged that Clinton's original promise would be honoured. However, King Hussein was forced to visit the USA the following month in an attempt to persuade Congress to permit the debt-cancellation plan to proceed. In September an agreement was finally signed by the USA and Jordan, cancelling $420m. of Jordan's outstanding debt. In August 1995, as King Hussein broke openly with Iraq (see below), President Clinton immediately promised to support Jordan if any threat was made to its security. Joint manoeuvres were held between US and Jordanian armed forces, although Jordan maintained that these had been arranged some time before. Nevertheless, efforts by the USA to persuade Jordan to sever all of its economic links with Iraq were rejected. In January 1996 the US Secretary of Defense announced that the USA would supply Jordan with 12 F-16A and four F-16B fighter aircraft, and in late February President Clinton authorized the supply of military equipment worth $100m. as a grant to Jordan. After King Hussein visited Washington, DC, in March, the USA announced that military co-operation between the two countries would be expanded, a move interpreted by some as a warning to other states in the region not to attempt to destabilize Jordan. In April 34 US F-15 and F-16 fighter aircraft were stationed in Jordan for an indefinite period in order to undertake flights over southern Iraq.

Some observers interpreted Jordan's *rapprochement* with Saudi Arabia and the Gulf states and the break with Iraq as part of a plan orchestrated by the USA to redraw the political map of the region, with the aim of further isolating Iraq, politically and economically, and linking the Jordanian economy more closely with that of Israel. In April 1996, when it was revealed that Turkey had signed a secret military agreement with Israel in February, some analysts argued that a new strategic partnership was emerging in the region to replace the long-promised Middle East peace accords, bringing together the USA, Israel, Turkey and Jordan in a military alliance designed to protect Israeli and US interests in the region and to isolate those states opposed to them. In May US and Jordanian forces carried out joint military exercises in the south of the kingdom.

In June 1996 King Hussein was the first Arab leader to visit Washington, DC, after the right-wing Likud victory in the Israeli elections. Discussions focused on the Middle East peace process and on Jordan's strategic relationship with the USA. Soon after the King's visit another series of joint military manoeuvres were carried out in southern Jordan, and at the end of the month the Chairman of the US Joint Chiefs of Staff, General Shalikashvili, visited Jordan to strengthen the military relationship between the two countries. In October, after violent clashes between Israelis and Palestinians following Israel's decision to open a tunnel in Jerusalem close to Muslim holy places (see below), President Clinton invited King Hussein, the Palestinian leader, Yasser Arafat, and the new Israeli Prime Minister, Binyamin Netanyahu, to Washington in order to reduce tensions. Little progress was made at their meeting, although it was agreed that direct talks would be resumed between Israel and the Palestine National Authority on the redeployment of Israeli troops in Hebron. Before the meeting, King Hussein held private talks with Prime Minister Netanyahu. In November President Clinton announced that Jordan was being granted special military status, thus making the kingdom eligible for increases in US military aid. In December Jordan received the first $100m. instalment of a $300m.-package of military equipment as part of a US commitment to help modernize the Jordanian armed forces. In early March 1997, when the US vetoed a UN Security Council resolution criticizing Israel's plans to build a new housing complex on the outskirts of Arab East Jerusalem, King Hussein protested and claimed that the veto had damaged the credibility of the USA as an honest broker in the Middle East. Nevertheless, joint exercises between Jordanian and US forces continued, and the first group of F-16 fighter aircraft, pledged under the rearmament agreement that had been signed with the USA at the end of 1996, arrived in December 1997, with the rest of the aircraft scheduled for delivery in early 1998. In

September 1997 the US Secretary of State, Madeleine Albright, met King Hussein for discussions in Amman, as part of her first visit to the Middle East since taking office. The talks in Jordan were very cordial; however, Albright's visit to the region failed to resolve the deadlock in the Middle East peace process. In October the US Government accorded Irbid in northern Jordan, where there were a number of Jordanian-Israeli joint ventures, the status of 'qualifying industrial zone', thereby allowing all goods exported from it duty-free access to the US market. In November Jordan dispatched a high-level delegation, headed by Jawad al-Anani, to the US-sponsored Middle East and North Africa economic conference in Doha, Qatar, while both Egypt and Saudi Arabia decided to boycott the meeting, owing to Israeli participation. Despite the close alliance with the US Government and the suppression of pro-Iraqi demonstrations during the increased tension between the USA and Iraq in early 1998, Jordan indicated that it would not allow its territory or airspace to be used for an attack on Iraq. During his visit to Washington in March King Hussein was reported to have requested that the US Government increase aid to Jordan and exert pressure on Israel to make concessions over the West Bank. There was a limited response from US officials to the King's suggestion that Jordan assist in the organization of discussions between the Governments of the USA and Iraq. A senior Jordanian naval officer was present at a joint exercise between the naval forces of the USA, Israel and Turkey (the first time that the three countries had co-operated in a military exercise).

RELATIONS WITH ARAB STATES

Since the end of the 1990–91 Gulf War, Jordan has continued to distance itself from Saddam Hussain's regime in Iraq and has tried to improve relations with the Gulf states. In 1992 King Hussein spoke publicly of the need for change in Iraq, but denied that he had discussed ways of removing the Iraqi leader with the director of the CIA. Jordan protested at the harassment of Iraqi refugees in Jordan by the Iraqi secret service and at the execution of Jordanian merchants in Iraq accused of economic crimes. Jordan welcomed the decision of Iraq, in November 1994, to recognize the sovereignty and territorial integrity of Kuwait. However, Jordan continued to favour the international rehabilitation of Iraq, including the relaxation of UN sanctions. In June 1995 King Hussein was openly critical of US policy towards Iraq. After a visit to Amman later that month by Viktor Possovalyuk, the Russian Deputy Minister of Foreign Affairs, both Jordan and Russia agreed to co-operate to end UN sanctions against Iraq.

At the end of November 1993 King Hussein made his first official visit to Egypt since the Gulf crisis. Relations with Egypt had slowly improved after diplomatic efforts by the King who made an unofficial visit to Cairo in October 1992 to offer condolences just after the Egyptian capital suffered a serious earthquake. During a visit to Amman by the Egyptian Minister of Foreign Affairs in October 1993 it was agreed to reconvene the Higher Jordanian-Egyptian Joint Committee which had not met since the Gulf crisis. In January 1995 President Mubarak of Egypt made his first official visit to Jordan since the Iraqi invasion of Kuwait, and in February Jordan, together with representatives of the PLO and Israel, attended a summit meeting in Cairo, in an attempt to avert a breakdown in the peace process. In March the Higher Jordanian-Egyptian Joint Committee convened in Cairo, where it was agreed to co-ordinate the activities of the two countries' respective interior ministries, a decision apparently aimed at increasing co-operation against the threat of Islamic extremists.

Following visits by Crown Prince Hassan to Doha in late 1993 and by Sheikh Hamad bin Jaber ath-Thani, the Qatari Minister of Foreign Affairs, to Amman at the beginning of 1994, normal relations between Jordan and Qatar were restored after being strained by Jordan's support for Saddam Hussain in the Gulf War. In March 1994 King Hussein made his first visit to Doha since the Gulf crisis. However, the normalization of relations with Qatar did not include the resumption of financial aid to Jordan from the emirate. King Hussein also visited Oman, where discussions included the efforts by both countries to mediate between the two factions in Yemen, but visits to Bahrain and the UAE were cancelled.

In November 1994 a three-year programme of bilateral co-operation in education, science and culture was agreed with Qatar, and in January 1995 King Hussein made a private visit to Oman for talks with Sultan Qaboos. There were also signs of some improvement in relations with Bahrain and the UAE. After the coup in Qatar in June 1995 in which Sheikh Hamad bin Khalifa ath-Thani deposed his father, King Hussein offered his congratulations to the new Amir, who had been largely responsible for the policy of improving relations with Jordan. During the second half of 1995 relations with Yemen were also strengthened.

In 1994–95 there was some improvement in relations with Kuwait, which had been severely strained since the Iraqi invasion of Kuwait in 1990. A senior Jordanian diplomat visited Kuwait in September 1994, and it was later announced that the Jordanian embassy in Kuwait would reopen and that Kuwait had agreed to allow several thousand Jordanians who had been expelled in 1991 to return. Nevertheless, relations remained difficult.

In late 1994 and 1995 relations with Saudi Arabia began to improve, despite the personal animosity believed to exist between King Fahd and King Hussein. The refusal of King Fahd to meet King Hussein in March 1995, when the Jordanian monarch was performing the *umra* (minor pilgrimage), was defused by the Jordanian leadership, anxious not to escalate tensions with its powerful neighbour. In addition to the serious rift in relations caused by the Gulf crisis, it is believed that the Saudi monarch may have a particular animosity towards King Hussein because of the long rivalry between the Hashemites and the House of Sa'ud. Nevertheless, tentative signs of a *rapprochement* were evident in late 1994. In September co-operation on border issues resumed. A ban on granting residence permits to the dependants of all Jordanians and Palestinians working in Saudi Arabia, which had been imposed since the Gulf Crisis, was partly revoked in March 1995, when residence permits were granted to the families of those Jordanians employed in 'vital positions'. After a visit to Riyadh by the Jordanian Minister of Foreign Affairs in July there were signs that Saudi Arabia was ready to restore diplomatic representation with Jordan to ambassadorial level.

BREAKDOWN IN RELATIONS WITH IRAQ

In early August 1995 King Hussein granted political asylum to Hussain Kamel al-Majid, his brother Saddam Kamel and their wives after they fled from Baghdad to Amman. Hussain and Saddam Kamel had been senior figures in the Iraqi regime and were married to daughters of Saddam Hussain, the Iraqi leader. Their defection marked a sharp deterioration in relations between Jordan and Iraq. At a press conference shortly after arriving in Jordan, Hussain Kamel appealed for the removal of Saddam Hussain and spoke of his hopes of leading an Iraqi opposition movement to rescue Iraqis from their worsening plight. Later that month King Hussein delivered a speech in which he praised Hussain Kamel as a great patriot and strongly criticized the Iraqi leader, although he stopped short of seeking the fall of the Iraqi regime. He also denied speculation, especially rife in the Egyptian and Syrian press, that he was seeking to revive Hashemite claims to Iraq. In response, Iraq denounced Hussain Kamel as a traitor and a US agent, but carefully avoided attacks on King Hussein. Despite the political rupture, economic co-operation continued, with Iraq remaining Jordan's main source of oil supplies. Jordan continued to provide Iraq with a vitally important link with the outside world. In October King Hussein renewed his attack on the Iraqi regime, denouncing the presidential elections in Iraq as a farce. He also established contact with Iraqi opposition groups in London, United Kingdom, and promoted the idea of holding a congress in Amman to bring the different factions together in order to discuss political change in Iraq. However, the proposed congress drew criticism, especially from Syria, and the idea was abandoned. The King was also criticized for appearing to favour a federal approach to Iraq's political future as this might have threatened the country's unity. In any case, his support for Hussain Kamel was short-lived. It quickly became clear that Kamel had few supporters in Iraq, while his appeals to the Iraqi opposition-in-exile were firmly rejected. By the end of 1995 his presence in Jordan had become something of an embarrassment.

When Hussain Kamel and his brother decided to return to Iraq in February 1996, after Iraq announced that they had been pardoned, rumours circulated that the Jordanian authorities may have encouraged them in their decision. Nevertheless, the brutal murder of the two men by order of Saddam Hussain only days after their return was strongly condemned by Jordan.

In April 1996, after US aircraft were stationed at Azraq to enforce the air exclusion zone in southern Iraq, the Jordanian Government insisted that it would not permit the country to be used as a base for attacks against Iraq. Nevertheless, King Hussein met with Iraqi opposition leaders in London, United Kingdom, in March and gave permission for the Iraqi National Accord (INA) to open an office in Amman. In March there was another high-level defection from Iraq when Gen. Nizar Kazraji, a former Chief of Staff of the Iraqi army, arrived in Jordan and associated himself with the INA. In late March, amid speculation that Iraqi agents operating in Jordan might be seeking to target Jordanians, the first expulsion of an Iraqi diplomat from Jordan occurred, although no explanation for it was made public. In retaliation, Iraq expelled a Jordanian diplomat. At the end of June it was reported that US, British, Saudi Arabian and Jordanian intelligence officers meeting in Saudi Arabia in January had agreed that Amman should become the centre of operations for the Iraqi opposition. They had agreed to support the INA, which claimed to be in contact with high-ranking officers in the Iraqi armed forces, and which favoured a swift *coup d'etat* that would remove Saddam Hussain from power but leave the country intact. It was also reported that US President Clinton had authorized a grant of some $6m. to finance the INA's operations in Amman, with additional funds being provided by Saudi Arabia, Kuwait and several other Arab countries. Speaking in Washington, DC, in June, the Jordanian Minister of Information stated that Jordan preferred to support the INA because its rival, the Iraqi National Congress (INC), had no credibility in either Iraq or Jordan.

Jordan's new policy on Iraq was welcomed by Saudi Arabia and relations between the two countries continued to improve. Shortly after Hussain Kamel's defection, the Jordanian Minister of Foreign Affairs was invited to visit Riyadh where he was received by King Fahd. Full diplomatic relations were restored with the appointment of a new Saudi Arabian ambassador to Amman in November 1995. In January 1996 the Saudi Arabian Minister of Foreign Affairs visited Jordan, the first visit by a senior member of the Saudi Arabian regime since the 1990–91 Gulf crisis, and offered to resume supplies of some 40,000 b/d of crude oil (cut off in September 1990) to Jordan. Relations with Bahrain, which, like Saudi Arabia, had taken a hard line on relations with Jordan since 1990, also improved after Jordan's political rupture with Iraq. In November 1995 two high-level Jordanian delegations visited Manama and there was speculation that Jordanian assistance in Bahrain's internal security was one of the main topics of discussion. In early 1996 Jordan's new Prime Minister reaffirmed the country's support for the Bahrain Government and did not exclude the dispatching of Jordanian troops to assist its security forces. During the second half of 1995 relations with Qatar and Oman were further strengthened. King Hussein visited Doha and Muscat in August, and in September the new Amir of Qatar visited Amman. Jordan's efforts to improve its relations with the Gulf states were rewarded when the GCC countries agreed to take part in an economic summit meeting held in Amman in October. However, relations with Kuwait remained uneasy. The Jordanian Minister of Foreign Affairs met his Kuwaiti counterpart in Cairo in September 1995, but was told that it was still too early for normal diplomacy between the two countries to resume. In December, however, the Kuwaiti Minister of Foreign Affairs urged the resumption of diplomatic relations with Jordan following the political break with Iraq and the improvement in Jordan's relations with other Gulf states. In a public disagreement, the Kuwaiti Prime Minister opposed the move, arguing that public opinion in Kuwait was still against normalization. In order to resolve their differences, telephone and postal links were restored, but Jordan was informed that the re-establishment of diplomatic relations would require the agreement of the Kuwaiti Government, its people and its press.

Jordan's new policy towards Iraq caused disquiet in Egypt and Syria, which feared that it could lead to a new, US-backed strategic reorientation in the region. The Egyptian and Syrian press accused King Hussein of pursuing his own ambitions in Iraq. The King had talks with President Mubarak of Egypt in Washington, DC, at the end of September 1995 during the signing of the Israel-Palestinian Interim agreement on the West Bank and Gaza Strip, and in late December President Mubarak visited Amman. At the end of his visit to Jordan the two leaders issued a joint statement in which they emphasized the need to ensure the unity of Iraq and to allow the Iraqi people to decide their own future. Nevertheless, while King Hussein appeared to have gone some way towards reassuring the Egyptian President, relations between the two countries remained uneasy owing to Egypt's sensitivities about its regional status. In contrast, Syria's attitude provoked strong criticism from Jordan, and resulted in a further deterioration in relations which had been poor since Jordan signed a separate peace agreement with Israel. At the end of June 1996 President Mubarak of Egypt attempted to mediate between the two countries during the emergency Arab League summit meeting in Cairo, encouraging King Hussein to hold talks with President Assad of Syria to try to resolve their differences. Jordan had accused Syria of sponsoring terrorist organizations in order to destabilize the kingdom, while Syria had denounced Jordan for working with Israel and Turkey to undermine President Assad's regime. Jordanian officials claimed that some progress had been made during the talks, and further contacts between the two leaders in July indicated an improvement in bilateral relations.

After the right-wing Likud victory in the Israeli elections, King Hussein urged other Arab leaders not to judge the new Prime Minister, Binyamin Netanyahu, until his policies concerning the peace process were announced. In order to review the new situation, King Hussein held talks with President Mubarak of Egypt and the Palestinian leader, Yasser Arafat, in Aqaba in early June 1996, but was not invited to the mini-summit between the leaders of Egypt, Syria and Saudi Arabia in Damascus. At the full Arab League summit in Cairo during 21–23 June, King Hussein joined other moderate Arab leaders to ensure that the final communiqué to be adopted was more restrained than many had predicted.

The tense relations that had existed with Iraq since August 1995 improved slightly in December 1996, when the Iraqi Ministers of Trade and Foreign Affairs held talks in Amman with senior Jordanian officials, marking a resumption in high-level contacts between the two countries. It was reported that King Hussein had been opposed to any relaxation of sanctions against Saddam Hussain's regime, but, after Baghdad accepted UN Security Council Resolution 986 allowing Iraq to sell limited quantities of oil in order to purchase food and medicine, he was willing to adopt a less confrontational stance to protect Jordan's economic interests. In addition, the invasion of Iraqi Kurdistan by Saddam Hussain's forces in August 1996, and the destruction of the Iraqi opposition based there, may have convinced the King that an early removal of the Iraqi leader was extremely unlikely. The Jordanian Government deliberately refrained from commenting on the Iraqi invasion, but voiced concern over the US missile attacks against Iraq. The Jordanian National Assembly, in contrast, strongly condemned the American action. The Iraqi National Accord (INA) was allowed to keep its office in Amman, despite reports that the group had been infiltrated by Iraqi agents, but the Jordanian Government repeatedly asserted that Jordan would not be used as a base for operations against the Iraqi regime.

In December 1997 relations between the two countries once again became strained, after the Iraqi authorities executed four Jordanian nationals who had been convicted of smuggling offences. King Hussein condemned the executions, expelled a number of Iraqi diplomats from Amman, and recalled the Jordanian chargé d'affaires from Baghdad. In an attempt to improve relations, Iraq announced that it would commute the death sentence of a fifth Jordanian convicted of smuggling and release a number of Jordanians held in Iraqi prisons. The killing of Iraq's chargé d'affaires in Amman in January 1998 prompted rumours that Iraqi government agents may have been responsible. In May, however, the Jordanian Minister of the Interior announced that a number of Jordanian nationals had been arrested in connection with the killing, which, he insisted, had not been politically motivated and did not involve 'neighbouring countries'. During the Gulf crisis in early 1998 there was widespread popular support for Iraq in Jordan, but the authorities banned pro-Iraqi demonstrations. Despite Jordan's close alliance with the US Government, however, the authorities indicated that they would not allow Jordanian territory or airspace to be used for air strikes against Iraq, but they urged the Iraqi Government to comply with all UN resolutions and allow UN weapons inspectors access to all suspect sites. Jordanian support for the Arab League's efforts to resolve the crisis by diplomatic means contributed to an improvement in relations with some other Arab states, notably Egypt. Although relations with Iraq remained uneasy, economic co-operation continued, and in February 1998 the two countries renewed the 1991 oil agreement.

During the second half of 1997 there were indications that King Hussein wished to achieve an improvement in relations with Syria. Speaking at Irbid, in northern Jordan, the King praised President Assad, but also urged the Syrian Government to reciprocate by ceasing to support some Jordanian opposition parties and professional associations. For their part, the Jordanian authorities ordered the head of the Syrian branch of the MB's information office in Amman to leave the country. President Liamine Zéroual of Algeria made an official visit to Amman in September. In December a high-level Jordanian delegation attended the summit conference of the Organization of the Islamic Conference (OIC, see p. 261) in the Iranian capital, Teheran, resulting in an improvement in relations with Iran.

The normalization of relations with Saudi Arabia was sealed in mid-August 1996 by a visit by King Hussein and a senior delegation to Riyadh, where the Jordanian monarch held his first talks with King Fahd since the 1990–91 Gulf crisis. Their discussions covered issues including the Middle East peace process and co-operation against terrorism. Both leaders agreed to strengthen bilateral relations, and agreements were concluded on the employment of Jordanians in Saudi Arabia and on resuming Jordanian agricultural exports to the kingdom. In July 1996 a meeting of the Jordanian-Qatari Higher Committee, attended by the foreign ministers of the two countries, and visits by other senior officials indicated a further consolidation of relations between Jordan and Qatar. In December King Hussein made his first visit to the United Arab Emirates since the Gulf crisis and held talks with the UAE President, Sheikh Zayed bin Sultan an-Nahyan. Relations with Kuwait remained problematic, and a dispute over Jordanian prisoners held in Kuwait since the Iraqi invasion threatened to destroy the limited progress that had been made to reconcile the two countries. In January 1997 the Jordanian press reported that Jordanian prisoners in Kuwait were being ill-treated. The press criticized their own Government for not taking action. Tension mounted after official exchanges on the issue, but the crisis was defused when the Amir of Kuwait included 10 Jordanians in a group of prisoners released to mark the Id al-Fitr celebrations in the following month. In June the Kuwaiti Minister of Foreign Affairs declared that Kuwait was prepared to normalize relations with Jordan, Sudan and Yemen, the three Arab states which it had accused of supporting Iraq during the 1990–91 Gulf crisis. In the following month the Kuwaiti Government indicated that it favoured the normalization of relations with Jordan proceeding at a faster pace, but emphasized that the Jordanian press would have to modify its strongly critical attitude towards Kuwait. Relations with Saudi Arabia continued to improve, with a visit by the Saudi Arabian Minister of Foreign Affairs to Amman in June, while good relations with the other Gulf states, especially Oman and Qatar, were consolidated. A high-level Jordanian delegation attended the Middle East and North Africa economic conference in Doha, the Qatari capital, in November, and Jordan benefited from increased economic co-operation with Qatar.

RELATIONS WITH ISRAEL AND THE PALESTINE NATIONAL AUTHORITY

In May 1995 the Government banned a conference (organized by the IAF) to oppose the normalization of relations with Israel, claiming that it posed a threat to national security and to the image of the country. In June 1995 Israel began to pipe 30m. cu m of drinking water a year from Lake Tiberias to Jordan as agreed in the peace treaty signed by Jordan and Israel in October 1994. The project aims to help Jordan overcome a growing shortage of drinking water and was promoted by the

Jordanian authorities as one of the dividends of the peace process. However, there was some embarrassment when Israel indicated that the flow of water to Jordan could not be guaranteed in the event of shortages in Israel due to drought. Opposition within many sections of Jordanian society to the peace treaty with Israel continued. In July, under the terms of the peace treaty, Jordan finally annulled laws banning Jordanians from having contact with, doing business with or selling land to Israelis, but only after several weeks of angry debate in the House of Representatives. After the assassination of the Israeli Prime Minister, Itzhak Rabin, in early November, King Hussein made his first visit to Jerusalem since 1967 in order to attend the funeral, at which he delivered an emotional oration. Clearly shocked by Rabin's murder, the King emphasized the need to continue the peace process. In December Jordan expelled an Iranian diplomat and there was speculation that he may have been involved in planning an attack on Israeli tourists visiting the country. In order to strengthen bilateral relations, Shimon Peres, the new Israeli Prime Minister, visited Jordan in December, and King Hussein made a state visit to Israel in January 1996. A transport agreement was signed in January establishing direct road and air links between the two countries. King Hussein and senior members of the Government condemned the spate of suicide bomb attacks which were carried out in Israel during February and repeatedly criticized the actions of Hamas militants. Claims by some Palestinian sources that the attacks might have been organized from Jordanian territory were immediately rejected by the Jordanian Minister of Information. King Hussein attended the anti-terrorism summit meeting in Sharm esh-Sheikh, Egypt, in March, which was held in response to the suicide bomb attacks in Israel, and it was subsequently reported that the Jordanian authorities had adopted a tough line with Hamas representatives and had carried out new arrests of Hamas sympathizers.

Relations with Palestinian leader Yasser Arafat continued to improve during 1995. Arafat received a warm reception when he visited Amman in May, and King Hussein used the opportunity to express his firm support for the Palestinian leader, who was under pressure from his opponents because of serious setbacks to the peace accord with Israel, and to reject claims that he was forming an alliance with Hamas. At the beginning of June the Jordanian authorities expelled two members of Hamas' political bureau who had been based in Jordan. The Jordanian authorities welcomed the Israel-Palestinian Interim Agreement on the West Bank and the Gaza Strip (see p. 136) signed in Washington, DC, on 28 September. Conscious of the tensions that had arisen between Jordan and the PLO during earlier negotiations between the Palestinians and Israel, Arafat visited Amman to inform the Jordanian leadership about the main provisions of the new accord and thanked King Hussein for his support during the long negotiations.

After the surprise victory of the Likud in the Israeli elections at the end of May 1996, and the creation of a new right-wing Israeli Government, King Hussein declared that the implications of this did not worry him. He was the only Arab leader to have met Netanyahu when he led the Israeli opposition and had maintained contacts with the Likud leader for some two years. An Israeli source indicated that the new Israeli Prime Minister expected the process of normalization with Jordan to continue, and revealed that Dore Gold, Netanyahu's political adviser, had visited Amman several times in recent months in order to assure King Hussein that the new Likud Government would seek to promote Jordan's role in the West Bank. Other analysts also argued that Netanyahu's victory had revived talk of the so-called 'Jordanian option', provoking fears among Palestinians that Israel would encourage Jordan to share in the administration of the West Bank, leaving the Palestine National Authority in full control of only the vulnerable Gaza Strip. King Hussein's optimism about the new Israeli administration soon transformed into despair and frustration at the intransigence of Netanyahu's Government with regard to the peace process. The Israeli Government did not inform Jordan in advance about its decision in September to reopen an ancient tunnel in East Jerusalem, a decision that resulted in violent clashes between the Israeli security services and Palestinian demonstrators. King Hussein tried to defuse the crisis by requesting an international inquiry to examine whether the opening of the tunnel had damaged nearby Muslim religious sites and urged Israel to resume peace talks with the Palestinians. After his discussions with Netanyahu in Washington, DC, in October, the King attempted to persuade the Israeli Prime Minister to adopt a more constructive position on the redeployment of Israeli forces on the West Bank, set out in the Declaration of Principles but not yet implemented. As the peace process appeared to be expiring, protests against the normalization of relations with Israel intensified and succeeded in delaying the opening of the first Israeli trade fair in Amman by several weeks. The eventual opening of the fair, in January 1997, was attended by a demonstration organized by a 'national committee' consisting of political parties and trade unions, in which more than 2,500 Jordanians participated. Also in January 1997 King Hussein intervened to support US efforts to secure an agreement between Israel and the Palestinian leadership on the issue of redeployment outlined in the Declaration of Principles. The King apparently persuaded Yasser Arafat to compromise on the timing of the second redeployment of Israeli forces from rural areas in the West Bank in order not to jeopardize the deal already made on Hebron. Israel's rapid redeployment of most of its forces from Hebron was welcomed by the Jordanian Government, and the release of three Jordanian prisoners held in Israel also helped to reduce tension between the two countries. At the end of February Prime Minister Netanyahu visited Amman to discuss bilateral relations, but the Israeli Prime Minister's decision to continue with the construction of a large new Jewish settlement at Jabal Abu Ghunaym (Har Homa) on the outskirts of Jerusalem, plunged relations between the two countries into a new crisis: the completed Har Homa project would result in Arab East Jerusalem becoming virtually surrounded by Jewish settlements, thereby prejudicing the future status of the city which is due to be discussed when 'final status' negotiations between Israel and the Palestinians begin. After the visit, in an exchange of letters, King Hussein stated that Netanyahu's policies threatened to destroy the peace process and could lead to violence. Shortly afterwards Crown Prince Hassan cancelled a visit to Israel where he had been due to attend a ceremony in memory of Itzhak Rabin. On 13 March, two days after the publication of the King's outspoken letter, a Jordanian soldier opened fire on a party of Israeli schoolgirls at Nayarayim, on the border with Jordan, killing seven of the girls and wounding six others. King Hussein, who cut short a visit to Spain to return to Amman, and Crown Prince Hassan immediately expressed their sorrow and distress at the killings and promised a full investigation. Three days after the attack the King, together with Prime Minister Netanyahu, visited the relatives of the deceased to offer their condolences. Some Israelis argued that the King's letter had provoked the massacre of the schoolgirls, an allegation strongly denied by the Jordanian King who insisted that he had written more in sorrow than in anger and pledged to continue to work for peace in the region. The perpetrator of the attack, Ahmad Dakamsa, went on trial at the end of May and his case was taken up by those Jordanians opposed to the normalization of relations with Israel. Several committees were established to support the soldier and his family. A military court later sentenced Dakamsa to 25 years' imprisonment.

Despite the increasing strain on political relations between the two countries, an agreement was reached in May 1997 on the transfer of drinking water from Israel to Jordan (under the provisions of the 1994 peace treaty), following talks between King Hussein and Netanyahu in Aqaba. At the end of August the two countries signed an accord to divert international flights from the airport serving Israel's Red Sea resort at Eilat, which is heavily congested, to nearby Aqaba airport in Jordan. Jordan's Minister of Transport stated that the agreement established the foundations for further co-operation in the future, and there was speculation that, if the arrangement proved successful, it could lead to the first jointly-managed airport in the region. In July Israel's Chief of Staff, Lt-Gen. Amnon Lipkin-Shahak, visited Jordan, the first official visit by the head of Israel's armed forces to an Arab country. The two countries were reported to

have extended their co-operation in the fields of security and intelligence. However, the attempted assassination of Khalid Meshaal, the head of the political bureau of Hamas, in Amman in late September by agents of the Israeli secret service, Mossad, created further tension between the two countries. The attack was apparently ordered by the Israeli Prime Minister and was only agreed to reluctantly by Mossad leaders. King Hussein demanded and secured the release of Sheikh Ahmad Yassin, the spiritual leader of Hamas, and a number of other Palestinians who had been imprisoned in Israel, in exchange for the return of the two Mossad agents. There were reports that King Hussein threatened to suspend diplomatic relations if the Israeli authorities failed to meet his demands. Following the attack on Meshaal, there were few high-level political contacts between the two countries for some months, although economic co-operation continued. After the resignation of the Mossad chief, Danny Yatom, in February 1998 and his replacement by Ephraim Halevy, who had been closely involved in the negotiations which had resulted in the 1994 peace treaty between Israel and Jordan, relations between the two countries improved. In early March Ariel Sharon, the Israeli Minister of National Infrastructure, and the senior Israeli responsible for relations with Jordan, visited Amman, followed by the Israeli Minister of Trade and Industry. Also in March a high-level Jordanian delegation, led by Crown Prince Hassan, visited Israel. Crown Prince Hassan held talks with Netanyahu and the Israeli Minister of Defence, Itzhak Mordechai, during the visit. Shortly afterwards, however, Ariel Sharon angered the Jordanian authorities by stating, in an Israeli news broadcast, that Israel was still determined to kill Khalid Meshaal. Abdullah an-Nusur, then the acting premier, condemned the statement and reminded Israel that Meshaal was a Jordanian national. Sharon subsequently wrote to Crown Prince Hassan, claiming that his comments had been misinterpreted and insisting that he respected Jordan's sovereignty. There was further embarrassment for the Jordanian authorities when Israeli radio reported that King Hussein had donated US $1m. to the families of the Israeli schoolgirls killed by a Jordanian soldier in March 1997 (see above). (In view of the strong opposition in Jordan to the normalization of relations with Israel, King Hussein had requested that no publicity should be given to the donation.)

As the Jordanian leadership became increasingly critical of the Netanyahu Government, its relations with the Palestine National Authority (PNA) improved. At his meeting with Yasser Arafat in Aqaba in June 1996, King Hussein emphasized that under no circumstances would Jordan seek to replace the Palestinian leadership in negotiations with Israel over the 'final status' of the West Bank. When King Hussein visited Washington in the same month, the Jordanian Minister of Information stressed that Jordan's role was to assist negotiations between the Israelis and the Palestinians and not to supplant the PNA. President Arafat visited Amman at the end of December when the Jordanian leadership reiterated its full support for Palestinian independence. In November the two sides had reached agreement over the controversial issue of responsibility for the holy sites in East Jerusalem. It was agreed that Jordan would retain formal jurisdiction over the sites until the 'final status' negotiations between Israel and the Palestinians had been successfully completed. The management of the sites, however, would be transferred from Jordan's Ministry of Awqaf and Islamic Affairs to the PNA.

The summit of the OIC, which took place in Teheran in December 1997, unanimously recognized Jordan's role in preserving Jerusalem's Muslim identity. Also in December al-Majali held discussions with President Arafat in Ramallah, on the West Bank; the Jordanian Government angered the Israeli authorities by suggesting that Jewish West Jerusalem, as well as occupied Arab East Jerusalem, should be discussed during 'final status' negotiations between Israel and the Palestinian leadership. On the occasion of his visit to Israel in March 1998 Crown Prince Hassan also met Arafat, although the meeting was viewed as one of courtesy rather than an opportunity for substantive talks.

Economy

Revised for this edition by ALAN J. DAY

Having twice been completely disrupted by war between the Arab states and Israel (first in 1948, and then in 1967), Jordan's economy was again severely affected by a regional conflict during the Gulf crisis and hostilities of 1990–91. This latest dislocation of established patterns of trade, aid and labour migration had a negative short-term impact on the vulnerable Jordanian economy, but failed to produce the sustained downturn that was widely predicted at the height of the crisis. By 1992 a strong recovery was under way, and it was clear that the restored Kuwaiti Government's expulsion of large numbers of Palestinians in 1991 had (because these 'returnees' were relatively affluent) provided Jordan with a timely economic stimulus. For its part, the Jordanian Government had, by adhering closely to IMF-approved economic policies, exerted a strong stabilizing influence throughout the crisis and its aftermath. From September 1993 onwards, Jordan's planners had to modify all medium- and long-term forecasts to take account of the implications of the PLO-Israel peace agreement. A further radical reappraisal was prompted by the Jordan-Israel peace treaty of October 1994, the potential economic consequences of which were a major topic of discussion in Jordan in 1995. However, initiatives to strengthen regional economic co-operation were generally scaled down in 1996 and 1997, following the re-emergence of regional political tensions. By 1998 it was widely acknowledged that Jordan had derived only limited economic benefit from the peace process. Although its macroeconomic position remained strong, initial government claims of healthy economic growth in 1996–98 were revised sharply downwards in mid-1998.

In the 1948–49 Arab–Israeli War, Jordan acquired some 5,600 sq km of new territory—the vast salient which juts out into Israel west of the River Jordan, and the country's population increased more than threefold. Before the war broke out, the country's population was perhaps 400,000. The number of those living on the West Bank of the River Jordan in the territory acquired in 1948 was well over 800,000. This territory was occupied by Israel in 1967, and perhaps 350,000 of the inhabitants fled to non-occupied Jordan. Jordan's 1979 census gave a total population for the East Bank of 2,100,019, which implied an annual growth rate between 1961 and 1979 of 4.8%. Natural increase accounted for 3.8% and immigration for 1.0%. The rate of growth in the mid-1980s was estimated at 4%. By the end of 1986 the population of the East Bank was officially estimated to have risen to 2,796,100 and by 1992 to 3.9m., the annual rate of increase in 1980–90 being 3.7%, compared with 4.3% in 1965–80. Of the present population, 32% reside in the capital Amman, and a further 15% in the cities of Zarqa and Irbid. The World Bank assessed the urban population proportion as 61% in 1990, in which year the crude birth rate was 43 per 1,000 (compared with 53 per 1,000 in 1965) and the crude death rate, 6 per 1,000 (compared with 21 per 1,000 in 1965). These levels of population increase are making themselves felt particularly in the major towns, where water shortages are becoming one of the most severe of the country's economic problems. The World Bank estimated Jordan's 1992 GNP per caput at $1,130 on a conventional exchange-rate basis or $4,220 using an 'international dollar' calculation based on a current Jordanian rating of 18.3 in the World Bank's 'purchasing power parity' (PPP) index (USA = 100). The World Bank's estimates for 1994 were a GNP per caput of $1,390 on the conventional basis and $4,290 on the PPP basis. Jordan's estimated GDP at current prices in 1996 totalled $7,300m. ($1,721 per caput).

The total work-force was estimated at 535,444 in 1986 by the Government's Department of Statistics, with a further 276,000 working in Arab countries and 52,000 elsewhere abroad. As of the end of 1986 it was reported that there were about 180,000 non-Jordanians working in the country and 80% of those were Arab nationals. At the end of 1987 the Jordanian Government announced that it was to stop issuing work permits, in order to stem the growth in unemployment. The rate of unemployment was unofficially estimated at 17% of the work-force in September 1987 and at just under 20% in August 1990, when Iraq occupied Kuwait.

The absorption of the refugees of 1948 and of 1967 caused problems which were accentuated by ethnic, cultural and religious differences. Jordanians before 1948 were mainly Bedouin and mostly engaged in pastoral, and even nomadic, activities. They therefore had little in common with the Palestinians, many of whom established themselves in Jordan as traders and professional men. In April 1994 there were 1,176,208 Palestinian refugees registered with the United Nations Relief and Works Agency (UNRWA) in Jordan, and a further 324,250 in the West Bank. The vast majority of the country's inhabitants are Sunni Muslims, but about 6% are Christians, mostly Greek Orthodox. Jordan's December 1994 census enumerated a population of 4,095,579 in the East Bank area. The authorities did not release statistics on the number of Palestinians within this total, stating that it would not be in the national interest to do so. The categories listed in the published census results were 'Jordanians' (92.4%), 'Gulf returnees' (5.2%) and 'foreigners' (2.4%). The average rate of population growth between 1952 and 1994 was 4.7% per annum.

The loss of the West Bank of Jordan to Israel in the summer of 1967 created a whole series of new economic problems. The result was the loss not only of some efficiently farmed agricultural land, but also of a large part of the important and growing tourist industry, and the large sums in foreign exchange received from the people who annually visited the old city of Jerusalem and Bethlehem. Some of the immediate problems caused by the war of 1967 were met by aid from Arab countries, but Jordan's economic future, in the long term, obviously depended on the evolution of the Arab–Israeli dispute and of regional relations generally.

During 1979 and the early part of 1980, Jordan moved closer to Iraq in both political and economic terms. The war between Iran and Iraq, which began in September 1980, further strengthened this alliance, notably by increasing trade for Iraq through Aqaba. Towards the end of 1980, Iraq and Jordan signed agreements to confirm their closer economic links, which were strengthened by various trade and aid protocols in 1981, in which year Jordanian exports to Iraq increased to US $186.8m. (compared with $42.3m. in 1979). Owing to war-induced cutbacks in Iraq, Jordanian exports declined to $180m. in 1982 and to $72.9m. in 1983. At Jordan's proposal, an oil-for-goods barter system was instituted. This facilitated a rise in Jordanian exports to $176.5m. in 1984 and, after a further downturn in 1986–87 (due to lower world oil prices and the continuing Iran–Iraq War), a further rise, to $216m., in 1989.

Jordan, its economy underpinned by foreign aid and by remittances from Jordanian workers abroad, enjoyed sustained economic growth from the mid-1970s into the early 1980s, although difficulties were encountered thereafter. Between 1974 and 1984 it had one of the highest growth rates in the world, with the East Bank region's GDP expanding, in real terms, at an average annual rate of more than 8%. In spite of the problems brought about by the conflicts with Israel and the uncertainty caused by the Iran–Iraq War, real GDP increased by 17.6% in 1980 and by 9.8% in 1981, but the growth rate slowed to 5.6% in 1982, 2.5% in 1983 and 0.8% in 1984. A major cause of this deceleration was the non-receipt of three-quarters of the special development aid of $1,250m. per year that was promised to Jordan at the 1978 Baghdad Arab Summit Conference, which had condemned the Camp David accords between Israel and Egypt: of the seven Arab states party to the pledge, only Saudi Arabia honoured its commitments to Jordan in full. In consequence, the targets of Jordan's 1981–85 Development Plan were not attained, while in 1981 Jordan recorded its first current account deficit for five years and continued to record deficits in 1982–85. These shortfalls, combined with Jordan's customary trade deficit (generally in excess of $2,000m. per year during the 1980s), obliged the Government to obtain new foreign development loans, which, in turn, assisted a partial recovery of

GDP growth to 2.7% in 1985, 2.4% in 1986 and 1.9% in 1987. Meanwhile, the annual rate of inflation had fallen steadily, from 12% in 1981 to 0% in 1986, but then rose steeply to 14% in 1988, in which year the national budget deficit increased to 24% of GDP. Moreover, the current account balance, having recorded a small surplus in 1986, showed deficits of 7% and 6% of GDP in 1987 and 1988 respectively. Against this background, the Government submitted to the disciplines of the IMF in mid-1989, agreeing to a five-year structural adjustment programme aiming, by 1993, to bring inflation down to 7%, to reduce the budget deficit to 5% of GDP and to eliminate the current account deficit (see Finance, below).

Immediate slippage on these targets included, in 1989, a rise of inflation to 25% and a budget deficit still around 20% of GDP, compared with the IMF target of 12.4%. Nevertheless, the current account recorded a surplus of $335m. in 1989 and the Government was able to conclude interim debt-rescheduling agreements with its major foreign creditors. Jordan's foreign debt remained high, at $8,400m. in early 1990, but by then the Government believed that economic prospects had improved; inflation was running at only 8%, the budget deficit was on course to fall and substantial GDP growth was expected. Moreover, exports, particularly of vegetables, were buoyant, while remittances and foreign aid were expected to exceed budgeted figures. This relatively hopeful scenario was, however, changed dramatically by the onset of the new Gulf crisis in August 1990.

AFTERMATH OF THE 1990–91 GULF CRISIS

At the time of Iraq's occupation of Kuwait, in August 1990, Iraq was Jordan's principal trading partner, taking at least 23% of Jordan's exports and supplying more than 80% of Jordan's petroleum. Total adherence by Jordan to the UN sanctions against Iraq, imposed by UN Security Council Resolution 661 on 6 August, therefore threatened the whole basis of Jordan's already troubled economy. On 25 August the Jordanian Ministry of Transport issued a circular stating that Jordan adhered to UN Security Council Resolution 661, but Jordan continued to import oil from Iraq by road tanker. Indeed, following the cessation of Saudi Arabian oil deliveries in late September, Jordanian imports from Iraq increased, until the outbreak of hostilities in the Gulf, in mid-January 1991, forced Jordan to find alternative suppliers and also to introduce petrol rationing (see Industry and Mining, below).

Loss of trade with Iraq was not the only problem facing Jordan's economy as a result of the Gulf crisis. Remittances from Jordanians working in the Gulf states (estimated at JD 470m. in 1989) dwindled to almost nothing as activity in Kuwait slowed or ceased, and business in the other Gulf states became affected. Moreover, many of these Jordanians returned to Jordan, as did thousands of Palestinians with Jordanian passports, raising the level of unemployment to 30%, increasing the population by 10% and putting an additional strain on health and education budgets. A further problem was the passage of thousands of migrants through Jordan, many of them attempting to return to the Indian sub-continent and South-East Asia. According to Jordanian officials, about 470,000 foreigners fled to Jordan in the five weeks following the Iraqi invasion of Kuwait on 2 August 1990. Many of these, particularly non-Arab Asians, remained stranded in overcrowded camps on the Iraqi-Jordanian border, suffering severe privations (including shortages of food, water and medical supplies), while awaiting repatriation. Conditions improved in early September, as new camps were established and chartered aircraft carried some of the refugees to their countries of origin. Moreover, fears that the outbreak of hostilities in January 1991 would lead to a furthur massive influx of refugees proved to be unfounded: although confirmed figures were scarce, it appeared that not more than a further 20,000 refugees were processed through Jordanian border camps in January–February.

Official Jordanian statistics showed that other negative effects of the crisis included a rise in inflation to more than 16% in 1990 as a whole and a nominal GDP growth rate of only 1.1%, which, according to the IMF, amounted to a fall in real terms of 7.9%, while GNP fell by 4% in nominal terms and by 17% in dollar terms. According to a UNICEF survey published in March 1991, nearly one-third of the Jordanian population were living in poverty (defined as a family income of less than JD 86 per

month), compared with 20% before the crisis. Because of the crisis, disbursements to Jordan, under the IMF stand-by facility and under an associated $150m. World Bank structural loan, were suspended from September 1990. Subsequent negotiations resulted in a new agreement with the IMF in October 1991, through which Jordan was to undertake a seven-year economic reform programme (1992–98) and as part of which the 1992 budget envisaged a reduced deficit and GDP growth of 3% compared with 1% in 1991 (see Finance, below).

A 'worst-case' forecast, produced by the Jordanian Ministry of Finance in October 1990, predicted the country's possible crisis-related losses in the 12 months from August 1990 to be $2,144m., itemized as follows: exports to Iraq and Kuwait, $280m.; exports to other countries, $160m.; budget support from Kuwait and Iraq, $185m.; repayment of Iraqi loans, $169m.; transit business, $250m.; tourism, $230m.; remittances from Jordanians in Kuwait, $320m.; increased import bill, $220m.; oil imports, $180m.; increased freight and insurance premiums, $120m.; emergency relief for evacuees, $30m. By the beginning of 1991 new estimates had inflated the potential loss over the same period to as much as $8,300m. (equivalent to twice Jordan's GDP), by assuming much higher oil import costs and allowing for a total write-off of the assets of Jordanians resident in Kuwait. By March 1991 pledges of special aid for Jordan in 1991, channelled mainly through the Gulf Financial Crisis Co-ordination Group (GFCCG), totalled $1,230m., of which $470m. had already been received. Having weathered the 1990/91 crisis and its immediate aftermath with the help of external emergency aid, Jordan experienced an unexpectedly strong recovery in 1992, prompting a radical, reappraisal of the medium-term economic outlook. The effective fiscal deficit, estimated to have equalled 14% of GDP in 1991, was cut to about 6% of GDP in 1991 (when domestic revenue exceeded current expenditure for the first time in Jordan's history), while GDP increased by 10.1% in real terms in 1992, as against 1.6% in 1991. The return of some 300,000 Palestinians, expelled by Kuwait in 1991, brought new capital resources into Jordan and helped to boost construction activity to 220% of its 1990 level by 1992, with consequential growth in many related areas of the economy. As UN sanctions against Iraq continued into a third year, it was clear that Jordan's external trading position had not been undermined to the extent that many 'worst-case' scenarios had predicted.

While acknowledging in mid-1993 that serious structural problems remained, including an external debt burden equivalent to 140% of GDP (down from 200% of GDP in the late 1980s) and an unemployment rate of around 25%, Jordanian ministers and business leaders were generally optimistic about the prospects for continued progress in meeting IMF economic targets. The IMF subsequently extended substantial new assistance to support the process of structural reform, while Jordan's main creditors arranged a major debt rescheduling package. In addition, a new Five-Year Economic and Social Development Plan, drafted for the period 1993–97, provided for a major extension of the private sector through the privatization of state enterprises (see Planning and Development, below).

The unemployment rate was officially stated to have fallen from a high of 18.8% in 1991, to 13% in 1997. Official figures also estimated the GDP growth rate in 1996 and 1997 as 5.2% and 5.3% respectively (above the regional average). In July 1998, however, external and internal pressure persuaded the Government to revise the figures to 1% and 2.5% respectively, whilst local economists estimated that GDP would actually fall in 1998. The revision in mid-1993 coincided with the increase in concern at the slow pace of privatization, resulting from the lack of clear and consistent government proposals, combined with strong parliamentary opposition to foreign ownership of Jordanian industries (see Industry and Mining, below).

THE REGIONAL PEACE PROCESS

A wide-ranging economic co-operation agreement between Jordan and the PLO was signed in Amman on 7 January 1994 to provide a framework for future approaches to specific issues 'as the peace process progresses'. It was agreed in principle that trade, investment, industry, agriculture, energy, water, electricity, telecommunications and private-sector enterprises were all fields of activity in which Jordan might be expected to co-operate closely with a developing PLO administration. It was predicted that Jordan could develop new trade flows of the order of $250m. to $500m. per year if Israel relinquished its dominant role in the Palestinian market.

On an issue of immediate concern to Jordan, the agreement in principle confirmed the Jordanian dinar as legal tender in the West Bank, gave the Central Bank of Jordan (CBJ) supervisory powers over Jordanian banks operating in the West Bank, and set up a joint Jordan-PLO committee to co-ordinate financial policy in the Occupied Territories.

A follow-up meeting in May 1994 re-examined the outlook for Jordanian-Palestinian co-operation in the light of a recently signed Israeli-Palestinian economic agreement which gave the Palestinian economy a measure of independence from Israel. The latter agreement's provision for the creation of a Palestinian Monetary Authority (PMA) had raised many questions in Jordan about the PMA's role and intended relationship with the CBJ. Jordan maintained that CBJ supervision of banking in the Occupied Territories was essential as long as the Jordanian currency was in use, in order to preserve control over the expansion of credit and ensure proper regulation of the money supply in Jordan. However, economists at the Palestinian Economic Council for Development and Reconstruction insisted that the PMA must assume a genuinely influential position within the regulatory process, and that key issues of bank licensing, currency management and payments administration should be examined in great detail before any binding agreements were concluded. Other topics discussed at this inconclusive meeting included trade, tariffs, tourism, transit rights and private Jordanian investment in the occupied territories.

In June 1994 Jordanian and Israeli delegations held two days of talks in Washington as part of the US-sponsored peace process, resulting in agreement in principle that all aspects of the emerging economic arrangements for the area needed to be discussed constructively between Jordan and Israel (and later in a tripartite forum with Palestinian representatives) with due regard for the long-term interests of all parties involved.

In January 1995 a Jordanian-Palestinian co-operation protocol was signed under which agreements were to be drawn up in areas of economic policy, trade, finance, banking, education, cultural affairs, transport, telecommunications, information and administration. Under the protocol the Palestine National Authority (PNA) undertook to accept the Jordanian dinar as legal tender in all official and private dealings and to use it 'to the fullest degree possible, pending the issue of the new Palestinian currency'. Neither Jordan nor the PNA would 'under any circumstances enforce any sudden unilateral monetary policy that would undermine the monetary stability and the economic security of either country'.

In March 1995 the PMA and the CBJ completed guidelines for an agreement on banking supervision in the West Bank and the Palestinian self-rule areas. Drawn up in consultation with the IMF, the guidelines confirmed the CBJ's predominant supervisory role in the self-rule areas until such times as the PMA developed its own expertise, while in the West Bank the CBJ's role would become liable to review in the context of any future Israeli-Palestinian agreement on a transfer of power. By the end of May 1995 seven Jordanian banks were operating a total of 32 branches in Gaza and the West Bank and others were in the process of establishing a presence. The level of direct local lending was as yet relatively low, partly because it was difficult for banks to organize loan security in the absence of a land registry and an established judicial framework, and it remained common practice for Palestinians with access to collateral in Jordan to obtain loans from bank branches within Jordan. In March 1996 the CBJ agreed to allow the PMA to invest about JD 55m. of its Jordanian dinar holdings in short-term debt instruments on the Amman market. In April 1996 the Jordanian Government set a target of $900m. for Jordan's foreign currency reserves, partly to allow for any future decision by the PMA to issue its own currency. At the time the target was announced Jordan's foreign reserves totalled around $500m., while a total of between $500m. and $800m. of savings in Jordanian dinars was believed to be held in the Palestinian territories.

In May 1995, as 'a first step towards a free-trade agreement', a detailed Palestinian-Jordanian trade accord was signed after three months of talks in which officials had had to heed the terms of an Israeli-Palestinian accord of April 1994 limiting the number of products the Palestinians could import from Jordan. The May 1995 accord covered trade in about 50 products, including cement, steel and electrical products. The Palestinians were permitted to export 25 categories of product to Jordan free of customs duties and import fees and another 25 free of customs duties only, all the products being ultimately subject to Jordan's sales tax. About 50 Jordanian product categories were exempted from Palestinian customs duties but were subject to the levies payable on locally produced products. In the first two months after the signing of the accord, Palestinian-Jordanian trade was worth about $8m. In June 1995 Jordan and the PNA signed an agreement guaranteeing freedom of movement by land and air for nationals and vehicles from both sides (although in practice control over the border between Jordan and the West Bank remained in Israel's hands at this time).

The Jordan-Israel peace treaty signed on 26 October 1994 included a number of economic provisions. Each country recognized the other's 'rightful allocation' of water resources from the Jordan and Yarmouk rivers and the Araba groundwater source and agreed to co-operate in the management and development of existing and potential water resources. Economic relations were to be normalized by removing discriminatory barriers and ending economic boycotts, and talks 'aimed at establishing a free trade area' were to be organized at an early date. There was to be free cross-border movement of nationals and vehicles, and talks were to be held about the building of a highway between Egypt, Jordan and Israel near Eilat. Arrangements on freedom of navigation and access to seaports were to be normalized, a civil aviation agreement was to be drawn up, and an international air corridor was to be negotiated. Both countries would work for the creation of a Jordan Rift Valley development master plan. Talks would be held on the joint development of the towns of Aqaba and Eilat, including the interconnection of their electricity grids. Co-operation agreements would be drawn up covering tourism, posts and telecommunications, environmental issues, energy, health and agriculture.

Agreements on border crossings, tourism and security were initialled in February 1995 and agreements on agriculture, energy and the environment in May 1995. Topics covered by the draft energy agreement included the transit of neighbouring states' oil and gas, trade in oil and gas products, and exchange of information on oil exploration. Negotiations on trade were deadlocked in mid-1995 because Jordan and Israel disagreed over the wording of a preferential trade agreement. Israel favoured an agreement incorporating a stated goal of free trade within 12 years, whereas Jordan did not at this point wish to commit itself to a specific timetable for achieving free trade, preferring to defer a decision until a preferential trading system had been in operation for three years.

An annex to the October 1994 treaty specified that Jordan should receive 215m. cu m of water per year from resources currently controlled by Israel and outlined means of achieving this aim. A joint Jordan-Israel water committee began to meet weekly from November 1994, when it agreed to prioritize the building of a 3.3-km-pipeline to transfer up to 30m. cu m of water per year from Lake Tiberias in Israel to the King Abdullah canal in Jordan. The newly completed pipeline was brought into operation on 20 June 1995. It was agreed in February 1995 to initiate a feasibility study for a dam on the Yarmouk river which would restrict the annual flow of water to Israel from this source to 25m. cu m, leaving the remainder available to Jordan. Also under consideration was a scheme to build a storage facility and conveyer system at the confluence of the Yarmouk and Jordan rivers. In 1996 Israel delivered a total of 31.5m. cu m of water (1.5% of Israel's water supply) to Jordan. A commitment to build a desalination plant to the west of Lake Tiberias to treat salty spring water remained unfulfilled in 1998 because of difficulties in drawing up an agreement on the division of financial contributions and operational responsibilities. Under an interim arrangement introduced in May 1997, Israel began pumping fresh water to Jordan in lieu of the projected supply from the delayed desalination plant. Jordan reportedly claimed an entitlement to 30m. cu m per year under this arrangement, whereas Israel maintained that the arrangement covered a maximum of 25m. cu m per year.

Israel and Jordan signed a transport agreement on 16 January 1996 which included provisions for the direct transfer of goods from Jordan to the Palestinian territories and for Palestinian access to the port of Aqaba. Agreements relating to the normalization of other aspects of Jordanian–Israeli economic relations (including definition of the maritime boundary at the Gulf of Aqaba) were signed on 18 January 1996. Commercial air services between Jordan and Israel began in April 1996, as did tourist bus services, with public bus services starting up in the following month and road haulage of goods in late June. It was, however, apparent in early July that Israel was in breach of an undertaking to grant visas to Jordanians within five days of receiving their applications. In 1996 Israel exported $12.25m. worth of goods to Jordan and imported $7.75m. worth of goods from Jordan. Israeli and Jordanian ministers met in June 1997 to discuss border-crossing problems and other obstacles to trade. In September, in a measure which was designed to reduce non-tariff barriers between the two countries, Israel announced a doubling of its quota of cement imports from Jordan, to 30,000 tons per year.

At further high-level meetings in March 1998 Jordan and Israel agreed to expand co-operation in the development of water resources and storage facilities in the Jordan Valley, to accelerate plans for the inter-connection of the electricity grid between Aqaba and Eilat, and to develop joint solar and wind energy projects. The two sides also agreed to examine joint tourism projects in the Wadi Araba and Umm Qais regions, and the feasibility of a canal between the Red and Dead Seas. Bilateral trade between Jordan and Israel in 1997 was valued at $31m. by Jordan, and at $32.5m. by Israel.

AGRICULTURE

The loss of the relatively fertile West Bank in the 1967 war, and subsequent events on the East Bank, caused major disruption to the agricultural sector, which was compounded by severe drought conditions from 1974 to late 1979. In the 1980s, however, major investment in irrigation, particularly in the Jordan Valley, began to show results, and agricultural output increased by an average of 6% per year in 1980–88, owing mainly to the rapid expansion in the output of vegetables and of dairy and poultry products, much of it exported. Whereas the 1981–85 Five-Year Plan had originally envisaged a decline in agriculture's share of GDP from 8.5% to 7.2%, non-attainment of industrial growth targets in that period, combined with greater emphasis on agricultural expansion in the 1986–90 Plan, in fact resulted in agriculture's retaining an average 10% share of GDP through the 1980s, although the proportion later fell to 8% in 1990, and to less than 7% in 1991 and 1992. Under the 1986–90 Plan, increases in the output of cereals, red meat and dairy produce were the major targets, and spending on agricultural projects was estimated at JD 337m. (about 10% of total investment), supplemented by JD 130m. for dam construction and JD 105m. for irrigation. A specific objective was to reduce the share of food imports (mainly cereals) in domestic consumption, which in the late 1970s had risen to 66% and in the late 1980s remained above 50%. In the 1980s migration away from the agricultural sector reduced its importance as an employer within the economy: in the late 1970s approximately 18% of the labour force were employed in agriculture, but by the late 1980s the proportion had declined to 10%.

A contrast can be drawn between the rain-fed upland zone (comprising about 90% of the cultivable land) and the irrigated Jordan Valley, which, since 1973, has been subject to its own development plan. As a result of irrigation and the production of high-value crops, the productivity of the Jordan Valley is far higher than that of the uplands, where cultivation is concentrated mainly on wheat and barley. Before the Jordan Valley Development Plan, only about 10% of the country's land was considered suitable for cultivation because of the low rainfall and vast areas of desert or semi-desert. The Jordan Valley, with its more favourable sub-tropical climate and available water, has been intensively exploited by small farmers who, using plasticulture and drip irrigation, obtained huge increases in production (particularly of fruit and vegetables). The development of irrigation in the Jordan Valley began in 1958, and between then and 1963 work on the East Ghor canal, carrying water from the Yarmouk river and running parallel to the

Jordan, added about 120,000 ha to the country's irrigated area. The installations were severely damaged by Israeli bombardment in 1967 and repairs were not carried out until after the 1970–71 civil war. Stage I of the Jordan Valley Development Plan, funded by a great variety of foreign aid bodies, finished at the end of 1979. Irrigation projects centred mainly on the extension of the East Ghor canal and the Zarqa river complex. The King Talal dam was constructed between 1972 and 1978, the East Ghor canal extended between 1975 and 1978, and the Zarqa Triangle Irrigation Project finished in 1978. Other irrigation works include the Hisban Kafrein project, constructed between 1976 and 1978, and the North-East Ghor complex. Many of the irrigation projects undertaken in the second stage of the Plan have been completed or are under implementation. Projects under way include the construction of the Wadi al-Arab dam, the raising of the King Talal dam, the extension of the 98-km East Ghor main canal, and the irrigation of 4,700 ha in the Southern Ghor (see below). The Jordan Valley Development scheme is, however, more than just a complex of irrigation projects, and includes the development of transport links, grading, packing and marketing centres, the development of schools and health centres, and also a housing programme. In 1981 the Jordan Valley Authority (JVA) was responsible for 22,000 ha of irrigated land. The use of plastic tunnels, greenhouses and drip-irrigation has greatly expanded within the valley and by 1978 6,000 dunums (1 dunum = 1,000 sq m) had plastic tunnels and 741 dunums had greenhouses. Most of the JD 42m. allocated to agricultural development in the 1976–80 Five-Year Plan was to be used for development of the valley. As well as irrigation, crop-raising has also been improved by the introduction of special strains of seed, inorganic fertilizers and mechanization.

Attempts to alleviate the critical problems of water supply, most recently highlighted by severe drought in 1984 (the worst for 37 years), have been given high priority by the Government. Developments begun by the JVA in 1983 include the beginning of the second phase of the Southern Ghor project, costing JD 30m., which involves the construction of a diversion weir on the Mujib river and the building of a 3.5-km canal to irrigate 4,000 ha. A dam is to be constructed in Wadi Hasa, at Tanur, to store water which will be used to irrigate the upland area to the east of the Jordan Valley. In 1983 work started on the $50m. project to raise the height of the King Talal dam by 16 m to 108 m. This has increased the capacity of the dam to 85m.–90m. cu m and, in addition to the construction of a 2.5-MW hydroelectric power station, has enabled 8,200 ha to be irrigated. Following the discovery of a major artesian well, estimated to be capable of producing 75m. cu m of water per year, at al-Muhaibeh in the north during 1982, an 11.6-km canal was rapidly constructed to take the water to join the East Ghor canal at Adasiya. This was opened in March 1983 at a cost of JD 3m. South Korea's Hanbo Corpn, who built this canal, are also constructing a dam of 20m. cu m capacity in the Wadi al-Arab, which will cost JD 17m. The dam is part of the Wadi al-Arab irrigation project, which began in early 1986 and is planned to increase the irrigated area between Wadi al-Arab, the Yarmouk river and the Jordan Valley by 2,800 ha. Elsewhere in the country, the National Resources Authority drilled 54 wells in 1982 in its search for new supplies of water. In 1989 the Ministry of Water and Irrigation announced plans to invest $20m. in a water exploration project in southern Jordan. It was estimated that by the year 2000 daily consumption of water per person (for all purposes) would rise to 300 litres.

The largest of 18 new agricultural projects to be started is a scheme to develop 830,000 dunums in the Zarqa river catchment area, at an estimated cost of JD 18.6m. The Water Authority of Jordan was established in 1984, and JD 521.7m. of the 1981–85 Development Plan budget was allocated to increase the irrigated area by 180,000 dunums. One of the major schemes for the 1980s was to have been the construction of the Maqarin dam and an associated hydroelectric power station on the Yarmouk river. However, plans for the dam were deferred. Under the 1986–90 Plan, an additional 114,000 dunums (11,400 ha) were to be brought under irrigation in the Jordan Valley, the Southern Ghor and the Wadi al-Arab. The Maqarin dam project was revived in 1988 as the al-Wahdeh ('Unity') dam and hydroelectric power station scheme, a joint Jordanian-Syrian venture to build a dam 100 m high on the Yarmouk river, to store 225m. cu m of water for drinking, irrigation and electricity generation. Plans were finalized in September 1988. Concern was expressed that the cost of building the dam was to be borne exclusively by Jordan but water stored therein was to be used to irrigate both Jordanian and Syrian land and 78% of the electricity to be generated by the dam was to be taken by Syria. The official estimate of the project's cost is $230m., compared with $450m. allocated in the 1975–80 Plan, and independent estimates of $300m.–$500m. In mid-1990 Jordan was seeking assistance from Arab and Islamic organizations in financing the al-Wahdeh dam.

Programmes initiated in 1991 included the North Ghor Conversion Project, involving the conversion of 7,300 ha in the Jordan Valley from surface to pressurized irrigation (with a consequential 20% water saving) at an estimated cost of $25m.–$30m., of which 80% was to be provided by Japan. Final preparations were under way in 1993 to implement a programme to raise the storage capacity of the Kafrein dam on the Jordan river, from 4.3m. cu m to 7.5m. cu m, and to construct new dams at Walah, Mujib, Karameh and Tannour. The overall goal of this programme was to create a total of 115m. cu m of additional storage capacity by 1996, at an estimated cost of over $200m. The Kafrein dam project, and an associated scheme to reduce leakage from irrigation canals, was expected to bring an additional 1,830 ha of land into cultivation.

In early 1992 a series of contracts for water projects included the Marhib wells scheme, involving the pumping of water from the wells to the existing Marhib and Awaja reservoirs and to a projected new reservoir at Berain. There was a further project to research water-harvesting at Muwaqar, east of Amman.

Describing the water supply outlook in early 1993, the Secretary-General of the Water Authority of Jordan said that 60% of current supply came from groundwater reserves, mainly in the desert areas in the east of the country; that farmers currently used two-thirds of Jordan's total water supply; and that the total supply was expected to increase from 550m. cu m per year to 700m. cu m per year during the decade 1990 to 2000, over which period the underlying level of annual demand was expected to rise from 900m. cu m to 1,600m. cu m, necessitating increasingly harsh restrictions on water use (already rationed for up to seven months of the year). He added that there was considerable scope for improving the efficiency of water use in the agricultural sector (e.g. by discouraging diversification into water-intensive crops like bananas, which currently provided farmers with higher profit margins than crops requiring far less irrigation).

Details of Jordan's water development strategy to the year 2011, which was published by the Government in November 1997, listed 61 projects, involving total investment of some $5,000m. The strategy was based on a projected growth in water consumption from 1,451m. cu m in 1995 to 1,720m. cu m in 2010, of which agriculture would account for a constant share of 1,088m. cu m. Even taking account of the new projects, Jordan's water deficit for all users was expected to increase from 220 cu m in 1995 to 250 cu m by 2011. Efforts to meet future needs would include the development of new ground water resources (including the Disi aquifer in southern Jordan), the transfer of water from Israel in accordance with the 1994 peace treaty, and the construction of new dams and desalination projects. In the last respect, the programme represented a departure from Jordan's previous rejection of the desalination option as too expensive.

Cereals, fruit and vegetables are the mainstays of Jordan's agriculture. Production levels vary widely, depending on the prevailing weather conditions. For example, after 1974 (a record year) yields of wheat and barley (which is used as animal fodder) were severely reduced, owing to drought, so that by 1979, despite similar areas being under cultivation, wheat production on the East Bank fell to what was then a record low of only 16,500 tons. As a result of the rains in November 1979, there was a great increase in the cultivated area and, following the excellent harvest produced in 1980, the government banned imports of wheat, barley and lentils, and paid farmers almost double the normal price for imports. Field crop production rose appreciably from 32,400 tons in 1979 to 204,000 tons in 1980. In January 1980 the King Talal dam was full for the first time since

its completion in 1978. In addition, the heavy rainfall also replenished depleting groundwater resources. Towards the end of 1980 grain storage was also greatly improved with the opening of new silos at Aqaba, with a storage capacity of 50,000 tons. The 1981 harvest, though, was 60% down on that of 1980, with a wheat production of 50,600 tons and barley, 19,200 tons. The 1982 harvest was generally worse and production in subsequent years continued to fluctuate as conditions alternated between rainfall and drought. Following favourable winter rains, annual production of wheat reached 80,000 tons in 1987/88 and in 1988/89. Although this was a relatively high yield, compared with the all-time low of less than 10,000 tons in 1983/84, it was still less than one-quarter of Jordan's annual requirement of 450,000 tons, which by 1990 had risen to 500,000 tons. The barley crop reached 40,000 tons in 1988/89, compared with an all-time low of 3,500 tons in 1983/84. Jordan continued to rely heavily on imports of food, which cost about $400m. per year (JD 155.7m.– $450m.– in 1987). Wheat consumption reached 627,000 tons in 1993 (50% higher than in 1988), owing partly to the increase in population after the Kuwait crisis and partly to Jordan's low bread prices.

The loss of the West Bank had a serious effect on cereal production, but its effect on fruit and vegetable cultivation was disastrous, removing some 80% of the fruit-growing area and 45% of the area under vegetables, and depriving Jordan of an important and expanding source of some of its major export commodities. Production of fruit and vegetables on the East Bank fluctuated widely in the 1970s, partly because of the weather and partly as a result of political instability. However, the general trend recently has been for increases in fruit and vegetable production, particularly in citrus fruits, tomatoes, melons and cucumbers. Between 1973 and 1986, overall vegetable production increased by 149%, fruit production by 546% and field crops by 88%, according to the US Agency for International Development. Under the 1986–90 Plan, up to 200,000 dunums (20,000 ha) of government land in southern and eastern Jordan were to be cultivated for the first time to produce cereals, forage and red meat, while output of fruit was set to increase as areas planted since 1979 began to produce. Increases in fruit and vegetable production, however, were not matched by a corresponding development in the areas of sales and marketing. The country was also faced with the problem of excessive production of tomatoes, cucumbers and aubergines, which cost the Ministry of Agriculture substantial sums each year in support for growers who could not sell their produce. In early 1985 the Ministry introduced an optional cropping system for irrigated vegetable growing. Under the system, farmers could be fined if they exceeded their allocation of tomato production, and the maximum production of tomatoes for 1985 was fixed at 242,000 tons, 158,000 tons less than production in 1984. Emphasis has been placed on the growing of other crops and Jordan is now self-sufficient in potatoes and 80% self-sufficient in onions. The establishment of a government-owned public marketing organization (the Agricultural Marketing and Processing Co) to handle agricultural produce, which had been decided on in March 1983, was achieved in 1984.

Production of fruit and vegetables increased in the late 1980s, as did exports, especially after the devaluation of the currency in 1988. Moreover, the signature of the Iran–Iraq cease-fire agreement of August 1988 led to a rapid expansion of deliveries to Iraq, Kuwait and other gulf markets. A record 522,000 tons of vegetables were exported in the 1989/90 season, and a further record of 650,000 tons had been anticipated in 1990/91, before trade was disrupted by the latest Gulf crisis in August 1990. The value of vegetable exports in 1991 was JD 43.5m., compared with JD 36.8m. in 1990 and JD 27.9m. in 1989.

In a crisis-induced move to increase domestic agricultural production, the Government decided in November 1990 to offer unused state-owned land for lease at a rent of JD 1 per dunum. Another measure affecting farmers was the enactment, in December 1990, of a law specifying that women could inherit only half as much land as their brothers could, rather than an equal share. The Government explained that equal shares for women, which had been guaranteed under legislation dating from the Ottoman period, was contrary to Islamic law.

The Jordanian Minister of Agriculture said in January 1993 that dependence on uncertain rainfall patterns had helped to engender a 'low-risk' approach to farming, and that higher levels of productivity could be achieved if Jordan improved its standards of resource management. Endorsing the findings of a policy study drawn up with FAO assistance, he accepted that there had been excessive state regulation of agriculture in the past, and that farmers' interests would be better served if the Government devoted itself more to broad policy-making and co-ordination. He advocated a further shift from cereals into the growing of 'off-season' vegetables for export; criticized the spread of restrictive trade policies in many export markets; and proposed an expansion of local food-processing capacity to provide new market outlets for farmers, particularly those producing highly perishable commodities.

The aggregate value of agricultural output rose from JD 213.3m. in 1995 to JD 232.9m. in 1996, and to JD 250.5m. in 1997. Among field crops, production of wheat increased to 58,500 tons in 1995 but fell to 42,700 tons in 1996, while barley production fell to 29,200 tons in 1996 (from 31,700 tons in 1995). Of the vegetable crops, production of tomatoes fell sharply from 439,700 tons in 1995 to 291,300 tons in 1996, whereas output of melons, potatoes and cucumbers remained relatively stable in 1996, at 106,400, 95,200 and 74,200 tons respectively. In the tree fruits' category, citrus fruits remained the most important, with production of 133,100 tons in 1996, followed by olives, at 88,600 tons. Under the livestock heading, output of eggs totalled 726m. in 1996 (compared with 871m. in 1994 and 715m. in 1995); milk production increased to 165,100 tons (from 147,000 tons in 1995); and poultry-meat output fell to 100,000 tons (from 107,000 tons in 1995). The value of Jordan's exports of agricultural produce (including oil and fats) rose from JD 224.5m. in 1996 to JD 268.0m. in 1997, with live animals and vegetables forming the two largest categories. Imports of agricultural produce (including oil and fats) were valued at JD 636.3m. in 1997, significantly less than the 1996 value of JD 759.6m.

INDUSTRY AND MINING

Manufacturing industry, which is almost entirely of recent origin, is concentrated around Amman (following the loss of the Nablus industrial centre on the West Bank in 1967). During the 1976–80 Plan period, it experienced an average growth rate of 13.6% per annum, which was only one-half of the planned rate. Moreover, the targets of the 1981–85 Plan period, during which manufacturing and mining were, together, expected to achieve an annual growth rate of 17.8%, fell even further short of being achieved. By 1990, according to World Bank figures, industry (including mining, manufacturing, construction and power) still contributed only 26% of GDP (compared with 66% from services and 8% from agriculture). Industrial investment in 1993 totalled JD 271m., up from JD 161m. in 1992, and remained buoyant in the first half of 1994, helping to allay Jordanian concern about the possible diversion of new investment to the West Bank and Gaza. The majority of factories produce food products, clothing or consumer goods but the major industrial income derives from the three heavier industries—phosphate extraction, cement manufacture and petroleum refining.

In a country which is short of natural resources, Jordan's mineral wealth lies predominantly in its phosphate reserves, which are estimated at more than 2,000m. tons, providing the country with its main export commodity, accounting for 24.5% of export value in 1987. The proportion was 40% in 1983 but later returns were affected by the low world price for phosphates. Jordan is the fifth largest producer of phosphate rock, after the USA, the countries of the former USSR, Morocco and the People's Republic of China, and the third largest exporter, after Morocco and the USA. The mining and marketing of phosphate is handled by the Jordan Phosphate Mines Co (JPMC). The expansion of the phosphate industry has been a major element in successive Development Plans. Quantities of uranium and vanadium are now known to be mixed in with the phosphate reserves. There are also known to be deposits of good-quality copper ore at Wadi Arabeh. Other minerals include gypsum, manganese ore, abundant quantities of glass sand and the clays and feldspar required for manufacturing ceramics. Foreign investors have been found to finance the establishment of companies to produce ceramics and sheet glass and also to exploit

potash deposits in the Dead Sea. The Arab Potash Co (APC), formed in 1956 as one of the earliest Arab joint ventures, is 57% owned by the Jordanian Government. The company was reconstituted in 1983 and produced 486,868 tons of potash in 1984, its first full year of operation, selling 450,000 tons, worth $36.4m. In 1986 production reached 1.1m. tons, compared with 932,000 tons and revenue of $77m. in 1985. In 1990 the APC recorded its first profit (of JD 39.6m.) since it began commercial operations in 1983. In 1996 the annual capacity of the APC's Ghor as-Safi extraction plant on the Dead Sea totalled 1.8m. tons, comprising 1.4m. tons of hot leach capacity and 400,000 tons of cold crystallization capacity. It was planned to add a further 200,000 tons of cold crystallization capacity by 1999. In 1996 the APC made a net profit of JD 34.2m. on sales of JD 131.3m. Production in 1996 totalled 1.76m. tons. The company's main markets in 1996 were India (27.5% of sales); the European Union (19.7%); Korea (9.3%); and Malaysia (9%).

Diversification plans under active consideration by the APC in 1993 included a salt plant on the Dead Sea with a capacity of 1.2m. tons of industrial salt and 31,000 tons of table salt per year; a chemical plant at Aqaba with a capacity of 75,000 tons of potassium sulphate and 50,000 tons of dicalcium phosphate; a $140m.-scheme to produce bromine derivatives from the Dead Sea (the world's richest bromine lake); and a plant to produce 50,000 tons of magnesium oxide per year. The APC holds a 20% interest in a joint-venture project set up in 1993 in partnership with a Japanese consortium (60%) and the JPMC (20%). The project involves the establishment of plant at Aqaba to produce 300,000 tons of compound fertilizers and ammonium phosphates per year, the fertilizers to be produced using 80,000 tons of potash and 50,000 tons of imported ammonia. By mid-1997 the Jordan Dead Sea Salt Company had started production, while other proposed projects were undergoing detailed evaluation.

Rich beds of phosphates exist at Rusaifa, a few kilometres north-east of Amman, and, from 1963 onwards, were exploited by a local company financed partly by the Government. Other deposits in the Wadi Hasa area, south of Amman, have been developed by US and Italian interests, and phosphates are also produced at Wadi al-Abyad. For many years production was centred on these three sites. However, in mid-1985 the JPMC was forced to close its Rusaifa mine because of falling demand for low-grade phosphate. In the longer term, the industry will focus on a major new, low-cost, mine at Shidiya, near Ma'an, in the south-east, which the JPMC is developing in two stages. The World Bank is contributing $31m. to the $71m. first stage and a further $25m. loan was announced in February 1990. The Shidiya mine has proven phosphate reserves of 1,200m. tons, and started production in the second half of 1988.

In 1968 the country's total production of natural phosphates was 1,162,000 tons, more than five times the production in 1956. By 1976 annual production exceeded 1.76m. tons. Export earnings from phosphates, constant in 1974 and 1975 at JD 19.5m., dropped to JD 19.2m. in 1976. This was due to a fall in the international price of phosphate rock and prompted Jordan in 1976 to join with Morocco, Tunisia and Senegal in an association of phosphate exporters. In 1985, when the Rusaifa mine was closed, output totalled 5.92m. tons. At the beginning of 1986 the JPMC secured a 10-year contract with Thailand to supply 650,000 tons of phosphates per year. Phosphates output rose to 6.25m. tons (exports 5.2m. tons) in 1986 and 6.7m. tons (exports 5.7m. tons) in 1987. Production in 1988 was 6.5m. tons (exports 5.5m. tons). Revenue from exports of phosphates amounted to $262m. in 1988, compared with $176m. in 1986. In 1989 the JPMC exported 6.4m. tons of phosphates and reported profits of JD 107.2m., but in 1990 exports decreased to 4.9m. tons and profits to JD 41.4m. (compared with a target of JD 108m.). While the Gulf crisis contributed to this decline in 1990, its major cause was a sharp fall in demand in Eastern Europe, exports to which were only 580,000 tons, compared with 2m. tons in 1989. By 1992 the JPMC's phosphate exports amounted to only 4.26m. tons (out of its total production of 5.2m. tons), although the company's share of the shrinking world market was, at 15.2%, slightly higher than before. The value of exports in 1992 was JD 206.1m. ($300m.), while the JPMC's net profit was JD 16.1m. In 1993 the JPMC recorded a loss of JD 20m., but was able to achieve a profit of JD 2.3m. in 1994 after reducing stock levels and introducing cost-cutting measures. In 1995 the company made a profit of JD 4.1m. on sales of JD 237m. Its largest phosphate export markets in 1995 were India (1.2m. tons), Indonesia (543,000 tons) and the Netherlands (448,000 tons). In 1996 the JPMC made a net profit of JD 15.8m. on sales of JD 254m. In April 1997 JPMC shareholders approved a plan to raise $100m. through the international capital markets in order to finance part of the cost of a $250m. expansion programme at the Shidiya mine, designed to raise the mine's annual capacity to nearly 8m. tons by 1998.

Allied industries form an important part of Jordan's industrial development programme. A $400m.-phosphate fertilizer plant south of Aqaba began production in June 1982. The 1981–85 Five-Year Plan allocated JD 15m. to the development of the plant. It was designed to produce 750,000 tons of diammonium phosphate and 105,000 tons of phosphoric acid per year, but has failed to produce to more than 65% of its phosphoric acid capacity. The plant is now undergoing restructuring to take production beyond present design capacity. The original project, which was managed by the Jordan Fertilizer Industries Co (JFIC), cost $410m. and included an aluminium fluoride plant with an annual capacity of 12,000 tons, which entered production in mid-1984. The JFIC made a JD 12.9m. loss in 1984, its first full year of trading, owing to a slump in world fertilizer prices; production reached 568,968 tons, of which 524,900 tons were sold. However, in 1986 the JPMC bought the JFIC (which had accumulated losses of JD 40.3m. by the end of 1985) for JD 60m. A loss of JD 1.3m. ($1.9m.) at the Aqaba plant in 1992 was attributed by the JPMC partly to depressed world prices (blamed on dumping by US and Russian producers), and partly to the plant's high staffing level.

The JPMC's plans for future 'downstream' development are centred on joint ventures with foreign partners who would provide investment funds and guarantee long-term export markets. The ventures would be designated as 'free-zone' industries in order to allow foreign majority participation. The Indo-Jordan Chemicals Co (60% Southern Petrochemical Industries Corpn of India, 40% JPMC) was established in 1993 to set up a plant at Shidiya capable of producing 200,000 tons of phosphoric acid from an annual input of 750,000 tons of rock phosphate, to create a 20,000-ton storage facility at Aqaba, and to export the acid to India for on-processing into fertilizer. A similar scheme was under discussion in 1993 with Fauji Fertilizer of Pakistan to produce sufficient phosphoric acid in Jordan to support annual production of 445,000 tons of diammonium phosphate and 346,000 tons of urea in Pakistan. It was envisaged that the Jordanian end of this project would be developed in parallel with the Indo-Jordan venture.

Jordan is almost wholly dependent on imports of crude petroleum for its energy needs. Its main sources, before the onset of the Gulf crisis in August 1990, were Iraq and Saudi Arabia, the former having replaced the latter as Jordan's main supplier in the late 1980s. Output of petroleum products from Jordan's only oil refinery, at Zarqa, increased steadily from 445,800 tons in 1970 to 748,000 tons in 1974, and to 1,114,600 tons in 1976. Production capacity was scheduled to reach 3.5m. tons per year by the end of 1979. This would have been more than sufficient to satisfy Jordan's domestic requirements. In 1980 the refinery, in fact, produced only 1,760,000 tons, but by 1982 it had an output capacity of 3m. tons per year (60,000 b/d). Between 1982 and 1984, maximum daily throughput was raised to 12,300 tons (about 86,000 b/d), an annual capacity of about 4.3m. tons, probably enough to satisfy domestic demand until 2000. In 1985, when the refinery's capacity was raised to 5m. tons (100,000 b/d), output rose to 2.6m. tons, compared with 2.3m. tons in 1984. Of this total, 1.8m. tons came from Saudi Arabia, 698,600 tons from Iraq and 2,800 tons from Jordan's Hamzah oilfield. In addition, 10,000 tons of LPG and 395,000 tons of fuel oil were imported from Iraq for domestic needs. The country's oil import bill was $8m. in 1974, but higher prices and greater domestic consumption caused the cost to increase to $540m. in 1983, and to $610m. in 1984. Under an agreement designed to relieve pressure on reserves of foreign exchange, Jordan imported from Iraq, in payment for goods, about one-sixth of its crude oil requirements in 1984 and 395,000 tons of fuel oil in 1985. Imports of crude petroleum amounted to 2.5m. tons, averaging 48,743 b/d, in 1988. Of this, 33,415 b/d was imported from Iraq and 15,000 b/d from Saudi Arabia.

In an attempt to reduce petroleum imports, attention has been given to the possibility of exploiting the estimated 40,000m. tons of shale oil deposits in the south of the country. Consequently, in September 1980 an agreement was signed with Technopromexport of the USSR for an oil-shale survey at Lajjoun. By the end of 1983 15 of the 55 wells to be drilled, to extract the oil from the shale, were reported to have been finished. In March 1984 the Qarma One oil-well, in the field near Azraq, was reported to be producing at a rate of 600 b/d. In November 1984 a Ministry of Energy and Mineral Resources was created, and in the following month the Government announced a plan to double investment in oil exploration, following promising oil strikes in the Azraq area on the border with Iraq and Saudi Arabia, and to reduce oil consumption by cutting oil subsidies and by increasing the prices of electricity and petroleum-based products. However, no commercial oil discoveries were made in the late 1980s, while production from the Azraq area declined to 315 b/d in 1988 and to only 40 b/d by mid-1990. Over this period, the cost of imported oil declined in relative terms, owing to reductions in world prices and to the availability of Iraqi oil at preferential prices.

The deferment, in 1985, of plans to construct a pipeline to convey crude petroleum from Iraq to Aqaba contributed to the decision to renew an agreement to receive Saudi Arabian crude petroleum, via the Trans-Arabian Pipeline (Tapline), at the Zarqa refinery. Tapline had been due to close in November 1983 and, again, in 1985. Transit dues rose threefold, however, and the total annual cost of the agreement to Jordan was calculated at $26m. In mid-1985 the Jordanian Ports Corpn awarded a $20m.-contract to Sosema Matex (a consortium of international firms) for the construction and management of an oil terminal at Aqaba port. The terminal consists of a permanently docked oil tanker, capable of exporting 7,000 b/d–10,000 b/d, and became operational before the end of 1985. In July 1990 Jordan opened talks on the construction of a new pipeline linking the Iraq-Saudi Arabia Petroline with Tapline, which would save Jordan the $50m. per year that it spent on importing Iraqi oil by road tanker. However, the subsequent Gulf conflict resulted in the suspension of this plan, at least temporarily.

At the outbreak of the Gulf crisis in August 1990, Jordan was importing more than 80% of its oil requirements from Iraq, with almost all the remainder coming from Saudi Arabia. When Jordan, in late August, announced its acceptance of the UN trade embargo on Iraq, Saudi Arabia pledged itself to supply at least half of Jordan's oil needs through Tapline. However, Jordan's reluctance to apply the UN embargo resulted in Saudi Arabia's suspension of all oil supplies to Jordan in late September (the official reason given was non-payment of outstanding oil bills of $46m.). Jordan accordingly became entirely dependent on Iraqi supplies by road tanker, which rose to some 60,000 b/d by mid-January 1991. The start of hostilities then resulted in the virtual cessation of such supplies, obliging Jordan to impose petrol rationing and to conclude emergency agreements to import oil from Yemen and Syria (at a higher price than the preferential rate charged by Iraq). In April 1991 it was announced that Iraqi supplies to Jordan would be resumed, but the after-effects of the war in Iraq were expected to inhibit normal trade for some time. Official Jordanian figures, issued in April 1991, showed that Iraq had supplied 86% (2.3m. tons) of Jordan's oil imports in 1990, and Saudi Arabia 13.2%, and that the Zarqa refinery had processed 2.7m. tons in the year, an increase of 11% over the 1989 level. Jordan's domestic oil production remained minimal, although it rose to 120,000 barrels in 1990, compared with 75,000 barrels in 1989. In mid-1993 the only commercial oil exploration activity was being carried out by Hanbo Corpn of South Korea. Some state-funded exploration was being undertaken by the Natural Resources Authority.

In March 1995 the Government approved the establishment of a National Petroleum Co to be owned by the Jordan Investment Corpn (JIC). The JIC would contribute JD 2m. of working capital, while the new company would take over ownership of JD 18m.-worth of oil and gas exploration and production equipment from the National Resources Authority. Half of the Government's $10m. per year revenues from the ar-Risha gas field would be used to fund the new company's initial activities. The company would function as an independent entity, with no government involvement in day-to-day management, and would be free to co-operate with foreign oil companies. State investment in hydrocarbon exploration in Jordan in the period 1980 to 1994 had amounted to $300m. In March 1996 two US companies, Andarko Petroleum Corpn and Trans Global Resources, signed agreements to explore for oil and gas in Jordan. In February 1997 another US company, Union Texas Petroleum, reached an agreement with Andarko to take a 50% interest in Andarko's 4.2m.-acre Safawi exploration block in north-eastern Jordan. Proposals were announced in the first half of 1995 to develop a 250,000 b/d-export refinery at Aqaba, to be located in a free zone and financed and operated by foreign investors, with the Government receiving a royalty on exported oil and a discount on prices of any refined products supplied to Jordan. Following the withdrawal of a US company which had signed a preliminary agreement in 1996, new bids were invited in 1997 for a modified scheme with 210,00 b/d of capacity, to be developed on a 'build-own-operate' basis. The Jordan Petroleum Refining Co, whose monopoly rights to supply refined products within Jordan were valid until 2008, was drawing up plans in 1997 to upgrade and expand its Zarqa refinery. It was estimated that an investment of $500m. would be required to diversify the refinery's product range and increase its total capacity to 140,000 b/d by 2002.

The discovery of reserves of natural gas at locations around ar-Risha in north-east Jordan in 1987 and 1988 encouraged speculation that the deposits would be sufficient to satisfy a significant proportion of Jordan's energy requirements in the future. By 1989 gas from the new discoveries was fuelling a 60-MW electricity generating plant at ar-Risha, employing two 30-MW gas turbines (ultimately to rise to six, producing 180 MW), which is connected to the main grid by a 220-km high-voltage transmission line. The plant was supplying 15% of national power requirements by 1990, when plans were announced to transfer to it two turbines from the South Amman station, with the aim of increasing its capacity to 25% of national power requirements. Domestic gas production in 1990 rose to 340m. cu m (compared with 160m. cu m in 1989). Production capacity at the ar-Risha field was due to reach 475m. cu m per year in mid-1993.

Jordan also has a thermal power station at Aqaba, which currently consists of two 130-MW oil-fired steam units, and is undergoing a $75m.-expansion with the addition of two more 130-MW units capable of burning coal as well as oil, which will give a potential reduction in operating costs of 28% when the scheme is completed. A 400-kV transmission line, extending for 320 km, has been constructed, joining the power plant to Amman. In April 1996 the Government announced a 12% increase in electricity charges for consumers using more than 160 kWh of electricity per month. A link between the Egyptian and Jordanian electricity grids (the first phase of a regional inter-connection project supported by the Arab Fund for Economic and Social Development) was due to be completed by the end of 1997. Arrangements were being finalized in 1997 for the start of work on a link between the Jordanian and Syrian grids. In September 1996 the Jordan Electricity Authority was superseded by the state-owned National Electric Power Company (Nepco), established with a share capital of JD 230m. The assets transferred to Nepco had an estimated value of JD 270m. Jordan's electricity supply legislation had earlier been amended to encourage future private-sector participation, and it was government policy to seek private finance for all new power generation projects. Jordan's installed generating capacity in 1997 totalled 1,268 MW.

Cement production reached 964,300 tons in 1981. Within the 1981–85 Plan, 37% of the money allocated to mining and manufacturing was set aside for four cement projects, including the construction of a cement works in the south, at Rashidiya. The existing plant at Fuheis, near Amman, owned by the Jordan Cement Factories Co (JCFC), has undergone an expansion, bringing its capacity up to 4.2m. tons per year. By the end of 1983 the first production line at the South Cement Co (SCC) works at Rashidiya was completed, and the second line was finished in the autumn of 1984, giving a total plant capacity of 2m. tons per year. The production of cement, having declined to 793,400 tons in 1982, rose in each of the subsequent three years, reaching 2,023,000 tons in 1985. Local demand rose by 5% in 1987, to 1.6m. tons. In 1987 and 1988 Egypt agreed to

buy 750,000 tons of cement annually from Jordan. Total exports, which reached 800,000 tons in 1987, increased to 1m. tons in 1988. The struggling SCC merged with the JCFC in September 1985. The discovery in the Tafila area of gypsum reserves totalling an estimated 1.5m. tons, sufficient to satisfy demand for 10 years, was announced in March 1985. In 1990 the JCFC achieved record exports of 1.4m. tons of cement and clinker, and also sold 1.5m. tons of cement in the domestic market.

Construction was the fastest growing sector of the economy in 1993, when its share of GDP reached 8.3% (up from 7.6% in 1991). Stimulated mainly by the influx of 'returnees' from Kuwait, new building projects totalled 5.9m. sq m in 1992, as against 4.4m. sq m in 1991 and 2.7m. sq m in 1990. In 1994 domestic demand for cement declined, but a 19% increase in cement exports (to 887,000 tons, shipped mainly to Saudi Arabia and Yemen) enabled the JCFC to maintain total production at the 1993 level of 3.4m. tons. JCFC production in 1995 was 3.1m. tons. RMC Jordan (a wholly-owned subsidiary of the British company RMC) opened its first plant in 1996. Situated near Amman, the plant had a capacity of 100 cu m of ready-mixed concrete per hour. In October 1996 the state-owned Jordan Investment Corpn (JIC), which held 49.5% of the shares in the JCFC, invited bids for 22% of JCFC shares. A total of 16 international cement companies submitted bids, but none was accepted. The JCFC had made a net profit of JD 9.8m. on sales of JD 104.3m. in 1995. In April 1997 the Government approved an increase in Jordan's basic cement price (held at JD 44 per ton since 1992) to JD 48 per ton. In June 1997 the JIC indicated its intention to make a 50% increase (from 22% to 33% of JCFC shares) in the number of shares to be offered when it next invited bids from interested companies. In June 1997 the JIC invited bids for all of its minority shareholdings in four companies: Jordan Tanning Co (a 15% holding), Jordan Worsted Mills (14.1%), Jordan Himmeh Mineral Co (34.7%) and Jordan Paper and Cardboard Factories (19.6%). The JIC was already seeking buyers for all of its shares in listed companies in which it had holdings of less than 5%.

In 1981 construction began on the 225-ha Sahab industrial estate, 18 km south-east of Amman, which is being built at a cost of JD 18m. The first phase of the estate, covering 85 ha, was opened at the end of 1982, and will include 15 ready-built factories and 15 other factories that are being built by the companies which are to use them. Work on the second phase of the Sahab industrial estate began in 1985. Nevertheless, the main focus of the 1981–85 and 1986–90 Plans appeared to be decentralization, putting emphasis on locating industries in geographically underdeveloped areas, especially the Soputj. An example of this is the Encouragement of Investment Law, which was enacted in February 1984. This divides the country into the following three zones: (a) Amman and its suburbs; (b) the other major cities; and (c) the remainder of the country. The Government hopes to encourage dispersal of investment by regulating the amount of assets required by companies setting up in each zone, with the minimum requirement of fixed assets for zone (a) being almost three times that for zone (c). The 1981–85 Plan, with a centrepiece in the construction of the $1,000m.-Yarmouk University (which received its first students in 1985), concentrated on manpower, technology transfer and regional development. Export industries were also to be promoted. The industrial plans for the region around Irbid (where an industrial estate is to be built at a cost of $20m.) and the Ma'an-Aqaba area will form magnets for attracting benefits away from the industrial core of Amman. However, plans to build an iron and steel plant at Irbid were postponed in November 1990. The Middle East Complex for Engineering, Electronics and Heavy Industry—a conglomerate formed in 1994 through the merger of three companies with manufacturing and trading interests in electrical equipment, household goods and related products and components—announced in late 1996 that it had reached an agreement for the local assembly of four-wheel-drive vehicles supplied in kit form by Ssangyong Motor Company of South Korea. Output of Musso and Korando models was planned to rise from 1,000 units per year in 1997 to more than 4,000 units per year from 2000.

In an effort to boost Jordan's role as an entrepôt, a free trade zone was introduced at Aqaba in 1976, and a second free trade zone was opened at Zarqa in February 1983. The amount of goods which passed through these zones totalled 350,000 tons in 1984. In March 1985 it was announced that two more duty-free zones would be established, at Queen Alia international airport and at the port of Aqaba. There is another free trade zone at Ramtha, on the Syrian border, while an industrial free zone was planned for the Shidiya phosphates-producing area (see above). All the zones are operated by the Free Zones Corpn under the aegis of the Ministry of Finance. In 1995, when 668,000 tons of goods passed through the zones, the Corporation made a profit of JD 4.7m. In May 1997 the Government agreed that the Aqaba region should be converted into a fully fledged free zone offering special incentives for the development of manufacturing and service industries in addition to the existing free-trade facilities. A ministerial committee was established to draft a detailed development plan for Aqaba.

By mid-1998 the major state-owned enterprises designated for complete or partial privatization included the Jordan Tele-communications Company (see Transport and Communications, below), the National Electric Power Company, Amman Water and Wastewater, the Disi Water Conveyor Company, the Jordan Cement Factories Corporation, Royal Jordanian Airline (the national airline), the Civil Aviation Authority, the Aqaba Railway Corporation, Zerqa Light Rail and the Public Transport Corporation. For most of these, considerable interest in purchasing the shares on offer was expressed by both local and foreign investors. However, delays resulted from uncertainty over the Government's precise intentions as to desired post-privatization arrangements, on which conflicting statements were made by officials. There was also opposition to the disposals within some of the enterprises concerned, backed by a sizeable contingent of parliamentary deputies, who feared that privatized concerns would be acquired by wealthy and well-connected businessmen rather than a wider share-owning public. Another concern was that strategic Jordanian industries would pass into foreign ownership.

TRANSPORT AND COMMUNICATIONS

The transport sector has contributed around 15% of Jordan's GDP since the early 1970s, and provided direct or indirect employment for over 20% of the private-sector workforce in the early 1990s.

Jordan's only seaport is situated at Aqaba on the country's 20-km Red Sea coastline. Cargo-handling facilities expanded rapidly during the 1980s, an important factor being the re-routing through Aqaba of much Iraqi trade when the Iran–Iraq War of 1980–88 severely dislocated trade through Iraq's own Gulf outlets. In 1989 Aqaba handled 2,446 vessels and 18.7m. tons of cargo, of which 8.7m. tons were Jordanian exports and 2.5m. tons were Jordanian imports. In mid-1990 the port had over 20 berths, one container terminal, two 40-ton gantry cranes and 299,000 sq m of storage facilities.

Aqaba's transit trade was severely affected by the imposition of UN sanctions against Iraq from August 1990. According to the Jordan Shipping Agents Association, the cumulative loss of transport revenues (including government port fees) amounted to $570m. by the end of 1992. The total cargo loaded at Aqaba in 1992 was 13.4m. tons, of which only 2.1m. tons was transit cargo (mainly Iraqi government imports of basic foods). Iraqi exports via Aqaba, which had amounted to about 1.15m. tons a year before the imposition of sanctions, ceased entirely. The estimated reduction in Aqaba's Iraq-bound imports as a result of sanctions was about 3.5m. tons per year, while up to 2.85m. tons of transit cargo for countries other than Iraq were being re-routed to non-Jordanian ports by shippers who did not wish to suffer the delays and inconveniences of UN monitoring of Aqaba-bound cargoes. For the same reason, some shippers were also routing part of Jordan's own import trade via Mediter-ranean ports in Syria and Lebanon. Although the number of ships calling at Aqaba in 1992 was, at 2,430, only 16 fewer than in 1989, the proportion of cargo vessels in the total fell from 64% in 1989 to 52% in 1992, while the number of shipping lines calling regularly at Aqaba fell from 41 to 26.

The US-led naval patrol responsible for enforcing the UN monitoring of shipping at Aqaba was discontinued in late April 1994 in favour of land-based inspections by agents of Lloyd's Register of Shipping. The change occurred after repeated and vigorous protests to the US Government by King Hussein,

citing estimates that diversions and delays caused by the naval blockade had cost the port about US $440m. in lost revenue in 1993. A US spokesman acknowledged in April 1994 that only six of the 460 ships turned away from Aqaba by the naval patrol had been carrying embargoed goods, while the remainder had merely lacked correct documentation. Between 1993 and 1994 Aqaba's annual trade volume declined from 11.63m. tons to 10.47m. tons, leaving about 50% of the port's capacity unused in the latter year. There was an 11% increase in the tonnage of cargo passing through Aqaba in 1995. From June 1996 the port authorities implemented cuts of 20% to 25% in overall handling fees; an additional 5% reduction in port fees on goods in transit; a 50% cut in fees for any cargoes transshipped from Aqaba to Eilat; and (by arrangement with Egypt's Suez Canal Authority) discounts on Suez Canal tolls of 20% for Aqaba-bound container vessels and 10% for Aqaba-bound bulk-cargo vessels. In 1996 the volume of cargo passing through Aqaba increased from 11.8m. tons to 12.2m. tons. The number of containers handled rose from 55,783 in 1995 to 75,333 in 1996. Design work was under way in 1997 for an expansion of port capacity (to include a new 400-m industrial wharf for vessels of up to 50,000 tons) to keep pace with the planned growth of Jordan's mineral exports. In mid-1997 the port authorities announced new cuts in Aqaba's handling fees, designed, in part, to stimulate the growth of transit trade.

A ferry service between Aqaba and the Egyptian port of Nuweibeh, opened in 1985, is one of the main low-cost passenger links between North Africa and the Gulf region (and as such carried most of the Egyptian workers who left Kuwait and Iraq in August 1990). In 1992 this service carried a total of 1.2m. passengers (many of them *en route* to Saudi Arabia), and its operator (the Arab Bridge Maritime Co) made a record profit of $9m.

The Jordanian section of the narrow-gauge Hedjaz railway runs from the Syrian border, via Amman and Ma'an, to the Saudi border. A 115-km link to a phosphate export terminal at Aqaba was added in the 1970s. A further 68 km of track, including a 48-km link to the Shidiya phosphate mines, is to be added in the mid-1990s. Freight (mainly phosphates) accounts for virtually all Jordan's current rail traffic, but future diversi-fication into passenger services has not been ruled out. Plans to build a 1,000-km standard-gauge railway from Aqaba to Baghdad were approved in principle in 1989 but were shelved in the following year when Iraq's development plans were over-taken by political events. In February 1995 Austria agreed to finance a pre-feasibility study for a proposed new rail link between Jordan and Syria. Proposals to build a 41.7-km light rail link between Amman and Zarqa were being drawn up in 1996 with a view to seeking foreign investment in a 'build-own-operate' or 'build-operate-transfer' project. The Aqaba Railway Corpn (ARC, established in 1972 to manage the rail transport of rock phosphate and related products) made a net loss of JD 11.6m. in 1995. Plans to privatize the ARC were being prepared in 1997 with the assistance of international consul-tants.

The Jordanian road system includes a number of major national and international transit routes, among which the main north-south desert highway from Amman to Aqaba had, by 1993, been upgraded along all but 71 km of its 330-km length. Improvements to the dilapidated section of the highway, between Ras an-Naqb and Wadi Yutm in a mountainous area in the south, were scheduled for completion by the end of 1996. Even after the suspension of much of Iraq's trade through Aqaba, an estimated 300,000 trucks were using the port in 1991, due in part to the fact that all of Jordan's potash exports, and about half of its phosphate exports, are transported to Aqaba by road. An estimated 22,000 Turkish trucks used Jordan as a freight transit route in 1992, while Jordan's own sizeable haulage fleet was increasingly active on routes to North Africa, Turkey and Eastern Europe to replace export business lost through the UN embargo on Iraq and a decline in some Jord-anian markets in other Gulf states. The Iraqi-Jordanian Land Transport Co, operating exclusively between these two coun-tries, cut its fleet from 900 to 336 trucks in 1992. In 1997 the Government announced plans to privatize the Public Transport-ation Corpn (responsible for bus services in Amman).

The national airline, Royal Jordanian, operates passenger and freight services from Queen Alia international airport at Zizya, 40 km south of Amman. It carried 44,520 tons of freight in 1992 (compared with a peak of 55,170 tons in 1990 and a decline to 41,637 tons in 1991 as a result of the Gulf crisis). Passenger numbers in 1992 totalled 1,109,000, compared with 798,000 in 1991 and a recent peak of 1,226,800 in 1988. The airline's operating profit reached a 5-year peak of JD 37.9m. in 1992, but its (unpublished) net profit position was believed to reflect an annual debt service requirement of around $40m. (which would have been even greater had the airline not cancelled an option on four additional European Airbus aircraft in 1991). Plans to privatize Royal Jordanian, first put forward in 1987, had still to be finalized in 1993, when a consultants' report recommended a major increase in capital to resolve cash-flow problems. A financial restructuring plan was understood to be nearing completion in mid-1995. Revenue in 1994 totalled around $400m. following a 3.9% increase in passenger numbers (to 1.22m.) and a 1.3% increase in freight (to 55,000 tons), but operating profits fell by 36% to JD 26.63m. ($38m.). In early 1995 the airline raised about $30m. through sales of shares in its hotel and duty-free shopping interests.

A telecommunications law enacted in August 1995 provided for the licensing of private-sector competitors to the state-owned Telecommunications Corporation. During 1996 private companies were granted licences to develop new mobile communications, data communications and public payphone systems, although the Telecommunications Corporation remained the sole provider of basic fixed-line services. With effect from January 1997 the Telecommunications Corporation was restructured as the Jordan Telecommunications Company (JTC), with a share capital of JD 250m., and advisers were appointed to organize the proposed sale of 26% of the company's shares to the private sector. The share offer was expected to attract major telecommunications companies with international interests. In 1995 Jordan's basic fixed-line telephone network comprised 335,000 exchange lines (about 80 per 1,000 people) and met about three-quarters of current demand. An expansion programme was in progress in 1996/97 with the aim of raising basic network capacity to 615,000 lines by 1998.

EXTERNAL TRADE

For a long time, phosphates have dominated Jordan's exports but, in spite of increasing in overall value, they fell in relative importance, accounting for only 22.6% of total export earnings in 1981 and 1982, compared with 43.6% in 1979. The proportion rose to 32.2% in 1983 (though this was principally due to a 40% fall in total export earnings), but fell to 26.6% (JD 69.6m.) in 1984 and 25.9% (JD 66.1m.) in 1985. It rose again to 28.7% (JD 64.8m.) in 1986 but fell to 24.5% (JD 61m.) in 1987. Phosphates and potash together accounted for 38.5% (JD 146.9m.) of the value of total exports in 1988 and 35.2% (JD 224.9) in 1989. In 1992, phosphates valued at JD 206.1m. (24.9% of total exports), and potash valued at JD 95.3m. (11.5% of exports), together accounted for 36.4% of Jordan's export earnings. The overall contribution of mineral resources to exports in 1992 was estimated to exceed 60% after taking account of processed derivatives (fertilizers and fertilizer inputs). Jordan's exports of phosphoric acid and other derivatives were forecast to increase substantially after the mid-1990s, when joint ventures with several Asian importers were scheduled to come into production. Cement, tomatoes, vegetables and fruit are other important exports.

Saudi Arabia was Jordan's principal supplier between 1979 and 1985. Saudi Arabia's share of imports rose to a peak of 20.4% in 1982, when it sold goods to Jordan worth JD 233.5m. The proportion declined to 5.8% in 1986, when sales to Jordan were valued at JD 49.7m. and the USA became Jordan's principal supplier, though its share of total imports in that year declined from 11.9% (JD 128m.) in 1985 to 8.9% (JD 75.5m.). The USA's share rose to 10.2% (JD 93.4m.) in 1987, but Iraq became Jordan's leading supplier with 10.9% (JD 99.4m.) of total imports. Other leading suppliers are, traditionally, Germany, Italy, Japan and the United Kingdom. Iraq overtook Saudi Arabia as the largest purchaser of Jordan's exports in 1980, when it accounted for 23.6% of the total. Iraq's share rose to 26% (valued at JD 63.5m.) in 1981 and declined slightly

to 25.2% (worth JD 66.6m.) in 1982. Jordan's exports to Iraq slumped to only 16% (JD 26m.) of the total in 1983, and Saudi Arabia once more became the principal customer for Jordanian exports, though only for one year, as Iraq accounted for 26% (JD 67.8m.) of Jordanian imports in 1984 and 25.8% (JD 65.9m.) in 1985. Iraq's share declined to 18.8% in 1986 and rose to 24.1% in 1987. Iraq, Saudi Arabia (with 10.5% of the total, in 1987) and India (8.9%) are by far the most important purchasers of Jordanian exports.

Iraq's position as Jordan's main trading partner made it inevitable that the UN sanctions against trade with Iraq, imposed after Iraq's occupation of Kuwait in August 1990, would be fulfilled only with reluctance by Jordan. In 1989 Jordan exported approximately JD 147.9m. worth of goods to Iraq (about 23% of its total commodity exports), while imports from Iraq totalled approximately JD 221.8m. (mainly petroleum). More than 80% of Jordan's petroleum is normally imported from Iraq. By the end of August 1990 transit trade with Iraq through the port of Aqaba had virtually ceased (see Transport, above), and the outbreak of hostilities in January 1991 resulted in the virtual cessation of Iraqi oil deliveries. Following the end of hostilities, Iraq declared in April that it wished to resume normal trade with Jordan, which it proposed to make its main channel to the outside world. However, while some Jordanian food exports resumed to Iraq, a restoration of full bilateral trading links depended on the repeal of the UN embargo.

In mid-1993 Jordan's full oil import requirement was supplied by road from Iraq under a bilateral arrangement (then in its third year) which was deemed by Jordan to fall outside UN sanctions because it involved no financial transfers. Just over half of the supply was free of charge, while the remainder (valued at $16 per barrel, inclusive of transport) was counted as a repayment of Iraqi debt to Jordan. The agreement, which was understood to cover 55,000 b/d of crude oil in 1993, was informally monitored by UN sanctions administrators but did not have the formal approval of the UN sanctions committee. Following widespread reports in early 1993 that there was a growing barter element (mainly involving the supply of Jordanian food to Iraq) in this trade, the US Government began to exert pressure on Jordan to contribute 30% of the value of its oil imports to the UN-administered compensation fund for claims arising out of the Iraqi invasion of Kuwait. (This was the percentage levy which the UN intended to impose on UN-supervised oil exports from Iraq under a scheme which Iraq had so far declined to implement.) Iraq continued to supply all of Jordan's oil imports in 1994 and 1995, and it was announced in April 1995 that Jordan and Iraq planned to build a 590-km. pipeline to supply up to 70,000 b/d of Iraqi crude to Jordan's Zarqa refinery by about 1998 (although Jordan would not begin to operate the proposed pipeline while Iraq remained subject to UN sanctions). Import costs via such a pipeline were expected to be at least 50% less than the current trucking cost of $10 per ton. In January 1996 the Government announced its intention to reduce Jordan's annual exports to Iraq (latterly worth $400m.) to $200m. 'in the interests of reinforcing Jordan's foreign currency reserves'. Jordan's total exports to Iraq from 1989 to 1995 were estimated to be worth JD 1,525m. ($2,170m.), comprising mainly foodstuffs and detergents.

Jordan's trade with Egypt has increased annually since the two countries resumed diplomatic relations in 1984. Trade protocols with Egypt set bilateral trade at $250m. in 1988, compared with JD 150m. in 1985. In 1989 Jordan and Egypt joined Iraq and the Yemen Arab Republic to form the Arab Co-operation Council. Although this organization effectively disintegrated during the Gulf crisis of 1990–91, Jordan and Egypt remained committed to increased bilateral trade in the 1990s. In June 1996 Jordan and Saudi Arabia signed a trade protocol abolishing tariffs on over 160 products making up most of the trade flow between the two countries. In 1995 Jordan had a trade deficit of $30m. with Saudi Arabia (exports $99m., imports $129m.).

Jordan's traditionally large trade deficit is offset, somewhat variably, by expatriate remittances, re-exports, international aid and tourism. In 1985 import duties were raised by between 11% and 50% in an effort to cut the import bill by $30m. Exports declined by 2.2% in 1985 to JD 255.3m., and imports rose by 0.3%, to JD 1,074,445m., giving a visible trade deficit of JD 819.1m. In 1986 exports declined by 11.6% to JD 225.6m., and imports declined by 20.9% to JD 850.2m., a deficit of JD 624.6m. In 1987 the trade deficit narrowed to JD 596.9m. (exports JD 315.7m., imports JD 912.6m.), but in 1988 it widened again, to JD 638.5m. (exports JD 381.5m., imports JD 1,020m.). In 1989 a rise in exports of phosphates and chemicals was largely responsible for narrowing the trade deficit to JD 576.5m. (exports JD 637.6m., imports JD 1,214.2m.). Devaluations of the Jordanian dinar in 1988–89 made Jordanian exports more competitive and restricted Jordanian consumers' ability to buy imported goods. From a deficit of JD 1,008.6m. in 1990, the visible trade balance improved slightly to a deficit of JD 994.1m. in 1991, when exports totalled JD 770.7m. and imports JD 1,764.8m. In 1992 imports rose sharply to JD 2,291m. ($3,363.2m.), mainly because of additional demand generated by 'returnees' from Kuwait, leaving a visible trade deficit of JD 1,461.7m. ($2,144m.) after taking account of exports worth JD 829.3m. ($1,217.4m.). In 1993 the visible trade deficit reached JD 1,593m. (imports totalling JD 2,234m. while exports totalled JD 641m.).

In 1994 import spending totalled $3,543m. (3.9% less than in 1993) and export earnings totalled $1,437m. (14.7% more than in 1993), leaving a visible trade deficit of $2,106m. Customs tariffs, whose weighted average rate had already been cut from 35% to 21% in two years as part of the Government's economic restructuring programme, were further adjusted in May 1995 to eliminate or reduce the import duties on many industrial raw materials and intermediate products, although at the same time many agricultural products became subject to higher duties. In 1995 Jordan recorded a visible trade deficit of $1,518.2m. and an overall current-account deficit of $258.6m. (compared with a current-account deficit of $550m. in 1994). In mid-1996 the Ministry of Supply, which for the previous 22 years had acted as the monopoly importer of basic foodstuffs, with responsibility for controlling the retail prices of 25 food items, announced plans to open the import trade in rice and sugar to the private sector as the first stage in the phasing-out of its monopoly. The ministry was responsible for JD 320m. of food imports in 1995. The trade deficit widened to $2,473m. in 1996, with imports of $4,287m. and exports of $1,817m., producing a current-account deficit (net of grants) of $253.9m. The 1997 account showed a slightly reduced trade deficit of $2,383m. (imports $4,495m., exports $2,010m.), but the 1998 figures were expected to produce a widening deficit of some $2,500m. Jordan's most important trading partner continued to be the European Union (EU), although the single biggest exporter by value remained Iraq, by virtue of its supply of oil products.

In January 1997 Jordan and Iraq signed a protocol covering their bilateral trade in the coming year. Iraqi petroleum supplies to Jordan were to total 25m. barrels of crude oil and 7m. barrels of refined products, the agreed value of these supplies being $611.2m. Within this total, $300m. represented oil supplied free of charge, $225m. represented payment for Jordanian goods and services to be supplied to Iraq, and the remaining $56.2m. represented a partial repayment of Iraq's accumulated debt to Jordan. In addition to the goods supplied under the terms of the bilateral protocol, Jordanian exports to Iraq in 1997 included humanitarian supplies within the framework of the UN 'oil-for-food' programme which came into operation in December 1996. In the first 180-day phase of the UN programme Jordanian firms obtained UN approval for an estimated $146m.-worth of humanitarian exports to Iraq. A Jordan-Iraq trade protocol for 1998 provided for the supply of 4.8m. tons of Iraqi petroleum and petroleum products (an increase of 12% compared with 1997), in exchange for Jordanian goods valued at $255m. In July 1998 Jordan and Iraq agreed to resume talks on the feasibility of an oil pipeline from Haditha in Iraq to the Zarqa refinery and Aqaba in Jordan, to transport supplies currently moved to Jordan by road, and to provide Iraq with a Red Sea outlet for its crude oil. In the same month Jordan signed an agreement with Egypt, providing for the establishment of bilateral free trade by the year 2005. In 1997 Jordan's exports to Egypt were valued at only $20.3m., and its imports from Egypt at $36m.

In April 1997, following two years of negotiations, Jordanian and EU representatives initialled an association agreement providing for the progressive liberalization of trading arrangements over a 10-year period. If ratified on schedule, the agreement was expected to take effect from January 1999. A Jordanian application for membership of the World Trade Organization was under negotiation in 1997-98, when the agenda included aspects of Jordanian copyright and patents law which were not consistent with current international standards.

FINANCE

Today, Jordan's main exports are phosphates, potash and fertilizer, but before 1967 net earnings from the tourist trade and income from private donations constituted the only important invisible export. After 1967 income from tourism and private transfers fell dramatically. In 1974, however, the Jordanian Government decided to allow its visitors to cross over the West Bank and the number of tourists arriving in the country that year rose by 79% on the 1973 total to reach 554,913, nearly regaining the 1966 level of 617,000, while income from tourism exceeded it, reaching JD 17.3m., compared with JD 11.3m. Tourism continued to expand during the 1970s and 1980s, reaching 2,677,021 in 1985. Earnings from tourism reached a record JD 310m. ($546m.) in 1989, when the number of European long-stay visitors totalled 130,000. In 1990 the Gulf crisis effectively ended all tourism from September onwards, while a slow recovery in the latter part of the following year took total European arrivals to 57,000 in 1991. In 1992, when European arrivals rose to 121,000, a strong revival of tourism (at least among non-Arab visitors) generated estimated net receipts of around $300m.

Strong overseas marketing campaigns by the government, private-sector tour operators and the national airline, Royal Jordanian Airline, produced significant increases in tourism from 1993 to 1996, but from 1997 the number of visitors began to decline, reportedly owing to fears concerning Islamic fundamentalism and rising Israeli-Palestinian tensions. A main aim of government tourism development policy for the 1990s has been to provide a varied range of attractions in different parts of the country, while taking steps to prevent over-development of Jordan's world heritage site at Petra. In 1994 a total of 696,760 visitors generated an estimated JD 443m. of tourism revenue, representing increases of 12% in visitor numbers and 13.6% in revenue compared with 1993. Moves towards a regional peace settlement greatly enhanced Jordan's appeal to overseas tourists, while the opening of the border with Israel prompted a significant influx of Israeli tourists from late 1994 onwards. Income from tourism in 1995 was estimated as JD 568m. ($800m.). At the end of the year 23 new hotels were under construction and many more were plannned. Total visitor numbers in 1995 exceeded 1m., of whom 400,000 were classed as leisure and culture tourists. An estimated 100,000 Israelis visited Jordan in 1995, while tourist arrivals from Japan and Korea began to feature significantly in the tourism statistics for the first time. The re-emergence of regional political tensions in 1996 led to a significant decline in visitor numbers, with some hotels reporting occupancy rates as low as 10% at some points in that year. The number of European and US visitors totalled 444,600 in 1996, declining to 429,700 in 1997 and showing no sign of recovering in 1998. Nevertheless, the Ministry of Tourism and Antiquities pursued an expansion of tourist facilities, including hotels, on the basis of a $44m. development programme announced in May 1997. In November, moreover, the Government announced the establishment of a new Jordanian Tourism Board as a public-private venture to promote Jordan as a tourist destination. Major new private tourism projects initiated in 1998 included a 6,000-bed hotel complex at Aqaba, at a projected cost of $452m.

An important source of foreign exchange in recent years has been remittances from Jordanians working abroad. In 1979 these totalled JD 180.4m. (including transfers through the banking system but not those through 'black market' money changers or by hand, which, it is estimated, would increase the total by at least 50%) and by 1981 had risen to $987m. In real terms the income from foreign remittances fell in 1982, but rose by 5% (JD 20m.) to JD 402m. ($1,040m.) in 1983. In 1984 remittances from the 340,000 Jordanians working abroad were worth JD 475m. ($1,228m.). However, the world oil glut and a fall in oil prices have adversely affected the economies of oil-producing countries in the Middle East, in particular the Gulf states where 85% of expatriate Jordanian workers are employed, and this, in turn, has affected the level of remittances. These fell, accordingly, by 17%, to JD 403.5m. ($1,204m.) in 1985. Although they recovered to JD 414.5m. ($1,243.5m.) in 1986, they declined to JD 317.7m. ($953.1m.) in 1987. The decline in Gulf economies also added to the number of the unemployed as workers returned from abroad. Remittances rose to JD 335.7m. in 1988, and to an estimated JD 470m. in 1989. Statistics issued by the Central Bank in May 1993 gave remittances in the years 1990, 1991 and 1992 as JD 331.8m., JD 306.3m. and JD 573.1m. respectively. The 1992 total was believed to include a large element of deferred transfers by workers who had returned to Jordan from Kuwait in 1991. Total remittances rose to JD 720.7m. in 1993, JD 763.7m. in 1994, JD 871.7m. in 1995, JD 1,094.8m. in 1996 and JD 1,173.5m. in 1997. The steady growth reflected the reopening of job opportunities for Jordanian nationals in the oil-rich Gulf states; in June 1998 the Government gave initial approval to the establishment of Jordan's first private employment agency, specializing in placing applicants in the Gulf.

For many years, Jordan's trade deficit has been offset, mainly by capital imports and subventions. Before 1967 these came principally from the United Kingdom and the USA, but since 1967 there have been similar payments from Saudi Arabia and other Arab states. These subventions enabled the country's exchange reserves to be maintained and even increased. At the end of 1979 net foreign assets stood at JD 363.9m., compared with JD 177.4m. at the end of 1976, and international reserves (excluding gold) were $1,140m., compared with $458.9m. at the end of 1976. The JD 57.4m. balance-of-payments surplus in 1979 was increased to a surplus of JD 144.9m. in 1980. However, aid from Arab states fixed at the Baghdad summit meeting in 1978 was not maintained at the agreed level (see below). The first balance-of-payments deficit for five years was recorded in 1981, followed by further small deficits in 1982, 1983, 1984 ($219m.) and 1985 ($260.5m.). These deficits led the Government to seek new loans. In 1984 and 1985 it obtained Euroloans of $200.8m. and $215m., respectively, both with eight years' credit, and in 1987 one of $150m., with seven years' credit. Consequently, the burden of debt financing was expected to increase over the next few years. The level of government debt and government guaranteed foreign debt rose to JD 1,100m. in 1986. By May 1987, as a result of debt servicing and reduced aid from other Arab countries, reserves of foreign exchange held by the Central Bank had fallen to JD 51m. ($153m.), sufficient to cover the cost of imports for less than one month. In 1986, owing to an increase in the level of remittances and Arab grant aid, a surplus of JD 35m. ($104.6m) was recorded in the balance of payments. Total foreign aid, however, declined from JD 377m. ($1,127m.) in 1985 to JD 304m. ($908m.) in 1986. The continuing decline in Arab aid, remittances from Jordanians working abroad, and low world prices for phosphates and potash contributed to a balance-of-payments deficit of JD 42.4m. ($140m.) in 1987.

Jordan's economic problems created a lack of confidence in the Jordanian dinar on the currency market and the dinar declined in value from US $1 = JD 0.33 in May 1988 to US $1 = JD 0.39 in June. On 4 June, in support of the dinar, the Government established a special committee to consider new foreign exchange regulations. Two days later, a fixed exchange rate system was introduced, with a commercial bank rate of US $1 = JD 0.356/0.360 and a rate of $1 = JD 0.370/0.375 for money-changers. Foreign currency reserves rose to $36m. in May and an aid instalment of $60m. from Saudi Arabia helped to calm the market. New regulations, introduced in June, permitted Jordanians working abroad to bring back as much foreign currency as they wished and to dispose of it as they chose; allowed citizens to import any amount of local or foreign currency; and increased the amount that local residents were allowed to hold in foreign currencies, from JD 30,000 to JD 50,000.

In early November 1988 the combination of a shortage of foreign currency reserves, a decline of more than 30% in the value of the dinar since mid-October, and the deteriorating balance-of-payments position prompted the Government to introduce various austerity measures. Bans were imposed on the import of several luxury items, and customs duties on non-essential items, airport tax and fees payable for work permits were increased. The Government hoped to save at least US $350m. by the measures. In February 1989, amid increasing pressure on the currency, the Government cancelled all licences for money-changers.

In March 1989 representatives of the IMF visited Jordan to discuss the Government's efforts to revive the economy and reschedule its foreign debt, which was estimated at $6,500m. The Government had reportedly been reluctant to enter into negotiations with the IMF, but had concluded that an agreement with the IMF was the only means by which it could maintain its reserves of foreign exchange and finance its budget deficit. The cost of servicing the foreign debt in 1989 was estimated at $900m., including interest payments of $500m. As a result of these negotiations, the IMF granted Jordan a stand-by credit of $125m. in mid-July 1979, conditional upon the implementation of a five-year economic adjustment programme, drafted in consultation with the Fund. The adjustment programme aimed to reduce Jordan's budget deficit from 24% of GDP in 1988 to 5%, to reduce the annual rate of inflation from 14% to 7%, and to achieve a current account surplus. In order to achieve this, the Government agreed to reduce state expenditure, to increase revenues and to reduce imports. In late April, however, the Government's announcement of substantial increases in taxes and in the prices of some commodities (staples such as bread, milk and rice were not affected) led to widespread rioting throughout the country and to the resignation of the Prime Minister, Zaid ar-Rifai, and his Cabinet. Nevertheless the new Government, under the leadership of Field Marshal Sharif Zaid ibn Shaker, remained committed to the programme agreed with the IMF.

Although the former Prime Minister, Zaid ar-Rifai, had assured bankers that the agreement between Jordan and the IMF would not affect the value of the dinar, a further devaluation, of 5.5%, was announced in May 1989, bringing the total devaluation of the dinar against the US dollar since October 1988 to 42.5%. It was announced that the value of the dinar would henceforth be determined against a 'basket' of currencies, although the dollar would remain the most important of these currencies. At the same time, it was reported that as much as one-third of the Central Bank's gold reserves had been exchanged for foreign currency in 1988, and the Governor of the Bank, Muhammad Said Nabulsi, confirmed reports that Jordan's foreign debt amounted to $8,100m.

On 31 July 1989 the Central Bank introduced a two-tier exchange rate for the dinar, formalizing a system that had already been operating informally. While the Government continued to provide dollars at a fixed rate for imports of basic commodities, commercial banks were permitted to trade dollars at free-market rates for other foreign currency requirements.

By September 1989 a renewed influx of financial aid from Arab states, together with the intervention of the Central Bank, had enabled the dinar to stabilize at around $1.20, and it was hoped to be able to maintain its value at about $1.60 by the end of 1989. On 11 September the Ministry of Finance announced that the 'London Club' of commercial bank creditors had agreed to reschedule $575m. of Jordan's debts, which were due to be repaid between the beginning of 1989 and mid-1991. Reserves of foreign currency were reported to have risen to $500m. by September. In July the 'Paris Club' of creditor countries had agreed to the rescheduling of Jordan's debt for 1989 and 1990 ($656m. and $622m. respectively) over a 10-year period. As a result of these financial measures, and increased aid from abroad, Jordan recorded a JD 223m. surplus on its current account for 1989, although the annual rate of inflation increased to 25%, and little impression was made on the budget deficit.

The Jordanian Minister of Finance, Basil Jardaneh, visited London in April 1990 to work for the completion of Jordan's debt-rescheduling arrangements with the 'London Club'. Foreign debt had by then reached $8,400m. and there was a probable deficit of $95m. on foreign reserves. The country's problems were subsequently exacerbated by the onset of the latest regional crisis in August 1990. Having immediately stopped all repayments on its foreign debts, Jordan had to cope with the suspension, from September 1990, of disbursements to it under the 1989 IMF agreement. When it became clear, in December 1990, that the original 1993 target for completion of the structural adjustment programme was not feasible, a two-year extension to

1995 was provisionally agreed with IMF negotiators. However, rescheduling of foreign debt due for repayment by mid-1991 was contingent upon a formal reactivation of the IMF agreement, with revised content and timetable. An agreement was concluded in October 1991, involving an IMF stand-by credit of SDR 44m. over 18 months in support of an economic and financial reform programme covering the seven-year period 1992–98. Elements of the new IMF agreement included cuts in state subsidies of food and other basic commodites and a progressive reduction of the budget deficit. This enabled Jordan, in early 1992, to reach new debt-rescheduling agreements with both the 'Paris Club' and the 'London Club', involving in the former case the deferral of payments due in 1991–93 on total foreign debt estimated at $7,200m.

Jordan's balance of payments showed a current-account deficit of JD 148.2m. in 1990, a surplus of JD 269m. in 1991 and a deficit of JD 520m. in 1992. The main factor in the 1991 surplus was a sharp dip in outgoings on the invisibles account, while the main factor in the 1992 deficit was the steep rise in spending on visible imports (see External Trade, above). External debt was reduced to $6,600m. by the end of 1992, when the country's foreign exchange reserves exceeded $800m.

Jordan's persistent financial problems in the 1980s had culminated in a budget deficit of 24% of GDP in 1988, but thereafter, in accordance with IMF prescriptions, efforts were made to improve matters. Budget proposals for 1989 envisaged total expenditure of JD 1,035.0m. (a reduction of 16% compared with the budget for 1988, due mainly to the decline in the value of the dinar), incorporating development spending of JD 346.5m., compared with JD 451.5m. in 1988, a reduction of 23%. The budget deficit was originally projected at JD 122.3m., but the Government subsequently introduced measures to reduce the budget deficit by 4.5% of GDP in 1989. Budget estimates for 1990 envisaged expenditure at JD 1,105.8m. and revenue at JD 906.7m., resulting in a deficit of JD 199.1m. Capital and development expenditure was reduced to only JD 253.3m., compared with JD 346.5m. in 1989. Projected current expenditure was subsequently reduced by JD 15.1m., before the budget proposals received legislative approval. A further revision in the course of 1990 reduced total budgeted expenditure to JD 1,033.7m. and increased forecast revenues to JD 938.7m. resulting in a deficit of JD 182.4m. after loan repayments of JD 87.4m. up to August 1990. The 1991 budget, as adopted by the House of Representatives, envisaged total expenditure of JD 1,109.2m. and loan repayments of JD 135.2m., compared with revenues of JD 902.5m., resulting in a projected deficit of JD 341.9m. It was noted, however, that the expenditure total excluded certain debit items (notably oil subsidies), which, if included, would produce a deficit of at least 16% of GDP. The Government also presented a separate emergency budget of JD 120m., intended to assist the economy to overcome the effects of the Gulf crisis, its implementation being dependent on receipts of special aid (see below).

The 1992 budget proposals reflected the terms of the October 1991 IMF agreement; government subsidies being cut by 30%, and new consumption taxes imposed, in order to reduce the deficit to JD 107m. In the event, there was an overall budget surplus of JD 149m. in 1992 (due mainly to additional revenue from 'returnees'), total domestic revenue (JD 1,098m.) being higher than current expenditure (JD 932m.) for the first time in Jordan's history. The 1993 budget envisaged an excess of domestic revenue over current expenditure of JD 87m. and an overall budget deficit of JD 55m. Despite the achievement of a budget surplus in 1992, the effective fiscal deficit for the year (as cited in discussions with international financial institutions) was put at about 6% of GDP. Total GDP was JD 3,189m. ($4,600m.) in 1992, up 10.1% in real terms on 1991 after allowing for inflation of 3%. Pledges of $380m. in aid to close Jordan's 1993 financing gap were made by international donors at a meeting organized by the World Bank in January 1993.

Of the structural reform measures proposed in the 1993 budget, price increases on selected oil products (including fuel for electricity generation and aviation fuel supplied to Royal Jordanian) were implemented in June. However, a new sales tax, which should have superseded existing consumption taxes in May 1993, was deferred following strong protests from private businesses which claimed that they would be subject to an

unfair burden, notwithstanding the Government's intention to raise only an extra JD 30m. per year, as against JD 100m. when the sales tax was first proposed. In the event the Government amended the scope of the consumption tax system to raise an additional JD 3.5m., a step that was accepted by the IMF as 'a temporary alternative'.

The 'London Club' of commercial bank creditors signed a debt rescheduling agreement in December 1993 covering US $740m. in principal and $150m. in interest owed by the Jordan Government to more than 80 lenders. The details of the agreement had been negotiated in July of that year.

The 1994 budget provided for revenue of JD 1,488m. (including domestic revenue of JD 1,311m.) and expenditure of JD 1,488m. (JD 1,124m. on current account and JD 364m. on capital account). Excluded from the budget were an unspecified amount of military spending, to be met by 'friendly Arab states', and the cost of servicing Jordan's foreign debt, which would have to be covered by fresh domestic and foreign borrowing to raise some JD 300m. In addition to the normal budget, the Government drew up an emergency budget providing for JD 66m. of development expenditure if sufficient foreign grants and/or soft loans could be raised. The controversial sales tax, after being strongly attacked during parliamentary debates, was finally approved on 14 May 1994 and took effect at the beginning of July 1994.

The parliamentary passage of the sales tax legislation paved the way for the IMF executive board to announce on 25 May 1994 its formal approval of a three-year extended Fund facility (EFF) to support the next stage of the Government's structural adjustment programme. Worth SDR 127.8m. ($178.9m.), the EFF would be used to further a programme whose main 1994 objectives were stated as real GDP growth of 5.5%, an annual inflation rate held at 5%, a reduction of the current-account deficit to 9.7% of GDP (compared with 12.5% in 1993), and an increase in the Central Bank's foreign exchange reserves to $665m. or the equivalent of 2.4 months' import cover. The aim of fiscal policy should be 'to enhance efficiency and revenue-elasticity' through tax reform. Areas of structural change which the Government should address more convincingly included the formulation of action plans for the agriculture and water sectors. The IMF said that the Government's on-target achievements in 1993 had included real growth of 5.8% of GDP, an inflation rate of 4.8% and a fiscal deficit of 6.4% of GDP.

The IMF agreement paved the way for successful negotiations with the 'Paris Club' of official creditors, culminating in an agreement on 29 June 1994 to reschedule $1,215m. of debt payments over 20 years, including 10 years' grace. Jordan's Prime Minister described the terms as very favourable and designed to alleviate pressure on the Jordanian economy during the EFF period. World Bank statistics for 1992 gave Jordan's total debt as $6,914m., of which $3,454m. (including $2,704m. in concessional loans) was owed to official bilateral creditors. Prior to the IMF and 'Paris Club' announcements, the Government had, on 18 May, obtained $200m. of aid from the Jordan consultative group of donors to finance the 1994 balance-of-payments deficit.

The IMF augmented Jordan's EFF allocation by SDR 25m. (about $37m.) in September 1994 and by a further SDR 36.5m. (about $54m.) in February 1995. A favourable IMF review of the economy in June 1995 showed that Jordan was on course to achieve 6.2% economic growth in 1995, with inflation of less than 4% and a current-account deficit equal to 5% of GDP, bettering its planning targets in each case. In 1994 the real GDP growth rate had been 5.7% (virtually unchanged from 1993) and the end-1994 foreign debt (totalling $5,644m.) had been equivalent to 91.8% of GDP, compared with a debt to GDP ratio of 109% at the end of 1993. Net foreign reserves in the banking system totalled $2,430m. at end-1994, compared with $2,280m. at end-1993.

In July 1994, when Jordan and Israel first committed themselves to an early peace agreement, the World Bank advocated substantial foreign debt relief for Jordan to strengthen its economic position during the early stages of the peace, thereby reinforcing popular support for the peace process and providing a more attractive climate for foreign investment. While early Jordanian hopes of a major debt forgiveness initiative worth up to $3,300m. proved to be groundless, some further relief was secured through bilateral agreements with various creditor countries.

The full writing-off of some $700m. of debts owed to the USA was approved by the US Congress in July 1995. As most of these debts had already been rescheduled through the 'Paris Club', Jordan did not gain an immediate cash-flow benefit from this development. The United Kingdom agreed in July 1994 to convert $92m. of loans into grants to support Jordan's peace initiatives. In mid-1995 Jordan's outstanding debts to the United Kingdom totalled $531m., of which $348m. had been rescheduled (including $267m. rescheduled under the terms of the June 1994 'Paris Club' agreement). Germany agreed in November 1994 to restructure $101.3m. of Jordanian debt under the 'Paris Club' agreement and to cancel $32.9m. of debt, half of this through a debt-equity swap to provide investment funds for environmental projects. In August 1994 France cancelled $4.6m. of Jordanian debts and provided a $5.6m.-line of credit for Franco-Jordanian joint ventures. In October 1994 France agreed to reschedule $200m. of Jordanian debt under the 'Paris Club' agreement and to finalize a debt-equity swap programme worth $100m. Jordan's total debt to France (excluding outstanding aircraft leasing payments) totalled around $600m. in 1994. Jordan's largest bilateral creditor, Japan, was owed around $1,800m. at the end of 1994. In mid-1995 Jordan requested $500m. of balance-of-payments support loans for 1995/96 and an increase in Japanese grant aid to $50m. per year from 1996. In October 1995 Japan extended a $135m.-balance-of-payments support loan to Jordan. In the same month the World Bank made an $80m.-economic reform and development loan, while a further $20m. was loaned by France. In December 1995 Japan signed agreements to loan $80m. to Jordan in support of its economic reform programme and to reschedule $101m. of government debt and $51m. of commercial debt, bringing the total amount of Jordanian debt rescheduled by Japan since 1989 to $400m.

Jordan's 1995 budget provided for expenditure totalling JD 1,674m. (JD 1,231m. on current account and JD 443m. on capital account). Debt servicing of JD 300m. was not included in this total. The budgeted revenue totalled JD 1,624m., including domestic revenue of JD 1,400m. A supplement to the main budget provided for JD 390m. of spending on development projects, dependent on the availability of international assistance. The 1996 budget provided for total spending of JD 1,798m. (of which JD 1,328m. was recurrent expenditure and JD 470m. was capital expenditure) and total revenue of JD 1,635m. (of which JD 1,575m. was classed as local revenue and JD 60m. as repaid loans), leaving a deficit of JD 163m. to be covered by foreign grants and loans.

In February 1996 the IMF approved a Jordanian request for new credits totalling SDR 200.8m. (about $195m.) to support the Government's economic and structural reform programme over the period 1996 to 1998. This new EFF arrangement replaced the previous arrangement approved in 1994, which the IMF regarded as broadly successful. The Government's economic targets for the period to 1998 included average GDP growth of at least 6% per annum (with an initial target of 6.5% growth in 1996); achievement of low inflation rates similar to those in industrialized countries (with an initial target of less than 3.5% inflation in 1996); a reduction in the balance-of-payments deficit on the current account to less than 3% of GDP (with a 1996 target of less than 4% of GDP); the accumulation of sufficient gross official reserves to cover about three months' expenditure on imports; and the reduction of the budget deficit to no more than 2.5% of GDP by 1998 (compared with 4.8% of GDP in 1995 and a target level of 3.8% for 1996). The IMF recommended that maintenance of a tight monetary policy should be combined with the use of 'flexible interest rates geared to maintaining the relative attractiveness of dinar-denominated assets'. The ongoing process of structural reform was to include further reductions in public subsidies, including in 1996 the subsidies on water charges, wheat prices and animal feed prices. A wide-ranging privatization programme was to be introduced, with five major sales of government shareholdings planned for 1996. The top rate of customs levy on all imports except cars, alcohol and tobacco was to be cut to 30% by 1998. (From the beginning of 1996 the maximum levy on goods other than cars, alcohol and tobacco, inclusive of any fees and taxes imposed in addition to customs duty, was reduced to 50%, with many categories of goods becoming subject to a ceiling of 40%.)

A 1996 IMF report on Jordan's economic strategy included an overview of the main fiscal trends in recent years. From the mid-1970s to 1988, about 12% of GDP had been made up of grants from oil-producing countries, while an average 10% of GDP was devoted to servicing foreign debts and a further 10% to military spending. Over the period 1976 to 1994, deficit budgeting had inhibited economic growth by an estimated 2% per annum after allowing for foreign grants of budgetary aid (without which growth would have been inhibited by 5% per annum). Between 1988 and 1994, the Government had cut the budget deficit from about 18% of GDP to less than 6% of GDP through a 65% cutback in expenditure and a 35% increase in revenue (notably from postal and telecommunication services). Public-sector employment had risen by 15% between 1991 and 1994, while the public-sector wage bill increased by 40% in real terms and accounted for about 25% of total budget expenditure in 1994. However, overall government spending was equal to only 35% of GDP in 1994, compared with 47% of GDP in 1989. The report concluded that the Government's 'remarkable fiscal adjustment in recent years' had greatly improved the kingdom's investment climate and growth prospects.

Jordan's 1997 budget provided for total spending of JD 1,916m. (of which JD 1,481m. was recurrent expenditure and JD 435m. was capital expenditure) and total revenue of JD 1,860m. (of which JD 1,691m. was local revenue and JD 169m. was foreign grant aid), leaving a deficit of JD 56m. Included in the recurrent spending estimates was an allocation of JD 72m. to alleviate the impact on low-income groups of recent subsidy reductions (including a cut in the wheat subsidy from August 1996). In February 1997 the IMF increased the total amount of credit available to Jordan under the current (1996–98) extended fund facility by SDR 37.2m. to SDR 238m. ($330.5m.). In 1996 the 'Paris Club' creditor group had agreed to reschedule $308m. of Jordanian official debt ($250m. of principal and $58m. of interest) falling due between July 1996 and May 1997. Repayment over 15 years would begin in June 1999. In 1997 the 'Paris Club' agreed to reschedule $450m. of Jordanian debt falling due between June 1997 and September 1999. The repayment period would be 22 years (with 10 years' grace) for bilateral debt and 20 years (with 5 years' grace) for export credits. In September 1997 the USA agreed to cancel Jordan's remaining US debt of $63.4m., following two earlier agreements under which $1,100m. had been cancelled. Jordan's total foreign debt at the end of 1997 was $6,469.7m. (81.7% of GDP), of which about $4,000m. was owed to bilateral creditors. A rescheduling agreement, signed with Germany in March 1998, provided for the cancellation of about $22m. if Jordan spent half of that amount on poverty-alleviating or environmental projects. The 1998 budget provided for expenditure of JD 1,950m. and a net deficit (after aid receipts) of only JD 37m. In April of that year, Jordan's official foreign-currency reserves stood at JD 1,110.9m., equivalent to 4.8 months' export cover.

Jordan's banking sector grew with the economy, but recent changes in the country's economic fortunes have enforced a new caution. The number of institutions grew nearly three-fold to 36 between 1973 and 1983. In January 1984 the Central Bank announced measures to 'Jordanize' foreign banks operating in Amman. They were given three (later extended to five) years to comply with regulations requiring that 51% of their equity be held by Jordanian nationals. The only foreign bank to respond was the Arab Land Bank. However, in April 1985, the new Government of Prime Minister Zaid ar-Rifai abandoned the regulation, though this did not affect another requirement for all banks to raise their capital from JD 3m. to JD 5m. in line with local commercial banks. ('Jordanization' would have taken the capital of foreign banks above the new minimum requirement.) In July Said Nabulsi resigned as Governor of the Central Bank of Jordan, a decision thought to have been influenced by the Government's rejection of his measures to 'Jordanize' foreign banks. The Chase Manhattan Bank decided to withdraw from Jordan in 1986, rather than comply with the direction to increase its capital. In February 1984 new Central Bank regulations stated that all banks must invest at least 4% of their total deposits either in government bonds or in government-guaranteed public corporation bonds, together with a further

4% in treasury bills. In addition, banks must now also invest at least 15%, but not more than 75%, of paid-up capital and domestic reserves in public shares. In July 1990 the financially-troubled Petra Bank went into liquidation, as did the Syrian-Jordanian Bank in May 1991, only 12 years after its creation as a joint venture of the Damascus and Amman Governments.

In January 1986 the Government lifted most of the restrictions preventing non-Jordanian Arabs from investing in the Jordanian economy. The only restriction to remain in force was that permitting a 49% maximum shareholding for non-Jordanian Arabs in retail trade, banking, finance and insurance companies. The change of policy was seen as an attempt to attract private capital to Jordan to offset the decline in Arab aid.

In December 1984 insurance companies were instructed to raise their capital to JD 600,000 by the end of 1986 or to merge with other companies. The regulation affected nine of the country's 21 insurance companies. Two mergers, between the Arab Belgium Insurance Co and the United Insurance Co, and the National Insurance Co and Al-Ahlia (Jordan) Insurance Co took place between October 1985 and August 1986.

In August 1991 the Central Bank imposed new credit ceilings in accordance with the IMF-decreed reforms. These included a 9% per annum limit on the increase in commercial credit and a specification that, in extending credit, commercial banks should not exceed ten times their capital and reserves, or 90% of total customer deposits. In May 1993 an overall ceiling of JD 400m. was imposed on the growth of bank credit in the current year. This followed a surge in lending as banks sought to make profitable use of the strong inflow of deposits from 'returnees' over the previous two years. By the beginning of July the 1993 loan total already exceeded JD 300m. The Central Bank had earlier imposed restrictions on bank lending to finance customers' share purchases following signs that the Amman stock market was overheating in mid-June 1993 (when daily trading volumes of JD 16m. were recorded, compared with the normal average of JD 4m.).

At the beginning of 1993 the Central Bank ordered commercial banks to increase their bad debt provisions on around JD 2,200m. of outstanding loans. This move (which occurred at a time when bank profits were at record levels) effectively paved the way for the writing off of nearly JD 400m. of bad debts dating from the late 1980s. The banks had until 1995 to bring their loan cover up to new minimum levels. In January 1995 the Central Bank set an end-1996 deadline for 16 small banks to increase their capital to JD 20m. ($28m.), making it clear that it would prefer banks to achieve this through mergers rather than increases in individual capital. At the same time Jordanian banks were warned that a July 1993 law limiting loans to 70% of total deposits was to be more strictly enforced than hitherto.

A new investment law introduced at the end of 1995 permitted foreign investors to buy shares on the Amman stock market without applying for government permission. A limit of 50% was set on the proportion of an existing listed company's shares that could be owned by foreign interests. In the case of companies whose shares were being publicly floated for the first time, foreign buyers could purchase holdings of up to 100% with the government's permission (which was required for any bid for foreign ownership of more than 50% of a newly floated company's shares). The minimum level for foreign investment through the stock market was reduced from JD 5,000 to JD 1,000. The minimum level for direct foreign investment in Jordan was set at JD 50,000. A limit of 25% was imposed on foreign participation in local printing and publishing companies (previously prohibited under Jordanian law). In mid-1997 the Higher Council for Investment recommended that the 50% ceiling on foreign ownership of shares be abolished in selected sectors, including banking and insurance. The proposal was made in order to encourage sustained foreign interest after the Government abolished a 15% tax on capitalized reserves in May 1997. At the end of June the authorities abolished exchange-control restrictions, allowing free movement of currency for the first time in Jordan. In early July the Central Bank reduced interest rates for the first time since 1989.

In July 1998 the inaugural meeting was held of the Jordan Investment Trust (Jordinvest), which had been established by the Kuwait-based Gulfinvest International investment holding company to provide investment and financial services to local and foreign investors in the Jordanian economy. With initial paid-in capital of some $22m. (including $5m. raised through a public share offering), Jordinvest was to specialize in recapitalizations and mergers of local banks and companies.

DEVELOPMENT

Jordan's first Five-Year Development Plan, for 1962–67, aimed to invest JD 137m. in the economy, to raise GDP to JD 144m. This plan, however, was superseded by a Seven-Year Plan that was due to run from 1964 to 1970. In its turn, this was disrupted and abandoned after the loss of the West Bank in 1967, and a new Three-Year Plan, covering the period 1973–75, was introduced, with a total proposed expenditure of JD 179m. The three largest items of expenditure were transport, housing and government buildings and mining and industry. The 1976–80 Plan, which followed the 1973–75 Plan, envisaged total expenditure of JD 756m., with the public and private sectors contributing in equal proportions. The Government felt that the Jordanian economy was too heavily biased towards the services sector, and one of the chief aims of the plan was the development of the commodity-producing sector and its increased contribution to GDP. In the event, although GDP failed to rise at the planned rate of 11.9% per annum, by 1980 it had risen by a substantial 62% compared with its 1976 value.

During the 1976–80 Plan period, the growth of agriculture was below target, but the 1981–85 Five-Year Plan still set goals. Agriculture was planned to have an annual growth rate of 7.5%, mining and manufacturing 17.8%, electricity and water supply 18.9% and construction 12.6%. These compare with an annual industrial growth rate of 13.6% during the 1976–80 Plan. In contrast, investment during the period 1976–80 overshot planned levels by 150%, largely owing to high levels of private investment. The initial planned investment for the 1981–85 Plan was JD 2,800m. ($8,446m.). Industry was to account for 21%, water and irrigation 18%, transport 18% and housing 11%. By October 1981, however, Iraq had promised financial support of JD 500m., and this led to an increase in the planned level of investment to JD 3,300m., of which JD 1,162m. was to be from overseas assistance. Over the period there was planned to be an annual growth rate in GDP of 10.4%, compared with the 8.5% rate of the 1976–80 Plan. However, the targets of the 1981–85 Plan were not met.

Under the 1986–90 Plan, expenditure was set at JD 3,115m. ($9,727m.), 52% of which was allocated to projects in the public sector and 48% to the private sector. Of total expenditure, 33% was to be provided by foreign borrowing. The Plan aimed for real economic growth of 5% per year and, with 39% of total investment to be allocated to the services sector (compared with less than 30% in the previous Plan), it was hoped that as many as 100,000 jobs would be created during its term. Agriculture was allocated 10% of total investment, compared with 5% and 7% in the previous two Plans, and agricultural production was expected to increase at an annual rate of 7%–8%. The phosphate industry was to be expanded with development plans focusing on the Shidiya phosphate deposits (see Industry and Mining), while potash mining and other important export industries were also to be developed with the aim of increasing the value of exports by an annual rate of 8.3%. At the same time, it was planned to reduce the annual growth of imports to 2.8% for goods and 3.6% for services. These measures were intended to reduce the deficit on the current account of the balance of payments—one of the Plan's key objectives. However, major slippages on the Plan's targets were compounded towards the end of its term by the onset of the 1990–91 Gulf crisis. According to World Bank figures, Jordan's GDP increased, in real terms, by an annual average of 4.2% in 1980–88, in which period agricultural output increased by 6% per year, industry by 3.6% and services by 4.4%.

A Five-Year Development Plan for the Occupied Territories (1986–90) was launched in November 1986. With total required investment of JD 461.5m. ($1,292.3m.) for projects in the West Bank and the Gaza Strip, the aim of the plan was to enable the 1.3m. Palestinians living in these areas to achieve a greater degree of economic independence; creating 20,000 jobs, constructing 8,500 homes and limiting the movement to Israel and, more especially, to Jordan (where immigrants might contribute to social, economic and political problems) of Palestinians deprived of work and opportunities. (About 850,000 West Bank Palestinians are entitled to Jordanian citizenship.) About 654,000 residents of the Occupied Territories left or were forced to leave between 1967 and 1984 (most of them to Jordan), and more than 100,000 Arab workers from the Territories, about one-third of the labour force, work in Israel. Israel took measures to facilitate the implementation of the Plan, such as the appointment in September 1986 of Arab mayors in four West Bank towns, and agreeing to the opening of four branches of the Cairo-Amman Bank, which were to provide the main channel for the transfer of funds to development projects. The Plan had singularly failed to attract sufficient investment from abroad and appeared to be struggling for financial viability when, on 28 July 1988, it was abandoned by King Hussein on political grounds (see History, above). On 31 July King Hussein severed Jordan's legal and administrative links with the West Bank. The practical effects of this were that 5,300 teachers and civil servants, and other government workers employed by Jordan in the West Bank before the Israeli occupation in 1967, and fully paid by Jordan, were retired on full pension; subsidies from the Jordanian Government, including salaries, to some 10,000 teachers and 5,000 civil servants, employed since 1967, were removed (although most of these received a salary from Israel and only a monthly bonus from Jordan). An additional 2,000 employees, working in departments of religious affairs and Islamic law, were to continue to be employed in order to preserve an Islamic cultural identity in the area. It was estimated that the removal of subsidies would save Jordan $60m. per year. The PLO undertook to compensate all former Jordanian employees for the loss of their jobs but, owing to the restrictions imposed by Israel on the movement of funds into the Occupied Territories, this promise has proved difficult to honour.

Following the 1990–91 Gulf crisis, Jordan's 1991 budget estimates included an allocation of JD 230.2m. for capital expenditure, as well as an emergency budget of JD 120m., intended to assist the recovery of important economic sectors such as industry, transport, agriculture and tourism. Substantial additional aid commitments from external sources (see Finance, above) made it possible to implement this emergency budget, but the Government came under domestic criticism for using the extra aid to reduce the budget and external deficits, as required by the IMF, rather than to compensate the sectors that had been damaged during the recent crisis.

In May 1991 Jordan signed its fourth financial co-operation protocol with the EC, which undertook to provide a total of 126m. ECUs in development grants and loans over a five-year period from November 1991. Under the three previous protocols, covering the period 1977–91, Jordan had received a total of 203m. ECUs.

In conjunction with IMF-decreed structural adjustment, the Government in 1993 introduced a further Five-Year Economic and Social Development Plan, covering the period to 1997. Allotting a major role to the private sector through the disposal of stakes in government-owned concerns, the plan also aimed to encourage export-oriented investment and production; to stabilize the exchange rate of the dinar; to increase Jordan's foreign currency reserves to at least three months' export cover; to shift revenue generation from income to consumption, while eliminating taxation on investments and savings; to remove market distortions arising from price-fixing agreements and monopolies; to reduce and restructure subsidies; to dismantle trade and investment barriers; and to alleviate the associated problems of poverty and unemployment. Following the completion of the 1993–97 plan period, the Government drafted a rolling National Economic and Development Strategy, capable of being adjusted on a year-by-year basis.

In 1996 James Wolfensohn, President of the World Bank, visited some of the poorest areas of Jordan. In 1997 it was reported that the Government was collaborating with the World Bank to establish a two-phase programme to improve living conditions for the poor and to create jobs for impoverished Jordanians and for skilled middle class workers. The first stage, expected to last three years, includes the enlargement of the National Aid Fund (NAF), which provides direct financial aid to the poor; expansion of basic infrastructure; provision of credit for small enterprises through private and commercial banks; development of private work placement agencies; and the establishment of training for former armed services and civil services personnel for future employment in the private sector.

Statistical Survey

Source: Department of Statistics, POB 2015, Jabal Amman, 1st Circle, POB 2015, Amman; tel. 24313.

Area and Population

AREA, POPULATION AND DENSITY
(East and West Banks)

Area (sq km)	97,740*
Population (UN estimates at mid-year)†	
1994	5,143,000
1995	5,373,000
1996	5,581,000
Density (per sq km) at mid-1996	57.1

* 37,738 sq miles.

† Source: UN, *World Population Prospects: The 1996 Revision.*

(East Bank only)

Area (sq km)	89,342*
Population (census results)	
10–11 November 1979	2,100,019
10 December 1994	
Males	2,135,883
Females	1,959,696
Total	4,095,579
Population (official estimates at mid-year)	
1994	4,066,000
1995	4,215,000
1996	4,368,000
Density (per sq km) at mid-1996	48.9

* 34,495 sq miles.

GOVERNORATES
(East Bank only; estimated population at 31 December 1996)

Amman	1,696,300
Irbid	802,200
Zarqa	687,000
Balqa	301,300
Mafraq.	191,900
Karak	182,200
Jarash	132,500
Madaba	110,700
Ajlun	101,400
Aqaba	85,700
Ma'an	85,300
Tafiela	67,500
Total	**4,444,000**

PRINCIPAL TOWNS (including suburbs)

Population at 31 December 1991: Amman (capital) 965,000; Zarqa 359,000; Irbid 216,000; Russeifa 115,500.

BIRTHS, MARRIAGES AND DEATHS (East Bank only)*

	Registered live births		Registered marriages		Registered deaths	
	Number	Rate (per 1,000)	Number	Rate (per 1,000)	Number	Rate (per 1,000)
1989 .	115,742	n.a.	31,508	n.a.	9,695	n.a.
1990 .	116,520	n.a.	32,706	n.a.	10,569	n.a.
1991 .	120,554	n.a.	35,926	n.a.	10,605	n.a.
1992 .	125,395	n.a.	37,216	n.a.	11,820	n.a.
1993 .	134,489	n.a.	40,391	n.a.	11,915	n.a.
1994 .	140,444	34.5	36,132	8.9	12,290	3.0
1995 .	141,319	33.5	35,501	8.4	13,018	3.1
1996 .	142,404	32.6	34,425	7.9	13,302	3.0

* Data are tabulated by year of registration rather than by year of occurrence. Registration of births and marriages is reported to be complete, but death registration is incomplete. Figures exclude foreigners, but include registered Palestinian refugees.

Expectation of life (UN estimates, years at birth, 1990–95): Males 66.16; Females 69.84. Source: UN, *Demographic Yearbook*.

ECONOMICALLY ACTIVE POPULATION (Jordanians only)

	1990	1991	1992
Agriculture	38,266	40,848	44,400
Mining and manufacturing . .	53,468	56,856	61,800
Electricity and water . . .	6,815	7,176	6,600
Construction	51,895	54,096	60,000
Trade	52,944	56,856	63,000
Transport and communications .	44,557	48,576	52,200
Financial and insurance services .	16,774	17,664	19,800
Social and administrative services	259,478	269,928	292,200
Total employed . . .	524,197	552,000	600,000
Unemployed	106,000	128,000	106,000
Total civilian labour force . .	630,197	680,000	706,000

Source: Ministry of Labour, *Annual Report*.

Agriculture

PRINCIPAL CROPS (East Bank only; '000 metric tons)

	1994	1995	1996
Wheat	47	58	51
Barley	27	32	45
Potatoes	49	97	147
Olives	94	63	82
Cabbages	13	24	22
Tomatoes	439	440	475
Cauliflowers	39	32	32*
Pumpkins, squash and gourds .	28	36	38*
Cucumbers and gherkins . .	35	66	68*
Eggplants (Aubergines) . .	38	73	74*
Green peppers . . .	11	18	19*
Onions (dry)	21	31	79
Green beans	8	8	8*
Other vegetables . . .	47	120	125*
Watermelons	123	99	105*
Melons	22	19	20*
Grapes	26	24	84
Apples	28	42	45
Oranges	30	21	26
Tangerines, mandarins, clementines and satsumas . .	85	47	55
Lemons and limes . . .	30	32	44
Bananas	25	29	39
Other fruits and berries . .	49	37	46
Tobacco (leaves)	2	5	3

* FAO estimate.

Source: FAO, *Production Yearbook*.

LIVESTOCK
(East Bank only; FAO estimates, '000 head, year ending September)

	1994	1995	1996
Horses	4	4	4
Mules	3	3	3
Asses	19	19	19
Cattle	42	43	43
Camels	18	18	18
Sheep	2,100	2,100	2,100
Goats	555	555	555

Poultry (FAO estimates, million): 77 in 1994; 78 in 1995; 78 in 1996.

Source: FAO, *Production Yearbook*.

LIVESTOCK PRODUCTS (East Bank only; '000 metric tons)

	1994	1995	1996*
Beef and veal	1†	1*	1
Mutton and lamb . . .	12†	13*	13
Goat meat	3†	3*	3
Poultry meat	94	95*	95
Cows' milk	89†	90*	90
Sheep's milk	38†	39*	39
Goats' milk	24†	24*	24
Cheese	4*	4*	4
Butter	2*	2*	2
Poultry eggs	53	44	50
Wool: greasy	4*	4*	4
clean . . .	2*	2*	2
Sheepskins	2*	2*	n.a.

* FAO estimate(s). † Unofficial figure.

Source: FAO, *Production Yearbook*.

Forestry

ROUNDWOOD REMOVALS
('000 cubic metres, excluding bark)

	1993	1994	1995
Industrial wood	4	4	4
Fuel wood	6	5	7
Total	10	9	11

Source: FAO, *Yearbook of Forest Products*.

Fishing

(metric tons, live weight)

	1993	1994	1995
Freshwater fishes . . .	60	86	170
Marine fishes	2	2	2
Total catch	62	88	172

Source: FAO, *Yearbook of Fishery Statistics*.

Mining

('000 metric tons)

	1994	1995	1996
Crude petroleum	1.2	1.5	1.9
Phosphate rock . . .	4,216.5	4,983.9	5,424.2
Potash salts* . . .	1,550.3	1,780.0	1,765.5
Salt (unrefined) . . .	19	57	50

* Figures refer to the K_2O content.

Industry

SELECTED PRODUCTS ('000 metric tons, unless otherwise indicated)

	1993	1994	1995
Liquefied petroleum gas	127	126	138
Motor spirit (petrol)	430	471	483
Aviation gasoline	21	20*	30
Kerosene	237	222	215
Jet fuels	220	198	244
Distillate fuel oils	880	859	872
Residual fuel oils	962	901	995
Lubricating oils	21*	24	28
Petroleum bitumen (asphalt)	140	136	129
Nitrogenous fertilizers (a)†	85	135	n.a.
Phosphate fertilizers (b)†	470	750	729
Potassic fertilizers (c)†	822	930	n.a.
Cement	3,437	3,392	3,415
Cigarettes (million)	3,465	4,191	3,675
Electricity (million kWh)	4,761	5,075	5,616

† Estimated production.

* Production in terms of (a) nitrogen; (b) phosphoric acid; and (c) potassium oxide.

Source: mainly UN, *Industrial Commodity Statistics Yearbook*.

1996: Cigarettes 2,769 million.

Source: Central Bank of Jordan.

Finance

CURRENCY AND EXCHANGE RATES

Monetary Units
1,000 fils = 1 Jordanian dinar (JD).

Sterling and Dollar Equivalents (31 May 1998)
£1 sterling = JD 1.1562;
US $1 = 709.0 fils;
JD 100 = £86.49 = $141.04.

Average Exchange Rates (US $ per JD)
1995	1.4276
1996	1.4104
1997	1.4104

Note: An exchange rate of US $1 = 709 fils (JD1 = $1.4104) has been maintained since October 1995.

BUDGET (East Bank only; JD million)*

Revenue†	1993	1994	1995
Taxation	812.5	871.1	976.4
Taxes on income, profits and capital gains	118.8	136.6	152.4
Taxes on property	51.0	54.8	66.8
Taxes on financial and capital transactions	49.7	53.1	65.3
Domestic taxes on goods and services	227.1	278.9	351.7
Excises	174.3	222.4	263.6
Taxes on international trade and transactions	353.4	340.2	336.4
Import duties	337.7	324.2	318.7
Other current revenue	306.5	290.4	354.7
Entrepreneurial and property income	235.7	221.8	272.7
Administrative fees and charges, non-industrial and incidental sales	28.5	30.9	41.3
Capital revenue	0.6	0.9	1.5
Total	1,119.6	1,162.4	1,332.6

Expenditure‡	1993	1994	1995
General public services	84.8	82.5	97.8
Defence	258.6	272.0	296.0
Public order and safety	101.1	105.4	121.0
Education	201.2	205.7	227.8
Health	87.1	98.5	103.7
Social security and welfare	189.3	187.6	246.3
Housing and community amenities	16.2	24.0	26.0
Recreational, cultural and religious affairs and services	22.3	27.9	31.5
Economic affairs and services	144.0	161.9	179.5
Agriculture, forestry, fishing and hunting	33.0	53.7	65.7
Transport and communications	71.3	61.4	60.9
Other purposes	131.7	147.4	141.9
Interest payments	122.0	109.4	132.7
Sub-total§	1,236.4	1,312.8	1,471.5
Adjustment	−1.3	—	—
Total	1,235.1	1,312.8	1,471.5

* Figures represent a consolidation of the Current, Capital and Development Plan Budgets of the central Government. The data exclude the operations of the Health Security Fund and of other government agencies with individual budgets.

† Excluding grants received from abroad (JD million): 163.3 (current 160.2, capital 3.1) in 1993; 175.6 (current 168.3, capital 7.3) in 1994; 182.8 (current 175.4, capital 7.4) in 1995.

‡ Excluding lending minus repayments (JD million): −21.9 in 1993; −20.0 in 1994; −5.4 in 1995.

§ Comprising (in JD million): current expenditure 992.3 in 1993, 1,052.8 in 1994, 1,187.9 in 1995; capital expenditure 244.1 in 1993, 260.0 in 1994, 283.6 in 1995.

Source: IMF, *Government Finance Statistics Yearbook*.

1996 (JD million): Revenue 1,518.0, excl. grants received (191.3); Expenditure 1,648.3, excl. net lending (−14.9).
1997 (JD million): Revenue 1,574.0, excl. grants received (217.2); Expenditure 1,786.9, excl. net lending (−10.0).
Source: IMF, *International Financial Statistics*.

INTERNATIONAL RESERVES (US $ million at 31 December)

	1995	1996	1997
Gold*	195.9	197.7	200.7
IMF special drawing rights	1.2	0.8	0.2
Foreign exchange	1,971.7	1,758.5	2,125.4
Total	2,168.8	1,957.0	2,326.3

* National valuation.

Source: IMF, *International Financial Statistics*.

MONEY SUPPLY (JD million at 31 December)

	1995	1996	1997
Currency outside banks	1,050.9	952.1	987.6
Demand deposits at commercial banks	664.7	578.1	636.1
Total money (incl. others)	1,738.7	1,532.8	1,626.1

Source: IMF, *International Financial Statistics*.

COST OF LIVING (Consumer Price Index; base: 1990 = 100)

	1994	1995	1996
Food (incl. beverages)	123.5	126.3	135.1
Fuel and light	122.3	122.3	125.9
Clothing (incl. footwear)	132.8	142.5	156.9
Rent	117.2	121.4	126.3
All items (incl. others)	120.4	123.1	131.2

Source: Central Bank of Jordan.

1997: Food 144.1; All items 135.1 (Source: UN, *Monthly Bulletin of Statistics*).

NATIONAL ACCOUNTS (East Bank only; JD million at current prices)

Expenditure on the Gross Domestic Product (provisional)

	1994	1995	1996
Government final consumption expenditure	990.2	1,081.2	1,194.0
Private final consumption expenditure	2,774.3	3,023.2	3,393.5
Increase in stocks	60.0	67.5	84.4
Gross fixed capital formation	1,391.0	1,479.9	1,716.9
Total domestic expenditure	5,215.5	5,651.8	6,388.8
Exports of goods and services	2,093.4	2,438.2	2,597.1
Less Imports of goods and services	3,107.6	3,435.4	3,839.2
GDP in purchasers' values	4,201.3	4,654.6	5,146.7
GDP at constant 1990 prices	3,601.4	3,851.3	4,052.8

Source: IMF, *International Financial Statistics*

Gross Domestic Product by Economic Activity (provisional)

	1994	1995	1996
Agriculture, hunting, forestry and fishing	197.2	213.3	232.9
Mining and quarrying	102.4	128.1	153.6
Manufacturing	561.4	618.7	688.6
Electricity, gas and water	84.0	90.8	98.2
Construction	300.2	327.8	341.1
Trade, restaurants and hotels	377.0	423.3	480.1
Transport, storage and communications	494.0	531.7	591.8
Finance, insurance, real estate and business services	658.6	705.6	766.8
Government services	671.2	732.9	792.7
Other community, social and personal services	110.6	121.9	138.3
Private non-profit services to households	47.0	51.8	56.6
Domestic services of households	6.0	6.4	7.0
Sub-total	3,609.6	3,952.3	4,347.7
Less Imputed bank service charge	73.9	79.2	87.3
GDP at factor cost	3,535.7	3,873.1	4,260.4
Indirect taxes *Less* Subsidies	665.6	781.5	886.3
GDP in purchasers' values	4,201.3	4,654.6	5,146.7

BALANCE OF PAYMENTS (US $ million)

	1994	1995	1996
Exports of goods f.o.b.	1,424.5	1,769.6	1,816.9
Imports of goods f.o.b.	−3,003.8	−3,287.8	−3,818.1
Trade balance	−1,579.4	−1,518.2	−2,001.1
Exports of services	1,562.0	1,709.2	1,846.3
Imports of services	−1,392.7	−1,614.9	−1,597.7
Balance on goods and services	−1,410.1	−1,424.0	−1,752.6
Other income received	72.7	115.7	111.7
Other income paid	−387.5	−394.5	−412.7
Balance on goods, services and income	−1,724.9	−1,702.8	−2,053.6
Current transfers received	1,447.4	1,591.8	1,970.2
Current transfers paid	−120.5	−147.6	−138.5
Current balance	−398.0	−258.6	−221.9
Capital account (net)	—	197.2	157.7
Direct investment abroad	23.1	27.3	43.3
Direct investment from abroad	2.9	13.3	15.5
Other investment assets	62.5	−313.4	−5.9
Other investment liabilities	100.4	502.8	181.0
Net errors and omissions	−55.8	−339.9	−357.9
Overall balance	−264.9	−171.3	−188.2

Source: IMF, *International Financial Statistics*.

External Trade

PRINCIPAL COMMODITIES (distribution by SITC, US $ million)

Imports c.i.f.	1994	1995	1996
Food and live animals	586.2	598.2	967.4
Crude materials (inedible) except fuels	102.4	130.0	130.7
Mineral fuels, lubricants, etc.	430.2	480.0	525.4
Crude petroleum	332.5	355.7	n.a.
Animal and vegetable oils and fats	118.1	135.1	103.9
Chemicals	400.6	453.3	464.2
Basic manufactures	618.4	719.2	722.8
Machinery and transport equipment	859.1	905.7	1,114.1
Miscellaneous manufactured articles	217.0	210.0	220.2
Total (incl. others)	3,380.9	3,696.1	4,292.7

Exports f.o.b.	1994	1995	1995
Natural calcium phosphates	143.7	150.5	179.0
Natural potassic salts, crude	132.5	173.5	177.2
Chemicals	375.5	431.1	467.0
Fertilizers	127.5	161.4	n.a.
Cement	39.1	42.2	58.5
Vegetables, fruit and nuts	95.4	97.3	115.7
Basic manufactures	83.8	95.7	109.1
Machinery and transport equipment	56.4	65.5	34.5
Miscellaneous manufactured articles	57.9	68.9	72.1
Total (incl. others)	1,136.1	1,433.3	1,466.6

Sources: Central Bank of Jordan and IMF, *Jordan — Statistical Appendix* (March 1997).

PRINCIPAL TRADING PARTNERS
(countries of consignment, US $ million)

Imports c.i.f.	1994	1995	1996*
Argentina	16.1	48.0	14.0
Australia	29.8	40.1	108.2
Bahrain	22.3	40.4	28.6
Belgium-Luxembourg	100.6	74.2	61.8
Brazil	37.7	52.6	56.7
China, People's Republic	89.5	84.1	89.7
Egypt	43.0	46.2	93.0
France	159.0	170.0	210.5
Germany	263.9	311.6	341.6
India	55.7	69.5	74.3
Indonesia	35.2	54.8	50.9
Iraq	417.1	451.3	505.6
Italy	199.0	197.7	251.6
Japan	134.0	130.5	179.0
Korea, Republic	83.4	109.6	133.0
Lebanon	25.8	42.5	51.6
Malaysia	94.8	107.8	85.6
Netherlands	129.0	102.1	115.4
Romania	39.4	30.7	47.1
Russia	24.3	43.9	51.2
Saudi Arabia	102.4	129.5	129.1
Spain	54.4	58.1	48.1
Switzerland	32.2	38.2	63.1
Syria	69.1	78.4	140.3
Turkey	90.0	127.0	152.3
Ukraine	71.2	55.4	33.7
United Kingdom	162.9	167.1	187.7
USA	332.2	342.6	415.9
Total (incl. others)	3,368.6	3,664.4	4,292.7

* Source: Central Bank of Jordan.

Exports f.o.b.	1993	1994	1995
Bahrain	20.8	23.0	21.5
China, People's Republic . . .	24.3	12.0	19.5
Ethiopia	2.5	5.5	17.0
France	21.3	35.5	30.3
India	95.8	126.5	162.9
Indonesia	54.8	40.0	39.2
Iran	14.5	6.4	27.9
Iraq	140.2	165.0	301.7
Italy	10.7	16.4	28.9
Japan	14.3	18.3	19.1
Korea, Republic	11.0	20.8	18.6
Lebanon	27.9	29.2	38.9
Malaysia	16.3	18.9	21.2
Netherlands	16.6	19.1	25.9
Philippines	4.6	5.6	21.5
Qatar	14.8	13.3	14.7
Russia	37.4	8.8	8.2
Saudi Arabia	124.7	110.5	108.2
Sudan	9.0	15.1	18.4
Syria	36.4	49.8	63.2
Turkey	20.5	15.7	30.4
United Arab Emirates . . .	48.5	68.8	67.2
United Kingdom	13.9	13.8	20.6
USA	38.6	47.5	68.3
Yemen	17.3	11.1	15.8
Total (incl. others)	1,225.2	1,411.1	1,768.8

Source (unless otherwise indicated): UN, *International Trade Statistics Yearbook*.

Transport

RAILWAYS (traffic)

	1993	1994	1995
Passenger-km (million) . . .	2	2	1
Freight ton-km (million) . . .	711	676	698

Source: UN, *Statistical Yearbook*.

ROAD TRAFFIC ('000 motor vehicles in use)

	1993	1994	1995
Passenger cars	175.3	164.0	188.0
Commercial vehicles	63.8	75.3	69.1

Source: UN, *Statistical Yearbook*.

SHIPPING

Merchant Fleet (registered at 31 December)

	1995	1996	1997
Number of vessels	4	4	7
Displacement (grt)	21,288	40,829	42,799

Source: Lloyd's Register of Shipping, *World Fleet Statistics*.

International Sea-borne Freight Traffic ('000 metric tons)

	1988	1989	1990
Goods loaded	913	832	739
Goods unloaded	762	725	514

Source: UN, *Monthly Bulletin of Statistics*.

CIVIL AVIATION (traffic on scheduled services)

	1994	1995	1996
Kilometres flown (million) . .	36	38	42
Passengers carried ('000) . . .	1,220	1,270	1,299
Passenger-km (million) . . .	4,155	4,395	4,750
Total ton-km (million) . . .	627	695	731

Sources: Jordan Civil Aviation Authority and Royal Jordanian Airline.

Tourism

	1994	1995	1996
Foreign tourist arrivals . . .	2,781,617	2,934,116	2,793,375
Tourist receipts (US $ million) .	581.6	659.9	743.6

Source: Central Bank of Jordan.

Communications Media

(East Bank only)

	1993	1994	1995
Radio receivers ('000 in use) .	1,200	1,265	1,350
Television receivers ('000 in use) .	375	395	430
Telephones ('000 main lines in use) .	290*	317.3†	328.4†
Telefax stations ('000 in use)* . .	29	31	32
Mobile telephones (subscribers)* .	1,456	1,446	11,500
Book production: titles . . .	500‡	n.a.	465
Daily newspapers:			
Number of titles	n.a.	4	4
Average circulation ('000 copies) .	n.a.	250	250§
Non-daily newspapers:			
Number of titles	n.a.	n.a.	34
Average circulation ('000 copies) .	n.a.	n.a.	90

1996: Telephones ('000 main lines in use) 356.2†.

* Source: UN, *Statistical Yearbook* (data on telefax stations are estimates).
† Source: Jordanian Department of Statistics.
‡ First editions only, not including pamphlets.
§ Estimate.

Source (unless otherwise indicated): UNESCO, *Statistical Yearbook*.

Education

(East Bank, 1995/96)

	Schools	Teachers	Pupils
Kindergarten	828	2,848	63,250
Basic	2,531	51,721	1,074,877
Secondary: general	n.a.	8,615	143,014
Secondary: vocational . . .	n.a.	2,306	33,109
Universities and equivalent . .	n.a.	3,511	76,375
Other higher education . . .	n.a.	1,310	22,645

Directory

The Constitution

The revised Constitution was approved by King Talal I on 1 January 1952.

The Hashemite Kingdom of Jordan is an independent, indivisible sovereign state. Its official religion is Islam; its official language Arabic.

RIGHTS OF THE INDIVIDUAL

There is to be no discrimination between Jordanians on account of race, religion or language. Work, education and equal opportunities shall be afforded to all as far as is possible. The freedom of the individual is guaranteed, as are his dwelling and property. No Jordanian shall be exiled. Labour shall be made compulsory only in a national emergency, or as a result of a conviction; conditions, hours worked and allowances are under the protection of the state.

The Press, and all opinions, are free, except under martial law. Societies can be formed, within the law. Schools may be established freely, but they must follow a recognized curriculum and educational policy. Elementary education is free and compulsory. All religions are tolerated. Every Jordanian is eligible for public office, and choices are to be made by merit only. Power belongs to the people.

THE LEGISLATIVE POWER

Legislative power is vested in the National Assembly and the King. The National Assembly consists of two houses: the Senate and the House of Representatives.

THE SENATE

The number of Senators is one-half of the number of members of the House of Representatives. Senators must be unrelated to the King, over 40, and are chosen from present and past Prime Ministers and Ministers, past Ambassadors or Ministers Plenipotentiary, past Presidents of the House of Representatives, past Presidents and members of the Court of Cassation and of the Civil and *Shari'a* Courts of Appeal, retired officers of the rank of General and above, former members of the House of Representatives who have been elected twice to that House, etc. . . . They may not hold public office. Senators are appointed for four years. They may be reappointed. The President of the Senate is appointed for two years.

THE HOUSE OF REPRESENTATIVES

The members of the House of Representatives are elected by secret ballot in a general direct election and retain their mandate for four years. General elections take place during the four months preceding the end of the term. The President of the House is elected by secret ballot each year by the Representatives. Representatives must be Jordanians of over 30, they must have a clean record, no active business interests, and are debarred from public office. Close relatives of the King are not eligible. If the House of Representatives is dissolved, the new House shall assemble in extraordinary session not more than four months after the date of dissolution. The new House cannot be dissolved for the same reason as the last.

GENERAL PROVISIONS FOR THE NATIONAL ASSEMBLY

The King summons the National Assembly to its ordinary session on 1 November each year. This date can be postponed by the King for two months, or he can dissolve the Assembly before the end of its three months' session. Alternatively, he can extend the session up to a total period of six months. Each session is opened by a speech from the throne.

Decisions in the House of Representatives and the Senate are made by a majority vote. The quorum is two-thirds of the total number of members in each House. When the voting concerns the Constitution, or confidence in the Council of Ministers, 'the votes shall be taken by calling the members by name in a loud voice'. Sessions are public, though secret sessions can be held at the request of the Government or of five members. Complete freedom of speech, within the rules of either House, is allowed.

The Prime Minister places proposals before the House of Representatives; if accepted there, they are referred to the Senate and finally sent to the King for confirmation. If one house rejects a law while the other accepts it, a joint session of the House of Representatives and the Senate is called, and a decision made by a two-thirds majority. If the King withholds his approval from a law, he returns it to the Assembly within six months with the reasons for his dissent; a joint session of the Houses then makes a decision, and if the law is accepted by this decision it is promulgated. The Budget is submitted to the National Assembly one month before the beginning of the financial year.

THE KING

The throne of the Hashemite Kingdom devolves by male descent in the dynasty of King Abdullah Ibn al Hussein. The King attains his majority on his eighteenth lunar year; if the throne is inherited by a minor, the powers of the King are exercised by a Regent or a Council of Regency. If the King, through illness or absence, cannot perform his duties, his powers are given to a Deputy, or to a Council of the Throne. This Deputy, or Council, may be appointed by Iradas (decrees) by the King, or, if he is incapable, by the Council of Ministers.

On his accession, the King takes the oath to respect and observe the provisions of the Constitution and to be loyal to the nation. As Head of State he is immune from all liability or responsibility. He approves laws and promulgates them. He declares war, concludes peace and signs treaties; treaties, however, must be approved by the National Assembly. The King is Commander-in-Chief of the navy, the army and the air force. He orders the holding of elections; convenes, inaugurates, adjourns and prorogues the House of Representatives. The Prime Minister is appointed by him, as are the President and members of the Senate. Military and civil ranks are also granted, or withdrawn, by the King. No death sentence is carried out until he has confirmed it.

MINISTERS

The Council of Ministers consists of the Prime Minister, President of the Council, and of his ministers. Ministers are forbidden to become members of any company, to receive a salary from any company, or to participate in any financial act of trade. The Council of Ministers is entrusted with the conduct of all affairs of state, internal and external.

The Council of Ministers is responsible to the House of Representatives for matters of general policy. Ministers may speak in either House, and, if they are members of one House, they may also vote in that House. Votes of confidence in the Council are cast in the House of Representatives, and decided by a two-thirds majority. If a vote of 'no confidence' is returned, the ministers are bound to resign. Every newly-formed Council of Ministers must present its programme to the House of Representatives and ask for a vote of confidence. The House of Representatives can impeach ministers, as it impeaches its own members.

AMENDMENTS

Two amendments were passed in November 1974 giving the King the right to dissolve the Senate or to take away membership from any of its members, and to postpone general elections for a period not to exceed a year, if there are circumstances in which the Council of Ministers feels that it is impossible to hold elections. A further amendment in February 1976 enabled the King to postpone elections indefinitely. In January 1984 two amendments were passed, allowing elections 'in any part of the country where it is possible to hold them' (effectively, only the East Bank) and empowering the National Assembly to elect deputies from the Israeli-held West Bank.

The Government

HEAD OF STATE

King HUSSEIN IBN TALAL (proclaimed King on 11 August 1952; crowned on 2 May 1953).

CABINET*
(September 1998)

Prime Minister and Minister of Defence: Dr FAYEZ AT-TARAWNEH.

Minister of Information: NASSER JUDEH.

Minister for Development Affairs: Dr TAHER KANA'AN.

Minister of Foreign Affairs: ABUL ILAH AL-KHATIB.

Minister of Justice: JAWDAT SBOUL.

Minister of Posts and Telecommunications: SULEIMAN AL-HAFEZ.

Minister of Awqaf (Religious Endowments) and Islamic Affairs: ABD AS-SALAM AL-ABBADI.

Minister of Planning: NABIL AMMARI.

Minister of Municipal, Rural and Environmental Affairs: Dr TAWFIQ KREISHAN.

Minister of Education: FAWZI GHARAIBCH.

Minister of Public Works and Housing, and Transport: NASSER LOZI.

Minister of the Interior: NAYEF AL-QADI.

Minister of Health: Dr NAYEL AJLOUNI.

Minister of Water and Irrigation, and Minister of Energy and Mineral Resources: Dr HANI AL-MULQI

Minister of Industry, and Trade and Supply: MUHAMMAD SALEH HOURANI.

Minister of Finance: MICHEL MARTO.

Minister of Culture and Youth: TALAL SATA'AN AL-HASSAN.

Minister of Labour: MAHDI AL-FARHAN.

Minister of Agriculture: MIJHEM KHREISHA.

Minister of Social Development: Dr MOH'D KHEIR MAMSER.

Minister of Tourism and Antiquities: AQEL BELTAJI.

Minister of Parliamentary Affairs, and Minister of Administrative Development: BASSAM AL-UMUSH.

Minister of State in the Office of the Prime Minister: SAMIH BINO.

Chief of the Royal Court: Dr JAWAD AL-ANANI.

* The Head of Intelligence and the Governor of the Central Bank also have full ministerial status.

MINISTRIES

Office of the Prime Minister: POB 1577, 35216, Amman; tel. (6) 4641211; telex 21444; fax (6) 4687420.

Ministry of Agriculture: POB 961043, Amman; tel. (6) 4686151; telex 24176; fax (6) 4686310.

Ministry of Awqaf (Religious Endowments) and Islamic Affairs: POB 659, Amman; tel. (6) 5666141; telex 21559; fax (6) 5602254.

Ministry of Culture and Youth: POB 6140, Amman; tel. (6) 5604701; fax (6) 5622214.

Ministry of Defence: POB 1577, Amman; tel. (6) 5644361; telex 21200.

Ministry of Development Affairs: POB 1577, Amman; tel. (6) 4644361; fax (6) 4648825.

Ministry of Education: POB 1646, Amman 11118; tel. (6) 5607181; telex 21396; fax (6) 5666019.

Ministry of Energy and Mineral Resources: POB 140027, Amman; tel. (6) 5817900; fax (6) 5818336.

Ministry of Finance: POB 85, Amman 11118; tel. (6) 4636321; telex 23634; fax (6) 4618528.

Ministry of Foreign Affairs: POB 1577, Amman; tel. (6) 5642359; telex 21255; fax (6) 5648825.

Ministry of Health: POB 86, Amman; tel. (6) 5665131; telex 21595; fax (6) 5688373.

Ministry of Industry, and Trade and Supply: POB 2019, Amman; tel. (6) 6507191; telex 21163; fax (6) 6603721.

Ministry of Information: POB 1794, Amman; tel. (6) 4641467; fax (6) 4648825.

Ministry of the Interior: POB 100, Amman; tel. (6) 4653533; telex 23162; fax (6) 5606908.

Ministry of Justice: POB 6040, Amman; tel. (6) 4653533; fax (6) 4629949; e-mail moj@amra.nic.gov.jo.

Ministry of Labour: POB 9052, Amman; tel. (6) 5607481; fax (6) 5667193.

Ministry of Municipal, Rural and Environmental Affairs: POB 1799, Amman; tel. (6) 4641393; fax (6) 4649341.

Ministry of Planning: POB 555, Amman; tel. (6) 4644466; fax (6) 4649341.

Ministry of Posts and Telecommunications: POB 35214, Amman; tel. (6) 5607111; fax (6) 5606233.

Ministry of Public Works and Housing, and Transport: POB 1220, Amman; tel. (6) 5607481; telex 21944; fax (6) 5684759.

Ministry of Social Development: POB 6720, Amman; tel. (6) 5931391; fax (6) 5931518; f. 1956.

Ministry of Tourism and Antiquities: POB 224, Amman 11118; tel. (6) 4642311; telex 21741; fax (6) 4648465.

Ministry of Transport: POB 35214, Amman; tel. (6) 5607111; telex 21541; fax (6) 5607233.

Ministry of Water and Irrigation: Amman; tel. (6) 5689400; fax (6) 5642520.

Legislature

MAJLIS AL-UMMA
(National Assembly)

Senate

The Senate (House of Notables) consists of 40 members, appointed by the King. A new Senate was appointed by the King on 18 November 1993.

Speaker: ZAID AR-RIFAI.

House of Representatives

General Election, 8 November 1993

Party	Seats
Independent centrists	44
Islamic Action Front	16
Independent Islamists	6
Independent leftists	4
Al-Ahd.	2
Jordanian Arab Democratic Party	2
Others	6
Total	**80**

Speaker: SAED HAYEL AS-SROUR.

Political Organizations

Political parties were banned before the elections of July 1963. In September 1971 King Hussein announced the formation of a Jordanian National Union. This was the only political organization allowed. Communists, Marxists and 'other advocates of imported ideologies' were ineligible for membership. In March 1972 the organization was renamed the Arab National Union. In April 1974 King Hussein dissolved the executive committee of the Arab National Union, and accepted the resignation of the Secretary-General. In February 1976 the Cabinet approved a law abolishing the Union. Membership was estimated at about 100,000. A royal commission was appointed in April 1990 to draft a National Charter, one feature of which was the legalization of political parties. In January 1991 King Hussein approved the National Charter, which was formally endorsed in June. In July 1992 the House of Representatives adopted draft legislation which formally permitted the establishment of political parties, subject to certain conditions. In the same month a joint session of the Senate and the House of Representatives was convened to debate amendments to the new legislation, proposed by the Senate. The political parties which achieved representation in the general election in November 1993 were: the Islamic Action Front (Sec.-Gen. Dr ISHAQ FARHAN); al-Mustaqbal; the Jordanian Arab Socialist Baath Party; al-Yakatha; al-Ahd; the Jordan National Alliance; the Jordan People's Democratic Party (Leader TAYSIR AZ-ZABRI); the Jordan Social Democratic Party; and the Jordanian Arab Democratic Party. In early May 1997 nine centre parties, including Pledge and the Jordan National Alliance, announced that they had united to form the National Constitutional Party (NCP), which became the country's largest political grouping. The formation of the NCP, together with the establishment in 1996 of the Unionist Arab Democratic Party (a coalition of three leftist parties), reduced the total number of political parties from 24 to 14. In July 1997 the establishment of new Jordanian political party, the Popular Democratic Pan-Arab Movement, was announced.

Diplomatic Representation

EMBASSIES IN JORDAN

Algeria: 3rd Circle, Jabal Amman; tel. (6) 5641271; Ambassador: ABDERRAHMAN SHRAYYET.

Australia: POB 35201, Amman 11180; tel. (6) 5930246; telex 21743; fax (6) 5931260; e-mail ausemb@nets.com.jo; Ambassador: M. S. WICKES.

Austria: POB 830795, 36 Mithqal al-Fayez St, Jabal Amman 11183; tel. (6) 4644635; telex 22484; fax (6) 4672725; e-mail austemb@go.com.jo; Ambassador: Dr PHILIPP HOYOS.

Bahrain: Amman; tel. (6) 5664148; Ambassador: IBRAHIM ALI IBRAHIM.

Belgium: POB 942, Amman 11118; tel. (6) 5675683; telex 22340; fax (6) 5697487; Ambassador: GUIDO COURTOIS.

Bosnia and Herzegovina: POB 850836, Amman 11185; tel. (6) 856921; fax (6) 856923; Chargé d'affaires: MUHAMMAD MRAHOROVIĆ.

Brazil: POB 5497, Amman; tel. (6) 5642183; telex 23827; fax (6) 5612964; Ambassador: FERNANDO SILVA ALVES.

Bulgaria: POB 950578, Al-Mousel St 7, Amman 11195; tel. (6) 5699391; telex 23246; fax (6) 5699393; Ambassador: (vacant).

Canada: POB 815403, Pearl of Shmeisani Bldg, Shmeisani, Amman; tel. (6) 5666124; telex 23080; fax (6) 5689227; Ambassador: MICHAEL J. MOLLOY.

Chile: POB 830663, 73 Suez St, Abdoun, Amman; tel. (6) 814263; telex 21696; e-mail echilejo@go.com.jo; Ambassador: JORGE IGLESIAS.

China, People's Republic: Shmeisani, Amman; tel. (6) 5666139; telex 21770; Ambassador: WANG SHIJIE.

Egypt: POB 35178, Zahran St, 3rd Circle, Jabal Amman; tel. (6) 5641375; Ambassador: IHAB SEID WAHBA.

France: POB 5348, Jabal Amman; tel. (6) 4641273; telex 21219; fax (6) 4659606; Ambassador: BERNARD BAJOLET.

Germany: POB 183, 25 Benghazi St, Jabal Amman; tel. (6) 7930351; telex 21235; fax (6) 7932887; Ambassador: PETER MENDE.

Greece: POB 35069, Jabal Amman; tel. (6) 5672331; telex 21566; fax (6) 5696591; Ambassador: THEODOROS N. PANTZARIS.

Holy See: POB 5364, Amman 11183; tel. (6) 5694095; fax (6) 5692502; Apostolic Nuncio: Most Rev. GIUSEPPE LAZZAROTTO.

Hungary: POB 3441, Amman 11181; tel. (6) 5925614; telex 21815; fax (6) 5930836; Chargé d'Affaires: Dr ATTILA SZANTO.

India: POB 2168, 1st Circle, Jabal Amman; tel. (6) 4622098; telex 21068; fax (6) 4659540; e-mail indembjo@go.com.jo; Ambassador: HER CHARAN SINGH DHODY.

Indonesia: South Um-Uthaina, 6th Circle, Amman; POB 811784, Amman; tel. (6) 828911; telex 23872; fax (6) 828380; Ambassador: EDDY SUMANTRI.

Iran: POB 173, Jabal Amman; tel. (6) 5641281; telex 21218; Ambassador: G. ANSARI.

Iraq: POB 2025, 1st Circle, Jabal Amman; tel. (6) 5639331; telex 21277; Ambassador: NORI AL-WAYES.

Israel: POB 950866, Amman 11195; tel. (6) 5524680; fax (6) 5524689; e-mail isrem@go.com.jo; Ambassador: ODED ERAN.

Italy: POB 9800, Jabal Luweibdeh, Amman; tel. (6) 4638185; telex 21143; fax (6) 4659730; e-mail italemb@go.com.jo; Ambassador: FRANCESCO CERULLÌ.

Japan: POB 2835, Jabal Amman; tel. (6) 5672486; telex 21518; fax (6) 5672006; Ambassador: AKIRA NAKAYAMA.

Korea, Democratic People's Republic: Amman; tel. (6) 5666349; Ambassador: CHOE GWANG RAE.

Korea, Republic: POB 3060, Amman 11181; tel. (6) 5660745; telex 21457; fax (6) 5660280; Ambassador: JUNG-IL OH.

Kuwait: POB 2107, Jabal Amman; tel. (6) 5641235; telex 21377; Chargé d'affaires: FAYSAL MUKHAYZIM.

Lebanon: POB 811779, 2nd Circle, Jabal Amman 11181; tel. (6) 5641381; telex 21330; fax (6) 5929111; Ambassador: Dr WILLIAM HABIB.

Morocco: Jabal Amman; tel. (6) 5641451; telex 21661; Chargé d'affaires: SALEM FANKHAR ASH-SHANFARI.

Norway: POB 830510, 33 Qais bin Sa'ida St, 3rd Circle, Jabal Amman; tel. (6) 4644932; fax (6) 4644894; e-mail noremb@go.com.jo; Ambassador JAN G. JØLLE.

Oman: Amman; tel. (6) 5661131; telex 21550; Ambassador: KHAMIS BIN HAMAD AL-BATASHI.

Pakistan: POB 1232, Amman; tel. (6) 5638352; fax (6) 5611633; Ambassador: TARIQ KHAN AFRIDI.

Poland: POB 2124, 3rd Circle, 1 Mai Zeyadeh St, Jabal Amman; tel. (6) 5637153; telex 21119; fax (6) 5618744; Chargé d'affaires: BOGUSLAW REKAS.

Qatar: Amman; tel. (6) 5644331; telex 21248; Ambassador: Sheikh HAMAD BIN MUHAMMAD BIN JABER ATH-THANI.

Romania: POB 2869, 21 Abdullah Bin Massoud St, Shmeisani, Amman; tel. (6) 5667738; telex 21860; fax (6) 5684018; Ambassador: IOAN AGAFICIOAIA.

Russia: Amman; tel. (6) 5641158; Ambassador: ALEKSANDR VLADIMIROVICH SALTANOV.

Saudi Arabia: POB 2133, 5th Circle, Jabal Amman; tel. (6) 5644154; Ambassador: ABDALLAH SUDEIRI.

South Africa: POB 851508, Sweifieh 11185, Amman; tel. (6) 811194; fax (6) 810080; Ambassador: H. B. B. DE BRUYN.

Spain: Zahran St, POB 454, Jabal Amman; tel. (6) 5614166; telex 21224; fax (6) 5614173; Ambassador: JUAN MANUEL CABRERA HERNÁNDEZ.

Sudan: Jabal Amman; tel. (6) 5624145; telex 21778; Ambassador: AHMAD DIAB.

Sweden: POB 830536, 4th Circle, Jabal Amman; tel. (6) 5931177; telex 22039; fax (6) 5930179; Ambassador: AGNETA BOHMAN.

Switzerland: Jabal Amman; tel. (6) 5931416; fax (6) 5930685; Ambassador: GIAN-FEDERICO PEDOTTI.

Syria: POB 1377, 4th Circle, Jabal Amman; tel. (6) 5641935; Chargé d'affaires: MAJID ABOU SALEH.

Tunisia: Jabal Amman; tel. (6) 5674307; telex 21149; fax (6) 5605790; Ambassador: HATEM BEN OTHMAN.

Turkey: POB 2062, Islamic College St, 2nd Circle, Jabal Amman 11181; tel. (6) 5641251; telex 23005; fax (6) 5612353; Ambassador: SÜHA UMAR.

United Arab Emirates: Jabal Amman; tel. (6) 5644369; telex 21832; Ambassador: ABDULLAH ALI ASH-SHURAFA.

United Kingdom: POB 87, Abdoun, Amman; tel. (6) 5923100; telex 22209; fax (6) 5923759; e-mail British@nets.com.jo; Ambassador: CHRISTOPHER BATTISCOMBE.

USA: POB 354, Amman 11118; tel. (6) 5920201; fax (6) 5920121; Ambassador: WILLIAMS BURNS.

Yemen: Amman; tel. (6) 5642381; telex 23526; Ambassador: ALI ABDULLAH ABU LUHOUM.

Yugoslavia: POB 5227, Amman; tel. (6) 5665107; telex 21505; Ambassador: ZORAN S. POPOVIĆ.

Judicial System

With the exception of matters of purely personal nature concerning members of non-Muslim communities, the law of Jordan was based on Islamic Law for both civil and criminal matters. During the days of the Ottoman Empire, certain aspects of Continental law, especially French commercial law and civil and criminal procedure, were introduced. Due to British occupation of Palestine and Transjordan from 1917 to 1948, the Palestine territory has adopted, either by statute or case law, much of the English common law. Since the annexation of the non-occupied part of Palestine and the formation of the Hashemite Kingdom of Jordan, there has been a continuous effort to unify the law.

Court of Cassation. The Court of Cassation consists of seven judges, who sit in full panel for exceptionally important cases. In most appeals, however, only five members sit to hear the case. All cases involving amounts of more than JD100 may be reviewed by this Court, as well as cases involving lesser amounts and cases which cannot be monetarily valued. However, for the latter types of cases, review is available only by leave of the Court of Appeal, or, upon refusal by the Court of Appeal, by leave of the President of the Court of Cassation. In addition to these functions as final and Supreme Court of Appeal, the Court of Cassation also sits as High Court of Justice to hear applications in the nature of habeas corpus, mandamus and certiorari dealing with complaints of a citizen against abuse of governmental authority.

Courts of Appeal. There are two Courts of Appeal, each of which is composed of three judges, whether for hearing of appeals or for dealing with Magistrates Courts' judgments in chambers. Jurisdiction of the two Courts is geographical, with the Court for the Western Region (which has not sat since June 1967) sitting in Jerusalem and the Court for the Eastern Region sitting in Amman. The regions are separated by the River Jordan. Appellate review of the Courts of Appeal extends to judgments rendered in the Courts of First Instance, the Magistrates' Courts, and Religious Courts.

Courts of First Instance. The Courts of First Instance are courts of general jurisdiction in all matters civil and criminal except those specifically allocated to the Magistrates' Courts. Three judges sit in all felony trials, while only two judges sit in misdemeanour and civil cases. Each of the seven Courts of First Instance also exercises appellate jurisdiction in cases involving judgments of less than JD20 and fines of less than JD10, rendered by the Magistrates' Courts.

Magistrates' Courts. There are 14 Magistrates' Courts, which exercise jurisdiction in civil cases involving no more than JD250 and in criminal cases involving maximum fines of JD100 or maximum imprisonment of one year.

Religious Courts. There are two types of religious court: The *Shari'a* Courts (Muslims): and the Ecclesiastical Courts (Eastern Orthodox, Greek Melkite, Roman Catholic and Protestant). Jurisdiction extends to personal (family) matters, such as marriage, divorce, alimony, inheritance, guardianship, wills, interdiction and, for the Muslim community, the constitution of Waqfs (Religious Endowments). When a dispute involves persons of different religious communities, the Civil Courts have jurisdiction in the matter unless the parties agree to submit to the jurisdiction of one or the other of the Religious Courts involved.

Each *Shari'a* (Muslim) Court consists of one judge (*Qadi*), while most of the Ecclesiastical (Christian) Courts are normally composed of three judges, who are usually clerics. *Shari'a* Courts apply the doctrines of Islamic Law, based on the Koran and the *Hadith* (Precepts of Muhammad), while the Ecclesiastical Courts base their law on various aspects of Canon Law. In the event of conflict between any two Religious Courts or between a Religious Court and a Civil Court, a Special Tribunal of three judges is appointed by the President of the Court of Cassation, to decide which court shall have jurisdiction. Upon the advice of experts on the law of the various communities, this Special Tribunal decides on the venue for the case at hand.

Religion

Over 80% of the population are Sunni Muslims, and the King can trace unbroken descent from the Prophet Muhammad. There is a Christian minority, living mainly in the towns, and there are smaller numbers of non-Sunni Muslims.

ISLAM

Chief Justice and President of the Supreme Muslim Secular Council: Sheikh MUHAMMAD MHELAN.

Director of Shari'a Courts: Sheikh SUBHI AL-MUWQQAT.

Mufti of the Hashemite Kingdom of Jordan: Sheikh MUHAMMAD ABDO HASHEM.

CHRISTIANITY
The Roman Catholic Church

Latin Rite

Jordan forms part of the Patriarchate of Jerusalem (see chapter on Israel).

Vicar-General for Transjordan: Mgr SELIM SAYEGH (Titular Bishop of Aquae in Proconsulari), Latin Vicariate, POB 1317, Amman: tel. (6) 5637440.

Melkite Rite

The Greek-Melkite archdiocese of Petra (Wadi Musa) and Philadelphia (Amman) contained 31,000 adherents at 31 December 1997.

Archbishop of Petra and Philadelphia: Most Rev. GEORGES EL-MURR, Archevêché Grec-Melkite Catholique, POB 2435, Jabal Amman, Amman 11181; tel. (6) 5624757; fax (6) 5628560.

Syrian Rite

The Syrian Catholic Patriarch of Antioch is resident in Beirut, Lebanon.

Patriarchal Exarchate of Jerusalem: Mont Achrafieh, Rue Barto, POB 10041, Amman; Exarch Patriarchal Mgr PIERRE ABD AL-AHAD.

The Anglican Communion

Within the Episcopal Church in Jerusalem and the Middle East, Jordan forms part of the diocese of Jerusalem. The President Bishop of the Church is the Bishop in Jerusalem (see the chapter on Israel).

Assistant Bishop in Amman: Rt Rev. ELIA KHOURY, POB 598, Amman.

Other Christian Churches

The Coptic Orthodox Church, the Greek Orthodox Church (Patriarchate of Jerusalem) and the Evangelical Lutheran Church in Jordan are also active.

The Press

Jordan Press Association: Amman; Pres. RAKAN AL-MAJALI.

DAILIES

Al-Akhbar (News): POB 62420, Amman; f. 1976; Arabic; publ. by the Arab Press Co; Editor RACAN EL-MAJALI; circ. 15,000.

Al-Aswaq: POB 11117, Amman 11123; tel. (6) 5687690; fax (6) 5687292; f. 1992; Editor MUSTAFA ABU LIBDEH.

Ad-Dustour (The Constitution): POB 591, Amman; tel. (6) 5664153; telex 21392; fax (6) 5667170; e-mail dustour@go.com.jo; f. 1967; Arabic; publ. by the Jordan Press and Publishing Co; owns commercial printing facilities; Chair. KAMEL ASH-SHERIF; Editor NABIL ASH-SHARIF; Man. Dir SAIF ASH-SHARIF; circ. 100,000.

Al-Mithaq: Amman; f. 1993; Arabic.

Ar-Rai (Opinion): POB 6710, Amman; tel. (6) 5667171; fax (6) 5661242; f. 1971; Arabic; independent; published by Jordan Press Foundation; Chair. ABD AS-SALAM TARAWNEH; Gen. Dir MOHAMAD AL-AMAD; Editor-in-Chief SULEIMAN QUDA; circ. 90,000.

The Jordan Times: POB 6710, Amman; tel. (6) 5667171; telex 21497; fax (6) 5661242; f. 1975; English; published by Jordan Press Establishment; Editor-in-Chief GEORGE HAWATMEH; circ. 15,000.

Sawt ash-Shaab (Voice of the People): POB 3037, Amman; tel. (6) 5667101; fax (6) 5667993; f. 1983; Arabic; Editor-in-Chief: HASHEM KHAISAT; circ. 30,000.

PERIODICALS

Akhbar al-Usbou (News of the Week): POB 605, Amman; tel. (6) 5677881; telex 21644; fax (6) 5677882; f. 1959; weekly; Arabic; economic, social, political; Chief Editor and Publr ABD AL-HAFIZ MUHAMMAD; circ. 100,000.

Al-Aqsa (The Ultimate): POB 1957, Amman; weekly; Arabic; armed forces magazines.

Al-Ghad al-Iqtisadi: Media Services International, POB 9313, Amman; tel. and fax (6) 5648298; telex 21392; fortnightly; English; economic; Chief Editor RIAD AL-KHOURI.

BYTE Middle East: POB 91128, Amman 11191; tel. (6) 5650444; fax (6) 5650888; f. 1995; monthly; Arabic; information technology; Editor-in-Chief KHALDOON TABAZA.

Huda El-Islam (The Right Way of Islam): POB 659, Amman; tel. (6) 5666141; telex 21559; f. 1956; monthly; Arabic; scientific and literary; published by the Ministry of Awqaf and Islamic Affairs; Editor Dr AHMAD MUHAMMAD HULAYYEL.

Jordan: POB 224, Amman; telex 21497; f. 1969; published quarterly by Jordan Information Bureau, Washington; circ. 100,000.

Al-Liwa' (The Standard): POB 3067, Jabal Amman-2nd Circle, Amman 11181; tel. (6) 5642770; fax (6) 5656324; f. 1972; weekly; Arabic; Chief Editor HASAN AL-TAL.

Military Magazine: Army Headquarters, Amman; f. 1955; quarterly; dealing with military and literary subjects; published by Armed Forces.

As-Sabah (The Morning): POB 2396, Amman; weekly; Arabic; circ. 6,000.

Shari'a: POB 585, Amman; f. 1959; fortnightly; Islamic affairs; published by Shari'a College; circ. 5,000.

Shihan: POB 96-654; Amman; tel. (6) 5601511; fax (6) 5656324; weekly; Editor-in-Chief HASAN AL-TAL.

The Star: Media Services International, POB 9313 Amman; tel. and fax (6) 5648298; telex 21392; e-mail star@arabia.com; f. 1982, formerly The Jerusalem Star; weekly; English; Publr and Editor-in-Chief OSAMA ASH-SHERIF; circ. 10,000.

NEWS AGENCIES

Jordan News Agency (PETRA): POB 6845, Amman; tel. (6) 5644455; telex 21220; f. 1965; government-controlled; Dir-Gen. ABDULLAH AL-UTUM.

Foreign News Bureaux

Agence France-Presse (AFP): POB 3340, Amman; tel. (6) 4642976; telex 21469; fax (6) 4654680; e-mail randa@afp.index.com.jo; Bureau Man. Mrs RANDA HABIB.

Agenzia Nazionale Stampa Associata (ANSA) (Italy): POB 35111, Amman; tel. (6) 5644092; telex 21207; Correspondent JOHN HALABI.

Associated Press (AP) (USA): POB 35111, Amman 11180; tel. (6) 4614660; telex 23514; fax (6) 4614661; e-mail jamal-halaby@ap.org; Correspondent JAMAL HALABY.

Deutsche Presse Agentur (dpa) (Germany): POB 35111, Amman; tel. (6) 5623907; telex 21207; Correspondent JOHN HALABI.

Reuters (UK): POB 667, Amman; tel. (6) 5623776; telex 21414; fax (6) 5619231; Bureau Chief JACK REDDEN.

Informatsionnoye Telegrafnoye Agentstvo Rossii—Telegrafnoye Agentstvo Suverennykh Stran (ITAR—TASS) (Russia): Jabal Amman, Nabich Faris St, Block 111/83 124, Amman; Correspondent NIKOLAI LEBEDINSKY.

Central News Agency (Taiwan), Iraqi News Agency, Middle East News Agency (Egypt), Qatar News Agency, Saudi Press Agency and UPI (USA) also maintain bureaux in Amman.

Publishers

Alfaris Publishing and Distribution Co: POB 9157, Amman 11191; tel. (6) 5605432; fax (6) 5685501; e-mail mkayyali@nets.com.jo; Dir MAHER SAID KAYYALI.

Aram Studies Publishing and Distribution House: POB 997, Amman 11941; tel. (6) 835015; fax (6) 835079; art, finance, health, management, science, business; Gen. Dir SALEH ABOUSBA.

El-Nafa'es: POB 211511, Amman 11121; tel. (6) 5693940; fax (6) 5693941; education, Islamic.

Jordan Book Centre Co Ltd: POB 301, Al-Jubeiha, Amman 11941; tel. (6) 5606882; telex 21153; fax (6) 5602016; e-mail jbc@nets.com.jo; f. 1982; fiction, business, economics, computer science, medicine, engineering, general non-fiction; CEO I. SHARBAIN.

Jordan House for Publication: Basman St, POB 1121, Amman; tel. (6) 24224; fax (6) 51062; f. 1952; medicine, nursing, dentistry; Man. Dir MURSI EL-ASHKAR.

Jordan Press and Publishing Co Ltd: POB 591, Amman; tel. (6) 5664153; telex 21392; fax (6) 5667170; e-mail dustour@go.com.jo; f. 1967 by *Al-Manar* and *Falastin* dailies; publishes *Ad-Dustour* (daily), *Ad-Dustour Sport* (weekly) and *The Star* (English weekly); Chair. KAMEL ASH-SHARIF; Dir-Gen SEIF ASH-SHERIF.

Jordan Press Foundation: POB 6710, Amman; tel. (6) 5667171; telex 21497; fax (6) 5661242; publishes *Ar-Rai* (daily) and the *Jordan Times* (daily); Chair. MAHMOUD AL-KAYED; Gen. Dir MOHAMAD AMAD.

Other publishers in Amman include: Dairat al-Ihsaat al-Amman, George N. Kawar, Al-Matbaat al-Hashmiya and The National Press.

Broadcasting and Communications

TELECOMMUNICATIONS

Telecommunications Regulatory Commission (TRC): POB 850967, Amman 11185; tel. (6) 862020; fax (6) 863641; e-mail trc@amra.nic.gov.jo; Dir-Gen. YOUSEF ABU JAMOUS.

Jordan Mobile Telephone Service Company (JMTSC): Amman; holds a monopoly on the operation of the mobile telecommunications network until Nov. 1998.

Jordan Telecommunications Company (JTC): Amman; Chair. ALI SHUKRI.

RADIO AND TELEVISION

Jordan Radio and Television Corporation (JRTV): POB 1041, Amman; tel. (6) 773111; telex 23544; fax (6) 751503; e-mail general@jrtv.gov.jo; internet http://www.jrtv.com; f. 1968; government TV station broadcasts for 90 hours weekly in Arabic and English; in colour; advertising accepted; Dir-Gen. IHSAN RAMZI SHIKIM; Dir of Television NASSER JUDEH; Dir of Radio HASHIM KHURAYSAT.

Finance

(cap. = capital; p.u. = paid up; dep. = deposits; m. = million; res = reserves; brs = branches; JD = Jordanian dinars)

BANKING

Central Bank

Central Bank of Jordan: POB 37, King Hussein St, Amman 11118; tel. (6) 4630301; telex 21250; fax (6) 4638889; e-mail rdep@cbj.gov.jo; internet http://www.cbj.gov.jo; f. 1964; cap. JD 18m., res JD 11.2m., dep. JD 2,193.6m. (Dec. 1996); Gov. Dr ZIAD FARIZ; 2 brs.

National Banks

Arab Bank PLC: POB 950545, Shmeisani, Amman 11195; tel. (6) 5607115; telex 23091; fax (6) 5606793; internet http://www.arabbank.com; f. 1930; cap. JD 88m., res JD 676m., dep. JD 9,131.6m. (Dec. 1997); Chair. ABD AL-MAJID SHOMAN; 88 brs in Jordan, 82 brs abroad.

Bank of Jordan PLC: POB 2140, South Sayegh Commercial Centre, Jabal Weibdeh, Amman; tel. (6) 5644327; telex 22033; fax (6) 5656642; f. 1960; cap. JD 10.5m., res JD 15.6m., dep. JD 493.7m., (Dec. 1996); Chair. TAWFIK SHAKER FAKHOURI; Gen. Man. FAYEZ ABUL ENEIN; 42 brs.

Cairo Amman Bank: Cairo Amman Bank Bldg, Wadi Saqra St, Amman 11195; POB 950661, Amman 11195; tel. (6) 5616910; telex 24049; fax (6) 5642890; f. 1960; cap. JD 10m., res JD 11.6m., dep. JD 648m. (Dec. 1996); Chair. KHALIL TALHOUNI; Gen. Man. YAZID MUFTI; 37 brs in Jordan, 16 brs abroad.

Jordan Gulf Bank: POB 9989, Shmeinsani-Al Burj Area, Amman 11191; tel. (6) 5603931; telex 21959; fax (6) 5664110; f. 1977; cap JD 20m., res JD 3.2m., dep. JD 161.8m. (Dec. 1996); Chair. ZUHAIR F. AWARIANI.

Jordan Islamic Bank for Finance and Investment: POB 926225, Amman; tel. (6) 5677377; telex 21125; fax (6) 5666326; f. 1978; cap. JD 14.6m., res JD 27.3m., dep. JD 534m. (Dec. 1996); Chair. MAHMOUD HASSOUHAH; Gen. Man. MUSA A. SHIHADEH; 35 brs.

Jordan Kuwait Bank: POB 9776, Abdali, Amman 11191; tel. (6) 5688814; telex 21994; fax (6) 5687452; f. 1976; cap. JD 20m., res JD 12.2m., dep. JD 263.3m. (Dec. 1997); Chair. ABD AL-KARIM KABARITI; Gen. Man. M. YASSER AL-ASMER; 25 brs.

Jordan National Bank PLC: POB 3103, Amman 11118; tel. (6) 702282; telex 23501; fax (6) 5687067; f. 1955; cap. JD 42m., res JD 25.8m., dep. JD 536.5m. (Dec. 1996); Chair. Dr RAJAI MUASHER; 54 brs in Jordan, 4 brs in Lebanon, 1 br. in Cyprus and 5 brs in the Gaza Strip and the West Bank.

Middle East Investment Bank: POB 560, Amman 11118; tel. (6) 5695470; telex 22174; fax (6) 5693410; cap. JD 10m., res 1.9m., dep. 44.8m. (Dec. 1996); Chair. ALI MANGO.

Foreign Banks

ANZ Grindlays Bank: POB 9997, Shmeisani, Amman 11191; tel. (6) 5607201; telex 21980; fax (6) 5679115; cap. p.u. JD 10m., dep. JD 185m., total assets JD 208m. (Dec. 1997); Gen. Man. in Jordan HUGH FERGUSON; brs in Amman (8 brs), Aqaba, Irbid (2 brs), Zerka, Northern Shouneh and Kerak.

Arab Banking Corpn: POB 926691, Queen Nour St, Amman 11110; tel. (6) 5664183; telex 21114; fax (6) 5686291; f. 1990; cap. p.u. JD 20m., dep. JD 164m., total assets JD 212m. (Dec. 1997); Chair. ABDUL WAHAB AT-TAMMAR; 22 brs.

Arab Islamic International Bank: Amman; f. 1997; cap p.u. JD 40m.

Arab Land Bank (Egypt): POB 6729, Queen Musbah St, 3rd Circle, Jabal Amman 11118; tel. (6) 4656508; telex 21208; fax (6) 4646274; e-mail arlb@go.com.jo; wholly-owned subsidiary of the Central Bank of Egypt; cap. JD 10m., dep. JD 103.3m., res JD 5.5m., total assets JD 136.1m. (Dec. 1997); Chair. ALA AL-ALOSSIYA; Gen. Man. SAMIR MAHDI; 19 brs in Jordan, 4 brs abroad.

The British Bank of the Middle East: POB 925286, Khalid Bin Walid St, Jebel Hussein, Amman 11110; tel. (6) 5607471; telex 21253; fax (6) 692964; f. 1889; cap. JD 5m., dep. JD 150m., total assets JD 169m. (Dec. 1994); Chair. Sir WILLIAM PURVES; Area Man. J. S. GIBSON; 6 brs.

Citibank NA (USA): POB 5055, Prince Muhammad St, Amman; tel. (6) 564227; telex 21314; fax (6) 5658693; cap. p.u. JD 5m., dep. JD 56.2m., total assets JD 75.4m. (Dec. 1992); Chair. and CEO JOHN S. REED.

Rafidain Bank (Iraq): POB 1194, Amman; tel. (6) 5624365; telex 21334; fax (6) 5658698; f. 1941; cap. p.u. JD 5m., res JD 2.1m., dep. JD 31.4m. (Dec. 1992); Pres. and Chair. DHIA HABEEB AL-KHAYOON; 3 brs.

Bank Al-Mashrek (Lebanon) also has a branch in Amman.

Specialized Credit Institutions

Agricultural Credit Corporation: POB 77, Amman; tel. (6) 5661105; telex 24194; fax (6) 5698365; e-mail agri-cc@nets.com.jo; f. 1959; cap. p.u. JD 24m., res JD 7.5m., total assets JD 96.4m. (Dec. 1997); Chair. MEGHIM AL-KHRIESHA; Dir-Gen. NIMER AN-NABULSI; 20 brs.

The Arab Jordan Investment Bank: POB 8797, Arab Jordan Investment Bank Bldg, Shmeisani Commercial Area, Amman 11120; tel. (6) 5607126; telex 22087; fax (6) 5681482; f. 1978; cap. JD 10m., res JD 15.6m., dep. JD 195.7m. (Dec. 1996); Chair. and CEO ABD AL-KADER AL-QADI; 10 brs in Jordan, 1 br abroad.

Cities and Villages Development Bank: POB 1572, Amman; tel. (6) 5668151; telex 22476; fax (6) 5668153; f. 1979; cap. p.u. JD 23m., gen. res JD 9.5m., total assets JD 68.1m. (Dec. 1996); Gen. Man. Dr HAMMAD AL-KASASBEH; 1 br. in Irbid.

Housing Bank: POB 7693, Parliament St, Abdali, Amman 11118; tel. (6) 5607315; telex 21693; fax (6) 5678121; f. 1973; cap. JD 100m., res JD 112.9m., dep. JD 987.9m. (Dec. 1997); Chair. ZUHAIR KHOURI; Gen. Man. ABDUL QADER DWEIK; 120 brs.

Industrial Development Bank: POB 1982, Islamic College St, Jabal Amman, Amman 11118; tel. (6) 5642216; telex 21349; fax (6) 5647821; f. 1965; cap. JD 11.6m., res JD 19.4m., dep. JD 33.5m. (Dec. 1996); Chair. MUNZER EL-FAHOUM; Gen. Man. RAJAB AS-SA'AD.

Jordan Co-operative Organization: POB 1343, Amman; tel. (6) 5665171; telex 21835; f. 1968; cap. p.u. JD 5.2m., dep. JD 11.5m., res JD 6.8m. (Nov. 1992); Chair. and Dir-Gen. JAMAL AL-BEDOUR.

Jordan Investment and Finance Bank (JIFBANK): Issam Ajlouni St, Shmeisani, Amman; POB 950601, Amman; tel. (6) 5665145; telex 23181; fax (6) 5681410; f. 1982 as Jordan Investment and Finance Corpn, name changed 1989; cap. JD 3.3m., dep. JD 234.2m. (Dec. 1998); Chair. NIZAR JARDANEH.

Social Security Corporation: POB 926031, Amman; tel. (6) 5643000; telex 22287; fax (6) 5610014; f. 1978; Dir-Gen. MUHAMMAD S. HOURANI.

Union Bank for Savings and Investment: Prince Shaker Bin Zeid St, Shmeisani, Amman; tel. (6) 5607011; telex 21875; fax (6) 5666149; f. 1978 as Arab Finance Corpn, named changed 1991; cap. JD 11m.; res 11.6m., dep. 167.1m. (Dec. 1996); Chair. HALIM SALFITI; 16 brs.

STOCK EXCHANGE

Amman Financial Market: POB 8802, Amman; tel. (6) 5607179; telex 21711; fax (6) 5686830; e-mail afm@go.com.jo; f. 1978; Gen. Man. WAHIB SHAIR.

INSURANCE

Jordan Insurance Co Ltd: POB 279, Company's Bldg, 3rd Circle, Jabal Amman, Amman; tel. and fax (6) 4634161; telex 21486; e-mail jicjo@go.com.jo; f. 1951; cap. p.u. JD 5m.; Chair. and Man. Dir

KHALDUN ABU HASSAN; 6 brs (3 in Saudi Arabia, 3 in the United Arab Emirates).

Middle East Insurance Co Ltd: POB 1802, Shmeisani, Yaqoub Sarrouf St, Amman; tel. (6) 5605144; telex 21420; fax (6) 5605950; f. 1963; cap. p.u. US $3.3m.; Chair. WASEF AZAR; 1 br. in Saudi Arabia.

National Ahlia Insurance Co: POB 6156-2938, Sayed Qutub St, Shmeisani, Amman 11118; tel. (6) 5671169; telex 21309; fax (6) 5684900; e-mail info@nationalahlia.com; internet http://www .nationalahlia.com; f. 1965; cap. p.u. JD 2m.; Chair. MUSTAFA ABU GOURA; Gen. Man. GHALEB ABU GOURA.

United Insurance Co Ltd: POB 7521, United Insurance Bldg, King Hussein St, Amman 11118; tel. (6) 4648513; telex 23153; fax (6) 4629417; e-mail united@go.com.jo; f. 1972; all types of insurance; cap. JD 2m.; Chair. and Gen. Man. RAOUF SA'AD ABUJABER.

There are 17 local and one foreign insurance company operating in Jordan.

Trade and Industry

DEVELOPMENT ORGANIZATIONS

Jordan Valley Authority: POB 2769, Amman; tel. (6) 5642472; telex 21692; projects in Stage I of the Jordan Valley Development Plan were completed in 1979. In 1988 about 26,000 ha was under intensive cultivation. Infrastructure projects also completed include 1,100 km of roads, 2,100 housing units, 100 schools, 15 health centres, 14 administration buildings, 4 marketing centres, 2 community centres, 2 vocational training centres. Electricity is now provided to all the towns and villages in the valley from the national network and domestic water is supplied to them from tube wells. Contributions to the cost of development came through loans from Kuwait Fund, Abu Dhabi Fund, Saudi Fund, Arab Fund, USAID, Fed. Germany, World Bank, EC, Italy, Netherlands, UK, Japan and OPEC Special Fund. Many of the Stage II irrigation projects are now completed or under implementation. Projects under way include the construction of the Wadi al-Arab dam, the raising of the King Talal dam and the 14.5-km extension of the 98-km East Ghor main canal. Stage II will include the irrigation of 4,700 ha in the southern Ghor. The target for the Plan is to irrigate 43,000 ha of land in the Jordan Valley. Future development in irrigation will include the construction of the Maqarin dam and the Wadi Malaha storage dam; Pres. MUHAMMAD BANI HANI.

CHAMBERS OF COMMERCE AND INDUSTRY

Amman Chamber of Commerce: POB 1800, Amman 11118; tel. (6) 5666151; e-mail aci@amra.nic.gov.jo; f. 1923; Pres. HAIDER MURAD; Sec.-Gen. MUHAMMAD AL-MUHTASSEB.

Amman Chamber of Industry: POB 1800, Amman; tel. (6) 5643001; telex 22079; fax (6) 5647852; f. 1962; 7,000 industrial companies registered (1992); Pres. KHALDUN ABU HASSAN; Dir.-Gen. WALID KHATIB.

UTILITIES
Electricity

Jordanian Electric Power Company (Jepco): Amman.

National Electric Power Company (Nepco): Amman.

Water

Water Authority of Jordan (WAJ): Amman.

MAJOR COMPANIES

Adnan Sha'lan & Co: POB 1428, King Hussein St, Amman; tel. (6) 5621122; telex 21613; fax (6) 5626946; f. 1953; manufacturers of paints, glues, refrigerators, gas cookers, dairy products and cosmetics; sales US $10m. (1982); cap. US $3m.; Chair. ADNAN SHA'LAN; Man. Dir GHALEB SHA'LAN; 400 employees.

Agricultural Marketing and Processing Co of Jordan: POB 7314, 38 Muhammad Ali-Janah St, Amman; tel. (6) 819161; telex 23796; fax (6) 819164; f. 1984; govt-owned; Chair. Dr ABDULHADI ALAWEEN; Gen. Man. SALEH AR-REFAI.

Arab Breweries Co Ltd: POB 168, Amman; tel. (6) 5660730; telex 24303; f. 1969; brewers of Henninger beer under licence; sales JD 1m. (1982); cap. p.u. JD 220,000; Chair. SAID I. MUASHER; Brewmaster MUHAMMAD ABED FATTAH.

Arab Centre for Pharmaceutical and Chemical Industries (ACPC): POB 22, Sahab; tel. (6) 818567; telex 23489; fax (6) 827282; f. 1984; manufacturers of pharmaceuticals and chemicals; cap. JD 5m.; Dir Gen. BADIE QAWASAMI; 300 employees.

Arab Investment and International Trade Co Ltd: POB 94, ar-Raqim, Amman; tel. 731191; telex 23216; f. 1976; manufacturers of toiletries; sales JD 6.2m. (1992); cap. p.u. JD 3.5m.; Chair. RAJAB ELSAAD; Gen. Man. OMAR HIKMAT; 150 employees.

Arab Pharmaceutical Manufacturing Co Ltd: POB 1695, Amman; tel. (6) 5685121; telex 21315; fax (6) 5685131; f. 1962; manufacturers of pharmaceuticals; sales JD 18m. (1990); cap. p.u. JD 5m.; Chair. AMIN SHOUQAIR; 362 employees.

Arab Potash Co Ltd: POB 1470, Amman; tel. (6) 5666165; telex 21683; f. 1956; production of potash and potassium chloride, with a by-product of salt; production 1.2m. tons (1987); 51% State-owned; Chair. OMAR ABDULLAH DAQHAN; Dir-Gen. ALI NSOUR; 1,200 employees.

Elba House Co: POB 3449, Amman; tel. (6) 842600; telex 22060; fax (6) 842603; f. 1976; manufacturers of prefabricated buildings, caravans, steel structures, vehicle bodies and construction plant; 500 employees.

General Investment Co Ltd: POB 312, Prince Muhammad St, Amman; tel. (6) 4625161; telex 21323; fax (6) 4657679; f. 1986 by merger of Jordan Brewery Co (f. 1955) and its subsidiary the General Investment Co; producers of beer and soft drinks and investment and real estate brokers; sales US $9m.; cap. US $10m. (1997); Chair. FARHAN ABUJABER; Gen. Man. KHALIL LAHLER.

Industrial, Commercial and Agricultural Co Ltd (ICA): POB 6066, Amman; tel. 951945; telex 41434; fax 951198; f. 1961; industrial, commercial and agricultural investment; operates factories producing (under licence) soap, detergents, toiletries, paints, biscuits, ice-cream and containers; sales JD 31m. (1993); cap. p.u. JD 5m.; Chair. MOHD. A. R. ABU HASSAN; Man. Dir Eng. YAHYA AL-ALAMI; 550 employees.

International Contracting and Investment Co: POB 19170, Amman; tel. (6) 5666133; telex 21977; f. 1977; building, civil construction, etc.; sales JD 10m. (1982); cap. p.u. JD 4m.; Chair. FAKHRY ABU SHAKRA; Vice-Pres. HASSAN SHIHABI; 176 employees.

Jordan Cement Factories Co: Amman; merged with South Cement Co Sept. 1985; annual production at two works 3.5m. tons (1987).

Jordan Petroleum Refinery Co: POB 1079, Amman; tel. (6) 4657600; telex 21246; fax (6) 4657934; f. 1956; petroleum refining and distribution of refined petroleum products (lube oil blending and canning; fmr of LPG cylinders); production 3.3m. tons (1997); sales 4.2m. tons (JD 516.2m.); profits JD 6.8m. ($9.6m.) (1997); Chair. ABD AL-MAJID SHOMAN; Dir-Gen. ABD AL-WAHAB ZU'BI; Refinery Man. M. KHALIFEH; 3,533 employees.

Jordan Phosphate Mines Co Ltd (JPMC): POB 30, Amman; tel. (6) 5660141; telex 21223; f. 1930; engaged in production and export of rock phosphate; absorbed Jordan Fertilizer Industries 1991; Chair. HUSSAIN AL-QASIM; Gen. Man. WASIF AZAR; three mines in operation; production 6.5m. tons (1988); exports 4.3m. tons (1992).

Jordan Plastics Co: POB 2394, Amman; tel. 793144; telex 21712; manufacturers of plastics (household goods); Chair. TAWFIQ G. ABUEITA.

Jordan Tobacco and Cigarette Co Ltd: POB 59, Ras El-Ain St, Amman; tel. (6) 5677112; telex 21204; f. 1931; manufacturers of cigarettes; tobacco growers; Chair. HE FARID SA'AD.

Metal Industries Co Ltd: POB 134, Amman Industrial Estate, Amman; tel. (6) 723015; fax (6) 723621; f. 1976; manufacturers of steel panel radiators and boilers; sales US $2.5m. (1995); cap. p.u. US $1.5m.; Chair. Eng. M. A. JARDANEH; Gen. Man. M. GHARAIBEH; Prodn Eng. S. OMRAN.

TRADE UNIONS

The General Federation of Jordanian Trade Unions: POB 1065, Amman; tel. (6) 5675533; f. 1954; 33,000 mems; member of Arab Trade Unions Confederation; Chair. KHALIL ABU KHURMAH; Gen. Sec. ABDUL HALIM KHADDAM.

There are also a number of independent unions, including:

Drivers' Union: POB 846, Amman; tel. (6) 4765637; fax (6) 4765829; Sec.-Gen. MAHMOUD ABD AL-HADI HAMMAD.

Engineers' Association: Amman; Sec.-Gen. LEITH SHBELAT.

Union of Petroleum Workers and Employees: POB 1346, Amman; Sec.-Gen. BRAHIM HADI.

Transport

RAILWAYS

Aqaba Railway Corporation: POB 50, Ma'an; tel. (3) 2132114; telex 64003; fax (3) 2131861; f. 1975; length of track 292 km (1,050-mm gauge); Dir-Gen. ABDULLAH KHAWALDIH.

Formerly a division of the Hedjaz–Jordan Railway (see below), the Aqaba Railway was established as a separate entity in 1972; it retains close links with the Hedjaz but there is no regular through traffic between Aqaba and Amman. It comprises the 169-km line south of Menzil (leased from the Hedjaz–Jordan Railway) and the 115-km extension to Aqaba, opened in October 1975, which serves phosphate mines at el-Hasa and Wadi el-Abyad.

Hedjaz–Jordan Railway (administered by the Ministry of Transport): POB 4448, Amman; tel. (6) 895414; telex 21541; fax (6) 894117; f. 1902; length of track 496 km (1,050-mm gauge); Chair. A. HALASA; Dir-Gen. B. AL-SHRYDEH.

This was formerly a section of the Hedjaz Railway (Damascus to Medina) for Muslim pilgrims to Medina and Mecca. It crosses the Syrian border and enters Jordanian territory south of Dera'a, and runs for approximately 366 km to Naqb Ishtar, passing through Zarka, Amman, Qatrana and Ma'an. Some 844 km of the line, from Ma'an to Medina in Saudi Arabia, were abandoned for over sixty years. Reconstruction of the Medina line, begun in 1965, was scheduled to be completed in 1971 at a cost of £15m., divided equally between Jordan, Saudi Arabia and Syria. However, the reconstruction work was suspended at the request of the Arab states concerned, pending further studies on costs. The line between Ma'an and Saudi Arabia (114 km) is now completed, as well as 15 km in Saudi Arabia as far as Halet Ammar Station. A new 115-km extension to Aqaba (owned by the Aqaba Railway Corporation (see above) was opened in 1975. In 1987 a study conducted by Dorsch Consult (Federal Republic of Germany) into the feasibility of reconstructing the Hedjaz Railway to high international specifications to connect Saudi Arabia, Jordan and Syria, concluded that the reopening of the Hedjaz line would be viable only if it were to be connected with European rail networks.

ROADS

Amman is linked by road with all parts of the kingdom and with neighbouring countries. All cities and most towns are connected by a two-lane paved road system. In addition, several thousand km of tracks make all villages accessible to motor transport. In 1996, the latest inventory showed the East Bank of Jordan to have an estimated 2,940 km of main roads, 1,970 km of secondary roads (both types asphalted) and 1,740 km of other roads.

Joint Land Transport Co: Amman; joint venture of Govts of Jordan and Iraq; operates about 750 trucks.

Jordanian-Syrian Land Transport Co: POB 20686, Amman; tel. (6) 5661134; telex 21384; fax (6) 5669645; f. 1976; transports goods between ports in Jordan and Syria; Chair. and Gen. Man. HAMDI AL-HABASHNEH.

SHIPPING

The port of Aqaba is Jordan's only outlet to the sea and has more than 20 modern and specialized berths, and one container terminal (540 m in length). The port has 299,000 sq m of storage area, and is used for Jordan's international trade and regional transit trade (mainly with Iraq). There is a ferry link between Aqaba and the Egyptian port of Nuweibeh.

The Ports Coporation: POB 115, Aqaba; tel. (3) 314024; fax (3) 316204.

Arab Bridge Maritime Co: Aqaba; f. 1987; joint venture by Egypt, Iraq and Jordan to improve economic co-operation; an extension of the company that established a ferry link between Aqaba and the Egyptian port of Nuweibeh in 1985; Chair. Eng. KHALID SALEH AMAR; Dir-Gen. TAWFIQ GRACE AWADALLA.

T. Gargour & Fils: POB 419, 4th Floor, Da'ssan Commercial Centre, Wasfi at-Tal St, Amman; tel. (6) 5524142; telex 21213; fax (6) 5530512; e-mail tgf@tgf.com.jo; f. 1928; shipping agents and owners; Chair. JOHN GARGOUR.

Jordan Maritime Navigation Co: Amman; privately owned.

Jordan National Shipping Lines Co Ltd: Nasir Ben Jameel St, Wadi Saqra, POB 5406, Amman 11183; tel. (6)5511500; telex 21730; fax (6) 5515119; e-mail JNL@nets.com.jo; POB 657, Aqaba; tel. (3) 2018738; telex 62276; fax (3) 318738; 75% govt-owned; service from Antwerp, Bremen and Tilbury to Aqaba; daily passenger ferry service to Egypt; land transportation to destinations in Iraq and elsewhere in the region; Chair. Dr FOTI KHAMIS; Gen. Man. Y. EL-TAL.

Amin Kawar & Sons Co W.L.L.: POB 222, 24 Abd al-Hamid Sharaf St, Shmeisani, Amman 11118; tel. (6) 5603703; telex 21212; fax (6) 5672170; e-mail aks@nets.com.jo; chartering and shipping agents; Chair. TAWFIQ A. KAWAR; Gen. Man. GHASSOUB F. KAWAR; Liner Man. JAMIL SAID.

Orient Shipping Co Ltd: POB 207, Amman 11118; tel. (6) 5641695; telex 21552; fax (6) 5651567.

Petra Navigation and International Trading Co Ltd: POB 8362, White Star Bldg, King Hussein St, Amman 11121; tel. (6) 5607021; telex 21755; fax (6) 5601362; e-mail petranav@jo.com; general cargo, ro/ro and passenger ferries; Chair. ALI H. ARMOUSH.

Syrian-Jordanian Shipping Co: POB 148, rue Port Said, Latakia, Syria; tel. (41) 471635; telex 451002; fax (41) 470250; Chair. OSMAN LEBBADI.

PIPELINES

Two oil pipelines cross Jordan. The former Iraq Petroleum Co pipeline, carrying petroleum from the oilfields in Iraq to Haifa, has

not operated since 1967. The 1,717-km (1,067-mile) pipeline, known as the Trans-Arabian Pipeline (Tapline), carries petroleum from the oilfields of Dhahran in Saudi Arabia to Sidon on the Mediterranean seaboard in Lebanon. Tapline traverses Jordan for a distance of 177 km (110 miles) and has frequently been cut by hostile action. Tapline stopped pumping to Syria and Lebanon at the end of 1983, when it was first due to close. It was later scheduled to close in 1985, but in September 1984 Jordan renewed an agreement to receive Saudi Arabian crude oil through Tapline. The agreement can be cancelled by either party at two years' notice.

CIVIL AVIATION

There are international airports at Amman and Aqaba. The Queen Alia International Airport at Zizya, 40 km south of Amman, was opened in 1983.

Civil Aviation Authority: POB 7547, Amman; tel. (6) 892282; telex 21325; fax (6) 891653; e-mail jcaa@com.jo; f. 1950; Dir-Gen. AHMAD JUWEIBER.

Royal Jordanian Airline: Head Office: POB 302, Housing Bank Commercial Centre, Shmeisani, Amman 11118; tel. (6) 5667618; telex 21501; fax (6) 5660787; internet http://www.rja.com.jo; f. 1963; govt-owned; scheduled and charter services to Middle East, North Africa, Europe, USA and Far East; Pres. and CEO NADER DAHABI.

Arab Wings Co Ltd: POB 341018, Amman; tel. (6) 891994; telex 21608; fax (6) 894484; f. 1975; subsidiary of Royal Jordanian; executive jet charter service, air ambulances, priority cargo; Man. Dir RAMZI SHUWAYHAT.

Royal Wings Co Ltd: POB 314018, Amman 1134; tel. (6) 875206; fax (6) 875656;f. 1995; subsidiary of Royal Jordanian; operates scheduled and charter regional and domestic services; Pres. and Gen. Man. AHED QUNTAR.

Tourism

The ancient cities of Jerash and Petra, and Jordan's proximity to biblical sites, have encouraged tourism. In 1996 there were 2,793,375 foreign visitors to Jordan. Income from tourism in 1996 was US $743.6m.

Ministry of Tourism and Antiquities: Ministry of Tourism, POB 224, Amman; tel. (6) 4642311; telex 21741; fax (6) 4648465; f. 1952; Minister of Tourism and Antiquities AQEL BELTAJI; Sec.-Gen. Ministry of Tourism MUHAMMAD AFFASH AL-ADWAN.

Defence

Commander-in-Chief of the Armed Forces: Maj.-Gen. FATHI ABU TALIB.

Assistant Commander-in-Chief of the Armed Forces: Brig. TAYSEER ZAROUR.

Chairman of Joint Chiefs of Staff: Gen. ABD AL-HAFIZ MARI AL-KAABINAH.

Commander of the Royal Jordanian Air Force: Lt-Gen. IHSAN HAMID SHURDUM.

Chief of the General Staff: Lt-Gen. ABDEL HADI AL-MAJAH.

Defence Budget (1996): JD 381m. (US $537m.).

Military Service: conscription, two years authorized.

Total Armed Forces (August 1997): 104,050: army 90,000; navy 650; air force 13,400. Reserves 35,000 (army 30,000).

Paramilitary Forces: 30,000 (10,000 Public Security Force, 20,000 Civil Militia).

Education

The Ministry of Education adopted the principle of decentralization from the beginning of 1980. It divided the East Bank into 18 districts, called Offices of Education, distributed over five Directorates of Education, each one run by a Director-General who is in charge of implementing educational policies and procedures in his own area. The Ministry of Education's Central Office is still responsible for all major educational decisions related to planning curricula, projects and examinations.

Education in Jordan is provided by public and private sectors. In 1982/83, 70.6% of school enrolment was provided by the Ministry of Education, 1% by other governmental agencies (such as the Ministries of Defence, Health, Labour and Islamic Affairs), 9.9% by the private sector and 15.9% by UNRWA, which offers educational facilities and services for Palestinian refugees in collaboration with UNESCO. The University of Jordan, Yarmouk University and Mo'ata University provided 2.6% of total school enrolment. In 1985/86 there were 3,205 schools in the East Bank, attended by 894,695 pupils and staffed by 37,516 teachers.

A child is admitted to the first grade of the elementary school at the age of five years and eight months. The duration of this cycle is six years. Most of the students are promoted to the seventh grade, which, with the eighth and ninth grades, constitutes the preparatory cycle.

The secondary school cycle, which follows the preparatory cycle, lasts three years, and is divided into three types: general school, vocational school and comprehensive school. At the end of this cycle all students sit the General Secondary Examination, and those who pass are entitled to continue their higher education by enrolling either in the universities of Jordan (at Amman, Irbid and Mo'ata) or in Community Colleges—or in foreign universities and colleges. In 1991 a total of 36,668 students were enrolled at Jordan's universities. In 1986 Yarmouk University, at Irbid, was divided into two separate institutions to create the University of Science and Technology. An open university, Al-Quds University, opened in October 1988.

Community Colleges, of two-year post-secondary duration, include 12 colleges controlled by the Ministry, 22 colleges controlled by the private sector and supervised by the Ministry, and seven other colleges controlled by other governmental agencies such as the Ministries of Health and Social Development, the armed forces, the Department of Statistics and the Central Bank of Jordan.

Education was allocated a total of JD 215m. (US $620m.) under the 1986–90 Development Plan. Budgetary expenditure on education by the central Government in 1995 was JD 227.8m. (15.5% of total spending).

The Ministry of Education, in accordance with law No. 16 of 1964, provides textbooks free of charge for the compulsory cycle, and at cost price for the secondary cycle.

In 1989 a 10-year programme to reform the state education system was announced. The programme, which was to be implemented in three phases (1989–92, 1993–95 and 1996–98), aimed to revise curricula; to produce new textbooks and teaching aids; to train 4,000 new primary school teachers, 1,500 new secondary school teachers and 360 new school principals and supervisors; and to construct 420 schools.

In 1995/96 there were 51,721 teachers and 1,074,877 pupils at primary level. At secondary level (including both general and vocational secondary education) in 1995/96 there were 10,921 teachers and 176,123 pupils. There were 4,821 teachers and 99,020 students in higher education in 1995/96. There are 10 universities in Jordan.

Bibliography

Abdullah of Transjordan, King. *Memoirs,* trans. G. Khuri, ed. P. Graves. London and New York, 1950.

Abidi, A. H. H. *Jordan, a Political Study 1948–1957.* Delhi, Asia Publishing House, 1966.

Day, Arthur. *East Bank, West Bank.* Council on Foreign Relations, 1986.

Dearden, Ann. *Jordan.* London, Hale, 1958.

Foreign Area Studies. *Jordan: A Country Study.* Washington, DC, American University, 1980.

Glubb, J. B. *The Story of the Arab Legion.* London, 1948.

 A Soldier with the Arabs. Hodder and Stoughton, 1957.

 Britain and the Arabs: A Study of Fifty Years 1908–1958. London, Hodder and Stoughton, 1959.

 War in the Desert. London, 1960.

 The Middle East Crisis—A Personal Interpretation. London 1967.

 Syria, Lebanon, Jordan. London, 1967.

 Peace in the Holy Land. London, 1971.

Goichon, A. M. *L'Eau: Problème Vital de la Région du Jourdain.* Brussels, Centre pour l'Etudes des Problèmes du Monde Musulmane Contemporain, 1964.

 Jordanie réelle. Paris, Maisonneuve et Larose, 1972.

Gubser, Peter. *Jordan: Crossroads of Middle Eastern Events.* Boulder, Colorado, Westview Press, 1983.

Hussein, His Majesty King. *Uneasy Lies the Head.* London, 1962.

 Ma guerre avec Israel. Paris, Albin Michel, 1968.

 Mon métier de roi. Paris, Laffont, 1975.

International Bank for Reconstruction and Development. *The Economic Development of Jordan.* Baltimore, Johns Hopkins Press, 1957.

Jarvis, C. S. *Arab Command: the Biography of Lt-Col. F. W. Peake Pasha.* London, 1942.

Johnston, Charles. *The Brink of Jordan.* London, Hamish Hamilton, 1972.

Kohn, Hans. *Die staats- und verfassungsrechtliche Entwicklung des Emirats Transjordanien.* Tübingen, 1929.

Konikof, A. *Transjordan: An Economic Survey.* 2nd edn, Jerusalem, 1946.

Layne, Linda. *Home and Homeland: the dialogues of tribal and national identities in Jordan.* Chichester, Princeton University Press, 1994.

Lowi, Miriam R. *Water and Power: The Politics of a Scarce Resource in the Jordan River Basin.* Cambridge, Cambridge University Press, 1994.

Luke, Sir Harry C., and Keith-Roach, E. *The Handbook of Palestine and Transjordan.* London, 1934.

Lunt, James. *Hussein of Jordan.* London, Macmillan, 1989.

Lyautey, Pierre. *La Jordanie Nouvelle.* Paris, Juillard, 1966.

Marashdeh, Omar. *The Jordanian Economy.* Al-Jawal Corpn, 1996.

Mishal, Shaul. *West Bank/East Bank: The Palestinians in Jordan 1949–67.* New Haven, London, Yale University Press.

Morris, James. *The Hashemite Kings.* London, Faber, 1959.

Patai, R. *The Kingdom of Jordan.* Princeton, 1958.

Peake, F. G. *History of Jordan and Its Tribes.* Univ. of Miami Press, 1958.

Perowne, Stewart. *The One Remains.* London, 1954.

 Jerusalem and Bethlehem. South Brunswick, New Jersey, A. S. Barnes Ltd, 1966.

Phillips, Paul G. *The Hashemite Kingdom of Jordan: Prolegomena to a Technical Assistance Programme.* Chicago, 1954.

Rogan, Eugene L., and Tell, Tariq (Eds). *Village, Steppe and State: the social origins of modern Jordan.* London, British Academic Press, 1994.

Sanger, Richard H. *Where the Jordan Flows.* Washington, DC, Middle East Institute, 1965.

Shipler, David K. *Arab and Jew: Wounded Spirits in a Promised Land.* London, Bloomsbury, 1987.

Shlaim, Avi. *Collusion Across the Jordan.* Oxford, Oxford University Press, 1988.

Shwadran, B. *Jordan: A State of Tension.* New York, Council for Middle Eastern Affairs, 1959.

Smith, Sir G. A. *Historical Geography of the Holy Land.* 25th edn, London, 1931.

Snow, Peter. *Hussein: A Biography.* London, Barrie and Jenkins, 1972.

Sparrow, Gerald. *Hussein of Jordan (the authorized biography).* London, Harrap, 1961.

 Modern Jordan. Allen and Unwin, 1961.

Toukan, Baha Uddin. *A Short History of Transjordan.* London, 1945.

US Government Printing Office. *Area Handbook for the Hashemite Kingdom of Jordan.* Washington, DC, 1970.

Vatikiotis, P. J. *Politics and the Military in Jordan 1921–57.* New York, Praeger, 1967.

Verdes, Jacques Mansour. *Pour les Fidayine.* Paris, 1969.

Wilson, Rodney (Ed.). *Politics and Economy in Jordan.* London, Routledge, 1991.

KUWAIT

Physical and Social Geography

Kuwait lies at the head of the Persian (Arabian) Gulf, bordering Iraq and Saudi Arabia. The area of the State of Kuwait is 17,818 sq km (6,880 sq miles), including the Kuwaiti share of the Neutral or Partitioned Zone (see below) but without taking into account the increase in territory resulting from the adjustment to the border with Iraq that came into effect in January 1993.

Although, for some time, the Gulf was thought to extend much further north, geological evidence suggests that the coastline has remained broadly at its present position, while the immense masses of silt brought down by the Tigris and Euphrates cause irregular downwarping at the head of the Gulf. Local variation in the coastline is therefore likely, with possible changes since ancient times. The development of Kuwait (which means 'little fortress') owed much to its zone of slightly higher, firmer ground (giving access from the Gulf inland to Iraq) and to its reasonably good and sheltered harbour, away from nearby sandbanks and coral reefs.

The territory of Kuwait is mainly flat desert with a few oases. An annual rainfall of 1 cm–37 cm, falls almost entirely between November and April, and there is a spring 'flush' of grass. Summer shade temperature may reach 49°C (120°F), although in January, the coldest month, temperatures range between –2.8°C and 28.3°C (27°F–85°F), with a rare frost. There is little inland drinking water, and supplies are largely distilled from sea-water, and brought by pipeline from the Shatt al-Arab waterway, which runs into the Gulf.

According to census results, the population of Kuwait increased from 206,473 in February 1957 to 1,357,952 by April 1980 and to 1,697,301 by April 1985. Based on the results of the 1985 census, the population was estimated to be 2,062,275 at mid-1990. It was estimated that in 1991, following the war to end the Iraqi occupation, the population had declined to only 1.2m., mainly as a result of the departure of a large proportion of the former non-Kuwaiti residents, who had previously formed a majority of the inhabitants (see below). Provisional census results for April 1995 indicated a total population of 1,575,983, including 655,820 Kuwaiti nationals. During 1963–70 the average annual increase in Kuwait's population was 10%, the highest growth rate recorded in any independent country. The average annual increase in 1970–80 was 6.3%, although in 1985–90 the rate of growth slowed to 4.0% per year, and the population actually declined by 4.8% per year during 1990–96.

Much of Kuwait's population growth resulted from immigration, although the country also had one of the highest natural increase rates in the world. Between 1957 and 1983 the non-Kuwaiti population grew from less than 93,000 (45% of the total) to about 870,000 (57.4%), most of them from other Arab states. At the 1995 census the non-Kuwaiti population, based on the definition of citizenship then in use, represented 58.4% of the total. In 1994 there were 38,868 recorded births (24.0 per 1,000 inhabitants) and only 3,464 deaths (2.1 per 1,000). In 1995 females comprised only 42% of the country's population, including non-Kuwaitis. The birth rate for the Kuwaiti population alone exceeded 50 per 1,000 each year in 1973–76.

According to the provisional results of the 1995 census, Kuwait City, the capital and principal harbour, had a population of 28,859 (compared with 44,335 in 1985 and 60,525 in 1980), although the largest town was Salmiya, with 130,215 inhabitants. Other sizeable localities were Jaleeb ash-Shuyukh (population 102,178) and Hawalli (population 82,238).

Apart from the distinction between Kuwaiti citizens and immigrants, Kuwaiti nationals can be divided into six groups. These groups reflect the tribal origins of Kuwaiti society. The first tribe of settlers, the Anaiza (led by the Sabah family) and later settlers, including the Bahar, Hamad and Babtain families, originated in the Nejd (central Arabia). Another group, the Kenaat (including the Mutawa family and its offshoot, the Saleh), came to Kuwait from Iraq, and remain distinct from the Nejdi families. There are also a few large families of Persian (Iranian) origin, including the Behbanis. The remaining citizens may be described as 'new Kuwaitis'; a few are former Palestinians, although most are bedouin who have been granted second-class citizenship. The majority of the Kuwaitis (including the ruling family) are Sunni Muslims, but most of the Persian families belong to the Shi'a sect. They, together with other Persians, comprise an estimated 150,000 (or one-quarter) of all Kuwaiti citizens. About 30% of the total population are thought to be Shi'ites.

Kuwait is the only Gulf country with a National Assembly entirely elected by popular vote. Suffrage, however, was, until 1994, confined to first-class male citizens (those who can prove Kuwaiti ancestry from before 1920), who in 1992 comprised only 15% of the population. Legislation promulgated in 1994 enfranchised sons of naturalized Kuwaitis, and in July 1995 the National Assembly approved a bill reducing the minimum period after which naturalized Kuwaitis become eligible to vote, from 30 years to 20 years.

Immediately to the south of Kuwait, along the Gulf, is a Neutral or Partitioned Zone of 5,700 sq km (2,200 sq miles), which is divided between Kuwait and Saudi Arabia. Each country administers its own half as an integral part of the state. However, the oil wealth of the whole Zone remains undivided and production from the onshore concessions in the Neutral/Partitioned Zone is normally shared equally between the two states.

History

Revised for this edition by KAMIL MAHDI

The origin of the present city of Kuwait is usually placed about the beginning of the 18th century, when a number of families of the Anaiza tribe migrated from the interior to the Arabian shore of the Gulf. The foundation of the present Sabah ruling dynasty dates from about 1756, when the settlers of Kuwait decided to appoint a sheikh to administer their affairs, provide them with security and represent them in their dealings with the Ottoman Government. The town prospered and in 1765 it was estimated to contain some 10,000 inhabitants possessing 800 vessels and engaged in trading, fishing and pearling.

Between 1776 and 1779, during the Persian occupation of Basra, the East India Company moved the southern terminal of its overland mail route to Aleppo from Basra to Kuwait, and much of the trade of Basra was diverted to Kuwait. At around the same time Kuwait was repeatedly threatened by raids from the Wahhabis, fanatical tribesmen from central Arabia, and the need for protection led to closer contacts with the East India Company, which had a depot in the town. Ottoman dominion over the mainland was accepted in return for recognition of British trading interests along the route from the Mediterranean to India through the Gulf. The depredations of pirates and the threat from the Wahhabis caused a decline in prosperity during the early years of the 19th century, but the British navy restored peace to the Gulf, and by 1860 prosperity had returned.

In order to retain their autonomy the Kuwaitis had to maintain good relations with the Turks. Although not under direct

Turkish administration, the Sheikh of Kuwait recognized a general Ottoman suzerainty over the area by the payment of tribute and Sheikh Abdullah bin Sabah al-Jabir (1866–92) accepted the title of Qa'immaqam (commandant) under the Turkish Vali (Governor) of Basra in 1871. His successor, Sheikh Mubarak 'the Great', feared that the Turks would occupy Kuwait, and in 1899, in return for British protection, he signed an agreement with the British not to cede, mortgage or otherwise dispose of parts of his territories to anyone except the British Government, nor to enter into any relationship with a foreign government other than the British without British consent.

The reign of Sheikh Mubarak, from 1896 to 1915, was notable for the development of Kuwait from a sheikhdom of undefined status to an autonomous state. In 1904 a British political agent was appointed, and in 1909 Great Britain and Turkey discussed proposals which, although never ratified because of the outbreak of the First World War, in practice secured the autonomy of Kuwait.

Sheikh Mubarak's second son, Sheikh Salim, who succeeded to the sheikhdom in 1917, supported the Turks in the First World War, thus incurring a blockade of Kuwait. Sheikh Salim was succeeded in 1921 by his nephew, Sheikh Ahmad al-Jabir. Kuwait prospered under his rule, and by 1937 the population had risen to about 75,000. Sheikh Ahmad laid the foundation of Kuwait's great petroleum industry. After considerable prospecting, he granted a joint concession in 1934 to the Gulf Oil Corpn of the USA and the Anglo-Persian Oil Co of Great Britain, which formed the Kuwait Oil Co Ltd. Deep drilling started in 1936, and was just beginning to show promising results when the Second World War began in 1939. The oil wells were plugged in 1942 and drilling was suspended until the end of the war.

After the war the petroleum industry in Kuwait was revived on an extensive scale (see Economy) and in a few years Kuwait Town had developed from an old-fashioned dhow port to a thriving modern city, supported by the revenues of the petroleum industry. In 1950 Sheikh Ahmad died and was succeeded by Sheikh Abdullah as-Salim. His policy was to use the petroleum revenues substantially for the welfare of his people, and in 1951 he inaugurated a programme of public works and educational and medical developments which transformed Kuwait into an organized and well-equipped country.

THE MODERN STATE

Kuwait has gradually built up what are probably the most comprehensive welfare services in the world, and for the most part free of charge, at least to native Kuwaitis. Education is completely free in Kuwait, and, despite the introduction of health charges in 1984, the country's health service is considered to be of a very high standard. A heavily subsidized housing programme has provided accommodation for many residents who satisfy the country's generous criteria of 'poverty'.

In 1961 the 1899 agreement, which had given the United Kingdom responsibility for the conduct of Kuwait's foreign policy, was terminated; Kuwait became a fully independent state on 19 June of that year. The ruling Sheikh took the title of Amir, and Kuwait was admitted to the League of Arab States (Arab League).

Shortly after attaining independence, Kuwait was threatened by an Iraqi claim to sovereignty over the territory. In response to a request from the Amir for assistance British troops landed in Kuwait. The Arab League met in July and agreed that an Arab League Force should be provided to replace the British troops as a guarantor of Kuwait's independence. This force, composed of contingents from Saudi Arabia, Jordan, the United Arab Republic (UAR) and Sudan, arrived in Kuwait in September 1961. The UAR contingent was withdrawn in December 1961, and those of Jordan, Saudi Arabia and Sudan before the end of February 1963. On 14 May 1963 Kuwait became the 111th member of the United Nations.

In December 1961, for the first time in Kuwait's history, an election was held to choose 20 members of the Constituent Assembly (the other members being ministers). This Assembly drafted a new Constitution under which a National Assembly of 50 members was elected in January 1963, and the first session was held, with Sheikh Sabah as-Salim as-Sabah, brother of the Amir and heir apparent, as the Prime Minister of a new Council of Ministers.

In October 1963 the new Iraqi Government announced its decision to recognize Kuwait's complete independence, in an attempt to dispel the tense atmosphere between the two countries, created by the previous regime. Kuwait was thought to have made a substantial grant to Iraq at this juncture.

In January 1965 a constitutional crisis, reflecting the friction between the ruling house and the National Assembly, resulted in the formation of a strengthened Council of Ministers under the heir apparent, Sheikh Sabah as-Salim as-Sabah. In July 1965 Kuwait decided not to ratify the agreement to establish an Arab common market with Iraq, Jordan, Syria and the UAR. On 24 November 1965 Sheikh Abdullah died and was succeeded by Sheikh Sabah. His post as Prime Minister was assumed by another member of the ruling family, Sheikh Jaber al-Ahmad, who became heir apparent in May 1966.

Although Kuwait had played a neutral role in inter-Arab conflicts during 1966 and 1967, it declared its support for the Arab countries in the 1967 war with Israel, and joined in the oil embargo imposed against the USA and the United Kingdom. However, the cease-fire had been announced before any Kuwaitis entered the conflict. The Government donated KD 25m. to the Arab war effort. At the Khartoum Conference in September 1967 Kuwait joined Saudi Arabia and Libya in offering financial aid to the UAR and Jordan, to help their economies to recover from the June 1967 war. The Kuwaiti share of this amounted to KD 55m. annually.

In 1968 it was announced that the agreement of June 1961—whereby Britain had undertaken to give military assistance to Kuwait if asked to do so by its ruler—would terminate by 1971. This followed an earlier announcement that Britain would withdraw all troops from the Gulf region by the end of 1971. At this time, Kuwait continually solicited support for the formation of a federation of Bahrain, Qatar and the Trucial States, but it failed to convince the first two states to join what eventually became the United Arab Emirates (UAE).

Following the June 1967 war, Kuwait ceased to be a target of radical Arab criticism, largely because of its financial support for the countries affected by war, and of the Palestinian guerrillas. A factor in this assistance was the large Palestinian community, totalling more than 350,000, in Kuwait; many of the most able and educated Palestinians had made a career in the country. Financial aid to Jordan, on the other hand, was suspended in September 1970, following the armed conflict between the Jordanian Government and Palestinian guerrilla forces.

During the 1960s the Kuwaiti leadership's policies led to extensive redistribution of income, through the use of oil revenues in public expenditure and through the land compensation scheme. At the same time, however, there was popular discontent about corruption and inefficiency in public services and the manipulation of the press and the National Assembly.

In response to public opinion, the ruling family permitted the assembly elections of January 1971 to be held on the basis of a free vote, although women, illiterates and all non-Kuwaitis were excluded, and remain so today. There was a lively election campaign, with 184 candidates contesting the 50 seats, despite the absence of political parties, which were still illegal. Several members and supporters of the Arab Nationalist Movement, founded in the 1950s by Dr George Habash (now leader of the Popular Front for the Liberation of Palestine), were elected. This radical group, led by Dr Ahmad al-Khatib, was generally regarded as the principal opposition to the Government.

After the 1971 elections the Crown Prince was reappointed Prime Minister and formed a new Council of Ministers. The representation of the ruling family was reduced from five to three and, for the first time, the Council of Ministers included two ministers drawn from the elected members of the National Assembly.

In August 1976 the Amir suspended the National Assembly for four years on the grounds that, amongst other things, it had been delaying legislation. A committee was ordered to be formed to review the Constitution.

On 31 December 1977 the Amir (Sheikh Sabah) died and was succeeded by his cousin, the Crown Prince, Sheikh Jaber al-Ahmad as-Sabah, who had been Prime Minister since 1966. The new heir apparent was Sheikh Saad al-Abdullah as-Salim as-Sabah, who became Prime Minister as well as Crown Prince.

Both the Amir and the Prime Minister publicly reaffirmed the Government's intention to reconvene the National Assembly and to restore democratic government by August 1980. In response to increasing public pressure, a 50-member committee was established in early 1980 to consider constitutional amendments and a revised form of legislature. Following its recommendations, an Amiri decree provided for the election of a new assembly before the end of February 1981. Despite the uncertainty generated by the Iran–Iraq War, the election campaign proceeded, with 448 candidates contesting the 50 seats. The franchise was limited to 90,000 'first-class' Kuwaiti citizens, and of these fewer than half (or about 3% of the population) registered to vote. A moderate assembly was returned, containing 23 conservative tribal leaders, sympathetic to the ruling sheikhs, and 13 young technocrats. The radical Arab nationalists, the fiercest opposition to the Government in the previous Assembly, failed to win any seats, while the Shi'a minority's representation was reduced to four seats. However, five Islamic fundamentalists of the Sunni sect were elected. The Crown Prince was subsequently reappointed Prime Minister and formed a new 15-member Council of Ministers in which the ruling family retained the major posts. There were seven new ministers, including the only member of the Council of Ministers to have been elected to the new Assembly, and the finance and planning ministries were merged.

Of all the Gulf states, Kuwait has been the most vulnerable to regional disruption. In March 1973 Iraqi troops and tanks occupied a Kuwaiti outpost at Samtah, on the border with Iraq. Iraq later withdrew its troops, but a source of potential dispute remained over Iraq's territorial claim on Bubiyan Island. Following the crisis in 1973, Kuwait allocated larger sums for the expansion of its armed forces and established its own navy. Legislation to introduce conscription was approved in 1975.

During the Arab–Israeli war of October 1973 Kuwaiti forces stationed along the Suez Canal were involved in fighting, and Kuwait contributed considerable financial aid, totalling KD 100m., to other Arab states. While the war was still in progress, Kuwait called for a meeting of the Organization of Arab Petroleum Exporting Countries (OAPEC) to draw up a common Arab policy for the use of oil as a weapon to put pressure on Western countries, particularly the USA, to force an Israeli withdrawal from occupied Arab territory. Kuwait also joined other Gulf states in announcing a unilateral increase of 70% in the posted price of crude petroleum (the reference price used for tax and royalty purposes) from 1 November 1973. The OAPEC meeting took place in Kuwait, where the organization's 10 member states decided to reduce petroleum production by at least 5% progressively each month. Kuwait also imposed a total embargo on petroleum shipments to the USA and, later, to the Netherlands.

In November oil ministers from the Arab states also agreed on an extra 5% reduction in output, which effectively led to an overall drop in supply of 25% compared with September levels, to be followed by further reductions. Later in November the Arab group in the Organization of the Petroleum Exporting Countries (OPEC) agreed on the next 5% cut for December, but exempted countries of the European Community (EC, now European Union—EU) except the Netherlands.

At the next OAPEC meeting, held in Kuwait in December, an additional 5% cut, without exemptions, was agreed for January 1974. A second December meeting, also in Kuwait, partly reversed earlier decisions to reduce oil production. Just before this, the Gulf states belonging to OPEC had agreed on a further sharp increase in the posted price of oil, effective from 1 January 1974.

Kuwait played a leading part in all these moves and made considerable reductions in national oil output. Monthly production (in million metric tons) fell from 13.4 in September 1973 to 12.0 in October and 9.8 in November. There was later a reversal in this trend and monthly output was more than 10m. tons in the first half of 1974.

Following the January conclusion of a disengagement agreement between Egypt and Israel and the consequent improvement in Arab relations with the USA, seven of the Arab oil-producing states (including Kuwait) agreed in March to lift the embargo on supplies to the USA. In July 1974 the Arab countries also lifted the oil embargo on the Netherlands. None the less, Kuwait's policy of conserving petroleum reserves, and the fall

in the world demand, meant that production fell from a peak of 3.3m. barrels per day (b/d) in 1972 to an average of 1.5m. b/d in 1980, and below 1m. b/d in 1981. Since then, OPEC agreements have imposed a maximum quota on every member country's production (see Economy).

Following the division of the Ministry of Finance and Oil, petroleum affairs became the sole responsibility of the Ministry of Oil. In April 1975 the Government decided to take over the Kuwait Oil Company (KOC), which was already 60% government-owned. The Government holding company, Kuwait National Petroleum Co (KNPC) came under the authority of the Supreme Oil Council and its co-ordinating committee and controlled all oil operations. The KOC was therefore limited to production. Nationalization of the oil industry was almost complete when, in 1977, the Government acquired Aminoil and created the Kuwait Wafra Oil Co.

Until 1973 Kuwait's financial support for the leading Palestinian organizations had protected the country from active involvement in the guerrilla struggle. However, the activities of extremist groups resulted in embarrassing incidents for the Government. In September 1973 Arab gunmen occupied the Saudi Arabian embassy in Paris and later flew to Kuwait with five hostages. The gunmen surrendered to the Kuwaiti authorities, who later handed them over to the Palestine Liberation Organization (PLO), which had condemned the incident.

At the Baghdad Arab summit in November 1978 Kuwait pressed for unanimity among the Arab nations in condemning the Egypt-Israeli peace agreement and supported the use of sanctions against Egypt. The Kuwaiti ambassador was recalled from Cairo and all aid, except for specific development projects, was withdrawn. Anxious to preserve Arab unity, Kuwait mediated successfully in the conflict between the Yemen Arab Republic and the People's Democratic Republic of Yemen in 1979, eventually bringing about a cease-fire, and was instrumental in resolving the crisis in the UAE. In the war between Iran and Iraq, which began in September 1980, Kuwait supported Iraq, allowing access to its strategic ports, and, with Saudi Arabia, exporting up to 310,000 b/d (250,000 b/d from the Neutral Zone and the remainder from Saudi Arabia), on Iraq's behalf, and providing generous financial aid, which by the end of 1983 was thought to have reached US $30,000m. (donated by both Kuwait and Saudi Arabia). Relations with Iran were, however, maintained. In May 1981 Kuwait, with Saudi Arabia, the UAE, Qatar, Oman and Bahrain, founded the Co-operation Council for the Arab States of the Gulf (Gulf Co-operation Council—GCC). By encouraging economic and social integration, it was hoped that the GCC would increase the security of the small oil-producing states of the Gulf.

In September 1981 Kuwaiti oil installations at Umm al-Aish, near the Iraqi border, were bombed by Iran. Kuwait's ambassador to Iran was temporarily withdrawn, but in February 1982 Kuwait announced its willingness to mediate in the continuing conflict between Iran and Iraq. Attempts at mediation were, however, unsuccessful.

Events at the end of 1983 and in early 1984 highlighted Kuwait's vulnerability to attack, and increased concern for the country's security. In December 1983 six bombs exploded in Kuwait City, killing five people and wounding 61. The principal targets were the French and US embassies, but a power station and an airport were also bombed. Responsibility was claimed by the al-Jihad al-Islami (Islamic Holy War) organization, a group of militant Shi'ite Muslims with widely acknowledged connections in Iran. The potential threat of domestic agitation by the country's own fundamentalist Shi'ites was coupled with the authorities' suspicion that the attacks were directed by Iran in retaliation for Kuwaiti support of Iraq in the Iran–Iraq War. As a result of the bombings, more than 600 Iranian workers were deported from Kuwait in early 1984.

In May 1984 two Kuwaiti and several Saudi Arabian tankers were bombed in a series of attacks by unidentified aircraft on shipping in the Gulf. Although both Iran and Iraq were known to have been firing at shipping, Iran was blamed for the attacks on Kuwaiti tankers. The bombings were seen as a warning to Kuwait to reduce its aid to Iraq and to put pressure on Iraq to desist from attacking tankers carrying Iranian oil. The GCC withdrew offers to mediate in the Iran–Iraq War and condemned Iran. Much concern arose as to whether the GCC countries could defend themselves unaided, and at the GCC summit conference in November 1984 the member states agreed to form a joint military force, capable of rapid deployment and aimed at combating any spread of the Iran–Iraq War.

Kuwait's attempts to mediate in the Iran–Iraq War in 1984 were hampered by Iran's increasing suspicion about the outcome of outstanding border disputes between Iraq and Kuwait. Iran believed that Kuwait was about to transfer three strategically important islands (Bubiyan, Warba and Failaka) to Iraq. In January 1985, however, Kuwait announced plans to build its own military bases on Bubiyan and Warba, and two months later Bubiyan was declared an out-of-bounds war zone. Kuwaiti forces were put on alert in February 1986, when Iranian forces crossed the Shatt al-Arab waterway and captured the Iraqi port of Faw, near Kuwait's north-eastern border. Iran pledged that Kuwait would not become embroiled in its war with Iraq provided that it maintained its military neutrality.

In an attempt to improve its own defences, Kuwait approached the USA in 1984 concerning the purchase of armaments, but, although it was prepared to sell other weapons, the USA refused to provide the *Stinger* anti-aircraft missiles which Kuwait had particularly requested. In July 1984 Kuwait signed a military training agreement with the USSR, and by January 1985, despite unwillingness among the GCC countries to allow either of the superpowers to become directly involved, Kuwait had taken delivery of a consignment of Soviet surface-to-air missiles. In November 1985 a trade agreement was signed between Kuwait and the USSR, and in early 1986 a $230m. arms sale was agreed between the two countries.

In May 1985 an Iraqi member of the banned ad-Dawa al-Islamiya (the Call of Islam) organization attempted to assassinate the Amir of Kuwait by driving a car-bomb into a royal procession. The attack resulted in appeals for even greater security measures in Kuwait, and the Government responded by agreeing to introduce appropriate legislation and by temporarily suspending the issue of entry visas and residence permits. In July the National Assembly unanimously approved legislation to impose the death penalty for terrorist acts which result in loss of life, and the Government announced plans to establish popular security committees in all districts. In June 1986 four simultaneous explosions occurred at Kuwait's main oil export refinery at Mina al-Ahmadi. A hitherto unknown organization, calling itself the 'Arab Revolutionaries Group', later claimed responsibility for the attacks, which had been intended to force Kuwait to reduce its petroleum output.

In 1985 and 1986 almost 27,000 expatriates, many of whom were Iranian, were deported, and concern over the security of the country continued. In June 1987 six Kuwaiti Shi'a Muslims were sentenced to death for their part in sabotaging oil installations and plotting against the Government. There were further explosions in May and July.

The Council of Ministers submitted its resignation to the Amir in July 1986, following 15 months of increasing confrontation with the National Assembly. The Amir subsequently issued a decree accepting the Council's resignation, dissolving the National Assembly and suspending some articles of the Constitution. Crown Prince Sheikh Saad al-Abdullah as-Salim as-Sabah was immediately reappointed to the post of Prime Minister and charged with the task of nominating a new government, which would be given greater powers of censorship, including the right to close down newspapers for up to two years. Ten days later the Amir named a 22-man Council of Ministers, which included seven new ministers and three new portfolios.

Between October 1986 and April 1987 Iranian forces attacked merchant ships sailing to or from Kuwait and seized cargoes, as a punishment for loading petroleum sold on Iraq's behalf and for the use of Kuwait's ports for Iraqi imports. In an attempt to deter Iranian attacks in the Gulf, Kuwait re-registered most of its fleet of oil tankers under the flags of the USA, Liberia, the USSR and the United Kingdom. Kuwait received help from the USA and Saudi Arabia in clearing mines from the channel leading to its main oil-loading facilities at Mina al-Ahmadi. On 24 July the *Bridgeton,* the first tanker to be re-registered by the USA, struck a mine in the Gulf, 30 km from Farsi Island, while under US naval escort to Mina al-Ahmadi. The US naval force in the Gulf was ill-equipped for minesweeping operations,

and in August France and the United Kingdom, having initially refused a request for assistance to clear the shipping lanes, sent minesweeping vessels to the Gulf. These were followed in September by vessels from the Netherlands, Belgium and Italy.

Six Iranian diplomats were expelled from Kuwait in September 1987, following Iranian attacks on Kuwaiti installations. Kuwait's main offshore oil-loading terminal, at Sea Island, was closed between October and December, after an Iranian missile attack in which three workers were injured. In November Kuwait resumed full diplomatic relations with Egypt, following a decision taken by the League of Arab States that permitted member states to restore relations with Egypt at their own discretion. The GCC held a summit meeting in December 1987, when the six member states urged the UN Security Council to enforce its Resolution 598, which ordered a cease-fire to be observed in the Iran–Iraq War, and approved a pact to increase security co-operation between the member states.

Two Kuwaiti soldiers were wounded in March 1988 as Iranian and Kuwaiti armed forces clashed for the first time during the eight-year Iran–Iraq War, when three Iranian gunboats attacked Bubiyan island, situated 25 km from the southern coast of Iraq. In the following month an Iranian missile landed at al-Wafra oilfield, 80 km south of Kuwait City. The launching of the missile was believed to represent an Iranian warning to Kuwait for allegedly permitting Iraqi armed forces to use Bubiyan island in an attempt to recapture the Iranian-occupied Faw peninsula.

In April 1988 a Kuwaiti airliner was hijacked over the Arabian Sea by a group believed to belong to pro-Iranian Shi'ite Muslim organizations in Lebanon. The hijackers demanded the release of 17 Shi'ite Muslims who were imprisoned in Kuwait. Two hostages were killed during the 15-day hijack, which ended when the Algerian Government negotiated the release of the hostages and the safe passage of the hijackers to an unknown destination in the Middle East. In the same month a bomb exploded outside the offices of Saudia (the Saudi Arabian national airline) in Kuwait City. In May it was reported that a hitherto unknown group, calling itself 'Kuwaiti Hezbollah', had announced that it intended to commence a 'holy war' against Kuwait's ruling family and other pro-Western rulers in the Gulf region. Two bomb explosions followed this announcement, one of which killed two Kuwaitis.

The cease-fire in the Iran–Iraq War in August 1988 brought stability to the region and a revival of economic growth in Kuwait. Relations between Kuwait and Iran improved, despite Kuwait's support for Iraq in the war, and in April 1989 the Prime Minister, Saad al-Abdullah as-Salim as-Sabah, announced that relations with Iran were 'moving towards stability and normalization'. Co-operation with Iraq appeared to increase, despite the continuing dispute over Bubiyan Island. In domestic affairs, concern about Iranian influence over the Shi'ite minority (about 30% of the population) led to severe measures to curb subversion. In June 1989 a Kuwaiti court sentenced 22 people, accused of plotting to overthrow the royal family, to prison terms of up to 15 years. A programme of 'Kuwaitization' was vigorously pursued; the aim was to achieve a majority of Kuwaitis in the population by 2000. The programme was most successful in the public sector, where 90% of Kuwaiti workers were employed, but the private sector continued to be dominated by expatriates, who formed 60% of the population.

In December 1989 a number of former members of the National Assembly campaigned for its re-establishment. In mid-January 1990 the Amir appealed for political dialogue, and in March the Prime Minister declared that he would welcome the restoration of an elected legislature. On 10 June 62% of the electorate voted at a general election for 50 members of a new National Council. The Council was to be an interim body and its members were to hold office for four years. It comprised 75 members, of whom 25 were appointed by the Amir.

Following the election, the Kuwaiti Government resigned. On 13 June 1990 the Amir reappointed the Crown Prince, Sheikh Saad al-Abdullah as-Salim as-Sabah, as Prime Minister. Sheikh Ali al-Khalifa as-Sabah became Minister of Finance, and Rashed Salim al-Ameeri became Minister of Oil. On 23 June a government reshuffle resulted in 10 new appointments to the Council of Ministers. Only three ministers not belonging to the as-Sabah family retained their posts, while the new members of the

Council were technocrats with no previous experience of government. The Council was believed to have been reshuffled in an attempt to satisfy domestic demands for new government policies. However, the fact that the as-Sabah family retained the majority of important positions in the Government, and that restoration of the National Assembly did not seem a realistic prospect, undermined the attempt to placate critics of the Government. In late June it was announced that five ministers from the reshuffled Council of Ministers had been appointed by the Amir to the National Council, the first session of which was held on 9 July.

IRAQ'S INVASION OF KUWAIT: THE GULF CRISIS

In July 1990 President Saddam Hussain of Iraq publicly criticized unspecified states for exceeding the petroleum production quotas that had been established by OPEC in May in order to increase prices. He accused Kuwait of having 'stolen' $2,400m.-worth of Iraqi oil reserves from a well in disputed territory. The Iraqi Minister of Foreign Affairs, Tareq Aziz, declared that Kuwait should not only cancel Iraq's war debt, but also compensate it for losses of revenue incurred during the war with Iran, and as a result of Kuwait's overproduction of oil, to which he attributed a decline in prices. Later in July Iraq began to deploy armed forces on the Kuwait-Iraq border, immediately before a meeting of the OPEC ministerial council in Geneva, Switzerland. At the meeting the minimum reference price for petroleum was increased, as Iraq had demanded. On 31 July representatives of Kuwait and Iraq conferred in Jeddah, Saudi Arabia, in an attempt to resolve the dispute over Iraq's territorial claims and demands for financial compensation. Kuwait was reportedly prepared to contribute one-half of the amount demanded, but would not concede any territory. Consequently, the negotiations collapsed.

On 2 August 1990 Iraq invaded Kuwait with 100,000 troops (compared with Kuwait's total military strength of about 20,000). The Iraqi Government claimed that its forces entered Kuwait at the invitation of insurgents who had overthrown the Kuwaiti Government, but there was no evidence to verify this. The Amir and other members of the Government escaped to Saudi Arabia, along with many other Kuwaiti citizens. The immediate response of the UN Security Council to the invasion of Kuwait was to adopt a series of resolutions which condemned the invasion, demanded the immediate and unconditional withdrawal of Iraqi forces from Kuwait, and appealed for a negotiated settlement of the conflict. A trade embargo was also imposed on Iraq and Kuwait. Immediately after the invasion, the USA and the members of the EC 'froze' all Kuwaiti assets to prevent an Iraqi-imposed regime from transferring them back to Kuwait.

On 7 August 1990, at the request of the Saudi Arabian Government, President Bush of the USA ordered the deployment of US troops and aircraft in Saudi Arabia, stating that his aim was to secure the country's borders with Kuwait in the event of an Iraqi attack. The British and other European Governments, together with some members of the Arab League, agreed to provide military support for the US forces (see chapter on Iraq). On 8 August the Iraqi Government announced the formal annexation of Kuwait, and ordered the closure of foreign diplomatic missions there. On 28 August most of Kuwait was officially declared to be the 19th governorate of Iraq, while a northern strip was incorporated into the Basra governorate. Successive diplomatic efforts to achieve a peaceful solution to the crisis in the Gulf region proved futile. Attempts to pursue a diplomatic solution were complicated by the detention of Western citizens resident in Kuwait and Iraq. At the end of August, however, Iraq announced that foreign women and children were free to leave Iraq and Kuwait. By early December all hostages had been released.

Following the Iraqi invasion, there were widespread reports that Iraqi forces were plundering Kuwait City, looting goods from shops and warehouses, and searching for Kuwaiti resistance fighters and Westerners in hiding. Iraqi troops, in an attempt to subjugate the population of Kuwait, reportedly burned houses and tortured or summarily executed persons suspected of opposing the occupation forces. Many installations were dismantled and removed to Iraq. By early October an estimated 430,000 Iraqi troops had been deployed in southern

Iraq and Kuwait. There was evidence of attempts to alter the demographic character of Kuwait, by settling Iraqis and Palestinians in the country, and by forcing Kuwaiti citizens to assume Iraqi citizenship. By October it was believed that a considerable number of Kuwaitis had died as a result of acts of brutality perpetrated by Iraqi occupation forces. The population was estimated to have decreased from approximately 2m., prior to the invasion, to about 700,000, of whom Kuwaitis constituted an estimated 300,000 and Palestinians 200,000, while the remainder comprised other Arab expatriate workers and Asians.

In early October 1990 a conference was held in Jeddah, Saudi Arabia, where the exiled Crown Prince and Prime Minister of Kuwait, Sheikh Saad al-Abdullah as-Salim as-Sabah, addressed approximately 1,000 distinguished Kuwaiti citizens, including 'opposition' members of the dissolved National Assembly. He agreed to establish committees to advise the Government on political, social and financial matters, and pledged that, after the liberation of Kuwait, the country's constitution and legislature would be restored, and that free elections would be held.

In late November 1990 the UN Security Council adopted a resolution which authorized the multinational force, stationed in Saudi Arabia and the Gulf region, to use 'all necessary means' to liberate Kuwait. Iraq was allowed until 15 January 1991 to begin to implement the 10 resolutions that had so far been adopted, including that stipulating unconditional withdrawal from Kuwait. Upon the expiry of this period, it was implied, military force would be employed against Iraq in order to remove its troops from Kuwait. In the interim, various unsuccessful diplomatic attempts were made, by the UN Secretary-General and the Governments of the USA, the USSR, the EC members and Arab states, to avert a military confrontation between the multinational and Iraqi forces. On 17 January 1991 the UN-backed, US-led multinational force launched its military campaign to liberate Kuwait by an intensive aerial bombardment of Iraq, with the aim of disabling that country's economic and military infrastructure. Soviet attempts to mediate were deemed unacceptable by the USA and its allies, as they proposed that a cease-fire should be declared before Iraq began to withdraw from Kuwait. On 24 February the US-led ground forces entered Kuwait, encountering relatively little effective Iraqi opposition. Within three days the Iraqi Government had agreed to accept all the resolutions of the UN Security Council concerning Kuwait, and on 28 February the US Government announced a suspension of military operations. In March the UN Security Council set out the terms for a permanent cease-fire. These included the release of all allied prisoners of war and of Kuwaitis who had been detained as potential hostages. They also required Iraq to repeal all laws and decrees concerning the annexation of Kuwait. Iraq promptly announced its compliance with these conditions. Another resolution, adopted in April, provided for the establishment of a demilitarized zone, supervised by the UN Iraq-Kuwait Observer Mission (UNIKOM, see p. 000), between the two countries. The UNIKOM mandate was subsequently renewed at six-monthly intervals.

In mid-January 1991 a conference in Jeddah, Saudi Arabia, was attended by members of the Kuwaiti Government-in-exile, including the Prime Minister, and opposition delegates. Islamic and Arab nationalist groups had collaborated in forming a 'National Constitutional Front' and demanded an immediate return of parliamentary and press freedom, while the more radical elements in the movement demanded the resignation of the as-Sabah family from all important positions in the Government, and the establishment of a constitutional monarchy. In February, despite the expression of discontent among the exiled Kuwaiti community, the Kuwaiti Government-in-exile excluded the possibility of early elections after Kuwait had been liberated, on the grounds that the need to rebuild and repopulate the country took precedence. The opposition parties were further frustrated by the stated aim of the UN resolutions to reinstate Kuwait's 'legitimate' Government prior to the invasion by Iraq, namely the as-Sabah family. In late February, immediately after the liberation of Kuwait, the Amir decreed that martial law would be enforced in Kuwait for the subsequent three months. The decree was contested by some members of Kuwait's opposition-in-exile, who expressed the need for the legislature to reconvene before any such decision could be made. In early March the opposition groups in exile made public their intention to form a coalition against the Government of the as-Sabah family. In the same month, the Amir announced the formation of a committee to administer martial law and to supervise the state's security internally and abroad. The committee's domestic objectives were to identify people who had collaborated with Iraq, to prevent the formation of 'vigilante' groups, and to identify civilians brought by the Iraqi authorities to settle in the emirate. On 4 March the Prime Minister and other members of the exiled Government returned to the emirate, followed by the Amir 10 days later. The country was in a condition of instability because of the enormous structural and environmental damage caused by the war, and also owing to the bitter resentment felt by the Kuwaiti people against many members of the Palestinian community who were suspected of having collaborated with Iraq; it was alleged by human rights groups that Palestinians suspected of collaboration were being tortured by the Kuwaiti security forces. Later in March the Government announced that elections would take place within six to 12 months, following the return of Kuwaiti exiles and the compilation of a new electoral roll. The Government also declared its intention to reduce the number of foreign workers in Kuwait. On 20 March the Council of Ministers resigned, apparently in response to public discontent at the Government's failure to restore supplies of electricity, water and food. On 20 April 1991 the formation of a new Council of Ministers by the Crown Prince was announced. Although several technocrats were appointed to important positions within the Council (in charge of the economic portfolios), the major portfolios—foreign affairs, defence and the interior—were all retained by members of the as-Sabah family. Members of illegal opposition groups immediately denounced the new Council of Ministers as 'unrepresentative'.

In May 1991 it was reported that 900 people were under investigation in connection with crimes committed during the Iraqi occupation. In late May a human rights organization, Amnesty International, alleged that trials were being conducted in Kuwait without the provision of adequate defence counsel, and that, in some cases, torture had been used in order to extract confessions from defendants. In the same month, the Prime Minister admitted that the abduction and torture of non-Kuwaiti nationals resident in Kuwait was taking place. He promised that the matter would be investigated.

In June 1991 the Amir formally decreed that elections to a new National Assembly would be held in October 1992, and he ordered the National Council (which had been elected in a provisional capacity in June 1990) to reconvene on 9 July 1991 in order to prepare for the elections. However, the announcement failed to satisfy the illegal opposition groups, whose members continued to demand the immediate introduction of democracy into Kuwait, and an end to the dominance of the as-Sabah family.

It was reported in June 1991 that 29 of a total of 200 defendants in trials for alleged collaboration during the occupation of Kuwait had been sentenced to death. The sentences were condemned by international human rights organizations as having resulted from the abuse of the judicial system. On 26 June, however, the Government repealed martial law and quashed all of the death sentences which had been imposed in recent trials. Subsequent trials of those accused of collaboration were to be referred to civilian courts.

In late June 1991, with British and US armed forces expected to leave Kuwait in July and September respectively, the Minister of Defence announced that an agreement had been reached for their replacement by a united Arab force, to comprise contingents from the GCC states, Egypt and Syria. In September, however, it was announced that US armed forces would remain in the country for several more months, owing to the slow progress that Kuwait had made in rebuilding its own security forces.

In July 1991 it was estimated that the Kuwaiti population had fallen to about 600,000 since August 1990. The Palestinian population, which had totalled an estimated 400,000 prior to the Iraqi invasion, was estimated to have declined to 150,000. International human rights organizations produced a report critical of the continued deportation of non-Kuwaiti nationals, citing the Fourth Geneva Convention, which prohibits such action against civilians who are justified in fearing persecution for their political or religious beliefs.

THE AFTERMATH OF THE GULF CRISIS

In August 1991 Kuwait protested against the alleged landing of 80 Iraqi troops on Bubiyan Island and appealed for further international safeguards. The Government also ordered that the trials of all detainees should be completed within six months and that courts of appeal be established, following international criticism of recent war trials. Further Palestinians were airlifted to Jordan (bringing the total to 3,000 by mid-August), as part of a policy of limiting non-Kuwaitis to less than 50% of the population.

On 19 September 1991 the Kuwaiti Minister of Defence signed a 10-year defence pact with the USA. The agreement included provisions for the stockpiling of US military equipment in Kuwait, the use of Kuwaiti ports by US troops, and joint training exercises. US companies were awarded lucrative contracts to 'rebuild' Kuwait. The Amir made visits to Saudi Arabia, Oman, the UAE, Qatar, Egypt and Syria in order to discuss defensive and economic co-operation. In October he visited Washington, DC (USA), London (United Kingdom) and Paris (France), where he expressed his country's gratitude and proposed closer defence ties. The Government protested at Iraq's lack of co-operation with the UN Iraq-Kuwait Boundary Demarcation Commission and at its failure to release prisoners. According to estimates, only 80,000 Palestinians (less than 25% of the pre-war total) were still resident in Kuwait, and there was international criticism of official sanctions and aggression against Palestinians, especially those suspected of collaboration.

In January 1992 the Government finally revoked its pre-publication censorship of written (but not broadcast) media. However, it retained the right to close publications printing articles to which it objected. The following month was the deadline for registration for the October elections to the National Assembly. Only 'first-class' Kuwaiti male citizens, who numbered about 81,400 (just under 15% of the adult population), were eligible to vote. The Minister of Justice and Legal Affairs excluded the possibility of foreign observers monitoring the elections. On 11 February Kuwait signed a defence pact (similar to that with the USA) with the United Kingdom. A defence pact with France was signed in August. On 16 April the UN Iraq-Kuwait Boundary Demarcation Commission adjudged that the border should be set 570m to the north of its present position. This had the effect of awarding part of the port of Umm Qasr and several of the Rumaila oilwells to Kuwait. This decision, the validity of which was now rejected by Iraq, seemed certain to provoke further conflict between the two countries.

The first half of 1992 was characterized by an unprecedented breakdown of law and order in Kuwait, with regular shootings and other incidents of violence. Many of these were directed against expatriate communities, especially the Palestinians. On 25 June there was a bomb attack on the home of Sheikh Mubarak Sabah an-Nasser, a member of the ruling family. One man was killed in the incident, which was the culmination of two months of violence. There were widespread allegations that the Government was using the shootings, and the fear of further Iraqi aggression, as a pretext to restrict the press and opposition meetings.

In August 1992, after the Iraqi Government had refused to allow inspections of weapons facilities by the UN (as stipulated by the 1991 cease-fire agreement), the US Government deployed missiles in Kuwait, and some 7,500 US troops participated in a military exercise in the emirate. At the end of the month, the UN Security Council adopted a resolution guaranteeing the new land frontier between Kuwait and Iraq. Demarcation was to take place before the end of the year, and the new border was to come into force on 15 January 1993. In the week leading up to this deadline, however, Iraqi forces made several incursions into Kuwaiti territory. In the course of these they recovered armaments left behind at the end of the Gulf War. At the same time, as US aircraft led air attacks on Iraq, more than 1,000 US troops were dispatched to Kuwait. Following the deadline for enforcement of the border, Iraqi operatives began to dismantle installations on what was now Kuwaiti territory. Nevertheless, the US Government deployed further missiles in Kuwait, and in early February the UN Security Council agreed to strengthen

UNIKOM by approving the dispatch of an initial 750-strong multinational contingent of armed troops (in addition to the existing unarmed personnel in the force) to patrol the Kuwaiti border with Iraq. In the same month Kuwait and Russia signed a memorandum of understanding, which, in the following month, led to a defence pact between the two countries.

In March 1993 the UN Iraq-Kuwait Boundary Demarcation Commission announced that it had completed demarcation of the maritime border between the two countries along the median line of the Khor Abdullah waterway. In May Kuwait announced that construction was to begin of a trench, to be protected by mines and a wall of sand, along the entire length of the land border. Allegations by Kuwait of Iraqi violations of the border intensified during the second half of 1993, and there were reports of exchanges of fire in the border region. In mid-November it was reported that some 300 Iraqi civilians had crossed the border in the Umm Qasr region to protest against the digging of the trench, while Iraqi troops were reported to have attacked a border post. These incursions coincided with the beginning of the evacuation, under UN supervision, of Iraqi nationals and property from the Kuwaiti side of the border. In November a 775-strong armed UNIKOM reinforcement was deployed in northern Kuwait, with authorization (under specific circumstances) to use its weapons to assist the unarmed force already in the demilitarized zone.

In September 1994 the UN Security Council agreed to extend the international sanctions against Iraq for a further period. On 6 October the leader of the UN's Special Commission on Iraq (responsible for inspecting the country's weapons) announced that a system for monitoring Iraqi defence industries was ready to begin operating. On the same day, however, there were reports of a large movement of Iraqi forces towards the border with Kuwait, apparently to draw attention to Iraq's demands for swift action to ease UN sanctions (not due to be considered by the Security Council until mid-November). Over the next few days, the accumulation of Iraqi military units in the border area reached as much as 70,000 troops and 700 tanks. In response to the apparent threat, Kuwait dispatched some 20,000 troops to the border region. The USA sent reinforcements (including combat aircraft and warships) to Kuwait and other parts of the Gulf region, to support the 12,000 US troops already stationed there. France and the United Kingdom deployed naval vessels, and some 1,200 British troops were dispatched to support the US military presence. On 10 October, as the first unit of additional US forces arrived in Kuwait, Iraq announced that it would withdraw its troops northward from their positions near the Kuwaiti border. On 13 October, as a result of mediation by the Russian Minister of Foreign Affairs, the Iraqi Government reportedly offered to comply with the Security Council's demands to recognize the UN-demarcated border with Kuwait and to acknowledge Kuwait's sovereignty. In return, the Russian Government agreed to urge the relaxation of the UN sanctions against Iraq. On 15 October the Security Council demanded that Iraq grant unconditional recognition to Kuwait and that all the Iraqi forces recently transferred to southern Iraq be redeployed to their original positions. Later in the month the USA (in a statement also signed by the United Kingdom and several GCC states) indicated that 'appropriate action' would be taken if Iraq deployed its forces south of latitude 32°N (the boundary of the southern air-exclusion zone in force since August 1992), and in late October 1994, during a visit to Kuwait, the US President, Bill Clinton, reiterated his country's commitment to the defence of Kuwait. On 10 November Iraq officially recognized Kuwait's sovereignty, territorial integrity and political independence, as well as its UN-defined borders. Although the declaration was welcomed by the Kuwaiti authorities, they continued to demand the release of all Kuwaiti citizens detained in Iraq and appealed for international sanctions against Iraq to be maintained until that country had complied with all pertinent UN resolutions. In mid-August 1995 the Kuwaiti Minister of Defence announced that events in Iraq were being closely monitored and that Kuwait's armed forces had been placed on alert following the defections from Iraq of the former Minister of Industry and Minerals, his brother and their wives (daughters of the Iraqi leader, Saddam Hussain), which threatened to destabilize the Iraqi regime. Joint Kuwaiti-US military exercises in the Gulf began in that month.

In mid-1993 it was announced that Kuwait was willing to restore relations with Arab states that had supported Iraq during the Gulf crisis, with the exception of Jordan and the leadership of the PLO. Despite the lack of progress towards a wider Gulf-Arab defence force, ministers responsible for defence in the GCC countries, meeting in Abu Dhabi (UAE) in November, agreed on the need to strengthen and extend the capabilities of the Peninsula Shield Force (the GCC's Saudi-based rapid deployment force). In the same month Kuwait signed a defence co-operation agreement with Russia, and in December the two countries participated in joint naval exercises in the Gulf. In late 1994, as part of a series of bilateral agreements on technological and military matters, Kuwait contracted to purchase military equipment valued at some $750m. from Russia. By the end of the year most of the US and British troops that had been stationed in the Gulf region in October had been withdrawn. Pre-positioned heavy equipment and aircraft remained in the region, together with the multinational forces present prior to the October incident.

In September 1996 the Kuwaiti Government agreed to the deployment, in Kuwait, of US military aircraft and troops in support of a US initiative to force the withdrawal of Iraqi armed forces from the Kurdish 'safe haven' in northern Iraq. However, this initiative attracted little regional support, and the threat of further retaliatory US attacks on Iraqi targets (a missile attack on targets in southern Iraq had been launched from aircraft based in Guam in early September) receded later in the month when Iraq announced that it would cease targeting allied aircraft enforcing the air exclusion zones.

In late May 1994 the governing body of the UN commission responsible for considering claims for compensation arising from the 1990–91 Gulf crisis approved the first disbursements (to 670 families or individuals in 16 countries), totalling $2.7m. In 1996 the UN approved $610m. to be paid to the KOC in compensation for the oil fires caused by Iraq and in December of that year, the long-delayed resumption of Iraqi oil exports under UN Security Council Resolution 986 (the 'oil-for-food' arrangement) made substantial funds available for the settlement of compensation claims. All personal claims, totalling $3,200m., were expected to be settled in 1998, before the more controversial corporate and government claims, mostly concerning Kuwaitis, totalling more than $80,000m. In July 1998 Iraq protested at the reported sale by Kuwait of five Iraqi oil tankers stranded in Kuwaiti ports since the cease-fire in 1991. Iraq threatened legal action although Kuwait claimed that it had been awarded the tankers by the compensation commission.

The Kuwait National Committee for Missing People and Prisoners of War claimed in 1994 that 625 Kuwaiti nationals were still in detention, or missing, in Iraq, and the fate of missing persons remains a major obstacle to any future normalization of relations between the two countries. Since mid-1996 Iraqi and Kuwaiti officials have held meetings in the mutual border area to discuss the fate of those not accounted for. The meetings have been conducted in closed sessions under the auspices of the International Committee of the Red Cross (ICRC), and have been attended by international observers. Although the Iraqi Government stated that it was holding no Kuwaiti prisoners of war, in late 1997 Kuwait claimed to be in possession of documentation, given to the ICRC by Iraq, relating to 126 Kuwaiti prisoners of war. In July 1998 delegations from both countries met in Geneva, Switzerland, for 'highly confidential' discussions on this issue.

Notwithstanding these difficult negotiations, relations between Iraq and Kuwait have demonstrated no discernable improvement. During early 1997 several allegations of attacks on shipping were made by both countries, and in July Kuwaiti pressure resulted in Iraq's exclusion from the Pan-Arab Games. Kuwait has continued to urge the GCC states to maintain an uncompromising stance towards Iraq, and to continue fully to enforce UN sanctions imposed against Iraq. At a meeting of GCC foreign ministers in Riyadh, Saudi Arabia, in June 1998, extreme concern was expressed at a recent statement made by the Vice-Chairman of Iraq's Revolutionary Command council which dismissed the terms of the UN resolution (844) which had demarcated the boundary between Iraq and Kuwait, following the 1990–91 crisis in the Persian (Arabian) Gulf.

From late October 1997 Kuwait expressed its support for the UN Security Council's resolution threatening punitive actions should Iraq continue to obstruct the work of weapons inspectors of the UN Special Commission (UNSCOM). However, while the Kuwaiti Government stated that it would hold the Iraqi regime wholly responsible for any escalation of the situation, it emphasized that any consequent military action would exacerbate hardship suffered by the Iraqi people and increase regional instability. Kuwait indicated, furthermore, that its territory would not be used as a base for an eventual US-led attack on Iraq. As the crisis involving UNSCOM inspections deepened in February 1998, Kuwait reiterated its support for the USA's stance with regard to Iraq, and urged a diplomatic solution to the situation. However, fears were expressed for Kuwait's security—in particular that an attack on Iraq might result in the use of chemical or other weapons of mass destruction against Kuwait. Early in the month it was announced that some 24,000 reservists were to be mobilized to reinforce the regular armed forces. The USA led a military deployment in the Gulf region at this time: by the end of the month, when the UN Secretary-General and the Iraqi Government reached a compromise agreement regarding weapons inspections, some 6,000 US ground troops had been dispatched to Kuwait. Kuwait maintained a military alert and conducted joint exercises with US forces in March. In June the USA announced its intention to reduce US forces in the Gulf to pre-1990 levels, but relations with Iraq remained volatile; in July a US F-16 fighter aircraft launched a missile at an Iraqi radar station near Basra, alleging that the base had locked its tracking systems onto the flightpath of allied aircraft patrolling the southern air exclusion zone near the Kuwaiti border.

Relations between Kuwait and Jordan (which had been severely strained since Jordan's adoption of a pro-Iraqi stance during the 1990–91 Gulf crisis) improved in early 1996 with the exchange of correspondence between the two countries' ruling families and in early 1997 Kuwait pardoned 10 Jordanian prisoners as part of a wider amnesty. In late April 1998 a further group of Jordanian prisoners (many of whom had been imprisoned on charges of collaboration with the occupying Iraqi authorities, following the return of the Kuwaiti Government in 1991) were released from detention and expelled from Kuwait. There was speculation that a further 25 Jordanian prisoners (including several journalists imprisoned on similar charges of collaboration) would be deported on a collective passport at a later date. These developments received favourable coverage in the media and in political circles, in contrast to earlier Jordanian reports of ill treatment of Jordanian nationals in Kuwaiti prisons. By July 1997 direct air links between the two countries were restored for the first time since 1990, and in June 1998 Jordan's Minister of Planning, Dr Rima Khalaf, visited Kuwait and delivered a conciliatory message from the Jordanian Crown Prince to his Kuwaiti counterpart. However, the Jordanian embassy in Kuwait remained closed, and the issue of reconciliation with Jordan remained controversial within Kuwait. It had previously caused divisions within the Kuwaiti Government when, in December 1995, Sheikh Sabah al-Ahmad al-Jaber as-Sabah, who favoured *rapprochement*, resigned as First Deputy Prime Minister and Minister of Foreign Affairs, in protest at the reluctance of the Crown Prince and the Prime Minister to seek a restoration of good relations with Jordan. Sheikh Sabah subsequently withdrew his resignation, and in March 1996 announced that the normalization of relations between the two countries was imminent. However, Kuwaiti policy towards Jordan and other Arab states was thought to have been one of the reasons for Sheikh Sabah's temporary resignation in May 1998.

During the first half of 1998 there was a discernable shift in Kuwaiti foreign policy. The First Deputy Prime Minister and Minister of Foreign Affairs declared that Kuwait no longer opposed Iraqi participation in Arab summit meetings and in May the Kuwaiti Red Crescent offered to send humanitarian supplies to Iraq. In 1997 Kuwait, in keeping with Arab League policy, condemned Israel's decision to construct a Jewish settlement in a disputed area of East Jerusalem, and in 1998 a visit to Kuwait by the Hamas leader, Sheikh Ahmad Yassin, provoked the consternation of the USA. Following the Amir's attendance at the Organization of the Islamic Conference (OIC) summit

meeting in Teheran in November 1997, several Iranian ministers visited Kuwait, and proposals for joint naval exercises with Iran were made, indicating a significant improvement in relations with that country.

THE ELECTIONS OF 1992 AND BEYOND

A total of 280 candidates, many of them affiliated to one of several quasi-political organizations, contested elections to the new National Assembly on 5 October 1992. The franchise was restricted to about 81,400 male citizens, and groups of women staged protests against their exclusion from the political process. Anti-Government candidates, in particular representatives of Islamic groups, secured 31 of the Assembly's 50 seats, and several of those elected had been members of the legislature dissolved in 1986. The Prime Minister submitted the resignation of his Government, and in the following week named a new administration. The revised Council of Ministers included six members of the new National Assembly. Among these was Ali Ahmad al-Baghli, the new Minister of Oil and a critic of the economic policy of the previous Government; members of the Assembly were also given responsibility for education, Islamic affairs and justice. The ruling family, however, retained control of the important defence, foreign affairs and interior portfolios.

In December 1992 the National Assembly voted to set up a commission of inquiry into the circumstances surrounding the 1990 invasion and Kuwait's preparedness for it. In January 1993, in an attempt to curb financial corruption, the Assembly adopted a law that all state companies and investment organizations must produce accounts for the auditor-general, who must pass them on to a commission of members of the Assembly. The law also provided for harsher penalties for those who misused public funds. In February a delegation of members of the Assembly travelled to London to investigate allegations that millions of dollars had been embezzled via the Kuwait Investment Office (KIO) in London. In March the Assembly voted to rescind a law of secrecy, which had been regarded as a legal mechanism to facilitate corruption. In the same month there were reports of criticism from members of the Assembly after the Government estimated defence spending for 1992/93 at $6,200m. Moreover, in July a report of the National Assembly's finance and economy commission was highly critical of the Government's management of overseas investments and its failure to ensure the accountability of officials. In mid-August the Prime Minister submitted a proposal to the National Assembly, according to which future budgets would contain, for the first time, details of purchases of defence equipment. In January 1994 the National Assembly abrogated an earlier decree demanding that, in the case of legal proceedings, government ministers be tried by a special court. In the same month Sheikh Ali al-Khalifah as-Sabah, a former Minister of Finance and of Oil, and Abd al-Fatr al-Bader, a former Chairman of the company, were among five people brought to trial in connection with alleged embezzlement from the Kuwait Oil Tanker Co; hearings were subsequently adjourned, and legal proceedings continued into 1996. (Meanwhile, in November 1995 a criminal court had ruled that the trial of the former would be held in a special court for cases involving ministers, in spite of the National Assembly's earlier ruling.) In July 1996 three of the four former executives to be tried by the criminal court were found guilty of corruption, and received prison sentences of between 15 and 40 years. In addition, they were ordered to repay the embezzled funds, together with fines totalling more than US $100m. The fourth defendant, a British national, was acquitted. The charges against the former oil and finance minister were later withdrawn—it was ruled that the correct proceedings had not been followed to bring the case to trial.

On 9 April 1994 the Prime Minister submitted the resignation of his Government, and in the following week named a new administration. The revised Council of Ministers included five new members, the Ministers of Defence and of the Interior exchanged portfolios, and a new Minister of Oil was appointed. It was subsequently announced that the new Government would persevere with economic reforms, including privatization.

Relations between the Government and the National Assembly became increasingly strained during late 1994 and early 1995, not least because of the discord which existed between the Crown Prince and Prime Minister, Sheikh Saad al-Abdullah as-Salim as-Sabah, and the Speaker of the National Assembly, Ahmad Abd al-Aziz as-Saadun, who appealed for a government composed only of elected members. A potential constitutional crisis developed in early 1995, moreover, with regard to the interpretation of Article 71 of the Constitution. Article 71 regulates the Amir's power to rule by decree during parliamentary recesses or when the Assembly is dissolved for new elections: the National Assembly is obliged to endorse all such legislation when it reconvenes. The Assembly argued that the Article did not apply to the 1976–81 or 1986–92 periods, when the Assembly was closed unconstitutionally by the Amir. Following these periods, a political agreement was reached with the Amir, whereby the Assembly would review the Amiri decrees, rejecting, approving or amending the legislation accordingly. In February 1995, however, the Constitutional Court had overruled the National Assembly's rejection of a 1986 decree which allowed the Government to close down newspapers; in the following month the Government exercised its right to do so, temporarily suspending publication of a newspaper, *Al-Anbaa*. In April the Government referred Article 71 to the Constitutional Court for interpretation in the light of the ruling on press censorship. If the Court ruled in the Government's favour, the authority of the Assembly would effectively be threatened, as the Amir could force through controversial legislation by dissolving and subsequently reconvening the Assembly. The Assembly protested by suspending consideration of more than 200 Amiri decrees until late May, when the Government withdrew its request for the interpretation of the Article.

In April 1995 the report of a parliamentary inquiry into state purchases of weapons alleged widespread waste and corruption in defence expenditure, and urged the Government to instigate judicial proceedings against those said to be involved. In the following month the report of the parliamentary commission of inquiry into the circumstances surrounding the 1990 invasion revealed profound negligence on the part of government and military officials, who had apparently ignored warnings of an imminent invasion. The report was critical of the flight of members of the royal family and the Council of Ministers immediately after the invasion, effectively depriving the country of political leadership and military organization. However, despite criticisms levelled against the Government, some observers noted that the balance of power within the National Assembly favoured the Government, as Islamist groups, which had been the Government's most vociferous opponents, failed to gain sufficient support to secure adoption of their proposed bills, and had lost control of parliamentary select committees.

In June 1995 the National Assembly approved legislation designed to increase the electorate by amending the 1959 nationality law to allow sons of naturalized Kuwaitis to vote. In July the Assembly approved a bill reducing the minimum period after which naturalized Kuwaitis would become eligible to vote from 30 years to 20 years. In July 1996 the Ministry of the Interior announced that a recorded total electorate of 107,169 was enfranchised to vote in elections to the National Assembly, on 7 October 1996. Pro-Government candidates were the most successful at the elections, securing an estimated 19 of the 50 legislative seats. A number of small demonstrations, organized and attended by women in support of demands for female enfranchisement, were reported in the days preceding the poll. Following the elections, Sheikh Saad al-Abdullah as-Salim as-Sabah was reappointed Prime Minister. On 15 October, he announced the composition of the Council of Ministers, which included four new members. The new legislature convened on 20 October.

In May 1997 a new political grouping, the National Democratic Rally (NDR), was formed, prompting debate on the legalization of political parties. The NDR, which is secular and liberal, is already popular, with a reported 2,000 supporters. The NDR is also the only political grouping to have a woman among its leaders. On 6 June, an assassination attempt was made on Abdullah an-Nibari, an opposition member of the National Assembly, and a former Chairman of the Committee for the Protection of Public Funds. Police charged five men with the offence (three Kuwaitis and two Iranians) one of whom was discovered to be related to the Minister of Finance, and had earlier been named by an-Nabari as an official involved in embezzlement. Answering suggestions that he should resign,

the Minister of Finance insisted that he had had no knowledge of the attack and was therefore under no obligation to stand down. In November an incendiary bomb attack on an-Nibari's office destroyed the building but resulted in no casualties. There was widespread belief that a conspiracy linked to state corruption lay behind the attacks on an-Nibari, and these suspicions exacerbated tensions between the Government and the National Assembly. Later that month, the Minister of Finance, Nasir ar-Rodhan, was reported to have tendered his resignation, although the Prime Minister apparently asked him to remain in office. In December three of the suspects detained in connection with the June assassination attempt were sentenced to life imprisonment; a fourth suspect was awarded a 10-year prison sentence, while a fifth suspect was acquitted.

Further tension between the Government and the National Assembly became apparent in early 1998, when a motion expressing 'no confidence' in the Minister of Information, Sa'ud Nasir as-Sabah, was brought by the legislature, following his decision to allow allegedly anti-Islamic publications to be displayed at the 1997 Kuwait Book Fair. On 15 March, however, two days before the vote was scheduled to take place in the National Assembly, the Council of Ministers resigned. The Crown Prince again formed a new Government. Sa'ud Nasir as-Sabah was transferred to the Ministry of Oil, while Nasir ar-Rodhan retained the post of Deputy Prime Minister and became Minister of State for Cabinet Affairs. It was widely considered that such a reallocation had frustrated the opposition's desire to question certain ministers over their earlier decisions. Four new appointments were also made, including Sheikh Ali Salim as-Sabah as Minister of Finance and Communications, bringing to six the number of members of the ruling family in the Council of Ministers. The sensitive portfolios of defence, foreign affairs and the interior were unchanged.

The National Assembly continued to monitor closely defence contracts (including a missile contract with British Aerospace), and other matters concerning public funds, including the alleged loss of KD 300m. in stock options speculation by the Public Institution for Social Security. In May 1998 the National Assembly approved a bill requiring public officials to declare their finances in order to aid transparency and to facilitate moves to counter corruption. In June 1998 there was evidence that the authorities were seeking to further restrict the freedom of the press. The Government brought legal proceedings against the independent newspaper, *Al-Qabas*, accusing the paper of religious defamation; the paper was closed for one week, and its Editor-in-Chief received a six-month prison sentence. Also in June, an edition of an Egyptian newspaper, which contained an article examining the crisis between the National Assembly and the Prime Minister, was removed from circulation. In mid-June meetings involving the Speaker of the National Assembly, the Amir and the Government, appeared to have averted an imminent confrontation over the cross-examination of the Interior Minister on matters relating to crime and the narcotics trade, although underlying problems remained unresolved. Later in that month the National Assembly refused to endorse the privatization of the communications sector, and in July a draft foreign investment law was announced which would permit majority foreign share holdings in the 'upstream' petroleum sector, subject to the approval of the Council of Ministers.

A collapse in petroleum prices in 1998 did not prompt a radical alteration of economic policy, but it did fuel persistent demands for reform. However, a lack of cohesion and resolve among the ranks of the Government and the opposition, increased the unlikelihood of the introduction of any unpopular measures. Meanwhile, significant areas of dissent persist between the Crown Prince and the First Deputy Prime Minister and Minister of Foreign Affairs, who acted as Prime Minister for seven months in 1997 during the Crown Prince's absence for medical treatment. Attempts to further enfranchise the population met with very limited success. While a legal and legislative committee of the National Assembly approved draft legislation providing for the lowering of the minimum voting age from 21 to 18 in May 1997, the law has yet to be endorsed by the Amir or the National Assembly. In early 1998 the same legal and legislative committee rejected draft legislation providing for the enfranchisement of women.

Economy

ALAN J. DAY (based on an original essay by P. T. H. UNWIN)

Revised for this edition by the Editor

Kuwait is a relatively small, arid country with a severe climate. Fresh water is scarce, and agriculture limited. However, the discovery of extremely rich deposits of petroleum transformed the economy and gave the country a high level of material prosperity. Kuwait's population increased from approximately 200,000 in 1957 to 1,697,301 in 1985, of whom only 40% were Kuwaiti nationals; the remainder were non-Kuwaitis, mainly immigrant workers and their families. At mid-1990 the population was estimated to be 2,062,275, of whom 1,473,054 were non-Kuwaiti nationals (based on the definition of citizenship in use in 1992). Twelve months later the estimated population had fallen to 1.2m., but census results for April 1995 indicated a total population of 1,575,983, of whom 655,820 were Kuwaiti nationals. The population increase also intensified demands on the infrastructure of the country; for example, total water consumption in Kuwait increased from 255m. gallons in 1954 to 40,306m. gallons in 1987. In August 1987 the Government initiated a five-year plan to reduce the number of expatriates in the Kuwaiti work-force. Taking advantage of the displacement caused by the Iraqi invasion, the Government subsequently announced its intention to restrict the level of non-Kuwaiti residents to less than 50% of the pre-crisis total. In pursuit of this policy, the Government attracted censure for its use of deportation and the treatment of expatriate groups, especially Palestinians, within the country. In March 1994 it was officially reported that a total of 34,000 persons had been deported from Kuwait since June 1991. In 1993 it was reported that non-Kuwaiti workers were being encouraged to leave the emirate on the expiry of their contracts and that unskilled workers would no longer be allowed to invite their families to join them unless they were earning a fixed minimum monthly salary.

Kuwait's level of gross national product (GNP) per head was the third highest in the world in 1980 and 1981, exceeded only by that of Qatar and the United Arab Emirates (UAE). According to estimates by the World Bank, Kuwait's GNP was US $33,150m. (equivalent to $24,160 per head) in 1980 and $30,600m. ($20,900 per head) in 1981 (at 1979–81 prices). By 1986 Kuwait ranked fourth (behind Bermuda, Switzerland and the USA), with a GNP of $29,472m. ($16,600 per head, at average 1984–86 prices). Kuwait's GNP (at current prices), which had been KD 7,364m. ($25,100m.) in 1992, was KD 8,283m. ($27,450m.) in 1993 and KD 8,272 m. ($27,800m.) in 1994. Kuwait's gross domestic product (GDP) fluctuated over the period 1980–89, falling by 0.7% per year. More severe contractions in 1990 and 1991 were brought about by the disruption of the Iraqi invasion. However, GDP has since recovered, rising to KD 5,826m. in 1992, KD 7,134m. in 1993, KD 7,214m. in 1994, and (according to figures published by the IMF) KD 7,952m. in 1995. The strong growth in GDP in 1995 reflected a significant increase in the value of output from the oil sector caused by higher oil prices.

After 1972 (the year of Kuwait's peak petroleum production of 1,201.6m. barrels), output of petroleum fluctuated, rising from 760.8m. barrels in 1975 to 911.2m. barrels in 1979, accounting for 4.5% of the world's oil output, and falling to 607m. barrels in 1980, 3% of world oil output. The oil glut and the implementation of OPEC quota allocations led to lower prices and fluctuating production after 1982. In common with most OPEC members, Kuwait tended to exceed its petroleum production quota. In 1987 Kuwait's production (excluding output from the Neutral/Partitioned Zone, shared with Saudi Arabia) averaged 1.1m. b/d, compared with 1.2m. b/d in 1986. Average production for 1988 was 1.4m. b/d. During the first half of 1989 Kuwait consistently exceeded its OPEC quota. At the beginning of June the oil ministers of OPEC member states convened and agreed on a quota increase of 5.8% for Kuwait. Kuwait rejected this allocation and requested a quota of 1.35m. b/d, but was allocated 1.12m. b/d under a pro-rata distribution of the 18.5m. b/d ceiling then in force, which was judged to be

sufficient to stabilize prices. The Kuwaiti Minister of Oil, Sheikh Ali al-Khalifa as-Sabah, presented a claim for an amendment to the final OPEC resolution, excluding Kuwait from the accepted production quotas. The production ceiling was raised by 1m. b/d to 19.5m. b/d.

In September 1989 the ceiling was raised to 20.5m. b/d. Kuwait nevertheless rejected its quota of 1.149m. b/d for late 1989. Overproduction persisted, and by the end of 1989 total OPEC output amounted to approximately 24m. b/d. At the following OPEC meeting, held in late November, Kuwait was authorized to produce 6.82% of the organization's entire output, compared with 5.61% previously.

In August 1990 Kuwait's OPEC production quota was fixed at 1.5m. b/d, but, owing to the invasion by Iraq, output averaged 1.065m. b/d for that year. In the aftermath of the Gulf crisis, Kuwait argued persistently within OPEC for a rise in the production ceiling and an increase in the country's quota, in order to offset losses and to finance reconstruction.

Following the liberation of Kuwait from the Iraqi occupation in February 1991, it was estimated that some 800 of the country's 950 oil wells had been damaged, some 600 having been set alight by Iraqi troops shortly before their retreat. The rehabilitation of the petroleum sector became the Government's highest economic priority. By June 1991 about 140 of the burning wells had been 'capped', and by late July onshore production of crude petroleum had resumed at a level of 115,000 b/d, while offshore production from fields in the Neutral/Partitioned Zone was estimated at 70,000 b/d. Exports of petroleum had also resumed by late July.

By the end of 1991 total production had reached 500,000 b/d and was increasing at a monthly rate of 100,000 b/d. By mid-1992 production had exceeded 1m. b/d, and was projected to reach 1.5m. by 1993 and 2m. thereafter. In June 1993 a meeting of OPEC oil ministers was obliged to exempt Kuwait from an agreement on production quotas, effectively allowing Kuwait to increase production to 2m. b/d in the third quarter of that year. In September, at the following OPEC meeting, this allocation was confirmed for a further period of six months. Kuwait, however, rejected suggestions that it was seriously jeopardizing its reserves by forcing such a rapid rise in output. At the same time, the major work of repairing Kuwait's infrastructure had been completed. In 1997 current capacity was 2.4m. b/d and was expected to rise to 3m. b/d by 2000. In November 1997 Kuwait's OPEC quota increased to 2.19m. b/d although in March 1998, as a result of declining world prices, and in conjunction with other major petroleum producers, petroleum output was reduced by 125,000 b/d.

In 1997 Kuwait's proven recoverable reserves of petroleum were 96,500m. barrels, representing about 9.3% of world reserves. Income from Kuwait's petroleum sales has been channelled mainly to five areas: industrial diversification, the development of substantial social service provision, the creation of the Reserve Fund for Future Generations (RFFG), overseas investment, and aid to poorer countries through the Kuwait Fund for Arab Economic Development (KFAED).

The immediate costs of the military operation to liberate Kuwait (about US $22,000m.) and of rebuilding the country's infrastructure (some $20,000m.) were, in large part, met by liquidating about one-half of Kuwait's overseas investment portfolio (including about one-half of the RFFG) and by external borrowing totalling $5,500m. In 1994 it was reported that the Kuwaiti economy had fully recovered from the effects of the Gulf crisis and rebuilding, and that the Government did not envisage further international borrowing. Economic growth in 1994 was primarily attributable to a recovery in the non-petroleum sector. However, Kuwait's contribution to the cost of the international military response to Iraqi troop movements in October 1994 increased spending obligations for 1994/95 by an estimated $500m. Earlier in the year the Government had announced its intention to eliminate the budget deficit by 2000. Proposals to reduce the deficit included an increase in customs fees, the imposition of a direct tax on commercial and industrial profits, the reform of the welfare system, the gradual withdrawal of subsidies on public services, the ending of protectionism, and the expansion of the privatization programme, anticipated to include the sale of the telecommunications, power and water industries, although in 1998 the National Assembly failed to endorse a law for the privatization of the communications sector.

PETROLEUM

In 1938 the Kuwait Oil Co (KOC), operated jointly by the Anglo-Persian Oil Co (now the British Petroleum Co PLC—BP) and the Gulf Oil Corpn, discovered a large oilfield at Burgan, about 40 km south of the town of Kuwait. The onset of the Second World War delayed development until 1945. In 1948, however, 6m. metric tons of crude petroleum were produced, although the main impetus to development was the Abadan affair in 1951, which effectively denied Iranian production to the rest of the world for three years. By 1956 Kuwait's annual production had increased to 54m. tons, and was then the largest in the Middle East. Further fields were discovered, notably at Raudhatain, north of Kuwait, and annual production had reached over 148m. tons by 1972. To handle this vast production, a huge tanker port was constructed at Mina al-Ahmadi, not far from the Burgan field. From a terminal about 15 km off shore, the port can now handle the largest tankers. Kuwait was the first Arab petroleum-producing nation to achieve complete control of its own output, buying out Gulf Oil and BP in March 1975 for approximately £32m.

Kuwait was also the first OPEC state to restrict petroleum production for reasons of conservation. Until December 1976, when Kuwait (together with 10 other OPEC countries) decided to raise petroleum prices by 10% (compared with a 5% increase by Saudi Arabia and the UAE), the country was generally regarded as moderate with regard to oil pricing. Subsequently Kuwait became increasingly 'hawkish', and during 1979 and 1980 the country was one of the first to set still higher prices every time that Saudi Arabia raised its prices in an attempt to achieve some kind of parity within OPEC.

The petroleum industry was reorganized in 1980, when the Kuwait Petroleum Corpn (KPC) was established to co-ordinate the four companies involved: the KOC, the Kuwait National Petroleum Co (KNPC), the Petrochemical Industries Co (PIC), and the Kuwait Oil Tanker Co (KOTC). This led to the centralization of oil sales and improved Kuwait's market competitiveness. In the early 1990s KPC was the twelfth largest petroleum company in the world. In addition to its oil refineries in Kuwait, it owns refineries abroad (in the Netherlands, Denmark and Italy). The sale of KPC stocks of oil was vital in supporting the Kuwaiti community in exile during the Iraqi occupation. In 1987/88 profits were KD 120.7m., and in 1988/89 profits reached a record KD 341m. In 1989/90 profits were KD 136.5m. In 1990/91 KPC's budgeted profits were KD 177.5m. Profits totalled KD 410m. in 1993/94 and increased to KD 729m. in 1994/95, largely owing to increased oil prices.

The KOC is currently developing capacity in the north and west of the country with the aim of boosting crude production capacity to 3.5m. b/d by 2005. The construction of gathering centres 27 and 28 in the Minagish and Umm Gudair fields, at a cost of nearly $400m., is expected to raise the production capacity of the fields from 110,000 b/d to 500,000 b/d. Also, in July 1997, KOC awarded contracts for two enhanced oil recovery (EOR) projects at the Raudhatain field, costing an estimated $200m. each, which will increase production at the field by 250,000 b/d.

There are three oil refineries in Kuwait: one at Mina al-Ahmadi, built in 1946; one at Mina Abdullah, built in 1958; and one at Shuaiba, completed in 1969. Expansion of Mina al-Ahmadi was completed in February 1986, and a programme of modernization at Mina Abdullah, costing $2,100m., was completed in February 1989. This project increased the refinery's capacity to 200,000 b/d, and raised total capacity in Kuwait to 670,000 b/d, mainly in high-quality products for export. Plans by KPC subsidiaries to expand and upgrade production prior to the Iraqi invasion were subsequently revised, but the Government remained committed to increasing Kuwait's petroleum

assets as part of its reconstruction and development strategy. The Mina al-Ahmadi refinery had resumed operations by June 1991, but the Mina Abdullah and Shuaiba refineries were reported to be more seriously damaged. The $47m. contract for repairs to the refineries was awarded to a US company, ...ter Wheeler. By May 1992 local refining capacity had excee. 300,000 b/d, although this was still less than one-half of the pre-invasion level. However, by early 1995 the refineries at Mina al-Ahmadi, Mina Abdullah and Shuaiba were producing at a rate of 400,000 b/d, 245,000 b/d and 155,000 b/d respectively, and in February 1997 the KNPC announced that total refining capacity had risen to 895,000 b/d. In 1996 KNPC invited bids for work on a series of contracts to increase the capacity of steam systems at the three refineries, and awarded a contract for the design and construction of an acid gas removal plant at Mina al-Ahmadi. It is also pursuing an ongoing programme to upgrade and expand export facilities at Shuaiba and Mina al-Almadi.

A further development in Kuwait's petroleum industry has been the expansion of downstream interests overseas. In 1981 the Kuwait Foreign Petroleum Exploration Co (KUFPEC) was established as a subsidiary of KPC. Later that year, it purchased a 22.5% interest in a 22,000-sq km concession in Morocco. KPC purchased the Santa Fe International Corpn, allowing the country to secure wider rights and facilities in exploration, and to develop downstream facilities. Through KUFPEC and Santa Fe, Kuwait now has interests in concessions in Australia, China, Egypt, Oman, the North Sea and the USA. In 1984 an agreement was signed for an offshore concession in Bahrain, and in February 1985 the USA reversed a two-year-old ruling by allowing Kuwait to acquire mineral leases on federal land.

Since 1981, Kuwait has been expanding facilities for the distribution, marketing and retail of its refined products. A joint venture to supply petroleum products to the Pacific area was agreed with Pacific Resources of Honolulu, Hawaii, in that year. In 1982 a 24% stake in a West German petrochemicals company, Hoechst, was acquired, and in 1983 KPC purchased Gulf Oil's network of petrol stations in Belgium, the Netherlands and Luxembourg, distribution outlets in Sweden and Denmark, and the refineries at Rotterdam, in the Netherlands, and at Skaelskor, in Denmark. In 1984 KPC acquired Gulf Oil's Italian interests, including a 75% share of the Bertonico refinery, near Sarni, and 1,500 service stations. In August 1985 the Belgian subsidiary of KPC acquired a further 53 retail service stations from Elf, bringing its total to more than 400. Kuwait Petroleum International (KPI), a subsidiary of KPC, was established at the end of 1983 to manage the newly-acquired distribution outlets (see Oil in the Middle East and North Africa, p. 000). Already successful in Scandinavia and other parts of Europe, KPI sought to extend its operations to Asia. In 1986 KPC adopted a new trade name, Q8, for its petroleum products distributed in Europe, and in March 1987 KPI acquired the British marketing branch of Ultramar, Golden Eagle Petroleum, thereby bringing its total number of petrol stations in Europe to 4,800. In 1988 Kuwait Petrolia Italia, a KPC subsidiary, enlarged the company's portfolio by purchasing the lubricants divisions of Italy's Raffineria Olii Lubrificante and Feruzzi-Montedison, despite their operating losses in 1987. KPC's downstream overseas expansion programme continued during the Iraqi occupation. In 1991 an agreement was signed with KPC to provide Hungary with 17 Q8 petrol stations. This agreement was in accordance with KPC's plans to expand its East European and Far Eastern operations. By mid-1995 KPI was marketing more than 400,000 b/d in Western Europe through a total of 6,400 Q8 petrol stations. Kuwait continued to pursue a policy of developing foreign refinery projects in the form of joint ventures, particularly in India, Pakistan and Thailand. In mid-1995 KPC and the Indian Oil Corpn agreed a joint venture to establish a refinery in the Indian state of Orissa, at a cost of $2,600m. In July 1997 it was reported that a feasibility study for the project had been completed. The proposed refinery is expected to process about 184,000 b/d.

NATURAL GAS

In November 1976 the Amir inaugurated the KOC's Gas Project. This involves the construction of extensive facilities to make use of the gas associated with the output of crude petroleum for the production of liquefied natural gas (LNG) and such derivatives as propane and butane. A three-train plant for the production of liquefied petroleum gas (LPG), together with a gas-gathering system (which came into operation in 1979), collects the gas, which is produced together with petroleum, at well-heads, removes LPG components and natural gasoline, then treats and distributes them to fuel users and to pressure-maintenance facilities.

The plant, built at a cost of over $1,000m., has a capacity of 2.2m. metric tons of LPG per year (60% propane, 40% butane) at a crude oil production rate of 1.5m. b/d. It was originally designed to take crude oil production of 3m. b/d. However, Kuwait's production of gas is limited by the absence of any known reserves independent of petroleum. Owing to the association of gas with petroleum, much of the gas produced is flared to facilitate oil production, or reinjected, to maximize the production of petroleum by maintaining pressure in the reservoir. From the early 1980s the LPG plant was forced to operate substantially below capacity, exporting 1.05m. metric tons of products in 1982/83 (compared with 1.7m. tons per year previously). In 1985 one in three of the trains at the plant was operating at a level below capacity.

Other projects which suffered as a result of decreased production of gas included the expansion of an ammonia and urea plant, where the annual capacity had been increased to about 900,000 tons of ammonia and various by-products. The lack of feedstock, however, meant that in early 1984 the plant was operating at about 50% of capacity, and certain lines had been suspended. On 1 January 1997 Kuwait's reserves of gas were estimated to be 1,500,000m. cu m (1.1% of world reserves). Gas production in 1996 totalled 6,048m. cu m.

OTHER INDUSTRIES

Although oil-related activities still contribute the overwhelming proportion of Kuwait's total industrial output, the Government has tried to foster other industries in order to diversify the economy and to provide alternative sources of employment. Petroleum's share of GDP fell from 61% in 1977 and almost 70% in 1980 to around 50% in 1983, and has since remained at roughly the same level. Between 1974 and 1984 the manufacturing sector in Kuwait registered an average annual rate of growth of 6.4%, although it subsequently suffered a decline as the downturn in the economy became more pronounced in the mid-1980s. In 1994 manufacturing contributed an estimated 10.5% of Kuwait's GDP. The major branch of manufacturing has been the production of building materials and related projects such as aluminium extrusion. Fertilizer manufacturers have a substantial production capacity, mainly in the form of urea and ammonia products. The profitability of these products has, however, proved difficult to maintain because of technical problems and a weak market. In addition, in 1986 the European Community (EC, now European Union—EU) imposed an 11% tariff on imports of urea from Kuwait after it had exceeded its duty-free allocation. The construction of a 150,000-ton capacity salt plant in Shuaiba, and a chlorine plant with an annual capacity of 27,000 tons, was approved in 1985. The expansion of Kuwait's petrochemicals industry gathered momentum in the mid-1990s, beginning with a $2,000m. petrochemicals complex at Shuaiba, which commenced operations in mid-1997. The contract for the development of the complex was given to Equate, a joint venture between PIC and Union Carbide of the USA. The plant will have an annual production capacity of 650,000 tons of ethylene, 450,000 tons of polyethylene and 350,000 tons of ethylene glycol. A $1,200m. project-financing agreement between a consortium of international, regional and local banks was signed in September 1996. PIC's plans for a new aromatics plant alongside the Shuaiba complex are currently under consideration.

Unlike its neighbours, Kuwait has hesitated to undertake heavy industrial projects, fearing both for their viability and the excess of foreign labour which they involve. It has favoured, instead, joint projects with Bahrain, Saudi Arabia and other Gulf countries, including agreements with the Gulf Aluminium Rolling Co and Gulf Petrochemical Industries Co to establish aluminium, ammonia and methanol plants in Bahrain. At the end of 1982 a joint venture was established between PIC and the Tunisian state-owned Maghrebia Chemical Industries to build a 1,000 tons-per-day diammonium phosphate fertilizer plant in Kuwait, at a cost of KD 16m. Towards the end of 1987, KPC also agreed to take a majority shareholding in Bahrain's ailing Iron and Steel Co (see chapter on Bahrain). In early 1989 PIC announced a joint venture, with Union Carbide, for the production of polypropylene. In July 1996 the local Kuwait Industries Co applied for a licence from the Commerce and Industry Ministry to establish a 900,000 tons-per-year alumina factory to supply producers in the UAE and Bahrain. In the following November the Finance Ministry approved the business plan proposed by the US company, Raytheon Corpn, to build a 230,000 tons-per-year aluminium smelter with foreign and local partners. Both projects are estimated to cost about $1,000m.

The construction industry is considerable, owing to the vast amount of infrastructural development since the early 1970s. During the 1970s major projects were carried out by foreign contractors, but in February 1981 the National Housing Authority (NHA) announced that 80% of future housing contracts would be awarded to local firms. Between 1974 and 1989 the NHA recorded 27,000 housing units built. In other sectors of construction, however, foreign companies continued to predominate. An indication of Kuwait's heavy reliance on foreign labour is the 2.4-km bridge from Subiya to Bubiyan island, completed in 1982 by Chinese migrant workers. The economic recession of the mid-1980s damaged the construction industry considerably, and the collapse of petroleum prices in 1986 exacerbated the situation. In 1988, however, there was a distinct recovery, particularly in the private residential sector, where expansion was stimulated by the availability of cheap bank credits, as well as the completion of highway improvements in suburban Kuwait. In 1989 work began on the Amiri Diwan, a government facility which was to cost an estimated KD 65m.–80m. and was completed in 1992. In the aftermath of the Iraqi occupation, the Kuwaiti Government worked with the international construction companies with which it was familiar, in particular US companies, in order to rebuild Kuwait's infrastructure, and in the mid-1990s work that had been traditionally undertaken by the public sector was increasingly allocated to the private sector. In mid-1994 the Government approved the construction of three new cities, at Subiya, Doha and Khiran, in order to alleviate the state's housing shortage. The cities were to be built by private-sector companies, and were scheduled for completion in 1998. The biggest concentration of construction work currently in progress is at the new campus for Kuwait University at Shuwaikh, while the most advanced build-operate-transfer (BOT) project is the development of Kuwait City waterfront by Kuwait's National Real Estate Co (NREC). Designs for a prestigious new headquarters for the Kuwait Petroleum Co (KPC) are under consideration, and a number of new public buildings are at various stages of construction.

Many of the smaller industrial projects have been promoted by the Industrial Bank of Kuwait (IBK), founded in 1973, which is 49% government-owned. By 1984, however, four leading commercial banks had combined with IBK to form a more specific concern, the Industrial Investment Company (IIC), to make new investments. During 1985 the Government took a further step in assisting local industry when it announced the introduction of protectionist trade measures for local industries which satisfy three criteria. Such industries should meet at least 40% of domestic requirements; should have a substantial added value and should contribute to national income; and the consumer should not be affected by any inflationary results of tariff protection.

In accordance with its aim of diversifying the economy, Kuwait has entered the international hotel industry at an accelerated rate. In 1988 Kuwait began to consolidate its assets by collecting them under one group, namely the Kuwait Hotels Co (KHC). The company was founded in 1962, soon after independence, and its main objectives were to assume control of all hotel management duties, and to take charge of all financial holdings. KHC will initially concentrate on Kuwait and other Arab countries, before venturing into the wider international market. Substantial staff-training will be a determining factor of the Government's intention to have all Kuwait-owned hotels managed by KHC in the next 10–15 years.

In mid-1996 the NREC was appointed to manage Kuwait's first free-trade zone, to be established at the port of Shuwaikh. Activities will be limited to transhipment initially, but will be expanded later to include light manufacturing. The establishment of the free-trade zone was approved by the Government in May 1998.

PUBLIC UTILITIES AND TRANSPORT

All of the industrial developments referred to above, and the demographic growth associated with the necessary immigration, have required great increases in power generation. (The annual increase in power demand is estimated at some 7%.) The increasingly harsh economic climate led the Government to introduce higher electricity rates in April 1986. This was the first increase since 1966 and meant that consumers would pay 27% of actual power costs, compared with their previous payment of about 6%. By the end of 1987 the five power stations, at Shuwaikh, Shuaiba North, Shuaiba South, Doha East and Doha West, had a total installed capacity of 5,230 MW. A sixth power station, with an installed capacity of 2,511 MW, came into full production at az-Zour South in 1988. In mid-1990 the Ministry of Electricity and Water decided to provide desalination units for the Subiya thermal power station. Two 6m.-gallons-per-day units are required for the 2,400-MW station. Subiya's first unit began operation in 1992. Substantial damage to Kuwait's power stations was reported as a result of the Iraqi occupation; az-Zour South was the least damaged power station. By mid-1993 installed generating capacity remained 30% below the pre-invasion level of 7,100 MW, although Shuaiba North was the only station not to have resumed operations. In mid-1995 Cogelex Alsthom of France finalized a contract with the Ministry of Communications, Electricity and Water to supply and install an electricity substation at the Shuaiba petrochemical complex. Germany's AEG and Switzerland-based Asea Brown Boveri were contracted to supply and install a further three substations, representing the first phase of the expansion of Kuwait's grid following a series of contracts aimed primarily at repairing damage sustained during the Iraqi invasion. Installed capacity in Kuwait in 1996 totalled 6,898 MW. Plans to rebuild the Shuaiba North power station were abandoned in mid-1996, in favour of a proposal to construct a new 2,400-MW thermal power plant at az-Zour. Tenders for construction of the plant are to be invited exclusively from US contractors. The project will also include a water desalination plant with a capacity of 48m. gallons per day. A new station is under construction at Subiya; the station will increase Kuwait's total installed capacity to 9,280 MW and is due for completion by 1999.

Increased water demands have been met by the distillation plants at Shuwaikh, Shuaiba North, Shuaiba South, Doha East and Doha West, which, in 1986, gave Kuwait a total installed capacity of 35,286m. gallons per year. The rapid increase in water demand was reflected in the rise in average daily water consumption, from 3.8m. gallons in 1960, to 18.2m. gallons in 1970, 64.1m. gallons in 1980, 130.3m. gallons in 1990, and 184.3m. gallons in 1996. Traditionally, Kuwait had concentrated on distillation methods for obtaining fresh water, but at the end of 1984 the Doha reverse osmosis plant was inaugurated, with an annual capacity of 220m. gallons. The pumping of fresh water from underground aquifers declined from 700m. gallons in 1970 to 126m. gallons in 1980, and to 14m. gallons in 1990, and ceased in 1991, following damage caused by the Iraqi invasion which has yet to be repaired. The pumping of brackish water, however, increased from 11,319m. gallons in 1980 to 21,366m. gallons in 1989. By 1991, however, following the Iraqi invasion, production had decreased to 2,787m. gallons. By 1996, however, annual production had recovered to 22,010m. gallons. The fresh water and brackish water systems are piped through separate networks, and the latter is used primarily for blending with distilled water, for irrigation, watering livestock, construction and in the household. Oil released into the Persian (Arabian) Gulf by Iraq caused considerable damage to Kuwait's desalination facilities.

The harbour of Kuwait City was completely reconstructed to accommodate the surge in imports after 1973. A new international airport was opened in 1980, and there is a national airline with an international service, Kuwait Airways Corpn (KAC). In 1990 KAC owned 19 aircraft, flying to 41 destinations. KAC lost two-thirds of its fleet during the Iraqi occupation, and six KAC airliners were held by Iran (until the end of July 1992), which demanded reparation for their upkeep. The airport infrastructure was also seriously damaged, but by 1993 the refurbished airport was operating normally. A major programme of aircraft replacement and fleet expansion began in 1992. By 1997 KAC owned 23 aircraft and served 47 destinations. It was anticipated that KAC would be privatized by 2000.

The Kuwait Oil Tanker Co (KOTC) was fully nationalized in 1979. The oil ministry then started to include the use of Kuwaiti tankers in the terms of sale of its crude petroleum. In 1983 the displacement of Kuwait's merchant fleet was 2,542,490 gross tons, and this included 23 oil tankers and 47 general cargo ships, as well as a considerable number of smaller vessels. In January 1987 the company signed a contract, valued at $131m., with the Samsung Heavy Industries Corpn of the Republic of Korea for the purchase of six new product carriers, two with a capacity of 120,000 dwt and four of 35,000 dwt, to be delivered in 1988 and 1989. In early 1990 KOTC commissioned the Republic of Korea to supply a third 280,000-dwt very large crude carrier (VLCC) by 1992. Similarly, the company finalized a contract with Japan for the supply of two liquefied gas carriers, each with a capacity of 78,000 cu m, under a plan to enlarge its fleet of 28 oil tankers and 6 gas carriers, in order to enhance its position in the world tanker market. Kuwait's two main container ports are at Shuwaikh and Shuaiba. Despite the devastation caused by the Iraqi forces during their occupation of Kuwait, the Shuaiba port resumed operations in March 1991. The 1990–95 Ports Public Authority programme contained plans to expand both ports. During 1981 the conflict between Iraq and Iran led to greatly increased trade between Iraq and Kuwait, with ports becoming severely congested, but in 1983 exports to Iraq fell by 73.3%. This was largely due to a cessation of cement sales, but it nevertheless caused a reappraisal of plans for port expansion. Worsening relations with Iran had a serious influence on Kuwaiti shipping, and between October 1986 and April 1987, 15 Kuwaiti ships were attacked in the Gulf. As a result of these attacks, Kuwaiti ports were given similar status to those of Iran and Iraq for insurance purposes, and 11 Kuwaiti tankers were re-registered under the US and British flags. Since the ending of hostilities, most of these have been reflagged to Kuwait. At the end of 1996 Kuwait's merchant fleet numbered 211 vessels, with a total displacement of 2,027,884 gross registered tons. The total included 25 oil tankers (displacement 1,342,512 grt). In January 1997 KOTC awarded a $610m. contract to South Korea's Hyundai Heavy Industries to build two 309,000-ton oil tankers.

The Government undertook a $2,000m. expressway road development (despite a recorded decline of 6.3% in traffic in 1983), which was completed in 1988. Plans were announced for a new KD 300m. causeway to link Shuwaikh with Bubiyan Island.

In recent years telecommunications have become increasingly important in Kuwait. At the end of 1996 Kuwait had 500,000 fixed telephone lines. It also has an extensive mobile network. As part of its ongoing programme to upgrade the country's fixed line system, the communications ministry awarded a contract in July 1997 to Germany's Siemens to install 100,000 new telephone lines at five exchanges at Surra, Qurain, Sulaibikhat, Salwa and Old Samiya. Earlier, in 1994, Sweden's Ericsson won two contracts to upgrade 15 local exchanges, and in February 1996 the UK's GPT was contracted to install 40,000 lines.

AGRICULTURE AND FISHERIES

Owing to the scarcity of water in Kuwait, little grain is produced, and, as a result, most of the country's food has to be imported. In 1994 agriculture contributed less than 1% of Kuwait's GDP. The principal agricultural crops are tomatoes, melons, onions and cucumbers.

A five-year development plan for agriculture, initiated in 1982, was intended to increase the area under vegetables to 3,500 ha by 1986, raising overall vegetable production from 42,000 tons in 1981—supplying 24% of vegetable requirements—to 98,000 tons. Experiments with hydroponics gave Kuwait the confidence to set these optimistic targets, and the Public Authority for Agriculture and Fish Resources agreed to continue to subsidize agricultural products during 1986 and

1987. A considerable amount was also invested in the development of methods of using treated effluent for irrigation purposes.

The Government also encouraged animal husbandry, the main activity of the bedouin before the development of the oilfields. Subsidies were introduced in 1983 to assist farmers using artesian wells and greenhouses, and for the owners of small fishing boats. The Government also owned a 36-ha experimental farm. In the private sector the poultry and dairy industries expanded, as has the cultivation of dates, production of which totalled 1,000 tons in 1996. In 1996 milk production was estimated at 37,000 tons and there were an estimated 25,000 cattle, 350,000 sheep, 75,000 goats and 22m. poultry in Kuwait. Kuwait also invested in livestock overseas, but it still needed to import considerable numbers. In 1989 plans were announced to develop self-sufficiency in food production by expanding irrigated farms and agricultural facilities in the north of Kuwait.

Fishing, particularly of prawns and shrimps, is also widely practised. Four fishing companies were amalgamated into Kuwait United Fisheries in 1972. A 20-year plan to develop the industry, at an estimated cost of $1m., was announced in 1987, when local production was sufficient to satisfy only 25% of domestic demand. The Public Authority for Agriculture and Fish Resources was allocated KD 8.6m. for construction projects in its 1988/89 budget. The total catch in 1995 was 8,400 tons, compared with 8,000 tons in 1994 and 7,100 tons in 1993.

FOREIGN TRADE AND BALANCE OF PAYMENTS

Kuwait's foreign trade is dominated by exports of crude petroleum and petroleum products, which generally account for over 90% of the value of export earnings each year. In 1985 the total value of exports was KD 3,185.1m. According to the IMF, total export earnings in 1990, the year of the Iraqi invasion, were reduced to KD 2,031.4m. (of which petroleum accounted for KD 1,842.0m.), from KD3,378.0m. in 1989, and in 1991 the total slumped to KD 309.4m. Kuwait was liberated from Iraqi occupation at the end of February in that year, but the country's petroleum-production facilities were severely damaged, and it was not possible to resume exports at pre-war levels. In 1992, however, export revenue recovered to KD 1,931.1m., with the petroleum sector providing KD 1,824.9m. (94.5% of the total). By 1994 total export earnings had increased to KD 3,342.3m., of which petroleum accounted for KD 3,112.7m. (93.1% of the total). In 1995 export revenues increased again (by 14.1%), to KD 3,814.4m., of which petroleum exports accounted for KD 3,597.1m. (94.3% of the total), and in 1996, exports earnings were KD 4,448.0m., of which petroleum exports accounted for KD 4,221.3m. (94.9% of the total).

The total value of imports reached KD 1,849.4m. in 1989. According to the IMF, Kuwait's imports fell to KD 1,145.7m. in 1990, but rose to KD 1,353.3m. in 1991 and to KD 2,129.2m. in 1992. Imports declined to KD 1,988.2m. in 1994. However, imports recovered slightly in 1995, to KD 2,323.1m., and in 1996 reached KD 2,507.2m. The most important commodity group in Kuwait's imports is usually machinery and transport equipment (which accounted for 41.6% of total imports in 1996), followed by basic manufactures (19.8% in 1996). In 1996 Kuwait's main source of imports was the USA, which supplied 16.7% of total imports. Japan, France, Germany and the United Kingdom are also important suppliers. Details concerning the destination of Kuwait's petroleum exports are not available for recent years. In 1996 the main customers for the country's non-petroleum exports (totalling KD 226.7m.) included India (which took 18.6% of the total), Saudi Arabia (16.9%) and the UAE (15.0%). In 1992 KPC signed an agreement with the National Iranian Oil Co to supply 700,000 tons of petroleum products per year. This was the first such agreement since the outbreak of the Iran–Iraq war in 1980. Kuwait subsequently took delivery of the first of 40 F-18 aircraft from the USA. Agreements were also concluded for the purchase of tanks, armoured vehicles and more aircraft from the allies. In mid-1992 Kuwait purchased a number of *Ammon* missiles from Egypt. In early 1995 Kuwait contracted to purchase eight naval missile-carrying patrol boats from France to replace those destroyed during the Iraqi invasion, together with a $54m. air-defence radar system.

The current account surplus on the balance of payments was US $4,602m. in 1988, increasing to $9,136m. in 1989. The surplus declined to $3,886m. in 1990, when trade was disrupted by the Iraqi invasion and occupation. In 1991 Kuwait paid huge amounts to the countries that contributed to ending the occupation, resulting in a current deficit of $26,478m. By 1994 there was a surplus on the current accout of $2,489m. which increased to $5,019m. in 1995, $7,071m. in 1996 and $7,671m. in 1997. The rise in 1988 was a result of increased income from investments, although the sharp decline in world petroleum prices caused a reduction in the visible trade surplus to $1,709m. in that year (from $3,280m. in 1987). The trade surplus rose to $4,987m. in 1989, but was reduced to $3,179m. in 1990. In 1991 Kuwait registered a visible trade deficit of $3,993m. By 1994 a trade surplus, of $4,460m., was recorded. The surplus increased to $5,582m. in 1995 and to $6,964m. in 1996, declining to $6,296m. in 1997.

BANKING AND FINANCE

In 1979 the Central Bank of Kuwait imposed tighter controls on the banking sector and demanded a significant reduction in overdrafts. Despite this, the banking sector continued to flourish in the early 1980s, with a 20% rise in total assets during 1982. However, the collapse of the Souk al-Manakh in 1982 (see below), the uncertainties caused by the Iran–Iraq War, and the problems associated with the falling price of oil led to severe difficulties for Kuwait's banking sector in the mid-1980s. In 1983 the banks' total assets rose by only 9.3%, and the decline in the commercial banking sector also led to the introduction of a two-tier exchange rate between April and August 1984. The foreign exchange market was effectively closed in June, when the Central Bank halted sales of US dollars, except for genuine commercial transactions.

In 1985 the banks faced a burgeoning debt crisis. Court cases involving bank debtors rose from 169 in 1981 to 437 in 1984, and in May 1985 bad debts held by commercial banks amounted to approximately KD 2,200m. ($7,200m.). At the end of 1984 the Central Bank asked for full documentation on all commercial bank loans in excess of KD 250,000. By the end of 1985 its survey of the country's financial institutions revealed that, as of 11 September 1985, Kuwait's banks had gross claims against foreign banks totalling KD 1,534m. ($5,192m.), a sum which exceeded their corresponding obligations by KD 93m. The survey also revealed that Kuwait's banks had lent a total of KD 275.9m. to their own directors. At the end of 1985 three banks recorded zero net profits, and the National Bank of Kuwait (NBK—the country's largest bank) was the only bank to record an increase (of 11.1%) in net profits over the previous year's figure. The dissolution of the National Assembly was widely regarded as providing an opportunity for seeking a solution to the debt crisis, and a series of measures, approved by the Council of Ministers in August 1986, facilitated a 'rescue programme' whereby debtors should repay as much as they could afford, and the Government would pay the remainder of the debt. In 1989 the majority of the commercial banks in Kuwait remained dependent on this scheme for debt-restructuring. A range of other radical changes in the policy of the Central Bank were made between 1987 and 1989, promoting the further revival of the banking sector.

Following the Iraqi invasion of Kuwait, all Kuwaiti bank deposits were frozen, paralysing the operations of the country's banks. The Bank of England allowed individuals and organizations from Kuwait to operate in Britain, but all of the banks had to seek permission from the Bank of England to pay out Kuwait-controlled assets. The NBK was instrumental in efforts to resume operations. With the support of the Kuwait Investment Office (see Investment, below), it was able to free most of its blocked accounts, and to restore its liquidity position, by quickly selling $2,000m. of its loan portfolio at little or no discount. The NBK played a central role in stabilizing the position of the other Kuwaiti banks. By early 1991 the Commercial Bank of Kuwait, the Al-Ahli Bank, the Industrial Bank of Kuwait (IBK), the Gulf Bank, the Kuwait Real Estate Bank (KREB), the Bank of Kuwait and the Middle East and Burgan Bank had resumed operations outside Kuwait and Iraq, as had Kuwait's main investment banks, the Kuwaiti Investment Co (KIC), the Kuwaiti Foreign Trading, Contracting and Investing Co (KFTCIC) and the Kuwait International Investment Co (KIIC).

Following the liberation of Kuwait, the Kuwaiti banks resumed domestic operations, but NBK was the only bank able to participate in the reconstruction process. The Government encouraged rationalization and the merger of some of the numerous domestic banks. By mid-1996, however, little progress had been made in this direction, and the proposed merger of the IBK and the KREB was reported to have been suspended. In March 1991 some branches of banks began to reopen, mainly to distribute the Government's cash grant to Kuwaiti citizens who had remained in the country during the occupation. Depositors were initially limited to cash withdrawals of $14,000 per month until the end of June. By August all currency restrictions had been removed. In April 1991 an Amiri decree instructed the banks to cancel debts totalling $4,900m., and so cleared the debts of 180,000 people. As a result, many local bad debts that had been incurred in the stock market crisis of the mid-1980s were cancelled. On 20 May 1992 it was announced that the Government was to buy the entire domestic loan portfolio of the domestic banking system, covering credits to residents worth $20,400m. In the first half of 1993 there was intense debate between the Government and the National Assembly over the terms under which the loans should be repaid. As long as the issue remained unresolved, Kuwaiti banks were unwilling to approve loans, and investment outside the petroleum industry was very limited. In August 1993 the National Assembly approved legislation requiring debtors to register their preferred method of repayment by March 1994; debtors could either settle their accounts by September 1995 in exchange for debt forgiveness of up to 46%, or pay over a period of 12 years with no debt forgiveness. Even though the majority of debtors opted to repay their debts by September 1995, the rate of repayment was slow and the Government came under increasing pressure to extend the repayment period as any rapid liquidation of assets could undermine the economy. In June 1995 the Council of Ministers reviewed a draft law proposing significant amendments to the difficult debts law, which would allow debtors several more years in which to make their repayments. The National Assembly initially opposed the amendments, as it was feared that the extension of the terms of repayment would benefit politically powerful debtors, including members of the royal family, at the expense of the economy. In August, however, preliminary approval was granted to a bill which would ease repayment terms. Hopes for the success of the latest repayment programme were encouraged by the high proportion (77%) of obligations repaid on 6 April 1996, the first of five annual payment instalments.

In 1988 the NBK had total assets of KD 3,476m. and estimated profits of KD 30.9m. Total assets of the Central Bank fell to KD 1,443m. at the end of the year, from KD 1,649m. in December 1987. A fall of 63% in foreign assets was partially offset by an increase in holdings of local bonds and public debt instruments. By 1989 the NBK had increased its total assets by 10.1%, to KD 3,867m., and had recorded a profit of KD 35m., representing an increase of 11.4% in comparison with the previous year. The other principal banks of Kuwait all reported an increase in assets and profits in 1989. NBK was the only commercial bank able to issue balance sheet figures for 1990. NBK's assets, which totalled KD 3,267m. at the end of 1993, had risen to KD 3,821m. by the middle of 1996, and net profits of KD 71.3m. were recorded for the year as a whole. At end-1997 NBK's assets had increased to KD 4,118m. and net profits for that year were KD73.5m. In that year, most local commercial banks had recorded an increase in net profits, and their total assets were KD11,458,000m. in 1996.

Prior to the Iraqi invasion, there were plans to develop Kuwait as an international, rather than a regional, financial centre. KIC incurred losses of $195m. over the period 1983–85, and, following a small recovery in 1986, foreign stocks were adversely affected by the world-wide decline in share prices in October 1987. Its total assets rose dramatically in 1988, from KD 9.8m. to KD 60.9m. KFTCIC announced losses of $213m. in the same year, bringing total losses to $613m. over four years. A capital injection in November 1988 helped to improve the situation. KIIC has been involved in the property market, and recent operations include a $40m. investment in real estate in Portugal, through the Kuwait-Portugal Fund. In 1994 foreign equity interests of up to 40% were allowed in the banking sector.

CAPITAL MARKET

A significant capital market has been developed in Kuwait through the activities of the leading investment companies and the IBK, and with the encouragement of the Government. An active bond market developed after 1973, mostly for international borrowers from the Third World and Eastern Europe. The Central Bank then closed the new issue market in November 1979 as part of its efforts to boost liquidity in Kuwait's money market, but by July 1981 the Kuwaiti dinar international bond market had reopened. Despite the issue of a number of new bonds, the market was to close again in September 1982. It reopened in June 1983 with a KD 5m. floating rate note bond for the United Bank of Kuwait's subsidiary, UBK Finance, and there followed a KD 14m. two-tranche bond offer for KFTCIC in November. However, following the collapse of the stock market (see below), the bond market also lost its appeal, and in 1985 and 1986 only solitary domestic bonds were issued. In the last quarter of 1987 and the first quarter of 1988 the Government issued a series of bonds and treasury bills, in an attempt to finance the budget deficit. During 1987 the Central Bank's total assets fell by 31%, to KD 1,458.7m., mainly as a result of a decline in foreign deposits, which decreased by 44%, to KD 681.8m., by the end of the year.

In 1952 Kuwait had established what was, prior to the Iraqi invasion of August 1990, the world's twelfth largest stock exchange. The amount of capital holders seeking investment outlets in Kuwait, and the innate entrepreneurial spirit of locals, generally pushed the prices of shares far above their real value. In April 1978, in an attempt to stem this unhealthy trend, the Government sanctioned the reduction in nominal value of shares to one dinar, a move which resulted in a split of share values to 10%–13% of their current value. This broadened the base of the market. In 1981 247m. shares, worth $6,854m., were traded in Kuwait's stock market, representing a 72% increase by volume, and a 47% increase by value, over 1980's figures.

Alongside the official market, an unofficial stock market, the Souk al-Manakh, also developed. After 1978 many Kuwaitis had invested in Iraq, and, as a result of the Iran–Iraq War, a severe cash-flow crisis emerged in Kuwait. In 1982 the liquidity shortage which this caused was particularly severe for the Souk al-Manakh. The unofficial market had been based on the use of post-dated cheques and the hope of continuously rising share prices. Then in September 1982 the system collapsed, as smaller creditors prematurely presented their post-dated cheques (perfectly legal under Kuwaiti law) at a time when many dealers were unable to pay. The collapse of the Souk al-Manakh initiated a major crisis in Kuwait's financial system, the impact of which lasted for several years.

Government measures to alleviate the crisis involved the immediate formation of the Kuwait Clearing Co, to register and process all cheques involved, and the establishment of a KD 500m. fund to protect, and pay, the smaller debtors whose investors were bankrupt. In August 1983 the Government urged the settlement of debts at the market price at the time of transaction, and set a maximum premium of 25% on post-dated cheques. Disagreement over the handling of the crisis led to the resignation of the Minister of Finance, Abd al-Latif Yousuf al-Hamad. In October the Government appointed an arbitration panel to revalue the debts of the 17 leading dealers in the Souk al-Manakh. These accounted for about $78,000m., or 82% of the estimated total of outstanding debts at the time of the crisis, and the dealers' assets were valued at between 20% and 30% of their liabilities. Since then, a new investment company has been established, with a capital of KD 300m. (in which the Government has a 40% share), to convert the debtors' non-liquid assets into payment for the creditors. In April 1984 the Council of Ministers announced further financial measures to resolve the crisis, including the division of assets into three categories. Bonds to repay creditors were issued in July, and, of the 254 people referred to the receivership, 88 were declared bankrupt, three restored their solvency and 163 reached agreements with their creditors.

In August 1984 the official stock exchange moved to new premises, and its permanent floor officially opened in April 1985. The Souk al-Manakh stock market was closed on 1 November 1984, and trading in shares was restricted to the official stock exchange and to a parallel market which it operated. To avoid a repetition of the Souk al-Manakh crisis, measures were introduced to limit the activities of brokers on the official market. Before being allowed on the floor, brokers had to pay a registration fee and provide a guarantee for KD 1m., while a percentage of brokers' commissions had to be paid to the exchange. By mid-January 1985 creditors who had been owed money by Souk al-Manakh defaulters had received cash and bonds totalling KD 759m., accounting for about three-quarters of the net debts. At the end of 1987, however, 17% of the debts resulting from the collapse of the Souk al-Manakh remained outstanding.

The Government bore the brunt of the crisis and was forced to inject large sums into the banking system to restore liquidity. However, its share-supporting operation after the collapse of the Souk al-Manakh, when it spent KD 755m. on shares worth KD 230m. at the beginning of 1986, led to losses of KD 528m. ($1,820m.).

At the end of November 1985, the Minister of Finance and Economy made the following recommendations: 33 companies should be dissolved; a number of the remaining 47 companies should be merged; from March 1986 the KIC was to purchase the companies that closed, on behalf of the Government; and companies registered in the Gulf that fell outside the jurisdiction of Kuwait were urged to comply with the Government's recommendations. These measures appeared to be necessary, owing to the fact that 24 of the 36 companies that had closed, and were under consideration for purchase by the Government, had incurred losses exceeding 50% of the paid-up capital invested in them. It was estimated that by mid-1986 this scheme had cost the Government approximately KD 121m. In May 1989 it was reported that stock market activity was disappointing, and measures to deregulate the stock market to some extent were to be introduced before the end of the year in the hope that a reduction in restrictions would encourage investors. Also in May it was announced that the Souk al-Manakh stock exchange was to be re-opened in June, to allow trading in companies that had failed to meet the minimum capital requirements of the official stock exchange.

In May 1988 the Government permitted citizens of all GCC members states to purchase shares on the Kuwait stock exchange. (Previously only Kuwaiti citizens had been permitted to do so.) Then, in 1992, the exchange was opened to international firms for the first time. In 1995 the exchange became the most active share market in the Arab world. Strong corporate earnings, excess liquidity and the privatization policy launched by the Kuwait Investment Authority (KIA) have maintained the buoyancy of the stock market, and in June 1997 it was reported that the average market price of shares had increased by some 30% since the start of the year. The privatization programme began in mid-1994, and by early 1997 the KIA had sold KD 653m. worth of shares. In January 1997 it was announced that a further KD 1,000m. worth of shares were available for sale at current prices.

PUBLIC FINANCE

The cumulative costs of the Gulf conflict (1990–91) to the Kuwaiti Government inevitably increased its budget deficits. By the end of July 1991 the cost to Kuwait of paying the expenses of Kuwaitis living abroad during the Iraqi occupation, and of financing 'Operation Desert Storm', had increased to $22,000m., which had been drawn from its reserves, with further expenditure expected. A further $6,000m.–$7,000m. was spent after liberation on stabilization measures, such as the cancellation of personal debts and cash grants to nationals who remained in Kuwait during the Iraqi occupation. The Kuwaiti Government stated that it had no intention of making large-scale sales of investments to create revenue, but it was nevertheless reported in mid-1993 that the value of Kuwait's overseas investments had more than halved in the previous three years (see also Investment). At the end of 1991 a $5,500m. international loan to Kuwait was announced, as well as export credit facilities worth the same amount with the USA, Japan, the UK, the Netherlands and France. Kuwait began repayments on the international loan in 1996.

In the 1980s, in response to fluctuating oil revenues, Kuwait sought ways of reducing public expenditure. In 1982, as a result of a decrease in subsidies, the price of petrol doubled, and in 1983

the supply of free school meals and uniforms was withdrawn. Charges for other formerly free services, such as health, were introduced, and the price of electricity was increased. The 1985/86 budget contained the first projected spending cut in Kuwait's recent history and the 1987/88 budget deficit was only KD 554m., as expenditure for the year was 20% below the projected figure, while overproduction of petroleum led to a 30% rise in revenues, to KD 2,252m. In September 1987 the Council of Ministers approved legislation enabling the Government to borrow as much as KD 1,400m. over 10 years through direct loans, treasury bills and medium- and long-term treasury bonds, to finance its budget deficit. However, the limit of KD 1,400m. was reached by June 1988 and was raised in March 1989 to KD 3,000m. By 1992/93 the budget deficit had decreased to KD 1,572.6m. In March 1994 the finance and economy committee of the National Assembly approved KD 3,500m. in extraordinary defence spending over the 12 years from 1992 to 2004. At the same time an increase in the budget deficit was forecast, although much of this was accounted for by the inclusion in the budget for the first time of allocations for arms procurement. A deficit of KD 1,773m. was forecast for 1994/95. The 1995/96 budget envisaged expenditure at KD 4,230m. and revenues at KD 2,910m., although higher petroleum revenue and lower state spending resulted in a much smaller deficit (an estimated KD 653m.) than forecast. The budget for 1997/98 put expenditure at KD 4,378m. and revenues at KD 3,105m., although the deficit out-turn is again likely to be far lower than government predictions. Estimates for 1998/99 envisaged revenues of KD3,127m., expenditure of KD4,409m. and a budget deficit of KD1,282m., although actual revenues appeared likely to be less than estimated owing to declining petroleum prices; in June 1998 several government departments were asked to make reductions in their budgets for 1998/99. A target of balancing the budget by 2000 was announced in 1995.

INVESTMENT

Kuwait's main priority for spending its income from petroleum has been the development of its own economy and the provision, through the investment of surplus funds, of an income for its citizens in the future when the oil-wells have run dry. In the mid-1970s, in addition to the general reserve, the Government established a Reserve Fund for Future Generations (RFFG), to which at least 10% of total revenue must be added annually, by law, and which was not intended to be used until 2001. From 1 July 1984 (the beginning of the 1984/85 fiscal year) the National Investment Authority began to assume the management of all of Kuwait's reserves. By the end of 1986 it was clear that Kuwait's investments were not performing as well as had been expected. Income from investments declined from KD 1,289m. in 1984 to KD 1,154m. in 1985. The interest on investments held by the RFFG totalled KD 747m. in 1985, which was equivalent to a return of 6.9%. During 1985 it was reported that Kuwait held 44% of its total reserves of KD 23,027.1m. in non-Arab countries. The RFFG was estimated at KD 14,000m. before the world-wide collapse of prices on stock markets in October 1987.

Kuwait had a budget surplus for some years before 1973 and therefore developed an investment strategy considerably earlier than other petroleum-producing countries did. This strategy was implemented when Kuwait established the Kuwait Investment Office (KIO) in the 1950s, with the aim of providing for its future generations by investing part of the Government's share of profits from the country's petroleum industry. The KIO in London (which was formally merged with its parent, the KIA, in March 1993) handled much of the nation's investment in Europe and elsewhere. In 1979 the KIO also started to buy small interests in leading Japanese electronics companies. Many of Kuwait's investments are in the USA, and involve almost every one of the 500 leading US companies. Kuwait also has some major real estate projects there. Exceptions to Kuwait's traditional preference for small shares in foreign companies included its outright purchase of the St Martin's Property Corpn of the UK, and its purchase of substantial holdings in Daimler-Benz of Germany, the USA's Korf Industries and a Canadian copper-molybdenum mine. During 1983 it was announced that the Kuwait Real Estate Investment Consortium (KREIC), together with the Arab General Investment Co of Dubai and other private investors, was to establish an offshore investment company in the Cayman Islands, with a capital of $25m., in order to invest mainly in advanced technology industries in the USA. However, in June 1985 the KREIC defaulted on a $60m. syndicated loan, signed in 1981, and had to be rescued by the KIO, which bought KD 30m. of its assets and increased its capital by 50%. In 1984 the KIO acquired one-fifth of the Hong Leong Co in Hong Kong. Investments made in 1986 included the purchase of a share of 5% in the Banco Central of Spain through a Spanish holding company, Cartera Central.

Investment income from abroad increased to $8,074m. in 1986, overtaking income from petroleum for the first time. In 1987 the KIO acquired further considerable shareholdings in Europe: in particular, it acquired a major stake in BP, and by August 1988 had obtained 21.68% of BP's total shares. In October 1988, after a report by the Monopolies and Mergers Commission in Britain, the KIO was forced to reduce its interest in BP to 9.9%. This disposal produced a profit of $700m. for the KIO, as the BP management raised its buy-back price for the shares in response to hostile bids from rival oil companies. (A further 3% stake in BP was sold by the KIA in May 1997 for about $2,000m.) By October 1987 the KIO had accumulated investments in Spain with a value of $2,400m., and, as a result of its acquisition of 37% of Torras Hostench, it established itself as a major force in Spain's chemicals industry; it also acquired 35% of Explosivos Rio Tinto (ERT) and further shares in several Spanish media groups. In 1988 ERT was merged with Cros to form a new company, Ercros, with capital of $225m. ERT was listed as unacceptable by the Arab League Boycott Office, causing some embarrassment to the KIO. The KIO also purchased Ebro, a large Spanish food manufacturer. Other investments by the KIO included the purchase of a 51% share in First Capital Corpn, a Singapore property developer, and a 10% interest in Avimo Singapore, a manufacturer of military optics. In June 1989 the KIO disclosed a 5.2% share in the United Kingdom's Midland Bank. In early 1989 the KIO sold its interest in Cartera Central, which included shares in three Spanish banks, for $360m., following considerable public pressure in Spain.

In 1993 the dealings of the KIO were the subject of an inquiry by a commission comprising members of the new National Assembly. It was alleged that officials of the KIO had lost $5,000m. in Spain since 1986, of which some $1,000m. had been embezzled through the collapsed Grupo Torras company. In mid-1993 it was reported that legal proceedings were being prepared against former KIO officials in the United Kingdom and Spain. In July a report of the National Assembly's finance and economy commission was critical of the Government for failing to ensure the accountability of KIO officials. A series of legislative measures in 1993 attempted to ensure greater accountability from state investment organizations and to increase penalties for the misuse of public funds.

Kuwaiti private investment is substantial. It is predominantly in real estate and high-yielding equities. Although this investment is concentrated in the USA, Europe and Japan, Kuwaitis have shown an interest in investment in other non-Arab countries in Asia, Africa and South America, as well as in the Arab world.

From August 1990 until July 1991, Kuwait's sole sources of income were earnings from its international financial investments and profits from Kuwait Petroleum International, which operates Kuwaiti petroleum companies in Europe and Asia. It was estimated that Kuwait's international investments in August 1990 were worth as much as $100,000m., comprising the RFFG and the State General Reserve. The rate of return on these investments was estimated at 5% per year. Although the Kuwaiti Government refused to disclose any details concerning the sale of assets to fund its activities during the 1990–91 Gulf crisis, it was estimated in mid-1993 that the value of Kuwait's overseas investments had more than halved since August 1990. Following the liberation of Kuwait, the Government indicated that it did not envisage the sale of large-scale investments, especially of important strategic assets such as its interests in Daimler-Benz, Hoechst, Metallgesellschaft, Hogg Robinson, Midland Bank UK and BP. In mid-1994 Kuwait submitted a claim of almost $41,000m. to the UN Compensation Committee for losses incurred by the KIA during the Iraqi invasion. The claim was part of a total of $94,800m. worth of compensation claims made by Kuwait by the end of June 1994, with further submissions expected. Income from overseas investments increased by almost 30%, to $5,153m., in 1995.

After its own development, Kuwait's next priority is that of the rest of the Arab and Islamic world, and then of the Third World in general. It pioneered foreign aid in the Arab world, setting up the Kuwait Fund for Arab Economic Development (KFAED) in 1961. Kuwait later raised the KFAED's capital considerably, and extended operations to Africa and Asia. Its capital in 1997 was KD 1,925m. The country also helped set up the Arab Fund for Economic and Social Development in Kuwait, and it is a member of various Arab, Islamic and OPEC aid organizations, notably the Islamic Development Bank, the Arab Bank for Economic Development in Africa (BADEA) and the OPEC Fund for International Development. It has also contributed to IMF and World Bank facilities.

Kuwait's total foreign aid, which was substantially more than that given on projected aid by the KFAED, ranged between about 8% and 15% of GNP during the second half of the 1970s. As a proportion of GNP, Kuwait gave more aid than any other country, at 4.86% of GNP in 1982. However, Kuwait's official contribution to development assistance declined over the period 1984–87, and Kuwaiti foreign aid further decreased in the post-liberation period of reconstruction. Overall, between 1962 and June 1997 it was estimated that the KFAED disbursed 514 loans, valued at KD2,640m. Annual disbursements had increased from KD69.7m. in 1987/88 to KD140.3m. in 1996/97.

Statistical Survey

Source (unless otherwise stated): Central Statistical Office, Ministry of Planning, POB 26188, 13122 Safat, Kuwait City; tel. 2454968; telex 22468; fax 2430464.

Note: Unless otherwise indicated, data refer to the State of Kuwait as constituted at 1 August 1990, prior to the Iraqi invasion and annexation of the territory and its subsequent liberation. Furthermore, no account has been taken of the increase in the area of Kuwait as a result of the adjustment to the border with Iraq that came into force on 15 January 1993.

Area and Population

AREA, POPULATION AND DENSITY

Area (sq km) .	17,818*
Population (census results)†	
21 April 1985 .	1,697,301
20–21 April 1995 (provisional)	
Males .	914,324
Females .	661,659
Total .	1,575,983
Density (per sq km) at April 1995 .	88.4

* 6,880 sq miles.

† Figures include Kuwaiti nationals abroad. Based on the definition of citizenship in use in 1992, the total population at the 1985 census included 474,200 Kuwaiti nationals (240,068 males; 234,132 females). On the same basis, the population at the 1995 census comprised 655,820 Kuwaitis and 920,163 non-Kuwaitis.

GOVERNORATES (population at 1995 census)

Governorate	Area (sq km)*	Population†	Capital
Capital . .	199.8	192,800	Kuwait City
Hawalli . . }	368.4 {	466,923	Hawalli
Farwaniya . . }		428,249	Farwaniya
Al-Jahra . .	11,230.2	224,205	Jahra
Al-Ahmadi . .	5,119.6	263,806	Ahmadi City

* Excluding the islands of Bubiyan and Warba (combined area 900 sq km).
† Provisional.

PRINCIPAL TOWNS (population at 1995 census)*

Kuwait City (capital) .	28,859	South Kheetan . .	63,628
Salmiya . . .	130,215	Farwaniya . . .	53,100
Jaleeb ash-Shuyukh .	102,178	Sabahiya . . .	50,535
Hawalli . . .	82,238		

*Provisional results

BIRTHS, MARRIAGES AND DEATHS

	Registered live births		Registered marriages		Registered deaths	
	Number	Rate (per 1,000)	Number	Rate (per 1,000)	Number	Rate (per 1,000)
1989 . .	52,858	26.7	10,108	5.1	4,628	2.3
1990* . .	12,358	n.a.	n.a.	n.a.	1,177	n.a.
1991 . .	20,609	9.9	6,907	3.3	3,380	1.6
1992† .	34,817	24.5	10,803	7.6	3,369	2.4
1993† .	37,379	25.6	10,077	6.9	3,441	2.4
1994† .	38,868	24.0	9,550	5.9	3,464	2.1
1995 . .	41,169	n.a.	9,515	n.a.	3,781	n.a.
1996 . .	44,005	n.a.	n.a.	n.a.	3,549	n.a.

* Figures relate only to the first quarter of year.
† Rates are based on unrevised estimates of mid-year population.

Expectation of life (UN estimates, years at birth, 1990–95): 74.9 (males 73.3; females 77.2) (Source: UN, *World Population Prospects: The 1994 Revision*).

ECONOMICALLY ACTIVE POPULATION
(sample survey, persons aged 15 years and over, March 1988)*

	Males	Females	Total
Agriculture, hunting and fishing .	9,122	132	9,254
Mining and quarrying . . .	6,329	201	6,530
Manufacturing	53,231	1,433	54,664
Electricity, gas and water. . .	7,527	86	7,613
Construction	112,926	1,608	114,534
Trade and restaurants . .	79,278	4,057	83,335
Transport, storage and communications . . .	35,119	2,653	37,772
Finance, insurance, real estate and business services . .	17,780	3,782	21,562
Other services (including defence)	224,328	159,256	383,584
Total	545,640	173,208	718,848
Kuwaitis	81,270	31,689	112,959
Non-Kuwaitis	464,370	141,519	605,889

* Figures exclude persons seeking work for the first time, totalling 11,067 (males 6,930; females 4,137), but include other unemployed persons.

Agriculture

PRINCIPAL CROPS ('000 metric tons)

	1994	1995	1996
Tomatoes	14	16	20
Cucumbers and gherkins . .	16	20*	26*
Onions (dry)*	16	18	20
Other vegetables	23	25	27
Melons*	5	5	5
Dates*	1	1	1

* FAO estimate(s).

Source: FAO, *Production Yearbook*.

LIVESTOCK ('000 head, year ending September)

	1994	1995	1996*
Cattle	15	20	25
Camels*	7	8	9
Sheep	216	308	350
Goats	42	69	75

Poultry (million): 20 in 1994; 20 in 1995; 22* in 1996.
* FAO estimate(s).

Source: FAO, *Production Yearbook*.

LIVESTOCK PRODUCTS ('000 metric tons)

	1994	1995	1996
Beef and veal	1*	1	1*
Mutton and lamb*	33	33	36
Poultry meat	25	26	28*
Cows' milk	29	33	35
Goats' milk	1†	2†	2*
Poultry eggs†	8	9	9
Sheepskins*	12	12	13

* FAO estimate(s).   † Unofficial figure(s).

Source: FAO, *Production Yearbook*.

Fishing

('000 metric tons, live weight)

	1993	1994	1995
Fishes	4.8	6.1	6.9
Shrimps and prawns . . .	2.3	1.9	1.5
Total catch	7.1	8.0	8.4

Mining*

	1993	1994	1995
Crude petroleum ('000 metric tons)	94,530	100,917	100,920
Natural gas (petajoules) . . .	243	233	354†

* Including an equal share of production with Saudi Arabia from the Neutral/Partitioned Zone.
† Provisional or estimated figure.

Source: UN, *Industrial Commodity Statistics Yearbook*.

Industry

SELECTED PRODUCTS ('000 metric tons, unless otherwise stated)

	1993	1994	1995
Wheat flour	127	136	133
Sulphur (by-product)	175	175	n.a.
Chlorine	14	14	16
Caustic soda (Sodium hydroxide) .	16	16	18
Nitrogenous fertilizers* . . .	293	n.a.	n.a.
Jet fuels†	1,932	4,668	7,853‡
Motor spirit (petrol)†	1,307	1,751	1,902
Naphthas†‡	2,000	2,200	2,500
Kerosene†	1,097	1,373	1,440‡
Gas-diesel (Distillate fuel) oils† .	6,541	13,101	12,300
Residual fuel oils†	6,954	9,688	10,111‡
Petroleum bitumen (asphalt)† . .	49	66	70‡
Liquefied petroleum gas† . . .	2,671‡	2,930‡	3,312
Quicklime	42	84	89
Cement	956	1,232	2,000‡
Electric energy (million kWh)†‡ .	18,200	23,152	24,126

* Production in terms of nitrogen.
† Including an equal share of production with Saudi Arabia from the Neutral/Partitioned Zone.
‡ Provisional or estimated figure(s).

Source: UN, *Industrial Commodity Statistics Yearbook*.

Finance

CURRENCY AND EXCHANGE RATES

Monetary Units
 1,000 fils = 10 dirhams = 1 Kuwaiti dinar (KD).

Sterling and Dollar Equivalents (31 May 1998)
 £1 sterling = 499.1 fils;
 US $1 = 306.1 fils;
 100 Kuwaiti dinars = £200.34 = $326.70.

Average Exchange Rate (US $ per KD)
 1995　3.3509
 1996　3.3399
 1997　3.2966

GENERAL BUDGET (estimates, KD million, year ending 30 June)*

Revenue	1992/93	1993/94	1994/95
Oil revenues	2,085.2	2,324.2	2,784.7
Taxes on non-oil companies . .	15.5	33.8	22.8
Custom duties and fees . . .	61.0	67.4	64.9
Service charges	183.4	345.3	222.3
Electricity and water . . .	19.9	34.3	46.7
Transport and communications .	75.1	86.6	82.1
Total revenue (incl. others) . .	2,363.7	2,775.1	3,100.7

Expenditure	1992/93	1993/94	1994/95
Ministries and departments			
Foreign affairs	41.8	37.6	41.5
Finance	1,632.8	1,265.3	1,744.0
Oil	9.1	9.2	10.7
Defence	493.0	479.1	517.8
Interior	282.3	257.7	274.6
Education	301.2	305.0	312.0
Information	61.2	58.1	58.0
Public health	241.7	232.7	253.5
Social affairs and labour . .	87.2	83.0	98.1
Electricity and water . . .	302.5	292.6	322.4
Communications	71.1	71.3	75.5
Public works	130.7	136.2	175.4
National Guards	51.8	55.6	63.7
Complementary credit . . .	n.a.	371.5	n.a.
Total expenditure (incl. others) .	3,193.2	4,241.7	4,193.2

* Figures exclude investment income.

1995/96 (estimates, KD million, year ending 30 June): Total revenue 2,910 (of which oil revenues 2,490); Total expenditure 4,230.
1996/97 (estimates, KD million, year ending 30 June): Total revenue 3,000 (of which oil revenues 2,560); Total expenditure 4,210.
1997/98 (estimates, KD million, year ending 30 June): Total revenue 3,105 (of which oil revenues 2,555); Total expenditure 4,378.
1998/99 (estimates, KD million, year ending 30 June): Total revenue 3,127 (of which oil revenues 2,577); Total expenditure 4,409.

INTERNATIONAL RESERVES (US $ million at 31 December)

	1995	1996	1997
Gold*	106.0	105.7	104.0
IMF special drawing rights . .	91.1	98.0	100.0
Reserve position in IMF . . .	206.6	196.3	226.1
Foreign exchange	3,263.2	3,220.8	3,125.7
Total	3,666.8	3,620.8	3,555.8

* National valuation of gold reserves (2,539,000 troy ounces in each year).
Source: IMF, *International Financial Statistics*.

MONEY SUPPLY (KD million at 31 December)

	1995	1996	1997
Currency outside banks . . .	311.5	350.1	345.3
Demand deposits at deposit money banks	873.5	892.5	902.2
Total money	1,185.0	1,242.6	1,247.5

Source: IMF, *International Financial Statistics*.

COST OF LIVING (Consumer Price Index; base: 1978 = 100)

	1993	1994	1995
Food	148.1	150.6	153.7
Beverages	187.4	185.1	185.5
Fuel and light	121.0	119.0	119.8
Clothing (incl. footwear) . . .	213.3	213.1	239.3
Rent	190.1	193.6	197.1
All items (incl. others) . . .	181.5	186.1	191.1

NATIONAL ACCOUNTS (KD million at current prices)
Expenditure on the Gross Domestic Product

	1994	1995	1996
Government final consumption expenditure . . .	2,504	2,615	2,608
Private final consumption expenditure . . .	2,756	3,241	3,909
Increase in stocks . . . } Gross fixed capital formation . . }	1,192	1,086	1,103
Total domestic expenditure .	6,452	6,942	7,620
Exports of goods and services . .	3,753	4,234	4,883
Less Imports of goods and services	2,825	3,233	3,226
GDP in purchasers' values .	7,380	7,942	9,277
GDP at constant 1985 prices .	9,633	9,732	n.a.

Source: IMF, *International Financial Statistics*.

Gross Domestic Product by Economic Activity

	1994	1995*	1996*
Agriculture, hunting, forestry and fishing	31	34	38
Mining and quarrying . .	2,830	3,137	4,127
Manufacturing	784	887	1,036
Electricity, gas and water. .	−44	−32	2
Construction	238	243	244
Trade, restaurants and hotels. .	587	610	627
Transport, storage and communications . . .	364	387	397
Finance, insurance, real estate and business services . .	871	895	951
Community, social and personal services	1,797	1,878	1,953
Sub-total	7,458	8,039	9,375
Import duties	66	68	93
Less Imputed bank service charges	144	165	191
GDP in purchasers' values . .	7,380	7,942	9,277

* Figures are provisional.

BALANCE OF PAYMENTS (US $ million)

	1995	1996	1997
Exports of goods f.o.b. . . .	12,833	14,913	14,208
Imports of goods f.o.b. . . .	−7,251	−7,949	−7,912
Trade balance	5,582	6,964	6,296
Exports of services . . .	1,401	1,516	1,764
Imports of services . . .	−5,381	−5,103	−5,238
Balance on goods and services.	1,602	3,377	2,822
Other income received . .	6,125	6,409	7,744
Other income paid . . .	−1,243	−1,229	−1,467
Balance on goods, services and income	6,484	8,557	9,098
Current transfers received . .	54	57	158
Current transfers paid . .	−1,518	−1,543	−1,586
Current balance . . .	5,019	7,071	7,671
Capital account (net) . . .	−194	−207	−211
Direct investment abroad . .	1,022	−1,740	−616
Direct investment from abroad .	7	347	16
Portfolio investment assets . .	−2,064	−788	−5,469
Portfolio investment liabilities .	−50	27	—
Other investment assets . .	−221	−745	3,580
Other investment liabilities . .	1,464	−4,733	−4,094
Net errors and omissions . .	−5,123	745	−870
Overall balance . . .	−140	−24	7

Source: IMF, *International Financial Statistics*.

External Trade

PRINCIPAL COMMODITIES (distribution by SITC, KD million)

Imports c.i.f.	1994	1995	1996
Food and live animals . . .	295.7	317.3	351.5
Dairy products and birds' eggs .	45.2	46.6	55.1
Cereals and cereal preparations .	40.2	49.7	59.8
Vegetables and fruit	71.9	76.3	78.7
Chemicals and related products	150.4	169.7	181.2
Basic manufactures . .	382.5	454.1	496.6
Textile yarn, fabrics, etc. . .	72.7	78.6	75.4
Non-metallic mineral manufactures . . .	74.7	103.1	107.4
Iron and steel	73.4	98.2	119.6
Machinery and transport equipment	758.3	958.0	1,042.3
Power-generating machinery and equipment.	37.8	53.5	154.0
Machinery specialized for particular industries . .	70.5	55.7	189.7
General industrial machinery, equipment and parts . .	88.6	97.9	110.8
Telecommunications and sound equipment	58.4	66.4	69.7
Other electrical machinery, apparatus, etc. . . .	102.5	87.3	108.0
Road vehicles and parts . .	272.7	300.5	353.4
Passenger motor cars (excl. buses)	165.9	193.8	217.8
Parts and accessories for cars, buses, lorries, etc. . .	45.8	52.3	55.6
Other transport equipment and parts	89.8	255.8	14.6
Miscellaneous manufactured articles	307.9	325.0	323.5
Clothing and accessories (excl. footwear)	86.7	95.1	96.5
Total (incl. others) . . .	1,988.2	2,323.1	2,507.2

Exports f.o.b.	1994	1995	1996
Mineral fuels, lubricants, etc. .	3,122.8	3,608.8	4,235.4
Petroleum, petroleum products, etc.*	3,112.7	3,597.1	4,221.3
Chemicals and related products	45.3	77.8	67.4
Machinery and transport equipment	102.8	54.4	57.4
Total (incl. others)* . . .	3,342.3	3,814.4	4,448.0

* Estimates by the Central Bank of Kuwait.

PRINCIPAL TRADING PARTNERS (KD million)*

Imports c.i.f.	1994	1995	1996
Australia	31.0	26.7	49.1
Belgium-Luxembourg . . .	22.6	22.5	26.9
China, People's Republic .	45.8	53.5	61.8
France (incl. Monaco) . .	126.2	258.8	100.7
Germany	163.5	168.4	175.6
India	57.7	67.1	80.5
Indonesia	23.3	22.5	27.2
Iran	26.1	24.6	19.8
Italy	119.0	137.1	174.2
Japan	233.1	217.3	302.9
Korea, Republic . . .	40.0	45.4	54.4
Malaysia	23.4	30.3	31.0
Netherlands	47.1	34.3	42.6
Saudi Arabia . . .	114.2	141.7	166.9
Singapore	22.5	20.5	18.5
Spain	23.2	33.9	34.0
Sweden	25.0	23.0	18.7
Switzerland-Liechtenstein .	28.8	28.3	46.5
Thailand	26.4	30.4	31.6
Turkey	48.3	42.0	45.6
United Arab Emirates . .	40.1	51.2	46.9
United Kingdom . . .	138.0	139.2	153.7
USA	289.1	374.3	418.7
Total (incl. others) . . .	1,988.2	2,323.1	2,507.2

Exports f.o.b.†	1994	1995	1996
Bahrain	4.4	5.1	5.3
China, People's Republic . .	7.5	25.9	11.2
France (incl. Monaco) . .	36.0	0.4	0.7
India	30.9	35.6	42.1
Philippines	4.6	7.9	6.0
Saudi Arabia	33.3	33.7	38.4
United Arab Emirates . .	31.6	22.6	34.0
Total (incl. others) . . .	229.6	217.3	226.7

* Imports by country of production; exports by country of last consignment.
† Excluding petroleum exports.

Transport

ROAD TRAFFIC (motor vehicles in use at 31 December)

	1993	1994	1995
Passenger cars	599,951	629,702	662,946
Buses and coaches . . .	12,513	11,600	11,937
Goods vehicles	112,417	114,085	116,813

SHIPPING

Merchant Fleet (registered at 31 December)

	1994	1995	1996
Number of vessels . . .	212	213	211
Displacement ('000 grt) . .	2,017	2,057	2,028

Source: Lloyd's Register of Shipping, *World Fleet Statistics*.

International Sea-borne Freight Traffic* ('000 metric tons)

	1988	1989	1990
Goods loaded	61,778	69,097	51,400
Goods unloaded	7,123	7,015	4,522

* Including Kuwait's share of traffic in the Neutral/Partitioned Zone.

Source: UN, *Monthly Bulletin of Statistics*.

Goods unloaded ('000 metric tons): 746 in 1991 (July–December only); 2,537 in 1992; 4,228 in 1993.

CIVIL AVIATION (traffic on scheduled services)

	1993	1994	1995
Kilometres flown (million) . .	33	35	38
Passengers carried ('000) . . .	1,554	1,756	1,951
Passenger-km (million) . .	4,054	4,509	5,124
Total ton-km (million) . .	632	696	797

Source: UN, *Statistical Yearbook*.

Tourism

	1993	1994	1995
Tourist arrivals ('000) . . .	73	73	72
Tourism receipts (US $ million) .	83	101	107

Source: UN, *Statistical Yearbook*.

Communications Media

	1993	1994	1995
Radio receivers ('000 in use) . .	725	726	800
Television receivers ('000 in use) .	615	620	625
Telephones ('000 main lines in use)	358	373	382
Telefax stations (number in use) .	25,000	30,000	35,000
Mobile cellular telephones (subscribers)	64,311	85,195	117,609
Daily newspapers Number	n.a.	9	9*
Average circulation ('000 copies)*	n.a.	655	655

Book production (titles published): 196 in 1992 (government only).

* Provisional or estimated figure(s).

Sources: UNESCO, *Statistical Yearbook*; UN, *Statistical Yearbook*.

Education

(state-controlled schools, 1995/96)

	Schools	Teachers	Students
Kindergarten	143	2,534	37,020
Primary	175	6,989	93,844
Intermediate	157	7,385	86,910
Secondary	111	7,824	63,435
Religious institutes . . .	6	246	1,542
Special training institutes . .	30	471	1,629

Private education (1990/91): 35 kindergarten schools (165 teachers, 3,509 students); 51 primary schools (1,204 teachers, 31,222 students); 53 intermediate schools (818 teachers, 19,168 students); 33 secondary schools (606 teachers, 11,508 students).

Directory

The Constitution

The principal provisions of the Constitution, promulgated on 16 November 1962, are set out below. On 29 August 1976 the Amir suspended four articles of the Constitution dealing with the National Assembly, the Majlis al-Umma. On 24 August 1980 the Amir issued a decree ordering the establishment of an elected legislature before the end of February 1981. The new Majlis was elected on 23 February 1981, and fresh legislative elections followed on 20 February 1985. The Majlis was dissolved by Amiri decree in July 1986, and some sections of the Constitution, including the stipulation that new elections should be held within two months of dissolving the legislature (see below), were suspended. A new Majlis was elected on 5 October and convened on 20 October 1992.

SOVEREIGNTY

Kuwait is an independent sovereign Arab State; its sovereignty may not be surrendered, and no part of its territory may be relinquished. Offensive war is prohibited by the Constitution.

Succession as Amir is restricted to heirs of the late MUBARAK AS-SABAH, and an Heir Apparent must be appointed within one year of the accession of a new Amir.

EXECUTIVE AUTHORITY

Executive power is vested in the Amir, who exercises it through the Council of Ministers. The Amir will appoint the Prime Minister 'after the traditional consultations', and will appoint and dismiss ministers on the recommendation of the Prime Minister. Ministers need not be members of the Majlis al-Umma, although all ministers who are not members of parliament assume membership *ex officio* in the legislature for the duration of office. The Amir also formulates laws, which shall not be effective unless published in the *Official Gazette*. The Amir establishes public institutions. All decrees issued in these respects shall be conveyed to the Majlis. No law is issued unless it is approved by the Majlis.

LEGISLATURE

A National Assembly, the Majlis al-Umma, of 50 members will be elected for a four-year term by all natural-born Kuwaiti males over the age of 21 years, except servicemen and police, who may not vote. Candidates for election must possess the franchise, be over 30 years of age and literate. The Majlis will convene for at least eight months in any year, and new elections shall be held within two months of the last dissolution of the outgoing legislature.

Restrictions on the commercial activities of ministers include an injunction forbidding them to sell property to the Government.

The Amir may ask for reconsideration of a bill that has been approved by the Majlis and sent to him for ratification, but the bill would automatically become law if it were subsequently adopted by a two-thirds' majority at the next sitting, or by a simple majority at a subsequent sitting. The Amir may declare martial law, but only with the approval of the legislature.

The Majlis may adopt a vote of 'no confidence' in a minister, in which case the minister must resign. Such a vote is not permissible in the case of the Prime Minister, but the legislature may approach the Amir on the matter, and the Amir shall then either dismiss the Prime Minister or dissolve the Majlis.

CIVIL SERVICE

Entry to the civil service is confined to Kuwaiti citizens.

PUBLIC LIBERTIES

Kuwaitis are equal before the law in prestige, rights and duties. Individual freedom is guaranteed. No one shall be seized, arrested or exiled except within the rules of law.

No punishment shall be administered except for an act or abstaining from an act considered a crime in accordance with a law applicable at the time of committing it, and no penalty shall be imposed more severe than that which could have been imposed at the time of committing the crime.

Freedom of opinion is guaranteed to everyone, and each has the right to express himself through speech, writing or other means within the limits of the law.

The press is free within the limits of the law, and it should not be suppressed except in accordance with the dictates of law.

Freedom of performing religious rites is protected by the State according to prevailing customs, provided it does not violate the public order and morality.

Trade unions will be permitted and property must be respected. An owner is not banned from managing his property except within the boundaries of law. No property should be taken from anyone, except within the prerogatives of law, unless a just compensation be given.

Houses may not be entered, except in cases provided by law. Every Kuwaiti has freedom of movement and choice of place of residence within the state. This right shall not be controlled except in cases stipulated by law.

Every person has the right to education and freedom to choose his type of work. Freedom to form peaceful societies is guaranteed within the limits of law.

The Government

HEAD OF STATE

Amir of Kuwait: His Highness Sheikh JABER AL-AHMAD AS-SABAH (acceded 31 December 1977).

COUNCIL OF MINISTERS
(September 1998)

Crown Prince and Prime Minister: Sheikh SAAD AL-ABDULLAH AS-SALIM AS-SABAH.

First Deputy Prime Minister and Minister of Foreign Affairs: Sheikh SABAH AL-AHMAD AL-JABER AS-SABAH.

Deputy Prime Minister and Minister of State for Cabinet Affairs: NASIR ABDULLAH AR-RODHAN.

Deputy Prime Minister and Minister of Defence: Sheikh SALIM SABAH AS-SALIM AS-SABAH.

Minister of the Interior: Sheikh MUHAMMAD KHALID AL-HAMAD AS-SABAH.

Minister of Electricity and Water, and Public Works: Dr HAMOUD AR-ROQBA.

Minister of Finance and Communications: Sheikh ALI SALIM AS-SABAH.

Minister of Information: YOUSUF MUHAMMAD AS-SAMIT.

Minister of State for Parliamentary Affairs: MUHAMMAD DHAI-FALLAH SHARAR.

Minister of Health: ADIL KHALID AS-SABIH.

Minister of Justice, Awqaf (Religious Endowments) and Islamic Affairs: AHMAD KHALID AL-KULAID.

Minister of Commerce and Industry: ABD AL-AZIZ AD-DAKHIL.

Minister of Labour and Social Affairs, and Minister of State for Housing Affairs: JASEM MUHAMMAD AL-AOUN.

Minister of Education and Higher Education: Dr ABD AL-AZIZ GHANIM ABD AL-WAHAB AL-GHANIM.

Minister of Planning and Minister of State for Administrative Affairs: ALI MUSA AL-MUSA.

Minister of Oil: Sheikh SA'UD NASIR AS-SA'UD AS-SABAH.

PROVINCIAL GOVERNORS

Ahmadi: ALI JABER AL-AHMAD AS-SABAH.

Farwaniya: IBRAHIM JASSEM AL-MUDHAF.

Hawalli: DAUD MUSAED AS-SALIH.

Jahra: IBRAHIM DUAIJ AL-IBRAHIM AS-SABAH.

Kuwait: Sheikh ALI ABDULLAH AS-SALIM AS-SABAH.

MINISTRIES

Ministry of Awqaf and Islamic Affairs: POB 13, 13001 Safat, al-Morkab St, Ministries Complex, Kuwait City; tel. 2466300; telex 44735; fax 2449943.

Ministry of Commerce and Industry: POB 2944, 13030 Safat, Kuwait City; tel. 2463600; telex 22682; fax 2424411.

Ministry of Communications: POB 318, 11111 Safat, Kuwait City; tel. 4819033; telex 22197; fax 4847058.

Ministry of Defence: POB 1170, 13012 Safat, Kuwait City; tel. 4819277; telex 22784; fax 4846059.

Ministry of Education: POB 7, 13001 Safat, Hilali St, Kuwait City; tel. 4836800; telex 23166; fax 2423676.

Ministry of Electricity and Water: POB 12, 13001 Safat, Kuwait City; tel. 4896000; telex 30060; fax 4897484.

Ministry of Finance: POB 9, 13001 Safat, al-Morkab St, Ministries Complex, Kuwait City; tel. 2468200; telex 22527; fax 243462.

Ministry of Foreign Affairs: POB 3, 13001 Safat, Gulf St, Kuwait City; tel. 2425141; telex 22042.

Ministry of Health: POB 5, 13001 Safat, Arabian Gulf St, Kuwait City; tel. 4842795; telex 22729; fax 4840056.

Ministry of Higher Education: POB 27130, 13132 Safat, Kuwait City; tel. 2407334; fax 2406224.

Ministry of State for Housing: POB 2935, 13030 Safat, Kuwait City; tel. 2428802; fax 2428801.

Ministry of Information: POB 193, 13002 Safat, as-Sour St, Kuwait City; tel. 2415300; telex 46151; fax 2419642.

Ministry of the Interior: POB 11, 13001 Safat, Kuwait City; tel. 2524199; telex 22507; fax 2561268.

Ministry of Justice and Administrative Affairs: POB 6, 13001 Safat, al-Morkab St, Ministries Complex, Kuwait City; tel. 2467300; telex 44660; fax 2466957.

Ministry of Labour and Social Affairs: POB 563, 13006 Safat, al-Morkab St, Ministries Complex, Kuwait City; tel. 2464500; telex 30329; fax 2419877.

Ministry of Oil: POB 5077, 13051 Safat, Fahd as-Salem St, Kuwait City; tel. 2415201; telex 22363; fax 2417088.

Ministry of Planning: POB 21688, 13122 Safat, Kuwait City; tel. 2428100; telex 22468; fax 2414734.

Ministry of Public Works: POB 8, 13001 Safat, Kuwait City; tel. 2449301; fax 2424335.

Legislature

MAJLIS AL-UMMA
(National Assembly)

Speaker: AHMAD ABD AL-AZIZ AS-SAADUN.

Elections to the Majlis took place on 7 October 1996.

Political Organizations

Political parties are not permitted in Kuwait. However, several quasi-political organizations are in existence. Among those that have been represented in the Majlis since 1992 are:

Islamic Constitutional Movement: Sunni Muslim; moderate.

Kuwait Democratic Forum: secular; liberal.

Salafeen: Sunni Muslim.

National Democratic Rally (NDR): f. 1997; secular, liberal; Sec.-Gen. Dr AHMAD BISHARA.

National Islamic Coalition: Shi'a Muslim.

Constitutional Group: supported by merchants.

Diplomatic Representation

EMBASSIES IN KUWAIT

Afghanistan: POB 22944, 13090 Safat, Rawdah, Block 1, 7 Mishref St, House 17, Kuwait City; tel. 5396916; telex 30165; fax 5396915; Chargé d'affaires: TAZAKHAN WIAL.

Algeria: POB 578, 13006 Safat, Istiqlal St, Kuwait City; tel. 2519987; telex 44750; fax 2563052; Ambassador: MUHAMMAD QADRI.

Austria: POB 15013, Diiya, 35451 Kuwait City; tel. 2552532; fax 2563052; Ambassador: Dr HAIMO KELLNER.

Bahrain: POB 196, 13002 Safat, Jabriya, Plot 312, Area 10, Kuwait City; tel. 5318530; telex 22649; fax 5330882; Ambassador: ABD AR-RAHMAN M. AL-FADHEL.

Bangladesh: POB 22344, 13084 Safat, Khaldya, Block 1, St 14, House 3, Kuwait City; tel. 4834078; telex 22484; fax 4831603; Ambassador: M. RUHUL AMIN.

Belgium: POB 3280, 13033 Safat, Salmiya, Baghdad St, House 15, Kuwait City; tel. 5722014; fax 5748389; Ambassador: PHILIPPE-HENRI ARCQ.

Bhutan: POB 1510, 13016 Safat, Qortuba, Area 4, Jadda 7, Street 1, Villa 5, Kuwait City; tel. 5331506; fax 5338959; Ambassador: SONAM TOBDEN RABGYE.

Botswana: Kuwait City.

Brazil: POB 21370, 13074 Safat, Plot 2, Istiqlal St, Villa 1, Kuwait City; tel. 2562086; telex 22398; fax 2562153; Ambassador: ADERBAL COSTA.

Bulgaria: POB 12090, 71651 Shamiya, Jabriya, Block 11, St 107, Kuwait City; tel. 5314459; telex 31550; fax 5321453; Ambassador: DIMITAR A. DIMITROV.

Canada: POB 25281, 13113 Safat, Diiya, Block 4, 24 al-Motawakell St, Villa 4, Kuwait City; tel. 2563025; telex 23549; fax 2564167; Ambassador: J. CHRISTOPHER POOLE.

China, People's Republic: POB 2346, 13024 Safat, Dasmah, Sheikh Ahmad al-Jaber Bldgs 4 & 5, Kuwait City; tel. 5333340; fax 5333341; Ambassador: WANG JINGQI.

Cyprus: POB 22034, Al-Mogil Commercial Centre, 9th Floor, Abdullah Mubarak St, 13081 Safat, Kuwait City; tel. 2448725; fax 2402971.

Czech Republic: POB 1151, 13012 Safat, Kuwait City; tel. 2575018; fax 2529021; e-mail czechemb@ncc.moc.kw; Ambassador: JOSEF RYCHTAR.

Egypt: POB 11252, 35153 Dasmah, Istiqlal St, Kuwait City; tel. 2519955; telex 22610; fax 2553877; Ambassador: AMIN NAMMAR.

Finland: POB 26699, 13127 Safat, Surra, Block 4, St 1, Villa 8, Kuwait City; tel. 5312890; telex 44948; fax 5324198; Ambassador: PERTTI KAUKONEN.

France: POB 1037, 13011 Safat, Mansouriah, Block 1, St 13, No. 24, Kuwait City; tel. 2571061; telex 2571058; fax 2571058; Ambassador: JEAN FÉLIX-PAGANON.

Germany: POB 805, 13009 Safat, Dahiya Abdullah as-Salem, Plot 1, St 14, Villa 13, Kuwait City; tel. 2520857; fax 2520763; e-mail 113061.3166@compuserve.com; Ambassador: Dr GÜNTER HELD.

Greece: POB 23812, 13099 Safat, Khaldiya, Block 4, St 44, House 4, Kuwait City; tel. 4817101; fax 4817103; Ambassador: STELIOS MALLIKOURTIS.

Hungary: POB 5671, 13057 Safat, Surra, Block 3, St 2, House 120, Kuwait City; tel. 5312600; fax 5313782; Ambassador: Dr G. GÉZAFEHÉREÁRI.

India: POB 1450, 13015 Safat, 34 Istiqlal St, Kuwait City; tel. 2530600; telex 22273; fax 2525811; Ambassador: PREM SINGH.

Indonesia: POB 21560, 13076 Safat, Keifan, Block 5, As-Sebhani St, House 21, Kuwait City; tel. 4839927; telex 22752; fax 4819250; Ambassador: D. SOESJONO.

Iran: POB 4686, 13047 Safat, 24 Istiqlal St, Kuwait City; tel. 2560694; telex 22223; fax 2529868; Ambassador: GHOLAMALI SANATI.

Italy: POB 4453, 13045 Safat, Shuwaikh 'B', Block 5, Villa 1, Kuwait City; tel. 4817400; telex 22356; fax 4817244; Ambassador: Dr LUCIO FORATTINI.

Japan: POB 2304, 13024 Safat, Jabriya, Area 9, Plot 496, Kuwait City; tel. 5312870; telex 22196; fax 5326168; Ambassador: TSUYOSHI KUROKAWA.

Jordan: POB 15314, 35305 Diiyah, Istiqlal St, Embassies Area, Kuwait City; tel. 2533500; telex 30412; Ambassador: NABIL TAWFIQ AT-TAHOUNI.

Korea, Republic: POB 20771, 13068 Safat, Kifan, Block 2, St 29, Villa 3, Kuwait City; tel. 2570342; telex 22606; fax 2526874; Ambassador: SAE HOON-AHN.

Lebanon: POB 253, 13003 Safat, 31 Istiqlal St, Kuwait City; tel. 2562103; telex 22330; fax 2571682; Ambassador: MUHAMMAD ISA.

Libya: POB 21460, 13075 Safat, 27 Istiqlal St, Kuwait City; tel. 2562103; telex 22256; fax 2571682; Chargé d'affaires: IDRIS DAHMANI BU DIB.

Malaysia: POB 4105, 13042 Safat, Surra Block 6, St 4, Villa 5, Kuwait City; tel. 5342091; telex 22540; fax 5341783; Ambassador: ISMAIL BIN MUSTAPHA.

Morocco: POB 784, 13008 Safat, Shuwaikh 'B', Block 4, Nil St, Kuwait City; tel. 4813912; telex 22074; fax 4814156; Ambassador: ABD AL-WAHED BEN MASOUD.

Netherlands: POB 21822, 13079 Safat, Jabriya, Area 9, St 1, Plot 40A, Kuwait City; tel. 5312650; telex 22459; fax 5326334; Ambassador: ANTHONIE PIJPERS.

Niger: POB 44451, 32059 Hawalli, Salwa, Block 5, St 9, Villa 22, Kuwait City; tel. 5652943; telex 23365; fax 5640478; Ambassador: ADAMOU SEYNI.

Nigeria: POB 6432, 32039 Hawalli, Surra, Area 1, St 14, House 25, Kuwait City; tel. 5320794; telex 22864; fax 5320834; Chargé d'affaires: SUMAILA ADAMU.

Oman: POB 21975, 13080 Safat, Istiqlal St, Villa 3, Kuwait City; tel. 2561962; telex 22057; fax 2561963; Ambassador: SALIM BIN ABDULLAH BA'OMAR.

Pakistan: POB 988, 13010 Safat, Jabriya, Plot 5, Block 11, Villa 7, Kuwait City; tel. 5327649; telex 44117; fax 5327648; Ambassador: ZAHID SAID KHAN.

Philippines: POB 26288, 13123 Safat, Jabriya, Police Station St, Area 10, House 363, Kuwait City; tel. 5329316; fax 5329319; Ambassador: SHULAN O. PRIMAVERA.

Poland: POB 5066, 13051 Safat, Jabriya, Plot 8, St 20, House 377, Kuwait City; tel. 5311571; telex 50800; fax 5311576; Ambassador: JAN NATKANSKI.

Qatar: POB 1825, 13019 Safat, Diiyah, Istiqlal St, Kuwait City; tel. 2513599; telex 22038; fax 2513604; Ambassador: AHMAD G. AR-RUMAIHI.

Romania: POB 11149, 35152 Dasmah, Kifan, Zone 4, Mouna St, House 34, Kuwait City; tel. 4843419; telex 22148; fax 4848929; Ambassador: DORU COSTEA.

Russia: POB 1765, 13018 Safat, Rawdah, Kuwait City; tel. 2560427; telex 22945; fax 2524969; Ambassador: PYOTR STEGNYI.

Saudi Arabia: POB 20498, 13065 Safat, Istiqlal St, Kuwait City; tel. 2400250; telex 23258; fax 2426541; Ambassador: Sheikh ABDULLAH ABDU-AZIZ AS-SUDAIRY.

Senegal: POB 23892, 13099 Safat, Rawdah, Parcel 3, St 35, House 9, Kuwait City; tel. 2542044; telex 22580; fax 2542044; Ambassador: ABDOU LAHAD MBACKE.

Somalia: POB 22766, 13088 Safat, Shuwaikh, Nasir St, Villa 7, Kuwait City; tel. 4815433; telex 23280; fax 5394829; Ambassador: MUHAMMAD S. M. MALINGUR.

Spain: POB 22207, 13083 Safat, Surra, Block 3, St 14, Villa 19, Kuwait City; tel. 5325827; telex 22341; fax 5325826; Ambassador: JOSÉ LUIS ROSELLÓ.

Sri Lanka: POB 13212, 71952, Keifan, House 381, St 9, Block 5, Salwa; tel. 5612261; fax 5612264; e-mail lankemb@kuwait.net; Ambassador: DARSIN SERASINGHE.

Sweden: POB 21448, 13075 Safat, Faiha, Area 7, ash-Shahba St, Kuwait City; tel. 2523588; fax 2572157; Ambassador: THOMAS GANSLANDT.

Switzerland: POB 23954, 13100 Safat, Qortuba, Block 2, St 1, Villa 122, Kuwait City; tel. 5340175; fax 5340176; Ambassador: DANIEL WOKER.

Syria: POB 25602, 13112 Safat, Diiyah, Parcel 4, Area 33, St 46, Kuwait City; tel. 5396560; telex 22270; fax 5396509; Ambassador: Dr ISA DARWISH.

Thailand: POB 66647, 43757 Bayan, Surra, Area 3, Block 49, Ali bin Abi-Taleb St, Building No 28, Kuwait City; tel. 5317531; telex 44339; fax 5317532; e-mail thaiemkw@ncc.moc.kw; Ambassador: SURIYA ROCHANABUDDHI.

Tunisia: POB 5976, 13060 Safat, Nuzha, Plot 2, Nuzha St, Villa 45, Kuwait City; tel. 2542144; telex 22518; fax 2528995; Ambassador: RIDHA TNANI.

Turkey: POB 20627, 13067 Safat, Block 16, Plot 10, Istiqlal St, Kuwait City; tel. 2531785; telex 44806; fax 2560653; Ambassador: AHMET ERTAY.

United Arab Emirates: POB 1828, 13019 Safat, Plot 70, Istiqlal St, Kuwait City; tel. 2518381; telex 22529; fax 2526382; Ambassador: YOUSUF A. AS-SIRKAL.

United Kingdom: POB 2, 13001 Safat, Arabian Gulf St, Kuwait City; tel. 2403334; fax 2426799; e-mail britemb@ncc.moc.kw; Ambassador: GRAHAM H. BOYCE.

USA: POB 77, 13001 Safat, Arabian Gulf St, Kuwait City; tel. 5395307; fax 2407368; Ambassador: JAMES LAROCCO.

Venezuela: POB 24440, 13105 Safat, Surra, Parcel 2, Ali bin Abi-Taleb St, Villa 11, Kuwait City; tel. 5324367; telex 22782; fax 5324368; Ambassador: RAFAEL OSUNA LOZADA.

Yugoslavia: POB 20511, 13066 Safat, Jabriya, Block 7, St 12, Plot 382, Kuwait City; tel. 5327548; fax 5327568; e-mail yuembakuw@kuwait.net; Ambassador: STANISLAV STAKIĆ.

Judicial System

SPECIAL JUDICIARY

Constitutional Court: Comprises five judges. Interprets the provisions of the Constitution; considers disputes regarding the constitutionality of legislation, decrees and rules; has jurisdiction in challenges relating to the election of members, or eligibility for election, to the Majlis al-Umma.

ORDINARY JUDICIARY

Court of Cassation: Comprises five judges. Is competent to consider the legality of verdicts of the Court of Appeal and State Security Court. Chief Justice: MUHAMMAD YOUSUF AR-RIFA'I.

Court of Appeal: Comprises three judges. Considers verdicts of the Court of First Instance. Chief Justice: RASHED AL-HAMMAD.

Court of First Instance: Comprises the following divisions: Civil and Commercial (one judge), Personal Status Affairs (one judge), Lease (three judges), Labour (one judge), Crime (three judges), Administrative Disputes (three judges), Appeal (three judges), Challenged Misdemeanours (three judges). Chief Justice: MUHAMMAD AS-SAKHOBY.

Summary Courts: Each governorate has a Summary Court, comprising one or more divisions. The courts have jurisdiction in the following areas: Civil and Commercial, Urgent Cases, Lease, Misdemeanours. The verdict in each case is delivered by one judge.

There is also a **Traffic Court**, with one presiding judge.

Attorney-General: MUHAMMAD ABD AL-HAIH AL-BANNAIY.

Advocate-General: HAMED AL-UTHMAN.

Religion

ISLAM

The Kuwaiti inhabitants are mainly Muslims of the Sunni and Shi'a sects. The Shi'ites comprise about 30% of the total.

CHRISTIANITY
The Roman Catholic Church

Latin Rite

For ecclesiastical purposes, Kuwait forms an Apostolic Vicariate. At 31 December 1996 there were an estimated 152,000 adherents in the country.

Vicar Apostolic: Mgr FRANCIS ADEODATUS MICALLEF (Titular Bishop of Tinisa in Proconsulari), Bishop's House, POB 266, 13003 Safat, Kuwait City; tel. 2434637; fax 2409981.

Melkite Rite

The Greek-Melkite Patriarch of Antioch is resident in Damascus, Syria. The Patriarchal Vicariate (now Exarchate) of Kuwait had an estimated 4,500 adherents at 31 December 1996.

Exarch Patriarchal: Archimandrite BASILIOS KANAKRY, Vicariat Patriarcal Melkite, POB 1205, Salmiya; tel. 5733633.

Syrian Rite

The Syrian Catholic Patriarch of Antioch is resident in Beirut, Lebanon. The Patriarchal Exarchate of Iraq and Kuwait, with an estimated 1,100 adherents at 31 December 1996, is based in Basra, Iraq.

The Anglican Communion

Within the Episcopal Church in Jerusalem and the Middle East, Kuwait forms part of the diocese of Cyprus and the Gulf. The Anglican congregation in Kuwait is entirely expatriate. The Bishop in Cyprus and the Gulf is resident in Cyprus, while the Archdeacon in the Gulf is resident in the United Arab Emirates.

Other Christian Churches

National Evangelical Church in Kuwait: Rev. NABIL ATTALLAH, pastor of the Arabic-language congregation; Rev. JERRY A. ZANDSTRA, senior pastor of the English-speaking congregation; POB 80, 13001 Safat, Kuwait City; tel. 2407195; fax 2431087; e-mail elc@ncc.moc.kw; internet http://home.tct.net; an independent Protestant Church founded by the Reformed Church in America; services in Arabic, English, Korean, Malayalam and other Indian languages; combined weekly congregation of some 20,000.

The Armenian, Greek, Coptic and Syrian Orthodox Churches are also represented in Kuwait.

The Press

Freedom of the press and publishing is guaranteed in the Constitution, although press censorship was in force between mid-1986 and early 1992 (when journalists adopted a voluntary code of practice); in February 1995 a ruling by the Constitutional Court effectively endorsed the Government's right to suspend publication of newspapers (see Recent History). The Government provides financial support to newspapers and magazines.

DAILIES

Al-Anbaa (The News): POB 23915, 13100 Safat, Kuwait City; tel. 4834772; telex 22622; fax 4837914; f. 1976; Arabic; general; Editor-in-Chief FAISAL YOUSUF AL-MARZOOQ; circ. 106,827; publication temporarily suspended in March 1995.

Arab Times: POB 2270, 13023 Safat, Kuwait City; tel. 4813566; fax 4833628; f. 1977; English; political and financial; no Friday edition; Editor-in-Chief AHMAD ABD AL-AZIZ AL-JARALLAH; Man. Editor MISHAL AL-JARALLAH; circ. 41,922.

Kuwait Times: POB 1301, 13014 Safat, Kuwait City; tel. 4833199; telex 23843; fax 4835621; f. 1963; (weekend edition also published); English; political; Owner and Editor-in-Chief YOUSUF ALYYAN; Man. Editor CLEMENT MESENAS; circ. 28,000.

Al-Qabas (Firebrand): POB 21800, 13078 Safat, Kuwait City; tel. 4812822; telex 23370; fax 4834320; f. 1972; Arabic; independent; Gen. Man. FOUZAN AL-FARES; Editor-in-Chief MUHAMMAD J. AS-SAGER: circ. 79,700.

Ar-Ra'i al-'Aam (Public Opinion): POB 695, 13007 Safat, International Airport Rd, Shuwaikh Industrial Area, Kuwait City; tel. 4813134; telex 22636; fax 4849298; f. 1961; Arabic; political, social and cultural; Editor-in-Chief FAHAD A. AL-MUSSAEED; circ. 86,900.

As-Seyassah (Policy): POB 2270, Shuwaikh, Kuwait City; tel. 4816326; fax 4833628; f. 1965; Arabic; political and financial; Editor-in-Chief AHMAD ABD AL-AZIZ AL-JARALLAH; circ. 70,000.

Al-Watan (The Homeland): POB 1142, 13012 Safat, Kuwait City; tel. 4840950; telex 22565; fax 4835426; internet http://www.alwatan.q8.net/alwatan; f. 1962; Arabic; political; Editor-in-Chief JASSEM AL-MUTAWA; Gen. Man. YOUSUF BIN JASSEM; circ. 59,940.

WEEKLIES AND PERIODICALS

'Alam al-Fann (World of Art): POB 13341, 71953 Keifan; tel. 4810526; Editor-in-Chief MUHAMMAD A. NASHMI DAWASH.

Arab Business Report: POB 6000, Safat, Kuwait City; telex 3511; fortnightly; English; business management.

Al-'Arabi (The Arab): POB 748, 13008 Safat, Kuwait City; telex 44041; f. 1958; monthly; Arabic; cultural; publ. by the Ministry of Information for distribution throughout the Arab world; Editor-in-Chief Dr MUHAMMAD AR-RUMAIHI; circ. 350,000.

Al-Balagh (Communiqué): POB 4558, 13046 Safat, Kuwait City; tel. 4818606; telex 44389; fax 4819008; f. 1969; weekly; Arabic; general, political and Islamic; Editor-in-Chief ABD AR-RAHMAN RASHID AL-WALAYATI; circ. 29,000.

Ad-Dakhiliya (The Interior): POB 12500, 71655 Shamiah, Kuwait City; monthly; Arabic; official reports, transactions and proceedings; publ. by Public Relations Dept, Ministry of the Interior; Editor-in-Chief Lt-Col Dr ADEL AL-IBRAHIM.

Al-Hadaf (The Objective): POB 2270, 13023 Safat, Kuwait City; tel. 4813566; fax 4833628; f. 1964; weekly; Arabic; social and cultural; Editor-in-Chief AHMAD ABD AL-AZIZ AL-JARALLAH; circ. 268,904.

Hayatuna (Our Life): POB 1708, Safat, Kuwait City; f. 1968; fortnightly; Arabic; medicine and hygiene; publ. by Al-Awadi Press Corpn; Editor-in-Chief YOUSUF ABD AL-AZIZ AL-MUZINI; circ. 6,000.

Iftah Ya Simsim (Open Sesame): POB 44247, Safat, Kuwait City; telex 44090; monthly; Arabic; children.

Al-Iqtisadi al-Kuwaiti (Kuwaiti Economist): POB 775, 13008 Safat, Kuwait City; tel. 2433854; fax 2412927; e-mail kcci@kuwait-chamber.com.kw; internet http://www.kuwait.chamber.com.kw; f. 1960; monthly; Arabic; commerce, trade and economics; publ. by Kuwait Chamber of Commerce and Industry; Editor MAJED JAMAL AD-DIN; circ. 6,000.

Journal of the Gulf and Arabian Peninsula: POB 17073, Khaldiya, Kuwait University, Kuwait City; tel. 4833215; fax 4833705; f. 1975; quarterly; Arabic; English.

Al-Khaleej Business Magazine: POB 24166, 13102 Safat, Kuwait City; tel. 2449890; telex 23384.

Al-Kuwait: POB 193, Safat, Kuwait City; tel. 2415300; telex 46151; f. 1961; monthly; Arabic; Islamic culture; publ. by Ministry of Information; Editor HAMED Y. AL-GHARABALLY; circ. 50,400.

Kuwait al-Youm (Official Gazette): POB 193, 13002 Safat, Kuwait City; tel. 2415300; telex 46151; fax 2421926; f. 1954; weekly; Arabic; statistics, Amiri decrees, laws, govt announcements, decisions, invitations for tenders, etc.; publ. by the Ministry of Information; circ. 5,000.

Al-Kuwaiti (The Kuwaiti): Information Dept, POB 9758, 61008 Ahmadi, Kuwait City; tel. 3989111; telex 44211; fax 3983661; e-mail kocinfo@koc.com.kw; internet http://www.moc.kw/kemscust.html; f. 1961; monthly journal of the Kuwait Oil Co; Arabic; Editor-in-Chief ALI H. MURAD; circ. 6,500.

The Kuwaiti Digest: Information Dept, POB 9758, 61008 Ahmadi, Kuwait City; tel. 3989111; telex 44211; fax 3983661; e-mail kocinfo@koc.com.kw; internet http://www.moc.kw/kemscut.html; f. 1972; quarterly journal of Kuwait Oil Co; English; Editor-in-Chief ALI H. MURAD; circ. 7,000.

Kuwait Medical Journal (KMJ): POB 1202, 13013 Safat, Kuwait City; tel. 5317972; fax 5333276; e-mail kmj@kma.org.kw; f. 1967; quarterly; English; case reports, articles, reviews; Editor-in-chief Dr ABD AR-RAHMAN AL-AWADI; circ. 10,000.

Al-Majaless (Meetings): POB 5605, 13057 Safat, Kuwait City; tel. 4841178; fax 4847126; telex 44728; weekly; Arabic; current affairs; Editor-in-Chief HEDAYA SULTAN AS-SALEM; circ. 60,206.

Mejallat al-Kuwait (Kuwait Magazine): POB 193, 13002 Safat, Kuwait City; tel. 2415300; telex 46151; f. 1961; fortnightly; Arabic; illustrated magazine; science, arts and literature; publ. by Ministry of Information.

Mirat al-Umma (Mirror of the Nation): POB 4299, 13043 Safat, Kuwait City; tel. 4813567; telex 22332; fax 4814481; weekly; Arabic; Editor-in-Chief ALI BIN YOUSUF AR-ROUMI; circ. 79,500.

An-Nahdha (The Renaissance): POB 695, 13007, Safat, Kuwait City; tel. 4813133; telex 22636; fax 4849298; f. 1967; weekly; Arabic; social and political; Editor-in-Chief AHMAD ABU SIDO; circ. 170,000.

Osrati (My Family): POB 2995, 13030 Safat, Kuwait City; tel. 4813233; telex 44438; fax 4838933; f. 1978; weekly; Arabic; women's magazine; publ. by Fahad al-Marzouk Establishment; Editor GHANIMA F. AL-MARZOUK; circ. 76,450.

Ar-Ressaleh (The Message): POB 2490, Shuwaikh, Kuwait City; f. 1961; weekly; Arabic; political, social and cultural; Editor JASSIM MUBARAK.

Ar-Riyadhi al-'Arabi (The Arab Sportsman): POB 1693, 13017 Safat, Kuwait City; tel. 4845307; telex 44728; weekly; Arabic; sports; circ. 101,822.

Sa'd (Good Luck): POB 695, Ismail Wasi, ar-Racalam, Kuwait City; tel. 813133; telex 22636; weekly; Arabic; children's magazine; Editor MANAL AL-MOSAFED; circ. 60,000.

Sawt al-Khaleej (Voice of the Gulf): POB 659, Safat, Kuwait City; tel. 815590; telex 2636; fax 4839261; f. 1962; politics and literature; Arabic; Editor-in-Chief CHRISTINE KHRAIBET; Owner BAKER ALI KHRAIBET; circ. 20,000.

At-Talia (The Ascendant): POB 1082, 13011 Safat, Kuwait City; tel. 4840470; fax 4815611; f. 1962; weekly; Arabic; politics and literature; Editor SAMI AHMAD AL-MUNAIS; circ. 10,000.

Al-Yaqza (The Awakening): POB 6000, 13060 Safat, Kuwait City; tel. 4831318; telex 44513; fax 4840630; f. 1966; weekly; Arabic; political, economic, social and general; Editor-in-Chief AHMAD YOUSUF BEHBEHANI; circ. 91,340.

NEWS AGENCIES

Kuwait News Agency (KUNA): POB 24063, 13101 Safat, Kuwait City; tel. 2412040; telex 22658; fax 2410972; f. 1976; public corporate body; independent; also publishes research digests on topics of common and special interest; Chair. and Dir-Gen. YOUSUF AS-SUMAIT.

Foreign Bureaux

Informatsionnoye Telegrafnoye Agentstvo Rossii—Telegrafnoye Agentstvo Suverennykh Stran (ITAR—TASS) (Russia): POB 1765, 13018 Safat, Kuwait City; Correspondent VIKTOR D. LEBEDEV.

Middle East News Agency (MENA) (Egypt): POB 1927, Safat, Fahd as-Salem St, Kuwait City; Dir REDA SOLIMAN.

Reuters Middle East Ltd (UK): POB 5616, 13057 Safat, Mubarak al-Kabir St, Kuwait Stock Exchange Bldg, 4th Floor, Kuwait City; tel. 2431920; telex 22428; fax 2460340; Country Man. EDWARD MANLEY.

Xinhua (New China) News Agency (People's Republic of China): POB 22168, Safat, Sheikh Ahmad al-Jaber Bldg, 10 Dasman St, Kuwait City; Correspondent HUANG JIANMING.

Agence Arabe Syrienne d'Information, Anatolian News Agency (Turkey), JANA (Libya), QNA (Qatar) and RIA—Vesti (Russia) are also represented in Kuwait.

PRESS ASSOCIATION

Kuwait Journalist Association: POB 5454, Safat, Kuwait City; tel. 4843351; fax 4842874; Chair. YOUSUF ALYYAN.

Publishers

Al-Abraj Translation and Publishing Co WLL: POB 26177, 13122 Safat, Kuwait City; tel. 2426686; fax 2407024; Man. Dir Dr TARIQ ABDULLAH.

Gulf Centre Publishing and Publicity: POB 2722, 13028 Safat, Kuwait City; fax 2458833; Propr HAMZA ISMAIL ESSLAH.

Al-Jeel Publishing Co: POB 44247, 32057 Hawalli, Kuwait City; tel. 4843183; telex 44090; children's education; Chair. and Gen. Man. OSSAMA EL-KAOUKJI.

Kuwait Publishing House: POB 5209, 13053 Safat, Kuwait City; tel. 2414697; telex 22771; Dir AMIN HAMADEH.

Kuwait United Advertising, Publishing and Distribution Co WLL: POB 29359, 13154 Safat; tel. 4817747; fax 4817757.

At-Talia Printing and Publishing Co: POB 1082, Airport Rd, Shuwaikh, 13011 Safat, Kuwait City; tel. 4840470; Man. AHMAD YOUSUF AN-NAFISI.

Government Publishing House

Ministry of Information: POB 193, 13002 Safat, as-Sour St, Kuwait City; tel. 2415300; telex 46151; fax 2421926.

Broadcasting and Communications

TELECOMMUNICATIONS

In early 1998 there were plans to privatize the state telecommunications sector, and to reorganize the Ministry of Communications as a company, designated the **Kuwaiti Communications Corporation.**

Mobile Telecommunications Co (KSC): POB 22244, Safat, 13083 Kuwait City; tel. 4842000; fax 4837755; Chair. and Man. Dir ABD AL-AZIZ AL-AYOUB.

BROADCASTING

Radio

Radio of the State of Kuwait: POB 397, 13004 Safat, Kuwait City; tel. 2423774; fax 2456660; e-mail radiokuwait@radiokuwait. org; internet http://www.radiokuwait.org; f. 1951; broadcasts for 70 hours daily in Arabic, Farsi, English and Urdu, some in stereo; Dir of Radio Dr ABD AL-AZIZ ALI MANSOUR; Dir of Radio Programmes ABD AR-RAHMAN HADI.

Television

Kuwait Television: POB 193, 13002 Safat, Kuwait City; tel. 2413501; fax 2438403; f. 1961 (transmission began privately in Kuwait in 1957); transmits in Arabic; colour television service began in 1973; has a total of five channels; Head of News Broadcasting MUHAMMAD AL-KAHTANI.

Plans were announced in early 1998 for the establishment of a private satellite broadcasting television channel, with administrative offices in Kuwait and transmission facilities in Dubai, United Arab Emirates.

Finance

(cap. = capital; res = reserves; dep. = deposits; m. = million; brs = branches; amounts in Kuwaiti dinars unless otherwise stated)

BANKING

Central Bank

Central Bank of Kuwait: POB 526, 13006 Safat, Abdullah as-Salem St, Kuwait City; tel. 2449200; telex 22101; fax 2402715; f. 1969; cap. 5m., res 293.6m., dep. 407.1m. (June 1997); Governor Sheikh SALEM ABD AL-AZIZ SA'UD AS-SABAH.

National Banks

Al-Ahli Bank of Kuwait KSC: POB 1387, 13014 Safat, Ahmad al-Jaber St, Safat Sq., Kuwait City; tel. 2400900; telex 22067; fax 2424557; f. 1967; wholly owned by private Kuwaiti interests; cap. 80.6m., res 50.9m., dep. 1,020.8m. (Dec. 1996); Chair. MORAD YOUSUF BEHBEHANI; Dep. Chair. Sheikh TALAL KHALID AL-AHMAD AS-SABAH; 13 brs in Kuwait.

Bank of Bahrain and Kuwait: POB 24396, 13104 Safat, Kuwait City; tel. 2417140; fax 2440937; f. 1977; owned equally by the Govts of Bahrain and Kuwait; cap. BD56.9m., res BD35.0m., dep. BD737.0m. (Dec. 1997); Chair. RASHED AZ-ZAYANI; Gen. Man. MICHEL KHAZEN.

Bank of Kuwait and the Middle East KSC: POB 71, 13001 Safat, Darwazat Abd ar-Razzak, Kuwait City; tel. 2459771; telex 22045; fax 2461430; f. 1971; 49% state-owned; cap. 53.3m., res 28.8m., dep. 795.4m. (Dec. 1996); Chair. and Man. Dir SALEH MUBARAK AL-FALAH; 12 brs.

Burgan Bank SAK: POB 5389, 13054 Safat, Ahmad al-Jaber St, Kuwait City; tel. 2439000; telex 22730; fax 2461148; f. 1975; cap. 74.3m., res 75.9m., dep. 967.1m. (Dec. 1997); merger with Commercial Bank of Kuwait approved 1998; Chair. and Man. Dir ABD AL-AZIZ IBRAHIM AN-NABHAN; Chief Gen. Man. JAMES MCNIE; 10 brs.

Commercial Bank of Kuwait SAK: POB 2861, 13029 Safat, Mubarak al-Kabir St, Kuwait City; tel. 2411001; telex 22004; fax 2450150; f. 1960 by Amiri decree; cap. 106.4m., res 54.1m., dep. 1,083.7m. (Dec. 1997); merger with Burgan Bank approved 1998; Chair. Sheikh MUHAMMAD JARRAH AS-SABAH; Gen. Man. DAVID BERRY; 23 brs.

Gulf Bank KSC: POB 3200, 13032 Safat, Mubarak al-Kabir St, Kuwait City; tel. 2449501; telex 22001; fax 2445212; f. 1960; cap. 78.2m., res 87.8m., dep. 1,408.8m. (Dec. 1996); Chair. Dr ALI AL-HILAL AL-MUTAIRI; CEO JOHN D. HARRIS; 15 brs.

Industrial Bank of Kuwait KSC: POB 3146, 13032 Safat, Joint Banking Centre, Commercial Area 9, Kuwait City; tel. 2457661; telex 22406; fax 2462057; 31.4% state-owned; f. 1973; cap. 20.0m., res 50.9m., dep. 63.6m. (Dec. 1995); Chair. and Man. Dir SALEH MUHAMMAD AL-YOUSUF.

Kuwait Finance House KSC (KFH): POB 24989, 13110 Safat, Abdullah al-Mubarak St, Kuwait City; tel. 2445050; telex 23331; fax 2455135; f. 1977; Islamic banking and investment company; 49% state-owned; cap. 50.6m., res 77.9m., dep. 1,202.2m. (Dec. 1997); Chair. and Man. Dir BADER AL-MUKHAISEEM; Gen. Man. WALEED AR-RUWAIH; 18 brs.

Kuwait Real Estate Bank KSC: POB 22822, 13089 Safat, West Tower—Joint Banking Centre, Darwazat Abd ar-Razzak, Kuwait City; tel. 2458177; telex 22321; fax 2462516; f. 1973; wholly owned

by private Kuwaiti interests; cap. 31.2m., res 40.9m., dep. 298.7m. (Dec. 1997); Chair. and Man. Dir Sheikh ALI KHALIFA AL-ATHBI AS-SABAH; Dep. Chair EMAD JAWAD BU KHAMSEEN; 2 brs.

National Bank of Kuwait SAK (NBK): POB 95, 13001 Safat, Abdullah al-Ahmad St, Kuwait City; tel. 2422011; telex 22451; fax 2431888; internet http://www.nbk.com; f. 1952; cap. 140.4m., res 226.4m., dep. 3,571.02m. (Dec. 1997); Chair. MUHAMMAD ABD AR-RAHMAN AL-BAHAR; Chief Gen. Man. IBRAHIM S. DABDOUB; 39 brs.

Savings and Credit Bank: POB 1454, 13015 Safat, ash-Shuhada St, Kuwait City; tel. 2411301; telex 22211; f. 1965; nominal cap. 1,000m.; Chair. and Gen. Man. Dr JASSEM M. AL-DABBOUS.

INSURANCE

Al-Ahleia Insurance Co SAK: POB 1602, as-Sour St, 13017 Safat, Kuwait City; tel. 2448870; telex 23585; fax 2430308; f. 1962; all forms of insurance; cap. 11.2m.; Chair. YOUSUF IBRAHIM AL-GHANIM; Man. Dir OSAMAH MUHAMMAD AN-NISF; Gen. Man. TALAL SAKIR AL-QATAMI.

Al-Ittihad al-Watani Insurance Co for the Near East SAL: POB 781, 13008 Safat, Kuwait City; tel. 4843988; telex 22442; fax 4847244; Man. JOSEPH ZACCOUR.

Arab Commercial Enterprises (Kuwait): POB 2474, 13025 Safat, Kuwait City; tel. 2413854; telex 22076; fax 2409450.

Gulf Insurance Co KSC: POB 1040, 13011 Safat, Kuwait City; tel. 2423384; telex 22203, fax 2422320; f. 1962; cap. 11.3m.; all forms of insurance; Chair. FAISAL HAMAD AL-AYYAR.

Kuwait Insurance Co SAK (KIC): POB 769, 13008 Safat, Abdullah as-Salem St, Kuwait City; tel. 2420135; fax 2428530; f. 1960; cap. 18.5m.; all life and non-life insurance; Chair. MUHAMMAD SALEH BEHBEHANI; Gen. Man. ALI HAMAD AL-BAHAR.

Kuwait Reinsurance Co KSC: POB 21929, 13080 Safat, as-Sahab Tower, 14th and 15th Floor, as-Salhia, Kuwait City; tel. 2432011; telex 22058; fax 2427823; f. 1972; Gen. Man. AMIR AL-MUHANNA.

Kuwait Technical Insurance Office: POB 25349, 13114 Safat, Kuwait City; tel. 2413986; telex 23583; fax 2413986.

Mohd Saleh Behbehani & Co: POB 370, 13004 Safat, Kuwait City; tel. 2412085; telex 22194; fax 2412089.

New India Assurance Co: POB 370, 13004 Safat, Kuwait City; tel. 2412085; telex 22194; fax 2412089.

The Northern Insurance Co Ltd: POB 579, 13006 Safat, Kuwait City; tel. 2427930; telex 22367; fax 2462739.

Oriental Insurance Co Ltd (Al Mulla Group): POB 22431, 13085 Safat, Kuwait City; tel. 2424016; telex 22012; fax 2424017; Man. V. HARSHAVARDHAN.

Sumitomo Marine & Fire Insurance Co (Kuwait Agency): POB 3458, 13055 Safat, Kuwait City; tel. 2433087; telex 23754; fax 2430853.

Warba Insurance Co SAK: POB 24282, 13103 Safat, Kuwait City; tel. 2445140; telex 22779; fax 2466131; f. 1976; Chair. ABDULLAH HASSAN JARALLAH; 1 br.

Some 20 Arab and other foreign insurance companies are active in Kuwait.

STOCK EXCHANGE

Kuwait Stock Exchange: POB 22235, 13083 Safat, Mubarak al-Kabir St, Kuwait City; tel. 2423130; telex 44015; fax 2420779; f. 1984; 75 companies listed in January 1998; Pres. HISHAM AL-OTAIBI; Vice-Pres. ABDULLAH AS-SDAIRAWI.

Trade and Industry

DEVELOPMENT ORGANIZATIONS

Arab Planning Institute (API): POB 5834, 13059 Safat, Kuwait City; tel. 4843130; telex 22996; fax 4842935; e-mail api@kuwait.net; f. 1966; 50 mems; publishes annual directory and proceedings of seminars and discussion group meetings, offers research, training programmes and advisory services; Dir ESSA ALGHAZALI.

General Board for the South and Arabian Gulf: POB 5994, Safat, Kuwait City; tel. 2424461; wholly state-owned; provides assistance to developing countries in the Arab world; Del. Mem. AHMAD AS-SAKKAF.

Industrial Investments Company (IIC): POB 26019, 13121 Safat, Kuwait City; tel. 2429073; telex 23132; fax 2448850; f. 1983; invests directly in industry; partly owned by the Kuwait Investment Authority; privatization initiated in April 1996; Man. Dir TALEB A. ALI.

Kuwait Fund for Arab Economic Development (KFAED): POB 2921, 13030 Safat, cnr Mubarak al-Kabir St and al-Hilali St, Kuwait City; tel. 2468800; telex 22613; fax 2436289; e-mail info@kuwait-fund.org; f. 1961; cap. KD 1,850m.; state-owned; provides and administers financial and technical assistance to the countries of the developing world; Chair. Minister of Finance; Dir-Gen. BADER M. AL-HUMAIDHI.

Kuwait Investment Authority (KIA): POB 64, 13001 Safat, Kuwait City; tel. 2439595; telex 46089; fax 2454059; oversees the Kuwait Investment Office (London); responsible for the Kuwaiti General Reserve; Chair. Minister of Finance; Gen. Man. MAURICE FINAN.

Kuwait International Investment Co SAK (KIIC): POB 22792, 13088 Safat, as-Salhia Commercial Complex, Kuwait City; tel. 2438273; fax 2454931; 30% state-owned; cap. p.u. 31.9m., total assets KD 146.9m. (1988); domestic real estate and share markets; Chair. and Man. Dir JASSIM MUHAMMAD AL-BAHAR.

Kuwait Investment Co SAK (KIC): POB 1005, 13011 Safat, 5th Floor, al-Manakh Bldg, Mubarak al-Kabir St, Kuwait City; tel. 2438111; telex 22115; fax 2444896; f. 1981; 88% state-owned, 12% owned by private Kuwaiti interests; total resources KD 50.1m. (1996); international banking and investment; Chair. and Man. Dir BADER A. AR-RUSHAID AL-BADER.

Kuwait Planning Board: c/o Ministry of Planning, POB 21688, 13122 Safat, Kuwait City; tel. 2428200; telex 22468; fax 2414734; f. 1962; supervises long-term development plans; through its Central Statistical Office publishes information on Kuwait's economic activity; Dir-Gen. AHMAD ALI AD-DUAIJ.

National Industries Co SAK (NIC): POB 417, 13005 Safat, Kuwait City; tel. 4815466; telex 22165; fax 4839582; f. 1960; 22.7% owned by KIA; cap. p.u. KD 24.3m.; has controlling interest in various construction enterprises; privatization initiated in March 1995; Chair. and Man. Dir SAUD M. AL-OSMANI

Petrochemical Industries Co KSC (PIC): POB 1084, 13011 Safat, Khalid Bin al-Walid St, Kuwait City; tel. 2422141; telex 22042; fax 2447159; f. 1963; state-owned; produced 851,700 metric tons of urea and 569,800 tons of ammonia in 1987/88; Chair. and Man. KHALED SALEH BOUHAMRA.

Fertilizer Plants: POB 1084, 13011 Safat, Kuwait City; tel. 2422141; telex 44212; fax 2447159; production of ammonia, urea, sulphuric acid and ammonium sulphate; four ammonia plants, three urea plants and one ammonium sulphate plant.

Salt and Chlorine Plants: POB 10277, 65453 Shuaiba, Kuwait; tel. 3261590; fax 3261587; f. 1986; production of salt, chlorine, caustic soda, hydrochloric acid, sodium hypochlorite and compressed hydrogen; Plants Man. HUSSAIN AD-DAMKHI.

Shuaiba Area Authority SAA: POB 4690, 13047 Safat, Kuwait City; POB 10033, Shuaiba; tel. 3260903; telex 44205; f. 1964; an independent governmental authority to supervise and run the industrial area and Port of Shuaiba; has powers and duties to develop the area and its industries which include an oil refinery, cement factory, fishing plant, power stations and distillation plants, chemical fertilizer and petrochemical industries, sanitary ware factory, asbestos plant and sand lime bricks plant; Dir-Gen. SULAYMAN K. AL-HAMAD.

CHAMBER OF COMMERCE

Kuwait Chamber of Commerce and Industry: POB 775, 13008 Safat, Chamber's Bldg, Ali as-Salem St, Kuwait City; tel. 2433864; fax 2404110; e-mail kcci@kuwait-chamber.com.kw; internet http://www.kuwait_chamber.com.kw; f. 1959; 45,000 mems; Pres. ABD AR-RAZZAK KHALID ZAID AL-KHALID; Dir-Gen. AHMAD RASHED AL-HAROUN.

STATE HYDROCARBONS COMPANIES

Kuwait Petroleum Corpn (KPC): POB 26565, 13126 Safat, Salhia Complex, Fahed as-Salem St, Kuwait City; tel. 2455455; telex 44875; fax 2423371; f. 1980; co-ordinating organization to manage the petroleum industry; controls companies listed below; Chair. Minister of Oil; Deputy Chair. NADER SULTAN.

Kuwait Aviation Fuelling Co KSC: POB 1654, 13017 Safat, Kuwait City; tel. 4330482; telex 23056; fax 4330475; Gen. Man. ABD AL-AZIZ AS-SERRI.

Kuwait Foreign Petroleum Exploration Co KSC (KUFPEC): POB 5291, 13053 Safat, Kuwait City; tel. 2421677; telex 50021; fax 2420405; f. 1981; state-owned; overseas oil and gas exploration and development; Chair. and Man. Dir MAHMOUD A. AR-RAHMANI.

Kuwait National Petroleum Co KSC (KNPC): POB 70, 13001 Safat, Ali as-Salem St, Kuwait City; tel. 2420121; telex 22006; fax 2433839; f. 1960; oil refining, production of liquefied petroleum gas, and domestic marketing and distribution of petroleum by-products; output of 855,000 b/d of refined petroleum in 1996/97; Chair. and Man. Dir AHMAD ABD AL-MOHSIN AL-MUTAIR.

Kuwait Oil Co KSC (KOC): POB 9758, 61008 Ahmadi; tel. 3989111; telex 44211; fax 3983661; e-mail kocinfo@koc.com.kw; internet http://www.moc.kw/kemscut.html; f. 1934; state-owned; Chair. and Man. Dir KHALID Y. AL-FULAIJ.

Kuwait Oil Tanker Co SAK (see Transport—Shipping).

Kuwait Petroleum International Ltd (KPI): 80 New Bond St, London, W1, England; tel. (0171) 491-4000; marketing division of KPC; controls 6,500 petrol retail stations in Europe, under the trade name 'Q8' (adopted in 1986), and European refineries with capacity of 235,000 b/d; Pres. KAMEL HARAMI.

Petrochemical Industries Co KSC (PIC) (see Development Organizations).

UTILITIES

In 1998 there were plans to create regulatory bodies for each of Kuwait's utilities, with a view to facilitating their privatization.

Ministry of Electricity and Water (see Ministries, above): provides subsidized services throughout Kuwait.

MAJOR COMPANIES

Kirby Building Systems Kuwait: POB 23933, 13100 Safat, Mina Abdullah Industrial Area, Kuwait City; tel. 4734439; fax 4734538; f. 1976; pre-engineered steel buildings and accessories for industrial and commercial use; an affiliate of Alghanim Industries; Vice-Pres. MARWAN KARADSHEH.

Kuwait Aluminium Co KSC: POB 5335, 13054 Safat, ar-Rai Industrial Area, Plot 1636, St No. 13, Kuwait City; tel. 4734600; telex 23025; fax 4734419; f. 1968; sales about KD 1.5m.; cap. p.u. KD 4m.; design, manufacture, erection and maintenance of aluminium and glass works for construction industry; Chair. NASSER NAKI; 190 employees.

Kuwait Cement Co KSC: POB 20581, 13066 Safat, Safat New Exhibition Bldg, 1st Floor, as-Sour St, Salhiya, Kuwait City; tel. 2414033; telex 22205; fax 2432956; f. 1968; 34.6% govt-owned; manufacture and marketing of cement; cap. p.u. KD 25.6m.; Chair. ABD AL-MOHSIN ABD AL-AZIZ AR-RASHID; 525 employees.

Kuwait Food and Beverage Co WLL: POB 22528, 13086 Safat, Kuwait City; tel. 4818862; canned food, soft drinks, juices, mineral water; Chair. MUHAMMAD RADWAN LUTHFI.

Kuwait Food Co (Americana) SAK: POB 5087, 13051 Safat, Safat Shuwaikh and Sabhan Industrial Area, Kuwait City; tel. 4815900; telex 22125; fax 4839337; f. 1963; cap. p.u. KD 11.3m.; chain of restaurants, meat industry, bakery plant for oriental sweets and English cakes; Man. MOATAZ AL-ALFI; 2,000 employees.

Kuwait Metal Pipe Industries Co KSC: POB 3416, 13035 Safat, Kuwait City; tel. 4675622; fax 4675897; f. 1966; sales KD 10.8m. (1982); 16.6% govt-owned; manufacture of various pipes, tanks and coatings; cap. p.u. KD 15.2m.; Chair. AHMAD YOUSUF M. AR-ROUDAN.

Kuwait Pharmaceutical Industrial Co (KPICO): POB 5846, 13059 Safat, Sabhan Industrial Area 4, Kuwait City; tel. 4748011; telex 23091; fax 4714150; f. 1980; cap. p.u. KD 10m. (1987); began production in 1987; owned 34.9% by the govt, 25% by ACDIMA (Arab Co for Drug Industries and Medical Appliances), 20% by GIC (Gulf Investment Corporation) and 20.1% by private shareholders; cap. p.u. KD 5.5m.; MAN. DIR SULAYMAN S. ATH-THERBAN.

Kuwait Prefabricated Building Co SAK: POB 5132, 13052 Safat, Kuwait City; tel. 4733055; telex 22201; fax 4749908; f. 1964; sales KD 18.5m. (1982); cap. p.u. KD 6m.; design and manufacture of pre-cast structures, pre-stressed hollowcore slabs, claddings, beams, welded wire mesh, terrazzo tiles, structural steel items; hot dip galvanization; Chair. ABDULLAH ABD AL-AZIZ OBAIDAN; 1,446 employees.

Kuwaiti Danish Dairy Co WLL: POB 835, 13009 Safat, Sabhan Industrial Area 1, St 104, Kuwait City; tel. 4717911; telex 23054; fax 4747029; dairy products, ice cream, fruit juices and tomato paste; Chair. and Gen. Man. EZZAT MUHAMMAD JAAFAR.

Packaging and Plastic Industries Co: POB 1148, 15462 Dasman, Kuwait City; tel. 2435841; fax 2435839; f. 1974; production of polypropylene woven bags for packaging fertilizers, polyethylene agricultural sheets, co-extruded flexible film packaging; Chair. Dr ABD AL-AZIZ SULTAN AL-ESSA; 200 employees.

United Fisheries of Kuwait KSC: POB 22044, 13081 Safat, Kuwait City; tel. 2445021; fax 2447970; f. 1972; sales KD 3.4m. (1995); cap. KD 7m.; production, export and import of frozen fish and shrimps; Chair. and Man. Dir FAISAL M. BIN SABT; 500 employees.

TRADE UNIONS

General Confederation of Kuwaiti Workers: POB 5185, Safat, 13052 Kuwait City; tel. 5616053; fax 5627159; f. 1968; central authority to which all trade unions are affiliated.

KOC Workers Union: Kuwait City; f. 1964; Chair. HAMAD SAWYAN.

Federation of Petroleum and Petrochemical Workers: Kuwait City; f. 1965; Chair. JASSIM ABD AL-WAHAB AT-TOURA.

Transport

RAILWAYS

There are no railways in Kuwait.

ROADS

Roads in the towns are metalled, and the most important are motorways or dual carriageways. There are metalled roads linking Kuwait City to Ahmadi, Mina al-Ahmadi and other centres of population in Kuwait, and to the Iraqi and Saudi Arabian borders, amounting to a total road network of 4,273 km in 1989 (280 km of motorways, 1,232 km of other major roads and 2,761 km of secondary roads).

Kuwait Public Transport Co SAK (KPTC): POB 375, 13004 Safat, Murghab, Safat Sq, Kuwait City; tel. 2469420; telex 22246; fax 2401265; f. 1962; state-owned; provides internal bus service; regular service to Mecca, Saudi Arabia; Chair. and Man. Dir MAH-MOUD ABD AL-KALEQ AN-NOURRI.

SHIPPING

Kuwait has three commercial seaports. The largest, Shuwaikh, situated about 3 km from Kuwait City, was built in 1960. By 1987 it comprised 21 deep-water berths, with a total length of 4 km, three shallow-water berths and three basins for small craft, each with a depth of 3.35m. In 1988 3.6m. metric tons of cargo were imported and 133,185 tons were exported through the port. A total of 1,189 vessels passed through Shuwaikh in 1988.

Shuaiba Commercial Port, 56 km south of Kuwait City, was built in 1967 to facilitate the import of primary materials and heavy equipment, necessary for the construction of the Shuaiba Industrial Area. By 1987 the port comprised a total of 20 berths, plus two docks for small wooden boats. Four of the berths constitute a station for unloading containers. Shuaiba handled a total of 3,457,871 metric tons of dry cargo, barge cargo and containers in 1988.

Doha, the smallest port, was equipped in 1981 to receive small coastal ships carrying light goods between the Gulf states. It has 20 small berths, each 100 m long. Doha handled a total of 20,283 metric tons of dry cargo, barge cargo and containers in 1988.

The oil port at Mina al-Ahmadi, 40 km south of Kuwait City, is capable of handling the largest oil tankers afloat, and the loading of over 2m. barrels of oil per day. By 1987 the port comprised 12 tanker berths, one bitumen-carrier berth, two LPG export berths and bunkering facilities.

At 31 December 1996 Kuwait's merchant fleet numbered 211 vessels, with a total displacement of 2,027,884 grt.

Arab Maritime Petroleum Transport Co (AMPTC): POB 22525, 13086 Safat, OAPEC Bldg, Shuwaikh, Airport St, Kuwait City; tel. 4844500; fax 4842996; f. 1973; 3 tankers and 5 LPG carriers; sponsored by OAPEC and financed by Algeria, Bahrain, Iraq, Kuwait, Libya, Qatar, Saudi Arabia and the UAE; Chair. AHMAD M. AR-RAHMA (UAE); Gen. Man. SULAYMAN I. AL-BASSAM.

Kuwait Maritime Transport Co KSC: POB 22595, 13086 Safat, Nafisi and Khatrash Bldg, Jaber al-Mubarak St, Kuwait City; tel. 2420519; telex 30967; fax 2420513; f. 1981.

Kuwait Oil Tanker Co SAK (KOTC): POB 810, 13009 Safat, as-Salhia Commercial Complex, Blocks 3, 5, 7 and 9, Kuwait City; tel. 2455455; telex 44755; fax 2445907; f. 1957; state-owned; operates 4 crude oil tankers, 20 product tankers and 6 LPG vessels; sole tanker agents for Mina al-Ahmadi, Shuaiba and Mina Abdullah and agents for other ports; LPG filling and distribution; Chair. and Man. Dir ABDULLAH AR-ROUMI.

Kuwait Ports Authority: POB 3874, 13039 Safat, Kuwait City; tel. 4812774; telex 22740; fax 4819714; f. 1977; there are plans to expand the ports to handle the increased cargo traffic projected for the 1990s; Dir-Gen. ABD AR-RAHMAN AN-NAIBARI.

Kuwait Shipbuilding and Repairyard Co SAK (KSRC): POB 21998, 13080 Safat, Kuwait City; tel. 4830308; fax 4815947; ship repairs and engineering services, underwater services, maintenance of refineries, power stations and storage tanks; maintains floating dock for vessels up to 35,000 dwt; synchrolift for vessels up to 5,000 dwt with transfer yard; five repair jetties up to 550 m in length and floating workshop for vessels lying at anchor; Chair. and Man. Dir MUSA J. MARAFI; Commercial Man. BILL PURDIE.

United Arab Shipping Co SAG (UASC): POB 3636, 13037 Safat, Shuwaikh, Airport Rd, Kuwait City; tel. 4843150; telex 22176; fax 4845388; f. 1976; national shipping company of six Arabian Gulf countries; services between Europe, Far East, Mediterranean ports, Japan and east coast of USA and South America, and ports of participant states on Persian (Arabian) Gulf and Red Sea; 46 vessels; subsidiary cos: Kuwait Shipping Agencies, Arab Transport Co (Aratrans), United Arab Chartering Ltd (United Kingdom), Middle East Container Repair Co (Dubai), Arabian Chemicals Carriers (Saudi Arabia), United Arab Agencies Inc. (USA) and United Arab Shipping Agencies Co (Saudi Arabia); Pres. and CEO ABDULLAH MAHDI AL-MAHDI.

CIVIL AVIATION

Kuwait International Airport opened in 1980, and was designed to receive up to 4.5m. passengers per year; in 1997 3.61m. arrivals and departures were recorded.

Directorate-General of Civil Aviation: POB 17, 13001 Safat, Kuwait City; tel. 4335599; telex 31945; fax 4713504; e-mail aviation@ kuwait.net; internet http://www.kuwait.net/-aviation/met1.html; Dir-Gen. YACOUB Y. AS-SAQER.

Kuwait Airways Corpn (KAC): POB 394, Kuwait International Airport, 13004 Safat; tel. 4345555; telex 23036; fax 4314726; f. 1954; services to the Arabian peninsula, Asia, Africa and Europe; Chair. AHMAD AL-MISHARI; Dir-Gen. AHMAD AZ-ZABIN.

Tourism

Department of Tourism: Ministry of Information, POB 193, 13002 Safat, as-Sour St, Kuwait City; tel. 2463400; fax 2464460.

Touristic Enterprises Co (TEC): POB 23310, 13094 Safat, Kuwait City; tel. 5652775; telex 22801; fax 5657594; f. 1976; 92% state-owned; manages 23 tourist facilities; Chair. BADER AL-BAHAR; Vice-Chair. YACOUB AR-RUSHAID.

Defence

In August 1997 the armed forces numbered an estimated 15,300, including 11,000 in the army, 2,500 in the air force, and 1,800 in the navy. Paramilitary forces include a National Guard of 5,000, and a coastguard. The defence budget for 1997 was KD 805m. In August 1992 an Amiri decree authorized the Government to withdraw KD 3,500m. from state reserves to cover potential expenditure on defence over the following 12 years. There is a period of military service lasting two years (one year for university students), compulsory since March 1979.

Chief of Staff of Armed Forces: Gen. ALI AL-MOUMEN.

Education

In recent years a comprehensive system of kindergarten, primary, intermediate and secondary schools has been developed, and compulsory education for children between 6 and 14 years of age was introduced in 1966–67. However, many children spend two years prior to this in a kindergarten, and go on to complete their general education at the age of 18 years. It is government policy to provide free education to all Kuwaiti children from kindergarten stage to the University. In 1995/96 a total of 244,189 pupils attended 443 government schools (175 primary, 157 intermediate and 111 secondary). In 1990/91 a total of 65,407 pupils attended 172 private schools. Education was allocated an estimated KD 312.4m. in the Government's 1994/95 budget, or 7.1% of total expenditure.

Primary education lasts four years, after which the pupils move on to an intermediate school for another four years. Secondary education, which is optional and lasts four more years, is given mainly in general schools. There are also commercial institutes, a Faculty of Technological Studies, a health institute, religious institutes (with intermediate and secondary stages) and 11 institutes for handicapped children. In 1995 enrolment at primary schools included 65% of children in the relevant age-group (males 65%; females 65%), while at secondary schools the rate was equivalent to 64% of children in the relevant age-group (males 64%, females 64%).

Two-year courses at post-secondary teacher training institutes provide teachers for kindergartens and primary schools and the University provides for intermediate and secondary schools. The number of graduates is not enough to meet all the teaching staff requirements and so the Ministry of Education meets this shortage by recruiting teachers from other Arab countries.

Scholarships are granted to students to pursue courses which are not offered by Kuwait University. Such scholarships are mainly used to study in Egypt, Lebanon, the UK and the USA. There are also pupils from Arab, African and Asian states studying in Kuwait schools on Kuwait Government scholarships. Kuwait University has about 15,500 students, and also provides scholarships for a number of Arab, Asian and African students. In May 1996 the National Assembly approved a draft law to regulate students' behaviour, dress and activities, with regard to observance of the teachings of *Shari'a* (Islamic) law, and to eradicate coeducational classes at Kuwait University over a five-year period. In 1989 a national library was being built, at an estimated cost of KD 4m. Following the Iraqi occupation of Kuwait, and the country's subsequent liberation, it was reported that 300 schools and colleges were in need of repair.

Between 1969 and 1985, 60,000 men and women graduated from the country's centres for illiteracy eradication and adult education, which in 1986 totalled 105, catering for 32,000 students. In 1995 the average rate of adult illiteracy was estimated by UNESCO at 21.4% (males 17.8%; females 25.1%).

Bibliography

Chisholm, A. H. T. *The First Kuwait Oil Concession: A Record of the Negotiations 1911–1934*. London, Cass.

Daniels, John. *Kuwait Journey*. Luton, England, White Crescent Press, 1972.

Department of Social Affairs. *Annual Report*. Kuwait.

Dickson, H. R. P. *Kuwait and her Neighbours*. London, Allen and Unwin, 1956.

El Mallakh, Ragaei. *Economic Development and Regional Co-operation: Kuwait*. University of Chicago Press, 1968.

Finnie, David. *Shifting Lines in the Sand*. London, I. B. Tauris, 1992.

Gardiner, Stephen, and Cook, Ian. *Kuwait: The Making of a City*. London, Longman, 1983.

Government Printing Press. *Education and Development in Kuwait*. Kuwait.

Port of Kuwait Annual Report. Kuwait.

Hakima, Abu A. M. *The Modern History of Kuwait: 1750–1966*. UK, The Westerham Press, 1983.

Hay, Sir Rupert. *The Persian Gulf States*. Washington, DC, Middle East Institute, 1959.

International Bank for Reconstruction and Development. *The Economic Development of Kuwait*. Baltimore, Johns Hopkins Press, 1965.

Khouja, M. W., and Sadler, P. G. *The Energy of Kuwait: Development and Role in International Finance*. London, Macmillan, 1978.

Kochwasser, Friedrich H. *Kuwait. Geschichte, Wesen und Funktion eines modernen Arabischen Staates*. Tübingen, Eldmann, 1961.

Kuwait Oil Co Ltd. *The Story of Kuwait*. London.

Mansfield, Peter. *Kuwait: Vanguard of the Gulf*. London, Hutchinson, 1990.

Marlowe, John. *The Persian Gulf in the 20th Century*. London, Cresset Press, 1962.

Mezerik, Avraham G. *The Kuwait-Iraq Dispute, 1961*. New York, 1961.

Ministry of Planning. *Kuwait in Figures: Twenty-Five Years of Independence*. Kuwait, Central Statistical Office, 1986.

Rahman, H. *The Making of the Gulf War*. Reading, Garnet, 1997.

Rush, Alan. *Al-Sabah History and Genealogy of Kuwait's Ruling Family 1752–1987*. London, Ithaca Press, 1987.

Al-Sabah, Y. S. F. *The Oil Economy of Kuwait*. Henley-on-Thames, Routledge and Kegan Paul, 1981.

Saldanha, J. A. *The Persian Gulf: Administration Reports 1873–1957*. London, Archive Editions, 1986.

The Persian Gulf Precis 1903–1908. London, Archive Editions, 1986.

Sandwick, John A. *The Gulf Co-operation Council: Moderation and Stability in an Interdependent World*. London, Mansell Publishing Ltd.

Winstone, H. V. F., and Freeth, Zahra. *Kuwait: Prospect and Reality*. London, Allen and Unwin, 1972.

LEBANON

Physical and Social Geography

W. B. FISHER

The creation, after 1918, of the modern state of Lebanon, first under French mandatory rule and then as an independent territory, was designed to recognize the nationalist aspirations of a number of Christian groups that had lived for many centuries under Muslim rule along the coast of the eastern Mediterranean and in the hills immediately adjacent. At least as early as the 16th century AD there had been particularist Christian feeling that ultimately resulted in the granting of autonomy, though not independence, to Christians living in the territory of 'Mount Lebanon', which geographically was the hill region immediately inland and extending some 30 km–45 km north and south of Beirut. The territory of Mount Lebanon was later expanded, owing to French interest, into the much larger area of 'Greater Lebanon' with frontiers running along the crest of the Anti-Lebanon mountains, and reaching the sea some miles north of Tripoli to form the boundary with Syria. In the south there is a frontier with Israel, running inland from the promontory of Ras an-Naqoura to the head of the Jordan Valley. In drawing the frontiers so as to give a measure of geographical unity to the new state, which now occupies an area of 10,452 sq km (4,036 sq miles), large non-Christian elements of Muslims and Druzes were included, so that at the present day the Christians of Lebanon form less than one-half of the total population.

PHYSICAL FEATURES

Structurally, Lebanon consists of an enormous simple upfold of rocks that runs parallel to the coast. There is, first, a very narrow and broken flat coastal strip—hardly a true plain—then the land rises steeply to a series of imposing crests and ridges. The highest crest of all is Qurnet as-Sauda, just over 3,000 m high, lying south-east of Tripoli; Mount Sannin, north-east of Beirut, is over 2,700 m. A few miles east of the summits there is a precipitous drop along a sharp line to a broad, trough-like valley, known as the Beka'a (Biqa), about 16 km wide and some 110 km–130 km long. The eastern side of the Beka'a is formed by the Anti-Lebanon mountains, which rise to 2,800 m, and their southern continuation, the Hermon Range, of about the same height. The floor of the Beka'a valley, though much below the level of the surrounding mountain ranges, lies in places at 1,000 m above sea-level, with a low divide in the region of Baalbek. Two rivers rise in the Beka'a—the Orontes, which flows northwards into Syria and the Gharb depression, ultimately reaching the Mediterranean through the Turkish territory of Antioch; and the River Litani (Leontes). This latter river flows southwards, and then, at a short distance from the Israeli frontier, makes a sudden bend westwards and plunges through the Lebanon mountains by a deep gorge.

There exists in Lebanon an unusual feature of geological structure which is not present in either of the adjacent regions of Syria and Israel. This is the occurrence of a layer of non-porous rocks within the upfold forming the Lebanon mountains; and, because of this layer, water is forced to the surface in considerable quantities, producing large springs at the unusually high level of 1,200 m–1,500 m. Some of the springs have a flow of several thousand cu ft per second and emerge as small rivers; hence the western flanks of the Lebanon mountains, unlike those nearby in Syria and Israel, are relatively well watered and cultivation is possible up to a height of 1,200 m or 1,500 m.

With its great contrasts of relief, and the configuration of the main ranges, which lie across the path of the prevailing westerly winds, there is a wide variety in climatic conditions. The coastal lowlands are moderately hot in summer, and warm in winter, with complete absence of frost. But only 10 km or so away in the hills there is a heavy winter snowfall, and the higher hills are covered from December to May, giving the unusual vista for the Middle East of snow-clad peaks. From this the name Lebanon (laban—Aramaic for 'white') is said to originate. The Beka'a has a moderately cold winter with some frost and snow, and a distinctly hot summer, as it is shut off from the tempering effect of the sea.

Rainfall is generally abundant but it decreases rapidly towards the east, so that the Beka'a and Anti-Lebanon are definitely drier than the west. On the coast, between 750 mm and 1,000 mm (30 ins to 40 ins) fall annually, with up to 1,250 mm (50 ins) in the mountains; but only 380 mm (15 ins) in the Beka'a. As almost all of this annual total falls between October and April (there are three months of complete aridity each summer), rain is extremely heavy while it lasts, and storms of surprising intensity sometimes occur. Another remarkable feature is the extremely high humidity of the coastal region during summer, when no rain falls.

ECONOMIC LIFE

The occurrence of high mountains near the sea, and the relatively abundant supplies of spring water, had a significant influence on economic development within Lebanon. Owing to the successive levels of terrain, an unusually wide range of crops can be grown, from bananas and pineapples on the hot, damp coastlands, olives, vines and figs on the lowest foothills, cereals, apricots and peaches on the middle slopes, to apples and potatoes on the highest levels. These last are the aristocrats of the Lebanese markets, since they are rarest, and, with the growing market in the oilfield areas of Arabia and the Persian (Arabian) Gulf, they are sold for the highest price. Export of fruit is therefore an important item. In addition, abundant natural water led to the development of pinewoods and evergreen groves, which add greatly to the already considerable scenic beauty of the western hill country. Prior to the prolonged civil conflict in Lebanon (see History), there was an important tourist trade in the small hill villages, some of which have casinos, luxury hotels and cinemas. The greatest activity was during the summer months, when wealthy Middle Easterners and others arrived; but there was a smaller winter sports season, when skiing was pursued.

In addition, the geographical situation of Lebanon, as a 'façade' to the inland territories of Syria, Jordan, and even northern Iraq and southern Turkey, enabled the Lebanese ports to act as the commercial outlet for a very wide region. The importance of Beirut as a commercial centre was due in large part to the fact that Lebanon was a free market. More than one-half of the volume of Lebanon's former trade was transit traffic, and Lebanon used to handle most of the trade of Jordan. Byblos claims to be the oldest port in the world; Tyre and Sidon were for long world-famous, and the latter was reviving as the Mediterranean terminal of the Tapline (Trans-Arabian Pipeline) from Saudi Arabia until the Lebanese branch of the pipeline was closed at the end of 1983. Another ancient centre, Tripoli, was also a terminal of the pipeline from Iraq. Beirut is now, however, the leading town of the country, and contains more than one-half of the total population, including many displaced persons. Although local resources are not in general very great (there are no minerals or important raw materials in Lebanon), the city in normal times lived by commercial activity on a surprising scale, developed by the ingenuity and opportunism of its merchant class.

Beirut, of recent years, came to serve as a financial and holiday centre for the less attractive but oil-rich parts of the Middle East. Transfer of financial credit from the Middle East to Zürich, Paris, London, New York and Tokyo; a trade in gold and diamonds; and some connection with the narcotics trade of the Middle East—all these gave the city a very special function. Whether the traditional economic basis of the country—extreme individualism and 'laissez-faire' for entrepreneurs—can revive is uncertain, but strenuous efforts began in 1977 to bring about reconstruction and redevelopment, assisted by loans from outside. During 1980 a large contribution of 'front-line aid' was made by Arab League states, and this showed signs of producing significant economic recovery. However, the abrupt intensification of military activity in 1981–82, the effects of the subsequent Israeli invasion and the prolonged sectarian conflict negated these hopes. Production declined because of damage and disruption; the south was virtually disconnected from the remainder of the Lebanese state until Israeli forces withdrew to just inside the border in June 1985; such was the extent of factional division within the country that, in the early years of the recent civil conflict, the Government's authority was barely felt outside Beirut; by the late 1980s, if not before, even the capital had effectively lapsed into anarchy; the impossibility of controlling customs and tax collection caused a substantial reduction in government income.

RACE AND LANGUAGE

It is difficult to summarize the racial affinities of the Lebanese people. The western lowlands have an extremely mixed population possibly describable only as 'Levantine'. Basically Mediterranean, there are many other elements, including remarkably fair individuals—Arabs with blonde hair and grey eyes, who are possibly descendants of the Crusaders. The remaining parts of the country show a more decided tendency, with darker colouring and more pronounced facial features. In addition, small refugee groups, who came to the more inaccessible mountain zones in order to escape persecution, often have a different racial ancestry, so that parts of Lebanon form a mosaic of highly varying racial and cultural elements. Almost all Middle Eastern countries are represented racially within Lebanon.

Arabic is current throughout the whole country, but owing to the high level of education (probably the highest in any Middle Eastern country) and to the considerable volume of temporary emigration, English, French and even Spanish are widely understood. French is probably still the leading European language (though English is tending to replace it) and some of the higher schools and one university teach basically in this language. In addition, Aramaic is used by some religious sects, but only for ritual—there are no Aramaic speaking villages as in Syria.

History

ANCIENT AND MEDIEVAL HISTORY

In the ancient world Lebanon was important for its pine, fir and cedarwood, much coveted by neighbouring powers, and during the long period of Egyptian, Assyrian, Persian and Seleucid rule the exploitation of the forests of Lebanon was normally a royal privilege. The area was also mined for its iron and copper in the time of the Ptolemies and the Romans. Gradually Lebanon came to have a distinct history of its own, for the mountainous character of the region prevented any complete subjugation to outside authority. It is probable that the Arab conquest of Syria did not include the 'Mountain', to which fled all those who were opposed to the Arab domination. The Caliph Mu'awiya (661–80) made some effort to assert a greater control, but the resistance of the native Aramaean Christians was reinforced by the arrival of the Mardaites from the fastnesses of the Taurus and the Amanus. These Christian nomads, led by Byzantine officers, made determined advances into Lebanon late in the seventh century, and seem to have united with the Maronite Christians who were later to become a Uniate Church of the Roman communion and to have a predominant role in the history of Lebanon. The Caliph Abd al-Malik (685–705) paid tribute to Byzantium in return for a withdrawal of most of the Mardaite forces; but it is clear that the 'Mountain' had begun to assume its historic function of providing a sure refuge for racial and religious minorities.

Lebanon maintained its Christian character until the ninth century when, among other elements, the Arab tribe of Tanukh established a principality in the region of al-Gharb, near Beirut, acting as a counterpoise to the Maronites of northern Lebanon and as a bulwark against Byzantine threats from the sea. Gradually Islam and, more slowly still, the Arabic language penetrated the 'Mountain' where, however, Syriac lingered on in the Maronite districts until the 17th century (it is still spoken in three villages of the Anti-Lebanon). In the ninth and 10th centuries Muslim sects began to establish themselves in the 'Mountain' as, for example, the Shi'a, known in Lebanon under the name of Mitwali, and, in the 11th century, the Druze, which won a firm hold in southern Lebanon.

The Crusaders established in this area the County of Tripolis and the lordships of Gibelet and Batron, which enjoyed considerable support from the Christian population of northern Lebanon and were protected by a network of fortresses, the most famous being Hisn al-Akrad (Crac des Chevaliers). In the Mamluk period the rulers of Lebanon, by continued political ma-

noeuvring, maintained for themselves a considerable degree of autonomy. The Tanukhid amirs, after a long period in which they had matched the Crusaders against the Islamic amirates, had eventually taken the Mamluk side. In northern Lebanon the Maronites, under their bishop, maintained contact with the Italian republics and also with the Roman Curia. Less fortunate were the Druzes and the Mitwali who, in the last years of the 13th century, took advantage of the Mamluk preoccupation with the Mongol threat from Persia and began a protracted revolt which led to widespread devastation in central Lebanon.

THE OTTOMAN PERIOD

In the 16th century the Turcoman family of Assaf and, after them, the Banu Saifa rose to prominence in the area from Beirut to the north of Tripoli; while in the south the Druze house of Ma'an supplanted the Tanukhid amirs. After the conquest of 1516–17 the Ottoman Sultan Selim I had confirmed the amirs of Lebanon in their privileges and had imposed only a small tribute; yet not infrequently there was open conflict with the Ottomans, as in 1584–85 when, after an attack on a convoy bearing the tribute from Egypt to Constantinople, the Sultan Murad III sent a punitive expedition to ravage the lands of the Banu Saifa and of the Druzes.

The power of the House of Ma'an now reached its zenith in the person of Fakhr ad-Din II (1586–1635), who by means of bribery, intrigue, foreign alliance and open force, set out to establish an independent power over the whole of Lebanon and parts of Palestine to the south. To this end he entered into close relations with the Grand Duke of Tuscany, negotiating in 1608 a commercial agreement that incorporated a secret military clause directed against the Sultan. In 1613 a naval and military expedition sent from the Porte (the Ottoman administration in Constantinople) compelled Fakhr ad-Din to seek refuge with his Tuscan ally. He returned in 1618, and within a few years had restored his power to become virtual ruler from Aleppo to the borders of Egypt. The Sultan, heavily engaged in repressing revolt in Anatolia, and in waging a long struggle with Persia, could do no more than recognize the *fait accompli*. Fakhr ad-Din embarked on an ambitious programme of development for Lebanon. He sought to equip a standing army with arms imported from Tuscany. Italian engineers and agricultural experts were employed to promote a better cultivation of the land and to increase production of silk and olives. The Christian peasantry were encouraged to move from northern to southern

Lebanon. Beirut and Sidon flourished as a result of the favour he showed to commerce, and religious missions from Europe (Capuchins, Jesuits, Carmelites) were allowed to settle throughout Syria—a development of great importance for France, which strove to assert a 'protectorate' over all the Catholic and other Christian elements in the Ottoman Empire. However, the ambitions of Fakhr ad-Din were doomed to failure, as by 1632 the Sultan Murad IV assumed effective control at Constantinople. The Pasha of Damascus, supported by a naval squadron, began a campaign to end the independent power of Lebanon, and in 1635 Fakhr ad-Din was executed at Constantinople.

In 1697 the Ma'an family became extinct and was succeeded by the House of Shihab, which maintained its predominance until 1840. In the course of the 18th century, the Shihab amirs gradually consolidated their position against the other factions of the 'Mountain' and for a while recovered control of Beirut. While normally the Shihab took care to remain on good terms with the Turkish pashas of Tripoli, Sidon and Damascus, the pashas themselves strove to exercise an indirect control by fomenting the family rivalries and religious differences that marked the course of Lebanese politics. With the advent of Bashir II (1788–1840) the House of Shihab attained the height of its influence. Not until the death of Ahmad Jazzar, Pasha of Acre (1804), was he free to develop his power, which he maintained by the traditional methods of setting one pasha against the other, and by bribing the officials of the Porte whenever it seemed expedient. In 1810 he helped the Ottomans to repel an invasion by the Wahhabi power of Arabia; but in 1831 he sided openly with Muhammad Ali of Egypt, when that ruler invaded Syria. Holding Lebanon as the vassal of Egypt, he was compelled, however, to apply to the 'Mountain' the unpopular policy imposed by Ibrahim Pasha, the son of Muhammad Ali, with the result that a revolt broke out, which, after the Egyptian withdrawal of 1840, led to his exile. The age of the Lebanese amirs was now at an end: the Ottomans assumed control of the 'Mountain', appointing two Kaimakams to rule there, one Druze and the other Maronite, under the supervision of the pashas of Sidon and Beirut.

The period of direct Ottoman rule saw the rapid growth between the Druzes and the Maronites of a mistrust already visible during the time of the Egyptian dominance, and now fostered by the Ottomans as the only means of maintaining their influence over Lebanon. As a result of social and economic discontent, due to the slow disintegration of the old feudal system which had existed in Lebanon since the Middle Ages, the Maronite peasantry revolted in 1858 and destroyed the feudal privileges of the Maronite aristocracy, thus facilitating the creation of a system of independent smallholdings. The Druze aristocracy, fearing the consequences of a similar discontent among their own Maronite peasantry, made a series of attacks on the Maronites of northern Lebanon, who, owing to their own dissensions, could offer no effective resistance. The dubious attitude of the Turkish pashas, in the face of these massacres of 1860, led to French intervention, and in 1864 to the promulgation of an organic statute for Lebanon, which was now to become an autonomous province under a non-Lebanese Ottoman Christian governor, appointed by the Sultan and approved by the Great Powers. He was to be aided by an elected administrative council and a locally recruited police force. The statute also abolished legal feudalism in the area, thus consolidating the position won by the Maronite peasantry in 1858. The period from 1864 to 1914 was one of increasing prosperity, especially among the Christian elements, who also played an important role in the revival of Arab literature and Arab national feeling during the last years of the 19th century.

THE FRENCH MANDATE

Lebanon's privileged status ended when the Turks entered the war of 1914–18; by 1918 the coastal areas of Lebanon were occupied by British and French forces. In September 1920 the French created the State of Greater Lebanon—which included not only the former autonomous province but also Tripoli, Sidon, Tyre and Beirut, some of which had in earlier times been under the control of the amirs of Lebanon. A Constitution, devised in 1926, proved unworkable and was suspended in 1932, from which time the President of the Republic carried on the admin-

istration. The President was, by convention, a Christian, while the Prime Minister was a Muslim, and both worked towards the achievement of a careful balance between the various religious communities of the new state. Lebanon was not unaffected by the growth of the nationalist movement in Syria, some sections of which demanded the reduction of Lebanon to its pre-war limits and even the abolition of its existence as a separate state. These demands found some support amongst the Sunni Muslims of the areas added to Lebanon proper in 1920, with the result that the Syrian revolt of 1925–26 spread to parts of southern Lebanon. The Maronite Christians, on the whole, supported the idea of a separate Lebanon, but were not united in their attitude towards France on the one hand, and the Arab states on the other. The Franco-Lebanese Treaty of 1936 differed little from that which France negotiated at the same time with Syria, the chief difference being that the military convention gave France wider military powers in Lebanon than in Syria. A reformed Constitution was promulgated in 1937; but the French refusal to ratify the treaty in 1938, and the advent of war prolonged a situation which, if outwardly calm, concealed a considerable discontent beneath the surface. In November 1941 the Free French Commander, General Catroux, formally proclaimed Lebanon a sovereign independent state. In September 1943 a new Parliament with a strong nationalist majority soon came into conflict with the French authorities over the transfer of the administrative services. When, in November 1943, the Lebanese Government approved legislation removing from the Constitution all provisions considered to be inconsistent with the independence of Lebanon, the French delegate-general arrested the President and suspended the Constitution. The other Arab states, together with the United Kingdom and the USA, supported the Lebanese demands, and in 1944 France began to transfer to Lebanese control all important public services, save for the Troupes spéciales (local units under French command), whose transfer the French authorities at first made conditional on the signing of a Franco-Lebanese Treaty. But in 1945 the Troupes spéciales were handed over to Lebanon without such conditions, and an agreement between France and the Lebanese Government in 1946 provided for the withdrawal of French troops.

ECONOMIC DIFFICULTIES

Like the other Arab states, Lebanon was at war with the new State of Israel from May 1948; but negotiated an armistice in March 1949. Just as in Syria the failure of the Arab arms had led eventually to the *coup d'état* of March 1949, so in Lebanon the widespread disillusionment of Arab nationalist hopes prepared the ground for a conspiracy against the Government. This conspiracy was easily suppressed in June 1949 and its leader, Antun Sa'ade, was executed.

The Lebanese Government encountered considerable economic and financial difficulties soon after the end of the 1939–45 war. When, in January 1948, France devalued the franc (to which both the Lebanese and the Syrian currencies were linked) Lebanon, economically weaker than Syria, felt obliged to sign a new agreement with France (February 1948). Syria refused to do so and began a long and complex dispute with Lebanon over the precise nature of the economic and financial arrangements which were to exist between the two states. In March 1950 the Lebanese Government refused a Syrian demand for full economic and financial union. The severance of economic relations which now ensued did not end until the signing, in February 1952, of an agreement for the division of royalties due from oil companies, and for the status, for customs purposes, of agricultural and industrial products passing between the two states.

In September 1952 Lebanon experienced a severe crisis in its internal affairs. Political and economic unrest brought about the fall of the Government and the resignation of President al-Khouri, who had held office since 1943. Charges of corruption were made against the President. During his long tenure of power he had indeed used all the arts of political influence and manoeuvre in order to impose a real degree of unity on a state where the divergent interests of Maronites, Sunni and Shi'a Muslims, Druzes and other religious communities underlined the need for firm and coherent rule. To an even greater degree, however, the crisis was due to causes of an economic order.

Lebanon had attained its independence in the period of war-time prosperity. The end of the war meant a progressive diminution of foreign expenditure in Lebanon, and the gradual disappearance of war shortages which had favoured Lebanese trade. The devaluation of the French franc, the unsuccessful war with Israel, and above all the economic rupture with Syria (the chief source of agricultural goods and principal customers for Lebanese industrial products) gave rise to further difficulties. By 1952 there was much discontent arising from the high cost of living and from considerable unemployment, and it was a loose coalition of all the elements of opposition, both political and economic, which brought about the fall of the al-Khouri regime.

CONSTITUTIONAL REFORM

Camille Chamoun became the new President of the republic. His administration, with the Amir Khalid Chehab as Prime Minister, pledged reforms including changes in the electoral laws, the enfranchisement of women, revision of the press laws and the reorganization of justice. Elections in July 1953 led to the formation of a 44-member chamber of deputies composed on a sectarian basis according to the electoral law of 1952.

Since the foundation of the republic, all seats in the Chamber of Deputies had been distributed among the various religious communities in proportion to their numerical strength. The chamber was thus intended as an institution reflecting the religious and social structure of the state, and was capable of harmonious function provided that the electoral system which maintained a delicate balance between the communities suffered no violent and prejudicial change. At the same time the Chamber contained a strong 'feudal' element—the tribal and religious leaders who, with their trusted retainers, formed powerful groups within the chamber and were often criticized as being 'anti-national' in their aims and methods. To end or at least weaken this 'feudalization' of Lebanese political life, without, however, impairing the equilibrium between the Muslim and Christian communities, had long been the purpose of those who advocated a reasonable and well-considered policy of reform. The law of 1952 created 33 electoral districts (during the previous life of the republic the number had been, as a rule, five) and allotted to 11 of them two seats, and to the remainder one seat each. Of the total of 44 seats, the Maronites were now to receive 13, the Sunni Muslims nine, the Shi'a Muslims eight, the Greek Orthodox Christians five, the Druzes three, the Greek-Melkite Catholics three, the Armenian Catholics two, and the other confessions (Protestant, Jewish, Nestorian, etc.) one seat.

FOREIGN RELATIONS 1953–56

In the period 1953–56 financial and economic relations with Syria remained on a provisional basis much the same as that which had prevailed since 1950, with earlier short-term arrangements being renewed as the need arose. Discussions with Syria in November 1953 over problems of currency, loan policy, banks and exchange difficulties made no effective progress. The Lebanese Government was more successful, however, in its efforts to promote internal development. It was announced in August 1955 that the World Bank had granted to Lebanon a loan of $27m. for the Litani river scheme, which was expected to more than double the electric power available within the republic and also to irrigate a large area in the coastal region. A number of commercial treaties at this time bore witness to the growing penetration of the Eastern bloc into Arab lands.

THE EISENHOWER DOCTRINE

A state of emergency was declared in Lebanon during the Sinai-Suez crisis at the end of October 1956. The Chamber of Deputies announced its support for Egypt, but Lebanon did not break off diplomatic relations with the United Kingdom and France. In November there were disturbances, however, at Tripoli and Beirut against the attitude of the Government. The 'Eisenhower Doctrine', a new programme, announced in January 1957, of US economic and military aid intended as a means of ensuring an anti-Soviet front in the Middle East, evoked a favourable response in Lebanese official circles. Some of the political groups in Lebanon protested against this pro-Western alignment, asserting that it could not fail to isolate Lebanon from the other Arab states (which had declined to accept the terms of the

Doctrine) and thus impair Arab solidarity. None the less, in April the Government obtained from the Chamber of Deputies a vote expressing confidence in its policies. Military equipment granted under the Doctrine began to reach Beirut in June.

The problem of electoral reform had been under consideration in Lebanon in the course of 1956. The main proposal now to be given effect was that the number of seats in the Chamber of Deputies should be raised from 44 to 66. As election time drew near in the summer of 1957, riots in Beirut compelled the Government to call out troops for the maintenance of order. According to reports at this time more than 100 communists were arrested for their part in the disturbances. The tense electoral campaign of June 1957 resulted in a marked triumph for the Government: a first estimate suggested that it might count on the adherence of some three-quarters of the deputies in the new chamber. Of the total of 66 seats, the Maronites now received 20, the Sunni Muslims 14, the Shi'a Muslims 12, the Greek Orthodox Christians seven, the Druzes four, the Greek-Melkite Catholics four, the Orthodox Armenians three, the Armenian Catholics one, and the other religious minorities also one seat.

It became clear that unrest, especially among those elements of the population which opposed the pro-Western policies of the Lebanese Government and favoured an alignment with Egypt and Syria, had not been quelled when further incidents (bombings and assassinations) occurred in November 1957. The Government, in its desire to halt these subversive activities, now imposed a close control over all Palestinian refugees in Lebanon. Indeed, after renewed outbreaks of violence in December, the northern area of Lebanon was declared to be a military sector.

The Lebanese Government stated in March 1958 that it would not join the United Arab Republic (UAR) of Egypt and Syria; the Arab Federation of Iraq and Jordan, or indeed any association that might limit its own independence and sovereignty. Large sections of the Muslim population, both in the north (at Tripoli) and in the south (at Tyre and Sidon), were inclined to be pro-Arab rather than pro-Lebanese in sentiment—a mood greatly stimulated by the emergence of the new UAR and by the propaganda emitted from Cairo and Damascus for the return to Syria of those predominantly Muslim areas that had been joined to the old Lebanon in the time of the French mandate. There was conflict, too, between those who, although reluctant to see Lebanon lose its separate political existence, were none the less strongly opposed to the pro-Western attitude of the Lebanese Government and those who, fearing the possible absorption of Lebanon into the framework of a larger Arab state, felt themselves bound to support fully the policies of the Beirut regime. The danger was real that these complex tensions might escalate in the form of a 'confessional' conflict between Muslims and Christians, in which, if not the continued independence, then at least the entire political orientation of Lebanon would be at stake.

THE CRISIS OF 1958

A reorganization of the Government, carried out in March 1958 and designed to remove those critical of the pro-Western policies of Lebanon who favoured closer co-operation with the UAR, brought no relief to the grave situation then developing. Serious disturbances, originating in Tripoli and the northern areas adjacent to the Syrian border, broke out in the second week of May and spread rapidly to Beirut and also to Tyre and Sidon in southern Lebanon. The Druze population in the south-east was also involved in the disorders, being sharply divided into pro- and anti-Government factions. Hostile demonstrations led to the destruction of the US information service centres at Tripoli and Beirut. At the request of the Lebanese Government, the USA agreed to dispatch in all haste supplies of arms and police equipment and decided at the same time to reinforce the US Sixth Fleet stationed in the Mediterranean. The USSR accused the USA of interference in Lebanese affairs and declared that Western intervention might have grave consequences. The Lebanese Government itself charged the UAR with interference in its internal affairs and appealed for redress to the Arab League—which, meeting at Benghazi in June, failed to agree on a course of action. The problem was brought before the UN, which resolved to send an observer corps to Lebanon.

The Lebanese Government was now, in fact, confronted with a widespread insurrection, in which the Muslim elements in the population were ranged against the Christian elements. The forces opposed to the existing regime controlled parts of Beirut, Tripoli and Sidon, as well as large areas in the north and the south of Lebanon. Attempts to negotiate a settlement led to no favourable result. The Prime Minister, Sami as-Sulh, gave an assurance that President Chamoun did not intend to ask for a constitutional amendment enabling him to seek re-election in September 1958, the date when his present tenure was due to end. To this assurance the leaders of the insurrection replied with a firm demand for the immediate resignation of the President, who made it clear, however, that he would not relinquish his office until September.

On 14 July 1958 (the date of the *coup d'état* which led to a change of regime in Iraq) President Chamoun requested the USA to send US troops into Lebanon to maintain security and preserve Lebanese independence. About 10,000 US troops were dispatched to the Beirut area, and the USA made it known that action on the part of forces under the control of the UAR against US troops in Lebanon might lead to most serious consequences. The USSR and the People's Republic of China made strong protests against the US intervention and asked for the prompt withdrawal of the US forces landed in Lebanon. On 18 August the USA gave a written undertaking to withdraw its troops, either at the request of the Lebanese Government, or in the event of the UN's taking appropriate measures to ensure the integrity and peace of the country. The UN General Assembly thereupon adopted a resolution, framed by its Arab members, providing for the evacuation of US troops under the auspices of the UN and the Arab League.

PRESIDENT CHEHAB, 1958–64

Meanwhile, the Lebanese Chamber of Deputies had, on 31 July 1958, elected as the new President of the state Gen. Fouad Chehab, the Commander-in-Chief of the Lebanese army—a choice supported by members from both sides involved in the internal conflict. He assumed office on 23 September, in succession to President Chamoun, and at once invited Rashid Karami, the leader of the insurgents at Tripoli, to become Prime Minister. An agreement was made on 27 September to the effect that the US forces were to leave Lebanon by the end of October.

In October 1959 the Lebanese Cabinet was increased from four to eight members, so that greater representation might be given to the various political groups. The Chamber of Deputies approved in April 1960 an electoral reform bill, which imposed for the first time the principle of the secret ballot in Lebanese elections and also enlarged the Chamber itself from 66 to 99 deputies—a total figure that maintained the existing ratio (laid down in 1943) of six Christian to every five Muslim (including Druze) deputies in the Chamber. The Chamber was dissolved by President Chehab on 5 May 1960, the Government of Rashid Karami resigning nine days later. A general election was then held in four separate stages on 12, 19 and 26 June and 3 July. The election took place in an atmosphere of complete calm, strict security measures being enforced throughout the various stages of the electoral process. In the new Chamber of Deputies there were 30 Maronite Christians, 20 Sunni Muslims, 19 Shi'a Muslims, 11 Greek Orthodox Christians, six Greek-Melkite Catholics, six Druzes, four Armenian Orthodox Christians, one Armenian Catholic, one Protestant and one member representing other elements. A large number of the 'rebel' personalities prominent in the events of 1958 and hitherto not seated in the Chamber were now returned as members.

A new Government, under the leadership of Saeb Salam, took the oath of office on 2 August 1960. The Cabinet, which included several personalities active on one side or the other in the troubles of 1958, was prompt to reaffirm the traditional policies of non-expropriation, of minimal government intervention in private enterprise, of encouragement for private investment both foreign and domestic, and of currency convertibility. By 1960 Lebanon had recovered, in economic terms, almost completely from the disturbances in 1958.

CABINET REFORM

It had come to be felt, since August 1960, that the Lebanese Cabinet, 18 members strong, was too large for the maintenance of an efficient administration and so, on 22 May 1961, the Prime Minister established a new Cabinet consisting of eight ministers only. However, on 24 October, as the result of a dispute with some members of his Government (notably Kamal Joumblatt, the Druze leader, who was Minister of Works and Planning), Salam resigned. Rashid Karami, a former Prime Minister, formed a new Government on 31 October.

Military elements, acting in conjunction with civilians described as supporters of the extremist Parti socialiste nationaliste, made an unsuccessful attempt, on 31 December 1961, to overthrow the Lebanese Government. The Parti socialiste nationaliste was in fact the old Parti populaire syrien, founded in the 1930s by Antoine Saadé with the aim of uniting several Arab states into a Greater Syria. Its current leader, Dr Abdallah Saadé, was now arrested and the party dissolved by the Lebanese Government on 1 January 1962. The Lebanese Government took firm action against all the elements suspected of involvement in the revolt, and crushed it within a few days.

On 19 February 1964 the Cabinet led by Rashid Karami resigned, after President Chehab had signed a decree dissolving the Chamber of Deputies (elected in 1960) and ordering elections to be held on four successive Sundays from 5 April to 3 May 1964. A caretaker Cabinet was appointed to supervise the elections for the new Chamber of Deputies.

PRESIDENT HÉLOU

Gen. Chehab, whose six-year term of office as President of the republic was due to end in September 1964, rejected all appeals that he should submit himself as a candidate for a second time. Even when the Chamber of Deputies approved a motion in favour of an amendment to the Constitution which would enable him to stand for a further term of office, Gen. Chehab persisted in his refusal. On 18 August Charles Hélou, Minister of Education in the caretaker administration, succeeded Gen. Chehab as President, pledging himself to follow the policies and reforms introduced under his predecessor.

On 25 September 1964 Hussein Oweini, the head of the caretaker Cabinet, formed an administration at the request of President Hélou. The new administration aroused dissatisfaction, however, in the Chamber of Deputies, since, deriving from the Cabinet appointed originally to act as a caretaker during the period of the 1964 elections, it was in fact composed wholly of non-members of the Chamber. Oweini resigned on 13 November and, five days later, gathered together a new Cabinet which, save for himself and the Minister of Foreign Affairs, consisted of members drawn from the Chamber of Deputies and reflected in itself all the main trends of opinion within the Chamber.

FOREIGN RELATIONS

On 20 July 1965 Prime Minister Oweini resigned. There had been much debate in the Chamber of Deputies about a proposed agreement to guarantee private US investment in Lebanon against expropriation, war or revolution—an agreement construed in some political circles as giving to the USA a possible excuse for intervention, at need, in Lebanese affairs. On 26 July Rashid Karami became the new Prime Minister, with a Cabinet of nine ministers, all chosen from outside the Chamber of Deputies.

There was friction during the first months of 1965 between the Federal Republic of Germany and the Arab states because of the decision by Bonn to enter into formal diplomatic relations with Israel. Anti-German demonstrations occurred at Tripoli and Beirut, and on 13 May 1965 Lebanon severed diplomatic relations with West Germany. In May 1965 Lebanon signed an agreement on trade and technical co-operation with the European Economic Community (or European Community—EC). There was some friction between Israel and Lebanon over border incidents during the summer and autumn of 1965. Members of the main Palestinian guerrilla organization, al-Fatah (the Palestine National Liberation Movement), made raids into Israel, provoking Israeli reprisals against the Lebanese village of Noule.

FINANCIAL CRISIS

Rashid Karami modified his Cabinet in December 1965 and January 1966, these changes arising from difficulties which hindered the full implementation of an administrative and judicial reform programme, one of the main advocates of which was President Hélou. Between December 1965 and March 1966 an estimated 150 officials including 100 civil servants were compelled to withdraw from public life. This sustained attempt to curb corruption and the abuse of office in government circles inevitably caused considerable tension. There was strong pressure in the Chamber of Deputies for a return to a Cabinet chosen mainly from the Chamber itself. This and other difficulties obliged Karami to offer his resignation to President Hélou, who appointed Dr Abdallah al-Yafi as the new Prime Minister. Dr al-Yafi assembled a 10-man Cabinet drawn entirely from the Chamber of Deputies with the exception of himself and Philippe Takla, the new Minister of Foreign Affairs. The constitution of the Cabinet represented a balance between the various religious interests and, from the point of view of politics, between the left-wing and right-wing elements in the Chamber of Deputies.

In October 1966 the Intra Bank of Lebanon was compelled to suspend operations, owing to a series of withdrawals amounting to more than £L11m. in the preceding month. One result of that financial crisis was that the Government resolved to discourage the creation of new commercial banks, foreign or Lebanese, for a period of five years. Hitherto there had been an almost complete freedom to establish new banks in Lebanon and there had been a large expansion of the banking system based on the flow into Lebanon of vast oil revenues from Saudi Arabia and from the states of the Persian (Arabian) Gulf.

On 2 December 1966 Dr Abdallah al-Yafi offered the resignation of his Government to President Hélou. Rashid Karami formed a new administration on 7 December. It was composed of figures drawn from outside Parliament, six of whom held ministerial posts for the first time.

In June 1967 the Lebanese Government aligned itself with the Arab states then engaged in war against Israel. On 8 June the Government asked the ambassadors of the United Kingdom and the USA to leave Lebanon. However, the months following the war witnessed a gradual easing of the tensions, and in September 1967 the Lebanese Cabinet agreed to reinstate its ambassadors in Washington and London.

POLITICAL INSTABILITY

Rashid Karami's Cabinet resigned from office in February 1968, whereupon President Hélou asked Dr Abdallah al-Yafi to form an interim administration, whose main task was to be the preparation and conduct of the general election in March 1968. The two most successful parties elected in the Chamber of Deputies were the Maronite-dominated Triple Alliance, of a right-wing complexion, and the Democratic Bloc, aligned further to the left. However, Dr al-Yafi's interim administration remained in office until October, when it was forced to resign, owing to bitter rivalry between the two main political groups, the 'Chamounists' and the 'Chehabists' (both named after former Presidents), disputes over sectional representation in the Cabinet, and the Government's inability to command a majority in the Chamber of Deputies. After a week of confusion, a new four-man Government was announced on 20 October, still headed by Dr al-Yafi.

THE GUERRILLAS AND ISRAEL

The first clash between Lebanese and Israeli forces on the border for over two years took place in May 1968. As the activities of the Palestinian guerrillas intensified, however, Lebanon became increasingly involved as a target for Israel's grievances against the Palestinians. On 26 December an Israeli airliner was machine-gunned by Arab guerrillas at Athens airport. Two days later, Israeli commandos raided Beirut airport and destroyed 13 aircraft, all belonging to Lebanese airlines. The Israeli Government stated that the raid should be regarded as a reprisal for the Athens attack, a warning to the Arab world not to make any repetition of it, and a further warning to Lebanon to police more effectively the activities of Palestinian *fedayin* (freedom fighters) in the country. The financial cost to Lebanon was relatively small, as most of the aircraft were insured abroad. The major after-effects of the raid were, firstly, the widespread criticism that it attracted even from countries normally favourable to Israel. Lebanon was viewed as a country

which had taken little active part in the campaign against Israel, while the Palestinian *fedayin* within it were only enjoying the freedom available to them in Lebanon's open, tolerant society. The UN Security Council unanimously condemned Israel for the raid. The second effect was the fall of the Government on 7 January 1969, its alleged lack of preparedness for Israeli aggression dealing the final blow to a weak administration. On 20 January, after much political manoeuvring, a new Government was formed under Rashid Karami, who thus became Prime Minister for the seventh time.

This Government was immediately confronted with the basic problems underlying the Lebanese situation, foremost among these the Christian-Muslim balance. In theory, both religions were equally represented in Lebanon, but no census had been held since 1939 mainly because the authorities feared that the balance had shifted to a 60% Muslim predominance, which would seriously affect the political situation. (Indeed, according to 1983 estimates, the Muslim population of Lebanon, both Shi'a and Sunni, was 1.95m., while the combined Maronite and Greek Orthodox Christian communities numbered 1.15m.) The Christian community had a disproportionate share of the wealth and important positions, was generally conservative by Arab standards and took a moderate position on the Israel question. The less privileged Muslim majority was more in favour of both domestic reform (Lebanon had, for example, only the beginnings of a welfare state) and of a more militant position towards Israel. Early in 1969 numbers of Syrian guerrillas entered the country and spent as much time in action against the Lebanese army as against Israel. Unrest also appeared amongst the 260,000 Palestinian refugees in the Sidon camp; part of the frontier with Syria was eventually closed. Numerous strikes and demonstrations continued. The Karami Government felt unable to maintain the necessary coalition from the two communities and their various factions and resigned on 25 April. However, it continued to function as a caretaker administration as no stronger government could be formed.

In the late summer of 1969 a number of guerrilla groups were reported to have moved to new bases better sited for attacks on Israel, which continued to raid these bases in reprisal; the combination of these factors created some friction between the guerrillas and the Lebanese army. In October the army apparently attacked some of these camps in an attempt to restrict or direct their activities. This caused a political crisis in which the caretaker Government resigned, claiming that it had not authorized the army's actions, and the President and the armed forces administered the country directly. Radical elements and guerrillas took over Tripoli, the second largest city, for several days, and most of the Palestinian refugee camps were fully converted into military training and equipment centres. Militant support for the guerrillas was voiced throughout the Arab world, and there were threats of military intervention by Syria and Iraq.

On 2 November 1969 the Lebanese Commander-in-Chief and Yasser Arafat, the leader of al-Fatah, signed a cease-fire agreement in Cairo. This restricted the guerrillas' freedom of movement to certain areas; as further defined in January 1970, it also provided that camps had to be set up some distance from towns, that military training must cease in refugee camps, and that guerrillas must enter Israel before engaging in hostilities. The intention was not to impede guerrilla attacks, but to prevent innocent Lebanese from being injured, and their property from being damaged, by Israeli counter-attacks. The calmer atmosphere that followed the cease-fire enabled Karami to form another Cabinet towards the end of November. There was much concern about the weakness of the country's southern defences, and in January 1970 the new ministry felt strong enough to dismiss the Commander-in-Chief of the army, appointing instead Brig. Jean Njeim. In March there was a series of street battles in the Beirut area between the Palestinian guerrillas and militant right-wing Phalangist groups, but the Government and the army managed to avoid becoming involved. In May Israel launched a major air and ground attack on guerrilla positions in southern Lebanon, and occupied a substantial area for nearly two days. Syria sent air assistance for the small Lebanese air force.

POLITICAL CRISES

Sulayman Franjiya was elected President in August 1970, and a new Cabinet was formed by Saeb Salam. Some measures of political liberalization, such as the relaxation of media censorship and the removal of the ban on extremist parties, did little to curb domestic unrest. Strikes and demonstrations against unemployment and inflation, student disorders and fighting between Phalangists and the Parti populaire syrien continued throughout 1971. The parliamentary elections of April 1972 reflected a marked swing towards left-wing political groups.

The Palestinian guerrillas remained Lebanon's major problem. Their bases in the refugee camps became more important following the expulsion of the guerrillas from Jordan in July 1971, and guerrilla operations against Israel produced violent Israeli reprisals. The villages of southern Lebanon bore the brunt of Israeli raids, and their inhabitants secured a greater measure of Lebanese army control over guerrilla activities in March 1972. Arab terrorist actions still provoked Israeli reprisals against Lebanon, even when there was little connection between the terrorists and Israel's vulnerable northern neighbour. The killing of Israeli athletes at the Olympic Games in Munich, West Germany, in September 1972 led to Israeli ground and air attacks on guerrilla bases, in which the Lebanese army suffered a number of casualties. The Lebanese Government was unable to persuade the guerrillas to suspend their activities against Israel, and several clashes between the Lebanese army and the guerrillas occurred.

In February 1973 Israeli commandos attacked guerrilla training bases in refugee camps about 160 km north of the Lebanese frontier, and escaped virtually unopposed. A further Israeli raid, in which three guerrilla leaders were shot in their homes in the centre of Beirut, and an attempt to blow up oil storage tanks at the Zahrani terminal, attributed to Palestinian extremists, resulted in the fall of the Salam Government. Salam resigned, frustrated at the inability of the Lebanese armed forces to prevent an Israeli military action in the capital, and Dr Amin Hafez formed a new Government. Several members of the Salam Cabinet remained in office, the new Government including representatives of most of the major political and religious groups.

Tension between the Lebanese army and the guerrillas culminated in May 1973 in Lebanese ground and air attacks on the refugee camps. An invasion by guerrillas based in Syria was repulsed, and a cease-fire was brought about by the mediation of other Arab states. The guerrillas apparently agreed to stop their terrorist activities within Lebanon and to cease using the camps for training guerrillas.

The Hafez Government lasted only seven weeks. The Prime Minister resigned on 14 June 1973, unable to settle the Sunni Muslim claim for a greater share in the allocation of government posts, and it was not until 8 July that Taki ed-Din Solh was able to form a new administration. A moderate, Solh enjoyed the support of many Sunni factions, and his Cabinet included representatives of all the main religious blocs. Outside Parliament, however, violent disorders continued, with industrial disputes resulting in demonstrations and clashes with police.

The potential religious hostility within Lebanon, and the political implications of the division of government and administrative posts on a confessional basis, were again evidenced in February 1974. Civil service reforms, intended to overcome the sectarian nature of certain appointments, were opposed by Maronites who feared that they would lose posts traditionally reserved for their community. The liberal reformist Parti national libéral threatened to withdraw its three cabinet members, and the proposed reforms were also condemned by the Phalange and the Bloc national. The Shi'a Muslims of southern Lebanon also made demands for increased representation and more investment and development in the south. The Shi'a leader, Imam Moussa as-Sadr, implied that he would organize his followers and arm them as protection against Israeli raids—as, indeed, he later did.

Although Lebanon was not directly involved in the October 1973 Arab–Israeli war, southern regions had continued to serve as a guerrilla base and to suffer Israeli reprisals. Southern villages were shelled intermittently, and small-scale raids across the border and acts of terrorism became commonplace.

In July 1974 there were clashes between Palestinians and Phalangists who continued to demand more government controls on guerrilla activities. Throughout 1974 and into 1975 Israeli shelling, air raids and incursions into Lebanon persisted, as did guerrilla attacks against the Israelis. Consequently the situation on the border remained tense. In September 1974, unable to curb internal sectarian violence by its ineffective ban on the possession of firearms, Taki ed-Din Solh's Cabinet resigned. In October a new Government was formed under Rashid Solh, although violence continued, finally erupting in a bloody clash between troops and citizens of the port of Sidon. The Cabinet split over the granting of a Muslim demand to confer citizenship to long-time residents of the country. Letter-bomb and dynamite explosions and further border fighting between the Israelis and guerrilla groups were followed by further fierce conflict between the Phalangists and Palestinians, in which over 150 died. Much damage was caused in Beirut, and, after an agreement by Solh to normalize relations with the Palestinians and the fact that the security forces had not intervened in the fighting, the Phalangists appeared to be on the defensive.

CIVIL WAR

Intercommunal strife had never been far from the surface in Lebanon. In February 1975 a demonstration in Sidon by a group of Muslim fishermen, in protest at the granting of what they perceived to be unduly advantageous fishing rights to a Christian-owned company (chaired by former President Camille Chamoun), escalated into clashes with the Lebanese army. Tensions were heightened as the apparent intervention of Palestinian elements on the side of the Muslims convinced Christian groups, notably the Phalangists, that the Palestinians—whose presence in Lebanon was already making the country vulnerable to Israeli attack—were now interfering in internal Lebanese affairs. Following an incident in April 1975, when Palestinians made an attack on some Phalangists, the Phalangists killed the passengers of a bus, who were mainly Palestinians. Intercommunal fighting between Christians and Muslims quickly spread. At this point the official policy of Yasser Arafat's Palestine Liberation Organization (PLO) was to stand aloof from the conflict, and Arafat himself was, in fact, instrumental in securing some of the many cease-fires of subsequent months.

In May 1975, shortly after the fighting began, Rashid Solh resigned as Prime Minister, and was replaced by Rashid Karami, who continued as Prime Minister through an exceedingly turbulent period until December 1976. In September 1975 a national dialogue committee was formed, consisting of 20 members from all political and confessional groups, to try to restore 'normal life'—a task in which they were unsuccessful. By October there was evident dissatisfaction with President Franjiya and his inability to bring the fighting to an end, and it also became increasingly evident that, in spite of the official policy of the PLO not to interfere in the internal affairs of Lebanon, members of extremist Palestinian groups, particularly those of the 'rejectionist front', were being drawn into the fighting on the side of the Muslims. It was also, at this point, the official policy of the Lebanese army not to intervene, although, later, breakaway groups became involved in the fighting. By early 1976 the PLO was becoming increasingly embroiled in the conflict, and several Syrian-based units of the Palestine Liberation Army were fighting in Lebanon on the side of the Muslims. Under these increasingly ominous conditions the term of the Chamber of Deputies was extended by a year (later increased to two years) and the general elections scheduled for April 1976 were postponed for up to 26 months. In January 1978 the Chamber's term was extended until June 1980. In March 1979 the Chamber was renamed the National Assembly and in April 1980 its term was further extended to the middle of 1983.

A temporary cease-fire gave a brief respite in January 1976, but by March no agreement had been reached on political reforms, fighting had flared up again, and 70 deputies signed a petition seeking President Franjiya's resignation. Further weight was given to this request in April, when a parliamentary session took place and 90 deputies voted unanimously to amend Article 73 of the Constitution to allow presidential elections to be held up to six months before the expiry of the incumbent's term of office. Franjiya signed this amendment on 23 April, but, in spite of the election of his successor, refused to resign until the completion of his term of office in September 1976, when he was succeeded by Elias Sarkis, who had been Governor of the central bank.

INCREASED SYRIAN INTERVENTION

By May 1976 Syria was becoming increasingly involved in Lebanese affairs: it was estimated that about 40,000 Syrian-controlled troops were in Lebanon at this time. Yasser Arafat had ordered pro-Damascus Palestinian units to withdraw, and it now became clear that Arafat and the PLO had become entirely sympathetic to the Lebanese left-wing. In early June Syria launched a full-scale invasion of Lebanon officially to end the civil war and restore peace, but unofficially, it became clear, to crush the Palestinians. The conflict threatened to assume an international dimension, and an emergency meeting of Arab ministers of foreign affairs was convened in Cairo under the sponsorship of the Arab League. It was agreed to send a joint Arab peace-keeping force to Lebanon, to be accompanied by a phased, but not complete, withdrawal of Syrian troops. The force was to include participants from Syria, Libya, Algeria, Sudan, Saudi Arabia and the PLO, under an Egyptian Commander-in-Chief, but by the end of June 1976 the 1,000-strong force was effectively made up of 500 Syrian troops and 500 Libyans. Meanwhile, fierce fighting broke out in the area of two Palestinian refugee camps, Tal az-Zaatar and Jisr al-Basha, and most of Beirut was without water or electricity. The Arab League took steps to hasten the arrival of further contingents of the peace-keeping force, but fighting continued unabated until October 1976, when Arab summit meetings in Riyadh and Cairo secured a lasting cease-fire. During the course of the fighting there had been more than 50 abortive cease-fires and it was estimated that some 60,000 people had been killed and around 100,000 injured.

The Riyadh and Cairo summits arranged for a 30,000-strong, mainly-Syrian Arab Deterrent Force (ADF) to police Lebanon, and a four-party disengagement committee was established to attempt to implement the terms of the 1969 Cairo agreement between the Lebanese Government and the Palestinian guerrillas—considered to be one of the keys to an enduring peace. The committee began by restricting the level of heavy weapons allowed to the various factions, and then sought an agreement on the proportion of armed elements allowed in the Palestinian guerrilla camps. The Shtaura Agreement of July 1977 attempted to settle this problem by endeavouring to regulate the Palestinian base camps and to introduce a reconstituted Lebanese army into the border area.

In December 1976 President Sarkis appointed as Prime Minister Dr Selim al-Hoss, who formed a Cabinet of eight technocrats charged with rebuilding and reconstruction; and the Government was granted the power to rule by decree for six months, subsequently extended. A Council for Development and Reconstruction was established, and this council took over the functions of the former Ministry of Planning. In January 1977 censorship was imposed on the press, initially both on Lebanese and foreign journalists, but restrictions on foreign dispatches were soon removed.

The Druze chief and leader of the Lebanese left, Kamal Joumblatt, was assassinated on 16 March 1977. Although his murder was followed by a wave of revenge killings, it did not lead to any renewed outbreak of major fighting. However, the southern area of Lebanon, between the Litani river and the Israeli border, became the scene of renewed fighting during 1977. This area was largely spared during the civil war, and fighting developed when the Palestinians moved to the hills of southern Lebanon after being subdued by the Syrians in the civil war. A war 'by proxy' developed, with Syria allied with the Palestine guerrillas and Israel supporting the Lebanese Government. The Shtoura Agreement of July and a later cease-fire in September, arranged with the intervention of the USA, were ineffective.

The volatile situation flared up in March 1978 as a result of a raid by al-Fatah guerrillas into Israel on 11 March, when, in an attack on a bus near Tel-Aviv, more than 35 people were killed. In retaliation, and in order to prevent further raids, Israeli forces advanced into southern Lebanon three days later.

On 19 March the UN Security Council adopted a Resolution (425) demanding that Israel cease its military action against Lebanese territorial integrity and withdraw its forces from Lebanese territory forthwith, and establishing a United Nations Interim Force in Lebanon (UNIFIL) to confirm the withdrawal and assist in the restoration of peace and the restoration of Lebanese government authority in the affected area. In May the Security Council endorsed a proposal to increase the eventual strength of UNIFIL from the 4,000 troops originally envisaged to 6,000. Israeli forces withdrew from southern Lebanon in June 1978, but relinquished control in southern border areas not to UNIFIL but to a right-wing, mainly-Christian Lebanese militia under the command of Maj. Saad Haddad.

In July 1978 fighting erupted again in Beirut between the Syrian troops of the Arab deterrent force and right-wing Christian militias. A cease-fire was proclaimed in early October and the ministers responsible for foreign affairs of the states participating in the Arab deterrent force (Kuwait, Lebanon, Qatar, Saudi Arabia, Sudan, Syria and the UAE) met at Beiteddin, near Beirut, and agreed on a declaration intended to bring peace to the area. It maintained that Lebanese central authority must be imposed, that armed militias must be curbed and that a truly national army must be formed.

LEBANON AFTER THE BEITEDDIN DECLARATION

The aims of the Beiteddin Declaration were not realized. In April 1979 Maj. Haddad proclaimed 'independent free Lebanon'—a slice of territory, covering about 1,800 sq km, next to the Israeli border. Encouraged and supplied by Israel, Haddad was able to maintain his 'independence'. In July 1980 the Phalangist Commander, Bachir Gemayel, consolidated his power by overcoming the militia of the Parti national libéral. This led to a strengthening of the Phalangist militia, with the result that Phalangist forces occupied the town of Zahle in the Beka‘a valley. In April 1981 fighting developed between Syrian troops of the ADF and Christian militias in the Beirut area, and Syrian and Palestinian forces besieged Zahle. Syria maintained that Zahle and the Beka‘a valley were essential for the security and defence of Syria against Israel, whereas the Phalangist forces sought the removal of Syrian forces from Lebanon.

During the remainder of April 1981 Israeli forces made frequent raids into southern Lebanon and Israeli aircraft strafed Palestinian guerrilla targets. When, at the beginning of May, two Syrian helicopters were destroyed by Israeli aircraft, Syria introduced surface-to-air missle (SAM) launchers into the Beka‘a valley. Although it was thought that Israeli aircraft already had the capacity to withstand the outdated SAM missiles, the Israeli Prime Minister, Menachem Begin, adopted a very belligerent stance and threatened to destroy the missiles. An international crisis developed, but on 30 June Syrian forces ended the siege on Zahle, after mediation by the Saudi and Kuwaiti ambassadors to Lebanon. Regular troops of the Lebanese army then occupied positions in the town as the Phalangist militia withdrew. The US Middle East peace envoy, Philip Habib, was able to arrange a cease-fire which became effective on 24 July.

As during previous crises, the Lebanese Government, undermined by the divided interests imposed on its composition by the Constitution, was not able to exert its authority. In July 1979 Prime Minister al-Hoss introduced a Cabinet of 12 members, seven of whom were deputies, to replace the Government which had been in office since December 1976. In April 1980 the National Assembly voted to extend its term by three years, to 30 June 1983 (rather than by 18 months as the Government desired). President Sarkis tried to formulate a national accord. On 5 March 1980 he issued a 'message to the nation' which reiterated his policy for the future: the unity, independence and sovereignty of the whole territory; total opposition to ministates and militias; allegiance to parliamentary democracy; acknowledgement that Lebanon was an Arab country; rejection of the Camp David agreements between Egypt and Israel; support for a future Palestinian state; co-operation with Syria; and support for UN resolutions concerning Lebanon.

On 7 June 1980 Dr al-Hoss offered his resignation, on the grounds that no progress had been made towards achieving accord on those principles. On 16 July Sarkis accepted al-Hoss's resignation; he appointed Takieddin Solh as Prime Minister, but the latter soon resigned, unable to form a government. It was not until October that Chafic al-Wazzan was able to form a Cabinet.

ISRAEL'S 1982 INVASION OF LEBANON

The 1981 cease-fire lasted until the following spring, when fresh Israeli air raids, which provoked PLO shelling of northern Israel, culminated in a full-scale invasion of Lebanon by the Israeli army. On 6 June 1982 Israeli forces attacked on three fronts. While one column pursued the Syrian army, which was retreating up the Beka'a valley, the most serious fighting took place against PLO forces around Beaufort Castle and along the coast. The Israelis preceded their attacks with bombardments that devastated many Lebanese towns and villages. Parts of Tyre, Sidon, Damour and Nabatiyah were almost obliterated by Israeli bombing raids. Civilian casualties among both Lebanese and Palestinians were enormous—according to *The Times* of London's correspondent in Beirut, about 14,000 people, at least 80% of them civilians, were killed during the first fortnight of the war.

The confrontation between the Maronite Christians and the alliance of radical Arab nationalists and Palestinians, which had been at the heart of the civil war of 1975–76, survived the Israeli invasion. The militia of the National Movement, in particular the Sunni Murabitoun and the Shi'ite Amal, fought alongside the PLO in the south and later in Beirut. The Phalangists, however, welcomed the invasion, although they did not take part in the actual fighting. During Israel's siege of west Beirut, which lasted two months, the Phalangists and Maj. Saad Haddad's militiamen acted as auxiliaries for the Israelis. The Maronites also shared Israel's political aims, demanding the expulsion of the PLO from Lebanon and the removal of Syrian troops. During July and August, while the Israelis kept up an almost continuous bombardment of west Beirut, negotiations took place between Americans, Israelis, Lebanese and Palestinians. The PLO commitment to withdrawal from the city, effected at the end of August, was negotiated by US diplomats through the mediation of former Lebanese Prime Minister Saeb Salam.

PRESIDENTIAL ELECTIONS

Bachir Gemayel, the younger son of Pierre Gemayel (the founder of the Phalangist Party and commander of the Lebanese Forces—LF—militia), had announced his presidential ambitions well in advance of the election. In peace-time there would have been no chance of his winning, but in the aftermath of the Israeli invasion he emerged as the obvious candidate. He was the strongest Maronite leader and the one most acceptable to the Israelis. Although Gemayel faced considerable opposition from the Muslim deputies, many of whom boycotted the voting, he succeeded in being elected on 23 August. Three weeks later, before he had assumed power, he (with up to 60 others) was killed in a bomb explosion at the Phalangist Party headquarters. On the following day, 15 September, the Israeli army moved into Beirut, and on 16 September Phalangist militiamen, unhindered by the Israelis, entered the Palestinian refugee camps of Sabra and Chatila and began a massacre of their inhabitants (see Arab-Israeli Relations 1967–98, p. 45).

A week after the assassination of Bachir Gemayel, his elder brother, Amin, was elected President. Amin was a Phalangist deputy with a reputation as a moderate, and his election was welcomed by many Muslims who hoped that he would be able to control the extremist elements inside the Phalangist Party. The problems confronting him were enormous. Lebanon was still occupied by two foreign armies and violence was continuing in many areas. After the Sabra/Chatila massacre the Israelis withdrew from Beirut—but only as far as the airport, just south of the city, from where they consolidated their hold on the southern half of the country. The north of Lebanon was still dominated by the Syrian army which refused to withdraw from the country until the Israelis did so. Towards the end of the year there was savage fighting between pro- and anti-Syrian forces in Tripoli, while in the Chouf area, where the Israelis were in control, there were frequent battles between Phalangists and Druze militiamen. The Government was in control of only a small area of central Lebanon, but even there it was often unable to assert authority.

TALKS BETWEEN ISRAEL AND LEBANON

After insistent pressure from the US Government, talks between the Israeli and Lebanese Governments finally commenced at the beginning of 1983. The Israelis eventually dropped their insistence that talks should take place in Jerusalem, and it was agreed that the two sides would meet alternately at Khalde in Lebanon and Kiryat Shmona in Israel. Israel's demands included security arrangements that would allow Israel to keep military bases inside Lebanon, a predominant role for Saad Haddad in the reconstituted Lebanese army, and relations with Lebanon that stopped only just short of a formal peace treaty. All these demands were rejected by the Lebanese, and the USA also considered them to be excessive. On 22 February US President Ronald Reagan offered to guarantee the security of Israel's northern border once the army had withdrawn, but the proposal was rejected by the Israeli Government.

The negotiations remained stalled until the end of April 1983, when the US Secretary of State, George Shultz, made his first visit to the area. He was able to persuade the two sides to sign an agreement on 17 May which provided for the withdrawal of Israeli forces from Lebanon. However, the Israeli Government announced that it would not be bound by the agreement unless Syria also agreed to withdraw its forces from the Beka'a valley. Shultz returned to the Middle East in July, but during a visit to Damascus he was unable to persuade President Assad to agree to a withdrawal. The Syrian Government declared that it would not accept an agreement which it believed was in the interest only of Israel and the USA; nor was it prepared to support President Gemayel's attempt to extend his control over the areas occupied by Syrian and Israeli forces. In July, as violence between Phalangist and Druze militias intensified in the Chouf, an opposition front was established to confront Gemayel. Calling itself the National Salvation Front, and relying entirely on Syrian support, it consisted of Walid Joumblatt, the Druze leader, former Prime Minister Rashid Karami and ex-President Sulayman Franjiya, one of the chief opponents of the Gemayel family.

ISRAELI REDEPLOYMENT

In July 1983 Israel, its casualties at the hands of the contending militias increasing, decided to redeploy its forces south of Beirut along the Awali river. The Israeli redeployment took place at the beginning of September, and by the end of the year the Israeli troop presence had been reduced from 30,000 to 10,000. However, owing to a lack of co-ordination between the Israeli and Lebanese armies in the handing over of military control of the vacated areas, a full-scale war erupted between the Druze and Christian militias in the Chouf mountains. In the southern, Israeli-occupied part of what had become, effectively, a partitioned country, Maj. Saad Haddad's 'South Lebanon Army' (SLA), armed and trained by Israel, was employed as a police force, intended progressively to assume the duties of the Israeli forces. (Haddad died in December 1983 and his successor, Maj.-Gen. Antoine Lahad, was appointed in March 1984.) Israeli personnel were a constant target of guerrilla attacks and, in order to reduce their exposure, as well as the burden of military supervision, the Israelis resorted to arming local militias, of whatever religious character, so that they could be responsible for the policing of their own areas. However, this effectively meant that arms provided by the Israelis were turned on them. Israel launched several punitive air raids against Palestinian positions in the Syrian-controlled Beka'a valley, in retaliation against the attacks of PLO guerrillas infiltrating from the north, and there were rumours that PLO fighters were returning to Beirut.

THE REVOLT AGAINST ARAFAT

From September 1983 the struggle for control of al-Fatah between the forces of its leader, Yasser Arafat (Chairman of the PLO), and those of the Syrian-backed rebels Abu Musa and Abu Saleh, which had begun in the Beka'a valley in May, was concentrated around Arafat's last stronghold, the northern Lebanese port of Tripoli. After months of bitter fighting, in which many Lebanese civilians, as well as Palestinian guerrillas, were killed or wounded, a truce was arranged through Saudi and Syrian mediation. This allowed Arafat and 4,000 of his supporters to leave Tripoli in December aboard five Greek-registered ships, under UN protection, bound for Algeria, Tunisia and the Yemen Arab Republic.

THE NATIONAL RECONCILIATION CONFERENCE

After the Israeli withdrawal, the 5,800-strong multinational force (comprising mainly French, Italian and US personnel), left to keep the peace between the various factions in Beirut, in the absence of an effective Lebanese army, was gradually drawn into the fighting. It came under attack from Muslim militiamen who were suspicious of its role in bolstering a Christian-led government, and of the presence off shore of massive, predominantly US, naval support. In the two most devastating incidents, 241 US and 58 French marines were killed in almost simultaneous suicide bombings, responsibility for which was claimed by two militant Shi'a groups, on 23 October 1983.

The inter-factional fighting in Beirut was punctuated by numerous short-lived cease-fires. The most successful of these began on 26 September 1983 and was accompanied by the resignation of Chafic al-Wazzan, who hoped to make way for a government of national unity. He was persuaded to remain in office, but these events were the prelude to a Conference of National Reconciliation, held in Geneva, Switzerland, from 31 October to 4 November. These talks were attended by most of the interested Lebanese parties, including the Shi'ite Amal militia, led by Nabih Berri, and the representatives of the National Salvation Front, which had been proclaimed, with Syrian backing, in July by the Druze leader, Walid Joumblatt (the son of Kamal Joumblatt, assassinated in 1977), in alliance with ex-President Franjiya, a pro-Syrian Maronite Christian, and former Prime Minister Rashid Karami, a Sunni Muslim. The conference effectively foundered on President Gemayel's refusal to do more than 'freeze' the 17 May agreement with Israel, rather than to abrogate the pact (as Syria wished) and risk losing US support for his Government. Broad agreement was reached, however, on the need for constitutional changes which would give Muslims representation in the Government commensurate with their majority status in the country.

In early February 1984, following abortive Saudi-mediated attempts to implement a comprehensive security agreement in Beirut, factional fighting developed with greater intensity than before, with the multinational force and the Lebanese army apparently powerless to prevent it. To the Muslim community, the reconstituted Lebanese army, armed and trained by the USA, appeared to be nothing more than an instrument to be used against them by the Christian President in co-operation with the Christian Phalangist militia. President Gemayel had refused to give the Amal leader, Nabih Berri, a post in the Cabinet, while Walid Joumblatt was openly committed to the President's removal. Muslim members of the army, unwilling to fight against their co-religionists, began to defect to the militias, while the Druze and Shi'ite forces co-operated in fighting the army. Chafic al-Wazzan (a Sunni Muslim) and the entire Cabinet tendered their resignation on 5 February. Shortly afterwards the USA, Italy and the United Kingdom decided to withdraw their peace-keeping troops from the multinational force. (The French troops were withdrawn in March.)

LEBANON ABROGATES THE 17 MAY AGREEMENT

By February 1984, Beirut was divided by the militias, east and west, along the so-called 'Green Line', into Christian- and Muslim-controlled sectors. On 16 February, with west Beirut in Shi'ite hands, with the army sustaining defeats south of the capital, and with his Government in effective control only of the eastern part of the city, Amin Gemayel offered, under the terms of a Saudi peace plan, to abrogate the 17 May agreement with Israel and to give greater government representation to Muslims; the President also proposed the formation of a government of national unity to institute the planned reforms of the Constitution. These proposals, which entailed the simultaneous withdrawal of all foreign forces from Lebanon and new security arrangements with Israel for southern Lebanon, proved to be unacceptable not only to Syria and to Gemayel's Muslim opponents, who largely took their lead from Syria (which equipped the Druze militia), but also to the Christian parties

which were committed to the agreement with Israel as a means to preserve their dominance in Lebanese politics.

Finally, on 5 March 1984, bowing to Syria's influence in Lebanese affairs, President Gemayel abrogated the 17 May agreement in return for guarantees of internal security from President Assad of Syria. On the same day, Chafic al-Wazzan's Cabinet withdrew its resignation, and one week later the National Reconciliation Conference was reconvened in Lausanne, Switzerland. It failed to produce the results for which Syria had hoped. Moreover, it saw the beginning of the disintegration of the Lebanese National Salvation Front, as former President Franjiya vetoed Syrian plans for constitutional changes in Lebanon involving the diminution of the powers of the President, by convention a Maronite Christian post. The Conference broke up, having agreed another cease-fire and recommended the formation of a government of national unity—though the composition of such a government was still undecided. (A movement replacing the National Salvation Front was announced in Damascus in March, including Walid Joumblatt, George Hawi, leader of the Parti communiste libanais, Assem Qansou, leader of the al-Baath party, Inaam Raad, leader of the Parti nationaliste syrien, and representatives of the Socialist Union and Arab Democratic parties, but not Nabih Berri of Amal.)

THE GOVERNMENT OF NATIONAL UNITY

At talks in Damascus in April 1984, President Assad of Syria approved plans for a Lebanese government of national unity, giving equal representation to Christians and Muslims, proposed to him by President Gemayel. Gemayel chose Rashid Karami, who had held the post on 10 previous occasions, as Prime Minister of the new Government, which was proclaimed on 30 April. Karami announced his principal aims as being the ending of the Israeli occupation of the south; the restoration of civil order; and the reformation of the Constitution to reflect the majority status of Lebanon's Muslims. On 30 April, without first consulting the appointees, Prime Minister Karami announced a 10-member Cabinet consisting of five leading members each from the Christian and Muslim communities. Nabih Berri, designated Minister of Water and Electrical Resources and Justice, refused to participate in the Government unless some provision were made in it for dealing with the predominantly Shi'ite area of southern Lebanon occupied by the Israelis. A Ministry of State for Affairs of the South and Reconstruction was duly created, to which Nabih Berri was appointed on 7 May. The other appointees having accepted their posts, the Cabinet thus included the leaders of all Lebanon's main religious groups: only former President Franjiya, who was bitterly opposed to Pierre Gemayel and Camille Chamoun, both of whom were included in the Cabinet, refused to give his support to the Government. His son-in-law, Abdullah ar-Rassi, who had been made Minister of the Interior, boycotted Cabinet meetings in support of Franjiya's call for the dismissal of these two.

The new Government won the approval of the National Assembly in June 1984. Fighting in Beirut between Christian and Muslim militias had not ceased, however, and it was not until Syrian Vice-President Abd al-Halim Khaddam intervened to mediate between the two sides that a cease-fire took effect; this finally allowed the terms of a security plan, providing for the reorganization of the army and the disengagement of the rival militias, to be drawn up. An all-party Military Council, consisting of one member from each of the main religious groups, was established to supervise the reintegration of the 37,000-strong army and the disengagement of the militias. Brig.-Gen. Michel Awn (a Maronite Christian) was made Commander-in-Chief of the armed forces, with a Druze, Maj.-Gen. Nadim Hakim, as Chief of Staff. (Hakim died in a helicopter crash in August and was replaced by Maj.-Gen. Abu Dargham.) A new body, the Directorate of Internal Security, was placed under the control of a Shi'ite general, Uthman Uthman. Future appointments in the army would be distributed equally between Christians and Muslims.

The security plan was put into operation at the beginning of July 1984. Three army brigades began to take control of militia positions along the 'Green Line' and in the port and airport of Beirut. The militias had earlier removed their heavy weaponry from the area and there was virtually no opposition to the implementation of the plan, even from the Phalangist militia which had bitterly opposed what it viewed as pro-Syrian, anti-Christian developments in Lebanese politics. The port and airport, closed since February, were reopened in mid-July, and more crossing points between the east and west of Beirut were also cleared.

However, Muslim and Druze dissatisfaction with the Government's lack of progress on constitutional reform, despite the Syrian influence on President Gemayel, led to sporadic fighting between rival Muslim and Christian militias and, occasionally, between Shi'a and Sunni Muslims belonging, respectively, to the Amal and Murabitoun militias. Troops of the Lebanese army failed to gain control of the city, although they reduced fighting along the 'Green Line'. President Gemayel's efforts to gain agreement on constitutional reform, already constrained by his fear of alienating his Christian supporters, were further handicapped by disagreements within the Cabinet. Walid Joumblatt maintained a torrent of vituperation against Gemayel, and in September 1984 vetoed the extension of the security plan along the southern coastal road and into the Druze bastion of the Chouf mountains, as he regarded the Lebanese army as merely a tool of the Christian Phalangists.

In September 1984 the Cabinet, which was agreed on the principle of increasing the number of members in the National Assembly to allow an equal representation for Christians and Muslims, appeared to have approved a total membership of 122 (from 99) but then failed to reach agreement on the number of members who would represent the various groups within the two major religious communities. Joseph Hashim, who became Minister of Posts, Telecommunications, Health and Social Affairs in September (succeeding Pierre Gemayel, who had died in August), caused further protest by demanding that the Maronite Christians form the largest single group in the Assembly. A 40-member committee, representing Muslims and Christians in equal numbers, was appointed to draw up proposals for political reforms. Ex-President Franjiya agreed to be represented on this committee, thus ending his boycott of the Government of National Unity.

Also in September 1984, Syrian mediation settled a feud in the northern port of Tripoli between the pro-Syrian Arab Democratic Party (known as the 'Red Knights') and the anti-Syrian, Sunni Muslim, Tawheed Islami (the Islamic Unification Movement), enabling a security plan to be implemented there.

In Beirut, sporadic violence continued and, at the end of October 1984, Walid Joumblatt (who was boycotting Cabinet meetings) and Nabih Berri threatened to resign from the Cabinet unless more progress was made on constitutional reform. A new security plan, effectively dictated by Syria, was introduced at the end of November. It was designed initially to put the whole of Beirut under the control of the Lebanese army, and then to extend the Government's authority north to Tripoli, south to Israeli-occupied territory and east to the Chouf mountains, demonstrating to the Israelis the ability of the Lebanese army to maintain security in the event of an Israeli withdrawal from the south of the country. Joumblatt's Druze militia repeatedly objected to the eastward deployment and obstructed the implementation of the plan. The army moved into Tripoli on 21 December, but a plan for the coastal areas to the north and south of Beirut was not agreed by all parties until 31 December. The army was deployed along the coast road to southern Lebanon in mid-January 1985.

ISRAEL'S WITHDRAWAL FROM LEBANON

With the cost of keeping a force in southern Lebanon proving a drain on a drastically weakened economy, and with its personnel increasingly the target of attacks by Lebanese resistance groups, Israel's Government of national unity, which was formed in September 1984, pledged itself to a withdrawal from Lebanon. Israel abandoned an unrealistic demand for a simultaneous withdrawal of Syrian forces from north-east Lebanon and, in November, entered into a series of talks at an-Naqoura, in southern Lebanon, with representatives of the Lebanese Government, who participated with Syrian approval. Israel's concern was that adequate security arrangements should be agreed to prevent the vacated areas from becoming bases for terrorist attacks on Israeli soldiers or territory, while the Lebanese Government wished to co-ordinate the withdrawal so as to

prevent intercommunal fighting (such as occurred in the Chouf mountains in September 1983). The talks repeatedly foundered on the question of which forces should take the place of the Israeli Defence Force (IDF). The Lebanese, influenced by Syria, wanted UNIFIL to police the border with Israel (as it had been mandated to do in 1978) and the Lebanese army to deploy north of the Litani river, between UNIFIL and the Syrian army. Israel did not consider the Lebanese army to be a credible security force, and wanted UNIFIL to deploy north of the Litani with the southern Lebanese border patrolled by the Israeli-backed SLA. In the absence of any agreement, Israel withdrew from talks, and on 14 January 1985 the Israeli Cabinet voted to take unilateral steps towards a complete withdrawal, which was to be effected in three phases. The first phase involved the evacuation of the IDF from the western occupied sector, covering about 500 sq km around Sidon, to the Litani river area, around Nabatiyah, and was implemented in February 1985. Israel was prepared to test the competence of the Lebanese army in handing over responsibility for security in the evacuated area to it, operating in tandem with UNIFIL. The Lebanese Government, however, rejected a peace-keeping role for the UN force, and the Lebanese army moved into Sidon in mid-February.

The second phase of the Israeli withdrawal, designed to evacuate the IDF from the occupied central and eastern sector, including the Beka'a valley, to redeploy around Hasbayyah, began on 3 March 1985 with no fixed deadline. The process was accelerated during April as the majority Shi'ite community of the south (which, antipathetic towards the PLO, had initially welcomed the IDF) now attacked it in retreat. This prompted the Israelis to pursue an 'Iron Fist' policy, attacking Shi'ite villages, killing many inhabitants and detaining hundreds of suspected guerrilla fighters. Instead of abating, the level of guerrilla activity against the IDF, orchestrated by the Shi'ite National Resistance Movement, intensified. After the evacuation of Tyre, the second phase of the Israeli withdrawal was completed on 29 April. The third and final phase, taking the IDF behind Israel's northern border and leaving a buffer zone between 10 km and 20 km wide along the border controlled by the SLA, was completed on 10 June, three months ahead of the original schedule. However, several hundred Israeli troops remained inside Lebanon to support the SLA, whose numbers had been depleted since the start of the withdrawal operation by desertion and defection to the southern Lebanese resistance movement. The role of the SLA was not recognized by the Lebanese Government, Syria or Lebanese Muslims, and friction between it and UNIFIL increased.

The Israeli invasion succeeded in that (at the cost of 654 Israeli lives) it temporarily removed the threat of attack by the PLO from within Lebanon (although internal divisions contributed equally to the diminution of PLO strength) and, by a coincidence of interest, the Shi'tes of southern Lebanon were unwilling to allow the PLO to re-establish a military power-base in the region. In the Shi'ites themselves, though, Israel created an enemy across its northern border which was more firmly entrenched and, potentially, more dangerous. In July 1985, less than one month after Israel completed its withdrawal from southern Lebanon, Syria withdrew 10,000–12,000 troops from the Beka'a valley, leaving some 25,000 in position.

CHRISTIAN REVOLT

After the initial euphoria of the Israeli departure from Sidon in February 1985, during the first phase of the IDF's withdrawal, fighting broke out between Christian Phalangists on one side and Druze and Shi'ite militias on the other, with the Lebanese army manifestly unable to keep the peace. In early March President Gemayel had approved a Syrian security plan which had the long-term aim of granting more political and constitutional power to Lebanon's Muslim majority, and which would immediately deprive Christian militias of revenues from illegal ports and the control of a key checkpoint on the road from Beirut to Tripoli. Samir Geagea, a commander in the LF militia, rebelled against what he viewed as a capitulation to Syrian and Muslim influence, and attracted substantial support from units of the LF in east Beirut and north of the capital. Geagea demanded the end of party control of the LF and the introduction of a collective leadership for the Phalange. He also requested a democratically elected council to be established in areas controlled by the LF, to decide on any political reforms. Geagea soon controlled most of the LF in east Beirut, and street battles were fought between pro- and anti-Gemayel Christian factions. At the same time, fighting was renewed between Christian and Muslim militias along the 'Green Line' dividing east and west Beirut. The split in the Christian militia and the partitionist sentiments implicit in Geagea's proposals raised the possibility of Syrian military intervention in Beirut, to bolster President Gemayel and prevent the first stage in what might prove to be the inexorable sectarian fragmentation of Lebanon (thus creating a threat to Syria's internal stability). However, Geagea's revolt ended, as suddenly as it had begun, on 9 May, when Elie Hobeika was elected Commander of the LF. He pronounced himself ready to open a dialogue with Druze and Shi'ite leaders, acknowledged the role of Syria in creating a stable Lebanon, and pledged to evacuate the LF from the last Christian enclave in southern Lebanon at Jezzine.

It was to Jezzine that at least 60,000 Christian refugees from Sidon had gone to escape the fighting around Sidon. At the end of March 1985, units of the rebel Christian militia had launched an offensive, allegedly with Israeli encouragement, against the Palestinian refugee camp of Ain al-Hilweh (to which PLO guerrillas had been returning) and Muslim militiamen and troops of the Lebanese army in Muslim suburbs of Sidon. The exodus of Christians from Sidon began when, at the end of April, prior to the evacuation of the IDF from Jezzine, the LF removed some 300 men from the area to reinforce Christian forces involved in battles with Muslim militias in Beirut, and the remaining Christian militiamen retreated. The retiring IDF were followed into the buffer zone along the Lebanese border by 60,000 Christians from Jezzine.

On 10 April 1985 Prime Minister Rashid Karami, angered by the Government's inability to restore peace to Sidon and its failure to reinforce the beleaguered Lebanese army there, announced that he would boycott cabinet meetings until a cease-fire was agreed. Then, on 17 April, he announced, but was persuaded to withdraw, his resignation after west Beirut had been overwhelmed by fighting, instigated by the Shi'ite Amal militia and their Druze allies to crush the Sunni Murabitoun militia and its Palestinian allies, and to prevent the revival of a pro-Arafat PLO force in Beirut.

ATTEMPTED SYRIAN SUPPRESSION OF THE PLO IN BEIRUT

In May and June 1985, through its proxy, the Shi'ite Amal militia, and with the assistance of the largely Shi'ite Sixth Brigade of the Lebanese army, Syria renewed its attempt to prevent Yasser Arafat from re-establishing a power-base in Lebanon. Most of the estimated 5,000 PLO guerrillas who returned to Lebanon in anticipation of and after the Israeli withdrawal from the south were thought to be loyal to Yasser Arafat. The Palestinian refugee camps of Sabra, Chatila and Bourj el-Barajneh in Beirut were besieged by Amal guerrillas (without the assistance of the Druze militia, who helped the Palestinians to take in supplies and reinforcements), but they failed to gain control of the camps or to quell PLO resistance. Furthermore, Palestinians belonging to the Palestine National Salvation Front (PNSF) of pro-Syrian guerrilla organizations joined with Arafat supporters in resisting the Shi'ites, many of whom were among the 640 people killed in the fighting. An uneasy cease-fire agreement was arranged in Damascus on 17 June between Amal and the pro-Syrian Palestinian element in the camps, but it subsequently collapsed repeatedly.

HIJACK CRISIS IN BEIRUT

On 14 June 1985 two Lebanese Shi'ite Muslims, reputedly members of Hezbollah (the Party of God), hijacked a TWA passenger aircraft, with 153 people on board, on a flight from Athens to Rome. After twice taking it to Beirut and Algiers, and releasing more than 100 hostages, the hijackers landed for the third time in Beirut on 16 June. On 17 June Nabih Berri, who was acting as spokesman for the hijackers, announced that the remaining 42 hostages, mostly Americans, had been taken to secret locations in Beirut, pending response to the hijackers' demand for the release of 766 Lebanese prisoners, mostly Shi'ites, who were being held in Israeli prisons. Israel said that it would not release its prisoners unless asked to do so by the US

Government. The USA declared that it would not use force to secure the release of the hostages, but threatened to impose sanctions against Lebanon. President Assad of Syria became involved in the negotiations for the release of the hostages (now reduced to 39 after further releases), through his links with Nabih Berri and Amal, and his influence was crucial in securing their freedom on 30 June.

ANOTHER SECURITY PLAN FOR BEIRUT

Weeks of fighting between Shi'ite, Sunni and Druze militias in west Beirut preceded another attempt by Syria to initiate the process of political reform. A security plan was introduced in July 1985, after 13 spiritual and temporal leaders of the Lebanese Muslim community had met for talks with Syrian leaders in Damascus. Under the terms of the plan, west Beirut was to be divided into five security zones, each controlled by its own security committee. The Muslim militias were asked to leave the streets and to close their offices. The plan was designed to lay the basis for its extension to Christian east Beirut, and for a renewal of inter-sectarian dialogue on political and constitutional reform, but its implementation was almost immediately disrupted by further fighting.

On 6 August 1985, in the central Lebanese town of Shtoura, representatives of most of the religious communities in the country (but, crucially, no one of stature representing the Sunni population and no Maronite Christians) announced the formation of a pro-Syrian national unity front. It had first been proclaimed in July, after meetings between the Syrian Vice-President, Abd al-Halim Khaddam, the Druze leader, Walid Joumblatt, and the leader of Amal, Nabih Berri. The front was committed to the end of the civil war and 'to the final liquidation of the sectarian regime' under disproportionate Maronite control. In mid-July, meanwhile, the LF settled its differences with ex-President Franjiya, President Gemayel's Christian rival in northern Lebanon, in order to oppose any attempt to implement political reforms without the consent of the Christian community.

Four weeks of intensive fighting between rival militias in Tripoli in September and October 1985 were interpreted as part of Syria's campaign to prevent the re-emergence in Lebanon of the pro-Arafat wing of the PLO. The pro-Arafat, Sunni Muslim Tawheed Islami (Islamic Unification Movement) and the pro-Syrian, Alawite, Arab Democratic Party fought for control of the city and its port, which was allegedly being used to distribute armaments and supplies to Arafat loyalists in other parts of the country. More than 500 people were killed and 500,000 were driven from their homes in Tripoli before a cease-fire was agreed in Damascus at the beginning of October, and the Syrian army moved into the city.

THE ABORTIVE NATIONAL AGREEMENT

A month of negotiations between the three main Lebanese militias (the Druze forces, Amal and the LF), beginning in October 1985, led to the preparation of a draft accord for a politico-military settlement of the civil war. Objections by the Christians to the curbing of presidential powers and a reduction in their political influence delayed approval of the accord, but on 28 December it was finally signed in Damascus by the three militia leaders (Joumblatt, Berri and Hobeika). It provided for an immediate cease-fire and for an end to the state of civil war within one year; the militias would be disarmed and disbanded, and responsibility for security would pass to a reconstituted and religiously integrated Lebanese army, supported by Syrian forces. The accord envisaged the immediate establishment of a national coalition government under a council of six ministers representing the main religious sects, for a transitional period of three years, after which the confessional system of power-sharing government would be abolished and a secular administration created. A new National Assembly would be elected within the three-year period to enact the necessary legislation. The number of deputies in the new assembly would be increased from 99 to 198, with the total divided equally between Christians and Muslims, and an upper house would be added to the legislature. For the period of transition, a Maronite would continue to hold the office of President, but some of his executive powers would pass to the Prime Minister. The agreement recognized Lebanon's community of interest with Syria and envisaged a 'strategic integration' of the two countries in the fields of military relations, foreign policy and security.

The agreement seemed to offer some hope for Lebanon, as it had been negotiated by the actual combatants in the civil war and not merely by politicians. However, the Shi'ite Hezbollah and the Sunni Murabitoun militias were not parties to the accord, the Christian community was divided over it, and it made no provision for dealing with the problem of Palestinian refugees. Muslim support for the agreement was not widespread. The Sunni community had been virtually ignored during negotiations, and under the agreement the Druzes (although Joumblatt had signed it) would be likely to lose their autonomy in the Chouf region. Only Amal appeared to be wholly in favour of the accord. President Gemayel, who had not been involved in drafting the agreement, refused to endorse it, and at the end of December 1985 clashes erupted in east Beirut between elements of the LF who supported the accord and those who resented the concessions that had been made on their behalf by Elie Hobeika. In January 1986 Hobeika was forced into exile; Samir Geagea, the LF's Chief of Staff, was elected Chairman of the Executive Committee of the LF on 24 January, and urged the renegotiation of the Damascus accord. This effectively ended all hope that the peace agreement with the Muslim militias could be implemented.

President Gemayel, who regained much support among the Christian community for his opposition to the Damascus accord, was blamed for its failure by Muslim leaders. By January 1986 the Cabinet had not met for five months, and Muslim ministers subsequently refused to have any dealings with the President. They rejected his request for the Damascus agreement to be referred to the National Assembly and persisted in attempts to engineer his downfall. Inter-sectarian clashes in Beirut resumed in earnest on 22 January.

THE RESURGENCE OF THE PLO CONTINUES

In the south of the country Israel was faced with the consequences of the failure of its invasion. During 1986 rocket attacks on Israeli settlements in northern Israel were resumed by Palestinian guerrillas, who had been gradually returning to the refugee camps around Tyre and Sidon after the Israeli withdrawal in 1985, and had established a number of mobile bases in the south. Israel responded with air raids on Palestinian targets in southern Lebanon, mostly in the Syrian-occupied Beka'a valley, during 1986 and 1987. The Amal militia, while contributing to the southern Lebanese resistance movement within the Israeli-imposed security zone, north of the international border, was more concerned to liberate south Lebanon than to carry the struggle against Israel into Israel itself. It attempted, therefore, to keep PLO guerrillas and radical Lebanese groups as far away from the zone as possible, in order to prevent them from launching rocket and mortar attacks against Israeli territory or from infiltrating the zone and then Israel itself, which might provoke Israeli reprisals inside Lebanon. Amal's controlling influence in the south was coming under threat from the pro-Iranian Hezbollah, which was attracting increasing support. Hezbollah intensified resistance to the SLA, attacking its positions within the security zone along the border with Israel, and fired rockets into Israel itself. Despite the backing of Amal, the role of UNIFIL was cast into doubt by the increasing number of clashes between the peace-keeping force and the SLA and, in particular, Hezbollah, which viewed UNIFIL as an obstacle to the pursuit of war against Israel. In May it was reported that the Syrians, ignoring Israeli warnings, were constructing fortifications and tank and gun emplacements in the Lake Karoun area, in the southern Beka'a, immediately to the north of the SLA-patrolled security zone.

Fighting between Palestinian guerrillas and Shi'ite Amal militiamen for control of the refugee camps in the south of Beirut, which had continued sporadically ever since the nominal cease-fire of June 1985, erupted into major exchanges on 19 May 1986. The refugee camps of Sabra, Chatila and Bourj el-Barajneh were increasingly under the control of guerrillas loyal to Yasser Arafat, who were continuing to return to Lebanon. Sunni and Druze militias continued to lend discreet support to the Palestinians, and there was serious fighting in June between Sunni forces and the Syrian-backed Amal.

THE SYRIAN ARMY'S RETURN TO BEIRUT

Leaders of the Muslim communities in Lebanon met Syrian government officials in Damascus, and agreed to impose a cease-fire around the Beirut refugee camps on 14 June 1986. The cease-fire, which succeeded in reducing the fighting to the level of sniper exchanges, proved to be the first element in a Syrian-sponsored peace plan for Muslim west Beirut. About 1,000 Lebanese troops were deployed in west Beirut at the end of June. The Amal, Druze and Sunni militias were ordered to close their offices and to remain off the streets. Crucial to their co-operation was the appearance in Beirut, for the first time since 1982, of uniformed Syrian soldiers (several hundred of them), supported by members of the Syrian *Muhabarat* (security service) under the command of Brig.-Gen. Ghazi Kena'an. The security plan was temporarily successful in its limited objective of curbing the activities of militias in west Beirut, but the plan (and Syria's active involvement in it) was strongly opposed in Christian east Beirut, and only in August, after lengthy negotiations with Amal and Hezbollah, was it tentatively extended to the predominantly Shi'ite southern suburbs, which contained the majority of the city's Palestinian refugees. The Syrian presence failed to end fighting across the 'Green Line', or to prevent a wave of car bombings and abductions of Westerners by extremist Islamist groups.

On 19 August 1986 the Prime Minister, Rashid Karami, urged the resumption of peace talks between the various Lebanese communities, and on 2 September, after a meeting of Government Ministers (excluding President Gemayel), a new truce (reportedly the 191st since the civil war broke out in April 1975) was agreed. At the same time, the drafting of a national charter, aiming to end the civil war and to reform the confessional system of political representation, was to be put in train.

THE WAR OF THE CAMPS

Resistance to the re-emergence of the pro-Arafat PLO in Lebanon spread from Beirut to the Palestinian refugee camps around Tyre and Sidon at the beginning of October 1986. Amal forces besieged Rashidiyah camp, to the south of Tyre, and the camps at Miyeh Miyeh and Ain al-Hilweh, outside Sidon, cutting off access to food and medical supplies. According to the Palestine Red Crescent relief organization, 1,924 Palestinians died in the Beirut camps between November 1986 and the following February. In February 1987, after the plight of the Palestinians in Beirut, Tyre and Sidon had attracted worldwide sympathy, Amal agreed to allow supplies into Bourj el-Barajneh and to permit women from Rashidiyah to leave the camp to buy food. Syria reportedly asked Amal to abandon the siege of the camps but the respite for the inhabitants of Bourj el-Barajneh and Rashidiyah proved to be brief, and the siege of the other camps remained strictly in force.

PAX SYRIANA

In February 1987 fierce fighting took place in west Beirut between Amal forces and an alliance of the Druze, Murabitoun and Communist Party militias. Muslim leaders appealed for Syria to intervene to restore order, and, with the consent of Karami, Berri and Joumblatt, about 4,000 Syrian troops were deployed in west Beirut on 22 February. The Syrian force (which was soon increased to some 7,500 troops) succeeded in enforcing a cease-fire in the central and northern districts of west Beirut, but, once again, its leaders hesitated to attempt to extend its control to the predominantly Shi'ite southern suburbs, which Syrian-backed Lebanese security forces had failed to secure in July 1986 when Syrian troops first re-entered Beirut. President Gemayel initially opposed the latest deployment of Syrian troops in Beirut as being 'unconstitutional', but in March he welcomed several clauses in a Syrian-sponsored agreement on political reform, which had been approved by Lebanese Muslim leaders and which would give Lebanon's Muslim majority a greater role in the government of the country and reduce the powers of the Christian President.

On 24 February 1987 Syrian troops moved into areas of west Beirut occupied by Hezbollah militiamen, killing 23 of them, but did not venture into the southern suburbs where Hezbollah had its greatest influence. On the following day Syria claimed that all 75 militia offices in west Beirut had been closed. The remaining Hezbollah fighters in west Beirut moved to the southern suburbs, while hundreds of Amal militiamen left Beirut to pursue the struggle against Israel in the south of Lebanon.

A Syrian-supervised cease-fire at all the embattled Palestinian refugee camps in Beirut began on 6 April 1987, and the siege of Chatila and Bourj el-Barajneh was suspended to allow supplies to be taken into the camps. The cease-fire agreement was negotiated by representatives of Syria, Amal and the pro-Syrian PNSF, who had made common cause with pro-Arafat PLO members to defend the camps. However, in Sidon, outside effective Syrian jurisdiction, renewed fighting broke out between Amal and members of the PLO loyal to Yasser Arafat. Amal maintained that it would only agree fully to end the siege of the camps if Arafat loyalists withdrew from villages near Sidon that they had captured from Amal in October and November 1986. Some 150 Syrian troops were deployed around Sidon in mid-April.

Prime Minister Karami announced his Government's resignation on 4 May 1987, following the failure of the Cabinet (which had recently held its first meeting for seven months) to agree on a course of action to alleviate Lebanon's acute economic problems. President Gemayel rejected Karami's resignation (although Karami, who had refused to have any dealings with President Gemayel since January 1986, did not formally submit it), and it seemed that he would remain in office until a suitable (i.e. Sunni) replacement could be found. On 1 June, however, Karami was killed when a bomb exploded in the helicopter in which he was travelling. President Gemayel appointed the Minister of Labour, Education, and Fine Arts, Dr Selim al-Hoss, as acting Prime Minister. It was not clear who was responsible for Karami's assassination, though the Christian section of the divided Lebanese army and the Christian LF were considered by the Muslim community to be the leading suspects. Karami, a Sunni Muslim, had been a firm ally of Syria and had been instrumental in the deployment of Syrian troops in Beirut in February. On 5 June Hussain al-Hussaini, the Shi'ite President of the National Assembly, resigned, alleging that President Gemayel was trying to conceal the truth about the circumstances, and authors, of Karami's death. Muslim leaders demanded a full investigation into the assassination.

On 21 May 1987 the National Assembly had voted to abrogate the agreement, signed by Lebanon and Yasser Arafat (for the PLO) in Cairo in 1969, that defined and regulated the PLO's activities and legitimized its presence in Lebanon. The annulment cancelled any theoretical right of the PLO to official Lebanese protection while it operated in Lebanon. In practice any such protection had long been withheld or had been impracticable. The abrogation of the Cairo accord was strongly suspected of being Syrian-inspired, coming, as it did, in the wake of the reunification of the PLO under Arafat's leadership at the 18th session of the Palestine National Council in Algiers in April, which had deprived the Syrian-sponsored PNSF of the support of the largest groups that had rebelled against Arafat in 1983. Although the divided Lebanese security forces were incapable of enforcing a withdrawal of PLO forces from Lebanon, in line with the abrogation of the Cairo accord, Syria, which had effectively assumed responsibility for security in Beirut, through its own forces and those of Amal was certainly in a position to attempt to do so. Such a policy would be merely a logical continuation of Syria's attempt to prevent the re-establishment of the PLO in Lebanon, and one which Syria could claim was sanctioned by the Lebanese National Assembly. (The Assembly also finally and formally cancelled the peace treaty of 17 May 1983 between Lebanon and Israel, abrogated by President Gemayel in March 1984 but on which the Assembly had never voted.)

Although the most intense fighting between Amal and PLO guerrillas had ended, and the removal of the blockade of the Palestinian refugee camps had been proclaimed in April 1987, the camps remained effectively under siege, apparently under the supervision of Syrian troops, and freedom of movement in and out of them was confined to women and children. On 11 September an agreement was announced between Amal (as part of the largely Muslim Unification and Liberation Front, which had been formed under Syrian auspices in July, and also included Walid Joumblatt's mainly Druze Parti socialiste prog-

ressiste—PSP) and the PLO in the camps, purportedly ending the 'war of the camps', in which more than 2,500 people had died. The agreement provided for the ending of the siege of the camps and for the withdrawal of Palestinian fighters from strategic positions outside the Ain al-Hilweh refugee camp, east of Sidon. However, neither measure was implemented, and in October differences over the withdrawal of some 5,000–8,000 Palestinian guerrillas led to renewed fighting around the disputed positions to the east of Sidon. On 16 January 1988, avowedly as a gesture of support for the uprising by Palestinians resident in Israeli-occupied territories, which had begun in December 1987, Nabih Berri, the leader of Amal, announced the ending of the siege of the Palestinian refugee camps in Beirut and southern Lebanon: Amal fighters and soldiers from the predominantly Shi'ite Sixth Brigade of the Lebanese army withdrew their positions around Bourj el-Barajneh and Chatila camps, to be replaced by Syrian troops, and the 14-month siege of Rashidiyah camp, near Tyre, was ended. However, PLO guerrillas loyal to Yasser Arafat still refused to withdraw from their positions overlooking Ain al-Hilweh camp near Sidon, disrupting the withdrawal of Amal from around Rashidiyah.

AMAL AND HEZBOLLAH CLASH

In cynical terms, it was politically inexpedient for Syria to continue to employ its proxy, Amal, in its attempt to suppress the PLO in Lebanon, at a time when the Palestinian uprising in the Israeli-occupied territories was attracting the sympathy of the world (in particular, the Arab world) to the plight of the Palestinians. By suspending Amal's campaign against the pro-Arafat PLO, Nabih Berri's forces could be deployed against the Hezbollah, whose ultimate aim was to establish an Islamic state in Lebanon on the Iranian model and whose strength was viewed by Syria as a threat to its own ambitions to control Lebanon. Amal's attacks were initially directed against Hezbollah bases in southern Lebanon, and clashes (the first military confrontation between the two groups) occurred at the end of March in the Nabatiyah area. On 9 April 1988 Amal claimed to have captured Hezbollah's last stronghold in the south, at Siddiqin, while Iranian Revolutionary Guards stationed at Sharqiyah and Jibshit had been ordered to leave the area.

In Beirut, Syria had demonstrated its opposition to hostage-taking by preventing a Kuwaiti Boeing 747, which had been hijacked by Islamic fundamentalists (alleged to be Lebanese), from landing at the city's airport in early April 1988. On 5 May fighting broke out between the Amal and Hezbollah militias (the latter supported by Iranian Revolutionary Guards) in the southern suburbs of Beirut. Attempts to impose a cease-fire through Iranian and Syrian mediation failed, and Syrian troops became involved in the fighting on 13 May, when Hezbollah guerrillas, who had wrested control of about 90% of the southern suburbs from Amal, briefly advanced into a Syrian-controlled area of west Beirut. On 15 May Syrian troops encircled the southern suburbs, while intensive negotiations took place between Syria and Iran. On 27 May several hundred Syrian troops moved into the southern suburbs of Beirut to enforce a cease-fire agreement reached by Syria, Iran and their militia proxies on the previous day. When the Syrian deployment was complete, Amal and Hezbollah were to close down their military operations in all parts of the southern suburbs, except in areas adjoining the 'Green Line', where they would continue to be allowed to post their men. On 3 June, in accordance with the agreement, Nabih Berri announced the disbandment of the Amal militia in Beirut and the Beka'a valley (areas under Syrian control) and all other areas of the country except the south (which was not controlled by Syrian troops).

ARAFAT LOYALISTS DRIVEN OUT OF BEIRUT

At the end of April 1988, following a partial reconciliation between Yasser Arafat and President Assad of Syria, Arafat loyalists in the Palestinian refugee camps of Chatila and Bourj el-Barajneh, attempted to drive out the fighters belonging to the Syrian-backed group, al-Fatah Intifada (Fatah Uprising) of Abu Musa. The Syrian troops who had surrounded the camps in April 1987 did not attempt to intervene in the fighting but, with Amal (Syria's other surrogate in Lebanon's factional conflict) otherwise occupied, they allowed reinforcements to reach the rebel Fatah group. On 27 June 1988 the Arafat loyalists in Chatila were overrun and surrendered to the forces of Abu Musa. The following day Syria granted 100 PLO guerrillas safe passage from Chatila to the Palestinian camp at Ain al-Hilweh, near Sidon, although their entry into the camp was allowed by the local Sunni Muslim militia (the Popular Liberation Army, led by Mustafa Saad) only after the personal intervention of the Libyan leader, Col Qaddafi. On 7 July Bourj el-Barajneh, Yasser Arafat's last stronghold in Beirut, was captured by the forces of Abu Musa, and 120 Arafat loyalists were evacuated to Ain al-Hilweh.

LEBANON FAILS TO ELECT A NEW PRESIDENT

President Gemayel's term of office was due to expire on 23 September 1988, and the National Assembly was required to elect a new President before that date. As the election approached, political manoeuvring began in an attempt to find a candidate for the post (under the confessional tradition a Maronite Christian) who would be acceptable to both Christians and Muslims. The question was complicated by divisions within the Maronite community and the unwillingness of most Christians to accept a candidate who was thought to represent the interests of Syria. Discussions between Syrian representatives and the US Under-Secretary of State for Near East Affairs, Richard Murphy, seeking a suitable candidate, failed to produce a compromise choice.

By mid-August 1988 more than two dozen candidates for the presidency had declared themselves, but the three main contenders were: Gen. Michel Awn, the Commander-in-Chief of the Lebanese army; Raymond Eddé, the leader of the Maronite Bloc national libanais, who had been in exile in France since 1976; and former President Sulayman Franjiya. The latter did not announce his candidacy until 16 August 1988, two days before the date of the election, and the news immediately united President Gemayel and Samir Geagea, the commander of the LF, who opposed Franjiya's candidature on the grounds that he represented Syrian interests. (It was Franjiya who, as President, had invited Syria to intervene militarily in Lebanon to end the civil war in 1976.) President Gemayel and Geagea asserted that they would do everything legally in their power to prevent Franjiya from being elected. The reaction of Walid Joumblatt, the Druze leader, was to withdraw the presidential candidate of his own PSP and to support Franjiya's candidacy.

Votes for the presidency were to be cast in two ballots. To be elected, the successful candidate had to receive a majority vote of two-thirds of the members of the National Assembly in the first ballot and a simple majority in the second. Prior to the session at which the election was to be held, a quorum of the Assembly was deemed by its President, Hussain al-Hussaini, to be 51, or two-thirds of the surviving 76 members of the original 99-member National Assembly (whose mandate had been repeatedly renewed since 1972, owing to the impossibility of holding parliamentary elections). In the event, only 38 members (10 of the 41 Christian deputies and 28 of the 35 Muslim deputies) attended the session on 18 August 1988 at the temporary parliamentary premises on the 'Green Line'; al-Hussaini thus declared the session to be inquorate, and the election was postponed. (It was strongly alleged that several of the Christian absentees had been intimidated, threatened or forcibly prevented from attending the election by the Christian LF and soldiers under the command of Gen. Awn, while it was thought that the failure of some Muslim deputies to arrive was due to the perennial difficulty of travelling across factional boundaries in Beirut.)

On 2 September 1988 the acting Prime Minister, Dr Selim al-Hoss, withdrew the Government's resignation which had been tendered by the late Rashid Karami in May 1987. President Gemayel claimed that al-Hoss's action was unconstitutional, insisting that his Government held office only in a caretaker capacity. Consultations between Syria and the USA resumed during September 1988 in an attempt to agree upon a compromise presidential candidate who might be acceptable to the majority in Lebanon. It was reported that they had agreed to support the candidacy of Mikhail ad-Daher, a parliamentary deputy, but Christian army and LF leaders repeated their rejection of any candidate imposed upon Lebanon by foreign powers. A second attempt at a presidential election was scheduled for 22 September but, again, the session of the National

Assembly failed to achieve a quorum. Only 14 deputies gathered for the vote in the old parliament building in west Beirut. Christian deputies assembled, instead, at a villa in east Beirut to repeat their opposition to a Syrian-imposed presidential candidate (i.e. Mikhail ad-Daher) and to the siting of the venue for the election in Syrian-controlled, Muslim west Beirut.

President Gemayel's term of office expired at midnight on 22 September 1988, and, only minutes before, in accordance with his constitutional privilege, he appointed a six-member interim military Government, composed of three Christian and three Muslim officers, led by Gen. Awn, to rule until a new President was elected. His choice of a military government was made after Muslim politicians had refused to participate in an interim civilian government which was to be headed, contrary to the National Covenant of 1943 (which divided power between the Christian and Muslim communities), by a Maronite Prime Minister, Pierre Hélou, instead of by a Sunni Muslim. The three nominated Muslim officers refused to accept their posts in the interim military administration (which were assumed by the remaining Christian ministers on 4 October 1988), while the two Christian members of the Government of Dr Selim al-Hoss (Joseph Hashim and Victor Qasir) surrendered their posts in recognition of the authority of the interim military administration. Dr al-Hoss appointed a Greek Orthodox Christian, Abdullah ar-Rassi, as Deputy Prime Minister on 24 September.

Lebanon was plunged into a constitutional crisis, with two governments (one Christian, in east Beirut, and one predominantly Muslim, in west Beirut) claiming legitimacy. Syria, for its part, refused to recognize the interim military Government. Concern over the stability of Lebanon's central institutions increased in October 1988, when the National Assembly failed to elect a successor to Hussain al-Hussaini, or to renew his one-year mandate. Meanwhile, each of the two governments claiming legitimacy warned the other not to encroach upon its jurisdiction. The authority of Gen. Awn's military administration was regarded as having been strengthened when Geagea's LF seized control of Gemayel's base in the Metn region, north of Beirut, in early October. Of Lebanon's central institutions, only the central bank remained intact, and it continued to make funds available to both governments for basic supplies of food and fuel.

In November 1988 Gen. Awn was dismissed as Commander-in-Chief of the army by Adel Osseiran, the Minister of Defence in Dr Selim al-Hoss's Government. However, since Awn retained the loyalty of large sections of the military, he remained its *de facto* leader. Fighting broke out in southern Beirut between rival Shi'a groups of the Syrian-supported Amal in that month, and between Amal and the Iranian-sponsored Hezbollah in January 1989. In the latter instance the two militias were reported to have agreed to a cease-fire on 30 January. In February a major confrontation occurred between the LF and the Lebanese army, when Gen. Awn attempted to restore the Government's authority over the illegal, militia-controlled ports. While neither side achieved a decisive victory, the authority of the Lebanese army, which had been steadily eroded, was restored as a result of the clashes. The balance of power in Beirut was perceived as gradually altering, and there were hopes that the success of the Lebanese army in its encounters with the LF would lead to the reunification of Beirut.

AWN'S ATTEMPT TO EXPEL SYRIAN FORCES FROM LEBANON

In March 1989, however, the most violent clashes for two years erupted in Beirut between Christian and Muslim forces positioned on either side of the 'Green Line'. While the immediate cause of the fighting was the blockade of illegal ports in west and south Beirut by Christian forces, it was Gen. Awn's declared intention to take all measures for the immediate expulsion of Syrian forces from Lebanon. On 29 March a cease-fire, agreed in response to an appeal from a six-member Arab League committee on Lebanon, was declared. However, exchanges of artillery fire resumed within a matter of hours.

Throughout most of April 1989 Awn's forces and Syrian troops exchanged artillery fire on an almost daily basis, and by the end of the month almost 300 people had been killed. On 19 April, despite Awn's claim that he had a popular mandate to pursue the expulsion of Syrian forces from Lebanon, 23 Christian members of the National Assembly demanded an immediate cease-fire and appealed to the Arab League, the UN and the EC to intervene to end the fighting. In late April, following an emergency meeting of Arab League Ministers of Foreign Affairs, further proposals for a comprehensive peace plan were announced, recommending a cease-fire, under the supervision of an Arab cease-fire monitoring force. The cease-fire took effect on 28 April, but renewed exchanges of fire were reported on 30 April.

RENEWED DIPLOMATIC INITIATIVES AS THE CONFLICT ESCALATES

Further fighting between Christian and Muslim forces erupted at the beginning of May 1989, and on 3 May a delegation from the Arab League (consisting of the League's Assistant Secretary-General, Lakhdar al-Ibrahimi, and the Kuwaiti ambassador to Syria, Ahmed Abd al-Aziz Jassem) arrived in Beirut with the aim of enforcing the 28 April cease-fire and to arrange for the arrival of an Arab monitoring force. The delegation met the leaders of the rival Lebanese Governments, who were reported to have consented to the withdrawal of all land, sea and air blockades. Following a further outbreak of fighting, an urgent meeting was held between the Arab League delegation, the Syrian Government and the leaders of the rival Lebanese Governments. On 11 May it was announced that a further cease-fire had been agreed, but this collapsed on the same day.

At an emergency summit meeting of Arab leaders, held in Casablanca, Morocco, between 23 May and 26 May 1989 (subsequently extended by two days in order to achieve a unified position on the Lebanese question), a tripartite Arab Committee, consisting of King Hassan of Morocco, King Fahd of Saudi Arabia and President Chadli of Algeria, was formed to supplement the efforts of the Arab League Committee on Lebanon. Its aims were: to implement a cease-fire agreement in Lebanon within six months; to install an Arab observer force to supervise the cease-fire; and to act as an intermediary between the conflicting forces in Lebanon in order to facilitate an agreement on the question of political reform and the election of a new President. However, many observers doubted that the newly-formed Committee, presided over by King Hassan, could achieve these aims, not least because there had been no indication at the summit meeting in Casablanca of any willingness on the part of either Syria or Iraq to resolve their conflicting interests in Lebanon. Since the cease-fire in the Iran–Iraq War of August 1988, the traditional enmity between Iraq and Syria (which had intensified as a result of Syria's support for Iran during the war) had increasingly found expression by proxy in the conflict within Lebanon. By mid-1989, as Gen. Awn pursued his campaign to expel Syrian forces from Lebanon, Iraq had become the principal supplier of weapons to the Lebanese army.

As in its attempt to persuade other Arab leaders to condemn Syria's role in Lebanon, Iraq was unsuccessful in its demand, made at the Casablanca summit, for the withdrawal of Syrian troops from Lebanon. Other Arab leaders, while reportedly willing to condemn Syria's 'negative' role in Lebanon in private, were believed to fear Iraqi ambitions and to have sought to maintain a balance between Iraq and Syria. Egypt, Iraq, Jordan and the PLO all supported a proposal for the withdrawal of Syrian troops from Lebanon and for their replacement by an Arab peace-keeping force, but the plan was abandoned, in response to Syrian opposition.

At the beginning of June 1989 the Tripartite Arab Committee on Lebanon issued a renewed appeal for a cease-fire, but further exchanges of artillery fire took place the following day. At the same time King Hassan, King Fahd and President Chadli were reported to have instructed their Ministers of Foreign Affairs to begin the implementation of a 'plan of action' for Lebanon. On 10 June the three ministers travelled to Damascus, delivering to President Assad a letter from the Tripartite Arab Committee and receiving assurances from President Assad of Syria's willingness to co-operate with the Committee. Lakhdar al-Ibrahimi also made further attempts to mediate between the opposed parties in Lebanon, holding talks with both President Assad and Gen. Awn. By mid-June, however, it had not been possible to reach an agreement regarding the composition of the proposed Arab cease-fire monitoring committee.

On 28 June 1989 the Tripartite Committee renewed its appeal for a cease-fire and announced details of its peace plan for Lebanon. The new plan proposed a cease-fire, the removal of blockades of Muslim and Christian ports in Lebanon and the opening of roads between east and west Beirut prior to a meeting of the Lebanese National Assembly in an unspecified foreign country. The last component of the new plan for peace was immediately rejected by Gen. Awn, however, on the grounds that such a meeting would 'contradict the principles of sovereignty and national unity'. Despite the appeal for a cease-fire, exchanges of artillery fire continued.

Evidence of Soviet support for the new peace plan emerged in early July 1989, when Aleksandr Bessmertnykh, the USSR's First Deputy Minister of Foreign Affairs, travelled to Damascus with a message to President Assad from President Mikhail Gorbachev, which reportedly appealed for an end to the fighting in Beirut. Iraq had previously responded to a similar communication by stating that it was prepared to halt all supplies of armaments to Gen. Awn's forces. However, while some observers optimistically attached their hopes for the salvation of Lebanon to the USSR, the extent of Soviet influence on Syria, as its principal supplier of arms, was limited. Despite the prolonged ferocity of the hostilities since March, it had long been inconceivable that either of the 'superpowers' would commit itself to the resolution of the Lebanese conflict. On 31 July the Tripartite Committee abruptly suspended its work and blamed Syrian intransigence for the lack of progress on the Lebanese question. The Committee issued a communiqué accusing Syria of having a concept of Lebanese sovereignty that was inconsistent with the independence of Lebanon.

By August 1989 more than 600 people had been killed since Gen. Awn had begun his attempt to expel Syrian forces from Lebanon. In mid-August France dispatched senior government envoys to Middle Eastern capitals in a new diplomatic initiative to halt the fighting. Since the escalation of hostilities in March France had evacuated badly-wounded victims from both Christian and Muslim communities and had urged its partners in the EC to join forces in an urgent humanitarian mission. Because a substantial number of Lebanese Christians enjoyed dual French-Lebanese nationality, the French Government was faced with increasing domestic pressure to send such a mission. However, the suspicions of Muslim Lebanese regarding France's true intentions, and its possible future extension of military support to Gen. Awn's forces, were only partially allayed by the French policy of providing aid to both Muslim and Christian communities. The new French diplomatic moves were made in response to a further, dramatic escalation of the fighting in Beirut. On 13 August Syrian forces made their first attempt for more than 14 years to penetrate Christian-held territory, launching an attack on the town of Souk el-Gharb. This assault, combined with increased artillery bombardments of east Beirut, was regarded as an attempt by Syria to compensate, by military means, for its increasing diplomatic isolation: at the end of July the Arab League had formally referred to Syria as the principal obstacle to a settlement in Lebanon, while the USA had condemned Syria's renewed use of heavy-calibre weapons in Beirut. Syria, however, claimed that Gen. Awn bore full responsibility for the escalation of hostilities since he had earlier rejected an offer of a cease-fire by Lebanese militias allied to Syria.

The French diplomatic initiative was strongly condemned by the Iranian-backed Hezbollah militia, which described it as a French 'military adventure' to assist Gen. Awn. While France emphasized repeatedly that it was not considering any military intervention in Lebanon, the Beirut-based Revolutionary Justice Organization warned that such intervention by French forces (eight French naval vessels had been dispatched towards Lebanon by 22 August 1989, in anticipation of a renewed onslaught against Christian-held positions in Beirut) would rebound upon US hostages held in Beirut.

On 16 August 1989 the UN Secretary-General, Javier Pérez de Cuéllar, summoned an emergency meeting of the Security Council to discuss means of achieving a cease-fire in Lebanon. This meeting, convened under emergency powers of the Secretary-General which had been invoked on only two previous occasions, followed reports that both Syrian- and Iranian-backed militias in Beirut were preparing to join regular Syrian forces to defeat the Lebanese army.

In late August 1989 French diplomatic pressure was reported to have led to an offer by Gen. Awn to meet his Muslim rivals at a conference, with no reference to his previous condition that political reform in Lebanon could be discussed only after Syrian forces had withdrawn from the country. On 27 August a French peace plan for Lebanon was formally presented to Syria's Minister of Foreign Affairs, Farouk ash-Shara', by the Director-General of the French Ministry of Foreign Affairs, François Scheer. The plan proposed: a cease-fire; a halt to deliveries of armaments to either side involved in the conflict; the introduction of political reforms to end the predominance of the Christians in Lebanon; and the phased withdrawal of foreign forces from Lebanon, beginning with the withdrawal of Syrian forces from west Beirut. While there was no immediate official response to these proposals by Gen. Awn's Government, Christian Lebanese sources in Beirut dismissed the proposals as 'Syrian-inspired' and as seeking to distract the international community from the primary issue of ending the siege of east Beirut.

On 7 September 1989, following allegations by the USA that its ambassador to Lebanon, John McCarthy, and his staff had been threatened with 'Christian terrorism', the USA announced its decision to evacuate its ambassador to Cyprus and close its embassy in Beirut. (The US embassy had been under a peaceful siege of civilians demonstrating in favour of increased US involvement in resolving the problems of Lebanon.) Prior to the embassy's closure, meetings between US diplomats and the head of the LF, Samir Geagea, had prompted accusations by Gen. Awn that the USA was seeking to divide Lebanese Christians as a prelude to concluding an agreement with Syria to end the fighting in Lebanon. The withdrawal of US diplomatic representation was regarded as signalling the failure of Gen. Awn's attempt to 'internationalize' the Lebanese conflict and to win Western support to expel Syrian forces.

On 18 September 1989 the Tripartite Arab Committee on Lebanon resumed its efforts to bring peace to Lebanon, following a meeting in Tripoli, Libya, at the beginning of September between President Assad and President Chadli, at which Assad agreed to have the Syrian presence in Lebanon debated. The Committee appealed for an 'immediate and comprehensive cease-fire'. A new peace plan was announced, under the terms of which a Lebanese security committee was to be established (under the auspices of the Assistant Secretary-General of the Arab League) to supervise the cease-fire. The new plan envisaged the removal of the Syrian naval blockade of Beirut's Christian enclave, while the committee would retain the right to inspect any ship reported to be carrying arms. At the same time, Beirut's international airport was to be reopened. Finally, the plan envisaged a meeting of the Lebanese National Assembly to discuss a 'charter of national reconciliation' drafted by the Tripartite Arab Committee. Members of the National Assembly were to assemble on 30 September at a venue to be announced. Unlike the Committee's previous plan for peace in Lebanon, the new plan made no appeal for the withdrawal of Syrian troops, and was thus welcomed by the Syrian Government. Gen. Awn rejected the proposal for an exclusively Lebanese security committee, arguing that, since Syrian forces were directly involved in the conflict, Syria should be represented on any committee established to supervise a cease-fire. However, due to his diplomatic isolation (the charter was supported by the USA, the USSR, the United Kingdom, France and almost every Arab nation), Awn subsequently relented. The cease-fire accordingly took effect from 23 September.

THE TA'IF AGREEMENT

At the end of September the Lebanese National Assembly met in Ta'if, Saudi Arabia, to discuss the charter of national reconciliation. The session was attended by 31 Christian deputies and 31 Muslim deputies. (Of the 99 deputies elected in May 1972, only 73 still survived.) At a further meeting on 22 October 1989, the charter of national reconciliation was endorsed by 58 of the 62 deputies attending the session. Subsequent to its first being announced, the charter had been amended at informal sessions of the National Assembly. However, the section dealing with Syria's role in Lebanon was the result of a prior agreement between the Tripartite Committee and Syria, and Lebanese deputies were prohibited from altering it. With regard to political reform, the charter now provided for the transfer of executive

power from the presidency to a cabinet, with portfolios divided equally among Christian and Muslim ministers. The appointment of the Prime Minister would remain the prerogative of the President, to be exercised in consultation with the members and President of the National Assembly. The charter further provided for an increase in the number of seats in the National Assembly, from 99 to 108, to be divided equally among Christian and Muslim deputies. A further provision was the implementation of two security plans in Lebanon, one within six months and the other within 24 months. Following the endorsement of the charter, the election of a President and the formation of a new government, all Lebanese and non-Lebanese militias were to be disbanded within six months, while the internal security forces were to be strengthened. For a maximum period of two years the Syrian army would then assist the new government in implementing the security plan.

The endorsement of the charter of national reconciliation (the Ta'if agreement) by the National Assembly was immediately denounced by Gen. Awn as a betrayal of Lebanese sovereignty. Prior to their departure for Ta'if, Christian deputies to the Assembly had reportedly assured Gen. Awn that they would permit concessions on the question of political reform only in exchange for a full withdrawal of Syrian forces from Lebanon. While there was some support for Gen. Awn's position in east Beirut, the agreement had, to a large extent, been facilitated by the co-operation of Lebanon's Maronite leaders, most notably Georges Saadé, the leader of the Phalangist Party, who had played an important role in the Ta'if negotiations.

In an annex to the Ta'if agreement, the Tripartite Arab Committee on Lebanon had appealed to the National Assembly to meet in November 1989 to ratify the charter and to elect a new President. This session of the Assembly was duly held in the northern town of Qlaiaat on 5 November, when René Mouawad, a Maronite Christian deputy and a former Minister of Education and Arts, was elected as President. (Of the 58 votes cast in the second round of voting in the presidential election, Mouawad received 52; Georges Saadé and Elias Hrawi, another Maronite Christian deputy, withdrew after the first round of voting.) Deputies also unanimously endorsed the Ta'if agreement and re-elected Hussain al-Hussaini as President of the National Assembly. Prior to the meeting Gen. Awn had appealed to all Christian deputies to consult with him before attending. In response to the news that Muslim deputies had departed for Qlaiaat, Gen. Awn had announced the dissolution of the National Assembly. His reaction to the presidential election was to declare it unconstitutional, and the result null and void.

On 13 November 1989 President Mouawad invited Dr Selim al-Hoss to form a 'government of national reconciliation'. However, Maronite leaders were reluctant to participate in such an administration and thus openly oppose Gen. Awn. On 22 November, only 17 days after his election, President Mouawad was assassinated in a bomb explosion. Two days later, in the town of Shtaura, 52 deputies of the National Assembly convened and elected Elias Hrawi as the new President. At the same session, deputies voted to extend the term of office of the National Assembly until the end of 1994. A new Government was formed by Dr al-Hoss on 25 November, and received a unanimous vote of confidence from the National Assembly.

Following a meeting of the new Cabinet on 28 November 1989, it was announced that Gen. Awn had again been dismissed as Commander-in-Chief of the Lebanese army, and that Gen. Emile Lahud had been appointed in his place. It was feared that Syrian forces would now launch a major assault on Awn's stronghold in Baabda, east Beirut. Geagea announced that, in the event of such an assault, the LF would fight beside Gen. Awn. In December, in an attempt further to isolate Gen. Awn, the central bank halted all transfers of funds to areas of Beirut controlled by him, and the Ministry of Defence was reported to have ceased paying the salaries of Awn's troops and officials.

On 31 January 1990 Gen. Awn ordered his forces to close all the barracks of the LF in east Beirut. There followed intense fighting between Awn's forces and the LF for control of the Christian enclave, precipitated by the refusal of Geagea to reject the Ta'if agreement, thus isolating Gen. Awn within the Christian community. Awn had accordingly declared the LF to be an ally of Syria. (Maronite leaders had sought to avoid open conflict with Gen. Awn by minimizing their approval of the Ta'if agreement, and on 29 January Georges Saadé, who had been appointed Minister of Posts and Telecommunications in November 1989, announced that he would not serve in the administration, thus damaging its credibility as a government of national unity.) By early March 1990 more than 800 people had been killed, and more than 2,500 wounded, in the inter-Christian fighting since 31 January. In March Gen. Awn declared a halt to the conflict between Christian factions, and expressed willingness to negotiate with his opponents, implying that he was willing to accept the Ta'if agreement in a modified form. Inter-Christian fighting resumed, however, later in the month.

In April 1990 Geagea announced his recognition of the al-Hoss Government, formally accepting the Ta'if agreement, and in June Georges Saadé resumed his duties in the same administration as Minister of Posts and Telecommunications. In early June President Hrawi visited Egypt, Libya and Tunisia, where he reportedly sought Arab backing for the implementation of the resolutions agreed at Ta'if.

In July 1990 there were reports of fierce fighting between Amal and Hezbollah in southern Lebanon. Clashes between the rival Shi'ite groups had occurred in March in southern Beirut, prompting the intervention of Syrian forces. At the beginning of August Israel warned that it would intervene if its interests were endangered by the hostilities.

Meanwhile, at the end of July 1990, the al-Hoss administration began an attempt to pressurize Gen. Awn into relinquishing his power base in east Beirut by seeking to prevent essential supplies from reaching his forces. In the last week of July Awn had conferred with the Assistant Secretary-General of the Arab League, Lakhdar al-Ibrahimi, but had rejected the suggestion—which had already been proposed in a diplomatic initiative pursued by the French Government and the Vatican in June—of joining the al-Hoss Government under the terms of the Ta'if agreement.

THE IMPLEMENTATION OF THE TA'IF AGREEMENT

The crisis in the Gulf region, which was precipitated by Iraq's invasion of Kuwait in August 1990, had serious repercussions for Lebanon. Iraq's Lebanese allies—Gen. Awn and the PLO—hoped that Iraq's challenge to US and Saudi power would serve to weaken that power and subsequently undermine the regional and international consensus that supported the Ta'if agreement. The pro-Ta'if parties in Lebanon were apprehensive about the fate of the agreement, in view of the crisis developing in the Gulf. In response, they succeeded, on 21 August, in convening a session of the National Assembly at which the Constitution was amended to incorporate the reforms agreed at Ta'if.

The reforms stipulated that new deputies (40 in all, taking account of the 32 vacant seats in the old assembly) were to be appointed, rather than elected, for one term, owing to the 'extraordinary situation' in the country. The powers of the National Assembly were increased to the point where it became virtually impossible to dissolve it. The term of office of the President of the National Assembly was increased from one to four years, and the holder of that office would in future play a role in appointing the Prime Minister. The President, meanwhile, was divested of his autonomous prerogatives. Presidential decisions now required the co-signature of the Prime Minister, except in two instances: the appointment of a Prime Minister, and when accepting the Government's resignation. Nominally the President continued to be Commander-in-Chief of the armed forces, but the army remained subject to the full authority of the Cabinet. In appointing a Prime Minister, the President could only follow the choice of deputies to the National Assembly. He no longer enjoyed the right to chair meetings of the Cabinet, to determine the agenda of such meetings or to vote at them.

With the stipulations of the Ta'if agreement incorporated into the Constitution, executive power was effectively transferred to the Lebanese Cabinet. The main beneficiary of the changes was the office of the Prime Minister, who became the head of the Government, speaking in its name, implementing its policies and co-ordinating the various ministries. In the event of a vacancy in the office of the President, the Cabinet, under the chairmanship of the Prime Minister, would assume the privileges and responsibilities of the presidency. The speed with

which the National Assembly was convened on 21 August 1990 reflected an evolution in Syria's attitude towards the process of constitutional reform. Syria's renewed interest in the Ta'if agreement came in response to US assurances regarding Syria's continued dominance in Lebanon and US support to that end.

On 28 September 1990 units of the Lebanese army loyal to the Government imposed an economic blockade on the areas of Beirut which were under the control of Gen. Awn. The blockade, which enjoyed Syrian and US support, was designed to force Awn into either co-operating with the al-Hoss Government, or evacuating his base at the presidential palace at Baabda. On 13 October Syrian forces commenced a military assault against the presidential palace at Baabda and other strategic areas under Awn's control. In a clear breach of the 'Red Lines' agreement between Syria and Israel, which regulated the parameters within which each country could operate in Lebanon, the Syrian air force shelled the presidential palace. That Israel did not retaliate in response to such a breach of the agreement reflected the USA's support of the Syrian offensive. The Syrian military operation was the first of the repercussions of the Gulf crisis in Lebanon, where Syria had effectively been granted freedom of action as a reward for its participation in the US-led multinational force deployed in Saudi Arabia. Awn's forces were completely defeated, and the areas under his control overrun. During the fighting Awn had departed for the French embassy in Beirut, in order to negotiate a cease-fire. As soon as Baabda had fallen under Syrian control, he was advised to remain in the embassy for his own safety, and the French Government, considering his protection to be a matter of honour, offered him and his family political asylum. The Lebanese Government, however, refused to allow Awn to depart for France, seeking to place him on trial for embezzlement of funds and crimes against the state.

Following Awn's defeat, the Government began to implement a security plan for the Greater Beirut area. On 24 December 1990 a new Government of national reconciliation was formed under the Minister of Education and Arts. It was the first Lebanese administration to be formed since the amendment of the Constitution in August 1990 and was intended to continue with the implementation of the Ta'if agreement, begun under the previous Government. The new Prime Minister enjoyed exclusive Syrian support. The 30-member Cabinet included various militia and party leaders as well as traditional political figures. Cabinet posts were divided equally between Muslims and Christians: six Sunni Muslims, six Maronite Christians, six Shi'a Muslims, three Druzes, four Greek Orthodox Christians, three Greek Catholics, one Armenian Catholic and one Armenian Orthodox Christian.

The composition of the new Government attracted considerable criticism. Deputies in the National Assembly complained at their under-representation in the Cabinet, while the Lebanese press questioned the merits of ministers whose only qualifications for office were those of being either a military leader or the son of a prominent politician. Other commentators accused the President of nepotism. The Phalangist Party and the LF complained that the Government lacked 'national balance'. Druze representatives complained at the dilution of their influence, while Hezbollah, the Parti communiste libanais and the Parti national libéral were not represented in the Cabinet at all.

The new Cabinet presented a statement of policy to the National Assembly and received a vote of confidence on 4 January 1991. However, representatives of the Phalangist Party and the LF boycotted sessions of the Cabinet, complaining that more than two-thirds of its members were, either directly or indirectly, susceptible to Syrian influence. However, their boycott did not result in their outright resignation and was intended, rather, to gain certain assurances and guarantees. By the same token, on 11 January the Druze leader, Walid Joumblatt, withdrew from the Cabinet in protest at the dilution of Druze influence in the Government, and at the fate of the so-called 'people's army' and the civilian administration that had been established in the Chouf mountains by his PSP. The Government, meanwhile, adhered to the four-point programme which it had presented to the National Assembly, aiming to extend its authority over the whole of Lebanon; to disband the militias; to formalize Lebanon's 'special relations' with Syria;

and to appoint deputies to the vacant seats in the National Assembly and fill senior military and civilian posts.

On 6 February 1991 Lebanese army battalions were dispatched to the south of the country for the first time since the Israeli invasion of 1978. They were deployed in the wake of a serious escalation in Palestinian guerrilla operations in the south, and consequent Israeli retaliation, as a 'buffer' between the 6,000 Palestinian fighters in and around Sidon and units of the Israeli-backed SLA. However, the inadequacy of the army's capabilities in relation to the size of the area which it was meant to patrol meant that its deployment was largely symbolic. Its presence was nevertheless welcomed by the Shi'ite militia, Amal. The Iranian-backed Hezbollah reacted cautiously. Israel welcomed the deployment of the army in principle, but warned that swift and severe retaliation would ensue if it failed to suppress attacks against Israel.

On 28 March 1991 a full session of the Cabinet approved a plan to dissolve all Lebanese and non-Lebanese militias in the country and to appoint 40 new deputies to the National Assembly. All militias were to surrender their weapons and equipment to the Government during the period 28 March–30 April. Between the end of April and 20 June the army was to deploy in the region of Mount Lebanon, outside Greater Beirut, and to assume responsibility for the security of the rest of the country during 20 June–20 September. The new momentum in the Government's extension of its authority was a result of the defeat of Iraq by the multinational force in February. The USA, Saudi Arabia, Egypt and Syria, which had all contributed to the multinational force, were all also proponents of the Ta'if agreement. Ministers in the Government who had boycotted sessions of the Cabinet while awaiting the outcome of the war in the Gulf region (Samir Geagea, Georges Saadé, Michel Sassine and Walid Joumblatt) now began to adjust their positions. On 7 March Joumblatt retracted his resignation, and by 20 March the representatives of the LF in the Government—Sassine and Saadé—had ended their boycott of the Cabinet sessions. Geagea refused to accept a post in the Cabinet, but nominated an adviser, Roger Deeb, in his place.

Not surprisingly, the larger militias viewed their own disbandment with little enthusiasm. The LF urged the creation of a national guard to assume responsibility for the security of certain regions, while the PSP argued that the militias should be incorporated into official military structures. Palestinian representatives, meanwhile, announced that they would not comply with the Government's decision, as the presence of Palestinian militias was a regional, rather than a domestic, issue. However, strong regional and international pressure ultimately compelled Lebanon's major militias to comply with the Government's order to disband, and army units were deployed in areas previously controlled by the LF and the PSP.

Apprehension remained, none the less, with regard to armed groups which had refused to disband. These included the 6,000-strong pro-Arafat PLO; the 2,000-strong Iranian Revolutionary Guards, stationed in and around the town of Ba'albeck in the Beka'a valley; the 5,000-strong, Iranian-backed Hezbollah in the Beka'a valley and the south; and the 3,000-strong, Israeli-backed SLA. Arafat's al-Fatah group, based in Sidon, refused to disband, on the grounds that it did not constitute a militia, but, rather, a 'resistance movement' or, even, the regular army of the Palestinian state. It accordingly refused to surrender its weapons, but indicated its willingness to come to an agreement with the Lebanese Government regarding their location and use. The Government, for its part, refused to negotiate an agreement similar to the one signed in Cairo in 1969 and abrogated by the National Assembly in 1987. It also rejected the PLO's demands for its own embassy in Beirut; for a Palestinian brigade within the Lebanese army, with responsibility for the security of the Palestinian refugee camps; and for the right to launch attacks against Israel. After much pressure, however, the PLO finally declared that it would not impede the deployment of Lebanese troops in the south of the country.

The commander of the Iranian Revolutionary Guards, Hadi Rida Askari, insisted that they did not constitute a militia within Lebanon and that their withdrawal could take place only following a decision by the Iranian Government, made in consultation with Syria. Hezbollah, meanwhile, agreed to dismantle its military structure in Beirut, but insisted on main-

taining armaments in the Beka'a valley and in southern Lebanon, in order to continue the struggle against Israel's occupation. The SLA rejected any suggestion that it would disarm or that Israel was ready to comply with the appeals of the Lebanese Government for the implementation of UN Security Council Resolution 425, which demanded the unconditional withdrawal of Israeli forces from Lebanon. Indeed, the fact that the Government had begun to disband Lebanese militias before their non-Lebanese counterparts aroused fears that its decision would be only partially applied and that the extension of its authority would encounter the perennial obstacle of the armed Palestinian presence in Lebanon, exacerbated by the presence of armed groups backed by Iran.

In accordance with the four-point political programme of the Government of national reconciliation, relations between Lebanon and Syria became closer, culminating in the signing, in May 1991, of a treaty of 'fraternity, co-operation and co-ordination'. The treaty was the natural outcome of the stipulations of the Ta'if agreement, establishing a formal structure for developing and implementing policies on a wide range of issues, and creating links between Lebanon and Syria in political, military, security and economic affairs. It received a mixed welcome, however. Georges Saadé and Roger Deeb abstained from voting at the Cabinet session at which the treaty was approved, and refused to join the official delegation which travelled to Damascus for its signing. The Maronite Patriarch, Nasrallah Sfeir, complained that such a treaty should not have been negotiated or signed before the Government had regained full sovereignty over the whole of Lebanon. He further warned that the treaty contravened the National Covenant of 1943.

The treaty declared that Syria and Lebanon had 'distinctive brotherly relations', based on their 'geographic propinquity, similar history, common belonging, shared destiny and common interests'. Moreover, it specified the executive mechanism by which these 'distinctive relations' were to be managed and developed. Five joint councils were established, which were to meet regularly in order to develop and execute policies affecting Lebanon. The most important of these was the Higher Council, comprising the Presidents of Lebanon and Syria, their Prime Ministers, Deputy Prime Ministers and the presiding officers of their respective legislatures. The Higher Council assumed responsibility for the co-ordination and co-operation of the two states in political, economic, security, military and other spheres. Its decisions were to be binding, albeit within the constitutional and legal frameworks of both countries. Opponents of the treaty claimed that the joint councils constituted a violation of Lebanese sovereignty and amounted, in effect, to Syria's annexation of Lebanon. In view of Syria's military strength, they regarded the treaty as unbalanced, and predicted grave consequences for Lebanon's independence, its democratic practices and its traditional freedoms. They considered to be even more alarming the Syrian Government's refusal to formalize its recognition of Lebanese sovereignty through the establishment of diplomatic relations. The supporters of the treaty, however, argued that it did not affect Lebanese freedoms, and that close relations with Syria were necessary for Lebanon's stability and prosperity.

On 9 May 1991 the National Assembly approved an amendment to Lebanon's electoral law, allowing the exceptional appointment by the Cabinet of 40 deputies to the National Assembly. The appointments were made to the 31 seats in the assembly which had become vacant since 1972, and to the nine new seats created in accordance with the Ta'if agreement. On 7 June 1991 the 40 deputies were selected (from a list of 384 candidates who had presented their credentials for office to the Ministry of the Interior) by the President, the Prime Minister and the President of the National Assembly, in close consultation with Syria. The term of office of the new assembly was to be four years. The appointed deputies were representative of the political and confessional breadth of the Cabinet. All except four (who represented the Phalangist Party and the LF) enjoyed close relations with Syria. Hezbollah and a new, popular 'Awnist' grouping remained unrepresented in the National Assembly.

Following the appointments to the National Assembly, the Government began to compile a list of militia members who would be enrolled into the state's security and administrative structures, and to establish a schedule and locations for their 'rehabilitation'. On 29 May 1991 the Government had decided that some 20,000 militia members would be incorporated into the structures of the state. The decision stipulated that equal numbers of Muslims and Christians would be assimilated, among them 6,500 members of the LF, 2,800 members of Amal and 2,800 members of the PSP. The remainder would be absorbed from other militias. All were to undergo retraining courses, lasting up to six months, before being assigned to employment in the service of the state.

In early June 1991 Israel launched its fiercest attacks on Palestinian bases in southern Lebanon since its invasion of the country in 1982. The attacks coincided with statements by Israeli officials that Israel had no intention of withdrawing from its self-declared 'security zone', nor of reducing its support for the SLA. The escalation of the fighting in the south appeared to serve the interests of both Israel and the Palestinians. It supported the Palestinians' assertion that they needed to retain their weapons in order to fight a war against Israel; and it allowed Israel to claim that its northern border remained insecure and that it needed to maintain an armed presence in southern Lebanon.

On 1 July 1991 the Lebanese army began to deploy in and around Sidon, encountering some armed resistance from pro-Arafat Palestinian guerrillas. On 4 July the Government and the PLO concluded an accord whereby the latter agreed to allow the army peacefully to impose the Government's authority in the area. The deployment of the army in southern Lebanon was subsequently reported to have proceeded according to plan, although its jurisdiction did not include the village of Jezzine, where, although the locality was technically outside Israel's buffer zone, units of the SLA occupied positions.

The release, in August 1991, of John McCarthy, a British citizen who had been held hostage in Lebanon by Islamic Jihad (a pro-Iranian fundamentalist guerrilla group) since 1986, signalled the beginning of intensive diplomatic efforts by the UN to achieve a comprehensive exchange of hostages who were being detained, respectively, by Israel and by various sectarian groups in Lebanon. By June 1992 the release of all of Western hostages in Lebanon had been secured.

In August 1991 the National Assembly approved a general amnesty for crimes committed during the civil war; several specified crimes committed during 1975–90 were not covered by the amnesty. Under the terms of a presidential pardon, Gen. Michel Awn was finally allowed to leave the French embassy compound (where he had been sheltering since his defeat in 1990) and depart for exile in France. A condition of the amnesty was that he remain in exile for at least five years and refrain from political activities during that time.

At the beginning of September 1991 Lebanon and Syria formally concluded a security agreement, as envisaged in the bilateral treaty of May 1991. The agreement permitted Lebanon and Syria to seek mutual military assistance in the event of a challenge to the stability of either country. In mid-October President Hrawi travelled to Damascus for the first session of the Lebanese-Syrian Higher Council, established by the May accord. The chief topic of discussion at the first session of the Council was reportedly the opening session (in October) of the Middle East peace conference in Madrid, Spain, which Lebanese and Syrian delegations had been invited to attend.

In early November 1991 Karami announced that the USA had requested Israel to cease military activity in southern Lebanon, since it jeopardized the newly-begun peace process. However, Israeli military activity intensified in late November, in response to alleged attacks by Hezbollah fighters. A further, more serious, escalation of the conflict in southern Lebanon was precipitated in February 1992 by the assassination, by the Israeli air force, of Sheikh Abbas Moussawi, the Secretary-General of Hezbollah. Retaliation by Hezbollah fighters prompted an incursion by Israeli armed forces beyond the southern Lebanese buffer zone in order to attack alleged Hezbollah positions. Although the Lebanese army had begun to occupy positions in southern Lebanon that had been vacated by UNIFIL, Hezbollah had retained its freedom to conduct military operations, in an apparent reflection of Syria's belief that only by continued coercion would Israel withdraw from occupied Arab territories. In late March Syrian forces began to withdraw from Beirut, in preparation for their withdrawal to eastern Lebanon by September (in accordance with the Ta'if agreement).

During the early months of 1992 Lebanon's economic situation worsened dramatically, and the value of the Lebanese pound depreciated sharply; general strikes took place in April and May. There were widespread allegations of corruption and incompetence within the Government, and on 6 May Omar Karami and his Cabinet were forced to resign. Following discussions in Damascus between President Hrawi and Syrian leaders, Rashid Solh was appointed Prime Minister (a position he had held in 1974–75), and on 13 May his appointment was approved by 70 of the National Assembly's 108 deputies. A new Cabinet, announced on 16 May, included 15 members of its predecessor. It was regarded as insufficiently different in character from Karami's Government to modify the widespread perception of Lebanon as a Syrian protectorate, which many, including Karami, had blamed for the reluctance of Western countries to provide the country with significant economic assistance.

ELECTIONS TO THE NATIONAL ASSEMBLY

In addition to efforts to alleviate the economic crisis, a principal task of the Lebanese Government in mid-1992 was to prepare the country for its first legislative election since 1972. In order to comply with the terms of the Ta'if agreement (see above), this had to take place before November 1992, and in early April the Karami Government had indicated that the election would be held in the summer of 1992—although it was not certain that Syrian forces would have withdrawn to the eastern area of the Beka'a valley by this time, as the Ta'if agreement stipulated that they should. Lebanese Christian groups accordingly threatened to boycott the election, on the grounds that the continued Syrian presence would prejudice its outcome. The USA, too, urged the withdrawal of Syrian armed forces before the election took place. The Lebanese Government, for its part, argued that the Lebanese army was still unable to guarantee the country's security in the absence of Syrian armed forces.

On 16 July 1992 the National Assembly approved a new electoral law whereby the number of seats in the Assembly was raised from 108 (as stipulated by the Ta'if agreement) to 128, to be divided equally between Christian and Muslim deputies. On 24 July the timetable for the election was announced. Voting was to take place in three phases: on 23 August in constituencies in North Lebanon and the Beka'a area; on 30 August in Beirut and Mount Lebanon governorates; and on 6 September in constituencies in the South and in Nabatiyah. By mid-August it was clear that most Maronite Christian groups, in particular the Phalangist Party, would not present candidates. In July Syria had indicated that its troops would not withdraw to the Beka'a area until the process of constitutional reform was complete, in accordance with its interpretation of the Ta'if agreement. Christian groups continued to maintain that a fair election could not take place until the Syrian armed forces had withdrawn. As the Lebanese Prime Minister and Cabinet had been chosen in close consultation with Syrian leaders, the Government continued to invoke the inability of the Lebanese army to guarantee the country's security in the absence of Syrian armed forces: the position of Christian ministers in the Cabinet thus appeared more compromised than ever.

The first round of the election to the National Assembly proceeded, as planned, on 23 August 1992. Voting in the first round was to elect a total of 51 deputies—28 to represent North Lebanon and 23 the Beka'a area. A total of 273 candidates contested the first round, in which the participation of the estimated 900,000-strong electorate was described as high in Muslim districts and very low in Christian ones. There were widespread allegations of electoral malpractice both during and after the first round, prompting the resignation of the incumbent President of the National Assembly, Hussain al-Hussaini. All the candidates presented by the Iranian-backed Hezbollah, which contested the election as a political party, were elected. The religious denominations of the deputies elected to the National Assembly in the first round of voting were as follows: 16 Maronite Christians; 16 Sunni Muslims; 8 Shi'ite Muslims; 8 Greek Orthodox; 3 Greek Catholics; 2 Alawites; 1 Druze and 1 Armenian Orthodox.

The second round of voting in the election to the National Assembly—to elect 54 deputies to represent constituencies in the Beirut and Mount Lebanon areas—took place on 30 August 1992, characterized by the low participation of the electorate especially in Christian districts. Indeed, in the Maronite district of Kesrouan voting was postponed, owing to a boycott by all candidates for election to its five seats. (All five seats were subsequently won by Maronite candidates in a by-election held on 11 October.) As in the first round of voting, there were widespread allegations of bribery and intimidation of the electorate. The religious denominations of the deputies elected to the National Assembly in the second round of voting were: 20 Maronite Christians; 8 Sunni Muslims; 6 Druze; 5 Shi'ite Muslims; 5 Greek Orthodox; 4 Armenian Orthodox; 1 Greek-Melkite Catholic; 1 Armenian Catholic; and 4 minority denominations.

The third round of voting, in constituencies in the South and in Nabatiyah, took place on 6 September 1992. The religious denominations of the deputies elected to the National Assembly in the third round of voting were as follows: 14 Shi'ite Muslims; 3 Sunni Muslims; 2 Maronite Christians; 2 Greek-Melkite Catholics; 1 Greek Orthodox; and 1 Druze. In October the Amal leader, Nabih Berri, was appointed President of the National Assembly.

LEBANON UNDER HARIRI

On 22 October 1992 Rafik Hariri was invited by President Hrawi to form a government. A new, 30-member Cabinet was appointed on 31 October. Hariri, a Lebanese-born Saudi Arabian entrepreneur, included many technocrats in his new Cabinet, and offices were not, as previously, distributed on an entirely confessional basis. His appointment was viewed as likely to restore some confidence in the country's economy and to facilitate its reconstruction. On 12 November the new Government secured a vote of confidence in the National Assembly.

On 16 December 1992, in response to the deaths in the Occupied Territories of five members of the Israeli security forces, and to the abduction and murder by the Islamic Resistance Movement (Hamas) of an Israeli border policeman, the Israeli Cabinet ordered the deportation to Lebanon of more than 400 alleged Palestinian supporters of Hamas. Owing to the Lebanese Government's refusal to co-operate in this action, the deportees were stranded in the territory between Israel's self-declared southern Lebanese security zone and Lebanon proper.

Serious escalations of the conflict in southern Lebanon between Hezbollah fighters, the SLA and Israeli armed forces occurred in October and November 1992, and fighting continued at a lower degree of intensity during the early months of 1993. In July the Government was reported to be attempting to curtail the activities of the Damascus-based Popular Front for the Liberation of Palestine—General Command (PFLP—GC), which had begun to mount guerrilla attacks on the positions of Israeli armed forces and Israeli-backed militias from southern Lebanon. On 25 July Israeli armed forces launched their heaviest artillery and air attacks on targets in southern Lebanon since 1982, with the declared aim of eradicating the threat posed by Hezbollah and Palestinian guerrillas and, moreover, of creating a flow of refugees so as to compel the Lebanese and Syrian authorities to take action to curb Hezbollah and the Palestinians. Syrian troops in Lebanon were also reported to have come under fire. According to Lebanese figures, Israel's so-called 'Operation Accountability' displaced some 300,000 civilians towards the north and resulted in 128 (mainly civilian) deaths. What was termed a cease-fire 'understanding', brokered by the USA, entered into effect at the end of the month, ending the week-long Israeli campaign, but this proved short-lived, and mutual offensives continued in subsequent months. In August, meanwhile, apparently as part of the cease-fire understanding, units of the Lebanese army took up positions, assigned to UNIFIL since the late 1970s, near the Israeli security zone.

A sudden cessation of attacks by Hezbollah units on Israeli targets in January 1994, during the approach to a meeting between US President Bill Clinton and President Assad of Syria, was cited as evidence, by Israeli observers, of Syrian control of Hezbollah. Hezbollah resumed attacks on Israeli targets in February, giving rise to the usual pattern of Israeli reprisals against Hezbollah targets. In June Israeli forces mounted an air attack on an alleged Hezbollah training camp in the Beka'a valley, close to the Syrian border. In early August further armed attacks by Israeli armed forces against Hezbollah targets in southern Lebanon caused the death of eight civilians, for which Israel subsequently made a formal apology. Israel claimed that Hezbollah had been involved in the planning of bomb attacks against Jewish targets in the United Kingdom and Argentina in July. An Israeli attack on the southern town of Nabatiyah on 19 October, in which seven civilians were killed, was unusual in that it was not a response to guerrilla activity in and around the southern Lebanese security zone, but, rather, appeared to have been made in retaliation for operations by Hamas in Israel itself. Hezbollah responded with rocket attacks on targets in northern and western Israel. There was a further escalation of the southern conflict in December, during which some six Israeli soldiers and eight members of the SLA were reported to have been killed.

Israeli attacks on targets south of Beirut in January 1995 caused a brief closure of the city's international airport (for the first time since 1987). In February 1995 Israel imposed a blockade on southern Lebanese fishing ports, in retaliation for the imposition, by the Lebanese army, of stricter security controls between the southern Lebanese security zone and sovereign Lebanese territory. These were enforced owing to the alleged involvement of Israeli agents in the planning of a car-bomb explosion in Beirut in December 1994. At the end of March 1995 the assassination of a Hezbollah leader by Israeli forces in southern Lebanon gave rise to fierce fighting between Hezbollah and Israeli forces in the area east of Sidon, and to rocket attacks by Hezbollah on Israeli targets in Galilee. In late April a Hezbollah fighter carried out a suicide bomb attack on an Israeli military convoy inside the Israeli 'security zone' in southern Lebanon, in which 11 Israeli soldiers were injured. Hostilities continued throughout May and June. On 8 July, in response to an attack three days earlier by Hezbollah fighters in which two Israeli soldiers were killed, Israeli armed forces reportedly attacked Nabatiyah with *fléchette* anti-personnel missiles—which were subject to an international ban; three children died in the attack. Hezbollah fighters retaliated with rocket attacks on targets in northern Israel. Israeli armed forces launched air and artillery attacks against Hezbollah targets in August, which were reported to have resulted in heavy casualties.

In March 1994 the National Assembly approved legislation instituting the death penalty for what were termed 'politically-motivated' murders. Shortly afterwards the Phalangist LF was proscribed, on the grounds that the organization had promoted the establishment of a Christian enclave and, hence, the country's partition. In the following month the LF leader, Samir Geagea, was arrested; he and several of his associates were subsequently charged in connection with the murder, in October 1990, of Dany Chamoun, son of former President Camille Chamoun and the leader of the right-wing Maronite National Liberal Party, and with the bombing of a Maronite church outside Beirut in January 1994. In September it was reported that the LF had temporarily relieved Geagea of the organization's leadership, and that it had revoked Geagea's recognition of the Ta'if agreement; the LF command was also reported to have countermanded Geagea's formal dissolution, in 1991, of the organization's militia status. In June 1995 Geagea and a co-defendant were convicted of instigating the murder of Chamoun, and were (together with seven others convicted *in absentia*) sentenced to death; the sentences were immediately commuted to life imprisonment with hard labour. Hearings in connection with the Maronite church bombing had been postponed. In early May 1994 Hariri withdrew from all his official duties owing to a dispute with President Hrawi, and with the President of the National Assembly, Nabih Berri, who both reportedly opposed his proposals to give the Government a measure of credibility with Lebanon's Maronite community by incorporating some of its representatives into the Cabinet. The dispute appeared to be resolved by President Assad of Syria's reported assurance to Hariri that pro-Syrian ministers within the Lebanese Cabinet would not seek to undermine the efficiency of the Government. Hariri resumed his duties later in May. At the beginning of September there was a minor reorganization of the Cabinet in which Michel Murr, the Deputy Prime Minister, replaced Beshara Merhej as Minister of the Interior. It was reported that this change represented an attempt to increase the unity of the Government. In early December Hariri abruptly announced his resignation, a decision which was apparently due to his frustration at perceived attempts within the National Assembly to obstruct Lebanon's economic reconstruction. Hariri withdrew his resignation on 6 December, but not before it had caused a dramatic decline in the value of the Lebanese pound and emphasized the fragility of the recovery process. In May 1995 Hariri again resigned as Prime Minister, but was subsequently persuaded by the President to remain in office and reappointed on 21 May. It was reported that Hariri had resigned this time as a result of a dispute concerning the Constitution, which stipulated that the President should serve a single, six-year term of office after which he was not eligible for re-election. Hariri had reportedly sought the amendment of the Constitution in order to allow President Hrawi to serve a second term of office, which Hariri believed was necessary to guarantee stability in the continued early phase of economic reconstruction. While Hariri favoured discussion of the issue before the expiry of the parliamentary session at the end of May, Nabih Berri, who was opposed to such an amendment, stated that he would use his authority as President of the National Assembly to delay discussion of the issue. Hariri and Berri travelled to Syria, where it was agreed that Hariri would be able to form a new Cabinet, while discussion of the renewal of the presidential mandate would be postponed. Hariri thus formally resigned, and was immediately reappointed; a new Government was named shortly afterwards, and its programme was approved by the National Assembly in June. In October the National Assembly voted to amend Article 49 of the Constitution, thereby extending Hrawi's mandate for a further three years.

In late February 1996 it was announced that elections to the National Assembly would be held in September 1996. On 29 February the Confédération Générale des Travailleurs du Liban (CGTL) organized a general strike in support of its demand for a 76%-increase in public-sector salaries and for a 100%-increase in the minimum wage. In response the Government placed the army in charge of national security for a three-month period and imposed a curfew in the country's principal cities and towns.

'OPERATION GRAPES OF WRATH'

On 11 April 1996 Israeli armed forces began an intense, sustained campaign of air and artillery attacks on what they claimed to be positions occupied by the Hezbollah militia. These included, for the first time since 1982, attacks on the southern suburbs of Beirut. The declared aim of the Israeli campaign (code-named 'Operation Grapes of Wrath') was to achieve the complete cessation of rocket attacks by Hezbollah on settlements in northern Israel. Immediately prior to the Israeli campaign such attacks had caused injuries to some 13 Israeli civilians. Hezbollah claimed, in turn, that the rocket attacks had been provoked by deliberate attacks on Lebanese civilians by Israeli armed forces or their proxies. (An important element of the 1993 cease-fire 'understanding' had been that Hezbollah and Israel had effectively largely confined their conflict to the region of the security zone by agreeing to halt unprovoked attacks on civilian targets.) As a result of the Israeli operation some 400,000 Lebanese were displaced northwards after the Israeli military authorities warned that they would be endangered by the attacks on Hezbollah targets in the south. However, not all of the Israeli air attacks targeted alleged Hezbollah positions: one was made on a power-station in Bselim, a village north of Beirut in the Maronite heartland of the country where Hezbollah had never been established and there was nothing that could be construed as a Hezbollah target.

The Israeli campaign could be regarded as having been determined by the proximity of a general election in Israel and by the need of Israeli Prime Minister Shimon Peres to restore some of the confidence with the electorate which he had lost as a result of suicide bomb attacks perpetrated earlier in the year by Hamas in Israel. It could also be interpreted as an attempt to pressurize Syria into exerting increased control over Hezbollah. On 18 April 1996 an Israeli attack on a UN base at Qana resulted in the death of more than 100 Lebanese refugees who had been sheltering there. The attack (in which four UNIFIL soldiers were also killed) led to an intensification of efforts to find a diplomatic solution to the conflict, especially by

the USA—Secretary of State, Warren Christopher, was dispatched to the region—and France. A cease-fire 'understanding' between Israel and Hezbollah took effect on 27 April. As in 1993, this was effectively a compromise confining the conflict to the area of the security zone in southern Lebanon, recognizing both Hezbollah's right to resist Israeli occupation and Israel's right to self-defence; the 'understanding' also envisaged the establishment of an Israel-Lebanon Monitoring Group (ILMG), comprising Israel, Lebanon, Syria, France and the USA, to supervise the cease-fire. According to the Israeli authorities, 'Operation Grapes of Wrath' resulted in no Israeli deaths, while 170–200 Lebanese civilians, in addition to some 50 fighters, were killed. For its part, Hezbollah claimed to have sustained minimal casualties, and its military capacity appeared largely undiminished. A UN report on the killing of Lebanese civilians at Qana, presented to the Security Council in May 1996, concluded that it was 'unlikely' that the shelling of the UNIFIL base had, as claimed by the Israelis, been accidental. The first meeting of the ILMG took place in July; the group was to be based in Cyprus, and would meet in Naqurah, near Lebanon's southern border. Prior to the meeting Israel and Hezbollah were reported to have exchanged prisoners and bodies of members of their armed forces for the first time since 1991.

ELECTIONS TO THE NATIONAL ASSEMBLY

In June 1996 the Cabinet approved a new electoral law in preparation for the legislative elections later in the year. Under the new legislation, the Beka'a valley was reunified as a single electoral area, having been divided into three areas for the 1992 legislative elections. In the forthcoming elections the 128 seats of the National Assembly would be divided among the country's five governorates as follows: Beirut, 19; the Beka'a valley, 23; the South and Nabatiyah, 23; the North, 28, and Mount Lebanon, 35.

In mid-July 1996 it was reported that Christian opposition leaders were urging the country's Christian communities to participate in the forthcoming elections, and that there had been relatively few appeals for a boycott such as had occurred in 1992. However, leading figures within the Christian community continued to criticize the new electoral legislation for its division of Mount Lebanon, where Lebanon's Maronite community was concentrated, into five electoral constituencies (thereby effectively dividing the Maronite vote, to the advantage of other, i.e. Druze, communities).

In early August 1996 Lebanon's Constitutional Court decided that the amendments to the electoral law (which had been approved by the National Assembly in July) were unconstitutional. The National Assembly subsequently approved an amendment to the new electoral law which, while it retained the controversial division of Mount Lebanon governorate, stated that this was an exceptional measure to be employed solely for the 1996 election.

In the first round of voting in the legislative elections, which took place in Mount Lebanon governorate on 18 August 1996, supporters of the Hariri Government achieved a comprehensive victory, winning 32 of the 35 seats. Some 189 candidates were reported to have contested the seats and the participation of the electorate was reported to have been relatively high—compared with that in the elections of 1992—at 45%. In the second round of voting, in the North, on 25 August, by contrast, opposition candidates were reported to have enjoyed greater success. In the third round of voting, in Beirut governorate, on 1 September, candidates contesting the elections on the list headed by the Prime Minister secured 14 of the 19 seats. Hariri himself won a larger number of votes than any other candidate contesting the Beirut governorate. However, prominent opponents of the Government, such as former Prime Minister Selim al-Hoss, also took seats in Beirut, where the participation of the electorate, at 30%, was relatively low. There was speculation that the marginalization of Hezbollah (through the creation of stronger links between Hariri and the President of the National Assembly and leader of Amal, Hezbollah's Shi'a rival, Nabih Berri) was taking place at Syria's insistence in order to appease Israel. In the fourth round of voting, in the South and Nabatiyah on 8 September, Hezbollah retained all four of its seats, having entered into an electoral alliance with Amal. Amal and Hezbollah, together with parties counted as their supporters, were reported to have won all of the 23 seats in the

South. (In the previous rounds of voting Hezbollah had lost two of the eight seats it had held in the outgoing National Assembly.) The participation of the electorate in the fourth round of voting was reported to have been 48%.

Prior to the fifth round of voting (in the Beka'a valley), it was reported that Syria had redeployed some 12,000 of its estimated 30,000 troops in Lebanon to the eastern part of the Beka'a valley. There was speculation that the redeployment had been made for fear of Israeli attacks. Under the terms of the Ta'if agreement the redeployment should have taken place before the legislative elections in 1992. In the final round of voting on 16 September 1996, the Amal-Hezbollah alliance won 22 of the governorate's 23 seats. The participation of the electorate, at 52%, was higher than in any of the previous rounds of voting. This brought the average turn-out in the five governorates to 45%, a marked improvement on the 32% average in 1992. (In May 1997 the Constitutional Court annulled the results of voting for four seats, having found evidence of electoral malpractice. By-elections took place in June, at which all but one of the deputies elected in 1996 were returned to office.)

Nabih Berri was re-elected President of the incoming National Assembly when it convened in October 1996. In late October Rafik Hariri was appointed for his third term as Prime Minister. Disputes reportedly ensued between the President, Prime Minister and President of the National Assembly regarding the composition of the Cabinet, and when this was named, in early November, following consultations with Syrian leaders, the distribution of portfolios among the country's various interests remained largely unchanged. The new Government's statement of policy, as delivered to the National Assembly in that month, emphasized a continuation of economic recovery efforts, and made reference to controversial proposals to prohibit public demonstrations, and to close private radio and television stations. The partial implementation of this last measure had already provoked considerable controversy. In September the Government had announced a ban on political broadcasts by about 150 radio and 50 television stations, and ordered the closure of these stations by the end of November; licences to broadcast political items had been granted to only a small number of stations, most of which were owned by prominent political figures, including Hariri and Berri.

In December 1996 there was a spate of attacks against Syrians in Lebanon, including one in which a bus carrying Syrian workers was hit with machine-gun fire in a predominantly Christian area. Consequently, Syrian Vice-President Abd al-Halim Khaddam indirectly accused Christian opposition leaders, hostile to the incumbent Lebanese Government and to Syria's presence in Lebanon, of collaborating with Israel. In late November seven Christians were sentenced by a military court to up to 15 years' imprisonment, convicted of espionage on behalf of Israel.

INTERNAL AFFAIRS

A further death sentence (commuted to life imprisonment) was imposed on Geagea in May 1996, following his conviction for ordering the assassination of another Maronite rival in 1990. In July 1996 he was acquitted of involvement in the Maronite church bombing of February 1994, although he received a 10-year prison sentence for attempting to recruit and arm militiamen after 1991 (when all militias had been banned). In August 1996 Geagea was further charged with orchestrating the death of Prime Minister Rashid Karami in 1987; his trial on this charge began in December 1997. Meanwhile, in May 1997 Geagea received yet another death sentence, (which was again commuted to life imprisonment), having been convicted of an assassination attempt in 1991 against Michel Murr (now Deputy Prime Minister and Minister of the Interior), who was at the time Minister of Defence.

Long-standing tensions between the Government and the Chairman of the CGTL, Elias Abu Rizq, apparently precipitated a split in the labour movement in April 1997. Prior to the CGTL's leadership elections, in that month, the Minister of Labour approved the admission of five new syndicates, each with voting rights, into the organization. Rizq refused to recognize the new members, and consequently two separate leadership polls took place—one attended by the incumbent and his supporters, the other by his rival, Ghneim az-Zoghbi, whose supporters

included the five new syndicates. The Government was swift to recognize az-Zoghbi as the official leader of the CGTL. At the end of May Rizq was arrested and detained for eight days, charged with usurping a civil office. The new leadership subsequently demonstrated a less confrontational approach towards the Government. In mid-November, none the less, the CGTL organized a one-day general strike, in support of its demand for public-sector pay increases of as much as 20%, and for a 200% increase in the minimum wage.

In July 1997 Sheikh Sobhi Tufayli, Hezbollah Secretary-General in 1989–91, launched a campaign of civil disobedience (designated 'revolution of the hungry') in the Beka'a valley, in protest against the Government's perceived neglect of the region. At a demonstration held in Ba'albek in early July, Tufayli addressed some 10,000 people, urging them to withhold taxes and abstain from paying for utilities in order to force the Government to reduce income taxes and increase development spending in the Beka'a. (Shortly before the rally the Government announced plans to invest some US $98m. in the most deprived areas of the valley.) Unrest continued, and in early November Tufayli instructed the residents of Beka'a to deny all ministers access to the region. In response, the Government ordered the deployment of troops in the eastern Beka'a valley for a three-month period, and it was announced that residents who had joined the protests would be liable to prosecution by the Military Court. In early December Tufayli announced an end to the blockade, after the Government announced development projects for the Beka'a; later in the month, however, he threatened a resumption of the disobedience campaign if investment was not increased. In late January 1998 Hezbollah announced the expulsion of Tufayli from the organization, although the former Secretary-General, who had been criticial of Hezbollah's assimilation under its current Secretary-General, Hasan Nasrallah, into 'mainstream' politics, maintained that he represented the 'true' spirit of Hezbollah. At the end of January at least eight people were killed as a result of a confrontation in Ba'albek involving Tufayli and his supporters and local Hezbollah officials and subsequent intervention by the army. In mid-February Tufayli and 19 of his associates were charged with offences including undermining national security, forming an armed group, and causing the deaths of three soldiers; Tufayli, who had evaded capture following the Ba'albek incident, was charged *in absentia*. Meanwhile, in late 1997 Hezbollah announced the formation of what it called Lebanese Brigades for the Resistance of the Israeli occupation, which it invited all Lebanese, regardless of their religion or political persuasion, to join.

The issue of government restrictions on the broadcast media again provoked controversy in the second half of 1997. In September the authorities began to close down unlicensed broadcasters, and two people were killed when security forces opened fire on members of the fundamentalist Tawheed Islami who were attempting to prevent the closure of a private station in Tripoli. In mid-December the Minister of the Interior prohibited a televised broadcast, from France, by Gen. Michel Awn, on the grounds that such transmissions were undermining national security. (The private satellite company that was to have transmitted the interview was owned by Murr's brother.) The ban provoked a violent demonstration in Beirut: a number of arrests were made, and it was subsequently announced that 10 people were to be tried by the Military Court for attacking the security forces, while civil charges were to be brought against a further 23 protesters who had defied a ban (imposed in 1993) on public demonstrations. Awn's interview was eventually broadcast in January 1998 by a private terrestrial channel. In that month the Government announced a ban on the broadcast of all news and political programmes by privately-owned satellite channels, after a company owned by prominent Maronite interests transmitted an interview with a National Assembly deputy who was an outspoken critic of the Government. It was stated that, henceforth, the stations in question (including a company owned by Prime Minister Hariri) would be authorized only to transmit a news bulletin prepared by the state-controlled Télé-Liban.

EVENTS IN THE SOUTH

Despite the cease-fire 'understanding' of April 1996, clashes continued, and numerous complaints were made to the ILMG by both sides throughout 1996 and 1997. In mid-June 1997 Lebanon welcomed the adoption by the UN General Assembly of a resolution demanding that Israel should pay US $1.7m. in damages for the shelling of the UN base at Qana in April 1996. Tensions were exacerbated in mid-1997 after Hezbollah, which according to the ILMG, had not previously violated the agreement, launched a series of rocket attacks against Israeli targets. On 8 August it was reported that Katyusha rockets were aimed at the Israeli town of Kiryat Shmona in retaliation for Israeli attacks which had caused the deaths of several Lebanese civilians, and an attack on 4 August in which five Hezbollah members were killed. Violence continued to escalate in mid-August, following the deaths of two civilians (the children of a deceased SLA commander) in a bomb explosion in Jezzine, an SLA stronghold north of the security zone. In reprisal, the SLA launched an artillery attack on Sidon, killing at least six civilians. Hezbollah in turn violated the cease-fire 'understanding' with rocket attacks into northern Israel, prompting the Israeli military to direct its most intensive air strikes against presumed Hezbollah and PFLP—GC targets since Operation Grapes of Wrath in April 1996. In late August 1997 four Amal fighters and four members of the Israeli security forces were killed following an ambush by the Israeli military on the edge of the occupied zone; this followed the death of an Amal commander by a car-bomb in central Beirut. In early September 12 members of an élite Israeli commando unit were killed (reportedly the highest Israeli death toll in a single operation since 1985) after Amal fighters and the Lebanese army foiled an operation, apparently against an Amal base, south of Sidon. Later in the month there was intense fighting within the security zone: among those killed was a son of the Hezbollah Secretary-General, Hasan Nasrallah. Reciprocal attacks by Hezbollah and Israeli forces continued into October, with Israel additionally targeting PFLP—GC bases.

Meanwhile, the extent of Israeli casualties as a result of the occupation of southern Lebanon prompted a vocal campaign within Israel for a unilateral withdrawal from the security zone. In late 1997 and early 1998 Israel's Minister of Defence, Itzhak Mordechai, indicated that Israel would be prepared to withdraw, in accordance with UN Security Council Resolution 425 (of March 1978), but with the stipulation that Lebanon provide guarantees of the security of Israel's northern border. On 1 April 1998 the Israeli 'inner' Security Cabinet voted to adopt Resolution 425, on this condition. However, Lebanon emphasized that Resolution 425 demanded an unconditional withdrawal, and stated that neither would it be able to guarantee Israel's immunity from attack, nor would it be prepared to deploy the Lebanese army in southern Lebanon for this purpose; furthermore, Lebanon could not support the continued presence there of the SLA (whose integration with the Lebanese army was sought by the Israelis). Concern was also expressed that a unilateral withdrawal from Lebanon in the absence of a comprehensive Middle East peace settlement might foment regional instability. Israel's demand that Hezbollah be disarmed prior to any Israeli withdrawal was, moreover, unacceptable not only to Lebanon but also to Syria, which regarded its support for the resistance in southern Lebanon as essential leverage in its efforts to secure a parallel Israeli withdrawal from the Golan Heights.

Clashes persisted throughout mid-1998, as did protests to the ILMG of violations of the April 1996 cease-fire 'understanding'. In mid-May 1998 at least 10 people were killed in an Israeli air raid on an al-Fatah training camp in the central Beka'a valley. At the end of the month, following a week of intense fighting in the south, as a result of which five Hezbollah fighters and four members of the SLA had died, two Israeli soldiers were killed in an ambush on their patrol. The deaths of two further Israeli soldiers were reported in late June. However, an exchange of remains of victims of the conflict and prisoners of war proceeded at this time, following 10 months of negotiations under the auspices of the International Committee of the Red Cross: the return to Israel of the remains of a naval commander killed in the abortive operation against Amal in September 1997 facilitated the return to Lebanon of the remains of 40 mainly Hezbollah fighters (including the son of Hasan Nasrallah) and the release of some 60 detainees. In late August 1998 rockets were fired into northern Israel, in retaliation for the death of a local Amal commander near Tyre; at least nine Israelis were

injured, prompting the Israeli Cabinet to approve a proposal by the Minister of Internal Security that in future such attacks be countered with action targeting Lebanese infrastructure.

In late July 1997 the US Secretary of State, Madeleine Albright, announced an end to her country's ban on travel to Lebanon, in response to a commitment by Hariri to increase co-operation in combating terrorism. (The USA had halted flights following the hijacking to Beirut of the TWA flight in 1985, and, in view of fears for the safety within Lebanon of nationals of the USA, had announced in 1987 that US passports were invalid for travel to Lebanon.) Albright visited Beirut in mid-September, as part of a tour of the Middle East; this was the first visit to Beirut by a US Secretary of State since 1983. Prime Minister Rafik Hariri visited Washington, DC, in mid-June 1998, where he met with President Clinton, Madeleine Albright and other US officials; the Lebanese Prime Minister also held discussions with the UN Secretary-General, Kofi Annan, in New York. Following Hariri's visit, the US Administration ended the ban on the sale of tickets to US citizens travelling to Lebanon. This proceeded despite a rocket-grenade attack near the US embassy in Beirut. Some 10 people were arrested in Lebanon in connection with the attack, which was denounced by the Lebanese authorities as an Israeli-inspired attempt to undermine security in the capital.

MUNICIPAL ELECTIONS

Lebanon's first local elections since 1963 were scheduled to take place in June 1997. In early April, however, Hariri withdrew from parliamentary debate draft legislation regulating the elections, on the grounds that the strength of opposition to the proposed law necessitated its reconsideration. It was reported that Hrawi was strongly opposed to the postponement of the elections, while critics of the Prime Minister stated that his action, apparently taken without consulting the Cabinet, was in violation of the Constitution. Later in April it was announced that legislation was to be prepared to extend the mandates of the existing local authorities for a maximum period of 12 months. Additional legislation was to extend the term of the present National Assembly by a further eight months. A new draft law for the municipal elections was approved in late December. In April 1998 it was announced that voting for new local authorities (in all areas except the Israeli-occupied zone and deserted villages in the Chouf region) would take place in four rounds, beginning on 24 May.

Voting proceeded according to this schedule. At the first round, in Mount Lebanon governorate on 24 May 1998, convincing victories for Hezbollah in the southern suburbs of Beirut frustrated an attempt by Hariri and Berri to moderate the influence of the opposition by supporting joint lists of candidates, while Dory Chamoun's PNL, which had boycotted the 1992 and 1996 legislative elections, was among the Government's right-wing opponents to take control of councils in the governorate. The second round, in the North on 31 May 1998, was notable for the failure of attempts to achieve an inter-community balance in Tripoli, where a council comprising 23 Muslims and only one Christian was elected, and (elsewhere in the governorate) for the success of candidates loyal to Samir Geagea. However, a joint list of candidates supported by Hariri and Berri, devised in a stated attempt to reflect the sectarian balance, did win control of the Beirut municipal council at the third round on 7 June. Candidates supported by the Prime Minister fared well in Sidon, while the National Assembly President's Amal won overall control in Tyre. The final stage of voting took place in the Beka'a valley on 14 June, where Hezbollah candidates were largely defeated by candidates of pro-Syrian secular parties and by representatives of the governorate's principal families. Other than in Beirut, turn-out at all stages was high (at about 70% of registered voters), and most political interests expressed broad satisfaction at the conduct and outcome of the elections.

THE ISSUE OF DECONFESSIONALIZATION

In mid-March 1998 Hrawi presented legislation to the Cabinet that would enable marriages to be conducted by civil authorities. Supporters of the President's bill stated that this would facilitate inter-faith marriages and thus erode sectarian divisions. However, the legislation was strongly opposed not only by religious leaders of all faiths (all marriages were hitherto regulated by the religious authorities), but also by the Prime Minister. Following the failure of his efforts to persuade government members to reject the legislation, Hariri refused to sign the bill, on the grounds that it would offend religious sensibilities and create divisions at a time when it was essential to preserve a consensus in order to facilitate the implementation of the Government's economic programme. The National Assembly President, Nabih Berri, was reported to have lent his support to Hrawi's legislation after the latter sought the establishment of a parliamentary committee to consider the 'deconfessionalization' of public life—a process that, it was generally considered, would be to the advantage of the Shi'ite community.

Rafik Hariri's refusal to submit President Hrawi's proposal to the National Assembly was in itself regarded as exemplifying what many Lebanese now regarded as the need for a reform of the confessional system on which Lebanese politics was based. It was increasingly recognized that, while this system had undoubtedly preserved civil peace since the conclusion of the Ta'if agreement, it had also fostered institutional paralysis and cronyism and thus hindered post-war recovery. Many thus believed that the power-sharing arrangement between the President, Prime Minister and President of the National Assembly could not endure into the next presidency.

Despite frequent speculation that Elias Hrawi's presidential term would be extended for a second time, he emphasized on several occasions during 1998 that he would stand down at the expiry of his mandate in November. As this time approached, debate surrounding the issue of succession intensified. While many still felt that Hrawi would finally extend his presidency, others suggested that the Commander-in-Chief of the armed forces, Gen. Emile Lahoud, might be a strong contender for the presidency (although this too would require amendment of the Constitution). However, it was not certain whether, while Syria undoubtedly trusted Lahud, President Assad would favour a Maronite Christian President who was likely to be considerably more authoritarian than his predecessor. Moreover, any future President would have to be acceptable to Prime Minister Hariri, whose continued presence at the head of the Lebanese Government was considered vital to the country's economic reconstruction. By early October Lahoud's candidacy had received full endorsement from the Syrian Government, and on 8 October the Lebanese Government initiated the necessary procedures to amend the article of the Constitution which prohibits individuals currently (or recently) employed in senior state positions from assuming the Presidency. Lahoud was duly elected President on 15 October and was to take office on 24 November.

LEBANON AND THE PEACE CONFERENCE

The Government's decision to send a Lebanese delegation to the opening session of a Middle East peace conference, held in Madrid, Spain, in October 1991, and to participate in subsequent rounds of bilateral negotiations, was criticized in both governmental and non-governmental circles. Critics argued that, since the terms of reference for the conference were UN Security Council Resolutions 242 and 338 only, Lebanon's participation was tantamount to a repudiation of UN Security Council Resolution 425, which demanded a comprehensive withdrawal of all Israeli armed forces from southern Lebanon; and that the implementation of Resolution 425 would henceforth be linked to the implementation of other UN resolutions. They asserted, moreover, that Lebanon had nothing to discuss in bilateral negotiations with Israel, since its relations with that country were regulated by the Armistice agreement of 1949, which remained valid.

Before the opening session of the Middle East peace conference was convened, Lebanon sought assurances from the USA on the following issues: that the implementation of UN Security Council Resolution 425 would not be linked to the implementation of other UN resolutions; that the country would receive support for the establishment of an international fund for Lebanon; that restrictions imposed by the US Government on its citizens with regard to travelling and investing in Lebanon would be removed; that the US Consulate in Beirut would be reopened; that the Lebanese national carrier, Middle East Airlines, should be allowed to resume flights to New York; and that arms paid for by the Government during Amin Gemayel's presidency would be delivered by the USA, and US-based training programmes for Lebanese army officers would be resumed.

With regard to Resolution 425, Lebanon's diplomacy was rewarded by a written US commitment to support its implementation in isolation from the wider Middle East peace process. On the other issues that Lebanon had raised, however, the USA remained non-committal, pending the release of all Western hostages being held in Lebanon. Some observers, too, regarded the US assurance on Resolution 425 to be unclear, since the US Government's letter of intent failed to distinguish between the nature of the Israeli and the Syrian armed presence in Lebanon. Another potential point of contention was the USA's demand that the activities of the Hezbollah militia in southern Lebanon should cease before the peace conference commenced, while the Government insisted that Hezbollah's resistance would continue until the Israeli armed forces had withdrawn from Lebanese territory.

Lebanon reacted cautiously to the Declaration of Principles on Palestinian Self-Rule in the Occupied Territories, signed by Israel and the PLO on 13 September 1993 (for details of the Declaration of Principles, see Documents on Palestine, p. 128). Fears were expressed, for instance, that, if the Declaration of Principles were to provoke violent confrontations between rival Palestinian factions, most of the violence would be likely to occur in Lebanon, endangering the country's reconstruction. There was also concern about the ultimate fate of the estimated 350,000 Palestinian refugees residing in Lebanon.

In late February 1994 Lebanon, together with the other Arab parties, withdrew from the Middle East peace process, following the murder, by a right-wing Jewish extremist, of some 30 Muslim worshippers in a mosque in Hebron on the West Bank. Together with Syria and Jordan, Lebanon agreed to rejoin the peace process in March. As before, any significant progress in negotiations between Lebanon and Israel remained dependent on the conclusion of a peace agreement between Syria and Israel.

Israel's proposal to withdraw from southern Lebanon, as approved by its Security Cabinet in April 1998 (see above), was deemed incompatible with Resolution 425 by Lebanon and Syria, and also by the Arab League, which rejected the proposal on 2 April. Both Lebanon and Syria declared their willingness to resume negotiations with Israel at the point at which they had been interrupted by Israel, but were opposed to completely new talks, as demanded by the Netanyahu administration in Israel.

In early September 1998, reportedly at Gen. Antoine Lahad's direct order, a Lebanese former communist activist was, amid considerable publicity, released from detention: Soha Bishara had spent 10 years in custody for an attempt on the SLA commander's life. It emerged that the Lebanese woman had been offered a visa by France (although it was uncertain whether she would take up President Chirac's offer of asylum). Asylum had, moreover, been offered by France to Lahad and other senior officers of the SLA, prompting speculation that Chirac was seeking to increase Frence influence in the Middle East peace process.

Economy

Revised for this edition by SIMON CHAPMAN

INTRODUCTION

Lebanon's role as the Middle East's leading centre for trade and financial services was destroyed by the civil war which erupted in 1975. Attempts to prepare plans for reconstruction were frustrated by recurring outbreaks of violence, culminating in the Israeli invasion of June 1982, which added a new dimension to the country's devastation. Lebanon's gross domestic product (GDP) expanded, in real terms, at an average annual rate of 6%–6.5% between 1964 and 1974. Average income per head in 1974 was estimated at US $1,300, one of the highest levels among developing countries at the time. With the outbreak of the civil war, however, real GDP declined sharply. Expressed in constant 1974 prices, it was estimated to have averaged £L4,800m. per year in 1975–81. The Israeli invasion caused a further sharp decline in GDP, which, again expressed in constant 1974 prices, was estimated at £L3,080m. in 1982. Despite the intervening years of turmoil, Lebanon's GDP, expressed in constant 1974 prices, was estimated to have recovered to £L8,600m. in 1987. However, although the banking sector actually thrived after 1975, the development of alternative Middle East banking and financial centres, particularly in the Persian (Arabian) Gulf region, made it unlikely that an unstable Lebanon would regain its position as the commercial centre of the Arab world. After Amin Gemayel became President in September 1982 and formed a Cabinet comprising technical experts, it was hoped that the process of rehabilitating the country could begin in earnest. Although detailed programmes were prepared, they could not be implemented, owing to the continued civil conflict and to the unwillingness of potential aid donors to commit themselves before the restoration of stability. In the late 1980s, after years of relative resilience to political events, the deterioration of the political situation, combined with a high level of unemployment, major shifts in population, the breakdown of the infrastructure and the perpetual postponement of reconstruction and development projects, plunged the economy to new depths of depression, and it teetered on the verge of collapse. Those who could afford to leave the country made efforts to establish themselves abroad, often in Cyprus, the USA or Australia. For those with no escape route, however, the outlook was grim. Hopes of an economic revival were raised when the civil war effectively ended in 1991. GDP for that year has been estimated at £L4,132,000m., measured at current prices, or £L3,720m. in constant 1974 prices, compared with an estimated £L1,973,000m. in 1990 (£L2,690m. in constant 1974 prices), and £L1,350,000m. in 1989 (£L3,107m. in constant 1974 prices). In 1992, however, the Government failed to narrow the budget deficit and, amid allegations of corruption and incompetence on the part of ministers, the value of the local currency collapsed, leading to a sharp rise in inflation and the resignation of Omar Karami's Government. The legislative elections held in mid-1992 and the subsequent appointment of an entrepreneur, Rafik Hariri, as Prime Minister paved the way for a serious start to economic reconstruction, which was to be based on higher receipts of foreign aid. In 1992 it is estimated that Lebanon's GDP, expressed in current prices, amounted to £L9,499,000m. (£L3,887m. in constant 1974 prices). In 1993 GDP increased to an estimated £L13,122,000m., or £L4,161m. in real (1974) terms. Lebanon's GDP increased by 8.0% in 1994 and by 6.5% in 1995, but growth slowed to 4% in 1996. According to estimates by a leading commercial bank, GDP increased, in real terms, by 3.5% in 1997, to total $14,957m. at current prices (compared with $13,240m. in 1996). The IMF estimated that GDP amounted to $11,400m. in 1995, indicating GDP per caput of $3,260 (still considerably lower, in real terms, than in 1974).

Lebanon's economic life after the outbreak of the civil war in 1975 was intimately shaped by the violence, which included the Israeli invasions of the south in March 1978 and of the area up to and including Beirut in 1982. According to the Lebanese authorities, of a total of more than 100,000 people killed between 1975 and 1982, up to and including the Israeli invasion, 19,085 people were killed and 30,302 wounded between 4 June and 31 August 1982, and the Council for Development and Reconstruction (CDR—created in 1977 as the main co-ordinator of reconstruction efforts) estimated the cost of material damage at US $1,900m., with damage to housing alone of $670m.

In 1979 the CDR disclosed proposals for a five-year reconstruction programme that envisaged expenditure of £L22,000m. However, following the Israeli invasion, the CDR produced a revised, 10-year programme, covering the period 1982–91, with plans for estimated spending of £L68,000m. The CDR's proposals stressed that the private sector would continue to be the main generator of economic activity, and that credit programmes for the private sector would be strengthened. Of the total planned expenditure, one-quarter was to be raised locally, and the rest from Arab oil states, international lending agencies and foreign governments. As a result of fighting from September 1983, however, and the consequences of the Israeli invasion of the south, the cost of the 10-year plan had to be revised on more than one occasion: in mid-1984 it was estimated by the CDR at more than £L100,000m. (US $17,000m.), compared with the March 1983 revision (£L62,200m. or $13,000m.) of the original 1978 plan (see below); and at the beginning of 1985 the estimated cost had soared to £L530,000m. ($33,000m.), taking account of new damage and the fall in the value of the Lebanese pound. In March 1983 the World Bank published a report on the country's reconstruction needs and detailed a programme which allocated £L4,130m. to telecommunications, £L3,854m. to energy, £L2,941m. to roads, £L2,121m. to urban development and £L2,222m. to education. The Bank also emphasized the need for a separate, $223.5m.-reconstruction project to cover urgent requirements, especially in Greater Beirut. In late 1991 a US engineering company, Bechtel, and a Lebanese consultancy, Dar al-Handasah, completed a government-commissioned plan for the country's emergency reconstruction needs. The $3,000m.-plan covered 133 projects, most of them for completion within three years. Of the total, $819m. was allocated to road schemes, $461.9m. to housing, $320m. to sewerage schemes, $234.9m. to health sector schemes and $200m. to water supply projects. The emergency reconstruction plan, covering 1992 to 1995, formed part of a 10-year programme called Horizon 2000. This originally envisaged public expenditure totalling $11,700m. (at constant prices of 1992). Of the total, $10,200m. was for physical infrastructure, $300m. for investments in institutions and planning and $1,200m. for grant and credit support for private sector enterprises. Horizon 2000 aims to double real GDP per caput in the 1995–2007 period.

Mobilizing resources for investment is one of the greatest challenges facing the Lebanese Government; flows of aid have been far smaller than the amounts pledged. The end of the civil war in early 1991 seemed likely to lead to an increase in foreign aid. In December of that year the World Bank sponsored a meeting of potential donors to Lebanon in Paris, at which the Lebanese Prime Minister, Omar Karami, reportedly requested $4,450m. for urgent projects in the subsequent three to five years. Following the meeting, it was confirmed that as much as $700m. in concessionary loans and grants had been pledged for the 1992–94 period, albeit mainly in earlier, bilateral meetings.

In late 1991 and early 1992 Lebanon secured a series of other aid commitments, although it was unclear whether these were included in the $700m. figure which had emerged after the Paris donors' meetings. In November 1991, for example, the Kuwait Fund for Arab Economic Development (KFAED) had agreed to make a $36.2m.-loan for power projects, and in the following month the Arab Fund for Economic and Social Development (AFESD) granted a $73m.-loan, also for power schemes. In February 1992 it was announced that Italy had agreed to provide $460m. in loans and grants for electricity, water, telecommunications, refuse collection, health, agricultural and transport projects. Italy thus emerged as by far the biggest Western contributor to Lebanon's reconstruction.

By mid-1992 the International Fund for Assisting Lebanon (for the establishment of which an agreement had been concluded at the Arab summit meeting held in Baghdad in May 1990) had still not been formed, although in October 1991 the Minister of Foreign Affairs, Faris Bouez, announced that the Fund would have a capital of $2,000m., of which $500m.–$600m. would come from Gulf states and a further $500m. from Japan, France, Germany and Italy. Subsequently, however, Lebanon descended into a deep economic crisis which, the Government claimed, was partly due to the fact that foreign aid had not been arriving at the rate anticipated.

The Government's hopes that expatriate Lebanese might use some of their substantial funds to invest in their country's reconstruction meanwhile appeared too optimistic. In 1991 the IMF estimated that between $10,000m. and $15,000m. was held abroad by expatriates. Although there was a significant influx of private funds after the end of the fighting in 1991, these were mainly invested in property rather than in more directly productive areas.

The end of the civil war in 1991 did, nevertheless, allow the launch of some reconstruction work, although this was constrained by shortages of funds. The Italian company Emit, for example, began work on a $30m.-Italian Government-funded project to improve Beirut's water supply system, and in February 1992 French companies submitted offers for three French Government-funded contracts to repair and upgrade telecommunications and power installations. Local and international contracting firms were meanwhile preparing studies for a range of other schemes. There was a marked increase in the amount of foreign aid granted to Lebanon following the legislative elections which took place in mid-1992, and the appointment of a new Government under Rafik Hariri. In March 1993 the World Bank agreed to grant the country $175m. for the reconstruction of its infrastructure. While this loan encouraged other lenders to grant aid, the World Bank made clear its concern at the Government's continued inability to bring state finances under control. In particular, the Bank was concerned at its failure to reduce the country's budget deficit. During 1993 and 1994 international confidence in Lebanon's new-found stability increased, and was reflected in a major influx of development aid from governments and lending agencies. During a visit to London in early 1994 Prime Minister Hariri said that the country had secured about $1,500m. in foreign funding and that a further $920m. was being negotiated. He commented that the Horizon 2000 programme could be completed in as little as five years if sufficient funding was available. Private capital, mostly from expatriate Lebanese, had also begun to return on a large scale. Within one month of Hariri's appointment as Prime Minister and during the first nine months of 1993 aggregate bank deposits increased by a further $1,500m. In early 1995, however, according to the CDR, the total contribution of funds by donors to the Lebanese economic recovery programme amounted to $1,900m. Of this, $1,500m. was in loans and the remainder in grants. The total was disappointingly close to the one announced by Hariri in early 1994 and suggested that the CDR would be obliged to seek funds from other sources if it was to meet its financing needs. The European Union (EU), the World Bank, Saudi Arabia, Kuwait, the AFESD and Italy had provided most of the funds to date. In 1995 the World Bank, concerned about Lebanon's rapidly growing public debt, suggested that the Government should scale down its commitments under Horizon 2000, identify a core investment programme of no more than $3.5m. for the next two years and increase the role of the private sector in financing infrastructure, public health and education.

The Israeli attack on southern Lebanon and Beirut in April 1996 is estimated to have cost Lebanon some $500m. in damage and disruption to business and to have reduced economic growth by up to 2% of GDP. The instability caused by the bombing and by the election of a right-wing Government in Israel in May further depressed investor confidence.

After the cease-fire agreement between Hezbollah and Israel, Prime Minister Hariri sought to establish a consultative committee including the USA and EU member states to assist Lebanon's development. At the same time, he announced that his Government needed to raise $5,000m. for reconstruction during the period 1997–2001, of which $270m. was to be spent on basic infrastructure; $216m. on social services including health, education and housing; $324m. on public services; $150m. on agriculture and industry; and $40m. on public facilities. This was the first indication that the Government acknowledged its inability to secure the scale of financing originally envisaged for Horizon 2000. The CDR reported that by April 1996 $2,700m. had been received from foreign donors; $2,303m. in loans, and the rest in grants. In December 1996, at the 'Friends of Lebanon' meeting held in Washington and attended by some 30 countries, and many international organizations, the Lebanese Government claimed to have received pledges of $3,200m. for the period to the end of 2001. The donations, $1,800m. less than the $5,000m. requested for a total of 31 projects, and the subsequent lack of detail concerning such projects raised speculation about the true extent of funding commitments made at the meeting. Moreover, the collapse of the Middle East peace process further jeopardized Lebanon's plans to re-establish Beirut as a regional services centre.

In late 1997 further doubt was cast on the viability of Lebanon's reconstruction programme when members of the Cabinet refused to endorse a proposal by the Prime Minister that petrol prices should be increased in order to raise $800m. in bonds on international markets to finance domestic social projects. This measure was part of an emergency plan proposed by Hariri to service Lebanon's foreign debt through revenue from taxes and price rises. Increasing concern had been expressed at the Government's financial management, in particular at its failure to reduce the huge, persistent budget deficit (see below). (Some 80% of government expenditure is absorbed by public-sector salaries and debt-servicing, while the collection of revenues is complicated by widespread tax evasion.) It was also noted that growth in Lebanon's GDP remained alarmingly low for a country engaged in infrastructural renewal, and it remained uncertain to what extent the funding commitments that the Government claimed to have secured in December 1996 had been honoured. Increasing public disquiet at the unavailability of funds for welfare spending were reported to have acted as a further catalyst for Hariri's emergency proposals.

POPULATION AND EMPLOYMENT

No proper census has been held in Lebanon since 1932, for fear of upsetting the delicate political balance between the various sects or confessions. Until 1991 all political and administrative offices were allocated on the basis of the 1932 census, which showed Christians in the majority by six to five over non-Christians. It has been widely recognized for many years, however, that Muslims account for about 60% of the total population. (In 1983 the combined Shi'a and Sunni Muslim population was estimated at 1.95m., while the combined Maronite and Greek Orthodox Christian communities were numbered at 1.15m.) The increase in the Muslim proportion occurred partly because of the higher ratio of Muslims in the Palestinian population in Lebanon and partly because Muslims tended to have a higher birth rate and to emigrate less than Christians. Demographic changes strained to the limit the delicate system of allocating offices on a sectarian basis which was adopted under the National Covenant of 1943. They were finally recognized in the Ta'if agreement of 1989, which stipulated, among other things, that Christians and Muslims should be represented by an equal number of deputies in the National Assembly.

The effects of the civil war on the size, composition and geographical distribution of Lebanon's population have been dramatic. From an estimated 3.1m. inhabitants in 1974 (which made Lebanon one of the most densely populated countries of the Middle East), the total is believed to have declined to 2.7m. in 1979, thereafter rising slightly, to reach about 2.9m. in 1990. By mid-1995, owing to the return of many Lebanese from exile, the population was estimated to have increased to about 3m. and was projected to increase to 4m. in 2000 and 4.5m. in 2010. According to Ministry of Health figures for 1996, 29.2% of the population were aged 14 or under, 63.8% 15–64 years, and 7% 65 years or over. The labour force was estimated at 1m. in 1996.

The total of those killed or disabled during 1975–76 was estimated by the Lebanese Chamber of Commerce, Industry and Agriculture at 30,000 but other estimates were as high as 60,000, while thousands more were killed or wounded during the spring and autumn of 1978. By the Lebanese Government's reckoning, a further 19,085 people died as a result of the Israeli invasion of 1982. Each round of violence tended to trigger a fresh wave of movement of population, whether within Lebanon, for example from the south into Beirut, or abroad. Those who went abroad often joined relatives or friends already there, for Lebanese emigration was considerable from the 1890s onwards, and by 1960 an estimated 2.5m. Lebanese, or people of Lebanese descent, were living outside the country. The biggest migrant community has traditionally been in the USA, and other favourite settling places were West Africa, Latin America and Australia. Remittances from Lebanese working abroad have traditionally been a staple source of national income. On average, the remittances from the 250,000–300,000 Lebanese workers abroad provided up to 35% of Lebanon's gross national product (GNP). However, returns slumped in 1983, according to US observers, with the usual monthly remittance of $125m.–$200m. falling to $75m.–$100m., reflecting the recession in the Gulf, where many Lebanese worked, caused by the world oil glut.

A study carried out at the American University of Beirut (AUB) showed the impact of the civil war and its aftermath on the labour force. It stated that in 1974 the non-agricultural labour force was 597,778, and had there been no civil war, the number would have reached 791,354 in 1979, instead of which it was only 426,239. The number of Lebanese working abroad in 1975 was 98,000, but by 1979 the number had risen to 210,000. Of these, 73,400 were in Saudi Arabia, 15,800 in Kuwait, and smaller numbers in other Arab states. Outside the Arab world, 17,300 were in West Africa, 27,000 in Europe, 17,000 in Latin America, 11,600 in North America and 14,000 in Australia. While Lebanon's recovery was hampered by the drain of skills and brains, there was at the same time a pool of unemployed, estimated at more than 200,000 in 1979. The sectors in which there was the greatest contraction of the work-force between 1974 and 1979 were industry (from 138,359 to 86,941), construction (from 46,517 to 18,942) and transport and communications (from 47,113 to 25,256). Many of those not in regular employment were engaged in paramilitary activities, or were part of the thriving 'black' economy. The exodus of thousands of Palestinian and Syrian workers from Lebanon, as a result of the Israeli invasion, caused a shortage of skilled and unskilled labour. The construction industry, in particular, was seriously affected. In 1985 it was estimated that 28% of the active population (18–68 years old) were unemployed, whereas before the civil war the rate had been 5%. Unemployment was estimated at almost 50% in 1987 and at 35% in 1990. According to official estimates, unemployment declined from almost 50% in 1987, to 35% in 1990 and to 18.5% in 1996.

AGRICULTURE

Of the total area of the country, about 52% consists of mountain, swamp or desert, and a further 7% of forest. Only 23% of the area is cultivated, although a further 17% is considered cultivable. In late 1996, however, the Ministry of Agriculture warned that soil erosion and groundwater pollution had reached critical levels and that a reafforestation programme would be launched in order to prevent desertification. The coastal strip enjoys a Mediterranean climate and is exceedingly fertile, producing mainly olives, citrus fruits and bananas. Many of the steep valleys leading up from the coastal plain are carefully terraced and very productive in olives and soft fruit. In the Zahleh and Shtoura regions there are vineyards, while cotton and onions are grown in the hinterland of Tripoli. The main cereal-growing district is the Beka'a, the fertile valley between the Lebanon and the Anti-Lebanon ranges, to the north of which lies the source of the river Orontes. The River Litani also flows southwards through the Beka'a before turning west near Marjayoun to flow into the Mediterranean just north of Tyre. This valley is particularly fertile and cotton is now grown there with some success. Throughout the country the size of the average holding is extremely small and, even so, a small-holding, particularly in the mountains, may be broken up into several fragments some distance apart. The agricultural sector contributed over 9% of GDP between 1972 and 1974, but the proportion declined to about 8.5% during the civil war, when depopulation of the countryside occurred and both public and private investment in agriculture declined. The number of people employed in the agricultural sector fell from 147,724 in 1975 to an estimated

103,400, or 23% of the labour force, in 1985. In 1996 the FAO estimated that only 3.7% of the total labour force were employed in agriculture. The Hariri Government, which took office in 1992, was criticized for giving the agricultural sector a low priority in its investment plans, but by early 1997 the necessity of agricultural development had been recognized. Indeed, the Government encouraged commercial bank lending to the agricultural sector by subsidizing interest rates. The Ministry of Agriculture's budget was also increased so that it could finance more agricultural research and also supply farmers with basic needs. From October 1997 a list of prohibited agricultural imports was to be introduced to protect local producers. Cereals and products used by the food processing industry would be exempt. By early 1997 agriculture was estimated to account for 10% of GDP.

In early 1997 the CDR announced a number of projects, including the development of 5,600 ha of farmland by terracing hillslopes, building 300 km of roads in remote rural areas and assisting the Ministry of Agriculture with staff training, to be supported by a $31m. grant from the World Bank.

Lebanon's wheat crop totalled an estimated 45,000 metric tons in 1996, compared with an estimated 49,000 tons in 1995. Fruit-growing increased substantially from the early 1950s and played an important part in the economy during the civil conflict. A rush to plant apple trees in the 1950s resulted in gluts, followed by a reduction in output in the late 1960s. Production of apples was estimated at 136,000 tons in 1996, compared with an estimated 135,000 tons in 1995. Production of grapes was estimated at 350,000 tons in 1996, compared with an estimated 330,000 tons in 1995. Other significant crops include citrus fruits, sugar beet, potatoes, tomatoes, cucumbers and olives. A small quantity of tobacco is also produced.

Agriculture was the sector worst affected by the Israeli attacks in April 1996, when the south and the western Beka'a valley experienced heavy bombardment. It was estimated that almost half of the 1996 tobacco crop was lost, together with 20% of the area's vegetable crop, and that citrus production had also been badly damaged. Losses to tobacco and vegetable crops were estimated at $26m.

The relative lack of security in Lebanon has allowed two crops to flourish: hemp (*Cannabis sativa*), the source of hashish; and the opium poppy (*Papaver somniferum*), the source of opium and its derivatives, heroin and morphine. Before the civil war, Lebanon's annual hashish production was estimated at 100 tons. Between 1987 and 1989 output averaged 700–900 tons, although production declined to 100 tons per year in 1990–91, owing to inclement weather. In 1988–91 annual opium production averaged 40 tons. More recently, the Government has tried to encourage farmers to substitute other crops for hemp and the opium poppy. As part of this programme, plans were announced in June 1996 to establish a crop substitution office for the north-eastern Baalbek-Hermel region in the Beka'a valley. In late February 1997 the Government and the UN Development Programme (UNDP) reportedly signed an agreement to implement the second phase of the programme at a cost of $12m. The Government and the UNDP were to contribute $4m. and $3.8m., respectively, while $2.2m. was to be invested by France, $595,000 by Italy and $690,000 by the EU.

INDUSTRY

Until the time of the first sudden increase in petroleum prices, in 1973–74, the only minerals which were exploited in Lebanon were lignite and some iron ore, smelted in Beirut. There have been hopes of petroleum discoveries for a number of years but, so far, these hopes have been unfulfilled.

Even before hopes of a petroleum discovery were raised, Lebanon was of considerable importance to the petroleum industry. Two of the world's most important oil pipelines cross the country, one from the Kirkuk oil wells in Iraq to Tripoli and the other from Saudi Arabia to Zahrani near Sidon. At each terminal there is an important petroleum refinery. Both the pipelines and the refineries have, however, been the subject of disputes.

Revenues from the Kirkuk–Tripoli pipeline, which was managed by the Iraq Petroleum Company (IPC), were reduced after both Iraq and Syria nationalized IPC assets in their countries on 1 June 1972. After the Iraqi Government and IPC had reached a settlement on the nationalization in 1973, a dispute over the ownership of the IPC refinery in Lebanon followed, as a result of which the Lebanese Government appropriated the refinery and agreed to compensate IPC. In April 1976, however, Iraq suspended pumping, choosing to direct its Kirkuk petroleum to the Persian (Arabian) Gulf instead. Lebanon was thus faced with a loss of around £L30m. per year in royalties as well as the loss of cheap petroleum. During the early part of 1977 the refinery at Tripoli was processing only 5,000 barrels per day (b/d), compared with an average of 36,000 b/d in 1975. By 1978, however, it was operating at around 75% of capacity on petroleum which reached Tripoli by sea or from nearby Zahrani. Iraq finally resumed pumping to Syria through the former IPC pipeline in early 1979, but the transfer of Kirkuk crude petroleum via Lebanon remained dependent on the conclusion of a new bilateral transit and supply agreement. It was reported in March 1981 that Iraq had agreed to start re-pumping after a break of five years. The initial rate of delivery was to be about 200,000 b/d, doubling after two months. Of this, 35,000 b/d were to be used domestically, with the remainder exported. At the time of the agreement, the Tripoli refinery was using 26,000 b/d of Saudi Arabian crude petroleum, which was pumped to Zahrani and then transported to Tripoli by tanker.

On 24 December 1981 Iraqi petroleum started to flow through the pipeline, but within days it was damaged by a bomb blast. Although the pipeline was repaired, its vulnerability to sabotage was underlined when, in March 1982, it was blown up again. Politics intervened when, on 10 April, the trans-Syria pipeline was closed and Iraqi deliveries to Tripoli were suspended. The refinery subsequently processed Iraqi petroleum which had been transported via Turkey. The fighting between PLO loyalists and anti-Arafat factions in Tripoli in December 1983 caused damage to the refinery which was estimated at $120m., while $60m.-worth of petroleum products were destroyed when 29 of the refinery's 36 major tanks, and 16 of its smaller tanks, were hit. The refinery began to receive shipments of Iraqi oil again in April 1984, when repairs were completed. Supplies of Iraqi oil ceased in 1990, as a result of the economic sanctions imposed on Iraq. In October 1990 Syria agreed to supply Lebanon with 20,000 b/d of light crude petroleum, to be delivered through the pipeline linking Tripoli with the Syrian oil terminal at Banias. In early 1991, after the completion of repairs and modifications, the Tripoli refinery resumed operations.

The Zahrani refinery was, until 1986, operated by the Mediterranean Refinery Co (Medreco), jointly owned by Caltex and Mobil. Mobil, Caltex's two parent firms (Texaco and Standard Oil of California) and Exxon also own the Trans-Arabian Pipeline Co (Tapline), which formerly operated the Saudi-Lebanese pipeline. Tapline suspended its pumping operations in early February 1975 because oil tankers found it cheaper to load petroleum directly from the Saudi terminal at Ras Tanura in the Gulf. This suspension cost Lebanon more than £L20m. in royalties. The company also demanded that the Lebanese Government pay for the higher cost of Saudi petroleum (previously supplied to the Zahrani refinery at a price of $5 per barrel), claiming that it was owed $100m. in back payments. A settlement was reached in August 1975, but when the refinery, which had been out of action for much of 1976, recommenced operations at the end of November 1976, the question of back payments arose again. Accumulated debts for 1975/76 were estimated at $120m., and in August 1977 it was finally agreed that these would be settled by the Saudi Arabian Government. However, it was not until early 1979, in the wake of the Iranian Revolution and the decline in Iran's exports of petroleum, that Tapline resumed operations on its former scale.

In early August 1981 Tapline suspended all deliveries of crude petroleum to the Zahrani refinery because of non-payment of debts, but a few weeks later Saudi Arabia announced that it would pay most of Lebanon's petroleum bill. The Israeli invasion of Lebanon in 1982 presented further complications. The Zahrani refinery was out of action from June to November, after it had been bombed. Tapline's oil pipeline passed through Israeli-held territory, so Saudi crude petroleum was delivered by tanker. In February 1982 Tapline announced that it had lost some $350m. on its Lebanese operations since 1975, and that it had decided to close the damaged pipeline, which, for political and security reasons, would not be repaired. In September 1983 Tapline gave 90 days' notice that it was to stop operating in

Lebanon and Syria and in early 1984 the Government took control of Tapline's installations. In 1986 Medreco ceased operations and the Government took control of the Zahrani refinery. In 1991, with the civil war apparently concluded, the Government announced its intention to bring the Zahrani refinery back into operation. Nevertheless, by late 1996 plans to renovate the Zahrani refinery and the refinery near Tripoli appeared to have been abandoned when it was announced that preliminary studies had been completed for an oil refinery in Syria to supply Lebanon with petroleum products. In August 1998, however, a joint French–Iranian proposal that could reactivate the Tripoli refinery, out of service since 1993, was announced. Under the plan, the Iranian Government would finance a feasibility study, and, if rehabilitation was recommended, French contractors would undertake the work.

The civil war had a dramatic impact on Lebanese industry. Between 1975 and 1982, up to and including the Israeli invasion, some 400 industrial units were destroyed or seriously damaged, according to the CDR. During their invasion, Israeli forces were said to have destroyed 25 of the country's major industrial units and to have damaged many smaller enterprises. Damage to the textile industry was particularly severe. Before the invasion, fewer than 50% of the 1,200 textile factories which were operating before 1975 remained active, and during the invasion a further 70 enterprises were completely destroyed and more than 150 others damaged.

The Chouf war of autumn 1983 cost local industry an estimated £L10m. per day; 140 factories, employing 25,000 workers, in the Choueifat-Kfarchima district of southern Beirut were forced to close. The Israeli occupation of southern Lebanon also posed serious problems for industrialists, who had to compete with a large influx of Israeli goods entering the country. This not only meant that local goods were competing with cheaper Israeli items, but it also led to problems between Lebanon and its Arab neighbours, who suspected that Israeli goods were being exported to them via Lebanon and imposed an embargo on some Lebanese products. Other factors which hampered industrial development were the shortage of skilled workers (owing to emigration to the Gulf), ageing machinery, and the weak and damaged infrastructure.

Much of Lebanon's remaining industry is located in the Christian Zone, which until 1989 was relatively free of widespread violence. During the period 14 March–10 May 1989, however, 170 Lebanese factories were damaged in Gen. Awn's 'war of liberation' against Syria, 20 of them being completely destroyed. Factories sustained further damage during inter-Christian fighting in early 1990.

Industry in Lebanon traditionally consisted of small-scale operations run by individuals who employed a handful of people. Food processing, yarn and textile firms accounted for about 44% of industrial output and furniture and woodworking factories for about 29%. Mechanical industries accounted for only about 7% of total production and the remainder was contributed by the cement, ceramics, pharmaceutical and plastic industries. With the exception of petroleum companies, the largest industrial employers prior to the civil conflict were probably the food-processing industries, followed by the well-developed textile industries.

The civil conflict prevented any sustained revival of industry during the 1980s. The value of industrial exports in 1980 was 15% higher than in 1979, and in 1981 there was a further increase, of 25%, to £L2,290m. However, these increases were mainly due to the depreciation of the Lebanese pound. The major buyers of Lebanese industrial exports in 1981 were Iraq, Syria, Saudi Arabia and Jordan, which together accounted for 86% of all sales. The invasion of Lebanon by Israel in 1982 caused the value of industrial exports to decline to £L1,924m. in 1982 and to £L1,296.4m. in 1983. In 1984 their value fell to £L984m. Assisted by the rapid depreciation in the value of the Lebanese pound, the value of industrial exports subsequently increased sharply: to $372m. in 1985, $438m. in 1986 and $690m. in 1987. In 1988, however, it amounted to only $274m., and in 1989—a year in which factories in east Beirut sustained particularly heavy damage—only $174m. The 1990 figure was $127m. With the end of the fighting in 1991, the value of industrial exports recovered to $206m.; the 1992 figure was $210m. The Israeli occupation of the south, the cumulative effect of years of violence, the recession in the Gulf, which was Lebanon's principal export market, and competition from cheap, smuggled goods, all contributed to the decline of industry. The new industrial zone around Sidon, which developed after 1976, was effectively throttled by the Israeli presence and the influx of subsidized Israeli goods. Lebanon's industrial sector was estimated to be operating at only 40% of capacity in early 1986, with textiles, leather goods and finished wood products accounting for the bulk of production, while the labour force employed in manufacturing industry had declined to an estimated 45,000 in 1985. The Hariri Government, which took office in 1992, was criticized both for giving the industrial sector a low priority in its investment plans and for implementing monetary policies which prevented the expansion of industrial production.

The lack of adequate sources of power hindered industrial development in the 1960s, but Lebanon gradually achieved the position of having excess capacity. In 1972 it began to supply power through a 100-kWh line to southern Syria, and in March 1976 the two countries agreed on the exchange of power through a similar line between Tripoli and Tartous. Work on implementing the power link-up project began in 1977 as part of moves to repair the country's badly damaged electricity network. A seven-year electrification scheme, costing some £L1,260m., was drafted, which was expected to be financed by the World Bank and the AFESD. An important feature of the plan was the upgrading of the Zouk power station, and in 1980 the European Investment Bank (EIB) lent around $4.3m. for two 125-MW generators for the station. In early 1982 Electricité du Liban (EDL) obtained a further loan of 7m. ECUs to help to finance the expansion of the Zouk power station. Generating capacity in 1990 totalled 515 MW, with thermal stations accounting for 465 MW and hydroelectric plants for 50 MW. By comparison, a capacity of 1,200 MW was required to satisfy the peak level of 1991 demand. In early 1991 officials from EDL outlined plans for a series of projects to expand existing power facilities and establish new ones. The projects included the construction of a 200-MW gas turbine station in the Beka'a valley; the installation of a 200-MW gas turbine and a 100-MW steam turbine at Zahrani; the addition of a 150–180-MW steam turbine at the Zouk station; the installation of 100-MW and 150-MW steam turbines at the Jiyyeh power station; the construction of a 100-MW steam turbine at the Harisha power station; and the construction of a new power station, with a 250-MW steam turbine, at Batroun. According to EDL, Lebanon required an additional 2,400 MW of capacity in order to satisfy projected demand in the 1990s. Owing to the decline in the value of the local currency and the ending of subsidies on the prices of fuel oil and electricity to industry, raw materials and energy now cost more, and these higher costs will hamper any industrial recovery. In 1993 the Italian firm Ansaldo Energia, South Korea's Hyundai Corpn and two French firms, Bouygues and Clemessy, won contracts to repair and rehabilitate the electricity sector. The work is being financed by the AFESD, the KFAED and the World Bank. Also in 1993 Electricité de France was appointed to prepare tender documents for the construction of two 415-MW combined-cycle power stations, one in the south, at Zahrani (near Sidon), the other in the north, at Beddawi (near Tripoli). In 1996 it was reported that a number of local banks had agreed to lend the Government $60m. towards the cost of the two stations, which are being built by an Italian and German consortium, at a projected total cost of $536m. The plant at Beddawi was expected to begin operations in September 1998, with the Zahrani plant scheduled to follow in May 1999. Another two 77-MW gas turbine stations were completed at Tyre and Baalbek in June 1996. The Government has also begun a $300m. plan to expand and upgrade the electricity grid, including the construction of several substations linked to the four new power plants, in order to fulfil demand until 2005. By the beginning of 1997 international banks and financial institutions, including the EIB, had pledged some $184m. towards the cost of expanding the country's electricity grid. In early 1997 EDL launched a $100m. Eurobond to provide additional funds for the expansion programme.

Despite Israeli bombing in April 1996 which damaged two electricity transformer stations in Greater Beirut, electricity rationing was avoided and repairs were completed by July with French assistance, at an estimated cost of $30m. Nevertheless, in early 1997 it was reported that 15% of all power generated was being lost, not only because equipment was out-dated, but also because of damage to the electricity network during the many years of civil conflict. The privatization of EDL's consumer billing and collection service was also being considered because the company itself was able to collect only some 40% of revenues owed to it. Meanwhile it was reported that Lebanon had joined a project to connect the electricity grids of Jordan, Iraq, Egypt, Turkey and Syria, being partly financed by the AFESD.

In 1998 it was reported that, in order to reduce the cost of fuel imports, the Government was considering a plan to convert the power stations at Beddawi and Zahrani to using natural gas, rather than fuel oil, for the generation of electricity. One potential means of supplying the new fuel is a project, with an estimated cost of $200m., to pipe gas to the Lebanese plants from the Homs natural gas refinery in Syria. Under the scheme, Syria was expected to supply at least 3m. cu m of gas per day. A second stage would provide Syrian gas to the Lebanese power stations at Harisha and Jiyyeh.

EXTERNAL TRADE AND BALANCE OF PAYMENTS

Reflecting the post-war increase in reconstruction activity, the value of Lebanon's merchandise exports (valued f.o.b. at the official dollar rate) increased from US $455m. in 1990 to $546m. in 1991, while imports (valued f.o.b. at the customs dollar rate) rose from $2,528m. in 1990 to $3,748m. in 1991. The trade deficit thus increased from $2,073m. in 1990 to $3,202m. in 1991. Net transactions in services, other income and private unrequited transfers (including workers' remittances from abroad) produced a surplus of $303m. in 1991, resulting in a deficit on the current account of the balance of payments (excluding official transfers) of $2,899m. in that year. However, there was a surplus on the capital account (including net errors and omissions) of $3,973m. in 1991, leaving the overall balance in surplus by $1,074m. In 1992 there was a trade deficit of $3,185m. (exports $601m., imports $3,786m.) and a current account deficit of $2,798m. The capital account was in surplus by $2,851m., resulting in an overall surplus of $53m. Meanwhile, the customs dollar rate, used to calculate to value of imports in terms of US currency, was adjusted in July 1992 to $1 = £L800 (having been $1 = £L200 since the beginning of the year). The new rate remained in operation until July 1995, although throughout this period the free market exchange rate was about £L1,700 per US dollar.

In 1993 Lebanon's expenditure on imports surged, reflecting the gathering pace of reconstruction, but, as in previous years, the current account deficit was more than offset by capital inflows. The overall balance of payments (defined as net change in foreign assets of the banking system) was $1,169m. in surplus in 1993, although there was a trade deficit of $4,222m. (exports $686m., imports $4,908m.) in that year. In 1994 the trade deficit was $4,798m. (exports $743m., imports $5,541m.), while the deficit on the current account was $4,103m., compared with $3,806m. in 1993. However, net capital inflows in 1994 were $5,234m., leaving an overall surplus of $1,131m. The c.i.f. value of total Lebanese imports in that year was $5,990m. On that basis, Lebanon's principal suppliers of goods in 1994 were Italy ($799m.), Germany ($598m.), the USA ($555m.) and France ($534m.). In 1995 the deficit in Lebanon's balance of trade increased to $5,770m. (exports $985m., imports $6,755m.) although the overall balance of payments recorded a surplus of $256m., owing to a surplus of $872m. on other current transactions and the inflow of $5,154m. in net capital receipts. In 1995 Lebanon's total export earnings included $161m. from re-exports (net of transit values). Of total domestic exports ($824m.) in that year, 28.7% were consigned to the United Arab Emirates (UAE), compared with 18% in 1994, while Italy and the USA were the principal suppliers of goods in 1995, accounting for 13% and 11%, respectively, of total imports (about $7,300m. on a c.i.f. basis). In July 1995 the use of differential exchange rates for valuing imports and exports was discontinued. Since that date the value of all external trade in US currency has been calculated on the basis of the official dollar rate (the previous month's average market rate).

The trade deficit remained high in 1996, with the value of total imports (on a c.i.f. basis) rising by 3.5%, to $7,559m., and exports increasing to $1,018m. Some 54% of all imports came from Western Europe, 11.9% from North America and only 6.3% from the Arab world. The principal supplying countries in 1996 were Italy ($915m. or 12.1% of total imports), the USA ($824m. or 10.9%), Germany ($644m. or 8.5%) and France ($588m. or 7.8%). Machinery (including electrical) and transport equipment accounted for almost one-third of the value of total imports. Government measures to protect domestic industry resulted in a slight fall in the value of textile imports. Almost two-thirds of exports were to the Arab world and just under 20% to Western Europe. In 1996, as in the previous year, the UAE was the main destination for Lebanese exports (accounting for $238.4m. or 23.4% of the total), followed by Saudi Arabia ($139.0m. or 13.7%). Pulp, paper and paper products accounted for almost one-third of the value of exports. Once again the trade deficit was offset by an increase in capital inflows, estimated at $6,500m., giving an overall balance-of-payments surplus of $786m. In late 1996 it was reported that some progress had been made in negotiations to establish an association agreement between Lebanon and the EU, involving access to European markets for Lebanese agricultural products. In 1997 Lebanon recorded another substantial trade deficit, with total imports (c.i.f.) valued at $7,456.6m. and exports declining to $642.3m. The principal suppliers of imports in that year were Italy ($987m. or 13.2%), France ($709m. or 9.5%), the USA ($685m. or 9.2%), Germany ($648m. or 8.7%) and Switzerland ($493m. or 6.6%), while the principal markets for Lebanese exports were Saudi Arabia ($96.9m. or 15.1%), the UAE ($57.7m. or 9.0%), France ($45.9m. or 7.2%), the USA ($38.6m. or 6.0%) and Syria ($37.6m. or 5.9%). From October 1997 the Government prohibited imports of certain foodstuffs in order to encourage local farmers and to reduce imports which cost the country some $1,400m. annually. In 1997, overall, Lebanon recorded a surplus of $419.8m. on the balance of payments. In February 1998 it was reported that Lebanon and Syria had agreed gradually to abolish customs tariffs, reducing them by 25% annually from 1999. During the period January–June 1998 total imports (c.i.f.) were valued at $3,481.5m., while exports totalled $320.0m.) The overall balance of payments registered a decline of $26.5m. in the first six months of the year. In July it was reported that the Lebanese Government was shortly to apply for observer status at the World Trade Organization.

CURRENCY AND FINANCE

The importance of Beirut as the commercial and financial centre of the Middle East derived, in the 1950s and onwards, from the almost complete absence of restrictions on the free movement of goods and capital, and from the transference of the Middle Eastern headquarters of many foreign concerns from Cairo to Beirut after 1952. Moreover, large sums were earned in the Gulf by Arabs who sought to invest locally, especially in property, and for them Beirut was a convenient centre. Its dominance was further strengthened later by the massive increases in surplus oil revenue earned by the producing states, much of which was channelled through Lebanon.

The growing competitiveness of financial centres in Europe and the Gulf region had, even before the disruption caused by the civil conflict, led the Government to seek ways of enhancing Beirut's attractions as a banking centre. A banking free-zone law which took effect in April 1977, exempted non-residents' foreign currency accounts from taxes on interest earned, from payment of a deposit guarantee tax and from reserve requirements. Moreover, in June 1977 the Government decided to lift the moratorium on new bank licences which had been imposed in the wake of the collapse of the Intra Bank in 1966. In 1977 a new specialized bank, the Banque de l'Habitat, was set up and in 1978 two new commercial banks, the International Commerce Bank and Universal Bank, were granted licences bringing the total number of banks operating in Lebanon to 81 as of mid-1979. In April 1980 the American Express International Banking Corpn became the first foreign bank to open a new branch in Beirut since 1975. In the spring of 1983 the central bank raised the minimum capital requirement for new banks from £L50m. to £L75m., and that for new financial institutions from £L5m. to £L15m. This was the third such increase since 1977.

Lebanon's banking system withstood the years of conflict surprisingly well, but by 1985 the strains were evident: non-performing loans accounted for 45% of banks' total loan portfolios, compared with 25% in 1984; costs were rising, while revenues were static or falling; and interest rates were extremely high, as a result of fierce competition in a depressed market. In addition, robberies were a serious problem. In 1985 50 banks were robbed, with losses of £L4,000m. The number of banks operating in Lebanon rose to 88 in 1986. The balance sheet of Beirut's commercial banks for 1985 and 1986 looked impressive, but it had to be interpreted with care. Total assets/ liabilities amounted to £L455,614m. in 1986, a rise of 181% compared with 1985 (during which a rise of 61.9%, compared with 1984, had been recorded). Loans to the private sector rose by 120.3%, and treasury bill holdings by 32.8%. Loans to non-resident banks rose by 446.4%, private-sector deposits by 184.2%, and liabilities to non-resident banks rose by 281.7% compared with 1985. Even more impressive apparent growth was recorded between the first quarter of 1986 and the first quarter of 1987. Total assets/liabilities rose by 229.3%. Loans to the private sector increased by 158%, and treasury bill holdings by 82.6%. Loans to non-resident banks rose by 452.9%, private sector deposits by 22.7% and liabilities to non-resident banks by 389.9%. However, the rise in private-sector deposits was almost entirely attributable to the collapse in the value of the Lebanese pound, as almost all such deposits were in foreign currencies. The rise in loans to the private sector were more indicative of the high rate of inflation than of any general economic recovery. Loans to non-residents and non-resident banks had risen (hugely) because these advances were almost all in foreign currencies. The expansion in treasury bill holdings merely reflected the Government's increasing use of such bills to finance its growing deficits.

The remarkable resistance of the Lebanese pound to the pressures of the civil conflict was chiefly due to the absence of restrictions on withdrawals or foreign exchange transactions, to an increase in the supply of foreign currencies to finance the conflict, and to the pound's strong gold backing and the flow of remittances safeguarding the balance of payments. Shortly before the war, in October 1974, the pound had reached a record high value, standing at £L2.22 against the US dollar. It lost just over 30% of this value during the war in 1975–76, but quickly recovered to £L3 after the cease-fire. Although the Lebanese pound declined in value in the two months following the beginning of the Israeli invasion in June 1982, from £L5.00 to the US dollar to £L5.20, it had strengthened to £L4.11 to the dollar by mid-November. Although officially valued at $389.4m. in March 1982, the 9.22m. ounces of gold that were held by the central bank were worth some $4,000m. at mid-1987 market prices. In view of the legendary strength of the Lebanese pound, the rapid erosion of its value from late 1983 onwards was a considerable psychological blow. In July 1983 the exchange rate stood at $1 = £L4.15; by late June 1984 it had dropped below $1 = £L6, and by March 1985 it stood at $1 = £L20.00, at that time its lowest level ever. Excluding gold, Lebanon's official reserves declined from $1,903m. to $672m. in 1984. They recovered to $1,074m. at the end of 1985, owing to new import controls and a net inflow of capital, but fell to $488m. at the end of 1986, as imports began to rise again, and totalled only $368m. at the end of 1987. The appreciation of the Lebanese pound during much of 1988 prompted a recovery. By the end of 1988 reserves stood at $978m. They exceeded $1,000m. for most of the first three quarters of 1989, but by the end of the year they had declined to $938m. After further falls in the value of the Lebanese pound, the value of reserves was only $659.9m. by the end of 1990. During 1991 the stabilization of the exchange rate, the growth in exports and an influx of private funds from expatriate Lebanese combined to produce an increase in reserves to $1,276m. by the end of the year. At the end of November 1992 the value of reserves was $1,588m. During 1993 reserves continued to expand, to reach $1,900m. In April 1994 foreign reserves were $1,300m. but had increased again, to $5,885.6m., at the end of December 1996. At 31 December 1997 the central bank's gross reserves of foreign exchange totalled $5,932m.

By July 1986 the Lebanese pound had fallen to $1 = £L38, or by about 50% since the end of 1985. This included an official devaluation of the pound by 16.35% against the US dollar in March 1986. The exchange rate fell below $1 = £L100 for the first time in February 1987 and continued to fall, reaching $1 = £L455 at the end of 1987 and $1 = £L530 at the end of 1988, following the failure to elect a new President in September of that year. During much of 1989 the exchange rate was stable, at about $1 = £L510, despite the violence of Gen. Awn's 'war of liberation' against Syria. With Awn's acceptance of the Arab League peace plan in September, however, the pound strengthened, to $1 = £L460, and it appreciated further, to $1 = £L410, after the approval of the Taif agreement on 23 October and the election of President Mouawad. This was the highest level that the pound had reached since the spring of 1988. By mid-January 1990, following President Mouawad's assassination, the pound had declined again, to $1 = £L544. The continuing political deadlock between east and west Beirut; the inter-Christian fighting in east Beirut; and the impact of the crisis in the Gulf region from August all caused further deterioration in the value of the Lebanese pound. In September the average rate of exchange was $1 = £L1,080. Following the defeat of Gen. Awn in October, the reunification of Beirut and the disbandment of the militias, the Lebanese pound gained in strength. In January and February 1991 the exchange rate averaged $1 = £L1,000, but by the end of the year it had strengthened to about $1 = £L880. On 19 February 1992, however, the central bank resolved to cease its currency support operations, prompting a dramatic slide in the value of the Lebanese pound. By 5 May the exchange rate was $1 = £L1,600. The central bank claimed that it had withdrawn its support from the pound because the currency had become overvalued. It was widely believed, however, that the real reason was the central bank's concern over the Government's inability to reduce its deficit (see below). Rising tensions in the prelude to the legislative elections held in mid-1992, and the implications of the Maronite boycott of the elections, gave rise to a further decline in the value of the currency. On 21 July 1992 the exchange rate was $1 = £L2,050, and on 7 September it was almost $1 = £L2,800. Post-electoral stability and the establishment of the Government of Rafik Hariri caused the currency to strengthen, and in 1993 the exchange rate averaged $1 = £L1,741. In 1994 the average exchange rate appreciated to $1 = £L1,680. During the Israeli attacks on southern Lebanon and Beirut in April 1996 the exchange rate of the Lebanese pound to the US dollar remained stable, and moves by the central bank to support the national currency proved largely unnecessary. During 1996 the exchange rate averaged $1 = £L1,571, some 3% higher than the average of $1 = £L1,621 recorded in 1995. In early 1997 the central bank announced that it would intervene in the exchange rate only when there was a rise or fall of £L10 against the dollar. The Lebanese pound continued to appreciate against the US dollar in 1997, when an average rate of $1 = £L1,539.5—some 2% higher than the average for 1996—was recorded. The currency strengthened further in the first six months of 1998, with the exchange rate moving from $1 =£L1,527.0 at the beginning of the year to $1 = £L1,516.3 at the end of June.

Government budget deficits have risen in recent years (see Public Finance and Development, below). The 1987 deficit was projected at £L65,000m.; that for 1988 at £L60,300m.; that for 1989 at £L89,500m.; and that for 1990 at £L387,000m. The Government accordingly borrowed heavily from the central bank and the commercial banks. At the end of May 1984 the public debt amounted to £L35,529m. ($2,250m.). By the end of 1987 it had risen to £L194,100m., of which £L127,200m. represented outstanding treasury bills. At 31 October 1988 the debt totalled £L504,500m., but one year later it had risen to £L755,000m. By November 1990 it had reached £L1,442,000m., and by March 1992 it was reportedly £L2,800,000m. Net total debt at the end of 1993 reached £L4,993,900m. Debt-servicing became a heavy burden on state finances, with interest payments totalling £L784,000m. in 1993 and £L1,488,000m. in 1994. The public debt continued to increase, despite warnings from independent financial organizations, and reached £L16,317,800m. by the end of 1996, equivalent to about 78% of that year's GDP. By the end of 1997 Lebanon's net public debt had increased to £L22,097,800m., and by the end of June 1998 it amounted to £L23,640,400m. During the first six months of 1998 the public debt increased by 6.98%, compared with an increase of 15.03% in

the corresponding period of 1997. In April 1998 the Government converted part of the debt into foreign currency by borrowing on the Eurodollar market, in order to reduce debt-servicing obligations. Of total public debt at the end of June 1998, £L18,239,600m. (77.2%) was domestic debt. External debt increased from $1,304.6m. at the end of 1995 to $1,907.0m. at the end of 1996. It rose to $2,434.0m. at the end of 1997 and reached $3,561.9m. at the end of June 1998. According to official figures, interest payments in 1995 totalled £L1,875,204m. (£L1,744,518m. on domestic debt and £L130,686m. on foreign debt), accounting for 32.0% of all government budgetary expenditure. The central bank reported that interest payments in 1996 totalled £L2,692,930m. (£L2,507,950m. on domestic debt and £L184,980m. on foreign debt), accounting for 37.2% of all budget spending. In 1997 interest payments increased to £L3,380,000m. (36.9% of total expenditure). Almost all of Lebanon's domestic debt is in the form of treasury bills. During the early months of 1997 interest rates on treasury bills declined steadily and there was an increase in the proportion of longer-term bills, easing the pressure somewhat on repayments. The central bank was continuing to issue new treasury bills but was concentrating on those with longer maturities in order to restructure the domestic debt and make it more manageable. At the end of 1997 the share of long-term bonds in domestic debt had risen to 67%, compared with 54% at the end of 1996. During the first seven months of 1998 government expenditure on debt-servicing was £L1,914,000m., compared with £L1,941,000m. during January–July 1997.

In October 1987, for the first time in Lebanese history, the commercial banks refused to co-operate with the monetary policies of the central bank (Banque du Liban). For the previous two years the central bank had tried to increase its control over the banking sector, in a vain attempt to halt the depreciation in the Lebanese pound. The commercial banks refused to continue to subscribe to treasury bills, which financed the majority of government spending, and initiated legal proceedings against the central bank, in respect of fines imposed on them in 1986 and 1987. The central bank was forced to concede, cancelling the fines and revoking some of its recently-promulgated measures.

Renewed signs of problems in the banking sector emerged in late 1988, when rumours of a liquidity crisis caused a sudden withdrawal of deposits from Bank al-Mashrek, the banking arm of the partly state-owned Intra Investment Co. The bank's chairman, Roger Tamraz, was forced to resign and, amid controversy over Tamraz's role, the central bank agreed to underwrite only the claims of local non-institutional depositors. In early 1989 the Swiss and French banking authorities withdrew the licences of two of Bank al-Mashrek's affiliates, the Paris-based Banque de Participations et de Placement (BPP) and the Lugano-based BPP, because of their failure to satisfy liquidity requirements. In May 1989 another Lebanese-controlled French bank, United Banking Corpn, had its licence withdrawn because of an apparent fraud combined with over-lending to high-risk countries. In July the French authorities rescinded the licence of a third Lebanese-controlled bank, the Lebanese Arab Bank, again because of over-lending to high-risk creditors. The difficulties in France seriously undermined confidence in the entire Lebanese banking system, and in early August it was disclosed that more than $200m. had been withdrawn from Lebanese banks, most of the funds having been transferred to France.

Currency speculation had become a major source of profit for commercial banks, especially the smaller ones, and the relative stability of the exchange rate in 1991 and the first weeks of 1992 caused renewed problems in the banking sector. In 1991 some 20 of Beirut's 90 banks were reported to be in serious difficulty and late in the year four small banks ceased operations. In February 1992 the Banque Libano-Brésilienne and the Banque Tohme both closed, and in March the Globe Bank also ceased trading.

In late 1991 the central bank ordered commercial banks to increase their capital and reduce their 'hard' currency loan exposure by restricting lending to 55% of their 'hard' currency deposits by mid-September 1992. Beirut newspaper reports, however, suggested that the banks' foreign currency loans in September 1991 totalled $1,380m.—equivalent to 48% of their 'hard' currency deposits. The banks were also instructed to make extra capital provisions for their head offices and for each branch. At the same time, the central bank informed commercial banks that they would soon be able to revalue their fixed assets. Their nominal value had remained constant for several years and had been rendered virtually meaningless by inflation.

In 1991 the Lebanese Bankers' Association proposed a series of reforms, including new procedures for the liquidation and merging of banks. New banking and investment legislation required all Lebanese banks to meet the Bank for International Settlements' capital-asset ratio of 8% by February 1995.

In 1996 commercial banks announced record profits, in some cases 50% higher than in 1995, achieved largely through the purchase of treasury bills issued by the central bank. However, with Lebanon experiencing mounting public debt and decelerating economic growth (owing to low levels of investment), the central bank attempted to make the banks less dependent on treasury bills for their income and to encourage them to lend more. At 31 March 1998 the commercial banks had total deposits to the value of £L39,650,496m. ($26,064m.) held for customers, of which 33.7% were held in local currency. Loans to the private sector in local currency were worth only £L1,967,622m. ($1,293m.) or a mere 12.1% of all loans. Most lending was in foreign currency. In the first half of 1997 the Lebanese Banks' Association reduced the interest rate on the Lebanese pound from 24% to 16%, and the central bank abolished the regulation requiring banks to hold at least 40% of their local currency deposits in treasury bills. In April 1997 the central bank also attempted to reduce the high cost of credit by introducing a programme to subsidize short and medium-term loans by commercial banks to the private sector for productive projects. Independent financial analysts, however, argued that interest rates were still too high and doubts were expressed that banks would find new investment outlets. It was argued that Lebanon was unlikely to re-establish itself as a major financial centre while there were more than 70 commercial banks, since many of them are family-owned and previous government efforts to force them to merge have proved unsuccessful. At the end of 1996 the Government introduced a regulation allowing banks to list up to 30% of their shares on the Beirut Stock Exchange but by mid-1997 only three banks had decided to do so.

Well before the civil war, inflationary pressures had been one of Lebanon's most serious economic problems, and the conflict removed all vestiges of price restraint. The minimum monthly wage was increased to £L310 in 1977, then to £L415, and from that to £L525 in 1979, but this did little to relieve the chronic post-war hardship afflicting much of the population. In April 1982 the Cabinet approved a 17% pay rise for private and public sector workers. In 1983 the minimum wage was raised by 18.9% to £L1,100 per month, and by January 1987 it had been raised to £L3,200 per month. Inflation, which was estimated at 20% in 1982, fell marginally, to between 16% and 18%, in 1983, but reached an annual rate of 50% or more in early 1985. The 1986 figure was well over 100%. By the end of August 1987, the annual rate of inflation was about 200% (though the cost of many basic consumer items, such as sugar, milk, meat and cheese, was estimated to have risen by 300% since the beginning of the year), and the disastrous depreciation in the value of the Lebanese pound meant that the minimum monthly wage of £L4,300 was worth only $15. Demonstrations combining protests against poverty and against the continuing civil conflict became more frequent. Lebanon's reserves of foreign exchange declined to $300m. in August, but the Government was reluctant to reduce state subsidies on basic commodities (which cost about $100m. per year) for fear of provoking greater unrest. Despite substantial increases in the heavily subsidized domestic prices of petroleum products in June 1986 and January 1987, the IMF estimated that the cumulative deficit on the oil trade account would reach about £L17,000m. by the end of 1986, while the deficit for 1986 alone was expected to reach about £L4,000m. In September 1987 the government subsidy on petroleum was substantially reduced with the result that the price of petrol more than doubled. At the beginning of October the minimum monthly salary was raised to £L8,500 in order to compensate for the high rate of inflation, but in the same month the prices of bread and fuel were raised by 43% and 15%, respectively. Declines in standards of living prompted the Confédération Générale des Travailleurs du Liban (CGTL), the country's leading independent labour union, to call a five-day general strike in November, which was generally supported in an unprecedented display of national unity. During 1987, according to official estimates, the consumer price index rose by 420% (though a survey of the prices of 30 basic commodities showed that they had risen by an average of 624% up to mid-December).

In 1988–93 the value of the Lebanese pound continued to fall, giving rise to further price increases. In two months, from mid-February 1992, the value of the currency declined by 65%, causing the price of food and that of many other commodities to double. Strikes and street demonstrations followed, culminating in the resignation, in May, of Omar Karami's Government. During 1992 the inflation rate was estimated to have averaged 100%. In March 1991 the Government finally removed subsidies on bread and fuel, although, at the same time, it levied a tax of 18% on petrol. In August 1991 public-sector salaries were increased by 60% (the increase backdated to the beginning of the year) and in December they were increased again, by 120%. In the same month the remaining subsidies on wheat and flour were removed. Early in 1996 the CGTL requested a 76% increase in salaries and an increase in the minimum monthly wage from £L250,000 to £L500,000 but its demands were rejected by the Government. However, in May the Government did decree salary increases for workers in the private sector effective from the beginning of the year. The minimum monthly wage was increased to £L300,000, the wages of those earning over £L250,000 and £L800,000 were increased by 10%, and those earning over £L800,000 by 5%. The CGTL declared that the wage increases were too small, and private sector employers, who normally set their own wage levels, did not welcome government interference.

The stabilization of the exchange rate in 1992–93 resulted in lower inflation. In 1993 prices rose by about 10%. As of January 1994 the minimum monthly wage was increased to £L200,000, from £L118,000. According to the Beirut Chamber of Commerce, the annual rate of inflation averaged 6.8% in 1994, 9.4% in 1995 and 6.1% in 1996. The rate of inflation was projected at 9% for 1997. In early 1997 the Government declared that, although it was determined to boost economic growth, it was also committed to maintaining annual inflation at less than 10%. The mid-1997 inflation level reportedly presented problems for the two-thirds of workers on fixed incomes. According to the central bank, the annual rate of inflation had fallen to less than 5% by August 1998.

In June 1994 a secondary share market opened, dealing mainly in shares of Solidère, the company established to redevelop Beirut's war-ravaged commercial centre. It was the first time that stock had been traded in Lebanon since before the civil war. In order to counter speculation, no stock is permitted to rise or fall by more than 5% in one day. Solidère, sponsored by Rafik Hariri before he became Prime Minister, has a capital of $1,820m. Of this, $1,170m. has been allocated to the owners and tenants of properties affected by the development, which covers 160 ha. The other $650m. was raised by public subscription in January 1994. Solidère commenced work on its redevelopment programme in 1994. On completion in 2018, the development should have 40,000 residents and accommodate businesses and government offices employing 100,000 people. By mid-1997 a number of major buildings had already been restored, but, generally, work has proceeded far more slowly than was initially envisaged, owing to the shortfall in funds committed to Lebanon's reconstruction. Solidère's net profits for 1996 were $58.9m., an increase of 81% on the previous year's level. The company distributed a dividend of $0.25 per share in 1996, with nominal value of $10, an increase of 25% on the 1995 level. During the early months of 1997 a steady appreciation was reported in Solidère's global depositary receipts (GDRs), which are listed on the London Stock Exchange. In May 1998, however, the company cancelled its plans to issue GDRs worth about $70m. For 1997, despite a 32% increase in profits, Solidère proposed to pay an unchanged dividend of $0.25 per share. The company's ultimate success largely depends on whether Lebanon can re-establish its role as a financial services centre serving the surrounding region.

TOURISM AND COMMUNICATIONS

Beirut's hotels, its port and airport, as well as Lebanon's largest non-government employer, Middle East Airlines (MEA), were all severely affected by the civil conflict, which erupted just as tourism was beginning to recover from the effects of the October 1973 war. As the civil conflict progressed the prosperous hotel district in the centre of Beirut became the scene of some of the fiercest fighting. According to the Lebanese Hotel Owners' Association, 145 hotels were damaged, incurring losses of some £L218m. In Beirut alone the number of hotels had fallen from 130 (with 10,486 beds) in 1975 to 44 (with 4,631 beds) by 1979. The contribution of tourism to GNP, which was 20% before 1975 declined to 7.4% in 1977. Visitors spent only 469,272 nights in Beirut in 1979, compared with 2,307,122 nights in 1974. In 1980 there was some improvement, with a 15% rise in the number of visitors to 135,548, who spent a total of 585,531 nights in Beirut. Overall occupancy was only 27%, however. The cost of damage sustained by Beirut's hotels during the Israeli invasion in 1982 was estimated at £L400m.

The National Council for Tourism in Lebanon (NCTL) undertook a massive promotional campaign through its nine offices in Europe, the USA and the Middle East, issuing a glossy monthly bulletin and preparing brochures, books and other materials. In the spring of 1983 the newly-formed National Council for External Economic Relations (NCEER) took over all the activities of the NCTL (until the disbandment of the NCEER in 1985). The Ministry of Tourism and the CDR drew up plans to rebuild the four international-class seaside hotels in Beirut at a cost of around $100m. They also outlined schemes to clean up the beaches. Although the security problem made it difficult to move from area to area within Lebanon, inside those areas domestic tourism flourished during the years of the civil conflict. The Ministry of Tourism reported a significant rise in investment in hotel construction from the beginning of 1994 to the middle of 1996, with total investment for that period reported at $325m. A number of leading pre-war hotels, such as the Phoenicia Intercontinental in Beirut, are to be refurbished and expanded, and new hotels built. Although the number of tourists visiting Lebanon, mainly Lebanese living abroad, increased after the end of the civil war in 1990, by 1996 tourist numbers had decreased and hoteliers reported very low occupancy rates. The Israeli attacks on southern Lebanon and Beirut in April 1996 exacerbated the problem of diminished tourism levels, and a marketing campaign, launched by the Ministry of Trade and Industry in February 1997, to attract tourists from the Gulf states produced only modest results.

MEA suffered a loss of £L14m. in 1975, and of £L69.1m. in 1976. A recovery occurred in 1977, with profits reaching £L22m., but 1978 was again disappointing, with staff prevented by the fighting from reporting for duty and passenger traffic some 16% lower than had been expected. In 1979 MEA made a startling recovery, recording a profit of £L51.14m., its highest ever. However, the MEA Chairman, Asad Nasr, warned that inflation and increases in fuel prices meant the airline must expect narrower profit margins in the future. In 1980 profits slumped to £L9m., and in 1981 the airline's losses were £L88m.

In October 1981 MEA increased its capital from £L100m. to £L150m. Shortly beforehand, plans had been announced to introduce new routes, including a service to New York.

The Israeli invasion in 1982 plunged MEA into its worst-ever crisis. The airline was closed for 115 days, losing almost £L140m., and five aircraft were destroyed. The airline recorded a loss of £L187.5m. in 1982. The fighting in the Chouf in September 1983 led to the closure of Beirut airport. In that year MEA made a loss of about £L250m., and its problems continued in 1984. In that year Beirut airport was closed from February until July, during which time MEA lost $250,000 per day.

MEA's losses in 1985 amounted to £L454m., and they were expected to total £L50m. in 1986. In 1987 the airline's losses were £L452m., and in 1988 they totalled £L500m. In 1989 MEA was badly affected by a further, prolonged closure of Beirut airport during Gen. Awn's 'war of liberation' against the Syrian presence in Lebanon. Losses of $15m. were forecast for 1990.

In 1987 MEA suffered from a dispute over the new, privately-developed Halat airport, sited in Christian-held territory to the north of Beirut and intended to enable Christians to travel to and from the country without having to enter Muslim-controlled west Beirut. The Government refused to recognize Halat as an international airport, and in January 1987 Christian LF militiamen closed Beirut airport by shellfire, in order to put

pressure on the Government over the issue of Halat. One of MEA's Boeing 707s was destroyed and the airline dispersed its fleet outside the country for fear of further losses. Beirut airport reopened in May, after the LF accepted assurances from the Minister of Transport that a newly established government commission, examining the feasibility of converting military airstrips to civilian use, would grant Halat airport official status. The destruction of the 707 in 1987 reduced MEA's active fleet to 11 aircraft. In addition, the company owns three Boeing 747s which, for several years, were leased to other airlines, generating annual revenues of about $17m. In November 1989, however, the company decided to take the 747s back into service with MEA. One of the leased aircraft was returned in 1990, and another in 1991, when, the civil conflict apparently having concluded, MEA was achieving high occupancy rates for its services to and from Beirut. In 1991 the airport handled 825,000 passengers, compared with 638,000 in 1990. In early 1992 it was reported that MEA had leased two Airbus A310s from the Dutch airline KLM for three years. In 1992 MEA's losses amounted to $6m., but in mid-1993 the company's Chairman, Yousuf Lahoud, announced that it was hoping to make a small profit in 1993. MEA continued to renew its fleet and embarked on a programme to restructure the company in order to improve efficiency. Passenger numbers increased slightly in 1996 but the company recorded losses of $50m., two-thirds higher than the figure for 1995. MEA expected losses of $20m. in 1997. At the end of 1996 it was reported that the central bank controlled a 90% stake in the company and in early 1997 it was announced that MEA had increased its capital by $47.4m.

There was an increase in airfreight, due to companies' reluctance to store goods in Lebanon, which in turn necessitated a faster turnaround that could be provided only by air. Lebanon's chief cargo-carrier, Trans-Mediterranean Airways (TMA), in operation since 1953, hoped to profit from this transport trend, although in 1982 the company made a loss of £L57m., of which £L50m. was attributable to the Israeli invasion. The airline was also badly affected by the discontinuation of its round-the-world service as a result of disputes over lost traffic rights in northern Europe, the USA and Japan. In 1983 TMA's losses totalled £L61m., and in May 1984 the company asked for immediate government financial assistance to assure its survival. In mid-1985 TMA suffered serious losses as a result of a three-week ban on its aircraft entering Saudi Arabian airspace. It failed to recapture the lost volume of freight when the ban was lifted, and was forced to request further financial help from the Government. Flights were suspended in July, when pilots organized a strike in protest at the company's failure to pay salaries. In August the airline was placed under government control. In July 1986 a majority stake in TMA was acquired by Jet Holdings, an east Beirut group headed by the financier Roger Tamraz. In December the airline resumed flights between Europe and the Middle and Far East. Following the collapse, in late 1988, of Roger Tamraz' business interests, the Lebanese central bank effectively took control of Jet Holdings and, through it, TMA. The move was resisted by Tamraz' partners in Jet Holdings, and in early 1990 TMA's ownership was still disputed. In early 1991 it was reported that a committee, established by the Ministry of Transport to decide TMA's future, had estimated the company's debts at $80m., while its assets amounted to only $45m. The committee proposed three options for TMA: a merger with MEA; the company's takeover by MEA; or a substantial grant of funds by the Government to enable the airline to resume operations in its own right. In March 1993 the 74% stake in TMA, formerly controlled by Roger Tamraz, was bought for $8m. by a holding company, the Lebanese Co for Aviation Investment (LCAI). The main shareholder in LCAI is Banque Libano-Française SAL. In approving the acquisition, the court handling the bankruptcy of the Tamraz-controlled Al-Mashrek Bank also waived TMA's $39m.-debt to the bank. TMA's fleet comprises seven Boeing 707s, one of which is on lease to Saudi Arabian Airlines and another to the Kuwait Airways Corpn. TMA continues to suffer from serious financial problems and this largely accounted for a decline in the volume of air cargo recorded in 1996 compared with 1995. In 1996 the company employed 450 workers. In May TMA announced that it had debts of $80m. and was unable to pay its employees. In mid-1994 a joint venture, comprising the German company Hochtief and Athens-based Consolidated Contractors International Co, won an estimated $490m.-contract to expand Beirut international airport to handle 6m. passengers per year. The new runway was originally scheduled for completion by the end of 1997 and the rest of the work by late 1998. However, the number of passengers that the airport handled totalled 1,672,657 in 1995, 1,715,434 in 1996 and 2,006,950 in 1997, suggesting that the expansion plan was overambitious and could be subject to delays.

During the early 1970s Beirut port suffered substantial congestion, owing, mainly, to the volume of goods bound for Saudi Arabia, Kuwait and Iraq, where petroleum revenues had boosted development expenditure. Shortly before the outbreak of the civil conflict in 1975 British consultants Peat, Marwick Mitchell & Co and consulting engineers Coode & Partners conducted a major study of Beirut and Tripoli ports and drafted a master plan. In 1977, the British consultants revised their forecasts to include reconstruction, and the CDR appointed a port committee in August 1977 to oversee the reconstruction and modernization process, the total cost of which was estimated at more than $144m. Although work on the port continued, there were frequent disruptions, owing to the civil conflict.

With the reunification of Beirut after the siege of 1982, the reign of snipers and political factions at the port was ended for a while. A temporary strengthening of government authority began to ease the problem of illegal ports, of which at least 17 had begun operating as a result of the civil war. These ports imposed tariffs which were only a fraction of those payable at the official ports, and the official ports, for their part, were seriously affected by smuggling. Of particular significance was the appropriation by the Lebanese army, in March 1983, of the notorious fifth basin of Beirut port, which had been a valuable source of revenue for right-wing Lebanese militias for a number of years. According to some sources, it had accounted for 90% of the country's illegal trade. Import duties and airport and seaport charges, which had formerly accounted for more than 45% of government revenues, contributed less than 15% in 1983. Tripoli port remained under the control of pro-Syrian militias or was the scene of fierce fighting between rival groups, while Israeli forces continued to occupy the ports of Sidon and Tyre in the south. Fighting between rival militias intensified, however, and, after the withdrawal from Beirut of the multinational peace-keeping force in March 1984, the Government was unable to impose its authority over the operation of the ports. A brief expansion of government control took place during 1984, after the formation of an administration that was more representative of the country's diverse factions. This helped to increase customs' revenues from the ports, but the improvement was short-lived (see Public Finance and Development, below). In February 1989 Gen. Awn, the head of Lebanon's Christian Government, ousted the Lebanese Forces militia from the fifth basin of Beirut port and then, acting in the name of state legitimacy, moved to close illegal militia ports in the Muslim parts of the country, imposing an aerial and maritime blockade. Several weeks of bitter Christian–Muslim battles followed, and, during Gen. Awn's 'war of liberation' against Syrian forces, ports were a major target. The port of Tripoli made a significant recovery following the deployment there of Syrian troops at the end of 1985. After a two-year closure, Beirut port reopened on 15 March 1992, and in the first half of the year it handled 671 vessels and just over 1m. tons of cargo. This represented about one-quarter of pre-civil war traffic levels.

In late 1980 the CDR recommended to the Cabinet that the concession for a new port at Sidon should be granted to a Sidon businessman, Rafik Hariri. The CDR advised that Hariri should be granted the concession for 30 years, and that he should set up a joint company with the CDR, with capital of £L250m. It was a controversial decision, because the British consultants who had prepared the plans for Beirut port said that, in a politically unified Lebanon, only two ports, Beirut and Tripoli, were needed, and that if the South must have a port, then Tyre, further south, would be more suitable than Sidon. In 1985, however, Hariri's Paris-based company, Oger International, invited bids for the construction of the first phase of a new port at Sidon. The problem of illegal ports seemed, finally, to have been solved in May 1991, when, in an assertion of its authority, the new Government of national reconciliation disbanded the country's militias, and units of the Lebanese army were deployed in the ports. In May 1998 it was reported that bids were expected to be invited in the near future for the development of a new port in Sidon, requiring total projected investment of $400m. The project, to be implemented in four stages, involves land reclamation, dredging and the construction of two breakwaters and two berths.

In November 1993 Port Autonome de Marseille, of France, won a $1m.-contract to advise on a scheme to redevelop Beirut port. Work began on the project in early 1997. Entrecanales of Spain secured a $102m.-contract to expand the four existing docks, to increase facilities for containers and to prepare a feasibility plan for a fifth dock. A loan worth $57m. was made by the EIB towards the cost of the project, which is also being financed by the private company managing the port, the Compagnie de Gestion et d'Exploitation du Port de Beyrouth (CGEPB). The work is scheduled for completion in 1999, when the port authority intends to spend some $40m. on new port equipment. The port's free-trade zone, closed since the mid-1970s, has reopened. The port handles some three-quarters of Lebanon's imports, but port traffic declined in 1996. The number of ships visiting the port declined from 3,443 in 1995 to 3,227 in 1996, and the volume of freight handled also decreased, from 6,904,000 metric tons in 1995 to 6,307,000 tons in 1996. In 1997 the number of vessels using Beirut port was 3,040 (a fall of 5.8%, compared with 1996), while the volume of freight handled was 6,010,000 tons (a decline of 4.7% from the previous year's total). In 1995 the port of Tripoli handled 938 vessels and 3,344,000 tons of freight, while Sidon handled 203 vessels and 306,000 tons of freight. In 1996 the Minister of Transport announced that these two ports would also be expanded.

In April 1983 the Ministry of Posts and Telecommunications confirmed that it intended to establish an autonomous body to administer the country's telephone and telecommunications services, as recommended by the World Bank. The deterioration of the telecommunications system during the civil war led many businesses to turn to private satellite communications systems. In early 1990 it was reported that 85 such systems were in use. In addition, international links were being maintained via cellular telephone systems operating through Cyprus, while private telephone systems were also in use for internal communications. In 1993 a major telecommunications rehabilitation project was launched, involving the replacement of existing exchanges and the installation of more than one million lines. As part of this, Siemens of Germany won an estimated $40m.-contract to install 420,000 new lines in and around Beirut, while the French company Alcatel is installing telephone exchanges with 270,000 new lines in the Beirut and Tripoli areas. Sweden's Ericsson was appointed to repair telephone switching systems in the south, the Beka'a valley and parts of Mount Lebanon. By early 1997 significant progress had been made but many lines were still not working and the Government estimated that an investment of some $500m. would be needed to repair and modernize the system. Nevertheless, in mid-1997 it was reported that the installation of some 250,000 new fixed telephone lines using local contractors to reduce the cost had begun. The use of mobile phones has increased, and Lebanon has the highest use of mobile phones per head of any Arab country. In early 1997 two local companies, France Telecom Mobile Liban and Libancell, signed contracts with Ericsson of Sweden and Siemens of Germany respectively, to expand their network capacity to a total of 240,000 subscribers. In September 1998 the Ministry of Posts and Telecommunications invited tenders for the supply of a national network of 4,000 public telephones.

Meanwhile, in July 1998 the CDR awarded a 12-year postal concession to two Canadian companies. As a result, a new operating company, to be called Liban Poste, was to provide the national postal service. The new company's seven-member board of directors, comprising three Canadians and four Lebanese, would be responsible for the management and upgrading of Lebanon's postal services.

In 1994 plans were announced for a $500m.-scheme to rebuild Lebanon's coastal railway. The 170-km line links Tyre and Sidon in the south with Beirut and Tripoli in the north. The southern section of the line ceased operating in 1948, during the first Arab-Israeli War. Services on the section from Beirut to Tripoli stopped at the start of the Lebanese civil war. An east-west railway line from Beirut to the Syrian border also ceased operating during the civil war, but no plans have been announced for its reconstruction.

PUBLIC FINANCE AND DEVELOPMENT

The draft state budget for 1987 forecast total expenditure of £L27,250m., compared with £L17,937m. in 1986, an increase of 52%. In addition, there was a supplementary budget of £L42,000m., covering posts and telecommunications, the national lottery, and wheat, fuel and sugar subsidies. Moreover, the supplementary budget allocated £L20,000m. for the under-subscription of treasury bills. Revenue was expected to total £L4,250m., compared with £L12,712m. in the 1986 budget. In previous years, the Government's estimates of customs revenues had been wildly optimistic, given the authorities' continuing inability to wrest control of the ports from militias. The sharp fall in revenues projected in the draft 1987 budget indicated greater realism. The 1987 draft budget forecast a deficit of £L65,000m., about twice the actual shortfall during 1986.

In some years there was an alarming discrepancy between the budget proposals and the actual course of economic events, largely as a result of the political turbulence in the country. Thus, in 1986, the actual deficit was an estimated £L34,000m. (expenditure £L36,000m.; revenue £L2,000m.), compared with the £L5,225m. for which the budget had allowed. This was largely due to a huge shortfall in customs revenues. In more settled times, these would have been a major source of government revenue. From the mid-1970s, losses of revenue from taxation and customs duties, caused by the inability of the Government to impose taxes and the proliferation of illegal ports, deprived it of valuable income. As a result of stricter government control of the ports in 1983, customs revenues rose to £L1,280m. in that year, compared with only £L403m. in 1982. However, in 1984, when the Government might have expected to earn some £L3,000m. in customs duty, income from this source amounted to only £L452m., or nearly 65% less than in 1983. The Government introduced further measures to close illegal ports in October 1984, but parts of Beirut port were again under the control of the Christian militias by April 1985. In 1985 customs receipts totalled £L481m., compared with the budget projection of more than £L3,000m. (about 35% of total revenue). The 1986 budget estimate for customs revenue (about £L4,000m.) proved equally unrealistic. In the event, customs receipts for the year totalled only £L373m. The draft 1987 budget allocated £L8,836m., or one-third of the ordinary budget (the largest single portion of expenditure), to servicing the national debt (an estimated £L98,000m. in March 1987), while a further £L20,000m. was allocated in a supplementary budget for the undersubscription of treasury bills.

The draft budget for 1988 estimated expenditure at £L70,000m. with a deficit of £L38,030m. A revised budget set expenditure at £L167,000m. and revenue at £L106,700m. The increase in revenue was occasioned by central bank earnings which were much higher than had been anticipated. The draft budget for 1989 was presented by the Cabinet of Prime Minister Dr Selim al-Hoss at the beginning of October 1988, despite the appointment of a military government by President Gemayel to administer the country during the transition from the end of his tenure until the election of a new President. Such was the political uncertainty during 1989, however, that the actual spending and revenue of the country's two governments probably bore only a slight resemblance to the al-Hoss draft budget. However, it forecast total expenditure during 1989 of £L219,500m. and total revenue of £L130,000m., leaving a deficit of £L89,500m. (the figures, as in the 1988 budget, were distorted by the huge depreciation in the value of the Lebanese pound). The allocation for servicing the national debt (£L194,100m. in January 1988) was again the largest single item of expenditure, accounting for 32% (£L70,240m.) of the total. In April 1990 Ali

Khalil, the Minister of Finance in the Cabinet of Dr Selim al-Hoss, presented a draft budget for 1990, in which expenditure was fixed at £L597,000m. and revenues at £L210,000m., leaving a deficit of £L387,000m. Debt service was, again, by far the biggest spending category, accounting, at £L183,557m., for 30% of the total. Defence was the second largest spending category, at £L97,486m., and education, at £L66,454m., the third largest. The 1991 budget, approved by the National Assembly in September of that year, set spending of £L1,158,000m., of which one-quarter was allocated to debt-servicing, 17% to public works and 12% to defence. After criticism, the Government, in February 1992, recalled a draft 1992 budget which had projected spending at £L2,500,000m. It was subsequently replaced by a draft budget that forecast spending at £L1,550,190m. A draft budget for 1993, prepared before the appointment of Rafik Hariri's Government, projected spending at £L2,271,791m. and forecast revenues of more than £L1,500,000m., giving a deficit of about £L770,000m. The biggest spending category in the draft budget for 1993 was debt-servicing, which accounted for 26.3% of projected total spending. The 1993 budget, approved in December 1993, set spending at £L3,400,000m. and provided for a deficit of £L1,698,700m. Actual revenues in 1993 totalled £L1,800,000m., which was 82% higher than in 1992. Customs duties accounted for £L662,000m. (twice the 1992 figure), while income tax receipts, at £L126,000m., were three times the level of the year before, underlining the Government's success in establishing its authority.

Expenditure in the 1994 budget was projected to total £L4,106,000m., and revenues forecast at £L2,246,000m. Actual expenditure amounted to £L5,204,048m., while revenues, at £L2,241,028m., fell slightly short of target. The draft budget for 1995 envisaged total revenues of £L3,150,000m., while expenditure was estimated at £L5,630,000m. In fact, in 1995 expenditure amounted to £L5,856,049m., while revenues totalled £L3,033,059m., resulting in a deficit equivalent to almost 50% of expenditure. In the budget for 1996 total expenditure was projected at £L6,458,000m., while revenues were forecast at £L4,022,000m. Actual revenues in 1996 were only £L3,536,060m., while expenditure increased to £L7,244,840m., resulting in an overall deficit of £L3,708,780m., equivalent to about 18% of GDP. In the draft budget for 1997 expenditure was forecast at £L6,570,000m., while it was estimated that revenues would total £L4,100,000m. Expenditure was projected to decrease by some 11%, compared with actual expenditure for 1996, with 40% allocated to interest payments on domestic debt, 35% to wages and salaries and only 7.4% to capital projects, almost one-half of the proportion projected for 1996. According to the central bank, actual revenues in 1997 increased by 6.1%, compared with 1996, to £L3,752,340m.—8.5% less than had been forecast. Actual expenditure rose by 26.4% to £L9,161,000m., 39.4% greater than had been forecast. Lebanon's budget deficit in 1997 thus amounted to £L5,408,660m., equivalent to 59.0% of total expenditure (compared with 51.2% in 1996). For 1998 the Government drafted a budget which forecast revenues of £L4,600,000m. and expenditure of £L7,920,000m. The budget deficit for 1998 was thus forecast at £L3,320,000m., equivalent to 41.9% of expenditure. Between January and August, according to the Ministry of Finance, actual expenditure totalled £L4,827,000m., compared with revenues of £L2,997,000m., resulting in a deficit of £L1,830,000m. (37.9% of total expenditure and so within the target for the whole of 1998). Meanwhile, a report by Banque Audi estimated that the budget deficit for the first half of the year was equivalent to 10.7% of the country's GDP, compared with 18.3% for the corresponding period of 1997.

In addition to its budgetary deficit, the Government has to secure financing for extrabudgetary capital expenditures by the CDR. These increased from £L175,026m. in 1994 to £L486,057m. in 1995 and to about £L550,700m. in 1996.

Statistical Survey

Source (unless otherwise stated): Direction Centrale de la Statistique, Ministère du Plan, and Direction Générale des Douanes, Beirut.

Area and Population

AREA, POPULATION AND DENSITY

Area (sq km)	10,452*
Population (official estimate)	
15 November 1970†	
Males	1,080,015
Females	1,046,310
Total	2,126,325
Population (UN estimates at mid-year)‡	
1994	2,915,000
1995	3,009,000
1996	3,084,000
Density (per sq km) at mid-1996	295.1

* 4,036 sq miles.

† Figures are based on the results of a sample survey, excluding Palestinian refugees in camps. The total of registered Palestinian refugees was 497,958 at April 1994.

‡ Source: UN, *World Population Prospects: The 1996 Revision.*

PRINCIPAL TOWNS (estimated population in 1975)

Beirut (capital) 1,500,000; Tarabulus (Tripoli) 160,000; Zahleh 45,000; Saida (Sidon) 38,000; Sur (Tyre) 14,000.

BIRTHS AND DEATHS (UN estimates, annual averages)

	1980–85	1985–90	1990–95
Birth rate (per 1,000) . . .	29.3	27.9	26.9
Death rate (per 1,000) . . .	8.8	7.8	7.1

Expectation of life (UN estimates, years at birth, 1990–95): 68.5 (males 66.6; females 70.5).

Source: UN, *World Population Prospects: The 1994 Revision.*

EMPLOYMENT (ISIC Major Divisions)

	1975	1985*
Agriculture, hunting, forestry and fishing .	147,724	103,400
Manufacturing	139,471	45,000
Electricity, gas and water.	6,381	10,000
Construction.	47,356	25,000
Trade, restaurants and hotels. . . .	129,716	78,000
Transport, storage and communications . .	45,529	20,500
Other services	227,921	171,000
Total	744,098	452,900

* Estimates.

Source: National Employment Office.

Agriculture

PRINCIPAL CROPS ('000 metric tons)

	1994	1995	1996
Wheat	53	49*	45*
Barley	20	22†	22†
Potatoes	322	325†	320†
Pulses	38	39†	39†
Olives	78	50†	85†
Cabbages	70	70†	73†
Tomatoes	233	236†	240†
Cauliflower†	32	33	33
Pumpkins, squash and gourds†	27	28	28
Cucumbers and gherkins† . .	158	160	160
Aubergines (Eggplants)† . . .	37	37	37
Onions (dry)	71	71†	72†
Garlic†	29	29	29
Green beans†	30	30	30
Carrots	33	33†	34†
Other vegetables	119	123†	123†
Watermelons†	71	72	72
Melons†	27	27	27
Grapes	328	330†	350†
Sugar beet	229	230†	235†
Apples	120	135†	136†
Pears†	46	46	46
Peaches and nectarines† . . .	44	44	44
Plums†	24	24	24
Oranges	137	180†	190†
Tangerines, mandarins, clementines and satsumas . .	23	24†	24†
Lemons and limes	99	99†	100†
Grapefruit and pomelo . . .	47	49†	50†
Apricots†	56	56	56
Bananas	98	99†	95†
Other fruits and berries . . .	128	131†	132†
Tobacco (leaves)	5	6†	6†

* Unofficial figure.   † FAO estimate(s).

Source: FAO, *Production Yearbook.*

LIVESTOCK ('000 head, year ending September)

	1994	1995*	1996*
Horses	13*	13	13
Mules	8*	9	9
Asses	23*	24	24
Cattle	77	79	80
Pigs	53	54	55
Sheep	243	245	246
Goats	419	420	425

Poultry (million): 26 in 1994; 28* in 1995; 29* in 1996.

* FAO estimate(s).

Source: FAO, *Production Yearbook.*

LIVESTOCK PRODUCTS ('000 metric tons)

	1994	1995	1996
Beef and veal*	20	20	20
Mutton and lamb*	14	14	14
Goat meat*	2	2	2
Poultry meat	42	43*	45*
Cows' milk*	133	135	138
Sheep's milk*	19	20	20
Goats' milk*	28	29	29
Cheese*	14	14	15
Poultry eggs*	64	65	65
Honey	2	2*	3*
Cattle hides*	3	3	3
Sheepskins*	2	2	2

* FAO estimate(s).

Source: FAO, *Production Yearbook*.

Forestry

ROUNDWOOD REMOVALS ('000 cubic metres, excluding bark)

	1993	1994	1995
Industrial wood	7	7	7
Fuel wood	471	491	508
Total	478	498	515

Source: FAO, *Yearbook of Forest Products*.

SAWNWOOD PRODUCTION
('000 cubic metres, including railway sleepers)

	1993	1994	1995
Total (all broadleaved)	9	9	9

Source: FAO, *Yearbook of Forest Products*.

Fishing

(metric tons, live weight)

	1993	1994	1995
Inland waters	200	220	320
Mediterranean Sea	2,000	2,205	4,065
Total catch	2,200	2,425	4,385

Source FAO, *Yearbook of Fishery Statistics*.

Mining

(provisional or estimated figures, '000 metric tons)

	1993	1994	1995
Salt (unrefined)	3	3	3

Source: US Bureau of Mines in UN, *Industrial Commodity Statistics Yearbook*.

Industry

SELECTED PRODUCTS
(estimates, '000 metric tons, unless otherwise indicated)

	1993	1994	1995
Olive oil	2	6	5
Wine ('000 hectolitres)	170*	300	300*
Plywood ('000 cubic metres)	34	34	34
Paper and paperboard	42	42	42
Quicklime†	15	15	15
Cement	2,591	2,948	3,470
Electric energy (million kWh)	4,860‡	5,150‡	5,573

* Estimate by the FAO.
† Estimates by the US Bureau of Mines.
‡ Provisional or estimated figure.

Source: mainly UN, *Industrial Commodity Statistics Yearbook*.

Finance

CURRENCY AND EXCHANGE RATES
Monetary Units
100 piastres = 1 Lebanese pound (£L).

Sterling and Dollar Equivalents (31 May 1998)
£1 sterling = £L2,476.2;
US $1 = £L1,518.5;
£L10,000 = £4.038 sterling = $6.585.

Average Exchange Rate (£L per US $)
1995   1,621.4
1996   1,571.4
1997   1,539.5

BUDGET (£L million)*

Revenue†	1993	1994	1995
Tax revenue	1,208,030	1,655,820	2,100,160
Taxes on income, profits and capital gains	175,000	249,900	190,700
Taxes on property	197,880	218,520	265,360
Taxes on financial and capital transactions	168,380	197,420	199,090
Domestic taxes on goods and services	104,980	176,350	157,440
Excises	78,990	103,470	98,080
Import duties	662,840	791,400	1,320,000
Other current revenue	646,970	585,160	932,510
Entrepreneurial and property income	74,420	98,120	238,330
Administrative fees and charges, non-industrial and incidental sales	70,650	129,110	26,610
Total	1,855,000	2,240,980	3,032,670

Expenditure*	1993	1994	1995
General public services . . .	238,490	259,780	567,700
Defence	468,570	639,230	725,630
Public order and safety . . .	183,820	274,400	301,680
Education	242,400	463,220	425,480
Health	105,490	155,030	188,580
Social security and welfare . .	239,700	447,740	410,710
Housing and community amenities	25,840	31,320	114,000
Recreational, cultural and			
religious affairs and services .	16,450	37,440	83,640
Economic affairs and services .	764,150	1,582,840	1,163,380
Fuel and energy . . .	122,570	275,230	228,510
Transport and communications	241,800	248,300	281,680
Other purposes	784,090	1,488,000	1,875,200
Interest payments . . .	784,000	1,488,000	1,815,000
Total	3,069,000	5,379,000	5,856,000
Current	2,624,000	3,954,000	4,829,000
Capital	445,000	1,425,000	1,027,000

* Figures, which are rounded, represent the consolidated operations of the central Government's General Budget and the Council for Development and Reconstruction. The accounts of other central government units with individual budgets (including the general social security scheme) are excluded.
† Excluding grants received from abroad (£L million): 197,000 in 1993; 507,000 in 1994.
Source: IMF, *Government Finance Statistics Yearbook*.

1996 (£L million): Revenue 3,536,060; Expenditure 7,244,840.
1997 (£L million): Revenue 3,752,340; Expenditure 9,161,000.
1998 (projections, £L million): Revenue 4,600,000; Expenditure 7,920,000.

INTERNATIONAL RESERVES (US $ million at 31 December)

	1995	1996	1997
Gold*	3,571.8	3,410.0	2,670.3
IMF special drawing rights . .	18.3	19.2	19.3
Reserve position in IMF . .	28.0	27.1	25.4
Foreign exchange	4,487.0	5,885.6	5,931.6
Total	8,105.1	9,341.9	8,646.7

* Valued at US $387.30 per troy ounce in 1995, at $369.75 per ounce in 1996 and at $289.55 per ounce in 1997.
Source: IMF, *International Financial Statistics*.

MONEY SUPPLY (£L '000 million at 31 December)

	1995	1996	1997
Currency outside banks . . .	1,046.2	1,160.7	1,210.0
Demand deposits at commercial			
banks	508.0	568.7	685.5
Private-sector demand deposits at			
Banque du Liban . . .	6.4	24.0	33.8
Total money	1,560.6	1,753.4	1,929.4

Source: Banque du Liban.

COST OF LIVING
(Consumer Price Index; base: previous year = 100)

	1994	1995	1996
All items	106.8	109.4	106.1

Source: Beirut Chamber of Commerce.

NATIONAL ACCOUNTS
Expenditure on the Gross Domestic Product
(official estimates, £L million at current prices)

	1980	1981	1982
Government final consumption			
expenditure	3,515	4,219	4,850
Private final consumption			
expenditure	12,905	15,488	15,840
Increase in stocks . . . }			
Gross fixed capital formation . }	2,196	3,459	1,179
Total domestic expenditure .	18,616	23,166	21,869
Exports of goods and services .	5,460	5,724	5,255
Less Imports of goods and services	10,076	12,090	14,525
GDP in purchasers' values .	14,000	16,800	12,599
GDP at constant 1974 prices .	4,900	4,923	3,082

GDP (estimates, £L'000 million at current prices): 4,132 in 1991; 9,499 in 1992; 13,122 in 1993 (Source: IMF, Occasional Paper 120: *Economic Dislocation and Recovery in Lebanon*, February 1995).
GDP (estimates, US $ million at current prices): 7,535 in 1993; 9,112 in 1994; 11,122 in 1995; 12,568 (provisional) in 1996 (Sources: Arab Monetary Fund; UN Economic and Social Commission for Western Asia).

Gross Domestic Product by Economic Activity
(official estimates, £L million at current prices)

	1980	1981	1982
Agriculture, hunting, forestry and			
fishing	1,288	1,435	1,076
Manufacturing	1,702	2,192	1,644
Electricity, gas and water . .	708	911	683
Construction	447	575	431
Trade, restaurants and hotels. .	4,008	4,753	3,565
Transport, storage and			
communications	530	628	471
Finance, insurance, real estate			
and business services . .	2,349	2,785	2,089
Government services . . .	1,443	1,712	1,284
Other community, social and			
personal services . . .	1,526	1,809	1,357
GDP in purchasers' values .	14,000	16,800	12,600

(unofficial estimates, US $ million at current prices*)

	1987
Agriculture	287
Manufacturing	483
Energy and water	28
Construction	158
Commerce	1,127
Financial services	286
Non-financial services	756
Public administration	171
GDP in purchasers' values	3,296†

* Source: Gaspard, Toufic. *The Gross Domestic Product of Lebanon in 1987* in Banque du Liban Quarterly Bulletin, July–December 1988–December 1989.
† £L740,743 million.

BALANCE OF PAYMENTS (US $ million)

	1993	1994	1995
Exports of goods f.o.b. . . .	686	743	985
Imports of goods f.o.b. . . .	−4,908	−5,541	−6,755
Trade balance	−4,222	−4,798	−5,770
Services (net)	−382	−369	−449
Balance on goods and services	−4,604	−5,167	−6,219
Other income received . . .	378	559	777
Other income paid	−145	−179	−292
Balance on goods, services and income	−4,371	−4,788	−5,734
Private unrequited transfers (net)	565	685	836
Current balance*	−3,806	−4,103	−4,898
Direct investment from abroad (net)	902	826	949
Other capital (net) . . .	982	573	485
Net errors and omissions . .	3,091	3,835	3,720
Overall balance	1,169	1,131	256

* Excluding official unrequited transfers.

Source: Banque du Liban, *Annual Report*.

External Trade

PRINCIPAL COMMODITIES (US $ million)*

Imports c.i.f.	1993	1994	1995
Live animals and animal products	236	264	291
Vegetable products . . .	360	390	470
Prepared foodstuffs; beverages, spirits and vinegar; tobacco and manufactured substitutes . .	388	486	573
Mineral products	586	600	646
Products of chemical or allied industries	319	398	487
Plastics, rubber and articles thereof	161	211	258
Paper-making material; paper and paperboard and articles thereof .	144	159	230
Textiles and textile articles . .	441	455	507
Articles of stone, plaster, cement, asbestos, mica, etc.; ceramic products; glass and glassware .	129	165	203
Natural or cultured pearls, precious or semi-precious stones, precious metals and articles thereof; imitation jewellery; coin	141	196	369
Base metals and articles thereof .	455	547	715
Machinery and mechanical appliances; electrical equipment; sound and television apparatus	620	931	1,140
Vehicles, aircraft, vessels and associated transport equipment .	556	688	831
Optical, photographic, cinematographic, measuring, precision and medical apparatus; clocks and watches; musical instruments . .	104	129	159
Total (incl. others)	4,940	5,990	7,304

Exports f.o.b.†	1993	1994	1995
Vegetable products . . .	35	48	70
Prepared foodstuffs; beverages, spirits and vinegar; tobacco and manufactured substitutes . .	52	49	59
Products of chemical or allied industries	33	42	48
Paper-making material; paper and paperboard and articles thereof .	22	87	215
Textiles and textile articles . .	77	68	81
Footwear, headgear, umbrellas, walking-sticks, whips, etc.; prepared feathers; artificial flowers; articles of human hair .	17	20	18
Articles of stone, plaster, cement, asbestos, mica, etc.; ceramic products; glass and glassware .	23	30	32
Natural or cultured pearls, precious or semi-precious stones, precious metals and articles thereof; imitation jewellery; coin	40	52	69
Base metals and articles thereof .	39	54	66
Machinery and mechanical appliances; electrical equipment; sound and television apparatus	42	43	65
Vehicles, aircraft, vessels and associated transport equipment .	27	23	29
Total (incl. others)	458	572	824

* Figures for exports are calculated on the basis of the official dollar rate, which is the previous month's average exchange rate of Lebanese pounds per US dollar. Data for imports have been based on the same method since July 1995. Previously the value of imports was calculated by using the customs dollar rate, which was fixed at US $1 = £L 800 between July 1992 and July 1995. On the basis of prevailing exchange rates, the value of total imports (in US $ million) was: 2,215 in 1993; 2,856 in 1994; 5,335 in 1995.

† Figures refer to domestic exports only. Adding re-exports and subtracting transit values, the value of total exports (in US $ million) was: 482 in 1993; 743 in 1994; 985 in 1995.

1996 (US $ million): Total imports c.i.f. 7,559.1; Total exports f.o.b. 1,018.0.
1997 (US $ million): Total imports c.i.f. 7,456.6; Total exports f.o.b. 642.3.

Source: mainly Banque du Liban.

PRINCIPAL TRADING PARTNERS (US $ million)*

Imports c.i.f.†	1994	1995	1996
Belgium	109	138	111.5
Brazil	84	96	76.6
China, People's Republic . . .	185	239	219.9
Czech Republic	n.a.	n.a.	95.9
France	534	555	588.3
Germany	598	611	643.6
Greece	160	227	190.4
Italy	799	946	914.1
Japan	253	288	292.4
Korea, Republic . . .	114	145	134.1
Netherlands	105	121	114.2
Romania	95	65	61.5
Russia	83	119	88.2
Saudi Arabia	84	126	112.4
Spain	130	145	141.9
Sweden	65	101	93.7
Switzerland	209	333	257.9
Syria	261	236	307.4
Taiwan	83	89	91.3
Turkey	132	154	172.9
Ukraine	139	184	190.2
United Kingdom	247	285	304.5
USA	555	773	824.0
Total (incl. others)	5,990	7,304	7,553.8

Exports f.o.b.		1994‡	1995‡	1996
Bahrain .	. . . . .	n.a.	n.a.	11.3
Belgium	. . . . .	6	7	11.3
Cyprus .	. . . . .	12	11	8.3
Egypt .	. . . . .	12	16	16.8
France .	. . . . .	26	50	46.9
Germany	. . . . .	10	18	22.9
Italy .	. . . . .	11	12	38.5
Jordan .	. . . . .	23	29	49.9
Kuwait .	. . . . .	32	32	77.7
Libya .	. . . . .	7	11	13.5
Netherlands .	. . . .	9	13	16.0
Qatar .	. . . . .	6	7	6.9
Romania	. . . . .	11	13	9.2
Russia .	. . . . .	12	12	7.8
Saudi Arabia	. . . .	87	92	138.7
Switzerland .	. . . .	13	10	14.8
Syria .	. . . . .	62	70	70.1
Turkey .	. . . . .	5	16	12.7
United Arab Emirates	. . .	103	237	238.3
United Kingdom .	. . .	11	14	15.9
USA .	. . . . .	21	31	30.6
Total (incl. others)	. . .	572	824	1,017.1

* Imports by country of production; exports by country of last consignment.
† Based on a fixed rate of US $1 = £L 800 until July 1995.
‡ Domestic exports only.

Sources: Banque du Liban; Beirut Chamber of Commerce.

Transport

ROAD TRAFFIC (motor vehicles in use)

	1994*	1995	1996*
Passenger cars (incl. taxis) .	1,180,000	1,197,521	1,217,000
Buses and coaches . . .	5,410	5,514	5,640
Lorries and vans . .	77,700	79,222	81,000
Motorcycles and mopeds . .	52,300	53,317	54,450

* IRF estimates.

Source: International Road Federation, *World Road Statistics*.

SHIPPING

Merchant Fleet (registered at 31 December)

	1995	1996	1997
Number of vessels . . .	128	122	116
Total displacement ('000 grt) . .	285.0	275.2	297.4

Source: Lloyd's Register of Shipping, *World Fleet Statistics*.

International Sea-borne Freight Traffic ('000 metric tons)

	1988	1989	1990
Goods loaded	148	150	152
Goods unloaded	1,120	1,140	1,150

Source: UN, *Monthly Bulletin of Statistics*.

CIVIL AVIATION (revenue traffic on scheduled services)

	1993	1994	1995
Kilometres flown (million) . .	18	19	20
Passengers carried ('000) . .	677	706	770
Passenger-km (million) . .	1,459	1,588	1,720
Total ton-km (million) . . .	260	284	287

Source: UN, *Statistical Yearbook*.

Tourism

	1993	1994	1995
Tourist arrivals ('000) . . .	265.7	335.2	409.7
Tourism receipts (US $ million)	600	672	710

Sources: UN, *Statistical Yearbook*; Banque du Liban, *Annual Report*.

Communications Media

	1993	1994	1995
Radio receivers ('000 in use) .	2,490	2,590	2,680
Television receivers ('000 in use) .	970	1,050	1,100
Daily newspapers:			
Number	n.a.	16	14
Average circulation ('000 copies)	n.a.	500*	330*

* Estimate.
Non-daily newspapers (estimates, 1988): 15 titles; average circulation 240,000 copies.

Source: UNESCO, *Statistical Yearbook*.

Telephones ('000 main lines in use): 330 (estimate) in 1992.
Telefax stations (number in use): 2,000 in 1991; 3,000 in 1992.
Mobile cellular telephones (subscribers): 120,000 (estimate) in 1995.

Source: UN *Statistical Yearbook*.

Education

	Teachers			Pupils		
	1993	1994	1995	1993	1994	1995
Pre-primary . .	n.a.		n.a.	148,400	157,083	161,590
Primary* . .	n.a.	67,935	n.a.	360,858	365,174	367,862
Secondary:						
General* . .	n.a.		n.a.	261,341	277,646	289,024
Vocational .	3,866	6,065	6,102	39,933	45,776	47,946
Higher . .	n.a.	n.a.	10,444	n.a.	n.a.	81,588

* Including schools operated by the UN Relief and Works Agency for Palestine Refugees in the Near East (UNRWA). The number of pupils at UNRWA primary schools in Lebanon was: 23,481 in 1986; 22,700 in 1988. The number of pupils enrolled in general education at UNRWA secondary schools was: 10,521 in 1986; 10,126 in 1988.

Schools (1994): Pre-primary, primary and secondary general 2,469; Secondary vocational 275.

Sources: Banque du Liban, *Annual Report*; UNESCO, *Statistical Yearbook*.

Directory

The Constitution

The Constitution was promulgated on 23 May 1926 and amended by the Constitutional Laws of 1927, 1929, 1943, 1947 and 1990.

According to the Constitution, the Republic of Lebanon is an independent and sovereign state, and no part of the territory may be alienated or ceded. Lebanon has no state religion. Arabic is the official language. Beirut is the capital.

All Lebanese are equal in the eyes of the law. Personal freedom and freedom of the press are guaranteed and protected. The religious communities are entitled to maintain their own schools, on condition that they conform to the general requirements relating to public instruction, as defined by the state. Dwellings are inviolable; rights of ownership are protected by law. Every Lebanese citizen over 21 is an elector and qualifies for the franchise.

LEGISLATIVE POWER

Legislative power is exercised by one house, the National Assembly, with 108 seats (raised, without amendment of the Constitution, to 128 in 1992), which are divided equally between Christians and Muslims. Members of the National Assembly must be over 25 years of age, in possession of their full political and civil rights, and literate. They are considered representative of the whole nation, and are not bound to follow directives from their constituencies. They can be suspended only by a two-thirds majority of their fellow-members. Secret ballot was introduced in a new election law of April 1960.

The National Assembly holds two sessions yearly, from the first Tuesday after 15 March to the end of May, and from the first Tuesday after 15 October to the end of the year. The normal term of the National Assembly is four years; general elections take place within 60 days before the end of this period. If the Assembly is dissolved before the end of its term, elections are held within three months of dissolution.

Voting in the Assembly is public—by acclamation, or by standing and sitting. A quorum of two-thirds and a majority vote is required for constitutional issues. The only exceptions to this occur when the Assembly becomes an electoral college, and chooses the President of the Republic, or Secretaries to the National Assembly, or when the President is accused of treason or of violating the Constitution. In such cases voting is secret, and a two-thirds majority is needed for a proposal to be adopted.

EXECUTIVE POWER

With the incorporation of the Ta'if agreement into the Lebanese Constitution in August 1990, executive power was effectively transferred from the presidency to the Cabinet. The President is elected for a term of six years and is not immediately re-eligible.* He is responsible for the promulgation and execution of laws enacted by the National Assembly, but all presidential decisions (with the exception of those to appoint a Prime Minister or to accept the resignation of a government) require the co-signature of the Prime Minister, who is head of the Government, implementing its policies and speaking in its name. The President must receive the approval of the Cabinet before dismissing a minister or ratifying an international treaty. The ministers and the Prime Minister are chosen by the President of the Republic in consultation with the members and President of the National Assembly. They are not necessarily members of the National Assembly, although they are responsible to it and have access to its debates. The President of the Republic must be a Maronite Christian, and the Prime Minister a Sunni Muslim; the choice of the other ministers must reflect the level of representation of the communities in the Assembly.

* In October 1995 the National Assembly approved the amendment of Article 49 of the Constitution to allow a three-year extension of President Elias Hrawi's term of office.

The Government

HEAD OF STATE

President: ELIAS HRAWI (elected 24 November 1989).

CABINET
(September 1998)

Prime Minister, Minister of Finance and of Posts and Tele-communications: RAFIK HARIRI.

Deputy Prime Minister and Minister of the Interior: MICHEL MURR.

Minister of Foreign Affairs: FARIS BOUEZ.

Minister of Defence: MUHSIN DALLOUL.

Minister of Agriculture: CHAWKI FAKHOURY.

Minister of Culture and Higher Education: FAWZI HABISH.

Minister of Information: BASEM AS-SABAA.

Minister of Justice: BAHIJ TABBARA.

Minister of National Education, Youth and Sports: JEAN OBEID.

Minister of Technical and Vocational Training: FAROUK BERBEER.

Minister of Labour: ASAAD HARDAN.

Minister of Health: SULAYMAN FRANJIYA.

Minister of Tourism: NICHOLAS FATOUSH.

Minister of Public Works: ALI HRAJLI.

Minister of Transport: OMAR MISKAWI.

Minister of Electricity and Water Resources: ELIE HOBEIKA.

Minister of Industry and Oil: CHAHE BARSOUMIAN.

Minister of Economy and Trade: YASSINE JABER.

Minister of Housing and Co-operatives: MAHMOUD ABU HAMDAN.

Minister of Municipal and Rural Affairs: (vacant)

Minister for the Affairs of Displaced Persons: WALID JOUMBLATT.

Minister of Emigrant Affairs: TALAL ARSLAN.

Minister of Social Affairs: AYYOUB HAMID.

Minister of the Environment: AKRAM CHEHAYEB.

Minister of State for Financial Affairs: FOUAD SINIORA.

Minister of State for Administrative Reform: BESHARA MURHEJ.

Minister of State for Industrial Affairs: NADIM SALEM.

Ministers of State without portfolio: MICHEL EDDE, ELIAS HANA, GHAZI SAYFUDDINE.

MINISTRIES

Office of the President: Baabda, Beirut; tel. (1) 220000; telex 21000.

Office of the President of the Council of Ministers: Grand Sérail, rue des Arts et Métiers, Sanayeh, Beirut; tel. (1) 862001; fax (1) 602020.

Ministry of Agriculture: blvd Camille Chamoun, Beirut; tel. (1) 455631; fax (1) 455475.

Ministry for the Affairs of Displaced Persons: Beirut; internet http://www.ministryofdisplaced.gov.lb/ministryofdisplaced/the-ministry.html/.

Ministry of Economy and Trade: rue Artois, Beirut; tel. (1) 340503; e-mail postmaster@economy.gov.lb; internet http://www.economy.gov.lb/.

Ministry of Education and Fine Arts: Campus de l'Unesco, Beirut; tel. (1) 866430; fax (1) 645844.

Ministry of the Environment: Beirut; internet http://www.moe.gov.lb.

Ministry of Finance: rue de l'Etoile, Beirut; tel. (1) 251600.

Ministry of Foreign Affairs: rue Sursock, Achrafiyé, Beirut; tel. (1) 333100; telex 20726.

Ministry of Housing and Co-operatives: Grand Sérail, rue des Arts et Métiers, Sanayeh, Beirut; tel. (1) 336002.

Ministry of Information: rue Hamra, Beirut; tel. (1) 345800; telex 20786.

Ministry of the Interior: Grand Sérail, rue des Arts et Métiers, Sanayeh, Beirut; tel. (1) 863910.

Ministry of Justice: rue Sami Solh, Beirut; tel. (1) 422953; e-mail justice@ministry.gov.lb.

Ministry of Labour: Shiah, Beirut; tel. (1) 274140.

Ministry of Defence: Yarze, Beirut; tel. (1) 452400; telex 20901.

Ministry of Posts and Telecommunications: rue Sami Solh, Beirut; tel. (1) 424400; telex 23700; fax (1) 423111.

Ministry of Public Health: place du Musée, Beirut; tel. (1) 645087; fax (1) 645062; e-mail mphealth@cyberia.net.lb; internet http://www.public-health.gov.lb/moh/data.html.

Ministry of Public Works and Transport: Shiah, Beirut; tel. (1) 428980; internet http://www.public-works.gov.lb.

Ministry of State for Administrative Reform: Beirut; tel. (1) 371508; fax (1) 371599; internet http://www.omsar.gov.lb.

Ministry of State for Affairs of the South and Reconstruction: Beirut.

Ministry of Tourism: POB 11-5344; rue Banque du Liban 550, Beirut; tel. (1) 340940; telex 20898; fax (1) 343279.

Ministry of Water and Electrical Resources: Shiah, Beirut; tel. (1) 270256.

Legislature

MAJLIS ALNWAB
(National Assembly)

The equal distribution of seats among Christians and Muslims is determined by law, and the Cabinet must reflect the level of representation achieved by the various religious denominations within that principal division. Deputies of the same religious denomination do not necessarily share the same political, or party allegiances. In the general election of 1996 constituencies were based on the country's five traditional governorates: Mount Lebanon, the North, Beirut, the South and Nabatiyeh, and the Beka'a valley. In 1996, with the stipulation that this was an exceptional measure, Mount Lebanon was subdivided into five voting districts. The term of office of the National Assembly is four years.

President: NABIH BERRI.

Vice-President: ELIE FERZLI.

Religious Groups in the National Assembly (General election, 18 August, 25 August, 1 September, 8 September and 15 September 1996)

Maronite Catholics	34
Sunni Muslims	27
Shi'a Muslims	27
Greek Orthodox	14
Druzes	8
Greek-Melkite Catholics	8
Armenian Orthodox	5
Alawites	2
Armenian Catholics	1
Protestants	1
Others	1
Total	**128**

Political Organizations

Armenian Revolutionary Federation (ARF): POB 11-587, rue Spears, Beirut; f. 1890; principal Armenian party; also known as Tashnag Party, which was the dominant nationalist party in the independent Armenian Republic of Yerevan of 1917-21, prior to its becoming part of the USSR; socialist ideology; collective leadership.

Al-Baath: f. in Syria, 1940, by MICHEL AFLAK; secular pro-Syrian party with policy of Arab union, branches in several Middle Eastern countries; Sec.-Gen. ABDULLAH AL-AMIN, Beirut.

Al-Baath: pro-Iraqi wing of Al-Baath party; Sec.-Gen. ABD AL-MAJID RAFEI.

Bloc national libanais: rue Pasteur, Gemmayze, Beirut; tel. (1) 584585; fax (1) 584591; f. 1943; right-wing Lebanese party with policy of power-sharing between Christians and Muslims and the exclusion of the military from politics; Leader RAYMOND EDDÉ; Pres. SÉLIM SALHAB; Sec.-Gen. JEAN HAWAT.

Ad-Dustur (Constitutional Party): rue Michel Chiha, Kantari, Beirut; f. 1943; led struggle against French mandate, established 1943 National Covenant; Leader MICHEL BECHARA AL-KHOURY.

Al-Harakiyines al-Arab: Beirut; f. 1948 by GEORGES HABASH; Arab nationalist party, with Marxist tendencies.

Al-Hayat al-Wataniya: Beirut; f. 1964 by AMINE ARAYSSI.

Al-Hizb ad-Damuqratiya al-Ishtiraqi al-Masihi (Christian Social Democratic Party): Beirut; f. 1988; formerly Christian Social Democratic Union; Sec.-Gen. WALID FARIS.

Al-Jabha ad-Damuqratiya al-Barlamaniya (Parliamentary Democratic Front): Beirut; advocates maintenance of traditional power-sharing between Christians and Muslims; mainly Sunni Muslim support; Leader (vacant).

Al-Katae'b (Phalanges Libanaises, Phalangist Party): POB 992, place Charles Hélou, Beirut; tel. (1) 584107; telex 42245; f. 1936 by the late PIERRE GEMAYEL; nationalist, reformist, democratic social party; largest Maronite party; 100,000 mems; announced merger with Parti national libéral, May 1979; Leader GEORGES SAADÉ; Vice-Pres. MOUNIR EL-HAJJ; Sec.-Gen. JOSEPH ABOU KHALIL.

Mouvement de l'action nationale: POB 5890, Centre Starco, Bloc Sud, Beirut; f. 1965; Founder and Leader OSMAN MOSBAH AD-DANA.

An-Najjadé (The Helpers): c/o Sawt al-Uruba, POB 3537, Beirut; f. 1936; Arab socialist unionist party; 3,000 mems; Founder and Pres. ADNANE MUSTAFA AL-HAKIM.

An-Nida' al-Kawmi (National Struggle): Immeuble Chammat, Ramlet el-Beida, Beirut; f. 1945; Founder and Leader KAZEM AS-SOLH.

Parti communiste libanais (Lebanese Communist Party): POB 633, Immeuble du Parti Communiste Libanais, rue al-Hout, Beirut; f. 1924; officially dissolved 1948-71; Marxist, much support among intellectuals; Leader and Sec.-Gen. FARUQ DAHRUJ (acting).

Parti démocrate: Immeuble Labban, rue Kantari, Beirut; f. 1969; supports a secular, democratic policy, private enterprise and social justice; Sec.-Gen. JOSEPH MUGHAIZEL; Co-founder ÉMILE BITAR.

Parti national libéral (Al-Wataniyin al-Ahrar): POB 165576, rue du Liban, Beirut; tel. (1) 338000; fax (1) 200335; e-mail ahrar@ahrar.org.lb; internet http://www.ahrar.org.lb; f. 1958; liberal reformist secular party; Pres. DORY CHAMOUN.

Parti socialiste nationaliste syrien: f. 1932, banned 1962-69; advocates a 'Greater Syria', composed of Lebanon, Syria, Iraq, Jordan, Palestine and Cyprus; Leader DAWOUD BAZ; Chair. HAFIZ AS-SAYEH; Sec.-Gen. ANWAR AL-FATAYRI.

Parti socialiste progressiste (At-Takadumi al-Ishteraki—PSP): POB 2893, Zkak el-Blat, Beirut; f. 1949; progressive party, advocates constitutional road to socialism and democracy; over 25,000 mems; mainly Druze support; Pres. WALID JOUMBLATT; Sec.-Gen. SHARIF FAYAD.

Wa'ad Party: Beirut; Leader ELIE HOBEIKA.

The **Lebanese Front** (f. 1976; Sec. DORY CHAMOUN) is a grouping of right-wing parties (mainly Christian). The **National Front** (f. 1969; Sec.-Gen. KAMAL SHATILA) is a grouping of left-wing parties (mainly Muslim). Other parties include the **Independent Nasserite Movement** (Murabitoun; Sunni Muslim Militia; Leader IBRAHIM QULAYAT) and the **Union of Working People's Forces** (Sec.-Gen. KAMAL SHATILA). The **Nasserite Popular Organization** and the **Arab Socialist Union** merged in January 1987, retaining the name of the former (Sec.-Gen. MUSTAFA SAAD). **Amal** (Hope) is a Shi'ite politico-military organization (Principal Controller of Command Council Sheikh MUHAMMAD MANDI SHAMS AD-DIN, Chair. SADR AD-DIN AS-SADR, Leader NABIH BERRI). The **Islamic Amal** is a breakaway group from Amal, based in Baalbek (Leader HUSSEIN MOUSSAVI). **Islamic Jihad** (Islamic Holy War) is a pro-Iranian fundamentalist guerrilla group (Leader IMAAD MOUGNIEH). **Hezbollah** (the Party of God) is a militant Shi'ite faction which was founded by Iranian Revolutionary Guards who were sent to Lebanon (Sec.-Gen. HASAN NASRALLAH). The **Popular Liberation Army** is a Sunni Muslim faction, active in the south of Lebanon (Leader MUSTAFA SAAD). **Tawheed Islami** (the Islamic Unification Movement; f. 1982; Sunni Muslim) and the **Arab Democratic Party** (or the Red Knights; Alawites; pro-Syrian; Leader ALI EID) are based in Tripoli.

Diplomatic Representation

EMBASSIES IN LEBANON

Algeria: POB 4794, face Hôtel Summerland, rue Jnah, Beirut; tel. (1) 826711; telex 21382; fax (1) 826712; Ambassador: LAHSSAN BOUFARES.

Argentina: POB 11-5245, Immeuble Antoun Saad, 5e étage, rue de l'Eglise Mar-Takla, Hazmieh, Beirut; tel. and fax (1) 428960; telex 40687; Ambassador: GUSTAVO ALBERTO URRUTIA.

Armenia: Beirut; tel. (1) 412733; fax (1) 402952; Chargé d'affaires: YERVAND MEKLONIAN.

Australia: POB 1860, Farra Building, rue Bliss, Beirut; tel. (1) 789010; telex 21754; fax (1) 789018; Ambassador: I. PARMETER.

Austria: 9th Floor, Tour Sadat, rue Sadat, Ras Beirut, Beirut; tel. (1) 801574; telex 23255; Ambassador: ANTON PROHASKA.

Bahrain: Sheikh Ahmed ath-Thani Bldg, Raoucheh, Beirut; tel. (1) 805495; telex 21686; Ambassador: MUHAMMAD BAHLOUL.

Belgium: Baabda, Beirut; tel. (5) 920551; fax (5) 923987; e-mail beirut@diplobel.org; Ambassador: MICHEL CZETWERTYNSKI.

Brazil: POB 166175, rue des Antonins, Baabda, Beirut; tel. (1) 921137; telex 41330; fax (1) 923001; Ambassador: BRIAN MICHAEL FRASER NEELE.

Bulgaria: Immeuble Hibri, rue de l'Australie, Beirut; tel. (1) 861352; Ambassador: VENTZISLAV KANEV.

Chad: Immeuble Kalot Frères, Pine Forest, ave Sami Solh, Beirut; Ambassador: (vacant).

Chile: Immeuble Antoine Boukhater, Beirut; tel. (4) 418670; fax (4) 418672; Ambassador: MARIO HAMUY.

China, People's Republic: rue Nicolas Ibrahim Sursock 72, Mar Elias, Beirut; tel. (1) 830314; telex 21344; Ambassador: AN HUIHOU.

Colombia: POB 1496, Corniche Chouran, Immeuble Jaber al-Ahmad as-Sabbah, Beirut; tel. (1) 810416; telex 44260; Ambassador: ROBERTO DELGADO SAÑUDO.

Cuba: Immeuble Ghazzal, rue Abd as-Sabbah, entre rue Sakiet el-Janzir and rue de Vienne, Beirut; tel. (1) 805025; fax (1) 810339; Ambassador: ROBERTO BLANCO DOMÍNGUEZ.

Czech Republic: POB 40195, Baabda, Beirut; tel. (5) 468763; fax (5) 922120; e-mail czechemb@cyberia.net.lb; Ambassador EVA FILIPIOVA.

Egypt: POB 690, rue Thomas Eddison, Beirut; tel. (1) 801769; Ambassador: SAYED ABUZEID OMAR.

Finland: POB 113-5966, Tour Sadat, 5e étage, rue Sadat, Ras Beirut, Beirut; tel. (1) 802276; fax (1) 803136; Ambassador: HEIKKI LATVANEN.

France: Résidence des Pins, Mar-Takla, Beirut; tel. (1) 429629; telex 41530; fax (1) 424426; Ambassador: DANIEL JOUANNEAU.

Germany: POB 2820, Hôpital Notre Dame du Liban, Jounieh, Beirut; tel. (4) 914444; telex 48040; fax (4) 914450; Ambassador: PETER WITTIG.

Greece: Immeuble Sarras, 11e étage, ave Elias Sarkis, Achrafiyé, Beirut; tel. (1) 219217; telex 40131; fax (1) 201324; Ambassador: ATHANASSIOS KANILLOS.

Haiti: Immeuble Sarkis, rue du Fleuve, Beirut; Ambassador: (vacant).

Holy See: POB 1882, Harissa, Kesrouan (Apostolic Nunciature); tel. (1) 903102; fax (1) 903763; Apostolic Nuncio: Most Rev. ANTONIO MARIA VEGLIÒ; Titular Archbishop of Eclano.

Hungary: POB 90618, Centre Massoud, Fanar, Beirut; tel. (1) 898857; fax (1) 873391; Chargé d'affaires: GABOR VIDA.

India: POB 113-5240, Immeuble Sahmarani, rue Kantari 31, Hamra, Beirut; tel. (1) 353892; telex 20229; Ambassador: S. SIVAS-WAMI.

Iran: Immeuble Sakina Mattar, Jnah, Beirut; tel. (1) 300007; Ambassador: (vacant).

Italy: POB 211, Immeuble Cosmidis, rue de Rome, Beirut; tel. (1) 868301; telex 48347; Ambassador: CARLO CALIA.

Japan: POB 3360, Baabda Mountain Bldg, Yarze, Officers' Club St, Beirut; tel. (1) 922001; fax (1) 922003; Ambassador: MATSUSHIRO HORIGUCHI.

Jordan: POB 109, Baabda; tel. (5) 922500; fax (5) 922502; Ambassador: FAKHRI ABU TALEB.

Korea, Democratic People's Republic: rue Selim Salaam, Moussaitbé, Beirut; tel. (1) 311490; Ambassador: JONG CHUN GUN.

Kuwait: Rond-point du Stade, Bir Hassan, Beirut; tel. (1) 345631; telex 22105; Ambassador: AHMAD GHAITH ABDALLAH.

Libya: Hôtel Beau Rivage, Ramlet el-Baida, Beirut; tel. (1) 866240; telex 22181; Chair. of People's Bureau: ASHOUR ABD AL-HAMID AL-FOURTAS.

Morocco: Bir Hassan, Beirut; tel. (1) 832503; telex 20867; Ambassador: MUHAMMAD FREDJ DOUKKALI.

Netherlands: Centre Sasco, Tabaris 2, rue Sursock, Achrafieh, Beirut; tel. (1) 204663; Ambassador: R. A. MOLLINGER.

Norway: Immeuble Taher et Fakhry, rue Bliss, Ras Beirut, Beirut; tel. (1) 353730; telex 22690; Ambassador: PER HANGESTAD.

Pakistan: 11th Floor, Immeuble Shell, Raoucheh, Beirut; tel. (1) 863041; fax (1) 864583; e-mail pak.emb.bey@t-net.com.lb; Ambassador: ANEESUDIN AHMED.

Poland: POB 3667, Immeuble Nassif, rue Souraty, Ras Beirut; tel. (1) 345278; fax 746620; e-mail polamb@cyberia.net.lb; Ambassador: TADEUSZ STRULAK.

Qatar: POB 6717, Beirut; tel. (1) 865271; telex 23727; Ambassador: MOHAMED ALI SAEED an-NUAIMI.

Romania: Manara, Beirut; tel. (1) 867895; telex 21661; Ambassador: ION BESTELIU.

Russia: rue Mar Elias et-Tineh, Wata Mseitbeh, Beirut; tel. (1) 300041; fax (1) 314168; Ambassador: OLEG PERESSYPKINE.

Saudi Arabia: rue Bliss, Manara, Beirut; tel. (1) 804272; telex 20830; Ambassador: AHMAD IBN MAHMOUD MAHMOUD AL-KAHEIMI.

Spain: POB 11-3039, Palais Chehab, Hadath Antounie, Beirut; tel. (5) 464120; fax (5) 464030; Ambassador: MARIANO GARCÍA MUÑOZ.

Switzerland: POB 2008, Centre Debs, 9e étage Kaflik, Beirut; tel. (1) 916279; telex 45585; Ambassador: GIANFREDERICO PEDOTTI.

Tunisia: Hazmieh, Mar-Takla, Beirut; tel. (1) 453481; telex 44429; Ambassador: MOHAMED HADI BELKHODJA.

Turkey: POB 11-5031, zone II, rue 3, Rabieh, Beirut; tel. (4) 520929; fax (4) 407557; e-mail trbebeyr@intracom.net.lb; Ambassador: NAZIM DUMLU.

Ukraine: Centre Commercial Hazmieh, Autostrade Damascus, Beirut; tel. and fax (1) 455324; Ambassador: VALENTYN NOVYKOV.

United Arab Emirates: Immeuble Wafic Tanbara, Jnah, Beirut; tel. (1) 646117; Ambassador: MUHAMMAD ABDULLAH AMER EL-FILACI.

United Kingdom: POB 60180, Immeuble Coolrite, Autostrade Jal ed-Dib, Beirut; tel. (4) 402035; telex 44104; fax (4) 402032; e-mail britemb@cyberia.net.lb; Ambassador: DAVID ROSS MACLENNAN.

USA: Aoucar, Beirut; tel. (1) 417774; Ambassador: RICHARD H. JONES.

Uruguay: Immeuble Muhammad Hussein Ben Moutahar, rue Verdun, Ain et-Tineh, Beirut; tel. (1) 803620; telex 45280; Ambassador: MANUEL SOLSONA-FLORES.

Venezuela: POB 603, Immeuble Sahmarani, rue Kantari, Beirut; tel. (1) 888716; telex 44599; fax (1) 4036670; Ambassador: NELCEN VALERA.

Yemen: Bir Hassan, Beirut; tel. (1) 832688; Ambassador: ABDALLAH NASSER MOUTHANA.

Yugoslavia: POB 742, Beirut; tel. (1)739633; fax (1) 739638; Chargé d'affaires: VELIBOUR DULOVIĆ.

Note: Lebanon and Syria have very close relations but do not exchange formal ambassadors.

Judicial System

Law and justice in Lebanon are administered in accordance with the following codes, which are based upon modern theories of civil and criminal legislation:

Code de la Propriété (1930).

Code des Obligations et des Contrats (1932).

Code de Procédure Civile (1933).

Code Maritime (1947).

Code de Procédure Pénale (Code Ottoman Modifié).

Code Pénal (1943).

Code Pénal Militaire (1946).

Code d'Instruction Criminelle.

The following courts are now established:

(a) Fifty-six **'Single-Judge Courts'**, each consisting of a single judge, and dealing in the first instance with both civil and criminal cases; there are seventeen such courts at Beirut and seven at Tripoli.

(b) Eleven **Courts of Appeal**, each consisting of three judges, including a President and a Public Prosecutor, and dealing with civil and criminal cases; there are five such courts at Beirut.

(c) Four **Courts of Cassation**, three dealing with civil and commercial cases and the fourth with criminal cases. A Court of Cassation, to be properly constituted, must have at least three judges, one being the President and the other two Councillors. The First Court consists of the First President of the Court of Cassation, a President and two Councillors. The other two civil courts each consist of a President and three Councillors. If the Court of Cassation reverses the judgment of a lower court, it does not refer the case back but retries it itself.

First President of the Court of Cassation: AMIN NASSAR.

(d) **The Council of State**, which deals with administrative cases. It consists of a President, Vice-President and four Councillors. A Commissioner represents the Government.

President of the Court of the Council of State: YOUSUF SAAVOLLAH EL-KHOURY.

(e) **The Court of Justice**, which is a special court consisting of a President and four judges, deals with matters affecting the security of the State; there is no appeal against its verdicts.

In addition to the above, the Constitutional Court considers matters pertaining to the constitutionality of legislation. Military courts are competent to try crimes and misdemeanours involving the armed and security forces. Islamic (*Shari'a*), Christian and Jewish religious courts deal with affairs of personal status (marriage, death, inheritance, etc.).

Religion

The largest single religious community in Lebanon was formerly the Maronite Christians, a Uniate sect of the Roman Catholic Church. Estimates for 1983 assessed the sizes of communities as: Shi'a Muslims 1.2m., Maronites 900,000, Sunni Muslims 750,000, Greek Orthodox 250,000, Druzes 250,000, Armenians 175,000. The Maronites inhabited the old territory of Mount Lebanon, i.e. immediately east of Beirut. In the south, towards the Israeli frontier, Shi'a villages are most common, while between the Shi'a and the Maronites live the Druzes (divided between the Yazbakis and the Joumblatis). The Beka'a valley has many Greek Christians (both Roman Catholic and Orthodox), while the Tripoli area is mainly Sunni Muslim. Altogether, of all the regions of the Middle East, Lebanon probably presents the closest juxtaposition of sects and peoples within a small territory.

CHRISTIANITY
The Roman Catholic Church

Armenian Rite

Patriarchate of Cilicia: Patriarcat Arménien Catholique, rue de l'Hôpital Libanais, Jeitawi, 2400 Beirut; tel. (1) 583520; fax (1) 449160; f. 1742; established in Beirut since 1932; includes patriarchal diocese of Beirut, with an estimated 12,000 adherents (31 December 1996); Patriarch: Most Rev. JEAN-PIERRE XVIII KASPARIAN; Protosyncellus Rt Rev. MANUEL BATAKIAN, Titular Bishop of Caesarea in Cappadocia (Armenian Rite).

Chaldean Rite

Diocese of Beirut: Evêché Chaldéen-de Beyrouth, POB 373, Hazmieh, Beirut; tel. (1) 429088; 10,000 adherents (31 December 1995); Bishop of Beirut Rt Rev. YOUSSIF THOMAS.

Latin Rite

Apostolic Vicariate of Beirut: Vicariat Apostolique, POB 11-4224, Beirut; tel. (9) 909420; 20,000 adherents (31 December 1996); Vicar Apostolic PAUL BASSIM, Titular Bishop ad Libanum.

Maronite Rite

Patriarchate of Antioch and all the East: Patriarcat Maronite, Bkerké; tel. (9) 915441; telex 45140; fax (9) 938844; e-mail jtawk@bkerke.org.lb; includes patriarchal dioceses of Batrun and Sarba, and Jobbé; Patriarch: Cardinal NASRALLAH PIERRE SFEIR. The Maronite Church in Lebanon comprises four archdioceses and six dioceses. At 31 December 1996 there were an estimated 1,569,866 adherents in the country.

> **Archbishop of Antélias:** Most Rev. JOSEPH MOHSEN BÉCHARA, POB 70400, Archevêché Maronite, Cornet-Chahouane, Beirut; tel. (4) 925005; fax (4) 921313.

> **Archbishop of Beirut:** Most Rev. PAUL YOUSSEF MATAR, Archevêché Maronite, 10 rue Collège de la Sagesse, Beirut; tel. (1) 200234; fax (1) 424727; also representative of the Holy See for Roman Catholics of the Coptic Rite in Lebanon.

> **Archbishop of Tripoli:** Most Rev. YOUHANNA FOUAD EL-HAGE, Archevêché Maronite, rue al-Moutran, Karm Saddé, Tripoli; tel. (6) 602567; fax (6) 629393.

> **Archbishop of Tyre:** Most Rev. MAROUN SADER, Archevêché Maronite, Tyre; tel. (7) 740059.

Melkite Rite

Patriarchate of Antioch: Patriarcat Grec-Melkite-Catholique, POB 50076, Beirut, or POB 22249, Damascus, Syria; tel. (Beirut) (1) 413111; fax (1) 407388; jurisdiction over an estimated 2.0m. Melkites throughout the world; Patriarch of Antioch and all the East, of Alexandria and of Jerusalem: Most Rev. MAXIMOS V HAKIM. The Melkite Church in Lebanon comprises seven archdioceses. At 31 December 1997 there were an estimated 320,000 adherents in the country.

> **Archbishop of Baalbek:** Most Rev. CYRILLE SALIM BUSTROS, Archevêché Grec-Catholique, Baalbek; tel. (8) 370200; fax (8) 373986.

> **Archbishop of Baniyas:** Most Rev. ANTOINE HAYEK, Archevêché de Panéas, Jdeidet Marjeyoun; tel. (3) 814487.

> **Archbishop of Beirut and Gibail:** Most Rev. HABIB BACHA, Archevêché Grec-Melkite-Catholique, Sabdeh-Firdaous, Beirut; tel. (1) 880866.

> **Archbishop of Sidon:** Most Rev. GEORGES KWAÏTER, Archevêché Grec-Melkite-Catholique, POB 247, rue el-Moutran, Sidon; tel. (7) 720100; fax (7) 722055.

> **Archbishop of Tripoli:** Most Rev. GEORGE RIASHI, Archevêché Grec-Catholique, POB 72, Tripoli; tel. (6) 431602; fax (6) 441716.

> **Archbishop of Tyre:** Most Rev. JEAN ASSAAD HADDAD, Archevêché Grec-Melkite-Catholique, Tyre; tel. (7) 740015.

> **Archbishop of Zahleh and Furzol:** Most Rev. ANDRÉ HADDAD, Archevêché Grec-Melkite-Catholique, Saidat en-Najat, Zahleh; tel. (8) 820540; fax (8) 806496.

Syrian Rite

Patriarchate of Antioch: Patriarcat Syrien-Catholique, rue de Damas, POB 116-5087, Beirut; tel. (1) 381532; jurisdiction over about 150,000 Syrian Catholics in the Middle East, including (at 31 December 1996) 25,000 in the diocese of Beirut; Patriarch: Most Rev. IGNACE ANTOINE II HAYEK; Protosyncellus Rt Rev. ELIAS TABÉ, Titular Bishop of Mardin (Syrian Rite).

The Anglican Communion

Within the Episcopal Church in Jerusalem and the Middle East, Lebanon forms part of the diocese of Jerusalem (see chapter on Israel).

Other Christian Groups

Armenian Apostolic Orthodox: Armenian Catholicosate of Cilicia, Antélias, POB 70317, Beirut, Lebanon; tel. (1) 523461; fax (1)

410002; e-mail cathcil@inco.com.lb; f. 1441 in Cilicia (now in Turkey), transferred to Antélias, Lebanon, 1930; Leader His Holiness ARAM I (KESHISHIAN), Catholicos of Cilicia; jurisdiction over an estimated 1m. adherents in Lebanon, Syria, Cyprus, Kuwait, Greece, Iran, the United Arab Emirates, the USA and Canada.

Greek Orthodox: Leader His Beatitude IGNATIUS IV, Patriarch of Antioch and all the East, Patriarcat Grec-Orthodoxe, POB 9, Damascus, Syria.

National Evangelical Synod of Syria and Lebanon: POB 70890, Antélias, Beirut; tel. (1) 525030; e-mail nessl@inco.com.lb; 80,000 adherents (1997); Gen. Sec. Rev. ADEEB AWAD.

Protestants: Leader Rev. Salim Sahiouny, Pres. of Supreme Council of the Evangelical Community in Syria and Lebanon, POB 5224, rue Eglise Evangélique, Beirut; tel. (1) 980051; fax (1) 980050; e-mail nec.beirut@t-net.com.lb.

Syrian Orthodox: Leader IGNATIUS ZAKKA I IWAS, Patriarch of Antioch and all the East, Patriarcat Syrien Orthodoxe, Bab Toma, POB 22260, Damascus, Syria; tel. 5432401; telex 411876; fax 5432400.

Union of the Armenian Evangelical Churches in the Near East: POB 11-377, Beirut; tel. (1) 443547; fax (1) 582191; e-mail uaecne@cyberia.net.lb; f. 1846 in Turkey; comprises about 30 Armenian Evangelical Churches in Syria, Lebanon, Egypt, Cyprus, Greece, Iran, Turkey and Australia; 7,500 mems (1990); Pres. Rev. HOVHANNES KARJIAN; Gen. Sec. (vacant).

ISLAM

Shi'a Muslims: Leader Imam SAYED MOUSSA AS-SADR (went missing in August 1978, while visiting Libya), President of the Supreme Islamic Council of the Shi'a Community of Lebanon, Sheikh MUHAMMAD MEHDI SHAMSEDDINE, Beirut; Deputy Pres. Sheikh ABD AL-AMIR QABALAN.

Sunni Muslims: Leader SG Sheikh Dr MUHAMMAD RASHID QABBANI, Grand Mufti of Lebanon, Dar el-Fatwa, rue Ilewi Rushed, Beirut.

Druzes: Leader SG Sheikh MUHAMMAD ABOUCHACRA, Supreme Spiritual Leader of the Druze Community, rue Abou Chacra, Beirut.

Alawites: a schism of Shi'ite Islam; there are an estimated 50,000 Alawites in northern Lebanon, in and around Tripoli.

JUDAISM

Jews: Leader CHAHOUD CHREIM, Beirut.

The Press
DAILIES

Al-Amal (Hope): POB 959, rue Libérateur, Beirut; tel. (1) 382992; telex 22072; f. 1939; Arabic; organ of the Phalangist Party; Chief Editor ELIAS RABABI; circ. 35,000.

Al-Anwar (Lights): POB 1038, Beirut; tel. (1) 450933; telex 44224; e-mail alanwar@alanwar.com.lb; internet http://www.alanwar@alanwar.com.lb; f. 1959; Arabic; independent; supplement, Sunday, cultural and social; published by Dar Assayad SAL; Propr SAID FREIHA; Editor ISSAM FREIHA; circ. 25,000.

Ararat: POB 756, Nor Hagin, Beirut; f. 1937; Armenian; Communist; Editor KRIKOR HAJENIAN; circ. 5,000.

Aztag: POB 11–587, rue Selim Boustani, Beirut; tel. (1) 366607; f. 1927; Armenian; circ. 6,500.

Al-Bairaq (The Standard): POB 1800, rue Monot, Beirut; f. 1911; Arabic; published by Soc. Libanaise de Presse; Editor RAYMOND KAWASS; circ. 3,000.

Bairut: POB 7944, Beirut; f. 1952; Arabic.

Ach-Chaab (The People): POB 5140, Beirut; f. 1961; Arabic; Nationalist; Propr and Editor MUHAMMAD AMIN DUGHAN; circ. 7,000.

Ach-Chams (The Sun): POB 7047, Beirut; f. 1925; Arabic.

Ach-Charq (The East): POB 838, rue Verdun, Beirut; f. 1945; Arabic; Editor AOUNI AL-KAAKI.

Ad-Diyar (The Homeland): Immeuble Shawki Dagher, Hazmieh, Beirut; tel. (1) 427440; Arabic; Propr CHARLES AYYUB.

Ad-Dunya (The World): POB 4599, Beirut; f. 1943; Arabic; political; Chief Editor SULIMAN ABOU ZAID; circ. 25,000.

Al-Hakika (The Truth): Beirut; Arabic; published by Amal.

Al-Hayat (Life): POB 11–987, Immeuble Gargarian, rue Emil Eddé, Hamra, Beirut; tel. (1) 352674; telex 43415; fax (1) 866177; f. 1946; Arabic; independent; circ. 31,034.

Al-Jarida (The (News) Paper): POB 220, place Tabaris, Beirut; f. 1953; Arabic; independent; Editor ABDULLA SKAFF; circ. 22,600.

Al-Jumhuriya (The Republic): POB 7111, Beirut; f. 1924; Arabic.

Journal al-Haddis: POB 300, Jounieh; f. 1927; Arabic; political; Owner GEORGES ARÈGE-SAADÉ.

Al-Khatib (The Speaker): POB 365, rue Georges Picot, Beirut; Arabic.

Al-Kifah al-Arabi (The Arab Struggle): POB 5158–14, Immeuble Rouche-Shams, Beirut; f. 1974; Arabic; political, socialist, Pan-Arab; Publr and Chief Editor WALID HUSSEINI.

Lisan ul-Hal (The Organ): POB 4619, rue Châteaubriand, Beirut; f. 1877; Arabic; Editor GEBRAN HAYEK; circ. 33,000.

Al-Liwa' (The Standard): POB 2402, Beirut; tel. 865080; telex 43409; f. 1963; Arabic; Propr ABD AL-GHANI SALAM; Editor SALAH SALAM; circ. 79,000.

An-Nahar (The Day): POB 11-226, rue Banque du Liban, Hamra, Beirut; tel. (1) 340960; fax (1) 344567; f. 1933; Arabic; independent; Publr, Pres. GHASSAN TUENI; Editor-in-Chief ONSI EL-HAJ; circ. 55,000.

An-Nas (The People): POB 4886, ave Fouad Chehab, Beirut; tel. (1) 308695; f. 1959; Arabic; Editor-in-Chief HASSAN YAGHI; circ. 22,000.

An-Nida (The Appeal): POB 4744, Beirut; f. 1959; Arabic; published by the Lebanese Communist Party; Editor KARIM MROUÉ; circ. 10,000.

Nida' al-Watan (Call of the Homeland): POB 6324, Beirut; f. 1937; Arabic.

An-Nidal (The Struggle): POB 1354, Beirut; f. 1939; Arabic.

L'Orient-Le Jour: POB 166495, rue Banque du Liban, Beirut; tel. (1) 340560; telex 42590; f. 1942; French; independent; Chair. MICHEL EDDÉ; Dir CAMILLE MENASSA; Editorial Dir AMINE ABOU-KHALED; Editor ISSA GORAÏEB; circ. 23,000.

Raqib al-Ahwal (The Observer): POB 467, rue Patriarche Hoyek, Beirut; f. 1937; Arabic; Editor SIMA'N FARAH SEIF.

Rayah (Banner): POB 4101, Beirut; Arabic.

Le Réveil: POB 8383, blvd Sinn el-Fil, Beirut; f. 1977; French; Editor-in-Chief JEAN SHAMI; Dir RAYMOND DAOU; circ. 10,000.

Ar-Ruwwad: POB 2696, rue Mokhalsieh, Beirut; f. 1940; Arabic; Editor BESHARA MAROUN.

Sada Lubnan (Echo of Lebanon): POB 7884, Beirut; f. 1951; Arabic; Lebanese Pan-Arab; Editor MUHAMMAD BAALBAKI; circ. 25,000.

As-Safir (The Ambassador): POB 113/5015, Immeuble as-Safir, rue Monimina, Hamra, Beirut; tel. (1) 350080; telex 21484; fax (1) 349430; e-mail co-ordinator@assafir.com; internet http://www .assafir.com; f. 1974; Arabic; Propr and Editor-in-Chief TALAL SALMAN; circ. 50,000.

Sawt al-Uruba (The Voice of Europe): POB 3537, Beirut; f. 1959; Arabic; organ of the An-Najjadé Party; Editor ADNANE AL-HAKIM.

Le Soir: POB 1470, rue de Syrie, Beirut; f. 1947; French; independent; Dir DIKRAN TOSBATH; Editor ANDRÉ KECATI; circ. 16,500.

At-Tayyar (The Current): POB 1038, Beirut; Arabic; independent; circ. 75,000.

Telegraf—Bairut: POB 1061, rue Béchara el-Khoury, Beirut; f. 1930; Arabic; political, economic and social; Editor TOUFIC ASSAD MATNI; circ. 15,500 (5,000 outside Lebanon).

Al-Yaum (Today): POB 1908, Beirut; f. 1937; Arabic; Editor WAFIC MUHAMMAD CHAKER AT-TIBY.

Az-Zamane: POB 6060, rue Boutros Karameh, Beirut; f. 1947; Arabic.

Zartonk: POB 617, rue Nahr Ibrahim, Beirut; tel. (1) 226611; fax (1) 448982; f. 1937; Armenian; official organ of Armenian Liberal Democratic Party; Man. Editor BAROUYR H. AGHBASHIAN.

WEEKLIES

Al-Alam al-Lubnani (The Lebanese World): POB 462, Ministry of Foreign Affairs, Beirut; f. 1964; Arabic, English, Spanish, French; politics, literature and social economy; Editor-in-Chief FAYEK KHOURY; Gen. Editor CHEIKH FADI GEMAYEL; circ. 45,000.

Achabaka (Network): POB 1038, Dar Assayad, Beirut; f. 1956; Arabic; society and features; Founder SAID FREIHA; Editor GEORGE IBRAHIM EL-KHOURY; circ. 108,000.

Al-Ahad (Sunday): POB 1462, rue Andalouss, Chourah, Beirut; Arabic; political; organ of Hezbollah; Editor RIAD TAHA; circ. 32,000.

Al-Akhbar (The News): Beirut; f. 1954; Arabic; published by the Lebanese Communist Party; circ. 21,000.

Al-Anwar Supplement: POB 1038, Beirut; cultural-social; every Sunday; supplement to daily *Al-Anwar*; Editor ISSAM FREIHA; circ. 90,000.

Argus: Bureau of Lebanese and Arab Documentation, POB 16–5403, Beirut; tel. (1) 219113; Arabic, French and English; economic bulletin; circ. 1,000.

Assayad (The Hunter): POB 1038, Dar Assayad, Beirut; f. 1943; news magazine; Propr SAID FREIHA; Editor RAFIQUE KHOURY; circ. 94,700.

Le Commerce du Levant: POB 687, Immeuble de Commerce et Financement, rue Kantari, Beirut; tel. (1) 297770; f. 1929; weekly and special issue quarterly; French; commercial and financial; publ. by Société de la Presse Economique; Pres. MAROUN AKL; circ. 15,000.

Dabbour: POB 5723, place du Musée, Beirut; f. 1922; Arabic; Editors MICHEL RICHARD and FUAD MUKARZEL; circ. 12,000.

Ad-Dyar: POB 959, Immeuble Bellevue, rue Verdun, Beirut; f. 1941; Arabic; political; circ. 46,000.

Al-Hadaf (The Target): POB 212, Immeuble Esseilé, rue Béchir, Beirut; f. 1969; tel. (1) 420554; organ of Popular Front for the Liberation of Palestine (PFLP); Arabic; Editor-in-Chief SABER MOHI ED-DIN; circ. 40,000.

Al-Hawadess (Events): POB 1281, rue Clémenceau, Beirut; published from London (183–185 Askew Rd, W12 9AX; tel. (181) 740-4500; telex 261601; fax (181) 749-9781); f. 1911; Arabic; news; Editor-in-Chief MELHIM KAVAM; circ. 120,000.

Al-Hurriya (Freedom): POB 857, Beirut; f. 1960; Arabic; organ of the Democratic Front for the Liberation of Palestine; Editor DAOUD TALHAME; circ. 30,000.

Al-Iza'a (Broadcasting): POB 462, rue Selim Jazaerly, Beirut; f. 1938; Arabic; politics, art, literature and broadcasting; Editor FAYEK KHOURY; circ. 11,000.

Al-Jumhur (The Public): POB 1834, Moussaitbé, Beirut; telex 21541; f. 1936; Arabic; illustrated weekly news magazine; Editor FARID ABU SHAHLA; circ. 45,000, of which over 20,000 outside Lebanon.

Kul Shay' (Everything): POB 3250, rue Béchara el-Khoury, Beirut; Arabic.

Al-Liwa' (The Standard): POB 11-2402, Immeuble Saradar, ave de l'Indépendance, Beirut; tel. (1) 865050; telex 43409; fax (1) 644761; Arabic; Editor-in-Chief SALAH SALAM; Propr ABD AL-GHANI SALAAM; circ. 15,000.

Magazine: POB 1404, Immeuble Sayegh, rue Sursock, Beirut; tel. (1) 202070; telex 41362; fax (1) 202663; e-mail info@magazine .com.lb; internet http://www.magazine.com.lb; f. 1956; French; political and social; published by Editions Orientales SAL; Pres. CHARLES ABOU ADAL; circ. 18,000.

Massis: c/o Patriarcat Arménien Catholique, rue de l'Hôpital Libanais Jeitawi, 2400 Beirut; Armenian; Catholic; Editor Fr ANTRANIK GRANIAN; circ. 2,500.

Al-Moharrir (The Liberator): POB 5366, Beirut; f. 1962; Arabic; circ. 87,000; Gen. Man. WALID ABOU ZAHR.

Al-Ousbou' al-Arabi (Arab Week): POB 1404, Immeuble Sayegh, rue Sursock, Beirut; f. 1959; tel. (1) 202070; telex 41362; fax (1) 202663; e-mail info@arabweek.com.lb; internet http://www .arabweek.com.lb; Arabic; political and social; published by Editions Orientales SAL; Pres. CHARLES ABOU ADAL; circ. 88,407 (circulates throughout the Arab World).

Ar-Rassed: POB 11–2808, Beirut; Arabic; Editor GEORGE RAJJI.

Revue du Liban: POB 165612, rue Issa Maalouf, Beirut; tel. (1) 200961; telex 20303; fax (1) 334116; e-mail rdl@rdl.com.lb; internet http://www.rdl.com.lb; f. 1928; French; political, social, cultural; Publr MELHEM KARAM; Gen. Man. MICHEL MISK; circ. 22,000.

Sabah al-Khair (Good Morning): Beirut; Arabic; published by the Syrian Nationalist Party.

Ash-Shira' (The Sail): POB 13-5250, Beirut; tel. (1) 70300; telex 42073; fax (1) 866050; Arabic; Editor HASSAN SABRA; circ. 40,000.

OTHER SELECTED PERIODICALS

Alam at-Tijarat (Business World): Immeuble Strand, rue Hamra, Beirut; f. 1965; monthly; commercial; Editor NADIM MAKDISI; international circ. 17,500.

Al Computer, Communications and Electronics: POB 1038, Beirut; tel. (1) 4527000; telex 44224; fax (2) 452957; f. 1984; monthly; computer technology; published by Dar Assayad SAL; Chief Editor ANTOINE BOUTROS.

Arab Construction World: POB 13–5121, Chouran, Beirut; tel. (1) 352413; fax (1) 352419; f. 1985; every two months; published by Chatila Publishing House; Editor-in-Chief RIYADH CHEHAB; circ. 10,165.

Arab Defense Journal: POB 1038, Hazmieh, Beirut; tel. (1) 452700; telex 44224; fax (1) 452957; monthly; published by Dar Assayad SAL; Chief Editor Gen. WADIH JUBRAN.

Arab Economist: POB 11–6068, Beirut; telex 21071; monthly; published by Centre for Economic, Financial and Social Research and Documentation SAL; Chair. Dr CHAFIC AKHRAS.

Arab Water World: POB 13–5121, Chouran, Beirut; tel. (1) 352413; fax (1) 352419; f. 1977; every two months; published by Chatila Publishing House; Editor-in-Chief FATHI CHATILA; circ. 9,159.

The Arab World: POB 567, Jounieh; tel. and fax (9) 935096; f. 1985; 24 a year; published by Dar Naaman lith-Thaqafa; Editor NAJI NAAMAN.

Fairuz: POB 1038, Hazmieh, Beirut; tel. (1) 452700; telex 444224; fax (1) 429884; f. 1982; monthly; Arabic; for women; published by Dar Assayad SAL; Chief Editor ELHAM FREIHA; international circ. 84,000.

Fann at-Tasswir: POB 16-5947, Beirut; tel. (1) 498950; telex 41146; monthly; Arabic; photography.

Al Fares: POB 1038, Hazmieh, Beirut; tel. (1) 452700; telex 44224; fax (1) 452927; f. 1991; monthly; Arabic; men's interest; published by Dar Assayad SAL; Chief Editor ELHAM FREIHA.

Al-Idari (The Manager): POB 1038, Hamzieh, Beirut; tel. (1) 452700; telex 44224; fax (1) 452957; f. 1975; monthly; Arabic; business management and public administration; published by Dar Assayad International; Pres. and Gen. Man. BASSAM FREIHA; Chief Editor HASSAN EL-KHOURY; circ. 25,819.

Al-Intilak (Outbreak): Al-Intilak Printing and Publishing House, POB 4958, Beirut; f. 1960; monthly; Arabic; literary; Chief Editor MICHEL NEHME.

Al-Khalij Business Magazine: POB 11-8440, Beirut; tel. (1) 345568; telex 20680; fax (1) 602089; f. 1981; fmrly based in Kuwait; 9 a year; Arabic; Editor-in-Chief ZULFICAR KOBFISSI; circ. 16,325.

Lebanese and Arab Economy: POB 11-1801, Sanayeh, Beirut; tel. (1) 341328; fax (1) 602374; e-mail info@ccib.org.lb; internet http://www.ccib.org.lb; f. 1951; monthly; Arabic, English and French; Publr Beirut Chamber of Commerce and Industry.

Majallat al-Iza'at al-Lubnaniat (Lebanese Broadcasting Magazine): c/o Radio Lebanon, rue des Arts et Métiers, Beirut; tel. (1) 863016; telex 20786; f. 1959; monthly; Arabic; broadcasting affairs.

Al-Mouktataf (The Selection): POB 11–1462, rue Andalous, Chouran, Beirut; monthly; Arabic; general.

Qitâboul A'lamil A'rabi (The Arab World Book): POB 567, Jounieh; tel. and fax (9) 935096; f. 1991; 6 a year; Arabic; published by Dar Naaman lith-Thaqafa; Editor NAJI NAAMAN.

Rijal al-Amal (Businessmen): POB 6065, Beirut; f. 1966; monthly; Arabic; business; Publr and Editor-in-Chief MAHIBA AL-MALKI; circ. 16,250.

As-Sihafa wal I'lam (Press and Information): POB 567, Jounieh; tel. and fax (9) 935096; f. 1987; 12 a year; Arabic; published by Dar Naaman lith-Thaqafa; Editor NAJI NAAMAN.

Siyassa was Strategia (Politics and Strategy): POB 567, Jounieh; tel. and fax (9) 935096; f. 1981; 36 a year; Arabic; published by Dar Naaman lith-Thaqafa; Editor NAJI NAAMAN.

Tabibok (Your Doctor): POB 90434, Beirut; tel. (11) 2212980; fax (11) 3738901; f. 1956; monthly; Arabic; medical, social, scientific; Editor Dr SAMI KABBANI; circ. 90,000.

Takarir Wa Khalfiyat (Background Reports): POB 1038, Hamzieh, Beirut; tel. (1) 452700; telex 44224; fax (1) 452957; f. 1976; tri-monthly; Arabic; politics and economics; published by Dar Assayad SAL.

At-Tarik (The Road): Beirut; monthly; Arabic; cultural and theoretical; published by the Parti communiste libanais; circ. 5,000.

Welcome to Lebanon and the Middle East: POB 4204, Centre Starco, Beirut; f. 1959; monthly; English; on entertainment, touring and travel; Editor SOUHAIL TOUFIK ABOU-JAMRA; circ. 6,000.

NEWS AGENCIES

Foreign Bureaux

Agence France-Presse (AFP): POB 4868, Immeuble Najjar, rue de Rome, Beirut; tel. (1) 347460; telex 20819; fax (1) 350318; Dir M. GAY-PARA; POB 166827, Immeuble Georges Massoud, rue d'Athènes, Achrafiye, east Beirut; tel. (1) 422445; telex 44279.

Agenzia Nazionale Stampa Associata (ANSA) (Italy): POB 1525, 2nd Floor, Immeuble Safieddine, rue Rashid Karame, Beirut; tel. (1) 810155; telex 20539; fax (1) 810201; Correspondent VITTORIO FRENQUELLUCCI.

Allgemeiner Deutscher Nachrichtendienst (ADN) (Germany): POB 114–5100, Immeuble Bitar-Rawas, Ramat el-Beida, Beirut; Correspondent HARALD DITTMAR.

Associated Press (AP) (USA): POB 3780, Immeuble Commodore, rue Ne' Meh Yafet, Beirut; tel. (1) 352310; telex 20636; Chief Middle East Correspondent (vacant).

Kyodo Tsushin (Japan): POB 13-5060, Immeuble Makarem, rue Makdessi, Ras Beirut, Beirut; tel. (1) 863861; telex 21203; Correspondent IBRAHIM KHOURY.

Middle East News Agency (MENA) (Egypt): POB 2268, 72 rue al-Geish, Beirut.

Reuters (United Kingdom): POB 11-1006, Immeuble Union Nationale, 5e étage, rue Spears, Sanayeh, Beirut; e-mail beirut.newsroom@reuters.com; Bureau Chief JACK REDDEN.

Rossiiskoye Informatsionnoye Agentstvo—Vesti (RIA–Vesti) (Russia): POB 11-1086, Beirut; tel. (1) 300219; fax (1) 314168; e-mail vesti@cyberia.net.lb; Dir KONSTANTIN MAXIMOV.

United Press International (UPI) (USA): Immeuble An-Nahar, Hamra, Beirut; telex 20724; Bureau Man. RIAD KAJ.

Xinhua (New China) News Agency (People's Republic of China): POB 114-5075, Beirut; tel. (1) 830359; telex 21313.

BTA (Bulgaria), INA (Iraq), JANA (Libya) and Prensa Latina (Cuba) are also represented in Lebanon.

PRESS ASSOCIATION

Lebanese Press Syndicate: POB 3084, Immeuble Press Order, ave Saeb Salam, Beirut; tel. (1) 865519; fax (1) 865516; f. 1911; 18 mems; Pres. MUHAMMAD AL-BAALBAKI; Vice-Pres. FADEL SAID AKL; Sec. HASSAM SABRA.

Publishers

Chatila Publishing House: POB 13-5121, Chouran, Beirut; tel. (1) 352413; fax (1) 352419; publishes *Arab Construction World* (every two months), *Arab Water World* (every two months), *Middle East Food* (quarterly), *Middle East and Water World Directory* (bi-annual).

Dar al-Adab: POB 11-4123, Beirut; tel. and fax (1) 861633; e-mail d-aladab@cyberia.net.lb; f. 1953; literary and general; Man. RANA IDRISS; Editor-in-Chief SAMAH IDRISS.

Dar Assayad SAL: POB 1038, Hazmieh, Beirut; tel. (1) 456373; fax (1) 452700; f. 1943; publishes in Arabic *Al-Anwar* (daily, plus weekly supplement), *Assayad* (weekly), *Achabaka* (weekly), *Background Reports* (three a month), *Arab Defense Journal* (monthly), *Fairuz* (monthly), *Al-Idari* (monthly), *Al Computers, Communications and Electronics* (monthly), *Al-Fares* (monthly); has offices and correspondents in Arab countries and most parts of the world; Chair. ISSAM FREIHA; Pres. and Man. Dir BASSAM FREIHA.

Arab Institute for Research and Publishing (Al-Mouasasah al-Arabiyah Lildirasat Walnashr): POB 11–5460, Tour Carlton, Saqiat el-Janzeer, Beirut; tel. (1) 807900; telex 40067; fax (1) 685501; f. 1969; Dir. MAHER KAYYALI; works in Arabic and English.

Editions Orientales SAL: POB 1404, Immeuble Sayegh, rue Sursock, Beirut; tel. (1) 202070; telex 41362; fax (1) 202663; e-mail info@ediori.com.lb; internet http://www.ediori.com.lb; political and social newspapers and magazines; Pres. and Editor-in-Chief CHARLES ABOU ADAL.

Dar el-Ilm Lilmalayin: POB 1085, Centre Metco, rue Mar Elias, Beirut; tel. (1) 306666; fax (1) 701657; e-mail malayin@cyberia .net.lb; f. 1945; dictionaries, encyclopaedias, reference books, textbooks, Islamic cultural books; CEO TAREF OSMAN.

Institute for Palestine Studies, Publishing and Research Organization: POB 11-7164, rue Nsouli-Verdun, Beirut; tel. and fax (1) 868387; telex 23317; e-mail ipsbrt@cyberia.net.lb; f. 1963; independent non-profit Arab research organization; to promote better understanding of the Palestine problem and the Arab–Israeli conflict; publishes books, reprints, research papers, etc.; Chair. Dr CONSTANTINE ZURAYK; Exec. Sec. Prof. WALID KHALIDI.

The International Documentary Center of Arab Manuscripts: POB 2668, Immeuble Hanna, Ras Beirut, Beirut; f. 1965; publishes and reproduces ancient and rare Arabic texts; Propr ZOUHAIR BAALBAKI.

Dar al-Kashaf: POB 112091, rue A. Malhamee, Beirut; tel. (1) 815527; f. 1930; publishers of *Al-Kashaf* (Arab Youth Magazine), maps and atlases; printers and distributors; Propr M. A. FATHALLAH.

Khayat Book and Publishing Co SAL: 90–94 rue Bliss, Beirut; Middle East, Islam, oil, Arab publications and reprints; Man. Dir PAUL KHAYAT.

Librairie du Liban: POB 945, place Riad es-Solh, Beirut; tel. (1) 217944; telex 21037; fax (1) 217734; f. 1944; fiction, children's books, dictionaries, Middle East, travel, Islam; Proprs KHALIL and GEORGE SAYEGH.

Dar al-Maaref Liban SAL: POB 2320, Immeuble Esseilé, place Riad es-Solh, Beirut; f. 1959; children's books and textbooks in Arabic; Gen. Man. JOSEPH NASHOU.

Dar al-Machreq SARL: c/o Librairie orientale, POB 946, Beirut; tel. (1) 202423; fax (1) 329348; f. 1848; religion, art, Arabic and Islamic literature, history, languages, science, philosophy, school books, dictionaries and periodicals; Man. Dir CAMILLE HÉCHAIMÉ.

Dar Naaman lith-Thaqafa: POB 567, Jounieh; tel. and fax (9) 935096; f. 1979; publishes *Encyclopedia of Contemporary Arab World*, *Qitâboul A'lamil A'rabi*, *Siyassa was Strategia*, *As-Sahafa wal I'lam* in Arabic and *The Arab World* in English; Propr NAJI NAAMAN; Exec. Man. MARCELLE AL-ASHKAR.

Dar an-Nahar SAL: POB 11-226, rue de Rome, Hamra, Beirut; f. 1967; tel. (1) 347176; fax (1) 738159; e-mail fadit@annahar.com.lb; a Pan-Arab publishing house; Pres. GHASSAN TUÉNI; Dir FADI TUÉNI.

Naufal Group: POB 11-2161, Immeuble Naufal, rue Sourati, Beirut; tel. (1) 354898; fax (1) 354394; f. 1970; subsidiary cos

Macdonald Middle East Sarl, Les Editions Arabes; encyclopaedias, fiction, children's books, history, law and literature; Man. Dir. TONY NAUFAL.

Rihani Printing and Publishing House: rue Jibb en-Nakhl, Beirut; f. 1963; Propr ALBERT RIHANI; Man. DAOUD STEPHAN.

Dar as-Safir: POB 113-5015, Immeuble as-Safir, rue Monimina, Hamra, Beirut; tel. (1) 802444; telex 21484; fax (1) 861807; f. 1974.

Broadcasting and Communications

TELECOMMUNICATIONS

Regulatory Authority

Direction Générale des Télécommunications pour l'Exploitation et la Maintenance: Ministry of Posts and Telecommunications (see above); Dir-Gen. ABDUL M. YOUSSEF.

Service Providers

France-Télécom Mobile Liban: Beirut; operates Cellis mobile cellular telephone service; Chief Exec. SALAH BOURAAD.

Libancell: Beirut; provides mobile cellular telephone services.

BROADCASTING

Radio

Radio Lebanon: rue Arts et Métiers, Beirut; part of the Ministry of Information; tel. (1) 346880; telex 29786; f. 1937; Dir-Gen. QASSEM HAGE ALI.

The Home Service broadcasts in Arabic on short wave, and the Foreign Service broadcasts in Portuguese, Armenian, Arabic, Spanish, French and English.

Television

Lebanese Broadcasting Corporation International SAL: POB 111, Zouk; tel. (9) 937919; fax (9) 937916; e-mail lbci@lbci.com.lb; f. 1985; programmes in Arabic, French and English; Chair. Sheikh PIERRE ED-DAHER.

Télé-Liban (TL) SAL: POB 11-5054, Hazmieh, Beirut; tel. (1) 793000; fax (1) 786931; e-mail tl.@teleliban.com.lb; f. 1959; commercial service; programmes in Arabic, French and English on three channels; Chair. and Dir-Gen. JEAN-CLAUDE BOULOS; Dep. Dir-Gen. MUHAMMAD S. KARIMEH.

During 1996–98 the Government took measures to close down unlicensed private broadcasters, and to restrict the activities of those licensed to operate. In particular, the broadcasting of news and political programmes by private satellite television channels has been banned.

Finance

(cap. = capital; dep. = deposits; res = reserves; m. = million; brs = branches); amounts in £L)

BANKING

Beirut was, for many years, the leading financial and commercial centre in the Middle East, but this role was destroyed by the civil conflict. To restore the city as a regional focus for investment banking is a key element of the Government's reconstruction plans.

Central Bank

Banque du Liban: POB 11-5544, rue Masraf Loubnane, Beirut; tel. (1) 341230; telex 20744; fax (1) 12124782740; internet http://www.bdl.gov.lb/; f. 1964 to take over the banking activities of the Banque de Syrie et du Liban in Lebanon; cap £L312,700m., dep. £L8,158,500m. (Dec. 1996); Gov. RIAD SALAMEH.

Principal Commercial Banks

Allied Business Bank SAL: POB 113-7165 Beirut; tel. (1) 323116; telex 41738; fax (1) 200660; f. 1962; cap. £L7,196m., res £L7,878m., dep. £L178,161m., res £L7,877m. (Dec. 1995); Chair. ABDULLAH S. ZAKHEM; Gen. Man. HABIB F. ABU FADIL.

Al Marawid Bank SAL: POB 113-6260; Immeuble Yared, rue Abdul Aziz, Beirut; tel. (1) 350612; telex 21375; fax (1) 350585; f. 1980; cap. £L3,000m., res £L2,418m., dep. £L119,698m. (Dec. 1995); Chair. and Gen. Man. SALIM KHEIREDDINE; 10 brs.

Al-Moughtareb Bank SAL: POB 11-5508, Immeuble Sehnaoui, rue Banque du Liban, Beirut; tel. (1) 350066; telex 22106; fax (1) 602009; e-mail almoughtareb@inco.com.lb; f. 1974; cap. £L12,000m., dep. £L112,448m. (Dec. 1997); Chair. SAFI HARB.

Bank of Beirut SAL: Centre Gefinor, Bloc A, rue Clémenceau, Beirut; tel. (1) 738767; telex 23640; fax (1) 612166; f. 1973; cap. £L11,000m., res £L6,418m., dep. £L654,532m. (Dec. 1996); Chair. and Gen. Man. SALIM G. SFEIR.

Bank of Beirut and the Arab Countries SAL: POB 11-1536, Immeuble de la Banque, 250 rue Clémenceau, Beirut; tel. and fax (1) 867142; telex 20761; f. 1956; cap. £L40,000m., res £L32,030m., dep. £L1,055,989m. (Dec. 1996); Chair. and Gen. Man. TOUFIC S. ASSAF.

Bank of Kuwait and the Arab World SAL: POB 113-6248, Immeuble Belle Vue, Ain at-Tineh, Verdun, Beirut; tel. (1) 866305; telex 23778; fax (1) 86529; e-mail bkaw@sodetel.net.lb; f. 1959; cap. £L18,000m., res £L3,191m., dep. £L216,740m. (Dec. 1997); Chair. and Gen. Man. ABDUL RAZZAK ACHOUR.

Bank al-Madina SAL: POB 113-7221, Immeuble Banque al-Madina, rue Commodore, Hamra, Beirut; tel. (1) 351296; telex 23105; fax (1) 351297; e-mail madinabk@inco.com.lb; f. 1982; cap. £L33,000m., dep. £L74,716m. (Dec. 1997); Chair. and Gen. Man. Sheikh IBRAHIM BOU AYYASH; 6 brs.

Banque Audi SAL: POB 11-2560, ave Charles Malek, St Nicolas, Beirut; tel. (1) 200250; telex 42393; fax (1) 200955; e-mail bkaudi@inco.com.lb; internet http://www.audi.com.lb; f. 1962; cap. £L33,720m., dep. £L3,235,356m. (Dec. 1997); Chair. and Gen. Man. RAYMOND W. AUDI; 33 brs.

Banque de la Beka'a SAL: POB 117, Centre Fakhoury, Zahleh, Beirut; tel. (8) 803217; telex 42828; fax (8) 429387; f. 1965; cap. £L2,000m., dep. £L112,650m. (Dec. 1996); Chair. and Gen. Man. CHAOUKI W. FAKHOURY.

Banque de Crédit National SAL: POB 110204, Immeuble Beirut-Riyad Bank, 5e étage, rue Riad es-Solh, Beirut; tel. (1) 980120; telex 22161; fax (1) 980123; f. 1920; cap. £L1,000m., res £L2,490m., dep. £L48,309m. (Dec. 1996); Chair. and Gen. Man. EDMOND J. SAFRA.

Banque de l'Industrie et du Travail SAL: POB 11-3948, Immeuble BIT, rue Riad es-Solh, Beirut; tel. (1) 980170; telex 20698; fax (1) 980182; f. 1960; cap. £L18,850m., res £L3,579m., dep. £L275,414m. (Dec. 1997); Chair. and Gen. Man. Sheikh FOUAD JAMIL EL-KHAZEN; Exec. Dir and Gen. Man. NABIL N. KHAIRALLAH; 12 brs in Lebanon.

Banque du Liban et d'Outre-Mer SAL: POB 11-1912, Immeuble BLOM, rue Rachid Karameh, Verdun, Beirut; tel. (1) 743300; telex 94015829; fax (1) 738946; e-mail blommail@inco.com.lb; internet http://www.blom.com.lb; f. 1951; cap. £L185,000m., res £L18,102m., dep. £L5,088,913m. (Dec. 1997); Chair. and Gen. Man. Dr NAAMAN AZHARI; 33 brs in Lebanon.

Banque Libanaise pour le Commerce SAL: POB 11-1126, rue Riad es-Solh, Beirut; tel. (1) 445450; telex 41020; fax (1) 581927; f. 1950; cap. £L10,080m., res £L95,044m., dep. £L943,299m. (Dec. 1996); Chair. and Gen. Man. FÉLIX ABOUJAOUDE; 34 brs.

Banque Libano-Française SAL: POB 11-808, Immeuble Liberty Plaza, Hamra, Beirut; tel. (1) 340350; telex 42317; fax (1) 340355; internet http://www.blf.com.lb; f. 1967; cap. £L100,000m., dep £L2,636,528m. (Dec. 1997); Pres. and Chair. FARID RAPHAEL; 21 brs.

Banque de la Méditerranée SAL: POB 11-348, rue Verdun, Ain et-Tineh, Beirut; tel. (1) 866925; telex 20826; fax (1) 790250; f. 1944; cap. £L330,000m., res £L4,681m., dep. £L3,720,005m. (Dec. 1996); Chair. and Gen. Man. Dr MUSTAPHA H. RAZIAN.

Banque Misr-Liban SAL: POB 11-7, rue Riad es-Solh, Beirut; tel. (1) 867397; telex 22783; fax (1) 868490; f. 1929; cap. £L18,000m., res £L5,422m., dep. £L412,251m. (Dec. 1997); Pres. and Gen. Man. IBRAHIM NOUR ED-DINE; 14 brs.

Banque Saradar SAL: POB 11-1121, Immeuble Saradar, rue 31, Rabyé, Beirut; tel. (4) 416804; telex 41803; fax (4) 404490; e-mail saradar@saradar.com.lb; internet http://www.saradar.com.lb; f. 1948; cap. £L16,500m., dep. £L1,064,110m. (Dec. 1997); Gen. Man. MARIO JOE SARADAR; 6 brs.

Beirut-Riyad Bank SAL: POB 11-4668, Immeuble de la Banque Beirut-Riyad, rue Riad es-Solh, Beirut; tel. (1) 980222; telex 20610; fax (1) 980358; f. 1958; cap. £L14,400m., res £L6,540m., dep. £L699,028m. (Dec. 1996); Chair. and Gen. Man. ANWAR M. EL-KHALIL; Dep. Chair. and Man. Dir HASSAN H. MANSOUR; 12 brs.

BEMO (Banque Européenne pour le Moyen-Orient) SAL: POB 11-7048, Immeuble BEMO, place Sassine, Achrafieh, Beirut; tel. (1) 200505; telex 44881; fax (1) 330779; f. 1964; cap. £L7,600m., res £L1,219m., dep. £L176,734m. (Dec. 1996); Pres. and Gen. Man. HENRY Y. OBEGI; Gen. Man. JEAN V. HAJJAR.

Byblos Bank SAL: POB 11-5605, Centre Commercial Aya, Dora, Beirut; tel. (1) 255620; telex 43364; fax (1) 255606; e-mail byblosbk@byblosbank.com.lb; f. 1959; absorbed Banque Beyrouth pour le Commerce 1997; cap. £L48,455m., res £L34,990m., dep. £L1,941,620m. (Dec. 1996); Chair. and Gen. Man. Dr FRANÇOIS SEMAAN BASSIL; 50 brs.

Crédit Bancaire SAL: POB 16-5795, Immeuble Crédit Bancaire SAL, blvd Bachir Gemayel, Achrafieh, Beirut; tel. (1) 218183; telex 40032; fax (1) 200483; f. 1981; cap. £L5,800m., res £L597m., dep. £L104,610m. (Dec. 1996); Chair. PAUL A. KEBBE; Man. Dir TAREK KHALIFEH; 8 brs.

Crédit Libanais SAL: POB 166729, Centre Sofil, ave Charles Malek, Beirut; tel. (1) 200028; telex 40706; fax (1) 602615; f. 1961; cap. £L80,000m., res £L16,547m., dep. £L1,061,588m. (Dec. 1996); Chair. and Gen. Man. Dr JOSEPH M. TORBEY; 44 brs.

Federal Bank of Lebanon SAL: POB 11-2209, Immeuble Antoine Gebara, Dora, Beirut; tel. (1) 896183; telex 42307; fax (1) 268711; e-mail federal@cyberia.net.lb; f. 1952; cap. £L2,410m., res £L0.3m., dep. £L47,425m. (Dec. 1996); Pres. and Chair. AYOUB FARID MICHEL SAAB; 7 brs.

Fransabank SAL: POB 11-0393, Centre Sabbag, rue Hamra, Hamra, Beirut; tel. (1) 340180; telex 20631; fax (1) 354572; e-mail fsb@fransabank.com.lb; internet http://www.fransabank .com.lb; f. 1978 as merger of Banque Sabbag and Banque Française pour le Moyen Orient SAL; cap £L90,000m., res £L14,517m., dep. £L2,137,952m. (Dec. 1997); Chair. ADNAN KASSAR; Vice Chair. ADEL KASSAR; 40 brs.

Innash Bank SAL: POB 80938, Centre Moucarri, 3e étage, Autostrade Dora, Beirut; tel. and fax (1) 582420; telex 42887; f. 1988 as Banque de l'Essor Economique Libanais SAL, name changed 1997; cap. £L15,000m., dep. £L150,182m. (Dec. 1997); Chair. and Gen. Man. IMAD M. JAFFAL; 10 brs.

Intercontinental Bank of Lebanon SAL: POB 90263, Immeuble Ghantous, Dora, Beirut; tel. (1) 883464; telex 43467; fax (1) 255111; f. 1961; cap. £L5,072m., res £L1,582m., dep. £L67,863m. (Dec. 1997); Chair. and Gen. Man. RIAD TAKY; 2 brs.

Jammal Trust Bank SAL: POB 11-5640, Immeuble Jammal, rue Verdun, Beirut; tel. (1) 864170; telex 20939; fax (1) 864161; e-mail jammal@sodetel.net.lb; internet http://www.jammalbank .co.lb; f. 1963 as Investment Bank, SAL; cap. £L23,672m., res £L19,125m., dep. £L134,823m. (Dec. 1996); Chair. and Gen. Man. ALI A. JAMMAL; 21 brs.

Lebanese Canadian Bank: POB 11-2520, Immeuble Ghantous, blvd Dora, Beirut; tel. (1) 250222; telex 43430; fax (1) 250777; f. 1960; cap. £L3,528m., res £L2,922m., dep. £L196,325m. (Dec. 1995); Pres., Chair. and Gen. Man. GEORGES ZARD ABOU JAOUDE; 6 brs.

Lebanese Swiss Bank SAL: POB 11-9552, Immeuble Hoss, rue Emile Eddé, Hamra, Beirut; tel. (1) 354501; telex 20934; fax (1) 346242; f. 1973; cap. £L10,000m., res £L7,309m., dep. £L173,697m. (Dec. 1997); Chair. and Gen. Man. Dr TANAL SABBAH; 7 brs.

Lebanon and Gulf Bank SAL: POB 113-6404, 585 rue de Lyon, Hamra, Beirut; tel. (1) 340190; telex 41093; fax (1) 602085; f. 1963; cap. £L12,000m., res £L457m., dep. £L346,123m. (Dec. 1995); Chair. and Gen. Man. ABDUL HAFIZ MAHMOUD ITANI; 9 brs.

Metropolitan Bank SAL: POB 70216, Immeuble Nihako, Antélias, Beirut; tel. (1) 415824; telex 42130; fax (1) 406861; f. 1979; cap. £L12,000m., dep. £L104,635m. (Dec. 1997); Chair. and Gen. Man. MERSHED BAAKLINI.

National Bank of Kuwait (Lebanon) SAL: POB 11-5727, place Sanayeh, rue Justinien, Beirut; tel. (1) 741111; telex 22083; fax (1) 602328; f. 1965 as Rifbank, name changed 1996; cap. £L16,036m., res £L170m., dep. £L166,584m. (Dec. 1996); Chair. IBRAHIM DABDOUB; Gen. Man. MICHAEL ROWIHAB; 8 brs.

Near East Commercial Bank SAL: POB 16-5766, Centre Sofil, ave Charles Malek, Beirut; tel. and fax (1) 200331; telex 44664; f. 1978; cap. £L7,000m., res £L4,042m., dep. £L49,923m. (Dec. 1996); Chair. and Gen. Man. PAUL CALAND; 4 brs.

North Africa Commercial Bank SAL: POB 11-9575, Centre Aresco, rue Justinien, Beirut; tel. (1) 346320; telex 20712; fax (1) 346322; f. 1973; cap. £L10,358m., res £L15m., dep. £L123,344m. (Dec. 1996); Chair. ABDULLATIF EL-KIB.

Saudi Lebanese Bank SAL: POB 11-6765, Centre Justinien, rue Justinien, Beirut; tel. (1) 345866; telex 43587; f. 1979; cap. £L20,000m., res £L1,057m., dep. £L489,693m. (Dec. 1995); Chair. and Gen. Man. MUSTAFA RAZIAN; 5 brs.

Société Bancaire du Liban SAL: POB 165192, place Sassine, Achrafieh, Beirut; tel. (1) 200451; telex 48265; fax (1) 200455; e-mail sbl-dg@dm.net.lb; f. 1899; cap. £L2,200m., res £L9,847m., dep. £L105,136m. (Dec. 1997); Chair. SELIM LEVY.

Société Générale Libano Européenne de Banque SAL: POB 11-2955, rond-point Salomé, Sin el-Fil, Beirut; tel. (1) 483001; telex 44453; fax (1) 502820; e-mail sgleb@sgleb.com.lb; f. 1953; cap. £L10,620m., res £L3,993m., dep. £L2,160,712m. (Dec. 1997); Chair. and Gen. Man. MAURICE SEHNAOUI; 30 brs.

Société Nouvelle de la Banque de Syrie et du Liban SAL (SNBSL): POB 11-957, rue Riad es-Solh, Beirut; tel. (1) 405563; fax (1) 405564; f. 1963; cap. £L7,000m., res £L19,221m., dep. £L355,472m. (Dec. 1996); Chair. RAMSAY A. EL-KHOURY; Gen. Man. ANTOINE ADM; 22 brs.

Syrian Lebanese Commercial Bank SAL: POB 11-8701, Immeuble Cinéma Hamra, rue Hamra, Hamra, Beirut; tel. (1) 341262; telex 20853; fax (1) 341208; f. 1974; cap. £L15,750m., res. £L2,791m., dep. £L98,902m. (Dec. 1996); Chair. and Gen. Man. MOHAMMED RIAD EL-HAKIM; 3 brs.

Transorient Bank SAL: POB 11-260, rue Sérail, Bauchrieh, Beirut; tel. (1) 888630; telex 44925; fax (1) 897705; f. 1966; cap. £L17,280m., res £L8,959m., dep. £L400,071m. (Dec. 1996); Chair. ADIB S. MILLET; Gen. Man. ADIB F. MILLET; 13 brs.

Universal Bank SAL: POB 217, Immeuble Unigroup, place Sayyad, Hazmieh, Beirut; tel. (1) 450350; telex 43404; fax (1) 457312; f. 1978; cap. £L5,000m., res £L89m., dep. £L210,854m. (Dec. 1995); Chair. and Gen. Man. GEORGE H. HADDAD; 5 brs.

Wedge Bank Middle East SAL: POB 16-5852, Centre Sofil, 4e étage, ave Charles Malek, Achrafieh, Beirut; tel. (1) 201182; telex 43570; fax (1) 201184; f. 1983; cap. £L10,770m., res £L1,633m., dep. £L193,455m. (Dec. 1996); Pres. MICHEL I. FARES; Gen. Man. BADIH A. HOBEICHE; 6 brs.

Development Bank

Audi Investment Bank SAL: POB 16-5110, ave Charles Malek, Achrafieh, Beirut; tel. (1) 200951; telex 42297; fax (1) 255722; f. 1974 as Investment and Finance Bank, present name since 1996; medium- and long-term loans, 100% from Lebanese sources; owned by Banque Audi SAL (99.3%); cap. £L25,820m., res £L772.3m., dep. £L491,507.4m. (Dec. 1996); Chair. and Gen. Man. RAYMOND WADIH AUDI.

Principal Foreign Banks

ABN AMRO Bank Lebanon (Netherlands): POB 113-5162, ABN AMRO Tower, ave Charles Malek, Achrafieh, Beirut; tel. (1) 219200; telex 48088; fax (1) 217756; e-mail aabbei@cyberia.net.lb; internet http://www.abnamro.com; f. 1954; cap. £L17,262m., res £L4,622m., dep. £L637,703m. (Dec. 1997); Man. Dir. ELIA NAHAS; 4 brs.

American Express Bank (USA): POB 113-5160, Centre Mirna Chalouhi, rue Sin el-Fil, Beirut; tel. (1) 491470; telex 44481; fax (1) 444830; dep. £L125,326m., total assets £L138,700m. (Dec. 1995); Gen. Man. GABY KASSIS; 2 brs.

Arab Bank plc (Jordan): POB 11-1015, rue Riad es-Solh, Beirut; tel. (1) 981155; telex 20704; fax (1) 980803; f. 1930; cap. £L31,700m., res £L20.4m. (Dec. 1997); Exec. Vice-Pres. and Regional Man. Dr HISHAM BSAT.

Banque Nationale de Paris Intercontinentale SA (France): Tour el Ghazal/BNPI, ave Fouad Chehab, Beirut; tel. (1) 333717; telex 41401; fax (1) 200604; f. 1944; cap. £L7,027m. (Dec. 1993); Gen. Man. HENRI TYAN.

British Bank of the Middle East (Hong Kong): POB 11-1380, Immeuble SNA, 9e étage, place Tabaris, Beirut; tel. (1) 647611; telex 48043; fax (1) 425295; f. 1946; cap. £L1,400m. (Dec. 1996); CEO DEREK KELLY; 4 brs.

Habib Bank (Overseas) Ltd (Pakistan): POB 5616, Fadlallah Centre, 1st Floor, blvd el-Shiah, Musharaffieh, Beirut; tel. (1) 558992; fax (1) 558995; e-mail habibbkbey@t-net.com.lb; Sr Vice-Pres. and Man. MASOOD ALAM.

Jordan National Bank SA: POB 5186, Immeuble Sehnaoui, rue Banque du Liban, Hamra, Beirut; tel. (1) 340451; telex 20512; fax (1) 353185; cap. £L7,961m., dep. £L121,964m. (Dec. 1997); Regional Gen. Man. RAFIC ARAMOUNI; 3 brs.

The National Commercial Bank (Saudi Arabia): POB 11-2355, place Verdun, Corniche al-Mazra'a, Beirut; tel. (1) 860863; telex 43619; fax (1) 867728; cap. £L6,000m., res £L1,501m., dep. £L69,435m. (Dec. 1996); Gen. Man. HANI HOUSSAMI.

Numerous other foreign banks have representative offices in Beirut.

Banking Association

Association des Banques du Liban: POB 80536, Bourj Hammoud, Centre Moucarri, Autostrade Dora, Beirut; tel. and fax (1) 240601; telex 43069; e-mail abl@abl.org.lb; internet http://www .abl.org.lb; f. 1959; serves and promotes the interests of the banking community in Lebanon; mems: 83 banks and 11 banking rep. offices; Pres. FARID RAPHAEL; Gen. Sec. Dr MAKRAM SADER.

STOCK EXCHANGE

The Beirut Stock Exchange recommenced trading in January 1996.

Beirut Stock Exchange: POB 13-6690, Tour Soudat, 2e étage, rue Soudat, Hamra, Beirut; tel. (1) 786501; fax (1) 786499; e-mail bse@bse.com.lb; internet http://www.bse.com.lb; f. 1920; 10 cttee mems; Cttee Chair. GABRIEL SEHNAOUI.

INSURANCE

Almost 88 insurance companies were registered in Lebanon in the late 1990s, although only about one-half of these were operational.

Arabia Insurance Co SAL: POB 11-2172, rue de Phénicie, Beirut; tel. (1) 363610; telex 40060; fax (1) 365139; f. 1944; cap. £L40,800m.; Chair. and Gen. Man. BADR S. FAHOUM.

Commercial Insurance Co SAL: POB 4351, Centre Starco, Beirut; tel. (1) 643873; telex 40006; fax (1) 869084; f. 1962; Chair. MAX R. ZACCAR.

Compagnie Libanaise d'Assurances SAL: POB 3685, rue Riad es-Solh, Beirut; tel. (1) 868988; telex 20379; f. 1951; cap. £L3,000m. (1991); Chair. JEAN F. S. ABOUJAOUDÉ; Gen. Man. MAMDOUH RAHMOUN.

Al-Ittihad al-Watani: POB 1270, Immeuble Al-Ittihadia, ave Fouad Chehab, St Nicolas, Beirut; tel. (1) 330840; telex 20839; f. 1947; cap. £L30m.; Chair. JOE I. KAIROUZ; Exec. Dir TANNOUS FEGHALI.

Al-Mashrek Insurance and Reinsurance SAL: POB 16-6154, Immeuble Amir, 65 rue Aabrine, Beirut; tel. (1) 200541; telex 43244; fax (1) 418578; f. 1962; cap. £L1,500m., (1994); Chair. and Gen. Man. ABRAHAM MATOSSIAN.

Libano-Suisse Insurance Co SAL: POB 90302, Immeuble Cité Dora, Dora, Beirut; tel. (1) 256060; telex 43766; fax (1) 255944; e-mail libanosu@dm.net.lb; f. 1959; cap. £L4,050m. (1991); Chair. MICHEL PIERRE PHARAON; Gen. Man. NAJI HABIS.

'La Phénicienne' SAL: POB 11-5652, Immeuble Hanna Haddad, rue Amine Gemayel, Sioufi, Beirut; tel. (1) 425484; telex 42357; fax (1) 424532; f. 1964; Chair. and Gen. Man. TANNOUS C. FEGHALI.

Trade and Industry

DEVELOPMENT ORGANIZATIONS

Council for Development and Reconstruction (CDR): POB 116-5351, Tallet es-Serail, Beirut; tel. (1) 643982; fax (1) 647947; f. 1977; an autonomous public institution reporting to the Cabinet, the CDR is charged with the co-ordination, planning and execution of Lebanon's public reconstruction programme; it plays a major role in attracting foreign funds; Chair. NABIL AL-JISR; Sec.-Gen. NOUHAD BAZOUDI.

Investment Development Authority of Lebanon (IDAL): Beirut; internet http://www.idal.com.lb; state-owned; Dir YOUSSEF CHOUCAIR.

CHAMBERS OF COMMERCE AND INDUSTRY

Beirut Chamber of Commerce and Industry: POB 11-1801, Sanayeh, Beirut; tel. (1) 341328; fax (1) 602374; e-mail info@ccib .org.lb; internet http://www.ccib.org.lb; f. 1898; 32,000 mems; Pres. ADNAN KASSAR; Dir-Gen. Dr WALID NAJA.

Tripoli Chamber of Commerce and Industry: POB 27, blvd Tripoli, Tripoli; tel. 622790; telex 46024; Pres. HASSAN EL-MOUNLA.

Chamber of Commerce and Industry in Sidon and South Lebanon: POB 41, rue Maarouf Saad, Sidon; tel. 720123; telex 20402; fax 722986; f. 1933; Pres. MOHAMAD ZAATARI.

Zahleh Chamber of Commerce and Industry: POB 100, Zahleh; tel. (8) 802602; telex 48042; fax (8) 800050; f. 1939; 2,500 mems; Pres. EDMOND JREISSATI.

EMPLOYERS' ASSOCIATION

Association of Lebanese Industrialists: POB 1520, Chamber of Commerce and Industry, rue Justinian, Beirut; fax (1) 351167; Pres. JACQUES SARRAF; Sec.-Gen. GHAZI YAHYA.

UTILITIES

Electricity

Electricité du Liban (EdL): POB 131, Immeuble de l'Electricité du Liban, 22 rue du Fleuve, Beirut; tel. (1) 442720; fax (1) 583084; state-owned.

Water

In early 1998 the Government was in the process of establishing five new regional water authorities (in the governorates of the North, South, Beka'a, Beirut and Mount Lebanon), to replace the existing water authorities and committees. The new authorities were to operate under the supervision of the Ministry of Electricity and Water Resources.

MAJOR COMPANIES

Arabian Construction Co Group: POB 11-6876, Immeuble Sucam, 1er étage, Sucam, Ain al-Tineh, Beirut, Beirut; tel. (1) 861962; telex 20385; f. 1971; construction of multi-storey buildings, hotels, houses, etc.; cap. US $1m.; Chair. GHASSAN ABDALLAH AL-MEREHBI; Man. Dirs TAHA MIKATI, ANAS MIKATI; 1,500 employees.

Caves de Ksara SAL: Immeuble Nakhle Hanna, ave Charles Malek, POB 16-6184, Beirut; tel. (1) 200715; telex 41456; fax (1) 200716; f. 1857; wines and spirits (incl. Ksarak); Pres. ZAFER CHAOUI; Gen. Man. CHARLES GHOSTINE; 75 employees.

Contracting and Trading Co (CAT) International Ltd: POB 11-1036, Immeuble CAT, rue al-Arz, Saifi, Beirut; tel. (1) 449910; telex 44275; f. 1942; civil, mechanical, electrical, pipeline and marine works contractors; sales US $7m. (1995); total assets US $17m.; Man. Partners SHOUKRI H. SHAMMAS, Mrs LAURA BUSTANI, Mrs NADIA EL-KHOURY; 800 employees.

Filature Nationale de Coton SAL, Asseily & Cie: Immeuble Asseily, place Riad es-Solh, POB 11-4126, Beirut; tel. (1) 890610; telex 20018; production of textiles; Dir. G. ASSEILY.

Fonderies Ohannes H. Kassardjian SAL: POB 11-4150, Beirut; tel. (1) 462462; telex 44062; fax (1) 462948; f. 1939; production of brass and gun-metal valves and fittings for pipes, chromium-plated bathroom fittings and floor drains, cast iron valves, fittings for ductile iron pipes manhole covers and gratings, etc.; Pres. JOSEPH O. KASSARDJIAN; 300 employees.

Al-Hamra Engineering Co SAL: POB 116040, Beirut; tel. and fax (1) 483275; telex 22211; e-mail hameng@bignet.com.lb; f. 1966; part of the Al-Hamra Group; construction work on industrial projects, airports, hospitals, housing schemes, reservoirs, power stations, etc.; sales US $75m. (1981/82); cap. $4.8m.; total assets $70m.; CEO HANNA AYOUB; Gen. Man. TONY HANANIA; 600 employees.

Industrial Development Co SARL (INDEVCO): POB 11-2354, Immeuble Frem, Tallat al-Ansafir, Ajaltoun, Beirut; tel. (9) 953600; telex 45736; fax (9) 953503; f. 1963; mfrs of tissue and paperboard, kitchen cabinets and doors, carton boxes, consumer tissue products, diapers and disposable products; sales US $500m. (1995); Chair. GEORGES FREM; 5,000 employees (Lebanon, Saudi Arabia, Arabian Gulf, Brazil and the USA).

Karoun Dairies SAL: Immeuble Baghdassarian Centre Industriel, Bauchrieh, POB 11-9150, Beirut; tel. (1) 497325; fax (1) 497080; e-mail dairies@karoun.com; internet http://www.karoun.com; f. 1931; dairy products; Chair. and Gen. Man. ARA BAGHDASSARIAN.

Lahoud Engineering Co Ltd: POB 55366, ave Charles de Gaulle, Sin el-Fil, Beirut; tel. (1) 424828; telex 40469; fax (1) 496540; construction of industrial plants.

Mothercat Ltd: POB 11-1036, Immeuble CAT, rue al-Arz, Saifi, Beirut; tel. (1) 449910; telex 44275; fax (1) 446931; f. 1963; civil, mechanical, electrical, pipeline, storage tanks and marine works contractors; sales US $13.5m. (1995); cap. US $7.5m.; total assets US $14.6m.; Chair. Mrs LAURA BUSTANI; Man. Dir SHUKRI H. SHAMMAS; 500 employees.

Société Industrielle des Produits Pioneer-Jabre SAL: POB 369, Beirut; tel. (1) 395053; telex 20988; f. 1874; production of wafers, chocolates, halva, pasta, biscuits, confectionery, cartons, tins; Chair. EDWARD NASSAR; 250 employees.

Zahrani Oil Installations: POB 11-1925, Beirut; tel. (1) 345702; telex 20442; oil refining; Gen. Man. G. A. AHMAD; 300 employees.

TRADE UNION FEDERATION

Confédération Générale des Travailleurs du Liban (CGTL): POB 4381, Beirut; f. 1958; 300,000 mems; only national labour centre in Lebanon and sole rep. of working classes; comprises 18 affiliated federations including all 150 unions in Lebanon; Chair. GHNEIM AZ-ZOGHBI.

Transport

RAILWAYS

Office des Chemins de Fer de l'Etat Libanais et du Transport en Commun: Gare St Michel, Nahr, Beirut; tel. (1) 587211; telex 43088; fax (1) 447007; since 1961 all railways in Lebanon have been state-owned. The original network of some 412 km no longer transports passengers. However, Lebanese authorities have planned a rail reconstruction project, costing US $40m.–$60m. Pres. BASAM ABDEL-MALAK.

ROADS

At 31 December 1995 Lebanon had 6,359 km of roads, of which 2,170 km were highways, main or national roads and 1,372 km were secondary or regional roads. The two international motorways are the north–south coastal road and the road connecting Beirut with Damascus in Syria. Among the major roads are that crossing the Beka'a and continuing south to Bent-Jbail and the Shtaura–Baalbek road. Hard-surfaced roads connect Jezzine with Moukhtara, Bzebdine with Metn, Meyroub with Afka and Tannourine.

SHIPPING

A two-phase programme to rehabilitate and expand the port of Beirut is currently under way. In the second phase, due to commence in 1996, the construction of an industrial free zone, a fifth basin and a major container terminal are envisaged, at an estimated cost of US $1,000m. Tripoli, the northern Mediterranean terminus of the oil pipeline from Iraq (the other is Haifa, Israel—not in use since 1948), is also a busy port, with good equipment and facilities. Jounieh, north of Beirut, is Lebanon's third most important port. A new deep-water sea port is to be constructed south of Sidon. The reconstructed port of an-Naqoura, in the 'security zone' along the border with Israel, was inaugurated in June 1987.

Port Authorities

Compagnie de Gestion et d'Exploitation: POB 1490, Beirut; tel. (1) 580211; Harbour Master JIHAD MENHEM.

Service d'Exploitation du Port de Tripoli: Tripoli; tel. (6) 601955; Harbour Master VICTOR GHAZI.

Principal Shipping Companies

Abbotswood Holding SAL: POB 16-6792, Immeuble Molderne, rue el-Arz, Beirut; tel. (1) 283004; telex 40115; fax (1) 601060.

Ets Paul Adem: Centre Moucari, 6e étage, autostrade Doura, Beirut; tel. (1) 582421; telex 41889; fax (1) 582421.

Agence Générale Maritime (AGEMAR) SARL: POB 9255, Centre Burotec, 7e étage, rue Pasteur, Beirut; tel. (1) 583885; telex 40915; fax (1) 583884; Dirs S. MEDLEJ, N. MEDLEJ.

Arab Shipping and Chartering Co: POB 1084, Beirut; tel. (1) 371044; telex 20711; fax (1) 373370; agents for China Ocean Shipping Co.

Associated Levant Lines (SAL): POB 110317, Garage Mercedes, Doura, Beirut; tel. (1) 899371; telex 43993; fax (1) 899218; Dirs T. GARGOUR, N. GARGOUR, H. GARGOUR.

Wafic Begdache: Immeuble Wazi, 4e étage, rue Mousatbe, Beirut; tel. (1) 632310; telex 48391; fax (1) 632688.

Bulk Traders International: POB 70-152, Centre St Elie, Bloc A, 6e étage, Antélias, Beirut; tel. (1) 410724; telex 40068; fax (1) 610539.

Continental Shipmanagement SARL: POB 901413, Centre Dora Moucarri, 8e étage, appt 804, Beirut; tel. (1) 583654; telex 42921; fax (1) 584440.

O. D. Debbas & Sons: Head Office: POB 166678, Immeuble Debbas, 530 blvd Corniche du Fleuve, Beirut; tel. (1) 585253; fax (1) 602515; e-mail debbason@attmail.com; f. 1892; Man. Dir OIDIH ELIE DEBBAS.

Dery Shipping Lines Ltd: POB 5720-113, Immeuble Eldorado, salle 607, rue Hamra, Beirut; tel. (1) 862442; telex 22842; fax (1) 344146.

Fauzi Jemil Ghandour: POB 1084, Beirut; tel. (1) 373376; telex 20711; fax (1) 360048; e-mail alifgand@dm.net.lb; agents for Denizçlik Bankasi TAO (Denizvollari); Ecuadorian Line, Festival Shipping and Tourist Enterprises Ltd.

G S Shipping Ltd: POB 55509, Sin el-Fil, Hayek, Beirut; tel. (1) 493961; telex 48111; fax (1) 423232.

Geizairi Chartering and Shipping Co (GEZACHART): POB 11-1402, Immeuble Attieh, rue Labban, Beirut; tel. (1) 803814; telex 48478; fax (1) 867136; e-mail gezair@beirut.com.

Issa, Issam & Toufic: El-Mina, Tripoli; tel. (6) 601265; fax (6) 610348.

Mediterranean Feedering Co SARL: POB 70-1187, Immeuble Akak, autostrade Dbayeh, Beirut; tel. (1) 403056; fax (1) 403047; e-mail mfcbeirut@attmail.com; Man. Dir EMILE AKEF EL-KHOURY.

Orient Shipping and Trading Co SARL: POB 11-2561, Immeuble Moumneh; no 72, rue Ain al-Mraisseh 54, Beirut; tel. (1) 644252; telex 22882; fax (1) 364455; Dirs ELIE ZAROUBY, EMILE ZAROUBY.

Rassem Shipping Agency: Immeuble Agha, Raoucheh, Beirut; tel. (1) 866372; telex 48442; fax (1) 515485.

G. Sahyouni & Co SARL: POB 175452, Immeuble Hafiz el-Hashem, 3e étage, Pont Karantina, rue de Tripoli, Beirut; tel. (1) 257046; fax (1) 241317; e-mail lloydsbey@attmail.com; f. 1989; agents for Baltic Control, Lloyd's Lebanon Ltd., SARL; Financial Man. HENRY CHIDIAC; Man. Dir. GEORGE SAHYOUNI.

Sinno Trading and Navigation Agency: POB 113-6977, Immeuble Rebeiz, 4e étage, rue du Port, Beirut; tel. (1) 446698; telex 48638; fax (1) 446707; Chair. MUHIEDDINE F. SINNO; Man. Dir AHMED JABBOURY.

Sioufi Transport SARL: POB 175-383, Beirut; tel. (1) 581124; telex 447761; fax (1) 583893.

Co A Sleiman & Sons: Immeuble Saroulla, 3e étage, rue Hamra, Beirut; tel. (1) 354240; telex 21221; fax (1) 340262.

Union Shipping and Chartering Agency: POB 2856, Beirut; tel. (1) 373376; telex 20768; e-mail un.chart@dm.net.lb; agents for Croatia Line, Jadroslobodna, Jugo Oceania, Atlanska Plovidba, Jadrolinija, Jadroplov, Norasia Line.

CIVIL AVIATION

Services from the country's principal airport, in Beirut, were subject to frequent disruptions after 1975; its location in predominantly Muslim west Beirut made it virtually inaccessible to non-Muslims. In 1986 a new airport, based on an existing military airfield, was opened at Halat, north of Beirut, by Christian concerns, but commercial operations from the airport were not authorized by the Government. Services to and from Beirut by Middle East Airlines (MEA) were suspended, and the airport closed, at the end of January 1987, after the Christian LF militia shelled the airport and threatened to

attack MEA aircraft if services from their own airport, at Halat, did not receive official authorization. Beirut airport was reopened in May, after the LF accepted government assurances that Halat would receive the necessary authorization for civil use. However, the commission concluded that Halat did not possess the facilities to cater for international air traffic. More than 2m. passengers used Beirut International Airport in 1997.

MEA (Middle East Airlines, Air Liban SAL): POB 206, Immeuble MEA, blvd de l'Aéroport, Beirut; tel. (1) 629250; telex 20820; fax (1) 629260; internet http://www.mea.com.lb; f. 1945; took over Lebanese International Airways in 1969; regular services throughout Europe, the Middle East, South America, North and West Africa and the Far East; Chair. MUHAMMAD EL-HOUT; Man. Dir YOUSUF LAHOUD.

Trans-Mediterranean Airways SAL (TMA): Beirut International Airport, POB 11–3018, Beirut; tel. (1) 820540; fax (1) 629218; e-mail cargo@tma.com.lb; f. 1953; scheduled cargo services, charter activities and aircraft lease operations covering Europe, the Middle East, Africa and the Far East; Chair. FADI SAAB.

Tourism

Before the civil war, Lebanon was a major tourist centre, and its scenic beauty, sunny climate and historic sites attracted some 2m. visitors annually. In 1974 tourism contributed about 20% of the country's income. Since the end of the civil conflict tourist facilities, in particular hotels, have begun to be reconstructed, and the Arab Tourist Organization designated 1994 as the International Year of Tourism in Lebanon. The annual total of tourist arrivals increased from 177,503 in 1992 to 409,735 in 1995. Tourism receipts reached an estimated US $710m. in the latter year. Of total arrivals in 1995, 37.1% were from Europe and 36.9% from Arab countries.

National Council of Tourism in Lebanon (NCTL): POB 11-5344, rue Banque du Liban 550, Beirut; tel. (1) 343196; fax (1) 343279; e-mail mot@lebanon-tourism.gov.lb; internet http://www.lebanon-tourism.gov.lb; government-sponsored autonomous organization responsible for the promotion of tourism; overseas offices in London (United Kingdom), Paris (France), Frankfurt (Germany), Cairo (Egypt), and Jeddah (Saudi Arabia); Pres. SAMY MAROUN; Dir-Gen. NASSER SAFIEDDINE.

Defence

Commander-in-Chief of the Armed Forces: Gen. EMILE LAHOUD (Maronite Christian).

Chief of Staff of Armed Forces: Maj.-Gen. ABU DIRGHAM (Druze).

Commander of the Air Force: Brig.-Gen. FAHIM AL-HAJJ.

Director-General of the Internal Security Forces: Brig.-Gen. UMAR MAKHZUMI (Shi'ite) (acting).

Total armed forces (August 1997): 55,100: army (estimated) 53,300; air force (estimated) 800; navy 1,000.

There is also an internal security force of some 13,000 (under reorganization), attached to the Ministry of the Interior. The strengths of the principal sectarian militias (before they, with the exception of Hezbollah, began to disband in March 1991) were estimated as follows: Lebanese Forces (Christian) 18,500 regulars (16,500 reserves); Druze 8,500 regulars (6,500 reserves); Amal (Shi'ite) 10,200 regulars (4,800 reserves); Hezbollah (Shi'ite) 3,500 regulars (11,500 reserves). The Israeli-backed South Lebanon Army, patrolling the buffer zone along the border with Israel, numbered an estimated 2,500. In March 1978 a 6,000-strong UN Interim Force in Lebanon (UNIFIL), (increased to 7,000 in February 1982 but numbering some 4,488 in August 1997), was deployed to try to keep the peace near the border with Israel. An estimated 30,000 Syrian troops remain in Lebanon.

Education

Education is not compulsory. Primary education has been available free of charge in state schools since 1960, but private institutions still provide the main facilities for secondary and university education. Private schools enjoy almost complete autonomy, except for a certain number which receive government financial aid and are supervised by inspectors from the Ministry of National Education.

Primary education begins at six years of age and lasts for five years. It is followed either by the four-year intermediate course or the three-year secondary course. The baccalaureate examination is taken in two parts at the end of the second and third years of secondary education, and a public examination is taken at the end of the intermediate course. Technical education is provided mainly at the National School of Arts and Crafts, which offers four-year courses in electronics, mechanics, architectural and industrial drawing, and other subjects. There are also public vocational schools providing courses for lower levels. In 1995 the total enrolment at primary and secondary schools was equivalent to 93% of all school-age children (92% of boys; 95% of girls); enrolment at secondary schools in that year was equivalent to 81% of the appropriate age-group (males 84%; females 77%).

Higher education is provided by 13 institutions, including six universities. Teacher training is given at various levels. A three-year course which follows the intermediate course trains primary school teachers and another three-year course which follows the second part of the baccalaureate trains teachers for the intermediate school. Secondary school teachers are trained at the Higher Teach-ers' College at the Lebanese University. Two agricultural schools provide a three-year course for pupils holding the intermediate school degree.

Lebanon has the highest literacy rate in the Arab world. In 1970 the rate of illiteracy among people aged 10 years and over was 21.5% for males and 42.1% for females. In 1995, according to estimates by UNESCO, the average rate of adult illiteracy was 7.6% (males 5.3%; females 9.7%). Expenditure on education by the Central Government in 1995 was £L425,480m. (7.3% of total budgetary expenditure).

Bibliography

Abouchdid, E. E. *Thirty Years of Lebanon and Syria (1917–47)*. Beirut, 1948.

Agwani, M. S. (Ed.). *The Lebanese Crisis, 1958: a documentary study*. Asia Publishing House, 1965.

Ajami, Fouad. *The Vanished Imam: Musa al-Sadr and the Shi'a of Lebanon*. London, I.B. Tauris; New York, Cornell University Press, 1986.

Atiyah, E. *An Arab tells his Story*. London, 1946.

The Beirut Massacre: the complete Kahan Commission Report. New York, Karz-Cohl, 1983.

Besoins et Possibilités de Développement du Liban. Étude Préliminaire, 2 Vols. Lebanese Ministry of Planning, Beirut, 1964.

Beydoun, Ahmad. *Le Liban. Itinéraires dans une guerre incivile*. Paris, Karthala and CERMOC, 1993.

Binder, Leonard (Ed.). *Politics in Lebanon*. New York, Wiley, 1966.

Bulloch, John. *Death of a Country: The Civil War in Lebanon*. London, Weidenfeld and Nicolson, 1977.

   Final Conflict: The War in Lebanon. London, Century Publishing Co.

Burckhard, C. *Le Mandat Français en Syrie et au Liban*. Paris, 1925.

Catroux, G. *Dans la Bataille de Méditerranée*. Paris, Julliard, 1949.

Chamoun, C. *Les Mémoires de Camille Chamoun*. Beirut, 1949.

Fisk, Robert. *Pity the Nation: Lebanon at War*. London, André Deutsch, 1990.

France, Ministère des Affaires Etrangères. *Rapport sur la Situation de la Syrie et du Liban*. Paris, annually, 1924–39.

Gaunson, A. B. *The Anglo-French Clash in Lebanon and Syria, 1940–45*. London, Macmillan, 1987.

Ghattas, Emile. *The monetary system in the Lebanon*. New York 1961.

Giannou, Chris. *Besieged: a doctor's story of life and death in Beirut*. Toronto, Key Porter, 1990.

Gilmour, David. *Lebanon: the Fractured Country*. London, Martin Robertson, 1983.

Glass, Charles. *Tribes with Flags: A Journey Curtailed*. London, Secker and Warburg, 1990.

Gulick, John. *Social Structure and Culture Change in a Lebanese Village*. New York, 1955.

Haddad, J. *Fifty Years of Modern Syria and Lebanon*. Beirut, 1950.

Halawi, Majed. *A Lebanon Defied: Mosa al-Sadr and the Shi'a community*. Oxford, Westview Press, 1993.

Harik, Iliya F. *Politics and Change in a Traditional Society— Lebanon 1711–1845*. Princeton University Press, 1968.

Hepburn, A. H. *Lebanon*. New York, 1966.

Himadeh, Raja S. *The Fiscal System of Lebanon*. Beirut, Khayat, 1961.

Hitti, Philip K. *Lebanon in History*. 3rd edn, London, Macmillan, 1967.

Hollis, Rosemary, and Shehadi, Nadim (Eds). *Lebanon on Hold: Implications for Middle East Peace*. London, Royal Institute for International Affairs, 1996.

Hourani, Albert K. *Syria and Lebanon*. London, 1946.

Hudson, Michael C. *The Precarious Republic: Political Modernization in the Lebanon*. New York, Random House, 1968.

Jaber, Hala. *Hezbollah*. London, Fourth Estate, 1997.

Kapeliouk, Amnon. *Sabra et Chatila: enquête sur un massacre*. Paris, Editions du Seuil.

Kassir, Samur. *La guerre du Liban. De la dissension nationale au conflit régional*. Paris, Karthala and CERMOC, 1994.

Lecerf, Marie-Ange. *Comprendre le Liban*. Paris, Karthala, 1988.

Longrigg, S. H. *Syria and Lebanon under French Mandate*. Oxford University Press, 1958.

Mills, Arthur E. *Private Enterprise in Lebanon*. American University of Beirut, 1959.

Picard, Elizabeth. *Lebanon: a Shattered Country*. New York and London, Holmes and Meier, 1996.

Puaux, G. *Deux Années au Levant; souvenirs de Syrie et du Liban*. Paris, Hachette, 1952.

Qubain, Fahim I. *Crisis in Lebanon*. Washington, DC, Middle East Institute, 1961.

Randal, Jonathan. *The Tragedy of Lebanon*. London, Chatto and Windus, 1983.

Rondot, Pierre. *Les Institutions Politiques du Liban*. Paris, 1947.

Saba, Elias S. *The Foreign Exchange Systems of Lebanon and Syria*. American University of Beirut, 1961.

Safa, Elie. *L'Emigration Libanaise*. Beirut, 1960.

Salem, Elie A. *Violence and Diplomacy in Lebanon*. London, I. B. Tauris, 1995.

Salibi, K. S. *The Modern History of Lebanon*. New York, Praeger, and London, Weidenfeld and Nicolson, 1964.

   Cross Roads to Civil War: Lebanon 1958–76. New York, Caravan Books, 1976.

Sayigh, Y. A. *Entrepreneurs of Lebanon*. Cambridge, Mass., 1962.

Stewart, Desmond. *Trouble in Beirut*. London, Wingate, 1959.

Suleiman, M. W. *Political Parties in Lebanon*. Ithaca, NY, Cornell University Press, 1967.

Sykes, John. *The Mountain Arabs*. London, Hutchinson, 1968.

Tibawi, A. L. *A Modern History of Greater Syria, including Lebanon and Palestine*. London, Macmillan, 1969.

Vallaud, Pierre. *Le Liban au Bout du Fusil*. Paris, Librairie Hachette, 1976.

Zarmi, Meir. *The Foundation of Modern Lebanon*. London, Croom Helm, 1985.

Ziadeh, Nicola. *Syria and Lebanon*. New York, Praeger, 1957.

LIBYA

(THE GREAT SOCIALIST PEOPLE'S LIBYAN ARAB JAMAHIRIYA)

Physical and Social Geography

W. B. FISHER

The Great Socialist People's Libyan Arab Jamahiriya (as Libya has been known since April 1986) is bounded on the north by the Mediterranean Sea, on the east by Egypt and Sudan, on the south and south-west by Chad and Niger, on the west by Algeria and on the north-west by Tunisia. The three component areas of Libya are: Tripolitania, in the west, with an area of 285,000 sq km (110,000 sq miles); Cyrenaica, in the east, which has an area of 905,000 sq km (350,000 sq miles); and the Fezzan, in the south, with an area of 570,000 sq km (220,000 sq miles)—giving a total for Libya of 1,760,000 sq km (680,000 sq miles). The independence of Libya was proclaimed in December 1951; before that date, following conquest by the Italians, Tripolitania and Cyrenaica had been ruled by a British administration, at first military, then civil; and the Fezzan had been administered by France. The revolutionary Government which came to power in September 1969 renamed the three regions: Tripolitania became known as the Western provinces, Cyrenaica the Eastern provinces, and the Fezzan the Southern provinces.

The political and economic capital of Libya is Tripoli. However, as part of a radical government decentralization programme undertaken in September 1988, all but two of the secretariats of the General People's Committee (ministries) were relocated in other parts of the country.

PHYSICAL FEATURES

The whole of Libya may be said to form part of the vast plateau of North Africa, which extends from the Atlantic Ocean to the Red Sea; but there are certain minor geographical features which give individuality to the three component areas of Libya. Tripolitania consists of a series of regions at different levels, rising in the main towards the south, and thus broadly comparable with a flight of steps. In the extreme north, along the Mediterranean coast, there is a low-lying coastal plain called the Jefara. This is succeeded inland by a line of hills, or rather a scarp edge, that has several distinguishing local names, but is usually alluded to merely as the Jebel. Here and there in the Jebel occurs evidence of former volcanic activity—old craters, and sheets of lava. The Jefara and adjacent parts of the Jebel are by far the most important parts of Tripolitania, since they are better watered and contain most of the population, together with the capital town, Tripoli.

South of the Jebel there is an upland plateau—a dreary desert landscape of sand, scrub, and scattered irregular masses of stone. After several hundred km the plateau gives place to a series of east-west running depressions, where artesian water, and hence oases, are found. These depressions make up the region of the Fezzan, which is merely a collection of oases on a fairly large scale, interspersed with areas of desert. In the extreme south the land rises considerably to form the mountains of the central Sahara, where some peaks reach 3,500 m in height.

Cyrenaica has a slightly different physical pattern. In the north, along the Mediterranean, there is an upland plateau that rises to 600 m in two very narrow steps, each only a few km wide. This gives a bold, prominent coastline to much of Cyrenaica, and so there is a marked contrast with Tripolitania where the coast is low-lying, and in parts fringed by lagoons. The northern uplands of Cyrenaica are called the Jebel Akhdar (Green Mountain), and here, once again, are found the bulk of the population and the two main towns, Benghazi and Derna. On its western side the Jebel Akhdar drops fairly steeply to the shores of the Gulf of Sirte; but on the east it falls more gradually, and is traceable as a series of ridges, about 100m in altitude,

that extend as far as the Egyptian frontier. This eastern district, consisting of low ridges aligned parallel to the coast, is known as Marmarica, and its chief town is Tobruk.

South of the Jebel Akhdar, the land falls in elevation, producing an extensive lowland, which, except for its northern fringe, is mainly desert. Here and there occur a few oases—Aujila (or Ojila), Jalo and Jaghbub in the north; and Jawf, Zighen and Kufra (the largest of all) in the south. These oases traditionally supported only a few thousand inhabitants and were less significant than those of the Fezzan, though some are now in petroleum-producing areas and, consequently, increasing in importance. In the same region, and becoming more widespread towards the east, is the Sand Sea—an expanse of fine, mobile sand, easily lifted by the wind into dunes that can sometimes reach about 100 m in height and more than 150 km in length. Finally, in the far south of Cyrenaica, lie the central Saharan mountains—the Tibesti Ranges, continuous with those to the south of the Fezzan.

The climate of Libya is characterized chiefly by its aridity and by its wide variation in temperatures. Lacking mountain barriers, the country is subject to the climatic influence of both the Sahara and the Mediterranean Sea, and, as a result, there can be abrupt transitions in climatic conditions. In winter it can be fairly raw and cold in the north, with sleet and even light snow on the hills. In summer it is extremely hot in the Jefara of Tripolitania, reaching temperatures of 40°C–45°C. In the southern deserts, conditions are hotter still; Gharian has recorded temperatures in excess of 49°C. Several feet of snow can also fall here in winter. Northern Cyrenaica has a markedly cooler summer of 27°C–32°C, but with high air humidity near the coast. A special feature is the *ghibli*—a hot, very dry wind from the south that can raise temperatures in the north by 15°C or even 20°C in a few hours, sometimes resulting in temperatures of 20°C or 25°C in January. This sand-laden, dry wind (which can cause considerable crop damage) may blow at any time of the year, but spring and autumn are the usual seasons.

The hills of Tripolitania and Cyrenaica annually receive as much as 400 mm–500 mm of rainfall, but in the remainder of the country the rainfall is usually 200 mm or less. Once every five or six years there is a pronounced drought, sometimes lasting for two successive seasons.

ECONOMIC LIFE

Such conditions imposed severe restriction on all forms of economic activity. Although petroleum was discovered in considerable quantities in Libya, physical and climatic conditions made exploitation difficult and, until the closure of the Suez Canal in 1967, the remote situation of the country, away from the currents of international trade, was a further handicap. However, production of crude petroleum increased rapidly and proximity to southern and central Europe presented a considerable advantage over the costly Suez passage that was reflected in the price. The introduction of petroleum revenues transformed the economic situation of Libya. Extensive development was undertaken, with the aim of improving housing, and the fostering of industries to produce consumer goods. Roads, electricity, improved water supplies, telecommunications links and reorganized town planning were all targeted by development initiatives, and the construction of a number of sizeable industrial plants was approved.

In the better-watered areas of the Jefara and, to a smaller extent, in northern Cyrenaica, cultivation of barley, wheat, olives and Mediterranean fruit is practised.

The Fezzan and the smaller oases in Cyrenaica are almost rainless, and cultivation depends entirely upon irrigation from wells. Millet is the chief crop, and there are several million date palms, which provide the bulk of the food. Small quantities of vegetables and fruit—figs, pomegranates, squashes, artichokes and tubers—are produced from gardens. Along the northern coast, and especially on the lower slopes both of the Tripolitanian Jebel and the Jebel Akhdar, vines are grown, though less so than formerly because of the prohibition of wine-making since independence.

Over much of Libya, pastoral nomadism, based on the rearing of sheep and goats (and some cattle and camels), is the only possible activity. In Cyrenaica, nomads outnumbered the remainder of the population for many years, but in Tripolitania the main emphasis is on agriculture, although herding is still practised. Several industries have developed—petroleum refining, of course, plus some petrochemical activity, iron and steel production and some light industries. Overall, the scale of industrial activity is still small, but growing. Major efforts have been made to improve agriculture, with debatable success. One increasing difficulty is the exodus of rural workers to jobs in the developing towns, and foreign labour has had to be introduced on some rural development schemes. Another limitation is over-use of artesian water in the Jefara. In certain areas near the coast, the water-table has fallen by 3 m–5 m per year, resulting in invasion of the aquifers by sea-water.

The population of Libya seems to have been Berber in origin, i.e. connected with many of the present-day inhabitants of Morocco, Algeria, and Tunisia. The establishment of Greek colonies, from about 650 BC onwards, seems to have had little ethnic effect on the population; but in the ninth and 10th centuries AD there were large-scale immigrations by Arabic-speaking tribes from the Najd of Arabia. This latter group, of relatively unmixed Mediterranean racial type, is now entirely dominant, ethnically speaking, especially in Cyrenaica, of which it has been said that no other part of the world (central Arabia alone excepted) is more thoroughly Arab.

A few Berber elements do, however, survive, mainly in the south and west of Libya; while the long-continued traffic in Negro slaves (which came to an end in the 1940s) has left a visible influence on peoples throughout Libya and especially in the south.

Arabic, introduced by the 10th century invaders, is the one official language of Libya, but a few Berber-speaking villages remain.

History

Revised for this edition by SIMON CHAPMAN

PRE-ISLAMIC LIBYA

In earliest historical times two races inhabited Libya—the 'Libyans' and the 'Ethiopians'—the former, of Mediterranean stock, inhabited the coastal areas; the latter, of negroid and African stock, inhabited the interior. Phoenician sailors began to visit Libya in about 1000 BC to trade for gold and silver, ivory, apes and peacocks, and established the permanent colonies of Leptis, Uai'at (Tripoli) and Sabratha on the coast. A more famous Phoenician colony, Carthage, was established to the west of what is now called Libya, and by 517 BC had come to dominate the others. During the Punic wars between Rome and Carthage the Tripolitanian half of Libya fell under the control of the Numidians until Julius Caesar created the province of Africa Nova.

In about 600 BC the Greeks had colonized Cyrene, and raised it to be a powerful city. Cyrene later fell under the domination of Alexander the Great, came under the Ptolemies in about 322 BC and was bequeathed to Rome in 96 BC. Libya then enjoyed several centuries of prosperity under Roman rule, but, by the middle of the fourth century AD, decline had set in. In AD 431 the Vandals, under Genseric, conquered the country, but a hundred years later the Emperor Justinian's general Belisarius reconquered the country for the Byzantine Empire. Repeated rebellions by Berber tribes, however, soon reduced the country to anarchy.

ARAB INVASION

Arab invaders overran the country and captured Tripoli in 643. The majority of the invaders embraced Islam, but mainly in its schismatic forms as Kharijites, Ibadites and Shi'ites. Continual rebellion induced the Caliph of Baghdad, Haroun ar-Rashid, to appoint, in 800, Ibrahim ibn al-Aghlabid as governor, with his capital at Qairawan (now Kairouan, in Tunisia). This Aghlabid dynasty, virtually independent of the Abbasid caliphate of Baghdad, ended in the 10th century when a Shi'ite uprising founded the Shi'ite Fatimid Dynasty, which from Tunisia conquered Egypt, transferring the seat of government to Cairo in 972. Bulukkin ibn Ziri was made governor of Ifriqiya, and at the beginning of the 11th century the Zirid Amir returned to orthodox Sunnism and acknowledged the sovereignty of the Caliph of Baghdad.

The Fatimid Caliph of Baghdad reacted by invading Libya in 1049, and the next five centuries witnessed little but inter-tribal wars. By the 16th century the northern coast of Africa had become infested with the dens of pirates, and was attracting the crusading and imperialistic designs of Christian Spain. Ferdinand the Catholic sent an expedition which took Tripoli in 1510. The Muslim world had now become, under the Ottoman Turks, more united than it had been for 600 years, and Sinan Pasha was able to wrest Tripoli from the Knights Hospitallers of St John (to whom it had been confided by Charles V) in 1551. Ottoman rule was loose but oppressive. The professional soldiers, the Janissaries, became a power within the state, and the activities of the pirate corsairs, often with the blessing of the Ottoman pashas, attracted reprisals from the European naval powers.

In 1711 a local notable, Ahmad Karamanli, of Ottoman origin and an officer in the Janissaries, was proclaimed *dey,* (originally, deys were high officers of the Ottoman army of occupation) and eventually recognized as pasha. The Karamanli dynasty lasted until 1835. Piracy had again contributed much to its finance, and when European naval action suppressed piracy after the Napoleonic wars, the Karamanlis were ruined. In 1835, probably through fear of the extension of French power in Algiers and Tunis, the Sultan decided to reoccupy Libya and to bring it once more under the direct rule of the Porte (the Ottoman administration in Constantinople). The years that followed were marked by corruption, oppression and revolts, but also by the rise of the Sanusi religious brotherhood.

ITALO–TURKISH CONFLICTS

On 29 September 1911 Italy declared war on Turkey for reasons largely of national prestige. After a short bombardment, Italian troops landed at Tripoli on 3 October. Italy knew the Turks to be involved in the Balkans, and knew, through its commercial infiltration of Libya, their weakness in Africa. But the attack on Libya was not the easy exercise which Italy expected. The Turks withdrew inland but the Libyans organized themselves and joined the Turks, to whom the Porte sent assistance in the form of arms and of two senior officers, Ali Fethi Bey and Enver Pasha. The presence in the Italian army of Eritrean troops was a spur to the pride of the Libyans. In October and November a number of actions were fought around Tripoli in which the Italians had little success. A seaborne Italian force then descended on Misurata and seized it, but could make no progress inland. At ar-Rumeila they suffered a considerable reverse.

Turkey, however, defeated in the Balkan War, was anxious for a peace, which was signed on 18 October 1912. One of the conditions of this peace was that the Libyans should be allowed 'administrative autonomy'. This was never realized.

Peace with Turkey did not, however, mean peace in Libya for the Italians. Although most of the Tripolitanians submitted and were disarmed within two years, the Sanusiya of Cyrenaica under Said Ahmad ash-Sharif, and their adherents in the Fezzan and Tripolitania, refused to yield. The Sanusiya maintained a forward post at Sirte under Sayyid Ahmad's brother, Sayyid Safi ad-Din as-Sanusi. The extent of contact between the latter and one Ramadan as-Sueihli of Misurata is not clear. Ramadan had been in the resistance to the Italians and two years later had appeared to be submissive. At all events, he found himself commanding Libyans in an action started by the Italians at al-Qaradabia in 1914, to push back Said Safi ad-Din. Ramadan and his Misuratis changed sides in this action, to the discomfiture of the Italians. By the time that the First World War had started, the Italians held only the coastal towns of Tripoli, Benghazi, Derna and Tobruk, and a few coastal villages near Tripoli.

The First World War gave Turkey and its German allies the opportunity of fomenting trouble against Italy in Libya. Arms and munitions were sent by submarine. Nuri Pasha from Turkey and Abd ar-Rahman Azzam from Egypt joined Said Ahmad ash-Sharif in Cyrenaica. Ramadan as-Sueihli became head of a government at Misurata. The Sultan, to prevent quarrels, sent Osman Fu'ad, grandson of Sultan Mourad, as Amir, and Ishaq Pasha as commander-in-chief in Tripolitania. The strategic objective of these efforts was to engage Italian forces in Libya and British forces in the Western Desert. The climax of Nuri Pasha's efforts with the Sanusi was a disastrous action in the Western Desert against the British, as a result of which Said Ahmad ash-Sharif handed over the leadership to Said Muhammad Idris. He was compelled to make the treaty of az-Zawiatna with the British and the Italians, who recognized him as Amir of the interior of Cyrenaica, provided that he desisted from attacks on the coastal towns and on Egypt.

The end of the war in 1918 left Italy weak and the Libyans, deserted by the Turks, weary. The Tripolitanians attempted to form a republic with headquarters at Gharian and with Abd ar-Rahman Azzam as adviser. The Italians made a truce with them at Suani ibn Adam, permitting a delegation to go to Rome, and entertaining the idea of 'administrative independence'. Ramadan as-Sueihli visited Tripoli. In Cyrenaica, Said Muhammad Idris as-Sanusi likewise attempted to come to terms; in 1921, at Sirte, the Tripolitanian leaders agreed with him to join forces to obtain Libya's rights and to pay homage to him as Amir of all Libya. Meanwhile the delegation to Rome had returned empty-handed and Ramadan as-Sueihli had been slain in a tribal fight.

ITALIAN COLONIZATION

The advent of the Fascists to power in Italy (1922) coincided with the appointment in Tripoli of a vigorous governor, Count Volpi. Thereafter, it took until 1925 to occupy and pacify the province of Tripolitania and to disarm the population. In Cyrenaica, however, the famous Said Omar al-Mukhtar, representing the Amir Muhammad Idris, whose health had collapsed, maintained the struggle. The Italians realized that the only effective policy was to deprive the Sanusiya of their bases, the oases of the south. Jaghbub was occupied in 1925, Zella, Ojila and Jalo in 1927. In 1928 Marshal Badoglio was appointed Governor-General and in 1929 he occupied Mizda in the Fezzan. Omar al-Mukhtar still resisted. The Italians removed into concentration camps at al-Aqeila the tribes of the Jebel Akhdar. In 1930 Rodolfo Graziani, an experienced Italian military commander, was dispatched to Cyrenaica, and the infamous barbed-wire fence was erected along the frontier with Egypt. Finally, in 1931, isolated from all support, Omar al-Mukhtar, now an old man, was surrounded, wounded, captured, and hanged.

Starting in the early 1920s, the Italians proceeded to colonize parts of Libya which they had occupied, and which geographical and ecological conditions rendered profitable for development. They enlarged and embellished the coastal towns. They extended throughout the cultivable areas an excellent network of roads. They bored wells, planted trees, and stabilized sand-dunes. But their civilizing policy was weighted heavily in favour of their own race. The object was clearly the settlement in Africa of as much as possible of Italy's surplus peasant population. These were encouraged to come in large numbers. Skilled cultivators of olives, vines, tobacco and barley, they needed the best lands and were provided with them. The priority given to the progress of the Libyans was a low one. Primary education for the Libyans was encouraged, and schools provided for them, but the main medium of instruction was Italian. Very few Libyans were accepted into Italian secondary schools.

INDEPENDENCE

There followed the Second World War, and the occupation in 1942 of Cyrenaica and Tripolitania by a British military administration and of the Fezzan by French forces. Thereafter, until 1950, the country was administered with the greatest economy on a care and maintenance basis. Its final fate was long in doubt, until the UN decreed its independence by 1952. On 24 December 1951 Libya was declared an independent united kingdom with a federal constitution under King Idris, the former Amir Muhammad Idris, hero of the resistance.

According to the Constitution promulgated in October 1951, the State of Libya was a federal monarchy ruled by King Muhammad Idris al-Mahdi as-Sanusi and his heirs, and divided into the three provinces of Tripolitania, Cyrenaica and the Fezzan. The federal Government consisted of a bicameral legislature, i.e. a Chamber of Deputies, to which was responsible a Council of Ministers appointed by the King, and a Senate of 24 members (eight for each province). The King had the right to nominate 12 of the senators, to introduce and to veto legislation, and to dissolve the Lower House at his discretion. The Constitution also provided that provincial legislatures should be created for the subordinate provinces of the new realm.

On the attainment of full independence, serious political, financial and economic problems confronted Libya. Not the least of these was the task of fostering amongst the population a sense of national identity and unity. The loyalties of the people were still given to the village and the tribe, rather than to the new federal state.

These rivalries revealed themselves in the next two years. The Party of Independence, which supported the Constitution, won control in the February 1952 elections for the Federal Chamber of Deputies. The National Congress Party of Tripolitania, however, was opposed to the federal principle and advocated a unitary state, with elections based on proportional representation (which would have given Tripolitania the main voice). Disorders arising from this disagreement led to the outlawing of the Tripolitania party and the deportation of its leader, Bashir Bey as-Sa'adawi. A Legislative Council for Tripolitania was formed in 1952 but had to be dissolved in 1954 because of continued friction with the federal Government and the King.

Efforts were undertaken, with Western technical aid, to increase the economic resources of Libya, e.g. to improve irrigation and initiate schemes for water catchments, to extend reafforestation, to teach better methods of farming, and to explore the possibilities of extending industries which could process local products and raw materials such as edible oils, fruits, vegetables, fish, etc.

FOREIGN RELATIONS IN THE 1950s

The first important development in the sphere of foreign relations was the admission of Libya to the League of Arab States in March 1953. The second development reflected the economic difficulties of the new state and its close links with Western Europe. In July 1953 Libya concluded a 20-year treaty with the United Kingdom. In return for permission to maintain military bases in Libya, the United Kingdom undertook to grant the new state £1m. annually for economic development and a further annual sum of £2.75m. to offset budgetary deficits.

In September 1954 a similar agreement was signed with the USA. A number of air bases were granted to the USA in return for economic aid amounting to $40m. over 20 years, an amount which was later substantially increased. Libya also consolidated relations with France and Italy, signing a friendship pact with France in 1955 and a trade and financial agreement with Italy in 1957. In addition Libya was attempting to cement relations with its Arab neighbours. In May 1956 Libya concluded a trade and payments pact with Egypt, arranging the exchange of Libyan cattle for Egyptian foodstuffs.

The critical problem for Libya was to ensure that enough funds from abroad should be available to meet the normal expenses of the Government and to pay for much-needed improvements. At this time, its strategic position was all Libya had to sell, hence its involvement with the Western military alliance. The Libyan attitude to the communist world was much more reserved. Reliance on income from foreign military bases continued, therefore, to dominate foreign policy, and in the late 1950s and early 1960s Libya received subsidies and military assistance from both the United Kingdom and the USA in return for the use of military bases.

PETROLEUM DISCOVERIES

After 1955–56, when Libya granted concessions for petroleum exploration to several US companies, the search for petroleum resources became one of the main interests of the Libyan Government. By the end of 1959 some 15 companies held petroleum concessions in Libya. An oilfield at Zelten in Cyrenaica was discovered in June 1959. By the end of the year, six productive wells had been found in Tripolitania, four in Cyrenaica and one in the Fezzan. By the beginning of July 1960 there were 35 petroleum wells in production, yielding altogether a little less than 93,000 barrels of petroleum per day. Petroleum production showed a tremendous increase in the 1962–66 period, with exports rising from 8m. tons in 1962 to more than 70m. tons in 1966.

A UNITARY REALM

A general election was held in Libya on 17 January 1960. Most of the 55 seats were contested, but there was no party system in operation. The election was fought mainly on a personal basis. Secret balloting, limited in earlier elections to the urban areas, was now extended to the rural districts. The Prime Minister, Abd al-Majid Koubar, and the other members of his Cabinet retained their seats.

Libya's increasing wealth was making the business of government more complex and several changes of administration ensued between 1960 and 1963. Finally, in March 1963, a new Cabinet was appointed under the premiership of Dr Mohieddin Fekini.

Dr Fekini stated in April 1963 that his Government intended to introduce legislation designed to transform Libya from a federal into a unitary state—a change which would mean increased efficiency and considerable administrative economies. On 15 April the Prime Minister presented to the Chamber of Deputies a bill which contained a number of important reforms: (1) the franchise was to be granted to women; (2) Libya would have (as before) a bicameral parliamentary system, but henceforward the King was to nominate all the 24 members of the Senate (previously one-half were nominated and the other half were elected); (3) the Kingdom of Libya would cease to be a federal state comprising three provinces (Tripolitania, Cyrenaica and the Fezzan), becoming instead a unitary realm divided into 10 administrative areas; (4) the administrative councils established in each of the three provinces were to be abolished, the exercise of executive power residing now in the Council of Ministers. Libya became a unitary state by royal proclamation on 27 April 1963.

THE REALITY OF INDEPENDENCE

In the field of foreign relations, Libya was by now helped by the prospect of financial independence and was making its voice heard in international affairs, particularly in Africa. As a result of decisions taken at the Addis Ababa conference of African Heads of State in May 1963, Libya closed its air and sea ports to Portuguese and South African ships. The signing of pacts with Morocco (1962) and Algeria (1963) meant that Libya now had closer links with all the Maghreb countries. Libya was also showing signs of ending its dependence on the West. The 1955 agreement with France had allowed France to retain certain military facilities in Libya—notably in the field of communications—for the defence of French African territories, but Dr Fekini felt that, with the coming of independence to French

African territories in the early 1960s, the matter should be reconsidered.

The question of foreign military bases in Libya now came to the fore. Dr Fekini resigned in January 1964 and the new Prime Minister was Mahmoud Muntasser, formerly Minister of Justice. The Government issued a statement on 23 February, stating that it did not propose to renew or extend its military agreements with the United Kingdom and the USA and that it supported the other Governments of the Arab world in the resistance to imperialism. Muntasser defined the aim of his Government as the termination of the existing agreements with the United Kingdom and the USA and the fixing of a date for the evacuation of the bases in Libya. The Chamber of Deputies then passed a resolution calling for the achievement of this aim and providing that, if negotiations were unsuccessful, the Chamber would pass legislation to abrogate the treaties and close the bases.

The Anglo-Libyan treaty of 1953 was due to expire in 1973. Under the treaty, the United Kingdom maintained a Royal Air Force staging post near Tobruk, an Air Force detachment at Idris airport in Tripoli and Army District Headquarters at Tripoli and Benghazi. The American-Libyan agreement of 1954 was to expire in 1971. Near Tripoli was situated the largest American air-base outside the USA. Under the treaties, Libya had received large amounts of financial, economic and military aid from the USA and from the United Kingdom. Petroleum revenues had greatly reduced Libyan dependence on such aid. The United Kingdom withdrew the bulk of its forces in February and March 1966.

At elections for the Libyan Parliament, held in October 1964, in which women voted for the first time, moderate candidates won most of the 103 seats. King Idris dissolved the Parliament, however, on 13 February 1965, because of complaints about irregularities in the election procedure. The Prime Minister resigned, to be succeeded by Hussain Maziq, Minister for Foreign Affairs. A new election for Parliament was held on 8 May 1965, with over 200 candidates contesting the 91 seats and 16 members being returned unopposed.

The outbreak of the six-day Arab–Israeli war in June 1967 was followed by serious disturbances in Tripoli and Benghazi, in which port and oil workers and students, inflamed by Egyptian propaganda, played a prominent part. The British and US embassies were attacked and the Jewish minorities were subjected to violence and persecution which resulted in the emigration of most of them to Italy, Malta and elsewhere. The Prime Minister, Hussain Maziq, proved unable to control the situation and was dismissed by the King on 28 June. Firm measures by his successor, Abd al-Qadir Badri, brought a return to order but the antagonisms which he aroused forced him, in turn, to resign in October. He was succeeded as Prime Minister on 28 October by the Minister of Justice, Abd al-Hamid Bakkoush.

An immediate result of the June 1967 war was a decline of about 80% in the Libyan output of crude petroleum, owing to the boycott of oil supplies from Arab countries to the United Kingdom, the USA and the Federal Republic of Germany. There was a gradual return to full production in the months following the conflict, however, and the ban on the export of petroleum was lifted in September. The closure of the Suez Canal brought about a considerable increase in Libya's petroleum exports and general prosperity, although the Libyan Government agreed to make annual aid payments totalling £30m. to the United Arab Republic (UAR) and Jordan to alleviate the consequences of the war. Libya's petroleum output increased by about 50% in 1968 and the country became, after only seven and a half years, the second largest producer in the Arab world, with the great advantage, as a supplier to Europe, of being on the more convenient side of the Suez Canal.

The new Prime Minister, Abd al-Hamid Bakkoush, initiated a programme of progressive change, seeking to modernize Libya's administration, reform the civil service and improve the educational system. He also sought to provide the armed forces with modern equipment, and, under a contract announced in April 1968, the purchase from a British firm of a surface-to-air missile defence system, costing £100m., was arranged. An agreement to buy British heavy arms followed, but in September 1968 Bakkoush was replaced as premier by Wanis al-Qaddafi, since the pace of Bakkoush's reforms had apparently alienated some conservative elements. Both Cabinets enjoyed close relationships with Western countries but played little part in Arab politics.

THE 1969 COUP

On 1 September 1969 a military coup was staged in Tripoli while the King was in Turkey for medical treatment. Within a few days the new regime gained complete control of the entire country. The coup was remarkable for the absence of opposition, relatively few arrests, virtually no fighting and no deaths at all being reported. A Revolution Command Council (RCC) took power and proclaimed the Libyan Arab Republic. The RCC initially remained anonymous but was soon revealed as a group of young army officers, the leader, Col Muammar al-Qaddafi, being only 27. The aged King Idris refused to abdicate but accepted exile in Egypt when it became obvious that the revolution had been completely accepted by his people. He remained there until his death, aged 93, in May 1983.

A provisional Constitution, announced in November, stated that supreme power would remain in the hands of the RCC, which appointed the Cabinet; there was no provision for a future general election or national assembly, and the royal ban on political parties was to continue. A largely civilian Cabinet was appointed, under close military supervision. The Ministers of Defence and of the Interior were accused of organizing an abortive counter-revolution in December, and were tried and sentenced in 1970. In January Col Qaddafi himself became Prime Minister and several of his colleagues also joined the Cabinet.

The principal force underlying the regime's policies was undoubtedly that of professed Arab nationalism. Internally, this led to the strict enforcement of the royal law requiring businesses operating in Libya to be controlled by Libyans—banks being particularly affected. The remaining British military establishment in Libya, requested to leave as soon as possible, was finally removed in March 1970, and the much larger US presence at Wheelus Field was removed in June. Most of the European and American specialists (managers, teachers, technicians and doctors), were replaced by Arabs, mainly from Egypt. English translations disappeared from street signs, official stationery and publications, and most hoardings, the use of Arabic alone being permitted; similarly, the Islamic prohibitions on alcoholic drinks and certain Western clothes were officially revived. In July 1970 the property of all Jews and Italians still living in Libya—some 25,000 people—was sequestered by the Government, and both communities were encouraged to leave without delay; some Jews were, however, offered compensation in government bonds. In the same month the three main petroleum marketing companies—Shell, Esso and an ENI subsidiary—had their distribution facilities nationalized.

Another anti-government plot was reported to have been crushed in July 1970. In the autumn two ministers resigned and there were signs of a power struggle developing within the RCC. The internal dissension apparently increased in the first part of 1970 over the proposed federation with the UAR, Syria and Sudan, and over Qaddafi's promises of a constitution and political institutions, including an elected President. A step towards introducing these was the announcement in June 1971 that an Arab Socialist Union (ASU) was to be created as the state's sole party.

FOREIGN POLICY AFTER THE COUP

The new regime almost immediately received enthusiastic recognition from the radical Arab countries and the USSR, and the rest of the world also granted recognition within a few days. As would be expected from the Arab nationalist inspiration behind the revolution, the monarchy's close ties with Western powers were abandoned in favour of close relations with the Arab world and Egypt in particular; this friendship became the basis of a triple alliance announced late in 1969, Sudan being the third member. The alliance was intended to develop both politically—as a strong bulwark against Israel and the West—and economically, in that the economies of the three countries complemented each other to a considerable extent. However, when a federation agreement was signed in April 1971, it was Syria which became

the third member. Libya also adopted a militant position on the Palestine question, and this created some diplomatic problems regarding arms contracts, particularly with the United Kingdom.

Although in July 1970 the Libyan Government followed Egypt in accepting US proposals for a cease-fire with Israel, it continued its militant statements on the Middle East problem. Qaddafi stated that a peaceful solution was impossible and rejected the UN Security Council resolution on which the US initiative was based. During the fighting between Palestinian guerrillas and the Jordanian army in September 1970, Libya redirected its financial aid from the Jordan Government to the guerrillas and severed diplomatic relations with King Hussein's government.

The coup appeared to have reoriented Libya away from the Maghreb; in the summer of 1970 Libya withdrew from the Maghreb Permanent Consultative Committee. Relations with Tunisia improved in the latter half of 1970, after initial concern in Tunis in 1969 at the radical leanings of the new regime, and Qaddafi headed a delegation which visited Tunisia in February 1971. Relations with Morocco were severed in July 1971, after the Libyan Government prematurely gave its support to an attempt to overthrow King Hassan, which failed within 24 hours.

There was little evidence of any closer relationship with the communist powers, although the People's Republic of China was recognized in June 1971 and the USSR was given due credit for its Middle East policies. However, communism was regarded in Libya as a 'foreign' ideology, antipathetic to more 'progressive' Arab socialism (as in Sudan). Hence, in July 1971, Qaddafi was ready to help President Nimeri of Sudan to regain power after a coup, led by communists, had ousted him. A regular BOAC flight from London to Khartoum was forced down over Libya and two leaders of the Sudanese coup (one of whom, Col Babiker an-Nur, was travelling back to become Head of State), were taken from the plane and deported to Sudan, where they were promptly executed by the restored regime.

PETROLEUM POWER

In April 1971 the negotiations with the oil companies operating in Libya, which had begun soon after the 1969 coup, finally ended in a new five-year agreement raising the total posted price for Libyan crude petroleum to US $3.447 per barrel. In the last stage of the negotiations, conducted in Tripoli, the Libyan Government also represented the interests of the Algerian, Iraqi and Saudi Arabian Governments. Threats of an embargo on the export of crude petroleum were used as a lever in the negotiations.

In 10 years Libya's position had changed from one of penury and dependence to one of power, based entirely on the country's ability to interrupt petroleum supplies. The pronouncements of Qaddafi were, therefore, by now of greater significance to the West. In July 1971 the Deputy Prime Minister, Maj. Abd as-Salam Jalloud, visited the Federal Republic of Germany, France and the United Kingdom: Federal Germany, which bought a particularly large proportion of its crude petroleum from Libya, needed to maintain good relations; France was anxious to discover the use to which Libya would put the *Mirage* jet-engined fighter aircraft that were being supplied under the 1970 agreement; the same anxiety was revealed in the United Kingdom over the supply of armaments, but none of these countries could afford to alienate Libya.

In December 1971, avowedly in retaliation for the United Kingdom's failure to prevent the Iranian occupation of the Tunb islands in the Gulf, Libya nationalized the assets of British Petroleum (BP). This began the process of nationalizing the foreign oil companies (described in more detail in the Economy section; see below).

Relations with the United Kingdom became very strained in the winter of 1971–72, not only because of the nationalization of BP but also because of Libyan intervention in the dispute with Malta over the British bases there. Libya had, for some time, been actively fostering relations with Malta, and talks on possible Libyan aid to Malta were held in August 1971. In January 1972 the British naval training mission was ordered to leave Libya, and in February the 1954 agreement with the USA was abrogated.

Libya's attitude towards the USSR had remained cool, and the Government was violently opposed to the Iraqi-Soviet treaty, signed in April 1972. Nevertheless, in February 1972, Maj. Jalloud visited Moscow and in March an agreement on petroleum co-operation was signed. It was also reported that the USSR might supply arms to Libya.

At home, Qaddafi continued his attempts to run the legislature and the Government entirely in accordance with Islamic principles. At the end of March 1972 the ASU held its first national congress. At subsequent sessions, the ASU adopted resolutions to clarify its position and policies, and to abolish censorship of the press, while, at the same time, maintaining financial control of newspapers.

In July 1972 disagreement within the RCC led to Qaddafi's replacement as Prime Minister by Maj. Jalloud, who formed a new Cabinet in which all but two of the ministers were civilians.

ARAB UNITY

A recurrent feature of Qaddafi's foreign policy has been the announcement of proposals for the union of Libya with neighbouring states, and the subsequent collapse of such planned mergers. The Tripoli Charter of December 1969, establishing a revolutionary alliance of Libya, Egypt (then the UAR) and Sudan, was followed by gradual moves towards federation and the adhesion of Syria. Sudan withdrew, but in September 1971 referenda in Libya, Egypt and Syria approved the constitution of the Federation of Arab Republics, which officially came into existence on 1 January 1972, but which had few practical consequences.

The Federation was not Qaddafi's only attempt to export his ideals by means of merger. At the time of Malta's dispute with the United Kingdom over the use of bases, in 1971, he proposed a union of Malta with Libya, but was rebuffed. In December 1972, in a speech in Tunis, he proposed the union of Libya and Tunisia, much to the surprise of his audience, not least President Bourguiba, who immediately rejected the idea, making some pointed remarks about Qaddafi's inexperience.

A merger of Libya and Egypt was agreed in principle in August 1972 but, as the date of implementation approached, certain difficulties became apparent. Qaddafi, who had recently launched his 'Cultural Revolution' of April 1973, was seen as a reactionary Muslim puritan in Egypt, and he was openly critical of Egyptian moral laxity. Egyptian suspicion of Libyan revolutionary enthusiasm, notwithstanding, the union came into effect on 1 September 1973, with the establishment, in theory, of unified political leadership and economic policy and a constituent assembly. The union soon fell apart, wrecked by Qaddafi's opposition to Egypt's conduct of the October 1973 Arab–Israeli war.

President Qaddafi's attitude towards the Palestine problem had long been a source of discord between Libya and other Arab states. He gave financial support to the Palestinian guerrillas, and a number of Libyan volunteers were sent to assist them, Qaddafi's objective being the complete destruction of Israel. He was extremely critical of what he saw as the lack of total commitment to the Palestinian cause on the part of Egypt and Syria, and frequently expressed the opinion that the Arab states could not, and did not deserve to, defeat Israel. He accused Egypt and Syria of being more interested in the recovery of territory lost in the 1967 war than in aiding the Palestinian resistance movement, which was being 'destroyed by the Arabs in co-operation with Israel'. Qaddafi was not informed of the Egyptian and Syrian plan to attack Israel in October 1973, was strongly critical of their battle plan, and refused to attend the Algiers meeting of Arab Heads of State after the war, declaring that it would only ratify Arab capitulation. Libya was nevertheless an enthusiastic proponent of the use of the Arab petroleum embargo against countries which were considered to be pro-Israel. During the war, Libya's participation had been limited to the supply of arms and equipment, and its conclusion seemed only to complete Qaddafi's disillusionment concerning the union with Egypt.

Presidents Qaddafi and Bourguiba announced the union of Libya and Tunisia on 12 January 1974, following two days of talks. A referendum to approve the decision was to be held on 18 January, but was almost immediately postponed. The decision had been taken in the absence of the Tunisian Prime Minister, Hedi Nouira. When he returned to Tunisia, the pro-merger Minister of Foreign Affairs was dismissed, and Tunisia's attitude changed, to support the indefinite deferment of the union. Qaddafi's impetuous action aimed to produce a unified state, but Tunisia now treated the agreement as merely a declaration of principle, without any practical effect.

Qaddafi's enthusiasm for Arab unity continued unabated, but the failure of political mergers led him to propound a new course. His speeches attacked the Arab leaders who blocked unity and failed to 'liberate' Palestine, and he spoke of Libyan aid for revolution and the achievement of Arab union by popular pressure on the Governments of Tunisia, Egypt, Algeria and Morocco. Libya had, for some time, been providing money, arms and training for subversive or 'liberation' organizations operating in Ireland, Eritrea, the Philippines, Rhodesia, Portuguese Guinea, Morocco and Chad, as well as providing aid for sympathetic countries such as Pakistan, Uganda, Zambia, Togo and, after May 1973, Chad. Now it appeared that Libya was supporting subversion in Egypt and Sudan. Attempted coups in Egypt in April and Sudan in May 1974 were believed to have had Libyan support, and relations between Libya and other Arab states became increasingly hostile. Qaddafi's failed mergers and his interference in the internal affairs of other countries were believed to have been major factors in his withdrawal from an active political role in April 1974, when it was seen that he had failed in his policy of exporting the ideals of the Libyan 'Cultural Revolution'.

THE 'CULTURAL REVOLUTION'

President Qaddafi's somewhat idiosyncratic political and social philosophy first obtained full expression in a speech in April 1973, when he called for the immediate launching of a 'cultural revolution to destroy imported ideologies, whether they are eastern or western' and for the construction of a society based on the tenets of the Koran. The form which this revolution was to take was laid down in a five-point programme: 'people's committees' would be set up to carry out the revolution, the 'politically sick' would be purged, the revolutionary masses would be armed, a campaign would begin against bureaucracy and administrative abuses, and imported books which propagated communism, atheism or capitalism would be burned. The people's committees set about their task of supervising all aspects of social and economic life, criticizing and dismissing officials and business executives who failed to show the required revolutionary fervour, and destroying offensive books and magazines.

In May 1973 Qaddafi presented his 'third international theory', which was 'an alternative to capitalist materialism and communist atheism'. In effect, it appeared to be an appeal for a return to Islamic fundamentalism (an appeal which was subsequently echoed in other Middle Eastern countries), together with a rather confused combination of socialism and respect for private property, and much talk of tolerance and the rights of oppressed nationalities. While the 'Cultural Revolution' proceeded apace in Libya, Qaddafi seemed more concerned with foreign policy and his new-found role as a revolutionary philosopher, who had proposed a universally applicable theory which would replace existing ideologies. Qaddafi concentrated on the formulation and propagation of his theory, and on his erratic, unsuccessful attempts to export the Libyan revolution by merger or by subversion, while the mundane details of administration were increasingly referred to Maj. Jalloud, the Prime Minister.

The return to the teachings of the Koran and the rejection of external influences took several forms, some of them petty, such as the insistence upon the use of Arabic in foreigners' passports, and some macabre, as in the revival of such features of Koranic law as the dismembering of thieves' hands. The theory was also invoked in the disputes with foreign oil companies in 1973 (dealt with in detail in the Economy section), presented as an expression of Libyan independence.

On 5 April 1974 it was announced that Qaddafi, while remaining Head of State and Commander-in-Chief, had been relieved of political, administrative and ceremonial duties, and was to devote himself to ideological and mass organization work. It appeared that, willingly or otherwise, Qaddafi had effectively been replaced by Prime Minister Jalloud. After a five-month withdrawal from active direction of the Government, Qaddafi re-emerged in the autumn of 1974 and it soon became apparent that he was more firmly in command than ever.

THE CREATION OF THE SOCIALIST PEOPLE'S LIBYAN ARAB JAMAHIRIYA

President Qaddafi's theories had, since 1973 (when he presented his third international theory), demonstrated a strong desire to foster 'people's assemblies' at all levels of Libyan life. Under a decree promulgated by the ruling RCC in November 1975, provision was made for the creation of a 618-member general national congress of the Arab Socialist Union (ASU), the country's only permitted political party. The congress, which held its first session in January 1976, comprised members of the RCC, leaders of existing 'people's congresses' and 'popular committees', and trade unions and professional organizations. Subsequently the General National Congress of the ASU became the General People's Congress (GPC), which first met in November 1976. Qaddafi announced plans for radical constitutional changes and these were endorsed by the GPC in March 1977. The official name of the country was changed to The Socialist People's Libyan Arab Jamahiriya, and power was vested in the people through the GPC and the groups represented in it. The RCC disappeared and a General Secretariat of the GPC, with Qaddafi as Secretary-General, was established. The Council of Ministers was replaced by the General People's Committee, with 26 members, each a secretary of a department. People's committees were set up at local level, ostensibly to give citizens control over their own affairs. In reality, their creation enabled Qaddafi to dispose of governors, ministers and local officials, some of whom were beginning to resist his more radical reforms. In March 1979 Qaddafi resigned from the post of Secretary-General of the General Secretariat of the GPC, so that he could devote more time to 'revolutionary work'. The General Secretariat was reorganized, as was the General People's Committee, which was reduced to 21 members.

In late 1979 Qaddafi urged Libyans living abroad to take over Libyan embassies; diplomats were ousted and 'people's bureaux' established in most Western countries. At the fifth meeting of the GPC, in January 1980, several government ministers were dismissed, notably the experienced Petroleum Secretary, Izzedin Mabrouk, who was accused of inefficiency in nationalizing the petroleum industry. The sixth meeting of the GPC, in January 1981, reshuffled several ministerial appointments, discussed the 1981–85 economic plan, and made further proposals for transforming Libyan society along the lines described in Qaddafi's 'Green Book' (published in three volumes over the period 1976–79). The Ministry of Foreign Affairs was abolished and replaced by a Bureau of Foreign Liaison.

QADDAFI'S EXTERNAL INVOLVEMENTS

Relations with Egypt deteriorated after Qaddafi boycotted the Rabat summit meeting of Arab Heads of State in October 1974. Qaddafi was unhappy about the decision to recognize the PLO, under Yasser Arafat, as the sole legitimate representative of the Palestinians. He subsequently demonstrated support for the 'rejectionist front'—the wing of the Palestinian guerrilla movement which rejected the concept of a possible settlement of the Arab–Israeli conflict under terms which could be acceptable to Arafat, Jordan and Egypt.

The war of words with Egypt continued in 1975, with articles in the Libyan press containing bitter personal attacks on President Sadat and with the Egyptian press accusing Qaddafi of preparing to mount an invasion of Egypt. A delegation from the National Assembly of the Federation of Arab Republics, which visited Tripoli and Cairo in May, was able to bring about a temporary reconciliation but, at the end of May, relations deteriorated again after reports that Libya was to allow the establishment of Soviet military bases on its territory in return for huge supplies of Soviet weapons. It later appeared that the arms deal did not include the establishment of Soviet military bases in Libya, and was, in fact, smaller than at first reported. Libya, in turn, condemned Egypt for signing the second interim disengagement agreement between Egypt and Israel in September 1975. Relations with Egypt did not improve in 1976 or 1977, and in July 1977 for a while, frontier clashes had the appearance of open war.

Relations with Egypt were not improved when, in November 1977, President Sadat of Egypt launched his peace initiative by visiting Israel. Qaddafi condemned Sadat's move and was a leading instigator of the Tripoli summit of 'rejectionist' states which formed a 'front of steadfastness and confrontation' against Israel in December 1977. Qaddafi remained strongly opposed to Sadat's peace initiative throughout 1978 and following the signing of the Egyptian-Israeli treaty in March 1979, Qaddafi withdrew from the Baghdad summit meeting of Arab states on the grounds that the sanctions which were being contemplated against Egypt were insufficiently far-reaching.

In early 1980 a serious rift developed between Qaddafi and Arafat, leader of the PLO, who was accused of having abandoned the armed struggle in favour of a strategy of diplomacy and moderation. In January relations were formally broken with al-Fatah, the largest component organization of the PLO, and all aid was suspended, although Libya continued to support other wings of the movement. The Libyan authorities began to organize Palestinians in the country into 'people's congresses' to pursue war against Israel independently, and by May about 27 such groups were reported to have been set up. However, a summit meeting of the 'steadfastness front' in Tripoli in April seemed to restore a measure of solidarity, and the PLO representative returned to Tripoli in May.

Relations with the USA were erratic throughout 1979 and the first half of 1980. In early 1979 Qaddafi threatened to cut off petroleum exports unless US President Jimmy Carter lifted a ban on sales to Libya of agricultural and electronic equipment and transport aircraft. The sacking of the US embassy in Tripoli, by mobs protesting at the presence in the USA of the exiled Shah of Iran, led to the withdrawal of the US ambassador in December 1979. In May 1980 Qaddafi announced that he was exacting compensation to the value of thousands of millions of dollars from the USA, the United Kingdom and Italy for damage which had been sustained by Libya during the North African campaigns of the Second World War. These countries were threatened with a petroleum embargo and the withdrawal of Libyan assets from their banking systems if the demands were not met. In mid-1979 Libyan petroleum accounted for an estimated 600,000 of the 8m. barrels per day which were being imported by the USA.

Although Qaddafi strenuously denied Libyan involvement, a guerrilla raid on the Tunisian mining town of Gafsa in January 1980, with the presumed intent to incite a popular rebellion, was attributed to Libya. France sent military aid to support the Tunisian Government against the potential Libyan threat, and in February the French embassy in Tripoli and consulate in Benghazi were burned as a demonstration of Libya's anger at this action. The incident prompted Qaddafi to pledge publicly his determination to counter French intervention in Africa by any means. In February 1982, however, relations between Libya and Tunisia improved when Qaddafi visited Tunisia and a co-operation agreement between the two countries was signed.

In March and April 1979 a Libyan military presence in Uganda was unable to prevent the overthrow of Idi Amin, and heavy losses were incurred. Morocco severed diplomatic relations in April 1980, following the decision by Libya to recognize the independence of the Western Sahara.

During the early months of 1981 there was a build-up of Soviet and East European military advisers in Libya, and in March 1983 it was announced that Qaddafi was to sign a treaty of friendship and co-operation with the USSR. The treaty was not expected, however, to contain military clauses which would commit the USSR to supporting Libya in the event of armed clashes. This increasing interest in the USSR closely paralleled worsening relations with the USA. The US embassy in Tripoli was closed down in May 1981 and relations deteriorated further in August, when US aircraft shot down two Libyan aircraft which had intercepted them over the Gulf of Sirte, claimed by Libya as its territorial waters. In November 1981 President Ronald Reagan alleged that a Libyan 'hit-squad' had been sent to assassinate him.

In February 1983 relations with the USA deteriorated further with the discovery of an alleged Libyan coup plot against the Sudanese Government. US naval vessels moved into Libyan waters and four US surveillance aircraft were spotted over the Libyan-Sudanese border. The US Administration, however, denied that these events were anything more than routine military movements, and said that US troops were merely training Egyptian forces.

LIBYA'S INVOLVEMENT IN CHAD: 1973–88

For many years Libya had been supporting the Front de libération nationale du Tchad (FROLINAT) in its rebellion against the Chad Government. In 1973 Libya occupied the Aozou strip, a region of 114,000 sq km (reputed to contain valuable deposits of minerals) in the north of Chad, basing its action on an unratified treaty of 1935, whereby Italy and France altered the frontiers between their two colonies and, according to Libya, sovereignty over the strip passed to Italy and subsequently to Libya, when it achieved independence in 1951. Chad raised this grievance at the OAU conference in Gabon in July 1977, and an *ad hoc* committee of reconciliation was established to regulate affairs in the disputed area, but Libya consistently refused to attend its sessions. In March 1978 the FROLINAT rebels were achieving such success against the Chad army that Gen. Félix Malloum (the President of Chad) was forced to appeal to Libya to arrest the progress of the rebels. A cease-fire was arranged at reconciliation meetings, held in the Libyan towns of Sebha and Benghazi, at the end of March. Sporadic fighting continued, however, amid allegations that certain factions of FROLINAT were still receiving substantial Libyan support.

A series of military reverses resulted in the downfall of the Malloum Government in March 1979 and, following an initiative by Nigeria, a cease-fire was signed at Kano by the four opposing Chadian factions. With the prospect of a share in the government of Chad at last, the mainstream of FROLINAT and, earlier, certain splinter groups withdrew their support from Libya over its annexation of the Aozou strip. Although a signatory of the Kano agreement, Libya engaged in a series of retaliatory attacks deep inside the northern border in mid-April. In June a 2,500-strong Libyan army invaded northern Chad and was driven back after several days' fierce fighting by FROLINAT forces. Chad's new coalition Government, formed in late April, was dominated by former FROLINAT insurgents and excluded the extreme factions from the south. The secessionist movement which subsequently appeared in the south was soon known to be receiving considerable support from Libya, while Libyan military aid continued to be received by certain guerrilla groups in the north. Dissent by the south and external pressure led to the disintegration of the coalition Government, but a second attempt to implement a 'Government of National Unity' foundered as, parallel to the north-south conflict, the inter-Muslim conflict intensified between President Goukouni Oueddei and the Minister of Defence, Hissène Habré. By March 1980 the Chad capital, N'Djamena, was the site of a pitched battle between Habré's forces and the armies of the President and his allies. In May Libya responded to an appeal from President Goukouni (some of whose Muslim rivals had received Libyan backing a year earlier) for reinforcements to help in stemming the rapid advance of Habré's forces in the capital.

During the latter half of 1980 an increasing number of Libyan troops were engaged in Chad, eventually helping President Goukouni to overcome the forces of Hissène Habré in December. In January 1981 it was announced that Libya and Chad had resolved to work for 'complete unity'. This could have been interpreted either as an agreed merger or as an occupation which was imposed on Chad by Libya. Some Libyan units withdrew from Chad in May 1981, but others remained because of a supposed threat from Sudan, which distrusted Qaddafi's African intentions. Some observers considered that Qaddafi had plans for the creation of a vast 'Saharan Republic', comprising Libya, Niger, Chad, Algeria, Tunisia and Mauritania, but, if so, this plan received a set-back in October 1981, when President Goukouni of Chad requested the removal of some 10,000 Libyan troops from his country. They were subsequently replaced by an OAU peace-keeping force, although Libya maintained troops in the Aozou strip. Despite Libyan support, Goukouni was unable to keep control of Chad, and the capital, N'Djamena, was captured by Habré's forces in June 1982.

Qaddafi persistently denied the charge of interfering in Chad's internal affairs, but in June 1983 Libyan aircraft supported troops of ex-President Goukouni Oueddei in capturing the city of Faya-Largeau, in northern Chad, from Chadian government

forces. Government troops repossessed the town at the end of July but, after prolonged bombing by Libyan aircraft, it again fell to the rebel forces in August. France responded to a request for aid from President Habré by deploying 3,000 troops in Chad from August, ostensibly in the role of military instructors, although they had orders to retaliate if fired upon. A defensive line across Chad at latitude 15° N, secured by French troops, caused a military stalemate, and serious fighting did not resume until after the collapse of peace negotiations in January 1984, when French troops extended the defensive line 100 km northwards to latitude 16° N. By April 1984 Libya was reported to have annexed the northern desert area of Chad and to have 6,000–7,000 troops in the region. The French force remained to the south, in the hope of a political solution. Libya, having made the Aozou strip secure, seemed to have achieved its main objective and to have abandoned all pretence of simply supporting the rebels. In May Qaddafi offered to withdraw Libyan troops from Chad if France would, in turn, withdraw its forces. In September, without consulting the Government of Chad, France and Libya reached an agreement providing for the evacuation of both countries' forces. In November it was reported that the joint withdrawal had been completed, although US and Chadian intelligence reports maintained that some 4,000–5,000 Libyan troops remained in northern Chad. In December 1984 President Mitterrand of France declined to intervene to remove Libyan forces from Chad by force, except in the event of their moving south of latitude 16° N.

Libyan forces allegedly supported the rebel army of Goukouni Oueddei, when it ended a lull in the civil war in February 1986, by launching an offensive southwards, across latitude 16° N. France sent a small 'deterrent' force to support President Habré, and French fighter-bombers attacked the Libyan-built rebel airfield at Ouadi Doum. In October Libya transferred its support from the Chadian rebels who were led by Goukouni to those led by Acheikh Ibn Oumar, the leader of the Conseil démocratique révolutionnaire (CDR), one of the factions in the loose GUNT coalition of opposition groups. The latter replaced Goukouni as the leader of the GUNT in November. Goukouni had been pursuing a conciliatory policy towards President Habré, and at the end of October he was reportedly wounded while resisting arrest in Tripoli. Goukouni's Forces armées populaires (FAP) declared allegiance to Habré's Government, in opposition to the Libyan presence in Chad. The FAP lost control of the oasis town of Zouar, in north-western Chad, in December, but recaptured it in January 1987, with the assistance of government troops, who had earlier occupied the Libyan garrison town of Fada, near latitude 16°N. At the end of March Libyan forces abandoned their last important base in Chad, at Faya-Largeau (after it had been rendered indefensible by the government troops' capture of the airbase at Ouadi Doum, 150 km to the north-west), and retreated towards Aozou. An estimated 4,000 Libyan soldiers were killed between January and the end of March, and Libya was forced to abandon Soviet-made aircraft, valued at $500m., at Ouadi Doum. Libyan troops in Chad (whose involvement in the fighting Col Qaddafi publicly continued to deny) were supported by the Islamic Pan-African Legion, a force consisting of mercenaries and volunteers from many African countries, which was formed in Libya.

President Habré's forces advanced into the Aozou strip and captured the town of Aozou in a new offensive on 8 August 1987. France, which maintained a force of 2,400 troops to the south of latitude 16° N, refused to provide protective fighter aircraft, or to deploy troops north of that latitude, in support of the Chadian Government offensive, which it had counselled against. Libya responded to the loss of Aozou by bombing towns in northern Chad, including Faya-Largeau, Ouadi Doum and Aozou itself. Libyan counter-attacks on Aozou on 14 and 20 August were both repulsed, but on 28 August Libyan forces recaptured the town, and advanced on Ouninga-Kebir, 100 km south of the disputed strip. Chadian forces responded by capturing and destroying an airbase at Maaten as-Sarra, 100 km inside Libya (claimed to be a base for Libyan raids on Chad), on 6 September. France criticized the Chadian incursion into Libya, reiterating its opinion that the question of sovereignty over the Aozou strip should be determined by international arbitration. On 11 September Chad and Libya agreed to observe a cease-fire proposed by the OAU. Later in the month Col

Qaddafi refused to attend a session in Lusaka, Zambia, of the six-nation *ad hoc* committee established by the OAU to consider the conflict in Chad. However, President Habré was present, and Libya was represented by the Secretary for Foreign Liaison, Jadallah Azouz at-Tali.

In November 1987 the UN General Assembly refused to debate the Aozou issue, concluding that its resolution was the responsibility of the OAU. The OAU *ad hoc* committee accordingly proposed a summit meeting of the Libyan and Chadian Heads of State, which, after several postponements, was finally scheduled for 24 May 1988. However, on the eve of the summit, it was announced that Col Qaddafi would not be attending, in protest at Chad's treatment of prisoners of war. Qaddafi had continued to state his terms for a peaceful settlement of the dispute as: the recognition of Libyan sovereignty over the Aozou strip; the withdrawal of 'foreign troops' from Chad; the conclusion of an armistice between President Habré and the opposition forces led by Goukouni; and the release of prisoners of war. On 25 May, however, in a speech delivered in Tripoli to celebrate the 25th anniversary of the foundation of the OAU, Col Qaddafi announced his willingness to recognize the Government of Hissène Habré. He also invited Habré and Goukouni to hold reconciliation talks in Libya and offered to provide financial aid for the reconstruction of bombed towns in northern Chad. In June Habré said that he was ready to re-establish diplomatic relations with Libya, which had been severed in 1982. The Ministers of Foreign Affairs of Libya and Chad held further talks in Gabon in July but, apart from reaching agreement, in principle, on the restoration of diplomatic links, no progress was made on the crucial issues of sovereignty over the Aozou strip, the return of Libyan prisoners of war and the future security of common borders.

On 3 October 1988 Libya and Chad announced the resumption of diplomatic relations and an undertaking to settle their differences by peaceful means and to co-operate with the OAU committee appointed for that purpose.

SETTLEMENT OF CHAD CONFLICT

On 31 August 1989 a peace accord was signed in Algiers by the Libyan Secretary for Foreign Liaison, Jadallah Azouz at-Tali, and Chad's Minister of Foreign Affairs, Acheikh Ibn Oumar, envisaging an end to fighting over the disputed Aozou strip. The agreement, concluded with the help of Algerian mediation, envisaged that the parties would attempt to resolve their dispute through a political settlement within one year. It further provided for the withdrawal of all forces from the disputed region, which was to be placed under the administration of a group of African observers, pending a settlement. All hostilities were to cease, and all prisoners being detained by both sides were to be released.

In October 1989 Chad claimed that its forces had killed 600 members of the Libyan-backed Islamic Pan-African Legion near its border with Sudan. Libya denied Chadian claims that it was involved in the activities of the Legion, including border violations contrary to the peace accord signed in Algiers. In November a joint commission, composed of delegations from Chad and Libya, held its first meeting to consider the provisions of the Algiers agreement.

In March 1990 Chad claimed that a further violation of its borders by mercenaries belonging to the Islamic Pan-African Legion had taken place with the support of the Sudanese Government, which was alleged to have allowed its territory to be used to launch the incursion. In April the Chadian Government claimed to have intercepted and destroyed forces belonging to the legion within Chadian territory, and accused Libya of reinforcing its military presence in the Aozou strip with Palestinian mercenaries. Libya again denied any involvement in the activities of the Legion. Following a meeting in August in the Moroccan capital, Rabat, between Col Qaddafi and President Habré, the Chadian Minister of Foreign Affairs announced that the dispute over the Aozou strip would be referred to the International Court of Justice and that both countries would continue to seek a political settlement to the conflict.

In December 1990 the Government of President Habré was overthrown, following a three-week campaign by the rebel Mouvement patriotique du salut (MPS), led by Col Idris Déby. Déby, who proclaimed himself President, had used Sudan as a base

for his activities and had been supplied with weapons and other equipment by Libya. He received immediate congratulations from Col Qaddafi, who welcomed the new regime's decision to repatriate 2,000 Libyan prisoners of war, detained in Chad since the end of the 1986–87 war. However, some 700 Libyan prisoners of war who opposed Qaddafi and who had reportedly been training at a camp near Lake Chad that was operated by the US Government's Central Intelligence Agency (CIA), were evacuated by the USA, arousing protests from Tripoli. Despite President Déby's denials of involvement, the incident resulted in a sharp decline in relations between Chad and Libya. In May 1991 the USA was reported to have offered asylum to some 350 of the former Libyan soldiers.

QADDAFI'S ATTEMPTS TO QUELL OPPOSITION AT HOME AND ABROAD

In February 1980 the third meeting of the revolutionary committees, bodies dominated by students and young male adults, which are responsible for ensuring the progress of the revolution at popular level (and which, effectively, impose Qaddafi's will on the popular, or people's committees), called for the 'physical liquidation' of opponents of the revolution who were living abroad and of 'elements obstructing change' inside Libya. An extensive anti-corruption campaign was launched in the same month, ostensibly to eradicate 'economic' crime. Between February and April, more than 2,000 people were arrested, mainly on charges of bribery, to be tried by members of the revolutionary committees. However, the arrests of several senior military officers introduced political overtones. In April Qaddafi issued an ultimatum to Libyan exiles abroad to return to Libya by 10 June, beyond which date he could not undertake to protect them from the revenge of the revolutionary committees. Since February 1980 several Libyans who were known to be hostile to the regime have been killed in Western countries.

Of the two new ministerial posts created at the ninth meeting of the GPC in February 1984, one was that of Secretary for External Security (the other being Secretary of Universities), to which Col Younis Bilqassim Ali was appointed. Although the functions of the post were not officially described, its creation appeared to formalize the activities of the Libyan Government to protect its representatives abroad and to silence opponents of the regime inside Libya and elsewhere, which had already been pursued for some time. An office, attached to the Bureau of Foreign Liaison, to combat international terrorism was also established in early 1984. The chief of the people's bureau in Rome had been assassinated in January, and generally the Libyan authorities seemed sensitive to the growth of opposition groups abroad. The National Front for the Salvation of Libya, which came to the fore in 1984, had been formed in 1981 and was based in Sudan under the leadership of Muhammad Yousuf Mugharief, a former Libyan ambassador to India, but it was only one of several such groups opposed to Qaddafi, which he accused foreign governments of nurturing.

Early in March 1984, following a repetition of the official exhortation to Libyans, first made in 1980, to liquidate enemies of the revolution, seven bombs exploded in the United Kingdom, in Manchester and London. It was believed that these attacks were aimed at Libyan dissidents whom Qaddafi had recently accused the United Kingdom of harbouring. Then, on 17 April, during a demonstration outside the Libyan People's Bureau in London by Libyans opposed to Qaddafi's regime, a policewoman was killed and 11 people were injured by shots fired from inside the Bureau. A 10-day siege of the Bureau ensued, during which the United Kingdom broke off diplomatic relations with Libya and ordered its diplomats to leave the country—which they did on 27 April. Revolutionary students had taken over the Bureau in February with the tacit approval of the Libyan Government. Qaddafi denied responsibility for the murder of the policewoman but, after the United Kingdom broke off diplomatic relations, he was understood to have ordered so-called 'hit-squads' to suspend their activities in Europe for fear of economic or other sanctions. In April 1996 a documentary broadcast on British television challenged claims that the policewoman had been shot from inside the Libyan embassy and suggested that the US intelligence service might have been responsible for the killing in order to win British support against Libya. A subsequent British television programme, broadcast in June 1997, suggested that the policewoman might have been killed by al-Burkan, a Libyan opposition group, which, it was claimed, might have operated from a building close to the Libyan embassy, in order to discredit the Qaddafi regime. It was also suggested that al-Burkan's efforts to unseat Qaddafi may have received support from US intelligence services, and that both British intelligence services and the CIA might have been aware, on the day before the shooting, of the group's plan to kill a British police officer.

Inside Libya, Qaddafi's opponents had been active during 1984. In March an explosion at an ammunition dump in al-Abyar had killed or wounded several hundred Libyan soldiers, but the most serious incident took place on 17 May, when up to 20 commandos belonging to the National Front for the Salvation of Libya attacked Qaddafi's residence in a heavily fortified barracks in the suburbs of Tripoli. According to the Front, 15 of the commandos were killed but heavy casualties were inflicted on Libyan soldiers.

The actions of Qaddafi's opponents were the signal for a wave of arrests of suspected dissidents in the first half of 1984, and several students were hanged.

QADDAFI'S CONFUSED FOREIGN POLICY

With visits to Jordan, the Yemen Arab Republic, Saudi Arabia, Algeria and Morocco during the second half of 1983, Qaddafi seemed intent on ending Libya's diplomatic isolation, but there was no compromise on his support for Goukouni Oueddei in Chad and for the Polisario Front in the Western Sahara, issues on which he had ignominiously failed to win backing at the OAU summit in June. Libya, with Syria and the People's Democratic Republic of Yemen, again found itself in a minority by dissenting from the decision of the Organization of the Islamic Conference, taken in January 1984, to readmit Egypt to membership. Qaddafi was also open in his support of the revolt against Yasser Arafat's leadership of the Palestine National Liberation Movement (Fatah), and of Iran in the Iran–Iraq War. Iraq severed diplomatic relations with Libya in June 1985, after Qaddafi had signed a 'strategic alliance' with Iran.

After the attack on his Tripoli headquarters in May 1984, Qaddafi accused Tunisia of being involved with Sudan and the United Kingdom in the incident. Libyan agents had previously sabotaged an oil pipeline from Algeria to Tunisia. Tunisia withdrew its ambassador to Tripoli for a time before relations were restored. In May 1984, in common with other Arab countries, Libya 'froze' diplomatic relations with Liberia and the former Zaire after they had restored their relations with Israel. Libya's support of the Fatah rebels and the secessionist movement in southern Sudan put it at variance with Jordan and Egypt, the leaders of an emergent moderate Arab tendency. The sacking of the Jordanian embassy in Tripoli in February caused Jordan to break off diplomatic relations with Libya.

On 13 August 1984 Libya and Morocco unexpectedly signed a treaty of union in Oujda (Morocco). The proposed 'Arab-African Federation' was unanimously approved by the Libyan GPC on 31 August and endorsed by an overwhelming majority in a Moroccan referendum on the same day. From the outset, the incongruous partnership of King Hassan's moderate, pro-Western Morocco and Col Qaddafi's maverick Libya had an air of impermanence, particularly in the light of previous and, on the surface, more likely 'unions' of Arab states which had proved abortive. The union, which Qaddafi envisaged as the first step towards the creation of a politically united 'Greater Maghreb', soon demonstrated the weakness of its foundations. The first meeting of the joint parliamentary assembly of Libya and Morocco, which was due to take place in Rabat in July 1985, was cancelled by King Hassan in anger over Col Qaddafi's announcement of a treaty between Libya and Iran. King Hassan abrogated the treaty of union with Libya at the end of August 1986, following violent criticism by Qaddafi of his meeting in July with the Israeli Prime Minister, Shimon Peres.

A previous agreement establishing a confederation of Arab states involving Libya, which had been dormant for years, was effectively dissolved in October 1984, when Egypt unilaterally withdrew from the putative 'Union of Arab Republics' which it had entered into with Libya and Syria in 1971. Egypt had accused Libya and Iran of laying mines in the Red Sea and the Gulf of Suez, which had damaged 18 vessels in July and August

1984, and suspected it of other terrorist and espionage activities. Colonel Qaddafi caused Egypt further alarm when he visited Sudan in May 1985 to endorse the new regime of Lt-Gen. Abd ar-Rahman Swar ad-Dahab, who overthrew President Nimeri in a bloodless coup in April 1985. Nimeri had been one of the very few Arab leaders who had supported President Sadat's peace initiative with Israel in 1978, which was anathema to Qaddafi, who was repeatedly accused of supporting plots to topple the Nimeri Government. Qaddafi urged the rebels in southern Sudan (the Sudanese People's Liberation Army), whom he had supported against Nimeri, to surrender their weapons and to begin negotiations with the new Government. He also advocated the overthrow of 'reactionary regimes' in the region, presumably a reference to Egypt and Jordan. Diplomatic relations between Libya and Sudan were restored in April, and a military protocol, whereby Libya was to aid Sudan in training its armed forces and supplying equipment, was signed in Tripoli in July. By 1988 Libya had emerged as Sudan's principal supplier of armaments. At the same time, Libyan troops and members of the Islamic Legion, recruited by Libya, were alleged to have crossed into Sudan, in the region of Northern Darfur which has borders with Libya and Chad, at will, while Chadian rebel forces, supported by Libya, launched raids into Chad from Southern Darfur. Following a military coup in Sudan in June 1989, the new regime announced its intention to negotiate a peace settlement with the rebels in southern Sudan. At a meeting in Libya in March 1990 the Sudanese military leader, Gen. Omar Hassan Ahmad al-Bashir, and Col Qaddafi discussed the framework for a possible union between their two countries. An agreement on integration, signed in Tripoli in August 1990, was intended to facilitate a full merger. Neighbouring countries reacted with concern at this development. A charter linking the Libyan province of Tahadi and the Darfur region of Sudan was scheduled to be considered at a meeting in October 1990. Little significant progress towards a merger has since been achieved, although 'minutes of integration' and an agreement on freedom of movement, residence, work and ownership were signed by Libya and Sudan in June 1991.

In December 1984 Libya and Malta signed a five-year security and economic co-operation treaty, whereby Libya was required to defend Malta if requested to do so by the Maltese Government. In June 1985 a ruling by the International Court of Justice in The Hague, on a maritime boundary dispute between Libya and Malta, extended Libya's territorial waters 18 nautical miles (33 km) northwards towards Malta.

In July 1985 Col Qaddafi barred Egyptians from working in Libya, in retaliation against a similar measure preventing Libyans from working in Egypt. In the following month, Tunisia expelled 283 Libyans (including 30 diplomats) for alleged spying. Earlier, Libya had begun to expel Tunisian workers from Libya. About 30,000 Tunisians were deported between August and October, and thousands of others from Mali, Mauritania, Niger and Syria were also expelled, officially as part of a policy to achieve self-sufficiency in labour. Tunisian imports were halted, and Col Qaddafi urged the overthrow of Tunisia's President Bourguiba. On 26 September Tunisia severed its diplomatic relations with Libya.

CONFLICT WITH THE USA

Details of a plan by the CIA to undermine the Qaddafi regime in Libya were revealed in the American press in November 1985, and the growing US conviction that Libya was promoting international terrorism contributed to a serious worsening of relations between the two countries towards the end of 1985. Libya had already been accused by Egypt of co-ordinating the hijacking of an Egyptian airliner to Malta in November, as a result of which 60 people had died. The incident led to an increase of military tension along the Libyan-Egyptian border. On 27 December Palestinian terrorists killed 19 people in simultaneous attacks on passengers at the departure desks of the Israeli airline, El Al, in Rome and Vienna airports. The US Government accused Libya of harbouring and training the members of Abu Nidal's Fatah Revolutionary Council, who were believed to be responsible for the attacks, and of being a centre for international terrorism. On 7 January 1986 President Reagan ordered the severance of all economic and commercial relations with Libya, and, on the following day, 'froze' Libyan assets in the USA. However, he was unsuccessful in persuading the USA's European allies to impose economic sanctions against Libya. A meeting of the Ministers of Foreign Affairs of Arab countries belonging to the Organization of the Islamic Conference gave verbal support to Libya in January.

A dispute over navigational rights was the ostensible cause of the eventual clash between US and Libyan forces in 1986, though, as far as the USA was concerned, it had the appearance of a pretext for the clash itself, and the naval manoeuvres which led up to it, despite the fact that Libya was the first actually to use military force. Libya had maintained since 1973 that the entire Gulf of Sirte, and not merely the 12 nautical miles (22 km) off its coast that were recognized by international law, constituted Libyan territorial waters. In December 1985 Col Qaddafi drew a notional 'line of death' across the north of the Gulf of Sirte, along latitude 32° 30′ N, which he warned US and other foreign shipping not to cross. At the end of January 1986, ostensibly in the exercise of its right to navigation in the area under international law, the US Navy's Sixth Fleet was deployed off the Libyan coast, though it appears that at no time did any US vessel cross the 'line of death'. On 24 March, the day after the Sixth Fleet had begun its fourth set of manoeuvres in the area since January (and the eighteenth since 1981), Libya fired Soviet SAM-5 missiles (which had been operational only since January) at US fighter aircraft flying over the Gulf of Sirte and inside the 'line of death'. In two retaliatory attacks on 24 and 25 March, US fighter aircraft destroyed missile and radar facilities in the coastal town of Sirte, and sank four Libyan patrol boats in the Gulf. A meeting of the League of Arab States (Arab League) criticized the US action, but rejected a Libyan appeal for Arab economic sanctions to be imposed against the USA.

On 5 April a bomb exploded in a discotheque in West Berlin, killing a US soldier and a Turkish woman. The USA gathered what it considered to be irrefutable evidence connecting Libya with this and a catalogue of other incidents and plots against US targets in Europe and the Middle East. On 15 April US military aircraft (including 18 F-111 fighter-bombers from bases in the United Kingdom and planes from the Sixth Fleet) bombed military installations, airports, government buildings (among them Col Qaddafi's own residential compound) and suspected terrorist training camps and communication centres in the Libyan cities of Tripoli and Benghazi. A total of 37 people were reported to have died in the raids, including many civilians, who were the inevitable victims of bombs and missiles which were directed against military or terrorist targets in largely civilian areas. On 16 April Libya fired two missiles at the Italian island of Lampedusa, the site of a US coastguard station.

The US raids were generally deplored as a new round in an escalation of violence in the Middle East, and an upsurge in terrorist activity in Europe and the Middle East was feared. However, there was little sympathy for Libya. Most other Arab countries confined themselves to verbal condemnation of the USA, and Libya was disappointed by the Soviet reaction, which was purely rhetorical. A meeting of the League of Arab States failed to take place after a disagreement over the agenda, which Qaddafi demanded should only include discussion of the US raid. Libya expelled about 250 foreign journalists at the end of April 1986, and in May, after the EC had decided to limit the size of Libyan diplomatic and commercial delegations within the Community, to restrict the movement of Libyan diplomats, and to tighten immigration regulations against Libyans, Col Qaddafi ordered the expulsion from Libya of 36 diplomats representing seven West European countries.

In the weeks following the US raids, Col Qaddafi was only rarely seen in public. There were rumours that he had lost overall control of the Government to Maj. Abd as-Salam Jalloud, who, although he held no formal government post, was accepted to be Qaddafi's deputy and was head of Libya's revolutionary committees (popular organizations throughout the country, which exist independently of the government bureaucracy) and the revolutionary guard corps, which were entrusted with responsibility for preserving the integrity of the revolution. The US Government had hoped that the raids on Libya would destabilize the regime of Col Qaddafi and create the conditions in which opposition groups could stage a coup. However, as the year progressed, Qaddafi gradually emerged from his retreat

and appeared to remain firmly in control of government. At the end of May 1986, the USSR promised to continue sales of military equipment to Libya, but urged the condemnation of terrorism.

Conflict with the USA erupted again in January 1989, when US aircraft shot down two Libyan fighter aircraft in 'self-defence' over international waters in the Mediterranean. The incident occurred at a time when the USA was becoming concerned that Libya was about to produce chemical weapons at a plant near Rabta, 60 km south of Tripoli. Qaddafi claimed that the plant was a pharmaceutical factory, being built with West German and Japanese help.

MAGHREB UNITY

In March and June 1986, in an attempt to consolidate its good relations with Algeria, Libya proposed a union of the two countries. The proposal was submitted to President Chadli of Algeria by Col Qaddafi's deputy, Maj. Jalloud, in June 1987. At the end of Jalloud's visit to Algiers, the parties issued a joint communiqué stating that President Chadli and Col Qaddafi would meet to discuss the proposal, although Algeria, reacting unenthusiastically to Libya's approaches, emphasized the need for 'compatibilities' between the countries—apparently a reference to Algeria's concern over Libya's intervention in Chad and its policy towards Tunisia. Algeria subsequently suggested that a framework for a new Algerian-Libyan relationship (and, by definition, one not going as far as actual union) already existed in the Maghreb Fraternity and Co-operation Treaty of 1983, between Algeria, Mauritania and Tunisia. Later in June, at short notice, Col Qaddafi arrived in Algeria in an attempt to persuade President Chadli to accede to the union proposals. However, he succeeded only in achieving agreement on several minor co-operation issues.

Economic links between Libya and Algeria expanded, and in early October 1987 the two Governments agreed in principle on a treaty of political union. The accord was to be announced officially on 1 November, but, owing to political opposition in Algeria, the announcement was not made. Instead, the Algerian Government proposed that Libya should sign the Maghreb Fraternity and Co-operation Treaty. This eventuality was made more likely by the re-establishment of diplomatic relations (at consular level) between Libya and Tunisia at the end of December.

In February 1988 Col Qaddafi, President Chadli and President Ben Ali of Tunisia held discussions concerning a proposed regional political accord, following which the border between Libya and Tunisia was reopened.

An expansion of economic co-operation was treated as the first stage towards regional integration in other fields. On 22 March 1988 Libya and Algeria signed two agreements relating to industrial development. The first was for a tripartite project to supply an estimated 90,000m. cu m of Algerian natural gas to Libya, via a trans-Tunisian pipeline. The second provided for the construction of a combined aluminium and petroleum coke complex in Zuwarah, Libya, to generate electricity for both countries, and the establishment of a joint company to undertake petrochemical projects. In April Libya and Tunisia signed a co-operation pact encompassing political, economic, cultural and foreign relations. Few details were released, but plans included the construction of an oil pipeline between Libya and Tunisia. Colonel Qaddafi announced that, from the date of the pact, Tunisians would be given priority among foreign nationals seeking employment in Libya, while the border posts on the frontier with Tunisia would be dismantled and Libyans and Tunisians would be guaranteed freedom of movement in both directions.

The leaders of the five countries of the Maghreb (Algeria, Morocco, Tunisia, Libya and Mauritania) held a meeting in Algiers (the first of its kind since they achieved independence), after the Arab summit there in June 1988, to discuss the prospects for 'a Maghreb without frontiers'. After the meeting, the participants issued a joint communiqué announcing the creation of a Maghreb commission, comprising a delegation from each of the five countries, to concentrate on the establishment of a semi-legislative, semi-consultative council which would co-ordinate legislation in the region and prepare joint economic projects. At the end of June, Algeria and Libya announced that they would each be holding a referendum on a proposed union of the two countries. The proposition to be considered by the peoples of Algeria and Libya, however, fell short of the total merger for which Col Qaddafi had hoped, and envisaged, instead, a federation of the two states, within a Great Arab Maghreb.

In July 1988 the Maghreb commission met for the first time, in Algiers, and announced the creation of five working parties to examine areas of regional integration (including education, finance, economy and regional security), which would report to the second meeting of the commission in October. In August President Ben Ali of Tunisia visited Libya, and he and Col Qaddafi signed a series of co-operation agreements and established a technical commission to examine means of accelerating co-operation and the merger process, as a prelude to the creation of the Great Arab Maghreb.

In February 1989, at a summit meeting in Morocco of North African Heads of State, the participants concluded a treaty proclaiming the formation of a 'Union of the Arab Maghreb' (UAM), comprising Algeria, Libya, Mauritania, Morocco and Tunisia. The treaty envisaged the establishment of a council of Heads of State, regular meetings of Ministers of Foreign Affairs, and the eventual free movement of goods, services and capital throughout the countries of the region. At the second summit meeting of the Union of the Arab Maghreb, held in Algiers in July 1990, it was decided that Libya would hold the annual presidency of the Union in 1991.

A third summit meeting of the UAM was held in Ras Lanuf, Libya, on 10 March 1991 and was opened by Col Qaddafi in his role as President of the organization for the first six months of that year. This was the first meeting of the UAM states since the invasion of Kuwait by Iraq in August 1990 and it reflected the difficulty they had encountered in maintaining a united response towards the conflict in the Gulf region. The final communiqué expressed 'deep pain over the tragic developments in the Gulf' and urged that the economic sanctions imposed on Iraq by the UN should be lifted. Agreement was reached on the establishment of a Maghreb Bank of Investment and Foreign Trade, and on co-operation in other fields. At a subsequent UAM summit meeting in Casablanca in September 1991 the forthcoming Middle East peace conference was discussed and the UN was urged to lift the economic sanctions that it had imposed on Libya.

GOVERNMENT CHANGES AND DOMESTIC REFORM

At its annual meeting in 1986, the GPC reduced the number of secretariats in the General People's Committee from 22 to 10. Several Committee posts were merged or abolished. Changes of personnel were also made in the composition of the General Secretariat of the GPC. The object of the changes was, apparently, greater administrative efficiency. The public service functions of the secretariats which were dismantled were, in future, to be handled by specially created national companies, such as already existed for the administration of the petroleum industry, the secretariat for which was among those to be abolished. The GPC also resolved to form 'suicide squads to strike at the enemy'. According to the human rights organization, Amnesty International, Libya assassinated at least 25 of its political opponents abroad between 1980 and 1987. In March 1987 the GPC elected a new General People's Committee. Only three Secretaries were re-elected from the previous Committee, and only two of these retained their former posts.

Increasing dissatisfaction at home with political repression, a deteriorating economy and shortages of basic commodities, combined with opposition to the military involvement in Chad and pressure from abroad to improve the image of his Government and ease his political isolation, caused Col Qaddafi to embark on a series of liberalizing economic and political reforms during 1988. In foreign policy, Qaddafi openly admitted the error of his involvement in Chad and adopted a more pragmatic approach to his ambition of union within the Maghreb and to his relations with other Arab and African countries, eliminating barriers to trade and tourism with neighbouring countries and declaring his opposition to terrorism. At home, he accused Libya's revolutionary committees of murdering political opponents of his regime. In early March Qaddafi began to encourage the reopening of private businesses, in recognition of the failure of the state-sponsored supermarkets to satisfy the

demand for even the most basic commodities, which had caused a thriving 'black market' to emerge. At the same time, all prisoners (including foreigners), except those convicted of violent crimes or of conspiring with foreign powers, were released; Libyan citizens were guaranteed freedom of travel abroad; and the revolutionary committees were deprived of their powers of arrest and imprisonment, which had often been indiscriminately and arbitrarily used. A new secretariat (ministry) was formed in May for Jamahiri ('masses') Mobilization and Revolutionary Guidance, apparently to monitor and regulate the revolutionary committees. In June the General People's Congress (GPC) approved a charter of human rights, guaranteeing freedom of expression and condemning violence. In March the GPC had created a people's court and a people's prosecution bureau to replace the 'revolutionary courts'.

At the end of August 1988, Col Qaddafi announced the abolition of the army and the police force. The army was to be replaced by a force of Jamahiri Guards, comprising conscripts and members of the existing army and police force, which would be supervised by 'people's defence committees' located in strategic areas. The most obvious sign of the practical implementation of a new policy of government decentralization was the decision in September to relocate all but two of the secretariats of the General People's Committee (ministries) away from the capital, Tripoli, mostly in Sirte, 400 km east of Tripoli. Further reform was promised when, in January 1989, Qaddafi announced that all state institutions, including the state intelligence service and the official Libyan news agency, were to be abolished.

There were reports, in November 1989, of a challenge to Col Qaddafi's leadership by Muslim fundamentalists. Armed clashes between them and the Libyan security forces were reported to have occurred, prompting Col Qaddafi to urge the GPC to consider legislation to suppress fundamentalist groups.

At the meeting of the 16th session of the GPC, held in Tripoli during 2–10 March 1990 to consider future government policy, Col Qaddafi strongly criticized corruption in government administration. The Secretary for Higher Education subsequently tendered his resignation, following criticism from delegates, and the Secretary for Transport also resigned, in protest at corruption and the exorbitant fares charged by the state-controlled Jerma Bus Company.

In October 1990 the GPC implemented the most extensive changes to the General People's Committee since March 1987. The appointment of the uncompromising Abu Zaid Omar Dorda as the new Secretary-General (Prime Minister) and of 11 new secretaries was approved, increasing the number of secretariats in the GPC from 19 to 22. The opposition National Front for the Salvation of Libya claimed that several of those promoted had been involved in purges against dissidents and had been expelled from European countries. The former Secretary-General, the moderate Umar Mustafa al-Muntasser, was appointed Secretary of a new combined Economic and Planning Secretariat. The new Strategic Industries Secretariat was to be headed by another moderate, Jadallah Azouz, who was replaced as Secretary for Foreign Liaison by Ibrahim Muhammad Bashari. The Secretariats for Electricity, Social Security and Youth and Sports, which had been abolished in 1986, were revived. The Secretariat for Jamahiri Mobilization and Revolutionary Guidance, formed in 1988, was abolished, and a new secretariat was created to promote co-operation with the Union of the Arab Maghreb. At the same time, three of the five-member General Secretariat of the GPC were replaced, Abd ar-Raziq Sawsa becoming Secretary-General of the GPC in place of Dr Muftah al-Usta Omar.

DEVELOPMENTS IN EXTERNAL RELATIONS

Following his reconciliation with Yasser Arafat's wing of the PLO in March 1987, Col Qaddafi sponsored efforts to reunite the divided Palestinian movement prior to the 18th session of the Palestine National Council in Algiers in April, although this strained relations with Syria, which had supported the revolt against Arafat's leadership of the PLO in 1983. It appeared that, after years of relative political isolation, Col Qaddafi found it expedient to realign Libyan policy with that of the majority of Arab states. After the Palestinian uprising (*intifada*) in the Israeli Occupied Territories began in December 1987, Col

Qaddafi intensified his efforts to reconcile the opposing factions within the PLO, and in June 1988, at the request of Yasser Arafat, he sent Libyan representatives to Lebanon to mediate between Palestinian guerrillas loyal to Arafat and members of 'Abu Musa's' rebel Fatah, who were fighting for control of Beirut's Palestinian refugee camps. He subsequently intervened personally to persuade the Sunni Muslim militia in southern Lebanon to allow Arafat loyalists, who had been driven out of Beirut, to enter the Palestinian camp of Ain al-Hilweh, near Sidon. Yasser Arafat and representatives of the dissident, Syrian-backed PLO factions visited Tripoli in September 1988 to attend the anniversary celebrations of the Libyan revolution, and their presence gave rise to speculation of a reconciliation, engineered by Col Qaddafi. In June Col Qaddafi had attended an Arab summit meeting in Algiers (the first such summit that he had attended for 18 years), which had been arranged to discuss Arab support for the Palestinian uprising.

In May 1987 Australia ordered the closure of the Libyan people's bureau in Canberra, accusing Libya of trying to destabilize the South Pacific region. Libya had been providing paramilitary training to dissident groups in the French territory of New Caledonia and the Indonesian provinces of Irian Jaya and East Timor, and, according to the Australian Government, had been involved in subversive activities in Australia.

In September 1987 Libya re-established 'fraternal' links with Iraq, modifying its support for Iran in the Iran–Iraq War and urging the observance of a cease-fire, according to the terms of UN Security Council Resolution 598. Later in the same month, Jordan restored its diplomatic relations with Libya. However, Libyan support for Iran had not completely ceased. Col Qaddafi refused to attend the extraordinary summit meeting of the League of Arab States which took place in Amman in November to discuss the war. His representative quickly dissociated Libya from an apparently unanimously supported resolution, which censured Iran for its occupation of Arab (i.e. Iraqi) territory and for failing to accept UN cease-fire proposals. Libya also dissented from the League's decision to remove the prohibition on diplomatic relations between member states and Egypt.

Libya attended an emergency summit meeting of the Arab League in Casablanca, Morocco, in May 1989, but not a meeting of the Ministers of Foreign Affairs of member states (held immediately prior to the summit meeting), at which Egypt was formally readmitted to the Arab League. Meetings between Col Qaddafi and President Mubarak of Egypt in October were thought to signal the countries' imminent reconciliation, but by mid-1991 Libya remained the only Arab state not to have restored full diplomatic relations with Egypt following its diplomatic and economic isolation by Arab states in 1979. Meeting in Cairo in February 1990 for the fourth time since May 1989, Col Qaddafi and President Mubarak agreed to strengthen financial and economic ties between Egypt and Libya.

In March 1990 both the USA and the Federal Republic of Germany claimed that Libya had commenced production of mustard gas at a plant near Rabta, 60 km south of Tripoli (see above, 'Conflict with the USA'). When a fire broke out at the plant during the same month, Libya accused these countries, together with Israel, of involvement in sabotage. All three countries denied any involvement. The Federal German Government stated that it would take measures, in accordance with international law, to halt the production of chemical weapons at Rabta, while the US Government refused to discount future military action against the plant. In June the US Government alleged that the plant at Rabta had not been destroyed by fire, as Libya had claimed, and voiced suspicions that a second such plant, for the production of chemical weapons, was under construction. In July the US Government claimed that members of a Muslim movement, which was trying to overthrow the Government of Trinidad and Tobago, had received training in Libya.

Libya's relations with France improved in April 1990, after the release of three Europeans who had been held hostage in Lebanon. The French Government formally thanked the Libyan Government for its role in obtaining their release. In March France had returned to Libya three *Mirage* jet fighter aircraft which it had impounded in 1986 after their delivery to France for repairs. However, the French Government denied that the return of the aircraft had played any part in securing the release

of the hostages. However, in September, following an official investigation, France alleged that Col Qaddafi, together with President Assad of Syria and the leader of the Popular Front for the Liberation of Palestine, Ahmad Jibril, had been responsible for planning the bombing of a French passenger aircraft over the Sahara in September 1989.

In June 1991, following a secret visit to Tripoli by a member of the United Kingdom Parliament, it was revealed that Col Qaddafi had offered £250,000 to a British police charity, together with a letter of regret for the killing of a policewoman outside the Libyan people's bureau in London in 1984 (see Qaddafi's Attempts to Quell Opposition at Home and Abroad, above). The Member of Parliament was reported to have discussed with Col Qaddafi a series of proposals aimed at restoring diplomatic relations between the United Kingdom and Libya, which had been severed at the time of the incident. However, the proposal was rejected by the UK Foreign and Commonwealth Office (FCO), which said that there could be no possibility of a resumption of relations until there was convincing evidence that the Libyans had renounced their support for groups engaged in international terrorism, including the Irish Republican Army (IRA). In addition, the FCO emphasized that Libya should co-operate in bringing to justice those responsible for the murder of the policewoman.

Early in 1992 Col Qaddafi was reported to have given assurances, through intermediaries, that he would reveal to the United Kingdom Government information about his dealings with the IRA, in return for improved relations with the United Kingdom. However, in an interview with a British newspaper in May 1992 he appeared to renege on this promise, claiming that he feared that the revelation of such information might be used to 'trick' him. He admitted that Libya had supplied the IRA with arms and explosives, but denied that IRA members had trained in Libya. All links with the IRA had now been severed, he maintained.

THE GULF CONFLICT 1990–91

Col Qaddafi attended the emergency summit meeting of the League of Arab States, held in Cairo on 10 August 1990 to discuss the Arab response to the invasion of Kuwait by Iraq. Subsequently, 12 Arab nations voted in favour of a motion condemning the invasion and advocating the deployment of a pan-Arab force for the defence of Saudi Arabia and other states from possible Iraqi aggression. Libya voted against the measure, and in September Libyan aircraft were reported to be transporting food supplies to Iraq in violation of UN Security Council Resolution 661 (of 6 August 1990) which imposed mandatory economic sanctions on Iraq. Libya also announced that its ports were at Iraq's disposal for the purpose of importing food supplies. Following the commencement, on 16 January 1991, by a multinational armed force, of 'Operation Desert Storm' to secure the liberation of Kuwait, anti-war demonstrations occurred in Libya. The Saudi Arabian ambassador in Tripoli urged Col Qaddafi to support the concerted action, but during February the Libyan Government offered to supply food, medicine and blankets to Iraq.

President Mubarak of Egypt was thought to have persuaded Col Qaddafi to exercise restraint during the war between Iraq and the multinational force, and relations between Egypt and Libya continued to improve in its aftermath. Talks were held on moves towards greater economic integration, and in March 1991 Col Qaddafi abolished immigration and customs controls for Egyptians travelling to Libya. However, the subsequent flood of visitors resulted in the reimposition of checkpoints. Col Qaddafi visited Cairo in early July 1991 for the ratification of 10 integration agreements, and on 6 August the Egyptian Government announced the opening of Egypt's border with Libya, removing all obstacles to travel and trade. A security agreement on border movements was signed on 23 August.

INAUGURATION OF THE GREAT MAN-MADE RIVER

The first phase of Libya's 'Great Man-made River' project (GMR), begun in 1984 and designed to carry water from Saharan wells through 2,400 miles of 13ft-diameter pipes to the more populous coastal regions, and to provide irrigation for agriculture, was inaugurated by Col Qaddafi on 28 August 1991 in a ceremony near Benghazi, attended by several Arab and African leaders,

PLO leader Yasser Arafat and the Secretary-General of the League of Arab States. Few Western leaders were present. The scheme, the largest irrigation project in the Middle East, will take 25 years to complete, at an estimated cost of $25,000m. During his visit for the ceremony, President Mubarak of Egypt held further talks with Col Qaddafi on economic co-operation. Libya had offered to resettle up to one million Egyptian farmers on lands to be irrigated by the GMR project.

THE LOCKERBIE AFFAIR AND THE IMPOSITION OF UN ECONOMIC SANCTIONS

In December 1988 all 259 people aboard a Pan Am Boeing 747, en route to New York, died when the aircraft exploded over Lockerbie, Scotland. Eleven people in the village also died. The plane had been flying from Frankfurt, Germany, where it was believed that a suitcase containing a bomb had been loaded on board. Investigations had revealed that this suitcase had arrived at Frankfurt on a flight from Malta, where an employee of Libyan Arab Airlines, Al-Amin Khalifa Fahima, was stationed. On 13 November 1991 Scotland's Lord Advocate and the acting US Attorney-General issued international warrants for the arrest of Fahima and the former security chief of the Libyan airline, Abd al-Basset al-Megrahi, accusing them of responsibility for the bombing of the Pan Am aircraft. Two days later the Libyan Secretariat for Foreign Affairs issued a statement denying any Libyan involvement in the bombing, condemning all forms of terrorism and urging the investigation of the charges by a neutral international body or the International Court of Justice (ICJ). A British demand for the extradition of the two men, presented by the Italian ambassador in Tripoli on 18 November, was refused, as was a repeated demand by the British and US authorities on 27 November.

A campaign was mounted by Libya among its Arab neighbours to enlist their support in countering the allegations, and it continued to resist pressure for the extradition of the two Lockerbie suspects and also for the arrest of four other Libyans sought by France in connection with the bombing of a French DC-10 airliner over the Sahara (in Niger) in September 1989, in which 171 people had died. One of those accused over the latter incident, Abdallah Sannousi, was the brother-in-law of Col Qaddafi himself and deputy head of the Libyan intelligence services. On 5 December 1991, the Arab League Council, meeting in Cairo, expressed solidarity with Libya and urged the avoidance of sanctions. However, on 26 December President Bush extended economic sanctions, which the USA had imposed on Libya in January 1986, for a further year.

Meanwhile, Libya had announced that it would conduct its own inquiry into the Lockerbie allegations under the chairmanship of Judge Taher az-Zawi. He was reported to have stated, on 7 December 1991, that the two suspects had been detained and would stand trial in Libya. An offer by the Libyan Secretary for Foreign Liaison, Ibrahim Muhammad al-Bishari, to send Libyan judges to London or Washington to discuss the case was rejected.

A unanimous resolution (No. 731) by the UN Security Council, adopted on 21 January 1992, demanded the extradition of the Lockerbie suspects to the USA or the United Kingdom as well as Libya's full co-operation with France's inquiry into the loss of its aircraft in Niger in 1989. Libya declined to extradite the men, but did offer to place them on trial in Libya. It also offered to allow French officials to interrogate the four men suspected of complicity in the Niger bombing. On 18 February al-Megrahi and Fahima appeared in court in Tripoli, where the judge refused to allow their extradition, claiming that there were no grounds for it in international or criminal law. The Libyan response to UN Security Council Resolution 731 was rejected by the USA, the United Kingdom and France, which urged the UN to impose sanctions on Libya.

On 23 March Libya applied to the ICJ for an order confirming its right to refuse the extradition of the Lockerbie suspects by applying the terms of the 1971 Montreal Convention on airline terrorism. It was claimed that the convention allowed Libya the option of trying the suspects in its own courts, a view opposed by lawyers acting for the United Kingdom and the USA, who claimed that Libya was 'wriggling, twisting and turning' in its attempts to evade the surrender of the suspects and the imposition of UN sanctions. A judgment was not expected for

another two years but the ICJ nevertheless ruled, on 14 April, that it had no power to prevent the UN from enacting sanctions against Libya.

An offer in late March 1992 by Col Qaddafi to place the suspects under the jurisdiction of the Arab League was subsequently withdrawn. Intensive diplomacy by the League, spearheaded by President Mubarak of Egypt (who, at the request of the PLO, met Col Qaddafi in Tripoli on 12 April), came to nothing. On 31 March the UN Security Council adopted Resolution 748, imposing mandatory economic sanctions against Libya. From 15 April 1992 all civilian air links and arms trade with Libya were to be prohibited and its diplomatic representation reduced. An embargo on the sale of Libyan petroleum was not imposed. There was widespread hostility in the Arab world to the imposition of sanctions against a fellow Arab and Muslim state. The UN was accused of hypocrisy for not enforcing similar measures against Israel over its failure to comply with UN Security Council Resolution 242 (1967), which demands Israeli withdrawal from the Occupied Territories. It was also feared that Islamic fundamentalists in countries such as Egypt, Algeria, Tunisia and Morocco might exploit the ensuing economic hardships for their own political ends.

In Libya itself demonstrators immediately took to the streets to condemn the West, and Col Qaddafi threatened to cut off oil supplies to, and withdraw all business from, those countries which complied with Resolution 748. On 2 April demonstrators besieged several Western embassies in Tripoli. The embassy of Venezuela (which had held the presidency of the Security Council when Resolution 748 was passed) was ransacked and burned. It was reported that exit visas had been refused to a number of foreign nationals, despite earlier assurances, and fears were expressed that Col Qaddafi might seek to use some of them as hostages. Speaking in Tripoli's Green Square on 4 April at a dawn rally to mark the end of the month of Ramadan, Col Qaddafi rejected Resolution 748 and sought to depict the situation as a new crusade against Islam by the Christian West. 'Muslims all over the world, the battle being waged by modern Western crusading forces, having ended against communism, is now being directed against Islam,' he declared.

UN sanctions took effect on 15 April 1992, the anniversary of the US air strikes against Tripoli and Benghazi in 1986 (see above). The previous day Col Qaddafi had severed all international communications and travel links in a day of self-imposed isolation to mark the anniversary. Prior to the imposition of sanctions, Libya was reported to have been stockpiling food and medicines and to have transferred liquid capital from Europe to banking centres in the Gulf region and the Far East. Arab neighbours rallied to find new land and sea routes to circumvent the air embargo, and it was announced that a hydrofoil service from Malta to Tripoli would operate five times a week instead of weekly. The immediate effect of the sanctions was thus primarily psychological and it was thought that this would cause little more than inconvenience, rather than actual hardship, in the foreseeable future.

In May 1992, at Col Qaddafi's instigation, 1,500 people's congresses were convened in Libya and abroad, to enable ordinary citizens to debate the fate of the two Lockerbie suspects and their response to the UN sanctions. Arab diplomats and the more pragmatic members of Qaddafi's circle had begun to urge a compromise, fearing that the imposition of further UN sanctions, particularly an embargo on sales of petroleum (Libya earns 95% of its income from such sales), would be disastrous. Observers concluded that Qaddafi was seeking to resolve his dilemma and save face by using the people's congresses as a means of distancing himself from any eventual 'surrender'. In late June the GPC announced its decision to allow the two Lockerbie suspects to stand trial abroad, provided the proceedings were 'fair and just'. It suggested that such a trial might take place under the auspices of either the Arab League or the UN. In August, at a meeting with Col Qaddafi, UN Under-Secretary-General Vladimir Petrovsky warned that, if Libya continued to refuse to comply with Resolution 731, the UN might strengthen the sanctions already in force against it. On 12 August, however, the UN Security Council merely renewed the sanctions for a further 120 days.

In early January 1993 Libya closed all of its land borders for three days in protest at the UN's decision, taken in early

December 1992, to renew the sanctions in force against Libya. In mid-February an article appeared in the US press that alleged that Libya was constructing an underground factory for the manufacture of chemical weapons at Tarhuna, west of Tripoli. In January Libya refused to a sign a UN convention banning chemical weapons, on the grounds that not all Middle Eastern and North African states were party to the convention.

During the approach to the UN Security Council's sanctions review in April 1993, Libya attempted to rally Arab support and announced in late March that it was tabling new proposals to try and break the deadlock. In the USA a group of senators, led by Edward Kennedy, urged the US Senate Foreign Relations Committee to seek the expansion of UN sanctions against Libya. At the same time, there were new allegations in the US press that Libya was building a second chemical weapons plant. Despite the USA's efforts to secure a tightening of the economic embargo, at its April meeting the Security Council did not modify the original sanctions which were retained for a further 120 days. Following the meeting, the USA stated that it would continue to consult its allies about tougher sanctions, including a possible ban on Libyan oil exports. However, the main European importers of Libyan crude petroleum, in particular Germany, Italy and Spain, remained firmly opposed to an oil embargo. In July the French Minister of Foreign Affairs, Alain Juppé, stated that France would demand tougher sanctions if Libya failed to comply with Resolution 731 before the next Security Council review in early August.

At its meeting on 13 August the Security Council decided to maintain existing sanctions. The USA, the United Kingdom and France, increasingly frustrated at Qaddafi's defiance, issued an ultimatum to Libya stating that if the two suspects were not surrendered for trial by 1 October 1993, they would propose a UN Security Council resolution imposing tougher sanctions, covering oil-related, financial and technical sectors. Libya rejected the deadline but repeated its offer to discuss holding the trial in a country other than the USA or the United Kingdom. In a television interview, Qaddafi claimed that 'all the sanctions in the world or even in the universe will never make Libya submit'.

As the 1 October 1993 deadline approached, pressure on Libya had mounted. US President Bill Clinton, in his first speech to the UN General Assembly, vowed to bring the perpetrators of the Lockerbie bombing to justice. When Libya failed to comply with Western demands, the USA, the United Kingdom and France introduced a draft resolution at the Security Council, seeking to impose tighter sanctions. After further negotiations had failed to break the deadlock, the Security Council finally yielded to the demands of the USA, the United Kingdom and France. On 11 November UN Security Council Resolution 883 was adopted, imposing new sanctions against Libya. The resolution provided for the freezing of all Libyan assets abroad, with the exception of earnings from hydrocarbon exports, placed a ban on the sale to Libya of certain equipment for the 'downstream' oil and gas sectors and placed further restrictions on Libyan civil aviation, including the immediate closure of all Libyan Arab Airlines offices abroad. The new measures came into force on 1 December 1993. Resolution 883 states that sanctions will be lifted as soon as the two Libyans accused of responsibility for the Lockerbie bombing are handed over for trial in the United Kingdom or the USA and Libya co-operates fully with the French authorities investigating the bombing of a UTA airliner over the Sahara in 1989. It also made provision for the reimposition of sanctions within 90 days if Libya failed to comply with all the demands set out in Resolutions 731 and 748.

In response to Resolution 883, Qaddafi declared that he was prepared to destroy Libya's oilfields and ports as a gesture of defiance to the West. In a series of public speeches he urged the Libyan people to make sacrifices in the cause of national dignity and rejected all further negotiations with the UN and the Western powers on the Lockerbie affair. Through editorials in *Ash-Shams*, Qaddafi criticized his own foreign secretariat for urging the surrender of the two accused Libyans. This was interpreted as an attack on Omar al-Muntasser, the Libyan Secretary for Foreign Liaison and International Co-operation. Nevertheless, al-Muntasser retained his post in the reshuffle of the General People's Committee at the end of January 1994. When the General People's Congress met in January 1994, the

Lockerbie affair was high on the agenda but the statement issued at the end of the session contained no hint that a compromise was possible and instead accused the USA of using sanctions to continue its policy of oppressing Libya and causing suffering to the Libyan people. In a speech in Misurata in February 1994 Qaddafi declared that the Lockerbie affair was closed, but two weeks later he proposed that the two accused men be tried by an Islamic court either in the USA, the United Kingdom or any other country, provided that the court officials were Muslims. The proposal was rejected by the British Foreign Office. After the Secretary-General of the League of Arab States held talks in Tripoli at the end of February, JANA, the official Libyan press agency, accused the Arab League of submitting to US pressure over UN sanctions and declared that Libya wished to play no further part in the organization. In February 1994 President Clinton renewed US sanctions against Libya, originally imposed in 1986, and reaffirmed his determination to see the two Libyans accused of the Lockerbie bombing extradited to face trial. He described Libya as an exceptional threat to US national security and interests.

On 12 June 1994 the Ministers of Foreign Affairs of the OAU member states adopted a resolution urging the UN Security Council to revoke the sanctions that it had imposed on Libya. The following day a member of the Palestinian Fatah Revolutionary Council, who was on trial in Lebanon (accused of the assassination of a Jordanian diplomat), claimed that the Council had been responsible for the explosion which destroyed the aircraft over Lockerbie in December 1988. At various times since February 1992 various parties had alleged that Iranian, Syrian and Palestinian agents—sometimes separately, sometimes in collaboration—had been responsible for the explosion. Nevertheless, both the US and the British authorities remained convinced that there was still sufficient evidence to continue to seek the extradition of the two Libyan suspects who had been formally indicted for the offence in the USA and Scotland.

In mid-February 1995 the Government announced that it would not assume the chairmanship of the UAM, as it was due to do later in the year, because other UAM member states were enforcing the sanctions which the UN had imposed on Libya. In late March the US Secretary of State announced that the USA would seek to persuade the UN Security Council to apply a ban on Libyan sales of petroleum before its forthcoming review of the sanctions already in force. At the end of the month, however, the Security Council did no more than renew the existing sanctions, prompting the USA to announce that it would impose more stringent unilateral sanctions on Libya.

In April 1995 Col Qaddafi successfully defied UN sanctions by ordering a Libyan aircraft carrying 150 pilgrims to leave Tripoli for Jeddah in Saudi Arabia. His decision came only hours after the UN had agreed to allow 6,000 Libyan pilgrims to visit Saudi Arabia for the annual *hajj* on 45 EgyptAir flights. The UN immediately condemned the Libyan action as a 'flagrant violation of the UN air embargo' and criticized Egypt and Saudi Arabia for their involvement. Both countries appeared to have had prior knowledge of the flight. However, the UN Security Council did not withdraw its permission for the EgyptAir flights. At the request of President Mubarak of Egypt, Col Qaddafi did not proceed with further Libyan flights to Saudi Arabia, but he claimed that the Libyan people had won a victory through their 'steadfastness and determination to die for the sacred right of the *hajj*'. Qaddafi himself declined to make the pilgrimage to Mecca.

In May 1995 Qaddafi adopted a new strategy over the extradition of the two Libyan Lockerbie suspects (see above) by insisting that the UN Security Council should first investigate the US bombing of Tripoli in 1986 and that Israel should first comply with some 40 UN resolutions. However, at the end of July 1995 the UN decided not to lift the sanctions in force against Libya, although it rejected persistent US demands for stronger sanctions, including an oil embargo. In November the USA again failed to convince its European allies to impose an embargo on Libyan oil, but despite appeals from Egypt and the Arab League for some relaxation in the sanctions, the existing embargo was once again renewed. The USA nevertheless continued its uncompromising stance towards Libya, and in December introduced domestic legislation to strengthen economic sanctions against both Libya and Iran, targeting in particular oil companies that invest in the two countries. In May 1996 it was reported that the EU Council of Ministers had protested against sanctions planned by the USA to penalize non-US companies investing in oil and gas projects and supplying refinery equipment to Libya. At the end of June Col Qaddafi once again flouted UN sanctions by flying to Cairo in order to attend the Arab summit meeting convened by President Mubarak following the victory of Likud leader Binyamin Netanyahu in the Israeli legislative elections. The summit meeting urged the UN to lift sanctions against Libya, and appealed to the United Kingdom and the USA to accept an Arab proposal that the two Libyan suspects in the Lockerbie affair should be given a neutral and fair trial in The Hague, the Netherlands, (rather than in the United Kingdom) but with Scottish judges in session and in accordance with Scottish law. Despite appeals by Russia, the People's Republic of China, Egypt, Indonesia and Botswana for sanctions to be lifted, and for the trial of the two Libyan suspects to be held in a third country, the UN renewed existing sanctions against Libya at the end of July 1996, and there seemed to be little prospect of them being lifted in the foreseeable future.

In October 1995 Libya withdrew its candidacy for a seat on the UN Security Council after the USA, the United Kingdom and France had organized a campaign to prevent its election. Libya relinquished its candidacy in favour of Egypt, stating that it did not wish to sit on the Council because the UN had become a tool of the USA. In November Libya was excluded from the summit meeting of Mediterranean countries in Barcelona, Spain, after strong pressure from the UK Government. Later in that month a Libyan dissident, Ali Mehmed Abuzeid, a founder member of the National Front for the Salvation of Libya (NFSL), was killed in London amidst reports that he had given information to the Italian police about arms smuggling to Libya. Although it was claimed that Abuzeid was the victim of a Libyan 'hit squad', British intelligence sources dismissed the theory that the killing was political. Nevertheless, in December the British Government accused the senior Libyan diplomat in London of intimidating Libyan dissidents in exile there and expelled him. In retaliation, Libya immediately expelled a British diplomat.

At the beginning of 1996 there were acrimonious exchanges with the US authorities after Col Qaddafi appeared to support the actions of Palestinian Islamists responsible for a series of devastating suicide bomb attacks in Israel, and reports that Libya had donated US $1,000m. to Louis Farrakhan, the controversial leader of the US Nation of Islam movement, who had visited Tripoli in the previous December. In February the US Central Intelligence Agency (CIA) repeated its claim that Libya was developing a secret chemical plant at Tarhuna for the manufacture of poison gas, in order to replace the Rabta facility (see above), and in March the US Secretary of Defense, William Perry, during a visit to Cairo, told the Egyptian authorities that, if necessary, the USA would use force to close down the plant. In early April President Mubarak indicated that Egypt had requested detailed data from the USA and that, if reports about the plant were confirmed, he might offer to mediate with Libya. In May the Libyan Secretary for Foreign Liaison and International Co-operation, Omar al-Muntasser, complained to the UN Security Council that the USA was preparing an attack on Libya, on the pretext of destroying the plant at Tarhuna, and strongly denied the existence of a chemical weapons facility there. Libya instead insisted that the plant formed part of the Great Man-made River project (see 'Inauguration of the Great Man-made River,' above). The USA repeated that it would take whatever action necessary to prevent the plant's completion, but excluded the use of chemical weapons. However, US efforts to win support for its proposal to destroy the alleged plant met with little success. Despite reports of photographic evidence confirming the plant's existence, many observers remained sceptical, although the arrest, in August, of two Germans accused of exporting computerized equipment often used in the manufacture of poison gas to Libya, reinforced the opinions of a number of US officials. Similar concerns had been expressed by the USA in June, when it was reported that Libya had signed a clandestine co-operation pact with Ukraine, which was understood to provide for the transfer of advanced weapons' technology to Libya. In December the US press published additional claims, which alleged that Ukraine had agreed to provide

Libya with a package of military equipment, including missiles, valued at $500m., in contravention of the UN arms embargo. The charges, allegedly founded on a CIA report, were denied by Ukranian officials.

The Libyan leader's stance on the suicide bomb attacks in Israel also soured relations with the EU, which had begun to show some signs of improvement at the beginning of the year when Libyan and EU representatives held talks in Brussels. At the international anti-terrorism summit meeting hastily convened in Egypt in March—the so-called 'Summit of Peacemakers'—the British Prime Minister, John Major, condemned Libya and Iran for sponsoring terrorism, although the final communiqué failed to mention any state by name. Qaddafi denounced those Arab states which participated in the summit, with the exception of Egypt. In April the South African Minister of Foreign Affairs, Alfred Nzo, on an official visit to Tripoli, called for the lifting of 'unjust sanctions' against Libya, incurring the displeasure of Britain, the USA and France. South Africa's President Nelson Mandela had earlier insisted that he would stand by countries that had supported the ANC in its struggle against apartheid and in February had issued an invitation to the Libyan leader to make an official visit to South Africa. South Africa announced that it was to appoint a non-resident ambassador to Libya. In February 1997 it was reported that President Mandela had ordered an inquiry into allegations that South Africa had illegally supplied chemical weapons to Libya since his Government had come to power.

USA IMPOSES SECONDARY SANCTIONS

In July 1996 the USA increased its pressure on Libya when the US Congress unanimously approved a controversial Iran and Libya sanctions act, which aimed to further weaken the Libyan economy as a penalty for that country's alleged support of international terrorism. The legislation had originally targeted only Iran, but had been amended to include Libya, and involved the imposition of sanctions on any non-US country investing more than $40m. in Libya's oil and gas industry in any one year (see Economy, below). European Governments protested vociferously against the legislation, and promptly lodged a protest with the World Trade Organization (WTO). Trade between the EU and Libya at that time was worth some $20,000m. each year, while almost 90% of Libya's oil exports went to Western Europe where they provided around 10% of all petroleum supplies. European oil companies, particularly those of Italy and Spain were heavily involved in the Libyan oil industry, and were, therefore, the countries most likely to suffer as a result of the new sanctions. In response to the European challenge, the USA invoked article 21 of the General Agreement on Tariffs and Trade (GATT), which permits a signatory to break the agreement if national security interests are involved. In November a Libyan-sponsored resolution which called for the repeal of the Iran and Libya sanctions act was adopted by the UN General Assembly. Libyan diplomatic efforts, however, failed to make any progress towards the removal of UN sanctions, which were once again renewed, unchanged, in mid-November. The appointment in February 1997 of Abu Zaid Omar Dorda, a former Prime Minister, as the new Libyan representative to the UN, was interpreted by a number of observers as an indication that Libya intended to make no further concessions, but would instead adopt an uncompromising approach to the Lockerbie affair. In January it had been reported that Libya had once more defied the UN-imposed air embargo, when an official delegation flew to Accra in Ghana. Moreover, in late March Libyan aircraft again transferred worshippers to Saudi Arabia for the annual pilgrimage, despite the fact that the UN had permitted EgyptAir to organize flights for the Libyan pilgrims. In May Qaddafi travelled by air to Niger and Nigeria, and was welcomed at the airport of the latter country by the military leader, Gen. Abacha. The violations were strongly condemned by the UN, but no action was taken against the Libyan regime. In April the EU and the USA came to an agreement to limit the impact of the Iran and Libya sanctions act upon European countries. Under the new arrangement the US Administration promised to protect European companies from the adverse effects of the legislation, while in return the EU agreed to withdraw its complaint to the WTO regarding an earlier US law, the Helms-Burton Act, which imposed sanctions on non-US companies involved in business with Cuba. By that time no charges had been brought against any foreign company by the USA. In July, in protest at the UN Security Council's renewal of existing sanctions and the unanimity requirement which enabled the USA to veto the lifting of sanctions, Abu Zaid Omar Dorda announced Libya's intention to no longer respect those sanctions.

EU protests at new US sanctions did not imply any change in Europe's position on Libya, and despite the visit by an EU delegation to Tripoli in June 1996, relations remained strained. Nevertheless, Qaddafi appeared to be seeking to take advantage of the divisions between the USA and the EU by working to improve European relations, particularly with France. He praised France for its pursuit of an independent foreign policy and allowed the French judge investigating the 1989 bombing of a French airliner over Niger unprecedented access to Libyan evidence during his visit to Tripoli in July, which led to the judge's decision to try *in absentia* the Libyans suspected of the attack. However, the announcement, in November, of the decision to create a rapid reaction force, EUROFOR, a joint project involving France, Italy, Spain and Portugal, which was to respond to humanitarian crises and undertake peace-keeping missions in the Mediterranean, was unreservedly denounced by Qaddafi. A declaration by German authorities in October that clear evidence was available to prove the Libyan Government's direct involvement in a 1986 bomb attack on a Berlin disco-theque, which provided a pretext for the US raids against Libya 10 days later was also a major set-back; it was announced that arrest warrants had been issued for the three Libyans believed to have been involved in the attack. Despite this development, three German deputies, who visited Libya in March 1997 as members of a parliamentary delegation responsible for relations with the UAM, recommended that regular contact between the German Parliament and the GPC should continue. In the same month Libya achieved rare success in foreign policy when the Vatican resisted US pressure and established formal diplomatic relations with Libya. Pope John Paul II had often spoken out against the imposition of UN sanctions on Libya, and his officials stated that the establishment of diplomatic links with Libya took place in recognition of that country's efforts to protect freedom of religion and the Vatican's wish to see a peaceful and stable Mediterranean region. Archbishop José Sebastián Laboa became the Pope's first envoy to Tripoli, while Libya was to open a 'people's bureau' in Vatican City. In contrast, Libya remained excluded from co-operation initiatives between the EU and southern Mediterranean states, which were launched in Barcelona in 1995.

In October 1996 the Libyan leader provoked diplomatic outrage during the visit of Necmettin Erbakan, Turkey's first Islamist Prime Minister, when he criticized Turkey's member-ship of NATO and its close association with the West, urging the establishment of an independent Kurdish state. There was an angry response from Ankara and Turkey's ambassador to Tripoli was recalled. After a few months, however, the situation improved and the Turkish ambassador returned, but in June 1997 Turkey again withdrew its ambassador, after Qaddafi reportedly made remarks on Libyan television criticizing the Turkish army and Government, and denouncing military agree-ments between Turkey and Israel.

In February 1997 the OAU Ministerial Council met in Tripoli for the first major meeting of the organization to be convened outside Addis Ababa, Ethiopia. The delegates called for an end to UN sanctions against Libya, and a committee of five ministers was established to mediate between Libya and the Western states in order to try to resolve the Lockerbie affair.

FURTHER DEVELOPMENTS IN THE LOCKERBIE AFFAIR

In July 1997 the Arab League, which had previously been criticized by Qaddafi for its lack of support, formally proposed that the two Libyan suspects in the Lockerbie affair be tried by Scottish judges under Scottish law in a neutral country. At an Arab League meeting in September the member states urged a relaxation of the air embargo on Libya and voted to defy UN sanctions by permitting aircraft carrying Qaddafi, and other flights for religious or humanitarian purposes, to land on their territory. In October the President of South Africa, Nelson Mandela, visited Libya, despite US disapproval, and publicly expressed support for the proposals to hold a trial of the Lock-erbie suspects in a third country. Later that month the United Kingdom requested the UN to send envoys to examine the Scottish legal system, and in December, following the renewal of sanctions by the UN in November, the UN issued a report concluding that the Libyan suspects would receive a fair trial under the Scottish system. However, in February 1998 the ICJ ruled that it was competent to hear Libya's complaints that the USA and the United Kingdom were acting unlawfully by insisting on the extradition of the two Libyan suspects. The USA and the United Kingdom had attempted to prevent the case from being heard, on the grounds that intervening UN Security Council resolutions had rendered it unnecessary. Libya declared that the ICJ ruling had given its claims legitimacy and that UN sanctions should now be disregarded. Nevertheless, sanctions were renewed in March and no progress towards lifting them was achieved at a debate within the Security Council later in the same month.

In April 1998 a representative for the families of the British victims of the Lockerbie bombing and a professor of Scottish law travelled to Libya, where they met Col Qaddafi. The Libyan leader was reported to have agreed to the trial of the two Libyan suspects in The Hague, the Netherlands. In the following month US and EU representatives concluded an agreement under which European companies would be able to invest in Iran, Libya and Cuba without incurring sanctions as set out in the so-called 'Iran-Libya sanctions act' of 1996 and the Helms-Burton Act. In return for this concession, which had been negotiated with reference to the involvement of Total of France in Iran, EU states were reported to have agreed to monitor more carefully their exports to Libya. In July commitments expressed following a meeting between the Italian Minister of Foreign Affairs and the Libyan Secretary for Foreign Liaison and International Co-operation appeared to imply significant improvement in relations between Libya and Italy.

In August 1998 Libya was reported to be considering a pro-posal by the UK Government to seek the suspension of the sanctions in force against Libya in return for the release of the two Lockerbie suspects for trial in The Hague before Scottish judges. Both the UK and US Governments had earlier indicated their willingness to accept such an arrangement. In September Col Qaddafi stated that he would allow such a trial to take place provided that The Hague was the final destination of the two suspects. It remained unclear what this implied with regard to any possible attempt to extradite the two men to Scotland in the event of their being found guilty by the extraterritorial Scottish court.

RUMOURS OF AN ABORTIVE ARMY COUP AND INTERNAL DISSENT

During the second week of October 1993 rumours began to circulate in the Western media that a revolt by a number of army units had been crushed by the Libyan air force which had remained loyal to Qaddafi. It was claimed that the most serious clashes had occurred around Misurata and Tobruk where there had been scores of casualties. There were unconfirmed reports that Libya had closed its borders and that after three days of unrest 2,000 people had been arrested and 12 officers executed. Qaddafi's Second-in-Command, Abd as-Salam Jalloud, was reported to have been placed under house arrest. There was speculation that the coup, described in the media as the most serious challenge to the Libyan leader since 1986, had arisen as a result of differences between Qaddafi and Jalloud over the handling of the Lockerbie crisis and that the armed forces may have divided along tribal lines. Throughout the Lockerbie affair, Jalloud, who belongs to the al-Megaha tribe, has been firmly opposed to surrendering the two suspects, both of whom are members of his tribe. The London-based daily *Al-Hayat* named Col Hassan al-Kabir and Col ar-Rifi Ali ash-Sharif as the leaders of the uprising and stated that while al-Kabir had been arrested, ash-Sharif had fled to Switzerland. However, doubts have been expressed that a major uprising did in fact occur. Qaddafi himself condemned the rumours of an army coup in a speech on 30 October describing them as a plot by British intelligence to humiliate the Libyan people. Nevertheless, it is perhaps significant that the government changes announced at the end of January 1994 placed men known for their personal loyalty to Qaddafi in key positions, suggesting that the Libyan leader felt the need to tighten his grip on power. Abu Zaid Omar Dorda, the Secretary-General of the General People's Committee and a close associate of Jalloud, was replaced by Abd al-Majid al-Qaoud. Ahmed Ibrahim was appointed Secretary for Information and Culture and Muhammad al-Hijazi Secretary for Justice and Public Security. Both are members of Qaddafi's personal entourage.

Libyan opposition groups in exile remain weak and divided and there is little evidence that they command significant support within the country. In October 1993 Muhammad Megarief, the leader of the NFSL, Maj. Abd al-Moneim al-Houni of the Co-operation Bureau for Democratic and National Forces, and Mansour Kikhia of the Libyan National Alliance (LNA) are reported to have met in either Algiers or Geneva to discuss forming a united front against the Qaddafi regime. Abd al-Hamid al-Bakkush, the leader of the Libyan Liberation Organization, did not attend and the meeting appeared to have failed to resolve the differences between the various opposition groups. This was confirmed in February 1994 when some leading members of the NFSL announced that they had formed a breakaway movement and criticized the NFSL for failing to co-operate with other opposition groups in creating a united front against the Qaddafi regime.

Qaddafi has regularly demonstrated his intolerance of these opposition groups and has urged that his opponents abroad be hunted down and liquidated. Therefore in early December 1993, when Mansour Kikhia, a former Secretary for Foreign Liaison and, since the early 1980s, leader of the opposition LNA, disappeared while attending a meeting of the Alliance in Cairo, it was widely assumed that he had been abducted by Libyan security agents. The affair proved particularly embarrassing because Kikhia had been living in the USA, had an American wife and had only agreed to attend the meeting in Cairo after receiving personal assurances from senior Egyptian officials about his safety there. The Libyan Secretariat for Foreign Liaison and Libya's representative to the Arab League in Cairo, Ibrahim Beshari, denied Libyan involvement in the affair. Beshari stated that Kikhia presented no threat to the Libyan Government. Qaddafi himself told Egyptian journalists that Libya was co-operating with the Egyptian authorities to discover what had happened. Both President Clinton and Dr Boutros Boutros-Ghali, the UN Secretary-General, appealed to President Mubarak of Egypt to investigate Kikhia's disappearance. However, although Mubarak dispatched one of his advisors to Tripoli he failed to make any progress and the Egyptian police admitted at the end of January that they had no information about Kikhia's whereabouts. Kikhia's wife continued to claim that her husband had been kidnapped by Libyan agents assisted by Egyptian security officers. In April 1995 the Arab Organization of Human Rights urged the Egyptian Government to investigate the matter and to punish those responsible for Kikhia's abduction. In late 1996 the LNA stated that it would continue to investigate Kikhia's disappearance, but many were convinced that he had been murdered.

In early March 1994 Libyan television broadcast 'confessions' by three army officers and a student, all members of the Warfallah tribe, who had been arrested in the Bani Walid region during the army revolt in October 1993. It was the first official acknowledgement of the attempted coup. During their 'confessions' the men admitted to supplying information to the CIA, and to Muhammed Megarief, the leader of the NFSL, on military deployment, the Rabta plant, nuclear research and Col Qaddafi's own movements. The accused men stated that they had met Megarief in Zurich, Switzerland, and Madrid, Spain, in order to pass on information. The NFSL claimed that after calls for the execution of the four men, demonstrations erupted in the Bani Walid region where several protestors were arrested after setting fire to government buildings. The Libyan opposition abroad stated that 55 army officers arrested after the abortive coup had been condemned to death. At the beginning of 1996 it was reported that Col Qaddafi had overturned a court's ruling on 12 army officers of the Warfallah tribe accused of leading the abortive coup because the sentences were too lenient, and that the men had been condemned to death. According to one source, the death sentences had not been carried out in order not

to antagonize the Warfallah, which had threatened retaliation if the men were killed.

Early in 1996 rumours circulated that Col Qaddafi had concentrated power within the armed forces almost exclusively in the hands of members of his own tribe and that the increasing involvement of two of his sons in government business, including financial and commercial affairs, had alienated tribal leaders, such as Cols Khalifa Ahneish, Masoud Abdel-Haft and Ahmad Qadhaf ad-Dam, who in the past had played key roles in internal security and foreign affairs. It was also claimed that the Libyan revolutionary committees were preparing to bring to trial those responsible for corruption and financial mismanagement in order to absolve Qaddafi and his immediate family of any responsibility for the country's economic problems and to provide a pretext for the elimination of opponents of the regime.

In addition to reports of continued dissent within the armed forces and the destabilizing effects of tribal rivalries, some observers argued that the Islamist opposition was the most dangerous threat to the Qaddafi regime. Despite being subjected to harsh repressive measures by the security forces for some years, Islamist opposition to the regime, strongly rooted in Cyrenaica, appears to have increased in strength, although little is known about the groups involved. In June 1995 there were a number of armed confrontations between police and Islamist militants in and around Benghazi, Libya's second city and economic capital. The regime blamed the unrest on 'extremist infiltrators' from Egypt and Sudan and independent sources confirmed that the large number of immigrants, mainly from Egypt and Sudan, seeking work in Benghazi, had created instability in the region.

There were reports of further clashes between the security services and Islamist militants in September 1995 in Benghazi, Derna and al-Bayda, in which a senior officer in the security services, Lt-Col al-Faydi, was ambushed and killed. Islamist militants calling themselves the Jama'at al-Islamiyah al-Muqatila, or Militant Islamic Group, claimed responsibility for the September incidents and stated that it was the duty of all Muslims to overthrow the Qaddafi regime and impose *Shari'a* law. In response to these incidents, thousands of Sudanese and Egyptian workers were expelled (see below), the regime tightened its control over the country's mosques and hundreds of suspected Islamist militants were arrested. The regime also made moves to re-Islamize Libyan society, adopting laws based on the *Shari'a*. In October 1995 the London daily, *The Independent*, claimed that Col Qaddafi was fighting an underground war against the Islamist militants who threatened the stability of his regime. An attack on the Abu Saleem prison in Tripoli in November, in which some 15 dissidents escaped, was also regarded as the work of Islamist militants. In February 1996 it was reported that militants from the Militant Islamic Group had attempted to assassinate Col Qaddafi in Sirte. After the assassination attempt, security forces carried out further arrests of suspected Islamist militants. In March, following a mass escape from the al-Kuwaifiyya prison near Benghazi during which police shot dead many of the prisoners, unrest erupted once again in and around Benghazi, Derna and al-Bayda, and there were reports of over 20 deaths in clashes between militants and the security forces. At the end of April, the Militant Islamic Group issued a statement claiming to have killed 15 security officers in Sirte during the previous month and to have seized weapons from police stations in Ras al-Hilal and al-Qubba. In May violent clashes were reported in Benghazi between security forces and supporters of a new opposition group, the Islamic Martyrs' Movement (IMM), which has claimed responsibility for the assassinations of a number of high-ranking government officials. The movement's leader, Muhammed al-Hami was killed in July in clashes with security forces, and was later replaced by Hamzah Abu Shaltilah. In March 1997 press reports stated that Shaltilah had been dismissed and replaced by a new leader, referred to as 'Khalifah'. In June a third Islamist group, the Libya Islamic Group, claimed responsibility for the murders of eight policemen during an attack on a police training centre in Derna. A fourth group, known as the Supporters of God, was formed in September. Claims by the Militant Islamic Group that they had carried out an assassination attempt on Col Qaddafi in November were denied by the authorities. Throughout the second half of 1996 there were reports of clashes between Islamist groups and Government forces, especially in the eastern part of the country, where several hundred people were estimated to have been killed. Few details are available about the Islamist opposition, and the degree of popular support for the various militant groups that have emerged is difficult to estimate, though the Militant Islamic Group, which is believed to have links with the extremist Groupe islamique armé in Algeria, appears to be the most important. There is little evidence of co-operation between the different groups or between the Islamists and the secular opposition, and it is understood that the groups' resources are limited.

The threat from the growing number of militant Islamist groups was accompanied by continued unrest within the armed forces and the alienation of tribal support for the regime. In July 1996 it was reported that an attempted coup organized by Col Khalifa Haftar, an officer who had taken part in the overthrow of the monarchy in 1969, but who had later gone into exile, had been quashed after fierce fighting in the Jabal al-Akhdar, near Derna. In the same month bodyguards of Qaddafi's son, Saadi, opened fire on crowds at Tripoli's football stadium, apparently after fans began to chant anti-Government slogans following a decision by the referee which ruled in favour of a team sponsored by Saadi Qaddafi. Official Libyan reports stated that eight people were killed and 39 injured as a result of the incident. However, Western reports citing diplomatic sources put the death toll at between 20 and 50, with many others injured. At the end of August another coup attempt was uncovered, involving some 45 army officers, and said to include members of the Libyan leader's own tribe, the Qadhadhifa. Three of the coup leaders were believed to have been executed. Tight security was maintained in and around Bani Walid, the home town of officers from the powerful Warfallah tribe purportedly accused of leading the abortive coup of 1993, who were put on trial at the Supreme Military Court at the end of the year. After being convicted of spying for the CIA and trying to overthrow the regime, six senior army officers and two civilians were executed at the beginning of January 1997. The eight remaining suspects were acquitted. US officials considered the reports to be a propaganda exercise by the Libyan Government. The executions took place against the wishes of the leaders of the Warfallah tribe, and were strongly condemned by several exiled opposition groups. Some members of the Warfallah tribe, however, continued to hold senior positions in the army. In March it was reported that Maj.-Gen. Abd as-Salam Jalloud, who had been Qaddafi's Second-in-Command for some years, had resumed an important government role, after being removed from office in 1993 and placed under house arrest.

In late 1996 there were reports that the two exiled opposition groups, the LNA and the NFSL, had once again agreed to co-operate to bring down the Qaddafi regime, and had rejected overtures from the Libyan leader to take part in negotiations. In January 1997 Muhammed as-Sanusi, the grandson of the late King Idris who was deposed in 1969, and the heir to the Libyan throne who was living in exile in Britain, claimed to have received death threats from Qaddafi's agents. He later condemned the regime for threatening Libyan exiles and accused the security forces of having used chemical weapons in attacks against insurgents in the Jabal al-Akhdar in August 1996. A new secular opposition group, the Libyan Patriots Movement, emerged in January 1997. The group claimed to have supporters among the Libyan armed forces and announced its commitment to overthrow the Qaddafi regime by force.

At its annual meeting at Sirte in March 1997 the GPC approved legislation imposing collective punishment upon the families or tribal clans of Libyans convicted of crimes including sabotage, trafficking in arms, drugs smuggling and assisting 'terrorists, criminals, saboteurs and heretics'. Collective punishment was to include the possibility of denial of access to water, food supplies and fuel. The so-called 'Charter of Honour' was directed principally at opponents of the regime and was strongly condemned by the leading opposition group in exile, the NFSL.

Following the GPC meeting, a number of cabinet changes were made, involving the restructuring of two secretariats (or ministries). The most significant change was the division of the Secretariat of Justice and Public Security into two parts. Muhammad al-Hijazi retained the public security portfolio while Muhammed Belgacem Zwai, formerly Libya's representative

at the UN, became Secretary for Justice. The Secretariat of Education, Youth, Scientific Research and Vocational Training, on the other hand, was divided in three. Mehdi Meftah Mediresh became Secretary for Education and Scientific Research, Maatouq Muhammed Maatouq retained the labour and training portfolio and Ali Chaari was appointed Secretary for Youth and Sports. Baghdadi Ali al-Hinshiri retired from his post as Secretary for Health and Social Security and was replaced by Suliman Muhammad al-Ghomari, while Nouri Hamad replaced Mahmoud Badi as Secretary for the Supervision of Public Accounting and Control. A further reorganization of the GPC took place in December, in which Muhammad Ahmad al-Manqush replaced Abd al-Majid al-Aoud as Secretary-General.

In June 1998 government officials denied reports by French and Egyptian press agencies that Col Qaddafi had been injured in an attack by members of an unidentified Islamic opposition group. In August an allegation by a former UK intelligence officer that UK agents had plotted to assassinate Col Qaddafi in 1996 was denied by the UK Secretary of State for Foreign and Commonwealth Affairs, Robin Cook.

In June 1995 the regime passed a law forbidding foreign workers without contracts to remain in Libya, and in July began a programme of mass expulsions. Only a fraction of the Egyptian community, believed to number between 700,000 and 1m. was affected, with Sudanese and other African workers bearing the brunt of the deportations. According to the French daily Le Monde, by October some 40,000 Sudanese, out of a community of 400,000, had already been expelled from the country and almost half a million African workers were threatened with expulsion. The regime blamed Egyptian and Sudanese infiltrators for the outbreak of disturbances involving armed Islamist militants (see above) and justified the expulsions as a means of ridding the country of 'contagious diseases'. The expulsions were also regarded as a response to popular discontent over mounting unemployment, especially among young Libyans. However, it was the plight of Palestinian workers which caused international controversy. In a speech on 1 September Col Qaddafi repeated his threat to expel all 30,000 Palestinians resident in Libya. By the end of the month only 2,500 Palestinians had been issued with deportation orders, but their expulsion created a political crisis for the newly-formed Palestine National Authority (PNA) in Gaza. Lebanon, Israel and Egypt refused to receive the expelled Palestinians and many were stranded on ferries trying to cross the Mediterranean to Lebanon, and at Libya's border with Egypt, without adequate supplies of water or food. In the case of the expulsions of the Palestinians, Col Qaddafi stated that their ordeal demonstrated the weakness of the Oslo peace accords because the PNA lacked the power to assist them. At the end of October, after appeals from the Arab League, the Egyptian President and PLO Chairman Yasser Arafat, Col Qaddafi temporarily suspended the expulsion of Palestinians. Most of those expelled were allowed to return to Libya but, according to the UN High Commissioner for Refugees, at the end of 1996 some 200 people remained stranded on the Libyan-Egyptian border, surviving in desperate conditions. The deportation of Sudanese workers continued. In January 1996 Libya announced that it had expelled some 70,000 Sudanese and that a further 200,000 would be expelled by the end of February. However, Libya stopped the expulsion of Egyptians after President Mubarak promised to strengthen his efforts to find a solution to the Lockerbie affair and to Libya's international isolation. According to a Libyan official, some 335,000 foreign workers had been expelled by the beginning of 1996. In May 1996 Qaddafi once again threatened to expel Palestinians living in Libya, despite a new appeal from President Mubarak of Egypt. However, by October the Libyan leader appeared to reconsider his decision, and in November Libya invited Arab workers to apply to live in that country, due to a reported labour shortage. In January 1997 the GPC formally revoked the expulsion order, though few Palestinians appeared willing to return to Libya, and there were reports that some Palestinians still living in Libya were trying to leave the country. Subsequent reports in April 1997 suggested that the Government had, in an unexpected move, forced Palestinians remaining in refugee camps to return to Libya, and had dismantled their camps.

ICJ RULING ON AOZOU STRIP

On 3 February 1994 the International Court of Justice (ICJ) ruled against Libya's claim to the Aozou strip in northern Chad. Libya and Chad had agreed in 1989 to accept the ICJ's ruling over the disputed territory. Libya's border with its southern neighbour, Chad, had been defined in 1955 in an agreement between the newly-independent State of Libya and France, then the colonial power in Chad. However, in 1973 Libya unilaterally abrogated the treaty and annexed the Aozou strip. Libya based its claim to northern Chad on the fact that the area had been part of the vast domain of the Sanusi order which had ruled much of Libya before the Italian colonial conquest in 1911. Most of the disputed strip is desert and sparsely populated. Chad regained control of the area in 1987 with the exception of a large military base built by Libya at the oasis of Aozou. After the court's ruling was announced, Libya appeared unwilling to relinquish its claim to the disputed territory and the Government of Chad reported that Libya had strengthened its military forces there. When negotiations between the two countries did begin in March, Libya demanded the release of some 500 prisoners of war captured in Chad in 1987. Then, Qaddafi suddenly announced that Libya was willing to abandon its claim to the disputed territory and a draft agreement on the withdrawal of Libyan forces was signed in Sirte on 5 April. Under the terms of the agreement the withdrawal was completed by the end of May 1994. In early June Libya signed a treaty of friendship and co-operation with Chad, but in January 1995 the President of Chad strongly denied reports in the Libyan press that plans for a union between Chad, Libya and Sudan had been agreed at a meeting of the leaders of the three countries held in Tripoli in October 1994. A communiqué issued at the end of the meeting had merely announced that a committee had been set up to study the question of integration. It was clear that neither Chad nor Sudan had any intention of forming a union with Libya, but had agreed to discuss integration in the hope of securing Libyan financial and military assistance. In January 1997 the Chadian Government announced its intention to protest to the UN Security Council against the appearance of an official Libyan publication which contained a map showing the Aozou strip within Libyan territory.

RELATIONS WITH EGYPT AND THE MAGHREB

Although President Mubarak has consistently resisted Qaddafi's plans for Arab unity, relations between Libya and Egypt have continued to improve in recent years. Egypt firmly opposed the UN sanctions imposed on Libya and has made strenuous diplomatic efforts to mediate between Libya and the West over the Lockerbie affair. In November 1993 President Mubarak told the newspaper *Al-Ahram* that it was in Egypt's interest for 'stability' to prevail in Libya and that relations between the two countries should remain cordial. Qaddafi's regime is seen as a bulwark against the spread of militant Islamist movements in the region and offers the prospect of much needed economic opportunities for Egypt, especially the employment of Egyptian manpower. Libya has offered to resettle one million Egyptian farmers on lands to be irrigated by the Great Man-made River scheme. For Libya, which has become increasingly isolated internationally through the efforts of the USA and the United Kingdom, Egypt serves as a valuable intermediary with the outside world. The close relationship between the two countries appeared to have survived the embarrassment resulting from the disappearance of Libyan opposition leader Mansour Kikhia in Cairo in December 1994 and Libya's strong condemnation of the Israel-PLO accord signed in September 1993. Early in 1994 the Libyan press agency, JANA, declared that Libya and Egypt were continuing to co-operate in many areas and acknowledged Egyptian efforts to persuade the West to ease sanctions against Libya. In February the Egyptian Minister of Foreign Affairs, Amr Moussa, condemned the latest round of sanctions against Libya as 'unfair' and 'coercive' and reiterated his Government's commitment to seeking a peaceful solution to the Lockerbie affair. However, Egypt's close relations with Libya provoked strong criticism from the US media at the end of 1994. Egypt was accused of abusing US aid by defending a state involved in terrorism against the USA. The Libyan Secretary of Foreign Liaison and International Co-operation, Omar al-Muntasser, condemned the attacks as an attempt to build a 'Berlin Wall' between Libya and Egypt and argued that this was yet another US media campaign to denounce Libya as a 'terrorist state' just before UN sanctions came up for review. In November 1994 Libya supported Egypt's application to join the UAM. However, political differences emerged between the states during 1995, especially as a result of Libya's outspoken opposition to the normalization of relations between a growing number of Arab states and Israel. Col Qaddafi was critical of Egypt's role in promoting economic co-operation between Israel and its Arab neighbours. Libya's expulsion of Egyptian workers during the second half of 1995 further soured relations, although the Egyptian Government carefully avoided any public condemnation of Libya's actions. Moreover, in October 1995 Col Qaddafi made a number of public statements criticizing Egypt and President Mubarak for not doing enough to help Libya obtain the lifting of UN sanctions. In January 1996 the Libyan leader agreed to stop the expulsion of Egyptian workers after the Egyptian President agreed to step up his mediation efforts on behalf of Libya, although observers noted that Libya's outspoken opposition to Israel and the Middle East peace process had made Egyptian efforts at mediation over UN sanctions even more difficult. In March Col Qaddafi condemned the 'Summit of Peacemakers' held at Sharm esh-Sheikh, but carefully avoided any criticism of Egypt. In May Col Qaddafi held talks in Cairo with President Mubarak, but caused some embarrassment to his host by issuing a new threat to expel Palestinians living in Libya. In late June, however, the Libyan leader flouted the UN-imposed air embargo and flew to Cairo to attend the Arab League summit convened by President Mubarak in response to the election of a right-wing Government in Israel, while during Libya's debate with the USA over allegations that it was involved in the construction of a chemical weapons plant at Tarhuna (see above), Egypt refused to endorse the US claims. Recognizing Egypt as Libya's only real ally in the Arab world and as a vitally important intermediary, especially with the West, the Libyan leader continued to maintain close relations with its eastern neighbour. Several meetings took place between Col. Qaddafi and President Mubarak throughout the second half of 1996 and in early December the Egyptian President paid an official visit to Tripoli, at the head of a large delegation. Co-operation in security, principally directed against militant Islamist groups, was agreed during the meeting. At the end of 1996 Col Qaddafi announced that after liquidating a number of investments in Europe, Libya was to reinvest in Egypt, where Libyan government holdings were believed to total some US $440m. However, differences between the two countries, particularly regarding Egypt's relations with Israel and Col Qaddafi's outspoken opposition to the Middle East peace process, continued to put their relationship under strain.

Egypt had also been suspicious of Libya's close relations with Sudan, which supports Libyan opposition to the peace process and offers shelter to Islamist militants from Egypt. In April 1995 a Libyan delegation attended the Popular Arab and Islamic Conference in Khartoum, along with representatives of Islamist opposition groups from Algeria, Morocco and Tunisia. The meeting avoided any criticism of the Libyan Government's harsh repression of its Islamist opposition and appealed for the lifting of UN sanctions against Tripoli. However, relations between Libya and Sudan became strained during the second half of 1995, owing to Libya's expulsion of large numbers of Sudanese workers (see above). Nevertheless, the Sudanese President, Omar Hassan al-Bashir, attended the 26th anniversary of the Libyan revolution in September 1995 as an honoured guest, and in early January 1996 Abu Bakr Yunes, the Libyan statesman responsible for defence, attended Sudan's independence celebrations. Early in 1996 Libya continued to mediate in disputes between Sudan and neighbouring Uganda and Ethiopia.

Although Libya joined the UAM and Col Qaddafi assumed the presidency of the organization on 1 January 1991 for a period of six months, the Libyan leader appeared to show little interest in further integration with his country's western neighbours and preferred to look east to Egypt. The union itself has made little progress and few of the agreements adopted have actually been ratified. At the sixth summit meeting, held in Tunis in April 1994, Libya, represented by Maj. Khoeldi al-Hamidi, threatened to leave the organization unless the other member states ceased to comply with the UN sanctions imposed against Libya. Of the UAM leaders, only the Algerian President, Lamine Zéroual, attended the celebrations marking the 25th anniversary of the Libyan revolution held in Tripoli in September 1994. At the beginning of 1995 Libya announced that it would not, in future, take over the presidency of the UAM nor chair any of its institutions. However, despite its threats to leave the organization, Libya continued to attend UAM meetings. It was suggested that renewed interest in the UAM may have been due to its desire to support Egypt's application for membership and its recognition that the UAM provided Libya with a rare opportunity for contact with the EU. In June the UAM expressed its solidarity with Libya by appealing for an end to UN sanctions. Early in 1996, however, Col Qaddafi's outspoken opposition to Israel strained relations with other members of the UAM. By the end of the year Libya had made some efforts to improve relations with its Maghreb neighbours and revive the UAM, largely in order to ensure their support for Libyan efforts to obtain the lifting of UN sanctions. Relations with Tunisia on the other hand, though often strained and sometimes hostile, have become friendly since the imposition of UN sanctions. Libya has come to depend increasingly on transit facilities through Tunisia as the air embargo imposed by the UN has tightened. Tunisia has profited greatly from this transit traffic, and the remittances from the 20,000 Tunisians working in Libya represent another valuable source of foreign exchange. Despite Tunisia's strict implementation of UN sanctions and the large profits that it has made out of its role as Libya's main transit route to Europe, relations remained friendly for most of 1995. In July Tunisia requested that the UN General Assembly lift sanctions against Libya, and Tunisia was among those countries which supported Libya's unsuccessful request to attend the EU summit in Barcelona, Spain, in November. During the second half of the year, Tunisians were not included in the mass expulsion of foreign workers from Libya. However, relations deteriorated at the beginning of 1996 after Tunisia agreed to establish low-level diplomatic relations with Israel, a move that was sharply condemned by Libya. Relations were further soured in February 1996, when Tunisia placed on trial an opposition leader, Muhammad Mouada of the Mouvement des démocrates socialistes. One of the charges against him was that he had links with Libyan intelligence. Relations, however, improved towards the end of 1996 when Col Qaddafi made two visits to Tunis and signed a number of bilateral co-operation agreements. The Libyan leader also declared that Tunisians were welcome to work and invest in Libya. Despite misunderstandings with Algeria over Col Qaddafi's attitude towards the Front islamique du salut (FIS), the Islamist opposition in Algeria, Algeria has continued to support Libya in the UN and the Arab League. In April 1995 Col Qaddafi visited Algeria for talks with President Lamine Zéroual. The talks were concluded with a joint statement reviewing bilateral and economic relations and urging the UN to end sanctions against Libya. Relations between the two countries were increasingly focused on co-operation over security and the containment of Islamist militancy, and these matters were discussed when the Algerian Minister of the Interior, Mustapha Benmansour, visited Tripoli in August 1995. In April 1996 the two countries signed a security agreement to co-operate in the struggle against the threat posed by militant Islamist groups, and shortly afterwards there was speculation that the Libyan authorities had handed over some 500 Algerian members of the FIS who had taken refuge in Libya. However, relations became strained in January 1997 when it was announced that the FIS had asked Libya to mediate in their conflict with the Algerian authorities, since Libya had ostensibly broken off all links with the FIS in 1994 when Col Qaddafi had pledged to cease all support for the Islamist opposition in Algeria. Morocco supported Libya in the UN by abstaining during the vote in the Security Council in November 1993 to impose tougher sanctions on Libya. After Libya criticized Morocco for its moves towards normalizing its relations with Israel, relations improved somewhat in 1995 when King Hassan, on a visit to Washington, DC, in March, urged the US Administration to re-examine its position on sanctions against Libya in the light of their impact on the Libyan people. During 1996 both countries called for a revival of the UAM. In November 1995, after Mauritania established diplomatic relations with Israel, Libya expelled some 10,000 Mauritanian workers, withdrew its ambassador to Nouakchott, severed economic links and threatened Mauritania's status as a member of the UAM and the Arab League. In March 1997 however, diplomatic relations between the two countries were restored, despite accusations by the Mauritanian authorities earlier in the year that Libya had maintained links with a number of opposition leaders, ostensibly for the purpose of destabilizing the Mauritanian regime. Although all of Libya's neighbours remain deeply suspicious of the Qaddafi regime, they have more to fear from its collapse, an event that could have serious consequences for the stability of the whole of North Africa.

Economy

Revised for this edition by ALAN J. DAY

Petroleum has transformed Libya from the poorest country in the world in 1951 into the country with the highest living standards in Africa (according to World Bank figures). Before the discovery of oil in commercial quantities in the 1950s, agriculture was the basis of the economy and domestic revenue covered only about one-half of the Government's ordinary and development expenditure. Between 1962 and 1968, however, national income increased from LD 131m. to LD 798m. and gross national product (GNP) increased from LD 163m. to LD 909m. Exports of petroleum during this period increased by 835%, accounting for 51% of gross domestic product (GDP) in 1968. As a result of the dramatic rise in oil prices in the 1970s, the country's GNP, according to official estimates, rose to LD 3,534m. in 1974 before falling slightly to LD 3,497m. in 1975, when petroleum exports accounted for 46.3% of GDP. Oil revenues then rose steeply, reaching a peak of US $22,000m. in 1980, but fell equally sharply in the 1980s, as world oil prices declined rapidly. Estimated GNP fell from $25,984m. in 1985 to $22,300m. in 1987 and $18,400m. in 1988, before rising again, in 1989, to $23,333m., measured at average 1987–89 prices. The country's population increased at an average annual rate of 3.6% in 1985–95. During the greater part of the 1980s the petroleum sector accounted for 65% of GDP and 99% of export earnings, although it provided employment for less than 10% of the labour force. In 1989, according to estimates by the World Bank, Libya's GNP per head, measured at average 1987–89 prices, was $5,310. This was the highest level to be recorded among African countries, but represented an average annual decline, in real terms, of 9.2% over the period 1980–89. Libya's financial position deteriorated further in 1988–89, but then improved significantly following the Gulf crisis of 1990–91, when world oil prices rose sharply, albeit for a brief period, and generated an increase in Libyan oil revenues of nearly 25% in 1990, compared with 1989.

After the 1969 revolution, state intervention in the economy increased, in accordance with Col Qaddafi's ideas of 'Islamic socialism'. Apart, however, from the nationalization of distribution and marketing of petroleum in Libya in 1970, the Government refrained from directly taking over petroleum company assets until the dispute with BP in 1971. In September 1978 and the first two months of 1979, a large number of private companies were taken over by workers' committees. Similarly, in 1979, all direct importing business was transferred to 62 public corporations, and the issuing of licences was stopped. In March 1981, it was announced that all licences for shops selling clothes, electrical goods, shoes, household appliances and spare parts were to be cancelled, and that by the end of the year all retail shops would have to close. Retail activity became controlled by state-administered supermarkets. The whole private sector was to be completely abolished by the end of 1981, to be replaced by people's economic committees. These plans were never implemented according to schedule, and by the late 1980s Qaddafi was extolling the virtues of private enterprise.

Until the country's petroleum resources began to be exploited, not more than 25% of the population lived in the towns. This is no longer true: by 1990, according to the World Bank, the urban population comprised 70% of the total. Approximately one-half of the non-urban population is settled in rural communities, and the remainder are semi-nomads, who follow a pastoral mode of life. According to the results of the census carried out on 31 July 1984, Libya's population was 3.6m., compared with 2,249,237 at the census of July 1973; by mid-1996 the total was estimated by the UN to have risen to 5.6m. The country's labour force totalled an estimated 800,000 in 1981. By the end of 1982 it was estimated that there were 569,000 foreigners living in Libya, representing 18% of the total population. Egyptians accounted for 174,158 of these, while 73,582 were Tunisians and 44,546 were Turkish. In July 1985, however, Col Qaddafi barred Egyptians (whose numbers in Libya had fallen by 20,000 since January) from working in Libya, in retaliation against a similar measure preventing Libyans from working in Egypt. Tunisia ordered 283 Libyans (the majority of Libya's diplomats and more than 250 other Libyan nationals), accused of spying, to leave the country in August 1985, after Libya decided to expel some 30,000 Tunisian workers from Libya. It was estimated that Libya expelled or laid off more than 120,000 foreign workers during 1985 (including workers from Mali, Mauritania, Niger, and 10,000–20,000 Syrians, between August and October). Col Qaddafi maintained that the expulsions were part of a policy to achieve self-sufficiency in Libya's labour force, and not the result of economic stringency. However, remittances by foreign workers to their own countries were a substantial drain on Libya's reserves of foreign exchange, totalling some $2,000m. in 1983, when the number of expatriate workers was at its highest level. Libya began to reduce the number of these workers in 1984, and remittances in that year were estimated to have fallen to $1,500m. According to figures released by the International Labour Organization, there were 583,900 migrant workers in Libya in July 1985.

Since 1980 planned mergers with Syria, Morocco and Algeria, and the military adventure into Chad, have had adverse effects on the economy. The latter episode resulted in diplomatic relations being broken off with a number of West African countries. In the economic sphere, for example, Nigeria cut off uranium sales to Libya, which amounted to 500 tons in 1980. The purge on corruption in February 1980 increased payment delays and so deepened the reluctance of foreign companies to invest in Libya. In practical terms, little progress was made towards the 'merger' with Syria, although Libya paid off all Syria's debts to the USSR, and appeared to be moving closer to the USSR.

Relations with the USA worsened, and in March 1982 President Reagan banned imports of Libyan petroleum to the USA, and halted all exports to Libya other than food and medical supplies. Libya's perceived interference in the affairs of other nations (notably Chad) and its alleged association with international terrorism had further significant economic repercussions in January 1986, when President Reagan 'froze' Libyan assets in the USA and banned all trade between the USA and Libya. However, the effectiveness of this action was vitiated by the unwillingness of the USA's allies in Japan and Western Europe to institute a complementary economic boycott of Libya, and by the fact that assets worth some $1,000m.–$2,000m. would have been surrendered to Libya by the US oil companies operating there if they had ceased operations immediately. These companies were given until 30 June 1986 to sell their assets to Libyan concerns, but only tenuous agreements had been reached by the time the deadline arrived. The assets were not nationalized and the companies signed agreements with Libya giving them the right to negotiate their return when circumstances allowed.

The US sanctions, rather than harming Libya, had their greatest impact on the departing oil companies, which estimated their annual losses from the oil operations that they had transferred to Libya at $2m.–$2.5m. The withdrawal of the US oil companies had a greater negative effect on Libya's ability to market its petroleum than on actual levels of production, which were lower than capacity, owing to weak world demand. Petroleum lifted by US companies was formerly guaranteed an outlet through their refineries, mainly in Europe. Following the US withdrawal, Libya had to compete with other countries for sales to refineries. In June 1986 the USA banned the export to third countries of goods and technology destined for use in the Libyan petroleum industry. A three-year 'standstill agreement' between the Libyan Government and the US oil companies officially expired at the end of June 1989, but continued to be observed by Libya, which confirmed in March 1991 that it had no plans to dispose of the US companies' Libyan areas to third parties. In January 1991 US sanctions were renewed for a further 12-month period, and in April the US Government published a list of 48 companies, based in various countries, which it believed to be acting as agents or 'fronts' for Libyan nationals and which were therefore to be subject to the US sanctions. A supplementary list published in August 1991 added 12 companies to the total. According to the US Department of the Treasury, the mid-1993 value of Libyan assets 'frozen' in the USA since 1986 was $903m.

In addition to Libya's increasingly isolated position among both African and Arab states, during the 1980s Libya's economy was severely restricted by the effect of the low prices for oil consequent on the global oil glut. Revenue from sales of petroleum declined from $22,000m. in 1980 to $5,000m. in 1988. Decreasing revenues caused serious cash-flow problems and necessitated a major revision of the 1981–85 Development Plan. Although in January 1986 the Central Bank claimed that 80% of projects under the Plan were either completed or under way, the slump in the price of oil in 1986 led to the suspension or cancellation of almost all new development projects (an outstanding exception being the 'Great Man-made River' scheme—see Agriculture, below). In the period 1980–89 GDP declined from $35,500m. to $23,000m. The crisis in the economy prompted Col Qaddafi to introduce a series of economic and political liberalization measures in March and April 1988. The state supermarket network, which was established in the early 1980s, was poorly organized and many basic commodities were usually unavailable, giving rise to a thriving black market. Subsequently, however, private shops were encouraged to reopen, and Col Qaddafi adopted measures to dismantle obstacles to trade and tourism with Libya's neighbours, closing customs and immigration posts along the borders with Egypt and Tunisia. Thousands of Tunisians entered Libya in 1988 to work on Libyan farms, while, along the border, a 'free zone' developed where Libyans could purchase items that were scarce in their own country. In September 1988 Qaddafi proposed an increase in 'privatization' and announced that Libyans would be able to import and export in complete freedom. In December the Government announced plans to reduce its budget deficit by removing subsidies on wheat, flour, sugar, tea and salt. However, controls on prices and on interest and exchange rates were maintained, and all important sectors of the economy remained under the effective control of the state (which in 1990 retained 70% of all Libyan salaried workers on its payroll).

At the second summit meeting of the Union of the Arab Maghreb (formed in February 1989 and comprising Algeria, Libya, Mauritania, Morocco and Tunisia), held in Algiers in July 1990, closer economic ties between the member states were proposed, including the establishment of a customs union before 1995. Moreover, a *rapprochement* with Egypt in October 1989 facilitated plans for wide-ranging economic integration and cross-border co-operation. This new relationship was one factor in Libya's decision ultimately to abide by the UN embargo that was imposed on Iraq in August 1990 because of its invasion of Kuwait (although Col Qaddafi opposed the US-led military action against Iraq). Another factor was Libya's need to take full advantage of the sudden rise in world oil prices, caused by the crisis. By increasing its output in the third and fourth quarters of the year, Libya recorded total oil revenues of $9,700m. in 1990 (compared with $7,846m. in 1989) and achieved a 9.4% increase in GDP, to LD 7,816m. ($27,370m.). It also converted the 1989 current account deficit estimated at US $940m. into an estimated surplus of $2,230m. in 1990. Libya thus emerged from the Gulf crisis of 1990–91 with its position enhanced both economically and diplomatically, notably in its relations with the EC, to which it was the second largest supplier of oil. The value of oil revenues in 1991 amounted to about $10,000m.

Libya's economic relations with the West nevertheless continued to be complicated by allegations of official Libyan involvement in international terrorism, including the 1988 Lockerbie airliner bombing and the destruction in 1989 of a French airliner over the Sahara (see History section, above). Under Resolution 748, adopted by the UN Security Council on 31 March 1992, Libya became subject to certain mandatory sanctions, in view of its failure to comply with Resolution 731 (of 12 January 1992) requiring Libyan co-operation in bringing those responsible for the terrorist actions to justice. As imposed from 15 April 1992, the sanctions included an arms embargo and the severance of air transport links with Libya, but did not, at that time, encompass a general trade embargo or any moves against Libya's exports of petroleum. Prior to their imposition, the Libyan authorities took the precaution of transferring substantial Libyan assets from West European to Middle Eastern banks.

In response to Libya's continuing non-compliance with Resolution 731, the Security Council extended the existing provisions of Resolution 748 for successive 120-day periods. The extension agreed in August 1993 was accompanied by a warning from three Council members (the United Kingdom, France and the USA) that they would seek to extend the scope of the sanctions if the situation remained deadlocked at the end of September 1993. Libyan claims that the country had suffered direct and indirect revenue losses totalling $2,200m. during the first year of the sanctions regime were generally believed to be greatly exaggerated, the main reported trade effect of the sanctions being an increase in imports of priority items (including inputs for development projects) as a safeguard against a future UN decision to widen the scope of the sanctions.

A law promulgated by the General People's Congress in September 1992 formally authorized the privatization of Libyan industries and permitted 'individuals or groups to exercise the liberal professions and to invest freely in the private sectors'. In July 1993 the General People's Committee issued a decree ending state control of wholesale trade, which was opened up to partnerships and limited companies. In the previous month the Committee had banned state employees from concurrently engaging in private employment. The national debate on economic reform had, in 1992, been widened by Col Qaddafi to include the proposal that 50% of the state's oil revenues should be distributed directly to citizens, and that the 'very, very big octopus' of state administration should be cut back to a minimum by privatizing most educational and health-care facilities, shutting down unprofitable state economic enterprises and devolving many defence responsibilities to local administrative units. Other leading figures, including the Governor of the Central Bank, spoke out strongly in favour of a more orthodox transition to a mixed economy. (In 1995 the General People's Congress approved a budget provision for a direct revenue distribution scheme. The first measures towards its implementation were reported in the following year.)

In May 1993 Col Qaddafi advocated the introduction of a law to guarantee foreign capital investment in Libya. In July 1993 representatives of some 250 Libyan and Tunisian companies met in Tripoli to discuss proposals for improving economic co-operation between the two countries, including the possible establishment of new joint ventures. Delegates stressed the desirability of standardizing investment laws, pointing out that any Libyan move to introduce laws on the current Tunisian model would be consistent with the liberalization policies of the Libyan leadership.

Following the August 1993 extension of UN Security Council Resolution 748 and the subsequent circulation by the USA, France and the United Kingdom of draft proposals for stronger international action against Libya, the Libyan Government stepped up its efforts to minimize its exposure to harsher sanctions. Libya's liquid assets overseas (estimated to total $17,000m.), if not already located in financial 'safe havens', were constantly monitored to avoid unnecessary exposure to seizure. According to the Bank for International Settlements, Libya withdrew $2,800m. of its overseas deposits in the third quarter of 1993, including an estimated $430m. from OECD countries. The stockpiling of imported equipment for use in part-completed projects, and of spares for existing plants, was speeded up and carefully targeted on priority areas. The functions and ownership structures of Libya's fixed assets overseas (which had an estimated worth of up to $4,000m.) were analysed to assess their exposure to sanctions, and a number of deals were struck with foreign (predominantly Italian) equity partners whereby Libya relinquished control of high-profile companies.

In particular Oilinvest, the holding company through which Libya had controlled an extensive European oil refining and distribution network, was in September 1993 restructured with minority (45%) Libyan ownership, while Oilinvest's shareholding in its principal subsidiary company, Tamoil Italia, was in turn reduced to 45% and two Tamoil subsidiaries (Tamoil Transport and Chempetrol Overseas) were taken over by new owners.

The crucial Security Council vote on Libyan sanctions was delayed until 11 November 1993 because Russia (which was owed up to $3,000m. for Soviet arms and other supplies to Libya in the 1970s and 1980s) was reluctant to endorse any measure that might prompt Libya to default on agreed payment obligations. This objection was dropped after the draft resolution was expanded to include an explicit reference to Libya's 'duty scrupulously to adhere to all its obligations concerning the servicing or repayment of foreign debt'.

Security Council Resolution 882 called on UN member states to 'freeze' all Libyan-controlled funds and financial resources abroad and to require the use of separate bank accounts for specified trade transactions; to prohibit the supply to Libya of specified items for use in the 'downstream' oil and gas sector; to shut down overseas offices of Libyan Arab Airlines and to ban the supply of civil aviation equipment and services and the renewal of aircraft insurance; and to reduce staffing levels at Libyan diplomatic missions.

The 'freeze' on Libyan funds prohibited withdrawals from, but not payments into, existing overseas bank accounts. The new 'external' bank accounts specified by the Resolution were to be set up to handle payments to foreign contractors and suppliers to the Libyan market, using revenue derived from Libyan exports of hydrocarbons and agricultural products. All transactions through such accounts had to be supported by evidence of compliance with the sanctions regulations. The oil and gas equipment specified in a detailed annex to Resolution 883 included pumps, loading equipment and various essential items of oil refining equipment.

The Resolution came into force on 1 December, but the complicated administrative arrangements meant that Libyan export revenues did not begin to reach the new 'external' accounts in overseas banks until mid-January 1994, delaying payments to many foreign contractors for some weeks beyond the due dates. Over-zealous actions by sanctions enforcers included the 'freezing' of the US assets of a Bahrain-based financial services company with a Libyan minority shareholder. This decision was rescinded in early February 1994. The UN Security Council renewed the terms of Resolution 883 for a further 120 days on 8 April.

In mid-1994 the current sanctions appeared to have had no effect on the functioning of Libya's established oil and gas production facilities or the progress of development projects which had been under way when the sanctions were imposed. Many hydrocarbon facilities were not dependent on embargoed items, while others were fully supplied with stockpiled equipment. Some future projects had to be shelved for the duration of the current sanctions because they required embargoed items, but all were low-priority schemes for which no firm contracts had been awarded. There was, nevertheless, a marked decrease in the overall tempo of economic activity in Libya, and it was estimated that the country's GDP declined by 7% in both 1993 and 1994, to stand at about $26,000m. in the latter year.

The UN sanctions remained in force in August 1995 on the same terms that applied in December 1993, the USA having failed to win UN Security Council backing for a proposal (tabled at the March and July 1995 sanctions reviews) to tighten them by imposing a total embargo on Libyan oil exports. European opposition to the US proposal had been strongest in Italy (which obtained 28% of its crude oil supplies from Libya). The US

Government announced in April 1995 that it would examine the scope for further tightening of the USA's own unilateral sanctions against Libya.

In August 1995 the Government launched a series of mass expulsions of foreigners accused of working illegally in Libya, those affected being mainly Sudanese, Egyptians and Palestinians (the latter apparently included to make a political point about the current status of the Middle East peace process). Libya's foreign work-force was estimated to number between 1m. and 2.5m. in 1995. Unemployment was believed to have become a significant problem (with some Western estimates putting it as high as 30%) and was known to have affected increasing numbers of Libyan nationals. The expulsion of Palestinians was suspended for six months in October 1995, after which time the main targets of the government crackdown were Sudanese workers. The Palestinian expulsion order was formally rescinded in January 1997.

Having risen slightly in 1995, Libya's oil output showed another small increase in the first half of 1996 as the country's principal export industry continued to demonstrate that the UN sanctions regime (which remained unchanged in mid-1996) posed no significant threat to the implementation of its normal production schedules. Nor were there any reports of a slowdown in the pace of work on the huge infrastructural project (the 'Great Man-made River') which accounted for a large proportion of government spending on economic development. The level of state investment on lower-priority projects remained depressed, however, with some delays being explicitly attributed to the effects of sanctions. In certain cases (e.g. a major desalination scheme) the Government said it was unable to proceed to the contract stage because sanctions had made it impossible to arrange satisfactory project financing. In other cases (e.g. an oil refinery upgrading scheme) implementation of completed plans was deferred because the import of essential equipment was directly blocked by UN sanctions. There were also instances of international companies modifying their Libyan contract bids to allow for non-standard items to be installed instead of embargoed equipment (one example being some of the automated equipment normally installed in cement plants).

In January 1996 President Clinton extended the duration of all existing US sanctions against Libya, including 1980s measures that would otherwise have expired. Some weeks earlier the US Senate had added Libya to a bill (previously applicable only to Iran) designed to inhibit hydrocarbon investments in these countries by non-US companies. In April 1996 EU Ministers of Foreign Affairs made a formal protest to the USA about the 'extra-territoriality' of the draft legislation, which the EU regarded as a formula for a 'secondary embargo' against the mainly European companies whose commercial freedom was under threat. The Ways and Means Committee of the US House of Representatives nevertheless failed to remove the most controversial aspects of the proposed legislation when it approved a modified draft in June 1996. The Iran and Libya sanctions act completed its passage through the US Congress in the following month and was signed into law by President Clinton on 5 August 1996. It specified six forms of sanction available to the US Government: denial of access to US Export-Import Bank facilities; denial of export licences in respect of goods ordered from the USA; imposition of a ceiling of $10m. per year on company loans from US financial institutions; withholding of permission to conduct primary dealings in US government bonds; exclusion from bidding for US government contracts; and exclusion from the US import market. A non-US company was liable to have two of these sanctions (selected by the President) imposed on it if it invested $40m. or more in the hydrocarbons industries of Libya or Iran in any one year, or if it violated current UN embargoes on Libya. However, the US President could decide to waive sanctions if a company's home country had 'agreed to undertake substantial measures, including economic sanctions' to prevent Libya or Iran from supporting terrorism or acquiring weapons of mass destruction, or if it had encouraged Libya to comply with UN Security Council Resolution 731 on the bringing to justice of terrorist suspects.

A resolution calling for the repeal of the US legislation was adopted by the UN General Assembly in November 1996, with EU member countries abstaining. Following the inauguration of the second Clinton Administration in January 1997, US officials indicated that there was no early intention to issue detailed guidelines on the implementation of the August 1996 legislation. A formal EU challenge to US sanctions laws, alleging violations of World Trade Organization rules, was suspended in April 1997 in order to seek a compromise settlement through informal discussions. There was minimal US reaction to reports during the first half of 1997 that the Italian company Agip, which had signed a major gas development agreement with Libya's National Oil Co some weeks before the Iran and Libya sanctions act came into force, was continuing to move towards the detailed design stage of this project.

The multilateral UN sanctions on Libya were renewed in 1996, 1997 and 1998. The Libyan Government claimed in October 1996 that UN sanctions had cost the country $19,000m. in lost revenue by the end of 1995 (including $5,900m. from potential agricultural exports) and had contributed to the deaths of up to 21,000 Libyans (including 16,000 patients unable to obtain urgent medical treatment abroad). Preliminary estimates of Libya's economic performance in 1996 indicated a return to positive GDP growth (at a rate of 3.5% per annum) for the first time since the imposition of UN sanctions in 1992. A 'purification' campaign against allegedly corrupt import-export traders led to the closure of many privately-owned small businesses in 1996.

A relaxation in May 1998 of the threat of US sanctions against countries whose companies invested in Iran was widely seen in Europe as also applying to dealings with Libya, although substantial opposition was evident in the US Congress to ending the US ban on investment in the Libyan oil industry. Following talks in Rome in July between the Italian and Libyan foreign affairs ministers, the Italian Government declared that normalization of relations between the two countries would assist Libya to return to 'co-operation with the international community', while also asserting that Libyan adherence to UN resolutions would assist the process. It was subsequently stated in Tripoli that Col Qaddafi had decreed that Italian companies should be 'given priority in all sectors' in the awarding of new government contracts.

AGRICULTURE

Agriculture dominated the economy until the discovery of petroleum. Even now, the petroleum industry gives direct employment to less than 10% of the total labour force (800,000 in 1981) and the present Government regards the agricultural sector as of primary importance, with Col Qaddafi himself regularly stating that more emphasis must be put on agriculture. Nevertheless, by 1982, the percentage of the population employed in agriculture had fallen to 16% from around 50% in the early 1970s. It is ironic that, despite having regularly received one-fifth of all state investment since 1970 (totalling an estimated $24,000m. in the period 1970–88), the contribution of the agricultural sector to GDP declined, in real terms, from 2.3% in 1975 to 1.9% in 1980, and Libya continued to be a major food importer. The appointment of the former Mayor of Tripoli, Abd al-Majid al-Aoud, as GPC Secretary for Agriculture, in March 1989, indicated the Government's determination to give support to the agricultural sector. This objective was reaffirmed in Col Qaddafi's decision to make 1990 the 'year of agriculture', but the aim of achieving self-sufficiency in food remained a distant prospect.

About 95% of Libya's land area is desert. Of the remainder, a high percentage is used for grazing, only 1.4% is arable, and 0.1% is irrigated. In mid-1970 all Italian-owned land and property in Libya, including 37,000 ha of cultivated land, was confiscated and plans were made to distribute the expropriated lands to Libyan farmers, with government credits for seed, fertilizers and machinery. Several very large contracts were awarded for reclamation and irrigation work in various scheduled areas. The best-known schemes, dating from the 1970s, are the Kufra oasis project to irrigate 10,000 ha; the Tawurgha project to reclaim 3,000 ha; the Sarir reclamation project; the Jebel al-Akhdar project; the Jefara plain project; and the Wadi Qatara reclamation project. The Wadi Jaref dam, one of the biggest in Libya, went into operation in 1976. All projects are meant to be fully integrated, providing for the establishment of farms, the building of rural roads, irrigation and drainage facilities and, in some cases, the introduction of agro-industries.

The Government invested a total of LD 700m. in agriculture over the 10-year period 1973–83. The Three-Year Plan, as revised in February 1975, provided LD 566.9m. for agricultural development and agrarian reform. The revised 1976–80 Development Plan provided LD 498m. plus LD 977m. for integral developments. Indeed, an important feature of Libya's economic planning in the 1970s was the high priority which was being given to agriculture. In 1975 agricultural development absorbed 21% of total budget expenditure whilst in 1976 it had risen to a corresponding 30%. In the 1978 financial year, the agricultural sector was allocated 18.9% of budgeted development expenditure and 14.6% of overall budget spending. In most other oil-rich countries, agriculture hardly received more than 10% of development funds. In 1979, however, investment in agriculture decreased, receiving only 6.4% of the general budget. In relative terms, the budget allocated to agriculture was expected to continue to decrease slightly during the 1980s, as the 1981–85 Five-Year Plan gave greater priority to industry. Nevertheless, the absolute level of expenditure on the agricultural sector was scheduled to increase. Thus, in the 1976–80 Development Plan LD 1,600m., or 21% of expenditure, were allocated to agriculture, whereas in the 1981–85 Plan the estimated expenditure on agriculture was LD 3,000m., representing about 20% of the total. This latest plan also envisaged that the proportion of the working population employed in agriculture would decline from 18.9% in 1980 to 16.8% in 1985. However, between 1983 and 1985, successive development budgets were underspent, and despite the official priority awarded to agricultural development, the agricultural sector was one of the most seriously affected, receiving 81.3% of budgeted investment in 1983, 86.9% in 1984, and only 66.7% in 1985.

In spite of the money invested in the sector, results in terms of production have been largely unsatisfactory. Climatic and soil factors will, it is hoped, cease to play such a large part in fluctuations of output, once irrigation schemes are operational and the distribution and use of fertilizers is well established. There have been signs in the production figures that this is indeed happening; according to the UN Food and Agriculture Organization (FAO), output of cereals increased from 62,000 metric tons in 1970 to 299,000 tons in 1988, while, over the same period, annual production of meat rose from 48,000 tons to 171,000 tons, root crops from 10,000 tons to 115,000 tons, oil crops from 20,000 tons to 31,000 tons and pulses from 2,000 tons to 12,000 tons. Nevertheless, in overall terms, the agricultural sector has not fulfilled expectations, and Libya continues to import around 80% of its food requirements, the value of which totalled US $1,117.3m. in 1987 (compared with $123.4m. in 1970). Problems, such as the lack of trained technicians and administrators and poor education among the farming communities, are not easily solved; Libya is obliged for the present to rely heavily on foreign expertise. The implementation of the various proposed agricultural projects has been particularly slow. In 1996 Libyan grain production amounted to some 360,000 tons, sufficient to supply about 20% of the country's cereal consumption.

Libya's most ambitious project is the so-called 'Great Manmade River' project (GMR), first announced in November 1983. Under the first stage of the irrigation and water-supply project, the Dong Ah Construction Industrial Co, from the Republic of Korea, was contracted to build a man-made river, at a cost of $3,300m., to carry 2m. cu m of water per day along 2,000 km of pipeline from natural underground reservoirs at Tazerbo and Sarir, in the south-east Sahara desert, to Sirte and Benghazi and agricultural projects and towns on the Mediterranean coast, via Agedabia. A total of 270 wells are being drilled in the Tazerbo and Sarir areas, with the aim of irrigating approximately 280,000 ha, on which some 37,000 model farms are to be established. This is possibly the largest single contract ever awarded in the Middle East, and its cost had risen to $4,200m. by 1986. The $5,300m. second stage of the GMR will eventually pipe 2m. cu m of water per day from Sawknah to Tripoli, a distance of 600 km. Three additional stages are planned, including the extension of the first phase southwards to Kufra oasis (doubling its capacity to 4m. cu m per day) and the construction of pipelines to serve the north-eastern coastal town of Tobruk (from Agedabia) and to link the eastern and western systems of the first two stages along the coast (Tripoli–Sirte),

thereby creating a national water grid. If all phases are completed, there will be a total of 4,040 km of pipeline, with a water-carrying capacity of 6m. cu m per day. The eventual cost of the GMR, including agricultural infrastructure, could be as high as $25,000m., and it is thought that Libya may have difficulties in paying for it, particularly following Saudi Arabia's refusal to contribute aid. In September 1989 the Dong Ah Construction Industrial Co was also awarded the main contract for the second stage of the GMR, on which it began preparatory road construction in mid-1990.

With 25% of the first phase still to be completed, the entire project came under review in March 1991, owing to various unforeseen problems, including the production of heavily contaminated water from some test pumping, as a result of collapsing well screens. Nevertheless, at a grand ceremony held near Benghazi on 28 August 1991 and attended by various Arab and African leaders, the first phase of the GMR was inaugurated by Col Qaddafi, who turned on a tap starting the flow of water into one of the project's reservoirs. The increase in Libya's oil revenues in 1990–91 had eased the burden of financing this priority project, which continued to be supported by a consortium of Arab banks. The Government also remained committed to the original objective that 80% of the water supplied by the GMR would be allocated to agriculture (which already accounted for 85% of total water consumption), despite evidence that, taking into account the real unit cost of irrigation water, the cost of using it to cultivate cereals was currently some six times the prevailing world market price. Another problem was shortage of labour for the newly-created agricultural land, in the light of which the Government hoped to attract large numbers of Egyptian and Moroccan nationals to work on GMR farms. Other uncertainties surrounded the post-inauguration cost and practicalities of maintaining the GMR, it being suggested in some quarters that the weaknesses of Libya's socio-political system would result in the project falling into disrepair. Among the special projects being assisted by the GMR Water Utilization Authority in mid-1991 were joint horticultural ventures with both private and state bodies from the Netherlands, in which particular emphasis was to be placed on the development of potato production for the lucrative north European market.

In mid-1993 the Dong Ah Construction Industrial Co, which had thus far completed 33% of the engineering and 20% of the construction work on its phase-two GMR contract, was instructed to modify certain pipeline routes and specifications in its future work schedule in ways which indicated a shift of priorities away from agricultural development in favour of accelerating the supply of water to coastal towns. The modifications effectively brought forward about half of the work originally included in phase three of the GMR plans, and would route an initial flow of 1.166m. cu m of water per day to the towns of Misurata and Khoms by 2000. Dong Ah, which at that time employed 10,000 staff on GMR projects, expected the modifications (costing an estimated $760m.) to add substantially to its labour requirement. At the Benghazi end of the GMR system, Dong Ah expected to link the Benghazi reservoir to the city's supply system by the end of the third quarter of 1993. The depletion rate of local groundwater sources in the Libyan coastal region was reported to be alarmingly high in 1993. By 1995 the GMR's phase-one transmission system was supplying Benghazi with 500,000 cu m of water per day, while further well-drilling was in progress to increase the volumes of water extracted at Sarir and Tazerbo. There was, however, no prospect of full utilization of the eastern trunk pipeline's transmission capacity of 2m. cu m per day until a planned network of branch pipelines was built to feed irrigation schemes. In 1995, agricultural usage of GMR water was restricted to a few small pilot schemes.

In 1995 the GMR's status as the centrepiece of Libya's economic development programme was highlighted by the inclusion in the national budget of allocations of $1,300m. for water transmission work and $300m. for associated irrigation projects. Dong Ah was now employing 13,000 people on GMR works in Libya, including 2,500 at a plant manufacturing the world's largest pipes (4 metres in diameter) and 4,000 involved in pipe-laying activities. Tripoli received its first supplies of GMR water via the western (phase-two) pipeline system at the beginning of September 1996. Final completion of phase two of the GMR project was scheduled for 1999. In all, the phase-two project specification, as modified in 1993, involved a total of 1,287 km of pipeline (of which 85% had been manufactured and about 70% had been laid by the start of 1996) with a daily transmission capacity of 2.5m. cu m of water drawn from 484 desert wells. The $310m. contract to drill the last 247 of these wells was awarded to Dong Ah in April 1996 for completion within two years. In the same month Col Qaddafi informed Dong Ah that it would be awarded the contracts to build phases three and four of the GMR once designs were finalized. Phase three was intended to link Tobruk (500 km to the east) and Kufra (325 km to the south) to the phase-one supply system and to create a 180-km coastal link between the phase-one system serving Sirte and the phase-two system serving Tripoli. Phase three had an estimated cost of $5,100m. and a target completion date of 2006. Phase four would involve the development of a new complex of desert wells at Waw al-Kabir, to be linked to Sirte via a 715-km pipeline system at an estimated cost of $4,900m. The total value of Dong Ah's past and existing GMR contracts amounted to $3,700m. for phase-one work and $6,700m. for phase-two work.

Despite having issued a letter of intent to Dong Ah in November 1996, Libya opened phase three of the GMR to international bidding in March 1997. The position was complicated by the severe difficulties experienced by Dong Ah's parent company in South Korea as a result of the Asian economic crisis. In December 1997 the French company Dumex was reported to be the lowest bidder for the first of seven contracts for phase three of the GMR project, involving construction of a water conveyance system from Sirte to As-Sadadah linking phases one and two. However, the slump in world oil prices in early 1998, and the consequential fall in Libyan oil revenues, served to delay the award of further GMR contracts.

Animal husbandry is the basis of farming in Libya and is likely to remain so until irrigation and reclamation measures really start to take effect. During the mid-1970s the breeding of cattle for dairy produce was expanded and livestock was imported on an increasing scale from a number of sources. Breeding cattle have been supplied by the United Kingdom, and stock-raising co-operation agreements signed with Argentina, Romania and Australia. There has also been a substantial expansion in camel and poultry numbers. In 1996 livestock farming contributed about half of the value of Libya's total agricultural output of $1,100m.

In July 1990 FAO held a special conference to raise funds to launch an emergency programme to eradicate from Libya the screw-worm fly, a parasitic insect which attacks livestock and wildlife. The fly was reported to have made its first appearance outside the western hemisphere in Libya some two years earlier, and the extent of its spread had raised fears that it would quickly infest the whole of the African continent. In January 1991 IFAD launched a $3m. pilot project as part of the programme, to which some $46m. had been pledged by February 1991. In October 1991 FAO was able to report that the screw-worm eradication programme in Libya had been successful and that the forecast continental infestation had been averted.

Of the cereal crops, barley, which is the staple diet of most of the population, is the most important, although, despite wide fluctuations from year to year in the yields of both crops, production of wheat now equals barley output. Olives and citrus fruit are grown mainly in the west of the country, and other important food crops are tomatoes, almonds, castor beans, groundnuts and potatoes, also grown mainly in the west. Dates are produced in oases in the south and on the coastal belt. As part of the Jebel al-Gharbi project, 1.5m. fig, olive and apple trees are to be planted, thus expanding the country's fruit production capacity. Esparto grass, which grows wild in the Jebel, is used for the manufacture of high-quality paper and banknotes and was formerly Libya's most important article of export.

The 1976–80 Development Plan envisaged an annual growth of 15.8% in domestic production, so that Libya would be self-sufficient in vegetables and dairy products by 1980 and would also be able to produce 92% of its fruit requirements and 75% of its meat and wheat consumption. However, these targets were too optimistic and were not achieved. In September 1984 Col Qaddafi said that, for climatic reasons, Libya had achieved only 66% self-sufficiency in wheat and barley and that 60% of meat and 40% of milk requirements were produced locally.

The Government is continuing to further land development and reform. Polish assistance has been used to develop new farms in eastern Libya and in 1986 the Government claimed that during the preceding 17 years the ownership of 14,853 farms had been transferred to farmers. An interesting development in the 1970s, and one that is practicable only in an oil-rich economy, was the growth of hydroponic farming.

Although the Government has attempted some desert reclamation and afforestation projects, many have proved to be based on over-optimistic estimates of long-term environmental potential and economic return. Government-financed irrigation projects, for example, have resulted in serious groundwater depletion in north-western Libya.

The offshore waters abound in fish, especially tunny and sardines, but most of the fishing is done by Italians, Greeks or Maltese. Of special importance are the sponge-beds along the wide continental shelf. These are exploited by foreign fishermen and divers, mainly Greeks from the Dodecanese. As part of the expansion of Libya's fishing industry, the Zliten fishing port was opened in October 1983 at a cost of $16.8m. It is designed for use by 40 trawlers and provides storage for 200 tons of fish, together with refrigeration facilities for up to 20 tons of fish per day. In early 1990 the Arab Fund for Economic and Social Development (AFESD) agreed to lend Libya 11m. Kuwaiti dinars for the construction of two fish canning factories. An $18m. project to construct a fishing harbour at Susa was due to be undertaken by Greek contractors in 1993–94. A $20m.-project to establish a fishing port at Marsa Zuaga with a capacity for 10 trawlers and up to 70 smaller boats was at an advanced planning stage in 1996. The Marine Wealth Secretariat planned eventually to establish up to 24 new fishing ports along the Libyan coast. In 1997 the greater part of a $66.9m. loan from the Islamic Development Bank was allocated to fisheries projects.

PETROLEUM

That petroleum was present in both Tripolitania and Cyrenaica had long been suspected and, for several years after Libya became independent, a large number of the bigger oil companies carried out geological surveys of the country. In 1955 a petroleum law came into force setting up a petroleum commission, which was empowered to grant concessions on a 50–50 profit-sharing basis, with parts of each concession being handed back to the Government after a given period. Under this law, concessions were granted to many US companies and to British, French and other foreign groups.

Important petroleum strikes first began to be made in 1957, and 10 years later Libya was already the fourth largest exporter in the world. The initial expansion of the Libyan petroleum industry was particularly rapid, owing to political stability, proximity to the Western European markets, and to the petroleum's lack of sulphur, which made it especially suitable for refining. The closure of the Suez Canal in 1967 was also an important factor in the growth of the industry. Production rose from 20,000 barrels per day (b/d) in 1962 to a peak of 3.3m. b/d in 1970, or 159.7m. metric tons in annual terms, equivalent to 13.6% of total output by OPEC members (then and future) and to 6.8% of world oil production. Output declined steadily to 71.3m. tons in 1975 (partly because of the reopening of the Suez Canal in 1974), rose again to 100.7m. tons in 1979, but then fell in the 1980s, reaching 47.9m. tons in 1987 (its lowest level since 1964), when Libya accounted for only 5% of OPEC production and 1.7% of world output. In 1988–89 a higher level of output was recorded, however. Production accelerated in 1990, as Libya took advantage of the rise in world oil prices caused by the 1990–91 Gulf crisis, and in mid-1993 the production level remained well above the depressed levels of the mid-1980s.

Oil is exported from five different sea terminals connected to the various fields by pipelines built by the five groups which have made the major finds. The pipeline system and the terminals are, however, available to other groups. The first of the five terminals to be opened was at Mersa Brega on the Gulf of Sirte, in 1961. The pipeline was built to Bir Zelten, in Cyrenaica, about 300 km south of Benghazi, where Esso Standard (Libya) had found oil in 1959. This group also operated a refinery at Mersa Brega and a gas liquefaction plant to prepare gas for shipment to Italy and Spain. The terminal for the Oasis group's Hofra field is at Ras as-Sidr, to the west of Mersa Brega. The Mobil/Gelsenberg group also found petroleum near Hofra, but built another pipeline to Ras Lanouf, just east of Ras as-Sidr. From a fourth terminal at Mersa al-Hariga, near Tobruk, a pipeline about 500 km long runs to Sarir, then the BP/Bunker Hunt concession. The terminal at Zuetina was opened in 1968 to serve the Augila and Idris fields. Here a US company, Occidental, which did not even obtain its concession until early in 1966, had found petroleum in large quantities. The Amoseas group, which produced petroleum from the Nafoora field, not far from Augila, had a pipeline connected to the Ras Lanouf terminal.

Libya has been a leader of those petroleum producers which demanded participation in petroleum activities, the National Oil Co (NOC) having been founded in 1968 for that express purpose. Extensive negotiations took place between the Libyan Government and the various petroleum producers in the early 1970s, with the result that, in 1973, the Libyan Government acquired a 51% share in the Libyan operations of Agip, Conoco/Marathon/Amerada Hess, Exxon, Mobil and Occidental, while it completely nationalized the holdings of Amoseas, BP/Bunker Hunt, Shell, Texaco, California Asiatic and Atlantic Richfield. Most outstanding claims by the companies were settled in 1977, following arbitration.

At the beginning of 1980, the experienced Secretary for Petroleum, Izzedin Mabrouk, was replaced by Abd as-Salam Muhammad Zagaar, for failing to accelerate full Libyanization of the oil industry. In a restructuring of the management of state oil concerns during the previous year, the NOC's operational responsibilities had been devolved to specialist subsidiary companies, leaving the NOC as a holding company responsible for strategic planning and supervision of the state oil sector. By the end of 1982 the Libyan state had an 81% interest in the Libyan operations of Elf Aquitaine, 59.2% in Oasis, 51% in Occidental and 50% in Agip. All of Exxon's Libyan interests were taken over by the state when the company withdrew in 1981, and, after a year's prevarication, Mobil, which first began operating in Libya in 1955, announced its withdrawal from exploration and production activities at the end of 1982. In mid-1985 Occidental agreed to sell 25% of its oil production and exploration facilities in Libya to the Austrian state oil company ÖMV AG. These holdings provided about one-half of Occidental's net income in 1979 and 1980, but the proportion fell to less than 20% of the total in 1984. By 1988, following the withdrawal of US companies from their Libyan operations (see below), the overall state share in oil output was 82%, with Italian, German, Austrian and French operators producing the remaining 18%.

During 1979 Libya aligned itself with Iran as a 'hawk' in terms of the international oil market, and at the beginning of 1980 raised its oil price by 28% to $30 per barrel, only to raise it to $34.50 two weeks later. A further increase in May brought the price to $36.12 per barrel. This aggressive pricing policy continued throughout 1980, and in January 1981, the price of top-grade Zuetina was raised to $41 per barrel. In 1979 Libya's export revenue from petroleum and derivatives totalled $16,000m., and in 1980 it amounted to a record $21,919m. With the world oil glut persisting, the price of Zuetina and Brega crude was lowered to $39.9 per barrel in mid-1981, but this was still higher than most other world oil prices. In the summer of 1981 BP suspended liftings of Libyan oil, owing to its high price, and the 'spot' market price of Libyan oil then fell rapidly to $33 per barrel. Total Libyan output declined to 58.7m. tons in 1981 (equivalent to 1.22m. b/d), while oil revenues fell to $15,500m.

During 1982 OPEC set Libya's production ceiling at 750,000 b/d but actual production averaged 1.135m. b/d (54.7m. tons in annual terms). At the end of 1982 spot prices for Libyan crude petroleum were as much as $4 per barrel below the official price. The March 1983 OPEC agreement gave Libya a quota of 1.1m. b/d, which represented some recognition of Libya's determination to continue with relatively high levels of production. The meeting set prices for Libyan oil at $30.5 per barrel for Brega 40° crude and $29.2 for Amna 36°. During most of 1983 Libya was producing only slightly more than the set OPEC quota, and the Government's eventual petroleum revenues for the year

were some $13,500m. The downward trend in oil prices on the spot market continued in 1984, during which Libyan production continued at just more than 1.1m. b/d. In October OPEC decided to reduce its collective production to 16m. b/d, as a result of which Libya accepted one of the largest quota reductions, of 990,000 b/d. The country dissociated itself from the OPEC agreement on a new price structure, which was reached in January 1985, and the cost of Libya's Brega blend was held at $30.40 per barrel. However, as a large proportion of Libyan sales at the time were accounted for by barter deals involving discounts, the fact that its official price remained unchanged was of limited significance. During 1985 Libya consistently exceeded its OPEC production quota (average output during the year was 1.11m. b/d), but petroleum revenues continued to decline, falling to about $10,000m. in 1985, from $13,000m. in 1984. As market prices fell in 1986, Libya, Iran and Algeria opposed OPEC's majority policy of abandoning production restraint and seeking a 'fair' share of the world market as compensation for lower prices, advocating instead reductions in production as a means to revive prices. Accordingly, Libyan production was reduced in 1986 to an average of 1.01m. b/d (49.9m. tons), effectively anticipating the reintroduction of an OPEC production ceiling in the last four months of the year, when Libya's quota averaged some 995,000 b/d. Nevertheless, a decline in spot prices to under $10 per barrel in mid-1986 led to a severe fall in Libya's oil revenues for the year, to about $5,000m.

Another important development in 1986 was the enforced withdrawal of US oil companies from Libya. Having banned imports of Libyan petroleum in 1982, the US Government complemented this with a ban on imports of petroleum products in November 1985. Then, in January 1986, convinced of Libya's involvement in international terrorism, President Reagan 'froze' Libyan assets in the USA, and ordered all commercial transactions between US companies and Libya to cease by the beginning of February. The instruction was modified in February to allow about one dozen US companies in Libya (including five oil companies with equity holdings there) to continue their operations for a transitional period, while they terminated their activities. The oil companies (Occidental, Conoco, Marathon, Amerada Hess and W. R. Grace) ceased operations in Libya on 30 June, the new deadline that President Reagan had set in May. A three-year 'standstill period' officially expired at the end of June 1989, but has continued to be observed by Libya as a means of exerting pressure for the repeal of the US sanctions. Amid reports of renewed negotiations between Libya and the US companies, the Libyan Secretary for Petroleum confirmed, in March 1991, that the Government had no plans to sell the US companies' assets in Libya, adding that the companies were free to resume operations at any time.

In December 1986 OPEC imposed a ceiling of 15.8m. b/d on collective production for the first half of 1987, incorporating a reduction of 7.25% in members' quotas, which, it was hoped, would support a fixed price for OPEC oil of $18 per barrel, which was applied from 1 February 1987. Libya's quota was reduced to 948,000 b/d. In June 1987 OPEC decided to retain the $18 reference price but to increase collective production by 800,000 b/d, to 16.6m. b/d, during the second half of the year, giving Libya a quota of 996,000 b/d. Although quota violations by some member states and the non-participation of Iraq made the ceiling on output a purely notional one, Libya's production in 1987 was close to its quota, at about 975,000 b/d (47.9m. tons in the year, its lowest output since 1964), and revenues fell below $5,000m. At meetings of OPEC held in December 1987 and May 1988, it was agreed to retain the output ceiling of 16.6m. b/d and the reference price of $18 per barrel for two further periods of six months, despite widespread quota violations, which had contributed to a renewed decline in the price of petroleum on the spot market. The price of the Brent blend, a widely traded North Sea crude (to which the Libyan blends Zuetina, Brega, Sirtica, es-Sidr, Sarir and Amna were linked in July 1988), declined to $11.20 per barrel in early September 1988. Libya's production of crude petroleum during 1988 averaged 1.055m. b/d (50.6m. tons), slightly above its OPEC quota, again yielding revenues of less than $5,000m. In November 1988 OPEC agreed to an output ceiling of 18.5m. b/d, to be imposed from January 1989. Libya's share of the total was to be 1.037m. b/d. In June 1989 oil ministers from OPEC member states met and agreed a new production ceiling of 19.5m. b/d, of which Libya was allocated a quota of 1.093m. b/d. Actual Libyan production in 1989 averaged 1.145m. b/d (54.8m. tons), yielding revenues of $7,846m., according to Libyan data. At the OPEC meeting of November 1989, quotas for the first half of 1990 were redistributed within a raised production ceiling of 22m. b/d, Libya's share being set at 1.233m. b/d. Actual Libyan output was, however, raised to 1.65m. b/d in early 1990 (allegedly to test sustainable production capacity), before being reduced to 1.35m. b/d from mid-March. At the OPEC meeting of July 1990, Libya pressed for quota parity with Kuwait but was again allocated 1.233m. b/d within an overall production ceiling of 22.5m. b/d, designed to underpin a minimum reference price of $21 per barrel.

However, the situation was then transformed by the onset of the Gulf crisis in August 1990 and by a rapid rise in world oil prices to more than $30 per barrel. Libya refused to attend an emergency OPEC meeting held in Vienna in late August, at which it was decided to suspend quotas to allow members to take advantage of the embargoes imposed on Iraqi and Kuwaiti oil production. While expressing opposition to this decision, Libya proceeded to raise its production as quickly as possible, to almost 1.5m. b/d by October, with the result that its total oil revenues in 1990 increased by 23%, compared with 1989, to $9,700m. The average production level for 1990 was 1.355m. b/d (the highest annual average since 1980). Following the end of the Gulf conflict in February 1991 and the stabilization of world oil prices at pre-crisis levels, OPEC reimposed quotas from the second quarter of 1991, Libya's allocation being 1.425m. b/d within an overall production ceiling of 22.3m. b/d. For 1992 Libya's OPEC quota was set at 1.409m. b/d, later reduced to 1.35m. b/d from 1 April 1993 and adjusted to 1.39m. b/d from 1 October 1993. Actual Libyan output averaged 1.54m. b/d in 1991 and 1.475m. b/d in 1992 (producing revenue of at least $10,000m. per year). During 1993 Libyan oil production averaged 1.4m. b/d, a level that was steadily maintained in the first half of 1994. The monthly average spot price of Brega crude, which had fallen from over $18 per barrel to under $14 per barrel during the course of 1993, had recovered to more than $16 per barrel by the second quarter of 1994. In 1994 Libyan oil output averaged 1.43m. b/d, rising slightly to 1.44m. b/d in 1995 and 1996. Libya's proven oil reserves (the largest of any African country) rose by nearly 30% in 1995 to 29,500m. barrels, sufficient to last for 56.4 years at the current rate of production.

In March 1989 the Petroleum Secretariat was revived, after a three-year period in which control of the oil industry had been in the hands of the national companies. The revived Petroleum Secretariat then drafted plans to reorganize and develop Libya's oil sector, which were implemented following the appointment as Secretary for Petroleum, in October 1990, of Abdullah al-Badri, hitherto Chairman of the NOC. The changes involved a drastic reduction of the NOC's powers and the elevation to a dominant role of the Secretariat for Petroleum, to which all state oil companies were now required to report directly.

Although there was an increase in exploration activity in the early 1980s, sharp reductions in oil revenues from 1986 onwards resulted in a decline not only in exploration but also in development work on discovered fields. Moreover, the deficiencies in expertise and technology resulting from the withdrawal of US operators in 1986 (and compounded by the subsequent imposition of sanctions by the USA on Libya) were only partially compensated by European, Canadian and Asian companies. Over the decade as a whole, only some 20% of current output was replaced by new proven reserves, while, as a result of poor state management, several established fields fell substantially below their theoretical production capacity.

Against this background, the Libyan authorities have, in the light of the 1990–91 Gulf crisis, re-emphasized the need for an active exploration campaign, to which LD 200m. (US $700m.) were allocated in the NOC's 1991/92 budget.

In particular, the Government is keen to evaluate the oil potential of parts of the country outside the Sirte Basin in north-central Libya, where the commercial fields are currently grouped. There are two main areas of interest—western Libya (formerly Tripolitania) and offshore, with particular stress on the Tripolitanian offshore. Indeed, exploration interest in areas off the Tripolitanian coast has been stimulated in recent years by

the discovery and successful development of the Bouri offshore oilfield, the largest so far discovered, in the Mediterranean, situated some 125 km north-west of Tripoli. Test production of 10,000 b/d at Bouri, Libya's first offshore oilfield (containing total reserves of up to 5,000m. barrels), began in August 1988, and output had risen to 75,000 b/d by mid-1990. In April 1989 Libya's NOC and the Tunisian state oil enterprise ETAP formed a Joint Oil Co (JOC) to exploit the '7 November' oilfield straddling the two countries' continental shelf boundary, but did not finalize a development programme until May 1997, when a production-sharing contract was awarded to a Saudi-Malaysian consortium. A subsidiary of Saudi Arabia's Nimr Petroleum Co held a 55% interest and was to act as operator. Nimr's partner in this venture was a subsidiary of the Malaysian state oil company Petronas. New exploration concessions awarded to, or under negotiations with, Canadian, British, Austrian, Yugoslav, South Korean and other companies in late 1990 and early 1991 included substantial offshore areas north-west of Tripoli.

Exploration also continues in other parts of the country, with some work being undertaken in the largely unexplored south. New finds continue to be made in the Sirte Basin, despite the intensive exploration of previous years. In 1976, Occidental brought the new Almas field into production and the Libyan Umm al-Jawaby company also had two commercial finds, one on the eastern side of the Sirte Basin and one on the west. In 1984 an oilfield with reserves estimated at 624m. barrels was discovered north-west of the Abu at-Tifl field.

In the Murzuk basin, in south-western Libya, Rompetrol of Romania was the original foreign contractor for the development of a new field (NC-115) with estimated reserves of up to 2,000m. barrels, exploitation of which will involve the construction of extensive oilfield storage facilities, some 900,000 barrels of new coastal storage facilities at Zawia, a new refinery at Sebha and a pipeline network to connect the new facilities. By 1993 implementation of this $1,000m. project (originally approved in 1989) was seriously behind schedule because of financial constraints, prompting Rompetrol to sell its stake in the NC-115 field to Spain's Repsol Exploración, which subsequently opened negotiations with the NOC on the terms of a formal transfer of development rights. Also being given priority were water-injection projects to increase output from certain established fields. These included the giant Sarir field in the Sirte basin, where production has seldom exceeded one-half of its capacity since nationalization but which was scheduled to be raised from a current output of 200,000 b/d to 600,000 b/d by 1994; the field was also to supply associated gas to power stations driving the GMR irrigation project (see Agriculture, above). In June 1992 ÖMV of Austria announced a promising new oil discovery in a block some 350 km south of Benghazi. It was officially claimed in 1994 that Libya was currently investing 23% of its oil revenues in oil exploration, production and development operations. In mid-1996 seven seismic crews were actively exploring for oil in Libya, compared with three or four crews in the previous year. Development of the Murzuk basin field NC-115 was meanwhile proceeding under the management of a consortium led by Repsol Exploración, which started commercial production in December 1996 and was expected to reach an output level of 200,000 b/d by the end of 1998. In June 1996 a 5,000-sq km concession in the Sirte basin was awarded to a consortium led by PanCanadian Petroleum, which undertook to spend $17m. on exploration over a period of five years.

In February 1998 UK operator Lasmo announced that a strike the previous year in the Murzuk basin was possibly the largest oil discovery in Libya since the mid-1980s. Designated the Elephant field, the discovery was thought to contain possible reserves of over 500m. barrels, it being hoped that production would begin in 1999 via the existing pipeline from Murzuk to the coast. Further finds were announced by Petrofina of Belgium in February 1998 and by Lundin Oil of Sweden in April. At the end of 1997 Libya's proven oil reserves stood at 29,500m. barrels, representing 2.8% of the Middle East and North Africa regional total and capable of sustaining production for 55.6 years at current average rates.

Libya's production of crude oil rose from an average of 1,415m. b/d in 1994 to 1,442m. b/d in 1997, slightly above its existing OPEC quota of 1,396m. b/d. Under an upward revision of OPEC output quotas decided in November 1997, Libya's share was increased to 1,522m. b/d, effective from January 1998. However, in light of the concurrent slump in world oil prices, Libya supported the emergency reduction in OPEC quotas decided in March, the Libyan cut being 80,000 b/d, to 1,442m. b/d (its actual production level in 1997). Having fallen to $8,300m. in 1997 (from $9,000m. in 1996), Libya's oil revenues were projected to decline further, to $6,000m., in 1998.

Libya's reserves of natural gas at the beginning of 1997 were estimated at 1,310,000m. cu m. Marketed gas output (excluding gas flared or reinjected into the oilwells from which most Libyan gas is derived) totalled 6,780m. cu m in 1992—its highest level since 1979. Output in 1996 was 6,200m. cu m. Inaugurated in 1971, a liquefaction plant at Mersa Brega was the world's first scheme to convert flared gas into liquefied natural gas (LNG), annual exports of which, mainly to Italy and Spain, reached more than 4,000m. cu m in the mid-1970s, although they fell to under 1,500m. cu m in the 1980s, as Italy switched to cheaper Algerian supplies by gas pipeline. Further trade with Italy became impractical in 1990, when the Italian LNG import terminal was converted to accept normal-grade LNG. Spain, which still has import facilities for the high-calorie LNG currently exported by Libya, now takes the greater part of Libya's LNG exports; a new 20-year contract, for the supply of at least 1,000m. cu m per year, was signed with Enagás of Spain in March 1991. Exports to Spain totalled 1,800m. cu m in 1992 and were predicted to reach 2,500m. cu m by 2000. A contract to supply Turkey with 1,500m. cu m of LNG over 25 years was signed in 1988, but implementation awaits the completion of a terminal at Marmara Ereglisi. Libya announced plans in 1993 to convert the Mersa Brega plant (which has a nominal daily capacity of 10.8m. cu m) to produce normal and low grades of LNG, rather than the high-calorie grade produced hitherto. However, when contractors who had submitted bids for this $200m.-project studied the latest UN sanctions on Libya, it was clear that it would be impossible to carry out the work without importing equipment included on the list of embargoed items. Eager to link its own gas network with that of Algeria, Libya, in 1990, initiated preparatory studies to extend its existing 670-km Mersa Brega–Homs coastal pipeline westward to the Tunisian border, with the eventual aim of linking up with the Algeria–Sicily pipeline running through Tunisia. The existing coastal pipeline had been completed by a Soviet company in 1988 and had opened in September 1989, with a capacity of 4m. cu m per year. At the same time, the concept of a direct pipeline linking Libya to Italy remained under consideration, despite previous assessments that its cost would be prohibitive. In December 1990 it was confirmed that Agip of Italy and the NOC were engaged in feasibility studies for a direct pipeline, which could form part of a massive gas development programme in Libya, costing up to US $13,000m. Meanwhile, the NOC's priority plans included the development of the Kabir gas field close to the Tunisian border, at an estimated cost of $80m., and the use of gas output from other fields to fuel the GMR irrigation project. In mid-1992 the French company Total signed a contract to take 300,000 tons of liquefied petroleum gas from Libya starting in 1993 (the personal authorization of President Mitterrand was needed in view of the current UN sanctions against Libya). Agip revealed in March 1996 that it had drawn up plans to build a sub-sea pipeline to transport 8,000m. cu m of gas per year from Libya to Italy. In June 1996 (shortly before the implementation of the US 'secondary sanctions' legislation) Agip signed an addendum to a 1974 agreement with the NOC to cover gas development in onshore and offshore fields, the onshore gas to be marketed within Libya and the offshore gas to be piped to Italy. It was estimated that the export project would entail an investment of $3,500m. and would take four years to complete. Agip said in January 1997 that it had concluded 20-year sales agreements with Italian buyers for the full 8,000m. cu m which it planned to export each year. In June 1997 detailed feasibility studies were on schedule for completion within six months. Because its development rights stemmed from agreements dating back to 1974, Agip said that it did not consider its Libyan gas development programme to be open to challenge as a 'new investment' under US sanctions laws.

In further gas development activity in 1998, bids were submitted to the Sirte Oil Company in June for the construction of a 160-km gas pipeline from Homs to Tripoli with a capacity of about 10m. cu m per day. Also involving the construction of two compressor stations, one to feed a power plant and the other a cement factory, the contract had an estimated value of $200m. The Sirte Oil Company was also negotiating with several companies for the construction of a 150-km gas pipeline from Zueitina to Benghazi, also at an estimated cost of $200m.

On the marketing side, Libya has concluded various agreements involving the exchange of crude petroleum for specific goods or services. During recent years, France, Italy, Poland, the USSR, Yugoslavia and a number of other countries concluded barter deals with Libya, involving purchases of petroleum. Libya also has special petroleum arrangements with Brazil and Greece, and, together with Algeria, Nigeria and Gabon, remains theoretically committed to reserve 4% of its output for delivery to African states. Libya's attempts to establish itself in the 'downstream' marketing of oil products in developed countries have included the purchase, in 1986, of a 70% stake in the Italian Tamoil group, which subsequently provided an important overseas marketing outlet when the international oil glut developed in the late 1980s. Such overseas marketing investments are directed by the state-owned Oil Investments International Co (Oilinvest), established in 1988, while sales are effected through Chempetrol, a wholly-owned subsidiary, based in Malta.

In common with other large oil producers, Libya would much prefer to refine and process its own oil, rather than export it in the crude state. Owing to its freedom from sulphur, Libya's oil is particularly suited to refining. A report by the General People's Committee for Economies and Planning, published in June 1985, stated that, since 1970, 56 chemical projects and 21 oil refineries, capable of producing 5.7m. tons of petroleum products per year, had been completed. Zawia refinery was opened in 1974, enlarged in 1977, and has a capacity of 120,000 b/d. An upgrading programme was in preparation in 1993. The other main refinery locations are at Tobruk, where a refinery with a capacity of 20,000 b/d was opened in 1986, and Ras Lanouf. Previously supplied by tanker with crude petroleum shipped from Mersa Brega, the Zawia refinery will eventually draw all of its materials from fields near the Algerian frontier. The country's largest oil refinery, at Ras Lanouf, which was begun by Italian contractors in 1978, finally started production in February 1985 and had a capacity of 201,000 b/d at 1 January 1988, compared with planned capacity of 220,000 b/d. At the end of 1989 Libya had a total installed refinery capacity of 380,000 b/d, having achieved an output of refined products in 1988 of 255,600 b/d, of which 110,000 b/d were consumed domestically. Plans were announced in 1991 to build a refinery at Hymed, to be supplied from the Bouri offshore field. In the following year plans were announced for a 20,000 b/d refinery at Sebha to process crude from oilfields under development in the Murzuk basin.

In the petrochemical sphere, NOC has built one ammonia plant and one ethanol plant, each with a capacity of 1,000 tons per day, at Mersa Brega. These came into production in September 1977. In 1978 NOC awarded a contract worth $150m. to an Italian company for the construction of a new ammonia plant, with a capacity of 1,000 tons per day, at Mersa Brega. A further $150m. contract has been granted at Mersa Brega for a urea plant with a capacity of 1,000 tons per day. (Most of the urea currently produced in Libya is exported to China, India, Turkey and Italy.) Sited near Exxon's LNG plant, the new units will process natural gas and are expected to make Mersa Brega the country's foremost centre for the production of petrochemicals. Local methanol production capacity, most of which is located at the Mersa Brega complex, was supplemented by the inauguration in September 1987 of a factory at al-Burayqah with a capacity of 2,000 tons per day. Libyan methanol production totalled 660,000 tons in 1987. In 1980 an Italian firm received a contract worth $60m. for the construction of an ethylene plant with a capacity of 330,000 tons per year at the Ras Lanouf refinery and petrochemical complex, and this, comprising, with the refinery, the first phase of the Ras Lanouf development, began production in 1987. A US company signed a contract for a monoethylene glycol plant at the same refinery. In addition, the contract for a 1,750 tons-per-day urea plant was won by a joint Federal German/Italian venture. The Abu

Kammash chemical complex was opened in September 1980. Reductions in government revenues from petroleum in the 1980s necessitated some rationalization of the plans for the Ras Lanouf project, which is co-ordinated by the Ras Lanouf Oil and Gas Processing Co (Rasco). In early 1993 a $130m. second-phase development contract, awarded in 1990 to a consortium from former Yugoslavia, was cancelled on grounds of non-performance and the work reopened to new tenders. Rasco's third-phase development project, involving the construction by South Korea's Hyudai Engineering and Construction Co of two 80,000 tons-per-year units to produce high-density and low-density polyethylene, was 20% complete by mid-1993. Plans were also in hand to build a 68,000 tons-per-year polypropylene plant.

INDUSTRY

Manufacturing in Libya has been largely confined to the processing of local agricultural products and such traditional crafts as carpet weaving, tanning and leather working and shoe making. Plans were made several years ago for a whole range of factories to make such diverse articles as prefabricated construction materials, cables, glass, pharmaceuticals, woollen and synthetic textiles, among others. Most of these factories did not get past the tendering stage, but efforts have been made, in successive development plans since the 1970s, to diversify the non-oil sector of industry and to increase its contribution to GNP.

Contracts for industrial plants have in the past been awarded mainly to Western European and US companies, but Japanese firms are becoming more active in Libya. Under the 1981–85 Development Plan, LD 1,200m. (of the total investment figure of $62,500m.) were allocated to light industry. Notwithstanding its support for smaller projects, the Government has given more attention, and resources, to a few major ventures in heavy industry and in infrastructure development. In January 1975 Col Qaddafi announced that Libya had plans for the establishment of a heavy industry sector involving vehicle and tractor assembly plants, shipbuilding and iron and steel works. In this context the master plan for the Misurata industrial city, due to house 180,000 people at a cost of $1,290m., was submitted in September 1979.

According to the OPEC news agency, some $62,500m. were spent by Libya between 1970 and 1983 to develop industry and reduce the country's dependence on the petroleum sector. The result has been that the value of non-oil production activities rose from $1,610m. in 1970 to $15,280m. in 1983, and their contribution to GDP from 37% to 50%, reducing the share of the petroleum sector from 63% to 50%. An economic report covering the years 1970–86, which was released by JANA, the Libyan news agency, in September 1986, claimed that investment in the industrial sector during the period totalled LD 3,959.8m., enabling 139 projects to reach the production stage (52 food industry projects; 23 chemical and petrochemical industry factories; 17 mineral and engineering industry factories; 16 textile, clothing and leather goods factories; eight wood and paper industry factories). However, as oil revenues declined in the 1980s, the industrial sector, in common with other parts of the economy, suffered from underspending compared with budgeted figures. Although heavy industry traditionally attracts the largest proportion of total development investment, actual spending in this sector in 1983, 1984 and 1985 was, respectively, 96.2%, 84.4% and 83.4% of the budgeted allocation. Light industry was even more seriously affected, with expenditure on the sector in the three years in question reaching only 74.6%, 76.5% and 75% of the budgeted level. (No official figures have been issued in recent years.)

Iron ore reserves, estimated at over 700m. metric tons, were discovered in 1974 at Wadi Shatti, in southern Libya, and plans for their exploitation are under way. Work was initially planned to begin in November 1979 on the construction of a steelworks at Misurata for completion in 1985 at a cost of some $1,000m. However, it was not until 1981 that Libya started awarding contracts for the Misurata steelworks. Kobe Steel of Japan was awarded a contract worth $751m. for a section mill and a rod mill; a consortium of Korf Engineering of the Federal Republic of Germany and Voest Alpine of Austria won a $540m. contract for a steel production plant, while a $674m. contract for a second production plant was won by Friedrich Krupp of Federal Germany; and two consortia, both led by Voest Alpine, won

contracts for hot and cold rolling mills. In 1982 the Hyundai Engineering and Construction Co of South Korea won a contract worth $520m. to build a 480-MW power station and a desalination plant, with a capacity of 31,500 cu m per day, to serve the steel complex. However, the repeated deferment of payments to contractors, caused by declining oil revenues, seriously delayed work on the project, which did not start full operations until September 1990. A 900-km railway is also to be built, linking the iron ore mines in the south to Misurata. The contract for a port to handle imports of iron ore was won by Sezai Türkes Feyzi of Turkey. It was originally planned that subsequent developments would increase production at Misurata to 5m. and 7m. tons per year (by 2005). However, in view of the shortage of revenue from petroleum to fund this expansion, these plans were deferred. The proposals to build a town to house 50,000 people at Misurata were scaled down, envisaging an initial phase to house 20,000 people, with possible later stages bringing the population to 40,000. In late 1990 all the production units at the Misurata steel plant were reported to be operating, employing 3,500 Libyan nationals and 1,000 expatriate workers.

In 1991 the Misurata complex operated at about two-thirds of design capacity, producing an estimated 800,000 tons of steel during that year. A $224m.-contract to add a 650,000 tons-per-year direct reduction plant, which would increase total capacity at Misurata to nearly 2m. tons per year, was awarded in January 1993 to a consortium led by Voest Alpine, but it was not until October 1994 that the consortium secured a down-payment which enabled it to schedule the start of construction for early 1995. Most of the new plant's output of hot briquetted iron was to be exported to Italy and Spain. In the first nine months of 1993 raw steel output at Misurata totalled 709,000 tons, nearly one-third more than in the corresponding period of 1992. A contract to build a 400,000 tons-per-year reinforcing bar mill was awarded in early 1994 to an Italian company which planned to begin construction before the end of 1995 if acceptable payment arrangements were in place at that time. In March 1997 the technical director of the Libyan Company for Iron and Steel announced that Libya was seeking foreign joint-venture partners for the development of iron-ore mining at Wadi Shatti.

In 1983 plans were announced for the construction of a 120,000 tons-per-year aluminium smelter complex at Zuwara, 120 km west of Tripoli, at a cost of $1,250m. to be run by a joint company, Libal, formed by Yugoslavia's Energoinvest and Libya's heavy industries secretariat. Eventually it is hoped that a petroleum coke plant and an associated industrial port will be built at Zuwara. Under an agreement signed by Algeria and Libya in July 1987, Algeria was to have constructed a pipeline, via Tunisia, to supply an 800-MW power station forming part of the Zuwara smelting complex. However, the smelter project was postponed in 1987, pending a revival in Libya's revenues from sales of oil, on which it depends to finance industrial development. At the end of 1982 plans were revived to build a $1,000m. fertilizer complex at Sirte in two stages. Talks with the USSR on the construction of the delayed first stage began at the end of 1984, and it was hoped that it would come into production by the end of 1987. However, the second stage of the Sirte complex was postponed in April 1986, and the first stage was itself postponed in 1987, owing to the decline in oil revenues. The contractors (from the United Kingdom, Italy, Spain, the Federal Republic of Germany and the Republic of Korea) blamed the postponement on the abrupt fall in the price of oil, and the consequent shortage of funds. A second urea plant capable of producing 1,850 tons of fertilizer per day was opened at the new town of al-Brega in September 1984.

The construction work carried out under the development programme gave rise to a rapidly increasing demand for cement. In 1987 cement production rose by 30%, compared with 1986, to 2.7m. tons, some 2m. tons less than the domestic requirement and more than 3m. less than rated capacity. In 1995 Libyan cement production exceeded local demand, with the surplus being exported to Egypt and Algeria. In November 1995 plans were announced to add 3,300 tons per day of new production capacity to a cement works at Zliten in order to meet an expected growth in demand when the GMR project entered its next phase. The Danish company FLOTEC was awarded a contract in October 1985 to build a gypsum factory. The gypsum, which is used in cement production, will be exported to Europe. The project includes the establishment of a natural gas energy plant at the factory and terminal facilities at the port of Tripoli. Other industrial diversification projects signed in 1991–92 included one with Candy Elettrodomestici of Italy for a refrigerator construction plant at Zuwara with a projected capacity of 80,000 units a year, and another with Gold Star of South Korea for a video-cassette recorder factory at Benghazi with a capacity of 70,000 recorders a year. A truck assembly plant at Tripoli, owned 75% by the Libyan Government and 25% by Iveco Fiat of Italy, produced 2,961 vehicles in 1993. Investment of $120m. was planned to increase the proportion of locally manufactured components to 40% by 1997 and to achieve a production volume of 4,000 vehicles in that year. Over 20,000 passenger cars were scheduled to be imported into Libya from South Korea and Japan in 1995. Daewoo Corpn (the South Korean supplier) was believed to have examined the feasibility of establishing a Libyan assembly plant and found that it would not be possible to match the current prices for imported cars. In mid-1997 Libya was involved in separate talks with prospective Egyptian and Moroccan partners, with a view to establishing car assembly plants. A large pharmaceuticals plant, built by a Libyan state company in co-operation with Egyptian and Moroccan companies, opened at Rabta in September 1995.

Many of the contracts at the peak of the construction boom in the 1970s were awarded to Turkish firms. In 1981 there were 102 Turkish companies operating in Libya, with an estimated 80,000 Turkish workers. Falling oil revenues, though, forced Libya to inform Turkey early in 1982 that it wanted to deduct $70m. in oil debts from $100m. owed to various Turkish firms. By early 1991 debts owed to Turkish contractors had reached some $600m., adversely affecting Libyan–Turkish relations, which remained strained until the following year, when a schedule of oil deliveries in lieu of debt payments was agreed in bilateral talks. By January 1995 (previously the target date for full repayment) Libya's outstanding debts to Turkish contractors were reported to have been reduced to $180m. In October 1996 Turkish government officials said that total payments arrears totalled $600m. (of which $160m. was principal and the remainder interest charges and other costs), for which the Libyan Government had issued promissory notes after a visit to Tripoli by the Turkish Prime Minister. These notes were to be honoured within three months, although it was not clear whether all payments would be made in convertible currency. The Turkish Contractors Association said in October 1996 that its members had so far carried out a total of $6,880m. worth of work in Libya and were currently contracted to work on projects worth $1,650m. South Korean companies, such as the Daewoo Corpn, have also been involved in the implementation of new contracts in Libya. In May 1981 100 South Korean dockers were used to clear severe congestion at Benghazi port. The Daewoo Corpn was awarded a $337m. contract in 1985 to build sewer and water facilities, roads, pumping stations and a telephone system in Benghazi. The employment of Indian workers in Libya declined from 40,000 in the early 1980s to around 10,000 in the early 1990s, many Indian contractors having pulled out after disputes over non-payment for work carried out. In April 1995 the Libyan authorities agreed to settle $100m. of claims by Indian companies (most of them state-owned) over the next 12 months and to increase the recruitment of Indian workers in the future. At the end of 1996, when the contract to expand cement capacity at Zliten (see above) was awarded to an Iranian company, it was reported that Iranian companies were involved in negotiations for several other Libyan contracts, including reservoir and water pipeline building, railway and tramway schemes and a cattle-rearing project.

Infrastructure expenditure has put great emphasis on power generation. Since 1974 the Government has awarded several large contracts for power stations, some in association with desalination plants. During the 1976–80 period $3,195m. were spent on power schemes. Installed generating capacity rose from 879 MW in 1975 to 1,700 MW in 1979. Under the 1980–85 plan, capacity was projected to increase from 1,950 MW to 3,878 MW. However, there have been delays in power station construction schemes, owing to lack of finance, and, according to the UN, installed capacity had declined to 1,460 MW in 1985. In 1982 an agreement was concluded with the USSR, designed

to help to establish a national electricity grid by 1995. A 10-MW Soviet nuclear research reactor became operational at Tajura, near Tripoli, in 1982, but subsequent plans to develop a major nuclear generating plant were shelved in the mid-1980s. Work was expected to start in late 1993 on a three-year project to add more than 1,000 MW of new gas-turbine generating capacity at five Libyan power stations, several of them scheduled for expansion since the mid-1980s. The AFESD announced a $107m. loan package in April 1996, partly to finance improvements in Tripoli's power distribution system and partly to finance the construction of a connection to the Egyptian electricity grid. The cross-border power line (between As-Saloum in Egypt and Tobruk in Libya) was scheduled for completion by the end of 1997. Preparations were ongoing in 1997 for the construction of new gas pipelines in connection with the expansion of Libya's gas-fired power generating capacity.

Scarcity of water is a continuing problem, and in 1982, in addition to the GMR project (see Agriculture, above), plans were announced for a 462,000 cu m-per-day desalination plant (Tripoli 1) to provide Tripoli with drinking water. Plans for a further 150,000 cu m-per-day desalination plant at Janzour, 20 km west of Tripoli, were also announced at the end of 1982. The site of Tripoli 1 was moved to Janzour in mid-1984. A water purification plant in Tobruk, with a daily capacity of 5,000 cu m for agricultural purposes (from 13,000 cu m of sewage), was inaugurated in April 1988. Plans for the power and water complex at Zuweitina (Zuetina), initially due to have been completed in 1987, have now been scaled down from a planned capacity of 40,000 cu m of water per day to 20,000 cu m, although still maintaining a power capacity of 720 MW. Bids for a further desalination plant, at the Zawia oil refinery, were submitted in October 1991 by Italian, Dutch and German companies. In 1993 the Hyundai Engineering and Construction Co signed a letter of intent to build Libya's largest power and desalination complex at Sirte. Costing an estimated $1,600m. and designed to provide 1,260 MW of generating capacity and 20,000 cu m per day of desalination capacity, this project had formed part of Libya's development plans since the early 1980s, when its intended location was Mlita, west of Tripoli. Having failed to finalize a contract on the basis of the 1993 letter of intent, the Libyan Government invited fresh bids for the Sirte complex in 1997.

In November 1995 the Government announced its intention to commission comprehensive five-year 'infrastructural master-plans' for several regions of Libya from international consultancy firms. In March 1996 Russia (which was currently negotiating terms for the settlement of debts owed by Libya) declared a willingness to participate in infrastructural joint-venture projects worth a total of more than $10,000m., particular areas of interest being railway building, power generation and transmission, gas pipeline repair and the upgrading of industrial plants.

TRANSPORT AND COMMUNICATIONS

As might be expected, the large and increasing volume of imports has led to severe congestion at the main ports of Tripoli and Benghazi. Worsening port conditions have resulted in increases in surcharges. In addition, Darna and Misurata ports are being reconstructed. Tripoli, Mersa Brega and Benghazi are undergoing large-scale expansion. In 1986, according to the Libyan news agency, JANA, the handling capacity of the nation's ports was 9.5m. tons.

Port expansion is necessarily a long-term process and the development of rail, road and to some extent air freight is very important. There is an extensive road-building programme, and a number of large road-building contracts, such as the Sebha-Wadden road and the Mirzuk link, were awarded to Egyptian companies. In 1980 an Indian company won a $129m.-contract for the construction of desert roads at a variety of locations throughout the country. The road from Tripoli to Sebha was opened at the end of 1983, providing 770 km of metalled surface. In September 1986 the Government claimed to have built 10,990 km of paved roads, and 6,250 km of rural roads during the preceding 17 years. There have been no railways in Libya since 1964, when the Benghazi-Barce line was abandoned, but during 1981 and 1982 plans were developed to link Tripoli with Tunisia, and to establish rail connections from Tripoli and Sebha to Misurata, and from Benghazi to Tobruk and Agedabia with a view eventually to the development of a national railway network of about 3,000 km in length. Following the *rapprochement* with Egypt in 1989, plans for bilateral co-operation included the construction of a 180-km rail link between the Egyptian border town of Salloun and Tobruk. In October 1994 the Libyan news agency announced that construction of the Salloun–Tobruk line had begun and that the start of work was 'imminent' on a line from Tripoli to Ras Adjir on the Tunisian border.

A new stage of railway development, for which tenders were expected to be invited in the second half of 1998, involved plans to construct 2,178 km of track running east to west and 992 km running north to south. The first phase of the project would be a 700-km rail link between Ras Jedir on the Tunisian border and Sirte on the Mediterranean coast, followed in the second phase by a line between Sirte and Omsaad on the Egyptian border. In mid-1998 talks were in progress between Libyan, Tunisian and Egyptian officials on linking the railway networks of the three countries.

The UN ban on international flights to Libya, which in April 1992 effectively shut down the international operations of the national carrier, Libyan Arab Airlines, led to increased use of airports in neighbouring countries. There was particularly strong demand for flights from Tunis (now the nearest available international airport to Tripoli) to the Tunisian island of Djerba, which is linked to Libya by a ferry service. Major users of this route included South Korean contractors working on large Libyan development projects, who were able to take advantage of regular Korean Airways flights into Tunis.

As part of Libya's aim to create a comprehensive telecommunications network, in mid-1991 Swedish companies were awarded contracts for new installations in the south-west of the country; however, other parts of the programme, notably plans for 20 new exchanges and 182,000 extra lines in Tripoli and Benghazi, were not finalized until mid-1993.

EXTERNAL TRADE

Until production of oil began, Libya's exports consisted almost entirely of agricultural products, and its imports of manufactured goods. In 1960, for instance, imports were valued at LD 60.4m. and exports at LD 4.0m., leaving an adverse balance of LD 56.4m. (although LD 21m. of the total value of imports in 1960 was accounted for by goods imported for the account of the petroleum companies). Petroleum was first exported in the autumn of 1961, and by 1969, according to IMF data, imports totalled LD 241.3m. and exports LD 937.9m., of which LD 936.5m. was officially accounted for by crude petroleum. Although there were fluctuations within the overall trend, petroleum exports rose from LD 2,109.5m. in 1974 to LD 4,419.2m. in 1979, when they represented 99% of all Libyan exports by volume. The minute proportion of remaining exports were mainly hides and skins, groundnuts, almonds, metal scrap and re-exports.

Imports consist of a wide variety of manufactured goods, such as textiles, motor vehicles and luxury consumer goods. In the last few years imports of timber, chemicals and raw materials and, in particular, cement and building materials, have been stepped up. In addition, many foodstuffs have to be imported, for example tea, sugar, coffee and, in years of drought, wheat and flour. The value of imports increased by over 500% betweeen 1971 and 1979, from LD 250.4m. to LD 1,572m., whereas over the same period exports by value grew by 400%.

Since petroleum has been exported, Libya has experienced a considerable trade surplus. In 1971 exports f.o.b. (including re-exports) were valued at LD 962.5m., and imports c.i.f. at LD 250.4m., leaving a trade surplus of LD 712.1m. The general trend of increasing surpluses continued during the 1970s, and in 1980, when Libya's imports totalled LD 2,006.2m., and its exports LD 6,489.2m., a trade surplus of LD 4,483m., was recorded. Declining demand and lower prices for petroleum reduced the trade surplus to LD 2,129.8m. in 1981, and to LD 2,006.7m. in 1982. The value of exports fell to LD 3,283m. in 1983 (imports LD 1,989.5m.), and stabilized at LD 3,295.4m. in 1984 (imports LD 1,811.8m.), but fell to LD 3,235.2m. ($10,841m.) in 1985 (imports LD 1,444.7m.), of which exports of crude petroleum accounted for LD 3,234.2m. The value of imports declined to LD 1,279m. in 1986, rising slightly, to LD 1,293.2m., in 1987. Estimated exports in 1989 totalled

US $7,320m., surpassing imports of $6,460m., a pattern which continued in 1990 (exports $11,530m., imports $7,250m.) and was forecast to be maintained in 1991 (projected exports $10,260m., projected imports $7,970m.). Libya had an estimated trade surplus of $3,300m. in 1993 (exports $10,000m., imports $6,700m.); $1,400m. in 1994 (exports $7,700m., imports $6,300m.); $3,600m. in 1995 (exports $10,100m., imports $6,500m.) and $4,700m. in 1996 (exports $11,400m., imports $6,700m.).

In 1982 Italy (with 25.4% of total imports by value) was Libya's main supplier, followed by the Federal Republic of Germany (14.4%) and the United Kingdom (8%). In 1981 the USA (with 27.4% of Libyan exports by value), Italy (23.8%), the Federal Republic of Germany (10.3%) and Spain (6.7%) were the principal customers for Libyan exports (almost exclusively, crude petroleum). In 1977 the USA took 25% of Libya's oil exports. The USA and Western Europe together accounted for almost 90% of total oil exports from Libya. However, in 1982 all imports of Libyan petroleum to the USA were banned. Libyan imports from the USA fell by $500m. from the level of $831m. in 1981. In January 1986, convinced of Libya's involvement in promoting international terrorism, President Reagan banned all trade between the USA and Libya. The USA succeeded in persuading some of its allies to reduce sharply their purchases of Libyan oil after the bombing of Tripoli and Benghazi in April 1986, but Italy, by far the largest customer for Libyan oil, actually increased its imports. The US embargo on bilateral trade with Libya reduced Libyan imports from the USA to $46.2m. in 1986, while Libyan exports to the USA amounted to a mere $1.6m.

As Libyan debts accumulated, imports from West European countries were also much reduced. Italian companies claimed outstanding credits of about $500m. from Libya in 1984. An agreement between Libya and Italy in August 1984 failed to solve the credits issue, and a new agreement was signed in Rome in July 1985. Several countries, including India, Turkey and Uganda, have accepted oil as payment for goods or debts owed to them by Libya. The Swedish export credit agency reached an agreement in 1991 under which it had recovered approximately $30m. through oil purchase arrangements by mid-1994. Libya agreed in July 1995 to settle $48m. of official debt to Bulgaria and to work towards a formula for the settlement of claims of $300m. by Bulgarian companies. Bulgarian trade with Libya had declined from $360m. in 1990 to $8m. in 1994. The Hungarian Government was reported in mid-1995 to be preparing an official approach to Libya on behalf of Hungarian companies which were owed $45m. for work carried out and goods supplied.

In the late 1980s imports from Japan showed a rapid rise, from $296m. in 1987 to $602m. in 1988, while exports to Japan rose from virtually zero in 1987 to more than $600m. in 1989. Libya remained Italy's largest regional trading partner in 1990, supplying exports (mainly oil) of $4,700m. and taking Italian exports of $1,083m. Following the Gulf crisis of 1990–91, Libya's efforts to improve relations with Western Europe were encouraged by the visit of the Italian Prime Minister in June 1991 (the first by an EC Head of Government for more than 10 years), when an agreement was signed with the objective of increasing bilateral trade and Italian participation in Libyan development projects, such as the GMR irrigation scheme (see Agriculture, above). After Italy, Libya's most important trading partners are Germany (to which Libyan exports in 1990 increased to $2,186m., compared with imports of $1,622m.), Spain (Libyan exports in 1990 of $1,163m., imports of $776m.) and France (Libyan exports in 1990 of $762m., imports of $466m.). By 1996 Libyan exports to Italy had reached $6,987m., while imports from Italy totalled $1,567m. In 1997 French imports from Libya were valued at $476m. and exports to Libya at $352m.

FINANCE

Before the 1969 coup most Libyan banks were subsidiaries of foreign banks. However, among the first decrees issued by the Revolution Council was one which required 51% of the capital of all banks operating in Libya to be owned by Libyans; the majority of directors, including the chairman, of each bank had to be Libyan citizens. Under the monarchy the Government had followed a similar policy without compulsion, and a number of foreign banks had accordingly already 'Libyanized' themselves. In December 1970 all commercial banks were nationalized, with government participation set at 51%.

In March 1993 legislation was passed authorizing Libyan citizens and companies to establish privately owned commercial banks with a minimum capitalization of LD 10m. ($37m.). Under the same law, Libyan nationals were permitted to apply to the Central Bank of Libya for authorization to hold foreign currency in local bank accounts and to make unrestricted use of such holdings. The heavily overvalued Libyan dinar was currently being unofficially traded for convertible currencies at about one-sixth of its official exchange rate (which had been pegged to the IMF's special drawing right since 1986). Speaking in May 1993, Col Qaddafi said that he favoured a move towards full convertibility of the Libyan dinar at such time as 'there was adequate production' in the Libyan economy to prevent 'catastrophic' consequences.

In early November 1994 the Central Bank devalued the official exchange rate by 15.5%, from $1 = LD 0.299 to $1 = LD 0.354, this being the fourth change in the official rate since 1992. The currency remained heavily overvalued, as its unofficial exchange rate was currently about $1 = LD 3. Later the same month the Central Bank introduced a second-tier official rate of $1 = LD 1.019 'for use by local companies'. Also in November 1994 a consortium of seven local banks set up a new financial services company in Tripoli to meet the foreign currency requirements of travellers, using exchange rates 'set by supply and demand'. In early 1995 it was reported that a widening gap between official and unofficial exchange rates in Libya was pushing up the rate of price inflation, which, according to some estimates, was as high as 50%, compared with an estimated 15% in 1994. In late 1995 the unofficial exchange rate was reported to be averaging about $1 = LD 3.40. Price inflation affected mainly the growing range of 'non-essential' items whose importation was now handled by private-sector companies with little or no access to foreign exchange at the official rate. The officially recorded rates of price inflation were 4.5% in 1994 and 6% in 1995. The estimated rate of inflation in 1996 was 5.8%. In an address to the General People's Congress in March 1997, Col Qaddafi acknowledged that the unofficial exchange rate at that time, of about $1=LD 3, represented a 'realistic' basis for foreign exchange transactions. However, the Central Bank's main official exchange rate was not devalued at that stage and it stood at $1=LD 0.38 in September 1997.

The growth in petroleum revenue in the 1970s allowed the Government to devote about one-half of its income to development expenditure, although this proportion declined in the 1980s, as oil revenues fell. Libya also gave generous aid abroad, in particular to the People's Democratic Republic of Yemen (PDRY), Egypt, Syria and Jordan, although the Government was somewhat capricious in implementing aid agreements. Aid was cut off from the Jordanian Government in September 1970 when it attacked the Palestinian guerrillas. Egypt was criticized over its conduct of the war with Israel and in 1974 Libya demanded the return of a loan to Sudan. Aid to Egypt was suspended as a result of Egypt's signing the peace treaty with Israel in March 1979. There is no comparable organization in Libya to the Kuwait Fund for Arab Economic Development (KFAED), but in 1974 Libya made a contribution to the Islamic Development Bank. In 1980 Libyan aid to developing countries was $281m., equivalent to 0.92% of GNP. This compares with the $261m. that was given in 1975, which then represented 2.3% of GNP.

Developments in the Libyan banking sector included the establishment of joint development banks with Algeria and Turkey and an agreement to establish a Libyan-Mali bank. In 1977 the Libyan Arab Foreign Bank (LAFB)—effectively the 'offshore' arm of the Central Bank of Libya, and a key institution in Libyan trade finance—bought a 15.2% stake in the equity of Fiat, the Italian motor car company, for $400m. The deal was backed by a loan to Fiat from the LAFB of $105m. repayable over 10 years (with two years' grace). Until this purchase the LAFB had pursued a cautious and selective policy of putting Libyan capital into banking, hotels and tourism in many countries, as well as joint-stock ventures in agriculture, fishing and forestry projects in some African countries. Libya appeared to regard the Fiat purchase as the vanguard of its investment in

industrial countries' manufacturing bases. Libya's holdings in Italy were enlarged at the end of 1981 when the LAFB bought the bankrupt Italian sugar and steel concern, Malradi, for $450m. In September 1986, however, Libya sold its shares in Fiat for $3,000m. The Libyan ambassador to Rome denied that the sale had been prompted by the collapse of oil prices and the consequent shortage of foreign exchange. Other Libyan assets in Italy were frozen in mid-1986 as guarantees for Italian companies awaiting payment of millions of dollars from Libya in debt arrears. In December 1979 Kuwait and Libya signed a $1,000m. agreement to set up an Arab investment company, and in April 1980 Libya, together with Kuwait and the United Arab Emirates, decided to establish a new international insurance company. This was finally established with a capital of $3,000m. in October 1981. In September 1987 the Bankers' Trust Co of New York was ordered by a British High Court judge to release $292m. of Libyan assets placed with the bank's London branch, that were 'frozen' by order of President Reagan in January 1986.

The LAFB increased its paid-up capital to LD156m. in the 1991/92 fiscal year, during which it made a pre-tax profit of LD15m. Its paid-up shares in international affiliates (including 28 international banks outside Libya) totalled LD169.3m. In mid-1993 a proposal by the LAFB to increase its shareholding in the Athens-based Arab Hellenic Bank from 30% to 86% (thereby opening the way to the establishment of Libyan-controlled bank branches in other EC countries) was effectively halted by the Greek banking authorities. In 1992/93 the LAFB reported an increase in paid-up capital to LD 192m., an increase in net profits to LD 18.3m. and a 25% increase in total assets to LD 1,398m. The Bank's assets abroad were frozen in December 1993 under the terms of UN Security Council Resolution 883. In 1993/94 the LAFB increased its paid-up capital to LD 222m. In November 1997 the LAFB acquired a 5% stake in the newly-privatized Banco di Roma, the governor of the Libyan Central Bank subsequently stating that the LAFB would seek a seat on the board of the Italian bank.

Although Libya enjoys a substantial trade surplus, it also experiences a considerable deficit on 'invisibles' (services and transfer payments). This deficit increased from $1,450m. in 1973 to $2,265m. in 1977. In the early 1970s this deficit partly offset the trade surplus, leaving a fluctuating surplus on the current account, but in 1975 (when the trade surplus was reduced) the current account was pushed into deficit. Aid payments and purchases of military equipment (in 1986 Libya was estimated to owe the USSR $4,000m.–$5,000m. for sales of arms) tended to bring about a substantial outflow on capital account—so that Libya's basic balance of payments often yielded a deficit. Government debts were estimated at $7,000m. in 1989, and the practice of paying debts in petroleum has become more common. International reserves totalled $4,208m. at 31 December 1978, compared with $2,131m. at the end of 1973, and by the end of 1979 the figure had risen to $6,449m. At mid-1981 foreign exchange reserves amounted to $13,444m. They declined to $3,266m. at the end of 1984, recovered to $5,465m. at the end of 1985, but had fallen to an estimated $3,923m. by May 1990. By May 1991, however, reserves were estimated at $4,635m. In 1980 the current account showed a surplus of $8,240m. but this was followed by a deficit of $2,978m. in 1981, and further deficits in 1982, 1983 and 1984. However, Central Bank figures show that a surplus of $2,016m. was recorded in 1985, following a decline of 33% in the value of merchandise imports and substantial reductions in capital expenditure (see Development). The Central Bank reported a deficit of $252m. in 1986. A deficit of $800m. in 1987 was followed by further deficits of $1,260m. in 1988 and $940m. in 1989. In 1990, however, the increase in oil revenues, due to the Gulf crisis of 1990–91, produced a current account surplus of $2,200m., but in 1991 the current account was roughly in balance as world oil prices reverted to their pre-crisis level. According to World Bank figures, Libya had gross international reserves of $7,225m. at the end of 1990. Recent Libyan initiatives to increase non-oil foreign currency earnings have included the abandonment of ideological objections to the development of a mass tourism industry. However, by mid-1995 no practical steps had been taken to attract the necessary foreign investment, there being very little scope for forward planning in this area while Libya remained subject to UN sanctions. In May 1996 the General Tourism Board released statistics predicting revenue of $3m. from tourism in that year. Despite the shutdown of its international air links, Libya was visited by 80,000 tourists in 1994 and 85,000 tourists in 1995. The Board said that the Government intended to invest $1,700m. over the next five years 'to rehabilitate the tourism infrastructure' with the aim of attracting up to 1.5m. visitors to Libya by 2000. In 1997 international consultants were appointed to draw up a plan for tourism development.

The Central Bank reported in early 1994 that Libya's foreign exchange reserves totalled $5,972m. at 31 March 1993; that external earnings in the year ending 31 March 1993 had totalled about $7,000m. (some 13% less than forecast) and that public debt stood at an estimated $20,818m. on that date. The Bank for International Settlements (BIS) said in early 1994 that Libyan funds in banks reporting to the BIS totalled $1,159m. on 30 September 1993. Libya had an estimated current-account deficit of $325m. in 1994 and an estimated external debt of $4,844m. at the end of that year. By the end of 1996 Libya had an estimated external debt of $4,200m. and estimated foreign exchange reserves of $4,900m. There was an estimated current-account surplus of $450m. in 1995 and $1,000m. in 1996.

DEVELOPMENT AND BUDGET

Libyan planning dates back to the 1960s, with the first Development Plan running from 1963/64 to 1967/68. The second Plan ran from 1969/70 to 1973/74, and the third Plan, with an investment of LD 2,200m. (of which 34% was for industry, petroleum and electricity), from 1973 to 1975. Development budgets in the 1970s favoured agriculture, and the 1976–80 Development Plan, known as the Economic and Social Transformation Plan, involved a total investment of LD 9,250m. with priority again given to agriculture. The Plan aimed at an annual increase of 10.5% in GNP and a 26% rise in industrial production. In 1978 GDP increased by 11%, which was above the planned rate of 10.7%, but the average growth for the period 1976–79 was only 9.5% a year. In 1978 the allocations of most sectors of the budget were increased, but it appears that by the end of the Plan only 80% of planned expenditure had been used. The overall aims of the Plan were to achieve diversity of production, thus reducing dependence on oil, to develop the economic and social infrastructure and to achieve a more equitable distribution of income and wealth.

The 1981–85 Five-Year Plan was regarded as part of a major 20-year development programme, aiming at structural change in the economy to reduce its dependence on petroleum. Expenditure was initially set at LD 18,500m., more than double the allocation for the previous Plan, and it was forecast that by 1985 the non-oil sector would contribute 53% of national income, compared with 35% in 1980. Industry was to be allocated 23% of investment, and rapid growth was planned for electricity, transport, communications and housing. Agriculture was to receive 16%. The overall annual growth rate was intended to be 9.4%, compared with the last Plan's achieved rate of 7.6%, but industry's annual growth rate was projected at 21.6%. Agriculture's annual growth rate, on the other hand, was forecast at 7.4%. By 1983, owing to the abrupt reversal in Libya's petroleum revenues, the targets of the Five-Year Plan for 1981–85 were not being met and major reassessments, involving substantial reductions in expenditure, had to be undertaken. The building of roads and houses worth US $1,000m. was cancelled, and plans for a $4,200m. Soviet-made nuclear power plant were shelved.

The decline in government revenues curtailed budget expenditure throughout the 1980s. For 1982 the administrative budget was endorsed at LD 1,255m., and the development budget at LD 2,600m. (5% less than in 1981). The development budget for 1983, at LD 2,370m., was a further LD 230m. less than that of 1982. The 1984 budgets reflected this continuing trend. The administrative budget of LD 1,440.2m. represented a cut of 7.1% on the allocation for 1983, while development projects in 1984 were allocated LD 2,110m., a decrease of 11%.

Further reductions in projected spending were recorded in

the budget allocations for 1985. The administrative budget totalled LD 1,200m. and the development budget LD 1,700m., representing reductions of 16.7% and 19.4%, respectively, compared with the previous year. In the event, actual capital expenditure on development was well below the planned allocation. During 1985 actual spending on development was LD 1,211m., 28.8% less than the budgeted figure of LD 1,700m., continuing the trend established in 1983 (when actual spending was LD 2,096.3m., a shortfall of 11.5%, compared with planned spending of LD 2,370m.) and 1984 (actual spending: LD 1,824.8m.; planned spending: LD 2,110m.—a shortfall of 13.5%). Owing to the loss of revenue as a result of the decline in oil prices, the budget for 1986 was deferred. The development budget for 1987 represented a reduction of 14.7% compared with the allocation for 1985, to LD 1,450m.

The budget for 1988 projected total expenditure of LD 2,300m. (administrative budget LD 1,243.5m.; development budget LD 1,056.5m.), an increase of 6%, compared with 1987. For 1989 there was a draft operational budget of LD 1,174m., together with a draft changeover budget of LD 900m. Few details of the 1990 budget were made available. It was reported that expenditure on defence and subsidies was to be reduced to LD 600m., compared with LD 750m. in 1989, in order to restrict the total budget deficit to LD 322m. With regard to expenditure on capital projects, LD 300m. was to be provided for the GMR project (see Agriculture, above). An estimated LD 380m. was to be allocated for the purchase of food imports and the hiring of foreign labour. As a result of the unexpected increase in income from oil exports in 1990, Libya's GDP increased by 9.4%, in comparison with 1989, to the equivalent of $27,370m., thereby enabling the Government to allocate additional funds for the development of the oil industry and other sectors during the 1990s.

The broad outlines of the Government's 1992/93 budget were revealed in February 1993 (the penultimate month of that fiscal year). Expenditure totalled LD 2,823m. ($9,700m.) and revenue LD 2,251m. ($7,735m.), leaving a deficit of LD 572m. ($1,965m.). Of the expected revenue, LD 1,284m. (57%) was derived from oil exports and the balance from taxes and duties. The total national oil revenue (including funds not earmarked for budgetary use) was expected to be about LD 3,000m. ($10,300m.). It was announced in January 1994 that Libya's budget year would henceforth coincide with the calendar year and that no budget had been in force in the nine months following the end of the last April–March budget year in 1993. No details of the 1994 budget were published, although the Government indicated that 'several billion dollars' of cutbacks had been made to take account of the impact of UN sanctions.

In July 1995 the Libyan authorities released details of the budget for that calendar year, stated partly in US dollars and partly in Libyan dinars. The foreign-currency part of the budget provided for revenue of $8,280m. and expenditure of $9,260m., leaving a deficit of $980m. The expenditure categories included $1,600m. on water-transmission and irrigation; $700m. on the oil industry; $1,260m. on imported goods; $1,700m. on 'operating costs'; $250m. on payments to foreign companies; and $750m. on membership of international organizations. The remaining $3,000m. was earmarked for the direct distribution of grants to local families. The dinar section of the budget provided for domestic revenue of LD 1,660m. and domestic recurrent expenditure of LD 2,000m. (including LD 1,155m. on public-sector salaries), leaving a deficit of LD 340m. The 1996 budget, approved by the General People's Congress in February of that year, provided for revenue of LD 4,518m. ($12,709m.) and expenditure of the same amount, this being Libya's first non-deficit budget for many years. The Government stated that the previous three years' budget deficits had been financed by drawings on the country's foreign reserves. The final size of the 1995 budget deficit was not revealed, although it was known that the Government had not implemented its plan to distribute lump-sum grants to Libyan families. In September 1996 the official Libyan news agency reported that 50,000 families were each to receive grants worth $5,000, under the Government's wealth redistribution programme. In March 1997 the Governor of the Central Bank told the General People's Congress that

Libya's foreign currency budget had a surplus of $680m. in 1996, when revenue on the foreign currency account had totalled $9,573m.

The sequence of balanced budgets was continued in 1997 and 1998, that for the latter year providing for a 1.3% reduction in expenditure and revenue to LD 5,311m. ($13,760m. at the official exchange rate). It was officially stated that the 1998 budget included the allocation of LD 1,133m. ($2,935m.) to the GMR project (see Agriculture, above). Figures released by the Government at the end of 1997 showed that Libya was owed some $3,273m. by various debtor nations. Debt rescheduling agreements had recently been concluded with Guinea, Guinea-Bissau and Burkina Faso, while negotiations were in progress with Pakistan and Sudan and were being sought with other debtors, including Algeria, Benin, Ethiopia, Madagascar, Mozambique, Nicaragua, Tanzania and Uganda.

Statistical Survey

Sources (unless otherwise stated): National Corporation for Information and Documentation; Census and Statistical Dept, Secretariat of Planning, 40 Sharia Damascus, 2nd Floor, Tripoli; tel. (21) 3331731.

Area and Population

AREA, POPULATION AND DENSITY

Area (sq km)	1,775,500*
Population (census results)	
31 July 1984	
Males	1,953,757
Females	1,688,819
Total	3,642,576
August 1995 (provisional)	
Total	4,811,902†
Density (per sq km) at August 1995	2.7

* 685,524 sq miles.

† Comprising 4,404,986 Libyan nationals (males 2,236,943; females 2,168,043) and 406,916 non-Libyans.

Estimated population (Libyan nationals only, mid-year): 4,394,732 in 1995; 4,519,367 in 1996; 4,647,520 in 1997.

POPULATION BY REGION
(1995 census, provisional figures)

Al-Batnan . . .	151,240	Misratah (Misurata)	.	488,573
Jebel Akhdar . .	381,165	Najghaza . . .	.	244,553
Banghazi (Benghazi)	665,615	Tarabulus (Tripoli) .		1,313,996
Al-Wosta . . .	240,574	Az-Zawiyah (Zawia)	.	517,395
Al-Wahat . . .	62,056	Jebel Gharbi . .	.	316,970
Al-Jufra . . .	39,335	Fazzan (Fezzan)	.	314,029
Sofuljin . . .	76,401	**Total** . . .	.	**4,811,902**

PRINCIPAL TOWNS (population at census of 31 July 1973)

Tarabulus (Tripoli,		Ajdabiyah . . .	.	31,047
the capital) . .	481,295	Darnah . . .	.	30,241
Banghazi (Benghazi)	219,317	Sabhah (Sebha)	.	28,714
Misratah (Misurata)	42,815	Tubruq (Tobruk)	.	28,061
Az-Zawiyah (Zawia)	39,382	Al-Marj . . .	.	25,166
Zawiyat al-Baida (Beida)	31,796	Zlitan (Zliten) .	.	21,340

BIRTHS AND DEATHS
(estimates, Libyan nationals only)

	1994	1995	1996
Birth rate (per 1,000) . . .	41.0	40.5	40.0
Death rate (per 1,000) . . .	7.0	7.0	7.0

Marriages: 19,190 in 1994; 21,358 in 1995; 18,743 in 1996.

Expectation of life (UN estimates, years at birth, 1990–95): 63.1 (males 61.6; females 65.0) (Source: UN, *World Population Prospects: The 1994 Revision*).

EMPLOYMENT (official estimates, '000 persons)

	1994	1996*
Agriculture, forestry and fishing .	213.4	219.5
Mining and quarrying	29.9	31.0
Manufacturing	124.1	128.5
Electricity, gas and water	33.7	35.5
Construction	168.3	171.0
Trade, restaurants and hotels .	70.7	73.0
Transport, storage and communications . .	97.7	104.0
Financing, insurance, real estate and business services	18.7	22.0
Other services	434.8	439.5
Total	**1,191.3**	**1,224.0**
Libyans	1,035.2	1,092.1
Non-Libyans	156.1	131.9

* Figures for 1995 are not available.

Agriculture

PRINCIPAL CROPS (FAO estimates, '000 metric tons)

	1994	1995	1996
Wheat	155	167	168
Barley	149	148	150
Potatoes	130	127	130
Dry broad beans	9	9	9
Groundnuts (in shell) . . .	13	13	13
Olives	60	52	52
Tomatoes	135	135	134
Pumpkins, squash and gourds .	27	27	26
Cucumbers and gherkins . .	16	16	16
Chillies and peppers (green) . .	13	13	13
Onions (dry)	75	75	75
Green peas	6	6	5
Carrots	22	22	22
Other vegetables	128	128	126
Watermelons	185	180	180
Melons	22	22	22
Grapes	32	30	30
Dates	70	68	68
Apples	8	8	8
Peaches and nectarines . . .	9	9	9
Oranges	82	80	80
Other citrus fruits	6	6	6
Apricots	15	15	15
Other fruits and berries . . .	35	34	34
Almonds	31	30	29

Source: FAO, *Production Yearbook*.

LIVESTOCK (FAO estimates, '000 head, year ending September)

	1994	1995	1996
Horses	22	22	22
Asses	55	55	55
Cattle	105	100	100
Camels	130	130	130
Sheep	4,500	4,400	4,400
Goats	800	800	800
Poultry	16,000	17,000	17,000

Source: FAO, *Production Yearbook*.

LIVESTOCK PRODUCTS (FAO estimates, '000 metric tons)

	1994	1995	1996
Beef and veal	20	20	20
Mutton and lamb	21	20	20
Goat meat	4	4	4
Poultry meat	68	68	68
Other meat	6	7	7
Cows' milk	87	85	85
Sheep's milk	21	21	21
Goats' milk	16	14	14
Hen eggs	33	33	33
Wool:			
greasy	7	7	7
clean	2	2	2
Cattle hides	3	3	3
Sheepskins	5	5	5

Source: FAO, *Production Yearbook*.

Forestry

ROUNDWOOD REMOVALS
('000 cubic metres, excl. bark)

	1994	1995	1996
Sawlogs, veneer logs and logs for			
sleepers	63	63	63
Other industrial wood	51	52	54
Fuel wood	536	536	536
Total	650	651	653

Source: FAO, *Yearbook of Forest Products*.

SAWNWOOD PRODUCTION
('000 cubic metres, incl. railway sleepers)

	1994	1995	1996
Total (all broadleaved)	31	31	31

Fishing

('000 metric tons, live weight)

	1993	1994	1995
Groupers*	3.7	4.0	4.1
Bogue*	2.3	2.5	2.6
Porgies and seabreams*	3.7	4.0	4.1
Red mullet*	3.7	4.0	4.1
Jack and horse mackerels	2.8*	3.0*	3.1
Sardinellas*	6.4	7.0	7.1
Northern bluefin tuna	0.5	1.3	1.5*
Bigeye tuna	1.1	0.5	0.4
'Scomber' mackerels*	2.8	3.0	3.1
Total catch (incl. others)*	31.2	34.1	34.5
Inland waters*	0.1	0.1	0.1
Atlantic Ocean	1.2	0.5	0.4
Mediterranean and Black Sea*	30.0	33.5	34.0

* FAO estimate(s).

Source: FAO, *Yearbook of Fishery Statistics*.

Mining

('000 metric tons, unless otherwise indicated)

	1993	1994	1995
Crude petroleum	65,478	66,854	67,299
Natural gas ('000 terajoules)	248	249*	246*
Salt (unrefined)*†	12	12	12
Gypsum (crude)*†	160	160	160

* Estimated figure(s).
† Data from the US Bureau of Mines.
Source: UN, *Industrial Commodity Statistics Yearbook*.

Industry

SELECTED PRODUCTS ('000 metric tons, unless otherwise indicated)

	1993	1994	1995
Olive oil (crude)	8	7	5
Paper and paperboard	6	6	6
Jet fuels*	1,510	1,520	1,540
Motor spirit (petrol)*	1,820	1,890	1,870
Naphthas*	2,100	2,300	1,935
Kerosene*	240	250	260
Gas-diesel (distillate fuel) oil	4,000	4,100	4,200
Residual fuel oils	4,900	4,900*	5,100*
Liquefied petroleum gas:			
from natural gas plants*	340*	470*	645
from petroleum refineries*	200	230	240
Petroleum bitumen (asphalt)*	90	100	90
Quicklime†	260	260	260
Cement	2,300†	2,300†	2,300*
Electric energy (million kWh)*	17,000	17,800	18,000

* Provisional or estimated figure(s).
† Estimate(s) by the US Bureau of Mines.
Source: mainly UN, *Industrial Commodity Statistics Yearbook*.

1996 (FAO estimate, '000 metric tons): Olive oil 6 (Source: FAO, *Production Yearbook*).

Finance

CURRENCY AND EXCHANGE RATES
Monetary Units
1,000 dirhams = 1 Libyan dinar (LD).

Sterling and Dollar Equivalents (31 May 1998)
£1 sterling = 641.1 dirhams;
US $1 = 393.2 dirhams;
100 Libyan dinars = £155.98 = $254.35.

Average Exchange Rate (US $ per Libyan dinar)
1995   2.8894
1996   2.7653
1997   2.6210
Note: Since March 1986 the value of the Libyan dinar has been linked to the IMF's special drawing right (SDR). Since November 1994 the official mid-point exchange rate has been SDR1 = 525 dirhams (LD1 = SDR 1.90476).

BUDGET (projections, LD million)

	1998
Total revenue	5,311
Total expenditure	5,311

INTERNATIONAL RESERVES (US $ million at 31 December)

	1990	1991	1992
Gold	152	152	152
IMF special drawing rights .	409	461	383
Reserve position in IMF . . .	346	348	439
Foreign exchange*	5,084	4,885	5,361
Total*	5,991	5,847	6,334

* Estimates.

1993 (US $ million at 31 December): IMF special drawing rights 417; Reserve position in IMF 438.
1994 (US $ million at 31 December): IMF special drawing rights 474; Reserve position in IMF 466.
1995 (US $ million at 31 December): IMF special drawing rights 520; Reserve position in IMF 474.
1996 (US $ million at 31 December): IMF special drawing rights 538; Reserve position in IMF 459.
1997 (US $ million at 31 December): IMF special drawing rights 538; Reserve position in IMF 430.

Source: IMF, *International Financial Statistics*.

MONEY SUPPLY (LD million at 31 December)

	1994	1995	1996
Currency outside banks . . .	1,989.8	2,035.4	2,419.8
Private-sector deposits at Central Bank	478.8	603.9	414.5
Demand deposits at commercial banks.	3,417.3	3,612.1	3,489.4
Total money	5,885.9	6,251.4	6,323.7

Source: IMF, *International Financial Statistics*.

COST OF LIVING
(Consumer Price Index, excluding rent, for Tripoli; base: 1979 = 100)

	1982	1983	1984
Food	134.9	152.9	169.5
Clothing	141.1	150.6	169.4
All items (incl. others) . . .	137.6	152.2	165.8

Source: ILO, *Yearbook of Labour Statistics*.

NATIONAL ACCOUNTS (LD million at current prices)
National Income and Product

	1983	1984	1985
Compensation of employees . .	2,763.1	2,865.8	2,996.2
Operating surplus	5,282.7	4,357.8	4,572.4
Domestic factor incomes . .	8,045.8	7,223.6	7,568.6
Consumption of fixed capital . .	436.1	457.5	481.6
Gross domestic product (GDP) at factor cost.	8,481.9	7,681.1	8,050.2
Indirect taxes	470.0	462.2	389.0
Less Subsidies	146.7	130.0	162.2
GDP in purchasers' values. .	8,805.2	8,013.3	8,277.0
Factor income from abroad . .	200.2	142.8	122.5
Less Factor income paid abroad .	989.0	727.7	397.9
Gross national product . .	8,016.4	7,428.4	8,001.6
Less Consumption of fixed capital .	436.1	457.5	481.6
National income in market prices	7,580.3	6,970.9	7,520.0
Other current transfers from abroad	8.6	2.3	2.6
Less Other current transfers paid abroad	25.2	27.9	16.0
National disposable income .	7,563.7	6,945.3	7,506.6

Source: UN, *National Accounts Statistics*.

Expenditure on the Gross Domestic Product (estimates)

	1990	1991	1992
Government final consumption expenditure	2,122	2,280	2,336
Private final consumption expenditure	2,658	2,887	2,957
Gross capital formation . . .	1,693	1,848	1,893
Total domestic expenditure .	6,473	7,015	7,186
Exports of goods and services .	4,105	3,931	4,218
Less Imports of goods and services	2,429	2,427	2,604
GDP in purchasers' values .	8,149	8,519	8,800
GDP at constant 1980 prices .	6,722	7,058	7,164

Source: UN Economic Commission for Africa, *African Statistical Yearbook*.

Gross Domestic Product by Economic Activity (estimates)

	1994	1995	1996
Agriculture, forestry and fishing .	601.5	680.5	782.5
Mining and quarrying . . .	2,728.5	2,840.0	3,036.5
Petroleum and natural gas .	2,559.5	2,675.0	2,822.0
Manufacturing	865.5	980.0	1,107.0
Electricity, gas and water. . .	191.0	213.5	240.5
Construction	604.5	580.5	797.0
Trade, restaurants and hotels .	1,100.0	1,190.5	1,345.5
Transport, storage and communications	846.0	925.5	1,025.5
Finance, insurance and real estate*	641.5	686.5	739.5
Public services	2,048.5	2,143.0	2,247.5
Other services	286.5	352.5	461.0
Total	9,913.5	10,592.5	11,782.5

* Including imputed rents of owner-occupied dwellings.

BALANCE OF PAYMENTS (US $ million)

	1988	1989	1990
Exports of goods f.o.b. . .	5,653	7,274	11,352
Imports of goods f.o.b. . .	−5,762	−6,509	−7,575
Trade balance	−109	765	3,777
Exports of services . . .	128	117	117
Imports of services . . .	−1,637	−1,481	−1,385
Balance on goods and services.	−1,617	−598	2,508
Other income received . . .	762	447	666
Other income paid . . .	−437	−388	−493
Balance on goods, services and income	−1,292	−539	2,682
Current transfers received . .	7	6	7
Current transfers paid . . .	−541	−493	−488
Current balance . . .	−1,826	−1,026	2,201
Direct investment abroad. . .	−56	−35	−105
Direct investment from abroad .	98	125	159
Portfolio investment assets . .	−222	−52	−115
Other investment assets . .	−670	320	−715
Other investment liabilities . .	1,013	830	−230
Net errors and omissions . . .	271	130	−37
Overall balance	−1,392	292	1,158

Source: IMF, *International Financial Statistics*.

External Trade

PRINCIPAL COMMODITIES
(distribution by SITC, US $ million, excl. military goods)

Imports c.i.f.	1989	1990	1991
Food and live animals	911.6	1,155.2	1,073.5
Dairy products and birds' eggs	99.1	113.5	80.8
Cereals and cereal preparations	365.6	479.6	439.1
Barley (unmilled)	53.7	149.7	80.4
Meal and flour of wheat and meslin	105.4	165.0	151.7
Flour of wheat or meslin	105.3	165.0	151.6
Sugar, sugar preparations and honey	85.4	101.0	107.7
Feeding-stuff for animals (excl. unmilled cereals)	74.2	188.8	141.7
Crude materials (inedible) except fuels	91.8	118.2	128.3
Animal and vegetable oils, fats and waxes	89.8	106.6	164.4
Fixed vegetable oils and fats	87.4	104.7	162.5
'Soft' fixed vegetable oils	86.6	103.0	161.0
Chemicals and related products	390.4	379.7	408.0
Basic manufactures	1,238.2	1,331.2	1,213.8
Textile yarn, fabrics, etc.	138.3	129.9	187.4
Non-metallic mineral manufactures	75.5	124.8	81.8
Iron and steel	476.3	516.2	401.4
Wire (excl. wire rod), not insulated	100.2	128.4	55.4
Tubes, pipes and fittings	143.1	117.4	144.3
Metal structures and parts	93.0	129.9	109.1
Machinery and transport equipment	1,715.8	1,936.6	1,813.4
Power-generating machinery and equipment	106.7	101.7	95.6
Machinery specialized for particular industries	241.1	334.1	268.8
Civil engineering and contractors' plant and equipment	88.2	146.9	98.1
Construction and mining machinery	56.0	118.9	53.0
General industrial machinery, equipment and parts	477.4	489.2	503.6
Telecommunications and sound equipment	99.9	104.7	111.8
Other electrical machinery, apparatus, etc.	243.9	292.9	262.9
Road vehicles and parts*	470.6	534.9	465.9
Passenger motor cars (excl. buses)	109.0	154.3	154.8
Motor vehicles for goods transport, etc.	116.6	107.2	68.7
Parts and accessories for cars, buses, lorries, etc.*	191.6	227.1	185.3
Miscellaneous manufactured articles	547.9	528.0	494.9
Clothing and accessories (excl. footwear)	134.6	88.2	165.8
Professional, scientific and controlling instruments, etc.	103.0	118.3	100.8
Total (incl. others)	5,048.7	5,598.6	5,357.5

* Data on parts exclude tyres, engines and electrical parts.

Exports f.o.b.	1989	1990	1991
Mineral fuels, lubricants, etc.	7,850.7	13,098.0	10,697.7
Petroleum, petroleum products, etc.	7,748.0	12,978.4	10,548.7
Crude petroleum oils, etc.	6,782.6	11,431.7	9,483.5
Refined petroleum products	965.5	1,546.7	1,065.2
Gas oils (distillate fuels)	198.4	—	—
Residual fuel oils	606.8	1,327.5	936.6
Chemicals and related products	388.0	524.7	375.8
Organic chemicals	311.3	439.8	272.2
Hydrocarbons and their derivatives	233.5	363.3	197.8
Acyclic hydrocarbons	185.9	256.2	118.9
Total (incl. others)	8,240.3	13,876.8	11,211.7

Source: UN, *International Trade Statistics Yearbook*.

Total imports c.i.f. (LD million); 1,422.1 in 1992; 1,711.3 in 1993; 1,487.9 in 1994; 1,728.5 in 1995; 1,914.8 in 1996.
Total exports f.o.b. (LD million): 3,038.8 in 1992; 2,477.6 in 1993; 3,117.2 in 1994; 3,222.1 in 1995; 3,578.7 in 1996.

PRINCIPAL TRADING PARTNERS (US $ '000)*

Imports c.i.f.	1989	1990	1991
Austria	96,626	108,452	155,205
Belgium-Luxembourg	136,839	156,065	110,505
Brazil	44,447	95,403	74,983
Canada	56,374	56,239	63,108
China, People's Republic	34,241	49,491	62,206
Cuba	3,587	56,463	28,547
Egypt	231	38,866	73,270
France (incl. Monaco)	344,532	412,513	333,183
Germany, Federal Republic†	745,055	819,436	700,983
Greece	53,285	81,209	65,160
Ireland	72,007	53,538	25,211
Italy	1,222,961	1,036,349	1,160,525
Japan	230,098	244,350	178,575
Korea, Republic	171,273	115,413	170,355
Malta	45,672	60,913	69,070
Morocco	83,115	120,941	191,038
Netherlands	167,215	313,237	207,038
Poland	68,772	36,913	20,159
Spain	62,047	53,751	47,943
Sweden	45,544	92,329	69,131
Switzerland-Liechtenstein	98,645	195,143	108,078
Tunisia	42,943	122,544	114,628
Turkey	243,053	290,231	340,255
United Kingdom	419,494	472,038	441,923
USA	76,932	69,962	69,643
Yugoslavia (former)	74,163	74,724	45,874
Total (incl. others)	5,020,587	5,579,291	5,339,275

Exports f.o.b.	1989	1990	1991
Belgium-Luxembourg	186,646	305,618	308,312
Bulgaria	176,252	242,489	84,397
France (incl. Monaco)	805,193	1,187,634	865,289
Germany, Federal Republic†	442,146	900,789	1,869,891
Greece	479,718	611,748	581,951
Italy	4,000,668	6,642,085	4,565,220
Morocco	8,431	115,392	122,441
Netherlands	454,529	387,915	194,593
Romania	21,187	241,994	87,103
Spain	719,734	1,276,599	1,077,736
Sudan	68,143	150,732	152,970
Switzerland-Liechtenstein	—	4,453	215,011
Turkey	264,612	506,589	246,231
USSR (former)	129,808	203,502	n.a.
United Kingdom	157,142	247,657	144,887
Yugoslavia (former)	149,750	369,874	347,195
Total (incl. others)	8,240,262	13,876,843	11,211,715

* Imports by country of origin; exports by country of destination. Figures exclude trade in gold.
† Figures for 1991 refer to the united Germany.

Source: UN, *International Trade Statistics Yearbook*.

Transport

ROAD TRAFFIC (motor vehicles in use)

	1994	1995	1996
Passenger cars	740,079	763,205	796,318
Buses	2,176	2,419	1,490
Goods vehicles	339,212	350,784	356,038

SHIPPING

Merchant Fleet (registered at 31 December)

	1995	1996	1997
Number of vessels . . .	153	150	151
Total displacement ('000 grt) . .	732.8	680.5	686.2

Source: Lloyd's Register of Shipping, *World Fleet Statistics.*

International Sea-borne Freight Traffic
(estimates, '000 metric tons)

	1991	1992	1993
Goods loaded	57,243	59,894	62,491
Goods unloaded	7,630	7,710	7,808

Source: UN Economic Commission for Africa, *African Statistical Yearbook.*

CIVIL AVIATION (traffic on scheduled services)

	1993	1994	1995
Kilometres flown (million) . .	6	4	3
Passengers carried ('000) . . .	853	641	623
Passenger-km (million) . .	565	425	398
Total ton-km (million) . . .	44	34	32

Source: UN, *Statistical Yearbook.*

Tourism

	1994	1995	1996
Tourist arrivals*	51,740	55,884	88,000

* Figures refer to overnight visitors, excluding residents of Arab countries in North Africa and the Middle East. Total arrivals from these areas (including tourists and same-day visitors) were: 1,441,000 in 1994; 1,776,000 in 1995; 1,188,000 in 1996.

Communications Media

	1993	1994	1995
Radio receivers ('000 in use) . .	1,140	1,180	1,250
Television receivers ('000 in use) .	504	525	550
Telephones ('000 main lines in use)	240	264	318
Book production: titles . .	n.a.	26	n.a.
Daily newspapers	n.a.	4	4
Average circulation ('000 copies)	n.a.	70*	71*

* Estimate.

Sources: UNESCO, *Statistical Yearbook;* UN, *Statistical Yearbook.*

Education

(1995/96, unless otherwise indicated)

	Institutions	Teachers	Students
Primary and preparatory:			
General	2,733*	122,020	1,333,679
Vocational . . .	168	n.a.	22,490
Secondary:			
General	n.a.	17,668	170,573
Teacher-training . . .	n.a.	2,760†	23,919
Vocational . . .	312	n.a.	109,074
Universities . . .	13	n.a.	126,348

* 1993/94.   † 1992/93.

Source: partly UNESCO, *Statistical Yearbook.*

Directory

The Constitution

The Libyan Arab People, meeting in the General People's Congress in Sebha from 2–28 March 1977, proclaimed its adherence to freedom and its readiness to defend it on its own land and anywhere else in the world. It also announced its adherence to socialism and its commitment to achieving total Arab Unity; its adherence to the moral human values; and confirmed the march of the revolution led by Col Muammar al-Qaddafi, the Revolutionary Leader, towards complete People's Authority.

The Libyan Arab People announced the following:

(i) The official name of Libya is henceforth The Socialist People's Libyan Arab Jamahiriya.

(ii) The Holy Koran is the social code in The Socialist People's Libyan Arab Jamahiriya.

(iii) The Direct People's Authority is the basis for the political order in The Socialist People's Libyan Arab Jamahiriya. The People shall practise its authority through People's Congresses, Popular Committees, Trade Unions, Vocational Syndicates, and The General People's Congress, in the presence of the law.

(iv) The defence of our homeland is the responsibility of every citizen. The whole people shall be trained militarily and armed by general military training, the preparation of which shall be specified by the law.

The General People's Congress in its extraordinary session held in Sebha issued four decrees:

The first decree announced the establishment of The People's Authority in compliance with the resolutions and recommendations of the People's Congresses and Trade Unions.

The second decree stipulated the choice of Col Muammar al-Qaddafi, the Revolutionary Leader, as Secretary-General of the General People's Congress.

The third decree stipulated the formation of the General Secretariat of the General People's Congress (see The Government, below).

The fourth decree stipulated the formation of the General People's Committee to carry out the tasks of the various former ministries (see The Government, below).

In 1986 it was announced that the country's official name was to be The Great Socialist People's Libyan Arab Jamahiriya.

The Government

HEAD OF STATE

Revolutionary Leader: Col MUAMMAR AL-QADDAFI (took office as Chairman of the Revolution Command Council 8 September 1969; he himself rejects this nomenclature and all other titles).

Second-in-Command: Maj. ABD AS-SALAM JALLOUD.

GENERAL SECRETARIAT OF THE GENERAL PEOPLE'S CONGRESS

(September 1998)

Secretary-General: AZ-ZINATI MUHAMMAD AZ-ZINATI.

Assistant Secretary-General: ABD AL-HAMID AS-SA'ID AZ-ZINTANI.

Secretary for Women's Affairs: NURA RAMADAN ABU SEFRIAN.

Secretary for Affairs of the People's Congresses: AHMAD MUHAMMAD IBRAHIM.

Secretary for Affairs of the People's Committees: AL-BAGHDADI ALI AL-MAHMUDI.

Secretary for Affairs of the Trade Unions, Syndicates and Professional Associations: ABDALLAH IDRIS IBRAHIM.

Secretary for Foreign Affairs: ABD AR-RAHMAN SHALGAM.

GENERAL PEOPLE'S COMMITTEE
(September 1998)

Secretary-General of the General People's Committee: Eng. MUHAMMAD AHMAD AL-MANQUSH.

Secretary for Finance: Dr MUHAMMAD ABDALLAH BAIT AL-MAL.

Secretary for Foreign Liaison and International Co-operation: OMAR MUSTAFA AL-MUNTASIR.

Co-ordinators of the General Provisional Committee for Defence: ABU BAKR JABER YUNES, MUSTAFA KHARRUBI, KHOUELDI HAMIDI.

Secretary for Public Security: MUHAMMAD MAHMUD AL-HIJAZI.

Secretary for Justice: MUHAMMAD ABU AL-QASIM AZ-ZUAI.

Secretary for Energy: ABDALLAH SALIM AL-BADRI.

Secretary for the Economy and Trade: Dr ABD AL-HAFIZ MAHMUD AZ-ZILITNI.

Secretary for Planning: Eng. JADALLAH AZUZ AT-TALAHI.

Secretary for Unity: JUMAA AL-MADHI AL-FAZZANI.

Secretary for Industry and Mines: Dr MUFTAH ALI AZUZA.

Secretary for Education and Scientific Research: Dr AL-MAHDI MUFTAH IMBARESH.

Secretary for Labour and Training: MAATUQ MUHAMMAD MAATUQ.

Secretary for Youth and Sports: ALI MURSI ASH-SHAARI.

Secretary for Information, Culture and Jamahiri (Mass) Mobilization: FAWZIYA BASHIR SHALABI.

Secretary for Marine Wealth: BASHIR RAMADAN BUJENAH.

Secretary for Agriculture: Eng. MUHAMMAD ALI IBN RAMADAN.

Secretary for Animal Resources: Dr MASUD SA'ID ABU SUWA.

Secretary for Transport and Communications: Eng. 'IZZ AD-DIN MUHAMMAD AL-HINSHIRI.

Secretary for Health and Social Security: SULAIMAN AL-GHOMARI ABDALLAH.

Secretary for Housing and Utilities: MUBARAK ABDALLAH ASH-SHAMIKH.

Secretary for the Great Man-made River Project: ABD AL-MAJID AL-AOUD.

Secretary for the Supervision of Public Accounting and Control: ABD AR-RAHMAN AL-ABARI.

Secretary for Tourism: Eng. AL-BUKHARI SALIM HAWDAH.

As part of a radical decentralization programme undertaken in September 1988, all General People's Committee secretariats (ministries), except those responsible for foreign liaison (foreign affairs) and information, were relocated away from Tripoli. According to diplomatic sources, the former Secretariat for Economy and Trade was moved to Benghazi; the Secretariat for Health to Kufra; and the remainder, excepting one, to Sirte (Surt), Col Qaddafi's birthplace. In early 1993 it was announced that the Secretariat for Foreign Liaison and International Co-operation was to be moved to Ras Lanouf.

Legislature

GENERAL PEOPLE'S CONGRESS

The Senate and House of Representatives were dissolved after the *coup d'état* of September 1969, and the provisional Constitution issued in December 1969 made no mention of elections or a return to parliamentary procedure. However, in January 1971 Col Qaddafi announced that a new legislature would be appointed, not elected; no date was mentioned. All political parties other than the Arab Socialist Union were banned. In November 1975 provision was made for the creation of the 1,112-member General National Congress of the Arab Socialist Union, which met officially in January 1976. This later became the General People's Congress (GPC), which met for the first time in November 1976 and in March 1977 began introducing the wide-ranging changes outlined in the Constitution (above).

Secretary-General: ABD AR-RAZIQ SAWSA.

Political Organizations

In June 1971 the Arab Socialist Union (ASU) was established as the country's sole authorized political party. The General National Congress of the ASU held its first session in January 1976 and later became the General People's Congress (see Legislature, above).

The following groups are in opposition to the Government:

Ansarollah Group: f. 1996.

Fighting Islamic Group: claimed responsibility for subversive activities in early 1996; seeks to establish an Islamic regime.

Islamic Martyrs' Movement (IMM): Spokesman ABDALLAH AHMAD.

Libyan Baathist Party.

Libyan Conservatives' Party: f. 1996.

Libyan Democratic Movement: f. 1977; external group.

Libyan Democratic Authority: f. 1993.

Libyan Democratic Conference: f. 1992.

Libyan Movement for Change and Reform: f. 1994; based in London, United Kingdom.

Libyan National Alliance: f. 1980 in Cairo, Egypt.

Movement of Patriotic Libyans: f. 1997.

National Front for the Salvation of Libya (NFSL): f. 1981 in Khartoum, Sudan; aims to replace the existing regime by a democratically-elected government; Leader MUHAMMAD MEGARIEF.

Diplomatic Representation

EMBASSIES IN LIBYA

Afghanistan: POB 4245, Sharia Mozhar al-Aftes, Tripoli; tel. (21) 75192; fax (21) 609876; Ambassador: (vacant).

Algeria: Sharia Kairauan 12, Tripoli; tel. (21) 4440025; Ambassador: MOHAMED SEBBAGH.

Argentina: POB 932, Sharia ibn Mufarrej al-Andalous, Tripoli; tel. (21) 72160; telex 20190; fax (21) 70597; Chargé d'affaires: MIGUEL ANGEL NICOLA MONDI.

Austria: POB 3207, Sharia Khalid ibn al-Walid, Garden City, Tripoli; tel. (21) 4443379; telex 20245; fax (21) 4440838; Ambassador: WERNER DRUML.

Bangladesh: POB 5086, Hadaba al-Khadra, Villa Omran al-Wershafani, Tripoli; tel. (21) 900856; fax (21) 901866; Ambassador: M. SHAFIULLAH.

Belgium: Tower 4, International Islamic Call Society Complex, Souk Ethulathah, Tripoli; tel. (21) 3350117; telex 20564; fax (21) 3350118; Ambassador: R. SCHRIJVERS.

Benin: Tripoli; tel. (21) 72914; Ambassador: El-Hadj ALASSANE ABOUDOU.

Bosnia and Herzegovina: POB 84373, Sharia ben Ashour, Tripoli; tel. and fax (21) 602162; Ambassador: MUHAMMAD KUPOSOVIĆ.

Brazil: POB 2270, Sharia ben Ashour, Tripoli; tel. (21) 607970; telex 20082; Chargé d'affaires: JOSÉ MARCOS NOGUEIRA VIANA.

Bulgaria: POB 2945, Sharia Talha ben Abdullah 5-7, Tripoli; tel. (21) 3609988; Ambassador: KRASTIO ILOV.

Burundi: POB 2817, Sharia Ras Hassan, Tripoli; tel. (21) 608848; telex 20372; Ambassador: ZACHARIE BANYIYEZAKO.

Chad: POB 1078, Sharia Muhammad Mussadeq 25, Tripoli; tel. (21) 4443955; Ambassador: IBRAHIM MAHAMAT TIDEI.

China, People's Republic: POB 5329, Andalous, Gargaresh, Tripoli; tel. (21) 830860; Ambassador: QIN HONGGUO.

Cuba: POB 83738, Al-Andalous, Gargaresh, Tripoli; tel. (21) 71346; telex 20513; Ambassador: RAÚL RODRÍGUEZ RÁMOS.

Czech Republic: POB 1097, Sharia Ahmad Lotfi Sayed, Sharia ben Ashour, Tripoli; tel. (21) 603444; fax (21) 609608; Ambassador: ALEXANDR KARYCH.

Egypt: The Grand Hotel, Tripoli; tel. (21) 605500; telex 20780; fax (21) 4445959; Ambassador: EL-SHAZLY.

Ethiopia: POB 12899, Sharia Jamahiriya, Tripoli; tel. (21) 608185; telex 20572; Ambassador: ABDULMENAN SHEKA.

Finland: POB 2508, Tripoli; tel. and fax (21) 4831132; Chargé d'affaires: ULLA-MAIJA SUOMINEN.

France: POB 312, Sharia Beni al-Amar, Hay Andalous, Tripoli; tel. (21) 607861; fax (21) 607864; Ambassador: JOSETTE DALLANT.

Germany: POB 302, Sharia Hassan al-Mashai, Tripoli; tel. (21) 3330554; telex 20298; fax (21) 4448968; Ambassador: PETER KIEWITT.

Ghana: POB 4169, Sharia G. ben al-Mafarah, Andalous, Tripoli; tel. (21) 4772366; telex 20879; fax (21) 4773557; Ambassador: Alhaji B. A. FUSEINI.

Greece: POB 5147, Sharia Jalal Bayar 18, Tripoli; tel. (21) 3336978; telex 20409; fax (21) 4441907; Ambassador: ELIAS DIMITRAKOPOULOS.

Guinea: POB 10657, Andalous, Tripoli; tel. (21) 72793; Ambassador: BAH KABA.

Holy See: Tripoli; Apostolic Nuncio: Most Rev. JOSÉ SEBASTIÁN LABOA, Titular Archbishop of Zaraï.

Hungary: POB 4010, Sharia Talha ben Abdullah, Tripoli; tel. (21) 605799; telex 20055; Chargé d'affaires: GYÖRGY BUSZTIN.

India: POB 3150, 16 Sharia Mahmud Shaltut, Tripoli; tel. (21) 4441835; telex 20115; fax (21) 3337560; Ambassador: SURENDRA KUMAR.

Iran: Sharia Gargaresh, Andalous, Tripoli; Ambassador: SEYYED MUHAMMAD QADEM KHUNSARI.

Iraq: Sharia ben Ashour, Tripoli.

Italy: POB 912, Sharia Uahran 1, Tripoli; tel. (21) 3334131; telex 20602; Ambassador: AUGUSTINO MATHIS; British interests section: POB 4206, Sharia Uahran, Tripoli; tel. (21) 3331191; telex 20296; Head of Section: (vacant).

Japan: Tower No. 4, That al-Imad Complex, Sharia Organization of African Unity, Tripoli; tel. (21) 607463; telex 20094; fax (21) 607462; Ambassador: AKIRA WATANABE.

Korea, Democratic People's Republic: Tripoli; tel. (21) 609529; telex 20110; fax (21) 607982; Ambassador: KIM YONG IL.

Korea, Republic: POB 4781, Gargaresh, Tripoli; tel. (21) 4831322; fax (21) 4831324; Ambassador: KONG SUN-SUP.

Kuwait: POB 2225, Beit al-Mal Beach, Tripoli; tel. (21) 4440281; telex 20328; fax (21) 607053; Chargé d'affaires: KHALED MOTLAQ AD-DUWAILA.

Lebanon: POB 927, Sharia Omar bin Yasser Hadaek 20, Tripoli; tel. (21) 3333733; telex 20609; Ambassador: MOUNIR KHOREISH.

Malaysia: POB 6309, Hay Andalous, Tripoli; tel. (21) 833693; telex 20387; fax (21) 833692; Chargé d'affaires a.i.: MOHAMED HUSNI BIN MOHD JAZRI.

Mali: Sharia Jaraba Saniet Zarrouk, Tripoli; tel. (21) 4444924; Ambassador: EL BEKAYE SIDI MOCTAR KOUNTA.

Malta: POB 2534, Sharia Ubei ben Ka'ab, Tripoli; tel. (21) 3611181; fax (21) 3611180; Ambassador: GEORGE DOUBLESIN.

Mauritania: Sharia Eysa Wokwak, Tripoli; tel. (21) 4443223; Ambassador: YAHIA MUHAMMAD EL-HADI.

Morocco: POB 908, Ave ben Ashour, Tripoli; tel. (21) 600110; telex 22009; fax (21) 4445757; Chargé d'affaires: MEHDI MASDOUKI.

Netherlands: POB 3801, Sharia Jalal Bayar 20, Tripoli; tel. (21) 4441549; telex 20279; fax (21) 4440386; Chargé d'affaires: G. J. VAN EPEN.

Nicaragua: Beach Hotel, Andalous, Tripoli; tel. (21) 72641; Ambassador: GUILLERMO ESPINOSA.

Niger: POB 2251, Fachloun Area, Tripoli; tel. (21) 4443104; Ambassador: KARIM ALIO.

Nigeria: POB 4417, Sharia Bashir al-Ibrahim, Tripoli; tel. (21) 4443038; telex 20124; Ambassador: Prof. DANDATTI ABD AL-KADIR.

Pakistan: POB 2169, Sharia Abdul Karim al-Khattabi 16, Maidan Al-Qadasia, Tripoli; tel. (21) 4440072; fax (21) 4444698; Ambassador: KHAWAR RASHID PIRZADA.

Philippines: POB 12508, Andalous, Gargaresh, Tripoli; tel. and fax (21) 4833966; telex 20304; Ambassador: MUKHTAR H. MUALLAM.

Poland: POB 519, Sharia ben Ashour 61, Tripoli; tel. (21) 607619; telex 20049; fax (21) 603641; Ambassador: WITOLD JURASZ.

Qatar: POB 3506, Sharia ben Ashour, Tripoli; tel. (21) 4446660; Chargé d'affaires: HASAN AHMAD ABU HINDI.

Romania: POB 5085, Sharia Ahmad Lotfi Sayed, Sharia ben Ashour, Tripoli; tel. (21) 607904; fax (21) 3615295; Ambassador: VICTOR DIACONU.

Russia: POB 4792, Sharia Mustapha Kamel, Tripoli; tel. (21) 3330545; telex 22029; Ambassador: ALEKSEI BORISOVICH PODTSEROB.

Rwanda: POB 6677, Villa Ibrahim Musbah Missalati, Al-Andalous, Tripoli; tel. (21) 72864; telex 20236; fax (21) 70317; Chargé d'affaires: CHRISTOPHE HABIMANA.

Saudi Arabia: Sharia Kairauan 2, Tripoli; tel. (21) 30485; Chargé d'affaires: MUHAMMAD HASSAN BANDAH.

Senegal: Tripoli.

Slovakia: POB 2764, Sharia Jallal Bayar 1–3, Tripoli; tel. (21) 3333312; fax (21) 3332568; Chargé d'affaires: JÁN KLINČOK.

Spain: POB 2302, Sharia el-Amir Abd al-Kader al-Jazairi 36, Tripoli; tel. (21) 3336797; telex 20184; fax (21) 4443743; Ambassador: PABLO BENAVIDES ORGAZ.

Sudan: Sharia Muhammad Ali Mosadak 68; tel. (21) 75387; fax (21) 74781; Tripoli; Ambassador: ABD AL-MAJID BASHIR AL-AHMADI.

Sweden: POB 437, 5th Floor, Tower No. 5, That al-Imad, Tripoli; tel. (21) 4447583; telex 20154; fax (21) 70357; Ambassador: NILS-ERIK SCHYBERG.

Switzerland: POB 439, Sharia ben Ashour, Tripoli; tel. (21) 607365; telex 20382; fax (21) 607487; Chargé d'affaires: JOSEF BUCHER.

Syria: POB 4219, Sharia Muhammad Rashid Reda 4, Tripoli (Relations Office); tel. 3331783; Head: MUNIR BORKHAN.

Togo: POB 3420, Sharia Khaled ibn al-Walid, Tripoli; tel. (21) 4449565; telex 20373; fax (21) 3332423; Ambassador: TCHAO SOTOU BERE.

Tunisia: POB 613, Sharia Bashir al-Ibrahimi, Tripoli; tel. (21) 3331051; telex 20217; fax (21) 4447600; High Representative: MANSOUR EZZEDDINE.

Uganda: POB 80215, Sharia ben Ashour, Tripoli; tel. (21) 604471; fax (21) 4831602; Ambassador: WILLIAM N. HAKIZA.

United Kingdom: (see Italy, above).

Venezuela: POB 2584, Sharia ben Ashour, Jamaa al sagaa Bridge, Tripoli; tel. (21) 3600408; fax (21) 3600407; Ambassador: JULIO CÉSAR PINEDA.

Viet Nam: POB 587, Sharia Talha ben Abdullah, Tripoli; tel. (21) 45753; Ambassador: DANG SAN.

Yemen: POB 4839, Sharia Ubei ben Ka'ab 36, Tripoli; tel. (21) 607472; Ambassador: ALI AIDAROUS YAHYA.

Yugoslavia: POB 1087, Sharia Turkia 14–16, Tripoli; tel. (21) 3334114; Ambassador: DRAGO MIRŠIČ.

Judicial System

The judicial system is composed, in order of seniority, of the Supreme Court, Courts of Appeal, and Courts of First Instance and Summary Courts.

All courts convene in open session, unless public morals or public order require a closed session; all judgments, however, are delivered in open session. Cases are heard in Arabic, with interpreters provided for aliens.

The courts apply the Libyan codes which include all the traditional branches of law, such as civil, commercial and penal codes, etc. Committees were formed in 1971 to examine Libyan law and ensure that it coincides with the rules of Islamic *Shari'a*. The proclamation of People's Authority in the Jamahiriya provides that the Holy Koran is the law of society.

Attorney-General: SALIM MUHAMMAD SALIM.

SUPREME COURT

The judgments of the Supreme Court are final. It is composed of the President and several Justices. Its judgments are issued by circuits of at least three Justices (the quorum is three). The Court hears appeals from the Courts of Appeal in civil, penal, administrative and civil status matters.

President: MUHAMMAD ALI AL-JADI.

COURTS OF APPEAL

These courts settle appeals from Courts of First Instance; the quorum is three Justices. Each court of appeal has a court of assize.

COURTS OF FIRST INSTANCE AND SUMMARY COURTS

These courts are first-stage courts in the Jamahiriya, and the cases heard in them are heard by one judge. Appeals against summary judgments are heard by the appellate court attached to the court of first instance, whose quorum is three judges.

PEOPLE'S COURT

Established by order of the General People's Congress in March 1988.

President: ABD AR-RAZIQ ABU BAKR AS-SAWSA.

PEOPLE'S PROSECUTION BUREAU

Established by order of the General People's Congress in March 1988.

President: ABD AR-RAZIQ ABU BAKR AS-SAWSA.

Religion

ISLAM

The vast majority of Libyan Arabs follow Sunni Muslim rites, although Col Qaddafi has rejected the Sunnah (i.e. the practice, course, way, manner or conduct of the Prophet Muhammad, as followed by Sunnis) as a basis for legislation.

Chief Mufti of Libya: Sheikh TAHIR AHMAD AZ-ZAWI.

CHRISTIANITY

The Roman Catholic Church

Libya comprises three Apostolic Vicariates and one Apostolic Prefecture. At 31 December 1996 there were an estimated 50,000 adherents in the country.

Apostolic Vicariate of Benghazi: POB 248, Benghazi; tel. (61) 96563; fax (61) 34696; Vicar Apostolic Mgr SYLVESTER CARMEL MAGRO, Titular Bishop of Babra (absent).

Apostolic Vicariate of Darna: c/o POB 248, Benghazi; Vicar Apostolic (vacant).

Apostolic Vicariate of Tripoli: POB 365, Dahra, Tripoli; tel. (21) 3331863; fax (21) 3334696; Vicar Apostolic Mgr GIOVANNI INNOCENZO MARTINELLI, Titular Bishop of Tabuda; also Apostolic Administrator of Benghazi.

The Anglican Communion

Within the Episcopal Church in Jerusalem and the Middle East, Libya forms part of the diocese of Egypt (q.v.).

Other Christian Churches

The Coptic Orthodox Church is represented in Libya.

The Press

Newspapers and periodicals are published either by the Jamahiriya News Agency (JANA), by government secretariats, by the Press Service or by trade unions.

DAILIES

Al-Fajr al-Jadid (The New Dawn): POB 2303, Tripoli; tel. (21) 3333056; f. 1969; since January 1978 published by JANA; circ. 40,000.

Ash-Shams: Tripoli.

PERIODICALS

Al-Amal (Hope): Tripoli; weekly; social, for children; published by the Press Service.

Ad-Daawa al-Islamia (Islamic Call): POB 2682, Sharia Tanta, Tripoli; tel. (21) 3332055; telex 20480; fax (21) 3338125; f. 1980; weekly (Wednesdays); Arabic, English, French; cultural; published by the World Islamic Call Society.

Economic Bulletin: POB 2303, Tripoli; tel. (21) 3337106; telex 20841; monthly; published by JANA.

Al-Jamahiriya: POB 4814, Tripoli; tel. (21) 4449294; f. 1980; weekly; Arabic; political; published by the revolutionary committees.

Al-Jarida ar-Rasmiya (The Official Newspaper): Tripoli; irregular; official state gazette.

Libyan Arab Republic Gazette: Tripoli; weekly; English; published by the Secretariat of Justice.

Risalat al-Jihad (Holy War Letter): POB 2682, Tripoli; tel. (21) 3331021; telex 20407; f. 1983; monthly; Arabic, English, French; published by the World Islamic Call Society.

Scientific Bulletin: POB 2303, Tripoli; tel. (21) 3337106; monthly; published by JANA.

Ath-Thaqafa al-Arabiya (Arab Culture): POB 4587, Tripoli; f. 1973; weekly; cultural; circ. 25,000.

Al-Watan al-Arabi al-Kabir (The Greater Arab Homeland): Tripoli; f. 1987.

Az-Zahf al-Akhdar (The Green Army): POB 15246, Tripoli; tel. (21) 4442598; fax (21) 602418; weekly; ideological journal of the Revolutionary Committees.

NEWS AGENCIES

Jamahiriya News Agency (JANA): POB 2303, Sharia al-Fateh, Tripoli; tel. (21) 3337106; telex 20841; branches and correspondents throughout Libya; main foreign bureaux: London, Paris, Rome, Beirut, Nairobi, Nouakchott and Kuwait; serves Libyan and foreign subscribers.

Foreign Bureaux

Informatsionnoye Telegrafnoye Agentstvo Rossii—Telegrafnoye Agentstvo Suverennykh Stran (ITAR—TASS) (Russia): Sharia Mustapha Kamel 10, Tripoli; Correspondent GEORG SHELENKOV.

ANSA (Italy) is also represented in Tripoli.

Publishers

Ad-Dar al-Arabia Lilkitab (Maison Arabe du Livre): POB 3185, Tripoli; tel. (21) 4447287; telex 20003; f. 1973 by Libya and Tunisia.

Al-Fatah University, General Administration of Libraries, Printing and Publications: POB 13543, Tripoli; tel. (21) 621988; telex 20629; f. 1955; academic books.

General Co for Publishing, Advertising and Distribution: POB 921, Sirte; tel. (54) 63170; telex 30098; fax (54) 62100; general,

educational and academic books in Arabic and other languages; makes and distributes advertisements throughout Libya.

Broadcasting and Communications

TELECOMMUNICATIONS

General Directorate of Posts and Telecommunications: POB 81686, Tripoli; tel. (21) 3604101; fax (21) 3604102; Dir-Gen. ABU ZAID JUMA AL-MANSURI.

BROADCASTING

Radio

Great Socialist People's Libyan Arab Jamahiriya Broadcasting Corporation: POB 3731, Tripoli; POB 119, al-Beida; tel. (21) 3332451; f. 1957 (TV 1968); broadcasts in Arabic and English from Tripoli and Benghazi; from September 1971 special daily broadcasts to Gaza and other Israeli-occupied territories were begun; External Service (Radio) and People's Revolution Broadcasting: POB 333, Tripoli; Dir-Gen. External Service ABDALLAH AL-MEGRI.

Television

People's Revolution Broadcasting TV: POB 333, Tripoli; f. 1968; broadcasts in Arabic; additional channels broadcast for limited hours in English, Italian and French; Dir YOUSUF DEBRI.

Finance

(cap. = capital; res = reserves; dep. = deposits; LD = Libyan dinars; m. = million; brs = branches)

BANKING

Central Bank

Central Bank of Libya: POB 1103, Sharia al-Malik Seoud, Tripoli; tel. (21) 3333591; telex 20661; fax (21) 4441488; f. 1955 as National Bank of Libya, name changed to Bank of Libya 1963, to Central Bank of Libya 1977; bank of issue and central bank carrying government accounts and operating exchange control; commercial operations transferred to National Commercial Bank 1970; cap. LD100m., res LD131m., dep. LD2,193m., total assets LD4,648m. (June 1984); Pres. Dr ABD AL-HAFIZ MAHMUD AZ-ZILITNI.

Other Banks

Jamahiriya Bank: POB 65155, Martyr St, Megarief, Gharian; tel. 3331964; telex 20889; fax (41) 3339402; f. 1969 as successor to Barclays Bank International in Libya; known as Masraf al-Jumhuriya until March 1977; wholly-owned subsidiary of the Central Bank; throughout Libya; cap. LD25m., res LD22.1m., dep. LD946.8m., total assets LD1,446.6m. (Dec. 1987); Chair. MUSTAFA SALAH GEBRIL; 53 brs.

Libyan Arab Foreign Bank: POB 2542, Tower No. 2, That al-Imad Administrative Complex, Tripoli; tel. (21) 3350155; telex 20200; fax (21) 3350164; f. 1972; offshore bank wholly owned by Central Bank of Libya; cap. LD222m., res LD49.6m., dep. LD2,993.8m. (Dec. 1997); Chair. and Gen. Man. MUHAMMAD H. LAYAS.

National Commercial Bank SAL: POB 543, Beida; tel. (21) 4446705; telex 50433; fax (21) 30340; f. 1970 to take over commercial banking division of Central Bank (then Bank of Libya) and brs of Aruba Bank and Istiklal Bank; wholly owned by Central Bank of Libya; cap. LD35m., res LD49.9m., dep. LD931m. (March 1994); Chair. and Gen. Man. BADER A. ABU AZIZA; 46 brs.

Sahara Bank: POB 270, 10 Sharia 1 September, Tripoli; tel. (21) 3339804; telex 20009; fax (21) 3337922; f. 1964 to take over br. of Banco di Sicilia; cap. LD525,000, res LD52.5m., dep. LD488.4m. (March 1988); Chair. and Gen. Man. OMAR ALI ASHABU; 20 brs.

Umma Bank SAL: POB 685, 1 Giaddat Omar el-Mokhtar, Tripoli; tel. (21) 3334031; telex 20256; fax (21) 3332505; f. 1969 to take over brs of Banco di Roma; state-owned; cap. LD23m., res LD16.7m., dep. LD1,212.1m. (March 1997); Chair. and Gen. Man. SADIQ OMAR AL-QABIR; 42 brs.

Wahda Bank: POB 452, Fadiel Abu Omar Sq., El-Berkha, Benghazi; tel. (61) 24709; telex 40011; f. 1970 to take over Bank of North Africa, Commercial Bank SAL, Nahda Arabia Bank, Société Africaine de Banque SAL, Kafila al-Ahly Bank; state-owned; cap. LD36m., res LD91.5m., dep. LD1,051.6m. (Dec. 1995); Chair. and Gen. Man. MUHAMMAD MUSTAFA GHADBAN; 49 brs.

INSURANCE

Libya Insurance Co: POB 2438, Osama Bldg, Sharia 1 September, Tripoli; tel. (21) 4444151; telex 20071; fax (21) 4444178; POB 643, Benghazi; tel. (61) 9090055; f. 1964 (merged with Al-Mukhtar Insurance Co in 1981); cap. LD30m.; all classes of insurance; Gen. Commr and Chair. K. M. SHERLALA.

Trade and Industry

There are state trade and industrial organizations responsible for the running of industries at all levels, which supervise production, distribution and sales. There are also central bodies responsible for the power generation industry, agriculture, land reclamation and transport.

GOVERNMENT AGENCY

Great Man-made River Authority (GMRA): Tripoli; supervises construction of pipeline carrying water to the Libyan coast from beneath the Sahara desert, to provide irrigation for agricultural projects; Sec. for the Great Man-made River Project ABD AL-MAJID AL-AOUD.

DEVELOPMENT ORGANIZATIONS

General National Organization for Industrialization: POB 4388, Sharia San'a, Tripoli; tel. (21) 3334995; telex 200990; f. 1970; a public organization responsible for the development of industry.

Kufra and Sarir Authority: Council of Agricultural Development, POB 50651, Benghazi; f. 1972 to develop the Kufra oasis and Sarir area in south-east Libya.

CHAMBERS OF COMMERCE

Benghazi Chamber of Commerce, Industry and Agriculture: POB 208 and 1286, Benghazi; tel. (61) 82857; telex 40077; fax (61) 80761; f. 1956; Pres. Dr SADIQ M. BUSNAINA; Gen. Man. YOUSUF AL-JIAMI; 45,000 mems.

Tripoli Chamber of Commerce, Industry and Agriculture: POB 2321, 6–8 Sharia Najed, Tripoli; tel. (21) 3336855; telex 20181; fax (21) 3332655; f. 1952; Pres. ABDALLAH AL-BARONE; Dir-Gen. RAMADAN A. ZEREG; 60,000 mems.

STATE HYDROCARBONS COMPANIES

Until 1986 petroleum affairs in Libya were dealt with primarily by the Secretariat of the General People's Committee for Petroleum. This body was abolished in March 1986, and sole responsibility for the administration of the petroleum industry passed to the national companies which were already in existence. The Secretariat of the General People's Committee for Petroleum was re-established in March 1989 and incorporated into the new Secretariat for the General People's Committee for Energy in October 1992. Since 1973 the Libyan Government has entered into participation agreements with some of the foreign oil companies (concession holders), and nationalized others. It has concluded 85%–15% production-sharing agreements with various oil companies.

National Oil Corporation (NOC): POB 2655, Tripoli; tel. (21) 4446180; telex 61508; f. 1970 as successor to the Libyan General Petroleum Corpn, to undertake joint ventures with foreign companies; to build and operate refineries, storage tanks, petrochemical facilities, pipelines and tankers; to take part in arranging specifications for local and imported petroleum products; to participate in general planning of oil installations in Libya; to market crude oil and to establish and operate oil terminals; Chair. HAMUDA AL-ASWAD.

Agip North Africa and Middle East Ltd—Libyan Branch: POB 346, Tripoli; tel. and fax (21) 3335135; telex 20282; Sec. of People's Cttee A. M. CREUI.

Arabian Gulf Oil Co (AGOCO): POB 263, Benghazi; telex 4440033; Sec. of People's Cttee H. A. LAYASS.

Azzawiya Oil Refining Co: POB 6451, Tripoli tel. (21) 605389; telex 30423; and POB 15715, Az-Zawiya; tel. (23) 20125; fax 605948; f. 1973; Gen. Commr HAMUDA M. AL-ASWAD.

Brega Petroleum Marketing Co: POB 402, Sharia Bashir es-Saidawi, Tripoli; tel. (21) 4440830; telex 20090; f. 1971; Sec. of People's Cttee Dr DOKALI B. AL-MEGHARIEF.

International Oil Investments Co: Tripoli; f. 1988 with initial capital of $500m. to acquire 'downstream' facilities abroad; Chair. MUHAMMAD AL-JAWAD.

National Drilling and Workover Co: POB 1454, 208 Sharia Omar Mukhtar, Tripoli; tel. (21) 3332411; telex 20332; f. 1986; Chair. IBRAHIM BAHI.

Ras Lanouf Oil and Gas Processing Co (RASCO): POB 1971, Ras Lanouf, Benghazi; tel. (21) 3605177; telex 50613; fax (21) 607924; f. 1978; Chair. MAHMUD ABDALLAH NAAS.

Sirte Oil Co: POB 385, Tripoli; tel. (21) 602052; telex 30120; fax (21) 601487; f. 1955 as Esso Standard Libya, taken over by Surt Oil Co 1982; absorbed the National Petrochemicals Co in October 1990; exploration, production of crude oil, gas, and petrochemicals, liquefaction of natural gas.

Umm al-Jawaby Petroleum Co: POB 693, Tripoli; Chair. and Gen. Man. MUHAMMAD TENTTOUSH.

Waha Oil Co: POB 395, Tripoli; tel (21) 3331116; telex 20158; fax (21) 3337169; Sec. of People's Cttee SALEH M. KAABAR.

Zueitina Oil Co: POB 2134, Tripoli; tel. (21) 3338011; telex 20130; fax (21) 3339109; Chair. of People's Cttee Dr N. A. ARIFI.

TRADE UNIONS

General Federation of Producers' Trade Unions: POB 734, 2 Sharia Istanbul, Tripoli; tel. (21) 4446011; telex 20229; f. 1952; affiliated to ICFTU; Sec.-Gen. BASHIR IHWIJ; 17 trade unions with 700,000 members.

General Union for Oil and Petrochemicals: Tripoli; Chair. MUHAMMAD MITHNANI.

Pan-African Federation of Petroleum Energy and Allied Workers: Tripoli; affiliated to the Organization of African Trade Union Unity.

Transport

Department of Road Transport and Railways: POB 14527, Sharia Az-Zawiyah, Secretariat of Communications and Transport Bldg, Tripoli; tel. (21) 609011; telex 20533; fax (21) 605605; Secretary for Public Works, Utilities, Transport and Communications MUBARAK ASH-SHAMIKH; Dir-Gen. Projects and Research MUHAMMAD ABU ZIAN.

RAILWAYS

There are, at present, no railways in Libya. In mid-1998, however, the Government invited bids for the construction of a 3,170 km-railway, comprising one branch, 2,178 km in length, running from north to south, and another, 992 km in length, running from east to west. The railway may eventually be linked to other North African rail networks.

ROADS

The most important road is the 1,822-km national coast road from the Tunisian to the Egyptian border, passing through Tripoli and Benghazi. It has a second link between Barce and Lamluda, 141 km long. Another national road runs from a point on the coastal road 120 km south of Misurata through Sebha to Ghat near the Algerian border (total length 1,250 km). There is a branch 247 km long running from Vaddan to Sirte (Surt). A 690-km road, connecting Tripoli and Sebha, and another 626 km long, from Ajdabiyah in the north to Kufra in the south-east, were opened in 1983. The Tripoli–Ghat section (941 km) of the third, 1,352-km long national road was opened in September 1984. There is a road crossing the desert from Sebha to the frontiers of Chad and Niger.

In addition to the national highways, the west of Libya has about 1,200 km of paved and macadamized roads and the east about 500 km. All the towns and villages of Libya, including the desert oases, are accessible by motor vehicle. In 1996 Libya had 47,590 km of paved roads.

SHIPPING

The principal ports are Tripoli, Benghazi, Mersa Brega, Misurata and as-Sider. Zuetina, Ras Lanouf, Mersa Hariga, Mersa Brega and as-Sider are mainly oil ports. A 30-inch crude oil pipeline connects the Zelten oilfields with Mersa Brega. Another pipeline joins the Sarir oilfield with Mersa Hariga, the port of Tobruk, and a pipeline from the Sarir field to Zuetina was opened in 1968. A port is being developed at Darna. Libya also has the use of Tunisian port facilities at Sfax and Gabès, to alleviate congestion at Tripoli.

At 31 December 1997 Libya's merchant fleet consisted of 151 vessels, with a combined displacement of 686,160 grt.

General National Maritime Transport Co: POB 80173, 2 Sharia Ahmad Sharif, Tripoli; tel. (21) 3333155; telex 20208; fax (21) 6361664; f. 1970 to handle all projects dealing with maritime trade; Chair. SAID MILUD AL-AHRASH.

CIVIL AVIATION

There are four civil airports: Tripoli International Airport, situated at ben Gashir, 34 km (21 miles) from Tripoli; Benina Airport 19 km (12 miles) from Benghazi; Sebha Airport; Misurata Airport (domestic flights only). In the late 1980s there were plans for a new international airport to be built at Ras Lanouf and for airports at Brak and al-Waigh. Since April 1992 international civilian air links with Libya have been suspended, in accordance with UN Security Council Resolution 748 of 31 March 1992.

Jamahiriya Libyan Arab Airlines: POB 2555, ben Fernas Bldg, Tripoli; tel. (21) 602083; telex 20845; fax (21) 602085; f. 1989 by merger of Jamahiriya Air Transport (which in 1983 took over operations of United African Airlines) and Libyan Arab Airlines (f. 1964 as Kingdom of Libya Airlines and renamed 1969); passenger and cargo services from Tripoli, Benghazi and Sebha to destinations in Europe, North Africa and the Middle East; domestic services throughout Libya; Chief Exec. MUHAMMAD SAAD AISSA.

Tourism

The principal attractions for visitors to Libya are Tripoli, with its beaches and annual International Fair, the ancient Roman towns of Sabratha, Leptis Magna and Cyrene, and historic oases. Excluding visitors from Arab countries, international tourist arrivals totalled an estimated 88,000 in 1996.

Department of Tourism and Fairs: POB 891, Sharia Omar Mukhtar, Tripoli; tel. (21) 3332255; telex 20179.

Defence

Commander-in-Chief of Armed Forces: Brig. ABU-BAKR YOUNIS JABER.

Chief of Staff of Armed Forces: Brig. MUSTAPHA KHARROUBI.

Commander of the Navy: ABD AL-LATIF AHMAD SHAKSHOUKI.

Estimated Defence Budget (1997): US $1,300m.

Military Service: selective conscription; 1–2 years.

Total Armed Forces (August 1997): 65,000: army (estimated) 35,000; navy 8,000; air force 22,000.

People's Militia: 40,000.

Education

A steady increase in educational facilities has taken place since 1943 and, according to UNESCO estimates, the average rate of adult literacy was 76.2% in 1995 (males 87.9%, females 63%), compared with 60.1% in 1984. In 1992 the number of pupils attending primary and secondary schools was 1,564,798, compared with 1,042,917 (including kindergartens) in 1982/83. The number of teachers rose similarly, from 67,246 in 1982/83 to an estimated 121,636 in 1991. In 1985 there were 4,164 primary schools with 63,122 teachers and 1,011,952 pupils. By 1991 the total number of students at all educational establishments was 1,527,393. Education is officially compulsory for nine years between six and 15 years of age. Primary education begins at the age of six and lasts for nine years. Secondary education, beginning at 15 years of age, lasts for a further three years. In 1992 primary enrolment included 97% of the relevant age-group (males 98%; females 96%). In that year secondary enrolment was equivalent to 97% of pupils in the relevant age-groups. The teaching of French was abolished in Libyan schools in 1983.

In 1958 the University of Libya opened in Benghazi with Faculties of Arts and Commerce, followed the next year by the Faculty of Science near Tripoli. Faculties of Law, Agriculture, Engineering, Teacher Training, and Arabic Language and Islamic Studies have since been added to the University. In 1973 the University was divided into two parts, to form the Universities of Tripoli and Benghazi, later renamed Al-Fatah and Ghar Younis universities. The Faculty of Education at Al-Fatah University became Sebha University in 1983. There is a University of Technology (Bright Star) at Mersa Brega and the Al-Arab Medical University at Benghazi.

Bibliography

di Agostini, Col Enrico. *La popolazione della Tripolitania*. 2 vols; Tripoli, 1917.

La popolazione della Cirenaica. Benghazi, 1922–23.

Amministrazione Fiduciaria all'Italia in Africa. Florence, 1948.

Archivio bibliografico Coloniale. Florence, Libia, 1915–21.

Allan, J. A. *Libya: the Experience of Oil*. London, Croom Helm, 1981.

Ansell, Meredith O. and al-Arif, Ibrahim M. *The Libyan Revolution*. London, The Oleander Press, 1972.

Arnold, Guy. *The Maverick State: Qaddafi and the New World Order*. London, Cassell, 1997.

Baruni, Omar. *Spaniards and Knights of St John of Jerusalem in Tripoli*. Tripoli, Arabic, 1952.

Berlardinalli, Arsenio. *La Ghibla*. Tripoli, 1935.

Blunsum, T. *Libya: the Country and its People*. London, Queen Anne Press, 1968.

Cachia, Anthony J. *Libya under the Second Ottoman Occupation, 1835–1911*. Tripoli, 1945.

Colucci Massimo. *Il Regime della Proprieta Fondiaria nell'Africa Italiana: Vol. I. Libia*. Bologna, 1942.

Cooley, John. *Libyan Sandstorm*. London, Sidgwick and Jackson, 1983.

Corò, Francesco. *Settantasei Anni di Dominazione Turca in Libia*. Tripoli, 1937.

Curotti, Torquato. *Gente di Libia*. Tripoli, 1928.

Davis, John. *Libyan Politics: Tribe and Revolution*. London, I. B. Tauris, 1987.

Deeb, Mary-Jane. *Libya's Foreign Policy in North Africa*. Boulder, CO, Westview Press, 1991.

Despois, Jean. *Géographie Humaine*. Paris, 1946.

Le Djebel Nefousa. Paris, 1935.

La Colonisation italienne en Libye; Problèmes et Méthodes. Paris, Larose-Editeurs, 1935.

Epton, Nina. *Oasis Kingdom: The Libyan Story*. New York, 1953.

Evans-Pritchard, E. E. *The Sanusi of Cyrenaica*. London, 1949.

Farley, Rawle. *Planning for Development in Libya*. London, Pall Mall, 1971.

First, Ruth. *Libya—the Elusive Revolution*. London, Penguin, 1974.

Franca, Pietro, and others. *L'Italia in Africa: Incivilimento e Sviluppo dell'Eritrea, della Somalia, e della Libia*. Rome, 1947.

Gurney, Judith. *Libya: The Political Economy of Oil*. Oxford University Press, 1996.

Hajjaji, S. A. *The New Libya*. Tripoli, 1967.

Herrmann, Gerhard. *Italiens Weg zum Imperium*. Leipzig, Goldman, 1938.

Heseltine, Nigel. *From Libyan Sands to Chad*. London, Museum Press, 1960.

Hill, R. W. *A Bibliography of Libya*. University of Durham, 1959.

Khadduri, Majid. *Modern Libya, a Study in Political Development*. Johns Hopkins Press, 1963.

Khalidi, I. R. *Constitutional Developments in Libya*. Beirut, Khayat's Book Co-operative, 1956.

El-Kikhia, Mansour O. *Libya's Qaddafi: The Politics of Contradiction*. University of California Press, 1997.

Kubbah, Abdul Amir Q. *Libya, Its Oil Industry and Economic System*. Baghdad, The Arab Petro-Economic Research Centre, 1964.

Legg, H. J. *Libya: Economic and General Conditions in Libya*. London, 1952.

Lethielleux, J. *Le Fezzan, ses Jardins, ses Palmiers: Notes d'Ethnographie et d'Histoire*. Tunis, 1948.

Lindberg, J. A. *General Economic Appraisal of Libya*. New York, 1952.

Martel, André. *La Libye 1835–1990: Essai de géopolitique historique*. Paris, Presses Universitaires de France, 1991.

Mattes, Hans-Peter. *Die innere und aussere islamische Mission Libyens*. Munich/Mainz, Kaiser-Gruenewald, 1987.

Micacchi, Rodolfo. *La Tripolitania sotto il dominio dei Caramanli*. Intra, 1936.

Murabet, Mohammed. *Tripolitania: the Country and its People*. Tripoli, 1952.

Norman, John. *Labour and Politics in Libya and Arab Africa*. New York, Bookman, 1965.

Owen, R. *Libya: a Brief Political and Economic Survey*. London, 1961.

Pelt, Adrian. *Libyan Independence and the United Nations*. Yale U.P., 1970.

Pichou, Jean. *La Question de Libye dans le règlement de la paix*. Paris, 1945.

Qaddafi, Col Muammar al-. *The Green Book*. 3 vols, Tripoli, 1976–79; Vol. I: The Solution of the Problem of Democracy, Vol. II: The Solution of the Economic Problem, Vol. III: The Social Basis of the Third Universal Theory.

Lord Rennell. *British Military Administration of Occupied Territories in Africa during the years 1941–47*. London, HMSO, 1948.

Rivlin, Benjamin. *The United Nations and the Italian Colonies*. New York, 1950.

Rossi, P. *Libya*. Lausanne, 1965.

Royal Institute of International Affairs. *The Italian Colonial Empire.* London, 1940.

Rushdi, Muhammad Rasim. *Trablus al Gharb.* Tripoli, Arabic, 1953.

Schlueter, Hans. *Index Libycus.* Boston, G. K. Hall, 1972.

Schmeider, Oskar and Wilhelmy, Herbert. *Die faschistische Kolonisation in Nordafrika.* Leipzig, Quelle and Meyer, 1939.

Steele-Greig, A. J. *History of Education in Tripolitania from the Time of the Ottoman Occupation to the Fifth Year under British Military Occupation.* Tripoli, 1948.

Vandewalle, Dirk (Ed.). *North Africa: Development and Reform in a Changing Global Economy.* New York, St Martin's Press Inc, 1996.

(Ed.) *Qadhafi's Libya: 1969–1994.* London, Macmillan, 1996.

Villard, Henry S. *Libya: The New Arab Kingdom of North Africa.* Ithaca, 1956.

Waddams, Frank C. *The Libyan Oil Industry.* London, Croom Helm, 1980.

Ward, Philip. *Touring Libya.* 3 vols, 1967–69.

Tripoli: Portrait of a City. 1970.

Williams, G. *Green Mountain, an Informal Guide to Cyrenaica and its Jebel Akhdar.* London, 1963.

Willimott, S. G. and Clarke, J. I. *Field Studies in Libya.* Durham, 1960.

Wright, John. *Libya: a Modern History.* London, Croom Helm, 1982.

MOROCCO

Physical and Social Geography

The Kingdom of Morocco is the westernmost of the three North African countries known to the Arabs as Jeziret al-Maghreb or 'Island of the West'. It occupies an area of 458,730 sq km (177,117 sq miles), excluding Western (formerly Spanish) Sahara (252,120 sq km or 97,344 sq miles), a disputed territory under Moroccan occupation. Morocco has an extensive coastline on both the Atlantic Ocean and the Mediterranean Sea. However, owing to its position and intervening mountain ranges, Morocco remained relatively isolated from the rest of the Maghreb and served as a refuge for descendants of the native Berber-speaking inhabitants of north-west Africa.

According to census results, the population at 2 September 1994 was 26,073,717. About 35% of the total were Berber-speaking peoples, living mainly in mountain villages, while the Arabic-speaking majority was concentrated in towns in the lowlands, particularly in Casablanca (which was the largest city in the Maghreb, with a population of 2,940,623 at the 1994 census), Marrakesh, the old southern capital (population 745,541), Fez (population 774,754), and Rabat (population 1,385,872, including Salé), the modern administrative capital.

PHYSICAL FEATURES

The physical geography of Morocco is dominated by the highest and most rugged ranges in the Atlas Mountain system of north-west Africa. They are the result of mountain-building in the Tertiary era, when sediments deposited beneath an ancestral Mediterranean Sea were uplifted, folded and fractured. The mountains remain geologically unstable and Morocco is liable to severe earthquakes.

In Morocco the Atlas Mountains form four distinct massifs, which are surrounded and partially separated by lowland plains and plateaux. In the north, the Rif Atlas comprise a rugged arc of mountains that rise steeply from the Mediterranean coast to heights of more than 2,200 m above sea level. There, limestone and sandstone ranges form an effective barrier to east–west communications. They are inhabited by Berber farming families who live in isolated mountain villages and have little contact with the Arabs of Tétouan (estimated population, including Larache, 878,000 at mid-1993) and Tangier (579,000) at the north-western end of the Rif chain.

The Middle Atlas lie immediately south of the Rif, separated by the Col of Taza, a narrow gap which affords the only easy route between western Algeria and Atlantic Morocco. They rise to about 3,000 m and form a broad barrier between the two countries. They also function as a major drainage divide and are flanked by the basins of Morocco's two principal rivers, the Oum er-Rbia which flows west to the Atlantic and the Moulouya which flows north-east to the Mediterranean. Much of the Middle Atlas consists of a limestone plateau dissected by river gorges and capped here and there by volcanic craters and lava flows. The semi-nomadic Berber tribes spend the winter in villages in the valleys and move to the higher slopes in summer to pasture their flocks.

To the south the Middle Atlas chain merges into the High Atlas, the most formidable of the mountain massifs, which rises to about 4,000 m and is heavily snow-clad in winter. The mountains extend from south-west to north-east, and rise precipitously from both the Atlantic lowland to the north and the desert plain of Saharan Morocco to the south. There are no easily accessible routes across the High Atlas, but numerous mountain tracks allow the exchange of goods by pack animal between Atlantic and Saharan Morocco. A considerable Berber population lives in the mountain valleys in compact, fortified villages.

The Anti-Atlas is the lowest and most southerly of the mountain massifs. Structurally it forms an elevated edge of the Saharan platform which was uplifted when the High Atlas was formed. It consists largely of crystalline rocks and is joined to the southern margin of the High Atlas by a mass of volcanic lavas which separates the valley of the river Sous, draining west to the Atlantic at Agadir, from that of the upper Draa, draining south-east towards the Sahara. On the southern side of the chain, barren slopes are trenched by gorges from which cultivated palm groves protrude.

Stretching inland from the Atlantic coast is an extensive area of lowland, enclosed on the north, east and south by the Rif, Middle and High Atlas. It consists of the Gharb plain and the wide valley of the River Sebou in the north and of the plateaux and plains of the Meseta, the Tadla, the Rehamna, the Djebilet and the Haouz farther south. Most of the Arabic-speaking people of Morocco live in this region.

CLIMATE AND VEGETATION

Northern and central Morocco experience a 'Mediterranean' climate, with warm, wet winters and hot, dry summers, but to the south this gives way to semi-arid and eventually to desert conditions. In the Rif and the northern parts of the Middle Atlas mean annual rainfall exceeds 75 cm and the summer drought lasts only three months, but in the rest of the Middle Atlas, in the High Atlas and over the northern half of the Atlantic lowland rainfall is reduced to between 40 cm and 75 cm and the summer drought lasts for four months or more. During the summer intensely hot winds from the Sahara, known as the Sirocco or Chergui, occasionally cross the mountains and desiccate the lowland. Summer heat on the Atlantic coastal plain is tempered, however, by sea breezes.

Over the southern half of the Atlantic lowland and the Anti-Atlas semi-arid conditions prevail and rainfall decreases to 20 cm–40 cm per year, becoming very variable and generally insufficient for the regular cultivation of cereal crops without irrigation. East and south of the Atlas Mountains, which act as a barrier to rain-bearing winds from the Atlantic, rainfall is reduced still further and regular cultivation becomes entirely dependent on irrigation.

The chief contrast in the vegetation of Morocco is between the mountain massifs, which support forest or open woodland, and the surrounding lowlands, which tend to be covered only by scrub growth of low, drought-resistant bushes. The natural vegetation has been depleted, and in many places actually destroyed, by excessive cutting, burning and grazing. The middle and upper slopes of the mountains are often quite well wooded, with evergreen oak dominant at the lower and cedar at the higher elevations. The lowlands to the east and south of the Atlas Mountains support distinctive species of steppe and desert vegetation, among which esparto grass and the argan tree (which is unique to south-western Morocco) are conspicuous.

NEWLY-ANNEXED TERRITORY

After independence the Moroccan Government claimed a right to administer a large area of the western Sahara, including territory in Algeria and Mauritania, and the whole of Spanish Sahara. The claim was based on the extent of Moroccan rule in medieval times. The existence of considerable deposits of phosphates in Spanish Sahara and of iron ore in the Algeria-Morocco border region further encouraged Moroccan interest in expansion. After Spanish withdrawal from the Sahara in 1976, Morocco and Mauritania divided the former Spanish Sahara (now known as Western Sahara) between them, with Morocco annexing the northern part of the territory, including the phosphate mines of Bou Craa. In August 1979 Mauritania renounced its share, which was immediately annexed by Morocco and incorporated as a new province, Oued ed-Dahab.

828

The current population of Western Sahara are of Moorish or mixed Arab-Berber descent with some negro admixture, who depend for their existence on herds of sheep, camels and goats which they move seasonally from one pasture to another. The main tribes are the R'gibat, Uld Delim, Izargien and Arosien. At the census of September 1982 the population of Western Sahara was estimated at 163,868; at the census of September 1994 the population had increased to 252,146. The principal towns in the area are el-Aaiún, es-Smara (formerly Smara) and Dakhla (Villa Cisneros).

The relief of most of the area is gentle. The coast is backed by a wide alluvial plain overlain in the south by extensive sand dunes aligned from south-west to north-east and extending inland over 250 km (155 miles). Behind the coastal plain the land rises gradually to a plateau surface broken by sandstone ridges that reach 300 m in height. In the north-east, close to the Mauritanian frontier, isolated mountain ranges, such as the Massif de la Guelta, rise to over 600 m. There are no permanent streams and the only considerable valley is that of the Saguia el-Hamra which crosses the northernmost part of the area to reach the coast at el-Aaiún north of Cape Bojador. The whole region experiences an extreme desert climate. Nowhere does mean annual rainfall exceed 100 mm and over most of the territory it is less than 50 mm. Vegetation is restricted to scattered desert shrubs and occasional patches of coarse grass in most depressions. Along the coast, summer heat is tempered by air moving inland after it has been cooled over the waters of the cold Canaries current which flows offshore from north to south.

History

Revised for this edition by RICHARD I. LAWLESS

EARLY HISTORY

The Phoenicians and Carthaginians established trading posts on Morocco's coasts, and later the Romans established the province of Mauritania Tingitana in the north of the country. Muslim warriors made raids in AD 684–85 and had conquered Morocco by the eighth century. The Berber tribes of Morocco rallied to Islam, but adopted Kharijite heresies, which, together with Berber particularism, led to a great rebellion in 739–40 and the subsequent fragmentation of Morocco into small Muslim principalities.

Idris, a descendant of the Prophet Muhammad, founded the first of the great ruling Muslim dynasties in Morocco. The regime lasted from 788–89 to 985–86 but, after the death of Idris' son (828–29), it fell into decline. There followed two centuries of internal conflict and tribal revolt, as well as pressures from the Umayyad Caliphate in Spain and from the Fatimid Caliphate in Ifriqiya (Tunisia and eastern Algeria) in 908–69. Subsequently, Morocco entered a glorious era, with the rise of the Almoravid religious movement among the nomadic Berbers of Sanhaja descent. The Almoravids declared Holy War (Jihad) and established control, under Yousuf ibn Tashufin (d. 1106), over all Morocco and much of Algeria, and also annexed Muslim lands in Spain. After the death of Tashufin's successor in 1142, however, Almoravid power declined rapidly.

A new religious force emerged after the death in 1130 of Muhammad ibn Tumart, a religious teacher who had gathered Berber adherents, called Almohads, around himself in the High Atlas. One of his disciples, Abd al-Mumin, led the Almohads in their conquest of the Maghreb as far east as Tripolitania and Cyrenaica in 1151–59. The Almohads prospered in the reign of al-Mansur (1184–98), who brought Muslim Spain under his control, but in 1212 they suffered a serious defeat at the hands of the Spanish Christians, and thereafter the Almohad empire began to decline. A new Berber house, the Merinids, became prominent, and by the mid-13th century they had eclipsed the Almohads. Their influence lasted for about 100 years but their attempts to reconstitute the Almohad empire were largely unsuccessful.

Nomadic tribes of Arab origin had penetrated the Maghreb in the 11th and 12th centuries, along with other Badawi elements during the later Almohad period. With the disintegration of the Merinid state, the Badawi tribes invaded, contributing greatly to the Arabization of the Maghreb. Until 1465 Morocco was prey to internal discords, which persisted until the emergence of the Wattasids, another Berber regime. Their pre-eminence was, however, short-lived, and they failed to halt the Portuguese and the Spaniards, who were establishing outposts along the Moroccan coasts.

A new movement of resistance to the Spaniards and Portuguese was born among the religious confraternities who now led the Jihad against the Christians. The Saadian regime arose, originating in a line of Sharifs from the Saharan side of the Atlas mountains. Ahmad al-Mansur (1578–1603) reorganized the Saadian regime under a system which exempted various Arab tribes from taxation, in return for armed services to the State. Under this system, much depended on the character of the Sultan, as tribal rivalries erupted whenever the central government was weak or ill-directed. The period of Saadian rule, which ended in 1668, was, however, one of considerable prosperity.

Yet another wave of popular religious feeling brought to power the house of Alawi (Hasani or Filali), which originated among the Saharan Berbers and continues to reign in Morocco. Rashid II (1664–72) and Mulai Ismail (1672–1727) firmly established the regime, under which Morocco was more peaceful and united than it was ever to be again until French occupation. Mulai Ismail successfully repelled the Sanhaja Berbers, but a period of uncertainty followed his death, in the course of which one of his sons, Abdullah, was dethroned four times. His son, Sharif Muhammad ibn Abdallah (1757–90), and his immediate successors strove to maintain their power in the face of tribal dissidence and the threat of foreign intervention. However, the French conquest of Algiers in 1830 had repercussions in Morocco. Mulai Abd ar-Rahman, who was then Sultan of Morocco, gave military assistance to Abd al-Qadir, the Algerian Amir who led Muslim resistance to France, and Moroccan troops were later defeated by a French force at Wadi Isly in 1844.

A dispute over the limits of the Ceuta enclave, which had been under Spanish rule since 1580, led to a brief war between Morocco and Spain in 1860. Spanish troops defeated the Moroccans and, under the terms of the peace settlement, the Ceuta enclave was enlarged and Spain was given indemnities. Morocco also granted to Spain a territorial enclave on the Atlantic coast opposite the Canaries (Santa Cruz de Mar Pequeña, now Ifni). In 1884 Spain claimed a protectorate over the coastal zone to the south of Morocco, from Cape Bojador to Cape Blanco, the future Spanish Sahara. The borders between this territory, known as the Río de Oro, and the French possessions to the south and east were agreed between France and Spain in June 1900. A convention between France and Spain in October 1904 assigned to Spain two zones of influence, one in northern and the other in southern Morocco. The southern border of Morocco was set at 27° 40′N, beyond which were Spain's Saharan territories. The Germans now sought to intervene in Moroccan affairs and, at the conference of Algeciras in 1906, they secured the agreement of the Great Powers to the economic 'internationalization' of Morocco. A crisis in 1911, precipitated by the appearance of a German gun-boat off Agadir, ended in a Franco-German settlement whereby the Germans recognized Morocco as a French sphere of influence. In March 1912 Morocco became a protectorate of France, with a French Resident-General empowered to direct foreign affairs, control defence and introduce domestic reforms.

FRENCH RULE

Under an agreement of 1912, Spain retained its zones of influence (somewhat reduced), but these were now granted by France as the protecting power rather than by the Sultan. General Lyautey, the first French Resident-General in Morocco, established effective control, before 1914, over the plains and lower plateaux of Morocco from Fez to the Atlas mountains south of Marrakesh; then, before 1918, over the western Atlas, the Taza corridor as far as Algeria and some areas of the northern highlands. French troops helped Spain to subdue a formidable rebellion (1921–26) of the Rif tribe under Abd al-Krim. This resulted in the subjugation of the northern mountains and allowed the French to concentrate on gaining control of the Middle Atlas and the Tafilalet—a task that was accomplished by 1934, when the pacification of Morocco could be regarded as complete.

From this time, nationalist sentiment began to make itself felt in Morocco. A 'comité d'action marocaine' asked for a limitation of the protectorate. This 'comité' was dissolved in 1937, but nationalist propaganda against the French regime continued. Morocco supported France in 1939 and the Free French movement in 1942. A Party of Independence (Istiqlal), formed in 1943, demanded independence for Morocco, with a constitutional government under Sultan Muhammad ibn Yousuf, who supported the nationalist movement. Although Istiqlal had a large following in the towns, the party had little support among the conservative tribes of Morocco, who favoured Thami al-Glawi, the Pasha of Marrakesh. As a result, tension between the new and the old ideologies in Morocco increased in 1953. Sultan Muhammad ibn Yousuf had quarrelled with the French administration, and in May 1953 a number of Pashas and Cadis, led by al-Glawi, asked for his removal. The Berber tribes began to converge in force on the main urban centres in Morocco, and on 20 August 1953 the Sultan agreed to go into exile in Europe, but not to abdicate. Muhammad ibn Arafa, a prince of the Alawi house, was subsequently recognized as Sultan. The situation remained tense, with assassination attempts on the Sultan in 1953 and 1954, outbreaks of violence throughout Morocco in 1954–55 and intense nationalist fervour.

INDEPENDENCE—1956

Sultan Muhammad ibn Arafa renounced the throne and withdrew to Tangier in 1955. Muhammad ibn Yousuf, on 5 November in that year, was recognized once more as the legitimate Sultan. A joint Franco-Moroccan declaration of 2 March 1956 stated that the protectorate agreement of 1912 was obsolete and that the French Government now recognized the independence of Morocco. A protocol of the same date covered the transitional phase before new agreements could come into effect. The Sultan would now have full legislative powers in Morocco. Henceforth a high commissioner was to represent France in the new State. France also undertook to assist Morocco in the organization of its armed forces and the reassertion of Moroccan control over the zones of Spanish influence. On 12 November 1956 Morocco became a member of the UN.

In August 1956 Istiqlal proclaimed the need to abrogate the Convention of Algeciras (1906), which had 'internationalized' the economic life of Morocco, and also to secure the withdrawal of all foreign troops from the land. Following an international conference in October, Tangier was restored to Morocco. A royal charter of August 1957 preserved the former economic and financial system in force at Tangier, which included a free money market, quota-free trade with foreign countries and a low level of taxation. In 1959 Tangier lost its special status and was integrated financially and economically with Morocco, but a royal decree of January 1962 made it once more a free port. In 1956, prior to independence, Istiqlal had envisaged the creation of a 'Great Morocco' which would include certain areas in south-west Algeria, the Spanish territories in north-west Africa and also Mauritania, together with the French Sudan (i.e. the Republic of Mali). These claims were to be reiterated by Morocco in the following years, beginning in 1960, with an intensive propaganda and diplomatic campaign against Mauritania.

The problem of the Spanish territories in north-west Africa also came to the fore at this time. Spain had recognized the independence of Morocco and had renounced the northern zone of the protectorate assigned to it in Morocco under the terms of the Franco-Spanish convention of 1912. No agreement was reached, however, on the enclaves of Ceuta and Melilla in the north, the enclave of Ifni in the south, or the Spanish territories to the south of Morocco. Since 1934 these territories had been divided in two parts—the northern Saguia el-Hamra and the southern Río de Oro—both administered jointly with Ifni, and separately from the contiguous southern zone of Spain's protectorate in Morocco. Raids on Ifni and the western Sahara by Moroccan irregular forces (the 'Armée de libération du Grand Sahara') caused serious internal unrest during 1956–58, although the Moroccan Government denied responsibility. Negotiations between Morocco and Spain, held in Portugal, led in April 1958 to an agreement whereby Spain, in accordance with the settlement reached in April 1956, relinquished the southern zone of its former protectorate. Spain retained possession of the enclaves and of Saguia el-Hamra and Río de Oro, which were renamed Spanish Sahara and separated from Ifni.

KING HASSAN II AND ROYAL DOMINANCE OF GOVERNMENT

After independence, Istiqlal remained the dominant political force and obtained a majority in the Government. At the same time Sultan Muhammad strengthened the position of the monarchy. In July 1957 Prince Moulai Hassan was proclaimed heir to the throne and in August the Sultan assumed the title of King. Istiqlal's efforts to curb the power of the monarchy were hampered by internal division. Tension between the conservative and radical wings culminated in December 1958, when a Government was formed by Abdullah Ibrahim, a leader of the radical tendency. In the following months Ben Barka led a movement to establish a radical party organization independent of the conservative Istiqlal leadership of Allal al-Fassi. In September 1959 this new organization became an independent party, the Union nationale des forces populaires (National Union of Popular Forces—UNFP). Although the UNFP supported Ibrahim's Government, it was subjected to repressive measures by the police and the army who were under the control of the King or of 'King's men' in the Cabinet. In May 1960 a new Government was formed with the King himself as Prime Minister and Prince Hassan as his deputy. Consequently the UNFP went into opposition. On the death of King Muhammad in February 1961 the Prince ascended the throne as King Hassan II, and also became Prime Minister. In December 1962 a new Constitution, which established a constitutional monarchy and guaranteed personal and political freedoms, was approved by referendum. In January 1963 a cabinet reshuffle deprived the Istiqlal leaders of their posts in the Government, and when elections for the Chamber of Representatives were held in May, both Istiqlal and the UNFP appeared as opposition parties. The King was represented by the newly formed Front pour la défense des institutions constitutionnelles (FDIC). The election, by universal direct suffrage, failed to produce the expected clear majority for the government party, the results being: FDIC 69 seats; Istiqlal 41 seats; UNFP 28 seats; independents six seats. In the following months repressive action was taken against both opposition parties. Several Istiqlal deputies were arrested for protesting against corruption and mismanagement of the election, leading the party to boycott further elections later in the year. Almost all the leaders of the UNFP were arrested in July in connection with an alleged coup attempt. Many of them were held in solitary confinement, tortured and eventually sentenced to death. In November the King relinquished the premiership and installed an FDIC Government to represent his interests.

RELATIONS IN THE MAGHREB

In July 1962 Moroccan troops entered the region south of Colomb-Béchar in Algeria—a region never officially demarcated. The Moroccan press also launched a strong campaign in support of the view that the Tindouf area in the extreme south-west of Algeria should belong to Morocco—a claim of some importance, since the area contained large deposits of high-grade iron ore and also considerable resources of petroleum and natural gas.

An arbitration commission was established by the Organization of African Unity (OAU), and Algeria and Morocco submitted evidence in support of their respective territorial claims. In

February 1964 an agreement was reached to establish a demilit-arized zone. Subsequently there was a swift improvement in relations between the two countries.

Relations between Morocco and Mauritania also became more amicable. The ministers of information of the two States met at Cairo in July 1964 during an African Summit Conference. An understanding was reached to bring an end to the 'war' of radio propaganda and criticism hitherto conducted between Morocco and Mauritania.

INTERNAL UNREST

In August 1964 the Moroccan Government was reorganized, although it remained composed largely of FDIC members. The reshuffle was part of an attempt to attract the opposition parties back into a coalition government, since the FDIC had an inade-quate majority in the Chamber of Representatives and was itself split into two factions, the Parti socialiste démocratique and the mainly Berber Mouvement populaire (MP). The weak-ness of the Government contributed to the tension which de-veloped in early 1965, as unemployment and rising prices generated discontent among the urban working class. In June King Hassan proclaimed a state of emergency, whereby he himself assumed full legislative and executive powers. Fresh elections, it was stated, would be held after the Constitution had been revised and submitted to a referendum. In October the UNFP leader, Ben Barka, disappeared in France, never to be seen again. At a subsequent French trial, Gen. Oufkir, one of the King's sturdiest supporters, was found guilty *in absentia* of complicity in Ben Barka's disappearance. Relations between Morocco and France became very strained and there were anti-government protest strikes in Morocco.

In July 1967 King Hassan relinquished the post of Prime Minister in favour of Dr Muhammad Benhima, and in 1967 and 1968 there were eight major cabinet reshuffles. Considerable student and trade union unrest continued during this period, but the King won some approval for extensive nationalization measures and a degree of land redistribution.

There was a gradual return to normal political activity in 1969, albeit under royal direction. Communal elections were held in October, although these were boycotted by opposition parties, and the successful candidates were mostly independ-ents. Following these elections, Benhima was replaced as Prime Minister by Dr Ahmad Laraki, formerly the Minister of Foreign Affairs. A national referendum on a new Constitution was held in July 1970; official figures claimed that over 98% of the votes were affirmative, despite general opposition from the main political parties, trade unions and student organizations. Elec-tions for a new unicameral legislature were held in August. Of the 240 members, 90 were elected by direct suffrage, 90 by local councils and 60 by an electoral college. The results were that 158 elected members were independents, 60 were from the MP and 22 were from opposition parties.

In July 1971 there was an unsuccessful attempt, apparently engineered by right-wing army officers, to overthrow the King and establish a republic. A series of talks ensued between the Government and members of Istiqlal and the UNFP, who had united to form a National Front in July 1970, but the parties refused to compromise on government policies.

In March 1972 a new Constitution was promulgated, under which executive power was vested in the King. Legislative power was held by the Chamber of Representatives, with two-thirds of its members elected by universal suffrage, compared with one-half under the previous Constitution. In late April, however, King Hassan announced that the Chamber would remain dis-solved, and that elections for a new Chamber would be postponed until new electoral lists had been prepared.

In August 1972 King Hassan, after surviving another attempt on his life, assumed command of the armed forces and responsi-bility for defence. He again appealed to opposition parties to co-operate in supervising general elections and to collaborate with the Government. However, both Istiqlal and the UNFP dem-anded extensive reforms, which were unacceptable to the King. The elections were postponed indefinitely, and a new Cabinet was formed in November without opposition participation.

FOREIGN RELATIONS 1967–72

Morocco continued to press its claim to Spanish-held territories in north-west Africa. In December 1967 the UN General Assembly adopted a resolution urging Spain to hold a refer-endum in Spanish Sahara to allow the population to determine its future. Spain accepted the principle of self-determination, but in June 1970 progress was halted, after the violent repression of riots in the Saharan town of el-Aaiún resulted in numerous deaths. Further UN resolutions in support of decolonization were adopted, and Morocco, Mauritania and Algeria each sup-ported a rival Saharan liberation movement. In contrast, the question of Ifni was settled amicably in June 1969, when Spain ceded the small coastal enclave to Morocco.

Morocco abandoned its claim to Mauritania in 1969. Full diplomatic recognition and an exchange of ambassadors followed in 1970, and the two countries signed a treaty of solidarity and co-operation in June. Relations with France improved, and in December 1969 the diplomatic missions in Paris and Rabat were returned to full ambassadorial status for the first time since the Ben Barka affair in 1966.

In May 1970 a final agreement (ratified in May 1973) was reached in the frontier dispute with Algeria, and a joint commis-sion agreed to maintain the boundaries of the colonial period. The disputed region of Gara-Djebilet, rich in iron ore deposits, thus became the property of Algeria, but Morocco was to be a partner in a joint company to be established to exploit the depo-sits.

HASSAN IN CONTROL

In March 1973 the King announced plans for the Moroccaniza-tion of sectors of the economy within two years. He also rein-forced his traditional support in the rural areas by ordering the confiscation of foreign-owned lands and their redistribution among the peasantry. Since most of the landowners were French, relations between France and Morocco deteriorated again and French aid was suspended for a year, pending an agreement on compensation. In the same month relations with Spain became strained when Morocco announced the extension of its territorial waters from 12 to 70 nautical miles; in January 1974 the two countries concluded an agreement allowing a limited number of Spanish vessels to fish in Moroccan waters. Hassan's new nationalist policy also led Morocco to take a more active part in the Arab-Israeli conflict. In February 1973 troops were dispatched to the Syrian front, and during the October War further detachments were sent to Egypt; this resulted in a partial *rapprochement* between Morocco and the more extremist Arab states.

Political trials continued in early 1974. Further arrests fol-lowed the discovery, in February, of a plot to free prisoners in Kénitra jail. The King, however, made some conciliatory ges-tures: in March he announced plans for university and judicial reforms, and in April several imprisoned UNFP leaders were released.

Meanwhile, Morocco pursued its claim to Spanish Sahara. The development of phosphate mining in the territory presented a threat to the Moroccan economy, which was itself dependent on revenue from phosphate exports. In July 1974 the King held consultations with military chiefs, ministers and leaders of all the political parties to prepare an international campaign for the annexation of the Sahara. Discussions with Spain in August were inconclusive, and Morocco and Mauritania rejected Spain's proposal to hold a referendum in the Sahara under UN supervi-sion. In October the issue was debated in the UN General Assembly at the initiative of Morocco. Two months later the Assembly formally approved Morocco's suggestion that the matter be brought before the International Court of Justice (ICJ) in The Hague, and the UN Special Committee on Coloni-alism was instructed to send a mission to the territory. The referendum that Spain had proposed was to be postponed.

In the atmosphere of national unity produced by the Sahara issue in the second half of 1974 there was a revival of political activity. New parties were formed and existing parties reorgan-ized. Most notably the split in the UNFP (which occurred in mid-1972) was confirmed, as the Rabat section of the party became the Union socialiste des forces populaires (USFP). King Hassan again promised elections for the following year, and once more postponed them indefinitely, but even the opposition were content to give priority to the Sahara dispute. Although some political prisoners were released, harassment of opposition parties continued and they remained unrepresented in the Government.

SAHARAN TAKE-OVER

After Spain reiterated its readiness to withdraw from Spanish Sahara, it became clear that the chief conflict was between the rival North African countries and liberation movements. In October 1974 Morocco and Mauritania reached a secret agreement on the future division of the territory, which came to light in July 1975. Meanwhile, Algeria became the main target of Moroccan invective for its support of the Frente Popular para la Liberación de Saguia el-Hamra y Río de Oro (Popular Front for the Liberation of Saguia el-Hamra and Río de Oro—the Frente Polisario or Polisario Front), a Saharan liberation movement, founded in 1973, which aimed to establish an independent, non-aligned state in Spanish Sahara.

In October 1975 a UN investigative mission reported that almost all the people whom it had consulted in the territory were 'categorically for independence and against the territorial claims of Morocco and Mauritania'. Two days later the ICJ ruled in favour of self-determination for the Sahrawi people. King Hassan immediately ordered a march of 350,000 unarmed civilians to take possession of Spanish Sahara. The Green March, as it was called, began on 6 November. The Spanish authorities allowed the marchers to progress a short distance across the border before halting their advance. On 9 November Hassan abandoned the march, and on 14 November a tripartite accord was signed in Madrid, whereby Spain agreed to withdraw from Western Sahara (as the territory was redesignated) in 1976 and transfer the territory to a joint Morocco-Mauritanian administration. Algeria reacted angrily, increasing its support for the Polisario Front and making veiled threats of direct military intervention. Moroccan armed forces swiftly occupied the territory, and entered the capital, el-Aaiún, on 11 December. They encountered fierce resistance from Polisario guerrillas, and many Sahrawis fled to the Algerian border to avoid the Moroccan advance. The last Spanish troops left in January 1976, a month before they were due to depart under the terms of the tripartite agreement.

The Moroccan Prime Minister, Ahmad Osman, visited France in January 1976, and French deliveries of military equipment to Morocco were increased. In late January Algerian and Moroccan forces clashed at Amgalla, inside Western Sahara, and there was further fighting in February. On 27 February the Sahrawi Arab Democratic Republic (SADR) was proclaimed, a Saharan government-in-exile was formed in Algeria and in March Morocco severed diplomatic relations with Algeria. The prospect of outright war between the two countries receded, however, as Algeria contented itself with arming and training Polisario guerrillas for raids into Western Sahara and providing camps for civilian refugees from the area, believed to number some 60,000.

In April 1976 Morocco and Mauritania reached agreement on the division of Western Sahara. The greater part of the territory, containing most of the known mineral wealth, was allotted to Morocco, which subsequently divided it into three provinces and absorbed it into the kingdom. By placing strong army garrisons in the territory's few scattered urban settlements, the Moroccans were able to secure them against guerrilla attacks, but incursions by forces of the Polisario Front into the surrounding desert areas could not be prevented. The conveyor belt from the important Bou Craa phosphate mines to the sea was sabotaged, and clashes between the Moroccan army and Polisario forces resulted in heavy casualties on both sides. Polisario units were too strong for Mauritania's very limited armed forces in the south, and Morocco took increasing responsibility for the defence of that region. The two countries formed a joint defence committee in May 1977, following a successful Polisario raid on the Mauritanian mining town of Zouérate, in which two French nationals were killed and six captured. In November King Hassan warned Algeria that Moroccan troops would pursue Polisario forces into Algerian territory if necessary; the Algerian Government retorted that any such incursion would result in war between the two countries.

Tension was increased when France, following the release of the French captives in December 1977, launched three air attacks on the Polisario Front. Although the French Government maintained that its action was for the protection of French nationals working at the Saharan mines, and had been undertaken at the request of Mauritania, it was clear that France favoured the expansion of Moroccan interests in the area rather than those of Algeria, for both economic and strategic reasons. During 1978 intermittent fighting continued, and there was a further French air-raid in April. Proposed meetings of the OAU to discuss the issue were postponed on three occasions, revealing an apparent unwillingness on the part of many African leaders to commit themselves. The intransigence of both Morocco and Algeria was partly due to the fact that their Governments relied to a great extent on their respective Saharan policies for domestic popular support. In Morocco the various opposition parties remained united in support of the King in this respect, despite the enormous expense of the war, which accounted for at least one-quarter of the 1979 budget, and the cost of confirming Morocco's control over the Saharan provinces by installing schools, hospitals and housing for those inhabitants remaining in the area. In January 1978 the Government had announced a Sahara Development Programme, involving proposed expenditure of US $292m., and envisaging the settlement of Saharan nomads and the creation of a sedentary economy.

The war was having an even more severe effect on the Mauritanian economy, and this was the chief reason for the coup which took place there in July 1978. The Polisario Front immediately announced a suspension of its hostilities against Mauritania; it was soon clear that the new President, Lt-Col (later Col) Moustapha Ould Salek, would be willing to renounce the Saharan province altogether, were it not for the 10,000 Moroccan troops still stationed in Mauritania. Salek's coup was followed by renewed diplomatic activity, in which France played an important role. President Félix Houphouët-Boigny of Côte d'Ivoire offered to act as mediator, proposing the creation of a Saharan Republic in the Mauritanian sector of Western Sahara alone, a suggestion which was rejected by all parties. In September King Hassan accepted the proposal by the President of the OAU, President Gaafar Mohammed Nimeri of Sudan, that the heads of state of six African countries (Guinea, Côte d'Ivoire, Mali, Nigeria, Tanzania and Sudan) should form a committee of 'wise men' to mediate in the dispute. Spain also became increasingly involved, although it had to safeguard its fishing rights in Moroccan waters and, more importantly, its claim to the enclaves of Ceuta and Melilla. Nevertheless, in December 1980, following harassment of Spanish fishing boats by Polisario forces, the Spanish Government gave official recognition to the Polisario Front (though not to the SADR itself) and declared its support for Saharan self-determination.

Fighting continued, and in January 1979 Polisario forces attacked the town of Tan-Tan, some distance inside Morocco's pre-1975 borders. In March the Chamber of Representatives approved the formation of a National Defence Council to formulate defence policy. This council included members of all the main political groups: independents, Istiqlal, the MP, the USFP, the Mouvement populaire constitutionnel et démocratique (MPCD), and the Parti du progrès et du socialisme (PPS). This suggested that the King was seeking to strengthen support for the war by enlarging the number and the variety of those responsible for its direction. At the same time, the Chamber of Representatives showed that its attitude was still belligerent by reaffirming Morocco's right to its Saharan territory, and recommended that the right of pursuit into foreign (i.e. Algerian) territory should be exercised.

In July 1979 Polisario forces broke their cease-fire agreement with Mauritania, and the OAU summit conference passed a resolution urging the holding of a referendum on self-determination in Western Sahara. Mauritania withdrew from the war, signing a peace treaty with the Polisario Front in August and renouncing its territorial ambitions in Western Sahara. King Hassan immediately claimed the former Mauritanian sector, and proclaimed it a Moroccan province, to be known as Oued ed-Dahab. In May 1981 elections were held for representatives from the province to the Moroccan Chamber of Representatives. Nevertheless, outside the towns, only a small area of this newly-annexed territory could strictly be said to be under Moroccan control, and, as a result, Morocco's military resources were considerably stretched. Polisario forces swiftly retaliated, and numerous battles took place during the next 18 months, often within Morocco's original borders and particularly around the garrison town of Zak. In 1980 Morocco resorted to defensive tactics, concentrating on the *triangle utile* between the towns of el-Aaiún, Bou Craa and es-Smara. This area, containing most of the population and the chief phosphate mines, was to be protected by a line of defences about 600 km long, which was completed in May 1982, and the sand wall was further extended, from Zak to the Mauritanian frontier, in 1984.

In early 1981 there were reports that Polisario, previously based only in Algeria, had established bases in Mauritania, while in March the Mauritanians blamed Morocco for an attempted coup and suspended diplomatic relations. In April Col Muammar al-Qaddafi, the Libyan leader, proposed that Mauritania and Western Sahara should unite, and the two countries issued a joint condemnation of Morocco's occupation of the territory.

DIPLOMATIC INITIATIVES

During the early years of the Western Sahara conflict, the international community gradually recognized the SADR. In November 1979 the UN General Assembly adopted a resolution confirming the legitimacy of the Polisario Front's struggle for independence, and a year later it urged Morocco to end its occupation of Western Sahara. By February 1981, the fifth anniversary of the declaration of the republic, the SADR had been recognized by about 45 Governments. Earlier, at the OAU's annual summit meeting in July 1980, a majority (26 out of 50 countries) approved the admission of the SADR. Morocco, however, argued that a two-thirds majority was necessary, and threatened to leave the OAU if the SADR was admitted. The decision was referred to the committee of 'wise men', who recommended that a cease-fire be established by December, followed by a referendum, to be supervised jointly by the OAU and the UN. In June 1981, at the OAU summit conference, King Hassan agreed for the first time to a referendum, to be held according to OAU recommendations. However, Morocco still refused to negotiate directly with the Polisario Front, and insisted that the proposed referendum be based on the 1974 Spanish census of the area, which enumerated only 74,000 inhabitants. The Polisario Front stipulated that, before the poll could take place, Morocco must withdraw its troops and administration to a considerable distance inside its original borders, and allow refugees living in Algeria to return and participate in the referendum; and that an interim international administration be established. However, the conditions of the referendum were never finally agreed by all the parties concerned.

In October 1981 Moroccan aircraft were shot down near Guelta Zemmour by what Morocco claimed to be Soviet-built SAM-6 surface-to-air missiles. Mauritania was accused of allowing Polisario forces to establish bases on its soil, and of taking part in the attack itself. In response, King Hassan asked the USA for increased military assistance. In February 1982 talks were held between the Moroccan Government and Alexander Haig, then US Secretary of State, as a result of which US military aid to Morocco was tripled. In May the USA and Morocco signed a military co-operation accord providing for the establishment of US military aircraft bases on Moroccan territory in the event of crises in the Middle East or Africa. The accord, initially for six years, was to be automatically renewed unless either country gave two years' notice of cancellation.

The situation deteriorated further during that month, when the SADR delegation was admitted to a meeting of the OAU Council of Ministers in Addis Ababa, Ethiopia. The Moroccan delegation withdrew in protest, and was followed by representatives of 18 other countries. Observers considered this to be the most serious crisis within the OAU since its inception, and it was feared that the organization's very future might be at risk. Subsequent OAU meetings often had to be postponed, since no quorum could be reached. However, in June 1983 the SADR delegation agreed not to attend an OAU summit meeting in Addis Ababa, thus ending the Moroccan boycott. The issue of the continuing conflict in Western Sahara was considered again at this summit, and the meeting adopted a resolution appealing for an immediate cease-fire; for direct negotiations to be held between the Polisario Front and the Moroccan Government; and

for the proposed referendum on the issue of self-determination to be held in Western Sahara before the end of the year. Morocco refused to hold talks with the Polisario Front, but once again agreed in principle to a referendum, although King Hassan stated that he would not necessarily consider Morocco to be bound by its result. Morocco and the Polisario Front failed to agree on who should be allowed to vote, and the referendum, scheduled for December 1983, did not take place.

PROGRESS TOWARDS DEMOCRACY

King Hassan won great domestic prestige and popularity from the Saharan take-over. The staging of the Green March had particularly captured the imagination of the Moroccan people. At last, Hassan felt himself secure enough to hold the long-awaited elections. With the exception of the UNFP, the opposition parties agreed to participate, despite the continuation of political trials arising from the March 1973 uprising, which resulted in heavy prison sentences for many of the accused in early 1977. Municipal elections were held in November 1976, followed by provincial elections in January 1977 and elections for professional and vocational chambers in March. At each election, independents, mostly pro-government and conservative, won more than 60% of the seats. Istiqlal and the USFP protested against electoral irregularities and administrative interference. On 1 March four party leaders, including Muhammad Boucetta of Istiqlal and Abd ar-Rahim Bouabid of the USFP, agreed to join the Government as Ministers of State without portfolio, in the hope of ensuring that the national elections would be fairly conducted. Prior to the national elections, press censorship was abolished. In June a new Chamber of Representatives was elected, signifying a return to parliamentary democracy after 12 years of direct rule. Of the Chamber's 264 members, 176 were directly elected on 3 June and 88 chosen by an electoral college on 21 June. Independents won 141 seats (including 60 by indirect election), while Istiqlal and the MP won 49 and 44 respectively, the USFP won 16 and other opposition parties 14. The new Government, announced in October, included former opposition members, notably Muhammad Boucetta as Minister of Foreign Affairs, with seven other members of Istiqlal, four members of the MP and Maati Bouabid of the UNFP, whose party, however, subsequently disowned him. Thus, the King gained the co-operation of the major part of the opposition, and appeared to have succeeded in his plan to combine democracy with strong royal authority.

Among the Moroccan people support for the war appeared solid, but there were signs of discontent which could be partly attributed to the heavy cost of the fighting. During early 1979 there were strikes by many different sections of the work-force, demanding higher wages. On 21 March the Prime Minister, Ahmad Osman, resigned, ostensibly to devote himself to the organization of the newly-formed Rassemblement national des indépendants (RNI; in 1980 the rural branch of this party seceded to form the Parti des indépendants démocrates (PID), which included several Cabinet ministers). He was replaced by Maati Bouabid, the Minister of Justice and a former trade union leader. The new Prime Minister held talks with union leaders, after which wage rises were announced, including an increase of 40% in the minimum wage. Although this provided a temporary respite from social unrest, it could only add to the burden on the economy.

During 1980 attempts were made to cut spending on education, which accounted for nearly one-quarter of the current budget. Student strikes ensued, supported by the USFP and the PPS, and unrest continued in 1981–83. In June 1981 at least 66 people were killed in Casablanca during a general strike against reductions in food subsidies. The USFP and the trade union organization, the Confédération Démocratique du Travail (CDT), were accused of fomenting this unrest. All CDT offices were closed, and union activists were arrested. Following USFP criticism of government Saharan policy in September, its leader Abd ar-Rahim Bouabid, and other senior officials were sentenced to terms of imprisonment, and the two USFP newspapers were suspended.

Further opposition was aroused in October 1981 by the implementation of the constitutional changes approved by referendum in May 1980, particularly the clause extending the maximum period between elections to the Chamber of Representatives from four to six years: the next parliamentary elections were thus postponed until 1983. The opposition parties were angered by the prolonged life of a body which, they maintained, had been irregularly elected, and in which the majority parties were guilty of absenteeism and passivity. Consequently, all 14 USFP deputies withdrew temporarily from the Chamber of Representatives, and in November all RNI ministers lost their portfolios in a cabinet reshuffle.

Abd ar-Rahim Bouabid was pardoned in March 1982, and CDT and USFP offices were allowed to reopen in April. However, many CDT activists remained in prison and the ban on USFP newspapers was not withdrawn until 1983, when the USFP commenced publication of a new newspaper.

The result of the June 1983 municipal elections, decisively won by pro-government centre-right parties, was challenged by the opposition parties on the grounds of electoral irregularities. A general election for a new Chamber of Representatives was due to take place in September 1983 but was postponed until after the proposed referendum on Western Sahara. However, as the date of the referendum remained uncertain, legislative elections were eventually announced for September 1984. The existing Government reached the end of its six-year mandate in November 1983 and was replaced by a caretaker 'Government of national unity', formed by King Hassan. The new Government was headed by Muhammad Karim Lamrani, an administrator chosen for his lack of party affiliation (who had also been Prime Minister in 1971–72), and included representatives of the six main political parties. It was to be responsible for organizing the general election and for drafting an economic programme for 1984.

In January 1984 the Government announced imminent increases in the prices of basic foodstuffs and in education fees, prompting violent street riots in several northern towns. Troops were summoned to quell the disturbances and, in several instances, opened fire on demonstrators. Unofficial estimates of the number of civilians killed in the riots were as high as 110. The rioting eventually subsided after King Hassan announced the suspension of the planned price increases. An estimated 1,800 people were detained during the riots, many of whom subsequently received prison sentences of up to 10 years.

TEMPORARY IMPROVEMENTS IN REGIONAL RELATIONS

Relations between Morocco and Algeria improved considerably in early 1983, following a summit meeting in February between King Hassan and President Ben Djedid Chadli of Algeria. This meeting resulted in the opening in April of the Morocco-Algeria border to Moroccans resident in Algeria and Algerians resident in Morocco. The *rapprochement* continued in April with a meeting in Tangier of political parties from Morocco, Algeria and Tunisia, at which representatives appealed for the creation of a Great Arab Maghreb—a political and economic union in north-west Africa.

In August 1984 King Hassan and Col Qaddafi of Libya signed the Arab-African Federation Treaty at Oujda, Morocco, which established a 'union of states' between their countries as the first step towards the creation of a Great Arab Maghreb. The Oujda Treaty, as it became known, provided for close economic and political co-operation between Morocco and Libya, and for mutual defence in the event of attack. The treaty was to take effect only after approval by the peoples of each country. A referendum was therefore held in Morocco on 31 August, and the treaty was approved by 99.97% of voters. Libya's General People's Congress backed the agreement unanimously. Following the alliance of Algeria, Tunisia and Mauritania, through the Maghreb Fraternity and Co-operation Treaty, initiated in March 1983, and Mauritania's recognition of the SADR in February 1984, Morocco had found itself isolated in the Maghreb. By signing the treaty of union with Libya, Morocco not only gained an ally (though an unlikely one, considering the contrast between Morocco's pro-Western stance and Libya's radicalism under Qaddafi), but also persuaded Col Qaddafi to end Libyan aid to Polisario.

Polisario responded to the *rapprochement* with Libya by launching the 'Greater Maghreb Offensive', a major military initiative which resulted in widespread fighting in southern Morocco. At the same time, Muhammad Abd al-Aziz, President of the SADR, undertook an extensive African tour to gather support prior to the November 1984 summit of the OAU in Addis Ababa. As a result, the SADR delegation was seated at the summit with few objections from other states. However, Morocco resigned from the OAU in protest, thus becoming the first State to leave the organization.

Although Polisario claimed to have killed 5,673 Moroccan soldiers during 1982–85, decisive victories proved elusive, owing to Morocco's defensive strategy of building a 2,500-km wall of sand, equipped with electronic detectors, to surround Western Sahara. At the UN General Assembly in October 1985, Morocco announced a unilateral cease-fire in Western Sahara on the condition that there was no aggression against territories under its jurisdiction, and that it would be ready to hold a referendum in the territory in January 1986. However, the latter offer was withdrawn in November, after the UN Decolonization Committee supported a settlement of the conflict through direct negotiations between Morocco and the Polisario Front. The Moroccan Minister of Foreign Affairs, Abd al-Latif Filali, announced that Morocco would boycott all UN discussions on Western Sahara, as the Government considered such discussions to be futile. In April and May 1986 a series of proximity talks between Morocco and Polisario took place through the UN and OAU, but failed to reach a resolution. By the end of 1985, Morocco appeared to be increasingly isolated, as 64 countries had officially recognized the SADR, and US-Moroccan relations remained uneasy, following Morocco's signature of the Oujda Treaty with Libya.

DOMESTIC AFFAIRS

About 67% of the electorate participated in elections to the Chamber of Representatives on 14 September 1984. Despite widespread gains by the USFP (which won 36 seats), the legislature was again dominated by the centre-right parties, which together controlled 206 of the 306 seats. In October King Hassan invited the leaders of the six main parties to submit their planned programmes to enable him to choose a coalition Government. Meanwhile, the previous 'Government of national unity' remained in office. King Hassan finally named a new Government in April 1985. The Government, again led by Muhammad Karim Lamrani, was a coalition of four centre-right parties: the Union constitutionnelle (UC), the RNI, the MP and the Parti national démocrate (PND, as the PID had been renamed). It did not include any members of Istiqlal or the USFP, which had participated in the previous Government. The new Government's programme included increased privatization, the decentralization of health and education, and reforms of the civil service and the education system. In September 1986 Lamrani resigned, owing to ill health, and was replaced by the Deputy Prime Minister and Minister of Education, Az ad-Dine Laraki.

Meanwhile, the Government mounted a campaign of repression against organizations which it deemed to pose a threat to internal security. In August 1985 26 members of a left-wing movement, Jeunesse Islamique (Islamic Youth), were charged with plotting to overthrow the monarchy and to establish an Islamic state; in September 14 were sentenced to death. A further 28 people were charged in October with membership of a clandestine fundamentalist group, the Moudjahedine Movement, and with subversive activities. In February 1986 27 left-wing activists were imprisoned for subversion. At their trial, the prosecuting counsel had claimed that the defendants were financed by the Polisario Front. Following Arab antipathy to the Morocco-Israeli initiative in July (see below), the Government introduced anti-terrorist measures in August, including entry restrictions for visitors from Arab countries. In the same month, four foreigners were arrested on charges of possessing explosives and plotting to bomb a synagogue in Casablanca. In November three people were imprisoned for membership of an illegal Marxist-Leninist organization, al-Kaaidiyine, and for disturbing public order.

In late 1986 and early 1987 King Hassan granted a series of pardons to both political and non-political detainees. In October 1987 the authorities announced that the family of Gen. Oufkir, who had staged an abortive coup attempt in 1972, would be allowed to emigrate, after 15 years in detention. However, the family were not released until mid-1996 (see below), although

Muhammad Ait Kaddour, who had been involved in one of the attempts to shoot down the King's aircraft, was pardoned after his return to Morocco.

In 1988 Morocco joined the UN Human Rights Commission and subsequently attempted to improve its reputation concerning human rights. For several years, political prisoners had held sporadic hunger strikes to focus attention on poor prison conditions, and in January 1988 the Paris-based Moroccan human rights group, the Association des Droits de l'Homme au Maroc (ADHM), organized demonstrations in France, Belgium, the Netherlands and the Federal Republic of Germany against alleged abuses of human rights in Morocco. The ADHM also drew attention to clashes between students and government forces in Fez earlier that month. The Moroccan authorities had claimed that one person died and 21 were wounded during the disturbances, but the ADHM alleged that casualties had been much more numerous, and that more than 400 subsequent arrests had been made. In May it was reported that about 12 suspected members of Ilal Amam, who had been arrested during the previous two months in a government campaign against Ilal Amam activists, had been released, along with Abdullah Zaidy, a lawyer whose arrest in December 1987 and sentence to three years' imprisonment for attacking 'sacred institutions' had attracted condemnation from the International Commission of Jurists. In the same month living conditions for political prisoners were reported to have been improved. However, the first meeting of the newly-formed human rights association, the Organisation Marocaine des Droits de l'Homme (OMDH), scheduled for late May, was postponed until the end of June, owing to government objections that some of its members were also members of 'banned extremist groups'. In August 1988 King Hassan ordered the release of 341 detainees to commemorate the 25th anniversary of the exile of Sultan Muhammad ibn Yousuf. The release of political prisoners continued, and about 2,000 were freed in the first six months of 1989. The most notable were 50 extremists, including 31 of those who had been imprisoned in February 1977 for complicity in the alleged scheme to establish a republic under the Jewish mining engineer, Abraham Serfaty. The others, some of whom were religious fundamentalists, had been arrested after the Marrakesh riots of 1984.

The question of political prisoners in Morocco attracted considerable international attention during 1989 and early 1990. Between June 1989 and April 1990 a total of 2,163 political prisoners were released, despite the authorities' denial that any such prisoners existed. In June 1989 six of the Ilal Amam prisoners in Rabat jail went on hunger strike in an abortive attempt to gain the status of political prisoners. They were transferred to hospitals, where one of them died after 64 days.

The imprisonment of Islamist activists provoked condemnation from other quarters, including the Iranian Government, which had seemed unconcerned about the fate of left-wingers. As far back as 1974 Abd as-Salam Yassin had criticized the State for failing to observe Islamic precepts, and later he was imprisoned several times. It was not until 1989, however, that his followers, who had formed a group called Al Adl wa-'l Ihsan (Justice and Charity), seemed to alarm the Government, although the group had been refused official registration in 1982. In November 24 of its members were charged with belonging to an unauthorized organization, holding illicit meetings and possessing documents which threatened state security. The conviction of 17 of the accused and the placing of Sheikh Yassin under house arrest led to demonstrations by the organization's followers and further arrests. Although the King denounced the intolerance of 'non-progressive' fundamentalists and, in particular, their attitude to women, militant fundamentalists dominated the universities. In January 1990 the Government ordered the dissolution of Al Adl wa-'l Ihsan, arrested five of its members who were presumed to be its executive committee and sentenced them to terms of imprisonment ranging from nine months to two years. Four were released on appeal, while the fifth had his sentence commuted. In May thousands of Islamists demonstrated in Rabat; an estimated 2,000 were reportedly arrested, and later released.

In April 1988, prompted in part by World Bank pressure, the King told the Chamber of Representatives that the State should retain sole control of strategic industries and sell the remainder, including sugar refineries, bus services and possibly water and electricity. There was considerable debate over which industries should be retained in the public sector, while the trade unions were concerned about job losses resulting from privatization of state companies. Thus, it was not until October 1989 that real progress was made, following the appointments of a new Governor of the Central Bank and of a minister in charge of privatization. In December the Chamber of Representatives approved a list of 113 enterprises to be privatized, including four leading banks, 37 hotels, the Nador steelworks and the tea and sugar monopolies. The legislation ensured that the monopolies would not fall under foreign control and that there would be opportunities for employees to buy shares in their firms; the process was expected to take six years. While foreign capital would be welcomed, the Government's priority was to create a larger national share-owning class. The moribund Bourse at Casablanca was revived. Morocco already had one of the most liberal economies in the developing world, and there were emerging plans for free-trade zones.

In late 1988 the country suffered a period of industrial unrest, as strikes took place in mines, flour mills, the petroleum refinery at Mohammadia and Air Maroc, until a series of pay settlements restored order. Mahjoub Ben Seddiq, who had led the largest trade union, the Union Marocaine du Travail (UMT), since its foundation in 1955, was re-elected Secretary-General. After the King's Throne Day speech in March 1990 (in which he appealed to the people to accept austerity because of the economic situation), demands for a general strike were ignored, following Government promises that food subsidies would be retained and that grievances would be discussed. On May Day the minimum wage was raised by 10%.

In December 1989 Hassan proposed a two-year postponement of the forthcoming general election, in order to accommodate the referendum to be held in Western Sahara. A referendum which showed that only 0.05% opposed the plan demonstrated the lack of popular interest in party politics at a time when no members of the Cabinet were party politicians. In May 1990, for the first time in the 26-year history of the Chamber of Representatives, the opposition proposed a motion expressing 'no confidence' in the Government, criticizing its record on human rights and the revised budget. Although the motion was defeated by 200 votes to 82, it remained a significant precedent.

In December 1990 more than 20 people were alleged to have been killed in Fez during a general strike, the first in Morocco since 1984. Demonstrators demanded a wage increase commensurate with rapidly rising prices; following two days of rioting, security was increased in Fez and Rabat, where tanks patrolled the streets and security forces guarded government buildings. The Government announced that a commission was to be established to ascertain the number of persons who had been killed and the circumstances of their deaths. In late December more than 100 people were accused of rioting, and received prison sentences. In March 1991 it was estimated by a prominent human rights organization, Amnesty International, that more than 1,500 people had been detained in connection with the riots. It was widely accepted that rising frustration at the country's socio-economic problems had precipitated these events. This was confirmed when the commission published its report, which showed that the outbreak could not be attributed to organized subversion.

Industrial unrest continued throughout 1991 and into 1992. There were numerous strikes by government employees, health workers, teachers, the post office and nationalized industries. There was also violence as in June 1991, when 104 workers were injured in a clash with police at a textile factory. Despite the establishment of a National Council for Youth and the Future (which aimed to provide 300,000 new jobs), the problem of youth unemployment was highlighted in October, when 100,000 out-of-work graduates established a national association to present their case. Wage rises failed to keep pace with inflation, and a government announcement in early 1991 that the minimum wage would be raised by 15% was rejected by two of the trade unions, which demanded that it be doubled to 2,000 dirhams (about $250) per month. In January 1992 three trade union militants received prison sentences ranging from five to 10 months.

As in other Maghreb countries, many of the unemployed saw their salvation in Islamic fundamentalism. Some of the leaders of the banned group Al Adl wa-'l Ihsan, including Sheikh Yassin, remained in detention, and in April 1991 eight other members were arrested (although subsequently released). In May Adl and other opposition groups participated in a rally in Casablanca, in which some 100,000 demonstrators demanded measures to enshrine the sovereignty of the people and reduce the powers of the King. At the same time, they denounced the proposed referendum in Western Sahara, asserting that the territory should simply be annexed to Morocco. The repression of the Front islamique du salut in Algeria was welcomed by the Government, despite apprehension that local militants might conclude that their aims were not to be achieved by the democratic process. In September the Government approached the imprisoned Adl leaders, offering recognition as a legitimate party on certain conditions, including acceptance of the monarchy and a petition for pardon. However, the leaders made their release a pre-condition of any negotiations, and the initiative foundered.

Despite the creation (in May 1990) of the Consultative Council on Human Rights, humanitarian organizations continued to criticize the Government. In May 1991 the OMDH, headed by Khalid Nauri, held its inaugural conference, at which speakers denounced the arbitrary treatment, and even torture, of prisoners, and the lack of contact with their families. In July the Government refused to defend its record before a UN panel in Geneva, Switzerland, because of the presence of French television cameras. In March 1991 Amnesty International claimed that 1,500 people had been detained in the previous few months, many for demonstrating against the dispatch of troops to the Gulf War. In September Abraham Serfaty, the longest-serving political prisoner in Africa, was freed and expelled from the country. In the same month 119 prisoners were released, bringing the total for the year to more than 5,000, and the notorious Tazmamart jail, whose existence the Government never admitted, was destroyed. During the winter of 1991–92 most of the remaining prisoners who had been condemned for the attempts on the King's life in 1971 and 1972 were freed. In December representatives of 23 political and humanitarian organizations, meeting in Casablanca, demanded the release of political prisoners and an amnesty for exiles.

AN ACTIVE PERIOD IN FOREIGN AFFAIRS: 1986–92

In 1986 and 1987 Morocco made determined efforts to improve its relations with the USA and other Western nations, in order to increase military and diplomatic support for its policy in Western Sahara. In April 1986 King Hassan, as chairman of the Arab League, suspended a summit meeting, following Libya's insistence that the US raids on Libya in April should be the sole topic on the agenda. In June King Hassan proposed the foundation of a 'Maghreb Community Consultative Committee', comprising Algeria, Morocco and Tunisia, thus isolating Libya.

In July 1986 King Hassan held talks with Shimon Peres, the Israeli Prime Minister, at Ifrane, in Morocco, in an effort to salvage the peace initiative in the Middle East; he thus became the first Arab head of state to meet an Israeli leader since the late President Anwar Sadat of Egypt. However, the meeting merely highlighted the divisions between Israel and the moderate Arab states on means of resolving the conflict in the Middle East. Arab reaction was mixed: Syria immediately suspended diplomatic relations with Morocco; Libya condemned Morocco; while Egypt, Kuwait and Jordan supported the initiative. Following criticism of the meeting, King Hassan resigned as chairman of the Arab League. In August Libya attempted to improve relations with Morocco by reaffirming support for the Oujda Treaty, but this was abrogated by Hassan at the end of the month. The Moroccan-Israeli initiative and the abrogation of the Oujda Treaty resulted in a dramatic improvement in US-Moroccan relations by September. The two countries held joint military exercises in November, and in July 1987 the US Defense Department approved the sale to Morocco of 100 M-48A5 tanks, suitable for use in desert terrain, along with other military equipment. Morocco re-emphasized its status as a moderate pro-Western Arab state by re-establishing diplomatic relations with Egypt in November, and in January 1988 the USA announced that Morocco was willing to allow US forces to resume 'partial activities' on Moroccan territory.

In the hope of gaining wider European support for its policy in Western Sahara and improved trading links, Morocco applied to join the European Community (EC) in July 1987. In August an accord was reached with the EC, whereby Morocco extended, for a further five months, the 1983 fishing treaty with Spain, which was due to expire at the end of the month. During this period, negotiations on a new fishing agreement were held with the EC, as Spain had joined the Community in 1986. In October, however, the EC rejected Morocco's application for membership, on the grounds that Morocco was not a European country.

Hassan insisted that the movement towards a unified Maghreb did not preclude Morocco's ambition to join the EC. The European Parliament had on several occasions criticized Morocco for its policy in Western Sahara and for domestic repression, but in May 1988 the West German Minister of Foreign Affairs stated that the reforms which were to be implemented in 1992 would provide Morocco with great opportunities for trade and, consequently, EC aid was substantially increased to $392m. During a visit to Morocco in March 1989 the British Prime Minister, Margaret Thatcher, said that there was no realistic possibility of Morocco's joining the EC, and in the following month, in Luxembourg at a meeting of the EC's Moroccan Co-operation Council, the Moroccan Minister of Foreign Affairs, Abd al-Latif Filali, blamed Europe for protectionism which had damaged Moroccan exports.

In January 1987 King Hassan proposed the creation of a 'reflection cell' to consider the future of the Spanish African enclaves of Ceuta and Melilla, but Spain showed no willingness to discuss their sovereignty. In July, however, the Spanish Minister of Foreign Affairs visited Rabat and agreed to further discussions on the future of the enclaves. In June 1988 a bilateral trading agreement was signed; in July discussions were held over the installation of an electric cable under the Strait of Gibraltar, and in September an agreement was signed for the construction of a pipeline across Moroccan territory, connecting the petroleum fields of Algeria with consumers in Europe. Although Spain refused to allow Polisario to reopen its office in Madrid, in October it voted against Morocco at the UN debate on Western Sahara; in protest Hassan cancelled an official visit scheduled for November. Morocco could not, however, afford to pursue the quarrel, when Spain was about to assume the presidency of the EC and a visit by Prime Minister Felipe González in May 1989 showed that amicable relations had been restored. In September King Hassan visited Spain and signed accords on defence, including joint military exercises, technology transfers and bilateral summits to be held annually.

Hassan has also played a prominent role in Arab relations. The Arab League summit meeting, held in Casablanca in May 1989, was a considerable triumph for Moroccan diplomacy since it brought Syria, with which diplomatic relations had been restored through the mediation of the Saudi Arabian Crown Prince in January, together with Iraq, while Col Qaddafi of Libya consented to meet President Muhammad Hosni Mubarak of Egypt. The meeting itself was less successful, for there was acrimonious disagreement over Lebanon. However, consensus was reached on the Palestinian *intifada,* which had evoked strong emotions in Morocco. The King was appointed, together with King Fahd of Saudi Arabia and President Chadli of Algeria, to head a Tripartite Arab Committee on Lebanon in order to seek a solution to the Lebanese conflict and to advocate the Palestinian case to the world. In practice the work was realized by their respective ministers of foreign affairs. In April 1990, following a meeting with the King, Yasser Arafat announced Hassan's intention to request the Heads of State Committee to work towards the convening of an international conference on the plight of Palestinians. He also stated that the King intended to visit the capitals of the five permanent members of the UN Security Council to draw their attention to the growing number of Soviet Jews settling in Israel. As Chairman of the Organization of the Islamic Conference (OIC), Hassan was also expected to try to persuade the US Government not to recognize Jerusalem as the capital of Israel.

THE WESTERN SAHARA CONFLICT: 1986–87

During 1986 Polisario forces attacked several foreign fishing vessels in the Atlantic, off the Western Saharan coast, which the Polisario Front terms a 'war zone'. After an outbreak of fighting between Moroccan troops and Polisario forces in February 1987, Morocco claimed to have repelled a major Polisario offensive near the Algerian border. In the same month the SADR representative in Algiers claimed that an attempted assassination of the SADR President, Muhammad Abd al-Aziz, had been foiled, and alleged that the Moroccan Minister of the Interior was implicated in the plot.

Tension in Western Sahara increased in April 1987, when Morocco completed the construction of its defensive wall on the southern border of the territory, parallel with the Mauritanian frontier. Mauritania protested that its neutrality was threatened, since Polisario troops might have to pass through Mauritanian territory to reach the Atlantic; Algeria expressed concerns and confirmed its support for Mauritania.

A *rapprochement* between Morocco and Algeria was effected in May 1987, at a summit meeting attended by King Hassan and President Chadli of Algeria, under the auspices of King Fahd of Saudi Arabia. The two leaders discussed the conflict in Western Sahara and issued a joint communiqué stating that they would remain in consultation. Before the meeting, Polisario urged Morocco to enter into direct dialogue, and attacked King Fahd's role as mediator. Later in the month, 102 Algerian prisoners in Morocco were exchanged for 150 Moroccan prisoners in Algeria, and King Hassan sent an emissary to President Chadli with proposals to establish two joint commissions to settle various bilateral disputes.

TOWARDS A SOLUTION IN WESTERN SAHARA

Meanwhile, the UN and the OAU made a concerted effort to settle the conflict in Western Sahara. In July 1987 UN missions visited Morocco, Algeria and the Congo to examine the possibility of organizing a UN-sponsored referendum on the question of self-determination in Western Sahara. In the same month there were signs of a *rapprochement* between Polisario and Morocco, following indirect talks in Geneva, under the auspices of the UN and the OAU. Afterwards, King Hassan announced that he would be willing to accept the results of the referendum, and Polisario issued a statement which welcomed some of Hassan's proposals. However, after the talks, there were clashes between Moroccan and Polisario forces near the Mauritanian border.

Polisario announced a three-week truce in November 1987 to coincide with a visit by a UN-OAU technical mission to Morocco, Western Sahara and Polisario refugee camps in Algeria, in order to assess conditions for holding a referendum. Although both Morocco and Polisario agreed on the need for a referendum, Morocco rejected Polisario's demand that the Moroccan armed forces and administration should withdraw from Western Sahara, and that the territory should be placed under an interim UN administration before the referendum. Morocco also refused to hold direct talks with Polisario representatives (a Polisario precondition of negotiations), as officially it continued to view Polisario as a front organization for Algerian mercenaries. In January 1988 Polisario renewed attacks on Moroccan positions in Western Sahara. Meanwhile, the UN announced that it was drafting detailed proposals for a cease-fire and a referendum. In April the President of the OAU, Dr Kenneth Kaunda of Zambia, visited Morocco, Western Sahara and Polisario refugee camps to discuss the conclusions of the UN technical mission. By mid-1988 a total of 71 countries had granted diplomatic recognition to the SADR.

RESTORATION OF DIPLOMATIC RELATIONS WITH ALGERIA AND MOVES TOWARDS MAGHREB UNITY

The conflict in Western Sahara was regarded by the other Maghreb nations as an obstacle to regional unity, and in late 1987 and 1988 they attempted to isolate Morocco, with the aim of forcing the kingdom to negotiate with the Polisario Front. Meanwhile, Morocco reiterated its commitment to Maghreb unity, at meetings with President Chadli of Algeria in November 1987 and with President Zine al-Abidine Ben Ali of Tunisia in February 1988, and took no part in attempts by Algeria, Libya, Mauritania and Tunisia to create a four-country Great Arab Maghreb. However, the emergence of such a power bloc was forestalled by Libya's refusal to sign the Maghreb Fraternity and Co-operation Treaty without the addition of several conditions, and in May King Hassan received the Algerian deputy

leader with an invitation from President Chadli for Morocco to attend the Arab League summit in June. Hassan promptly dispatched two of his senior advisers to Algiers to hold further discussions with Chadli, and in mid-May both countries announced the re-establishment of full diplomatic relations. In May 1989 a 1972 treaty with Algeria, on the demarcation of the joint border, was ratified by Morocco. These developments were considered to be a victory for Morocco and an apparent retreat by Algeria from its previous position that diplomatic relations could be resumed only if Morocco held direct talks with Polisario. Following the *rapprochement* with Algeria, Morocco became fully involved in regional efforts to establish a Great Arab Maghreb, and in June 1988 attended the first Maghreb summit.

Diplomatic relations improved further, as it became clear that Hassan and Chadli shared similar views on Maghreb unity. They rejected the Libyan concept of a vast 'superstate' but agreed on practical steps such as the abolition of visas, harmonization in economic, cultural and technical matters and joint ventures, which had been discussed at a bilateral meeting of Algeria and Morocco in October 1988. In February 1989, at a meeting in Marrakesh, of North African Heads of State, the Union of the Arab Maghreb (UAM), grouping Morocco with Algeria, Libya, Mauritania and Tunisia, was inaugurated. The new body aimed to promote unity by allowing free movement of goods, services and labour. King Hassan was appointed the first President of the UAM for the 1989/90 year. In October, at the first meeting of delegates from each national legislature, the former Prime Minister and brother-in-law of King Hassan, Ahmad Othman, was elected President of the UAM Assembly. In the same month the respective ministers of foreign affairs met in Rabat and agreed to establish committees to discuss food, security, economic affairs, human resources and infrastructure. In January 1990 the national employers' organizations discussed closer co-operation, and in February a committee was created to co-ordinate petroleum policies. Plans were also drafted for the introduction of a common identity card which would serve as a travel document within the UAM. The Moroccan Chamber of Representatives endorsed two accords with Algeria, providing for the establishment of joint ventures to consider creating a second gas pipeline to transport Algerian gas through Morocco to Europe, and for closer economic and industrial relations. Morocco also increased its ties with Tunisia and Libya, which the King had visited for the first time in September 1989.

During late 1989 and early 1990 the renewal of the Polisario campaign provoked criticism of the Government within Morocco. Meanwhile, King Hassan stressed that the new alignment would not preclude Morocco's membership of the EC. Further divisions in the UAM surfaced in August 1990, following the invasion of Kuwait (see Kuwait and Iraq chapters). Whereas the other UAM members were slow to react, Morocco issued a vehement condemnation of the invasion, voted for the resolutions at the Arab summit denouncing Iraq's action and agreed to contribute to the pan-Arab force defending Saudi Arabia. In September Hassan was host in Rabat to King Hussein of Jordan and President Chadli of Algeria in an attempt to launch a new peace initiative and avoid armed conflict. Although they failed to persuade the Iraqi President, Saddam Hussain, to withdraw his troops from Kuwait, in October the Iraqi President sent his Minister of Foreign Affairs, Tareq Aziz, and a Deputy Prime Minister, to Rabat in an attempt to find a resolution. When these discussions failed, King Hassan attempted unsuccessfully to convene a summit meeting of the Arab League in November. By December some 1,500 Moroccan troops were stationed in Saudi Arabia, as part of the multinational alliance attempting to enforce Iraq's withdrawal from Kuwait.

However, in late January 1991, after pro-Iraqi demonstrations in Morocco, the Government gave implicit support to a one-day general strike (in an apparent attempt to ease domestic political pressure), organized by the principal Moroccan trade unions to express solidarity with the Iraqi people. Other members of the anti-Iraq alliance expressed concern that the Moroccan Government was not fully committed to the military campaign. In February an estimated 300,000 people demonstrated in Rabat, where they denounced the war against Iraq and demanded that the Moroccan contingent withdraw from the multinational force. The Government stressed that its troops were in the region to defend Saudi Arabia and not to force the withdrawal of Iraq from Kuwait. By late February the multinational force had liberated Kuwait from Iraqi occupation, and shortly afterwards Morocco, together with its fellow members of the UAM, demanded that the sanctions which the UN had imposed on Iraq in August 1990 be repealed immediately.

UN PEACE PLAN FOR WESTERN SAHARA

In August 1988 the UN Secretary-General, Javier Pérez de Cuéllar, who had visited Morocco in May, announced that a detailed peace plan for Western Sahara had been drafted and appealed for its prompt approval by Morocco and Polisario. The plan contained proposals for a cease-fire and a referendum to determine the status of Western Sahara, while a UN representative with wide-ranging powers and a 2,000-strong UN monitoring force were to oversee their implementation. Prior to the referendum, Morocco was to reduce its presence in Western Sahara from 100,000 to 25,000 troops, who would then be confined to barracks, while Polisario forces (totalling an estimated 8,000) were to withdraw to their bases. Eligibility to vote in the referendum was to be decided by a UN team and was expected to be limited to those enumerated in the 1974 Spanish census of the then Spanish Sahara and to those born in Western Sahara. The referendum was to offer a choice between complete independence for the territory and its integration into Morocco; it was hoped that a further option would be added, offering a large measure of autonomy for the Sahrawi people under the Moroccan crown. On 30 August Morocco and the Polisario Front formally accepted the UN peace plan, although both sides expressed reservations.

However, the UN's expectation that a cease-fire could be secured within a month, and the referendum held within six months, seemed increasingly optimistic. Moreover, the belief that the UN proposals had been unconditionally accepted by both parties was undermined when in early September 1988 the Polisario Front declared that the UN could arrange a cease-fire by the end of 1988 if Morocco was prepared to hold direct talks with its representatives. In mid-September Polisario forces attacked Moroccan troops at the Oum Dreiga section of the defensive wall, near the Mauritanian border. Polisario was reported to have deployed 2,500 men, and there were more than 200 Moroccan casualties. There was speculation that Polisario had launched the offensive to demonstrate its ability to inflict substantial damage on Morocco without Algerian support, and to emphasize the need for Morocco to hold direct negotiations before a solution could be reached. Polisario representatives maintained that all Moroccan troops, administrators and colonists must be withdrawn before the proposed referendum, but two cabinet reshuffles within a month suggested serious differences within their leadership. Meanwhile, the Moroccan Minister of Foreign Affairs, Abd al-Latif Filali, stated that, since both sides had accepted the UN proposal for a cease-fire, there was no need for direct talks. In October the UN General Assembly agreed, by 87 votes to nil with 58 abstentions (which included Morocco and the USA), that direct talks should be held, followed by a cease-fire and a referendum. Pérez de Cuéllar appointed a personal representative, Héctor Gros de Espiel (a Uruguayan), to visit the area in November or December.

In December 1988 there was a significant change in Morocco's stance on Western Sahara, when King Hassan agreed to meet officials of Polisario and the SADR. The meeting, held in Marrakesh in January 1989, was the first direct contact for 13 years and was reported to have been limited to exchanges of goodwill; no negotiations took place. In February Polisario announced a unilateral cease-fire. A second meeting, scheduled to take place in February, was postponed by King Hassan. Polisario put further pressure on Morocco for full negotiations by threatening to take fresh military action. By mid-March no more discussions had taken place, and Polisario resumed hostilities, bringing the six-week cease-fire to an end. In May 1989 the Polisario politburo, meeting in Tindouf, sent a message to the King complaining that the projected second round of talks had not been held and asking him to assist the peace process; at the same time it dismissed two of its members for 'infantile attitudes'. At the seventh Polisario Front Congress, held in May, Polisario reiterated its own willingness to pursue direct dialogue, and announced that, as a gesture of goodwill, 200 Moroccan soldiers

would be released. Their release, however, was postponed 'for technical reasons'.

In June 1989 Pérez de Cuéllar, who had held talks with the King and the Polisario leadership in Tindouf, and visited Algeria and Mauritania, declared himself 'confident of progress in the near future.' The UN established a technical commission to expedite the peace plan which both sides had formally accepted in August 1988. The issue of entitlement to vote in any referendum on the future of Western Sahara remained unresolved, however, owing to the ambiguous status of the Moroccan settlers in the area, who now outnumbered the original inhabitants by three to two.

Hassan's vacillation was probably due, in part, to the defection, in August 1989, of Omar Hadhrami (one of the six founders of the Polisario Front), two leading guerrilla commanders and the chief propagandist in Algiers. This seemed to underline splits in the movement between authentic Sahrawis and new members from Algeria and Mauritania. In addition, mass arrests had taken place in the camps, aid from Eastern Europe had ceased, and assistance from other Maghreb states was diminishing, with the result that rationing had been introduced. Hassan welcomed these 'lost sheep' back into the fold, and other defections followed. The Moroccan Government let it be known that it was ready to consider any approach from oil companies seeking concessions to prospect for petroleum deposits in Western Sahara.

In October 1989 Polisario forces launched a series of major attacks, which continued unabated for more than a month. During the offensive, 15 km of the defensive wall facing the Mauritanian border was reportedly destroyed and hundreds of Moroccan soldiers were killed. The Government claimed that only 45 soldiers had been killed. The extent of the onslaught suggested that it could not have been launched without Algerian support. During the campaign the Polisario Front demanded direct talks with the Government, but the King refused to 'negotiate with his own subjects' and announced his readiness to order his troops across international borders in pursuit of Polisario forces.

In March 1990 Pérez de Cuéllar commented that he was pleased to find 'a more propitious atmosphere' than he had encountered during his June 1989 visit, but expressed caution over any practical outcome. In mid-1990 a special UN technical commission visited Western Sahara and the neighbouring states to investigate the practical difficulties of conducting a referendum on the territory's future. In April 1991 the UN Security Council approved a resolution (No. 690) which authorized the establishment of a UN Mission for the Referendum in Western Sahara (MINURSO, see p. 224), which was to implement the plan for a referendum on self-determination, proposed by the UN Secretary-General in 1988. A UN peace-keeping force, comprising contingents from 36 countries (including the five permanent members of the UN Security Council), was to supervise the operation. In May 1991 the Security Council approved plans for a referendum in the disputed territory, which was scheduled to take place in January 1992.

In May 1991 King Hassan visited Western Sahara (his third visit to the region since 1976), where he was met by approximately 100,000 people. In recognition of the contribution of local tribes in the conflict between Moroccan forces and the Polisario Front, the King created a new province, Assa-Zag, on the Algerian border. The royal visit coincided with the preparations for the referendum. It was announced that a peace-keeping force of 200,000 Moroccan troops would be stationed in the area in the interim. In the same month Pérez de Cuéllar met King Hassan to discuss the UN peace plan for Western Sahara. In June Hassan granted an amnesty to all Sahrawi opponents, including members of Polisario and refugees abroad. A further unspecified number of prisoners, including left-wing leader Abraham Serfaty, were released in the following months. It was believed that the amnesty to refugees abroad was part of a campaign to persuade Sahrawis who were disillusioned with the Polisario Front to vote for integration into Morocco.

In July 1991 it was announced that a cease-fire in Western Sahara would come into effect on 6 September, from which date the UN special representative, Johannes Manz, would supervise the preparations for a referendum. The Moroccan presence would be reduced from about 190,000 to 65,000 troops, and

MINURSO would commence operation. Morocco rejected any role for the OAU in the area, while Istiqlal and other political parties declared the referendum futile, as the return of the Saharan provinces was irreversible. The Polisario Front promised to abide by the result. Morocco, however, continued a building programme to develop the Saharan provinces—an auto-route from Tangier to Nouadhibou (Mauritania), a university and housing at es-Smara.

In August 1991 a significant increase in hostilities developed, with the Polisario Front denouncing Moroccan air strikes, while the Moroccan Government stated that it was engaged in clearing 'no man's land': each side was trying to intimidate rival elements into leaving the area before the cease-fire. In addition, Polisario demanded the release of men allegedly held as prisoners of war: Morocco denied that there were any, but some 200 detainees were nevertheless released.

The main obstacle to holding the referendum was that Manz had prepared an electoral roll of about 74,000, based on the Spanish census of 1974. The Moroccans presented an alternative list of about 120,000 who, they claimed, were natives of the area or their children who had been omitted from the census because, at the time, they were refugees. The UN representatives ruled that, while applications from individuals could be considered, a block list could not. The Moroccans used this dispute as a pretext to prevent the deployment of MINURSO; the Polisario Front countered by repeating its former claim that the total population was 207,000, of whom 167,000 were in 'liberated areas' or in refugee camps in Algeria and Mauritania. King Hassan appealed for a postponement of the referendum, but, after meeting Polisario representatives, Pérez de Cuéllar insisted that it should go ahead.

The first 100 members of MINURSO flew into el-Aaiún, and the cease-fire took effect, as planned, on 6 September 1991. Within a fortnight, however, each side had accused the other of violating the cease-fire, while the Polisario Front alleged that the Moroccan Minister of the Interior, Driss Basri, was organizing a 'second Green March' of 170,000 people for whom temporary accommodation was being built. There were few signs that Moroccans were reducing their military presence. Algerian support for the Polisario Front effectively ceased, and there were important defections from its ranks. Both sides also complained of UN bias. By the end of November MINURSO had only 240 men in the territory. Manz resigned from his post in December. The Polisario Front complained that Morocco was planting mines in 'no man's land' and arresting its supporters. Pérez de Cuéllar appeared to side with Morocco by recommending that a vote be given to anyone whose father had been born in the territory or who had had intermittent residence there for 12 years before 1974. However, this proposal was delayed in the UN Security Council and on 1 January 1992 his successor, Dr Boutros Boutros-Ghali, was asked for a report within two months; it became clear that the vote could not take place before September.

In March 1992 Boutros-Ghali's report concluded that, unless there were progress by the end of May, the whole UN policy should be reconsidered. He also stated that, of the 77 violations of the cease-fire reported by MINURSO, Morocco had been responsible for 75. It was not until the end of the month that a veteran Pakistani diplomat, Yaqub Khan, was appointed as successor to Manz. He visited the area in April, and in May Boutros-Ghali announced that the two sides were to hold indirect talks under his auspices. These took place in Geneva, but proved inconclusive.

In June 1992 Driss Basri visited Western Sahara to encourage the population to enroll on the electoral register. This message was repeated by Ibrahim Hakim, who, as a former Minister of Foreign Affairs of the SADR and ambassador to Algeria, was a significant defector to Morocco in August. Hakim claimed that the Algerian Government was no longer committed to the foundation of an autonomous state in Western Sahara. He was subsequently appointed as the King's itinerant ambassador. Polisario threatened to resume hostilities if the Moroccan referendum on constitutional reform, in September, were extended to Western Sahara. In the event, however, the Ministry of the Interior announced a 100% participation of the electorate in the area, unanimously in favour of the amendments. King Hassan stated that Western Sahara would receive priority in the allocation of

development funds and also that Morocco would abide by the result of the UN referendum. Polisario claimed that demonstrations in Western Sahara against the communal elections in October had been forcibly suppressed, but once more the Moroccan Ministry of the Interior announced an overwhelming rate of voter participation in the region.

Following the assassination of Muhammad Boudiaf, the Algerian Head of State, in June 1992, relations between Morocco and Algeria were strained, and the latter was reported to be increasing its aid to Polisario. In December two groups of Sahrawi notables, composed of equal numbers of representatives from within the wall and from the camps at Tindouf in Algeria, travelled to Geneva for a meeting under the chairmanship of Yaqub Khan. The Tindoufis, however, refused to negotiate, claiming that the other delegation had altered its composition. In January 1993 a *rapprochement* between Morocco and Algeria was reported.

The President of the SADR accused the UN Security Council of losing interest in the Western Sahara dispute, and in January 1993 Boutros-Ghali reported that there was little prospect of success from continuing talks on their present basis. In March he suggested three alternatives to the Council: efforts to organize talks could continue; the UN could impose the Pérez de Cuéllar list; or there could be an entirely fresh initiative. Under Resolution 809, the Council decreed that the referendum should take place before the end of 1993, with or without Polisario co-operation, that further efforts should be made to compile a satisfactory electoral list, and that Boutros-Ghali should undertake a new round of negotiations. Morocco accepted the resolution at once and, after some delay, Polisario agreed to do likewise.

In April 1993 Yaqub Khan held talks in Algiers with senior Algerian officials before meeting King Hassan in Rabat in order to prepare a report on the situation in Western Sahara. In May a senior UN diplomat, Erik Jensen, was appointed to begin work on registering voters prior to the referendum. Morocco nevertheless included its 'Saharan provinces' in the kingdom's general election, held in June. Talks in July at el-Aaiún were the first to be held in the disputed territory itself, but proved inconclusive. Morocco had enjoyed a propaganda success on the eve of the talks when a notable Sahrawi chief defected.

According to a communiqué issued by Polisario in Algiers in September 1993, the SADR President, Muhammad Abd al-Aziz, nominated a new Government for the region in that month. Bouchraya Hammoudi Bayoun was appointed to lead the Government, with the uncompromising Grahim Ghali as his Minister of Defence. In the same month it was reported that, of 1,600 UN military personnel appointed to Western Sahara, only 360 were stationed in the territory.

In November 1993 Boutros-Ghali informed the UN Security Council that, because of unresolved differences as to voter eligibility, the referendum could not take place before mid-1994. In March 1994 he announced a new approach, involving three options: to proceed with the referendum by the end of 1994, even if one or both sides in the dispute disagreed; to cancel the referendum and withdraw most of the UN peace-keeping force; or to continue with talks between Morocco and the Polisario Front in order to compile acceptable voter lists. In April Jensen stated that Polisario, after some initial misgivings, had accepted a voter registration plan proposed under Security Council Resolution 907, and that voter registration would begin in June.

In May 1994 Jensen and Driss Basri issued a joint statement that voter registration would start in el-Aaiún in early June; however, the registration of voters did not begin until late August. Morocco had adopted familiar blocking techniques and at first refused to allow the presence of observers from the OAU at the process of identification of voters. After registration began it proved to be a slow process. In November, the date set for the completion of voter registration, the UN announced that plans to hold the referendum in February 1995 would have to be delayed because of problems of identifying potential voters. During a visit to the region at the end of November, Boutros-Ghali warned Morocco and Polisario of serious consequences if progress was not achieved in preparations for the referendum. At a meeting with Muhammad Abd al-Aziz, Boutros-Ghali tried to persuade him of the importance of encouraging voter registration. In December the UN Secretary-General stated that the referendum could be held in October 1995 but told the Security Council that a major reinforcement of UN personnel was essential if identification and registration of the large number of applications already received were to be completed in time. By February 1995 the UN had identified about 11,000 eligible voters, but differences between Morocco and Polisario over exactly who was eligible to vote remained. Polisario claimed that Morocco had settled large numbers of Moroccans in the disputed territory in order to influence the outcome of the referendum. There were violent clashes between Sahrawis and Moroccans in February during voter registration at the town of Ksabi. Although a delegation from the UN Security Council visited the territory in June to try and resolve the problems concerning voter registration, new disputes resulted in the announcement that the referendum would be delayed until January 1996. Meanwhile, during June and early July Polisario stopped co-operating with the UN commission identifying voters after a Moroccan court sentenced eight young Sahrawis to lengthy terms of imprisonment for organizing a demonstration in support of independence for Western Sahara. The sentences were subsequently commuted after the intervention of King Hassan, and Polisario resumed co-operation over voter identification. In August it was reported that Morocco had opened 40 new voter identification centres, not only in Western Sahara but also in some Moroccan towns and in its embassies abroad.

Muhammad Abd al-Aziz, who was re-elected as Polisario's Secretary-General at the organization's ninth congress held in Tindouf in August 1995, repeated that the struggle for sovereignty and independence would continue whatever the result of the referendum. Algeria reaffirmed its support for Polisario by sending three ministers to the congress but, preoccupied with its own political and economic crises, seemed unlikely to offer much practical assistance. In September it was reported that the SADR Government had been reshuffled and in the following month the first elected Saharan National Assembly, comprising 101 members elected by secret ballot, was inaugurated in Tindouf under the chairmanship of Abd al-Aziz. Polisario persisted with its campaign against Morocco by urging Spanish fishermen to ignore warnings from Morocco not to operate in Atlantic waters off Western Sahara, claiming that the fishing zone belonged to the Sahrawi people.

Progress towards a peaceful solution to the dispute was hampered by the deterioration in relations between Morocco and Algeria. Liamine Zéroual, the Algerian President, appeared to adopt a less flexible position on Western Sahara, and in August 1994 angered Morocco by referring to the territory as 'an illegally occupied country'. In December 1995, after Algeria objected to UN proposals to expedite voter registration in Western Sahara, Morocco responded angrily by obstructing the activities of the UAM of which Algeria currently held the presidency.

At intervals the UN Security Council voted to extend MINURSO's mandate on a short-term basis, although it did not set a new date for the referendum, which failed to take place in January 1996. Meanwhile, the registration process continued to be hampered by disputes between Morocco and Polisario on the identification of voters. In May 1996 the Security Council agreed to renew MINURSO's mandate until the end of November, although it voted to reduce its personnel in the territory. By November MINURSO's military component had decreased from 288 to 230, and the civilian police from 91 to nine. As the identification process remained suspended, the number of civilian posts was reduced from 410 to 170. Despite Polisario's threat to resume the armed struggle, the cease-fire remained in force, although MINURSO reported a number of violations on both sides. Both the Moroccan army and Polisario's forces conducted live-fire exercises, suggesting that they were preparing for combat when MINURSO's mandate expired. Although some progress was made on the exchange of prisoners of war, the identification process did not resume. MINURSO's mandate was extended in November (and again in March and September 1997), and in that month King Hassan confirmed that senior-level direct talks between his representatives and Polisario had taken place in August and September but had failed to reach any conclusive agreements.

In March 1997 the new UN Secretary-General, Kofi Annan, appointed James Baker (a former US Secretary of State) as the UN's special envoy to Western Sahara. Between June and September Baker chaired a series of direct talks between the Moroccan Government and representatives of Polisario in Lisbon (Portugal), London (United Kingdom) and Houston (USA), which he admitted had been difficult, but in mid-September a compromise agreement was reached on the highly contentious issue of who would be eligible to vote in the long-delayed referendum, which was scheduled to be held in December 1998. He appeared to have persuaded the Moroccans to accept a lower figure for the number of eligible voters than they had originally demanded. Agreement was also reached on the reduction of military forces of the two sides in the disputed territory, the repatriation of refugees and the release of detainees. Prime Minister Filali subsequently declared that the referendum would merely reaffirm Moroccan sovereignty over the Western Sahara, which he insisted would always remain an integral part of the kingdom. In March 1998 King Hassan referred to 'an affirmative referendum', that would put an end to 'an artificial problem' that had prevented Morocco from achieving its 'territorial unity'. Morocco also continued its campaign to weaken support for Polisario in the OAU, and by September 1997 10 member states had withdrawn recognition of the SADR in return for financial assistance from Morocco. In January 1998 changes to the SADR Government appeared to strengthen the position of intransigent members of the Polisario leadership and possibly pointed to a greater control over the movement by Algerian military intelligence. Some observers, however, predicted that if Polisario failed to win the referendum, the movement would split, with much of its leadership defecting to Morocco. By the end of 1997 the UN had begun reopening voter registration centres at el-Aaiún and es-Smara, but the process of voter identification was not completed by 31 May 1998, the closing date set by Annan for finalizing electoral lists, and in June it was reported that the referendum, scheduled for early December 1998, had been postponed for at least two months. In September the UN announced that some 147,000 potential voters had been identified to date.

FOREIGN POLICY IN THE 1990s

Morocco has determined to play a full part in world affairs in the 1990s, and in the first two years of the decade it established diplomatic relations with Namibia, South Africa (the first Arab country to do so), Viet Nam, Estonia, Ukraine and Kyrgyzstan. In August 1990 the Minister of Foreign Affairs, Filali, visited all five permanent members of the UN Security Council, and in the same month, at a meeting in Turkey of OIC Ministers of Foreign Affairs, Morocco presented proposals to increase the group's international scope. In September Morocco and the People's Republic of China signed an agreement on co-operation in energy and mining. In the following year Crown Prince Sidi Mohammed became the most important Moroccan to visit Beijing since the establishment of diplomatic relations in 1958. The visit was returned by the Chinese President, Yang Shangkun. In October 1991 Morocco was elected to the UN Security Council for a two-year term beginning on 1 January 1992 (it had previously been a member in 1962–63).

Morocco was quick to capitalize on the goodwill that it had generated in the USA by its strong support during the Gulf War. It benefited from both bilateral aid and credits from US-dominated agencies, receiving more from the World Bank than any other country in the Middle East or North Africa. Wheat and vegetable oil were provided on credit, and Morocco acquired 20 used F-16 military aircraft for $250m. In return, it supported the US peace initiative in the Middle East, and the King offered Morocco as a venue for the Arab-Israeli peace conference and expressed willingness to receive Prime Minister Itzhak Shamir of Israel. In August 1991 the Chairman of the Palestine Liberation Organization (PLO), Yasser Arafat, and the US Secretary of State, James Baker, visited Morocco within a few days of each other. The King made a fruitful visit to Washington, DC, in September, establishing closer relations with President George Bush, and apparently securing US support for Morocco's policy on Western Sahara. He announced that a US university, specializing in science, would be established in Ifrane, with financial support from the USA and Saudi Arabia. The former US President Ronald Reagan visited the King, to the outrage of Col Qaddafi, who was even more enraged when Morocco, as a member of the UN Security Council, did not veto the imposition of sanctions on Libya for its refusal to surrender the suspects wanted for trial in connection with the 1988 Lockerbie bombing. In August 1992, after Yasser Arafat had visited Rabat to discuss the forthcoming round of Middle East peace negotiations, Filali held talks with Baker in the USA. In December Morocco sent a contingent of 1,250 troops to support 'Operation Restore Hope' in Somalia. Five Moroccan soliders were killed during incidents in Mogadishu, Somalia, in June 1993. In April 1994 King Hassan held talks with the US Vice-President, Albert Gore, during meetings culminating in the signing of the Final Act of the Uruguay Round of the General Agreement on Tariffs and Trade (GATT), which took place in Marrakesh.

As expectations of the UAM diminished, Morocco intensified its efforts to become, if not a full member, at least a 'separate partner' of the EC. In September 1991 a proposal of the European Parliament to send observers to monitor the cease-fire and referendum in Western Sahara was officially denounced in Rabat as 'shameful blackmail'. In January 1992 the European Parliament voted against a four-year programme of aid, worth $600m., for Morocco, in protest against alleged human rights abuses. Morocco responded by refusing to renegotiate its fishing agreement with the EC, which was due to expire in February. There were separate visits to Rabat by the EC Commissioners for European Integration and for Mediterranean Policy, to discuss a new relationship based on a free-trade zone. A new fishing agreement was signed in May, whereby Morocco would receive annual compensation of ECU 102m. In December the European Commission approved loans worth $590m. to Morocco over four years, and the European Investment Bank made a loan to improve the telecommunications system. In March 1993 the EC announced that negotiations on a form of partnership, which would include permanent political dialogue, economic co-operation, financial aid and progressive moves towards a free-trade zone, should start within a year. In December the EC ministers of foreign affairs gave their approval for the European Union (EU), as the EC had become, to negotiate with Morocco on a new Europe-Maghreb association agreement. In February 1996 Morocco signed an economic association agreement as part of the EU's plan for a 'Euro-Mediterranean partnership', leading to the gradual introduction of free trade in manufactured goods with the EU. (When the European Parliament ratified the agreement in June, it insisted on inserting a clause allowing for the accord's suspension should concerns arise regarding the violation of human rights in Morocco.) In November 1995 Morocco participated in the first Euro-Mediterranean conference held in Barcelona, Spain, at which there were appeals for greater EU investment in the Maghreb countries in order to create jobs and provide housing, thus stemming emigration and the growth of Islamist militancy. Morocco offered to host the next conference planned for 1997. Yet despite Morocco's desire for closer ties with Europe, and a series of high-level ministerial visits from EU member states during 1997, drugs-trafficking and fisheries remained sources of friction. Morocco also expressed concern that Eastern Europe rather than the countries of the southern Mediterranean had become the EU's main priority.

Morocco continued to rely on France for diplomatic support in the UN Security Council and within the EC. In August 1991 Filali visited Paris, and in November 1992 Pierre Bérégovoy became the first French premier to visit Morocco since 1986. He promised to support Moroccan interests in the EC as far as he could without prejudice to French farmers. His visit was followed by that of the Minister of Foreign Trade, who announced a 50% increase in French aid. In July 1993 Edouard Balladur, the new French Prime Minister, made an official visit to Morocco, where he met King Hassan. In January 1994 the French Minister of the Interior, Charles Pasqua, visited Rabat for talks, which were believed to have covered the crisis in Algeria, Islamist terrorism, immigration, and an offer by the French Government to mediate in the dispute between Morocco and the Polisario Front. Pasqua made a private, but nevertheless controversial, visit to el-Aaiún, the first time that a senior French minister had visited the disputed territory.

After the murder of two Spanish tourists in Marrakesh in August 1994 (see below), the search for suspects spread to France, and in September French police arrested several Islamist activists, including Moroccan, Algerian and French

nationals, who were alleged to have been implicated in the incident. It was claimed that they were part of Islamist terrorist cells operating on both sides of the Mediterranean. In October France expelled two Moroccan religious leaders for allegedly collecting funds for arms purchases by Islamist militant groups. In late August Morocco imposed visa requirements on Algerian nationals and others of Algerian origin, including French nationals. However, the visa requirement for French nationals of Algerian origin was quickly withdrawn, following protests from the French authorities. Filali (now Prime Minister and Minister of Foreign Affairs and Co-operation) visited Paris in October. An agreement on military co-operation was signed, and France promised to support Morocco in its negotiations with the EU on a partnership accord. In July 1995, moreover, the new French President, Jacques Chirac, visited Morocco. This was his first official foreign visit in his capacity as Head of State. Chirac emphasized the good relations that existed between the two countries and pledged to assist Morocco in combatting Islamist extremism. The Chirac administration subsequently strengthened relations further by assisting with Morocco's external debt and by increasing project aid. In May 1996 King Hassan made a successful state visit to Paris where he was granted the rare honour of addressing the National Assembly, an invitation criticized by France's left-wing parties because of Morocco's questionable record on human rights. After a socialist Government assumed office in May 1997, the new administration sought to show that Morocco remained an important partner in France's Mediterranean strategy. The Minister of Foreign Affairs, Hubert Védrine, visited Rabat in July, followed by the Prime Minister, Lionel Jospin, accompanied by the Minister of the Economy, Finance and Industry, in late December. In March 1998 the Minister of the Interior, Jean-Pierre Chevènement, held talks with his Moroccan counterpart on security issues, notably illegal immigration and drugs-smuggling. Chevènement again emphasized the great importance that France attached to its relations with Morocco which he referred to as a country 'firmly on the path of progress and modernization'.

Discussions continued with the Spanish Government on a proposed bridge or tunnel link across the Strait of Gibraltar, and official relations remained good. In July 1991, during a visit to Rabat by King Juan Carlos, the two countries signed a treaty of friendship. The sources of former conflict over fishing and immigration remained, but Spain seemed no longer to be concerned about its former colony of Western Sahara. Economic links between Morocco and Spain were strengthened, and Spain overtook France as the principal foreign investor in the kingdom. In July 1992 the two countries signed a 25-year agreement to build and operate the second trans-Mediterranean gas pipeline, extending from Algeria to Spain, via Morocco. In March 1993 the ministers of energy of Spain, Morocco and Algeria met in Rabat to discuss details, and a joint Moroccan-Spanish company, the Société pour le Pilotage de la Construction du Gazoduc Maghreb-Europe (Metragaz), was founded, with its headquarters in Casablanca. Despite improving economic links, diplomatic relations became strained in 1994, primarily because of Spanish intransigence over improved access to EU markets for Moroccan agricultural products. Morocco countered with demands for drastic reductions in EU fishing quotas, which largely affect Spanish fishermen, who hold most of the fishing licences for Moroccan waters (see Economy). Relations were not improved when, in September, Morocco criticized Spain at the UN General Assembly for its autonomy plans for the Spanish enclaves of Ceuta and Melilla. Morocco intensified its diplomatic campaign to obtain sovereignty over the territories following the final approval by the Spanish Parliament, in February 1995, of the statutes of autonomy for the two enclaves. In April responsibility for two bomb explosions in Ceuta was claimed by the Organización 21 de Agosto para la Liberación de los Territorios Marroquíes Usurpados, a group which had apparently remained inactive during the previous two decades, and which, the Spanish Government suspected, was now receiving clandestine support from the Moroccan authorities. Relations remained strained through much of 1995, partly because of the prolonged dispute over Spanish fishing rights, but improved in early 1996, following a visit by Prime Minister González of Spain in February. Spain offered financial credits and proposed a joint committee on bilateral disputes, including the sensitive issue of Ceuta and Melilla. Later in the year the new Spanish premier, José María Aznar, visited Morocco for his first overseas engagement. Crown Prince Sidi Mohammed made a state visit to Spain in May 1997 and was received by King Juan Carlos. In June a ministerial delegation, led by Prime Minister Filali, visited Madrid where talks focused on economic relations. But the issue of Spanish fishing vessels operating in Moroccan territorial waters remained a source of friction between the two countries and in July Morocco detained a Spanish vessel, claiming that it was fishing illegally. Morocco indicated that it would not review the EU fisheries accord in 1999, an issue primarily affecting Spain. In January 1998 a joint commission was established with Spain to examine security issues, particularly illegal immigration and drugs-smuggling. Meanwhile, relations with Portugal were strengthened following a visit by Aníbal Cavaco Silva, the Portuguese Prime Minister, in May 1994, and the signing of a friendship and co-operation agreement. The Portuguese premier offered his support for Morocco in its negotiations with the EU. Co-operation agreements dealing with civil defence, organized crime, narcotics and visas were signed during a state visit by the Portuguese Prime Minister, António Guterres, in late 1997. In February 1998 Morocco and Italy signed a security accord covering issues such as illegal immigration, drugs-smuggling and organized crime.

The UAM itself made halting progress towards its avowed goal of economic union. The Casablanca summit meeting of September 1991 was dominated by the need to agree a common policy for the forthcoming Madrid Peace Conference, to which it sent a joint delegation. The summit also advocated the creation of a charter of rights for UAM citizens working in Europe. Headquarters of the various UAM institutions were allocated, with Morocco hosting the General Secretariat, Algeria the Consultative Assembly, Mauritania the Supreme Court, Tunisia the Investment Bank, and Libya the Maghreb University and Academy of Science. In December the ministers responsible for foreign affairs, the economy and agriculture met to discuss the co-ordination of policies: there were agreements on the Maghreb Autoroute, and trade union representatives from the five countries presented a joint plea for a social charter. In February 1993, however, Filali announced that, at a recent meeting of the ministers of foreign affairs within the UAM, it had been decided that there should be a 'pause' in the development of a closer union; it was noted that, of the 15 conventions signed since the inauguration of the UAM, none had as yet been fully applied. The organization was further weakened during 1994 by the sharp deterioration in relations between Morocco and Algeria, including the closure of the border between the two countries, and tensions between Morocco and Tunisia over Tunisia's expulsion of several hundred alleged illegal Moroccan immigrants. The Moroccan Government protested that some of its nationals had been maltreated by the Tunisian authorities and there were mutual recriminations. In December 1995 Morocco threatened to obstruct UAM activities, accusing Algeria of interfering in the Western Sahara dispute (see above). Morocco condemned a meeting in January 1996 between the Tunisian and Mauritanian foreign ministers and Liamine Zéroual, who continued to hold the UAM presidency. The meeting had been convened to resolve the dispute with Morocco. Morocco was especially critical that the UAM's Secretary-General, Mohamed Amamou, was present. As Libya did not attend, some observers believed that there was the possibility of renewed polarization in the region if the current UAM crisis was not resolved.

Morocco and Algeria restored diplomatic relations in 1988, and the two countries maintained particularly strong links during early 1992, while Muhammad Boudiaf, who had lived in Morocco for more than 20 years, was Algerian Head of State. The two states collaborated on security matters, and the Algerian Government urged the Polisario Front to make peace. Following the assassination of Boudiaf, relations deteriorated, the frontier was closed and Algerian supplies to Polisario were resumed. In January 1993, however, there was a reconciliation. Ambassadors were exchanged and the border was reopened. Relations deteriorated again in 1994, reaching their lowest ebb for many years. When the alleged leader of the Algerian Groupe islamique armé (GIA), Abd al-Hak Layada, stood trial in Algiers, he stated that, before being extradited from Morocco in September 1993,

senior Moroccan army officers had asked him to eliminate certain members of the Moroccan opposition living in Algeria, together with the Polisario Secretary-General, Muhammad Abd al-Aziz. In August, after the murder of two Spanish tourists at Marrakesh (see below), the Moroccan Ministry of the Interior issued a public statement alleging that two of the suspects sought for the killings were in the pay of the Algerian secret services, which it accused of sponsoring terrorism to destabilize the kingdom. During a massive security alert following the incident Moroccan police targeted the country's Algerian community in its search for terrorists. Morocco imposed entry visas on Algerian nationals and others of Algerian origin, including French nationals, visiting Morocco. The Algerian Government strongly denied that it was sponsoring terrorism against its neighbour, and sealed its border with Morocco. By mid-September, however, the tension between the two countries had eased somewhat, and in a gesture of goodwill Algeria appointed a permanent ambassador to Rabat. In October the Moroccan Minister of Energy and Mines visited Algeria to attend the ceremony marking the formal start of work on the Maghreb–Europe gas pipeline. But the frontier remained closed and visa requirements for Algerian nationals continued to be enforced. In December it was claimed that Algerian forces had killed a Moroccan at one of the border posts. Talks between King Hassan, the Algerian premier, Mokdad Sifi, and Abd al-Latif Filali, during the OIC summit held in Casablanca in December, failed to make any significant progress. Relations remained strained throughout 1995 and at the end of the year deteriorated sharply as Morocco accused Algeria of interfering in the Western Sahara dispute. Differences between the two countries seriously threatened the future of the UAM (see above). It was widely believed that the appointment of a former Moroccan minister to the presidency of the African Development Bank in August 1995 had also angered Algeria, which regarded the appointment as a further attempt by Morocco to increase its international influence. In December 1996 the Algerian Minister of the Interior held talks in Rabat with his Moroccan counterpart. This was the first meeting of senior ministers since the border was closed in August 1994. The Western Sahara remained a source of tension between the two countries and in February 1998 Gen. Khaled Nezzar, a former Algerian Minister of Defence and a powerful figure in the regime, accused Morocco of demanding that Algeria end its support for Polisario in return for the extradition of Abd al-Hak Layada. Gen. Nezzar also accused the Moroccan authorities of providing covert assistance to armed opposition groups in Algeria and allowing weapons to be smuggled across the border. Morocco strenuously denied the allegations.

In the Arab world as a whole Morocco benefited both from the personal prestige of its monarch as an experienced statesman and from its support for the liberation of Kuwait. In January 1992 Arab ministers of foreign affairs met in Marrakesh to agree a common strategy for the Moscow session of the Middle East peace talks. In October, just before the seventh round of the talks (held in Washington, DC), King Hassan made his most extensive tour of the Islamic world in 30 years, visiting Jordan (for the first time), Syria, Saudi Arabia, the Gulf states and Egypt. In December 1994 Morocco hosted a summit of the OIC at the request of Saudi Arabia, but King Hassan failed to engender any reconciliation between Iraq and Saudi Arabia and Kuwait, despite lengthy negotiations.

In September 1993, following the mutual recognition and signature of a peace accord between Israel and the PLO, the Israeli Prime Minister, Itzhak Rabin, and the Minister of Foreign Affairs, Shimon Peres, visited Rabat for talks with King Hassan. Apart from Egypt, Morocco was the only Arab state to receive the two Israeli leaders. In October a group of Moroccan industrialists, including King Hassan's economic consultant, visited Israel to attend a business conference, the first official Moroccan delegation to visit the Jewish state. Commercial links developed rapidly, and tourism was expected to expand. The Moroccan-Jewish community constitutes more than 10% of the Israeli population, and large numbers visit their country of origin every year. After talks with King Hassan in June 1994, Shimon Peres announced that the two countries had agreed to establish telecommunications links and, at a later date, to establish 'representations of some kind'. In September, as the peace process gained momentum, Morocco and Israel agreed to open 'liaison offices' in Rabat and Tel-Aviv. King Hassan has maintained discreet contacts with Israeli leaders since the 1970s. The latest move towards Israel was criticized by the opposition parties, which urged caution until a comprehensive Middle East peace settlement had been achieved. Morocco also became the first Arab state to announce that it would open a 'liaison bureau' in the Gaza autonomous area. In October 1994, during an historic appearance on Israeli television, King Hassan declared that the peace process would lead to the establishment of full diplomatic relations between Morocco and Israel, but carefully avoided stating when this would take place. He repeated Morocco's position on the restoration of Arab lands and rights, while insisting that the unconditional recognition of Israeli sovereignty within internationally agreed borders was essential. Also in October Israeli companies participated for the first time in an international trade fair in Morocco, and at the end of the month Israel was one of the principal countries represented at the Casablanca Middle East Regional Conference sponsored by the US and Russian Presidents, which brought together politicians and businessmen to discuss the economic implications of the Arab-Israeli peace process. In early 1995 Morocco opened a small bureau in Tel-Aviv, making it the third Arab country after Egypt and Jordan to have a representative office in Israel. However, King Hassan continued to stress that full normalization of relations between the two countries would only be achieved after the conclusion of a comprehensive Middle East peace settlement. In May King Hassan hosted talks between Shimon Peres and Yasser Arafat. In February 1996 an Israel-Moroccan chamber of commerce was opened in Tel-Aviv. King Hassan did not attend the emergency Arab League summit in Cairo in June, convened by President Mubarak of Egypt after the new Israeli premier, Binyamin Netanyahu, and his right-wing government rejected the 'land for peace' policies of the previous administration. It was reported that the King had taken umbrage when he was not consulted about the planning of the conference. In February 1997, as the Middle East peace process seemed close to collapse, King Hassan indicated that visits to Morocco by either Prime Minister Netanyahu or Israel's Deputy Prime Minister and Minister of Foreign Affairs, David Levy, would not be appropriate. In March the King organized a meeting in Rabat of the OIC's Jerusalem committee, of which he is the Chairman. The committee demanded that the Israeli Government stop construction of the controversial Jewish settlement at Har Homa on the outskirts of Arab East Jerusalem, and appealed to Arab states that had begun to establish relations with Israel to reconsider these links. A threat by Morocco in April to close the Moroccan-based Bureau for Economic Development in the Middle East, established to promote economic relations between the Arab states and Israel, was withdrawn in May after US intervention. Morocco did not close its liaison office in Tel-Aviv despite Hassan's continued refusal to have any contact with the Netanyahu administration. Although two Euro-Mediterranean summits were scheduled to be held in Marrakesh to discuss co-operation between the EU and Mediterranean countries, including Israel, the meeting planned for October was cancelled by the Moroccan Government; nevertheless, the second went ahead as scheduled in November. Along with most Arab League members, Morocco boycotted the fourth US-sponsored Middle East and North Africa Economic Conference held in Qatar in November, arguing that while the Middle East peace process remained deadlocked there was little to be gained from discussing economic co-operation with Israel. Notwithstanding, commercial and business links between Morocco and Israel remained strong.

THE 1993 GENERAL ELECTION

In October 1991 various opposition parties allied to form the Mouvement national populaire (MNP), an opposition grouping under a veteran Berber politician, Mahjoubi Aherdane; in November Istiqlal and the USFP formed a united front, demanding a separation of powers, a reduction in the minimum voting age to 18 years, new electoral lists and constituency boundaries, and improvements in civil rights. The USFP was, however, weakened by the death of its veteran leader, Abd ar-Rahim Bouabid. His successor, Abd ar-Rahman Youssouf, did not have the same close links with the monarchy. In April 1992 a 16th

political party, the Parti de l'avant-garde démocratique socialiste (PADS, a breakaway from the USFP), was legalized. In March a trade union official and USFP politburo member, Nubir Amaoui, was sentenced to two years' imprisonment for his public criticism of the Government. In late 1992 trade union activists demonstrating to demand Amaoui's release were forcibly dispersed. Meanwhile, a prominent member of the ADHM, Ahmed Belaichi, was sentenced to three years' imprisonment for making derogatory remarks about the armed forces. In February 1993 the ADHM alleged that as many as 750 political prisoners were being detained in Morocco. However, in July, following the legislative elections, Amaoui was released, along with the leader of another, pro-Istiqlal, union, Driss Laghnimi.

In April 1992, in an address to a conference of local government bodies, the King declared that parliamentary elections would be preceded by those for regional and local councils. There was disagreement on the text of the electoral law, and the opposition parties (Istiqlal, the USFP, the PADS and the PPS) refused to enter discussions, complaining that their previous recommendations had always been ignored. Hassan, fearing that these parties would boycott the poll (rendering it meaningless), asked them to negotiate with his close associate, Reda Guedira. It was agreed that a new Constitution should be submitted to a referendum. Declaring that his status as a religious, as well as a national, leader empowered him to arbitrate, King Hassan announced the establishment of two committees: one to draft the law and the other to monitor the electoral process. In May he chaired a conference of three ministers and the leaders of five pro-government and four opposition parties, allowing them 10 days to agree on an electoral law. A law comprising 99 articles was approved, and Hassan reiterated his promise of 'transparency'. A commission, chaired by a judge and consisting of members of local authorities and party representatives, was established, with direct access to the King or to Guedira.

In June 1992 the Chamber of Representatives adopted a new electoral law, in spite of a boycott by all opposition parties. The law reduced the minimum voting age to 20 years and the minimum candidate age to 23 from 25. It also made provision for equal funding and media exposure for all parties, and was approved by 162 votes in favour, with two abstentions. The opposition parties had earlier formed the Bloc démocratique (or Koutla Dimocratya), whose expressed aims were: a minimum voting age of 18 years; a minimum age of 21 for candidates; a two-tier voting system; and an independent chairman of a new body to supervise elections.

In July 1992 King Hassan announced preparations for elections to the Chamber of Representatives, and by the end of the month registration had taken place, increasing the electorate from 7m. to 11.7m. voters. In mid-August an interim Government was appointed to ensure the fairness of the political process. The new Prime Minister, Karim Lamrani, had held the office on two previous occasions. Lamrani's Government contained just one member with party political affiliations, although the major portfolios were unchanged.

In an address to the nation in August 1992 King Hassan stated that the revised Constitution would give more responsibilities to the legislature, but emphasized that this did not mean a reduction in the sovereign's prerogatives. Under the proposed changes, ministers would be chosen by the premier but appointed by the King. A new Constitutional Council of eight members, one-half of them appointed by the King, would be created to arbitrate at the request of one-quarter of the parliamentary deputies. The revised Constitution also reaffirmed the King's commitment to human rights.

On 4 September 1992 the revised Constitution was endorsed by the Moroccan electorate. According to official results, 99.96% voted in favour (increasing to 100% in main cities, and three of the four 'Saharan provinces') and 97.25% of the 11.7m. registered voters participated. The opposition claimed that the results destroyed all credibility in the democratic process. The revised Constitution required the government to reflect the composition of the Chamber of Representatives and to submit its programme to a vote. New legislation would be promulgated automatically one month after approval by the Chamber.

Despite protests over the result of the referendum, the Bloc démocratique contested the communal elections that took place in October 1992. The RNI became the largest party in local government, winning 18.1% of the votes cast and 21.7% of the 22,282 seats contested. The independent list, Sans appartenance politique, which, despite its name, was loyal to the Government, obtained 13.8% of the votes, and the UC 13.4%. Istiqlal emerged as the largest opposition party (with 12.5% of the votes cast), followed by the USFP, which confirmed its strength in Casablanca and Rabat. The opposition parties, however, failed to improve on their performance in the previous communal elections, despite contesting many more seats, and complained of widespread malpractices by local authorities in favour of 'loyalist' parties.

In December 1992 it was announced that the long-awaited national legislative election, the first since 1984, would not be held until 30 April 1993, to allow time for the compiling of new electoral registers. The opposition demanded that the lists should be radically revised, and the boundaries of constituencies redrawn. The authorities stated that the registers would include newly-eligible voters but rejected proposals for any other changes. In February 1993 the four leading opposition parties that formed the Bloc démocratique—Istiqlal, the USFP and two smaller parties, the PPS and the Organisation de l'action démocratique et populaire (OADP)—withdrew from the multiparty national commission responsible for overseeing the election, and threatened to boycott the poll unless the Government agreed to changes in the electoral law and register, and responded to their demands for the release of all political prisoners. Meanwhile, there were strikes by teachers and health workers and a week-long campaign of stoppages over unemployment, pay and living conditions, supported by the UMT. In late March King Hassan announced that the election would be postponed until 25 June, to allow more time to update electoral lists and to redefine electoral boundaries. The opposition parties welcomed the King's decision and agreed to participate in the election. Following boundary revisions (completed in late April), the Government announced that the number of seats in the Chamber of Representatives had been increased from 306 to 333. Of the total, 222 would be elected by universal adult suffrage, and the remainder by local councils and professional organizations.

At the general election, on 25 June 1993, the two main opposition parties, Istiqlal and the USFP, substantially increased the number of their seats in the Chamber (from 57 in 1984 to 91) to become the leading parties at the end of the first stage of the electoral process. The parties of the Bloc démocratique won a total of 99 seats. Although the five loyalist parties won more seats overall, the UC and the RNI secured fewer seats than in 1984. The UC had been the largest single party at the 1984 election, with 55 seats, but won only 27 seats in 1993. The MP emerged with 33 seats, two more than in 1984. According to official figures, 62.8% of the electorate voted, but observers suggested that the level of participation may have been even lower. Despite reports of abuses by local officials, polling was judged to have been fairer than in previous elections. Nevertheless, the opposition parties demanded that the election of four cabinet ministers be annulled. In the second stage of the election, held on 17 September 1993, the loyalist parties made significant gains, winning 79 of the 111 seats contested. The UC alone won 27 seats, making it the second largest party in the new Chamber (after the USFP). The USFP and Istiqlal gained only 17 seats, and accused the authorities of 'falsifying the popular will.' Abd ar-Rahman Youssouf, the USFP leader, resigned in protest at the attitude of the administration during the election. At the end of the second stage the five loyalist parties had 195 seats in the new Chamber, while the Bloc démocratique had 120 seats, with independents holding the remaining 18 seats.

After the election it was reported that King Hassan had agreed that the USFP and Istiqlal, as the main components of the Bloc démocratique, could form a government on condition that he appointed three principal ministers. The two parties rejected the offer and announced that they would not participate in the new Government. On 9 November 1993 the King therefore asked Karim Lamrani, who had led the interim Government appointed in August 1992 to oversee the election, to form a new Government. This was the fourth occasion on which the 74-year-old Lamrani, one of the most trusted members of the King's inner circle, had been named Prime Minister. Lamrani

announced a Government largely composed of technocrats and independents. None of the ministers from the previous administration who had stood for election in June were included. Ten new ministers and five new junior ministers were appointed. Mohamed Saghou replaced Mohamed Berrada as Minister of Finance, a post that Berrada had held for eight years, and Serge Berdugo, appointed Minister of Tourism, became the first Jewish minister since 1957. Omar Azziman, a co-founder of the OMDH, was appointed to the new post of Minister-delegate responsible for Human Rights. The appointment was welcomed by Amnesty International, a persistent critic of Morocco's record in observing human rights. Amnesty appealed to the Government to release all prisoners of conscience, and presented a list of 80 Moroccans and 485 Sahrawis, whom it claimed to have 'disappeared.' In late November 1993 the Chamber of Representatives adopted the Government's new programme, promising economic reforms and greater social justice.

In February 1994 there were clashes between radical Islamist and leftist students at Fez University, and courses were suspended indefinitely after the security forces intervened. At the end of the month the Government banned a 24-hour general strike (planned for 25 February), organized by the CDT to protest against declines in the standard of living. On 24 February, after 11 of its activists had been arrested in Casablanca, the CDT announced its decision to postpone the strike. The banning order was condemned by most opposition parties and by the three national trade unions. A number of parliamentary by-elections were held in April, following a judicial decision to reorganize polling after complaints of irregularities during the 1993 legislative election. Of the 14 seats contested by 88 candidates in the by-elections, the USFP won two, and Istiqlal three. The RNI, which had won five of the seats in June 1993, retained only two. Nevertheless, the opposition parties again complained of irregularities during the voting.

FILALI BECOMES PRIME MINISTER AND EFFORTS TO DRAW THE OPPOSITION INTO GOVERNMENT FAIL

On 25 May 1994 Lamrani was replaced as Prime Minister by Abd al-Latif Filali, formerly the Minister of Foreign Affairs and Co-operation and another member of the King's inner circle. Filali, a former diplomat, had first held government office in 1968. The new premier was expected to promote economic liberalization more vigorously and, within a few days of his appointment, announced that he had begun consultations with all the political parties with members in the Chamber of Representatives about the political, economic and social situation of the country. After a week of consultation, however, Filali made no changes to the list of ministers presented to the King in early June. The Prime Minister retained control of the Ministry of Foreign Affairs and Co-operation. However, Ali Yata, the Secretary-General of the PPS, stated that Filali had proposed the formation of a Government of national consensus within three or four months. In July King Hassan again appealed to the opposition to join a 'government of change and renewal'. After less than a year in office, the Minister of Finance, Mohamed Saghou, was dismissed in July, for a budget policy deemed to be too lenient, and replaced by Mourad Cherif, hitherto Minister of Foreign Trade. In October Hassan continued his efforts to draw the parliamentary opposition parties into a coalition government by announcing his intention to select a Prime Minister from the ranks of the opposition. He held separate discussions with Muhammad Boucetta, the Secretary-General of Istiqlal, and with Abdelwahed Radi of the USFP. The two main opposition parties agreed to the King's proposal in principle and looked to the RNI and to one of the two Berber groups as potential partners in an alternative government. But talks between the palace and the opposition parties collapsed over the appointment of the Minister of State for the Interior and Information in the new Government. The King insisted on retaining the long-serving Driss Basri in this sensitive post, but the opposition demanded that they be allowed to make their own appointment to the ministry. The King had also insisted that the opposition should support the economic liberalization measures agreed with the IMF, implementing the privatization programme and reducing the budget deficit. In December the opposition parties rejected the Government's 1995 budget, claiming that it would adversely affect living standards and increase unemployment. They also criticized the Government for placing too great a dependence on the private sector in economic development. However, support from the loyalist parties ensured that the budget was accepted by the Chamber of Representatives.

In late January 1995 King Hassan reappointed Filali as Prime Minister and Minister of Foreign Affairs and Co-operation, and once again chose a Government drawn from loyalist parties. In February he approved a new Cabinet drawn from three of the main centre-right parties, the UC, the MP and the PND. The other two main centre-right parties, the RNI and the MNP declined an offer to join the administration but confirmed that they would continue to support the Government in the Chamber of Representatives. Of the 35 cabinet posts, 20 portfolios were allocated to political parties, the rest to palace-appointed technocrats. Yet despite an attempt to give the political process greater legitimacy by drawing more than one-half of the ministers from elected political parties, the King retained control of appointments to important cabinet posts. Driss Basri remained at the Ministry of the Interior and although he ceded the information portfolio—a new Ministry of Communications was created headed by Driss Alaoui M'Daghri—the King could be assured that internal security would remain tightly controlled. Abderrahmane Saaidi was retained as head of the Ministry of Privatization, and the politically sensitive posts of housing and education also went to non-party palace appointees. Nine of the portfolios given to political parties went to the UC including tourism, human rights and the important post of finance and foreign investments. The MP received eight posts of which the most important were the portfolios of agriculture and foreign trade, and the PND three posts.

In June 1994 Prime Minister Filali announced that the national television service would begin broadcasting news bulletins in Tamazight, the Berber language. Since August a short news programme has been broadcast on Moroccan television with a different presenter for each of the three main Berber dialects, Tarifit (spoken in the Rif), Tamazight (centre-east) and Tachlahit (south). A few days before the broadcasts began King Hassan declared that Berber 'dialects' were an integral part of Morocco's authenticity and history and would soon be taught in state schools, at least at elementary level. He stressed, however, that Arabic remained the official language as detailed in the Moroccan Constitution. Nevertheless, these developments appeared to mark a major change in policy towards the Berber-speaking minority which constitutes more than one-third of the country's population. Berber cultural associations have flourished in recent years, attracting many young activists. Six of these associations had signed the Agadir charter in August 1991 deploring the marginalization of the Berber language and culture, appealing for the teaching of Tamazight in Moroccan schools and for Tamazight to be given national status in the Constitution alongside Arabic. By 1994 some 11 associations had signed the charter. In May 1994, after a peaceful Berberist demonstration by the Tilelli (Liberty) association at er-Rachidia demanding official recognition of Tamazight, and for the Berber language to be taught in schools, seven supporters were arrested and charged with threatening state security. The authorities claimed to have discovered documents implicating the President of Tilelli in links with 'foreign organizations'. Three of those arrested were given prison sentences but were released in July when King Hassan granted an amnesty to 424 prisoners following appeals by international and local human rights groups.

The regime remained nervous of any challenge to its authority and determined to act against organized labour, students and other dissenting groups. In June 1994 several unemployed graduates were given two-year prison sentences after holding an unauthorized demonstration to protest against corruption in local government. The penal code was also revised so that trade unionists involved in strike action over pay would be subject to prison sentences or fines. In August, after gunmen shot and killed two Spanish tourists in Marrakesh, a massive security operation was launched amidst fears that the vitally important tourist industry was being targeted as part of a wider attempt to destabilize the country. Within days, two French nationals of North African origin, Algerian-born Stephane Ait-Idir and Moroccan-born Redouane Hammadi, were arrested and charged with the murders, and in the following months several hundred suspects, most of them Algerian-French or Moroccan-French, were arrested and accused of terrorist activities. The net spread to France where French police arrested alleged associates of the two men charged and claimed that they belonged to Islamist terrorist cells. Seven main suspects were brought to trial in early 1995 for the Marrakesh murders. The Moroccan authorities alleged that they formed three terrorist groups: the Marrakesh group led by Ait-Idir and Hammadi, the Casablanca group led by Hamel Marzouk, and the Fez group which included a French-Algerian and three Moroccan nationals. Ait-Idir, Hammadi and Marzouk were condemned to death, the first death sentences given for political or security offences since the early 1970s, and three of the other main defendants were given life imprisonment. Twelve other suspects received prison sentences ranging from six months to 10 years. At their trial the three main defendants admitted to belonging to an Islamist terrorist group and being converted to *jihad* by a Moroccan known as Abdelilah Ziad. In August Ziad was extradited from Germany to stand trial in France on charges of involvement in terrorist acts in both Morocco and France. Tarek Falah, also accused of taking part in the Marrakesh murders, had been extradited from Germany to France in July. The incident at Marrakesh had a damaging effect on Morocco's relations with Algeria after Morocco accused the Algerian security forces of financing terrorist groups in Morocco with the aim of destabilizing the country (see above). At his trial in Paris in December 1996 Ziad claimed that his terrorist group (the outlawed Mouvement de la jeunesse islamique marocaine) based in Paris was responsible for organizing the Marrakesh operation and had also smuggled arms to the Armée islamique du salut in Algeria, the armed wing of the banned Front islamique du salut.

In mid-1995 the Minister of Higher Education, Driss Khalil, admitted publicly for the first time that Islamist militants were gaining strength among university students. The authorities announced their intention to continue to target the ringleaders, while they would encourage other student organizations in order to counter the Islamist threat. In October 12 Moroccans and five Algerians were arrested near the Algerian border and charged with smuggling arms to the Algerian GIA. In January 1996 they received prison sentences of up to 14 years. In December 1995 Abd as-Salam Yassin, the leader of the banned Islamist movement Al Adl wa-'l Ihsan, was released after spending six years under house arrest. A week later, after addressing worshippers at a mosque and denouncing certain aspects of government policy, he was placed once again under house arrest; the authorities insisted that he was under 'police protection'. Some observers argued that this episode illustrated the Government's ambivalent attitude towards the Islamist opposition: a measure of tolerance was displayed towards the more moderate Islamist opposition (although they were refused permission to form a political party), while armed Islamist groups were severely repressed. Although small extremist Islamist groups certainly exist and are supported in particular by young militants, since the 1980s the main currents of the Islamist movement have evolved towards an 'Islamism of compromise' with the Government. Islamist groups such as Al Adl wa-'l Ihsan and Al Islah wa Attajdid (Reform and Renewal) insist that they wish to be integrated into the political system, rejecting violence and favouring the peaceful re-Islamization of society. They conduct a range of socio-cultural activities, including charitable work in the most disadvantaged quarters of the major cities, and seek to gain influence in trade unions and in major political parties such as the USFP and Istiqlal. Poor employment prospects (especially among young people), low pay, redundancies owing to the privatization of state companies, declining living standards and a severe drought not only provided fertile ground for the Islamist movement but also led to widespread strike action by many, including teachers and workers in the phosphate industry and on the railways. Although the Government attempted to promote dialogue between employers and workers, several trade unionists were imprisoned, and, amidst allegations of police brutality, both unions and human rights groups condemned the Government's repressive policy in labour disputes. In mid-1995 the police presence in major cities was heightened to combat increasing levels of robbery and violence. Opposition parties accused the police of exceeding their authority by making arbitrary arrests and intimidating suspects, and in September both the police and the judiciary were strongly criticized when 26 unemployed graduates staging a peaceful demonstration at El Jadida were arrested and sentenced to six months in prison. At the end of the year the King warned that the civil service and national and local administration would have to be reformed to enable the country to confront the challenges of the next century. But conscious that retrenchment and redundancies would be strongly opposed, he appealed for dialogue with political parties and trade unions to discuss potential reforms. In December 1996 senior officials reiterated the King's message, insisting that the country could not become a modern market economy unless its bureaucracy was reformed.

In June 1995 charges against Muhammad Basri, former leader of the USFP, who had lived in exile for some 28 years after being sentenced to death (*in absentia*) for plotting against the State, were dropped, allowing him to return to Morocco. Abd ar-Rahman Youssouf, who had resigned as Secretary-General of the USFP in 1993, agreed to resume the post in July. In the same month the PPS held its first congress for four years, at which Ali Yata was re-elected as Secretary-General.

In August 1995 King Hassan announced plans to hold a referendum to decide whether to create a second parliamentary chamber. The referendum, held on 13 September 1996, confirmed overwhelming support for the new parliamentary system, under which all members of the Chamber of Representatives would be directly elected and their term would be reduced from six to five years. A new upper house, the Chamber of Advisers, was to be established and its members chosen by electoral colleges, representing mainly local councils, with the remainder selected from professional associations and trade unions. The Chamber of Advisers would be competent to initiate legislation, issue 'warning' motions to the government and, by a two-thirds' majority vote, force its resignation. Moroccan officials denied that the role of the new upper house was to neutralize the Chamber of Representatives. The USFP and Istiqlal, together with the PPS, gave a guarded welcome to the reforms, but the OADP, their partner in the Bloc démocratique, condemned them. The USFP had either boycotted or urged its supporters to vote against the four previous revisions to the Constitution. After the referendum the OADP split when a group of officials left to form the Parti socialiste démocratique. The Ministry of Information reported that 10.17m. people had voted in favour of the King's proposal, representing 99.56% of the votes cast. Some 82.95% of the electorate participated. In early December the Government announced that it was beginning to reform electoral procedures in preparation for the forthcoming elections; a commission, on which all officially recognized political parties were allowed representation, commenced examining electoral lists to identify irregularities. Within days the commission had identified more than 400,000 voters whose names appeared twice on the electoral lists. In mid-December a draft law was approved, providing for the establishment of elected councils in 16 new regions, including the disputed Western Sahara. Each regional council would be elected for a six-year period and would have responsibility for tax collection and the construction of schools and hospitals.

In February 1997 11 political parties, including five from the opposition, signed a political pact with the Minister of State for the Interior, Driss Basri, with the aim of 'strengthening the democratic regime based on the monarchy'. All the signatories agreed to abide by the law. The authorities conceded that they would treat all political parties equally and ban illegal practices. For their part the political parties promised to mobilize their supporters in 'a positive spirit' and not to contest, in advance, the integrity of future voting. After lengthy negotiations the authorities and the opposition parties agreed that new electoral lists would be prepared, and a national commission established to oversee the elections. The scale of irregularities in previous elections was revealed when the Moroccan press published figures indicating that 4.5m. voter registrations out of an electorate of 12m. were unreliable. The authorities appeared to have entered into the pact because they calculated that the successful integration of Morocco into the world economy required political reforms, if only to satisfy international organizations such as the World Bank and the IMF. While the official media welcomed the pact with enthusiasm, some leading members of the opposition expressed caution. There were also doubts as to whether the task of reviewing and correcting all the electoral lists could be completed in time for the general election. The Bloc démocratique announced that it would present joint candidates in some 25,000 municipal districts. The 'loyalist' parties (including the UC, the MP and the PND) which held a majority of seats in the current Chamber of Representatives, also formed a common front, the Entente nationale (or Wifaq), and adopted the same strategy. However, the small parties of the radical left felt excluded from the political process as did the Islamists. Several radical Islamist groups demanded the right to form political parties and to contest the forthcoming elections. But although Al Islah wa Attajdid gained legal status in January 1997 after its merger with the MPCD, the authorities rejected Al Adl wa-'l Ihsan's bid for recognition as a political party.

The Moroccan authorities strongly condemned the publication of a report by the Observatoire géopolitique des drogues (based in France) presented to the EU in October 1995 on the Moroccan drugs trade, which implicated members of the royal family, former cabinet ministers, members of parliament and local government officials. Nevertheless, as part of the Government's campaign against drugs-trafficking, action was taken against several officials allegedly involved in the trade; however, some observers argued that this was merely an attempt to divert attention away from others close to the King. In April 1996 some 30 drugs-traffickers were sentenced to up to 10 years' imprisonment by a court in Salé after the country's biggest drugs trial. Other drugs trials were held in Casablanca, Tétouan, Tangier and Al-Hoceima. In the following months the Government intensified its campaign against drugs-trafficking and a record number of arrests were made. In January 1996 the Ministry of the Interior launched its largest campaign against smuggling, which targeted corrupt customs officials and resulted in the prosecution of the head of the customs and excise department and his predecessor. The campaign against the smuggling trade, believed to be extensive in Tangier and around the Spanish enclaves of Ceuta and Melilla, provoked strong criticism from opposition parties and human rights organizations for being arbitrary and unduly harsh. It also led to the resignation of the Minister-delegate to the Prime Minister, in charge of Human Rights, who described the Government's tactics against smugglers as 'collective lynching'. In June, in an attempt to placate the business community, the Government promised the employers' association that future campaigns against smuggling would be less disruptive to business. Also in June there was renewed criticism of Morocco's human rights record by the French media after three members of Gen. Oufkir's family escaped to France (see above). The family was released from detention in 1991, but had been placed under surveillance and forbidden to travel abroad. Following the much publicized escape, passports were issued to the remaining family members, including Oufkir's widow.

In early 1996 there was renewed speculation about the health of King Hassan after he became seriously ill during late 1995; meanwhile, rumours circulated that the King favoured the succession of his second son, Moulay Rachid, rather than the Crown Prince, Sidi Mohammed.

During early 1996 there was renewed labour unrest leading to strikes and demonstrations by public-sector employees demanding better working conditions. The unrest culminated in a general strike in June, the first since 1990, during which there were serious clashes between demonstrators and the security services. In the Beni Makada district of Tangier (where violent confrontations had occurred in 1990) demonstrators damaged businesses and other properties. The strike was organized by the Union Générale des Travailleurs Marocains (UGTM) and the CDT, which urged the Government to increase the minimum wage and establish a national fund for the unemployed. Fearing more violence, the Government made concessions, and in July agreed a new accord on labour relations with employers' associations and trade unions. The Government accepted a 10% increase in minimum wages, and rises in family allowances, pensions and social security allowances; recognized the unions' right to take strike action; and agreed to consult the unions on new legislation concerning employment. In future a permanent committee representing the Government, employers' associations and unions is to meet regularly to monitor labour relations. The accord was signed by representatives of the UGTM, the CDT, the Confédération Générale des Entreprises du Maroc and Driss Basri. The UMT indicated that it accepted most of the points in the accord, but rising unemployment continued to provoke demonstrations against the Government, especially by unemployed graduates. In October 1,200 unemployed graduates demonstrated outside the UMT office in Rabat and then launched a hunger strike when the authorities prevented them from protesting outside the Chamber of Representatives. In January 1997 three unemployed graduates were arrested and sentenced to six months' imprisonment after participating in a small, peaceful protest in Marrakesh. After further demonstrations by unemployed graduates in May, Prime Minister Filali met their repesentatives in June and promised to address their grievances. Nevertheless, further protests were staged in August. Although the July 1996 accord on labour relations was confirmed in July 1997, some state-sector workers expressed dissatisfaction at the new pay levels, and in September public-sector health workers went on strike for the fifth time since the beginning of the year to demand an increase in their salaries. In January 1998 the police forcibly dispersed a march by miners who were protesting about the proposed closure of a coal mine at Jerada; trade unionists accused security forces of attacking their headquarters in Jerada.

In March 1996 clashes occurred at Casablanca University between Islamist undergraduates and students affiliated to the USFP; the latter accused the Islamists of trying to 'assassinate democracy in Morocco'. There was speculation that the rift between the two student groups may have been instigated by the authorities in an attempt to weaken the Islamists' position on the campus. In January 1997 Islamist students protesting against poor facilities on campus clashed with security forces at Casablanca University and the violence quickly spread to other universities. Many students were injured in the rioting and numerous arrests were made. Some 50 undergraduates, most of them members of Al Adl wa-'l Ihsan, were later sentenced to between three months and two years in prison for their part in the disturbances. (In March the Court of Appeal substantially reduced the sentences of 25 of the students.) However, a strike in late January organized by the Union Nationale des Etudiants du Maroc, which is controlled by Al Adl wa-'l Ihsan, to protest against Government repression, did not precipitate further clashes with the security forces. In February the authorities tried to prevent Islamist students at Casablanca University from holding Friday prayers on the campus; the incident did not escalate, thanks to the intervention of the Minister of Higher Education. The Government blamed the campus unrest on poor staff–student relations, and in late January King Hassan dismissed eight university rectors and replaced them with his own appointees. In November there were further clashes between Islamist students and the security forces after the students tried to organize a strike at Casablanca and Mohammadia universities. In January 1998 supporters of Adl wa-'l Ihsan appealed to the Government to release the movement's leader, Abd as-Salam Yassin, who remained under house arrest.

THE 1997 LOCAL AND LEGISLATIVE ELECTIONS

The political pact signed in February 1997 (see above) was first tested in local elections held in June. A national commission, chaired by the President of the Supreme Court and including members of political parties as well as government representatives, was established to monitor the election process. Despite some complaints of irregularities, the elections for 24,253 seats on municipal councils and communes were judged to have been relatively fair with the turnout officially estimated at 75.0%. Although the opposition Bloc démocratique achieved a much better result than in the 1992 elections, winning 31.7% of the seats, overall control of local councils was retained by the right-wing Entente nationale and the centrist grouping led by the RNI, which took 30.3% and 26.4% of the seats, respectively. During the election campaign the Bloc démocratique outlined for the first time its economic programme in an attempt to reassure the business community. In addition to the three main political groupings, five other political parties presented

candidates and there were many independent condenders. The MPCD refused to take part in the elections on the grounds that it was not represented on the national election commission; however, there were claims that the authorities had put pressure on the party to withdraw because they feared that there would be strong support for radical Islamists. Notwithstanding, Al Islah wa Attajdid presented a number of independent candidates. Prior to the elections more than 100 left-wing activists were arrested, including 67 members of the PADS, for campaigning for a boycott of the electoral process. Some 26 PADS supporters were subsequently sentenced to short terms of imprisonment, having been found guilty of violating electoral and press codes.

In mid-August 1997 King Hassan appointed a new Cabinet (in which several portfolios were merged) primarily comprising technocrats, after ministers with formal party affiliation resigned at his behest in order to concentrate on their electoral campaigns for the forthcoming legislative elections. Significantly, Driss Basri retained his post as Minister of State for the Interior. Legislation promulgated later in the month detailed the composition of the future bicameral parliament: the Chamber of Representatives would comprise 325 members, directly elected for a five-year term: the Chamber of Advisers would have 270 members, selected by indirect election, of whom 162 would represent local authorities, 81 trade chambers, and 27 employees' associations. The King again appealed for legislative elections free of irregularities and repeated that his goal was to include members of opposition parties in the Government. In September the Assistant Secretary-General of Istiqlal stated that the parties of the Bloc démocratique planned to present joint candidates in the legislative elections. However, observers noted that deep rivalries still existed between its two main parties, the USFP and Istiqlal. One of the bloc's smaller parties, the PPS, which performed poorly in the local elections, lost 40 of its members in June when they established the Front des forces démocratiques (FFD), a rival grouping. In August the PPS suffered another reverse when its long-serving leader, Ali Yata, died in a car accident.

Elections to the country's 16 new regional councils, established in December 1996 (see above), took place in October 1997. Centrist parties won control over nine of the councils. Members of the councils, elected for six years, were chosen indirectly by an electoral college comprising local provincial and prefectoral councils, salaried workers and chambers of commerce and industry, agriculture, artisans and fisheries.

Voting for the wholly-elected 325-member Chamber of Representatives in the new bicameral parliament took place on 14 November 1997. The legislative elections were considered to have been fairer than previous polls, although some complaints were registered. Of the country's legalized political parties, only the extreme left-wing PADS boycotted the elections, but the rate of voter participation was officially estimated at only 58.3% of the electorate. The Bloc démocratique, which had been widely predicted to dominate the new Chamber, won only 102 seats, 57 of which went to the USFP, while Istiqlal secured only 32 seats. The Bloc démocratique hardly improved on the number of seats it gained by direct voting in the 1993 elections and won fewer seats overall. The Entente nationale secured 100 seats, one-half of which were won by the UC, and parties of the centre-right took 97 seats (including 46 obtained by the RNI). Right-wing and centre-right parties performed much better than in direct voting in the 1993 elections. The Bloc démocratique won 34.3% of the vote, compared with 27.3% by the centre-right parties and 24.8% by the Entente nationale. The MPCD won nine seats and the leader of Al-Islah wa Attajdid, Abdelilah Benkiarane, stated that the party was opposed to violence and would use its presence in the Chamber of Representatives to defend Islamic values and oppose corruption. The newly-formed FFD won nine seats, equal to the number obtained by the PPS, from which the new party had split. In an attempt to appeal to young voters, many political parties presented young candidates, with the result that 43% of deputies in the new lower chamber were under 45 years old, compared with only 14% in the previous parliament. Relatively few women stood as candidates and, as in the previous assembly, only two were elected.

Indirect elections for the new Chamber of Advisers took place on 5 December 1997. As predicted, the right and centre-right parties gained a dominant position in the upper house, winning 166 of the 270 seats. Centrist parties secured 90 seats, with the RNI emerging as the largest single party in the Chamber with 42 seats, while the Entente nationale took 76 seats. The Bloc démocratique obtained only 44 seats, of which 21 were won by Istiqlal. Smaller parties made significant gains, winning 33 seats, of which 13 went to the Parti de l'action and 12 to the FFD. Some observers anticipated that the King would use the Chamber of Advisers (which has the power to dismiss the Government) to control the Government and thereby avoid the need to intervene directly, which might damage the country's new democratic credentials. The new bicameral parliament met for the first time in January 1998 when Abdelwahed Radhi of the USFP was voted President of the Chamber of Representatives, and Mohamed Yalal Esaid (UC) was chosen as President of the upper chamber.

With the three main political groupings gaining roughly the same number of seats in the Chamber of Representatives, on 4 February 1998 King Hassan named Abd ar-Rahman el-Youssoufi, the veteran leader of the USFP, as Prime Minister. This was the first time that the King had chosen an opposition politician as premier. In mid-March, after weeks of difficult negotiations, Youssoufi announced his Cabinet in which 13 of the 22 ministerial posts went to members of the Bloc démocratique: the largest number of ministers (seven) being appointed from the USFP, five from Istiqlal, and one from the PPS. Istiqlal, which had been the dominant political force in the early years of Moroccan independence, had not been represented in govern-

ment since the early 1960s. After Istiqlal's poor performance in the legislative elections, the party's first national congress for nearly 10 years, meeting in February, had voted Abbas el-Fassi as leader in place of Muhammad Boucetta. El-Fassi had immediately reversed the party's earlier decision not to participate in a new coalition Government. Of the remaining posts, six went to centre-right parties, five to the RNI and one to the MNP. Parties of the Entente nationale were not represented in the Cabinet. Youssoufi's administration was hailed as the country's first 'government of alternance', but while ministers from opposition parties had taken charge of economic and social policy, loyalist government members retained control of portfolios concerning domestic and foreign affairs and defence. Driss Basri remained as Minister of State for the Interior, and former Prime Minister Filali retained control of the foreign affairs and co-operation portfolio. Technocrats without party affiliation who had served in Filali's administration remained in charge of the ministries of justice and Islamic affairs. King Hassan formally approved the new Cabinet, but warned the political parties represented in the Government that they had a duty to control their supporters in the interest of social stability. Youssoufi announced that the new administration would focus on three main issues, namely the Western Sahara dispute, employment and social problems.

In April 1998 Mary Robinson, the UN Commissioner for Human Rights, made a visit to Morocco during which she signed a memorandum to open a North Africa and Middle East centre in Rabat to promote and protect human rights in the region. She stated that Rabat had been chosen for the new centre because of Morocco's efforts to address human rights issues.

Economy

ALAN J. DAY

Revised for this edition by RICHARD I. LAWLESS

By the late 1970s, Morocco was seriously in debt and had a current account deficit on its balance of payments equivalent to nearly 17% of gross domestic product (GDP). In 1978 the Government introduced a three-year stabilization programme, but external factors (such as the petroleum price rise in 1979, increasing international interest rates, and a decline in revenues from phosphate exports and from migrant workers' remittances), combined with a continuing commitment to heavy expenditure on the war in Western Sahara and on subsidies for basic goods, ensured that the programme was largely ineffective. In early 1983 the Government imposed emergency import controls and reduced its expenditure. Inflation was high in the early 1980s, with increases in food prices and rising levels of unemployment particularly aggravating the living conditions of the urban poor. Reductions in public expenditure exacerbated mounting discontent, and in 1981 and 1984 provoked major strikes and violent street demonstrations.

With the support of the World Bank and the IMF, the Government introduced policies of structural adjustment in 1984 and was able to reschedule its debts towards the end of 1985. Despite good harvests in 1985 and 1986, and the fall in petroleum prices, the trade balance deteriorated. At the beginning of 1986 the World Bank expressed its concern about the underlying structural weakness of the Moroccan economy and argued that stronger corrective measures were needed, including reductions in public expenditure and food subsidies. The IMF was equally concerned by the Government's fiscal and economic performance. Measures that were adopted during late 1986 and 1987 renewed confidence in Morocco's economic prospects. A firm commitment to a radical reform of the economy, involving a new emphasis on export production, trade liberalization, attraction of foreign investment and development of tourism, together with a domestic programme of privatization and encouragement of the private sector, was expressed in the 1988–92 Development Plan (see Development below). Between 1988 and 1990 new IMF and World Bank support arrangements were negotiated, and debt rescheduling agreements were reached with the 'Paris

Club' of creditor governments and the 'London Club' of official creditors (see Banking and Finance). In May 1989 the text of the proposed law on privatization was published, committing the Government to the transfer of the majority of state enterprises to the private sector, and in October a Ministry of Privatization was created. The law came into effect in January 1990.

In November 1991 the Minister of Finance stated that policies of structural adjustment, introduced since 1983, had produced a significant upturn in the economy. He forecast that the rescheduling cycle would end by 1993, by which date the dirham would be made convertible and Morocco would return to international capital markets. In February 1992 it was announced that the IMF had approved a further credit in support of the Government's economic programme for the following year, which according to the IMF, aimed at promoting investment and increasing productivity, and strengthening the budgetary position and reorientating of credit towards the private sector. The programme aimed at an annual 4% growth in GDP, a decline in inflation to 5% per year and a reduction in the current account deficit. The World Bank's vice-president for the Middle East and North Africa visited Rabat in April and stated that the Bank would give full support to the country's adjustment programme. He emphasized that high priority should be given to the development of the capital and financial markets, and expressed concern about some social indicators, notably the high rates of infant mortality and illiteracy. In that month the Minister in charge of Planning maintained that the number of poor people in Morocco had declined from 6.6m. to 3.9m. between 1985 and 1991, and that there had been a significant reduction in the gap between rich and poor. The opposition parties disputed these claims, and argued that liberalization had widened the gap. A survey by the United Nations Development Programme and Morocco's Direction de la Statistique in 1993 estimated that 6.3m. Moroccans (almost one-quarter of the population) lived below the poverty line.

A study compiled by the IMF and released in late 1994 concluded that financial balances had been restored and the economy's structural weaknesses substantially resolved in 1993, a year which it stated 'marked a watershed for the Moroccan economy'. According to the IMF, inflation fell from 8.7% in 1986 to 5.2% in 1993, there was an overall balance of payments surplus of US $378m. in that year and the current account deficit was equivalent to 2.5% of GDP. But growth was constrained in 1992 and 1993 as a result of drought and external pressures. The study stated that the Moroccan economy still faced significant challenges that needed to be addressed in order to move to a higher sustainable growth path, which in turn would reduce chronic unemployment and raise living standards. It identified four policy priorities: strengthening the fiscal system and accelerating financial sector reforms to free more private sector resources for investment; further liberalizing the trade and payments system and accelerating privatization to promote competition and improve resource allocation; improving the legal and regulatory environment; and elaborating a medium-term strategy to alleviate poverty and provide social protection.

In his first statement on economic policy on his appointment as Prime Minister in May 1994, Abd al-Latif Filali pledged to expedite Morocco's ambitious programme of privatization. At that time it was estimated that the debt owed by state enterprises was equivalent to about one-third of total public debt. During 1994 receipts from the sale of state assets reached 3,700m. dirhams. This was 200m. dirhams above target, and included the showpiece of the privatization programme, the holding company Société Nationale d'Investissement, which was sold for 1,669m. dirhams. In an interview that month, the Minister of Privatization, Abderrahmane Saaidi, insisted that the divestment process had the support of the general public and that it had caused minimum social upheaval. Investors in privatized companies had to agree not to dismiss workers for a period of five years, and Saaidi claimed that employees, for their part, had mostly co-operated, purchasing shares and accepting management changes. He did admit, however, that problems might arise in the future as the Government proceeded to sell less profitable companies. In December 1994 Saaidi stated that out of a total of 112 companies set aside for sale to the private sector by the end of 1995, 37 had already been sold.

In March 1995 the Ministry of Privatization announced that the privatization schedule had been extended beyond 1995 and that new companies would be added to the list, including those previously considered as 'strategic' and excluded from the programme. During that month the first privatizations in the mining sector were announced (see Mining), and in April the Government and the Office Chérifien des Phosphates (OCP) stated that they were working on plans to bring private capital into Morocco's important phosphate industry (see Industry). Receipts from privatization in 1995 were estimated at 3,500m. dirhams. In January 1996 the Government launched its first issue of a new privatization bond, which was oversubscribed and raised 1,700m. dirhams (see Banking and Finance). The bonds could be converted into shares in newly-privatized companies. A second tranche of bonds was issued the following May. In November 1996 it was reported that Morocco was the market leader in Arab privatizations, although its programme had been affected by wrangles between the Ministry of Privatization and the Evaluation Organization, established to set a minimum price for privatizations. Government efforts to accelerate the privatization programme during 1997 met with some success, notably the sale of the state's remaining 62% holding in the national steel company, the Société Nationale de Sidérurgie (SONASID). Following the appointment of a new Government in March 1998, the new Minister of the Economy and Finance, Fathallah Oualalou of the left-wing Union socialiste des forces populaires (USFP), stated that privatization would continue as an important source of income and might eventually raise enough to cover some 15% of government spending. It was announced that a new programme would be launched in which the major element would be the sale of a share of the state telecommunications company, Itissalat al-Maghrib, created following the dismantling of the Office National des Postes et Télécommunications. When the new Prime Minister Abd ar-Rahman el-Youssoufi (the USFP leader) presented his Government's policy plan to parliament in April he stated that the privatization programme would be completed 'in transparency and speed' in order to raise funds for investment in infrastruc-

ture. Local surveys suggested that on the whole the business community welcomed the appointment of an opposition-led Government, probably because it anticipated no major changes in economic policy. However, tensions were expected to arise between loyalists, who remained committed to a market-driven economy, and members of the opposition, who were determined to reduce social inequalities. In March King Hassan had declared that the state alone would be unable to eliminate all social deprivation and that local and national government would need to seek private capital to finance infrastructure, educational and social projects.

On a visit to Rabat in late April 1998 to open the World Bank's first resident mission in the Maghreb, the Bank's Vice-President, Kemal Dervis, stated that he expected Morocco to register significantly stronger economic growth over the following decade—averaging 6% in real terms—but emphasized the need to divide the profits of that growth more equitably. Morocco is currently a major borrower from the World Bank, with loans totalling $8,100m.

Having grown by 10.4% in 1994 after a good harvest, Morocco's economy suffered a sharp downturn of 7.0% in 1995 primarily because of a severe drought. GDP growth of 12.0% was recorded in 1996, but the economy was again adversely affected by poor rainfall in 1997 when GDP contracted by 2.2%. In February 1998 the Government projected GDP growth for 1998 at 8%–11%, but this figure was revised to 6.8% in April. Average inflation fell from 6.1% in 1995 to 3.0% in 1996 and 1.0% in 1997. Unemployment, which according to official figures was 17.8% at the end of 1997, remains one of the Government's most urgent problems. Some trade union sources insisted that unemployment stood at 23%.

AGRICULTURE AND FISHERIES

About 55% of the Moroccan population live in rural areas, and in 1997 some 40% of the working population were employed in agriculture, livestock-raising and fishing. In 1996 the agricultural sector (including forestry and fishing) accounted for an estimated 22.1% of GDP. The principal crops are cereals (especially wheat, barley and maize), citrus fruit, as well as olives, beans, chick-peas, tomatoes and potatoes. Canary seed, cumin, coriander, linseed and almonds are also grown. Sugar beet and cane are cultivated on a large scale to substitute for imports; sugar is one of Morocco's principal food imports owing to the high level of domestic consumption. Changing climatic conditions cause substantial year-to-year variations in agricultural output. These variations, moreover, have a significant impact on the economy, affecting the level of GDP growth or decline. Severe drought in 1981—the worst for 35 years—caused cereal production to fall by 50% from 4.5m. metric tons in 1980. In 1985, when rainfall was good, cereal production increased by 41%, compared with the previous year, and in 1986 production rose again by about 47% to a record 7.7m. tons. However, the 1987 harvest was very disappointing, with cereal production reaching only 4.2m. tons. 1988 was another record year, with a bumper harvest of nearly 8m. tons. Production declined from 7.4m. tons in 1989 to 6.3m. tons in the following year. After good rains in 1991, it rose to 8.5m. tons, of which 2.2m. tons was durum wheat, 2.7m. tons soft bread wheat, 3.3m. tons barley and 335,000 tons maize. The cereal harvest decreased to 2.7m. tons in 1992, following a severe drought. It was estimated that as much as 4m. tons of wheat and barley needed to be imported as a result. In 1993 the harvest was again depleted by drought, with rainfall 60% below average. It was forecast that production of wheat, barley and maize would total approximately 2.5m. tons in that year. A record 9.4m. tons of cereals were produced in 1994 but severe drought struck again in 1995. In March 1995 it was reported that there had only been one-third of the normal rainfall and that only 60% of acreage had been planted. In May King Hassan announced that wheat production would reach only 1.6m. tons, one-quarter of the normal figure. He appealed to the public to contribute some $200m. to a solidarity fund of $441m. to finance wheat imports. A record cereal harvest of 10m. tons was reported in 1996 when the agricultural sector grew by 78.8% in real terms, but poor rains in 1997 resulted in cereal output of only 3.4m. tons and caused a fall of 24% in agricultural value added. Grain imports between June 1997 and May 1998 were expected to total 3.3m.

tons. In addition, the Caisse Nationale de Crédit Agricole was forced to reschedule the debts of some 250,000 farmers during 1997. After heavy rains, cereal production in 1998 was expected to be above average, with estimates varying between 6m. and 11m. tons. In early 1998 the King admitted that agricultural policies would have to be revised if Morocco was to achieve self-sufficiency in food and provide stable incomes for the country's farmers.

In 1987 Morocco produced 2.8m. metric tons of sugar beet and 848,000 tons of cane, resulting in total sugar output of 412,000 tons. In 1988 sugar production rose to nearly 500,000 tons, which covered more than two-thirds of domestic requirements in 1989. By 1993 production of beet was 3.2m. tons, and cane production was 946,000 tons. A slight decline in production was recorded in 1994. Brazil and Thailand have been the main suppliers of sugar imports. In October 1997 the Ministry of Privatization offered for sale three state sugar producers for the second time. The first attempt at sale failed in 1994 because investors balked at government fixing of sugar prices. However, the sugar regime has since been liberalized, with reforms culminating in the abolition of price controls in January 1997. It is envisaged that Morocco's seven other sugar companies, one of which owns two plants, will also be privatized in due course.

Morocco is also a major food exporter. Agricultural produce accounted for 59% of total export revenue in the period 1969–73, but its importance was later eclipsed by phosphate earnings. During the late 1980s agricultural products accounted for about 25% of total exports. The main agricultural exports are citrus fruit (mainly oranges), tomatoes, and fresh and processed vegetables. A fruit processing industry is being developed, and exports of preserved fruit, jam and fruit juice contribute to foreign exchange earnings. In 1988 citrus production rose by 35% from the 1987 level, reaching a total of around 1.2m. tons, about one-half of which was exported. Other crops, including legumes, vegetables, grapes and industrial crops (sugar beet, cane and cotton), all performed well in 1988. In 1989/90 citrus fruit production increased slightly, with exports totalling 436,500 tons. In 1990/91 record exports of citrus fruits and vegetables were reported, with citrus sales rising to 648,500 tons. Maroc late oranges represented about one-half of the total citrus sales. Tomato exports increased from 91,400 tons in 1989/90 to 132,000 tons in 1990/91, potatoes from 60,500 tons to 110,000 tons, and vegetables from 9,400 tons to 9,500 tons. Morocco exports approximately 40% of its citrus products, of which about 70% goes to the European Union (EU, formerly the European Community, EC). In 1990/91 France was the largest importer, accounting for almost 250,000 tons. However, it is feared that Morocco's agricultural exports may be adversely affected by growing competition from other Mediterranean countries in the EU, in particular Spain and Portugal. Under the terms of the free-trade agreement with the EU, initialled in November 1995 and signed in February 1996 (see also Balance of Payments and Trade), both parties agreed to increase trade in agricultural products; however, the controversial question of free movement of agricultural products will not be discussed until 2000. Morocco won some concessions, and the EU agreed to raise import quotas and loosen restrictions on trading periods for tomatoes, oranges and other products, but in return EU agricultural exporters are to receive favourable tratment in Morocco. Morocco also sought financial assistance from the EU to eradicate the cultivation of cannabis in the Rif mountains by creating alternative forms of employment for the rural population in an isolated and poorly-developed part of the country. In February 1998 the EU allocated $10m. for pilot projects to encourage the cultivation of almond trees, apiculture and livestock-rearing in this region.

Livestock numbers remained relatively static until the mid-1980s, when they increased from 24.2m. in 1986 to 28.6m. in 1989. Subsequently, however, numbers have declined (reaching a high of 27.5m. in 1992) and in 1996 they totalled an estimated 25.0m. Numbers of sheep—the most numerous species—rose from 14.6m. in 1986 to 17.5m. in 1989 before declining in the early 1990s and totalling 16.3m. in 1996. Meat and dairy production have been increasing accordingly; meat production rose from 293,000 tons in 1987 to 474,000 tons in 1996. Morocco produces virtually all of its national meat requirements. Output of dairy products totalled 1,015,600 tons in 1987, increasing to 1,127,000 tons in 1996. In February 1992 the Ministry of

Agriculture and Agrarian Reform announced a $50m. emergency programme to save some 22m. cattle, sheep and goats that were threatened by the severe drought. Some 60,000 tons of livestock feed was distributed to those areas worst affected, and a further 100,000 tons was distributed to farmers at half the price. A further drought-related rescue plan for local farmers, launched in early 1995, involved importing 70,000 tons of barley for livestock consumption.

Financial assistance was secured for the first phase of the Upper Abda-Doukkala irrigation scheme, south-west of Casablanca, from the African Development Bank (ADB), the European Investment Bank (EIB) and the Arab Fund for Economic and Social Development (AFESD), which pledged $181m., $74.8m. and $130m., respectively. The new scheme aimed eventually to irrigate a total of some 64,000 ha in the Doukkala region, to increase food production for Casablanca and Rabat; all four phases were estimated to cost some 6,000m. dirhams ($705m.). The first phase of the work involves building a main canal and pumping station to draw water from the Im Fout reservoir, on the Oued Oum er Riba, which will be carried some 60 km to irrigate an area of 16,000 ha. In March 1996 it was reported that in the second half of the year international contractors would be invited to bid for four contracts under the second phase of the project, estimated to cost some $153m., and involving the irrigation of 19,000 ha. A $129m. low-interest loan was agreed with Japan in December 1995 to finance part of the second phase. A third phase, estimated to cost $120m., is to begin in late 1997 when the first phase is due to be completed. The fourth and final phase will cost $103m.

In July 1991 it was reported that work had started on the Wahada dam scheme, to irrigate 100,000 ha in the Sebou and Ouerrgh valleys. Financial support is being provided by Italy, the AFESD and the Kuwait Fund for Arab Economic Development (KFAED). In January 1996 it was announced that the AFESD had agreed to lend $56.2m. to help finance the dam's construction. The OPEC Fund for International Development agreed in February 1992 to provide a loan of $7.5m. for the Tassaouat project, which involves irrigating 44,000 ha with a new canal system and the rehabilitation of existing irrigation canals. Financial support is also being provided by the AFESD, the Saudi Fund for Development, the KFAED and the EU. In December 1992 King Hassan inaugurated the $195m. Matmata gallery project, designed to channel 600m. cu m of water per year, to irrigate 25,000 ha of the Gharb valley. In August 1993 Japan agreed to provide a loan of $127m. to the Caisse Nationale de Crédit Agricole for agriculture and fisheries projects. In February 1994 the World Bank announced that it would lend $34.7m. to provide irrigation services to some 200,000 small farmers in order to raise production in irrigated areas. In May, in one of the last major allocations from the EU's fifth financial protocol, the EIB agreed to provide $24.7m. for a five-year project to irrigate 23,000 ha in the Haouz region. The KFAED was to lend $66m. towards the project which was part of a government plan to irrigate an additional 250,000 ha by 2000. The Ministry of Agriculture reported that at the end of 1997 the total area of irrigated farmland had increased to 1m. ha, just over 10% of the country's total cultivated area of 9.3m. ha. In July 1994 the World Bank provided a $121m. loan, repayable over 20 years, to support the government's agricultural investment programme (estimated at $993m. in 1994–97) and to be used for projects in poorer regions of the country. A loan agreement was signed with the AFESD in September to provide $10m. towards the total cost of remaining works on a project for agricultural development in the Loukos basin. In November 1997 the EU approved a loan of $13.5m. to combat soil erosion in the Middle Atlas as well as credits worth $4.5m. to increase agricultural production in the Doukkala plain.

Fishing has become increasingly important. A separate Ministry of Fisheries, formerly the responsibility of the Ministry of Commerce, Industry and Tourism, was established in April 1981. Special financial concessions were granted to the fishing industry in 1984 to improve its export potential; in addition, state control over exports was removed. Since 1984 annual landings have surpassed 400,000 metric tons; about one-half of the fish caught are sardines, which are mainly canned for export. In 1988 exports of fish and fish products totalled 179,000 tons and accounted for 50% of all food exports and 11% of total exports. In 1990 the volume of fish available for canning decreased by an estimated 8%, largely as a result of reductions in sardine catches landed at Agadir. In 1983 the Government signed a treaty with Spain, granting Spanish vessels certain rights in Moroccan waters in exchange for finance for infrastructural development. Bilateral agreements with Spain were renegotiated in 1987 as accords with the EC, following Spanish accession to the Community in 1986. An agreement reached in February 1988 restricted EC vessels to a catch of 95,000 tons annually in Moroccan waters, in return for licence fees and compensation worth $48.3m. a year. Morocco also gained improved access to the European market for its canned sardine exports, the annual volume of which was to rise to 17,500 tons, compared with 14,000 tons in 1988. In February 1992, however, it was reported that the Moroccan Government had suspended talks with the EC about fishing rights for EC fleets, in retaliation for the EC's refusal to approve Morocco's fourth financial protocol in January. The 1988 agreement expired in March 1992. After lengthy negotiations, a new three-year accord came into force in May 1992 allowing 650 Spanish, 50 Portuguese and 36 other trawlers into Moroccan waters, in return for increased compensation of 102m. ECUs ($131m.). The accord also envisaged new conservation measures, the expansion of port facilities and the creation of joint marketing companies. Negotiations with the EU began at the end of March 1995 to renew the three-year fisheries agreement due to expire on 30 April. The Moroccan Government pressed for a reduction in the number of European fishing vessels allowed to operate in Moroccan waters in order to allow fish stocks to be replenished and for the local fishing industry to take a greater part in the industry, including European fishing boats landing catches at Moroccan ports. No agreement had been reached when the accord lapsed, but a new round of talks began in Brussels in May. The accord is the EU's most important external fisheries agreement and sustains an estimated 28,000 people working in the Spanish fishing and fish processing industry. Moroccan demands met with strong resistance from the Spanish fishing industry which holds most of the fishing licences for Moroccan waters. Spanish fishermen attempted to block imports of Moroccan fish at several ports. After lengthy negotiations, a new fisheries accord was initialled with the EU in November. The four-year agreement came into effect in December when European (mainly Spanish) fishing boats were allowed back into Moroccan waters for the first time since the end of April. Morocco won substantial concessions from the EU, which it claimed would boost the country's fishing industry and safeguard endangered fish stocks. Catches by EU fishing vessels are being reduced by up to 40% for certain species, and European trawlers must unload part of their catches of squid and octopus at Moroccan ports—the proportion will rise to 30% after four years. Total compensation payments from the EU was set at $355m. over four years, and payment during the first year was increased to $162.5m., compared with $133m. under the previous agreement. In order to deal with the increase in business expected as a result of the accord, the Government announced a $233m. investment programme in April 1996 to modernize fishing ports to meet additional demand. In addition, the Government embarked on a $151m. investment programme to renew the country's fishing fleet over the next four years. The programme aims to replace up to 400 fishing boats with more powerful vessels with better refrigeration equipment, enabling them to operate in the open sea and to remain at sea for longer periods. Most of the investment is expected to be provided by the private sector, although the Government agreed to contribute $23.3m. in the form of grants to finance 10%–20% of the cost of each new boat and to provide bank loan guarantees to shipowners. In February 1996 it was reported that $7.2m. in aid from Japan would be invested in equipment to improve fishing conditions and warehouses in the provinces of Agadir and El-Hoceima. By the end of 1997 some $21m. had been spent upgrading 320 refrigerated fishing vessels to meet EU standards. In November of that year the Government announced that it planned to invest $315m. developing fishing off its southern coasts. In April 1998 the Ministry of Public Works began evaluating bids for a $46m.–$51m. fishing harbour at Boujdour in the disputed Western Sahara. After the fish catch declined significantly in 1997, the Moroccan Government announced that it was extending the closed season for fishing

in its territorial waters from two to four months. Despite the 1996 EU fisheries accord, tensions between the Moroccan authorities and the mostly Spanish vessels fishing in Moroccan waters continued. Morocco indicated that it did not intend to renew the EU accord when it expires at the end of 1999, seeking instead to exploit the fish stocks in its territorial waters through joint ventures with foreign companies. In early 1998 it was reported that talks about joint ventures had begun with France and Japan.

In June 1992 ONA, Morocco's largest private company, signed an agreement with the Union des Coopératives de Pêcheurs de France to establish a fish-canning and marketing enterprise to market canned sardines and mackerel. In August 1995 Morocco and Russia renewed a three-year fishing accord, permitting Russian vessels to catch fish in the coastal waters off Western Sahara. The accord allows 28 Russian trawlers to fish some 200,000 tons in these waters in the first year, a substantial increase on 1994 when 17 trawlers were given permission to fish 80,000 tons. Fishing quotas for the remaining two years are to be determined by the size of fish stocks. Under the agreement all Russian catches would be marketed by a joint Russian-Moroccan company. In February 1997 Morocco signed a fisheries accord with Canada.

MINING

The mining sector accounted for 2.6% of GDP in 1989 and almost one-third of Morocco's total exports, but there has been a progressive decline in the relative importance of the sector, which only accounted for an estimated 1.9% of GDP in 1996. There has also been a shift from the export of minerals to mineral derivatives. In 1997 phosphates accounted for about 95% of the total volume of mineral output.

Morocco has about two-thirds of the world's known reserves of phosphate rock. Proven reserves are 10,600m. tons, and probable reserves 57,200m. tons. Major deposits are located at Khouribga, Youssoufia and Ben Guerir. Morocco also controls production at Bou Craa in Western Sahara, which was reopened in July 1982. Morocco is the world's third largest producer of phosphate rock, after the USA and the former USSR, producing 20.4m. tons in 1994, compared with 18.3m. tons in the previous year. With the opening of mines at Ben Guerir in 1981 and at Sidi Hajjaj in 1984, annual output capacity has gradually increased and there are long-term plans to exploit large phosphate deposits at Meskala. In March 1995 the OCP stated that it had the capacity to produce 30m. tons of phosphate rock a year from four open-cast mines. Morocco is the world's largest exporter of phosphate rock, and its exports account for about one-third of world trade. As a result of high phosphate prices in the early to mid-1970s, there was a decline in demand, and the volume of Moroccan exports of phosphate fell by 22% between 1979 and 1982. In the early 1980s there was a slow recovery in world demand, but international phosphate prices fell from $49.50 per ton in 1980 to less than $40 by 1983, to $34.80 in 1986 and to $31.95 in 1987, before rising in 1988 and 1989 to $40.50. Morocco, as a result, invested heavily in the 'downstream' phosphate derivatives industry, to increase the value of its exports (see Industry). Phosphate rock production increased from 20.9m. tons in 1996 to 23.1m. tons in 1997, while prices rose from $39.00 per ton to $40.83 per ton.

Between 1982 and 1986 coal production ranged between 735,000 and 835,000 metric tons a year, but declined in 1988 and 1989 to 640,000 tons. Production declined further in the early 1990s, to 550,800 tons in 1991, but then increased steadily to reach 603,800 tons in 1993. From 1983 the Jerrada anthracite mine in north-east Morocco was expanded, with the aim of increasing total annual production to 1m. tons by 1992. Output, however, has failed to meet these targets and consequently coal and coke imports have grown dramatically. Diversification into coal represents an attempt to become less heavily reliant on petroleum imports.

Production of crude petroleum is negligible, reaching at most around 23,000 tons a year. Exploration for hydrocarbons intensified following the creation of the Office National de Recherches et d'Exploitations Pétrolières (ONAREP) in 1981. By mid-1986 agreements had been reached with numerous foreign oil companies for exploration both onshore and offshore. However, the collapse in oil prices in 1986 prompted many of these companies to relinquish their interests; in any case, no major discovery had yet been made, apart from a gasfield owned by ONAREP in the Essaouira area. Even this, which was originally expected to satisfy 40% of Morocco's energy needs, proved, during 1985, to be more limited than anticipated. In 1991 incentives for international companies to explore for oil and gas were approved by the Chamber of Representatives, following the revision of laws which reduced the state's minimum share in agreements with international companies to 35% from 50%, reduced the minimum size of an exploration permit to 2,000 sq km from 5,000 sq km and reduced the minimum duration of an accord to eight years from 15. Two US oil companies, Ashland Exploration and Santa Fe Energy Co, were the first to sign an exploration and production-sharing agreement with ONAREP under the revised hydrocarbons code, which came into force in April 1992. The companies are exploring in a 6,000 sq km area off shore of Essaouira and Agadir, with each company holding 50% in its part of the venture and with Ashland Exploration as operator. Renewed efforts have been made to attract foreign investment in oil exploration and in early 1998 ONAREP signed agreements with Enterprise Oil Exploration of the United Kingdom, Shell Prospecting Africa, the Roc Oil Co of Australia and Lasmo Overseas Nederland covering offshore areas in southern Morocco. Between June 1997 and June 1998 ONAREP signed exploration agreements with seven prospecting companies involving total investments of $7.5m. Extensive deposits of oil-bearing shale are known to exist, with a potential output of 100,000m. tons (15% of world reserves). In February 1995 the Office Nationale de l'Electricité (ONE) signed an agreement with Pama of Israel to test oil shale from the Tarfaya deposit for power generation. Preliminary estimates suggested that the Tarfaya deposit contains some 80,000m. tons of oil shale. Under the agreement, some 400 tons of oil shale are being shipped to Pama's testing plant in Israel and if successful a shale-fired power plant could be built in Tarfaya. In early 1996 it was reported that results of the initial tests were encouraging and that ONE was considering whether to begin the next phase in the development of the project to define the process parameters. Gas production in the early 1980s ranged between 78,800m. cu m in 1982 and 86,600m. cu m in 1985. Four major gasfields are in production, with two others, including the Meskala field in the Essaouira area, being developed. Gas treatment facilities have been developed at Meskala. In October 1997 ONAREP announced that it had discovered reserves of some 300m. cu m of natural gas in the Gharb region near Kénitra and that after the drilling of a second well, production might reach 75,000 cu m a day. Also in October Lasmo of the United Kingdom signed an agreement to carry out surveys in the Essaouira basin in southern Morocco, which currently produces small quantities of oil and gas but where known reserves are almost exhausted.

In August 1991 Gaz de France (GdF) signed two agreements with Morocco's Ministry of Energy and Mines and the Société Nationale des Produits Pétroliers (SNPP), in preparation for the second trans-Mediterranean pipeline to carry Algerian natural gas across Morocco to Europe. The SNPP, Algeria's state energy company SONATRACH, Spain's Enagas, GdF, and Germany's Ruhrgas were each to have a 19% interest, while Gas de Portugal was allocated the remaining 5%. In July 1992 Morocco and Spain signed a 25-year agreement to build and exploit the new Maghreb–Europe gas pipeline to run from Hassi R'Mel in Algeria across Morocco and the Strait of Gibraltar to Spain. The first phase of the project was to supply 6,000m. cu m of natural gas to Spain, 1,300m. cu m to Morocco, with another 1,000m. cu m being used in Algeria. The cost of the entire pipeline was estimated at $2,500m. Enagas was to provide an estimated $1,300m. to finance the 525 km Moroccan section. In January 1994 the pipeline's capacity reportedly had been increased by 30% to 10,000 m. cu m per year because of a new contract to supply 2,500m. cu m per year to Portugal. Following widespread reports that the work on the project was delayed and might even be cancelled because of the security situation in Algeria and rising tensions between Morocco and Algeria, the ministers of energy of Morocco, Spain, Portugal and Algeria met in September 1994 and reaffirmed their governments' commitment to completing the pipeline. In October 1994 the Moroccan Minister of Energy and Mines visited Algeria to attend a ceremony marking the formal start of work on the pipeline. In

March 1996 it was reported that Enagas had acquired total control of Sagane, the company responsible for the construction and operation of the Moroccan section of the pipeline, by purchasing the 91% stake from the Spanish public-sector Sociedad Estatal de Participaciones Industriales for $513m. The Maghreb–Europe gas pipeline became operational in November 1996 when the first gas supplies were delivered to Spain, and the link to Portugal was completed in early 1997. The pipeline's initial capacity of 7,000 cu m a year was expected to be expanded to 10,000 cu m a year by 2000.

Production of iron ore, mainly from mines in the north-east of Morocco, was as high as 1.5m. metric tons in 1958, but during the next 20 years annual output declined considerably. After 1982 there was an increase in production and in 1987 total output reached 280,000 tons, although it slumped in 1988 to 156,000 tons. Production in 1990 was 149,500 tons, but by 1994 had declined to 63,500 tons. There are plans to open new mines in the Rif mountain area. Production of iron ore is currently undertaken by the Société d'Exploitation des Mines du Rif.

Other minerals produced include barytes, lead, copper, zinc and manganese. Production of most other, non-ferrous ores had been falling, but there were signs of a recovery by the late 1980s. Apart from a sharp decline in estimated output in 1986, production of lead ore has generally increased, and the capacity of the lead smelter at Oued Heimer, operated by the Société des Mines de Zellidja, was to be expanded, following studies which indicated a high lead content in nearby deposits. Zinc production has also been increasing. In 1991 Morocco's total output of zinc ore concentrate was 47,709 tons, with exports worth $13.3m. Production of zinc ore concentrates increased dramatically in 1993, totalling 125,700 tons, and in 1994 output was 147,200 tons. Production of fluorspar at el-Hammam, near Meknès, and of barytes and cobalt concentrate also increased. Another barytes mine was opened at Zelmou, with a production capacity of 100,000 tons a year. Production of barytes rose to 322,000 tons in 1988 from 127,000 tons in 1987; output increased to 434,700 tons in 1991, but subsequently declined, totalling 264,500 tons in 1994. In the late 1980s and early 1990s output of lead has averaged around 100,000 tons, and copper around 40,000 tons. The production of silver rose from 76 tons in 1987 to 132 tons in 1988. In an attempt to increase copper production, which had fallen in the 1980s, a major mine was developed at Bleida. Interest has been shown in the possibility of recovering uranium from the phosphate rock reserves, and exploration by the Bureau de Recherches et de Participation Minières (BRPM) has revealed traces of uranium in the upper Moulouya valley, east of Zeida, in the High Atlas. In late 1987 the BRPM signed an agreement with its French counterpart for survey work on deposits of copper, zinc and lead in the Anti-Atlas region. As a result of a recent project by the US Agency for International Development (USAID), US and Moroccan researchers have identified traces of nickel, cobalt and gold in the Foum Zguid region of the Anti-Atlas. There were also reports from OPEC sources that deposits of up to 20m. tons of bauxite had been discovered in Morocco. The Guemassa polymetallic mine in the High Atlas was officially opened in December 1992. In July 1993 ONA (formerly Omnium Nord Africain), which owns and operates the mine, was seeking a $100m. loan to increase annual production to 130,000 tons of zinc, 32,000 tons of copper and 12,000 tons of lead. In May 1994 BRPM signed an agreement with Placer Outokumpu Exploration, a Canadian/Finnish company, which will invest $2m. in mineral exploration work and drilling in the Marrakesh region where the Guemassa mine is located. In November 1995 the BRPM announced that it was to appoint a contractor to develop a gold mine at Iourirn and that it was evaluating bids from international companies. In May 1998 the BRPM signed a convention with Odyssey Resources of Canada, granting the firm a four-year lease for copper exploration in Alous, a town in the southern province of Taroudant. Also in May the BRPM signed a preliminary joint venture agreement with Ennex International of Ireland to develop zinc production in the Middle and High Atlas. In March 1995 the Ministry of Privatization announced its intention to sell the state's shareholdings in five mines: the Compagnie de Tifnout et Tighanimine, producing cobalt, in which the government holds 40% of shares; the Société Minière de Bougaffer (SOMIFER), producing 35,700 tons of copper a year, in which the state's shareholding is 34.2%;

the Société Métallurgique d'Imiter (SMI), producing 236,000 tons of silver ore a year, in which the state's holding is 69.07%; the Société Anonyme Chérifienne des Etudes Minières (SACEM), producing 42,600 tons of manganese a year, in which the state's holding is 42.99%; and the Société Anonyme d'Entreprise Minière (SAMINE), producing 70,100 tons of fluorite a year, in which the state's holding is 35%. The sale, which represented the first privatization in the mining sector, had been timed to take advantage of rising international metal prices. However, the Ministry of Privatization failed to sell its shares to ONA (which holds a minority stake in the companies), after they were unable to agree on a sale price during 1995. Thus, in March 1996 the Government announced that it had put all mining companies on its privatization list on the market and was planning to sell its shares in the SMI, the Compagnie de Tifnout et Tighanimine, the SAMINE and the SOMIFER to a single bidder at a minimum price of 648.8m. dirhams ($75.3m.). The SMI, in which two-thirds of its shares were sold to ONA in 1996, recorded profits of 83.4m. dirhams in 1997, compared with 43.2m. dirhams in 1996.

INDUSTRY

In the 1980s the Government made particular efforts to promote industrial development, in order to reduce Morocco's dependence on agriculture and phosphate-mining, to create employment and to reduce imports. Official policy has been to promote export-oriented industry and to encourage private-sector investment; this has been supported by the World Bank. As a result of the investment code promulgated in 1983, and amended in 1988, which provided attractive incentives for both national and foreign investors, investment rose considerably. In 1987 investment in the industrial sector increased by 32%, following growth of 25% the previous year. Investment then rose by 23% in 1988, by 39% in 1989 and by about 35% in 1990. Three-quarters of the invested funds were from private Moroccan investors; foreign investors accounted for 16% of the total in 1987 and 20% in 1988. Foreign investment (principally from France, followed by Spain and Italy) fell markedly in the early 1990s, mainly as a result of recession in Europe. Investment recovered in 1995, growing by 26%. Industrial growth slowed during 1996 to 2.6%, compared with 3.7% in 1995, but recovered in the first half of 1997 to 5.2%. However, industrial growth during the first quarter of 1998 fell to 1%. The main industry, in terms of investment and foreign exchange earnings, is the processing of phosphates, which continues to be undertaken by the state-controlled OCP. The phosphate sector was originally excluded from the government's privatization programme but in early 1995 plans were being considered to open this strategic sector to private capital (see below). Other industries, in order of importance, are petroleum refining, cement production, food processing, textiles and chemicals. Manufacturing remains a relatively small sector, and is primarily concerned with the processing of export commodities and the production of consumer goods. A number of state-owned industrial concerns were among the first to be offered for sale in the privatization programme. Among these were the Société des Dérivés du Sucre, in late 1992, and the Cimenterie de l'Oriental (Cior) and the Société Nationale d'Electrolyse et de Petrochimie, in early 1993. In March 1994 it was announced that three sugar companies would be offered for privatization: Sucrerie de Beni Mellal, SUTA and Sucrerie du Tadla (see also Agriculture and Fisheries). The Minister of Privatization announced that the state's remaining 22.2% share in the General Tire and Rubber Co would be sold, along with the Société Nationale de Sidérurgie (SONASID, the national steel company), the Société Marocaine de Constructions Automobiles (SOMACA) and the Société Marocaine des Fertilisants, a subsidiary of the OCP. The Government sold its remaining stake in the General Tire and Rubber Co in October, and in late September announced the privatization of the Société des Industries Mécaniques et Electriques de Fès, which makes diesel and electric motors. In January 1995 the General Tire and Rubber Co raised its capital by 20% in a stock market offering, the first newly-privatized company to do so. In February the privatization programme was expanded to incorporate some of the so-called strategic industries, including the country's two oil refineries (see below). The possibility of opening the key phosphate industry to private investment was

also announced. The privatization programme experienced its first reverse in February 1995, when the Government failed to find a buyer for SONASID; however, in 1996 a 35% share was floated on the Casablanca stock exchange, and in October 1997 the state's remaining 62% holding was sold to a consortium of local financial institutions, notably the Société Nationale d'Investissement (SNI), and Marcial Ucin, a Spanish steel company. The divestment of other less profitable industries have continued to prove troublesome. In late 1997 the Government made a new attempt to sell part of the state-owned sugar refineries, which were first offered for sale in 1994. In April 1996 the Government invited private investors to develop three new industrial zones at Tangier, Jorf Lasfar and Nouasser. International developers were asked to equip the zones and take responsibility for attracting companies to them, with the Government providing infrastructure. Total investment of some $186m. was sought. Priority was given to the Tangier industrial zone in order to attract jobs to a deprived area. There were plans to develop a 200 ha site at an estimated cost of $87m. and to attract 1,100 enterprises, one-third of them international companies. The Nouasser zone was to cover 200 ha and Jorf Lasfar 135 ha. However, the state-owned Office de Développement Industriel failed to attract international developers and in mid-1997 the Government announced that it had asked local financial institutions to establish the Tangier and Nouasser zones on a non-commercial basis. In July three privately-owned institutions, the Banque Marocaine de Commerce Extérieur (BMCE), Banque Commerciale du Maroc (BCM) and the SNI announced that they would finance the Tangier zone which would be located near the airport and cover some 120 ha. Construction work was scheduled for completion within two years. The consortium hoped to attract foreign investment in manufacturing and warehousing. The same institutions, together with Al-Wataniya and Mutuelle Centrale Marocaine d'Assurances, two local insurance companies, were also to develop the Nouasser zone, covering 270 ha.

Following the conclusion of a new EU association agreement in February 1996 (see Balance of Payments and Trade) the Ministry of Trade, Industry and Handicrafts published a report which claimed that some 45,000m. dirhams ($5,287m.) would be needed over the next five years if local industries were to survive competition from EU markets after the free-trade accord became effective in 1997. Under the accord, Morocco agreed to phase out protective customs barriers on all its manufactured products over a 12-year period, with the most sensitive industries being given the longest time to adjust. The report recommended reducing energy prices, liberalizing road transport, opening public services to the private sector (so as to lower production costs for local industries), developing professional training better adapted to the needs of the private sector, reforming further the financial system, and simplifying bureaucratic procedures for manufacturers. Morocco, along with other signatories of this type of agreement, will receive EU funds to help their industries adapt to increased competition. In April 1996 the EU pledged ECU 450m. ($570m.) in grants to help Moroccan industries restructure to meet the challenge of European competition. The grant forms part of some ECU 4,685m. ($5,932m.) to be distributed by the EU to signatories of the new association agreements over a period of four to five years. It will be distributed mainly to private manufacturing companies on a project basis rather than through government agencies, with the aim of assisting them to modernize, expand and improve training. Morocco could receive additional funds in 1999 when the EU intends to offer further grants with the largest amounts being allocated to those countries with the most successful industrial restructuring programme. In August 1997 it was reported that the EU was to start disbursing aid promised under the free-trade accord following the initialling in July of a framework agreement. In addition, Moroccan industries were to receive another ECU 450m. ($570m.) in loans from the EIB. During 1997 the Government embarked on a plan to provide financial assistance to small and medium-sized firms, which accounted for about 90% of Moroccan industry, in order to prepare them for increased competition from the EU after 2008. Companies would be offered long-term credits at preferential rates so that they could invest in new equipment and training. In November USAID approved a loan of $10m. to support the programme, which received a further $5.5m. from the Moroccan Government.

Morocco has invested heavily in the 'downstream' phosphates industry. Four phosphate-processing plants are in operation at Safi: Maroc Chimie I, producing phosphoric acid and fertilizers; Maroc Chimie II, producing phosphoric acid; Maroc Phosphore I—a much larger plant, opened in 1976—producing phosphoric acid and mono-ammonium phosphate; and Maroc Phosphore II—opened in 1982, with three sulphuric acid lines and three phosphoric acid lines. A new facility is planned at Safi with a capacity to produce 2,300 tons a day of sulphuric acid which will be fed into the phosphoric acid plants at the complex. The project is part of the rehabilitation and modernization programme at Safi. The contract to prepare detailed designs for the facility was awarded in March 1997 to the French company Krebs. The phosphoric acid treatment plant at Jorf Lasfar began production in 1986. In 1987 the commissioning of two plants for phosphate calcination took place, as well as the entry into production of the fertilizer-manufacturing units of the Maroc Phosphore III and IV factories at Jorf Lasfar, producing a new type of fertilizer-diammonia. Maroc Phosphore III and IV were expected to add a further 784,000 tons of phosphoric acid per year to total production. In 1991 the OCP announced a project to develop the Maroc Phosphore V and VI fertilizer and acid production units at Jorf Lasfar, with the aim of doubling annual capacity, estimated at 4.5m. tons of sulphuric acid, 1.4m. tons of phosphoric acid and 1.2m. tons of fertilizers. In April 1995 it was announced that construction of the Maroc Phosphore units could be opened to private capital. OCP declared in July 1997 that it planned to build a sodium tripolyphosphate plant at Jorf Lasfar, as a joint venture with Prayon-Rupel of Belgium. The $30m. plant will have an initial capacity of 50,000 tons, rising to 100,000 tons. In 1987 the value of exports of phosphate derivatives (mainly phosphoric acid) surpassed that of phosphate rock for the first time, and in 1988 the combined value of phosphoric acid and fertilizers accounted for almost two-thirds of total exports of phosphates and phosphate derivatives. The value of exports by the OCP rose from 9,855m. dirhams in 1990 to 10,048m. dirhams in 1991. Phosphoric acid and phosphate fertilizers accounted for some 70% of sales. Exports by the OCP in 1992 declined to 8,491m. dirhams, but phosphoric acid and fertilizers continued to account for about 70% of sales revenue. After a four-year slump, OCP exports of phosphates and phosphate products rose to $1,060m. in 1994, a 13% increase over 1993. OCP exports accounted for 28% of the country's total foreign currency earnings in 1994, compared with 25% in 1993. Exports of phosphoric acid rose from 1.6m. tons in 1996 to 1.8m. tons in 1997. Production capacity for phosphoric acid was 1.8m. tons a year in 1998 and was expected to expand in 1999, when a new 300,000 tons-per-year phosphoric acid plant opens at Jorf Lasfar. OCP has pursued a number of joint venture phosphate projects with foreign partners. In early 1996 the company signed a five-year contract with Pardeed Phosphates of India to supply 80% of its phosphate requirement, amounting to 250,000–500,000 tons a year. Also in 1996, the Indian Farmers Fertilizer Co-operative (IFFCO) and OCP discussed the setting up of a joint venture phosphoric acid manufacturing facility, the entire output of which was to have been bought by the IFFCO to use as feedstock for its phosphoric fertilizer plants in India. However, this project did not proceed. In July 1997 it was reported that OCP and India's Chambal Fertilizers & Chemicals were also in discussions about a joint venture phosphoric acid plant, estimated to cost some $230m. Having signed a partnership agreement with Troy of Mexico in August 1995, OCP agreed a joint venture in December 1995 with Prayon-Rupel for a 130,000 tons-per-year phosphoric acid plant (to commence operations in 1997). OCP also agreed to supply Grande Paroisse of France with sufficient phosphate to feed its 180,000 tons-per-year phosphoric acid plant.

The largest industrial project in the 1980s, outside the phosphates industry, was the Nador steel rod and bar mill, with an annual capacity of 420,000 metric tons, built by a British company, Davy Loewy, with a £75m. contract agreed in 1980. The plant began production in 1984 with an output that included wire and reinforcing rods and bars. In May 1994 it was reported that SONASID was seeking foreign investors to finance its expansion. The steel mill required considerable modernization

and needed a private sector company to provide capital and technological assistance to increase its capacity of 420,000 tons a year by building an electric arc furnace and continuous caster. Earlier, in May 1992, it was reported that SONASID planned to build a steel mini-mill near Jorf Lasfar port consisting of a 258,000 tons-per-year continuous caster and a 250,000 tons-per-year bar mill. The Government was disappointed when no buyer was found for the state's 51% holding in SONASID, which was put up for sale in early 1995. In a new attempt at a sale, SONASID was 35% privatized on the Casablanca stock exchange in July 1996, and in October 1997 the state's remaining 62% holding was sold to a consortium of local financial institutions. The consortium planned to modernize and expand the Nador plant. SONASID increased its capacity from 480,000 tons a year to 600,000 tons a year in February 1998 when it acquired Longometal Industries of Casablanca. The company recorded profits of 188m. dirhams ($20m.) in 1997.

In late 1994 the privately-owned Maroc Sidérurgie (Masid) announced that it was to build a steel mini-mill near Casablanca to produce 125,000 tons a year of steel bars and rods. The plant would include a 30 ton electric furnace, continuous billet caster and rolling mill. Masid planned to involve a European company as a partner in the project with about one-third of equity. The Banque Nationale pour le Développement Economique (BNDE) announced that it was to participate in financing the $82m. project by providing a long-term loan of $13m. The local mining group OISMINE was to invest $27m. Liquigaz GPL of Canada and MN Dastur of India were also involved in the project, which was due to become operational in April 1997.

Petroleum refining is another major industry. The biggest refinery, located at Mohammadia and owned by the Société Anonyme Marocaine de l'Industrie du Raffinage (SAMIR), has a design capacity of 4m. tons per year but has been producing at more than 5m. tons per year. CTIP of Italy has a contract to raise the refinery's capacity to 6m. tons a year, to be completed in late 1996. The other oil refinery, at Sidi Kacem (owned by the Société Chérifienne des Pétroles, SCP), has a capacity of 1.2m. tons a year. The two refineries, which satisfy 80% of local demand, were originally considered part of the strategic sector and not included on the list of companies listed for privatization. An auditor was appointed for the refineries in March 1995. In March 1996 the Government offered for sale 25% of its holding in SAMIR worth an estimated 1,730m.–2,070m. dirhams ($200m.–$240m.); 70% of the shares were reserved for small investors. The offer was fully subscribed with some 75% of buyers using the new privatization bonds (see below). The Government planned to sell a further 25% of its holdings in SAMIR through the stock exchange at a later date. The demand for SAMIR shares was encouraged by reports that both the Royal Dutch/Shell Group and Total of France were interested in buying a controlling stake. In early 1996 petrol distributors expressed concern that the privatization of SAMIR might lead to an increase in the company's prices. Local distributors complained that their profit margins were already too low owing to government control of petrol prices. As a result, Mobil Oil Maroc, which had previously announced a programme to double its investment to $5m. a year, stated that it would not increase investment. In May 1997 it was announced that a Saudi-owned company (Corral Petroleum Holdings) had purchased majority stakes in SAMIR and SCP (67.7% of SAMIR's capital and 73.9% of SCP) in a privatization deal that would generate $420m. in revenues for the Government. Corral also made a commitment to invest a similar amount in the local refining industry over five years. In early 1998 Corral announced plans to merge the operation and administration of the two companies. In April the Government declared that it was to sell its remaining shares in the two companies to Corral, bringing the company's total shareholdings to 74.47% in SAMIR and 81.29% in SCP in a transaction estimated at 400m. dirhams ($40.7m.). In May SAMIR announced plans to invest $500m. over the next five years in development projects including an expansion of its refinery at Mohammadia and modernizing port links.

One of Morocco's major import-substitution industries is cement production. The country's cement works produced a total of 3.9m. tons in 1987. Virtually all plants were working below capacity (average utilization of capacity was 70% in 1987), but amid indications of renewed growth in the construction industry domestic production reached 4.6m. tons in 1988 and 5.4m. tons in 1990. Cement production rose from 6.6m. tons in 1996 to 7.2m. tons in 1997. In 1990 consumption of cement increased by 16.7%, compared with the previous year, and all the country's cement production units indicated consistent growth. Cement plants have attracted increased foreign investment in recent years, especially from France. Lafarge-Coppée of France holds a 65% interest in Cementos Marroquíes (Cemenmar), a 26.5% interest in the Cimenterie Nouvelle de Casablanca (Cinouca) and a 40% interest in Cimenterie de Meknès. Annual capacity at the Cinouca plant increased to 1.9m. tons, following the opening of a new 700,000-ton production line. Production capacity at Cemenmar's Tétouan plant, currently 250,000 tons per year, may also be increased. Lafarge-Coppée has also taken an equity share in Readymix Maroc. Another French company, Ciments Français, has a 51% share in Société des Ciments d'Agadir, which has a production capacity of 1m. tons per year, and controls 60% of Cimenterie de Safi, a 600,000 tons-per-year plant. The International Finance Corpn (IFC) has provided financial assistance for the new Safi plant ($20.3m.) and for Cinouca's expansion programme ($17m.). In May 1994 the IFC agreed to provide $10m. to modernize Ciment du Maroc's plant at Agadir. A further $4.2m. was to be provided by a syndicate led by Banque Indosuez of France. Among the largest privatizations to have been completed by mid-1994 were holdings of the ODI, including the Cior. In August 1996 the local Laraqui group sold its majority shareholding in the Asment de Temara cement plant to Portugal's Cimpor-Cimentos for $70m. The Laraqui group had earlier planned a 30% increase in production capacity at the 900,000 tons-per-year plant, but other shareholders failed to agree to the necessary capital increase. Cior is planning a $8.5m. expansion project, involving a distribution centre and a crushing plant, in the north of the kingdom. In February 1998 Lafarge Coppée announced an expansion project at its Casablanca plant, where capacity will be increased from 1.6m. tons to 2m. tons.

The food-processing industry remains of considerable importance. It produces both for export and for domestic consumption. A large quantity of grain is processed into flour locally, but imported wheat is processed at a number of mills. There are also extensive sugar processing facilities in the country (see Agriculture and Fisheries). Other food industries include fruit and vegetable processing and canning—mainly for export—and fish canning. Fruit and vegetable processing recorded low growth rates in the mid-1980s, despite the fact that manufacturers could market directly, rather than through the Office de Commercialisation et d'Exportation, which was dismantled as part of the Government's privatization programme. This sector encountered restrictions on exports by the EC from 1986, when Spain and Portugal acceded to the Community.

The textile industry suffered from over-stocking in the mid-1960s, but in the 1970s its turnover grew at an annual rate of about 10%, and by 1981 it employed some 55,000 workers. Investment in textiles and leather increased from 361m. dirhams in 1982 to 717m. dirhams in 1984, and 966m. dirhams in 1986; in 1987 the level of investment nearly doubled, to 1,857m. dirhams. In 1988 textiles and leather accounted for 22% of total investment and 58% of projected employment, virtually all of this coming from textiles rather than leather. In 1990 investments in textiles and leathers increased by 45% (to 3,583m. dirhams, compared with 2,466m. dirhams in 1989). Textiles were at the forefront of export-led industrial growth, and export earnings increased significantly in the 1980s. Whereas in 1983 clothing exports were worth 683m. dirhams, by 1987 their value was 2,347m. dirhams. In 1988 Moroccan exports of textiles and leather goods together accounted for 38% of all manufactured exports. Owing to the Gulf crisis of 1990–91, Moroccan textile exports to Gulf markets were reported to have suffered. European markets for Moroccan products, however, had not been severely affected, although there has been a tendency for preference to be given to Portuguese and Eastern European goods. Spanish and Italian textiles firms have invested in Morocco in recent years. Tavex of Spain is majority shareholder in the Settavex textile scheme in Settat, which now employs 300 staff and produces 13.5m. metres of denim fabric a year. In January 1992 Carrera, an Italian textile firm, established a joint venture in Tangier with the local Nasco group to produce 2m. pairs of jeans per year. In September 1994 it was reported that an Irish company, Fruit of the Loom, had signed an agreement to build a $6.5m. textile plant at Salé employing 680 workers and making hosiery, mainly for export. Rising labour costs are presenting problems for the textile industry which remains Morocco's major exporter of manufactured goods. Some 85% of total production of some 1,500 companies is exported, mainly to Europe. The sector employs some 180,000 people, about one-quarter of the total manufacturing labour force. There are fears that some European-owned textile plants may transfer their operations to Asia if labour costs continue to rise. In January 1996 the British company Marks and Spencer denied allegations that Morocco's Société Industrielle de Confection à Mèknes—which makes clothes for Marks and Spencer—was using child labour.

In the engineering sector, there are four plants assembling cars and small utility vehicles: Renault Maroc, the Société de Promotion Industrielle et Automobile au Maroc (Peugeot-Talbot), SOMACA (Fiat), and the Société Méditerranéenne pour l'Industrie Automobile (Land Rover). Heavy trucks (16.5 metric tons and over) are manufactured by Berliet Maroc and Saida; smaller capacity vehicles are assembled by Berliet, Auto-Hall and Siab. Berliet also assembles buses, and Somami-Rahali, a Casablanca-based firm, has manufactured bus bodies for Daf chassis imported from the Netherlands. A limited range of motor vehicle components is made locally, as are tyres. Railway goods wagons, and mineral and tanker wagons are assembled by SCIF of Casablanca. In April 1994 the Ministry of Commerce, Industry and Privatization invited tenders to build and operate a plant producing an economy car for the local market and to develop the local components industry.

In May 1996 the French/Italian electronics company, SGS-Thomson, announced that it was to spend $300m. over the next five years expanding its two factories near Casablanca which assemble electronic components and currently employ more than 2,000 people. In October 1997 South Korea's Daewoo Corpn signed an agreement with the Government to build a car assembly plant and a semiconductor plant at the Nouasser industrial complex near Casablanca, involving an investment of $500m. The two plants were expected to create almost 6,000 jobs and generate exports of $300m. during the next five years. Daewoo launched a holding company, Daewoo-Maghreb, in June 1998 in order to implement the agreement. The two plants were expected to start production by the end of 1999.

After severe droughts in 1992 and 1993 had exacerbated serious power shortages, the state power company, ONE, was forced to develop an emergency plan to increase generating capacity. Contracts for several new power stations were awarded in 1993 including the installation of 100 MW new capacity at the CTZ-ZI power plant at Casablanca to be built by Technip of France at a cost of $88m. In October 1993 an agreement was signed between ONE and Tractabel of Belgium and AES of the USA to build and operate a 500 MW oil-fired power station at Mohammadia. Output from the $600m. plant was to be sold exclusively to ONE under a long-term contract. In July 1994 the EIB approved a loan of $96m. to ONE to help finance the interconnection of the Moroccan and Spanish power grids, the first power link between North Africa and Europe. The 400-kV undersea electricity link with Spain under the Strait of Gibraltar, which cost $250m., was inaugurated in June 1998. In November 1994 it was reported that ONE had failed to meet payment to local distribution companies for oil shipments. State companies, including the Office National des Chemins de Fer and the Office National de l'Eau Potable, had fallen into arrears amounting to an estimated $194m. A special payment of $107m. was made to ONE in the 1995 budget to help the company overcome its payment problems.

In September 1994 it was reported that the first of two 330 MW units at the Jorf Lasfar power station had reached full load in late August and had been linked to the national grid in July, and that the second 330 MW unit would be linked to the grid in early 1995. In June 1994 the Minister of Privatization had stated that the full or partial privatization of power distribution was under consideration, and in October ONE invited tenders to build and operate Morocco's first private power project, the Jorf Lasfar III and IV units. It was announced that the successful bidders would also receive contracts to manage the two existing units at Jorf Lasfar on a concession basis and a letter of intent to build and operate the planned Jorf Lasfar V and VI units. The contract for the privatization and expansion of the Jorf Lasfar power station was awarded to ABB Asea Brown Boveri of Switzerland and CMS Energy Corpn of the USA in February 1995; however, the final agreements were not initialled with ONE until April 1996. ONE indicated that the deal would be finalized when the financial arrangements had been made; these arrangements were outlined at the end of 1996. Under the agreements, two additional 348-MW units will be constructed to double the power station's capacity to 1,362 MW, the first unit to be completed in September 1999 and the second in March 2000. All the electricity generated at the plant will be purchased by ONE, which retains its monopoly over distribution. Construction work, carried out by subsidiaries of ABB Asea Brown Boveri, began in September 1997 and when completed the plant will be operated and maintained by CMS Energy Corpn for 30 years under the build-operate-transfer formula. The $1,500m. project is being financed mainly by commercial bank loans, supported by export credit facilities from Italy and Switzerland and loans from the US Export-Import Bank and the US Overseas Private Investment Corpn. In early 1998 it was reported that ABB Asea Brown Boveri and CMS Energy Corpn were discussing a further expansion of the power station involving the addition of 700 MW of capacity.

In November 1996 it was reported that ONE was revising its plan to build two new gas-fired power stations in Mohammadia and Kénitra in Morocco's industrial heartland. It was instead considering the construction of one installation at a northern location because of immediate access to the Europe–Maghreb gas pipeline, saving on fuel transport costs. Morocco currently receives 1,000m. cu m of gas a year from Algeria instead of transit fees. Building a station further south would require the construction of a 240-km branch pipeline to feed the plant with gas. ONE confirmed in January 1997 that it wanted the facility to be built in Tahaddart near Tangier rather than in Mohammadia or Kénitra as originally planned. The Tahaddart station was expected to be a combined cycle facility of up to 475 MW, costing an estimated $500m., and use up to 500 cu m of gas a year from the Maghreb–Europe pipeline. ONE hopes to attract a private consortium to finance and build the new station on a build-operate-transfer basis similar to the Jorf Lasfar project.

In August 1995 Lyonnaise des Eaux-Dumez of France signed an agreement with the Moroccan authorities to manage Casablanca's power and water distribution network; the agreement was approved in principle in March 1996. Opposition parties criticized the deal, arguing that it was a privatization and would lead to higher prices for consumers. Lyonnaise des Eaux-Dumez rejected these claims and stated that the agreement was neither a sale nor a privatization. The company announced that agreement would require an investment of $2,212m., substantially less than the sum envisaged when the agreement was signed. A Moroccan company, capitalized at $93.1m., will be established to run the network with Lyonnaise as the operator and major shareholder. Other shareholders in the company will be France's Elyo and Electricité de France, and Spain's Endesa and Aguas de Barcelona. In May 1998 a consortium of Spanish, Portuguese and local companies signed a 30-year concession agreement to operate power, water and wastewater systems in Greater Rabat (including Salé and Temara), involving investment of 14,000m. dirhams ($1,500m.) over the concession period. Other cities were reported to be contemplating contracting private operators to manage water and sewerage services, but the Casablanca and Rabat contracts proved highly controversial and met with resistance from the employers' federation.

In April 1995 ONE announced that it was to appoint a consortium of contractors to build and operate a 50-MW wind-driven power plant at Tétouan. The consortium will operate the plant for 19 years, after which ownership will pass to ONE, which is responsible for the construction of the transmission lines and associated substations. The plant will cost an estimated $60m. Construction of the plant by Denmark's Vestas Wind Systems began in early 1998 and was expected to be completed in 1999. The consortium appointed to operate the plant included Electricité de France and Compagnie Eolienne du Detroit/Banque Paribas. It was reported in January 1997 that ONE was working on a plan to invite private investors to build a 200-MW wind power station in the south (likely to be near Agadir). The project will be the second wind power scheme, following the facility at Tétouan in the north. The construction of dams with hydroelectric complexes, a programme which began in the 1960s, remains an important element in the Government's strategy to increase generating capacity. In mid-1997 the AFESD agreed a loan of $100m. for the Dchar el-Oued and Aït Messaoud hydroelectric dams in the Tadla region. Construction of the dams was scheduled to begin in 1998. In November 1995 it was reported that the Association Marocaine pour la Gestion de l'Energie was preparing a study on solar power. In October 1997 Germany's development agency Kreditanstalt für Wiederaufbau agreed to contribute $5.6m. to a solar energy project in the Tensift region near Marrakesh operated by ONE.

In May 1995 ONE and Sonelgaz of Algeria renewed a contract for 1995–96 under which Sonelgaz would supply 50 MW of electricity to Morocco at a cost of $25m. Also in May ONE stated that it expected the Government to approve a $119m.-a-year investment programme to accelerate rural electrification as part of a plan to provide electricity to all rural households by 2010. Currently only 35% of rural households have electricity. The new programme is to co-ordinate two schemes for rural electrification already in progress; one financed by ONE, the other financed by local communities by creating a central fund to which both rural communities and ONE contribute. Some 1,255 villages were linked to the electricity grid in 1996. In May 1998 it was reported that negotiations were taking place with Japan for a $45.8m. loan to ONE to finance its rural electrification programme. In February 1996 ONE stated that investment of 30,000m. dirhams ($3,462m.) would be required between 1996 and 2000 to satisfy a growth in demand of some 7% a year. Additional generating capacity of 1,900 MW would be required over this period. Under the company's 1996–2000 operational plan, it aims to reduce its own power production by almost one-half, from 9,106 GWh to 4,757 GWh, and to increase the amount of electricity it buys in from 2,494 GWh in 1996 to 10,343 GWh in 2000. The private sector is to be more heavily involved in power generation with ONE buying in electricity to resell to its customers. Expenditure of 4,460m. dirhams ($515m.) was planned for 1996. Some 1,814m. dirhams is to be spent on boosting production (935m. dirhams on hydroelectric plants, 379m. dirhams on thermal power stations and 500m. dirhams on coal facilities), 1,831m. dirhams on transmission (including 933m. dirhams on the submarine link with Spain), 522m. dirhams on expanding the distribution network and 393m. dirhams on the rural electrification programme. In 1997–99 ONE was to spend 2,500m. dirhams expanding the national transmission network, including the cost of completing the link with Spain. Despite the fact that ONE no longer receives a government subsidy, the company reported that it was in profit in 1995 because of the success in making its operations cheaper and more effective. In February 1996 ONE introduced a new pricing system for electricity to standardize and control pricing practices and make the power sector more commercially competitive.

BALANCE OF PAYMENTS AND TRADE

Morocco's main sources of revenue are earnings from exports of phosphate rock and phosphate derivatives, agricultural products and manufactured goods, receipts from tourism and workers' remittances from abroad. The country's expenditure is mainly on imports of capital equipment, food and crude petroleum. After 1976 the deficit on the current account widened, as export earnings rose slowly while the cost of imports soared. In 1983 the Government took strong measures to close the export/import gap by reducing budget expenditure and by restricting imports. This reduced the trade deficit from 13,552m. dirhams in 1982 to 11,218m. dirhams in 1983. However, the continuing decline in phosphate exports (by volume and value), and the high level of food and energy imports, resulted in further increases in the trade deficit, to 15,278m. dirhams in 1984 and to 16,938m. dirhams in 1985. Only the collapse of petroleum prices during 1986 enabled the trade deficit for that year to fall by 26%, to 12,505m. dirhams. In 1987 the trade deficit fell by a further 5%, to 11,881m. dirhams. Imports in 1987 rose by only 1.9%, to 35,271m. dirhams, while exports increased in value by 5.8%, to 23,390m. dirhams. The trade deficit continued to fall in 1988, to 9,382m. dirhams, with imports of foodstuffs down by 3.9%

and energy imports by 14.9%, while exports rose by 20%. The precarious nature of this improvement was revealed, however, by a sharp increase in the trade deficit in 1989, when exports declined by 5% and imports rose by 19%, compared with 1988. Even so, the improvements in the export performance of some sectors were encouraging, particularly the increase of more than 30% in export earnings from manufactured consumer goods in the first quarter of 1989. Results for the whole year, however, indicated that the trade deficit almost doubled, to 18,323.8m. dirhams. The decline in exports in 1989 was largely the result of a sharp drop in sales of phosphoric acid. In 1990 the trade deficit grew by 21% (despite an increase of 19% in exports), to 22,165m. dirhams. Imports increased by 22% in 1990, to 57,022m. dirhams. The 1990 trade deficit was equivalent to 10.5% of GDP. In 1991 the trade deficit rose to 22,437m. dirhams, despite a 7% increase in exports (to 37,283m. dirhams) and a decline in expenditure on energy imports. Imports rose to 59,720m. dirhams, of which more than one-half were semi-finished products and industrial equipment. Food exports rose by 20.6% and there was a steady growth in sales of manufactured products. Exports of phosphates and derivatives accounted for 27% of total sales. The trade deficit increased in 1992 by almost 30%, to 28,846m. dirhams. Invisible earnings (remittances from migrant workers and tourist revenues) also increased, however, so that balance-of-payment problems were not anticipated. Sales of phosphates and products decreased from 10,047m. dirhams in 1991 to 8,491.7m. dirhams in 1992. Clothing sales remained constant at 4,137m. dirhams. Oil imports increased by almost 22%, and those of wheat nearly doubled as a result of the drought, totalling 2.4m. tons in 1992. Imports of industrial machinery rose from 2,460.7m. dirhams in 1991 to 2,711m. dirhams in 1992. Figures published by the Central Bank record exports of 34,238m. dirhams in 1993 and imports of 56,368m. dirhams, giving a trade deficit of 22,130m. dirhams and a current account deficit of 4,899m. dirhams. In 1994 exports rose to 36,546m. dirhams, while imports increased by 17% to 65,963m. dirhams, resulting in a trade deficit of 29,417m. dirhams. The trade deficit continued to widen in 1995; although exports increased by 10.1% to reach 40,240m. dirhams, imports rose by 10.5% to total 72,869m. dirhams (primarily owing to a substantial increase in food imports following the severe drought), giving a deficit of 32,629m. dirhams. In 1996 the trade deficit narrowed slightly to 30,600m. dirhams as exports rose to 41,300m. dirhams and imports declined to 71,900m. dirhams. Revenue from tourism increased by almost one-quarter, to 9,000m. dirhams, and remittances from Moroccan migrants in Europe also rose, to 17,500m. dirhams. In March 1998 the IMF estimated that exports totalled $6,900m. in 1997, with imports declining to $8,900m., resulting in a narrowing of the trade deficit. The current account deficit was estimated to have fallen from $627m. in 1996 to $405m. in 1997.

Morocco's GDP is heavily dependent on agricultural performance. GDP grew at an average annual rate of 2.9%, in real terms, during 1978–84, although growth was depressed during several of those years, owing largely to poor harvests. Improved agricultural output in 1985 allowed GDP to rise by 6.3% in real terms, and an exceptional harvest in 1986 contributed substantially to the 8.4% growth in GDP for that year. In 1987 GDP declined by 2.6%, largely as a result of poor harvests, forcing agricultural output down by 13%, and stagnation in the phosphate sector, contributing to a 1.2% fall in output from the mining sector. A record harvest in 1988 boosted GDP growth to an estimated 10.4%. Other strong areas were manufacturing, energy production, commerce, transport and other services. In 1989, despite a good harvest, GDP grew by only 1.8%. According to Moroccan official figures, GDP fell by approximately 3% in 1992, largely as a result of the drought, which reduced agriculture's share of GDP from 21% to 15%. However, according to the IMF, GDP declined by 4.1% in 1992 and grew by only 0.2% in 1993. Official estimates suggested that the economy grew by 11% in 1994 as a result of a good harvest following two years of economic decline. However, severe drought in 1995 caused a sharp contraction in the economy, with GDP declining by 7%. Heavy rainfall resulted in a marked improvement in the economy in 1996, with GDP growth of 12.0%. The economy contracted again in 1997 following a poor harvest; GDP declined by 2.2%.

In 1996 the EU remained Morocco's largest trading partner, accounting for 61.4% of all exports and 54.1% of imports, although its share of the market has declined slightly in recent years. France remained the largest source of goods, providing 20.8% of imports, followed by Spain (8.8%), the USA (7.4%), Italy (7.2%) and Germany (6.1%). France also remained Morocco's largest export market, taking 28.3% of exports, followed by Spain (9.9%), Japan (6.9%), India (6.3%) and Italy (6.3%). Trade with the other Maghreb countries remains limited but was expected to increase, following the creation in 1989 of the Union of the Arab Maghreb (UAM). Numerous initiatives have been taken to encourage closer economic collaboration and integration with other members of the UAM, including the lowering of customs and tariff barriers and promotion of trade and joint ventures. Despite a great deal of rhetoric, by late 1995 the UAM had largely failed to promote greater economic co-operation between its members, and in December Morocco threatened to bring UAM activities to a standstill after it accused Algeria of interfering in the Western Sahara dispute (see History).

In April 1994 Morocco hosted the signing of the GATT Uruguay round trade pact in Marrakesh. Morocco had been one of the principal supporters of the GATT agenda in the Arab world. In July 1993 the maximum customs duty on imported goods was reduced from 40% to 35%, and, in line with the government's commitment to GATT, rates on some 2,300 products (including textiles, fibres, paper and packaging, and foodstuffs) were reduced. In March 1995 the liberalization of cereal, vegetable oil and oilseed imports was postponed from April and May until July in order to give time for measures to be put in place to protect local industries. The existing quantitative restrictions are to be replaced by tariff barriers, in accordance with GATT. Measures to liberalize sugar imports were also delayed until mid-1995. In June the Government announced that it had approved the ending of the state's monopoly on petroleum imports, as part of its policy of liberalizing the energy sector. In March 1998 customs duties on imported wheat were increased significantly in an attempt to protect local farmers.

Morocco's trade is likely to remain crucially dependent on Europe. In view of the importance of its trade relations with the EU, Morocco has continually sought more favourable trade agreements. A five-year agreement conferring 'partial association' on Morocco was negotiated in 1968 and came into force in 1969. A new agreement for an unlimited period was finalized in January 1976, whereby most Moroccan agricultural and industrial products were allowed free access to the EC, but with restrictions on a few crucial items, such as olive oil, citrus fruit, wine, textiles and refined petroleum products. In 1984 Morocco applied to join the EC, but, in the absence of European approval for its application, urged the Community to liberalize its trade policies; new quota agreements were signed in January 1985. The entry of Spain and Portugal into the EC in 1986 stimulated a series of discussions, in which Morocco, as one of the countries most affected, was deeply involved. It was later agreed that the voluntary quota system on manufactured goods should be abandoned, but no agreement was reached concerning agricultural exports. Proposals by the EC Commission covered the five-year transitional period up to 1990. However, ministers of foreign affairs from EC member states were unable to agree on the Commission's proposals, while Morocco also expressed serious concern at what it regarded as the 'protectionism' of the EC and the inadequacy of the Community's arrangements for relations with Morocco. In July 1987 Morocco made a second application for full membership of the EC, which was rejected in October. In 1991 it was announced that the EC would provide a financial aid programme of $5,800m. for eight Mediterranean countries, of which Morocco was to be the largest benefactor (receiving $534m. in total funds). Concessionary loans would comprise 50%. In January 1992 the European Parliament decided to block $600m. of development aid, in protest at abuses of human rights in Morocco and in the disputed Western Sahara. Morocco then refused to agree a new fishing accord, and agreement was not reached until May. In April the EC Commission approved a policy document envisaging a new Euro-Maghreb partnership. In October the European Parliament eventually ratified a fourth financial protocol, according to which Morocco was to receive $580m. in new funding over four years. In March

1993 the President of the EC Commission, Jacques Delors, held talks with King Hassan during a visit to Morocco. In July it was reported that the EU had proposed an annual increase of 3% in quotas of citrus fruit, orange juice, fruit and vegetables from Morocco in 1997–2000. In January 1995 the Government signed an agreement with the EU to bring agricultural trade regulations closer to the provisions of GATT. Under the new agreement, Morocco's preferential status in tomato exports to the EU was reduced, but exports would be allowed to maintain their traditional level of 140,000–145,000 tons per year. A minimum price was imposed for the months from November to March, Morocco's busiest export period. Moroccan farmers were prevented from selling tomatoes at less than ECU 560 ($693) per ton, compared with minimum prices stipulated under the GATT of ECU 700–750 ($866–$928) in the period from November to March and ECU 920 ($1,138.5) for the months January to March. After two years of negotiations, in February 1996 Morocco became the third Mediterranean country to sign a free-trade accord with the EU. The accord had been initialled in November 1995 after delays due to Morocco's bitter dispute with the EU over fishing rights. Under the terms of the new agreement, Morocco will phase out protective tariffs on EU manufactured goods entering the country over a period of 12 years, and will receive financial help from the EU to assist local industries adapt to new competition. No detailed financial package was written into the agreement, but the EU pledged to give signatories of this type of accord priority access to some ECU 4,695m. ($5,983m.) over the period 1996–2000. The sensitive issue of free trade in agricultural products will not be discussed until 2000, although both parties agreed to increase agricultural trade and in the short-term Morocco will benefit from a number of concessions. The accord forms part of the EU's wider plan to foster a new political and economic force in the Mediterranean based on free trade and political co-operation.

TOURISM

The tourist industry has become an increasingly important source of foreign exchange. By 1987 the total revenue earned from tourism had reached 8,000m. dirhams, representing 23% of total exports of goods and services. Only phosphates and their derivatives, and workers' remittances, brought in more foreign exchange. Tourism was undoubtedly one of the growth areas of the Moroccan economy in the 1980s, and government incentives played a significant part in its development. Special conditions drawn up in 1983 govern investment in tourism, including tax exemptions on capital goods imports, interest-free loans and, in certain circumstances, income tax exemptions for a 10-year period. Major tourist complexes were constructed at Casablanca, Agadir, Tangier and Restinga, near Tétouan. By the end of 1988 there were more than 79,000 beds available in nearly 500 hotels, pensions and holiday villages. Most tourists stay on the southern, Atlantic coast. The total number of foreign tourist arrivals in 1987 was 1,566,254, an increase of 6.5% on the 1986 total. In 1989 the number of tourists visiting Morocco increased by 27% (to 2,515,251, compared with 1,978,420 in 1988). In 1990 some 3m. foreigners visited Morocco, increasing tourist remittances by 22%, to 10,500m. dirhams. This advance was due to a rise in the number of Algerian visitors, taking advantage of the 'open frontiers' that had been authorized by the UAM. In 1991 tourist receipts declined to 8,822.2m. dirhams, despite a 3.1% increase in arrivals, mainly accounted for by more visitors from other Maghreb countries. In 1992 the number of visitors increased to 3.3m. Tourist arrivals from Italy increased by 67.9%, and from Spain by 43.4%. There was also an increase in the number of tourists from Germany, the USA and Japan, although tourist arrivals from Algeria decreased by 19%. Tourist arrivals decreased by 9.4% in 1993 and by 22.1% in 1994 (to 2.3m.) as a result of the recession in Europe, tensions between Morocco and Algeria and the fear of terrorist attacks following the Marrakesh shooting (see History). There was a further sharp decline in 1995 when the number of tourists fell to 1.5m., resulting in a decline of 12% in revenue to 10,000m. dirhams. In late 1995 the Ministry of Tourism reported that it had closed 36 hotels and downgraded 53 as part of a programme to raise the standard of tourist facilities. Foreign tourist arrivals increased from 1.6m. in 1996 to 1.8m. in 1997, but revenue fell slightly as a result of a decline in per caput expenditure.

In March 1993 it was reported that five state-owned hotels in Tangier, Meknès and Casablanca (the first of 37 hotels owned by the Office National Marocain du Tourisme scheduled for privatization) had been sold. A new approach to the privatization of state holdings in hotels was announced in April, according to which the Government would sell its holdings in four- and five-star hotels to international companies as a comprehensive transaction. The 1993 budget included a reduction in the allocation to the Office National Marocain du Tourisme to 90m. dirhams, indicating the Government's commitment to disengage from the tourist industry. In May 1994 local investors purchased the Transatlantique hotel in Meknès. In January 1998 the Ministry of Privatization announced that nine state-owned hotels would be offered for sale in 1998, including seven hotels that had failed to attract buyers when they were first offered for sale in November 1997.

Recent foreign investment is providing an opportunity to revive the flagging tourist industry. In July 1996 South Korea's Daewoo Corpn announced that it would buy the Rabat Hyatt Regency hotel for $40m. and build an extension for an additional estimated $50m. In February 1997 it was reported that the French hotel management company Accor was to open subscriptions in March for its planned $100m. fund to invest in tourism development projects in Morocco. The funds will be spent to acquire hotels, spas and other facilities. In July Accor purchased the local Moussafir hotel chain for $5m., the company's first purchase under its current investment programme in Morocco. In April it was reported that the company was in talks with the Government about financing and building a trade and leisure centre in Casablanca and a 1,200-room hotel complex in Agadir. In addition, Germany's Paradiana is to invest in two separate tourism projects (a 600-bed hotel and a holiday club) in the Agadir region, where the Société d'Aménagement de la Baie d'Agadir is trying to attract some $450m. of private investment to develop tourist facilities there.

TRANSPORT AND COMMUNICATIONS

There are 10 major ports: Casablanca, Safi, Mohammadia, Agadir, Kénitra, Jorf Lasfar, Tan Tan, Dakhla in the disputed territory of Western Sahara, along the Atlantic coast, and Nador in the north-east and Tangier in the north-west, both on the Mediterranean. Since early 1985 the major ports have been controlled by the Office d'Exploitation des Ports (ODEP). In 1985 ODEP began modernizing port equipment and facilities in a two-year development plan. In the period to 1990 ODEP planned to spend 1,350m. dirhams, more than half of which was to finance the development of ports. In 1991 several projects were announced, including a new container terminal at Casablanca, at a cost of 610m. dirhams, a 160m. dirham coal terminal at Jorf Lasfar and modernization of port equipment at ports controlled by ODEP. The World Bank was to provide loans of $99m. to ODEP and $33m. to the central Government for the financing of these projects. The volume of traffic through all ports in 1988 reached 39.6m. tons, an increase of 12.7% over the 1987 total. In 1990 the volume was 37.9m. tons. The major goods handled include hydrocarbons and phosphates, sulphur and ammonia, triple superphosphate and phosphoric acid, citrus and other fruit, and vegetables. Of the total cargo handled in 1988, 42% went through Casablanca, 17% through Jorf Lasfar, 15% through Safi and 12% through Mohammadia. The volume of cargo traffic through Moroccan ports increased to 40.5m. tons, in 1993; the 22.1m. tons of imports included 9.5m. tons of hydrocarbons and 3.9m. tons of cereals. In March 1994 work began on a new harbour at Dakhla in Western Sahara as a centre for coastal and deep-sea fishing, including a 1,300-ha free-trade zone. In March 1996 it was reported that ODEP planned to invest 1,700m. dirhams ($200m.) in port development over the period 1996–2000. Its plans included investment of 328m. dirhams for the purchase of equipment and 144m. dirhams for infrastructure development at Casablanca, 361m. dirhams at Dakhla and 145m. dirhams at Jorf Lasfar. ODEP reported a rise in its turnover of 23% to 1,127m. dirhams in the year to the end of September 1995. In February 1996 shipping firms reported severe congestion at Casablanca owing to the Government's campaign against smuggling, which led to the arrest of a number of senior customs officials. In November 1996 the Government launched an initiative to raise interest in a $300m. investment project to build a new multi-purpose deep water port in Tangier. The aim of the project is to divert all merchandise traffic from the existing port, which is expected to suffer from serious congestion by 2002, despite short-term expansion projects in 1996–98. The contract for the project, known as Tangier-Atlantique, was expected to be awarded in 1998. It involves the design, construction, operation and financing of the new port under a 50-year concession. The second port at Tangier is scheduled for completion by 2003. In November 1997 Spain agreed credits of $4m. towards the cost of a new port at Agadir. In February 1998 ODEP announced that it was planning to spend $220m. on modernizing and expanding the country's port facilities during 1998–2002.

The railways are operated by the Office National des Chemins de Fer (ONCF). In 1989 the company planned to invest nearly 1,000m. dirhams in rail development, including projects to double the Rabat–Kénitra line and the construction of a connection between Casablanca and the city's King Muhammad V airport. Also considered were an extension of the rapid transit system which runs between Casablanca and Rabat south to El Jadida, a rail link between Taourirt and Nador in the northeast, and a controversial plan to link Marrakesh and el-Aaiún, in Western Sahara. In mid-1992 it was announced that the ADB had agreed to contribute $84m. towards an estimated $270m. programme to improve main railway routes, in particular the Casablanca–Fez line. In January 1997, following a two-and-a-half-year period of almost no new investment, it was reported that ONCF was to start work on a $591m. (5,200m. dirhams) four-year restructuring and investment plan after securing loans to cover part of it. The plan includes rehabilitating installations, modernizing the rolling stock and reorganizing the company. In April ONCF awarded a contract to double the Kénitra–Meknès railway line to a local/Spanish consortium as part of the investment programme. The World Bank agreed in May to lend ONCF $85m. to expand the domestic network and purchase seven new locomotives, while in July the EIB approved a loan for rehabilitation and upgrading work on the Marrakesh–Casablanca and the Rabat–Fez–Oujda lines. The ADB has also pledged $85m. to support ONCF's investment programme. In September 1997 Cegelec of France was awarded contracts to electrify the Kénitra–Sidi Kacem line, improve lines serving Casablanca and rehabilitate the Sidi el Aidi–Oued Zem phosphate line. In October ONCF announced that it was interested in granting concessions to private investors to build and operate new railway lines of which the first would probably be a 120-km line from Taourit to Nador and Beni Enzar where a new port was planned. In 1996 ONCF for the first time reported an operational profit, of 7,000m. dirhams, though the company still incurred an overall loss of 206m. dirhams. The company was expected to become profitable in 1997. In February 1998 three French companies began a feasibility study financed by France for a 28-km metro for Casablanca. The $588m. project (aimed to ease congestion in Casablanca) has been under consideration for some years but the Government has been unable to raise the necessary finance for it.

The road network is well developed, comprising more than 60,000 km of road, of which 50.3% is paved. Most of the roads are built to design standards appropriate for a volume of traffic substantially in advance of that which they are currently carrying. In 1996 there were 1,021,515 passenger cars and 363,533 commercial vehicles in use, as well as 19,417 motorcycles and scooters. Tonnage carried by public road freight transport under the auspices of the Office National des Transports virtually doubled between 1976 and 1986, from 6.8m. tons to 13.4m. tons, and rose to an estimated 14.7m. tons in 1988. In 1991 the Government approved a decree permitting the Société Nationale des Autoroutes du Maroc to collect tolls on Moroccan motorways. The revenue received from the tolls on the Casablanca–Rabat motorway was to be used to finance the construction of the projected Tangier–Casablanca motorway. In April 1991 four international groups were invited to rebid for the construction of the central section of the Tangier–Casablanca motorway, between Rabat and Larache, and the contract was awarded to a group of Italian companies. The $220m. road project was to be funded by the AFESD and Italy. The AFESD agreed to a grant of $1.7m. for a study of the Maghreb Unity highway linking Nouadhibou, in Mauritania, with Benghazi, in Libya.

In March 1996 contractors submitted bids for a 50-km section of the Rabat–Fez motorway between Khemisset and Sidi Allal Bahraoui, estimated to cost some $50m.–$60m. This was the fourth of five contracts for the motorway, and in August 1996 it was awarded to Spain's OCP Construcciones. An Italian consortium was working on the section between Meknès and Khemisset, under a $75m.-contract signed in November 1995. Invitations to bid for the final section of the Rabat–Fez motorway—a 15-km section from Sidi Allal Bahraoui to Rabat—were expected to be made in 1997. The EIB and the AFESD agreed long-term loans in 1995 to cover most of the cost of the Rabat–Fez motorway. In March 1995 Japan's Overseas Economic Co-operation Fund agreed to a loan of $86.7m. towards the cost of modernizing 2,400 km of roads throughout the country and of constructing roads linking central Morocco with the northern and southern provinces. The loan is to be repaid over 10 years with a 10-year grace period. The World Bank is also contributing $140m. to the $226m. road programme, parts of which are now under construction. In June the World Bank approved a $57.6m. loan for road maintenance and management. It was reported in March and April 1997 that the Ministry of Public Works was evaluating bids for a project to build a four-lane, 112-km motorway from Casablanca to Jorf Lasfar on a build-operate-transfer-basis, and that a technical study for a 560-km road along the Mediterranean coast was to be undertaken. In February 1998 the Government announced that it was proceeding with the construction of a Mediterranean coastal highway which would link Tangier with Saidia, near the border with Algeria. Much of the construction costs would be financed by the state, but certain stretches were to be privately financed on a build-operate-transfer basis. In March bids were invited for a contract to build a 72-km highway between Casablanca and Azemmour, which forms part of the Casablanca–Jorf Lasfar motorway. In February work began on the construction of a motorway between Casablanca and Settat, a project part-financed by the AFESD and Japan's Overseas Economic Co-operation Fund. Japan is also helping to finance a 35-km motorway between Casablanca and Mohammadia. The state-owned road transport company, Compagnie de Transports du Maroc-Lignes Nationales (CTM-LN), Morocco's biggest bus company, was privatized in 1993. The Government's remaining 18.9% holding in the company was sold on the Casablanca stock exchange in October 1994, raising $5.5m. The offer was nearly three times oversubscribed. In May 1995 the company announced a major expansion plan over the next three years, and in November claimed that it would double its profit in 1995 to 23.9m. dirhams ($2.9m.). The company also increased its capital by 23% to 122.6m. dirhams ($14.7m.) in order to purchase new buses.

In February 1996 plans to construct a fixed link across the Strait of Gibraltar received new impetus when Spain and Morocco issued a joint communiqué stating their commitment to the project and announcing that they had agreed that the fixed link would be a tunnel rather than a bridge, the latter option previously favoured by Morocco. The link would involve building a 22-km single rail tunnel 900 m under the seabed; a second main tunnel would be added after the first no longer satisfied demand. The first phase, estimated to take five years and cost $403m., would be to dig an exploratory tunnel in order to gain a better understanding of technical difficulties. It was hoped that the EU would cover just over one-third of the cost of this phase, with the private sector financing the remainder under a concession scheme. The tunnel link was expected to create jobs in Morocco and Spain and encourage the establishment of passenger and freight transport networks from other European countries to the tunnel's Spanish terminal.

There are 10 major airports in Morocco, as well as about 50 landing strips for light aircraft. In addition, el-Aaiún in Western Sahara has an airport. In 1991 a four-year programme to expand and modernize Moroccan airports, at an estimated cost of 1,200m. dirhams, was announced. The Office National des Aéroports (ONDA) and the ADB were each to provide a 25% loan to finance the project. The remaining 50% of the cost of the programme was to be negotiated. Marrakesh-Menara airport reopened in August 1991, after the extension of the runway and work on airport buildings at a cost of $8m. A new passenger terminal was opened in July 1992 at Casablanca's King

Muhammad V airport. The airport handled 1.8m. passengers in 1991 and it was forecast that some 3.3m. passengers would pass through the airport in 1993. The ONDA plans the creation of a major industrial and commercial zone, occupying 200 ha, as the latest phase in the expansion of the airport. In 1993 a $36m. contract to build an aircraft maintenance centre at the airport was awarded to a group of US firms, led by Westinghouse Electric Corpn. In December 1992 the ADB approved a loan of $102m. to support the ONDA's plans to upgrade the infrastructure of Morocco's airports. Royal Air Maroc (RAM), which was formed in 1953, is the national airline. It operates services to European and African countries, as well as to the USA. In 1988 RAM handled 1.7m. passengers, compared with 1.2m. in 1983. The number of passengers travelling by RAM increased steadily in the early 1990s, reaching 2.3m. in 1994. Tourism accounts for a significant proportion of passengers carried, although flights for business-related purposes are increasingly important. Total freight carried by air has also continued to rise. As at November 1996 RAM operated 27 aircraft, most of them Boeings. The airline's current renewal and expansion plan envisaged the purchase of two new aircraft every year until 2001. Two Boeing 737–800 aircraft ordered in 1996 were delivered in May 1998 with financing arranged by the Banque Nationale de Paris. Also in May RAM signed a co-operation agreement with Spain's national carrier, Iberia. An independent Moroccan company, Regional Airlines, was set up in October 1997; it will compete with RAM on internal and eventually some international routes.

Television and most radio services are controlled by the State, which runs a nationwide television network (Radiodiffusion-Télévision Marocaine) and nine regional radio stations broadcasting in the Arabic, French and Berber languages. There is also a commercial radio network, which broadcasts from Tangier and Nador to North Africa (Radio Méditerranée Internationale). In 1995 there were 6.0m. radios and 2.5m. television sets in Morocco. A commercial television channel for subscribers opened in 1989. In December 1994 a contract was signed between the Office Nationale des Postes et Télécommunications (ONPT) and Siemens of Germany to install 230,000 telephone lines as part of ONPT's programme to install a total of 400,000 new lines. The company plans to increase telephone density from 3.5 lines to 10 lines per 100 inhabitants by 2000. Negotiations were taking place with Ericsson of Sweden and Alcatel of France for the remaining lines. Under an agreement signed with ONPT in March 1995 AT&T of the USA is preparing a plan for the modernization of the country's telecommunications network. ONPT stated that it wants to double the capacity of its network and introduce the latest technology. AT&T will study ways to digitalize the network and expand the use of fibre optic links and satellites. When the study has been completed AT&T will begin negotiating to carry out part of the recommendations. In early 1996 ONPT announced that it was to invest 4,300m. dirhams ($505.7m.) in that year on a programme to modernize and expand its network. There were plans for an additional 250,000 switching units to extend the automation system to more than 300 towns, the expansion of the global standard for mobiles network to remote provinces, and increasing the number of subscribers from 1m. to 1.3m. The EIB is funding fibre optic links between Tétouan and Agadir and a link across the Strait of Gibraltar. In February 1996 it was reported that Glenayre Electronics of the USA had been awarded a $2.6m. contract to supply and install a pager system for ONPT, initially serving 50,000 subscribers in Rabat, Casablanca, Tangier, Marrakesh, Agadir, Tétouan, Fez and Larache, to be completed in March 1997. In April 1996 it was announced that, as part of a project to restructure and modernize the country's telecommunications network funded by the World Bank, Société Eton of France had been awarded a $1m. contract to supply connection equipment, and Acome/CEAC a $2.2m. contract to supply cable.

In June 1997 the Chamber of Representatives adopted a new law heralding the liberalization of the fixed and mobile telecommunications sector. The law would allow for the split of the state-owned ONPT into two enterprises—Itissalat al-Maghrib and Barid al-Maghrib, handling telecommunications and postal services respectively. Itissalat al-Maghrib's capital was to be open to private investors and was expected to form the major element of the Government's privatization programme

in 1998. ONPT planned to expand its fixed telephone network by another 56,000 lines and to double its mobile phone network by 1999. Tenders for Morocco's first private global standard for mobiles licence were expected to be issued in July 1998.

BANKING AND FINANCE

Morocco's foreign debt rose sharply during the second half of the 1970s. In October 1980, in an attempt to control its escalating debt burden, Morocco negotiated a three-year loan from the IMF, totalling $1,000m., the largest loan ever granted to a developing country by the Fund at that time. The terms of the loan were modified in 1982, when the progress of the economy failed to meet the IMF conditions. By 1983 Morocco's debt had reached unmanageable proportions, and a new IMF agreement was negotiated as part of a debt-rescheduling arrangement with all of Morocco's creditors. Outstanding debt to the 'Paris Club' creditor countries and the Arab states was rescheduled in 1983, but negotiations with creditor banks continued until 1985. In 1985 Morocco negotiated a new arrangement with the IMF, but this encountered difficulties, as Morocco failed to achieve IMF targets in early 1986. Eventually, a new programme, with less stringent terms, was agreed in November 1986, to run until April 1988. The 'Paris Club' and the creditor banks agreed to reschedule debt repayments until the end of the IMF agreement. Meanwhile, during 1984–87 the World Bank provided finance for several sectoral adjustment programmes within a general programme to restructure and reorient the Moroccan economy. The major elements of this restructuring programme included a shift to export-oriented production, privatization, a reduction in public expenditure, fiscal reform and tighter control over the economy as a whole. In September 1987 the World Bank declared that Morocco was 'well-poised' for economic success, as a result of its stabilization and structural adjustment programmes, and it subsequently increased its lending, to make Morocco the Bank's third largest recipient after Turkey and Pakistan, during 1987. In mid-1988 the IMF approved a new stand-by facility of SDR 220m. for the period from June 1988 to the end of 1989. The Fund generally approved of Morocco's macroeconomic performance, but was somewhat critical of fiscal policy implementation. Debt owing to the 'Paris Club' of creditor countries was rescheduled in October 1988 and again in September 1990. In December 1988 the World Bank made further finances available as part of the structural adjustment support to assist Morocco with debt management. In early 1989 negotiations began for the rescheduling of $1,400m. owing to the commercial banks of the 'London Club' and continued until April 1990, when an agreement was reached. The new accord rescheduled about $3,200m. of medium-term debt over a period of up to 20 years and reduced the interest to be paid on the debt. The existing IMF stand-by agreement expired in December 1989 but was renewed for a further eight months in July 1990. In May 1991 Spain rescheduled official debt within Morocco's 'Paris Club' accords, which included credits provided by the concessionary lending agency Fondo de Ayuda al Desarrollo, repayable over 20 years. Total debt to Spain was then estimated at 110,000m. pesetas ($1,012m.). In July the World Bank approved a $235m. loan to the financial sector, which would permit Morocco to develop domestic financial markets and to invest in private export-orientated industries. Morocco is also one of a small group of heavily indebted countries to benefit from a World Bank Export Credit Enhanced Leverage, which provides bank guarantees and some funds for private-sector projects already receiving support from credit agencies. According to the Ministry of Finance, Morocco's external debt at the end of 1991 totalled $21,000m., of which $10,600m. was outstanding to 'Paris Club' Governments, $3,600m. to the 'London Club', $3,300m. to the World Bank, $1,600m. to the USA and $600m. to the IMF. Morocco's economic prospects improved signficantly in late 1991, when Saudi Arabia and other Gulf states agreed to cancel bilateral debts estimated at around $3,600m. In February 1992 the IMF approved a stand-by credit authorizing drawings of up to SDR 91.98m. ($129m.) to support the Government's economic programme from January 1992 to March 1993. At the end of this period the Government expected to be able to return to the international capital markets and to make no further demands on IMF resources. In February the 'Paris Club' Governments agreed to reschedule official debt worth $1,500m., and in March the World Bank approved a $275m. structural adjustment loan, the final loan in Morocco's economic rehabilitation, according to the country's official news agency. In August 1992, under the terms of the 'Paris Club' agreement signed in February, the USA announced that it would reschedule bilateral debt worth $101.1m. incurred up to 1983. Some $32.5m. in official development assistance was to be repaid over 20 years with a 10-year grace period and $68.6m. in consolidated debt and arrears was to be repaid over 15 years with an eight-year grace period. Figures released in May 1993 by the Ministry of Finance revealed that Morocco's external debt in 1993 was $21,305m. 'Paris Club' member states accounted for $10,549m. (about one-half of the total debt), the 'London Club' $3,525m. (17%) and international financial institutions $5,700m. (27%). Debt-service repayments in 1992 increased to $3,000m., but were projected to decrease from $2,848m. in 1993 to $2,126m. in 2000. Announcing the 1995 budget in December 1994, the Minister of Finance, Mourad Cherif, stated that the cost of servicing the external debt remained a burden with repayments in 1994 equivalent to 4.2% of gross national product. In June 1993 the Ministry of Finance introduced new rules whereby Moroccan banks or private enterprises were allowed to raise credits with foreign financial institutions to finance imports of goods and services without prior authorization.

In 1992 Morocco became the major recipient of concessionary financing from the Caisse Française de Développement, with loan commitments during the year totalling 274.5m. francs, compared with 160m. francs for Algeria and 110m. francs for Tunisia. In November it was announced that France would increase the value of its 1992 financial protocol to 1,220m. francs from 800m. francs. In mid-1993, however, the French Ministry of Finance indicated that the level of support offered under the 1993 protocol would probably be less than that for 1992. In December Spain agreed to provide a new five-year credit programme worth $1,056m., renewing the credit line originally signed in 1988. The EU was to lend Morocco a total of ECU 438m. in 1992–96, together with funds for structural adjustment and EIB loans for the Europe-Maghreb gas pipeline. In February 1995 it was reported that Spain had renewed a credit line of $1,125m. as part of an economic and financial co-operation agreement signed in 1994. The credit line involved $375m. to be disbursed in five equal annual tranches and $750m. in export credits.

In late 1995 the Ministry of Finance estimated debt-servicing at 35% of foreign currency income and indicated that it was considering ways of reducing debt-service payments for the financial year starting 1 July 1996, including debt-equity swaps, refinancing and debt buy-backs. In January 1996 representatives of Morocco and France signed a series of bilateral agreements under which France agreed to forgive or convert 1,000m. French francs ($203m.) of Moroccan debt, and promised further aid and technical assistance. France agreed to forgive 400m. francs of government debt on condition that this money be invested in development projects in the Rif (Morocco's main marijuana producing region); a further 600m. francs of sovereign debt was to be converted into equity of financial support for French companies investing in Morocco. In addition France would provide 340m. francs to assist with water and railway development projects, offer training and assistance to modernize and liberalize the administration, and help in the development of the country's tourist industry. Under the terms of the final accord, French and Moroccan investors were guaranteed equal treatment in both countries. France agreed to offer further financial aid in May, following a visit by King Hassan to Paris. The Caisse Française de Développement was to underwrite government bonds issued on the international market to the value of 1,500m. francs, and France would provide 1,200m. francs in aid over the next two years to support the Government's campaign against drugs smuggling. France's aid budget to Morocco is currently 1,500m. francs a year. Although the underwriting agreement was welcomed, it was unlikely to have a significant impact on the country's overall foreign debt. During the visit of the then Spanish Prime Minister, Felipe González, in February 1996, the disbursement of a 150,000m. peseta ($1,198m.) credit package for the period to 2000 was discussed together with options for easing the terms of Morocco's $1,400m. debt to Spain. In October Spain agreed to convert

$50m. of bilateral debt into investments in a similar deal to that concluded with France. In October 1997 France agreed to convert a further 1,400m. francs ($245m.) of bilateral debt into investments along the lines of the initiative concluded in January 1996 (see above). Morocco's total bilateral debt to France was estimated at $4,000m. At the same time, Spain offered to convert a further $38m. of its bilateral debt into local investment. In March Italy offered to convert $75m. of debt into local investment, and it was reported that similar debt-conversion deals were being discussed with Germany, Austria and the United Kingdom. In December 1997 Morocco returned to international capital markets for the first time since 1981 when Commerzbank of Germany and Sumitomo Bank Ltd of Japan started arranging a five-year loan of $200m. The Euroloan was fully subscribed when it closed in February 1998. There was speculation that Morocco would seek to raise up to $400m. with a debut Eurobond issue later in 1998. In March Moody's Investors Service and Standard Poor's awarded Morocco its first international credit ratings.

Servicing the foreign debt remained a serious burden, with debt-service payments accounting for 31.8% of export income in 1996 and 25.4% in 1997 according to World Bank figures. After the appointment of a new opposition-led Government in March 1998, the Minister of the Economy and Finance, Fathallah Oualalou, stated that the Government would go to the capital markets to refinance its most expensive debt. Morocco's total external debt stood at $21,767m. at the end of 1996, of which $20,774m. was long-term public debt. In July 1997 the Government admitted that domestic debt was escalating and had reached 110,000m. dirhams, or 34% of GDP. It was hoped that the ratio would be reduced to 25% of GDP. In early 1998 figures released by the World Bank put domestic debt at 39.1% of GDP in 1997.

In December 1995 it was reported that the ADB had agreed a loan of $225m., repayable over 12 years with a five-year grace period to support financial reforms in 1995–96. The loan agreement required the creation of a foreign exchange market, the establishment of an indirect system of currency controls, and the further development of commercial financing instruments. In January 1996 a committee comprising members of the Bank Al-Maghrib, the Ministry of Finance and commercial banks announced a number of reforms. Interest rates were freed to encourage competition between banks and to make it easier for companies to secure loans, bank reserve requirements were reduced by 5% to 15% of sight deposits and the proportion of a bank's equity that can be lent to a single client was increased from 7% to 10%. In April the Bank Al-Maghrib informed local banks that it would cease currency fixing on 2 May and allow banks to trade in foreign currencies from that date. However, local banks were reported to have requested a delay in the start of a domestic foreign exchange market as they needed time to obtain clarification on guidelines for certain types of transactions.

Morocco's central bank, the Bank Al-Maghrib, is the sole issuer of currency, holds and administers the State's foreign currency reserves, controls the commercial banking sector and advises the Government on its financial policies. Associated with the bank are six specialized credit institutions with specific sectoral responsibilities. There are 15 commercial banks, of which one of the most important is the Banque Marocaine du Commerce Extérieur SA (BMCE). In 1989 a new development bank, the Bank al-Amal, was established; three-quarters of its capital was to be made available in shares to Moroccans working abroad to encourage more investment from the expatriate community. The Banque Centrale Populaire (BCP, also known as Crédit Populaire du Maroc), which has specialized in handling the remittances of migrant workers for many years, was to be joined by the major Moroccan private bank, the Banque Commerciale du Maroc (BCM), which in 1989 acquired 10% of the capital of the Banque Méditerranéenne de Dépôts (BMD) in order to attract the savings of the 27,000 Moroccan workers in France who use the BMD. Several other Moroccan banks have heeded an appeal from the Minister of Finance and are extending their international activities. In February 1992 it was reported that the IFC had arranged a $110m. credit line for four commercial banks (BCM, BMCE, Crédit du Maroc and Wafabank), the major source of term finance for the private sector. The credit lines were to be used to make five 10-year loans to small and medium-sized private-sector firms. In December the Government approved a banking law, which increased the scope for regulation in domestic banking. All local credit institutions were brought under the legislation, which also gave greater protection for savers and borrowers. In addition, the law codified rules governing business banks and other credit institutions previously excluded from legislation. In the same month it was announced that Wafabank, one of Morocco's leading privately-owned banks, was increasing its capital through the issue of shares on the Casablanca stock exchange. Other banks have been seeking foreign shareholders and increasing their capital to meet the growing demand for local banking services as the economy develops. In June 1993 the Banco Exterior de España became the first wholly-owned foreign company authorized to open a subsidiary in Morocco since the country won its independence. The BMCE took a small stake in the Banco Exterior de España and opened a branch in Madrid under a reciprocal arrangement. The long-established Citibank Maghreb offers retail banking services and has the same status as a local bank. Nevertheless the Central Bank has proved cautious in licencing foreign institutions. In August 1993 it was reported that the Banco Central Hispano-Americano of Spain was to purchase a 15% interest in Morocco's largest bank, the BCM, subject to the approval of the Moroccan and Spanish monetary authorities, in an agreement valued at $48.8m. In October 1994 the Minister of Privatization announced the sale of most of the state's 50.4% holding in the BMCE. Some 14% of the bank's shares were offered for sale on the Casablanca stock exchange in January 1995 and another 26% were offered for sale by international tender in April, one-half restricted to local non-bank institutions and the remainder was open to all bidders. The sale of 26% of BMCE shares raised $144m., 42% more than the Government's minimum price. The new shareholders included the Royale Marocaine d'Assurances, London-based Morgan Grenfell and Co, and Morgan Stanley of the USA. The last publicly-owned shares in the BMCE were sold to the private sector in May 1997.

In March 1996 the BMCE issued a global depository receipt (GDR) to boost share capital. The issue was more than four times oversubscribed and raised $52m.; 48% of the issue was placed in Europe, 30% in the USA and 22% in Asia. It represented the first international equity issue from Morocco and North Africa and the largest GDR transaction in the Arab world. Although small on an international scale, it was significant in Morocco where total foreign investment was estimated at $200m. Financial analysts argued that demand was high because investors were attracted by the progress made by the bank since its privatization. The funds raised by the offer will be used to expand the bank's lending activities in Morocco. In 1995 the BMCE registered assets of 33,957m. dirhams and net profits increased by 19.2% to 301m. dirhams in that year. In March 1998 BMCE established its own merchant bank, capitalized at $10.2m. The Government confirmed that it would privatize the BCP and the BNDE before 1999. BNDE was put on the market in May 1998 when the Government announced the sale of most of the state's 34.2% holding in the bank.

The Government launched the first issue of its new privatization bond in January 1996. The issue originally had been planned by the Ministry of Privatization for November 1995, but was delayed when the Ministry of Finance claimed jurisdiction on the grounds that it would constitute sovereign debt. The bonds may be exchanged for shares in any of the companies to be privatized on the stock exchange in the next three years, and to make the bonds attractive to the public, holders are given priority access to shares in newly privatized companies. Individual investors were offered the majority of the bonds, while companies, especially investment funds, were offered the remainder. The issue was handled by the BCM and Wafabank. Some 1,700m. dirhams ($200m.) was raised through the sale of the first issue which was oversubscribed by 25%. The first test of the new bond came in March 1996 when the Government offered for sale on the stock exchange 25% of its stake in SAMIR. The offer was fully subscribed with about three-quarters of the buyers using privatization bonds. A second tranche of privatization bonds was issued in May under the same terms and conditions as the first tranche in January, although this time one-

half of the bonds were reserved for institutional investment. Preliminary results indicated that demand for the second issue was lower than the first. The Ministry of Privatization had hoped to raise 1,000m. dirhams from the second issue.

By 1992 the volume of transactions on the Casablanca stock exchange had risen to 1,520m. dirhams, but this increased more than threefold in 1993 (to 4,870m. dirhams) as a result of the privatization of state companies, including CTM-LN and Cior. In July 1993 it was reported that a number of decrees had been approved to convert the Casablanca exchange into a private company with stock held by brokers, to create new stock-trading bodies, to channel small savers' funds into share issues and unit trusts, and to create a stock exchange commission. A major boost to stock exchange activity in 1994 was the issue of shares worth 1,500m. dirhams in Morocco's leading private company, ONA. Local companies have turned increasingly to the stock market to raise capital through local share offers. In January 1995 the General Tire and Rubber Co raised its capital by 20% in a stock market offering, becoming the first newly-privatized company to do so. In November 1994 the bourse Director forecast a turnover of 9,000m. dirhams in 1994, almost double the figure for 1993. In new moves to modernize the exchange, the Government announced in November 1994 that it had authorized the operations of the country's first stockbrokers. An agreement signed in February 1995 provided for the Société Française des Bourses and Société Interprofessionelle de Compensation des Valeurs Mobilières to conduct a $1.2m. study on the modernization and computerization of the stock exchange and establish a central depositary and clearing house. The stock market crises affecting several Asian countries during the second half of 1997 had little impact on the Casablanca stock exchange because only some 5% of transactions involved foreign investors. In mid-1997 the Société Marocaine de Dépôt et Crédit and the Crédit Immobilier et Hôtelier both issued bonds on the exchange. At the end of 1997 the exchange began a campaign to attract new listings, especially from small and medium-sized firms, and aimed to increase the number of companies listed from the current 49 to 100.

In August 1991 Tangier became the kingdom's first 'offshore' banking zone. It is intended to attract major international banks, and their local operations must have a minimum capital of $500,000. Banks are offered exemption from corporation tax for 15 years, and during this period they pay a $25,000 annual licence fee. The zone is intended to compete with other Mediterranean 'offshore' zones to attract capital into the kingdom. In April 1992 Crédit Lyonnais of France became the first bank to announce its participation in the zone followed by the Banque Nationale de Paris, both with local partners. In January 1995 Attijari International, a joint venture between the local BCM and Spain's BCH capitalized at $3m., became the third bank to open in the zone. In mid-1994 it was reported that the new Euratlas Capital Development Fund, and a new investment bank, the Maghreb International Bank, would also be based in the Tangier zone.

DEVELOPMENT

The 1978 Five-Year Development Plan never came into effect, largely because of the disruption caused to the economy by the war in Western Sahara and the fall in phosphate revenues after 1975. Instead, a three-year transitional plan, which was to emphasize agriculture and industry, and attempt to reduce public expenditure, was introduced as part of the austerity measures adopted by the Government. The target for annual GDP growth was set at a modest 4.6%. Only 3% annual growth was, however, achieved in 1978 and 1979. In April 1981 a new Five-Year Development Plan came into operation, whose general aims were similar to that of its predecessor, but which envisaged a more rapid rate of GDP growth, at 6.5% a year. The level of investment was over-ambitious and, following the decision to reschedule the country's external debt in 1983, many of the Plan's targets were abandoned. The Government was obliged to make severe reductions in public expenditure in order to satisfy the terms of the IMF programme. Not only were the 1983 budget commitments for capital expenditure cut by more than 20%, but even the revised targets for 1984 were reduced further. All major projects were postponed, except those already under way and likely to enhance export earnings or import savings.

The proposed 1986–88 Three-Year Plan, announced in April 1985, suggested further cuts in expenditure. Investment was to be reduced from the 1984 level of 20% of GDP to only 16.7%, while it was projected that GDP would rise by 2.9% per year. However, in late 1985 it was announced that this transitional plan was to be delayed, and a new set of proposals for a more expansionary programme was produced. These plans, however, were also deferred, largely as a result of IMF pressure, and a policy of bringing government spending more closely into balance with revenues was eventually pursued. Measures geared mainly towards tighter spending controls and the gradual reform of the fiscal system helped to reduce the treasury deficit in 1986. In October 1987 a new Five-Year Plan for 1988–92 was presented, in which 52% of funding was expected to come from the private sector. A large proportion of the investment funds was to be directed towards the newly-formed local authorities (collectivités locales), which were allocated 36,000m. dirhams. The Plan was expected to transform the current account deficit into a surplus, equivalent to 2.9% of GDP by 1992, and to enable exports to increase by 5.5% per annum. It also aimed to mobilize domestic savings for investment at a rate of 16.6% of GDP per year and to create jobs for the estimated 300,000 people entering the labour market every year. The Plan also included a reform of the public sector, envisaging the privatization of many state companies. Appropriate legislation for a privatization programme was approved by the Chamber of Representatives in April 1988 and came into force from January 1990. The six-year privatization programme was subsequently extended beyond 1995.

The 1989 budget aimed to reduce further the budget deficit, mainly by increasing tax revenue, and to limit the increase in overall state expenditure to around 7%. In the event, however, revenues failed to increase as expected, and the budget deficit was greater than had been anticipated. The treasury deficit in 1989 was equivalent to 5.7% of GDP, rather than the projected 4.4%. The 1990 budget, which had been endorsed by the Chamber of Representatives at the end of 1989, was radically revised during early 1990, while a variety of austerity measures were implemented, including a devaluation of the dirham in an attempt to improve the balance-of-payments deficit.

In accordance with the anticipated results of the 1988–92 Five-Year Plan, the main economic objectives for 1991 were to increase the rate of GDP growth to 4%–4.5%, a reduction in the annual rate of inflation to 5% (from a rate of 7%–8% in 1990) and a reduction of the budget deficit to 2% of GDP. The rise in investment in 1990 produced a more optimistic outlook for 1991. In early 1991 the Government announced that domestic savings would be encouraged, that investment would be made more efficient and that foreign trade and the public and financial sectors would be reformed, in an attempt to realize the year's economic objectives. The budget proposals for 1992 envisaged a substantial rise in social spending. Education was allocated 1,600m. dirhams (an increase of 21%), and health 552m. dirhams (an increase of more than 25%). Defence spending was to rise by 13.6%, to 10,000m. dirhams. Total spending was projected at 86,440m. dirhams, 5.5% higher than for 1991, and the deficit was to remain stable, at 1,450m. dirhams. To increase revenues, it was forecast that direct taxation would rise by 23.8%, and indirect taxes by 15.3%.

The budget proposals for 1993 envisaged a 6% increase in GDP. Overall revenue was expected to rise to 77,220m. dirhams, despite reductions in taxation. Expenditure was forecast at 80,000m. dirhams. Priority was to be given to education, public health, employment, irrigation and electric power generation. A reduction of the budget deficit was forecast, to 1% in 1993, compared with 2% in 1992 and 3% in 1991. Inflation was regarded as stable at 5.7% and foreign reserves had risen. Public investment was to increase by 11%. Debts totalling 2,700m. dirhams owed by farmers were to be rescheduled, and the Government was to pay off public-sector arrears worth 2,603m. dirhams to ease cash-flow problems besetting local suppliers. Some 800m. dirhams was allocated to increase youth employment, and more than 15,000 jobs were to be created in public administration. Under the 1994 budget proposals, expenditure was projected to increase to 110,553m. dirhams. Of recurrent expenditure of 47,111m. dirhams, 12,900m. dirhams were allo-

cated to education, and 9,400m. dirhams to defence. Revenues were projected at 105,352m. dirhams, including 23,719m. dirhams from indirect taxes, 17,098m. dirhams from direct taxes and 18,002m. dirhams from customs duties. The increase in recurrent expenditure was to be financed by an estimated 16% increase in tax revenues. The total projected deficit was 5,202m. dirhams. The Minister of Finance reported that debt-reservicing costs would increase by 17.3% in 1994, to 27,168m. dirhams. There was speculation that the Government's commitment to keep the budget deficit to 1.5% of GDP would be difficult to achieve because of pressure on state spending to maintain social stability. Under the 1995 budget, announced in December 1994, state spending was to be cut in most sectors in order to bring the budget deficit under control, a major priority for the Government. The Minister of Finance, Mourad Cherif, announced that the 1995 deficit would be around 7,000m. dirhams ($781m.) and insisted that recourse to bank lending had to remain at reasonable levels. Official figures forecast revenues of 88,900m. dirhams in 1995 and expenditure of 91,471m. dirhams. Current spending was forecast to rise only slightly in an attempt to halt inflationary pressures in the public sector. The figure given for inflation was 4%, but other official sources put it at 5.1% in 1994. Investment spending was cut from 19,147m. dirhams in 1994 to 16,624m. dirhams in 1995. Receipts from the privatization programme, estimated at 3,500m. dirhams ($391m.) in 1995 were to be allocated to financing the investment budget and special provisions. Foreign investment was expected to reach $700m. in 1995, which, it was hoped would help cover the current account deficit. Cherif told the Chamber of Representatives that in order to reduce state spending, private sector involvement in infrastructure development would be extended to sectors such as telecommunications and communications. The budget also included incentives for stock market investment with a reduction of the tax on share earnings from 15% to 10%. While the budget was welcomed by the business community it was critized by the opposition because it offered little help to the majority of the population. In late 1995 the Government approved a mini-budget for January–June 1996 to bridge the gap between December 1995 and the start of the new financial year in July 1996. Expenditure was projected at 47,900m. dirhams, of which the major item was debt-servicing and repayment, forecast at 13,700m. dirhams. Revenue was projected at 43,400m. dirhams, of which 13.2m. dirhams would be provided by indirect taxes and 5,800m. dirhams from customs duties. Value-added tax was to be raised to 20% to compensate for an anticipated fall in income and corporate tax. Revenue from customs duties was also projected to decline as the Government began to comply with the GATT. The projected deficit was 4,500m. dirhams and was expected to be somewhat lower than the actual figure for the same period in 1995, which was higher than planned owing to the severe drought. In June 1996 the Chamber of Representatives approved the budget for July 1996–June 1997. Expenditure was forecast at 117,180.3m. dirhams, while revenue was expected to total 107,744.1m. dirhams, giving a deficit of 9,436.2m. dirhams. The draft budget for 1997/98, presented to the Chamber of Representatives in May 1997, envisaged expenditure of 126,700m. dirhams, with revenue forecast at 114,300m. dirhams, leading to a 32% increase in the fiscal deficit. In February 1998 the Government was more optimistic about the budget deficit for 1997, forecasting that if the agricultural harvest was good the overall deficit would not exceed 3.5% of GDP. Nevertheless, in a report published in March, the IMF urged the Government to cut current spending and reduce the budget deficit. The IMF stated that the projected widening of the budget deficit in 1997/98, mainly as a result of public-setor pay increases granted in 1996, was not consistent with the need for stronger fiscal consolidation. It encouraged the Government to reduce the size of the civil service and replace food subsidies with better targeted assistance. Fathallah Oualalou, the recently-appointed Minister of the Economy and Finance, stated that he aimed to eliminate the budget deficit early next century and that the first loser would be the consumer. In April Prime Minister Youssoufi announced that public-sector spending would be cut in order to reduce the budget deficit.

Statistical Survey

Source (unless otherwise stated): Direction de la Statistique, BP 178, Rabat 10001; tel. (7) 773606; telex 32714; fax (7) 773042.

Note: Unless otherwise indicated, the data exclude Western (formerly Spanish) Sahara, a disputed territory under Moroccan occupation.

Area and Population

AREA, POPULATION AND DENSITY

Area (sq km) .	710,850*
Population (census results)†	
3 September 1982	
Males .	10,205,859
Females .	10,182,358
Total .	20,388,217
2 September 1994	26,073,717
Density (per sq km) at 1994 census .	36.7

* 274,461 sq miles. This area includes the disputed territory of Western Sahara, which covers 252,120 sq km (97,344 sq miles).
† Including Western Sahara, with a population of 163,868 (provisional) at the 1982 census and 252,146 at the 1994 census.

REGIONS (population at 1994 census)

	Area (sq km)	Population	Density (per sq km)
Sud* .	394,970	3,234,024	8.2
Tensift .	38,445	3,546,768	92.3
Centre .	41,500	6,931,418	167.0
Nord-Ouest .	29,955	5,646,716	188.5
Centre-Nord .	43,950	3,042,310	69.2
Oriental .	82,820	1,768,691	21.4
Centre-Sud .	79,210	1,903,790	24.0
Total .	710,850	26,073,717	36.7

* Including the prefectures of Boujdour, el-Aaiún, es-Smara and Oued ed-Dahab, which comprise the disputed territory of Western Sahara (area 252,120 sq km; population 252,146).

PRINCIPAL TOWNS (population at 1994 census)

Casablanca .	2,940,623	Meknès .	530,171
Rabat (capital)*	1,385,872	Tanger (Tangier) .	526,215
Fès (Fez) .	774,754	Kénitra .	448,785
Marrakech		Beni-Mellal .	386,505
(Marrakesh) .	745,541	Safi .	376,038
Oujda .	678,778	Tétouan .	367,349
Agadir .	550,200	Khouribga .	294,680

* Including Salé.

BIRTHS AND DEATHS (UN estimates, annual averages)

	1980–85	1985–90	1990–95
Birth rate (per 1,000) .	35.2	31.7	29.1
Death rate (per 1,000) .	11.2	9.5	8.1

Source: UN, *World Population Prospects: The 1994 Revision*.

Expectation of life (estimates, years at birth, 1997): 68.8 (males 67.1; females 70.7).

ECONOMICALLY ACTIVE POPULATION (1994 census)*

	Males	Females	Total
Agriculture, hunting, forestry and fishing .	2,341,887	461,469	2,803,356
Mining and quarrying .	51,207	2,424	53,631
Manufacturing .	661,449	363,398	1,024,847
Electricity, gas and water .	40,703	3,535	44,238
Construction .	497,627	9,999	507,626
Trade, restaurants and hotels .	923,948	65,650	989,598
Transport, storage and communications .	199,374	11,110	210,484
Financing, insurance, real estate and business services .	256,540	205,131	461,671
Community, social and personal services .	671,145	223,210	894,355
Activities not adequately defined .	8,989	1,616	10,605
Total .	5,652,869	1,347,542	7,000,411

* Figures are based on a 1% sample tabulation of census returns. The data relate to employed persons aged 7 years and over and unemployed persons (excluding those seeking work for the first time) aged 15 years and over.

Mid-1996 (estimates in '000): Agriculture, etc. 4,225; Total labour force 10,564 (Source: FAO, *Production Yearbook*).

Agriculture

PRINCIPAL CROPS ('000 metric tons)

	1994	1995	1996
Wheat .	5,523	1,091	5,916
Rice (paddy) .	70	3	53
Barley* .	3,720	608	3,831
Maize .	203	50	235
Oats .	85	10	28
Sorghum .	14	3	10
Other cereals .	26	27	27
Potatoes .	1,038	774	1,125
Sweet potatoes .	12	9	9
Dry broad beans .	111	36	100*
Dry peas .	29	4	28
Chick-peas .	47	12	29
Lentils .	36	8	9†
Other pulses .	62	58	65
Soybeans (Soya beans) .	4	4†	2
Groundnuts (in shell) .	30	14	17
Sunflower seed .	61	11	95
Cottonseed .	2*	1*	2
Olives .	500	436	800
Artichokes .	34	34*	34*
Tomatoes .	850	624	935
Cauliflowers .	16	16*	16*
Pumpkins, squash and gourds .	201	201*	200*
Cucumbers and gherkins .	26	26*	26*
Aubergines (Eggplants) .	26	26	26*
Green chillies and peppers .	93*	94	94*
Onions (dry) .	367	406	360
Green beans .	13	13*	13*
Green peas .	61	62*	62*
Carrots .	166	224	300
Other vegetables .	506	515	514
Watermelons .	226	226†	230*
Melons .	415	415†	415*
Grapes .	282	174	270
Dates .	62	98	81
Sugar cane .	903	1,031	899
Sugar beets .	3,144	2,717	2,717
Apples .	270	310	360
Pears .	29	26	35*
Peaches and nectarines .	36	30	35*
Plums .	57	33	40*
Oranges .	939	673	972

— continued	1994	1995	1996
Tangerines, mandarins, clementines and satsumas . .	343	276	403
Lemons and limes . . .	20†	12	20
Apricots	88	88*	90*
Bananas	100	90	88
Other fruits and berries . .	178	165	174
Almonds	31	46	50*
Tobacco (leaves) . . .	4†	4†	6
Cotton (lint)	1†	n.a.	1

* FAO estimate(s).   † Unofficial figure.

Source: FAO, *Production Yearbook*.

LIVESTOCK ('000 head, year ending September)

	1994	1995	1996
Cattle	2,343	2,490	2,420
Sheep	13,309	16,586	16,267
Goats	3,973	4,424	4,658
Camels*	37	40	37
Horses	165	162	162*
Mules	527	540	540*
Asses	916	954	954*

* FAO estimate(s).

Poultry (FAO estimates, million): 82 in 1994; 90 in 1995; 115 in 1996.

Source: FAO, *Production Yearbook*.

LIVESTOCK PRODUCTS ('000 metric tons)

	1994	1995	1996
Beef and veal	125	122	105
Mutton and lamb . . .	105	112	80
Goat meat	20	20	20
Poultry meat	160	180	230
Other meat	38	39	39
Cows' milk	845	855	850
Sheep's milk* . . .	27	27	27
Goats' milk*	34	34	34
Butter*	13	14	14
Cheese*	7	7	7
Poultry eggs* . . .	190	195	195
Honey	3	2	4
Wool (greasy)* . . .	36	36	36
Wool (clean)* . . .	17	17	17
Cattle hides (fresh)* . .	21	21	21
Sheepskins (fresh)* . .	12	12	21
Goatskins (fresh)* . . .	3	3	3

* FAO estimates.

Source: FAO, *Production Yearbook*.

Forestry

ROUNDWOOD REMOVALS ('000 cubic metres, excluding bark)

	1994	1995	1996
Sawlogs, veneer logs and logs for sleepers	225	247	288
Pulpwood	521	339	337
Other industrial wood . .	299	304	316
Fuel wood	1,416	1,520	1,484
Total	2,460	2,410	2,425

Source: FAO, *Yearbook of Forest Products*.

SAWNWOOD PRODUCTION
('000 cubic metres, including railway sleepers)

	1987	1988	1989
Coniferous (softwood) . . .	40	26	43
Broadleaved (hardwood) . . .	40	27	40
Total	80	53	83

1990–96: Annual production as in 1989.

Source: FAO, *Yearbook of Forest Products*.

Fishing

('000 metric tons, live weight)

	1993	1994	1995
Jack and horse mackerels . .	28.8	28.8	30.5
European pilchard (sardine) . .	382.2	492.3	570.9
Chub mackerel	18.3	39.2	30.1
Other fishes (incl. unspecified) .	95.0	99.7	115.1
Total fish	524.3	660.0	746.6
Crustaceans	6.5	8.6	9.2
Cuttlefishes and bobtail squids .	9.3	14.3	12.4
Octopuses	63.9	56.3	57.8
Other molluscs	18.8	12.8	20.1
Total catch	622.8	752.0	846.2
Inland waters	1.8	1.9	2.2
Atlantic Ocean	590.9	717.2	805.8
Mediterranean Sea . . .	30.2	32.9	38.2

Source: FAO, *Yearbook of Fishery Statistics*.

Mining

('000 metric tons)

	1994	1995	1996
Hard coal	650.4	649.6	505.6*
Crude petroleum	7.9	4.8	4.7*
Iron ore†	65.2	47.2	11.8*
Copper concentrates† . . .	36.0	35.8	37.6*
Lead concentrates† . . .	104.5	101.6	107.5
Manganese ore† . . .	31.5	31.3	29.5*
Zinc concentrates† . . .	150.2	153.1	152.4*
Phosphate rock	20,335.0	20,314.0	20,792
Fluorspar (acid grade) . . .	85.0	106.5	96
Barytes	229.6	289.5	282.5*
Salt (unrefined)	176.4	173.0	165.3*
Clay	8.9	15.0	17.2*

* Preliminary figure.
† Figures refer to the gross weight of ores and concentrates. The estimated metal content (in '000 metric tons) was: Iron 38 in 1994, 24 in 1995; Copper 10.0 in 1994, 8.3 in 1995; Lead 72.1 in 1994, 70.1 in 1995; Manganese 15.7 in 1994; Zinc 78.1 in 1994, 79.5 in 1995 (Source: UN, *Industrial Commodity Statistics Yearbook*).

Industry

SELECTED PRODUCTS*
('000 metric tons, unless otherwise indicated)

	1993	1994	1995
Cement	6,175	6,284	6,391
Electric energy (million kWh)	9,903	11,100	11,724†
Passenger motor cars ('000)‡	72	n.a.	n.a.
Phosphate fertilizers§	434	461	530
Carpets and rugs ('000 sq m)	900	780	754
Wine ('000 hl)‖	400	240	280
Olive oil (crude)	38	40	45
Motor spirit—petrol	397	409	365
Naphthas	449	359	417
Kerosene	43	43	49
Distillate fuel oils	1,919	2,167	2,019
Residual fuel oils	2,459	2,540	2,330
Jet fuel	223	238	239
Petroleum bitumen—asphalt	101	136	137
Liquefied petroleum gas	247	263	235

* Major industrial establishments only.
† Preliminary figure.
‡ Assembly only.
§ Estimated production in terms of phosphoric acid.
‖ Source: FAO, *Production Yearbook*.

Source: partly UN, *Industrial Commodity Statistics Yearbook*.

Finance

CURRENCY AND EXCHANGE RATES

Monetary Units
100 centimes (santimat) = 1 Moroccan dirham.

Sterling and Dollar Equivalents (31 May 1998)
£1 sterling = 15.846 dirhams;
US $1 = 9.717 dirhams;
1,000 Moroccan dirhams = £63.11 = $102.91.

Average Exchange Rate (dirhams per US $)
1995   8.540
1996   8.716
1997   9.527

GENERAL BUDGET (million dirhams)*

Revenue	1995	1996†	1996/97‡
Tax revenue	60,885	33,236	67,903
Taxes on income and profits	15,927	10,480	20,075
Corporate profit tax	5,148	3,972	7,316
Individual income tax	7,706	4,450	8,959
Taxes on international trade	11,843	5,781	11,956
Import duties and taxes	11,811	5,762	11,931
Domestic taxes on goods and services	30,299	15,004	32,394
Value-added tax	15,821	8,609	18,105
Excises	14,243	6,395	14,289
Tobacco products	4,546	2,293	4,473
Petroleum products	8,656	3,653	8,835
Registration and stamp taxes	2,816	1,971	3,478
Non-tax revenue	6,577	5,331	11,844
Entrepreneurial income	3,660	1,494	3,490
Receipts from privatization	1,241	1,607	4,558
Total	**67,462**	**38,567**	**79,747**

Expenditure	1995§	1996†	1997‡
General public services	6,967	1,914	3,509
Defence	13,245	6,190	12,823
Public order and safety	6,958	3,249	6,858
Education	15,542	7,962	16,013
Health	3,001	1,450	2,898
Social security and welfare	353	204	435
Housing	341	133	284
Recreational, cultural and religious affairs and services	852	331	604
Economic affairs and services	8,699	4,629	9,728
Agriculture	3,283	1,600	3,320
Mines and energy	645	221	444
Transport and communications	3,936	537	1,091
Other current expenditure	21,623	15,106	32,906
Capital transfers to local authorities	4,800	n.a.	n.a.
Total	**82,381**	**41,168**	**86,058**
Current	62,335	32,761	67,699
Capital	20,046	8,407	18,359

* Figures refer to the budgetary operations of the central Government. The accounts of the National Social Security Fund are excluded.
† Figures refer to the transitional fiscal year January–June 1996.
‡ Figures refer to the fiscal year ending in June 1997.
§ Figures for capital expenditure are provisional. The revised totals for 1995 (in million dirhams) are: 82,015 (capital 19,680).

Source: IMF, *Morocco: Statistical Appendix* (April 1998).

INTERNATIONAL RESERVES (US $ million at 31 December)

	1995	1996	1997
Gold*	230	222	201
IMF special drawing rights	26	7	1
Reserve position in IMF	45	44	40
Foreign exchange	3,530	3,743	3,951
Total	**3,831**	**4,016**	**4,193**

* National valuation of gold reserves (704,000 troy ounces in each year).
Source: Bank Al-Maghrib.

MONEY SUPPLY (million dirhams at 31 December)

	1995	1996	1997
Currency outside banks	43,261	46,581	48,792
Private sector deposits at Bank of Morocco	1,308	1,882	2,126
Demand deposits at deposit money banks	84,606	87,323	95,313
Checking deposits at post office	1,701	1,721	1,871
Private sector checking deposits at treasury	5,088	6,311	6,435
Total money	**135,964**	**143,818**	**154,537**

Source: Bank Al-Maghrib.

COST OF LIVING (Consumer Price Index; base: 1990 = 100)

	1995	1996	1997
Food	142.5	143.5	141.9
Fuel and light	129.5	142.4	142.8
Clothing	130.8	135.2	140.3
Rent	135.3	143.7	147.8
All items (incl. others)	134.0	138.0	139.4

NATIONAL ACCOUNTS (million dirhams at current prices)
Expenditure on the Gross Domestic Product

	1994	1995	1996
Government final consumption expenditure	47,853	48,336	52,591
Private final consumption expenditure	197,170	200,758	226,511
Increase in stocks	1,722	−2,397	1,255
Gross fixed capital formation . .	57,900	62,899	64,744
Total domestic expenditure .	304,645	309,597	345,101
Exports of goods and services . .	58,197	65,796	68,867
Less Imports of goods and services	83,518	94,185	93,049
GDP in purchasers' values . .	279,323	281,207	320,919
GDP at constant 1980 prices .	121,170	112,738	126,228

Source: IMF, *Morocco: Statistical Appendix* (April 1998).

Gross Domestic Product by Economic Activity

	1994	1995	1996*
Agriculture, hunting, forestry and fishing	51,579	41,545	65,478
Energy and water . . .	21,305	23,845	24,568
Other mining and quarrying . .	5,151	5,057	5,539
Other manufacturing. . . .	47,586	51,681	54,384
Construction.	12,061	12,433	13,515
Wholesale and retail trade . .	32,168	31,707	35,755
Transport and communications .	16,631	17,509	18,153
Government services . . .	34,136	36,740	39,350
Other services	35,421	37,296	39,725
GDP at factor cost . . .	256,217	257,812	296,468
Indirect taxes, *less* subsidies . .	23,106	23,395	24,452
GDP in purchasers' values . .	279,323	281,207	320,920

* Figures are provisional.

BALANCE OF PAYMENTS (US $ million)

	1994	1995	1996
Exports of goods f.o.b. . . .	5,541	6,871	6,886
Imports of goods f.o.b. . . .	−7,648	−9,268	−8,997
Trade balance	−2,107	−2,397	−2,111
Exports of services . . .	2,014	1,996	2,360
Imports of services . . .	−1,730	−2,063	−1,984
Balance on goods and services.	−1,822	−2,464	−1,734
Other income received . . .	224	251	189
Other income paid . . .	−1,394	−1,569	−1,498
Balance on goods, services and income	−2,992	−3,782	−3,043
Current transfers received . .	2,355	2,339	2,498
Current transfers paid . . .	−86	−78	−82
Current balance	−723	−1,521	−627
Capital account (net). . . .	−3	−6	73
Direct investment abroad. . .	−24	−12	−27
Direct investment from abroad .	551	290	311
Portfolio investment liabilities .	238	20	142
Other investment assets . .	344	216	238
Other investment liabilities .	139	−378	−483
Net errors and omissions . . .	−39	615	568
Overall balance	483	−776	194

Source: IMF, *International Financial Statistics*.

External Trade

PRINCIPAL COMMODITIES (million dirhams)

Imports c.i.f.	1994	1995	1996
Foodstuffs, beverages and tobacco	7,348	11,630	11,223
Wheat	1,491	3,997	4,137
Energy and lubricants . .	10,239	10,053	11,199
Crude petroleum . . .	6,902	6,721	7,397
Raw products	7,497	9,067	7,745
Vegetable oil and oilseeds . .	1,899	2,080	2,030
Timber	1,734	1,964	n.a.
Textile fibres and cotton . .	1,428	1,587	1,350
Sulphur	1,126	1,585	1,234
Semi-finished products . .	16,671	17,882	16,840
Chemicals, fertilizers, dyes and disinfectants . . .	4,302	4,534	n.a.
Artificial plastic materials . .	1,961	2,297	2,132
Iron and steel	1,166	1,784	n.a.
Capital goods	16,990	16,257	15,375
Industrial equipment . .	16,158	15,742	14,419
Consumer goods	7,275	7,980	9,581
Cotton yarn and fabrics . .	1,347	1,496	n.a.
Total (incl. others)	66,028	72,869	71,963

Exports f.o.b.	1994	1995	1996
Foodstuffs, beverages and tobacco	10,352	12,393	13,079
Citrus fruit	1,383	1,716	2,700
Vegetables	1,008	1,421	1,275
Canned fish	1,440	1,542	1,535
Fresh fish	742	763	811
Crustaceans and molluscs . .	3,521	4,310	4,110
Canned fruit and vegetables .	977	1,308	1,346
Energy and lubricants . .	770	886	673
Raw animal and vegetable products	1,429	1,631	1,572
Raw mineral products . .	4,005	4,014	4,551
Phosphates	2,515	2,426	3,030
Semi-finished products . .	9,105	10,472	10,630
Phosphoric acid . . .	3,937	4,699	4,598
Natural and chemical fertilizers	2,489	3,076	3,321
Capital goods	1,296	1,312	1,334
Consumer goods	9,595	9,532	9,517
Clothing	3,804	3,640	3,412
Hosiery	2,708	2,856	3,046
Total (incl. others)	36,552	40,240	41,356

PRINCIPAL TRADING PARTNERS (US $ million)*

Imports c.i.f.	1993	1994	1995
Algeria	107.9	119.3	111.4
Argentina	50.4	74.5	44.3
Belgium-Luxembourg . .	154.3	166.0	238.6
Brazil	143.6	150.6	241.9
Canada	102.6	63.3	162.9
China, People's Republic . .	125.7	123.6	166.6
France	1,528.8	1,626.8	1,868.0
Gabon	24.4	85.4	53.4
Germany	395.3	506.7	535.6
Iran	166.9	195.2	208.0
Italy	417.9	485.7	489.9
Japan	114.1	122.4	124.4
Kuwait	80.4	16.0	10.3
Libya	17.3	82.6	55.7
Netherlands	145.6	156.2	207.4
Poland	69.1	85.8	134.6
Russia	83.3	110.1	285.2
Saudi Arabia	373.8	385.0	449.6
Spain	699.3	631.4	729.4
Sweden	119.2	126.1	175.8
Switzerland	75.0	89.2	93.0
United Arab Emirates . .	110.9	86.5	17.3
United Kingdom . . .	180.7	202.1	311.9
USA	672.3	620.4	559.9
Total (incl. others) . . .	6,658.8	7,193.7	8,551.5

Exports f.o.b.		1993	1994	1995
Algeria	. . . .	77.8	96.6	56.1
Belgium-Luxembourg	. . .	110.3	135.3	146.9
France	. . . . .	1,227.5	1,279.2	1,402.9
Germany	. . . .	163.4	172.6	194.3
India	. . . . .	143.6	258.2	310.2
Iran	. . . . .	54.0	49.5	22.6
Italy	. . . . .	193.2	231.1	269.2
Japan	. . . .	217.3	268.1	362.5
Liberia	. . . .	41.8	0.2	0.1
Libya	. . . .	136.9	99.0	161.8
Mexico	. . . .	39.0	34.1	37.7
Netherlands	. . . .	96.6	118.2	114.3
Saudi Arabia	. . .	48.3	54.7	60.7
Spain	. . . .	326.6	373.8	444.0
Tunisia	. . . .	39.3	41.9	53.1
Turkey	. . . .	41.5	33.7	47.3
United Kingdom	. . .	133.8	155.4	211.8
USA	. . . .	126.0	141.7	160.0
Total (incl. others)	. . .	3,696.0	4,034.6	4,728.1

* Imports by country of production; exports by country of last consignment.

Source: UN, *International Trade Statistics Yearbook*.

Transport

RAILWAYS (traffic)*

	1994	1995	1996
Passenger-km (million) . .	1,922	1,613	1,776
Freight ton-km (million) . .	4,677	4,621	4,757

* Figures refer to principal railways only.

Source: Ministère du Transport et de la Marine Marchande, du Tourisme, de l'Energie et des Mines.

ROAD TRAFFIC (motor vehicles in use at 31 December)

	1994	1995	1996
Passenger cars	942,684	989,508	1,021,515
Goods vehicles	335,530	350,875	363,533
Motorcycles and scooters . .	19,144	19,297	19,417

Source: Ministère du Transport et de la Marine Marchande, du Tourisme, de l'Energie et des Mines.

SHIPPING

Merchant Fleet (registered at 31 December)

	1995	1996	1997
Number of vessels . . .	475	481	495
Total displacement ('000 grt) . .	382.6	403.4	416.7

Source: Lloyd's Register of Shipping, *World Fleet Statistics*.

International Sea-borne Freight Traffic ('000 metric tons)

	1994	1995	1996
Goods loaded	19,690	25,255	20,482
Goods unloaded	21,969	29,758	22,144

Source: Ministère du Transport et de la Marine Marchande, du Tourisme, de l'Energie et des Mines.

CIVIL AVIATION (traffic on Royal Air Maroc scheduled services)

		1994	1995	1996
Kilometres flown (million)	. .	47.8	48.4	47.4
Passengers carried ('000) .	. .	2,264	2,205	2,363
Passenger-km (million)	. . .	4,831	4,815	4,912
Total ton-km (million)	. . .	383	391	408

Source: Ministère du Transport et de la Marine Marchande, du Tourisme, de l'Energie et des Mines.

Tourism

FOREIGN TOURIST ARRIVALS

Country of Origin		1994	1995	1996
Algeria	. . . . . .	699,763	11,178	14,794
France	. . . . .	439,493	424,378	429,730
Germany	. . . .	214,195	162,151	212,538
Italy	. . . . .	103,691	101,212	91,485
Spain	. . . .	212,636	199,133	196,511
United Kingdom	. . .	113,904	128,916	103,082
USA	. . . .	85,834	80,168	77,356
Total (incl. others)	. . .	2,293,744	1,527,877	1,637,972

Communications Media

	1993	1994	1995
Radio receivers ('000 in use) . .	5,670	5,800	6,000
Television receivers ('000 in use) .	2,050	2,100	2,500
Telephones ('000 main lines in use) .	821	993	1,128
Mobile cellular telephones (subscribers)	6,725	13,794	29,511
Book production:			
Titles	n.a.	354	940
Copies ('000)	n.a.	1,380	2,861
Daily newspapers	14	13	13

Telefax stations (estimated number in use): 7,500 in 1993.
1996: 1,208,000 main telephone lines in use.

Sources: mainly UNESCO, *Statistical Yearbook*; UN, *Statistical Yearbook*.

Education

(1996/97, unless otherwise indicated)

	Insti-tutions	Teach-ers	Pupils/Students		
			Males	Females	Total
Pre-primary . . .	33,617	40,301	577,432	269,043	846,475
Primary . . .	5,329	109,311	1,753,709	1,280,699	3,034,408
Secondary					
General* . .	1,273	78,004	754,534	553,507	1,308,041
Vocational† . .	63	1,561	11,863	8,231	20,094
University level‡ . .	53	8,562	141,775	100,278	242,053

* State schools only.
† Data exclude professional schools.
‡ 1994/95 figures (Source: mainly UNESCO, *Statistical Yearbook*).

Source: mainly Ministère de l'Education Nationale.

Directory

The Constitution

The following is a summary of the main provisions of the Constitution, as approved in a national referendum on 4 September 1992, and as amended by referendum on 13 September 1996.

PREAMBLE

The Kingdom of Morocco, a sovereign Islamic State whose official language is Arabic, shall be a part of the Great Maghreb. As an African State, one of its aims shall be the realization of African unity. It will adhere to the principles, rights and obligations of those international organizations of which it is a member and will work for the preservation of peace and security in the world.

GENERAL PRINCIPLES

Morocco shall be a constitutional, democratic and social monarchy. Sovereignty shall pertain to the nation and be exercised directly by means of the referendum and indirectly by the constitutional institutions. All Moroccans shall be equal before the law, and all adults shall enjoy equal political rights including the franchise. Freedoms of movement, opinion and speech and the right of assembly shall be guaranteed. Islam shall be the state religion. All Moroccans shall have equal rights in seeking education and employment. The right to strike, and to private property, shall be guaranteed. All Moroccans shall contribute to the defence of the Kingdom and to public costs. There shall be no one-party system.

THE MONARCHY

The Crown of Morocco and its attendant constitutional rights shall be hereditary in the line of HM King Hassan II, and shall be transmitted to the oldest son, unless during his lifetime the King has appointed as his successor another of his sons. The King is the symbol of unity, guarantees the continuity of the state, and safeguards respect for Islam and the Constitution. The King shall have the power to appoint and dismiss the Prime Minister and other Cabinet Ministers (who are nominated by the Prime Minister), and shall preside over the Cabinet. He shall promulgate adopted legislation within a 30-day period, and have the power to dissolve the Chamber of Representatives and or the Chamber of Advisers. The Sovereign is the Commander-in-Chief of the Armed Forces; makes appointments to civil and military posts; appoints Ambassadors; signs and ratifies treaties; presides over the Supreme Council of the Magistracy, the Supreme Council of Education and the Supreme Council for National Reconstruction and Planning; and exercises the right of pardon. In cases of threat to the national territory or to the action of constitutional institutions, the King, having consulted the President of the Chamber of Representatives, the President of the Chamber of Advisers and the Chairman of the Constitutional Council, and after addressing the nation, shall have the right to declare a State of Emergency by royal decree. The State of Emergency shall not entail the dissolution of Parliament and shall be terminated by the same procedure followed in its proclamation.

LEGISLATURE

This shall consist of a bicameral parliament: the Chamber of Representatives and the Chamber of Advisers. Members of the Chamber of Representatives shall be elected by direct universal suffrage for a five-year term. Three-fifths of the members of the Chamber of Advisers shall be elected by electoral colleges of local councils; the remainder shall be elected by electoral colleges representing chambers of commerce and trade unions. Members of the Chamber of Advisers shall be elected for a nine-yearterm, with one-third renewable every three years. Deputies in both chambers enjoy parliamentary immunity. Parliament shall adopt legislation, which may be initiated by members of either chamber or by the Prime Minister. Draft legislation shall be examined consecutively by both parliamentary chambers. If the two chambers fail to agree on the draft legislation the Government may request that a bilateral commission propose a final draft for approval by the chambers. If the chambers do not then adopt the draft, the Government may submit the draft (modified, if need be) to the Chamber of Representatives. Henceforth the draft submitted can be definitively adopted only by absolute majority of the members of the Chamber of Representatives. Parliament shall hold its meetings during two sessions each year, which shall commence on the second Friday in October and the second Friday in April.

GOVERNMENT

The Government, composed of the Prime Minister and his Ministers, shall be responsible to the King and Parliament and shall ensure the execution of laws. The Prime Minister shall be empowered to initiate legislation and to exercise statutory powers except where these are reserved to the King. He shall present to both parliamentary chambers the Government's intended programme and shall be responsible for co-ordinating ministerial work.

RELATIONS BETWEEN THE AUTHORITIES

The King may request a second reading, by both Chambers of Parliament, of any draft bill or proposed law. In addition, he may submit proposed legislation to a referendum by decree; and dissolve either Chamber or both if a proposal that has been rejected is approved by referendum. He may also dissolve either Chamber by decree after consulting the Chairman of the Constitutional Council, and addressing the nation, but the succeeding Chamber may not be dissolved within a year of its election. The Chamber of Representatives may force the collective resignation of the Government either by refusing a vote of confidence or by adopting a censure motion. The election of the new Parliament or Chamber shall take place within three months of its dissolution. In the interim period the King shall exercise the legislative powers of Parliament, in addition to those conferred upon him by the Constitution. A censure motion must be signed by at least one-quarter of the Chamber's members, and shall be approved by the Chamber only by an absolute majority vote of its members. The Chamber of Advisers is competent to issue 'warning' motions to the Government and, by a two-thirds' majority, force its resignation.

THE CONSTITUTIONAL COUNCIL

A Constitutional Council shall be established, consisting of six members appointed by the King (including the Chairman) for a period of nine years, and six members appointed for the same period—three selected by the President of the Chamber of Representatives and three by the President of the Chamber of Advisers. One-third of each category of the Council shall be renewed every three years. The Council shall be empowered to judge the validity of legislative elections and referendums, as well as that of organic laws and the rules of procedure of both parliamentary chambers, submitted to it.

JUDICIARY

The Judiciary shall be independent. Judges shall be appointed on the recommendation of the Supreme Council of the Magistracy presided over by the King.

THE ECONOMIC AND SOCIAL COUNCIL

An Economic and Social Council shall be established to give its opinion on all matters of an economic or social nature. Its constitution, organization, prerogatives and rules of procedure shall be determined by an organic law.

THE HIGH AUDIT COUNCIL

The High Audit Council shall exercise the general supervision of the implementation of fiscal laws. It shall ensure the regularity of revenues and expenditure operations of the departments legally under its jurisdiction, as it shall assess the management of the affairs thereof. It is competent to penalize any breach of the rules governing such operations. Regional audit councils shall exercise the supervision of the accounts of local assemblies and bodies, and the management of the affairs thereof.

LOCAL GOVERNMENT

Local government in the Kingdom shall consist of establishing regions, governorships, provinces and communes.

REVISING THE CONSTITUTION

The King, the Chamber of Representatives and the Chamber of Advisers shall be competent to initiate a revision of the Constitution. The King shall have the right to submit the revision project he initiates to a national referendum. A proposal for a revision by either parliamentary chamber shall be adopted only if it receives a two-thirds' majority vote by the chamber's members. Revision projects and proposals shall be submitted to the nation for referendum by royal decree; a revision of the Constitution shall be definitive after approval by referendum. Neither the state, system of monarchy nor the prescriptions related to the religion of Islam may be subject to a constitutional revision.

The Government

HEAD OF STATE

HM King HASSAN II (acceded 3 March 1961).

CABINET
(September 1998)

A coalition of the Union socialiste des forces populaires (USFP); Rassemblement national des indépendants (RNI); Istiqlal; Parti du progrès et du socialisme (PPS); Mouvement national populaire (MNP); Front des forces démocratiques (FFD); Parti socialiste démocratique (PSD).

Prime Minister: ABD AR-RAHMAN EL-YOUSSOUFI (USFP).

Minister of State and Minister of Foreign Affairs and Co-operation: ABD AL-LATIF FILALI.

Minister of State for the Interior: DRISS BASRI.

Minister of Justice: OMAR AZZIMAN.

Minister of Religious Endowments (Awqaf) and Islamic Affairs: ABD AL-KAEBIR M'DAGHRI ALAOUI.

Minister of Territorial Administration, the Environment, Urban Planning and Housing: MOHAMED EL-YAZGHI (USFP).

Minister of the Economy and Finance: FATHALLAH OUALALOU (USFP).

Minister of Agriculture, Rural Development and Maritime Fishing: HABIB MALKI (USFP).

Secretary-General of the Government: ABDESSADEK RABII.

Minister of Industry, Commerce and Handicrafts: ALAMI TAZI (RNI).

Minister of Social Development, Solidarity, Employment and Vocational Training, and Government Spokesman: KHALID ALIOUA (USFP).

Minister of Tourism: HASSAN SEBBAR (USFP).

Minister of Equipment: BOUAMAR TIGHOUANE (Istiqlal).

Minister of Transport and Merchant Navy: MUSTAPHA MANSOURI (RNI).

Minister of Energy and Mining: YOUSSEF TAHIRI (Istiqlal).

Minister of National Education: ISMAÏL ALAOUI (PPS).

Minister of Higher Education, Graduate Training and Scientific Research: NAJIB ZEROUALI (RNI).

Minister in charge of Relations with Parliament: MOHAMED BOUZOUBAA (USFP).

Minister in charge of Human Rights: MOHAMED AOUJAR (RNI).

Minister of Cultural Affairs: MOHAMED ACHAARI (USFP).

Minister of Health: ABDELWAHED EL-FASSI (Istiqlal).

Minister of Youth and Sports: AHMED MOUSSAOUI (MNP).

Minister of Communications: LARBI MESSARI (Istiqlal).

Minister of Public Service and Administrative Reform: AZIZ HOCINE (RNI).

Minister in charge of the Public Sector and Privatization: RACHID FILALI (Istiqlal).

Minister-delegate to the Prime Minister, in charge of the Administration of National Defence: ABDERRAHMANE SBAI.

Minister-delegate to the Prime Minister, in charge of General Affairs of the Government: AHMED LAHLIMI (USFP).

Minister-delegate to the Prime Minister, in charge of Economic Provision and Planning: ABDELHAMID AOUAD (Istiqlal).

Minister-delegate in charge of Maghreb, Arab and Islamic Affairs: ABDESLAM ZNINED (RNI).

Minister-delegate in charge of Maritime Fishing: THAMI KHIARI (FFD).

Minister-delegate in charge of Water Resources and Forests: SAÏD CHBAATOU (MNP).

Minister-delegate in charge of Secondary and Technical Education: ABDELLAH SAAF (PSD).

There are also nine Secretaries of State.

MINISTRIES

Ministry of Agriculture, Public Works and the Environment: Quartier Administratif, Rabat; tel. (7) 769529; fax (7) 763318.

Ministry of Communications: Rabat; tel. (7) 766591; fax (7) 768755.

Ministry of Cultural Affairs: rue Gandhi, Rabat; tel. (7) 66054.

Ministry of Economic Encouragement and Privatization: 47 ave Ibn Sina, BP 6552, Agdal, Rabat; tel. (7) 672017; fax (7) 673299; e-mail minpriv@mtds.com.

Ministry of Finance, Trade, Industry and Handicrafts: ave Muhammad V, Quartier Administratif, Rabat; tel. (7) 760661; telex 31820; fax (7) 764081.

Ministry of Foreign Affairs and Co-operation: ave Franklin Roosevelt, Rabat; tel. (7) 761763; telex 31007; fax (7) 764679.

Ministry of Higher Education, Professional Training and Scientific Research: Rabat; tel. (7) 737233; fax (7) 737236.

Ministry of Housing: Quartier Administratif, Rabat; tel. (7) 763539; telex 32744; fax (7) 767973.

Ministry of the Interior: Quartier Administratif, Rabat; tel. (7) 765145; telex 31015; fax (7) 766489.

Ministry of Justice: rue Beyrout, Rabat; tel. (7) 721589; telex 31888.

Ministry of National Education: place Louklere, Rabat; tel. (7) 771822; telex 36016; fax (7) 779029.

Ministry of Ocean Fisheries, Administrative Affairs and Parliamentary Relations: Nouveau Quartier Administratif, Haut Agdal, BP 476, Rabat; tel. (7) 770144; fax (7) 778540.

Ministry of Religious Endowments (Awqaf) and Islamic Affairs: Al-Mechouar Essaid, Rabat; tel. (7) 762361; telex 36771; fax (7) 765257.

Ministry of Social Affairs (Health, Youth and Sports, and National Cohesion): Quartier Administratif, Rabat; tel. (7) 761855; fax (7) 768801.

Ministry of Telecommunications: blvd Muhammad V, Rabat; tel. (7) 703895; fax (7) 705641.

Ministry of Transport, Merchant Navy, Tourism, Energy and Mines: rue Maa al-Ainane, Casier Officiel, BP 759, Agdal, Rabat; tel. (7) 774822; fax (7) 774578.

Legislature

MAJLIS AN-NUAB
(Chamber of Representatives)

President: ABDELWAHED RADHI (USFP).

General Election, 14 November 1997

Party	Votes	% of votes	Seats
Union socialiste des forces populaires (USFP) . .	884,061	13.87	57
Union constitutionnelle (UC) .	647,746	10.17	50
Rassemblement national des indépendants (RNI) . .	705,397	11.07	46
Mouvement populaire (MP) .	659,331	10.35	40
Istiqlal	840,315	13.19	32
Mouvement démocratique et social (MDS)	603,156	9.47	32
Mouvement national populaire (MNP)	431,651	6.77	19
Parti national démocrate (PND)	270,425	4.24	10
Mouvement populaire constitutionnel et démocratique (MPCD) .	264,324	4.15	9
Parti du progrès et du socialisme (PPS) . .	274,862	4.31	9
Front des forces démocratiques (FFD) .	243,275	3.82	9
Parti socialiste démocratique (PSD) .	188,520	2.96	5
Organisation de l'action démocratique et populaire (OADP) . .	184,009	2.89	4
Parti de l'action (PA) .	89,614	1.41	2
Parti démocratique pour l'indépendance (PDI) .	76,176	1.20	1
Mouvement populaire pour la démocratie (MPD) . .	8,768	0.14	0
Total	**6,371,630**	**100.00**	**325**

MAJLIS AL-MUSTASHARIN
(Chamber of Advisers)
President: MOHAMED YALAL ESAID (UC).

Election, 5 December 1997

	Seats
Rassemblement national des indépendants (RNI) . .	42
Mouvement démocratique et social (MDS)	33
Union constitutionnelle (UC)	28
Mouvement populaire (MP)	27
Parti national démocrate (PND)	21
Istiqlal.	21
Union socialiste des forces populaires (USFP) . .	16
Mouvement national populaire (MNP)	15
Parti de l'action (PA)	13
Front des forces démocratiques (FFD)	12
Parti du progrès et du socialisme (PPS) . . .	7
Parti social et démocratique (PSD)	4
Parti démocratique pour l'indépendance (PDI) .	4
Trade unions	
Confédération Démocratique du Travail (CDT) . .	11
Union Marocaine du Travail (UMT) . .	8
Union Générale des Travailleurs Marocains (UGMT)	3
Others	5
Total	270

Note: Of the Chamber of Advisers' 270 members, 162 were elected by local councils, 81 by chambers of commerce and 27 by trade unions.

Political Organizations

Bloc démocratique (Koutla Dimocratya): f. 1992; opposition alliance currently comprising the USFP, Istiqlal, the OADP and the PPS; supported by trade unions and other groupings.

Entente nationale (Wifaq): loyalist, centre-right coalition currently comprising the UC, the MP and the PND.

Front des forces démocratiques (FFD): 13 blvd Tariq lbn Ziad, Rabat; tel. (7) 661623; fax (7) 661626; f. 1997 after split from PPS; Sec.-Gen. THAMI EL KHIARI.

Istiqlal: 4 charia Ibnou Toumert, Rabat; tel. (7) 730951; fax (7) 725354; f. 1944; aims to raise living standards and to confer equal rights on all; stresses the Moroccan claim to Western Sahara; Sec.-Gen. ABBAS EL-FASSI.

Mouvement démocratique et social (MDS): f. 1996 as Mouvement national démocratique et social after split from MNP; adopted current name in Nov. 1996; Leader MAHMOUD ARCHANE.

Mouvement national populaire (MNP): f. 1991; centre party; Leader MAHJOUBI AHERDANE.

Mouvement populaire (MP): 12 rue Marinin Hassan, Rabat; tel. (7) 730808; fax (7) 200165; f. 1959; conservative; Sec.-Gen. MUHAMMAD LAENSER.

Mouvement populaire constitutionnel et démocratique (MPCD): 352 blvd Muhammad V, Rabat; tel. (7) 702347; f. 1967; breakaway party from MP; formally absorbed members of the Islamic assen Al Islah wa Attajdid in 1997; Leader ABDELILAH BENKIARANE.

Mouvement populaire pour la démocratie (MPD): Leader M. EL-KHATIB.

Organisation de l'action démocratique et populaire (OADP): 29 blvd Lalla Yakout, BP 15797, Casablanca; tel. (2) 278442; f. 1983; Sec.-Gen. MUHAMMAD BEN SAÏD.

Parti de l'action (PA): 113 ave Allal ben Abdallah, Rabat; tel. (7) 24973; f. 1974; advocates democracy and progress; Sec.-Gen. ABDALLAH SENHAJI.

Parti de l'avant-garde démocratique socialiste (PADS): an offshoot of the USFP; legalized in April 1992.

Parti démocratique pour l'indépendance (PDI): Casablanca; tel. (2) 223359; f. 1946; Leader THAMI EL-OUAZZANI.

Parti national démocrate (PND): 18 rue de Tunis, Rabat; tel. (7) 30754; f. 1981 from split within RNI; working within the framework of the constitutional monarchy, aims to support the democratic process, defend Morocco's territorial integrity and reduce social and economic disparities; Leader ARSALANE EL-JADIDI.

Parti du progrès et du socialisme (PPS): 32 rue Lédru Rollin, BP 13152, Casablanca; tel. (2) 222238; f. 1974; successor to the Parti communiste marocain (banned in 1952), and the Parti de la libération et du socialisme (banned in 1969); left-wing; advocates nationalization and democracy; 35,000 mems; Sec.-Gen. ISMAIL ALAOUI.

Parti socialiste démocratique (PSD): Salé; f. 1996; breakaway party from OADP; Leader ISSA OURDIGHI.

Rassemblement national des indépendants (RNI): rue Laos, Rabat; tel. (7) 721420; f. 1978 from the pro-govt independents' group that formed the majority in the Chamber of Representatives; Leader AHMED OUSMAN.

Union constitutionnelle (UC): Rabat; tel. (7) 76935; telex 24645; f. 1983; 25-member Political Bureau; Leader ABD AL-LATIF SAMLALI.

Union nationale des forces populaires (UNFP): 28–30 rue Magellan, BP 747, Casablanca 01; tel. (2) 302023; fax (2) 319301; f. 1959 by MEHDI BEN BARKA from a group within Istiqlal; left-wing; in 1972 a split occurred between the Casablanca and Rabat sections of the party; Leader MOULAY ABDALLAH IBRAHIM.

Union socialiste des forces populaires (USFP): 17 rue Oued Souss, Agdal, Rabat; tel. (7) 773905; fax (7) 773901; f. 1959 as UNFP, became USFP in 1974; left-wing progressive party; 100,000 mems; First Sec. ABD AR-RAHMAN EL-YOUSSOUFI.

The following group is active in the disputed territory of Western Sahara:

Frente Popular para la Liberación de Saguia el-Hamra y Río de Oro (Frente Polisario) (Polisario Front): BP 10, el-Mouradia, Algiers; tel. and fax (2) 747820; f. 1973 to gain independence for Western Sahara, first from Spain and then from Morocco and Mauritania; signed peace treaty with Mauritanian Govt in 1979; supported by Algerian Govt; in February 1976 proclaimed the Sahrawi Arab Democratic Republic (SADR), since recognized by 30 member-states of the OAU (to which it was admitted in February 1982 as the 51st member) and by more than 75 countries worldwide; its main organs are a 33-member National Secretariat, a 101-member Sahrawi National Council (Parliament) and a 13-member Govt; Sec.-Gen. of the Polisario Front and Pres. of the SADR MUHAMMAD ABD AL-AZIZ; Prime Minister of the SADR MAHFOUD ALI BEÏBA.

Diplomatic Representation

EMBASSIES IN MOROCCO

Algeria: 46–48 blvd Tariq Ibn Ziad, BP 448, Rabat; tel. (7) 765474; telex 31074; fax (7) 762237; Chargé d'affaires a.i.: SALAH BOUCHA.

Argentina: 12 rue Mekki Bitaouri, Souissi, Rabat; tel. (7) 755120; telex 31017; Ambassador: ADOLFO ENRIQUE NANCLARES.

Austria: 2 rue Tiddas, BP 135, Rabat; tel. (7) 764003; fax (7) 765425; e-mail autrich@mtds.com; Ambassador: Dr MICHAEL FITZ.

Belgium: 6 ave de Marrakech, BP 163, Rabat; tel. (7) 764746; telex 31087; Ambassador: MARC VAN RYSSELBERGHE.

Brazil: 1 ave de Marrakech, Rabat; tel. (7) 765522; telex 31628; fax (7) 766705; Ambassador: ANTÔNIO S. CANTUARIA GUIMARÃES.

Bulgaria: 4 ave de Meknès, Rabat; tel. (7) 764082; telex 31761; fax (7) 763201; Ambassador: KOSSIO PROYKOV KITIPOV.

Cameroon: 20 rue du Rif, Souissi, Rabat; tel. (7) 754194; fax (7) 750540; Ambassador: MAHAMAT PABA SALÉ.

Canada: 13 bis rue Jaafar as-Sadik, BP 709, Agdal, Rabat; tel. (7) 672880; telex 31964; fax (7) 672187; Ambassador: JEAN-GUY SAINT-MARTIN.

Central African Republic: Villa 42, ave Pasteur, Agdal, Rabat; tel. (7) 70203; telex 31920; Ambassador: JULES KOUALEYABORO.

China, People's Republic: 16 ave al-Fahs, Rabat; tel. (7) 54056; telex 31023; Ambassador: MU WEN.

Congo Democratic Republic: 34 ave de la Victoire, BP 537, Rabat-Chellah; tel. (7) 734862; telex 31954; Ambassador: TOMONA BATE TANGALE.

Côte d'Ivoire: 21 rue Tiddas, BP 192, Rabat; tel. (7) 63151; telex 31070; Ambassador: AMADOU THIAM.

Czech Republic: rue Ait Melloul, BP 410, Souissi, Rabat; tel. (7) 55421; telex 32941; fax (7) 55420; Ambassador: VLADIMIR SATTRAN.

Denmark: 4 rue de Khémisset, BP 203, Rabat; tel. (7) 769293; telex 31077; fax (7) 769709; Ambassador: JØRGEN REIMERS.

Egypt: 31 rue al-Jazair, Rabat; tel. (7) 31833; Ambassador: MUHAMMAD BESHR.

Equatorial Guinea: 30 ave des Nations Unies, BP 723, Agdal, Rabat; tel. (7) 74205; telex 31796; Ambassador: RESURRECCIÓN BITA.

Finland: 16 rue de Khémisset, BP 590, Rabat 10002; tel. (7) 62352; Ambassador: DIETER VITZTHUM.

France: 3 rue Sahnoun, Rabat; tel. (7) 689706; telex 31013; fax (7) 689720; e-mail michel.bonnecorse@diplomatie.fr; Ambassador: MICHEL DE BONNECORSE BENAULT DE LUBIÈRES.

Gabon: ave des Zaërs, km 3.5, Rabat; tel. (7) 51968; telex 31999; Ambassador: CLAUDE ROGER OWANSANGO.

Germany: 7 rue Madnine, BP 235, Rabat; tel. (7) 709662; telex 36026; fax (7) 706851; Ambassador: Dr HERWIG BARTELS.

Greece: 23 rue d'Oujda, Rabat; tel. (7) 723839; telex 31953; fax (7) 702270; Ambassador: ELEFTHERIOS DANELLIS.

Guinea: 15 rue Hamzah, Rabat; tel. (7) 674148; telex 31796; fax (7) 672513; Ambassador: El Hadj GUIRANE NIDIAYE.

Holy See: rue Béni M'tir, BP 1303, Souissi, Rabat (Apostolic Nunciature); tel. (7) 772277; fax (7) 756213; Apostolic Nuncio: Most Rev. DOMENICO DE LUCA, Titular Archbishop of Teglata in Numidia.

Hungary: 21B rue Ouled Jerrar, Souissi, BP 5026, Rabat; tel. (7) 750757; telex 32718; fax (7) 754123; Ambassador: Dr JÁNOS TERÉNYI.

Indonesia: 63 rue Béni Boufrah, Rabat; tel. (7) 757860; telex 32783; fax (7) 757859; Ambassador: ISKANDAR DINATA.

Iran: route des Zaërs, Kacem, Souissi, Rabat; tel. (7) 752167; fax (7) 659118; Ambassador: JA'FAR SHAMSIAN.

Iraq: 39 rue Béni Iznassen, Souissi, Rabat; tel. (7) 54466; telex 31663; Ambassador: FADHIL AL-SHAHIR.

Italy: 2 rue Idriss al-Azhar, BP 111, Rabat; tel. (7) 706597; telex 32731; fax (7) 706882; Ambassador: GUIDO MARTINI.

Japan: 70 ave des Nations Unies, Agdal, Rabat; tel. (7) 674163; telex 31901; fax (7) 672274; Ambassador: KYOICHI OMURA.

Jordan: Villa al-Wafae, Lot 5, Souissi II, Rabat; tel. (7) 59270; telex 31085; fax (7) 58722; Ambassador: HUSSEIN HAMMAMI.

Korea, Republic: 41 ave Mehdi Benbarka, Souissi, Rabat; tel. (7) 751767; fax (7) 750189; Ambassador: KIM DONG-HO.

Kuwait: Rm 413, ave Iman Malik, Rabat; tel. (7) 56423; telex 31955; Ambassador: ABD AL-MUHSIN SALEM AL-HAROUN.

Lebanon: 19 ave de Fès, Rabat; tel. (7) 760728; telex 31060; fax (7) 766667; Ambassador: SAMI OMAR KRONFOL.

Libya: 1 rue Chouaïb Doukkali, BP 225, Rabat; tel. (7) 68828; telex 31957; Chargé d'affaires a.i.: MUHAMMAD ZWAI.

Mauritania: 9 rue Taza, Souissi, Rabat; Ambassador: SIDNA OULD CHEIKH TALEB BOUYA.

Mexico: 6 rue Cadi Mohamed Brebi, Souissi, Rabat; tel. (7) 631969; fax (7) 631971; e-mail embamexmar@techno.net.ma; Ambassador: FRANCISCO JOSÉ CRUZ GONZÁLEZ.

Netherlands: 40 rue de Tunis, BP 329, Rabat; tel. (7) 733512; fax (7) 733333; e-mail nlgovrab@mtds.com; Ambassador: H. J. VAN PESCH.

Nigeria: 70 ave Omar ibn al-Khattab, BP 347, Agdal, Rabat; tel. (7) 671857; telex 31976; fax (7) 672739; Ambassador: Y. USMAN.

Oman: 21 rue Hamza, Agdal, Rabat; tel. (7) 71064; telex 31747; Ambassador: MUHAMMAD BIN SALIM AL-SHANFARI.

Pakistan: 11 rue Zankat Azrou, Rabat; tel. (7) 762402; telex 31918; fax (7) 766742; Ambassador: SYED AZMAT HASSAN.

Peru: 16 rue d'Ifrane, Rabat; tel. (7) 723236; fax (7) 702803; e-mail embaperu@acdim.net.ma; Ambassador: TOMÁS CASTILLO MEZA.

Poland: 23 rue Oqbah, Agdal, BP 425, Rabat; tel. (7) 771791; fax (7) 775320; e-mail apologne@onpt.net.ma; Ambassador: PIOTR SZYMANOWSKI.

Portugal: 5 rue Thami Lamdouar, Souissi, Rabat; tel. (7) 756446; telex 31711; fax (7) 756445; Ambassador: ANTÓNIO VALENTE.

Qatar: 4 ave Tarik ibn Ziad, BP 1220, Rabat; tel. (7) 65681; telex 31624; Ambassador: ALI AHMED AS-SULAITI.

Romania: 10 rue d'Ouezzane, Rabat; tel. (7) 738611; telex 31079; fax (7) 700196; Ambassador: Dr ÉMILIAN MANCIUR.

Russia: Km 4, route des Zaërs, Souissi, Rabat; tel. (7) 753509; telex 31602; fax (7) 753590; Ambassador: VASSILII KOLOTOUCHA.

Saudi Arabia: 43 place de l'Unité Africaine, Rabat; tel. (7) 30171; telex 32875; Ambassador: ALI MAJED KABBANI.

Senegal: 17 rue Cadi ben Hamadi Senhaji, Souissi, Rabat; tel. (7) 754171; telex 31048; fax (7) 754149; Ambassador: DOUDOU DIOP.

South Africa: 34 rue des Saadiens, Rabat; tel. (7) 706760; fax (7) 706756; e-mail sudaf@mail.sis.net.ma; Ambassador: M. M. MOTALA.

Spain: 3 rue Madnine, Rabat; tel. (7) 707600; telex 31073; fax (7) 707387; e-mail infembsp@mtds.com; Ambassador: JORGE DEZCALLAR DE MAZAREDO.

Sudan: 5 ave Ghomara, Souissi, Rabat; tel. (7) 52863; Ambassador: ABDALLA MAGHOUB.

Sweden: 159 ave John Kennedy, BP 428, Rabat; tel. (7) 759303; telex 36541; fax (7) 758048; e-mail swedrab@mtds.com; Ambassador: CECILIA MAMSTEN.

Switzerland: Sq. de Berkane, BP 169, Rabat 10001; tel. (7) 706974; fax (7) 705749; Ambassador: HENRI CUENNET.

Tunisia: 6 ave de Fès et 1 rue d'Ifrane, Rabat; tel. (7) 730636; telex 31009; fax (7) 730637; Ambassador: SALAH BACCARI.

Turkey: 7 ave de Fès, Rabat; tel. (7) 762605; telex 36164; fax (7) 704980; Ambassador: ONDER OZAR.

United Arab Emirates: 11 ave des Alaouines, Rabat; tel. (7) 30975; telex 31697; Ambassador: ISSAA HAMAD BUSHAHAB.

United Kingdom: 17 blvd de la Tour Hassan, BP 45, Rabat; tel. (7) 720905; fax (7) 704531; e-mail britemb@mtds.com; Ambassador: WILLIAM FULLERTON.

USA: 2 ave de Marrakech, Rabat; tel. (7) 762265; fax (7) 765661; Ambassador: EDWARD M. GABRIEL.

Yemen: 11 rue Abou-Hanifa, Agdal, Rabat; tel. (7) 74363; telex 32855; Ambassador: ABDUL WAHAB ASH-SHOWKANI.

Yugoslavia: 23 ave Beni Iznassen, Souissi, BP 5014, Rabat; tel. (7) 52201; telex 31760; Ambassador: DIMITRIJE BABIĆ.

Judicial System

The **Supreme Court** (al-Majlis al-Aala) is responsible for the interpretation of the law and regulates the jurisprudence of the courts and tribunals of the Kingdom. The Supreme Court sits at Rabat and is divided into six Chambers.

First President: DRISS DAHAK.

Attorney-General: AHMAD ZEGHARI.

The 15 **Courts of Appeal** hear appeals from lower courts and also comprise a criminal division.

The **Courts of First Instance** pass judgment on offences punishable by up to five years' imprisonment. These courts also pass judgment, without possibility of appeal, in personal, civil and commercial cases involving up to 3,000 dirhams.

The **Regional Tribunals** pass judgment in the first and last resort in cases of personal property of 1,000 dirhams. The Regional Tribunals also pass judgment, subject to appeal before the Court of Appeal, in cases of minor offences in penal matters, punishable by a fine of 10 to 800 dirhams.

Labour Tribunals settle, by means of conciliation, disputes arising from rental contracts or services between employers and employees engaged in private industry. There are 14 labour tribunals in the Kingdom.

The **High Court of Justice**, one-half of whose members are elected from the Chamber of Representatives and the remainder from the Chamber of Advisers, considers crimes and felonies allegedly committed by government members in the exercise of their functions. The Court's president is appointed by royal decree.

Religion

ISLAM

About 99% of Moroccans are Muslims (of whom about 90% are of the Sunni sect), and Islam is the state religion.

CHRISTIANITY

There are about 69,000 Christians, mostly Roman Catholics.

The Roman Catholic Church

Morocco (excluding the disputed territory of Western Sahara) comprises two archdioceses, directly responsible to the Holy See. At 31 December 1996 there were an estimated 23,266 adherents in the country, representing less than 0.1% of the population. The Moroccan archbishops participate in the Conférence Episcopale Régionale du Nord de l'Afrique (f. 1985), based in Algiers (Algeria).

Archbishop of Rabat: Most Rev. HUBERT MICHON, Archevêché, 1 rue Zerhouni, BP 258, Rabat 10001; tel. (7) 709239; fax (7) 706282.

Archbishop of Tangier: Most Rev. JOSÉ ANTONIO PETEIRO FREIRE, Archevêché, 55 rue Sidi Bouabid, BP 2116, Tangier; tel. (9) 932762; fax (9) 949117.

Western Sahara comprises a single Apostolic Prefecture, with an estimated 140 Catholics (1996).

Prefect Apostolic of Western Sahara: Fr ACACIO VALBUENA RODRÍGUEZ, Misión Católica, BP 31, el-Aaiún 70001; tel. 893270.

The Anglican Communion

Within the Church of England, Morocco forms part of the diocese of Gibraltar in Europe. There are Anglican churches in Casablanca and Tangier.

Protestant Church

Evangelical Church: 33 rue d'Azilal, Casablanca 20000; tel. (2) 302151; fax (2) 444768; f. 1920; established in 6 towns; Pres. Pastor ETIENNE QUINCHE; 1,000 mems.

JUDAISM

There is a Jewish community of 6,000–7,000.

Grand Rabbi of Casablanca: CHALOM MESSAS, President of the Rabbinical Court of Casablanca, Palais de Justice, place des Nations Unies.

The Press

DAILIES

Casablanca

Al-Bayane (The Manifesto): 62 blvd de la Gironde, BP 13152, Casablanca; tel. (2) 307666; Arabic and French; organ of the Parti du progrès et du socialisme; Dir ISMAIL ALAOUI; circ. 5,000.

Al-Ittihad al-Ichtiraki (Socialist Unity): 33 rue Emir Abdelkader, Casablanca 05; tel. (2) 241538; telex 24961; Arabic; organ of the Union socialiste des forces populaires; Dir ABDALLAH BOUHLAL; circ. 110,000.

Maroc Soir: 34 rue Muhammad Smiha, Casablanca; tel. (2) 268860; telex 23845; fax (2) 262969; f. 1971; French; Dir DRISSI EL-ALAMI; circ. 50,000.

Le Matin du Sahara et du Maghreb: 88 blvd Muhammad V, Casablanca; tel. (2) 301271; telex 27794; fax (2) 317535; f. 1971; French; Dir ABD AL-HAFID ROUISSI; circ. 100,000.

Rissalat al-Oumma (The Message of the Nation): 158 ave des Forces Armées Royales, Casablanca; tel. (2) 310427; Arabic; weekly edition in French; organ of the Union constitutionnelle; Dir MUHAMMAD ALAOUI MUHAMMADI.

Rabat

Al-Alam (The Flag): 11 ave Allal ben Abdallah, BP 141, Rabat; tel. (7) 32419; fax (7) 733896; f. 1946; organ of the Istiqlal party; Arabic; literary supplement on Fridays; weekly edition on Mondays; monthly edition on foreign policy; Dir ABD AL-KRIM GHALLAB; circ. 100,000.

Al-Anba'a (Information): 21 rue Patrice Lumumba, Rabat; tel. (7) 24644; f. 1970; Arabic; publ. by Ministry of Information; Dir AHMAD AL-YAAKOUBI; circ. 15,000.

Assyassa al-Jadida: 43 rue Abou Fares al-Marini, BP 1385, Rabat; tel. (7) 208571; fax (7) 208573; e-mail assassjdid@maghrebnet .net.ma; f. 1997; Arabic; organ of the Parti socialiste démocratique; Dir ABD AL-LATIF AOUAD: Editor TALAA ASSOUD ALATLASSI.

Al-Maghrib: 6 rue Laos, BP 469, Rabat; tel. (7) 722709; telex 31916; fax (7) 722765; f. 1977; French; organ of the Rassemblement national des indépendants (RNI); Dir MUSTAPHA IZNASNI; circ. 15,000.

Al-Mithaq al-Watani (The National Charter): 6 rue Laos, BP 469, Rabat; tel. (7) 722709; telex 31916; fax (7) 22765; f. 1977; Arabic; organ of the RNI; Dir MED AUAJJAR; circ. 15,000.

An-Nidal ad-Dimokrati (The Democratic Struggle): 18 rue de Tunis, Rabat; tel. (7) 30754; Arabic; organ of the Parti national démocrate; Dir MUHAMMAD ARSALANE AL-JADIDI.

L'Opinion: 11 ave Allal ben Abdallah, Rabat; tel. (7) 727812; fax (7) 732181; f. 1965; French; organ of the Istiqlal party; Dir MUHAMMAD IDRISSI KAÏTOUNI; circ. 60,000.

SELECTED PERIODICALS

Casablanca

Assahra Al-Maghribia: 88 blvd Muhammad V, Casablanca; tel. (2) 268860; telex 27794; fax (2) 203935; f. 1989; Arabic; Dir ABD AL-HAFID ROUISSI.

Bulletin Mensuel de la Chambre de Commerce et d'Industrie de la Wilaya du Grand Casablanca: 98 blvd Muhammad V, BP 423, Casablanca; tel. (2) 264327; telex 24630; monthly; French; Pres. LAHCEN EL-WAFI.

Cedies Informations: angle ave des Forces Armées Royales et rue Muhammad Arrachid, Casablanca 20100; tel. (2) 252696; fax (2) 253839; e-mail cgem@mail.cbi.net.ma; weekly; French; Admin. MOUHCINE AYOUCHE.

Construire: 25 rue d'Azilal, Immeuble Ortiba, Casablanca; tel. (2) 305721; fax (2) 317577; f. 1940; weekly; French; Dir TALAL BOUCHAIB.

Les Echos Africains: Immeuble SONIR, angle blvd Smiha, rue d'Anjou, BP 13140, Casablanca; tel. (2) 307271; fax (2) 319680; f. 1972; monthly; French; news, economics; Dir MUHAMMAD CHOUFFANI EL-FASSI; Editor Mme SOODIA FARIDI; circ. 5,000.

Al-Ittihad al-Watani Lilkouate ach-Chaabia (National Union of Popular Forces): 28-30 rue Magellan, Casablanca 01; tel. (2) 302023; fax (2) 319301; weekly; Arabic; organ of the Union nationale des forces populaires; Dir MOULAY ABDALLAH IBRAHIM.

Lamalif: 6 bis rue Defly Dieude, Casablanca; tel. (2) 220032; f. 1966; monthly; French; economic, social and cultural magazine; Dir MUHAMMAD LOGHLAM.

La Mañana: 88 blvd Muhammad V, Casablanca; tel. (2) 268860; telex 27794; fax (2) 203935; f. 1990; Spanish; Dir ABD AL-HAFID ROUISSI.

Maroc Fruits: 22 rue Al-Messaoudi, Casablanca 02; tel. (2) 363946; fax (2) 364041; f. 1958; fortnightly; Arabic, French; organ of the

Association des Producteurs d'Agrumes du Maroc; Dir NEJJAI AHMED MANSOUR; circ. 6,000.

Maroc Soir: 88 blvd Muhammad V, Casablanca; tel. (2) 301271; telex 23845; fax (2) 317535; f. 1971; French; Dir ABD AL-HAFID ROUISSI.

Matin Hebdo: 34 rue Muhammad Smiha, Casablanca; tel. (2) 301271; telex 27794; weekly; Dir AHMAD AL-ALAMI.

Matin Magazine: 88 blvd Muhammad V, Casablanca; tel. (2) 268860; telex 23845; fax (2) 262969; f. 1971; weekly; French; Dir ABD AL-HAFID ROUISSI.

An-Nidal (The Struggle): 10 rue Cols Bleus, Sidi Bousmara, Médina Kédima, Casablanca; f. 1973; weekly; Dir IBRAHIMI AHMAD.

Les Nouvelles du Maroc: 28 ave des Forces Armées Royales, Casablanca; tel. (2) 203031; fax (2) 277181; weekly; French; Dir KHADIJA S. IDRISSI.

Al-Ousbouaa al-Maghribia: 158 ave des Forces Armées Royales, Casablanca; f. 1984; organ of the Union constitutionnelle; Dir A. MUHAMMADI.

Panorama Interview: 17 rue Lapebie, Casablanca; tel. (2) 277396; monthly; French; Dir BOUJEMAÀ AMARA.

La Quinzaine du Maroc: 53 rue Dumont d'Urville, Casablanca; tel. (2) 302482; fax (2) 440426; f. 1951; monthly; English/French; Dir HUBERT MAURO.

Revue Douanes Marocaines: 69 rue Muhammad Smiha, Casablanca; tel. (2) 301613; f. 1959; monthly; French; general economic review; Dir MOHAMED KABOUS.

Revue Marocaine de Droit: 24 rue Nolly, Casablanca; tel. (2) 273673; telex 22644; quarterly; French and Arabic; Dirs J. P. RAZON, A. KETTANI.

Les Temps du Maroc: 88 blvd Muhammad V, Casablanca; tel. (2) 301271; telex 27794; fax (2) 262969; f. 1995; weekly; French; Dir ABD AL-HAFID ROUISSI.

La Vie Economique: 5 blvd ben Yacine, Casablanca; tel. (2) 443868; telex 28045; fax (2) 304542; f. 1921; weekly; French; Pres. and Dir JEAN LOUIS SERVAN-SCHREIBER.

La Vie Industrielle et Agricole: 142 blvd Muhammad V, Casablanca; tel. (2) 274407; 2 a month; French; Dir AHMAD ZAGHARI.

La Vie Touristique Africaine: 142 blvd Muhammad V, Casablanca; tel. (2) 274407; telex 21721; fortnightly; French; tourist information; Dir AHMAD ZAGHARI.

Rabat

Al-Aklam (The Pens): Rabat; monthly; Arabic; Dir ABD AR-RAHMAN BEN AMAR.

Anoual: 5 bis ave Hassan II, BP 1385, Rabat; tel. (7) 26733; fax (7) 738259; f. 1979; weekly; Arabic; organ of the Organisation de l'action démocratique et populaire; Dir ABD AL-LATIF AOUAD.

Ach-Chorta (The Police): BP 437, Rabat; tel. (7) 23194; monthly; Arabic; Dir MUHAMMAD AD-DRIF.

Da'ouat Al-Haqq (Call of the Truth): al-Michwar as-Said, Rabat; publ. by Ministry of Religious Endowments (Awqaf) and Islamic Affairs; tel. (7) 60810; f. 1957; monthly; Arabic.

Al-Haraka: 8 Sahat al-Alaouiyine, Rabat; tel. (7) 64493; weekly; Arabic; organ of the Mouvement populaire; Dir ALI ALAOUI.

Al-Imane: rue Akenssous, BP 356, Rabat; f. 1963; monthly; Arabic; Dir ABOU BAKER AL-KADIRI.

Al-Irchad (Spiritual Guidance): al-Michwar as-Said, Rabat; publ. by Ministry of Religious Endowments (Awqaf) and Islamic Affairs; tel. (7) 60810; f. 1967; monthly; Arabic.

Al-Khansa: 154 ave Souss Mohamedia, Rabat; monthly; Arabic; Dir ABOUZAL AICHA.

Al-Maghribi: Rabat; tel. (7) 68139; weekly; Arabic; organ of the Parti de l'action; Dir ABDALLAH AL-HANANI.

At-Tadamoun: Rabat; monthly; Arabic; Dir ABD AL-MAJID SEMLALI EL-HASANI.

Tangier

Actualités Touristiques: 80 rue de la Liberté, Tangier; monthly; French; Dir TAYEB ALAMI.

Le Journal de Tanger: 11 ave Moulay Abd al-Aziz, BP 420, Tangier; tel. (9) 46051; fax (9) 45709; f. 1904; weekly; French, English, Spanish and Arabic; Dir BAKHAT ABD AL-HAQ; circ. 10,000.

NEWS AGENCIES

Maghreb Arabe Presse (MAP): 122 ave Allal ben Abdallah, BP 1049, Rabat 10000; tel. (7) 764083; telex 36044; fax (7) 765005; e-mail map@map.co.ma; internet http://www.map.co.ma; f. 1959; Arabic, French, English and Spanish; state-owned; Dir-Gen. ABDEL-JALIL FENJIRO.

Foreign Bureaux

Agence France-Presse (AFP): 2 bis rue du Caire, BP 118, Rabat; tel. (7) 768943; telex 31903; fax (7) 700357; f. 1920; Dir IGNACE DALLE.

Agencia EFE (Spain): 14 ave du Kairouane, Rabat; tel. (7) 723218; telex 32806; fax (7) 732195; Bureau Chief ALBERTO MASEGOSA GARCÍA-CALAMARTE.

Agenzia Nazionale Stampa Associata (ANSA) (Italy): Rabat; tel. (7) 311083; telex 31044; Dir RAFFA HOUCINE.

Informatsionnoye Telegrafnoye Agentstvo Rossii—Telegrafnoye Agentstvo Suverennykh Stran (ITAR—TASS) (Russia): 32 rue de la Somme, Rabat; tel. (7) 750315; telex 31018; Dir OLEG CHIROKOV.

Inter Press Service (IPS) (Italy): Rabat; tel. (7) 756869; fax (7) 727183; Dir BOULOUIZ BOUCHRA.

Reuters (United Kingdom): 509 Immeuble es-Saada, ave Hassan II, Rabat; tel. (7) 726518; fax (7) 722499; Chief Correspondent (North Africa) JOHN BAGGALEY.

Rossiiskoye Informatsionnoye Agentstvo—Vesti (RIA-Vesti) (Russia): BP 281, Rabat; tel. (7) 69784; telex 31069; Dir BORIS BOUKAREV.

Xinhua (New China) News Agency (People's Republic of China): 4 rue Kadi Mekki el-Bitaouri, Souissi, Rabat; tel. (7) 755320; telex 31674; fax (7) 754319; Dir ZHUGE CANGLIN.

Publishers

Dar el-Kitab: place de la Mosquée, quartier des Habous, BP 4018, Casablanca; tel. (2) 305419; fax (2) 304581; f. 1948; philosophy, history, Africana, general and social science; Arabic and French; Dir BOUTALEB ABDOU ABD AL-HAY; Gen. Man. KHADIJA EL KASSIMI.

Editions La Porte: 281 ave Muhammad V, Rabat; tel. (7) 709958; fax (7) 706476; law, guides, economics, educational books; Man. Dir MUHAMMAD RAFII DOUKKALI.

Editions Maghrébines: 5–13 rue Soldat Roch, Casablanca; tel. (2) 245148; telex 22994; f. 1962; general non-fiction.

Government Publishing House

Imprimerie Officielle: ave Yacoub El Mansour, Rabat-Chellah; tel. (7) 765024; fax (7) 765179.

Broadcasting and Communications

TELECOMMUNICATIONS
Regulatory Authority

Agence Nationale de Réglementation des Télécommunications: f. 1997; Dir MUSTAPHA TERRAB.

Principal Operators

Office National des Postes et Télécommunications (ONPT): ave Annakhil, Rabat 10100; tel. (7) 714855; telex 0407; fax (7) 779123; Dir MUHAMMAD OUAKRIM.

Itissalat al-Maghrib: f. 1998 to take over telephone services from the ONPT; scheduled for transfer to private ownership in 1998; Dir ABDESSALEM AHIZOUNE.

BROADCASTING

Morocco can receive broadcasts from Spanish radio stations, and the main Spanish television channels can also be received in northern Morocco.

Radio

Radiodiffusion-Télévision Marocaine: 1 rue el-Brihi, BP 1042, Rabat 1000; tel. (7) 709613; telex 0407; fax (7) 703208; internet http://www.maroc.net/rc; govt station; Network A in Arabic, Network B in French, English and Spanish, Network C in Berber and Arabic; Foreign Service in Arabic, French and English; Dir-Gen. MUHAMMAD TRICHA; Dir Radio ABD AR-RAHMAN ACHOUR; Dir Foreign Service AHMAD RAYANE.

Radio Méditerranée Internationale: 3–5 rue Emsallah, BP 2055, Tangier; tel. and fax (9) 936363; telex 33771; Arabic and French; Man. Dir PIERRE CASALTA.

Voice of America Radio Station in Tangier: c/o US Consulate-General, chemin des Amoureux, Tangier.

Television

Radiodiffusion Télévision Marocaine: 1 rue el-Brihi, BP 1042, Rabat 1000; tel. (7) 709613; telex 0407; fax (7) 703208; internet http://www.maroc.net/rc; govt station; transmission commenced 1962; 45 hours weekly; French and Arabic; carries commercial advertising; Dir-Gen. MUHAMMAD TRICHA; Dir Television MUHAMMAD LISSARI.

2M International: Société d'études et de réalisations audio-visuelles, km 7, 3 route de Rabat, Ain-Sebaa, Casablanca; tel. (2) 354444; fax (2) 354071; f. 1988, transmission commenced 1989; private television channel, jointly owned by Moroccan interests

(85%) and by foreign concerns; broadcasting in French and Arabic; Dir-Gen. ANTONIO FILALI.

Finance

(cap. = capital; res = reserves; dep. = deposits; m. = million; brs = branches; amounts in dirhams unless otherwise indicated)

BANKING
Central Bank

Bank Al-Maghrib: 277 ave Muhammad V, BP 445, Rabat; tel. (7) 702626; telex 31006; fax (7) 706677; f. 1959 as Banque du Maroc; bank of issue; cap. 500m., res 4,212.5m., dep. 10,408.6m., total assets 68,384.7m. (Dec. 1996); Gov. MUHAMMAD SEQAT.

Other Banks

ABN AMRO Bank (Maroc) SA: 47 rue Allal ben Abdallah, BP 13478, Casablanca 21000; tel. (2) 209191; telex 45687; fax (2) 209099; f. 1948 as Société Hollandaise de Banque et de Gestion; 97% owned by ABN AMRO Bank NV (Netherlands); cap. 500.0m., res 481.2m., dep. 1,725.6m., total assets 3,204.8m. (Dec. 1996); Pres. Hadj ABDERRAHMANE BOUFTAS; Vice-Pres. and Gen. Man. A. RUTGERS; 20 brs.

Arab Bank Maroc: 174 blvd Muhammad V, BP 13810, Casablanca; tel. (2) 223152; telex 22942; fax (2) 200233; f. 1975; owned by Arab Bank PLC; cap. 100m., res 15.8m., dep. 1,404.6m., total assets 1,632.8m. (Dec. 1995); Pres. ABD AL-LATIF LARAKI; Gen. Man. Dr SALAH EDDINE HAROUN; 3 brs.

Banque Commerciale du Maroc SA (BCM): 2 blvd Moulay Youssef, BP 11141, Casablanca 20000; tel. (2) 298888; telex 22863; fax (2) 268829; f. 1911; 20.3% owned by Banco Central Hispano; cap. 1,325.0m., res 1,788.0m., dep. 26,563.3m., total assets 32,387.0m. (Dec. 1996); Chair. ABD AL-AZIZ ALAMI; Gen. Man. ALI IBN MANSOUR; 112 brs.

Banque Marocaine du Commerce Extérieur SA (BMCE): 140 ave Hassan II, BP 13425, Casablanca 20000; tel. (2) 200496; telex 21635; fax (2) 200512; f. 1959; transferred to majority private ownership in 1995; cap. 1,443.2m., res 1,790.7m., dep. 28,284.2m., total assets 34,780.3m. (Dec. 1996); Chair. and CEO OTHMAN BEN JELLOUN; 171 brs.

Banque Marocaine pour l'Afrique et l'Orient: 1 place Bandoeng, Casablanca 20000; tel. (2) 307070; telex 26720; fax (2) 301673; f. 1975 to take over British Bank of the Middle East (Morocco); cap. 200.0m., res 1.4m., dep. 2,042.0m., total assets 2,578.8m. (Dec. 1996); Chair. FARID DELLERO; Gen. Man. SAID IBRAHIMI; 29 brs.

Banque Marocaine pour le Commerce et l'Industrie SA: 26 place des Nations Unies, BP 573, Casablanca; tel. (2) 224101; telex 23727; fax (2) 299402; f. 1964; transferred to majority private ownership in 1995; cap. 742.5m., res 583.2m., dep. 10,656.0m. (Dec. 1997); Chair. MUSTAPHA FARIS; Gen. Man. JEAN-CLAUDE TRÉMOSA; 77 brs.

Banque Nationale pour le Développement Economique (BNDE): 12 place des Alaouites, BP 407, Rabat 10000; tel. (7) 706040; telex 31942; fax (7) 703706; f. 1959; transfer to private ownership pending; cap. 600.0m., res 825.7m., dep. 3,767.7m., total assets 9,332.9m. (Dec. 1996); Chair. and Man. Dir FARID DELLERO; 14 brs.

Crédit Immobilier et Hôtelier: 187 ave Hassan II, Casablanca; tel. (2) 202480; telex 23038; fax (2) 223748; f. 1920; transferred to majority private ownership in 1995; cap. 1,020.5m., res 119.5m., dep. 7,977.7m., total assets 22,074.0m. (Dec. 1995); Pres. MOULAY ZINE ZAHIDI; Gen. Man. ABDELOUAHED SOUHAÏL; 72 brs.

Crédit du Maroc SA: 48–58 blvd Muhammad V, BP 13579, Casablanca 20000; tel. (2) 477000; telex 46678; fax (2) 277127; f. 1963; cap. 833.8m., res 457.9, dep. 10,137.2m., total assets 12,421.8m. (Dec. 1996); Chair. and CEO JAWAD BEN BRAHIM; Dir YVES KERROS; 117 brs.

Crédit Populaire du Maroc (Banque Centrale Populaire): 101 blvd Muhammad Zerktouni, BP 10622, Casablanca 02; tel. (2) 202533; telex 21723; fax (2) 222699; f. 1961; 51% state-owned, 49% privately-owned; cap. 1,267.6m., res 3,151.1m., dep. 46,852.1m., total assets 57,300.7m. (Dec. 1996); Chair. and CEO ABD AL-LATIF LARAKI; Exec. Gen. Man. FAYÇAL ZEMMAMA.

Société Générale Marocaine de Banques SA: 55 blvd Abd al-Moumen, Casablanca 21100; tel. (2) 200972; telex 24898; fax (2) 200948; f. 1962; cap. 975.0m., res 386.2m. dep. 12,388.9m. (Dec. 1996); Pres. ABD AL-AZIZ TAZI; 115 brs.

Société Marocaine de Dépôt et Crédit: 79 ave Hassan II, BP 296, Casablanca 20000; tel. (2) 224114; telex 21013; fax (2) 271590; f. 1974; cap. 625.9m., res 729.4m., dep. 3,048.7m. (Dec. 1996); Pres. ABD AL-LATIF LARAKI; Gen. Man. MOHAMED TAZI; 21 brs.

Wafabank: 163 ave Hassan II, Casablanca 01; tel. (2) 224105; telex 21051; fax (2) 266202; f. 1964 as Compagnie Marocaine de Crédit et de Banque; cap. 553.2m., res 1,342m., total assets 20,807m. (Dec. 1996); Pres. and CEO ABD AL-HAK BENNANI; 89 brs.

Bank Organizations

Association Professionnelle des Intermédiaires de Bourse du Maroc: 71 ave des Forces Armées Royales, Casablanca; tel. (2) 314824; telex 22821; fax (2) 314903; f. 1967; groups all banks and brokers in the stock exchange of Casablanca, for studies, inquiries of general interest and contacts with official authorities; 11 mems; Pres. ABD AL-LATIF JOUAHRI.

Groupement Professionnel des Banques du Maroc: 71 ave des Forces Armées Royales, Casablanca; tel. (2) 314824; telex 22821; fax (2) 314903; f. 1967; groups all commercial banks for studies, inquiries of general interest, and contacts with official authorities; 18 mems; Pres. ABD AL-LATIF JOUAHRI.

STOCK EXCHANGE

Bourse des Valeurs de Casablanca: ave de l'Armée Royale, Casablanca; tel. (2) 452626; telex 23698; fax (2) 452625; f. 1929; Pres. ZOUHEIR BENSAÏD; Sec.-Gen. DRISS BENCHEIKH.

INSURANCE

Al-Amane: 122 ave Hassan II, Casablanca 20000; tel. (2) 267272; telex 46473; fax (2) 265664; f. 1975; cap. 120m.; Pres. and Dir-Gen. MOHAMED BOUGHALEB.

Al-Wataniya: 83 ave de l'Armée Royale, Casablanca; tel. (2) 314850; telex 22674; fax (2) 313137; Dir-Gen. ABD AL-JALIL CHRAIBI.

Alliance Africaine: 63 blvd Moulay Youssef, Casablanca 20000; tel. (2) 200690; telex 45737; fax (2) 200694; f. 1975; cap. 20m.; Pres. ABD AR-RAHIM CHERKAOUI; Dir-Gen. KHALID CHEDDADI.

Atlanta: 49 angle rues Othman ben Affane et Saâd Ben-Abi Ouakkas, Casablanca; tel. (2) 491448; telex 21644; fax (2) 203011; f. 1947; cap. 40m.; Dirs-Gen. MOHAMED REYAD, OMAR BENNANI.

Cie Africaine d'Assurances: 120 ave Hassan II, Casablanca 21000; tel. (2) 224185; telex 21661; fax (2) 260150; f. 1950; Pres. FOUAD FILALI; Dir-Gen. JAMAL HAROUCHI.

Cie d'Assurances SANAD: 3 blvd Muhammad V, BP 13438, Casablanca; tel. (2) 260591; telex 21927; fax (2) 293813; f. 1975; Chair. MUHAMMAD AOUAD; Dir-Gen. ABDELTIF TAHIRI.

Cie Nordafricaine et Intercontinentale d'Assurances (CNIA): 216 blvd Muhammad Zerktouni, Casablanca; tel. (2) 224118; telex 21096; fax (2) 267866; f. 1949; cap. 30m.; Man. Dir SAÂD KANOUNI.

Garantie Générale Marocaine: 106 rue Abd ar-Rahman Sahraoui, Casablanca; tel. (2) 279015; telex 24885; Dir-Gen. DIDIER LAMBERT.

La Marocaine Vie: 37 blvd Moulay Youssef, Casablanca; tel. (2) 206320; telex 46462; fax (2) 261971; f. 1978; cap. 12m.; Pres. H. KETTANI.

Mutuelle Centrale Marocaine d'Assurances: 16 rue Abou Inane, BP 27, Rabat; tel. (7) 766960; telex 31739; Pres. ABD AS-SALAM CHERIF D'OUEZZANE; Dir-Gen. YACOUBI SOUSSANE.

Mutuelle d'Assurances des Transporteurs Unis (MATU): 215 blvd Muhammad Zerktouni, Casablanca; tel. (2) 367097; Dir-Gen. M. BENYAMNA MOHAMED.

La Royale Marocaine d'Assurances (RMA): 67–69 ave de l'Armée Royale, Casablanca; tel. (2) 312163; telex 21818; fax (2) 313884; f. 1949; cap. 100m.; Chair. OTHMAN BEN JELLOUN; Dir-Gen. SÉBASTIEN CASTRO.

Es-Saada, Cie d'Assurances et de Réassurances: 123 ave Hassan II, BP 13860, Casablanca; tel. (2) 222525; telex 21791; fax (2) 262655; f. 1961; cap. 50m.; Pres. MEHDI OUAZZANI; Man. Dir SAÏD OUAZZANI.

Société Centrale de Réassurance: Tour Atlas, place Zallaqa, BP 13183, Casablanca; tel. (2) 308585; telex 28084; fax (2) 308672; e-mail s.c.r@elan.net.ma; f. 1960; cap. 30m.; Chair. KHALID KADIRI; Man. Dir AHMED ZINOUN.

Société Marocaine d'Assurances à l'Exportation: 24 rue Ali Abderrazak, BP 15953, Casablanca; tel. (2) 982000; fax (2) 252070; f. 1988; insurance for exporters in the public and private sectors; assistance for export promotion; Pres., Dir-Gen. ABD AL-HAMID JOUAHRI; Asst. Dir-Gen. ABD EL-KADER DRIOUACHE.

WAFA Assurance: 1–3 blvd Abd al-Moumen, Casablanca; tel. (2) 224575; telex 21867; fax (2) 209103; Dir-Gen. JAOUAD KETTANI.

INSURANCE ASSOCIATION

Fédération Marocaine des Sociétés d'Assurances et de Réassurances: 154 blvd d'Anfa, Casablanca; tel. (2) 391850; telex 45524; fax (2) 391854; f. 1958; 22 mem. cos; Pres. ABD AL-JALIL CHRAIBI; Dir ABD AL-FETTAH ALAMI.

Trade and Industry

GOVERNMENT AGENCIES

Bureau de Recherches et de Participations Minières (BRPM): 5 ave Moulay Hassan, BP 99, Rabat; tel. (7) 05005; telex 31066; fax (7) 09411; f. 1928; a state agency conducting exploration, valorization and exploitation of mineral resources; Gen. Man. ASSOU LHATOUTE; Sec.-Gen. ALI BENNANI.

Centre Marocain de Promotion des Exportations (CMPE): 23 blvd Bnou Majid el-Bahar, BP 10937, Casablanca; tel. (2) 302210; telex 27847; fax (2) 301793; f. 1980; state org. for promotion of exports; Dir-Gen. MOUNIR M. BENSAID.

Société de Gestion des Terres Agricoles (SOGETA): 35 rue Daïet-Erroumi, BP 731, Agdal, Rabat; tel. (7) 72834; telex 31704; f. 1973; oversees use of agricultural land; Man. Dir OMAR AL-HEBIL.

DEVELOPMENT ORGANIZATIONS

Caisse de Dépôt et de Gestion: place Moulay El-Hassan, BP 408, Rabat; tel. (7) 765520; telex 31072; fax (7) 763849; f. 1959; finances small-scale projects; cap. and res 1,126m. dirhams (Dec. 1995); Gen. Man. KHALID EL-KADIRI; Sec.-Gen. MUSTAPHA MECHAHOURI.

Caisse Marocaine des Marchés (Marketing Fund): Résidence El Manar, blvd Abd al-Moumen, Casablanca; tel. (2) 259118; telex 24740; fax (2) 259120; f. 1950; cap. 10m. dirhams; Man. HASSAN KISSI.

Caisse Nationale de Crédit Agricole (Agricultural Credit Fund): 2 ave d'Alger, BP 49, Rabat; tel. (7) 725920; telex 31657; fax (7) 732580; f. 1961; cap. 1,573.5m. dirhams, dep. 3,471.9m. dirhams; Dir-Gen. SAID IBRAHIMI.

Office pour le Développement Industriel (ODI): 10 rue Gandhi, BP 211, Rabat; tel. (7) 708460; telex 31053; fax (7) 67695; f. 1973; a state agency to develop industry; Man. Dir ABD EL-HAMID BELAHSEN.

Société de Développement Agricole (SODEA): ave Hadj Ahmed Cherkaoui, BP 6280, Rabat; tel. (7) 770825; telex 31675; fax (7) 774798; f. 1972; state agricultural development org.; Man. Dir M. SABBARI HASSANI LARBI.

Société Nationale d'Investissement (SNI): 60 rue d'Alger, BP 38, Casablanca; tel. (2) 484288; telex 22736; fax (2) 484303; f. 1966; transferred to majority private ownership in 1994; cap. 10,900m. dirhams; Pres. N'FADEL LAHLOU; Sec.-Gen. YOUSSEF IRAQUI.

CHAMBERS OF COMMERCE

La Fédération des Chambres de Commerce et d'Industrie du Maroc: 6 rue d'Erfoud, Rabat-Agdal; tel. (7) 767078; telex 36662; fax (7) 767076; f. 1962; groups the 26 Chambers of Commerce and Industry; Pres. AHMED M'RABET; Dir-Gen. MOHAMED LARBI EL HARRAS.

Chambre de Commerce et d'Industrie de Rabat-Salé et de Skhirat-Temara: 1 rue Gandhi, BP 131, Rabat; tel. (7) 706444; telex 36898; fax (7) 706768; Pres. MOULAY LAHCEN EL-IDRISSI; Dir MUHAMMAD NAJIB AFFANE.

Chambre de Commerce et d'Industrie de la Wilaya du Grand Casablanca: 98 blvd Muhammad V, BP 423, Casablanca; tel. (2) 264327; telex 24630; Pres. LAHCEN EL-WAFI.

INDUSTRIAL AND TRADE ASSOCIATIONS

Office National Interprofessionnel des Céréales et des Légumineuses: 25 ave Moulay Hassan, BP 154, Rabat; tel. (7) 701735; telex 31930; fax (7) 709626; f. 1937; Dir-Gen. ABD AL-HAI BOUZOUBAA.

Office National des Pêches: 15 rue du Lieutenant Mahroud, BP 16243, Casablanca 20300; tel. (2) 240551; fax (2) 242305; e-mail onp@onp.co.ma; internet http://www.onp.co.ma; f. 1969; state fishing org.; Man. Dir TOUFIQ IBRAHIMI.

EMPLOYERS' ORGANIZATIONS

Association Marocaine des Industries Textiles et de l'Habillement (AMITH): 92 blvd Moulay Rachid, Casablanca; tel. (2) 942085; fax (2) 940587; e-mail amith@mail.winner.net.ma; f. 1958; mems 700 textile, knitwear and ready-made garment factories; Pres. MOHAMED LAHLOU; Dir-Gen. ABDE LALI BERRADA.

Association des Producteurs d'Agrumes du Maroc (ASPAM): 22 rue al-Messaoudi, Casablanca; tel. (2) 363946; fax (2) 364041; f. 1958; links Moroccan citrus growers; has its own processing plants; Chair. AHMED MANSOUR NEJJAI.

Association Professionnelle des Cimentiers: 239 blvd Moulay Ismail, BP 3096, Casablanca; cement manufacturers.

Confédération Générale des Entreprises du Maroc (CGEM): angle aves des Forces Armées Royales et rue Muhammad Arrachid, Casablanca 20100; tel. (2) 252696; fax (2) 253839; e-mail cgem@mail.cbi.net.ma; Pres. ABD AR-RAHIM LAHJOUJI; Dir MOUHCINE AYOUCHE.

Union Marocaine de l'Agriculture (UMA): 12 place des Alaouites, Rabat; Pres. M. NEJJAI.

UTILITIES
Electricity

Office National de l'Electricité (ONE): 65 rue Othman Ben Affan, BP 13498, Casablanca 20100; tel. (2) 224165; telex 22780; fax (2) 220038; f. 1963; state electricity authority; Dir-Gen. ABERRAHMANE NAJI.

Water

Office National de l'Eau Potable (ONEP): 6 bis rue Patrice Lumumba, Rabat; tel; (7) 734004; telex 31982; fax (7) 731355; f. 1972; responsible for drinking-water supply; Dir LAHOUCINE TIJANI.

MAJOR COMPANIES

Brasseries du Maroc: ave Pasteur, BP 87, Casablanca; tel. (2) 245726; telex 25931; f. 1919; distillery, brewery and producer of soft drinks; Chair. BACHIR BELABBES TAARJI; Dir-Gen. HAMID BEN CHEKROUN.

Charbonnages Nord Africains: 27 ave Moulay Hassan, BP 255, Rabat; tel. (7) 24147; telex 31923; f. 1946; coal mining; 5,000 employees.

Chérifienne de Travaux Africains: 1 blvd du Fouarat, Casablanca; tel. (2) 614684; telex 25782; fax (2) 614689; f. 1960; building and civil engineering contractors; cap. 10m. dirhams; Dir-Gen. SARGA BERDUGO; 2,000 employees.

Compagnie Marocaine des Hydrocarbures: BP 6180, angle rond Point des Sports et rue Point du Jour, blvd Abd al-Latif Benkaddour, Casablanca; tel. (2) 296786; telex 46695; fax (2) 207955; marketing of petroleum and oil products; cap. 33m. dirhams; Dir-Gen. HASSAN AGZENAI.

Compagnie Sucrière Marocaine et de Raffinage SA (COSUMAR): 8 rue el Mouatamid ibnou Abbad, BP 3098, Casablanca; tel. (2) 247345; telex 25032; fax (2) 241071; f. 1967; sugar refining and trading; cap. 60m. dirhams; Chair. FOUAD FILALI; Gen. Man. MUHAMMAD AL-BAZ; 2,854 employees (April 1989).

Complexe Textile de Fès (COTEF): Quartier Sidi Brahim, route de Sefrou, BP 2267, Fez; tel. (6) 41309; telex 51606; f. 1967; production of yarns and textiles; Dir-Gen. ABD AL-HAMID SEDDIKI.

Conserveries Chérifiennes: route du Djorf el-Youdi, BP 96, Safi; tel. (4) 472513; telex 71774; f. 1949; fish and food processing and canning; cap. 16.2m. dirhams; Gen. Man. MUHAMMAD EL-JAMALI; 2,500 employees.

Manufacture Nationale de Textiles (MANATEX): 164 blvd de la Gironde, Casablanca; tel. (2) 246565; telex 26734; f. 1957; manufacture of textiles and furnishings; Chair. ALI KETTANI; Dirs LARBI AS-SAKALLI, MUHAMMAD LAHLOU, MUHAMMAD LAZRAK; 1,250 employees.

Office Chérifien des Phosphates (OCP): blvd de la Grande Ceinture, route d'el Jadida, Casablanca; tel. (2) 360025; telex 21630; f. 1921; a state co to produce and market rock phosphates and derivatives; Dir-Gen. MUHAMMAD FETTAH.

ONA: 52 ave Hassan II, BP 657, Casablanca; tel. (2) 224102; telex 21859; fax (2) 261064; f. 1919; fmrly Omnium Nord Africain; largest private co in Morocco, owns subsidiaries in food, mining, distribution, real estate and insurance industries; cap. 1,720m. dirhams (1996); Pres. FOUAD FILALI; Dir-Gen. GILLES DENISTY.

Phosphates de Boucraa SA (PHOSBOUCRAA): Immeuble OCP, angle route d'el Jadida et blvd de la Grande Ceinture, Casablanca; tel. (2) 360025; telex 24033; f. 1962; production and processing of phosphate rock; cap. 328m. dirhams; Pres. MUHAMMAD KARIM LAMRANI; Dirs ALFONSO ALVAREZ MIRANDA, MUHAMMAD BEN HAROUGA; 1,146 employees.

SATFILAGE SA: route de l'Aviation, BP 1059, Tangier; tel. (9) 34049; telex 33047; f. 1962; production of synthetic fibres and textiles; 1,500 employees; Pres. Agha ADAL TALEB.

Société d'Exploitation des Mines du Rif (SEFERIF): 30 Abou-Faris el-Marini, BP 436, Rabat; tel. (7) 66350; telex 31708; nationalized 1967; open and underground mines produce iron ore for export and for the projected Nador iron and steel complex; Man. Dir MUHAMMAD HARRAK.

Société Marocaine de Constructions Automobiles (SOMACA): km 12, autoroute de Rabat, BP 2628, Casablanca; tel. (2) 353924; telex 25825; f. 1959; assembly of motor vehicles; owned by Moroccan Govt, Fiat, Peugeot and SNI; Pres. MEHDI BEN BOUCHTA; Dir-Gen. MUHAMMAD A. BELARBI; 1,011 employees.

Société Nationale de Sidérurgie (SONASID): Route RP 18, Mont Arouit, BP 151, Nador; tel. (6) 609441; telex 65787; fax (6) 609442; f. 1974; iron and steel projects; cap. 390m. dirhams; transferred to private ownership in 1997; Dir-Gen. ABDALLAH SOUIBRI.

Société Nouvelle des Conduites d'Eau (SNCE): Résidence Kays Sahat Rabia, Al Adaouiya Agdal, Rabat; tel. (7) 723424; telex 31028; fax (7) 776674; f. 1961; manufacture of steel and cast-iron pipes and materials; cap. 67.2m. dirhams; Chair. OMAR LARAQUI; Dir-Gen. MUHAMMAD ABDELLAOUI; 2,600 employees.

TRADE UNIONS

Confédération Démocratique du Travail (CDT): 64 rue al-Mourtada, Quartier Palmier, BP 13576, Casablanca; tel. (2) 994470; fax (2) 258162; f. 1978; 400,000 mems; Sec.-Gen. MOHAMED NOUBIR AMAOUI.

Union Démocratique de l'Agriculture: f. 1997; Sec.-Gen. ABD AR-RAHMAN FILALI.

Union Générale des Travailleurs Marocains (UGTM): 9 rue du Rif, angle Route de Médiouna, Casablanca; tel. (2) 282144; f. 1960; associated with Istiqlal; supported by unions not affiliated to UMT; 673,000 mems; Sec.-Gen. ABD AR-RAZZAQ AFILAL.

Union Marocaine du Travail (UMT): Bourse du Travail, 232 ave des Forces Armées Royales, Casablanca; tel. (2) 302292; telex 27825; left-wing and associated with the UNFP; most unions are affiliated; 700,000 mems; Sec. MAHJOUB BEN SEDDIQ.

Union Syndicale Agricole (USA): agricultural section of UMT.

Union Marocaine du Travail Autonome: Rabat; breakaway union from UMT.

Transport

Office National des Transports (ONT): rue al-Fadila, Quartier Industriel, BP 596, Rabat-Chellah; tel. (7) 797842; telex 36090; fax (7) 797850; f. 1958; Man. Dir AHMED EL YOUSFI.

RAILWAYS

In 1997 there were 1,907 km of railways, of which 271 km were double track; 1,003 km of lines were electrified and diesel locomotives were used on the rest. The network carried some 10.7m. passengers and 27.3m. metric tons of freight in 1996. All services are nationalized. A feasibility study was begun in early 1998 for the construction of a 28-km metro system in Casablanca.

Office National des Chemins de Fer (ONCF): 8 bis rue Abderrahmane El Ghafiki, Rabat-Agdal; tel. (7) 774747; telex 36474; fax (7) 777857; f. 1963; administers all Morocco's railways; Pres. Minister of Transport; Dir-Gen. MOHAMED EL ALJ.

ROADS

In 1996 there were 60,369 km of classified roads, of which 49.4% were paved. There were 10,336 km of main roads and 10,627 km of regional roads.

Cie de Transports au Maroc 'Lignes Nationales' (CTM−LN): 23 rue Léon l'Africain, Casablanca; tel. (2) 312061; telex 28962; agencies in Tangier, Rabat, Meknès, Oujda, Marrakesh, Agadir, El Jadida, Safi, Casablanca, es-Saouira, Ksar es-Souk, Fez and Ouarzazate; privatized in mid-1993 with 40% of shares reserved for Moroccan citizens; Man. Dir MOHAMED EL ALJ.

SHIPPING

Morocco's 21 ports handled 42.6m. tons of goods in 1996. The most important ports, in terms of the volume of goods handled, are Casablanca, Mohammadia, Jorf Lasfar and Safi. Tangier is the principal port for passenger services. Construction work on new ports at Tangier (to handle merchandise traffic) and Agadir was expected to begin in 1998.

Office d'Exploitation des Ports (ODEP): 4 rue Mossa Ibnou Noussair, Casablanca; tel. (2) 317111; telex 46790; fax (2) 313501; f. 1985; Man. Dir MUHAMMAD HALAB.

Principal Shipping Companies

Agence Gibmar SA: 3 rue Henri Regnault, Tangier; tel. (9) 935875; fax (9) 933239; e-mail agemcemed@mamnet.net.ma; also at Casablanca; regular services from Tangier to Gibraltar; Chair. JAMES PETER GAGGERO; Dir YOUSSEF BENYAHIA.

Cie Chérifienne d'Armement: 5 blvd Abdallah ben Yacine, Casablanca 21700; tel. (2) 309455; telex 27054; fax (2) 301186; f. 1929; regular services to Europe; Man. Dir MAX KADOCH.

Cie Marocaine d'Agences Maritimes (COMARINE): 45 ave des Forces Armées Royales, Casablanca 21000; tel. (2) 311941; telex 21851; fax (2) 312570; f. 1969; Pres. YVES PERRIN; Dir-Gen. THIERRY LABARRE.

Cie Marocaine de Navigation (COMANAV): 7 blvd de la Résistance, BP 628, Casablanca; tel. (2) 303012; telex 26093; fax (2) 308455; f. 1946; regular services to Mediterranean, North-west European, Middle Eastern and West African ports; tramping; Chair. MOHAMED BENHAROUGA.

Intercona SA (Transmediterránea and Isleña de Navegación): 31 ave de la Résistance, Tangier; tel. (9) 41101; telex 33005; fax (9) 43863; f. 1943; daily services from Algeciras (Spain) to Tangier and Ceuta (Spanish North Africa); Dir-Gen. ANTONIO FERRE CASALS.

Limadet-ferry: 3 rue Ibn Rochd, Tangier; tel. (9) 33639; telex 33013; fax (9) 37173; f. 1966; operates between Algeciras (Spain) and Tangier, six daily; Dir-Gen. RACHID BEN MANSOUR.

Société Marocaine de Navigation Atlas: 81 ave Houmane el-Fatouaki, Casablanca 21000; tel. (2) 224190; telex 23067; fax (2) 274401; f. 1976; Chair. HASSAN CHAMI; Man. Dir M. SLAOUI.

Société Marocaine de Navigation Fruitière (SOFRUMA): Casablanca; tel. (2) 310003; telex 23097; fax (2) 310031; f. 1962; Dir-Gen. KHAMMAL ABD EL-HAMID.

Union Maritime Maroc-Scandinave (UNIMAR): 12 rue de Foucauld, BP 746, Casablanca; tel. (2) 279590; telex 22996; fax (2) 223883; f. 1974; chemicals; Dir-Gen. ABD AL-WAHAB BEN KIRANE.

Voyages Paquet: Hotel Royal Mansour, rue Sidi Belyout, Casablanca 20000; tel. (2) 311065; fax (2) 442108; f. 1970; Pres. MUHAMMAD ELOUALI ELALAMI; Dir-Gen. NAÏMA BAKALI ELOUALI ELALAMI.

CIVIL AVIATION

The main international airports are at Casablanca (King Muhammad V), Rabat, Tangier, Marrakesh, Agadir Inezgane, Fez, Oujda, Al-Hocima, el-Aaiún, Ouarzazate and Agadir al-Massira.

Regional Airlines: f. 1997; privately-owned; domestic flights and services planned to southern Spain and the Canary Islands.

Royal Air Maroc (RAM): Aéroport de Casablanca-Anfa; tel. (2) 912000; telex 21880; fax (2) 912087; f. 1953; 94.4% state-owned; domestic flights and services to 35 countries in western Europe, Scandinavia, the Americas, North and West Africa, the Canary Islands and the Middle East; Chair. and Dir-Gen. MOHAMED HASSAD.

Tourism

Tourism is Morocco's second main source of convertible currency. The country's attractions for tourists include its sunny climate, ancient sites (notably the cities of Fez, Marrakesh, Meknès and Rabat) and spectacular scenery. There are popular holiday resorts on the Atlantic and Mediterranean coasts. In 1997 tourist arrivals totalled an estimated 1.8m., compared with 2.9m. in 1993. Tourist receipts in 1996 totalled 11,500m. dirhams.

Office National Marocain du Tourisme: 31 angle ave al-Abtal and rue Oued Fas, Agdal, Rabat; tel. (7) 681531; fax (7) 777437; f. 1918; Dir SAMIR KHELDOUNI SAHRAOUI.

Defence

Commander-in-Chief of the Armed Forces: HM King HASSAN II.
Estimated Defence Budget (1997): 14,700m. dirhams.

Military Service: 18 months.
Total Armed Forces (August 1997): 196,300 (army 175,000; navy 7,800; air force 13,500); royal guard 12,000. Paramilitary forces: 42,000. Reserves: 150,000.

Education

Since independence in 1956, Morocco has tried to solve a number of educational problems: a youthful and fast-growing population, an urgent need for skilled workers and executives, a great diversity of teaching methods between French, Spanish, Muslim and Moroccan government schools, and, above all, a high degree of adult illiteracy. In 1995, according to UNESCO estimates, adult illiteracy averaged 56.3% (males 43.4%; females 69.0%). Under the 1995 budget, expenditure on education by the central Government was projected at 15,542m. dirhams (18.9% of total spending).

In 1996/97 there were 3,034,408 pupils in primary schools. At this level most instruction is given in government schools, where syllabuses have been standardized since 1967. Great progress was made in providing new schools during 1957–64, but since then the increase in the number of places has decelerated. A decree of November 1963 made education compulsory for children between the ages of seven and 13 years, and this has now been applied in most urban areas, but throughout the country only 72% (81% of boys; 62% of girls) of the age-group attended school in 1995. All primary teachers are Moroccan. Instruction is given in Arabic for the first two years and in Arabic and French for the next three years, with English as the first additional language.

Secondary education, beginning at the age of 13, lasts for up to six years (comprising two cycles of three years), and in 1996/97 provided for 1,328,135 pupils (excluding those in private and professional schools). In 1988 the secondary school graduation examination, the *baccalauréat*, was replaced by a system of continuous assessment. Most secondary teachers are Moroccan, but in 1986 there were 1,461 from abroad, chiefly from France. Secondary enrolment in 1995 included 39% of the relevant age-group (boys 44%; girls 33%).

There are eight universities in Morocco, including the Islamic University of al-Quarawiyin at Fez (founded in 859), the Muhammad V University at Rabat (opened in 1957), and an English-language university, inaugurated at Ifrane in 1995. In addition, there are institutes of higher education in business studies, agriculture, mining, law, and statistics and advanced economics. In 1994/95 there was a total of 242,053 students engaged in higher education.

Adult education is supplemented by radio programmes, simplified type, and a newspaper for the newly literate. In recent years increasing attention has been given to education for girls. There are now a number of mixed and girls' schools, notably in urban areas.

Bibliography

Abu-Lughod, Janet L. *Rabat: Urban Apartheid in Morocco.* Guildford, England, Princeton University Press, 1981.

Amin, Samir. *The Maghreb in the Modern World.* Harmondsworth, Penguin, 1971.

Ashford, D. E. *Political Change in Morocco.* Princeton U.P., 1961.

Perspectives of a Moroccan Nationalist. New York, 1964.

Ayache, A. *Le Maroc.* Paris, Editions Sociales, 1956.

Baduel, Pierre-Robert. *Enjeux Sahariens.* Paris, CNRS, 1984.

Barbier, Maurice. *Le Conflit du Sahara occidental.* Paris, L'Harmattan, 1982.

Barbour, Nevill. *Morocco.* London, Thames and Hudson, 1964.

Ben Barka, Mehdi. *Problèmes de l'édification du Maroc et du Maghreb.* Paris, Plon, 1959.

Option Révolutionnaire en Maroc. Paris, Maspéro, 1966.

Bennett, Norman Robert. *A study guide for Morocco.* Boston, 1970.

Bernard, Stephane. *Le Conflit Franco-Marocain 1943–1956,* 3 vols. Brussels, 1963; English translation, Yale University Press, 1968.

Berque, Jaques. *Le Maghreb entre deux guerres.* Paris, Edns. du Seuil, 1962.

Brown, Kenneth. *People of Salé.* Manchester University Press, 1976.

Cohen, M. I., and Hahn, Lorna. *Morocco: Old Land. New Nation.* New York, Praeger, 1964.

Coulau, Julien. *La paysannerie marocaine.* Paris, 1968.

Eickelman, Dale F. *Moroccan Islam: Tradition and Society in a Pilgrimage Center.* Princeton University Press, 1986.

Hall, L. J. *The United States and Morocco, 1776–1956.* Metuchen, NJ, Scarecrow Press, 1971.

Halstead, John P. *Rebirth of a Nation: the Origins and Rise of Moroccan Nationalism.* Harvard University Press, 1967.

Hassan II, King of Morocco. *Le Défi.* Paris, Albin Michel, 1976.

Hodges, Tony. *Western Sahara: the Roots of a Desert War.* London, Croom Helm, 1983.

Historical Dictionary of Western Sahara. London, Scarecrow Press, 1982.

Horton, Brendon. *Morocco: Analysis and Reform of Foreign Policy.* Economic Development Institute of the World Bank, 1990.

Julien, Charles-André. *Le Maroc face aux Impérialismes (1415–1956).* Paris, Editions Jeune Afrique, 1978.

Kay, Shirley. *Morocco.* London, Namara Publications, 1980.

Kininmonth, C. *The Travellers' Guide to Morocco.* London, Jonathan Cape, 1972.

Lacouture, J. and S. *Le Maroc à l'épreuve.* Paris, du Seuil, 1958.

Landau, Rom. *The Moroccan Drama 1900–1955.* London, Hale, 1956.

Morocco Independent under Mohammed V. London, Allen and Unwin, 1961.

Hassan II, King of Morocco. London, Allen and Unwin, 1962.

The Moroccans — Yesterday and Today. London, 1963.

Morocco. London, Allen & Unwin, 1967.

Landau, Rom, and Swann, Wim. *Marokko.* Cologne, 1970.

MOROCCO

Le Tourneau, Roger. *Evolution politique de l'Afrique du Nord musulmane*. Paris, Armand Colin, 1962.

Maxwell, Gavin. *Lords of the Atlas*. London, Longmans, 1966.

Metcalf, John. *Morocco—an Economic Study*. New York, First National City Bank, 1966.

Mumson, Henry, Jr. *Religion and Power in Morocco*. London, Yale University Press, 1993.

Perrault, Gilles. *Notre Ami le Roi*. Paris, Editions Gallimard, 1991.

Perroux, F., and Barre, R. *Développement, croissance, progrès— Maroc-Tunisie*. Paris, 1961.

Robert, J. *La monarchie marocaine*. Paris, Librairie générale de droit et de jurisprudence, 1963.

Sutton, Michael. *Morocco to 1992 (Growth against the Odds)*. London, Economist Intelligence Unit, 1987.

Terrasse, H. *Histoire du Maroc des origines à l'établissement du protectorat français*, 2 vols. Casablanca, 1949–50; English trans. by H. Tee, London, 1952.

Thompson, Virginia, and Adloff, Richard. *The Western Saharans*. London, Croom Helm, Totowa, NJ, Barnes and Noble, 1980.

Tiano, André. *La politique économique et financière du Maroc indépendant*. Paris, Presses universitaires de France, 1963.

Trout, Frank E. *Morocco's Saharan Frontiers*. Geneva, 1969.

Waterbury, John. *The commander of the Faithful. The Moroccan political élite*. London, 1970.

Waterson, Albert. *Planning in Morocco*. Baltimore, Johns Hopkins Press, 1963.

World Bank. *The Economic Development of Morocco*. Baltimore, Johns Hopkins Press, 1966.

Growing Faster, Finding Jobs: Choices for Morocco. 1997.

Zartman, I. W. *Morocco: Problems of New Power*. New York, Atherton Press, 1964.

OMAN

Geography

The Sultanate of Oman occupies the extreme east and southeast of the Arabian peninsula. It is bordered by the United Arab Emirates (UAE) to the north and west, by Saudi Arabia to the west and by Yemen to the south-west. A detached area of Oman, separated from the rest of the country by UAE territory, lies at the tip of the Musandam peninsula, on the southern shore of the Strait of Hormuz. Oman is separated from Iran by the Gulf of Oman, and it has a coastline of more than 1,600 km (1,000 miles) on the Indian Ocean. The total area of the country is 309,500 sq km (119,500 sq miles). Oman's frontiers with all its neighbours have yet to be clearly demarcated, although agreement exists on their general course. In mid-1995 Oman completed the demarcation of its joint borders with both Yemen and Saudi Arabia. In May 1997 Oman and Yemen signed international border demarcation maps in Muscat, Oman.

The first full census in Oman was held in 1993. Previous estimates of the country's population varied widely between official Omani figures and those of independent international organizations. The UN Population Division, basing its assessment on a mid-1965 figure of 571,000, estimated totals of 654,000 for mid-1970 and 984,000 for mid-1980. By 1990 the UN estimated that Oman's mid-year population had grown to 1,502,000. World Bank estimates indicated annual average population growth of 4.8% during 1990–96. According to the census of 1 December 1993, the population totalled 2,018,074, comprising 1,483,226 Omani nationals (73.5%) and 534,848 non-Omanis (26.5%). In 1996 the UN estimated the mid-year population to be 2,302,000. The majority of the population are Ibadi Muslims, and about one-quarter are Hindus.

At Muscat the mean annual rainfall is 100 mm and the mean temperature varies between 20°C and 43°C (69°F and 110°F). Rainfall on the hills of the interior is somewhat heavier, and the south-western province of Dhofar is the only part of Arabia to benefit from the summer monsoon.

Oman may be divided into nine topographical areas. The largest urban area in the country is the capital region, around Muscat. Although most of the country is arid, the Batinah plain, which lies between the Gulf of Oman and the Hajar al-Gharbi range of mountains, comprises a fertile coastal region, and is among the most densely populated areas of the country. Another such plain is found between Raysut and Salalah, on the south-west coast in the Dhofar region, which, in total, occupies one-third of the country's area and extends northwards into the Rub al-Khali, or 'empty quarter', on Oman's western border: a rainless, unrelieved wilderness of shifting sand, almost entirely without human habitation.

Irrigation has been developed in some parts of the country, including the Dhahira area, a semi-desert plain between the south-western Hajar mountains and the Rub al-Khali, which also provides clusters of cultivable land near the wadis Dank and Ain, and the Buraini oasis. From Jebel al-Akhdar, at the southern tip of the Hajar al-Gharbi range, towards the desert in the south, lies the Interior, the country's central hill region and the most densely populated zone. The area has four main valleys, two of which (Halafein and Samail) provide the traditional route to Muscat.

The less hospitable regions are sparsely populated by groups of tribal settlers. The Hajar al-Gharbi, running parallel to the coast southwards from Oman's border with the UAE, is the home of the Rostaq, Awabi and Nakhe tribes. To the east of the Hajar range, the Sharqiya area extends south towards the Arabian Sea. It is an area of sandy plains and the home of the various Bani tribes. Musandam, separated from Oman by the UAE, is a mountainous area inhabited by the ash-Shahouh tribes. Around the eastern coast of the Arabian Sea, the Barr al-Hekkman, a group of islands and salt-plains of 650 sq km (250 sq miles), is inhabited by fishing communities.

For administrative purposes, the Sultanate is divided into eight governorates, comprising 59 *wilayat* (provinces), each under the jurisdiction of a *wali*, or provincial governor.

History

Revised for this edition by YOUSSEF CHOUEIRI

Oman was probably the land of Magan (mentioned in Sumerian tablets) with which cities such as Ur of the Chaldees traded in the third millennium BC. The province of Dhofar also produced frankincense in vast quantities, which was shipped to markets in Iraq, Syria, Egypt and the West. Roman geographers mention the city of Omana, although its precise location has not been identified, and Portus Moschus, conceivably Muscat. Oman, at various times, came under the influence of the Himyaritic kingdoms of southern Arabia and of Iran, which are believed to have been responsible for the introduction of the *falaj* irrigation systems, although legend attributes them to Sulaiman ibn Daud (Solomon).

The people of Oman come from two main ethnic stocks, the Qahtan, who immigrated from southern Arabia, and the Nizar, who came in from the north. According to tradition, the first important invasion from southern Arabia was led by Malik ibn Faham, after the final collapse of the Marib dam in Yemen in the first or second century AD. Oman was one of the first countries to be converted to Islam by Amr ibn al-As, who later converted Egypt. Omanis of the tribe of al-Azd played an important part in the early days of Islam in Iraq. They subsequently embraced the Ibadi doctrine, which holds that the caliphate in Islam should not be hereditary or confined to any one family, and established their own independent Imamate in Oman in the eighth century AD. Subsequently, although subject to invasions by the Caliphate, Iranians, Moguls and others, Oman has largely maintained its independence.

During the 10th century Sohar was probably the largest and most important city in the Arab world, while Omani mariners, together with those from Basra and other Gulf ports, went as far afield as China. When the Portuguese arrived in 1507, on their way to India, Affonso d'Albuquerque and his forces found the Omani seaport under the suzerainty of the King of Hormuz, himself of Omani stock. The towns of Qalhat, Quryat, Muscat and Sohar were already prosperous.

However, the arrival of the Portuguese in the Indian Ocean radically altered the balance of power in the area. The Portuguese established themselves in the Omani ports, concentrating principally on Sohar and Muscat, where they built two great forts, Merani (1587) and Jalali (1588). British and Dutch traders followed in the wake of the Portuguese, though they did not establish themselves by force of arms in Oman. In 1650 the Imam Nasir ibn Murshid of the Yaariba dynasty, who was also credited with a period of Omani renaissance during which learning flourished, effectively expelled the Portuguese from Muscat and the rest of Oman. The Omanis then extended their

879

power, and by 1730 had conquered the Portuguese settlements on the east coast of Africa, including Mogadishu (now in Somalia), Mombasa (Kenya) and Zanzibar (now part of Tanzania).

The country was, however, ravaged by civil war in the first half of the 18th century, when the authority of the Imam diminished. During this period the Iranians were summoned to assist one of the contenders for the Imamate, but they were subsequently ousted by Ahmad ibn Said, who was elected Imam in 1749 and founded the al-Bu Said dynasty, one of the oldest dynasties in the Middle East, which still rules Oman. The country prospered under the new dynasty and its maritime influence revived. In about 1786 the capital of the country was transferred from Rostaq to Muscat, a move which led to a dichotomy between the coast and the interior, creating political problems between the two regions at various times.

The Imam, Said bin Sultan, ruled Oman from 1804 until 1856. He was a strong and popular ruler, who also gained the respect and friendship of European nations, in particular the British. Treaties providing for the establishment of consular relations were negotiated with the British in 1839 (there had been earlier treaties of friendship in 1798 and 1800), the USA in 1833, France in 1844 and the Netherlands in 1877. British relations with Oman were maintained almost uninterrupted from the early 18th century until the present day, while relations with the other states concerned were less continuous.

Said bin Sultan revived Omani interest in Zanzibar and, in the latter part of his reign, spent an increasing amount of his time there. He started the clove plantations which later brought great wealth to the islands of Zanzibar and Pemba, and he founded the dynasty which ruled there until the revolution in 1964. During Said's reign, Omani dominions expanded to their greatest extent. In 1829 Dhofar became one of the constituent parts of the Sultanate and has remained so ever since.

The latter half of the 19th century was a difficult period for Oman. Not only had it lost its East African possessions, but a series of treaties with Britain to curb the slave trade also brought about a decline in the local economy, as Muscat had been an important port for this lucrative traffic.

Several insurrections took place towards the end of the 19th century, and in 1913 a new Imam was elected in the interior, in defiance of the Sultan who ruled from Muscat. This led to the expulsion of the Sultan's garrisons from Nizwa, Izki and Sumail. In the same year Sultan Faisal bin Turki, who had ruled since 1888, died, to be succeeded by his son Taimur. Efforts to come to terms with the rebels failed until 1920, when an agreement was reached between the Sultan and the principal dissidents, led by Isa bin Salih. It provided for peace, free movement of persons between the interior and the coast, limitation of customs duties and non-interference by the government of the Sultan in the internal affairs of the signatory tribes. A Treaty of Friendship with Britain, signed on 20 December 1951, recognized the full independence of the sultanate, officially called Muscat and Oman. Relations between the Imam, Muhammad bin Abdullah al-Khalili, and the Sultan remained good until the Imam's death in 1954, when rebellion again broke out under the Imam's successor, Ghalib bin Ali, who sought external assistance to establish a separate principality. In December 1955 forces under the Sultan's control entered the main inhabited centres of Oman without resistance. The former Imam was allowed by the Sultan to retire to his village, but his brother, Talib, escaped to Saudi Arabia and thence to Cairo. An 'Oman Imamate' office was established there, and the Imam's cause was supported by Egyptian propaganda. In the summer of 1957 Talib returned and established himself, with followers, in the mountain areas north-west of Nizwa. The Sultan appealed for British help, and fighting continued until early 1959, when the Sultan's authority was fully re-established. In October 1960, despite British objections, 10 Arab countries succeeded in placing the 'question of Oman' on the agenda of the UN General Assembly. In 1961 a resolution in support of separate independence for Oman failed to secure the necessary majority, and in 1963 a UN Commission of Inquiry refuted the Imamate's charges of oppressive government and public hostility to the Sultan. Nevertheless, a committee was formed to study the problem and, after its report had been submitted to the General Assembly in 1965, a resolution was adopted which, among other things, demanded the elimination of British domination in any

form. The question was debated on several further occasions until, more than a year after Sultan Qaboos's accession, Oman (as Muscat and Oman was renamed in 1970: see below) became a member of the UN in October 1971.

THE SULTANATE SINCE 1970

By 1970 Sultan Said's Government had come to be regarded as the most reactionary and isolationist in the area. Slavery was still common, and many medieval prohibitions were in force. The Sultan's insistence that petroleum revenues be used exclusively to fund defence was embarrassing for Britain, the oil companies and the neighbouring states, and provoked the rebellion that began in Dhofar province in 1964. On 23 July 1970 the Sultan was deposed (and later exiled) in a coup, led by his son, Qaboos bin Said, at the royal palace in Salalah. Qaboos, who was then 29 years of age and had trained at Britain's Royal Military Academy (Sandhurst), thus became Sultan amid general acclaim, both within the country and abroad. (The new Sultan's mother remained in residence in Oman until her death in August 1992.) Sultan Qaboos intended to transform the country, using petroleum revenues for development, following the model of the Gulf sheikhdoms to the north. He asked the rebels for their co-operation, but only the Dhofar Liberation Front responded favourably. The Popular Front for the Liberation of the Occupied Arabian Gulf (reported to control much of Dhofar, and to be receiving aid, via Southern Yemen, from the People's Republic of China) and its ally, the National Democratic Front for the Liberation of the Occupied Arab Gulf, appeared to think that the palace coup changed little.

In August 1970 'Muscat' ceased to be part of the title of the country, which became simply the 'Sultanate of Oman'. Sultan Qaboos appointed his uncle, Tariq bin Taimur, as Prime Minister. Tariq resigned his office in December 1971, since which time the Sultan has himself presided over cabinet meetings and acted as his own Prime Minister, Minister of Defence and Minister of Foreign Affairs. Priority was given to providing the basic social and economic infrastructure which the former Sultan had rigidly opposed—housing, education, communications, health services, etc. In addition, restrictions on travel were abolished, many prisoners were released, and many Omanis returned from abroad. None the less, a substantial proportion of the annual budget continued to be devoted to defence and to quelling the Dhofar insurgency.

Oman's admission to the UN in 1971 was achieved despite opposition from the People's Democratic Republic of Yemen (PDRY, formerly Southern Yemen), which supported the Popular Front for the Liberation of Oman and the Arab Gulf (PFLOAG), formed in 1972 by the unification of the two nationalist liberation fronts. The name of this organization was changed in July 1974 to the People's Front for the Liberation of Oman (PFLO). Oman's relationship with Britain also compromised Oman's candidature for UN membership. Britain continues to supply weapons, ammunition and military advisers to the Omani Government.

The progress which was achieved after the palace coup of 1970 did have some impact on the insurgents' following, with a number of defections to the Sultan's forces, but fighting continued until 1975. Omani forces attacked the border area of the PDRY for the first time in May 1972. In 1973 Iranian troops entered the conflict on the side of the Sultan, who also received assistance from Jordan, Saudi Arabia, the UAE, Pakistan and India. Although the Sultan's forces gradually gained the upper hand, the war was prolonged, and during October 1975 the rebels used sophisticated weapons such as Soviet-made SAM-7 missiles. In December 1975, after an offensive, the Sultan claimed a complete victory over the insurgents. Saudi Arabia helped to negotiate a cease-fire in 1976, and an amnesty was granted to the Omanis who had been fighting for the PFLO.

Since then, only desultory conflicts have taken place and many rebels have returned to their homes in Oman. In January 1977 Iran withdrew the bulk of its forces from Dhofar, but a token force remained until the Iranian revolution in early 1979. A renewal of the insurrection against Sultan Qaboos occurred in June 1978, when a party of British engineers was attacked in the Salalah region of Dhofar. The PFLO became largely an external force, however, and had little success in attracting adherents within Oman, despite the assassination, in 1979, of the Governor of Dhofar, and reports of renewed insurgency. In January 1981 Oman closed its border with the PDRY, and more British officers were seconded to the Omani forces as the frontier defences were put on the alert. However, by October 1982, after talks at which Kuwait and the UAE mediated, Oman and the PDRY had re-established diplomatic relations, signing an agreement on 'normalization'.

Oman's relations with its other Arab neighbours have improved rapidly over the last few years. During the reign of Sultan Said, the Omani dependence on British military forces was viewed with disfavour by its neighbours, increasing Oman's isolation in the Arab world. However, since the accession of Sultan Qaboos, and more especially since the defeat of the Dhofar insurgents, relations have improved considerably. Both Kuwait and the UAE have supplied much-needed financial support to Oman, while Iraq, formerly a supporter of the PFLO, has established diplomatic relations. The establishment of economic and diplomatic links with Saudi Arabia was particularly significant. Oman's support for the Israeli-Egyptian peace treaty of 1979 threatened to damage relations with some of the more uncompromising members of the League of Arab States (Arab League), but promised closer ties with the USA and with Egypt, which has undertaken to respond to any request from Oman for military aid. Concern over regional security prompted Oman to join the Co-operation Council for the Arab States of the Gulf (Gulf Co-operation Council—GCC), founded in May 1981.

The strategic importance of military bases in Oman has long been recognized. The United Kingdom withdrew its forces from Masirah Island in 1977, and since then the USA has shown keen interest. In February 1980 Oman began negotiations with the USA concerning a defence alliance whereby, in exchange for US military and economic aid and a commitment to Oman's security, Oman would grant the USA use of port and air base facilities in the Gulf (including Masirah Island). Although direct alignment with a superpower is contrary to Oman's foreign policy, the agreement was finalized in June, and was bitterly condemned by the Arab People's Congress in Libya as a concession to 'US imperialism'. The outbreak of the Iran–Iraq War in September 1980 only served to underline Oman's strategic importance, particularly with regard to the Strait of Hormuz, a narrow waterway at the mouth of the Persian (Arabian) Gulf, between Oman and Iran, through which about two-thirds of the world's sea-borne trade in crude petroleum passes. The fact that Oman possesses export outlets other than the Strait brought some economic advantages to the country in May 1984, as its ports handled some trade which was destined for countries within the Gulf whose commerce was threatened by an escalation of the Iran–Iraq War.

In 1981 the USA established a communications centre in Oman, and US President Ronald Reagan pledged more than US $200m. in 1981–83 to develop port and airport facilities in return for the right to stockpile supplies in Oman for possible use by the US Rapid Deployment Force. By 1985 the total sum spent on the improvement of facilities in Oman had risen to $300m. United States forces were permitted to make landings in Oman during the massive 'Bright Star' military exercises, held in the region in December 1981. This aroused protest from the PDRY, as it contravened a clause of the 'normalization' agreement previously made. As a result, the other Gulf states, particularly Kuwait, attempted to discourage both countries' links with the superpowers by reportedly offering Oman $1,200m. to withdraw the US military facility. In a preliminary attempt to co-ordinate the Gulf's own independent defence system, the GCC focused its attention on Oman, awarding a five-year defence grant to the country in July 1983 and holding joint military exercises there in October.

Oman was keen to maintain relations with the GCC countries, and in November 1983 it joined with them in urging Iran to grant safe passage to traffic in the Strait of Hormuz. The Sultanate also continued to develop its own defences, with the support of the GCC, and by the end of 1984 had acquired two squadrons of *Chieftain* tanks and two squadrons of *Jaguar* aircraft.

In September 1985 Oman established diplomatic relations with the USSR. The move was encouraged by the peaceful relations which had been maintained between Oman and the PDRY since the resumption of diplomatic contact in 1982, and

was interpreted as an indication of Oman's desire to preserve its political independence. However, an American presence was discreetly maintained, and US troops were allowed to use military bases in Oman only with the agreement of the Omani Government. The USA continued to make improvements to existing installations in the Sultanate, expanding fuel, ammunition, power and water facilities at Seeb airfield. In October 1988 Oman and the PDRY signed an agreement to increase co-operation in the sectors of trade and communications. The signing took place during the first visit to the Sultanate by a President of the PDRY since the PDRY attained independence in 1967. In January 1989 the Omani Minister of Petroleum and Minerals, Said ash-Shanfari, became the first Omani minister to visit the USSR since the establishment of diplomatic relations between the two countries in 1985. The USSR's potential role in the stabilization of the global oil market was discussed. In early 1989 Oman adopted a more conciliatory policy towards Iran (in November 1987 Oman had supported the League of Arab States' condemnation of Iran's prolonging hostilities with Iraq), and in March the two countries established an economic co-operation committee. However, Oman's support for Iran was conditional upon the latter's efforts to achieve political stability in the Gulf region.

After the invasion of Kuwait by Iraqi troops in August 1990, the Omani Government stated that the dispute should be resolved without the use of force. When it became clear that Iraq would not withdraw from Kuwait, Oman, together with the other members of the GCC, gave its support to the deployment of a US-led defensive force in Saudi Arabia. The Omani Government expressed the view that the imposition of economic sanctions would force Iraq to withdraw from Kuwait. Oman was, however, prepared to tolerate the continuation in office of the Iraqi President, Saddam Hussain. In late November there was evidence that Oman had attempted to mediate in the crisis, when the Iraqi Minister of Foreign Affairs, Tareq Aziz, made the first official Iraqi visit to a GCC state, other than Kuwait, since August 1990.

In the aftermath of the Gulf crisis, Sultan Qaboos supported further integration among the GCC's members, and in December 1991, at the annual meeting of GCC Heads of State, he unsuccessfully proposed the creation of a 100,000-strong GCC army. By March 1995, following Iraq's deployment in October 1994 of troops and artillery near the border with Kuwait in what was widely regarded as an attempt to effect the easing of UN economic sanctions imposed in August 1990, Oman's stance on the prolongation of economic restrictions against Iraq appeared ambivalent: Oman and Qatar were, notably, absent from talks held in March 1995 between the US Secretary of State, Warren Christopher, and other members of the GCC on the continued maintenance of sanctions against Iraq. Oman has since maintained a degree of ambivalence with regard to this issue, urging the prompt political rehabilitation of Iraq in the region, while continuing to support the indefinite maintenance of economic sanctions. In March 1998 Sultan Qaboos met the Iraqi Minister of Justice, Shabib al-Malki, and urged him to recognize that full co-operation with the UN was the most effective way to ensure a swift removal of sanctions.

Oman has expressed a particular desire to promote relations between the GCC states and Iran, and to support gradual political reform in the latter. In March 1991 Oman hosted a meeting at which diplomatic relations between Saudi Arabia and Iran were restored. In September 1992 the Governments of Oman and Iran signed an agreement to increase trade and economic co-operation, in particular in the sectors of transport and shipping.

In January 1992 President Mitterrand of France arrived in Muscat for talks on increasing political ties and bilateral commerce, particularly in the defence, energy and banking sectors. In April Oman and the UAE agreed to relax travel regulations to enable nationals to travel between the countries with identity cards, rather than passports. In May the President of the UAE, Sheikh Zayed an-Nahyan, visited the Sultan for talks, as a result of which diplomatic representation between the two countries was raised to ambassadorial level.

In October 1992 Oman signed an agreement with Yemen (the Yemen Arab Republic–YAR–and the PDRY were unified in May 1990) to establish the demarcation of their border. The agreement was officially ratified in December, and in October 1993 Sultan Qaboos pledged $21m. to finance the construction of a border road between the two countries. Normalization of relations were restored and in March 1994 Oman hosted talks with Yemen to discuss the furthering of bilateral co-operation. The efforts of Sultan Qaboos to mediate a settlement to the conflict in Yemen ended in disappointment when fighting broke out again between the two rival Yemeni factions in late April. However, the Sultanate was elected to be a non-permanent member of the UN Security Council for a two-year term from January 1994, in tribute to its mediatory role in the Middle East. In June 1995 Oman and Yemen completed the demarcation of their joint border; in the following month Oman and Saudi Arabia officially demarcated their common border. At the end of July 1996 Oman withdrew an estimated 15,000 troops from the last of the disputed territories on the Yemeni border, in accordance with the 1992 agreement. In May 1997 official representatives from both countries signed the international border demarcation maps at a ceremony in Muscat. It was also agreed to promote bilateral trade by building a new 245-km road linking the two countries.

In January 1994 bilateral talks were held with Egypt to promote the exchange of expertise between their respective armed forces. In March the Pakistani Prime Minister, Benazir Bhutto, made an official visit to Oman which resulted in an agreement to increase co-operation in various fields, especially in the sectors of economics and regional security. In April the Israeli Deputy Minister of Foreign Affairs, Yossi Beilin, participated in talks in Oman. This constituted the first official visit by an Israeli minister to an Arab Gulf state since Israel's declaration of independence in 1948. In late September 1994, moreover, Oman and the other GCC member states announced the partial ending of their economic boycott of Israel. In December the Israeli Prime Minister, Itzhak Rabin, made an official visit to the Sultanate to discuss the Middle East peace process, and in February 1995 it was announced that low-level diplomatic relations were to be established between Oman and Israel with the opening of interests sections, respectively, in Tel-Aviv and Muscat.

The agreement to establish interests sections was signed in January 1996, and in April relations between the two countries were consolidated further by a two-day official visit to Oman by Shimon Peres, the new Israeli Prime Minister. An Omani trade office was opened in Israel in August 1996, despite concerns that relations with Israel would be undermined by the uncompromising international stance adopted by the new Netanyahu Government in Israel. However, in April 1997, in accordance with an Arab League resolution adopted in March in protest at Israel's decision to construct a Jewish settlement in a disputed area of East Jerusalem, Oman suspended diplomatic links with Israel, resumed the economic boycott and withdrew from multilateral peace talks. As the Middle East peace process faltered, Oman suspended all commercial and business activities with Israel; the Government barred Israeli companies from taking part in an annual computer fair in Muscat, and two Israeli Ministry of Foreign Affairs officials were refused visas to enter Oman in order to find a permanent site for the Israeli diplomatic mission in Muscat. In late July, the Omani Ministry of Foreign Affairs announced the opening of a representative office in the Palestine National Authority (PNA)-administered city of Gaza, to be headed by an ambassador, and in October, in an address to the UN General Assembly, the Minister of State for Foreign Affairs, Yousuf bin al-Alawi bin Abdullah, urged UN members to encourage Israel to withdraw from the Golan Heights and southern Lebanon. Bin al-Alawi also reiterated the Government's support for the PNA. In November Oman attended the Middle East and North Africa economic conference in Doha, which was widely boycotted by Arab nations, owing to Israel's participation. In December Oman recalled its representative from its trade office in Tel-Aviv.

A 45-member Consultative Assembly (consisting of 17 representatives of the Government, 17 representatives of the private sector and 11 regional representatives) was created in October 1981 in response to suggestions that Sultan Qaboos was not being made sufficiently aware of public opinion. In 1983 the Assembly's membership was expanded to 55, including 19 representatives of the Government. Its role, however, was confined

to comment on economic and social development and recommendations on future policy. In November 1990 Sultan Qaboos announced that a new Consultative Council, comprising regional representatives, was to be established within one year, in order to allow 'wider participation' by Omani citizens in national 'responsibilities and tasks'. In March 1991 he announced that the Council would consist of 59 elected members. The President of the Council was to be appointed by the Government. In April 21 prominent figures met to nominate three candidates (of whom one was to be appointed to the Council) for each of the country's *wilayat* (provinces). On taking office, the members of the Council were to appoint committees and executive officers. An annual meeting between the Council and members of the Government would also be held. Although the Council has no legislative power, ministers are obliged to present annual statements to it and to answer any questions addressed to them.

In December 1991 a cabinet reshuffle produced wide-ranging ministerial changes and the amalgamation of several ministries. This was followed by a further reshuffle in May 1992. The inaugural session of the Consultative Council, created to replace the former State Consultative Assembly, was held in January 1992. The new body's 59 members were appointed for a three-year term. Three new ministries were created in the cabinet reshuffle in January 1994, and in July it was announced that membership of the Consultative Council would be increased to 80 in 1995, allowing constituencies of 30,000 or more inhabitants to have two seats while the remaining regions would each be represented by one member. Women were to be permitted, for the first time, to be nominated as candidates in six regions in and around the capital. In early 1995 two women were appointed to the Consultative Council. On 6 November 1996 Sultan Qaboos issued a decree promulgating what was termed a Basic Statute of the State, a constitutional document defining, for the first time, the organs and guiding principles of the State. Article 58 of the Statute provided for a Council of Oman, to be composed of the Consultative Council (Majlis ash-Shoura) and a new Council of State (Majlis ad-Dawlah). The latter was to be appointed from among prominent Omanis, and would act in a liaison capacity between the Government and the people of Oman. Later in November it was reported that 23 senior government ministers had resigned as directors of public joint-stock companies, in accordance with a stipulation in the Basic Statute that ministers should not abuse their official position for personal gain. In December a Defence Council was established by Royal Decree, comprising the Minister of the Royal Court, the heads of the branches of the armed and police forces and the head of internal security. The process of succession to the Sultan, as defined by the Basic Statute, required that the ruling family determine a successor within three days of the throne's falling vacant, failing which the Defence Council would confirm the appointment of a successor pre-determined by the Sultan.

Voting was organized on 16 October 1997 to select candidates for appointment to the Consultative Council. Of a total of 736 candidates, 164 were chosen, from whose number the Sultan selected the 82 members of the new Council on 24 November. The two female members of the outgoing Council were returned to office. (Women from all regions had been permitted to seek nomination in the October poll.) In mid-December the Sultan issued a decree appointing the 41 members of the Council of State, which was reportedly dominated by former politicians, business leaders and academics. A further decree established the Council of Oman, which was formally inaugurated by the Sultan on 27 December.

In mid-1994 the Omani Government was reported to be employing stringent measures to curb an apparent rise in Islamic militancy in the country. In late August the security forces announced the arrest of more than 200 members of an allegedly foreign-sponsored Islamic organization, most of whom were later released. Among the persons arrested were two junior ministers, university lecturers, students and soldiers. In November several detainees were sentenced to death, having been found guilty of conspiracy to foment sedition; the Sultan subsequently commuted the death sentences to terms of imprisonment.

In 1997 there were public signs of growing impatience with the slow pace of progress on political reform and economic development. Civil disturbances were reported in al-Hajer, 180 km west of Muscat, in May; troops were eventually deployed to end the demonstrations and disperse the crowds. University students also protested against the introduction of severe security measures on campus, which included a ban on public gatherings. Hitherto, such demonstrations had been virtually unknown in Oman and it is widely believed that budget cuts and privatization plans have created anxiety about employment prospects among the younger generation.

In September 1995 Qais bin Abd al-Munim az-Zawawi, Deputy Prime Minister for Financial and Economic Affairs and Oman's principal financial policy-maker, was killed in a traffic accident when travelling in the same vehicle as the Sultan (who escaped unharmed). A week later Ahmad bin Abd an-Nabi Macki, the Minister of the Civil Service, was appointed acting Minister of Finance and the Economy. In a cabinet reshuffle in December Macki was relieved of the civil service portfolio and appointed to head the newly-created Ministry of National

Economy; it was announced that he would continue to 'supervise' the former Ministry of Financial and Economic Affairs, now restyled the Ministry of Finance. In early November 1996 Fahar bin Taimour as-Said, Deputy Prime Minister for Security and Defence, died. In a cabinet reorganization in December 1997 the portfolio of Justice, Awqaf (Religious Endowments) and Islamic Affairs was separated into two ministries; Sheikh Muhammad bin Abdullah bin Zahir al-Hinai, previously Minister of Agriculture and Fisheries, was appointed Minister of Justice, and Sheikh Abdullah bin Muhammad bin Abdullah as-Salimi entered the Council of Ministers as Minister of Awqaf and Religious Affairs. Three other ministers were replaced following their retirement. All the new ministers were Western-educated, with a strong academic background, and their appointment seemed to suggest a move towards technocratic rule in Oman.

Economy
Updated for this edition by ALAN J. DAY

Oman's economy is based largely on revenue from the petroleum sector. Petroleum was first produced commercially in 1967, but it was not until 1970, when Sultan Qaboos bin Said assumed power, that income from petroleum was invested in the country's economic development. Subsequently, Oman's economy expanded considerably under a prudent policy of avoiding external debt while developing both public and private sectors.

In 1995, according to estimates by the World Bank, Oman's gross national product (GNP), measured at average 1993-95 prices, was US $10,578m., equivalent to $4,820 per head. Between 1985 and 1995 it was estimated, GNP per head increased, in real terms, at an average rate of 0.3% per year. Oman's economic growth since the mid-1960s has been rapid but uneven. Between 1965 and 1980, according to World Bank estimates, the country's gross domestic product (GDP) increased, in real terms, by 12.5% per year, one of the highest national growth rates in the world. The comparable increase between 1973 and 1984 was 6.1% per year, a rate that was maintained at 6% during 1985. Measured in current prices, Oman's annual GDP rose from an estimated mere $60m. in 1965 to $8,980m. in 1985. However, real GDP rose by only 3.3% in 1986 and it declined by 3.4% in 1987. During 1990–95 the average annual growth rate for GDP, measured at constant prices, was 6.0%. In 1996 there was a marked increase in GDP of 11% and in 1997, according to the Central Bank of Oman, GDP growth was 12.5%.

Revenues from petroleum have been used to underpin a series of five-year development plans, covering 1976–80, 1981–85, 1986–90, 1991–95 and, currently, 1996–2000. These plans have aimed to provide the country with necessary social amenities while investing further in the petroleum sector, but in recent years there has been a strong emphasis on diversification within the economy. The third five-year Plan aimed to achieve greater industrial diversification and the construction of several major industrial estates. Agricultural development was also an important objective. However, the crisis in the oil industry led to some delays in the implementation of the third Plan. In January 1991 the Government announced details of a fourth development plan, covering 1991–95. The plan imposed strict limits on projected external borrowing, and again emphasized the diversification of the economy, which was to be achieved through the expansion of the private sector, and renewed stress on industry, agriculture and fisheries, mining and services. In July 1994 the Government initiated a wide-ranging privatization programme to attract private investment, particularly for infrastructure projects. In November an investment law was introduced to allow foreign nationals to own as much as 100% of 'projects contributing to the development of the national economy', particularly if they pertained to infrastructure. A new tax law was introduced in October 1996, reducing the rate of tax paid by Omani companies with 49% or less foreign ownership as part of the Government's efforts to promote foreign investment and

strengthen the role of the private sector in the economy. All companies working in industry, mining, fishing, tourism and agriculture now benefit from tax exemptions which previously applied only to firms that were entirely Omani-owned. Early in 1997 the Minister of Commerce and Industry announced that all new Omani companies would be required to offer 49% of their shares to foreign ownership, a move that was not welcomed by a number of the country's major trading families who felt that this initiative would undermine their dominant position.

Under the fifth Development Plan (1996–2000), announced in January 1996, emphasis was placed on the elimination of the budget deficit by 2000 through the reduction of public expenditure, the development of the non-petroleum sector and the expansion of the privatization programme. The policy of 'Omanizing' the work-force (to reduce the country's dependence on expatriate labour, thereby providing opportunities for Oman's rapidly expanding population) was given fresh impetus when, in June 1996, the Government stated that it would assume the full cost of training Omani nationals employed in the private sector and announced that a schedule of charges would be imposed on private sector companies employing foreign workers. Yet despite the Government's 'Omanization' policy, figures for the end of 1996 revealed that expatriates made up almost two-thirds of the workforce and continued to dominate the private sector. (Indian nationals form the largest group of expatriates, comprising almost one-half of all foreign workers in 1993.) The Ministry of Social Affairs and Labour had given private sector companies until the end of 1996 to submit plans indicating how they intended to replace expatriate staff with Omanis so as to meet government quotas, but under pressure from the business community the deadline was extended to the end of 1997. Quotas for the number of Omanis employed have been set by sector: 60% of all employees in transport and storage; 45% in banks, insurance companies and estate agents; 35% in manufacturing industry; 30% in hotels and restaurants and 20% in the wholesale industry. However, finding employment for the growing number of Omanis leaving school every year is becoming an increasingly urgent problem. Between 1998 and 2002 the annual number of school leavers is projected to total 48,000, rising to 53,000 between 2003 and 2007. At the end of 1996 almost 80% of all employees in the public sector, but only 25% of private-sector workers, were Omanis. It will be difficult for the Government to increase this percentage, as the monthly salary of the majority of foreign workers in the private sector is much less than an Omani would expect to earn, and many jobs in the private sector, especially those involving manual work, are unattractive to Omani nationals.

Oman is neither a member of the Organization of the Petroleum Exporting Countries (OPEC), nor of the Organization of Arab Petroleum Exporting Countries (OAPEC). However, its agreements on concessionary terms ensure that concession-holders are obliged to grant it the same privileges as those granted to members of OPEC. Oman is not, therefore, subject to controls on petroleum production and pricing, although it generally respects OPEC's policies. In the 1980s Oman benefited from its freedom to raise production levels to compensate for any loss of income resulting from the existence of large surplus stocks of petroleum during the first half of the decade. Owing to Oman's position on the southern shore of the Persian (Arabian) Gulf, the country was less vulnerable to the disruption of petroleum traffic caused by the 1980–88 war between Iran and Iraq. Annual Omani production of crude petroleum fell from 135m. barrels in 1976 to 103m. barrels in 1980, but the opening of new fields brought a recovery, with the result that production reached 137m. barrels in 1983, at a rate of 375,000 barrels per day (b/d). After the collapse in petroleum prices in 1986, Oman supported OPEC's decision to reduce output in September and October (in order to bring about an increase in prices) by announcing a reduction of 50,000 b/d in its own production. Further reductions of 5% in production were introduced in February 1987 and February 1988, limiting output to 550,000 b/d, as its contribution to OPEC's attempt to support an international oil price of $18 per barrel. However, over-production depressed the price of oil on the 'spot' market in September 1988, and in January 1989 Oman announced that it would reduce production of crude petroleum by a further 5% from 1 April. In June 1990 the level of oil production was 650,000 b/d and the Ministry of Petroleum and Minerals planned to raise it by an additional 50,000 b/d. However, in July 1990 the Omani Government suspended these plans in an attempt to co-operate with OPEC's efforts to raise international oil prices. In 1992 the price of Omani oil averaged $18 per barrel, but by the end of 1993 the price had sunk to less than $12 per barrel. In January 1994 Oman cut its output by 5% in the hope that other oil-producing countries would follow suit in order to raise the price of oil. By April, however, Oman abandoned its unilateral stance, resuming production to 800,000 b/d to average $14 per barrel by mid-1994. Production averaged 865,000 b/d in 1995 and 895,000 b/d in 1996, increasing to 910,000 b/d in 1997 at an average price of nearly $19 per barrel. In March 1998 Oman agreed a modest cut in production as its contribution to international efforts to arrest a decline in prices. Although petroleum remains the predominant feature in all aspects of the Omani economy, the development of the country's gas reserves for export and as the basis for energy-intensive industrial projects is seen as the main hope for transforming the economy in the future.

Oman's development has been aided by grants from the Gulf Co-operation Council (GCC—see p. 246). Among GCC regulations is an agreement to abolish tariffs on home-produced goods that are traded between member countries. Oman has retained these tariffs, however, in order to protect the country's developing industrial sector. In 1986 the Omani Government requested other members of the GCC to reveal the level of subsidy being applied to goods that they exported to Oman, in order to enable the tariff system to be updated.

In mid-1991 the annual rate of inflation was estimated at 3%, decreasing to 1.4% in 1992, and annual economic growth averaging 6% was recorded for the period 1991–95. Annual inflation averaged 1.5% in 1990–94, reportedly falling to 0.3% by 1996; consumer prices declined by 0.7% in 1994.

AGRICULTURE AND FISHERIES

Since the development of the petroleum industry, the relative importance of agriculture has declined sharply. However, it remains a significant source of employment and income. The 1993 census indicated that 60% of arable land was under cultivation and that some 9.4% of the working population were engaged in the agricultural sector. Most agriculture currently takes the form of subsistence farming by traditional methods. The 1981–85 Development Plan allocated about RO 43m. for the development and modernization of farming methods, particularly irrigation. Total expenditure on agriculture and fisheries in the Plan was estimated at RO 110m. As a result, the sector's contribution to GDP in 1985 rose by 7.6% to RO 93.7m., and in 1986 the sector contributed RO 95.9m. to GDP. Agricultural GDP increased by an annual average of 8.9%, in real terms, during 1978–92, and by 5.2% and 3.2%, respectively, in 1993 and

1994. The 1986–90 Five-Year Plan emphasized the expansion of the fishing industry and the encouragement of production for export and the urban market. This was intended to reduce Oman's dependence on food imports, which cost RO 131m. (18.6% of Oman's total imports) in 1987 and RO 162.6m. in 1990. The Oman Bank for Agriculture and Fisheries (established in 1981 with the intention of curbing rural-to-urban migration) provides loans to farmers, and there is a state marketing authority, the Public Authority for Marketing Produce, which aims to increase domestic consumption of local products. In 1987 Japan granted a concessionary loan of $200m. to Oman for the development of agriculture and infrastructure. By the end of 1988, which was declared to be 'Agricultural Year' by the Sultan, about 2,500 government-owned research and experimental farms had been established. In January 1989 a 10-year plan was announced for the development of the agricultural and fishing industries. In March a loan of up to $186m. was secured from the Export-Import Bank of Japan for agricultural and infrastructural projects under the 1986–90 Plan. In 1989 government expenditure on agriculture, forestry and fishing was only RO 27.1m. (less than 2% of the total). By 1993 government expenditure on the sector had increased to RO 40.7m., representing 3.7% of the total. Expenditure on the sector decreased in 1994 to RO 30.8m., equivalent to 2.8% of total expenditure.

About 60% of the area under cultivation is planted with dates. Other crops include lucerne (alfalfa), limes, mangoes, melons, bananas, papaya and coconuts. Oman is almost self-sufficient in tomatoes, cucumbers, onions and peppers. Imports of cereals increased from 52,000 metric tons in 1974 to 287,000 tons in 1987 and 445,800 tons in 1995. In 1988 405 ha of new land were brought under wheat cultivation. Livestock farming is practised in Dhofar, which benefits from monsoon rains between June and September. Cattle are raised in the hills north of Salalah, and goats in the Hajar mountains. The development of livestock was one of the principal aims of the 1981–85 Plan. In an effort to reduce the total cattle herd in Dhofar, and thereby protect the environment, the Government announced in 1985 that, for every 20 sheep purchased from overseas, importers would have to buy one cow from Dhofar.

During 1992–96 agricultural output rose from 784,200 tons to 1,181,800 tons, reflecting an expansion of modern techniques and intensification methods. As a result of the increase in production, the value of agricultural produce increased from RO 85.1m. in 1992 to RO 100.8m. in 1996, registering an annual increase of 4.6% (although the rate targeted in the 1991–96 Development Plan was 6.3%). Over the same period, the value of agricultural exports increased from RO 31.8m. to RO 50.8m.— an average annual growth of 14.5%.

Agriculture is heavily dependent on irrigation. In 1985 the Government announced that rural power and water networks were to be greatly expanded over the next five years, and in that year new dams at Khour ar-Rassagh and Wadi al-Koudh came into operation. By early 1988 a dam with a capacity of 3.6m. cu m was under construction at Wadi Jizzi in Sohar. In August 1989 three schemes to improve and expand the water distribution networks were announced: two in Nizwa and Sur, costing RO 2m. each, and one on Masirah island, at a cost of RO 500,000. In May 1990, contracts were awarded to improve water supply systems in Nizwa and Sur. The Nizwa project consisted of laying 45 km of pipeline, construction of a new section for the reservoir and the establishment of a telemetry system at a cost of RO 741,000. The Sur project involved a RO 688,000 contract to lay 10 km of transmission pipeline, 30 km of distribution pipeline and install a pumping station. In April 1991 the Ministry of Agriculture and Fisheries awarded a contract worth $8.3m. to build two recharge dams in the Batinah coastal region. Dams already constructed at Wadi Rubkah and Wadi Taww will eventually have respective capacities of 5m. cu m and 3.7m. cu m. The Ministry of Agriculture and Fisheries commissioned a recharge dam to be built at Wadi al-Fuleij, in Sur, at a cost of RO 1.2m., enabling a saving of 2.2m. cu m of flood water which would normally flow from the wadi into the sea. In May 1990 the newly-created Ministry of Water Resources announced a programme for water rationalization which introduced new regulations for the registration of wells and a permit requirement for new wells. Nevertheless, irrigation still accounts for an estimated 90% of the country's water consumption and as the crops produced are of relatively low value the high rate of water usage by the agricultural sector remains a matter of concern for the Government. Oman's consumption of fresh water currently exceeds that replaced naturally by rainfall, and the depletion of groundwater supplies and sea-water intrusion into coastal aquifers have become a serious problem. A conference organized by Sultan Qaboos University in Muscat in April 1997 urged all the GCC states to reduce the volume of water allocated to agriculture in order to conserve scarce supplies. However, for the Omani Government to impose additional restrictions on water use would present difficulties, given that agriculture is such a politically sensitive sector; figures for the end of 1996 indicate that agriculture employs almost half of all Omanis in the work-force and provides jobs for at least some young Omanis living in the countryside where alternative forms of employment are limited.

Fishing is a traditional industry in Oman, and during the 1970s it employed about 10% of the working population. In 1980 the Oman National Fisheries Co (ONFC) was formed to organize concession agreements, government trawlers and land facilities. By 1996 the ONFC was operating nine deep-sea trawlers, an onboard fish meal plant and a processing and freezing plant at Mutrah. The inshore waters are rich in marine animals (mainly rock-cod, snapper and cuttlefish, together with some shellfish), which are the main source of protein in the diet of many Omanis, and provide some export revenue. In August 1991, however, new regulations to curb excess fishing of shellfish were introduced. The Government's Fishermen's Fund grants substantial subsidies to the sub-sector, while the Bank for Agriculture and Fisheries encouraged small-scale fishing, and had helped to provide about 500 boats and 2,000 outboard motors by early 1984. Most of those engaged in the sub-sector, however, were reluctant to change from subsistence to commercial fishing, despite the expansion of facilities for the storage and marketing of fish. During the late 1970s the annual catch was about 60,000 metric tons. The total catch in 1985 was 101,180 tons and in 1988 it increased by 22% compared with the previous year, to 165,576 tons. By 1992, however, the total catch had declined to 112,313 tons, but it rose to 116,469 tons in 1993 and 118,568 tons in 1994 (comprising 97,531 tons landed by traditional fishing methods and 21,037 tons landed by the ONFC). In 1995 the total catch increased to 139,860 tons, although in 1996 it decreased to 121,615 tons, about a third of which was exported. In March 1989 the Government held discussions with the US Agency for International Development (USAID) concerning the provision of finance for a project to develop and manage the local fishing industry. In July 1990 representatives of the USA and Oman concluded discussions concerning an agreement on the provision of aid. The USA pledged $75m. for a water programme already under way, and contributed approximately $40m. to a fisheries scheme. In November 1991 the newly-renamed Ministry of Agriculture and Fisheries Wealth announced the awarding of contracts for consultancy work on four fishing-harbour projects: at Qurayat, Bukha, Al-Lakbi and Mirbat. Construction of the fishing harbour at Qurayat was due to commence in April 1995. In 1992 electricity charges for the agriculture and fishery sectors were reduced as an incentive. In the fourth Five-Year Plan (1991–1995) RO 200m. was allocated to the fishing industry with the objective of raising its annual growth rate to account for 9.9% of GDP.

PETROLEUM AND NATURAL GAS

Since the early 1970s the economy of Oman has been dominated by the petroleum industry. Petroleum currently accounts for about 75% of government revenue and around 40% of GDP. Proven oil reserves totalled 5,100m. barrels in 1996, sufficient to sustain production at present rates until 2012. Estimates of reserves have since been revised upwards to 5,400m. barrels. In 1937 Petroleum Concessions (Oman) Ltd, a subsidiary of the Iraq Petroleum Co, was granted a 75-year concession to explore for petroleum, extending over the whole area except for the district of Dhofar. A concession covering Dhofar was granted in 1953 to Dhofar Cities Service Petroleum Corpn. However, petroleum was not discovered until 1964, when deposits were found near Fahud. Commercial production began in 1967, and average output increased to around 300,000 b/d in the 1970s. Production is managed by Petroleum Development Oman

(PDO), in which the Government holds a 60% share, while Royal Dutch/Shell has 34%. In 1997 PDO was responsible for about 94.5% of Oman's crude oil output, the remainder being produced by a number of foreign concerns. PDO operates two main production areas: a group of central oilfields, south-west of Muscat, and a group of southern oilfields in Dhofar. The central area was the first to be developed, and four connected oilfields together produced crude petroleum at an average rate of 341,000 b/d in 1975. When production from the three Ghaba fields started in 1976, output from the total central area reached a peak level of 368,000 b/d. From then on, production declined, averaging about 250,000 b/d in early 1984. Development of the oilfields in the south has compensated for this fall. Production started at the Marmul field in 1980, and the Rima field came 'on stream' in 1982, producing 45,000 b/d in early 1984. Further fields, at Marmul, Nimr and Sayyala, were brought into production in late 1985. Output from the southern fields totalled some 150,000 b/d in early 1984. A north–south pipeline connects the oilfields to the port of Mina al-Fahal, near Muscat. In June 1988 the Rajaa oilfield, situated in the Balija region of central Oman, commenced production. Also in mid-1988 78 new wells were being drilled in the Yibal region of northern Oman, where 168 producing wells and 43 water-injection wells were already in operation.

In mid-1995 the Government revealed plans to offer at least 10 largely untapped petroleum exploration areas (mostly in southern Oman) to international companies before the end of the year in order to stimulate exploration activity. In the first half of 1996 four major concessions for exploration were granted by PDO to the US companies Triton Energy and Phillips Petroleum Oman, the Japan Petroleum Exploration Co (Japex) and a joint venture between the US company, Arco, and the Portuguese-owned Partex (Oman) Corpn. Early in 1997 it was announced that the Saudi Arabian company, Nimr Petroleum, had been granted a concession to drill for oil on the south-east coast near Masirah island. In June 1998 the Government signed three exploration and production agreements with US companies—Amoco, Occidental Petroleum Corpn, and Triton—securing a minimum investment of US $80m. in exploration activities. Yet despite the Government's claims that it wishes to encourage greater foreign involvement in developing the country's oil reserves, the most productive fields are operated by the PDO. In March 1997 the petroleum minister reiterated that the Government was not planning to change the ownership structure of the PDO, which remains heavily dependent on managerial and technical assistance from Shell, and the complete nationalization of Oman's petroleum industry appears to be unlikely in the immediate future.

In 1987 petroleum exports were estimated to be worth RO 1,194m., representing 82% of total revenue, and in 1988 they were worth RO 1,141.0m., according to estimates by the Central Bank. Japan is the principal recipient of Omani petroleum, taking 40.4% of the total in 1992, compared with 52.6% in 1986. Following the rise in petroleum prices occasioned by the Gulf crisis, the Government's net oil revenues rose by almost 58%, to RO 1,538m., in 1990. Oil exports rose to 252.5m. barrels in 1992 from 243.7m. in 1991. Net oil revenues fell to RO 1,241m. in 1991, rising slightly to RO 1,276m. in 1992, accounting for 79% and 77% of total revenue respectively. In January 1994 production was reduced to 720,000b/d following an attempt by the Government to raise prices. The plan was abandoned when it became apparent that production quotas set by OPEC would not be reduced and the PDO subsequently resumed production of an average of 800,000 b/d in 1994. In late 1994 the Government announced that it was to invest $6,000m. in the crude petroleum production sector during 1995–98, in an attempt to increase petroleum reserves. In 1993 exports of crude petroleum provided 72.2% of total export earnings, and in 1994 the proportion increased to 74%. Petroleum exports rose from 778,000 b/d in 1995 to 811,000 b/d in 1996. However, exports to Japan fell from 272,000 b/d to 247,000 b/d. Exports to South Korea rose slightly from 147,000 b/d to 156,000 b/d while exports to the People's Republic of China increased from 90,000 b/d to 116,000 b/d. Figures for the first quarter of 1997 revealed a further decrease in exports to Japan while exports to the People's Republic of China more than doubled compared with the same period in 1996 (making the latter Oman's leading customer in this period). As a result of increased levels of production and higher prices, the value of petroleum exports, which currently account for some 75% of total export revenues, rose substantially from $4,752m. in 1995 to $5,889m. in 1996. The value of exports for the first quarter of 1997 was $1,587m. compared with $1,247m. during the same period in 1996. By September 1997 export earnings for the year were RO 1,678m. ($4,358m.). In that year production increased to 910,000 b/d, from 895,000 b/d in 1996 and 865,000 b/d in 1995.

Oman's recoverable reserves of natural gas were estimated to total 263,500m. cu m (9,310,000m. cu ft) in 1987. By 1996, after further discoveries, known reserves had risen to 777,290m. cu m (27,450,000m. cu ft). The Yibal gas fields are thought to be capable of a daily yield of 4m. cu m (140m. cu ft). In September 1984 PDO embarked on a 10-year programme of exploration for unassociated gas, which, it was hoped, would enable more petroleum to be released for export. By September 1985 a total of 19 new discoveries of gas deposits had been reported. Gas production in 1985 reached 3,930m. cu m, of which 1,290m. cu m was reinjected, 900m. cu m was flared, 190m. cu m was lost and 1,550m. cu m was consumed. In 1985 PDO discovered gas reserves in Lekhwair, where it was planned, in 1989, to construct a gas injection plant in order to improve recovery levels, using surplus gas. The plant was part of a larger project to upgrade facilities at the Lekhwair field and its cost was estimated at $100m.–$130m. In June 1990 PDO announced that it was initiating several oil pipelines and gas lift projects. In August 1990 PDO awarded a contract to develop a water flood scheme at the Lekhwair oilfield. This project was allocated $500m., enabling the scheme to have a daily capacity of 200,000 barrels of crude petroleum and 4m. cu ft of gas. In June 1986 offshore gas was discovered in the Bukha field, in the Musandam Peninsula region. Its reserves were estimated at 31.2m. barrels of condensate, 500,000m. cu ft (14,000m. cu m) of dry gas and 7.3m. barrels of associated gas. A contract to develop the gas field was negotiated with a group led by a Canadian company, International Petroleum (IPL). At the end of 1987 natural gas was being extracted at the rate of 3.90m. cu m (140m. cu ft) per day, and by the end of the decade this was increased to between 14m. and 17m. cu m per day. A pipeline links Yibal to Muscat and Sohar, and an extension of the gas pipeline network from Yibal to Izki has been completed. The scheme is intended to provide sufficient supplies from Yibal to the coast until 2010. PDO also initiated a programme to build a 10-in pipeline, 26 km in length, from Natih to Fahud. Other projects have included pipeline links from Qaharir to Marmul and Jalmu to Rima. Schemes are under way to convert domestic fuelling systems to natural gas in order to release more petroleum for export, and gas is also used to enhance the rate of petroleum recovery (by reinjection), and to power the country's copper smelter (see below). Gas liquefaction plants have been built at Yibal. In July 1989 a proposal to expand the plant producing natural gas liquids (NGL) at Yibal was announced. In 1987 output of liquefied petroleum gas (LPG) by the National Gas Co was 35,000 tons, increasing to 37,000 tons in 1988. The Government has exclusive rights to revenue from gas, and in 1988 the National Gas Co's profits reached RO 649,000, 17.5% higher than in 1987. In April 1989 Oman agreed terms for a 10-year contract to supply natural gas for the world's first floating methanol plant, beginning production by 1991. The Government agreed to sell as much as 6,343m. cu m (224,000m. cu ft) of natural gas over the period of the agreement to the consortium owning the plant, which has a capacity of 2,200 metric tons per day. In July 1989 PDO announced its largest gas discovery for 22 years, at the Saih Nihayda field in the central region. Recoverable reserves were estimated at 10,000m. cu m (350,000m. cu ft), making it Oman's fifth biggest gas field. A further large discovery of gas, at the Saih Rawl field, was announced in March 1991. In 1992 gas revenues peaked at RO 63.1m. (equivalent to 3.3% of total revenue), only to decrease again to RO 57.9m. (3.3%) in 1993 and to RO 52.5m. (2.9%) in 1994. In 1991 it was announced that more than RO 44m. had been allocated for exploration and exploitation of new gas discoveries. In February 1992 plans were announced for massive investment (estimated at $9,000m.) in a project to produce liquefied natural gas (LNG), to be implemented by Oman LNG, a consortium led by the Government (51% share), Shell, Total, and various Japanese and Korean companies. The liquefaction plant is being constructed at al-Ghalilah near Sur, on the coast 150 km south of the capital by the Chiyoda Corporation of Japan and Foster Wheeler of the USA. The plant, which is expected to cost $2,250m., will have a capacity of 6.6m. tons per year (t/y) and production is scheduled to start in 2000. Oman LNG is raising the bulk of the finance for the plant through loans from commercial firms and the balance through equity. A 25-year agreement with the Korea Gas Corpn has been signed to supply 4.1m. t/y of LNG from 2000. However, a preliminary sales and purchase agreement with the Petroleum Authority of Thailand, which would have accounted for most of the remainder of the new LNG plant's planned output, was suspended in November 1997. In May 1998 it was reported that negotiations on alternative long- and medium-term supply deals were underway with China, India and Turkey. At the same time, Oman LNG approved a sales and purchase agreement with Japan's Osaka Gas for 700,000 t/y from 2000 to 2025. Plans are underway to drill new wells at three of the country's central gasfields, Barik, Saih Rawl and Saih Nihayda, in order to supply the amount of gas that will be required by the new liquefaction plant. Revenues from gas are still relatively small, little more than 3% of total revenues, but they are expected to increase rapidly when the LNG project becomes operational and could eventually rival earnings from petroleum exports.

Oman's first petroleum refinery came into production at Mina al-Fahal, near Muscat, in late 1982. As a result, the value of imports of refined products was reduced from RO 49.5m. in the first half of 1982 to RO 7m. in the comparable period of 1983. It was hoped that the new refinery would satisfy domestic demand for petrol. The refinery's average throughput was 38,000 b/d in 1983, and by 1988, its capacity had risen to 80,000 b/d. In July 1989 it was reported that the French oil group Total had begun refining 10,000 b/d of crude petroleum at Mina al-Fahal, utilizing the extra capacity. The Government is planning the construction of a new refinery at Salolah. In June 1992 Oman signed an agreement with Kazakhstan to explore for, develop and produce petroleum and gas in the republic. Later that year Oman agreed to collaborate with Kazakhstan, Azerbaijan and Russia in the 'Caspian Pipeline Consortium'. This project envisaged the construction of a pipeline to transport about 1.5m. b/d of petroleum from the former Soviet republics. Azerbaijan later withdrew from the project and after five years of disputes Russia, Kazakhstan and Oman, together with eight major oil companies, signed an agreement in April 1997 to build the pipeline. In the restructured consortium the Russian Government is the biggest shareholder, Kazakhstan holds 24% and Oman 7%. Construction work on the pipeline will cost $2,000m. In 1993 the Governments of Oman and India signed a memorandum that envisaged the construction of a $5,000m. submarine pipeline, to transport Omani natural gas to the subcontinent. The project, promoted by the state-owned Oman Oil Company (OOC), was to have been carried out in two stages involving the construction of two pipelines with a total capacity of 2,000 cu ft of gas a day and was to have been completed by 2001. In 1996, however, it was reported that the project would not proceed in the immediate future because of complex technical problems and concern that Oman would not have sufficient reserves to provide adequate supplies of gas, given its other commitments. The proposed Oman–Sharjah pipeline faces similar constraints but Amoco, the company promoting the project, insists it will be able to obtain the gas. A preliminary accord was signed with Caltex of the USA in 1993 to construct a $1,900m. refinery in Thailand which would have the capacity to refine 130,000 barrels of crude per day. Under the agreement Oman would reserve the right to export 80,000 b/d for refinement. The OOC plans to build two refineries in India with Indian partners. In late 1996 it was reported that plans were proceeding for the first refinery to be built in Madhya Pradesh (with Bharat Petroleum). The refinery, with a capacity of 6m. t/y is expected to cost $1,600m.

INDUSTRY AND MINERALS

Before 1964, industry in Oman was confined to small traditional handicrafts, such as silversmithing, weaving and boat-building. The development of petroleum generated activity in the construction sector, but it was not until the change of regime in

1970 that government investment in infrastructure projects and private spending on housing started a boom in construction. Some of the new projects were not well conceived, resulting in the drain of resources abroad to foreign contractors. By 1984, however, the construction industry in Oman was still healthy, at a time of relative inactivity in other Gulf states. This situation altered radically at the end of 1985, as major projects under the 1981–85 Plan, such as the Sultan Qaboos University, were completed. In 1986 petroleum prices declined sharply, and virtually all construction projects were brought to a halt.

With smaller petroleum revenues than many other Middle Eastern states, Oman is not well placed to develop heavy industry or manufacturing on a large scale. The Government is, accordingly, concentrating more on the development of agriculture and fisheries, and encouraging construction in the rural areas, with the emphasis on social projects and roads. Small-scale industrial ventures in the private sector are also being promoted, and the Government offers incentives to private enterprise, such as cheap land and energy, exemption from duty on imports of raw materials and plant, and low-interest loans. The 1981–85 Development Plan aimed to quadruple industrial output, giving the industrial sector an average growth rate of 36.2% per year over the Plan's term and between 1982 and early 1984, more than 640 small and medium-sized enterprises went into operation. A large proportion of Oman's labour force in construction and industry was provided by immigrant workers from India and Pakistan. During 1984, however, as the recession worsened and tenders for projects were fewer, many contractors reduced the numbers of their employees by between 20% and 50%. The 1986–90 Development Plan aimed to diversify Oman's economic base as a provision against an eventual exhaustion of hydrocarbon reserves. In 1990 industry (including mining, manfacturing, construction and power) provided 56.5% of Oman's GDP, although the proportion was reduced to 51.7% in the following year which was designated the 'Year of Industry'. In that year the Government allocated RO 24m. for industrial projects. These included a plant to manufacture 200m. glass bottles per year and another to produce 300,000 car batteries per year. The latter began production in 1992, which was also declared a 'Year of Industry' by the Sultan. In that year the Government adopted a 15-year industrial strategy, which included a liberalization of credit provision, regulations to simplify administrative procedures for business executives and development of the infrastructure. An industrial estate was established in 1983 at Rusayl, near Muscat, and two new industrial estates were opened in November 1992 at Sohar and Raysut. Further industrial estates are planned at Nizwa, Sur, Khasab and al-Buraimi. During 1980–94 industrial GDP increased by an annual average of 6.2%. Manufacturing industry grew by 11.6% in 1995 and 5.4% in 1996. However, the Government plans to expand and diversify its small industrial sector during the 1996–2000 Development Plan. Proposals prepared by the Japan International Co-operation Agency envisage ambitious growth rates in manufacturing during the current five-year plan (13% per year) and advocates the development of energy-based industries—in particular petrochemicals, fertilizers and aluminium smelting—together with hi-tech, capital intensive industries, all of which will export most of their production. Two major projects are already well advanced. In early 1997 Oman and India signed an agreement to construct a fertilizer plant at Sur, next to the LNG complex. The plant, which will cost an estimated $1,100m., will produce ammonia and urea and have a capacity of 1.7m. t/y. It will be constructed and managed by the Oman-India Fertilizer Project in which the state-owned OOC will have a 50% stake and the two Indian partners 25% each. Gas feedstock for the plant will be provided by PDO and the two Indian partners will take most of the output. A consortium of Western companies is expected to build the plant. Plans are also going ahead for an aluminium smelter to be built, possibly at Sohar, north-east of Muscat. The smelter will have an initial capacity of 240,000 t/y which may be expanded later to 480,000 t/y and production is scheduled to begin in 2000. Gas will be supplied by PDO from its inland fields and most of the output will be exported to the People's Republic of China. Sohar may also be the site of a planned ethylene cracker and polyethylene plant and it is hoped to develop other new industries at Sur around the LNG plant and

fertilizer complex. Alongside these major projects the Government is encouraging small-scale industries to locate on the industrial estates which now cover some 200 ha. Government incentives to private industry include interest-free loans and exemption from customs duties on capital goods and raw material imports.

Geological surveys are being undertaken to locate mineral deposits other than petroleum and natural gas. So far, sizeable reserves of copper and chromite (chromium ore) have been found. Chromite reserves, estimated at 2m. tons of medium-grade ore, exist on the coastal side of the Jebel Akhdar. The concession to develop the deposit is held by a Canadian-based company. The government-owned Oman Mining Co (OMC) began mining chromite in early 1984, and in 1986 about 5,000 tons were produced. In 1989 OMC was ordered to suspend the mining and export of chromite while a joint committee of the Ministries of Commerce and Industry and Petroleum and Minerals established priorities for the sector. In 1991 the new Oman Chromite Co, owned jointly by the Government (15%), private companies (45%) and public subscribers (40%), announced plans to exploit the country's chromite reserves at a rate of approximately 15,000 tons per year. By 1992 it was estimated that Oman had reserves of about 200m. tons of chromite ore at as many as 600 sites. OMC has exploited three copper mines, at Bayda, Avga and Lassail, near Sohar, north-west of Muscat, where drilling had indicated the presence of about 12m. tons of ore. In 1990 about 3,000 tons of copper ore per day was being handled from these pits. A complex for the smelting and refining of the copper ore, at Sohar, began operation in July 1983. The project cost more than $200m., of which Saudi Arabia provided more than one-half. In 1994 bids were invited to expand the copper smelter at an estimated cost of RO 2m.–3.5m. The Yibal–Ghubra gas pipeline has been extended to the Sohar region to provide fuel, both for the smelter and for cement manufacturing. The privatization of the OMC was expected to provide sufficient funds to expand the copper refinery at Sohar, increasing its capacity from 22,000–24,000 tons a year to 33,000 tons a year. Preliminary results from a joint study between OMC and Minproc Engineers (Australia) have indicated that the mining of copper at Hail as-Safil and Ar-Raki in Yanqul province would be economically viable, with total potential reserves of 15.25m. tons. The OMC developed a new gold mine at Yanqul in 1994, which was expected to produce 500kg of gold annually. In July 1989 plans were announced for the construction of a plant to produce ferro-chrome near Sohar, on the Batinah coast, to begin after 1991. In August 1990, a French geological company won a RO 98,800 contract to explore for lead and zinc in the Saih Hatat and Jebel Akhdar regions. In 1991 the UN Development Programme agreed to co-operate with the Ministry of Petroleum and Minerals in a study of Oman's coal resources. The study, the cost of which was estimated at $1m., was to examine the possibility of using coal at Al-Kamil, near Sur, to generate electricity. Coal deposits exceeding 122m. tons have been discovered in the province of Bani Bu Ali, south of Sur. Estimated recoverable reserves at the two coalfields in Wadi Muswa and Wadi Fisaw are sufficient to meet the power generation needs of the Sharqiya region for the next 35–40 years.

The economic and industrial changes which have taken place in the country since 1970 have led to a need for major increases in power and water supply. As a result, production of electricity in the capital area alone rose from 8m. kWh in 1970 to 642m. kWh in 1980, and in 1981 an extensive rural electrification scheme was completed. In 1985 there were plans for the extension of the Sohar power station, and by the end of the year about one-half of the country was connected to the National Grid. Net installed generating capacity in Oman rose from 479 MW in 1981 to 1,250 MW in 1993, while actual production rose from 1,148m. kWh in 1981 to more than 6,000m. kWh in the early 1990s. In 1991 the Ministry of Electricity was preparing to evaluate bids for a number of major projects in the electricity sector, including a consultancy contract for the fourth-phase, 160 MW expansion of the Ghubrah power and desalination plant. In late 1994 Hitachi Zozen of Japan and ABB Turbinen Nuernberg of Germany signed a contract for the construction of a desalination plant at Ghubrah 5. The plant will have a desalination capacity of up to six million gallons per day, and a

30-MW back-pressure steam turbine will also be built. In early 1995 the Government announced it was to proceed with a large-scale power and desalination project at Barqa which, by 2010, would provide an extra 1,880 MW of power and a desalination capacity of 56m. gallons per day. The first phase of the project will include the construction of a 388-MW power plant and a 14m.-gallons-per-day desalination plant. In 1996 it was announced that the project would be completed in four stages on a build-own-operate basis and that the main developer would be selected by the Ministry of Electricity and Water. In 1996 the Government announced its decision to privatize the electricity industry. This policy has resulted in the Government involving the private sector in projects that the state is unable to fund but has not meant selling off any of the existing publicly-owned facilities. The 90-MW Manah power station in Muscat, which was completed in 1996, was the first project to involve the private sector and was built on a build-operate-transfer basis. The Government will assume ownership of the plant after 20 years. Another privately-owned and operated 200-MW power station is to be built at Salalah in Dhofar. The project will include power generation and expansion of the transmission and distribution systems. The Government invited tenders for the project in early 1997. The Manah project included power purchase agreements, but the Government has indicated that future privately-funded projects will not be given the same guarantees which may make it more difficult to attract private investors. By 1995 some 87% of Oman's regions were connected to the National Grid.

Other heavy industrial projects currently under consideration include plans for a hydrochloric acid plant, a silicon plant (using locally mined quartz), a salt production plant and a new sugar refinery. Tourism is in the early stages of development in Oman, and private-sector initiatives are being encouraged. In 1996 the number of hotels, motels and resthouses totalled about 50, compared with 32 in 1991. The present target is to have over 10,000 rooms by the year 2005.

FINANCE AND DEVELOPMENT

Expenditure on defence and national security in Oman has increased rapidly, with the total doubling between 1979 and 1984. In 1979 the budget allocation for defence spending was RO 238m. By 1986 this figure had risen to RO 665m., representing 42% of total expenditure. Although the allocation for 1988 was reduced to RO 519m., it still placed considerable strain on the country's finances. By 1994, defence expenditure had increased to RO 779.3m. (34.8% of total expenditure). In view of Oman's strategic importance within the GCC, defence expenditure is supported by other Council countries, which, in July 1983, agreed to make a grant of $150m. per year to Oman for general military purposes, to be paid until 1995.

Infrastructural and communications projects are gradually being completed. Port facilities are being improved by the expansion of Mina Raysut at Salalah, and 12 new berths have been completed at Mina Qaboos. In June 1990 a contract was awarded for work on the third phase of a scheme to improve facilities at Nizwa. The project involved the construction of a 140-metre bridge and a 900-metre by-pass. Mina Qaboos handled 1.9m. tons of cargo in 1988. In April 1992 an RO 11.7m. contract for further development of Mina Qaboos was awarded to a British company, Wimpey Alawi. Construction has begun on a new container port at Mina Raysut at Salalah in the southern province of Dhofar. The first phase of the project consists of two berths to be completed by mid-1998 with a second and third phase bringing the total number of berths to four by 2000. The Omani Government, together with Sea-Land of the USA and Maersk of Denmark, have formed Salalah Port Services Company to carry out the port's development. Maersk have stated that they will probably transfer much of their business from Jebel Ali port in Dubai to Mina Raysut when the new terminal opens, and the Government hopes that it will prove competitive in attracting the growing volume of regional container traffic. Roads link Seeb and Nizwa, and Salalah and Thumrait. A $30m. project to build roads in the Sharqiya region is under way. In 1990 the Ministry of Communications announced proposals to build 140 km of roads and to upgrade a further 158 km, in addition to constructing 58 km of road in Al-Qabil, Ibra and Briddayah. The Dhofar Transport Co was awarded a contract

in May 1990 to build a 13-km link road connecting Al-Ayjah and Sur, at a cost of RO 2.5m. Another project under consideration in 1990 was the construction of a 16-km road linking the Thumrait airforce base to the main Salalah–Thumrait highway, at a cost of RO 400,000. Between 1970 and 1985 an estimated 6,000 km of asphalt roads and 18,500 km of dirt roads were built in Oman. In 1989 243 km of roads were built, at a total cost of RO 36m. In late 1985 the World Bank announced a $30m. loan to Oman for further improvements to the road network. By 1994 a road linking Salalah with Sarfait, near the border with Yemen, had been completed. Air services to rural and outlying areas have been increased: by the end of 1984 there were rural air services to Khassab, Bayah, Buraimi, Sur and Masirah island. A major expansion programme at Seeb International Airport was completed in 1985, and in the following year more than 1.4m. passengers passed through the airport. In 1993 five international airlines began operating regular flights to Oman. In 1996 on estimated 2.2m. passengers passed through Seeb Airport. Oman's second largest airport is at Salalah and has been upgraded to receive cargo and passenger aircraft of all sizes.

The targets of the 1976–80 Development Plan were relatively modest, concentrating on establishing a workable basis for light industry and agriculture. The Omani Development Bank was established in December 1977 to encourage private sector investment. The 1981–85 Development Plan envisaged total expenditure of RO 7,400m., of which RO 3,300m. was to be allocated to development projects. The general aim was to reduce economic dependence on petroleum, in favour of private-sector industry. The Plan included development of tourism, education, health, welfare, housing and roads. In 1984 it was announced that total spending on projects undertaken during the 1981–85 Development Plan would total RO 1,800m., 28% more than was originally envisaged.

At the end of 1985 the 1986–90 Development Plan was approved, with proposed expenditure totalling RO 9,250m. ($26,780m.). Early in 1986, however, proposed spending was reduced to RO 8,830m. as a result of falling oil prices. The revised total was based on an estimated average petroleum price of $20 per barrel. The subsequent decline in oil prices, to less than $10 per barrel in July, necessitated further revision of proposed expenditure. Although oil prices rose above $17 per barrel by the end of 1986, the Plan was postponed for re-evaluation. In January 1991 the Government announced a fourth Development Plan, covering the period 1991–95. The plan envisaged total expenditure of RO 9,450m. The projected rate of annual GDP growth in the five years was about 6.3%. In April 1991 total development spending for the Plan period was reportedly budgeted at RO 2,107m. Of this, some RO 319m. was to be allocated to construction projects, including a hospital, housing and schools; to a $78m. extension of the airport at Seeb; to the $65m. development of the port of Mina Qaboos, gas fields and fishing ports; and to the upgrading of the Rusayl–Nizwa highway and the renovation of the Muscat water networks.

Despite the world oil surplus in the early 1980s, Oman raised its petroleum output during the 1981–85 Plan period, maintaining adequate revenues, but at a lower level than originally expected. From 1982, falling oil prices led to deficits in the annual budget. In January 1986 the rial was devalued by 10.2%, to compensate for the reduction in petroleum revenues. By 1987 the effect of the decline in oil prices was evident as expenditure decreased from RO 1,587.2m. in 1986 to RO 1,330.1m. Revenue from the petroleum sector increased from RO 521.2m. in 1986 to RO 998.0m. in 1990 (an increase of 45% over the previous year). This resulted in a reduction in the budget deficit to RO 32.8m., compared with a deficit of RO 289.5m. in 1989. In 1991 oil revenue declined to RO 777.0m., and total revenue to RO 1,261.4m. Total expenditure was 1,575.1m. The budget for 1995 anticipated an increase in total revenue to RO 1,847.0m., of which RO 1,352.4m. was oil revenue, and an increase in total expenditure to RO 2,159.0m., resulting in a deficit of RO 312.0m. The budget for 1996 envisaged total revenue of RO 1,934m. and expenditure of RO 2,152m., with a budget deficit forecast of RO 218m. Actual revenue and expenditure figures for the year were, however, estimated at RO 1,990.2m. and RO 2,253.7m. respectively, resulting in a deficit of RO 263.5m. The 1997 budget anticipated increases in revenue to RO 2,003m. (including RO 1,502m. from petroleum) and in expenditure to

RO 2,266m., leaving a deficit of RO 263m. However, according to figures released by the National Economy Ministry in April 1998, actual revenue for the year, at RO 2,270m., was about 13% higher than the budgeted figure (largely attributable to increased earnings from petroleum). Although actual expenditure was also more than forecast (RO 2,292.5m.), the budget deficit of RO 21.7m. was considerably lower than anticipated. Projected petroleum revenue is based on a relatively low average price of $15 a barrel (the Government's forecasts having become increasingly conservative after it based the 1986–1990 Development Plan on oil prices that were unrealistically high). The Government maintains its policy of putting any extra petroleum revenue derived from a price over $15 a barrel, and up to $17, into the State General Reserve Fund. Any revenue resulting from a price over $17 can be used for extra capital expenditure. The current Development Plan envisages the elimination of the budget deficit by the year 2000. However, the 1998 budget has predicted a deficit of RO 295m. (based on proposed revenue of RO 2,012m. and expenditure of RO 2,307m.). A bleaker outlook for the price of petroleum in 1998, compared with the previous two years, may require cuts in spending if the target of balancing the budget by the turn of the century is to be achieved.

Oman's trade pattern continues to reflect the dominance of petroleum in the economy. In 1987 the value of non-oil exports and re-exports was RO 123.9m., equivalent to 8.3% of the value of total exports. Although by 1990, their value had risen to RO 176.2m., this represented just 8.3% of total exports. In 1991, however, the Government's efforts at diversifying the economy began to demonstrate a degree of success and non-oil exports and re-exports were valued at RO 244.2m., accounting for 13.0% of the total exports of RO 1,873.9m. Their value continued to increase and in 1994, they accounted for RO 503.9m. (23.6% of total exports of RO 2,132.0m.) The value of recorded imports in 1987 (when unrecorded imports were estimated at RO 55m.) was RO 700.7m. By 1990, this had risen to RO 1,030.9m. Their value continued to rise until 1994 when a 4.8% decrease (to RO 1,505.3m.) was recorded. Oman's major trading partner is Japan, which in 1987 received 41.3% of petroleum exports. The UAE was the principal supplier of imports in that year, providing 21% of the total, followed by Japan (15%) and the United Kingdom (14%). In 1990 Oman's balance of trade showed an improvement of 56.1% compared with 1989, with recorded imports totalling RO 1,030.9m., compared with exports of RO 2,116.4m. The UAE remained the main source of imports, while Japan, followed by the Republic of Korea, was the main purchaser of Omani petroleum. A trade surplus was recorded each year between 1991 and 1993, and in 1994 a 29.7% increase in the trade surplus, was recorded with an increase in exports, to RO 2,132.0m., and a decrease in imports, to RO 1,505.3m. In the period 1991–94 the UAE continued to be Oman's principal supplier of imports, followed by Japan, the United Kingdom and the USA. The principal markets for exports during this period were Japan, the Republic of Korea, the UAE and Thailand. In 1994 the principal sources of imports were the UAE (29.1%) and Japan (19.9%) while the principal markets for exports were Japan (34.8%) and the Republic of Korea (14.2%). The value of exports rose from RO 2,330.5m. in 1995 to RO 2,820.0m. in 1996, due to an increased volume of oil exported, as well as higher prices. Imports rose more slowly from RO 1,633.0m. in 1995 to RO 1,760.0m. in 1996, resulting in an increase in the trade surplus from RO 697.5m. in 1995 to RO 1,060.0m. in 1996. In mid-June 1996 the World Trade Organization agreed to establish a working party to negotiate terms of entry for Oman. The decision followed a commitment made by the Omani Undersecretary for Commerce and Industry to co-operate with other GCC countries in the promotion of liberal trade. In March 1997, Oman became one of the founder members of the Indian Ocean Rim Association for Regional Co-operation (IORARC) which seeks to promote co-operation in trade, investment and economic development between the countries of the region. During a state visit to India in April, Sultan Qaboos signed a number of co-operation agreements to promote trade between India and Oman. India is an important source of imports to Oman, but Oman is keen to increase its small volume of exports to India.

Between 1981 and 1982 Oman's balance-of-payments surplus fell by 40.3%, and in the following year it declined by a further 52.8%, to US $ 351m., despite GDP growth of 16.0%. In 1986 a deficit of $1,040m. was recorded on the current account of the balance of payments. A major reason for the deficit on the current account, in addition to the decline in revenue from petroleum, was the level of remittances being transferred abroad by foreigners working in Oman. This increased by 52.5% between 1981 and 1982, to RO 236m., and reached RO 300m. in 1984. A surplus of $784m. was recorded on the current account of the balance of payments in 1987, followed by a $309m. deficit in 1988, a $305m. surplus in 1989 and in 1990 Oman's balance of payments recorded a current account surplus of $1,106m. However a deficit of $244m. was recorded in 1991 and by 1993 this had increased sharply to $1,069m. In June 1990 the Government pledged that foreign workers would retain their tax-free status. The announcement was made after the Government had expressed its intention to impose a levy on foreign remittances, in an attempt to increase revenues. In October 1993 it was announced that income tax would be collected from all companies, whether Omani or foreign, from 1 January 1994 in order to increase government revenue. Despite its balance-of-payments surpluses, Oman has also received a substantial amount of foreign aid and loans, mainly in order to finance development projects. Oman's foreign debt declined from $1,931m. (with a debt-service ratio of 4.6%) in 1984 to $1,875m. at the end of 1985. Until 1986, Oman enjoyed an excellent credit rating, and in 1983 the country was able to raise a Eurodollar loan of $300m. with no difficulty. The sharp fall in petroleum prices altered this position, and an application for a Euroloan of $500m. in 1986 encountered difficulty in attracting a sufficient number of subscribers. According to World Bank data, Oman's total foreign debt increased to $2,959m. at the end of 1986, but declined to $2,848m. in 1987. However, petroleum prices revived in 1988, and the Government secured a syndicated loan of $500m. in June 1989, and another of $300m. in October 1991. At the end of 1995 Oman's total external debt was $3,107m., of which $2,563m. was long-term public debt. In that year the cost of servicing the external debt was equivalent to 7.5% of the total value of exports of goods and services. In January 1994 four international banks were awarded a mandate to raise a $300m. five-year syndicated sovereign loan to finance the fiscal deficit.

In comparison with some other countries in the region, Oman has a small banking sector. At the end 1997 there were 18 banks (eight national institutions and the rest branches of foreign banks) operating in the Sultanate. The largest bank is the National Bank of Oman, which reportedly has 30% of the market in retail and corporate banking, and recorded profits of $36m. in 1996. Other large institutions are Bank Muscat Al-Ahli Al-Omani and Oman International Bank. Mergers have been officially encouraged to strengthen the banking sector (see below). In April 1997, mergers were approved between the Oman Development Bank and the Oman Bank for Agriculture and Fisheries, and the Commercial Bank of Oman and the Oman Savings and Finance Bank (the latter being finalized the following August). A new bank, the Oman Alliance Bank, was launched in May and the Industrial Bank of Oman was due to be launched in October. It was announced in June 1998 that the Commercial Bank of Oman (Combank) had undertaken a further merger with the Bank of Oman, Bahrain and Kuwait (BOBK). At the end of 1995 the Central Bank of Oman's total assets stood at RO 912.4m. Between 1973 and 1986 the rial Omani was linked to the US dollar at a rate of $1 = RO 0.3454, but in January 1986 the rial was devalued by 10.2%, with the exchange rate adjusted to $1 = RO 0.3845. The Central Bank raised interest rates in April 1989, with the annual rate payable on non-government deposits increased by 1%, to 9.5%, and that on rial loans raised by 0.75%, to 11.25%. In mid-1983 only 40% of bank staff were Omani; however, government efforts to reduce the number of foreign staff in the banking sector succeeded in reducing their number to 19.4% by mid-1994. By the end of 1995 banks had to reduce their foreign staff to 10% of their work-force or face heavy penalties. In May 1992 the Government introduced a new law increasing the minimum requirement for a bank's paid-up capital to RO 10m., in order to encourage smaller banks to merge and thereby rationalize the banking system. Measures introduced to strengthen the banking sector included the creation of a fund in March 1995 to guarantee bank deposits. In an effort to broaden the base of local financial institutions, the Central Bank announced in early 1997 that it will impose limits on the voting shares that any individual or company can hold in a local bank. In 1989 Oman's first stock exchange—the Muscat Securities Market (MSM)—was opened, trading in shares in local companies with a potential total value of RO 250m. Oman's first investment fund open to non-GCC nationals was listed on the London and Muscat stock exchanges in March 1994. Subscriptions for the Oryx fund, launched to raise $52m., closed in June. A second investment fund set up in 1994 was the UAE-Omani Joint Holding Co with a capital of $78m. Both funds were fully subscribed. In March 1995 the stock exchanges of Muscat and Bahrain were formally linked. The Government's first Eurobond was launched in March 1997 and was heavily oversubscribed. Oman is the first GCC country to venture into the Eurobond market.

The Iraqi invasion of Kuwait on 2 August 1990 prompted panic withdrawals of deposits and increased demand for foreign currency during a 10-day period following the invasion. By late August 1990, however, the local banking system had stabilized, and by April 1991, encouraged by uncompromising government action and by encouraging reports of economic growth, deposits at local commercial banks had fully recovered from the impact of the Gulf crisis. Following the collapse of the Bank of Credit and Commerce International (BCCI) in July 1991, substantial support from the Omani Government enabled depositors and creditors in the country to be paid in full. On 15 February 1992 the Bank Dhofar al-Omani al-Fransi acquired the 12 BCCI branches in the Sultanate.

HEALTH

Oman has a free National Health Service, and in 1995 there were 47 hospitals and 82 health centres, with a total of more than 3,578 beds. There were also 96 preventive health centres, five mobile rural health centres and three maternity centres in 1990. The number of health centres was expected to increase to 120 by the end of 1995 and the number of hospitals to 51. In 1994 there were 1,658 physicians working in Oman. The Royal Hospital of Oman, with 629 beds, was completed in 1987 and became fully operational in 1988, with a staff of more than 2,000, including more than 220 doctors and 1,000 nurses, mainly recruited from overseas. The Ministry of Health has announced plans to construct a paediatric hospital, with 200 beds, in Muscat. In March 1989 it was announced that citizens of other GCC member-states would be eligible to the same health services as Omani citizens. In June 1990 the Ministry of Health announced a programme to construct children's wards at four hospitals at an estimated cost of RO 800,000. In April 1992 Oman and the People's Republic of China signed an agreement for co-operation in the health sector. A 140-bed hospital in Buraimi and a 248-bed hospital at Rustaq were opened in May 1994. A regional hospital at Ibri was due for completion in 1994 and work had begun on a 248-bed hospital in Sohar, a 280-bed hospital at Nizwa, and an extension of Sultan Qaboos hospital. Of total expenditure by the central Government in 1994, RO 154.2m. (8.8%) was for health services, and a further RO 97.7m. (5.6%) for social security and welfare.

Statistical Survey

Source (unless otherwise stated): Oman Directorate-General of National Statistics, Development Council, POB 881, Muscat; tel. 698900; telex 5384.

Area and Population

AREA, POPULATION AND DENSITY

Area (sq km)	309,500*
Population (census results)	
1 December 1993	
Total	2,018,074†
Population (UN estimates at mid-year)	
1994.	2,116,000
1995.	2,207,000
1996.	2,302,000
Density (per sq km) at mid-1996.	7.4

* 119,500 sq miles.

† Comprising 1,483,226 Omani nationals and 534,848 non-Omanis.The provisional total was 2,017,591, comprising 1,480,531 Omani nationals (males 755,071; females 725,460) and 537,060 non-Omanis.

GOVERNORATES (1993 census)

	Area (sq km)	Population	Density (per sq km)
Muscat	3,500	549,150	156.9
Al-Batinah.	12,500	564,677	45.2
Musandam	1,800	28,727	16.0
Adh-Dhahira	44,000	181,224	4.1
Ad-Dakhliya	31,900	229,791	7.2
Ash-Sharqiya	36,800	258,344	7.0
Al-Wosta	79,700	17,067	0.2
Dhofar	99,300	189,094	1.9
Total	309,500	2,018,074	6.5

BIRTHS AND DEATHS (official estimates, Omani nationals only)

	1994	1995	1996
Birth rate (per 1,000). . .	39.0	34.0	30.0
Death rate (per 1,000) . .	7.2	6.1	4.4

Expectation of life (official estimates, years at birth, Omani nationals, 1996): 71.6.

ECONOMICALLY ACTIVE POPULATION
(persons aged 15 years and over, 1993 census)

	Omanis	Non-Omanis	Total
Agriculture and fishing . .	21,993	40,789	62,782
Mining and quarrying . .	8,076	5,991	14,067
Manufacturing	4,212	55,825	60,037
Electricity, gas and water. .	942	3,481	4,423
Construction.	4,412	103,291	107,703
Trade, hotels and restaurants. .	12,201	91,041	103,242
Transport, storage and communications . . .	11,339	12,989	24,328
Finance, insurance and real estate	5,857	11,287	17,144
Public administration and defence	134,714	25,610	160,324
Other community, social and personal services . . .	34,178	76,205	110,383
Activities not adequately defined	2,056	3,786	5,842
Total employed . . .	239,980	430,295	670,275
Unemployed	32,417	2,106	34,523
Total labour force . . .	272,397	432,401	704,798
Males	248,917	387,473	636,390
Females.	23,480	44,928	68,408

Agriculture

PRINCIPAL CROPS (FAO estimates, '000 metric tons)

	1994	1995	1996
Cereals	5	5	5
Potatoes	6	6	6
Tomatoes	33	33	33
Onions (dry)	9	9	9
Other vegetables	84	84	84
Watermelons	30	30	30
Dates	133	133	133
Lemons and limes	29	29	29
Mangoes	11	11	11
Bananas	26	26	26
Tobacco (leaves)	2	2	2

Source: FAO, *Production Yearbook*.

LIVESTOCK (FAO estimates, '000 head, year ending September)

	1994	1995	1996
Asses	26	26	26
Cattle	142	142	142
Camels	94	94	94
Sheep	148	148	148
Goats	735	735	735

Poultry (FAO estimates, million): 3 in 1994; 3 in 1995: 3 in 1996.

Source: FAO, *Production Yearbook*.

LIVESTOCK PRODUCTS (FAO estimates, '000 metric tons)

	1994	1995	1996
Beef and veal	3	3	3
Mutton and lamb	11	11	11
Goat meat	5	5	5
Poultry meat	4	4	4
Cows' milk	19	19	19
Goats' milk	63	63	63
Hen eggs	6	6	6

Source: FAO, *Production Yearbook*.

Fishing

('000 metric tons, live weight)

	1993	1994	1995
Groupers	2.1	3.8	4.0
Croakers and drums	3.4	3.9	4.1
Emperors (Scavengers)	4.4	3.5	6.0
Porgies and seabreams	4.9	5.8	5.1
Jacks and crevalles	1.9	4.0	3.4
Indian oil sardine	29.2	31.2	33.1
Narrow-barred Spanish mackerel	3.1	3.8	6.2
Longtail tuna	5.8	5.2	4.0
Yellowfin tuna	22.7	13.9	28.6
Hairtails and cutlassfishes	3.0	3.9	8.2
Sharks, rays, skates, etc.	4.8	3.7	7.0
Other marine fishes (incl. unspecified)	28.0	32.0	26.4
Total fish	113.4	114.9	135.9
Crustaceans and molluscs	3.1	3.7	3.9
Total catch	116.5	118.6	139.9

Source: FAO, *Yearbook of Fishery Statistics*.

1996: Total catch ('000 metric tons, live weight) 121.6 (Source: Central Bank of Oman, *Al-Markazi*).

Mining

	1993	1994	1995
Crude petroleum ('000 metric tons)	38,571	40,150	42,324
Natural gas (petajoules)	159*	260	92

* Estimate.

Source: UN, *Industrial Commodity Statistics Yearbook*.

1994 ('000 metric tons, unless otherwise indicated): Gold (kg) 137; Chromium 6.2; Gypsum 446.1; Salt 13.1; Limestone 1,929.8; Marble 70.4.

1995 ('000 metric tons, unless otherwise indicated): Gold (kg) 523; Chromium 5.3; Gypsum 70.0; Salt 14.3; Limestone 2,098.2; Iron ore 9.4; Marble 144.3.

Source: Ministry of Petroleum and Minerals.

Industry

SELECTED PRODUCTS ('000 metric tons, unless otherwise indicated)

	1993	1994	1995
Jet fuels	150	163*	166
Motor spirit (petrol)	368	561	555
Kerosene*	5	5	0
Gas-diesel (distillate fuel) oils	448	792	738
Residual fuel oils	1,314	2,055	2,044*
Electric energy (million kWh)	7,298	7,856	8,258*

* Estimate(s).

Source: UN, *Industrial Commodity Statistics Yearbook*.

Finance

CURRENCY AND EXCHANGE RATES

Monetary Units

1,000 baiza = 1 rial Omani (RO).

Sterling and Dollar Equivalents (31 May 1998)

£1 sterling = 627.0 baiza;
US $1 = 384.5 baiza;
100 rials Omani = £159.49 = $260.08.

Exchange Rate

Between February 1973 and January 1986 the value of the rial Omani was fixed at US $2.8952 ($1 = 345.4 baiza). In January 1986 the currency was devalued by about 10.2%, with the exchange rate fixed at 1 rial = $2.6008 ($1 = 384.5 baiza).

BUDGET (RO million)*

Revenue†	1994	1995	1996
Taxation on income, profits, etc.	281.6	305.5	342.8
Oil companies	248.2	n.a.	n.a.
Import duties	41.5	45.3	47.6
Taxes on payroll or work-force	12.4	22.5	30.3
Other tax revenue	18.3	20.8	22.0
Entrepreneurial and property income	922.7	968.4	1,030.7
Petroleum	825.0	n.a.	n.a.
Fees, charges, etc.	17.0	18.9	20.7
Other current revenue	86.5	94.8	96.9
Capital revenue	6.7	11.7	11.8
Total	1,386.7	1,487.9	1,602.8

Expenditure‡	1994	1995	1996
General public services . . .	172.7	187.7	145.7
Defence	699.0	681.3	653.7
Public order and safety . . .	103.2	116.1	103.6
Education	238.5	253.3	254.9
Health	122.8	124.5	134.4
Social security and welfare . .	60.5	62.2	98.1
Housing and community amenities	149.3	157.8	138.7
Recreational, cultural and religious affairs	48.1	46.4	41.6
Economic affairs and services . .	217.9	226.2	187.5
Fuel and energy	123.4	131.5	113.4
Agriculture, forestry and fishing	31.6	30.7	31.2
Mining, manufacturing and construction	5.3	5.0	3.2
Transport and communications .	37.9	36.7	23.0
Other economic affairs and services	19.7	22.3	16.7
Interest payments	100.7	115.7	121.2
Total	**1,912.7**	**1,971.2**	**1,879.4**
Current	1,612.2	1,674.2	1,651.9
Capital	300.5	297.0	227.5

* The data refer to the consolidated accounts of the central Government, including ministries, regional government offices and municipalities.
† Excluding grants received from abroad (RO million): 29.9 in 1994; 13.2 in 1995; 10.8 in 1996.
‡ Excluding lending minus repayment (RO million): −10.2 in 1994; −2.0 in 1995; −6.1 in 1996.

Source: IMF, *Government Finance Statistics Yearbook*.

1997 (forecasts, RO million): Total revenue 2,003.0; Total expenditure 2,266.0.
1998 (forecasts, RO million): Total revenue 2,012.0; Total expenditure 2,307.0.

INTERNATIONAL RESERVES (US $ million at 31 December)

	1995	1996	1997
Gold*	68.3	68.3	68.3
IMF special drawing rights . .	11.1	12.7	13.6
Reserve position in IMF . .	51.2	48.8	42.0
Foreign exchange	1,075.9	1,327.8	1,493.1
Total	**1,206.6**	**1,457.7**	**1,617.1**

* Valued at RO 90.8 per troy ounce.
Source: IMF, *International Financial Statistics*.

MONEY SUPPLY (RO million at 31 December)

	1995	1996	1997
Currency outside banks . .	235.9	231.2	242.2
Demand deposits at commercial banks	235.4	272.1	307.5
Total money	**471.3**	**503.4**	**549.7**

Source: IMF, *International Financial Statistics*.

COST OF LIVING (Consumer Price Index for Muscat; base: 1990 = 100)

	1993	1994	1995
Food (incl. beverages and tobacco)	100.8	99.8	101.3
Fuel, light and water . . .	96.8	97.4	98.2
Clothing, textiles and footwear .	98.3	97.0	98.2
Rent	122.1	118.1	104.9
All items (incl. others) . .	**106.8**	**106.1**	**104.7**

1996: Food 103.6; All items 105.0 (Source: UN, *Monthly Bulletin of Statistics*).

NATIONAL ACCOUNTS (RO million in current prices)
Expenditure on the Gross Domestic Product

	1994	1995	1996
Government final consumption expenditure	1,428.7	1,462.4	1,446.9
Private final consumption expenditure	2,346.6	2,599.7	2,824.5
Increase in stocks . . .	−5.6	3.6 ⎱	818.9
Gross fixed capital information	787.6	791.4 ⎰	
Total domestic expenditure .	**4,557.3**	**4,857.1**	**5,090.3**
Exports of goods and services .	2,136.0	2,337.0	2,827.0
Less Imports of goods and services	1,726.0	1,887.0	2,027.0
GDP in purchasers' values . .	**4,967.3**	**5,307.2**	**5,890.3**
GDP at constant 1990 prices .	**5,136.7**	**5,384.8**	**5,574.9**

Source: mainly IMF, *International Financial Statistics*.

Gross Domestic Product by Economic Activity

	1993	1994	1995*
Agriculture and livestock† . .	88.2	94.9	100.1
Fishing†	26.9	30.9	51.9
Mining and quarrying . . .	1,792.8	1,826.1	2,038.1
Crude petroleum . . .	1,720.5	1,749.4	1,974.1
Natural gas	61.8	65.4	46.8
Manufacturing	202.0	215.7	240.8
Electricity, gas and water . .	42.5	49.1	49.1
Construction	158.2	149.7	137.6
Trade, restaurants and hotels .	661.3	664.6	716.1
Transport, storage and communications† . . .	287.0	311.6	332.9
Financing, insurance, real estate and business services‡ . . .	574.2	592.5	572.7
Public administration and defence	630.3	689.4	705.6
Other community, social and personal services . . .	375.6	396.8	414.1
Domestic services of households	14.4	13.4	15.5
Sub-total	**4,853.3**	**5,034.8**	**5,374.5**
Import duties	43.6	41.5	45.3
Less Imputed bank service charge	93.2	109.0	131.6
GDP in purchasers' values . .	**4,803.6**	**4,967.3**	**5,288.2**

* Provisional figures.
† Excluding activities of government enterprises.
‡ Including imputed rents of owner-occupied dwellings.

BALANCE OF PAYMENTS (US $ million)

	1994	1995	1996
Exports of goods f.o.b. . . .	5,542	6,065	7,339
Imports of goods f.o.b. . . .	−3,693	−4,050	−4,385
Trade balance	**1,849**	**2,015**	**2,954**
Exports of services . . .	13	13	13
Imports of services . . .	−900	−985	−1,037
Balance on goods and services .	**962**	**1,043**	**1,930**
Other income received . . .	257	325	218
Other income paid . . .	−724	−699	−754
Balance on goods, services and income	**495**	**669**	**1,394**
Current transfers received . .	65	68	49
Current transfers paid . . .	−1,365	−1,537	−1,709
Current balance	**−805**	**−801**	**−265**
Direct investment from abroad .	76	46	67
Other investment assets . .	−174	−52	−23
Other investment liabilities . .	328	−13	146
Net errors and omissions . .	−86	388	264
Overall balance	**−661**	**−432**	**189**

Source: IMF, *International Financial Statistics*.

External Trade

PRINCIPAL COMMODITIES (distribution by SITC, US $ '000)

Imports c.i.f.	1993	1994	1995
Food and live animals . .	482,082	499,080	568,135
Meat and meat preparations . .	70,553	75,197	86,791
Dairy products and birds' eggs .	83,530	87,807	97,725
Cereals and cereal preparations	102,554	104,673	137,836
Vegetables and fruit . . .	126,176	118,153	102,310
Beverages and tobacco. .	243,627	251,955	228,323
Tobacco and tobacco manufactures	195,813	202,175	193,006
Manufactured tobacco . .	195,465	201,937	192,867
Cigarettes	186,790	201,647	192,518
Crude materials (inedible) except fuels . . .	84,603	96,640	115,911
Mineral fuels, lubricants, etc.	131,496	42,111	64,628
Petroleum, petroleum products, etc.	125,952	37,076	60,922
Refined petroleum products. .	123,902	35,206	58,954
Chemicals and related products	231,762	228,541	279,074
Basic manufactures . .	616,787	560,356	655,954
Textile yarn, fabrics, etc. . .	131,297	129,435	162,621
Woven fabrics of man-made fibres (excl. narrow or special fabrics). . .	63,633	59,704	91,033
Non-metallic mineral manufactures . . .	89,357	84,418	88,835
Machinery and transport equipment	1,778,458	1,670,041	1,672,316
Power-generating machinery and equipment	95,087	126,752	126,476
Machinery specialized for particular industries . .	244,590	216,716	210,454
Civil engineering and contractors' plant and equipment. . . .	197,861	173,326	151,056
General industrial machinery, equipment and parts . .	160,170	146,821	139,076
Telecommunications and sound equipment . . .	99,464	88,731	126,201
Other electrical machinery, apparatus, etc. . . .	129,144	132,770	201,402
Road vehicles and parts* . .	898,993	854,856	787,522
Passenger motor cars (excl. buses)	632,760	500,877	406,062
Motor vehicles for goods transport, etc. . . .	67,514	107,360	127,277
Goods vehicles (lorries and trucks) . . .	59,582	104,268	105,609
Parts and accessories for cars, buses, lorries, etc.* . . .	159,209	158,990	182,703
Miscellaneous manufactured articles	259,617	267,256	309,548
Special transactions and commodities not classified according to kind . .	179,524	127,441	187,843
Gold, non-monetary (excl. gold ores and concentrates) . .	80,375	137,884	123,154
Total (incl. others) . . .	4,114,043	3,915,035	4,248,557

Exports f.o.b.	1993	1994	1995
Food and live animals . .	98,334	112,069	149,681
Beverages and tobacco. .	124,576	119,947	112,918
Tobacco and tobacco manufactures	121,457	117,190	107,549
Manufactured tobacco . . .	120,427	116,311	106,849
Cigarettes	120,345	116,311	106,673
Mineral fuels, lubricants, etc.	4,181,741	4,144,268	4,650,589
Petroleum, petroleum products, ets.	4,181,741	4,144,252	4,650,580
Crude petroleum oils, etc. . .	4,147,979	4,107,703	4,606,883
Basic manufactures . .	102,762	127,645	161,596
Machinery and transport equipment . . .	619,712	695,964	569,815

Exports f.o.b. — *continued*	1993	1994	1995
Road vehicles and parts* . .	514,562	578,645	460,939
Passenger motor cars (excl. buses)	401,329	417,992	246,401
Parts and accessories for cars, buses, lorries, etc.* . . .	82,716	94,508	121,240
Miscellaneous manufactured articles	94,611	115,351	150,393
Total (incl. others) . . .	5,299,511	5,418,298	5,917,390

*Data on parts exclude tyres, engines and electrical parts.

Source: UN, *International Trade Statistics Yearbook*.

PRINCIPAL TRADING PARTNERS

Imports c.i.f. (RO '000)	1994	1995	1996
Australia	33,579	43,968	40,818
Belgium.	9,076	20,182	16,938
France	40,772	62,990	59,720
Germany	73,879	82,907	90,759
India	46,956	54,374	69,945
Indonesia	13,899	25,466	11,825
Italy	28,512	31,512	41,969
Japan	299,533	257,602	302,411
Korea, Republic . . .	19,529	41,918	58,898
Malaysia	27,826	20,412	24,983
Netherlands	38,876	40,719	34,737
Saudi Arabia . . .	37,362	62,177	54,024
Switzerland	12,962	15,727	23,604
United Arab Emirates . .	438,098	389,240	417,857
United Kingdom . . .	133,127	170,991	155,265
USA	101,423	106,169	132,812
Total (incl. others) . . .	1,505,171	1,629,708	1,760,162

Exports f.o.b. (US $ '000)	1993	1994	1995
China, People's Republic . .	432,697	436,365	573,491
Hong Kong	143,365	222,089	129,020
Iran.	131,378	119,661	124,838
Japan	1,418,662	1,887,088	1,688,468
Korea, Republic . . .	1,069,683	769,435	936,340
Saudi Arabia . . .	42,035	54,698	55,240
Singapore	276,802	29,200	161,204
Thailand	274,839	447,270	506,590
United Arab Emirates . .	505,430	549,058	604,566
USA	210,476	53,451	163,875
Yemen	189,431	250,768	167,403
Total (incl. others) . . .	5,299,505	5,417,679	5,911,123

Source (for Exports): UN, *International Trade Statistics Yearbook*.

Transport

ROAD TRAFFIC (vehicles in use at 31 December)

	1994	1995	1996
Private cars	158,629	166,085	176,637
Taxis	11,812	13,390	15,494
Commercial	88,512	89,256	92,002
Government	22,021	22,349	23,525
Motor-cycles	4,494	4,365	4,246
Private hire	1,491	1,676	1,996
Diplomatic	511	572	532
Other	1,896	2,116	2,354
Total	289,012	299,799	316,786

SHIPPING
Merchant Fleet (registered at 31 December)

	1994	1995	1996
Number of vessels . . .	20	21	21
Total displacement ('000 grt) .	15	16	16

Source: Lloyd's Register of Shipping, *World Fleet Statistics*.

International Sea-borne Freight Traffic ('000 metric tons)

	1994	1995	1996
Goods loaded	40,174	41,586	43,525
Goods unloaded	4,475	4,799	5,303

CIVIL AVIATION (traffic on scheduled services)

	1993	1994	1995
Kilometres flown (million) . .	19	26	26
Passengers carried ('000) . .	1,180	1,512	1,453
Passenger-km (million) . .	2,275	2,802	3,226
Total ton-km (million) . .	303	386	436

Note: Figures include an apportionment (one-quarter) of the traffic of Gulf Air, a multinational airline with its headquarters in Bahrain.

Source: UN, *Statistical Yearbook*.

Tourism

	1993	1994	1995
Tourist arrivals*	344,000	358,000	350,000
Tourist receipts (US $ million) .	86	88	92

* Figures refer to international arrivals at hotels and similar establishments.

Source: UN, *Statistical Yearbook*.

Communications Media

	1993	1994	1995
Radio receivers ('000 in use) . .	1,155	1,210	1,280
Television receivers ('000 in use) .	1,300	1,375	1,450
Telephones ('000 main lines in use)	148	158	170
Mobile cellular telephones			
(subscribers)	5,616	6,751	8,052
Daily newspapers			
Number	4	4	4*
Average circulation ('000 copies)	n.a.	63	63*

1992: Telefax stations (number in use) 1,560; Book production (excl. pamphlets) 24 titles, 25,000 copies; Non-daily newspapers 5; Other periodicals 15.

1996: Daily newspapers 5; Non-daily newspapers and other periodicals 23.

* Estimate.

Sources: mainly UNESCO, *Statistical Yearbook*, and UN, *Statistical Yearbook*.

Education

(1994/95)

	Insti-tutions	Teachers	Pupils/Students		
			Males	Females	Total
Nursery . . .	23	66	282	287	569
Pre-primary . .	6	280	2,933	2,302	5,235
Primary . . .	425	11,586	156,927	145,072	301,999
Preparatory . .	438	6,285	63,595	53,682	117,277
Secondary . . .	140	3,814	28,744	31,335	60,079
Higher . . .	n.a.	n.a.	3,152	1,537	4,689
University . . .	1	563	1,949	2,347	4,296

1995/96: *Pre-primary:* Institutions 5, Teachers 268, Pupils 5,265 (males 2,911; females 2,354); *Primary:* Institutions 416, Teachers 11,925, Pupils 307,050 (males 159,542; females 147,508); *Total Secondary:* Teachers 11,231, Pupils 193,113 (males 100,013; females; 93,100). (Source: UNESCO, *Statistical Yearbook*.)

Directory

The Constitution

The Basic Statute of the State was promulgated by Royal Decree on 6 November 1996, as Oman's first document defining the organs and guiding principles of the State.

Chapter 1 defines the State and the system of government. Oman is defined as an Arab, Islamic and independent state with full sovereignty. Islamic law (*Shari'a*) is the basis for legislation. The official language is Arabic. The system of government is defined as Sultani (Royal), hereditary in the male descendants of Sayyid Turki bin Said bin Sultan. Article 6 determines the procedure whereby the Sultan is designated.

Chapter 2 defines the political, economic, social, cultural and security principles of the State. Article 11 (economic principles) includes the stipulation that 'All natural resources and revenues therefrom shall be the property of the State which will preserve and utilize them in the best manner taking into consideration the requirements of the State's security and the interests of the national economy'. The constructive and fruitful co-operation between public and private activity is stated to be the essence of the national economy. Public property is inviolable, and private ownership is safeguarded. Article 14 (security principles) provides for a Defence Council to preserve the safety and defence of the Sultanate.

Chapter 3 defines public rights and duties. Individual and collective freedoms are guaranteed within the limits of the law.

Chapter 4 concerns the Head of State, the Council of Ministers, Specialized Councils and financial affairs of the State. Article 41 defines the Sultan as Head of State and Supreme Commander of the Armed Forces. The article states that 'His person is inviolable. Respect for him is a duty and his command must be obeyed. He is the symbol of national unity and the guardian of its preservation and protection.' The Sultan presides over the Council of Ministers,

or may appoint a person (Prime Minister) to preside on his behalf. Deputy Prime Ministers and other Ministers are appointed by the Sultan. The Council of Ministers and Specialized Councils assist the Sultan in implementing the general policy of the State.

Chapter 5 comprises a single Article (58). This states that the Council of Oman shall consist of the Majlis ash-Shoura (Consultative Council) and the Majlis ad-Dawlah (Council of State). The jurisdiction, terms, sessions, rules of procedure, membership and regulation of each shall be determined by the law.

Chapter 6 concerns the judiciary. Articles 59 and 60 state that the supremacy of the law shall be the basis of governance, and enshrine the dignity, integrity, impartiality and independence of the judiciary. Article 66 provides for a Supreme Council of the judiciary.

Chapter 7 defines the general provisions pertaining to the application of the Basic Statute.

The Government

HEAD OF STATE

Sultan: QABOOS BIN SAID (assumed power on 23 July 1970, after deposing his father).

COUNCIL OF MINISTERS
(September 1998)

Prime Minister and Minister of Foreign Affairs, Defence and Finance: Sultan QABOOS BIN SAID.

Deputy Prime Minister for the Council of Ministers: Sayyid FAHD BIN MAHMOUD AS-SAID.

Personal Representative of the Sultan: Sayyid THUWAINI BIN SHIHAB AS-SAID.

Special Adviser to the Sultan: Sayyid HAMAD BIN HAMOUD AL-BUSAIDI.

Minister of National Economy and Supervisor of Ministry of Finance: AHMAD BIN ABD AN-NABI MACKI.

Minister for Security and Defence: Sayyid BADR BIN SAUD BIN HAREB.

Minister of State for Legal Affairs: MUHAMMAD BIN ALI AL-ALAWI.

Minister of Petroleum and Gas: Dr MUHAMMAD BIN HAMAD BIN SAIF AR-RUMHI.

Minister of Justice: Sheikh MUHAMMAD BIN ABDULLAH BIN ZAHIR AL-HINAI.

Minister of Awqaf (Religious Endowments) and Religious Affairs: Sheikh ABDULLAH BIN MUHAMMAD BIN ABDULLAH AS-SALIMI.

Minister of State for Foreign Affairs: YOUSUF BIN AL-ALAWI BIN ABDULLAH.

Minister of Information: ABD AL-AZIZ BIN MUHAMMAD AR-ROWAS.

Minister of Electricity and Water: Sheikh MUHAMMAD BIN ALI AL-QATABI.

Minister of Posts, Telegraphs and Telephones: AHMAD BIN SUWAIDAN AL-BALUCHI.

Minister of Communications: SALIM BIN ABDULLAH AL-GHAZALI.

Minister of Education: Sayyid SAUD BIN IBRAHIM AL-BUSAIDI.

Minister of Higher Education: YAHYA BIN MAHFOUZ AL-MANTHARI.

Minister of Social Affairs, Labour and Vocational Training: Sheikh AMIR BIN SHUWAIN AL-HOSNI.

Minister of Housing: MALEK BIN SULAYIMAN AL-MA'AMARI.

Minister of National Heritage and Culture: Sayyid FAISAL BIN ALI AS-SAID.

Minister of the Interior: ALI BIN HAMUD BIN ALI AL-BUSAIDI.

Minister of Commerce and Industry: MAQBOOL BIN ALI BIN SULTAN.

Minister of Agriculture and Fisheries: AHMAD BIN KHALFAN BIN MUHAMMAD AR-RAWAHI.

Minister of Water Resources: HAMID BIN SAID AL-AUFI.

Minister of Health: Dr ALI BIN MUHAMMAD BIN MOUSA AR-RAISI.

Minister of Regional Municipalities and of the Environment: Dr KHAMIS BIN MUBARAK BIN ISA AL-ALAWI.

Minister of the Civil Service: Sheikh ABD AL-AZIZ BIN MATAR BIN SALIM AL-AZIZI.

Governor of Muscat and Minister of State: Sayyid AL-MUTASIM BIN HAMOUD AL-BUSAIDI.

Governor of Dhofar and Minister of State: Sayyid MUSALLAM BIN ALI AL-BUSAIDI.

Minister of the Royal Court: Sayyid SAIF BIN HAMAD BIN SAUD.

Minister of Palace Office Affairs and Head of the Office of the Supreme Commander of the Armed Forces: Maj-Gen. ALI BIN MAJID AL-MA'AMARI.

Secretary-General to the Council of Ministers: Sayyid HAMOUD BIN FAISAL BIN SAID.

Secretary-General to the Ministry of Defence: SAIF BIN HAMAD AL-BATASHI.

Secretary-General to the Ministry of National Economy: MUHAMMAD BIN NASSER AL-KHOSAIBI.

MINISTRIES

Diwan of the Royal Court: POB 632, Muscat 113; tel. 738711; telex 5016.

Ministry of Agriculture and Fisheries: POB 467, Ruwi 113; tel. 696300; telex 3503.

Ministry of Awqaf and Religious Affairs: POB 354, Ruwi 112; tel. 697699.

Ministry of the Civil Service: POB 3994, Ruwi 112; tel. 696000.

Ministry of Commerce and Industry: POB 550, Muscat 113; tel. 7717238; telex 3665; fax 7713500; e-mail moci123@gto.net.om.

Ministry of Communications: POB 684, Muscat 113; tel. 702233; telex 3390; fax 701776.

Ministry of Defence: POB 113, Muscat 113; tel. 704096; telex 3228.

Ministry of Education: POB 3, Muscat 113; tel. 775209; telex 3369; fax 704465.

Ministry of Electricity and Water: POB 1491, Ruwi 112; tel. 603906; telex 3358; fax 699180.

Ministry of Finance: POB 506, Muscat 113; tel. 738201; telex 5663; fax 737028.

Ministry of Foreign Affairs: POB 252, Muscat 113; tel. 699500; telex 3337.

Ministry of Health: POB 393, Muscat 113; tel. 602177; telex 5294.

Ministry of Higher Education: POB 82, Ruwi 112; tel. 693148.

Ministry of Housing: POB 173, Muscat 113; tel. 693333; telex 3694.

Ministry of Information: POB 600, Muscat 113; tel. 603222; telex 5265; fax 601638; e-mail inform@omanet.com.

Ministry of the Interior: POB 127, Ruwi 112; tel. 602244; telex 5650.

Ministry of Justice: POB 354, Ruwi 112; tel. 697699.

Ministry of Legal Affairs: POB 578, Ruwi 112; tel. 605802.

Ministry of National Economy: POB 506, Muscat 113; tel. 738201; fax 738140.

Ministry of National Heritage and Culture: POB 668, Muscat 113; tel. 602555; telex 5649.

Ministry of Palace Office Affairs: POB 2227, Ruwi 112; tel. 600841.

Ministry of Petroleum and Gas: POB 551, Muscat 113; tel. 603333; telex 5280.

Ministry of Posts, Telegraphs and Telephones: POB 338, Ruwi 112; tel. 697870; telex 5625; fax 696817.

Ministry of Regional Municipalities and of the Environment: POB 323, Muscat 113; tel. 696444; telex 5404; fax 602320.

Ministry of Social Affairs, Labour and Vocational Training: POB 560, Muscat 113; tel. 602444; telex 5002.

Ministry of Water Resources: POB 2575, Ruwi 112; tel. 703552.

COUNCIL OF OMAN
Majlis ash-Shoura
(Consultative Council)

President: ABD AL-QADIR BIN SALIM ADH-DHAHAB.

The Majlis ash-Shoura was established by Royal Decree in November 1991. Members of the Majlis are appointed by the Sultan from among nominees selected at national polls. Two representatives are appointed from four candidates in each *wilaya* (region) of more than 30,000 inhabitants, and one from two candidates in each *wilaya* of fewer than 30,000 inhabitants. Members of the Majlis are appointed for a single three-year term of office. The Majlis appointed in November 1997 comprised 82 members. The Majlis is an advisory body, the duties of which include the review of all social and economic draft laws prior to their enactment; public-service ministries are required to submit reports and answer questions regarding their performance, plans and achievements. The President of the Majlis ash-Shoura is appointed by Royal Decree.

Majlis ad-Dawlah
(Council of State)

President: Sheikh HAMUD BIN ABDULLAH AL-HARITHI.

The Majlis ad-Dawlah was established in December 1997, in accordance with the terms of the Basic Statute of the State. It is also an advisory body, comprising 41 members appointed by the Sultan. Its function is to serve as a liaison between the government and the people of Oman.

Political Organizations

There are no political organizations in Oman.

Diplomatic Representation

EMBASSIES IN OMAN

Algeria: POB 216, Muscat 115; tel. 601698; fax 694419; e-mail algeria@gto.net.om; Ambassador: CHÉRIF DERBAL.

Austria: Moosa Complex Bldg, No 477, 2nd Floor, Way No. 3109, POB 2070, Ruwi 112; tel. 793135; telex 3042; fax 793669; Ambassador: Dr RUDOLF BOGNER.

Bahrain: POB 66, Madinat Qaboos, Al-Khuwair; tel. 605912; fax 605072; Chargé d'affaires: AHMAD MUHAMMAD MAHMOUD.

Bangladesh: POB 3959, Ruwi 112; tel. 707462; telex 3800; fax 708495; Ambassador: AMIN AHMED CHOWDHURY.

Brunei: POB 91, Ruwi 112; tel. 603533; fax 693014; Ambassador: Pehin Dato' Haji MAHDINI.

China, People's Republic: Madinat Al-Ilam, Way No. 1507, House No. 465, POB 315, Muscat 112; tel. 696698; telex 5114; fax 602322; Ambassador: ZANG SHIXIONG.

Egypt: Diplomatic City, Al-Khuwair, POB 2252, Ruwi 112; tel. 600411; telex 5438; fax 603626; Ambassador: MAHMOUD HUSSEIN ABD AN-NABY.

France: Diplomatic City, Al-Khuwair, POB 208, Muscat 115; tel. 604266; telex 5163; fax 604300; Ambassador: GEORGES GAUTIER.

Germany: POB 128, Ruwi 112; tel. 702482; telex 3440; fax 705690; Ambassador: Dr PETER DASSEL.

India: POB 1727, Ruwi 112; tel. 702960; telex 3429; fax 797547; Ambassador: INDRAJIT SINGH RATHORE.

Iran: Madinat Qaboos East, Dal, POB 3155, Ruwi 112; tel. 696944; telex 5066; fax 696888; Ambassador: SIAVASH ZARJAR YAGHOUBI.

Iraq: POB 262, 115 Madinat Qaboos, Ruwi 112; tel. 604178; telex 5110; fax 605112; Ambassador: KHALID ABDULLAH SALEH AS-SAMIRA'I.

Italy: Qurum Area, No. 5, Way No. 2411, House No. 842, POB 3727, Muscat 112; tel. 564832; telex 5450; fax 564832; Ambassador: ANACLETO FELICANI.

Japan: Madinat Qaboos West, POB 3511, Ruwi 112; tel. 601028; telex 5087; fax 698720; Ambassador: AKIO LJUIN.

Jordan: Diplomatic City, Al-Khuwair, POB 2281, Ruwi 112; tel. 786350; telex 5518; Ambassador: SAMIR AR-RAFAI AL-HAMOUD.

Korea, Democratic People's Republic: Muscat; Ambassador: KIM HAK YONG.

Korea, Republic: POB 2220, Ruwi 112; tel. 702322; fax 706250; Ambassador: WOO JONG-HO.

Kuwait: Diplomatic City, Al-Khuwair, Block No. 13, POB 1798, Ruwi 112; tel. 699626; telex 5746; fax 600972; Ambassador: ABD AL-MOHSIN SALIM AL-HAROUN.

Lebanon: Al-Harthy Complex, POB 67, Ruwi 118; tel. 695844; fax 695633; Ambassador: Sheikh ADIB ALAMUDDIN.

Malaysia: Shati al-Qurum, Villa 1611, Way 3019, POB 3939, Ruwi 112; tel. 698329; fax 605031; e-mail wakilnct@gto.net.om; Ambassador: ISMAIL BIN MUSTAPHA.

Morocco: Al-Ensharah Street, Villa No. 197, POB 3125, Ruwi 112; tel. 696152; telex 5560; fax 601114; Ambassador: ALAOUI M'HAMDI MUSTAPHA.

Netherlands: O.C. Centre, 7th Floor, POB 3302, Ruwi 112; tel. 705410; telex 3050; fax 799020; e-mail nethmus@gto.net.om; internet http://www.hollandpromo.com/oman/; Ambassador: W. WILDEBOER.

Pakistan: POB 1302, Ruwi 112; tel. 603090; telex 5451; fax 697462; Ambassador: KHALID MAHMOOD.

Philippines: POB 420, Madinat Qaboos 115; tel. 684002; fax 686718; Chargé d'affaires a.i.: JOHN M. BUSTRIA.

Qatar: Al-Mamoura Road, POB 802, Muscat 113; tel. 691152; telex 5661; Ambassador: SAAD NASSER AL-HOMIDI.

Russia: Shati al-Qurum Way 3032, Surfait Compound, POB 80, Ruwi 112; tel. 602894; telex 5493; fax 604189; Ambassador: ALEKSANDR K. PATSEV.

Saudi Arabia: Al-Khuwair, Al-Alaam Area, POB 1411, Ruwi 112; tel. 601744; telex 5406; Chargé d'affaires: NASIR MUHAMMAD AR-RUSHAYDAN.

Somalia: Mumtaz Street, Villa Hassan Jumaa Baker, POB 1767, Ruwi 112; tel. 564412; telex 3253; fax 564965; Ambassador: MUHAMMAD SUBAN NUR.

Sri Lanka: POB 95, Madinat Qaboos 115; tel. 697841; telex 5158; fax 697336; Ambassador: TIKIRI BANDARA MADUWEGEDERA.

Sudan: Diplomatic City, Al-Khuwair, POB 3971, Ruwi 112; tel. 697875; fax 699065; Ambassador: ABD AL-AZIZ MARHOUM AHMAD.

Syria: Madinat Qaboos, Al-Ensharah Street, Villa No. 201, POB 85, Muscat 115; tel. 697904; telex 5029; fax 603895; Chargé d'affaires: ANWAR WEBBI.

Tanzania: Muscat.

Thailand: Villa No. 33–34, Madinat Qaboos East, POB 60, Ruwi 115; tel. 602684; telex 5210; fax 605714; Ambassador: PENSAK CHARALAK.

Tunisia: Al-Ensharah Street, Way No. 1507, POB 220, Muscat 115; tel. 603486; telex 5251; fax 697778; Ambassador: FATHI TOUNSI.

Turkey: Bldg. No. 3270, Street No. 3042, Shatti al-Qurm, POB 47, Mutrah 115; tel. 697050; telex 5571; fax 697053; e-mail turem mus@gto.net.om; Ambassador: ERDAL TÜMER.

United Arab Emirates: Diplomatic City, Al-Khuwair, POB 551, Muscat 111; tel. 600302; telex 5299; fax 604182; Ambassador: HAMAD HELAL THABIT AL-KUWAITI.

United Kingdom: POB 300, Muscat 113; tel. 693077; fax 693087; e-mail becomu@gto.net.om; Ambassador: RICHARD JOHN SUTHERLAND MUIR.

USA: Diplomatic City, POB 202, Muscat 115; tel. 698989; telex 3785; fax 699778; Ambassador: FRANCES D. COOK.

Yemen: Shati al-Qurum, Area 258, Way No. 2840, Bldg No. 2981, POB 105, Madinat Qaboos 115; tel. 600815; telex 5109; fax 605008; Ambassador: AHMAD DAIFALLAH AL-AZEIB.

Judicial System

Oman's Basic Statute guarantees the independence of the judiciary. The foundation for the legal system is *Shari'a* (Islamic law), which is the basis for family law, dealing with matters such as inheritance and divorce. Separate courts have been established to deal with commercial disputes and other matters to which *Shari'a* does not apply.

Courts of the First Instance are competent to try cases of criminal misdemeanour; serious crimes are tried by the Criminal Courts; the Court of Appeal is in Muscat. There are district courts throughout the country. Special courts deal with military crimes committed by members of the armed and security forces.

The Basic Statute provides for a Supreme Council to supervise the proper functioning of the courts.

Religion

ISLAM

The majority of the population (estimated at 53.5% in 1994) are Muslims, of whom approximately three-quarters are of the Ibadi sect and about one-quarter are Sunni Muslims.

HINDUISM

According to 1994 estimates, 28.0% of the population are Hindus.

CHRISTIANITY

It was estimated that in 1994 14.7% of the population were Christians.

The Anglican Communion

Within the Episcopal Church in Jerusalem and the Middle East, Oman forms part of the diocese of Cyprus and the Gulf. In Oman there are inter-denominational churches at Ruwi and Ghala, in Muscat, and at Salalah, and the congregations are entirely expatriate. The Bishop in Cyprus and the Gulf is resident in Cyprus, while the Archdeacon in the Gulf is resident in the United Arab Emirates.

Chaplaincy: POB 1982, Ruwi 112; tel. 702372; fax 789943; joint chaplaincy of the Anglican Church and the Reformed Church of America; Chaplain Rev. GERARD STOREY.

The Press

Article 31 of Oman's Basic Statute guarantees the freedom of the press, printing and publishing, according to the terms and conditions specified by the law. Published matter 'leading to discord, harming the State's security or abusing human dignity or rights' is prohibited.

NEWSPAPERS

Oman Daily Newspaper: POB 6002, Ruwi 112; tel. 701555; telex tel. 790524; 3638; daily; Arabic; Editor-in-Chief HABIB MUHAMMAD NASIB; circ. 15,560.

Ash-Shabibah: POB 6112, 112 Ruwi; tel. 795373; fax 796711; daily; Arabic; leisure and sports.

Al-Watan (The Nation): POB 643, Muscat 113; tel. 591919; telex 5643; fax 591280; e-mail alwatan@gto.net.om; f. 1971; daily; Arabic; Editor-in-Chief MUHAMMAD BIN SULAYMAN AT-TAI; circ. 32,500.

English Language

Oman Daily Observer: POB 6002, Ruwi 112; tel. 703055; telex 3638; fax 790524; f. 1981; daily; publ. by Oman Newspaper House; Editor SAID BIN KHALFAN AL-HARTHI; circ. 22,000.

Times of Oman: POB 3770, Ruwi 112; tel. 701953; telex 3352; fax 799153; f. 1975; daily; Founder, Propr and Editor-in-Chief MUHAMMAD AZ-ZEDJALI; Man. Dir ANIS BIN ESSA AZ-ZEDJALI; circ. 15,000.

PERIODICALS

Al-Adwaa' (Lights): POB 580, 113 Muscat; tel. 704353; telex 3376; fax 798187; weekly; Arabic; economic, political and social; Editor-in-Chief HABIB MUHAMMAD NASIB; circ. 15,600.

Al-'Akidah (The Faith): POB 1001, 112 Ruwi; tel. 701000; telex 3399; fax 709917; weekly illustrated magazine; Arabic; political; Editor SAID AS-SAMHAN AL-KATHIRI; circ. 10,000.

The Commercial: POB 2002, Muscat; tel. 704022; telex 3189; fax 795885; monthly; Arabic and English; advertising.

Al-Ghorfa (Oman Commerce): POB 1400, Ruwi 112; tel. 707674; telex 3389; fax 708497; e-mail pubrel@omanchamber.com; internet http://www.omanchamber.com; f. 1973; bi-monthly; English and Arabic; business; publ. by Oman Chamber of Commerce and Industry; Editor RASHID AHMAD AS-SAWAFI; circ. 10,500.

Jund Oman (Soldiers of Oman): POB 113, Muscat; tel. 613615; telex 5228; fax 613369; monthly; illustrated magazine of the Ministry of Defence; Supervisor: Deputy Prime Minister for Security and Defence.

Al-Markazi (The Central): POB 1161, Ruwi 112; tel. 702222; telex 3794; fax 707913; f. 1975; bi-monthly economic magazine; English and Arabic; publ. by Central Bank of Oman.

Al-Mawared at-Tabeey'iyah (Natural Resources): POB 551, Muscat; publ. by Ministries of Agriculture and Fisheries and of Petroleum and Minerals; monthly; English and Arabic; Editor KHALID AZ-ZUBAIDI.

Al-Mazari' (Farms): POB 467, Muscat; weekly journal of the Ministry of Agriculture and Fisheries; Editor KHALID AZ-ZUBAIDI.

An-Nahda (The Renaissance): POB 979, 113 Muscat; tel. 563104; fax 563106; weekly illustrated magazine; Arabic; political and social; Editor TALEB SAID AL-MEAWALY; circ. 10,000.

Oman Today: Apex Publishing, POB 2616, Ruwi 112; tel. 799388; fax 793316; e-mail 104677,1072@compuserve.com; f. 1981; bi-monthly; English; leisure and sports; Editor ANJU VISEN SINGH.

Al-Omaniya (Omani Woman): POB 6112, Ruwi 112; tel. 792700; telex 3758; fax 707765; monthly; Arabic; circ. 10,500.

Risalat al-Masjed (The Mosque Message): POB 6066, Muscat; tel. 561178; fax 560607; issued by Diwan of Royal Court Affairs Protocol Dept (Schools and Mosques Section); Editor JOUMA BIN MUHAMMAD BIN SALEM AL-WAHAIBI.

Ash-Shurta (The Police): Muscat; tel. 569216; telex 5377; fax 562341; quarterly magazine of Royal Oman Police; Editor Director of Public Relations.

Al-Usra (The Family): POB 440, Mutrah 114; tel. 794922; fax 795348; f. 1974; weekly; Arabic; socio-economic illustrated family magazine; Chief Editor SADEK ABDOWANI; circ. 12,680.

NEWS AGENCY

Oman News Agency: Ministry of Information, POB 3659, Ruwi 112; tel. 696970; telex 5256; Dir-Gen. MUHAMMAD BIN SALIM AL-MARHOON.

Publishers

Apex Publishing: POB 2616, Ruwi 112; tel. 799388; fax 793316; e-mail 104677,1072@compuserve.com; trade directory and maps, leisure and business magazines and guidebooks; Man. Dir SALEH M. TALIB.

Arabian Distribution and Publishing Enterprise: Mutrah; tel. 707079; telex 3085.

Dar al-Usra: POB 440, Mutrah 114; tel. 794922; fax 795348; e-mail admeds@gto.net.om.

Muscat Press and Publishing House: SAOC: POB 3112, 112 Ruwi; tel. 795373; fax 796711.

National Publishing and Advertising LLC: POB 3112, Ruwi 112; tel. 793098; fax 708445; e-mail NPAnet@USA.net; f. 1987; Man. ASHOK SUVARNA.

Oman Newspaper House: POB 3002,112 Ruwi; tel. 701555; fax 790523.

Oman Publishing House: POB 580, Muscat; tel. 704353.

Omani Establishment for Press, Printing and Publishing: POB 463, 113 Muscat; tel. 591919; fax 591280.

Ash-Shahmi Publishers and Advertisers: POB 6112, Ruwi; tel. 703416; telex 3564.

Broadcasting and Communications

TELECOMMUNICATIONS

General Telecommunications Organization (GTO): POB 789, Ruwi 112; tel. 692888; telex 5522; fax 696868; f. 1980; state-owned; transfer to private ownership planned; Exec. Pres. ALI BIN AHMAD AL-ANSARI.

BROADCASTING

Radio

Radio Sultanate of Oman: Ministry of Information, POB 600, Muscat 113; tel. 603222; telex 3265; fax 601393; internet http://www.oman-tv.gov.com; f. 1970; transmits in Arabic 20 hours daily, English on FM 15 hours daily; Dir-Gen. ALI BIN ABDULLAH AL-MUJENI.

Radio Salalah: f. 1970; transmits daily programmes in Arabic and the Dhofari languages; Dir MUHAMMAD BIN AHMAD AR-ROWAS.

The British Broadcasting Corpn (BBC) has built a powerful medium-wave relay station on Masirah island. It is used to expand and improve the reception of the BBC's Arabic, Farsi, Hindi, Pashtu and Urdu services.

Television

Oman Television: Ministry of Information, POB 600, Muscat; tel. 603222; telex 5454; fax 605032.

Finance

(cap. = capital; res = reserves; dep. = deposits; m. = million; brs = branches; amounts in rials Omani unless otherwise stated)

BANKING

At 31 December 1996 there were 18 licensed banks, with a network of more than 300 branch offices, operating throughout Oman. In 1993 the Central Bank of Oman issued instructions whereby the minimum capital for licensed banks was increased to RO 10m., and incentives were offered to encourage mergers, in an effort to rationalize the domestic banking system.

Central Bank

Central Bank of Oman: POB 1161, Ruwi 112; tel. 702222; telex 3794; fax 702253; f. 1974; cap. 539.8m., res 217.4m., dep. 8.4m. (Dec. 1996); 100% state-owned; Exec. Pres. HAMOUD SANGOUR AZ-ZADYALS; Deputy Chair. Dr ALI BIN MUHAMMAD BIN MOUSA; 2 brs.

Commercial Banks

Bank Dhofar al-Omani al-Fransi SAOC: POB 1507, Ruwi 112; tel. 790466; telex 3900; fax 797246; f. 1990; cap. 15.0m., res 1.0m., dep. 115.0m. (Dec. 1996); acquired 12 branches of former Bank of Credit and Commerce International in 1992; Gen. Man. AHMAD ALI ASH-SHANFARI; 20 brs.

Bank Muscat Al-Ahli Al-Omani SAOG: POB 134, Ruwi 112; tel. 703044; telex 3450; fax 707806; f. 1993 by merger; 84.6% owned by Omani shareholders; cap. 20.0m., res 29.5m., dep. 524.9m. (Dec. 1997); Chair. AHMAD BIN SAIF AR-RAWAHY; CEO ABD AR-RAZAK ALI ISSA; 41 brs.

Commercial Bank of Oman Ltd SAOG: POB 550, Ruwi 112; tel. 793226; telex 3275; fax 793229; reorg. 1993 (when it absorbed Oman Banking Corpn); absorbed Oman Savings and Finance Bank 1997; merged with Bank of Oman, Bahrain and Kuwait June 1998; cap. 55.4m. (June 1998); Chair. AMER BIN SHUWAIN AL-HOSNI; Gen. Man. WILLIAM S. HARLEY; 66 brs.

National Bank of Oman SAOG (NBO): POB 751, Ruwi 112; tel. 708894; telex 3281; fax 707781; f. 1973; 100% Omani-owned; cap. 29.0m., res 18.5m., dep. 489.6m. (Dec. 1997); Chair. KHALFAN BIN NASSER AL-WOHAIBI; Gen. Man. AUBYN R. HILL; 52 brs.

Oman Alliance Bank: f. 1997; private sector housing bank; cap. 20m.

Oman Arab Bank SAO: POB 5010, Ruwi 112; tel. 700161; telex 3285; fax 797736; f. 1984; purchased Omani European Bank SAOG in 1994; 51% Omani-owned, 49% by Arab Bank Ltd (Jordan); cap. 14.0m., res 7.1m., dep. 233.7m., (Dec. 1997); Chair. JUMA BIN ALI AL-JUMA; Gen. Man. ABD AL-QADER ASKALAN; 14 brs.

Oman Industrial Bank: Muscat; f. 1997; cap. 10m.; to commence operations in early 1998.

Oman International Bank SAOG: POB 1727, Muscat 111; tel. 682500; telex 5406; fax 682800; e-mail omintbnk@gto.net.om; f. 1984; 100% Omani-owned; cap. 46.6m., res 36.3m., dep. 496.3m. (Dec. 1997); Chair. NOOR BIN MUHAMMAD BIN ABD AR-RAHMAN; Gen. Man. YAHYA SAID ABDULLAH AL-JABRI; 81 brs.

Foreign Banks

Bank of Baroda (India): POB 231, Mutrah 114; tel. 714549; telex 5470; fax 714560; f. 1976; Man. N. RAMANI; 3 brs.

Bank Melli Iran: POB 2643, Ruwi 112; tel. 701579; telex 3295; fax 793017; f. 1974; Gen. Man. ALI JAFFARI LAFTI.

Bank Saderat Iran: POB 1269, Ruwi 112; tel. 793923; fax 796478; Man. M. SEFIDARI.

Banque Banorabe (France): POB 1608, Ruwi 112; tel. 704274; telex 3666; fax 707782; f. 1981; fmrly Banque de l'Orient Arabe et d'Outre Mer; Man. (Oman) PETER S. CARVALHO.

British Bank of the Middle East (Channel Islands): POB 240, Ruwi 112; tel. 799920; telex 3110; fax 704241; f. 1948; CEO IAN W. GILL; 4 brs.

Citibank NA (USA): POB 8994, Mutrah; tel. 795705; telex 3444; fax 795724; f. 1975; Vice-Pres. MUHAMMAD ZAHRAN.

Habib Bank AG Zurich (Switzerland): POB 3679, Ruwi 112; tel. 701736; telex 3931; fax 703613; f. 1967; Exec. Vice-Pres. WAZIR MUMTAZ AHMAD; Asst Vice-Pres. MUHAMMAD IQBAL MUMAL; 2 brs.

Habib Bank Ltd (incorporated in Pakistan): POB 3538, Ruwi 112; tel. 705272; telex 3305; fax 795283; f. 1972; Sr Vice-Pres. and Gen. Man. S. FAZAL MABOOD; 13 brs.

National Bank of Abu Dhabi (UAE): POB 2293, Ruwi 112; tel. 798842; telex 3740; fax 794386; f. 1976; Man. DAVID J. RUNDLE.

Standard Chartered Bank (UK): POB 2353, Ruwi 112; tel. 703999; telex 3217; fax 796864; f. 1968; Man. MURTADHA MUHAMMAD ALI KUKOOR; 4 brs.

Development Banks

Oman Development Bank SAOG: POB 309, Muscat 113; tel. 738021; telex 5179; fax 738026; f. 1977; absorbed Oman Bank for Agriculture and Fisheries in 1997; short-, medium- and long-term finance for development projects in industry, agriculture and fishing; state-owned; cap. 20m., dep. 53.6m., total assets 62m. (Dec. 1997); Chair. Sheikh YACOUB BIN HAMAD AL-HARTHY; Gen. Man. MURTADHA BIN MUHAMMAD FADHIL.

Oman Housing Bank SAOC: POB 2555, Ruwi; tel. 704444; telex 3077; fax 704071; f. 1977; medium- and long-term finance for housing development; 100% state-owned; cap. 30m., res 22m., dep. 1.4m.; total assets 133m. (1994); Chair. MALIK BIN SULAYMAN BIN SAID AL-MA'MARI; Gen. Man. MAHMOUD BIN MUHAMMAD OMAR BAHRAM; 9 brs.

STOCK EXCHANGE

Muscat Securities Market: POB 3265, Muscat 112; tel. 702607; telex 3220; fax 799266; f. 1989; Dir-Gen. MAHMOUD AL-JARWANI.

INSURANCE

Al-Ahlia Insurance Co SAO: POB 1463, Ruwi; tel. 709331; telex 3518; fax 797151; f. 1985; cap. 2m.; Chair. MOHSIN HAIDER DARWISH; Gen. Man. G. V. RAO.

Dhofar Insurance Co SAOG: POB 1002, 112 Ruwi; tel. 705305; fax 793641.

Al-Ittihad al-Wattani: POB 2279, 112 Ruwi; tel. 700715; fax 705595.

Muscat Insurance Co SAOG: POB 72, 112 Ruwi; tel. 695897; fax 695847.

National Life Insurance Co SAOC: POB 798, 117 Wadi Kabir; tel. 791330; fax 791350.

Oman National Insurance Co SAOG (ONIC): POB 2254, Ruwi; tel. 795020; telex 3111; fax 702569; f. 1978; cap. 2m.; Chair. MUHAMMAD BIN MUSA AL-YOUSUF; Gen. Man. MICHAEL J. ADAMS.

Oman United Insurance Co SAOG: POB 1522, Ruwi 112; tel. 703990; telex 3652; fax 796327; f. 1985; cap. 2m.; Chair. SAID SALIM BIN NASSIR AL-BUSAIDI; Gen. Man. KHALID MANSOUR HAMED.

Trade and Industry

GOVERNMENT AGENCY

Omani Centre for Investment Promotion and Export Development (OCIPED): Muscat; f. 1996 as an autonomous body under the aegis of the Ministry of Commerce and Industry; promotes private-sector investment.

CHAMBER OF COMMERCE

Oman Chamber of Commerce and Industry: POB 1400, Ruwi 112; tel. 707684; telex 3389; fax 708497; f. 1973; Pres. Sheikh SALIM AL-KHALILI; 77,000 mems (1996).

HYDROCARBONS COMPANIES

Petroleum Development Oman LLC (PDO): POB 81, Muscat 113; tel. 678111; telex 5212; fax 677106; incorporated in Sultanate of Oman since 1980 by royal decree as limited liability co; 60% owned by Oman Govt, 34% by Shell, 4% by Total-CFP and 2% by Partex; production (1996) averaged 830,000 b/d from 89 fields, linked by a pipeline system to terminal at Mina al-Fahal, near Muscat; Man. Dir B. J. WARD.

Amoco Oman Petroleum Co: POB 1690, Ruwi 112; tel. 698402; fax 698408; no production recorded to date; Pres. and Man. LARRY R. MARKS.

BP Middle East: POB 92, 116 Mina al-Fahal; tel. 561801; telex 5419; fax 561283; CEO CHRIS BROOKS.

Elf Petroleum Oman: POB 353, Ruwi; tel. 694655; fax 694663; concession granted in 1975 for exploration in the onshore region of Butabul; area of 7,000 sq km; converted to a production sharing agreement in October 1976; 48% owned by Elf, 32% by Sumitomo and 20% by Wintershall; present concession area 4,033 sq km (1992) at Butabul; production 6,000 b/d.

Japex Oman: POB 543, Ruwi 112; tel. 602011; telex 5695; fax 602181; f. 1981; operates a concession at Wahibah; 49.6% owned by JNOC, 35.3% by JAPEX and 10.1% by CIECO; present concession area 992 sq km (1996) at Wadi Aswad; production 10,000 b/d; Gen. Man. Y. ARAI.

National Gas Co SAOG: POB 95, CPO Seeb Airport; tel. 626073; fax 626307; f. 1979; bottling of liquefied petroleum gas; Gen. Man. P. K. BAGCHI; 83 employees.

Occidental of Oman Inc.: POB 2271, Ruwi 112; tel. 603595; telex 5258; fax 603358; fmrly Occidental Petroleum Corpn (Occidental Oman); succeeded Gulf Oman Petroleum as majority shareholders

in Suneinah concession in 1983; total area of 9,717 sq km; US $11m. oil stabilization plant completed 1989.

Oman LNG LLC: POB 560, 116 Mina al-Fahal; tel. 707807; fax 707656; f. 1992; 51% state-owned; construction and management of 5,000 tons-per-year liquefied natural gas plant at Bimma, shipping and marketing.

Oman Oil Co (OOC): POB 261, 118 al-Harthy Complex; tel. 567392; fax 567386; f. late 1980s; to invest in foreign commercial enterprises and oil trading operations; 100% state-owned; Chair. MAQBOOL BIN ALI BIN SULTAN.

Oman Refinery Co LLC: POB 3568, Ruwi 112; tel. 561200; telex 5123; fax 561384; production of light petroleum products; Gen. Man. JAY RODNEY MCINTIRE; 298 employees.

The Government has granted exploration rights over a large area of western and south-western Dhofar to BP, Deminex, AGIP, Hispanoil, Elf/Aquitaine I, the Adolph Lundin Group, Quintana/Gulf and Cluff Oil.

UTILITIES

As part of its privatization programme, the Omani government is divesting the utilities on a project-by-project basis. Private investors have already been found for several municipal waste water projects, desalination plants and regional electricity providers. Listed below are the state agencies currently responsible for each utility.

Ministry of Electricity and Water: (see The Government); plans and supervises the development of the utilities in Oman.

Electricity

Oman National Electric Co SAO: POB 1393, 112 Ruwi; tel. 796353; telex 3328; fax 704420; f. 1978; Chair. HAMOUD BIN SONGOR BIN HASHIM; Gen. Man. M. OSMAN BAIG.

Water

Ministry of Water Resources: (see The Government); to assess, manage, develop and conserve water resources.

MAJOR COMPANIES

Al-Felaij Trading and Contracting: POB 2266, Ruwi; tel. 704481; telex 3448; fax 708352; f. 1978; sales RO 6.5m. (1991); cap. and res RO 8m.; manufacture of household and industrial plastic products; Gen. Man. SHAHID BASHIR; 120 employees.

Arabian Trade and Industry Est.: POB 3437, Ruwi 112; tel. 697032; fax 697038; f. 1980; sales RO 1.5m. (1992); cap. and res RO 127,000; manufacture of tissue paper; Chief Exec. RAZAK MAHMOUD; 22 employees.

Construction Materials Industries SAOG: POB 1791, Ruwi 112; tel. 704603/4; fax 799203; e-mail cmioman@gto.net.oni; f. 1977; sales RO 1.3m. (1997); cap. and res RO 3m.; manufacture and supply of calcium silicate bricks, paving and hydrated lime and limestone products; Gen. Man. ADIL MANSOUR AL-JUMA; 120 employees.

National Detergent Co SAOG: POB 3104, Ruwi; tel. 603824; telex 5635; fax 602145; f. 1980; cap. and res RO 1.7m.; manufacture and marketing of detergents; Chair. ABD AL-HUSSAIN BHACKER; Gen. Man. V. SUNDARESAN; 210 employees.

Oman Cement Co SAO: POB 560, 112 Ruwi; tel. 626626; telex 5139; fax 626414; f. 1977; development and production of cement; partial privatization commenced in mid-1994; Chair. Dr ALYQDHAN AL-HINAI.

Oman Chromite Co SAOG: POB 1313; 114 Mutrah; tel. and fax 680058; production of chromite.

Oman Fisheries Co SAOG: POB 2900, Ruwi 112; tel. 693032; fax 697304; f. 1980 as Oman National Fisheries Co; responsible for commercial development of fishing, processing and marketing of marine products; operates 9 deep-sea trawlers, a processing and freezing plant and an onboard fishmeal plant; Gen. Man. MUHAMMAD ALAWI.

Oman Flour Mills Co SOAG: POB 566, Ruwi 112; tel. 711155; telex 5422; fax 714711; f. 1976; sales US $70m. (1994/95); cap. $40m.; 60% state-owned; produces 600 tons per day (t/d) of various flours and 600 t/d of animal feedstuffs; Chair. RASHID BIN SALIM AL-MASROORY; 167 employees.

Oman Mining Co LLC: POB 758, 113 Muscat; tel. 850777; telex 3041; fax 850865; f. 1978; cap. RO 25m.; state-owned; development of copper, gold and chromite mines; Chair. MOHSIN HAIDER DARWISH.

Oman Organic Fertilizer and Chemicals Industries SAO: POB 6781, Ruwi; tel. 591013; telex 5407; fax 590120; f. 1981; cap. RO 2m.; manufacture of organic fertilizers commenced 1986; Gen. Man. TEJ B. SARAF; 28 employees.

Oman Refreshment Co Ltd SAOG: POB 301, Seeb Airport; tel. 591455; telex 5583; fax 591389; f. 1974; cap. RO 2m. (1995); bottling and distribution of soft drinks; Chair. ANWAR ALI SULTAN; Man. Dir ABDULLAH MOUSA; 360 employees.

Poly Products LLC: POB 2561, Ruwi 112; tel. 626044; telex 5182; fax 626046; f. 1979; sales US $20m. (1996); cap. and res $8m.; manufacture of flexible and rigid polyurethane foam and spring mattresses, divan and upholstered beds; Man. Dir SAID AL-HINAI; Gen. Man. SAYED ANWAR AHSAN; 350–400 employees.

Yahya Costain LLC: POB 2282, 112 Ruwi; tel. 591366; telex 5218; fax 591981; f. 1977; mechanical, electrical, civil and process engineering, building and geotechnical investigation, furniture manufacture and joinery; Gen. Man. S. C. MARSHALL; 2,000 employees.

Transport

Directorate-General of Roads: POB 7027, Mutrah; tel. 701577; Dir-Gen. of Roads Sheikh MUHAMMAD BIN HILAL AL-KHALILI.

ROADS

A network of adequate graded roads links all the main centres of population and only a few mountain villages are not accessible by Land Rover. In 1995 there were an estimated 6,020 km of asphalt road and 24,300 km of graded roads.

Oman National Transport Co SAOG: POB 620, Muscat; tel. 590046; telex 5018; fax 590152; operates local, regional and long-distance bus services from Muscat; Chair. TARIQ BIN MUHAMMAD AMIN AL-MANTHERI; Man. Dir SULAYMAN BIN MUHANA AL-ADAWI.

SHIPPING

Port Sultan Qaboos, at the entrance to the Persian (Arabian) Gulf, was built in 1974 to provide nine deep-water berths varying in length from 250 ft to 750 ft (76 m to 228 m), with draughts of up to 43 ft (13 m), and three berths for shallow-draught vessels drawing 12 ft to 16 ft (3.7 m to 4.9 m) of water. A total of 12 new berths have been opened and two of the existing berths have been upgraded to a container terminal capable of handling 60 containers per hour. The port also has a 3,000-ton-capacity cold store which belongs to the Oman Fisheries Co. In 1994 1,418 ships visited Port Sultan Qaboos, and 2.8m. tons of cargo were handled. In 1992 work commenced on the upgrading and expansion of Port Sultan Qaboos.

Directorate General of Ports and Maritime Affairs: POB 684, 113 Ruwi; tel. 700986; fax 702044; e-mail dgpma@gto.net.one; Dir-Gen. Eng. JAMAL T. AZIZ.

Oman National Shipping Line: POB 1479, 114 Jibroo; tel. 792316; fax 792317.

Port Services Corporation SAOG: POB 133, Muscat 113; tel. 714001; telex 5233; fax 714007; e-mail pscco@gto.net.com; f. 1976; cap. RO 4.8m.; jointly owned by the Govt of Oman and private shareholders; Chair. (acting) Eng. MAJID BIN SAID AR-RAWAHI; ABDULLAH AL-GHAZALI; Pres. SAUD AHMAD AN-NAHARI.

The oil terminal at Mina al-Fahal can also accommodate the largest super-tankers on offshore loading buoys. Similar facilities for the import of refined petroleum products exist at Mina al-Fahal. Mina Raysut, near Salalah, has been developed into an all-weather port, and, in addition to container facilities, has four deep-water berths and two shallow berths. During 1994 203 ships called at the port. Loading facilities for smaller craft exist at Sohar, Khaboura, Sur, Marbet, Ras al-Had, Kasab, Al-Biaa, Masirah and Salalah. In 1997 work began on a major project for the development of the Mina Raysut container facilities.

CIVIL AVIATION

Domestic and international flights operate from Seeb International Airport. Oman's second international airport, at Salalah, was completed in 1978. In 1996 some 2.2m. passengers passed through Seeb International Airport. There are airports at Salalah, Sur, Masirah, Khasab and Diba; most other sizeable towns have airstrips.

Directorate-General of Civil Aviation: POB 1, CPO Seeb Airport; tel. 519210; telex 5418; fax 510122; Dir-Gen. Eng. AHMAD BIN SAID BIN SALIM AR-RAWAHY.

Gulf Aviation Ltd (Gulf Air): POB 138, Bahrain; tel. 531166; telex 8255; fax 530385; internet http://www.gulfair.com; f. 1950; jointly owned by the Govts of Bahrain, Oman, Qatar and Abu Dhabi (UAE); international services to destinations in Europe, the USA, Africa, the Middle East and the Far East; Chair. YOUSUF AHMAD ASH-SHIRAWI; Pres. and Chief Exec. ALI IBRAHIM AL-MALKI.

Oman Aviation Services Co SAOG: POB 1058, Seeb International Airport; tel. 519223; telex 5424; fax 510805; f. 1981; cap. RO 7m.; 35% of shares owned by Govt, 65% by Omani nationals; air-charter, maintenance, handling and catering; operators of Oman's domestic airline; international services to India, Kuwait, Pakistan and Sri Lanka; Chair. SALIM BIN ABDULLAH AL-GHAZALI.

Tourism

Tourism, introduced in 1985, is strictly controlled. Attractions, apart from the capital itself, include Nizwa, ancient capital of the interior, Dhofar and the forts of Nakhl, Rustaq, and Al-Hazm. In 1995 there were 350,000 visitor arrivals in Oman, and tourist receipts for that year totalled US $92m.

Director-General of Tourism: J. H. SAYYID FATIK.

Defence

Chief of Staff of the Sultan's Armed Forces: Lt-Gen. KHAMIS BIN SALIM AL-KABANI.

Defence Expenditure (1997 budget): 698m. Omani rials.

Military service: voluntary.

Total armed forces (August 1997): 43,500: army 25,000; navy 4,200; air force 4,100. There is a 6,500-strong Royal Guard.

Paramilitary forces: 4,400: tribal Home Guard (*Firqat*) 4,000; police coastguard 400.

Education

Great advances have been made in education since 1970, when Sultan Qaboos came to power. Although education is still not compulsory, it is provided free to Omani citizens from primary to tertiary level, and attendance has greatly increased. Primary education begins at six years of age and lasts for six years. The next level of education, divided into two equal stages (preparatory and secondary), lasts for a further six years. As a proportion of the school-age population, the total enrolment at primary, preparatory and secondary schools increased from 25% (boys 36%; girls 14%) in 1975 to 74% (boys 76%; girls 72%) in 1995/96. Primary enrolment in 1995/96 included 71% of children in the relevant age-group (boys 72%; girls 70%), while preparatory and secondary enrolment included 56% of children in the relevant age-group (boys 56%; girls 55%). In 1994/95 there were eight teacher-training colleges and 9 vocational institutes, together with institutes of health sciences and banking and five technical institutes. There were also eight Islamic colleges. Oman's first national university, named after Sultan Qaboos, was opened in late 1986, and had 4,296 students (males 1,949; females 2,347) in 1994/95. In 1970 an estimated 80% of Oman's adult population were illiterate; however, government literacy centres for adults (first opened in 1973) have largely redressed this problem. In 1994/95 such centres were attended by 6,654 students (635 males; 6,019 females); some 192 adult education centres were attended by 18,179 students (8,493 males; 9,686 females). Of total expenditure by the central Government in 1996, RO 254.9m. (13.6%) was allocated to education.

Bibliography

Aitchison, C. U. (Ed.) *Government of India Foreign Department—Collection of Treaties Relating to India and Neighbouring Countries. Volume XII.* Calcutta, 1932, reprint 1973.

Akehurst, John. *We Won a War: The Campaign in Oman 1965–75.* London, Michael Russell, 1982.

Allen, Calvin H. *Oman: the Modernization of the Sultanate.* London, Croom Helm, 1987.

Arkless, David C. *The Secret War: Dhofar 1971/72.* London, W. Kimber, 1988.

Badger, G. P. *The History of the Imams and Sayyids of Oman, by Salilbin-Razik, from AD 661 to 1856.* Hakluyt Society, 1871, reprint 1967.

Bailey, Ronald (Ed.) *Records of Oman 1867–1960.* Slough, Archive Editions, 1988 (12 vols).

Barrault, M. *Sultanate of Oman.* Paris, M. Hetier, 1994.

Bhacker, M. *Trade and Empire in Muscat and Zanzibar.* London, Routledge, 1992.

Busch, B. C. *Great Britain and the Persian Gulf 1894–1914.* University of California Press, 1967.

Clements, F. A. *Oman: A Bibliography* (2nd edn). Oxford, Clio Press, 1994.

Oman: The Reborn Land. London, Longman, 1980.

Düster, J., and Scholz, F. *Bibliographie über das Sultanat Oman.* All texts in both German and English. Hamburg, Deutsches Orient-Institut, 1980.

Eickelman, Christine. *Women and Community in Oman.* New York University Press, 1984.

Graz, Liesl. *The Omanis: Sentinels of the Gulf.* London, Longman, 1982.

Hawley, Donald. *Oman and its Renaissance* (5th edn). London, Stacey International, 1995.

Hill, Ann and Daryl. *The Sultanate of Oman: A Heritage.* London, Longman, 1977.

Kechichian, J. *Oman and the World.* Rand, 1997.

Kelly, J. B. *Great Britain and the Persian Gulf, 1793–1880.* London, 1968.

Eastern Arabia Frontiers. London, Faber and Faber, 1964.

Landen, R. G. *Oman Since 1856.* Princeton University Press, 1967.

Lorimer, J. C. *Gazetteer of the Persian Gulf, Oman and Central Arabia.* 2 vols. Calcutta, 1908 and 1915, reprint 1970 in 5 vols, and in 1986 in 9 vols.

Maurizi, Vincenzo. *History of Seyd Said.* Cambridge, Oleander Press, 1984.

Miles, S. B. *The Countries and Tribes of the Persian Gulf.* 3rd edition, London, Frank Cass, 1966.

Morris, James (now Jan). *Sultan in Oman.* London, Faber, 1957.

Newcombe, Ozzie. *The Heritage of Oman.* Reading, Garnet, 1995.

Oman Studies Bibliographic Info. Oman Studies Centre, Pforzheim, Germany.

Peterson, J. E. *Oman in the Twentieth Century.* London, Croom Helm, 1978.

Phillips, Wendell. *Unknown Oman.* London, Longman, 1966, reprint 1971.

Oman. A History. London, Longman, 1967, reprint 1971.

Pridham, Brian R. (Ed.). *Oman: Economic, Social and Strategic Developments.* London, Croom Helm, 1987.

Risso, Patricia. *Oman and Muscat: An Early Modern History.* London, Croom Helm, 1986.

St Albans, Duchess of. *Where Time Stood Still: A portrait of Oman.* London, Quartet, 1980.

Saleh, N. A. *The General Principles of Saudi Arabian and Omani Company Laws.* London, Namara Publications, 1981.

Shannon, M. O. *Oman and Southeastern Arabia: A Bibliographic Survey.* Boston, Hall, 1978.

Sirhan, Sirhan ibn Said ibn. *Annals of Oman.* Cambridge, Oleander Press, 1985.

Skeet, Ian. *Oman: Politics and Development.* London, Macmillan, 1992.

Oman before 1970: The End of an Era. London, Faber, 1985.

el-Solh, Raghid (Ed.) *Oman and the South-Eastern Shore of Arabia.* Reading, Ithaca Press, 1997.

Thesiger, Wilfred. *Arabian Sands.* London, Longman, 1959.

Townsend, John. *Oman: The Making of the Modern State.* London, Croom Helm, 1977.

Vine, Peter. *The Heritage of Oman.* London, Immel, 1995.

Ward, Philip. *Travels in Oman: on the Track of the Early Explorers.* Cambridge, Oleander Press, 1986.

Wikan, U. *Behind the Veil in Arabia: Women in Oman.* London, Johns Hopkins Press, 1982.

Wilkinson, John C. *Water and Tribal Settlement in South-East Arabia.* Oxford University Press, 1977.

The Imamate Tradition of Oman. Cambridge University Press, 1987.

al-Yousuf, Muhammad bin Musa. *Oil and the Transformation of Oman 1970–1995.* London, Stacey International, 1995.

QATAR

Geography

The State of Qatar occupies a peninsula (roughly 160 km long, and between 55 km and 90 km wide), projecting northwards from the Arabian mainland, on the west coast of the Persian (Arabian) Gulf. Its western coastline joins onto the shores of Saudi Arabia, and to the east lie the United Arab Emirates (UAE) and Oman. The total area is 11,427 sq km (4,412 sq miles), and at the census of 16 March 1986 the population was 369,079, of whom fewer than one-third were native Qataris. At mid-1995, according to official estimates, the population was 640,846, but a census in 1997 enumerated a provisional total of only 520,500. About 60% of the total were concentrated in the town of Doha, on the east coast. Two other ports, Zakrit on the west coast and Umm Said on the east, were developed after the discovery of petroleum. Zakrit is a convenient, if shallow, harbour for the import of goods from Bahrain, while Umm Said affords anchorage to deep-sea tankers and freighters.

The climate of Qatar is hot and humid in summer, with temperatures reaching 44°C between July and September, and humidity exceeding 85%. There is some rain in winter, when temperatures range between 10°C and 20°C. Qatar is stony, sandy and barren; limited supplies of underground water are unsuitable for drinking or agriculture because of high mineral content. More than one-half of the water supply is now provided by sea-water distillation processes.

History

Revised for this edition by KAMIL MAHDI

Qatar was formerly dominated by the Khalifa family of nearby Bahrain. The peninsula became part of Turkey's Ottoman Empire in 1872, but Turkish forces evacuated Qatar at the beginning of the First World War (1914–18). The United Kingdom recognized Sheikh Abdullah ath-Thani as Ruler of Qatar, and in 1916 made a treaty with him, in accordance with its policy in Bahrain, the Trucial States (now the United Arab Emirates) and Kuwait. The Ruler of Qatar undertook not to cede, mortgage or otherwise dispose of parts of his territories to anyone except the British Government, nor to enter into any relationship with a foreign government, other than the British, without British consent. In return, Britain undertook to protect Qatar from all aggression by sea, and to provide support in case of an overland attack. A further treaty, concluded in 1934, extended fuller British protection to Qatar.

The discovery of petroleum in 1939 promised greater prosperity for Qatar, but further development was delayed by the onset of the Second World War, and production did not begin on a commercial scale until 1949. The country used the revenues from the export of petroleum to finance an ambitious development programme. In January 1961 Qatar joined the Organization of the Petroleum Exporting Countries (OPEC), and in May 1970 it also became a member of the Organization of Arab Petroleum Exporting Countries (OAPEC). Qatar is a relatively minor oil-exporting country, but its development needs and its standard of living are highly dependent upon its small oil (and, more recently, gas) reserves.

In October 1960 Sheikh Ali ath-Thani, who had been Ruler of Qatar since 1949, abdicated in favour of his son, Sheikh Ahmad ath-Thani. In 1968 the British Government announced its intention to withdraw British forces from the Persian (Arabian) Gulf area by 1971. As a result, Qatar attempted to associate itself with Bahrain and the Trucial States in a proposed federation. In April 1970 the Ruler, Sheikh Ahmad, announced a provisional Constitution for Qatar, providing for a partially elected consultative assembly. Effective power remained, however, in the monarch's hands. In May 1970 the Deputy Ruler, Sheikh Khalifa ath-Thani (a cousin of Sheikh Ahmad), was appointed Prime Minister. After the failure of negotiations for union with neighbouring Gulf countries, Qatar became fully independent on 1 September 1971, when the Ruler took the title of Amir. The 1916 treaty was replaced by a new treaty of friendship with the United Kingdom. In February 1972 a bloodless coup, led by Sheikh Khalifa, the Crown Prince and Prime Minister, deposed the Amir during his absence abroad. Claiming support from the royal family and the armed forces, Sheikh Khalifa proclaimed himself Amir, while retaining the premiership.

Qatar has generally maintained close links with Saudi Arabia, with which it signed a bilateral defence agreement in 1982. It opposed the Camp David agreements between Egypt, Israel and the USA, and the subsequent Egyptian-Israeli treaty, signed in March 1979. In early 1981 Qatar joined the newly-established Co-operation Council for the Arab States of the Gulf (Gulf Co-operation Council—GCC). By May 1983 member countries were implementing new GCC regulations, including the abolition of import tariffs between member states, reduced restrictions on travel between GCC countries, and more favourable investment conditions for business. Co-operation on defence was also a priority, as was underlined by the threat to the security of GCC states of an escalation of the war between Iran and Iraq, which had begun in 1980. In October 1983 Qatari forces participated in the GCC's 'Peninsula Shield' joint military exercise in Oman, and in November Qatar was the venue for a three-day GCC summit meeting.

After his accession in 1972, the Amir pursued reform while preserving the Islamic pattern of life. In accordance with the 1970 Constitution, Sheikh Khalifa decreed the first Advisory Council, to complement the ministerial Government. Its 20 members, selected from representatives elected by limited suffrage, were increased to 30 in December 1975. The Advisory Council's term of office was extended by four years in May 1978 and by further terms of four years in 1982, 1986, 1990, 1994 and 1998. The Advisory Council's constitutional entitlements include power to debate legislation drafted by the Council of Ministers before ratification and promulgation. It also has power to request ministerial statements on matters of general and specific policy, including the draft budget.

Using the wealth that it acquired through petroleum sales, the Qatari Government made significant social and infrastructural improvements. By 1983 an estimated 6,000 families were housed by the state, a welfare and non-contributory pension scheme had been introduced, and a programme to construct schools and clinics was almost complete. In May 1989 the Supreme Council for Planning (SCP) was formed to co-ordinate plans for Qatar's social and economic development. Under the direction of the heir apparent (Sheikh Hamad bin Khalifa ath-Thani), the council promoted industrial diversification and agricultural development in order to reduce dependence on the petroleum sector.

In April 1986 Qatar raided the island of Fasht ad-Dibal, which had been artificially constructed on a coral reef in the Persian (Arabian) Gulf, and seized 29 foreign workers who were constructing a Bahraini coastguard station on the island. Officials of the GCC met representatives of both states in an attempt to reconcile them, and to avoid a division within the Council. In May the workers were released, and the two Governments agreed to destroy the island. In July 1991 Qatar referred the demarcation of its maritime border with Bahrain and the issue of ownership of the potentially oil-rich Hawar islands (held by Bahrain) to the International Court of Justice (ICJ) in The Hague. In mid-1992 the Qatari Government rejected Bahrain's attempt to broaden the issue to include sovereignty over an area around Zubara on the Qatari coast, while in April 1992 Qatar had issued a decree redefining its maritime borders to include territorial waters claimed by Bahrain. A hearing of the ICJ opened in February 1994 with the aim of determining whether the court had jurisdiction to give a ruling on the dispute. In July the ICJ invited the two countries to resubmit their dispute by 30 November, either jointly or separately. However, the two countries failed to reach agreement on presenting the dispute to the Court, and at the end of November Qatar submitted a unilateral request to continue its case through the ICJ. In February 1995, while the ICJ declared that it would have authority to adjudicate in the dispute (despite Bahrain's refusal to accept the principle of an ICJ ruling), Saudi Arabia also proposed to act as mediator between the two countries. Sheikh Hamad, then Deputy Amir and Heir Apparent, subsequently indicated that Qatar would be willing to withdraw the case from the ICJ if Saudi arbitration proved successful. In September, however, relations between Qatar and Bahrain soured following the Bahraini Government's decision to construct a tourism resort on the Hawar islands despite controversy over their sovereignty. In late December, furthermore, Qatar's deposed Amir visited Bahrain and suggested that sovereignty of the Hawar islands would be returned to that country if he were restored to power. Qatar retaliated by televising interviews with exiled Bahraini Shi'ites and by publishing articles alluding to abuses of human rights in Bahrain. In mid-1996 the Qatari Government reiterated not only its rejection of Bahraini exhortations to withdraw the case from the ICJ, but also its willingness to consider Saudi involvement in negotiations, provoking renewed Bahraini claims of sovereignty over the disputed territory in July 1996. During August the Bahraini authorities continued to promote a regional settlement to the dispute, proposing the convention of a bilateral summit meeting to be followed by Saudi mediation. Relations between Qatar and Bahrain deteriorated at the end of 1996 following an announcement, made by the Bahrain Government in early December, that two Qatari nationals had been arrested in Bahrain and charged with spying. (The two men were subsequently acquitted.) Qatar retaliated with public accusations of Bahraini involvement in the failed February coup attempt. Bahrain boycotted the GCC annual summit convened in Doha in December, at which it was decided to establish a quadripartite committee (comprising those GCC countries not involved in the dispute) to facilitate a solution. Attempts by the committee to foster improved relations between Bahrain and Qatar achieved a degree of success, and meetings between prominent government ministers from both countries in London (United Kingdom) and Manama (Bahrain) in February and March 1997 resulted in the announcement that diplomatic relations at ambassadorial level were to be established between the two countries by mid-1997. Qatar announced its choice of ambassador to Bahrain in early April, but Bahrain has yet to approve this choice and to announce its ambassador to Qatar. Previously hostile media coverage of the dispute diminished as a result of these contacts, although little further progress was made. In April 1998 Bahrain alleged that the 82 documents submitted by Qatar to the ICJ in 1997 in support of its claims to sovereignty and territorial rights were forgeries. Qatar maintained that such judgement should be reserved for the Court. Later in the same month, the opening of a Bahraini hotel on the islands provoked renewed Qatari protests, and in June Bahrain announced its intention to build a 22.5-km causeway connecting the group's principal island to Bahrain. In July 1998 the ICJ had yet to make a ruling on the dispute.

In May 1989 Iran's Minister of Oil, Gholamreza Aqazadeh, declared that one-third of the Qatari-controlled North Field, the world's largest natural gas field, was beneath Iranian waters.

Aqazadeh provoked a hostile response from the Qatari Government by announcing that Iran planned to appropriate its share of the field and to pipe gas to an Iranian gas-processing plant.

In July 1989, in the first government reshuffle since 1978, seven ministers were replaced and 11 new members were appointed to a new 16-member Council of Ministers. Five new portfolios were created. The Ministry of the Economy and Commerce, which had been vacant, became the Ministry of Economy and Trade, and the Agriculture and Industry portfolio was divided. Agriculture was amalgamated with Municipal Affairs, while Industry was linked with Public Works and was expected to play a major role in the planning of industrial development. The Minister of Foreign Affairs, Abdullah bin Khalifa al-Attiyah, resigned in May 1990 and was replaced by Mubarak Ali al-Khatir, the former Minister of Electricity and Water.

In January 1992 50 leading Qatari citizens petitioned the Amir to demand the establishment of a consultative assembly with legislative powers. They also expressed concern at abuse of power in the emirate and proposed reforms of the economy and the education system. In September there was another extensive reorganization of the Council of Ministers, expanding its membership from 14 to 17.

Qatar, as a member of the GCC, the League of Arab States (Arab League) and the UN, condemned Iraq's occupation of Kuwait in August 1990, although it had previously supported Iraq in its 1980–88 war with Iran. In late 1990 Qatar permitted the deployment of foreign forces on its territory, as part of the multinational attempt to force Iraq to withdraw from Kuwait. Units of the Qatari armed forces subsequently participated in the military operation to liberate Kuwait in January–February 1991. Qatar resumed tentative contact with Iraq in 1993. In February 1994 the Kuwaiti Government temporarily recalled its ambassador from Qatar in protest at the *rapprochement* between Qatar and Iraq. In April Qatar stressed that co-operation with Iraq would depend on Iraq's implementation of the UN resolutions. In the same month an Iraqi cultural delegation was welcomed to Qatar. In March 1995, during the first official visit to the country by a senior Iraqi official since the 1990–91 crisis, the Iraqi Minister of Foreign Affairs, Muhammad Saeed as-Sahaf, attended a meeting with his Qatari counterpart, Sheikh Hamad bin Jaber ath-Thani, to discuss the furtherance of bilateral relations. At a press conference at the end of the visit, the Qatari minister indicated Qatar's determination to pursue a foreign policy independent from that of its GCC neighbours when he announced his country's support for the ending of UN sanctions against Iraq. Notwithstanding Qatar's close alliance with the USA, the Amir expressed dismay at US policy towards both Iraq and Iran during meetings with the US President, Bill Clinton, in Washington, DC (USA), in June 1997. Qatar also sent humanitarian aid to Iraq and continued to do so during the weeks of military crisis in February 1998 (see chapter on Iraq). At that time the Qatari Minister of Foreign Affairs made a visit to Baghdad to relay messages between the Iraqi President and the Amir, following which the Amir himself travelled to Saudi Arabia for a meeting with King Fahd to discuss the deepening crisis. After the easing of tensions in the region, the Amir met the Iraqi Minister of Foreign Affairs during the latter's presence at a meeting of foreign ministers of the Organization of the Islamic Conference in Doha in March.

In May 1992 Qatar signed six agreements with Iran for co-operation in various sectors, including customs, air traffic and the exchange of information. In July 1993 the Deputy Amir, Sheikh Hamad, visited Teheran and in October an agreement was signed to establish a joint committee for co-operation in the oil and gas sector. In January 1994 Qatar hosted talks with Iran to discuss security issues and draw up plans to curb drugs-trafficking in the Persian Gulf. Qatar chose to pursue good relations with Iran despite adverse reaction from its Arab neighbours and the USA. In April further discussions were held with regard to a proposed water pipeline from Iran to Qatar. Iran's relations with the Arab states of the Gulf showed a marked improvement during 1997 and 1998, and as a result, both the Amir and the Minister of Foreign Affairs urged an end to the US isolation of Iran during their respective visits to the USA in June 1997 and March 1998.

In June 1992 Qatar followed Kuwait and Bahrain in signing a defence pact with the USA. In mid-1993 Qatar and the United

Kingdom signed a memorandum of understanding on defence. The Ministers of Foreign Affairs of Qatar and Tunisia signed an agreement in January 1994 to further political and economic relations. On 7 April Qatar became a contracting party to the General Agreement on Tariffs and Trade (GATT), and a week later the Qatari Minister of Foreign Affairs travelled to Bonn, Germany, for three days of talks on expanding mutual co-operation. The following month military co-operation was discussed with a Russian military official. Sheikh Hamad, the Deputy Amir, voiced Qatar's continuing support for the Palestinian reconstruction programme when a Palestinian delegation visited in June. In August Qatar and France signed a defence agreement which would entail Qatar receiving a number of *Mirage* 2000-5 aircraft. In the same month the Qatari Minister of Foreign Affairs met King Hussein of Jordan in London to discuss the Middle East peace process and ways of boosting bilateral relations. In March 1995 Qatar signed an agreement with the USA, in which the USA was given permission to pre-position military equipment in the emirate.

At the end of September 1992 tensions arose with Saudi Arabia when Qatar accused a Saudi force of attacking the al-Khofous border post, killing two soldiers and capturing another. As a result, Qatar announced the suspension of a 1965 agreement with Saudi Arabia on border demarcation (which had never been fully ratified) and withdrew its 200-strong contingent from the GCC 'Peninsula Shield' force in Kuwait. The Saudi Government denied the involvement of its armed forces. Qatar registered its disaffection by boycotting meetings of the GCC ministers in Abu Dhabi and Kuwait in November. However, on 20 December, following mediation by President Mubarak of Egypt, Sheikh Khalifa and King Fahd of Saudi Arabia signed an agreement whereby a committee was to be established to demarcate the border between the two states by the end of 1993. Qatar subsequently resumed attendance of GCC sessions but its border with Saudi Arabia has yet to be officially demarcated. In November 1994 Qatar boycotted a meeting in Saudi Arabia of GCC ministers of the interior, in protest at what it alleged to have been armed incidents on the border with Saudi Arabia in March and October, during one of which a Qatari citizen was reported to have been wounded by Saudi border guards.

The foreign policy adopted by Qatar in 1994 differed from that of its GCC allies on a number of key issues. Qatar declined to support a final communiqué, issued by seven other Arab states, demanding an immediate cease-fire in Yemen, arguing that it was not their place to interfere in the domestic affairs of another country. Similarly, Qatar made early contact with the Israeli Government without waiting for the peace process to be firmly established: in January 1994 discussions took place with regard to the supply of natural gas to Israel. Following Arab protests, Qatar conceded that a sales agreement would depend on a feasibility study and on Israel's withdrawal from all Arab territories occupied in 1967. In September, however, Qatar, along with the other GCC states, revoked aspects of the economic boycott of Israel. In early November the Israeli Deputy Minister of Foreign Affairs, Yossi Beilin, made an official visit to Qatar, and in December negotiations were reported to be in progress on the establishment of an Israeli interests office in Doha. A trade office was established, and in October 1995 Qatar's Minister of Foreign Affairs was reported to have expressed his country's support for the cancellation of the direct economic boycott of Israel, even if a compromise peace settlement in the Middle East were not achieved. In the following month Israel signed a memorandum of intent to purchase Qatari liquefied natural gas, and in April 1996 Shimon Peres made the first official visit to Qatar by an Israeli Prime Minister. However, relations deteriorated in late 1996, when Israel declared that the memorandum of intent to purchase Qatari gas had expired, although negotiations would continue. In early November, Qatar announced that any gas sales to Israel would be dependent on the peace process and would be conducted through a US company. In December, Qatar condemned the expansion of Israeli settlements into Arab-occupied territories, and in March 1997 Qatar 'froze' relations with Israel. At the end of that month, the Arab League passed a resolution recommending the restoration of the economic boycott against Israel and withdrawal from multilateral peace talks with that state. Qatar was heavily pressed by Arab and Islamic interests to cancel the Middle East

and North Africa economic summit planned for November 1997, to be held in Doha. (This was to be the fourth in a series of meetings gathering Israeli and Arab leaders to discuss the development of economic links in the region.) Recent set-backs in the peace process with Israel had cast doubt over the future of the summit, although the USA was determined that the meeting should go ahead. The Amir, who received a kidney transplant in the USA in mid-1997 and spent nearly three months until October convalescing in that country, had also ruled out cancellation. The conference, downgraded from a 'summit', owing to the widespread Arab boycott, proceeded on 16–18 November, with the participation of an Israeli delegation. The Qatari Government emphasized the economic rather than the political aspects of the conference, and attempted to attract foreign investment for joint industrial projects in the country. Following the Doha conference, a dispute erupted with Egypt when the Qatari Minister of State for Foreign Affairs accused the Egyptian Government (which had been vociferous in its demands for the cancellation of the conference) of conducting a campaign of denigration against Qatar. The dispute continued in the media and in the political arena for several months, and about 700 Egyptian workers, including almost all those employed by the Ministry of the Interior, had their employment in Qatar terminated. A meeting in December between the Amir and President Mubarak in Riyadh did not appear to have settled matters completely, but in early March 1998, it was announced that differences between Qatar and Egypt were to be resolved, with an exchange of ministerial visits. Later in March, the Qatari Amir visited Cairo for talks on bilateral relations. Qatar's relations with the UAE also soured at the time of the Doha meeting, but they improved following a visit by the Amir to the UAE in March 1998. Since the conference, the Qatari Government has been distancing itself from Israel and has criticized the intransigence of the Israeli Government. Statements issued in early 1998 concerned the possible closure of the Israeli trade office in Doha. A visit to Qatar by the Hamas leader Sheikh Ahmad Yassin in June 1998 was criticized by the Israeli Government.

On 27 June 1995 the Deputy Amir, Heir Apparent, Minister of Defence and Commander-in-Chief of the Armed Forces, Maj.-Gen. Sheikh Hamad bin Khalifa ath-Thani, deposed the Amir in a bloodless coup. Sheikh Hamad proclaimed himself Amir, claiming the support of the royal family and the Qatari people. Sheikh Khalifa, who was in Switzerland at the time of the coup, immediately denounced his son's actions, and vowed to return to Qatar. Although Sheikh Khalifa had effectively granted Sheikh Hamad control of the emirate's affairs in 1992 (with the exception of the treasury), a power struggle was reported to have emerged between the two in the months preceding the coup: Sheikh Khalifa was particularly opposed to his son's notably independent foreign policy (which had led to the strengthening of relations with both Iran and Iraq, and with Israel, thereby jeopardizing relations with Saudi Arabia and the other Gulf states), and had attempted to regain influence in policy decisions. The United Kingdom and the USA quickly recognized the new Amir; Saudi Arabia endorsed the regime shortly afterwards. In mid-July Sheikh Hamad reorganized the Council of Ministers and appointed himself Prime Minister, while retaining the posts of Minister of Defence and Commander-in-Chief of the Armed Forces. Sheikh Abdullah, Sheikh Hamad's brother, was appointed Deputy Prime Minister and Minister of the Interior. Speculation that Sheikh Abdullah might be named heir apparent was swiftly curbed by alterations made to the rules of succession, specifying that thenceforth the hereditary line would pass through the sons of the Amir. The new Amir instituted a number of reforms including the relaxation of press censorship and greater transparency of government procedures. There was also discussion of the separation of the financial affairs of the state from those of the ruling family, and in August 1997 the Amir announced that a draft law was being prepared to ensure this separation. Women's issues have also assumed greater prominence; in May 1998 the Amir's wife gave a newspaper interview in which she advocated reform to facilitate the participation of women in political life.

In November 1995 Sheikh Hamad announced his intention to establish elected municipal councils, and in May 1997 it was announced that elections for these would be held by November of that year. By mid-1998, the elections had still not taken place, although voter registration was due to begin on 3 October. Women were to be allowed to participate in the elections and to serve on the councils. (In April 1998 elections were held for the first time to the board of directors of the Qatar Chamber of Commerce and Industry.) In early June 1997, the justice minister resigned, reportedly owing to conflict within the Council of Ministers over the municipal elections. Meanwhile, the deposed Amir took residence in the UAE, and visited Bahrain, Kuwait, Saudi Arabia, Egypt and Syria in an apparent attempt to assert his legitimacy as ruler of Qatar. In January 1996, moreover, Qatar's Minister of Foreign Affairs confirmed that Sheikh Khalifa had gained control of a substantial part of Qatar's financial reserves. In the following month security forces in Qatar were reported to have foiled an attempted coup. As many as 100 people were arrested, and a warrant was issued for the arrest of Sheikh Hamad bin Jasim bin Hamad ath-Thani, a former Minister of Economy and Trade. There were conflicting reports as to the origin of the coup plot, including suggestions that other Gulf states might be implicated. Sheikh Khalifa denied any involvement; however, he was quick to imply that the alleged plot indicated popular support for his return. The trial began in December 1997 of seven people on charges of selling state military secrets. In early February 1998 two of the defendants, including a military officer, were convicted and sentenced to 10 years' imprisonment; another military officer was imprisoned for one year for failing to report a capital offence. All seven were acquitted of charges of forming an illegal society with the intention of overthrowing the Government. In November 1997, meanwhile, the trial began of 110 people (40 of whom were charged *in absentia*), accused of involvement in the attempted coup of February 1996. Hearings were immediately adjourned. Another seven individuals, including a member of the ruling family, were charged with involvement in the attempted coup, in February 1998. In June of that year seven men were charged with an attempted bomb attack on the passport administration building in Doha in October 1996.

Meanwhile, the Government had requested the suspension of several bank accounts held in the names of Sheikh Khalifa and a former office director, Isa al-Kawari, in five countries, pending the outcome of legal proceedings, initiated in Qatar and abroad in late July 1996, to determine the ownership of some $3,000m.–$8,000m. in overseas assets, which were asserted by the new Amir to have been amassed by his father from state oil and investment revenues. By mid-October, however, it was reported that Sheikh Hamad and Sheikh Khalifa had been reconciled, and in February 1997 all legal proceedings were formally withdrawn. Although there was much speculation surrounding the possibility of Sheikh Khalifa returning to Qatar, he indicated that this would not happen in the near future. Sheikh Khalifa was expected to return to Qatar by the end of 1996. On 22 October Sheikh Hamad named the third eldest of his four sons, Sheikh Jasim bin Hamad bin Khalifa ath-Thani, as heir apparent. Shortly afterwards, Sheikh Hamad appointed his younger brother, Sheikh Abdullah bin Khalifa ath-Thani (the Minister of the Interior), as Prime Minister. On 30 October a new Government, which included five newly-appointed ministers, was formed. A Ministry of Housing and the Civil Service was established, while the Ministry of Information and Culture was abolished. The Council of Ministers was reorganized in January 1998. Notable changes included the appointment of Sheikh Muhammad bin Khalifa ath-Thani as Deputy Prime Minister; he was succeeded as Minister of Finance, Economy and Trade by Yousuf Hussein Kamal (previously an undersecretary at the finance ministry). The justice portfolio, which had been undertaken by the Minister of Electricity and Water, Ahmad Muhammad Ali as-Subay'i, in an acting capacity following the resignation of the Minister of Justice in June 1997, was not reassigned. In March 1998 it was reported that the Ministry of Information had been reinstated, and that a National Council for Culture, Arts and Heritage had been created.

Economy

Dr P. T. H. UNWIN

Revised for this edition by ALAN J. DAY

Qatar is a largely barren peninsula, with stony and sandy soil which is generally unsuitable for arable farming. There are numerous coastal saline flats, known as *sabkha*, and the only agricultural soils are found in small depressions in the centre of the country and towards the north. Traditionally the Qatari economy was based on the nomadic farming of livestock, and on fishing and pearling. Since the discovery of significant reserves of petroleum in 1939, however, the exploitation of these deposits has transformed Qatar into one of the richest countries in the region, measured in terms of average income. In 1984, according to estimates by the World Bank, Qatar's gross national product (GNP), calculated on a 1982–84 base period (to adjust for fluctuations in prices and exchange rates), was US $5,780m., equivalent to $19,010 per head. As in 1983, Qatar's GNP per head in 1984 was the second highest national level in the world, exceeded only by that of its neighbour, the United Arab Emirates (UAE). In 1985, however, Qatar's GNP per head (at average 1983–85 prices) declined to $16,220, the sixth highest level in the world (exceeded by the UAE, Bermuda, Brunei, the USA and Switzerland). According to World Bank estimates, Qatar's GNP in constant prices, i.e. adjusted for inflation, actually diminished between 1973 and 1985, owing to declines in petroleum output and prices in the early 1980s. Over this period, real GNP per head declined by 8.5% per annum. Over the 12 years to 1985, it is estimated, the country's population increased at an average rate of 6.8% per year, mainly because of an influx of immigrant labour. This rate was estimated to have declined to 5.8% per year during 1985–95. The World Bank estimated the average rate of decline in Qatar's real GNP per head as 2.6% per annum over the period 1985–95. In 1995 the World

Bank estimated Qatar's GNP, measured at average 1993–95 prices, as $7,448m., equivalent to $11,600 per head on a conventional exchange-rate basis.

The economic changes that have taken place within Qatar in recent years have been made possible by the high level of labour immigration. In 1991 the number of indigenous Qataris was estimated at 350,000, while the World Bank estimated the total mid-year population at 506,000. The mid-year population in 1996 was estimated at 585,000. In May 1997 the Government issued a directive advising private sector businesses to ensure that Qatari nationals constituted at least 20% of their workforce. By the mid-1980s the economy still relied heavily on petroleum revenues, but a policy of diversification meant that between 1979 and 1983 the percentage of government revenues derived from crude oil fell from 93% to 80%. The collapse in world prices for crude petroleum during 1986 nevertheless placed an increased burden on an already stressed economy. Despite a recovery in the price of oil in the second half of the year, Qatar's total revenue from petroleum in 1986 was approximately $1,720m., compared with $3,068m. in 1985. Oil revenues remained at low levels during the second half of the 1980s. In 1984 the petroleum sector's contribution to GDP was 45%, but by 1988 the proportion had fallen to an estimated 27%. Qatar has a reputation for caution in its economic policy, but in the late 1980s moves towards economic restructuring were made, and reforms took place, in anticipation of a sharp reduction in Qatar's output of crude oil after 2010. As a result, in 1987 the Government introduced a programme of industrialization, centred on ambitious plans for the development of the North Field, the world's largest single natural gas deposit.

The ending of the Iran–Iraq War in August 1988 improved conditions of trade in the region, in particular by removing from neutral merchant shipping the threat of attack and by restoring confidence in local export industries, especially the petroleum industry. By 1990 the first phase of the North Field development programme was close to completion, but Iraq's invasion of Kuwait in August led to the suspension of major investment projects. Although the crisis raised oil revenues to an estimated $2,500m. in 1990, its overall impact was to depress economic activity. Since the liberation of Kuwait in February 1991, Qatar has revived its programme of industrial projects, the cost of which has been estimated at $8,000m. Production from the North Field began on 3 September 1991, the 20th anniversary of Qatar's independence. In view of the huge capital cost of implementing the full industrialization programme, availability of financing is expected to be one of the major factors determining the pace of Qatar's economic development during the 1990s. In 1995 Qatar's estimated GDP at current prices was QR 27,355m., of which QR 8,900m. (32.5%) was contributed by the petroleum sector and QR 3,120m. (11.4%) by non-oil manufacturing industries. By mid-1995 Qatar had secured an estimated $4,000m. of international project finance for its industrialization programme, early implementation of which was one of the main priorities of the new Head of State who took power in June 1995. By mid-1998 the total amount of project finance secured by Qatar was estimated to have exceeded $6,000m., as international bankers continued to respond positively to the emirate's development programme.

A 1997 IMF survey of Qatar's economy indicated that, whereas there had been a 2.4% increase in real GDP in 1994, 1995 had witnessed an estimated 1.2% overall decline in real GDP (the oil and gas component having declined by 2.6% and the non-oil component by 0.7% in that year). The IMF's estimates for 1996 showed that there had been 23.8% growth in the oil and gas sector and 5% growth in other sectors, predicting real GDP growth of 9.9% overall in that year. In 1996, according to the Governor of the Central Bank, the economy grew by 9.7% (and inflation was restricted to 2.2%), although some confusion was created by the Central Bank's annual report for 1996, which asserted that GDP had increased by only 3% in that year. The IMF's predictions of real GDP growth rates of 15.5% in 1997 and 11.5% in 1998, based on an average oil export price of $17.70 per barrel, proved to be over-optimistic, as a slump in world oil prices from late 1997 reduced Qatari receipts to $12.40 per barrel in the first quarter of 1998. In mid-1998 local economists estimated that the growth rate in 1998 would be no more than 3% if the oil price did not rise before the end of the year. Nevertheless, the Government and the IMF remained optimistic that the anticipated inauguration of major gas production developments in the early 21st century would yield substantial new revenues.

Total external debt, including project finance, grew from $4,508m. at the end of 1995 to $7,342m. at the end of 1996. It was expected to exceed $10,000m. by the end of 1997. The IMF expected external debt to reach the equivalent of 108% of GDP in 1998 before falling back to 76% of GDP in 2000 as externally-financed development projects begin to show a profit. There were official foreign-exchange reserves of $1,456m. at the end of 1996, when the Government's share of Qatar's external debt (representing borrowing to finance the fiscal deficit) amounted to $2,870m. Total external debt at end-1996 was estimated at $7,342m. (representing 82% of GDP) and was expected to reach $12,000m. in 1998 as borrowing for gas development peaked. In 1997, the Government had an investment-grade credit rating in the syndicated loan markets through which it regularly arranged sovereign borrowing (see Budget and Finance, below).

PETROLEUM AND NATURAL GAS

The first concession to explore for petroleum in Qatar was granted to the Anglo-Persian Oil Co in 1935, and was later transferred to Petroleum Development (Qatar) Ltd. Deposits of petroleum were first discovered in Qatar in 1939, although exploration and production was delayed during the Second World War. By 1949 a pipeline had been constructed from the Dukhan oilfield, on the west coast, to Umm Said in the east, where terminal facilities had also been built, and in December of that year the first shipment of Qatari petroleum was exported.

In 1952 the Shell Co of Qatar acquired a concession to develop the entire continental shelf offshore area, and by 1960 petroleum had been discovered at Idd ash-Shargi, 100 km to the east of Qatar. Soon afterwards, a second offshore oilfield was discovered, to the north-east of the first, at Maydan Mahzam, and in 1970 a third offshore field, Bul Hanine, was discovered nearby. In 1953 Petroleum Development (Qatar) Ltd was renamed the Qatar Petroleum Co, and by 1960 Qatar's onshore production had reached 60,360,000 barrels, compared with 800,000 barrels in 1949. Qatar was admitted to membership of the Organization of the Petroleum Exporting Countries (OPEC) in 1961. In 1969 Qatar and Abu Dhabi agreed to a joint production scheme for the al-Bunduq field which straddles the border between Qatar and the UAE.

Following Qatar's attainment of full independence in 1971, the petroleum industry was reorganized, and in 1972 the Qatar National Petroleum Co was created to supervise the country's oil operations. In 1974 the Qatar General Petroleum Corpn (QGPC) was established, and new participation agreements were signed with the foreign oil companies operating in the country, to give the Government a 60% share in profits. In December 1974 the Government announced its intention to purchase the remaining 40% share in the ownership of QGPC and the Shell Co of Qatar. After lengthy negotiations, the state took over the assets and rights of QGPC in September 1976, and acquired those of the Shell Co of Qatar in February 1977.

Qatar's oil production varied considerably during the 1970s and the early 1980s, falling from 570,300 barrels per day (b/d) in 1973 to 437,600 b/d in 1975. By 1979 production had risen to 508,100 b/d, but it subsequently declined rapidly, and in 1982 output averaged only 332,000 b/d. However, even this reduced level of production was higher than Qatar's recommended OPEC quota of 300,000 b/d. In October 1984 a meeting of OPEC members reduced the production quota for the country to 280,000 b/d. In spite of falling prices, OPEC effectively abandoned the October 1984 production 'ceiling' in December 1985, when it was decided to seek a larger share of the world market. Qatar's production rose in order to offset a fall in revenue, caused by the decline in petroleum prices, which fell below $10 per barrel in July 1986. In August OPEC decided to reduce its collective production in an attempt to stabilize prices, and a return to the production quotas which had been allocated in October 1984 was approved for two months beginning in September, permitting Qatar to produce at an average rate of 280,000 b/d. Oil prices rose in response to production restraint and, at a meeting held in October, OPEC's output 'ceiling' was raised, with Qatar's production quota increased to 300,000 b/d for November and December. The extent of its current budget deficit led to demands for Qatar's quota to be increased from the level of 285,000 b/d, which it was allocated by OPEC in December 1986, as part of a programme to support a fixed price for the organization's oil of $18 per barrel in the first half of 1987. Qatar's quota was duly increased to 299,000 b/d for the second half of 1987, and the 'ceiling' on OPEC production was raised by an overall 5%, reflecting the success of the organization's production programme in stabilizing prices. By July 1990 Qatar's OPEC quota had been raised to 371,000 b/d. However, Iraq's invasion of Kuwait in August led to the suspension of quotas in order to allow OPEC member states to compensate for the loss of Iraqi and Kuwaiti production. Between August 1990 and February 1991 Qatari production averaged 420,000 b/d. After the liberation of Kuwait, Qatar's production quota was set by OPEC at 399,000 b/d and by the fourth quarter of 1993 Qatar's OPEC production quota was 378,000 b/d. Total oil production (including natural gas liquids) averaged 450,000 b/d in 1994, 460,000 b/d in 1995 and 570,000 b/d in 1996, rising sharply to a record level of 695,000 b/d in 1997 and 700,000 b/d in the first quarter of 1998. Output continued to be well above Qatar's official OPEC quota, which was set at 414,000 b/d in November 1997 and reduced to 384,000 b/d under the March 1998 Riyadh agreement, but Qatar attracted little criticism because of its relatively small share in overall OPEC production. In notional observance of the OPEC cuts, Qatar reduced its production by 30,000 b/d from 1 April and by a further 20,000 b/d from 1 July (in accordance with the Amsterdam accord of early June). Nevertheless, the Government continued to plan for an increase in oil output to 854,000 b/d by the end of 1999 and thus for a doubling of production from its 1993 level. The value of Qatar's oil exports rose from $3,100m. in 1996 to $3,500m. in 1997, but was expected to decrease to $3,000m. in 1998. Qatar's proven crude oil reserves at 1 January 1998 totalled 3,700m. barrels (sufficent for 15 years' production at 1997 levels), while probable reserves were estimated at some 5,400m. barrels.

Among the concessions that Qatar granted for petroleum exploitation in the 1980s was Amoco's 25-year production-sharing agreement for an 8,000-sq km area covering most of the country, except the Dukhan field and part of the north-east, which was concluded at the beginning of 1986. A six-year offshore exploration permit for 2,800 sq km was granted to Elf Aquitaine in 1988. An offshore concession agreement with the group of companies headed by Wintershall was terminated in June 1985, with the discovery of substantial quantities of gas in the area, but the consortium won a partial award against Qatar at the International Arbitration Tribunal at The Hague, after which a production-sharing agreement was concluded. The consortium announced plans in early 1994 for the development of facilities to produce gas and condensate for export before the end of the century. In 1995 it opened negotiations with the Dubai Government on a proposal to export gas via pipeline to Jebel Ali in Dubai. In late 1994 Wintershall had reduced its interest in the consortium from 50% to 15% and had relinquished the role of operating company. The revised participation was Atlantic Richfield (operator) 27.5%, Gulfstream Resources 27.5%, British Gas 25%, Wintershall 15% and Preussag 5%. This consortium brought the Ar-Rayyan field into production in November 1996 at an initial rate of 32,000 b/d. Under a July 1997 agreement with QGPC, the consortium was granted the right to develop up to 23m. cu m (800m. cu ft) per day of gas production from a defined sector of the North Field for export (via pipeline) after separation of liquids for separate marketing.

In September 1994 Occidental Petroleum secured a five-year contract, worth an estimated $1.9m. per year, to supply technical and support services to QGPC in onshore and offshore fields. At the same time Occidental concluded a 25-year production-sharing agreement for the Idd ash-Shargi offshore field, whereby the US company would invest an estimated $700m. to raise output from around 20,000 b/d to over 90,000 b/d and would have an entitlement to 19% of the field's output. Production from this field averaged 75,000 b/d in early 1996, and was expected to reach 110,000 b/d by 2000. Under QGPC's timetable for making available new exploration blocks to foreign oil companies, agreements were in force in respect of 90% of Qatar's territorial area by mid-1995. A subsidiary of the US company Pennzoil signed a four-year offshore exploration agreement on production-sharing terms in July 1994, this being Qatar's first new exploration agreement for two years. Maersk Oil began oil production in an offshore concession area in late 1994. It was hoped to increase output at Maersk's Ash-Shaheen field from 30,000 b/d to 150,000 b/d by the end of 1998, upon completion of new production facilities. An agreement on the development of another offshore oilfield (Al-Khalij) was concluded in July 1995 between QGPC and the concession holders, Elf Aquitaine (55% and operator) and Agip International (45%). Production from this field, which had estimated reserves of 70m. barrels, began in 1997 at an initial rate of 30,000 b/d. In April 1996 QGPC signed an exploration and production-sharing agreement with Chevron Overseas Petroleum (the operator and majority partner in a 60%–40% venture with the Hungarian Oil and Gas Co) pertaining to a 7,500-sq km offshore concession area. Output from the onshore Durkhan field was expected to rise from 280,000 b/d in mid-1997 to 335,000 b/d in 1999, as the result of a programme to enhance recovery methods and to install new facilities.

Qatar's first major refinery, at Umm Said, was commissioned in 1974 for the National Oil Distribution Co (NODCO), which had been founded in 1968 to manage the refining and distribution of oil products. Umm Said refinery had an initial capacity of 6,200 b/d, compared with an earlier refinery, built in 1953, which had a capacity of only 600 b/d. Expansion at Umm Said increased total capacity to 12,000 b/d in 1977. A second refinery, with a capacity of 50,000 b/d, was built by a French company, Technip, and commenced operations in 1984. It is situated close to the original Umm Said refinery and is linked to it. The new

refinery was structured to allow for further expansion, to meet the expected increase in local consumption without any need for major modifications or additional equipment. In 1988 two new pipelines were constructed to carry light and heavy products from Umm Said to QGPC's export terminal. In April 1990 the two refineries at Umm Said were processing 62,000 b/d of crude petroleum and exporting 50,000 b/d of oil products. Modifications were being planned that would make it possible to include a proportion of North Field gas condensates in the refineries' mix of feedstocks. In 1995 QGPC was examining the feasibility of building a new refinery at Ras Laffan to process up to 120,000 b/d of condensate which would become available if North Field gas development proceeded according to current plans. About 27,000 b/d of condensate-processing capacity was planned at Umm Said as part of a refinery expansion project which would increase total refinery throughput at Umm Said to 80,000 b/d. In June 1998 Lurgi of Germany and LG of the Republic of Korea signed a US $686m.-contract to carry out further expansion of the Umm Said refinery over a three-year period, intended to increase overall capacity to 137,000 bld.

Qatar's proven reserves of natural gas at the start of 1998 were estimated to total 10,600,000m. cu m, representing almost 5% of total world reserves at that date. The major part of Qatari reserves are in the offshore North Field (the world's largest single deposit of non-associated gas), which was discovered in the 1970s and subsequently assumed a central position in the Government's development plans. Prior to the inauguration of the North Field in 1991, Qatar's gas output was drawn from a relatively small onshore deposit of non-associated gas (used mainly for power generation) and from the onshore and offshore oilfields, whose output of associated gas is processed at two plants at Umm Said. Annual gas output averaged less than 10,000m. cu m during the 1980s, when low output of associated gas at periods of weak oil demand prevented some gas-dependent industries from achieving optimum production levels.

The first phase of Qatar's North Field Development Project (NFDP) is designed to produce a constant 22.6m. cu m per day of gas for domestic use, together with 1.65m. tons per year of liquefied petroleum gas and condensate for export. Having been completed at a cost close to the budgeted $1,300m., the first-phase facilities went into production in September 1991.

The second phase of the NFDP involves the construction of an integrated liquefied natural gas (LNG) complex and associated export facilities at Ras Laffan, at an estimated total cost of as much as $5,000m. The liquefaction plant will have an annual capacity of up to 6m. tons of LNG, of which 4m. tons are to be shipped to Japan under a 25-year agreement with Chubu Electric Power Co. Contracts for most of the 'downstream' construction work were signed in July 1993, when the shareholders in the Qatargas company which would operate the LNG plant were QGPC (65%), Mobil (10%), Total (10%), Marubeni Corpn (7.5%) and Mitsui & Co (7.5%). Construction work on the liquefaction plant began in April 1994. A $2,000m. 'downstream' financing package (funded by four Japanese and two European financial institutions) became available for disbursement in October 1995. A $570m. 'upstream' financing package was syndicated in September 1996. Qatargas made its first condensate exports in September 1996 and dispatched its first LNG shipment to Japan in December 1996.

In a separate venture, QGPC (70%) and Mobil (30%) agreed in December 1992 to establish a new company, subsequently incorporated as the Ras Laffan Liquefied Natural Gas Co (RASGAS), with a view to developing another LNG export facility by the end of the decade, at a cost of up to $7,500m. Output of about 10m. tons per year was envisaged, and the most likely export markets were seen as Japan, the Republic of (South) Korea and Taiwan. In August 1995 RASGAS was close to signing a sales and purchase agreement with the Korea Gas Corpn for the supply of 2.4m. tons of LNG per year from August 1999 (with an option for a further 1.6m. tons per year), which would effectively guarantee implementation of the project. Discussions with other potential customers had so far yielded letters of intent in respect of at least 6.6m. tons per year (from companies in Taiwan, Turkey and China) and memoranda of understanding in respect of up to 4.5m. tons per year (from Thailand and India). Having signed the Korea Gas agreement, RASGAS awarded construction contracts worth an estimated

$1,390m. in April 1996. In June 1997 Korea Gas Corpn signed an agreement to double its LNG purchases from RASGAS to 4.8m. tons per year by 2001. RASGAS subsequently scaled up its construction programme to add the required production capacity. Details of a project to export dry gas directly to Pakistan by pipeline were being finalized in 1994 by a consortium whose main sponsors were Crescent Petroleum (based in Sharjah, UAE), Brown & Root (the US company which would handle the construction work) and TransCanada PipeLines. The consortium proposed to raise $3,200m. of private funding to finance the building of a 1,600-km pipeline with a capacity of 1,600 cu ft per day. The proposed pipeline route would cross about 100 km of land in the far north-east of the UAE (where a compressor station would be sited) but would otherwise run offshore. In May 1995 Pakistan and Qatar established a joint committee to examine the technical and economic feasibility of the project. In late 1996 the French company Total joined the consortium (now named the Gulf-South Asia Gas Corpn) to take responsibility for 'upstream' development work. Qatar's exports of natural gas rose to 13,500m. cu m in 1996 (double the 1990 figure), so that gas exploitation was on course to join oil as a major source of income by the early 21st century. Budgetary constraints arising from the sharp downturn in oil prices from late 1997 resulted in delays in the provision of state investment for a range of current gas projects; but development was largely unaffected because the bulk of new funds came from external sources, including a number of 'blue chip' international hydrocarbons companies for whom Qatar remained a favoured investment destination.

INDUSTRY

Qatar's hydrocarbon-based industrialization strategy has centred on the development of 'downstream' processing facilities for oil and gas feedstocks, coupled with some diversification into heavy industry, using local gas as a low-cost fuel source. Three core schemes were initiated at Umm Said in the late 1970s and early 1980s. These are the Qatar Fertilizer Co (QAFCO), the Qatar Petrochemicals Co (QAPCO) and the Qatar Steel Co (QASCO).

The first of these projects was QAFCO, which was established in 1969 and which, since 1975, has been owned jointly by QGPC (75%) and Norsk Hydro of Norway (25%). Production of fertilizers began in 1973, with gas feedstocks being supplied from the Dukhan field. Work on a second plant, QAFCO II, began in 1976 and was completed in 1979. QAFCO made substantial profits in the first half of the 1980s, experienced a downturn in 1986 and 1987, as a result of difficult conditions in the world market, and made a steady recovery in succeeding years, after taking action to improve productivity. In 1990 production totalled 708,000 tons of ammonia and 761,000 tons of urea. Major export markets included India and China. In 1992 QAFCO's profits reached a record QR 172m. Plans are proceeding to increase QAFCO's production capacity by using gas from the North Field. A third QAFCO plant with a capacity of 1,500 tons per day of ammonia and 2,000 tons per day of urea came into production in March 1997. In 1995 QAFCO produced 885,966 tons of urea (a 3.3% increase over 1994) and 794,074 tons of ammonia (a 1.2% increase over 1994). In excellent market conditions, the company made a net profit of QR 289.6m. in 1994 on total sales worth QR 583.8m., representing year-on-year increases of 124% in profits and 39% in turnover. About four-fifths of QAFCO's ammonia output and two-fifths of its urea output were exported to India in 1994. QAFCO was in 1995 examining proposals for a future diversification into melamine production.

The petrochemical facilities of QAPCO were commissioned at Umm Said during 1980 and 1981. The company was established in 1974. The plant had an initial design capacity of 280,000 tons of ethylene per year, but in its first year of production it produced only 132,679 tons. The plant also produces low-density polyethylene and sulphur. Sales, particularly of ethylene, were substantially below production, and in 1983 plans were cancelled for a high-density polyethylene plant at the complex. In 1984, despite increases in production to 204,000 tons of ethylene, 150,000 tons of low-density polyethylene and 33,000 tons of sulphur, QAPCO operated at a loss of QR 69m. ($19m.). The company suffered from a shortage of ethane-rich gas, and there-

fore construction of an ethane recovery plant was completed in 1985. Nevertheless, QAPCO made a record loss of QR 156m. in 1985, as a result of the world-wide decline in prices of polyethylene, and a reduction in output of one-third. In early 1986 QAPCO's financial difficulties forced it to renegotiate a $100m. Euroloan which was signed in 1984. However, despite a loss of QR 57m. in 1986, QAPCO recorded a profit of QR 85m. in 1987. In 1988 production of ethylene declined by 2.3%, compared with the previous year, to 256,550 tons, sulphur production fell by 23%, to 36,900 tons, and production of linear low-density polyethylene (LLDPE) fell by 1.8%, to 170,700 tons. In early 1989 the rehabilitation of the value-control system at the ethylene plant was completed. QAPCO's performance in 1989 was much improved, with profits estimated at a record QR 420m., and production of ethylene increasing to 295,000 tons, LLDPE to 181,000 tons and sulphur to 52,000 tons. In September 1990 the French company Elf Atochem, and in June 1991 the Italian company Enichem, each acquired a 10% interest in QAPCO. QGPC holds the remaining 80%. Another initiative in the field of petrochemicals was taken in 1991, when the QGPC and a Canadian company, International Octane, established the Qatar Fuel Additives Co (QAFAC), which was to build a plant to produce methyl tertiary butyl ether (MTBE) and methanol. Following several restructurings, in June 1996 shareholdings in QAFAC were distributed as follows: QGPC 50%, International Octane 15%, Lee Chang Yung Chemical Industrial Corpn 15% and China Petroleum Corpn 20% (the two last-named being Taiwanese companies). Construction work began in 1997 on a plant with an annual capacity of 830,000 tons of methanol and 610,000 tons of MTBE. The work was expected to take 26 months at an estimated cost of $425m. In June 1992 QAPCO announced a programme of expansion, involving estimated expenditure of $385m., under which ethylene capacity at Umm Said was scheduled to reach 450,000 tons in October 1995 and 525,000 tons in April 1996, while polyethylene capacity would be nearly doubled, to 365,000 tons per year, in April 1996. In 1994 QAPCO produced a record 357,000 tons of ethylene and 186,000 tons of polyethylene (representing year-on-year increases of 1.5% and 2.5% respectively) and achieved a 44% increase in profits to QR 260m. In 1995 QAPCO's net profits reached QR 325m. In May 1996 QGPC signed a preliminary agreement with a group of European companies with existing interests in Qatar (Norsk Hydro, Elf Atochem and Enichem) for a project to produce an annual 338,000 tons of ethylene dichloride, 200,000 tons of vinyl chloride monomer and 260,000 tons of caustic soda, using ethylene feedstock supplied by QAPCO. Participation in the new venture, to be called Qatar Vinyl Co, was finalized in January 1997. The project, estimated to cost $500m., was scheduled for completion in 2000. In May 1997 QGPC signed an outline agreement with Phillips Petroleum to develop a plant at Umm Said which would include a 500,000 tons-per-year ethylene cracker, 467,000 tons-per-year of polyethylene capacity and 50,000 tons-per-year of hexene-I capacity. Feedstock would be supplied from a natural gas liquids plant at Umm Said. The target date for completion of the project, costing an estimated $750m., was the end of 2000.

The Qatar Steel Co (QASCO) began commercial production in 1978, and processes imported iron ore and local scrap for export, mainly to Saudi Arabia, Kuwait and the UAE. The government is now the sole owner of QASCO, having acquired the holdings of the original Japanese partners (a total of 30%) in May 1997. Production levels have risen continuously, from 378,544 tons of steel bars in 1979 to 475,000 tons in 1984. In 1985, however, there was a growing stockpile, due to falling demand and lower world prices, and profits were smaller than anticipated. In an attempt to solve this problem, QASCO reduced its prices in 1985 and placed a 20% import duty on steel from non-GCC countries. In 1985 production reached 510,000 tons, exceeding consumption by 55%. QASCO made a loss of $13.7m. for the year, bringing the plant's accumulated loss since 1978 to about $109m. Following a decline in the level of production of steel bars to 493,000 tons in 1986, QASCO's production rose to 500,000 tons in 1987, and to 533,000 tons (53% above installed capacity) in 1988. The plant made a profit for the first time in 1988, despite a 12.14% increase in prices of raw materials. Production reached more than 550,000 tons in 1989, and a record 565,000 tons in 1990. QASCO assumed the management of the Umm Said steel mill in early 1989, although Japan's Kobe Steel Co, the former managers, maintained a consultancy at the plant. In June 1992 QASCO decided to commission a feasibility study with the aim of increasing capacity at the Umm Said plant by 140,000 tons per year, as the first stage of a plan to raise Qatari steel production to 1m. tons per year. QASCO's output in 1991 was 561,000 tons, yielding a profit of QR 127m. In 1992 production totalled 588,000 tons, yielding a profit of QR 155m., and in 1993 output reached 608,626 tons. A contract was awarded in early 1995 for the supply and installation of a 140,000-tons-per-year rolling mill to raise reinforced steel bar capacity to 470,000 tons per year. A contract was signed in May 1996 for the installation, over a period of 18 months, of an electric arc furnace with an annual output capacity of 500,000 tons of molten steel. In 1995 QASCO produced 601,000 tons of concrete-reinforcing bars and recorded a net profit of QR 210m. In February 1997 QASCO set up a new company called Qabico (Qatar Hot Briquetted Iron Company) to build a 2m. tons-per-year hot briquetted iron plant at Umm Said at an estimated cost of $408m. Qabico was owned 31% by QASCO, 10% by Qimco (see below) and 10% by the Qatar Shipping Co, with the remaining shares divided equally between Kuwait's Gulf Investment Corpn, Kuwait's National Industries Co and Duferco (a holding company based in the Channel Islands). A further seven major development projects, involving total investment of more than $1,000m., were included in QASCO's development plans for the period to 2005.

In addition to these major industrial schemes, many small enterprises have been established, mainly at Umm Said, now the industrial centre of the country. In 1973 the Industrial Development Technical Centre (IDTC) was founded to co-ordinate the development of non-oil related industry, and by 1983 it had reported the establishment of 72 industrial ventures. The Qatar Flour Mills Co began production at Umm Bab in 1969, and by 1985 output had reached a level of about 1,700 tons per day. Cement production began in Qatar at a rate of 330,000 tons per year, and was aimed solely at the domestic market. By the mid-1980s cheap imports, particularly from the UAE, had forced the Qatar National Cement Manufacturing Co (QNCMC) to reduce its prices by as much as 30%, but in 1984 production rose by 26%, to 313,000 tons, and profits for the year were QR 13.8m. In 1985 production increased further, to 319,740 tons, which was 1% above the capacity for which the plant was designed. In 1992 output of cement totalled 354,133 tons, output of clinker totalled 313,287 tons, and net profits were QR 25.8m. In 1994 net profits were QR 40m., an increase of 27% over 1993. Work began in 1995 on a new 2,000-tons-per-day cement plant at Umm Bab, designed to increase Qatar's total cement capacity to 3,200 tons per day by mid-1997. The new capacity would eliminate Qatar's net import requirement for cement (of up to 700 tons per day in 1995), placing it instead in a position to become a net exporter. Other industries in the country include a ready-mix concrete factory, a plastics factory, a paint factory, a detergents company and several light industrial ventures.

Much of Qatar's initial industrial development depended on the operation of a power and desalination complex at Ras Abu Aboud, which can produce 11.5m. gallons of water per day and 210 MW of power. In 1983 a new power and desalination complex came into production at Ras Abu Fontas. Domestic demand for water in Qatar is among the highest per head in the world, and the Government has initiated several schemes to upgrade the water network. Qatar had an installed electricity generating capacity of 1,284 MW, and water desalination capacity of 68m. gallons per day, in mid-1993. The joint-stock Qatar Electricity and Water Co (QEWC) was founded in 1990 to manage the generating installations and associated facilities, leaving distribution under the control of the Ministry of Electricity and Water.

The joint-stock Qatar Industrial Manufacturing Co (QIMCO), established in 1990 to promote industrial joint ventures, made a net profit of QR 7m. in 1992, when it held investments of QR 64.5m. in eight industrial projects. By the end of 1994 QIMCO held investments totalling QR 90.6m. in 10 projects (seven of them in the local market). There was a 29% increase in net profits (to QR 16.7m.) and a 4.6% increase in shareholders' equity (to QR 138.1m.) in 1994. In 1995 QIMCO recorded a net profit of QR 23m. Its investments totalled QR 102m., while its

operating companies' aggregate sales revenue exceeded QR 200m. In 1996, QIMCO's net profit was QR 21.5m. In June 1993, in an attempt to attract foreign investment for industrial projects, the Government approved legislation to reduce the maximum rate of taxation on profits earned by foreign partners in joint ventures from 50% to 35%. In June 1997 the Government announced plans to establish a purpose-built light industrial zone to the west of Doha and to introduce a new investment law incorporating incentive schemes for companies setting up plants in designated industrial zones. The new investment law would also allow non-Qatari entities to take majority shareholdings in joint-venture projects (which were currently required to be at least 51% Qatari-owned).

AGRICULTURE AND FISHING

Qatar's agricultural activity increased steadily during the 1970s, with the number of producing farms rising from 338 in 1975 to 406 in 1979. However, during the same period the number of non-producing farms also rose, owing to increased problems of water supply and water salinity. Agriculture (including fishing) provided 1.0% of Qatar's GDP in 1996. All agricultural land in the country is owned by the Government, and most farm owners participate only indirectly in the farming process, having permanent positions in other sectors of the economy. Consequently, most farms in Qatar are administered by immigrant managers employing Omani, Palestinian, Iranian and Egyptian labour. Vegetable production has been the most successful sector of the agrarian economy, and Qatar is now thought to be self-sufficient in winter vegetables, and nearly self-sufficient in summer vegetables, with some being exported to other Gulf countries. In 1985 date and other fruit trees accounted for 38% of cultivable land, vegetables for 37%, green fodder for 13% and cereals for 12%. In 1986 the value of agricultural production reached QR 318.1m. ($87.4m.), of which QR 87.3m. ($24m.) was accounted for by farm production; and cereal imports declined from 105,449 tons in 1985 to 95,936 tons in 1986, when 6% of Qatar's cereal requirements were met by local production. The Arab Investment and Agricultural Development Organization (AIADO) established the Arab-Qatari Company for Vegetable Production (AQCVP) in 1989. A dairy farm, completed in 1984, can satisfy about 60% of the local demand for dairy products. Egg production averaged about 1m. per year in 1985, which was sufficient to meet 80% of local demand. In 1988 the Arab-Qatari Dairy Co, in a joint venture with the Arab Company for Livestock Development, initiated a scheme to produce green fodder on 637 ha. In 1985 a study by the Arab Organization for the Development of Agriculture pointed out that the main problems facing the farming sector were lack of irrigation, soil infertility, harsh weather conditions, lack of pasture land and the unwillingness of Qataris to invest in agriculture. At the end of 1986, the Government announced a three-year programme to drill 77 wells, to a depth of 70 m, in order to increase the water resources available for agricultural purposes. At the end of 1991 Qatar and Iran announced plans for a $13,000m. pipeline to carry drinking water to Qatar from Iran's Karum river. In April 1992 the AQCVP signed a $5m. contract with Dace of the Netherlands for the supply of greenhouses, sufficient to treble the company's covered growing area.

In May 1992 the Government announced the provision of interest-free loans of up to QR 500,000 to farmers and fishermen, to encourage production by promoting modernization. The loans, repayable over 10 years, were to be administered by a special committee, established by the Ministry of Agriculture and Municipal Affairs. In 1994 Qatar's imports of food and live animals were valued at QR 927.7m., representing about 13% of total import spending. In 1995 Qatar produced 5,000 tons of cereals, 40,000 tons of vegetables and melons and 13,000 tons of fruit and dates, as well as 13,000 tons of milk, 4,000 tons of poultry meat, 3,000 tons of eggs, and 14,000 tons of mutton and lamb. In 1996 5,000 tons of cereals were produced, as well as 42,000 tons of vegetables and melons and 14,000 tons of fruit and dates. In that year Qatar produced 13,000 tons of milk, 4,000 tons of poultry, 3,000 tons of eggs and 14,000 tons of mutton and lamb.

Most of the country's fishing is undertaken by the Qatar National Fishing Co (QNFC), which was formed in 1966 and was nationalized in 1980. By 1985 the company had a refrigeration and processing plant near Doha, capable of handling 7 tons of shrimps per day. From the mid-1970s until 1980 the annual catch was estimated at about 2,000 tons. The total rose to 2,604 tons in 1981, but fell to 2,114 tons in 1983. In 1984 the QNFC achieved net profits of QR 1.9m., representing an increase of 24% compared with 1983's profits, and its total catch constituted 17% of local consumption. The catch in 1987 totalled 2,678 tons, increasing by 13.2% in 1988, to 3,086 tons. By 1994 the total catch had reached 5,086 tons, declining in 1995 to 4,271 tons.

BUDGET AND FINANCE

Since 1979 the Qatari riyal has been officially pegged to the IMF special drawing right (SDR) at a rate of QR 4.7619 = SDR 1 within a permitted fluctuation margin of plus or minus 7.25%. Since 1986, however, the riyal has in reality been linked to the US dollar at a rate of QR 3.64 = $1.

The increases in petroleum revenue which occurred in the 1970s resulted in large budget surpluses, which enabled Qatar to embark on its impressive programme of industrial and infrastructural projects. However, after achieving a budget surplus of QR 7,993m. in 1980, the country recorded a deficit of QR 566m. in 1983. This was largely due to the fall in petroleum exports, and, in order to alleviate the problem, government current expenditure was reduced from QR 10,980m. in 1982 to QR 8,496m. in 1983. As a result of these cutbacks, less foreign investment was attracted to the country, and liquidity levels consequently suffered. In 1984/85, in an attempt to solve this problem, the government increased expenditure to QR 12,173m. As a result of the collapse of petroleum prices, no budget was announced for 1986/87, but it was understood that ministries were asked not to exceed the previous year's budget. In early 1986 the Government deferred $80m. worth of contracts. The 1987/88 budget envisaged total expenditure of QR 12,217m., 22% less than in the 1985/86 budget, and revenue of QR 6,745m., 30% less than in the previous budget. A deficit of QR 5,472m. was predicted, to be financed from foreign reserves and assets. The budget proposals contained no provisions for any substantial investment in the areas of gas, power or desalination, but placed more emphasis on social services, in an attempt to stimulate the depressed contracting sector. Expenditure on defence, however, continued to increase, and in 1986 France agreed to supply Qatar with four *Mirage* F-1 fighter aircraft, missiles and a radar system, at a cost of $243m. Nevertheless, the actual deficit for 1987, according to the Qatar Monetary Agency (QMA), was 34% below the predicted figure. The 1988/89 budget forecast total expenditure of QR 12,442.5m., revenue of QR 6,335.8m. and a budget deficit of QR 6,106.7m., the highest level yet projected. From 1989 Qatar's financial year began on 1 April.

The 1993/94 budget envisaged expenditure of QR 13,076.5m., of which QR 2,708.2m. was to be capital spending, and revenue of QR 10,373.2m., resulting in a deficit of QR 2,703.3m. The 1994/95 budget made provision for a 20% fall in revenue to QR 8,359m. (mainly because of low oil prices). Total expenditure was set to fall by 10% to QR 11,830m. (including a capital budget of QR 2,320m.), while the budget deficit was projected to rise by 28% to QR 3,471m. Cutbacks in expenditure were to include a halt to property loans for citizens, an accelerated shift from expatriate to local labour, and closures of some overseas information offices. The capital spending allocations for 1994/95 were public services and infrastructure projects QR 1,031m. (including QR 151m. for roads, QR 174m. for sewerage and QR 135m. for land purchases); economic services and industrial projects (including water and power supplies and airport expansion) QR 1,022m.; and health, social services, education and youth welfare QR 267m. The official budget out-turn for 1994/95 showed substantially higher revenue receipts of QR 10,210m. and total expenditure of QR 12,780m., producing a lower-than-anticipated deficit of QR 2,570m. The 1995/96 budget provided for a 10.1% rise in revenue to QR 9,204m. (assuming an average crude oil price of $15 per barrel) and a 7.7% rise in total expenditure to QR 12,735m. (including slightly lower capital spending of QR 2,224m.). Capital spending allocations for 1995/96 were public works and infrastructure QR 931m. (including QR 198m. for roads, QR 251m. for sewerage and QR 120m. for land purchases); economic services QR 928m.; and health, social services, education and youth welfare QR 365m. The budget out-turn for that year showed an 18.2% increase in revenues

(mainly owing to higher oil prices), which totalled QR 12,068m., compared with expenditure of QR 13,138m., resulting in a deficit of QR 1,070m.

The 1996/97 budget provided for total expenditure of QR 13,750m. (QR 11,530m. on current account and QR 2,220m. on capital account) and total revenue of QR 10,800m., resulting in a projected deficit of QR 2,950m. A QR 500m. package of increases in public-sector pay and allowances was announced in late June 1996. The provisional 1996/97 out-turn, published by the Central Bank, showed higher revenues of QR 11,159m. and expenditure of QR 13,970m., producing a deficit of QR 2,811m.

The 1997/98 budget forecast provided for total expenditure of QR 16,387m. (including a 20% increase in spending on capital projects) and revenues of QR 13,397m., producing an anticipated deficit QR 2,990m. In mid-1998 analysts suggested that the loss of budgeted revenue caused by the sharp downturn in oil prices from late 1997 would result in a significantly higher deficit than planned. The 1998/99 budget, tabled in April, took account of the continuing slump in oil prices, providing for a 4.4% cut in overall expenditure (including a 35% reduction in capital spending) to QR 15,660m., a 7.7% reduction in revenues to QR 12,350m. and a resultant deficit of QR 3,310m. (10% higher than the previous year's budgeted figure). The rise in the anticipated deficit in 1998/99 seemed likely to prevent the Government from meeting its target of a balanced budget by 2000; achievement of this goal now seems dependent on revenues from large new gas and petrochemicals projects, planned for the early 21st century.

The inauguration of the Qatar Bank for Industrial Development (QBID) in November 1997 brought the number of banks operating in Qatar to 15 (excluding the Central Bank), including eight foreign banks. Structured as a joint venture between the Qatar Government and local private-sector interests (mainly banks and insurance companies), the QBID will provide soft loans to fund the fixed capital requirements of small- and medium-sized industrial ventures. In October 1993 the QMA was superseded by the Qatar Central Bank, with paid-up capital of QR 50m. and overall capital and reserves totalling QR 156m. The Central Bank's end-1993 assets totalled QR 2,875.1m. (including QR 2,599.2m. of foreign assets), while the principal liabilities on its end-1993 balance sheet were currency issued to the value of QR 1,517.7m. and local banks' deposits totalling QR 662.9m. The Central Bank has supervisory powers over all banks, foreign exchange houses, investment companies and finance houses operating in Qatar. In August 1997 the Central Bank was empowered to license Qatar-based banks and finance companies to establish 'offshore' banking units (OBUs), with effect from October 1997. Bahrain had previously been the only GCC member state with an 'offshore' banking sector.

Until April 1997 trading in local companies' shares was conducted through an unofficial stock exchange which had a turnover of some $89.3m. in 1996. In May 1997 an official Doha Securities Market (DSM), supervised by the Ministry of Finance, Economy and Trade, began trading in the shares of 17 companies and banks, the number rising to 18 by February 1998, when their market capitalization totalled QR 9,902m. ($2,720m.) and weekly turnover was averaging QR 8.4m. ($2.3m.). The DSM is currently restricted to Qatari nationals, but there are plans to launch a mutual fund offering non-Qataris indirect access, and direct access by non-Qatari GCC nationals was expected to be permitted within a few years, followed eventually by universal access. In May 1998 the Qatar Arabian Investment Company (QAIC) was launched with plans for its shares to be listed on the DSM—the first listing of a dollar-denominated stock and the first open to non-Qatari investment. The market's start-up costs were funded by the Government, which planned to organize a series of share offers as part of a future privatization programme. Currently conducting business by floor trading, the DSM is to be relocated in 2000 to a purpose-built exchange with a fully computerized trading system.

In 1997 the Government continued its practice of contracting syndicated overseas loans for general funding purposes, taking out loans of $300m. and $200m. from consortia of international banks in the latter months of the year. A new public debt law approved in March 1998 was intended to facilitate the issue of treasury bills and bonds to finance the Government's budget deficit, the Central Bank Governor stating that the new law would also enable the bank to influence money supply and interest rates by market intervention. Under a Central Bank directive which came into force on 1 April, the maximum 6.5% interest rate on riyal deposits was abolished and banks were permitted to set their own interest rates on deposits of over 15 months' duration. Recommended by the IMF as part of desirable financial sector reform, the changes were intended to attract more local capital into the domestic banking system and to encourage depositors to hold funds on a longer-term basis.

In May 1998 the Commercial Bank of Qatar (CBQ) became the first local bank to secure a syndicated credit facility, signing an agreement with a group of regional and international banks under which it would borrow $60m. for the financing of forthcoming industrial projects. At the end of June, however, the Qatari authorities postponed the Government's first Eurobond issue, expected to be for at least $500m. and possibly double that amount, because of unfavourable conditions in emerging debt markets.

In addition to investment in industrial diversification at home, Qatar also allocated considerable sums of aid to poorer countries during the 1970s. In 1975 the level of aid was $339m., but in 1980 the total declined to $277m., representing 4.2% of GNP. In October 1990 the Government announced that the debts owing to it by 10 Arab and African countries (Cameroon, Egypt, Guinea, Mali, Mauritania, Morocco, Somalia, Syria, Tunisia and Uganda) were to be cancelled. The World Bank estimated that Qatar extended net aid of around $1m. (0.01% of GNP) in 1991 and that its cumulative net aid over the five years 1987–91 amounted to just $4m.

In December 1995 IMF statistics for Qatar indicated total official reserves of $694m. and total foreign assets of $787m. However, it was confirmed by the Government in the following month that a substantial tranche of Qatar's reserves had remained under the control of the former Amir, Sheikh Khalifa, following his removal from office in June 1995. The sum involved was widely reported to be in the region of $3,000m. A settlement agreement was signed in February 1997 whereby Sheikh Khalifa was understood to have formally ceded control over disputed assets.

TRADE, TRANSPORT AND COMMUNICATIONS

A primary objective in development has been to diversify Qatar's economic base away from dependence on petroleum. However, despite an overall downward trend in world oil prices since 1986, oil revenues have continued to dominate the country's export earnings.

During the 1970s imports and exports grew quickly, but in the early 1980s there was a fall in Qatar's levels of trade. Imports were reduced over the period 1982–84, and in 1985 their value declined to QR 4,146.5m., the lowest annual total since 1976. The value of exports fell from QR 20,787m. in 1980 to QR 12,002m. in 1983, reflecting the reduction in petroleum exports. By 1989, the value of imports had risen to QR 4,827m. They continued to rise and were valued at QR 6,169m. in 1990 and to QR 6,261m. in 1991. Export earnings were QR 9,967m. in 1989 and QR 14,161m. in 1990, but fell to QR 11,684m. in 1991. In 1991 Japan provided 13.6% of Qatar's imports, the United Kingdom 11.8%, and the USA 11.6%. According to analysts, Japan's imports of Qatari crude petroleum in 1988 accounted for more than one-half of the estimated value of Qatar's total oil exports. In 1994 the principal source of imports (13.4%) was Japan; other important suppliers in that year were the USA and the United Kingdom. Preliminary figures for exports in the same year suggested that Asia (excluding Arab countries) was the principal market for exports (80.8%). The principal commodities that Qatar imports are electrical items and machinery, and there is also considerable importation of basic manufactures, food and live animals, and chemicals. Apart from its exports of petroleum, most of Qatar's export trade is with its Arab neighbours.

In 1992 Qatar's exports were valued at QR 13,980m. (68% of this from petroleum) and its imports at QR 7,336m., leaving a visible trade surplus of QR 6,644m. Net outgoings of QR 6,675m. on the services account placed the current account in deficit by QR 31m., while net capital transfers of QR 400m. raised the overall balance-of-payments deficit to QR 431m. The visible

trade surplus fell progressively, to QR 5,154m. in 1993, QR 4,729m. in 1994 and QR 1,714m. in 1995. In that year net services expenditure and private transfers increased the current account deficit to QR 6,727m., while net capital transfers of QR 4,849m. produced an overall balance-of-payments deficit of QR 1,849m. Provisional Central Bank figures for 1996 showed a significantly bigger trade surplus of QR 4,095m., from exports of QR 14,939m. (71.5% from oil) and imports of QR 10,844m., while net services expenditure and private transfers produced a current-account deficit of QR 5,287m. However, lower net capital transfers of QR 2,863m. resulted in an increased overall balance-of-payments deficit for 1996 of QR 2,424m. Japan remained Qatar's most important trading partner in 1996, taking 56.6% of its exports by value, although its share of Qatari imports was only 6.8%.

The first contracts for a major port development project at Doha were awarded in mid-1993. Extensive dredging work on the 17-km port approach channel would serve the dual purpose of upgrading the maritime access facility and providing landfill material to create 360,000 sq m of new quayside space at the port and to fill some 3.55m. sq m of reclaimed land, which was designated as the site of a new international airport. Also under development at Doha was a new container terminal with two berths and a roll-on, roll-off facility. At Ras Laffan, major new port facilities for LNG and condensate carriers and roll-on roll-off vessels were completed in 1995. The development plan for Ras Laffan proposed the linking of the port area to a 50 sq km industrial area which would be surrounded by a buffer zone. In April 1996, Ras Laffan was officially designated an industrial city. In late 1997 a US firm was selected as consultant for a $450m. roads project involving the reconstruction and upgrading of 280 km of the primary road network and the construction of 19 interchanges, including numerous bridges and underpasses. However, falling oil revenues in 1998 compelled the Government to modify its original plans and to split the construction work into several packages to be phased over a number of years.

The Qatar Shipping Co, established in 1992, was scheduled to inaugurate a passenger and car ferry service between Doha and Bahrain in late 1994, while expanding its cargo-carrying capabilities to include the transport of crude oil, liquefied petroleum gas, petrochemicals and iron ore. A QR 350m. fleet expansion programme was approved in June 1996. The Qatar Government is a co-owner of the regional airline Gulf Air. Qatar Airways was established by Qatari business interests in 1993 and introduced its inaugural services (on routes to the UAE and at fares which undercut Gulf Air) in January 1994. By July 1994 the new airline had added services to Colombo, Amman, Bombay, London, Kuwait and Cairo and expected to add Damascus and Beirut to its list of destinations. Initially, the airline was wholly dependent on leased aircraft but by mid-1995 five aircraft had been purchased and the number of destinations served increased to 21. In February 1997 Qatar Airways embarked on an extensive restructuring programme following a decision to double its capital to $50m. through the sale of new shares to local institutions and individuals. In April 1997 legislation was introduced authorizing a $19m.-government loan to Qatar Airways. A Doha airport departure tax of QR 20 per passenger, introduced in June 1996, was expected to generate revenue of QR 13m. per year. In April 1998 Qatar Airways confirmed its intention to acquire a listing on the Doha Securities Market by the end of 1999, when the 1997 state loan to the airline would be converted into stock. Results for 1997 showed that Qatar Airways had achieved a 46% increase in passenger volume, to 630,000 and a 71% increase in revenue, and the airline was expected to break even in the near future. Under a five-year $400m. expansion plan, the airline was to increase its fleet to 15 aircraft (including at least six European Airbus A320s) and to expand its services to Europe, Asia and the Middle East. In May 1998, bids were received for the construction of a new $125m. international terminal at Doha airport; the successful bidder was to be announced in early 1999.

The state-owned Qatar Public Telecommunications Corpn (Q-Tel) made a net profit of QR 307m. on a turnover of about QR 1,000m. in 1996, when it had a public network with a design capacity of 350,000 lines. The main Q-Tel network had 150,000 subscribers in 1996, while there was rapid growth in the provision of ancillary services, including mobile telephones (29,000 users in 1996), cable television (30,000 users) and a paging network (60,000 users). Q-Tel held a 10% share in the Ath-Thurraya satellite programme being developed by a consortium headed by Emirates Telecommunications Corpn.

SOCIAL SERVICES

In 1995 Qatar had four government hospitals, with a total of 1,122 beds, and there were 715 physicians working in official medical services. In 1988, according to the World Health Organization, there were 20 physicians, three dentists and 51 nurses for every 10,000 inhabitants in Qatar, the highest ratios for any Arab country. The Hamad General Hospital (opened in 1982) has 598 beds. In 1995 there were 25 health centres and four out-patient clinics. There is a hospital for women, offering 272 maternity beds. Social welfare developments within the country have been a high priority. Education has expanded, and by 1994/95 there were 169 primary schools in the country. The University of Qatar was established in 1977, and new campus buildings were completed in February 1985.

Under the 1993/94 government budget, social services and health were allocated a total of QR 552m. plus an additional QR 235m. of capital funding from outside the budget. Major health facilities under development included a children's hospital and an outpatients' clinic, while there was a house-building target of more than 3,000 new dwellings in 1993/94. The 1994/95 capital budget for health and social services totalled QR 200.3m., to include broadcasting transmission stations as well as health centres and housing projects. The 1995/96 budget of QR 280m. focused primarily on housing and health centres. A capital allocation of QR 103m. for education and youth welfare

in 1993/94 envisaged the construction of 13 schools and a new science faculty building at the University of Qatar. There was a continuing emphasis on school and university premises within the 1994/95 allocation of QR 66.7m. and the 1995/96 allocation of QR 85m.

Construction of Qatar's first privately-financed hospital (the 116-bed Al-Ahli hospital in Doha) was scheduled to begin in August 1996 and to continue for 18 months at a projected cost of QR 100m. The Government announced, in March 1996, that local private-sector funding would also be sought for other health projects, inlcuding the expansion of 14 existing facilities. Other government proposals include the introduction of compulsory health cards costing QR 50 per five-year period for Qatari nationals, QR 100 per annum for expatriate civil servants and diplomats and QR 200 per annum for other expatriates. Visitors to Qatar would be liable to pay 15% of the cost of local medical treatment.

The 1997/98 budget provided funding for government housing schemes, including the completion of 900 houses already under construction and the building of 700 additional houses. In 1998 the Government was considering several initiatives to improve access to housing for Qatari nationals entering private-sector employment, including the establishment of a new bank to provide housing loans. Consideration was also being given to the introduction of pension schemes and other social security provisions to encourage Qatari nationals to take up private-sector employment. The 1998/99 budget contained provision for spending of QR 241m. in the health and social services sector, of which QR 190m. would finance the completion of the 700 houses provided for under the previous budget as well as the construction of 700 new housing units. The 1998/99 budget also allocated QR 77.4m. to education and youth welfare.

Statistical Survey

Source (unless otherwise stated): Press and Publications Dept, Ministry of Education, POB 80, Doha; telex 4552.

AREA AND POPULATION

Area: 11,427 sq km (4,412 sq miles).

Population: 369,079 (males 247,852; females 121,227) at census of 16 March 1986; 640,846 (official estimate) at mid-1995; 520,500 (provisional) at census of 1997.

Density (1997): 45.6 per sq km.

Principal Towns (estimated population of municipalities, mid-1995): Doha (capital) 392,384; Rayyan 165,127; Al-Wakrah 33,891; Umm Salal 19,194; Al-Khor 10,618.

Births, Marriages and Deaths (1995): Registered live births 10,371 (birth rate 16.2 per 1,000); Registered marriages 1,488 (marriage rate 2.3 per 1,000); Registered deaths 1,000 (death rate 1.6 per 1,000).

1996: Registered live births 10,317; Registered deaths 1,015 (Source: UN, *Population and Vital Statistics Report*).

Expectation of Life (UN estimates, years at birth, 1990–95): 70.5 (males 68.8; females 74.2). Source: UN, *World Population Prospects: The 1994 Revision.*

Economically Active Population (persons aged 15 years and over, March 1986): Agriculture and fishing 6,283; Mining and quarrying 4,807; Manufacturing 13,914; Electricity, gas and water 5,266; Building and construction 40,523; Trade, restaurants and hotels 21,964; Transport and communications 7,357; Finance, insurance and real estate 3,157; Community, social and personal services 96,466; Activities not adequately defined 501; Total employed 200,238 (Qatari nationals 20,807; non-Qataris 179,431). Figures include 1,025 unemployed persons with previous work experience, but exclude 944 persons seeking work for the first time.

Mid-1996 (estimate): Agriculture, etc. 8,000; Total labour force 305,000 (Source: FAO, *Production Yearbook*).

AGRICULTURE, ETC.

Principal Crops (FAO estimates, '000 metric tons, 1996): Barley 5; Cabbages 2; Tomatoes 9; Cauliflowers 1; Pumpkins 8; Cucumbers 2; Aubergines (Egg-plants) 4; Onions (dry) 3; Carrots 1; Other vegetables 7; Watermelons 2; Melons 3; Dates 13; Citrus fruits 1. Source: FAO, *Production Yearbook.*

Livestock (FAO estimates, '000 head, year ending September 1996): Horses 2; Cattle 13; Camels 47; Sheep 187; Goats 168; Chickens (million) 4. Source: FAO, *Production Yearbook.*

Livestock Products (FAO estimates, '000 metric tons, 1996): Mutton and lamb 14; Goat meat 1; Poultry meat 4; Cows' milk 4; Sheep's milk 4; Goats' milk 5; Hen eggs 3; Sheepskins 2. Source: FAO, *Production Yearbook.*

Fishing (metric tons, live weight): Total catch 6,994 in 1993; 5,086 in 1994; 4,271 in 1995. Source: FAO, *Yearbook of Fishery Statistics.*

MINING

Production ('000 metric tons, unless otherwise indicated, 1995): Crude petroleum 18,706; Natural gas (petajoules) 531. Source: UN, *Industrial Commodity Statistics Yearbook.*

INDUSTRY

Production (estimates, '000 metric tons, unless otherwise indicated, 1995): Wheat flour (including bran) 42 (1994); Nitrogenous fertilizers (nitrogen content) 858 (1994); Jet fuels 399; Motor spirit (petrol) 558; Gas-diesel (Distillate fuel) oils 770; Residual fuel oils 1,010; Liquefied petroleum gas 1,327; Cement 580; Steel bars 601 (official figure); Electric energy 5,738 million kWh. Source: mainly UN, *Industrial Commodity Statistics Yearbook.*

FINANCE

Currency and Exchange Rates: 100 dirhams = 1 Qatar riyal (QR). *Sterling and Dollar Equivalents* (31 May 1998): £1 sterling = 5.936 riyals; US $1 = 3.640 riyals; 100 Qatar riyals = £16.85 = $27.47. *Exchange Rate:* Since June 1980 the rate has been fixed at US $1 = QR 3.64.

Budget (QR million, year ending 31 March): 1994/95: *Revenue* 10,210; *Expenditure* 12,780 (Current 9,926, Capital 2,854); 1995/96 (provisional): *Revenue* 12,068; *Expenditure* 13,138 (Current 10,432, Capital 2,706); 1996/97 (provisional): *Revenue* 13,970 (Current 11,247, Capital 2,723); 1997/98 (forecasts): *Revenue* 13,397; *Expenditure* 16,387 (Current 12,026, Capital 4,361). Note: Figures exclude net lending and equity participation. Source: Qatar Central Bank, *Annual Report.*

International Reserves (US $ million at 31 December 1994): Gold 41.6; IMF special drawing rights 29.0; Reserve position in IMF 44.7; Foreign exchange 584.0; Total 699.3. Source: IMF, *International Financial Statistics.*

Money Supply (QR million at 31 December 1997): Currency outside banks 1,555; Demand deposits at commercial banks 2,575; Total money 4,131. Source: IMF, *International Financial Statistics.*

Cost of Living (Consumer Price Index for Doha; base: 1988 = 100): 115.0 in 1994; 118.4 in 1995; 127.2 in 1996. Source: Qatar Central Bank, *Annual Report.*

Expenditure on the Gross Domestic Product (QR million at current prices, 1995): Government final consumption expenditure 9,010; Private final consumption expenditure 8,015; Increase in stocks 50; Gross fixed capital formation 6,850; *Total domestic expenditure* 23,925; Exports of goods and services 12,550; *Less* Imports of goods and services 9,120; *GDP in purchasers' values* 27,355. Note: Figures are provisional. The revised total (in QR million) is 29,622.

Gross Domestic Product by Economic Activity (preliminary estimates, QR million at current prices, 1996): Agriculture and fishing 315; Petroleum and natural gas 11,120; Manufacturing 2,737; Electricity and water 415; Construction 1,968; Trade, restaurants and hotels 2,320; Transport and communications 1,167; Finance, insurance, real estate and business services 3,405; Other services (including import duties, *less* imputed bank service charges) 7,071; Total 30,518. Source: Qatar Central Bank, *Annual Report.*

Balance of Payments (estimates, QR million, 1996): Exports f.o.b. 14,939; Imports f.o.b. –10,844; *Trade balance* 4,095; Services, private and official transfers (net) –9,382; *Current balance* –5,287; Capital (net) 2,863; *Overall balance* –2,424. Source: Qatar Central Bank, *Annual Report.*

EXTERNAL TRADE

Imports f.o.b. (QR million): 6,122 in 1994; 9,737 (estimate) in 1995; 10,844 (estimate) in 1996.

Exports f.o.b. (QR million): 10,851 in 1994; 11,451 (estimate) in 1995; 14,939 (estimate) in 1996.

Principal Commodities (distribution by SITC, QR million, 1994): *Imports c.i.f.:* Food and live animals 927.7 (Dairy products and birds' eggs 144.2, Vegetables and fruit 219.4); Crude materials (inedible) except fuels 240.3 (Metalliferous ores and metal scrap 140.6); Chemicals and related products 489.6; Basic manufactures 1,525.2 (Textile yarn, fabrics, etc. 356.2, Non-metallic mineral manufactures 319.3, Iron and steel 271.6); Machinery and transport equipment 2,785.0 (Power-generating machinery and equipment 214.7, Machinery specialized for particular industries 390.1, General industrial machinery, equipment and parts 520.5, Telecommunications and sound equipment 162.4, Other electrical machinery, apparatus, etc. 343.0, Road vehicles and parts 989.2); Miscellaneous manufactured articles 871.2; Total (incl. others) 7,015.6. *Exports f.o.b.:* Mineral fuels and lubricants 9,297.4 (Petroleum, petroleum products, etc. 8,148.9, Gas (natural and manufactured) 1,148.5); Chemicals and related products 1,187.9 (Manufactured fertilizers 420.2, Plastics in primary forms 372.3); Basic manufactures 676.0 (Iron and steel 673.6); Total (incl. others) 11,452.8 (excl. re-exports 242.3).

Principal Trading Partners (QR million, 1994): *Imports c.i.f.:* Australia 138.3; Bahrain 112.3; Brazil 109.9; People's Republic of China 103.0; France 276.3; Germany 466.4; India 229.9; Italy 304.2; Japan 938.1; Republic of Korea 139.8; Netherlands 209.9; Saudi Arabia 347.3; Switzerland 144.4; United Arab Emirates 486.7; United Kingdom 720.5; USA 743.3; Total (incl. others) 7,015.6. *Exports f.o.b.* (incl. re-exports): States of the Co-operation Council for the Arab States of the Gulf (Gulf Co-operation Council—GCC) 1,170.0; USA 233.5; Asia (except Arab countries) 9,448.0; Australia and New Zealand 475.3; Total (incl. others) 11,695.1.

TRANSPORT

Road Traffic (licensed vehicles, 1995): Private 141,679; Public transport 65,926; Heavy vehicles 4,881; Taxis 1,747; Motorcycles 2,952; Trailers 2,329; General transport 2,769; *Total* 222,283 (excl. government vehicles, totalling 5,169 in 1993).

Shipping (international sea-borne freight traffic, '000 metric tons, 1994): *Goods loaded:* 5,853; *Goods unloaded:* 2,500. *Merchant Fleet* (registered at 31 December 1996): 59 vessels; 561,739 gross registered tons (Source: Lloyd's Register of Shipping, *World Fleet Statistics.*)

Civil Aviation (scheduled services 1995): Kilometres flown 21 million; Passengers carried 1,073,000; Passenger-km 2,766 million; Total ton-km 395 million. Figures include an apportionment (one-quarter) of the traffic of Gulf Air, a multinational airline with its headquarters in Bahrain. Source: UN, *Statistical Yearbook.*

TOURISM

Tourist arrivals (hotel occupants only): 159,982 in 1993; 241,295 in 1994; 309,216 in 1995.

Hotel beds (1995): 2,667.

COMMUNICATIONS MEDIA

Radio Receivers (1995): 240,000 in use*.

Television Receivers (1995): 220,000 in use*.

Telephones (1995): 146,980 lines in use.

Telefax stations (1995): 9,400 in use†.

Mobile Cellular Telephones (1995): 18,469 subscribers†.

Daily Newspapers (1995): 6.

Non-daily Newspapers (1995): 1.

Book Production (1995): 419 titles*.

* Source: UNESCO, *Statistical Yearbook.*

† Source: UN, *Statistical Yearbook.*

EDUCATION

Pre-primary (1994/95): 64 schools; 302 teachers; 6,786 pupils.

Primary (1994/95): 169 schools; 5,853 teachers; 52,130 pupils.

Secondary (1994/95): 126 schools (general 123, vocational 3—1993/94); 3,858 teachers (general 3,738, vocational 120); 37,635 pupils (general 36,964, vocational 671).

University (1995/96): 1 institution; 645 teaching staff; 8,271 students.

Source: partly UNESCO, *Statistical Yearbook.*

Directory

The Constitution

A provisional Constitution was adopted on 2 April 1970. Executive power is vested in the Amir, as Head of State, and exercised by the Council of Ministers, appointed by the Head of State. The Amir is assisted by the appointed Advisory Council of 20 members (increased to 30 in 1975 and 35 in 1988), whose term was extended for six years in 1975, for a further four years in 1978, and for further terms of four years in 1982, 1986, 1990 and 1994. All fundamental democratic rights are guaranteed. In 1975 the Advisory Council was granted power to summon individual ministers to answer questions on legislation before promulgation. Previously the Advisory Council was restricted to debating draft bills and regulations before framing recommendations to the Council of Ministers. In November 1997 it was announced that elections were to take place, by universal adult suffrage, for a 29-member central council with authority over Qatar's municipalities.

The Government

HEAD OF STATE

Amir: Maj.-Gen. Sheikh HAMAD BIN KHALIFA ATH-THANI (assumed power 27 June 1995).

Crown Prince: Sheikh JASIM BIN HAMAD BIN KHALIFA ATH-THANI.

COUNCIL OF MINISTERS
(September 1998)

Amir, Minister of Defence and Commander-in-Chief of the Armed Forces: Maj.-Gen. Sheikh HAMAD BIN KHALIFA ATH-THANI.

Prime Minister and Minister of the Interior: Sheikh ABDULLAH BIN KHALIFA ATH-THANI.

Deputy Prime Minister: Sheikh MUHAMMAD BIN KHALIFA ATH-THANI.

Minister of Foreign Affairs: Sheikh HAMAD BIN JASIM BIN JABER ATH-THANI.

Minister of Finance, Economy and Trade: YOUSUF HUSSEIN KAMAL.

Minister of Awqaf (Religious Endowments) and Islamic Affairs: AHMAD BIN ABDULLAH SALEM AL-MARRI.

Minister of Municipal Affairs and Agriculture: ALI SAID AL-KHAYARIN.

Minister of Communication and Transport: Sheikh AHMAD BIN NASSER ATH-THANI.

Minister of Education, Culture and Higher Education: MUHAMMAD ABD AR-RAHIM KAFOUD.

Minister of Electricity and Water and Acting Minister of Justice: AHMAD MUHAMMAD ALI AS-SUBAYI.

Minister of Energy and Industry: ABDULLAH BIN HAMAD AL-ATTIYA.

Minister of Public Health: ABD AR-RAHMAN AS-SALEM AL-KAWARI.

Minister of Housing and the Civil Service: Sheikh FALAH BIN JASIM ATH-THANI.

Minister of State for Foreign Affairs: AHMAD ABDULLAH AL-MAH-MOUD.

Minister of State for Council of Ministers' Affairs: ALI MUHAMMAD AL-KHATIR.

Minister of State for the Interior: Sheikh ABDULLAH BIN KHALID ATH-THANI.

Ministers of State without Portfolio: Sheikh AHMAD BIN SAIF ATH-THANI, Sheikh HASSAN BIN ABDULLAH BIN MUHAMMAD ATH-THANI, Sheikh HAMAD BIN SAHIM ATH-THANI, Sheikh HAMAD BIN ABDULLAH ATH-THANI, Sheikh MUHAMMAD BIN KHALID ATH-THANI.

MINISTRIES

Ministry of Amiri Diwan Affairs: POB 923, Doha; tel. 468333; telex 4297; fax 416773.

Ministry of Awqaf (Religious Endowments) and Islamic Affairs: POB 422, Doha; tel. 466222; fax 466266; internet http://www.islam.gov.qa.

Ministry of Communication and Transport: POB 22228, Doha; tel. 464000; telex 4800; fax 835101.

Ministry of Defence: Qatar Armed Forces, POB 37, Doha; tel. 404111; telex 4245.

Ministry of Education: POB 80, Doha; tel. 413444; telex 4316; fax 413886.

Ministry of Electricity and Water: POB 41, Doha; tel. 437633; telex 4478; fax 355312.

Ministry of Energy and Industry: POB 3212, Doha; tel. 832121; telex 4323; fax 832024.

Ministry of Finance, Economy and Trade: POB 83, Doha; tel. 427444; telex 4315; fax 446294.

Ministry of Foreign Affairs: POB 250, Doha; tel. 415000; telex 4577; fax 426279.

Ministry of Information and Culture: POB 1836, Doha; tel. 831333; fax 416356.

Ministry of the Interior: POB 2433, Doha; tel. 330000; telex 4383; fax 429565.

Ministry of Justice: POB 917 (Dept of Legal Affairs), Doha; tel. 427444; telex 4238; fax 832868.

Ministry of Municipal Affairs and Agriculture: POB 820, Doha; tel. 413535; telex 4476; fax 439177.

Ministry of Public Health: POB 42, Doha; tel. 441555; telex 4261; fax 446294.

ADVISORY COUNCIL

The Advisory Council was established in April 1972, with 20 nominated members. It was expanded to 30 members in December 1975, and to 35 members in November 1988.

Speaker: MUHAMMAD BIN MUBARAK AL-KHALIFA.

Diplomatic Representation

EMBASSIES IN QATAR

Algeria: POB 2494, Doha; tel. 662900; telex 4604; fax 663658; Ambassador: HADEF BOUTHALDJA.

Bangladesh: POB 2080, Doha; tel. 671927; fax 671190; Ambassador: (vacant).

Bosnia and Herzegovina: POB 876, Doha; tel. 670194; fax 670595; Ambassador: NUSRET CANCAR.

China, People's Republic: POB 17200, Doha; tel. 824200; telex 5120; fax 873959; Ambassador: GAO WENXIAN.

Cuba: POB 12017, Doha; tel. 672072; fax 672074; Ambassador ORLANDO REQUEIJO GUAL.

Egypt: POB 2899, Doha; tel. 832555; telex 4321; fax 832196; Ambassador: MUHAMMAD MUHAMMAD MINESSI.

France: POB 2669, Doha; tel. 832281; telex 4280; fax 832254; Ambassador: BERTRAND BESANCENOT.

Germany: POB 3064, Doha; tel. 876959; telex 4528; fax 876949; Ambassador: WALTER WEINBERGER.

India: POB 2788, Doha; tel. 672021; telex 4646; fax 670448; Ambassador: KALARICKAL PRANCHU FABIAN.

Iran: POB 1633, Doha; tel. 835300; telex 4251; fax 831665; Chargé d'affaires: BAHMAN AGARAZI.

Iraq: POB 1526, Doha; tel. 672237; telex 4296; fax 673347; Ambassador: ANWAR SABRI ADL AR-RAZZAQ.

Italy: POB 4188, Doha; tel. 436842; telex 5133; fax 446466; Ambassador: IGNAZIO DI PACE.

Japan: POB 2208, Doha; tel. 831224; telex 4339; fax 832178; Ambassador: SHINYA NAGAI.

Jordan: POB 2366, Doha; tel. 832202; telex 4192; fax 832173; Ambassador: TRAD EL-FAYEZ.

Korea, Republic: POB 3727, Doha; tel. 832238; fax 833264; Ambassador: JIN HO KIM.

Kuwait: POB 1177, Doha; tel. 832111; telex 4113; fax 832042; Ambassador: FAISAL ABDULLAH AL-MASHAAN.

Lebanon: POB 2411, Doha; tel. 444468; telex 4404; fax 324817; Ambassador: ZOUHER AL-CHOKER.

Libya: POB 574, Doha; tel. 429546; fax 429548; Chargé d'affaires: MUHAMMAD RAJAB AL-FAYTOUR.

Mauritania: POB 3132, Doha; tel. 836003; telex 4379; fax 836015; Ambassador: OUTHMAN OULD SHAIKH AHMED ABU AL-MAALY.

Morocco: POB 3242, Doha; tel. 831885; telex 4473; fax 833416; e-mail moroccoe@qatar.net.qa; Ambassador: MUHAMMAD BEN LARBI DILAI.

Oman: POB 1525, Doha; tel. 670744; telex 4341; fax 670747; Ambassador: (vacant).

Pakistan: POB 334, Doha; tel. 832525; fax 832227; Ambassador: LIAQUAT MAHMOOD.

Philippines: POB 24900, Doha; tel. 831585; fax 831595; Ambassador: ANTONIO B. MAGTIBAY.

Romania: POB 22511, Doha; tel. 426740; fax 444346; Chargé d'affaires: CONSTANTIN SANDU.

Russia: POB 15404, Doha; tel. 329117; fax 329118; Ambassador: NIKOLAI K. TIKHOMIROV.

Saudi Arabia: POB 1255, Doha; tel. 832030; telex 4483; fax 832720; Ambassador: ABD AR-RAHMAN ASH-SHUBAILI.

Somalia: POB 1948, Doha; tel. 832200; telex 4275; fax 832182; Ambassador: SHARIF MUHAMMAD OMAR.

Sudan: POB 2999, Doha; tel. 423007; telex 4707; fax 351366; Ambassador: OSMAN NAFIE HAMAD.

Syria: POB 1257, Doha; tel. 831844; telex 4447; fax 832139; Chargé d'affaires: MAMDOUH ZAAROUR.

Tunisia: POB 2707, Doha; tel. 832645; telex 4422; fax 832649; Ambassador: M. HEDI DRISSI.

Turkey: POB 1977, Doha; tel. 835553; telex 4406; fax 835206; Ambassador: SELCUK TARLAN.

United Arab Emirates: POB 3099, Doha; tel. 885111; fax 882837; Ambassador: MUHAMMAD SULTAN EL-ZA'ABI.

United Kingdom: POB 3, Doha; tel. 421991; fax 438692; Ambassador: DAVID ALAN WRIGHT.

USA: POB 2399, Doha; tel. 864701; fax 861669; Ambassador: PATRICK N. THEROS.

Yemen: POB 3318, Doha; tel. 432555; telex 5130; fax 429400; Ambassador: SHARAF AD-DIN SALEH AS-SAIDI.

Judicial System

Justice is administered by five courts (Higher Criminal, Lower Criminal, Commercial and Civil, Labour and the Court of Appeal) on the basis of codified laws. In addition the *Shari'a* Court decides on all issues regarding the personal affairs of Muslims, specific offences where the defendant is Muslim, and civil disputes where the parties elect to have them adjudicated upon, by recourse to Islamic Law of the Holy Quran and the Prophet's Sunna or tradition. Non-Muslims are invariably tried by a court operating codified law. Independence of the judiciary is guaranteed by the provisional Constitution.

Presidency of Shari'a Courts and Islamic Affairs: POB 232, Doha; tel. 452222; telex 5115; Pres. Sheikh ABD AR-RAHMAN BIN ABDULLAH AL-MAHMOUD.

Chief Justice: MUBARAK BIN KHALIFA AS-ASARI.

Public Prosecutor: Col ABDULLAH AL-MAL.

Religion

The indigenous population are Muslims of the Sunni sect, most being of the strict Wahhabi persuasion.

The Press

Al-'Arab (The Arabs): POB 6334, Doha; tel. 325874; telex 4497; fax 440016; f. 1972; daily; Arabic; publ. by Dar al-Ouroba Printing and Publishing; Editor-in-Chief KHALID NAAMA; circ. 25,000.

Ad-Dawri (The Tournament): POB 310, Doha; tel. 328782; fax 447039; f. 1978; weekly; Arabic; sport; publ. by Abdullah Hamad al-Atiyah and Ptnrs; Editor-in-Chief Sheikh RASHID BIN OWAIDA ATH-THANI; circ. 6,000.

Gulf Times: POB 2888, Doha; tel. 350478; fax 350474; e-mail editor@gulf-times.com; internet http://www.gulf-times.com; f. 1978; daily and weekly editions; English; political; publ. by Gulf Publishing and Printing Org.; Editor-in-Chief ABD AR-RAHMAN SAIF AL-MADHADI; circ. 15,000 (daily).

Al-Jawhara (The Jewel): POB 2531, Doha; tel. 414575; telex 4920; fax 671388; f. 1977; monthly; Arabic; women's magazine; publ. by al-Ahd Est. for Journalism, Printing and Publications Ltd; Editor-in-Chief ABDULLAH YOUSUF AL-HUSSAINI; circ. 8,000.

Nada (A Gathering): POB 4896, Doha; tel. 445564; telex 4234; fax 433778; f. 1991; weekly; social and entertainment; published by Akhbar al-Usbou'; Editor-in-Chief ADEL ALI BIN ALI.

Al-Ouroba (Arabism): POB 663, Doha; tel. 325874; telex 4497; fax 429424; f. 1970; weekly; Arabic; political; publ. by Dar al-Ouroba Printing and Publishing; Editor-in-Chief YOUSUF NAAMA; circ. 12,000.

The Peninsula: POB 3488, Doha; tel. 663945; fax 663965; e-mail penqatar@qatar.net.qa; f. 1996; daily; English; political; publ. by Dar ash-Sharq Printing, Publishing and Distribution; Editor-in-Chief MALCOLM WARD; circ. 13,000.

Qatar Lil Inshaa (Qatar Construction): POB 2203, Doha; tel. 424988; telex 4877; fax 432961; f. 1989; publ. by Almaha Trade and Construction Co; Gen. Man. MUHAMMAD H. AL-MIJBER; circ. 10,000.

Ar-Rayah (The Banner): POB 3464, Doha; tel. 466555; telex 4600; fax 350476; f. 1979; daily and weekly editions; Arabic; political; publ. by Gulf Publishing and Printing Org.; Editor NASSER AL-OTHMAN; circ. 25,000.

Saidat ash-Sharq: POB 3488, Doha; tel. 662445; fax 662450; f. 1993; monthly; Arabic; women's magazine; publ. by Dar ash-Sharq Printing, Publishing and Distribution; Editor NASSER AL-OTHMAN; circ. 15,000.

Ash-Sharq (The Orient): POB 3488, Doha; tel. 662444; fax 662450; f. 1985; daily; Arabic; political; publ. by Dar ash-Sharq Printing, Publishing and Distribution House; Gen. Supervisor NASSER AL-OTHMAN; circ. 45,018.

At-Tarbiya (Education): POB 9865, Doha; tel. 861412; telex 4672; fax 880911; f. 1971; quarterly; publ. by Qatar National Commission for Education, Culture and Science; Editor-in-Chief ABD AL-AZIZ FARAJ AL-ANSARI; circ. 2,500.

This is Qatar and What's On: POB 4015, Doha; tel. 413813; telex 4787; fax 413814; f. 1978; quarterly; English; tourist information; publ. by Oryx Publishing and Advertising Co; Editor-in-Chief YOUSUF J. AL-DARWISH; circ. 10,000.

Al-Ummah: POB 893, Doha; tel. 417510; telex 4999; monthly; news and current affairs.

Al-Wattan: POB 22345, Doha; tel. 354466; fax 351138; f. 1995; daily; Arabic; political; publ. by Dar al-Wattan Printing, Publishing and Distribution; Editor-in-Chief AHMAD ALI AL-ABDULLAH.

NEWS AGENCY

Qatar News Agency (QNA): POB 3299, Doha; tel. 322725; telex 4493; fax 442282; f. 1975; affiliated to Ministry of Foreign Affairs; Dir and Editor-in-Chief AHMAD JASSIM AL-HUMAR.

Publishers

Qatar National Printing Press: POB 355, Doha; tel. 448451; telex 4072; fax 449660; Propr KHALED BIN NASSER AS-SUWAIDI; Dir ABD AL-KARIM DIB.

Ali bin Ali Printing and Publishing: POB 75, Doha; tel. 445565; telex 4234; fax 433778.

Dar al-Ouroba Printing and Publishing: POB 52, Doha; tel. 423179.

Dar ash-Sharq Printing, Publishing and Distribution: POB 3488, Doha; tel. 662445; fax 662450.

Gulf Publishing and Printing Organization: POB 533, Doha; tel. 466555; fax 424171; Gen. Man. MUHAMMAD ALLAM ALI.

Oryx Publishing and Advertising Co: POB 3272, Doha; tel. 413813; fax 413814.

Broadcasting and Communications

TELECOMMUNICATIONS

Qatar Telecommunications Corpn (Q-Tel): POB 217, Doha; tel. 400400; telex 4468; fax 413904; f. 1987; state-owned; provides telecommunications services within Qatar; Gen. Man. MUHAMMAD ISMAIL AL-EMADI.

BROADCASTING
Regulatory Authority

Qatar Radio and Television Corpn (QRTC): Doha; f. 1997; autonomous authority reporting directly to the Council of Ministers.

Radio

Qatar Broadcasting Service (QBS): POB 3939, Doha; tel. 894444; telex 4597; fax 882888; f. 1968; govt service transmitting in Arabic, English, French and Urdu; programmes include Holy Quran Radio and Doha Music Radio; Dir MUBARAK JAHAM AL-KUWARI.

Television

Al Jazeera Satellite Station: POB 23123, Doha; tel. 890890; fax 885333; f. 1996; Pres. HAMAD BIN THAMER ATH-THANI; Dir MUHAMMAD JASIM AL-ALI.

Qatar Television Service: POB 1944, Doha; tel. 894444; telex 4040; fax 874170; f. 1970; operates two channels; Dir MUHAMMAD JASIM AL-ALI (acting); Asst Dir ABD AL-WAHAB MUHAMMAD AL-MUTAWA'A.

Finance

(cap. = capital; res = reserves; dep. = deposits; m. = million; brs = branches; amounts in Qatar riyals unless otherwise stated)

BANKING
Central Bank

Qatar Central Bank: POB 1234, Doha; tel. 456456; telex 4335; fax 413650; f. 1966 as Qatar and Dubai Currency Board; became Qatar Monetary Agency in 1973; renamed Qatar Central Bank in 1993; cap. and res 709.2m., currency in circulation 1,610.9m. (Sept. 1997); Gov. ABDULLAH BIN KHALID AL-ATTIYA; Dep. Gov. Sheikh ABDULLAH BIN SAID ABD AL-AZIZ ATH-THANI.

Commercial Banks

Al-Ahli Bank of Qatar QSC: POB 2309, Doha; tel. 326611; telex 4884; fax 444652; f. 1984; cap. 90.0m., res 69.3m., dep. 1,589.3m. (Dec. 1996); Chair. Sheikh MUHAMMAD BIN HAMAD ATH-THANI; Gen. Man. FAROOQ ABD AL-MAJEED; 3 brs.

Commercial Bank of Qatar QSC: Grand Hamad Ave, POB 3232, Doha; tel. 490222; telex 4351; fax 438182; e-mail cbqitech@qatar .net.qa; internet http://www.cbqbank.com; f. 1975; owned 20% by board of directors and 80% by Qatari citizens; cap. and res 429.1m., dep. 2,595.4m. (Dec. 1997); Chair. Sheikh ALI BIN JABER ATH-THANI; Gen. Man. TIMOTHY P. NUNAN; 8 brs.

Doha Bank Ltd: Grand Hamad Ave, POB 3818, Doha; tel. 456600; telex 4534; fax 416631; f. 1979; cap. 78.8m., res 209.8m., dep. 3,382.3m. (Dec. 1996); Chair. FAHAD BIN MUHAMMAD BIN JABER ATH-THANI; Gen. Man. MUHAMMAD JAMJOUM; 9 brs in Qatar and 3 brs overseas.

Qatar Industrial Development Bank: POB 22789, Doha; tel. 421600; fax 350433; f. 1996; inaugurated Oct. 1997; owned 50% by Govt of Qatar; to provide long-term low-interest industrial loans; cap. 200m.

Qatar International Islamic Bank: POB 664, Doha; tel. 332600; telex 4161; fax 444101; f. 1990; cap. 100m., total assets 1,095.7m. (1996); Gen. Man. ABD AL-BASIT ASH-SHAIBEI (acting); 3 brs.

Qatar Islamic Bank SAQ: POB 559, Doha; tel. 409409; telex 5177; fax 412700; f. 1983; cap. 150m., res 67.5m., dep. 2,549.9m. (Dec. 1996); Chair. and Man. Dir KHALID BIN AHMAD AS-SUWAIDI; 5 brs.

Qatar National Bank SAQ: POB 1000, Doha; tel. 407407; telex 4212; fax 413753; internet http://www.qatarbank.com; f. 1965; owned 50% by Govt of Qatar and 50% by Qatari nationals; cap. 553.7m., res 2,053.7m., dep. 14,516.1m. (Dec. 1997); Chair. Minister of Finance, Economy and Trade; Gen. Man. J. P. FINIGAN; 20 brs in Qatar and 3 brs abroad.

Foreign Banks

ANZ Grindlays Bank PLC (Australia): POB 2001, Rayyan Rd, Doha; tel. 418222; telex 4209; fax 428077; f. 1956; total assets 706.3m. (1989); Gen. Man. J. F. MURRAY.

Arab Bank PLC (Jordan): POB 172, Doha; tel. 437979; telex 4202; fax 410774; f. 1957; total assets 1,100m. (31 Dec. 1996); Regional Man. GHASSAN BUNDAKJI; Dep. Man. SAAD AD-DIN ELAYAN; 2 brs.

Bank Saderat Iran: POB 2256, Doha; tel. 414646; telex 4225; fax 430121; f. 1970; Man. MUHAMMAD ZAMANI.

Banque Paribas (France): POB 2636, Doha; tel. 433844; telex 4268; fax 410861; f. 1973; Gen. Man. PIERRE IMHOF.

The British Bank of the Middle East (UK): POB 57, Doha; tel. 335222; telex 4204; fax 416353; internet http://www.british bank.com; f. 1954; total assets 1,166m. (1994); CEO CHRIS MEARES; Gen. Man. J. P. PASCOE; 3 brs.

Mashreq Bank PSC (UAE): POB 173, Doha; tel. 413213; telex 4235; fax 413880; f. 1971; Gen. Man. KHALED GAMAL ELDIN.

Standard Chartered PLC (UK): POB 29, Doha; tel. 414252; telex 4217; fax 413739; f. 1950; total assets 428.6m. (1991); Gen. Man. A. R. PARRY.

United Bank Ltd (Pakistan): POB 242, Doha; tel. 416930; telex 4222; fax 424600; f. 1970; Gen. Man. and Vice-Pres. RAI MANSOOR AHMAD KHAN.

STOCK EXCHANGE

Doha Securities Market (DSM): Al-Khaleej Insurance Co Bldg, Doha; f. 1997; operations began in May 1997; 18 cos initially listed; Dir HUSSEIN ABDULLAH.

INSURANCE

Al-Khaleej Insurance Co of Qatar (SAQ): POB 4555, Doha; tel. 414151; telex 4692; fax 430530; f. 1978; cap. 9m. (1995); all classes except life; Chair. ABDULLAH BIN MUHAMMAD JABER ATH-THANI; Gen. Man. MUHAMMAD NOOR AL-OBAIDLY.

Qatar General Insurance and Reinsurance Co SAQ: POB 4500, Doha; tel. 417800; telex 4742; fax 437302; f. 1979; cap. 15m. (1995); all classes; Chair. Sheikh ALI BIN SAUD ATH-THANI; Gen. Man. GHAZI ABU NAHL.

Qatar Insurance Co SAQ: POB 666, Doha; tel. 490490; telex 4216; fax 831569; f. 1964; cap. 36m. (1995); all classes; the Govt has a majority share; Chair. Sheikh KHALID BIN MUHAMMAD ALI ATH-THANI; Gen. Man. KHALIFA A. AS-SUBAYI; br. in Dubai.

Qatar Islamic Insurance Co: POB 12402, Doha; tel. 413413; fax 447277; f. 1993; cap. 20m. (1995).

Trade and Industry

DEVELOPMENT ORGANIZATION

Department of Industrial Development: POB 2599, Doha; tel. 832121; telex 4323; fax 832024; govt-owned; conducts research, development and supervision of new industrial projects; Dir-Gen. MAJID ABDULLAH AL-MALKI.

CHAMBER OF COMMERCE

Qatar Chamber of Commerce and Industry: POB 402, Doha; tel. 621491; telex 4078; fax 622538; e-mail qcci@qatar.net.qa; f. 1963; 17 elected mems; Pres. Sheikh HAMAD BIN JASIM BIN MUHAMMAD ATH-THANI; Dir-Gen. Dr MAJID ABDULLAH AL-MALKI.

STATE HYDROCARBONS COMPANIES

Qatar General Petroleum Corpn (QGPC): POB 47, Doha; tel. 402400; telex 4201; fax 831125; f. 1974; cap. QR 5,000m.; the State of Qatar's interest in companies active in petroleum and related industries has passed to the Corpn. In line with OPEC policy, the Govt agreed a participation agreement with the Qatar Petroleum Co and Shell Co of Qatar in 1974 to secure Qatar's interest and obtained a 60% interest in both. In late 1976, under two separate agreements, the Govt secured a 100% interest in both companies. The Qatar Petroleum Producing Authority (QPPA) was established in 1976 as a subsidiary, wholly owned by the Corpn, to undertake all operations previously conducted by the two companies. In February 1980 the QPPA was merged with the Corpn.

Qatar General Petroleum Corpn wholly or partly owns: National Oil Distribution Co (NODCO), Qatar Fertilizer Co Ltd (QAFCO), Qatar Liquefied Gas Co (QATARGAS), Qatar Petrochemical Co Ltd (QAPCO), Ras Laffan LNG Co, Compagnie Pétrochimique du Nord (COPENOR), Arab Maritime Petroleum Transport Co Ltd, Arab Petroleum Pipelines Co (SUMED), Arab Shipbuilding and Repair Yard Co (ASRY), Arab Petroleum Services Co and Arab Petroleum Investments Corpn (APICORP); Chair. Minister of Energy and Industry; Vice-Chair. HUSSAIN KAMAL.

National Oil Distribution Co (NODCO): POB 50033, Umm Said; tel. 776555; telex 4324; fax 771232; operates two refineries with a capacity of 62,000 b/d; responsible for the nationwide distribution of petroleum products; wholly owned by QGPC; Gen. Man. MUHAMMAD KHALIFA TURKYSOBAI.

Qatar Liquefied Gas Co (QATARGAS): POB 22666, Doha; tel. 327121; telex 4500; fax 327144; f. 1984 to develop the North Field of unassociated gas; cap. QR 500m.; QGPC has a 65% share; Mobil and Total—Cie Française des Pétroles hold 10% each; the Marubeni Corpn and Mitsui and Co of Japan hold 7.5% each; Chair. Minister of Energy and Industry; Gen. Man. ABD AR-REDHA ABD AR-REHMAN.

QGPC (Onshore Operations): POB 47, Doha; tel. 343287; telex 4253; fax 444554; produces and exports crude petroleum from the Dukhan oilfield and processes and exports natural gas liquids from the onshore and offshore oilfields in Qatar; also responsible

for the internal distribution of fuel gas and support services; 182.6m. US barrels of condensate, 223,384 metric tons of butane and 362,180 tons of propane produced in 1987; Man. Dir JABER AL-MARRI; Dep. Exec. Man. AJLAN ALI AL-KUWARI.

QGPC (Offshore Operations): POB 47, Doha; tel. 402000; telex 4201; fax 402584; state-owned organization for offshore oil/gas exploration and production; (now merged with QGPC) average production in 1990 was 188,000 b/d, total approximately 68.7m. barrels; Man. Dir JABER A. AL-MARRI; Exec. Man. MUHAMMAD SAUD AD-DOLAIMI.

Qatar Petrochemicals Co (QAPCO) SAQ: POB 756, Doha; tel. 321105; telex 4871; fax 772674; f. 1974; QGPC has an 80% share; 10% is held by ELF-ATOCHEM (France); the remaining 10% is held by ENICHEM (Italy); total assets QR 3,110m.; operation of petrochemical plant at Umm Said (tel. 777111; telex 4871; fax 772674); produced 525,000 tons of ethylene, 360,000 tons of low-density polyethylene, and 70,000 tons of solid sulphur in 1997; Gen. Man. HAMAD RASHID AL-MOHANNADI.

UTILITIES

Qatar Electricity and Water Co (QEWC): POB 22046, Doha; tel. 858585; fax 831116; e-mail qewc@qatar.net.qa; f. 1990; manages privately-owned utilities, generation of power and water and desalination.

MAJOR COMPANIES

AK Group Contracting: POB 1991, Doha; tel. 440474; telex 4138; fax 444594; f. 1975; building, plumbing, joinery, landscaping, etc.; sales QR 59m. (1992); Man. Dir Sheikh ABD AL-AZIZ BIN KHALIFA ATH-THANI; Gen. Man. MARK P. GOLDING; 700 employees.

Arab-Qatari Co for Dairy Production: POB 8324, Doha; tel. 601107; telex 4972; fax 600516; f. 1981; production of dairy products, ice creams and fruit juices; cap. p.u. QR 45m.; Gen. Man. (Commercial) KAMAL KANDALAFT.

Arab-Qatari Co for Poultry Production: POB 3606, Doha; tel. 729042; fax 729028; produces between 1m. and 2.5m. broiler chickens, and between 10m. and 25m. eggs, per year; Dir ISMAIL FAITI AL-ISMAIL.

Kassem Darwish Fakhroo & Sons (KDS): POB 350, Doha; tel. 422781; telex 4298; fax 426378; f. 1911 (corporate group 1971); electrical, mechanical and civil contractors, general trading, manufacturers; Chair. KASSEM DARWISH FAKHROO; Man. Dir HASSAN K. DARWISH; 1,000 employees.

Mideast Constructors Ltd (MECON): POB 3325, Doha; tel. 415025; telex 4293; fax 415174; e-mail mecon@qatar.net.qa; f. 1975; mechanical and electrical instrumentation, heating, ventilating and air-conditioning, and civil engineering and contracting; annual sales QR 220m.; Chair. AHMAD AL-MANNAI; Gen. Man. SAMIR E. DWIDAR; 550 employees.

National Industrial Gas Plants: POB 1391, Doha; tel. 422116; telex 4408; fax 435030; f. 1954; production of industrial gases (oxygen, carbon dioxide, nitrogen, argon and acetylene), liquid gases (oxygen, nitrogen and argon), and dry ice, hydrostatic pressure testing of high-pressure cylinders; Pres. M. H. ALMANA; 125 employees.

Qatar Dairy Co: POB 4770, Doha; tel. 689009; telex 4365; fax 689922; production of dairy products.

Qatar Fertilizer Co (QAFCO) SAQ: POB 50001, Umm Said; tel. 779779; telex 4215; fax 770347; e-mail info@qafco.com; internet http://www.qafco.com; f. 1969; produced 1,147,505 tons of ammonia and 1,439,579 tons of urea in 1997; owned by QGPC (75%) and Norsk Hydro (25%); Chair. ABDULLAH H. SALATT; Man. Dir KHALIFA AS-SUWAIDI.

Qatar Flour Mills Co SAQ: POB 1444, Doha; tel. 671816; telex 4285; fax 671611; f. 1968; produced 33,000 metric tons of flour and 11,500 tons of bran in 1993; Chair. Sheikh AHMAD BIN ABDULLAH ATH-THANI; Gen. Man. GHAZI ABD AL-SALIMI.

Qatar Industrial Manufacturing Co: POB 16875, Doha; tel. 672212; fax 670344; f. 1989 to establish domestic and international industrial ventures; operates seven subsidiaries; Qatar Saudi Gypsum Co, Qatar Jet Fuel Co, Qatar Metal-Coating Co, Modern Detergent Co, Gulf Ferro Co, National Paper Co, Qatar Sand-Treatment Plant.

Qatar National Cement Co SAQ: POB 1333, Doha; tel. 350800; telex 4337; fax 417846; f. 1965; produced 470,000 tons of ordinary Portland and salt-resisting cement in 1994; Chair. KHALIFA ABDULLAH AS-SUBAYI; Gen. Man. SAEED M. AL-KUWARI.

Qatar National Plastic Factory: POB 5615, Doha; tel. 689977; telex 4365; fax 689922; production of polyethylene bags, film and UPVC pipes.

Qatar Steel Co (QASCO): POB 50090, Steel Mill, Umm Said; tel. 778778; telex 4606; fax 771424; the plant was completed in 1978, and produced 601,000 tons of concrete-reinforcing steel bars in 1995; the Govt owns a 70% share, with Kobe Steel (20%) and Tokyo Boeki (10%); Chair. Aḥmad Muhammad Ali as-Subayi; Man. Dir Nasser Muhammad al-Mansouri.

Qatar Hot Briquetted Iron Co (Qabico): f. 1997 by QASCO (31%), Duferco (16.3%), Gulf Investment Corpn (16.3%), National Industries Co (16.3%), Qatar Industrial Manufacturing Co (10%), Qatar Shipping Co (10%); capacity 2m. tons.

Readymix (Qatar) Ltd: POB 5007, Doha; tel. 653070; telex 4668; fax 651534; f. 1978; production of ready-mixed concrete; Gen. Man. W. D. Forde.

Qatar Quarry Co Ltd: POB 5007, Doha; tel. 653070; telex 4668; fax 651534; f. 1983; production of aggregates, road materials and armour rock; Gen. Man. W. D. Forde.

Transport

ROADS

In 1991 there were some 1,191 km (740 miles) of surfaced road linking Doha and the petroleum centres of Dukhan and Umm Said with the northern end of the peninsula. A 105-km (65-mile) road from Doha to Salwa was completed in 1970, and joins one leading from Al Hufuf in Saudi Arabia, giving Qatar land access to the Mediterranean. A 418-km (260-mile) highway, built in conjunction with Abu Dhabi, links both states with the Gulf network.

SHIPPING

Doha Port has nine general cargo berths of 7.5m–9.0m depth. Total length of berths is 1,699 m. In addition, there is a flour mill berth, and a container terminal (with a depth of 12.0m and a length of 600m) with a roll-on roll-off berth at the north end, is currently under construction. Cold storage facilities exist for cargo of up to 500 tons. At Umm Said Harbour the Northern Deep Water Wharves consist of a deep-water quay 730 m long with a dredged depth alongside of 15.5 m, and a quay 570 m long with a dredged depth alongside of 13.0 m. The General Cargo Wharves consist of a quay 400 m long with a dredged depth alongside of 10.0 m. The Southern Deep Water Wharves consist of a deep water quay 508 m long with a dredged depth alongside of 13.0 m. The North Field gas project has increased the demand for shipping facilities. A major new industrial port was completed at Ras Laffan in 1995, providing facilities for LNG and condensate carriers and roll-on-roll-off vessels.

Department of Ports, Maritime Affairs and Land Transport: POB 313, Doha; tel. 457457; telex 4378; fax 413563; Dir of Ports G. A. Genkeer.

Qatar National Navigation and Transport Co Ltd (QNNTC): West Bay, Al-Tameen St, POB 153, Doha; tel. 468666; telex 4206; fax 468777; f. 1957; 100%-owned by Qatari nationals; shipping agents, stevedoring, chandlers, forwarding, shipowning, repair, construction, etc.; Chief Exec. Abd al-Aziz H. Salatt.

Qatar Shipping Co, SAQ: POB 22180; Doha; tel. 436777; telex 4888; fax 329692; e-mail qshipwdm@qatar.net.qa; f. 1992; oil and bulk cargo shipping; Chair. Abd al-Aziz H. Salat; Gen. Man. Bryan S. Archer.

CIVIL AVIATION

Doha International Airport is equipped to receive all types of aircraft. In 1995 the total number of passengers using the existing airport was 2,263,287. Construction of a new terminal, at a cost of QR 350m., began in 1997.

Department of Civil Aviation: POB 3000, Doha; tel. 428177; telex 4306; fax 429070; Dir of Civil Aviation Abd al-Aziz an-Noaimi.

Doha International Airport: POB 73, Doha; tel. 622222; fax 622044; Dir Abdullah bin Ahmad ath-Thani.

Gulf Air Co Ltd: POB 3394, Doha; tel. 455455; telex 5150; fax 449955; internet http://www.gulfair.com; jointly owned by the Govts of Bahrain, Oman, Qatar and Abu Dhabi; flights world-wide; Pres. and CEO Ahmad bin Saif an-Nahiyan.

Gulf Helicopters: POB 811, Doha; tel. 333888; fax 352287; e-mail gulfheli@qatar.net.qa; f. 1974; owned by QGPC; Chair. Abdullah bin Hamad al-Attiya.

Qatar Airways: POB 22550, Doha; tel. 621717; fax 621533; f. 1993; services to 20 international destinations; CEO Akbar al-Baker.

Defence

Estimated Defence Budget (1997): QR 4,100m.

Total armed forces (August 1997): 11,800: army 8,500; navy 1,800 (incl. marine police); air force 1,500.

Education

All education within Qatar is provided free of charge, although it is not compulsory, and numerous scholarships are awarded for study overseas. In 1994/95 there were 6,786 children receiving private pre-primary education. Primary schooling begins at six years of age and lasts for six years. In 1994/95 the 169 primary schools were attended by 52,130 pupils. The next level of education, beginning at 12 years of age, is divided between a three-year preparatory stage (with 20,701 pupils at 70 schools in 1993/94) and a further three-year secondary stage (14,817 pupils at 53 schools in 1993/94). General secondary education facilities are complemented by a technical school, a school of commerce and an institute of religious studies. Specialized instruction is also available at an institute of administration and a language teaching institute. In 1994/95 there were 3,858 teachers employed and 37,635 pupils enrolled at secondary level in Qatari schools. In 1994 the equivalent of 87% of all children in the relevant age-group (boys 89%; girls 84%) were enrolled at primary schools, while the comparable ratio for secondary enrolment was equivalent to 82% (boys 82%; girls 82%). In 1994/95 some 1,193 Qataris were sent on scholarships to higher education institutions abroad, in other Arab countries, Britain, France or the USA. In October 1973 the first two Higher Teacher Training Colleges were opened, providing education to university level. In 1993/94 the University of Qatar comprised the faculties of education, science, humanities and social studies, administration and economics, technology, engineering and *Shari'a*. In the academic year 1995/96 there were 8,271 students and a teaching staff of 645 at the University of Qatar. The 1998/99 budget allocated QR 77.4m. to education and youth welfare. The average rate of adult illiteracy in 1995 was estimated by UNESCO to be 20.6% (males 20.8%; females 20.1%).

Bibliography

Abu Nab, Ibrahim. *Qatar: A Story of State Building*. Ministry of Information, Qatar, 1977.

Al-Abdulla, Yousof Ibrahim. *A Study of Qatari-British Relations 1914–1945*. Orient Publishing and Translation, 1981.

Graham, Helga. *Arabian Time Machine: Self-Portrait of an Oil State*. Heinemann, 1978.

El-Mallakh, Ragaei. *Qatar, Energy and Development*. Croom Helm, 1985.

Nafi, Zuhair Ahmed. *Economic and Social Development in Qatar*. Frances Pinter, 1983.

Al-Othman, Nasser. *With Their Bare Hands: the Story of the Oil Industry in Qatar*. Longman, 1984.

For further titles, see Bibliography sections on Bahrain and the United Arab Emirates.

SAUDI ARABIA

Physical and Social Geography
of the Arabian Peninsula

The Arabian peninsula is a distinct geographical unit, delimited on three sides by sea—on the east by the Persian (Arabian) Gulf and the Gulf of Oman, on the south by the Indian Ocean, and on the west by the Red Sea—while its remaining (northern) side is occupied by the deserts of Jordan and Iraq. This isolated territory, extending over some 2.5m. sq km (about 1m. sq miles), is divided politically into several states. The largest of these is Saudi Arabia, which occupies 2,240,000 sq km (865,000 sq miles); to the east and south lie much smaller territories where suzerainty and even actual frontiers are disputed in some instances. Along the shores of the Persian Gulf and the Gulf of Oman there are, beginning in the north, the State of Kuwait, with two adjacent zones of 'neutral' territory; then, after a stretch of Saudi Arabian coast, the islands of Bahrain and the Qatar peninsula, followed by the United Arab Emirates and the much larger Sultanate of Oman. Yemen occupies most of the southern coastline of the peninsula, and its south-western corner.

PHYSICAL FEATURES

Structurally, the whole of Arabia is a vast platform of ancient rocks, once continuous with north-east Africa. Subsequently a series of great fissures opened, as the result of which a large trough, or rift valley, was formed and later occupied by the sea, to produce the Red Sea and Gulf of Aden. The Arabian platform is tilted, with its highest part in the extreme west, along the Red Sea, and it slopes gradually down from west to east. Thus the Red Sea coast is often bold and mountainous, whereas the Persian Gulf coast is flat, low-lying and fringed with extensive coral reefs which make it difficult to approach the shore in many places.

Dislocation of the rock strata in the west of Arabia has led to the upwelling of much lava, which has solidified into vast barren expanses, known as *harras*. Volcanic cones and flows are also prominent along the whole length of the western coast as far as Aden, where peaks rise to more than 3,000 m above sea-level. The mountains reach their highest in the south, in Yemen, with summits at 4,000 m, and the lowest part of this mountain wall occurs roughly halfway along its course, in the region of Jeddah, Mecca, and Medina. A principal reason for the location of these three Saudi Arabian towns is that they offer the easiest route inland from the coast, and one of the shortest routes across Arabia.

Further to the east the ancient platform is covered by relatively thin layers of younger rocks. Some of the strata have been eroded to form shallow depressions; others have proved more resistant, and now stand out as ridges. This central area, relieved by shallow vales and upstanding ridges and covered in many places by desert sand, is called the Najd, and is considered to be the homeland of the Wahhabi sect, which now rules the whole of Saudi Arabia. Farther east, practically all the land lies well below 300 m in altitude, and both to the north and to the south are desert areas. The Nefud in the north has some wells, and even a slight rainfall, and therefore supports a few oasis cultivators and pastoral nomads. South of the Najd, however, lies the Rub' al-Khali, or Empty Quarter, a rainless, unrelieved wilderness of shifting sand, too harsh for occupation even by nomads.

Most of the east coast of Arabia (al-Hasa) is low-lying, but an exception is the imposing ridge of the Jebel al-Akhdar ('Green Mountain') of Oman, which also produces a fjord-like coastline along the Gulf of Oman. Another feature is the large river valleys, or *wadis*, cut by river action during an earlier geological period, but in modern times almost, or entirely, dry and partially filled with sand. The largest is the Wadi Hadramawt, which runs parallel to the southern coast for several hundred km; another is the Wadi Sirhan, which stretches north-westwards from the Nefud into Jordan.

CLIMATE

Because of its land-locked nature, the winds reaching Arabia are generally dry, and almost all the area is arid. In the north there is a rainfall of 100 mm–200 mm annually; further south, except near the coast, even this fails. The higher parts of the west and south do, however, experience appreciable falls—rather sporadic in some parts, but copious and reliable in areas adjacent to the Red Sea.

Because of aridity, and hence relatively cloudless skies, there are great extremes of temperature. The summer is overwhelmingly hot, with maxima of more than 50°C, which are intensified by the dark rocks, while in winter there can be general severe frost and even weeks of snow in the mountains. Another result of the wide variations in temperature is the prevalence of violent local winds. Also, near the coast, atmospheric humidity is particularly high, and the coasts of both the Red Sea and the Persian Gulf are notorious for their humidity. Average summer temperatures in Saudi Arabia's coastal regions range from 38°C to 49°C (100°F–120°F), sometimes reaching 54°C (129°F) in the interior, or falling to a minimum of 24°C (75.2°F) in Jeddah. The winters are mild, except in the mountains. Winter temperatures range from 8°C (46.4°F) to 30°C (86°F) in Riyadh, and reach a maximum of 33°C (91.4°F) in Jeddah.

Owing to the tilt of the strata eastwards, and their great elevation in the west, rain falling in the hills near the Red Sea apparently percolates gradually eastwards, to emerge as springs along the Persian Gulf coast. This phenomenon, borne out by the fact that the flow of water in the springs greatly exceeds the total rainfall in the same district, suggests that water may be present underground over much of the interior. Irrigation schemes to exploit these supplies have been developed, notably in the Najd at al-Kharj, but results have been fairly limited.

ECONOMIC LIFE

Over much of Arabia, life is based around oases. Many wells are used solely by nomads for watering their animals, but in some parts, more especially the south, there is regular cultivation. Yemen, in particular, has a well-developed agriculture, showing a gradation of crops according to altitude, with cereals, fruit, coffee and qat (a narcotic) as the chief products. Other agricultural districts are in Oman and in the large oases of the Hedjaz (including Medina and Mecca). However, conditions in Arabia are harsh, and the population depends partly on resources brought in from outside, such as revenues from pilgrims. A major change in the economy of Saudi Arabia and the Gulf States resulted from the exploitation of petroleum, the revenues from which transformed those States.

RACE, LANGUAGE AND RELIGION

The inhabitants of the centre, north and west are of almost unmixed Mediterranean stock—lightly built, long-headed and dark. In coastal districts of the east, south and south-west, intermixture of broader-headed and slightly heavier peoples of Armenoid descent is a prominent feature; and there has been some exchange of racial type with the populations on the Iranian shores of the Persian Gulf and Gulf of Oman. Owing to the long-continued slave trade, negroid influences from Africa are also widespread. On this basis it is possible to delimit two ethnic zones within Arabia: a northern, central and western area, geographically arid and in isolation, with a relatively unmixed racial composition; and the coastlands of the south, south-west and east, showing a mixed population. A recent result of the rapid economic growth in the petroleum-producing countries has been the influx of large numbers of expatriates from the developed countries of the Western world, and labourers from developing countries further east. Arabic, however, is the sole language of Arabia. Unlike many other parts of the Middle East, European languages are not current.

As its borders enclose the holy cities of Mecca and Medina, Saudi Arabia is the centre of the Islamic faith. About 85% of Saudi Muslims belong to the Sunni sect of Islam, the remainder being Shi'ites. Except in the Eastern Province, Sunni rites prevail.

History

Revised for this edition by the Editor

ANCIENT AND MEDIEVAL HISTORY

For the most part, Arabian history has been the account of small pockets of settled civilization, subsisting mainly on trade, in the midst of nomadic tribes. The earliest urban settlements developed in the south-west, where the flourishing Minaean kingdom is believed to have been established in the 12th century BC. This was followed by the Sabaean and Himyarite kingdoms, which lasted until the sixth century AD. The term 'kingdom' in this connection implies a loose federation of city states rather than a centralized monarchy. As an important trading station between east and west, southern Arabia was brought into early contact with the Persian and Roman empires, and thereby with Judaism, Zoroastrianism, and later Christianity. Politically, however, the south Arabian principalities remained independent.

By the end of the sixth century the centre of power had shifted to the west coast, to the Hedjaz cities of at-Ta'if, Mecca and Medina. While the southern regions fell under the control of the Sasanid rulers of Persia, the independent Hedjaz grew in importance as a trade route between the Byzantine Empire, Egypt, and the East. From the fifth century, Mecca was dominated by the tribe of Quraish. Meanwhile, the central deserts remained nomadic, and the inhospitable east coast remained, for the most part, under Persian influence.

The flowering and development of Arabism from the 7th century AD, inspired by the Prophet Muhammad (the founder of Islam) proceeded, for the most part, outside the Arabian peninsula itself. The Islamic unification of the Near and Middle East reduced the importance of the Hedjaz as a trade route. Mecca retained a unique status as a centre of pilgrimage for the whole Islamic world, but Arabia as a whole, temporarily united under Muhammad and his successors, soon drifted back into disunity. Yemen was the first to break away from the weakening Abbasid Caliphate in Baghdad, and from the ninth century onwards a variety of small dynasties established themselves in San'a, Zabid, and other towns. Mecca also had its semi-independent governors, though their proximity to Egypt made them more cautious in their attitude towards the Caliphs and the later rulers of that country, particularly the Fatimids of the 10th to 12th centuries. In Oman, in the south-east, a line of spiritual Imams arose who before long were exercising temporal power. To the north the Arabian shores of the Persian Gulf provided a home for the fanatical Carmathian sect, whose influence at times extended as far as Iraq, Syria, Mecca, and Yemen.

THE OTTOMAN PERIOD

Arabia remained unsettled until the beginning of the 16th century, when the whole peninsula came nominally under the suzerainty of the Ottoman Sultans in Istanbul. It was a hold that was never very strong, even in the Hedjaz, and in Oman and Yemen native lines of Imams were once again exercising unfettered authority before the end of the century. More important for the future of the peninsula was the appearance of European merchant adventurers in the Indian Ocean and the Persian (Arabian) Gulf. The Portuguese were the first to arrive, in the 16th century, and they were followed in the 17th and 18th centuries by the British, Dutch and French. By the beginning of the 19th century Britain had supplanted its European rivals and had established its influence firmly in the Gulf and, to a lesser extent, along the southern coast.

The political structure of Arabia was now beginning to develop along its modern lines. Yemen was already a virtually independent Imamate; Lahej broke away in the middle of the 18th century, only to lose Aden to Britain in 1839 and to become the nucleus of the Aden Protectorate. To the north of Yemen was the principality of the Asir, generally independent, though both countries were occupied by the Turks from 1850 until the outbreak of the First World War. The Hedjaz continued to be a province of the Ottoman Empire. In 1793 the Sultanate of Oman was established with its capital at Muscat, and during the 19th century all the rulers and chieftains along the Persian Gulf coast, including Oman, the sheikhdoms of the Trucial Coast, Bahrain and Kuwait, entered into 'exclusive' treaty relations with the British Government. Britain was principally concerned with preventing French, Russian and German penetration towards India, and suppressing the trade in slaves and weapons.

Meanwhile, the Najd, in the centre of Arabia, was the scene of another upheaval with religious inspirations. The puritanical and reforming Wahhabi movement, launched in the middle of the 18th century, had by 1800 grown so powerful that its followers were able to capture Karbala and Najaf in Iraq, Damascus in Syria, and Mecca and Medina in the Hedjaz. They were defeated by Muhammad Ali of Egypt, acting in the name of the Ottoman Sultan, in 1811–18 and again in 1838, but the Wahhabi ruling house of Sa'ud continued to rule in the interior until 1890, when the rival Rashidi family, which had Turkish support, seized control of Riyadh.

In 1901 a member of the deposed Sa'udi family, Abd al-Aziz ibn Abd ar-Rahman, set out from Kuwait, where he had been living in exile, to regain the family's former domains. In 1902, with only about 200 followers, Abd al-Aziz captured Riyadh, expelled the Rashidi dynasty and proclaimed himself ruler of the Najd. Later he recovered and consolidated the outlying provinces of the kingdom, resisting Turkish attempts to subjugate him. Having restored the House of Sa'ud as a ruling dynasty, Abd al-Aziz became known as Ibn Sa'ud. To strengthen his position, Ibn Sa'ud instituted the formation of Wahhabi colonies, known as Ikhwan ('Brethren'), throughout the territory under his control. The first Ikhwan settlement was founded in 1912, and about 100 more were established, spreading Wahhabi doctrines to communities in remote desert areas, over the next 15 years. These colonies formed the basis of a centralized organization which was to prove a powerful instrument in later years. By the outbreak of the First World War (1914–18), Ibn Sa'ud was effectively the master of central Arabia, including the Hasa coast of the Persian Gulf.

EVENTS, 1914–26

When Turkey entered the war on the side of Germany in October 1914, Arabia inevitably became a centre of intrigue, if not necessarily of military action. British influence was paramount along the eastern and southern coasts, where the various sheikhs and tribal chiefs from Kuwait to the Hadramawt lost no time in severing their remaining connections with the Ottoman Empire. On the other hand, the Turks had faithful allies in Ibn Rashid of the Shammar, to the north of the Najd, and in Imam Yahya of Yemen. The Turks also maintained garrisons along the west coast. In the centre, Ibn Sa'ud, who, in 1913, had accepted Turkish recognition of his occupation of the Hasa coast, enjoyed friendly relations with the British-controlled Government of India.

British military strategy developed, as the war dragged on, into a two-pronged thrust against the Turks from both Egypt and the Persian Gulf. In the implementation of this plan opinions were divided on the extent to which use could be made of the Arab population. The Indian Government on the eastern wing, while favouring the pretensions of Ibn Sa'ud, preferred to see the problem in purely military terms, and opposed any suggestion of an Arab revolt. This, however, was the scheme favoured by the Arab Bureau in Cairo, whose views eventually prevailed in London. They were alarmed at the Ottoman declaration of a *jihad* (holy war) and possible repercussions in Egypt and North Africa. Negotiations were started at a very early stage with Arab nationalist movements in Syria and Egypt, but these met with comparatively little success. More progress was made when the British negotiators turned their attentions to the Sharif of Mecca, Hussein, a member of the Hashimi family which had ruled in Mecca since the 11th century AD. The support of such a religious dignitary would be an effective counter to Turkish claims. Hussein was inclined to favour the Allied cause, but it was only after he had elicited from the British (in the MacMahon correspondence—see Documents on Palestine, p. 108) promises which he believed would meet Arab nationalist aspirations that he decided to move. On 5 June 1916 he proclaimed Arab independence and declared war on the Turks. By November things had gone so well that he felt able to claim the title of King of the Hedjaz. Military operations continued throughout the winter, and in July 1917 the port of Aqaba was captured and the Hedjaz cleared of Turkish troops except for a beleaguered garrison in Medina.

Arabia thereafter remained comparatively peaceful, and was not even greatly disturbed by the complicated post-war political manoeuvres in the Middle East. Hussein was a rather ineffectual spokesman for the Arab point of view at the peace conferences and over the allocation of mandates, and as a result forfeited the favour of the British Government. When, therefore, he was unwise enough to challenge the growing power of his former rival Ibn Sa'ud, he found himself entirely without support. Ibn Sa'ud's stature had been steadily growing since the end of the war. In November 1921 he had succeeded in supplanting the house of Ibn Rashid and annexing the Shammar, and a year later he was recognized by the Government of India as overlord of Hayil, Shammar and Jawf. On 5 March 1924 Hussein laid claim to the title of Caliph, made vacant by the deposition of the Ottoman Sultan. His claims were nowhere recognized, and Ibn Sa'ud overran the Hedjaz in a campaign of a few months, captured Mecca and forced Hussein's abdication. Hussein's eldest son, Ali, continued to hold Jeddah for another year, but was then ousted, and on 8 January 1926 Ibn Sa'ud proclaimed himself King of the Hedjaz. At first the Najd and the Hedjaz formed a dual kingdom, but on 23 September 1932 they were merged to form the Kingdom of Saudi Arabia.

THE KINGDOM OF SAUDI ARABIA*

Ibn Sa'ud's new status was recognized by Britain in the Treaty of Jeddah of 1927, while Ibn Sa'ud, in his turn, acknowledged his rival Hussein's sons, Abdullah and Faisal, as rulers of Transjordan and Iraq, and also the special status of the British-protected sheikhdoms along the Gulf coast. The northern frontier of his domains had previously been established by the Hadda and Bahra agreements of November 1925, which set the Mandate boundaries as the limit of his expansion. The border with Yemen was settled in 1934 after protracted negotiations and a brief war.

In the years that followed, the new king's priority remained the unification and development of his country. The colonization policy which he had begun in 1912 was pursued vigorously; land settlements were established and unruliness among the bedouin was suppressed. The modernization of communications was initiated, and the need for economic development emphas-

ized. The main damage that Saudi Arabia suffered during the Second World War was economic. The pilgrimage traffic declined to almost nothing, and in April 1943 it was necessary to include Saudi Arabia as a beneficiary of Lend-Lease, the arrangement whereby the USA supplied equipment to allied countries.

Saudi Arabia's production of crude petroleum increased steadily as new oilfields were developed. In October 1945 a petroleum refinery opened at Ras Tanura, and two years later work started on the Trans-Arabian Pipeline (Tapline), to connect the Arabian oilfields with ports on the Mediterranean Sea in Lebanon. Petroleum first reached the Lebanese port of Sidon on 2 December 1950. In the same month the Saudi Arabian Government and the Arabian-American Oil Co (Aramco) signed a new agreement providing for equal shares of the proceeds of petroleum sales. In 1956 a government-owned National Oil Co was formed to exploit areas not covered by the Aramco concession.

Saudi Arabia was a founder member of the League of Arab States (Arab League), formed in 1945, and initially played a loyal and comparatively inconspicuous part. Ibn Sa'ud sent a small force to join the fighting against Israel in the summer of 1948. When the solidarity of the League began to weaken, it was natural that he should side with Egypt and Syria rather than with his old dynastic enemies, the rulers of Iraq and Jordan. In the course of time, however, he began to turn once more to internal development, and to forget his political quarrel with the USA in his need for economic advice and aid; in 1950 and 1951 a US \$15m. loan was agreed, as well as a four-point agreement and a mutual assistance pact. However, the real basis of development was the revenue from the developing petroleum industry. This was sufficient to justify the announcement, in July 1949, of a \$270m. Four-Year Plan, whose main feature was an ambitious programme of railway development. Apart from this, the King's policy was one of cautious modernization at home, and the enhancement of Saudi Arabian prestige and influence in the Middle East and in world affairs generally.

AFTER IBN SA'UD

On 9 November 1953 King Ibn Sa'ud died, at the age of 71, and was succeeded by one of his many sons, Sa'ud ibn Abd al-Aziz, hitherto the Crown Prince, who had been appointed Prime Minister in the previous month. Another of the late King's sons, Faisal ibn Abd al-Aziz, replaced Sa'ud as Crown Prince and Prime Minister. The policy of strengthening the governmental machine, and of relying less on one-man rule, was continued by the formation of new ministries and a regular Council of Ministers. In March 1958, bowing to pressure from the royal family, King Sa'ud conferred on Crown Prince Faisal full powers over foreign, internal and economic affairs, with the professed aim of strengthening the machinery of government and of centralizing responsibilities. In December 1960, however, the Crown Prince resigned as Prime Minister, and the King assumed the premiership himself. In the following month, a high planning council, with a team of international experts, was formed to survey the country's resources, and there followed steady progress in the modernization of the country.

Throughout his reign, King Sa'ud regarded his role as that of a mediator between the conflicting national and foreign interests in the Arab Middle East. He refused to join either the United Arab Republic (UAR) or the rival Arab Federation. Relations with Egypt ranged from the mutual defence pacts between Egypt, Syria and Saudi Arabia in October 1955 (which Yemen and Jordan also signed a year later) to the open quarrel in March 1958 over an alleged plot to assassinate President Nasser. Subsequently, relations improved. The Saudi Government also played a leading role in bringing the Arab Governments together after Egypt's nationalization of the Suez Canal in July 1956 and the Israeli, British and French military action in the Sinai peninsula in November. In 1961 Saudi Arabia supported the Syrians in their break with the UAR, and in general, relations with that country deteriorated. By 1964, however, in spite of the tensions over the revolution in Yemen, King Sa'ud attended the Cairo conference on the Jordan waters dispute in January, and in March, after a meeting in Riyadh, diplomatic relations with the UAR were resumed. In September Prince Faisal attended the Arab Summit Conference in Alexandria, and after-

---

* For subsequent developments in the rest of the Arabian peninsula, see separate chapters on Bahrain, Kuwait, Oman, Qatar, the United Arab Emirates and Yemen.

wards had talks with President Nasser on the situation in Yemen.

FAISAL IN POWER

In March 1964 King Sa'ud relinquished all real power over the affairs of the country to his brother, Crown Prince Faisal, who had again acted as Prime Minister intermittently during 1962, and continuously since mid-1963. The rule of Prince Faisal was expected to result in many concessions to 'Westernization', such as more cinemas and television, with more profound social and economic reforms to follow. The change of power, by which King Sa'ud retired as active monarch, was supported in a statement by the *ulema* council of religious leaders 'in the light of develop- ments, the King's condition of health, and his inability to attend to state affairs'. In November 1964 Sa'ud was forced to abdicate in favour of Faisal. The new King retained the post of Prime Minister, and in March 1965 appointed his half-brother, Khalid ibn Abd al-Aziz, to be Crown Prince. On 24 August 1965 King Faisal confirmed his stature as an important Arab leader when he concluded an agreement at Jeddah with President Nasser of the UAR on a peace plan for Yemen.

Although the Yemen issue remained unresolved, there was evidence of Saudi Arabia's genuine anxiety that a solution should be found, even though in April 1966 the construction of a military airfield near the frontier brought protests from the Republican Government of Yemen and the UAR. Representat- ives of Saudi Arabia and the UAR met in Kuwait in August 1966 in an attempt to implement the Jeddah agreement, but relations with both the UAR and the Arab League continued to be tense.

THE SIX-DAY WAR, AND AFTER

In the June 1967 Arab–Israeli war, Saudi forces collaborated with Jordanian and Iraqi forces in action against Israel. At a summit conference of Arab leaders held in Khartoum at the end of August 1967 Saudi Arabia agreed to provide £50m. of a total £135m. fund to assist Jordan and the UAR in restoring their economic strength after the hostilities with Israel. An agreement was also concluded with President Nasser on the withdrawal of UAR and Saudi military support for the warring parties in Yemen. By way of recompense for these concessions, the Saudi Arabian Government persuaded other Arab states that it was in their best interests to resume shipments of petroleum to Western countries—supplies had been suspended for political reasons after the war with Israel.

Although outwardly calm, the internal political situation was disturbed by abortive coups in June and September 1969. Plans for both seem to have been discovered in advance, the only visible evidence being the arrests of numbers of army and air force officers. A flight of private capital abroad was also reported. In Yemen the royalist cause, which the Saudi Government had strongly supported, appeared to be within sight of victory early in 1968. By mid-1969, however, its remaining adherents had largely been driven into exile and the civil war seemed to have come to an end, although further hostilities were reported during the 1969/70 winter. Dissension amongst the royalists, which led to the withdrawal of Saudi assistance, was a principal factor in this decline. Discussions between San'a representatives and Saudi officials took place in 1970, and the Yemen Arab Republic (YAR) was officially recognized in July. Relations with Southern Yemen (subsequently the People's Democratic Republic of Yemen—PDRY) deteriorated, however, and in December 1969 the two countries fought an extensive battle on the disputed frontier: Saudi Arabia won easily, owing mainly to its superior air power.

REPERCUSSIONS OF THE OCTOBER WAR

When the Arab–Israeli war of October 1973 broke out and US aid to Israel continued, Saudi Arabia, despite its traditionally good relationship with the West, led a movement by all the Arab petroleum-producing countries to exert political pressure by cuts in petroleum production. Since there was no immediate response from the USA, OPEC members placed an embargo on petroleum supplies to that country and to several other de- veloped Western countries. Supplies to the western world were not cut off entirely, but it was announced that production would

be progressively reduced until attitudes towards support for Israel changed. Western nations attempted to repair their links with the petroleum-producing countries, who were debating among themselves how far they should wield the 'oil weapon' to achieve their ends.

As the possessor of 40% of the Middle East's petroleum reserves, and one-quarter of world reserves, Saudi Arabia, to- gether with Egypt, was in the very forefront of negotiations. It soon became apparent, however, that the Saudis held different views from those of other producer nations (notably Libya, Algeria and Iran) on the extent to which their control of petro- leum supplies could safely be used to put pressure on the West. It was feared in Riyadh that too much of this pressure would have unwanted economic repercussions. The more radical OPEC members wanted to retain the petroleum embargo until a satis- factory outcome to the October hostilities was reached. At a meeting in March 1974, however, Saudi Arabia pressed for a resumption of supplies to the USA and, when this was agreed, resisted any moves to increase prices for petroleum, which had risen to nearly four times the pre-hostilities level. It was reported that, in order to achieve their aim, the Saudis had threatened to leave OPEC and to lower prices unilaterally. Reluctantly, therefore, the more radical OPEC members agreed to a price freeze.

Meanwhile, in negotiations with consumer countries, the Saudis made it clear that the continued supply of petroleum was dependent not only on a change in attitudes towards Israel but on assistance to Saudi Arabia itself in industrializing and diversifying its economy, in preparation for the time when reserves of petroleum would be depleted. The USA, in particular, showed itself eager to satisfy these conditions, and an important economic and military co-operation agreement was signed in May 1974.

ASSASSINATION OF FAISAL, ACCESSION OF KHALID

On 25 March 1975 King Faisal was assassinated by one of his nephews, Prince Faisal ibn Masaed ibn Abd al-Aziz. There were fears of a conspiracy but it soon became clear that the assassin had acted on his own initiative. King Faisal was succeeded by his half-brother, Khalid, hitherto Crown Prince. The new King Khalid also became Prime Minister, and appointed one of his brothers, Fahd ibn Abd al-Aziz (Minister of the Interior since 1962), to be Crown Prince and First Deputy Prime Minister.

No major change of policy followed Khalid's succession. He quickly announced that Saudi Arabia would follow the late King Faisal's policies of pursuing Islamic solidarity and the strengthening of Arab unity, and that Saudi Arabia's objectives remained 'the recovery of occupied Arab territories' and the 'liberation of the City of Jerusalem from the claws of Zionism'.

In March 1976 Saudi Arabia established diplomatic relations with the PDRY. Although the two countries had been ideological enemies since the PDRY achieved independence (as Southern Yemen) in 1967, they were both concerned about the presence of Iranian forces in Oman. A Saudi Arabian loan was made to the needy PDRY, and it was expected that, in return, the Yemenis would abandon their support for the People's Front for the Liberation of Oman.

An indication of the growth in stature of Saudi Arabia in Arab affairs in the late 1970s was the key role which the country played in October 1976 in bringing about the Riyadh summit— a meeting which was instrumental in ending the civil war in Lebanon and also brought about reconciliation between Egypt and Syria. Saudi Arabia also asserted itself at the OPEC summit in Doha in December 1976, when the country, along with the United Arab Emirates, showed itself firmly committed to a petroleum price rise of only 5%, while the other OPEC countries insisted on a 10% rise.

Saudi Arabia supported President Sadat of Egypt, fearing that his fall from power would result in Egypt's moving to the left. When Sadat visited Israel in November 1977, Saudi Arabia gave him discreet support in his peace initiative. This position, however, was abandoned following the signing of the Egyptian- Israeli treaty in the following spring. At the Arab summit meeting held in April 1979, Saudi Arabia aligned itself with the 'moderate' states in supporting the sanctions against Egypt which had been outlined at the Arab League meeting in the previous November. In July 1979 the Saudi Government withdrew from its arms manufacturing consortium with Egypt. Nevertheless, flights between Egypt and Saudi Arabia continued, and there was no ban on the employment of Egyptian workers in Saudi Arabia.

In domestic affairs, the Saudi Government was content to allow social change to unfold gradually, although the country's vast petroleum wealth and the development plans of 1975–80 and 1980–85 brought about a great improvement in communications, welfare services and the standard of living in general. The Saudi royal family received a severe shock in November 1979, when the Grand Mosque in Mecca was occupied by about 250 armed followers of Juhaiman ibn Seif al-Oteibi, a Sunni Muslim extremist, who had come to proclaim a Mahdi on the first day of the Islamic year 1400. The siege continued for two weeks, until the extremists were defeated; 102 insurgents and 127 Saudi Arabian troops died.

SAUDI ARABIA IN THE 1980s

The siege of the Mecca Mosque revealed unease in Saudi Arabia. Although the royal family was firmly in control, the existing system entitled as many as 5,000 Saudi princes to royal privileges, and there were murmurings against the royal family's conspicuous consumption and privilege. An eight-man committee under the chairmanship of Prince Nayef, Minister of the Interior, was appointed in March 1980 to draft a 200-article 'system of rule' based on Islamic principles. Saudi Arabia's geopolitical position, however, added to the unease. With the former PDRY already in the Soviet orbit, with the former YAR concluding an agreement to purchase armaments from the USSR in November 1979, and with the Soviet invasion of Afghanistan in December 1979, Saudi Arabia came to feel increasingly vulnerable. This feeling was intensified by the outbreak of war between Iran and Iraq in September 1980, which caused further instability in the region. Saudi Arabia initially supported Iraq, but later came to fear that Iranian retaliation might take the form of agitating Saudi Arabia's Shi'a minority. Saudi Arabia therefore concentrated on consolidating its position in the early 1980s. Defence spending became a major feature of Saudi Arabia's current expenditure, largely involving the purchase or loan of armaments and military equipment from the USA. In March 1981 President Ronald Reagan of the USA, in spite of congressional opposition, agreed to sell to Saudi Arabia five AWACS (airborne warning and control systems) aircraft in addition to the four that were supplied under US control after the outbreak of the Iran–Iraq War.

In May 1981 Saudi Arabia joined five other Gulf states in setting up the Co-operation Council for the Arab States of the Gulf (Gulf Co-operation Council—GCC), a pact for economic co-operation but also with some emphasis on the formation of a military alliance and a collective security agreement. The GCC made preliminary moves towards the co-ordination of its members' defences in November 1982, when it was agreed that its own Rapid Defence Force (RDF) would be formed. This decision was ratified in October 1983, when member countries participated in the 'Peninsula Shield' joint military exercises in Oman. Saudi Arabia's defence forces form a large part of the RDF's military strength.

Saudi Arabia was one of the leading mediators in the negotiations which ended the 1981 missile crisis in Lebanon, and has become increasingly involved in trying to find a solution to the whole Arab–Israeli question and the issue of Palestinian autonomy. The basis of Saudi Arabia's policy with regard to these questions was the eight-point 'Fahd Plan', first publicized by Prince (later King) Fahd in August 1981. The plan (reproduced on p. 124) caused concern in the remainder of the Arab world because it recognized the legitimacy of Israel, by implication, although Saudi Arabia was reluctant to admit this. The plan was due to be discussed at an Arab summit meeting at Fez, in Morocco, in November, but there was disagreement over its implications and the summit quickly broke up in disarray.

ACCESSION OF FAHD

King Khalid died suddenly on 13 June 1982 and was succeeded by his younger brother, Fahd, hitherto Crown Prince. Owing to Khalid's ill-health, Fahd had already exercised considerable power. The new King Fahd also became Prime Minister, and he appointed a half-brother, Abdullah ibn Abd al-Aziz (Commander

of the National Guard since 1962), to be Crown Prince and First Deputy Prime Minister. The previous Saudi policy of positively seeking a solution to the Palestine question, inflamed still further by the Israeli move into Lebanon in June, was continued. The Saudi Government was unwilling to exercise the political influence over Syria (particularly concerning Syrian involvement in Lebanon) which Western countries assumed it to have, demonstrating clearly its priority of Arab unity. In February 1984 Crown Prince Abdullah expressed support for the Syrian position in Lebanon, demanding a withdrawal of US marines from the area.

After 1982 there was a considerable slump in government revenues from petroleum (see Economy, below). Supportive loans to other Arab countries, including Syria and Iraq, proved to be a significant burden on the kingdom's finances. Donations to Iraq were widely thought to have totalled $25,000m. by April 1984, and there seemed little likelihood that Saudi Arabia would abrogate the responsibility which it had assumed for supporting Iraq in its war with Iran. Under an agreement reached in the first year of the Iran–Iraq War, Saudi Arabia and Kuwait sold up to 310,000 b/d of oil (250,000 b/d from the Neutral/Partitioned Zone and the remainder from Saudi Arabia) through the Arabian Oil Co, the proceeds of which went to Iraq, to compensate it for lost export capacity. In mid-1987, however, Saudi Arabia assured Iran that it was selling only a negligible amount of oil on Iraq's behalf.

As the war between Iran and Iraq showed signs of escalating towards the end of 1983 and in early 1984, Saudi Arabia appeared to be in danger of becoming involved militarily in the conflict. In April 1984 a Saudi Arabian merchant ship, a tanker loading at Iran's Kharg Island oil terminal, was struck by missiles from Iraqi fighter aircraft. In retaliatory incidents in May, Iranian aircraft attacked two more tankers, one of which was travelling in Saudi Arabian waters. In response, Saudi Arabia approached the USA to request help in improving its defence systems, by extending its air defence zone (with the new 'Fahd Line'), and by mobilizing its defences to patrol the region. At a meeting of the UN's Security Council in May, the GCC countries tried unsuccessfully to secure a general condemnation of Iran's behaviour in the war. However, they were supported by Egypt, a move which heralded an improvement in relations between Egypt and the more moderate Arab countries. The willingness of the USA to become involved in safeguarding the Strait presented problems for the Gulf countries, since GCC policy countenanced the intervention of either superpower only in a case of urgent need, and the Gulf States retained certain reservations in their otherwise good relations with the USA concerning, for example, US policy in Lebanon. Therefore, Saudi Arabia refused to give the USA access to military facilities on its territory in the event of a major escalation of the war between Iran and Iraq.

Saudi Arabia's concern for the development of its own defences was apparent in 1985, and was reflected particularly in the announcement of the 'Peace Shield' defence programme in February. The project, which was not expected to be complete before the mid-1990s, aimed to provide Saudi Arabia with a computerized command, control and communications system for all of its air defences, and also involved the establishment of factories producing avionics and telecommunications equipment. Other defence projects under way in 1985 included plans for the formation of a joint strike force involving Saudi Arabia and its allies in the Gulf region, and the construction of the King Khalid military city, which was eventually to accommodate 70,000 people. Arrangements were also being made in 1985 for the introduction of military conscription. This was one of the aims of the country's fourth Development Plan (1985–90), and reflected growing concern over the dependence of Saudi Arabian military forces upon foreign recruits.

In June 1986 a controversial sale of military equipment was agreed between Saudi Arabia and the USA. The deal, which was initially valued at $3,000m., was reduced to $265m. when plans to supply 800 *Stinger* anti-aircraft missiles and 60 advanced fighter aircraft were cancelled, owing to strong Congressional opposition. Also in June, another controversial agreement was signed between the two countries for the sale of five US-built AWACS aircraft, worth $8,600m. Saudi Arabia's co-operation became essential to the US naval convoys, which began to escort reflagged Kuwaiti tankers through the Persian Gulf in June, following an increase in attacks on shipping in the Gulf by Iran and Iraq during the year. Saudi minesweepers also helped to clear Iranian mines from the shipping lanes in the Gulf in June, when Saudi Arabia agreed to extend the area of operation of its AWACS aircraft, which had been carrying out surveillance operations in the region, monitoring Iranian and Iraqi military movements in the Iran–Iraq War. The escalation of tension in the Gulf, exacerbated by the presence of US and Soviet naval forces, resulted in the adoption of Resolution No. 598 by the UN Security Council on 20 July 1987, which urged an immediate cease-fire. Iraq agreed to observe a cease-fire if Iran would also, but Iran prevaricated, attaching conditions to its acceptance of the Resolution. In November, at an extraordinary meeting of the League of Arab States in Amman, Jordan, representatives of the member nations, including Saudi Arabia, unanimously condemned Iran for prolonging the war against Iraq, deplored its occupation of Arab (i.e. Iraqi) territory, and urged it to accept Resolution No. 598 without pre-conditions. (For more detailed coverage of the Iran–Iraq War and of the events that led to a cease-fire in August 1988, see chapters on Iran and Iraq.)

In early 1985, following a visit by the Saudi Minister of Foreign Affairs, Prince Sa'ud al-Faisal, to Teheran, Ali Akbar Velayati, his Iranian counterpart, visited Riyadh in an attempt to improve relations between the two countries. However, in May two bombs exploded in the Sulmaniya district of Riyadh, killing one person and injuring three others. The Iranian-based Islamic Jihad group claimed responsibility and threatened that this was the beginning of a major bombing campaign within the country. Relations between Saudi Arabia and Iran deteriorated further in 1987, following clashes on 31 July between Iranian pilgrims and Saudi security forces during the *Hajj* (the annual pilgrimage of Muslims to the Islamic holy city of Mecca). Saudi Arabia reported that 402 people, of whom 275 were Iranians, were killed in the disturbances. Confusion surrounded exactly what took place in Mecca. Iran alleged that Saudi security forces opened fire on Iranian pilgrims, and accused Saudi Arabia and the USA of planning the incident. Mass demonstrations took place in Teheran, the Saudi embassy was sacked and Iranian leaders vowed to avenge the pilgrims' deaths by overthrowing the Saudi ruling family. Saudi Arabia, on the other hand, denied that any shooting took place, and insisted that the deaths occurred during a stampede caused by Iranian pilgrims, following unlawful political demonstrations in support of Ayatollah Khomeini. The Mecca incident renewed fears in Saudi Arabia, which had first been aroused after the Islamic revolution in Shi'ite Iran in 1979, that the minority Saudi Shi'ite community would rebel against the Sunni majority, to which the Saudi royal family belongs. A more pressing concern was that Saudi Arabia might become directly involved in the war between Iran and Iraq, if Iran carried out its threats of armed retaliation. In March 1988 the Saudi Arabian Government announced its intention of temporarily limiting the number of pilgrims to Mecca from abroad during the *Hajj* season, which was to begin in mid-July. National quotas would be allocated on the basis of 1,000 pilgrims for every million citizens. This formula gave Iran a quota of 45,000. Iran's religious leader, Ayatollah Khomeini, insisted that 150,000 Iranians, the same number as in 1987, would perform the *Hajj,* and that he would not prevent them from staging political protests at Mecca. In the event, Iran decided not to send pilgrims on the *Hajj,* and the pilgrimage passed without incident. Saudi Arabia severed its diplomatic relations with Iran in April 1988.

In October 1986 Sheikh Ahmad Zaki Yamani was dismissed from office by King Fahd, after serving for 24 years as Minister of Petroleum and Mineral Resources. His dismissal was interpreted as a sign of King Fahd's dissatisfaction with the OPEC 'fair share' policy, adopted at the end of 1985, whereby OPEC abandoned its system of official quotas for petroleum production in an attempt to regain its share of the world market. Sheikh Hisham Nazer, the Minister of Planning, was subsequently confirmed by King Fahd as the new Minister of Petroleum and Mineral Resources, and in April 1988 he was appointed as the first Saudi Arabian chairman of Aramco, the largest oil company operating in Saudi Arabia.

In November 1987 Saudi Arabia resumed full diplomatic relations with Egypt, following a decision taken by the League of Arab States that permitted member states to restore relations with Egypt at their own discretion. Relations had been severed in 1979, following the signing of a peace treaty between Egypt and Israel.

In March 1988 the disclosure that Saudi Arabia had taken delivery of an unspecified number of Chinese DF-3 (CSS-2) medium-range missiles provoked threats by Israel of a pre-emptive strike on the missiles' base at al-Kharj. The USA subsequently warned Israel against taking such action. In April, however, it was reported that King Fahd, in an unprecedented move, had requested the replacement of the US ambassador, following his delivery of an official complaint from the USA concerning Saudi Arabia's purchase of the missiles. In the same month Sino–Saudi relations were further strengthened when the Deputy Minister of Foreign Affairs of the People's Republic of China became the first Chinese leader to undertake an official visit to the kingdom. In May 1988 the US Senate voted to ban sales of military equipment to Saudi Arabia (or to any other nation which had taken delivery of CSS-2 missiles), unless the President could certify that the country purchasing the missiles had no chemical, biological or nuclear warheads with which to equip them.

Following the refusal of the US Congress to sanction an arms agreement, valued at an estimated $1,000m., to supply military equipment to Saudi Arabia, the kingdom signed an agreement with the United Kingdom, valued at a record $20,000m., for the supply of 50 *Tornado* fighter-bomber aircraft, 60 *Hawk* trainer aircraft, 80 helicopters manufactured by Westland, minesweepers and two huge airbases to be built in collaboration with Ballast Nedam of the Netherlands.

In October 1988 four Saudi Arabian Shi'a Muslims, convicted of sabotaging a petrochemical plant and collaborating with Iran, were executed. In an attempt to demonstrate Saudi Arabia's intention of improving relations with Iran, it was decreed that the Saudi official media would halt their campaign of attacks on that country. However, in late 1988 and early 1989 two senior Saudi Arabian intelligence officers, posing as diplomats in an attempt to trace members of the pro-Iranian Shi'a group believed to be responsible for the aforementioned sabotage, were assassinated in Turkey and in Thailand.

In December 1988 the Soviet Deputy Minister of Foreign Affairs visited Saudi Arabia to discuss the conflict in Afghanistan. Saudi Arabia, along with Sudan, recognized the Afghan *mujahidin* Government-in-exile, formed following the Soviet withdrawal, and, at a meeting of the Organization of the Islamic Conference (OIC) in March, it urged other countries to do likewise. However, the exclusion by the Government-in-exile of the eight *mujahidin* opposition groups based in Iran angered the Iranians. Relations between Saudi Arabia and Iran were further strained at the OIC meeting by King Fahd's tolerance on the controversial question of Salman Rushdie's novel, *The Satanic Verses.* Moreover, the issue of compensation for the families of the Iranian pilgrims who died in the July 1987 riots remained unresolved. Iran boycotted the pilgrimage for the second time in July 1989, owing to Saudi Arabia's refusal to abandon the quota system agreed in March 1988 by the OIC (see above). Two explosions, which killed one pilgrim and wounded 16 in Mecca during the *Hajj,* widened the rift between the two countries. Iran blamed the USA and Saudi Arabia for the bombings, while the Saudis accused Iran of promoting terrorism. Saudi Arabia neglected to send condolences upon the death of Ayatollah Khomeini, illustrating the deterioration in relations with Iran. Iranian pilgrims boycotted the *Hajj* for the third successive year in 1990, and Iran claimed that the Saudi Arabian Government opposed their participation. However, Saudi Arabian officials said that Iranian pilgrims were welcome on condition that Iran observed the allocated quota.

Relations between Saudi Arabia and other Gulf states improved in 1989. In March King Fahd signed a non-aggression pact with Iraq, a development apparently designed to ease concerns among conservative Arab Gulf states about Iraq's political ambitions following the war between Iran and Iraq. In April Saudi Arabia announced that it would help Iraq to rebuild the nuclear reactor that had been destroyed by Israel, if the installation were used for peaceful purposes. In August documents ratifying the November 1988 agreement concluded by Kuwait and Saudi Arabia, concerning the property of citizens of the two countries in the Neutral Zone, were signed and exchanged at the Kuwaiti Ministry of Foreign Affairs. King Fahd's visit to Egypt in March 1989 was viewed as signifying the end of Egypt's isolation from the Arab world. Saudi Arabia and Egypt agreed to increase co-operation in trade, transport, insurance and cultural relations, but no decision regarding economic aid to Egypt was announced by King Fahd. Both countries declared their support for efforts to create a Palestinian state and denounced Israeli repression of the Palestinians in the occupied West Bank and Gaza Strip.

Defence remained a major concern in Saudi Arabia. In February 1989 the US Department of State announced that the USA was considering the sale of a large volume of military equipment to the Middle East, of which Saudi Arabia would be the main recipient. In March British Aerospace revealed that the value of the defence agreements signed by Saudi Arabia and Britain in 1985 and 1988 (see above) could ultimately reach £150,000m., representing one of the biggest arms contracts in history. In the same month, allegations that bribery was used to secure the contract led to an official investigation in Britain. Saudi Arabia denied the allegations, stating that the sale was agreed by the two Governments without the use of intermediaries.

OPERATION DESERT SHIELD AND ITS IMPLICATIONS

Saudi Arabia's concern about its capacity to defend itself and its fears of Iraqi expansionism were substantiated in August 1990, when Iraq invaded and annexed Kuwait and proceeded to deploy armed forces along the Kuwaiti-Saudi Arabian border. Following consultations with the US Secretary of Defense, Richard Cheney, King Fahd decided that he had no option but to invite—in accordance with Article 51 of the UN Charter—multinational armed forces to Saudi Arabia in order to deter an attack on the country by Iraq. Thus 'Operation Desert Shield' was launched (see chapters on Jordan, Kuwait and Iraq).

King Fahd condemned the Iraqi invasion of Kuwait and offered refuge to the Amir of Kuwait. Kuwait established a Government-in-exile at Ta'if, Saudi Arabia. Meanwhile, Saudi Arabia stressed the role of Egyptian, Moroccan, Pakistani, Bangladeshi, Kuwaiti and Syrian contingents in the multinational force. By so doing, it sought to counter allegations—made by President Saddam Hussein of Iraq principally, but also by the Palestine Liberation Organization (PLO) and all those opposed to the USA's policies in the Middle East—that, by allowing the deployment of US forces in its defence, it had allowed itself to become an instrument of US strategic interests in the Gulf. The perception, in the Arab world, of Saudi Arabia as such an instrument threatened the whole of its diplomacy, by which it set great store, and which was based not only on the country's wealth, its leading role in OPEC and its custodianship of the holy cities, but also on the standing of King Fahd. Saudi Arabia stressed that the presence of the multinational defensive force was temporary.

There was a shift in the pattern of Saudi Arabia's foreign relations after the onset of the Gulf crisis in August 1990. The co-operation of the USSR, within the structures of the UN, was regarded as vital to the defence of Saudi Arabia, and in September Saudi Arabia and the USSR re-established diplomatic relations after a rupture lasting 50 years. Syria, aware of the diplomatic benefits that it could gain, committed forces to the defence of Saudi Arabia.

Meanwhile, Saudi Arabia implemented retaliatory measures against Jordan and Yemen for the equivocal stance that they had adopted towards Iraq's invasion of Kuwait. In late September 1990 Saudi Arabia expelled some diplomats from Iraq, Jordan and Yemen, while emergency supplies of oil to Jordan were terminated. Privileges enjoyed by the estimated 1.5m. Yemeni expatriate workers in Saudi Arabia were withdrawn, which resulted in the return to Yemen of more than 300,000 of the expatriates. In early November discussions on the restoration of diplomatic relations were held between Saudi Arabia and Iran. In the same month President George Bush of the USA visited Saudi Arabia, where he conferred with King Fahd and the exiled Amir of Kuwait.

By early January 1991 some 30 countries had contributed ground troops, aircraft and warships to the multinational force based in Saudi Arabia and the Gulf region, although the USA played the principal logistical role in the operation. The entire Saudi Arabian armed forces (numbering about 67,500 men) were mobilized in defence of the country. Financial contributions to the cost of the multinational force were received from all over the world.

In mid-January 1991, following the failure of international diplomatic efforts to effect Iraq's withdrawal from Kuwait, the US-led multinational force launched a military campaign ('Operation Desert Storm') to liberate Kuwait, as authorized by the UN Security Council's Resolution 678, which had been adopted in late November 1990. As part of its response to the aerial bombardment which began the campaign, Iraq launched 35 *Scud* missiles (not carrying chemical warheads, as had been feared) against mainly urban targets in Saudi Arabia, and made similar attacks against Israel. Most of the missiles were intercepted by advanced air defence systems that had been installed by the USA, although one of those that struck Saudi Arabia demolished a US barracks near Dhahran, killing 28 soldiers, in February. A potentially more damaging retaliatory measure was taken by Iraq in late January, when it released an estimated 4m. barrels of petroleum from Kuwaiti storage tanks into the Gulf, thus causing what was believed to be the largest spillage ever to have occurred. Although the flow of petroleum was contained by US aerial action, the resultant slick caused extensive ecological damage and threatened many Saudi Arabian coastal installations, including desalination plants. However, the long-term effects of the spillage were eventually seen to be less devastating than had been feared. In late January Iraqi forces entered Saudi Arabia, briefly occupying the town of Ras al-Khafji, close to Saudi Arabia's border with Kuwait, before being repelled by US, Saudi Arabian and Qatari units. Other Iraqi incursions in the same region were likewise repelled, and there was no further fighting on Saudi Arabian territory. In early February Iraq formally severed diplomatic relations with Saudi Arabia. By the end of February, when hostilities were suspended, Saudi Arabian casualties included at least 26 men killed and 10 missing.

Following the liberation of Kuwait and the declaration of a cease-fire in late February 1991, the Kuwaiti Prime Minister and other members of his Government returned to Kuwait from Saudi Arabia in early March, followed subsequently by the Amir. Also in early March, Saudi Arabia and seven other Arab states in the anti-Iraq coalition (the remaining members of the GCC, Egypt and Syria) agreed to form an Arab peace-keeping force in the Gulf region, as part of a draft plan on security and economic co-operation. Later in the month the withdrawal of coalition forces from bases in Saudi Arabia began. The return to Iraq of an estimated 62,000 Iraqi prisoners of war, held in camps in Saudi Arabia, also began in March. In April Saudi Arabia announced its decision to give refuge to an estimated 50,000 Iraqis, many of whom had participated in an unsuccessful revolt against Saddam Hussein's regime in the previous month. In early May the GCC member states endorsed US proposals for an increased Western military presence in the Gulf region, as a deterrent to any future military aggression. Meanwhile, diplomatic relations between Saudi Arabia and Iran were re-established in late March 1991, and Iranian pilgrims resumed attendance of the *Hajj*, their numbers regulated in accordance with Saudi Arabia's quota system.

DOMESTIC AND FOREIGN CHALLENGES SINCE 1991

In February and May 1991 two petitions, presented to King Fahd, appealed for more extensive Islamization in areas as diverse as the armed forces, the press and all administrative and educational systems. The first petition bore the signatures of as many as 100 senior Saudi religious dignitaries, including that of Sheikh Abd al-Aziz ibn Baz, the most influential Saudi theologian. Following the second petition, the Government immediately sent security force personnel to visit leading signatories, some of whom were forbidden to travel abroad. In June the Government's Higher Judicial Council issued a statement warning the signatories of the consequences of issuing any further criticism against the King. The creation of the Higher Judicial Council, within the Ministry of Justice, is considered to be an institutional challenge to the judicial powers of the *ulama* (religious scholars) in Saudi Arabia. Reform of the judicial system was one of the principal aims of the petition, as it stipulated the establishment of a supreme judiciary council with the authority to implement Islamic laws, which would conflict with the powers of the existing Higher Judicial Council. The petitions illustrated the growing assertiveness and restlessness of Islamic conservatives in the domestic debate on the political future of the country, which intensified after the Gulf crisis of 1990–91. On the other hand, the growth of liberal opposition was illustrated in April, when 43 intellectuals and businessmen published an open letter requesting the King to establish national and municipal councils and to curb the excesses of the Islamic religious police, the *mutaween*.

In early September 1991 it was revealed that 37,000 of the 541,000 US troops who had been deployed in Saudi Arabia during the Gulf War remained, in a non-military capacity, in the country. However, resistance to closer military co-operation came from both Islamic fundamentalists within the kingdom, and from pro-Israeli elements in the US Congress. Nevertheless, in September President Bush announced that he was authorizing the sale of 72 F-15 aircraft to Saudi Arabia.

At the end of January 1992 there were widespread reports of repression of fundamentalist dissent. On 29 January it was reported that the Minister of Justice had ordered the deposition of Sheikh Abd al-Ubaykan, the president of Riyadh's main court, who had criticized government policies in his Friday sermons and opposed the deployment of US troops on Saudi Arabian soil and the Middle East peace conference, which had begun in October 1991. At the end of the month the French news agency, Agence France-Presse, reported that 20 Muslim clerics had been arrested in recent weeks, and a preacher dismissed and condemned to 80 lashes for criticizing the Saudi women's association. Sheikh ibn Baz exhorted the people of Saudi Arabia to ignore the 'smear campaign' against the Government and praised the implementation of *Shari'a* law in the kingdom. In February 15 Iraqi opposition leaders met in Riyadh in an attempt to form a united front to depose Saddam Hussain. The conference was held amid strict security and indicated that Saudi Arabia was prepared to be more forthright in its opposition to the Iraqi President. In March a royal decree announced the creation of a Consultative Council within six months. Its members were to be selected by the King every four years, but were not to have any legislative powers. Two further decrees provided the framework for the creation of regional authorities and for a 'basic law of government', equivalent to a written constitution. However, in an interview with the Kuwaiti newspaper *As-Seyassa*, King Fahd stated that the 'prevailing democratic system' in the world was unsuited to the Gulf region, and that Islam favoured 'the consultative system and openness between a ruler and his subjects', rather than free elections. In September Sheikh Muhammad al-Jubair, hitherto the Minister of Justice, was appointed Chairman of the Consultative Council.

In November 1992 a major reorganization of the 18-member Council of Ulema was instigated by royal decree. Among 10 new members appointed by the King was the new Minister of Justice, Abdullah ibn Muhammad ash-Sheikh. In a speech in December King Fahd warned the religious community not to use public platforms to discuss secular matters. He also denounced the spread of Islamic fundamentalism, and referred to attempts by 'foreign currents' to destabilize the kingdom. In May 1993 Saudi authorities disbanded the Committee for the Defence of Legitimate Rights (CDLR), established by a group of six prominent Islamic scholars and lawyers, less than two weeks after its formation. The six founders of the committee were also dismissed from their positions, and their spokesman, Muhammad al-Masari, was arrested. In the following month it was reported that an accommodation had been reached between the Saudi authorities and an opposition Shi'a organization, the Reform Movement, whereby members of that organization undertook to cease 'dissident' activities, in return for permission to return to Saudi Arabia and for the release of a number of Shi'a Muslims held in detention there. In April 1994 members of the CDLR, including al-Masari (who had recently been released from custody), relocated their organization to London, United Kingdom.

In August 1993 four royal decrees had defined the membership and administration of the new Consultative Council (*Majlis*

ash-Shoura), and outlined new rules governing the composition and procedure of the Council of Ministers. The Consultative Council was to consist of 60 men selected by King Fahd from the educated and professional classes. It was to meet regularly in full session, and eight committees were to be established to review the activities of Government. The composition of the Council did not lead observers to expect many challenges from it to government policies. In relation to the Council of Ministers, King Fahd set fixed limits for the cabinet's term of office and that of each cabinet member. Many ministers had occupied the same portfolio since the mid-1970s.

In September 1993 a further decree concerned a provincial system of government, the last of the constitutional reforms promised in March 1992. The decree defined the nature of government for the 13 regions, as well as the rights and responsibilities of their governors, and created councils of officials and citizens for each province to monitor development and to advise the government. Each council was to meet four times a year under the chairmanship of its governor, who will be an amir with ministerial rank. By the end of 1993 both the Consultative Council and the provincial councils had been opened.

During 1994 the Saudi Government was the subject of a series of accusations of corruption and malpractice, made by foreign journalists and Saudi citizens residing abroad. In June Muhammad al-Khiweli, a high-ranking diplomat at the Saudi mission to the UN headquarters in New York, sought political asylum in the USA, accusing the Saudi Government of human rights violations, terrorism and corruption. In the same month another Saudi diplomat residing in the USA, Ahmad az-Zahrani, levelled similar accusations against the Government and sought asylum in the United Kingdom. The defections caused embarrassment to the US and British Governments, which appeared averse to jeopardizing commercial and political ties with Saudi Arabia. In August, none the less, al-Khiweli was granted asylum in the USA. Meanwhile, az-Zahrani was denied political asylum in the United Kingdom, and in November the British authorities announced their intention to deport him. During 1995 the British Government sought, unsuccessfully, to deport Muhammad al-Masari. In January 1996 the British authorities renewed their attempt to expel al-Masari from the United Kingdom by ordering his deportation to the Caribbean island of Dominica. The Saudi Government was reported to have demanded his expulsion, and prominent British defence and aerospace companies were believed to have exerted pressure on the Government to concede to Saudi Arabia's demands in order to secure the continuation of lucrative trade agreements with that country. In March the Chief Immigration Adjudicator in the United Kingdom rejected the deportation order (finding that diplomatic and trade reasons had led to the British Government's attempt to circumvent the UN 1951 Convention on Refugees) and recommended that the Government should reconsider al-Masari's application for political asylum. In April 1996 al-Masari was granted exceptional leave to remain in the United Kingdom for a period of at least four years, although he was not granted asylum. Meanwhile, reports emerged of a split within the CDLR; in April it was announced that al-Masari would continue to lead the reorganized CDLR, while Dr Saad al-Faqih, the former Secretary-General of the CDLR, would lead the rival Islamic Reform Movement.

In September 1994 the CDLR was among organizations to report the arrest of more than 1,000 people, including clerics and academics, most of whom had attended a demonstration in Buraidah, 300 km to the north-west of Riyadh, to protest at the arrest of two religious leaders who had allegedly been agitating for the stricter enforcement of *Shari'a* (Islamic) law. The Government subsequently confirmed that 110 arrests had been made, but in mid-October announced that 130 of the 157 people arrested in September had since been released. In early October the King approved the creation of a Higher Council for Islamic Affairs, under the chairmanship of Prince Sultan ibn Abd al-Aziz, the Second Deputy Prime Minister and Minister of Defence and Civil Aviation, in what was widely interpreted as a measure to limit the influence of militant clerics and to diminish the authority of the powerful Council of Ulema.

The Government's plan eventually to replace the expatriate work-force with Saudi nationals was given fresh impetus in late 1994 with the strict enforcement of the kingdom's residency law, which resulted in the expulsion or voluntary repatriation of more than 100,000 illegal immigrants between December 1994 and February 1995. In May 1995 it was reported that expatriate communities in Saudi Arabia had expressed their concern at the closure of dozens of foreign schools which, according to Saudi authorities, were not officially licensed. Consequently some 10,000 non-Saudi children (including 5,000 pupils from the Indian school) were reported to be left without schooling.

In June 1995 Abdullah Abd ar-Rahman al-Hudhaif, an opposition activist, was sentenced to 20 years' imprisonment for his part in an attack on a security officer and for maintaining links with the CDLR in London. In mid-August, however, Abdullah al-Hudhaif was reported to have been executed. No explanation was given for the increase to his sentence, and Western human rights groups alleged that al-Hudhaif had been denied access to lawyers and that his trial had been conducted in secrecy. A further nine opposition activists were reported to have received prison sentences ranging from three to 18 years, and, according to Amnesty International, as many as 200 'political suspects' remained in detention in the kingdom.

The increase in the number of executions in Saudi Arabia during 1995—primarily for those convicted of drugs-smuggling or murder—provoked international criticism. Between January and October 1995 a total of 191 people (including six women) received the death penalty, compared with 53 during the whole of 1994, and 85 in 1993. In August the Turkish Government appealed to King Fahd to halt the executions of four Turks convicted of smuggling aphrodisiacs into the kingdom. The executions were carried out, however, prompting public outcry in Turkey, where the press condemned the beheadings as excessive and barbaric; it was feared that as many as 40 other Turks imprisoned in Saudi Arabia would suffer the same fate.

In August 1995 King Fahd announced the most far-reaching reshuffle of the Council of Ministers for two decades, although no changes were made to the portfolios held by members of the royal family. The key portfolios of finance and national economy and of petroleum and mineral resources were allocated to younger, though highly experienced, officials. Dr Sulaiman Abd al-Aziz as-Sulaim, hitherto Minister of Commerce, replaced Sheikh Muhammad Ali Aba al-Khail (who had managed the kingdom's finances for 20 years) as Minister of Finance and National Economy. Sheikh Hisham Mohi ad-Din Nazer was replaced as Minister of Petroleum and Mineral Resources by Ali ibn Ibrahim an-Nuaimi, hitherto President of the government-controlled oil company, Saudi Aramco. Nevertheless, the portfolio changes were not expected to result in any major alterations to the kingdom's strategic policies. Some observers regarded the appointment of a new, Western-educated, Minister of Information, Dr Fouad ibn Abd as-Salam ibn Muhammad Farsi, as more significant, possibly signalling the imminent liberalization of Saudi Arabia's press regulations. In October the new Minister of Finance and National Economy resigned, citing ill health; he was replaced by an experienced government official, Dr Abd al-Aziz al-Abdullah al-Khuwaiter, hitherto Minister of State and erstwhile Minister of Education, Agriculture and Water, who was, in turn, replaced by Dr Ibrahim Abd al-Aziz al-Assaf (hitherto Minister of State) in January 1996. In early July 1997 King Fahd issued a decree increasing the membership of the Majlis from 60 to 90 when it began its second term later that month. In early November the Islamic Reform Movement reported that a senior military commander had resigned from the Majlis, dissatisfied at the council's lack of political influence. Following the expiry of an amnesty for illegal immigrants in mid-October, the Government announced that more than 500,000 immigrant workers without valid documentation had left the country, while a further 300,000 had obtained the necessary work permits.

In November 1995 a car-bomb exploded outside the offices of the Saudi Arabia National Guard in Riyadh, which was being used temporarily by US civilian contractors to train Saudi personnel. Seven foreign nationals (including five US citizens) were killed as a result of the explosion, and a further 60 were injured. Responsibility for the bomb was claimed by several organizations, including the Islamic Movement for Change, which earlier in the year had warned that it would initiate attacks if non-Muslim Western forces did not withdraw from

the Gulf region. (In mid-1995 King Fahd had replaced six of the seven University chancellors and more than one-half of the members of the Council of Ulema, in an attempt to counter the perceived spread of Islamist zealotry.) In April 1996 four Saudi nationals were arrested in connection with the attack; in their confessions they claimed to have been influenced by Islamist groups outside the kingdom. The accused were executed at the end of the following month, despite anonymous threats of retaliation if the sentences were carried out. According to Amnesty International, their trial had been conducted in secret and they had been denied access to lawyers. The reliability of their confessions was also questioned. Amnesty International issued a report in 1997 in which the organization condemned the Saudi justice system as 'blatantly unfair', denouncing a lack of judicial supervision which permitted the widespread use of torture, amputation and execution. The report alleged that many defendants were denied access to defence lawyers, and assessed that appeals procedures were inadequate. Furthermore, the organization considered that the increasing exaction of the death penalty had been facilitated by the 'summary and secretive' nature of trials.

In late November 1995 King Fahd was admitted to hospital in Riyadh. Few details concerning the monarch's health were officially revealed, and, when Crown Prince Abdullah was entrusted with responsibility for the affairs of state on 1 January 1996, many observers expressed doubts as to whether the King would ever resume his duties. However, on 21 February King Fahd officially resumed control of the affairs of state. During 1998 there was renewed speculation concerning the state of health of King Fahd; in August it was revealed that he had undergone minor surgery.

In April 1997 some 343 pilgrims, largely from India, Pakistan and Bangladesh, died in a fire at a tent encampment near Mecca. More than 1,000 pilgrims were injured. According to official figures, 118 pilgrims died as a result of a stampede in Mina during the *Hajj* in April 1998.

In late June 1996 19 US personnel were killed, and as many as 400 others (including 147 Saudi, 118 Bangladeshi and 109 US citizens) were injured, when an explosive device attached to a petroleum tanker was detonated outside a military housing complex in al-Khobar, near Dhahran. Saudi officials pledged increased security measures in the kingdom, and offered a substantial reward for information leading to the arrest and prosecution of those responsible for the explosion (believed to be Islamist militants). Earlier in the year US officials had reportedly been critical of the Saudi authorities' investigation of the November 1995 bomb explosion, and of the swift execution of the alleged perpetrators. It was reported in early November 1996 that some 40 Saudis were being held on suspicion of involvement in the bombing. Scant information regarding the Saudi authorities' investigation into the attack emerged in late 1996, prompting speculation that Saudi Shi'a groups with possible links to Iran were being held responsible for the atrocity, rather than the same Sunni extremist factions that were widely believed to have been responsible for the November 1995 car bomb (see above).

Saudi–US relations had been placed under increasing strain as a result of the bomb attack and subsequent investigation. However, in May 1997 a Canadian court ruled that a Saudi citizen, Hani Abd ar-Rahim as-Sayegh, could be deported to the USA to face charges in connection with the June 1996 bombing; he was deported in mid-June 1997. Suspicions of Iranian involvement in the explosion were repeatedly denied by Iran. In September, however, the USA announced that there was insufficient evidence to secure a conviction, and as-Sayegh would thus not be tried in the USA. Saudi Arabia declared its intention to apply for as-Sayegh's extradition; however, his subsequent application for political asylum in the USA was expected to delay the process. In May 1998 Saudi Arabia declared that the bombing had been perpetrated by independently-acting Saudi Arabians, although the USA continued to investigate alleged Iranian involvement.

In late 1997, as tensions mounted between the Iraqi authorities and the weapons inspectors of the UN Special Commission (UNSCOM), Saudi Arabia firmly advocated a diplomatic solution. In February 1998 Saudi Arabia stated that it would not allow the USA to use Saudi territory as a base for air-strikes against Iraq, and reiterated its desire for a diplomatic solution.

In mid-1992 there were signs of a *rapprochement* between Saudi Arabia and Jordan, as well as the PLO; King Fahd sent best wishes to King Hussein for a speedy recovery from an operation in the USA, and the Saudi Arabian Minister of Foreign Affairs received the Palestinian envoy to Riyadh, the first indication of a reconciliation since the outbreak of the Gulf crisis. In January 1994 King Fahd met PLO leader Yasser Arafat for the first time since the Gulf crisis and pledged $100m. towards the reconstruction of the Gaza Strip and Jericho, the two sites for Palestinian interim self-rule agreed by Israel and the PLO in their 1993 Declaration of Principles (see Documents on Palestine—p. 128). In February 1994 Saudi Arabia pledged $53,000 to the families of each Palestinian victim of the Hebron massacre. In January 1995 King Fahd held a meeting in Mecca with Yasser Arafat, and in April Saudi Arabia became the first Arab country to recognize passports issued by the Palestine National Authority (PNA) for Palestinians in Gaza and Jericho. In June the Council of Ministers approved the import of goods made within the area controlled by the PNA. In July Jordan's Minister of Foreign Affairs met his Saudi counterpart in Riyadh, the first high-level visit made by a Jordanian official since the Gulf crisis. The normalization of relations between the two countries began in November with the appointment of a Saudi ambassador to Jordan. Relations were consolidated in February and August 1996 when King Hussein of Jordan met Crown Prince Abdullah in Saudi Arabia.

In September 1992 the Government sent a memorandum to the Government of Yemen in an attempt to expedite demarcation of the Saudi-Yemeni border. Sporadic negotiations, through the medium of a joint border commission, continued into 1993 but stalled in 1994 as a result of renewed civil war between north and south in Yemen. It became apparent that the Saudi Government's allegiance lay with the secessionists and, following their defeat in July 1994, tensions between the two countries increased. In early December Yemen accused Saudi Arabia of encroaching on its territory by erecting monitoring posts and constructing roads on Yemeni territory, and alleged that three Yemeni soliders had been killed during clashes earlier in that month. Relations deteriorated further in January 1995, when the two countries failed to renew the 1934 Ta'if agreement (renewable every 20 years), which delineated their *de facto* frontier. Following military clashes between the two sides, and intense mediation by Syria, a joint statement was issued in mid-January 1995, in which Saudi Arabia and Yemen undertook to halt all military activity in the border area; it was subsequently agreed to pursue the demarcation of the disputed border area by a joint committee. In late February the Saudi and Yemeni Governments signed a memorandum of understanding that reaffirmed their commitment to the legitimacy of the Ta'if agreement and provided for the establishment of six joint committees to delineate the land and sea borders and to develop economic and commercial ties. In mid-March, shortly after the Saudi Council of Ministers approved the memorandum of understanding, the joint Saudi-Yemeni military committee, also established by the memorandum, held its first meeting in Riyadh. In June President Saleh of Yemen visited the kingdom, accompanied by a high-ranking delegation. This was the first official Yemeni visit since February 1990. In a joint statement, issued at the end of the visit, the two Governments agreed to promote economic, commercial and cultural co-operation between the two countries. In December 1995 both countries denied that there had been further military clashes on the land border. Meetings of the joint committees continued into 1996, and in July the two countries signed a border security agreement. Despite further reported tensions, negotiations on border demarcation continued in 1997. In November, however, armed clashes on the border resulted in the deaths of three Saudis and one Yemeni border guard. In early 1998 both countries expressed their desire to resolve the border issue, and in May Saudi Arabia began issuing visas to Yemeni expatriate workers for the first time since 1990. During June and July, however, there were further land and sea clashes around a group of Red Sea islands in the disputed maritime border region. In July it was reported that three armed Yemenis had been killed on the island of Duwaima (area 6 sq km), as a result of an exchange of

gunfire with a Saudi border patrol. According to the Saudi authorities, the patrol had acted in self-defence against the men, who were part of a small military presence that Yemen had established on the island during June and early July. The Saudi Government maintained, moreover, that some three-quarters of the island is marked as Saudi territory under the terms of the Ta'if agreement. In late July the Saudi Minister of Foreign Affairs visited his Yemeni counterpart to discuss the escalation of hostilities. A joint military committee meeting was convened in early August, but limited significant progress was made.

At the end of September 1992 trouble flared with Qatar, which accused a Saudi military force of attacking a border post at al-Khofous, killing two soldiers and capturing a third. In October Qatar announced the suspension of the 1965 border agreement with Saudi Arabia, and in the same month it was reported that Qatar was to withdraw its contingent of 200 troops from the GCC 'Peninsula Shield' force, stationed in Kuwait. However, in late December 1992, following mediation by president Hosni Mubarak of Egypt, the Qatari Amir, Sheikh Khalifa, signed an agreement in Medina with King Fahd to establish a committee which was to demarcate the border between the two states by the end of 1994. In late November 1994 Qatar boycotted a GCC ministerial session in Riyadh, in protest at alleged armed incidents on the Saudi-Qatari border earlier in that year (in one of which, it was claimed, a Qatari citizen had been wounded by Saudi border guards); the Saudi Government, however, denied the allegations. In August 1995, following the coup in Qatar, the new Amir, Sheikh Hamad, visited Saudi Arabia to hold talks with King Fahd. Some observers argued that the visit, the Amir's first trip abroad since assuming power, demonstrated Sheikh Hamad's willingness to resume good relations with the kingdom. However, in December relations were again strained when Qatar boycotted the closing session of the annual GCC summit, in protest at the selection of a Saudi national as the new GCC Secretary-General (in preference to a Qatari candidate). In January 1996, in apparent retaliation, Crown Prince Abdullah received Qatar's deposed Amir in Riyadh. None the less, in March Qatar formally announced its acceptance of the new GCC Secretary-General, and in the following month Qatar and Saudi Arabia agreed to precipitate the completion of their border demarcation (initially scheduled for the end of 1994).

In March 1993 the leaders of eight Afghan *mujahidin* factions travelled to Mecca, at the instigation of King Fahd, to discuss their differences. The leaders subsequently ratified the Islamabad peace accord for Afghanistan, which aimed at achieving a peaceful settlement in the region, and which was also signed by King Fahd and the Pakistani Prime Minister, Nawaz Sharif, as co-guarantors. However, with the resurgence of fighting soon after, Saudi Arabia appealed for a mediation effort by the OIC and a UN-sponsored cease-fire plan.

In July 1995 officials from Saudi Arabia and Oman signed documents to demarcate their joint borders. In the same month it was reported that Saudi Arabia and Kuwait had made progress on the demarcation of their mutual sea border.

In September 1994 Saudi Arabia, in common with the other GCC members, agreed to a partial removal of the economic boycott of Israel. Relations with Israel deteriorated in 1997, however, owing to Israeli plans to recommence construction of Jewish settlements in East Jerusalem. At the end of March the Arab League (of which Saudi Arabia is a member) passed a resolution recommending a number of sanctions against Israel. In common with most other Arab League and GCC members, Saudi Arabia did not attend the Middle East and North Africa conference in Doha, Qatar, in November 1997: the boycott was in protest at the presence of a delegation from Israel.

Relations with Iran, which were strained at the beginning of the year owing to allegations of Iranian involvement in the al-Khobar bombing, subsequently improved, and by mid-1997 it was announced that a Saudi–Iranian summit was planned for later in the year. In September Iran Air resumed flights to Saudi Arabia for the first time since the 1979 revolution. The installation of the new Government of President Sayed Muhammad Khatami in Iran, in August 1997, facilitated further *rapprochement*; the new Minister of Foreign Affairs, Kamal

Kharrazi, toured Saudi Arabia and other GCC states in November, and Crown Prince Abdullah attended the Conference of Heads of State of the OIC in Teheran in December. There was considerable speculation that the improvement in relations reflected the desire of the two countries, as the region's principal petroleum producers, to co-operate in maintaining petroleum prices and in efforts to curtail over-production by OPEC members. An Iranian delegation, led by former President Ali Akbar Hashemi Rafsanjani, began a 10-day visit to Saudi Arabia in late February 1998. The formation of a joint ministerial committee for bilateral relations was announced at the end of the visit. Some tensions remained, however, notably with regard to Saudi Arabia's insistence that there should be no political rallies as part of the *Hajj*: Iran had urged its pilgrims to protest against the USA and Israel. In May, in what was widely seen as an attempt to maintain good relations with Iran, the Minister of the Interior stated that the Saudi Government was satisfied that the al-Khobar bombing had been carried out by Saudi nationals with no foreign assistance.

Economy

Revised for this edition by ALAN J. DAY

The economy of Saudi Arabia is dominated by petroleum, of which the country is by far the largest producer within the Organization of the Petroleum Exporting Countries (OPEC). Saudi Arabia has received massive revenues from petroleum exports (particularly since the dramatic increase in international petroleum prices in 1973–74), which it has used in part to finance an ambitious programme of infrastructural development and modernization, as well as far-reaching programmes for health, social and educational purposes. Substantial budgetary allocations have also been made to the country's armed forces and to the purchase of sophisticated weaponry from abroad. Conservative and strictly Islamic in orientation, the Saudi ruling family has consistently favoured a pro-Western, market-orientated economic strategy and has placed great reliance on Western and Japanese expertise for the development of the country's petroleum and other sectors. There remains a substantial expatriate contribution to the management of various economic sectors, although Saudi nationals have come increasingly to the fore, especially in the petroleum and gas industries. Emphasis has been placed, under recent development plans, on the promotion of 'downstream' oil industries, such as refining and petroleum derivatives, and progress has also been made in developing the country's non-oil industries and in overcoming climatic obstacles to agricultural production.

Whereas in the 1970s and early 1980s Saudi Arabia's exports consisted almost entirely of petroleum, by the late 1980s non-oil exports represented more than 10% of total value. A similar pattern was apparent in the structure of gross domestic product (GDP), enhanced by a sharp fall in petroleum production in the mid-1980s. Having achieved an average annual growth rate of 10.6% in the period 1968–80, Saudi Arabia's GDP declined, in real terms, at an average rate of 1.2% per year over the decade 1980–90, largely because petroleum output was reduced from a peak of almost 10m. barrels per day (b/d) in 1980 to 3.6m. b/d in 1985 (see Petroleum, below). Although production rose to more than 5m. b/d in 1988 and 1989, depressed international prices resulted in substantially reduced revenues, with adverse consequences for the current account and national budget, both of which moved into deficit. The situation was transformed by the Gulf crisis of 1990–91, as a result of which Saudi Arabia entered a new period of economic growth. The cost of the conflict to the Saudi Government was substantial, being estimated at between US $50,000m. and $65,000m., with the result that the current account and budget deficits rose sharply in 1990–91. However, partly to compensate for the loss of Iraqi supplies, Saudi Arabia was able to increase its petroleum production to more than 8m. b/d, as international petroleum prices rose sharply because of the crisis. Overall GDP exceeded $100,000m. in 1990, for the first time since 1983, and stood at $108,640m. in 1991. The growth rate of GDP, in real terms, was estimated to be around 1% in 1992. GDP declined by 0.6% in 1993, but increased again by 0.5% in 1994, compared with 10.8% in 1990 and 9.8% in 1991. GDP increased, in real terms, by an annual average of 1.7% in 1990–96. The Government reactivated a range of major projects under the 1990–95 Five-Year Plan, aiming, in particular, at industrial diversification and import substitution. In 1991, according to World Bank figures, Saudi Arabia's gross national product (GNP) per head was $7,820

(assuming a mid-year population of 15.4m.), having declined at an average annual rate of 3.4%, in real terms over the period 1980–91 (when the population increased by an estimated 4.6% per year). During 1985–95, it was estimated, GNP per head declined, in real terms, at an average rate of 1.9% per year. In the same period the population increased by an annual average of 4.0%. In 1995, according to World Bank estimates, GNP, measured at average 1993–95 prices, was $133,540m., equivalent to $7,040 per head.

In 1993 and 1994 the Saudi Government came under increasing pressure to place the public finances on a sounder footing, many years of deficit budgeting having helped to boost the Government's net outstanding domestic debt to an estimated 318,000m. riyals (equivalent to about 76% of annual GDP) in the latter year. An attempt to achieve a balanced budget in 1994 was unsuccessful, despite reductions in planned spending and lengthy delays in payments to contractors. The 1995 budget, introduced at the start of the year, combined further spending cuts with an unprecedented initiative to increase domestic revenues through the imposition of higher charges for a range of state-subsidized goods and services. This tightening of fiscal discipline coincided with favourable external factors in 1995 (notably a year-on-year rise of about 20% in the average oil export price at a time of strong growth in non-oil exports). In the 1996 budget total expenditure was 'frozen' at the 1995 level, while total revenue was expected to fall by nearly 3% if oil export prices declined as forecast. However, oil prices increased in 1996 to their highest average levels since 1990, with the result that total government revenue exceeded the budget forecast by some $12,100m. (34.6%). Most of the additional revenue was used to fund increased spending, and some $5,900m. of payments arrears to domestic creditors were settled by the Government. Saudi Arabia's estimated GDP in 1996 was $136,000m., and the finance ministry estimated the rate of real GDP growth to be 5% in that year, although IMF estimates were lower, at 2.5%.

Estimated GDP in 1997 was $145,600m., said by the Government to represent nominal year-on-year growth of about 7% (the IMF estimated that real GDP had grown by only 2%). The official inflation rate for the year was less than 1%. Oil export prices remained relatively strong in 1997, and the Saudi Arabian balance of payments showed a small current-account surplus for the second successive year. Government revenue was significantly above the budget forecast and was estimated to have slightly exceeded total expenditure for the year. In sharp contrast to the two preceding budgets, Saudi Arabia's 1998 budget seriously over-estimated the level of oil export prices, which in the first half of the year suffered their steepest decline since 1986. It was clear in mid-1998 that efforts were being made throughout the public sector to hold capital and recurrent expenditure below the levels originally budgeted. Some large projects were scaled down or postponed, public-sector wages and recruitment were 'frozen', and payments to contractors were withheld for the maximum allowable settlement periods (often 180 days).

AREA AND POPULATION

The area of Saudi Arabia has been estimated at 2,240,000 sq km (864,869 sq miles), but, since not all of the borders have been defined, it is not possible to arrive at a precise figure. The preliminary results of a census held in September and October 1992 recorded the total population as 16,929,294, of whom 12,304,835 (males 50.5%, females 49.5%) were Saudi Arabian citizens and 4,624,459 (males 70.4%, females 29.6%) were for-eign nationals. The census results reflected the country's dep-endence on foreign contract labour in most areas of employment outside administration, banking and certain state enterprises. By mid-1996 the population was estimated to have increased to 18,836,000. Total civilian employment in Saudi Arabia was estimated at 5,771,800 in 1991 and by 1995 had increased to 5,839,000. It was estimated that more than three-quarters of Saudi Arabia's population resided in urban areas in 1990 (com-pared with less than one-half at the end of the 1960s).

A comprehensive socio-economic survey of the royal capital, Riyadh, published by the Ar-Riyadh Development Authority (ADA) in 1992, provided detailed examples of recent trends in the composition of the urban population and labour force in Saudi Arabia. Between 1986 and 1991, the survey showed, the area of land under development in Riyadh had almost doubled, while the population had likewise risen by 49%, to 2,073,800, comprising 1,334,800 Saudi nationals and 739,000 non-nationals. Net migration into the city accounted for more than one-third of the total population increase over this period. Some 153,000 Egyptians constituted the largest group of foreign nationals in Riyadh in 1991, a large number of Yemenis having been forced to leave the country after Iraq's invasion of Kuwait in 1990. The next largest group of non-nationals in 1991 comprised Syrians, Jordanians and Iraqis. The survey showed that 60% of Riyadh's 1991 population was aged less than 20 years, and just 2% aged more than 60, and that the average age of the Saudi nationals was 17.1 years. Total employment in the city was 584,779 in 1991, nearly 40% higher than in 1986, with Saudi nationals filling 254,182 jobs in 1991. The employment of women (severely restricted by Islamic law and custom) nearly doubled to 83,000 (of whom 72,000 were non-nationals) between 1986 and 1991, virtually all of the employed Saudi females in Riyadh being engaged in professional and technical positions. Riyadh's unskilled work-force (accounting for 28% of all jobs in the city) was almost entirely composed of foreign nationals in 1991, whereas Saudi citizens held nearly 50% of professional and technical jobs and about 73% of clerical jobs.

In February 1995 the Saudi Government stated that more than 100,000 illegal immigrants had left the country in the preceding four months, which had seen strict enforcement of the residency laws. Saudi employers were reminded that they could be fined as much as $13,000 and imprisoned for up to three months for employing illegal workers. In July 1995 the Government announced that its 'strategic goal' was the eventual elimination of expatriate labour, which would entail acceptance by Saudi citizens of employment 'in all kinds of work and at all levels'. In December 1995 the Ministry of the Interior estimated the expatriate population at 6.2m., drawn from 190 different countries. Of these, some 4m. were employees and the remainder were dependants of employees. Expatriate remit-tances abroad totalled 38,100m. riyals ($10,160m.) in the first nine months of 1995. The Government urged the private sector to create 660,000 new jobs for Saudi citizens by the end of the decade. From the beginning of 1996 the Government began to enforce quotas for the employment of Saudi citizens in various sectors of the economy, including some types of manual and clerical employment. The minimum Saudi element which the affected industries were required to employ varied from 5% to 40% of the company work-force. Local private-sector employers held consultations in 1996 with a view to adopting standard contracts of employment and standard salary ranges for dif-ferent occupations, the suggested minimum salaries for Saudi citizens being significantly higher than the suggested maximum salaries for expatriates doing similar work. In December 1996 government figures estimated the expatriate population to be 6.5m. Employment sectors targeted for 'Saudiization' in 1997 included the shipping industry (employing 8% of the total labour force) where in 1996 only 2% of the work-force were Saudi citizens. The number of expatriates employed by the Govern-ment in that year was 104,000 (including 51,000 in the health sector and 44,000 in education), compared with 119,500 in 1992. A three-month amnesty for illegal foreign residents in mid-1997 led to 500,000 people leaving the kingdom; a further 300,000 obtained the necessary work permits. The issuing of entry visas to Yemeni citizens, suspended since the 1990–91 Gulf crisis, was resumed in 1998, although Yemenis were now required to comply with standard Saudi work permit regulations which had previously been waived. More than 400,000 Yemenis were believed to be working in Saudi Arabia in early 1998. In July 1998 the Saudi Government restricted the duration of public-sector employment contracts for expatriates to a maximum of 10 years in most categories of employment.

DEVELOPMENT PLANS

Since 1970 the development of the Saudi economy has been guided by a series of five-year plans. The first Plan (1970–75) was a relatively modest programme costing 56,223m. riyals, of which 32,762m. riyals was allotted to economic and social development. However, after the rise in petroleum revenues in 1973–74 (see Petroleum, below), the Government found itself in possession of vast financial resources and determined to embark on a massive programme of industrialization and moderniza-tion. Hence the second Five-Year Plan (1975–80) provided for expenditure of no less than 498,230m. riyals (about $142,000m.). It was described by the Saudi Minister of Planning, Hisham Nazer, as an 'experiment in social transformation'. The largest single investment item in the second Plan was defence, put at 78,157m. riyals, followed by education at 74,161m. riyals, urban development at 53,328m. riyals and industrial and mineral production at 45,058m. riyals.

A major feature of the second Plan was a project to increase industrial output, creating two new industrial cities, one at Jubail on the Gulf coast and the other at Yanbu on the Red Sea. Development of the two sites was to take 10 years and cost around $70,000m. Jubail was to have three petroleum refineries, six petrochemical plants, an aluminium smelter and a steel mill, as well as support industries, an industrial port and large-scale urban development. Yanbu was planned on a slightly smaller scale: two petroleum refineries, a natural gas processing plant, a petrochemical complex, other lighter industries, an industrial port and a new urban area. The Yanbu industries were to be supplied by an oil pipeline and a gas pipeline across the Arabian peninsula from the Eastern Province. There were also plans to expand existing industrial and commercial sites, at Dammam in particular.

Despite the pessimism of most foreign commentators, the Saudi Arabian Government pursued the goals of the second Plan with great determination, and the results were, on the whole, successful. Although the main industrial projects fell behind schedule, infrastructure grew apace, endowing the country with the basic transport and communications facilities which are required by a modern industrial state.

Consequently, the third Five-Year Plan (1980–85) was intended to shift the emphasis from infrastructure projects to the productive sectors, with particular importance accorded to agriculture and the aim of achieving 'food security' by being less dependent on imported foodstuffs. The Plan stressed the need for manpower training, to reduce reliance on foreign labour, and for Saudi private investors to be encouraged to play a more prominent role in the economy. Planned investment for the five-year period was set at 782,000m. riyals (about $235,000m.), but this total did not include defence spending, the largest item of expenditure under the previous Plan.

The fourth Five-Year Plan (1985–90), published in March 1984, envisaged a total expenditure of 1,000,000m. riyals at current prices, of which 500,000m. riyals were allocated to development projects in the civilian sector. Four essential policy themes underlay the Plan: greater operational efficiency; an emphasis on non-oil revenue-generating activities, particularly industry, agriculture and financial services; a campaign to de-velop private-sector involvement and initiatives; and the need for further economic and social integration among the countries of the Co-operation Council of the Arab States of the Gulf (Gulf Co-operation Council—GCC). Within the details of the Plan, considerable emphasis was also given to raising desalination capacity, the expansion of irrigation and power facilities, a review of subsidies, the reduction of expatriate labour, the development of new industrial estates, and the expansion of Saudi Arabia's health services.

By mid-1988, the fourth Development Plan was widely considered to have fallen short of its targets, mainly as a result of the steep decline in oil revenues following the collapse in oil prices in 1986. The implementation of many projects, in particular those involving public utilities, had been delayed.

Direct military spending was to receive 312,500m. riyals of the fourth Plan's allocation, sustaining the emphasis already given to defence by the Government. As a consequence of the Iran–Iraq War, large sums of money had already been spent on defence, in particular on the Peace Shield defence system, which was announced in 1985. In the early part of that year the Boeing Aerospace Corpn of the USA was chosen to complete the project at a cost of $3,700m. The programme would provide a computerized command, control and communications system for Saudi Arabia's air defences. In July 1991 the Hughes Aircraft Co of the USA was awarded a contract to complete the Peace Shield air defence project, and so replaced the original contractor, Boeing. The scheme was estimated to cost $837m. Boeing was replaced because of substantial delays in implementing the programme. In early 1986 another major defence contract, worth about £7,500m., was signed with the British Government for the supply of 48 *Tornado* fighter-bomber aircraft from the European Panavia consortium, 30 *Hawk* trainer aircraft from British Aerospace and 30 *Pilatus* trainers. In July 1988 a new agreement, which more than doubled the value of the orginal contract, was signed. It included a revised £1,000m. offset programme which involved bilateral investments by Saudi and British companies. In addition to aircraft, the agreement envisaged the supply of ships and the construction of two huge airbases. It is expected that the provisions of the agreement will not be fulfilled until the late 1990s.

The fifth Five-Year Development Plan (1990–95) envisaged a total expenditure of 753,000m. riyals. Owing to the crisis in the Gulf following the invasion of Kuwait by Iraq, Saudi Arabia increased military spending, and about 34% (255,000m. riyals) of total expenditure in the fifth Plan was to be allocated to defence, with education receiving 19% and health and social services 12%.

The six major themes of the 1990–95 Plan were: the expansion of government revenue, in particular from non-oil sources; increased reliance on the private sector; further job opportunities and training for the Saudi Arabian labour force; import substitution and the promotion of exports; the diversification of economic activities into non-oil areas; and a balanced development of the regions. Under the Plan, the encouragement of Saudi Arabian industry, notably in the construction sector, was to be reinforced by the '30% rule', according to which at least 30% of the value of government contracts has to be awarded to Saudi Arabian companies.

A development plan for the period 1995–2000, designed to achieve average annual growth of 3.8%, was approved by the Council of Ministers in July 1995. Priority was to be given to measures to balance the national budget by the end of the planning period (including reductions in direct and indirect price subsidies); to the development of a privatization programme; to increasing the proportion of Saudi nationals in the private-sector work-force; and to bringing about greater private-sector participation in infrastructural and other development projects. The planning ministry published a survey in 1996 which forecast average sectoral growth rates during the 1995–2000 planning period of 3.8% per annum for oil and gas and 8.3% per annum for petrochemicals.

An IMF assessment of the Saudi economy, prepared in early 1995, advocated a radical restructuring of established institutions and practices through privatization, deregulation and modernization measures. In the IMF's view, an early transition to an efficient market economy would attract new foreign investment to Saudi Arabia while encouraging repatriation of part of the estimated $300,000m. of private Saudi capital held abroad. The IMF saw a pressing need for a new inflow of funds following an estimated 46% reduction in the state's overseas assets since the 1990–91 Gulf conflict. The IMF estimated the nominal end-1994 value of the Saudi Government's overseas assets as $64,900m., but noted that more than one-third of this total comprised assets needed to cover the issue of the Saudi currency. About one-half of the remaining assets were currently committed against letters of credit, while many of the uncommitted assets had a paper value only (e.g. because Saudi Arabia's claims on certain poorer countries were not recoverable in practice). Saudi Arabia's existing capital spending commitments were estimated by the IMF as $80,000m., including $30,000m. for US defence equipment, more than $20,000m. for British defence equipment and (under a contract signed in November 1994) $3,700m. for French defence equipment. Major non-military commitments included $6,000m. to re-equip the state airline; $4,000m. to update and expand the telecommunications system; and $10,000m. to install additional power-generation and water-desalination capacity.

AGRICULTURE AND FISHING

Agriculture (including forestry and fishing), contributed only 6.3% of GDP in 1996, although the sector employed an estimated 13% of the working population in that year. Its contribution to GDP increased from 3.3% in 1984, mainly as the result of the decline in revenue from petroleum that Saudi Arabia began to experience in the mid-1980s. During the third Five-Year Plan (1980–85), the output of the agricultural sector expanded, in real terms, at an average of 8.7% per year, compared with its projected growth rate of 5.4%. Agricultural production increased by an annual average of 7.4% in 1985–93; however, in 1994 output declined by 11.7%. Cultivation is confined to oases and to irrigated regions, which comprise only 2% of the total land area. About 39% of land is used for low-grade grazing. In 1988 the Ministry of Agriculture and Water reported that, over the previous 10 years, the area of cultivated land in Saudi Arabia had increased to approximately 2.5m. ha, at a time when the agricultural labour force was falling in numbers. A considerable area of this land lies fallow, however, and only about 600,000 ha are under regular cultivation. In mid-1988 a total of 776,111 ha of agricultural land was distributed amongst the kingdom's farmers. The annual harvest of wheat increased from 142,000 metric tons in 1979/80 to a record level of 3.9m. tons in 1990/91, of which 1.7m. tons were exported. The Grain Silos and Flour Mills Organization (GSFMO), the state-owned body responsible for overseeing the cereals sector, has storage capacity for about 2m. tons. These increases in production have been heavily subsidized by the Government, which, through the GSFMO, paid farmers about $1,000 per ton of wheat produced in the 1984 season; approximately six times the average world price. In 1985 a plan to reduce the volume of wheat bought by the GSFMO to 60% received a hostile response and was abandoned. Levels of subsidy subsequently declined. In 1988/89 farmers were paid $533 per ton to produce wheat that was available on the world market for $120. However, government policy concerning the reduction of subsidies remained cautious, in order to maintain the stability of the agricultural sector and ensure its continued contribution to the diversification of the economy. Production of sorghum fell from 110,000 tons in 1979/80 to 63,000 tons in 1981/82, but recovered to an estimated 87,000 tons in each of the following two seasons, and by 1996 had risen to an estimated 210,000 tons. Levels of barley and millet production have remained low. Indeed, imports of barley have become a new problem, with record levels of barley being imported in 1986/87. A system of subsidies was introduced for domestic barley cultivation in 1986, in an attempt to reduce imports of barley, in particular from the USA and the United Kingdom, which reached 1,434,000 tons in the year to March 1987, compared with 506,000 tons in the year to March 1986. In early 1989 the remaining import subsidy of 100 riyals per ton was abolished, despite a barley harvest in 1988 estimated at only 187,000 tons. In an attempt to increase the barley harvest, the Government required the kingdom's six large publicly-owned farms to cultivate one-third of their crop-land with barley. By 1990/91 the annual output of barley had risen to more than 400,000 tons. In 1987 Saudi Arabia became the world's sixth-largest exporter of cereals. By 1990 output from Saudi Arabia's flour mills had reached almost 1m. tons per year, compared with 748,000 tons in 1985. In 1993 a noticeable tightening of government agricultural policy—enforced partly through deliberate delays in payments to some cereal farmers—reduced the wheat harvest to 3.6m. tons (down from a record

4.07m. tons in 1992), while increasing the barley harvest to 1.1m. tons (up from 406,000 tons in 1992). In 1995, according to unofficial figures, 2m. tons of wheat and 1.2m. tons of barley were harvested. In 1993 exports of wheat had totalled nearly 2.2m. tons, while imports of barley (mainly for livestock feed) totalled 3.7m. tons. The GSFMO had announced in August 1993 that it would buy no wheat in 1994 from the six main commercial producers, while imposing quota restrictions on purchases from smaller commercial farmers, who would be entitled to an 'incentive' price of $400 per ton. The aggregate government subsidy to wheat farmers was estimated to have reached $1,300m. per year before the production cutbacks started. The GSFMO budget for 1994 was 2,697.8m. riyals, compared with 3,336.2m. riyals in 1993. At the end of 1994 the Government announced that its planned levels of wheat purchases from farmers were 2.3m. tons in 1995/96 and 2m. tons in 1996/97, with wheat exports being discontinued in 1996/97. Thereafter, annual wheat production would be maintained in balance with the prevailing level of domestic consumption (expected to be around 1.8m. tons annually in coming years), with a limited margin of surplus production for the country's strategic stockpile of grain. However, the estimated yield of the 1996 wheat harvest was 500,000 tons below the 1.7m. tons forecast demand for that year, partly as a result of reduced plantings by farmers experiencing delays in payment. Any consequent shortfall was expected to be covered by drawing down local stocks.

Watermelons, tomatoes, dates and grapes are produced in significant numbers. In 1996 the Government embarked on the third phase of a programme to combat red beetle infestation in date palms (which had caused the European Union—EU—to ban the importation of Saudi dates). Some 850,000 trees were to be cut down over a period of four months, bringing the total number felled since the launch of the programme to more than 1m. In 1998 the Government allocated 74.25m. riyals for the purchase of 21,000 tons of locally-grown dates (most of which were to be distributed to the poor).

The importance of developing the agricultural sector as a means of reducing imports has been emphasized by the Government. In 1987 an increase in local output reduced food imports to 65% of total food requirements, compared with 83% in 1980. The cost of imported food declined from $4,669m. in 1984 to $2,799m. in 1987 and increased to $5,023m. in 1990 and $5,500m. in 1991. By 1994 the cost of food imports had fallen to $3,035m. At the start of 1998 the Government banned imports of specified fruits and vegetables from five countries—Egypt, Jordan, Lebanon, Syria and Turkey—which did not themselves permit the import of Saudi Arabian fruit and vegetables. Syria had been an important supplier of Saudi Arabia's tomato imports (worth $53m. in 1996), while Turkey and Egypt had provided most of Saudi Arabia's onion imports (worth $38m. in 1996). In February 1998 the Government announced new import tariffs on food products to protect local farmers. It subsequently banned the importation of 10 types of vegetable during Saudi Arabia's own harvesting seasons for the crops concerned.

Saudi Arabia is subject to important natural limitations on the development of agriculture, principally the scarcity of water. Agriculture accounts for 89% of water demand in the kingdom. The Government has initiated an ambitious programme to improve the country's water supply, including surveys for underground water resources (20 main aquifers had been established by 1983, nine of which were being exploited), construction of dams, irrigation and drainage networks, combined with distribution of fallow land, settlement of bedouin and the introduction of mechanization. The eventual aim of the programme is to raise agricultural production to the level of near self-sufficiency in all foods. Consequently, budgetary allocations for the agricultural sector have increased considerably in recent years. The third Five-Year Plan (1980–85) projected spending on agriculture at 7,975m. riyals, and on water (mainly desalination plants) at no less than 52,979m. riyals, although much of this was to be used for developing urban water supplies. Surveys that were conducted in the 1960s indicated a potential for greatly increasing agricultural output by means of irrigation. Under the 1985–90 Plan, 50,000 ha of land were to be drained or irrigated, and 8,000 ha were to be converted into pasture land.

In 1981, according to FAO estimates, 395,000 ha of land were irrigated. Important projects which have been undertaken by the Government include the al-Hasa irrigation scheme, the Faisal Model Settlement scheme, the Wadi Gizan and Najran dam projects and the Abha dam. The al-Hasa irrigation and drainage scheme, inaugurated in December 1971, was completed over five years at a cost of 260m. riyals. It is the country's largest agricultural scheme and about 50,000 people benefit from it. The Faisal Model Settlement scheme, which cost 100m. riyals, has involved extensive land reclamation and irrigation, and provided permanent farmland and housing for 1,000 bedouin families. The Wadi Gizan dam, inaugurated in March 1971, has a reservoir with a capacity of 71m. cu m of water and was built at a cost of 42m. riyals. A second dam at Wadi Najran, completed in 1980, has added a further 68m. cu m to water storage capacity in the Gizan Najran area. The Abha dam, in the Asir region, was opened in April 1974, with a reservoir capacity of 2.4m. cu m. In all, the kingdom operated a total of 104 dams in 1983.

Apart from lack of water, the major constraint on Saudi agriculture is shortage of labour, as the population is drawn away from rural areas by the attractions of urban development, and most farm workers are expatriates. The Government is countering the drift to the towns by improving rural facilities, but the future of Saudi agriculture must lie in capital-intensive, large-scale farming, highly mechanized and requiring only a small work-force. A major success has been achieved with dairy farming, using the most modern technical expertise from Sweden, Denmark and Ireland. In 1988 Masstock Saudia, a joint venture established by Ireland and Saudi Arabia in 1976, had 12 farms throughout the kingdom, and a herd of 11,000 cows, yielding an average 7,900 litres of milk per year. The Saudi Arabian Agriculture and Dairy Co (SAADCO) was formed in 1980, and by the end of 1984 had 15,000 cows and a 60 sq km farm at al-Kharj. By 1986 Saudi Arabia was self-sufficient in eggs and broiler chickens, and by 1991 it was self-sufficient in fresh milk and *laban* (a yoghurt drink), milk production being 550m. litres in 1990/91. Subsidized milk powder from the EU constitutes the main competition to local production.

Government encouragement to farmers is substantial. Interest-free loans are available through the Agricultural Bank, set up in 1963, and a total of 9,209 loans, valued at 1,551m. riyals were disbursed by the bank in 1985/86. Chemical fertilizers, domestic or imported, are distributed at half-price. There are also large subsidies available to local farmers for the purchase of farm machinery (amounting to 45% of the total cost of the item), irrigation pumps and imported rearing stock. In response to these incentives, the agricultural sector has made rapid progress in recent years, and grew at over 6% per year in the early 1980s. As a result of declining revenue from petroleum in the early 1980s, expenditure on agriculture was reduced. In the 1985/86 financial year the total amount of loans by the Agricultural Bank was 33% lower than in the previous year, and less than one-half the level of four years earlier. Total planned lending under the fifth Development Plan was set at 14,411m. riyals, compared with 61,000m. riyals disbursed during the third Plan.

Criticism of Saudi Arabia's agricultural policy has concentrated on the high depletion rate of the non-renewable fossil aquifers from which farmers draw most of their water supply. It was estimated in 1992 that the water table in Qassim (the principal wheat-growing area) had fallen by 100 m in the previous decade. The export of subsidized wheat has also been criticized, and it has been calculated that dairy farming in Saudi Arabia uses 1,500 litres of water per litre of milk production. In March 1997 the Minister of Agriculture and Water outlined the Government's progress in implementing more responsible policies. Cutbacks in the production of cereal crops (see above) had reduced the extraction of groundwater for irrigation from 6,990m. cu m in 1992 to 1,850m. cu m in 1996, while 500 cattlefeed projects had been phased out because of their high water requirement. In 1998 the authorities were studying the feasibility of installing water meters on artesian wells used by agricultural enterprises. The Ministry of Agriculture and Water planned to spend 1,100m. riyals on water development projects in that year.

The fishing industry has grown in recent years, and in 1988 Saudi Arabia's total catch was 46,773 tons, an amount which satisfied about one-half of total local demand. The Saudi Fisheries Co (SFC) recorded a net profit of 33.1m. riyals in 1988. Sales increased in that year by 22%, in comparison with 1987, and included exports to seven countries. The company announced an increase in sales from 221m. riyals in 1989 to 235.5m. riyals in 1990. It recorded a minor decrease in net profit, to 30.2m. riyals, owing to the crisis in the Gulf region, which forced 3m. riyals of extra expenditure to be incurred on emergency measures. New projects launched by the company included a facility to convert fish to fodder, a processing factory and the purchase of shrimping vessels. The SFC reported in June 1992 that stocks of shrimps in the Gulf had been almost destroyed by pollution, caused by the Gulf hostilities. The SFC recorded losses of 18.4m. riyals in 1993. Saudi Arabia's total catch in 1993 was 49,420 tons and by 1995 this had increased to 54,486 tons. In late 1995 another Saudi company signed a joint-venture agreement with a US aquaculture business to establish an indoor salt-water shrimp farm in the kingdom's Eastern Province. Costing some $60m., the farm would comprise 22 nursery buildings, each with an annual production capacity of as much as 1,800 tons of prime tiger shrimps. The venture was scheduled to begin operations by early 1997.

PETROLEUM

The most important industry in Saudi Arabia is the production of crude petroleum and petroleum products. Saudi Arabia is the major petroleum-producer in OPEC, accounting for 31.3% of the organization's output in 1997, and is one of the three principal producers in the world, with 12.9% of global oil output in 1997, ahead of the USA (10.9%) and Russia (8.8%). Saudi Arabia's proven reserves of petroleum at the start of 1998 totalled 261,500m. barrels (25.2% of the world total and 32.8% of the OPEC total), sufficient to maintain production at 1997 levels for 79.5 years. Production is from 14 major oilfields, in particular Ghawar, Abqaiq, Safaniya and Berri. Ghawar is generally accepted as the world's largest oilfield, while Safaniya is the world's largest offshore field. The kingdom also enjoys equal rights with Kuwait to the petroleum reserves of the Saudi Arabia-Kuwait Neutral Zone, which totalled 5,000m. barrels at the start of 1993.

In 1933 a concession was granted to Standard Oil Co of California to explore for petroleum in Saudi Arabia. The operating company, the Arabian-American Oil Co (Aramco), began exploration in that year, and discovered petroleum in commercial quantities in 1938. By the end of the Second World War, four oilfields had been discovered, and the necessary facilities had been established to satisfy post-war demands for crude petroleum and refined products. Other US companies gradually acquired shares in Aramco, bringing the ownership structure in 1948 to: Standard Oil 30%, Texaco 30%, Exxon 30% and Mobil 10%.

In November 1962 the Government created the General Petroleum and Mineral Organization (PETROMIN) as the instrument for increasing state participation in the petroleum and gas industries. In accordance with the action of other Arab petroleum-producing states, the Saudi Government acquired a 25% share in Aramco in January 1973. A 100% takeover of the company was agreed in 1980 (for the subsequent creation of Saudi Aramco, see below).

The expansion of Saudi Arabia's petroleum output in the 1960s and 1970s was spectacular. Production increased from about 62m. metric tons (equivalent to 1.3m. b/d) in 1960 to 178m. tons (3.8m. b/d) in 1970, and to 412m. tons (8.5m. b/d) in 1974. This growth in output was accompanied by rising prices for petroleum, culminating in the huge increases of October and December 1973, which almost quadrupled the cost per barrel. The Saudi Government's petroleum revenues increased dramatically, from $1,214m. in 1970 to $22,573m. in 1974. The price rises reflected OPEC's collective will to exploit a favourable market situation. The industrialized countries' fear of a shortfall in petroleum supplies placed them completely at the mercy of OPEC.

After the events of 1973–74, however, Saudi Arabia emerged as a powerful conservative and pro-Western influence in OPEC, using its high potential output to hold down the price of petroleum. In the depressed market of 1975, the country's production of crude petroleum declined to 344m. tons (7.1m. b/d), but in

1977 it rose to a new peak of 455m. tons (9.2m. b/d), with government revenues at $36,540m. This increase in output resulted from a disagreement within OPEC over pricing. By raising output, Saudi Arabia put pressure on the market to depress prices, because countries charging higher prices would find it difficult to sell their petroleum. A compromise on OPEC pricing policy was reached in July 1977.

For most of 1978, the supply of petroleum was plentiful, prices remained steady, and Saudi Arabia kept its production below 8.5m. b/d. With the outbreak of the Iranian revolution in late 1978, however, the situation was transformed. To compensate for the Iranian shortfall, Saudi Arabia increased production to more than 10m. b/d. The country's total output for 1978 was 410m. tons (8.3m. b/d), with government revenue from petroleum reaching $32,234m., but 919m. barrels were produced in the last quarter alone. Output was maintained at around 9.5m. b/d for most of 1979, but prices increased sharply, as intense anxiety over petroleum supplies seized the industrialized West. Despite Saudi efforts, the price of the country's petroleum rose rapidly. The price of one grade, Saudi light crude, increased from $13.3 per barrel at the start of 1979 to $28 per barrel in May 1980, the most rapid rise since 1973–74. Since Saudi Arabia's total output for 1979 was 470m. tons (9.5m. b/d) and prices doubled in the course of the year, government revenues from petroleum reached a new peak of $48,435m.

The Saudi Government raised production in the last quarter of 1980 to 10.3m. b/d to compensate for output lost as a consequence of the Iran–Iraq War, giving a record total production for the year of 493m. tons (9.99m. b/d), which remains the peak output level for any one year. Prices continued to drift upwards, Saudi light crude reaching $32 per barrel by the end of 1980, and total government revenues from petroleum in that year were $84,466m., which represented an increase of 74% over the previous year's figure. During the first nine months of 1981, however, Saudi efforts to hold down prices finally began to have a real effect. Slack demand in the West, combined with the continued high level of Saudi output (maintained at more than 10m. b/d), made it difficult to sell petroleum at the official level and impossible for prices to rise any further. In October 1981, in an attempt to restore a unified price structure, Saudi Arabia induced OPEC to accept a package involving a $2 rise in the market price to $34 per barrel, accompanied by a cut in Saudi output to a ceiling of 8.5m. b/d. Total Saudi output for 1981 fell marginally, to 491m. tons (9.98m. b/d), but government revenues from petroleum reached a record level of about $102,000m.

During 1982 world demand for petroleum continued to fall and, after a further OPEC meeting in March, the Saudi Government declared a new upper limit of 7.5m. b/d for the country's production. In reality, output had already dropped below that figure. Total production for 1982 was 328m. tons, an average of only 6.6m. b/d, and the petroleum sector's output, as a proportion of real GDP, declined by 36.1% during the year 1982/83. Finally, in March 1983, OPEC bowed to market pressure. The member states agreed to reduce the market price by 15%, to $29 per barrel, and to limit total OPEC output to 17.5m. b/d. Total Saudi output for 1983 was 256m. tons (5.2m. b/d), and in 1984 production levels fell once again, to 233m. tons (4.8m. b/d), yielding revenues of $46,000m. Since 1984 Saudi Arabia has been involved in barter agreements, whereby petroleum is exchanged for other goods, particularly aircraft and military equipment.

Saudi Arabia's petroleum is mostly exported by tanker from terminals on the Gulf coast. In 1981 PETROMIN completed construction of a Trans-Arabian pipeline to Yanbu on the Red Sea coast. The pipeline, designed to carry some 1.9m. b/d (mainly for export from a Red Sea tanker terminal), shortens the export route to Western Europe and North America by about 3,500 km. A new pipeline, linking the Iraqi oilfields to the Trans-Arabian pipeline, was completed in 1985, allowing Iraq and Saudi Arabia to share the pipeline until 1989, when a direct pipeline, with a capacity of 1.6m. b/d, was planned to link Iraqi oilfields to Yanbu. A former 1,200-km line from the Saudi oilfields to Lebanon and Jordan is no longer in use.

In the 1980s Saudi Arabia acted as a 'swing producer' within OPEC, adjusting its own production levels in order to keep overall production by OPEC member states within the organization's recommended limits. However, the lack of agreement among OPEC members on pricing and production, and the loss of revenue resulting from Saudi Arabia's much lower production levels, culminated in a major change of policy in late 1985. Saudi Arabia abandoned its former role and increased sales, with petroleum exports in the last quarter of 1985 at their highest since the end of 1983. Nevertheless, total production in 1985 was only 173m. tons (3.6m. b/d), yielding revenues of $27,000m. At the end of 1985 OPEC decided to end its official quota policy and to seek a greater share of the world market, to offset falling prices. As a result of a surge in production, international prices for crude petroleum fell precipitously in 1986, dipping below $10 per barrel in July. Accordingly, although Saudi Arabian output in 1986 rose to 251m. tons (5.2m. b/d), oil revenues fell to $20,000m.

In October 1986 the veteran Minister of Petroleum and Mineral Resources, Sheikh Ahmad Zaki Yamani, was dismissed by King Fahd. He was replaced by Sheikh Hisham Nazer, the former Minister of Planning, and a policy aimed at limiting production and increasing prices was implemented. The policy was proposed by Sheikh Nazer at an OPEC meeting held in December, whereby a target price for crude petroleum of $18 per barrel was to be supported by an arrangement ensuring strict output quotas, with a production ceiling for the first half of 1987 of 15.8m. b/d, a reduction of 7.25% in each country's quota compared with December. Saudi Arabia, which was allotted a nominal quota of 4,133,000 b/d, was again effectively the 'swing producer'. The new production agreement came into effect on 1 January 1987. In practice, however, production in the first half of 1987 was consistently below the ceiling and prices stabilized at slightly above the reference level of $18 per barrel.

In June 1987 OPEC members agreed to maintain the reference price of $18 per barrel in the second half of that year, but to increase their collective production by 800,000 b/d, to 16.6m. b/d. Under the revised arrangements, Saudi Arabia was allocated a quota of 4,343,000 b/d, its actual average output in 1987 being close to the quota, at 4.36m. b/d (annual production 212m. tons), yielding revenues of $25,000m. The agreement was extended for further six-month periods at OPEC meetings in December 1987 and May 1988. The ceiling for the other 12 members of OPEC was 15.06m. b/d. However, consistent over-production caused a renewed decline in the price of crude petroleum, which fell below $12 per barrel in September 1988. Total Saudi Arabian production in 1988 rose to 257m. tons (5.26m. b/d), but revenues fell to around $20,000m. In November 1988 OPEC agreed to form a committee, comprising representatives of eight member states, to monitor the production quotas of all members and to supervise adherence to the agreed production levels. At the same meeting OPEC agreed a collective production quota of 18.5m. b/d, of which Saudi Arabia's share was to be 4,524,000 b/d, to take effect from January 1989 and to operate for the first six months of the year. At the mid-1989 OPEC conference the production ceiling was raised to 19.5m. b/d, and in November quotas were redistributed within a new ceiling of 22m. b/d. Total Saudi Arabian output for the year was slightly reduced, at 256m. tons (5.2m. b/d), with revenues at $24,000m.

The OPEC meeting in Geneva in July 1990 was held in an atmosphere of increasing tension, caused by Iraq's threats of military action against those countries—principally the UAE and Kuwait—which it had accused of exceeding their production quotas. At the meeting Iraq sought to raise OPEC's minimum reference price for crude petroleum to $25 per barrel, but, in the event, OPEC's ministerial council adopted a price of $21 per barrel and fixed a new production ceiling of 22.5m. b/d for the remainder of 1990. Quotas for individual countries remained unchanged (Saudi Arabia's at 5.38m. b/d), except that of the UAE, which was raised to 1.5m. b/d.

Prior to the full OPEC meeting in July 1990, the five principal Gulf petroleum producers had met in Jeddah and agreed to curb over-production, thus facilitating the agreement that was reached in July. Prices had increased by about $2 per barrel as a result of the Jeddah meeting. Demand for OPEC crude petroleum was forecast at more than 22.5m. b/d for the second half of 1990, and it was hoped that restrained OPEC production would allow surplus supplies to be absorbed. However, by mid-August 1990 'panic buying' of crude petroleum, following Iraq's

invasion of Kuwait at the beginning of the month, had caused 'spot' market prices to almost double. On 20 August Saudi Arabia announced that it would increase its production of crude petroleum by 2m. b/d unless OPEC agreed to hold an emergency meeting. Saudi Arabia claimed that the Geneva agreement was now obsolete. Petroleum prices had risen to about $28 per barrel, and OPEC production—since Iraqi and Kuwaiti supplies could no longer be marketed—was some 4m. b/d below the ceiling agreed at the July meeting.

Saudi Arabia was initially concerned that soaring petroleum prices would damage the world economy and, in turn, weaken future demand. While stressing its willingness to achieve an agreement within the framework of OPEC, Saudi Arabia left no doubt that it would act unilaterally if an emergency meeting was not held, and also urged the major Western countries to draw upon their strategic reserves of petroleum in order to stabilize the market. An emergency meeting of OPEC was duly held in August 1990, at which it was agreed to allow members to increase production rates above the quotas fixed in July. Iraq and Libya were absent from the meeting, and Iran refused to endorse the agreement. By early September petroleum prices had risen above $30 per barrel in London and New York. Saudi Arabia was reported to have increased production to 7.4m. b/d, and to be exporting more than 7m. b/d. Despite OPEC's decision to increase production, the fear of hostilities in the Gulf caused prices to rise above $40 per barrel for the first time in almost a decade. Over 1990 as a whole, Saudi Arabian production averaged 6.4m. b/d (annual production 312m. tons), producing revenues of $31,500m.

OPEC quotas remained in effective suspension throughout 1991, and Saudi Arabia took advantage of the absence of Iraqi and Kuwaiti petroleum to increase its output to an average of 8.2m. b/d (annual production was almost 400m. tons, the highest level since 1981), of which only 1m. b/d was for domestic use. Although international petroleum prices eventually fell, they remained higher than the pre-crisis level, so that Saudi oil revenues rose to $43,450m. in 1991. In mid-February 1992 Saudi Arabia protested at an OPEC decision to allocate a ceiling of 7,887,000 b/d to the kingdom for the remainder of the year, demanding that it be allotted a minimum quota of 8m. b/d. In the event, Saudi crude oil production remained significantly above 8m. b/d throughout 1992, its final average for the year being 8,377,800 b/d. Saudi Arabia accepted an OPEC ceiling of 8,395,000 b/d for the first quarter of 1993, and 8m. b/d thereafter. Average oil export earnings were estimated at $3,568m. per month for the first half of 1993 and around $3,040m. per month for the remainder of the year, when prices weakened significantly. Saudi Arabia's 1993 crude oil production averaged 8,131,700 b/d, having been cut back to fractionally over 8m. b/d by the last quarter of the year. Output averaged 8,006,700 b/d in 1994 and 8,018,000 b/d in 1995. In 1996 Saudi Arabia's output of crude oil averaged 8,150,000 b/d, while the kingdom's total oil production (including natural gas liquids) averaged 8,920,000 b/d.

Prior to the stimulus to its petroleum industry that the Gulf crisis provided, Saudi Arabia had undertaken a major reorganization of state structures responsible for the sector. This included the conversion of PETROMIN into a holding company and the creation of several affiliated operating companies with responsibilities for exploration, refining, marketing and shipping. The first of these, Petrolube, was established in February 1988, to operate the lubricating oil blending plants in Jeddah, Riyadh and Jubail. The most important of the successor companies was the Saudi Arabian Marketing and Refining Co (SAMAREC), formed in 1989 to manage petroleum refining and distribution for the Saudi domestic market and to handle state exports of refined products.

In April 1989 the Saudi Arabian Oil Co (Saudi Aramco) was formed to take control of the nationalized Aramco assets. It is an independent enterprise with the right to establish companies and initiate projects. In addition, a new Supreme Oil Council was formed to take responsibility for the country's petroleum industry. Chaired by King Fahd, the council's members include private businessmen as well as government ministers: an indication of the Government's determination to involve the private sector in the management of the economy. In June 1993 the Government effectively abolished SAMAREC, and placed its operations, together with other PETROMIN oil interests, under the management of Saudi Aramco.

In June 1989 Saudi Aramco announced that three major development projects would be proceeding as planned: the expansion of the east-west pipeline to carry crude petroleum (Petroline); the upgrading of facilities at the Safaniya and Uthmaniya oilfields; and the development of two wet crude handling and gas-gathering facilities at the onshore Uthmaniya field. The expansion of Petroline's overall capacity from 3.6m. to 4.8m. b/d (completed in mid-1993) was the largest scheme to have been undertaken in the petroleum sector for several years. In the same month it was stated that new oilfields in the al-Hawtah region, south of Riyadh, were commercially viable, and that further exploration would be undertaken; subsequent evaluation indicated a production capacity of up to 170,000 b/d of high-quality crude. In June 1991 a US company, McDermott International, was awarded a contract for work on offshore pipelines at the Zuluf oilfield, as part of the kingdom's plan to raise petroleum production capacity to 10m. b/d by the mid-1990s. By mid-1994 sustainable production capacity had reached the target level, representing a very substantial margin of excess capacity in current market conditions.

Saudi Aramco nevertheless decided in May 1995 to initiate a major development programme in the Shayba oilfield, situated on the border with Abu Dhabi, some 600 km. from the closest gathering facility in the established Saudi oilfields. Discovered in 1968, the Shayba field contained estimated reserves of up to 7,000m. barrels of very light (40°–42° API gravity) crude containing only 0.7% sulphur. Development of the field had first been considered in 1989, since when the pattern of world oil demand had undergone a significant shift towards premium-priced light crudes. Saudi Aramco expected this trend to continue, assuring the company of a relatively rapid recovery of its development costs (estimated at $2,500m.) when the field was brought into production. Meanwhile, Saudi Aramco's policy of reducing production of heavy crude in favour of lighter grades was facilitated by the inauguration of the al-Hawtah field in late 1994, with a production capacity of 150,000 b/d of 44°–50° API 'super-light' crude. An adjacent 'super-light' field was discovered in early 1995. The Haradh oilfield, containing 34° API crude, was due to begin producing in 1996, with an initial capacity of 300,000 b/d (to be doubled by late 1998).

In 1997 Saudi Arabia's output of crude oil (excluding Neutral Zone output) averaged 8,358,000 b/d, while total Saudi Arabian oil production (including natural gas liquids and the Saudi share of Neutral Zone crude oil output) averaged 9,375,000 b/d. Saudi Arabia's OPEC crude oil production quota, which had stood at 8m. b/d since April 1993, was raised to 8,761,000 b/d at the start of January 1998 in line with an OPEC agreement on 9.5% quota increases for most member states. World oil prices subsequently fell sharply (touching their lowest levels for 12 years in 'spot' trading in March 1998) against a background of depressed demand in key Asian import markets, prompting OPEC members to undertake a fresh review of quotas. Under revised OPEC quota agreements (supported by several non-OPEC exporting countries) Saudi Arabia introduced a reduced crude oil output ceiling of 8,461,000 b/d with effect from the start of April 1998, with a further reduction of 225,000 b/d from the start of July 1998. Estimates of Saudi Arabia's average crude oil production in the second quarter of 1998 gave Saudi Aramco's own-account output as 8,250,000 b/d (including 150,000 b/d of natural gas liquids produced at the well-head); Saudi Aramco's Abu Saafa output (produced for the benefit of Bahrain) as 150,000 b/d; and the Saudi share of Neutral Zone output as 290,000 b/d. Saudi Aramco's own-account production comprises 59% light crude, 16% medium crude, 12% heavy crude, 11% extra-light crude and 2% super-light crude. The recently developed Shayba oilfield was scheduled to start commercial production in August 1998 and to reach its full capacity of 500,000 b/d by the end of the year. With Saudi Arabia continuing to make full use of its agreed OPEC production ceiling, the proportion of extra-light crude in Saudi Aramco's output was set to rise in the second half of 1998 as output of other grades was cut back to accommodate the Shayba output. Saudi Aramco decided in June 1998 (while prospective contractors were drawing up tenders for the work) to postpone implementation of a project to double the production capacity

of the Haradh oilfield. There were no other 'upstream' oil development projects on Saudi Aramco's current planning agenda.

INDUSTRY, GAS AND MINING

Saudi Arabia is making determined efforts to achieve major industrial development, financed mainly by government revenues from petroleum, under the aegis of successive development plans (see Development Plans, above). The cornerstone of the industrialization programme is the construction of refineries and processing industries to exploit the country's huge reserves of petroleum and natural gas (Saudi Arabia had published proven gas reserves of 5,400,000m. cu m at the end of 1997). The major projects are being undertaken as joint ventures between the State and foreign companies.

Following its absorption of SAMAREC in mid-1993, Saudi Aramco took charge of the management of the entire range of state petroleum-refining and product-marketing interests. As well as handling the marketing of products from Saudi Aramco's Ras Tanura plant, SAMAREC had operated refineries at Jeddah, Riyadh and Yanbu and had been responsible for marketing the state share of output from export-oriented refineries at Jubail, Yanbu and Rabigh. Saudi Arabia's installed refinery capacity totalled 1,865,000 b/d in 1992, an increase of 1m. b/d since 1984. At the refineries' aggregate throughput level of about 1.5m. b/d of crude oil in 1992, the volume of refined products available for marketing through state channels was slightly more than 1m. b/d., of which about two-thirds was sold on the home market and the remainder exported. In 1997 Saudi Arabia had an installed refining capacity of 1,720,000 b/d and a domestic demand for refined products of 1,205,000 b/d.

One effect of the reorganization was the deferment of a proposed $4,000m. programme to upgrade the oil-refining facilities which had fallen within SAMAREC's sphere of influence for planning purposes. A separate $1,000m. upgrading programme for the Ras Tanura refinery received final approval in late 1993 and was under way by mid-1994. In 1995 Saudi Aramco acquired full ownership of the Rabigh export refinery (built in 1985 as a joint venture with a Greek company) and announced plans for a $2,000m. upgrading programme at this plant. A heavily modified programme (costed at $800m.) was put out to tender in June 1998. At that time the current phase of upgrading work at the Ras Tanura refinery was completed. It now had sufficient gasoline capacity to supply the kingdom's expected domestic demand until 2002. Recent shortfalls in Saudi gasoline production had been covered by imports from one of Saudi Aramco's overseas refining affiliates. The Petromin Lubricating Oil Refining Co (LUBEREF, owned 70% by Mobil and 30% by PETROMIN) announced in 1994 that it was to build a new lubricant basestock refinery at Yanbu. Scheduled for completion in 1997, the Yanbu plant would have an annual capacity of 2m. barrels, compared with 1.8m. barrels at LUBEREF's existing plant at Jeddah, and would aim primarily to supply the domestic market. Contracts were awarded in 1996 for the construction of two 'multi-products' (multiple petroleum products pipelines, one running 380 km from Dhahran to a new bulk-handling plant at Riyadh and the other running 360 km from Riyadh to Saudi Aramco's existing bulk-handling plant in Qassim Province. The new pipelines (scheduled for completion in 1999) would greatly reduce the role of road transport in Saudi Aramco's domestic product distribution system. The pipelines were expected to be linked to Saudi Arabia's strategic oil storage caverns, the first two of which (at Jeddah and Riyadh) were completed in early 1996. Originally administered by the Ministry of Defence and Civil Aviation but later entrusted to Saudi Aramco, the strategic storage programme (financed with the proceeds of 200,000 b/d of the country's crude oil production) provided for the creation of a total of six underground storage facilities for crude oil and refined products, each requiring the excavation of nearly 1m. cu m of rock.

An important element of Saudi Arabia's overall product-marketing strategy for the 1990s is the acquisition by Saudi Aramco of refining interests in petroleum-importing countries. In November 1988 Saudi Aramco entered into a joint venture with Texaco, whereby it gained access to a refining and marketing network spanning 26 states in the southern and eastern USA. In 1991 Saudi Aramco acquired a 35% equity interest in

South Korea's largest refining company, Ssangyong Oil, which had 265,000 b/d of installed capacity.

In 1993 Saudi Aramco was actively studying proposals for further joint ventures with established refiners in Asia, Europe and the USA, with a view to raising its effective overseas refining capacity to around 3m. b/d. There was also a complementary programme to acquire oil storage capacity in major overseas importing centres, in furtherance of which Saudi Aramco announced in mid-1993 that it was to buy a 34.35% interest in a 17m.-barrel import terminal at the Dutch port of Rotterdam. In February 1994 Saudi Aramco acquired a 40% shareholding in the Philippine company Petron, which, through its 155,000 b/d Bataan refinery and its associated transportation and retailing network, currently supplied 41% of the Philippine market for refined products. In the following month a Saudi businessman acquired Sweden's largest oil firm, OK Petroleum, which had a refining capacity of 265,000 b/d and which obtained part of its current crude supply from Saudi Aramco. In March 1996 Saudi Aramco acquired a 50% shareholding in a Greek company, Motor Oil Hellas Corinth Refineries, and its marketing affiliate, Avin Oil. The refining company's 100,000 b/d Corinth plant supplied a chain of 700 Avin petrol stations.

A plan to build a refinery and associated facilities in northern India, conceived as a joint venture by Hindustan Petroleum Corpn and Saudi Aramco (which would supply 115,000 b/d of Saudi crude), was approved in principle by the Indian Government in mid-1996. Saudi Aramco was a minority partner in two Chinese joint-venture refineries in 1995. In early 1996 its efforts to acquire a majority share in one of these ventures were blocked by China's state petrochemical company SINOPEC (the existing majority partner), which also rejected Saudi Aramco's proposals for creating a third joint venture. The stumbling-block in the latter case was the Chinese Government's requirement for joint-venture refineries to export at least 70% of their output in order to generate foreign currency earnings. In September 1997 Saudi Aramco cancelled plans to acquire a minority interest in Portugal's state oil company Petrogal. In July 1997 an agreement was reached between Texaco, Shell Oil Co and Saudi Aramco to merge their refining and marketing operations in the eastern and Gulf coast regions of the USA. A new jointly-owned company was to be set up in 1998 to take control of the 820,000 b/d of US refining capacity and the various service-station networks covered by the merger. The merger would entail the dissolution of Star Enterprise (Saudi Aramco's current 50:50 joint venture with Texaco). In mid-1998 the new company, Motiva Enterprises, became fully operational. Saudi Arabia's Minister of Petroleum and Mineral Resources said in June 1997 that the volume of Saudi crude oil supplied to overseas refining affiliates was projected to rise from 3.2m. b/d to 4m. b/d as Saudi Aramco continued to expand its worldwide interests.

The Saudi Basic Industries Corpn (SABIC), founded in 1976, is Saudi Arabia's main non-oil industrial enterprise, including among its holdings many major gas-utilization projects. Chief among them is the petrochemical development at Jubail, Jeddah and Yanbu. In 1983 the Saudi Methanol Co (ar-Razi) plant at Jubail, which cost 900m. riyals and has a capacity of 500,000 tons per year, became the first venture to begin production. It was followed by a further four new projects in 1984: the National Methanol Co (Ibn Sina) plant at Jubail, the Saudi Petrochemical Co (Sadaf) plant at Jubail, producing ethylene, ethylene dichloride, styrene, ethanol and caustic soda; the Al-Jubail Petrochemical Co (Kemya) plant, producing linear low-density polyethylene (LLDPE); and the Saudi Yanbu Petrochemical Co (Yanpet) plant, producing ethylene, ethylene glycol, LLDPE and high-density polyethylene. In 1985 two new plants also came into operation at Jubail: the Arabian Petrochemical Co (Petrokemya) plant, producing ethylene; and the Eastern Petrochemical Co (Sharq) plant, producing LLDPE and ethylene glycol. In March 1989 it was reported that the production of methyl-tertiary-butyl ether (MTBE), a lead substitute for petrol, had been initiated by one of SABIC's joint ventures, the Saudi-European Petrochemical Co (Ibn Zahr), at Jubail. In the same month Petrokemya began the production of plastic resin polystyrene, with the aim of producing 100,000 tons per year, while the annual output of ethylene was scheduled to reach 500,000 tons in 1993, increasing total ethylene capacity to 2.9m. tons per year. In July PVC production capacity at Ibn Hayyan was

100,000 tons per year. SABIC experienced severe problems in selling its products, as major market areas began to impose tariff restrictions in 1985. The company has, however, been able to sell a large volume of products in the Far East and in Europe, despite the tariffs. In 1988 SABIC's profits tripled to a record 3,553m. riyals. In 1989 SABIC's medium-term plans envisaged the expansion of existing ventures, rather than the creation of new affiliates.

In March 1991 SABIC expanded its marketing network when it opened a new ethylene glycol terminal in Livorno, Italy, to improve service to Italian and other southern European clients. In 1991 SABIC owned two European terminals for liquid products (in Italy and in the Netherlands), as well as three storage terminals for plastic resins, situated in Belgium, France and the United Kingdom. In June Ibn Zahr signed contracts for the construction of a polypropylene plant with a capacity of 200,000 tons per year and a new MTBE plant with a capacity of 700,000 tons per year. Ibn Zahr is Saudi Arabia's only producer of MTBE, pending construction of a new plant at Ibn Sina expected to commence production in July 1994. The Italian company Snamprogetti, which built the original plant at Jubail, was awarded part of the $250m. contract to build the MTBE plant, and the United Kingdom's John Brown Engineers and Constructors was to build the polypropylene plant. Features of SABIC operations in 1991 included the completion of expansion at the National Plastics Co (Ibn Hayyan), to a capacity of 300,000 tons per year, and of the Saudi Methanol Co (ar-Razi), to a capacity of 1.2m. tons per year. Following the start of polypropylene production at Jubail, SABIC was in 1994 manufacturing all five thermoplastics and was inviting joint-venture proposals to produce more than 30 categories of finished product, ranging from cling film to footwear. Saudi Arabia's consumption of plastic resins per caput was forecast to approach European levels by 2000.

SABIC's total production volume in 1994 amounted to 20.94m. tons, comprising 11.01m. tons of petrochemicals and chemicals, 4.22m. tons of fertilizer, 2.04m. tons of plastics, 2.61m. tons of metals and 1.06m. tons of industrial gases. There was a record net profit of 4,202m. riyals (almost double the 1993 profit) in 1994. Strong growth continued in 1995, when SABIC raised its total production volume to 22m. tons, its turnover to 23,590m. riyals, and its net profit to 6,280m. riyals. Half of SABIC's 1995 export sales went to Asian markets. Significant developments in 1995 included the start of polyester fibre production by the Arabian Industrial Fiber Co, whose future plans included the installation by mid-1997 of an aromatics and purified terephthalic acid complex at Yanbu. This and other expansion and diversification projects within the SABIC group were expected to increase SABIC's annual production capacity to 25m. tons by 2000. Corporate strategy options under active consideration in 1996 included the encouragement of mergers between some subsidiary companies with identical product lines (such restructuring being subject to negotiation with foreign joint-venture partners) and participation by SABIC in overseas petrochemicals ventures (the main focus of SABIC's interest being the south-east Asian region). In 1996 SABIC marketed 17m. tons of products, having increased its total production volume to 23m. tons (including 12.3m. tons of chemicals, more than 2m. tons of plastics, 2.8m. tons of steel and more than 4m. tons of fertilizer). A fall in international prices for many petrochemical products caused SABIC's profits to fall by almost 30% to 4,412m. riyals in 1996.

In 1997 SABIC's total production rose by 3% to 23.7m. tons, while its marketed production rose by 4.5% to 18.39m. tons, comprising 9.2m. tons of petrochemicals, 2.85m. tons of steel, 2.8m. tons of fetilizers, 2.3m. tons of plastics, 1.1m. tons of industrial gases and 140,000 tons of polyester products. Turnover rose by 15.3% to 24,023m. riyals in 1997, while net profits rose by 4.3% to 4,600m. riyals. In the first six months of 1998 SABIC recorded year-on-year increases of 11% in total output and 7% in marketed production while suffering an 18% drop in sales revenue and a 42% slump in net profits. A company spokesman said that SABIC's competitive position had been eroded in 1998 because the decline in world oil prices (which benefited overseas petrochemical manufacturers using oil-derived feedstocks) had occurred at a time when Saudi Arabia's gas-based factories were absorbing a 50% rise in their own feedstock costs. (With effect from January 1998 Saudi Aramco increased its charge to industrial users of ethane and methane.)

A joint venture with Taiwan Fertilizer Co, Saudi Fertilizer Co (Samad), has an annual capacity of 500,000 tons of urea. In August 1983 its production was 167,760 tons, but by the beginning of 1985 it had reached its full capacity. In early 1985 the Saudi Arabian Fertilizer Co (SAFCO) and SABIC formed a company to build a 1,500 tons-per-day ammonia plant at Jubail. In April 1989 SAFCO's annual output was 450,000 tons in Dammam. In 1988 SAFCO produced 176,591 tons of ammonia, 284,994 tons of urea, approximately 91,728 tons of sulphuric acid and 17,839 tons of melamine. In 1991 SAFCO had a net income of 167m. riyals and announced plans for the construction of a new fertilizer complex at Jubail, at an estimated cost of 1,400m. riyals. Saudi Arabia's third fertilizer manufacturer, the National Chemical Fertilizer Co, opened a factory at Jubail in 1987. The aggregate annual capacity of Saudi Arabian fertilizer plants exceeded 3m. tons in 1993 and was targeted to reach 4m. tons before the end of the decade. The producing companies (all affiliates of SABIC) signed a 'services agreement' in January 1994 to consolidate many of their operational and management functions. SAFCO made net profits of 312m. riyals in 1994 and 607m. riyals in 1995. In 1996 SAFCO made a net profit of 613m. riyals on a turnover of 904m. riyals. In 1997 its net profit fell by 29% to 438m. riyals, reflecting (notably) the impact of China's termination of fertilizer imports in the latter part of the year. SAFCO's net profit for the first half of 1998 was 110m. riyals, some 62% lower than the first-half profit in 1997.

The Saudi Iron and Steel Co (Hadeed), based in Jubail, is a joint venture with Germany's Korf-Stahl. In 1991 Hadeed began exporting iron products to Far East and South-East Asian countries. In July a shipment of about 10,000 tons of reinforcing bars and wire rod coils was exported to Japan, and further sales to Singapore, Taiwan and South Korea, in July and August, raised exports to more than 40,000 tons. The Jeddah Steel Rolling Mill (Sulb) has a capacity of 140,000 tons of steel rods and bars per year, and in 1984 sold 317,000 tons of steel billets. In 1985 production of steel was 1.18m. tons, and in 1986 output increased to 1.9m. tons. An expansion programme, for which a seven-year loan of 500m. riyals was signed in August 1991, was intended to increase steel capacity at Hadeed's Jubail plant to 2m. tons per year. In 1991, owing to Hadeed exports, self-sufficiency was achieved within the Saudi Arabian steel industry, which expanded to satisfy construction requirements within the kingdom and other GCC countries. Steel output from the expanded Hadeed plant reached a record 2.54m. tons in 1996 and was predicted to reach 2.9m. tons in 1997. A contract to build a rolling mill with an annual capacity of 850,000 tons of flat steel products was awarded in 1996 with a view to completion by early 1999. Existing Hadeed facilities undergoing expansion and upgrading in 1997 included a rod mill, a section and bar mill and an electric arc furnace. In mid-1988 the National Industrialization Co (NIC) announced plans to construct a steel foundry at Dammam with a capacity of 10,000 tons per year, at an estimated cost of 117m. riyals. Construction work was expected to reach completion in 1991. NIC is also planning the construction of a steel wire plant at Jubail, with a provisional capacity of about 50,000 tons per year, to produce specialized steel wires and related wire products. In 1990 profits fell from 17m. in 1989 to 14m. riyals. This decline was attributed to the failure of certain companies, in which NIC has shareholdings, to announce dividends. The reduction in profits continued to reflect NIC's poor performance in its delayed implementation of the many industrial projects that it had initiated. In 1994 NIC reported a net profit of 9.4m. riyals (55% less than in 1993).

One of the most interesting developments in SABIC's proposals for joint ventures was agreed in 1983 between SABIC and private Saudi Arabian investors. Called the National Gas Co (Gas), it was expected to produce 146,000 tons of nitrogen and 438,000 tons of oxygen per year by 1985. Further joint ventures, agreed in 1984, included a partnership with Italy and Finland to produce fractionated gases.

The success of these ventures depends, to a large extent, on effective marketing, and all partners are bound to market at least 40% of production in their own countries. The basis for such ambitious heavy industrial schemes is a gas-gathering project, Master Gas System (MGS), which is being implemented by Saudi Aramco. Natural gas will provide the raw material for the petrochemical industry and an energy source for the steel plant. The scheme was initiated in 1975, when it was expected to cost $5,000m. and to produce 156m. cu m per day (cm/d) (5,500m. cu ft per day—cf/d). By the time of its completion in 1982, however, the first phase of the scheme had cost an estimated $12,000m., with a capacity of 98m. cm/d (3,460m. cf/d). In January 1998 Saudi Aramco increased its charge to industrial users of ethane and methane. The new tariff covered about two-thirds of the estimated replacement cost to Saudi Aramco as operator of the MGS. Three processing plants have been built (at Berri, Shedgum and Uthmaniyah) to separate out natural gas liquids (NGLs) from methane, and two fractionation plants, at Juaymeh on the Gulf coast and at Yanbu on the Red Sea, process the NGLs into ethane, liquefied petroleum gas (LPG) and condensate. Gas is carried to Yanbu through a 1,200-km trans-Arabian pipeline which came into operation in 1981. The Berri, Shedgum and Juaymeh plants had all started production by mid-1980, the Uthmaniyah plant began operating in 1981, and the Yanbu plant started in 1982. Apart from fuelling industrial development, the scheme should make Saudi Arabia one of the world's largest exporters of LPG, with shipments of about 650,000 b/d. In 1991, however, SAMAREC amended its LPG price-indexing mechanism, owing to the exceptional volatility of the LPG market. As a result, SAMAREC introduced an upper limit on the permitted volume of exported LPG, in order to compensate for any rapid change in prices. In June 1992 SAMAREC signed 15 five-year contracts for the supply of a total of 42m. tons of LPG to Japanese, South Korean, British and Saudi Arabian companies. There are also facilities for the recovery of sulphur: three plants, with a combined annual capacity of about 1.3m. barrels, came into operation in 1981, and total sales in 1982 reached 800,000 tons.

Most of the gas which is produced in Saudi Arabia is associated gas (i.e. it is found in conjunction with petroleum), so the decline in petroleum output in the mid-1980s led to shortfalls in the production of gas and its 'downstream' products. Work on the second phase of the MGS scheme is under way, aiming to exploit associated gas from offshore fields and to reduce the problem of gas shortages created by declines in production of petroleum. The installed processing capacity of the MGS in 1993 was estimated at 121.8m. cm/d, based on crude oil output of about 8.2m. b/d. During 1985 a major new gasfield was discovered in the onshore Farhah and Sabha area. Saudi Aramco's refinery at Ras Tanura has been producing NGLs since 1962, and production totalled 155m. barrels in 1982. Recovery of NGLs from associated gases rose by 27%, from 420,946 b/d in 1989, to 533,229 b/d in 1990. Similarly, production of refined products at Ras Tanura increased from 174m. barrels in 1989 to 192m. barrels in 1990, with significant increases in the output of jet fuel and fuel oil. There were plans to exploit unassociated gas, independent of petroleum extraction, by 1986. The Khuff reservoir of unassociated gas in the Ghawar oilfield, estimated to contain more than one-half of Saudi Arabia's natural gas reserves, was scheduled to yield 20m. cm/d (700m. cf/d). Saudi Arabia's marketed output of natural gas in 1997 (excluding gas flared or reinjected into oil wells) totalled 43,900m. cu m. Expansion schemes under way in 1997 (including the development of a major new gathering facility at Hawiya for unassociated gas) were designed to increase the installed processing capacity of the MGS to 195m. cm/d (6,900m. cf/d) by 2001. However, the programme began to fall behind schedule in early 1998 when the bids submitted for the main phases of the installation work were unacceptably high. (The lowest bid for the installation of the key gas treatment plant was, at $1,000m., some 60% above Saudi Aramco's budgeted figure.) Saudi Aramco subsequently re-examined the project specifications and invited contractors to submit new tenders for the work by mid-September 1998.

The Government is encouraging Saudi private enterprise to develop smaller-scale industries. A total of eight industrial estates offer basic infrastructure and services at minimal charge, credit is available on favourable terms, and selected products are protected by duties on imports. The Saudi Industrial Development Fund (SIDF) was established in 1974 to provide concessionary loans to private investors, and the NIC was established in 1984, by private investors, to develop and control investment by private individuals. By 1991 the SIDF had an authorized capital of 8,000m. riyals and had granted 1,404 loans, amounting to 18,738m. riyals. During 1996 the SIDF approved 109 loans totalling 2,429m. riyals. The building materials sector, and in particular the cement industry, is flourishing, as are electrical equipment manufacturing, the production of chemical rubber and plastics, and food processing and soft drinks. National cement output of 14.1m. tons in 1992 covered only 98% of the rapidly rising domestic demand, prompting five of the kingdom's seven publicly-traded cement companies to announce expansion plans, which would increase total cement production capacity by almost one-third, to 18.5m. tons per year. Some 1m. tons of cement and 1.6m. tons of clinker were imported in 1993. Cement imports increased to 2m. tons in 1994. Saudi Arabia's annual demand for all types of cement in 1996 was 17.3m. tons (including 16m. tons of Portland cement). In 1997 Saudi cement production fell by 6% to 15.4m. tons; 14m. tons were consumed locally, 1.3m. tons were exported and the remainder stockpiled. Saudi Arabia's installed cement production capacity rose to 22.7m. tons per year in 1998, following the establishment of an eighth producing company.

Between 1975 and 1978 about 70% of the industrial projects which were authorized were wholly Saudi-owned, the rest being joint ventures, and during 1982 a total of 2,689 new licences for privately-owned enterprises were approved. In 1991 the Ministry of Industry and Electricity approved a licence for the newly-established Saudi Industrial Development Co (SIDC) to build a ceramics plant in the Western Province. The scheme would involve a total investment of 311m. riyals. The output of the new plant and that of the Saudi Ceramics Co, based in Riyadh, was expected to satisfy 80% of the domestic market. As part of its policy to stimulate the Saudi private sector, the Government sold 30% of SABIC's capital in 1984, and aims ultimately to transfer 75% into private control. At the end of 1986 the Government reported that there were 3,345 licensed factories in the kingdom, of which 2,022 were operating, with a total work-force of 130,494. In 1990 there were 2,255 factories in operation, of which the metal industry accounted for 28.1%, building materials 24.8%, and food and beverages 16%. Total investment in factories for 1990 was 96,900m. riyals, of which the largest amount (52,900m. riyals) was invested in the chemicals industry. A public flotation of shares in the SIDC in mid-1992, intended to raise 250m. riyals, was oversubscribed by more than three times. The SIDC planned to invest in various industrial projects, including a $64m. pharmaceuticals factory. In June 1994 the Government published figures showing that new factories had recently been opened at an average rate of six per month, representing an average job creation rate of 395 per month and an average capital investment of 90m. riyals per month.

At the end of 1994 the Minister for Industry and Electricity stated that the Saudi manufacturing sector currently had an invested capital of more than $40,000m., annual production of more than $15,000m. and annual exports of more than $3,000m., although its share of GDP was less than half of the Government's 22% planning target. Nearly $26,000m. was currently invested in chemicals and plastics enterprises; nearly $5,300m. in the manufacture of building materials, ceramics and glass; $3,500m. in production of machine tools and finished metal goods; $2,400m. in food and beverage production; $1,100m. in basic metal industries; $1,100m. in paper and printing; and $533m. in the manufacture of textiles, clothing and leather. In 1997 Saudi Arabia's first sugar refinery, with the capacity to produce 500,000 tons a year from imported raw sugar, began production at Jeddah. Plans for a second refinery at Al-Jouf, to process locally grown sugar beet, were announced in 1997.

Non-oil mineral production includes limestone (for cement manufacture), gypsum, marble, clay and salt. Substantial deposits of bauxite, iron ore and magnesite, as well as copper, gold, lead, zinc, silver and some uranium, are known to exist. A mine at Mahd adh-Dhahab, with 1.2m. tons of ore (including gold), was inaugurated in 1983. At the end of 1984 work started on the construction of a gold-mining town at Mahd adh-Dhahab, and annual output of gold from the mine reached 3.5 tons in 1991, with estimated reserves of 1,123,000 tons. In 1997 the mine's reserves were estimated to be more than 2m. tons and

in 1996 157,000 ounces (oz) of gold, 479,000 oz of silver and 900 tons of copper were produced. Production of zinc concentrate, at an annual rate of up to 10,000 tons, was due to begin in 1997. In 1991 there were 495 known sites of gold deposits in Saudi Arabia (and 800 'indications' of gold occurrence), of which 31 were estimated to contain more than 1,000 kg each and a further 99 were estimated to contain at least 100 kg each. In 1986 large quantities of gold were discovered in the Sukhaybarat area, and in 1991 the Saudi Company for Precious Metals (a joint venture between PETROMIN and a Swedish company, Boliden) began gold production, which reached 978 kg by the end of the year. By the end of 1996 cumulative production had reached 13,000 kg of fine gold. Reserves at Sukhaybarat were estimated at 8.4m. tons. The private-sector Arabian Shield Development Co was awarded a 30-year mining lease in 1993 for the Al-Masane area of south-western Saudi Arabia, where substantial deposits of copper, zinc, gold and silver were known to exist. Feasibility studies were in progress in 1994 for a proposed $50m. mining project and associated plans to create zinc-processing facilities at Yanbu. At the end of 1996 the project was granted an industrial licence after preparing plans which envisaged annual yields of 31,270 tons of zinc, 8,750 tons of copper, 13,100 oz of gold, 550,000 oz of silver and 12 tons of bullion (98% silver and 2% gold). At the end of 1997 the US-owned Arabian Shield Development Co set up the Arabian Shield Company for Mining Industries as a joint venture with the Saudi-owned Al-Mashreq Company for Mining Investments. Financial backers of the Arabian Shield project now included the Saudi Industrial Development Fund, which agreed to provide a $38m. interest-free loan. In 1994 the Government invited applications to develop a recently evaluated iron ore deposit at Wadi Sawawin in north-western Saudi Arabia. It was estimated that an investment of $550m. would be needed to develop an open-pit mine and ore beneficiation facility for the production of pellets at an annual rate of 2.2m. tons for 25 years. During 1984 a large coal field was discovered in central Qassim Province. In early 1989 the Compagnie Générale des Matières Nucléaires (COGEMA) of France secured mineral-prospecting rights in an area of 500,000 sq km from the Ministry of Petroleum and Mineral Resources. There are 213m. tons of proved phosphate-bearing ore (averaging 21% phosphoric anhydride content) at Al-Jalamid in the far north of Saudi Arabia. In May 1994 the Government invited proposals for the extraction from these reserves of 4.5m. tons of phosphate concentrate per year, to be transported by slurry pipeline to Jubail as feedstock for a proposed 2.9m. tons-per-year diammonium phosphate plant. A feasibility study was initiated in 1993 on proposals to establish a 150,000 tons-per-year copper smelter and refinery at Yanbu. Strategic control of the minerals sector is exercised by the Directorate-General of Mineral Resources (DGMR). In 1997 the state-owned Saudi Arabian Mining Company (Ma'aden) was established to take over existing state interests in the non-oil mining sector and to serve as a vehicle for future state mining ventures. Ma'aden had an initial capital of 4,000m. riyals. In addition to taking sole ownership of the Mahd adh-Dhahab mine, where 1997 gold production was around 170,000 oz, Ma'aden inherited PETROMIN's 50% interest in the Sukhaybarat gold mine, whose 1997 production was around 90,000 oz. Ma'aden was granted a 30-year gold mining lease at Al-Amar (220 km south-west of Riyadh) in September 1997 and a 30-year gold and silver mining lease at Al-Hajar (350 km south-east of Jeddah) in May 1998. The company said that it aimed to double Saudi Arabia's gold production by 2001. Demand for gold in Saudi Arabia (one of the top five consuming countries) increased by 8% to 199 tons in 1997.

ELECTRICITY AND WATER

Saudi Arabia's electricity system has to satisfy rapidly growing urban and industrial demand, and also to supply power for small, widely-scattered rural settlements. Until the 1970s, generation was controlled by a large number of small companies: 26 of them were operating in the Eastern Province alone. The main aim was to create regional grids, each operated by a single company. In 1977 the companies operating in the Eastern Province merged into a single Saudi Consolidated Electric Co (SCECO-East), managed by Aramco. A unified company for the southern region (SCECO-South) was formed in 1979. The other unified regional companies are SCECO-West and SCECO-Central. Northern areas continued to be supplied by separately-controlled local plants in 1994. SCECO-Central imports about 40% of its supply from SCECO-East via the only connection between two regional grids. Total sales of electric power increased from 1,690m. kWh in 1970 to 55,201m. kWh in 1988/89, of which 15,524m. kWh were used by industry. Electricity generation capacity was 16,850 MW at the end of 1991, and there were 2.4m. subscribers. Industry accounts for about 30% of total consumption. An increasing amount of electricity is now produced in association with sea-water desalination. By the end of 1992 the kingdom's installed electricity generating capacity totalled 17,049 MW, and the combined power capacity of water desalination projects was 2,825 MW. Peak load in 1992 was 14,389 MW. Industrial users accounted for 27% of total power consumption in 1992. By 1994 peak load was approaching 19,000 MW, following steep rises in demand, attributable in part to low tariff levels, which covered less than one-half of the costs of production. A major programme for the expansion of capacity was planned, coupled with a campaign to reduce wasteful consumption (accounting for an estimated 30% of current electricity usage). In 1994 the standard monthly tariff for electricity supply was 0.05 riyal per unit for the first 4,000 kWh, 0.08 riyal per unit for the next 2,000 kWh, and 0.15 riyal per unit for consumption in excess of 6,000 kWh. From January 1995 a surcharge of 0.05 riyal per unit was imposed on all monthly consumption in excess of 2,000 kWh. Electricity consumption continued to increase rapidly in 1995, however, causing power cuts in Jeddah in August (the month of peak demand for air-conditioning). During August 1996 Saudi oil exports were subject to reductions of up to 5% in order to make supplementary fuel supplies available to the kingdom's power stations. Installed generating capacity totalled 21,300 MW in mid-1996.

In 1996, the number of electricity subscribers rose by 122,000 to 3.34m., and by 1997, according to government estimates, demand was growing at an annual rate of 16% (the Government's long term forecast for 1995–2020 envisaged annual growth of 4.5%). A wide range of development options, including national and international private sector participation, were under review in 1997 as the Government considered the practicalities of sustaining an expansion of generating capacity at an average rate of 1,500 MW–2,000 MW per year. In April 1997 contractors were invited to bid for a new power station development on a 'build-own-operate' basis, although in mid-1998 it was reported that a conventional 'turnkey' bidder seemed likely to win the contract.

The state body with overall responsibility for the Saudi electricity system is the General Electricity Corpn, founded in 1976. The Corporation has been especially active in establishing power networks in rural areas. These networks will, where possible, be integrated into one of the regional grids under the control of the appropriate unified company. By 1982 SCECO-South was implementing its own rural schemes, including the largest single rural project, Tihama rural electricity supply programme, costing an estimated 4,000m. riyals. By August 1984 the overall target of the 1980–85 Development Plan, which was to provide 80% of the population with electricity and water, had already been reached. Under the fifth Five-Year Plan, electricity generating capacity was to be increased by 3,500 MW between 1990/91 and 1994/95, and daily water production from desalination plants to 3m. cu. m. By mid-1992 approval had been given for some 300 water projects across the kingdom, involving the drilling of 450 wells, the improvement of 100 others, the construction of 49 dams and the installation of 350 pumping units.

Urban water supply has been a major challenge. At one time, the exploitation of underground sources appeared to be the best solution, but this method has encountered technical difficulties. However, aquifers at depths as great as 1,700 m are to be tapped. The largest projects are at Riyadh: the Minjur aquifer began supplying the city in 1979, and the huge Wasia aquifer produced 200,000 cu m of water per day in 1983, while an additional 110,000 cu m per day were supplied by Salbakh and Buwaib. In June 1989 a drinking water project was inaugurated in Khamis Mushait, to be completed in three years, and a project to build reservoirs and a sanitary disposal network near Medina was being planned. The construction of dams throughout the kingdom, as a means of preserving rainwater, has also expanded

in recent years. By 1986 a total of 169 dams had been built, and in 1987 work began on a project, costing an estimated 239.8m. riyals, to construct a dam at Bisha, with the capacity to store 325m. cu m of water. The dam was expected to be completed in 1992.

Desalination projects are the responsibility of the Saline Water Conversion Corpn (SWCC), which is the world's largest producer of desalinated water. Jeddah already receives 350,000 cu m per day, or 91% of its water, from the SWCC, and massive new plants at Jubail and al-Khobar are due to supply the Eastern Province. In 1991 the Western Province Water and Sanitary Disposal Department approved contracts worth 327m. riyals to undertake three maintenance programmes in Mecca and Jeddah. A pipeline carries water from the Jubail plant inland to Riyadh. In the mid-1990s the Shuaiba desalination plant was pumping 35m. gallons to Mecca and 15m. gallons to Ta'if daily. The 1985–90 Plan foresaw investment of 31,789m. riyals in water projects. The aim was to increase desalination capacity to 1.8m. cu m per day by 1990. Emphasis will be placed on developing reclaimed and surface water resources for direct use and for recharging aquifers. In 1991 a contract worth 31m. riyals was awarded to As-Saiqh Trading to implement an expansion project in Yanbu, and a contract worth 15m. riyals was awarded to Al-Fahd Corporation for Trading, Contracting and Industry to work on one of a series of projects to dispose of rising ground water in Riyadh. In 1994 the SWCC had 24 plants in 15 locations, with a combined capacity of about 2m. cu m (450m. gallons) per day; was in the process of constructing 1m. cu m per day of additional capacity; and was considering plans for 15 new units with a combined capacity of 1.2m. cu m per day. The SWCC had a 1996 project budget of 1,900m. riyals (unchanged from 1995), of which an estimated 800m.–1,000m. riyals was required for maintenance work on existing installations. Water output in 1996 was around 2.36m. cu. m (520m. gallons) per day, while the SWCC's electricity generating capacity was around 3,000 MW (due to rise to 4,500 MW on completion of the current expansion programme).

TRANSPORT, COMMUNICATIONS AND TOURISM

Until 1964 the only surfaced roads, besides those in the petroleum network, were in the Jeddah-Mecca-Medina area. Since then, roads have been given priority, and at the end of 1994 there were about 150,000 km of roads, of which about 42% were paved. In early 1992 there were about 60 road-building projects in progress in the kingdom. During the third Plan period (1980–85), the length of paved roads increased at an annual average rate of 15.8%, a major project being the 317-km Riyadh–Qassim highway, which was completed in the late 1980s. In 1991 Kuwait was awarded a contract worth $25.8m. to implement part of a project which would link Mecca by road with the Riyadh–Ta'if expressway. Some 1,840 km of major roads were built in 1993. Saudi Arabia's national bus operator, the Saudi Public Transport Co (SAPTCO, whose 1,700 vehicles serve mainly inter-city routes), made a net profit of 82.6m. riyals in the first half of 1994.

The main sea ports are at Jeddah, Yanbu and Gizan on the Red Sea and at Dammam and Jubail on the Gulf. A programme of rapid expansion and modernization was undertaken by the Saudi Ports Authority in the late 1970s which improved facilities, particularly at Jubail, Yanbu and Gizan. In 1988 the expansion of exports from the agricultural and industrial sectors led to a revival in cargo-handling, despite the continuing decline in the volume of imports. The emergence of the industrial ports of Jubail and Dammam as important export centres has been prompted by the decision, in 1987, to reduce port tariffs for industrial and some agricultural goods produced locally by 50% and to extend the period of free storage from two to 10 days. Jeddah port, however, has continued to suffer from the decline in imported cargo, and therefore SEAPA agreed in late 1988 to revise the regulations to allow transhipment. In 1995 9,967 vessels used Saudi Arabian ports, which, by 1996 had a total of 183 berths (137 at six commercial ports and 46 at two industrial ports). The volume of cargo (excluding crude petroleum) handled by Saudi ports in 1996 totalled 86.28m. tons (60.24m. tons of exports and 26.04m. tons of imports). A programme was introduced in 1997 to 'commercialize' the operation of the main ports by offering 10-year operations, maintenance and management leases to private-sector contractors, who would derive their income from stevedoring fees charged to port users and would pay a proportion of their income to SEAPA as royalties. In 1983 Saudi Arabia became the 40th member of the London-based International Maritime (now Mobile) Satellite Organization (INMARSAT). Vela, the shipping arm of Saudi Aramco, owns one of the world's largest fleets of oil tankers, which in 1994 included 23 vessels classified as very large or ultra-large crude carriers. Operational management of the fleet, hitherto contracted out to various international companies, was due to be transferred during 1996 to an in-house ship operating division, based in Dubai. In 1997 the National Shipping Company of Saudi Arabia (NSCSA) made a net profit of 5m. riyals, compared with a net loss of 77.5m. riyals in 1996. Primarily an operator of container and general cargo services, the NSCSA also owned five very large crude carriers, currently on long-term charter to Vela.

In the late 1980s Saudi Arabia established satellite transmission and reception stations, facilitating direct telephone dialling to most of the rest of the world. About 50,000 new telephone lines became available in mid-1996, on completion of the first phase of a $3,950m. scheme to add 1.5m. digital lines to the system over a seven-year period. In early 1998 there were 2.2m. telephone lines installed (about 12 lines per 100 inhabitants), the current planning aim being to reach a 'teledensity' of at least 30 lines per 100 inhabitants within five years. The number of cellular phone users in the kingdom (190,700 in 1996) was forecast to reach 500,000 by the end of the century. In April 1998 a royal decree authorized the transfer of state-run telecommunications interests to a new Saudi Telecommunications Company (STC) with an initial capital of 12,000m. riyals. It was intended that STC, once established as a profitable commercial enterprise, should become the subject of Saudi Arabia's first major privatization exercise. Private involvement was meanwhile introduced into the provision of postal services in June 1998, when the first three-year licences were issued to applicants wishing to set up privately-run post offices in six areas of the kingdom.

There are 25 commercial airports in the kingdom. The principal international airports are at Jeddah (King Abd al-Aziz), Dhahran (the Eastern Province International Airport) and Riyadh (King Khalid). In the late 1970s plans were announced for new airports in the three main regions. King Fahd International Airport in Dhahran came into operation in 1990. The new Riyadh airport, inaugurated in November 1983, cost some $5,000m. to build and is one of the world's largest. More than 25m. passengers, including 16m. on domestic flights, passed through Saudi Arabian airports on normal flights in 1996. There were also 864,000 passengers on special flights for Muslim pilgrims. In July 1998 the Government drew up plans to introduce departure taxes for all non-pilgrim travellers on international routes, the proposed rates being 50 riyals at airports and 20 riyals at seaports.

The Government operates the national carrier, Saudi Arabian Airlines (Saudia), which links important Saudi cities and operates regular flights to many foreign countries. In 1993 the airline carried 11.86m. passengers, including 3.8m. on international services, and handled 195,833 tons of freight, 71% of it on international routes. It had a fleet of 108 aircraft, more than one-half of which were designated for replacement under plans announced in 1994. In October 1995 Saudia signed an agreement to purchase 61 new aircraft from the US companies Boeing and McDonnell Douglas at an estimated total cost of $7,500m. New hangars and maintenance facilities were expected to cost a further $600m. Delivery of the new fleet was to begin in September 1996 and be completed within three to five years, while payment for the aircraft would be made over a period of up to 10 years. It was intended that the introduction of the new fleet would be accompanied by a campaign to improve the airline's competitiveness (the Government's declared aim being to open Saudia to private investment as soon as its operations had been suitably restructured). Use of the name Saudia was phased out at the end of 1996 and replaced by the full name Saudi Arabian Airlines. In 1996 the airline carried 11.7m. passengers, including 3.87m. on international services, and handled 225,473 tons of freight, 65% of it on international routes. By mid-1998 the airline was taking delivery of new

aircraft at the rate of three to four per month, and expected to have 39 of its new fleet in operation by the end of 1998.

Saudi Arabia has the only rail system in the Arabian peninsula; in the year ending June 1994 it carried 402,570 passengers and 1.9m. tons of freight. Operating revenue in excess of 70m. riyals (28% from passengers and the balance from freight) was insufficient to cover costs, and the 1994 government subsidy totalled 192.4m. riyals. The principal lines are a 571-km single-track railway which connects the port of Dammam, on the Gulf, with Riyadh, and a 322-km line, linking Riyadh with Hufuf, which was inaugurated in May 1985. In early 1995 plans to create a 120-km rail link between Dammam and Jubail, at an estimated cost of 920m. riyals, were presented to potential industrial users and development authorities by the Saudi Railway Organization, which forecast an annual revenue yield of between 140m. and 170m. riyals if the scheme was implemented. In 1991 it was announced that an automated light railway service was to be built, to take pilgrims from parking areas to the Grand Mosque, as part of the project to develop the holy places in Mecca and Medina. The project was estimated to cost $100m.

A causeway linking Bahrain with the Saudi mainland was opened in late 1986. It is open for 24 hours per day, although trucks and lorries may only use it at off-peak times.

In June 1992 the Saudi Automotive Services Co (SASCO) approved plans to produce light and heavy trailers, refrigerated boxes, wagons and tankers. In the latter half of 1992 the company began manufacturing spares for the main makes of cars available in Saudi Arabia (i.e. for US, Japanese and German models).

In 1996 several tourism development projects, representing a total investment of some 15,000m. riyals, were under way in Saudi Arabia, many of them designed to appeal primarily to Saudi citizens wishing to holiday in their own country. (Saudi citizens spent an estimated 6,700m. riyals on foreign tourism in 1995.) The largest single tourism development was the new town of al-Buhairat, being built at a cost of 4,800m. riyals to provide a wide range of accommodation and leisure facilities on the Red Sea coast about 45 km north of central Jeddah (and about 15 km from Jeddah's international airport). Designed to house a population of about 18,000 when fully developed, al-Buhairat was due to receive its first residents before the end of 1996. Another town-sized development, Durrat al-Arus, was under construction on an island at the mouth of the Gulf of Salman, north of al-Buhairat. Costing 1,300m. riyals and including a racecourse, golf-course, marina, theme park and aqua park, Durrat al-Arus was scheduled to open in mid-1996 and to complete all its planned attractions by 1998. Most tourism facilities under development on Saudi Arabia's Gulf coast in 1996 were smaller in scale. Developments in the Half Moon Bay area, south of al-Khobar, included the al-Nakheel tourist village, a complex of 120 villas under construction at a cost of 124m. riyals.

FOREIGN TRADE

The total value of the country's exports, of which more than 90% was provided by petroleum before 1988, rose from 138,242m. riyals in 1978 to 362,885m. riyals in 1980, but by 1985 had decreased to 99,536m. riyals, before increasing again, to 166,339m. riyals in 1990. Total exports, including re-exports, increased to 159,590m. riyals in 1994, to 187,403m. riyals in 1995 and to 212,353m. riyals in 1996. Sales of petroleum and petroleum products accounted for 88.6% of total export revenue in 1996. The principal customers for Saudi Arabia's exports in 1995 were the USA (taking 16.9% of the total), Japan (16.2%), the Republic of Korea (9.8%), Singapore (5.3%) and the Netherlands (4.6%). Other important sources of foreign exchange are the local expenditure of foreign companies and the pilgrimage traffic.

The value of Saudi Arabia's imports increased from 69,180m. riyals in 1978 to 139,335m. riyals in 1982, but fell to 85,564m. riyals in 1985, and by 1990 had increased to 90,139m. riyals. The main categories of imports are machinery and transport equipment, consumer goods, and food and beverages. In 1996 the kingdom's major suppliers were the USA (accounting for 21.9% of total imports), the United Kingdom (9.0%), Germany (7.5%), Japan (7.0%) and Italy (5.7%). The main items to be imported from Japan are cars, pick-up trucks and spare parts. Cars and machinery are the main imports from the USA, and from the United Kingdom military equipment is pre-eminent. In 1990 the visible trade surplus increased by 150%, to US $22,889m., as a result of exports worth $44,414m. (an increase of 56.5% over 1989) and imports worth $21,525m. (an increase of 11.9%). In 1993 the visible trade surplus decreased to $16,522m. (exports $42,395m., imports $25,873m.), but recovered to $21,296m. (exports $42,614m., imports $21,318m.) in 1994, and $24,390m. (exports $50,041m., imports $25,650m.) in 1995. Non-oil exports were worth an estimated $5,700m. in 1995, having increased by about 50% since 1993 (mainly because of the rapid expansion of the petrochemicals sector). In 1996 the impact of a downturn in world petrochemical prices was more than offset by a strengthening of oil export prices. The visible trade surplus for 1996 was $35,370m. (exports $60,729m., imports $25,358m.), and in 1997 there was an estimated visible trade surplus of $33,530m. (exports $59,684m., imports $26,154m.).

Saudi Arabia's current-account surplus increased dramatically from US $2,520m. in 1973 to $23,025m. in 1974, under the influence of the increases in the price of petroleum, and in 1980 it reached $41,503m. The impact of the fall in petroleum output in 1982 was dramatic: the decline in export revenues was far greater than the drop in imports, and by 1983 a deficit of $16,852m. had been recorded. The deficit decreased to $12,932m. in 1985, and $4,152m. in 1990, but in 1991 extraordinary items arising out of the Gulf conflict were largely responsible for a sharp increase in the overall current-account deficit to $27,546m. (that year's deficit on services being $35,896m., while net transfers abroad totalled $20,235m. and net unearned income totalled $6,767m.). By 1994 the current-account deficit had been reduced to $10,487m. and it decreased further in 1995, to $5,324m. In 1996 the current account showed its first surplus (of $681m.) for 15 years. Preliminary estimates for 1997 showed a current-account surplus of $254m. The estimated deficit on services in 1997 was $20,993m., while net transfers abroad totalled an estimated $15,439m. and net unearned income an estimated $3,156m.

In June 1993 Saudi Arabia, which had held observer status in GATT since 1985, submitted an application for full GATT membership. In mid-1996 negotiations with GATT's successor body, the World Trade Organization, were at a preliminary stage and it subsequently became apparent that negotiations were unlikely to be completed before the end of the century.

FINANCE

Since mid-1977, and particularly since July 1978, the Saudi Arabian Monetary Agency (SAMA) has made a series of frequent small adjustments in the exchange rate of the Saudi riyal against the US dollar. At the end of June 1984 the rate was $1 = 3.505 riyals, and by the end of the year the riyal had been devalued seven times. Following three further adjustments in the first six months of 1985, the exchange rate stood at $1 = 3.645 riyals in June. This rate remained unchanged until June 1986, when a rate of $1 = 3.745 riyals was established. This remained in effect at mid-1993, after which the currency came under heavy pressure from speculators who maintained that it was overvalued at a time of weak oil prices. However, the Government ruled out any devaluation, accepting a rise in Saudi interest rates at the end of 1993 in order to defend the existing exchange rate. SAMA, established in 1952, acts as a central bank.

At the end of 1977 Saudi Arabia's international reserves totalled $30,034m. and were surpassed only by those of the Federal Republic of Germany. From April 1978 Saudi Arabia's reserves were redefined to exclude foreign exchange cover against the note issue, then about $5,300m. Under the new definition, reserves declined to $16,756m. in October 1979, but they then made a sharp recovery, rising to $32,422m. at the end of 1981. Reserves declined to $25,181m. in December 1985, and by December 1990 had declined further to $11,897m. (including gold valued at $229m.). By the end of 1993 total reserves stood at only $7,649m., following heavy expenditure to finance the international action against Iraq in 1990–91 and to purchase new military equipment in the aftermath of the crisis. At the end of 1995 reserves minus gold totalled $8,622m. de-

creasing to $6,794m. at the end of 1996 and recovering to $7,353m. at the end of 1997.

Until September 1997 there were 12 commercial banks in Saudi Arabia, of which three were wholly Saudi and nine joint ventures. The largest Saudi commercial bank is the National Commercial Bank (NCB). In 1988 the formalities were completed for the creation of the country's twelfth commercial bank, the Ar-Rajhi Banking and Investment Co (ARABIC), which had previously been the country's leading money-changing company, and had been endeavouring to become a commercial bank since 1984. In September 1997 the United Saudi Commercial Bank merged with the Saudi Cairo Bank to form the United Saudi Bank, making the total number of banks 11. In terms of its capital, the new bank is the third largest in the kingdom.

Specialized credit institutions provide project finance: the Saudi Industrial Development Fund (SIDF) is the major source, and was set up by the Government in 1974. It grants low-interest loans for up to 50% of the total cost of a project (up to 80% in the case of electricity projects). The SIDF is managed by Chase Manhattan Bank. The Public Investment Fund (PIF), established in 1972, finances large-scale commercial and industrial projects in the public sector. A new institution, the National Industrialization Co, was established in 1984 by private investors: its object is to encourage and plan development in the private sector.

Another major state financial institution which assists in the country's development is the Real Estate Development Fund (REDF), whose capital has been raised successively from 240m. riyals to 23,800m. riyals. The REDF provides a home-loan scheme under which purchasers are required to pay 80% of loan principal. The Saudi Agricultural Bank, set up in 1963, offers medium- and short-term loans for farmers. The Saudi Credit Bank was set up in 1973 to advance interest-free loans to low-income Saudis for purposes such as getting married or carrying out home repairs.

Saudi banks have become more outward-looking, and the most obvious example of this trend is the 55% Saudi-owned Saudi International Bank, which opened as a fully-fledged merchant bank in London in March 1976. SAMA holds 50% of the capital, while the NCB and Riyad Bank have 2.5% each. The principal non-Saudi partner in the enterprise is the Morgan Guaranty Trust Co, a US bank, which also provides management. The other shares are held by leading Western and Japanese banks. The first wholly private Saudi bank abroad—As-Saudi Banque—opened in Paris in the autumn of 1976. Riyad Bank has a share in the Paris-based Union de Banques Arabes et Françaises, and in the Gulf Riyad Bank in Bahrain. The NCB has small stakes in European-Arab Holding and the Compagnie Arabe et Internationale d'Investissement, both based in Luxembourg, and in the Amman-based Arab-Jordanian Investment Bank, which opened in the spring of 1978.

Total assets of Saudi banks grew by 12%, to 191,059m. riyals in 1987/88, and nearly one-half of these were held abroad. In 1988 the performance of the banking sector improved, although the recovery was not uniform among all the 12 commercial banks. The United Saudi Commercial Bank, Riyad Bank and the Arab National Bank increased their profits, but NCB recorded no profit and the Saudi Cairo Bank trebled its losses. The main reason for the poor performance of the banking sector in the mid-1980s was the domestic recession, but they also needed to make substantial provision against loan losses. In 1985 SAMA began requiring banks to report their non-performing loans. In March 1987 King Fahd ordered the central bank to establish a committee to arbitrate in bank loan disputes. By mid-1988 the outstanding loans and advances disbursed by the Saudi Agricultural Bank, the Saudi Credit Bank, the PIF, the SIDF and the REDF totalled 166,600m. riyals. In 1992 the Saudi commercial banking sector experienced very strong growth. The audited accounts released by the 11 publicly-quoted banks showed aggregate assets of 234,233m. riyals, an increase of 13.4% on the 1991 total, and aggregate profits of 3,712m. riyals, a rise of nearly 29% on the previous year's level. A 30% increase in Saudi banking profits in 1993 was followed by a 4% fall in 1994, when commercial banks' aggregate net income totalled 4,808m. riyals. In 1997 Saudi Arabia's 11 commercial banks had aggregate assets of 385,860.4m. riyals and aggregate net profits of 6,588m. riyals, representing an increase of 15.1% over 1996 (when there were 12 banks).

During the course of 1994 banks came under increasing pressure to provide short-term credit facilities to companies affected by delays in government payments to contractors undertaking public-sector projects. By the last quarter of the year, when some payments were more than 12 months overdue, a total of 18,750m. riyals was believed to be involved, causing senior bankers to appeal for urgent government action to resolve the situation. The Government subsequently undertook to release cash payments to contractors that were owed less than 10m. riyals, and had by late April 1995 reduced its debt to such contractors by an estimated 3,000m.–5,000m. riyals. Contractors that were owed more than 10m. riyals were, in March 1995, issued with government bonds maturing at different dates between March 1996 and September 1997 and carrying fixed coupons of between 6.5% and 7.25%. The bonds were negotiable through the banking system and could be used as security against commercial borrowing. The March 1995 bond issue covered a total of 5,200m. riyals owed to 120 local and foreign companies. Between January and March 1996 the Government issued negotiable non-interest-bearing certificates to the value of an estimated 9,500m. riyals to Saudi farmers who were awaiting official payments (mainly for grain production). Contractors' bonds worth an estimated 4,000m. riyals, and maturing between April 1998 and April 2002, were issued to corporate creditors in April 1996. In January 1998 the Saudi Government secured a seven-year sovereign loan of $4,330m. from a consortium of international banks to finance the purchase of a new fleet of US aircraft for the national carrier Saudi Arabian Airlines. (The airline was not in a position to raise its own finance, having incurred operating losses for many years because of the low level of domestic air fares for Saudi citizens.) In mid-1998 the state energy company Saudi Aramco renewed an existing $2,000m. five-year revolving credit facility and opened negotiations with international banks for a new $2,000m. syndicated loan repayable over four years.

In May 1987 Saudi Arabia opened its first stock-exchange trading floor in Riyadh, under the jurisdiction of SAMA. However, the Central Trading Hall was closed indefinitely less than a month after it had opened, owing to technical problems and to disagreement about procedures between the Ministry of Finance, which is responsible for SAMA, and the Ministry of Commerce. Shares are traded by banks and independent brokers, and in 1990 SAMA introduced an electronic trading system. Although the market is limited, the value of traded shares rose by 80% in 1991, compared with 1990, to some 8,000m. riyals, and share prices increased overall by about 70%. In 1995 shares were being traded in 69 companies with a market capitalization of 153,400m. riyals. In 1997 market capitalization was about 218,750m. riyals and the value of shares traded was 62,060m. riyals. It was estimated that the Government owned about 25% of all quoted shares in 1997 and that a single large corporation (SABIC) accounted for 21% of total market capitalization in that year. A Saudi Arabia Investment Fund was launched in June 1997 by Saudi American Bank as a vehicle for indirect market participation by non-GCC investors. Saudi Arabia's insurance market, in which about 80 companies and agencies were active in 1992, was worth some 1,870.5m. riyals in gross written premiums in that year. The only locally registered insurer, the National Company for Co-operative Insurance, wrote 619m. riyals of insurance premiums in 1993, when it had gross claims of 228.4m. riyals and made a net surplus of 61.6m. riyals.

In July 1989 Saudi Arabia signed a syndicated loan for $660m., apparently the first international borrowing by the Saudi Government for a quarter of a century. There has been a reluctance to raise funds publicly over the last two decades, due to the memory of the 1950s, when an excess of borrowing led to economic crisis. Economists in Saudi Arabia have speculated that the loan, raised in the name of the PIF, could be used to finance the budget deficit, while other observers claim that it will be used to refinance concessionary loans made by the Government to SABIC.

Owing to the Saudi Government's own budget deficit, in 1991 it was forced to sign a term-loan worth $4,500m. with international banks, in addition to borrowing $2,500m. in for-

eign currency from domestic banks. It was agreed that the larger Saudi banks would lend a maximum of $400m. each to the Government, while the smaller banks would lend $50m.–$100m. each. The major part of the foreign borrowing was believed to be needed to defray costs incurred as a result of the multinational military assistance provided to Saudi Arabia during the Gulf crisis in 1990–91. In November 1991 SAMA announced the kingdom's first issue of Treasury bills, starting with issues of up to 2,000m. riyals per week, to finance the budget deficit. The Government's other main public financing instrument is medium-term development bonds, first introduced in 1988. The first repayment of $900m. to international banks under the terms of the 1991 loan was made on schedule in May 1994. In April 1994 the Government had signed a new loan agreement under which a syndicate of local banks would lend the Ministry of Finance and National Economy $1,300m. over seven years, with two years' grace. Repayment of the international banks' 1991 loan was completed in May 1995. In 1996 SAMA accepted an invitation to join the Bank for International Settlements. In June 1998 the Government made its third issue of contractors' bonds, worth an estimated total of 5,000m.–6,000m. riyals; maturity periods ranged from one to five years and rates of interest payable ranged from 5.67% to 5.95%. The farmers' payment certificates issued in 1996 were redeemable in three instalments, the third of which (amounting to 3,000m. riyals in respect of the 1994 wheat crop) was due in August 1998. In July 1998 the Government indicated that wheat farmers would receive a total of 2,200 riyals for their 1996 harvest but did not specify whether payment would be made in cash or certificates.

INVESTMENT

SAMA is also Saudi Arabia's investment authority, responsible for managing the country's vast foreign assets. Most of this money is held in the USA and Europe. Although SAMA has recently been making more long-term investments, the vast bulk of its assets are still thought to be liquid. Very little official Saudi money goes into equities and almost nothing into property. Major Western banks seem to be the main beneficiaries of the vast funds at SAMA's disposal, and SAMA's investment department is advised by a small team which has been seconded from Baring Brothers & Co, a London merchant bank, and White Weld, a US investment bank. IMF figures reveal that SAMA's foreign assets increased from about 16,940m. riyals in December 1973 to 472,930m. riyals in December 1982, but declined to 202,760m. riyals ($54,140m.) in March 1991. These assets totalled 224,650m. riyals in September 1992.

AID

Between 1973 and 1989, grants and concessionary loans that Saudi Arabia made available to developing countries totalled $59,470m., representing 5.5% of GNP and placing the kingdom fourth in the world list of aid-donors. Among OPEC members, Saudi Arabia is by far the largest aid-donor, having contributed more than 80% of OPEC allocations in the period 1980–89. Between 1972 and 1983, aid totalling $25,568m. was provided to other Islamic states, where most aid is sent (in particular to the 'front-line' countries and Pakistan). Saudi contributions to the 'front-line' states after 1974 amounted to $1,000m. per year. The country has generally been the principal contributor to the various Arab funds that have been established to help poor Arab and poor African states, as well as to the IMF oil facilities. In April 1981 Saudi Arabia made a $10,000m. loan to the IMF for two years. Following further loans, the country was estimated to have advanced $15,000m. by 1984. It has also lent large sums to the World Bank at commercial rates. The Saudi Fund for Development (SFD), established in 1974, makes concessionary loans to Africa, Asia and Latin America, as well as to the Arab world. Financial support was given to Iraq during its war with Iran from 1980 to 1988, and in 1983 a substantial loan was granted to France. In March 1989 Saudi Arabia donated $85.5m. to the PLO, the last tranche of a 10-year programme of payments to the organization. A further $6m. per month during 1989 was pledged for Palestinians in the Israeli-occupied territories. In the period 1975–91 the SFD granted 277 loans to 61 countries, totalling 18,727m. riyals.

In May 1991 Saudi Arabia gave $3,650m. in cash payments towards the US military effort in the Gulf War in

January–February 1991. The USA had so far received $8,186m. in cash for its military contribution. In July the Saudi Government approved a loan worth 64m. riyals to Egypt by the SFD, to build an expressway from Asyut to Cairo. In the same month the US received a further $850m. for costs incurred during the Gulf crisis (1990–91). Saudi Arabia pledged to give $16,839m. in total, and as of August the outstanding balance was $4,110m. In August the Government announced its intention to give Turkey $1,000m. worth of free crude petroleum, in addition to supplies that Turkey had already received, worth $1,600m., to compensate for the adverse effects that the Gulf crisis had had on the Turkish economy. Bangladesh was to receive aid worth $100m. to help in the rebuilding of infrastructure which was destroyed during the flood disaster in May 1991. In mid-August Saudi Arabia paid $175m. of its $1,000m. pledge to the United Kingdom towards that country's military costs during the Gulf War. Aid allocations approved in 1993 included $100m. for reconstruction in Lebanon and $26m. for Bosnian refugee relief. In June 1997 $2.4m. of exceptional aid was given to the UN Relief and Works Agency for Palestine Refugees in the Near East.

BUDGETS

Government revenues from petroleum traditionally provide more than 90% of the State's budget revenue. In 1979/80 the unexpected sharp rise in petroleum prices, resulted in revenue of 220,000m. riyals (compared with a forecast of 160,000m. riyals). This was reflected in the budget estimates for 1980/81, 1981/82 and 1982/83, which projected expenditure rising to 245,000m. riyals, 290,000m. riyals and 313,400m. riyals respectively. Actual expenditure for 1982/83 was much lower than projected, however, at 244,900m. riyals, and revenue totalled 246,200m. riyals. The 1983/84 budget reflected the sharp decline in petroleum revenues: although both revenue and expenditure were lower than expected, at 206,400m. riyals and 230,200m. riyals respectively, they resulted in a budget deficit. Another deficit was recorded in 1984/85, and the effect of the growing economic crisis was shown in the provisional budget figures for 1985/86, which suggest that revenue may have been as low as 112,000m. riyals, and expenditure 180,900m. riyals. A deficit of 69,700m. riyals, to be financed from the kingdom's general reserve, was also recorded. Publication of the 1986/87 budget, due in March 1986, was postponed for 10 months, owing to uncertainty over the level of petroleum prices. The monthly government expenditure on essential items during the months continued at the same average monthly rate as in the 1985/86 financial year. Budget revenues from petroleum in the financial year 1986/87 were projected at 65,200m. riyals, representing 55.6% of total government revenues, and a 6.5% increase compared with the previous year. The budget for 1986/87 envisaged total expenditure of 170,000m. riyals, 6% less than in 1985/86, and a deficit of 52,720m. riyals was projected. Total expenditure for 1989 was set at 141,200m. riyals. The Government anticipated revenues, mainly from oil, of 105,300m. riyals, resulting in a deficit of 35,900m. riyals. The budget proposals for 1989 predicted total expenditure of 140,460m. riyals.

As originally presented in December 1989, the Government's budget proposals for 1990 envisaged expenditure of 143,000m. riyals, and a deficit of 25,000m. riyals. In view of the Gulf crisis, no separate 1991 budget was prepared, the 1990 provisions being extended through the year. In the event, official figures for 1990, published in April 1992, revealed that actual expenditure had reached 210,430m. riyals and revenue 154,721m. riyals, producing a deficit of 55,709m. riyals. Provisional figures for 1991 showed that expenditure increased to 261,570m. riyals, and the deficit to 77,000m. riyals. Budget deficits were recorded in 1992 and 1993, at 39,500m. riyals (revenue 165,400m. riyals, expenditure 204,900m. riyals) and 27,800m. riyals (revenue 169,150m. riyals, expenditure 196,950m. riyals) respectively.

The 1994 budget provided for the first balanced budget since 1982, at 160,000m. riyals. However, this revenue projection proved to be wholly unrealistic, and in the 1995 budget statement the Government's 1994 revenue was stated as 120,000m. riyals, leaving a deficit of 40,000m. riyals. In the 1995 budget provision was made for total expenditure of 150,056m. riyals (6.2% less than in 1994) and total revenue of 135,000m. riyals (12.5% more than the revised revenue total for 1994), leaving a

1995 budget deficit of 15,056m. riyals (over 60% lower than the previous year's recorded deficit). The expenditure total in the budget did not include spending of 1,088m. riyals by the municipal and water sector and 2,175m. riyals by the state telephone company, funded out of the service providers' charges to users. On the revenue side of the 1995 budget, the Government used a very conservative oil price forecast of $14 per barrel while imposing new or higher charges for a range of subsidized items, including fuel, power, water, telecommunications and transport. Other measures included substantial rises in visa fees for foreign workers. The total yield from domestic revenue-raising measures in 1995 was expected to exceed 9,000m. riyals. Oil export prices remained above budgeted levels in 1997, with the result that the Government's actual revenue for that year totalled 204,000m. riyals (including 153,000m. riyals from oil and gas). Expenditure was revised upwards to 200,600m. riyals (including 30,000m. riyals of capital spending), leaving a small surplus of 3,400m. riyals. The 1998 budget provided for total revenue of 178,000m. riyals and total expenditure of 196,000m. riyals, resulting in a deficit of 18,000m. riyals. Sectoral spending allocations itemized in the budget announcement were 45,595m. riyals (23.3% of total expenditure) for education, 19,700m. riyals (10%) for health and social development, 11,750m. riyals (6%) for transport and communications, 10,655m. riyals (5.4%) for infrastructure, industry and electricity, 7,640m. riyals (3.9%) for municipal services and water, 7,271m. riyals (3.7%) for domestic subsidies and social insurance and 5,000m. riyals (2.5%) for state development organizations and funds. Independent analysts estimated that around 31.5% of the total 1998 budget was earmarked for spending on defence and national security. The Government's 1998 revenue projections assumed an average oil export price of about $14.50 per barrel. However the actual price of the kingdom's main export grade averaged only $11.46 per barrel during the first 28 weeks of 1998, compared with an average of $17.05 per barrel for the whole of 1997.

The 1996 budget provided for total expenditure of 150,000m. riyals and total revenue of 131,500m. riyals, leaving a deficit of 18,500m. riyals. Less than half of the 1996 expenditure total was attributed to specific sectors in the budget announcement, the specified allocations being those for education (18.4%), health and social development (8.9%), transport and communications (6.1%), domestic subsidies (4.6%), infrastructure, industry and electricity (4.1%) and municipalities and water (3.6%). As in 1995, the revenue estimates assumed an average oil export price of $14 per barrel, whereas the actual price of Saudi Arabia's main export grade averaged $17.73 per barrel in the first half of 1996 (compared with $16.26 per barrel in the first half of 1995). This price increased further in the second half of 1996 to $18.56 per barrel, boosting the Government's actual revenue for 1996 to 177,000m. riyals. Expenditure was revised upwards to 194,000m. riyals, leaving a reduced deficit of 17,000m. riyals. Of the 44,000m. riyals of additional expenditure in 1996, some 22,000m. riyals were used to reduce the Government's indebtedness to domestic creditors. The Government's 1997 budget provided for revenue of 164,000m. riyals and expenditure of 181,000m. riyals, leaving a deficit of 17,000m. riyals. Levels of taxation and subsidy remained unchanged in the 1997 budget, which included no new revenue-raising measures. Sectoral spending allocations detailed in the 1997 budget were 41,692m. riyals (23% of total expenditure) for education, 17,763m. riyals (9.8%) for health and social development, 10,432m. riyals (5.7%) for transport and communications, 8,631m. riyals (4.8%) for infrastructure, industry and electricity, 7,133m. riyals (3.9%) for domestic subsidies and 6,473m. riyals (3.6%) for municipal services and water. The remaining 49.1% of the 1997 budget (including expenditure on defence and security) was aggregated as 'other spending'.

EDUCATION, HEALTH AND SOCIAL SECURITY

Within the Government's development policy, considerable emphasis has been placed on the improvement of education, health services and other aspects of social security. The number of schools and institutes of higher education increased from 3,107 in 1970 to 17,268 in 1991, with the number of students increasing from 547,000 to 3.1m. over the same period. There are plans to expand the universities at Umm al-Qura, Jeddah and Medina. The total number of students enrolled at all levels of education increased to 3.9m. in 1995/96. Illiteracy rates were officially estimated at 14.9% among males and 35.5% among females in 1995/96. UNESCO estimates for 1995, however, suggested much higher rates (28.5% for males and 49.8% for females). The number of hospitals under the control of the Ministry of Health increased from 47 in 1970 to 267 in 1994, with medical and paramedical personnel increasing from 4,494 to almost 100,000, and the number of beds to 36,000. In early 1991 there were four hospital beds for every 1,000 inhabitants, a ratio similar to that in the USA. In 1994 there were 1,668 health centres. In August 1994 the Ministry of Health announced that work would soon commence on the construction of 2,000 additional primary health care centres and that the possibility of establishing a comprehensive health insurance programme was being studied. In December 1995 the Government introduced a compulsory health insurance scheme for expatriate workers, 80% of the cost of contributions being borne by employers and 20% by employees. Social security payments are made available by the Deputy Ministry of Social Care, and total disbursements increased from 41.7m. riyals (to 198,000

beneficiaries) in 1970 to 1,537m. riyals (to 314,117 beneficiaries) in 1985/86. The budget allocation for expenditure on health and social services in 1990 was 11,239m. riyals, the same allocation applying to 1991. In the 1992 budget the allocation for health and social development was 12,200m. riyals, and the 1993 budget proposals allocated 14,087m. riyals. In 1994 the allocation was reduced by an unspecified amount (the IMF's estimate of 1994 spending on 'social development' being 11,300m. riyals). The 1995 budget allocated 13,366m. riyals for health and social services, and the 1996 allocation was fractionally lower at 13,329m. riyals. The 1997 health and social development budget of 19,700m. riyals included allocations of capital for the construction of 11 new hospitals. Housing has also been an important part of government policy, and since 1974 it is estimated that more than 500,000 housing units have been constructed throughout the kingdom: about half by the Government and half by the private sector. By late 1991 a total of 477,000 housing units had been wholly or partly funded by the REDF. All adult Saudi Arabians, if not independently wealthy, are entitled to a plot of land and a loan of $80,000 with which to build a home. In 1988 a total of 347,260 people received the loan.

Statistical Survey

Sources (unless otherwise indicated): Kingdom of Saudi Arabia, *Statistical Yearbook*; Saudi Arabian Monetary Agency, *Annual Report* and *Statistical Summary*.

Area and Population

AREA, POPULATION AND DENSITY

Area (sq km)	2,240,000*
Population (census results)	
9–14 September 1974	7,012,642
27 September 1992†	
Males	9,466,541
Females	7,462,753
Total	16,929,294
Population (UN estimate at mid-year)‡	
1994	17,765,000
1995	18,255,000
1996	18,836,000
Density (per sq km) at mid-1996	8.4

* 864,869 sq miles.

† Figures are provisional. Of the total population at the 1992 census, 12,304,835 (males 50.5%; females 49.5%) were nationals of Saudi Arabia, while 4,624,459 (males 70.4%; females 29.6%) were foreign nationals.

‡ Source: UN, *World Population Prospects: The 1996 Revision*.

SAUDI ARABIA-IRAQ NEUTRAL ZONE

The Najdi (Saudi Arabian) frontier with Iraq was defined in the Treaty of Mohammara in May 1922. Later a Neutral Zone of 7,044 sq km was established adjacent to the western tip of the Kuwait frontier. No military or permanent buildings were to be erected in the zone and the nomads of both countries were to have unimpeded access to its pastures and wells. A further agreement concerning the administration of this zone was signed between Iraq and Saudi Arabia in May 1938. In July 1975 Iraq and Saudi Arabia signed an agreement providing for an equal division of the diamond-shaped zone between the two countries, with the border following a straight line through the zone.

SAUDI ARABIA-KUWAIT NEUTRAL ZONE

A Convention signed at Uqair in December 1922 fixed the Najdi (Saudi Arabian) boundary with Kuwait. The Convention also established a Neutral Zone of 5,770 sq km immediately to the south of Kuwait in which Saudi Arabia and Kuwait held equal rights. The final agreement on this matter was signed in 1963. Since 1966 the Neutral Zone, or Partitioned Zone as it is sometimes known, has been divided between the two countries and each administers its own half, in practice as an integral part of the State. However, the petroleum deposits in the Zone remain undivided and production from the onshore oil concessions in the Zone is shared equally between the two states' concessionaires.

PRINCIPAL TOWNS (population at 1974 census)

Riyadh (royal capital)	.	666,840	Hufuf	.	101,271
Jeddah (administra-			Tabouk . . .	.	74,825
tive capital)	. .	561,104	Buraidah . .	.	69,940
Makkah (Mecca)	. .	366,801	Al-Mobarraz .	.	54,325
At-Ta'if	. . .	204,857	Khamis-Mushait	.	49,581
Al-Madinah (Medina)	.	198,186	Al-Khobar . .	.	48,817
Dammam . .	.	127,844	Najran . .	.	47,501
			Ha'il (Hayil)	. .	40,502

BIRTHS AND DEATHS (UN estimates, annual averages)

	1980–85	1985–90	1990–95
Birth rate (per 1,000) . . .	40.5	36.6	35.1
Death rate (per 1,000) . . .	7.9	5.4	4.7

Expectation of life (UN estimates years at birth, 1990–95): 69.7 (males 68.4; females 71.4).

Source: UN, *World Population Prospects: The 1994 Revision*.

ECONOMICALLY ACTIVE POPULATION
(ILO estimates, '000 persons at mid-1980)

	Males	Females	Total
Agriculture, etc.	1,289	43	1,333
Industry	387	9	395
Services	903	121	1,023
Total labour force . . .	2,579	172	2,751

Source: ILO, *Economically Active Population Estimates and Projections, 1950–2025*.

Mid-1996 (estimates in '000): Agriculture, etc. 807; Total 6,136 (Source: FAO, *Production Yearbook*).

Agriculture

PRINCIPAL CROPS ('000 metric tons)

	1994	1995	1996
Wheat	2,818	2,453	1,200*
Barley	2,011	2,021	450*
Millet	12	13	14†
Sorghum	185	207	210†
Potatoes	238	406	435†
Pulses†	7	7	7
Sesame seed†	2	2	2
Tomatoes	442	489	500†
Pumpkins, squash and gourds†	69	69	69
Cucumbers and gherkins†	113	115	115
Aubergines (Eggplants)†	69	69	69
Onions (dry)	43	239	250†
Carrots	27	30	30†
Other vegetables	1,583	1,428	1,428
Watermelons†	400	400	400
Melons†	130	130	130
Grapes	124	129	137†
Dates	568	589	597†
Citrus fruit†	40	41	41
Other fruits	200	200	200†

* Unofficial figure.   † FAO estimate(s).
Source: FAO, *Production Yearbook*.

LIVESTOCK ('000 head, year ending September)

	1994	1995	1996
Asses†	98	97	97
Camels	417*	420	422†
Cattle	214*	220*	225†
Sheep	7,578	7,753	7,800†
Goats	4,309	4,373	4,400†

Poultry (million)†: 81 in 1994; 83 in 1995; 83 in 1996.

* Unofficial figure.   † FAO estimate(s).

Source: FAO, *Production Yearbook*.

LIVESTOCK PRODUCTS ('000 metric tons)

	1994	1995	1996
Beef and veal*	30	26	20
Mutton and lamb†	64	66	66
Goat meat†	25	25	25
Poultry meat	297*	311*	311†
Other meat	41	42	42
Cows' milk†	345	350	350
Sheep's milk†	48	49	49
Goats' milk†	68	69	69
Poultry eggs	127	135	140†
Wool: greasy†	7	7	7
clean†	4	4	4
Cattle hides (fresh)†	4	4	4
Sheepskins (fresh)†	11	11	11
Goatskins (fresh)†	4	4	4

* Unofficial figures.   † FAO estimate(s).

Source: FAO, *Production Yearbook*.

Fishing

(metric tons, live weight)

	1993	1994	1995
Nile tilapia	2,175	2,200	2,435
Groupers and seabasses	5,752	5,707	3,514
Snappers and jobfishes	3,019	3,054	1,662
Emperor (Scavengers)	8,281	7,524	6,598
Porgies and seabreams	1,064	1,910	1,469
Spinefeet (Rabbitfishes)	1,388	1,887	2,341
Barracudas	1,990	2,249	1,065
Carangids	4,920	5,884	4,859
Seerfishes	10,374	10,851	12,378
Indian mackerel	1,741	3,240	3,069
Other fishes (incl. unspecified)	6,675	6,542	7,590
Penaeus shrimps	2,846	4,297	6,142
Other crustaceans and molluscs	299	1,502	1,364
Total catch	50,524	56,847	54,486
Inland waters	2,185	2,200	2,435
Indian Ocean	48,339	54,647	52,051

Source: FAO, *Yearbook of Fishery Statistics*.

Mining

('000 metric tons, unless otherwise indicated)

	1993	1994	1995
Crude petroleum*	401,132	401,197	399,915
Natural gasoline*†	6,051	6,060	n.a.
Natural gas (petajoules)	1,401	1,471	1,574
Gypsum (crude)‡	327	375	375

* Including 50% of the total output of the Neutral or Partitioned Zone, shared with Kuwait.
† Estimated production.
‡ Data from the US Bureau of Mines.

Source: UN, *Industrial Commodity Statistics Yearbook*.

1996: Crude petroleum 2,965.45 million barrels (404.95 million metric tons).

Industry

SELECTED PRODUCTS
(including 50% of the total output of the Neutral Zone; '000 metric tons, unless otherwise indicated)

	1993	1994	1995
Nitrogenous fertilizers (a)*†	832	1,068	n.a.
Phosphatic fertilizers (b)*†	132	165	n.a.
Jet fuel†	2,700	2,750	2,740
Motor spirit (petrol)	10,500	10,907	9,971
Naphtha†	5,200	5,700	5,600
Kerosene†	4,610	4,770	4,760
Distillate fuel oils	23,010	23,496	23,067
Residual fuel oils	26,000†	23,656	24,025
Lubricating oils	620	760	750
Petroleum bitumen (asphalt)†	1,100	1,310	1,400
Liquefied petroleum gas:			
from natural gas plants†	15,550	17,030	17,100
from petroleum refineries†	950	900	910
Cement†‡	15,300	16,000	n.a.
Crude steel‡	2,318	2,411	2,451
Electric energy (million kWh)	87,906	96,880	99,833

* Production in terms of (a) nitrogen or (b) phosphoric acid..
† Provisional or estimated figure(s).
‡ Data from the US Bureau of Mines.

Source: mainly UN, *Industrial Commodity Statistics Yearbook*.

Finance

CURRENCY AND EXCHANGE RATES

Monetary Units

100 halalah = 20 qurush = 1 Saudi riyal (SR).

Sterling and Dollar Equivalents (31 May 1998)

£1 sterling = 6.107 riyals;

US $1 = 3.745 riyals;

100 Saudi riyals = £16.375 = $26.702.

Exchange Rate

Since June 1986 the official mid-point rate has been fixed at US $1 = 3.745 riyals.

BUDGET ESTIMATES (million riyals)

Revenue	1995	1996	1997
Petroleum revenues . . .	101,461	99,606	129,444
Other revenues	33,539	31,894	34,556
Total	135,000	131,500	164,000

Expenditure	1995	1996	1997
Human resource development . .	26,912	27,536	41,595
Transport and communications .	6,199*	6,310	6,890
Economic resource development .	3,855	4,544	4,733
Health and social development .	10,161	10,110	14,366
Infrastructure development . .	1,395	1,356	1,588
Municipal services . . .	4,880	4,893	5,445
Defence and security . . .	49,501	50,025	67,975
Public administration and other government spending	39,706	37,952	30,836
Government lending institutions† .	476	415	439
Local subsidies	6,915	6,859	7,133
Total	150,000	150,000	181,000

* Excluding 2,175m. riyals for telephone system expansion project, to be financed directly from revenues.

† Including transfers to the Saudi Fund for Development (SFD).

1995 (revised figures, million riyals): Total revenue 146,500; Total expenditure 173,900.

1996 (revised figures, million riyals): Total revenue 179,100; Total expenditure 198,100.

1997 (revised figures, million riyals): Total revenue 204,000; Total expenditure 200,600.

1998 (estimates, million riyals): Total revenue 178,000; Total expenditure 196,000.

INTERNATIONAL RESERVES (US $ million in December)

	1995	1996	1997
Gold*	239	231	217
IMF special drawing rights . .	666	692	691
Reserve position in IMF . .	854	807	718
Foreign exchange . . .	7,101	5,295	5,944
Total	8,861	7,025	7,570

* Valued at SDR 35 per troy ounce.

Source: IMF, *International Financial Statistics*.

MONEY SUPPLY (million riyals in December)

	1994	1995	1996
Currency outside banks . .	44,965	43,087	43,038
Demand deposits at commercial banks	80,679	81,384	89,890
Total money	125,645	124,471	132,928

COST OF LIVING (Consumer Price Index for all cities; base: 1988 = 100)

	1994	1995	1996
Food, drink and tobacco . . .	115.7	116.7	118.6
Housing	114.9	123.2	124.0
Textiles and clothing . . .	96.5	95.7	94.1
House furnishing	99.7	100.4	104.0
Medical care	101.3	102.3	101.4
Transport and communications .	109.2	133.0	131.9
Entertainment and education . .	105.1	105.6	105.9
All items (incl. others) . . .	109.0	114.5	115.5

NATIONAL ACCOUNTS

Expenditure on the Gross Domestic Product

(million riyals at current prices)

	1993	1994	1995
Government final consumption expenditure	127,779	119,561	122,849
Private final consumption expenditure	193,909	194,831	198,099
Increase in stocks . . .	9,171	6,182	6,198
Gross fixed capital formation . .	98,450	83,707	85,595
Total domestic expenditure .	429,309	404,281	412,741
Exports of goods and services .	179,403	180,001	197,265
Less Imports of goods and services .	164,870	134,257	140,885
GDP in purchasers' values .	443,842	450,025	469,121
GDP at constant 1990 prices* .	433,960	436,180	438,230

* Source: IMF, *International Financial Statistics*.

Gross Domestic Product by Economic Activity

(million riyals at current prices)

	1994	1995*	1996†
Agriculture, forestry and fishing .	31,131	31,598	32,162
Mining and quarrying:			
Crude petroleum and natural gas	146,984	155,890	183,018
Other	2,104	2,114	2,172
Manufacturing:			
Petroleum refining . . .	15,689	16,639	19,535
Other	23,783	25,805	28,117
Electricity, gas and water . .	754	795	853
Construction	42,730	43,499	44,447
Trade, restaurants and hotels .	32,978	33,143	34,258
Transport, storage and communications . . .	30,456	30,913	31,507
Finance, insurance, real estate and business services:			
Ownership of dwellings . .	7,516	7,591	7,804
Other	20,098	19,888	20,189
Government services . . .	80,100	86,243	88,873
Other community, social and personal services . . .	13,362	13,562	13,800
Sub-total	447,676	467,680	506,744
Import duties	8,289	7,500	8,358
Less Imputed bank service charge	5,940	6,059	5,816
GDP in purchasers' values . .	450,025	469,121	509,284

* Estimates.   † Preliminary figures.

BALANCE OF PAYMENTS (US $ million)

	1995	1996	1997
Exports of goods f.o.b. . . .	50,041	60,729	59,684
Imports of goods f.o.b. . . .	−25,650	−25,358	−26,154
Trade balance	24,390	35,370	33,530
Exports of services . . .	3,480	2,772	4,484
Imports of services . . .	−19,083	−24,295	−25,477
Balance on goods and services .	8,787	13,848	12,537
Other income received . .	4,987	5,127	5,736
Other income paid . . .	−2,184	−2,681	−2,580
Balance on goods, services and income	11,591	16,294	15,692
Current transfers paid . .	−16,916	−15,613	−15,439
Current balance . . .	−5,325	681	254
Direct investment from abroad .	−1,877	−1,129	2,575
Portfolio investment assets .	4,025	−10,169	−7,358
Other investment assets . .	4,253	9,115	3,208
Other investment liabilities . .	142	−275	1,973
Overall balance . . .	1,217	−1,778	652

Source: IMF, *International Financial Statistics*.

External Trade

PRINCIPAL COMMODITIES (million riyals)

Imports c.i.f.	1994	1995	1996*
Live animals and animal products	3,334	5,233	5,071
Vegetable products . . .	5,511	6,615	7,674
Prepared foodstuffs, beverages, spirits, vinegar and tobacco .	2,079	4,421	4,411
Products of chemical or allied industries.	6,242	8,332	8,382
Plastics, rubber and articles thereof	3,456	4,033	3,777
Paper-making material; paper and paperboard, and articles thereof . .	2,018	2,828	2,295
Textiles and textile articles . .	6,410	7,913	7,589
Pearls, precious or semi-precious stones, precious metals, etc. .	2,954	4,237	4,399
Base metals and articles of base metal	8,108	10,857	10,396
Machinery and mechanical appliances; electrical equipment; sound and television apparatus	18,145	23,020	21,848
Vehicles, aircraft, vessels and associated transport equipment	18,058	15,171	15,903
Scientific instruments, photographic equipment, watches, musical instruments, recorders, etc. . .	2,588	2,813	2,897
Miscellaneous manufactured articles	1,947	2,028	1,935
Total (incl. others)	87,449	105,187	103,980

Exports†	1994	1995	1996*
Mineral products	142,829	163,083	188,170
Crude petroleum	117,200	132,990	153,448
Refined petroleum products. .	25,629	30,093	34,722
Petrochemicals	7,878	10,166	10,429
Construction materials . . .	1,151	2,706	2,964
Agricultural, animal and food products	1,430	1,589	1,342
Total (incl. others)	159,590	187,403	212,353

* Provisional.

† Including re-exports (million riyals): 1,312 in 1994; 1,762 in 1995; 2,320 (provisional) in 1996.

PRINCIPAL TRADING PARTNERS (million riyals)

Imports c.i.f.	1994	1995	1996*
Australia	758	804	1,263
Belgium.	1,678	1,913	1,812
Brazil	1,027	1,660	1,780
Canada	1,471	1,178	1,486
France	3,806	5,019	4,313
Germany	7,246	8,273	7,798
India	1,578	1,909	2,241
Indonesia	993	1,443	1,543
Italy	4,116	4,620	4,901
Japan	10,270	9,312	7,314
Korea, Republic	2,477	3,304	2,940
Netherlands		1,983	1,770
Spain	1,323	1,551	1,414
Sweden	1,273	1,494	1,288
Switzerland	3,634	5,198	4,856
Taiwan	1,402	1,515	1,547
Thailand	765	1,070	1,219
Turkey	1,726	1,574	1,123
United Arab Emirates . . .	1,115	247	1,510
United Kingdom	7,400	8,904	9,334
USA	18,657	22,633	22,771
Total (incl. others) . . .	87,449	105,187	103,980

Exports (incl. re-exports)	1993	1994	1995
Australia	1,535	1,443	2,212
Bahrain	4,991	5,017	5,541
Brazil	4,953	4,911	4,096
China, People's Republic . .	4,798	4,320	5,470
France	6,960	8,471	7,347
Germany	1,833	1,980	957
Greece	2,672	2,088	1,730
India	4,971	4,686	5,844
Indonesia	1,325	1,833	1,871
Italy	7,971	8,142	7,398
Japan	26,777	25,470	30,346
Korea, Republic	11,931	12,999	18,429
Morocco	1,537	1,674	1,648
Netherlands	6,821	7,685	8,703
Pakistan	1,838	1,744	1,998
Philippines	2,144	2,666	3,659
Singapore	7,833	7,735	9,972
Spain	2,392	2,141	4,359
Turkey	5,221	4,549	4,982
United Arab Emirates . . .	3,253	3,569	5,057
United Kingdom	5,167	3,148	2,747
USA	27,715	29,518	31,743
Total (incl. others) . . .	158,770	159,590	187,403

* Provisional figures.

Transport

RAILWAYS (traffic)

	1994	1995	1996
Passenger journeys ('000)	444.6	468.0	546.6
Freight carried ('000 metric tons)	1,844.1	1,581.6	1,610.0

ROAD TRAFFIC (motor vehicles in use at 31 December)

	1989	1990	1991
Passenger cars	2,550,465	2,664,028	2,762,132
Buses and coaches	50,856	52,136	54,089
Goods vehicles	2,153,297	2,220,658	2,286,541
Total	4,754,618	4,936,822	5,103,205

1994: Passenger cars 1,671,200; Buses and coaches 22,100; Goods vehicles 1,124,500; Total 2,817,800.

Source: IRF, *World Road Statistics*.

SHIPPING

Merchant Fleet (vessels registered at 31 December)

	1995	1996	1997
Oil tankers			
Vessels	37	35	31
Displacement ('000 grt)	238	258	203
Others			
Vessels	243	241	252
Displacement ('000 grt)	949	950	960
Total vessels	280	276	283
Total displacement ('000 grt)	1,187	1,208	1,164

Source: Lloyd's Register of Shipping, *World Fleet Statistics*.

International Sea-borne Freight Traffic ('000 metric tons*)

	1988	1989	1990
Goods loaded	161,666	165,989	214,070
Goods unloaded	42,546	42,470	46,437

* Including Saudi Arabia's share of traffic in the Neutral or Partitioned Zone.

Source: UN, *Monthly Bulletin of Statistics*.

1995 ('000 metric tons, excluding crude oil): Goods loaded 54,653; Goods unloaded 24,711.

CIVIL AVIATION (traffic on scheduled services)

	1993	1994	1995
Kilometres flown (million)	113	117	115
Passengers carried ('000)	11,864	12,142	11,525
Passenger-kilometres (million)	18,572	18,250	18,501
Total ton-km (million)	2,415	2,477	2,583

Source: UN, *Statistical Yearbook*.

Tourism

PILGRIMS TO MECCA FROM ABROAD*

Country of Origin	1984/85	1985/86	1986/87
Egypt	130,872	98,606	97,216
India	33,691	39,344	40,854
Indonesia	41,965	59,172	57,519
Iran	152,227	152,149	157,395
Iraq	33,856	14,551	29,522
Pakistan	87,889	92,305	93,013
Turkey	41,693	54,624	96,711
Yemen Arab Republic	41,121	43,512	61,416
Total (incl. others)	851,761	856,718	960,386

Total pilgrims: 762,755 in 1987/88; 774,560 in 1988/89; 827,236 in 1989/90; 720,102 in 1990/91; 1,015,664 in 1991/92; 992,813 in 1992/93.

* Figures relate to Islamic lunar years. The equivalent dates in the Gregorian calendar are: 26 September 1984 to 14 September 1985; 15 September 1985 to 4 September 1986; 5 September 1986 to 24 August 1987; 25 August 1987 to 12 August 1988; 13 August 1988 to 1 August 1989; 2 August 1989 to 22 July 1990; 23 July 1990 to 11 July 1991; 12 July 1991 to 30 June 1992; 1 July 1992 to 19 June 1993.

1993/94: more than 2m. pilgrims.

Communications Media

	1993	1994	1995
Radio receivers ('000 in use)	5,015	5,125	5,320
Television receivers ('000 in use)	4,370	4,455	4,700
Telephones ('000 main lines in use)	1,615	1,676	1,719
Mobile cellular telephones (subscribers)	15,910	15,959	16,008
Daily newspapers	n.a.	19	12

Non-daily newspapers: 3 in 1994.

Telefax stations (number in use): 75,000 in 1993.

Sources: UNESCO, *Statistical Yearbook*; UN, *Statistical Yearbook*.

Education

(1995/96)

	Institutions	Teachers	Students
Pre-primary*	968	7,479	85,802
Primary	13,917	169,321	2,248,122
Intermediate	4,895	69,310	887,520
Secondary (general)	2,316	35,746	497,857
Teacher-training*	n.a.	1,482	24,462
Vocational*	n.a.	2,991	24,570
University	7	9,490	143,787

* Source: UNESCO, *Statistical Yearbook*.

Directory

The Constitution

The Basic Law of Government was introduced by royal decree in 1992.

Chapter 1 defines Saudi Arabia as a sovereign Arab, Islamic state. Article 1 defines God's Book and the Sunnah of his prophet as the constitution of Saudi Arabia. The official language is Arabic. The official holidays are Id al-Fitr and Id al-Adha. The calendar is the Hegira calendar.

Chapter 2 concerns the system of government, which is defined as a monarchy, hereditary in the male descendants of Abd al-Aziz ibn Abd ar-Rahman al-Faisal as-Sa'ud. It outlines the duties of the Heir Apparent. The principles of government are justice, consultation and equality in accordance with Islamic law (*Shari'a*).

Chapter 3 concerns the family. The State is to aspire to strengthen family ties and to maintain its Arab and Islamic values. Article 11 states that 'Saudi society will be based on the principle of adherence to God's command, on mutual co-operation in good deeds and piety and mutual support and inseparability'. Education aims to instil the Islamic faith.

Chapter 4 defines the economic principles of the State. All natural resources are the property of the State. The State protects public money and freedom of property. Taxation is only to be imposed on a just basis.

Chapter 5 concerns rights and duties. The State is to protect Islam and to implement the *Shari'a* law. The State protects human rights in accordance with the *Shari'a*. The State is to provide public services and security for all citizens. Punishment is to be in accordance with the *Shari'a*. The Royal Courts are open to all citizens.

Chapter 6 defines the authorities of the State as the judiciary, the executive and the regulatory authority. The judiciary is independent, and acts in accordance with *Shari'a* law. The King is head of the Council of Ministers and Commander-in-Chief of the Armed Forces. The Prime Minister and other ministers are appointed by the King. It provides for the establishment of a Consultative Council (Majlis ash-Shoura).

Chapter 7 concerns financial affairs. It provides for the annual presentation of a state budget. Corporate budgets are subject to the same provisions.

Chapter 8 concerns control bodies. Control bodies will be established to ensure good financial and administrative management of state assets.

Chapter 9 defines the general provisions pertaining to the application of the Basic Law of Government.

The Government

HEAD OF STATE

King FAHD IBN ABD AL-AZIZ AS-SA'UD (acceded to the throne 13 June 1982).

Crown Prince: ABDULLAH IBN ABD AL-AZIZ AS-SA'UD.

COUNCIL OF MINISTERS
(September 1998)

Prime Minister: King FAHD IBN ABD AL-AZIZ AS-SA'UD.

First Deputy Prime Minister and Commander of the National Guard: Crown Prince ABDULLAH IBN ABD AL-AZIZ AS-SA'UD.

Second Deputy Prime Minister and Minister of Defence and Civil Aviation: Prince SULTAN IBN ABD AL-AZIZ AS-SA'UD.

Minister of Public Works and Housing: Prince MUTAIB IBN ABD AL-AZIZ AS-SA'UD.

Minister of the Interior: Prince NAYEF IBN ABD AL-AZIZ AS-SA'UD.

Minister of Foreign Affairs: Prince SA'UD AL-FAISAL AS-SA'UD.

Minister of Petroleum and Mineral Resources: Eng. ALI IBN IBRAHIM AN-NUAIMI.

Minister of Labour and Social Affairs: MUSAID IBN MUHAMMAD AS-SANNANI.

Minister of Agriculture and Water: Dr ABDULLAH IBN ABD AL-AZIZ IBN MUAMMAR.

Minister of Education: Dr MUHAMMAD IBN AHMAD AR-RASHID.

Minister of Higher Education: Dr KHALID IBN MUHAMMAD AL-ANGARI.

Minister of Transport: Dr NASIR IBN MUHAMMAD AS-SALOUM.

Minister of Finance and National Economy: Dr IBRAHIM IBN ABD AL-AZIZ AL-ASSAF.

Minister of Planning: Dr ABD AL-WAHAB IBN ABD AS-SALIM AL-ATTAR.

Minister of Information: Dr FOUAD IBN ABD AS-SALAM IBN MUHAMMAD FARSI.

Minister of Industry and Electricity: Dr HASHIM IBN ABDULLAH IBN HASHIM YAMANI.

Minister of Commerce: USAMA IBN JAFAAR IBN IBRAHIM FAQIH.

Minister of Justice: Dr ABDULLAH IBN MUHAMMAD IBN IBRAHIM ASH-SHEIKH.

Minister of Pilgrimage (Hajj) Affairs: Dr MAHMOUD IBN MUHAMMAD SAFAR.

Minister of Municipal and Rural Affairs: Dr MUHAMMAD IBN IBRAHIM AL-JARALLAH.

Minister of Awqaf (Religious Endowments), Dawa, Mosques and Guidance Affairs: Dr ABDULLAH IBN ABD AL-MOHSEN AT-TURKI.

Minister of Health: Dr USAMA IBN ABD AL-MAJID SHUBUKSHI.

Minister of Posts, Telegraphs and Telecommunications: Dr ALI IBN TALAL AL-JUHANI.

Ministers of State: Dr MUHAMMAD IBN ABD AL-AZIZ IBN ABDULLAH IBN HASSAN ASH-SHEIKH, Dr MUTLIB IBN ABDULLAH AN-NAFISA, Dr ABD AL-AZIZ IBN IBRAHIM AL-MANIE, Dr MUSAID IBN MUHAMMAD AL-AYBAN, Dr MADANI IBN ABD AL-QADIR ALAQI, Dr ABD AL-AZIZ AL-ABDULLAH AL-KHUWAITER.

MINISTRIES

Most ministries have regional offices in Jeddah.

Council of Ministers: Murabba, Riyadh 11121; tel. (1) 488-2444; telex 6655766.

Ministry of Agriculture and Water: Airport Rd, Riyadh 11195; tel. (1) 401-6666; telex 40690; fax (1) 404-4592.

Ministry of Awqaf (Religious Endowments), Dawa, Mosques and Guidance Affairs: Riyadh.

Ministry of Commerce: POB 1774, Airport Rd, Riyadh 11162; tel. (1) 401-2222; telex 401057; fax (1) 403-8421.

Ministry of Defence and Civil Aviation: POB 26731, Airport Rd, Riyadh 11165; tel. (1) 476-9000; telex 401188; fax (1) 405-5500.

Ministry of Education: POB 3734, Airport Rd, Riyadh 11481; tel. (1) 411-5777; telex 402650; fax (1) 411-2051.

Ministry of Finance and National Economy: Airport Rd, Riyadh 11177; tel. (1) 405-0000; telex 401021; fax (1) 401-0583.

Ministry of Foreign Affairs: Nasseriya St, Riyadh 11124; tel. (1) 401-5000; telex 405000; fax (1) 403-0159.

Ministry of Health: Airport Rd, Riyadh 11176; tel. (1) 401-5555; telex 404020; fax (1) 402-9876.

Ministry of Higher Education: King Faisal Hospital St, Riyadh 11153; tel. (1) 441-9849; telex 401481; fax (1) 441-9004.

Ministry of Industry and Electricity: POB 5729, Omar bin al-Khatab St, Riyadh 11432; tel. (1) 477-6666; telex 401154; fax (1) 477-5441.

Ministry of Information: POB 370, Nasseriya St, Riyadh 11161; tel. (1) 406-8888; telex 401461; fax (1) 404-4192.

Ministry of the Interior: POB 2833, Airport Rd, Riyadh 11134; tel. (1) 401-1111; telex 404416; fax (1) 403-1185.

Ministry of Justice: University St, Riyadh 11137; tel. (1) 405-7777; telex 4054443.

Ministry of Labour and Social Affairs: Omar bin al-Khatab St, Riyadh 11157; tel. (1) 477-8888; telex 401043; fax (1) 478-9175.

Ministry of Municipal and Rural Affairs: Nasseriya St, Riyadh 11136; tel. (1) 441-8888; telex 404018; fax (1) 441-7368.

Ministry of Petroleum and Mineral Resources: POB 247, King Abd al-Aziz Rd, Riyadh 11191; tel. (1) 478-1661; telex 400997; fax (1) 478-1980.

Ministry of Pilgrimage (Hajj) Affairs: Omar bin al-Khatab St, Riyadh 11183; tel. (1) 404-3003; telex 400189; fax (1) 402-2555.

Ministry of Planning: POB 1358, University St, Riyadh 11182; tel. (1) 401-3333; telex 402851; fax (1) 404-9300.

Ministry of Posts, Telegraphs and Telecommunications: Sharia al-Ma'azer, Intercontinental Rd, Riyadh 11112; tel. (1) 463-4444; telex 400200; fax (1) 405-2310.

Ministry of Public Works and Housing: POB 56095, Ma'ather St, Riyadh 11554; tel. (1) 407-3618; telex 400415.

Ministry of Transport: Airport Rd, Riyadh 11178; tel. (1) 404-3000; telex 401616; fax (1) 403-1401.

MAJLIS ASH-SHOURA
(Consultative Council)

In March 1992 King Fahd issued a decree to establish a Consultative Council of 60 members, whose powers include the right to summon and question ministers. The composition of the Council was announced by King Fahd in August 1993, and it was officially inaugurated in December of that year. Each member is to serve for four years. The Council's membership was increased to 90 when its second term began in July 1997.

Chairman: Sheikh MUHAMMAD IBN IBRAHIM AL-JUBAIR.

Diplomatic Representation

EMBASSIES IN SAUDI ARABIA

Afghanistan: Tariq al-Madina, Kilo No. 3, Jeddah; tel. (2) 53142.

Algeria: POB 94388, Riyadh 11693; tel. (1) 488-7171; telex 402828; fax (1) 482-1703; Ambassador: ABD AL-KARIM GHARIB.

Argentina: POB 94369, Riyadh 11693; tel. (1) 465-2600; fax (1) 465-1632; Ambassador: LUIS D. MENDIOLA.

Australia: POB 94400, Riyadh 11693; tel. (1) 488-7788; fax (1) 488-7973; Ambassador: PHILIP KNIGHT.

Austria: POB 94373, Riyadh 11693; tel. (1) 477-7445; fax (1) 476-6791; Ambassador: Dr OTTO DITZ.

Bahrain: POB 94371, Riyadh 11693; tel. (1) 488-0013; telex 407055; fax (1) 488-0208; Ambassador: ISSA MUHAMMAD AL-KHALIFA.

Bangladesh: POB 94395, Riyadh 11693; tel. (1) 465-5300; telex 406133; fax (1) 463-3555; Ambassador: Maj.-Gen. QUAZI GOLAM DASTGIR.

Belgium: POB 94396, Riyadh 11693; tel. (1) 488-2888; telex 406344; fax (1) 488-2033; Ambassador: JACQUES DE MONTJOYE.

Bosnia and Herzegovina: POB 94301, Riyadh 11693; tel. (1) 454-4360; fax (1) 465-7833; Ambassador: S. BISTRIĆ.

Brazil: POB 94348, Riyadh 11693; tel. (1) 488-0018; fax (1) 488-1075; Ambassador: SÉRGIO M. THOMPSON-FLORES.

Burkina Faso: POB 94330, Riyadh 11693; tel. (1) 465-2244; telex 403844; fax (1) 465-3397; Ambassador: HAROUNA KOUFLA.

Cameroon: POB 94336, Riyadh 11693; tel. (1) 488-0203; telex 408866; fax (1) 488-1463; Ambassador: MOHAMADOU LABARANG.

Canada: POB 94321, Riyadh 11693; tel. (1) 488-2288; fax (1) 488-0137; Ambassador: D. E. HOBSON.

Chad: POB 94374, Riyadh 11693; tel. (1) 465-7702; telex 406366; Ambassador: al-Hajji DJIME TOUGOU.

Chile: POB 94313, Riyadh 11693; tel. (1) 462-0481; fax (1) 462-4368.

China, People's Republic: POB 75231, Riyadh 11578; tel. (1) 482-4246; fax (1) 482-1123; Ambassador: ZHENG DAYONG.

Côte d'Ivoire: POB 94303, Riyadh 11693; tel. (1) 456-6943.

Denmark: POB 94398, Riyadh 11693; tel. (1) 488-0101; telex 404672; fax (1) 488-1366; Ambassador: POUL HOINESS.

Djibouti: POB 94340, Riyadh 11693; tel. (1) 454-3182; telex 406544; fax (1) 456-9168; Ambassador: IDRISS AHMAD CHIRWA.

Egypt: POB 94333, Riyadh 11693; tel. (1) 465-8425; fax (1) 465-2800; Ambassador: FATHY AL-SHAZLY.

Ethiopia: POB 94341, Riyadh 11693; tel. (1) 477-5285; telex 406633; fax (1) 476-8020; Ambassador: Ato MUHAMMAD ALI.

Finland: POB 94363, Riyadh 11693; tel. (1) 488-1515; fax (1) 488-2520; Ambassador: KAI GRANHOLM.

France: POB 94009, Riyadh 11693; tel. (1) 488-0880; telex 406967; fax (1) 488-2869; Ambassador: BERNARD POLETTI.

Gabon: POB 94325, Riyadh 11693; tel. (1) 463-2664; fax (1) 463-1817; Ambassador: NABIL KOUSSOU INAMA.

Gambia: POB 94322, Riyadh 11693; tel. (1) 465-1320; fax 462-1481; Chargé d'affaires: MOMODOU G. NJIE.

Germany: POB 94001, Riyadh 11693; tel. (1) 488-0700; telex 402297; fax (1) 488-0660; Ambassador: Dr RUDOLF RAPKE.

Ghana: POB 94339, Riyadh 11693; tel. and fax (1) 454-5122; telex 406599; fax 450-9819; Ambassador: ABUKARI SUMANI.

Greece: POB 94375, Riyadh 11693; tel. (1) 465-9094; telex 406322; fax (1) 465-3330; Ambassador: PAUL APOSTOLIDES.

Guinea: POB 94326, Riyadh 11693; tel. (1) 488-1121; telex 404944; fax (1) 482-6757; Ambassador: el-Hadj MAMADOU S. SYLLA.

Hungary: Riyadh; Ambassador TAMÁS VARGA.

India: POB 94387, Riyadh 11693; tel. (1) 488-4144; telex 408040; fax (1) 488-4750; e-mail 2168975@mcimail.com; Ambassador: MUHAMMAD ANSARI.

Indonesia: POB 94343, Riyadh 11693; tel. (1) 488-2800; telex 406577; fax (1) 488-2966; Ambassador: Dr ISMAIL SUNY.

Iran: POB 94394, Riyadh 11693; tel. (1) 488-1916; telex 406066; fax (1) 488-1890; Ambassador: MUHAMMAD REZA NURI-SHARUDI.

Ireland: POB 94349, Riyadh 11693; tel. (1) 488-2300; fax (1) 488-0927; Ambassador: MICHAEL COLLINS.

Italy: POB 94389, Riyadh 11693; tel. (1) 488-1212; telex 406188; fax (1) 488-1951; Ambassador: MARCO SORACE MARESCA.

Japan: POB 4095, Riyadh 11491; tel. (1) 488-1100; telex 405866; fax (1) 488-0189; Ambassador: MINORO TAMBA.

Jordan: POB 94316, Riyadh 11693; tel. (1) 488-0071; telex 406955; fax (1) 488-0072; Ambassador: HANI KHALIFAH.

Kenya: POB 94358, Riyadh 11693; tel. (1) 488-2484; telex 406055; fax (1) 488-2629; Ambassador: ALI MUHAMMAD ABDI.

Korea, Republic: POB 94399, Riyadh 11693; tel. (1) 488-2211; telex 406922; fax (1) 488-1317; Ambassador: KIM CHUNG-KI.

Kuwait: POB 94304, Riyadh 11693; tel. (1) 488-3500; telex 401301; fax (1) 482-1284; Ambassador: ABD AR-RAHMAN AHMAD AL-BAKR.

Lebanon: POB 94350, Riyadh 11693; tel. (1) 465-1000; telex 406533; fax (1) 462-6774; Ambassador: ZOUHEIR HAMDAN.

Libya: POB 94365, Riyadh 11693; tel. (1) 454-4511; telex 406399; Ambassador: MILOUD RAMADAN ERIBI.

Malaysia: POB 94335, Riyadh 11693; tel. (1) 488-7100; telex 406822; fax (1) 482-4177; Ambassador: Datuk Haji MOKHTAR BIN Haji AHMAD.

Mali: POB 94331, Riyadh 11693; tel. (1) 465-8900; telex 406733.

Malta: POB 94361, Riyadh 11693; tel. (1) 463-2345; fax (1) 463-3993.

Mauritania: POB 94354, Riyadh 11693; tel. (1) 465-6313; telex 406466; Ambassador: BABA OULD MUHAMMAD ABDULLAH.

Mexico: POB 94391, Riyadh 11693; tel. (1) 482-8218; fax (1) 482-8379; Ambassador: MARCELO VARGAS.

Morocco: POB 94392, Riyadh 11693; tel.(1) 481-1858; telex 406155; fax (1) 482-7016; Ambassador: ABD AL-KRIM SEMMAR.

Nepal: POB 94384, Riyadh 11693; tel. (1) 402-4758; telex 406288; fax (1) 403-6488; Ambassador: NARAYAN S. THAPA.

Netherlands: POB 94307, Riyadh 11693; tel. (1) 488-0011; fax (1) 488-0544; Ambassador: J. J. WIJENBERG.

New Zealand: POB 94397, Riyadh 11693; tel. (1) 488-7988; fax (1) 488-7912; Ambassador: DAVID PAYTON.

Niger: POB 94334, Riyadh 11693; tel. (1) 464-3116; telex 406722; fax (1) 456-6612.

Nigeria: POB 94386, Riyadh 11693; tel. (1) 482-3024; telex 406177; fax (1) 482-4134; Ambassador: Alhaji AHMAD AL-GAZALI.

Norway: POB 94380, Riyadh 11693; tel. (1) 488-1904; telex 406311; fax (1) 488-0854; Ambassador: SVEN ANDREASON.

Oman: POB 94381, Riyadh 11693; tel. (1) 465-0010; telex 206277; Ambassador: HAMAD H. AL-MO'AMARY.

Pakistan: POB 6891, Riyadh 11452; tel. (1) 476-7266; telex 406500; Ambassador: WALIULLA KHAN KHAISHGI.

Philippines: POB 94366, Riyadh 11693; tel. (1) 454-0777; telex 406377; fax (1) 454-2550; Ambassador: ROMULO M. ESPALDON.

Portugal: POB 94328, Riyadh 11693; tel. (1) 464-4688; telex 404477; fax (1) 464-4419; Ambassador: JOSÉ MANUEL WADDINGTON MATOS PARREIRA.

Qatar: POB 94353, Riyadh 11461; tel. (1) 482-5544; telex 405755; fax (1) 482-5694; Ambassador: M. ALI AL-ANSARI.

Russia: POB 94308, Riyadh 11693; tel. (1) 481-1875; telex 407890; fax (1) 481-1890; Ambassador: IGOR A. MELIKHOV.

Rwanda: POB 94383, Riyadh 11693; tel. (1) 454-0808; telex 406199; fax (1) 456-1769; Ambassador: SIMON INSONERE.

Senegal: POB 94352, Riyadh 11693; tel. (1) 454-2144; telex 406565; Ambassador: PAPA ABDOU CISSÉ.

Sierra Leone: POB 94329, Riyadh 11693; tel. (1) 463-3149; fax (1) 464-3982; Ambassador: Alhaji AMADU DEEN TEJAN.

Singapore: POB 94378, Riyadh 11693; tel. (1) 465-7007; telex 406211; fax (1) 465-2224; Chargé d'affaires a.i.: THIAGARAJAH THIRUNAGARAN.

Somalia: POB 94372, Riyadh 11693; tel. (1) 464-3456; fax (1) 464-9705; Ambassador: ABD AR-RAHMAN A. HUSSEIN.

South Africa: POB 94006, Riyadh 11693; tel. (1) 454-3723; fax (1) 454-3737; Ambassador: Dr SAMUEL MOTSUENYANE.

Spain: POB 94347, Riyadh 11693; tel. (1) 488-0606; fax 488-0420; Ambassador: FRANCISCO VIQUEIRA.

Sri Lanka: POB 94360, Riyadh 11693; tel. (1) 454-1745; telex 405688; fax (1) 454-9748; Ambassador: NOWFEL SALY JABIR.

Sudan: POB 94337, Riyadh 11693; tel. (1) 488-7979; fax (1) 488-7729; Ambassador: Dr ATTALLA H. BASHIR.

Sweden: POB 94382, Riyadh 11693; tel. (1) 488-3100; telex 406266; fax (1) 488-0604; Ambassador: LAVE JOHNSSON.

Switzerland: POB 94311, Riyadh 11693; tel. (1) 488-1291; fax (1) 488-0632; Ambassador: PETER HOLLENWEGER.

Syria: POB 94323, Riyadh 11693; tel. (1) 465-3800; telex 406677; fax (1) 465-1617; Ambassador: MUHAMMAD KHALID AT-TALL.

Tanzania: POB 94320, Riyadh 11693; tel. (1) 454-2839; telex 406811; fax (1) 454-9660; Ambassador: Prof. A. A. SHAREEF.

Thailand: POB 94359, Riyadh 11693; tel. (1) 488-1507; fax 488-1179; Chargé d'affaires: AMNUAY THAWORNWONG.

Tunisia: POB 94368, Riyadh 11693; tel. (1) 465-4585; telex 406464; Ambassador: KACEM BOUSNINA.

Turkey: POB 94390, Riyadh 11693; tel. (1) 482-0101; telex 407633; fax (1) 488-7823; Ambassador: TÜRKEKUL KURTTEKIN.

Uganda: POB 94344, Riyadh 11693; tel. (1) 454-4910; telex 406588; fax (1) 454-9260; Ambassador: al-Haj Prof. BADRU DDUNGU KATEREGGA.

United Arab Emirates: POB 94385, Riyadh 11693; tel. (1) 482-6803; telex 406222; fax (1) 482-7504; Ambassador: ISSA K. AL-HURAIMIL.

United Kingdom: POB 94351, Riyadh 11693; tel. (1) 488-0077; fax (1) 488-2373; Ambassador: Sir ANDREW FLEMING GREEN.

USA: POB 94309, Riyadh 11693; tel. (1) 488-3800; telex 406866; fax (1) 488-3278; e-mail usisriy@khaleej.net.bh; Ambassador: WYCHE FOWLER.

Uruguay: POB 94346, Riyadh 11693; tel. (1) 462-0739; fax (1) 462-0638; e-mail ururia@mcimail.com; Ambassador: CARLOS A. CLULOW.

Venezuela: POB 94364, Riyadh 11693; tel. (1) 476-7867; telex 405599; fax (1) 476-8200; Ambassador: NORMAN PINO.

Yemen: POB 94356, Riyadh 11693; tel. (1) 488-1757; Ambassador: Dr MUHAMMAD AHMAD AL-KABAB.

Judicial System

Judges are independent and governed by the rules of Islamic *Shari'a*. The following courts operate:

Supreme Council of Justice: consists of 11 members and supervises work of the courts; reviews legal questions referred to it by the Minister of Justice and expresses opinions on judicial questions; reviews sentences of death, cutting and stoning; Chair. Sheikh SALIH AL-LIHAYDAN.

Court of Cassation: consists of Chief Justice and an adequate number of judges; includes department for penal suits, department for personal status and department for other suits.

General (Public) Courts: consist of one or more judges; sentences are issued by a single judge, with the exception of death, stoning and cutting, which require the decision of three judges.

Summary Courts: consist of one or more judges; sentences are issued by a single judge.

Specialized Courts: Article 26 of the judicial system stipulates that the setting up of specialized courts is permissible by Royal Decree on a proposal from the Supreme Council of Justice.

Religion

ISLAM

Arabia is the centre of the Islamic faith, and Saudi Arabia includes the holy cities of Mecca and Medina. Except in the Eastern Province, where a large number of people follow Shi'a rites, the majority of the population are Sunni Muslims, and most of the indigenous inhabitants belong to the strictly orthodox Wahhabi sect. The Wahhabis originated in the 18th century but first became unified and influential under Abd al-Aziz (Ibn Sa'ud), who became the first King of Saudi Arabia. They are now the keepers of the holy places and control the pilgrimage to Mecca. In 1986 King Fahd adopted the title of Custodian of the Two Holy Mosques. The country's most senior Islamic authority is the Council of Ulema.

Mecca: Birthplace of the Prophet Muhammad, seat of the Great Mosque and Shrine of Ka'ba, visited by 993,000 Muslims in the Islamic year 1413 (1992/93).

Medina: Burial place of Muhammad, second sacred city of Islam.

CHRISTIANITY

The Roman Catholic Church

Apostolic Vicariate of Arabia: POB 54, Abu Dhabi, United Arab Emirates; responsible for a territory comprising most of the Arabian peninsula (including Bahrain, Oman, Qatar, Saudi Arabia, the United Arab Emirates and Yemen), containing an estimated 880,000 Roman Catholics at 31 December 1996 Vicar Apostolic GIOVANNI BERNARDO GREMOLI, Titular Bishop of Masuccaba.

The Anglican Communion

Within the Episcopal Church in Jerusalem and the Middle East, Saudi Arabia forms part of the diocese of Cyprus and the Gulf. The Anglican congregations in the country are entirely expatriate. The Bishop in Cyprus and the Gulf is resident in Cyprus, while the Archdeacon in the Gulf is resident in the United Arab Emirates.

Other Denominations

The Greek Orthodox Church is also represented.

The Press

Since 1964 most newspapers and periodicals have been published by press organizations, administered by boards of directors with full autonomous powers, in accordance with the provisions of the Press Law. These organizations, which took over from small private firms, are privately owned by groups of individuals experienced in newspaper publishing and administration (see Publishers).

There are also a number of popular periodicals published by the Government and by the Saudi Arabian Oil Co, and distributed free of charge. The press is subject to no legal restriction affecting freedom of expression or the coverage of news.

DAILIES

Arab News: POB 4556, Jeddah 21412; tel. (2) 669-1888; telex 604397; fax (2) 667-1650; f. 1975; English; publ. by Saudi Research and Marketing Co; Editor-in-Chief ABD AL-QADER-TASH; circ. 110,000.

Asharq al-Awsat: POB 45553, Madina Rd, Jeddah 21522; tel. (2) 669-1888; telex 604397; fax (2) 669-1649; Arabic; Editor-in-Chief OSMAN AL-OMAIR.

Al-Bilad (The Country): POB 7095, Jeddah 21462; tel. (2) 671-1000; telex 601526; fax (2) 671-1222; f. 1934; Arabic; publ. by Al-Bilad Publishing Org.; Editor-in-Chief QUINAN AL-GHOMDI; circ. 66,210.

Al-Iqh'ssadiah: POB 10421, Jeddah 21433; tel. (2) 664-1888; fax (2) 669-1505; Editor-in-Chief MUHAMMAD AT-TUNISI.

Al-Jazirah (The Peninsula): POB 354, Riyadh 11411; tel. (1) 441-9999; telex 401479; fax (1) 441-3826; Arabic; Dir-Gen. ABD AR-RAHMAN BIN FAHD AR-RASHAD; Editor-in-Chief MUHAMMAD ABD AL-AZIZ ABA HUSSEIN; circ. 94,000.

Al-Madina al-Munawara (Medina—The Enlightened City): POB 807, Makkah Rd, Jeddah 21421; tel. (2) 671-2100; telex 601356; fax 671-1877; f. 1937; Arabic; publ. by Al-Madina Press Est; Chief Editor USAMA AS-SIBA'IE; circ. 46,370.

An-Nadwah (The Council): Jarwal Sheikh Sayed Halabi Bldg, POB 5803, Mecca; tel. (2) 5200111; telex 401205; fax (2) 5203055; f. 1958; Arabic; publ. by Mecca Printing and Information Establishment; Editor Dr ABD AR-RAHMAN AL-HARTHI; circ. 35,000.

Okaz: POB 1508, Seaport Rd, Jeddah 21441; tel. (2) 672-2630; telex 601360; fax 672-4297; e-mail 104127.266@compuserve.com; f. 1960; Arabic; Editor-in-Chief HASHIM ABDU HASHIM; circ. 107,614.

Ar-Riyadh: POB 2943, Riyadh 11476; tel. (1) 442-0000; fax (1) 441-7417; f. 1965; Arabic; publ. by Al-Yamama Publishing Establishment; Editor TURKI A. AS-SUDARI; circ. 150,000 (Sat.–Thurs.), 90,000 (Friday).

Riyadh Daily NP: POB 2943, Riyadh 11476; tel. (1) 441-7544; fax (1) 441-7116; English; publ. by Yamama Publishing Establishment; Editor-in-Chief TALA'T WARFA.

Saudi Gazette: POB 5576, Jeddah 21432; tel. (2) 676-1869; telex 600920; fax (2) 672-7621; e-mail 104127.266@compuserve.com; f. 1976; English; publ. by Okaz Org.; Editor-in-Chief Dr AHMAD AL-YOUSSUF; circ. 32,699.

Al-Watan: Abha; f. 1998; publ. by Asir Organization for Press and Publication.

Al-Yaum (Today): POB 565, Dammam 31421; tel. (3) 834-5058; telex 801109; fax (3) 834-0064; f. 1965; Deputy Editor-in-Chief ATEEQ AL-KHAMMAS; circ. 50,000.

WEEKLIES

Al-Alam al-Islami: Arabic and English; Chief Editor M. IBRAHIM ABD AS-SATTAR.

Al-Muslimoon (The Muslims): POB 13195, Jeddah 21493; tel. (2) 669-1888; telex 601122; fax (2) 669-5549; Arabic; cultural and religious affairs; publ. by Saudi Research and Marketing Co; Editor-in-Chief Dr ABDULLAH AR-RIFA'E; circ. 68,665.

Saudi Arabia Business Week: POB 2894, Riyadh; English; trade and commerce.

Saudi Economic Survey: POB 1989, Jeddah 21441; tel. (2) 651-4952; fax (2) 651-4952; f. 1967; English; a weekly review of Saudi Arabian economic and business activity; Publr S. A. ASHOOR; Man. Editor ABD AL-HAKIM GHAITH; circ. 2,500.

Sayidati (My Lady): POB 4556, Madina Rd, Jeddah 21412; tel. (2) 639-1888; telex 401205; fax (2) 669-5549; Arabic; women's magazine; publ. by Saudi Research and Marketing Co; Editor-in-Chief MATAR AL-AHMADI.

Al-Yamama: POB 851, Riyadh 11421; tel. (1) 442-0000; fax 441-7114; f. 1952; Editor-in-Chief ABDULLAH AL-JAHLAN; circ. 35,000.

OTHER PERIODICALS

Ahlan Wasahlan (Welcome): POB 4288, Jeddah 21491; tel. (2) 643-2841; telex 601007; fax (2) 643-2821; monthly; flight journal of Saudi Arabian Airlines; Gen. Man. and Editor-in-Chief YARUB A. BALKHAIR; circ. 22,000.

Arabia Monthly: POB 5054, Jeddah 21422; tel. (2) 665-2056; telex 601090; English; publ. by Islamic Press Agency.

Al-Faysal: POB 3, Riyadh 11411; tel. (1) 465-3026; telex 402600; fax (1) 464-7851; monthly; f. 1976; Arabic; Editor-in-Chief HUSSEIN HASSAN AL-HUSSEIN.

Al-Manhal (The Spring): POB 2925, Jeddah; tel. (2) 643-2124; fax (2) 642-8853; f. 1937; monthly; Arabic; cultural, literary, political and scientific; Editor NABIH ABD AL-QUDOUS ANSARI.

Majallat al-Iqtisad wal-Idara (Journal of Economics and Administration): Research and Development Center, King Abd al-Aziz University, POB 1540, Jeddah; monthly; Chief Editor Dr MUHAMMAD M. N. QUOTAH.

The MWL Journal: Press and Publications Department, Rabitat al-Alam al-Islami, POB 537, Mecca; fax 5441622; monthly; English; Dir MURAD SULAIMAN IRQISOUS.

Ar-Rabita: POB 537, Mecca; tel. 5433583; telex 440009; fax 5431488; Arabic; Man. Editor MUHAMMAD AL-ASAD.

Saudi Review: POB 4288, Jeddah 21491; tel. (2) 651-7442; telex 601845; fax (2) 653-0693; f. 1966; English; monthly; newsletter from Saudi newspapers and broadcasting service; publ. by International Communications Co; Chief Editor SAAD AL-MABROUK; circ. 5,000.

Ash-Sharkiah-Elle (Oriental Elle): POB 6, Riyadh; telex 40112; monthly; Arabic; women's magazine; Editor SAMIRA M. KHASHAGGI.

As-Soqoor (Falcons): POB 2973, Riyadh 11461; tel. (1) 476-6566; f. 1978; 2 a year; air-force journal; cultural activities; Editor HAMAD A. AS-SALEH.

At-Tadhamon al-Islami (Islamic Solidarity): Ministry of Pilgrimage (*Hajj*) Affairs, Omar bin al-Khatab St, Riyadh 11183; monthly; Editor Dr MUSTAFA ABD AL-WAHID.

At-Tijarah (Commerce): POB 1264, Jeddah 21431; tel. (2) 651-5111; fax 651-7373; f. 1960; monthly; for businessmen; publ. by Jeddah Chamber of Commerce and Industry; Chair. Sheikh ISMAIL ABU DAUD; circ. 15,000.

NEWS AGENCIES

International Islamic News Agency (IINA): POB 5054, Jeddah 21422; tel. (2) 6652056; telex 601090; fax (2) 6659358; e-mail iina@mail.gcc.com.bh; internet http://www.islamicnews.org.

Saudi Press Agency: c/o Ministry of Information, POB 7186, Riyadh 11171; tel. (1) 462-3333; telex 401074; fax 462-6747; f. 1970; Dir-Gen. BADI KUIAYYEM.

Publishers

Asir Organization for Press and Publication: Abha; f. 1998; to publish *Al-Watan*; cap. 200m.; Chair. FAHD AL-HARITHI; Dir-Gen. ABDULLAH ABU MILHA.

Al-Bilad Publishing Organization: POB 6340, As-Sahafa St, Jeddah 21442; tel. (2) 672-3000; telex 601205; fax (2) 671-2545; publishes *Al-Bilad* and *Iqra'a*; Dir-Gen. AMIN ABDULLAH AL-QARQOURI.

Dar al-Yaum Press, Printing and Publishing Ltd: POB 565, Dammam 31421; tel. (3) 843-5058; telex 801109; fax (3) 843-0064; f. 1964; publishes *Al-Yaum*.

International Publications Agency (IPA): POB 70, Dhahran 31942; tel. (3) 895-4925; telex 871229; fax (3) 895-4925; publishes material of local interest; Man. SAID SALAH.

Al-Jazirah Organization for Press, Printing and Publishing: POB 354, Riyadh 11411; tel. (1) 441-9999; fax (1) 441-3826; f. 1964; 34 mems; publishes *Al-Jazirah* and *Al-Masaeyah* (both dailies); Editor-in-Chief MUHAMMAD ABA HUSSEIN.

Al-Madina Press Establishment: POB 807, Jeddah 21421; tel. (2) 671-2100; telex 605000; fax (2) 671-1877; f. 1937; publishes *Al-Madina al-Munawara*; Gen. Man. AHMED SALAH JAMJOUM.

Makkah Printing and Information Establishment: POB 5803, Jarwal Sheikh Sayed Halabi Bldg, Mecca; tel. (2) 542-7868; telex 540039; publishes *An-Nadwah* daily newspaper.

Okaz Organization for Press and Publication: POB 1508, Jeddah 21441; tel. (2) 672-2630; telex 402645; fax (2) 672-8150; publishes *Okaz*, *Saudi Gazette* and *Child*.

Saudi Publishing and Distributing House: Al-Jouhara Bldg, South Block, Bughdadia, Medina Road, POB 2043, Jeddah 21451; tel. (2) 642-4043; telex 601845; fax (2) 643-2821; publishers, importers and distributors of English and Arabic books; Chair. MUHAMMAD SALAHUDDIN.

Saudi Research and Publishing Co: POB 4556, Jeddah 21412; tel. (2) 669-1888; telex 604397; fax (2) 669-5549; publishes *Arab News*, *Asharq al-Awsat*, *Al-Majalla*, *Al-Muslimoon* and *Sayidati*.

Yamama Publishing Establishment: POB 2943, Riyadh 11476; tel. (1) 442-0000; fax (1) 441-7116; publishes *Ar-Riyadh* and *Al-Yamama*; Dir-Gen. SAKHAL MAIDAN.

Broadcasting and Communications

TELECOMMUNICATIONS

Ministry of Posts, Telegraphs and Telecommunications: (see Ministries, above); service regulator.

Saudi Telecommunications Co: Riyadh; f. 1998; provides telecommunications services in Saudi Arabia; to be privatized in 1999; cap. 12,000m. riyals.

BROADCASTING

Radio

Saudi Arabian Broadcasting Service: c/o Ministry of Information, POB 60059, Riyadh 11545; tel. (1) 401-4440; telex 401149; fax (1) 403-8177; 24 medium- and short-wave stations, including Jeddah, Riyadh, Dammam and Abha, broadcast programmes in Arabic and English; 23 FM stations; overseas service in Bengali, English, Farsi, French, Hausa, Indonesian, Somali, Swahili, Turkestani, Turkish and Urdu; Dir-Gen. MUHAMMAD AL-MANSOOR.

Saudi Aramco FM Radio: Bldg 3030 LIP, Dhahran; tel. (3) 876-1845; fax (3) 876-1608; f. 1948; English; private; for employees of Saudi Aramco; Man. A. A. AL-ARFAJ.

Television

Saudi Arabian Government Television Service: POB 7971, Riyadh 11472; tel. (1) 401-4440; telex 401030; fax (1) 404-4192; began transmission 1965; 112 stations, incl. six main stations at Riyadh, Jeddah, Medina, Dammam, Qassim, Abha, transmit programmes in Arabic and English; Dir-Gen. ABD AL-AZIZ AL-HASSAN (Channel 1).

Saudi Arabian Government Television Service Channel 2: POB 7959, Riyadh 11472; tel. (1) 442-8400; telex 401030; fax (1) 403-3826; began transmission 1983; Dir-Gen. ABD AL-AZIZ S. ABU ANNAJA.

Dhahran HZ-22 TV, Channel 3 TV: Bldg 3030 LIP, Dhahran; tel. (3) 876-4634; fax (3) 876-1608; non-commercial private co; started 1957, since 1969 English language film-chain operation only; Man. (Media Productions and Operations) A. A. AL-ARFAJ.

Finance

(cap. = capital; res = reserves; dep. = deposits; m. = million; brs = branches; amounts in Saudi riyals unless otherwise stated)

BANKING

In September 1997 the Saudi Arabian banking system consisted of: the Saudi Arabian Monetary Agency, as central note-issuing and regulatory body; 11 commercial banks (three national and eight foreign banks); and five specialist banks. There is a policy of 'Saudiization' of the foreign banks.

Central Bank

Saudi Arabian Monetary Agency (SAMA): POB 2992, Riyadh 11169; tel. (1) 463-3000; telex 404400 (English), 401466 (Arabic); f. 1952; functions include stabilization of currency, administration of monetary reserves, regulation of banking and issue of notes and coins; res 17,995m., dep. 49,120m., total assets 240,510m. (June 1997); Gov. Sheikh HAMAD SA'UD AS-SAYARI; 10 brs.

National Banks

National Commercial Bank (NCB): POB 3555, King Abd al-Aziz St, Jeddah 21481; tel. (2) 644-6644; telex 605571; fax (2) 644-6468; internet http://www.arabinternet.com/co/ncb; f. 1950; cap. 6,000m., res 1,787m., dep. 61,929m. (Dec. 1997); Chair. and Gen. Man. Sheikh KHALID IBN MAHFOUZ; 245 brs.

Ar-Rajhi Banking and Investment Corpn (ARABIC): POB 28, Riyadh 11411; tel. (1) 405-4244; telex 406317; fax (1) 403-6606; f. 1988; operates according to Islamic financial principles; 44% owned by Ar-Rajhi family; cap. 1,500m., res 3,662m., dep. 26,480m. (Dec. 1997); Chair. Sheikh SALEH IBN ABD AL-AZIZ AR-RAJHI; Man. Dir Sheikh SULAIMAN BIN ABD AL-AZIZ AR-RAJHI; 350 brs.

Riyad Bank Ltd: POB 22622, King Abd al-Aziz St, Riyadh 11416; tel. (1) 401-3030; telex 407409; fax (1) 404-1255; f. 1957; cap.

4,000m., res 3,550m., dep. 34,287m. (Dec. 1997); Chair. Sheikh OMRAN M. AL-OMRAN; Gen. Man. ALAN THOMSON; 179 brs.

Specialist Bank

Arab Investment Co SAA (TAIC): POB 4009, Riyadh 11491; tel. (1) 476-0601; telex 401011; fax (1) 476-0514; f. 1974 by 15 Arab countries for investment and banking; cap. and res US $366m., dep. $941m., total assets $1,386m. (1997); Chair. Dr MUHAMMAD SULAIMAN AL-JASSER, Dir-Gen. Dr SALIH AL-HUMAIDAN; 4 brs throughout Middle East.

Banks with Foreign Interests

Al-Bank as-Saudi al-Fransi (Saudi French Bank): POB 56006, Riyadh 11554; tel. (1) 404-2222; telex 407666; fax (1) 404-2311; f. 1977; Saudi Arabian shareholders 68.9%, Crédit Agricole Indosuez 31.1%; cap. 1,800m., res 1,132m., dep. 20,608m. (Dec. 1997); Chair. IBRAHIM A. AT-TOUQ; Man. Dir HENRI GUILLEMIN; 57 brs.

Arab National Bank (ANB): POB 56921, Riyadh 11564; tel. (1) 402-9000; telex 402660; fax (1) 402-7747; f. 1980; Arab Bank Ltd, Jordan, 40%, Saudi shareholders 60%; cap. 1,500m., res 1,400m., dep. 23,595m. (Dec. 1997); Chair. ABD AL-AZIZ AS-SAGHYIR; Man. Dir NEMEH SABBAGH; 116 brs.

Bank al-Jazira: POB 6277, Jeddah 21442; tel. (2) 651-8070; telex 601574; fax (2) 653-2478; 94.17% Saudi-owned; cap. and res 540m., dep. 1,807m., total assets 4,211m. (Dec. 1997); Chair. ABD AL-AZIZ MUHAMMAD AL ABDULKADER; Gen. Man. MISHARI I. AL-MISHARI; 12 brs.

Saudi American Bank (SAMBA): POB 833, Riyadh 11421; tel. and fax (1) 477-4770; telex 400195; 70% owned by Saudi nationals; cap. 2,400m., res 2,181m., dep. 34,534m. (Dec. 1997); Chair. ABD AL-AZIZ IBN HAMAD AL-GOSAIBI; Gen. Man. ROBERT EICHFELD; 43 brs.

Saudi British Bank: POB 9084, Riyadh 11413; tel. (1) 405-0677; telex 402349; fax (1) 405-0660; 60% owned by Saudi nationals; cap. 1,250m., res 1,702m., dep. 23,560m. (Dec. 1997); Chair. Sheikh ABDULLAH MUHAMMAD AL-HUGAIL; Man. Dir ALEXANDER FLOCKHART; 71 brs.

Saudi Hollandi Bank (Saudi Dutch Bank): POB 1467, Riyadh 11431; tel. (1) 401-0288; telex 401488; fax (1) 403-1104; a joint-stock co f. 1977 to take over the activities of Algemene Bank Nederland NV in Saudi Arabia; ABN AMRO Bank (Netherlands) 40%, Saudi citizens 60%; cap. 420m., res 901m., dep. 12,504m. (Dec. 1997); Chair. Sheikh SULEIMAN A. R. AS-SUHAIMI; Man. Dir HERMAN ERBE; 37 brs.

Saudi Investment Bank (SAIB): POB 3533, Riyadh 11481; tel. (1) 477-8433; telex 401170; fax (1) 477-6781; f. 1976; provides a comprehensive range of traditional and specialized banking services to business and individuals; foreign shareholders have provided 25% of cap.; cap. 720m., res 650m., dep. 7,360m. (Dec 1997); Chair. Dr ABD AL-AZIZ O'HALI; Gen. Man. SAUD AS-SALEH; 10 brs.

United Saudi Bank: POB 25895, Riyadh 11476; tel. (1) 478-4200; fax (1) 478-3197; f. 1997 by merger between Saudi Cairo Bank and United Saudi Commercial Bank; cap. 2,450m., res 732m., dep. 15,239m. (Dec. 1997); Chair. Prince ALWALEED BIN TALAL BIN ABD AL-AZIZ AS-SA'UD; Man. Dir MAHER AL-AUJAN; 85 brs.

Government Specialized Credit Institutions

Public Investment Fund (PIF): POB 6847, Riyadh 11452; tel. (1) 478-4466; fax (1) 477-8993; f. 1971; provides credit to public-sector enterprises; Gen. Man. MUHAMMAD AL-BASSAM.

Real Estate Development Fund (REDF): POB 5591, Riyadh 11139; tel. (1) 479-2222; fax (1) 479-0148; f. 1974; provides interest-free loans to Saudi individuals and cos for private or commercial housing projects; cap. 70,841 (1993); Gen. Dir AHMAD AL-AKEIL; 25 brs.

Saudi Arabian Agricultural Bank (SAAB): POB 11126, Riyadh; tel. (1) 402-2361; telex 401184; f. 1963; cap. 10,000m. (1982); Controller-Gen. ABDULLAH SAAD AL-MENGASH; Gen. Man. ABD AL-AZIZ MUHAMMAD AL-MANQUR; 71 brs.

Saudi Credit Bank: POB 3401, Riyadh 11471; tel. (1) 402-9128; f. 1973; provides interest-free loans for specific purposes to Saudi citizens of moderate means; Chair. SAID IBN SAIED; Dir-Gen. MUHAMMAD AD-DRIES.

STOCK EXCHANGE

The Saudi Arabian Monetary Agency (see Central Bank, above) operates the Electronic Securities Information System. At mid-1997 shares in 70 companies were being traded.

INSURANCE COMPANIES

In 1990 there were 38 insurance companies based in Saudi Arabia.

Al-Alamiya Insurance Co Ltd (E.C.): POB 2374, Jeddah 21451; tel. (2) 671-8851; telex 600941; fax (2) 671-1377; managed by Royal & Sun Alliance Insurance Group, London; total assets US $37m. (1997); Chair. ABDULAZIZ ZAID AL-QURAISHI; Man. Dir C. ROBERT BRADSHAW.

Amana Gulf Insurance Co (E.C.): POB 6559, Jeddah 21452; tel. and fax (2) 665-5692.

Arabia CIGNA Insurance Co Ltd (E.C.): POB 276, Dammam 31411; tel. (3) 832-4441; telex 801259; fax (3) 834-9389; internet http://www.Khereiji.com; f. 1976 as Pan Arabian Insurance Co; cap. US $1m.; Chair. Sheikh ABD AL-KARIM AL-KHEREIJI; Man. Dir TAJUDDIN HASSAN.

Independent Insurance Co of Saudi Arabia Ltd: POB 1178, Jeddah 21431; tel. (2) 651-7732; telex 601580; fax (2) 651-1968; f. 1977; all classes of insurance; cap. US $1m.; Pres. KHALID TAHER; Man. JULIAN D. SHARPE.

Insaudi Insurance Co (E.C.): POB 3984, Riyadh 11481; tel. (1) 476-7711, fax (1) 476-1213.

Islamic Arab Insurance Co: POB 430, Jeddah; tel. (2) 671-0000; fax (2) 667-1339.

Al-Jazira Insurance Co Ltd: POB 153, al-Khobar 31952; tel. and fax (3) 895-3445.

National Company for Co-operative Insurance (NCCI): POB 86959; Riyadh 11632; tel. (1) 482-6969; telex 406828; fax (1) 488-1719; f. 1985 by royal decree; owned by three govt agencies; auth. cap. SR500m.; Chair. SOLIMAN AL-HUMMAYYD; Man. Dir and Gen. Man. MOUSA AR-RUBAIAN; 12 brs and sales offices.

Ar-Rajhi Insurance Co: POB 22073, Jeddah 21495; tel. (2) 651-1017; fax (2) 651-1797.

Ar-Rajhi Islamic Co for Co-operative Insurance: POB 42220, Jeddah 21541; tel. (2) 651-4514; fax (2) 651-3185.

Red Sea Insurance Group of Cos: POB 5627, Jeddah 21432; tel. (2) 660-3538; telex 601228; fax (2) 665-5418; f. 1974; insurance, development, and reinsurance; cap. US $27.5m.; Chair. KHALDOUN B. BARAKAT.

Saudi Continental Insurance Co: POB 2940, Riyadh; tel. (1) 479-2141; telex 406325; fax (1) 476-9310; f. 1983; all classes of insurance; cap. US $3m.; Chair. OMAR A. AGGAD; Gen. Man. J.A. McROBBIE.

Saudi National Insurance Co EC: POB 5832, Jeddah 21432; tel. (2) 660-6200; fax (2) 667-4530; Gen. Man. SAMIR T. JABBOUR.

Saudi Union National Insurance Corpn: POB 2357, Jeddah 21451; tel. (2) 667-0648; fax (2) 667 2084.

Saudi United Insurance Co Ltd: POB 933, al-Khobar 31952; tel. (3) 894-9090; telex 871335; fax (3) 894-9428; f. 1976; all classes of insurance and reinsurance except life; cap. US $5m.; majority shareholding held by Ahmad Hamad al-Gosaibi & Bros; Chair. and Man. Dir Sheikh ABD AL-AZIZ HAMAD AL-GOSAIBI; Dir and Gen. Man. AHMAD MUHAMMAD SABBAGH; 6 brs.

U.C.A. Insurance Co (E.C.): POB 5019, Jeddah 21422; tel. (2) 653-0068; fax (2) 651-1936; f. 1974 as United Commercial Agencies Ltd; all classes of insurance; cap. US $6m.; Chair. JACQUES G. SACY; Dir and Gen. Man. MACHAAL A. KARAM.

Al-Yamamah Insurance Co Ltd: POB 41522; Riyadh 11531; tel. (1) 477-4498; fax (1) 477-4497.

Trade and Industry

DEVELOPMENT ORGANIZATIONS

Arab Petroleum Investments Corpn: POB 448, Dhahran Airport 31932; tel. (3) 864-7400; telex 870068; fax (3) 894-5076; f. 1975; affiliated to the Organization of Arab Petroleum Exporting Countries (see p. 214); specializes in financing petroleum and petrochemical projects and related industries in the Arab world and in other developing countries; shareholders: Kuwait, Saudi Arabia and the United Arab Emirates (17% each), Libya (15%), Iraq and Qatar (10% each), Algeria (5%), Bahrain, Egypt and Syria (3% each); authorized cap. US $1,200m.; subscribed cap. $460m. (Dec. 1996), Chair. ABDULLAH A. AZ-ZAID; Gen. Man. Dr NUREDDIN FARRAG.

General Investment Fund: c/o Ministry of Finance and National Economy, Airport Rd, Riyadh 11177; tel. (1) 405-0000; telex 401021; f. 1970; provides government's share of capital to mixed capital cos; 100% state-owned; cap. 1,000m. riyals; Chair. Minister of Finance and National Economy; Sec.-Gen. SULEIMAN MANDIL.

National Agricultural Development Co (NADEC): POB 2557, Riyadh 11461; tel. (1) 404-0000; fax (1) 405-5522; f. 1981; interests include 4 dairy farms, 39,760 ha for cultivation of wheat, barley, forage and vegetables and processing of dates; the govt has a 20% share; chief agency for agricultural development; cap. 400m. riyals; Chair. Minister of Agriculture and Water; Dir MUHAMMAD AL-BUBTAIN.

National Industrialization Co (NIC): POB 26707, Riyadh 11496; tel. (1) 476-7166; telex 406662; fax (1) 477-0898; f. 1984 to develop private investment in industry; cap. 600m. riyals; 86% of cap. owned by Saudi nationals (1985); Gen. Man. KHALID ATH-THUKAIR.

Saudi Consulting House (SCH): POB 1267, Riyadh 11431; tel. (1) 448-6500; telex 404380; fax (1) 448-1234; f. 1979; engineering, economic, industrial and management consultants; Chair. Minister of Industry and Electricity; Dir-Gen. MUHAMMAD ALI AL-MUSALLAM.

Saudi Fund for Development (SFD): POB 1887, Riyadh 11441; tel. (1) 464-0292; telex 401145; fax (1) 464-7450; f. 1974 to help finance projects in developing countries; cap. 31,000m. riyals (1991); had financed 320 projects by 1992; total commitments amounted to 25,814m.; Chair. Minister of Finance and National Economy; Vice-Chair. and Man. Dir MUHAMMAD A. AS-SUGAIR.

Saudi Industrial Development Fund (SIDF): POB 4143, Riyadh 11149; tel. (1) 477-4002; telex 401065; fax (1) 479-0165; f. 1974; supports and promotes industrial and electrical development in the private sector, providing long-term interest-free loans to industry; also offers marketing, technical, financial and administrative advice; cap. 7,000m. riyals (1995); Chair. Dr JOBARA IBN EID AS-SORAISRY; Dir-Gen. SALEH ABDULLAH AN-NAIM.

CHAMBERS OF COMMERCE

Council of Saudi Chambers of Commerce and Industry: POB 16683, Riyadh 11474; tel. (1) 405-3200; telex 405808; fax (1) 402-4747; comprises one delegate from each of the chambers of commerce in the kingdom; Chair. KHALID AZ-ZAMIL; Sec.-Gen. ABDALLAH T. DAB-BAGH.

Abha Chamber of Commerce and Industry: POB 722, Abha; tel. (7) 227-0092; telex 701125; fax (7) 227-1919; Pres. ABDULLAH SAEED ABU MELHA; Sec.-Gen. ABDULLAH IBRAHIM MUTAIN.

Al-Ahsa Chamber of Commerce and Industry: POB 519, al-Ahsa 31982; tel. (3) 852-0458; telex 861140; fax (3) 857-5274; Pres. ABD AL-AZIZ SULAIMAN AL-AFALIQ.

Ar'ar Chamber of Commerce and Industry: POB 440, Ar'ar; tel. (4) 662-6544; telex 812058; fax (4) 662-3868; Sec.-Gen. MATAB MOZIL AS-SARRAH.

Al-Baha Chamber of Commerce and Industry: POB 311, al-Baha; tel. (7) 725-0042 fax (7) 727-0146; Pres SAID ALI AL-ANGARI; Sec.-Gen. YAHYA AZ-ZAHRANI.

Eastern Province Chamber of Commerce and Industry: POB 719, Dammam 31421; tel. (3) 857-1111; telex 801086; fax (3) 857-0607; f. 1952; Pres. KHALID AZ-ZAMIL; Sec.-Gen. IBRAHIM ABDULLAH AL-MATRAF.

Federation of Gulf Co-operation Council Chambers (FGCCC): POB 2198, Dammam 31451; tel. (3) 826-4441; fax (3) 826-6794; e-mail FGCCC@sahara.com; Pres. ALI YOUSUF FAKHROO; Sec.-Gen. MUHAMMAD A. AL-MULLA.

Ha'il Chamber of Commerce and Industry: POB 1291, Ha'il; tel. (6) 532-1060; telex 311086; fax (6) 533-1366; Pres. SAAD AD-DAKHIL ALLAH AS-SAID; Sec.-Gen. KHADDAM AS-SALIH AL-FAYEZ.

Jeddah Chamber of Commerce and Industry: POB 1264, Jeddah 21431; tel. (2) 651-5111; telex 601069; fax (2) 651-7373; f. 1946; 26,000 mems; Chair. Sheikh ISMAIL ABU DAWOOD; Sec.-Gen. Dr MAJED A. AL-KASSABI.

Al-Jizan Chamber of Commerce and Industry: POB 201, al-Jizan; tel. (7) 322-2433; telex 911065; fax (7) 322-3635; Pres. Dr SALEH AZ-ZAIDAN.

Al-Jouf Chamber of Commerce and Industry: POB 585, al-Jouf; tel. (4) 624-9060; telex 821065; fax (4) 624-0108; Pres. MA'ASHI DUKAN AL-ATTIYEH; Sec.-Gen. AHMAD KHALIFA AL-MUSALLAM.

Al-Majma' Chamber of Commerce and Industry: POB 165, al-Majma' 11952; tel. (6) 432-0268; telex 447020; fax (6) 432-2655; Pres. FAHD MUHAMMAD AR-RABIAH; Sec.-Gen. ABDULLAH IBRAHIM AL-JAAWAN.

Mecca Chamber of Commerce and Industry: POB 1086, Mecca; tel. (2) 534-3838; telex 540011; fax (2) 534-2904; f. 1947; Pres. ADEL ABDULLAH KA'AKI; Sec.-Gen. ABDULLAH ABD AL-GAFOOR TOUJAR-ALSHAHI

Medina Chamber of Commerce and Industry: POB 443, Airport Rd, Medina; tel. (4) 822-5190; telex 470009; fax (4) 826-8965; Sec.-Gen. TARRIEF HUSSAIN HASHIM.

Najran Chamber of Commerce and Industry: POB 1138, Najran; tel. (7) 522-4019; telex 921066; fax (7) 522-3926; Sec.-Gen. MAKHFOOR ABDULLAH AL-BISHER.

Qassim Chamber of Commerce and Industry: POB 444, Buraydah, Qassim; tel. (6) 323-6104; telex 301060; fax (6) 324-7542.

Al-Qurayat Chamber of Commerce and Industry: POB 416, al-Qurayat; tel. (4) 642-3034; fax (4) 642-3172; Pres. OTHMAN ABDULLAH AL-YOUSEF; Sec.-Gen. JAMAL ALI AL-GHAMDI.

Riyadh Chamber of Commerce and Industry: POB 596, Riyadh 11421; tel. (1) 405-7596; telex 401054; fax (1) 402-4747; f. 1961; acts as arbitrator in business disputes, information centre; Chair. Sheikh ABD AR-RAHMAN AL-JERAISY; Sec.-Gen. HUSSEIN ABD AR-RAHMAN AL-AZAL; 23,000 mems.

Tabouk Chamber of Commerce and Industry: POB 567, Tabouk; tel. (4) 422-2736; telex 681173; fax (4) 422-7387; Pres. ABD AL-AZIZ M. OWADEH; Sec.-Gen. AWADH AL-BALAWI.

Ta'if Chamber of Commerce and Industry: POB 1005, Ta'if; tel. (2) 736-6800; telex 751009; fax (2) 738-0040; Pres. IBRAHIM ABDULLAH KAMAL; Sec.-Gen. Eng. YOUSUF MUHAMMAD ASH-SHAFI.

Yanbu Chamber of Commerce and Industry: POB 58, Yanbu; tel. (4) 322-7878; telex 661036; fax (4) 322-6800; f. 1979; produces quarterly magazine; 5,000 members; Pres. Dr TALAL ALI ASH-SHAIR; Sec.-Gen. OSMAN NAIM AL-MUFTI.

STATE HYDROCARBONS COMPANIES

Saudi Arabian Oil Co (Saudi Aramco): POB 5000, Dhahran 31311; tel. (3) 875-4915; telex 801220; fax (3) 873-8490; f. 1933; previously known as Arabian-American Oil Co (Aramco); in 1993 incorporated the Saudi Arabian Marketing and Refining Co (SAM-AREC, f. 1988) by merger of operations; holds the principal working concessions in Saudi Arabia; Pres. and CEO ABDULLAH S. JAMAAH; Exec. Vice-Pres. (Exploration and Production) SADAD AL-HUSSEINI.

Arabian Drilling Co: POB 708, Dammam 31421; tel. (3) 857-6060; telex 871212; fax (3) 857-7114; f. 1964; PETROMIN share-holding 51%, remainder French private cap.; undertakes contract drilling for oil (on shore and off shore), minerals and water both inside and outside Saudi Arabia; Chair. SULEIMAN J. AL-HERBISH; Man. Dir SAAD A. SAAB.

Arabian Geophysical and Surveying Co (ARGAS): POB 535, Al Khobar 31952; tel. (3) 857-7102; fax (3) 857-9042; f. 1966, with the General Petroleum and Mineral Organization (PETROMIN) having a shareholding of 51%; remainder provided by Cie Générale de Géophysique; geophysical exploration for petroleum, other minerals and ground water, as well as all types of land, airborne and marine surveys; Man. Dir HABIB M. MERGHELANI; Tech. Man. Dir ANDREW TUCKEY.

Jeddah Oil Refinery Co (JORC): POB 5000, Dhahran 31311; tel. (2) 669-5044; fax (2) 669-4033; f. 1967; Saudi Aramco share-holding 75%, remainder held by Saudi Arabian Refining Co (SARCO); the refinery at Jeddah, Japanese-built, has a capacity of 90,000 b/d; total production 30.7m. barrels (1990); responsible for distribution in the Western Province; Vice-Pres. (Saudi Aramco Jeddah) HASSAN A.YAMANY.

Petromin—Jet: POB 5518, Jeddah 21432; tel. (2) 636-7411; telex 601150; fax (2) 636-6932; f. 1979 as a subsidiary of the General Petroleum and Mineral Organization (PETROMIN); became wholly-owned by SAMAREC; supplies petroleum products, in particular jet fuel, to King Abd al-Aziz International Airport; Chair. and Exec. Asst ABDULLAH O. ATTAS (acting).

Petromin Lube Oil Blending and Grease Manufacturing Plant (SAUDI LUBE): POB 10382, Jubail 31961; tel. (3) 341-1209; telex 832168; f. 1987; wholly-owned by PETROLUBE; production and marketing of lubricants and grease, capacity 1m. barrels lubricants and 4,000 tons grease per year; Man. Dirs BADDAH S. AS-SEBAIE (Finance and Trade), ABD AR-RAHMAN M. AL-CABBANI.

Petromin Lubricating Oil Co (PETROLUBE): POB 1432, Jeddah 21431; tel. (2) 661-3333; telex 606175; fax (2) 661-3322; f. 1968; PETROMIN took a 71% share, Mobil Oil Investment owns 29%; for the processing, manufacture, marketing and distribution of lubricating oils and other related products; production 199m. litres (1988); cap. 110m.; Pres. M.A. TRABULSI.

Petromin Lubricating Oil Refining Co (LUBEREF): POB 5518, Jeddah 21432; tel. (2) 636-7411; telex 602781; fax (2) 636-6932; f. 1975; owned 70% by PETROMIN and 30% by Mobil; production 1,889,000 barrels (1992); Chair. SALIM S. AL-AYDH; Exec. Man. Dir BAKR A. KHOJA.

Petromin Marketing (PETMARK): POB 50, Dhahran Airport 31932; tel. (3) 890-3883; telex 870009; f. 1967; wholly-owned by SAMAREC; operates the installations and facilities for the distribution of petroleum products in the Eastern, Central, Southern and Northern provinces of Saudi Arabia; Pres. and CEO HUSSEIN A. LINJAWI.

Petromin Services Department (PETROSERVE): POB 2329, Jeddah 21451; tel. (2) 636-6309; telex 601867; f. 1968; operates all types of services in medical care, social and sports activities, telecommunications, computers, housing, security and training; Pres. HUSSAIN A. LINJAWI.

Rabigh Refinery: POB 5000, Dhahran 31311; wholly-owned by Saudi Aramco; capacity 325,000 b/d.

Riyadh Refinery: POB 5000, Dhahran 31311; tel. (2) 669-5044; fax (2) 669-4033; f. 1974; wholly-owned by Saudi Aramco; production capacity 140,000 b/d; total production 43.6m. barrels (1990); Vice-Pres. (Saudi Aramco Jeddah) HASSAN A. YAMANY.

Saudi Aramco Mobil Refinery Co Ltd (SAMREF): POB 30078, Yanbu as-Sinaiyah; tel. (4) 396-4000; fax (4) 396-0942; f. 1984; operated by Saudi Aramco and Mobil, capacity 360,000 b/d; CEO MUHAMMAD SAIB AL-GOSAIBI.

Saudi Aramco Shell Refinery Co (SASREF): POB 10088, Jubail 31961; tel. (3) 357-2000; telex 832060; fax (3) 3572235; e-mail k.al-buainain@pr.sasrefalj.simis.com; internet http://www.shell.com; operated by Saudi Aramco and Shell; capacity 300,000 b/d; exports began in 1985; Chair. ABD AL-AZIZ M. AL-HOKAIL.

Yanbu Refinery: POB 5000, Dhahran 31311; tel. (4) 321-8400; fax (4) 396-2756; f. 1983; wholly-owned by Saudi Aramco; production capacity of 190,000 b/d; production 60m. barrels (1990); Exec. Dir (Saudi Aramco) TALIB A. AD-DOSSARY.

Saudi Basic Industries Corpn (SABIC): POB 5101, Riyadh 11422; tel. (1) 406-9900; telex 401177; fax (1) 401-2045; f. 1976 to foster the petrochemical industry and other hydrocarbon-based industries through jt ventures with foreign partners, and to market their products; 70% state-owned; production 23.7m. tons (1997); Chair. Minister of Industry and Electricity; Vice-Chair. and CEO ABD AL-AZIZ A. ZAMIL.

Projects include:

Al-Jubail Petrochemical Co (Kemya): POB 10084, Jubail 31961; tel. (3) 357-6000; telex 832058; fax (3) 358-7858; f. 1980; began production of linear low-density polyethylene in 1984, of high-density polyethylene in 1985, and of high alfa olefins in 1986, capacity of 330,000 tons per year of polyethylene; jt venture with Exxon Corpn (USA) and SABIC; Pres. KHALIL I. AL-GANNAS; Exec. Vice-Pres. CLAY LEWIS.

Arabian Petrochemical Co (Petrokemya): POB 10002, Jubail 31961; tel. (3) 358-7000; telex 832053; fax (3) 358-4480; produced 1.2m. tons of ethylene, 135,000 tons of polystyrene, 100,000 tons of butene-1; 300,000 tons of propylene, 100,000 tons of butadiene and 70,000 tons of benzene in 1993; wholly-owned subsidiary of SABIC; owns 50% interest in ethylene glycol plant producing 203,000 tons per year of monoethylene glycol, 21,700 tons per year of diethylene glycol and 1,300 tons per year of triethylene glycol; Chair. IBRAHIM A. IBN SALAMAH; Pres. NABIL A. MANSOURI.

Eastern Petrochemical Co (Sharq): POB 10035, Jubail 31961; tel. (3) 357-5000; telex 832037; fax (3) 358-0383; f. 1981 to produce linear low-density polyethylene, ethylene glycol; total capacity 660,000 tons of ethylene glycol and 280,000 tons of polyethylene per year; a SABIC jt venture; Pres. IBRAHIM S. ASH-SHEWEIR.

National Industrial Gases Co (Gas): POB 10110, Jubail; tel. (3) 357-5700; telex 832082; fax (3) 358-8880; total capacity of 876,000 tons of oxygen and 492,750 tons of nitrogen per year; jt venture with Saudi private sector; Pres. ABDULLAH ALI AL-BAKR.

National Plastics Co (Ibn Hayyan): POB 10002, Jubail 31961; tel. (3) 358-7000; telex 832053; fax (3) 358-4736; produces 390,000 tons per year of vinylchloride monomer and 324,000 tons per year of polyvinylchloride; jt venture with Lucky Group (Republic of Korea), SABIC and three other cos; Pres. NABIL A. MANSOURI.

Saudi-European Petrochemical Co (Ibn Zahr): POB 10330, Jubail 31961; tel. (3) 341-5060; telex 832157; fax (3) 341-2966; f. 1985; annual capacity 1.4m. tons of methyl-tertiary-butyl ether (MTBE, 0.2m. tons of propylene); SABIC has a 70% share, Ecofuel, Nesté Corpn and APICORP each have 10%; Pres. ABD AR-RAHMAN A. AL-GARAWI.

Saudi Methanol Co (ar-Razi): POB 10065, Jubail Industrial City 31961; tel. (3) 357-7820; telex 832023; fax (3) 358-0838; f. 1979; capacity of 1,280,000 tons per year of chemical-grade methanol; total methanol exports in 1992 were 1,338,000 tons; jt venture with a consortium of Japanese cos; cap. 259m.; Pres. ABD AL-AZIZ I. ALAUDAH; Exec. Vice-Pres. T. SEKI.

Saudi Petrochemical Co (Sadaf): POB 10025, Jubail Industrial City 31961; tel. (3) 357-3000; telex 832032; fax (3) 357-3142; f. 1980; to produce ethylene, ethylene dichloride, styrene, crude industrial ethanol, caustic soda and methyl-tertiary-butyl ether (MTBE); total capacity of 3,190,000 tons per year; Shell (Pecten) has a 50% share; Pres. M. H. AL-MORISHED.

Saudi Yanbu Petrochemical Co (Yanpet): POB 30129, Yanbu; tel. (4) 396-5000; telex 662359; fax (4) 396-3236; f. 1980; to produce 820,000 tons per year of ethylene, 600,000 tons per year of high-density polyethylene and 340,000 tons per year of ethylene glycol; total capacity 1,692,200 tons per year by 1990; Mobil and SABIC each have a 50% share; Pres. ALI AL-KHURAIMI; Exec. Vice-Pres. P. J. FOLEY.

Foreign Concessionaires

Arabian Oil Co Ltd (AOC): POB 339, Jeddah 21411 (Head Office in Japan); tel. (2) 653-0912; telex 601484; f. 1958; holds concession (2,200 sq km at Dec. 1987) for offshore exploitation of Saudi Arabia's half-interest in the Kuwait-Saudi Arabia Neutral Zone; Chair. HIRO-MICHI EGUCHI; Man. BAKIR M. AS-SANIE.

Saudi Arabian Texaco Inc: POB 363, Riyadh; tel. (1) 462-7274; fax (1) 464-1992; also office in Kuwait; f. 1928; fmrly Getty Oil Co; holds concession (5,200 sq km at Dec. 1987) for exploitation of Saudi Arabia's half-interest in the Saudi Arabia-Kuwait Neutral Zone.

UTILITIES

Electricity

Electricity Corporation: Industry and Electricity Ministry Bldg, POB 1185, Riyadh 11431; tel. (1) 477-2722; telex 401393; f. 1976; state body; co-ordinates supply in areas not covered by companies below.

Saudi Consolidated Electric Co (Central): POB 57, Riyadh 11411; tel. (1) 403-2222; fax (1) 405-0723; f. 1979; supplies central region; cap. 8,000m.; CEO ABD AL-AZIZ AL-WAHED.

Saudi Consolidated Electric Co (East): POB 5190, 31422 Dammam; tel. (3) 857-2300 ; telex 802030; fax (3) 858-6601; f. 1977; supplies eastern region; cap. 5,000m.; Chair. YUSUF ABDULLAH AL-HAMMAD; Gen. Man. SULEIMAN A. AL-QADI.

Saudi Consolidated Electric Co (South): Abha; tel. (7) 227-1111; fax (7) 227-1627; f. 1979; supplies southern region; cap. 3,564m.; CEO MUHAMMAD ABDULLAH AZ-ZURA.

Saudi Consolidated Electric Co (West): POB 433, 21411 Jeddah; tel. (2) 651-1008; fax (2) 653-4139; f. 1981; supplies western region; cap. 8,000m.; CEO MAHMOUD ABDULLAH TAIBAH.

Water

Saline Water Conversion Corpn (SWCC): POB 4931, 21412 Jeddah; tel. (2) 6821240; telex 602300; fax (2) 682-0415; provides desalinated water; 24 plants; capacity 2m. cu m per day (1994); Dir-Gen. ABD AL-AZIZ OMAR NASSIEF.

MAJOR COMPANIES

Figures for sales and capital are in Saudi riyals.

Arabian Cement Co Ltd: POB 275, Jeddah; tel. (2) 682-8270; telex 600718; fax (2) 682-9989; f. 1956; produces ordinary Portland cement and sulphate-resistant cement; subsidiary company Cement Product Industry Co Ltd; cap. 600m.; Chair. Prince TURKI IBN ABD AL-AZIZ AS-SAUD; Dir-Gen. Eng. MUHAMMAD NAJIB KHEDER; 800 employees.

As-Safi Dairy Establishment: POB 10525, Riyadh 11443; tel. (1) 462-9643; fax (1) 462-9647; dairy products.

The Concrete Company LLP (CONCO): POB 5703, Jeddah 21432; tel. (2) 682-0305; telex 603023; f. 1977; manufacture and erection of pre-cast concrete; member of the Dallah Group; cap. p.u. 60m.; Chair. Sheikh SALEH ABDULLAH KAMEL; Gen. Man. MAGD H. TURKI; 450 employees.

Grain Silos and Flour Mills Organization: POB 5529, Jeddah 21432; tel. (2) 647-7633; fax (2) 647-1171; autonomous body formally responsible to the Ministry of Commerce; production of flour and animal feeds for domestic consumption; grain capacity 585,999 tons (1988); Chair. Minister of Agriculture and Water; Dir-Gen. SALEH AS-SULEIMAN.

Hoshanco: POB 25888, Riyadh; tel. (1) 477-2323; fax (1) 479-2588; f. 1964; office furniture and equipment; Chair. AHMAD AL-HOSHAN; Gen. Man. AHMAD AL-HARAFI; 2,000 employees.

Jeddah Steel Rolling Co (Sulb): POB 1826, Jeddah 21441; tel. (2) 636-7462; telex 602127; fax (2) 636-8161; f. 1967; capacity of 150,000 tons per year of reinforcing steel bars; cap. 62.4m.; Man. GERHARD JUNG.

Al-Jubail Fertilizer Co (Samad): POB 10046, Jubail 31961; tel. (3) 341-6488; telex 832024; fax (3) 341-7122; f. 1979; capacity of 620,000 tons per year of urea, 40,000 tons per year of ammonia, 150,000 tons per year of 2-ethyl hexanol, 50,000 tons per year of di-octyl phtalate and 180,000 tons per year of ISO-butaraldehyde; jt venture between SABIC and Taiwan Fertilizer Co; Pres. AHMAD A. AL-AHMAD.

Manufacturing and Building Co Ltd (MABCO): POB 1549, Riyadh 11441; tel. (1) 477-8421; telex 401364; fax (1) 498-1222; f. 1977; manufacture of pre-cast components for construction of buildings; also turnkey contractors for pre-cast construction; sales 830m. (1984); cap. p.u. 100m.; Chair. HASSAN MISHARI AL-HUSSEIN; Gen. Man. YOUSUF H. AL-HAMDAN; 2,800 employees.

National Fisheries Development Co Ltd: POB 4590, Riyadh 11515; tel. (1) 402-7904; fax (1) 402-1272.

National Methanol Co (Ibn Sina): POB 10003, Jubail 31961; tel. (3) 340-5500; telex 832033; fax (3) 340-5506; began commercial production of chemical-grade methanol in November 1984; capacity 1m. tons per year; began commercial production of methyl-tertiary-butyl ether (MTBE) in May 1994; capacity 900,000 tons per year; jt venture of SABIC, Hoechst-Celanese Corpn (USA) and PanEnergy Corpn (USA); Pres. K. S. RAWAF.

National Pipe Co Ltd: POB 1099, al-Khobar 31952; tel. (3) 857-0535; fax (3) 857-0962; f. 1978; manufacture and marketing of spiral-welded steel pipes for oil and gas transmission; sales 208m. (1996); cap. 50m.; Chair. TEYMOUR ALIREZA; Gen. Man. TOMOYAKI TAKI; 300 employees.

Qassim Cement Co: POB 345, Buraydah, Qassim; tel. (6) 381-0795; fax (6) 381-6187; production of 2,000 tons per day; Hon.

Chair. Prince ABDULLAH AL-FAISAL AS-SA'UD; Chair. Prince SULTAN AL-ABDULLAH AL-FAISAL AS-SA'UD.

Saudi Arabian Fertilizer Co (SAFCO): POB 553, Dammam 31421; tel. (3) 857-5011; telex 870117; fax (3) 857-4311; produced 353,744 tons of urea, 225,735 tons of ammonia, 98,535 tons of sulphuric acid and 20,240 tons of melamine in 1993; owned 41% by SABIC, 10% by its staff and 49% by private Saudi investors; Pres. AHM M. AN-NEKHILAN.

Saudi Arabian Mining Co (Ma'aden): Riyadh; f. 1997; produced 7 tons of gold in 1997; Pres. ABDULLAH AD-DABBAGH.

Saudi Cable Group of Companies: POB 4403, Jeddah 21491; tel. (2) 638-0080; telex 607151; fax (2) 637-7; f. 1975; manufacture of building wires, power and telecommunication cables including fibre optic cables, copper and aluminium rod, PVC compounds, information technology products, power transmission and distribution products, turnkey services; revenue 1,509m.; cap. 500m. (1997); Chair. KHALID ALIREZA; 2,000 employees.

Saudi Cement Co: POB 306, Dammam 31411; tel. (3) 834-4500; telex 801068; fax (3) 834-5460; f. 1955; cap. 3.2m.; Chair. Sheikh SALEH ABD AL-AZIZ AR-RAJHI; Gen. Man. ABD AL-AZIZ M. SHOWAIL; 1,750 employees.

Saudi Fisheries Co (SFC): POB 6535; Dammam 31452; tel. (3) 857-3979; telex 802020; fax (3) 857-2493; Chair. Minister of Agriculture and Water; Gen. Man. ABD AL-LATIF IBRAHIM AL-AJAJI.

Saudi Iron and Steel Co (Hadeed): POB 10053, Madinat al-Jubail as-Sinaiyah 31961; tel (3) 357-1702; telex 832022; fax (3) 358-7385; f. 1979; produced more than 2.7m. tons of steel reinforcing bars, coils of wire rod and light sections in 1996; Pres. SAMI A. AS-SUWAIGH.

Saudi Plastic Products Co Ltd (SAPPCO): POB 2828, Riyadh 11461; tel. (1) 448-0448; fax (1) 446-1392; f. 1969; manufacture and supply of UPVC pipes and fittings; cap. 75m.; total assets 194m.; Chair. Sheikh OMAR A. AGGAD; Gen. Man. SALEH M. AL-BARGAN; 170 employees.

Saudi United Fertilizer Co: POB 4811, Salaheldin Ayyoubi Rd, al-Malaz area, Riyadh 11412; tel. (1) 478-1304; telex 401865; fax (1) 478-9581; import and export of agricultural fertilizers, pesticides, forage seeds, field sprayers and agricultural machinery; Man. Dir SAMIR ALI KABBANI.

Southern Province Cement Co: (Head Office) POB 548, Gizan; tel. (7) 227-1500; telex 905010; fax (7) 227-1407; Chair. Prince KHALID IBN TURKI AT-TURKI; Gen. Man. Eng. AMER SAEED BARGAN.

Tamimi Co: POB 172, Dammam 31411; tel. (3) 857-4050; telex 801561; fax (3) 857-1592; e-mail tamimi.h.o@tamimi.geis.com; f. 1964; pipeline construction, mechanical and civil construction, industrial catering, real estate; cap. 20m.; Chair. TALAL A. TAMIMI.

Yanbu Cement Co: POB 5330, Jeddah; POB 467, Yanbu; tel. (4) 322-6652; fax (2) 653-1420; Chair. Prince MESHAL IBN ABD AL-AZIZ; Dir-Gen. Dr SAUD SALEH ISLAM.

Az-Zamil Group: POB 9, al-Khobar 31952; tel. (3) 894-4888; telex 670132; fax (3) 894-9336; f. 1930; involved in real estate and land development as well as the marketing of products from numerous subsidiary companies, including Az-Zamil Aluminium Factory Ltd, Zamil Soule Steel Building Co Ltd, Yamama Factories, Arabian Gulf Construction Co Ltd, Bahrain Marble Factory, Az-Zamil Nails and Screws Factory, Saudi Plastics Factory; Pres. MUHAMMAD A. AZ-ZAMIL; 2,500 employees.

TRADE UNIONS

Trade unions are illegal in Saudi Arabia.

Transport

RAILWAYS

Saudi Arabia has the only rail system in the Arabian peninsula. The Saudi Government Railroad comprises 719 km of single and 157 km of double track. In addition, the total length of spur lines and sidings is 348 km. The main line, which was opened in 1951, is 578 km in length; it connects Dammam port, on the Gulf coast, with Riyadh, and passes Dhahran, Abqaiq, Hufuf, Harad and al-Kharj. A 310-km line, linking Hufuf and Riyadh, was inaugurated in May 1985. A 933m.–riyal rail link to Jubail was under consideration in 1996. A total of 546,600 passengers travelled by rail in the kingdom in 1996, and 1.6m. metric tons of freight was carried by the railways in the same year.

Saudi Railways Organization: POB 36, Dammam 31241; tel. (3) 871-5151; telex 801050; fax (3) 833-6337; an independent entity with a Board of Dirs headed by the Minister of Transport; Pres. FAISAL M. ASH-SHEHAIL.

ROADS

Asphalted roads link Jeddah to Mecca, Jeddah to Medina, Medina to Yanbu, Ta'if to Mecca, Riyadh to al-Kharj, and Dammam to Hufuf

as well as the principal communities and certain outlying points in Aramco's area of operations. During the 1980s the construction of other roads was undertaken, including one extending from Riyadh to Medina. The trans-Arabian highway, linking Dammam, Riyadh, Ta'if, Mecca and Jeddah, was completed in 1967. A causeway linking Saudi Arabia with Bahrain was opened in November 1986. A 317-km highway linking Riyadh to Qassim was completed in the late 1980s. At the end of 1995 there were 141,716 km of roads, of which 22,416 km were main roads (including motorways) and 14,669 km were secondary roads. Metalled roads link all the main population centres. Some 443 km of asphalted roads were constructed during 1995.

Saudi Public Transport Co (SAPTCO): POB 7830, Jeddah 21472; tel. (2) 691-0019; telex 602222; fax (2) 691-2118; f. 1979; operates a public bus service throughout the country and to neighbouring countries; the Govt holds a 30% share; Chair. Dr NASIR AS-SALOOM; CEO Dr ABD AL-AZIZ AL-OHALY.

National Transport Co of Saudi Arabia: Queen's Bldg, POB 7280, Jeddah 21462; tel. (2) 643-4561; telex 401235; specializes in inward clearance, freight forwarding, general and heavy road haulage, re-export, charter air freight and exhibitions; Man. Dir A. D. BLACKSTOCK; Operations Man. I. CROXSON.

SHIPPING

The commercial ports of Jeddah, Dammam, Yanbu, Dhiba and Gizan, the King Fahd Industrial Ports of Jubail and Yanbu, and the oil port of Ras Tanura, as well as a number of minor ports, are under the exclusive management of the Ports Authority. In 1994/95 the total cargo handled by Saudi Arabian ports, excluding crude petroleum, was 79.4m. metric tons, compared with 68.2m. tons in 1990/91.

Jeddah is the principal commercial port and the main point of entry for pilgrims bound for Mecca. It has berths for general cargo, container traffic, 'roll on, roll off' (ro-ro) traffic, livestock and bulk grain shipments, with draughts ranging from 8 m to 14 m. The port also has a 200-ton floating crane, cold storage facilities and a fully-equipped ship-repair yard. In 1995 a total of 4,205 vessels called at Jeddah Islamic Port, and 17.1m. tons of cargo were handled.

Dammam is the second largest commercial port and has general cargo, container, ro-ro, dangerous cargo and bulk grain berths. Draughts at this port range from 9 m to 14 m. It has a 200-ton floating crane and a fully-equipped ship-repair yard. In 1995 a total of 2,091 vessels called at King Abd al-Aziz Port in Dammam, and 7.6m. tons of cargo were handled.

Jubail has one commercial and one industrial port. The commercial port has general cargo, bulk grain and container berths with ro-ro facilities, and a floating crane. Draughts at this port range from 12 m to 14 m. In 1995 a total of 134 vessels called at Jubail Commercial Port, and 1.3m. tons of imported goods were handled. The industrial port has bulk cargo, refined and petrochemical and ro-ro berths, and an open sea tanker terminal suitable for vessels up to 300,000 dwt. Draughts range from 6 m to 30 m. In 1995 King Fahd Industrial Port in Jubail handled 27.1m. tons of cargo.

Yanbu, which comprises one commercial and one industrial port, is Saudi Arabia's nearest major port to Europe and North America, and is the focal point of the most rapidly growing area, in the west of Saudi Arabia. The commercial port has general cargo, ro-ro and bulk grain berths, with draughts ranging from 10 m to 12 m. It also has a floating crane, and is equipped to handle minor ship repairs. In 1995 a total of 1,233 vessels called at Yanbu Commercial Port, and 0.9m. tons of cargo were handled. The industrial port has berths for general cargo, containers, ro-ro traffic, bulk cargo, crude petroleum, refined and petrochemical products and natural gas liquids, and a tanker terminal on the open sea. In 1995 a total of 991 vessels called at King Fahd Industrial Port in Yanbu; the port handled 25.1m. tons of cargo.

Gizan is the main port for the southern part of the country. It has general cargo, ro-ro, bulk grain and container berths, with draughts ranging from 8 m to 11 m. It also has a 200-ton floating crane. In 1995 a total of 991 vessels called at Gizan Port, and 0.2m. tons of cargo were handled.

Dhiba port, on the northern Red Sea coast, serves the Tabouk region. It has three general cargo berths with a ro-ro ramp, and passenger-handling facilities. Maximum draught is 10.5m. In 1995 a total of 419 vessels called at Dhiba, and 47,491 tons of cargo were handled.

In addition to these major ports, there are a number of minor ports suitable only for small craft, including Khuraiba, Haql, al-Wajh, Umlujj, Rabigh, al-Lith, Qunfoudah, Farasan and al-Qahma on the Red Sea coast and al-Khobar, Qatif, Uqair, Darin and Ras al-Khafji on the Gulf coast. Ras Mishab, on the Gulf coast, is operated by the Ministry of Defence and Civil Aviation.

Seaports Authority (SEAPA): POB 5162, Riyadh 11188; tel. (1) 476-0600; telex 401158; fax (1) 402-7394; f. 1976; partial privatization announced in 1997; Vice-Chair. and Dir-Gen. MUHAMMAD IBN ABD AL-KARIM BAKR.

Dammam: POB 28062, Dammam 31188; tel. (3) 833-2500; telex 801139; fax (3) 857-1727.

Jeddah: POB 9285, Jeddah; tel. (2) 647-1200; fax (2) 647-7411; Dir of Operations Capt. MARWAN AHMAD.

Jubail: POB 276, Jubail 31951; tel. (3) 361-2824; fax (3) 361-3337.

Gizan: POB 16, Gizan; tel. (7) 317-1000; fax (7) 317-0777; Dir MUHAMMAD A. ADAM.

Yanbu: POB 1019, Yanbu; tel. (4) 322-1163; fax (4) 322-7643; Man. HAMID MUHAMMAD ENEBSY.

Arabian Marine and Terminal Services Co Ltd: POB 10366, Jeddah 21433; tel. (2) 667-6052; fax (2) 667-6055; port services.

Arabian Petroleum Supply Co Ltd: POB 1408, Al-Qurayat St, Jeddah 21431; tel. (2) 637-1120; telex 602613; fax (2) 636-2366; Gen. Man. E. D. CONNOLLY.

National Shipping Co of Saudi Arabia (NSCSA): POB 8931, Riyadh 11492; tel. (1) 478-5454; telex 405624; fax (1) 477-8036; f. 1979; regular container, ro-ro and general cargo service from USA to the Middle East, South-East Asia and Far East; annual two-way capacity 188,880 20-ft equivalent units; Chair. SALEH A. AN-NAIM; CEO ABDULLAH ASH-SHURAIM.

Saudi Lines: POB 66, Jeddah 21411; tel. (2) 642-3051; regular cargo and passenger services between Red Sea and Indian Ocean ports; Pres. M. A. BAKHASHAB PASHA; Man. Dir A. M. BAKHASHAB.

Saudi Shipping and Maritime Services Co Ltd: POB 7522, Jeddah 21472; tel. (2) 644-0577; telex 601845; fax (2) 644-0932; Chair. Prince SA'UD IBN NAYEF IBN ABD AL-AZIZ; Man. Dir Capt. MUSTAFA T. AWARA.

Shipping Corpn of Saudi Arabia Ltd: POB 1691, Arab Maritime Center, Malik Khalid St, Jeddah 21441; tel. (2) 647-1137; telex 601078; fax (2) 647-8222; Pres. and Man. Dir ABD AL-AZIZ AHMAD ARAB.

CIVIL AVIATION

King Abd al-Aziz International Airport, which was opened in 1981, has three terminals, one of which is specifically designed to cope with the needs of the many thousands of pilgrims who visit Mecca and Medina each year. King Khalid International Airport, at Riyadh, opened in 1983 with four terminals. It handled 7.9m. passengers in 1993. A third major airport, King Fahd International Airport, (with an initial handling capacity of 5.2m. passengers per year), opened in the Eastern Province in 1994. The country's airports were used by more than 25m. passengers in 1996. There are 25 commercial airports in the kingdom.

Presidency of Civil Aviation (PCA): POB 887, Jeddah 21421; tel. (2) 640-5000; telex 601093; fax (2) 640-1477; Pres. Dr ALI ABD AR-RAHMAN AL-KHALAF.

Saudia—Saudi Arabian Airlines: POB 620, Jeddah 21231; tel. (2) 686-0000; telex 601007; fax (2) 686-4552; internet http:// www.saudiairlines.com; f. 1945 and began operations in 1947; in 1997 Saudia carried 12.2m. passengers, its fleet numbering 122 aircraft; regular services to 25 domestic and 47 international destinations; regular international services worldwide; Chair. Prince SULTAN IBN ABD AL-AZIZ; Dir-Gen. KHALED A. BEN-BAKR; Exec. Vice-Pres. (operations) ADNAN AD-DABBAGH.

Tourism

All devout Muslims try to make at least one visit to the holy cities of Medina, the burial place of Muhammad, and Mecca, his birthplace. In 1993/94 more than 2m. pilgrims visited Saudi Arabia. In 1994 there were 287 hotels in the kingdom, with a total of 24,740 rooms. A total of 1,132,344 foreign pilgrims performed the *Hajj* in 1998.

Saudi Hotels and Resort Areas Co (SHARACO): POB 5500, Riyadh 11422; tel. (1) 465-7177; telex 401173; fax (1) 465-7172; f. 1975; Saudi Govt has 40% interest; cap. SR500m.; Chair. Dr SOLIMAN AL-HUMAYYED; Dir-Gen. ABD AL-AZIZ AL-AMBAR.

Defence

Chief of the General Staff: Gen. SALEH IBN ALI AL-MUHAYA.

Director-General of Public Security Forces: Brig.-Gen. ABDULLAH IBN ASH-SHEIKH.

Commander of Land Forces: Lt-Gen. SULTAN IBN ALI AL-MUTAYRI.

Commander of Air Force: Maj. ABD AL-AZIZ IBN MUHAMMAD HUNAIYDI.

Defence Budget (estimate, 1997): 67,000m. riyals.

Military Service: male conscription (18–35 years of age).

Total Armed Forces (August 1997): 105,500 (army 70,000; navy 13,500; air force 18,000); air defence forces 4,000; national guard 57,000 active personnel.

Paramilitary Forces (August 1997): 10,500 frontier force and 4,500 coastguard.

Education

The educational system in Saudi Arabia resembles that of other Arab countries. Educational institutions are administered mainly by the Government. The private sector plays a significant role at the first and second levels, but its total contribution is relatively small compared with that of the public sector.

Pre-elementary education is provided on a small scale (with 85,802 children enrolled in 1995/96), mainly in urban areas. Elementary or primary education is of six years' duration and the normal entrance age is six. The total number of pupils at this stage in 1995/96 was 2,248,122, with 169,321 teachers. Intermediate education begins at 12 and lasts for three years. The total number of pupils at this stage in 1995/96 was 887,520, with teachers numbering 69,310. Secondary education begins at 15 and extends for three years. After the first year, successful pupils branch into science or arts groups. The total number of pupils at this stage in 1995/96 was 497,857, with 35,746 teachers. In that year the total number of students enrolled at all levels of education (including University level) was 3,912,120, with 295,819 teachers. Enrolment of children in the primary age-group increased from 32% in 1970 to 62% (boys 63%; girls 61%) in 1995. Over the same period enrolment at intermediate and secondary schools rose from 9% to 48% (boys 54%; girls 41%). The proportion of females enrolled in Saudi Arabian schools increased from 25% of the total number of pupils in 1970 to 46.7% in 1997.

Industrial and commercial schools can be entered after the completion of the intermediate stage. In 1990/91 there were eight industrial schools, 22 commercial schools and one agricultural school. In addition, there were seven higher technical and four higher commercial colleges offering two-year courses. Vocational craft-training institutes are maintained in 62 centres, providing courses in electrical, mechanical and allied trades. In 1993 a total of 30,686 students attended 101 technical and vocational institutes.

There are seven universities, with a total of 143,787 students in 1995/96, and 65 colleges. There are also 12 colleges and one higher institute for girls. Adult education continues for three years. In 1993 there were 117,357 students enrolled at adult education schools. According to estimates by UNESCO, adult illiteracy declined from 97.5% in 1962 to 37.2% (males 28.5%; females 49.8%) in 1995. Government expenditure on education in 1997 was provisionally estimated at 41,692m. riyals, equivalent to 23% of total expenditure.

Bibliography

Abir, Mordechai. *Saudi Arabia: Society, Government and the Gulf Crisis*. London, Routledge, 1993.

Al-Farsy, Fouad. *Saudi Arabia. A Case Study in Development*. London, Kegan Paul International Ltd, 1981.

Anderson, Irvine H. *Aramco, the United States, and Saudi Arabia: a study in the dynamics of Foreign Oil Policy, 1935–50*. Princeton University Press, 1982.

Anderson, Prof. Sir Norman. *The Kingdom of Saudi Arabia*. London, Stacey International, 1977.

Assah, Ahmed. *Miracle of the Desert Kingdom*. London, Johnson, 1969.

Atlas of Saudi Arabia. London, Edward Stanford, 1978.

Benoit-Méchin, S. *Ibn Séoud ou la naissance d'un royaume*. Paris, Albin Michel, 1955.

Brown, E. Hoagland. *The Saudi-Arabia-Kuwait Neutral Zone*. Beirut, 1964.

De Gaury, Gerald. *Faisal*. London, Arthur Barker, 1969.

Dequin, Horst. *Saudi Arabia's Agriculture and its Development Possibilities*. Frankfurt, 1963.

Field, Michael. *The Merchants: The Big Business Families of Arabia*, London, John Murray, 1984.

Gharaybeh, A. *Saudi Arabia*. London, 1962.

Helms, Christine Moss. *The Cohesion of Saudi Arabia*. Croom Helm, 1981.

Hobday, Peter. *Saudi Arabia Today: An Introduction to the Richest Oil Power*. London, Macmillan, 1978.

Holden, David, Johns, Richard, and Buchan, James. *The House of Saud*. London, Sidgwick & Jackson, 1981.

Howarth, David. *The Desert King: Ibn Sa'ud*. New York, McGraw Hill, 1964.

Lees, Brian. *Handbook of the Sa'ud family of Saudi Arabia*. London, Royal Genealogies, 1980.

Lipsky, George A., and others. *Saudi Arabia: Its People, Its Society, Its Culture*. New Haven, 1959.

Mackey, Sandra. *The Saudis*. London, Harrap, 1987.

McLoughlin, Leslie. *Ibn Saud, Founder of a Kingdom*. London, Macmillan, 1993.

Montague, Carolyn. *Industrial Development in Saudi Arabia*. London, Committee for Middle East Trade, 1987.

Niblock, Tim. *State, Society and Economy in Saudi Arabia*. London, Croom Helm, 1981.

Philby, H. St. J. B. *Arabia and the Wahhabis*. London, 1928.

   Arabia. London, Benn, 1930.

   Arabian Jubilee. London, 1951.

   The Empty Quarter. London, 1933.

   The Land of Midian. London, 1957.

   A Pilgrim in Arabia. London, 1946.

   Saudi Arabia. London, 1955.

Quandt, Willam B. *Saudi Arabia in the 1980s: Foreign Policy, Security and Oil*. Oxford, Basil Blackwell, 1982.

Robinson, Jeffrey. *Yamani: The Inside Story*. London, Simon and Schuster, 1988.

Sarhan, Samir (Ed.). *Who's Who in Saudi Arabia*. Jeddah, Tihama, and London, Europa, 3rd edn, 1984.

Troeller, Gary. *The Birth of Saudi Arabia: Britain and the Rise of the House of Sa'ud*. London, Frank Cass, 1976.

Van der Meulen, D. *The Wells of Ibn Sa'ud*. John Murray, 1957.

Wilkinson, John. *Arabia's Frontiers*. London, I. B. Tauris, 1991.

Williams, K. *Ibn Sa'ud: the Puritan King of Arabia*. London, Cape, 1933.

Winder, R. Bayly. *Saudi Arabia in the Nineteenth Century*. London, Macmillan, 1965.

SPANISH NORTH AFRICA

Geography

Spanish North Africa comprises Ceuta and Melilla, two enclaves within Moroccan territory, and several rocky islets off the Moroccan coast. The average temperature is 17°C.

CEUTA

The ancient port and walled city of Ceuta is situated on a rocky promontory on the North African coast overlooking the Strait of Gibraltar, the Strait here being about 25 km wide. Ceuta was retained by Spain as a plaza de soberanía (a presidio, or fortified enclave, over which Spain has full sovereign rights) when Morocco became independent from France in 1956, and is administered as part of Cádiz Province. The Portuguese first established a fort at Ceuta in 1415, and it was subsequently ceded to Spain by Portugal. It developed as a military and administrative centre for the former Spanish Protectorate in Morocco, and now functions as a bunkering and fishing port. Ceuta occupies an area of 19.7 sq km. In May 1996 its population was 68,796.

MELILLA

Melilla is situated north of the Moroccan town of Nador, on the eastern side of a small peninsula jutting out into the Mediterranean Sea. It was retained by Spain as a plaza de soberanía when Morocco became independent in 1956, and is administered as part of Málaga Province. The Spanish Crown assumed control in 1556, and the territory has served as a military stronghold ever since. Melilla is an active port. The territory's area totals 12.5 sq km. In May 1996 its population was estimated to be 59,576 (including the islets separately mentioned below).

THE PEÑÓN DE VÉLEZ DE LA GOMERA, PEÑÓN DE ALHUCEMAS AND CHAFARINAS ISLANDS

These rocky islets are administered with Melilla. The Peñón de Vélez de la Gomera is situated 117 km south-east of Ceuta, lying less than 85 m from the Moroccan coast, to which it is connected by a narrow strip of sand. This rocky promontory, of 1 ha in area, rises to an altitude of 77 m above sea-level, an ancient fortress being situated at its summit. Spain maintains a small military base on the rock. The Peñón de Alhucemas lies 155 km south-east of Ceuta and 100 km west of Melilla, being 300 m from the Moroccan coast and the town of al-Hocima. A military garrison of fewer than 100 men is stationed on the islet, which occupies an area of 1.5 ha. The uninhabited rocks of Mar and Tierra lie immediately to the east of the Peñón de Alhucemas. The three Chafarinas Islands (from west to east: Isla del Congreso, Isla de Isabel II and Isla del Rey) are situated 48 km east of Melilla and about 3.5 km from the Moroccan fishing port of Ras el-Ma (Cabo de Agua). The islands are of volcanic origin, their combined area being 61 ha. A garrison of about 100 Spanish soldiers is maintained on Congreso.

History

CEUTA

Ceuta was conquered by Juan I of Portugal in 1415. Following the union of the crowns of Spain and Portugal in 1580, Ceuta passed under Spanish rule and in 1694, when Portugal was formally separated from Spain, the territory requested to remain under Spanish control. During the 16th, 17th and 18th centuries Ceuta endured a number of sieges by the Muslims. Ahmad Gailan, a chieftain in northern Morocco, blockaded the town in 1648–55. The Sultan of Morocco, Mulai Ismail (1672–1727), attacked Ceuta in 1674, 1680 and 1694, after which he maintained a blockade against the town until 1720. Ahmad Ali ar-Rifi, a chieftain from northern Morocco, made yet another unsuccessful assault in 1732. A pact of friendship and commerce was negotiated between Spain and Morocco at Aranjuez in 1780, a peaceful agreement following in the next year over the boundaries of the Ceuta enclave. In 1844–45 there was a sharp dispute once more about the precise limits of Ceuta. Further disagreement led to the war of 1859–60. Spanish forces, after an engagement at Los Castillejos, seized Tetuán from Morocco. Following another battle at Wadi Ras in March 1860 the conflict came to an end. A settlement was then made, which enlarged the enclave of Ceuta and obliged Morocco to forfeit to Spain 100m. pesetas as war indemnities. In 1974 the town became the seat of the Capitanía General de Africa.

MELILLA

Spain secured control of Melilla in 1556, the town having been conquered in 1497 by the ducal house of Medina Sidonia, which had been empowered to appoint the governor and seneschal with the approval of the Spanish Crown. The Rif tribesmen attacked Melilla in 1562–64. Later still, the Sultan of Morocco, Mulai Ismail (1672–1727), assaulted the town in 1687, 1696 and 1697. Sultan Muhammad b. Abdallah (1757–90) besieged Melilla in 1771 and 1774. An agreement concluded between Spain and Morocco in 1780 at Aranjuez led, however, in the following year, to a peaceful delimitation of the Melilla enclave. There was a brief period of tension in 1844 and then, in 1861, under the terms of an agreement signed at Madrid, after Spain's Moroccan campaign of 1860, Melilla received an extension of its boundaries. Conflict with the Rif tribesmen gave rise in 1893–94 to the so-called 'War of Melilla', which ended with a settlement negotiated at Marrakesh. It was not until 1909 that Spanish forces, after a hard campaign, occupied the mountainous hinterland of Melilla between the Wadi Kert and and Wadi Muluya—a region in which, some 15 km behind Melilla, were situated the rich iron mines of Beni Bu Ifrur. In July 1921 the Rif tribes, under the command of Abd al-Krim, defeated a Spanish force near Annual and threatened Melilla itself. Only in 1926, with the final defeat of the Rif rebellion, was Spanish control restored over the Melilla region. Melilla was the first Spanish town to rise against the government of the Popular Front on 17 July 1936, at the beginning of the Spanish Civil War. Since 1939 both Ceuta and Melilla have been ruled as integral parts of Spain, though this arrangement is disputed in the territories.

OTHER POSSESSIONS

The Chafarinas Islands came under Spanish control in 1847. The Peñón de Alhucemas was occupied in 1673. The Peñón de Vélez de la Gomera, about 80 km farther west, came under Spanish rule in 1508, was then lost not long afterwards and reoccupied in 1564. All three possessions are, like Melilla, incorporated into the province of Málaga. Spanish sovereignty over the uninhabited island of Perejil, which lies north-west of Ceuta, is uncertain.

RECENT EVENTS

Those born in Ceuta, Melilla and the island dependencies, whether Christian or Muslim, are Spanish citizens and subjects. Both Ceuta and Melilla have municipal councils (ayuntamientos), and are administered as an integral part of Spain by an official (Delegado del Gobierno) directly responsible to the Ministry of the Interior in Madrid. This official is usually assisted by a government sub-delegate. There is also one delegate from each of the ministries in Madrid.

In October 1978 King Hassan of Morocco attempted to link the question of the sovereignty of Melilla to that of the return of the British dependent territory of Gibraltar to Spain. In November King Hassan stated his country's claim to Ceuta and Melilla. In October 1981 Spain declared before the UN that Ceuta and Melilla were integral parts of Spanish territory. In April 1982 the Istiqlal, a Moroccan political party, demanded action to recover the territories from Spain, and in March 1983 the Moroccan Government blocked the passage of goods across the frontiers of Ceuta and Melilla. In August the movement of Moroccan workers to Ceuta, Melilla and also Gibraltar was restricted.

From 1984 there was increasing unease over Spanish North Africa's future. The riots in Morocco in January 1984 and the signing of the treaty of union between Libya and Morocco in August gave rise to disquiet. Following the opening of the Spanish frontier with Gibraltar, in early 1985 Morocco reiterated its claim to Ceuta and Melilla. King Hassan indicated, however, that he desired a political solution to the problem. Spain continued to reject any comparison between the two enclaves and Gibraltar. In July 1985 the joint Libyan-Moroccan assembly passed a resolution calling for the 'liberation' of Ceuta and Melilla. In the same month the leaders of the nationalist parties of both Ceuta and Melilla visited Gibraltar for talks with the Chief Minister, in an effort to secure support for their cause.

Details of the enclaves' new draft statutes, envisaging the establishment of two local assemblies, with jurisdiction over such matters as public works, agriculture, tourism, culture and internal trade, were announced in August and approved by the central Government in December 1985. Unlike Spain's other regional assemblies, however, those of Ceuta and Melilla were not to be vested with legislative powers, and this denial of full autonomy was much criticized in the two enclaves. In March 1986 up to 20,000 people took to the streets of Ceuta in a demonstration to demand autonomy.

Meanwhile, the introduction of Madrid by a new aliens law in July 1985 required all foreigners resident in Spain to register with the authorities or risk expulsion. In Ceuta most Muslims possessed the necessary documentation. However, in Melilla (where the Muslim community was estimated to number 27,000, of whom only 7,000 held Spanish nationality) thousands of Muslims staged a protest against the new legislation in November 1985, as a result of which the central Government gave an assurance that it would assist the full integration into Spanish society of Muslims in Ceuta and Melilla, and promised to improve conditions in the territories. In December an interministerial commission, headed by the Minister of the Interior, was created to formulate plans for investment in the enclaves' transport, health services (in 1982 Ceuta had 112 doctors and Melilla 110) and other public facilities.

Tension in Melilla was renewed in December 1985, when 40,000 members of the Spanish community attended a demonstration in support of the new aliens law. In January 1986 the brutality with which the police dispersed a peaceful rally by Muslim women provoked outrage in all quarters. In addition to the hunger strike already being undertaken by a number of Muslims, a two-day general strike was called. In February 1986, however, the Ministry of the Interior in Madrid and the leaders of the Muslim communities of Ceuta and Melilla reached agreement on the application of the aliens law. A joint commission to study the Muslims' problems was to be established, and a census to determine those eligible for Spanish citizenship was to be carried out. The agreement was denounced as unconstitutional by the Spanish populations of the enclaves. The Minister of the Interior visited the territories in April and reiterated that the implementation of the aliens law (the deadline for registration having been extended to 31 March 1986, following three postponements) would not entail mass expulsions of Muslim immigrants.

After negotiations with representatives of the Muslim community, in May the Government agreed to grant Spanish nationality to more than 2,400 Muslims resident in the enclaves. By mid-1986, however, the number of Muslims applying for Spanish nationality in Melilla alone had reached several thousand. As a result of the delays in the processing of the applications by the authorities, Aomar Muhammadi Dudú, the leader of the newly-founded Muslim party, Partido de los Demócratas de Melilla (PDM), accused the Government of failing to fulfil its pledge to the Muslim residents.

At the general elections of June 1986 the ruling Partido Socialista Obrero Español (PSOE) was successful in Ceuta, but was defeated by the centre-right Coalición Popular (CP) in Melilla, the latter result indicating the strong opposition of local Spaniards to the Government's plan to integrate the Muslim population. Tight security surrounded the elections in Melilla, where 'parallel elections', resulting in a vote of confidence in the PDM leader, were held by the Muslim community. The elections were accompanied by several days of unrest, involving right-wing Christians and local Muslims, and there were further violent clashes between the police and Christian demonstrators demanding the resignation of the Government Delegate in Melilla, Andrés Moreno.

In August 1986 work began on the census of Muslim residents in Ceuta and Melilla. In the same month Juan Díez de la Cortina, Secretary-General of the extreme right-wing Partido Nacionalista (Español) de Melilla, was arrested on suspicion of planning a terrorist attack against the Government Delegate in Melilla. Following talks in Madrid between representatives of the main political parties in Melilla and the Ministry of the Interior, concessions to the enclave included the replacement of Andrés Moreno as Government Delegate by Manuel Céspedes. The Madrid negotiations were denounced by Aomar Muhammadi Dudú, the Muslim leader of Melilla, who nevertheless in September agreed to accept a senior post in the Ministry of the Interior in Madrid, with responsibility for relations with the Muslim communities of Spain.

In October 1986 it was reported that Dudú had travelled to Rabat for secret discussions with the Moroccan Minister of the Interior. In November Muslim leaders in Melilla announced that they wished to establish their own administration in the enclave, in view of the Madrid Government's failure to fulfil its promise of Spanish citizenship for Muslim residents. The Spanish Minister of the Interior, however, reiterated an assurance of the Government's intention to carry out the process of integration of the Muslim community. Later in the month, Muslim traders staged a four-day closure of their businesses to draw attention to their plight, and thousands of Muslims took part in a peaceful demonstration, reaffirming support for Dudú, who had resigned from his Madrid post after only two months in office. (Dudú subsequently went into exile in Morocco and lost the support of Melilla's Muslim community.) A similar protest, to have taken place in Ceuta in December, was banned by the Spanish authorities.

In January 1987 the Spanish Minister of the Interior paid an official visit to Morocco. King Hassan proposed the establishment of a joint commission to seek a solution to the problem of the Spanish enclaves, but the proposal was rejected by Spain. There was a serious escalation of tension in Melilla in early February, when a member of the Muslim community died from gunshot wounds, following renewed racial clashes. Police reinforcements were flown in from Spain to deal with the crisis. Numerous demonstrators were detained. Several prominent Muslims were charged with sedition and transferred to a prison in Almería on the Spanish mainland, but were released shortly afterwards. The indictment of a total of 27 Muslims was completed in mid-1988.

In March 1987 King Hassan of Morocco reaffirmed his support for the Muslims of the Spanish enclaves, and later warned that a serious crisis in relations between Rabat and Madrid would arise if Spain were to grant autonomy to the territories. King Hassan renewed his proposal for dialogue, ruling out the possibility of a 'green march' similar to the campaign organized in 1975, when 300,000 unarmed Moroccan volunteers had attempted to occupy the Spanish Sahara, which Spain had subsequently agreed to relinquish.

In April 1987 Spanish and Moroccan troops participated in joint manoeuvres on Moroccan territory adjacent to Melilla, as part of a programme of military co-operation. In early May thousands of Melilla residents attended a demonstration in favour of autonomy for the enclave. During a visit to Melilla a senior official of the ruling PSOE emphasized the need for the integration of Christians and Muslims, while asserting that Spanish sovereignty would continue and would form the basis of the territory's future autonomy statute. In July, following a visit to Rabat by the Spanish Minister of Foreign Affairs, King Hassan declared that agreement had been reached on the holding of talks on the question of Ceuta and Melilla. The Spanish Government, however, denied the existence of such an agreement, maintaining that the issue was not negotiable.

At the end of July 1987 Spain was obliged to order its fishing fleet to withdraw from Moroccan waters, upon the expiry of an agreement signed with Morocco in 1983 (prior to Spain's accession to the European Community—EC, now European Union—EU), allowing Spain access to the rich fishing grounds off the Moroccan coast in exchange for financial aid of US $550m. Having previously appeared unwilling to extend the treaty, in an attempt to link the issue of fishing rights to that of Spanish North Africa, Morocco unexpectedly agreed to a provisional renewal of the accord, whereby Spanish vessels would be permitted to continue operating in Moroccan waters until December 1987, pending the negotiation of a new agreement between Morocco and the EC. At the end of 1987, when the temporary accord expired, Spanish fishing vessels were once again expelled from Moroccan waters and were unable to resume operations until March 1988, upon the entry into force of a new four-year agreement between the EC and Morocco. This agreement was renewed for a further three years in May 1992 (see Morocco, p. 851).

In Ceuta, meanwhile, there was renewed unrest in August 1987, following the indiscriminate shooting dead of a Muslim by a member of the security forces. On a visit to that territory in September, the Spanish Minister of Justice emphasized the difficulty of elevating the status of the enclaves to that of an autonomous region. In February 1988 it was announced that, in accordance with EC regulations, Moroccan citizens would in due course require visas to enter Spain. Entry to Spanish North Africa, however, was to be exempt from the new ruling.

In March 1988 a group of seven Muslims began an indefinite occupation of the Melilla office responsible for the processing of applications for Spanish nationality, to protest against its alleged inefficiency. Of the 8,000 applications presented, it was claimed, fewer than one-half had been granted. After several months of negotiations, in March the central Government and main opposition parties in Madrid reached a broad consensus on the draft autonomy statutes for the Spanish External Territories.

Spain's relations with Morocco improved in June 1988, when the two countries signed an agreement on bilateral economic co-operation, whereby Spain was to grant credits totalling 125,000m. pesetas to Morocco. In the same month the Melilla representative to the Madrid Senate requested that the Government clarify all aspects of Spanish North Africa's security position, in view of the territories' exclusion from the NATO 'umbrella'.

In July 1988 a senior member of the ruling PSOE acknowledged that the party's Programme 2000 contained contradictory proposals regarding Ceuta and Melilla. Although it was envisaged that Spain would retain the territories, the possibility of a negotiated settlement with Morocco was not discounted. In late July, seven years after the enclaves' first official request for autonomy, the central Government announced that the implementation of the territories' autonomy statutes was to be accelerated. Revised draft statutes were submitted by the PSOE to the main opposition parties for consideration. The statutes declared Ceuta and Melilla to be integral parts of Spain and, for the first time, the Spanish Government undertook to guarantee financial support for the territories. A further innovation contained in the revised draft provided for the establishment of mixed commissions to oversee the movement of goods and services through the territories. As previously indicated by the Spanish Government, the two Spanish North African assemblies were to be granted 'normative' rather than legislative powers. Each new assembly would elect from among its members a city president.

It was subsequently revealed that the revised statutes encompassed only the enclaves of Ceuta and Melilla, thus excluding the associated Spanish North African islands (the Chafarinas Islands, the Peñón de Alhucemas, the Peñón de Vélez de la Gomera and the island of Perejil, Spanish sovereignty over the latter being uncertain), and that they had been erroneously incorporated in the preliminary statutes, approved by the Government in December 1985. Although remaining the responsibility of the Spanish Ministry of Defence, these islands were not, therefore, to become part of any Spanish autonomous region.

In August 1988 a Moroccan Minister of State asserted that Spain should negotiate a peaceful, political solution to the question of Ceuta and Melilla. In October the Moroccan Minister of Foreign Affairs formally presented his country's claim to Ceuta and Melilla to the UN General Assembly. An official visit by King Hassan to Spain, scheduled for November, was indefinitely postponed without explanation, and in Melilla a Muslim group acknowledged that it had been in receipt of financial assistance from the Moroccan Government. By December 1988 a total of 5,257 Muslims in Melilla had been granted Spanish citizenship since 1986, and a further 1,126 applications were pending. (By 1990 nearly all residents were in possession of an identity card.) On a visit to Ceuta in December 1988 a Spanish government official stated that the enclaves would be granted autonomy during the present Government's term of office.

In January 1989, however, King Hassan reiterated Morocco's claim to Ceuta and Melilla. A planned visit to Rabat by the Spanish Minister of Foreign Affairs was postponed, but in March Narcís Serra, the Spanish Minister of Defence, travelled to Morocco for consultations with King Hassan on security matters. In April the Spanish Government and the Partido Popular (PP), the main opposition party, reached agreement on the revised statutes for Ceuta and Melilla. In May the Spanish Prime Minister and King Hassan met in Casablanca for discussions on the situation in the Middle East. King Hassan paid an official visit to Spain in September 1989. The question of Spanish North Africa was not discussed, although the King of Morocco reiterated his country's claim to the territories, while discounting the use of force as a means of settling the dispute. Spain and Morocco agreed to hold annual summit meetings, in order to improve relations.

At the general election held in October 1989 the ruling PSOE retained its Ceuta seats, despite allegations by the opposition PP that many names on the electoral register were duplicated. In Melilla, however, the election results were declared invalid, following the discovery of serious irregularities. Melilla's one seat in the Congress of Deputies and one of its two seats in the Senate in Madrid had originally been allocated to the PSOE, the PP winning the second seat in the Senate. At the repeated ballot held in March 1990, however, at which 52% of the electorate voted, both Senate seats and the one Congress seat were won by the PP, the latter result stripping the PSOE of its overall majority in the Madrid lower chamber. The Government Delegate in Melilla claimed that voting irregularities had again occurred.

In January 1990, meanwhile, the Partido Comunista de España (PCE) and its Moroccan counterpart, the Parti du Progrès et du Socialisme (PPS), had issued a joint communiqué urging the Governments of Spain and Morocco to open dialogue and work towards a satisfactory solution to the question of Ceuta and Melilla. Relations between Spain and Morocco were strained in March, when Spanish fishermen blockaded Algeciras and other ports (thereby disrupting communications with Ceuta) in protest at the Moroccan authorities' imposition of greatly-increased penalties on Spanish fishing vessels found to be operating without a licence in Moroccan waters. Following negotiations between the EC and Morocco, Spain agreed to grant financial compensation to Morocco.

In a newspaper article in March 1990 a Moroccan government minister repeated his country's claim to Spanish North Africa, maintaining that, with the accession of Namibia to independence, Ceuta and Melilla were the last vestiges of colonialism in Africa. In April the Spanish Government decided to open negotiations with the political groupings of Ceuta and Melilla, the autonomy statutes being presented for discussion in the territories. It was confirmed that the enclaves were to remain an integral part of Spain, and that they were to be granted self-government at municipal, rather than regional, level. The Spanish Government's decision provoked a strong reaction from Moroccan political parties, which were united in their denunciation of the perceived attempt to legalize Spanish possession of the territories. In Ceuta a two-hour strike, in support of demands for full autonomy for the enclave, was widely observed.

In July 1990 the Istiqlal, the Moroccan opposition party, announced that it was initiating a new campaign to press for the 'liberation' of Ceuta and Melilla. In the following month the Istiqlal organized a protest march through the streets of Martil, a Moroccan town 40 km from Ceuta. The Muslim community of Ceuta, however, expressed its concern at these developments.

In mid-August 1990 Spain granted its Government Delegate in Melilla direct powers to expel illegal residents from the territory. In the same month King Hassan and the Spanish Prime Minister, met near Rabat for talks. Their discussions focused on the Gulf crisis, caused by Iraq's invasion of Kuwait, and on their bilateral relations, particularly increased co-operation and security. In December a Spanish delegation, led by Felipe González, travelled to Morocco, where the first of the planned regular summit meetings between the Spanish and Moroccan Prime Ministers took place. Among the topics discussed was the forthcoming implementation (in May 1991) of new visa requirements for North Africans entering Spain, which had caused dismay in the Muslim community. Special arrangements were to apply to Moroccan citizens who worked in, or travelled regularly to, Ceuta and Melilla. At the meeting a Spanish credit to Morocco of 25,000m. pesetas (in addition to that agreed in 1988) was also arranged.

The outbreak of the Gulf war in early 1991 gave rise to renewed disquiet in Spanish North Africa. In February 800 Muslims marched through the streets of Melilla to protest against the war, in which the US military bases in Spain were to play a crucial role. In the same month, as anti-Western sentiment in North Africa increased, the Spanish Minister of Foreign Affairs embarked on a tour of five Maghreb countries. Discussions with his Moroccan counterpart took place in Rabat.

Elections for the 25-member municipal councils of Ceuta and Melilla were held in May 1991, and in each territory the PSOE Mayor was replaced. In Ceuta Francisco Fraiz Armada of the Progreso y Futuro de Ceuta (PFC) became Mayor. In Melilla, where the PP had secured 12 of the 25 seats, Ignacio Velázquez Rivera of the right-wing Partido Nacionalista de Melilla (PNM) was elected Mayor of the enclave.

In July 1991, in Rabat, the Spanish and Moroccan heads of government signed a treaty of friendship. In addition to the promotion of co-operation in the fields of economy, finance, fisheries, culture and the judiciary, agreement was also reached on Spanish military aid to Morocco. Shortly afterwards the Moroccan Minister of the Interior, Driss Basri, and a cabinet colleague unexpectedly accepted an invitation from the Spanish Minister of the Interior to visit Ceuta, their brief trip being the first ever visit by members of the Government of King Hassan.

The draft autonomy statutes of Ceuta and Melilla were submitted to the Congress of Deputies in Madrid for discussion in October 1991. During the debate the PP accused the PSOE of supporting Moroccan interests. In November thousands of demonstrators, many of whom had travelled from the enclaves, attended a protest march in Madrid (organized by the Governments of Ceuta and Melilla), in support of demands for autonomy for the territories. In early 1992, however, the central Government confirmed that the assemblies of Ceuta and Melilla were not to be granted full legislative powers. In May a general strike in Ceuta, to protest against this denial of full autonomy, was widely supported.

In mid-1992 relations between Spain and Morocco were dominated by the issue of illegal immigration. In addition to the problem of the large numbers of Moroccans trying to enter mainland Spain (many drownings in the Strait of Gibraltar being reported), there had been a sharp increase in the numbers of those from other (mainly West African) countries attempting to gain entry to Europe via Morocco and the two Spanish enclaves. In July the Spanish Minister of Foreign Affairs flew to Rabat for discussions on the problem.

In March 1993 it was revealed that Spain would require the permission of NATO before employing its most modern military equipment in the defence of the enclaves. In the same month, in an attempt to bring about the transfer of powers to the territories, the PP submitted its own draft statute for Melilla to the central Government, which immediately condemned the document as unconstitutional. All political parties in Melilla, except the PSOE, demanded that a local referendum be held on the issue of autonomy. In September the Spanish Minister of Public Administration affirmed his commitment to the conclusion, within the next few months, of an agreement on the territories' statutes.

At the general election of June 1993, meanwhile, the PSOE of Ceuta lost its one seat in Congress and its two seats in the Senate to the PP. In Melilla the PSOE candidate defeated the incumbent PP Congress member; the PP also lost one of its two seats in the Senate.

In February 1994 the Mayor of Ceuta, Francisco Fraiz Armada, was obliged to resign, following the Supreme Court's ratification of a lower court ruling that barred him from holding public office for six years. His disqualification resulted from his involvement in irregularities in the housing sector in 1984, when unauthorized evictions had been carried out. He was replaced by Basilio Fernández López, also of the PFC.

In March 1994 King Hassan declared his opposition to the forthcoming adoption of the autonomy statutes, repeating Morocco's claim to the territories. By May, however, the final statutes had still not been presented to the Cortes in Madrid. Representatives of Ceuta were particularly critical of the dilatory conduct of the Minister of Public Administration, and urged the central Government and the opposition PP to bring the matter to a speedy conclusion. In the same month King Juan Carlos of Spain received a delegation from Melilla, led by the Mayor, Ignacio Velázquez Rivera, who emphasized the necessity for a swift adoption of the enclave's autonomy statute and conveyed his citizens' concern at the Moroccan monarch's recent statement.

In September 1994 the final statutes of autonomy were approved by the Spanish Government, in preparation for their presentation to the Cortes. The statutes provided for 25-member local assemblies with powers similar to those of the municipal councils of mainland Spain. Morocco, however, announced that it was initiating a new diplomatic campaign to reassert its claim over the territories. Spain rejected as 'inappropriate' the Moroccan Prime Minister's efforts, in a speech to the UN General Assembly, to draw a comparison between the position of the enclaves and the forthcoming return to Chinese sovereignty of the British dependent territory of Hong Kong and of the Portuguese territory of Macau.

The proposals for limited self-government were generally acceptable in Melilla but not in Ceuta, where, in October 1994, a general strike received widespread support. An estimated 20,000 residents of Ceuta participated in a demonstration to demand equality with other Spanish regions and full autonomy for the enclave. Earlier in the month, following expressions of concern regarding the territories' protection in the event of Moroccan aggression, the Minister of Defence confirmed that Spain would continue to maintain an appropriate military presence in Ceuta and Melilla. In December more than 2,000 citizens of Ceuta attended a demonstration in Madrid in support of their demands for full autonomy.

Following their approval by the Congress of Deputies in December 1994, the autonomy statutes were ratified by the Senate in February 1995. This approval of the statutes by the Spanish Cortes was denounced by the Moroccan Government, which, upon taking office in March, declared that the recovery of Ceuta and Melilla was to be one of its major objectives. In April responsibility for two explosions in Ceuta was claimed by the Organización 21 de Agosto para la Liberación de los Territorios Marroquíes Usurpados, a group that had apparently remained inactive since 1975, and which the Spanish Government suspected was now receiving covert assistance from the Moroccan authorities.

In September 1994 Morocco had demanded that the fishing accord with the EU be renegotiated and that quotas be drastically reduced. At the end of April 1995 hundreds of Spanish fishing vessels, including some from Ceuta, were obliged once again to withdraw from Moroccan waters, following the EU's failure to renegotiate the agreement with Morocco. In May, as anti-Moroccan sentiment grew, there were violent scenes when Spanish fishermen and farmers attempted to obstruct the entry of Moroccan produce into the ports of southern Spain. The protests were renewed in late August. Negotiations between the EU and Morocco continued intermittently in mid-1995. In October Morocco agreed to accept an irrevocable four-year accord (rather than a three-year arrangement as it had originally demanded) on the basis of decreases in fish catches. Morocco also agreed to reduce its claim for financial compensation. Following final agreement on issues such as the compulsory unloading of a certain percentage of fish in Moroccan ports, vessels from EU nations, mainly Spain, were able to return to Moroccan waters in late November. The accord entered into force in January 1996.

Elections for the new local assemblies were held in May 1995, to coincide with the municipal polls. At the latter, in Ceuta the PP won nine of the 25 seats, the PFC six, the nationalist Ceuta Unida four and the PSOE three. Basilio Fernández López of the PFC was re-elected Mayor/President, heading a coalition with Ceuta Unida and the PSOE. Mustafa Mizzian Ammar, leader of the Partido Democrático y Social de Ceuta (PDSC), became the first Muslim candidate ever to be elected in the territory. Fewer than 57% of those eligible voted in Ceuta. In Melilla, where the level of participation was less than 62%, the PP won 14 of the 25 seats, the PSOE five seats, Coalición por Melilla, a new Muslim grouping, four seats and the right-wing Unión del Pueblo Melillense (UPM) two seats. Ignacio Velázquez (PP/PNM) returned to the position of Mayor/President.

In Ceuta concern about the level of illegal immigration from sub-Saharan Africa increased during 1995. By mid-1995 these immigrants, many of whom were without documentation and claimed to have fled from war-ravaged countries such as Rwanda, were estimated to total more than 300. In October a violent confrontation occurred between about 150 Africans and the security forces, the latter being joined by citizens' vigilante groups. During the course of the affray a policeman was shot and seriously injured. An investigation into the shooting discounted the possibility that an African demonstrator had been responsible. Nevertheless, more than 100 illegal immigrants were transferred to a detention centre on the Spanish mainland, while 15 Africans who were alleged to have led the riot were imprisoned in Ceuta. In an attempt to curtail illegal immigration, Ceuta's frontier with Morocco was strengthened.

A general election was held in March 1996. In Ceuta the three PP delegates to the Cortes in Madrid were re-elected. In Melilla the PSOE lost its seat in the lower house to the PP, which also took both seats in the Senate. Following the installation of the PP administration in Madrid, both Government Delegates in the territories were replaced. In the same month, following the killing of a Spanish legionnaire in a bar brawl, which led to a rampage by hundreds of soldiers through the streets of a Muslim district of Melilla, more than 100 legionnaires were confined to barracks. At the end of March thousands of Muslims, organized by Coalición por Melilla, took part in a demonstration to protest against their position on the margins of society.

In February 1996, meanwhile, at a summit meeting in Rabat (the first since December 1993) the Spanish and Moroccan Prime Ministers concluded an agreement relating to a Spanish credit of 150,000m. pesetas, to be extended to Morocco over the next five years. An arrangement was also reached regarding Morocco's bilateral debt of 242,300m. pesetas. In May, however, on his first official overseas trip, José María Aznar, the newly-appointed Prime Minister, travelled from Spain to Morocco for discussions with King Hassan. The new head of government appeared to adopt a less conciliatory stance on the question of debt relief for Morocco. The issue of Ceuta and Melilla was not given prominence.

In July 1996 the Mayor/President of Ceuta, Basilio Fernández López of the PFC, resigned after seven months at the head of a minority administration, and was replaced by Jesús Fortes Ramos of the PP, who urged that the enclave be considered a full autonomous region. In September the Secretary-General of NATO confirmed that Ceuta and Melilla would remain outside the alliance's sphere of protection if Spain were to be fully integrated into NATO's military structure.

In mid-1996 attention focused once again on the issue of illegal immigration from Africa. Both Ceuta and Melilla appealed to the EU for financial assistance to counter the problems arising from the enclaves' attractive location as an entry point to Europe and from the recent implementation of the EU's Schengen Convention permitting the free movement of persons among the accord's signatory countries. In June, following disturbances involving refugees from Central Africa during which several people were injured, a total of 103 immigrants were flown from Melilla to detention centres on the

Spanish mainland and thence, only hours later in a clandestine operation, were expelled via the Canary Islands to various sub-Saharan countries. The Spanish Government's apparently peremptory procedure and dismissal of requests for asylum not only provoked criticism from humanitarian groups, but also led to demands from senior judges and politicians for clarification of the events. The General Prosecutor of Spain was ordered to initiate an inquiry. The Spanish Ministry of the Interior, having been obliged to admit that sedative drugs had been administered to the refugees prior to their deportation, also opened an investigation. The case was closed in July 1998, no charges having been brought.

As the exodus of emigrants from Africa continued, the Spanish authorities intercepted numerous small boats in the Strait of Gibraltar. In September 1996 the Red Cross declared that its supplies of rations were insufficient to feed the 406 (mainly Moroccan and Algerian) immigrants located at an encampment in Ceuta. In October the Spanish Minister of the Interior met his Moroccan counterpart in Madrid for discussions. The negotiations resulted in an agreement on the establishment of two joint commissions to address the specific problems of illegal immigration and drugs-trafficking.

In October 1996 two police-officers were injured in disturbances in Ceuta, the third such protest by disaffected citizens in that year. In November, for the first time in more than 14 years, the Spanish Minister of Defence paid an official visit to the enclaves which, upon Spain's proposed full integration into the military structure of NATO, were to remain outside the organization's sphere of protection. In early December it was reported that Spain was to convert part of Morocco's debt into investment projects. Later in the month the Spanish Minister of the Interior travelled to Rabat for further discussions on the issues of illegal immigration and drugs-trafficking. For the first time since the signing of a joint accord in 1992, Morocco agreed to the readmission of illegal immigrants held in the Spanish enclaves.

Between January and December 1996, according to the Spanish Ministry of the Interior, a total of 1,552 illegal Moroccan immigrants were detained in Ceuta, while 2,321 were detained in Melilla. The central Government allocated emergency funding of 28m. pesetas to meet the immediate needs of the immigrants. A sum of 30m. pesetas was granted to the Red Cross. In early 1997 concern grew that much of the illegal immigration from Morocco was being controlled by networks involved in the smuggling of drugs and tobacco. In April the Spanish Minister of the Interior expressed reservations regarding the likely success of the first joint police operation with Morocco against these networks. In May 1997 Morocco announced that its fishing accord with the EU (see above) would not be renewed upon its expiry in the year 2000.

In March 1997, in Melilla, a motion of censure against Ignacio Velázquez resulted in the Mayor/President's defeat, owing to the defection to the opposition of two PP councillors, Enrique Palacios and Abdelmalik Tahar. The latter subsequently absconded to the Canary Islands. The opposition then declared Enrique Palacios to be Mayor/President, although the central Government continued to recognize Ignacio Velázquez as the rightful incumbent. In May Enrique Palacios alleged that at the election of May 1995 that party had employed irregular tactics in its campaign for the support of Muslim voters. Also in May 1997, for the first time, the Mayor/Presidents of Ceuta and Melilla attended a conference of the autonomous regions' presidents, held in Madrid. Despite the attempted 'coup' in Melilla, the territory was represented by Ignacio Velázquez. In November 1997, from Tenerife, Abdelmalik Tahar accused Ignacio Velázquez and five associates of having subjected him to blackmail and threats, as a result of which he had relinquished his seat on the Council, thereby permitting the PP to replace him and to regain its majority. In December 1997 Tahar, who was now under police protection, declared to the investigating judge that he had been offered 50m. pesetas (of which he had received 3m.) and a monthly sum of 200,000 pesetas. Following an appeal by Enrique Palacios and a judicial ruling leading to the successful revival of the motion of censure against Ignacio Velázquez in February 1998, Palacios took office as Mayor/President of Melilla, accusing his predecessor, furthermore, of serious financial mismanagement. A new motion of censure, presented by the PP urging that (despite the bribery charges against him) Ignacio Velázquez be restored to office, was deemed to be illegal and therefore rejected in a decree issued by Enrique Palacios, who also ordered the temporary closure of the local assembly. In July Enrique Palacios accused the PP of having employed public funds, amounting to more than 200m. pesetas, to secure the votes of some 2,500 Muslims at the 1995 local elections, the bribes reportedly having taken the form of building materials for the purposes of residential repairs. The allegations were denied by the PP.

During 1997 there was increased concern regarding the numbers of illegal immigrants. In June police reinforcements were drafted into Melilla, following renewed disturbances in which one immigrant died. More than 100 illegal immigrants were immediately returned to Morocco as part of a special security operation, and on the same day of action a total of 873 Moroccans were denied entry to Melilla. (More than 10,000 Moroccans daily continued to cross the border legally, in order to work in the enclave.) In July a young Moroccan was shot and wounded, and two civil guards were injured, during a confrontation on the Melilla border. Meanwhile, many North Africans continued to risk their lives attempting to cross the Strait of Gibraltar, often in makeshift vessels, in the hope of gaining access to Europe; numerous drownings were recorded during 1997.

In August 1997 various non-governmental organizations condemned the rudimentary conditions in which more than 800 illegal immigrants, mainly from sub-Saharan Africa and Algeria, were being held in Melilla. Furthermore, it was announced that a Melilla reception centre housing about 100 Algerians was to close, owing to unsatisfactory conditions. It was envisaged that a new refuge, to accommodate 300 immigrants, would open in November 1997. In Ceuta 51 Moroccans and 43 Algerians were detained in August, as they tried to leave the enclave hidden in lorries bound for shipment to the Spanish mainland. They were swiftly repatriated. In the same month hundreds of Moroccan children, who had been begging on the streets of Melilla, were returned to their homeland. The increasing involvement of organized criminal gangs in such activities continued to cause disquiet. Following an incident involving Moroccan immigrants, in which 15 cars were destroyed by fire, the Melilla Government accused the Moroccan authorities of facilitating the entry of the illegal immigrants. In August the Spanish General Prosecutor demanded emergency measures to address the immigrant crisis, having already urged the Ministry of the Interior in June to find an immediate solution.

In September 1997, as Melilla commemorated the 500th anniversary of its foundation by the Spanish, various Moroccan political parties renewed their denunciation of Spain's 'colonial' occupation of the territory. In the same month, at the UN General Assembly in New York, the Moroccan Prime Minister denounced the situation in Ceuta and Melilla.

In Ceuta one Algerian man died during an altercation among immigrants at the Calamocarro camp in September 1997. As tension in the camps increased, by December 1997 the number of immigrants in Melilla alone totalled 930. In that month the Spanish Government announced that 1,206 sub-Saharan Africans were to be transferred from Ceuta and Melilla to the mainland. In late December the authorities effected the first transfers to Spain, where the illegal immigrants were received by various non-governmental organizations. The Minister of the Interior announced that two new reception centres were to be built in Ceuta and Melilla.

In January 1998 three police officers were injured and six immigrants were detained, as a result of a confrontation in offices of the Red Cross in Melilla, where about 50 immigrants from central Africa staged a demonstration against the criteria for transfer to mainland Spain. About 200 Algerians, protesting against delays in their transfer, demonstrated outside government offices. During the same month four members of the security forces were injured in three separate incidents, involving carriers of contraband, on the border with Morocco. As the territories' borders were strengthened and both maritime and street patrols increased, in February 1998 it was announced that during the course of the previous year 4,358 illegal immigrants had been expelled from Ceuta. In March 1998, in Melilla, a demonstration by Algerian

immigrants left three people injured. In April 1998 it was revealed that in the first three months of the year a total of 1,317 illegal immigrants, mostly from Morocco, had been detained in Cádiz, compared with 714 in the corresponding period of the previous year. On the occasion of the Spanish Prime Minister's visit to Morocco in April 1998, his newly-appointed Moroccan counterpart requested that Spain review its policy on Ceuta and Melilla.

In mid-1998 it was estimated that since 1990 some 2,000 people had drowned during unsuccessful attempts to cross the Strait of Gibraltar, while about 20,000 illegal immigrants had been arrested by the Spanish authorities. Improvements in the territories' border security continued. On Ceuta's frontier with Morocco a 2-m high double fence, incorporating a parallel patrol road and equipped with security cameras and fibre optic sensors, was approaching completion in late 1998, funding having been provided by the EU. In August it was reported that at least 38 Moroccans had been drowned several weeks previously when their boat capsized during an attempted illegal sea crossing. In Madrid the Ministry of the Interior was criticized for its apparent failure to assist in a rescue attempt. The Spanish Government, however, maintained that the disaster had taken place within Moroccan waters. Also in August 1998 some 40 illegal immigrants from sub-Saharan Africa broke through the security fence to reach Melilla, where an extensive police operation to capture them was immediately mounted.

In September 1998 the Government of Melilla was the first to reject Morocco's offer of dual nationality for the citizens of the two enclaves, urging the Spanish Government to lodge a protest with the Moroccan authorities.

Economy

CEUTA AND MELILLA

Ceuta and Melilla, both free ports, are in fact of little economic importance, while the other possessions, with a 1982 population of 312, mostly military personnel and fishermen, are of negligible significance. The basic reason for Spanish retention of these areas was their predominantly Spanish population. The registered populations of both Ceuta and Melilla have fallen since the 1960s, owing to the lack of economic opportunities in the towns, although the proportion of Arab residents has greatly increased, particularly in Melilla. There are large number of immigrants from Morocco.

In 1991 Ceuta's gross domestic product (GDP) was 33.6% below the average for the whole of Spain, while that of Melilla was 30.5% below. In the same year the average disposable family income of Ceuta was only 76.85% that of Spain, the figure in Melilla being 84.76%. Social security benefits accounted for 22.75% of the average family income in Ceuta and 24.25% in Melilla. In 1992 the GDP of the two territories totalled 133,767m. pesetas, equivalent to 1,072,607 pesetas per head. In 1995 the territories' combined GDP per head was 11.61% below the average for the whole of Spain. In that year, compared with 1994, the GDP of Ceuta and Melilla increased by 1.98%. In 1996 GDP per head was estimated to have increased by 1.58% in Ceuta and by 1.68% in Melilla. By 1996, although the two territories' income per head was below the average for Spain, family income per caput being 0.83% below the Spanish average in Ceuta and 6.04% above in Melilla, purchasing power was 3.03% higher in Ceuta and 6.55% higher in Melilla. An unofficial report issued in October 1996 classified Melilla as by far the poorest city in Spain. In 1997, compared with the previous year, the GDP of Ceuta increased by 2.82%, while that of Melilla expanded by 2.76%, among the lowest growth rates in Spain.

The hinterland of the two cities is small. Development is restricted by the lack of suitable building land. Ceuta, in particular, suffers from intermittent water shortages. In September 1995 tenders were invited for the construction of a desalination plant in the territory, which would be capable of processing 12,000 cu m of seawater per day (rising to 16,000 cu m). The apparent shortcomings of the territories' infrastructure were demonstrated in Melilla in November 1997 by the rupture of a large water-storage tank. The resultant flood killed 11 people, injured 41 and caused damage estimated at more than 1,350m. pesetas.

Most of the population's food has to be imported, with the exception of fish, which is obtained locally. Sardines and anchovies are the most important items. A large proportion of the tinned fish is sold outside Spain. More important to the economies of the cities is the port activity; most of their exports take the form of fuel supplied—at very competitive rates—to ships. Most of the fuel comes from the Spanish refinery in Tenerife. Ceuta's port is the busier, receiving a total of 8,203 ships in 1993. Apart from the ferries from Málaga and Almería in mainland Spain, Melilla's port is not so frequented and its exports are correspondingly low. Ceuta's main exports are frozen and preserved fish, foodstuffs and beer. Industry is limited to meeting some of the everyday needs of the cities. There is a local brewery in Ceuta.

In both cities a negligible percentage of the working population is employed in agriculture. In 1989 the economically active population of the two enclaves totalled 49,400, of whom 15,200 were unemployed, 1,800 were employed in the construction sector, 1,400 in industry and 100 in agriculture; 30,800 were employed in the services sector. In 1996 the civil service employed 2,904 workers in Ceuta and 2,877 in Melilla. In the same year the average rate of unemployment was estimated at 12.90% of the labour force in Ceuta and at 12.70% in Melilla. In July 1998 there were 3,462 registered unemployed in Ceuta and 3,730 in Melilla. The average annual rate of inflation in 1996 was 2.2% in Ceuta and 3.6% in Melilla, compared with 4.5% in the two enclaves in 1995. In the 12 months to December 1997 the inflation rate was 1.9% in Ceuta and Melilla combined.

In 1986 the Spanish Government announced that it was to grant 6,500m. pesetas to Ceuta and 8,500m. to Melilla for the purposes of infrastructural development. In 1989 a campaign to attract more investment to Ceuta began. Tax concessions and other incentives were offered. In the three years to 1990 the Spanish Government's investment in Melilla totalled 32,000m. pesetas. Ceuta received 9,000m. pesetas for the purposes of public works, and its health service was allocated 347m. pesetas. In early 1993 investment of a further 18,000m. pesetas for housing and transport projects in Melilla was announced. In Ceuta the apparent lack of banking controls and alleged corruption at senior levels drew criticism in April 1993, when evidence of the territory's use as a 'money-laundering' centre for the proceeds of drugs-trafficking was revealed. A sum of more than 25,000m. pesetas was believed to be involved. Furthermore, in December fraudulent operations, allegedly involving almost 100m. pesetas and in which two civil servants were implicated, were uncovered at the city hall of Ceuta. Following Spain's intensification of security at its frontier with Gibraltar in 1995–96, many drug and tobacco smugglers were believed to have relocated their bases to Ceuta.

Tourism makes a significant contribution to the territories' economies. Almost 1m. tourists visited Ceuta in 1986, attracted by duty-free goods. High ferry-boat fares and the opening of the Spanish border with Gibraltar, however, were expected to have an adverse effect on the enclaves' duty-free trade. Proposed defence cuts led not only to fears for Spanish North Africa's security but also to fears of losses in income from military personnel stationed in the territories.

Upon the accession of Spain to the European Community (EC, now European Union—EU) in January 1986, Ceuta and Melilla were considered as Spanish cities and European territory, and joined the Community as part of Spain. They retained their status as free ports. The statutes of autonomy, adopted in early 1995, envisaged the continuation of the territories' fiscal benefits. In June 1994 the EU announced substantial regional aid: between 1995 and 1999 Ceuta and Melilla were to receive totals of ECU 28m. and ECU 45m., of which ECU 20m. and ECU 18m., respectively, were to be in the form of direct aid. With assistance from the European Social Fund, a programme of employment and vocational training for Melilla was announced in 1996. In 1997 projected state investment in Ceuta and Melilla was 7,786m. pesetas, compared with 6,363m. pesetas in 1996. As a proportion of GDP per head in relation to the EU average, the estimate for Ceuta rose from 37.0% in 1960 to 66.2% in 1996, while that for Melilla increased from 30.8% in 1960 to 70.9% in 1996. The comparable figures for Spain as a whole were 57.2% in 1960 and 76.2% in 1996.

Statistical Survey

Ceuta

Area: 19.7 sq km.

Population (1 May 1996): 68,796 (34,229 males, 34,567 females).

Density (1 May 1996): 3,492.2 per sq km.

Births, Marriages and Deaths (1994): Live births 962; Marriages 440; Deaths 422.

Finance: Spanish currency: 100 céntimos = 1 peseta. *Sterling and Dollar Equivalents* (31 May 1998): £1 sterling = 246.7 pesetas; US $1 = 151.3 pesetas; 1,000 pesetas = £4.053 = $6.609. *Average exchange rate* (pesetas per US $): 124.69 in 1995; 126.66 in 1996; 146.41 in 1997.

External Trade: Ceuta is a duty-free port. Trade is chiefly with mainland Spain, the Balearic and Canary Islands and Melilla. Ceuta supplies fuel and water to ships entering the port. Other exports include frozen and preserved fish, beer and foodstuffs.

Transport: *Road Traffic:* vehicles registered (1994): 2,156; vehicles entered (1993): 205,886; vehicles departed (1993): 150,499. *Shipping* (1993): Ships entered 8,203. Goods unloaded 2,758,797 metric tons (of which fuel 685,117 metric tons, water 1,461,782 metric tons); Passenger departures 1,062,005; arrivals 1,215,010.

Education (1994/95): Pre-school 2,388 pupils, General basic 9,351 pupils, 24 schools; Secondary 3,438 pupils, 5 schools; Vocational (1987/88) 873 students, 3 centres.

Melilla

Area: 12.5 sq km.

Population: (1 May 1996): 59,576 (29,647 males, 29,929 females (incl., at March 1982, Peñón de Alhucemas 61, Chafarinas 191, Peñón de Vélez de la Gomera 60).

Density (1 May 1996): 4,766.1 per sq km.

Births, Marriages and Deaths (1988, provisional): Live births 997; Marriages 332; Deaths 396.

Finance: Spanish currency (see Ceuta).

External Trade: Melilla is a duty-free port. Most imports are from Spain but over 90% of exports go to non-Spanish territories. The chief export is fish.

Transport: *Road Traffic* (vehicles registered, 1987, provisional): 1,498. *Shipping* (1989): Ships entered 819; (1992, provisional): Goods loaded and unloaded 639,000 metric tons; Passenger departures and arrivals 476,000. *Civil Aviation* (1989): Goods loaded and unloaded 560 metric tons; Passenger departures and arrivals 168,000.

Education (1987/88): Pre-school 1,961 pupils, 61 centres; General basic 8,256 pupils, 245 schools; Secondary 1,863 pupils, 4 schools; Vocational 927 students, 1 centre.

Directory

Ceuta

GOVERNMENT
(September 1998)

Delegación del Gobierno: Beatriz de Silva 4, 51001 Ceuta; tel. (956) 512523; fax (956) 513671; Government Delegate in Ceuta LUIS VICENTE MORO DÍAZ.

Consejo de Gobierno: Plaza de Africa s/n, 51001 Ceuta; tel. (956) 528200; fax (956) 514470; Mayor/President of Ceuta JESÚS CAYETANO FORTES RAMOS (PP).

Deputy elected to the Congress in Madrid: FRANCISCO ANTONIO GONZÁLEZ PÉREZ (PP). Representatives to the Senate in Madrid: JOSÉ LUIS MORALES MONTERO (PP), FRANCISCO OLIVENCIA RUIZ (PP). Commandant-General: GONZALO RODRÍGUEZ DE AUSTRIA.

COUNCIL
Election, 28 May 1995

	Seats
Partido Popular (PP)	9
Progreso y Futuro de Ceuta (PFC).	6
Ceuta Unida (CEU)	4
Partido Socialista Obrero Español (PSOE) . . .	3
Partido Socialista del Pueblo de Ceuta (PSPC) . . .	2
Other	1
Total	**25**

POLITICAL ORGANIZATIONS

Ceuta Unida (CEU): Ceuta; nationalist party; Sec.-Gen. José Antonio Querol.

Iniciativa por Ceuta (INCE): Plaza de Africa 10, 1°, 11701 Ceuta; fax (956) 516890; f. 1993; Muslim party; 380 mems; Pres. Ahmed Subaire; Sec. Abdelkader Maimon.

Izquierda Unida: Ceuta; left-wing electoral alliance; Leader Rosa Rodríguez.

Partido Democrático y Social de Ceuta (PDSC): Ceuta; Leader Mustafa Mizzian Ammar.

Partido Humanista: B. Príncipe Alfonso, Ceuta; Leader Mohamed Ali.

Partido Nacionalista Ceutí (PNC): Ceuta; nationalist party; Leader Francisco Alcántara Trujillo.

Partido Popular (PP): Ceuta; fmrly Alianza Popular; centre-right; Leader Ricardo Muñoz Rodríguez.

Partido Socialista Obrero Español (PSOE): Ceuta; socialist workers' party; Leader Antonio Troyano Pérez.

Partido Socialista del Pueblo de Ceuta (PSPC): Carretera del Embalse 10, 11704 Ceuta; dissident group of PSOE; Leader Juan Luis Aróstegui.

Partido Socialista de los Trabajadores (PST): B. Príncipe Alfonso, Ceuta; Leader Sr Abbas.

Progreso y Futuro de Ceuta (PFC): Marina de Ceuta, Ceuta; Leader Francisco Fraiz Armada.

There are branches of the major Spanish parties in Ceuta, and also various civic associations. The **Asociación Ceuta y Melilla (Acyme)** is based in Granada (Pres. Francisco Godino), and is opposed to the limited autonomy of the enclaves. The **Organización 21 de Agosto para la Liberación de los Territorios Marroquíes Usurpados** resumed its activities in 1995.

JUDICIAL SYSTEM

Tribunal Superior de Justicia de Andalucía, Ceuta y Melilla: Plaza Nueva s/n, 18071 Granada; tel. (958) 242108; fax (958) 242156; Pres. Augusto Méndez de Lugo y López de Ayala.

RELIGION

The majority of the European inhabitants are Christians, almost all being adherents of the Roman Catholic Church. Most Africans are Muslims, totalling about 13,000 in 1991. The Jewish community numbers several hundred.

Christianity
The Roman Catholic Church

Bishop of Cádiz and Ceuta: Antonio Ceballos Atienza (resident in Cádiz); Vicars-General: Manuel de la Puente Sendón, Francisco Correro Tocón, Plaza de Nuestra Señora de Africa, 11701 Ceuta; tel. (956) 513208.

THE PRESS

El Faro de Ceuta: Sargento Mena 8, 51001 Ceuta; tel. (956) 511024; fax (956) 517603; f. 1934; morning; Dir Luis Manuel Aznar Cabezón; circ. 5,000.

El Pueblo de Ceuta: Independencia 11, 1°, 51001, Ceuta; tel. (956) 514367; fax (956) 517650; daily; Dir Salvador Vivancos Canales.

Press Association

Asociación de la Prensa: Sargento Mena 8, 51001 Ceuta; tel. (956) 524148.

BROADCASTING
Radio

Onda Cero Radio Ceuta: Grupos Alfau 4, 3°, 51001 Ceuta; tel. (956) 517887; fax (956) 517004; Dir Fernando José Silva López.

Radio Ceuta: Real 90, Portón 4, 1° Dcha, 51001 Ceuta; tel. (956) 511820; fax (956) 516820; f. 1934; commercial; owned by Sociedad Española de Radiodifusión (SER); Dir Beatriz Palomo Fernández.

Radio Nacional de España: Real 90, 51001 Ceuta; tel. (956) 519035; fax (956) 519067; Dir María Dolores Bex Barrera.

Radio Popular de Ceuta/COPE: Sargento Mena 8, 1°, 11701 Ceuta; tel. (956) 513233; fax (956) 517603; Dir José Manuel Domínguez.

Television

Antena Ceuta Televisión: Avda Marina Española 9 bis, Ceuta; tel. (956) 514417; Dir Manuel González Bolorino.

FINANCE

Banco Bilbao Vizcaya (BBV): Plaza de los Reyes s/n, 51001 Ceuta; tel. (956) 511611; 2 brs.

Banco Central Hispanoamericano (BCH): Paseo del Revellín 17, 51001 Ceuta; tel. (956) 511371.

Banco Crédit Lyonnais España: Sargento Coriat 5, 51001 Ceuta; tel. (956) 518040.

Banco de España: Plaza de España 2, 51001 Ceuta; tel. (956) 511805; fax (956) 513108.

Banco Español de Crédito (Banesto): Camoens 6, 51001 Ceuta; tel. (956) 513009.

Banco Exterior–Argentaria: Paseo del Revellín 5, 51001 Ceuta; tel. (956) 516746.

Banco Popular Español: Paseo del Revellín 1, 51001 Ceuta; tel. (956) 510740.

Banco Santander: Marina Española 10, 51001 Ceuta; tel. (956) 510015; 2 brs.

Caja Madrid: Plaza de los Reyes s/n, 51001 Ceuta; tel. (956) 510542.

Caja Postal Argentaria: Plaza Tte Ruiz 6, 51001 Ceuta; tel. (956) 516090.

TRADE AND INDUSTRY

Cámara Oficial de Comercio, Industria y Navegación: Muelle Cañonero Dato s/n, 11701 Ceuta; tel. (956) 509590; fax (956) 509589; Pres. Luis Moreno Naranjo; Sec.-Gen. Francisco Olivencia Ruiz.

Confederación de Empresarios de Ceuta: Teniente Arrabal 2, 11701 Ceuta; tel. (956) 516912; employers' confederation; Pres. José María Campos Martínez; Sec.-Gen. Évaristo Rivera Gómez.

TRANSPORT

Much of the traffic between Spain and Morocco passes through Ceuta; there are ferry services to Algeciras, Spain. Plans for an airport are under consideration.

TOURISM

Visitors are attracted by the historical monuments and museums, and by the availability of duty-free goods. In 1992 Ceuta had four hotels and 27 hostels and guest houses. Plans to build additional accommodation were under way.

Consejería de Turismo, Ferias y Fiestas: Paseo de las Palmeras 26, Ceuta; tel. (956) 518022.

Oficina de Información de Turismo: Muelle Cañonero Dato 1, 51001 Ceuta; tel. (956) 501410.

DEFENCE

Military authority is vested in a commandant-general (see Government). The enclaves are attached to the military region of Sevilla. In August 1997 Spain had 10,000 troops deployed in Spanish North Africa, compared with 21,000 in mid-1987. Two-thirds of Ceuta's land area are used exclusively for military purposes.

EDUCATION

The conventional Spanish facilities are available. In higher education, links with the University of Granada are maintained.

Melilla

GOVERNMENT
(September 1998)

Delegación del Gobierno: Avda de la Marina Española 3, 52001 Melilla; tel. (95) 2675840; fax (95) 2672657; Government Delegate in Melilla: Enrique Beamud Martín.

Consejo de Gobierno: Plaza de España 1, 52001 Melilla; tel. (95) 2681663; fax (95) 2674800; Mayor/President of Melilla ENRIQUE PALACIOS.

Deputy elected to the Congress in Madrid: ANTONIO GUTIÉRREZ MOLINA (PP). Representatives to the Senate in Madrid: CARLOS A. BENET CAÑETE (PP), AUREL-GHEORGHE SAVA. Commandant-General: FRANCISCO DÍAZ MORENO.

COUNCIL

Election, 28 May 1995

	Seats
Partido Popular (PP)	14
Partido Socialista Obrero Español (PSOE)	5
Coalición por Melilla	4
Unión del Pueblo Melillense (UPM)	2
Total	25

POLITICAL ORGANIZATIONS

Coalición por Melilla: Melilla; Leader MUSTAFA ABERCHAN HAMED.

Lucha por la Libertad de Melilla: Melilla; extreme right-wing; opposed to granting of Spanish citizenship to Muslims.

Movimiento para la Liberación de Melilla: Melilla; f. 1986; clandestine group; advocates use of violence.

Partido de Acción Social de Melilla: Melilla; favours full autonomy.

Partido de los Demócratas de Melilla (PDM): Melilla; f. 1985; Muslim party; Leader ABDELKÁDER MOHAMED ALÍ.

Partido Independiente Hispano Bereber: Melilla; Pres. LAARBI BUMEDIEN.

Partido Nacionalista de Melilla-Asociación Pro Melilla (PNM-Aprome): Miguel Zazo 30, 29804 Melilla; extreme-right-wing nationalist party; allied to PP; Pres. AMALIO JIMÉNEZ; Sec.-Gen. ANTONIO CIENDONES GARCÍA.

Partido Popular (PP): Gral Marina 11, 1° Dcha, POB 384, 52001 Melilla; tel. (95) 2681095; fax (95) 2684477; centre-right; Pres. IGNACIO VELÁZQUEZ RIVERA.

Partido Progresista Liberal de Melilla (PPLM): Melilla; Leader FRANCISCO CINTAS GARCÍA.

Partido Socialista de Melilla-Partido Socialista Obrero Español (PSME-PSOE): Cándido Lobera 7-1°, Melilla; tel. (95) 2681820; socialist workers' party; favours self-government but not full autonomy; Pres. JOSÉ TORRES VEGA; Sec.-Gen. JULIO BASSETS RUTLLANT.

Unión de Melillenses Independientes (UMI): Melilla; advocates independence; Spokesman JOSÉ IMBRODA DOMÍNGUEZ.

Unión del Pueblo Melillense (UPM): Ejército Español 7, 1°, Apdo 775, 29801 Melilla; tel. (95) 2681987; fax (95) 2673545; f. 1985; right-wing; Pres. JUAN JOSÉ IMBRODA ORTIZ; Gen. Sec. DANIEL CONESA MÍNGUEZ.

There are branches of the major Spanish parties in Melilla, and also various civic associations.

RELIGION

As in Ceuta, most Europeans are Roman Catholics. The registered Muslim community numbered 20,800 in 1990. The Jewish community numbered 1,300.

THE PRESS

Diario Sur: Edif. Monumental 3a, Oficina 17, Melilla; tel. (95) 2681854; fax (95) 2683908; Perm. Rep. AVELINO GUTIÉRREZ PÉREZ.

Guía del Ocio: Melilla; tel. (95) 2683734; leisure guide; Dir JOSÉ LUIS CÉSPEDES MERCADO.

Melilla Costa del Sol: Melilla; tel. (95) 2686848; f. 1985; Rep. LAUREANO FOLGAR VILLASENÍN; circ. 2,500.

Melilla Hoy: Polígono Industrial SEPES, La Espiga, Naves A-1/A-2, 52008 Melilla; tel. (95) 2690000; fax (95) 2675725; f. 1985; Dir IRENE FLORES SÁEZ; Editor-in-Chief MARÍA ANGELES JIMÉNEZ PADILLA; circ. 2,000.

El Telegrama de Melilla: Muelle Ribera s/n (Antigua Lonja Pesquera), 52001 Melilla; tel. (95) 2685613; fax (95) 2684814; Dir JOSÉ CARLOS RUIZ JAIME.

News Agency

Agencia EFE: Candido Lobera 4-1° Izq., 52001 Melilla; tel. (95) 2685235; fax (95) 2680043; Correspondent ANTONIO SOTO CRESPO.

Press Association

Asociación de la Prensa: Crtra Alfonso XII, Edif. Miguel de Cervantes, Bloque 5 Bajo, 52006 Melilla; tel. (95) 2679121; Pres. ANGEL MORÁN JIMÉNEZ.

BROADCASTING

Radio

40 Melilla: Muelle Ribera 18, 29805 Melilla; tel. (95) 2681708; fax (95) 2681573; Administrator YAMILA AMED.

Antena 3: Edif. Melilla, Urbanización Rusadir, 29805 Melilla; tel. (95) 2688840; Dir TOÑI RAMOS PELÁEZ.

Cadena Rato: Melilla; tel. (95) 2685871; Dir ANGEL VALENCIA.

Dial Melilla: Urbanización Rusadir, Edif. Melilla, 29805 Melilla; tel. (95) 2673333; fax (95) 2678342; Dir ANTONIA RAMOS PELÁEZ.

Onda Cero Radio Melilla: General Mola 26, 29804 Melilla; tel. (95) 2680706; fax (95) 2685572; Dir LEANDRO RODRÍGUEZ.

Radio Melilla: Muelle Ribera 18, 52001 Melilla; tel. (95) 2681708; fax (95) 2681573; commercial; owned by Sociedad Española de Radiodifusión (SER); Dir ANTONIA RAMOS PELÁEZ.

Radio Nacional de España (RNE): Mantelete 1, Apdo 222, 52801 Melilla; tel. (95) 2681907; fax (95) 2683108; state-controlled; Rep. MONTSERRAT COBOS RUANO.

Television

A fibre optic cable linking Melilla with Almería was laid in 1990. From March 1991 Melilla residents were able to receive three private TV channels from mainland Spain: Antena 3, Canal+ and Tele 5.

FINANCE

The following banks have branches in Melilla: Banco Bilbao Vizcaya (2 brs), Banco Central Hispanoamericano, Banco Español de Crédito (Banesto), Banco Meridional, Banco Popular Español and Banco de Santander (2 brs).

TRADE AND INDUSTRY

Cámara Oficial de Comercio, Industria y Navegación: Cervantes 7, 52001 Melilla; tel. (95) 2684840; fax (95) 2683119; f. 1906; Pres. MARGARITA LÓPEZ ALMENDÁRIZ; Sec.-Gen. MARÍA JESÚS FERNÁNDEZ DE CASTRO Y PEDRAJAS.

Confederación de Empresarios de Melilla: Paseo Marítimo Mir Berlanga 26—Entreplanta, Apdo de Correos 445, 29806 Melilla; tel. (95) 2678295; telex 79407; fax (95) 2676175; f. 1979; employers' confederation; Pres. MARGARITA LÓPEZ ALMENDÁRIZ; Sec.-Gen. JERÓNIMO PÉREZ HERNÁNDEZ.

TRANSPORT

There is a daily ferry service to Málaga and a service to Almería. Melilla airport, situated 4 km from the town, is served by daily flights to Málaga and Almería, operated by Iberia. There are also services to Madrid and Granada. Plans to extend the runway were approved in early 1993.

TOURISM

There is much of historic interest to the visitor. Melilla had 19 hotels in the late 1980s. Further hotels, including a luxury development, were under construction in 1990.

DEFENCE

See Ceuta. More than one-half of Melilla's land area is used solely for military purposes.

EDUCATION

In addition to the conventional Spanish facilities, the Moroccan Government finances a school for 600 Muslim children in Melilla, the languages of instruction being Arabic and Spanish. The curriculum includes Koranic studies. In 1982 only 12% of Muslim children were attending school, but by 1990 the authorities had succeeded in achieving an attendance level of virtually 100%. The Spanish open university (UNED) maintains a branch in Melilla.

The Peñón de Vélez de la Gomera, Peñón de Alhucemas and Chafarinas Islands

These rocky islets, situated respectively just west and east of al-Hocima (Alhucemas) and east of Melilla off the north coast of Morocco, are administered with Melilla. The three Chafarinas

Islands lie about 3.5 km off Ras el-Ma (Cabo de Agua). The Peñón de Alhucemas is situated about 300 m from the coast. The Peñón de Vélez de la Gomera is situated about 80 km further west, lying 85 m from the Moroccan shore, to which it is joined by a narrow strip of sand. Small military bases are maintained on the Peñón de Vélez, Peñón de Alhucemas and on the Isla del Congreso, the most westerly of the Chafarinas Islands. A supply ship calls at the various islands every two weeks. Prospective visitors must obtain the necessary military permit in Ceuta or Melilla.

Bibliography

Areilza, José María de, and Castiella y Maíz, Fernando María. *Revindicaciones de España*. Madrid, 1941.

Boucher, M. *Spain in Africa* (3 articles, *Africa Institute Bulletin*, May–July 1966).

Domínguez Sánchez, Constantino. *Melilla*. Madrid, Editorial Everest, 1978.

Habsbourg, Otto D. E. *Européens et Africains: L'Entente Nécessaire*. Paris, Hachette, 1963.

Lafond, Philippe. *Melilla*. Barcelona, Lunwerg Editores, 1997.

Mir Berlanga, Francisco. *Melilla en los Siglos Pasados y Otras Historias*. Madrid, Editora Nacional, 1977.

Resumen de la Historia de Melilla. Melilla, 1978.

Patronato Municipal de Turismo. *Ceuta—La España Inédita*. Madrid, 1988.

Pélissier, René. *Los Territorios Españoles de Africa*. Madrid, 1964.

SYRIA

Physical and Social Geography

W. B. FISHER

Before 1918 the term 'Syria' was rather loosely applied to the whole of the territory now forming the modern states of Syria, Lebanon, Israel and Jordan. To the Ottomans, as to the Romans, Syria stretched from the Euphrates to the Mediterranean, and from the Sinai to the hills of southern Turkey, with Palestine as a smaller province of this wider unit. Although the present Syrian Arab Republic has a much more limited extension, covering 185,180 sq km (71,498 sq miles), an echo of the past remains to colour the political thinking of some present-day Syrians and from time to time there are references to a 'Greater Syria' as a desirable but possibly remote aspiration. None the less, there is evidence of the attachment to the idea of a 'Greater Syria' in current Syrian policy towards Israel and, especially, Lebanon.

The frontiers of the present-day state are largely artificial, and reflect to a considerable extent the interests and prestige of outside powers—Britain, France and the USA—as these existed in 1918–20. The northern frontier with Turkey is defined by a single-track railway line running along the southern edge of the foothills—probably the only case of its kind in the world; whilst eastwards and southwards boundaries are highly arbitrary, being straight lines drawn for convenience between salient points. Westwards, the frontiers are again artificial, although less crudely drawn, leaving the headwaters of the Jordan river outside Syria and following the crest of the Anti-Lebanon hills, to reach the sea north of Tripoli.

PHYSICAL FEATURES

Geographically, Syria consists of two main zones: a fairly narrow western part, made up of a complex of mountain ranges and intervening valleys; and a much larger eastern zone that is essentially a broad and open platform dropping gently towards the east and crossed diagonally by the wide valley of the Euphrates river.

The western zone, which contains over 80% of the population of Syria, can be further subdivided as follows. In the extreme west, fronting the Mediterranean Sea, there lies an imposing ridge rising to 1,500 m above sea-level, and known as the Jebel Ansariyeh. Its western flank drops fairly gradually to the sea, giving a narrow coastal plain; but on the east it falls very sharply, almost as a wall, to a flat-bottomed valley occupied by the Orontes river, which meanders sluggishly over the flat floor, often flooding in winter, and leaving a formerly malarial marsh in summer. Farther east lie more hill ranges, opening out like a fan from the south-west, where the Anti-Lebanon range, with Mount Hermon (2,814 m), is the highest in Syria. Along the eastern flanks of the various ridges lie a number of shallow basins occupied by small streams that eventually dry up or form closed salt lakes. In one basin lies the city of Aleppo, once the second town of the Ottoman Empire and still close to being the largest city of Syria. In another is situated Damascus, larger, irrigated from five streams, and famous for its clear fountains and gardens—now the capital of the country. One remaining sub-region of western Syria is the Jebel Druse, which lies in the extreme south-west, and consists of a vast outpouring of lava, in the form of sheets and cones. Towards the west this region is fertile, and produces good cereal crops, but eastwards the soil cover disappears, leaving a barren countryside of twisted lava and caverns, for long the refuge of outlaws, bandits, and minority groups. Because of its difficulty and isolation, the Jebel Druse has tended socially and politically to act independently, remaining aloof from the rest of the country.

The entire eastern zone is mainly steppe or open desert, except close to the banks of the Euphrates, the Tigris and their larger tributaries, where recent irrigation projects have allowed considerable cultivation on an increasing scale. The triangularly-shaped region between the Euphrates and Tigris rivers is spoken of as the Jezireh (Arabic *jazira* = island), but is in no way different from the remaining parts of the east.

The presence of ranks of relatively high hills aligned parallel to the coast has important climatic effects. Tempering and humid effects from the Mediterranean are restricted to a narrow western belt, and central and eastern Syria show marked continental tendencies: that is, a very hot summer with temperatures often above 100°F (38°C) or even 110°F (43°C), and a moderately cold winter, with frost on many nights. Very close to the Mediterranean, frost is unknown at any season, but on the hills altitude greatly reduces the average temperature, so that snow may lie on the heights from late December to April, or even May. Rainfall is fairly abundant in the west, where the height of the land tends to determine the amount received; but east of the Anti-Lebanon mountains the amount decreases considerably, producing a steppe region that quickly passes into true desert. On the extreme east, as the Zagros ranges of Persia are approached, there is once again a slight increase, but most of Syria has an annual rainfall of less than 250 mm.

ECONOMIC LIFE

There is a close relationship between climate and economic activities. In the west, where up to 750 mm (30 ins) or even 1,000 mm (40 ins) of rainfall occur, settled farming is possible, and the main limitation is difficult terrain. From the Orontes valley eastwards, however, natural rainfall is increasingly inadequate, and irrigation becomes necessary. The narrow band of territory where annual rainfall lies between 200 mm and 380 mm (8 ins–15 ins) is sometimes spoken of as the 'Fertile Crescent', since it runs in an arc along the inner side of the hills from Jordan through western and northern Syria as far east as Iraq. In its normal state a steppeland covered with seasonal grass, the Fertile Crescent can often be converted by irrigation and efficient organization into a rich and productive territory. Such it was in the golden days of the Arab caliphate; now, after centuries of decline, it has been revived. From the 1950s onwards, a marked change was seen and, initially because of small-scale irrigation schemes and the installation of motor pumps to raise water from underground artesian sources, large areas of the former steppe began to produce cotton, cereals and fruit. Syria used to have a surplus of agricultural production, especially cereals, to export to Jordan and Lebanon, neither of which are self-sufficient in foodstuffs. It was expected that production would increase with the eventual doubling of Syria's irrigated area (by 640,000 ha) as the Euphrates Dam at Tabqa developed fully. However, only about 60,000 ha had been irrigated by 1988; difficulties have been experienced in irrigating part of the designated area and some experts believe that perhaps 300,000 ha may be impossible to develop according to the original plans. Over the last few years, production of cereals and cotton has declined, partly owing to lack of technical and management skills, and partly to drought. High military expenditure has also reduced available development funds.

Because of its relative openness and accessibility and its geographical situation as a 'waist' between the Mediterranean and the Persian (Arabian) Gulf, Syria has been a land of passage, and for centuries its role was that of an intermediary, both commercial and cultural, between the Mediterranean world and the Far East. From early times until the end of the Middle Ages there was a flow of traffic east and west that raised a number of Syrian cities and ports to the rank of international markets.

Since the 1930s, following a long period of decline and eclipse resulting from the diversion of this trade to the sea, there has been a revival of activity, owing to the new elements of air transport and the construction of oil pipelines from Iraq.

In addition, Syria was able to develop its own deposits of petroleum and phosphate; and its greatly improved political standing (as, temporarily at least, the successor of Egypt as the leading politically activist Arab state) brought economic benefits. The Syrian economy became stronger, and the country was able to 'balance' between the Soviet and Western political groups, although the cost of wars and internal political uncertainties eroded some development gains. After 1981, however, Syria became more isolated from its Arab neighbours, and the policy of balance, both in external and internal affairs, was less successful. In response to the collapse of communism in Eastern Europe and the diminution of Soviet influence, Syria's foreign policy has remained, above all, pragmatic. This was clearly illustrated by the country's allying itself with the Western powers and the 'moderate' Arab states against Iraq in 1990/91, in return for diplomatic and economic gains.

RACE AND LANGUAGE

Racially, many elements can be distinguished in the Syrian people. The nomads of the interior deserts are unusually pure specimens of the Mediterranean type, isolation having preserved them from intermixture. To the west and north there is a widely varying mosaic of other groups: the Kurds and Turkish-speaking communities of the north, and the Armenians, who form communities in the cities; groups such as the Druzes, who show some affinity to the tribes of the Persian Zagros, and many others.

As a result, there is a surprising variety of language and religion. Arabic is spoken over most of the country, but Kurdish is widely used along the northern frontier and Armenian in the cities. Aramaic, the language of Christ, survives in three villages.

History

Revised for this edition by RICHARD I. LAWLESS

ANCIENT HISTORY

From the earliest times, Syria has experienced successive waves of Semitic immigration—the Canaanites and Phoenicians in the third millennium BC, the Hebrews and Aramaeans in the second, and, unceasingly, the nomad tribes infiltrating from the Arabian peninsula. This process has enabled Syria to assimilate or reject, without losing its essentially Semitic character, the alien invaders who, time and again, in the course of a long history, have established their domination over the land. Before Rome assumed control of Syria in the first century BC, the Egyptians, the Assyrians and the Hittites, and, later, the Persians and the Macedonian Greeks had all left their mark to a greater or lesser degree. Damascus is claimed to be the oldest capital city in the world, having been continuously inhabited since about 2000 BC, and Aleppo may be even older. Under Roman rule the infiltration and settlement of nomad elements continued, almost unnoticed by historians, save when along the desert trade routes a Semitic vassal state attained a brief importance as, for example, the kingdom of Palmyra in the Syrian desert, which the Emperor Aurelian destroyed in AD 272 or, later still, when the Byzantines ruled in Syria, the Arab state of Ghassan, prominent throughout the sixth century AD as a bulwark of the Byzantine Empire against the desert tribes in the service of Sasanid Persia.

ARAB AND TURKISH RULE

When, after the death of the Prophet Muhammad in AD 632, the newly-created power of Islam began a career of conquest, the populations of Syria, Semitic in their language and culture and, as adherents of the Monophysite faith, ill-disposed towards the Greek-speaking Orthodox Byzantines, did little to oppose the Muslims, from whom they hoped to obtain a greater measure of freedom. The Muslims defeated the Byzantine forces at Ajnadain in 634, seized Damascus in 635, and, by their decisive victory on the River Yarmouk (636), virtually secured possession of all Syria. From 661 to 750 the Umayyad dynasty ruled in Syria, which, after the conquest, had been divided into four military districts or junds (Damascus, Homs, Urdun, i.e. Jordan, and Palestine). To these the Caliph Yazid I (680–83) added a fifth, Kinnasrin, for the defence of northern Syria, where in the late seventh century, the Mardaites, Christians from the Taurus, were making serious inroads under Byzantine leadership. Under Abd al-Malik (685–705), Arabic became the official language of the state, in whose administration, hitherto largely carried out by the old Byzantine bureaucracy, Syrians, Muslim as well as Christian, now had an increasing share. For Syria was now the heart of a great Empire, and the Arab army of Syria, well trained in the ceaseless frontier warfare with Byzantium, bore the main burden of imperial rule, taking a major part in the two great Arab assaults on Byzantium in 674–8 and in 717–18.

The new regime in Syria was pre-eminently military and fiscal in character, representing the domination of a military caste of Muslim Arab warriors, who governed on the basic assumption that a large subject population, non-Muslim and non-Arab in character, would continue indefinitely to pay tribute. But this assumption was falsified by the gradual spread of Islam, a process which meant the progressive diminution of the amount of tribute paid to the state, and the consequent undermining of the fiscal system as a whole. In theory, conversion meant for the non-Arab convert (*mawla*; in the plural, *mawali*) full social and economic equality with the ruling caste, but in practice it was not enough to be a Muslim, one had to be an Arab as well. The discontent of the *mawali* with their enforced inferiority expressed itself in an appeal to the universal character of Islam, an appeal which often took the form of religious heresies, and which, as it became more widespread, undermined the strength of the Arab regime.

To the ever present fiscal problems of the Arab state and the growing discontent of the *mawali* was added a third and fatal weakness: the hostility between those Arab tribes which had arrived in Syria with or since the conquest, and those which had infiltrated there at an earlier date. The Umayyad house strove to maintain a neutral position over and above the tribal feuds; but from the moment when, under the pressure of events, the Umayyads were compelled to side with one faction to oppose the other (Battle of Marj Rahit, 684), their position was irretrievably compromised.

When in AD 750, with the accession of the Abbasid dynasty, the centre of the Empire was transferred to Iraq, Syria, jealously watched because of its association with the former ruling house, became a mere province, where in the course of the next hundred years, several abortive revolts, inspired in part by the traditional loyalty to the Umayyads, failed to shake off Abbasid control. During the ninth century Syria was the object of dispute between Egypt and Baghdad. In 878 Ahmad ibn Tulun, Governor of Egypt, occupied it and, subsequently, every independent ruler of Egypt sought to maintain a hold, partial or complete, over Syria. Local dynasties, however, achieved from time to time a transitory importance, as did the Hamdanids (a Bedouin family from northern Iraq) who, under Saif ad-Daula, ruler of Aleppo from 946–967, attained a brief ascendancy, marked internally by financial and administrative ineptitude, and externally by military campaigns against the Byzantines which did much to provoke the great Byzantine re-conquest of the late 10th century. By the treaty of 997, northern Syria became Byzantine, while the rest of the country remained in the hands of the Fatimid dynasty which ruled in Egypt from 969. Fatimid control remained insecure and from about 1027 a new Arab house ruled at Aleppo—the Mirdasids, who were soon to disappear before the formidable power of the Seljuq Turks. The Seljuqs, having conquered Persia, rapidly overran Syria (Damascus fell to them in 1075) but failed to establish there a united state. As a result of dynastic quarrels, the Seljuq domination disintegrated into a number of amirates: Seljuq princes ruled at Aleppo and Damascus, a local dynasty held Tripoli and, in the south, Egypt controlled most of the littoral.

This political fragmentation greatly favoured the success of the First Crusade which, taking Antioch in 1098 and Jerusalem in 1099, proceeded to organize four feudal states at Edessa, Antioch, Tripoli and Jerusalem, but did not succeed in conquering Aleppo, Homs, Hama, and Damascus. From the death of Baldwin II of Jerusalem in 1131, the essential weakness of the crusading states began to appear. Byzantium, the Christian state of Lesser Armenia, and the Latin principalities in Syria never united in a successful resistance to the Muslim counter-offensive which, initiated by the energetic Turkish general Zangi Atabeg of Mosul, developed rapidly in the third and fourth decades of the century. Zangi, who seized Aleppo in 1128, and the Latin state of Edessa in 1144, was succeeded in 1146 by his able son Nur ad-Din, who by his capture of Damascus in 1154 recreated in Syria a united Muslim power. On Nur ad-Din's death in 1174, the Kurd Saladin, already master of Egypt, assumed control of Damascus and, in 1183, seized Aleppo. His victory over the Crusaders at Hattin (July 1187) destroyed the kingdom of Jerusalem. Only the partial success of the Third Crusade (1189–92) and, after his death in 1193, the disintegration of Saladin's empire into a number of separate principalities, made it possible for the Crusaders to maintain an ever more precarious hold on the coastal area of Syria. The emergence in Egypt of the powerful Mamluk sultanate (1250) meant that the end was near. A series of military campaigns, led by the Sultan Baibars (1260–77) and his immediate successors, brought about the fall of Antioch (1268) and Tripoli (1289), and, with the fall of Acre in 1291, the disappearance of the crusading states in Syria.

Before the last crusading states had been reduced, the Mamluks had to encounter a determined assault by the Mongols until, in 1260, the Mongol army of invasion was crushed at the Battle of Ain-Jalut, near Nazareth. The Mongol Il-Khans of Persia made further efforts to conquer Syria in the late 13th century, negotiating for this purpose with the papacy, the remaining crusader states, and Lesser Armenia. In 1280 the Mamluks defeated a Mongol army at Homs; but in 1299 were themselves beaten near the same town, a defeat which enabled the Mongols to ravage northern Syria and to take Damascus in 1300. Only in 1303, at the Battle of Marj as-Suffar, south of Damascus, was this last Mongol offensive finally repelled.

The period of Mamluk rule in Syria, which endured until 1517, was on the whole one of slow decline. Warfare, periodical famine, and not least, the plague (there were four great outbreaks in the 14th century, and in the 15th century 14 more recorded attacks of some severity) produced a state of affairs which the financial rapacity and misrule of the Mamluk governors and the devastation of Aleppo and Damascus by Timur (1400–01) served only to aggravate.

The ill-defined protectorate which the Mamluks asserted over Cilicia and considerable areas of southern Anatolia occasioned, in the late 15th century, a growing tension with the power of the Ottoman Turks, which broke out into inconclusive warfare in the years 1485–91. When to this tension was added the possibility of an alliance between the Mamluks and the rising power of the Safavids in Persia, the Ottoman Sultan Selim I (1512–20) was compelled to seek a decisive solution to the problem. In August 1516 the battle of Marj Dabik, north of Aleppo, gave Syria to the Ottomans, who proceeded to ensure their continued hold on the land by conquering Egypt (1517). Turkish rule, during the next three centuries, although unjustly accused of complete responsibility for a decay and stagnation which appear to have been well advanced before 1517, brought only a temporary improvement in the unhappy condition of Syria, now divided into the three provinces of Damascus, Tripoli, and Aleppo. In parts of Syria the Turkish pashas in reality administered directly only the important towns and their immediate neighbourhood; elsewhere, the older elements—Bedouin

emirs, Turcoman chiefs, etc.—were left to act much as they pleased, provided the due tribute was paid. The pashas normally bought their appointment to high office and sought in their brief tenure of power to recover the money and bribes they had expended in securing it, knowing that they might, at any moment, be replaced by someone who could pay more for the post. Damascus alone had 133 pashas in 180 years. As the control of the Sultan at Constantinople became weaker, the pashas obtained greater freedom of action, until Ahmad Jazzar, Pasha of Acre, virtually ruled Syria as an independent prince (1785–1804).

The 19th century saw important changes. The Ottoman Sultan Mahmoud II (1808–39) had promised Syria to the Pasha of Egypt, Muhammad Ali, in return for the latter's services during the Greek War of Independence. When the Sultan declined to fulfil his promise, Egyptian troops overran Syria (1831–33). Ibrahim Pasha, son of Muhammad Ali, now gave to Syria, for the first time in centuries, a centralized government strong enough to hold separatist tendencies in check and to impose a system of taxation which, if burdensome, was at least regular in its functioning. But Ibrahim's rule was not popular, for the land-owners resented his efforts to limit their social and political dominance, while the peasantry disliked the conscription, the forced labour, and the heavy taxation which he found indispensable for the maintenance of his regime. In 1840 a revolt broke out in Syria, and when the Great Powers intervened on behalf of the Sultan (at war with Egypt since 1839), Muhammad Ali was compelled to renounce his claim to rule there.

Western influence, working through trade, through the protection of religious minorities, and through the cultural and educational efforts of missions and schools, had received encouragement from Ibrahim Pasha. The French Jesuits, returning to Syria in 1831, opened schools, and in 1875 founded their University at Beirut. The American Presbyterian Mission (established at Beirut in 1820) introduced a printing press in 1834, and in 1866 founded the Syrian Protestant College, later renamed the American University of Beirut. Syria also received some benefit from the reform movement within the Ottoman Empire, which, begun by Mahmoud II, and continued under his successors, took the form of a determined attempt to modernize the structure of the Empire. The semi-independent pashas of old disappeared, the administration being now entrusted to salaried officials of the central Government; some effort was made to create schools and colleges on Western lines, and much was done to deprive the landowning classes of their feudal privileges, although their social and economic predominance was left unchallenged. As a result of these improvements, there was, in the late 19th century, a revival of Arabic literature which did much to prepare the way for the growth of Arab nationalism in the 20th century.

MODERN HISTORY

By 1914 Arab nationalist sentiment had made some headway among the educated and professional classes, and especially among army officers. Nationalist societies like al-Fatat soon made contact with Arab nationalists outside Syria—with the army officers of Iraq, with influential Syrian colonies in Egypt and America, and with the Sharif Husain of Mecca. The Husain-McMahon Correspondence (July 1915–January 1916) encouraged the Arab nationalists to hope that the end of the First World War would mean the creation of a greater Arab kingdom. This expectation was disappointed, for as a result of the Sykes-Picot Agreement, negotiated in secret between England, France, and Russia in 1916 (see Documents on Palestine, p. 108), Syria was to become a French sphere of influence. At the end of the war, and in accordance with this agreement, a provisional French administration was established in the coastal districts of Syria, while in the interior an Arab government came into being under Amir Faisal, son of the Sharif Husain of Mecca. In March 1920 the Syrian nationalists proclaimed an independent kingdom of Greater Syria (including Lebanon and Palestine); but in April of the same year the San Remo Conference gave France a mandate for the whole of Syria, and in July, French troops occupied Damascus.

By 1925 the French, aware that the majority of the Muslim population resented their rule, and that only amongst the Christian Maronites of the Lebanon could they hope to find support, had carried into effect a policy based upon the religious divisions so strong in Syria. The area under mandate had been divided into four distinct units; a much enlarged Lebanon (including Beirut and Tripoli), a Syrian Republic, and the two districts of Latakia and Jebel Druse. Despite the fact that the French rule gave Syria a degree of law and order which might have rendered possible the transition from a medieval to a more modern form of society, nationalist sentiment opposed the mandate on principle, and deplored the failure to introduce full representative institutions and the tendency to encourage separatism amongst the religious minorities. This discontent, especially strong in the Syrian Republic, became open revolt in 1925–26, during the course of which the French twice bombarded Damascus (October 1925 and May 1926).

The next 10 years were marked by a hesitant and often interrupted progress towards self-government in Syria, and by French efforts to conclude a Franco-Syrian treaty. In April 1928 elections were held for a Constituent Assembly, and in August a draft Constitution was completed; but the French High Commissioner refused to accept certain articles, especially Article 2, which, declaring the Syrian territories detached from the old Ottoman Empire to be an indivisible unity, constituted a denial of the separate existence of the Jebel Druse, Latakia, and the Lebanese Republic. After repeated attempts to reach a compromise, the High Commissioner dissolved the Assembly in May 1930 and, on his own authority, issued a new Constitution for the State of Syria, much the same as that formerly proposed by the Assembly, but with those modifications which were considered indispensable to the maintenance of French control. After new elections to a Chamber of Deputies (January 1932), negotiations were begun for a Franco-Syrian treaty, to be modelled on that concluded between the United Kingdom and Iraq in 1930, but no compromise could be found between the French demands and those of the nationalists who, although in a minority, wielded a dominant influence in the Chamber and whose aim was to limit both in time and in place the French military occupation, and to include in Syria the separate areas of Jebel Druse and Latakia. In 1934 the High Commissioner suspended the Chamber indefinitely. Disorders occurred early in 1936 which induced the French to send a Syrian delegation to Paris, where the new Popular Front Government showed itself more sympathetic towards Syrian aspirations than former French governments had been. In September 1936 a Franco-Syrian treaty was signed which recognized the principle of Syrian independence and stipulated that, after ratification, there should be a period of three years during which the apparatus of a fully independent state should be created. The districts of Jebel Druse and Latakia would be annexed to Syria, but would retain special administrations. Other subsidiary agreements reserved to France important military and economic rights in Syria. It seemed that Syria might now enter a period of rapid political development; but the unrest caused by the situation in Palestine, the crisis with Turkey, and the failure of France to ratify the 1936 treaty were responsible, within two years, for the breakdown of these hopes.

In 1921 Turkey had consented to the inclusion of the Sanjak of Alexandretta in the French mandated territories, on condition that it should be governed under a special regime. The Turks, alarmed by the treaty of 1936, which envisaged the emergence of a unitary Syrian state including, to all appearance, Alexandretta, now pressed for a separate agreement concerning the status of the Sanjak. After long discussion the League of Nations decided in 1937 that the Sanjak should be fully autonomous, save for its foreign and financial policies which were to be under the control of the Syrian Government. A treaty between France and Turkey guaranteed the integrity of the Sanjak, and also the Turco-Syrian frontier. Throughout 1937 there were conflicts between Turks and Arabs in the Sanjak, and in Syria a widespread and growing resentment, for it was clear that sooner or later Turkey would ask for the cession of Alexandretta. The problem came to be regarded in Syria as a test of Franco-Syrian co-operation, and when, in June 1939, under the pressure of international tension, Alexandretta was finally ceded to Turkey, the cession assumed in the eyes of Syrian nationalists the character of a betrayal by France. Meanwhile, in France itself, opposition to the treaty of 1936 had grown steadily; and in

December 1938 the French Government, anxious not to weaken its military position in the Near East, declared that no ratification of the treaty was to be expected.

Unrest in Syria led to open riots in 1941, as a result of which the Vichy High Commissioner, Gen. Dentz, promised the restoration of partial self-government; while in June of the same year, when in order to combat Axis intrigues the Allies invaded Syria, Gen. Catroux, on behalf of the Free French Government, promised independence for Syria and the end of mandatory rule. Syrian independence was formally recognized in September 1941, but the reality of power was still withheld, with the effect that nationalist agitation, inflamed by French reluctance to restore constitutional rule and by economic difficulties owing to the war, became even more pronounced. When at last elections were held once more, a nationalist Government was formed, with Shukri al-Kuwatli as President of the Syrian Republic (August 1943).

Gradually all important powers and public services were transferred from French to Syrian hands; but conflict again developed over the Troupes Spéciales, the local Syrian and Lebanese levies which had existed throughout the mandatory period as an integral part of the French military forces in the Levant, and which, transferred to the Syrian and Lebanese Governments, would enable them to form their own armies. Strongly supported by the newly-created Arab League, Syria refused the French demand for a Franco-Syrian Treaty as the condition for the final transfer of administrative and military services which had always been the main instruments of French policy. In May 1945 disturbances broke out which ended only with British armed intervention and the evacuation of French troops and administrative personnel. The Troupes Spéciales were now handed over to the Syrian Government, and with the departure of British forces in April 1946 the full independence of Syria was at last achieved.

UNSTABLE INDEPENDENCE

After the attainment of independence Syria passed through a long period of instability. It was involved in a complicated economic and financial dispute with the Lebanon (1948–50) and also in various schemes for union with Iraq—schemes which tended to divide political opinion inside Syria itself and, in addition, to disrupt the unity of the Arab League. Syria, in fact, found itself aligned at this time with Egypt and Saudi Arabia against the ambitions of the Hashemite rulers of Iraq and Jordan. These rivalries, together with the profound disappointment felt at Damascus over the Arab failures in the war of 1948–49 against Israel, were the prelude to three *coups d'état* in 1949. Dislike of continued financial dependence on France, aspirations towards a greater Syria, the resentments arising out of the unsuccessful war against the Israelis—all help to explain the unrest inside Syria.

The intervention of the army in politics was itself a cause of further tension. Opposition to the dominance of the army grew in the Syrian Chamber of Deputies to such an extent that yet another *coup d'état* was carried out in December 1951. Syria now came under the control of a military autocracy with Col Shishakli as head of state. The Chamber of Deputies was dissolved in December 1951; a decree of April 1952 abolished all political parties in Syria. After the approval of a new Constitution in July 1953 Shishakli became President of Syria in August of that year. The formation of political parties was now allowed once more. Members of the parties dissolved under the decree of April 1952 proceeded, however, to boycott the elections held in October 1953, at which President Shishakli's Movement of Arab Liberation obtained a large majority in the Chamber of Deputies. Politicians hostile to the regime of President Shishakli established in November 1953 a Front of National Opposition, refusing to accept as legal the results of the October elections and declaring as their avowed aim the end of military autocracy and the restoration of democratic rule. Demonstrations at Damascus and Aleppo in December 1953 led soon to the flight of Shishakli to France. The collapse of his regime early in 1954 meant for Syria a return to the Constitution of 1950. New elections held in September 1954 brought into being a Chamber of Deputies notable for the large number of its members (81 out of 142) who might be regarded as independents grouped around leading political figures.

INFLUENCE FROM ABROAD

There was still, however, much friction in Syria between those who favoured union or at least close co-operation with Iraq and those inclined towards an effective *entente* with Egypt. In August 1955 Shukri al-Kuwatli became President of the Republic. His appointment was interpreted as an indication that pro-Egyptian influence had won the ascendancy in Syria. On 20 October 1955 Syria made with Egypt an agreement for the creation of a joint military command with its headquarters at Damascus.

The USSR, meanwhile, in answer to the developments in the Middle East associated with the Baghdad Pact, had begun an intensive diplomatic, propaganda and economic campaign of penetration into the Arab lands. In the years 1954–56 Syria, the only Arab state where the Communist Party was legal, made a number of barter agreements with the USSR and its associates in Eastern Europe. A report from Cairo intimated, in February 1956, that Syria had joined Egypt in accepting arms from the USSR.

At the end of October 1956 there occurred the Israeli campaign in the Sinai peninsula, an event followed, in the first days of November, by the armed intervention of Great Britain and France in the Suez Canal region. On 30 October the President of the Syrian Republic left Damascus on a visit to the USSR. A state of emergency was declared in Syria. Reports from Beirut revealed on 3 November that Syrian forces had put out of action the pipelines which carried Iraqi oil to the Mediterranean. The damage that Syrian elements had done to the pipelines earned the sharp disapproval of such Arab states as Iraq and Saudi Arabia, both of whom were now faced with a severe loss of oil revenues. The Syrian Government declared that it would not allow the repair of the pipelines until Israel had withdrawn its troops from Gaza and the Gulf of Aqaba. Not until March 1957 was it possible to restore the pipelines, Israel having in the mean time agreed to evacuate its forces from the areas in dispute.

UNION WITH EGYPT

The Syrian National Assembly, in November 1957, passed a resolution in favour of union with Egypt and the formal union of Egypt and Syria to constitute one state under the title of the United Arab Republic (UAR) received the final approval of the Syrian National Assembly on 5 February 1958. President Nasser of Egypt, on 21 February, became the first head of the combined state. A central Cabinet for the UAR was established in October 1958, also two regional executive councils, one for Syria and one for Egypt. A further move towards integration came in March 1960, when a single National Assembly for the whole of the UAR consisting of 400 deputies from Egypt and 200 from Syria, was instituted.

Syrian dissatisfaction with the union grew over the next three years, as administrators and officials of Egyptian origin came to hold influential positions in the Syrian Region, and on 28 September 1961 there occurred in Syria a military *coup d'état* which aimed—successfully—at the separation of Syria from Egypt and at the dissolution of the UAR. Political figures representing most of the parties which existed in Syria before the establishment of the UAR in 1958 met at Damascus and Aleppo on 3 October 1961, issuing a declaration of support for the new regime and calling for free elections to a new legislature. President Nasser recognized the *fait accompli*. Most foreign states made haste to grant formal recognition to the Government at Damascus. On 13 October 1961 Syria became once more a member of the United Nations (UN). A provisional Constitution was promulgated in November and elections for a Constituent Assembly took place on 1 December 1961.

The regime thus established in Syria rested on no sure foundation. At the end of March 1962 the Syrian army intervened once more, bringing about the resignation of Dr Nazim Kudsi, the President of the Republic, and also of the ministers who had taken office in December 1961. After demonstrations at Aleppo, Homs and Hama in April 1962, Dr Kudsi was reinstated as President, but further ministerial resignations in May of that year pointed to the existence of continuing tensions within the Government.

THE REVOLUTION OF 1963

A military junta, styled the National Council of the Revolutionary Command, seized control in Damascus on 8 March 1963. In May the Baathists (members of the Arab nationalist socialist party) took measures to purge the armed forces and the administration of personnel known to favour a close alignment with Egypt. A new Government, formed on 13 May and strongly Baathist in character, carried out a further purge in June and at the same time created a National Guard recruited from members of the Baath movement. These measures led the pro-Egyptian elements to attempt a *coup d'état* at Damascus on 18 July 1963. The attempt failed, however, with a considerable loss of life. On 27 July Maj-Gen. Amin al-Hafiz, Deputy Prime Minister and Minister of the Interior, became President of the National Council of the Revolutionary Command, a position equivalent to head of state.

BAATH SOCIALISM

The nationalization of all Arab-owned banks in 1963, and of various industrial enterprises, also the transfer of land to the peasants—all had contributed to bring about much dissatisfaction in the business world and amongst the influential landed elements. The Baath regime depended for its main support on the armed forces which, however, had been recruited in no small degree from the religious minorities in Syria, including adherents of the Alawi faith (a schism of the Shi'ite branch of Islam)—most Syrians being, in fact, of Sunni or orthodox Muslim allegiance. In general, conservative Muslims tended to oppose the Baath Government under guidance of the *ulema* (scholars/lawyers) and of the Muslim Brotherhood. The mass of the peasant population was thought to have some pro-Nasser sympathies; the working class (small in number) was divided between pro-Nasser and Baathist adherents; the middle and upper classes opposed the domination of al-Baath. The unease arising out of these frictions and antipathies took the form of disturbances and finally of open revolt—soon suppressed—at Hama (April 1964).

On 25 April 1964 a provisional Constitution had been promulgated, describing Syria as a democratic socialist republic forming an integral part of the Arab nation. A Presidential Council was established on 14 May 1964, with Gen. Hafiz as Head of the State.

The, as yet, undeveloped petroleum and other mineral resources of Syria were nationalized in 1964, together with other industrial concerns. On 7 January 1965 a special military court was created with sweeping powers to deal with all offences, of word or deed, against the nationalization decrees and the socialist revolution. General Hafiz denounced the *ulema* and the Muslim Brotherhood as being involved in the resulting demonstrations. Further nationalization followed.

A National Council, almost 100 strong, was established in August 1965 with the task of preparing a new constitution which would be submitted to a public referendum. Meeting for the first time on 1 September 1965, it created a Presidential Council, of five members, which was to exercise the powers of a head of state.

RADICAL REACTION

The tensions hitherto visible in al-Baath were, however, still active. Two groups stood ranged one against the other—on the one hand the older, more experienced politicians in al-Baath, less inclined than in former years to insist on the unrestrained pursuit of the main Baathist objectives, socialism and Pan-Arab union, and, on the other hand, the extreme left-wing elements, doctrinaire in their attitude and enjoying considerable support amongst the younger radical officers in the armed forces.

The tensions thus engendered found expression in a new *coup d'état* on 23 February 1966. A military junta representing the extreme radical elements in al-Baath seized power in Damascus and placed under arrest a number of personalities long identified with al-Baath and belonging to the international leadership controlling the organization throughout the Arab world—amongst them Michel Aflaq, the founder of al-Baath; Gen. Hafiz, the Chairman of the recently established Presidential Council; and Salah ad-Din Bitar, the Prime Minister of the displaced administration.

ARAB–ISRAELI WAR OF 1967

The friction ever present along the frontier between Syria and Israel had provoked violent conflict from time to time during recent years, particularly in the region of Lake Tiberias. Now, in the winter of 1966–67, the tension along the border began to assume more serious proportions. Israel, in October 1966, complained to the Security Council of the UN about guerrilla activities from Syria across the frontier into Israeli territory. In April 1967 mortars, cannon and air force units from Syria and Israel were involved in fighting south-east of Lake Tiberias.

The continuing tension on the Syrian-Israeli frontier was now to become a major influence leading to the war which broke out on 5 June 1967 between Israel and its Arab neighbours Egypt, Syria and Jordan. During the course of hostilities, which lasted six days, Israel defeated Egypt and Jordan and then, after some stubborn fighting, outflanked and overran the Syrian positions on the hills above Lake Tiberias. With the breakthrough accomplished, Israeli forces made a rapid advance and occupied the town of Quneitra about 65 km from Damascus. On 10 June Israel and Syria announced their formal acceptance of the UN proposal for a cease-fire, but Syria effectively boycotted the Arab summit conference held at Khartoum in August 1967 and in September the Baath Party of Syria rejected all idea of a compromise with Israel. A resolution adopted by the UN Security Council in November, urging the withdrawal of the Israelis from the lands occupied by them during the June war and the ending of the belligerency which the Arab Governments had until then maintained against Israel, was rejected by Syria, which alone maintained its commitment to a reunified Palestine.

STRUGGLE FOR POWER 1968–71

The ruling Baath Party had for some years been divided into two main factions. Until October 1968 the dominant faction had been the 'progressive' group led by Dr Atassi and Dr Makhous, the premier and foreign minister respectively. This group was distinguished by its doctrinaire and Marxist-oriented public pronouncements and by the strong support it received from the USSR. It held that the creation of a strong one-party state and economy along neo-Marxist lines was of paramount importance, overriding even the need for a militant stand towards Israel and for Arab unity.

By October 1968 the Government felt particularly insecure, partly owing to a feud with the new Baath regime in Iraq, and at the end of the month a new Cabinet was formed including several members of the opposing 'nationalist' faction. This group took less interest in ideological questions and favoured a pragmatic approach to the economy, improved relations with Syria's Arab neighbours and full participation in the campaign against Israel, including support for the *fedayin* movement. Its leader was Lt-Gen. Hafiz al-Assad, who assumed control of the all-important Ministry of Defence. His critical attitude to the powerful Soviet influence on the Government, seen by some 'nationalists' as tantamount to colonialism in restricting Syria's freedom of action, led to a prolonged struggle with the 'progressive' leadership. Cabinet reshuffles took place in March and May, but both Dr Atassi and Gen. Assad retained their positions. During the spring of 1969 a number of communists were arrested or sent into exile, and the leader of the Syrian Communist Party, still technically an illegal organization, flew to Moscow.

General Assad attempted to take over the Government in February 1969 but was forestalled by Soviet threats that if he did so all military supplies (including spares), economic and technical aid, and trade agreements would end. This would have brought about a major disruption in the national economy and the armed forces, and the 'nationalists' were obliged to yield. In May Gen. Mustafa Tlass, the Chief of Staff of the army and Gen. Assad's principal assistant, led a military delegation to the People's Republic of China to negotiate the purchase of military equipment. The incident indicated a new independence from Moscow. Some observers also saw this independence in the creation of a joint military command with Iraq (with whom relations improved during the spring) and Jordan. Relations with Lebanon worsened, owing to Syria's support of the Lebanese *fedayin* movement, containing many Syrian members. In the 1968–70 period this appeared to direct much of its activity towards bringing down the precarious Lebanese Government, presumably in the hope that a more militantly anti-Israel ministry would take power.

In November 1970, following a reported coup attempt backed by Iraq in August, the struggle between the two factions of the Baath Party culminated in Gen. Assad's seizure of power. Dr Atassi, who was in hospital at the time, was placed under guard and a retired general, Salah Jadid, Assistant Secretary-General of the Baath Party and leader of the civilian faction, was arrested. Other members of the civilian wing were arrested or fled to Lebanon. The coup was precipitated by attempts of Jadid and his supporters to oust Assad and Tlass from their posts. This power struggle had become acute as a result of differences over support for the Palestine guerrillas during the fighting with the Jordanian army in September. Jadid and Yousuf Zeayen, a former Prime Minister, controlled the movement of tanks from Syria into Jordan to support the Palestinian guerrillas' efforts against the Jordanian army; this Assad and the military faction opposed. Their approach to the Palestinian problem was more akin to Nasser's and they wanted to avoid giving any provocation to Israel, because they considered the Syrian armed forces to be unready to offer adequate resistance.

ASSAD IN POWER

There was no obvious opposition to the military *coup d'état.* Ahmad Khatib became acting President and Gen. Assad Prime Minister and party secretary-general. A new Regional Command of the Baath Party was formed. The old leaders were removed from their posts in a purge which stretched into the new year. Following amendments to the 1969 provisional Constitution in February 1971, Gen. Assad was elected President for a seven-year term in March. In the following month Maj.-Gen. Abd ar-Rahman Khlefawi became Premier and Mahmoud al-Ayoubi was appointed Vice-President. In February the first legislative body in Syria since 1966, the People's Assembly, was formed. Of its 173 members, 87 represented the Baath Party.

The Nasserite leanings of the new regime in foreign policy soon became apparent. Although Syria continued to reject the November 1967 UN Security Council Resolution (No. 242), relations with the UAR and Jordan improved, and Syria's isolation in the Arab world was soon reduced. Syria's willingness to join a union with the UAR, Sudan and Libya almost immediately became apparent and agreement on federation with Libya and the UAR was reached in April 1971, but the Federation had little effect.

After coming to power, the Assad regime increased the Syrian army's control over the Palestinian guerrilla group, Saiqa (Vanguard of the Popular Liberation War). In April 1971 guerrilla operations against Israeli positions from the Syrian front were banned by the Government. Then, at the beginning of July, some guerrilla units were forced out of Syria into southern Lebanon and arms destined for them and arriving from Algeria were seized by the Syrian authorities. Yet, after the Jordanian Government's final onslaught on the Palestinian guerrillas in northern Jordan in July, Syria closed its border and in August severed diplomatic relations when the tension had become so great that tank and artillery clashes developed between the two armies. Egyptian mediation reduced the chances of a more serious conflict developing, but diplomatic links remained severed with Jordan until October 1973. Relations with the USSR improved during the last half of 1971 and in 1972, and in May Marshal Grechko, the Soviet Minister of Defence, visited Damascus. Syria was not prepared, however, at that time to sign a friendship treaty with the USSR, like Egypt and Iraq. On the other hand, the Syrian Government, which had been broadened in March 1972 to include representatives of parties other than the Baath, like the communists, did not follow Egypt's example in July and expel its Soviet advisers.

In December 1972 Maj.-Gen. Khlefawi resigned from the post of Prime Minister for health reasons, and a new Government was formed by Mahmoud al-Ayoubi, the Vice-President, who allotted 16 out of 31 government portfolios to the Baath Party. A new Syrian Constitution, proclaiming socialist principles, was approved by the People's Assembly in January 1973 and confirmed by a referendum in March. The Sunni Muslims were dissatisfied that the Constitution did not recognize Islam as the state religion, and, as a result of their pressure, an amendment was passed, declaring that the President must be a Muslim. Under the Constitution, freedom of belief was guaranteed, with the state respecting all religions, although the Constitution recognized that Islamic jurisprudence was 'a principal source of legislation'. In 1972 a National Charter created a National Progressive Front, a grouping of the Baath Party and its allies. Elections were held in March 1973 for the new People's Assembly, under the aegis of the Front, and 140 out of the 186 seats were won by the Progressive Front, while 42 seats were won by independents and four by the opposition.

THE FOURTH ARAB–ISRAELI WAR AND ITS AFTERMATH

On the afternoon of 6 October 1973, Egyptian and Syrian forces launched a war against Israel in an effort to regain territories lost in 1967. On both the Egyptian and Syrian fronts, complete surprise was achieved, giving the Arabs a strong initial advantage, much of which they subsequently lost. (The course of the war is described in 'Arab–Israeli Relations 1967–98', pp. 34–97.) Although Egypt signed a disengagement agreement with Israel on 18 January 1974, fighting continued on the Syrian front, in the Golan Heights area, until a disengagement agreement was signed on 31 May, after much diplomacy and travel by the US Secretary of State, Dr Henry Kissinger (see 'Documents on Palestine' p. 117).

Syria continued to maintain an uncompromising policy in the Middle East, especially regarding the Palestinian question, and after the 1973 war it received vast amounts of Soviet military aid in order to fully re-equip its forces. Contact with Moscow and Eastern European states remained close. Syria's strong support for the PLO was vindicated in October 1974 at the Arab summit meeting in Rabat, Morocco, where the PLO's claim to the West Bank was recognized. By June 1976, however, Syria was in the position of invading Lebanon to crush the Palestinians, and finding most of the remainder of the Arab world agreeing to send a peace-keeping force to the Lebanon to quell the conflict.

FOREIGN AFFAIRS 1975–78

This reversal for Syria arose out of a lengthy chain of events. An improvement in relations with Jordan took place in 1975, with King Hussein visiting Damascus in April and President Assad visiting Amman in June. A joint military and political command was set up between the two countries, and by the spring of 1977 their customs, electricity networks and education systems were unified. Plans were made for the eventual union of the two countries. Relations between Syria and Jordan deteriorated, however, after Jordan appeared to give guarded support to Sadat's peace initiative in November 1977.

The second Egyptian-Israeli disengagement agreement in Sinai, signed in September 1975, met with Syria's strong condemnation. Syria accused Egypt of acting without the agreement of other Arab states and, by agreeing to three years of peace with Israel, of weakening the general Arab position and betraying the Palestinians.

Syria had shown considerable interest in the Lebanese civil war since it began in April 1975. Initially, Syria wanted to protect the position of the Palestinians in Lebanon and perhaps also to further plans for a 'Greater Syria', sending in about 2,000 Saiqa troops in January 1976. After having secured a cease-fire, Assad pledged that he would control the Palestinians in Lebanon, and the core of the PLO, under Yasser Arafat, began to be apprehensive that they would be dominated by Syria. By early June 1976 the fighting in Lebanon was so fierce that Syria felt obliged to intervene militarily and overtly. This time, Syria's intervention was welcomed by the Christian right-wing parties and condemned by the Palestinians and the Muslim left (and also Egypt).

A meeting of the Arab League ministers of foreign affairs on 8–9 June agreed that an Arab peace-keeping force should be sent to Lebanon to effect a cease-fire. After some delay, a peace-keeping force, consisting of Syrian and Libyan troops in equal proportions, did arrive in Lebanon, but the fighting continued unabated until October 1976, when Arab summit meetings, at Riyadh and Cairo, secured a more lasting cease-fire. A 30,000-strong Arab Deterrent Force, consisting largely of Syrian troops, was given authority at the Arab summit meetings to maintain the peace. President Assad's prestige, in Syria and the Arab world, was considerably strengthened by this success. Relations with Egypt improved after a tacit understanding that Syria

would end its criticism of the September 1975 Egyptian-Israeli agreement on Sinai in return for Egypt's acceptance of Syria's intervention in Lebanon.

In August 1976 Syria's Prime Minister, Mahmoud al-Ayoubi, was replaced by his predecessor, Gen. Khlefawi. He held office until March 1978, when he was succeeded by Muhammad Ali al-Halabi, previously Speaker of the People's Assembly.

Relations with the USSR, which had been extremely poor during most of 1976, improved after the October 1976 summit meetings and were consolidated when Assad visited Moscow in April 1977. With Iraq, however, relations remained poor. Iraq shut off the flow of petroleum from its Kirkuk oilfield to the Syrian port of Banias in protest at Syria's intervention in Lebanon. Another Iraqi grievance was Syria's use of water from the Euphrates river for irrigation projects. When an attempt to assassinate the Syrian Vice-Premier and Minister of Foreign Affairs, Abd al-Halim Khaddam, was made in December 1976, sources in Syria were swift to blame terrorists trained in Iraq. Relations between Syria and Egypt deteriorated again as a result of President Sadat's peace initiative in November 1977. Syria's President Assad strongly criticized the move and diplomatic relations between the two countries were severed in December.

Syria's rift with Egypt grew even wider after Sadat and Prime Minister Begin of Israel signed the Camp David agreements (see p. 119 et seq.) in the USA in September 1978. The third summit meeting of the 'Steadfastness and Confrontation Front', comprising Arab countries strongly opposed to Egypt's attempt to make a separate peace with Israel, met in Damascus in late September 1978. When the Egyptian-Israeli peace treaty was finally signed in March 1979 (see p. 121), Syria joined most of the other Arab League member countries at a meeting in Baghdad which endorsed political and economic sanctions against Egypt.

Egypt's *rapprochement* with Israel led to a brief improvement in Syria's relations with Iraq. In October 1978 Syria and Iraq signed a 'national charter for joint action' in which the eventual intention was complete political and economic union between the two countries. Although the oil pipeline from Iraq to Banias was reopened, the scheme for union collapsed when an internal conspiracy in Iraq in July 1979 was attributed to Syrian intrigue.

DIFFICULTIES OF THE EARLY 1980s

Although President Assad was comfortably returned for a second seven-year term of office in February 1978, there was growing evidence of internal dissatisfaction in Syria. Important government posts were largely in the hands of Alawites, a minority Muslim sect to which Assad belongs, and after 1977, assassinations of Alawites became an increasing problem. In June 1979 more than 60 army cadets, most of them thought to be Alawites, were massacred. The slaughter was officially attributed to the Muslim Brotherhood, who were also held responsible for subsequent killings.

President Assad's attempts to end this violence met with little lasting success. In January 1980 he appointed a new Council of Ministers with Dr Abd ar-Rauf Kassem as Prime Minister, and 23 of the 37 ministers had never before held ministerial posts. Militias of workers, peasants and students were set up, but were ineffective in helping the regular authorities to curb violence.

During the spring of 1980 the number of Soviet advisers in the country grew to more than 4,000, and in October 1980 Syria signed a 20-year treaty of friendship and co-operation with the USSR. By 1986 Syria had received $2,000m. from the USSR in military loans since 1982, and a total of between $12,000m. and $13,000m. since 1973. A proposed merger between Syria and Libya, announced in September 1980, has not been achieved.

At the outbreak of war between Iraq and Iran in September 1980, Syria supported Iran, on account of its own long-standing distrust of the rival Baath Party in Iraq. A crisis with Jordan soon developed, partly because of Syrian allegations that Muslim Brotherhood treachery was being planned from within Jordan and partly because of Jordan's support for Iraq in the Iran–Iraq War. Towards the end of 1980 Syrian and Jordanian troops faced each other across the frontier and conflict was finally averted by Saudi mediation.

Syria's biggest distraction, however, was its involvement in Lebanon. The 30,000 Syrian troops of the Arab Deterrent Force had been in Lebanon since 1976, and had been a severe drain on Syrian resources. In the summer of 1980 the Phalangist militia consolidated its position in Lebanon and came to occupy the town of Zahle in the Beka'a valley, east of Beirut. Clashes developed in the Zahle area between Syrian troops and the Phalangist militia, and the Christian forces found themselves under siege in Zahle in April 1981. Syria maintained that Zahle and the Beka'a valley were vital to its security against Israel. Israeli aircraft made repeated sorties into Lebanon, and at the end of April Syria moved surface-to-air (SAM) missiles into the Beka'a valley after two Syrian helicopters had been shot down by Israeli planes. A prolonged international crisis developed, with a serious threat of war between Israel and Syria. After Saudi and Kuwaiti mediation, however, the siege of Zahle was lifted at the end of June, and the Phalangist militia withdrew. The SAM missiles remained in the Beka'a valley, as the Syrians maintained that this was a separate issue.

In the following year, however, there were a number of reversals for President Assad. In December Israel formally annexed the Golan Heights, a development which prompted Syria to try to obtain more arms from the USSR. A huge car bomb explosion in Damascus in November was attributed to the Muslim Brotherhood, and this was followed by further indications of incipient unrest, culminating in February 1982 in an uprising in Hama which lasted for nearly three weeks. This was eventually suppressed by Assad's forces with brutal ferocity, and, although it was again attributed to the Muslim Brotherhood, other opposition elements were also involved. On 20 February an opposition group called the National Alliance of the Syrian People was formed, consisting of 19 factions drawn from, among others, Baathists, Nasserites, Christians, Alawites and the Muslim Brotherhood.

These problems were completely overshadowed, however, by the Israeli invasion of Lebanon in June 1982. Israeli forces quickly reached Beirut, trapping the PLO guerrillas there; the Syrian missiles in the Beka'a valley were destroyed; and the Syrian presence in northern Lebanon, in the guise of the Arab Deterrent Force, was rendered impotent.

In August agreement was reached on the evacuation of PLO and Syrian forces from Beirut, and their withdrawal, supervised by an international peace-keeping force, took place between 21 August and 1 September. The number of evacuees was estimated to be more than 14,500. No change occurred in the relative positions of Syrian and Israeli forces in Lebanon as a whole, however.

In January 1983, shortly after the start of negotiations between Lebanon and Israel for an agreement covering the withdrawal of foreign forces from Lebanon, Syria took delivery of a number of Soviet SAM-5 anti-aircraft missiles. Soviet *Scud* ground-to-ground rockets were already deployed with Syrian forces, but the SAM missiles, with a range of 240 km, posed a potential threat to aircraft over Lebanon, parts of Jordan and over Israel almost as far as Jerusalem. Two bases were built to accommodate the missiles: one at Dumeir, north of Damascus, and the other at Shinshar, near Homs. These missiles had never before been deployed outside the USSR and Eastern Europe, and the arrival of the technicians who were employed to operate the system was thought to have increased the number of Soviet military personnel in Syria to 6,000.

Syria opposed all US-sponsored diplomatic initiatives towards a peace agreement between Lebanon and Israel, and categorically rejected President Reagan's proposed settlement of the Palestinian question, based on an eventual Palestine-Jordan confederation, which he announced on 1 September 1982. Finally, on 17 May 1983, after almost six months of talks, an agreement was reached between Lebanon and Israel announcing the end of hostilities and imposing a time limit of three months for the withdrawal of foreign troops from Lebanon. The agreement, formulated by the US Secretary of State, George Shultz, was rejected outright by President Assad, who refused to withdraw Syrian forces from northern Lebanon—thus creating a stalemate with Israel, which refused to leave Lebanon unless the Syrians and the PLO did so first. President Assad insisted on Israel's unconditional withdrawal, declaring that the status of Syrian troops, which had been invited into Lebanon by the Lebanese Government in 1976, was not to be compared with that of the invading Israeli forces. He stated that the agreement between Israel and Lebanon placed unacceptable limitations on Lebanon's sovereignty and threatened Syrian security. Support for the Syrian position from the rest of the Arab world was less than unanimous, with only Libya, the People's Democratic Republic of Yemen (PDRY) and Kuwait expressing outright opposition to the agreement.

THE STRUGGLE FOR CONTROL OF THE PLO

By July 1983 the position was little changed. About 40,000 Syrian troops, camped in the Beka'a valley, and between 8,000 and 10,000 PLO guerrillas, entrenched in the eastern Beka'a and northern Lebanon, faced some 25,000 Israelis in the south of the country. Neither side seemed eager for war, but, equally, neither was prepared to withdraw. Syria, which continued to supply, and, effectively, to control the militias of the Lebanese Druze and Shi'ite factions in their struggle with the Lebanese Government and the Christian Phalangists in and around Beirut, began to address itself to destabilizing the regime of President Amin Gemayel of Lebanon by trying to unite Lebanese opposition groups in a pro-Syrian 'national front'. Syria was also supporting Palestinian rebels involved in the struggle for power within the PLO which erupted in the Beka'a valley in May, fundamentally over dissatisfaction with what radical Fatah members viewed as the compromise diplomacy of the PLO Chairman, Yasser Arafat, which, they believed, had been responsible for the Palestinians' humiliation in Beirut in 1982. Arafat accused Syria and Libya of inspiring the revolt in order to win control of the PLO, and at the end of June he travelled to Damascus to receive a personal letter of support from President Andropov of the USSR, only to be ordered out of the country by the Syrian authorities. Syrian forces now faced armed opposition in Lebanon, not only from the Israeli army, but also from Sunni Muslims in Tripoli, Maronite Christians in the centre of the country, and guerrillas loyal to Arafat in the Beka'a valley.

Syrian and rebel PLO forces, led by 'Abu Musa' and 'Abu Saleh', finally trapped Arafat in the Lebanese port of Tripoli in November 1983. After fierce fighting, a truce, arrived at through the mediation of Saudi Arabia, allowed Arafat and some 4,000 of his followers to leave Lebanon in December, in five Greek ships, under UN protection. Syria had failed to gain control of the Palestine Liberation Movement, though it had been instrumental in effecting a dilution of Arafat's authority within the PLO. This became apparent in a series of reconciliation talks held between several of the rival Palestinian factions (though not those which had sent troops against Arafat in Tripoli) in the first half of 1984. The agreements reached at these talks saw the PLO wishing to move towards a more collective style of leadership. Whether this style would give rise to policies deferential to Syria's preferred role as leader of the Arab world remained to be seen.

Syria's progress towards a position of pre-eminence in the Arab world was eroded during 1984, as the rehabilitation of Egypt continued. Syria dissented from the decision to readmit Egypt to membership of the Organization of the Islamic Conference in March 1984, and opposed Jordan's restoration of diplomatic relations with Egypt in September and King Hussein's alliance with Yasser Arafat. Syria's attempt to wrest control of the PLO from Yasser Arafat succeeded in splitting the movement. Arafat retained his leadership of the bulk of the organization and manoeuvred it towards an emergent moderate Arab alliance including Egypt, Jordan, Iraq and Saudi Arabia.

SYRIAN INFLUENCE IN LEBANON

Although Israel withdrew its forces from Beirut, redeploying them along the Awali river, south of the capital, in September 1983, Syria's army remained entrenched in northern Lebanon. There were occasional exchanges of fire between Syrian forces around Beirut and aircraft and naval guns of the US fleet standing off shore in support of the US contingent in the multinational peace-keeping force in Beirut. The state of civil war existing in and around Beirut eventually compelled the evacuation of the multinational force in the first three months of 1984.

In March President Gemayel of Lebanon was forced to succumb to the controlling influence of Syria in Lebanese affairs.

He abrogated the 17 May agreement with Israel, as President Assad had always insisted that he should, and reconvened the National Reconciliation Conference of the rival Lebanese factions (which had first met in Geneva in November 1983) in Lausanne, Switzerland, under pressure from Syria to agree constitutional reforms which would give the majority Muslim community of Lebanon greater representation in government. In return, Gemayel received guarantees of internal security from Syria. These involved Syrian agreement to restrain the Druze and Shi'ite Amal militias (led by Walid Joumblatt and Nabih Berri, respectively) which relied on Syria to continue their armed struggle.

The National Reconciliation Conference failed to produce the results for which Syria had hoped and it marked the beginning of the rapid disintegration of the Lebanese National Salvation Front, comprising leading Lebanese opponents of President Amin Gemayel, which had been created, with Syrian backing, in July 1983. At the Conference, a member of the Front, the former Lebanese President, Sulayman Franjiya, vetoed Syrian plans for constitutional changes in Lebanon involving the diminution of the powers of the President, traditionally a Maronite Christian. So, despite careful Syrian orchestration, the Conference broke up without having agreed any reforms of the Lebanese system of government.

The reversal was short-lived, for, in April, President Gemayel returned to Damascus to gain approval from President Assad for plans for a government of national unity in Lebanon, giving equal representation in the cabinet to Muslims and Christians. Assad accepted the terms of composition of the government under the premiership of Rashid Karami (who had been Prime Minister of Lebanon on 10 previous occasions); Gemayel was to retain the presidency. Walid Joumblatt and Nabih Berri greeted their appointment to posts in the new Lebanese Cabinet on 30 April, and the very idea of a government of national unity under a Christian President, with scepticism. After consulting Syrian officials, however, both agreed to participate in the Government. Inter-factional fighting, which continued and intensified in Beirut despite the creation of the new Government, threatened its existence. It was only through the intercession of the Syrian Vice-President for Political Affairs (and former Minister of Foreign Affairs; see below), Abd al-Halim Khaddam, and the negotiation, with his help, of a comprehensive security agreement between the warring factions, that the Government survived, and some semblance of order was restored in Beirut. Although this agreement, like many before it, and the political basis on which the new Lebanese Government was built, seemed fragile and prone to collapse, still, the fact that they existed at all was testimony to the extent of Syrian influence in the country's affairs.

INTERNAL TENSION

In November 1983 President Assad suffered what was thought to be a heart attack, though this was denied by the Syrian authorities. He recovered, but his evidently weakened condition aroused speculation regarding his eventual successor. During Assad's illness, potential rivals for the succession made displays of military force in and around Damascus, involving various units of the armed forces, to establish the strength of their claims to power. Prominent among these was Rifaat Assad, the President's brother and commander of the 20,000–30,000-strong defence brigades which, effectively, controlled Damascus and defended the regime's authority. The defence brigades and units of the regular army confronted each other in further, similar displays up to March 1984.

On 4 March the Council of Ministers, under Prime Minister Abd ar-Rauf Kassem, resigned. Kassem was then invited to form a new Council of Ministers to fill four vacancies left as a result of the deaths of ministers. It was the first ministerial reshuffle for four years. At the same time as a new Council of Ministers was being formed, President Assad appointed an unprecedented three Vice-Presidents. Rifaat Assad was made Vice-President for Military and National Security Affairs; Abd al-Halim Khaddam, the former Minister of Foreign Affairs, was made Vice-President for Political Affairs; and Zuheir Masharkah was promoted from his post as a regional secretary of the Baath Party to become Vice-President for Internal and Party Affairs. Ostensibly, President Assad's intention was to ease his

workload after his debilitating illness, but another possible motive for the appointment of three Vice-Presidents was to distribute power evenly between his potential successors, giving none an overall advantage. Rifaat Assad thus gained some recognition of his claim to the succession and retained control of the defence brigades; but the regular army (Assad's power-base in what is, essentially, a military dictatorship) was still commanded by officers loyal to President Assad, including the Chief of Staff, Gen. Hikmat Shehabi, who was responsible for the appointment and dismissal of senior officers in the army, and a rival of Rifaat Assad.

In what was seen, in the event, as a disciplinary measure against those principally responsible for the confrontations between military units which took place in and around Damascus after President Assad's illness in November 1983, Rifaat Assad, Gen. Ali Haydar (commander of the special forces élite army unit), and Gen. Shafiq Fayyadh (commander of the third armoured division) were sent as part of a delegation to Moscow in June. While the rest of the delegation returned to Syria within one week, these three were, apparently, not permitted to do so. Rifaat Assad was sent to Geneva, Switzerland, and Gens Haydar and Fayyadh to Sofia, Bulgaria, into what appeared to be temporary exile. While Rifaat Assad was abroad, the defence brigades were absorbed into the army, with the exception of a few units which were put under the command of Rifaat Assad's son-in-law. Rifaat Assad was finally permitted to return to Syria in November 1984 and was given responsibility for national security affairs. President Assad was re-elected for a third seven-year term of office in February 1985 and appeared to have regained much of his former authority. In January 1985 he declared an amnesty for some members of the Muslim Brotherhood who were imprisoned in Syria, and invited those in exile to return to the country. A ministerial reshuffle took place in April 1985.

THE IRAN–IRAQ WAR AND OIL SUPPLIES

Syria's reliance on Iran for supplies of crude oil for processing at its oil refineries (see Economy), which occurred as a direct result of its support for Iran in the Iran–Iraq War, was exposed as a serious weakness in 1984, as hostilities in the conflict began to affect the passage of oil tankers in the Gulf. Attacks on shipping were made by both sides in the first half of the year, threatening Syria's oil link with Iran. President Assad attempted to restrain Iran from widening the conflict and endangering vital oil supplies. An agreement on the continued delivery of Iranian oil to Syria was reached in May, but attacks on Gulf shipping by both Iran and Iraq continued. A Soviet attempt to bring about a reconciliation between the rival Baathist regimes in Syria and Iraq, involving the reopening of the oil pipeline between Kirkuk, in Iraq, and Banias, in Syria, made no progress.

ISRAEL'S WITHDRAWAL FROM LEBANON

By dint of Syrian mediation, a security plan for Beirut was agreed and put into operation at the beginning of July 1984. The plan met with only limited success, and the extent of Syria's influence with its Lebanese allies came into question when, in September, even the threat of force failed to win Walid Joumblatt's unequivocal approval of an extension of the security plan to allow the Lebanese army into the Druze stronghold of the Chouf mountains. In September Syria arranged a truce to end fighting in Tripoli between the pro-Syrian Arab Democratic Party and the Sunni Muslim Tawheed Islami (Islamic Unification Movement). This prepared the way for the Lebanese army to enter the city in November, under the terms of an extended security plan, backed by Syria, to assert the authority of the Lebanese Government in Beirut, Tripoli and south of the capital. On this occasion, Walid Joumblatt's opposition to the plan's provisions for the army to take control of the coastal road south of Beirut appeared to have tacit Syrian approval. However, the plan finally went ahead in January 1985.

Syria's rejection of Israel's demand that any withdrawal from Lebanon should be undertaken by both sides simultaneously was vindicated as it became clear, during the latter half of 1984, that Israel would be forced by domestic economic, political and social pressures to withdraw unilaterally. Syria approved Lebanese participation in talks with the Israelis to co-ordinate the departure of the Israeli Defence Force (IDF) from southern

Lebanon with other security forces, in order to prevent an outbreak of civil violence. A series of talks began in Naqoura (Lebanon) in November and repeatedly foundered on the question of which forces should take the place of the IDF. Under Syrian influence, the Lebanese wanted the UN Interim Force in Lebanon (UNIFIL) to police the Israel–Lebanon border (as it had been mandated to do in 1978), and the Lebanese army to deploy north of the Litani river, between UNIFIL and the Syrians in the Beka'a valley. Israel was not convinced of the competence of the Lebanese army, and wanted UNIFIL to be deployed north of the Litani, while the Israeli-backed, so-called 'South Lebanon Army' (SLA) patrolled the southern Lebanese border. In the absence of an agreement, Israel withdrew from the talks, and on 14 January 1985 the Israeli Cabinet voted to take steps towards a three-phased unilateral withdrawal to the international border.

The first phase involved the evacuation of the IDF from the western sector of occupied southern Lebanon, covering about 500 sq km around Sidon, and this was carried out in February 1985. In the second phase the IDF left the occupied central and eastern sectors where it faced the Syrian army and its Palestinian allies in the Beka'a valley, completing the operation on 29 April. On 10 June Israel announced the accomplishment of the third and final phase of the withdrawal, taking its forces behind the southern Lebanese border and leaving a protective buffer zone inside Lebanon, policed by the SLA with IDF support. Although Syria was evidently determined to retain control of events in Lebanon, the Israeli withdrawal offered the opportunity of reducing its costly military presence in the north and east of the country. At the end of June and the beginning of July Syria withdrew an estimated 10,000 troops from the Beka'a valley, leaving some 25,000 in position.

SYRIA LOSES ITS GRIP ON LEBANON

In March 1985 Dr Samir Geagea, a regional commander of the Christian Lebanese Forces (LF) militia, rebelled against the Phalange Party leadership and the extent to which it was prepared to accept the Syrian influence in Lebanese affairs, particularly as manifested in President Gemayel's apparent willingness to accommodate Syrian-backed plans for constitutional reform favouring the Muslim majority in Lebanon. Geagea immediately secured the support of the greater part of the LF and threatened to set up an independent Christian administration. Syria, though unwilling to be drawn into the civil-military entanglement in Lebanon, feared the necessity of having to send troops into Christian east Beirut to quell the revolt, which threatened to precipitate the partition of Lebanon along sectarian lines, creating a number of unstable mini-states close to the Syrian border, in a condition of perhaps permanent conflict and vulnerable to exploitation by Syria's enemies. Indeed, Syria accused Israel of inciting the revolt. It ended, however, as suddenly as it had begun, in May, when the LF elected a new leader, Elie Hobeika, who announced his readiness to negotiate with Syria and its Druze allies.

The extent of Syria's diminishing influence over the actions of its allies in Lebanon was repeatedly demonstrated by its inability to prevent renewed inter-factional fighting in Beirut. If the members of the LF were alarmed by the prospect of constitutional reform, their Muslim counterparts were dissatisfied with the lack of progress towards it. This could account for continued fighting between Christians and Muslims, but other factors now led to conflict between rival Muslim factions. On 17 April Prime Minister Rashid Karami, a Sunni Muslim, tendered his resignation, partly over the failure of the Council of Ministers to agree to reinforce the army, which was engaged in heavy fighting against elements of Samir Geagea's rebel LF around Sidon, and partly over attacks on Sunni Muslims by the Shi'ite Amal militia. The Shi'ites had combined with the Druze in trying to eliminate the Sunni Murabitoun militia, which had joined forces with members of the PLO, whose numbers in Beirut were growing again. Amal hoped to prevent the re-emergence anywhere in Lebanon of a PLO power-base which might attract Israeli military retaliation. Karami withdrew his resignation later on 17 April and, on a subsequent visit to Damascus, was persuaded to remain as Prime Minister and ensure the survival of the Government of national unity.

In May and June, however, Syria itself backed Amal in attempting to suppress a resurgence of the PLO (in particular the pro-Arafat wing of the movement) in the Palestinian refugee camps of Sabra, Chatila and Bourj el-Barajneh in Beirut. Many of the estimated 5,000, mostly pro-Arafat, Palestinians who had infiltrated Lebanon since the Israeli withdrawal became inevitable, had made their way to Beirut. Walid Joumblatt's Druze militia refused to assist its former allies in imposing a siege on the camps, but Amal had the support of the predominantly Shi'ite sixth brigade of the Lebanese army. In the bloody battle for the camps, which spanned May and June, more than 600 people were killed, but Amal failed to take control of the camps. An unforeseen development was the extent to which pro- and anti-Arafat PLO factions united to resist the attack on the Palestinian community. On 17 June a fragile Syrian-sponsored cease-fire agreement was reached in Damascus between Amal and the Palestinian National Salvation Front (PNSF), representing the pro-Syrian, anti-Arafat element in the camps.

Weeks of fighting between Christians and Muslims along the 'Green Line' dividing east and west Beirut, and between Muslims and Druze in the west of the capital, preceded an attempt to enforce another Syrian-sponsored security plan for the city. The plan was introduced in July, after 13 Muslim and Druze leaders had met to discuss it in Damascus. Under the terms of the plan, Muslim west Beirut was to comprise five security zones; the militias were to leave the streets and close their offices, with the police taking their place, supported by a unit of the sixth army brigade. These measures were meant to lay the foundations for the extension of the plan to Christian east Beirut and the renewal of inter-sectarian dialogue on political and constitutional reform. However, more heavy fighting soon reduced the plan to utter ineffectiveness.

President Assad was able to demonstrate that he retained some command over events in Lebanon when his intercession was instrumental in securing the release of 39 American hostages from a hijacked TWA airliner, who had been detained at secret locations in Beirut since 17 June 1985 by members of the extremist Shi'ite group Hezbollah (the Party of God). Assad threatened to sever relations with Hezbollah and to provide no further aid if the hostages were not released. The hostages were freed and driven to Damascus on 30 June.

Four weeks of intensive fighting between rival militias in the Lebanese town of Tripoli in September and October were interpreted as part of Syria's campaign to prevent the re-emergence of the pro-Arafat wing of the PLO in Lebanon. The pro-Arafat, Sunni Muslim group, Tawheed Islami, and the pro-Syrian, Alawite Arab Democratic Party fought for control of the town and its port, which was allegedly being used to distribute weapons and supplies to Arafat loyalists in other parts of the country. A cease-fire was agreed in Damascus in November, and troops of the Syrian army moved into the town.

THE ABORTIVE NATIONAL AGREEMENT IN LEBANON

One month of negotiations, under Syrian auspices, between the three main Lebanese militias, the Druze forces, Amal and the LF, which began in October 1985, led to the preparation of a draft accord for a politico-military settlement of the civil war. The agreement was finally signed by the three militia leaders (Walid Joumblatt, Nabih Berri and Elie Hobeika) on 28 December, in Damascus. It provided for an immediate cease-fire and for an end to the state of civil war within one year; the militias would be disbanded, and the responsibility for security would pass to a reconstituted and religiously-integrated army, supported by Syrian forces. The accord sought the immediate establishment of a national coalition government which would preside over the abolition of the confessional system of power-sharing government and the creation of a secular administration. It also recognized Lebanon's community of interest with Syria and envisaged a 'strategic integration' of the two countries in the fields of military relations, foreign policy and security.

It was always doubtful that the Damascus accord could be implemented. The Shi'ite Hezbollah and the Sunni Murabitoun militias were not party to the agreement, the Christian community was divided over it, and it made no provision for dealing with the problem of Palestinian refugees or the PLO. Among the Muslim community, only Amal appeared to be wholly in favour of the accord. President Gemayel, who had not been consulted during the drafting of the agreement, refused to endorse it, and at the end of December 1985 clashes erupted in east Beirut between elements of the LF who supported the agreement and those loyal to President Gemayel, who resented the concessions that had been made on their behalf by Elie Hobeika. In January 1986 Hobeika was forced into exile, and Samir Geagea resumed command of the LF, urging the renegotiation of the Damascus agreement. The long round of intersectarian clashes in Beirut resumed in earnest on 22 January.

Fighting between Palestinian guerrillas and Shi'ite Amal militiamen for control of the refugee camps in the south of Beirut, which had continued sporadically ever since a cease-fire nominally took effect in June 1985, escalated into major exchanges on 19 May 1986. The Palestinian refugee camps of Sabra, Chatila and Bourj el-Barajneh were increasingly under the control of guerrillas loyal to Yasser Arafat, who were continuing to return to Lebanon. Concentrations of PLO guerrillas were also identified in and around the refugee camps on the outskirts of Tyre and Sidon, while mobile PLO bases resumed rocket attacks on settlements in the north of Israel during 1986, drawing retaliatory attacks from the Israeli air force. Syria appeared to be powerless to prevent the resurgence of the PLO in Lebanon, despite the efforts of the Syrian-backed Amal militia to keep Palestinian and radical pro-Iranian Hezbollah guerrillas, who were growing in strength, away from the Israeli security zone inside the southern Lebanese border. The PLO claimed that the number of guerrillas in Lebanon in 1986 exceeded the 14,300 who, according to its own figures, had been evacuated from Beirut in 1982. Independent estimates assessed the number in Beirut at several thousands. Syria itself apparently ignored Israeli warnings not to fill the military vacuum which had been left by their withdrawal in 1985. In May 1986 it was reported that Syrian forces were constructing fortifications and tank and gun emplacements in the Lake Karoun area, in the southern Beka'a, immediately to the north of the SLA-patrolled security zone.

THE SYRIAN ARMY RETURNS TO BEIRUT

Leaders of the Muslim communities in Lebanon met Syrian Government officials in Damascus, and agreed to impose a cease-fire around the Palestinian refugee camps in Beirut on 14 June. The cease-fire, which reduced the fighting to exchanges of sniper fire, proved to be the first element in a Syrian-sponsored peace plan for Muslim west Beirut. About 1,000 Lebanese troops were deployed in west Beirut at the end of June. The Amal, Druze and Murabitoun militias were ordered to close their offices and to leave the streets. Crucial to their co-operation in the plan was the appearance in Beirut, for the first time since 1982, of uniformed Syrian soldiers (several hundred in number), supported by members of the Syrian security service, *Muhabarat* (literally, 'information'), under the command of Brig.-Gen. Ghazi Kena'an. The security plan was successful in its limited objective of curbing the activities of militias in west Beirut, but the plan (and Syria's visible involvement in it) was strongly opposed in Christian east Beirut, and the Syrians hesitated over extending the plan into the southern suburbs, which contained the majority of the city's Palestinian refugees and was controlled by the radical Shi'ite Hezbollah, who were backed by Iran, which Syria was concerned not to offend. (See Histories of Israel and Lebanon.)

RAPPROCHEMENT WITH JORDAN

Syria opposed the joint Jordanian-Palestinian agreement, which was signed by King Hussein and Yasser Arafat in Amman in February 1985, and its proposals for a Middle East peace settlement. In August, with Algeria, Lebanon, Libya and the PDRY, Syria boycotted the extraordinary meeting of the League of Arab States in Casablanca, which was convened partly to consider the Amman accord. The PLO's persistent refusal to acknowledge the UN Security Council Resolutions (Nos 242 and 338) on the Palestinian issue, and a series of terrorist incidents in the second half of 1985 in which the PLO was implicated, reducing its credibility as a potential partner in peace negotiations, and reducing the prospects that the joint peace initiative would make progress, led King Hussein to seek a reconciliation

with Syria. (It was suggested in some quarters that factions of the PLO, and other Palestinian groups supported by Syria, were involved in a campaign to discredit Yasser Arafat's wing of the movement.) Relations between Jordan and Syria had been poor since 1979, when Syria had accused Jordan of harbouring anti-Syrian groups. Apart from their different sympathies in the struggle for control of the PLO, a further cause of contention was Syria's support for Iran in the Iran–Iraq War, in which Jordan openly backed Iraq. In November 1985 King Hussein admitted that Jordan had, unwittingly, been a base for the Sunni fundamentalist Muslim Brotherhood in its attempts to overthrow President Assad, but he stated that members of the group would no longer receive shelter in Jordan. The Prime Ministers of the two countries met in Damascus in November, and agreed on the need for 'joint Arab action' to achieve peace in the Middle East. At subsequent talks in Riyadh (Saudi Arabia) in October, Jordan and Syria rejected 'partial and unilateral' solutions (ruling out separate negotiations with Israel) and affirmed their adherence to the Fez plan, omitting all reference to the Jordanian-Palestinian peace initiative. President Assad and King Hussein confirmed the improved state of Syrian–Jordanian relations when they met in Damascus in December. In February 1986 King Hussein withdrew from his political alliance with Yasser Arafat, and in April Jordan appointed its first ambassador to Syria since 1980.

King Hussein acted as a mediator between President Assad and President Saddam Hussain of Iraq during the first half of 1986. However, a meeting between the Syrian and Iraqi Ministers of Foreign Affairs, which was heralded as the beginning of a reconciliation between the two countries, was cancelled by President Assad, shortly before it was due to take place, in June 1986. Only days before, Syria had concluded an agreement with Iran to renew purchases of Iranian petroleum, while in southern Lebanon the guerrilla activities of pro-Iranian groups (in particular, Hezbollah) had been threatening Syria's already tenuous hold on the region through its proxy, Amal.

Syria broke off diplomatic relations with Morocco in July 1986, after King Hassan held talks with the Prime Minister of Israel, Shimon Peres.

BOMB ATTACKS IN SYRIA

On 13 March 1986 a bomb exploded in Damascus causing casualties which were estimated at 60 dead and 110 wounded. Syria blamed Iraqi agents for the attack. Then, on 15 April, bombs exploded, almost simultaneously, in five Syrian towns. Several more bomb attacks were made on buses and trains in towns, including Damascus, before the end of the month. In May the Government admitted that 144 people had been killed, and 149 injured, during the campaign of bombings in April. According to the Voice of Lebanon radio station, a hitherto unknown Syrian group (the '17 October Movement for the Liberation of the Syrian People') claimed responsibility for the campaign, and its message suggested that it was a pro-Iraqi, Islamic fundamentalist organization.

SYRIA AND INTERNATIONAL TERRORISM

Although it failed to provide conclusive proof of Syrian involvement, the USA claimed that there was evidence of a link between Syria and the Palestinian terrorists who carried out attacks on Rome and Vienna airports in December 1985, and on a discotheque in West Berlin in April 1986. The USA attacked the Libyan cities of Tripoli and Benghazi in April 1986, as punishment for alleged Libyan involvement in international terrorism, and reserved the right to use force against other countries which had proven links with terrorist operations. President Assad denied that Syria was sponsoring terrorism, and refused to restrict the activities of Palestinian groups (including the Abu Nidal faction, the Fatah Revolutionary Council) on Syrian territory, which, he claimed, were 'cultural and political'.

In October 1986 a Jordanian, Nezar Hindawi, was convicted in the UK of attempting to plant a bomb on an Israeli airliner at London's Heathrow airport in the previous April. The British Government claimed that it had proof of the complicity of Syrian diplomats in the affair, and, on 24 October, severed diplomatic relations with Syria. One month later, three Syrian diplomats were expelled from the Federal Republic of Germany (FRG), after a court in West Berlin ruled that the Syrian embassy in East Berlin was implicated in the bombing of a discotheque in the West of the city in 1986. In November the UK and its partners in the EC (excluding Greece), and the USA and Canada, imposed limited diplomatic and economic sanctions against Syria (the US and Canadian ambassadors to Syria were both recalled). Syria persistently denied any involvement in international terrorism, and by April 1987 several EC countries had made tentative advances to Syria, seeking to upgrade diplomatic relations, and only the UK continued to insist on a ban on high-level (ministerial) contacts. It had always seemed unlikely that the isolation of Syria would last long. Several EC countries, in particular France, had been unenthusiastic supporters of the sanctions demanded by the UK, mindful of the crucial role that Syria had to play in the Middle East peace process, and of the need for its co-operation in securing the release of Western hostages being held by Islamic fundamentalist groups in Beirut. For its part, Syria appeared to be anxious to be seen to dissociate itself from terrorist groups and to use its influence in Lebanon to free Western hostages. In June 1987 it was reported that the offices of Abu Nidal's Fatah Revolutionary Council, near Damascus, had been closed, and many of its members expelled, by the Syrian authorities, and that Abu Nidal himself had moved to Libya. The EC, with the exception of the UK, lifted its ban on ministerial contacts with Syria in July, and financial aid was resumed in September, although a ban on the sale of arms to Syria remained in force. The UK, although it had withdrawn its opposition to its EC partners' restoration of contacts with Syria, remained sceptical as to the true extent of Syria's rejection of terrorism, and alleged that Abu Nidal's group was still active in Lebanon, in the Syrian-controlled Beka'a valley.

PAX SYRIANA IN LEBANON

In October 1986 the Syrian-backed resistance to the re-emergence of the pro-Arafat PLO in Lebanon spread from Beirut to the Palestinian refugee camps around Tyre and Sidon, which were besieged by the forces of Amal. In February 1987 Syria reportedly asked Amal to abandon the blockade of the camps, but the respite for the inhabitants of the camps of Bourj el-Barajneh, in Beirut, and Rashidiyah, near Tyre, where supplies were allowed in, proved to be brief, and the siege of the other camps remained in force.

In February 1987 fierce fighting took place in west Beirut between Amal forces and an alliance of Druze, Murabitoun and Communist Party militias. Muslim leaders appealed for Syria to intervene, to restore order, and about 4,000 Syrian troops were deployed in west Beirut on 22 February. The Syrian force (which was soon increased to some 7,500 troops) succeeded in enforcing a cease-fire in the central and northern districts of west Beirut, and moved into areas occupied by Hezbollah, killing 23 Hezbollah members and forcing others to return to their stronghold in the southern suburbs, into which the Syrians still declined to venture.

A Syrian-supervised cease-fire at the embattled Palestinian refugee camps in Beirut took effect on 6 April 1987. The cease-fire agreement was negotiated by representatives of Syria, Amal and the pro-Syrian Palestine National Salvation Front (PNSF), and brought an end to the worst fighting. Members of the PNSF and Arafat loyalists had made common cause in defence of the camps, and their alliance was a contributory factor in the reunification of the PLO under Arafat's leadership, which took place at the 18th session of the Palestine National Council (PNC) in Algiers in April, turning the Syrian-backed PNSF into a rump, depriving it of the support of the largest and most influential groups that had rebelled against Arafat in 1983. The PNC adopted a resolution committing itself to improving PLO relations with Syria.

It was not until September 1987 that the Arafat wing of the PLO and Amal reached a comprehensive cease-fire agreement, which provided for the lifting of the siege of the Beirut, Tyre and Sidon camps, in return for a withdrawal by PLO forces from the positions around Ain al-Hilweh camp in Sidon, which they had captured from Amal in October and November 1986. However, neither measure was implemented, and differences concerning the withdrawal of Palestinian guerrillas led to renewed fighting around the disputed positions to the east of

Sidon in mid-October. In January 1988, avowedly as a gesture of support for protests by Palestinians living in Israeli-occupied territories, Nabih Berri, the leader of Amal, announced the lifting of the siege of the Palestinian refugee camps in Beirut and southern Lebanon. On 21 January Syrian troops replaced Amal militiamen and soldiers of the Sixth Brigade of the Lebanese army in positions around the Beirut camps, and the 14-month siege of Rashidiyah camp, near Tyre, was lifted. However, PLO guerrillas loyal to Yasser Arafat refused to withdraw from their positions overlooking Ain al-Hilweh, interrupting the withdrawal of Amal from around Rashidiyah.

A new political crisis overtook Lebanon in mid-1987, which emphasized the division between the Muslim and Christian communities and the extent of the problem that Syria faced in its attempts to oversee a political settlement. The Lebanese Prime Minister, Rashid Karami, who had tendered his resignation on 4 May, as a result of the Cabinet's failure to agree on measures to alleviate the country's acute economic problems, was assassinated on 1 June. Although it was not clear who was responsible for Karami's death, the Muslim community strongly suspected the Christian section of the divided Lebanese army and the Christian LF militia. Karami, a Sunni Muslim, had been a firm ally of Syria and had been one of the leaders who invited Syrian troops into Beirut in February, in the face of Christian opposition. Syria had yet to confront the problem of Christian-controlled east Beirut, to which no attempt had been made to extend the security plan.

In July 1987 representatives of Walid Joumblatt's Druze Parti socialiste progressiste, Nabih Berri's Amal, the Communist, Baath and Arab Democratic parties, and the Popular Nasserite Organization formed a brittle-seeming Unification and Liberation Front (the third of its type to be formed under Syrian auspices since 1977). The stated aims of the new, largely Muslim, left-wing front were: the unification of Lebanon; the expulsion of Israeli forces from southern Lebanon: the abolition of the confessional system of government; and the reintegration of the army.

RELATIONS WITH IRAN AND IRAQ

A realignment of Syrian policy towards Iran, which became more apparent during 1987, led to an increasingly uneasy relationship between the two countries. As international opinion turned against Iran in the Iran–Iraq War and moves were made to engineer a diplomatic settlement of the conflict, Syria's support for Iran became more of a liability. The USSR was critical of Syria's stance (reportedly withholding sales of arms to Syria in July), and, as the only Arab country, apart from Libya, to support Iran, Syria attracted the displeasure of other Arab states. (Libya switched its allegiance to Iraq in September.) Syria, significantly, responded to Iranian threats of reprisals against Saudi Arabia and Kuwait, after the deaths on 31 July of 275 Iranian pilgrims in riots in Mecca, by stating that it would not stand by and allow a fellow Arab country to be attacked with impunity. Syria's concern to regain the favour of Western nations and to play a full role in proposed Middle East peace initiatives by distancing itself from Islamic fundamentalist and anti-Arafat terrorist groups, and by seeking the release of Western hostages in Lebanon, brought it into dispute with Iran. Syrian troops in Beirut did not venture into the southern suburbs where Hezbollah (a group inspired by the Islamic revolution and backed by Iran) was based, but, after their deployment in February and to Iran's obvious annoyance, they harassed Hezbollah members and limited their freedom of movement in the parts of Lebanon under the group's effective jurisdiction. Syria also controlled the entry of Iranians into the country, and in June sent tanks and 'special forces' to surround the camps of Hezbollah militiamen and several hundred Iranian Revolutionary Guards, who were stationed at Baalbek in the Beka'a valley. Syria was evidently concerned about the destabilizing influence of Hezbollah's brand of Islamic fundamentalism, which aimed to create in Lebanon an Islamic republic on the Iranian model.

Syria's relations with Iran were further strained by the kidnapping in June 1987 of Charles Glass, an American journalist, allegedly by Hezbollah. This was the first abduction of a Westerner in west Beirut since the Syrian army assumed responsibility for security there in February, and was the cause of annoyance and embarrassment to Syria, which was eager to improve its relations with the USA. When, four weeks later, Glass escaped from his captors, his freedom was attributed to Syrian mediation with Hezbollah. Syrian influence was also instrumental in securing the release in September of a West German hostage, one of 23 Western captives who were being held in south Beirut. At the beginning of September the US ambassador to Damascus, who had been recalled to Washington in November 1986, returned to Syria, and the US Government withdrew its opposition, of the preceding 10 months, to operations by US oil companies in Syria.

Rumours of a *rapprochement* between Syria and Iraq were revived by reports that President Assad and President Hussain had met secretly in Jordan in April 1987, at the instigation of King Hussein of Jordan and Crown Prince Abdullah of Saudi Arabia. It was confirmed that this meeting had taken place when, in November, the two leaders held talks with King Hussein and other leaders at an extraordinary summit meeting of the League of Arab States in Amman, Jordan. The summit, which had been organized by King Hussein to discuss the Iran–Iraq War, produced a unanimous statement expressing solidarity with Iraq, condemning Iran for prolonging the war and for its occupation of Arab (i.e. Iraqi) territory, and urging it to observe the cease-fire proposals contained in UN Security Council Resolution 598. Syria's acquiescence in the statement appeared to represent a significant modification in its support for Iran. It was widely reported that Syria had been offered financial inducements by Saudi Arabia (which is Syria's principal source of aid), Kuwait and other Gulf states to realign its policy on the Iran–Iraq War with majority Arab opinion, and compensatory supplies of oil, should such a realignment result in Iran's withholding oil shipments. However, after the summit meeting, Syria announced that it had succeeded in obstructing an Iraqi proposal that Arab states should sever diplomatic relations with Iran, that a reconciliation with Iraq had not taken place, and that Syrian relations with Iran remained fundamentally unchanged. Syria had used its veto to prevent the adoption of an Iraqi proposal to readmit Egypt to membership of the League of Arab States, but it could not prevent the inclusion in the final communiqué of a clause permitting individual member nations to re-establish diplomatic relations with Egypt. By mid-February 1988, 11 Arab countries, including Iraq, had resumed diplomatic links with Egypt.

In March 1988 the Minister of Information, Muhammad Salman, announced that two months of Syrian mediation between Iran and the Arab states of the Gulf (designed to prevent an escalation of the Iran–Iraq War), which had been fiercely criticized by Iraq, had produced an Iranian undertaking to desist from attacks on tankers belonging to the members of the Gulf Co-operation Council (GCC).

In July 1987 Syria and Turkey signed a security protocol in which both agreed to curb the activities on their soil of terrorist and separatist groups carrying out operations against the other. Turkey believed that guerrilla attacks in its south-eastern provinces had been organized by Kurdish exiles in Damascus. Turkey also assured Syria that the series of dams that it was building on the Euphrates river would not be deliberately used in such a way as to deprive Syria of vital water supplies further downstream.

GOVERNMENT CHANGES

A major government reshuffle took place in November 1987, following the resignation of the Prime Minister, Abd ar-Rauf al-Kassem. His Government had been accused of corruption and inefficiency, and of failure to solve the country's severe economic problems. Earlier, four ministers (in June those of Agriculture and of Construction; and, in October, those of Industry and of Supply and Internal Trade) had been forced to resign, following accusations of mismanagement, which led to votes of 'no confidence' in the People's Assembly. Mahmoud az-Zoubi, the Speaker of the People's Assembly, was appointed Prime Minister on 1 November. His Council of Ministers contained 15 new members.

SYRIAN AND IRANIAN SURROGATES CLASH IN LEBANON

The Syrian-inspired lifting of the siege of the Palestinian refugee camps in January 1988, was a carefully calculated move. In cynical terms it was politically inexpedient for Syria to continue to employ its proxy, Amal, in its attempt to suppress the PLO in Lebanon, at a time when the Palestinian *intifada* (uprising) in the Israeli-occupied territories (see below) was attracting the sympathy of the world (in particular, the Arab world) to the plight of the Palestinians and increasing support for Arafat's mainstream PLO. By suspending Amal's campaign against the (pro-Arafat) PLO, Nabih Berri's Amal forces could be deployed against the Iranian-backed Hezbollah, whose strength was viewed by Syria as a threat to its own ambitions to control Lebanon.

Amal's attacks were initially directed against Hezbollah bases in southern Lebanon, and clashes (the first military confrontation between the two groups) occurred at the end of March in the Nabatiyeh area. On 9 April Amal claimed to have captured Hezbollah's last stronghold in the south, at Siddiqin, while Iranian Revolutionary Guards stationed at Sharqiyah and Jibshit had been ordered to leave the area.

In Beirut, Syria had demonstrated its opposition to hostage-taking by preventing a Kuwaiti Boeing 747, which had been hijacked by Islamic fundamentalists (alleged to be Lebanese), from landing at the city's airport in early April 1988. On 5 May fighting broke out between the Amal and Hezbollah militias (the latter supported by Iranian Revolutionary Guards) in the southern suburbs of Beirut. Attempts to impose a cease-fire through Iranian and Syrian mediation failed, and Syrian troops became involved in the fighting on 13 May when Hezbollah guerrillas, who had wrested control of about 90% of the 36-sq-km southern suburbs from Amal, briefly advanced into a Syrian-controlled area of west Beirut. On 15 May 7,500 Syrian troops encircled the southern suburbs, ready to advance into the enclave to restore order, while intensive negotiations took place between Syria and Iran, neither of which, despite their divergent ambitions in Lebanon, was eager to alienate the other. On 27 May several hundred Syrian troops moved into the southern suburbs of Beirut to enforce a cease-fire agreement reached by Syria, Iran and their militia proxies on the previous day. When the Syrian deployment was complete, Amal and Hezbollah were to close down their military operations in all parts of the southern suburbs, except in areas adjoining the 'Green Line' which separated west Beirut from the Christian-controlled east of the city, where they would continue to be allowed to post their men. On 3 June, in accordance with the agreement, Nabih Berri announced the disbandment of the Amal militia in Beirut and the Beka'a valley (areas under Syrian control) and all other areas of the country except the south (which was not controlled by Syrian troops).

ARAFAT LOYALISTS DRIVEN OUT OF BEIRUT

In April 1988 a reconciliation was reported to have taken place between President Assad and Yasser Arafat, though Assad continued to insist on the severance of all relations between Arafat's Fatah and Egypt. The two leaders held discussions (their first since Arafat's expulsion from Syria in 1983) when Arafat attended the funeral in Damascus of Khalil al-Wazir ('Abu Jihad'), the military commander of the Palestine Liberation Army. At the end of April, Arafat loyalists in the Palestinian refugee camps of Chatila and Bourj el-Barajneh in Beirut, possibly interpreting Syria's support for the Palestinian *intifada* and subsequent indications of a *rapprochement* between their leader and Assad as evidence of the Syrian President's waning commitment to the revolt within the PLO, attempted to drive out the fighters belonging to the Syrian-backed group, al-Fatah Intifada (Fatah Uprising), led by PLO dissident 'Abu Musa'. The Syrian troops who had surrounded the camps in April 1987, did not attempt to intervene in the fighting but, with Syria's other surrogate in Lebanon's factional conflict, the Amal militia, otherwise occupied, they allowed reinforcements to reach the rebel Fatah group. On 27 June the Arafat loyalists in the camp of Chatila were overrun and surrendered to the forces of 'Abu Musa'. On the following day, Syria granted 100 PLO guerrillas safe passage from Chatila to the Palestinian camp at Ain al-Hilweh, near Sidon. On 7 July Bourj el-Barajneh, Yasser Arafat's last stronghold in Beirut, fell to 'Abu Musa' and 120 Arafat loyalists were evacuated to Ain al-Hilweh.

LEBANON FAILS TO ELECT A NEW PRESIDENT

Amin Gemayel's term of office as President of Lebanon was due to expire on 22 September 1988 and the National Assembly was required to elect a new President prior to that date. Syria, naturally, was concerned that a candidate sympathetic to its views should be elected. Talks between Syria and the US Under-Secretary of State for Near Eastern and South Asian Affairs, Richard Murphy, during the summer, failed to produce agreement on a candidate who would be acceptable to both sides and who would be likely to gain the support of both Muslims and Christians in Lebanon.

Three main contenders for the presidency (traditionally a post occupied by a Maronite Christian) emerged: Gen. Michel Awn, the Commander-in-Chief of the armed forces; Raymond Eddé, the exiled leader of the Maronite Bloc National; and Sulayman Franjiya, who was President of Lebanon between 1970 and 1976. The latter did not announce his candidacy until 16 August, two days before the election was scheduled to take place, and the news immediately united President Gemayel and Samir Geagea, the commander of the Christian LF militia, in opposition to Franjiya's candidature, on the grounds that he represented Syrian interests. It was Franjiya who, as President, had invited Syria to intervene militarily in Lebanon to end the civil war in 1976.

On 18 August, only 38 of the 76 surviving members of the National Assembly attended the session at which the new President was to be elected. The President of the National Assembly declared the session inquorate and the election was postponed. It was strongly alleged that a number of Christian deputies had been intimidated, threatened or forcibly prevented from attending the election by the LF and soldiers under the command of Gen. Awn.

Consultations between Syria and the USA resumed during September to find a compromise candidate for the presidency. It was reported that they had agreed to support the candidacy of Mikhail ad-Daher, a deputy in the National Assembly, but Christian leaders in Lebanon repeated their rejection of any candidate imposed upon them by foreign powers.

A second attempt to stage the presidential election was made on 22 September, but, again, the session of the National Assembly failed to achieve a quorum.

Only minutes before his term of office was due to expire, President Gemayel appointed a six-member interim military Government, composed of three Christian and three Muslim officers, led by Gen. Awn, to rule until a new President was elected. Muslim politicians had refused to participate in an interim civilian government headed, contrary to the Constitution, by a Maronite Prime Minister, Pierre Hélou, instead of a Sunni Muslim. The three Muslim officers named in the interim military Government refused to take up their posts, while the two Christian members of the existing civilian Government surrendered their posts in recognition of the authority of the interim military administration.

Lebanon was plunged into a constitutional crisis, with two Governments, one Christian, in east Beirut, and one predominantly Muslim, in west Beirut, claiming legitimacy. Syria refused to recognize the interim military Government and there were fears that, unless a new President could be elected, the fact of dual-authority would formalize what was already an effective partition of the country into Christian and Muslim cantons.

The new interim military Government was regarded with suspicion by the LF militia, which feared that it would seek an accommodation with Syria in order to further the presidential ambitions of Gen. Awn. In February 1989 there was a major confrontation between the LF and Lebanese army brigades (both Christian and Muslim) loyal to Gen. Awn. While neither side achieved a decisive victory, the authority of the Lebanese army (which had been steadily eroded) was restored as a result of the clashes. On 17 February, after having suffered heavy losses, the LF was ordered by its commander, Samir Geagea, to withdraw from many parts of east Beirut. In response to allegations by Gen. Awn that it was levying illegal taxes, the LF agreed to close its 'customs point' in east Beirut, and Geagea subsequently claimed that both the LF and the Lebanese army were united in the aim of expelling Syrian forces from Lebanon.

GENERAL AWN'S 'WAR OF LIBERATION'

In March 1989 the most violent clashes for two years erupted in Beirut between Christian and Muslim brigades of the Lebanese army, loyal to Gen. Awn, and Syrian-backed Muslim militia, positioned on either side of the 'Green Line'. While the immediate cause of the fighting was the blockade of illegal ports in west and south Beirut by Christian forces, Gen. Awn declared at a press conference on 14 March that his Government had decided to take all measures for the immediate withdrawal of Syrian forces from Lebanon.

During the ensuing six months, Gen. Awn's self-declared 'war of liberation' developed into one of the most violent confrontations of the Lebanese conflict, causing heavy casualties in both the Christian and Muslim communities. Syria's claim that its forces were not directly involved in the hostilities was regarded as highly disingenuous, but most observers doubted whether Gen. Awn realistically expected to achieve the withdrawal of Syrian forces from Lebanon by military means. Rather, his aim was perceived to be the 'internationalization' of the Lebanese conflict in order to increase diplomatic pressure on Syria to effect such a withdrawal.

The ferocity of the fighting and the scale of the casualties prompted several diplomatic initiatives to secure a peace settlement (for a full account, see chapter on Lebanon). However, successive plans for peace foundered on the question of the withdrawal of Syria's estimated 35,000–40,000 troops in Lebanon, on which Gen. Awn insisted as an essential condition of any cease-fire agreement. At an emergency summit meeting of Arab leaders in Casablanca during 23 May–28 May, the proposal (supported by Egypt, Iraq, Jordan and the PLO) that Syria should immediately withdraw its troops from Lebanon was abandoned in response to Syrian opposition. Indeed, as the 'war of liberation' progressed, it became apparent that no agency was able or willing to exert sufficient diplomatic pressure on Syria to gain such a concession. While the Arab League was on one occasion officially to condemn Syria as the principal obstacle to peace in Lebanon, and while many Arab leaders were reportedly ready to admit, in private, that this was so, the Arab world feared that Syria's withdrawal from Lebanon would be perceived as a victory by Iraq (for Syrian–Iraqi rivalry in Lebanon, see below) and that it might lead to a direct confrontation between Iraq and Syria. While the USSR endorsed the proposals of the Tripartite Arab League Committee on Lebanon (formed at the Arab League summit meeting in May 1989), and urged Syria to accept them, the influence that it was able to exert as Syria's principal supplier of arms was limited.

By August 1989 it had become clear that Syria was prepared to disregard international censure of its role in Lebanon and to wage a war of attrition against the Lebanese army. Its refusal to consider any compromise with regard to the withdrawal of its forces stemmed from the longstanding strategic consideration of its need to control Lebanon in order to guard against any Israeli strike in the Beka'a valley. However, Syria was restrained from using its overwhelming military superiority to impose its authority on 'Christian Lebanon' by several factors. Initially, Syria feared that Israel might come to the defence of Lebanese Christians in the event of a full-scale military assault on the Christian enclave. Also, for economic reasons, it was anxious to avoid any further deterioration of its relations with Western countries, and with the USSR, which such an assault might have provoked.

In September 1989 the Tripartite Arab Committee on Lebanon announced details of a seven-point plan for peace in Lebanon which, unlike its previous diplomatic initiatives, did not demand the withdrawal of Syrian forces from Lebanon. Rather, in recognition of the futility of attempting to persuade Syria to withdraw its forces, diplomatic efforts in support of the new peace plan now concentrated on persuading Gen. Awn to accept its terms. The new plan for peace envisaged a cease-fire (to be supervised by a Lebanese security committee under the auspices of the Assistant Secretary-General of the Arab League, Lakhdar al-Ibrahimi); the ending of the Syrian naval blockade of the Christian enclave; and the convening of the Lebanese National Assembly to discuss a 'charter of national conciliation' drafted by the Tripartite Committee. The new plan presented Gen. Awn with a dilemma, since he had already, on previous occasions, rejected its principal proposals. At the same time, it had become clear that the 'war of liberation' was being fought in vain. The evacuation in early September of US diplomatic personnel and the closure of the US embassy in Beirut, in response to alleged threats of 'Christian terrorism', were widely regarded as signalling the end of Awn's hopes of achieving his aim though international intervention. Moreover, by September more than 800 people were reported to have been killed, and more than 2,000 injured, in the six months since the escalation of the hostilities. The Christian population (those who had not already fled Beirut), which had at first enthusiastically supported the 'war of liberation', was badly demoralized. On 22 September, following reports that the French Minister of Foreign Affairs had warned him that he could expect no international assistance if he refused to accept the Tripartite Arab Committee's latest proposals, Gen. Awn announced that he had abandoned the 'war of liberation' against Syria and agreed to the seven points of the Committee's peace plan for Lebanon. However, he subsequently vowed to continue the war by political means until the liberation was complete. For Syria, therefore, the problem remained of how to impose its authority on Christian Lebanese by means other than military force, since, ultimately, it had been international pressure which had forced Gen. Awn to abandon his campaign. On 25 September it was announced that the Lebanese National Assembly would convene in Saudi Arabia on 30 September to discuss political reforms aimed at ending the Lebanese conflict. The proposed reforms envisaged, among other things the transfer of executive powers from the Christian Maronite President to the Sunni Muslim Prime Minister; the ending of sectarianism in the army and the civil service; and an increase in the number of seats in the National Assembly, from 99 to 108.

In October 1989 the Lebanese National Assembly endorsed a charter of national reconciliation (the Ta'if agreement—for full details, see chapter on Lebanon, p. 747), which envisaged a continuing role for the Syrian armed forces in Lebanon by stipulating that they should assist in the implementation of a security plan incorporated in the agreement. The endorsement of the charter by the National Assembly was denounced by Gen. Awn as a betrayal of Lebanese sovereignty, since Christian deputies to the Lebanese National Assembly had reportedly assured Gen. Awn that they would permit concessions on the question of political reform in Lebanon only in exchange for a full withdrawal of Syrian forces.

Following a meeting of the newly-formed Lebanese Cabinet on 28 November 1989, it was announced that Gen. Awn had again been dismissed as Commander-in-Chief of the Lebanese army, and that Gen. Emile Lahoud had been appointed in his place. It was feared that Syrian forces would now launch an assault on Awn's stronghold in Baabda, east Beirut. Samir Geagea, the commander of the LF, announced that, in the event of such an assault, the LF would fight beside Gen. Awn, even though the Ta'if agreement had, to a large extent, been facilitated by the co-operation of Lebanon's Maronite leaders. Geagea's refusal to reject the Ta'if agreement led Gen. Awn to declare the LF to be an ally of Syria, and precipitated intense fighting between Awn's forces and the LF in early 1990 for control of the Christian enclave in Beirut.

In October 1990 thousands of Syrian troops were deployed to evict Gen. Awn from the presidential palace at Baabda, after President Hrawi of Lebanon had requested their assistance.

THE INTIFADA AND THE SHULTZ PLAN

In December 1987 a violent Palestinian uprising (*intifada*) against Israeli occupation of the West Bank and Gaza Strip, erupted in the Occupied Territories. At the end of February 1988, with the *intifada* showing no sign of moderating in intensity, the US Secretary of State, George Shultz, embarked on a tour of Middle Eastern capitals, including Damascus, in an attempt to solicit support for a new peace initiative. The Shultz Plan proposed an international peace conference and direct talks between Israel and each of its adversaries (excluding the PLO), and an interim period of limited autonomy for Palestinians in the Occupied Territories, pending a permanent negotiated settlement (for full details, see Documents on Palestine, p. 125). President Assad stopped short of rejecting the plan outright, but, in certain fundamental respects, it was impossible for any Arab leader to accept: it failed to recognize the right of the PLO to participate in peace negotiations or the right of the Palestinians to self-determination. Further talks between Shultz and Assad in April failed to reconcile the two sides.

At the beginning of June 1988 an extraordinary summit meeting of the Arab League was held in Algiers to discuss the *intifada* and the Arab–Israeli conflict in general. The final communiqué of the summit, endorsed by all 21 League members, including Syria, rendered the Shultz Plan effectively moribund by demanding the participation of the PLO in any future peace conference, endorsing the Palestinians' right to self-determination and urging the establishment of an independent Palestinian state in the West Bank.

Syria, alone of all the Arab states, refused to recognize the independent Palestinian State (proclaimed at the 19th session of the PNC in Algiers in November 1988), in accordance with its long-standing policy of preventing any other force in Lebanon from acquiring sufficient power to challenge Syrian interests there (for full details of the Declaration of Palestinian Independence see Documents on Palestine, p. 125).

FOREIGN RELATIONS 1988–90

The cease-fire in the Iran–Iraq War, which came into force on 20 August 1988, created a number of problems for Syria. As the sole Arab supporter of Iran, Syria was already isolated, and the cessation of hostilities presented Iraq with an opportunity to settle old scores with its Baath rival, initially by attempting to thwart Syrian plans for domination over Lebanon. In September, Iraq was reportedly supplying arms and money to the Christian LF in Lebanon and, following the failure of the Lebanese National Assembly to elect a new President, Iraq proclaimed its support for the interim military administration appointed by President Gemayel, which was opposed by Syria. After March 1989, when the 'war of liberation' waged by the Lebanese army against Syrian forces in Lebanon began, Iraq became the principal supplier of arms to the Lebanese army. The expression of Syrian–Iraqi rivalry by proxy in Lebanon also complicated attempts by the Arab League to achieve a cease-fire there following the escalation of hostilities in March 1989, since it was feared that the withdrawal of Syrian forces from Lebanon might provoke a direct confrontation between Iraq and Syria.

Syria found itself on the same side as Iraq in a dispute with Turkey over the diversion of water from the Euphrates river in order to fill the reservoir supplying Turkey's newly-constructed Atatürk dam. In January 1990 Syria lodged a formal complaint with Turkey over the effects of the diversion on Syria's water and electricity supplies. However, the Turkish Government rejected the complaint, claiming that it had increased the supply of water to Iraq and Syria by 50% between November 1989 and January 1990 in order to make good the loss of water caused by the diversion in early 1990. The Syrian and Turkish Ministers of Foreign Affairs met in Turkey in June 1990 to discuss relations, in particular the sharing of the Euphrates waters.

SYRIA AND THE 1990–91 GULF CRISIS

In April 1990 Syria expressed support for Iraq's right to defend itself in any conflict with Israel, the ideological differences between Syria and Iraq notwithstanding. In August 1990, however, Syria was eager to exploit the diplomatic opportunities arising from Iraq's invasion of Kuwait, and, in particular, to improve its relations with the USA and Egypt. In December 1989 Egypt and Syria had agreed to re-establish diplomatic relations after a rupture lasting almost 12 years, and in May 1990 President Mubarak of Egypt visited Syria, the first such visit by an Egyptian leader since 1977. The talks he held with President Assad reportedly concentrated on the faltering Middle East peace process and on means of achieving Arab unity to oppose the increased emigration of Soviet Jews to Israel, a process which had begun in 1989 and accelerated in early 1990.

Syria supported Egypt's efforts to co-ordinate Arab responses to Iraq's invasion of Kuwait, and agreed, at an emergency summit meeting of the Arab League, held in Cairo on 10 August 1990, to send troops to Saudi Arabia as part of a pan-Arab deterrent force supporting the US effort to deter an Iraqi invasion of Saudi Arabia. Despite widespread popular support among Syria's Palestinian population for the Iraqi President, Saddam Hussain, Syria committed itself to the demand for an unconditional Iraqi withdrawal from Kuwait, and later in August the first contingent of Syrian troops was deployed in Saudi Arabia, joining a multinational force that was predominantly composed of US military personnel. In September the US Secretary of State, James Baker, made a visit to Damascus, where he held talks with President Assad. The USA emphasized the importance of establishing a dialogue with Syria, in view of its opposition to Iraq's occupation of Kuwait. Syria, for its part, claimed that its troops were in Saudi Arabia purely for defensive purposes. In late September President Assad visited Iran, where he held discussions with President Rafsanjani. They reportedly agreed on the desirability of a regional security system, but were unable to elaborate a common position regarding the deployment of Western forces in the Gulf region, which Iran had strongly condemned.

In late October 1990 the objections of the United Kingdom prevented the EC from removing the economic sanctions which it had applied against Syria since 1986. In late November 1990, however, it became apparent that Syria's participation in the US-led multinational force was transforming its relations with the West, when diplomatic ties were restored between Syria and the United Kingdom. By the beginning of December it was estimated that some 20,000 Syrian troops had been deployed in Saudi Arabia.

In mid-January 1991 President Saddam Hussain of Iraq rejected a message from President Assad, who sought to persuade him that Iraq's occupation of Kuwait benefited Israel alone. Following attacks by Iraqi *Scud* missiles on Israel, Syria warned Israel not to become militarily involved in the crisis in the Gulf region, and implied that it might be obliged to withdraw from the multinational force in the event of an Israeli attack on an Arab state. Subsequent statements, however, indicated that Syria would tolerate limited Israeli retaliation against Iraq for the missile attacks.

In early 1991 the overwhelming military defeat of Iraq by the US-led multinational force placed Syria in a stronger position with regard to virtually all of its major regional concerns, thus vindicating the pragmatic stance adopted by the Government with regard to the crisis in the Gulf region. Syria consolidated the improvement in relations with Egypt which had begun in December 1989, and laid the foundation for increased co-operation with Egypt in matters of regional security. In early March 1991 the Ministers of Foreign Affairs of the members of the GCC (Saudi Arabia, Kuwait, Qatar, Bahrain, the UAE and Oman) met the Egyptian and Syrian Ministers of Foreign Affairs in Damascus to discuss regional security issues. The formation of an Arab peace-keeping force, comprising mainly Egyptian and Syrian troops, was subsequently announced. In early May, however, Egypt announced its decision to withdraw all of its forces from the Gulf region within three months, thus casting doubt on the future of joint Syrian-Egyptian security arrangements. These have remained in doubt, although in May 1992 the Secretary of the GCC stated the determination of its member states to create a regional security role for Egyptian and Syrian forces.

Syria's decision to ally itself, in opposition to Iraq, with the Western powers and the so-called 'moderate' Arab states led the USA to realize that it could no longer seek to exclude it from any role in the resolution of the Arab–Israeli conflict. After the conclusion of hostilities with Iraq, US diplomacy focused on seeking to initiate negotiations between Israel, the Arab states, including Syria, and Palestinian representatives. The loss of credibility which the PLO had suffered as a result of its support for Iraq in the Gulf War left all the Arab states in a stronger position to dictate the final terms of a peace settlement with Israel, and was especially gratifying to Syria, which had long opposed Yasser Arafat's leadership.

In March 1991 the Israeli Prime Minister, Itzhak Shamir, indicated that Israel was prepared to take steps to reduce tension in the Middle East, and reaffirmed his commitment to the peace initiative which he had proposed in May 1989 (see chapter on Israel). However, he was dismissive of the prospects for peace with Syria. In late April, immediately prior to a visit to Damascus by the US Secretary of State, James Baker, the official Syrian newspaper, *Tishrin*, listed a number of Syrian conditions for a peace settlement with Israel. These included the unconditional withdrawal of Israel from the Occupied Terri-

tories; the safeguarding of Palestinian national rights; and a prominent role for the UN in any future peace conference. The Israeli Government had already made it clear that it regarded these conditions as unacceptable.

Despite attempts in early May 1991 by both the USA and the USSR to create sufficient common ground between Israel and Syria for peace negotiations to begin, Baker stated that there were still 'significant' differences between Israel and Syria regarding the holding of a Middle East peace conference. Syria remained adamant that talks with Israel should take place within the framework of an international conference, with the full participation of the UN, and that afterwards such a conference should reconvene at regular intervals. Israel remained opposed both to the participation of the UN and to the reconvening of the conference after an initial session had been held. The USA, for its part, excluded the possibility of holding a peace conference without Syrian participation.

On 18 July 1991, in a remarkable volte-face, President Assad agreed for the first time, following a meeting with the US Secretary of State, to participate in direct negotiations with Israel at a regional peace conference, for which the terms of reference would be a comprehensive peace settlement based on UN Security Council Resolutions 242 and 338. By agreeing to participate in a peace conference on the terms proposed by the USA, Syria decisively increased the diplomatic pressure on Israel to do likewise. However, the publicly-stated positions of the Syrian and Israeli Governments remained as far apart as ever. Each claimed, towards the end of July 1991, to have received confidential (and incompatible) assurances from the USA: Israel with regard to the composition of a Jordanian-Palestinian delegation to the peace conference; and Syria with regard to the return of the Israeli-occupied Golan Heights. On 4 August the Israeli Cabinet formally agreed to attend a peace conference on the terms proposed by the USA and the USSR.

NEGOTIATIONS WITH ISRAEL

By late October 1993—following an initial, 'symbolic' session of the conference held in Madrid, Spain, in October 1991, and attended by Israeli, Syrian, Egyptian, Lebanese and Palestinian-Jordanian delegations—11 sessions of bilateral negotiations had been held between Israeli and Syrian delegations. In April 1992 they had proceeded to debate the precise meaning of UN Security Council Resolution 242, but the Israeli Government continued firmly to reject any exchange of occupied land—including the Golan Heights—in return for a peace settlement. In May, owing to the failure of bilateral negotiations to achieve any progress towards a peace settlement, Syria and Lebanon refused to attend multilateral negotiations, convened in Belgium, Austria, Canada and Japan, to discuss, among other issues, water resources and the question of Palestinian refugees. In the aftermath of the further disintegration of the USSR, which took place in December 1991, and the consequent erosion of its position as a potential counterfoil to the USA's Middle Eastern policies, Syria remained obliged actively to support and participate in the US peace initiative. With regard to other regional issues, however, the Syrian Government appeared determined not to simply acquiesce in the interests of the USA, announcing, in mid-April 1992, that it would continue to maintain air links with Libya, in defiance of the sanctions which the UN had imposed on that country (see chapter on Libya). In late April, in an attempt to allay suspicions of its Middle Eastern policies, the US Administration formally assured the Syrian Government that it had no hostile intentions towards it.

The formation, in mid-July 1992, of a new Israeli coalition Government, in which the Labour Party was the dominant element, aroused fears in Syria that any improvement in such a government's relations with the USA might increase the pressure on Syria to make disadvantageous concessions in the ongoing Middle Eastern peace process. The sixth round of bilateral negotiations between Israeli and Syrian delegations, which commenced on 24 September in Washington, DC, and lasted for a month, seemed at times to be close to achieving real progress on the issue of the Israeli-occupied Golan Heights. The new Israeli Government was reported to have indicated its willingness to consider some form of compromise, although there was no sign that it was prepared to meet Syria's minimum demand: Israel's full and unconditional compliance with UN Security

Council Resolution 242, which requires, among other things, the withdrawal of Israeli armed forces from territories occupied in 1967.

Initially, the Declaration of Principles on Palestinian Self-Rule in the Occupied Territories, signed by Israel and the PLO on 13 September 1993, drew a guarded response from Syria. Subsequently, however, President Assad indicated that he had serious reservations about the agreement, and that he regarded the secret negotiations between Israel and the PLO which had led to it as having weakened the united Arab position in the ongoing peace process with Israel. It appeared that Syria would not actively oppose the agreement, but there was no sign that it would cease to support those Palestinian factions, such as the Damascus-based Popular Front for the Liberation of Palestine—General Command (PFLP—GC), which had vowed to do so. Syria was reported to fear that Israel might now view the terms of the Declaration of Principles concluded with the PLO as a model for an agreement with Syria on the Golan Heights (i.e. the exchange of only a partial withdrawal of Israeli armed forces from the Golan Heights for a comprehensive peace settlement).

In January 1994 Syria agreed to resume bilateral negotiations with Israel, claiming that it had secured a commitment from Jordan to delay the finalization of any agreement with Israel until Lebanon and Syria had negotiated their own agreements with Israel. On 16 January President Assad met with the US President Clinton for talks in Geneva aimed at giving fresh momentum to the negotiations. The Israeli Prime Minister, Itzhak Rabin, responded by announcing that a referendum would have to be held in Israel on the issue of the withdrawal from the Golan Heights; Syrian Minister of Foreign Affairs, Farouk ash-Shara', claimed that this would contravene international law. Talks between the two countries continued in Washington, DC, on 24 January, but were temporarily suspended on 27 February following the murder of some 30 Muslim worshippers at a mosque in Hebron on the West Bank by a right-wing Jewish extremist. Assad continued to reject proposals to hold secret talks with Israel and ignored Israeli demands to prevent attacks by Lebanese militia groups on the Israeli forces in south Lebanon. In late April Warren Christopher, the US Secretary of State, visited the Middle East in what was seen as an attempt to break the deadlock over the Golan Heights. Under the Israeli plan, which would be phased over a period of eight years, Syria would initially be granted control over the four Druze settlements in the Golan Heights, the next stage would involve the closure of Israeli settlements in the Golan, and the final phase would be a full-scale withdrawal. In May, when an agreement was signed between Israel and the PLO providing for Palestinian self-rule in the Gaza Strip and Jericho, Syrian officials remained sceptical, arguing in favour of a united Arab approach to the peace settlement. Syria similarly expressed dissatisfaction at the agreement reached between Israel and Jordan in early June, accusing the two sides of placing obstacles in the way of reaching a comprehensive peace settlement in the region.

In July and August 1994 Warren Christopher visited Damascus for further talks; following the August trip he acknowledged that major differences still remained between Israel and Syria, but claimed that a 'psychological barrier' had been broken through. The US envoy, Dennis Ross, met with Israeli and Syrian leaders in September as speculation grew about possible secret talks between the two countries. In Israel Itzhak Rabin faced growing public discontent over the prospect of withdrawal from the Golan Heights, and in late September a group of Labour party members submitted a proposal to the Knesset to table a law requiring the Government to secure an absolute majority in order to withdraw from the Golan. The Middle East peace process was again curtailed in mid-October following the events in the Gulf (see Kuwait). On 18 October a group of 300 Syrian Jews were allowed to emigrate to Israel in what was seen as a gesture of goodwill on the part of the Syrian Government towards its Israeli neighbour. President Clinton attended the signing of the peace treaty between Israel and Jordan on 26 October, and on the following day he visited Syria—the first visit to the country by a US President for 20 years. Pressure on President Assad to reach an agreement with Israel over the Golan Heights increased following the Israeli-Jordanian treaty and it was reported that Assad might be considering Israel's

proposal for a phased withdrawal but over a shorter period of time. In mid-March 1995—more than one year after their suspension—talks betwen Syria and Israel finally resumed. Initially they involved only the ambassador of each country to the USA, but were subsequently to include high-level Syrian and Israeli military delegations. In April the US special co-ordinator for the Middle East peace process visited the Middle East and indicated that the USA was trying to widen the scope of the talks taking place between Syria and Israel to include military officials. In mid-April, however, the Syrian Minister of Foreign Affairs stated that senior Syrian military officials would not participate because no agreement had been reached on security principles.

In late May 1995 Israel and Syria concluded a 'framework understanding on security arrangements', which, it was reported, would facilitate the participation in the negotiations of the two countries' chiefs of staff. Israel stated publicly, for the first time, that it had proposed a four-year timetable for the withdrawal of its armed forces from the Golan Heights, but that Syria had insisted on one of 18 months. In June the then Israeli Minister of Foreign Affairs, Shimon Peres, referred to the Golan as 'Syrian territory' while the Israeli President, Ezer Weizman, clearly stated that Israel was negotiating on the basis of a full withdrawal to the international border. Opinion polls in Israel, however, suggested that the majority of the population was against full withdrawal, in particular Jewish settlers on the Golan itself. President Assad spoke publicly about the peace process for the first time in June during a television broadcast and took the unprecedented step of actually referring to Israel by name. In late June the Israeli and Syrian chiefs of staff held talks in Washington, DC. Syria was reported to have proposed a means of demilitarization in the Golan Heights whereby Syria would demilitarize 10 km on its side of the border for every 6 km demilitarized by Israel. However, neither government was prepared to release further details of the negotiations. Syria's willingness to compromise on demilitarization failed to give the peace talks a new impetus, and it was reported that the talks had become blocked over Israel's insistence on retaining its early warning system on Mount Hermon. There were also differences over the delineation of the final border between the two countries, with Syria insisting on a return to the border that existed before the 1967 war, and Israel demanding a return to the pre-1948 border. Syria blamed Israel for the lack of progress, and many observers concluded that the Israeli Prime Minister Rabin had decided not to try to reach a full settlement with Syria until after the Israeli elections due to take place in 1996. Syria's attempts in August 1995 to persuade the EU to take a more active role in the peace talks met with only a limited response. In October President Assad stated that Syria was willing to accept Israeli air surveillance over the Golan Heights but not radar monitoring. Efforts by US Secretary of State, Warren Christopher, who met President Assad at the end of October, failed to achieve a resumption of peace talks. In November, on becoming Israeli Prime Minister after the assassination of Itzhak Rabin, Shimon Peres declared that peace talks with Syria would be his top priority. He immediately strengthened the Israeli negotiating team and called for the talks to be expanded to cover a range of political issues in addition to military questions. Syria welcomed Peres' initiative, and the two countries concluded a 10-point agreement to act as a framework for new negotiations. A new round of talks, hosted by the US Government, began at the end of December in Maryland and continued in January and February 1996. According to US officials some progress was made during the talks, and there were rumours that agreement had been reached in principle on border issues. US Secretary of State Christopher visited Damascus in February to assure President Assad that despite Peres' decision to call an early election in May, the Israeli Prime Minister remained determined to negotiate a settlement with Syria. The USA clearly hoped that a Labour victory in the elections would put Peres in a strong position to make concessions to Syria and that a preliminary agreement might be reached before the US presidential elections in November 1996.

A series of suicide bomb attacks in Israel in late February and early March 1996, in which more than 50 Israelis died, shattered support for the peace process in Israel. As part of the tough stance Prime Minister Peres adopted following the attacks, and against US advice, he broke off negotiations with Syria. Despite pressure from the USA and Egypt, President Assad refused to attend the 'summit of peacemakers' at Sharm esh-Sheikh which was convened in March in response to these attacks. Syria claimed that the summit meeting was simply an attempt to support the embattled Israeli Prime Minister and argued that the only effective means of saving the peace process was to reconvene the Madrid conference. After the summit Israel demanded that Syria should explicitly condemn terrorism before it would resume peace talks. Syria stated that it did condemn terrorism, but claimed that violent resistance to Israeli occupation was a legitimate right of the Palestinians. Syria also rejected demands by Israel and the USA that it should close down the offices in Damascus of radical Palestinian groups opposed to the peace process.

Negotiations received a further setback in April when Israel launched 'Operation Grapes of Wrath', a massive bombardment of Lebanon in response to Hezbollah rocket attacks on Kiryat Shmona and other northern settlements (see below). Some analysts argued that this offensive confirmed Syrian interpretations of the objectives of Prime Minister Peres, that neutralizing Hezbollah would not only bring advantages in terms of security, but would also allow Israel to take a tougher stance in its negotiations with Syria on the Golan Heights and southern Lebanon. Having failed to achieve these objectives, when both Syria and Lebanon refused to yield to Israeli and US demands, Peres gave priority once again to negotiations with the Palestinians and it appeared that talks with Syria might be suspended for a long time.

During the approach to the Israeli elections at the end of May 1996, Shimon Peres told voters that he doubted whether a peace agreement could be reached with Syria without returning all of the Golan Heights and added that he had always been prepared to make territorial compromises over the Golan. His right-wing challenger, Likud leader Binyamin Netanyahu, in contrast, repeated his pledge that he would only negotiate with Syria on the understanding that Israel retained control over the Golan Heights. Netanyahu's unexpected victory in the elections and the subsequent formation of a right wing Government in Israel was greeted with alarm in Syria which condemned the new administration as 'a cabinet of rabbis, racists and generals'. Addressing the Knesset in June, Prime Minister Netanyahu appealed for the reopening of unconditional peace talks with Arab states but rejected the land-for-peace policies of his Labour predecessor and told deputies that his emphasis would be on security. He insisted that retaining sovereignty over the Golan Heights must be the basis of any peace settlement with Syria. When the new Israeli Minister of Foreign Affairs, David Levy, suggested that Israel might meet Syria 'half-way' on the Golan problem, his statement was immediately disavowed by Netanyahu's spokesman, who insisted that only statements made by the Prime Minister reflected Israeli policy on these issues. The final communiqué of the emergency Arab League summit meeting held in Cairo at the end of June urged the new Israeli Government not to abandon the land-for-peace principle. It appealed for the removal of all Israeli settlements on the Golan Heights and its return to Syria. In response, however, the Israeli Prime Minister, and the Minister of Internal Security Avigdor Kahalani, stated that Israel should wait at least two generations before even discussing the possibility of giving up the Golan Heights, even if Syria agreed to normalize relations with Israel. In July Dennis Ross, the US special envoy to the Middle East, visited Damascus, and, after talks with President Assad, indicated that Syria still wanted to pursue peace talks with Israel. The French Minister of Foreign Affairs, Hervé de Charette, also visited Damascus as part of France's efforts to assume a more active role in the Middle East peace process. When Netanyahu visited Washington, DC, in July, he reiterated Israel's refusal to withdraw from Golan but stated that he was willing to resume talks with Syria without pre-conditions. His offer was rejected by the Syrian authorities which stated that renewed talks would only be possible if the new Israeli Government accepted the 'land-for-peace' principle. At the end of July a well-informed Israeli source predicted that Netanyahu would maintain an intransigent stance towards Syria and would strengthen and enlarge Jewish settlements on the Golan Heights. In exchange for peace, it was argued, the new Israeli Prime Minister would

promise to persuade the USA to remove Syria from its list of countries which support terrorism, but only after Syria had disarmed Hezbollah militants in Lebanon. As these conditions were likely to be rejected by Syria, some influential members of Likud suggested that Israel should wait for a new and weaker regime in Syria that would be more amenable to Israeli demands.

In early August 1996, during a visit to Israel's 'security zone' in southern Lebanon, Netanyahu warned that further attacks by Hezbollah guerrillas might provoke Israeli reprisals against Syria. Tensions mounted as the Syrian Chief of Staff claimed that the military option was still open to Syria in its dispute with Israel, and intelligence sources reported the redeployment of large numbers of Syrian troops from Lebanon to new positions in Syria, possibly to reinforce the western defences of the capital, Damascus. An offer by Netanyahu to withdraw Israeli troops from southern Lebanon, on condition that Hezbollah forces were disarmed and that both Lebanon and Syria agreed to prevent them launching any new attacks on northern Israel, was rejected by President Assad. Such a move would have denied Syria the option of using Hezbollah to exert pressure on Israel while leaving Israel firmly in control of Golan. The Syrian President insisted that peace negotiations could only resume if Netanyahu's Government honoured earlier agreements and understandings reached with Itzhak Rabin and Shimon Peres. President Assad stated that, before his assassination, Prime Minister Rabin had given a commitment to the USA that Israel would withdraw from the whole of the Golan Heights. However, Netanyahu declared that he was under no obligation to abide by what he referred to as 'theoretical statements' made by his predecessor during the course of negotiations, and insisted that peace talks must be without prior conditions. At the end of December Syria blamed Israel for a bomb attack on a bus in Damascus, although most observers believed that responsibility for the attack lay elsewhere (see below). During the early part of 1997 the Israeli Government's determination to proceed with the controversial Jewish settlement at Har Homa in Arab East Jerusalem, and the collapse in negotiations between Israel and the PNA, only served to reinforce obstructions to the resumption of the Syrian peace track. In February Israel announced that further Jewish settlements were to be constructed on the Golan, and in July withdrawal from the Golan was made conditional on approval by two-thirds of the Knesset. In April the Israeli press accused Syria of developing weapons of mass destruction, including missiles armed with lethal nerve gas capable of hitting targets inside Israel. The allegations were confirmed by the Israeli Minister of Defence, Itzhak Mordechai, but denied by Damascus. Nevertheless, during a visit to Paris in June Mordechai stated that he was keen to see peace talks with Syria resume, even if the two sides were not in agreement. He stressed that it was necessary to talk so that each side could understand the other's demands and try to find a formula to resolve their conflict. However, in July Syria withdrew from the Middle East and North Africa economic summit as a result of Israel's inclusion. Syria also urged other Arab countries to boycott the summit in Doha, Qatar, which went ahead, as scheduled, in November, but without the participation of leading Arab states. In August President Assad invited a delegation of Israeli Arabs, including members of the Knesset, to Damascus, only the second visit of its kind. Assad told them that he thought a withdrawal from the Golan was unlikely while Netanyahu remained Prime Minister. Meanwhile, Western military analysts reported that Syria had deployed new 200T-55MV main battle tanks, supplied by Ukraine, in forward positions near the Golan Heights. Nevertheless, there were reports in the Israeli press that Israeli, Syrian and US officials had begun preliminary talks in Washington, DC, in November and December, in an attempt to restart negotiations between the two countries.

SYRIAN DOMINANCE IN LEBANON

By aligning itself with the Western powers and the moderate Arab states against Iraq in August 1990, Syria had obtained a free rein to consolidate its interests in Lebanon. In October 1990 it had acted to suppress the revolt led by Gen. Michel Awn (see above) as the first step towards the implementation of the Ta'if agreement. The Ta'if agreement stipulated a formal role for Syrian forces in Lebanon, assigning to them the responsibility for maintaining security there until the various Lebanese militia had been disbanded and the Lebanese army could itself assume that role. The implementation of the Ta'if agreement accelerated in the aftermath of Iraq's military defeat by the US-led multinational force in February 1991, and it culminated in the signing, in May, of a treaty of 'fraternity, co-operation and co-ordination' between Syria and Lebanon.

In late May 1992 there was international concern at the escalating tension between Israel and Syria, as expressed in southern Lebanon. Syria feared that the USA might permit Israel to undermine, through military action, the implementation of the Ta'if agreement. The possibility of direct conflict between Syrian and Israeli armed forces arose from Syria's decision to allow Hezbollah fighters to continue to mount attacks on northern Israeli settlements, in the belief that only by continued coercion would Israel withdraw from occupied Arab territories. It is widely recognized that Syria has used its ability to control the supply of Iranian arms to Hezbollah in order to raise, or reduce, pressure on the Israeli Government in the context of the Middle East peace process. By the same token, the Israeli Government cited attacks by Hezbollah fighters in justification of its refusal to comply with UN Security Council Resolution 425 and withdraw its armed forces from the southern Lebanese 'buffer zone'. In July 1993 Israeli armed forces launched their most intense offensive against the positions of Hezbollah and other guerrilla factions in southern Lebanon since 'Operation Peace for Galilee' in 1982. Israeli aircraft were also reported to have attacked the positions of Syrian armed forces in the Beka'a valley. Many civilians were killed and more than a quarter of a million Lebanese were forced to flee from their homes. The Israeli Prime Minister, defying strong criticism from the UN and the EU, admitted that the operation, code-named 'Operation Accountability', had been deliberately intended to embarrass the Lebanese and Syrian Governments and to persuade them to stop their territory being used against Israel and Israel's so-called 'security zone' in southern Lebanon. Mediation by the USA and Syria produced an informal 'understanding' between Israel and Hezbollah under which fighting was to be confined to the southern 'security zone'. However, Hezbollah continued to strike at Israeli targets, provoking Israeli reprisals. In February 1994 four Israeli soldiers were killed by Hezbollah fighters in the 'buffer zone'. In May the leader of an Islamic resistance group was abducted by Israeli forces, and on 21 June, following an ambush by the Hezbollah in which three Israeli soldiers were killed, the Israeli forces conducted air raids over the 'buffer zone' and in the Beka'a valley close to the Syrian border. In October, after Israel attacked the southern Lebanese village of Nabatiyah killing seven civilians, Hezbollah launched rocket attacks on targets in northern and western Israel. In March 1995, after Hezbollah leader, Rida Yasin was assassinated by Israeli forces, fierce fighting erupted as Hezbollah fighters attacked Israeli military targets in the 'security zone' and fired rockets into Galilee. After the death of three children in an Israeli attack on Nabatiyah in July Hezbollah retaliated with further rocket attacks on settlements in northern Israel. In August Israel launched air and artillery attacks against Hezbollah strongholds during which heavy casualties were reported. Israel continued to blame Syria for not restraining Hezbollah.

In April 1996, little more than a month before the Israeli general elections, there was a new escalation in the conflict in southern Lebanon. After Hezbollah fighters fired rockets into northern Israel wounding 36 people, and killed an Israeli soldier in the security zone, Prime Minister Peres launched 'Operation Grapes of Wrath' during which, for almost two weeks, Israel attacked targets in the southern part of the 'security zone', the Beka'a valley and for the first time in 14 years the southern suburbs of Beirut. The massive bombardment resulted in many civilian casualties, and in the most serious incident more than 100 Lebanese civilians, who had taken refuge in the UN base at Qana, near Tyre, were killed when the base was hit by Israeli artillery fire. The Israeli air and artillery attacks provoked another exodus of refugees from southern Lebanon. However the Israeli bombardment failed to stop Hezbollah's rocket attacks on targets in northern Israel, and neither the Lebanese nor the Syrian Government yielded to Israeli and US demands. In the face of international pressure to bring about a cease-fire, US

Secretary of State Warren Christopher turned to Syria as the main power broker in Lebanon to resolve the crisis. After a week of shuttle diplomacy by Secretary of State Christopher between Jerusalem, Damascus and Beirut, a cease-fire agreement was reached, under which Hezbollah agreed to end its rocket attacks on settlements in northern Israel, but could still attack Israeli military targets inside the 'security zone'. Less than a month after the accord, Syria accused Israel of violating the cease-fire agreement after a Lebanese civilian was wounded in clashes between Israeli forces and Hezbollah in the security zone. Under the agreement both sides had pledged not to attack civilians but Israel claimed once again that Hezbollah units had sheltered in civilian areas. In late July 1996 representatives from Syria, Lebanon, Israel, the USA and France attended the first meeting of the international committee set up to monitor the cease-fire agreement.

In late March 1992 some Syrian armed forces began to withdraw from Beirut, in preparation for the withdrawal of all Syrian armed forces to eastern Lebanon by September 1992 (in accordance with the Ta'if agreement). However, Syrian influence on Lebanese internal affairs remained pervasive and was regarded by some observers as having contributed to the resignation of the Lebanese Government on 6 May. The former Lebanese Prime Minister, Omar Karami, alleged that, had it not been for Lebanon's close relations with Syria, Western economic aid to Lebanon would have been more substantial, and the economic crisis that had led to his Government's resignation less severe.

The decision of the new Lebanese Government to hold elections to the National Assembly in August and September 1992, before the redeployment of Syrian armed forces to eastern Lebanon had taken place, attracted strong criticism both in Lebanon and abroad. Lebanese Maronites and other Christian groups, and Western governments argued that the continued presence of the Syrian forces would prejudice the outcome of the elections. However, the Lebanese Government argued that its own army was still unable to guarantee the country's security in the absence of the Syrian armed forces, and that the timetable for elections, as stipulated by the Ta'if agreement, should be observed. Syria claimed that the continued presence of its forces did not contravene the Ta'if agreement, which allowed for them to remain to assist the Lebanese Government until constitutional reforms had been fully implemented. There was no doubt, however, that the electoral process had been severely compromised in the eyes of Christian, especially Maronite, Lebanese. In many Maronite constituencies the participation of the electorate was very low, although there was not—as some Maronite leaders urged—a total boycott. Other Maronite leaders adopted a more pragmatic approach, acknowledging Syria's domination of Lebanon as a *fait accompli*. However, more than six years after the Ta'if agreement, some 30,000–35,000 Syrian troops remained in Lebanon occupying highly visible positions in the capital, Beirut, and elsewhere. No decision of any importance is taken by the Lebanese Government without the agreement of the Syrian regime, resulting in regular visits by Lebanese officials to Damascus. Some analysts maintained that in order to ensure a key role for Syria in the Middle East, President Assad had strengthened his grip on Lebanon. To that end the Syrian President had, in October 1995, given his support to the Lebanese Prime Minister's proposal to extend Lebanese President Hrawi's term of office by another three years, a change subsequently approved by 110 of the 128 Lebanese deputies in the National Assembly. Parliamentary elections held in mid-1996 produced an Assembly dominated by pro-Syrian supporters of Prime Minister Hariri. The largely Christian opposition parties had little success, and there were allegations of vote-rigging. During the elections Syria redeployed an estimated 10,000–12,000 of its troops from Lebanon to more secure positions in Syria amidst speculation that Damascus feared Israeli attacks. In September the Commander of the Israeli-backed South Lebanon Army, General Antoine Lahd, suggested that Israel might carry out a unilateral withdrawal from southern Lebanon but would hold Syria responsible for any new attacks on northern Israel. Shortly before, the Israeli Prime Minister had put forward a similar proposal which had been immediately rejected by Syria (see above). In mid-December a bus carrying Syrian workers was attacked in a predominantly Christian area prompting swift action by the Lebanese authorities who arrested some 50 government opponents, although most of them were subsequently released. In response to the attack the Syrian Vice-President, Abd al-Halim Khaddam, accused Lebanese opposition leaders of conspiring with Israel against Syria.

During his visit to Lebanon in May 1997 Pope John Paul II called for the reconciliation of Christians and Muslims and for Lebanon's complete independence, voicing regret at the presence of non-Lebanese forces on Lebanese territory, but refraining from mentioning Syria or Israel. Lebanon's Constitutional Court overturned the results of the 1996 elections to four parliamentary seats, and accused Syria of intimidating voters. The defeated Maronite Christian candidate for one of the seats, Mikhael Daher, claimed that, at the request of President Hrawi, Syrian intelligence officers had arrested and abused voters in order to coerce them to vote for his opponent, the Minister of Culture and Higher Education, Fawzi Habish. The 1996 elections were described as the most corrupt in Lebanese history by the independent monitoring group, the Lebanese Association for the Democracy of Elections. Also in 1997 the Washington-based Human Rights Watch accused Syrian forces of seizing over 100 Lebanese and Palestinians in Lebanon and holding them in Syria. It called on the Lebanese President and Prime Minister publicly to condemn such abuses of human rights and for Syrian forces to be held accountable for crimes that they committed in Lebanon. In August fighting again escalated in southern Lebanon between Syrian-backed Hezbollah guerrillas and Israeli troops supporting the SLA. The rising death toll among Israeli soldiers in Israel's self-declared 'security zone' led to renewed calls within Israel for a unilateral withdrawal of its forces from Lebanon. Syrian support for Hezbollah in southern Lebanon remained part of a strategy by Damascus to put pressure on Israel to withdraw from the Golan Heights. In August the head of the Maronite Church, Cardinal Nasrallah Pierre Sfeir, an outspoken critic of the Syrian presence in Lebanon, stated that Damascus was interfering in every aspect of life and undermining the country's right to self-determination. Responding to Cardinal Sfeir's comments, the Lebanese Prime Minister, Rafik Hariri, repeated that the Syrian presence was necessary to guarantee domestic security and was in accordance with the 1989 Ta'if agreement. In September the US Secretary of State, Madeleine Albright, visited Beirut and pledged to support a 'free and democratic sovereign Lebanon', a comment which was interpreted as a reference to Syria's control over the country's internal and external affairs. Some days earlier Albright was reported to have annoyed President Assad by refusing to discuss Lebanese affairs during her talks with him in Damascus.

At the beginning of April 1998 the Lebanese and Syrian Governments rejected an offer by Israel to withdraw from its 'security zone' in southern Lebanon on the provision that there were adequate security guarantees for its northern border. Damascus dismissed the proposal as propaganda designed by the Netanyahu government to improve Israel's image in the West. At the same time, Israel's request for direct negotiations with Lebanon concerning security issues in southern Lebanon led Damascus to suspect that the Israeli authorities were seeking to undermine Syrian dominance in Lebanon. In July it was reported that President Assad was planning to visit Beirut later in that year. It would be his first visit to Lebanon since civil war broke out in 1976 and would represent a break with protocol, as it had become usual practice for Lebanese leaders to go to Damascus to receive their instructions.

FOREIGN RELATIONS SINCE 1995

Throughout 1995 Syria's relations with the USA were dominated by the US-sponsored peace negotiations with Israel (see above), with the Syrian official press praising the USA for its 'remarkable efforts' to achieve a just and comprehensive peace in the region. However, in August, after reports that the Damascus office of Hamas had threatened to attack US interests, the USA urged Syria to make every effort to prevent Syrian-based Palestinian groups opposed to the peace process from carrying out any such attack. Syria denied that any of these groups was planning to carry out 'military acts' against US targets. The expulsion of the Palestinian 'rejectionist' groups from its territory is believed to be the key prerequisite for Syria's removal from the US list of countries which sponsor terrorism. In early 1996 relations between the two countries deteriorated. The USA blamed the collapse of peace negotiations between Syria and Israel on President Assad's intransigence, and the US Department of State became increasingly exasperated with the Syrian regime as it attempted to broker a cease-fire in southern Lebanon. US officials began to question the priority given to Syria in US Middle East diplomacy, remarking that since 1993 Secretary of State Christopher had made 24 visits to Damascus, compared with six to Paris, two to Mexico and only one to China. There were demands from some members of both the US Senate and the US Congress to increase the pressure on Syria and a suggestion that, in the light of its continued support for terrorists and its intransigence in the peace negotiations, new sanctions might be imposed on it. Prospects for Middle East peace declined dramatically after the right-wing victory in the Israeli elections in May 1996 and Syria appealed to the USA to abandon its pro-Israeli bias in favour of a more balanced approach towards the peace process. However, although the US special envoy visited Syria in July the Syrian peace track remained deadlocked. US allegations of Syrian involvement in the bomb attack on a US military base in Saudi Arabia in June 1996 placed renewed strain on Syria's relations with the USA. In September 1997, during her first visit to the region, the US Secretary of State, Madeleine Albright, held talks in Damascus with President Assad. In mid-December the US Assistant Secretary of State for Near and South Asian Affairs, Martin Indyk, also met the Syrian leader. By the end of the year Washington appeared to have persuaded Syria to begin talks with Israel towards establishing a basis for the resumption of bilateral negotiations. In November 1997 efforts by Damascus to combat drugs production and trafficking in Lebanon's Beka'a valley, which was largely controlled by the Syrian army, were rewarded when President Clinton removed both Lebanon and Syria from the list of states allegedly producing or trafficking in illegal drugs. However, as long as Syria continues to support Hezbollah in southern Lebanon, it is likely to remain on the US list of countries which sponsor terrorism. Efforts by the Syrian Government to involve the EU in the peace negotiations with Israel, in order to counterbalance the USA's role, met with little success, although Syria was invited to participate in the first Euro-Mediterranean conference held in Barcelona, Spain, in November 1995. During the conference Syria's Minister of Foreign Affairs, Farouk ash-Shara, clashed with his Israeli counterpart over the Nuclear Non-proliferation Treaty. Syria continued to press for greater EU involvement in the Middle East peace process and in particular welcomed France's efforts to bring about a cease-fire in Lebanon after renewed fighting between Hezbollah and Israeli forces in April 1996, although it recognized that French influence was likely to be modest compared with that of the USA. The French foreign minister visited Damascus in July and his Syrian counterpart made several visits to Paris. In October 1996 President Chirac visited Damascus and announced the rescheduling of some 1,900m. French francs of debt arrears owed to France. In late 1997 Israeli officials visited Paris for talks with the French Government regarding the resumption of peace negotiations with Syria, and in November 1997 and January 1998 the French Minister of Foreign Affairs, Hubert Védrine, held talks in Damascus. In mid-July 1998 President Assad made a state visit to France, the first time that the Syrian leader had ventured outside the Middle East since 1976, with the exception of his meetings in Geneva with President Carter and President Clinton. Assad was accompanied by senior economic officials but the focus of his discussions with President Chirac was expected to be the stalled Middle East peace process. France supported Syria's rejection of Israel's proposal in April to withdraw from its 'security zone' in southern Lebanon. In November 1997 Jacques Poos, the Minister of Foreign Affairs of Luxembourg and leader of an EU mission to the Middle East, met President Assad in Damascus and indicated that the EU supported Syria's demand that Israel withdraw completely from the Golan Heights. Following a visit to Damascus in October 1997 by Manuel Marín, a Vice-President of the European Commission, Syria indicated that it was prepared to enter negotiations towards establishing a free-trade association agreement with the EU. At the end of 1997 Russia also joined diplomatic efforts to restart peace negotiations between Syria and Israel. The Russian Deputy Minister of Foreign Affairs, Viktor Posvalyuk, held talks in Damascus and Jerusalem in December 1997, but angered Israelis by supporting Syria's position that negotiations should begin at the point where they were broken off in February 1996 (see above). There were visits to Damascus by a number of senior Russian officials in early 1998, and the Syrian-Russian committee, which had been set up in 1993 to co-ordinate relations between the two countries, held its first meeting. There was speculation that the strong links that had existed between Damascus and Moscow during the Soviet era were being re-established and that a major arms deal with Russia might follow. There were reports that President Assad planned to visit Moscow later in the year. In March 1998 the President of Belarus, Alyaksandr Lukashenka, accompanied by his Minister of Defence, Alyaksandr Chumakou, visited Damascus, where they concluded a military agreement under which Belarus will help Syria to modernize its weapons systems and service the army's Soviet-manufactured equipment.

Following a meeting of the Syrian, Iranian and Turkish Ministers of Foreign Affairs in Teheran in September 1995, a statement was issued reaffirming their commitment to the territorial integrity of Iraq and warning against foreign interference in Iraq's internal affairs. Although Syria has become a centre for elements of the Iraqi opposition, the Syrian regime is concerned that the disintegration of Iraq could set a dangerous precedent for its own minorities and also fears that Saddam Hussein might be replaced by a pro-Western regime. In November 1995 the Syrian Minister of Foreign Affairs accused Israel of trying to destroy Iraq by plotting its division into Kurdish, Sunni and Shi'a regions. It was alleged that President Assad had conducted a clandestine meeting with the Iraqi President, Saddam Hussain, on the Syrian-Iraqi border in May 1996 to discuss common issues including Turkey's military agreement with Israel, although some sources maintained that the meeting was only attended by their representatives. In May 1997 an economic delegation from Syria, including the Chairman of the Federation of Syrian Chambers of Commerce, visited Baghdad for talks with the Iraqi trade minister, Muhammad Mahdi Salih, about securing contracts for Syrian exports to Iraq following implementation of the UN 'oil-for-food' agreement. A large Iraqi trade delegation, led by the head of the Baghdad Chamber of Commerce, visited Damascus the following month. Commenting on the visit, the Syrian Vice-President, Abd al-Halim Khaddam, stated that his Government's decision to reopen trade links with Baghdad, after an interlude of 18 years, was largely due to concern that Turkey was seeking to monopolize trade with Iraq in order to impose its economic domination over the country. However, it seemed more likely that the decision was influenced by Syria's concern about Turkey's military co-operation with Israel and Ankara's military operations against the Kurdish Workers' Party (PKK) in northern Iraq. On 2 June border crossings between the two countries were reopened, and each country closed down radio stations that had been broadcasting propaganda against the other since the late 1970s. By September 1997 several large contracts for Syrian exports of food and medical supplies to Iraq had been signed, and it was agreed that the Syrian ports of Tartous and Latakia would receive goods in transit for Iraq. Baghdad was also reported to have requested that Syria reopen the oil pipeline linking Iraq's Kirkuk oilfields to the Mediterranean terminal of Banias in Syria, which had been closed since 1982. At the end of 1997, as tension mounted between Baghdad and Washington, the Iraqi Deputy Prime Minister, Tareq Aziz, was received in Damascus by the Syrian Minister of Foreign Affairs, Farouk ash-Shara, the first public meeting between senior ministers of the two countries for 17 years. After the meeting there were reports that ash-Shara had gone to Riyadh with a letter from President Assad to King Fahd, setting out proposals for reintegrating Iraq into the Arab fold. In early February 1998, when the US sought regional support for renewed air strikes against Iraq, Syria strongly opposed such action. To emphasize this point, President Assad received the Iraqi Minister of Foreign Affairs in Damascus on 10 February, the first time that he had met publicly with a senior Iraqi official since the early 1980s. At the end of March 1998 the Syrian Minister of Health, Iyad ash-Shatti, became the first Syrian minister to visit Baghdad for almost 20 years.

Relations with Iran deteriorated in late 1995 after the Syrian regime voiced support for the UAE in its dispute with Teheran over Abu Musa and the Greater and Lesser Tunbs. In protest, Hassan Habibi, an Iranian Vice-President, and the Iranian Minister of Foreign Affairs cancelled a visit to Damascus, and there were attacks on Syria in the Iranian press. Since Iraq's invasion of Kuwait in 1990 Syria has continued to strengthen its links with Saudi Arabia and the Gulf states, while assuring Teheran that it is still committed to maintaining the 'strategic' relationship with Iran. There were signs of an improvement in relations with Iran in February 1996 when a joint committee to co-ordinate co-operation between the two countries was set up. A little later, when Syria expressed support for the Bahrain Government, it was careful to avoid any reference to alleged Iranian involvement in the unrest on Abu Musa. In August 1996 a Syrian delegation, led by the Prime Minister, met senior Iranian government officials in Teheran. During this visit, President Rafsanjani called for closer links between the two countries to confront the threat posed by the USA and Israel. There were further talks about economic co-operation, including a number of joint projects. In July 1997 President Assad visited Teheran. However, there were reports that Syrian interest in a triple alliance with Iran and Iraq, to counter growing military co-operation between Israel, Turkey and the USA, had not met with a positive response from Iranian officials, owing to continuing tensions between Iran and Iraq. Nevertheless, relations between Damascus and Teheran remained friendly.

Syria's relations with Turkey remained strained owing to continuing disagreements over cross-border water supplies, and over the Kurds. Although the two countries have a provisional accord for sharing water from the Euphrates river, whereby Turkey allows a flow of 500 cu m/second of water into Syria, they have failed to conclude a permanent accord, and both Syria and Iraq are concerned that new dam projects in Turkey, especially the Birecik dam, will reduce the volume of Euphrates water downstream. Both Syria and Iraq have also blamed Turkey for increased pollution levels in the water they receive. At the end of 1995 Syria retaliated by announcing that it would reduce the water supply to Turkey from the Orontes river. Syria also used its support for the rebel PKK to put pressure on its powerful neighbour. The PKK is known to have bases in the Syrian controlled Beka'a valley in Lebanon, and at the end of 1995 Kurdish fighters crossed the Turkish border from Syria and attacked Turkish military targets on several occasions. In February 1996 Turkey accused the Syrian Government of giving refuge to the PKK leader, Abdullah Ocalan, and demanded his extradition to Turkey. Relations between the two countries deteriorated sharply in April 1996 after an Israeli television broadcast revealed that Turkey and Israel had signed a military accord earlier in the year allowing the Israeli air force to use Turkish military airfields for training purposes. The Syrian press denounced the treaty, declaring that Israel had extended its 'zone militaire' to the borders of Iran and warning that Turkey would be better advised to respect its historical links with the Arab world. In mid-April, the Turkish Prime Minister, Mesut Yilmaz travelled to the frontier province of Hatay, the former *sanjak* of Alexandretta ceded by France to Turkey in 1939 and still claimed by Syria, where he urged President Assad to stop criticizing the military accord with Israel and Turkey's control over the regulation of Euphrates water. Two days later, the Turkish Deputy Prime Minister, Nahib Mentese, intensified the verbal conflict by accusing the Syrian Baathists of never abandoning their ambitions to create a 'Greater Syria' and promising to retaliate with force if they ever tried to reconquer the province of Hatay. He also denounced Syria's support for the PKK. Syria interpreted these threats as part of an Israeli-US attempt to pressurize the Syrian regime into being more accommodating and conceding Israeli demands in the peace negotiations. The crisis between Syria and Turkey was aggravated at the end of April when Turkey temporarily closed the flood gates of the Euphrates dams for 'technical reasons', resulting in water rationing in Damascus on the eve of the festival of Id al-Adha and provoking widespread concern in the Arab world. When a series of small bombs exploded in Syrian cities in May there was speculation that the Turkish Government might be responsible and that they were in response to Syria's support for the PKK separatist guerrillas, particularly as one of the attacks was reportedly made on the apartment of the PKK leader in Damascus. Although the Syrian Government denied that the bomb attacks had taken place, it was reported to have arrested several hundred ethnic Turks in retaliation. The Turkish media blamed Syria's banned Muslim Brotherhood for the explosions. Some commentators argued that the military accord between Turkey and Israel was part of an emerging strategic partnership in the Middle East (to replace the Middle East peace process) involving an alliance of Turkey, the USA, Israel and Jordan in order to form a military front against those states in the region perceived as enemies of the West. The new partnership would leave Syria, increasingly vilified by the USA for its intransigence in the peace negotiations, dangerously isolated. After Turkey's first Islamist-led Government took office in July 1996, the Syrian ambassador to Ankara was one of the first envoys to visit the new Turkish Prime Minister, Necmettin Erbakan. Whilst in opposition, Erbakan's Refah party had strongly criticized Turkey's military accord with Israel and had urged closer relations with neighbouring Arab and Muslim countries. Once in government, Erbakan did indicate his desire for a political solution to the dispute with the PKK but pressure from the military caused him to revert to the official line, condemning PKK terrorism. In addition, military co-operation with Israel was expanded, again at the insistence of the military, which regarded the accord as a means of exerting pressure on Syria for its support of the PKK. Relations with Turkey deteriorated once again in May 1997, when it launched another military operation against PKK bases in northern Iraq. It was reported that Syria mobilized troops on its border with Turkey and called on Ankara to withdraw its forces from Iraq. Also in May the Turkish authorities accused Syria of helping Kurdish dissidents to set up television transmitters along the border with Turkey so that Kurds living in south-eastern Anatolia could receive programmes broadcast by the pro-PKK Kurdish-language channel, MED-TV. During a meeting of the Organization of the Islamic Conference in Teheran in early December, at which Turkey faced implicit criticism for its military co-operation with Israel, the Syrian Minister of Foreign Affairs, Farouk ash-Shara, stated that Ankara had agreed not to renew its agreement with Israel. This was later denied by Turkish officials.

The election of a right-wing Government in Israel at the end of May 1996 resulted in closer contacts between Syria, Egypt, Jordan and the PNA. After informal talks between Syria, Egypt and Saudi Arabia, an Arab League summit was convened in Cairo at the end of June. Although Syria's more militant proposals, including a 'freeze' on existing relations with Israel and the reintroduction of the Arab economic boycott of Israel, were opposed by the moderate Arab states, the summit was widely seen as a success for Syria. The final communiqué stated that existing steps taken towards conciliation with Israel would be reconsidered in the light of Israeli government policies, and that any agreement was still dependent upon the principle of 'land-for-peace'. Also at the summit, Turkey was urged to reconsider its military agreement with Israel. The Egyptian President, Hosni Mubarak, had condemned this agreement fearing that it would further undermine Egypt's regional role, and had pledged his support for President Assad. In the following months, as hopes for the peace process collapsed, there were regular consultations between Syrian and Egyptian officials. At the Cairo summit King Hussein had accused the Syrian authorities of sponsoring terrorist operations in Jordan in an attempt to destabilize the kingdom. Syria's relations with Jordan had become increasingly acrimonious since Jordan signed a separate peace agreement with Israel in 1994, and Syrian officials claimed that Jordan was working with Israel and Turkey to undermine President Assad's regime. However, after direct talks between King Hussein and President Assad at the summit, relations between the two countries were reported to have improved, and in August the King met Assad again in Damascus—his first visit to Syria since 1994. Following this visit, the Syrian authorities arrested a number of Palestinians and other Arabs who were alleged to have been implicated in organizing attacks in Jordan or in Israel through Jordan, and the two countries agreed to reopen talks to resolve their differences over the use of water from the Yarmouk river. During the Cairo summit, Mubarak also persuaded Assad to meet the PNA

President, Yasser Arafat. The two men have been bitter rivals for many years and had not met since 1993 when Assad condemned Arafat for signing the Oslo accords, but the meeting improved relations between the two men. One month later Arafat visited Damascus and his foreign affairs adviser, Farouk Kaddoumi, held talks with leaders of Palestinian groups opposed to the Oslo accords which have their headquarters in the Syrian capital. Early in 1997 there were reports that the Syrian authorities had warned the PFLP and other Palestinian groups based in Damascus that if they continued to organize military operations against Israel from Syria their offices would be closed down.

INTERNAL AFFAIRS

In May 1990 elections were held to the People's Assembly, in which the number of seats had been increased from 195 to 250. Candidates representing the Baath Party were elected to 134 seats, 54% of the total, compared with 66% of the total in elections held in 1986. Other parties which had joined the Baath Party in the National Progressive Front, an electoral coalition, were elected to 32 seats, while independent candidates were elected to 84 seats. Some 60% of the electorate were reported to have participated in the elections, which were contested by 9,765 candidates.

There was speculation in late 1991 that President Assad was preparing to introduce a degree of liberalization into Syria's political system, which is widely regarded as one of the most autocratic in the world. In December it was announced that 2,864 political prisoners were to be released. In March 1992, in a speech to the People's Assembly, Assad indicated that new political parties might in future be established in Syria. However, he rejected the adoption by Syria of foreign democratic frameworks as unsuited to the country's level of economic development. In late June a reshuffle of the Council of Ministers took place in which most senior ministers retained their portfolios.

In January 1994 the future stability of the regime appeared to be in jeopardy when Assad's eldest son, Basel, who had been expected to succeed his father as President, died in a motor accident. The President's second son, Bashar, was instructed to take up the role played by his brother in a move to avoid a power struggle. In June the Minister of Electricity, Kamal al-Baba, was dismissed following two years of electricity shortages and power cuts. In August 16 senior officials, including the special forces commander, Ali Haidar, were removed from office in what was considered to be an attempt by Assad to consolidate his position, weaken the influence of the old guard and improve the country's international stance. At the People's Assembly elections held on 24 August more than 7,000 candidates were presented, but turnout at the polls was recorded at just over 50% of the electorate. The coalition parties in the National Progressive Front maintained their dominant position, winning 167 seats; the remaining seats were won by independent candidates. Leading business people were reported to be among the 158 newly-elected members. At the inaugural session of the new Assembly, on 14 November, the Prime Minister announced a programme of major economic reforms.

A team from the UK-based human rights organization, Amnesty International, visited Damascus in October 1994 and in its report, released in April 1995, it concluded that although some attempts had been made to improve human rights in Syria, further reforms were still urgently needed.

In November 1995 rallies were held across the country to mark President Assad's 25 years in power, and some 1,200 political prisoners, including members of the banned Muslim Brotherhood, were released. The Muslim Brotherhood is no longer seen as a threat to the regime and a number of the organizations's leading figures, among them the former Secretary-General, Abd al-Fattah Abu Ghuddah, have been allowed to return from exile. In November 1995 the Minister of Tourism, Amin Abu ash-Shamat, was replaced by Danhu Daoud, a Minister of State. Ash-Shammat was believed to have been dismissed because he had alienated influential figures in the private sector which controls much of the tourist sector. In May 1996 Syrian officials denied reports that a series of bomb explosions had taken place in Damascus, Aleppo and Latakia. Little reliable information emerged on the alleged bombings but there was speculation that the attacks had been carried out by Turkey (see above). However, a Jordanian source claimed that they were part of an army coup involving Sunni Muslim officers supported by the US and Israeli intelligence services. Later that month, Abd al-Majid at-Tarabulsi, the Minister of Awqaf (Islamic Endowments), died and was succeeded by Muhammad Abd ar-Ra'uf Ziyadah. Musallam Muhammad Hawwa was appointed Minister of State for Cabinet Affairs, but rumours of a major cabinet reshuffle, including the replacement of Mahmoud az-Zoubi as premier, proved unfounded. Towards the end of the year there were several reports that President Assad was ill, provoking more speculation about the succession. While the President is believed to be in poor health, there has been no definite confirmation that he has been seriously ill since 1983, when he is thought to have suffered a heart attack. Syrian officials quickly condemned the latest reports as 'malicious lies' aimed at destabilizing the country and stated that the President had undergone minor surgery but was expected to require a long period of convalescence. President Assad has continued to prepare his surviving son, Bashar, for high office but Bashar himself was reported to be reluctant to assume a leading role and it was unclear whether the President really intends him to become his successor. Nevertheless, in the early months of 1997 a poster campaign in support of Bashar appeared in towns and cities throughout the country, and, in a sermon during the festival of Id al-Fitr, the Mufti of Damascus referred to Bashar as his father's successor. The Mufti also acknowledged Bashar's role in heading the Government's campaign against corruption, which is known to be widespread and to involve the President's family, prominent government officials and members of the ruling Baath Party. In early 1997 President Assad's brothers, Jamil and Rifaat, both came under investigation for their business dealings, and, as a result, Jamil was sent into exile in Paris. Earlier, in June 1996, Nadir an-Nabulsi, then Minister of Petroleum and Mineral Wealth, was dismissed after corruption charges were made against him relating to the period when he headed the Al-Furat Petroleum Company. When a bomb exploded on a bus in Damascus at the end of December 1996, killing 11 people and wounding many others, some commentators argued that it may have been related to the Government's anti-corruption drive and the investigations into the business affairs of the President's family. Others thought that it was probably the work of Lebanese opposition groups (see above). Few details were released about the incident but an official statement accused Israel of responsibility for the attack. Towards the end of 1997 there were reports that Bashar, newly appointed to the rank of lieutenant-colonel in the army, had been given new responsibilities in economic policy-making, notably in the promotion of privatization and foreign investment, in addition to heading the campaign against corruption and overseeing Syrian interests in Lebanon, especially contacts with the Maronite Christian community, although he still had no specific political post. Speculation continued concerning the possibility that Bashar would succeed his father as President. Some analysts argued that President Assad was not preparing his son for the presidency but was seeking to strengthen Bashar's position so that he could protect the interests of the Assad family after his death. At the same time it was reported that, as a result of divisions within the Assad regime, the authorities had decided not to continue with negotiations with the exiled leadership of the Syrian branch of the Muslim Brotherhood. The reports indicated that the rehabilitation of the Brotherhood, although favoured by Vice-President Abd al-Halim Khaddam in order to promote national unity against Israel, was opposed by senior members of the security forces. In early 1998 President Assad dismissed his brother Rifaat from his position as one of Syria's three Vice-Presidents, a post which he had held since 1984. For much of this period, however, Rifaat had been out of favour and living in exile, but he had been allowed to return to Syria in 1992 for the funeral of his mother and had remained in the country. There were reports that Rifaat and his son Sawmar had recently become more active in politics and business and that Rifaat still enjoyed a measure of popularity with some sections of the armed forces. This may explain President Assad's decision to remove him. In early July Maj.-Gen. Hikmat ash-Shehabi retired as Chief of Staff of the Armed Forces, a post that he had held since 1973. He was replaced by his deputy, Maj.-Gen. Ali Aslan. There was speculation that ash-Shehabi, for many years a close associate of President Assad, might be appointed Vice-President. At the same time the head of the General Intelligence Directorate, Bashar an-Najjar, was dismissed from his post for unspecified irregularities and replaced by Gen. Mahmoud ash-Shaqqa, a former chief of military intelligence in the Quneitra region and commander of the Syrian troops sent to Saudi Arabia during the 1991 Gulf War. Some commentators interpreted these changes as the prelude to the appointment of Bashar Assad to a senior political post and a cabinet reshuffle that would bring younger people committed to economic reform into the Government. In mid-June 1998 there were press reports that some 225 political prisoners had been released since the beginning of the month, including leading members of the Syrian branch of the Muslim Brotherhood, communists and associates of Salah Jadid, the leader of the civilian branch of the Baath party ousted from power by Assad in 1970.

Economy

Revised for this edition by ALAN J. DAY

The Syrian economy must be viewed against a background of regional geopolitics and the internal political developments that have taken place since the Baath Party came to power in 1963. As a 'confrontation state', a portion of whose land has been under Israeli occupation since 1967, Syria bears a heavy burden of defence expenditure, which consumes more than one-half of current spending under the annual budget. At the same time, its position as a regional power has encouraged Syria to intervene elsewhere in the area, notably in Lebanon, where it has had a costly military presence since 1976. The continuing involvement in Lebanon, combined with the threat of outright war with Israel and the history of bad relations with neighbouring Iraq (which have, in turn, influenced relations with the moderate Arab states of the Persian (Arabian) Gulf), all affect the Syrian economy. In 1976–77, for example, Iraq decided to stop pumping petroleum through Syria to the Mediterranean coast, thus depriving the Government in Damascus of valuable transit revenues and the benefits of easily accessible petroleum supplies at a favourable price. The pipeline was closed again in 1982, but Syria was subsequently able to buy oil from Iran at concessionary rates. (An agreement to reopen the pipeline was reached between Syria and Iraq in July 1998.)

The internal political upheavals of the past three decades have also profoundly affected the Syrian economy and disrupted attempts at sustained development. During the three-year union with Egypt (the United Arab Republic—UAR) from 1958 to 1961, agrarian reform and nationalization were introduced. The country's first Five-Year Plan was inaugurated during the union, and covered the period 1961–65. The nationalization programme was reversed after the dissolution of the union, and the land reform law was amended in favour of the landowners. However, in June 1963, following the Baath-dominated coup, all amendments to the agrarian reform law were abrogated, and the law itself was made even stricter. The banks were nationalized in that year, and a rigorous nationalization of industry and trade was begun in 1965. By the time that Hafiz al-Assad seized power in November 1970, there had been a radical transformation of the country's economic structure, with the economic power of the landowners, merchants and industrialists greatly weakened, and the public sector dominant.

President Assad relaxed the economy somewhat after coming to power, partly in an attempt to widen his power base: he introduced some liberalization of foreign trade early in his presidency; a foreign investment law was promulgated in 1971; and this was followed by several related articles of legislation.

The Arab–Israeli war of October 1973 caused damage to Syria estimated at $1,800m. Latakia port, the Banias and Tartous oil terminals and the huge Homs complex in central Syria, which then housed the country's only petroleum refinery and generated more than 40% of its power needs, were virtually destroyed. The reconstruction effort necessary to restore the Syrian economy was immense, but the Government acted swiftly, introducing measures of economic liberalization, to encourage investment, in early 1974. Business confidence gradually began to return, to the extent that the third Development Plan (1971–75) ended with a flourish of unprecedented growth. This, in turn, prompted the Government to reinforce investment incentives in certain sectors and to initiate an ambitious fourth Development Plan for the period 1976–80, only to find itself confronted, once again, with the economic repercussions of regional political problems.

The fifth Development Plan (1981–85) and its successor (1986–90) concentrated on trying to finish projects already under way rather than launching ambitious new schemes. The growth targets set by the fifth Plan were noticeably more modest than those in the fourth, but even these were not achieved.

In the late 1980s, the economy was in a state of crisis, with the population suffering increasing hardship. According to the IMF, Syria's total reserves minus gold in mid-1986 stood at only $10m., although by the end of 1987 reserves had risen to $223m., the highest end-of-year total since 1984. At the end of 1988 reserves of foreign exchange amounted to $191m. The scarcity of foreign exchange caused a shortage of spare parts and raw materials for industry, and production was substantially below capacity, with some factories ceasing production altogether. Corruption and mismanagement in the state industrial and agricultural sectors also affected output. The economic crisis led to the imposition of strict curbs on the 'black market' and on the issuing of import licences, which created difficulties for the private sector.

Budget expenditure was reduced in real terms during the late 1980s, and zero or negative economic growth rates were recorded from 1986 to 1988. According to World Bank estimates, Syria's GNP per head in 1996 was $1,160, having increased in real terms at an average rate of 4.3% per year since 1990. Official statistics gave Syria's 1996 GDP as £S655,124m. at current prices.

In the absence of a Middle East peace settlement, Syria's best hope for economic progress lies in diversification of its sources of development finance and export revenues and in improved economic management to restore confidence in investment. The 1980 friendship treaty with the USSR and Syria's alleged links with international terrorism affected US aid to the country. In 1983 such aid was halted altogether. Syria's alleged involvement in international terrorism also affected the flow of aid from the EC and from individual European countries. Lending by multinational institutions, meanwhile, has been hampered by the slow rate of project implementation and, more recently, by Syria's debt arrears. Syria does, however, enjoy considerable support from the various Arab aid organizations.

Participation in the US-led multinational force against Iraq in 1990/91 was calculated to increase Syria's access to aid from the USA, the EC and the 'moderate' Arab states, among other diplomatic benefits. In the event, Syria was widely regarded as the main regional beneficiary of the war, particularly in the economic sphere. Bolstered by higher world oil prices, GDP grew by more than 5% in real terms in 1991 and the trade balance went into healthy surplus. At the same time there was a major influx of aid from various sources, while economic deregulation and new tax incentives helped to stimulate private investment by local and foreign businesses. On the negative side, the collapse of the USSR in 1991 presaged economic problems for Syria, to the extent that large sectors of its economy had been oriented towards exporting low-quality goods to the USSR.

Syria's leading exports remain petroleum, cotton and phosphates, which depend on the fickle world commodity markets and, in the case of cotton, on agricultural policies and the unreliable rainfall in much of the country. The services sector,

dependent on tourism and transit trade, remains extremely vulnerable to the political situation in the region.

In the first half of the 1990s, the main constraints on Syria's economic development were the poor condition of much of the physical infrastructure and the inefficient administration within highly centralized public-sector organizations. The disbursal of available funding for important public-sector projects was frequently delayed for long periods by procedural obstacles, while the financing of some private-sector projects was greatly complicated by Syria's complex foreign-exchange rules and limited banking services. Despite these and other impediments, the rate of real economic growth was estimated to have averaged 6% per annum over the five year period 1991-95. Over the same period Syria received about $2,500m. of project aid from abroad (including $855m. of loans from the Kuwait Fund for Arab Economic Development (KFAED)) and obtained provisional offers of up to $1,000m. of additional aid for proposed future projects. According to official figures, real economic growth slowed to 2.2% in 1996, and trade figures published for the first half of 1997 suggested a further decline in the growth rate for that year.

Japan's Overseas Economic Co-operation Fund lent more than $800m. between 1991 and 1995 for power generation projects. However, US aid to Syria (halted for political reasons in 1983) remained suspended, while Syria's access to up to $472m of EU aid funds was largely blocked because of disputes over Syria's debt arrears to certain EU member states. (At the end of 1995 only ECU 7.9m. in grants – for banking reforms and electricity sector management – had been extended to Syria under current EU aid protocols covering a total of ECU354m., the bulk of this total being European Investment Bank funding blocked by the freeze on new EU lending to Syria.) The Arab donors which provided the bulk of project aid to Syria in 1991-95 included the national development funds of Kuwait, Saudi Arabia and Abu Dhabi and various Gulf-based multilateral agencies, notably the Arab Petroleum Investments Corpn and the Arab Fund for Economic and Social Development. As well as extending development aid, Saudi Arabia reportedly provided substantial financial backing for Syrian purchases of Russian weapons after the 1990/91 Gulf crisis.

In September 1997 Syria made its largest ever single repayment of foreign debt, having reached an agreement with the World Bank to settle arrears accumulated since the 1980s (see below under Finance). An important bilateral debt settlement agreement had earlier been negotiated with France, bringing Syria closer to an unblocking of multilateral EU funds (In mid-1998 Germany was the only EU member with an unresolved Syrian debt dispute). At that time, the US legislature voted to curb the US President's discretionary powers, under a 1996 law, on the regulation of US companies' conducting business with countries accused of sponsoring international terrorism. As a result, such companies faced an increased risk of sanctions under US law. The pace of economic reform and government decision-making within Syria remained chronically slow in 1996 and 1997, prompting public criticism from several quarters. In April 1997 the Arab Fund for Social and Economic Development made it clear that Syria could not expect long-standing offers of project aid to be held open indefinitely. In the same month prominent members of the Syrian business community estimated that projects worth up to $1,300m. had been lost in recent years because prospective Arab investors had encountered severe difficulty conducting business in Syria.

AREA AND POPULATION

Syria covers an area of 185,180 sq km (71,498 sq miles), of which about 45% is considered to be arable land. The remainder consists of bare mountain, desert and pastures capable of sustaining only nomadic populations. Of the total cultivable area of 8.7m. ha, little more than about 70% is under cultivation. The average annual increase in Syria's population between 1980 and 1990 was estimated to be 3.6%. Census totals in September 1970, September 1981 and September 1994 were 6,304,685, 9,052,628 and 13,812,284 respectively. By mid-1996, according to official estimates, the population had increased to 14,619,000.

There has been a continuing movement from village to town. In 1965 about 40% of the population were classified as urban. By 1990 the proportion had risen to 50%. The urban population increased at an annual rate of 4.4% in 1980–90, almost identical to the 4.5% of 1965–80. The process of urbanization has put a strain on services in the cities. One of the achievements of President Assad's regime, however, has been to extend development projects to rural areas, notably through the ambitious rural electrification programme. The population of Damascus and its surrounding province approximately doubled between 1959 and 1973, from more than half a million to an estimated 1.46m. At the census of September 1994 the city had a population of 1,394,322. The population of Aleppo, estimated at 466,026 in 1959, had risen to 1,582,930 by 1994, while Homs had a population of 540,133. The distribution of employment changed markedly between the mid-1960s and the late 1980s, reflecting industrial growth and the expansion of the service sector. In 1989, of a total economically active population of 2,951,100, 23% were employed in agriculture, forestry and fishing, compared with 52% in 1965, while manufacturing and construction employed 28.8% in 1989, compared with 20% in 1965. It was estimated in 1993 that the public sector (excluding the armed forces) employed about 31% of the Syrian labour force, and that the total number of Syrians supported by public-sector employment (including employees' dependants) was approaching 6m.

AGRICULTURE

Agriculture retains its position as a mainstay of the Syrian economy, despite the existence of a traditionally strong trading sector and partially successful attempts at industrialization. The agricultural sector employed about 32% of the economically active population in 1996. The main areas of cultivation form a narrow strip of land along the coast, from the Lebanese to the Turkish frontiers, which enjoys a Mediterranean climate, is exceedingly fertile and produces fruit, olives, tobacco and cotton. East of this strip lies the northward continuation of the Lebanon range of mountains, which falls sharply on the east to the Orontes river valley, whose marshes have been reclaimed to form one of Syria's most fertile areas. In central Syria this valley joins the steppe-plain, about 150 km wide, which runs from the Jordanian borders north-eastward towards the Euphrates valley. The plain is traditionally Syria's major agricultural area, with cereals as the principal crops. Also in this region are the country's main cities, Damascus, Homs, Hama and Aleppo. The importance of this plain is now being rivalled by a fourth area, the Jezira, which lies between the Euphrates in Syria and the Tigris in Iraq. Although fertile lands along the banks of the Euphrates and its tributaries had previously been cultivated, the Jezira's value was recognized only in the early 1950s, when large-scale cotton cultivation was introduced in former pasture lands. It is now vastly increasing its output with the development of the Euphrates Dam, and the Government has made efforts to promote the social and economic development of this previously neglected area.

One of the chief characteristics of Syria's agricultural performance, in the absence of any established large-scale irrigation system, has been an extreme fluctuation in annual output, owing to wide variations in rainfall. Dependence on rainfall for good harvests is illustrated by the Central Bureau of Statistics' general indices for agricultural production, which show fluctuations from 78 in 1979 to 109 in 1983, to 99 in 1984, to 104 in 1985 and to 110 in 1986 (1980 = 100). In 1989 agricultural output by value fell by nearly 20%. By the early 1990s, however, the implementation of irrigation schemes and investment in modern techniques had begun to yield results in the shape of higher and more consistent output, especially of cereal crops. Between 1990 and 1993 the annual value of Syrian agricultural output increased by 27% in real terms, while the agricultural sector's share of GDP rose from 28.5% in 1990 to 30% in 1995. Agriculture was highlighted as the Government's top development priority in a 1994 economic policy statement.

An earlier prolonged decline in agriculture's share of GDP (which had stood at 32.2% in 1962) had stemmed initially from under-use of potential, caused by the discouraging effects of the 1958 agrarian reform law on investment and the removal of the large rural landowners and urban money-lenders who had formerly provided the traditional channels of credit. The area of unused cultivable land (excluding fallow) increased from 1,892,000 ha in 1963 to 2,825,000 ha by 1970. Suspicion of

government intentions was gradually tempered, however, by the relaxation of the reform law and, under the post-1970 Assad administration, by a number of significant amendments. Agriculture, forestry and fishing contributed £S10,935m. to GDP in 1980 and the annual growth rate for this sector was projected at 7.8% under the fifth Five-Year Development Plan (1981–85), which allocated £S17,200m. to its development. Agriculture's share of total investment in the sixth Plan (1986–90) was projected to rise to 18.9%, compared with 16.9% in the fifth Plan. Under the Government's 1992 budget, 26% of investment expenditure was allocated to agriculture and irrigation.

Extensive irrigation programmes, now under way, should eventually have the effect of steadying agricultural output as well as increasing it. It was with this in mind that, out of agricultural investments accounting for a sizeable 35% of total investment under the third Five-Year Plan (1971–75), the Government devoted the largest share to the Euphrates Dam project (see below under Economic Development). The main task for the fourth Development Plan, which ran from 1976 to 1980, was to put the dam's stored waters to work and to irrigate an additional 240,000 ha of land in the Euphrates basin by the end of the decade. However, statistics for 1984 showed that only some 60,000 ha had actually been irrigated, which means that it will be a very long time before the final Euphrates irrigation target of 640,000 ha (which, it was originally intended, would be achieved by the end of the century) is reached. In the mean time, emphasis has been placed not only on the Euphrates, but also on other irrigation schemes, including those on the Yarmouk river (on which three pumping stations and 400 km of canals are being constructed to irrigate about 300 ha of farmland) and in the Ghab, in order to increase the area available for the cultivation of cereals, sugar beet and cotton. In September 1987 Jordan and Syria signed an agreement on the use of the waters of the Yarmouk, whereby the countries undertook to share irrigation systems and the power from a hydroelectricity plant associated with the al-Wahdeh dam, which was to be built on the Yarmouk in Jordan.

With the Euphrates scheme having produced somewhat disappointing results, the Government gave increasing attention to the rain-fed areas, which account for 84% of the total cultivated area. In the southern provinces of Dera'a and Suweidiya a $76.3m. project began in the mid-1980s to increase food production and improve living standards on 25,400 ha of rain-fed land. The project was funded by the World Bank ($22m.), the International Fund for Agricultural Development (IFAD, $18m.), and the UN Development Programme ($2.2m.). Syria has benefited from the presence near Aleppo of the International Centre for Agricultural Research in the Dry Areas (ICARDA), one of the 13 centres throughout the world of the Consultative Group on International Agricultural Research (CGIAR). ICARDA is attempting to improve yields and farming systems in areas of low and medium rainfall throughout the Middle East.

In January 1993 the European Investment Bank agreed to finance the construction of the 65m. cu m Ath-Thawra earthfill dam on the Snobar river, designed to irrigate 10,500 ha of land in the Latakia area. Scheduled for completion in 1994, the project would stimulate cultivation of market-garden crops, mainly for local consumption, and would facilitate tree planting to combat soil erosion. Later in 1993, bids were invited from Western consultants for the redesign of unimplemented irrigation schemes originally drawn up by East European firms in the mid-1980s. The main redesign contract (to be funded by the KFAED) related to a proposed 5-km dam on the Khabour river, which formed part of a scheme to irrigate 40,000 ha of farmland in north-eastern Syria. The unimplemented designs for this scheme had been prepared by a Bulgarian firm in 1985.

Although medium-staple cotton had been grown in Syria for many years, it was the high prices prevalent after the Second World War and during the Korean War that provided the greatest impetus to cotton production. In the early 1950s the previously neglected Jezira area was opened up for large-scale agriculture on a new capital-intensive basis, relatively free from traditional agricultural relations, still semi-feudal in the rest of the country. Syria's output of unginned cotton increased from 38,000 tons in 1949 to 220,800 tons in 1954. The area under cotton increased from 25,300 ha in 1949, to 78,000 ha in 1950 and to 250,000 ha in 1971/72. By 1987/88, this area had declined to 128,000 ha, but in the following year it increased to 165,000 ha, and the area designated for cotton in 1989/90 was 170,000 ha.

Petroleum overtook cotton as Syria's most valuable source of export earnings in 1974, as cotton exports (raw, yarn and textiles) declined, both in value and volume. Output of cotton lint was 200,000–250,000 metric tons per year in 1968–73, but by the 1980/81 season it had declined to 117,800 tons. Production subsequently recovered, and in 1983/84 a record cotton crop of 523,418 tons yielded 194,000 tons of cotton lint, although there was a decline in cotton output, to 125,931 tons of lint in 1986/87. Cotton export earnings rose from £S453m. in 1982 to £S1,076m. in 1984, but dropped to £S391m. in 1986. The 1987/88 crop was affected by bad winter weather, and this, combined with the decrease in area, yielded only 95,000 tons of lint. The 1988/89 crop yielded 116,000 tons of lint, and total cotton production rose to 441,000 tons in 1989/90 and to 555,000 tons in 1990/91. The official prices payable to Syrian farmers for their cotton have been progressively increased in recent years, but the sector has suffered to some extent from competition from other major crops. The local textile industry (historically one of the Syrian economy's leading sectors) uses an appreciable proportion of the cotton crop, averaging about 50,000 tons a year in the early 1990s. Syria's cotton crop totalled 662,000 tons in 1994, 650,000 tons in 1995, 750,000 tons in 1996 and a record 1m. tons in 1997. The volume of ginned cotton reached 350,000 tons in 1997.

One of the crops that has competed with cotton is sugar beet. The Government has been keen to foster a domestic sugar industry, and the area planted with beet rose from 22,000 ha in 1980 to 35,700 ha in 1984. However, the failure of the domestic refining industry to perform as planned has led to a drastic reduction in the beet area, to 13,200 ha in 1986. The harvest of sugar beet declined from 1.3m. tons in 1984 to 412,000 tons in 1985, rising to 440,000 tons the following year. Production rose again, to 457,000 tons, in 1987, but declined to 222,000 tons in 1988. It rose again to 412,000 tons in 1989, to 422,000 tons in 1990 and to 637,000 tons in 1991. In 1992 production reached 1.4m. tons, declining slightly, to 1.2m. tons in 1993, and rising again, to 1.4m. tons, in 1994. Production rose to 1.5m. tons in 1995, then fell sharply to 975,000 tons in 1996 before recovering to 1.1m. tons in 1997. Production of refined sugar by local factories reached a peak of 206,000 tons in 1983 but dropped to 54,000 tons in 1985, rising only marginally to 57,000 tons in the following year. The decline in the sugar industry was partly the result of the fall in the world price of sugar. In the mid-1970s, when Syria started to develop the industry, prices were high, while those of cotton were low. Imports of sugar fluctuated during the 1980s. Those of raw sugar rose from 96,600 tons in 1985 to 261,200 tons in 1986, while those of refined sugar declined from 321,700 tons to 268,200 tons. In 1994 the state sugar refining company anticipated a local beet crop of 1.32m. tons, sufficient to cover 51% of its raw sugar requirement, and planned to import 128,000 tons of raw sugar in order to fulfil its 1994 production target of 260,000 tons of refined sugar (about 48% of current consumption). Construction of a new 129,000 tons-per-year sugar refinery was scheduled to begin in 1995. The Government gave its approval in 1995 to proposals to build Syria's first privately-owned sugar refinery, with an output capacity of 100,000 tons per year. The refinery would be sited at Tartous and would process imported raw sugar.

Syria's cereal crop is also of prime importance, accounting in 1993 for nearly 80% of the £S45,000m. spent on crop purchases by the agricultural marketing authorities. Wheat and barley together occupied 2.65m. ha in 1985, two-thirds of the total cropped area. Output of both crops has varied considerably from year to year, depending on the rainfall. In 1987/88 the cereal harvest more than doubled, to almost 5m. tons, including more than 2m. tons of wheat. However, low rainfall in early 1989 adversely affected the harvest, leading to substantial decreases. Wheat production was 2m. tons in 1990, 2.1m. tons in 1991 and 3m. tons in 1992. Barley production was 1m. tons in 1990, after which efforts were made to stabilize yields in marginal growing areas. (During the 1980s the average annual barley yield had ranged from as little as 235 kg per ha to as much as 1,044 kg per ha.) The Government's 1994 barley production target of

1.5m. tons was underfulfilled by 50% because of weather-related crop damage. About 300,000 tons of corn (sufficient to supply 60% of the state fodder company's requirement) were produced in 1993.

In 1993 the wheat harvest reached 3.6m. tons, placing a severe strain on available storage space despite the construction of 15 additional grain silos over the previous year. The state grain marketing authorities launched an emergency programme to build 13 more silos during 1994 and to expand local flour-milling capacity, which fell far short of current requirements. The main reasons for the strong upturn in wheat production in 1993 were favourable rainfall, improved cultivation techniques, and increases in areas planted (attributable partly to price liberalization to improve the financial returns to farmers). Syria's annual wheat consumption was around 2.2m. tons in the early 1990s, while national flour-milling capacity was around 1.35m. tons, necessitating a heavy reliance on Lebanese mills to process part of the Syrian wheat harvest. Despite some weather damage, the 1994 wheat harvest totalled 3.7m. tons. Wheat production in 1995 was just over 4m. tons. Contracts were awarded in late 1994 for the construction of five new flour mills to increase Syria's annual milling capacity by 750,000 tons by 1998. In 1996 the wheat harvest totalled 4.2m. tons and the barley harvest was 1.5m. tons. Up to 5.3m. tons of wheat were held in storage in 1996, when Syria exported cereals to the value of $150m. It was reported in May 1997 that Syria was to export $14m. worth of wheat to Bulgaria in settlement of debts owed to Bulgarian state enterprises. Cereal production declined in 1997, owing to low rainfall in the traditional wheat-growing areas. Wheat output was estimated at 3.2m. tons, while that of barley fell to 1.1m. tons. It was reported in December 1997 that the OPEC Fund for International Development had agreed to provide a loan of $6m. to help finance the construction of four new grain silos, each with a capacity of 100,000 tons.

There are several other actual and potential agricultural exports. Tobacco production has averaged around 15,000 tons per year, and exported about 3,000 tons per year, during the 1990s. There is also considerable scope for expansion in the production of fruit and vegetables. The fruit harvest in 1996 included 540,000 tons of grapes, 83,300 tons of apricots, 302,000 tons of apples and 25,300 tons of plums. Syria has embarked on a project to double production of citrus fruit. In 1990 it produced 171,000 tons of oranges. By 1996 production had risen to 372,000 tons. The production of tomatoes and onions in 1996 totalled 409,000 tons and 126,000 tons, respectively. Demand for fruit and vegetables is necessitating imports from other sources, including Lebanon. In recent years there have, at times, been shortages of fruit and vegetables, partly as a result of the official curbing of imports in general. Syria does export a certain amount of fruit and vegetables, and in 1986 such exports included 33,512 tons of potatoes, 415 tons of onions, 5,935 tons of lentils, 1,788 tons of dried figs and 4,183 tons of watermelons. Fruit growers who had expanded production for export to guaranteed markets in the former Soviet Union suffered some losses when trade was cut back after the late 1980s. Production of grape and apple juice was due to start in 1995 at a new processing plant near Damascus which aims to provide growers with an assured outlet for a proportion of these crops.

Stockraising is another important branch of agriculture. In 1996 there were 810,000 cattle, 1.1m. goats and 13.1m. sheep. More than 1.5m. tons of milk was produced in 1996.

PETROLEUM AND GAS

Syria was formerly thought to have no petroleum. The Iraq Petroleum Co group had rights throughout Syria but abandoned them in 1951 after failing to find petroleum in commercial quantities. Concessions were granted to an independent American operator in 1955 and to a West German-led consortium in 1956. These led to the discovery of petroleum, first of the Karatchouk field, in the north-eastern corner of the country, then of the Suweidiya field and finally of the field at nearby Rumelan. However, in addition to the cost of extraction being high, the petroleum from all three oilfields was of low quality. The petroleum which was found at Karatchouk had a density of 19° API and a sulphur content of 4.5%, while that found at Suweidiya had a density of 25° API and a 3.5% sulphur content. In 1964, several years before any of the three fields had begun production on a commercial basis, Syria became one of the first Arab states to discard the notion of petroleum concessions and to nationalize its petroleum operations. Even at that early stage, Syria's industrial planners were anxious to use the country's petroleum not only for export in its crude state, but also as a raw material for domestic industry. For the next 10 years all exploration and exploitation was conducted solely by the state-owned General Petroleum Authority and its offshoot, the Syrian Petroleum Co (SPC), with Soviet assistance.

Output from Suweidiya started in July 1968 and totalled 1m. tons in the first year, of which 833,000 tons were exported. Output in 1969, when the Karatchouk field began to produce, failed to reach expectations, totalling only 3.2m. tons, of which 2.3m. tons were exported. The October war in 1973 reduced production from a level of 6.3m. tons in the previous year to just 5.4m. tons, recovering in 1974 to 6.2m. tons. Production remained at about that level in the late 1970s; by the early 1980s, with oil prices falling and its known petroleum reserves being exhausted, Syria was actually a net importer of petroleum. From the mid-1980s, however, the petroleum industry was transformed by the discovery of large reserves of high-quality crude oil near Deir ez-Zor by a consortium of foreign oil companies.

The new discoveries were the result of the reversal of the Government's 'no-concessions' policy in the mid-1970s. In May 1975 the first Syrian concession to be won by any Western company for over 15 years was awarded to a US group, on production-sharing terms heavily tilted in the Government's favour and stipulating that $20m. be invested in exploration off shore. In June 1975 the Government took its new policy one stage further by offering a dozen onshore oil concessions for international bidding. Altogether, 50,000 sq km were to be made available. The oil companies' response to the invitation was initially slow and, when the first US group, Tripco, relinquished its concession in March 1976, no other company had come forward to join the search. In July 1977, however, a US-Syrian consortium called Samoco took up a concession in the Deir ez-Zor area, and in December another concession, in Raqqa province, was taken by Shell subsidiaries, Syria Shell Petroleum Development and Pecten Syria Co. Both Shell and Samoco insisted on a larger share of eventual petroleum production than was agreed between the Government and Tripco. This softening of terms reawakened the interest of other firms, including Chevron of the USA.

By 1983, however, Samoco, Chevron and Rompetrol of Romania (which was exploring west of Hassakeh) had all followed Tripco in relinquishing their concessions, leaving Pecten and Marathon of the USA as the only foreign operators in the country. In early 1983 Pecten, together with Royal Dutch Shell and Deminex of the Federal Republic of Germany, assumed control of Samoco's concession area. At the end of 1984 it was revealed that the consortium had discovered reserves of high-quality crude oil at ath-Thayyem, near Deir ez-Zor. In 1985 the three foreign partners and the SPC formed the Al-Furat Petroleum Co (AFPC) to develop the concession. Full commercial production began in September 1986, adding an initial 60,000 b/d (3m. tons per year) to Syria's total production capacity. Because the oil from the field is light crude (36° API), with a very low sulphur content, it has considerably reduced the need to import light crudes for blending with heavy Syrian ones at Syrian refineries. Previously Syria had imported between 5m. and 6.6m. tons of oil every year. Related to the main ath-Thayyem field are the later discoveries of the al-Ward, al-Asharah, ash-Shula and al-Kharata fields. In May 1989, it was reported that ath-Thayyem was producing 65,000 b/d, with output from the related fields bringing the total output of this system to 100,000 b/d out of total Syrian production in 1989 of 15.2m. tons (310,000 b/d).

Marathon had discovered gas reserves capable of producing 450m. cu m per day at a well named Cherrife 2 in 1982, and had made a further gas and condensate discovery in mid-1985, at ash-Shair. In December 1988, after a long period of resisting government pressure to develop gas reserves, Marathon agreed to a production-sharing scheme, with investment of up to $20m. in converting the oil-fired Muhardeh and Banias power stations to gas. The agreement was the first in Syria to include a gas sales clause. Turkey has expressed an interest in developing

Syrian gas reserves (which were estimated to total 225,000m. cu m in 1992) with a view to possible export to Turkey.

Syria's crude oil production reached 21m. tons (400,000 b/d) in 1990, 24.5m. tons (465,000 b/d) in 1991 and 25.2m. tons (475,000 b/d) in 1992, about two-thirds of the latter total being light crude and the balance heavy crude. Syria's proven oil reserves totalled 2,500m. barrels at the end of 1996, sufficient to maintain the previous year's rate of production for a further 11.3 years. Syrian oil output averaged 570,000 b/d in 1994, 600,000 b/d in 1995 and 605,000 b/d in 1996.

While AFPC continued to widen the scope of its own development programme (which included increasing use of water-injection techniques to maintain production from 'mature' oilfields), Elf Aquitaine was preparing to increase or commence production from new wells in the Atallah North and Jafra areas of the Deir ez-Zor field in 1993, while the Shell, Tullow Oil, Unocal and Occidental companies were engaged in active oil exploration programmes in other parts of the country. During the third quarter of 1994 Syrian oil output reached 615,000 b/d following the completion of current oilfield development programmes. Oil exploration activity was very limited and was currently yielding disappointing results. In late 1994 Shell (whose investment in Syria over the previous decade totalled about $3,000m., 90% of which had so far been recouped) signed a new exploration agreement covering areas previously relinquished by BP and Total. Unocal had ceased exploration in Syria by the end of 1994. Tullow Oil was in mid-1996 preparing to develop a small Euphrates Basin oilfield (the Kishma field) discovered in 1995. In mid-1996 about 66% of Syria's oil output was produced by AFPC, 24% by SPC and 10% by Elf Aquitaine. In February 1997 MOL was awarded a 5,000 sq km oil exploration block east of Palmyra. In March 1997 an exploration and production agreement covering a five-block exploration area totalling 4,201 sq km was concluded with a consortium made up of subsidiaries of France's Elf Aquitaine (40%), Japan's Sumitomo Development Co (30%) and Malaysia's Petronas (30%). In May 1997 Syria Shell Petroleum Development was granted a new exploration block in the Euphrates basin. At the end of 1997 the Government concluded two new agreements with international companies, Croatia's INA—Naftaplin and Sweden's Svenska Petroleum Exploration, to explore in the Palmyra and Deir ez-Zor areas, and was reported to be negotiating as many as three further such agreements. Government plans were subsequently revealed in June 1998 to invite companies to explore for oil and gas for the first time off shore in the Mediterranean.

Major gas development projects in progress or under active planning in 1993/94 included: the expansion of productive capacity in the Omar Field in the Deir ez-Zor region from 4.5m. cu m per day to about 7m. cu m per day, and the construction of pipelines to convey the Omar field's supplies to the 400-MW Tishrin power station in Damascus, the 650-MW Mhardeh power station near Homs and the 600-MW Jandar power station to be built also near Homs; a $300m.-programme for the Palmyra region fields designed to achieve production of 6m. cu m per day; and a $50m.-extension of the Jbeissa gas treatment plant, using gas from the SPC's Audeh field and aimed at increasing capacity from 1.7m. cu m per day to 3.5m. cu m per day (which was completed in early 1998); and a $200m.-programme to gather and treat gas from three fields in the Suweidiya region for use in a planned 150-MW power station in Suweidiya. By mid-1994 Syrian production of natural gas totalled 6.94m. cu m per day. It was scheduled to exceed 16.5m. cu m per day by the middle of 1995 on completion of current expansion projects. The actual output level attained by mid-1996 was estimated to be around 11.3m. cu m per day. Three new fields, with a combined output of 3m. cu m per day, were brought into production in mid-November 1996. Gas production is planned to increase to 18m. cu m per day by 2000.

The generally poor quality of Syrian petroleum until the late 1980s, together with opposition on the part of some of the major oil companies to Syria's nationalization experiment, combined, at the outset of the country's petroleum development, to cause considerable marketing difficulties. However, with increasing sales (particularly to Greece, France, Italy and the USSR), crude petroleum became Syria's most important export. The value of exports of petroleum and petroleum products soared from £S291.2m. in 1972 to £S1,607.5m. in 1974 and to £S6,253m. in

1980, but it fell subsequently as a result of the slump in world oil prices. In 1981 Syria became a net importer of petroleum by value for the first time since petroleum exports began in the mid-1970s, recording a deficit on its trade in petroleum of £S262m. There was a surplus of £S189m. in the petroleum account in 1982, although deficits of £S123m. and £S767m. were recorded in 1983 and 1984. In 1986 oil imports were halved, from 5.4m. tons in 1985, to 2.7m. tons, while exports fell from 7.4m. tons to 6.3m. tons—an oil trade surplus of 3.7m. tons, worth £S346m. (compared with a surplus of £S315m. in 1985). In 1986 sales of oil and oil products accounted for 42% of total exports by value, compared with 74% in 1985, the decline being caused by lower oil prices. By 1990 oil and other minerals accounted for 45% of Syria's merchandise exports by value, and in 1991 exports of oil were valued at £S17,218m. The volume of oil exports fluctuated within the range of 300,000 b/d to 360,000 b/d in early 1994, at which point the state marketing company had 21 term customers abroad and was seeking to conduct an increasing proportion of its business through term contracts rather than sales on the spot market. In mid-1995 the estimated volume of Syria's oil exports was 320,000 b/d. The country's oil export earnings totalled £S21,007m. (nearly 60% of total merchandise exports by value) in 1993 and £S20,190m. in 1994.

The capacity of petroleum refineries in Syria totalled 11.4m. tons per year (228,000 b/d) at 1 January 1988, comprising 5.4m. tons per year (102,000 b/d) at the Homs refinery and 6m. tons per year (126,000 b/d) at the Romanian-built refinery at Banias, which came 'on stream' in 1980. For a long time, however, the Banias plant operated at considerably below capacity, owing to repeated shortfalls in deliveries of crude petroleum. It was this problem which delayed construction of the refinery, as its specifications had to be altered to enable it to process different grades of crude and thus reduce its dependence on uncertain Iraqi supplies, which were subsequently discontinued by Syria's closure of the Kirkuk–Banias pipeline, which had a capacity of 500,000 b/d. The sixth expansion of the Homs refinery was carried out by Technoexport of Czechoslovakia. The seventh expansion was to have entailed construction of a base lube oil complex with a capacity of 100,000 tons per year (t/y) but, owing to Syria's budgetary constraints, this project was replaced by one for a plant to process used lubricating oils, with a capacity of 30,000 t/y, to be increased to 40,000 t/y. In 1994 the Government accepted the recommendations of a 1992 study by a US consultancy which advocated a major restructuring of both existing refineries in order to boost their output of light products. About half of the current refining capacity was devoted to the production of heavy fuel oil, Syrian demand for which was due to fall substantially in coming years as new gas-fired power stations were constructed. Also in 1994, a private-sector business backed by Saudi Arabian and other Gulf region investors announced plans (approved in principle by the Government) to build a new oil refinery in Syria with a capacity of about 100,000 b/d, while the Government put forward unrelated proposals for a new 60,000 b/d refinery near the Deir ez-Zor oilfields.

Royalties for the transit of foreign crude petroleum through Syrian territory were, for many years, more valuable than indigenous production. Two pipelines carry petroleum from the Kirkuk oilfield, in Iraq, through Syria. One, built in 1934, leads on to a terminal at Tripoli in Lebanon. The second, completed in 1952, branches off at Homs to the Syrian terminal at Banias. A third pipeline, belonging to the Trans-Arabian Pipeline Co (Tapline) which used to carry 24m. tons of Saudi crude petroleum per year to a terminal near Sidon in Lebanon, crosses about 150 km of Syrian territory, much of which was occupied by Israel in 1967. After nationalizing the Iraq Petroleum Company in June 1972, the Iraqi Government took over payment of royalties to Syria and in January 1973, after lengthy negotiations, Syria and Iraq signed a transit agreement which provided both for transit dues and the supply of petroleum for Syria's own domestic use. However, the flow of petroleum through the Kirkuk–Banias pipeline has been interrupted more than once since then. Throughput was suspended in 1976, when negotiations between Iraq and Syria on renewing the financial clauses of the transit agreement broke down, with Iraq demanding higher prices for its petroleum (to match the 1973–74 increases) and Syria seeking a proportionate increase in transit fees. For more than two years, Iraq refused to use the pipeline, instead

directing its petroleum southwards to the Gulf and also via Turkey, through a pipeline that came 'on stream' in 1977. The short-lived improvement in Iraqi–Syrian political relations in late 1978, combined with the world shortage of petroleum arising from the Iranian revolution, brought a resumption of pumping from Kirkuk to Banias in 1979, but this was halted yet again in September 1980 at the start of the Iran–Iraq War. When, despite the continuation of the war, Iraq recommenced exports of petroleum on a limited scale, the situation in the Gulf put Syria in a relatively stronger position and the Iraq–Syria pipeline came into use again in February 1981. However, Syria remained dissatisfied with the transit royalties, stating that in 1981 the pipeline cost $31m. to operate but brought revenues of only $25.7m. In April 1982, having signed an agreement to buy 8.7m. tons of petroleum per year from Iran, Syria closed the Kirkuk–Banias pipeline to Iraqi petroleum. With the closure of the pipeline, concessional supplies from Iran played an important part in fulfilling Syria's oil import needs. From 1982 onwards, yearly agreements were negotiated with Iran for the supply of oil; typically, 1m. tons supplied free to the Syrian army and the rest at a discount. The oil agreements were, however, plagued by political disagreements between the two countries, and by Syria's mounting oil debt to Iran, which was reported in mid-1986 to be at least $1,500m. For some periods Iranian oil supplies were halted altogether. In April 1987, 12-month agreements were signed for the supply of 1m. tons of oil free of charge to the Syrian army, and 2m. tons at OPEC prices on a cash-payment basis. A new one-year agreement, allowing for the supply of 1m. tons of free oil was reached in April 1988. The smaller quantity of oil involved in the recent agreements reflected the impact that the Deir ez-Zor production has had on Syria's oil import needs. In mid-June 1989, the Syrian Minister of Petroleum stated that Iran had made no deliveries of 'free' oil since the end of 1988.

From the late 1980s the Government's desire to maximize oil output was apparent in the easing of state bureaucratic constraints on the sector. Nevertheless, foreign companies continued to be deterred by the difficulties they experienced in Syria, added to which the prospects of major new discoveries were seen as limited. Against this background, the appointment in June 1992 of the AFPC Chairman, Nadir an-Nabulsi, as Minister of Petroleum and Mineral Wealth was seen as signalling a new commitment to commercial principles and to removing obstacles to oil development. An estimated 65% of Syria's geological structures remained unexplored in 1993, when the Government's policy on oil development terms was broadly based on prevailing Egyptian practices. According to a comparative survey of 101 oil-producing countries, published in February 1995 by the Swiss company Petroconsultants, Syria had the least attractive fiscal climate for oil exploration companies. The foreign oil companies operating in Syria in 1995 were understood to have urged the Government to allow 40% recovery of development costs (compared with Syria's existing 25% cost-recovery allowance) and to introduce accelerated cost-recovery procedures for existing operators (i.e. by allowing pro-duction from established wells to be offset against the development costs of new wells).

INDUSTRY AND TRANSPORT

A remarkable industrial boom, mainly based on textiles, occurred in Syria shortly after independence and was the principal cause of the dissolution of the customs union with Lebanon in 1959, since the protectionist policies which were adopted by the Syrian Government to safeguard this growth came into direct conflict with Lebanon's free-trade tradition. Since then the industrial (manufacturing and mining) sector has grown steadily. In 1971, for the first time, it replaced agriculture as the main generator of wealth, accounting for 19.5% of Syria's GDP, compared with 19.1% for agriculture. Manufacturing output expanded strongly in the early 1980s, with the index of production rising from 108 in 1982 to 167 in 1983 (1980 = 100). Until the early 1990s, however, production stagnated, with the industrial index standing at 163 in 1986. In some sectors, there was a marked decline in 1986: the wood and furniture index fell from 80 to 14; that for paper, printing and binding from 252 to 165; and that for the main mineral industries from 175 to 132. The target for average annual industrial growth under the

1976–80 Development Plan was an ambitious 15.4%, while the investment allocation for the industrial sector was £S11,289m., representing 20.8% of the total. There has been something of a change of heart since then, however, partly because of disappointing growth rates in this sector, and industry's allocation under the 1981–85 Plan fell to 16.6% of the total, or £S16,899m. In Syria's national accounts, the industrial sector comprises manufacturing, with mining, electricity, gas and water. In terms of GDP at constant 1980 prices, the value of mining, manufacturing and utilities fell by 17% in 1984, to £S7,622m. In 1985 it rose by 5%, to £S7,997m. Figures showed a further increase of 33% in 1986, to £S10,767m. However, this is likely to have been caused by increases in the output of oil and phosphates, rather than the result of an improvement in the performance of the manufacturing sector in general. According to the World Bank, in 1992 the industrial sector contributed 23% of GDP, compared with the agricultural sector's 30% and the service sector's 48%. In 1994, according to official sources, the industrial sector contributed 13.3% of GDP, compared with the agricultural sector's 28.4% and the service sector's 43.4%.

Production of phosphates started from mines in the Palmyra area in 1972. A sudden rise in world phosphate prices in 1974 took the price of Syrian rock up to $53 per metric ton, despite its high chlorine content and low quality. Prices and production subsequently fluctuated. Under the provisions of the 1981–85 Plan, phosphate production was expected to reach 5m. tons per year by 1985, but actual output was considerably less than this figure. Production declined from 1.46m. tons in 1982 to 1.23m. tons in 1983. It rose to 1.51m. tons in 1984 but fell to 1.2m. tons in 1985. In 1986 production rose to 1.6m. tons, and exports increased from 694,000 tons, worth £S75.6m., in 1985, to 1.3m. tons, worth £S150m. Production in 1987 amounted to almost 2m. tons. In 1997 phosphate output was expected to total 2.6m. tons, about 80% of which would be exported (mainly to Europe). Government planning targets advocated the modernization of equipment and the adoption of more efficient processing methods in order to increase annual output to 4m. tons by 2000. Syria's phosphate reserves have enabled the establishment of a phosphatic fertilizer industry. Production at a Romanian-built triple superphosphate (TSP) plant at Homs, costing $180m., began in 1981 with an annual capacity of 450,000 tons of TSP. Production of phosphatic fertilizers rose from 68,333 tons in 1981 to 192,720 tons in 1986. An ammonia urea plant was completed at Homs in 1979, with a daily capacity of 1,000 tons of ammonia, of which 600 tons was to be used to manufacture 1,050 tons of urea per day. Production of nitrogenous fertilizers increased from 59,607 tons in 1981 to 116,543 tons in 1982. In 1984 and 1985 production was 110,206 tons and 104,000 tons, respectively, rising to 109,919 tons in 1986. In December 1986 Syria and the USSR signed a protocol on co-operation in the phosphate industry, providing for the annual volume of Syrian phosphate exports to the USSR to rise to 6m. tons by 2000. (After the collapse of the USSR in 1991, Syria sought to renegotiate such contracts with the Russian Government and other successor republics.) Plans for the construction of a new TSP plant near Palmyra, which have been under study since the 1980s, were reported to have been revived in 1997. Estimated to cost between $350m. and $450m., the plant would have a capacity of 500,000 tons per year. In March 1998 international bids were invited for another long-delayed project for the construction of an ammonia and urea plant (with a daily production capacity of 1,000 tons and 1,750 tons respectively).

The iron and steel industry, centred on Hama, comprises a smelter (capacity 120,000 tons per year), a rolling mill and a steel pipe plant, built by firms from West Germany and Switzerland. The potential for developing Syria's own deposits of iron ore, estimated at about 530m. tons, has been studied by Indian consultants. After the 1990/91 Gulf crisis, Saudi Arabia pledged funding for a new $1,000m.-iron and steel complex at az-Zara (near Hama), which would have an annual capacity of 700,000 tons and specialize in coils, bars and industrial sections. Contract negotiations had not been concluded by the end of 1993. Syria's cement output (once targeted to reach 6m. tons by 1980) amounted to 2.85m. tons in 1982. However, completion of a big cement works at Tartous in 1983, together with other factories at Adra, Hama, Musulmiya and Aleppo, brought output to 4.3m. tons in 1985. In 1993 Syrian cement demand was

expected to total 5m. tons, which was roughly in balance with the country's current production capacity. An import requirement emerged again in 1994, when Jordan was among the sources of supplies to meet the shortfall. In 1995 Syria's estimated cement demand was between 6m. and 6.5m. tons, while local cement production was around 3.2m. tons. Annual demand was forecast to reach 10m. tons by the end of the century. Having allocated a total of £S1,810m. to modernize, expand and refurbish existing state-owned cement plants, the Government was in mid-1996 evaluating bids for a project to add 1m. tons per year of new capacity at Hama. By early 1998 the award of the construction contract for the Hama cement plant was thought to be imminent. The KFAED was to provide $71m. towards the project, the total cost of which was estimated at between $160m. and $200m. Syria's seven sugar refineries supplied nearly half of local demand of 550,000 tons in 1994, when plans were announced to build an eighth plant which would raise the country's total sugar refining capacity to 389,000 tons per year.

Other established industries include the manufacture of textiles, rubber, glass and paper, and the assembly of tractors, refrigerators and television receivers (including colour sets). Plans for a motor car assembly plant were postponed following the financial difficulties of 1976, and cars have since been imported in large numbers from Japan. However, a new private-sector scheme to assemble pick-up trucks, jeeps and small passenger vehicles was approved in principle by the Government in August 1994. To be based on the import of kits supplied by the US manufacturer General Motors, the proposed plant would begin production within two years of final approval for the project and would reach its full capacity of 30,000 vehicles per year within seven years. Food processing industries have also been developed. In April 1992 Alfamatex of Spain won a $125m.-contract to build a new textiles mill at Idleb, with Kuwait and Islamic Development Bank financial aid. At the same time, bids were invited for a $150m.-textiles mill at Latakia, to be funded in part by the Abu Dhabi Fund for Arab Economic Development and with a projected output of 150,000 tons a year of cotton products.

Despite the dominance of large-scale state industries, the private sector has continued to play an important role in industrial manufacture. In 1986 the private sector accounted for 56% of the production of refrigerators, 62% of paints, 23% of biscuits, 100% of olive oil and 34% of detergents. Under Law 10 of May 1991, encouragement was given to Syrian and foreign investment in industrial ventures, particularly in the light industry sector. To qualify for 'Law 10' status, a project had to involve investment of more than £S10m. and had to secure the approval of the Higher Council for Investment, whose project evaluation criteria took particular account of the amount of foreign capital to be invested; compatibility with national development plans; utilization of advanced or innovatory technology; the amount of new employment to be created; and the utilization of locally available resources. Approved projects were entitled to five or more years' exemption from profit, dividend and real-estate taxes and were subject to a liberalized regime of import regulations and exchange controls (including unrestricted repatriation of profits for foreign investors). At the start of 1995 the total number of approved 'Law 10' projects was 1,251, involving projected investment of £S232,800m. and the creation of up to 87,346 new jobs. Inward transfers of funds were expected to cover nearly 77% of the average amount invested, with expatriate Syrians providing much of this 'foreign' investment. (It was generally believed that a significant proportion of private capital investment from abroad was in reality a repatriation through legitimate channels of undeclared wealth that had originally left Syria through clandestine channels.) The transport sector accounted for nearly 53% of all projects approved (although only 25% of projected total investment), with car import schemes predominating. The agricultural sector accounted for just 26 projects costing an estimated £S17,800m. Some 565 projects, involving projected investment of £S155,300m., were approved in production industries, including food processing (217 projects worth £S45,900m.), metal goods and construction materials (146 projects worth £S69,400m.), chemical goods (104 projects worth £S14,300m.) and textiles and clothing (75 projects worth £S21,600m.). By early 1995 a total of 65 'Law 10' manufacturing enterprises had started production and a further 135 manufacturing projects were under active development. The generally slow implementation of approved manufacturing projects stemmed in part from the need to raise equity finance (often on a large scale) as a substitute for commercial loan finance, which was virtually unobtainable within Syria and very difficult to obtain from abroad. The first 'Law 10' project financed in part by a commercial loan was a chemicals plant (25% owned by the Syrian Ministry of Industry) that was due to start production in early 1997. A $4.4m. seven-year loan for this project was granted in August 1996 by the German investment agency DEG. One of the first 'Law 10' projects under majority foreign ownership (a food and beverages plant, 60%-owned by Nestlé of Switzerland) went into production in May 1997. In September 1994 the management of public-sector enterprises was placed on a new footing under the terms of a legislative decree empowering the directors of such enterprises to operate 'on a commercial basis' without the need to seek government approval for their business plans.

Infrastructural improvement to aid commercial activity included a plan to install 600,000 new telephone lines (double the existing number), for which a contract was awarded to Siemens of Germany in mid-1991. International telecommunications sevices were upgraded in December 1994 with the inauguration of a new submarine cable linking Syria and Lebanon with Cyprus. In 1996 Syria had an efficient modern telephone system with a total of over 2m. lines installed and was planning to establish a GSM (global standard for mobiles) system in the near future. In mid-1998, as part of a new programme to expand the telephone system by 1.65m. lines, Ericsson of Sweden signed a contract valued at $120m. for the supply and installation of digital switching systems for 1m. new lines. Samsung Electronics of South Korea was reported to have secured the contract for rural fibre optic links. The expansion programme was being financed by loans from the Arab Fund for Economic and Social Development, KFAED and the Abu Dhabi Development Fund.

Since its inauguration in 1978, the Euphrates Dam, with its eight 100-MW turbines, has made an important contribution to power generation in Syria. However, from an early stage extensive Turkish exploitation of the Euphrates waters often reduced the level of water in Lake Assad to such an extent that only three turbines could operate. In July 1987 Turkey undertook to use 500m. cu m of water from the Euphrates per year for irrigation until agreement was reached with Syria and Iraq on the use of the river's waters. Syria has considered various ways of overcoming its power shortage. There has long been talk of a nuclear power plant, possibly using uranium obtained from local phosphate deposits. Four Western companies were short-listed to carry out the pilot study for a 1,200-MW station in 1979/80, but none was ever given the go-ahead. In mid-1983 Syria and the USSR signed a protocol whereby both sides were to study the construction of Syria's first nuclear power station, but little progress appeared to have been made in this direction before the disintegration of the USSR in 1991. In 1995 Syria opened discussions with Argentina with a view to purchasing a 3-MW research reactor.

In recent years Syria has suffered frequent interruptions in the supply of electric power. Electricity demand soared, owing to rapid industrialization in the 1970s, and the Euphrates Dam (see above) did not, as was hoped, meet Syria's growing needs, as shortfalls in its water supply due to erratic rainfall and Turkish offtake upstream were compounded by an almost total lack of maintenance of the dam and its generating plant. By early 1993 the generating capacity of the dam was thought to be barely 150 MW, while its actual output fell below 100 MW at some points, contributing to chronic power shortages which led to electricity supplies being cut off for seven or more hours per day. Many Syrian businesses relied on diesel generators to keep factories running. An ambitious programme of power station construction, launched in the 1980s, was increasingly geared to the exploitation of local natural gas resources as a fuel source, but failed to keep pace with the growth of demand because of chronic delays between the planning and construction stages. (Only three contracts were finalized between 1983 and 1992.) In 1993 Syria was estimated to have a total of 1,900 MW of operational generating capacity (10.5% hydro, 63% thermal and 26.5% gas-turbine) out of a theoretical installed capacity of 3,002 MW (30% hydro, 51% thermal and 19% gas-turbine),

while the minimum operational capacity needed to meet current demand was estimated to be 2,500 MW. Demand was officially projected to rise to 3,284 MW in 1995 and 4,882 MW in 2000. In a bid to rectify the situation, the authorities approved heavy, aid-financed investment in electricity generation in the early 1990s. Work has since been completed on the 600-MW Jandar plant, financed by Japan, and is continuing on the Saudi-financed 1,000-MW plant in Aleppo. Another important generating project carried out in recent years has been the installation of eight 128-MW turbines in various locations by an Italian company, with finance from Kuwait. In early 1997 Mitsubishi Heavy Industries of Japan was awarded the contract to construct a 600-MW plant at Az-Zara. In August 1995 the Arab Fund for Economic and Social Development extended a $100m. loan for a project to link the Syrian and Jordanian electricity networks, and in June 1996 it made a further $86.7m. available to finance a link between the Syrian and Turkish electricity networks. It was reported in March 1998 that Siemens of Germany had secured the contract to construct two substations serving the grid interconnection with Jordan. Earlier, at the end of 1997, the Government issued a decree allowing Syria's first independent power project to proceed as a 100% private venture. The developers, a Belgian/Syrian partnership, plan to build a 600-MW plant at Al-Bardeh, 150 km north of Damascus.

The regional political situation has not helped Syria in encouraging private investment or in developing its ports. Free zones which were set up in the 1970s in Damascus, Aleppo, Homs, Latakia and Tartous, with the aim of attracting foreign investment in light industries, assembly plants and warehouses, failed to have the desired effect. Jordan's support for Iraq in the Iran–Iraq War compounded the discord between Syria and Jordan, and although in 1985 there was a dramatic improvement in relations, plans for a joint industrial free zone south of Dera'a had been undermined. Operations at the ports of Latakia and Tartous (both equipped to handle transit traffic bound for the Gulf) were adversely affected by the closure of the border with Iraq in 1982. The volume of goods handled at the two ports declined markedly after 1981, when it totalled 7.63m. tons. In 1985 the total was 5.5m. tons, and in 1986 4.37m. tons. In mid-1996 the Government announced plans for a major expansion of port capacity, as recommended in studies submitted by the Japan International Co-operation Agency. Total port capacity in Syria was targeted to reach 19.3m. tons per year by 2003 (6.2m. tons at Latakia, 5.4m. tons at Tartous and 7.7m. tons at a new port to be developed near Tartous), rising to 29.1m. tons per year by 2010 (11.4m. tons at Latakia, 7.7m. tons at Tartous and 10m. tons at the proposed new port). Existing port capacity in 1996 was 9.5m. tons per year (4.4m. tons at Latakia and 5.1m. tons per year at Tartous) and in that year, Latakia handled just under 3m. tons of cargo, and Tartous 4.14m. tons. In mid-1997 Tartous had two Finnish straddle carriers and four British dockside cranes on order, while Latakia (currently lacking specialized container-handling equipment) was negotiating to buy four ship-to-shore gantry cranes. The reopening of Syria's land border with Iraq at the start of June 1997 was followed by a Syrian request to the United Nations that Syrian seaports be added to the list of approved transit points for Iraq's humanitarian imports under the UN-administered 'oil-for-food' scheme.

At the start of 1997 the national airline, Syrian Arab Airlines, had a 16-strong fleet comprising two Boeing 747s, six Boeing 727s, three Tupolev 154s, two Tupolev 134s and three Caravelles. No new aircraft had been purchased since the early 1980s, although some Boeings had been obtained as gifts from Kuwait and Abu Dhabi. Six Airbus A320 aircraft have been ordered from Airbus Industrie for delivery in 1998. Syrian Arab Airlines, which reported profits of £S1,700m. in 1994 and £S2,400m. in 1995, is in the process of expanding its short- and long-haul international services.

In June 1997 the General Establishment for Syrian Railways signed a contract to purchase 30 new diesel locomotives from the Anglo-French company GEC Alsthom. Separate negotiations were in progress with other Western companies bidding for a contract to refit 32 of Syria's existing fleet of 140 (mainly Soviet-built) diesel locomotives. In 1997 Iranian consultants began an outline study of proposals to build a metro system in Damascus. Similar proposals had been studied by Soviet consultants in the early 1980s.

TRADE AND TOURISM

Commerce has traditionally been a major occupation of Syria's towns, especially of Damascus and Aleppo which lie on the main east-west trade route. There have been, however, some radical changes in both the direction and the composition of Syria's trade over the years. During the mid-1960s Syria's principal suppliers were among the Eastern European bloc. In 1968 the USSR and Czechoslovakia together provided more than 20% of all imported goods. In 1974, although the value of their supplies had increased, those two countries accounted for just under 7.2% of the total. Meanwhile, the value of Syria's imports over the six-year period had risen nearly four-fold, reaching £S4,571m. in 1974, and the bulk of the increase had resulted from flourishing trade ties with Western Europe. In the 1980s, the pendulum swung back in favour of the Eastern bloc again. The trend towards the East was reinforced during this period by trade agreements with Eastern bloc countries and by the willingness of some of these to accept barter deals and thereby accommodate Syria's shortage of foreign exchange. Yugoslavia, for example, agreed in 1985 to take almost one-third of Syrian phosphate exports in return for construction machinery, iron and steel, timber, pharmaceuticals and medical equipment. Czechoslovakia also agreed to exchange engineering equipment for phosphates and farm produce, while Romania was a close trading partner for some years. The USSR, after signing a friendship treaty with Syria in 1980, followed this up with an agreement to boost bilateral trade to the equivalent of some $2,600m. in the five years up to 1985. This was renewed for a further five years in 1985. The fields in which Soviet companies were active in Syria included transport, the oil industry, the phosphate industry, agriculture, power generation, and the search for reserves of water. Another friendship and co-operation treaty, this time with Bulgaria, was signed in May 1985. In 1980 socialist countries took 16.1% of Syria's exports, and in 1986 the proportion rose to 46.4%. The proportion of Syria's imports supplied by socialist countries rose from 14.6% in 1985 to 20.2% in 1986. However, the EC's share also increased, from 29.9% to 34.8%, while that of Iran declined from 17.8% to 6.8%, as a result of the fall in Iranian oil imports. After the post-1989 changes in Eastern Europe and the disintegration of the USSR in 1991, the pendulum swung again towards trade with the West. Exports to the USA increased to $206.6m. in 1991 (from $150.4m. in 1990), while imports fell from $52.1m. to $27.1m.

Syria's exports increased dramatically during the 1970s, mainly owing to large increases in the value of petroleum sales. Largely as a result of the decline in oil prices and the volume of exports, Syria's export earnings declined every year between 1980 and 1986. From £S8,273m. in 1980, the value of exports fell to £S6,427m. in 1985 and £S5,199m. in 1986. Exports in 1987 nearly trebled, in terms of local currency, to £S15,200m., although these figures used an exchange rate of US $1 = £S11.20, which did not replace the former rate of US $1 = £S4.05 until early 1988. In terms of US dollars, the value of exports in 1987 increased by only 6%, to $1,356m.

In view of the country's alarming shortage of foreign exchange, there have been strict curbs on imports (although large amounts of goods are smuggled into the country). In 1981 the value of imports totalled £S19,781m. In 1985 the figure was £S15,570m., and in 1986 there was a drop of 31.9%, to £S10,611m. The change in the exchange rate affected import figures, in local currency, with an almost three-fold increase in 1987 to £S27,900m. In terms of US dollars, however, there was a 6% drop, to $2,492m. The trade deficit declined from $1,360m. in 1986 to $1,136m. in 1987. The USSR was Syria's leading trade partner in 1986, taking 29.7% of Syria's exports, and providing 10.1% of its imports. Syria's second biggest customer was Italy (12.1%), followed by Romania (9.4%) and the Federal Republic of Germany (4.1%). Its second biggest supplier was the Federal Republic of Germany (9.1%), followed by France (8.7%) and Italy (7.5%). Iran, previously Syria's largest supplier, fell to fifth place, with a 6.8% share.

In March 1990 the Government announced a trade surplus of £S10,430m. for 1989. The value of exports was reported to

have totalled £S33,740m., while that of imports amounted to £S23,310m. However, local analysts cast doubt upon the accuracy of these figures, observing that few of the goods smuggled into Syria from Lebanon were recorded in trade statistics. Furthermore, it was noted that at least three exchange rates applied to imports: the official fixed rate of US $1 = £S11.225; an 'incentive' rate of $1 = £S20.22; and a free market rate of $1 = £S45. Since it was unclear on which rate the calculation of the trade balance had been based, it was impossible to ascertain the accuracy of the Government's figures in hard currency terms. The IMF estimated Syria's 1990 trade surplus as $2,094m. (exports $4,156m., imports $2,062m.). According to official statistics, a 1991 trade surplus of £S7,438m. (exports £S38,504m., imports £S31,066m.) was followed by a deficit of £S4,459m. in 1992 (exports £S34,719m., imports £S39,178m.) and a further deficit of £S11,151m. in 1993 (exports £S35,318m., imports £S46,469m.). Within the overall trade balance for 1991 there was a public-sector trade surplus of £S10,364m. and a private-sector deficit of £S2,926m. In 1992, public-sector trade was in surplus by £S12,713m. while private-sector trade was in deficit by £S17,172m. In 1993 the public-sector surplus fell to £S8,761m. while the private-sector deficit increased to £S19,912m. Law 10 of May 1991 (see above under Industry) was an important factor in a sharp rise in private-sector imports from £S16,575m. in 1991 to £S28,752m. in 1993. In June 1992 the Minister of Economy and Foreign Trade stated that there was a need to set up a special Syrian export bank. Five years later the Government was still 'studying the possibility' of such a step. IMF statistics gave Syria's 1993 visible trade deficit as $322m. (exports $3,153m., imports $3,475m.), the 1994 deficit as $1,275m. (exports $3,329m., imports $4,604m.), the 1995 deficit as $143m. (exports $3,858m., imports $4,001m.) and the 1996 deficit as $338m. (exports $4,178m., imports $4,516m.). In 1997 Syria recorded a trade surplus of $454m. (exports $4,057m., imports $3,603m.). The three largest suppliers of imports in 1996 were Germany, the USA and Italy.

In May 1993 the Government launched an unprecedentedly thorough clampdown on smuggling across the Lebanese border, causing the black-market price of illegally imported American cigarettes (the main indicator of the level of smuggling activity) to triple within a month. The Government subsequently announced that a state trading organization would in future import foreign cigarettes for sale at the prices which smugglers had been charging before the clampdown (when the trade in illegal cigarette imports had been worth an estimated $1m. per day).

Syria's entire system of foreign trade, based on laws dating back to 1952, was under review in 1993 as the Government studied the extent to which current import and export controls were hampering the growth of private-sector enterprises. In September 1997 the Government removed a £S300,000 ceiling on the total value of approved locally produced goods which Syrian travellers were permitted to carry abroad. This was interpreted as a move to encourage the growth of 'informal' trade across the recently reopened border with Iraq. It was reported in June 1998 that an agreement had been reached with Saudi Arabia to establish a free-trade regime under the Arab League free-trade protocol (which calls on Arab states to reduce tariffs on mutual trade by 10% per year from 1998). Earlier in 1998 the Syrian Government had agreed to establish a free-trade regime with Lebanon. Exports to Lebanon totalled $326m. in 1997, compared with imports of just $38m.

Tourist traffic declined from 774,500 tourists in 1979 to 346,800 in 1982, though it rose to 565,000 in 1984, largely because of an arrangement whereby Iranians visited Syria in part-payment for Iranian oil supplies. The number of Iranian visitors dropped from 157,200 in 1984 to 132,600 in 1985, and there was a decline in the overall number of tourists to 486,700. In 1986, however, the number of Iranian tourists rose to a record 174,000 and the total number of tourists reached 567,700. The number of tourists from Western Europe has remained modest—by far the largest number in 1986 came from West Germany (17,100) and France (14,800), followed by the United Kingdom and Italy, each with 5,600. Western tourists are doubtless deterred by the instability in the region and by fear of terrorist attacks. Since 1978, a number of joint public/private sector companies, in which the Government has a minority interest, have been set up.

In 1993 Syria was visited by 2.9m. tourists who generated $700m. of tourism revenue. A joint private and public sector consortium was in 1994 preparing to invite construction bids for a $70m. resort development near Tartous, to include hotel and bungalow accommodation, sports facilities, restaurants and shops. Work on this project had still to start in mid-1996 because of difficulties in arranging financing. Construction of a $10m. tourism complex in the Shabaa area (south of Damascus) began in early 1996. The main shareholder in the Shabaa complex was a Saudi Arabian company. The construction, with Saudi investment, of a 350-room five-star hotel and assocated facilities in Damascus was to proceed, and international contractors were expected to be invited to bid in early 1999. The first stage of the $25m. Happy Land amusement park opened near Damascus in April 1998.

FINANCE

The sudden increase in Syrian exports from 1972 onwards was one of the major results of a reform in the country's regulations on foreign exchange. The method of valuing exports, other than cotton and crude petroleum, was transferred from the official exchange rate (then US $1 = £S3.80) to the 'parallel' (free) market rate ($1 = £S4.30), which meant a *de facto* devaluation of Syrian currency in relation to most transactions. The 'parallel' market was discontinued in July 1973 and remained suspended for nearly eight years. In April 1981, in an attempt to mobilize remittances to finance imports by the private sector and thereby reduce pressure on the Syrian pound, the Government announced that remittances from abroad and other private sector 'invisible' earnings would be convertible into Syrian currency at a freely floating 'parallel' rate. At the same time, it imposed very tight restrictions on private businesses wishing to open letters of credit for imports. These were not eased until late 1984, and, even then, importers were advised that suppliers might have to wait nearly a year to receive payment. In late 1984 there was also an official reduction in the Syrian currency's value in terms of the tourist exchange rate, which was adjusted from $1 = £S7 to $1 = £S8. From September 1985, resident Syrians were permitted to open accounts in foreign currency at the Commercial Bank of Syria, to be used for imports. In the previous year this concession had been granted to foreigners and non-resident Syrians. In early 1986 there was a major currency crisis, with the value of the Syrian pound on the 'black' market dropping to $1 = £S17, or more. There were widespread arrests of currency dealers, and large quantities of gold and foreign currency were seized. The effect of these measures was to bring about a short-term appreciation in the value of the currency, but it soon began to depreciate once more, weakened by Syria's shortage of reserves of foreign exchange. Between October 1985 and October 1986 the Syrian pound lost 50% of its value against the US dollar. In August 1986 one of Syria's five exchange rates was devalued from $1 = £S11.75 to $1 = £S22, a level more comparable with the 'black' market rate, which fell to $1 = £S24–£S25 at the end of 1986, when the tourist exchange rate stood at $1 = £S9.75. The fixed official rate for government accounts and strategic imports remained at $1 = £S3.925, as it had been since April 1976. Decree 24 of September 1986 rendered currency smugglers liable to prison terms of 15–25 years, and smugglers of precious metals to terms of three to 10 years. Possession of hard currency was classed as a criminal offence punishable by imprisonment. Although it was rarely enforced, the latter provision was seen by Syrian businesses as a disincentive to legitimate trading activity and demands for its repeal were repeatedly made in the first half of the 1990s by advocates of economic liberalization. In September 1987 the Syrian pound, according to the official exchange rate, was devalued from $1 = £S3.925 (a level maintained since 1976) to $1 = £S11.20–£S11.25—a move that many observers considered to be long overdue.

Subsidies have been paid to Syria by other Arab countries since the Khartoum summit meeting of 1967. They were reinforced at the Rabat summit of 1974, which resulted in the promise of an annual $1,000m. to Syria in its capacity as a 'confrontation state'. The Baghdad summit of 1978 pledged to increase these subsidies to $1,800m. per year for a period of 10

years. The amount of Arab aid which Syria actually received reached $690m. in 1975 but dropped to only $355m. in 1976. The amounts received in 1979 and 1980 were estimated at $1,600m. and $1,400m., respectively, but donations were adversely affected by the Iran–Iraq War (in which Syria's former backers provided financial support to Iraq, while Syria sided with Iran) and by the erosion of the financial surpluses that OPEC countries accumulated before the decline in oil prices. Aid to Syria from the Gulf states was estimated to have dropped to $600m.–$700m. in 1986, although it has been difficult to gauge with any true accuracy the amount of aid from Gulf states under the Baghdad summit agreement. Saudi Arabia has been the most consistently conscientious of the Arab states in meeting its aid commitments to Syria.

Syrian political actions that have met with the approval of 'moderate' Arab states are often accompanied by reports of large sums being channelled from Saudi Arabia. Thus it was widely believed that Syria received a substantial 'reward' for attending the Arab summit held in Amman in November 1987, which was critical of Iran's actions in the Iran–Iraq War. Moreover, Syria's participation in the US-led multinational force which defeated Iraq in the Gulf War of 1991 led to further 'rewards' in the form of special aid totalling over $1,000m.

Syria also obtains considerable sums from multilateral and bilateral development aid sources, its receipts of official development aid (ODA) being in the $600m.–$700m. range in 1984–87, falling to $191m. in 1988 and to $127m. in 1989, rising to $650m. in 1990 (when ODA represented 4.4% of GNP) and falling to $373m. in 1991. Syria's debt arrears to funding institutions, particularly the World Bank, have, however, created problems. The arrears to the World Bank led to disbursements of new loans being 'frozen' in late 1986; in mid-1991 Syria's debt to the Bank was estimated at more than $300m. Political events have at times cast a shadow over Western governmental aid. In November 1983 the US Congress voted for US economic aid to Syria to be terminated; already in 1981 Congress had decided to 'freeze' $138.2m. in aid instalments totalling $227.8m. The Federal Republic of Germany cut off aid in late 1986, after two Jordanians were sentenced for a bomb attack in Berlin in which Syria was implicated—a line of credit suspended since 1980 had only been restored in 1985. In 1987 aid was restored. The EC imposed a *de facto* 'freeze' on its aid to Syria in late 1986, but aid was resumed after the visit of the EC's North-South commissioner, Claude Cheysson, to Damascus in September 1987. In the third EC protocol, which came into effect at the start of 1993, Syria was allocated ECU 146m. A fourth EC protocol, providing for an allocation of ECU 158m., failed to gain the necessary support when it was submitted to the European Parliament for approval in March 1993. Syria's total external debt (including military debt to the former Soviet bloc countries of about $10,000m.) was estimated by the World Bank to have been $16,815m. at the end of 1991, compared with $3,549m. in the early 1980s. However, the debt-service ratio as a percentage of exports was reduced from 15.6% in 1986 to 3.9% in 1990. The World Bank's estimate of Syria's end-1993 external debt was $19,975m. (over 70% of which was classified as 'bilateral concessional'), while total debt service paid during 1993 was estimated as $283m. Nearly $4,000m. of the end-1993 debt consisted of arrears to official creditors, about 10% of these arrears being owed to the World Bank, about 30% to OECD creditors and the balance to the former Soviet Union and other East European countries.

In May 1994 the Minister of Economy and Foreign Trade said that Syria was currently making interest payments of $6m. per month on its World Bank debt of about $500m., and was seeking to negotiate arrangements whereby the Government would pay off one-third of the debt while a 'friends of Syria' donor group would pay off the remainder. He ruled out the option of a formal IMF/Paris Club arrangement as 'unacceptable in our political climate'. He said Syria was currently settling its outstanding debts to the export credit agencies of several West European states; that it had reduced its indebtedness to commerical banks to about $500m. through repayments and restructuring agreements; and that it regarded its military debt to the former Soviet Union as a matter for discussion 'in its proper context as a mutual obligation'. It had been reported in April 1994 that Syria had sought an 80% write-off of military debt during exploratory talks with Russian officials. Sweden and Belgium were among the OECD countries whose export credit agencies reached agreements with Syria in 1994 in respect of relatively minor debts. However, Syria's main OECD bilateral creditors (among which France, Japan and Germany were each owed arrears of more than $100m.) were still seeking settlements in mid-1995. Negotiations with Germany were complicated by the inclusion of an estimated $500m. of Syrian debt to former East Germany within Syria's total debt of around $640m. to the unified state. The World Bank estimated Syria's end-1994 external debt as $20,557m., including arrears of principal totalling $4,563m. and arrears of interest totalling $1,400m. The Bank estimated that Syria paid $398m. in debt service in 1994 (out of a total of $1,530m. due for payment in that year).

In October 1996 France announced a debt settlement agreement involving the 'forgiving' of a reported 900m. French francs ($175m.) of arrears of interest and the rolling-over of a further 1,000 French francs ($195m.) of debt. In July 1997 the Syrian Government signed an agreement to settle its debt to the World Bank. Arrears of principal totalling $269.5m. were repaid in full on 1 September 1997, while arrears of interest totalling $256.9m. were to be repaid in instalments over five years from 1 October 1997. It was reported in September 1997 that Syria was negotiating with the Islamic Development Bank to settle around $300m. of payments arrears. By mid-1998 Syria's only remaining unresolved debt problems of significance were with Germany and Russia.

After the October 1973 war, state expenditure also clearly reflected the inflow of foreign funds. The general budget soared from a total of £S6,976m. in 1974 to £S16,564m. in 1976. The events of 1976, however, caused the authorities to reconsider and in 1977 and 1978 overall budget expenditure increased by only about 5% in absolute terms over each of the previous years. In 1979, as a result of the pledges made at the Baghdad summit, a big increase in defence spending raised total budget expenditure to £S22,600m. By 1985 the total had increased to £S42,984m. ($10,950m.), with defence, at £S13,000m., continuing to take a major share of current spending. The 4% nominal increase in total expenditure compared with an annual rate of inflation estimated at 10%. Investment expenditure under the 1985 budget was estimated at only £S19,436m., compared with £S17,886m. in 1984 and £S17,981m. in 1983. In the 1986 budget total spending amounted to £S37,091m., a substantial drop in real terms, taking inflation into account. In the 1987 budget, expenditure was cut by 4.4% to £S35,443m. Current expenditure was reduced by 14.1% to £S23,029m. Defence received the largest single allocation (£S14,327m., accounting for 62.2% of current expenditure), while agriculture was allocated about 20% (£S3,500m.) of total investment spending, compared with almost 25% in 1986. The 1988 draft budget was the first for a number of years to feature a substantial increase in spending. Total expenditure was raised by more than one-fifth to £S51,545m., compared with actual spending of £S35,443m. in 1987. Current expenditure rose from £S23,029m. to £S29,665m., and investment spending from £S12,414m. to £S21,880m. Of revenues of £S51,545m., taxes, aid and services were budgeted to provide £S34,848m. and the state sector surplus £S16,697m. The 1989 and 1990 budgets provided for expenditure of £S57,413m. and £S61,875m. respectively. The 1991 budget set expenditure at £S84,690m. and envisaged an effective deficit of £S13,676m., although this was treated as exceptional financing in order to achieve a technical balance. The 1992 budget was also technically balanced, providing for expenditure and revenue of £S93,043m.; this represented a nominal spending increase of almost 10% over 1991, although after allowing for inflation of 20% budgeted spending was lower in real terms. The 1992 expenditure total consisted of £S56,793m. in current spending and £S36,250m. in investment, with defence accounting for 26% of current spending (considerably less than in previous years), education 20% and health 5%. The largest allocation in the investment budget, some 26%, was for agriculture and irrigation. The effective deficit in the 1992 budget was equivalent to 20.9% of total revenue, to be funded by concessional loans totalling £S13,904m. and other foreign loans totalling £S5,607m.

The 1993 budget provided for total expenditure of £S123,018m., including £S27,869m. for defence (up 2.5% on 1992) and £S12,671m. for electricity, water and gas (up 157%

on 1992). Overall, investment spending was nearly twice as high as in 1992, and represented about half of total budgeted spending for 1993. The effective deficit was equal to 34.9% of the total budget in Syrian pounds, the borrowing elements on the revenue side being concessional loans of £S9,000m., other foreign loans totalling £S22,868m. and domestic loans of £S11,026m. (compared with a zero requirement for domestic loans in the 1992 budget). The real increase in foreign borrowing between 1992 and 1993 was estimated to be around 6.5% in dollar terms after allowance was made for the Government's use of an exchange rate of $1 = £S43 (rather than the official accounting rate of $1 = £S11.2) to calculate this component of the 1993 budget. The overall size of the deficit was nevertheless criticized by several deputies during the budget debate in the Syrian legislature (which formally adopted the Government's proposals on 9 May 1993). The 1994 budget provided for total expenditure of £S144,162m. (17.2% higher than in 1993) and total revenue of £S106,890m., leaving a deficit of £S37,272m. Current spending accounted for 53% of the 1994 expenditure total. Public-sector wages were raised by 30% in May 1994, while price increases were announced for electricity, petrol and many other items. In the same month the currency exchange rate used to levy customs duties on items other than basic commodities and most industrial raw materials was changed from $1 = £S11.2 to $1 = £S23. (The former rate continued to apply to the 'basic' import category.) There was a further selective modification of exchange-rate policy at the start of 1995, when the rate applicable to most sales or purchases of foreign currency through the Syrian banking system was changed from £S23 to £S42 per dollar. The free-market exchange rate for the Syrian pound (as determined by informal currency trading in Lebanon) averaged $1 = £S49 in the first half of 1995, having remained fairly stable for more than two years. From October 1995 the exchange rate of $1 = £S42 was applied to the prices charged to foreign visitors for hotel accommodation. It was estimated that four-fifths of all officially sanctioned foreign-exchange transactions in Syria were based on this rate of exchange at the end of 1995. The oil industry (hitherto required to use a rate of $1 = £S11.20) was permitted to switch to a rate of $1 = £S22.95 from January 1996 and to the main rate of $1 = £S42 from August 1996.

Syria's 1995 budget, approved by the legislature in April 1995, provided for expenditure of £S162,040m. (12.4% higher than in 1994) and revenue of £S125,718m. (17.6% higher than in 1994), leaving a deficit of £S36.322m. (2.5% less than the 1994 deficit). Recurrent items made up 54.3% of expenditure in the 1995 budget. The 1996 budget provided for total expenditure of £S187,450m. and total revenue of £S137,170m., leaving a deficit of £S50,280m. Recurrent spending totalled £S95,977m. (51.2% of total expenditure), including £S36,463m. (19.5% of total expenditure) for defence. Syria's 1997 budget provided for total expenditure of £S211,125m. and a supplementary allocation of £S10,200m. was announced in August 1997 to cover payments connected with Syria's debt settlement agreement with the World Bank.The 1998 budget provided for total expenditure of £S237,300m. (£S117,700m. for current expenditure and £S119,600m. for investment expenditure). This was 12.4% higher than in 1997, although 5.7% of that increase was the result of an adjustment to the exchange rate of the Syrian pound against the dollar.

In October 1996 the exchange rate applicable to most foreign exchange transactions was devalued from $1 = £S42 to $1 = £S43.50, and decreased further to $1 = £S45 in July 1997; the Government stated that it intended to use the latter rate to calculate the 1998 budget (previous budgets were based on multiple exchange rates). The free-market value of the currency in the latter part of 1997 averaged around $1 = £S50, having shown little variation over a long period of stable trading. From October 1996 Syrians were permitted to open hard-currency deposit accounts in Syria without declaring the origin of their funds, but there was no formal repeal of the 1986 law forbidding possession of hard currency and no measures were introduced to make it possible to buy hard currency through the Syrian banking system. In these circumstances, Syrians continued to rely on the Lebanese banking system for most foreign exchange transactions.

The current account of Syria's balance of payments was $959m. in surplus in 1979. In 1980 the surplus fell to $251m., and there was a deficit in every subsequent year until 1989. In that year a surplus of $1,222m. was recorded, followed by surpluses of $1,762m. in 1990, $699m. in 1991 and $55m. in 1992, when increased spending on imports coincided with reduced revenue from oil exports. Remittances from Syrians working abroad were estimated at $550m. in 1992, while capital inflows through government channels totalled $313m. In 1993 there was a current-account deficit of $607m. Inward official transfers in 1993 totalled only $40m. In 1994 Syria recorded a current-account deficit of $922m. According to Central Bank of Syria figures, Syria recorded a current-account surplus of $312m. in 1995 and $164m. in 1996. In 1997, according to IMF figures, the surplus was $564m.

Total official reserves (excluding gold) fluctuated considerably in the 1980s. At the end of the first half of 1986 they declined to only $10m., but by the end of 1988 they had increased to $191m. Net foreign assets rose from $2,000m. at the end of 1989 to $3,700m. at the end of 1990. At the end of 1996 Syria's net foreign assets totalled $8,901m., having risen by more than 50% since 1994, as world oil prices improved.

The Government was in mid-1994 finalizing a draft law to establish a stock market in Syria in order to facilitate a structured transition to a market economy. The Government was also coming under increasing pressure from the private business sector to relax the state monopoly on banking. Savers had recently been depositing funds with unlicensed finance houses, several of which had collapsed in circumstances which prompted the passage of legislation to shut down the remaining such operations in June 1994. Business customers' criticisms of the Commercial Bank of Syria focused mainly on the bank's negligible provision of loan finance for private businesses and its insistence on 100% cash cover for letters of credit. In 1998 the stock market law was still awaited (the Government was advising Syrian companies to apply to the Beirut stock exchange if they wanted market listings for their shares) and Western banking experts were conducting detailed appraisals of the Commercial Bank of Syria and the Central Bank of Syria as part of an EU-funded banking reform initiative.

ECONOMIC PLANNING

The most ambitious of the projects contained in the third Five-Year Plan (1971–75) was the Euphrates Dam project, on which construction work began in 1968. Most of the country's future industrial and agricultural development depends on this scheme, and nearly one-quarter of public investment over the Plan period was earmarked for its implementation, with £S950m. allocated for the dam itself and £S643m. for land reclamation and development in the Euphrates basin. The project involved the construction of a dam 4.6 km long and 60 m high, with a width of 500 m at the bottom. The reservoir thus created, Lake Assad, was designed to hold 12,000m. cu m of water, operating eight turbines and enabling the long-term irrigation of 640,000 ha of land, including 550,000 ha by 1990. The scheme was undertaken with the help of 1,200 Soviet technicians and about £S600m. in Soviet financial assistance, under an agreement reached with the USSR in April 1966. By 1977, however, only 100 Soviet experts remained on the site. In the spring of 1978 the entire project was formally opened, although the dam's first turbines had started to operate, ahead of schedule, in early 1974. Despite its advantages, the dam has exacerbated friction between Syria and Iraq, which also relies on water from the Euphrates river. Disputes over water rights

reached a crisis point in 1974–75, when Turkey started to fill the reservoir behind its Keban dam, also on the Euphrates, at the same time as Syria started to fill Lake Assad, leaving Iraq with much less water than usual. Tension over this issue subsided in 1977–78, but resurfaced in 1984 between Syria and Turkey after the latter had started work on its new Atatürk dam. It is thought that the Atatürk dam and the associated South East Anatolian project (GAP) could remove 5,000m. cu m of water per year, or more, from the Euphrates, once they are completed, in or around 2015.

The fourth Five-Year Plan started in 1976 but was interrupted by the events of that year and was reissued in 1977. It envisaged expenditure of nearly £S53,000m., comprising £S27,000m. for projects already under way, £S17,600m. for new projects and £S8,000m. to be held in reserve. Mining and manufacturing were to take 22% of the £S44,600m. allocated to specific projects, followed by energy and fuel development (17.8%) and Euphrates projects (16.6%). The target for the average annual growth of GDP during the Plan period was 12%, compared with 8.2% under the previous Plan. One important aspect of the Fourth Plan, in its original form, was its emphasis on tourism, which was expected to become the country's third main source of foreign currency, after petroleum and cotton, by 1980. This objective was not achieved, however, partly because of political factors.

Like its predecessor, the fifth Five-Year Plan (for 1981–85) started late, and details of its targets did not become available until 1982. Its main features included a decisive shift in investment from industry to agriculture, with the agricultural sector receiving a provisional allocation of £S17,200m., or 16.9% of the overall £S101,493m. spending target. The annual growth rate target for agriculture was set at 7.8%, compared with a projected 8% under the previous Plan and an average annual growth rate target of 7.7% for the economy as a whole.

The role that the private sector should play in the economy has been subject to debate. Private sector funding for the Fifth Plan was set at £S23,351m., compared with £S68,705m. from the public sector and £S59,437m. from foreign sources. However, the Baath Party Congress of January 1985 criticized public sector performance and specifically encouraged private sector investment. In 1986 the first joint public/private sector company in agriculture was established, 75% owned by the private sector and 25% by the state. Several other such ventures were subsequently created. Previously, these joint ventures had been found only in the tourist industry.

Few details on the Sixth Plan (1986–90) were released and, in view of Syria's economic constraints, five-year plans have tended to be a somewhat academic exercise anyway. Like its predecessor, the Plan concentrated on completing projects in hand and making those already complete operate efficiently, rather than embarking on a series of new projects. Syrian officials revealed that the share of agriculture in proposed investment was projected to increase from 16.9% to 18.9%, and that of industry from 12.2% to 13.7%. In real terms, spending under the Plan was to be only slightly more than under the fifth Plan. From 1991 onwards, Syria's economic policy was officially described as 'pluralist', a term indicating 'equal coexistence' of the public, private and mixed sectors of the economy. The Government's annual budgets for the years 1991 to 1994 provided for a total of £S42,000m. of public capital investment in public-sector production industries (equal to 27% of the projected private-sector investment in 'Law 10' production industries approved over the same period—see above under Industry.)

Statistical Survey

Source (unless otherwise stated): Central Bureau of Statistics, rue Abd al-Malek bin Marwah, Malki Quarter, Damascus; tel. (11) 335830; telex 411099; fax (11) 3322292.

Area and Population

AREA, POPULATION AND DENSITY

Area (sq km)	
Land	184,050
Inland water	1,130
Total	185,180*
Population (census results)†	
8 September 1981	9,052,628
3 September 1994	
Males	7,005,385
Females	6,806,899
Total	13,812,284
Population (official estimates at mid-year)†	
1995	14,186,000
1996	14,619,000
Density (per sq km) at mid-1996	78.9

* 71,498 sq miles.

† Including Palestinian refugees, numbering 193,000 at mid-1977.

PRINCIPAL TOWNS (population at census of 3 September 1994)

Damascus (capital)	1,394,322	Hama	264,348
Aleppo	1,582,930	Rakka	165,195
Homs	540,133	Al-Qamishli	144,286
Latakia	311,784	Deir ez-Zor	140,459

REGISTERED BIRTHS, MARRIAGES AND DEATHS

	Births	Marriages	Deaths
1990	385,316	99,705	39,897
1991	396,309	96,656	43,910
1992	404,948	106,545	46,308
1993	399,330	114,979	46,032
1994	407,395	115,994	43,981

Expectation of life (years at birth, 1981): males 64.42; females 68.05 (Source: UN, *Demographic Yearbook*).

ECONOMICALLY ACTIVE POPULATION

(sample survey, persons aged 10 years and over, April 1991)*

	Males	Females	Total
Agriculture, hunting, forestry and fishing	625,001	291,951	916,952
Mining and quarrying	6,651	—	6,651
Manufacturing	421,523	34,639	456,162
Electricity, gas and water	7,866	556	8,422
Construction	334,343	6,436	340,779
Trade, restaurants and hotels	368,955	9,295	378,250
Transport, storage and communications	158,358	8,607	166,965
Financing, insurance, real estate and business services	20,176	4,475	24,651
Community, social and personal services	767,428	183,676	951,104
Total employed	2,710,301	539,635	3,249,936
Unemployed	147,281	88,151	235,432
Total labour force	2,857,582	627,786	3,485,368

* Figures refer to Syrians only, excluding armed forces.

Source: ILO, *Yearbook of Labour Statistics*.

Agriculture

PRINCIPAL CROPS ('000 metric tons)

	1994	1995	1996
Wheat	3,703	4,184*	4,225*
Barley	1,482	1,705*	1,500*
Maize	203	200*	200*
Chick-peas	36	53	49
Dry broad beans	15	15†	16†
Haricot beans	3	3†	3
Lentils	116	128*	152*
Seed cotton	535	600	760
Tobacco	14	23*	23
Sesame seed	9	10†	10†
Grapes	362	384*	451
Olives	518	433*	600
Apricots	59	30*	80*
Apples	224	250*	235
Plums	24	24†	24†
Oranges	341	309*	361
Almonds	28	34*	35*
Watermelons	293	310†	320†
Melons	70	71†	75†
Cucumbers	132	150†	155†
Squash	144	150†	155†
Sugar beet	1,452	1,280*	1,227
Onions	110	124*	123
Cabbages	56	82	80
Cauliflowers	45	46†	48†
Aubergines (Egg-plants)	153	160*	165*
Green peppers	40	40†	40†
Tomatoes	426	431*	401
Potatoes	362	489*	478

* Unofficial figure. † FAO estimate.

Source: FAO, *Production Yearbook*.

LIVESTOCK ('000 head, year ending September)

	1994	1995*	1996*
Cattle	721	780	800
Horses	27	27	28
Camels	6	7	7
Asses	201	205	208
Mules	18	23	25
Sheep	11,257	11,800	12,000
Goats	1,035	1,200	1,250

Chickens (million): 18 in 1994; 19* in 1995; 18* in 1996.

* FAO estimate(s).

Source: FAO, *Production Yearbook*.

LIVESTOCK PRODUCTS ('000 metric tons)

	1994	1995*	1996*
Beef and veal	30	32	32
Mutton and lamb	102*	98	98
Goat meat	5	6	6
Poultry meat	82	86	82
Cows' milk	764	806	836
Sheep's milk	395	425	450
Goats' milk	67	68	70
Butter and ghee	12	14	14
Cheese	64	67	70
Hen eggs	103†	105	106
Wool:			
greasy	24	25	26
clean	12	13	13

* FAO estimate(s). † Unofficial figure.

Source: FAO, *Production Yearbook*.

Forestry

ROUNDWOOD REMOVALS ('000 cubic metres, excl. bark)

	1993	1994	1995
Sawlogs, veneer logs and logs for sleepers	16	16	16
Other industrial wood . . .	19	19	19
Fuel wood	19	19	20
Total	54	54	55

Sawnwood production ('000 cubic metres): 9 per year in 1991–95.

Source: FAO, *Yearbook of Forest Products*.

Fishing

('000 metric tons, live weight)

	1993	1994	1995
Freshwater fishes . . .	7.2	8.1	8.6
Marine fishes*	1.9	1.9	1.9
Crustaceans*	0.1	0.1	0.1
Total catch	9.2	10.0	10.5
Inland waters	7.2	8.1	8.6
Mediterranean Sea . . .	2.0	2.0	1.9

* FAO estimates.
Source: FAO, *Yearbook of Fishery Statistics*.

Mining

('000 metric tons, unless otherwise indicated)

	1994	1995	1996*
Crude petroleum ('000 cubic metres)	32,432	34,277	33,791
Phosphate rock	1,202	1,598	2,188
Salt (unrefined)	100	111	72
Natural asphalt	82	108	116

* Public-sector production only.

Source: Central Bank of Syria, *Quarterly Bulletin*.

Industry

SELECTED PRODUCTS ('000 metric tons, unless otherwise indicated)

	1994	1995	1996*
Cotton yarn (pure) . . .	37	40	43
Silk and cotton textiles . .	28	23	15
Woollen cloth (metric tons) . .	424	186	n.a.
Plywood ('000 cu metres) . .	4.5	3.2	4.3
Cement	4,344	4,804	4,817
Glass and pottery products .	54	70	53
Soap	18	18	4
Refined sugar	180	158	181
Olive oil	100	85	127
Vegetable oil and fats . .	33	39	36
Cottonseed cake . . .	103	118	117
Manufactured tobacco . .	8	10	9
Electricity (million kWh) . .	14,036	15,549	17,278
Refrigerators ('000) . .	148.3	156.2	65.3
Washing machines ('000) . .	49.8	77.6	n.a.
Television receivers ('000) . .	77.4	71.2	123.8
Beer ('000 hectolitres) . .	102	102	n.a.
Wine ('000 hectolitres) . .	2.6	n.a.	n.a.
Arak ('000 hectolitres) . .	24	n.a.	n.a.

* Public-sector production only.

Source: mainly Central Bank of Syria, *Quarterly Bulletin*.

Finance

CURRENCY AND EXCHANGE RATES

Monetary Units
100 piastres = 1 Syrian pound (£S).

Sterling and Dollar Equivalents (31 May 1998)
£1 sterling = £S18.305;
US $1 = £S11.225;
£S1,000 = £54.63 sterling = $89.09.

Exchange Rate
Between April 1976 and December 1987 the official mid-point rate was fixed at US $1 = £S3.925. On 1 January 1988 a new rate of $1 = £S11.225 was introduced. In addition to the official exchange rate, there is a promotion rate (applicable to most travel and tourism transactions) and a flexible rate.

BUDGET (estimates, £S million)

Revenue	1995	1996	1997
Taxes and duties . . .	48,903.0	57,371.0	69,296.0
Services, commutations and revenues from state properties and their public investments .	7,186.0	12,743.0	18,574.0
Various revenues . . .	46,157.0	53,929.0	48,108.0
Supply surplus . . .	23,147.3	32,870.4	44,516.1
Exceptional revenues . . .	36,646.7	31,136.6	30,630.9
Total	**162,040.0**	**188,050.0**	**211,125.0**

Expenditure	1995	1996	1997
Community, social and personal services	98,962.2	110,713.8	116,168.2
Agriculture, forestry and fishing .	15,281.4	19,442.9	24,220.0
Mining and quarrying . . .	5,099.3	5,856.0	8,471.0
Manufacturing . . .	10,833.6	11,524.4	14,033.4
Electricity, gas and water . .	17,813.8	24,056.4	27,004.4
Building and construction .	1,235.9	1,281.6	1,216.2
Trade	1,801.4	2,278.0	3,435.4
Transport, communications and storage	7,506.7	8,427.4	11,012.4
Finance, insurance and companies	655.7	1,119.5	1,164.0
Non-distributed funds . . .	2,850.0	3,350.0	4,400.0
Total	**162,040.0**	**188,050.0**	**211,125.0**

CENTRAL BANK RESERVES (US $ million at 31 December)

	1986	1987	1988
Gold*	29	29	29
Foreign exchange . . .	144	223	193
Total	**173**	**252**	**222**

* Valued at $35 per troy ounce.

Source: IMF, *International Financial Statistics*.

MONEY SUPPLY (£S million at 31 December)

	1994	1995	1996
Currency outside banks . .	135,021.3	143,800.4	153,251.8
Demand deposits at Central Bank	3,199.9	3,210.3	6,095.5
Demand deposits at commercial banks	68,884.9	78,028.3	84,685.3
Total money	**207,106.1**	**225,039.0**	**244,032.6**

Source: Central Bank of Syria, *Quarterly Bulletin*.

COST OF LIVING
(Consumer Price Index for Damascus; base: 1990 = 100)

	1994	1995	1996
Food	145	155	169
Fuel and light	198	274	278
Clothing	186	203	231
Rent	144	171	192
All items (incl. others)	154	170	185

Source: ILO, *Yearbook of Labour Statistics.*

1997: All items 188.2.

Source (for 1997): IMF, *International Financial Statistics.*

NATIONAL ACCOUNTS (£S million at current prices)
Expenditure on the Gross Domestic Product

	1994	1995	1996
Government final consumption expenditure	68,019	76,709	81,463
Private final consumption expenditure	348,865	377,110	447,480
Gross capital formation	151,622	154,824	169,444
Total domestic expenditure	568,506	608,643	698,387
Exports of goods and services	167,327	177,229	219,872
Less Imports of goods and services	229,732	216,610	263,135
GDP in purchasers' values	506,101	569,262	655,124
GDP at constant 1985 prices	119,828	127,904	130,770

Source: Central Bank of Syria, *Quarterly Bulletin*

Gross Domestic Product by Economic Activity

	1994	1995	1996
Agriculture, hunting, forestry and fishing	139,288	161,017	176,607
Mining and quarrying			
Manufacturing	70,452	79,386	135,359
Electricity, gas and water			
Construction	21,937	24,530	26,708
Trade, restaurants and hotels	136,138	146,406	142,103
Transport, storage and communications	56,296	66,361	72,680
Finance, insurance, real estate and business services	24,417	27,391	31,924
Government services	47,732	53,097	56,911
Other community, social and personal services	9,667	10,874	12,602
Non-profit private services	174	200	230
GDP in purchasers' values	506,101	569,262	655,124

Source: Central Bank of Syria, *Quarterly Bulletin.*

BALANCE OF PAYMENTS (US $ million)

	1995	1996	1997
Exports of goods f.o.b.	3,858	4,178	4,057
Imports of goods f.o.b.	−4,001	−4,516	−3,603
Trade balance	−143	−338	454
Exports of services	1,979	1,833	1,604
Imports of services	−1,537	−1,555	−1,489
Balance on goods and services	299	−60	569
Other income received	444	534	421
Other income paid	−983	−933	−925
Balance on goods, services and income	−240	−459	65
Current transfers received	610	630	504
Current transfers paid	−3	−6	−5
Current balance	367	165	564
Capital account (net)	20	26	18
Direct investment from abroad	100	89	80
Other investment assets	−787	−762	−997
Other investment liabilities	1,154	1,452	832
Net errors and omissions	−69	−173	−186
Overall balance	785	797	311

Source: IMF, *International Financial Statistics.*

External Trade

PRINCIPAL COMMODITIES (£S million)

Imports c.i.f.	1994	1995	1996
Cotton textiles, other textile goods and silk	5,945.4	3,781.9	3,750.3
Mineral fuels and oils	1,027.0	573.8	1,081.5
Live animals, meat and canned meat	1,236.8	1,532.7	978.2
Vegetables and fruit	2,329.6	1,074.3	545.9
Sugar	1,544.4	1,235.0	1,835.2
Other foodstuffs	4,503.8	4,377.6	4,905.6
Machinery and apparatus	11,331.4	9,908.6	13,107.3
Base metals and manufactures	7,195.4	10,304.7	10,890.4
Chemicals and pharmaceutical products	2,445.4	3,957.6	4,675.3
Transport equipment	5,444.5	6,626.5	5,895.0
Paper and paper products	815.2	1,169.4	1,025.0
Wood and wood products	1,175.3	1,467.4	976.2
Resins, artificial rubber, etc.	1,994.7	2,357.0	3,675.7
Total (incl. others)	61,374.1	52,856.0	60,385.4

Exports f.o.b.	1994	1995	1996
Raw cotton	2,181.1	2,390.8	1,913.7
Textiles	6,184.7	7,258.5	3,981.2
Vegetables and fruit (fresh and prepared)	4,124.2	2,801.8	3,107.7
Live animals and meat	858.2	537.2	1,079.5
Crude petroleum	20,605.4	24,752.4	28,519.8
Total (incl. others)	39,818.5	44,561.8	44,887.0

Source: Central Bank of Syria, *Quarterly Bulletin.*

PRINCIPAL TRADING PARTNERS (£S million)

Imports c.i.f.	1994	1995	1996
Austria	546.9	308.3	615.7
Belgium	1,717.6	1,616.9	1,637.4
Bulgaria	1,214.9	646.3	1,212.8
China, People's Republic . . .	2,247.3	2,029.0	1,806.0
Czechoslovakia (former) . . .	1,085.8	1,029.9	839.6
Egypt	779.4	782.4	928.9
France	3,038.2	1,854.2	3,576.2
Germany	5,228.4	5,507.5	4,859.4
India	359.3	410.2	603.0
Italy	5,324.3	3,993.0	4,042.9
Japan	6,205.8	2,308.2	2,962.7
Jordan	676.7	829.4	1,212.1
Lebanon	618.2	635.6	634.8
Netherlands	1,286.1	1,190.5	1,132.2
Romania	2,361.9	2,030.1	2,030.5
Russia	1,282.0	1,668.2	1,108.1
Saudi Arabia	841.7	875.9	1,023.0
Spain	857.2	707.2	809.8
Sweden	672.5	604.1	406.9
Turkey	2,917.7	2,961.6	3,491.2
United Kingdom	2,188.4	1,348.9	1,633.8
USA	3,534.1	3,578.2	4,373.9
Total (incl. others) . . .	61,374.1	52,856.0	60,385.4

Exports f.o.b.	1994	1995	1996
Cyprus	413.7	792.7	n.a.
France	4,943.5	6,494.1	6,995.6
Germany	992.1	1,184.3	467.5
Greece	246.6	1,413.3	1,127.6
Italy	10,731.8	10,412.7	12,939.4
Jordan	1,082.2	1,041.3	1,189.1
Kuwait	573.5	677.8	762.5
Lebanon	4,376.1	3,469.4	2,487.9
Libya	566.3	681.2	n.a.
Romania	328.4	521.7	244.8
Russia	2,751.9	1,793.9	1,388.0
Saudi Arabia	2,198.5	2,188.3	2,176.4
Spain	2,701.7	3,405.5	4,465.4
Turkey	982.0	2,582.9	3,220.8
United Kingdom	2,123.1	1,930.3	1,028.6
USA	478.5	400.4	172.9
Total (incl. others)	39,818.5	44,561.8	44,887.0

Source: Central Bank of Syria, *Quarterly Bulletin*.

Transport

RAILWAYS (traffic)

	1994	1995	1996
Passenger-km ('000) . . .	768,505	498,311	453,886
Freight ('000 metric tons) . . .	4,040	4,318	4,655

ROAD TRAFFIC (motor vehicles in use)

	1994	1995	1996
Passenger cars	130,829	136,160	139,592
Buses and coaches . . .	28,316	30,384	33,970
Lorries, trucks, etc. . . .	188,408	224,031	251,451
Motor cycles	87,070	89,038	88,453

SHIPPING

Merchant Fleet (registered at 31 December)

	1995	1996	1997
Number of vessels	190	220	219
Total displacement ('000 grt) . .	351.7	420.2	414.9

Source: Lloyd's Register of Shipping, *World Fleet Statistics*.

International Sea-borne Traffic

	1994	1995*	1996*
Vessels entered (number) . . .	3,433	2,884	2,901
Cargo unloaded ('000 metric tons)†	4,473	4,459	4,569
Cargo loaded ('000 metric tons)† .	19,532	1,898	1,794

* Excluding Banias.
† Excluding Arwad.

CIVIL AVIATION (traffic on scheduled services)

	1993	1994	1995
Kilometres flown (million) . .	10	10	10
Passengers carried ('000) . .	485	472	563
Passenger-km (million) . .	817	823	948
Total ton-km (million) . .	86	88	103

Source: UN, *Statistical Yearbook*.

Tourism

VISITOR ARRIVALS ('000 visitors)

	1994	1995	1996
Jordanians, Lebanese and Iraqis .	1,156	1,265	1,377
Other Arabs	293	369	441
Europeans	151	176	330
Asians	347	384	210
Others	65	59	78
Total visitors	2,012	2,253	2,436

Tourist Accommodation: 31,394 tourist hotel beds (1994).

Communications Media

	1993	1994	1995
Radio receivers ('000 in use) . .	3,515	3,640	3,750
Television receivers ('000 in use) .	850	880	950
Telephones ('000 main lines in use)	550	688	930
Telefax stations (number in use) .	n.a.	4,200	5,000
Daily newspapers:			
Number	n.a.	8	8
Average circulation ('000 copies)	n.a.	261	274

1992: Book production 598 titles.

Sources: UNESCO, *Statistical Yearbook*; UN, *Statistical Yearbook*.

Education

(1995/96)

	Insti-tutions	Teachers	Pupils/Students Males	Females	Total
Pre-primary . .	1,048	4,233	50,321	42,149	92,470
Primary . .	10,564	113,530	1,426,130	1,246,830	2,672,960
Secondary:					
General . .	n.a.	51,483*	463,028	381,750	846,778
Vocational . .	n.a.	12,200*	46,001	48,203	94,204
Higher:†					
Universities, etc.	n.a.	5,997	110,533	67,993	178,526
Others‡ . .	n.a.	n.a.	9,690	6,155	15,845

* Provisional figure.
† Figures refer to 1992/93.
‡ Excluding a part of vocational education.

Source: UNESCO, *Statistical Yearbook*.

Directory

The Constitution

A new and permanent Constitution was endorsed by 97.6% of the voters in a national referendum on 12 March 1973. The 157-article Constitution defines Syria as a 'Socialist popular democracy' with a 'pre-planned Socialist economy'. Under the new Constitution, Lt-Gen. al-Assad remained President, with the power to appoint and dismiss his Vice-President, Premier and government ministers, and also became Commander-in-Chief of the armed forces, Secretary-General of the Baath Socialist Party and President of the National Progressive Front. Legislative power is vested in the People's Assembly, with 250 members elected by universal adult suffrage (84 seats are reserved for independent candidates).

The Government

HEAD OF STATE

President: Lt-Gen. HAFIZ AL-ASSAD (elected 12 March 1971 for a seven-year term; re-elected 8 February 1978, 10 February 1985 and 2 December 1991).

Vice-Presidents: ABD AL-HALIM KHADDAM (responsible for Political and Foreign Affairs), ZUHEIR MASHARKAH (responsible for Internal and Party Affairs).

COUNCIL OF MINISTERS
(September 1998)

Prime Minister: MAHMOUD AZ-ZOUBI.

Deputy Prime Minister and Minister of Defence: Maj.-Gen. MUSTAFA TLASS.

Deputy Prime Minister in charge of Public Services: RASHID AKHTARINI.

Deputy Prime Minister in charge of Economic Affairs: SALIM YASSIN.

Minister of Foreign Affairs: FAROUK ASH-SHARA.

Minister of Information: MUHAMMAD SALMAN.

Minister of the Interior: Dr MUHAMMAD HARBAH.

Minister of Supply and Internal Trade: NADIM AKKASH.

Minister of Local Government: YAHYA ABU ASALAH.

Minister of Education: GHASSAN HALABI.

Minister of Higher Education: Dr SALIHAH SANQAR.

Minister of Electricity: MUNIB ASAAD SAIM AL-DAHER.

Minister of Culture: Dr NAJAH AL-ATTAR.

Minister of Transport: Dr MUFID ABD AL-KARIM.

Minister of Economy and Foreign Trade: Dr MUHAMMAD AL-IMADI.

Minister of Petroleum and Mineral Wealth: MUHAMMAD MAHIR HUSNI JAMAL.

Minister of Industry: Dr AHMAD NIZAM AD-DIN.

Minister of Finance: KHALID AL-MAHAYNI.

Minister of Housing and Utilities: Eng. HUSAM AS-SAFADI.

Minister of Justice: Dr ABDULLAH TULBAH.

Minister of Agriculture and Agrarian Reform: ASSAD MUSTAFA.

Minister of Irrigation, Public Works and Water Resources: Eng. ABD AR-RAHMAN MADANI.

Minister of Communications: Eng. RADWAN MARTINI.

Minister of Health: Dr IYAD ASH-SHATTI.

Minister of Construction: MAJID IZZU RUHAYBANI.

Minister of Awqaf (Islamic Endowments): MUHAMMAD ABD AR-RA'UF ZIYADAH.

Minister of Labour and Social Affairs: ALI KHALIL.

Minister of Tourism and Minister of State for Council of Ministers Affairs: Dr DANHU DAOUD.

Minister of State for Presidential Affairs: WAHIB FADEL.

Minister of State for Planning Affairs: Dr ABD AR-RAHIM SUBAYI.

Minister of State for Environmental Affairs: ABD AL-HAMID AL-MOUNAJJID.

Minister of State for Foreign Affairs: NASIR QADDOUR.

Minister of State for Cabinet Affairs: MUSALLAM MUHAMMAD HAWWA.

Ministers of State: Eng. YOUSUF AL-AHMAD, HUSSEIN HASSUN, NABIL MALLAH, Eng. HANNA MURAD.

MINISTRIES

Office of the President: Damascus.

Office of the Prime Minister: Damascus.

Ministry of Agriculture and Agrarian Reform: 29 rue Ayar, Damascus; tel. (11) 113613.

Ministry of Communications: nr Majlis ash-Sha'ab, Damascus; telex 411993.

Ministry of Economy and Foreign Trade: Damascus; tel. (11) 113513; telex 411982.

Ministry of Electricity: BP 4900, 41 rue al-Jamhourieh, Damascus; tel. (11) 227981; telex 411256; fax (11) 2227736.

Ministry of Finance: POB 13136, Jule Jamal St, Damascus; tel. (11) 2239624; telex 411932; fax (11) 2224701.

Ministry of Foreign Affairs: Damascus; telex 411922.

Ministry of Industry: POB 12835, place Yousuf al-Azmeh, Damascus; tel. and fax (11) 3720909.

Ministry of Information: ave al-Mazzeh, Imm. Dar al-Baath, Damascus; tel. (11) 6619396; fax (11) 6617665.

Ministry of Petroleum and Mineral Wealth: rue Moutanabbi, Damascus; tel. (11) 116783; telex 411006.

Ministry of Public Works and Water Resources: rue Saadallah Jabri, Damascus.

Ministry of Supply and Internal Trade: opposite Majlis ash-Sha'ab, Damascus; tel. (11) 720604; telex 412908; fax (11) 2219803.

Ministry of Tourism: rue Victoria, Damascus; tel. (11) 2215916; telex 411672; fax (11) 2242636.

Ministry of Transport: BP 134, rue Abou Roumaneh, Damascus; tel. (11) 336801; telex 411994.

Legislature

MAJLIS ASH-SHA'AB
(People's Assembly)

Speaker: ABD AL-QADIR QADDURAH.

Election, 24 August 1994

Party	Seats
Baath Party	135
Arab Socialist Unionist Party	7
Syrian Arab Socialist Union Party	7
Arab Socialist Party	6
Socialist Unionist Democratic Party	4
Communist Party	8
Independents	83
Total	**250**

Political Organizations

The **National Progressive Front**, headed by President Assad, was formed in March 1972 by the grouping of the following five parties:

Arab Socialist Party: Damascus; a breakaway socialist party; contested the 1994 election to the People's Assembly as two factions; Leader ABD AL-GHANI KANNOUT.

Arab Socialist Unionist Party: Damascus; Leader SAMI SOUFAN; Sec.-Gen. FAYIZ ISMAIL.

Baath Arab Socialist Party: National Command, BP 849, Damascus; Arab nationalist socialist party; f. 1947; result of merger of the Arab Revival (Baath) Movement (f. 1940) and the Arab Socialist Party (f. 1940); brs in most Arab countries; in power since 1963; supports creation of a unified Arab socialist society; Sec.-Gen. Pres. HAFIZ AL-ASSAD; Asst Sec.-Gen. ABDULLAH AL-AHMAR; Regional Asst Sec.-Gen. Dr SULEIMAN QADDAH; more than 800,000 mems in Syria.

Communist Party of Syria: Damascus; tel. (11) 448243; f. 1924; until 1943 part of joint Communist Party of Syria and Lebanon; Sixth Party Congress January 1987; contested the 1994 election to the People's Assembly as two factions; Sec.-Gen. YOUSUF FAISAL.

Syrian Arab Socialist Union Party: Damascus; tel. (11) 239305; Nasserite; Sec.-Gen. SAFWAN KOUDSI.

A sixth party, the **Socialist Unionist Democratic Party**, contested the elections held to the People's Assembly in May 1990 and August 1994 as a member of the National Progressive Front. There is also a **Marxist-Leninist Communist Action Party**, which regards itself as independent of all Arab regimes.

An illegal Syrian-based organization, the **Islamic Movement for Change (IMC),** claimed responsibility for a bomb attack in Damascus in December 1996.

Diplomatic Representation

EMBASSIES IN SYRIA

Afghanistan: BP 12217, ave Secretariat, West Villas, Mezzeh, Damascus; tel. (11) 6112910; fax (11) 6133595; Chargé d'affaires: Sheik ABDULLAH MOHSENI.

Algeria: Immeuble Noss, Raouda, Damascus; telex 411344; Ambassador: SALEM BOUJOUMAA.

Argentina: BP 116, rue Ziad ben Abi Soufian, Raouda, Damascus; tel. (11) 3334167; fax (11) 3327326; Ambassador: JUAN ANTONIO PARDO.

Australia: Immeuble Dakkak, 128A rue Farabi, East Villas, Mezzeh, Damascus; tel. (11) 6664317; telex 419132; fax (11) 6621195; Ambassador: JIM DALLIMORE.

Austria: Immeuble Mohamed Naïm ad-Deker, 152A rue Farabi, East Villas, Mezzeh, Damascus; tel. (11) 6624730; telex 411389; fax (11) 6624734; Ambassador: Dr ROBERT KARAS.

Belgium: Immeuble du Syndicat des Médecins, rue al-Jalaa, Abou Roumaneh, Damascus; tel. (11) 3332821; telex 411090; fax (11) 3330426; Ambassador: JACQUES VERMEULEN.

Brazil: BP 2219, 7 rue Kassem Amin, Damascus; tel. (11) 3335770; fax (11) 3330054; Ambassador: GUILHERME FAUSTO DA CUNHA BASTOS.

Bulgaria: 4 rue Chahbandar, Damascus; Ambassador: GEORGI YANKOV.

Canada: BP 3394, Damascus; tel. (11) 6116692; telex 412422; fax (11) 6114000; Ambassador: ALEXANDRA BUGAILISKIS.

Chile: BP 3561, 43 rue ar-Rachid, Damascus; tel. (11) 3338443; fax (11) 3331563; e-mail echilesy@cyberia.net.lb; Ambassador: JULIO LAGARINI.

China, People's Republic: 83 rue Ata Ayoubi, Damascus; Ambassador: LI QINGYU.

Cuba: Immeuble Oustwani and Charabati, 40 rue ar-Rachid, Damascus; tel. (11) 3339624; telex 419155; fax (11) 3333802; Ambassador: ERNESTO GÓMEZ ABASCAL.

Cyprus: BP 3853, rue Abd al-Malek al-Marouan, Jaded ar-Rais, Abou Roumaneh, Damascus; tel. (11) 332804; telex 411411; Ambassador: NICOLAS MACRIS.

Czech Republic: BP 2249, place Abou al-Ala'a al-Maari, Damascus; tel. (11) 3331383; fax (11) 3338268; Chargé d'affaires: PETR DUBOVEC.

Denmark: BP 2244, Immeuble Patriarcat Grec-Catholique, rue Chekib Arslan, Abou Roumaneh, Damascus; tel. (11) 3331008; telex 419125; fax (11) 3337928; Ambassador: LARS BLINKENBERG.

Egypt: Damascus; Ambassador: MOUSTAFA ABD AL-AZIZ.

Ethiopia: Damascus; Ambassador: ABD AL-MONEM AHMAD.

Finland: BP 3893, Immeuble Yacoubian, Hawakir, West Malki, Damascus; tel. (11) 3338809; fax (11) 3734740; Ambassador: HEIKKI LATVANEN.

France: BP 769, rue Ata Ayoubi, Damascus; tel. (11) 3327993; telex 411013; fax (11) 3338632; Ambassador: CHARLES DE BANCALIS DE MAUREL D'ARAGON.

Germany: BP 2237, Immeuble Kotob, 53 rue Ibrahim Hanano, Damascus; tel. (11) 3323800; telex 411065; fax (11) 3323812; Ambassador: Dr HEINRICH REINERS.

Greece: Immeuble Pharaon, 1 rue Farabi, East Villas, Mezzeh, Damascus; tel. (11) 6113035; telex 411045; fax (11) 6114920; Ambassador: YANNIS MOURIKIS.

Holy See: BP 2271, 82 rue Masr, Damascus (Apostolic Nunciature); tel. (11) 3332601; telex 411065; fax (11) 3327550; Apostolic Nuncio: Most Rev. PIER GIACOMO DE NICOLÒ, Titular Archbishop of Martana.

Hungary: BP 2607, 102 rue al-Fursan, East Villas, Mezzeh, al-Akram, Damascus; tel. (11) 6110787; fax (11) 6117917; e-mail hunemdam@cyberia.net.16; Ambassador: ZOLTÁN PERESZLÉNYI.

India: BP 685, Immeuble Noueilati, 40/46 ave Adnan al-Malki, Damascus; tel. (11) 3719580; telex 411377; fax (11) 3713294; Chargé d'affaires: R. S. AISOLA.

Indonesia: BP 3530, 10A rue East Villas, Mezzeh, al-Akram, Damascus; tel. (11) 6119630; telex 419188; fax (11) 6119632; Ambassador: DJAMARIS B. SULEMAN.

Iran: Mezzeh Autostrade, nr ar-Razi Hospital, Damascus; telex 411041; Ambassador: Hojatoleslam MUHAMMAD HASSAN AKHTARI.

Italy: 82 ave al-Mansour, Damascus; Ambassador: ANTONIO NAPOLITANO.

Japan: 15 ave al-Jala'a, Damascus; tel. (11) 339421; telex 411042; Ambassador: RYUJI ONODERA.

Jordan: rue Abou Roumaneh, Damascus; telex 419161; Ambassador: ALI KHURAIS.

Korea, Democratic People's Republic: rue Fares al-Khouri-Jisr Tora, Damascus; Ambassador: PAK UI CHUN.

Kuwait: rue Ibrahim Hanano, Damascus; telex 419172; Ambassador: AHMAD ABD AL-AZIZ AL-JASSEM.

Libya: Abou Roumaneh, Damascus; Head of People's Bureau: AHMAD ABD AS-SALAM BIN KHAYAL.

Mauritania: ave al-Jala'a, rue Karameh, Damascus; telex 411264; Ambassador: MUHAMMAD MAHMOUD OULD WEDDADY.

Morocco: Damascus; Ambassador: IDRIFF DHAHAQ.

Netherlands: BP 702, Immeuble Tello, rue al-Jalaa, Abou Roumaneh, Damascus; tel. (11) 3335119; telex 411032; fax (11) 3339369; Ambassador: R. H. MEYS.

Norway: BP 7703, rue Ahmad Shawki; tel. (11) 3322072; fax (11) 3337114; Ambassador: VIGLEIK EIDE.

Oman: BP 9635, rue Ghazzawi, West Villas, Mezzeh, Damascus; tel. (11) 6110408; fax (11) 6110944; Ambassador: Sheikh HILLAL BIN SALIM AS-SIYABI.

Pakistan: BP 9284, rue al-Farabi, East Villas, Damascus; tel. (11) 6132694; fax (11) 6132662; Ambassador: AFZAL AKBAR KHAN.

Panama: BP 2548, Apt 7, Immeuble az-Zein, rue al-Bizm, Malki, Damascus; tel. (11) 224743; telex 411918; Chargé d'affaires: CARLOS A. DE GRACIA.

Poland: BP 501, 21 rue Mehdi Ben Barakeh, Damascus; tel. and fax (11) 3333010; telex 412288; Ambassador: STANISŁAW PAWLAK.

Qatar: BP 4188, 20 Immeuble Allawi, place Madfa, Abou Roumaneh, Damascus; tel. (11) 336717; telex 411064; Ambassador: FAHD FAHD AL-KHATER.

Romania: BP 4454, 8 rue Ibrahim Hanano, Damascus; tel. (11) 3327570; telex 411305; fax (11) 3327571; Ambassador: DORU PANA.

Russia: rue d'Alep, Boustan al-Kouzbari, Damascus; telex 411221; Ambassador: ALEKSANDR I. ZOTOV.

Saudi Arabia: ave al-Jala'a, Damascus; telex 411906; Ambassador: ABDULLAH BIN SALEH AL-FADL.

Slovakia: BP 33115, place Mezzeh, East Villas, rue ash-Shafei, Damascus; tel. (11) 6132114; telex 421045; fax (11) 6132598; Chargé d'affaires a.i.: PETER JENDRUS.

Somalia: ave Ata Ayoubi, Damascus; telex 419194; Ambassador: (vacant).

South Africa: Damascus; Ambassador: (vacant).

Spain: BP 392, rue ash-Shafi, East Villas, Mezzeh, Damascus; fax (11) 6132941; Ambassador: MANUEL GÓMEZ DE VALENZUELA.

Sudan: Damascus; telex 411266.

Sweden: BP 4266, rue Chakib Arslan, Abou Roumaneh, Damascus; tel. (11) 3327261; telex 411339; fax (11) 3327749; e-mail ambassaden .damasku@foreign.ministry.se; Ambassador: TOMMY ARWITZ.

Switzerland: BP 234, 2 rue ash-Shafi, East Villas, Mezzeh, Damascus; tel. (11) 6111972; fax (11) 6111976; e-mail vertretung@dam .rep.admin.ch; Ambassador: CHRISTIAN FAESSLER.

Tunisia: BP 4114, 6 rue ash-Shafi, West Villas, Mezzeh, Damascus; tel. (11) 660356; telex 431302; Ambassador: MUHAMMAD CHERIF.

Turkey: 56–58 ave Ziad bin Abou Soufian, Damascus; tel. (11) 3331370; Ambassador: UGUR ZIYAL.

United Arab Emirates: Immeuble Housami, 62 rue Raouda, Damascus; telex 411213; Ambassador: SALIM RASHID AL-AQROUBI.

United Kingdom: BP 37, Immeuble Kotob, 11 rue Mohd Kurd Ali, Malki, Damascus; tel. (11) 3712561; fax (11) 3731600; Ambassador: BASIL EASTWOOD.

USA: BP 29, 2 rue al-Mansour, Damascus; tel. (11) 3333232; telex 411919; fax (11) 2247938; Ambassador: RYAN C. CROCKER.

Venezuela: BP 2403, Immeuble Tabbah, rue Zuheir Bin Abi Sulma, Abou Roumaneh, Damascus; tel. (11) 3335356; telex 411929; fax (11) 3333203; Ambassador: HERNANI ESCOBAR CABRERA.

Viet Nam: 9 ave Malki, Damascus; tel. (11) 333008; Ambassador: LE THANH TAM.

Yemen: Abou Roumaneh, Charkassieh, Damascus; Ambassador: ABDULLAH HUSSAIN BARAKAT.

Yugoslavia: BP 739, ave al-Jala'a, Damascus; tel. (11) 3336222; telex 412646; fax (11) 3333690; Ambassador: ZORAN S. POPOVIĆ.

Note: Syria and Lebanon have very close relations but do not exchange formal ambassadors.

Judicial System

The Courts of Law in Syria are principally divided into two juridical court systems: Courts of General Jurisdiction and Administrative

Courts. Since 1973 the Supreme Constitutional Court (Damascus; tel. (11) 3331902) has been established as the paramount body of the Syrian judicial structure.

THE SUPREME CONSTITUTIONAL COURT

This is the highest court in Syria. It has specific jurisdiction over: (i) judicial review of the constitutionality of laws and legislative decrees; (ii) investigation of charges relating to the legality of the election of members of the Majlis ash-Sha'ab (People's Assembly); (iii) trial of infractions committed by the President of the Republic in the exercise of his functions; (iv) resolution of positive and negative jurisdictional conflicts and determination of the competent court between the different juridical court systems, as well as other bodies exercising judicial competence. The Supreme Constitutional Court is composed of a Chief Justice and four Justices. They are appointed by decree of the President of the Republic for a renewable period of four years.

Chief Justice: NASRAT MOUNLA-HAYDAR.

COURTS OF GENERAL JURISDICTION

The Courts of General Jurisdiction in Syria are divided into six categories: (i) The Court of Cassation; (ii) The Courts of Appeal; (iii) The Tribunals of First Instance; (iv) The Tribunals of Peace; (v) The Personal Status Courts; (vi) The Courts for Minors. Each of the above categories (except the Personal Status Courts) is divided into Civil, Penal and Criminal Chambers.

(i) **The Court of Cassation:** This is the highest court of general jurisdiction. Final judgments rendered by Courts of Appeal in penal and civil litigations may be petitioned to the Court of Cassation by the Defendant or the Public Prosecutor in penal and criminal litigations, and by any of the parties in interest in civil litigations, on grounds of defective application or interpretation of the law as stated in the challenged judgment, on grounds of irregularity of form or procedure, or violation of due process, and on grounds of defective reasoning of judgment rendered. The Court of Cassation is composed of a President, seven Vice-Presidents and 31 other Justices (Councillors).

(ii) **The Courts of Appeal:** Each court has geographical jurisdiction over one governorate (Mouhafazat). Each court is divided into Penal and Civil Chambers. There are Criminal Chambers which try felonies only. The Civil Chambers hear appeals filed against judgments rendered by the Tribunals of First Instance and the Tribunals of Peace. Each Court of Appeal is composed of a President and sufficient numbers of Vice-Presidents (Presidents of Chambers) and Superior Judges (Councillors). There are 54 Courts of Appeal.

(iii) **The Tribunals of First Instance:** In each governorate there are one or more Tribunals of First Instance, each of which is divided into several Chambers for penal and civil litigations. Each Chamber is composed of one judge. There are 72 Tribunals of First Instance.

(iv) **The Tribunals of Peace:** In the administrative centre of each governorate, and in each district, there are one or more Tribunals of Peace, which have jurisdiction over minor civil and penal litigations. There are 227 Tribunals of Peace.

(v) **Personal Status Courts:** These courts deal with marriage, divorce, etc. For Muslims each court consists of one judge, the 'Qadi Shari'i'. For Druzes there is one court consisting of one judge, the 'Qadi Mazhabi'. For non-Muslim communities there are courts for Roman Catholics, Orthodox believers, Protestants and Jews.

(vi) **Courts for Minors:** The constitution, officers, sessions, jurisdiction and competence of these courts are determined by a special law.

PUBLIC PROSECUTION

Public prosecution is headed by the Attorney-General, assisted by a number of Senior Deputy and Deputy Attorneys-General, and a sufficient number of chief prosecutors, prosecutors and assistant prosecutors. Public prosecution is represented at all levels of the Courts of General Jurisdiction in all criminal and penal litigations and also in certain civil litigations as required by the law. Public prosecution controls and supervises enforcement of penal judgments.

ADMINISTRATIVE COURTS SYSTEM

The Administrative Courts have jurisdiction over litigations involving the state or any of its governmental agencies. The Administrative Courts system is divided into two courts: the Administrative Courts and the Judicial Administrative Courts, of which the paramount body is the High Administrative Court.

MILITARY COURTS

The Military Courts deal with criminal litigations against military personnel of all ranks and penal litigations against officers only. There are two military courts; one in Damascus, the other in Aleppo. Each court is composed of three military judges. There are other military courts, consisting of one judge, in every governorate, which

deal with penal litigations against military personnel below the rank of officer. The different military judgments can be petitioned to the Court of Cassation.

Religion

In religion the majority of Syrians follow a form of Islamic Sunni orthodoxy. There are also a considerable number of religious minorities: Shi'a Muslims; Ismaili Muslims; the Ismaili of the Salamiya district, whose spiritual head is the Aga Khan; a large number of Druzes, the Nusairis or Alawites of the Jebel Ansariyeh (a schism of the Shi'ite branch of Islam, to which President Assad belongs, who comprise about 11% of the population) and the Yezidis of the Jebel Sinjar, and a minority of Christians.

The Constitution states only that 'Islam shall be the religion of the head of the state'. The original draft of the 1973 Constitution made no reference to Islam at all, and this clause was inserted only as a compromise after public protest. The Syrian Constitution is thus unique among the constitutions of Arab states (excluding Lebanon) with a clear Muslim majority in not enshrining Islam as the religion of the state itself.

ISLAM

Grand Mufti: AHMAD KUFTARO.

CHRISTIANITY

Orthodox Churches

Greek Orthodox Patriarchate: His Beatitude IGNATIUS HAZIM, Patriarch of Antioch and all the Orient; BP 9, Damascus; has jurisdiction over Syria, Lebanon, Iran and Iraq.

Syrian Orthodox Patriarchate: BP 914, Bab Touma, Damascus; tel. (11) 447036; Syrian Orthodox Patriarch: His Holiness IGNATIUS ZAKKA I IWAS, Patriarch of Antioch and All the East; the Syrian Orthodox Church includes one Catholicose (of the East), 30 Metropolitans and one Bishop, and has an estimated 3m. adherents throughout the world.

The Armenian Apostolic Church is also represented in Syria.

The Roman Catholic Church

Armenian Rite

Patriarchal Exarchate of Syria: Exarcat Patriarcal Arménien Catholique, Bab Touma, Damascus; tel. (11) 5433438; fax (11) 5431988; represents the Patriarch of Cilicia (resident in Beirut, Lebanon); 3,200 adherents (31 December 1996); Exarch Patriarchal Bishop JOSEPH ARNAOUTIAN.

Archdiocese of Aleppo: Archevêché Arménien Catholique, BP 97, rue Tillel 120, Aleppo; tel. (21) 213946; fax (21) 235303; fax (11) 5431988; 17,000 adherents (31 December 1996); Archbishop BOUTROS MARAYATI.

Diocese of Kamichlié: Evêché Arménien Catholique, BP 97, Al-Qamishli; tel. (21) 220211; fax (21) 235303; 4,000 adherents (31 December 1996); Bishop (vacant).

Chaldean Rite

Diocese of Aleppo: Evêché Chaldéen Catholique d'Alep, BP 4643, Soulémaniyé; tel. (21) 441660; 15,000 adherents (31 December 1996); Bishop ANTOINE AUDO.

Latin Rite

Apostolic Vicariate of Aleppo: BP 327, 19 rue Antaki, Aleppo; tel. (21) 210204; fax (21) 219031; f. 1644; 9,500 adherents (31 December 1996); Vicar Apostolic ARMANDO BORTOLASO, Titular Bishop of Raphanea.

Maronite Rite

Archdiocese of Aleppo: Archevêché Maronite, BP 203, Aleppo; tel. (21) 248048; 3,700 adherents (31 December 1996); Archbishop YOUSSEF ANIS ABI-AAD.

Archdiocese of Damascus: Archevêché Maronite, Bab Touma, Damascus; tel. (11) 5403129; 8,000 adherents (31 December 1996); Archbishop ANTOINE-HAMID MOURANY.

Diocese of Latakia: Evêché Maronite, BP 161, rue Hamrat, Tartous; tel. (43) 223433; fax (43) 322939; 27,000 adherents (31 December 1996); Bishop ANTOINE TORBEY.

Melkite Rite

Melkite-Greek-Catholic Patriarchate: BP 22249, Damascus, or POB 50076, Beirut, Lebanon; tel. (11) 5433129; fax (11) 5431266 (Damascus), or 413111 (Beirut); jurisdiction over 1.5m. Melkites throughout the world (including 187,000 in Syria); Patriarch of Antioch and all the East, of Alexandria and Jerusalem MAXIMOS V HAKIM. The Melkite Rite includes the patriarchal sees of Damascus, Cairo and Jerusalem and four other archdioceses in Syria; seven archdioceses in Lebanon; one in Jordan; one in Israel; and five Eparchies (in the USA, Brazil, Canada, Australia and Mexico).

Archdiocese of Aleppo: Archevêché Grec-Catholique, BP 146, Aleppo; tel. (21) 213218; fax (21) 223106; 20,000 adherents (31 December 1996); Archbishop JEAN-CLÉMENT JEANBART.

Archdiocese of Busra and Hauran: Archevêché Grec-Catholique, Khabab, Hauran; tel. (15) 851082; 27,000 adherents (31 December 1996); Archbishop BOULOS NASSIF BORKHOCHE.

Archdiocese of Homs: Archevêché Grec-Catholique, BP 1525, rue El-Bahri, Boustan ad-Diwan, Homs; tel. (31) 482587; fax (31) 810114; 25,000 adherents (31 December 1996) Archbishop IBRAHIM NEHMÉ.

Archdiocese of Latakia: Archevêché Grec-Catholique, BP 151, Latakia; tel. (431) 223433; 10,000 adherents (31 December 1995); Archbishop FARES MAAKAROUN.

Syrian Rite

Archdiocese of Aleppo: Archevêché Syrien Catholique, Azizié, Aleppo; tel. (21) 241200; 8,800 adherents (31 December 1996); Archbishop DENYS ANTOINE BEYLOUNI.

Archdiocese of Damascus: Archevêché Syrien Catholique, BP 2129, rue Bab Charki, Damascus; 6,000 adherents (31 December 1996); tel. (11) 5432312; fax (11) 5434009; Archbishop EUSTACHE JOSEPH MOUNAYER.

Archdiocese of Hassaké-Nisibi: Archevêché Syrien Catholique, BP 6, Hassaké; tel. (52) 220052; 5,200 adherents (31 December 1996); Archbishop JACQUES BEHNAN HINDO.

Archdiocese of Homs: Archevêché Syrien Catholique, BP 368, rue Hamidieh, Homs; tel. (31) 221575; 9,800 adherents (31 December 1996); Archbishop BASILE MOUSSA DAOUD.

The Anglican Communion

Within the Episcopal Church in Jerusalem and the Middle East, Syria forms part of the diocese of Jerusalem (see the chapter on Israel).

Protestant

National Evangelical Synod of Syria and Lebanon: BP 70890, Antelias, Lebanon; tel. (04) 525030; e-mail nessl@inco.com.lb; f. 1920; 80,000 adherents (1997); Gen. Sec. Rev. ADEEB AWAD.

Union of the Armenian Evangelical Churches in the Near East: BP 110-377, Beirut, Lebanon; tel. 443547; fax 582191; f. 1846 in Turkey; comprises about 30 Armenian Evangelical Churches in Syria, Lebanon, Egypt, Cyprus, Greece, Iran and Turkey; 7,500 mems (1995); Moderator Rev. HOVHANNES KARJIAN; Sec. Rev. AVEDIS BOYNERIAN.

The Press

Since the Baath Arab Socialist Party came to power, the structure of the press has been modified according to socialist patterns. Most publications are published by organizations such as political, religious, or professional associations, trade unions, etc. and several are published by government ministries. Anyone wishing to establish a new paper or periodical must apply for a licence.

The major dailies are *Al-Baath* (the organ of the party), *Tishrin* and *Ath-Thawra* in Damascus, *Al-Jamahir al-Arabia* in Aleppo, and *Al-Fida'* in Hama.

PRINCIPAL DAILIES

Al-Baath (Renaissance): BP 9389, Autostrade Mezzeh, Damascus; tel. (11) 6622142; telex 419146; fax (11) 6622099; f. 1946; morning; Arabic; organ of the Baath Arab Socialist Party; Gen. Dir and Chief Editor TURKI SAQR; circ. 40,000.

Barq ash-Shimal (The Syrian Telegraph): rue Aziziyah, Aleppo; morning; Arabic; Editor MAURICE DJANDJI; circ. 6,400.

Al-Fida' (Redemption): BP 2448, rue Kuwatly, Hama; morning; Arabic; political; publishing concession holder OSMAN ALOUINI; Editor A. AULWANI; circ. 4,000.

Al-Jamahir al-Arabia (The Arab People): Al-Wihdat Press, Printing and Publishing Organization, Aleppo; Arabic; political; Chief Editor MORTADA BAKACH; circ. 10,000.

Al-Oroubat: Al-Wihdat Press, Printing and Publishing Organization, Homs; morning; Arabic; published by Al-Wihdat Printing and Publishing Organization; circ. 5,000.

Ash-Shabab (Youth): rue at-Tawil, Aleppo; morning; Arabic; Editor MUHAMMAD TALAS; circ. 9,000.

Syria Times: Tishrin Foundation for Press and Publication, BP 5452, Corniche Meedan, Damascus; tel. (11) 2247359; telex 411416; fax (11) 2247049; English; circ. 15,000.

Ath-Thawra (Revolution): Al-Wihdat Press, Printing and Publishing Organization, BP 2448, Damascus; morning; Arabic; political; circ. 40,000; Chief Editor M. KHAIR AL-WADI.

Tishrin (October): Tishrin Foundation for Press and Publication, BP 5452, Corniche Meedan, Damascus; tel. (11) 886900; telex 411916; Arabic; Chief Editor M. KHEIR WADI; circ. 50,000.

Al-Wihdat (Unity): Al-Wihdat Press, Printing and Publishing Organization, Latakia; Arabic; published by Al-Wihdat Press, Printing and Publishing Organization.

WEEKLIES AND FORTNIGHTLIES

Al-Ajoua' (The Air): Compagnie de l'Aviation Arabe Syrienne, BP 417, Damascus; fortnightly; Arabic; aviation; Editor AHMAD ALLOUCHE.

Al-Esbou ar-Riadi (The Sports Week): Immeuble Tibi, ave Fardoss, Damascus; weekly; Arabic; sports; Asst Dir and Editor HASRAN AL-BOUNNI; circ. 14,000.

Al-Fursan (The Cavalry): Damascus; Arabic; political magazine; Editor Major RIFAAT AL-ASSAD.

Homs: Homs; weekly; Arabic; literary; Publisher and Dir ADIB KABA; Editor PHILIPPE KABA.

Jaysh ash-Sha'ab (The People's Army): BP 3320, blvd Palestine, Damascus; f. 1946; fortnightly; Arabic; army magazine; published by the Political Department of the Syrian Army.

Kifah al-Oummal al-Ishtiraki (The Socialist Workers' Struggle): Fédération Générale des Syndicats des Ouvriers, rue Qanawat, Damascus; weekly; Arabic; labour; published by General Federation of Labour Unions; Editor SAID AL-HAMAMI.

Al-Masirah (Progress): Damascus; weekly; Arabic; political; published by Federation of Youth Organizations.

Al-Maukef ar-Riadi: Al-Wihdat Press, Printing and Publishing Organization, BP 2448, Damascus; weekly; Arabic; sports; published by Al-Wihdat Press, Printing and Publishing Organization; circ. 50,000.

An-Nas (The People): BP 926, Aleppo; f. 1953; weekly; Arabic; Publisher VICTOR KALOUS.

Nidal al-Fellahin (The Struggle of the Fellahin): Fédération Générale des Laboureurs, BP 7152, Damascus; weekly; Arabic; peasant workers; Editor MANSOUR ABU AL-HOSN.

Nidal ash-Sha'ab (People's Struggle): Damascus; fortnightly; Arabic; published by the Communist Party of Syria.

Ar-Riada (Sport): BP 292, near Electricity Institute, Damascus; weekly; Arabic; sports; Dir NOUREDDINE RIAL; Publisher and Editor OURFANE UBARI.

As-Sakafat al-Usbouiya (Weekly Culture): BP 2570, Soukak as-Sakr, Damascus; weekly; Arabic; cultural; Publisher, Dir and Editor MADHAT AKKACHE.

Tishrin al–Usbouiya October weekly): Damascus; weekly.

Al-Yanbu al-Jadid (New Spring): Immeuble Al-Awkaf, Homs; weekly; Arabic; literary; Publisher, Dir and Editor MAMDOU AL-KOUSSEIR.

OTHER PERIODICALS

Ad-Dad: rue Tital, Wakf al-Moiriné Bldg, Aleppo; monthly; Arabic; literary; Dir RIAD HALLAK; Publisher and Editor ABDALLAH YARKI HALLAK.

Ecos: BP 3320, Damascus; monthly review; Spanish.

Al-Fikr al-Askari (The Military Idea): BP 4259, blvd Palestine, Damascus; f. 1950; 6 a year; Arabic; official military review published by the Political Dept of the Syrian Army; Editor NAKHLE KALLAS.

Flash: BP 3320, Damascus; monthly review; English and French.

Al-Irshad az-Zirai (Agricultural Information): Ministry of Agriculture and Agrarian Reform, 29 rue Ayar, Damascus; tel. (11) 113613; 6 a year; Arabic; agriculture.

Al-Jundi al-Arabi (The Arab Soldier): BP 3320, blvd Palestine, Damascus; telex 411500; monthly; published by the Political Department of the Syrian Army.

Al-Kalima (The Word): Al-Kalima Association, Aleppo; monthly; Arabic; religious; Publisher and Editor FATHALLA SAKAL.

Al-Kanoun (The Law): Ministry of Justice, Damascus; monthly; Arabic; juridical.

Al-Ma'arifa (Knowledge): Ministry of Culture, Damascus; tel. (11) 331556; telex 411944; f. 1962; monthly; Arabic; literary; Editor ABD AL-KARIM NASIF; circ. 7,500.

Al-Majalla al-Batriarquia (The Magazine of the Patriarchate): Syrian Orthodox Patriarchate, BP 914, Damascus; tel. (11) 447036; f. 1962; monthly; Arabic; religious; Editor SAMIR ABDOH; circ. 11,000.

Al-Majalla at-Tibbiya al-Arabiyya (Arab Medical Magazine): rue al-Jala'a, Damascus; monthly; Arabic; published by Arab Medical Commission; Dir Dr Y. SAKA; Editor Prof. ADNAN TAKRITI.

Majallat Majma' al-Lughat al-Arabiyya bi-Dimashq (Magazine of the Arab Language Academy of Damascus): Arab Academy of

Damascus, BP 327, Damascus; tel. (11) 373145; fax (11) 3733363; f. 1921; quarterly; Arabic; Islamic culture and Arabic literature, Arabic scientific and cultural terminology; Chief Editor Dr SHAKER FAHAM; circ. 1,000.

Al-Mawkif al-Arabi (The Arab Situation): Ittihab al-Kuttab al-Arab, rue Murshid Khatir, Damascus; monthly; Arabic; literary.

Monthly Survey of Arab Economics: BP 2306, Damascus and BP 6068, Beirut; f. 1958; monthly; English and French editions; published by Centre d'Etudes et de Documentation Economiques, Financières et Sociales; Dir Dr CHAFIC AKHRAS.

Al-Mouallem al-Arabi (The Arab Teacher): Ministry of Education, Damascus; f. 1948; monthly; Arabic; educational and cultural.

Al-Mouhandis al-Arabi (The Arab Engineer): BP 2336, Immeuble Dar al-Mouhandisen, place Azme, Damascus; tel. (11) 214916; telex 411962; f. 1961; bi-monthly; Arabic; published by Inst. of Syrian Engineers; scientific and cultural; Dir Dr Eng. GHASSAN TAYARA; Editors Eng. ADNAN IBRAHIM and Dr Eng. AHMAD AL-GHAFARI; circ. 21,000.

Al-Munadel (The Militant): c/o BP 11512, Damascus; fax (11) 2126935; f. 1965; monthly; Arabic; magazine of Baath Arab Socialist Party; Dir Dr FAWWAZ SAYYAGH; circ. 100,000.

Risalat al-Kimia (Chemistry Report): BP 669, Immeuble al-Abid, Damascus; monthly; Arabic; scientific; Publisher, Dir and Editor HASSAN AS-SAKA.

Saut al-Forat: Deir ez-Zor; monthly; Arabic; literary; Publisher, Dir and Editor ABD AL-KADER AYACHE.

Ash-Shourta (The Police): Directorate of Public Affairs and Moral Guidance, Damascus; monthly; Arabic; juridical.

Souriya al-Arabiyya (Arab Syria): Ministry of Information, Immeuble Dar al-Baath, ave al-Mazzeh, Damascus; tel. (11) 6619396; fax (11) 6617665; monthly; publicity; in four languages.

Syrie et Monde Arabe: BP 3550, place Chahbandar, Damascus; f. 1952; monthly; French and English; economic, statistical and political survey.

Tabibok (Your Doctor): Damascus; tel. (11) 2212980; fax (11) 3738901; f. 1956; monthly; Arabic; medical, social, scientific; Editor Dr SAMI KABBANI; circ. 90,000.

At-Tamaddon al-Islami (The Spreading of Islam): Darwichiyah, Damascus; tel. (11) 2215120; telex 411258; f. 1932; monthly; Arabic; religious; published by At-Tamaddon al-Islami Association; Pres. of Asscn. MUHAMMAD ZAHIR KOUZBARI.

At-Taqa Wattanmiya (Energy and Expansion): BP 7748, rue al-Moutanabbi, Damascus; tel. (11) 233529; telex 411031; monthly; Arabic; published by the Syrian Petroleum Co.

Al-Yakza (The Awakening): Al-Yakza Association, BP 6677, rue Sisi, Aleppo; f. 1935; monthly; Arabic; literary social review of charitable institution; Dir HUSNI ABD AL-MASSIH; circ. 12,000.

Az-Zira'a 2000 (Agriculture 2000): Ministry of Agriculture and Agrarian Reform, 29 rue Ayar, Damascus; tel. (11) 213613; telex 411643; f. 1985; monthly; Arabic; agriculture; circ. 12,000.

PRESS AGENCIES

Agence Arabe Syrienne d'Information: Damascus; f. 1966; supplies bulletins on Syrian news to foreign news agencies; Dir-Gen. Dr SABIR FALHUT.

Foreign Bureaux

Agencia EFE (Spain): Damascus; Correspondent ZACHARIAS SARME.

Agence France-Presse (AFP): BP 2400, Immeuble Adel Charaj, place du 17 avril, Damascus; tel. (11) 428253; telex 419173; Correspondent JOSEPH GHASI.

Agenzia Nazionale Stampa Associata (ANSA) (Italy): Hotel Méridien, BP 2712, Damascus; tel. (11) 233116; telex 411098; f. 1962; Correspondent ABDULLAH SAADEL.

Allgemeiner Deutscher Nachrichtendienst (ADN) (Germany): BP 844, Damascus; tel. (11) 332093; telex 411010; Correspondent FRANK HERRMANN.

Associated Press (AP) (USA): c/o Hotel Méridien, BP 2712, Damascus; tel. (11) 233116; telex 411196.

Deutsche Presse-Agentur (dpa) (Germany): c/o Hotel Méridien, BP 2712, Damascus; tel. (11) 332924; telex 411098.

Reuters (UK) is also represented in Syria.

Publishers

Arab Advertising Organization: BP 2842-3034, 28 rue Moutanabbi, Damascus; tel. (11) 2225219; telex 411923; fax (11) 2220754; f. 1963; exclusive government establishment responsible for advertising; publishes *Directory of Commerce and Industry, Damascus*

International Fair Guide, Daily Bulletin of Official Tenders; Dir-Gen. MUHAMMAD RAZOUK.

Damascus University Press: Damascus; tel. (11) 2215100; telex 411971; fax (11) 2236010; arts, geography, education, history, engineering, medicine, law, sociology, economics, sciences, architecture, agriculture, school books.

Office Arabe de Presse et de Documentation (OFA-Edition): BP 3550, 67 place Chahbandar, Damascus; tel. (11) 3318237; telex 411613; fax (11) 4426021; f. 1964; numerous periodicals, monographs and surveys on political and economic affairs; Dir-Gen. SAMIR A. DARWICH. Has two affiliated branches, OFA-Business Consulting Centre (foreign company representation and services) and OFA-Renseignements Commerciaux (Commercial enquiries on firms and persons in Syria and Lebanon).

The Political Administration Press: BP 3320, blvd Palestine, Damascus; telex 411500; publishes *Al-Fikr al-Askari* (6 a year) and *Jaysh ash-Sha'ab* (fortnightly) and *Al-Jundi al-Arabi* (monthly).

Syrian Documentation Papers: BP 2712, Damascus; f. 1968; publishers of *Bibliography of the Middle East* (annual), *General Directory of the Press and Periodicals in the Arab World* (annual), and numerous publications on political, economic and social affairs and literature and legislative texts concerning Syria and the Arab world; Dir-Gen. LOUIS FARÈS.

Al-Wihdat Press, Printing and Publishing Organization (Institut al-Ouedha pour l'impression, édition et distribution): BP 2448, Dawar Kafr Soussat, Damascus; publishes *Al-Jamahir al-Arabia, Al-Ouroubat, Ath-Thawra, Al-Fida'* and *Al-Wihdat* (dailies), *al-Maukef ar-Riadi* (weekly) and other commercial publications.

Broadcasting and Communications

TELECOMMUNICATIONS

Syrian Telecommunications Establishment (STE): Damascus.

BROADCASTING

Radio

Directorate-General of Radio and Television: place Omayyad, Damascus; tel. (11) 720700; telex 411138; f. 1945; Dir-Gen. KHUDR OMRAN; broadcasts in Arabic, French, English, Russian, German, Spanish, Portuguese, Hebrew, Polish, Turkish, Bulgarian; Dir SAFWAN GHANIM.

Television

Directorate-General of Radio and Television: (see Radio); services started in 1960; Dir of Television: M. ABD AS-SALAM HIJAB.

Finance

(cap. = capital; res = reserves; dep. = deposits; m.= million; brs = branches; amounts in £S)

BANKING

Central Bank

Central Bank of Syria: POB 2254, Altajrida al-Mughrabia Sq., Damascus; tel. (11) 2212642; telex 411007; fax (11) 2227109; f. 1956; cap. 10m., dep. 22,689m., total assets 46,202m. (June 1987); 10 brs; Gov. Dr MUHAMMAD BASHAR KABBARA.

Other Banks

Agricultural Co-operative Bank: BP 4325, Immeuble General Administration, Jardin Al-Haanua, Damascus; tel. (11) 2213461; telex 412732; fax (11) 2238525.

Commercial Bank of Syria: BP 933, place Yousuf al-Azmeh, Damascus; tel. (11) 2219390; telex 411002; fax (11) 2216975; f. 1967; govt-owned bank; cap. and res 2,116.4m., dep. 185,345.7m., total assets 281,876.1m. (June 1995); Chair. and Gen. Man. MUHAMMAD RIYADH HAKIM; 48 brs.

Industrial Bank: BP 7578, Immeuble Dar al-Mohandessin, rue Maysaloon, Damascus; tel. (11) 2228200; fax (11) 228412; f. 1959; nationalized bank providing finance for industry; cap. 100m.; 13 brs; Chair. ABD AL-QADIR OBEIDO.

Popular Credit Bank: BP 2841, 6e étage, Immeuble Dar al-Mohandessin, rue Maysaloon, Damascus; tel. (11) 2227604; fax (11) 2218555; f. 1967; government bank; provides loans to the services sector and is sole authorized issuer of savings certificates; cap. 25m., dep. 2,313m., res 42,765m. (Dec. 1984); 43 brs; Chair. and Gen. Man. MUHAMMAD HASSAN AL-HOUJJEIRI.

Real Estate Bank: BP 2339, rue al-Furat, Damascus; tel. (11) 2218602; fax (11) 2237938; f. 1966; govt-owned bank; provides loans and grants for housing, schools, hospitals and hotel construction; cap. 750m.; 13 brs; Chair. and Gen. Man. MUHAMMAD A. MAKHLOUF.

Syrian Lebanese Commercial Bank: BP 2, rue Kastel Hajjarin, Aleppo.

INSURANCE

Syrian General Organization for Insurance: BP 2279, 29 rue Salhiah, Damascus; tel. (11) 2218430; telex 411003; fax (11) 2220494; f. 1953; auth. cap. 1,000m.; a nationalized company; operates throughout Syria; Chair. and Gen. Man. AMIN ABDULLAH.

Trade and Industry

STATE ENTERPRISES

Syrian industry is almost entirely controlled and run by the State. There are national organizations responsible to the appropriate ministry for the operation of all sectors of industry, of which the following are examples:

Cotton Marketing Organization: POB 729, rue Bab al-Faraj, Aleppo; tel. (21) 238486; telex 331210; fax (21) 218617; f. 1965; governmental authority for purchase of seed cotton, ginning and sales of cotton lint; Pres. and Dir-Gen. Dr AHMAD SOUHAD GEBBARA.

General Organization for Phosphate and Mines (GECO-PHAM): BP 288, Homs; tel. 20405; telex 441000; production and export of phosphate rock.

General Organization for the Exploitation and Development of the Euphrates Basin (GOEDEB): Raqqa; telex 31004; Dir-Gen. Dr Eng. Dr AHMAD SOUHAD GEBBARA.

General Organization for the Textile Industries: BP 620, rue Fardoss, Damascus; tel. (11) 116200; telex 411011; control and planning of the textile industry and supervision of textile manufacture; 13 subsidiary cos.

Syrian Petroleum Company (SPC): BP 2849, rue al-Moutanabbi, Damascus; tel. (11) 227007; telex 411031; f. 1958; state agency; holds the oil and gas concession for all Syria; exploits the Suweidiya, Karatchouk, Rumelan and Jbeisseh oilfields; also organizes exploring, production and marketing of oil and gas nationally; Dir-Gen. Dr Eng. ALI JEBRAN.

Al-Furat Petroleum Company: f. 1985; owned 50% by SPC and 50% by a foreign consortium of Syria Shell Petroleum Development B.V. and Deminex Syria GmbH; exploits oilfields in the Euphrates river area; Chair. JABER GHZAYYEL.

CHAMBERS OF COMMERCE

Federation of Syrian Chambers of Commerce: BP 5909, rue Mousa Ben Nousair, Damascus; tel. (11) 3311504; telex 411194; fax (11) 3331127; f. 1975; Chair. Dr RATEB ASH-SHALLAH.

Aleppo Chamber of Commerce: BP 1261, rue al-Moutanabbi, Aleppo; tel. (21) 238236; telex 331012; fax (21) 213493; f. 1885; Pres. M. SALEH AL-MALLAH; Sec. MUHAMMAD MANSOUR.

Alkalamoun Chamber of Commerce: BP 2507, rue Bucher A. Mawla, Damascus; telex 411061; fax (11) 778394; Pres. M. SOUFAN.

Damascus Chamber of Commerce: BP 1040, rue Mou'awiah, Damascus; tel. (11) 2211339; telex 411326; fax (11) 2225874; f. 1890; 11,000 mems.; Pres. Dr RATEB ASH-SHALLAH; Gen. Dir HISHAM AL-HAMWY.

Hama Chamber of Commerce and Industry: BP 147, rue al-Kouatly, Hama; tel. (33) 233304; telex 431046; fax (33) 517701; f. 1934; Pres. ABD AS-SALAM SABEH.

Homs Chamber of Commerce and Industry: BP 440, rue Abou al-Of, Homs; tel. (31) 469440; telex 441025; fax (31) 464247; f. 1938; Pres. Eng. WALID TULEIMAT; Dir M. FARES AL-HUSSAMY.

Latakia Chamber of Commerce: rue al-Hurriyah, Latakia; Pres. JULE NASRI.

CHAMBERS OF INDUSTRY

Aleppo Chamber of Industry: BP 1859, rue al-Moutanabbi, Aleppo; tel. (21) 339812; telex 331090; f. 1935; Pres. MUHAMMAD M. OUBARI; 7,000 mems.

Damascus Chamber of Industry: BP 1305, rue Harika Mou'awiah, Damascus; tel. (11) 2215042; telex 411289; fax (11) 2245981; Pres. Dr YEHYA AL-HINDI; Dir-Gen. Dr ABD AL-HAMID MALAKANI.

EMPLOYERS' ORGANIZATIONS

Fédération Générale à Damas: Damascus; f. 1951; Dir TALAT TAG-LUBI.

Fédération de Damas: Damascus; f. 1949.

Fédération des Patrons et Industriels à Lattaquié: Latakia; f. 1953.

UTILITIES

Electricity

Public Establishment for the Generation and Transmission of Electricity: Damascus.

TRADE UNIONS

Ittihad Naqabat al-'Ummal al-'Am fi Suriya (General Federation of Labour Unions): BP 2351, rue Qanawat, Damascus; f. 1948; Chair. 'IZZ AD-DIN NASIR; Sec. MAHMOUD FAHURI.

Transport

RAILWAYS

In 1990 the railway system totalled 1,918 km of track.

Syrian Railways: BP 182, Aleppo; tel. (21) 213900; telex 331009; fax (21) 228480; f. 1897; Pres. and Dir-Gen. MUHAMMAD GHASSAN AL-KADDOUR.

General Organization of the Hedjaz-Syrian Railway: BP 134, place Hedjaz, Damascus; tel. (11) 2215815; fax (11) 2227106; f. 1908; the Hedjaz Railway has 347 km of track (gauge 1,050 mm) in Syria; services operate between Damascus and Amman, on a branch line of about 24 km from Damascus to Katana, and there is a further line of 64 km from Damascus to Serghaya; Dir-Gen. S. AHMED.

ROADS

Arterial roads run across the country linking the north to the south and the Mediterranean to the eastern frontier. At 31 December 1996 there were 866 km of motorways, 27,799 km of main or national roads and 9,411 km of secondary or regional roads. In 1996 work was scheduled to commence on the first stage of a project costing £S1,800m. to improve the road linking Rakka with Deir ez-Zor.

General Co for Roads: BP 3143, Aleppo; tel. (21) 555406; telex 331403; f. 1975; Gen. Man. Eng. M. WALID EL-AJLANI.

PIPELINES

The oil pipelines that cross Syrian territory are of great importance to the national economy, representing a considerable source of foreign exchange.

Syrian Co for Oil Transport (SCOT): BP 13, Banias; tel. (43) 711300; telex 441012; fax (43) 710418; f. 1972; Dir-Gen. MUHAMMAD DOUBA.

SHIPPING

Latakia is the principal port; the other major ports are at Banias and Tartous. A project to expand the capacities of Latakia and Tartous, and to construct new port facilities near Tartous, commenced in 1997.

Syrian General Authority for Maritime Transport: BP 730, 2 rue Argentina, Damascus; tel. (11) 226350; telex 411012.

Ismail, A. M., Shipping Agency Ltd: BP 74, rue du Port, Tartous; tel. 20543; operates a fleet of 1 tanker and 9 general cargo vessels; Man. Dir MAHMOUD ISMAIL.

Sea Transport Agency: BP 78, Kamilieh Quarter, Harbour St, Latakia; tel. 33964; telex 510044; operates 3 general cargo vessels; Gen. Man. WADIH M. NSEIR.

Syrian Navigation Co: BP 314, rue Baghdad, Latakia; tel. (41) 233778; telex 451028; fax (41) 235781; f. 1975; state-owned company operating 4 general cargo ships; Chair. and Man. Dir MUHAMMAD A. HAROUN.

Syro-Jordanian Shipping Co: BP 148, rue Port Said, Latakia; tel. (11) 471635; telex 451002; fax (11) 470250; f. 1976; operates 2 general cargo ships; transported 70,551 metric tons of goods in 1992; Chair. OSMAN LEBBADY.

Tabalo, Muhammad Abd ar-Rahman: BP 66, rue al-Mina, Tartous; tel. 20906; telex 470008; operates 4 general cargo vessels (1 refrigerated); Man. Dir ABDULLAH TABALO.

CIVIL AVIATION

There is an international airport at Damascus, and the upgrading of Aleppo airport, to enable it to handle international traffic, is planned.

Directorate-General of Civil Aviation: BP 6257, place Nejmeh, Damascus; tel. (11) 3331306; telex 411928; fax (11) 2232201.

Syrian Arab Airlines (Syrianair): BP 417, 5th Floor, Social Insurance Bldg, Youssef al-Azmeh Sq, Damascus; tel. (11) 232154; telex 411593; fax (11) 224923; f. 1946, refounded 1961 to succeed Syrian Airways, after revocation of merger with Misrair; domestic passenger and cargo services (from Damascus, Aleppo, Latakia and Deir ez-Zor) and routes to Europe, the Middle East, North Africa and the Far East; Chair. Brig. OMAR ALI REDA.

Tourism

Syria's tourist attractions include a pleasant Mediterranean coastline, the mountains, the town bazaars and the antiquities of Damascus and Palmyra. About 2.4m. foreigners visited Syria in 1996.

Ministry of Tourism: rue Victoria, Damascus; tel. (11) 2215916; telex 411672; fax (11) 2242636; f. 1972; Dir of Tourist Relations and Ministerial Adviser Mrs SAWSAN JOUZY.

Middle East Tourism: BP 201, rue Fardoss, Damascus; tel. (11) 2211876; telex 411726; fax (11) 2246545; f. 1954; Pres. MUHAMMAD DADOUCHE; 7 brs.

Defence

Commander-in-Chief of the Armed Forces: Lt-Gen. HAFIZ AL-ASSAD.

Minister of Defence and Deputy Commander-in-Chief of the Armed Forces: Maj.-Gen. MUSTAFA TLASS.

Chief of Staff of the Armed Forces: Maj.-Gen. ALI ASLAN.

Deputy Chief of Staff: Maj.-Gen. HASAN AT-TURKMANI.

Air Force Commander: Gen. MUHAMMAD AL-KHOULI.

Special Forces Commander: Gen. ALI HABIB.

Defence Budget (1997): £S59,100m. (US $1,700m.).

Military Service: 30 months (Jewish population exempted).

Total Armed Forces (August 1997): 320,000 (army 215,000, air defence command (an army command; estimated) 60,000, navy (estimated) 5,000, air force 40,000); reserves 500,000.

Paramilitary Forces: 8,000 Gendarmerie (under control of Ministry of Interior).

Education

Primary education, which begins at six years of age and lasts for six years, is officially compulsory. Secondary education, beginning at 12 years of age, also lasts for six years. In 1995/96 there were 2,672,960 pupils in primary education in the public and private sectors, and 940,982 in secondary education. In 1995 enrolment at primary schools included 91% (males 95%; females 87%) of children in the relevant age-group. Secondary enrolment in that year included 39% (males 41%; females 37%) of pupils in the relevant age-group.

Agricultural schools prepare students mainly for work in agriculture and are open to the sons of peasants. Technical schools prepare students for work in all types of factories. Higher education is provided by the universities of Damascus, Aleppo, Tishrin (the October University, in Latakia) and Homs (the Baath University, formerly the Homs Institute of Petroleum). There were 178,526 students enrolled at the universities in 1992/93. The main language of instruction in schools is Arabic, but English and French are widely taught as second languages. In 1995, according to estimates by UNESCO, the average rate of adult illiteracy was 20.6%. Expenditure on education (excluding higher education) by all levels of government in 1995 amounted to £S18,182m.

Bibliography

Abd-Allah, Dr Umar. *The Islamic Struggle in Syria*. Berkeley, Mizan Press, 1984.

Abu Jaber, Kamal S. *The Arab Baath Socialist Party*. New York, Syracuse University Press, 1966.

Asfour, Edmund Y. *Syrian Development and Monetary Policy*. Harvard, 1959.

Degeorge, Gérard. *Syrie*. Paris, Editions Hermann.

Devlin, John F. *Syria: A Profile*. London, Croom Helm, 1982.

Drysdale, Alastair, and Hinnebusch, Raymond A. *Syria and the Middle East Peace Process*. New York, Council on Foreign Relations, 1992.

Ehteshami, A., and Hinnebusch, R. *Syria and Iran: Middle Powers in a Penetrated Regional System*. London, Routledge, 1997.

Fedden, Robin. *Syria: an Historical Appreciation*. London, 1946.

Syria and Lebanon. London, John Murray, 1966.

Glubb, J. B. *Syria, Lebanon, Jordan*. London, Thames and Hudson, 1967.

Haddad, J. *Fifty Years of Modern Syria and Lebanon*. Beirut, 1950.

Helbaoui, Youssef. *La Syrie*. Paris, 1956.

Hinnebusch, Raymond E. *Authoritarian Power and State Formation in Ba'thist Syria: army, party and peasant*. Oxford, Westview Press, 1990.

Hitti, Philip K. *History of Syria; including Lebanon and Palestine*. New York, 1951.

Homet, M. *L'Histoire secrète du traité franco-syrien*. New Ed., Paris, 1951.

Hopwood, Derek. *The Russian presence in Syria and Palestine 1843–1914*. Oxford, 1969.

Hourani, Albert H. *Syria and Lebanon: A Political Essay*. New York, 1946.

Hureau, Jean. *La Syrie aujourd'hui*. Paris, Editions Afrique.

Kienle, Eberhard (Ed.). *Contemporary Syria: Liberalization between Cold War and Cold Peace*. London, I. B. Tauris, 1994.

Lawson, Fred H. *Why Syria Goes to War: Thirty Years of Confrontation*. Cornell University Press, 1996.

Lloyd-George, D. *The Truth about the Peace Treaties, Vol. II.* (London, 1938).

Longrigg, S. H. *Syria and Lebanon Under French Mandate*. Oxford University Press, 1958.

Ma'oz, Moshe. *Syria and Israel: from war to peace-making*. Oxford University Press, 1995.

Mirza, Nasseh Ahmad. *Syrian Isma'ilism: The Ever Living Line of Imamate AD 1100–1260*. Richmond, Curzon Press, 1996.

Perthes, Volker. *The Political Economy of Syria Under Asad*. London, I. B. Tauris, 1995.

Petran, Tabitha. *Syria*. London, Benn, 1972.

Pipes, Daniel. *Greater Syria: the History of an Ambition*. New York, Oxford Unversity Press, 1990.

Rabbath, E. *Unité Syrienne et Devenir Arabe*. Paris, 1937.

Rathmell, Andrew. *Secret War in the Middle East: The Covert Struggle for Syria, 1949-1961*. London, I. B. Tauris, 1995.

Runciman, Steven. *A History of the Crusades*. London, Vol. I 1951, Vol. II 1952.

Seale, Patrick. *The Struggle for Syria*. London, 1965.

Springett, B. H. *Secret Sects of Syria and the Lebanon*. London 1922.

Stark, Freya. *Letters from Syria*. London, 1942.

Thubron, C. A. *Mirror to Damascus*. London, Heinemann, 1967.

Tibawi, A. L. *Syria*. London, 1962.

American Interests in Syria 1800–1901. New York, Oxford University Press, 1966.

A Modern History of Syria. London, Macmillan, 1969.

Torrey, Gordon H. *Syrian Politics and the Military*. Ohio, State University, 1964.

Tritton, A. S. *The Caliphs and their Non-Muslim Subjects*. London, 1930.

Van Dam, Nikolaos. *The Struggle for Power in Syria*. London, Croom Helm, 1979.

Weulersse, J. *Paysans de Syrie et du Proche Orient*. Paris, 1946.

Yamak, L. Z. *The Syrian Social Nationalist Party*. Cambridge, Mass., Harvard University Press, 1966.

Ziadeh, N. *Syria and Lebanon*. New York, Praeger, 1957.

TUNISIA

Physical and Social Geography

D. R. HARRIS

Tunisia is the smallest of the countries that comprise the 'Maghreb' of North Africa, but it is more cosmopolitan than Algeria or Morocco. It forms a wedge of territory, 163,610 sq km (63,170 sq miles) in extent, between Algeria and Libya. It includes the easternmost ridges of the Atlas Mountains but most of the country is low-lying and bordered by a long and sinuous Mediterranean coastline that faces both north and east. Ease of access by sea and by land from the east has favoured the penetration of foreign influences and Tunisia owes its distinct national identity and its varied cultural traditions to a succession of invading peoples: Phoenicians, Romans, Arabs, Turks and French. It was more effectively arabized than either Algeria or Morocco and remnants of the original Berber-speaking population of the Maghreb are confined, in Tunisia, to a few isolated localities in the south.

At the April 1994 census the population was 8,785,364 and the overall density was 57.9 per sq km. Most of the people live in the more humid, northern part of the country, and at the 1994 census about 7.7% (674,100) lived in Tunis. Situated where the Sicilian Channel links the western with the central Mediterranean and close to the site of ancient Carthage, Tunis combines the functions of capital and chief port. No other town approaches Tunis in importance, but on the east coast both Sousse (population 125,000 in 1994) and Sfax (population 230,900) provide modern port facilities, as does Bizerta (population 98,900) on the north coast, while some distance inland the old Arab capital and holy city of Qairawan, now known as Kairouan (population 102,600), serves as a regional centre. Other sizeable towns include Ariana (152,700), Ettadhamen (149,200) and Gabès (98,900). Provisional estimates indicated that the population had reached 9,092,000 by mid-1996.

The principal contrasts in the physical geography of Tunisia are between a humid and relatively mountainous northern region, a semi-arid central expanse of low plateaux and plains, and a dry Saharan region in the south. The northern region is dominated by the easternmost folds of the Atlas mountain system which form two separate chains, the Northern and High Tell, separated by the valley of the River Medjerda, the only perennially flowing river in the country. The Northern Tell, which is a continuation of the Algerian Tell Atlas, extends along the north coast at heights of between 300 m and 600 m. South of the Medjerda valley lies the broader Tell Atlas, which is a continuation of the Saharan Atlas of Algeria, and comprises a succession of rugged sandstone and limestone ridges. Near the Algerian frontier these reach a maximum height of 1,544 m at Djebel Chambi, the highest point in Tunisia, but die away eastward towards the Cap Bon peninsula which extends northeast to within 145 km of Sicily.

South of the High Tell or Dorsale ('backbone') central Tunisia consists of an extensive platform sloping gently towards the east coast. Its western half, known as the High Steppe, comprises alluvial basins rimmed by low, barren mountains, but eastward the mountains give way first to the Low Steppe, a gravel-covered plateau, and ultimately to the flat coastal plain of the Sahel. Occasional watercourses cross the Steppes, but they flow only after heavy rain and usually fan out and evaporate in salt flats, or sebkhas, before reaching the sea.

The central Steppes give way southward to a broad depression occupied by two great seasonal salt lakes or shotts. The larger of these, the Shott Djerid, lies at 16 m below sea-level and is normally covered by a salt crust. It extends from close to the Mediterranean coast near Gabès almost to the Algerian frontier and is adjoined on the north-west by the Shott ar-Rharsa, which lies at 21 m below sea-level. South of the shotts Tunisia extends for over 320 km into the Sahara. Rocky, flat-topped mountains, the Monts des Ksour, separate a flat plain known as the Djeffara, which borders the coast south of Gabès, from a sandy lowland which is partly covered by the dunes of the Great Eastern Erg.

The climate of northern Tunisia is Mediterranean in type, with hot, dry summers followed by warm, wet winters. Average rainfall reaches 150 cm in the Kroumirie Mountains, the wettest area in north Africa, but over most of the northern region it varies from 40 cm to 100 cm. The wetter and least accessible mountains are covered with forests in which cork oak and evergreen oak predominate, but elsewhere lower rainfall and overgrazing combine to replace forest with meagre scrub growth. South of the High Tell rainfall is reduced to between 20 cm and 40 cm annually, which is insufficient for the regular cultivation of cereal crops without irrigation, and there is no continuous cover of vegetation. Large areas of the Steppes support only clumps of wiry esparto grass, which is collected and exported for paper manufacture. Southern Tunisia experiences full desert conditions. Rainfall is reduced to below 20 cm annually and occurs only at rare intervals. Extremes of temperature and wind are characteristic and vegetation is completely absent over extensive tracts. The country supports only a sparse nomadic population except where supplies of underground water make cultivation possible.

History

Revised for this edition by RICHARD I. LAWLESS

EARLY HISTORY

By 550 BC Carthage had achieved a position of commercial and naval supremacy in the Mediterranean. The empire reached its height in the course of the fourth century BC but was later challenged by the Roman Republic. The Punic Wars (264–241 BC, 218–201 BC and 149–146 BC) ended in the total destruction of the Carthaginian Empire and its incorporation within the empire of Rome. Carthage was rebuilt by the Emperor Augustus and intensive colonization brought a new prosperity. During the first two centuries AD Carthage was accounted the empire's second city but, with the decline of Rome's power, the city was lost to the Vandals (AD 439), to be recovered for the Byzantine Empire in 533–34. Byzantine rule was by no means secure: the tendency of the local governors to reject the control of Constantinople was compounded by religious dissent among the native Berber population, who adopted Christian heresies in opposition to imperial rule. It was, however, the rise of Islam in Arabia and its rapid expansion after the death of the Prophet (632) that led to the destruction of Byzantine power and to the Arab invasion of North Africa. Arab control was finally established there with the conquest of Carthage in 698 and the foundation of Tunis. Islam spread rapidly among the Berbers, but they adopted Kharijite heresies; the eighth century was dominated by Berber-supported risings, manifestations of militant Islam against the central Government, and constant revolts among the occupying Arab forces. In the last years of the Umayyad dynasty (overthrown 748–50) Tunisia escaped completely from imperial control: the new dynasty of the Abbasids, ruling from Iraq, retook Qairawan, the centre of Arab rule in the Maghreb, but lost it in 767, and a period of complete anarchy ensued. Tunisia was restored to Abbasid control in 800 and Ibrahim ibn Aghlab was appointed tributary ruler of Ifriqiya—corresponding roughly to present-day Tunisia.

For most of the ninth century the country was relatively prosperous, but the Aghlabid dynasty began to decline from 874 and was finally overthrown between 905 and 909 by the Fatimids, fanatical adherents of the heretical doctrines of Shi'ism, who pursued a vigorous policy of expansion and conquest; by 933 Fatimid rule was established throughout the Maghreb. Between 943 and 947 a Berber revolt took place, but it was effectively suppressed, allowing Tunisia to enjoy a certain amount of prosperity for the subsequent 25 years. In 969–70 the Fatimids gained control of Egypt and Syria: three years later Mahdiya was abandoned for the new capital of Cairo, and the Government of Tunisia was handed over to the Berber Zirid family. The golden age of Zirid rule was brought to an end in 1050 when the dynasty transferred its allegiance to the orthodox caliph at Baghdad. The economy crumbled and the country lapsed into political fragmentation. In 1087 Italian forces from Pisa and Genoa took Mahdiya, allowing the Zirids to continue as its rulers. Early in the 12th century the Zirids renewed their loyalty to Cairo, but were expelled by the Normans in 1148. Norman rule in Tunisia was over by 1160, and for the next 50 years Tunisia formed part of the empire of the caliphs of Marrakesh (the Almohads). In the 13th century the authority of Baghdad was briefly restored over Tunisia: a strong provincial government was established in 1207 under the Berber family of the Hafsids, who had held the governorship of Tunis since 1184. For most of the 13th century they ruled over North Africa from Tripoli to central Algeria but, in the face of tribal and Arab unrest, the town of Jerba fell into Christian hands (1284–1337). In the reign of Abu'l-Abbas (1370–94) the fortunes of the dynasty revived, but by the end of the 15th century the Hafsid Empire was disintegrating and Tunisia had become involved in the struggle between the Spanish and Ottoman forces for control of the Mediterranean.

By 1520 Bougie, Tripoli and Jerba had fallen to Spain; then in 1534 Khair ed-Din (Barbarossa), high admiral of the Ottoman fleet, drove the Emir al-Hasan from Tunis. In 1535 a great Spanish naval expedition recaptured the town, and al-Hasan was returned as the Emperor's vassal. In 1542 he was deposed by his son Ahmad, who made a final attempt to reunite Tunisia against Spain. The defeat of Ahmad at the siege of Malta (1565) which, together with the Spanish naval victory of Lepanto six years later, ended the struggle for maritime supremacy. The Pasha of Algiers stationed a garrison in Tunis in 1564, only to be expelled briefly (1572) in the aftermath of Lepanto; but in 1574 an Ottoman expedition put an end to Spanish power in Tunis and to the Hafsid dynasty itself.

Direct Ottoman rule was brief, a military revolt in Tunisia in 1591 reducing the power of the Pasha, the representative of the sultan, to a cypher. State affairs were assumed by one of the 40 deys, or high officers of the Ottoman army of occupation. By about 1600 the diwan, or governing council, shared a pre-eminent place with the taifa, or guild of corsair chiefs. By about 1606 the *de facto* independence of Tunisia had been recognized, although it was to remain nominally part of the Ottoman Empire for more than 250 years.

In the first half of the 17th century trade and commerce flourished, but from about 1650 the deys' power declined, authority passing to the beys, originally subordinate in rank. Hammuda, bey from 1659–63, became master of the entire country, and his family—the Muradids—retained power until 1702. This was a period of decline, with tribal unrest and incursions from Algiers. With the accession of Hussain Ali Turki in 1705, a new line of beys brought some semblance of order. The remainder of the 18th century passed fairly uneventfully, with some prosperity, despite uncertain relations with Algeria and the growth of European naval power in the Mediterranean.

After the Napoleonic Wars the European powers forced the bey, Mahmud (1814–24), to suppress the activities of the corsairs, which had provided a considerable part of state revenues. The French occupied Algiers in 1830, and reduced Algeria to colonial status; for the next 50 years Tunisia desperately tried to avoid the same fate. Increasingly the influence of France and Britain, and later Italy, became apparent through the activities of their consuls. The beys Ahmad (1837–55) and Muhammad (1855–59) attempted reforms, but merely intensified dependence on France. The next bey, Muhammad as-Sadiq (1859–82), promulgated a constitution (suspended 1864). Increased taxes, however, provoked tribal rebellion, and in 1869 the bey was obliged to accept financial control by France, Britain and Italy. Imminent financial collapse prompted France to intervene, and French forces invaded Tunisia in April 1881. They encountered little resistance and the Treaty of Kassar Said was signed, under which the bey remained the nominal ruler, while French officials administered military, financial and foreign affairs.

FRENCH PROTECTORATE

The Treaty of Mersa (1883) formally established a French protectorate over Tunisia and brought the actual Government of the country under French control, effective power passing to the French Resident-General. The international control commission was abolished in 1884, the currency was reformed along French lines in 1891, and the extra-territorial privileges of other Europeans were abrogated. Encouraged by large-scale grants of land, there was a considerable influx of settlers from France, and also from Italy, especially after 1900. Besides being confronted with the task of sustaining the economy, which they tackled by investment in the development of the country's resources, the French encountered rivalry from Italy and a rise of Tunisian nationalism.

Tunisian cultural and political life absorbed many French ideas, but was also influenced by movements in other parts of the Islamic world. An attempt to emulate the Young Turk reformers in the Ottoman Empire was the foundation, in 1908, of the Young Tunisian Movement, which demanded the restoration of the authority of the bey together with democratic reforms. The achievement of independence in eastern Arab countries after the First World War, and the example of the nationalist movement in Egypt, inspired Tunisians with a greater national consciousness, and in 1920 the Destour (Constitution) movement was formed under the leadership of Sheikh ath-Tha'libi, one of the founders of the Young Tunisians.

The Destour appealed for a self-governing constitutional regime with a Legislative Assembly. French attempts to conciliate opinion by administrative reforms, dating from 1920 with the formation of economic councils on which Tunisians were represented, failed to satisfy the more radical elements, and, confronted with further nationalist activity, the French administration resorted to repressive measures. Sheikh ath-Tha'libi was exiled in 1923, and in 1925 the Destour movement was dissolved. It was revived in the early 1930s but soon split, the former leaders of the Destour being accused of collaboration with France by younger members eager for political action on a broad front. In 1934 the Néo-Destour (New Constitution) Party was formed, led by Habib Bourguiba, a Tunisian lawyer. The party employed methods of widespread political agitation as a result of which Bourguiba was exiled. After the victory of the Popular Front in France in 1936 he returned to Tunisia, but little was achieved in direct negotiations with the new French Government. The Néo-Destour became a powerful organization, its influence extending to all parts of the country, and its strength was proved in a successful general strike in 1938. Widespread clashes with the police followed, martial law was proclaimed, some 200 nationalists were arrested, and both the Destour and Néo-Destour parties were dissolved.

At the outbreak of the Second World War Tunisian opinion rallied in favour of France, and when Italy entered the war some 23,000 Italians in Tunisia were interned. With the fall of France Tunisia came under Vichy rule, and Bizerta, Tunis and other ports were used by Germany and Italy to supply their armies in Libya until the defeat of the Axis forces by the Allies in 1943 restored French authority. The bey, Muhammad al-Monsif, was accused of collaboration with the Axis powers and deposed; he was replaced by his cousin, Muhammad al-Amin.

GROWING AUTONOMY

The virtual restoration of peace in 1944 brought a relaxation of political restrictions and during the following years there was renewed agitation for political change. As a result of subsequent French repression, Habib Bourguiba went into exile in Cairo in 1945 but his chief lieutenant, Salah Ben Yousuf, remained in Tunisia. The French authorities turned their attention to political reforms, and by beylical decrees in 1945 the Council of Ministers and the Grand Council (an elected body with equal French and Tunisian representation) were reorganized, the authority of the latter being extended. These measures did not satisfy the nationalists, who demanded complete independence. Later in 1946 a government was formed under Muhammad Kaak, which included an increased number of Tunisians (moderate leaders being appointed after the Destour and Néo-Destour had refused to participate); the French, however, retained ultimate control.

Bourguiba returned to Tunisia in 1949. In April 1950 the Néo-Destour proposed the transfer of sovereignty and executive control to Tunisian hands, under a responsible government with a Prime Minister appointed by the bey and an elected National Assembly which would draft a democratic constitution. Local French interests would be protected by representation on municipal councils, and Tunisia would co-operate with France on equal terms. These proposals received a reasonable response in France, and a new Tunisian Government was formed in August 1950, composed of an equal number of Tunisian and French ministers, with Muhammad Chenik as Prime Minister and Salah Ben Yousuf as Minister of Justice. The object of the new Government was stated to be the gradual restoration of Tunisian sovereignty, in co-operation with France. Despite strong opposition to these developments from the European settlers (some 10% of the population), further reforms were effected in September 1950 and February 1951, when French advisers to the Tunisian ministers were removed and the Resident-General's control over the Council of Ministers was diminished.

Peaceful progress towards autonomy came to a halt, however, owing to growing settler opposition, procrastination on the part of the French Government and consequent alienation of the nationalists. Tunisian resentment erupted in strikes and demonstrations in early 1952. The Néo-Destour had formed an intimate alliance with the influential trade union movement, and many leaders held office in both organizations. In February Bourguiba and other Néo-Destour leaders were arrested on the order of the new Resident-General, Jean de Hautecloque, and a wave of violence spread throughout the country, culminating in the arrest and removal from office of the Prime Minister, and the imposition of French military control.

A new Government was formed under Salaheddine Baccouche, and a French-inspired scheme designed to lead to eventual internal autonomy was announced in April 1952. Meanwhile, the now-proscribed Néo-Destour took its case to Cairo and the UN General Assembly. Against a background of increasing terrorism, countered by French repressive action, and in the face of opposition from both the Néo-Destour and the settlers, little in the way of reform could be achieved. The bey at first refused to sign French reform decrees, and when he yielded in December under the threat of deposition, the proposals were promptly repudiated by the Néo-Destour.

Terrorist activities continued and a settler counter-terrorist organization, the 'Red Hand', came to prominence. The situation approached civil war in 1953, with bands of fellagha active in the western highlands and around Bizerta and terrorism and counter-terrorism in the towns. In July 1954 the newly-formed French Government, led by Pierre Mendès France, offered internal autonomy for Tunisia, with France retaining responsibility only for defence and foreign affairs. The French proposals were accepted, and in August a new Tunisian Government was formed, headed by Tahar Ben Ammar and containing three members of the Néo-Destour as well as moderate nationalists. Negotiations with the French Government opened in Carthage in September. The talks had reached deadlock when the Mendès France Government fell in February 1955, but they resumed in March and a final agreement was signed in Paris on 2 June.

The accord granted internal autonomy to Tunisia while protecting French interests and preserving Tunisia's close links with France. France retained responsibility for foreign affairs, defence (including the control of frontiers) and internal security. Although the agreement was supported by a majority of the Néo-Destour, the extremist wing, headed by the exiled Salah Ben Yousuf, and the old Destour and Communist elements, opposed it, as did the settlers' organizations. An all-Tunisian Council of Ministers was formed in September 1955 by Tahar Ben Ammar, with members of the Néo-Destour holding six of the 12 posts.

Habib Bourguiba had returned from three years' exile in June 1955, to be followed by Salah Ben Yousuf in September. In October Ben Yousuf was expelled from the Néo-Destour for opposition to the recent agreement and for 'splitting activities'. A Néo-Destour party congress at Sfax in November endorsed the agreement, but reaffirmed that the party would be satisfied only with independence and demanded the election of a constituent assembly. Clashes between 'Bourguibist' and 'Yousufist' factions followed, and in December a conspiracy to create a terrorist organization to prevent the implementation of the agreement was discovered. Ben Yousuf fled to Tripoli in January 1956, and many suspected 'Yousufists' were placed in detention. At the same time fellagha activity revived, rebel bands became active in the remoter parts of the country and acts of terrorism were committed against both French settlers and members of the Néo-Destour.

INDEPENDENCE

On 27 February 1956 a Tunisian delegation led by Bourguiba began independence negotiations with the French Government in Paris. In a protocol signed on 20 March, France formally recognized the independence of Tunisia and its right to exercise responsibility over foreign affairs, security and defence, and to raise a national army. A transitional period was envisaged during which French forces would gradually be withdrawn from Tunisia, including Bizerta.

Elections for the Constituent Assembly, held on 25 March 1956, resulted in all 98 seats being won by candidates of the National Front, all of whom acknowledged allegiance to the Néo-Destour. The elections were boycotted by the 'Yousufist' opposition. Habib Bourguiba became Prime Minister on 11 April, leading a government in which 16 of the 17 ministers belonged to the Néo-Destour.

In the early years of independence Tunisia's relations with France were dominated by the question of the evacuation of French forces. A Tunisian demand for their withdrawal was rejected in July 1956 by the French Government, which was preoccupied with the deteriorating situation in Algeria. Bourguiba visited Paris in September in an attempt to promote a mediated settlement in Algeria based on French recognition of Algeria's right to independence, but hopes of progress in this direction were shattered by the French kidnapping in October of five leading Algerian nationalists. Tunisia immediately severed diplomatic relations with France, anti-French riots erupted, and there were clashes between French troops and Tunisian demonstrators resulting in deaths on both sides.

Measures were taken in early 1957 to strengthen Tunisia's relations with its neighbours. In January a treaty of good-neighbourliness was signed with Libya, as a step towards establishing a 'Great Arab Maghreb', and in March a 20-year treaty of friendship was concluded with Morocco.

The bey, Muhammad al-Amin, had been the object of constant criticism from Tunisian nationalist leaders, who accused him of reluctance to participate actively in the struggle for independence. After independence his remaining powers were eroded and on 25 July 1957 the Constituent Assembly voted to abolish the monarchy, proclaim Tunisia a republic and invest Bourguiba with the powers of Head of State.

RELATIONS WITH FRANCE

Although diplomatic relations with France had been resumed in January 1957, differences between the two Governments concerning the Algerian revolt persisted. The most serious Franco-Tunisian incident during the Algerian war occurred in February 1958, when French aircraft from Algeria attacked the Tunisian border village of Sakhiet Sidi Yousuf, the scene of several clashes the previous month. The Tunisian Government's reaction was to sever diplomatic relations with France, to forbid all French troop movements in Tunisia, to demand the immediate evacuation of all French bases, including Bizerta, and to take the matter before the UN Security Council. French troops were blockaded in their barracks, and the extra-territorial status of Bizerta, from which French warships were banned, was abolished. In addition some 600 French civilians were expelled from the frontier area and five of the seven French consulates were closed.

British and US mediation was accepted, and on 15 April 1958 it was agreed that all French troops would be evacuated and Tunisian sovereignty over Bizerta recognized; at the same time the French consulates would be reopened and the cases of the expelled French civilians examined. When further clashes between Tunisian and French forces occurred in May, a state of emergency covering the whole country was proclaimed and Tunisia again took the matter to the UN Security Council.

A new phase in Franco–Tunisian relations began with the accession to power of Gen. de Gaulle in June 1958. An agreement was concluded on 17 June under which French troops stationed outside Bizerta were to be withdrawn during the next four months, while negotiations for a provisional agreement on Bizerta were to follow. Restrictions on French troops were removed and diplomatic relations resumed. By October the only French troops remaining in Tunisia were in Bizerta.

The eradication of French interests had meanwhile commenced. In June 1958 the French-owned transport services and in August the electricity services of Tunis were nationalized. In November President Bourguiba announced proposals for the purchase of all agricultural land in Tunisia owned by French citizens by 1960, and for its redistribution to landless Tunisians.

POLITICAL CONSOLIDATION

With the improvement of relations with France, the Tunisian Government was able to consolidate its internal position, by restructuring the Néo-Destour Party and by instituting court proceedings against members of the former regime and 'Yousufist' opponents. Prince Chadli, the eldest son of the bey, and former Prime Ministers Tahar Ben Ammar and Salaheddine Baccouche were among those tried in late 1958 on charges that included the misuse of public funds and collaboration with the French authorities; sentences imposed ranged from heavy fines to imprisonment and loss of civic rights. Salah Ben Yousuf (*in*

absentia) and 54 of his supporters were charged with plotting to assassinate President Bourguiba, smuggling arms from Libya, and aiming to overthrow the Government. Ben Yousuf and eight others were sentenced to death, with most of the remainder receiving long prison sentences.

This trial widened the breach between Tunisia and the United Arab Republic (UAR—Egypt), from where Ben Yousuf had been conducting his activities. In October 1958 Tunisia had joined the Arab League, only to withdraw from a meeting of its council 10 days later, after accusing the UAR of attempting to dominate the organization. Diplomatic relations with the UAR were severed later in the month on the grounds of its alleged complicity in the 'Yousufist' attempt to assassinate President Bourguiba. On the eve of Ben Yousuf's trial, Bourguiba announced the capture of Egyptian officers who had secretly entered Tunisia to assist subversive elements to overthrow his Government.

On 1 June 1959 a new Constitution was promulgated, providing for the election of a President with a five-year mandate (renewable three times consecutively). The President was empowered to formulate the general policy of the state, choose the members of the Government, hold supreme command of the armed forces and make all appointments to civil and military posts. The Constitution also provided for the election of a national assembly for five years and required the approval of the assembly for the declaration of war, the conclusion of peace and the ratification of treaties. In elections which followed on 8 November President Bourguiba was elected unopposed, and all 90 seats in the new National Assembly were won by the Néo-Destour, their only opponents being the Communists.

THE BIZERTA CRISIS

The forging of cordial relations with France continued during 1959–60. A trade and tariff agreement was signed in September 1959, and further agreements on technical co-operation and the transfer of property of the French State in Tunisia to the Tunisian Government were concluded. In October President Bourguiba announced his support for President de Gaulle's offer of self-determination for Algeria, and Tunisia subsequently acted as intermediary between France and the Algerian rebels in moves towards a negotiated settlement.

None the less, Tunisia continued to press for the return of the Bizerta base, and in July 1961 President Bourguiba made a formal demand for its return and repeated the claim (first made in 1959) to Saharan territory in Algeria adjacent to the south-western part of Tunisia. Demonstrations ensued against the continued French occupation of Bizerta, and fighting between Tunisian and French troops began around the Bizerta base and in the disputed area of the Sahara. In mid-July diplomatic relations were again severed, and Tunisia requested a meeting of the UN Security Council. The fighting ended on 22 July with the French in firm control of the base and town of Bizerta, more than 800 Tunisians having been killed. In the south a Tunisian attempt to seize the fort of Garat el-Hamel also failed. A subsequent visit to Bizerta by the UN Secretary-General, Dag Hammarskjöld, in an attempt to promote a settlement, was unsuccessful. According to a French statement released in late July, France wished to continue to use the base while a state of international tension persisted but was prepared to negotiate with Tunisia over its use during this period.

The immediate results of the Bizerta crisis were a *rapprochement* between Tunisia and other Arab states, a deterioration in relations with the West and an improvement of relations with the communist bloc. The final settlement of the dispute occupied the remainder of 1961 and much of 1962. The Algerian cease-fire in March 1962 benefited Franco-Tunisian relations, and the French installations at Menzel Bourguiba, near Bizerta, were handed over to Tunisia on 30 June. In March 1963 agreement was reached on the transfer of some 370,000 acres of French-owned agricultural land to the Tunisian Government. Other agreements, on trade and finance, were reached, in order to reduce Tunisia's balance-of-payments deficit with France.

Although Algerian independence had been warmly welcomed by Tunisia, the extremist doctrines of the new state conflicted with Tunisian moderation and relations quickly deteriorated. In January 1963 the Tunisian ambassador was recalled from Algiers on the grounds of alleged Algerian complicity in a recent unsuccessful attempt on the life of President Bourguiba, in which 'Yousufists' in Algeria, as well as supporters of the old Destour and army elements, were implicated. Moroccan mediation facilitated a conference of the Maghreb states in Rabat in February, at which the Tunisians demanded the cessation of 'Yousufist' activities in Algeria. After further negotiations a frontier agreement between Tunisia and Algeria was signed in July.

EXPROPRIATION

In May 1964 the Tunisian National Assembly enacted legislation which authorized the expropriation of all foreign-owned lands (some 300,000 ha). The French immediately suspended, then cancelled, all financial aid. This nationalization of foreign-owned land was a step towards the development of socialism in the agrarian sector of the economy. The Néo-Destour's commitment to 'Tunisian socialism' was emphasized in the change of the party's name to the Parti socialiste destourien (Destour Socialist Party—PSD) prior to the presidential and general elections in November 1964, in which President Bourguiba was again elected unopposed and the PSD, the only party to present candidates, won all 90 seats in the National Assembly. Subsequent cabinet changes included the appointment of the President's son, Habib Bourguiba, Jr, as Minister of Foreign Affairs.

From 1964 onwards, domestic politics became more settled and the Government concentrated its attention on economic development. The hold of the PSD on the country was strengthened and President Bourguiba's position was unchallenged.

FOREIGN POLICY

After 1964 Tunisia's relations with the world beyond the Arab states and Africa were influenced by the need for foreign aid, most of which was received from Western countries where the moderation of Tunisian policies inspired confidence. Tunisia also made cautious overtures towards the communist bloc. Some economic assistance was obtained from the USSR while Tunisia maintained its non-aligned position. Diplomatic relations with the People's Republic of China were established, following a visit to Tunisia by the Chinese Premier, Zhou Enlai, in January 1964. Nevertheless, President Bourguiba publicly criticized Chinese policies, in particular the policy of encouraging revolution in Africa.

Relations with the rest of the Arab world continued to be the focus of President Bourguiba's attention and the source of bitter controversy. In April 1965 he openly attacked Arab League policy on Palestine and advocated a more flexible approach, including direct negotiations with Israel over the UN partition plan of 1948. This provoked severe criticism from the Arab states (excepting Morocco, Libya and Saudi Arabia). After violent demonstrations in Cairo and Tunis, the UAR and Tunisia withdrew their respective ambassadors. Tunisia's refusal at the end of April to follow the example of other Arab League states in severing relations with the Federal Republic of Germany, which had exchanged ambassadors with Israel, widened the rift. A conference of Arab heads of state at Casablanca in May, at which Tunisia was not represented, categorically rejected Bourguiba's proposal that Israel should be asked to cede territory to the Palestinian refugees in return for recognition by the Arab states, and reaffirmed their determination to effect the complete overthrow of Israel. In an open letter to those attending, Bourguiba accused the Egyptian President, Gamel Abd an-Nasser, of attempting to use the Arab League as an instrument of UAR national policy and of interfering in the affairs of every Arab state; Tunisia was not prepared to take part in the debates of the Arab League under such circumstances. In October 1966 Tunisia announced the complete severance of diplomatic relations with the UAR.

The Six-Day War between Israel and the Arab states in June 1967 led to immediate reconciliation in the Arab world. Tunisian troops were dispatched to the front, but the Israeli success was so swift and the cease-fire came so soon that they were recalled before they had reached the scene of the fighting. Diplomatic relations between Tunisia and the UAR were restored, and Tunisia was represented at the Arab summit meeting in Khartoum in September, when Arab nations agreed to neither recognize nor negotiate with Israel.

In May 1968, however, following criticism of President Bourguiba by the Syrian Prime Minister, who charged him with having betrayed the Arab struggle in Palestine, the Syrian chargé d'affaires and his staff in Tunis were accused of inciting subversive activities and expelled. At a meeting in Cairo in September, the Arab League refused to hear a statement from the Tunisian delegate criticizing the Arab attitude, particularly that of the UAR, towards Israel. Tunisia subsequently announced its intention to boycott future meetings of the League. Nevertheless, Tunisia reaffirmed its support for the Palestine Liberation Organization (PLO).

An exchange of visits by the ministers of foreign affairs of Tunisia and Algeria in early 1969 resulted in an improved climate for negotiation on the demarcation of their common frontier and on economic matters, especially those arising from the nationalization by each country of property owned by nationals of the other. In January 1970 the two countries signed a treaty of co-operation and friendship.

THE FALL OF AHMAD BEN SALAH

During 1964–69 the chief issue in internal affairs was the campaign to collectivize agriculture, implemented under the leadership of Ahmad Ben Salah, Minister of Finance and Planning. The programme encountered widespread opposition in affected areas and disagreement within the ruling party itself. In September 1969 the policy was abandoned; Ben Salah was stripped of all office, arrested, tried and sentenced to 10 years' hard labour. However, he escaped from prison in February 1973 and took refuge in Europe, from where he issued statements condemning President Bourguiba for acting against the people in the interests of a privileged class, and became the leader of the radical Mouvement de l'unité populaire (Popular Unity Movement—MUP), which was declared illegal in Tunisia.

Ben Salah was the first of several ministers to experience a sharp reversal of fortune. In November 1969 President Bourguiba appointed Bahi Ladgham as Prime Minister, but in October 1970 replaced him by Hédi Nouira. A year later the President declared that Nouira would be his successor. In March 1973 Ladgham resigned from all his political posts. Mahmoud Mestiri was the next minister to fall into disgrace. As Minister of the Interior in 1970 and 1971, he demanded the liberalization of the Government. Consequently he was dismissed from the Council of Ministers in September 1971, expelled from the party in 1972 and from the National Assembly in May 1973. When a revision of the Constitution was finally proposed in March 1973, it included almost none of the measures suggested by Mestiri to modify the presidential nature of the Government. Indeed, during the next two years Bourguiba and Prime Minister Nouira consolidated their power. In September 1974 the ninth party congress of the PSD elected Bourguiba as President-for-life of the party and confirmed Nouira in the post of Secretary-General. Bourguiba appointed a new political bureau of 20 members, including 14 ministers, confirming a tendency to draw the PSD and the Government closer together. In November Bourguiba was re-elected unopposed as President of Tunisia, and in the National Assembly elections all 112 PSD candidates were returned, also without opposition. The Assembly voted amendments to the Constitution, designating the Prime Minister as the President's successor and allowing for the appointment of a President-for-life, a post to which the Assembly elected Bourguiba in March 1975. Constitutional reforms in December 1975 increased presidential powers still further.

UNION WITH LIBYA

In June 1970 the President's son, Habib Bourguiba, Jr, was replaced as Minister of Foreign Affairs by Muhammad Masmoudi. From that date relations with the more radical Arab states and with extremist powers outside the area improved. Normal relations were resumed with the UAR and Syria, and Tunisia rejoined the Arab League.

In January 1974, after a meeting between President Bourguiba and Col Muammar al-Qaddafi, the Libyan leader, on the island of Djerba, it was announced that Tunisia and Libya had agreed to form a union. The Djerba Agreement was greeted with general surprise for, despite an improvement in relations between the two countries in previous years, Bourguiba had always shown himself to be hostile to such a union. Bourguiba was to be president of the new state, with Qaddafi as his deputy. It would seem that the Djerba Agreement was managed by

Muhammad Masmoudi, without the consent of Prime Minister Nouira, who was out of the country at the time. Nouira returned swiftly to Tunisia, and Masmoudi was dismissed from his post in the Government and the PSD.

In the aftermath of this confused affair, relations with Libya were tense. The Libyans continued to urge fulfilment of the Djerba Agreement, and in 1975 Bourguiba expressed concern at the increase in strength of the Libyan army. Another source of contention between the two countries was the delimitation of their respective sectors of the continental shelf, in which important deposits of petroleum were to be found. In June 1977 both sides agreed to submit to arbitration by the International Court of Justice (ICJ) and agreement was finally reached in February 1982. In October 1977 a joint statement was issued, saying that Tunisia and Libya had agreed to 'reactivate mutual co-operation' and establish a scheme to link the electricity networks of the two countries, while experts were to discuss the possibility of other joint ventures. Relations with Algeria also improved in 1977, after Tunisia had abandoned its attempts at conciliation in the Western Sahara dispute (in which it sided with Morocco): a co-operation agreement was signed in July by the respective ministers of the interior.

DOMESTIC UNREST

By 1977, with President Bourguiba in his seventies and in poor health, there was growing uncertainty over the future of the system of government which he had dominated for so long. Hédi Nouira, his designated successor, appeared to lack the powerful personality which had kept Bourguiba in command of the country, and there were signs of a succession struggle in the increasing demands for the free development of a pluralist democracy from, among others, former ministers Ahmad Ben Salah, in exile, and Ahmad Mestiri, leader of the unofficial Mouvement des démocrates socialistes (Social Democrats—MDS). The arrest and trial (in mid-1977) of 33 members of the MUP, on charges of threatening state security and defaming the President, indicated the continuing hostility of the Government to any form of organized opposition.

Meanwhile, however, a more effective political force was beginning to make itself felt. After a number of strikes by workers in 1976, a 'social contract' was formulated in early 1977 between the Government and the Union Générale des Travailleurs Tunisiens (General Union of Tunisian Workers—UGTT) under the leadership of Habib Achour, involving inflation-linked pay rises for the duration of the 1977–81 Development Plan. In spite of this agreement there were further strikes in various sectors of industry in late 1977, demanding better pay and conditions, and backed by the UGTT, which was becoming (particularly through its weekly newspaper *Ach-Cha'ab*) an increasingly vocal critic of government policy and an outlet for political dissenters. In December Muhammad Masmoudi, the former Minister of Foreign Affairs, returned from exile in Libya and declared his support for the UGTT, thereby underlining its potential as a political force. Tahar Belkhodja, the Minister of the Interior, was dismissed in late December, after having suggested that the unrest should be attributed to social and economic problems, such as a rapidly increasing population and severe unemployment. Six other moderate members of the Council of Ministers resigned in sympathy, but President Bourguiba reaffirmed his support for Nouira by forming a new Government in which the dissidents were replaced mainly by civil servants and technocrats, all of whom could be expected to accept Nouira's tough policy; in addition, Bourguiba appointed his son, Habib Bourguiba, Jr, as special adviser.

In January 1978 Achour resigned from the political bureau and central committee of the PSD after pressure from members of the UGTT who felt that his dual role had become unacceptable. The UGTT national council appealed for urgent changes in the method of government and an end to the use of 'intimidation' in suppressing strikes and demonstrations. In late January the union organized a general strike as a warning to the Government and in retaliation for attacks on union offices. Rioting ensued in Tunis and several other cities, the army intervened and at least 51 people were killed, while hundreds more were injured; a state of emergency was declared and a curfew imposed. Hundreds of demonstrators were arrested, tried and

imprisoned, and Achour and other members of the UGTT executive were also taken into custody and charged with subversion. The Government accused the UGTT of a long-standing conspiracy against the State and hinted at foreign backing, presumably from Libya.

There was considerable international criticism of the irregular conduct of the trial of Achour and 30 other union leaders, which began in August 1978. Nevertheless, Achour was sentenced to 10 years' hard labour, and prison sentences were also passed on all but six of the other defendants. Under a new Secretary-General, Tijani Abid, the UGTT expressed regret at the recent events and declared its willingness to co-operate with the Government. Although Achour was pardoned by President Bourguiba in August 1979, he remained under house arrest; 263 others serving prison terms for their involvement in the riots had been pardoned in May, but it was nevertheless clear that the power of the UGTT as a source of opposition had, for the moment, been crushed.

In July 1979 the National Assembly approved an amendment to the electoral code, allowing, for the first time, the number of candidates in legislative elections to be twice the number of seats although it remained unclear whether members of parties other than the PSD would be permitted to stand. At the PSD congress in September, the need to 'open up' the party to new adherents and original ideas was emphasized, but the Prime Minister rejected the idea of a multi-party system and a 'national pact' proposed two years previously by the MDS. The main opposition groups—the MUP, the MDS and the Parti communiste tunisien (PCT—the Communist Party)—declared that they would boycott the legislative elections in November, since participation would indicate support of the present system (and would presumably not have been permitted in any case, since none of the groups had official party status). The rate of participation in the elections was substantially lower than on previous occasions, reaching only 81%, compared with an average of 95%.

In January 1980 there was an attack on the town of Gafsa in western Tunisia by guerrillas, originally estimated to number 300, although only 60 were later brought to trial. The Tunisian armed forces quickly regained control of the town, but 41 deaths were reported. Responsibility for the attack was claimed by a hitherto unknown group, the Tunisian Armed Resistance, who declared that they aimed to free Tunisia from the 'dictatorship' of the PSD. The Tunisian Government claimed that the attackers were Tunisian migrant workers who had been trained in Libya and encouraged to make the attack in order to destabilize the Bourguiba administration: diplomatic relations with Libya were suspended. Libya expressed its incredulity at these allegations, and referred to the incident as a 'popular uprising'. Nevertheless, the attack caused international concern, particularly in France, which sent military transport aircraft to Gafsa and naval vessels to the Tunisian coast, while the USA also offered to expedite military supplies. The Gafsa attack was condemned by the more established opposition groups within Tunisia, engendering a temporary national solidarity, although the same groups condemned the execution of 13 of the guerrillas which took place in April.

MOVES TOWARDS POLITICAL LIBERALIZATION

The sudden illness of Hédi Nouira in February 1980 renewed political uncertainty. The Minister of Education, Muhammad Mzali, was appointed as temporary government co-ordinator and in April as Prime Minister, thereby becoming Bourguiba's successor under the terms of the Constitution. The new Government headed by Mzali included a member of the MDS and three of the ministers who had resigned in 1977 in protest at the harsh measures taken against strikers. In December Tahar Belkhodja, the former Minister of the Interior who had been dismissed in 1977, was readmitted to the Government. Most political prisoners were released during 1980, and in January 1981 a pardon was granted to nearly 1,000 members of the UGTT who had been convicted of involvement in the 1978 riots. Greater tolerance was also shown towards opposition parties: in mid-1980 permission was granted to the MDS to publish two weekly periodicals, and in the following February an amnesty was granted to all members of the proscribed MUP, except its leader-in-exile, Ahmad Ben Salah. In April 1981 President Bourguiba declared that he saw no objection to the emergence of political parties provided that they rejected violence and religious fanaticism and were not dependent 'ideologically or materially' on any foreign group (which suggested that Islamic fundamentalists would not be welcome candidates). The congress elected a new PSD central committee of 80 representatives, some 75% of whom had not previously been members of the committee.

An extraordinary congress of the UGTT was also held in April 1981, the first since the riots of January 1978. Of the 13 members of the executive committee elected by the congress, 11 were former committee members who had been imprisoned in 1978. The new Secretary General—Taieb Baccouche—was the first non-PSD member to be elected to this post. Habib Achour was released in December 1981, when he was allowed to resume his position as leader of the UGTT.

The process of installing a multi-party system continued with the announcement of legislative elections for November 1981; Bourguiba promised that any participating group which gained a minimum of 5% of the votes cast would be officially recognized as a political party. Several parties refused to take part in the elections under these conditions. In July the one-party system ended with the official recognition of the PCT. As a former officially recognized political party (banned since 1963), the PCT was not required to fulfil the 5% condition laid upon the other groups. In contrast to this apparent political liberalization, as many as 50 leading members of the Mouvement de la tendance islamique (Islamic Tendency Movement—MTI) were arrested and given prison sentences in September. The Government continued to regard the MTI, a relatively moderate Islamic group, as a dangerous influence.

Although the PCT, the MUP and the MDS presented candidates in the November 1981 legislative elections, the result was an emphatic victory for the Front national, a joint electoral pact formed by the PSD and the UGTT, which gained 94.6% of votes cast and won all 136 seats in the new Assembly. The other parties all failed to win 5% of the vote, and consequently none was given official recognition. Formal protests of electoral irregularities were made by the three opposition groups. The MDS and the MUP were finally accorded official status in November 1983.

FURTHER UNREST

In January 1984 widespread rioting and looting broke out. The immediate cause was a substantial increase in the price of bread and the abolition of government subsidies on flour and other staple foods, but the disturbances were also linked to long-standing grievances, including the high level of unemployment (particularly among the young), and to unrest amongst Islamist groups. Rioting started in the south of the country, but spread to the northern cities of Sfax, Gabès and Tunis. On 3 January the Government declared a state of emergency, and troops were brought in to control street demonstrations. The resulting clashes between troops and demonstrators left 89 people dead and 938 injured, according to official figures, and more than 1,000 people were arrested. After a week of disturbances President Bourguiba personally intervened to reverse the price rises, and order was re-established.

An official inquiry into the cause of the riots accused the Minister of the Interior, Driss Guiga, of exploiting the violence for his own political ends and of failing to inform the President of the magnitude of the disturbances. Guiga had been dismissed by President Bourguiba in January 1984 and subsequently left the country. The vacant portfolio was granted to Prime Minister Mzali, whose position was considerably strengthened by the downfall of his former rival for the presidential succession. In June Guiga was tried *in absentia* for high treason and sentenced to 15 years' imprisonment.

Throughout 1984 and in early 1985 Tunisia was troubled by a series of strikes in the public sector. The strikers demanded increases in public-sector salaries, which had been frozen for two years. In April 1985 riot police surrounded the UGTT headquarters, after the union urged a general strike in support of the demands of public-sector strikers. The UGTT subsequently postponed the strike, pending talks with government negotiators. However, in early May, the UGTT announced that negotiations had collapsed and that it would refuse to participate in the municipal elections later that month. The MDS, the

PCT and the MUP also boycotted the elections. Nevertheless, there was a turn-out of 92.8% (compared with only 66.8% for the equivalent elections in 1980), which the PSD interpreted as a vote of support for its policies. In July the UGTT declared the start of a campaign of renewed strike action. In the same month the union's newspaper, *Ach-Cha'ab,* was suspended by the Government for six months. In October the police occupied the UGTT headquarters and arrested union leaders. Local UGTT committees were dissolved and replaced by pro-government committees. By early November about 100 UGTT leaders had been arrested, including the union's Secretary-General, Habib Achour, but many were released later in the month. In December the UGTT executive committee agreed to replace Achour with a provisional Secretary-General, on condition that the Government released the union members who were still in detention and reinstated workers who had been dismissed for taking industrial action. In January 1986 the UGTT's administrative commission, considering that these conditions had not been met, voted to reinstate Achour as Secretary-General. In the same month, however, Achour was imprisoned on a charge of theft, dating from 1982. (In April he was sentenced to a further two years' imprisonment for alleged mismanagement of union funds, and in December his sentence was extended by another four years.) In May the UGTT elected a 'moderate', Ismaïl Lajeri, as Secretary-General.

The Tunisian Government's refusal to condemn the US raid on Libya in April 1986 prompted considerable popular disquiet, and anti-US sentiment was suppressed by the authorities. Ahmad Mestiri, leader of the MDS, was jailed for organizing a demonstration, and several magazines (including the MDS weekly and two PCT periodicals) were seized by the Government. The authorities suspended publication of three magazines for six months. The appointment of Gen. Zine al-Abidine Ben Ali, who was regarded as immoderate, as Minister of the Interior, in late April, was considered a significant change in domestic policy.

BOURGUIBA ATTEMPTS TO TIGHTEN HIS GRIP ON POWER

In early 1986 Habib Bourguiba, Jr, was suspended from his post of special adviser, owing to his opposition to the series of arrests in late 1985. In the following months President Bourguiba announced several ministerial reshuffles, which gradually weakened the position of Muhammad Mzali, the Prime Minister, who had been regarded as Bourguiba's potential successor. During the 12th congress of the PSD in June, Bourguiba apparently confirmed Mzali's position as Secretary-General of the PSD, yet he dispensed with the ballot to elect the members of the PSD central committee, and personally appointed 90 members, none of whom was an associate of Mzali. In July Mzali was replaced in the premiership by Rachid Sfar (previously Minister of Finance), and was dismissed as Secretary-General of the PSD. Mzali subsequently fled to Algeria, and was later sentenced *in absentia* to one year's imprisonment for crossing the border illegally, to a further three years' imprisonment for defamatory comments against Tunisian leaders, and to 15 years' hard labour for mismanagement of public funds.

A general election for a new National Assembly was held in November 1986, but was boycotted by the opposition parties. The PSD won all 125 seats, opposed by only 15 independent candidates. There was a high level of participation (82.9% of the electorate), according to official figures, although these were disputed by the opposition.

By 1987 the Government had consolidated its control over the UGTT, and left-wing militancy was no longer perceived as a threat. In December 1986 the UGTT elected a new 18-member executive bureau, and an apparently moderate Secretary-General, Abd al-Aziz Bouraoui. In January 1987 Bourguiba presided over the opening of an extraordinary congress of the UGTT, during which the union confirmed its support of the PSD and approved a new union charter. Habib Achour was released on humanitarian grounds in May. In the same month, Bourguiba pardoned 13 members of the Rassemblement socialiste progressiste (RSP), who had been sentenced to six months' imprisonment for illegal assembly.

SUPPRESSION OF ISLAMIST ACTIVISTS

Meanwhile, President Bourguiba had become increasingly concerned that 'Islamic fundamentalism' was a threat to his regime, and attempts were made to suppress Islamist activity. In July 1986 four Islamist activists were sentenced to death, and about 22 others were imprisoned, for a series of offences. Numerous arrests were reported by human rights organizations, following clashes between Islamists and left-wing students at the University of Tunis in early 1987. In March 1987 the Secretary-General of the MTI, Rached Ghanouchi, was arrested on charges of violence and collusion with foreign powers to overthrow the Government. Later in the month, Tunisia severed diplomatic relations with Iran, after Tunisians, suspected of terrorist offences, were arrested in France and Djibouti. The Tunisian Government accused the Iranian Embassy in Tunis of subversive acts, including the recruitment of Tunisian Islamists to perpetrate terrorist acts abroad, and thus undermine Tunisia's relations with friendly states. The Government also claimed to have evidence of an Iranian plot to overthrow Bourguiba, and to establish a pro-Iranian fundamentalist administration in Tunisia. On this pretext, a series of arrests of Islamists ensued. According to the authorities, 1,500 people were detained, although opposition parties estimated that the total reached more than 3,000. The arrests were condemned by the Ligue tunisienne des droits de l'homme (Tunisian League of Human Rights—LTDH), and in April the opposition parties issued a communiqué, warning against a return to repressive practices and demanding guarantees for the freedom of the trade unions and the universities. There were further arrests after clashes between police units and Islamists during an anti-government demonstration in April. Later in the month, the Secretary-General of the LTDH, Khemais Chamari, was arrested and accused of disseminating false information and defaming the State. (Chamari was later released on parole, and was acquitted in January 1988.) In May the Government approved the creation of the Association for the Defence of Human Rights and Public Liberty, as a rival to the LTDH, which the Government accused of being pro-MTI. In June 37 Islamists, mostly students, were sentenced to terms of imprisonment of between two and six years for taking part in illegal demonstrations in April and for defaming Bourguiba. In August 13 foreign tourists were injured by bomb explosions, and the Government promptly insisted that the MTI was responsible, despite the publication of a statement from a radical group, Islamic Jihad, claiming responsibility. Six young Tunisians later confessed to planting the bombs, and stated that they were members of the MTI. They alleged that the bombings were part of an operation to damage the tourist trade on which Tunisia depended. In September the trial opened of 90 Islamists, accused of threatening state security and of plotting against the Government. The conduct of the trial was criticized by opposition parties and human rights groups. Despite the prosecution's demand that all 90 defendants should receive the death penalty, only seven were sentenced to death, five of them *in absentia*. Fourteen defendants were acquitted, and 69 (including Rached Ghanouchi) received prison sentences.

FOREIGN RELATIONS IN THE 1980s

In the 1980s President Bourguiba continued to pursue a moderate, pro-Western foreign policy. After the attack on Gafsa in January 1980, Tunisia strengthened its links with the USA and the two countries established a US-Tunisian military commission in November 1981.

Tunisian relations with other Maghreb countries improved considerably in the early 1980s. In March 1983 a meeting was held in Tunisia between President Bourguiba and President Ben Djedid Chadli of Algeria. Discussions on the normalization of relations between the two countries, the demarcation of the frontier and common industrial projects resulted in the drafting of the Maghreb Fraternity and Co-operation Treaty. At the subsequent ratification of the treaty by the Tunisian National Assembly, appeals were made for closer relations between the Maghreb states of Algeria, Libya, Mauritania, Morocco and Tunisia, and the introduction of a common political structure. Mauritania signed the treaty in December 1983.

However, relations with Libya reached a dangerously low ebb in August 1985 after Tunisia expelled 283 Libyan nationals, including most of the Libyan diplomats in Tunis, on charges of spying, in retaliation against Col Qaddafi's decision to expel some 30,000 Tunisians working in Libya. Qaddafi threatened to use military force to resolve the dispute, and Tunisia's armed forces were placed on alert before Morocco offered to mediate between the two countries. In September Tunisia severed diplomatic relations with Libya, following the expulsion of four Libyan diplomats who had been accused of sending letter-bombs to Tunisian journalists.

In response to the Libyan military threat, Tunisia's links with the USA were strengthened. However, in October 1985 relations between the two countries were soured, following the bombing by Israeli aircraft of the headquarters of the PLO, near Tunis. At the UN Security Council, the USA abstained on a Tunisian resolution condemning the raid, but resisted Israeli pressure to veto the motion. By March 1986 relations between the USA and Tunisia had improved, following a visit by US Vice-President George Bush. However, the US raid on Libya in the following month proved to be a further source of embarrassment for the Tunisian Government, which refused to condemn or to approve the US action and thus angered members of opposition parties and Islamists. Demonstrations ensued and many opposition figures were arrested (see above).

Meanwhile, there was growing Tunisian ambivalence over the PLO presence in Tunis. Following the Israeli raid on the PLO headquarters, a group of Palestinians 'hijacked' an Italian cruise liner, the *Achille Lauro*, off the Egyptian coast. The USA made it clear that it would not allow the hijackers to return to the PLO headquarters in Tunis, and the Tunisian authorities refused to let the Egyptian aircraft carrying the hijackers and a PLO official land in Tunisia (see chapter on Egypt). Although there was speculation in late 1986 that the PLO would move its headquarters out of Tunisia, as a result of increasing restrictions imposed on its activities by the Tunisian Government, in October the organization decided to remain in Tunisia but with a considerably reduced number of staff.

Relations with Libya began to improve in March 1987, when President Bourguiba met a representative of the Libyan Government to discuss the issue of compensation for Tunisian workers, and the restoration of capital to companies expelled from Libya in 1985. In early 1987 Libya produced a written undertaking not to interfere in Tunisia's internal affairs. In July flights were resumed by Tunisia's national airline, TunisAir, to Tripoli. Following Col Qaddafi's proposals to unify Libya and Algeria, Bourguiba and President Chadli of Algeria issued a joint communiqué in July, announcing that discussions had taken place on how to develop the unity of the Maghreb region, although it seemed that Bourguiba had agreed to increased co-operation between the Maghreb states, rather than merger. In September Tunisia announced that the dispute with Libya over the expulsion of the Tunisian workers had been resolved, and consular ties were resumed in the following month, when the border between the two countries was reopened.

BOURGUIBA'S DECLINE

In the second half of 1987 President Bourguiba's behaviour became increasingly erratic. In September the appointments were announced of a new Minister of Cultural Affairs, Director of the PSD Political Bureau, Director-General of the Tunisian broadcasting company, and editor of the state-owned newspaper, *al-Amal*. A few days later, in early October, Bourguiba revoked the appointments and dismissed Rachid Sfar from the premiership. Ben Ali was appointed Prime Minister, with responsibility for internal affairs, and Secretary-General of the PSD. A few weeks later, a new director of the PSD was appointed. In late October Bourguiba carried out a minor cabinet reshuffle in which the Ministry of Finance was divided into two portfolios and a Ministry of the National Economy was created.

Meanwhile, ministers, concerned about Bourguiba's behaviour, began to examine provisions in the Constitution which would allow for the retirement of the President. Reports emerged that Bourguiba was demanding a retrial of the Islamists who had been sentenced in September 1987 (see above), with the aim of having the death sentence imposed on all 90 defendants. A disagreement about the fate of the Islamists allegedly ensued between Bourguiba and Ben Ali, and it was rumoured in early November that Bourguiba intended to dismiss Ben Ali. Meanwhile, a plot to overthrow Bourguiba was disclosed, allegedly involving about 150 people, both military and civilian.

BEN ALI TAKES OVER

On 7 November 1987 seven doctors declared that President Bourguiba was unfit to govern, owing to senility and ill health, and, in accordance with the Constitution, the Prime Minister, Zine al-Abidine Ben Ali, was sworn in as President. There was no apparent opposition to Ben Ali's take-over, which had been approved in advance by the majority of ministers and senior military officers. President Ben Ali declared that he would continue to implement existing foreign and economic policies, but announced plans to revise the Constitution and to permit greater political freedom. He appointed Hedi Baccouche as Prime Minister, and a new Council of Ministers was announced, which omitted four ministers closely associated with Bourguiba. Later in November, Ben Ali formed a National Security Council (comprising himself, the Prime Minister, the Minister of State for Defence, the Minister of Foreign Affairs and the Minister of the Interior) to safeguard internal security. The Council subsequently announced that 76 people, including members of the army and national guard, police, customs officers and members of the MTI, had been arrested on suspicion of plotting against the State.

On assuming power, President Ben Ali immediately began to effect a policy of national reconciliation. The publication was permitted of opposition newspapers which had been suspended by the Bourguiba administration, although radio and television networks continued to be controlled. In late November 1987 the National Assembly approved legislation which limited to four days the length of time during which a person could be held in police custody without the authority of the public prosecutor: the length of time during which a person could be held on remand was limited to six months for most offences. In December the State Security Court was abolished, along with the post of Prosecutor-General. In the same month, 2,487 political and non-political detainees were released, including 608 MTI members and Ahmad Mestiri, the leader of the MDS. In January 1988 405 political prisoners were released, and in March Ben Ali granted amnesty to a further 2,044 political and common-law detainees.

Ben Ali also initiated attempts to normalize relations between the Government and the UGTT, as a result of which the two rivals for the leadership of the UGTT, Habib Achour and Abd al-Aziz Bouraoui, agreed to renounce their union responsibilities as a first step towards the reconciliation of the 'radical' and 'moderate' factions of the union. In May 1988 Ben Ali ordered the release of Rached Ghanouchi, the leader of the MTI. Ahmad Ben Salah, the exiled leader of the MUP, was also pardoned, and he returned to Tunisia in June.

Meanwhile, the new Government continued to consolidate its power. The size of the PSD political bureau was reduced from 20 to 13 members in December 1987. Nine new members were appointed, including seven members of the Council of Ministers formed in November, all of whom were close associates of President Ben Ali. In January 1988 the PSD won all the seats at five by-elections to the National Assembly with a comfortable majority, although the PCT alleged electoral malpractice. In a government reorganization in the following month, Ben Ali assumed the defence portfolio and appointed a Secretary of State for Security Affairs.

POLITICAL LIBERALIZATION

In accordance with his promises after assuming power, President Ben Ali introduced proposals to increase political freedom and to introduce a more democratic system of government. In February 1988 the central committee of the PSD announced that the party's name had been changed to the Rassemblement constitutionnel démocratique (Democratic Constitutional Assembly—RCD). In July the National Assembly approved a series of proposals to reform the Constitution. Under the amendments, the post of President-for-life was abolished, and the President was to be elected by universal suffrage every five years, and limited to two consecutive terms in office. A maximum age of 70 years was to be introduced for presidential candidates. If the presidency fell vacant before the end of the term of office, the President of the National Assembly, rather than the Prime

Minister, was to assume presidential powers until elections were held, but was himself prohibited from becoming a candidate. The reforms also redefined the role of the Prime Minister as a coordinator of government activities rather than as leader of the government.

In April 1988 legislation was passed by the National Assembly instituting a multi-party system, although, in order to gain legal recognition, political parties had to uphold the aims of, and work within the Constitution, and were not to be permitted to pursue purely religious, racial, regional or linguistic objectives. Gifts and donations to political parties were to be supervised by the Minister of the Interior, in order to prevent foreign interference. In July the National Assembly modified the Press Code, relaxing its repressive tendencies. In the same month, Tunisia became the first Arab nation to ratify the UN convention against torture and other inhumane or degrading treatment. In late July, as part of an amnesty extended to 932 detainees, Tunisia's remaining 180 classified political prisoners were released, and a further 1,075 people charged with political crimes or under police surveillance had their civil liberties restored. The beneficiaries of this amnesty included 50 Islamists arrested in 1987; members of the UGTT; Tunisians involved in the attack on Gafsa in 1980; and supporters of Salah Ben Yousuf, who had been arrested in 1963. (However, about 170 prisoners accused of terrorist acts remained in detention.)

In a major ministerial reshuffle in July 1988, seven ministers who had served under Bourguiba were dismissed, leaving Hedi Baccouche, the Prime Minister, as the only prominent member of the Council of Ministers to have served under the two Presidents. In an apparent move to separate the RCD from the state apparatus, as a prelude to a multi-party system, the Director of the RCD Political Bureau lost his right to sit in the Council of Ministers and the public health portfolio was allocated to Saadadine Zmerli, the President of the LTDH, who was not a member of the RCD. Ben Ali also divided the Ministry of Economy into a Ministry of Trade and Industry and a Ministry of Energy and Mines.

At the first congress of the RCD in late July 1988, President Ben Ali pledged that he would establish a multi-party system with fair elections and freedom of expression. In accordance with Ben Ali's appeal for pluralism, Ahmad Mestiri, the leader of the MDS, and Muhammad Belhadj Amor, the leader of the Parti de l'unité populaire (PUP), were invited to address the congress, and both endorsed the policies of the Ben Ali Government. Ben Ali was re-elected as president of the RCD, despite speculation, following the recent cabinet reshuffle, that he would relinquish his party post. The perpetuation of ties between the RCD and the Government was also reflected in the appointments of Hedi Baccouche, the Prime Minister, as Vice-President of the party, and of the Minister of Foreign Affairs, the Minister of the Interior and the Governor of the Central Bank (who held cabinet rank) as members of the new streamlined seven-member political bureau. There was also concern over the disclosure that Ben Ali had personally appointed 122 members of the RCD's enlarged 200-strong central committee.

Ben Ali restated his desire to 'open a new page of pluralism and democracy' at the beginning of consultations held in September 1988 on a Tunisian 'National Pact' to present the aims and values of the administration. Participants in the consultations included representatives from national organizations (the UGTT, employers' organizations, youth and womens' groups, etc), the Secretary-Generals of the RCD, the MDS, the PCT and the PUP, and the leaders of the unofficial political parties (the leftist RSP, the liberal Parti social pour le progrès—PSP, the MUP and the MTI). Later that month, the RSP and the PSP were granted legal recognition. Earlier in August, Rached Ghanouchi had announced that the MTI accepted the law on political parties and respected the Constitution, especially the personal status code enshrining womens' rights.

Ben Ali was faced with the problem of integrating the Islamists within the political system without totally abandoning the secularism of the Bourguiba regime, and he succeeded in establishing good relations with their leader. Following the release of leading fundamentalists in September and November 1988, Ghanouchi stated that the era of injustice was over. Stress was laid upon the Arab and Islamic identity of Tunisia, the *Azzan* and prayers were broadcast on television, *Hijri* dates appeared on official documents, and the seventh-century religious college, the Zeitouna, was given the status of a university. The MTI, transformed into a political party (Hizb an-Nahdah or Parti de la renaissance), was, none the less, denied official status.

On the first anniversary of his rise to power Ben Ali announced a National Pact, which was designed to show Tunisia as a country ready for democracy. Basic freedoms were guaranteed, although political parties could be formed only with the approval of the Minister of the Interior. Elections, not due until 1991, were brought forward to April 1989. In November 1988 a new political party, the union démocratique unioniste (UDU), was legalized, and began to develop Arab nationalist and unionist policies.

During this period old associates of Bourguiba were indicted for corruption and embezzlement of considerable sums: Mahmoud Skhiri was sentenced to five years' imprisonment, Tahar Belhodja (*in absentia*) to five years, Mahmoud Belhassine to 10 years and a heavy fine, while Mzali's request, from abroad, for rehabilitation was refused. Moreover, Ben Ali dismissed Habib Ammar, one of his oldest and closest associates (whose son had been involved in a smuggling case), from the Ministry of the Interior.

THE APRIL 1989 ELECTIONS

In February 1989, in an attempt to establish national consensus and also to guarantee the election of some non-RCD candidates, Ben Ali invited the leaders of the six opposition parties to present themselves to the electorate as a coalition. The offer was rejected, although the parties had previously agreed to support Ben Ali as sole candidate for the presidency. In a drastic purge conducted at local level, the RCD readopted only 20 of its 125 retiring members. The communists, fearing humiliation at the polls, declined to participate. Hizb an-Nahdah, forbidden from campaigning as a party, presented 'independent' candidates in 19 out of the 25 constituencies, in which a total of 480 candidates contested 141 seats. The National Assembly elections were the first multi-party elections in Tunisia since 1981; the level of participation was 76% of the 2,700,000 eligible voters. The RCD won all 141 seats, with 80% of the votes cast, while the Islamist independents replaced the MDS as the main opposition force, taking 13% of the total votes and 25% of votes in many constituencies. Opposition allegations of widespread electoral fraud were denied by the RCD. Ben Ali was confirmed as President by 99% of voters.

On 11 April 1989 a new Council of Ministers of 32 members was announced. Although the leading members, headed by Baccouche, were retained, the cabinet represented a new political generation. With an average age of 48 years, most ministers were too young to have taken part in the struggle for independence, and 28 of them had not held any office under Bourguiba. In addition, they were drawn from the whole country (one-third from the deprived south) rather than predominantly from Bourguiba's own Sahel area. Technocrats were given portfolios to address what Ben Ali defined as the main problems: foreign debts, expensive subsidies, a cumbersome and expensive public sector, unemployment and regional policies. As a conciliatory gesture to the opposition, the liberal Mohammed Charfi, a leading member of the LTDH, was placed in charge of Education and Scientific Research, while Daly Jazi, a founding member of the MDS, was appointed as Minister of Public Health.

POLITICAL DEVELOPMENTS

However, the National Pact failed to curb political dissent in the country, and tensions were exacerbated by the imposition of essential economic reforms. In April 1989 Ben Ali announced a general amnesty, which restored civil and political rights to 5,416 people condemned by the former regime, many of whom were Islamist activists. The remaining 48 Islamist prisoners, sentenced in 1987 for plotting against Bourguiba, were released in May 1989. In September Ben Ali dismissed his Prime Minister, Hedi Baccouche, following a disagreement over economic policy; Baccouche was replaced by Hamed Karoui, hitherto Minister of Justice. In November a further 1,354 people, including Bourguiba's close associates Mahmoud Skhiri and Tahar Belkhodja, were granted amnesty. In one of the few political trials, the leader of a breakaway faction of the MUP

was sentenced in August to one year's imprisonment for defamation of the President (but was released in November); six communists were later imprisoned for similar offences. In May 1990 an Islamist leader, Professor Moncef Ben Salem, was sentenced to three years' imprisonment for criticizing the Government in an Algerian fundamentalist newspaper.

In late 1989 taxes were lowered in an attempt to reduce evasion, and Ben Ali announced a 10% increase in wages. However, the President failed to gain popular support and appeared increasingly autocratic, declaring that he alone would decide the pace and course of reform. The conflict between the country's need for reform and modernization and the traditional Islamic values held by certain factions was seemingly insoluble. The Government was also concerned that Islamists were receiving financial aid from foreign sources. After the April 1989 elections, Rached Ghanouchi went into voluntary exile in Paris, and a lawyer, Abd al-Fatha Mourou, assumed the leadership of an-Nahdah within Tunisia. In June official recognition of an-Nahdah was refused, on the grounds that 15 of its leaders had not yet regained their civil rights. Ben Ali also demanded that an-Nahdah clarify its position on the rights of women, and reiterated his opposition to the concept of a religious political party. In December a second application for registration was refused, although an-Nahdah was permitted to publish a weekly journal, *al-Fajr*. (The an-Nahdah weekly, *al-Moustaqbal*, had been closed down in the previous year.)

Following their failure to secure legal recognition, the Islamists increased their political agitation and gained support among students. In December 1989 96 students began a hunger strike after the Government tried to divide its opponents by dissolving the Theological Faculty of the Zeitouna University. A campus police station in Kairouan was ransacked, and casualties were reported on the campus at Sfax. In February 1990 the protests culminated in clashes between police and students belonging to the Union Générale des Etudiants Tunisiens (UGET), an organization allied to an-Nahdah. About 600 student activists were detained, and some were briefly drafted into the army. The Government accused an-Nahdah of exploiting the students and of inciting unrest among the work-force, including a strike by 10,000 municipal workers. Political tension increased following severe floods in late January 1990, which killed 30 people and caused damage to property totalling more than US $400m. Some 800 demonstrators, incited by Islamist leaders who condemned the Government's dilatory relief efforts, attacked government offices in Sidi Bou Zid, and 26 were arrested. Ben Ali subsequently pledged $445m. towards relief work. (In April five men were sentenced to three months' imprisonment for leading the riots.) In a reshuffle of some prominent government posts in March, Abd al-Hamid Escheikh, hitherto Minister of Foreign Affairs, was appointed Minister of the Interior.

The Government was keen that municipal elections, due to be held in June 1990, should be viewed as a serious stratagem towards multi-party democracy. In January Prime Minister Karoui invited opposition leaders for discussions on the amendment of the electoral code and access to the media. However, the discussions were boycotted by three of the recognized opposition parties and by an-Nahdah, and little progress was made. In May the electoral law was amended to introduce a form of proportional representation in the forthcoming municipal elections. The winning party was to gain only 50% of the seats, while the remaining seats were to be divided between all the parties, according to the number of votes received. However, the six legal opposition groups and an-Nahdah boycotted the elections, held on 10 June, on the grounds that they were neither free nor fair. The RCD won control of all but one of the 245 municipal councils, taking 3,750 council seats. The remaining 34 seats were won by independent candidates, many of whom were former members of the RCD. According to official sources, an estimated 79.3% of the electorate voted. In the same month publication of *al-Fajr* was suspended, following an article by exiled leader Rached Ghanouchi which strongly criticized the Tunisian Government.

Disagreement over government policy regarding the Gulf crisis, and in particular the stance adopted concerning Iraq, was the apparent cause of the replacement, in late August 1990, of the Minister of Foreign Affairs, Ismaïl Khelil, by Habib

Boulares (a prominent journalist and a former Minister of Culture and Information under Bourguiba).

In October 1990 it was reported by the human rights organization Amnesty International that although more than 10,000 common-law and political prisoners had benefited from amnesty measures since Ben Ali's accession to the presidency, human rights abuses, of which members of unregistered political groups were often the victims, continued. In the following month Ben Ali pardoned 113 prisoners, and announced the formation of a national commission on human rights (to be known as the Comité supérieur des droits de l'homme et des libertés fondamentales—CSDHLF). In March 1991 an amnesty was announced for a further 836 prisoners. The human rights commission was inaugurated in April.

In November 1990 several members of an-Nahdah were arrested, following the discovery of explosives which were allegedly to have been used for terrorist activities. An-Nahdah's senior officials denied that the movement was involved in terrorism. In the same month it was announced that the authorities had dismantled an 'Islamic network' that had allegedly been planning an Islamist revolution. In late December senior officials of an-Nahdah were arrested, together with more than 100 other people, and accused of attempting to establish an Islamic state. The arrests provoked demonstrations by Islamist militants in January 1991, and in the same month thousands of Tunisians took part in pro-Iraqi demonstrations, following the outbreak of war between Iraq and the US-led multinational force. In February further demonstrations by Islamists were violently suppressed. In the same month the co-ordinator of the MUP, Brahim Hayder, was sentenced to three months' imprisonment on a charge of attempting to disturb public order (after having condemned the Government's banning of a pro-Iraqi demonstration in January).

In February 1991 the Minister of the Interior, Abd-al Hamid Escheikh, whose attitude towards recent Islamist manifestations of support for Iraq had apparently been regarded by his government colleagues as insufficiently uncompromising, was replaced by Abdallah Kallel, hitherto Minister of Defence. Habib Boulares assumed the defence portfolio. Escheikh's dismissal was announced within hours of an armed attack, allegedly by an-Nahdah supporters, on RCD offices in Tunis, as a result of which one person was said to have been burned to death. In March Abd al-Fatha Mourou and the two other members of the an-Nahdah executive committee who were still at liberty in Tunis (four members were reported to be in detention at this time, two had fled the capital to evade arrest, while Rached Ghanouchi remained in exile) responded to government pressure, denouncing violent acts committed in the name of an-Nahdah and 'freezing' their activities within the movement. However, tensions persisted, and in May two students were killed in a clash with the police. The students' union, UGET, was disbanded by the authorities after the police claimed to have found weapons and subversive material linked to an-Nahdah, and riot police were posted outside centres where the annual baccalaureate examinations were being held. Also in May some 300 people, including about 100 members of the security forces, were arrested in connection with an alleged Islamist plot: the Government claimed that it had been planned to assassinate Ben Ali and other government members in October. In June five Islamists were sentenced to death (two *in absentia*) for their part in the attack on the RCD headquarters. The executions of the three who were in detention took place in October, this reportedly being only the second occasion on which death sentences had been implemented since Ben Ali's accession to power.

In July 1991 Amnesty International reported that it had received accounts of the systematic torture of more than 100 prisoners, most of whom were suspected members of an-Nahdah. The Government requested the newly-created CSDHLF to investigate, and its findings, published in October, showed that there had indeed been abuses, but concluded that these had not been officially sanctioned. About 140 prisoners, many of them political, were released in November (on the anniversary of the President's accession to power), and the sentences of more than 900 other detainees were reduced. In March 1992 a further report by Amnesty International, which detailed the arrests of some 8,000 people—mostly suspected members of an-Nahdah—

over an 18-month period, and cited 200 cases of the torture and ill-treatment of detainees, as well as the deaths in custody of at least seven Islamists, was immediately condemned by the Tunisian authorities as 'baseless'. However, the Government, while denying that any detainee in Tunisia could be classified as a prisoner of conscience, later conceded that some violations of human rights had been committed, and announced that it would investigate allegations of the abuse of detainees. Meanwhile, new restrictions were imposed on organizations such as the LTDH, which in July 1991 had criticized restrictions on press freedom. In June 1992 the LTDH was dissolved by its leadership, following the introduction of legislation which, in establishing new distinctions between the competences of political parties and hitherto quasi-political associations such as the LTDH, effectively banned members of the latter from participation in political life.

In addition to an apparently unsuccessful attempt to persuade Abd al-Fatha Mourou and his supporters to form a 'moderate' Islamic party, Ben Ali began to court the legalized opposition. In March 1991 he received opposition leaders and ordered that they should receive funds for party expenses and propaganda and that the police should not harass their activities. Ben Ali also appeared anxious to end the RCD's monopoly of power in the National Assembly, and offered not to present RCD candidates for nine by-elections pending to the legislature. However, the opposition, demanding a wider reform of the electoral system, boycotted the elections, and the vacant seats were taken by RCD candidates. The relatively high level of participation by voters, ranging from 69.5% and 92.4%, was interpreted as an indication of popular support for the Government's uncompromising attitude towards an-Nahdah. In December Ben Ali announced that changes to the electoral code, to be formulated in co-operation with opposition parties, would be implemented during 1992, with the aim of ensuring greater representation at the national level for parties other than the RCD. The opposition resumed a dialogue with the Government in January 1992, although its cohesion was undermined by a number of incidents: Ahmed Ben Salah and Muhammad Mzali, both still in exile, were reported to have declared support for an-Nahdah, and Ahmad Mestiri resigned from the MDS in early 1992, apparently in response to internal party differences which resulted in the 'suspension' of the activities within the MDS of three members of the party's political bureau.

Government changes in October 1991 resulted in the promotion of Abdallah Kallel to the rank of Minister of State. At the same time Ben Ali appointed a close associate, Abd al-Aziz Ben Dhia, to replace Habib Boulares at the Ministry of Defence. (Boulares was subsequently appointed President of the National Assembly.) In March 1992, at the beginning of the Islamic month of Ramadan, a new Ministry of Religious Affairs was created. Further government changes in June included the creation of a Ministry of International Co-operation and Foreign Investment, as well as the appointment of Ben Ali's adviser on human rights, Sadok Chaabane, as Minister of Justice. In the following month the composition of the Council of Ministers was again modified.

Suppression of an-Nahdah continued, with widespread arrests and a large security presence on the streets. In July 1992 more than 100 people, said to belong to the Islamist terrorist group 'Commandos du sacrifice', were put on trial at the Tunis military tribunal. The accused, who included army, police and customs officials, were charged with conspiring to take power by force and plotting to assassinate the President. During the trial, an-Nahdah's official spokesman insisted that the Commandos du sacrifice were not part of the an-Nahdah movement and denied the existence of any plot to overthrow the State. Habib Laasoued, alleged to be the leader of the Commandos, also denied any link with an-Nahdah, which he described as a rival movement. At the same time, almost 200 alleged an-Nahdah members were put on trial for plotting to take power by force. Throughout both trials there were allegations of irregularities in the conduct of the hearings and of human rights abuses. Many of the accused claimed that torture had been used to extract a confession. In August the courts announced long prison sentences for the defendants. Among those receiving life sentences were three exiled an-Nahdah leaders, Rached Ghanouchi, Salah Karkar and Habib Moknil.

It was claimed that Ghanouchi had received funds from the Governments of Iran, Sudan and Saudi Arabia to overthrow the Tunisian regime and was organizing violent Islamist revolution. These mass trials were seen as the culmination of the Tunisian Government's long campaign against an-Nahdah, whose organizational structures within the country were largely destroyed and its leaders imprisoned or forced into exile. Abdallah Kallel claimed that 'a Tunisian terrorist network' had been completely dismantled. Some members of opposition parties accused President Ben Ali of using the threat of 'Islamic fundamentalism' as an excuse to delay long-promised democratic reforms.

FOREIGN POLICY UNDER BEN ALI

President Ben Ali continued to pursue a moderate, pro-Western foreign policy. Relations with the USA remained cordial, and, during discussions on political and economic issues in March 1988 with the Tunisian Government, the US Secretary of State, George Shultz, announced US support for Ben Ali's political reforms. In April the US Secretary of Defense, Frank Carlucci, visited Tunis to discuss Tunisia's military debt to the USA, which totalled $400m. In June the Tunisian administration authorized two US banks to refinance the debt. The Tunisian Government attempted to improve relations between the USA and Libya after the shooting down of two Libyan aircraft in January 1989. It was hampered by the strength of popular sentiment, with anti-US demonstrations occurring across the country. During an official visit to the USA in May 1990, Ben Ali met the US President, George Bush, to discuss the issue of peace in the Middle East. He also urged continued economic support from Western nations and an increase in US investment.

However, the new Tunisian Government was also interested in extending its co-operation with other Western nations. A military co-operation accord was reached with Spain in December 1987 and adopted by the Tunisian National Assembly in May 1988. Under the terms of the accord, the two countries were to establish joint ventures for the research, development and production of military equipment, to exchange military personnel and to conduct joint military exercises on each other's territory. Earlier, in January the United Kingdom announced that it was willing to assist in the training and equipping of Tunisian security forces. In April the Tunisian Government received a military delegation from the Federal Republic of Germany, with the intention of gaining German military co-operation. In September Ben Ali discussed economic co-operation with President François Mitterrand, during a state visit to France. Co-operation between France and Tunisia was strengthened following visits by Laurent Fabius, the President of the French National Assembly, in December, and by Roland Dumas, the Minister of Foreign Affairs, in May 1989. During a state visit to Tunisia in June President Mitterrand promised greater investment in Tunisia; in August four agreements concerning financial aid were reached. The Turkish Prime Minister, Turgut Özal, also visited Tunisia. Although the two countries reached some trade agreements, Tunisia refused a request to recognize the 'Turkish Republic of Northern Cyprus'. In March 1990 a military co-operation agreement was signed with Turkey.

Following Iraq's invasion of Kuwait in August 1990 (see chapter on Iraq), President Ben Ali condemned the deployment of a US-led multinational force in the Gulf region, arguing that it was neither in the interests of Arabs nor of world peace. He refused to attend an emergency summit meeting of the Arab League, held in Cairo, and, in an apparent attempt to undertake a central mediatory role, asked that the meeting be postponed while he visited Baghdad to persuade the Iraqi President, Saddam Hussain, of the need for a settlement. His official pronouncements against intervention by Western nations were apparently influenced by the growing Arab nationalist support for Iraq within Tunisia. This solidarity was reflected by the formation of a new political organization, the National Committee for Support to Iraq, which comprised most opposition parties and professional associations. The Committee demanded a suspension of diplomatic relations with countries, such as Egypt and Saudi Arabia, which supported intervention in the Gulf region, and the enlistment of Tunisian volunteers to be sent to Iraq. In late August Ben Ali sent a number of emissaries to Arab and Western nations, as part of a diplomatic initiative

to prevent war in the Gulf. In September Tunisia restored diplomatic relations with Iran, which had been suspended in 1987 after Tunisia had accused Iran of supporting fundamentalist opponents of then President Bourguiba.

RELATIONS WITHIN THE MAGHREB

Under the Ben Ali administration, relations with Libya improved dramatically, with the result that Tunisia was able to play a more active role in the development of Maghrebin unity. In December 1987 full diplomatic relations were resumed with Libya, after Libya had agreed to pay $10m. in indemnities to the Tunisian workers expelled in 1985 and to reimburse Tunisian assets, which had been frozen in Libya. Subsequently the Tunisian, Algerian and Mauritanian ministers responsible for foreign affairs met to discuss the possibility of Libya becoming a signatory to the Maghreb Fraternity and Co-operation Treaty of 1983, as a prelude to the creation of a Great Arab Maghreb. In January 1988 President Chadli of Algeria visited Tunisia and held further discussions with Ben Ali on the issues of the Great Arab Maghreb, bilateral co-operation and a lasting settlement for the Moroccan-occupied Western Sahara. Ben Ali discussed these matters again with the Moroccan Prime Minister, Az ad-Dine Laraki, at the beginning of February.

In January 1988 Col Qaddafi postponed a scheduled visit to Tunisia to demonstrate his displeasure at the Tunisian Government receiving the commanders of the US and French navies. In February, however, the visit took place, and, following talks, Ben Ali and Col Qaddafi stated that they had agreed to abolish entry visas for Tunisians and Libyans crossing the Tunisian–Libyan border, and to abide by the judgement of the ICJ concerning the delineation of their respective sectors of the continental shelf in the Gulf of Gabès. Several days later, Ben Ali, Col Qaddafi and President Chadli of Algeria met and expressed their determination to encourage co-operation between the Maghreb countries. In June Ben Ali attended the first summit meeting of the five heads of the Maghrebin countries in Algiers (for further details, see Algeria, History). In May Ben Ali and Col Qaddafi had held an unscheduled summit on the island of Djerba. The two leaders signed an agreement providing for a social and economic union of the two countries, the free movement of people and goods across their common frontier, the establishment of a common identity card system and the freedom to live, work and own property in the respective countries. A number of joint industrial, economic and cultural projects were initiated immediately after the summit. In August Ben Ali visited Col Qaddafi in Libya and signed a series of co-operation agreements and an agreement concerning the settlement of the dispute over the continental shelf in the Gulf of Gabès. During the visit, a technical commission was established to examine means of accelerating co-operation and merger between Tunisia and Libya. In September an agreement was signed establishing a joint Tunisian-Libyan company, which would exploit the '7 November' oilfield on the continental shelf in the Gulf of Gabès. An agreement to link the two countries' electricity grids was signed.

Taking advantage of the open frontier, an estimated 1m. Libyan tourists visited Tunisia, spending so much money that shortages of goods in the shops were reported. A new motorway from the frontier to Sfax was constructed to facilitate their entry. At least 30,000 Tunisians found employment in Libya. During a visit to Tunisia in December 1988, Col Qaddafi addressed the National Assembly, stating that he favoured 'constitutional unity' between the two countries but would not try to impose it. He returned with President Chadli of Algeria in February 1989.

Ben Ali was influential in the movement towards Maghreb unity, by convincing President Chadli that unity would be impossible without the participation of Morocco; he had no wish to continue in a subordinate role in the Maghreb Fraternity and Co-operation Treaty. Tunisia was put in charge of the working party dealing with human and social affairs and security, and played a significant role in all the meetings of ministers and heads of state, arguing for gradual progress towards unity.

Tunisia initially seemed the most committed member of the newly-created Union of the Arab Maghreb (UAM), while Col Qaddafi appeared reluctant to implement agreements, such as the joint exploration of the Gulf of Gabès and the financing of infrastructure programmes in Tunisia. The Tunisian Prime Minister, Hedi Baccouche, visited Tripoli in July 1989, in an attempt to promote economic co-operation, although little practical progress was achieved. During a preliminary meeting of ministers responsible for foreign affairs in January 1990 the Tunisian Foreign Minister proposed a series of measures, all of which were approved, including the creation of a permanent secretariat (preferably based in Tunis), the expansion of the Consultative Council to 100 members, the establishment of commissions to examine joint projects in food production, economy and finance, infrastructure and human resources, and negotiations with other groups, particularly the European Community (EC).

In February 1990 the Minister of the Economy proposed a single energy market for North Africa, with free trade in electricity, petroleum and natural gas, the linkage of grids and extension of pipelines. In the same month the first meeting of the Human Resource Committee, attended by ministers of education, was held, and special passport controls were provided for North African visitors at Tunis airports. In March a television service, broadcast throughout North Africa, was established in Tunis. Also in March the newly-appointed Tunisian Minister of Foreign Affairs, Ismaïl Khelil, proposed that the EC should reschedule debts to provide for training and the creation of jobs in North Africa, with the aim of reducing emigration to Europe. Official sources estimated that 1.8m. Maghrebis worked in Europe (with a further 600,000 working illegally), while the number of unemployed within the UAM totalled at least 2m. The UAM also raised the issue of racial attacks upon their citizens in the EC. In June 1990 President Ben Ali proposed an agreement between the EC and UAM, which would guarantee the rights of North Africans working in Europe.

RELATIONS WITH OTHER ARAB NATIONS

Tunisia's status as a moderate Arab state was maintained under Ben Ali. Following discussions with PLO representatives and members of the Egyptian Government, the Tunisian Government announced in January 1988 that it would be resuming diplomatic relations with Egypt. (Relations had been severed by Tunisia in 1979 after Egypt signed the Camp David Agreement with Israel.) Meanwhile, Hedi Baccouche, the Tunisian Prime Minister, toured the Arab Gulf states, which ranked among Tunisia's major sources of economic aid, to explain to Arab leaders the new administration's domestic and foreign policies. Baccouche reaffirmed Tunisia's support for the Gulf states, which feared an extension of the Iran–Iraq War, thus seeming to rule out the possibility that the Ben Ali Government would restore diplomatic relations with Iran in the near future. In April Baccouche visited Egypt and concluded several bilateral agreements. In January 1989 Dr Boutros Boutros-Ghali, then Minister of State for Foreign Affairs, became the first Egyptian minister to visit Tunisia for 10 years.

Meanwhile, Tunisia was the scene of another Israeli operation against the PLO. In April 1988 'Abu Jihad', the military commander of the PLO, was assassinated at his home near Tunis in a combined operation by the Israeli secret service, Mossad, and Israeli army and naval commando forces. The Israeli operation was a source of embarrassment for the Tunisian authorities, as it was revealed that Mossad operatives had been based in Tunisia for some time before the assassination was carried out. After discovering evidence that an Israeli military aircraft (apparently carrying sophisticated equipment with which to 'jam' telecommunications) had passed close to Tunisian airspace when 'Abu Jihad' was killed, the Tunisian Government lodged a complaint with the UN Security Council. Later in April, the Council adopted a resolution condemning 'the Israeli aggression against Tunisian territory'.

In March 1990 Ben Ali made the first visit to Cairo by a Tunisian President since 1965, and signed several agreements on bilateral co-operation with Egypt. Relations with Saudi Arabia also remained cordial; in March the Saudi-Tunisian Joint Commission met to discuss eight projects, financed by Saudi Arabia, and in July the Saudi Arabian Minister of Defence visited Tunis. Despite the high level of co-operation between the two countries, the Tunisian Government was concerned about the extent of Saudi support for Tunisian Islamists. In April the Iraqi Deputy Prime Minister visited Tunis, where he

signed a bilateral trade agreement. In September a majority of members of the Arab League decided to move the League's headquarters from Tunis (where it had been 'temporarily' established in 1979) back to its original site in Cairo. The Tunisian Government protested at the decision and the League's Tunisian Secretary-General, Chedli Klibi, resigned.

RELATIONS WITH THE ARAB WORLD SINCE THE GULF WAR

After the cease-fire in the Gulf War in February 1991, Tunisia sought to restore links that had been strained by its support for Iraq (a policy which probably prompted the replacement of the pro-Baathist Habib Boulares as Minister of Foreign Affairs by the less abrasive Habib Ben Yahia). Although Kuwait had withdrawn its ambassador from Tunis, Ben Ali sent a cordial message to the Amir, congratulating him upon regaining his sovereignty. Ben Ali undertook a tour of the Gulf region in November. Soon after his appointment Ben Yahia went to Cairo in an attempt to re-establish cordial relations. The Egyptian and Tunisian ministers responsible for the interior met twice to discuss the problems posed by Islamist activists, and made arrangements for the exchange of intelligence. A trade pact was signed with Syria in August 1991, following an earlier visit to Damascus by Ben Yahia. In February 1992 further bilateral agreements covered co-operation in education and other fields.

Conversely, when in April 1991 the Iraqi Deputy Prime Minister, Tareq Aziz, visited the Maghreb, Ben Ali, alone among the regional heads of state, refused to receive him, claiming fatigue and the need to prepare for a visit to the People's Republic of China. The Iraqi aircraft that had taken refuge in Tunis during the crisis were not returned, but Tunisia did join the other UAM countries in appealing for the ending of sanctions against Iraq. Sudan had co-operated closely with Tunisia in the attempt to prevent the outbreak of war in the Gulf region, and Lt-Gen. Omar Hassan Ahmad al-Bashir, the Sudanese Head of State, visited Tunis in March 1991. However, in October Tunisia withdrew its ambassador from Khartoum, alleging that Sudan had been supporting Islamist terrorists. In July 1992 Sudan announced the closure of its embassy in Tunis, in protest against the Tunisian authorities' alleged suppression of the Islamist movement. In December a series of agreements was signed with Oman and relations between the two countries were described as exemplary. In mid-1993 there were signs that relations with Kuwait, badly strained during the Gulf crisis, might improve. In June Habib Ben Yahia made his first visit to Kuwait since the crisis, and President Ben Ali, in a letter to the Amir of Kuwait, sought improved relations. After a hostile reception from Kuwaiti politicians and from the press, Ben Yahia was forced to cut short his visit. However, after a visit to Tunis in April 1994 by the Kuwaiti Minister of Foreign Affairs and First Deputy Prime Minister, Sheikh Sabah al-Ahmad al-Jaber as-Sabah, it was reported that normal diplomatic relations would be restored. Later in 1994 the first co-operation agreement with Kuwait since the Gulf crisis was signed during a visit to Tunis by the Kuwaiti Minister of Education. In early 1996, during a visit to Kuwait by Sadok Rabah, the Tunisian Minister of Social Affairs, to encourage more investment in Tunisia, Kuwait's Minister of Foreign Affairs spoke of his pleasure at the continuing improvement in relations between the two countries. Efforts to improve relations with Kuwait were finally rewarded in April 1996 when bilateral co-operation was restored during a visit to Tunis by a high-level Kuwaiti delegation led by Sheikh Saad al-Abdullah as-Salim as-Sabah, the Crown Prince and Prime Minister. During the visit agreements were signed with the Kuwait-based Arab Fund for Economic and Social Development for loans worth $45m., the first to Tunisia since the Gulf crisis. At the same time, Tunisia continued to maintain good relations with Iraq. In September 1995 Ben Ali had visited Jordan, Syria and Qatar as part of the Government's efforts to improve relations with other Arab states. In early 1997 the Egyptian Prime Minister, Kamal Ahmad al-Ganzouri, visited Tunis where he signed several economic and cultural co-operation agreements. Both countries pledged to work together to increase bilateral trade, and agreement was reached in principle on the creation of a free-trade zone. In early 1998 the two countries signed an agreement in Cairo at a meeting of the Tunisian-Egyptian Joint Higher Committee to dismantle customs duties over the next 10 years. A state visit to Tunis by the Amir of Qatar, Sheikh Hamad bin Khalifa ath-Thani, in June 1997, provided further evidence of the gradual improvement in Tunisia's relations with the Gulf states since the 1991 Gulf War. In January 1998 two small opposition parties, the RSP and the UDU, with the support of the UGTT, organized a meeting to express support for Iraq in its dispute with the UN. The Tunisian Government has regularly urged the UN to lift sanctions against Iraq. Also in January the Council of Arab Interior Ministers, meeting in Tunis, approved the draft of an Arab anti-terrorism agreement.

Tunisia claimed to have played a leading role, together with Norway, in the secret talks between the PLO and Israel which led to the signing of the Declaration of Principles on Palestinian Self-Rule in September 1993. The PLO headquarters were based near Tunis for more than 10 years. Tunisia welcomed the breakthrough in PLO-Israeli relations, and shortly afterwards an Israeli delegation arrived in Tunis for talks with Tunisian and PLO officials. Salah Masawi, the director-general of foreign relations, declared that there was no obstacle to Tunisia's establishing diplomatic relations with Israel, but that the Tunisian Government was waiting for another North African state to make the first move; it was assumed that he was referring to Morocco, which has maintained contacts with the Jewish state through the Moroccan Jewish community for some years (see chapter on Morocco). After meeting Ben Yahia in Tunis in December, Warren Christopher, the US Secretary of State, announced that progress was being made in the normalization of relations between Tunisia and Israel. The Tunisian Foreign Ministry welcomed the PLO-Israeli Cairo agreement of May 1994 on implementing Palestinian self-rule in Gaza and Jericho. The PLO offices in Tunis were closed in June, as Yasser Arafat and the Palestinian leadership prepared to move to Gaza, where the newly-appointed Palestine National Authority (PNA) was to be established. At a meeting with President Ben Ali at the end of June Chairman Arafat thanked Tunisia for the 'warm hospitality' the PLO had received since its offices were transferred from Beirut to Tunis in 1982. The official farewell ceremonies for Arafat in July were attended by Ben Ali.

As the Palestinians departed, Tunisia made new moves towards the normalization of relations with Israel. The first party of Israeli tourists to visit Tunisia since independence arrived in June 1994 (following an agreement made in October 1993 with Yossi Beilin, the Israeli Deputy Minister for Foreign Affairs—the first senior Israeli to visit Tunisia), and direct telephone links were established with Israel in July. In October the Tunisian and Israeli ministers responsible for foreign affairs met at the UN General Assembly in New York and agreed in principle to open interests sections (which Tunisia referred to as 'economic channels') in the Belgian embassies in Tunis and Tel-Aviv. At a meeting at the US State Department in Washington, DC, with Warren Christopher and the Israeli Minister of Foreign Affairs, Shimon Peres, Habib Ben Yahia stated that this was only the first step to full diplomatic relations. In October an agreement on co-operation in environmental affairs was signed between the two countries during a visit to Tunis by the Israeli Minister of the Environment. In December Haim Madar, the Grand Rabbi of Tunisia's small Jewish community, made his first visit to Israel. In February 1995 Tunisia, together with Israel, Morocco, Mauritania and Egypt, took part in talks with NATO in Brussels, Belgium, on security co-operation. Before the talks the Secretary-General of NATO, Willy Claes, had made the controversial statement that he saw Islamist extremism as the biggest single threat to the West since the collapse of communism. In March Tunisia participated in naval exercises off the Tunisian coast with Israel, Canada, Morocco, Algeria, Egypt and four of the Arab Gulf states. These attempts to co-operate with Israel provoked criticism from some Arab quarters. In April a Tunisian liaison office was opened in the Gaza Strip; a second office was expected to be installed in Jericho. In October Yasser Arafat met President Ben Ali in Tunis to review progress made on the implementation of Palestinian self-rule. After the Palestinian elections in January 1996, Tunisia indicated that it was satisfied that progress had been made in the peace process and an agreement was reached with Israel to proceed with low-level diplomatic relations from April. Tunisia thus became the fourth Arab state to establish diplom-

atic relations with Israel, after Egypt, Jordan and Morocco. The move, agreed in principle in October 1994, was opposed by only one of the six legal opposition parties, but strongly condemned by Rached Ghanouchi, the exiled leader of an-Nahdah. At the same time Tunisia agreed to recognize passports issued by the PNA. In April 1996 Israel opened an interests office in the Belgian Embassy in Tunis; however Tunisia delayed sending its own representative to Tel-Aviv in response to Israeli attacks on southern Lebanon. Nevertheless some contacts between the two countries were made. However, after the victory of Binyamin Netanyahu in the Israeli elections in May and the creation of a right-wing Government, the process of normalization was expected to decelerate. President Ben Ali attended the emergency Arab summit in Cairo in June and, as current Chairman of the Arab League, made one of the two keynote speeches. After the conference he defended the actions of those countries that had taken steps to normalize relations with Israel, stating that they were intended 'to push the peace process forward'. However, in November the Tunisian leadership condemned Israeli intransigence towards the peace process and criticized the building of Jewish settlements in the occupied territories. The normalization of relations was suspended, but the Israeli liaison office in Tunis remained open.

Within the UAM, Tunisia was chosen as the site of the new Maghreb Investment and Foreign Trade Bank. A Tunisian diplomat, Mohammed Amamou, was appointed UAM Secretary-General and represented the UAM at the opening session of the Middle East peace conference in Madrid, Spain, in October 1991. Tunisia was the only UAM member to contribute personnel to the UN monitoring body, MINURSO, in Western Sahara (see chapter on Morocco). In January 1993 Tunisia assumed the annual presidency of the UAM. The Government emphasized its determination to reactivate the process of Maghreb union, as well as dialogue with the EC. However, according to a statement made by the Moroccan Minister of Foreign Affairs, Abd al-Latif Filali, in February 1993, following a meeting of the five UAM member states in Tunis, it had been decided to allow a 'pause' for reflection in the process of developing Maghreb union. Tunisian officials stressed that Ben Ali's presidency had been a success and that 11 co-operation agreements had been signed during his one-year term of office, including plans for a Maghreb free-trade zone. Yet, in reality, he failed to give new impetus to the organization, largely because two of its members, Algeria and Libya, remained preoccupied with their own problems: Algeria plunged into civil war by escalating Islamist violence, and Libya subjected to even tighter UN sanctions. The summit meeting that should have marked the end of Tunisia's presidency was delayed three times and did not take place until April 1994. At the meeting, Ben Ali handed over the presidency to Liamine Zéroual, the new Algerian Head of State. Neither King Hassan of Morocco nor Col Qaddafi of Libya attended the summit. Although at least 40 accords had been adopted by the UAM, only five had been ratified by all five member states, indicating that little progress had been made in translating rhetoric into reality in developing a unified Maghreb. During 1994 tensions between Tunisia and Morocco (see below) and between Morocco and Algeria merely added to the problems affecting the UAM. There were reports that Tunisia was hostile to Egypt's request in November to join the UAM, and would oppose Egyptian membership. In February 1995 Ben Ali sent a letter to the leaders of the other four member states urging them to try to overcome the obstacles facing the UAM by joint action. However, little progress was made, and in late 1995 Morocco blocked UAM activities because of alleged Algerian interference in the Western Sahara dispute. Tunisia regretted Morocco's action and continued its diplomatic efforts to revive the Union. During 1996 Tunisia concentrated on attempting to engender a reconciliation between Algeria and Morocco. Its efforts appeared to have met with some success when in October Algeria proposed a new UAM summit and Morocco was reported to have agreed in principle to the meeting. By the end of 1996 both Algeria and Morocco appealed for a revival of the UAM. On a visit to Tunis in October Col Qaddafi also expressed renewed interest in the UAM.

The decision by the UN Security Council in April 1992 to impose sanctions against Libya over the Lockerbie affair (see chapter on Libya) was reluctantly accepted by Tunisia. Although flights to and from Libya were suspended, Tunisia acknowledged popular feeling and the close economic ties between the two countries by insisting that land and sea links would remain open. The Libyan sanctions created a mini-boom in southern Tunisia, amid a sharp increase in cross-border trade and in transit traffic, but relations deteriorated sharply in September, when the Libyan leader remarked that Tunisia had no future and was doomed to unite with either Libya or Algeria. This outburst provoked an indignant response from President Ben Ali, who drew attention to Tunisia's achievements and commented that the Libyan people were suffering from the consequences of a crisis for which they were not responsible. Despite these differences, the Tunisian Government made efforts to negotiate a solution to the Lockerbie affair. In April 1993 Ben Ali visited Libya and consulted with President Mubarak of Egypt in a further attempt to resolve the deadlock between Libya and the West in the approach to the UN Security Council's sanctions review. Failure to resolve the Lockerbie affair also frustrated Ben Ali's efforts to forge closer relations between the UAM and the European Union (EU). On a visit to Tunis in December 1993, the French Minister of Defence left the President in no doubt that Libya's membership of the UAM was a serious impediment to closer relations between the UAM and the EU. There were reports of a flourishing black market as Tunisian traders took advantage of the overvalued Libyan dinar and heavily subsidized prices to import cheap food into southern Tunisia. In July 1993 representatives of some 250 Libyan and Tunisian companies met in Tripoli to examine ways of strengthening business relations in the formal sector of the economy. As a result of UN sanctions, Tunisia has become the main point of entry for international companies working in Libya—international flights to Tunis link with Djerba, from where there are ferry services to Libya. But a new dispute occurred in October 1994 when Libya claimed that cholera had broken out in Tunisia and stated that all travellers from Tunisia would be vaccinated at the border if they did not possess a vaccination certificate. Tunisia retaliated by stating that bubonic plague had broken out in Libya and that anyone entering the country from Libya had to present a hospital certificate confirming that they did not have the disease. Some hundreds of travellers were stranded at the border with both countries blaming the other for the disruption. It was not until late November that the travel restrictions were lifted. There was speculation that Libya's actions in this affair may have been a response to Tunisian moves towards the normalization of relations with Israel announced in October. Discussions on economic co-operation resumed in July 1995 and relations improved in the second half of 1995. In September Tunisia appealed for the lifting of UN sanctions against Libya and also supported Libya's request to take part in the Euro-Mediterranean summit held in Barcelona, Spain, in November. A series of economic agreements were signed in October when the Tunis-ian Prime Minister met the Secretary-General of the Libyan General People's Committee. President Ben Ali held talks with Col Qaddafi in January 1996. However, relations between the two countries became strained after Libya criticized Tunisia's decision to establish low-level diplomatic relations with Israel. Nevertheless, a Tunisian delegation led by the Prime Minister attended a meeting in Tripoli in July, and relations between the two countries improved after a visit to Tunis by Col Qaddafi in October where he addressed the National Assembly. Several agreements on investment, trade and co-operation were signed subsequently and progress was made on a number of joint economic projects during 1997.

Tunisia's relations with Algeria continued to be dominated by the Islamist issue. In December 1991 Rached Ghanouchi and other senior an-Nahdah members were reportedly expelled from Algeria to Sudan. Relations with Algeria improved appreciably after the second round of Algerian elections were suspended in January 1992, and Tunisia welcomed the appointment of Muhammad Boudiaf as Chairman of the High Council of State, as well as the suppression of Algeria's Islamist movement. In February 1993 Boudiaf's successor, Ali Kafi, visited Tunis. During his stay he exchanged letters with President Ben Ali to ratify the official demarcation of the 1,000-km border between Tunisia and Algeria. Ben Ali and Kafi also expressed their determination to work together to counter the threat of terrorism in the region. In December the Algerian and Tunisian

ministers responsible for foreign affairs met at Tabarka, Tunisia, to celebrate the final demarcation of the frontier between the two countries, the precise line of which had been disputed for some years after independence. The new Algerian Head of State, Liamine Zéroual, visited Tunis for the UAM summit in April 1994 and held further talks with Ben Ali after the meeting ended. The two leaders issued a statement expressing their commitment to democracy, pluralism and the promotion of human rights; and condemning fanaticism and extremism. Zéroual's appeals for dialogue with Algeria's banned Front islamique du salut (FIS) seem certain to have alarmed Ben Ali, who had rejected any negotiations with the Tunisian Islamist opposition. During 1994 there were reports that several thousand Algerians, mainly professionals, had taken refuge in Tunisia since the conflict began in Algeria, many of whom had experienced difficulty in finding jobs. After the attack by Algerian Islamist militants against a Tunisian frontier post in February 1995, security along the border was strengthened and no further incidents were reported. The Tunisian Government welcomed Zéroual's victory in the Algerian presidential elections in November and the press hailed it as a triumph against terrorism and extremism. President Ben Ali continued to urge the Algerian Government to take decisive action against Islamist extremists. Some difficulties that had arisen over the employment of Algerians in Tunisia and over trade relations between the two countries appeared to have been resolved when Prime Minister Karoui visited Algiers in June 1996. The Algerian Prime Minister, Ahmed Ouyahia, paid a reciprocal visit to Tunis in December and indicated his support for Tunisia's efforts to revive the UAM.

Tunisia's normally good relations with Morocco were strained in May 1994 after Tunisia expelled some 600 Moroccans whom the authorities claimed were living there without permission or had broken Tunisian laws. Towards the end of the year the Tunisian authorities expelled several hundred Moroccans claiming that they were trying to enter Italy as illegal immigrants. The Moroccan Government protested that some of its nationals had been maltreated by the Tunisian police. Relations remained strained during 1995 as a result of further expulsions of Moroccan workers and students. In early 1996 Tunisia condemned Morocco for trying to block UAM activities in retaliation for alleged Algerian interference in the Western Sahara dispute. Relations were further strained by criticism from Moroccan non-governmental organizations of the prison sentences imposed on opposition politicians Muhammad Mouada and Khemais Chamari (see below). However, after a visit to Rabat by Karoui in September, a commitment was made to improve economic and political co-operation. In November both countries appealed for the revival of the UAM.

RELATIONS WITH THE NON-ARAB WORLD SINCE THE GULF WAR

For a brief period in the aftermath of the Gulf War, Tunisia's stance during the crisis was seen to have damaged relations with those countries that had participated in the effort to liberate Kuwait, while reports, most notably by Amnesty International, of abuses of human rights in Tunisia continued to cause international disquiet. In February 1991 the USA reduced the level of economic aid to Tunisia (see Economy), and military aid was entirely discontinued, although subsequent investment agreements with the USA indicated a rapid improvement in relations. A visit by François Mitterrand in July 1991 (the French President's first visit to an Arab country since the end of the Gulf War) was interpreted as a sign of French support for the Ben Ali administration's campaign against Islamist extremists. In December 1992 considerable anger was provoked in Tunisia by the trial, in Paris, of a group of mainly Tunisian suspects. Among these was the brother of President Ben Ali, who was sentenced *in absentia* to 10 years' imprisonment for drugs-trafficking offences. In February 1993 the Tunisian Minister of the Interior, Abdallah Kallel, on a visit to Paris, criticized the French authorities for providing asylum to Tunisian Islamist militants. The election of a new French Government in March 1993 was, however, well received in Tunisia. The French Minister of Foreign Affairs, Alain Juppé, visited Tunisia in June 1994 and after talks with Ben Ali, he stated that relations between the two countries were good but that he was anxious that Tunisia resolve the remaining cases of compensation to former French residents for property left behind in Tunisia after independence. When the French Minister of the Interior, Charles Pasqua, visited Tunis in October for a meeting on security co-operation, he pledged that the French Government would not allow France to become a rear base for Islamist activists. In January 1995 the French and Tunisian ministers responsible for the interior met in Tunis with their counterparts from Italy, Spain, Portugal, Algeria and Morocco to discuss security matters resulting from Islamist militancy. They condemned 'terrorism, fundamentalism and every form of extremism and fantacism' and agreed to exchange information on a regular basis. In their declaration at the end of the meeting the ministers sought to link illegal immigration into Europe and the growing traffic in drugs and arms to the rise in 'Islamist extremism'. Jacques Chirac's election to the French presidency was welcomed by the Tunisian authorities and it was hoped that the new French administration would support Tunisia in its negotiations with the EU and maintain an unyielding policy towards Islamist militants in France. In June the French police arrested a number of Tunisians and Algerians living in France who, it was alleged, were part of a network providing arms to Islamist groups in Algeria and to the Front islamiste tunisien, described as a splinter group of an-Nahdah. The new French Minister of the Interior, Jean-Louis Debré, visiting Tunis in September, urged all Mediterranean states to form a common front against 'these terrorists'. In October President Chirac made a state visit to Tunisia during which he praised Ben Ali for his achievements in promoting modernization, democracy and social harmony in the country. He promised that French aid to Tunisia during 1995 would be increased to 1,100m. French francs. In April 1996 the second Franco–Tunisian parliamentarians' conference met in Paris at which delegates discussed bilteral relations and EU co-operation with the Mediterranean states. However, Ben Ali's state visit to France, which should have taken place in September, was cancelled amidst speculation that the President feared public criticism of Tunisia's human rights record. There had been widespread criticism in France of the arrest and imprisonment of Mouada and Chamari (see below). Mouada had been arrested only three days after Chirac's visit to Tunis. The release of the two politicians in December together with promises of political reforms, helped to improve relations, and during a visit to Tunis in February 1997 by the French Minister of Defence, Charles Millon, agreement was reached on further military co-operation to include joint military manoeuvres, arms supply and the training in France of Tunisian army officers. In May Karoui held talks with Chirac in Paris, and in August the new French Minister of Foreign Affairs, Hubert Védrine, on his first visit to Tunis, stated that relations between the two countries remained close and that the French administration would continue to assist the Tunisian Government's political and economic reform programme. Ben Ali's state visit to Paris finally took place at the end of October. French leaders acknowledged Tunisia's difficult regional position and pledged continued support for economic reforms, but appealed for further progress in democracy and human rights. Although the French press was highly critical of the Ben Ali regime, which was also condemned in a petition signed by several prominent people, there were no hostile street demonstrations and during the visit two economic agreements were signed, providing additional French financial support for the Tunisian economy. The longstanding dispute over French-owned property in Tunisia was also resolved.

Robert Pelletreau, the US Assistant Secretary of State, visited Tunis in December 1995 for talks with President Ben Ali and leading ministers. He praised the country's economic reforms, stated that military co-operation between the two countries would continue and announced that any threat to Tunisia would be viewed 'with concern' by the US administration. In May 1997 a senior-level delegation, led by Tunisia's Minister of National Defence, visited Washington, DC, to attend a meeting of the joint committee for military co-operation.

President Oscar Luigi Scalfaro of Italy visited Tunis in November 1993 for a two-day visit to boost bilateral trade and to discuss Mediterranean security issues. Italy is Tunisia's second largest trading partner (after France) and the third biggest source of foreign investment. Italy was anxious to ensure the continued co-operation of the Tunisian authorities in trying to curb illegal immigration from Tunisia. During 1994 the Tunisian authorities made several well-publicized arrests of groups of illegal emigrants—including Tunisians, Moroccans and Libyans—who were trying to enter Italy from Tunisia. But the arrival in Tunisia of former Italian Prime Minister, Bettino Craxi, sentenced *in absentia* by the Italian courts to serve 18 years in prison for corruption, proved embarrassing for the Tunisian authorities. Craxi, who maintained close links with the Tunisian leadership, was reported to be too ill to leave his villa near Hammamet. The Italian authorities also began investigations into the Italian export credit agency's relations with the Maghreb states, which caused delays in Italian trade credits for Tunisia. In June 1995 Italy requested that Tunisia extradite Craxi; however, the matter proved complicated because the extradition agreement between the two countries excluded political offences. When the new Tunisian Minister of Foreign Affairs, Abd ar-Rahim Zouari, visited Rome in March 1997, Italian officials appealed for an agreement between the two countries on the repatriation of illegal immigrants from Tunisia. In May Tunisia and Italy signed a co-operation agreement following a meeting held in Rome between the two Heads of State. Later in the year relations became strained when Tunisia seized several Italian boats which it claimed were fishing illegally in Tunisian waters. Tensions between the two countries were exacerbated in mid-1998 following an influx of illegal immigrants from North Africa to Italy. However, in August Tunisia and Italy signed an agreement allowing for the repatriation of hundreds of illegal immigrants. In April 1996 Pope John Paul II visited Tunis where he celebrated mass in the cathedral and met President Ben Ali. President Kravchuk of Ukraine signed a treaty of friendship and co-operation with Tunisia during a visit in December 1993. Ukraine plans to open an embassy in Tunis with responsibility for all the Maghreb states and the EU through the creation of a free-trade zone. Relations with Spain were strengthened in October 1995 when a treaty of friendship and co-operation was signed during a visit to Tunis by the then Spanish Prime Minister, Felipe González. King Juan Carlos of Spain had visited Tunisia in November 1994 and President Ben Ali had made an official visit to Spain in May 1991. The first annual meeting between leaders of the two countries, as agreed under the 1995 treaty of friendship and co-operation, was held in Madrid in January 1997 and attended by the Tunisian Prime Minister, Hamed Karoui. Although the meeting dealt with economic co-operation, the Spanish Prime Minister, José María Aznar, appealed for a further improvement in Tunisia's record on human rights. Karoui insisted that there were no political prisoners in Tunisia, only Islamist militants convicted of terrorist acts. The issue of human rights and political freedoms had also been raised when the Tunisian Minister of Foreign Affairs held talks with his Spanish counterpart in Madrid in July 1996. In March 1995 Mário Soares, the President of Portugal, made a state visit to Tunisia, and in talks with Ben Ali discussed Maghreb-Europe relations and ways of containing Islamist extremism. Soares stated that the main source of 'Islamic fundamentalism' was to be found in economic and social imbalances and that Portugal wanted the EU to provide Tunisia and its neighbours with more aid to help maintain social stability. Ben Ali had made a state visit to Portugal in 1993. Germany's Minister of Defence visited Tunis in April 1996 and described Tunisia as a stabilizing influence in the region. In November Ben Ali paid a state visit to Germany in order to strengthen economic links between the two countries. However, the German President, Prof. Dr Roman Herzog, reminded Ben Ali that democracy, political tolerance and respect for human rights were the major characteristics of a modern state.

In December 1993 the EU's Council of Ministers mandated the European Commission to begin talks with Tunisia on a new partnership agreement to replace the co-operation agreement signed in 1976. The Tunisian Ministry of Foreign Affairs welcomed the talks, which it described as 'a political signal' marking European approval of Tunisia's progress towards political pluralism and its respect for human rights. During talks with the EU which began in Brussels in March 1994, Tunisian negotiators expressed their support for free entry of European goods into Tunisia but wanted tariffs to be lowered gradually, additional financial assistance to make its industries more competitive with their European counterparts and higher guaranteed quotas for its olive oil exports to Europe. The European Commission was reported to have impressed on EU governments that a new partnership agreement with the Maghreb states was essential, since strengthening their economies would lessen Islamist violence and stem the flow of emigrants to Europe. Negotiations were not completed until July 1995 when Tunisia became the first southern Mediterranean country to sign a new economic association agreement as part of the EU's plan for a 'Euro–Mediterranean partnership'. The agreement involves the gradual removal of tariffs on industrial imports from the EU, a high-risk strategy for the country's vulnerable manufacturing sector (see Economy). In May 1996 the European Parliament had for the first time passed a resolution condemning Tunisia's treatment of opposition politicians and strongly criticizing its human rights record. The resolution reiterated that the 1995 association agreement required Tunisia to respect democratic principles and human rights and urged the European Commission to persuade the Tunisian Government to meet these obligations. The resolution was greeted with an indignant response from the Tunisian Government and from several opposition parties. The association agreement was formally implemented in March 1998 after it had been ratified by all EU member states. In November 1996 the establishment of Eurofor, the rapid action force for the southern Mediterranean region, by France, Italy, Spain and Portugal, was criticized by the Tunisian authorities. Despite assurances that the force was for defence, peace-keeping and humanitarian missions, Tunisia's Minister of Foreign Affairs declared that it was incompatible with the tradition of dialogue his country had sought to create between the northern and southern shores of the Mediterranean.

In November 1993 Tunisia hosted a meeting of the ministers responsible for foreign affairs of the members of the Organization of African Unity (OAU). Shortly before the meeting, Tunisia invited the South African Minister of Foreign Affairs, Pik Botha, to make an official visit, at the end of which both countries agreed to establish diplomatic relations. In May 1994 Tunisia announced that diplomatic relations with South Africa would soon be established and ambassadors exchanged. In April President Ben Ali assumed the presidency of the OAU for 12 months and in June Tunis hosted the 30th annual summit meeting of the OAU. South Africa attended for the first time. As Chairman of the OAU, Ben Ali appealed for a new partnership between Europe and Africa and urged industrialized nations to assist African countries by improving their terms of trade and through debt rescheduling. Ben Ali made a state visit to South Africa in April 1995 where he had talks with President Nelson Mandela and addressed the South African Parliament. With Tunisia holding the chairmanship of the OAU, Tunis became the venue for a series of meetings sponsored by that organization in the first half of 1995 including a summit meeting held in April to discuss the prevention, management and solution of conflicts in Africa.

In July 1996 President Ben Ali made his first state visit to Japan which has become an important source of financial assistance in recent years. In March 1997 Ben Ali became the first Arab leader to make a state visit to Argentina, during which six co-operation agreements were signed. President Carlos Saúl Menem of Argentina had visited Tunis in 1991 and 1994.

THE ELECTIONS OF 1994

In December 1992 President Ben Ali announced that presidential and parliamentary elections would be held in March 1994. Promising a revised electoral law and an up-to-date voting register, the President predicted that political pluralism in Tunisia would be consolidated. The ruling RCD held its second congress at the end of July 1993 (the first was in 1988, following Ben Ali's take-over and the renaming of the party) and nominated Ben Ali as its candidate for the forthcoming presidential election. The party was reported to have 1.6m. members, including 60,000 elected cadres, linked through 321 federations and 27 co-ordinating committees in Tunisia and one in Paris. Leaders of the legal opposition parties, of which the largest was the MDS, were present at the congress, and Ben Ali used the opportunity to reiterate his commitment to bring the opposition into the new parliament. On 7 November 1993, the sixth anniv-

ersary of his take-over, Ben Ali formally announced that he would stand for a second term as President. Once again he was the only candidate and was supported by all the legal opposition parties. The UGTT endorsed the President's candidature at its December congress. Under the terms of the new electoral system, the number of seats to be contested in the National Assembly was increased to 163. Of these, 144 seats were to be contested according to the existing majority list or 'first past the post' system, which gave all 141 seats in the old chamber to the RCD, but the remaining 19 seats would be distributed at a national level among the parties according to their proportion of the total vote. Ben Ali commended the system as one that would 'achieve pluralism in the National Assembly through the representation of political parties according to their weight and influence in society'. Other reforms to the voting system brought to an end the controversial practice of sponsorship for candidates. The State also agreed to contribute to the election expenses of candidates. Some of the opposition parties felt that the long-awaited electoral reform did not go far enough and that the number of seats allocated on a proportional basis should have been larger. Nevertheless, all six legal parties, the MDS, the Mouvement de la rénovation (MR—which incorporated some of the members of the disbanded PCT), the RSP, the PUP, the UDU and the PSP, which had boycotted all elections since 1989 because they maintained that the results were rigged by the RCD, accepted the new formula and indicated that they would take part. There were appeals from the opposition for equal access to the state-controlled media during the election campaign and complete freedom to hold public meetings without interference by the authorities. Their acceptance of the extremely modest and largely cosmetic electoral reform measures were seen by many as a clear indication of the weakness of the legal and secular opposition parties, reduced to an obedient official opposition to the ruling party.

The President continued to reject any dialogue with an-Nahdah, referring to its members as 'enemies of democracy and apostles of sedition and terrorism'. In particular, he condemned those members of an-Nahdah who had obtained political asylum in Europe. In August 1993 it was reported that Rached Ghanouchi, the leader of an-Nahdah (sentenced to life imprisonment *in absentia* in 1992), had been granted political asylum in the United Kingdom despite the Tunisian Government's efforts to obtain his extradition. The British Foreign Office emphasized that the decision to grant Ghanouchi asylum was taken by the Home Office and was not a matter of foreign policy. In October Salah Karkar, one of the leaders of an-Nahdah who had lived in France since he was sentenced to death *in absentia* by a Tunisian court in 1987, was arrested by French police and served with an expulsion order for supporting a terrorist movement in France and in other European countries. In December, following a request from Tunisia, French police raided the homes of several alleged Tunisian Islamist activists who were suspected of planning attacks on people or property in France.

Despite government claims that an-Nahdah's organization had been destroyed in Tunisia, a high level of security was maintained. In early 1994 Noufal Ziadi, the Secretary-General of the UGET, condemned the permanent presence of police on university campuses and complained about restrictions placed on union activity. The LTDH (dissolved in June 1992) began rebuilding its regional networks in January 1994. In April, in an unusually outspoken declaration, some 200 intellectuals denounced the regime's paranoia about security and alleged a sharp decline in human rights and freedom of speech. In a report published in January Amnesty International had claimed that the Government's prominent role in international human rights organizations served to mask its own serious and systematic violations of human rights. Amnesty reported that, over the previous three years, thousands of suspected political opponents had been subjected to arbitrary arrest, held illegally, incommunicado, in prolonged detention, tortured or ill-treated and imprisoned after unfair trials.

The presidential and legislative elections on 20 March 1994 brought few surprises. President Ben Ali was re-elected for a second term, winning 99.9% of the vote, according to official sources, which also reported that 94.9% of eligible voters had participated in the election. Abderrahmane el-Hani, a lawyer and leader of a political party not recognized by the Government, and Moncef Marzouki, the former president of the LTDH and an obstinate critic of the regime's human rights record, had both been arrested after announcing their intention to stand for the presidency. In the parliamentary elections the RCD swept to victory, winning 97.7% of the vote and taking all 144 seats allocated under the majority list system. The six legal opposition parties secured only 2.3% of the vote, but, under the new electoral formula, the MDS was given 10 of the 19 'guaranteed' seats reserved for parties which did not secure a majority in the constituencies, the MR four seats, the UDU three seats, and the PUP two seats. In his address to the new National Assembly in April, Ben Ali proclaimed that Tunisia had achieved political pluralism and declared its commitment to strengthen democracy and human rights.

In contrast to the 1989 election, there were few complaints from opposition parties about the conduct of the 1994 poll. However, the LTDH claimed that secrecy of voting had not always been assured and accused the authorities of interfering with a number of opposition campaign meetings. When Boujamaa Rmili, an official of the MR, condemned the election as 'a scandal', he was quickly arrested and detained for a week. There were few foreign observers because, in the approach to the elections, the regime had moved to control the foreign press and television. Several French and British newspapers were banned, the BBC's correspondent in Tunis was expelled and a French television team deported for their alleged hostile attitude and 'intolerable attacks on Tunisia's dignity'. Local journalists who expressed criticism of the regime suffered harassment, dismissal and even imprisonment.

The opposition parties drawn into the National Assembly by the offer of a handful of seats had little power and did not threaten the dominant position of the ruling party and the President. Supporters of the regime claimed that democracy had to be introduced gradually or Tunisia would suffer the instability and violence that has engulfed neighbouring Algeria. There were appeals for further electoral reform from the leader of the largest opposition party, the MDS, and from the LTDH. Given its overwhelming victory in the elections, there was considerable speculation about why the regime was so unwilling to tolerate any criticism or opposition. Critics pointed, in particular, to the apparently vindictive arrests of el-Hani, Marzouki and Rmili, to the harsh sentence imposed in April 1994 on Hamma Hammani, the leader of the banned Parti des ouvriers communistes tunisiens (POCT), for belonging to an illegal organization, to press censorship and to the continued repression of Islamist sympathizers. Some argued that the Government was afraid to relax its strict controls in case this resulted in a resurgence of the Islamist threat. Others accused the Government of merely using the threat from militant Islam as an excuse to crush all opposition movements. Some felt that the regime was able to act in an increasingly arrogant manner because it could rely on the support of important foreign investors and the majority of Tunisians who, it was argued, were willing to accept restrictions on political freedoms and human rights in return for stability and economic prosperity. In March 1,793 prisoners were pardoned to mark the anniversary of independence, and a further 762 were released in July.

Criticism of the regime's human rights record continued both at home and abroad. In February 1994 the US State Department, reporting on human rights practices in Tunisia, referred to continuing widespread human rights abuses, including torture, and deplored the prosecution of critics of the regime and the restrictions imposed on press freedom. In April the LTDH renewed its request for greater freedom of opinion, expression and organization and in May expressed its support for a petition signed by more than 100 Tunisian women, mainly professionals, which deplored 'grave violations' of human rights in Tunisia, 'pressures imposed on the press' and restrictions on freedom of expression. The LTDH appealed for the release of all political prisoners and permission to publish its own annual report on human rights in the country. In July Moncef Marzouki was freed provisionally and there was speculation that his trial might be postponed indefinitely if he withdrew from politics. But in December he was not allowed to travel to New York to receive an award from the US-based Human Rights Watch. The French Government protested against the ban on the sale of certain French newspapers in Tunisia, and there was also

criticism of press restrictions from the Paris-based Reporters sans frontières. The Fédération internationale des ligues des droits de l'homme, which has its headquarters in Paris, strongly denounced the regime's attacks on individual liberty and restrictions on freedom of expression. In reply, the authorities maintained that fundamental liberties were guaranteed in Tunisia, and human rights respected. In November 1994 the UN's Commission on Human Rights praised Tunisia for the move to political pluralism and for its achievements in improving women's rights, but expressed disquiet at the harsh treatment of detainees, including the use of torture, the banning of several foreign newspapers and restrictions imposed on the activities of political parties. Also in November, in an address to the UN General Assembly, the US Assistant Secretary of State, Robert Pelletreau (a former US ambassador to Tunisia), appealed for greater political openness and improved human rights in Tunisia so that the political system would correspond more closely to economic prosperity now enjoyed by the Tunisian people. In December a petition signed by some 60 people, including human rights activists, was published. It urged the Government to release Hamma Hammani, the imprisoned leader of the POCT. Also in December the International Commission of Jurists accused the Government of forcing Tunisian magistrates who had attended one of the Commission's seminars to dissociate themselves from the meeting's conclusions because they questioned the independence of Tunisia's judicial system.

TUNISIA SINCE THE 1994 ELECTIONS

In August 1994, in interviews with the foreign press, President Ben Ali stated that democracy had to be introduced gradually in Tunisia and that freedom of expression on its own would not bring development or create employment. He renewed his attack on 'Islamic fundamentalists' and argued that religious extremists only found support where there was poverty. His Government sought to achieve political stability by pursuing policies that addressed social and economic problems and that helped the country's poorest regions and sections of society.

Following the transfer of the two leaders of the Algerian FIS from prison to house arrest in September 1994, the leader of an-Nahdah, Rached Ghanouchi, in exile in the United Kingdom, urged the Tunisian Government to follow Algeria's example and open dialogue with the Islamist opposition. In August Ghanouchi himself had been criticized by two senior members of an-Nahdah for favouring a policy of confrontation with the Tunisian authorities which they claimed had led to the imprisonment of large numbers of party members. From exile in Paris, El Azhar Abaab issued a statement urging an-Nahdah to disband and the Government to release imprisoned party activists and allow those living in exile to return to Tunisia. Some days later, another member of the an-Nahdah leadership, Fouad Mansour Kassem, resigned from the party which he claimed was on the verge of collapse. There were reports that another group of activists had established a radical Islamist party, committed to armed struggle against the Tunisian authorities. In early 1995 a Paris court ordered the deportation of Salah Karkar, the co-founder of an-Nahdah 'for active support for a terrorist movement'. Karkar had lived in exile in France since 1988 after being condemned to death *in absentia* by a Tunisian court in 1987.

In February 1995 there were reports of an attack on a Tunisian frontier post at Tamerza, near Tozeur in the south-west of the country, by an Islamist group based across the border in Algeria, in which six Tunisian soldiers were killed. Algeria's radical Groupe islamique armé (GIA) claimed responsibility for the attack. The Tunisian authorities initially denied that the incident had taken place; however, they later conceded that the guards had been killed, most probably by Islamist militants. They also denied a report in the London-based *al-Hayat* newspaper in March that Tunisian forces were assisting the Algerian Islamist guerrillas. Some observers considered the Tamerza attack as a GIA warning to the Tunisian Government against assisting Algeria in its struggle to destroy the Islamist opposition; others regarded it as an attempt to obtain weapons. Tunisia is known to have co-operated with Algeria on security matters for some years and the co-operation may have extended beyond sharing intelligence.

When the National Assembly reconvened in October 1994 some 14 of the 19 opposition members attending for the first time were elected to parliamentary committees. In January 1995 President Ben Ali made a number of ministerial changes, notably replacing Abdallah Kallel at the Ministry of the Interior with Muhammad Jegham. Kallel, who was given the new post of Minister of State and Special Adviser to the President, had been criticized both at home and abroad for his harsh treatment of opponents of the Government, and there was some speculation that his successor might adopt a more subtle approach, especially in dealing with the secular opposition. The transfer of influential Sadok Rabah, from the Ministry of National Economy to head the Ministry of Social Affairs, suggested that the President was giving greater priority to social problems in his efforts to maintain political stability. But Jegham appeared determined to continue an intransigent policy towards opponents of the regime. In February a number of trade union officials were arrested and detained for several days after a strike by school teachers, and in March Moncef Marzouki was prevented from travelling to Belgium where he was to have delivered a series of lectures. In June it was reported that a court order imposed on Marzouki, refusing him permission to leave the country, had been lifted.

At local elections held in May 1995 the RCD won control of all municipal councils and received 99.9% of the votes cast. Independent candidates and members of five legal opposition parties, represented in 47 of the 257 constituencies, won only six of the 4,090 seats; however, this was the first time since 1956 that the opposition had been represented on municipal councils. The RCD rejected allegations made by the MDS of irregularities in the electoral procedure, including inadequate access for observers. The result highlighted the impotence of the secular opposition parties which failed to offer an attractive alternative to the ruling party. Given the lack of interest in the elections, the official figure of a 92.5% turn-out appeared unrealistically high.

In July 1995 the Government introduced a law imposing strict controls on the use of satellite dishes and in September stopped broadcasts to Tunisia by the Italian television channel Rai Uno. Opposition deputies condemned the law on satellite dishes and accused the Government of imposing even tighter controls on the media. In September President Ben Ali reorganized the Ministry of Economic Development and appointed a new minister, Tawfik Baccar, to replace Mustapha Nabli. The ministry would thenceforth concentrate on the country's development plans; responsibility for the investment budget was transferred to the Ministry of Finance, where Mounir Jaidene was appointed to the new post of Secretary of State to the Finance Minister, in charge of the budget (responsible for both the administrative and investment budgets).

In September 1995 Muhammad Mouada, the Secretary-General of the MDS, sent a letter to President Ben Ali expressing disquiet at what he referred to as a return to 'a regime of a hegemonic and dominating single party', and complaining that the repressive measures introduced to control society were more extensive and systematic than under the Bourguiba regime. Mouada argued that the current climate encouraged public indifference to politics and provided favourable ground for violence and extremism. He proposed a political plan which, he argued, would lead gradually to political pluralism and democracy. Under Mouada's leadership the MDS had agreed to participate in the 1994 legislative elections, and had supported both the regime's intransigent approach to the Islamist opposition and its economic liberalization programme. Mouada's letter was regarded as an expression of the party's frustration at not receiving any reward for supporting the regime. In early October, the day after the MDS made the letter public, Mouada was arrested and charged with maintaining secret contacts with foreign agents, endangering the country's security and accepting money from a foreign country. The security forces claimed to have found documents at his home which indicated that he had received substantial sums of money from Libya. A Libyan informer alleged that the payments were for secret political and military information about Tunisia. In November Khemais Chamari, the deputy leader of the MDS, was stripped of his parliamentary immunity, in order to allow judicial charges (relating to Mouada's trial) to be brought against him. At his

trial, Mouada, who was known for his pan-Arab beliefs and sympathy for Libya, insisted that his contacts with Libya had been strictly within bounds acceptable for politicians. His lawyers argued that the incriminating documents found at his home had been falsified.

In November 1995 President Ben Ali promised electoral reform to enable the opposition parties to win more seats at the next municipal elections, and financial subsidies for the four opposition parties represented in the National Assembly. He also pardoned Hamma Hammani and Muhammad Kilani of the POCT, both serving long prison sentences, and in December held talks with the leaders of the two centrist opposition parties represented in the National Assembly, the UDU and the PUP. While these moves were considered to be an attempt to improve relations with the opposition, most observers were convinced that the treatment of Mouada was more indicative of the authoritarian nature of the regime, and its refusal to tolerate criticism or permit genuine political pluralism. In February 1996 Mouada was sentenced to 11 years in prison. Chamari was detained in May, and in July was sentenced to five years' imprisonment for breaching security proceedings relating to Mouada's trial. Both men denied the charges made against them and their harsh sentences were strongly condemned by international human rights organizations and the European Parliament. Mouada's arrest and detention provoked a bitter struggle for leadership of the MDS between supporters of Ismail Boulahya, a critic of Mouada's policies, and a faction led by Muhammad Ali Khalfallah. Boulahya, recognized as the new MDS Secretary-General by the Tunisian authorities, convened an extraordinary party congress in April 1997 at which it was decided to increase the MDS political bureau from nine to 11 members and to require the national council (rather than the congress) to elect future leaders.

In December 1996 President Ben Ali announced plans to amend the electoral law in an attempt to increase the number of opposition deputies in the National Assembly. Political parties would need to win only 3% of the vote to become eligible for parliamentary seats distributed by proportional representation (compared with 5% in the 1994 election). Opposition parties would also be represented in municipal councils owing to a proposed amendment preventing any one party from holding more than 80% of the seats. Ben Ali promised legislation to provide more state funds for recognized political parties. Observers interpreted these moves as an attempt by the Tunisian leadership to improve its image abroad without undermining the ruling party's dominant position in the political system. Ben Ali's announced reforms were followed by the conditional release of Mouada and Chamari at the end of December, together with Muhammad Hedi Sassi, imprisoned for being a member of the POCT. There were rumours that the French Government had made discreet approaches to the Tunisian authorities to grant the two MDS leaders a presidential pardon. Despite their release, Mouada and Chamari remained under police surveillance. Their prison sentences had only been suspended and their civil rights were not restored. In by-elections held at the end of 1996 the seat at Ben Arous (formerly held by Chamari) was won by a candidate presented by the PUP and the UDU, which had formed an alliance earlier in the year, while the seat at Medenine was won by the RCD. Voter turn-out at Ben Arous, which was not contested by the RCD, was less than 5%, demonstrating once again that the opposition parties lacked popular support among an increasingly cynical electorate.

During a reshuffle of the Council of Ministers in June 1996 President Ben Ali appointed Abd al-Aziz Ben Dhia (hitherto Minister of National Defence) as Secretary-General of the RCD, with a mandate to revitalize its structure and make it more attractive to young Tunisians. Neffati (the erstwhile RCD Secretary-General), who became Minister of Social Affairs, was also removed from the RCD's political bureau. Abdallah Kallel, who was known for his intransigence on security issues, was allocated the defence portfolio. The President also carried out a major reshuffle of senior civil servants and directors-general of state companies. In January 1997 Ben Ali again reorganized the Council of Ministers, notably appointing Habib Ben Yahia as Minister of National Defence, Muhammad Ben Rejeb as Minister of the Interior, and Abd ar-Rahim Zouari as Minister of Foreign Affairs. Most of the ministers were technocrats with little political power. Although some observers argued that the cabinet changes were effected in order to give the Government dynamism prior to the implementation of the EU association agreement, others insisted that Ben Ali reshuffled his ministers regularly so as to prevent them from establishing a personal power base in any one ministry. Changes were also made to the composition of the RCD's political bureau and the President sought to invigorate the ruling party by attracting more young people and women. In February a decree was issued giving the Ministry of the Interior greater powers of surveillance over political gatherings, and later in the year it was announced that the law was to be strengthened to restrict the activities of Tunisian critics who spread false information to 'foreign parties', a move clearly directed at Tunisian activists with links to international human rights organizations (see below). In April, when several trade unionists appealed for greater democracy and criticized the UGTT leadership for collaborating with the Government, a number were promptly arrested. In May the Council of Ministers approved draft legislation on constitutional amendments which included proposals to widen the scope of referendums, lowering the minimum eligible age for candidates for the National Assembly (from 25 to 23 years) and obliging political parties to denounce all forms of violence, extremism, racism and segregation. In August, just before the French Minister of Foreign Affairs visited Tunis, the authorities ended the house arrest of Mouada, and lifted police surveillance of him. However, in December, after returning from a visit to France and the United Kingdom, during which he met exiled members of the Tunisian opposition, including some from an-Nahdah, Mouada was arrested again and questioned by the police. He was due to be brought to trial in May 1998, charged with attempting to destabilize the regime in alliance with a 'terrorist network'. Meanwhile, the split in the MDS between the faction led by Ismail Boulahya and that led by Muhammad Ali Khalfallah, which was opposed to collaboration with the Ben Ali regime, deepened and virtually paralysed the party. The continuing detention of former head of state Habib Bourguiba, who remains under effective house arrest and is rarely permitted visitors, led to some public protest in late 1997. A further cabinet reshuffle took place in October, with Ali Chaouch (hitherto Minister of Equipment and Housing) taking over as Minister of the Interior and Said Ben Mustapha appointed as Minister of Foreign Affairs. Fouad Mebazaa replaced Habib Boulares as President of the National Assembly. Both Chaouch and Mebazaa took the place of their predecessors on the political bureau of the ruling RCD. Towards the end of 1997 a number of political reforms that had first been announced by Ben Ali in 1996 were approved by the National Assembly and incorporated into the Constitution. The reforms, which according to the Government would 'strengthen democracy', included a guarantee that opposition parties should win at least 20% of the seats in the National Assembly; no party was to be allowed to hold more than 80% of seats on municipal councils; the minimum age of parliamentary candidates was to be reduced form 25 to 23 years; citizens with Tunisian mothers (in addition to those with Tunisian fathers) were to be allowed to stand for parliament; all political parties would have to respect republican values, human rights and the rights of women and not be based on religion, language, race or region, or have links with foreign countries; and the President was to be allowed to hold a referendum on issues of national importance (there was speculation that Ben Ali might use such a referendum to change the Constitution in order to allow him to stand for a third term as President). In a speech in November, on the tenth anniversary of his takeover of power, Ben Ali announced further political reforms including a formula to increase the number of candidates at the presidential election scheduled to be held in March 1999; an extension to the powers of the Constitutional Council; and reform of the law on the issue of passports to improve freedom of movement. In the same speech, the President announced that the post of Secretary of State for Information (whose role had been to disseminate government propaganda and censor those who criticized the regime) had been abolished and told journalists that they should abandon self-censorship and help stimulate public debate on political issues. He also urged members of the National Assembly to engage in more vigorous debate in the Assembly

on policy issues. Given the strict controls over the press and the regime's intolerance of criticism from opposition politicians, genuine debate either in the press or in the Assembly seemed unlikely. Some commentators dismissed the proposals as a façade created by the authoritarian regime merely to impress Tunisia's European allies, notably France.

In early 1998 reports of high-level government corruption became more widespread and included claims that members of the country's political élite had profited unfairly from the recent privatization of public companies. As some of the reports came from within the Government, there was speculation that they were being spread by people who resented the wealth and privileges acquired by families close to President Ben Ali.

The Tunisian authorities continued to maintain that the country was immune to Islamist extremism because of progressive social policies and the strict application of the law. However, they were concerned that networks of Islamist militants still existed abroad, especially in certain European countries, and that these groups were determined to undermine Tunisia's stability. At a meeting in July 1995 with foreign ministers from several Mediterranean countries, President Ben Ali stated that Islamist militants granted political asylum in Western countries had abused their status, and he appealed for co-operation in containing 'fanaticism, extremism and terrorism'. In January 1996 the Arab League, meeting in Tunis, adopted a proposal sponsored by Tunisia for a 'code of conduct' to combat 'terrorism', referring primarily to Islamist extremism. The Tunisian Minister of Foreign Affairs, Habib Ben Yahia, appealed for an international code of conduct against terrorism at the 'Summit of Peace-makers', hastily convened in Egypt in March after the spate of suicide bomb attacks in Israel, and again criticized countries that gave asylum to Islamist extremists. From his exile in the United Kingdom, Rached Ghanouchi warned that unless all parties were allowed to participate in the political system, Tunisia could experience violent conflict in the future, like its neighbour Algeria. In November 1995 Ghanouchi was one of a group of Tunisian opposition leaders in exile who published a statement in *al-Hayat* petitioning for a return to democracy. In early 1996 Ghanouchi stated that he was working with other opposition leaders, including former premier Muhammad Mzali, to form an alliance committed to a democratic Tunisia. He declared that all Tunisians, whether or not they held Islamist sympathies, had become the victims of the authoritarian regime, and claimed that an-Nahdah differed from Tunisia's other Islamist groups in that it had rejected armed struggle and favoured peaceful political change. In December Ben Ali once again refused to legalize an-Nahdah and proposed constitutional amendments in order to proscribe political parties based on race, region or religion (see above).

During 1995–96 concern continued to be expressed over human rights violations in Tunisia. The US State Department's report on human rights in Tunisia during 1995 noted that serious problems still remained and that the Government continued to 'stifle freedoms of speech, press and association'. The LTDH's annual report included accounts of violations of the freedom of the press, the illegal detention of suspects, the banning of political parties, and poor conditions inside prisons—despite claims by an internal commission of inquiry into the country's prisons (established by the President) that conditions had greatly improved. In September 1995 the LTDH issued a statement which denounced the deaths in suspicious circumstances of two prisoners. Amnesty International's annual report on Tunisia, published in November, described widespread and systematic human rights abuses and argued that internal commissions of inquiry by the authorities were ineffectual. In January 1996 Najib Hosni, a lawyer who had defended an-Nahdah activists, was sentenced to eight years' imprisonment. It was alleged that he had falsified documents, but Amnesty International insisted that he had been prosecuted for his human rights activities and claimed that he had been tortured during the 18 months that he was detained without trial. In May two other leading human rights activists, Moncef Marzouki, a former President of the LTDH, and Frej Fennich, the Director of the Arab Institute of Human Rights, were arrested. Later that month a court ruling found that as a private association the LTDH could continue to select its members. The Ministry of the Interior had insisted that the organization should be open to anyone, leading to fears that it would be infiltrated by political opponents. Meanwhile, the European Parliament passed a resolution in May which strongly criticized Tunisia's human rights record and made special reference to Marzouki's treatment. Several of Tunisia's European allies also openly criticized Tunisia's record on human rights (see above). In October Reporters sans frontières condemned the Tunisian Government for stifling the press. In December Hosni was granted a presidential pardon at the same time as Mouada and Chamari were released from prison. Their release may have been a response to criticism from abroad, but it did not signal greater tolerance of political opponents. In early 1997 the head of Amnesty International's local branch was arrested and detained for several days, prompting renewed complaints of human rights abuses in Tunisia. In May an-Nahdah announced the death in prison of one of its founder members, Sheikh Mabrouk Zren, and cited other cases of political activists who had died or contracted illnesses while in detention. Ironically, Tunisia was unanimously elected to the UN Human Rights Commission in May, and soon afterwards the Government tried to improve relations with the LTDH, describing the organization as a 'national asset' but urging it to prove its 'patriotism and sense of responsibility'. In a report on Tunisia published in June, Amnesty International stated that while the Government expressed its commitment to human rights it was guilty of 'a widening circle of repression', affecting families (particularly wives) and associates of political opponents, and that large-scale human rights abuses continued to take place. Amnesty later joined several other international organizations in appealing to the regime to stop its 'campaign of intimidation' against human rights activists. After several Tunisian human rights activists were refused permission to

attend a conference at the European Parliament, a group of parliamentary members announced that they planned to introduce another resolution in the Parliament condemning Tunisia for human rights abuses. In July, during a speech to mark the 40th anniversary of the declaration of the Republic, President Ben Ali vigorously denounced critics of his regime, insisting that in every possible way Tunisia was a state of law and a country of human rights. He accused prominent Tunisian human rights activists of spreading lies about their country and stated that they were guilty of 'a form of high treason'. In September Khemais Ksila, the Vice-President of the LTDH, was arrested after publishing a statement attacking the Government and sending it to a French news agency. He was sentenced to three years' imprisonment in February 1998 for divulging false information likely to upset public order. At the end of March Radhia Nasraoui, a lawyer well-known for defending political and human rights activists, and married to Hamma Hammani of the POCT, was charged with several offences including links with a terrorist organization and incitement to rebellion. If found guilty she could spend up to 20 years in prison. Reporting on human rights practices in 1997, the US State Department recorded an improvement in the Tunisian Government's performance on human rights, but claimed that it continued to commit serious offences, including the physical abuse of prisoners, harassment of government critics, and significant restrictions on the freedom of speech and press, while demonstrating a pattern of intolerance to public criticism. In a report published in early 1998 the Arab Commission of Human Rights stated that there had been an increase in human rights abuses in Tunisia and claimed to have evidence relating to the torture of political opponents.

Economy

Revised for this edition by RICHARD I. LAWLESS

Tunisia covers an area of 163,610 sq km (63,170 sq miles). At the census of May 1975 the population was 5,572,193, of whom over one-half were less than 25 years old, and at the census of 30 March 1984 the population was 6,966,173. The annual rate of increase in the population in 1974–84 averaged 2.5%. According to World Bank estimates, the average annual rate of population growth during 1985–94 was 2.3%. The projected growth rate for the period 1992 to 2000 was 2.2% per annum. The results of a census carried out in April 1994 indicated that the population totalled 8,785,364. By 1997 the population was estimated to have reached 9,200,000, and it was projected to rise to 10,800,000 by 2007. Most of the towns, and also the greater part of the rural population, are concentrated in the coastal areas. In the centre and the south, the land is infertile semi-desert, the population scattered, the standard of living very low, and the rate of growth of the population even higher than in the north.

The capital and main commercial centre is Tunis (population 674,100, according to the 1994 census), which, together with the adjacent La Goulette, is also the chief port. There are about 50,000 Europeans in Tunis, mainly French and Italians, their numbers having decreased rapidly since independence. Other towns of importance include Sfax (population 230,900 in 1994), which is the principal town in the south, the second port and the centre for exports of phosphates and olive oil; Ariana (152,700); Ettadhamen (149,200); Sousse (125,000); and Kairouan (102,600). Just over 600,000 Tunisians are currently resident abroad, relieving the domestic employment situation and providing a source of foreign exchange earnings through workers' remittances from overseas. The Government is trying to encourage Tunisians to work in Saudi Arabia and in other countries bordering the Persian (Arabian) Gulf, in an attempt to offset the reduction in demand for Tunisian workers in traditional markets, especially France. Even greater efforts were needed to accommodate the 30,000 Tunisian workers who were expelled from Libya in 1985. However, the *rapprochement* with Libya in

1987–88 alleviated this problem, and a new agreement, signed in May 1988, included provisions allowing Tunisians to work, live and own property freely in Libya (see History).

Tunisia's development record in the 1970s was fairly impressive, with gross domestic product (GDP), measured in current prices, increasing from US \$4,339m. (\$773 per head) in 1975 to \$8,667m. (\$1,356 per head) in 1980. In the early 1980s, however, the economy entered a period of turbulence. Output of petroleum reached a peak level in 1980, and the countryside was devastated by a series of droughts. Measured at constant 1980 prices, GDP (in purchasers' values) declined from TD 3,736m. in 1981 to TD 3,718m. in 1982, but growth averaged 5.3% per year in 1983–85. Meanwhile, the deficit on the current account of the balance of payments remained at an unacceptably high level, resulting in a worrying increase in external debt (totalling \$4,880m. at the end of 1985). These problems culminated in 1986, when the sudden fall in the international price of petroleum resulted in a balance-of-payments crisis, which forced the Government to seek assistance from the IMF. As agricultural output declined, GDP fell by 1.4%, in real terms, in 1986. With the IMF's assistance, the Government adopted a radical economic programme for the 1987–91 period, designed to provide a secure basis for the economy until the next decade, by which time it was anticipated that Tunisia would have become a net energy importer. The strategy depended on an increase in exports of agricultural and manufactured goods, a rise in revenues from tourism, and severe reductions in the Government's investment budget. Meanwhile, trade was to be liberalized, and the Tunisian dinar was to be devalued, in an attempt to maintain export competitiveness. The economy recovered in 1987, as a result of an increase in the international price of petroleum, an abundant harvest and the success of government measures to control public spending and to encourage higher output, exports and foreign investment. Accordingly, GDP expanded by 5.5%, in real terms, and the current account deficit fell to the equivalent of 0.6% of GDP. However, in 1988 the combined effects of severe drought and locust damage on the harvest, and a fall in the oil price, reduced GDP growth to 1.5%, although the current account of the balance of payments showed an annual surplus (of $216m.) for the first time since 1974. In 1989 GDP increased by 3.5%, with the help of a substantial expansion in the tourism sector and higher remittances from workers abroad, although the current account was in deficit by $160m. (1.6% of GDP). In 1990 an ample harvest of cereals and a rise in the petroleum price contributed to real GDP growth of 6%, but the current account deficit increased to $523m. (4.1% of GDP).

In 1988 the IMF and the World Bank provided financial support for a medium-term adjustment programme for 1988–91. The policies of the 1987–91 programme were continued under the new programme, with emphasis being placed on the acceleration of the process of trade liberalization, the strengthening of the financial sector, the restructuring of state enterprises and the introduction of tax reforms. By 1989 substantial progress had been made and the programme was viewed as highly successful. In March 1991, however, it was announced that austerity measures would have to be adopted in order to counter the effects of the Gulf War on exports, tourism revenues and external funding sources. In protest at Tunisia's ambivalence at the time of the crisis, Kuwait and Saudi Arabia withdrew planned investment and aid totalling $412m. and $200m. respectively, while the USA reduced aid from $59m. in 1990 to a projected $19m. in 1991. Against this background the Government obtained a one-year extension to its agreement with the IMF and also secured balance-of-payments support from the World Bank and other sources. By the end of 1991 mid-year forecasts of zero GDP growth that year had been revised to projected growth of 3.5%, reflecting a record harvest, a recovery in tourism and an upturn in the industrial sector. As a result, both the trade deficit ($874m.) and the current account deficit ($191m. or 1.5% of GDP) showed improvements in 1991, and GDP growth of 6.5% was forecast for 1992. In July 1992 a new Five-Year (1992–96) Plan was inaugurated, amid optimism that Tunisia was set to become North Africa's leading centre of venture capital and technology. At the same time it was announced that the Government would not be seeking an IMF facility to replace the extended Fund facility (EFF) which had expired in mid-1992. GDP growth of 7.8% was recorded in 1992, followed by growth of only 2% in 1993, when there were falls in agricultural, mining and oil production. The economy grew by 3.3% in 1994, when the effects of an accelerated decline in agricultural output (due mainly to drought conditions) were offset by strong growth in tourism, transport and industry, including export-orientated manufacturing, and by 2.4% in 1995. GDP grew by 6.9% in 1996, a significant rise which in large part was the result of a good agricultural performance and, according to official estimates, by 5.6% in 1997, although some independent sources put the figure at just over 5%. GDP was forecast to grow by 5.4% in 1998. In 1994 the World Bank estimated Tunisia's gross national product (GNP) per head as $1,800 on a conventional exchange-rate basis or $4,960 using an 'international dollar' calculation based on a current Tunisian rating of 19.2 in the Bank's international 'purchasing power parity' index (USA = 100). The Vice-President of the World Bank praised Tunisia's economic performance in 1997, noting a marked recovery in investment and strong export growth. But he observed that investment in the non-energy sector was limited and warned of the serious problem posed by unemployment (15% of the economically active population, according to official figures). He argued that with an annual growth in GDP of at least 5%, more jobs could be created.

In July 1995 Tunisia signed a new trade agreement with the European Union (EU) under which Tunisian manufacturers would be exposed to increasingly strong competitive pressures from 1996 onwards. It was expected that there would be significant inflows of EU official assistance and European private investment during the 12-year trade liberalization period. According to government officials, Tunisia's closer association with Europe would help to ensure that a critical phase of the industrialization process was realistically planned and adequately funded. The agreement formally came into force in March 1998, although Tunisia began dismantling trade barriers to EU industrial goods in January 1996. In April 1998 it was announced that the EU had agreed to grant Tunisia $10.7m. to support the Government's privatization programme as part of its aid programme to assist the Tunisian economy adjust to growing competition from the EU under the free-trade agreement. The grant was to be disbursed over five years and was made on the condition that the Government accelerate the divestment of state-owned companies. Despite pressure from the World Bank, the IMF and Tunisia's own central bank, over the preceding decade the Government had moved relatively slowly to privatize public companies, fearing that this would lead to reductions in the workforce and aggravate unemployment. According to the Minister of Economic Development an annual average of six firms were privatized in 1987–94, and 15 per year in 1994–97. The Government raised around TD 350m. ($308m.) from the programme during 1987–97. At the end of May 1998 the Secretary of State for Privatization announced that 19 state-controlled companies had been targeted for flotation and that a further 49 would be put on sale by the end of 1999. He stated that the Société Tunisienne d'Entreprise de Télécommunications would be among the first companies to be sold and that others would include TunisAir and the Société Tunisienne de Banque. He estimated that the Government would raise some $600m. in revenues from these sales.

AGRICULTURE

About two-thirds of the total area of Tunisia is suitable for farming. For agricultural purposes the country is composed of five different areas: the mountainous north, with its large fertile valleys; the north-east, including the Cap Bon, where the soil is especially suitable for the cultivation of oranges and other citrus fruit; the Sahel, where olives grow; the centre, with its high tablelands and pastures; and the south, with oases and gardens, where dates are prolific. Harvests vary considerably in size, determined by the uncertain rainfall, since cultivation is largely by dry farming and irrigation is, as yet, limited. The main cereal crops are wheat, barley, maize, oats and sorghum. Fruit is also important, with grapes, olives, dates, oranges and figs grown for export as well as for the local market.

In recent years Tunisia has been importing increasing amounts of cereals, as local production has failed to keep pace with population growth. During the 1960s the agricultural sector grew at only about 1.5% per year, but exceptional weather conditions and improved irrigation in 1971 and 1972 resulted in excellent agricultural yields, and during the fourth Plan period (1973–76) good weather, except in 1974, led to an average annual growth rate of 3%. The 1977–81 Plan envisaged annual growth of 3.5% and the 1982–86 Plan projected average annual growth at 5%, as a higher proportion of investment was allocated to the agricultural sector. However, these targets were not reached, owing to poor crop conditions in 1977, 1982 and 1986. The collapse in agricultural output was particularly severe in 1986. The 1987–91 Plan projected annual growth of 6% per year, and directed even more investment to agriculture. In 1988, however, agricultural output declined drastically as a result of drought and a plague of locusts. Agriculture's contribution to GDP declined from 22% in 1965 to 12% in 1990. However, a record cereal harvest reversed the trend in 1991, when agriculture's share of GDP increased to 19.6%. Owing to population increase, the average index of food production per caput fell to 87 in the period 1988–90 (1979–81 = 100). By 1996 the proportion of the labour force engaged in agriculture had fallen to 22.6%, from 49% in 1965. In 1993 agriculture's share of GDP was 16.9%, and the total value of exports from this sector (TD 392.6m.) was some TD 7.4m. more than spending on agricultural and food imports. In 1994 the surplus in agricultural trade amounted to TD 48.4m. (exports TD 526.7m., imports TD 478.3m.). By 1995 agriculture's contribution to GDP had declined to 13.4%, increasing to 15.9% in 1996. During 1980–90 agricultural GDP rose by an annual average of 2.8%; however, agricultural GDP declined by an annual average of 0.1% in 1990–96.

The means by which self-sufficiency should be achieved has been the cause of political debate since the early 1970s. During 1960–69, at the instigation of the Minister of Planning, Ahmad Ben Salah, the basis of the Government's agrarian reform programme lay in the formation of collective 'agricultural units'. These units, consisting of at least 500 ha, were to be operated as collectives in order to consolidate small peasant holdings and, later, to exploit land expropriated from French farmers or acquired from owners of large or medium-sized farms. The system was controlled through credits provided by the Agricultural Bank. By 1968 some 220 state co-operatives were in existence and several hundred more were being created. However, opposition to the scheme was widespread, and there were revelations of unsatisfactory performance, heavy debts and misappropriation of state funds. These discoveries were instrumental in the downfall and disgrace of Ben Salah, whose position was already weakened by the displeasure of foreign aid donors with his agricultural policies.

Following Ben Salah's downfall, farmers were given a chance to opt out of the state co-operatives, which were later dismantled. Meanwhile, the National Assembly approved legislation allowing for the eventual division of large private estates, to be split among individual farmers or private co-operatives. The Government also introduced a number of measures to stimulate output, including the provision of funds for mechanization, a reduction in taxes, and the introduction of subsidies for purchases of fertilizers and seed. By 1975 about 50% of the total cultivated area of 9m. ha was privately owned, a further 2.1m. ha were worked by private co-operatives and the remainder was farmed by state or religious institutions. In April 1974 a 'supervised credits scheme' was announced, whereby small and medium-sized farms could be given supervised credits on a short-term basis to improve farming methods. It was hoped that this would encourage the cultivation of diversified crops rather than the traditional staple crops.

The Government's current agricultural policy reflects several concerns: one is to achieve self-sufficiency, thus saving on expensive food imports which the country can ill afford, and a second is to reduce regional imbalance by developing rural areas. By making funds available for agriculture, the authorities hope to stem rural depopulation. The 1982–86 Plan allocated about 16% of total investment to agriculture, compared with only 13% in the previous Plan. In the 1987–91 Plan, investment in agriculture increased further, to about 20% of total proposed investment, a particular aim being to increase the role of the private sector in the financing of agriculture.

In June 1989 the World Bank agreed to provide Tunisia with credit of $84m. to finance the second phase of a seven-year agricultural reform programme launched in 1986. During the second phase of the programme it was intended to increase the share of the private sector in agricultural production, fortify agricultural support services and reform pricing and marketing structures. The need to boost domestic production was regarded as increasingly urgent since, by the mid-1980s, the value of Tunisia's agricultural exports was less than one-half that of its agricultural imports. In June 1990 the Government introduced the first stage of a further reform programme, financed by the World Bank, to improve agricultural extension and research. Under the 1992–96 Plan emphasis was to be given to encouraging private investment in agro-industrial ventures, with a view to maximizing export and food-processing potential.

The fragmentation of land-holdings and the need to consolidate them into larger, more efficient units, remains a major obstacle to increasing the profitability of the agricultural sector. But after the experiences of the 1960s, attempts to consolidate small land-holdings have become a highly sensitive subject for the Government. Nevertheless, speaking in November 1997, President Ben Ali announced that there would be national debate on land reform to find ways of amalgamating small agricultural land-holdings into more efficient units. The scale of the problem was highlighted by the Ministry of Agriculture in early 1998 when it reported that while the area devoted to agriculture—some 5.3m. ha—was beginning to decline as farmland was taken over for urban and industrial uses, the number of land-holders had increased from 326,000 in 1962 to 471,000 in 1995, with the average size of land-holdings declining from 16 ha to 11 ha. According to government estimates, farms on non-irrigated land must be at least 50 ha to be efficient, but the vast majority of land-holdings are well below this threshold and just over one-half are under 5 ha. Consequently many farms are too small to be profitable, and this discourages investment and the use of modern farming methods. One-third of land-owners are part-time farmers and there are many absentee landlords. In January 1998 the Minister of Agriculture

announced that state-owned farms would be leased to foreign investors with expertise in livestock and vineyard management.

A major programme of water development, including the construction of a number of dams for irrigation and flood prevention, is being implemented under the supervision of the World Bank. The Sidi Salem dam, with a capacity of 500m. cu m per year, opened in May 1982, and the Sidi Saad dam, near Kairouan, irrigating more than 4,000 ha, formally opened in the following month. Germany is currently financing the construction of the Bou Heurtna dam in Jendouba, which will irrigate 20,000 ha. In 1988 construction was to begin of a pipeline linking the Sidi Salem dam and the partly-built Sejnane dam with the water plant at Mateur. The saline water from Sidi Salem was to be mixed with the water from Sejnane at the plant, and was to be used to supply Tunis and to irrigate the northern cereal- and citrus fruit-growing areas. In the mid-1980s Tunisia's national water storage capacity was 1,500m. cu m and some 80,000 ha of land were irrigated. In mid-1992 two major dam projects, at El-Houareb and Sejnane, were near completion. Plans were also announced to build a dam creating a reservoir with a capacity of 130m. cu m at Zouitine, in the Barbera complex, and one creating a reservoir of 250m. cu m at Sidi El-Barek. Zouitine and Sidi El-Barek and a number of small hill dams constitute the final phase of government plans to utilize all available water resources by the end of the century. Work on the TD 122m. Sidi El-Barek project began in 1994, with a scheduled completion date of 1998. The Ministry of Agriculture has stated that, by 2000, 2,600m. cu m of water will be impounded, mainly in the north-west. Large dams would account for almost 2,000m. cu m, of which about 1,200m. cu m have already been mobilized. After the discovery of a huge underground lake in the Sahara, there were moves to encourage 'desert farming' by developing new land.

In March 1992 the European Community (EC) approved a grant of ECU 45m. for soil and water conservation projects, including the production of 243 hill reservoirs, 1,000 small-scale sewage recycling schemes and several dam improvements. Other EC-funded water and agriculture schemes included the rehabilitation of 13 irrigated zones in Kasserine governorate, the construction of a new barrage at Hasi el-Fred and the provision of an ECU 12m. 'credit-line' for small and medium-sized farming. Two earlier EC-funded schemes, for agricultural development in Kef governorate and in the Sejnane region, were nearing completion in mid-1992.

Grown in a belt across the northern part of the country, wheat is the most important cereal crop. The Government guarantees the price to the grower and, among other incentives, pays the transport costs of merchants. The Government has encouraged the spread of the Mexican dwarf wheat, and this variety now accounts for more than one-tenth of Tunisia's output. Production of wheat and barley totalled 606,000 metric tons during the disastrous 1985/86 season, but output increased to 1.9m. tons in 1986/87. In 1987/88, however, production fell sharply, to 292,000 tons, as a result of severe drought and the worst plague of locusts to affect the country for 30 years. Total cereal production reached 636,000 tons in 1989, but increased to 1.6m. tons in 1990, despite floods in January 1990, which necessitated the import of large amounts of grain. In 1991 there was a record cereal harvest of 2.6m. tons, falling in 1992 to 2.2m. tons. The 1993 cereal harvest totalled 1.9m. tons, but in 1994 drought conditions reduced the harvest to 650,000 tons. There was another poor harvest in 1995, resulting in a substantial increase in food imports. Spending on imports of cereals was TD 124.1m. in 1990, TD 65m. in 1991, TD 80.1m. in 1992 and TD 95.2m. in 1993. Improved rainfall in the 1995/96 growing season boosted the size of the 1996 cereal harvest to around 2.8m. tons. However, poor rains in 1996/97 reduced the 1997 cereal harvest to just over 1m. tons. After heavy autumn rains in 1997, the Government forecast a cereal harvest of 1.7m. tons in 1998.

Grapes are grown around Tunis and Bizerta. Wine production reached a peak of 1,986,000 hl in 1963. However, annual output had declined to one-third of this amount by the end of the 1970s. Production increased from 513,000 hl in 1982 to 680,000 hl in 1984, but fell to only 210,000 hl in 1988. By the early 1990s average annual output was around 340,000 hl, and there was new investment in vineyards. Some 90,000 hl of wine, worth TD 12.5m., was exported in 1993.

The size of Tunisia's annual harvest of olives fluctuates considerably, owing partly to the two-year flowering cycle of the tree. Tunisia is usually the world's fourth largest producer of olive oil. Production reached a record 180,000 metric tons in 1975/76 but fell to only 80,000 tons in 1978/79. Output of olive oil declined from 145,000 tons in 1980/81 to 80,000 tons in 1981/82. There was another sharp fall in 1982/83, but production reached 150,000 tons in 1983/84, before declining to about 100,000 tons per year in 1984/85, 1985/86 and 1986/87. The value of Tunisia's exports of olive oil has fluctuated dramatically since the late 1960s, reaching a peak of TD 70m. in 1974, but falling steeply in the late 1970s. Exports recovered in the mid-1980s, totalling TD 54m. in 1986, TD 66m. in 1987 and TD 71m. in 1988. Output of olive oil in 1991/92 reached a record 280,000 tons, falling to less than half this tonnage in the following year. Exports of olive oil rose from 96,473 tons (worth TD 158.4m.) in 1992 to 122,630 tons (worth TD 179.1m.) in 1993. Radical reforms of the export marketing system for olive oil included the ending in 1994 of a requirement to negotiate all export contracts through the industry's national marketing board. In the 1993/94 season olive oil production totalled 210,000 tons. It then fell sharply to 75,000 tons in 1994/95 and declined further to between 60,000 and 70,000 tons in 1995/96 because of continuing drought conditions. Olive oil output in 1996/97 reached a record 310,000 tons, and a sharp increase in olive oil exports helped to boost agricultural and food exports during that year. There had been no exports of olive oil in the first half of 1996 as a result of the poor harvest of 1995/96. However, poor rains in early 1997 reduced olive oil production in 1997/98 to an estimated 95,000 tons. Production during the 1998/99 season is estimated at 200,000 tons and exports at 110,000 tons. Annual domestic consumption of olive oil is around 50,000–60,000 tons, and the bulk of exports are to the EU.

Citrus fruits are grown on the north-eastern coast. Production declined from 220,000 metric tons in 1980/81 to 165,000 tons in 1981/82. The annual crop rose to around 250,000 tons in 1985/86 and 1986/87. In 1992/93 citrus production totalled 281,000 tons, and in 1993 exports totalled 23,640 tons, worth TD 9.6m. Production then declined to 210,000 tons in 1993/94 and 194,000 tons in 1994/95. Although output recovered to 221,000 tons in 1995/96, there was a decline in production to 211,000 tons in the 1996/97 harvest, with exports totalling only 16,100 tons (a level below those achieved during the previous two seasons). Output was estimated to have risen to 229,000 tons in 1997/98 and the Ministry of Agriculture announced plans to increase production to 350,000 tons during the next 10 years. Tunisia's production of dates totalled 81,200 tons in 1990, 74,700 tons in 1991 and 74,800 tons in 1992, with average annual exports of 18,200 tons over the same period. Date exports of 18,510 tons in 1993 (in which year production totalled 90,000 tons) were worth TD 47.5m. Date production declined to 86,000 tons in 1994 (worth TD 55.5m.). There was a fall of about 12% in the 1996 date harvest (compared with a 13.5% increase in the previous year), output totalling 74,000 tons. Production in 1997/98 was estimated at a record 93,000 tons, with date exports expected to exceed the 21,000 tons recorded in 1996/97. Production of sugar beet was 291,000 tons in 1992 and totalled 300,000 tons in 1996. A sugar refinery at Béja is able to process 1,850 tons per day. A second refinery, at Ben Bechir in Jendouba governorate, was commissioned in 1983, with an annual capacity of 40,000 tons of sugar. Spending on sugar imports totalled $91.5m. in 1994 and $72.7m. in 1995. Other crops include tomatoes, chillies and peppers, melons, watermelons and almonds.

In 1996, according to FAO estimates, Tunisia's livestock included 1.3m. goats, 6.4m. sheep, 700,000 cattle and 39m. poultry (which produced 63,000 metric tons of eggs). During the drought in 1987–88 the Government introduced measures to protect livestock, including the distribution of state-subsidized fodder to farmers, a reduction of the price of animal feedstuffs, a programme to import lucerne and bran, and a vaccination campaign.

The fishing industry employs about 60,000 people. Sfax is the main centre of the industry, which has received substantial state investment in recent years, including finance for the modernization of the fishing fleet, the upgrading of some 30 fishing ports, and for research and training. The Government has also sought to reduce overfishing in the gulf of Gabès by developing fishing grounds in the north. The total catch rose steadily from 31,686 metric tons in 1975 to 102,570 tons in 1988, but declined steadily to 87,617 tons in 1991, mainly as a result of pollution and overfishing in the Gulf of Gabès. The total catch fell from 88,540 tons in 1992 to 83,353 tons in 1993, increasing to 85,992 tons in 1994, before declining to 83,754 tons in the following year. The total catch rose to 88,000 tons in 1997 and was projected to increase to 110,000 tons in 2001. During the 1990s exports have averaged 14,000 tons with a mean value of TD 80m. ($69m.).

A $69m. forestry development loan was approved by the World Bank in 1993 to finance the planting of trees on 25,000 ha of land, together with related schemes to promote the growth of forestry in Tunisia.

Two institutions have been established to address the problem of Tunisia's insufficient agricultural output. The Agence de Promotion des Investissements Agricoles was created in 1982 to channel funds into productive projects, notably the development of new cash crops. In early 1983 the Banque Nationale du Développement Agricole (BNDA) was founded to ease investment in the agricultural sector. Although fully Tunisian-owned, the BNDA's funds—initially TD 140m.—were subscribed equally by Kuwait and the EC. In 1990 the BNDA and the Banque Nationale de Tunisie (BNT) merged to form a new commercial bank based in the agricultural sector, designated the Banque Nationale Agricole (BNA).

MINERALS

Petroleum, formerly Tunisia's principal source of export earnings, was overtaken as a source of revenue by textiles and agricultural exports in the late 1980s. The collapse of petroleum prices in the mid-1980s resulted in a fall in export earnings from a peak of TD 665m. in 1980 to TD 341m. in 1986, although in 1987 earnings recovered to TD 418m. By 1990 exports of hydrocarbons were worth TD 533.4m., but in 1991, despite a 15% increase in oil output, export revenues fell to TD 489.8m., against energy imports of TD 365.8m. (TD 429.4m. in 1990). In 1992 there was a surplus of TD 141.3m. in energy-sector trade (exports TD 538.4m., imports TD 397.1m.), but in 1993 export earnings fell by 19.4% to TD 434.2m., some TD 22.9m. below spending on imports (up 15.1% to TD 457.1m.). Energy exports totalled TD 442m. in 1994, TD 437m. in 1995 and TD 563m. in 1996, when they accounted for 10% of the value of total exports. The Government expected energy exports to remain at around this level until 1999, but to decline to TD 367m. in 2000 and to TD 320m. in 2001, when they were forecast to account for only 4% of the value of total exports. In 1996 imports of petroleum and petroleum products totalled $482.4m.; imports of gas totalled $148.7m.

Intensive exploration for petroleum has been carried out in Tunisia since the discovery of hydrocarbons in neighbouring Algeria. In May 1964 a subsidiary of Ente Nazionale Idrocarburi (ENI), the Italian state energy enterprise, discovered petroleum at al-Borma, in southern Tunisia, near the Algerian border. When the discovery was announced, the Tunisian Government took a 50% share in the al-Borma operating company. The crude petroleum extracted from the al-Borma oilfield is transported to the terminal at La Skhirra on the Gulf of Gabès via a 'spur' pipeline which links with the pipeline from the oilfields at Zarzaitine and Edjeleh, in Algeria. The crude petroleum is then transported from La Skhirra to the refinery at Bizerta.

In 1968 Tunisia's second oilfield came into operation at Douleb, 200 km north of al-Borma. A pipeline was subsequently built, connecting the Douleb oilfield to the terminal at La Skhirra. Other oilfields include Tamesmida, on the Algerian border south-west of Douleb, which was joined to the Douleb-La Skhirra pipeline in 1969; and Bihrat and Sidi al-Itayem, both of which began producing in 1972. Important discoveries of petroleum were made off shore at Ashtart, east of Sfax in the Gulf of Gabès, and these deposits accounted for more than one-quarter of Tunisia's total output in the mid-1980s. The Ashtart oilfield was originally operated by Elf Hydrocarbures Tunisie (EHT—a wholly-owned subsidiary of Elf Aquitaine of France) and the Tunisian state oil company, Entreprise Tunisienne d'Activités Pétrolières (ETAP), which also operated the Douleb oilfield. In 1997 EHT was bought by Arco of the USA, which currently has a 50% holding in the Ashtart field. Production at Ashtart, Tunisia's second-largest oilfield with reserves of 800m. barrels, has more than doubled, to 19,000 barrels per day (b/d), as a result of a $200m. development programme which was completed in 1997.

Other new Tunisian oilfields include, in the south, Makhrouga, Larich and Debbech, which are being developed by the Société d'Exploitation des Permis du Sud, FINA of Belgium, and ETAP; the Tazerka field in the Gulf of Hammamet, operated by Shell with AGIP Africa, a subsidiary of ENI, and ETAP; the Isis field in the Gulf of Gabès, for which the concession is held by Shell, Tunirex, Total-CFP and AGIP; the Ezzaouia offshore field, operated by Marathon Oil of the USA; the Rhemoura onshore field, in the Karkemna concession of British Gas (BG) Tunisie; and the Belli field, also operated by Marathon Oil.

A dispute with Libya over demarcation of territorial waters in the Gulf of Gabès, where promising discoveries of petroleum had been made, was settled in February 1982. A ruling by the International Court of Justice (ICJ) delimited the two countries' offshore territories around a boundary approximately 26° east from the land border to latitude 34°10′30″ north, where it deviates 52° east. (In December 1985 Tunisia's application to the ICJ for a revision of its judgment was rejected.) In August 1989 a joint Tunisian-Libyan company was established to exploit the '7 November' oilfield in the Gulf of Gabès. However this company, known as Joint Oil, failed to attract any foreign partners, prompting the Libyan and Tunisian Governments to conclude a detailed agreement in early 1996 clarifying the legal status of the shared oilfield. After 1980, US oil companies began to obtain permits for drilling rights in Tunisia. Promising discoveries included the offshore Cosmos well, near Hammamet, located by EHT, gas and condensate discoveries in the Douz area, found by the US company Amoco, the el-Bibane well in the extreme south, discovered by Marathon Oil, and the two offshore Maamoura wells, near Hammamet, discovered by the Italian company AGIP. In mid-1991 Marathon Oil was given permission to explore for oil and gas in a new area of 1,760 sq km at Grombalia, which is situated close to the Abiod gas-production structure, south-east of Tunis; Marathon Petroleum Grombalia, a new subsidiary of Marathon Oil, will finance all exploration costs. In 1985 the Government improved the terms of its petroleum exploration law to encourage prospecting companies to develop new discoveries. In 1986, however, the collapse of energy prices prompted many oil companies to reduce the scale of their operations, and the Government was forced to introduce an even more favourable law in April 1987. In 1990 23 foreign companies held permits for drilling rights in Tunisia, attracted by the range of financial incentives offered by the Government to encourage exploration and development. By the late 1990s, despite the absence of a major oil strike for many years, foreign oil companies remained interested in Tunisia and at the end of 1997 Pluspetrol of Argentina, Anadarko Petroleum Corpn of the USA, AGIP of Italy and Mobil of the USA were among the companies engaged in exploration work. In early 1998 Germany's Preussag Energie announced the discovery of oil in a second well in the Guebiba field in which it had a 49% holding (the remainder being held by ETAP). In 1997 Preussag bought the oil interests of BG Tunisie in Guebiba along with four other small onshore fields, namely Al Ain, Gremda, Rhemoura and El Hajeb, as well as the Cercina offshore field. Production at the offshore al-Biban field began in March 1998, operated by Centurion Energy International of Canada. The field, with estimated recoveable reserves of 6m. barrels of oil, is currently producing 4,000 b/d and crude oil exports began in May. In April Petro-Canada signed a two-year exploration agreement for Tunisia's Berkane basin, working jointly with ETAP. The area is relatively unexplored, but substantial oil discoveries have been made recently in adjacent areas in Algeria. As part of an agreement signed in 1997, Tunisia and Libya were to develop the 'November 7' oilfield, which was estimated to contain recoverable reserves of 260m.–300m. barrels. Tunisia also agreed to import 1m. tons a year of crude oil and 580,000 tons of refined oil products from Libya.

At 1 January 1998 Tunisia's reserves of petroleum were estimated at 300m. barrels, sufficient to maintain output (at 1997 levels) for 9.4 years. Production has exceeded 4m. metric tons per year since 1970, and reached a peak level of 5.6m. tons

in 1980. Production fell to 5.4m. tons in 1981 and to 5.1m. tons in 1982, but rose again to 5.6m. tons in 1983 because of increased production from Ashtart. Production fell to 5.0m. tons in 1987, and declined to 4.5m. tons in 1990. In 1991 production from the Ezzaouia field reversed the downward trend of oil production, which by mid-1992 was running at 120,000 b/d, as against domestic consumption of 90,000 b/d. It was hoped that further exploration, and the development of known deposits, might result in an increase in output from the mid-1990s. Total output in 1992 was 5.2m. tons. ETAP concluded oil exploration agreements with 10 companies (three of them locally owned) in 1993 and aimed to reach a similar number of agreements in 1994. Tunisia's oil output totalled 4.7m. tons in 1993, 4.4m. tons in 1994 and 4.3m. tons in 1995. Spending on exploration declined from $123m. in 1992 to $94m. in 1993. Oil output in 1996 totalled 4.2m. tons and increased to 4.3m. tons in 1997 (90,000 b/d).

Tunisia's main petroleum refinery, at Bizerta, has a capacity of 1.7m. metric tons per year. Actual production has not approached rated capacity, however, and Tunisia has been forced to import around 50% of its needs, estimated to be about 1.9m. tons in 1986. Plans to double the capacity of the Bizerta refinery, suspended since 1989 because of financing difficulties, were once more under active discussion in 1993 (when the cost of the project was estimated at $77m.). However, an alternative project has since been conceived, and in March 1997 the Government selected the local Offshore-Mediterranean Refining Company (ORC) to establish and operate a new refinery at La Skhirra. The refinery's ultimate capacity will be 6m. tons a year, but construction may well be in phases.

Tunisia became a member of the Organization of Arab Petroleum Exporting Countries (OAPEC) in March 1982. In 1986, however, Tunisia withdrew from the organization, owing to the decline in the country's oil output. In September 1995 the Groupement des Industries Petrolières, a company formed by a group of Libyan private investors, signed a draft agreement to establish a 6m.-tons-a-year refinery at La Skhirra at a cost of $500m. It was anticipated that some 80% of the refinery's output would be exported.

In February 1998 an attempt by the Government to sell shares in Tunisia Oil Fields Contractors, in which the state had a majority holding, failed to meet an acceptable price and tenders were reissued in July. The Société d'Assistance et de Ravitaillement Offshore Tunisie and the Société Nationale de Distribution du Pétrole were among other state-owned companies to be offered for sale in 1998 as part of the Government's accelerated privatization programme (see above).

Tunisia's reserves of natural gas are estimated at about 100,000m. cu m. Almost all of the country's gas production originally came from the al-Borma field until 1995, when the offshore Miskar field was brought on stream by BG Tunisie, which invested $600m. to develop the field, the biggest foreign investment ever made in the country. The Miskar project, completed in early 1997, is now the country's major gasfield, supplying 80% of Tunisia's daily gas demand. BG Tunisie is under contract to deliver 4.5m. cu m of gas a day to the Société Tunisienne d'Electricité et du Gaz (STEG) for the first five years, rising to 5.7m. cu m per day thereafter. The 4.5m. cu m daily delivery rate was achieved on a sustained basis from June 1996, and by early 1998 production had reached 5.2 m. cu m per day. In March 1998 it was reported that BG was seeking a review of the price formula in its agreement with STEG to supply gas from the Miskar field. The gas price is currently indexed to that of high-sulphur fuel oil, which has fallen sharply along with other oil prices and has reduced BG's returns from the Miskar project. In May BG announced that it was prepared to invest $400m. in the development of a new offshore gas field, Hasdrubal, located just south of the Miskar field. Initial discoveries suggested that future production from the Hasdrubal field could average 5m. cu m per day. It was reported that a final decision was likely to be made by the end of 1998, subject to the fiscal and pricing terms set by the new hydrocarbons law. Both the Miskar and Hasdrubal fields are part of BG Tunisie's Amilcar permit, held jointly with ETAP. In 1997 CMS Nomeco International of the USA announced a $30m. investment programme to develop the El Franig and Baguel gasfields in the south-west of the country, where gas and condensates estimated at 1.7m. tons of oil equivalent have been discovered. The development programme was reported to include the construction of a processing and separation plant and a 155-km pipeline to link the fields to the national pipeline grid. The fields are owned jointly by Nomeco and ETAP. In early 1998 Preussag Energie of Germany announced that it was to develop the offshore Chergui gasfield in the Gulf of Gabès where recoverable reserves were estimated at 2,000m cu m of natural gas. Tunisia's total gas production rose to 1,300m. cu m during the first six months of 1997, a 19% increase on the same period for 1996. The Transmed gas pipeline constructed to supply Algerian natural gas to Italy crosses Tunisia and became operational in 1983. Tunisia's royalty was equivalent to 5.25% of all gas transported in the pipeline. Liftings from the pipeline became a new source of natural gas for STEG. Work to expand the annual capacity of the Transmed pipeline from 16,000m. cu m to 24,000m. cu m was completed during 1997. As part of an agreement signed in 1997, Tunisia and Libya are to build a gas pipeline to supply southern Tunisia with Libyan gas.

Tunisia is the world's fourth-largest producer of calcium phosphates, which are chiefly mined from six large deposits in central Tunisia. Output of calcium phosphates totalled 5.6m. metric tons in 1994. Phosphates and phosphatic fertilizers have long been an important source of export revenue. After remaining fairly static at 3.0m.–3.8m. tons per year in 1970–78, production of natural phosphates increased steadily after 1979, when it exceeded 4.1m. tons. Annual phosphate output reached a peak of 5.9m. tons in 1983, fell to 4.5m. tons in 1985, but recovered to 5.8m. tons in 1986 and to slightly more than 6m. tons annually in 1987–89. The phosphate sector was affected by low world prices in 1986, and a recovery plan was implemented, aiming to reduce production costs and to increase output to 6m. tons annually in 1986–88. Government policy is to develop new resources and to concentrate efforts on the local manufacture of highly profitable fertilizer and phosphoric acid. Only about 25% of phosphate output is exported as raw phosphate rock, and production of triple superphosphate (TSP) and phosphoric acid increased dramatically in the early 1980s. Output of TSP reached 956,800 tons in 1986, an increase of more than 400,000 tons in 10 years, and 985,800 tons in 1987, while production of phosphoric acid rose from 93,000 tons in 1973—the first year of production—to 593,300 tons in 1987, and to 856,100 tons in 1988. Because the phosphate rock is of low quality, the processing plants use special methods to produce phosphoric acid and phosphatic fertilizers. The Compagnie des Phosphates de Gafsa (CPG), which mines phosphate rock in the Gafsa area, plans to maintain annual production at less than 6m. tons, developing new mines as existing ones become exhausted. Most of the fertilizer plants are at Gabès, but in 1985 a new plant was opened at M'Dilla, near the Gafsa mines. A new plant to produce superphosphoric acid was due to open at La Skhirra in 1987. However, a project to exploit the phosphate reserves at Sra Ouertane, in the north-west, was postponed, owing to the Government's budgetary problems. In July 1989 Tunisia was granted a loan of $34m. by the Kuwait Fund for Arab Economic Development in order to finance the renovation of its phosphate fertilizer plants.

In 1991 production of raw phosphates fell by 30% compared with 1990, although export revenues fell by only 19%, to TD 14m. Exports of phosphatic fertilizers fell by 4% in 1991, to TD 241m., mainly owing to a 35% shortfall on sales of ammonium nitrate to the Iraqi market. The value of exports of phosphoric acid, however, increased by 27% to TD 156m. The 1991 results reflected continuing problems in the Tunisian phosphates industry, especially within the CPG, as well as the disappearance of traditional markets in Eastern Europe. In 1992 the CPG doubled the volume of its export sales from 425,888 metric tons to 956,109 tons, while its domestic sales (to the state processing company Groupe Chimique) totalled 5.1m. tons. In 1991 the two companies had recorded combined losses of TD 522m. A government restructuring programme, announced in 1993, envisaged plant closures among other rationalization measures, including an eventual merger of the two companies. The CPG's phosphate production totalled 6.1m. tons in 1992 and 6.4m. tons in 1993 (85% from underground mines and the balance from surface mines). Tunisia's exports of phosphorus pentoxide and phosphoric acid were worth TD 166.2m. in 1994, while exports

of phosphatic fertilizers totalled TD 112.1m. Initiatives to gain new export outlets in 1994 included co-operation with Brazilian agricultural research with a view to increasing that country's imports of Tunisian phosphates from 90,000 tons to 170,000 tons per year. Production of raw phosphate by the CPG reached 7.2m. tons in 1997, of which some 1.3m. tons were exported and the remainder was sold to Groupe Chimique for conversion into phosphoric acid and fertilizers.

Production of iron ore has steadily declined since independence, when it was more than 1m. metric tons per year. Output was 310,000 tons (gross weight) per year during 1984–86, compared with 275,000 tons in 1982 and 400,000 tons in 1981. In 1995 output was 225,000 tons. The ore's iron content is approximately 53%.

Lead is mined in the northern coastal region, and zinc in the north-west. In 1980 the Société Tunisienne d'Expansion Minière announced a $50m. investment programme to expand production. Output of zinc concentrates totalled 17,400 metric tons in 1989, but fell to 9,400 tons in 1991. Production declined to 4,100 tons in 1992 and 1,300 tons in 1993 before rising to 12,900 tons in 1994, and to 44,200 in 1995. Output of lead concentrates, which totalled 14,000 tons in 1980, has been falling steadily, and reached only 3,100 tons in 1986, increasing to 3,400 tons in 1987 before declining to 1,300 tons in 1991. Production totalled 1,400 tons in 1992 and 500 tons in 1993, increasing to 2,000 tons in 1994, and to 7,000 tons in 1995. The Bougrine lead and zinc mine, operated by the Société Minière de Bougrine (SMB), the country's first private mine, opened in 1994 after an investment of $80m., but was closed in October 1996 as a result of financial problems. In 1997 Inmet Mining Corpn of Canada sold its 49% holding in SMB to Breakwater Resources of Canada, which announced plans to invest $7m. to reopen the mine in 1998. Extractable reserves were estimated at 2.8m. tons. A joint Tunisian-Bulgarian mining company was formed in January 1990 to exploit lead and zinc mines in Lahdoum and Siliana. The Government postponed plans to exploit the country's uranium deposits until the world market improves. A pilot production plant was built at Gabès. About 90% of the salt that the Compagnie Générale des Salines de Tunisie produces (320,000–350,000 tons per year) is exported, chiefly to Japan.

INDUSTRY

Tunisia's industrial sector ranges from the traditional activities, such as textiles and leather, to 'downstream' industries based on the country's phosphate reserves. During the period of the 1973–76 Plan, the industrial sector grew by 7.4% instead of the 10.2% planned. In 1977 the sector grew by only 4.2%, mainly because of a sharp fall in agri-business and the food processing industries. Apart from a zero rate of growth in the textile industries, the sector's performance improved in 1978, with a 10.6% growth rate, mainly because of higher output in three sectors: construction materials, mechanical and electrical industries. The growth rate of manufacturing industries fell to 3% in 1982, but rose to around 9% per year in 1983, 1984 and 1985, in accordance with the 1982–86 Development Plan. In the late 1980s private sector small and medium-sized businesses became increasingly prominent, and the Government made considerable progress in attracting foreign venture capital to the industrial sector, as well as in promoting Tunisia as a regional centre for high technology. Figures issued by the Société de Participation et de Promotion des Investissements (SPPI) in early 1992 showed that in 1990–91 the SPPI had supported 22 joint venture projects involving total investment of TD 34m. According to the Agence de Promotion des Investissements (API), declarations of investment intent by local and international companies were 2% higher in 1991 than in 1990, although the impact of the Gulf crisis had contributed to a 20% decline in foreign investment applications in 1991. In June 1992 the new post of Minister of International Co-operation and Foreign Investment was created to signal the Government's commitment to industrial expansion. In 1992 new foreign investment in Tunisian manufacturing industry was estimated at TD 52m., out of total foreign investment of TD 160m. In 1996, however, new foreign investment in manufacturing industry was only TD 48m., out of total foreign direct investment of TD 296m., with the bulk of foreign investment going to the energy sector. In 1997 the Minister of International Co-operation and Foreign Investment reported that total foreign direct investment had risen to TD 310m., and while two-thirds was directed to the energy sector, foreign investment in manufacturing industry had risen significantly. Much of the new investment was reported to be in the high technology sector, particularly electronics. Officials forecast strong growth in foreign direct investment during 1998, with investment in textiles increasing by 50%. By 1996 manufacturing industry's share of GDP was 20.7%. During 1997 the manufacturing sector grew by 7%, stimulated by a rise in investment and the strong expansion of exports of textiles and mechanical and electrical goods. Manufacturing GDP increased by an annual average of 3.7% in 1980–90, and by 5.2% in 1990–96.

During the 1982–86 Development Plan, the Government concentrated on large investment projects, until it was forced by budgetary constraints to alter its strategy in 1986. The 1987–91 Plan reflected this change, with more investment in small projects and a greater emphasis on attracting private investment into industry. Exports of industrial goods (excluding energy) rose steadily in the period of the 1987–91 Plan, reaching TD 1,812.6m. in 1990. Textiles and leather contributed TD 1,325m. to this total, mechanical and electrical items TD 416.4m., and other industries TD 254.7m. Under the 1992–96 Plan, the 6% annual GDP growth target was to be achieved mainly by means of expansion in the manufacturing and services sector. Exports from the manufacturing sector rose from TD 2,240m. in 1992 (out of total exports of TD 3,550m.) to TD 3,794m. in 1996 (out of total exports of TD 5,372m.). In 1992 textiles and leather contributed TD 1,546m., mechanical and electrical goods TD 433m. and other industries TD 261m. In 1996 textiles and leather contributed TD 2,743m., mechanical and electrical goods TD 675m. and other industries TD 376m. Exports from this sector were forecast to grow from TD 3,985m. in 1997 (out of total exports of TD 5,945m.) to TD 6,306m. in 2001 (out of total exports of TD 8,803m.).

More than one-half of Tunisia's industry is located in Tunis. Other industrial centres are Sousse, Sfax, Gabès, Bizerta, Gafsa, Béja and Kasserine. Major new industrial estates were under development near Tunis and Sfax in 1994. In the past, manufacturing tended to concentrate on processing raw materials, especially foodstuffs, and was aimed at meeting local demand. In an attempt to attract foreign investment and to promote exports, the Government ratified a new industrial investment code during 1987. This law simplified and extended the provisions in the legislation of 1973 and 1981. A new code, adopted in November 1989, laid down guidelines for the activities of service companies, the aim being to increase private-sector investment; by mid-1992 some 600 new companies had been established in the services sector. Other government initiatives included the approval of special legislation early in 1992 for the creation of 'offshore' free-trade zones for new industries. Site preparation for the 46-ha Bizerta zone began in late 1993, with a view to completing the installation of infrastructure by 1996. The aim of the zone's shareholders (42% banks, 32% public-sector companies, 26% private-sector companies) was to attract TD 60m. of new investment from Europe, North America and South-East Asia and to generate TD 120m. of exports per year. In mid-1996 the Bizerta zone was on course to open by early 1997, initially with 20 businesses (10 industrial companies, four trading companies and six banks) on site. A free-trade zone at Zarzis (near Tunisia's border with Libya) was undergoing expansion from 12 ha to 20 ha in the second half of 1996, in response to strong demand for accommodation from manufacturing, trading and services companies. It was announced in February 1997 that the Government intended to invite private investors to equip and operate three industrial zones at sites in Bizerta, Menzel Bourguiba and M'Saken. The plan was part of a larger programme to establish 26 industrial zones throughout the country under the ninth five-year Plan covering 1997–2001 (see Planning). This would include 16 zones in coastal regions, five in central Tunisia and one in the interior. A shortage of prepared sites for manufacturing industry was reported to have been a factor in discouraging industrial expansion and thwarting efforts to increase foreign investment in this sector.

The textiles sector (including leather) contributed 21% of domestic manufacturing value in 1989 (compared with 18% in 1970) and accounted for 38.6% of total export value in 1991. By 1993 an estimated 216,000 workers were employed by 1,585 textile companies, about 500 of which were wholly export-orientated businesses. In 1993 textiles exports earned TD 1,773m. and accounted for some 70% of all exports of manufactured goods and 47% of total exports. By 1996 export earnings from textiles had risen to TD 2,743m., and textiles accounted for 72% of all exports of manufactured goods and 51% of all exports. Textiles were forecast to remain Tunisia's leading export and to increase their share of total exports to 54% by 2001. Earnings from textile exports were forecast to rise from TD 3,020m. in 1997 to TD 4,780m. in 2001. However, this performance would only be achieved if Tunisia could successfully meet growing competition from Asian and East European exporters in its vitally important markets in France, Germany and Italy. An increase in the minimum wage by 5% in November 1997 meant that Tunisian labour costs were then equal to or even greater than in countries such as Turkey, Morocco and Portugal, which could also affect the country's competitiveness. In early 1998 it was reported that Hualon, a Taiwanese textile company, was to build a $377m. integrated polyester plant in Tunisia, producing polyester granules, fibre, cloth and clothing for export to Europe.

In order of importance, the other leading sectors are: construction materials, mechanical and electro-mechanical, chemicals, and paper and wood. Tunisia also manufactures glass, furniture, batteries, paint and varnish, and rubber goods. Ceramics are made at Nabeul, while sugar is refined at Béja and carpets are hand-woven at Kairouan. A cellulose factory and paper pulp plant at Kasserine uses locally grown esparto grass. The metallurgical, mechanical and electrical industries are expanding steadily. The al-Fouladh steel complex at Menzel Bourguiba, near Bizerta, is supplied with iron ore from Tamera and Djerissa. It has an annual capacity of 175,000 metric tons of iron bars, wire and small sections. Plans were in progress to increase the complex's capacity to 400,000 tons per year. A further steel mill, with a capacity of 100,000 tons per year, is sited at Bizerta.

In 1983 a farm machinery complex, managed by the Complexe Mécanique de Tunisie, began production. Output will eventually total 2,200 tractors, 6,000 diesel engines, 100 combine harvesters and 700 small farm machines per year. A scheme to manufacture tyres for the local market and for export was commissioned in 1986, with the assistance of an Italian company, Pirelli, the Government having nationalized the largest US investment in Tunisia—the Firestone Tyre and Rubber Co's tyre factory at Menzel Bourguiba in 1980. In early 1988 production of diesel engines was scheduled to begin at a plant being constructed at Sakiet Sidi Youssef, on the Algerian-Tunisian border. The plant, managed by the Société Maghrebine de Fabrication de Moteurs Thermiques, has an annual capacity of 25,000 diesel engines. Later in 1988 it was announced that joint ventures with Mercedes and Volkswagen would be established to produce car components. In November 1991 General Motors of the USA announced the reopening of its joint venture vehicle assembly plant at Kairouan, which was to produce up to 4,000 light commercial vehicles per year for the North African market. Known as Industries Mécaniques Maghrébines, the joint venture had been launched in 1982 but suspended in 1988. Also active in vehicle assembly in Tunisia is Saab-Scania of Sweden. Local assembly of Mercedes-Benz buses, imported from Germany in kit form, began in 1994 at the rate of 60 vehicles per year. In 1995 Tunisia had 50 export-orientated automobile components manufacturers whose combined output was worth an estimated TD 22m. in that year. Although the total value of their output in 1996 rose to TD 28m., this still fell well short of the Government's ambitions for an industry whose development is a priority in Tunisia's industrial strategy. In early 1998 METS, a subsidiary of Germany's Draxlmaier, and Leonische Drahtwerke of Germany both announced plans to expand their production of electrical car components in Tunisia by building new plants at Sousse. In April United Technologies Corpn opened a factory producing wire harnesses for Peugeot's car assembly plant in Spain and announced plans to double output by the end of the year.

In the high technology sector, several computer companies have located operations in Tunisia. Plans for a special 'offshore' high technology zone, to be located in Tunis, were under consideration in mid-1992. By 1993 a 40-ha site near Tunis-Carthage airport had been earmarked for development, and financing of up to $100m. was being sought. Citing successful Malaysian 'technology parks' as its model, the Government regarded the venture as a means of encouraging the transfer of technology, creating jobs for graduates and attracting foreign investment.

Tunisian cement production averaged 4.2m. metric tons per year from 1990 to 1992. Production of cement totalled 4.6m. tons in 1996. Several new cement plants are planned or under construction, while existing ones are being expanded. A cement works at Oum al-Khelil, built by Fives-Cail Babcock of France, started production in 1980. A works at Enifida, constructed by Japan's Kawasaki Heavy Industries, Marubeni Corpn and C. Itoh, was commissioned in 1983. In January 1988 a white cement works at Feriana entered production. The plant, established as a joint project with Algeria, has an annual capacity of 210,000 tons, enough to meet both domestic and Algerian needs. In early 1998 two state-owned cement plants, the Société des Ciments d'Enfida (with a capacity of 1.2m. tons of cement per year) and the Société des Ciments de Jebel Oust (with a capacity of 1m. tons of cement per year) were offered for sale as part of the Government's privatization programme; three other cement plants, the Société des Ciments de Bizerte, Société des Ciments de Tajérouine and the Société des Ciments de Gabès were expected to be sold during 1998–99.

The chemical industry is receiving special attention from the Government, its share of industrial output having fallen from 13% in 1970 to 9% in 1989. The principal activity within this sector is the processing of phosphate rock into phosphatic fertilizers and phosphoric acid by the state-owned Industries Chimiques Maghrébines at Gabès and by 'mixed' (partly state-owned) companies at Sfax. In 1988 reforms for the chemical sector were announced, including consolidation of companies' capital, long-term restructuring of their debts and, possibly, plant closures. Paint, glue and detergents are also manufactured. Two works, each producing 650 metric tons of wet lime per day, are to be built at Thala and Mezuna, in the south.

Under the terms of Tunisia's association agreement with the EU, signed in July 1995 and formally implemented in March 1998, Tunisia will dismantle trade barriers to EU industrial goods in stages over a 12-year period; barriers to those products which would be most competitive with Tunisian manufactured goods were to be phased out over the full period. The Ministry of Industry estimated that as many as 2,000 companies could collapse as a result of increased competition from the EU unless efforts were made to improve productivity and the quality of their goods. Almost two-thirds of the 384 firms that applied for help from SOS Entreprise, a government body established in 1995 to assist ailing companies, were in the manufacturing sector. The vast majority were family-run businesses, suffering from poor management, a shortage of capital, low levels of training and outdated technology. The EU pledged to provide financial support to Tunisia for adjustment programmes designed to prepare the manufacturing industry for competition from EU member states. These included a 'mise à niveau' programme of industrial modernization to help private-sector firms reform their management and production processes to become competitive with European manufacturers. The programme planned to modernize 2,000 companies by 2001. In addition to receiving financial support from the EU, the programme was also funded by the World Bank and by two Tunisian state funds, the Fonds de Promotion et de Maîtrise de Technologie and the Fonds pour le Développement de la Compétitivité Industrielle. By early 1998 the Comité de Pilotage had approved the modernization plans of 218 companies, mainly manufacturing textiles, involving a total investment of TD 580m., and another 298 companies had registered to take part in the programme. In April the EU agreed a grant of TD 12.5m. ($10.7m.) for the 'mise à niveau' project and a further grant of TD 12.5m. to support the privatization of state-owned companies on condition that the Government's divestment programme is improved and accelerated. In May the Minister of Economic Development pledged to advance the programme and it was announced that more than 60 companies would be offered for sale by the end of 1999. Among the first companies to be sold were two large cement factories.

In early 1998 it was reported that the Government planned to strengthen craft industries, which currently employ some 220,000 workers, account for 3% of GDP and earn TD 177m. in export revenue. A training commission was to be established, and improvements made to the quality and diversity of products, to marketing, and to the provision of loans.

Production of electricity for public use was 4,536m. kWh in 1989, compared with 2,429m. kWh in 1980. Most of this was generated by thermal means; hydroelectric power is of lesser importance. The Government prepared ambitious plans for new generating units in the early 1980s. However, implementation of these plans was postponed, owing to budgetary constraints and a fall in demand, and funding was reallocated to development of the power distribution network. In the light of the economic upturn, which followed the Gulf crisis, the Government confirmed, in June 1992, that the British/French GEC Alsthom group had been contracted to build a 350-MW combined-cycle power station at Sousse, at an estimated cost of $250m. Completion of this plant (scheduled for late 1995) would raise Tunisia's total installed capacity to 1,680 MW. At the end of 1997 the General Electric Co of the USA completed the installation of two 120-MW gas turbines at the new Bir M'Cherga power station and won the contract to supply and install a 120-MW gas turbine at the Bouchemma power station near Gabès. At the same time ETAP announced that it was building a 16-MW power station on the Ezzaouia oilfield using gas that is currently flared. The electricity generated would be sold to STEG. The national electricity grid served over 75% of the country in 1994, and was due to provide 90% coverage by 1996 if current planning targets for rural electrification were met. In March 1996 legislation was introduced to end STEG's monopoly on power generation, current government policy being to open up power-station construction, operation and ownership to private investors. In early 1998 Carthage Power Co, a consortium of Community Energy Alternatives of the USA, Marubeni Corpn of Japan and Sithes Energies, a Franco-Japanese group, was awarded the contract for the country's first private power station at Radès. The 300–500-MW combined-cyle plant, which would run on natural gas and fuel oil, was due to start production in 2001. Carthage Power would build, own and operate the new plant and sell electricity to STEG, which retained its monopoly on prices and distribution. The projected growth rate of Tunisian electricity demand in the second half of the 1990s was 7% to 8% per annum. Production of electricity in 1996 totalled 7,553m. kWh, 90.7% of which was generated by STEG. Tunisia and Libya agreed to a 225-kV link between their electricity grids, to be part-financed by the Arab Fund for Economic and Social Development. In March 1998 contractors submitted bids for the project, which would include the construction of a new substation, the expansion of six others and a 700-km overhead line, most of which would be on Tunisian territory.

In late 1997 the Agence de Maîtrise de l'Energie announced plans to install 1m. sq m of solar panels to generate power equivalent to 120,000 tons of oil by 2010. A pilot project involving the installation of 50,000 sq m of solar panels was being funded by the International Fund for the Environment.

TRANSPORT AND COMMUNICATIONS

Tunisia inherited a relatively modern system of road and rail communications from the period of colonial rule. Substantial work is being carried out to modernize and extend the existing highway and railway networks. In mid-1991 it was announced that construction work on the motorway from Hammamet to M'Saken was due for completion by the end of 1993. By mid-1993 some 31 km (out of 90 km) of the road remained to be completed. In 1995 the Government announced a $88.7m. programme (including $51.5m. loaned by the World Bank) to improve over 1,000 km of rural roads. After 1995 the Government's policy on motorway building was to seek private-sector financing for the construction of toll roads. It was intended that public-sector investment should be channelled into the maintenance and improvement of existing roads, some 500 km of roads being scheduled for upgrading in 1996. In 1980 work began on the 30-km first phase of the Tunis city railway. A five-line 'metro' transport system was in operation in 1996; further lines were under construction. In early 1998 it was reported that the Government was planning to allow the state railway company, the Société Nationale des Chemins de Fer Tunisiens (SNCFT), to operate under a concession, with the state retaining control over track. SNCFT would be expected to cover its costs and would only receive state subsidies on a limited number of loss-making services. At the same time the European Investment Bank (EIB) announced a loan of ECU 25m. to help finance the modernization of the country's main railway line linking Tunis to Sfax.

There are international airports at Tunis-Carthage, Djerba, Monastir, Sfax, Tabarka, Thyna and Tozeur. The second phase of the Tunis-Carthage airport expansion project, to increase passenger capacity from 3.5m. to 4.5m. per year, was completed in April 1998. The country's airports handled 8m. passengers in 1997, an increase of 12.5% over 1996 as a result of a rise in the number of foreign tourists. The national airline, TunisAir, carried 3m. passengers in 1997. In 1995 the state's 85% shareholding in the company was reduced to 45.2% as part of the Government's privatization programme, and in mid-1995 the company announced that it would offer 20% of its capital to public subscription. In May 1998 TunisAir was listed for further privatization. The company, which recorded improved profits of TD 27m. ($24m.) in 1997, brought forward its plans to update its fleet and placed orders for 14 new aircraft with Airbus and Boeing; deliveries were due to begin in 1998. Its fleet currently comprises 24 aircraft.The state-owned shipping company, the Compagnie Tunisienne de Navigation (CTN), began operating in 1971 and carried around 25% of total trade in 1985. Although the Government announced in mid-1995 that it wanted to privatize the company, no action was taken. The CTN has not been profitable and in recent years has begun a restructuring programme, abandoning non-profitable routes and offering incentives to reduce the workforce by one-third. It has also started renewing its fleet. In April 1998 it was reported that the Government was considering several ways of opening the CTN to private capital, and was understood to favour the establishment of a holding company in partnership with private investors. In early 1984 a contract was awarded to a Turkish firm for the expansion of the port at Gabès. A new commercial port at Zarzis, near Djerba, was constructed shortly afterwards. In May 1990 the World Bank agreed to provide a loan of $17m. towards rural road improvement, and $80m. towards the development of railways and ports. In March 1992 the Office des Ports Nationaux Tunisiens announced a project to upgrade facilities in the Tunis-Goulette-Radès area. Following criticism from the business community about the inefficiency of Tunisian ports and the consequent long delays in handling cargo, in late 1997 the government stated that it planned to involve the private sector in port management and cargo handling, thereby ending the monopolies of the state-owned Office des Ports Nationaux Tunisiens and the Société Tunisienne d'Acconage et de Manutention. Under the 1997–2000 Development Plan, investment of TD 4,600m. ($4,000m.) was projected for the transport sector, including finance for the construction of 1,500 km of new roads, the extension of Tunis, Monastir and Djerba airports and the creation of a second railtrack between Tunis and Sousse.

Investment of some TD 1,500m. ($1,300m.) was allocated to the telecommunications sector under the 1997–2001 Development Plan, with the aim of increasing the number of telephone lines to 1m. In early 1998 the country's first global standard for mobiles (GSM) cellular phone system, installed by Alcatel of France for the state telecommunications company, Tunisie Télécom (at a cost of $20m.), started operating for 30,000 subscribers in the Tunis-Nabeul-Hammamet region. The service was expected to have been extended to all urban, industrial and tourist areas from Bizerta in the north to Djerba in the south by late 1998. The network was to be expanded to reach a capacity of 200,000 lines by 2001. In May 1998 the Government announced the privatization of the state telecommunications engineering company, Société Tunisienne d'Entreprises de Télécommunications; 40.6% of shares were to be offered for sale.

FINANCE AND BUDGET

The Banque Centrale de Tunisie (BCT) is the sole bank of issue of Tunisia's national currency, the dinar, and it performs all the normal central banking functions. On 1 March 1994 a new foreign exchange market opened in Tunis, bringing to an end the BCT monopoly on quoting prices for the dinar against hard currencies. Apart from the commercial banks, the Government has established several development institutions to channel aid

into the economy. The Banque de Développement Economique de Tunisie (BDET) is the largest development bank. There is also a specialist tourism bank, the Banque Nationale de Développement Touristique (BNDT), and an agricultural bank, the BNA, formed from a merger of the BNDA and the BNT. Agricultural aid from the EC is channelled through the BNA. Other development institutions, such as the World Bank, have established credit programmes with the BDET and the BNDT. A major development since 1981 has been the creation of six joint-venture banks with other Arab countries. These are: Banque Tuniso-Koweitienne de Développement, Société Tuniso-Saoudienne d'Investissement et de Développement, Banque de Coopération du Maghreb Arabe, Banque Tunisienne des Emirats et d'Investissement, Banque Tuniso-Qatarie d'Investissement and the Banque Arabe Tuniso-Libyenne pour le Développement et le Commerce Extérieur. In October 1991 it was announced that Tunis was to be the headquarters of the Banque Maghrebine d'Investissement et de Commerce Extérieur, a development bank established by the five members of the Union of the Arab Maghreb (UAM). The Government introduced legislation in 1994 to tighten the regulation of several areas of banking activity, and (in a separate initiative included in the 1994 budget) ordered Tunisian banks to set aside 50% of their profits to cover an estimated $3,000m. of bad debts. Thereafter, additional efforts were made to increase competition, improve efficiency and to bring the banking system up to international standards. Banks have improved their performance but many are still burdened by substantial bad debts. Reform of the banking system remains one of the Government's priorities and bank mergers are being encouraged to create stronger institutions. The Government particularly favoured the merger of less competitive development banks with commercial banks. In early 1998 the merger of the Union Internationale de Banques and the Banque de Tunisie et des Emirats d'Investissement was announced, followed by that of the Société Tunisienne de Banque and the BNDT. Also in 1998 the Banque Tunisienne de Solidarité was established, providing credit for small businesses.

The 'offshore' banking sector was regulated by legislation, enacted in 1976, which placed strict limits on the banks' activities. Offshore banks include Citibank, Tunis International Bank, Union Tunisienne de Banques and Arab African International Bank. Complaints from the offshore banks about lack of business led to reductions in staffing levels and to the withdrawal of National Bank of Abu Dhabi in 1984. These complaints were heeded by the Central Bank and the Ministry of Finance, and in March 1985 they approved the text of a law that was to give offshore banks a greater freedom to do business in the local currency and to participate in dinar treasury operations. The law was approved by the National Assembly towards the end of 1985. In June 1995 Tunisia's first merchant bank, International Maghreb Merchant Bank, began operating with a paid-up capital of TD 3m. Shareholders included the International Finance Corpn, French and Austrian banks, the local Maghreb Finance Group and private Saudi Arabian investors, together with the British-based initiator of the project, London Court Securities. The new bank's aim was to specialize in project and corporate finance and in privatization and stock market activities, intitially within Tunisia but with a view to subsequent expansion into the wider Maghreb region. A second merchant bank, the Banque d'Affaires de Tunisie, opened in 1998, with the Société Tunisienne de Banque as the major shareholder, together with the BDET and banks from Morocco, the United Kingdom, Spain, Italy and France. The new merchant bank specialized in privatization and in the restructuring of company finances. In February the Banque Internationale Arabe de Tunisie raised $40m. through the issue of global depository receipts. This was Tunisia's first international equity offering.

The availability of local savings for investment has meant, firstly, that the need for foreign borrowings to finance development projects has been greatly reduced; and, secondly, that the local financial markets have expanded and become more sophisticated to meet the demand for loans. To encourage domestic savings, interest rates on deposits and loans were raised in September 1977, and the official discount rate increased from 5% to 5.75%. Overall national savings accounted for about 80% of total investment in the fifth Plan (1977–81), compared with a projected 65%. Since the early 1980s, the

Government has been studying various proposals for tax reform, and in July 1988 64 taxes on turnover, production and consumer goods were replaced by a new value-added tax (VAT), which by 1991 was yielding 30% of tax receipts. However, with total tax receipts still only equivalent to 2.4% of GDP, the Government, in late 1991, introduced measures to increase the tax base, including a strengthened inspectorate. Other sources of government income include petroleum and gas revenues, profits from state monopolies and, increasingly, the proceeds from the privatization of state assets. In June 1994 the Government issued five- and 10-year treasury bonds which were open to the public for the first time. In 1996 the scope of VAT was extended to cover all retail activities (including those of small shops), and steps were taken to strengthen the tax inspection and enforcement systems. VAT and other indirect taxes were expected to play an increasingly important revenue-raising role as customs tariffs were progressively reduced under the terms of Tunisia's trade agreement with the EU (see External Trade, below).

In November 1994 a law was introduced to convert the state-run Tunis stock exchange, the Bourse des Valeurs Mobilières, (then dealing actively in only 20 companies' shares) into a private company, regulated by an independent monitoring body. The creation of an independently administered exchange with streamlined trading procedures was expected to facilitate the Government's privatization programme. Shares in various transport, hotel and industrial companies were initially scheduled for sale in the second half of 1995 at the rate of one flotation per month, but this timetable was modified when the market showed signs of over-rapid expansion. Regulations were introduced in mid-1995 to make it easier for foreign investors to do business on the Tunis stock exchange, with the proviso that no quoted company's share capital could be more than 10% foreign-owned without the permission of the Tunisian authorities. (The investment regulations allowed foreign ownership of non-quoted companies' shares to reach 30% before permission was required.) In 1997 the limit on foreign ownership of companies was raised to 49.9%. Yet despite government efforts to stimulate the stock market, by early 1998 only 38 firms were listed, many of them banks, and few foreign investors had shown interest. It was hoped that the acceleration of the privatization of state-owned companies through the stock market during 1998 and 1999 would significantly increase market activity.

Tunisia made use of the Eurocurrency market for the first time in 1977 and obtained a $125m. loan to finance industrial development. In early 1979 a $100m. loan was arranged, through a consortium of international banks, to finance the Tunisian section of the Algeria-Italy gas pipeline. In early 1981 the Compagnie Financière Immobilière et Touristique was able to raise $25m. for seven years at 0.5% above the London interbank offered rate—a very low spread for a developing country. During the period of the 1982–86 Plan, borrowing remained at a relatively high level, although the Government managed to attract concessionary loans for development projects, especially from France and the Federal Republic of Germany. In May 1986 the Government raised $120m. on the international markets, but this proved to be the last international loan before the balance-of-payments crisis in mid-1986.

Under a medium-term IMF-sponsored programme for 1988–91, the Government committed itself to the reduction of the central government deficit, which was to be achieved by liberalizing external trade and pricing mechanisms, and by restructuring and, in some cases, 'privatizing' state enterprises. In addition, as stated above, the Government attempted to enhance its revenue base by implementing various tax reforms. In 1989 the principal objectives of the IMF's three-year extended programme, including the reduction of the central government deficit, had been, in part, achieved. As a reflection of this success, Tunisia requested that the amount of credit available in the three-year EFF be reduced from $275m. to $183m. However, the effects of the 1991 Gulf crisis undermined adjustment efforts, and in June 1991 Tunisia became only the second country ever to request an extension of, and restoration of full access to, the IMF's EFF. This was granted, effectively extending the reform programme for a further year. In mid-1992 it was reported that the Government would not be seeking an IMF facility to replace the EFF, which had recently expired.

Following this extension, in December 1991 the World Bank approved a three-year loan of $250m. in support of Tunisia's restructuring programme, the total cost of which was put at almost $400m. In March 1992 a structural adjustment loan of ECU 40m. was granted by the EC, while the balance of funds required was made available by Japan and the Arab Monetary Fund. In addition, in December 1991 the Tunisian Government took the unprecedented step of issuing treasury bills to finance its budget deficit, while in June 1992 Tunisia raised a syndicated loan of $110m. on the international market. In March 1994 a further loan of ECU 20m. was granted by the EU. The World Bank approved a loan of $280m. in 1998, bringing the total value of its loans to Tunisia during 1996–98 to $750m. World Bank funds support projects in agriculture, health, education, transport, tourism and export promotion. In April 1998 the EU agreed to grant TD 12.5m. to support Tunisia's industrial restructuring programme. The EU pledged a further TD 12.5m. to support an accelerated privatization programme.

The Government's 1991 budget provided for a 10% rise in expenditure, to TD 4,080m., and a deficit of TD 410m., which, in the event, widened to over TD 500m. The 1992 budget envisaged an 11.4% increase in expenditure and a reduction in the deficit to TD 320m. The Five-Year Plan for 1992–96 set as a target the reduction of the budget deficit to 1.2% of GDP. The 1993 budget projected expenditure totalling TD 4,950m. Sources of revenue included TD 330m. ($352m.) in foreign credits, to be extended by the World Bank ($149m.), Japan ($59m.), the African Development Bank ($42.6m.), France ($42.6m.), the USA ($32m.) and Italy ($27m.). The average annual inflation rate in 1987–91 was about 7%, the aim being to reduce the rate to 5% over the period 1992–96. From 8.3% in 1991, the annual rise in the consumer price index fell to 5.8% in 1992 and to 4% in 1993. The 1994 budget provided for expenditure of TD 5,515m., of which 52% was current spending and 19% was capital investment, the remaining 29% being the debt-servicing requirement. Revenue was budgeted as TD 4,312m., leaving a deficit of TD 1,203m. to be financed by government borrowing, 28% of which would come from foreign loans. Over 47% of expenditure was linked to social policy, and spending to alleviate the impact of structural economic reform on the poorer sections of society included TD 230m. in price subsidies for basic commodities. Sectoral spending allocations included TD 304m. for agricultural projects. The 1995 budget provided for total expenditure of TD 6,595m. and total revenue of TD 4,951m., leaving an overall deficit of TD 1,644m. to be financed by government borrowing. Further liberalization measures in 1995 would reduce to 15% the proportion of domestic consumer items subject to retail price control, while there would be a reduction to 9.5% in the proportion of imported goods for which import permits were required. The Government's inflation target for 1995 was 4.5%, compared with recorded inflation of 4.7% in 1994. In May 1995 statutory minimum wages were increased by 4.6%, to TD 132.9 per 40-hour week in industry and to TD 4.5 per day in agriculture. The 1996 budget provided for total expenditure of TD 7,230m. and total revenue of TD 5,235m., leaving a deficit of TD 1,995m. Inflation dropped to 3.7% from 6.3% in 1995. In the budget for 1997, the Government planned a spending increase of 10.8% to TD 8,010m. and a deficit of TD 2,546m. Actual expenditure in 1997 was higher than budgeted (totalling TD 8,200m.) and there was a significant shortfall in revenue. In the budget for 1998 projected spending was increased to TD 9,000m., with revenues forecast to rise to TD 5,700m., leading to an increase in the overall deficit to TD 3,300m. Taxation was expected to account for some 83% of total revenue. Notably, VAT was to be increased by 1%, to 18%, in order to offset the loss of customs revenue following the implementation of Tunisia's trade agreement with the EU. The budget was based on inflation at 3.8% and real GDP growth of 5.4%.

Tunisia's deficit on its balance of trade (see External Trade, below) has normally been offset by earnings from tourism and remittances sent home by Tunisians working abroad, so that the overall position on current payments was roughly in balance until 1975. In that year the fall in petroleum prices and the slump in demand for phosphates widened the visible trade gap so seriously, despite continuing good harvests, that the current balance showed a deficit of TD 227.2m., compared with TD 90.9m. in 1974. Over the next decade, the deficit rose steadily, reaching TD 1,076m. in 1984. A severe cutback on imports reduced the deficit to TD 844m. in 1985, TD 50m. in 1986 and TD 78m. in 1987. In 1988 the trade deficit increased substantially as a result of a poor harvest and a low oil price; but, partly owing to a large increase in receipts from tourism, the current account of the balance of payments recorded a surplus of TD 52m. However, in 1989 the current account registered a deficit of TD 312.5m., equivalent to 3.6% of GDP, as a result of an increase in food imports after severe drought, and in capital goods imports, owing to the recovery of foreign investment. In 1990 the current account deficit widened to TD 580m. because of the negative impact of the Gulf crisis, which also contributed to the further large deficit of TD 527.3m. in 1991. A deterioration in the country's terms of trade contributed to an increase in the current-account deficit to TD 662.3m. in 1992. A current-account deficit of TD 860m. in 1993 was followed by an estimated deficit of TD 839m. in 1994. The current-account deficit increased by 36.7% in 1995, according to IMF figures, representing 4.3% of GDP. However, as a result of a decline in the trade deficit, together with higher receipts from tourism and worker remittances, the current-account deficit was reduced to TD 554m. in 1996, equivalent to 2.9% of GDP. According to government figures, the current-account deficit was held at 2.9% in 1997 and was forecast to fall to 2.8% in 1998. The Government launched a 30,000m.-yen ($295m.) placement on the Japanese bond market in early 1994 to help cover Tunisia's balance-of-payments deficit, having chosen to borrow in yen to obtain a favourable interest rate. Part of this yen borrowing was subsequently swapped into French francs. The Government returned to the Japanese bond market in February, April and September 1995 (to bring its cumulative borrowing from this source to 85,000m. yen—about $870m.) and again in October 1996 and August 1997. In September Tunisia launched its first Yankee bond for $400m. In December 1995 Tunisia sought a $100m. syndicated sovereign loan on the international market, where the response was such that the amount borrowed was doubled to $200m. when the loan was finalized in the following month. A further syndicated loan of $150m. (an amount 50% higher than the Government originally asked for) was signed in September 1996. Almost 600,000 Tunisians were resident abroad (about 80% of them in Europe) in 1993, when remittances from migrant workers amounted to TD 600m. ($588m.), some 18% higher than in 1992. Worker remittances increased from TD 696m. in 1994 to TD 712m. in 1995 and TD 798m. in 1996. The central bank reported that during the first quarter of 1998 the 610,000 Tunisians living abroad remitted $204.2m., compared with $193.2m. for the same period in 1997.

PLANNING

It was not until 1961, when the 10-year perspective plan was formulated, that the Government laid down comprehensive plans for development. The broad lines of policy which had been put forward in the perspective plan were embodied in the first Three-Year Plan (1962–64) and then successive Four-Year Plans (1965–68, 1969–72 and 1973–76). These were followed by successive Five-Year Plans covering 1977–81, 1982–86, 1987–91 and 1992–96. The ninth development plan, covering 1997–2001, was approved by the Council of Ministers in June 1997.

Although Tunisia has relied to a considerable extent on petroleum to underpin economic growth, it has to plan for a future in which it is likely to be a net importer of fuel. Because of petroleum, the country's exports during the 1977–81 Development Plan grew faster, in constant prices, than imports did—by 14.6% per year, compared with import growth of 8.9%. The 1982–86 Plan was designed to introduce the economic adjustments necessary to prepare Tunisia for an era of reduced income from petroleum. Stringent controls were to be maintained on the external debt and the balance of payments, while non-oil exports were to be encouraged, and various incentives given to increase employment. However, most of the Plan's targets were not achieved. Growth in real GDP averaged about 3% per year, instead of the projected figure of 6% per year, and job creation totalled about 200,000, compared with the Plan's target of 270,000. Investment spending rose above the targeted level, contributing to a worrying rise in the current-account deficit and the external debt. The need for revised measures became apparent in 1986, when the collapse of international

petroleum prices coincided with a poor harvest and a bad tourist season. In this situation, the Government brought forward its 1987–91 Plan, which constituted a radical attempt to restructure the economy and to reduce dependence on oil exports. The objectives of the 1987–91 Plan were more modest than those of its predecessors, with annual GDP growth targeted at 4% and job creation at 240,000, compared with the total expected demand of about 345,000 jobs during the Plan period. The various structural reforms, to be implemented with the assistance of the World Bank, were intended to promote non-oil exports, which were expected to increase by 8% per year, compared with the 2% growth rate achieved during 1982–86. One of the major instruments of economic reform has been the devaluation of the dinar, which has been maintained at a rate which competes with the currencies of other Mediterranean exporters, such as Greece, Spain and Portugal. As well as stimulating exports, the depreciation of the currency assists the tourism industry, which has become a major source of foreign exchange.

Investment was estimated to total about TD 10,400m. during the 1987–91 Development Plan, representing a substantial reduction, in real terms, compared with the 1982–86 period. A higher proportion of investment was directed into agriculture (20%, compared with 16% in the 1982–86 Plan). To compensate for reduced state investment, the Government envisaged that 52% of total investment would come from the Tunisian private sector, and also sought to attract TD 6,000m. in external investment support. The 1992–96 Plan was introduced in July 1992 and envisaged total investment of TD 17,400m., of which 52.3% would be generated by the private sector, and the creation of 320,000 jobs. Public expenditure would be focused on health, education, housing and services, with priority for investment in transport and communications, and emphasis would be placed on regional development, particularly in western Tunisia. Also planned were further reductions in subsidies on consumer and other products (which, the Government estimated, could cost TD 2,300m. per year by 1996); the disposal of all state assets except in strategic sectors such as electricity generation; the elimination of price controls on manufactured goods; and the introduction of selective charges for health, education and other services. Assuming the implementation of fundamental reforms (the introduction of free-trade zones and a relaxation of exchange controls, leading to full convertibility of the Tunisian dinar), it was projected that an average GDP growth rate of 6% per year could be attained in the period 1992–96. In reality, GDP grew at about 4.5% per year over the period, and the Government is seeking to improve economic performance on all fronts in the 1997–2001 Development Plan (see below).

There has been a notable change in Tunisian policy regarding foreign private investment since the fall of Ben Salah and Ladgham, who were widely reputed to favour economic policies tending towards socialism. The law of April 1972 provided a package of incentives to attract foreign and also domestic capital to establish manufacturing industries producing solely for export. By 1980 a total of about 250 export-orientated projects had been established under the 1972 decree, employing some 25,000 people. Companies from Germany, France, Belgium and the Netherlands predominated, with about 65% in the textile sector. In 1973 a special organization, the API, was established to centralize investment activities. Legislation was introduced in 1974 to promote investment in domestic-orientated manufacturing. In 1985 the API approved schemes with a total value of TD 504m., compared with a total of TD 583m. in 1984. Of the 1985 total, the largest single allocation was for the manufacture of construction materials, ceramics and glass, which took TD 142m. Mechanical and electrical industries received TD 123m. during the year, and food industries TD 100m. Investments receiving the API's approval created a total of 27,000 jobs in 1985, compared with nearly 30,000 in 1984. The private sector provided nearly two-thirds of the 1985 investment, and created nearly 90% of the jobs. In August 1987 the API was merged with the Centre Nationale d'Etudes and the Agence Foncière Industrielle. The newly-formed API was to conduct feasibility studies, organize industrial training schemes and establish industrial zones. In September 1990 Tunisia created an Employment and Training Bank, financed by the

World Bank, to help the country's labour force to adapt to changing patterns in employment.

A revised foreign investment law which took effect in January 1994 was designed to unify existing sectoral codes, to update legislation relating to investment and to stimulate investment in priority areas, including high-technology and export-orientated industries. Emphasis was placed on the fulfilment of broad policy objectives such as job creation, decentralization and technology transfer. Drafting of the law began in February 1992 as a condition of Tunisia's structural adjustment loan from the World Bank. In June 1995 the Government announced that major infrastructural projects would in future be open to private-sector investment. The first areas to be opened up would be power-station and motorway construction and management. Other areas listed by the Government included water and sewerage systems; desalination plants; solid waste treatment plants and controlled dumping facilities; land reclamation and pollution control schemes; and large-scale tourism developments. In early 1996 the Government was in negotiation with the World Bank over the conditions for obtaining loans of about $250m. per year over a period of three years. The Bank advocated in particular the early implementation of 'a serious programme of privatization'; a radical reform of the banking sector to improve its competitiveness and flexibility; and the removal of many remaining bureaucratic obstacles to foreign investment in Tunisia. In July the Government drafted a list of 112 companies to be offered for privatization and adopted a target of $500m. for sales of state-owned assets over the next three years. The World Bank subsequently announced its approval of three loans: $60m. to establish employment and training services for workers affected by economic restructuring; $38.7m. to strengthen institutions supporting private-sector industries; and $75m. to improve the competitiveness of Tunisian companies during the transition to freer trade with the EU.

In December 1996 the Government announced new measures to encourage foreign investment. The measures, to be implemented during the period 1997–2001, include allowing foreign investors to buy up to 49% of any local company without prior authorization (at present the limit is 10% for companies listed on the Tunis stock exchange and 30% for other companies); simplifying procedures for foreign investment in agricultural joint ventures; opening up engineering and technical consulting to foreign investment; and lowering interest rates on business loans and social welfare contributions by employers. The limit on foreign ownership of companies listed on the stock exchange was raised to 49.9% in 1997. Yet despite efforts to attract foreign investors, the level of investment outside the hydrocarbons sector has proved disappointing. Foreign direct investment fell from TD 544m. in 1994 to TD 313m. in 1995 and to TD 288m. in 1996, of which only TD 92m. was in non-energy sectors. However, in early 1998 the Minister of International Co-operation and Foreign Investment reported that foreign direct investment had increased significantly in 1997, to TD 360m., of which TD 120m. was in non-energy sectors. He predicted a further rise in foreign direct investment in 1998. The Government envisaged foreign direct investment to total $2,300m. between 1997 and 2001, an average of $460m. a year. Foreign direct investment during the first quarter of 1998 was reported to have reached $88.2m., compared with $82.6m. during the same period in 1997.

The 1997–2001 Development Plan has set the following economic targets. GDP is to grow an average 6% in real terms each year, a target which implies average annual growth of 7% in manufacturing and services and 4.3% in agriculture. The unemployment rate, at 15.5% in 1996, is to fall to 13% by 2001, while average inflation over the five-year period is targeted at 3.7%, down from 4.8% in 1992–96. The budget deficit is to be reduced to an average 2.6% of GDP from 3.5% in 1992–96, and the current-account deficit is to narrow to 2.2% of GDP in 2001. External debt (see Foreign Aid) is to increase in absolute terms but fall as a percentage of GDP (to 40.9%, compared with 51.1% in 1996). The investment plan envisages total spending of TD 42,000m. over the five-year period, of which the government budget will provide TD 33,775m.; the remainder is to be funded by external financing.

EXTERNAL TRADE

Tunisia's trade deficit grew steadily during the 1960s and 1970s. The deficit in 1987 totalled TD 738m., compared with TD 892m. in 1986 and TD 844m. in 1985. In 1988, as a result of severe drought and a plague of locusts, the cost of imports rose by 26.2% (with food imports up by 53% on those of 1987) and the trade deficit increased to TD 1,112m. (imports TD 3,167m., exports TD 2,055m.), despite a 16% rise in export revenues. The trade deficit for 1990 was TD 1,800m., which represented a 29% increase over the 1989 level, but in 1991 it narrowed to TD 1,372m., although rising in 1992 to TD 2,121.8m., primarily because of a rise in imports. According to World Bank estimates, the average annual growth rate of exports by value fell from 10.8% in 1965–80 to 4.8% in 1980–90, while the growth of imports showed a sharper decline, from 10.4% in 1965–80 to 1.1% in 1980–90. Exports in 1990 covered only 64% of imports, compared with 67% in 1989. The ratio of exports to imports has remained close to 60% for most of the period since 1960.

Petroleum and its derivatives were the main source of export earnings from the mid-1970s to the mid-1980s. However, the slump in oil prices in 1986 caused export earnings from petroleum to fall from TD 604m. in 1985 to TD 340m. in 1986. Oil was overtaken as the largest export, in terms of value, by textiles, worth TD 389m. in 1986, compared with TD 283m. in 1985. In 1987 oil prices recovered and Tunisian export earnings from petroleum accordingly increased to TD 418m., although declining to TD 331m. in 1988. Exports of crude petroleum were worth a total of TD 506m. in 1989, TD 451m. in 1990, and TD 411m. in 1991. Meanwhile, exports of textiles continued to grow, earning TD 511m. in 1987, rising to TD 1,325m. in 1991. Other major exports include agricultural products (such as seafood, olive oil, dates, citrus fruits and vegetables), leather goods and phosphates.

Tunisia's main imports are machinery, raw cotton and cotton yarn, chemicals and related products, food and live animals, crude petroleum (grades not produced locally) and petroleum products, clothing and accessories, iron and steel, and cereals and cereal preparations. In 1986 imports of capital goods were worth TD 505m., while food imports cost TD 288m. Semi-finished products cost TD 557m. in 1986, and energy imports TD 199m., a substantial reduction from TD 308m. in 1985. In 1987 total imports rose slightly to TD 2,509m., compared with TD 2,308m. in 1986. The value of total imports increased to TD 3,167m. in 1988, to TD 4,151m. in 1989, to TD 4,852m. in 1990 and to TD 4,789m. in 1991.

Under an agreement reached with the EC in January 1976, the import levy on Tunisian olive oil was abolished and tariffs on all other Tunisian agricultural products imported into EC countries were lowered. Nevertheless, Tunisia was disappointed with the way in which the agreement was implemented, and particularly with the delays in lifting the restrictions on imports of olive oil. In June 1977 the EC quota of textiles and clothing imports was reduced. This measure severely affected the Tunisian textile and clothing industries although Tunisia did not, in fact, fulfil its EC quotas in 1978, as a result of a two-month strike in the industry early in 1978. Nevertheless, negotiations on this issue continued into 1979, and in March Tunisia signed an agreement, under pressure from the EC, to limit its textile exports to EC countries in 1979 and 1980. In return, Tunisia sought a five-year freeze on its obligations to eliminate tariff barriers relating to goods imported from the EC. Tunisia registered its anxiety about the possible consequences of the entry of Spain and Portugal into the EC in January 1986, as the two countries are Tunisia's main agricultural competitors. In mid-1985 the Commission of the European Communities announced a plan to guarantee Tunisian exports to the EC at levels prevailing in the early 1980s. In December 1990 Tunisia was one of the states to benefit from a new 'horizontal' trade and co-operation agreement between the EC and Mediterranean non-Community countries. In September 1990 Tunisia had become a contracting party to the General Agreement on Tariffs and Trade (GATT), in a move designed to increase exports to foreign markets.

In 1995 Tunisia exported goods to the value of $5,474.6m. (19.4% up on the 1994 total) and imported goods to the value of $7,903.1m. (21.9% more than in 1994), leaving a visible trade deficit of $2,428.5m. (27.9% higher than in 1994). The 1995 import total was boosted by increased imports of foodstuffs (primarily as a result of Tunisia's continuing drought), chemicals and related products, and basic manufactures. The export total was improved by substantial increases in earnings from machinery and transport equipment, clothing and accessories, and chemicals and related products, which rose by 31.2%, 26.2% and 23.4%, respectively, compared to 1994. Exports of agricultural products declined markedly. The sectoral shares of 1995 export earnings were textiles and leather 47.5%; chemicals and related products 11.9%; machinery and transport equipment 9.4%; agriculture and food products 8.7%; and minerals, fuels and lubricants 8.5%. Of Tunisia's three largest trading partners, France had a surplus of $488.2m. in 1995 (exports to Tunisia $2,024.6m., imports from Tunisia $1,536.4m.); Italy had a surplus of $187.6m. (exports $1,209.0m., imports $1,021.4m.); and Germany had a surplus of $132.7m. (exports £993.7m., imports $861.0m.). Overall, the EU supplied 71.5% of Tunisian imports and bought 79.0% of Tunisian exports in 1995. Trade grew strongly in 1997, with total imports rising from TD 7,543m. in 1996 to TD 8,756m. (an increase of 16.1%), while exports increased from TD 5,372m. to TD 6,148m., a rise of 14.4%). In July 1997 the Government ended its 5% export duty and doubled the term of export licences to two years in order to stimulate exports. The Conseil Supérieur de l'Exportation was created, chaired by President Ben Ali, who stated that it was essential to reduce bureaucratic constraints on exporters. Exports were forecast to rise by an average of 13% a year to total TD 8,803m. ($7,707m.) by 2001, with textiles and leather, together with chemical and phosphate exports, increasing their share of the total and energy exports continuing to decline.

In July 1995 Tunisia signed a free-trade agreement with the EU, scheduled to take effect from the start of 1996. Its main provisions were as follows. EU capital goods and semi-finished goods not manufactured in Tunisia (at present accounting for 12% of Tunisia's imports from the EU) would be exempt from import duty from the date the agreement entered into force. EU exports of specified goods which were also manufactured in Tunisia (at present accounting for 28% of Tunisian imports from the EU) would be subject to a progressive phasing out of import duties over a period of five years after entry into force. Duties on EU exports of goods which were deemed to be 'more sensitive' in the Tunisian economic context (at present accounting for 30% of Tunisian imports from the EU) would be phased out over a period of 12 years. Duties on EU exports of goods which were deemed to be 'most sensitive' (29.5% of current Tunisian imports from the EU) would be maintained for the first five years of the agreement before being phased out over a seven-year period. Duties on traditional handicraft and textile products (constituting 0.5% of current Tunisian imports from the EU) would not be phased out under the agreement. During the 12-year transition period following the agreement's entry into force, Tunisia would have the option of reimposing import duties of up to 25% on EU exports which were considered to threaten emerging industries in Tunisia, provided that such duties did not affect more than 15% of all imports from the EU and were not maintained for more than five years. Tunisia (which already had duty-free access to the EU market for industrial goods) would benefit from a limited relaxation of EU quota and tariff restrictions on some Tunisian agricultural exports, although its olive oil exports to the EU remained subject to existing restrictions. Free trade in agricultural products remained a long-term objective on which the two sides agreed to reopen discussions in 2001.

The Tunisian Government expected that an investment of around TD 2,200m. (60% for the restructuring and modernization of businesses and 40% for infrastructural development and other initiatives to improve the business environment) would be required during the first five years of exposure to increased competition. Detailed preparatory studies had indicated that about one-third of Tunisian industrial companies were likely to be put out of business by the new trade measures, while a further third would find the transition difficult. Under the agreement, the EU pledged to provide financial assistance to help the Tunisian economy adjust to growing competition from EU member states, including support for the Government's industrial restructuring programme (see Industry), training and the promotion of the private sector. The EU was to provide ECU

330m. ($300m.) in loans over the period 1996–99 and by early 1998 it was reported that some ECU 250m. had already been allocated. It took more than two and a half years for all 15 EU member states to ratify the free-trade agreement, which did not come into force formally until March 1998. However, Tunisia began implementing the agreement from 1 January 1996, when import duties on EU capital goods were abolished.

TOURISM

During 1961–72, total tourist arrivals grew at a rate of 30% annually. Tourism was the nation's principal source of foreign currency from 1968 to 1976 (when it was overtaken by petroleum). In the 1980s the number of annual tourist arrivals fluctuated wildly, owing to the effects of recession in Western European countries on the whole Mediterranean tourist industry. Tunisia has experienced difficulties in competing with other holiday destinations, such as Greece, Spain and Morocco, and foreign tourists have been deterred from visiting Tunisia by terrorist incidents and the bombing of Libya by the USA in 1986. The number of foreign visitors totalled 3.3m. in 1989 and 3.2m. in 1990. The number of tourist arrivals increased steadily to 3.9m. in 1994, and 4.1m. in 1995. Although the number of tourist arrivals fell slightly to 3.9m. in 1996, numbers increased to 4.3m. in 1997 mainly as a result of a rise in arrivals from Europe. Germany is the main country of origin of tourists and, together with France, Italy and the United Kingdom, accounts for almost one-half of all tourist arrivals. There are four main centres for tourists: Hammamet, Sousse, Djerba and Tunis. A major tourist development was built along the coast north of Sousse, and in 1998 work began on the Marina Hammamet-Sud, a new development including a 740-berth marina, hotels and commercial buildings. The BNDT promotes and finances three types of ventures: construction of new hotels; modernization of existing hotels; and other activities related to tourism, such as transport, housing and real estate. The substantial devaluation of the dinar in mid-1986 enabled the Tunisian tourist industry to compete with Mediterranean rivals. In November 1987 the Government announced a series of incentives to encourage the development of tourism in the Sahara, with the aim of attracting tourists, who generally arrive in the summer to stay at the seaside resorts, to Tunisia throughout the year. However, Saharan tourism did not grow as rapidly as expected, with tourists continuing to choose coastal resorts and making only short excursions into the Sahara. As a result, by 1997 hotels in the Saharan region had accumulated debts of TD 35m. ($30m.). In January 1998 President Ben Ali announced a number of measures to expand tourism in the area, including the rescheduling of hotel debts and an increase in direct air connections from European cities to the regional capital, Tozeur. The 1987–91 Development Plan envisaged that tourism would overtake petroleum as the principal source of foreign exchange, providing Tunisia with an average of TD 600m. per year. In 1988 receipts from tourism amounted to about $1,300m. In 1989 receipts from tourism totalled $951m.; arrivals in 1990 declined slightly and tourist receipts in that year were $900m. Receipts from tourism were estimated at TD 950m. ($1,037m.) in 1992, up from $770m. in the previous year, and reached TD 1,114m. ($1,092m.) in 1993. In 1994 the tourism sector grew by 5.1% and accounted for one-half of all new jobs created in that year. Tourism receipts in 1994 amounted to TD 1,317m. ($1,404m.). In 1995 tourist arrivals rose by 7%, while estimated earnings from tourism increased to TD 1,323m. Tourist revenues grew from TD 1,413m. in 1996 to TD 1,540m. in 1997, an increase of 9%. The central bank reported that during the first quarter of 1998 tourism receipts rose by 8.4% over the same period in 1997. The Ministry of Tourism began implementing its own five-year plan in 1998 to improve training of employees in the tourism sector.

FOREIGN AID

The principal sources of economic aid for Tunisia continue to be Western countries and international institutions. The World Bank Group has been the most important multilateral donor, providing loans and credits for investment in a variety of projects—including participation in the BDET and the BNDT. The African Development Bank is another large multilateral donor. Tunisia's largest bilateral donor is France, which provides annual packages of mixed credits. In August 1989 an agreement was signed, under the terms of which France agreed to extend to Tunisia three new credit lines and a grant totalling 1,060m. French francs. In August 1990 Tunisia and France renewed the financial agreement, which comprised a loan of 1,000m. French francs. Protocols signed with France in late 1993 granted Tunisia a total of more than 900m. French francs. One of the agreements, signed in November, granted 277m. French francs for exceptional balance of payments aid. Other important bilateral donors are the USA and the Gulf Arab states, although these countries have reduced lending, owing to recent budgetary constraints. In February 1991 the US Government announced its decision to reduce sharply its aid to Tunisia, owing to the country's muted support for Iraq during the Gulf crisis (1990–91). In recent years Japan has extended substantial credit to Tunisia for the purchase of Japanese goods and services. Tunisia's receipts of official development aid rose from $178m. in 1984 to $316m. in 1988, $283m. in 1989, $393m. in 1990 and $322m. (2.5% of GNP) in 1991. Germany agreed to provide Tunisia with $33.4m. of development aid in 1994. During the second half of the 1990s Tunisia continued to obtain substantial external funds, principally from the World Bank,

the EU and OECD countries. The World Bank agreed loans of $750m. during 1996–98. In early 1998 the EIB announced new loans of $157m., and in March Japan's Overseas Economic Co-operation Fund signed loan agreements for infrastructure projects totalling $123m.

Tunisia's total foreign debt increased from $3,526m. in 1980 to $8,475m. in 1992. As a proportion of total exports of goods and services, the cost of debt-servicing rose correspondingly, from 14.8% to 20.6%. During the period of the 1982–86 Development Plan, Tunisia's total debt increased rapidly, owing partly to the appreciation of the US dollar in the early 1980s. As a proportion of Tunisia's GNP, the country's total external debt increased from 41.6% in 1980 to 73.9% in 1987. In 1991 the ratio stood at 66.2%. At the end of 1995 Tunisia's external debt was $9,938m., while the cost of debt-servicing was equivalent to 17.0% of the value of exports of goods and services. Total foreign debt fell to $9,886m. in 1996 and was estimated at $9,418m. in 1997. Most of it was public or publicly guaranteed medium- to long-term debt. Debt service payments totalled $1,444m. in 1996 when the debt-service ratio stood at 16.1%. Debt service payments were estimated to have risen to $1,585m. in 1997, with the debt-service ratio increasing to 17.3%.

Statistical Survey

Source (unless otherwise stated): Institut National de la Statistique, Ministère du Développement Economique, 70 rue ach-Cham, 1002 Tunis; tel. (1) 282-500; fax (1) 792-559.

Area and Population

AREA, POPULATION AND DENSITY

Area (sq km)	
Land	154,530
Inland waters	9,080
Total	163,610*
Population (census results)	
30 March 1984	6,966,173
20 April 1994	
Males	4,447,341
Females	4,338,023
Total	8,785,364
Population (official estimates at mid-year)	
1994	8,815,400
1995	8,957,500
1996	9,092,000
Density (per sq km) at mid-1996	58.8

* 63,170 sq miles.

PRINCIPAL COMMUNES (population at 1994 census)

Tunis (capital) . . .	674,100	Kairouan (Qairawan) .	102,600
Sfax (Safaqis) . . .	230,900	Gabès	98,900
Ariana	152,700	Bizerta (Bizerte) . .	98,900
Ettadhamen . . .	149,200	Bardo	72,700
Sousse. . . .	125,000	Gafsa	71,100

BIRTHS, MARRIAGES AND DEATHS*

	Registered live births		Registered marriages		Registered deaths	
	Number	Rate (per '000)	Number	Rate (per '000)	Number	Rate (per '000)
1988 . .	215,079	27.7	50,026	6.4	44,700	5.7
1989 . .	199,459	25.2	55,163	7.0	44,600	5.6
1990 . .	205,345	25.4	55,612	6.9	45,700	5.6
1991 . .	207,455	25.2	59,010	7.2	46,300	5.6
1992 . .	211,649	25.2	64,700	7.7	46,300	5.5
1993 . .	207,786	24.1	54,120	6.3	49,400	5.8
1994 . .	200,223	22.7	52,431	5.9	50,300	5.7
1995 . .	186,416	20.8	53,726	6.0	51,900	5.8

* Birth registration is reported to be 100% complete. Death registration is estimated to be about 73% complete. UN estimates for average annual death rates are: 8.4 per 1,000 in 1980–85, 7.2 per 1,000 in 1985–90, 6.4 per 1,000 in 1990–95. UN estimates for average annual birth rates are: 33.7 per 1,000 in 1980–85, 29.7 per 1,000 in 1985–90, 25.6 per 1,000 in 1990–95.

1996 (provisional): Registered live births 184,000 (birth rate 20.2 per 1,000); Registered deaths 54,000 (death rate 5.9 per 1,000) (Source: UN, *Population and Vital Statistics Report*).

Expectation of life (UN estimates, years at birth, 1990–95): 67.8 (males 66.9; females 68.7) (Source: UN, *World Population Prospects: The 1994 Revision*).

EMPLOYMENT ('000 persons aged 15 years and over at 20 April 1994)

	Males	Females	Total
Agriculture, forestry and fishing .	393.7	107.3	501.0
Manufacturing	244.7	211.0	455.7
Electricity, gas and water* . .	34.4	2.4	36.8
Construction	302.6	3.2	305.8
Trade, restaurants and hotels† .	277.8	37.8	315.6
Community, social and personal services‡	503.9	163.2	667.1
Activities not adequately defined .	28.6	10.0	38.6
Total employed	**1,785.7**	**534.9**	**2,320.6**

* Including mining and quarrying.
† Including financing, insurance, real estate and business services.
‡ Including transport, storage and communications.

Mid-1996 (estimates in '000): Agriculture, etc. 784; Total labour force 3,461 (Source: FAO, *Production Yearbook*).

Agriculture

PRINCIPAL CROPS ('000 metric tons)

	1994	1995	1996
Wheat	503	531	2,018
Barley	145	80	835
Other cereals . . .	12	27	26
Potatoes	210	250	290
Broad beans (dry) . . .	17	26*	37*
Chick-peas	6	9	30
Olives	350	350†	1,050*
Tomatoes	480	580	620
Green chillies and peppers . .	165	150	190*
Dry onions†	90	90	90
Watermelons	280†	230*	230†
Melons†	74	74	74
Grapes	103	106	107
Dates	74	84	86
Sugar beet	232	234	300
Apples	68*	63	70
Peaches and nectarines* . .	76	48	48
Oranges	105	101	148*
Tangerines, mandarins, clementines and satsumas . .	38	40	38*
Lemons and limes . . .	18	13	15*
Grapefruit and pomelo . .	47	41	55*
Apricots	27	26	25*
Almonds	52	35	42*
Tobacco (leaves) . . .	4	4	5

* Unofficial figure(s).   † FAO estimate(s).

Source: FAO, *Production Yearbook*.

LIVESTOCK ('000 head, year ending September)

	1994	1995	1996
Horses*	56	56	56
Mules*	81	81	81
Asses*	230	230	230
Cattle	662	654	700*
Camels*	231	231	231
Sheep	6,137	6,222	6,400*
Goats	1,351	1,205	1,250*

Poultry (million): 33* in 1994; 34* in 1995; 39* in 1996.

* FAO estimate(s).

Source: FAO, *Production Yearbook*.

LIVESTOCK PRODUCTS ('000 metric tons)

	1994	1995	1996
Beef and veal	43	44	45
Mutton and lamb . . .	38	46	47
Poultry meat	61	66	70
Other meat	15	14	15
Cows' milk	509	564	605
Sheep's milk	15	15	15
Goats' milk	11	11	11
Poultry eggs	55	62	63
Wool:			
greasy	9	9	9
clean*	6	6	6
Cattle hides*	5	5	5
Sheepskins*	7	7	7

* FAO estimates.

Source: FAO, *Production Yearbook*.

Forestry

ROUNDWOOD REMOVALS ('000 cu m, excluding bark)

	1994	1995	1996
Sawlogs, veneer logs and logs for sleepers	21	21	21
Pulpwood	75	75	75
Other industrial wood . .	111	113	114
Fuel wood	3,327	3,391	3,417
Total	**3,534**	**3,600**	**3,627**

Source: FAO, *Yearbook of Forest Products*.

SAWNWOOD PRODUCTION ('000 cu m, including sleepers)

	1994	1995	1996
Coniferous (softwood) . . .	7	7	7
Broadleaved (hardwood) . .	14	14	14
Total	**20**	**20**	**20**

Source: FAO, *Yearbook of Forest Products*.

Fishing

('000 metric tons, live weight)

	1993	1994	1995
Common pandora . . .	2.8	2.0	3.2
Flathead grey mullet . . .	2.8	2.2	2.1
Bluefish	2.0	1.3	0.7
Jack and horse mackerels .	2.4	3.7	4.1
Sardinellas	8.9	7.6	8.6
European pilchard . . .	9.6	13.1	11.9
Northern bluefish tuna . .	1.1	2.4	1.1
Chub mackerel . . .	3.3	2.3	2.6
Caramote prawn . . .	1.7	2.3	3.6
Common cuttlefish . . .	6.3	5.1	3.5
Common octopus . . .	3.4	1.8	1.9
Total catch (incl. others) . .	**83.5**	**86.0**	**83.8**

Source: FAO, *Yearbook of Fishery Statistics*.

Mining

('000 metric tons, unless otherwise indicated)

	1993	1994	1995
Iron ore*	190	155	122
Lead concentrates* . .	0.5	2.0	7.0
Calcium phosphate . .	5,476	5,565	6,302
Zinc concentrates* . . .	1.3	12.9	44.2
Crude petroleum . . .	4,650	4,378	4,251
Natural gas (million cu m) .	366	354	335
Salt (unrefined) . . .	435	528	319

* Figures refer to the metal content (Source: UN, *Industrial Commodity Statistics Yearbook*).

Industry

SELECTED PRODUCTS ('000 metric tons, unless otherwise indicated)

	1994	1995	1996
Superphosphates (16%)	20	16	19
Superphosphates (45%)	821	780	790
Phosphoric acid	973	1,017	1,063
Cement	4,605	4,997	4,560
Electric power—production by Société Tunisienne de l'Electricité et du Gaz (million kWh)	6,031	6,625	6,852
Electric power—other producers (million kWh)	683	680	701
Beer ('000 hl)	510	659	661
Cigarettes (million)	7,128	7,421	n.a.
Wine ('000 hl)	294	292	237
Olive oil	210	70	60
Semolina	566	601	597
Flour	800	892	679
Refined sugar	90	90	91
Crude steel	183	201	187
Lime	508	412	464
Petrol	310	303	325
Kerosene	137	134	131
Diesel oil	539	576	571
Fuel oil	581	645	645

Source: mainly Banque Centrale de Tunisie.

Finance

CURRENCY AND EXCHANGE RATES

Monetary Units
1,000 millimes = 1 Tunisian dinar (TD).

Sterling and Dollar Equivalents (31 May 1998)
£1 sterling = 1.886 dinars;
US $1 = 1.156 dinars;
100 Tunisian dinars = £53.03 = $86.48.

Average Exchange Rate (dinars per US $)
1995   0.9458
1996   0.9734
1997   1.1059

BUDGET (million dinars)*

Revenue†	1993	1994	1995
Taxation	3,593.3	3,961.1	4,263.9
Taxes on income, profits, etc.	698.1	733.8	807.4
Social security contributions	511.8	677.5	770.7
Taxes on payroll or work-force	56.7	58.1	61.5
Taxes on property	2.9	65.1	67.6
Domestic taxes on goods and services	914.5	996.7	1,029.3
Sales taxes	386.2	388.7	423.0
Excises	424.8	487.7	505.1
Taxes on international trade	1,239.1	1,338.3	1,427.3
Import duties	1,218.3	1,312.2	1,384.0
Export duties	9.1	9.7	8.6
Other current revenue	846.2	993.8	854.9
Capital revenue	2.6	3.8	3.1
Transfers from other levels of government	17.9	11.5	19.3
Total	4,460.0	4,970.2	5,141.2

Expenditure‡	1993	1994	1995
General public services	453.5	448.6	472.3
Defence	277.2	300.5	324.3
Public order and safety	314.9	352.6	381.5
Education	838.4	902.5	1,023.6
Health	315.9	359.1	392.1
Social security and welfare	693.0	809.2	891.0
Housing and community amenities	327.4	291.0	293.2
Recreational, cultural and religious affairs and services	161.2	159.6	156.3
Economic affairs and services	951.3	924.8	1,014.8
Agriculture, forestry and fishing	351.6	382.2	456.0
Mining (excl. fuel), manufacturing and construction	2.8	0.5	0.7
Transport and communications	116.3	110.3	120.1
Other purposes	517.8	553.3	635.1
Total	4,850.6	5,101.2	5,584.2
Current	3,839.3	4,114.4	4,481.2
Capital	1,011.3	986.8	1,103.0

* Figures refer to the consolidated accounts of the central Government, including administrative agencies and social security funds. The data exclude the operations of economic and social agencies with their own budgets.
† Excluding grants from abroad (million dinars): 35.4 in 1993; 51.9 in 1994; 25.3 in 1995.
‡ Excluding net lending (million dinars): 120.2 in 1993; 140.1 in 1994; 125.9 in 1995.

Source: Banque Centrale de Tunisie.

CENTRAL BANK RESERVES (US $ million at 31 December)

	1995	1996	1997
Gold*	4.8	4.4	3.8
IMF special drawing rights	7.0	15.9	16.3
Reserve position in IMF	0.1	0.1	0.1
Foreign exchange	1,598.2	1,881.7	1,961.7
Total	1,610.1	1,902.0	1,981.9

* National valuation.

Source: IMF, *International Financial Statistics*.

MONEY SUPPLY (million dinars at 31 December)

	1995	1996	1997
Currency outside banks	1,315	1,473	1,592
Demand deposits at commercial banks	2,092	2,371	2,847
Total money (incl. others)	3,637	4,109	4,643

Source: IMF, *International Financial Statistics*.

COST OF LIVING (Consumer Price Index; base: 1990 = 100)

	1994	1995	1996
Food	121.9	132.0	137.0
Fuel, light and water	126.9	132.1	136.4
Clothing	129.0	138.6	147.4
Rent	124.1	129.2	132.3
All items (incl. others)	124.6	132.4	137.4

Source: Banque Centrale de Tunisie.

1997: Food 142.8; All items 142.4 (Source: UN, *Monthly Bulletin of Statistics*).

NATIONAL ACCOUNTS (million dinars at current prices)
Expenditure on the Gross Domestic Product

	1995	1996	1997
Government final consumption expenditure	2,789	2,995	3,250
Private final consumption expenditure	10,716	11,586	12,617
Increase in stocks . . .	64	539	536
Gross fixed capital formation .	4,124	4,379	5,130
Total domestic expenditure	17,693	19,398*	21,533
Exports of goods and services .	7,657	7,969	9,100
Less Imports of goods and services	8,323	8,297	9,617
GDP in purchasers' values .	17,027	19,070	21,016
GDP at constant 1990 prices .	13,082	14,010	14,773

* Including adjustment.

Source: IMF, *International Financial Statistics*.

Gross Domestic Product by Economic Activity

	1994	1995	1996
Agriculture	1,985.9	1,938.2	2,636.0
Mining and quarrying . . .	617.0	584.1	659.5
Manufacturing	2,909.8	3,201.7	3,432.8
Electricity and water . . .	291.5	347.5	375.8
Construction	789.6	803.2	873.9
Wholesale and retail trade . .	2,686.2	3,032.1	3,277.1
Transport, storage and communications . . .	1,197.2	1,277.5	1,424.4
Hotels, cafés and restaurants . .	943.7	1,049.7	1,129.5
Government services . . .	2,124.2	2,338.5	2,525.6
Other services	201.3	254.5	279.6
GDP at factor cost . . .	13,746.4	14,827.0	16,614.2
Indirect taxes, *less* subsidies . .	2,060.6	2,185.1	2,346.8
GDP in purchasers' values . .	15,807.0	17,012.1	18,961.0

Source: Banque Centrale de Tunisie.

BALANCE OF PAYMENTS (US $ million)

	1994	1995	1996
Exports of goods f.o.b. . . .	4,643	5,470	5,519
Imports of goods f.o.b. . . .	−6,210	−7,459	−7,323
Trade balance	−1,567	−1,989	−1,804
Exports of services . . .	2,267	2,509	2,632
Imports of services . . .	−1,363	−1,352	−1,259
Balance on goods and services .	−663	−832	−431
Other income received . .	71	119	66
Other income paid . . .	−745	−835	−1,030
Balance on goods, services and income	−1,338	−1,548	−1,396
Current transfers received . .	816	843	876
Current transfers paid . .	−17	−32	−16
Current balance . . .	−539	−737	−536
Capital account (net) . . .	−3	−7	34
Direct investment abroad . .	−6	5	—
Direct investment from abroad .	432	264	253
Portfolio investment assets . .	−1	2	−5
Portfolio investment liabilities .	16	23	149
Other investment assets . .	−326	−327	−593
Other investment liabilities . .	1,029	990	1,002
Net errors and omissions . .	−76	−117	138
Overall balance . . .	527	97	441

Source: IMF, *International Financial Statistics*.

External Trade

PRINCIPAL COMMODITIES
(distribution by SITC, US $ million)

Imports c.i.f.	1993	1994	1995
Food and live animals . . .	385.2	478.3	787.6
Cereals and cereal preparations .	135.8	183.4	442.5
Wheat and meslin (unmilled) .	90.0	98.7	301.5
Crude materials (inedible) except fuels	297.2	372.2	486.1
Mineral fuels, lubricants, etc. .	488.0	496.3	575.2
Petroleum, petroleum products, etc.	352.3	340.8	358.7
Refined petroleum products . .	294.9	257.6	228.2
Gas (natural and manufactured) .	120.8	142.5	198.5
Petroleum gases, etc., in the gaseous state	89.8	115.4	159.3
Chemicals and related products	499.2	549.7	700.3
Medicinal and pharmaceutical products	129.5	144.2	161.4
Artificial resins, plastic materials, etc.	121.2	137.9	193.0
Basic manufactures . .	1,805.0	1,845.1	2,268.6
Textile yarn, fabrics, etc. . .	979.1	1,063.4	1,288.6
Woven cotton fabrics* . .	441.8	478.0	587.2
Bleached and mercerized fabrics*	410.7	447.9	548.5
Woven fabrics of man-made fibres*	252.5	284.7	363.9
Iron and steel	347.4	230.2	294.4
Tubes, pipes and fittings .	180.5	72.8	41.3
Machinery and transport equipment	1,987.5	1,893.7	2,043.2
Power-generating machinery and equipment	237.9	135.4	106.7
Machinery specialized for particular industries . .	371.7	288.9	351.8
General industrial machinery, equipment and parts . .	367.9	338.3	394.0
Other electrical machinery, apparatus, etc. . . .	324.8	364.9	415.8
Road vehicles and parts† . .	379.8	395.8	441.7
Passenger motor cars (excl. buses)	158.5	209.5	238.9
Other transport equipment† .	93.7	169.2	92.2
Miscellaneous manufactured articles	614.4	671.4	828.4
Clothing and accessories (excl. footwear)	268.1	335.6	434.9
Total (incl. others) . . .	6,214.0	6,483.9	7,903.1

* Excluding narrow or special fabrics.

† Excluding tyres, engines and electrical parts.

Exports f.o.b.	1993	1994	1995
Food and live animals . . .	213.3	224.5	247.1
Fish, crustaceans and molluscs .	85.9	79.0	76.7
Mineral fuels, lubricants, etc. .	436.2	434.6	463.7
Petroleum, petroleum products, etc.	434.3	434.1	462.5
Crude petroleum oils, etc. .	368.1	352.2	377.8
Animal and vegetable oils, fats			
and waxes	179.3	302.2	230.5
Fixed vegetable oils and fats . .	179.1	301.8	230.1
Olive oil	179.1	301.8	230.1
Chemicals and related products	421.4	527.6	651.2
Inorganic chemicals . . .	177.6	223.0	271.5
Inorganic chemical elements,			
oxides and halogen salts . .	121.5	167.1	204.6
Inorganic acids and oxygen			
compounds of non-metals .	120.6	166.6	204.2
Phosphorus pentoxide and			
phosphoric acids . .	120.4	166.2	201.9
Manufactured fertilizers . .	183.4	229.8	298.1
Phosphatic fertilizers . .	178.7	112.1	123.7
Superphosphates. . .	74.7	100.5	117.0
Basic manufactures . . .	419.8	557.8	660.5
Leather, leather manufactures			
and dressed furskins . .	67.7	94.6	110.8
Textile yarn, fabrics, etc. . .	125.8	153.7	165.5
Non-metallic mineral			
manufactures . . .	75.8	75.7	118.6
Iron and steel . . .	25.1	91.9	57.4
Other metal manufactures .	67.5	81.8	122.7
Machinery and transport			
equipment	366.4	392.5	515.1
Electrical machinery, apparatus,			
etc.	222.7	267.9	355.0
Equipment for distributing			
electricity . . .	103.7	119.9	149.8
Insulated electric wire, cable,			
etc. . . .	102.8	118.1	149.2
Miscellaneous manufactured			
articles	1,656.9	2,005.9	2,533.7
Clothing and accessories (excl.			
footwear)	1,503.9	1,839.5	2,322.1
Men's and boys' outer garments			
of non-knitted textile fabrics .	698.7	870.2	1,068.7
Women's, girls' and infants'			
outer garments of non-knitted			
textile fabrics . . .	353.6	441.8	580.5
Undergarments (excl.			
foundation garments) of non-			
knitted textile fabrics . .	105.5	130.9	155.3
Knitted or crocheted outer			
garments and accessories			
(excl. gloves, stockings, etc.),			
non-elastic	158.2	165.4	209.5
Knitted or crocheted			
undergarments (incl.			
foundation garments of non-			
knitted fabrics) . . .	149.2	190.1	262.2
Total (incl. others) . . .	3,804.5	4,584.5	5,474.6

Source: UN, *International Trade Statistics Yearbook*.

PRINCIPAL TRADING PARTNERS (US $ '000)*

Imports c.i.f.	1993	1994	1995
Algeria	99,032	124,931	179,838
Belgium-Luxembourg . . .	268,504	283,183	354,322
France	1,668,224	1,779,588	2,024,561
Germany	807,661	791,923	993,687
Italy	1,134,365	999,816	1,208,985
Japan	143,181	151,804	140,924
Libya	52,139	120,765	203,876
Netherlands	136,306	137,471	206,167
Russia	98,887	104,138	228,460
Spain	201,432	233,336	329,432
Sweden	80,615	69,489	82,678
Switzerland	69,650	80,437	98,445
Turkey	57,100	84,595	105,921
United Kingdom	140,506	144,260	159,182
USA	358,394	426,936	399,994
Total (incl. others) . . .	6,205,838	6,468,314	7,887,094

Exports f.o.b.	1993	1994	1995
Algeria	66,622	106,069	185,464
Belgium-Luxembourg . . .	276,451	297,729	357,095
France	1,142,804	1,232,176	1,536,353
Germany	660,847	712,824	860,978
Greece	2,761	54,340	31,441
India	49,268	81,204	98,293
Italy	620,748	885,921	1,021,370
Libya	188,520	156,468	192,377
Netherlands	117,293	141,091	156,071
Spain	96,030	216,846	221,489
Switzerland	20,385	49,399	48,187
Turkey	51,182	42,133	33,658
United Kingdom	50,375	68,841	81,569
USA	31,657	47,979	69,065
Total (incl. others) . . .	4,039,731	3,804,499	5,474,626

* Imports by country of production; exports by country of last destination.

Source: UN, *International Trade Statistics Yearbook*.

Transport

RAILWAYS (traffic)

	1995	1996	1997
Passenger-km (million) . .	997	989	1,022
Freight ton-km (million) . .	3,322	3,327	3,318

Source: Ministère du Transport.

ROAD TRAFFIC (estimates, motor vehicles in use at 31 December)

	1994	1995	1996
Private cars	243,000	248,000	269,000
Commercial vehicles . . .	275,000	283,000	312,000

Source: International Road Federation, *World Road Statistics*.

SHIPPING

Merchant Fleet (vessels registered at 31 December)

	1995	1996	1997
Number of vessels . . .	75	77	77
Total displacement ('000 grt) .	159.7	157.9	180.4

Source: Lloyd's Register of Shipping, *World Fleet Statistics*.

International Sea-borne Freight Traffic ('000 metric tons)

	1993	1995†	1996
Goods loaded*	6,060	7,500	6,888
Goods unloaded	10,200	11,880	11,136

* Excluding Algerian crude petroleum loaded at La Skhirra.
† Figures for 1994 are not available.
Source: UN, *Monthly Bulletin of Statistics*.

CIVIL AVIATION (traffic on scheduled services)

	1993	1994	1995
Km flown (million) . . .	17	19	19
Passengers carried ('000) . .	1,351	1,391	1,419
Passenger-km (million) . .	1,877	1,977	1,955
Total ton-km (million) . .	173	197	197

Source: UN, *Statistical Yearbook*.

Tourism

FOREIGN TOURIST ARRIVALS BY NATIONALITY ('000)

	1994	1995	1996
Algeria	672.4	988.6	669.9
Austria	71.6	65.1	90.3
Belgium	78.1	74.5	87.4
France	484.8	465.1	541.8
Germany	852.5	837.1	808.4
Italy	229.8	245.9	270.1
Libya	543.9	618.7	526.1
Morocco	399.9	26.7	30.8
Netherlands	80.3	70.5	71.7
Scandinavia	61.7	59.6	88.3
Switzerland	76.4	74.5	75.4
United Kingdom . . .	267.2	239.5	206.1
Total (incl. others) . . .	3,855.5	4,119.8	3,884.5

Source: Office National du Tourisme Tunisien.

Communications Media

	1993	1994	1995
Radio receivers ('000 in use) . .	1,700	1,740	1,800
Television receivers ('000 in use) .	690	710	800
Telephones ('000 main lines in use)	421	474	522
Telefax stations ('000 in use) . .	15	20	25
Mobile cellular telephones (subscribers)	2,269	2,709	3,185
Daily newspapers:			
Number	9	7	7*
Average circulation (000)* . .	410	403	400
Book production (titles)† . . .	539‡	569	n.a.

* Estimate(s).
† Excluding pamphlets.
‡ Figure refers to first editions only.
Non-daily newspapers (1988): 9 (estimated circulation 244,000 copies).
Sources: UNESCO, *Statistical Yearbook*; UN, *Statistical Yearbook*.

Education

	1993/94	1994/95	1995/96
Institutions			
Pre-primary	n.a.	n.a.	1,115
Primary	4,201	4,321	4,384
Secondary	655*	712*	n.a.
Teachers			
Primary	56,154	58,738	59,887
Secondary	38,891†	41,328†	n.a.
Higher‡	5,655	5,944	6,481
Pupils			
Pre-primary	n.a.	n.a.	68,108
Primary	1,476,329	1,481,759	1,468,998
Secondary	717,156	783,169	849,359
Higher	96,101	102,682	112,634

* Source: Ministère de l'Education et des Sciences.
† Data excludes teaching staff at professional schools.
‡ Data refers to full-time staff only.
Source: UNESCO, *Statistical Yearbook*.

Directory

The Constitution

A new Constitution for the Republic of Tunisia was promulgated on 1 June 1959 and amended on 12 July 1988. Its main provisions are summarized below:

NATIONAL ASSEMBLY

Legislative power is exercised by the National Assembly, which is elected (at the same time as the President) every five years by direct universal suffrage. Every citizen who has had Tunisian nationality for at least five years and who has attained 20 years of age has the right to vote. The National Assembly shall hold two sessions every year, each session lasting not more than three months. Additional meetings may be held at the demand of the President or of a majority of the deputies.

HEAD OF STATE

The President of the Republic is both Head of State and Head of the Executive. He must be not less than 40 years of age and not more than 70. The President is elected by universal suffrage for a five-year term which is renewable twice, consecutively. The President is also the Commander-in-Chief of the army and makes both civil and military appointments. The Government may be censured by the National Assembly, in which case the President may dismiss the Assembly and hold fresh elections. If censured by the new Assembly thus elected, the Government must resign. Should the

presidency fall vacant for any reason before the end of a President's term of office, the President of the National Assembly shall take charge of affairs of the state for a period of 45 to 60 days. At the end of this period, a presidential election shall be organized. The President of the National Assembly shall not be eligible as a presidential candidate.

COUNCIL OF STATE

Comprises two judicial bodies: an administrative body dealing with legal disputes between individuals and state or public bodies, and an audit office to verify the accounts of the state and submit reports.

ECONOMIC AND SOCIAL COUNCIL

Deals with economic and social planning and studies projects submitted by the National Assembly. Members are grouped in seven categories representing various sections of the community.

The Government

HEAD OF STATE

President: ZINE AL-ABIDINE BEN ALI (took office on 7 November 1987; re-elected 2 April 1989 and 20 March 1994).

COUNCIL OF MINISTERS
(September 1998)

Prime Minister: HAMED KAROUI.

Minister of National Defence: HABIB BEN YAHIA.

Minister of the Interior: ALI CHAOUCH.

Minister, Director of the Presidential Office: MUHAMMAD JEGHAM.

Minister of Justice: ABDALLAH KALLEL.

Minister of Foreign Affairs: SAID BEN MUSTAPHA.

Minister of Religious Affairs: ALI CHEBBI.

Minister of International Co-operation and Foreign Investment: MUHAMMAD GHANNOUCHI.

Minister of Finance: MUHAMMAD JERI.

Minister of Economic Development: TAWFIK BACCAR.

Minister of Industry: MONCEF BEN ABDALLAH.

Minister of Trade: MONDHER ZENAIDI.

Minister of Agriculture: SADOK RABAH.

Minister of State Domains: MUSTAPHA BOUAZIZ.

Minister of Equipment and Housing: SLAHEDDINE BELAID.

Minister of the Environment and Land Planning: MUHAMMAD MEHDI MELIKA.

Minister of Transport: HASSINE CHOUK.

Minister of Tourism and Handicrafts: SLAHEDDINE MAAOUIA.

Minister of Communications: AHMED FRIAA.

Minister of Education: RIDHA FERCHIOU.

Minister of Higher Education: DALY JAZI.

Minister of Culture: ABDELBAKI HERMASSI.

Minister of Public Health: HEDI M'HENNI.

Minister of Social Affairs: CHEDLI NEFFATI.

Minister of Professional Training and Employment: MONCER ROUISSI.

Minister of Children and Youth: RAOUF NAJAR.

Minister of Family and Women's Affairs: NEZIHA ZARROUK.

Government Secretary-General: RIDHA GRIRA.

Secretary of State in charge of Scientific Research and Technology: MONGI SAFRA.

Secretary of State in charge of Administrative Reform and the Civil Service: SLAHEDDINE CHERIF.

There are, in addition, seven Secretaries of State (without independent charge).

MINISTRIES

Ministry of Agriculture: 30 rue Alain Savary, Tunis; tel. (1) 660-088; telex 13378.

Ministry of Children and Youth: ave Muhammad Ali Akid, al-Menzah, Tunis; tel. (1) 286-704; fax (1) 789-047.

Ministry of Communications: Tunis.

Ministry of Culture: place du Gouvernement, la Kasbah, 1006 Tunis; tel. (1) 262-003; telex 1432; fax (1) 574-580.

Ministry of Economic Development: 25 bis rue Asdrubal, Lafayette, 1002 Tunis; tel. (1) 799-200; telex 14677; fax (1) 787-234.

Ministry of Education: place de la Kasbah, Tunis; tel. (1) 660-088; telex 13004.

Ministry of the Environment and Land Planning: Tunis.

Ministry of Equipment and Housing: Cité Jardin, Tunis; tel. (1) 680-088; telex 13565.

Ministry of Family and Women's Affairs: Tunis.

Ministry of Finance: place Alizouaui, Tunis; tel. (1) 650-621; telex 51922.

Ministry of Foreign Affairs: place du Gouvernement, la Kasbah, Tunis; tel. (1) 660-088; telex 13470.

Ministry of the Interior: ave Habib Bourguiba, Tunis; tel. (1) 333-000; telex 13994.

Ministry of International Co-operation and Foreign Investment: 149 ave de la Liberté, 1002 Tunis; tel. (1) 798-522; telex 18060; fax (1) 799-069.

Ministry of Justice: ave Bab Benat, Tunis; tel. (1) 660-088.

Ministry of National Defence: blvd Bab Menara, Tunis; tel. (1) 260-244; telex 12580.

Ministry of Public Health: Bab Saadoun, 1030 Tunis; tel. (1) 662-040; telex 15235; fax (1) 567-100.

Ministry of Religious Affairs: Tunis.

Ministry of Social Affairs: blvd Farhat Hached, Tunis; tel. (1) 660-088; telex 13711.

Ministry of Tourism and Handicrafts: ave Muhammad V, Tunis.

Ministry of Transport: 3 rue d'Angleterre, Tunis; tel. (1) 660-088; telex 13040.

President and Legislature

PRESIDENT

At the presidential election, which took place on 20 March 1994, the sole candidate, Zine al-Abidine Ben Ali, was re-elected to the presidency with 2,987,375 votes, 99.92% of the votes cast.

ASSEMBLÉE NATIONALE

President: FOUAD MEBAZAA.

Election, 20 March 1994

Party	Votes	%	Seats
Rassemblement constitutionnel démocratique	2,768,667	97.73	144
Mouvement des démocrates socialistes	30,660	1.08	10
Mouvement de la rénovation . .	11,299	0.39	4
Union démocratique unioniste . .	9,152	0.32	3
Parti de l'unité populaire . . .	8,391	0.30	2
Parti social libéral	1,892	0.07	0
Rassemblement socialiste progressiste	1,749	0.06	0
Independents	1,061	0.04	0
Total	2,832,871*	100.00	163†

* Excluding 8,686 spoilt ballot papers.

† Under the terms of an amendment to the electoral code adopted by the National Assembly in January 1994, 19 of the 163 seats in the National Assembly were reserved for candidates of opposition parties. These were allotted according to the proportion of votes received nationally by each party.

Political Organizations

Mouvement de l'unité populaire (MUP): Tunis; supports radical reform; split into two factions, one led by AHMAD BEN SALAH, living in exile until 1988; the other became the Parti de l'unité populaire (see below); Co-ordinator BRAHIM HAYDER.

Mouvement des démocrates socialistes (MDS): Tunis; in favour of a pluralist political system; participated in 1981 election and was officially recognized in Nov. 1983; Political Bureau of 11 mems, National Council of 60 mems, normally elected by the party Congress; Sec.-Gen. ISMAIL BOULAHYA.

Mouvement de la rénovation (MR): 6 rue Metouia, 1000 Tunis; tel. (1) 246-400; fax (1) 350-748; f. 1993; Sec.-Gen. MUHAMMAD HARMEL.

Parti de la renaissance—Hizb an-Nahdah: Tunis; formerly Mouvement de la tendance islamique (banned in 1981); Leader RACHED GHANOUCHI; Sec.-Gen. Sheikh ABD AL-FATHA MOUROU.

Parti des ouvriers communistes tunisiens (POCT): Tunis; illegal; Leader HAMMA HAMMANI.

Parti social libéral (PSL): 38 rue Gandhi, 1001 Tunis; tel. and fax (1) 341-093; f. 1988; officially recognized in Sept. 1988 as the Parti social pour le progrès; adopted present name in 1993; liberal; Pres. MOUNIR BEJI; Vice-Pres. HOSNI LAHMAR.

Parti de l'unité populaire (PUP): 7 rue d'Autriche, 1002 Tunis; tel. (1) 289-678; fax (1) 796-031; broke away from MUP (see above); officially recognized in Nov. 1983; Leader MUHAMMAD BELHADJ AMOR.

Rassemblement constitutionnel démocratique (RCD): blvd 9 avril 1938, Tunis; f. 1934 as the Néo-Destour Party, following a split in the Destour (Constitution) Party; renamed Parti socialiste destourien in 1964; adopted present name in Feb. 1988; moderate left-wing republican party, which achieved Tunisian independence; Political Bureau of nine mems, and a Cen. Cttee of 200, elected by the party Congress; Chair. ZINE AL-ABIDINE BEN ALI; Vice-Chair. HAMED KAROUI; Sec.-Gen. ABD AL-AZIZ BEN DHIA.

Rassemblement national arabe: Tunis; banned in 1981; Leader BASHIR ASSAD.

Rassemblement socialiste progressiste (RSP): Tunis; f. 1983, officially recognized in Sept. 1988; leftist; Sec.-Gen. NEJIB CHEBBI.

Union démocratique unioniste (UDU): Tunis; officially recognized in Nov. 1988; supports Arab unity; Sec.-Gen. ABDERRAHMANE TLILI.

Diplomatic Representation

EMBASSIES IN TUNISIA

Algeria: 18 rue de Niger, 1002 Tunis; tel. (1) 783-166; telex 14275; fax (1) 788-804; Ambassador: SMAÏL ALLAOUA.

Argentina: 10 rue al-Hassan et Houssaine, al-Menzah IV, 1004 Tunis; tel. (1) 231-222; fax (1) 750-058; e-mail etune@emb_argentina .intl.tn; Ambassador: MARCELO HUERGO.

Austria: 16 rue ibn Hamdiss, BP 23, al-Menzah, 1004 Tunis; tel. (1) 751-091; fax (1) 767-824; Ambassador: Dr KARL DIEM.

Bahrain: 72 rue Mouaouia ibn Soufiane, al-Menzah VI, Tunis; tel. (1) 231-811; telex 13733; Ambassador: JASSIM BUALLAY.

Belgium: 47 rue du 1er juin, BP 24, 1002 Tunis; tel. (1) 781-655; telex 14342; fax (1) 792-797; Ambassador: DANIEL LEROY.

Bosnia and Herzegovina: 23 ave de la République, 2016 Carthage, Tunis; tel. (1) 732-700; fax (1) 733-044; Ambassador NERKEZ ARIFHODŽIĆ.

Brazil: 37 ave d'Afrique, BP 64, al-Menzah V, 1004 Tunis; tel. (1) 232-538; fax (1) 750-367; Ambassador: LUIZ JORGE RANGEL DE CASTRO.

Bulgaria: 5 rue Ryhane, Cité Mahragène, 1082 Tunis; tel. (1) 798-962; telex 17289; fax (1) 791-667; Ambassador: TCHAVDAR TCHERV-ENKOV.

Canada: 3 rue du Sénégal, place d'Afrique, BP 31, Belvédère, 1002 Tunis; tel. (1) 796-577; telex 25324; fax (1) 792-371; Ambassador: MICHEL ROY.

China, People's Republic: 41 ave Jugurtha, Mutuelleville, Tunis; tel. (1) 282-090; telex 12221; Ambassador: WU CHUANFU.

Congo, Democratic Republic: 11 rue Tertullien, Notre Dame, Tunis; tel. (1) 281-833; telex 12429; Ambassador: MBOLADINGA KATAKO.

Côte d'Ivoire: 7 rue Fatma al-Fahria, BP 21, Belvédère, 1002 Tunis; tel. (1) 796-601; telex 18160; fax (1) 798-852; Ambassador: KOUASSI GUSTAVE OUFFOUÉ.

Cuba: 20 ave du Golfe Arabe, al-Menzah VIII, 1004 Tunis; tel. (1) 712-844; telex 14080; fax (1) 714-198; Ambassador: JORGE MAN-FUGAS-LAVIGNE.

Czech Republic: 98 rue de Palestine, BP 53, Belvédère, 1002 Tunis; tel. (1) 780-456; telex 14466; fax (1) 793-228.

Denmark: 5 rue de Mauritanie, BP 254, Belvédère, 1002 Tunis; tel. (1) 792-600; telex 14352; fax (1) 790-797; Ambassador: HERLUF HANSEN.

Djibouti: 5 rue Fatma al-Fahria, Mutuelleville, Tunis; tel. (1) 890-589; telex 13148; Ambassador: ALI ABDOU MUHAMMAD.

Egypt: ave Muhammad V, Quartier Montplaisir, Routhi 6, Tunis; tel. (1) 792-233; telex 13992; fax (1) 794-389; Ambassador: MOKHLES MUHAMMAD KOTB.

France: Les Berges du Lac, 2045 Tunis; tel. (1) 860-033; fax (1) 860-363; e-mail ambafran.tunis@planet.tn; Ambassador: JACQUES LANXADE.

Germany: 1 rue al-Hamra, Mutuelleville, Tunis; tel. (1) 786-455; fax (1) 788-242; Ambassador: Dr DIETMAR JOHANNES KREUSEL.

Greece: 9 impasse Antelas, Nord Hilton, BP 151, Mahrajane, 1002, Tunis; tel. (1) 288-411; telex 13742; fax (1) 789-518; Ambassador: VASSILIS PISPINIS.

Holy See: 22 rue Félicien Challaye, Belvédère, 1002 Tunis (Apostolic Nunciature); tel. (1) 849-364; fax (1) 845-280; Apostolic Nuncio: Most Rev. ANTONIO SOZZO, Titular Archbishop of Concordia.

Hungary: 12 rue Achtart, Nord Hilton, Tunis; tel. (1) 751-987; fax (1) 750-620; Ambassador: LÁSZLÓ NIKICSER.

India: 4 place Didon, Notre Dame, Tunis; tel. (1) 891-006; telex 18072; fax (1) 783-394; Ambassador: RAMESH CHANDRA SHUKLA.

Indonesia: BP 63, al-Menzah, 1004 Tunis; tel. (1) 860-377; telex 12513; fax (1) 861-758; e-mail ss.alink@kbritun.intl.tn; Ambassador: IS ISNAEDI.

Iran: 10 rue de Docteur Burnet, Belvédère, 1002 Tunis; tel. (1) 792-578; telex 15138.

Iraq: ave Tahar B. Achour, route X2 m 10, Mutuelleville, Tunis; tel. (1) 890-633; telex 12245; Ambassador: MUNDHIR AHMAD AL-MUTLAQ.

Italy: 37 rue Gamal Abd an-Nasser, 1000 Tunis; tel. (1) 321-811; telex 13501; fax (1) 324-155; Ambassador: ROCCO ANTONIO CANGELOSI.

Japan: 10 rue Mahmoud al-Matri, BP 95, Belvédère, 1002 Tunis; tel. (1) 285-937; telex 15456; fax (1) 786-625; Ambassador: YOSHI-KAZU SUGITANI.

Jordan: 87 ave Jugurtha, Mutuelleville, Tunis; tel. (1) 288-401; telex 13745; Ambassador: NABIH AN-NIMR.

Korea, Republic: 16 rue Caracalla, Notre Dame, BP 297, 1082 Tunis; tel. (1) 799-905; fax (1) 791-923; Ambassador: CHOI BONG-RHEUM.

Kuwait: 40 route Ariane, al-Menzah, Tunis; tel. (1) 236-811; telex 12332; Ambassador: MEJREN AHMAD AL-HAMAD.

Libya: 48 bis rue du 1er juin, Tunis; tel. (1) 236-666; telex 12275; Ambassador: ABD AL-ATTI OBEIDI.

Mauritania: 17 rue Fatma Ennechi, BP 62, al-Menzah, Tunis; tel. (1) 234-935; telex 12234; Ambassador: MOHAMED LAMINE OULD YAHYA.

Morocco: 39 ave du 1er juin, Tunis: tel. (1) 782-775; telex 14460; fax (1) 787-103; Ambassador: ABD AL-KADER BENSLIMANE.

Netherlands: 6–8 rue Meycen, Belvédère, BP 47, 1082 Tunis; tel. (1) 797-724; telex 15260; fax (1) 785-557; Ambassador: Baron BENTINCK VAN SCHOONHETEN.

Norway: 20 rue de la Kahéna, BP 9, 1082 Tunis; tel. (1) 802-158; fax (1) 801-944; e-mail noramb@planet.tn; Ambassador: KJELL ØSTREM.

Pakistan: 7 rue Ali ibn Abi Talib, BP 42, al-Menzah VI, 1004 Tunis; tel. (1) 234-366; telex 14027; fax (1) 752-477; Ambassador: Vice-Adm. (rtd) SHAMOON ALAM KHAN.

Poland: 4 rue Sophonisbe, Notre Dame, Tunis; tel. (1) 286-237; telex 14024; fax (1) 795-118; Ambassador: JANUSZ FEKECZ.

Portugal: 2 rue Sufétula, Belvédère, 1002 Tunis; tel. (1) 893-981; telex 18235; fax (1) 791-008; Ambassador: FILIPE GUTERRES.

Qatar: 2 Nahj al-Hakim Bourni, Belvédère, Tunis; tel. (1) 285-600; telex 14131; Chargé d'affaires: MAJID AL-ALI.

Romania: 18 ave d'Afrique, al-Menzah V, 1004 Tunis; tel. (1) 766-926; telex 15223; fax (1) 767-695; Ambassador: NICOLAE IORDACHE.

Russia: 4 rue Bergamotes, BP 48, 2092 el Manar I, Tunis; tel. (1) 882-446; fax (1) 882-478; e-mail russie@emb_rus.intl.tn; Ambassador: VENIAMIN V. POPOV.

Saudi Arabia: 16 rue d'Autriche, Belvédère, Tunis; tel. (1) 281-295; telex 13562; Ambassador: Sheikh ABBAS FAIK GHAZZAOUI.

Senegal: 122 ave de la Liberté, Tunis; tel. (1) 282-544; telex 12477; Ambassador: IBRA DEGUENE KA.

Somalia: 6 rue Hadramout, Mutuelleville, Tunis; tel. (1) 289-505; telex 13480; Ambassador: AHMAD ABDALLAH MUHAMMAD.

South Africa: 7 rue Achtart, Nord Hilton, BP 251, 1082 Tunis; tel. (1) 800-311; fax (1) 796-742; e-mail embassy.tunis@emb_safrica .intl.tn; Ambassador: E. M. SALEY.

Spain: 22-24 ave Dr Ernest Conseil, Cité Jardin, 1002 Tunis; tel. (1) 782-217; fax (1) 786-267; Ambassador: JOSÉ ANTONIO LÓPEZ ZATÓN.

Sweden: Les Berges du Lac, Lot 12-01-03, Tunis; tel. (1) 860-580; fax (1) 860-810; Ambassador: STAFFAN ÅBERG.

Switzerland: 10 rue ach-Chenkiti, BP 501, Mutuelleville, 1025 Tunis; tel. (1) 281-917; telex 14922; fax (1) 788-796; Ambassador: Dr LUCIANO MORDASINI.

Syria: Cité al-Manor III, No. 119, Tunis; tel. (1) 235-577; telex 13890; Ambassador: OMAR AS-SAID.

Turkey: 30 ave d'Afrique, BP 134, al-Menzah V, Tunis; tel. (1) 750-668; fax (1) 767-045; Ambassador: HÜSEYIN PAZARCI.

United Arab Emirates: 15 rue du 1er juin, Mutuelleville, Tunis; tel. (1) 783-522; telex 12168; Ambassador: HAMAD SALEM AL-MAQAMI.

United Kingdom: 5 place de la Victoire, Tunis; tel. (1) 341-444; fax (1) 354-877; e-mail british.emb@planet.tn; Ambassador: RICHARD EDIS.

USA: 144 ave de la Liberté, Tunis; tel. (1) 782-566; fax (1) 789-719; Ambassador: ROBIN L. RAPHEL.

Venezuela: 30 rue de Niger, 1002 Tunis; tel. (1) 285-075; telex 15091; Ambassador: JOSÉ ANTONIO QUIJADA SÁNCHEZ.

Yemen: rue Mouaouia ibn Soufiane, al-Menzah VI, Tunis; tel. (1) 237-933; telex 13045; Ambassador: RASHID MUHAMMAD THABIT.

Yugoslavia: 4 rue de Libéria, 1002 Tunis; tel. (1) 783-057; telex 18399; fax (1) 796-482; Chargé d'affaires a.i.: BRATISLAV KRSTIĆ.

Judicial System

The **Cour de Cassation** in Tunis has three civil and one criminal sections. There are three **Cours d'Appel** at Tunis, Sousse and Sfax, and 13 **Cours de Première Instance**, each having three chambers, except the **Cour de Première Instance** at Tunis which has eight chambers. **Justices Cantonales** exist in 51 areas.

Religion

The Constitution of 1956 recognizes Islam as the state religion, with the introduction of certain reforms, such as the abolition of polygamy. An estimated 7m., or 99% of the population, are Muslims. Minority religions include Jews (an estimated 2,000 adherents in 1993) and Christians. The Christian population comprises Roman Catholics, Greek Orthodox and French and English Protestants.

ISLAM
Grand Mufti of Tunisia: Sheikh MUHAMMAD HABIR BELKHODJA.

CHRISTIANITY
Reformed Church of Tunisia: 36 rue Charles de Gaulle, 1000 Tunis; tel. (1) 327-886; f. 1880; c. 100 mems; Pastor LEE DEHOOG.

Roman Catholic Church: 4 rue d'Alger, 1000 Tunis; tel. (1) 335-225; fax (1) 335-832; e-mail eveche.tunisie@gnet.tn; f. 1964; Bishop of Tunis Most Rev. FOUAD TWAL; 20,000 adherents (1997).

The Press

DAILIES

L'Action: 15 rue 2 mars 1934, Tunis; tel. (1) 264-899; telex 12163; f. 1932; French; organ of the Rassemblement constitutionnel démocratique (RCD); Dir MUSTAPHA MASMOUDI; circ. 50,000.

Al-Amal (Action): 15 rue 2 mars 1934, Tunis; tel. (1) 264-899; telex 12163; f. 1934; Arabic; organ of the RCD; Dir HUCINE MAGHREBI; circ. 50,000.

La Presse de Tunisie: 6 rue Ali Bach-Hamba, Tunis; tel. (1) 341-066; telex 13880; fax (1) 349-720; f. 1936; French; Dir MAHFOUZ MUHAMMAD; circ. 40,000.

As-Sabah (The Morning): 4 rue Ali Bach-Hamba, Tunis; tel. (1) 340-222; f. 1951; Arabic; Dir HABIB CHEIKHROUHOU; circ. 50,000.

PERIODICALS

Al-Akhbar (The News): 1 passage d'al-Houdaybiyah, Tunis; tel. (1) 344-100; f. 1984; weekly; general; Dir MUHAMMAD BEN YOUSUF; circ. 50,000.

Les Annonces: 6 rue de Sparte, BP 1343, Tunis; tel. (1) 350-177; telex 13206; fax (1) 347-184; f. 1978; 2 a week; French/Arabic; Dir MUHAMMAD NEJIB AZOUZ; circ. 170,000.

Al-Anouar at-Tounissia (Tunisian Lights): 10 rue ach-Cham, 1002 Tunis; tel. (1) 289-000; fax (1) 289-357; f. 1981; weekly; general; Dir SLAHEDDINE AL-AMRI; circ. 165,000.

L'Avenir: 26 rue Gamal Abd an-Nasser, BP 1200, Tunis; tel. (1) 258-941; f. 1980; weekly; organ of Mouvement des démocrates socialistes (MDS); Dir HASSIB BEN AMMAR; circ. 120,000.

Al-Bayan (The Manifesto): 87 ave Jughurta, Belvédère, 1002 Tunis; tel. (1) 791-098; fax (1) 796-400; f. 1977; weekly; general; Dir HÉDI DJILANI; circ. 120,000.

Al-Biladi (My Country): 15 rue 2 mars 1934, Tunis; telex 12163; f. 1974; Arabic; political and general weekly for Tunisian workers abroad; Dir HÉDI AL-GHALI; circ. 90,000.

Bulletin Mensuel de Statistiques: Institut National de la Statistique, BP 265, 1080 Tunis; tel. (1) 891-002; fax (1) 792-559; monthly.

Ach-Chourouk (Sunrise): 10 rue ach-Cham, Tunis; tel. (1) 834-000; fax (1) 830-337; weekly; general; Dir SLAHEDDINE AL-AMRI; circ. 70,000.

Conjoncture: 37 ave Khereddine Pacha, 1002 Tunis; tel. (1) 784-223; fax (1) 782-742; f. 1974; monthly; economic and financial surveys; Dir HOSNI TOUMI; circ. 5,000.

Démocratie: Tunis; f. 1978; monthly; French; organ of the MDS; Dir HASSIB BEN AMMAR; circ. 5,000.

Dialogue: Maison du RCD, blvd 9 avril 1938, Tunis; telex 12163; f. 1974; weekly; French; cultural and political organ of the RCD; Dir NACEUR BECHEKH; circ. 30,000.

Etudiant Tunisien: 11 rue d'Espagne, BP 286, Tunis; f. 1953; French and Arabic; Chief Editor FAOUZI AOUAM.

Al-Fajr (Dawn): Tunis; f. 1990; weekly; to become daily; Arabic; publ. of the Hizb an-Nahdah movement; Dir HAMADI JEBALI (imprisoned Jan. 1991).

Al-Falah: rue Alain Savary, al-Khadra, 1003 Tunis; tel. (1) 800-800; fax (1) 797-292; weekly; agricultural; Dir ABD AL-BAKI BACHA; Editor YAHIA AMOR; circ. 7,000.

Al-Fikr (Thought): 13 rue Dar al-Jel, BP 556, Tunis; tel. (1) 260-237; f. 1955; monthly; Arabic; cultural review.

Gazette Touristique: rue 8601, 40, Zone Industrielle, La Charguia 2, 2035 Tunis; tel. (1) 786-866; fax (1) 794-891; f. 1971; monthly; French; tourism; Dir TIJANI HADDAD; circ. 5,000.

L'Hebdo Touristique: rue 8601, 40, Zone Industrielle, La Charguia 2, 2035 Tunis; tel. (1) 786-866; fax (1) 794-891; f. 1971; weekly; French; tourism; Dir TIJANI HADDAD; circ. 5,000.

IBLA: Institut des Belles Lettres Arabes, 12 rue Jemaa el-Haoua, 1008 Tunis Bab Menara, Tunis; tel. (1) 560-133; fax (1) 572-683; f. 1937; 2 a year; French; social and cultural review on Maghreb and Muslim-Arab affairs; Dir J. FONTAINE.

Al-Idhaa wa Talvaza (Radio and Television): 71 ave de la Liberté, Tunis; tel. (1) 287-300; fax (1) 781-058; f. 1956; fortnightly; Arabic language broadcasting magazine; Dir Gen. ABD AL-HAFIDH HERGUEM; Editor WAHID BRAHAM; circ. 10,000.

Information Economique Africaine: 16 rue de Rome, BP 61, 1015 Tunis; tel. (1) 347-441; fax (1) 353-172; f. 1970; monthly; Dir MUHAMMAD ZERZERI.

Irfane (Children): 6 rue Mohammed Ali, 1000 Tunis; tel. (1) 256-877; fax (1) 351-521; f. 1965; monthly; Arabic; Dir-Gen. RIDHA EL OUADI; circ. 100,000.

Jeunesse Magazine: 6 rue Mohammed Ali, 1000 Tunis; tel. (1) 256-877; fax (1) 351-521; f. 1980; monthly; Arabic/French; Dir-Gen. RIDHA EL OUADI; circ. 30,000.

Journal Officiel de la République Tunisienne: ave Farhat Hached, 2040 Radès; tel. (1) 434-211; telex 14939; fax (1) 434-234; f. 1860; the official gazette; French and Arabic editions published twice weekly by the Imprimerie Officielle (The State Press); Pres. and Dir-Gen. ROMDHANE BEN MIMOUN; circ. 20,000.

Al-Maoukif: Tunis; tel. (1) 346-077; weekly; organ of the Rassemblement socialiste progressiste; Dir AHMAD NEJIB CHABI.

Al-Maraa (The Woman): 56 blvd Bab Benat, Tunis; tel. (1) 560-178; fax (1) 567-131; f. 1961; monthly; Arabic/French; political, economic and social affairs; issued by the Union Nationale de la Femme Tunisienne; Dir FAIZA KEFI; circ. 10,000.

Le Mensuel: Tunis; f. 1984; monthly; economic, social and cultural affairs.

Al-Moussawar: 10 rue ach-Cham, Tunis; tel. (1) 289-000; fax (1) 289-357; weekly; circ. 75,000.

Outrouhat: BP 492, 1049 Tunis; tel. (1) 230-092; monthly; scientific; Dir LOTFI BEN AISSA.

Ar-Rai (Opinion): Tunis; tel. (1) 242-251; f. 1977 by MDS; weekly; opposition newspaper; Dir HASSIB BEN AMAR; circ. 20,000.

Réalités: 85 rue de Palestine, Belvédère, BP 227, 1002 Tunis; tel. (1) 788-313; fax (1) 893-489; f. 1979; weekly; French/Arabic; Dir TAÏEB ZAHAR; circ. 25,000.

At-Tariq al-Jadid (New Road): 6 rue Metouia, Tunis; tel. (1) 246-400; fax (1) 350-748; f. 1981; organ of the Mouvement de la rénovation; Editor MOHAMED HARMEL.

Le Temps: 4 rue Ali Bach-Hamba, Tunis; tel. (1) 340-222; f. 1975; weekly; general news; French; Dir HABIB CHEIKHROUHOU; circ. 42,000.

Tounes al-Khadra: rue Alain Savary, 1003 Tunis; tel. (1) 800-800; fax (1) 797-292; f. 1976; monthly; agricultural, scientific and technical; Dir ABD AL-BAKI BACHA; Editor GHARBI HAMOUDA; circ. 5,000.

Tunis Hebdo: 1 passage d'al-Houdaybiyah, Tunis; tel. (1) 344-100; f. 1973; weekly; French; general and sport; Dir MUHAMMAD BEN YOUSUF; circ. 40,000.

NEWS AGENCIES

Tunis Afrique Presse (TAP): 7 ave Slimane Ben Slimane, 2092 al-Manar, Tunis; tel. (1) 889-000; telex 13400; fax (1) 883-500; f. 1961; Arab, French and English; offices in Algiers, Rabat, Paris and New York; daily news services; Chair. and Gen. Man. BRAHIM FRIDHI.

Foreign Bureaux

Agence France-Presse (AFP): 45 ave Habib Bourguiba, Tunis; tel. (1) 337-896; fax (1) 352-414; Chief MICHEL PIERRE DURIEUX.

Agencia EFE (Spain): 126 rue de Yougoslavie, 1000 Tunis; tel. (1) 321-497; fax (1) 325-976; e-mail manostos@gnet.tn; Chief MANUEL OSTOS LÓPEZ.

Agenzia Nazionale Stampa Associata (ANSA) (Italy): Tunis; tel. (1) 733-993; telex 12110; fax (1) 733-888; Chief MANUELA FONTANA.

Informatsionnoye Telegrafnoye Agentstvo Rossii— Telegrafnoye Agentstvo Suverennykh Stran (ITAR—TASS) (Russia): Tunis; tel. (1) 282-794; telex 12544; Chief VIKTOR LEBEDEV.

Inter Press Service (IPS) (Italy): 80 ave Tahar Ben Ammar, al-Menzah IX, 1013 Tunis; tel. (1) 880-182; fax (1) 880-848; f. 1976; Chief ABD AL-MAJID BEJAR.

Reuters (United Kingdom): BP 369, Belvédère, 1002 Tunis; tel. (1) 787-711; telex 13933; fax (1) 787-454; Senior Correspondent ABD AL-AZIZ BARROUHI.

Rossiiskoye Informatsionnoye Agentstvo—Vesti (RIA— Vesti) (Russia): 102 ave de la Liberté, Tunis; tel. (1) 283-781; telex 15448; Chief NICOLAS SOLOGUBOVSKII.

Xinhua (New China) News Agency (People's Republic of China): 6 rue Smyrne, Notre Dame, Tunis; tel. (1) 281-308; telex 12127; Dir XIE BINYU.

Publishers

Addar al-Arabia Lil Kitab: 4 ave Mohieddine El Klibi, al-Manar 2, BP 32, 2092 al-Manar 2, Tunis; tel. (1) 888-255; telex 14966; fax (1) 888-365; f. 1975; general literature, children's books, non-fiction; Dir-Gen. REBAH DEKHILI.

Agence de Promotion de l'Industrie (API): 63 rue de Syrie, Belvédère, 1002 Tunis; tel. (1) 792-144; telex 14166; fax (1) 782-482; e-mail api@api.com.tn; f. 1987 by merger; industrial investment; Gen. Man. TAHAR ENNEIFER.

Bouslama Editions: 15 ave de France, 1000 Tunis; tel. (1) 243-745; telex 14230; fax (1) 381-100; f. 1960; history, children's books; Man. Dir ALI BOUSLAMA.

Ceres Productions: 6 ave Abd ar-Rahman Azzam, BP 56, 1002 Tunis; tel. (1) 782-033; fax (1) 787-516; e-mail ceres@planet.tn; f. 1964; art books, literature, novels; Dir MUHAMMAD BEN SMAIL.

Dar al-Amal: rue 2 mars 1934, Tunis; tel. (1) 264-899; telex 12163; f. 1976; economics, sociology, politics; Man. Dir S. ZOGHLAMI.

Dar al-Kitab: 5 ave Bourguiba, 4000 Sousse; tel. (3) 25097; f. 1950; literature, children's books, legal studies, foreign books; Pres. TAIEB KACEM; Dir FAYÇAL KACEM.

Dar as-Sabah: Centre Interurbain, BP 441, al-Menzah, 1004 Tunis; tel. (1) 717-222; fax (1) 718-366; f. 1951; 200 mems; publishes daily and weekly papers which circulate throughout Tunisia, North Africa, France, Belgium, Luxembourg and Germany; Dir-Gen. MONCEF CHEIKHROUHOU.

Imprimerie al-Manar: 12 rue du Tribunal, Tunis; tel. (1) 260-641; telex 14894; fax (1) 560-641; f. 1938; general, educational, Islam; Man. Dir HABIB M'HAMDI.

Institut National de la Statistique: 70 rue ach-Cham, BP 265, 1080 Tunis; tel. (1) 891-002; fax (1) 792-559; publishes a variety of annuals, periodicals and papers concerned with the economic policy and devt of Tunisia.

Maison Tunisienne d'Edition: Tunis; tel. (1) 235-873; telex 12032; fax (1) 353-992; f. 1966; all kinds of books, magazines, etc.; Dir ABDELAZIZ ACHOURI.

An-Najah—Editions Hedi Ben Abd al-Gheni: 11 ave de France, Tunis; tel. (1) 246-886; Arab and French books, Koranic texts.

Société d'Arts Graphiques, d'Edition et de Presse: 15 rue 2 mars 1934, La Kasbah, Tunis; tel. (1) 264-988; telex 13411; fax (1) 569-736; f. 1974; prints and publishes daily papers, magazines, books, etc.; Chair. and Man. Dir HASSEN FERJANI.

Société Tunisienne de Diffusion (STD): 5 ave de Carthage, BP 440, Tunis; tel. (1) 255-000; telex 12521; general and educational books, office supplies; Man. Dir SLAHEDDINE BEN HAMIDA.

Sud Editions: Tunis; tel. (1) 785-179; telex 12363; fax (1) 792-905; f. 1976; Arab literature, art and art history; Man. Dir M. MASMOUDI.

Government Publishing House

Imprimerie Officielle de la République Tunisienne: ave Farhat Hached, 2040 Radès; tel. (1) 434-211; telex 14939; fax (1) 434-234; f. 1860; Man. Dir ROMDHANE BEN MIMOUN.

Broadcasting and Communications

TELECOMMUNICATIONS

Société Tunisienne d'Entreprise de Télécommunications (SOTETEL): Tunis; state-owned; scheduled for transfer to private ownership in 1998.

Tunisie Télécom: rue Asdrubal, 1002 Tunis; tel. (1) 801-717; telex 18118; fax (1) 800-777; Gen. Man. AHMED MAHJOUB.

BROADCASTING

Radio

Etablissement de la Radiodiffusion-Télévision Tunisienne (ERTT): 71 ave de la Liberté, 1002 Tunis; tel. (1) 287-300; telex 14560; fax (1) 785-146; e-mail info@radiotunis.com; internet http://www.radiotunis.com; govt service; broadcasts in Arabic, French and Italian; stations at Gafsa, El-Kef, Monastir, Sfax and Tunis (two); Dir-Gen. ABDELHAFIDH HARGUEM.

Television

Etablissement de la Radiodiffusion-Télévision Tunisienne: (see Radio).

Television was introduced in northern and central Tunisia in January 1966, and by 1972 transmission covered the country. A relay station to link up with European transmissions was built at al-Haouaria in 1967, and a second channel was introduced in 1983.

Finance

(cap. = capital; dep. = deposits; res = reserves; m. = million; brs = branches; amounts in dinars unless otherwise stated)

BANKING

Central Bank

Banque Centrale de Tunisie (BCT): 7 rue Hédi Nouira, BP 369, 1001 Tunis; tel. (1) 254-000; telex 15375; fax (1) 340-615; e-mail bct@bct.gov.tn; f. 1958; cap. 6.0m., dep. 1,978.5m., res 20.1m., total assets 3,867.1m. (Dec. 1996); Gov. MUHAMMAD EL BEJI HAMDA; Vice-Gov. MOHAMED DAOUAS; 10 brs.

Commercial Banks

AMEN Bank: 13 ave de France, BP 52, 1080 Tunis; tel. (1) 340-511; telex 14079; fax (1) 349-909; e-mail amenbank@com.tn; f. 1967

as Crédit Foncier et Commercial de Tunisie; cap. 40m., total assets 892.5m. (Dec. 1996); Chair. and Pres. RACHID BEN YEDDER; Gen. Man. AHMED EL KARM; 72 brs.

Arab Tunisian Bank: 9 rue Hédi Nouira, 1001 Tunis; tel. (1) 351-155; telex 14205; fax (1) 342-852; f. 1982; cap. 17.8m., total assets 642.1m. (Dec. 1995); Dir-Gen. HAMMOUDA BELKHODJA; 29 brs.

Banque de l'Habitat: 4 rue J. Jacques Rousseau, BP 242, 1002 Tunis; tel. (1) 785-277; telex 14349; fax (1) 784-417; f. 1984; 57.4% govt-owned; cap. 47.5m., total assets 1,175.9m. (Dec. 1996); Chair. TAHAR BOURKHIS; 49 brs.

Banque Internationale Arabe de Tunisie (BIAT): 70–72 ave Habib Bourguiba, BP 520, 1080 Tunis; tel. (1) 340-733; telex 14091; fax (1) 340-680; f. 1976; cap. 80.0m., dep. 1,320m., res 24.9m., total assets 1,947m. (Dec. 1997); Pres. MOKHTAR FAKHFAKH; 80 brs.

Banque Nationale Agricole: rue Hédi Nouira, 1001 Tunis; tel. (1) 791-000; telex 15436; fax (1) 793031; f. 1989 by merger of the Banque Nationale du Développement Agricole and the Banque Nationale de Tunisie; cap. 100m., dep. 2,225.7m., res 200.3m. (Dec. 1996); Pres. BERID BEN TANFOUS; 140 brs.

Banque du Sud: 95 ave de la Liberté, 1002 Tunis; tel. (1) 849-400; telex 14351; fax (1) 847-352; f. 1968; cap. 100m., dep. 627.6m., res 29.9m. (1997); Pres. LAROUSSI BAYOUDH; 85 brs.

Banque de Tunisie SA: 2 rue de Turquie, BP 289, 1001 Tunis; tel. (1) 332-188; telex 14070; fax (1) 349-401; f. 1884; cap. 25m., dep. 1,070.6m., res 29.4m. (Dec. 1997); Chair. and Man. Dir FAOUZI BELKAHIA; 77 brs and agencies.

Citibank N.A.: 3 ave Jugurtha, BP 72, Belvédère, 1002 Tunis; tel. (1) 790-066; telex 15139; fax (1) 785-556; f. 1989; cap. 10m., total assets 142.2m. (Dec. 1995); Dir-Gen. ERIC PHILIPPE STOCLET; 2 brs.

Société Tunisienne de Banque (STB): rue Hédi Nouira, 1001 Tunis; tel. (1) 340-477; telex 14135; fax (1) 348-400; f. 1957; 19.3% govt-owned; merged with BNDT (q.v.) in 1998; cap. 80m., dep. 1,373.0m., res 32.1m. (Dec. 1996); Chair. and Gen. Man. BÉCHIR TRABELSI; 113 brs.

Union Bancaire pour le Commerce et l'Industrie: 139 ave de la Liberté, 1002 Tunis; tel. (1) 842-000; telex 14990; fax (1) 846-187; f. 1961; cap. 30m., total assets 748.4m. (Dec. 1996); affiliated to Banque Nationale de Paris Intercontinentale; Chair. ABD AS-SALAM BEN AYED; 28 brs and agencies.

Union Internationale de Banques SA: 65 ave Habib Bourguiba, BP 109, 1001 Tunis; tel. (1) 247-000; telex 15397; fax (1) 780-440; f. 1963 as a merging of Tunisian interests by the Société Tunisienne de Banque with Crédit Lyonnais (France) and other foreign banks, including Banca Commerciale Italiana; merged with Banque de Tunisie et des Emirats d'Investissement in 1998; cap. 70m., dep. 633.9m., res 17.7m. (Dec. 1996); Pres. and Gen. Man. IBRAHIM SAADA; 94 brs.

Merchant Banks

Banque d'Affaires de Tunisie (BAT): Tunis; f. 1997; cap. 3m.; Gen. Man. ARNAUD DINASHIN.

International Maghreb Merchant Bank (IM Bank): blvd 7 novembre, 2035 Tunis; tel. (1) 708-220; fax (1) 708-020; f. 1995; auth. cap. 3m., total assets 3.1m. (Dec. 1995); Pres. MONCEF CHEIKH-ROUHOU; CEO ABDEL AWNI AZIZ DAJANI.

Development Banks

Banque Arabe Tuniso-Libyenne pour le Développement et le Commerce Extérieur: 25 ave Kheireddine Pacha, BP 102, Belvédère, 1002 Tunis; tel. (1) 781-500; telex 14938; fax (1) 782-818; f. 1983; promotes trade and devt projects between Tunisia and Libya, and provides funds for investment in poorer areas; cap. 53.7m., dep. 57.8m., res 12.9m. (Dec. 1996); Pres., Chair. and Gen. Man. SAID M'RABET.

Banque de Coopération du Maghreb Arabe: ave Muhammad V, BP 46, Belvédère, 1002 Tunis; tel. (1) 780-311; telex 13404; fax (1) 781-056; f. 1981, began operations 1982; finances jt devt projects between Tunisia and Algeria; cap. 30.0m., total assets 75.8m. (Dec. 1996); Pres. MUHAMMAD BEN HALIMA; Dir-Gen. CHEFIK BEN HAMZA.

Banque de Développement Economique de Tunisie (BDET): 34 rue Hédi Karray, al-Menzah 1004, BP 48, 1080 Tunis; tel. (1) 718-000; telex 14133; fax (1) 713-744; f. 1959; main source of long-term and equity finance for industrial and tourist enterprises; cap. 50.0m., dep. 662.4m., res 35.4m. (Dec. 1996); Pres. ALI DEBAYA.

Banque Nationale de Développement Touristique (BNDT): ave Muhammad V, 1002 Tunis; tel. (1) 785-322; telex 15265; fax (1) 784-778; f. 1969; merged with STB (q.v.) in 1998; cap. 30.9m., dep. 387.8m., res 34.9m. (Dec. 1996); Pres. SAID M'RABET.

Banque Tunisienne de Solidarité: 56 ave Muhammad V, 1001 Tunis; tel. (1) 844-040; fax (1) 845-537; f. 1997; provides long-term finance for small-scale projects; cap. 30m.; Pres. ABD AL-LATIF SADAM.

Banque Tuniso-Koweïtienne de Développement: 10 bis ave Muhammad V, BP 49, 1001 Tunis; tel. (1) 340-000; telex 14834; fax

(1) 343-106; e-mail fredj.abdelmajid@btkd.com.tn; f. 1981; provides long-term finance for devt projects; cap. 100m., total assets 441.7m. (Dec. 1996); Dir-Gen. ABDELMAJID FREDJ.

Société Tuniso-Séoudienne d'Investissement et de Développement (STUSID): 32 rue Hédi Karray, BP 20, 1002 Tunis; tel. (1) 718-233; telex 13594; fax (1) 719-233; f. 1981; provides long-term finance for devt projects; cap. 100m., total assets 247.3m. (Dec. 1996); Chair. Dr MAHSOUN BAHJET JALAL; Pres. ABDELGHAFFAR EZZEDDINE.

'Offshore' Banks

Alubaf International Bank: 90–92 ave Hédi Chaker, BP 51, Belvédère, 1002 Tunis; tel. (1) 783-500; telex 17471; fax (1) 801-395; f. 1985; cap. US $25.0m., dep. $69.4m., res $1.8m. (Dec. 1994); Dirs MUHAMMAD ABDULJAWAD, MICHEL MARTO; Gen. Man. FARAG ALI GAMRA.

Arab Banking Corpn BSC: 3 ave Jugurtha, BP 57, 1002 Tunis; tel. (1) 786-752; telex 17255; fax (1) 788-990; f. 1993; cap. US $6m., total assets $20.1m. (Dec. 1995); Pres. RACHID BEN YEDDER.

Beit Ettamwil Saudi Tounsi (BEST): 88 ave Hédi Chaker, 1002 Tunis; tel. (1) 790-000; telex 14084; fax (1) 780-235; f. 1983; cap. US $50m., total assets $156.0m. (Dec. 1996); Pres. Dr SALAH JEMIL MALAIKA.

North Africa International Bank: 25 ave Kheireddine Pacha, BP 485, 1080 Tunis; tel. (1) 785-200; telex 14940; fax (1) 782-537; f. 1983; cap. US $16.3m., total assets $131.0m. (Dec. 1996); Pres. MUHAMMAD ALI RIANY.

Tunis International Bank: 18 ave des Etats-Unis d'Amérique, BP 81, 1002 Tunis; tel. (1) 782-411; telex 14051; fax (1) 782-479; f. 1982; cap. US $25m., total assets $152.9m. (Dec. 1996); Chair. ZOUHAIR KHOURI.

STOCK EXCHANGE

Bourse des Valeurs Mobilières de Tunis: 19 bis Kemal Attaturk, 1002 Tunis; tel. (1) 299-411; fax (1) 347-256; Chair. AHMED HADDOUEJ.

INSURANCE

Caisse Tunisienne d'Assurances Mutuelles Agricoles: 6 ave Habib Thameur, 1000 Tunis; tel. (1) 340-933; telex 12451; f. 1912; Pres. MOKTAR BELLAGHA; Dir-Gen. SLAHEDDINE FERCHIOU.

Compagnie d'Assurances Tous Risques et de Réassurance (ASTREE): 45 ave Kheireddine Pacha, BP 780, 1002 Tunis; tel. (1) 792-211; telex 15149; fax (1) 794-723; f. 1950; cap. 4m. dinars; Pres. and Dir-Gen. MUHAMMAD HACHICHA.

Compagnie Tunisienne pour l'Assurance du Commerce Extérieur (COTUNACE): ave Muhammad V/Montplaisir I, rue 8006, 1002 Tunis; tel. (1) 783-000; telex 17373; fax (1) 782-539; f. 1984; cap. 5m. dinars; 50 mem. cos; Pres. and Dir-Gen. MONCEF ZOUARI.

Lloyd Tunisien: 7 ave de Carthage, 1000 Tunis; tel. (1) 340-911; telex 13293; fax (1) 340-909; f. 1945; fire, accident, liability, marine, life; cap. 1m. dinars; Chair. and Man. Dir M. ELTAIEF.

Société Tunisienne d'Assurance et de Réassurance (STAR): ave de Paris, Tunis; tel. (1) 340-866; fax (1) 340-835; f. 1958.

Tunis-Ré (Société Tunisienne de Réassurance): ave Muhammad V, 1002 Tunis; tel. (1) 844-011; telex 17303; fax (1) 787-573; f. 1981; all kinds of reinsurance; cap. 35m. dinars; Pres. and Dir-Gen. EZZEDINE SOUAI.

Trade and Industry

GOVERNMENT AGENCIES

Centre de Promotion des Exportations (CEPEX): 28 rue Ghandi, 1001 Tunis; tel. (1) 350-344; telex 14716; fax (1) 353-683; e-mail cepexedpue@attmail.com; f. 1973; state export promotion org.; Pres. and Dir-Gen. HAMDANE BEN OTHMAN.

Foreign Investment Promotion Agency (FIPA): 63 rue de Syrie, 1002 Tunis; tel. (1) 792-144; fax (1) 782-971; e-mail fipa.tunisia @mcl.gov.tn; internet http://www.investintunisia.tn; f. 1995; Dir-Gen. FAOUZI DHEMAIED.

Office du Commerce de Tunisie (OCT): 1 rue de Syrie, 1060 Tunis; tel. (1) 682-901; telex 14177; Dir-Gen. MUHAMMAD AMOR.

CHAMBERS OF COMMERCE AND INDUSTRY

Chambre de Commerce et d'Industrie de Tunis: 1 rue des Entrepreneurs, 1000 Tunis; tel. (1) 350-300; telex 14718; fax (1) 354-744; e-mail ccitunis@planet.tn; f. 1885; 25 mems; Pres. YOUNES MENNAI.

Chambre de Commerce et d'Industrie du Centre: rue Chadli Khaznadar, 4000 Sousse; tel. (3) 225-044; fax (3) 224-227; f. 1895; 25 mems; Pres. KABOUDI MONCEF; Dir FATEN BASLY.

Chambre de Commerce et d'Industrie du Nord-Est: 46 rue ibn Khaldoun, 7000 Bizerte; tel. (2) 431-044; telex 21086; fax (2) 432-379; f. 1903; 5 mems; Pres. KANEL BELKAHIA; Dir MOUFIDA CHAKROUN.

Chambre de Commerce et d'Industrie de Sfax: 10 rue Tahar, BP 794, 3018 Sfax; tel. (4) 296-120; telex 40767; fax (4) 296-121; f. 1895; 25,000 mems; Dir IKRAM MAKNI.

INDUSTRIAL AND TRADE ASSOCIATIONS

Agence de Promotion de l'Industrie (API): 63 rue de Syrie, 1002 Tunis; tel. and fax (1) 792-144; telex 14166; f. 1987 by merger; co-ordinates industrial policy, undertakes feasibility studies, organizes industrial training and establishes industrial zones; overseas offices in Belgium, France, Germany, Italy, the United Kingdom, Sweden and the USA; Pres. and Dir-Gen. MUHAMMAD BEN KHALIFA.

Compagnie des Phosphates de Gafsa (CPG): Cité Bayech, Gafsa; tel. (6) 22022; telex 60007; f. 1897; production and marketing of phosphates; Pres. MUHAMMAD AL-FADHEL KHELIL.

Entreprise Tunisienne d'Activités Petrolières (ETAP): 27 ave Kheireddine Pacha, BP 367, 1002 Tunis; tel. (1) 782-288; telex 15128; fax (1) 784-092; responsible for exploration and investment in hydrocarbons.

Office des Céréales: Ministry of Agriculture, 30 rue Alain Savary, Tunis; tel. (1) 790-351; telex 14709; fax (1) 789-573; f. 1962; responsible for the cereals industry; Chair. and Dir-Gen. A. SADDEM.

Office National des Mines: BP 215, 1080 Tunis; tel. (1) 787-366; telex 15004; fax (1) 794-016; f. 1963; mining of iron ores; research and study of mineral wealth; Pres. and Dir-Gen. ABD AR-RAHMAN TOUHAMI.

Office National des Pêches (ONP): Le Port, La Goulette, Tunis; tel. (1) 275-093; telex 12388; marine and fishing authority; Dir-Gen. L. HALAB.

Office des Terres Domaniales (OTD): 43 rue d'Iran, Tunis; tel. (1) 280-322; telex 13566; f. 1961; responsible for agricultural production and the management of state-owned lands; Dir BECHIR BEN SMAIL.

Société Générale des Industries Textiles (SOGITEX): Bir Kassaa, Ben Arous, Tunis; tel. (1) 297-100; telex 12444; responsible for the textile industry; Chair. BECHIR SAIDANE.

UTILITIES

Electricity and Gas

Société Tunisienne de l'Electricité et du Gaz (STEG): 38 rue Kemal Atatürk, BP 190, 1080 Tunis; tel.(1) 341-311; telex 14020; fax (1) 349-981; f. 1962; responsible for generation and distribution of electricity and for production of natural gas; Pres. and Gen. Man. MONCEF MOUELHI; 35 brs.

MAJOR COMPANIES

Entreprises Ali Mheni (EAM): 12 bis rue de Russie, BP 609, Tunis; tel. (1) 252-433; telex 12562; f. 1934; construction and civil engineering, public works, building; Chair. ALI MHENI; 3,500 employees.

Bata Tunisienne SA: route de Mornag, Km 7, Ben Arous, Tunis; tel. (1) 380-485; telex 12041; f. 1934; manufacture of shoes and sandals; Dir-Gen. ROGER SICCO.

Compagnie Générale des Salines de Tunisie (COTUSAL): 19 rue de Turquie, Tunis; tel. (1) 347-666; telex 15354; fax (1) 336-163; f. 1949; production of edible and industrial sea salt; Man. Dir NORBERT DE GUILLEBON.

Grands Ateliers du Nord SA: route de Mornag, GP 1 Km 12, az-Zahra Hammam-Lif, Tunis; tel. (1) 482-422; telex 13254; f. 1975; manufacture of agricultural and building equipment; sales TD 10m., cap. p.u. TD 1.4m. (1991); Pres. ABDELAZIZ GUIDARA; 1,000 employees.

Groupe Chimique Tunisien: 7 rue Royaume d'Arabie Saoudite, 1002 Tunis; tel. (1) 784-488; telex 14705; fax (1) 783-485; f. 1952; production of Phosphoric acid and fertilizers; Chair. RAFAA DKHIL.

Industries Maghrébines de l'Aluminium (IMAL): 2035 Tunis; tel. (1) 795-979; telex 15376; fax (1) 782-074; f. 1965; manufacture and distribution of aluminium products; cap. p.u. TD 57,000; Chair. T. OUNAIS; 50 employees.

Industries Mécaniques Maghrébines (IMM): Kairouan; tel. (7) 722-028; fax (7) 722-685; f. 1982; ownership 20% General Motors, 10% Isuzu Motors, 70% local investors; production of light commercial vehicles; Man. Dir TAHAR LATROUS.

Skanes Meubles: route de Sousse, 5000 Monastir; tel. (3) 61390; telex 30734; manufacture of furniture and hotel equipment, toys; Pres. AHMAD TRIMECH.

Société Industrielle de Pêches et de Conserves Alimentaires SA: ave Habib Bourguiba, Megrine-Riadh; tel. (1) 295-500; telex 12240; fish, fruit and vegetable processing and canning; Dir-Gen. ALI MABROUK.

Société Tunisienne Automobile, Financière, Immobilière et Maritime (STAFIM): 85 ave Louis Braille, 1003 Tunis; tel. (1) 785-055; fax (1) 782-467; f. 1932; sales of cars, spare parts, engines and mechanical machinery; Dir-Gen. DOMINIQUE DOUROUZE.

Tunisienne de Conserves Alimentaires (TUCAL): 15 rue Sidi Bou Mendil, Tunis; tel. (1) 241-617; manufacture and distribution of canned food products; Pres. and Gen. Man. AMOR BEN SEDRINE.

TRADE AND OTHER UNIONS

Union Générale des Etudiants de Tunisie (UGET): 11 rue d'Espagne, Tunis; f. 1953; 600 mems; Pres. MEKKI FITOURI.

Union Générale Tunisienne du Travail (UGTT): 29 place Muhammad Ali, Tunis; f. 1946 by FARHAT HACHED; affiliated to ICFTU; mems 360,000 in 23 affiliated unions; 18-member exec. bureau; Sec.-Gen. ISMAIL SAHBANI.

Union Nationale des Agriculteurs (UNA): 6 ave Habib Thameur, 1000 Tunis; tel; (1) 246-920; fax (1) 349-843; f. 1955; Pres. BACHA ABD AL-BAKI.

Union Nationale de la Femme Tunisienne (UNFT): 56 blvd Bab Benat, Tunis; tel. (1) 560-181; fax (1) 567-131; f. 1956; 100,000 mems; Pres. FAIZA KEFI; Vice-Pres. NADHIRA ERRAÏES.

Union Tunisienne de l'Industrie, du Commerce et de l'Artisanat (UTICAL): 103 ave de la Liberté, Belvédère, 1002 Tunis; tel. (1) 780-366; telex 18982; fax (1) 782-143; f.1946; mems: 15 national federations and 170 syndical chambers at national levels; Pres. HEDI JILANI.

Transport

RAILWAYS

In 1997 the total length of railways was 2,170 km. A total of 30m. passengers travelled by rail in Tunisia in that year.

Société du Métro Léger de Tunis (SMLT): 60–62 ave Jean-Jaurès, BP 4, 1002 Tunis; tel. (1) 348-555; telex 14072; fax (1) 338-100; f. 1981; operates light railway system in and around Tunis (total length 53 km); Pres. and Dir-Gen. MONCEF KAFSI.

Société Nationale des Chemins de Fer Tunisiens (SNCFT): 67 ave Farhat Hached, 1001 Tunis; tel. (1) 249-999; telex 14019; fax (1) 344-045; f. 1956; state org. controlling all Tunisian railways; Pres. and Dir-Gen. ALI CHEIKH KHALFALLAH.

ROADS

In 1996 there were an estimated 23,100 km of roads. Of these, 6,240 km were main roads and 7,900 km secondary roads.

Société Nationale des Transports (SNT): 1 ave Habib Bourguiba, BP 660, 1025 Tunis; tel. (1) 259-422; telex 15196; fax (1) 342-727; f. 1963; operates 166 local bus routes with 906 buses; Chair. and Man. Dir CHEDLY HAJRI; Gen. Man. HASSINE HASSANI.

Société Nationale de Transport Interurbain (SNTRI): ave Muhammad V, BP 40, Belvédère, 1002 Tunis; tel. (1) 784-433; telex 18335; fax (1) 786-605; f. 1981; Dir-Gen. SLAHEDDINE MZABI.

There are 12 **Sociétés Régionales des Transports**, responsible for road transport, operating in different regions in Tunisia.

SHIPPING

Tunisia has seven major ports: Tunis-La Goulette, Radès, Bizerta, Sousse, Sfax, Gabès and Zarzis. There is a special petroleum port at La Skhirra.

Office des Ports Nationaux Tunisiens: Bâtiment Administratif, Port de la Goulette, 2060 La Goulette; tel. (1) 735-300; telex 15386; fax (1) 735-812; maritime port administration; Pres. and Dir-Gen. HICHEM LAJNEF.

Cie Générale Maritime: Résidence Alain Savary, Bloc D7, Apt 74, 1003 Tunis; tel. and fax (1) 711-475; Chair. MOUFID CHIHEB ESSEFI.

Cie Tunisienne de Navigation SA (CTN): 5 ave Dag Hammarskjoeld, BP 40, 1001 Tunis; tel. (1) 341-777; telex 14202; fax (1) 350-976; f. 1959; state-owned; brs at Bizerta, Gabès, La Skhirra, La Goulette, Radès, Sfax and Sousse; Chair. HABIB DALDOUL.

Gabès Chimie Transport: 7–9 rue Khartoum, 1002 Tunis; tel. (1) 283-174; telex 13323; fax (1) 787-821; transportation of chemicals; fleet of 3 chemical tankers; Chair. HAFEDH EL-MOKHTAR.

Gabès Marine Tanker: Immeuble SETCAR, route de Sousse, km 13, 2034 Ez-Zahra; tel. (1) 445-644; fax (1) 454-650; Chair. FÉRID ABBES.

Gas Marine: Immeuble SETCAR, route de Sousse, km 13, 2034 Ez-Zahra; tel. (1) 454-644; fax (1) 454-650; Chair. HAMMADI ABBES.

Hannibal Marine Transport: 10 rue 8161, Cité Olympique, 1003 Tunis; tel. (1) 807-032; fax (1) 773-805; Chair. AMEUR MAHJOUB.

Société Tunisienne de Navigation Pétrolière (PETRONAV): Immeuble Saâdi, BP 84, 2080 Ariana; tel. (1) 717-576; fax (1) 718-811; Chair. HICHEM KHATTECH.

SONOTRAK: ave Mohamed Hédi Khafacha, Gare Maritime de Kerkenna, 3000 Sfax; tel. (4) 222-216; fax (4) 298-496; Chair. MUSTAPHA JABEUR.

Tunisian Shipping Transport Co: 9 rue Amilcar, 1001 Tunis; tel. (1) 346-766; fax (1) 345-545; Chair. ABDELHAMID DOUIK.

CIVIL AVIATION

There are international airports at Tunis-Carthage, Sfax, Djerba, Monastir, Tabarka, Gafsa and Tozeur.

Office de l'Aviation Civile et des Aéroports: BP 137, Aéroport International de Tunis-Carthage, 1090 Tunis; tel. (1) 754-000; telex 13809; fax (1) 755-133; f. 1970; air traffic control and airport administration; Pres. and Dir-Gen. HABIB ALLEGUE.

Nouvelair Tunisie: BP 66, Aéroport International, 5000 Monastir; tel. (3) 467-100; fax (3) 467-110; f. 1989 as Air Liberté Tunisie; name changed as above in 1995; Tunisian charter co; flights from Tunis, Djerba and Monastir airports to Scandinavia and other European countries; Chair. AZIZ MILAD; Gen. Man. SLAHEDDINE KASTALLI.

Tuninter: BP 1080, Immeuble Securas ZI Charguia 11, 1080 Tunis; tel. (1) 701-717; fax (1) 712-193; e-mail tuninter@mail.gnet.tn; f. 1992; Tunisian charter co; Man. Dir ABDERRAZAK OUERDANI.

TunisAir (Société Tunisienne de l'Air): blvd 7 novembre, 2035 Tunis; tel. (1) 700-100; telex 15283; fax (1) 700-008; f. 1948; 45.2% govt-owned; 20% of assets privatized in 1995; flights to Africa, Europe and the Middle East; Pres. and Dir-Gen. AHMED SMAOUI.

Tunisavia (Société de Transports, Services et Travaux Aériens): Immeuble Saadi Spric, Tour CD, 1082 al-Menzah, Tunis; tel. (1) 717-600; telex 13121; fax (1) 718-100; f. 1974; helicopter and charter operator; Pres. AZIZ MILAD; Man. Dir JILANI BENM'BAREK.

Tourism

The main tourist attractions are the magnificent sandy beaches, Moorish architecture and remains of the Roman Empire. Tunisia contains the site of the ancient Phoenician city of Carthage. Tourism, a principal source of foreign exchange, has expanded rapidly, following extensive government investment in hotels, improved roads and other facilities. The number of hotel beds increased from 71,529 in 1980 to 161,000 in 1995. In 1997 foreign tourist arrivals totalled 4.3m. (compared with 3.9m. in 1996). Receipts from tourism in 1997 totalled 1,540m. dinars.

Office National du Tourisme Tunisien: 1 ave Muhammad V, 1001 Tunis; tel. (1) 341-077; telex 14381; fax (1) 350-997; e-mail info@tourismtunisia.com; internet http://www.tourismtunisia.com; f. 1958; Dir-Gen. FAKHREDDINE MESSAI.

Defence

Chief of Staff of the Army: Gen. MUHAMMAD SAID AL-KATEB.

Chief of Staff of the Navy: Adm. HABIB FEDHILA.

Chief of Staff of the Air Force: Gen. RIDHA ATTAR.

Defence Budget (1997): 454m. dinars (US $418m.).

Military Service: 1 year (selective).

Total Armed Forces (August 1997): 35,000 (army 27,000; navy 4,500; air force 3,500).

Paramilitary Forces (August 1997): 12,000 National Guard).

Education

Education is compulsory in Tunisia for a period of nine years between the ages of six and 16. Primary education begins at six years of age and normally lasts for six years. Secondary education begins at 12 years of age and lasts for seven years, comprising a first cycle of three years and a second cycle of four years. In 1995 the total enrolment at primary and secondary schools was equivalent to 87% of the school-age population (90% of boys; 85% of girls). In that year an estimated 97% of children in the primary age-group (98% of boys; 95% of girls) were enrolled at primary schools; enrolment at secondary schools included 61% of children in the relevant age-group (63% of boys; 59% of girls). Proposed administrative budget expenditure on education was 1,023.6m. dinars in 1995, representing 18.3% of total government spending.

Arabic is the first language of instruction in primary and secondary schools, but French is also used. French is used almost exclusively in higher education. The University of Tunis was opened in 1959/60. In 1988 the university was divided into separate institutions: one for science, the other for arts. It has 54 faculties and institutes. In 1986 two new universities were opened, at Monastir and Sfax. In 1995/96 a total of 112,634 students were enrolled at universities in Tunisia. Adult illiteracy averaged 62.0% (males 48.9%; females 75.2%) in 1975, but, according to UNESCO estimates, the rate declined to 33.3% (males 21.4%; females 45.4%) in 1995.

Bibliography

Anthony, John. *About Tunisia.* London, 1961.

Ardant, Gavriel. *La Tunisie d'Aujourd'hui et Demain.* Paris, 1961.

Ashford, Douglas E. *Morocco-Tunisia: Politics and Planning.* Syracuse University Press, 1965.

Basset, André. *Initiation à la Tunisie.* Paris, 1950.

Ben Salem, Mohamed. *L'Antichambre de l'Indépendance.* Tunis, CERES Productions, 1988.

Bessis, Sophie, and Belhassen, Souhayr. *Bourguiba Tome 1: A la conquête d'un destin (1901–1957).* Paris, Jeune Afrique Livres, 1988.

Bourguiba, Habib. *La Tunisie et la France.* Paris, 1954.

   Hadith al-Jamaa. (Collected Broadcasts) Tunis, 1957.

Brunschvig, Robert. *La Tunisie au haut Moyen Age.* Cairo, 1948.

Camau, Michel. *Tunisie au présent. Une modernité au-dessus de tout soupçon?* Paris, Centre National de la Recherche, 1987.

Cambon, Henri. *Histoire de la régence de Tunisie.* Paris, 1948.

Depois, Jean. *La Tunisie, ses Régions.* Paris, 1959.

Duvignaud, Jean. *Tunisie.* Lausanne, Editions Rencontre, 1965.

Duwaji, Ghazi. *Economic Development in Tunisia.* New York, Praeger, 1967.

Garas, Felix. *Bourguiba et la Naissance d'une Nation.* Paris, 1956.

Guen, Moncef. *La Tunisie indépendante face à son économie.* Paris, 1961.

Joffe, E. G. H. Editor. *North Africa: Nation, State and Region.* London, Routledge, 1993.

Knapp, W. *Tunisia.* London, Thames and Hudson, 1972.

Laitman, Leon. *Tunisia Today: Crisis in North Africa.* New York, 1954.

Ling, Dwight D. *Tunisia, from Protectorate to Republic.* Indiana University Press, 1967.

Memmi, Albert. *Le Pharaon.* Paris, Julliard, 1988.

Micaud, C. A. *Tunisia, the Politics of Moderation.* New York, 1964.

Moore, C. H. *Tunisia since Independence.* Berkeley, University of California Press, 1965.

Nerfin, M. *Entretiens avec Ahmed Ben Salah.* Paris, F. Maspero, 1974.

Perkins, Kenneth J. *Historical Dictionary of Tunisia* (African Historical Dictionaries, No. 45). Metuchen, NJ, and London, The Scarecrow Press, 1989.

Raymond, André. *La Tunisie.* Series *Que sais-je,* No. 318, Paris, 1961.

Rudebeck, Lars. *Party and People: A Study of Political Change in Tunisia.* London, C. Hurst, 1969.

Salem, Norma. *Habib Bourguiba, Islam and the Creation of Tunisia.* London, Croom Helm, 1984.

Sylvester, Anthony. *Tunisia.* London, Bodley Head, 1969.

Tlatli, Salah-Eddine. *Tunisie nouvelle.* Tunis, 1957.

World Bank. *Tunisia's Global Integration and Sustainable Development: Strategic Choices for the 21st Century.* World Bank, 1997.

Ziadeh, Nicola, A. *The Origins of Tunisian Nationalism.* Beirut, 1962.

TURKEY

Physical and Social Geography

W. B. FISHER

Turkey is, in a remarkable sense, passage land between Europe and Asia, boasting land frontiers with Greece, Bulgaria, Armenia, Georgia, the Nakhichevan Autonomous Republic (part of Azerbaijan), Iran, Iraq and Syria. The west, the richest and most densely populated part of Turkey, looks towards the Aegean and Mediterranean seas and is very conscious of its links with Europe. However, in culture, racial origins and ways of life, there are frequent reminders of Turkey's geographical situation primarily as a part of Asia.

Turkey consists essentially of the large peninsula of Asia Minor, which has strongly defined natural limits; sea on three sides (the Black Sea to the north, the Aegean to the west, and the Mediterranean to the south), and high mountain ranges on the fourth (eastern) side. The small region of European Turkey, containing the cities of İstanbul (Constantinople) and Edirne (Adrianople), is, on the other hand, defined by a purely artificial frontier, the exact position of which has varied considerably since the 19th century, according to the fluctuating fortunes and prestige of Turkey itself. Another small territory, the Hatay, centred on İskenderun (Alexandretta) and lying as an enclave in Syrian territory, was acquired as part of a diplomatic bargain in 1939.

PHYSICAL FEATURES

The geological structure of Turkey is extremely complicated, and rocks of almost all ages occur, from the most ancient to most recent. Broadly speaking, Turkey consists of a number of old plateau blocks, against which masses of younger rock series have been squeezed to form fold mountain ranges of varying size. As there were several of these plateau blocks, rather than just one, the fold mountains run in many different directions, with considerable irregularity, and hence no simple pattern can be discerned—instead, one mountain range gives place to another abruptly, and we can pass suddenly from highland to plain or plateau.

In general outline Turkey consists of a ring of mountains enclosing a series of inland plateaux, with the highest mountains to the east, close to Armenia and Iran. Mount Ararat is the highest peak in Turkey, reaching 5,165 m, and there are neighbouring peaks almost as high. In the west the average altitude of the hills is distinctly lower, though the highest peak (Mount Erciyas or Argaeus) is over 3,900 m. The irregular topography of Turkey has given rise to many lakes, some salt and some fresh, and generally more numerous than elsewhere in the Middle East. The largest, Lake Van, covers nearly 4,000 sq km (1,100 sq miles).

Two other features may be mentioned. Large areas of the east and some parts of the centre of Asia Minor have been covered in sheets of lava which are often of such recent occurrence that soil has not yet been formed—consequently wide expanses are sterile and uninhabited. Secondly, in the north and west, cracking and disturbance of the rocks has taken place on an enormous scale. The long, indented coast of the Aegean Sea, with its numerous oddly shaped islands and estuaries, is due to cracking in two directions, which has split the land into detached blocks of roughly rectangular shape. Often the lower parts have sunk and been drowned by the sea. The Bosphorus and Dardanelles owe their origin to this faulting action, and the whole of the Black Sea coast is due to subsidence along a great series of fissures. Movement and adjustment along these cracks has by no means ceased, so that at the present day earthquakes are frequent in the north and west of Turkey.

Because of the presence of mountain ranges close to the coast, and the great height of the interior plateaux (varying from 800 m to 2,000 m), Turkey has special climatic conditions, characterized by great extremes of temperature and rainfall, with wide variation from one district to another. In winter, conditions are severe in most areas, except for those lying close to sea-level. Temperatures of minus 30°C to minus 40°C can occur in the east, and snow lies there for as many as 120 days each year. The west has frost on most nights of December and January, and (again apart from the coastal zone) has an average winter temperature below 1°C. In summer, however, temperatures over most of Turkey exceed 30°C, with 43°C in the south-east. There can hence be enormous seasonal variations of temperature—sometimes over 50°C, among the widest in the world.

Rainfall, too, is remarkably variable. Along the eastern Black Sea coast, towards the Georgian frontier, over 2,500 mm (100 ins) fall annually; but elsewhere, amounts are very much smaller. Parts of the central plateau, being shut off by mountains from the influence of sea winds, are arid, with annual totals of under 250 mm, and expanses of salt steppe and desert are frequent. Like Iran, Turkey also has a 'dead heart', and the main towns of Anatolia, including Ankara, the capital, are placed away from the centre and close to the hills, where rainfall tends to be greater and water supplies better.

It is necessary to emphasize the contrast that exists between the Aegean coastlands, which, climatically, are by far the most favoured regions of Turkey, and the rest of the country. Round the Aegean, winters are mild and fairly rainy, and the summers hot, but tempered by a persistent northerly wind, the Meltemi, or Etesian wind, which is of great value in ripening fruit, especially figs and sultana grapes.

ECONOMIC LIFE

The variety of geographical conditions within Turkey has led to uneven development, intensified by poor communications, due to the broken nature of the topography. Roads are relatively few, railways slow and often circuitous, and whole districts—sometimes even considerable towns—are accessible only by unsurfaced track. Many rivers flow in deep gorges near their sources and either meander or are broken by cascades in their lower reaches, so that none are navigable.

Thus, we find that the west of Turkey, situated close to the Aegean Sea, is by far the most densely peopled and the most intensively developed. Since 1923, however, attempts have been made to develop the Anatolian plateau and the districts in the extreme east, which, following the expulsion and massacre of the Armenians in 1914–18, for a time supported only a very scanty population. Development in the central plateau has been aided by the exploitation of several small, but on the whole valuable, mineral deposits, and by irrigation schemes to improve agriculture. A certain degree of industrialization (mainly undertaken by state-sponsored and -owned organizations) has also grown up, based on Turkish-produced raw materials—cotton, wool, mohair, beet-sugar, olive oil and tobacco. The eastern districts present a more intractable problem, and development so far has been slower.

The considerable increase of population in recent years (an annual average of 2.2% in 1985–90 and 1.5% in 1990–97) has led to intensification of settlement and to an increase in the use of available land for cultivation. Henceforth an important task for Turkey must be to improve yields from agriculture and industry. Because of the strategic importance of the country, there has been a considerable programme of road building, largely financed by the USA. Until recently, the absorption of Turkish labour in Western Europe (chiefly Germany) provided useful extra revenue from remittances. With the repatriation of many of these *gastarbeiter* during the recession of the last few years, however, there have been problems of reabsorption (the returning workers have higher expectations), together with the need to find other sources of revenue.

Latterly, Turkey has experienced severe economic crises, compounded by political uncertainty and social instability. In 1980 there were severe shortages, due to rampant inflation and the inability to finance necessary imports. Inflation, however, has fluctuated since 1981, while 'black market' activities have reduced, confidence has increased, export performance has improved and, most importantly, the country has returned to civilian rule. This has allowed the start of reform of the tax system, and a limited plan for land reform. Nevertheless, social problems (in part due to widespread unemployment, low credit-worthiness and the effects of military government) remain considerable handicaps, and doubts persist as to the real extent of civilian control and the ability of the Government to free itself from the legacy of the military regime. Corruption and bureaucratic inefficiency remain perennial problems.

RACE AND LANGUAGE

Racially, the bulk of the Turkish people show an inter-mixture of Mediterranean and Armenoid strains. In the western half of the country Mediterraneans and Armenoids are more or less equally represented; but further east the proportion of Armenoids steadily increases until, towards the former Soviet and Iranian borders, they become almost universal. Much of south-eastern Turkey is inhabited by Kurds, a people of Indo-

European descent; estimates of their number range from 3m. to more than 8m. Turkey also has less important racial elements; there would seem to be small numbers of proto-Nordics in the north and west, and some authorities suggest a racial relationship between Galatia (the modern district of Ankara) and ancient Gaul. The Ottoman Turks were, in the main, of Turki (western Mongoloid) ancestry but, in the view of some authorities, their contribution to the ethnic stocks of Turkey was small, since they were really an invading tribal group that became an aristocracy and soon intermarried with other peoples. There are also numbers of Caucasians—particularly Circassians and Georgians—who have contributed to the racial structure of Turkey; and during 1951 a further element was added by the arrival of many thousands of Bulgarian Muslims who had been deported from their own country.

The Turkish language, which is of central Asiatic origin, is spoken over most, but by no means all, of the country. This was introduced into Turkey in Seljuq times, and was written in Arabic characters, but, as these are not really well adapted to the sound of Turkish, Roman (i.e. European) script has been compulsory since 1928. In addition, there are a number of non-Turkish languages. Kurdish is widely spoken in the south-east, along the Syrian and Iraqi frontiers; and Caucasian dialects, quite different from either Turkish or Kurdish, occur in the north-east. Greek and Armenian were once widespread but, following the deportations which began in the 1920s, both forms of speech are now current only in the city of İstanbul, where considerable numbers of Greeks and Armenians still live.

History

Revised for this edition by ALAN J. DAY

ANCIENT HISTORY

The most ancient written records so far found in Asia Minor date from the beginning of the second millennium BC. They are in Assyrian, and reveal the existence of Assyrian trading colonies in Cappadocia. These documents, together with a growing amount of archaeological evidence, show an important Copper Age culture in Central Anatolia in the third and early second millennia. Later in the second millennium the greater part of Asia Minor fell under the rule of the Hittites, whose empire flourished from about 1600 BC to about 1200 BC, and reached its apogee in the 14th and 13th centuries, when it became one of the dominant states of the eastern Mediterranean. After the break-up of the Hittite Empire, Asia Minor was split up among a number of dynasties and peoples—Phrygians, Cimmerians, Lydians and others—about whom not very much is known. Towards the end of the Hittite period the Greeks began to invade the Aegean coast, and entered on a long struggle with the native states that is reflected in the story of the Trojan War. Greek culture spread in western Anatolia, which was gradually incorporated into the Hellenic world. A series of political changes, of which the most important are the Persian conquest in 546 BC, the conquest of Alexander in 334 BC, and the constitution of the Roman province of Asia in 133 BC, did not impede the steady spread of Greek language and culture in the cities.

In AD 330, the Emperor Constantine inaugurated the new city of Constantinople, on the site of the old Greek trading settlement of Byzantium. This city at once became the capital of the East Roman and then of the Christian Byzantine Empire. Asia Minor was now the metropolitan province of a great empire, and grew in wealth, prosperity and importance. Under Byzantine rule Greek Christianity, already firmly established in Roman times, spread over most of the peninsula.

SELJUQS AND OTTOMANS

At the beginning of the 11th century a new conquest of Anatolia began—that of the Turks. The early history of the Turkish peoples is still obscure. Some references in the ancient biography of Alexander show them to have been established in Central

Asia at the time of his conquests, and Turkish tribal confederacies played an important part in the invasions of Europe from late Roman times onwards. The name 'Turk' first appears in historical records in the sixth century AD, when Chinese annals speak of a powerful empire in Central Asia, founded by a steppe people called Tu-Kiu. It is from this state that the oldest surviving Turkish inscriptions have come. From the seventh century onwards the Central Asian Turks came into ever closer contact with the Islamic peoples of the Near East, from whom they adopted the Islamic faith and the Arabic script, and with them much of the complex civilization of Islam. From the ninth century Turks entered the service of the Caliphate in increasing numbers, and soon came to provide the bulk of its armies, its generals and, eventually, its rulers.

From the 10th century whole tribes of Turks began to migrate into Persia and Iraq, and in the 11th century, under the leadership of the family of Seljuq, the Turks were able to set up a great empire comprising most of the eastern lands of the Caliphate. The Muslim armies on the Byzantine frontier had long been predominantly Turkish, and in the course of the 11th century they began a great movement into Anatolia which resulted in the termination of Byzantine rule in most of the country and its incorporation in the Muslim Seljuq Sultanate. A Seljuq prince, Süleyman ibn Kutlumush, was sent to organize the new province, and by the end of the 12th century his successors had built up a strong Turkish monarchy in Anatolia, with its capital in Konya (the ancient Iconium). Under the rule of the Anatolian Seljuqs, which in various forms lasted until the 14th century, Anatolia gradually became a Turkish land. Masses of Turkish immigrants from further east entered the country, and a Turkish, Muslim civilization replaced Greek Christianity.

In the late 13th century the Sultanate of Konya fell into decay, and gradually gave way to a number of smaller principalities. One of these, in north-western Anatolia, was ruled by a certain Osman, or Othman, from whom the name Ottoman is derived. The Ottoman state soon embarked on a great movement of expansion, on the one hand in Anatolia, at the expense of its Turkish neighbours, on the other in the Balkans. Ottoman armies first crossed to Europe in the mid-14th century, and by

1400 they were masters of much of the Balkan peninsula as well as almost all of Anatolia. The capital was moved first from Bursa to Edirne and then, in 1453, to Constantinople, the final conquest of which from the last Byzantine emperor completed the process that had transformed a principality of frontier-warriors into a new great empire. Constantinople, called İstanbul by the Turks, remained the capital of the Ottoman Empire until 1922. The wave of conquest was by no means spent. For more than a century Ottoman arms continued to advance into Central Europe, while in 1516–17 Sultan Selim I destroyed the Mamluk Sultanate and incorporated Syria and Egypt into the Empire. During the reign of Sultan Süleyman I (1520–66), known as the Magnificent in Europe, the Ottoman Empire was at the height of its power. In three continents the Sultan held unchallenged sway over vast territories. A skilled and highly-organized bureaucracy secured for the peoples of the Empire peace, justice and prosperity; literature, scholarship and the arts flourished; and the Ottoman armies and fleets seemed to threaten the very existence of Western Christendom.

The decay of the Empire is usually dated from the death of Süleyman. In the West great changes were taking place. The Renaissance and the Reformation, the rapid development of science and technology, the emergence of strong, centralized nation states with constantly improving military techniques, the deflection of the main routes of international trade from the Mediterranean to the open seas, all combined to strengthen Turkey's Western adversaries while leaving her own resources unchanged or even diminished, and helped to relegate her into a backwater of cultural and economic stagnation. An imposing military façade for a while masked the internal decay that was rotting the Empire, but by the end of the 17th century the weakness of the Ottoman state was manifest. Then began the struggle of the powers for pickings of Turkish territory and for positions of influence in the Empire. During the 18th century it was Austria and Russia that made the main territorial advances in the Balkans and in the Black Sea area, while Britain and France were content with commercial and diplomatic privileges. In a succession of wars one province after another was lost, while internal conditions went from bad to worse. During the 19th century Britain and France began to play a more active role. British policy was generally to support the Turks against their impatient heirs. In 1854 Britain and France went to war at the side of Turkey in order to check Russian ambitions and in 1877–78 British diplomatic intervention was effective to the same end. Meanwhile the ferment of nationalist ideas had spread from the West to the subject peoples of the Empire, and one by one the Serbs, Greeks, Romanians and Bulgarians succeeded in throwing off Ottoman rule and attaining independent statehood.

The first stirrings of a new spirit among the Turks themselves, and the first serious attempts at reform, occurred during the reign of Selim III (1789–1807), and during the 19th century a series of reforming sultans and ministers worked on a programme of reform and modernization which, though it fell short of its avowed objectives, nevertheless transformed the face of the Ottoman Empire and began a process of change, the effects of which are still visible. In 1878 the reforming movement came to an abrupt end, and from that year until 1908 the Empire was subjected to the iron despotism of Abd al-Hamid II, who ruthlessly repressed every attempt at liberal thought and reform. In 1908 the secret opposition group known as the Young Turks seized power, and in a wave of revolutionary enthusiasm inaugurated a constitution, parliamentary government, and a whole series of liberal reforms. Unfortunately the Young Turks had little opportunity to follow up their promising start. First internal dissension, then foreign wars, combined to turn the Young Turk regime into a military dictatorship. In 1911 the Italians suddenly started a war against Turkey which ended with their gaining Libya and the Dodecanese Islands; in 1912–13 a Balkan alliance succeeded in wresting from the Empire most of its remaining possessions on the continent of Europe. Finally, in October 1914, Turkey entered the war on the side of the Central powers. During the reign of Abd al-Hamid, German influence had been steadily increasing in Turkey, and the process continued under the Young Turks. It was certainly helped by the growing friendship between the Western powers and Russia, which threw the Turks into the arms of the only power

that seemed ready to support them against Russian designs. German officers reorganized the Turkish army; German businessmen and technicians extended their hold on the economic resources of the country, and German engineers and financiers began the construction of the famous Baghdad railway which was to provide direct rail communication between Germany and the Middle East.

The Turkish alliance was of immense military value to the Central powers. The Turkish armies, still established in Syria and Palestine, were able to offer an immediate and serious threat to the Suez Canal and to the British position in Egypt. By their dogged and successful defence of the Dardanelles they prevented effective co-operation between Russia and the Western powers. Their position as the greatest independent Muslim state and their prestige among Muslims elsewhere created a series of problems in the British and French Empires.

Despite their weakness and exhaustion after two previous wars, the Turks were able to wage a bitter defensive war against the Allies. At last, after two unsuccessful attempts, one on the Dardanelles and the other in Mesopotamia, a new British attack from Egypt and from India succeeded in expelling the Turks from Palestine, Syria, and most of Iraq. Defeated on all sides, cut off from their allies by the Salonika expedition, the Turks decided to abandon the struggle, and signed an armistice at Mudros on 30 October 1918. French, Italian and British occupation forces moved into Turkey.

For some time the victorious powers were too busy elsewhere to attend to the affairs of Turkey, and it was not until the San Remo Conference of April 1920 that the first serious attempt was made to settle the Turkish question. Meanwhile the victors were busy quarrelling among themselves. Partly, no doubt, with the idea of forestalling Italian ambitions, the British, French, and US Governments agreed to a Greek proposal for a Greek occupation of İzmir (Smyrna) and the surrounding country, and on 15 May 1919 a Greek army, under cover of Allied warships, landed there. The integrity of this move later became a cause for concern within the Allied camp, and in October the Inter-Allied Commission in İstanbul condemned it as 'unjustifiable' and as 'a violation of the terms of the Armistice'. The consequences of the invasion for Turkey were momentous. Now, it was no longer the non-Turkish subject provinces and the Ottoman superstructure of the Turkish nation that were threatened, but the Turkish homeland itself. Moreover, the Greeks, unlike the Western Allies, showed that they intended to stay, and that they were aiming at nothing less than the incorporation of the territories they occupied into the Greek kingdom. The Turkish reaction to this danger was vigorous and immediate. The Nationalist movement, hitherto limited to a small class of intellectuals, became the mass instrument of Turkish determination to preserve the integrity and independence of the homeland. A new leader appeared to organize their victory.

THE RISE OF ATATÜRK

Mustafa Kemal, surnamed Atatürk in 1934, was born in Salonika, then an Ottoman city, in 1880. After a promising career as a regular army officer, he achieved his first active command in Libya in 1911, and thereafter fought with distinction in the successive wars in which his country was involved. After his brilliant conduct of the defence of Gallipoli, he fought on various fronts against the Allies, and at the time of the Armistice held a command on the Syrian front. A month later he returned to İstanbul, and at once began to seek ways and means of getting to Anatolia to organize national resistance. At length he was successful, and on 19 May 1919—four days after the Greek landing in İzmir—he arrived at Samsun, on the Black Sea coast, ostensibly in order to supervise the disbanding of the remaining Turkish forces. Instead he set to work at once on the double task of organizing a national movement and raising a national army.

Meanwhile the Allied powers were at last completing their arrangements for the obsequies of the Turkish Empire, which had long been known as 'the Sick Man of Europe'. After a series of conferences, a treaty was drawn up and signed by the Allied representatives and those of the Sultan's Government at Sèvres, on 10 August 1920. The Treaty of Sèvres was very harsh—far harsher than that imposed on Germany. The Arab provinces were to be placed under British and French Mandates, to prepare them for eventual independence. In Anatolia, Armenian and Kurdish states were to be set up in the east, the south was to be divided between France and Italy, and a truncated Turkish Sultanate confined to the interior. The Straits were to be demilitarized and placed under Allied administration, with a Turkish İstanbul surrounded by Allied forces. The rest of European Turkey was to be ceded to Greece, while the İzmir district was to be under 'Ottoman sovereignty and Greek administration'.

This treaty was, however, never implemented. While the Allies were imposing their terms on the Sultan and his Government in İstanbul, a new Turkish state was rising in the interior of Anatolia, based on the rejection of the treaty and the principles on which it was founded. On 23 July 1919 Mustafa Kemal and his associates convened the first Nationalist congress in Erzurum, and drew up a national programme. A second congress, held in September, was attended by delegates from all over the country. An Executive Committee, presided over by Kemal, was formed, and chose Ankara, then a minor provincial town, as its headquarters. Frequent meetings were held in Ankara, which soon became the effective capital of the Nationalist movement and forces. It was there that they issued the famous National Pact, the declaration that laid down the basic programme of the Kemalist movement, renouncing the Empire and the domination of the non-Turkish provinces, but demanding the total and unconditional independence of all areas inhabited by Turks. This declaration won immediate support, and on 28 January 1920 was approved even by the legal Ottoman Parliament sitting in İstanbul. The growth of the Nationalist movement in İstanbul alarmed the Allies, and on 16 March British forces entered the Turkish part of the city and arrested and deported many Nationalist leaders. Despite this setback, followed by a new anti-Nationalist campaign on the part of the Sultan and his political and religious advisers, the Kemalists continued to advance. On 19 March Kemal ordered general elections, and at the end of April a National Assembly of 350 deputies met in Ankara and voted the National Pact. The Sultan and his Government were declared deposed, a provisional constitution promulgated, and a government set up with Mustafa Kemal as President.

There remained the military task of expelling the invaders. The Greco–Turkish war falls into three stages, covering roughly the campaigns of 1920, 1921 and 1922. In the first campaign the Nationalists, hopelessly outmatched in numbers and material, were badly defeated, and the Greeks advanced far into Anatolia. Turkish resistance was, however, strong enough to impress the Allies, who, for the first time, accorded a certain limited recognition to the Nationalist Government and proclaimed their neutrality in the Greco–Turkish war. The second campaign began with Greek successes, but the Turks rallied and defeated the invaders first at İnönü—from which İsmet Pasha, who commanded the Turkish forces there, later took his surname—and then, on 24 August 1921, in a major battle on the Sakarya River, where the Turkish forces were under the personal command of Mustafa Kemal. This victory considerably strengthened the Nationalists, who were now generally realized to be the effective Government of Turkey. The French and Italians withdrew from the areas of Anatolia assigned to them, and made terms with the new Government. The Soviets, now established on Turkey's eastern frontier, had already done so at the beginning of the year.

A period of waiting and reorganization followed, during which the morale of the Greek armies was adversely affected by political changes in Greece. In August 1922 the third and final phase of the war of independence began. The Turkish Army drove the Greeks back to the Aegean, and on 9 September reoccupied İzmir. Mustafa Kemal now prepared to cross to Thrace. To do so he had to cross the Straits, still under Allied occupation. The French and Italian contingents withdrew, and, after a menacing pause, the British followed. On 11 October an armistice was signed at Mudanya, whereby the Allied Governments agreed to the restoration of Turkish sovereignty in Eastern Thrace. In November the Sultan's Cabinet resigned, and the Sultan himself went into exile. Turkey once more had only one Government, and İstanbul, the ancient seat of empire, became a provincial city, ruled by a governor appointed from Ankara.

The peace conference opened in November 1922. After many months of argument the treaty was finally signed on 24 July 1923. It recognized complete and undivided Turkish sovereignty and the abolition of the last vestiges of foreign privilege. The only reservation related to the demilitarization of the Straits, which were not to be fortified without the consent of the powers. This consent was given at the Montreux Conference in 1936.

THE TURKISH REPUBLIC

The military task was completed, and the demands formulated in the National Pact had been embodied in an international treaty. There remained the greater task of rebuilding the ruins of long years of war and revolution—and of remedying those elements of weakness in the Turkish state and society that had brought Turkey to the verge of extinction. Mustafa Kemal saw the solution of Turkey's problems in a process of Westernization—in the integration of Turkey, on a basis of equality, in the modern Western world. To do this it was necessary to change the very basis of society in Turkey, and to suppress, ruthlessly if need be, the opposition that was bound to come from the entrenched forces of the old order. Between 1922 and 1938, the year of his death, Kemal carried through a series of far-reaching reforms.

The first changes were political. After the deposition of Sultan Vahdeddin in November 1922, a brief experiment was made with a purely religious sovereignty, and Abd al-Mejid was proclaimed as Caliph but not Sultan. The experiment was not successful. Abd al-Mejid followed his predecessor into exile, and on 29 October 1923 Turkey was declared a Republic, with Kemal as President. The Kemal regime was effectively a dictatorship—though without the violence and oppression normally associated with that word in Europe. A single party—the Cumhuriyet Halk Partisi (CHP—Republican People's Party)—formed the main instrument for the enforcement of government policy. The Constitution of 20 April 1924 provided for an elected parliament which was the repository of sovereign power. Executive power was to be exercised by the President and a cabinet chosen by him.

The next object of attack was the religious hierarchy already weakened by the removal of the Sultan-Caliph. In a series of edicts the Ministry of Religious Affairs was abolished, the religious orders disbanded, religious property sequestrated and religious instruction forbidden. With the religious leaders in retreat, the attack on the old social order began. Certainly the most striking reforms were the abolition of the fez and the Arabic alphabet, and their replacement by the hat and the Latin alphabet. But these were probably less important in the long run than the abrogation of the old legal system and the introduction of new civil and criminal codes of law adapted from Europe. In 1928 Islam itself was disestablished, and the Constitution amended to make Turkey a secular state.

Not the least of the problems that faced Mustafa Kemal was the economic one. Turkey needed capital. Rather than risk the independence of Turkey by inviting in foreign capital at a time of weakness, Kemal adopted the principle of *étatisme*, and made it one of the cardinal doctrines of his regime. From 1923 to 1933 the State's main achievement was in railway construction, nearly doubling the length of line in that period. At the same time efforts were made towards establishing other industries. While often wasteful and inefficient, state-sponsored industry was probably the only form of development possible at the time without recourse to foreign aid. The progress achieved stood Turkey in good stead in the critical years that were to follow.

The foreign policy of the Republic was, for a long time, one of strict non-involvement in foreign disputes, and the maintenance of friendly relations with as many powers as possible. In 1935–36, however, Turkey co-operated loyally in sanctions against Italy, and thereafter the growing threat of German, and more especially Italian, aggression led to closer links with the West. In 1938 steps were taken to strengthen economic links between Turkey and the United Kingdom. A British credit of £16m. was granted to Turkey, and a number of contracts given to British firms by Turkey.

The establishment of the Republic also put an end to the prospect of Kurdish independence offered by the Treaty of Sèvres. The Kurds were opposed to Kemal's secularist and nationalist policies and in 1925 rose up in revolt after the abolition of the Caliphate. They were ruthlessly crushed. A more nationalist uprising in 1930 and a further revolt against the repressive actions taken by the Government were also suppressed. The Kurdish provinces remained rigorously policed, garrisons were established in larger towns and Kurdish leaders were exiled. The Kurdish language was made illegal and the Government refused to recognize any aspect of the Kurds' separate ethnic identity, calling them 'mountain Turks'.

The death of Kemal Atatürk in November 1938 was a great shock to Turkey. He was succeeded as President by İsmet İnönü, who announced his intention of maintaining and carrying on the work of his predecessor. The new President was soon called upon to guide his country through a very difficult time. As early as 12 May 1939 a joint Anglo-Turkish declaration was issued, stating that 'the British and Turkish Governments, in the event of an act of aggression leading to war in the Mediterranean area, would co-operate effectively and lend each other all the aid and assistance in their power'. This prepared the way for the formal Anglo-French-Turkish Treaty of Alliance, signed on 19 October. It had been hoped that this Treaty would be complemented by a parallel treaty with the USSR, but the equivocal attitude of the Soviet Government, followed by the Stalin-Hitler Agreement of August 1939, made this impossible, and the Turks proceeded with the Western alliance in the face of clearly expressed Soviet disapproval. They protected themselves, however, by Protocol II of the treaty, stipulating that nothing in the treaty should bind them to any action likely to involve them in war with the USSR.

TURKEY DURING THE SECOND WORLD WAR

The fall of France, the hostile attitude of the Soviet Government, and the extension of German power over most of Europe led the Turkish Government to the conclusion that nothing would be gained by provoking an almost certain German conquest. While continuing to recognize the Alliance, therefore, they invoked Protocol II as a reason for remaining neutral, and in June 1941, when German expansion in the Balkans had brought the German armies within 100 miles of İstanbul, the Turks further protected themselves by signing a friendship and trade agreement with Germany, in which, however, they stipulated that Turkey would maintain her treaty obligations to Britain.

The German attack on the USSR, and the consequent entry of that country into the Grand Alliance, brought an important change to the situation, and the Western powers increased their pressure on Turkey to enter the war. The main consideration holding Turkey back from active participation in the war was mistrust of the USSR, and the widespread feeling that Nazi conquest and Soviet 'liberation' were equally to be feared. While stopping short of actual belligerency, however, the Turks, especially after 1942, entered into closer economic and military relations with the West and aided the Allied cause in a number of ways. In August 1944 they broke off diplomatic relations with Germany, and on 23 February 1945 declared war on Germany in order to comply with the formalities of entry to the United Nations (UN) Conference in San Francisco.

The war years subjected Turkey to severe economic strains. These, and the dangers of armed neutrality in a world at war, resulted in the imposition of martial law, of closer police surveillance, and of a generally more authoritarian form of government. And then, between 1945 and 1950, came a further series of changes, no less remarkable than the great reforms of Atatürk. When the Charter of the UN was introduced for ratification in the Turkish Parliament in 1945, a group of members, led by Celâl Bayar, Adnan Menderes, Fuad Köprülü and Refik Koraltan, tabled a motion suggesting a series of reforms in the law and the Constitution which would effectively ensure inside Turkey those liberties to which the Turkish Government was giving its theoretical approval in the Charter. The motion was rejected by the Government, and its sponsors were forced to leave the party. In November 1945, however, under pressure of a by now active and informed public opinion, President İnönü announced the end of the single-party system, and in January 1946 the opposition leaders registered the new Democratic Party.

TURKEY UNDER THE DEMOCRATIC PARTY

In July 1946 new elections gave the Democrat opposition 70 out of 416 parliamentary seats and there can be little doubt that completely free elections would have given them many more. During the years that followed, the breach in the dictatorship grew ever wider, and a series of changes in both law and practice ensured the growth of democratic liberties. Freedom of the press and of association were extended, martial law was ended, and on 15 February 1950 a new electoral law was approved, guaranteeing free and fair elections. In May 1950 a new general election was held, in which the Democrats won an overwhelming victory. Celâl Bayar became President, and a new Cabinet was formed, with Adnan Menderes as Prime Minister and Fuad Köprülü as Foreign Minister. The new regime adopted a more liberal economic policy, involving the partial abandonment of *étatisme* and the encouragement of private enterprise, both Turkish and foreign. For a while, the stability and progress of the Republic seemed to be threatened by the growing activities of groups of religious fanatics, whose programme appeared to require little less than the abrogation of all the reforms achieved by the Turkish revolution. After an attempt on the life of the liberal journalist Ahmet Emin Yalman in November 1952, the Government took more vigorous action against what were called the 'forces of clericalism and reaction'. Many arrests were made, and in mid-1953 the National Party, accused of complicity in reactionary plots, was for a time outlawed and legislation was passed prohibiting the exploitation of religion for political purposes. The relations between the two main parties, after a temporary improvement in the face of the common danger of reaction, deteriorated again in the course of 1953–54, though not to such an extent as to imperil national unity. On 2 May 1954, in Turkey's third general election since the war, the Democrats won a resounding victory.

In view of the smallness and weakness of the opposition parties, and the immense parliamentary majority of the Democratic Party, it was inevitable that sooner or later splits would appear within it. In October 1955 a serious crisis culminated in the dismissal or resignation from the party of 19 deputies. These were later joined by others and formed a new party, the Freedom Party.

Conflict between the Government and opposition was sharpened by the decision taken to advance the date of the general elections by more than eight months, to 27 October 1957. The three opposition parties—Republicans, Freedom and National Parties—first intended to present a united front, but the electoral law was changed to make this impossible. They were therefore obliged to present separate lists in each constituency, and so, although the combined votes won by opposition candidates were slightly more than 50% of the total, the Democrats again emerged triumphant, though with a diminished majority.

FOREIGN AFFAIRS 1945–60

In foreign affairs, both the CHP and the Democrat Governments followed a firm policy of unreserved identification with the West in the Cold War. From May 1947 the USA extended economic and military aid to Turkey on an increasing scale, and in 1950 a first indication of both the seriousness and the effectiveness of Turkish policy was given with the dispatch of Turkish troops to Korea, where they fought with distinction. In August 1949 Turkey became a member of the Council of Europe, and early in 1952 acceded to full membership of the North Atlantic Treaty Organization (NATO), in which it began to play an increasingly important part. Thereafter other arrangements were made by which Turkey accepted a role in both Balkan and Middle Eastern defence. This culminated in November 1955 in Turkey's joining the Baghdad Pact, in which the country thereafter played a major role.

In January 1957 the President of the USA announced a new programme of economic and military assistance for those countries of the area which were willing to accept it. At a further meeting held in Ankara the Muslim states belonging to the Baghdad Pact expressed their approval of this 'Eisenhower Doctrine'. The USA in March made known its decision to join the military committee of the Baghdad Pact, and later in March Turkey promised to co-operate with the USA against all subversive activities in the Middle East. It was announced that financial aid would be forthcoming from the USA for the economic projects previously discussed between the members of the Baghdad Pact.

From 1958 Turkey was actively involved in settling terms for the constitution of an independent Cyprus. These were eventually agreed between Turkey, Greece, the United Kingdom and the Greek and Turkish Cypriots. Cyprus achieved independence in August 1960.

Fidelity to NATO and the Central Treaty Organization (CENTO) remained the basis of Turkey's foreign policy during the late 1950s. By the beginning of 1960, however, Turkey's relations with the USSR were becoming less frigid.

THE 1960 REVOLUTION

Economic difficulties continued to be one of the main preoccupations of the Turkish Government. The development plans envisaged since 1950 had been carried forward with financial aid from the USA and from such bodies as the World Bank. These policies had been accompanied by inflationary pressures, an unfavourable trade balance, decreased imports, a shortage of foreign exchange and, since the agricultural population was in receipt of subsidies from the Government, a higher demand for consumer goods which aggravated the prevalent inflation. Social and economic unease tended to reveal itself in a drift of people from the villages to the towns, the population of centres like Ankara, İstanbul, İzmir, Bursa and Adana being considerably increased during recent decades.

The influences which led to the revolution had long been at work. Hostility between the Democrats in power and the CHP in opposition grew steadily more marked, and was sharpened towards the end of 1959 by suspicions that the Democrats were planning to hold elections in the near future, ahead of schedule. It was feared that these would, if necessary, be rigged to keep the Democrats in power indefinitely.

In May 1959, political tension between the two main parties had already broken into violence during a political tour of Anatolia conducted by the opposition leader İsmet İnönü. The Government banned all political meetings. Blows were struck in the Grand National Assembly, and the opposition walked out.

Much the same pattern of events ushered in the final breakdown a year later. At the beginning of April 1960, İsmet İnönü undertook another political tour of Anatolia. At one point troops were called on to block his progress. The opposition tried, but failed, to force a debate in the Assembly. On their side the Democrats set up a commission of inquiry, composed entirely of their own supporters, to investigate 'the destructive and illegal activities of the CHP'. Again the Grand National Assembly was the scene of violence, and all political activity was suspended for three months.

At the end of April, student unrest led to the imposition of martial law. As administrator of martial law, the Turkish army found itself, contrary to its traditions, involved in politics. A group of officers decided that their intervention must be complete if Turkey was to return to Kemalist principles. In the early hours of 27 May they struck. President Bayar, Prime Minister Menderes, most Democratic deputies and a number of officials and senior officers were arrested. The Government was replaced by a Committee of National Unity headed by Gen. Cemal Gürsel, a much respected senior officer who had fought with Atatürk at Gallipoli.

The coup was immediately successful and almost bloodless. The accusation against the Menderes regime was that it had broken the Constitution and was moving towards dictatorship. The officers insisted that they were temporary custodians of authority and would hand over to the duly constituted civilian authorities. A temporary Constitution was quickly agreed, pending the drafting of a final new one. During this interval legislative power was vested in the Committee of National Unity, and executive power in a Council of Ministers, composed of civilians as well as soldiers. On 25 August, however, 10 of the 18 ministers were dismissed, leaving only three civilians in the Government. Gen. Gürsel was President of the Republic, Prime Minister and Minister of Defence. The courts were declared independent. Commissions were set up to inquire into the alleged misdeeds of the Menderes regime.

Although the new regime did not fail to meet political opposition, particularly among the peasants and around İzmir, a stronghold of Menderes, the main problems facing it were economic. The former regime had been heavily in debt. Austerity measures, including restrictions on credit, had to be put into

operation and an economic planning board was set up to work out a long-term investment plan with the aid of foreign experts.

THE COMMITTEE OF NATIONAL UNITY

The Committee of National Unity, which originally consisted of 37 members, was reduced to 23 on 13 November 1960. The 14 officers dismissed represented a group led by Col Alparslan Türkeş, who had been pressing for the army to retain its postrevolutionary powers and to introduce radical social reforms.

This purge completed, preparations for a return to political democracy continued. A new Assembly, to act as a temporary parliament, was convened at the beginning of January 1961. It consisted of the 23 members of the Committee of National Unity, acting jointly with a House of Representatives of 271 members, both elected and nominated. In this the CHP predominated. At the same time party politics were again legalized and a number of new parties emerged. Some of them proved short-lived, but one, the Adalet Partisi (AP—Justice Party), founded by Gen. Ragip Gümüşpala, who had been Commander of the Third Army at the time of the *coup d'état*, attracted the support of many former adherents of the Democratic Party, which had been declared illegal.

A special committee of the Assembly framed a new Constitution which had some significant changes from the 1924 version. It provided for a court to determine the constitutionality of laws, for a bicameral legislature, and it included a reference to 'social justice' as one of the aims of the State.

THE YASSIADA TRIALS

These constitutional developments took place against the background of the trial of the accused members of the Menderes regime. The trial was held on the small island of Yassiada in the Bosphorus, where the accused had been confined after arrest, and lasted from October 1960 to August 1961. The sentence of the court was pronounced on 15 September. There were 15 death sentences, 12 of which, including that on Bayar, were commuted to life imprisonment. Adnan Menderes, Fatin Zorlu, the former Foreign Minister, and Hasan Polatkan, the former Minister of Finance, were duly hanged. In September 1990, following a prolonged campaign by right-wing factions (including the ruling Anavatan Partisi—ANAP—Motherland Party), the bodies were exhumed and buried in İstanbul with state honours.

The trial, in 1960, inevitably absorbed the attention of the country, and there were many reminders that sympathy for the former regime and its leaders was far from dead. The most serious setback for the authorities, however, appeared in the results of the referendum on the new Constitution. This was approved by 6,348,191 votes against 3,934,370, and the large minority was taken as an indication of continuing loyalty to the Democrats.

The campaign preceding elections in October 1961, perhaps because Yassiada was ruled out as a subject for discussion, proved unexpectedly quiet. On 15 October the elections gave the CHP 173 seats and the AP 158 seats in the National Assembly, and 36 and 70 respectively in the Senate.

These figures were a blow to the hopes of the CHP that they would achieve an overall working majority. A coalition became necessary. The election results were also further evidence of latent support for the Democrats.

THE NEW GOVERNMENT

On 25 October 1961, Parliament opened and the transfer of power from military to civilians was made. The revolutionaries had kept their word and a new epoch began. The next day Gen. Gürsel, the only candidate, was elected President. But forming a government proved a much harder process. On 10 November İsmet İnönü, leader of the CHP, was asked to form a government, and after much hesitation and strong pressure from the army, the AP agreed to join forces with its rival. A new Cabinet was formed with İnönü as Prime Minister, Akıf İyidoğan, of the AP, as Deputy Prime Minister, and 10 more ministers from each of the two coalition parties.

The Government remained, as İnönü said, exposed to a double fire—from those who thought the army did too much (i.e. that civil liberties were still circumscribed) and those who thought it did too little (i.e. that it did not crush all signs of counter-revolution). The resignation of İnönü at the end of May 1962 weakened the extremists in the AP, who had wanted to grant an amnesty to former supporters of Menderes. They were now face to face with the army, the original architects of the 1960 revolution, and many of them felt it wise to moderate their demands.

By the end of June 1962 İnönü had formed a new coalition Government composed of 12 ministers from the CHP, six from the New Turkey Party, four from the Republican Peasants' Nation Party, and one independent minister. The new Government's programme expressed attachment to the principles of Western democracy and to the NATO alliance. It covered almost every sphere of national life, including education, taxation, employment and the problems of a rapidly rising birth-rate and an adverse balance of trade.

RAPPROCHEMENT WITH THE USSR

The first months of 1964 were overshadowed by an attempt on the life of İnönü in February, and by the situation in Cyprus, where the fate of the Turkish minority created strong feeling on the mainland. İnönü's critics claimed that he had displayed a considerable lack of foresight by failing to intervene on the island with force when the trouble started. Diplomatic efforts towards a solution failed and public disaffection grew, not only with Greece, but also with Turkey's western allies, in particular the USA and the United Kingdom, which were accused of being lukewarm in their support of Turkey's case. In August 1964 this disaffection exploded in İzmir, when rioters wrecked the US and British pavilions at the trade fair. İnönü, though moving with characteristic caution, gave a warning that the alliance with the West, the basis of Turkey's foreign policy since the war, was in danger. To reinforce his warning, several steps were taken to improve relations with the USSR. Initially, the Soviet Government had appeared to side with Greece on the question of Cyprus, and the Soviet trade pavilion had also been a target for the İzmir hooligans. Diplomatic approaches were made in both Moscow and Ankara, however, and at the end of October Erkin visited the USSR—the first Turkish Foreign Minister to make this journey for 25 years. Before leaving he invoked the memory of the early days of friendship between Atatürk and Lenin, and the same precedent was made much of by his hosts, who tactfully refrained from pressing Turkey into premature neutralism, as they had done in the past. On Cyprus, the USSR appeared to have moved closer to the Turkish point of view, the communiqué which ended Erkin's talks speaking favourably of a solution 'by peaceful means on the basis of respect for the territorial integrity of Cyprus, and for the legal rights of the two national communities'. Erkin's journey was followed up in January 1965 by the visit to Ankara of a Soviet parliamentary delegation. A trade pact between the two countries followed in March.

DEMIREL GOVERNMENT

For all this, Cyprus continued to give the opposition ammunition with which to harass the İnönü Government. At the Senate elections in June 1964, the AP won 31 out of the 51 seats contested, thus increasing its already large majority in this house. Its success was clouded by the death of the party's leader, Gen. Gümüşpala. In November Süleyman Demirel, a trained engineer and a former Director-General of the State Water Organization, was elected leader in his place, although he was without a seat in Parliament. İnönü survived more than one narrow vote of 'confidence', but was finally defeated on 13 February 1965, during voting in the Assembly on the budget—the first time that the term of a Turkish Government had been ended in this way. After a short delay, a coalition Government was formed from the four opposition parties—the AP, the New Turkish Party, the Republican Peasants' Party, and the Millet Partisi (National Party). An independent senator and former diplomat, Suat Ürgüplü, became Prime Minister.

At the general election of 11 October 1965, the AP under Süleyman Demirel won an overall majority. On introducing his AP Government to the Assembly, Demirel declared that the most important task would be to withstand communism 'by the realization of social justice and measures of social security'. Emphasis was to be put on industrialization. In spite of its

working majority, the Demirel Government proved only marginally more successful than its predecessors in getting things done. However, elections in June 1966 for one-third of the seats in the Senate showed that the AP was not losing popularity.

To some extent this success was attributed to the innate conservatism of the Turkish peasantry, who may have been alarmed by İnönü's statement that the CHP was left of centre. This position was not approved by all the party—some thought that it went too far, others not far enough. A convention of the party in October 1966 showed a victory for the left-wingers. Bülent Ecevit, Minister of Labour in 1961–65, was elected Secretary-General of the party, with the declared intention of turning it into a party of democratic socialism. Six months later 48 senators and congressmen, led by Turhan Feyzioğlu, a former minister, resigned from the party on the grounds that it was falling into a 'dangerous leftist adventure'. This was denied by Ecevit and İnönü, who supported him. They claimed that, on the contrary, their progressive policies would pre-empt the policies of and undermine support for other left-wing parties and therefore represented the best barrier against communism.

In May 1967 a majority of dissidents came together to form the new Reliance Party, which proclaimed its opposition to socialism and its belief in the 'spiritual values of the Turkish nation'. In June Ecevit forced a fresh election of the CHP executive, and by securing the elimination of two left-wing representatives he was able to emphasize that his party remained left of centre rather than left wing.

In March 1968 a new electoral law was approved, in spite of the protests of a united opposition, that abolished the so-called 'national remainder system'—a change which threatened the electoral chances of all the smaller parties but was thought to be particularly aimed at the Türkiye İşçi Partisi (TIP—Turkish Workers' Party), which was accused by the Government of using communist tactics.

In March 1966 President Gürsel was succeeded by Senator Cevdet Sunay. Turkey's relations with her allies in 1966 deteriorated. The Turkish press's campaign against US bases in Turkey led to a riot in Adana in March. Together with these manifestations against Turkey's formerly most stalwart ally, an effort by the Demirel Government to make its whole foreign policy more flexible was undertaken.

The touchstone of Turkey's foreign relations continued to be Cyprus. In 1967 this perennial problem oscillated between near settlement and near war. Later in the year the situation suddenly deteriorated as a result of attacks by Greek Cypriots on the island's Turkish enclaves on 15 November. Two days later the National Assembly voted by 432 votes to 1 to authorize the Government to send troops to foreign countries—in other words, to fight in Cyprus. There were daily Turkish flights over the island and the likelihood of war increased. As a result of strong intervention by US and UN intermediaries, however, a more serious conflict was avoided. On 3 December the Greeks undertook to withdraw their troops from the island and the Turks to take the necessary measures to ease tension. By February 1968 the situation had been so far restored that direct efforts to agree on a negotiated settlement for Cyprus were once again under way.

MILITARY INTERVENTION

Süleyman Demirel's AP Government was faced with the growing problem of political violence from early 1968 onward. Disorders in the universities, springing from non-political educational grievances and from clashes between political extremists of the right and the left, took an increasingly violent form. Students staged anti-US riots, and in June 1969 troops had to be summoned to prevent extremists disrupting examinations. The fighting between right- and left-wing factions became more serious in 1970, firearms and petrol bombs being used, and a number of political murders taking place.

Parliamentary politics also became rather confused. Elections in October 1969 produced an enlarged majority for the AP, but the party soon split, a number of Demirel's right-wing opponents forming the Demokratik Parti (DP—Democratic Party). Party strengths became almost impossible to calculate, as factions and alliances formed and dissolved, and on crucial votes the support of Government and the combined opposition parties was almost equally balanced. A new party, the Milli Nizam

Partisi (MNP—National Order Party), with right-wing policies and theocratic tendencies, was formed in January 1970 by Prof. Necmettin Erbakan.

Throughout 1970 and the early part of 1971, political and social unrest continued, with outbreaks of violence among students, in the trade unions and by Kurdish separatist groups. Factional bickering prevented the Government from taking effective action and on 12 March 1971, the Chief of the General Staff and the army, navy and air force commanders delivered a memorandum to the President. They accused the Government of allowing the country to slip into anarchy and of deviating from Atatürk's principles. They threatened that, unless 'a strong and credible government' were formed at once, the armed forces would take over the administration of the State. Later that day the Demirel Government resigned.

MILITARY DOMINATION OF POLITICS

A new Government was formed by Dr Nihat Erim, with the support of both the AP and the CHP. Bülent Ecevit, the CHP Secretary-General, resigned from office and refused to collaborate. Dr Erim's programme promised sweeping reforms in taxation, land ownership, education, power and industry, but the Government's attention was first directed to the suppression of political violence. The military ultimatum was followed by further bombings, kidnappings and clashes between right- and left-wing students and between students and police. On 28 April 1971, martial law was proclaimed, initially for one month, in 11 provinces, including Ankara and İstanbul.

Newspapers were suppressed, strikes were banned and large numbers of left-wing supporters were arrested. The MNP was dissolved in May 1971 and the Turkish Labour Party in July. The murder of the Israeli Consul-General in İstanbul by the Turkish People's Liberation Army provided the military authorities with an opportunity to round up nearly 1,000 suspects in İstanbul alone, including many journalists, writers and intellectuals. In September Dr Erim introduced a number of amendments to the Constitution, limiting individual civil rights and the autonomy of universities and radio and television stations as well as placing restrictions on the press and trade unions and giving the Government powers to legislate by decree. Dr Erim's proposal to use the new powers to introduce sweeping social and economic reforms, supported by the armed forces, was opposed by the AP. Cabinet crises in October and December led to the formation of a new coalition Government, again headed by Dr Erim, but his proposals for taking further executive powers were opposed by the four major parliamentary parties, and in April 1972 he resigned. A Government formed by Suat Ürgüplü was rejected by President Sunay, and in May a Government drawn from the AP, National Reliance Party and CHP, headed by Ferit Melen, was approved. There was a swing to the left within the CHP in May; the veteran party leader İsmet İnönü resigned after 34 years as Chairman, and was replaced by Bülent Ecevit. Meanwhile, the terrorist activities of the Turkish People's Liberation Army continued, and martial law was prolonged at two-month intervals.

In July 1972, dissident CHP members, opposing the dominance of the left wing led by Ecevit, formed the Republican Party. In November the CHP withdrew its support from the Melen coalition Government, but its five ministers preferred to leave the party and stay in the Council of Ministers. This caused further resignations from the CHP, including that of İsmet İnönü and 25 other deputies and senators. A number of these dissidents, together with the National Reliance Party and the Republican Party, joined to form the Cumhuriyetci Güven Partisi (CGP—Republican Reliance Party) in February 1973. The CHP, without its right wing, began actively to oppose the Melen Government, which it considered to be dominated by the armed forces, and martial law, under which, it was alleged with increasing frequency, arbitrary arrest and torture were practised. In March, for the first time, the CHP voted against the prolongation of martial law.

President Sunay's term of office expired in March 1973. Gen. Gürler resigned his post as Chief of Staff in order to stand for the presidency, his candidature receiving the strong support of the armed forces. He was opposed by members of the Justice and Democratic parties while the CHP decided to abstain from voting as a protest against military interference in the election and the censorship of electoral news in Ankara. Despite obvious military support for Gen. Gürler, 14 ballots failed to produce a result, and eventually the AP, CHP and CGP agreed on a compromise candidate, Senator Fahri Korutürk, former Commander-in-Chief of the Navy, who had not belonged to any political party. He was elected President on 6 April 1973. The following day Melen resigned, and was succeeded as Prime Minister by Naim Talû, an independent senator, who formed a Government with AP and CGP participation.

The Talû Government, although considered to be merely a caretaker administration to last until the general election, scheduled for October 1973, brought about a number of reforms, and during its term of office the armed forces gradually withdrew from political affairs. A Land Reform Law, distributing some 8m. acres to 500,000 peasants, was passed in June 1973, and measures were taken to prevent foreign domination of the mining and petroleum industries. A strong element within the armed forces felt that the time had come to return to a strictly military role, and that martial law had achieved its objective by duly eradicating extremism. Gen. Sancar, who became Chief of Staff when Gen. Gürler resigned to make his unsuccessful attempt to become President, was opposed to military intervention in politics, and retired 196 senior officers. Martial law was gradually lifted, and came to an end in September 1973.

FOREIGN POLICY DEVELOPMENTS

The traditional hostility between Turkey and Greece revived following the Greek announcement in February 1974 that oil had been found in Greek territorial waters in the Aegean. This led to a dispute over the extent of national jurisdiction over the continental shelf and territorial waters, with both sides making warlike moves in Thrace and the Aegean area. Turkey began a hydrographical survey of the continental shelf in this area, claiming oil exploration rights in the eastern Aegean. The Aegean issue contributed to making a preoccupation with the possibility of a confrontation with Greece rather than the USSR the dominating issue of Turkish foreign policy during the late 1970s. The potentially tense situation in the Aegean was overshadowed by a coup in Cyprus in July.

This coup was carried out by the Cypriot National Guard, led by officers from Greece, apparently with the support of the Greek military regime. Declaring its intention of protecting the Turkish community in Cyprus and preventing the union of Cyprus with mainland Greece, the Turkish Government proclaimed a right to intervene as a guarantor state under the Zürich agreement of 1959. On 20 July 1974 Turkish troops landed in Cyprus, and rapidly won control of the area around Kyrenia on the northern coast. The Turkish intervention in Cyprus was followed by negotiations in Geneva between Turkey, Greece and the United Kingdom. Turkey pressed for the creation of an independent federal Cypriot state, with population movements to give the Turkish community their own sector in the north. The intransigence of both Greeks and Turks, and Greece's rejection of a possible cantonal solution put forward by Turkey, led to a further successful advance by the Turkish forces in Cyprus. When a second cease-fire was called on 16 August, Turkey controlled about one-third of the total area of Cyprus.

The sector under Turkish control, all of Cyprus north of a line running from Morphou through Nicosia to Famagusta, contained more than half the livestock, citrus plantations and mineral reserves of Cyprus, with access to two major seaports. The flight of Greek Cypriot refugees from the north left the Turks a free hand to take over the administration and economy, and establish an effective partition of the island. Ecevit claimed that the Turkish military success had laid the foundation of a federal state with two autonomous administrations, allowing the Turkish Cypriot community to concentrate in the conquered area and establish their own government. On 13 February 1975, the Turkish Cypriots unilaterally declared a 'Turkish Federated State' in northern Cyprus and continued pressing for the establishment of a bi-regional federal state system in Cyprus. Greek and Turkish foreign ministers held talks in Rome in May on outstanding disputes between the two countries, with the future of Cyprus among the main topics. The Greek-Turkish Aegean dispute was also discussed, including the issue of ownership of the rights to oil exploration in the area, the equitable division of the Aegean continental shelf and the question of air space control in the area. The dispute was submitted to the International Court of Justice. In April 1978 Turkey refused to recognize the jurisdiction of the Court on this question, preferring to try to negotiate a political settlement, and in October the Court ruled that it was not competent to try the issue.

The USA imposed an embargo on military aid and the supply of arms to Turkey in February 1975 on the grounds that US military equipment had been used in the Turkish invasion of Cyprus in July 1974 and that Turkey had failed to make substantial progress towards resolving the Cyprus crisis. In July Turkey implemented counter-measures, including the take-over of US bases in Turkey. After lengthy negotiations a new bilateral defence agreement was reached between the two countries in March 1976, but the agreement was not ratified, owing to the strength of the Greek lobby in the US Congress.

In January 1978, at the beginning of his term of office, Bülent Ecevit stated that his foreign policy would be aimed at the exploration at the highest level of possible compromises between Greece and Turkey. A summit meeting took place at Montreux, Switzerland, on 9 March and the progress made in personal relations between Ecevit and the Greek Prime Minister, Konstantinos Karamanlis, contributed to a general lessening of tension in the Aegean.

In response to a US statement about the linkage of the arms embargo relaxation and US arms aid, Ecevit turned to the USSR to demonstrate that Turkey had alternatives for her national defence. In April 1978 a trade pact was agreed between the two countries and in June a friendship document was signed, which Ecevit claimed not to be in conflict with Turkey's NATO responsibilities. In response to this *rapprochement* with the USSR, the US Congress lifted the arms embargo in October and four key US bases in Turkey were reopened. Finally, after lengthy negotiations, a five-year defence and economic co-operation agreement was signed on 29 March 1980. In return for economic aid to help Turkey modernize her army and fulfil her NATO obligations, the US was to obtain access to over 25 military establishments, allowing expanded surveillance of the USSR. The eagerness of the USA to come to an agreement grew after the Soviet invasion of Afghanistan in December 1979, which increased Turkey's strategic importance.

Some progress was achieved in the Greek-Turkish Aegean dispute in February 1980. On 22 February Turkey revoked Notam 714 which claimed Turkish control of all air traffic over the eastern half of the Aegean. In response, Greece revoked its civil aviation notice of 1974 which declared the Aegean unsafe and banned all flights except its own. However, the dispute flared up again in June when Turkey held its annual NATO Sea Wolf air and naval manoeuvres in the Aegean, with Greece demanding flight plans for areas which Turkey did not regard as being within Greek airspace. In July Turkish Airlines resumed flights to Athens from İstanbul and Ankara.

Intercommunal talks on Cyprus, sponsored by the UN, were resumed in June 1979 but were adjourned after a week with no agreement reached. At mid-1997 little further progress had been made, despite the resumption of talks under UN auspices, and the issues appeared as intractable as ever. Turkey continued to maintain an estimated 30,000 troops in Cyprus.

ECEVIT GOVERNMENT

General elections for the National Assembly and for 52 Senate seats were held on 14 October 1973. In the National Assembly the CHP, with 185 seats, replaced the AP as the largest party, but failed to win an overall majority. The CHP was believed to have won many votes from former supporters of the banned TIP, while the AP lost support to the DP and a new organization, the Milli Selamet Partisi (MSP—National Salvation Party). The latter, led by Prof. Necmettin Erbakan, was founded in 1972 to replace his banned MNP, and shared its traditionalist, Islamic policies, and became the third largest party in the new National Assembly. Prime Minister Talû resigned, but then remained in office for a further three months while negotiations on the formation of a coalition government continued. Despite this parliamentary crisis, the armed forces remained aloof from politics. Eventually, on 25 January 1974, a Government was formed by the CHP and the MSP, with Bülent Ecevit as Prime Minister and Necmettin Erbakan as his deputy. The Council

of Ministers was composed of 18 CHP members and 7 from the MSP.

The new Government, an apparently unlikely coalition of the left-of-centre CHP and the reactionary MSP, proclaimed its reforming intentions, but made concessions to the demands of its Muslim supporters which tended to deviate from Atatürk's strictly secular principles. In March 1974, Turkey was for the first time represented at an Islamic Summit Conference. The appointment of an MSP deputy as Minister of the Interior brought about a number of petty manifestations of Islamic puritanism, but the main lines of the Ecevit Government's policy seemed to be of a reforming, liberal nature, intended to remove the more excessive aspects of the police state created during the period of military intervention. In May 1972, to mark the 50th anniversary of the founding of the Republic, the Government gave amnesty to 50,000 prisoners.

The land reform passed by the Talû administration came into operation in a pilot project in Urfa province, and in July 1974 the ban on opium production, introduced under US pressure in 1972, was rescinded: a move which, together with the successful handling of the Cyprus question, increased Ecevit's popularity. The differences between the MSP and the CHP had been submerged during the Cyprus crisis, but once more became apparent in September. On 16 September Ecevit announced that he had decided to resign, as the coalition was no longer viable, and to seek a stronger mandate in new elections. New elections, however, were not held immediately and President Korutürk sought to find a coalition government.

Following the resignation of Ecevit's Council of Ministers on 18 September 1974, Turkey remained without a parliamentarily approved government for more than six months. In November Prof. Sadi Irmak attempted unsuccessfully to form an interim coalition to prepare for new elections in 1975, but remained in office in an interim capacity while efforts were made to form a new government. Internal unrest increased during the lengthy government crisis, with serious clashes between opposing political factions and between students.

DEMIREL RETURNS TO POWER

In March 1975 Süleyman Demirel returned to power, leading a right-wing coalition, the Nationalist Front, consisting of four parties: Demirel's AP, the MSP, the CGP and the neo-fascist Milliyetçi Hareket Partisi (MHP—Nationalist Action Party) founded by Col Alparslan Türkeş, who became Deputy Prime Minister. Of the Council of Ministers of 30, the AP occupied 16 of the seats, the MSP eight, the CGP four, and the MHP two. However, the precarious nature of this coalition meant that the Government had to avoid taking radical measures which would upset the co-operation between the four parties. This prevented Demirel's Government from tackling the pressing problems of a deteriorating economy and increasing political violence, for Erbakan refused to countenance the austerity measures demanded by the IMF while Türkeş stood in the way of a crackdown on political violence, most of which the 'Grey Wolves' of the MHP were thought to have instigated. The weakness of the coalition also hampered progress towards a settlement of the Cyprus question, with Demirel having to make concessions to the militant views of the extreme right wing represented by Necmettin Erbakan's MSP. Between 1974 and 1977 the fortunes of the MSP changed drastically and their representation in the National Assembly was reduced from 48 to 24. Erbakan became increasingly discredited, although his deputy and chief rival, Korbut Özal, grew in influence. At the same time support for the MHP increased substantially. It combined anti-communism, Islamic values and a desire for centrally-directed free enterprise with a nationalism that would dispense with democracy. During Demirel's administration, the MHP was able to build up a system of militant cadres by placing its supporters in the police and civil service.

In spite of its difficulties, the Demirel Government continued in power by suspending all action over controversial issues, such as the economy, Cyprus and Greece and relations with the European Community (EC) and NATO, pending the general election scheduled for October 1977. Increasing political violence throughout Turkey and especially in the universities, between left- and right-wing groups, persuaded the authorities to bring forward the general election to June. The political inactivity was matched by economic paralysis as it became clear that the economy was overloaded with short-term debt and banks struggled to pay foreign currency bills of payment.

However, the election of June 1977 failed to produce the hoped-for decisive majority. While the CHP increased its share of seats in the National Assembly to 213 out of 450, the AP also increased its share from 149 to 189 seats. Bülent Ecevit, the leader of the CHP, formed a Council of Ministers but failed to agree a coalition with the smaller parties, and a week later was defeated in a vote of confidence in the Grand National Assembly. Süleyman Demirel, the leader of the AP, was subsequently invited to form a new Government and on 1 August a coalition came to power which gave key ministerial posts to members of the MSP and the MHP. As a result there was penetration of the university and college administrations by extreme right-wing factions and a consequent flare-up of violence on campuses. By mid-December one-third of the universities were shut and 250 people had died in political violence.

The MSP contributed to the country's deepening financial crisis by blocking attempts to follow IMF prescriptions for the economy, insisting on the maintenance of a 5.5% growth rate and refusing to implement monetarist curbs to reduce inflation. Failure to agree on economic remedies led to the withdrawal of an IMF team in December 1977, without agreeing the necessary restructuring for the foreign debt position.

Frustration at the coalition's powerlessness led to the progressive diminution of the AP's support in the Assembly between October and December 1977 as members resigned. By 27 December the coalition could muster only 214 votes and Bülent Ecevit was preparing a new coalition. Following a vote of 'no confidence' in the Grand National Assembly, the Demirel Government resigned on 31 December and formed a caretaker administration. On 2 January 1978 Bülent Ecevit formed a new Government.

ECEVIT RETURNS TO POWER

After the chaos of Demirel's administration, the appointment of Ecevit as Prime Minister was greeted with great popular enthusiasm and high hopes were entertained of his promise to deal with the economic crisis and the political violence. Ecevit's popular support, however, was not reflected in the National Assembly. His majority was dependent upon the support of defectors from the AP, to 10 of whom he gave places in the Council of Ministers, while the number of deputies who had 'crossed the floor' had resulted in a pool of about 20 independents with no set allegiances. Radical reforms were urged on Ecevit, but the insecure parliamentary majority, the country's economic weakness and the unwanted reputation of the CHP in the conservative rural areas as a radical party enjoined on him the necessity for caution. He began a painstaking, relentless purge of right-wing elements in the public administration in response to the cramming of their ministries by Demirel, Erbakan and Türkeş in 1975–77. He adopted an economic stabilization programme, signed a stand-by arrangement with the IMF (providing for a total of US $450m. over two years) and began work on restructuring the severe short-term debt burden. He was, however, unable to secure the huge amounts of international financial assistance necessary to make the stabilization programme work and few of the targets were reached. Inflation continued at about 60%–70%, unemployment reached 20% and, for lack of raw materials, industry was working half-time. Nevertheless, Ecevit was unwilling to take further austerity measures demanded by the IMF as a condition for further aid. Moreover, political violence continued to escalate. Although the universities returned to normal, elsewhere more and more people were killed in acts of terrorism. Both the police force and the internal security forces (MIT) were riven by factions of left and right which made them unable to intervene. Here, too, the process of purging extremists was begun and in September 1978 Ecevit replaced the Chief of Security but, while the civilian tools of authority remained weak and unreformed, the maintenance of law and order depended on the armed forces and Ecevit was forced to ask the *gendarmerie* to undertake policing duties in urban areas. By December more than 800 people had been killed, particularly in the eastern provinces. These new areas of violence reflected a change of tactics by the MHP, which during 1978 campaigned in central and eastern Anatolia, where the traditional elements of society had been least affected by modernization and were most threatened by its arrival. Türkeş's appeal to nationalism gained him supporters, particularly in areas where Turks lived with other ethnic groups, notably the Kurds. The violence culminated in December at the south-eastern town of Karamanmaraş in the most serious outbreak of ethnic fighting since the 1920s. There the historic enmity between the orthodox Sunni majority and the Alevi (Shi'a) minority had been exacerbated by the activities of right- and left-wing agitators. On 21 December the funeral of two members of the left-wing teachers' association, murdered the day before, was turned into a large-scale demonstration by the Alevis. The mourners were fired on by Sunni supporters of Türkeş and indiscriminate rioting erupted. After three days, more than 100 people had been killed, at least 1,000 had been injured and large parts of the Alevi quarters had been reduced to ruins. The MIT had failed to alert the Government to the incidents leading up to the massacre and order was not restored until the intervention of the army on 24 December.

MARTIAL LAW

The violence led to the imposition of martial law on 26 December 1978. Although he had long been urged to take this step by Demirel, Ecevit had refused in view of Turkey's previous experiences of martial law. Martial law was imposed for two months (renewed subsequently at two-monthly intervals) in 13 provinces, all, excepting İstanbul and Ankara, in the east, although the mainly Kurdish areas of the south-east were excluded to prevent friction. Ecevit announced that it was to be 'martial law with a human face' and instituted a co-ordination committee for its implementation comprising himself, Gen. Kenan Evren, the Chief of the General Staff, and Lt-Gen. Sahap Yardimoğlu, the Chief Martial Law Administrator. Special military courts were established to hear cases of those arrested for martial law violations. However, even these new measures proved insufficient to curb the violence, which was now endemic.

In April 1979 a crisis developed on the political front when six ministers, members of the group of defectors from the AP, issued a public memorandum criticizing Ecevit for taking insufficient account of their views and demanding tougher measures to combat political violence, particularly by left-wing groups, and Kurdish separatism. They also demanded a redirection of economic policies to allow more Western investment and greater freedom for private enterprise. The gulf between these views and those of Ecevit's left-wing supporters in the CHP became more and more pronounced and the impossibility of reconciling the left- and right-wing elements in the coalition became clear. In response to the growth of Kurdish separatism, and alarmed by Kurdish violence in Iran, Ecevit agreed to extend martial law into six more provinces, all in the Kurdish south-east. Three CHP deputies promptly resigned, reducing the party's minority representation in the National Assembly to 211 out of 450.

As violence continued, the authorities imposed an all-day curfew in İstanbul and Ankara on May Day in 1979, to prevent riots at the traditional parades. A march planned by the more radical of the union confederations, Devrimci İşçi Sendikaları Konfederasyonu (DİSK), was banned and the army ordered the arrest of its entire leadership, a severe blow to Ecevit's reputation as a champion of workers' rights and an indication of the army's increasing involvement in politics. During the next few months Ecevit's parliamentary majority gradually dwindled after a series of resignations by CHP deputies, and in the October by-elections the AP achieved substantial gains. Ecevit's Government resigned on 16 October.

On 24 October 1979 Demirel formed a new Government with the backing of the rightist MHP and the MSP, affording the Government a majority of four. His Council of Ministers was entirely composed of moderate and uncontroversial AP deputies in an effort to avoid antagonizing the left-wing faction in the National Assembly and jeopardizing his slender majority. Demirel promised a tough policy on terrorism and proposed new legislation to accelerate court procedure and give wider powers to regional governors for dealing with terrorist incidents. However, the elections gave rise to a wave of left-wing protest and the proposed measures gained little headway due to obstruction by the CHP, who objected to what they saw as fascist measures.

With no reduction in the level of violence by the beginning of 1980, the armed forces again intervened. On 2 January the Turkish generals issued a public warning to all political parties, criticizing them for arguing and urging them to reach a consensus of opinion on anti-terrorist measures. Under threat of greater military intervention, the National Assembly immediately began to debate the package of anti-terrorist legislation proposed by the Government. In spite of this threat, the bill was defeated on 15 January, when the MSP voted against it, and sectarian and political killings continued at an average rate of 10 per day. A state-owned factory in İzmir was the scene of fighting between left-wing strikers and the army for several weeks, leading to the imposition of martial law in İzmir and Hatay on 20 February. Twenty provinces were now under martial law. At this time a number of left-wing papers were shut down, including *Politika*, and in May the Türkiye Emekçi Partisi (Workers' Party of Turkey) was dissolved by the Constitutional Court. Once again May Day processions were banned and violence broke out.

The instability of the Government was illustrated by the Grand National Assembly's inability to choose a new President after Korutürk's term expired in April 1980. This again provoked criticism from Gen. Kenan Evren, Chief of the General Staff. Neither the right nor the left was prepared to compromise on the choice of candidate and after much indecision, Ihsan Sabri Çağlayangil took office as acting President. In June the CHP tabled a censure motion intended to force the resignation of the Government before the summer recess. It accused Demirel of allowing prices to rise and violence to continue. However, the 22 MSP deputies voted against the motion, in spite of their opposition to Demirel's pro-Western, pro-NATO stance, and the Government survived the motion by one vote. By August political violence had almost reached the proportions of civil war. Although martial law continued to be extended every two months in 20 out of the 67 provinces, clashes between right and left had caused some 2,000 deaths since the beginning of the year. Meanwhile, inflation and foreign debts continued to escalate, food and power shortages and unemployment were widespread and the political bickering continued. At the beginning of September Demirel attempted to bring forward the elections (scheduled for June 1981), which he hoped would give his party a majority and the power to deal with the country's crisis. However, this move was defeated by the opposition and the Government remained paralysed, unable to make important decisions or implement vital measures.

THE 1980 COUP AND ITS AFTERMATH

On 11 September 1980 the armed forces, led by Gen. Evren, seized power in a bloodless coup, the third in 20 years. There appeared to be three main reasons for their intervention: the failure of the Government to deal with the country's political and economic chaos, the ineffectiveness of the police force, and, more immediately, the sudden resurgence of Islamic fundamentalism, which was evident at a rally in August, during which Necmettin Erbakan and the MSP appealed for the restoration of the *Shari'a*, Islamic Holy Law. The leaders of the coup formed a five-man National Security Council (NSC), sworn in on 18 September. The Chairman of the NSC, Gen. Evren, became head of state. Martial law was extended to the whole country and the Grand National Assembly was dissolved. On 21 September the NSC appointed a mainly civilian Council of Ministers, with a retired naval commander, Bülent Ulusu, as Prime Minister and Turgut Özal as Deputy Prime Minister and Minister for Economic Affairs. The new Government's main aims were to eradicate all possible sources of terrorism and political violence and to reduce the power of political extremists, to uphold Kemalist principles, to honour all foreign debts and existing agreements, and to return the country to democratic rule after the establishment of law and order. Immediately former political leaders, suspected terrorists and political extremists were detained, while all political activity was banned and trade union activities were restricted. At the same time, a severe programme of austerity was introduced by Turgut Özal. In October the NSC drafted a seven-point provisional Constitution which provided the generals with unlimited powers for an indefinite period. In January 1981 the military junta announced its decision to establish a Consultative Assembly between 30 August and 29 October 1981, as the first stage in the promised return to parliamentary rule.

By February 1981 the new Government claimed to have eliminated the main left-wing terrorist groups, including the powerful guerrilla organization Dev Yol. By May 1982, according to varying reports, between 43,000 and 100,000 suspected left- and right-wing activists had been detained. The authorities also imposed harsh measures on Kurdish nationalist organizations, believing them to be supported by forces in the Eastern bloc. By May 1982 there had been a number of mass trials of Kurdish activists, especially members of the PKK, the left-wing separatist Kurdish Workers' Party. In December 1980 proceedings began against 2,000 members of the left-wing DİSK. In November 1981 a law was passed depriving the universities of their traditional administrative autonomy, and banning academics and students from political parties. In February 1982 there were 44 arrests in the biggest crackdown on left-wing intellectuals since the coup. Censorship of the press was not officially imposed but extremist publications were banned and the press and other media placed under strict self-censorship. By October more than 66,000 suspects were said to have been arrested, including the leaders of the MHP and the MSP, together with a large number of trade unionists and the editors of some leading newspapers. The new Government succeeded in reducing the level of political violence in Turkey and in establishing law and order. However, the likelihood that this had been achieved only at the expense of human rights caused concern among the Western Governments: Turkey was banned from the Council of Europe, EC aid was suspended, and fellow-members of NATO urged Turkey to return to democratic rule as soon as possible.

In October 1981 a Consultative Assembly was formed to draft a new Constitution and to prepare the way for a return to parliamentary rule. It comprised five members of the NSC and 160 others, of whom 40 were appointed directly by the NSC, while the remaining 120 were chosen by the NSC from candidates put forward by the governors of the 67 provinces. All former politicians (who had been banned from political activity in April 1981) were excluded and on 16 October all political parties were disbanded and their assets confiscated. A new Constitution was approved by referendum on 7 November 1982, with a 91% majority—despite widely-expressed objections that excessive powers were to be granted to the President, while judicial powers and the rights of trade unions and the press were to be curtailed. An appended 'temporary article' automatically installed Gen. Evren as President for a seven-year term. The opposition was not allowed to canvass openly against the new Constitution. Under the Constitution, power was vested in the President, enabling him to dissolve the National Assembly, delay laws, call elections and make all key public appointments.

Following the referendum, the military regime dismissed left-wing university professors, closed newspapers, tightened press censorship and held mass trials of labour leaders and prominent Turks. In May 1983 the President lifted a 30-month ban on political activity and allowed political parties to be formed under strict rules. All the former political parties, which had been dissolved in October 1981, were to remain proscribed, along with 723 former members of the Grand National Assembly and leading party officials who were banned from active politics for 10 years. By the end of May it was clear to President Evren that proscribed political parties were resurfacing under new names and with new titular leaders. The first new political party to be banned, on 31 May, was the Great Turkey Party, whose leader was Husamettin Cindoruk. This party was the reconstructed AP, with discreet support from Süleyman Demirel. In response, Demirel's supporters formed the Dogru Yol Partisi (DYP—True Path Party). The President gave support to the Milliyetçi Demokrasi Partisi (MDP—Nationalist Democracy Party), led by Gen. Turgut Sunalp, in the hope that it would become the main centre-right party in the new Parliament. On the centre-left the Sosyal Demokrasi Partisi (SDP—Social Democratic Party) was formed, under the leadership of Prof. Erdal İnönü, and won support from the former CHP, although the leader, Bülent Ecevit, recommended boycotting the new political system. The SDP was banned on 24 June. The Halkçi Parti (HP—Populist Party), led by Necdet Calp, had military approval as a centre-left party.

CIVILIAN RULE RETURNS UNDER ÖZAL

A general election was held on 6 November 1983, and parliamentary rule was restored, with a 400-seat National Assembly. Election was on the basis of proportional representation (with a minimum requirement of 10% of the total votes, to discourage small parties), voting was compulsory and every candidate had to be approved by the military council.

The President banned a total of 11 parties from participating in the general election. In a surprise result, the conservative ANAP, led by Turgut Özal, won 211 of the 400 seats in the unicameral National Assembly. The party had been allowed to participate only because the President felt that it would be no threat to the two parties that the military leadership favoured. However, the armed forces' preferred party, the centre-right MDP, was beaten into third place, with the centre-left HP coming second. The result reflected the great popularity of Turgut Özal, stemming from his performance while head of the State Trading Organization and later as Deputy Prime Minister and Minister for Economic Affairs. He was appointed Prime Minister and named his Council of Ministers in December.

The result of the election suggested a decisive rejection of military rule, and this view was strengthened when local elections were held on 25 March 1984. Three parties which had been banned from the general election (the SDP, the DYP and the Refah Partisi (RP—Welfare Party)) were allowed to contest the local elections. ANAP received about 40% of the total votes (almost identical to the November general election result), with the moderate left-wing SDP obtaining 23.3% of the votes. Thus, the main opposition in the country to ANAP was a party not represented in Parliament, a fact which gave rise to further speculation about the undemocratic nature of the general election. The HP and the MDP (the official parliamentary opposition) fared badly in the elections, winning less than 10% of the votes each. In November 1985 the HP and the SDP, the main opposition parties within and outside the National Assembly respectively, merged to form a single party, known as the Sosyal Demokrat Halkçı Parti (SHP—Social Democratic Populist Party). However, the left-wing opposition was split as a result of the formation, a few days later, of the Demokratik Sol Parti (DSP—Democratic Left Party), led by Rahsan Ecevit (wife of the former Prime Minister, Bülent Ecevit) and drawing support from the former CHP.

The civilian Government's main priorities were economic: to cut the inflation rate, which was around 40% at mid-1984; to lower taxes; to reduce drastically the cumbersome bureaucracy; to boost exports and to liberalize imports; to encourage private enterprise; to relax foreign exchange controls; and to slim down state-owned industries. Inflation was still running at an annual rate of around 55% in July 1985, and remained a major worry. Corruption continued to be a problem, and in October 1984 the Minister of Finance and Customs, Vural Arikan, was dismissed by President Evren after accusing the Minister of the Interior (who had resigned shortly before) of allowing the police to torture customs officials who had been accused of corruption. The press and labour unions were put under strict control, despite a few civilian appointments to important posts formerly held by the military. The police were given further widespread powers to maintain law and order and to ensure that there was no return to the political violence which was prevalent in Turkey during the late 1970s.

Widespread concern continued throughout the 1980s and the early 1990s regarding the persistent and widespread use of torture of political prisoners. In May 1984, 1,256 academics and leading figures petitioned the Prime Minister for the eradication of torture and the restoration of full democratic rights. In December 1985 a case brought before the Human Rights Commission of the Council of Europe by five European countries, alleging that Turkey had violated the European Convention for the Protection of Human Rights, was settled out of court when Turkey agreed to rescind all martial law decrees within 18 months, to introduce an amnesty for political prisoners, and to allow independent observers from the Council of Europe to monitor progress. In July 1987 all martial law decrees in Turkey were repealed when martial law was replaced with a state of emergency in the provinces of Diyarbakir, Mardin, Siirt and Hakkâri (making a total of nine provinces under an official state of emergency). The Government's signing, in January 1988, of

the UN's and Council of Europe's agreements denouncing torture, however, received a cynical response from both the local and the international media. In November the eight-year state of emergency in İstanbul was revoked.

In November 1987 Dr Nihat Sargin and Haydar Kutlu, the respective leaders of the banned Workers' Party of Turkey and the Turkish Communist Party, returned to Turkey after seven years of self-imposed exile, with the intention of merging their two parties to form a new Turkish United Communist Party. They were both arrested at the airport and were charged with offences under the Turkish penal code, which specifically outlaws communist organizations and the dissemination of Marxist-Leninist ideas. At their trial, which began in June 1988, both men alleged that they had been tortured by the Turkish police. In May 1990 they were released from detention for the remainder of the trial, in anticipation of significant changes to the articles of legislation that had declared communist parties illegal. In June it was reported that an application for legal status for the Turkish United Communist Party put forward by the two men, had been rejected. In July 1989, at the end of a seven-year trial of members of the banned Dev Yol, a military court sentenced seven left-wing extremists to death, 39 to life imprisonment and more than 300 to jail terms of up to 21 years for activities dating back to the time of the 1980 military coup. In April 1990 it was estimated that 25,000 people had been detained for political reasons since 1980.

A sharp increase in outbreaks of urban terrorism in early 1990, coupled with a perceived increase in the influence of fundamentalist thought, led to widespread fears of a return to the extremist violence of the late 1970s. In October 1990 a hitherto unknown terrorist group, the Islamic Movement, claimed responsibility for a bomb attack which killed Dr Bahriye Ucok, an outspoken critic of the 'fundamentalist perversion' of Islam and a staunch defender of the secular rights of women. The increase in terrorist attacks by Islamic and left-wing groups was exacerbated by the Government's stance in the conflict in the Persian (Arabian) Gulf. A series of attacks against Western targets in Turkey were unleashed, including US civilians, diplomatic missions and offices of several national airlines and banks in İstanbul and Ankara.

In early April 1991 a draft anti-terrorism bill was approved by the National Assembly. Presented as a move towards greater liberalization and democratization, the bill contained provisions for the abolition of controversial articles of the penal code which had proscribed the formation of religious or communist political parties, for the early release of as many as 35,000 prisoners, for the commuting of the death sentence for more than 250 prisoners and for a relaxation of the ban on the use of minority languages. By mid-April it was reported that some 5,000 political prisoners had already been released as a result of the new bill. In July Turkey's Constitutional Court again refused to afford legal status to the Turkish Communist Party.

The MDP voted to disband itself in May 1986. Many of its members joined the new right-wing Hür Demokrat Partisi (HDP—Free Democratic Party), which was formed by Mehmet Yazar, the former President of the Union of Chambers of Commerce and Industry. In December there was much political manoeuvring when the HDP merged with ANAP, and the right-wing Vatandas Partisi (VP—Citizen Party, formed earlier in the year) merged with the DYP (although the VP's leader, Vural Arikan, became an independent); the DSP became a legitimate parliamentary group (i.e. it had more than 20 deputies in the National Assembly) when several deputies from the SHP defected and joined its ranks. By the end of 1986, therefore, the number of recognized parliamentary groups in the National Assembly stood at four—ANAP, the SHP, the DSP and the DYP.

In May 1987 it became apparent that there were rifts within ANAP when its Secretary-General, Mustafa Tasar, resigned after criticizing the party's increasingly powerful Islamic fundamentalist wing. ANAP fared well, however, in the mayoral elections in June, winning 55 of the 84 seats contested. The DYP also proved its continuing popularity by winning 17 seats, whilst the SHP won only six seats and the DSP a mere three.

FURTHER STEPS TOWARDS DEMOCRACY

In a national referendum, held in September 1987, a narrow majority approved the repeal of the 10-year ban imposed on over 200 politicians in 1981, which prohibited them from taking an active part in public life. This result enabled Bülent Ecevit to assume the leadership of the DSP, while Süleyman Demirel was elected as leader of the DYP. As the polls for the referendum closed, the Prime Minister, who had campaigned against the repeal of the ban, immediately announced that a general election would be held on 1 November (a year earlier than required). A few days later, the National Assembly approved legislation enabling a general election to be held at such short notice, by eliminating the procedure of primary elections within each party. After protests and threats of an electoral boycott by the opposition parties, however, the Government postponed the general election until 29 November, thus enabling primary elections to be held. Seven parties contested the general election, which was the first free election in Turkey since the 1980 military coup. ANAP obtained 36.3% of the votes cast (which, because of the 'weighted' electoral system, meant that it was allotted 292 of the seats in the National Assembly, now enlarged from 400 to 450 seats), while the SHP (24.7% of the votes) won 99 seats and the DYP (19.1% of the votes) won 59 seats. Because of the country's proportional representation system, requiring a party to obtain at least 10% of the national vote in order to be represented in the National Assembly, none of the four other parties contesting the election (including the DSP, with 8.5% of the votes, and the RP, with 7.2%) won seats. Özal formed a new expanded Council of Ministers in December. In February 1988 the Sosyalist Parti (Socialist Party), the first overtly socialist political party in Turkey since the 1980 coup, was formally established.

In June 1988, an unsuccessful assassination attempt was made on Özal, as he addressed an ANAP meeting in Ankara. This incident raised fears of a right-wing conspiracy against the Prime Minister, since the would-be assassin had been a senior member of the neo-fascist 'Grey Wolves' group in the 1970s. In August Özal made an unsuccessful attempt to pass a new piece of legislation through the Constitutional Court, which would have enabled local elections (normally held every five years) to take place up to one year in advance. In the following month a national referendum was held to decide whether to adopt this amendment and to bring forward the holding of local elections (scheduled for March 1989) by five months, to November. The political situation became more tense when opposition parties insisted that the result of the referendum should be interpreted as reflecting the extent of confidence in the Prime Minister and ANAP. The widespread public dissatisfaction with the Government and its policies was reflected in the fact that only 35% of the total votes cast were in favour of Özal's proposed amendment, which was, consequently, not adopted.

At the local elections, which were held, as scheduled, throughout Turkey in late March 1989, ANAP obtained only 22% of the total votes, while the SHP and the DYP won 28% and 26%, respectively. The ruling party's defeat included the loss of control of the local councils in the country's three largest cities (Ankara, İstanbul and İzmir) to the SHP. A few days after these elections, Özal implemented an extensive ministerial reshuffle, which was aimed at restoring public confidence in the Government. In the following month, the Prime Minister requested and won a vote expressing confidence in the National Assembly.

ÖZAL BECOMES PRESIDENT

In mid-October 1989 Özal declared his candidacy for the presidential election to be held by members of the National Assembly on 31 October. Despite a boycott of the election by SHP and DYP deputies, who claimed that Özal no longer had a popular mandate, and attempts by a second ANAP candidate to divide support, Özal received the simple majority required in the third round of voting (having failed to secure the two-thirds majority of the 450 Assembly Deputies necessary for victory in the first two rounds), polling 263 of the votes. On 9 November Özal succeeded Gen. Kenan Evren as President and unexpectedly appointed Yıldırım Akbulut, the Speaker of the National Assembly and a former Minister of the Interior, as his successor to the premiership. Although Akbulut was considered by many ANAP supporters as likely to be an ineffectual leader, chosen to allow Özal a greater degree of control as President, a motion expressing confidence in the new Prime Minister was approved

by the National Assembly, and Akbulut was later elected as party leader. Towards the end of 1989 the parliamentary position of the SHP was seriously undermined when a number of SHP deputies resigned in protest at the expulsion of six Kurdish deputies who had attended a Kurdish conference in Paris earlier in the year. Rumours of division within ANAP were confirmed in early 1990, when the Ministers of Foreign Affairs and of Finance and Customs both resigned, expressing disenchantment with party policy and leadership. In March Bedrettin Dalan, a former Mayor of İstanbul and an ANAP party member, announced his intention of forming a new Demokratik Merkez Partisi (DMP—Democratic Centre Party) which was expected to attract many disaffected ANAP supporters.

Following the forcible annexation of Kuwait by Iraq in August 1990, the Government was afforded the *de facto* power to declare war at an emergency session of parliament where, despite strong opposition, a proposal allowing the Government to accept foreign troops in Turkey and deploy Turkish troops abroad in retaliation for acts of aggression against Turkey, was approved by 216 votes to 151.

Although Özal's visible and vociferous support for the UN's sanctions against Iraq (and for US initiatives in particular) did much to enhance Turkey's international standing, political opponents accused the President of jeopardizing Turkey's position in the conflict unnecessarily. In mid-January 1991 a resolution expanding existing war powers, which had been granted to the Government in September 1990, was approved by the National Assembly, despite strong opposition from the SHP and the DYP. The new resolution effectively sanctioned the unrestricted use of NATO air bases in Turkey by coalition forces. However, President Özal stressed that Iraq's 'territorial integrity' would be violated by Turkish forces only in the event of direct military aggression against Turkey or of territorial incursions into Iraq by Iran or Syria. At the end of January 1991 (in a move interpreted as an attempt to prepare the country for the possibility of war) the Government imposed a 60-day ban on strike action, hoping to curtail disruption in crucial industrial sectors.

At an ANAP party congress convened on 15 June 1991 Prime Minister Yıldırım Akbulut was defeated by former Minister of Foreign Affairs Mesut Yılmaz in a contest for the party leadership. The following day Akbulut resigned as Prime Minister, and on 17 June, in accordance with the Constitution, President Özal invited Yılmaz to head a new administration. On 23 June Yılmaz announced the composition of a new, radically-altered Council of Ministers and the next day he assumed the premiership. The appointment of Yılmaz (the leader of the liberal faction within ANAP) and the composition of the Council of Ministers was widely interpreted as an attempt to balance the influence of the liberal and Islamic fundamentalist movements within the Government. In early July the economic programme of the new administration (reaffirming ANAP's commitment to free-market policies and deregulation) was approved by the ANAP majority in the National Assembly. In August the Government announced that general elections (not legally required until November 1992) would be conducted in October 1991, in response to demands by the opposition SHP and DYP, who claimed that ANAP no longer commanded sufficient popular support to govern effectively.

THE 1991 GENERAL ELECTION

A general election was held on 20 October 1991. The DYP, under the leadership of Süleyman Demirel, received an estimated 27.3% of the votes cast, narrowly defeating ANAP (with 23.9%) and the SHP (with 20.6%). Although the DYP failed to attract the level of support necessary for the formation of a single-party government, it was expected that Demirel would assume the premiership at the head of a coalition government. The new coalition government comprising members of the DYP and the SHP was approved by the Assembly later in the month. The Council of Ministers was to include 12 SHP ministers (with the deputy premiership assigned to SHP party leader Erdal İnönü). The remaining 20 cabinet positions were to be occupied by DYP members. On 25 November the coalition partners announced a programme for political and economic reform that included the drafting of a new constitution, improvements in anti-terrorist legislation and matters of human rights, and increased levels of cultural recognition and of autonomy in local government for Kurds in Turkey. While international observers were impressed by Demirel's apparent commitment to human rights (the establishment of a separate ministry of human rights, to be headed by an ethnic Kurd, was promptly announced), the formal adoption of amendments to the criminal procedure code, designed to discourage torture (including a proposed reduction in the length of periods of legitimate police detention), were impeded by a lack of consensus within the coalition Government. Although the DYP and the SHP had performed well at municipal elections conducted in early June 1992 (increasing their combined share of national support to 58%, compared with 48% in the October 1991 general election), the reactivation of the CHP in September 1992 (as a result of the adoption of more lenient guidelines for the formation of political parties, proposed by the Government) threatened to undermine left-wing support for the Government.

At a special ANAP party conference, convened in early December, concern was expressed that right-wing extremism had become the dominant force behind the party leadership, prompting the emergence of a dissident, more conservative faction of the party. Some 70 deputies subsequently announced their intention to leave ANAP in order to form a new party, to be headed by President Özal. However, in April 1993, Özal died as a result of heart failure.

FOREIGN AFFAIRS, 1980–93

Turkey is recognized as a key member of NATO, both on account of its strategic position in Europe and because it is the only NATO member of the Organization of the Islamic Conference (OIC). This was illustrated in 1984 when the USA announced plans to provide Turkey with almost twice as much aid as Greece. In December 1981 the NATO countries were divided over support for the Turkish Government: while the USA promised to speed up aid to Turkey, EC countries were considering the suspension of aid. In January 1982 the European Parliament voted to suspend relations with Turkey, while, at the same time, the Council of Europe condemned military rule, in protest against human rights abuses and other repressive measures, the imprisonment of the former Prime Minister, Bülent Ecevit, and the delay in returning to democratic rule. In March 1982 the EC decided to 'freeze' aid to Turkey.

In September 1986 Turkey was readmitted to associate membership of the EC, when the Turkish-EC Association Council (which was established in 1963, but had been suspended since the army coup in 1980) met for talks in Brussels. Turkey, however, failed to gain access to the suspended EC aid, and to extend the rights of Turkish workers in Europe. In April 1987 Turkey made a formal application to become a full member of the EC. Overruling Greek objections, the EC Council of Ministers agreed to submit the application to the Commission of the European Communities to formulate its opinion on the merits of the case. In April 1988 a meeting of the Turkish-EC Association Council in Luxembourg was postponed indefinitely after objections by the Turkish delegation to a reference to Cyprus, which was inserted at the request of the Greek delegates, in the EC's opening statement (see below). In December 1989 Turkey's application was effectively rejected, at least until 1993, by the Commission of the European Communities. The Commission emphasized that the completion of a single European market was necessary before any enlargement could take place, and cited factors including Turkey's unsatisfactory human rights record, high rate of inflation, dependence upon the rural population and inadequate social security provisions as falling short of EC expectations.

Following negotiations lasting more than a year, an addendum to the 1980 US-Turkish defence and economic agreement, extending it until December 1990, was signed in March 1987 by the US Secretary of State, George Shultz, and the Turkish Minister of Foreign Affairs, Vahit Halefoğlu. The Turkish Government refused, however, to ratify this extension, in protest against what was perceived to be insufficient US military and economic aid, until February 1988, by which time Turkey had benefited significantly from supplies of arms from US surplus stocks.

The Turkish Government responded positively to requests from the USA for logistical aid following the forcible annexation of Kuwait by Iraq in August 1990, and in September the defence and economic co-operation agreement (which provides for the US military presence in Turkey) was extended. In mid-January 1991 a resolution to extend the war powers of the Government and effectively endorse the unrestricted use of Turkish air bases by coalition forces was agreed by the National Assembly (see above). On the following day US aircraft began bombing missions into north-east Iraq from NATO bases inside south-east Turkey. In February and March the US Government announced substantial increases in military and economic aid to Turkey for 1991 and 1992. In September 1991 the 1980 defence and economic co-operation agreement was extended for a further year.

Although Greece and Turkey had agreed to ease tensions in April 1982, relations were further strained when the Turkish-backed 'Turkish Federated State of Cyprus' made a unilateral declaration of independence in November 1983. Turkey is the only country to have recognized this state, the 'Turkish Republic of Northern Cyprus' ('TRNC'), and to have exchanged ambassadors with it (in May 1984). In July 1986 Turgut Özal became the first Turkish Prime Minister to make an official visit to the 'TRNC'. Tension between Greece and Turkey came to a head in March 1987 when a disagreement between the two countries over petroleum-prospecting rights in disputed areas of the Aegean Sea almost resulted in the outbreak of military conflict. Relations between Turkey and Greece improved considerably, however, in 1988: in February the Turkish Government officially annulled a decree, issued in 1964, which curbed the property rights of Greek nationals living in Turkey. In return, the Greek Prime Minister, Andreas Papandreou, officially accepted Turkey's status as an associate member of the EC by signing the Protocol of Adaptation (consequent on Greece's accession to the EC) to the EC–Turkey Association Agreement in April, which the Greek Government had, hitherto, refused to do. The situation deteriorated somewhat, however, later in the same month, when Greece insisted on linking the possibility of Turkey's entry into the EC with the ending of the Turkish presence in Cyprus. In May Melina Mercouri, the Greek Minister of Culture, became the first Greek minister to visit Turkey since 1974, and in the following month Özal became the first Turkish Premier to visit the Greek Prime Minister in Athens for 36 years. As regards Cyprus, Greece wanted the complete de-militarization of the island, on the basis of a set timetable, and the establishment of a joint Greek-Cypriot and Turkish-Cypriot police force under UN auspices. Özal insisted, however, that Turkey would remove its troops only after an overall peace settlement was reached (see chapter on Cyprus). In September 1988 the Turkish and Greek ministers of foreign affairs chaired a session of a joint political committee, which had been proposed in January, in Ankara, while a joint economic committee was convened concurrently in Athens. In February 1990 relations deteriorated again, following violent clashes between Christians and the Muslim minority in western Thrace, in Greece.

Other aspects of Turkey's foreign policy included neutrality in the Iran–Iraq War and commitment to full rights for the Palestinians. In late 1984 tension arose between the USA and Turkey over a congressional resolution condemning alleged massacres of Armenians by Turks during the First World War. The resolution eventually lapsed, and the USA granted military aid, but the tension remained. The Turkish Government was angered once again in February 1987 when the European Parliament adopted a report 'deploring' the alleged massacres. The controversial 'Ottoman Archives', which may help to clarify the circumstances surrounding the alleged killings, were officially opened to scholars for the first time in İstanbul in May 1989.

Turkey protested vehemently against the campaign of forced assimilation, launched by the Bulgarian authorities in late 1984, in which ethnic Turks living in Bulgaria (estimated to number about 1.5m.) were forced to adopt Slavonic names and were banned from practising Muslim religious rites. In February 1988 Turkey took part in a six-nation Balkan conference in Belgrade. During this conference, the ministers of foreign affairs of Turkey and Bulgaria signed a protocol to improve relations between the two countries. In May 1989, however, there were reports that ethnic Turks had been killed in Bulgaria during demonstrations against the continuing assimilation campaign, and the Bulgarian authorities began to deport hundreds of

Turks to Turkey. The Bulgarian Government, however, continued to deny the existence of a resident Turkish minority in their country. The official explanation was that the ethnic Turks were merely Slavs whose ancestors had been forcibly converted to Islam. In late May the Bulgarian authorities altered their policy and issued passports and exit visas to at least 150,000 Turks who wished to enter Turkey. In response, the Turkish Government opened the border and publicly stated its commitment to accepting all the ethnic Turks as refugees from Bulgaria. By mid-August an estimated 310,000 had crossed into Turkey, but more than one-third of that number had returned to Bulgaria by February 1990, as a result of disillusionment with conditions in Turkey and the proposed abolition of the assimilation campaign by a new Bulgarian administration.

Following the formal dissolution of the USSR in December 1991, the Turkish Government sought to further its political, economic and cultural influence in the Central Asian region, and to forge strong links with the six Muslim states of the former Soviet Union in particular. In April 1992 Prime Minister Demirel undertook an official visit to several of the former Soviet republics, pledging aid of more than $1,000m. in the form of credits for the purchase of Turkish goods and contracts. At the same time, programmes broadcast by the Turkish national television company were relayed, by satellite, to the region for the first time. In June leaders of 11 nations, including Turkey, Greece, Albania and six former Soviet republics, established a Black Sea economic alliance, and expressed their commitment to promoting greater co-operation with regard to transport, energy, information, communications and ecology.

TURKEY AND THE IRAQI KURDS

In August 1988 the Iraqi armed forces launched a major offensive against Kurdish separatists in northern Iraq. Thousands of Kurdish refugees (an estimated 100,000–150,000 by early September) fled to the Turkish border, where, after initial hesitation, the Turkish Government admitted them on 'humanitarian grounds' and provided asylum in makeshift camps. In addition, the Turkish Government refused a request by Iraq to allow Iraqi forces to pursue Kurdish guerrillas in Turkish territory. However, the Government made it clear that the refuge being given to the Iraqi Kurds was only temporary. The situation became more serious when many of the refugees claimed that the Iraqi armed forces had launched numerous chemical bomb attacks against them. Despite strenuous denials by Iraqi officials, the physical evidence clearly indicated the use of chemical warfare. The Turkish Government, however, claimed that no traces of the use of chemical weapons had been found, and it would not permit a proposed visit by UN medical experts to investigate the allegations. Iraq offered an amnesty to the Iraqi Kurds in Turkey in September, but very few returned. By August 1989 there were still about 36,000 Iraqi Kurds living in three camps in eastern Turkey, yet the Turkish authorities continued to refuse to recognize them officially as political refugees.

Following the Iraqi invasion of Kuwait in August 1990, the Turkish Government swiftly complied with UN proposals for economic sanctions against Iraq. The passage of Iraqi oil through pipelines (which had not been suspended by the Iraqis themselves) across the Turkish mainland to Mediterranean outlets was curtailed, all Iraqi assets in Turkey were 'frozen' and Turkey's border with Iraq was closed to the passage of all but essential supplies (and to all traffic in January 1991). Turkish nationals were swiftly evacuated from Iraq and Kuwait, and as many as 130,000 troops were redeployed along Turkey's border with Iraq. Despite the increase in the number of Turkish troops in the border region and the deployment of additional US and NATO aircraft in south-east Turkey in early 1991, President Özal continued to stress that Turkey had no intention of opening a second military front against Iraq and that Turkish forces would continue to guarantee Iraq's 'territorial integrity'. In January, following the Government's decision to allow US aircraft to conduct bombing missions into north-east Iraq from NATO bases in Turkey, the Iraqi Minister of Foreign Affairs accused the Turkish Government of committing 'unjustified aggression' against Iraq.

In early March 1991 President Özal revealed that high-level talks had been conducted in Turkey between senior Turkish

foreign ministry officials and the leaders of Kurdish groups within Iraq, during which Turkey had endorsed the notion of some form of autonomy for Iraqi Kurds within Iraqi territory. The Turkish Government had also agreed to open its border for humanitarian aid to areas of northern Iraq which had been reportedly liberated by Kurdish rebels in the aftermath of the conflict in the Persian (Arabian) Gulf. By the beginning of April, however, having suffered serious reversals at the hands of the Iraqi armed forces, more than 500,000 Iraqi refugees (mainly Kurds) were reported to be fleeing to the Turkish border. Although the Turkish Government formally announced the closure of the border, claiming that it was unable to accommodate such a large-scale exodus (some 10,000 refugees, many of them ethnic Turks, had already been recently received by Turkish authorities), and appealed to the UN Security Council to consider the plight of the refugees and to take immediate action to ensure their safety, by mid-April it was estimated that some 600,000 refugees (including 400,000 within Turkish borders) were encamped in the mountainous border region. While reports of the appalling conditions confronting the refugees gave rise to grave international concern and the initiation of an ambitious humanitarian aid programme (with US Air Force transport planes from the İncirlik air base distributing supplies to the refugees), the Turkish minister of state in charge of the relief effort criticized Western governments for their slow response to the crisis. Following intense international pressure, the Turkish authorities (who had contained the refugees in the border region in the hope that a protected buffer zone would be created to accommodate the Kurds on flatlands just inside the Iraqi border rather than on equivalent land at a much greater distance inside Turkey) began to make provision for the removal of up to 20,000 of those refugees in greatest need of medical attention to better conditions at an existing camp at Silopi, inside Turkey. Prime Minister Yıldırım Akbulut insisted that such initiatives were merely temporary measures and that the ultimate aim of the relief effort must be the complete repatriation of the Kurds. In mid-April, in accordance with a UN-approved proposal to establish temporary 'safe havens' for the refugees in northern Iraq, Turkey agreed to allow coalition forces to use Turkish facilities to help the refugees, under UN auspices. By mid-May it was estimated that some 200,000 refugees had returned to Iraq, while 89,000 remained in Turkey (65,000 at Hakkâri and 24,000 at Sirnak) and a further 162,000 were still encamped on the Iraqi side of the border with Turkey.

Following the completion of the first phase of the international relief effort for the Kurdish refugees and the subsequent withdrawal of coalition forces, the Turkish Government agreed to the deployment in south-east Turkey of a 3,000-strong multinational 'rapid reaction force' which would respond to any further act of aggression by Iraq against the Kurds in the newly-created 'safe havens'. The force, to be jointly commanded by the USA and Turkey (the latter would reserve the right to veto attacks against Iraq launched from Turkish territory or airspace) was to include a 1,000-strong Turkish battalion. In September 1991 the Government approved a 90-day extension for the presence, in south-east Turkey, of a small allied air-strike force, and subsequently its mandate was granted six-month extensions. All allied ground forces, however, were withdrawn in October.

POLICY TOWARDS THE TURKISH KURDS, 1980–93

During the 1980s the potential threat of separatism among the Kurds in the south-east of the country was a continuing problem. Despite the fact that there are an estimated 3m.–10m. Kurds in Turkey, they are not officially recognized as a separate ethnic group and it is illegal to speak Kurdish. In 1984 the outlawed PKK, which supports the creation of a Kurdish national homeland in Turkey and which is led by Abdullah Ocalan, launched a violent guerrilla campaign against the Turkish authorities in the south-eastern provinces. The Government responded by arresting suspected Kurdish leaders, dispatching more security forces to the region, establishing local militia groups, and imposing martial law in nine troubled provinces. By July 1987, however, martial law had been replaced by a state of emergency under a district governor in all of these provinces. In spite of this concession, the violence continued and the PKK began to concentrate their attacks on the local militia and civilians. In June 1988 the Government made no response to Abdullah

Ocalan's offer of a cease-fire and prisoner exchange and his demand for the legalization of the PKK. He threatened to spread the conflict to the cities and to attack Turkish politicians and diplomats if the Government continued to insist on a military solution. In April 1990 the Government introduced severe measures to combat ethnic unrest, including harsh restrictions on the media and an increase in the powers of local officials to outlaw strikes and impose internal banishment. Violence continued to escalate, however, and in April and May clashes between rebel Kurds, security forces and civilians left 140 dead, marking the bloodiest period of the conflict since August 1984.

In early 1991, in the context of the Kurdish uprising in Iraq, President Özal sought to alleviate mounting tension among Turkish Kurds by announcing the Government's decision to review existing legislation proscribing the use of languages other than Turkish and by allowing Kurds to celebrate openly the Kurdish new year for the first time. By mid-1991, however, a new wave of violence between the PKK guerrillas and the security forces had erupted in the south-eastern provinces. In July three people were killed and more than 100 wounded when security forces clashed with some 20,000 mourners attending the funeral of a murdered Kurdish rights activist in Diyarbakir. The conflict entered a new phase when, in late 1991 and early 1992 (in retaliation for continuing cross-border attacks on Turkish troops), government fighter aircraft conducted numerous sorties into northern Iraq in order to attack suspected PKK bases there. In the course of these raids many civilians and refugees (mainly Iraqi Kurds) were reportedly killed, prompting international observers and relief workers publicly to call into question the integrity of the exercises. In October 1991 the Iraqi Government lodged formal complaints with the UN, denouncing Turkish violations of Iraq's territorial integrity. In April 1992 negotiations with Syria resulted in the reactivation of a 1987 security agreement designed to curb the activities of the PKK in the border region.

In late 1992 Turkish air and ground forces (in excess of 20,000 troops), conducted further attacks upon PKK bases inside northern Iraq, hoping to taking advantage of losses inflicted upon the Kurdish rebels by a simultaneous offensive, initiated by Iraqi Kurdish *peshmerga* forces in October, with the aim of forcing the PKK from Iraq. By mid-December most Turkish ground forces had been withdrawn from Iraqi territory, and in January 1993, the Turkish military offensive was redirected against PKK strongholds in south-eastern Turkey.

ÇILLER BECOMES PRIME MINISTER

On 16 May 1993 Süleyman Demirel succeeded Turgut Özal as President, after being elected in the third round of voting by the National Assembly. In early June Minister of State Tansu Çiller was elected to the DYP party leadership, and subsequently assumed the premiership as Turkey's first woman Prime Minister. Çiller announced the composition of her Council of Ministers in late June. While all 12 SHP ministers retained their portfolios, the replacement of several prominent DYP ministers was interpreted as an attempt by the Prime Minister to consolidate support for her election to office.

On taking office as Prime Minister, Çiller was immediately confronted with a dramatic increase in separatist violence. The PKK ended its unilateral cease-fire, which had been announced in March 1993, by declaring 'war' on all Turkish targets. There followed a wave of bomb explosions in Turkish tourist resorts and abductions of foreign nationals by the PKK. There was also a series of attacks upon Turkish diplomatic missions and business interests in Europe. The Çiller Government responded by postponing measures to allow the use of the Kurdish language in schools and the media, and by withdrawing plans to give a degree of local autonomy to the south-eastern provinces. At the same time the armed forces, which numbered 150,000-200,000 in the south-east of the country, were given a virtual free hand against the PKK.

The pro-Kurdish Halkın Emek Partisi (HEP—People's Labour Party) was outlawed in July 1993. In September Mehmet Sincar, a deputy of the Demokrasi Partisi (DEP—Democratic Party), the successor to HEP, was assassinated. The PKK and the authorities each blamed the other for the assassination. The Government cancelled all public investment in the south-east of the country, while it was estimated that there had been 2,000

deaths in the region as a result of the conflict between June and December 1993. In March 1994 mainstream parliamentarians voted to strip seven members of the DEP (and one independent Kurdish deputy) of their parliamentary immunity from prosecution, and six deputies were subsequently detained. On 16 June Turkey's Constitutional Court banned the DEP and ruled that its 13 deputies should be expelled from the National Assembly, owing to associations with the PKK. In August the six deputies detained since March, along with two DEP deputies arrested in July, went on trial on charges of supporting separatist movements. In December they were found guilty and received prison sentences of between three-and-a-half and 15 years, despite international protests (although the length of time already served in prison was sufficient to enable the immediate release of two of the deputies). At the end of October 1995 the Supreme Court released two of the deputies. However, it upheld the sentences of the four deputies remaining in prison.

In March 1995 about 35,000 Turkish troops were sent into northern Iraq in a military operation aimed at forcing the PKK out of its bases near the border. The PKK was reported, however, to have obtained advance knowledge of the incursion and to have withdrawn to areas inaccessible to the Turkish forces. Under increasing international pressure, including the temporary suspension of relations by the Council of Europe parliamentary assembly and the suspension of military trade with Turkey by certain countries, Turkish troops withdrew by early May. However, there was a further incursion into northern Iraq, by some 3,000 Turkish troops in July 1995, by which time the official death toll arising from the PKK conflict was estimated at more than 19,000.

Even as Çiller struggled to contain and defeat the PKK, she was confronted by tensions within her governing coalition. Her minority coalition partner, the SHP, was suspicious of the Prime Minister's plans for privatization. It was widely expected that the Government would suffer heavy electoral defeats in the local elections of March 1994; however, at the elections, the beneficiary was not the main opposition party, ANAP, but the Islamic conservative RP. The RP, which had campaigned against inflation and high interest rates and against Turkey's ties to NATO and the European Union (EU, as the EC had then become), won 19% of the votes and took control of both Ankara and İstanbul.

In May 1994 Çiller sought to consolidate relations with the SHP, and simultaneously to deflect international criticism of Turkey's human rights record in the south-eastern provinces, by announcing plans to open up the political arena to groups that had been barred since the 1980 military coup. All restrictions on political activity by academics, students, labour unions and associations were to be abolished, the voting age was to be reduced to 18 from 21, and deputies were to be allowed to move between parties.

Despite continuing dissension within her Government, and the resignation of several cabinet ministers, Çiller's coalition held together throughout the remainder of 1994, sustained, not least, by mutual fear of the RP. In November legislation enabling the sale of some 100 state enterprises was approved by the National Assembly. Çiller's position appeared to be strengthened by the merger of the SHP and the CHP in February 1995, the merged party taking on the latter's name under the leadership of Hikmet Cetin (succeeded by Deniz Baykal in September 1995). The merger led to a new coalition agreement and a consolidation of the Government's parliamentary majority. However, Çiller encountered considerable resistance from the National Assembly in relation to her proposals for 'democratization', as first disclosed in May 1994. In June 1995 deputies from the RP and from within Çiller's own DYP successfully blocked the majority of these proposals. This placed in jeopardy the customs union between the EU and Turkey, the terms of which had been agreed in March and which was scheduled to come into effect at the end of the year, subject to ratification by the European Parliament (which had threatened to veto the agreement unless there was significant progress on raising standards of human rights in Turkey). At the end of July Çiller succeeded in gaining approval from the National Assembly for several democratization measures, including the lowering of the minimum voting age and the removal of certain restrictions on trade unions and political participation. In addition, the number of parliamentary seats was to be increased by 100, to 550.

In foreign affairs Çiller sought the creation of a UN peace-keeping force in Azerbaijan and a role for Turkey in the UN effort in the former Yugoslavia. In July 1994 around 1,455 Turkish troops were deployed in Bosnia and Herzegovina, strictly in support positions. Turkey advocated a removal of the UN embargo against the sale of armaments to Bosnia and Herzegovina and increased pressure on the international community to achieve this aim as a member of the contact group of the OIC (see p. 261). Relations with Greece deteriorated in 1994, owing to Greece's signing of the UN Convention on the Law of the Sea, which would permit the extension of its territorial waters in the Aegean Sea from six to 12 nautical miles. The Turkish Government, fearing the loss of shipping access to international seas, insisted that any expansion of territorial waters would be considered an act of aggression on the part of Greece, to which Turkey would respond. As the Convention entered into force in mid-November 1994, both sides conducted military exercises in the Aegean. Tensions between the two countries were manifest in early 1995 during negotiations to conclude a customs union between the EU and Turkey. Greece finally withdrew its opposition to the agreement in March, following the adoption of a formal timetable for accession negotiations to commence with Cyprus. In June the Turkish National Assembly granted the Government military powers to defend the country's interests in the Aegean, following ratification of the Law of the Sea Convention by the Greek parliament.

In early September 1995, following the election of Deniz Baykal as the new leader of the CHP, the party's government ministers submitted their resignation, to enable Baykal to rene-gotiate the coalition arrangement with the DYP. Talks between Baykal and Çiller revealed substantial differences between the two leaders, in particular with Baykal supporting trade union wage demands and demanding the resignation of the right-wing İstanbul Director of Security. In addition, Çiller rejected the possibility of conducting an early general election. By 20 September the leaders had failed to secure the future of the coalition, forcing President Demirel to accept the Prime Minister's resignation. On the following day Demirel asked Çiller to form a new government. In early October Çiller announced the composition of a new Government, having secured the backing of the Milliyetçi Hareket Partisi (Nationalist Movement Party) and the DSP parliamentary groups, although the latter was dependent on Çiller's resolution of the trade dispute (at that time involving an estimated 350,000 striking public-sector workers). A week later the new administration lost a vote of 'confidence' in the National Assembly by 230 to 191 votes, hindered by several defections from its own DYP party. (The 'rebel' deputies were subsequently expelled from the DYP.) On 16 October Baykal revealed that a tentative agreement had been reached with the DYP leadership for the re-establishment of the DYP-CHP coalition. On 17 October Demirel assigned Çiller the task of forming the next government. Çiller conceded that an early general election would have to be conducted, at the end of the year, in order to secure future political stability. At the end of October Demirel approved a new coalition administration, formed by Çiller with the CHP. The Council of Ministers, which included several independent deputies, secured a vote expressing confidence, in the National Assembly on 5 November, obtaining 243 votes to 171.

THE ISLAMISTS ENTER GOVERNMENT

The overriding objective of Tansu Çiller's caretaker administration prior to the general election, scheduled for 24 December 1995, was to secure endorsement by the EU of the long-proposed customs union. In October 1995 the Supreme Court cancelled the charges against four Kurdish former deputies, while the National Assembly voted to amend the 'anti-terror' laws, one of the outstanding concerns of the European Parliament, in order to permit greater freedom of expression. The customs union was finally approved by the European Parliament on 13 December, and entered into force on 1 January 1996. Çiller had warned European leaders that failure to secure the agreement could provoke a rise in Islamic fundamentalism in Turkey, and, indeed, approval of the customs union was granted shortly before the general election in which the RP, which opposed a

closer working arrangement with the EU, was expected to perform strongly.

During the election campaign domestic issues, such as the high rate of inflation, were the dominant concerns. The outcome of the election failed to resolve the country's political uncertainties: the RP won 158 of the 550 seats in the enlarged National Assembly, having obtained 21.4% of the votes cast, while the DYP secured 135 seats (19.2%), ANAP 132 seats (19.7%), the DSP 76 seats (14.6%) and the CHP 49 seats (10.7%). The remaining votes, 14.4%, were shared among smaller parties which gained no representation. The rate of voter participation was officially estimated at 85%.

President Demirel gave the RP, as the largest party in the new National Assembly, the first opportunity to form a government. Protracted negotiations between the parties ensued over the next two months. Despite RP leader Necmettin Erbakan's apparently conciliatory approach, the party failed to secure the secular coalition partner that it needed to form the first predominantly Islamic government in the history of modern Turkey. The question increasingly became whether the two secular right-wing parties, the DYP and ANAP, could agree on terms for a coalition that would prevent the formation of an RP administration. Finally, on 28 February 1996, ANAP and the DYP concluded an agreement. A rotating premiership arrangement was to be undertaken, according to which the ANAP leader, Mesut Yılmaz, was to occupy the office in the first year. The DYP was given most of the economic ministries, while ANAP took control of the defence and security portfolios. The new coalition still needed the support of the DSP if it was to control an absolute majority in the National Assembly, but a formal arrangement proved impossible to secure.

Within weeks it was evident that the DYP-ANAP coalition would not last long, not least because of the intense personal animosity between Yılmaz and Çiller. During April and May 1996 the RP won two parliamentary votes to initiate corruption investigations against Çiller, on both occasions with significant support from ANAP deputies. Meanwhile, the opposition parties questioned the credibility of the Government following a ruling of the Constitutional Court to annul the vote of confidence that the coalition received in March. By the end of May Çiller was publicly urging Yılmaz to resign. The political uncertainty was seriously damaging the economy. The atmosphere of crisis within the country was deepened by an unsuccessful attempt to assassinate President Demirel on 19 May. In early June the National Assembly, with the support of DYP deputies, voted to debate a censure motion on the Government; however, on 6 June Yılmaz resigned.

On 7 June 1996 Necmettin Erbakan was invited to form a government, and negotiations to establish a new coalition began. The DYP entered into discussions with the RP for the first time. On 28 June the two parties reached agreement, and the new coalition won a 'confidence' vote in the National Assembly on 8 July. Erbakan, as leader of the RP, became Prime Minister, while Çiller assumed the deputy premiership and foreign affairs portfolio. In addition, the DYP was awarded the defence, interior and education ministries and responsibility for the Treasury. The coalition's programme embraced pragmatism, perhaps in order to reassure a watchful army, long the guardian of Turkish secularism. The new Government announced that its objective was to secure political and economic stability; it promised to pursue further European integration and undertook to honour existing international and strategic agreements, providing that they did not threaten national interest.

Nevertheless, Turkey had entered a new, potentially contradictory, era. It had moved closer to Europe even as it had sworn in its first Islamist-led government. Almost immediately Erbakan embarked on a tour of Middle East and Asian Islamic countries, while there was continuing uncertainty over the future of the agreement reached in February 1996 between Turkey and Israel, providing for co-operation in military training, which had led Syria, Egypt and Iran to express anxiety that Turkey was abandoning the Islamic camp. It remained to be seen whether RP rank-and-file members would be willing to accept the continuation of this agreement without demur. Similar uncertainty prevailed over the long-term prospects for continued use of Turkish bases by allied forces engaged in 'Operation Provide Comfort' in northern Iraq, although at the end of July a five-month extension of the mandate was approved. Relations with the USA, however, became strained in the first months of the new administration. In August Turkey and Iran signed an agreement authorizing the construction of a pipeline between the two countries and enabling the sale of natural gas from 1999. The accord was concluded days after the entry into force of US legislation threatening punitive measures against countries undertaking substantial investment commitments in Iran. In early September Turkey was reportedly not consulted before US air strikes were launched against Iraqi government troops in northern Iraq, and the Turkish authorities refused permission for the use of Turkish bases to pursue the operation.

However, there were policy areas where continuity seemed more assured under a government led by the RP. The RP leadership pledged itself to firm action against the PKK. On 30 June 1996 a militant supporter of the Kurdish cause killed herself and six soldiers in a suicide bomb attack in Tunceli, eastern Turkey. In late June more than 30 members of the principal pro-Kurdish nationalist grouping, the Halkın Demokrasi Partisi (People's Democracy Party), including its leader Murat Bozlak, were detained following disturbances at a party congress and were subsequently charged with encouraging separatism. Civilian clashes with police occurred in Ankara and İstanbul during June and July at demonstrations of support for some 300 PKK prisoners who were on hunger strike as a protest against their treatment and conditions of confinement. Some 12 detainees died while refusing sustenance, prompting widespread international criticism at the Government's intransigence. Meanwhile, the National Assembly, at the end of July, approved an extension of the state of emergency in the south-eastern provinces, despite the RP's electoral campaign commitment to reverse the situation, and the Turkish army intensifed its efforts to combat the PKK in the south-east and in northern Iraq. In August the Government approved legislation granting extensive powers of martial law to the governors of all 76 provinces, in a move which suggested the imminent repeal of the controversial 'state of emergency' law, which in November was extended for a further four months in nine of the ten south-eastern provinces in which it had previously been applied. In August legislation was also endorsed which relaxed curbs on the Kurdish language and culture and facilitated increased investment in the south-east. In October, however, the European Parliament blocked aid to Turkey worth US \$470m., because of continuing concerns regarding the country's human rights record. Following the US raids on northern Iraq in early September, the Turkish Government proposed the establishment of an exclusion zone along its entire border with Iraq in order to prevent an influx of refugees and to eradicate separatist violence from the region. Turkey argued for the lifting of UN sanctions against Iraq, which would allow it to begin purchasing Iraqi oil, and the renegotiation of 'Operation Provide Comfort', which, it was claimed, had produced a political vacuum in northern Iraq, which was being exploited by the PKK. The 'Operation Provide Comfort' mandate expired on 31st December 1996, and a more limited aerial surveillance operation, 'Northern Watch', which was to monitor Iraq's compliance with UN resolutions, was established. In December, in accordance with the 'oil-for-food' agreement (Resolution 986) agreed between the UN and Iraq in May, a fixed quantity of Iraqi oil began to be exported through Turkey, in order to enable Iraq to purchase supplies of medicine and food.

Syria's alleged support for the PKK was likely to mean that its relations with Turkey would remain tense. A further source of tension between the two countries lay in Turkey's construction of hydroelectric dams on the Euphrates river, which Syria protested against, claiming that they would severely restrict its water supplies. In May Syria had accused Turkey of responsibility for a series of bomb explosions that had occurred in a number of its large cities. A further likely area of continuity in policy lay in Turkey's relations with Greece. In January confrontation flared up over rival territorial claims to the Kardak/Imia rocks in the Aegean Sea. UN and US mediation persuaded both sides to end a military and naval build-up in the area; however, the issue remained unresolved and in April 1997 Turkey rejected proposals to take the dispute to the International Court of Justice.

In October 1996 Erbakan was subjected to a vote of 'confidence', in the National Assembly, following severe criticism of his Government's foreign policy, which included a controversial visit to Libya by the Prime Minister. The censure motion was defeated. In early November the Minister of the Interior, Mehmet Ağar, resigned amid allegations by opposition parties of close links between senior DYP politicians, the police and organized crime. In December the chief of police in Istanbul was suspended, along with five other senior officers, pending an investigation into the allegations. In December 1996, the controversial visit of President Rafsanjani of Iran, during which a number of economic accords were signed, provoked widespread criticism, while tensions were further exacerbated following an anti-Israeli rally in Sincan, an Ankara suburb, on 31 January, during which the Mayor of Sincan publicly urged the introduction of *Shari'a* law in Turkey. The mayor was arrested and the Iranian ambassador, Muhammad Reza Bagheri, who also took part in the demonstration, left the country amid denials by senior parliamentary officials that his departure was related to the event. On 4 February the army paraded a tank unit through Sincan in what was widely considered to be a display of secular strength.

The Government suffered a serious legal defeat in December 1996 when the European Court of Human Rights (ECHR) ruled that Turkey, as the effective power in the 'TRNC', had breached the European Convention on Human Rights by denying a Greek Cypriot woman access to her property in Kyrenia since the 1974 invasion. The ruling was expected to open the way for compensation claims against Turkey (a signatory of the Convention) by other displaced Greek Cypriots.

YILMAZ REPLACES ERBAKAN

In the context of persistent rumours of an imminent military coup and a new censure motion against the Government, tabled in protest at proposals to introduce Islamic reforms, a meeting of the military-dominated National Security Council (NSC) on 28 February 1997 led to the publication of an 18-point memorandum setting out recommendations to ensure the protection of secularism in Turkey. On 5 March, under severe pressure, Erbakan reluctantly signed the memorandum, whereby the Government was committed to increasing the length of compulsory state education from five to eight years, to closing unauthorized Islamist schools and acting against Muslim brotherhoods; to halting the employment of soldiers expelled from the army for fundamentalist activities; and to reducing co-operation with Iran.

Although the immediate political crisis had been resolved, DYP dissidents began to call for the dissolution of the Government and the organization of early elections. At the end of April 1997 the NSC demanded that Erbakan accelerate implementation of the 18-point memorandum, stating that inadequate progress had been made. On 26 May Erbakan was also compelled to chair a special session of the Supreme Military Council and to counter-sign an order expelling 161 officers from the army for demonstrating Islamist sympathies. On 20 May a censure motion brought by four opposition parties was only narrowly defeated, and by 30 May the Government had lost its parliamentary majority as more DYP deputies defected (a number had resigned in April). Erbakan finally stepped down on 18 June, but President Demirel selected not Çiller (despite agreements concluded at the formation of the 1996 coalition) but ANAP leader Mesut Yılmaz to form a new coalition. On 30 June Yılmaz was appointed Prime Minister, having successfully gained the support of the DSP and the recently-founded Demokrat Türkiye Partisi (DTP—Democratic Turkey Party), along with several DYP defectors, to form a coalition with a nominal 12-seat majority. The new Government's programme, announced on 7 July, stressed its commitment to secularism and echoed many of the recommendations of the 18-point memorandum drawn up by the NSC (including the controversial education reforms). The Government received a vote of 'confidence' from the National Assembly on 12 July. Legislation promulgating the education reforms secured parliamentary approval in mid-August, as did a press amnesty law which suspended the sentences of imprisoned editors (believed to number at least six) who had been convicted of publishing articles posing a threat to national security. Later that month, the trial began of a total of 48 members of the security forces, including 11 officers, for the murder of a journalist in 1996. Doubts were raised about the effectiveness of the trial when the defendants failed to attend the court; delays to the case resulted in demonstrations in İstanbul in January 1998. In March, however, five of the officers were sentenced to more than seven years' imprisonment, while the remaining six were acquitted.

On 5 September 1997 the Human Rights Co-ordination High Council met in Diyarbakır to review measures introduced to prevent torture. At that time the international Committee to Protect Journalists visited the country and urged the relaxation of press laws. In early October the Government established a working council for freedom of thought and expression, and launched an initiative to promote human rights through radio and television broadcasts.

On 16 October 1997 Turkey agreed an out-of-court settlement in a case of alleged torture which had been taken to the ECHR. Later that month a human rights activist, Esber Yagmurdereli, was sentenced to 23 years' imprisonment for supporting terrorist activity and disseminating separatist propaganda. Following both foreign and domestic condemnation of his detention, he was released in November ostensibly on the grounds of ill health. At the end of November the ECHR ordered Turkey to pay compensation to six former DEP deputies who had been detained for two weeks without trial and to three Kurdish women whose homes had been destroyed by the army.

In March 1998 10 members of the security forces were acquitted of torturing 14 students who were subsequently convicted of belonging to a proscribed organization and sentenced to between five and 12 years' imprisonment. At the end of the month, five of the students were released, pending their retrial on lesser charges. During late 1997 and early 1998 detainees at Erzurum prison protested against prison conditions, staging an extended hunger strike and taking hostages to reinforce their claims.

Meanwhile, in May 1997 the armed forces launched their most ambitious military incursion into northern Iraq yet, in pursuit of PKK activists, in a move which involved the mobilization of some 50,000 troops. The army claimed that its intervention was invited by the Iraqi-Kurdish Democratic Party of Kurdistan (DPK), which was reported to have clashed ferociously with the PKK during 1996. The incursion prompted a muted international response, when compared with the military intervention of 1995; the USA had been 'disengaging' from northern Iraq for some months and appeared content for Turkey to assume some of its former responsibilities. The most severe critics of the exercise were Iran and Syria, who accused Turkey of seeking to establish a permanent military presence in northern Iraq. A further offensive against PKK positions in northern Iraq in October was accompanied by the lifting of the 10-year-old state of emergency in three of the nine south-eastern provinces (Bitlis, Batman and Bingöl). The continuing emergency rule in the other six provinces and the Turkish military presence in northern Iraq were seen as indicative of a Turkish intention to create an informal cross-border security zone to prevent further incursions by Kurdish rebels.

At the end of April 1997 the Greek and Turkish ministers responsible for foreign affairs held bilateral talks in Malta under EU auspices, during which it was agreed that each country would establish a committee of experts to help resolve bilateral disputes. The two committees were to be separate and independent and were to communicate through the EU. In July, at a NATO summit in Madrid, direct talks took place between Demirel and the Greek Prime Minister, Konstantinos Simitis (the first such meeting for three years). An agreement, known as the Madrid agreement, was signed in which both sides pledged to respect the other's sovereign rights and to renounce violence, and the threat of violence, in their dealings with each other. Later in July, following earlier statements from Turkey expressing the hope that Greece would revoke its veto on EU aid, Greece stated that the veto would not be removed unless Turkey agreed to international arbitration over the disputed islet of Imia/Kardak.

In July 1997 Turkey announced the formation of a joint committee to implement partial integration between Turkey and the 'TRNC', in response to the EU's agreement to commence accession talks with Cyprus. Turkey also declared in September that should the EU continue to conduct membership talks with the Greek Cypriot Government, then it would seek further integration with the 'TRNC'. Shortly afterwards Turkey banned all Greek-Cypriot ships from entering Turkish ports. Following the involvement of Greece in Greek Cypriot military exercises in October, in November Turkish forces engaged in military manoeuvres in the 'TRNC'. However, Yılmaz and Simitis held a cordial meeting later in November and agreed to explore confidence-building measures. Throughout 1997 and early 1998 relations were strained by accusations of violations of airspace and territorial waters, made by both Greece and Turkey. The most serious incident occurred in October when Greece accused Turkey of harassing a plane carrying the Greek Minister of Defence. In January 1998 Turkey declared that a Greek plan to extend its territorial waters from six to 12 miles under UNCLOS was unacceptable, as were plans to open several Aegean islets for settlement. Turkey also protested to the UN that the proposed opening of an airbase at Paphos in southern Cyprus would destabilize the military situation on the island. In April Greece again vetoed the release of aid promised to Turkey under the Turkish-EU customs union. In June new tensions arose over Cyprus when six Turkish military aircraft landed at a 'TRNC' airfield in response to the landing a week earlier of Greek military aircraft at Paphos. The following month President Demirel paid an official visit to the 'TRNC' (in response to an unprecedented visit to Greek Cyprus by President Stefanopoulos of Greece the previous month), amid a show of Turkish military force to mark the 24th anniversary of the 1974 intervention. At the same time, Yılmaz reiterated Turkey's threat to take retaliatory military action if the Greek Cypriot Government went ahead with its plan to deploy Russian-supplied S-300 missiles before the end of 1998.

Relations with the EU were further strained by announcements in December 1997 that Turkey would not be invited to join the EU, but that it would be invited to a newly-created EU Conference, which was to include both EU and non-EU states, Turkey stated that it would not attend such a conference and that it would also cease negotiations on Cyprus, human rights and the Aegean disputes. It further threatened to boycott EU goods and to withdraw its application to the EU if it was not included in a list of candidates by June. On 20 December Turkey announced a six-month 'freeze' in relations with the EU. The EU later announced it was withholding all aid to Turkey for 1998, owing to the situation in the south-east and human rights problems.

In January 1998 the EU called for Turkish action to halt the flow of Kurdish refugees arriving in the EU from Turkey. A meeting was held in Rome, Italy, by European police chiefs to discuss the problem, although Turkey refused to sign a communiqué issued at the meeting. A total of 2,646 refugees had arrived in Italy since July 1997 (1,200 of whom had arrived in the first week of January). The EU announced its willingness to help find a solution, and suggested establishing 'safe havens' for Kurdish refugees. Turkey, however, opposed this idea owing to fears that it would strengthen the position of the PKK and act as a base for terrorist activity.

Relations with Germany deteriorated in early March 1998 following Turkish accusations that Germany had blocked Turkish entry to the EU; it compared German policies to those of the Nazis. Turkey also officially declined its invitation to the EU Conference in that month.

At the end of 1997, as relations between Iraq and the UN deteriorated (see chapter on Iraq), Turkey announced that it opposed the use of its Incirlik air base for potential US-led strikes against Iraq and urged a peaceful solution to the crisis.

Meanwhile, following negotiations, it was announced at the end of September 1997 that full diplomatic relations were to be resumed with Iran. In September President Demirel called for talks with Syria and Iran on the use of the Euphrates' waters.

In December 1997 at a conference of the Organization of the Islamic Conference in Teheran, which Demirel attended, a resolution was passed condemning joint military action with Israel, although all specific references to Turkey were dropped; planned joint military exercises between Turkey, Israel and the USA took place in the Aegean in January 1998. They were condemned as provocative by many Arab states, particularly Syria and Iran. Official visits had previously been conducted by the Turkish and Israeli ministers responsible for defence, and Turkey had earlier awarded Israel several military contracts.

In January 1998 the Constitutional Court banned the RP on the grounds that it had a 'hidden' fundamentalist agenda and had conspired against the secular order. In addition, former Prime Minister Erbakan and six other RP officials were banned from holding political office for five years. A month later some 100 former RP Assembly deputies joined the new Virtue Party (FP), which had been founded in December 1997 under the leadership of Ismail Alptekin and by early March the FP had become the largest party in the Grand National Assembly.

Public demonstrations followed the military's insistence on the strict enforcement of the ban on wearing Islamic dress in public buildings, notably educational establishments. The largest of these demonstrations was attended by 10,000 people in İstanbul at the end of February 1998. In early March the University of İstanbul temporarily annulled the ban and the Government stated that the ban would not be strictly enforced. In mid-March the Government survived its third censure motion, which was presented against the Minister for Education for his handling of the issue of Islamic dress. A few days later 20 members of a proscribed Islamic organization were arrested for inciting the demonstrations. At the end of the month the NSC criticized the Government for advocating a relaxation of the enforcement of anti-Islamic legislation; the Government subsequently proposed further measures to curb Islamic radicalism, and the universities announced their decision to enforce the dress code. Further demonstrations were organized by the

trade unions in protest at legislation that they feared would erode union rights.

Also in March, the Court of Appeals ruled that former Prime Minister Çiller could not be prosecuted over allegations that she had misused government funds during her premiership. While admitting that she had withdrawn substantial sums from a secret government 'slush fund', Çiller had claimed that she could not disclose the destination of the money for reasons of national security. Nevertheless, the Grand National Assembly voted in April to open a new investigation of the former Prime Minister's finances, while the following month her husband, Özer Çiller, was given a five-year suspended prison sentence for having misled a parliamentary commission investigating the couple's wealth. In May the Assembly confirmed that an inquiry would be conducted into corruption allegations against Prime Minister Yılmaz connected with tendering for government contracts.

In early June 1998 Yılmaz announced that he would resign at the end of the year to make way for a broad-based caretaker government which would oversee the holding of early legislative elections in April 1999. In August the ministers responsible for Justice, the Interior, and Transport and Communications resigned and were replaced by independent deputies; this was in order to comply with constitutional requirements which state that prior to an election, key posts should be held by independents. Later that month the chief prosecutor began legal action against 12 former members of the RP, including Erbakan, on charges of fraud. Seven of those under investigation are currently FP deputies.

Economy

Dr DAVID SEDDON

Revised for this edition by Alan J. Day

Turkey is about 1,450 km (900 miles) long and some 500 km (300 miles) wide, covering an area of 779,452 sq km (300,948 sq miles). The October 1985 census recorded a population of 50,664,458, and that of October 1990 showed the population to be 56,473,035. These totals excluded Turks working abroad, the largest number of whom are in Germany. The census results indicated an average annual population increase between 1985 and 1990 of 2.2%, compared with 2.6% between 1980 and 1985. Turkey's population density was 65.0 per sq km in October 1985, and had increased to 80.4 per sq km by mid-1996. The results of the national census conducted in November 1997 showed the population to have increased to 62.9m., indicating an average annual rate of growth of 1.5% since 1990. İstanbul, the country's largest city, had a population of 9.2m. (7.2m. in 1990), followed by Ankara (the capital) with 3.7m. and Izmir with 3.1m.

The country possesses great natural advantages: the land yields good grain and a wide variety of fruit and other products; it is rich in minerals; and it has a number of natural ports. The climate is varied and, on the whole, favourable, but communications are hindered by the mountain ranges that ring the Anatolian plateau to the north, east and south.

Gross national product (GNP) expanded, in real terms, by an average of 7% annually between 1970 and 1978. However, in the severe economic and social crisis of the late 1970s, growth slowed to the extent that an actual decline of 1.1% was recorded in 1980. In 1980–90 GNP at constant 1987 prices increased by an annual average of 5.5%, with a growth rate of 9.2%, the highest for more than a decade, in 1990. In 1991 the adverse effects of the Gulf War contributed to growth of just 0.9%, with GNP amounting to $109,078m. The economy recovered in 1992, with GNP growth of 5.9%. This impressive growth performance continued in 1993, with a rate of 7.3%, owing essentially to a consumption boom fed by foreign borrowing. An official target growth rate of 4.5% was announced for 1994, but, after a severe financial crisis early in the year and an austerity programme in April, GNP, in fact, contracted by 6.1%. The decline in the

economy was successfully reversed during 1995, and a growth in GNP of 8% was achieved, which levelled out at 7.9% in 1996. The strongest sectoral growth in both 1995 and 1996 was recorded in trade and industry. Figures published by the OECD revealed that although per-capita income rose by 6.1% in 1995, to $2,928, the wealthiest 20% of the population had a per-capita income of $8,037, while the poorest had only $717, giving Turkey the worst income distribution of all OECD countries except Mexico. In 1997 GNP increased by some 7%, but was forecast to increase by only 4.5% in 1998 and 4.4% in 1999, according to the Government's IMF-monitored economic programme (see Finance, below).

AGRICULTURE

Turkey relies substantially on agriculture, although the sector's overall role is shrinking rapidly. According to ILO, 43.3% of the country's labour force was employed in the agricultural sector in 1996. Agriculture provided 59.4% of total export revenue in 1979, but the proportion declined to around 20% in the late 1980s and stood at 13.6% in 1994. The agricultural sector, including forestry and fishing, contributed 14.6% of GNP in 1995, 15.5% in 1996 and 13.8% in 1997. Nearly 25m. ha, or about one-third of total land area, are under cultivation. Most of the farms are small and the average size of a family farm is only 8 ha. The country is basically self-sufficient in foodstuffs. The principal agricultural exports are cotton, tobacco, wheat, fruit and nuts. Other important crops are barley, sunflower and other oilseeds, maize, sugar beet, potatoes, tea and olives.

During the period 1963–70 Turkey's agricultural output rose by only 2.5% per annum, mainly because insufficient emphasis had been placed on agriculture in both the first and second economic development plans. However, with the introduction of land reforms and the improved utilization of land, machinery and farmer education resources, agricultural production in 1971 increased by some 30%. In 1975 real expansion in agriculture was 10.9%, but such good results were infrequent. In 1978 the rise in output was only 2.7%, while in 1981 it was just 0.3%.

The rate of increase has fluctuated considerably in recent years and although inadequate rainfall in 1989 caused agricultural output to contract by 10.8%, during 1980–90 agricultural output grew by an annual average of 1.3%. In 1990–96 an average annual increase of 1.2% was recorded. In 1995 an increase in output of only 2% was attained, but growth was stronger in 1996, averaging 5.2%, largely due to exceptionally strong growth during the last three months of the year. Production then declined by about 1% in 1997, according to estimates from US Department of Agriculture officials in Ankara.

Government policy is to increase agricultural productivity, but budget constraints restrict project financing. The funds that are available come mainly from international sources, notably the World Bank. However, there is increasing foreign commercial interest in developing Turkish agro-industry, particularly for Middle Eastern export markets. In an attempt to alleviate the poverty of the south-eastern provinces of Turkey, the government drew up a south-east Anatolia programme (GAP) in the early 1980s, covering a total area of 74,000 sq km. Some 495 projects were integrated into GAP, which envisaged the construction of 22 dams on the Tigris and Euphrates rivers and their tributaries, 19 power plants and an irrigation network with the potential to cover 8.5m. ha. GAP has been affected by delays resulting from attacks by the PKK separatists and disputes over financing. In 1994 two water pipelines were opened. At the end of that year GAP had cost $11,000m. and required an estimated $21,000m. for its scheduled completion by 2005.

About one-half of the cultivated area is devoted to cereals, of which the most important is wheat. The principal wheat-growing area is the central Anatolian plateau but the uncertain climate causes wide fluctuations in production. Barley, rye and oats are other important crops grown on the central plateau. Maize is grown along the Black Sea coastal regions, and leguminous crops in the İzmir hinterland. Rice, normally sufficient for domestic needs, is grown in various parts of the country. Since 1977 the annual wheat harvest has usually stayed above the high level of 16m. metric tons, owing to good weather, improved cultivation methods and increased levels of irrigation. In 1993 there was a particularly good harvest of 21m. tons, although export earnings remained at a relatively low level of about $70m. In 1994 output was 17.5m. tons, with no improvement in export earnings. Output rose to 18.0m. tons in 1995 and 18.5m. tons in 1996, while provisional figures for 1997 suggested that output had again increased slightly, to 18.7m. tons.

Cotton has traditionally been Turkey's main export earner, grown mainly in the İzmir region and in the district round Adana, in southern Turkey. In recent years, however, it has lost some of its traditional importance. Production stood at 558,000 metric tons in 1993, when exports of cotton were valued at $123m., and 630,000 tons in 1994. The irrigation of agricultural land in the eastern Haran region was expected to enhance the production of cotton, and official figures indicated that production stood at 851,000 tons in 1995, 792,000 tons in 1996 and an estimated 779,000 tons in 1997.

Turkey produces a particularly fine type of tobacco. The three principal producing regions are the Aegean district, the Black Sea coast and the Marmara-Thrace region. The bulk of the crop is produced in the Aegean region, where the tobacco is notable for its light golden colour and mild taste. The finest tobacco is grown on the Black Sea coast, around Samsun. Although a traditional Turkish export, its relative position as an export has been declining in recent years. Most of Turkey's tobacco exports go to buyers in the USA and East European countries. The size of the crop fluctuates considerably: in 1993 it reached a record level of 324,000 metric tons (matched only in 1976) but fell to 227,000 tons in 1994 and 204,000 tons in 1995. In 1996 production increased to 232,000 tons, and estimates for 1997 showed a further increase in production, to 300,000 tons. In 1984 the Government permitted the first legal imports of foreign cigarettes in more than forty years, breaking the monopoly over sales and distribution held by the state-owned tobacco and beverages agency, Tekel. Several international tobacco companies have started negotiations to manufacture cigarettes locally, and one joint-venture operation has been established at Bitlis in the south-east of the country to produce cigarettes for export. A new cigarette factory in İzmir, as part of a joint venture between the US tobacco company Philip Morris and the local Sabanci group, produces popular US brands for the domestic market. Tekel, however, has responded by raising capacity and output and improving the quality of its brands.

The coastal area of the Aegean, with mild winters and hot, dry summers, produces grapes, figs and olives. Exports of dried figs were valued at $53m. in 1993. France is the main customer for figs. The outstanding product, however, is the sultana type of raisin, which is also grown in California and elsewhere. Turkey normally ranks second in the world as a sultana producer, but in good years becomes the largest producer in the world. Sultana harvests varied from 85,000 metric tons in 1976 to 138,000 tons in 1989, when exports were worth $72m. In 1996 the sultana harvest was 220,000 tons, falling to an estimated 211,000 tons in 1997. In 1994 total exports of dried fruits were valued at $747m.

The Black Sea area, notably around the Giresun and Trabzon, produces the greatest quantity of hazel-nuts (filberts) of any region in the world. A harvest of 455,000 metric tons was recorded in 1995, when exports of hazel-nuts (40% of which were sold to Germany) were valued at $771m. Substantial amounts of walnuts, chestnuts and almonds are also grown.

Tea is grown at the eastern end of the Black Sea, around Rize, and in other areas. Production of fresh leaves from state-owned tea plantations has steadily increased since the early 1980s to total 654,000 metric tons in 1994. Output declined to 524,000 tons in 1995, but increased to 600,000 tons in 1996. Provisional figures showed a further increase in 1997, to 752,000 tons.

Turkey is also an important producer of oilseeds, principally sunflower, cotton, sesame and linseed. It also produces olive oil, some of which is exported. Production fluctuates, partly because of the two-year flowering cycle of olive trees. In 1996 olive oil production increased substantially from 52,000 metric tons in 1995 to 220,000 tons, although provisional figures showed that production again fell to 40,000 tons in 1997.

Turkey was, until 1972, one of the seven countries with the right to export opium under the UN Commission on Narcotic Drugs. Much opium was, however, exported illegally, particularly to the USA and Iran; partly as a result of pressure from the US Government, the Turkish Government made the cultivation of opium poppies illegal in 1972, but the ban was ended in July 1974 and the flowers are grown in certain provinces under strict controls. Opium gum is no longer tapped from the living plant. The poppy pods (opium straw) are sold to the government, which processes them into concentrate for export as the basis for morphine and other drugs.

Sheep and cattle are raised on the grazing lands of the Anatolian plateau. Stock-raising forms an important branch of the economy. The sheep population (33.8m. in 1996) is mainly of the Karaman type and is used primarily as a source of meat and milk. The bulk of the clip comprises coarse wool suitable only for carpets, blankets and poorer grades of clothing fabric. However, efforts have been made in recent years to encourage breeding for wool, and there are some 200,000 Merino sheep in the Bursa region. The Angora goat produces the fine, soft wool known as mohair. Turkey is one of the world's largest producers of mohair, with an average output of about 9,000 metric tons per annum.

Although Turkey has for many years worked towards agricultural self-sufficiency, imports were set to rise in 1998, especially from the European Union. In January 1998 Turkey agreed to grant the EU major trade concessions on exports of EU food and farm products to the country. The Government agreed to unlimited imports of EU breeding cattle and up to 70% reductions on import duties for some 19,000 tons of frozen beef a year from the EU. Between September and the end of May every year, Turkey will accept imports, without duty, of 200,000 tons of wheat, 100,000 tons of barley, 52,000 tons of corn, 46,000 tons of malting barley, 28,000 tons of rice and 60,000 tons of soy oil. The EU can also export 80,000 tons of sugar to Turkey at half the normal duty rates. These concessions were agreed despite the EU's decision to exclude Turkey from the list of countries currently eligible to join the organization (see External Trade).

MINERALS

Turkey has a diversity of rich mineral resources, including large quantities of bauxite, borax, chromium, copper, iron ore, manganese and sulphur. The mining and quarrying sector employed some 162,000 workers in 1996. Mineral exports earned $2,316.6m. in 1994 and $2,243.0m. in 1995, representing about 10% of the value of total exports. About 60% of all mineral output, and all coal production, derives from state-owned enterprises. The most important state-owned enterprise in the mining sector is Etibank, which works through its subsidiaries, Eregli Coal Mines, East Chromium Mines, Turkish Copper, Keban Lead Mines and Keçiborlu Sulphur Mines. During the early 1960s state-owned enterprises increased their predominance over the private sector, with an investment programme that was supported by the Mining Investment Bank, established in 1962. The policy of encouraging the private sector to play a greater part in the mining industry, through the establishment of the Turkish Mining Bank Corpn in 1968, has failed to overcome the general reluctance of private investors to view mining as a worthwhile area for long-term investment, with the result that the private sector is under-capitalized. An additional factor militating against the development of mining has been the long-held suspicion of foreign investment in mining. A law enacted in 1973 restricted foreign participation in mining development projects. However, this restriction was relaxed in January 1980, allowing up to 49% foreign participation in mining ventures. Since then, negotiations have proceeded slowly between Etibank and potential foreign partners for copper, lead and other mineral mining. In 1983, Etibank entered into a joint venture agreement with a US company, Phelps Dodge, for copper mining. Etibank is scheduled for privatization, and in 1993 its banking and mining operations were separated in the initial phase of this process.

Bituminous coal is found at and around Zonguldak, on the Black Sea coast. The seams are steeply inclined, much folded and strongly faulted. The coal is generally mined by the longwall system or a variation of it. These mines constitute Etibank's largest operation, and the coalfield is the largest in this part of the world, including the Balkans. Most of the seams are of good coking quality, the coke being used in the steel mills at nearby Karabük. In both 1996 and 1997 total coke production amounted to 3.2m. metric tons, compared with 2.2m. tons in 1995. Lignite is found in many parts of central and western Anatolia, and total reserves are estimated at 5,000m. tons. In 1996 production of lignite by public-sector enterprises amounted to 52.5m. tons. Seams located in western Turkey are operated by the West Lignite Mines. The other main mines are at Soma, Degirmisaz and Tunçbilek. Lignite deposits at Afsin Elbistan are being developed, with extensive German and international financial assistance, as part of an ambitious integrated energy project designed to increase capacity by 1,360 MW.

Practically all of Turkish iron ore comes from the Divrigi mine, situated between Sivas and Erzurum, in the north-east of the country, and operated by the Turkish Iron and Steel Corpn. The average grade of ore is from 60% to 66%; reserves have been estimated at 28m. metric tons. Output of iron ore increased from 1.7m. tons in 1979 to 5.5m. tons in 1992. Production totalled 6.7m. tons in 1994.

Turkey is one of the world's largest producers of chromite (chromium ore). The richest deposits are in Güleman, south-eastern Turkey, in the vicinity of İskenderun; in the area around Eskişehir, north-west Anatolia; and between Fethiye and Antalya on the Mediterranean coast. The Güleman mines, producing 25% of the country's total, are operated by East Chromium Mines under Etibank. Other mines are owned and worked by private enterprise. Little chromium is used domestically and the mineral is the principal earner of foreign exchange among Turkey's mining exports. Output of chromite fell from a peak of 800,000 metric tons of ore, mined in 1977, to less than 500,000 tons per year in the early 1980s, but recovered to reach 1.5m. tons in 1989. However, production decreased again to around 600,000 tons in 1992 with exports valued at $32m. In 1993 output decreased further, and export earnings fell to $18m.

Copper has been mined in Turkey since ancient times. Current production, conducted entirely by Etibank, comes from the Ergani Mines, at Maden in Elâziğ, and the Morgul Copper Mine, at Borçka in Çoruh province. Production of blister copper has

tended to fluctuate, decreasing from 36,000 metric tons in 1986 to 28,578 tons in 1994. Most of the output is exported to Germany, the United Kingdom and the USA. Known reserves of copper ore are estimated at 90m. tons.

Eskişehir, in north-west Anatolia, is the world's leading centre for meerschaum mining. Meerschaum, a soft white mineral which hardens on exposure to the sun and looks like ivory, has long been used by Turkish craftsmen for pipes and cigarette holders.

Manganese, magnesite, lead, sulphur, salt, asbestos, antimony, zinc and mercury are important mineral resources. Of these, manganese ranks first in importance. Deposits, worked by private enterprise, are found in many parts of the country, but principally near Eskişehir and in the Eregli district. Lead is mined at Keban, west of Elâziğ. Production of sulphur (public sector only), mainly from the Keciborlu mine, in Isparta province, totalled 39,000 metric tons in 1987. Antimony is mined in small quantities near Balikesir and Nigde. An important find of mercury deposits, which may amount to 440,000 tons, has been made at Sizma, in Konya province. Large uranium deposits have been discovered in the Black Sea, between 1 km and 2 km below sea-level. Turkey's first commercially viable silver mine was opened in January 1988. In April 1996 a project to develop Turkey's first gold mine (reserves were discovered in 1990) near Bergama, in İzmir province, was finally approved.

The Uludağ (Bursa) tungsten deposits, carrying an average grade of 0.43% WO_3, are among the richest in the world. Etibank and the German firm of Krupp are jointly working these deposits. Output of tungsten ore reached 3,400 metric tons in 1979. Other minerals are barytes, perlite, phosphate rock, boron minerals, cinnabar and emery (Turkey supplies more than 80% of the world market for emery).

Turkey's bauxite deposits are now supplying the aluminium complex which was built, with Soviet aid, at Seydişehir. The plant's initial annual capacity was 60,000 metric tons of aluminium but this is to be expanded to 120,000 tons. The plant will also produce alumina for export, and semi-finished products. The reserves at Seydişehir are estimated at more than 30m. tons.

Petroleum was first discovered in Turkey in 1950, and all subsequent discoveries have been in the same area, in the south-east of the country. It is mostly heavy-grade petroleum with a fairly high sulphur content. Production of crude petroleum has fluctuated since it reached 3.5m. metric tons in 1973. Because of the small size of Turkey's main oilfields in the fractured terrain of the south-east, it declined steadily between 1980 and 1985. Production increased in the early 1990s and reached 3.9m. tons in 1993. In 1995 and 1996 production each year totalled 3.5m. tons and declined slightly to 3.4m. tons in 1997. Total domestic output of crude petroleum of about 49,000 barrels per day (b/d), in addition to about 1,500 m. cu m of natural gas, accounts for roughly 12% of the country's hydrocarbon requirements. Imports of petroleum and petroleum products rose from $2,807.5m. in 1994 to $3,290.5m. in 1995, when they accounted for almost 10% of the value of total imports. Saudi Arabia is Turkey's main supplier, with substantial volumes also imported from Iran and Libya. Prior to a UN embargo on trade with Iraq, that country was a major supplier of petroleum.

Three main companies produce petroleum: the Turkish Petroleum Corpn (TPAO), a 99% state-owned Turkish company, with an output of 26,000 b/d. Subsidiaries of the Royal Dutch/Shell Group and the US Mobil group produce 18,000 b/d and 5,000 b/d respectively. Ultimate reserves are estimated by TPAO at 10,000m. barrels. Exploration is continuing in the south-east and in the Aegean. In 1983 the Government passed a new law which was intended to liberalize conditions for foreign companies, enabling them to export up to 35% of any onshore petroleum which they discovered, and up to 45% of any offshore output. At first, major foreign oil companies were dubious about Turkey as a viable political and economic base, but in 1984 quickening interest resulted in the signing of several joint-venture exploration agreements by new foreign major oil companies with TPAO.

Refining and other 'downstream' operations are dominated by the state-owned Turkish Petroleum Refining Co (Tupras), which has four refining complexes: Batman in the southeast, Aliaga near İzmir, İsmit near İstanbul, and the Central Anatolian Refinery at Kirikkale near Ankara. Turkey's sole private refinery is ATAS, near Mersin on the Mediterranean coast, a joint venture of Mobil, Shell British Petroleum and a local company.

TPAO operates a 500-km pipeline, with a diameter of 45 cm (18 in), which runs from the oilfields around Batman to Dörtyol on the Gulf of İskenderun. A 986-km pipeline from Kirkuk, in northern Iraq, to Turkey has a capacity of 1.5m. b/d. Completion and full commissioning of a second pipeline, alongside the first, took place in July 1987. Until August 1990, when economic sanctions were imposed upon Iraq by the UN, the twin pipeline from Kirkuk to Turkey's Mediterranean terminal at Ceyhan carried about one-third of Iraq's oil exports. The closure of the pipeline for more than six years is estimated to have cost the Turkish state oil and gas pipeline authority, Botas, more than $400m. per year in lost revenues. In March 1996 Turkey and Iraq signed a memorandum of understanding determining conditions for the future reopening of the pipeline. Following Iraqi acceptance, in May, of a UN proposal to permit limited oil sales (up to a value of $2,000m. over a six-month period, amounting to an estimated 800,000 b/d) in order to purchase humanitarian supplies, the pipeline was scheduled to open in mid-September. However, the agreement was postponed by the UN in early September, owing to Iraqi military activities against its Kurdish population, and oil did not start to flow through the pipeline until December.

Turkey is looking to Central Asia to provide the major proportion of its future oil needs, and has begun projects to develop supplies there. In 1994 TPAO became part of the Azerbaijan International Operating Company (AIOC), a consortium of foreign oil companies in an oil production-sharing agreement with Azeri state oil company Socar, to develop offshore oilfields in the Caspian Sea. TPAO also became a partner in the Azeri Shah Deniz field in 1996, and has established an oil exploration company with the Kazakhstan Government.

Oil and gas transportation is a controversial issue in the Caspian Sea/Central Asia regions. Turkey, Russia and Iran are competing to route the rich energy resources of Azerbaijan, Kazakhstan, Turkmenistan and Uzbekistan through their territories en route to Western markets. Turkey is advocating a pipeline that would run from Baku in Azerbaijan through Georgia and then across Turkey to the Mediterranean port of Ceyhan, at an estimated cost of $2,500m. Russia, meanwhile, is promoting a route across the Caucasus to the terminal at the Russian Black Sea port of Novorossiisk. Other proposals include a pipeline to Georgia's Black Sea port of Supsa, and a swap agreement with, or export pipeline through, Iran. The governments of Turkey, the USA and Azerbaijan have all declared their support for the Baku–Ceyhan route, which would reduce dependence of Caspian Sea energy exports on Russia. Turkey's position is based largely on its concern to restrict the use of the Bosphorus to export petroleum. In 1994 Turkey imposed stricter controls for ships transporting hazardous goods through the Bosphorus, effective from 1 July, following a collision in March. Russia, which exports some 70% of its oil exports by means of the Bosphorus protested at the measure. An agreement signed in April 1997, to build a pipeline with a capacity of 560,000 b/ d, rising to 1.5m. b/d, from the Kazakhstan oilfields to the Russian Black Sea port of Novorossiisk, was likely to increase tensions between Turkey and Russia regarding the use of the Bosphorus for the export of petroleum.

Demand for natural gas is projected to rise dramatically in Turkey over the next two decades, with the main consumers expected to be industry and power plants. Although natural gas production has risen steadily in recent years, it currently meets only about 3% of domestic consumption requirements. The bulk of Turkish gas demand is met by imports, nearly all from Russia. In December 1997 Turkey and Russia signed a 25-year contract (the so-called 'Blue Stream' agreement) for a large increase in Russian natural gas imports. The gas will mostly be delivered via a 1,210-km-long dual pipeline which, when built (at a cost of $13,500m.), will run from Isobilnoye in southern Russia under the Black Sea to the Turkish port of Samsun and on to Ankara. It may eventually be extended to Israel. The agreement includes the import of an additional 3,000m. cu m of gas per year through the pipeline, with its throughput rising to 16,000m. cu m by 2010. The rapid increase in Russian supplies through the Black

Sea pipeline and the existing route (crossing Ukraine, Moldova, Romania and Bulgaria) from the current annual level of 7,000m. cu m is expected to meet half of Turkey's total annual demand for imported gas of about 60,000m. cu m by 2010. An earlier agreement to ensure the supply of natural gas was concluded in August 1996, with Iran. Construction of a 1,400-km pipeline from Tabriz, in Iran, to Ankara was scheduled to commence at the end of 1996. Despite US disapproval, Turkey proceeded with the project and awarded the contract for the construction of the first section of the pipeline, from the Iranian border to Erzerum, in early 1997; the second section, from Erzerum to Ankara, was to be built at a later date. Iran was to be responsible for financing the section of the pipeline running through its own country. According to a further agreement, signed in December 1996 with Turkmenistan, from 1999 Turkey was to import 3,000m. cu m of natural gas each year from Turkmenistan, via the Tabriz–Ankara pipeline, in the place of Iranian gas, until such gas was available. In late July 1997 the US Administration announced that it would not oppose the construction of the $1,600m.-gas pipeline from Turkmenistan, because it would not technically violate US-imposed sanctions against Iran. US officials stated that Turkey's agreement to purchase Turkmen gas would make it less reliant on supplies from Iran, but an oil industry source maintained that the deal involved a gas swap, with Turkmenistan pumping gas into the Iranian pipeline and an equivalent amount of Iranian gas being sent to Turkey. Turkey has also signed a number of agreements to import supplies of liquefied natural gas (LNG). Imports of LNG from Algeria, equivalent to 3,000m. cu m a year of natural gas, began in 1994 and were to continue for a 20-year period, while plans exist for annual imports of LNG from Qatar, equivalent to 2,000m. cu m of natural gas, to begin in 1999. The state pipeline agency, Botas, is tendering a project to build a terminal at Alinga with the capacity to store 4,000 cu m of LNG. It is due for completion by 2000.

INDUSTRY

The leading role in the process of inaugurating industrialization was played by the State economic enterprises (SEEs). However, by the beginning of the 1970s the private sector accounted for nearly one-half of industrial output and its rate of capital investment had become almost equal to public sector investment. The Government announced its long-awaited plans for privatization of the SEEs in May 1987. Initially, the Government's stake in 22 private companies would be sold, followed by the denationalization of the more efficient and profitable SEEs. As a first step, one-half of the Government's shareholding of 40% in Teletas, a telecommunications company, was sold to the private sector in early 1988. A sharp fall in share prices on the İstanbul stock exchange then slowed the privatization programme. Five state-owned cement works were sold directly to a French company (although the completion of this sale was suspended in 1991), and USAS, an aircraft services firm, was sold directly to a Scandinavian airline in early 1989. The fact that these were sold directly to foreign companies, rather than to the public on the stock exchange, attracted widespread criticism. As the stock exchange recovered at the end of 1989, the Government proceeded with the sale of its minority shareholdings in private-sector companies. Such holdings in six companies were sold in early 1990. Subsequent privatizations enjoyed varying degrees of success. Small portions of state-owned shareholdings were sold in a number of major companies such as Petkim, the petrochemicals giant, and Erdemir, the iron and steel complex. In the first half of 1992 the Demirel Government undertook five such sales, with estimated total revenue of TL 552,000m. In July 1992 the Government announced the sale of 11 state cement companies which together accounted for 18% of total cement production in Turkey. In late 1992 and 1993 the privatization programme continued at a steady rate, but under the Çiller Government few sales were completed. In July 1994 legislation to accelerate privatization was declared to be unconstitutional by the Constitutional Court, although new legislation was approved in November. Nonetheless, the programme generated only $354m. in 1994, and $576m. in 1995 (of a target revenue figure for that year of $5,000m.). Although every government from the mid-1980s claimed that privatization was a key part of economic policy, only $3,500m. had been raised from the sale of state enterprises by 1997. However, proceeds from privatization in 1998 were projected to rise dramatically as the coalition Government under Mesut Yılmaz reactivated the process. In May 1998 the Privatization Administration (OIB) sold a 12.23% stake in Türkiye İş Bankası (one of the country's leading commercial banks) for $651m., while the sale of a 51% holding in the petrol distributor Petrol Ofisi in July raised $1,160m. Plans were also in hand for the sale of significant state holdings in Türk Telecom (Turkey's principal telecommunications operator), Turkish Airlines (THY) and Tupras. In the case of THY, it was reported that the Government was aiming to raise about $3,000m. from the sale of part of its share, which was expected to be completed by October. Significant proceeds were also realized from the sale of concessions to operate seven major power networks in central and western areas of the country and of two operating licences for mobile telephone networks. It was reported in August 1998 that the OIB had received five bids for the state's 84.52% stake in Turkbank, and that it had invited seven international banks to bid for the advisory contract on the sale of the steelmill Erdemir (in which the state holds 51.66%).

Turkey's recent high growth rates have been industry-led. The share of industry in the economy increased from 12% of gross domestic product (GDP) in 1952 to 32.4% in 1993. After a disastrous year for the economy, it fell to 27% in 1994, but recovered to 30.5% in 1995 before declining to 27.8% in both 1996 and 1997. Growth in the manufacturing sector has been the most noticeable, under the stimulus of the Government's export incentive scheme, although, latterly, domestic demand has equalled the demand made on manufacturing for exports. In 1986 the manufacturing sector expanded by a record 10.5%, followed by growth of 10.1% in 1987. In 1989 the growth rate decreased to 4.2%, but in 1990 it recovered to 9.7%, only to decrease again, to 6.7%, in 1993. The financial collapse in 1994 then caused the manufacturing sector to contract by 8.4%. The output of two leading sectors, textiles and chemicals, fell by 5.3% and 3.8%, respectively. An expansion in the manufacturing sector of 13.5% was reported in 1995, but during the first nine months of 1996, manufacturing production slowed to 6.5%.

Production of such goods as paper, cotton and woollen yarn, cotton and woollen fabrics, refined fuels and petroleum products, steel products and glassware began a significant recovery in the early 1980s. Overall, the average annual growth rate of industrial GDP was 7.8% in 1980–90, and 4.6% in 1990–96.

Textiles and clothing manufacture accounts for some 40% of Turkey's export sales. Exports of textiles rose by more than 10% in 1997 to $2,800m., while overseas sales of readywear clothing grew by 14% to more than $7,000m. The industry employs around one-fifth of Turkey's industrial workers, accounting for more than 8% of industrial production.

The iron and steel industry in Turkey is one of the fastest-growing in the world and prospects are good, compared with its difficulties in the early 1980s. However, following the liberalization of imports in 1989, the sector suffered a trade deficit of $895m., although this was reduced to $312m. in 1990, only to increase again, to $972m., in 1993. Both private and public manufacturers complain of dumping by European and Asian companies. Public sector capacity is 4.6m. metric tons per year and private sector capacity 2.7m. tons per year. Total output of crude steel reached 10.3m. tons in 1993. The value of exports of iron and steel totalled $2,160.1m., compared with $1,828.9m. in the previous year. In July 1996 an agreement was signed with the European Coal and Steel Community (part of the EU) for the elimination of duties by both sides, with effect from 1 August 1996.

Cement production, on the strength of the expansion in the construction industry (due largely to the Government's mass housing programme), rose to a record 20m. metric tons in 1986. Production has continued to increase, in spite of occasional declines in years when the economy as a whole has done badly, and output stood at 36.0m. tons in 1997. The industry is now almost totally privately-owned as a result of the privatization programme.

Among food industries, the state-controlled sugar industry is the most important. In 1994 total production of raw sugar was 1.7m. metric tons, with the private sector accounting for only slightly over 25% of this total. Total production in 1995 declined slightly to 1.3m. tons, but rose to 1.8m. tons in 1996.

The paper and board industry is dominated by the state-owned SEKA corporation, which has one old-established mill at İzmir, with an annual capacity of 126,000 metric tons of paper and board, plus six mills which have been opened since 1971. Total output of paper and board is relatively stable at around 400,000 tons annually (including 136,000 tons of newsprint and 78,000 tons of Kraft paper in 1994).

The motor vehicle industry was established after 1956, and by 1971 had become the largest industrial employer after the textile sector, accounting for about 5% of total industrial output. After several years of suppressed demand and low capacity utilization in the early 1980s, the outlook began to improve in 1983. In 1988 output of cars (local versions of certain Fiat, Ford and Renault models) increased by 12.7%, to 120,800. By 1993 output had nearly trebled to just under 345,000. However, in 1994 the automotive sector suffered a collapse in demand as a result of the currency crisis which hit the economy, and the output of cars fell to 201,000. Nevertheless, a number of foreign manufacturers have expressed interest in local production ventures in view of Turkey's expanding domestic market and, since the start of 1996, its advantageous trading relationship with the EU, under the customs union agreement. In 1994 a Toyota assembly plant began operations, and Honda and Mazda have more recently pledged to invest in production projects. In 1996 Honda was proceeding with the construction of a car plant, in association with Anadolu Endustri Holding AŞ, at a cost of $50m., while Oyak-Renault, the Turkish subsidiary of Renault of France, announced plans to build a $362m.-plant, which would employ over 1,000 workers. In early 1997 it was reported that Volvo of Sweden planned to invest DM 300m. in a factory at Bursa, to produce buses for export to the Middle East and Russia. The new plant, a joint venture with Ulosoy Holding, was to begin production by 2000. Suzuki and KIA were also reported to be considering the construction of car production plants in Turkey, though in 1996, the first year of customs union with the EU, car production fell by 11% to 207,575, while imported models increased their share of car sales. Total vehicle output for 1996 rose by 2% to 348,467, however, as a result of a sharp increase in the production of buses, tractors and trucks. The domestic car industry faced the prospect of further problems in 1997, following a decision taken by the Erbakan Government which allowed all Turkish citizens to import one foreign used car, on the condition that they deposited DM 50,000 in a state bank. Production of vehicles made by South Korea's Hyundai Motor Co was inaugurated in September 1997 at a plant near İzmit. The plant's initial output of 60,000 cars a year will eventually double when it reaches full capacity. It was announced in March 1998 that the US Ford Motor Co and the local Otosan had agreed in principle to build a $500m. car plant in Turkey, with a planned capacity of 120,000 vehicles a year. In 1997 car sales rose to 344,800, but while sales of imported cars rose by 118%, sales of those produced in Turkey increased by only 21%. Sales of light commercial vehicles increased to 118,800 units.

In 1970 Turkey's first petrochemicals complex, situated at İzmit, began production of ethylene, polythene, polyvinyl chloride (PVC), chlorine and caustic soda. There is another petrochemicals plant at Aliaga, while a third is planned at Yumurtalık. They are operated by the state-owned firm Petkim. In 1994 the output of artificial fertilizers (excluding potassic fertilizers) totalled 4.0m. metric tons, although this increased to 5.3m. tons by 1996. The state-owned Turkish Nitrates Corpn has a nitrate plant at Kutahya, a triple superphosphate plant at Samsun and a superphosphate plant at Elâziğ. There are several privately-owned fertilizer plants, including triple superphosphate plants at İskenderun and Yarimca. Turkey produces 75% of its requirements of fertilizers and, when new plants are completed, it will be self-sufficient.

Other manufacturing industries include tobacco, chemicals, pharmaceuticals, metal working, engineering, leather goods, glassware and ferrochrome.

The power sector, along with the transport, communications and tourism sector, has continued to hold priority in the Government's development programmes for every year since 1989. Nevertheless, together with other infrastructure projects, the power sector suffered from the attempt to cut back Government spending and progress was slow on power plant projects. In spite of the progress made in power plant construction in recent years, many more units will have to be built to meet an expected increase in demand to 170,000m. kWh annually by the end of the century, compared with 33,000m. kWh in 1986. Output from stations operated by the Turkish Electricity Board accounted for 62% of all electricity generated, while chartered companies and private generators provided the remainder. Total output stood at 78,256m. kWh in 1994, rising to 86,341m. kWh in 1995 and 94,863m. kWh in 1996. Thermal sources accounted for about 57% of the 1996 total power generation and hydroelectricity the remainder. In mid-1995 construction of a natural gas generating station in Marmara was initiated by a consortium of one Turkish and three foreign companies. The power plant, which was estimated to cost $540m., had a potential capacity of 3,600m. kWh. In November 1995 an agreement was signed with foreign creditors and contractors for the construction of the 672-MW-capacity Birecik hydroelectric plant on the Euphrates river. The agreement was the first of many planned build-operate-transfer schemes, under which the ownership of the plant was to be transferred to the Turkish government once it became fully operational and profitable, or after a period of 15 years. In mid-1996 preparations were being undertaken to provide for the construction of the country's first nuclear generator, at Akkuyu on the southern Mediterranean coast. The $1,500m.-plant was put out to tender in December 1996 and construction was expected to be completed in 2005. The plant, which is expected to have a capacity of 1,400 MW, should supply some 2% of Turkey's energy needs. Turkey has imported electricity from Bulgaria for some time, and in March 1997 Ankara signed a new five-year energy agreement with that country. Official sources indicated that domestic power production rose by 10.5% in 1996, but still failed to keep pace with increase in demand, which grew by 12%. The growth in energy consumption is estimated to require an additional 2,000 MW of new capacity annually, and the Energy Ministry has estimated that capacity must rise threefold to 65,000 MW between 1998 and 2010. Even with increasing private sector input, most new capacity will have to be provided by the state. The Turkish Electricity Generation & Transmission Corpn. (TEAŞ) awarded a $1,500m. contract in March 1998 to a consortium led by Japan's Mitsubishi Corpn to build the 1,400 MW Afsin-Elbistan B thermal power station. A decision on the award of a similar contract for the Afsin-Elbiston C plant had not been announced by August 1998. Most new capacity will be generated by gas-fired plants.

Joint-venture defence manufacturing with foreign partners is the next major development for foreign investment in Turkish industry (a development that began with the $4,000m. agreement concluded in 1983 with the US Government and a US company, General Dynamics, to assemble and later manufacture F-16 fighter aircraft at Murted outside Ankara). The Defence Industry and Support Administration (DIDA), established in 1985, was to co-ordinate Turkey's 10-year, $15,000m. programme to modernize the armed forces. The modernization was to involve, to a large extent, locally manufactured equipment and weapons. In July 1988 a joint-venture manufacturing agreement for multi-launch rocket systems was signed by a US company and a state-owned munitions company. According to the agreement, 180 rocket launchers were to be produced at a plant near Burda. Some of the launchers were to be bought by DIDA and the remainder were to be exported. In late 1988, a consortium (including a US company and the Turkish company Nurol) was awarded a contract to manufacture armoured personnel carriers in Turkey. Turkey currently exports a range of weapons including F-16 fighter aircraft and armoured personnel carriers. In August 1998 it was reported that Turkish Aerospace Industries (TAI) had awarded a $200m. contract to install radar systems on 80 F-16s to a joint venture between a local company and the US' Lockheed Martin Corpn. The Turkish firm was already working on a contract to install radar systems on another 160 Turkish F-16s. Earlier, in June, the Government suspended talks with France's Aerospatiale over a $441m. short-range anti-tank missile production contract after the French National Assembly voted in May to adopt a resolution recognizing the genocide of Armenians in Turkey in 1915. In July 1998 it was announced that the Ministry of Defence had signed

a $558m. contract with a German company for the construction of four 1,400-ton submarines.

Tourism is one of Turkey's fastest growing industries and is an important source of foreign currency. In 1995 an estimated 7.7m. tourists visited Turkey, generating some $4,957m. in revenue. While these figures represent a substantial improvement on the previous decade, a huge potential still remains unrealized. One problem over the past few years has been the escalation of Kurdish nationalist activity which frequently spills over into the tourist resorts of the West, severely damaging the prospects of the tourism industry. Some 8.6m. tourists visited Turkey during 1996, an increase of 11.5% over 1995, but capacity remained underutilized. In 1997 9.7m. tourists visited Turkey. Germany was the main source of tourists, followed by Russia, the UK, USA, France, Iran, Italy, Greece, Yugoslavia and Syria.

FINANCE

The Central Bank (Merkez Bankası), the sole bank of issue, started its operations on 3 October 1931. It controls exchange operations and ensures the monetary requirements of certain state-owned enterprises by the discounting of bonds which are issued by these institutions and guaranteed by the treasury. However, legislation that was adopted in 1987 awarded the Government wide-ranging powers over the Central Bank, that could, if they were applied, theoretically reduce the bank to the level of an ordinary state bank.

The monetary unit is the kuruş (piastre) by the law of April 1916. The Turkish lira (pound), which is, in practice, employed as the monetary unit, is equal to 100 kuruş.

The principal sources of budgetary revenue are income tax, import taxes and duties, taxes and fees on services, and revenues from state monopolies. In late 1984 the Government introduced value-added tax to replace the previous unwieldy system of production taxes.

In 1993 the budget deficit tripled that of the previous year to reach TL 122,000,000m., or 9.2% of GNP. In April 1994 the Government introduced stringent spending cuts as part of an austerity package designed in response to a financial collapse earlier in the year (see below). As a result, the budget deficit was substantially reduced in real terms and totalled TL 146,000,000m., or 3.7% of GNP, in 1994. None the less, the budget deficit continued to exert serious inflationary pressure on the economy and to attract much domestic and international criticism. The Government continued to borrow heavily on the domestic market, although foreign borrowing became prohibitively expensive because of the crisis and was reduced. The domestic debt stood at TL 799,100,000m. at the end of 1994 (compared with TL 356,555,000m. at the end of 1993). At the same time, Turkey's foreign debt came down to $65,601m., from more than $67,000m. in 1993. The pressure of servicing both the domestic and external debt indirectly fuels the rate of inflation. In 1993 the average annual rate of inflation was 66.1%, and in 1994 it rose dramatically to 106.3%.

Under these inflationary pressures, in early 1994 two US credit rating agencies downgraded Turkey's credit rating, which resulted in a 'run' on foreign currencies. The value of the lira was officially devalued by 12% against the dollar; however the currency contined to plummet. Interest rates rose to 150%–200% as the Government and the Central Bank desperately tried to bring the financial markets under control. In early April the Government announced a programme of austerity measures to reduce the budget deficit, lower inflation and restore domestic and international confidence in the economy. The programme included a 'freezing' of wages, price increases of up to 100% on state monopoly goods, as well as longer-term restructuring measures such as the closure of loss-making state enterprises and an accelerated privatization process. By May the lira stabilized at around TL 30,000 to the dollar, having stood at some TL 16,000 at the beginning of the year. In August the value of the lira fell once more but was steadied at a rate of TL 34,000 per dollar, following an increase in interest rates from 70% to 240%. The austerity measures then began to have a measure of success, the markets stabilized and the lira stayed below 40,000 to the dollar until the end of the year. The measures also helped to restore international confidence in the Turkish economy and to secure an IMF stand-by loan, approved in July, of SDR 610m. (approximately $873m.). However, the 14-month stand-by agreement was abandoned by Prime Minister Çiller in September 1995, after the collapse of the Government. The inflationary pressure on the economy remained strong during 1995, and the annual rate of inflation slowed only to 93.6%. The actual budget deficit rose to TL 320,000,000m. in 1995. In January 1997 the Prime Minister announced a budget deficit for the whole of 1996 of TL 1,215,000,000m., which represented 8.2% of GNP. In November 1996 the Government had ordered all state and local administrative spending to be suspended until the beginning of 1997, in an effort to reduce the size of the deficit. In October the Prime Minister had stated that he would balance the state budget for the first time in 50 years, increase investment and end domestic borrowing. This was to be achieved largely through the receipt of projected revenues from the extended privatization programme (see above), although an IMF team that visited Ankara that month warned that the Government was unlikely to reach its 1997 budgetary targets and called on the Government to take swift action to implement both major fiscal adjustment and structural reform. The widening budget deficit/GNP ratio was the main underlying factor inflicting inflationary pressure upon the economy and the annual rate of inflation was 82.4% in 1996. The IMF projections of still higher inflation and concern over the RP's ambitious budget predictions resulted in the Japanese and US credit rating agencies lowering Turkey's international credit rating at the end of 1996. The coalition Government of Prime Minister Yılmaz, which took office in mid-1997, made a determined effort in its first year to stem the rise in inflation and improve economic management. By July 1998, year-on-year inflation had fallen to 72% from 101% in January. The reduction was achieved largely through a 'freeze' in public sector prices. In June 1998 the Government signed an accord with the IMF under which the Fund would monitor the Turkish economy for 18 months. The agreement, which committed the Government to keeping a tight rein on public expenditure and boosting privatization and tax receipts, set targets for wholesale inflation of 50% by the end of 1998 and 20% by the end of 1999. Tax reform legislation, passed in July, reduced the tax burden for most people and aimed to encourage full declaration of earnings. However, in the same month the Government was forced to compromise on its pledge to keep down public sector pay rises when it agreed to an immediate 20% rise, with a further 10% for the three months from October. The overall fiscal deficit in 1998 was expected to be about 7.5% of GNP, similar to 1997. The target for 1999 was set at 5.6%.

A heavy burden of foreign debt, contracted in the late 1970s and extended through reschedulings in 1978, 1980 and 1981, has severely hampered the Government's structural adjustment programme. In January 1980 the Government introduced an austerity package which set the economy on a more open footing, in contrast to its previously insular, state-dominated growth; for example, a ban on foreign investment in mining (including petroleum) exploration was lifted. Turkey's foreign creditors responded with yet more large infusions of aid; the IMF pledged $1,650m. over three years. In both 1980 and 1981, successful debt rescheduling operations were carried out, which left Turkey with a manageable short-term debt load by converting much of Turkey's debt into medium- and long-term credits. Turkey's international credit rating steadily improved in the second half of 1985 (after a setback earlier in the year, with the slow syndication of a $500m. Eurodollar loan). However, the Government has not managed to control external borrowing and the country's foreign debt totalled $67,356m. at the end of 1993, $73,300m. by the end of 1995 and $79,767m. at the end of 1996. Some 52% of Turkey's foreign debt was incurred through bilateral financial protocols, 37% was raised from international bond issues, 8% by commercial banks and 3% from multinational agencies. $59,231m. consisted of medium- and long-term debt, while the rest consisted of short-term debt. Debt service payments of $9,880m. in 1995 and $9,410m. in 1996 were made. Turkey originally intended to borrow externally only $2,500m. in 1996, but this was increased to $5,000m. in May because of the widening budget deficit. By September 1997 Turkey's foreign debt stock stood at $84,500m. The Yılmaz Government's economic programme projected external debt rising to more than $100,000m. by the end of 1999. The debt service schedule for the second half of 1998 suggested that there would be more

redemptions than borrowings in aggregate. Turkey's domestic debt rose from TL 356,555,000m. in 1993 to TL 1,368,000,000m. in 1995, reaching TL 3,149,000,000m. by the end of 1996. In dollar terms domestic debt increased to $30,600m. in 1997.

Turkey's persistent trade deficit has been partly offset, for some time, by a net surplus on invisible earnings (services and transfers), particularly helped by expatriate workers' remittances. A major contributor to the invisibles balance since the early 1980s has been the contribution from Turkish contractors, who, although arriving late for the growth in the Middle East construction industry, quickly made their mark. Like other foreign firms, however, their fortunes have suffered as a result of the fall in the price of petroleum and the subsequent decrease in development revenues. In 1986 Turkish contractors won $1,430m. worth of new work in the Middle East, 82% more than in 1985. Most of this total, however, was accounted for by a single order—the $775m. Turkish share in the Bekme dam scheme in Iraq. However, in the context of economic sanctions imposed upon Iraq by the UN in August 1990, work on the scheme has been suspended indefinitely at enormous cost to the Turkish contractors. Since the collapse of the Soviet Union, Turkish contractors have been turning their attention to Russia, Azerbaijan and the Turkic republics of Central Asia, with considerable success. They have built hotels, factories, public buildings and lodgings for troops returning from East Germany. In March 1997 a Russian official stated that 150 Turkish contractors were working on 200 construction projects in Russia, worth some $5,000m., making Turks the leading foreign contractors in that country.

Workers' remittances have long been an important source of foreign exchange. These totalled $3,590m. in 1996 and $4,229m. in 1997. Receipts from tourism, also an important source of foreign exchange, totalled $5,650m. in 1996 and $7,002m. in 1997. The current account yielded a surplus of $2,631m. in 1994, following deficits of $974m. in 1992 and $6,433m. in 1993. The improvement was due largely to imports falling as a result of shrinking demand after the financial crisis. A current account deficit of $2,338m. was recorded in 1995, increasing to $2,437 in 1996 and $2,750 in 1997. However, Turkey receives large inflows of foreign currency from unrecorded trade with Eastern Europe and Russia, known as the 'suitcase trade', which do not appear in official current-account statistics. Estimates have suggested that these unrecorded revenues, which help to finance the current-account deficit, may be as high as $5,000m.–$10,000m.

EXTERNAL TRADE

Since 1947, Turkey has had a persistent foreign trade deficit. But, following the economic reforms of 1980 and the introduction of free-market, export-led policies, the deficit decreased for a few years in the early 1980s. In 1990 the deficit more than doubled, to $9,343m., owing to the overvalued lira, the continuing liberalization of the import regime and the phasing out of direct subsidies to exporters. Foreign trade performance was much improved by 1994, with exports of $18,106m. and imports of $23,268m., bringing the trade deficit down to $5,162m. In 1995, however, while exports increased to $21,975m., imports rose sharply to $35,187m., resulting in a trade deficit of $13,212m. Figures issued for 1996 showed that exports increased to $32,446m., but imports rose to $43,028m., resulting in a trade deficit of $10,582m. In 1997 a deficit of $15,446m. was recorded from exports of $32,631m. and imports of $48,097m. Turkey's principal imports are machinery, chemicals, petroleum and iron and steel. The principal exports are ready-to-wear clothing, textiles and agricultural products, principally fruit, vegetables and nuts. The EU is Turkey's principal trading partner, with Germany alone taking 20.0% of all Turkish exports in 1997 and supplying 16.5% of all imports. A customs union with the EU came into effect in January 1996 (see below) and a supplementary agreement on trade in iron and steel products, concluded in July 1996, means that, in theory, there is free trade between Turkey and EU countries in all goods, except agricultural products. As analysts had predicted, there was a rapid increase in imports from the EU in 1996, with imports rising by 19%, as Turkey removed remaining trade tariffs, with the result that the trade gap between Turkey and the EU widened. Turkey's trade with Russia and with the Turkic-speaking Central Asian republics, Azerbaijan, Uzbekistan, Kazakhstan and Kyrgyzstan, grew rapidly in 1995. While official Turkish exports to Russia totalled \$1,200m. in 1995, some analysts believed that the figure would rise to \$6,000m. if the so-called 'suitcase trade' (see above) were taken into account.

In 1963 the Government signed an association agreement with the EC, under which Turkey was granted financial aid and preferential tariff quotas. A package of minor improvements was introduced at the end of 1976 and the association agreement was revised in July 1980, offering Turkey a five-year financial aid package. Since the military coup of September 1980, aid from EC countries has become increasingly dependent upon the restoration of democracy and human rights in Turkey. NATO countries have been divided on support for the Ankara regime: in December 1981 the USA promised to accelerate aid to Turkey, but in March 1982 EC aid worth \$586m. was 'frozen'. This aid remained blocked, despite the reconvening of the Turkey-EC Association Council in September 1986. In 1987 Turkey submitted an application for full EC membership in March, followed by a concerted diplomatic effort to win support for its application in Europe. The 'frozen' aid was partly released in early 1988. At the end of 1989 the European Commission published its report in response to Turkey's application for full membership. The report drew attention to both economic and political problems in Turkey, as well as the country's unsatisfactory human rights record, and proposed that negotiations should not start until after 1992. Discussions between the two sides in 1993 secured an agreement to construct a customs union, which was scheduled to be effective on 1 January 1995. In December 1994 the EU-Turkey Association Council agreed to postpone the establishment of the customs union, owing to persisting concerns regarding the Turkish Government's record on human rights, democracy and the rule of law. Negotiations in early 1995 finally concluded an agreement, which was signed at a meeting of the EU-Turkey Association Council in March. The accord was formally ratified by the European Parliament in December, and came into effect on 1 January 1996. However, some \$470m. in EU adjustment funds to support the customs union was blocked in September 1996 by Greece, and by the European Parliament as a result of concern over Turkey's human rights record. Turkey's relations with the EU remained strained throughout 1996, and they suffered a further setback in December 1997 when the EU decided to exclude Turkey from the list of countries eligible to join the organization in the near future. Although the European Commission subsequently published a strategy in March 1998 for enhancing co-operation by building on the customs union which came into force in 1996, EU financial assistance to Turkey remained blocked at the insistence of Greece. In January 1997 Turkey signed a free-trade agreement with Hungary, under which virtually all tariffs on industrial goods were to be removed. A free-trade agreement with Israel was finally ratified by the Turkish parliament in April 1997 and there were predictions that trade between the two countries could grow rapidly to reach some \$2,000m. per year.

In recent years, the US Government's intended military and economic aid to Turkey has been affected by the determination of Congress to institute severe cuts in retaliation for the Turkish Government's refusal to modify its support for the 'Turkish Republic of Northern Cyprus'. The Congress has also attempted to withhold certain portions of aid in order to encourage greater respect for human rights in the Turkish Government's treatment of Kurdish separatists. In August 1994 Prime Minister Çiller refused US military and economic aid amounting to \$453m., owing to its conditional element. In June 1996 the US House of Representatives vetoed a \$25m. foreign aid allocation to Turkey, in part because of Turkey's land blockade of Armenia. However, the US Senate later authorized the release of some \$12m., without conditions. Turkey incurred further US displeasure when Ankara signed a trade agreement with Cuba in August 1996 and when Prime Minister Erbakan made controversial visits to Iran and Libya.

At the end of August 1997, following a recommendation by the National Security Council (NSC), the Government indicated that the illegal barter trade with northern Iraq would be brought under control, to raise urgently required tax revenues. For some years Turkish traders had exchanged a variety of goods for cheap Iraqi diesel oil, to be resold in Turkey at prices far lower than those recommended officially. Although this thriving border trade was in violation of UN sanctions against Iraq, it was tolerated, since it provided an important source of foreign currency for the Kurdish population of northern Iraq. Petrol Offisi, the state-owned petroleum distributor, was henceforth to buy, sell and tax the diesel, to raise an estimated \$900m. a year in revenue for the Government.

PLANNING

Successive Five-Year Economic Development Plans have aimed at the long-term target of self-sustained economic growth (independent of foreign loans), devoting a large proportion of investment to mining and manufacturing industry. During the years of the first Five-Year Plan (1962–67) a real growth rate of 6.6% per annum was achieved. The second Five-Year Plan, covering 1968–72, envisaged an annual growth rate of 7%, which was almost exactly achieved. An annual growth rate of 7.9% in GNP was aimed at in the third Five-Year Plan (1973–77) but many targets were only 60% achieved and, in real terms, the overall growth rate was below target. The start of the fourth Plan (1978–82) was delayed by the economic crisis of 1978, and later shelved. The Evren Government drew up a fifth Five-Year Plan, but in June 1983 decided to leave its formal introduction to the new civilian Government after the transition to civilian rule in the November general elections. In the event, Prime Minister Özal's Government unveiled its own modified fifth Five-Year Plan in mid-1984.

In May 1989 the Government published the sixth Plan (1990–94), which envisaged an average annual growth rate of 7%, reaching 8.3% in 1994. Private sector investments were targeted to grow at an annual average rate of 11%, with growth reaching 15% by the end of the Plan period. The surplus on the current account of the balance of payments was expected to increase throughout the period, to reach \$2,500m. in 1994, while exports were projected to grow at an average rate of 15% per year, and to exceed \$22,000m. by 1994. In September 1994 the preparation for the seventh Plan was postponed by one year; an intermediary target plan was implemented in 1995. In May 1995 the Government published the seventh Plan, for the period 1996–2000, which envisaged economic growth increasing to an annual 7.1%.

PROSPECTS

From 1989 onwards politial instability affected the Government's ability to implement its economic plans. The appointment of Tansu Çiller as Prime Minister in 1993 was a popular choice with the business community, and while she quickly identified economic priorities, internal problems hampered attempts to implement reform. The political uncertainty and negotiations which took place following the collapse of the coalition Government in 1995, were accompanied by the largest series of strikes since the 1970s, which caused the closure of ports and a halt in production at state-owned industrial and transport companies. By October the strike action was costing the country an estimated \$500m. in lost export revenue and production and threatened to undermine attempts to control inflation and restore economic stability. Prior to the general election in December, Çiller was able to settle the public-sector wage dispute, and, more importantly, to secure ratification of the EU customs union, which entered into force on 1 January 1996. The impact of the removal of commercial barriers (except those on agricultural goods) was expected to stimulate trade between the two sides and to promote greater competitiveness among Turkish industries. The EU was to provide ECU 1,800m. over a five-year period, in order to assist the implementation of the new trade regime and to alleviate any initial hardships resulting from the agreement. However, during 1996 the release of ECU 375m. in aid was blocked, until July, by Greece, following a deterioration in relations with Turkey, and, in September, by the European Parliament, expressing renewed concern at the human rights situation in Turkey.

The general election of December 1995 failed to produce a clear victory for any one party, and a period of uncertainty followed. In March 1996 the newly-established True Path Party (DYP)–Anavatan Partisi coalition administration announced measures to confront the expanding budget deficit, by implementing social security and tax reforms and reducing public-sector expenditure. However, the growing public discord between the two parties precluded the adoption of any stabilizing measures to improve the economic situation. In June a new Government was established, led by the Islamic fundamentalist Welfare Party (RP), with the DYP as a coalition partner. In early July the new administration approved an increase in the minimum wage and salary increases of 50% for state workers and pensioners. During his first five months in office, Erbakan announced three economic packages which, he claimed, would raise a total of $30,000m. in revenue, to meet the pay award and limit the budget deficit. They included the sale of state-owned land, housing and real estate, a 6% levy on short-term foreign financing of imports (mainly consumer goods), measures to attract hard currency held abroad by Turkish banks, and the leasing of uncompleted power plants. The new Government stated that the main aspects of its economic programme were: a commitment to a free-market economy; lower inflation and a steady growth rate; lower taxation for producers; greater efforts to attract foreign investment; an acceleration in the privatization programme; an emphasis on investment in infrastructure projects; and economic planning to achieve long-term solutions. According to the OECD, international reaction to the Government's fiscal performance was likely to be one of the most important factors in determining future economic stability and growth. In addition, it advised the Government to adhere to budget targets and to implement structural reforms, in order to stabilize inflation and control high interest rates, which were contributing to a disabling debt-servicing cost. At the end of November 1996 the National Assembly approved the Prime Minister's ambitious and controversial budget for 1997, in which he vowed to increase expenditure, end domestic borrowing and yet produce a 'zero-deficit' through a massive increase in government income from privatization. Dubbed the 'dream' budget, it totalled TL 6,254,920,000m., and encountered strong criticism from political opponents and from the country's business community. The IMF predicted that the Government would raise only a fraction of the revenue projected from privatization and warned that the Government could face a budget deficit of TL 3,014,000,000m. in 1997. The Government's privatization plans received a welcome boost in January 1997, when the Constitutional Court gave its approval to the sale of a major stake in the state company, Türk Telecom, though there were objections to a number of the Prime Minister's revenue-raising packages, notably his attempt to sell large public real estate holdings and lease state-owned power projects. Early in 1997 Erbakan made new promises of additional pay increases to state workers and pensioners, over and above those included in the 1997 budget, which did little to inspire confidence in the Government's economic competence.

Announcing the new Government's economic policy in July 1997, Mesut Yılmaz stated that priority would be given to countering inflation and accelerating privatization (see above). The new Minister of Finance, Zekeriya Temizel, announced revised economic targets for 1997, which included: growth in GNP of 5.5%–6%, compared with the previous target of 4%, based on a 5.7% increase in GNP during the first quarter of 1997; a reduction in the trade deficit, from $20,500m. to $20,000m.; and a budget deficit at the end of the year of TL 2,400,000m., including a supplementary budget of TL 2,000,000m. Inflation in 1997 was forecast at 75%–80%. Independent analysts viewed these goals as more realistic than those of the previous Government, and significant economic progress was recorded during the following year despite the Government's weak political base in the Grand National Assembly. In June 1998 the parties in the Government agreed to maintain the coalition until the end of 1998, when the Prime Minister would resign in favour of a caretaker leader who would take charge until fresh elections in April 1999.

Statistical Survey

Source (unless otherwise stated): Türkiye İş Bankası AS, Economic Research Dept, Atatürk Bul. 191, 06684 Kavaklıdere, Ankara; tel. (312) 4281140; telex 42082; fax (312) 4250750.

Area and Population

AREA, POPULATION AND DENSITY

Area (sq km)	779,452*
Population (census results)	
21 October 1990	
Males	28,607,047
Females	27,865,988
Total	56,473,035†
30 November 1997	62,870,030
Population (official estimates at mid-year)‡	
1995	61,644,000
1996	62,697,000
1997	63,745,000
Density (per sq km) at 30 November 1997	80.6

* 300,948 sq miles. The total comprises Anatolia (Turkey in Asia or Asia Minor), with an area of 755,688 sq km (291,773 sq miles), and Thrace (Turkey in Europe), with an area of 23,764 sq km (9,175 sq miles).
† Comprising 50,497,586 in Anatolia and 5,975,449 in Thrace.
‡ Not revised to take account of the 1997 census results.

PRINCIPAL TOWNS
(estimated population at mid-1996, within municipal boundaries)

Ankara (capital)	.	2,890,025	Urfa	. 381,938
İstanbul . .	.	8,023,329	Samsun . . .	. 335,886
İzmir (Smyrna)	.	2,073,669	Malatya . . .	. 323,429
Adana . .		1,099,154	Erzurum . . .	. 248,135
Bursa . .		1,057,016	Sivas . . .	. 247,566
Gaziantep .	.	. 758,438	Denizli . . .	. 247,560
Konya . .	.	. 600,062	Gebze . . .	. 247,412
Mersin (İçel)	.	. 557,400	Kahramanmaraş	. 245,221
Antalya . .		. 530,201	Tarsus . . .	. 238,814
Kayseri . .		. 471,463	Elâziğ . . .	. 228,933
Diyarbakır .	.	. 464,479	İzmit (Kocaeli) .	. 208,748
Eskişehir .	.	. 464,010	Van . . .	. 207,666

Source: UN, *Demographic Yearbook*.

BIRTHS AND DEATHS

	Registered live births		Registered deaths	
	Number	Rate per 1,000	Number	Rate per 1,000
1992	1,338,000	23.8	394,000	6.7
1993 . . .	1,385,000	23.3	398,000	6.7
1994 . . .	1,383,000	22.8	401,000	6.6
1995 . . .	1,381,000	22.4	405,000*	6.6*
1996* . . .	1,379,000	22.0	408,000	6.5
1997* . . .	1,377,000	21.6	412,000	6.5

* Provisional.

Expectation of life (UN estimates, years at birth, 1990–95): Males 65.0; Females 69.6.

Sources: UN, *Demographic Yearbook* and *Population and Vital Statistics Report*.

ECONOMICALLY ACTIVE POPULATION*
(sample survey, '000 persons aged 12 years and over, October 1996)

	Males	Females	Total
Agriculture, hunting, forestry and fishing	5,108	4,854	9,962
Mining and quarrying . . .	161	2	162
Manufacturing	2,607	527	3,134
Electricity, gas and water. . .	75	8	82
Construction.	1,322	34	1,356
Trade, restaurants and hotels. .	2,482	223	2,704
Transport, storage and communications . . .	882	35	917
Financing, insurance, real estate and business services . . .	331	121	453
Community, social and personal services	2,285	643	2,928
Total employed	15,252	6,446	21,698
Unemployed	956	376	1,332
Total labour force	16,208	6,821	23,030

* Excluding armed forces.

Source: ILO, *Yearbook of Labour Statistics*.

WORKERS ABROAD ('000)

	1995	1996	1997*
Australia	31	21	21
Austria	55	51	51
Belgium.	27	38	38
CIS	40	40	40
France	103	73	73
Germany	751	740	748
Libya	6	6	6
Netherlands	85	65	65
Saudi Arabia	120	120	120
Switzerland	40	35	34
Total (incl. others) . . .	1,331	1,264	1,315

* Figures at October.

WORKERS' REMITTANCES FROM ABROAD (US $ million)

	1995	1996	1997
Total	3,365	3,590	4,229

Agriculture

PRINCIPAL CROPS ('000 metric tons)

	1995	1996	1997*
Wheat	18,000	18,500	18,650
Spelt	15	14	13
Rye	240	245	235
Barley	7,500	8,000	8,200
Oats	250	275	280
Maize	1,900	2,000	2,080
Millet	6	6	5
Rice (milled)	250	280	275
Dry beans	225	230	235
Chick peas	730	732	720
Lentils	665	645	515
Vetch	167	160	165
Broad beans (dry) . . .	49	46	46
Potatoes	4,750	4,950	5,100
Onions (dry)	2,850	1,900	2,100
Garlic (dry)	75	80	85
Tomatoes	7,250	7,800	6,600
Cabbages (incl. black) . .	676	678	679
Melons and watermelons . .	5,400	5,800	5,550
Aubergines (Eggplants) . .	750	850	847
Apples	2,100	2,200	2,250
Grapes	3,550	3,700	3,700
Pears	410	415	400
Hazel-nuts (Filberts) . . .	455	446	410
Sultanas	179	220	211
Figs (dried)	50	50	45
Walnuts	110	115	115
Pistachios (in shell) . . .	36	60	70
Almonds	37	43	33
Chestnuts	77	65	61
Oranges	842	890	740
Lemons	418	401	270
Mandarins	453	450	365
Peaches	340	360	355
Plums	187	195	200
Apricots (incl. wild) . . .	250	206	270
Cherries (incl. sour) . . .	92	110	120
Cotton (lint)	851	794	779
Tobacco (leaves) . . .	204	232	300
Sugar beet	11,171	14,383	16,135
Sesame seed	30	30	28
Sunflower seed	900	780	900
Olives	515	1,800	510
Olive oil	52	220	40
Tea (fresh leaves) . . .	524	600	752

* Figures are provisional.

LIVESTOCK ('000 head, year ending September)

	1994	1995	1996
Horses	450	437	435*
Mules	172	169	165*
Asses	841	809	800*
Cattle	11,910	11,901	11,789
Buffaloes	316	305	255
Camels	2	2	2*
Pigs	9	8	5
Sheep	37,541	35,646	33,791
Goats	10,133	9,564	9,111

Chickens (million): 178 in 1994; 184 in 1995; 129 in 1996.
Turkeys (million): 3 in 1994; 3 in 1995; 4* in 1996.

* FAO estimate.

Source: FAO, *Production Yearbook*.

LIVESTOCK PRODUCTS ('000 metric tons)

	1994	1995	1996
Beef and veal	317	292	287*
Buffalo meat.	7	6	6*
Mutton and lamb	286*	273	260*
Goat meat*	62	61	61
Horse meat*.	3	3	3
Poultry meat	490	506	517*
Edible offals*	87	87	n.a.
Cows' milk	9,129	9,275	9,133
Buffalo milk.	144	115	108*
Sheep milk	992	934	922*
Goats' milk	297	277	280*
Butter and ghee*	116	114	117
Cheese*	137	136	139
Hen eggs	513	555	560*
Honey	55	69	60*
Wool:			
greasy.	39	37*	37*
clean	22	20*	20*
Cattle and buffalo hides* . . .	39	36	36
Sheepskins*.	62	59	56
Goatskins*	10	10	9

* FAO estimate(s).

Source: FAO, mainly *Production Yearbook*.

Forestry

ROUNDWOOD REMOVALS ('000 cubic metres, excl. bark)

	1994	1995	1996
Sawlogs, veneer logs and logs for			
sleepers	4,689	5,467	5,467
Pulpwood	1,577	1,558	1,558
Other industrial wood . . .	2,945	3,720	3,720
Fuel wood	7,634	8,534	8,534
Total	16,845	19,279	19,279

Source: FAO, *Yearbook of Forest Products*.

SAWNWOOD PRODUCTION ('000 cubic metres, incl. railway sleepers)

	1994	1995	1996
Coniferous (softwood) . . .	2,334	2,502	2,502
Broadleaved (hardwood) . . .	1,703	1,829	1,829
Total	4,037	4,331	4,331

Source: FAO, *Yearbook of Forest Products*.

Fishing

('000 metric tons, live weight)

	1993	1994	1995
Common carp	16.6	16.2	17.5
Whiting	20.5	16.6	18.1
Mullets	25.5	28.6	31.5
Bluefish	16.4	8.1	5.5
Atlantic horse mackerel . .	27.3	20.0	7.4
Mediterranean horse mackerel .	8.0	11.7	11.3
European pilchard (sardine) . .	32.9	26.4	33.8
European anchovy . . .	227.1	294.4	387.6
Atlantic bonito	19.5	10.1	8.9
Chub mackerel	15.9	16.7	17.4
Other fishes (incl. unspecified) .	98.1	101.3	84.8
Total fish	507.9	550.2	623.8
Crustaceans	4.8	4.1	2.7
Molluscs.	45.0	47.4	24.2
Frogs	0.8	0.9	0.9
Jellyfishes	0.8	0.8	0.5
Total catch	559.2	603.3	652.2
Inland waters	52.2	52.3	61.1
Mediterranean and Black Sea. .	507.0	551.0	591.1

Source: FAO, *Yearbook of Fishery Statistics*.

Mining

('000 metric tons)

	1995	1996	1997
Crude petroleum. . . .	3,514	3,499	3,428
Iron ore*	2,754	n.a.	n.a.
Lignite†	51,943	52,503	52,050
Coal†	2,248	2,424	2,412
Copper (blister)†	24	30	32

* Figures refer to the iron content of ores (Source: UN, *Industrial Commodity Statistics Yearbook*).

† Production in the public sector only.

Industry

SELECTED PRODUCTS
('000 metric tons, unless otherwise indicated)

	1995	1996	1997
Paper*	512	372	403
Cotton yarn*	32	26	29
Woollen yarn*	3	4	3
Cotton fabrics (million metres)* .	80	76	69
Woollen fabrics (million metres)* .	3	3	3
Raki ('000 litres)* . . .	66,549	73,277	71,995
Beer ('000 litres). . . .	672,965	689,895	723,516
Cigarettes*	81	74	75
Pig-iron	4,363	5,263	5,567
Cement	33,153	35,214	36,035
Sugar	1,290	1,842	2,013
Commercial fertilizers‡ . . .	5,123	5,300	5,270
Electrolytic copper† . . .	24	30	32
Polyethylene*	301	299	293
Coke	2,248	3,217	3,186
Motor spirit (petrol) . . .	3,554	3,373	3,383
Kerosene	78	94	72
Fuel oils.	7,786	7,408	7,185
Hydroelectricity (million kWh) .	35,541	40,475	39,750
Thermal electricity (million kWh) .	50,800	54,387	63,438

* Public sector only. † Private sector only.

‡ Excluding potassic fertilizers.

Finance

CURRENCY AND EXCHANGE RATES

Monetary Units

100 kuruş = 1 Turkish lira (TL) or pound.

Sterling and Dollar Equivalents (31 May 1998)

£1 sterling = 418,364 liras;
US $1 = 256,555 liras;
1,000,000 Turkish liras = £2.390 = $3.898.

Average Exchange Rate (liras per US $)

1995	45,845
1996	81,405
1997	151,865

GENERAL BUDGET (TL '000 million)*

Revenue†	1994	1995	1996
Taxation	588,058	1,084,941	2,245,290
Taxes on income, profits, etc.	246,580	435,999	865,909
Taxes on property . . .	32,643	16,775	3,333
Sales taxes	176,742	354,980	743,025
Excises	53,610	117,798	383,066
Other domestic taxes on goods and services	40,981	78,410	129,322
Import duties . . .	23,825	51,783	63,286
Stamp taxes . . .	13,677	29,196	57,349
Property income	11,769	20,243	52,323
Other current revenue . .	145,208	287,388	411,414
Capital revenue	5,638	9,275	17,138
Total	750,673	1,401,847	2,726,165

Expenditure‡	1994	1995	1996
General public services . .	318,972	790,645	1,950,126
Defence	85,377	167,798	333,434
Education	122,546	215,024	442,420
Health	26,886	45,112	89,526
Social security and welfare .	35,056	62,696	176,574
Housing and community amenities	11,254	17,362	44,856
Other community and social services	4,467	7,589	14,494
Economic services . . .	120,056	206,101	413,411
Fuel and energy . . .	25,337	53,914	111,454
Agriculture, forestry, fishing and hunting	10,142	17,833	33,568
Mining, manufacturing and construction	12,117	3,059	48,158
Transport and communications .	45,697	78,435	162,853
Other economic services .	26,763	52,860	57,378
Other expenditure . . .	177,463	211,509	496,467
Interest payments . . .	177,463	211,272	495,886
Adjustment to total expenditure	–	–	–138
Total	902,077	1,723,836	3,961,170
Current	825,167	1,577,411	3,642,488
Capital	76,910	146,425	318,682

* Figures exclude the operations of central government units with their own budgets.
† Excluding grants received (TL '000 million): 942 in 1994; 7,404 in 1995; 1,793 in 1996.
‡ Excluding net lending (TL '000 million): 376 in 1994; 358 in 1995; 138 in 1996.

Source: IMF, *Government Finance Statistics Yearbook*.

INTERNATIONAL RESERVES
(US $ million at 31 December)

	1995	1996	1997
Gold*	1,383	1,372	1,384
IMF special drawing rights . .	3	1	1
Reserve position in IMF . .	48	46	44
Foreign exchange . . .	12,391	16,388	18,614
Total	13,825	17,808	20,042

* National valuation.

Source: IMF, *International Financial Statistics*.

MONEY SUPPLY
(TL '000 million at 31 December)

	1995	1996*	1997*
Currency outside banks . . .	188,506	315,890	598,570
Demand deposits at deposit money banks	193,429	562,350	887,430
Total money (incl. others) . .	384,391	882,290	1,491,710

* Figures are rounded to the nearest 10,000 million liras.

Source: IMF, *International Financial Statistics*.

COST OF LIVING
(Consumer Price Index for urban areas; base: 1987 = 100)

	1995	1996	1997
Food	8,732.4	14,714.1	31,973.4
Clothing	9,788.4	17,638.7	31,833.2
Household expenditures . .	6,911.4	12,758.4	23,532.4
Medical and personal care .	9,688.1	19,599.0	36,263.7
Transport	8,088.2	16,686.0	34,250.4
Cultural and recreational expenditures	8,759.2	14,759.3	30,585.9
Dwelling expenditures* . .	5,666.4	11,848.4	22,279.3
All items	7,864.3	14,140.0	28,152.0

* Rent is assumed to be fixed.

NATIONAL ACCOUNTS (TL '000 million at current prices)

Expenditure on the Gross Domestic Product (provisional)*

	1994	1995	1996
Government final consumption expenditure	451,000	837,000	1,709,000
Private final consumption expenditure	2,706,000	5,551,000	9,938,000
Increase in stocks . . .	–121,000	33,000	–80,000
Gross fixed capital formation . .	952,000	1,814,000	3,706,000
Total domestic expenditure .	3,988,000	8,235,000	15,273,000
Exports of goods and services . .	826,000	1,541,000	3,182,000
Less Imports of goods and services	789,000	1,885,000	4,111,000
GDP in purchasers' values . .	4,026,000	7,891,000	14,345,00
GDP at constant 1990 prices .	431	460	494

* Except for GDP at constant prices, figures are rounded to the nearest 1,000,000 million liras.

Source: IMF, *International Financial Statistics*.

Gross Domestic Product by Economic Activity

	1995	1996	1997
Agriculture and livestock . .	1,066,439	2,176,433	3,862,523
Forestry and logging . . .	36,474	72,445	105,465
Fishing	43,485	71,284	122,270
Mining and quarrying . .	87,629	159,420	286,823
Manufacturing . . .	1,474,300	2,378,709	4,691,331
Electricity, gas and water . .	184,282	393,457	702,332
Construction	388,416	767,355	1,547,471
Wholesale and retail trade . .	1,361,826	2,497,309	5,004,360
Transport, storage and communications . . .	972,955	1,965,453	3,953,954
Financial institutions . .	281,105	657,828	1,369,266
Ownership of dwellings . .	210,905	380,781	708,080
Other private services . .	264,634	505,969	976,262
Government services . . .	619,785	1,238,527	2,579,910
Private non-profit institutions .	14,577	26,922	53,021
Gross domestic product at factor cost	7,006,813	13,291,893	25,963,067
Indirect taxes	846,230	1,723,626	3,552,447
Less Subsidies	93,586	243,409	377,960
GDP in purchasers' values . .	7,762,457	14,772,110	29,137,554

BALANCE OF PAYMENTS (US $ million)

	1995	1996	1997
Exports of goods f.o.b. . . .	21,975	32,446	32,631
Imports of goods f.o.b. . . .	−35,187	−43,028	−48,097
Trade balance	**−13,212**	**−10,582**	**−15,466**
Exports of services . . .	14,606	13,051	19,373
Imports of services . . .	−5,024	−6,426	−8,510
Balance on goods and services.	**−3,630**	**−3,957**	**−4,603**
Other income received . . .	1,489	1,577	1,900
Other income paid . . .	−4,693	−4,504	−4,913
Balance on goods, services and income	**−6,834**	**−6,884**	**−7,616**
Current transfers received .	4,512	4,466	4,909
Current transfers paid . .	−16	−19	−43
Current balance . . .	**−2,338**	**−2,437**	**−2,750**
Direct investment abroad. .	−113	−110	−251
Direct investment from abroad	885	722	805
Portfolio investment assets .	−466	−1,380	−710
Portfolio investment liabilities .	703	1,950	2,344
Other investment assets . .	−383	331	−1,750
Other investment liabilities .	4,017	7,250	8,178
Net errors and omissions . .	2,355	−1,782	−2,523
Overall balance . . .	**4,660**	**4,544**	**3,343**

Source: IMF, *International Financial Statistics*.

External Trade

PRINCIPAL COMMODITIES

(distribution by SITC, US $ million, excl. military goods)

Imports c.i.f. (excl. grants)	1993	1994	1995
Food and live animals . . .	838.6	465.1	148.0
Crude materials (inedible) except fuels . . .	2,490.0	2,272.5	3,512.2
Textile fibres (excl. wool tops) and waste.	578.2	489.7	808.7
Metalliferous ores and metal scrap	893.3	908.2	1,218.6
Waste and scrap metal of iron or steel	819.7	848.9	1,081.2
Mineral fuels, lubricants, etc. .	3,989.6	3,837.9	4,657.7
Petroleum, petroleum products, etc.	3,065.8	2,807.5	3,329.4
Crude petroleum oils, etc. .	2,550.3	2,432.1	2,917.2
Gas (natural and manufactured) .	587.2	628.6	1,007.0
Chemicals and related products	3,481.1	3,145.2	5,236.3
Organic chemicals . . .	865.0	890.1	1,521.0
Artificial resins, plastic materials, etc.	655.1	626.0	1,129.9
Basic manufactures . . .	5,054.0	4,063.2	6,732.2
Textile yarn, fabrics, etc.. . .	1,026.9	1,121.7	1,834.3
Iron and steel	2,003.1	1,315.8	2,115.3
Ingots and other primary forms .	730.7	424.6	612.9
Universals, plates and sheets .	775.5	434.8	959.7
Non-ferrous metals . . .	408.4	399.1	752.3
Machinery and transport equipment	11,196.2	7,657.0	11,470.3
Power-generating machinery and equipment	705.1	444.6	594.5
Machinery specialized for particular industries . . .	2,245.2	1,456.9	2,583.1
Textile and leather machinery .	1,111.2	685.2	1,541.2
General industrial machinery, equipment and parts . .	1,490.1	1,272.4	1,584.6
Office machines and automatic data-processing equipment . .	587.8	398.4	686.9
Telecommunications and sound equipment	440.7	537.3	633.8
Other electrical machinery, apparatus, etc.	1,505.5	1,173.1	1,469.4

Imports c.i.f. (excl. grants) — *continued*	1993	1994	1995
Road vehicles and parts* . . .	2,008.5	870.3	1,521.7
Passenger motor cars (excl. buses)	734.2	222.0	327.1
Parts and accessories for cars, buses, lorries, etc.* . . .	694.1	424.9	767.8
Other transport equipment* . .	1,864.5	1,186.7	2,022.8
Aircraft, associated equipment and parts*	1,404.9	802.4	1,377.6
Miscellaneous manufactured articles	1,506.5	1,130.7	1,727.1
Total (incl. others)	29,429.3	23,268.0	35,707.5

* Data on parts exclude tyres, engines and electrical parts.

Exports f.o.b.	1993	1994	1995
Food and live animals . . .	2,793.7	3,298.2	3,414.9
Cereals and cereal preparations .	284.6	383.1	450.2
Vegetables and fruit . . .	1,671.0	2,003.3	2,176.8
Fresh, chilled, frozen or simply preserved vegetables . .	444.7	452.7	470.4
Fresh or dried fruit and nuts (excl. oil nuts)	897.6	1,079.9	1,211.2
Edible nuts	440.5	523.8	610.3
Hazel-nuts	426.3	509.9	590.8
Beverages and tobacco. . .	465.6	471.2	467.3
Tobacco and tobacco manufactures	441.0	423.7	381.4
Unmanufactured tobacco (incl. refuse)	395.6	395.2	244.5
Crude materials (inedible) except fuels	554.5	604.9	774.2
Chemicals and related products	605.6	724.5	874.4
Basic manufactures . . .	4,486.4	5,707.4	6,262.9
Textile yarn, fabrics, etc.. . .	1,592.2	2,194.7	2,526.6
Textile yarn	347.2	597.7	505.8
Non-metallic mineral manufactures	422.0	529.7	632.5
Iron and steel	1,828.8	2,160.1	1,997.6
Ingots and other primary forms	491.6	599.8	483.4
Blooms, billets, slabs, etc. .	416.8	452.2	430.8
Bars, rods, angles, shapes and sections	1,135.3	1,284.6	1,094.6
Bars and rods (excl. wire rod).	852.3	1,036.1	811.4
Machinery and transport equipment	1,290.7	1,696.4	2,373.9
Electrical machinery, apparatus, etc.	617.0	726.3	991.1
Road vehicles and parts (excl. tyres, engines and electrical parts) .	295.2	413.5	725.9
Miscellaneous manufactured articles	4,779.2	5,165.5	6,801.1
Clothing and accessories (excl. footwear)	4,339.7	4,581.8	6,118.8
Men's and boys' outer garments of non-knitted textile fabrics .	333.9	366.8	525.5
Women's, girls' and infants' outer garments of non-knitted textile fabrics	779.2	846.6	1,220.7
Knitted or crocheted outer garments and accessories (excl. gloves, stockings, etc.), non-elastic	1,492.4	1,520.4	1,990.9
Jerseys, pullovers, etc.. .	554.0	705.3	860.2
Knitted or crocheted undergarments (incl. foundation garments of non-knitted fabrics) . . .	879.4	946.6	1,308.8
Cotton undergarments, non-elastic	790.7	805.1	1,086.2
Non-textile clothing and accessories, and headgear of all materials	498.3	473.9	471.7
Leather clothing and accessories	440.7	410.4	406.5
Total (incl. others)	15,348.9	18,106.1	21,598.7

Source: UN, *International Trade Statistics Yearbook*.

PRINCIPAL TRADING PARTNERS (US $ million, excl. military goods)

Imports c.i.f. (excl. grants)	1995	1996	1997
Austria	294	545	502
Belgium-Luxembourg	912	1,129	1,296
China, People's Republic	539	556	788
France	1,996	2,771	2,964
Germany	5,548	7,814	8,010
Iran	689	806	646
Italy	3,193	4,286	4,456
Japan	1,400	1,422	2,040
Korea, Republic	566	719	1,080
Libya	385	476	533
Netherlands	1,084	1,449	1,483
Romania	368	441	394
Russia	2,082	1,921	2,163
Saudi Arabia	1,385	1,708	1,017
Spain	591	1,034	1,275
Sweden	518	660	896
Switzerland	816	1,015	1,097
Ukraine	856	762	916
United Kingdom	1,830	2,510	2,758
USA	3,724	3,516	4,345
Total (incl. others)	35,709	43,627	48,657

Exports f.o.b.	1995	1996	1997
Algeria	269	278	316
Austria	275	291	300
Belgium-Luxembourg	452	493	564
Egypt	246	316	304
France	1,033	1,053	1,163
Germany	5,036	5,187	5,253
Hong Kong	217	219	238
Iran	268	298	307
Italy	1,457	1,446	1,388
Libya	238	244	187
Netherlands	737	770	779
Poland	273	253	255
Russia	1,238	1,512	2,056
Saudi Arabia	470	431	535
Singapore	143	248	366
Spain	354	363	434
Switzerland	238	276	318
Syria	272	308	269
United Arab Emirates	189	211	265
United Kingdom	1,136	1,261	1,505
USA	1,514	1,639	2,020
Total (incl. others)	21,636	23,224	26,246

Transport

RAILWAYS (traffic)

	1993	1994	1995*
Passenger journeys (million)	146	119	105
Freight (million metric tons)	16	14	15

* Estimates.
Source: Ministry of Transport and Communications.

ROAD TRAFFIC (motor vehicles at 31 December)

	1994	1995	1996
Passenger cars	3,028,064	3,231,562	3,456,850
Goods vehicles (incl. vans)	688,244	719,164	776,057
Buses and coaches	87,545	90,197	94,978
Motorcycles and mopeds	788,786	819,922	854,150

Source: IRF, *World Road Statistics*.

SHIPPING
Merchant Fleet (registered at 31 December)

	1995	1996	1997
Number of vessels	1,075	1,114	1,146
Total displacement ('000 grt)	6,267.6	6,425.7	6,567.3

Source: Lloyd's Register of Shipping, *World Fleet Statistics*.

International Sea-borne Freight Traffic ('000 metric tons)*

	1993	1994	1995
Goods loaded	22,946	21,089	22,812
Goods unloaded	61,556	46,374	56,186

* Excluding livestock.

CIVIL AVIATION (Turkish Airlines)

	1993	1994	1995*
Number of passengers ('000)	6,099	7,274	8,680
Freight handled (metric tons)†	70,004	85,111	89,696

* Figures are provisional.
† Cargo and mail.

Tourism

	1995	1996	1997
Number of foreign arrivals ('000)	7,726	8,614	9,689
Receipts from foreign travel (million US $)	4,957	5,650	7,002
Expenditures for foreign travel (million US $)	911	1,265	1,716

TOURISTS BY COUNTRY OF ORIGIN ('000)

Country	1995	1996	1997
France	252	252	334
Germany	1,656	2,142	2,339
Greece	154	147	170
Iran	361	378	332
Italy	108	160	208
Syria	112	92	99
USSR (former)	1,357	1,582	1,514
United Kingdom	735	758	915
USA	290	326	365
Yugoslavia (former)	70	105	151
Total (incl. others)	7,726	8,614	9,689

TOURIST ACCOMMODATION (registered by the Ministry of Tourism).
1994: 265,136 beds; **1995:** 286,463 beds; **1996:** 301,524 beds.

Communications Media

	1993	1994	1995
Radio receivers ('000 in use) . .	9,650	9,850	10,000
Television receivers ('000 in use) .	10,500	11,000	11,500
Telephones ('000 main lines in use)	10,936	12,212	13,228
Telefax stations (number in use) .	77,190	87,610	99,146
Mobile cellular telephones			
(subscribers)	84,187	174,780	437,130
Book production: titles* . . .	5,978	4,473	6,275
Daily newspapers			
Number	n.a.	57	400
Circulation ('000)	n.a.	2,679	7,000
Non-daily newspapers . . .	n.a.	1,100	1,321

* Of which pamphlets: 410 in 1993; 316 in 1994.

Sources: UNESCO, *Statistical Yearbook*, and UN, *Statistical Yearbook*.

Education

(1995/96)

	Institutions	Teachers ('000)	Pupils ('000)
Primary	49,240	232	6,403
Secondary:			
General	10,689	138	3,498
Technical and vocational . . .	3,678	71	1,309
Higher (incl. academies, teacher training and other higher technical and vocational schools, universities)	817	50	1,161

Source: State Institute of Statistics.

Directory

The Constitution

In October 1981 the National Security Council (NSC), which took power in September 1980, announced the formation of a Consultative Assembly to draft a new constitution, replacing that of 1961. The Assembly consisted of 40 members appointed directly by the NSC and 120 members chosen by the NSC from candidates put forward by the governors of the 67 provinces; all former politicians were excluded. The draft Constitution was approved by the Assembly in September 1982 and by a national referendum in November. Its main provisions are summarized below:

Legislative power is vested in the unicameral Turkish Grand National Assembly (TGNA), with 400 deputies, who are elected by universal adult suffrage for a five-year term. Executive power is vested in the President, who is elected by the TGNA for a seven-year term and is empowered to appoint a Prime Minister and senior members of the judiciary, the Central Bank and broadcasting organizations; to dissolve the TGNA; and to declare a state of emergency entailing rule by decree. Strict controls on the powers of trades unions, the press and political parties were also included. An appended 'temporary article' automatically installed the incumbent President of the NSC as Head of State for a seven-year term, assisted by a Presidential Council comprising members of the NSC.

An amendment adopted in June 1987 increased the number of deputies in the TGNA from 400 to 450. The number was increased to 550 in a further amendment adopted in July 1995.

The Government

HEAD OF STATE

President: SÜLEYMAN DEMIREL (took office 16 May 1993).

COUNCIL OF MINISTERS
(September 1998)

A coalition of the Anavatan Partisi (ANAP), the Demokratik Sol Partisi (DSP) and the Demokrat Türkiye Partisi (DTP).

Prime Minister: MESUT YILMAZ (ANAP).

Deputy Prime Minister and State Minister: BÜLENT ECEVIT (DSP).

Deputy Prime Minister and Minister of National Defence: İSMET SEZGİN (DTP).

Minister of Justice: HASAN DENIZKURDU (Independent).

Minister of the Interior: KUTLU AKTAS (Independent).

Minister of Foreign Affairs: İSMAİL CEM (DSP).

Minister of Finance and Customs: ZEKERIYA TEMIZEL (DSP).

Minister of National Education: HIKMET ULUĞBAY (DSP).

Minister of Public Works and Housing: YAŞAR TOPÇU (ANAP).

Minister of Health: HALİL İBRAHİM ÖZSOY (ANAP).

Minister of Transport and Communications: ARIF AHMET DENI-ZOLGUN (Independent).

Minister of Agriculture and Rural Affairs: MUSTAFA TAŞAR (ANAP).

Minister of Labour and Social Security: NAMİ ÇAĞAN (DSP).

Minister of Trade and Industry: YALIM EREZ (Independent).

Minister of Energy and Natural Resources: CUMHUR ERSÜMER (ANAP).

Minister of Culture: İSTEMIHAN TALAY (DSP).

Minister of Tourism: İBRAHIM GÜRDAL (ANAP).

Minister of Forestry: ERSİN TARANOĞLU (ANAP).

Minister of the Environment: İMREN AYKUT (ANAP).

Ministers of State: GÜNEŞ TANER (ANAP), HÜSAMETTİN ÖZKAN (DSP), YÜCEL SEÇKİNER (ANAP), IŞILAY SAYGIN (ANAP), HİKMET SAMİ TÜRK (DSP), MEHMET SALİH YILDIRIM (ANAP), RIFAT SERDAROĞLU (DTP), METIN GÜRDERE (ANAP), SÜKRÜ SİNA GÜREL (DSP), AHAT ANDICAN (ANAP), IŞIN ÇELEBİ (ANAP), MUSTAFA YILMAZ (DSP), BURHAN KARA (ANAP), CAVİT KAVAK (ANAP), RÜŞTÜ KAZIM YÜCELEN (ANAP), HASAN GEMİCİ (DSP), MEHMET BATALLI (DTP).

MINISTRIES

President's Office: Cumhurbaşkanlığı Köşkü, Çankaya, Ankara; tel. (312) 4407212.

Prime Minister's Office: Başbakanlık, Bakanlıklar, Ankara; tel. (312) 4189056; fax (312) 4180476.

Deputy Prime Minister's Office: Başbakan yard. ve Devlet Bakanı, Bakanlıklar, Ankara; tel. (312) 4191621; fax (312) 4191547.

Ministry of Agriculture and Rural Affairs: Tarım ve Köyişleri Bakanlığı, Şehit Adem Yavuz Sok. 10, 06140 Kızılay, Ankara; tel. (312) 4191677; fax (312) 4177168.

Ministry of Culture: Kültür Bakanlığı, Atatürk Bul. 29, Opera, Ankara; tel. (312) 3240322; fax (312) 3111431.

Ministry of Energy and Natural Resources: Enerji ve Tabii Kaynaklar Bakanlığı, Konya Yolu, Beştepe, Ankara; tel. (312) 2135330; fax (312) 2123816.

Ministry of the Environment: Gevre Bakanlığı, İstanbul Cad. 88, İskitler, Ankara; tel. (312) 3423900.

Ministry of Finance and Customs: Maliye Bakanlığı, Dikmen Cad., Ankara; tel. (312) 4250018; fax (312) 4250058.

Ministry of Foreign Affairs: Dişişleri Bakanlığı, Yeni Hizmet Binası, 06520 Balgat, Ankara; tel. (312) 2871665; fax (312) 2873869.

Ministry of Forestry: Orman Bakanlığı, Atatürk Bul., Bakanlıklar, Ankara; tel. (312) 4176000.

Ministry of Health: Sağlık Bakanlığı, Yenişehir, Ankara; tel. (312) 4312486; telex 42770; fax (312) 4339885.

Ministry of the Interior: İçişleri Bakanlığı, Bakanlıklar, Ankara; tel. (312) 4254080; fax (312) 4181795.

Ministry of Justice: Adalet Bakanlığı, 06440 Bakanlıklar, Ankara; tel. (312) 4192199; fax (312) 4191696.

Ministry of Labour and Social Security: Çalışma ve Sosyal Güvenlik Bakanlığı, Eskişehir Yolu 42, Emek, Ankara; tel. (312) 4170727; fax (312) 4179765.

Ministry of National Defence: Milli Savunma Bakanlığı, 06100 Ankara; tel. (312) 4254596; fax (312) 4184737.

Ministry of National Education: Milli Eğitim Bakanlığı, Ankara; tel. (312) 4255330; fax (312) 4177027.

Ministry of Public Works and Housing: Bayındırlık ve İskan Bakanlığı, Vekaletler Cad. 1, 06100 Ankara; tel. (312) 4255711; fax (312) 4180406.

Ministry of Tourism: Turizm Bakanlığı, İsmet İnönü Bul. 5, 06100 Bahçelievler, Ankara; tel. (312) 2128300; fax (312) 2128391.

Ministry of Trade and Industry: Sanayi ve Ticaret Bakanlığı, Eskişehir yolu üzeri 7 km Ankara; tel. (312) 2860365.

Ministry of Transport and Communications: Ulaştırma Bakanlığı, Sok. 5, Emek, Ankara; tel. (312) 2124416; fax (312) 2124930.

Legislature

TURKISH GRAND NATIONAL ASSEMBLY

Speaker: HİKMET ÇETİN.

General Election, 24 December 1995

Party	% of votes	Seats
Refah Partisi (RP)	21.4	158
Doğru Yol Partisi (DYP)	19.2	135
Anavatan Partisi (ANAP) . . .	19.7	132
Demokratik Sol Parti (DSP) . . .	14.6	76
Cumhuriyet Halk Partisi (CHP) . .	10.7	49
Others*	14.4	—
Total	**100.0**	**550**

* Including Milliyetçi Hareket Partisi (8.2%), Halkın Demokrasi Partisi (4.2%), Yeniden Doğuş Partisi (0.3%), Millet Partisi (0.5%), İşçi Partisi (0.2%), Yeni Demokrasi Hareketi (0.5%), Yeni Parti (0.1%), Independents (0.5%).

Note: Members of the Büyük Birlik Partisi (BBP) contested the election as part of ANAP; however, after the poll the elected deputies announced their intention to serve as representatives of the BBP. In January 1997 a new party, the Demokrat Türkiye Partisi (DTP), was established with representation in the TGNA. On 22 February 1998 the RP was officially dissolved by the Constitutional Court; the majority of its members joined the new Fazilet Partisi (FP).

Political Organizations

All activities by political parties were banned by the National Security Council (NSC) on 12 September 1980, and all political parties were dissolved on 16 October 1981, prior to the formation of a Consultative Assembly. From May 1983 new political parties were allowed to form, but their participation in the November general election was subject to strict rules. Legislation enacted in March 1986 stipulated that a party must have organizations in at least 45 provinces, and in two-thirds of the districts in each of these provinces, in order to take part in an election. A political party is recognized by the Government as a legitimate parliamentary group only if it has at least 20 deputies in the National Assembly.

In mid-1992, following the adoption of more lenient guidelines for the formation of political parties (proposed by the Demirel Administration), several new parties were established, and the left-wing CHP, dissolved in 1981, was reactivated.

Anavatan Partisi (ANAP) (Motherland Party): 13 Cad. 3, Balgat, Ankara; tel. (312) 2865000; fax (312) 2865019; f. 1983; supports free-market economic system, moderate nationalist and conservative policies, rational social justice system, integration with the EU, and closer ties with the Islamic world; Chair. MESUT YILMAZ; Sec.-Gen. YAŞAR OKUYAN.

Büyük Birlik Partisi (BBP) (Great Unity Party): Tuna Cad. 28, Yenişehir, Ankara; tel. (312) 4340920; fax (312) 4355818; f. 1993; Chair. MUHSİN YAZICIOĞLU.

Cumhuriyet Halk Partisi (CHP) (Republican People's Party): Çevre Sok. 38, Ankara; tel. and fax (312) 4685969; f. 1923 by Kemal Atatürk, dissolved in 1981 and reactivated in 1992; merged with Sosyal Demokrat Halkçı Parti (Social Democratic Populist Party) in February 1995; left-wing; Leader DENIZ BAYKAL; Sec.-Gen. ADNAN KESKIN.

Değişen Türkiye Partisi (DEPAR) (Changing Turkey Party): Aşağı Öveçler 6, Cad. 78, Sok. 15/2, Dikmen, Ankara; tel. (312) 4794875; fax (312) 4795964; f. 1998; Chair. GÖKHAN ÇAPOĞLU.

Demokrasi ve Barış Partisi (DBP) (Democracy and Peace Party): Menekşe 1, Sok. 10-A/7, Kızılay, Ankara; tel. (312) 4173587; f. 1996; pro-Kurdish; Leader REFİK KARAKOÇ.

Demokrat Türkiye Partisi (DTP) (Democratic Turkey Party): Mesrevi Sok 22, Ankara; tel. (312) 4421619; fax (312) 4386463; Leader HÜSAMETTİN CİNDORUK.

Demokratik Sol Partisi (DSP) (Democratic Left Party): Fevzi Çakmak Cad. 17, Ankara; tel. (312) 2124950; fax (312) 2213474; f. 1985; centre-left; drawing support from members of the fmr Republican People's Party; Chair. BÜLENT ECEVİT; Sec.-Gen. ZEKİ SEZER.

Doğru Yol Partisi (DYP) (True Path Party): Selanik Cad. 40, Kızılay, Ankara; tel. (312) 4172241; fax (312) 4185657; f. 1983; centre-right; replaced the Justice Party (f. 1961 and banned in 1981); Chair. TANSU ÇİLLER; Sec.-Gen. NURHAN TEKİNEL.

Fazilet Partisi (FP) (Virtue Party): Hanımeli Sok. 15/7, Sıhhıye, Ankara; tel. (312) 230 7780; f. 1997; replaced Refah Partisi (Welfare Party), dissolved by Constitutional Court; Islamic fundamentalist; interest in free-market economy; Leader RECAİ KUTAN.

Halkın Demokrasi Partisi (HADEP) (People's Democracy Party): Mithatpaşa Cad. 39/9, Kızılay, Ankara; tel. (312) 3602838; f. 1994; pro-Kurdish nationalist party; Chair. MURAT BOZLAK.

İşçi Partisi (IP) (Workers' Party): Mithatpaşa Cad. 10/8, Sıhhıye, Ankara; tel. (312) 4352999; fax (312) 4343386; f. 1992; Chair. DOĞU PERİNÇEK.

Liberal Demokratik Parti (LDP) (Liberal Democratic Party): Gazi Mustafa Kemal Bul. 108/18, Maltepe, Ankara; tel. (312) 2323374; f. 1994; Chair. BESİM TİBUK.

Millet Partisi (MP) (Nation Party): İstanbul Cad., Rüzgarlı Gayret Sok. 2, Ankara; tel. (312) 3127626; fax (312) 3127651; f. 1992; Chair. AYKUT EDİBALİ.

Milliyetçi Hareket Partisi (MHP) (Nationalist Action Party): Strazburg Cad. 36, Sihhiye, Ankara; tel. (312) 2318700; fax (312) 2311424; f. 1983; fmrly the Conservative Party; Sec.-Gen. KORAY AYDIN.

Ozgurluk ve Dayanisme Partisi (ODP) (Freedom and Solidarity Party): Necatibey Cad. 23/11, Ankara; f. 1996; Leader UFUK URAZ.

Türkiye Özürlüler Partisi (TÖP) (Turkish Party for the Handicapped): Bahçelerüstü 40, Sok. Cami Yanı 41, Saimekadın, Ankara; tel. (312) 3699082; Chair. MURAT DİILMEN.

Yeniden Doğuş Partisi (YDP) (Rebirth Party): Sağlık Sok 3, Sıhhıye, Ankara; tel. (312) 4356565; fax (312) 4356564; f. 1992; Chair. HASAN CELAL GÜZEL.

Yeni Parti (YP) (New Party): Rabat Sok 27, Gaziosmanpaşa, Ankara; tel. (312) 4469254; fax (312) 4469579; f. 1993; Leader YUSUF BOZKURT ÖZAL.

The following proscribed organizations were engaged in an armed struggle against the Government:

Partiya Karkere Kurdistan (PKK) (Kurdish Workers' Party): 57-member directorate; launched struggle for an independent Kurdistan in 1984; Leader ABDULLAH OCALAN.

Revolutionary People's Liberation Party–Front (DHKP–C): left wing faction of Dev-Sol; subsumed parent organization in 1996.

Diplomatic Representation

EMBASSIES IN TURKEY

Afghanistan: Cinnah Cad. 88, 06551 Çankaya, Ankara; tel. (312) 4381121; telex 46769; fax (312) 4387745; Ambassador: Dr ABDUL SALAM AUSEM.

Albania: Ebuziya Tevfik Sok 17, Çankaya, Ankara; tel. (312) 4411103; fax (312) 4466528; Ambassador: SAIMAR BALA.

Algeria: Şehit Ersan Cad. 42, 06680 Çankaya, Ankara; tel. (312) 4278700; telex 42053; fax (312) 4268959; Ambassador: RABAH HADID.

Argentina: Uğur Mumcu Cad. 60/3, 06700 Gaziosmanpaşa, Ankara; tel. (312) 4462062; telex 42373; fax (312) 4462063; Ambassador: JOSÉ PEDRO PICO.

Australia: Nenehatun Cad. 83, 06680 Gaziosmanpaşa, Ankara; tel. (312) 4461180; fax (312) 4461188; e-mail ausemank@ibm.tr; Ambassador: IAN FORSYTH.

Austria: Atatürk Bul. 189, Kavaklıdere, Ankara; tel. (312) 4190431; fax (312) 4189454; e-mail austramb@austria.org.tr; Ambassador: Dr RALPH SCHEIDE.

Azerbaijan: Cemal Nadir Sok 20, Çelikler Apt, Çankaya, Ankara; tel. (312) 4412621; telex 46404; fax (312) 4412600; Ambassador: MEHMET NEHROZODLU ALIEV.

Bangladesh: Cinnah Cad. 78, Çankaya, Ankara; tel. (312) 4392750; telex 46068; fax (312) 4392408; Ambassador: MAHBOOB ALAM.

Belarus: Resit Galip Cad. 85/3, 06200 Ankara; tel. (312) 4463042; fax (312) 4460150.

Belgium: Nenehatun Cad. 109, Gaziosmanpaşa, Ankara; tel. (312) 4468247; telex 46296; fax (312) 4468251; Ambassador: ALEXIS BROUHNS.

Bosnia and Herzegovina: Mahatma Gandhi Cad. 91, Gaziosmanpaşa, Ankara; tel. (312) 4464090; fax (312) 4466228; Ambassador: HAJRUDIN SOMUN.

Brazil: İran Cad. 47/1, Gaziosmanpaşa, Ankara; tel. (312) 4685320; fax (312) 4685324; Ambassador: LUIZ ANTÔNIO JARDIM GAGLIARDI.

Bulgaria: Atatürk Bul. 124, 06680 Kavaklıdere, Ankara; tel. (312) 4267455; fax (312) 4273178; Ambassador: VIKTOR VALKOV.

Canada: Nenehatun Cad. 75, 06700 Gaziosmanpaşa, Ankara; tel. (312) 4361276; fax (312) 4464437; Ambassador: MICHAEL T. MACE.

Chile: İran Cad. 45/2, Çankaya, Ankara; tel. (312) 4389444; telex 46673; fax (312) 4386145; Ambassador: JAIME PARDO.

China, People's Republic: Gölgeli Sok 34, 06700 Gaziosmanpaşa, Ankara; tel. (312) 4360628; telex 44582; fax (312) 4464248; Ambassador: YAO KUANGYI.

Croatia: Kelebek Sok 15/A, Gaziosmanpaşa, Ankara; tel. (312) 4469460; fax (312) 4366212; Ambassador: Dr I. TOMIĆ.

Cuba: Komşu Sok 7/2, 06690 Çankaya, Ankara; tel. (312) 4394110; fax (312) 4414007; Ambassador: JORGE CASTRO BENÍTEZ.

Czech Republic: Uğur Mumcu Cad. 100/3, 06700 Gaziosmanpaşa, Ankara; tel. (312) 4461244; fax (312) 4461245; Ambassador: TOMÁŠ LANÉ.

Denmark: Kırlangıç Sok 42, 06700 Gaziosmanpaşa, Ankara; tel. (312) 4667760; telex 46385; fax (312) 4684559; e-mail danemb@ada.net.tr; Ambassador: NIELS HELSKOV.

Egypt: Atatürk Bul. 126, 06680 Kavaklıdere, Ankara; tel. (312) 4261026; fax (312) 4270099; Ambassador: MAHDI FATHALLAH.

Estonia: Rävala 9, EE0100 Tallinn; tel. (372) 6317100; fax (372) 6317099; Ambassador: SVEN JÜRGENSON.

Finland: Kader Sok 44, 06700 Gaziosmanpaşa, Ankara; tel. (312) 4265921; fax (312) 4680072; Ambassador: BJÖRN EKBLOM.

France: Paris Cad. 70, 06540 Kavaklıdere, Ankara; tel. (312) 4681154; fax (312) 4679434; e-mail ambafr@ada.net.tr; Ambassador: DANIEL LEQUERTIER.

Georgia: Büyük Esat, Ulubey Sok 24, Ankara; tel. (312) 4471720; fax (312) 4471724; Chargé d'affaires: VICTOR CHIKAIDZE.

Germany: Atatürk Bul. 114, 06540 Kavaklıdere, Ankara; tel. (312) 4265465; telex 44394; fax (312) 4266959; Ambassador: HANS JOACHIM VERGAU.

Greece: Ziya ül-Rahman 9–11, 06610 Gaziosmanpaşa, Ankara; tel. (312) 4368860; telex 42146; fax (312) 4463191; Ambassador: DHIMITRIOS NAZARITIS.

Holy See: Birlik Mah. 3, Cad. 37, PK 33, 06552 Çankaya, Ankara (Apostolic Nunciature); tel. (312) 4953514; fax (312) 4953540; e-mail nunaptr@ibm.net; Apostolic Nuncio: Most Rev. PIER LUIGI CELATA, Titular Archbishop of Doclea.

Hungary: Sancak Mah. 1. Cad. 30, Yıldı, Çankaya, Ankara; tel. (312) 4422273; fax (312) 4415049; Ambassador: Dr GYÖRGY KÉRY.

India: Cinnah Cad. 77/A, 06680 Çankaya, Ankara; tel. (312) 4382195; telex 42561; fax (312) 4403429; Ambassador: K. GAJENDRA SINGH.

Indonesia: Abdullah Cevdet Sok 10, 06552 Çankaya, Ankara; tel. (312) 4382190; telex 46850; fax (312) 4382193; Ambassador: SOEMARSO H. SUEBROTO.

Iran: Tahran Cad. 10, Kavaklıdere, Ankara; tel. (312) 4274320; Ambassador: SAYED MUHAMMAD HUSEIN LAVASANI.

Iraq: Turan Emeksiz Sok 11, 06692 Gaziosmanpaşa, Ankara; tel. (312) 4687421; telex 46679; fax (312) 4684832; Ambassador: Dr SAAD AS-SEMARRAI.

Israel: Mahatma Gandhi Cad. 85, Gaziosmanpaşa, Ankara; tel. (312) 4463605; fax (312) 4261533; Ambassador: URI BAR-NER.

Italy: Atatürk Bul. 118, Kavaklıdere, Ankara; tel. (312) 4263461; telex 46603; fax (312) 4265800; e-mail itaamb@superonline.com; Ambassador: Dr MASSIMILIANO BANDINI.

Japan: Kırlangiç Sok 9, Gaziosmanpaşa, Ankara; tel. (312) 4660414; telex 42435; fax (312) 4660420; Ambassador: ATSUKO TOYAMA.

Jordan: Dede Korkut Sok 18, 06690 Çankaya, Ankara; tel. (312) 4402054; telex 43637; fax (312) 4404327; Ambassador: Dr MOUSA SULEIMAN BRAIZAT.

Kazakhstan: Ebuzziya Tevfik Sok 6, Çankaya, Ankara; tel. (312) 4412301; telex 46193; fax (312) 4412303; Ambassador: KANAT B. SAUDABAYEV.

Korea, Republic: Cinnah Cad., Alaçam Sok 5, 06690 Çankaya, Ankara; tel. (312) 4684822; telex 42680; fax (312) 4682279; Ambassador: BYUNG WOO YU.

Kuwait: Reşit Galip Cad. 110, Gaziosmanpaşa, Ankara; tel. (312) 4450576; fax (312) 4466839; Ambassador: ABDULLAH AL-MURAD.

Kyrgyzstan: Boyabat Sok 11, Eren Apt, Gaziosmanpaşa, Ankara; tel. (312) 4468408; fax (312) 4468413.

Lebanon: Kızkulesi Sok 44, Gaziosmanpaşa, Ankara; tel. (312) 4467486; telex 46063; fax (312) 4461023; Ambassador: JAFFER MUAVI.

Libya: Cinnah Cad. 60, 06690 Çankaya, Ankara; tel. (312) 4381110; telex 43270; fax (312) 4403862; Ambassador: MANSUR EL-BEDIR.

Macedonia, former Yugoslav republic: Filistin Sok 30/2, Gaziosmanpaşa, Ankara; tel. (312) 4469204; fax (312) 4469206.

Malaysia: Mahatma Gandhi 58, 06700 Gaziosmanpaşa, Ankara; tel. (312) 4468547; telex 43616; fax (312) 4464130; Ambassador: ABDUL JALIL HARON.

Mexico: Çankaya Cad. 20/2, Çankaya, Ankara; tel. (312) 4413204; fax (312) 4413203; e-mail enriqueb@dominet.in.com.tr; Ambassador: ENRIQUE BUJ FLORES.

Moldova: Gazi Osman Pasa, Captan Pasa 49, Ankara; tel. (312) 4465527; fax (312) 4465816; Ambassador: ION BOTNARU.

Morocco: Reşit Galip Cad., Rabat Sok 11, Gaziosmanpaşa, Ankara; tel. (312) 4376020; fax (312) 4468430; Ambassador: BABANA EL-ALAOUI.

Netherlands: Uğur Mumcu Cad. 16, 06700 Gaziosmanpaşa, Ankara; tel. (312) 4460170; telex 42612; fax (312) 4463358; e-mail nlgovank@domi.net.tr; Ambassador: Dr NIKOLAOS VAN DAM.

New Zealand: PK 162, İran Cad. 13/4, 06692 Kavaklıdere, Ankara; tel. (312) 4679054; fax (312) 4679013; e-mail newzealand@superonline.com; Ambassador: IAN KENNEDY.

Norway: Kelebek Sok 18, 06700 Gaziosmanpaşa, Ankara; tel. (312) 4379950; fax (312) 4376430; Ambassador: FINN K. FOSTERVOLL.

Oman: Mahatma Gandhi Cad. 63, 06700 Gaziosmanpaşa, Ankara; tel. (312) 4470630; fax (312) 4470631; Ambassador: MUHAMMAD AL-VAHIBI.

Pakistan: İran Cad. 37, 06700 Gaziosmanpaşa, Ankara; tel. (312) 4271410; fax (312) 4671023; e-mail pakinfo@ada.net.tr; Ambassador: HUMAYAN KHAN BANGASH.

Philippines: Mahatma Gandi Cad. 56, Gaziosmanpaşa, Ankara; tel. (312) 4465831; fax (312) 4465733; e-mail jochar@surf.net.tr; Ambassador: JOSE LINO B. GUERRERO.

Poland: Atatürk Bul. 241, 06650 Ankara; tel. (312) 4261694; fax (312) 4273987; Ambassador: MIROSLAW PALASZ.

Portugal: Kuleli Sok 26, 06700 Gaziosmanpaşa, Ankara; tel. (312) 4461890; fax (312) 4461892; Ambassador: JOSÉ STICHINI VILELA.

Qatar: Karaca Sok 19, 06610 Gaziosmanpaşa, Ankara; tel. (312) 4411364; fax (312) 4411544; Ambassador: Dr HASSAN ALI HUSSEIN EN-NIMAH.

Romania: Bükreş Sok 4, 06680 Çankaya, Ankara; tel. (312) 4271241; telex 42760; fax (312) 4271530; Chargé d'affaires a.i.: NIKOLAI DASKALU.

Russia: Karyağdı Sok 5, 06692 Çankaya, Ankara; tel. (312) 4392122; telex 46151; fax (312) 4401485; Ambassador: ALEKSANDR LEBEDEV.

Saudi Arabia: Turan Emeksiz Sok 6, Gaziosmanpaşa, Ankara; tel. (312) 4685540; fax (312) 4274886; Ambassador: NAJI MUFTI.

Slovakia: Atatürk Bul. 245, 06692 Kavaklıdere, Ankara; tel. (312) 4265887; fax (312) 4682689; Ambassador: JAN RITUCH.

South Africa: Filistin Cad. 27, Gaziosmanpaşa, Ankara; tel. (312) 4464056; fax (312) 4466434; Ambassador: OMAS WHEELER.

Spain: Abdullah Cevdat Sok 8, 06680 Çankaya, Ankara; tel. (312) 4380392; telex 46528; fax (312) 4395170; Ambassador: JESÚS ATIENZA.

Sudan: Koza Sok 51, Gaziasmanpaşa, Ankara; tel. (312) 4413885; telex 46719; fax (312) 4467516; Ambassador: HASSAN ADAM OMER.

Sweden: Katip Çelebi Sok 7, 06692 Kavaklıdere, Ankara; tel. (312) 4286735; telex 46273; fax (312) 4685020; Ambassador: Dr MICHAEL SAHLIN.

Switzerland: Atatürk Bul. 247, 06692 Kavaklıdere, Ankara; tel. (312) 4675555; fax (312) 4671199; e-mail 100634.3643@compuserve.com; Ambassador: ANDRÉ FAIVET.

Syria: Sedat Simari 10, 06680 Çankaya, Ankara; tel. (312) 4409657; telex 46688; fax (312) 4385609; Chargé d'affaires a.i.: MAMDOUH HAIDAR.

Tajikistan: Mahatma Gandhi Cad. 36, Gaziosmanpaşa, Ankara; tel. (312) 4461602; fax (312) 443620; Chargé d'affaires a.i.: ROUSTAM DODCNOV.

Thailand: Çankaya Cad. Kader Sok 45/3, 06700 Gaziosmanpaşa, Ankara; tel. (312) 4673409; fax (312) 4386474; Ambassador: YINGPONG NARUMITREKAGARN.

Tunisia: Kuleli Sok 12, 06700 Gaziosmanpaşa, Ankara; tel. (312) 4377100; Ambassador: AHMAD SAHNOUN.

'Turkish Republic of Northern Cyprus': Rabat Sok 20, 06700 Gaziosmanpaşa, Ankara; tel. (312) 4376031; fax (312) 4465238; Ambassador: NAZIF BORMAN.

Turkmenistan: Koza Cad. 28, Çankaya, Ankara; tel. (312) 4417122; telex 46085; fax (312) 4417125; Ambassador: NUR MUHAMMAD HANAMOV.

Ukraine: Cemal Nadir Sok 9, Çankara, Ankara; tel. (312) 4399973; fax (312) 4406815; Ambassador: OLEXANDER MOTSYK.

United Arab Emirates: Mahmut Yesari Sok 10, 06680 Çankaya, Ankara; tel. (312) 4408410; telex 46044; fax (312) 4389854; Ambassador: SALEM RASHED SALEM AL-AGROOBI.

United Kingdom: Şehit Ersan Cad. 46/A, Çankaya, Ankara; tel. (312) 4686230; telex 42320; fax (312) 4680113; Ambassador: DAVID LOGAN.

USA: Atatürk Bul. 110, Kavaklıdere, Ankara; tel. (312) 4686110; fax (312) 4409269; Ambassador: MARC PARRIS.

Uzbekistan: Ahmet Rasim Sok 14, 06550 Çankaya, Ankara; tel. (312) 4409269; telex 46028; fax (312) 4409222; Ambassador: OMAR ALI HUDAYBERDIYEV.

Venezuela: Cinnah Cad. 78/2, Çankaya, Ankara; tel. (312) 4387135; telex 46460; fax (312) 4406619; e-mail venezemb@dominet.in.com.tr; Ambassador: RAMÓN DELGADO.

Yemen: Fethiye Sok 2, 06700 Gaziosmanpaşa, Ankara; tel. (312) 4462637; fax (312) 4461778; Ambassador: MOHAMED ABDULLA AL-GAIFI.

Yugoslavia: Paris Cad. 47, Kavaklıdere, Ankara; tel (312) 4280664.

Judicial System

Until the foundation of the Turkish Republic, a large part of the Turkish civil law—the laws affecting the family, inheritance, property, obligations, etc.—was based on the Koran, and this holy law was administered by special religious (*Shari'a*) courts. The legal reform of 1926 was not only a process of secularization, but also a radical change of the legal system. The Swiss Civil Code and the Code of Obligation, the Italian Penal Code and the Neuchâtel (Cantonal) Code of Civil Procedure were adopted and modified to fit Turkish customs and traditions.

According to current Turkish law, the power of the judiciary is exercised by judicial (criminal), military and administrative courts. These courts render their verdicts in the first instance, while superior courts examine the verdict for subsequent rulings.

SUPERIOR COURTS

Constitutional Court: Consists of 11 regular and four substitute members, appointed by the President. Reviews the constitutionality of laws, at the request of the President of the Republic, parliamentary groups of the governing party or of the main opposition party, or of one-fifth of the members of the National Assembly, and sits as a high council empowered to try senior members of state. The rulings of the Constitutional Court are final. Decisions of the Court are published immediately in the Official Gazette, and shall be binding on the legislative, executive, and judicial organs of the state.

Court of Appeals: The court of the last instance for reviewing the decisions and verdicts rendered by judicial courts. It has original and final jurisdiction in specific cases defined by law. Members are elected by the Supreme Council of Judges and Prosecutors.

Council of State: An administrative court of the first and last instance in matters not referred by law to other administrative courts, and an administrative court of the last instance in general. Hears and settles administrative disputes and expresses opinions on draft laws submitted by the Council of Ministers. Three-quarters of the members are appointed by the Supreme Council of Judges and Public Prosecutors, the remaining quarter is selected by the President of the Republic.

Military Court of Appeals: A court of the last instance to review decisions and verdicts rendered by military courts, and a court of first and last instance with jurisdiction over certain military persons, stipulated by law, with responsibility for the specific trials of these persons. Members are selected by the President of the Republic from nominations made by the Military Court of Appeals.

Supreme Military Administrative Court: A military court for the judicial control of administrative acts concerning military personnel. Members are selected by the President of the Republic from nominations made by the Court.

Court of Jurisdictional Disputes: Settles disputes among judicial, administrative and military courts arising from disagreements on jurisdictional matters and verdicts.

The Court of Accounts: A court charged with the auditing of all accounts of revenue, expenditure and government property, which renders rulings related to transactions and accounts of authorized bodies on behalf of the National Assembly.

Supreme Council of Judges and Public Prosecutors: The President of the Council shall be the Minister of Justice, and the Under-Secretary to the Minister of Justice shall serve as an *ex-officio* member of the Council. Three regular and three substitute members from the Court of Appeals, together with two regular and two substitute members of the Council of State, shall be appointed to the Supreme Council by the President of the Republic for a four-year term. Decides all personnel matters relating to judges and public prosecutors.

Public Prosecutor: The law shall make provision for the tenure of public prosecutors and attorneys of the Council of State and their functions. The Chief Prosecutor of the Republic, the Chief Attorney of the Council of State and the Chief Prosecutor of the Military Court of Appeals are subject to the provisions applicable to judges of higher courts.

Military Trial: Military trials are conducted by military and disciplinary courts. These courts are entitled to try the military offences of military personnel and those offences committed against military personnel or in military areas, or offences connected with military service and duties. Military courts may try non-military persons only for military offences prescribed by special laws.

Religion

ISLAM

More than 99% of the Turkish people are Muslims. However, Turkey is a secular state. Although Islam was stated to be the official religion in the Constitution of 1924, an amendment in 1928 removed this privilege. After 1950 subsequent governments have tried to re-establish links between religion and state affairs, but secularity was protected by the revolution of 1960, the 1980 coup and the 1982 Constitution.

Diyanet İşleri Reisi (Head of Religious Affairs in Turkey): Prof. MUSTAFA SAIT YAZICIOĞLU.

CHRISTIANITY

The town of Antioch (now Antakya) was one of the earliest strongholds of Christianity, and by the the 4th century had become a patriarchal see. Formerly in Syria, the town was incorporated in Turkey in 1939. Constantinople (now İstanbul) was also a patriarchal see, and by the 6th century the Patriarch of Constantinople was recognized as the Ecumenical Patriarch in the East. Gradual estrangement from Rome developed, leading to the final breach between the Catholic West and the Orthodox East, usually assigned to the year 1054.

In 1986 it was estimated that there were about 100,000 Christians in Turkey.

The Orthodox Churches

Armenian Patriarchate: Ermeni Patrikliği, Şarapnel Sok 20–22; 34480 Kumkapı, İstanbul; tel. (212) 5170970; fax (212) 5164833; f. 1461; 45,000 adherents (1989); Patriarch KAREKIN BEDROS KAZANDJIAN.

Bulgarian Orthodox Church: Bulgar Ortodoks Kilisesi, Halâskâr Gazi Cad. 319, Şişli, İstanbul; Rev. Archimandrite GANCO ÇOBANOF.

Greek Orthodox Church: The Ecumenical Patriarchate (Rum Ortodoks Patrikhanesi), 34220 Fener-Haliç, İstanbul; tel. (212) 5319670; fax (212) 5349037; Archbishop of Constantinople New Rome and Ecumenical Patriarch BARTHOLOMEOS I.

The Roman Catholic Church

At 31 December 1996 there were an estimated 28,575 adherents in the country.

Bishops' Conference: Conferenza Episcopale di Turchia, Ölçek Sok 83, Harbiye, 80230 İstanbul; tel. (212) 2480775; fax (212) 2408801; f. 1978; Pres. Mgr LOUIS PELÂTRE (Vicar Apostolic of İstanbul).

Armenian Rite

Patriarchate of Cilicia: f. 1742; Patriarch JEAN-PIERRE XVIII KASPARIAN (resident in Beirut, Lebanon).

Archbishopric of İstanbul: Sakızağacı Cad. 31, PK 183, 80072 Beyoğlu, İstanbul; tel. (212) 2441258; fax (212) 2432364; f. 1830; Archbishop HOVHANNES TCHOLAKIAN.

Byzantine Rite

Apostolic Exarchate of İstanbul: Hamalbaşı Cad. 44, PK 259, 80070 Beyoğlu, İstanbul; tel. (212) 2497104; fax (212) 2411543; f. 1861; Vicar Delegate Rev. Archimandrite THOMAS VARSAMIS.

Bulgarian Catholic Church: Bulgar Katolik Kilisesi, Eski Parmakkapı Sok. 15, Galata, İstanbul.

Chaldean Rite

Archbishopric of Diyarbakır: Hamalbaşı Cad. 48, 80070 Beyoğlu, İstanbul; tel. (212) 2932713; fax (212) 2932064; Archbishop PAUL KARATAS.

Latin Rite

Metropolitan See of İzmir: Church of St Polycarpe, Necatibey Bul. 2, PK 267, 35212 İzmir; tel. (232) 4840531; fax (232) 4845358; Archbishop of İzmir GIUSEPPE GERMANO BERNARDINI.

Apostolic Vicariate of Anatolia: Uray Cad. 85, PK 35, 33001 Mersin; tel. (324) 2320578; fax (324) 2320595; f. 1990; Vicar Apostolic RUGGERO FRANCESCHINI, Titular Bishop of Sicilibba.

Apostolic Vicariate of İstanbul: Ölçek Sok 83, 80230 Harbiye, İstanbul; tel. (212) 2480775; fax (212) 2411543; f. 1742; Vicar Apostolic Louis Pelâtre, Titular Bishop of Sasima.

Maronite Rite

The Maronite Patriarch of Antioch is resident in Lebanon.

Melkite Rite

The Greek Melkite Patriarch of Antioch is resident in Damascus, Syria.

Syrian Rite

The Syrian Catholic Patriarch of Antioch is resident in Beirut, Lebanon.

Patriarchal Vicariate of Turkey: Sarayarkası Sok 15, PK 84, 80090 Ayazpaşa, İstanbul; tel. (212) 2432521; fax (212) 2490261; Vicar Patriarchal Rev. Yusuf Sağ.

The Anglican Communion

Within the Church of England, Turkey forms part of the diocese of Gibraltar in Europe. The Bishop is resident in England.

Archdeacon of the Aegean: Canon Jeremy Peake, (resident in Vienna, Austria).

JUDAISM

In 1996 it was estimated that there were about 25,000 Jews in Turkey.

Jewish Community of Turkey: Türkiye Hahambaşılığı, Yemenici Sok 23, Beyoğlu, 80050 Tünel, İstanbul; tel. (212) 2435166; fax (212) 2441980; Chief Rabbi David Asseo.

The Press

Almost all İstanbul papers are also printed in Ankara and İzmir on the same day, and some in Adana. Among the most serious and influential papers are the dailies *Milliyet* and *Cumhuriyet*. The weekly *Gırgır* is noted for its political satire. The most popular dailies are the İstanbul papers *Sabah, Hürriyet, Milliyet, Yeni Günaydın* and *Zaman; Yeni Asır,* published in İzmir, is the best-selling quality daily of the Aegean region. There are numerous provincial newspapers with limited circulation.

PRINCIPAL DAILIES

Adana

Yeni Adana: Abidinpaşa Cad. 56, Adana; tel. (322) 3599006; fax (322) 3593655; f. 1918; political; Propr Çetin Remzi Yüreğir; Chief Editor Ayten Çay; circ. 2,000.

Ankara

Ankara Ticaret: Rüzgârlı Sok O. V. Han 2/6, Ankara; tel. (312) 4182832; telex 42308; f. 1954; commercial; Man. Editor Nuray Tüzmen; Chief Editor Muammer Solmaz; circ. 1,351.

Belde: Rüzgarlı Gayret Sok 7/1, Ulus, Ankara; tel. (312) 3106820; f. 1968; Propr İlhan İşbilen; circ. 3,399.

Tasvir: Ulus Meydanı, Ulus İş Hanı, Kat 4, Ankara; tel. (312) 4111241; f. 1960; conservative; Editor Ender Yokdar; circ. 3,055.

Turkish Daily News: Hülya Sok 45, 06700 GOP, Ankara; tel. (312) 4475647; fax (312) 4468374; f. 1961; English language; Publisher İlhan Çevik; Editor-in-Chief İlnur Çevik; circ. 54,500.

Türkiye Ticaret Sicili: Karanfil Sok 56, Bakanlıklar, Ankara; f. 1957; commercial; Editor Yalçın Kaya Aydos.

Vakit: Konya Yolu 8km, 68 Balgat, Ankara; tel. (312) 2877906; f. 1978; Man. Editor Nali Alan; circ. 3,384.

Yeni Tanin: Ankara; f. 1964; political; Propr Burhanettin Göğen; Man. Editor Ahmet Tekeş; circ. 3,123.

Yirmidört Saat: Gazeteciler Cemiyeti Çevre Sok 35, Çankaya, Ankara; tel. (312) 1682384; f. 1978; Propr Beyhan Cenkçi.

Eskişehir

Istikbal: Köprübaşı Değirmen Cad. 19/4, Eskişehir; tel. (222) 2318975; fax (222) 2345888; f. 1950; morning; Editor Vedat Alp.

Gaziantep

Olay (Event): Gaziantep; Man. Erol Maras.

İstanbul

Apoyevmatini: İstiklâl Cad., Suriye Pasajı 348, Beyoğlu, İstanbul; tel. (212) 2437635; f. 1925; Greek language; Publr Dr Y. A. Adaşoğlu; Editor İstefan Papadopoulos; circ. 1,200.

Bugün: Medya Plaza Basın Ekspres Yolu, 34540 Güneşli, İstanbul; tel. (212) 5504850; fax (212) 5023340; f. 1989; Propr Önay Bilgin; circ. 184,884.

Cumhuriyet (Republic): Türkocağı Cad. 39, 34334 Cağaloğlu, İstanbul; tel. (212) 5120505; telex 22246; fax (212) 5138595; f. 1924; morning; liberal; Man. Editor Hikmet Çetinkaya; circ. 75,000.

Dünya (World): Yil Mahallesi 100, 34440 Bağcilar, İstanbul; tel. (212) 6290808; fax (212) 6200313; f. 1952; morning; economic; Editor-in-Chief Nezih Demirkent; circ. 50,000.

Fotomaç: Medya Plaza Basın Ekspres Yolu, 34540 Güneşli, İstanbul; tel. (212) 5504900; fax (212) 5028217; f. 1991; Chief Officer Yavuz Gürel; circ. 150,000.

Günaydın-Tan: Alayköşkü, Cad. Eryilmaz Sok 13, Cağaloğlu, İstanbul; tel. (212) 5120050; fax (212) 5260823; f. 1968; Editor-in-Chief Seckin Turesay.

Hürriyet: Babiali Cad. 15–17, Guneslikoy, 34540 Bakırköy, İstanbul; tel. (212) 5550050; telex 22249; fax (212) 5156705; f. 1948; morning; independent political; Propr Aydın Doğan; Chief Editor Ertuğrul Özkök; circ. 542,797.

Meydan (Nationalism): Yüzyıl Mahallesi, Mahmutbey Viyadüğü Altı, İkitelli, 34410 Cağaloğlu, İstanbul; tel. (212) 5056111; fax (212) 5056436; f. 1990; Propr Refik Aras; Ed. Ufuk Guldemir.

Milli Gazete: Çayhane Sok 1, 34040 Topkapı, İstanbul; tel. (212) 5674775; telex 23373; fax (212) 5674024; f. 1973; pro-Islamic; right-wing; Editor-in-Chief Ekrem Kızıltaş; circ. 51,000.

Milliyet: Doğan Medya Center, Bağcilar, 34554 İstanbul; tel. (212) 5056111; telex 22884; fax (212) 5056233; f. 1950; morning; political; Publr Aydın Doğan; Editor-in-Chief Derya Sazak; circ. 630,000.

Nor Marmara: İstiklâl Cad., Solakzade Sok 5, PK 507, İstanbul; tel. (212) 2444736; f. 1940; Armenian language; Propr and Editor-in-Chief Rober Haddeler; Gen. Man. Ari Haddeler; circ. 2,200.

Sabah (Morning): Medya Plaza, Basın Ekspres Yolu, Günesli, İstanbul; tel. (212) 5504810; fax (212) 5028143; Propr Dinç Bilgin; Editor Zafer Mutlu; circ. 550,000.

Tercüman: Sercekale Sok 4, 34370 Topkapı, İstanbul; tel. (212) 5017505; fax (212) 5446562; f. 1961; right-wing; Propr Sedat Colak; Chief Editor Nazif Okumus; circ. 32,869.

Türkiye (Turkey): Çatalçeşme Sok 17, 34410 Cağaloğlu, İstanbul; tel. (212) 5139900; telex 22000; fax (212) 5209362; f. 1970; Editor-in-Chief Kenan Akın; circ. 450,000.

Yeni Nesil (New Generation): Sanayi Cad., Selvi Sok 5, Yenibosna, Bakırköy, İstanbul; tel. (212) 5846261; telex 28620; fax (212) 5567289; f. 1970 as *Yeni Asya*; political; Editor-in-Chief Umit Simsek.

Yeniyüzyıl: Medya Plaza Basın Ekspres Yolu, 34540 Güneşli, İstanbul; tel. (212) 5028877; fax (212) 5028295.

Zaman (Time): Cobancesme, Kalendar Sok 21, 34530 Yenibosna, İstanbul; tel. (212) 5511477; fax (212) 5512822; f. 1962; morning; political, independent; Man. Editor Adem Kalac; circ. 210,000.

İzmir

Rapor: Gazi Osman Paşa Bul. 5, İzmir; tel. (232) 4254400; f. 1949; Owner Dinç Bilgin; Man. Editor Tanju Ateşer; circ. 9,000.

Ticaret Gazetesi: 1571 Sok 16, 35110 Çınarlı, 35110 İzmir; tel. (232) 4619642; fax (232) 4619646; e-mail ticinfo@unimedya.net.tr; f. 1942; commercial news; Editor-in-Chief Ahmet Sukûti Tükel; Man. Editor Cemal M. Tükel; circ. 5,009.

Yeni Asır (New Century): Yeni Asır Plaza, Ankara Cad. 3, İzmir; tel. (232) 4615000; fax (232) 4610757; e-mail yeniasır@yeniasır.com.tr; f. 1895; political; Man. Editor Aydın Bilgin; Editorial Dir Hamdi Türkmen; circ. 60,000.

Konya

Yeni Konya: Mevlâna Cad. 4, Konya; tel. (332) 2112594; f. 1945; political; Man. Editor M. Naci Gücüyener; Chief Editor Adil Gücüyener; monthly circ. 1,657.

Yeni Meram: Babu Aksaray Mah. Piroğlu Sok 4, Konya; tel. (332) 3512699; fax (332) 3507565; f. 1949; political; Propr M. Yalçın Bahçivan; Chief Editor Tufan Bahçivan; monthly circ. 25,000.

WEEKLIES

Ankara

EBA Briefing: Bestekar Sok 59/3, Kavaklıdere, Ankara; tel. (312) 4685376; telex 46836; fax (312) 4684114; f. 1975; publ. by Ekonomik Basın Ajansı (Economic Press Agency); political and economic survey; Publrs Yavuz Tolun, Melek Tolun.

Ekonomi ve Politika: Kavaklıdere, Ankara; f. 1966; economic and political; Publisher Ziya Tansu.

Türkiye İktisat Gazetesi: Karanfil Sok 56, 06582 Bakanlıklar, Ankara; tel. (312) 4184321; fax (312) 4183268; f. 1953; commercial; Chief Editor Mehmet Sağlam; circ. 11,500.

Turkish Economic Gazette: Atatürk Bul. 149, Bakanlıklar, Ankara; tel. (312) 4177700; telex 42343; publ. by UCCET.

Turkish Probe: Hülya Sok. 45, 06700 GOP, Ankara; tel. (312) 4475647; fax (312) 4468374; English language; Publr A. İlhan Çevik; Editor-in-Chief İlnur Çevik; circ. 2,500.

Antalya

Pulse: PK 7, Kemer, Antalya; tel. and fax (242) 8180105; e-mail uras@ada.net.tr; internet http://www.ada.net.tr/pulse; politics and business; English; published online; Publr VEDAT URAS.

İstanbul

Aktüel: Medya Plaza Basın Ekspres Yolu, 34540 Güneşli, İstanbul; tel. (212) 5504870; f. 1991; Gen. Man. GÜLAY GÖKTÜRK; Man. Editor ALEV ER.

Azadi Welat: İstanbul; f. 1996; pro-Kurdish nationalist.

Bayrak: Çatalçeşme Sok 50/5, 34410 Cağaloğlu, İstanbul; tel. (212) 5275575; fax (212) 5268363; f. 1970; political; Editor MEHMET GÜNGÖR; circ. 10,000.

Doğan Kardeş: Türbedar Sok 22, Cağaloğlu, İstanbul; f. 1945; illustrated children's magazine; Editor ŞEVKET RADO; circ. 40,000.

Ekonomik Panaroma: Büyükdere Cad. Ali Kaya Sok 8, 80720 Levent, İstanbul; tel. (212) 2696680; f. 1988; Gen. Man. AYDIN DEMIRER.

Ekonomist: Hürgüç Gazetecilik AŞ Hurriyet Tesisleri, Kireçocaği Mevkii, Evren Mah., Güneşli Köy, İstanbul; tel. (212) 5500050; f. 1991; Gen. Man. ADIL ÖZKOL.

Gırgır: Alayköşkü Cad., Çağaloğlu, İstanbul; tel. (212) 2285000; satirical; Propr and Editor OĞUZ ARAL; circ. 500,000.

Hıbır: İstanbul; satirical; circ. 250,000.

İkibine Doğru: Cağaloğlu, İstanbul; f. 1987; Propr MEHMET SABUNCU; Man. Editor FERIT ILSEVER.

İstanbul Ticaret: İstanbul Chamber of Commerce, Ragip Gümüşpala Cad. 84, 34378, Eminönü, İstanbul; tel. (212) 5114150; telex 31038; fax (212) 5131565; f. 1958; commercial news; Publr MEHMET YILDIRIM.

Nokta: Gelisim Yayinlari, Buyukdere Cad., Ali Kaya Sok 8, 80720 Levent, İstanbul; tel. (212) 2782930; fax (212) 2794378; Editor ARDA USKAN; circ. 60,000.

Tempo: Hürgüç Gazetecilik AŞ Hürriyet Tesisleri, Güneşli, İstanbul; tel. (212) 5500081; f. 1987; Dir SEDAT SIMAVI; Gen. Man. MEHMET Y. YILMAZ.

Türk Dünyası Araştırmalar Dergisi: Hürgüç Gazetecilik AŞ Hürriyet Tesisleri, Güneşli, İstanbul; tel. (212) 5500081; Dir SEDAT SIMAVI; Gen. Man. MEHMET Y. YILMAZ.

İzmir

Merhaba: Cumhuriyet Bul. 238/3, İzmir; f. 1979; magazine; Editor ÜMIT ÇELIKER; circ. 90,000.

PERIODICALS

Ankara

Azerbaycan Türk Kültür Dergisi: Vakıf İş Hanı 324, Anafartalar, Ankara; f. 1949; literary and cultural periodical of Azerbaizhanian Turks; Editor Dr AHMET YAŞAT.

Bayrak Dergisi: Bestckar Sok 44/5, Kavaklıdere, Ankara; f. 1964; Publr and Editor HAMI KARTAY.

Bilim ve Teknik: Bilim ve Teknik Dergisi Tübitak, Atatürk Bul. 221, Kavaklıdere, 06100 Ankara; tel. (312) 4270625; fax (312) 4276677; e-mail bteknik@tubitak.gov.tr; internet http://www.billek.-tubitak.gov.tr; f. 1967; monthly; science; Propr DINÇER ÜLKÜ; Man. Editor ZAFER KARACA.

Devlet Opera ve Balesi Genel Müdürlügü: Ankara; tel. (312) 3241476; telex 44401; fax (312) 3107248; f. 1949; state opera and ballet; Gen. Dir. RENGIM GOKMEN.

Devlet Tiyatrosu: Devlet Tiyatrosu Um. Md., Ankara; f. 1952; art, theatre.

Eğitim ve Bilim: Ziya Gökalp Cad. 48, Yenişehir, Ankara; tel. (312) 4313488; f. 1928; quarterly; education and science; publ. by the Turkish Educational Asscn (TED); Editor REFIK ÇÖLAŞAN; circ. 500.

Elektrik Mühendisliği Mecmuası: Gülden Sok. 2/A Güvenevler, Kavaklıdere, Ankara; f. 1954; publ. by the Chamber of Turkish Electrical Engineers; Pres. SEFA GÖMDENIZ.

Karınca: Türk Kooperatifçilik Kurumu, Mithatpaşa Cad. 38/A, 06420 Kızılay, Ankara; tel. (312) 4316125; fax (312) 4340646; f. 1934; monthly review publ. by the Turkish Co-operative Asscn; Editor Prof. Dr CELÂL ER; circ. 5,000.

Maden Tetkik Arama Enstitüsü Dergisi: İnönü Bul., Ankara; f. 1935; 2 a year; publ. by Mineral Research and Exploration Institute of Turkey; English Edition *Bulletin of the Mineral Research and Exploration Institute* (2 a year).

Mimarlık (Architecture): Konur Sok 4, Kızılay, Ankara; tel. (312) 4173727; fax (312) 4180361; e-mail mimarlar.odasi@service.raksnet.com.tr; f. 1963; every 2 months; publ. by the Chamber of Architects of Turkey, with a summary in English; Editor DERYA ÖZKAN; circ. 11,500.

Mühendis ve Makina: Sümer 2 Sok 36/1-A, 06640 Demirtepe, Ankara; tel. (312) 2313159; fax (312) 2313165; f. 1957; engineering; monthly; Publr Chamber of Mechanical Engineers; Propr MEHMET SOĞANCI; Editor EMIN KORAMAZ; circ. 30,000.

Teknik ve Uygulama: Konur Sok 4/4, 06442 Kızılay, Ankara; tel. (312) 4182374; f. 1986; engineering; every 2 months; publ. by the Chamber of Mechanical Engineers; Propr İSMET RIZA ÇEBI; Editor UĞUR DOĞAN; circ. 3,000.

Türk Arkeoloji Dergisi (General Directorate of Monuments and Museums): Kültür Bakanlığı, Anıtlar ve Müzeler Genel Müdürlüğü-II. Meclis Binası Ulus, Ankara; tel. (312) 3105363; fax (312) 3111417; archaeological.

Türk Dili: Türk Dil Kurumu, Atatürk Bul. 217, 06680 Kavaklıdere, Ankara; tel. (312) 4286100; fax (312) 4285288; e-mail tdili@tdk.gov.tr; internet http://www.tdk.gov.tr; f. 1951; monthly; Turkish literature and language; Editor Prof. Dr AHMET B. ERCILASUN.

Turkey—Economic News Digest: Karanfil Sok 56, Ankara; f. 1960; Editor-in-Chief BEHZAT TANIR; Man. Editor SADIK BALKAN.

Turkish Review: Atatürk Bul. 203, 06688 Kavaklıdere, Ankara; tel. (312) 4671180; telex 42384; fax (312) 4682100; f. 1985; 4 a year; cultural, social and economic; English; publ. by the Directorate General of Press and Information; Chief Officers MURAT ERSAVCI, OSMAN ÜNTÜRK, NAZAN ER, MINE CANPOLAT.

Türkiye Bankacılık: PK 121, Ankara; f. 1955; commercial; Publisher MUSTAFA ATALAY.

Türkiye Bibliyografyası: Milli Kütüphane Başkanlığı, 06490 Bahçelievler, Ankara; tel. (312) 2126200; fax (312) 2230451; f. 1928; monthly; Turkish national bibliography; publ. by the Bibliographical Centre of the Turkish National Library; Dir SEMA AKINCI.

Türkiye Makaleler Bibliyografyası: Milli Kütüphane Başkanlığı, 06490 Bahçelievler, Ankara; tel. (312) 2126200; fax (312) 2230451; e-mail bibli@kitap.mkutup.gov.tr; internet http://www.mkutup.gov.tr; f. 1952; monthly; Turkish articles, bibliography; publ. by the Bibliographical Centre of the Turkish National Library; Dir SEMA AKINCI.

İstanbul

Archaeology and Art Magazine: Hayriye Cad. 3/5 Çorlu Apt., Beyoğlu 80060, İstanbul; tel. (212) 2456838; fax (212) 2456877; f. 1978; bimonthly; publ. by Archaeology and Art Publications; Publr and Editor NEZIH BAŞGELEN.

Bankacılar: Nıspetiye Cad. Akmerkez, B3 Blok. Kat 13–14, 80630 Etiler, İstanbul; tel. (212) 2820973; fax (212) 2820946; publ. by Banks' Asscn of Turkey; quarterly.

İstanbul Ticaret Odası Mecmuası: Gümüşpala Cad. 84, 34378 Eminönü, İstanbul; tel. (212) 5114150; telex 22682; fax (212) 5131565; f. 1884; quarterly; journal of the İstanbul Chamber of Commerce (ICOC); English; Editor-in-Chief CENGIZ ERSUN.

Kulis: İstanbul; f. 1947; fortnightly arts magazine; Armenian; Publr HAGOP AYVAZ.

Musiki Mecmuası (Music Magazine): PK 666, 34435 İstanbul; tel. (216) 3306299; fax (216) 3306299; f. 1948; monthly; music and musicology; Editor ETEM RUHI ÜNGÖR.

Nûr (the Light): Nuruosmaniye Cad., Sorkun Han 28/2, 34410, Cağaloğlu, İstanbul; tel. (212) 5277607; fax (212) 5208231; e-mail sozler@ihlas.net.tr; internet www.sozler.com.tr; f. 1986; religion; Publr MEHMET NURI GÜLEÇ; Editor CEMAL UŞAK; circ. 10,000.

Pirelli Mecmuası: Büyükdere Cad. 117, Gayrettepe, İstanbul; tel. (212) 2663200; telex 26337; fax (212) 2520718; e-mail bilyay@ibm.net; f. 1964; monthly; Publr Türk-Pirelli Lâstikleri AS; Editor UĞUR CANAL; circ. 24,500.

Présence (Aylık Dergi): Ölçek Sok 82, 80230 Harbiye, İstanbul; tel. and fax (212) 2408801; f. 1986; 10 a year; publ. by the Apostolic Vicariate of İstanbul; Gen. Man. FUAT ÇOLLU.

Ruh ve Madde Dergisi (Spirit and Matter): Ruh ve Madde Publications and Health Services Co., PK 9, 80072 Beyoğlu, İstanbul; tel. (212) 2431814; fax (212) 2520718; e-mail bilyay@ibm.net; f. 1959; organ of the Foundation for Spreading the Knowledge to Unify Humanity; Editor ERGÜN ARIKDAL.

Sevgi Dünyası (World of Respect): Aydede Cad. 4/5, 80090 Taksim, İstanbul; tel. (212) 2504242; f. 1963; monthly; social, psychological and spiritual; Publr and Editor Dr REFET KAYSERILIOĞLU.

Turkey: Catalcesme Sok 17, 34410 Cağaloğlu, İstanbul; tel. (212) 5110028; telex 22000; fax (212) 5135195; e-mail turkey@ihlas.net.tr; internet http://www.turkeynewspaper.com.tr; f. 1982; monthly; English language, economics; Editor MEHMET SOZTUTAN; circ. 80,000.

Türkiye Turing ve Otomobil Kurumu Belleteni: Oto Sanayi Sitesi Yanı Gamlık Cad. 2, Levent, İstanbul; tel. (212) 2314631; f. 1930; quarterly; publ. by the Touring and Automobile Club of Turkey; Publr Prof. NEJAT ÖLCAY; Editor ÇELIK GÜLERSOY.

Varlık: Cağaloğlu Yokuşu 40/2, İstanbul; tel. and fax (212) 5226924; e-mail varlik@varlik.com.tr; internet http://www.varlik.com.tr;

f. 1933; monthly; literary; Editors FİLİZ NAYIR DENİZTEKİN, ENVER ERCAN; circ. 4,000.

İzmir

İzmir Ticaret Odası Dergisi: Atatürk Cad. 126, 35210 İzmir; tel. (232) 4417777; telex 52331; fax (232) 4837853; f. 1927; every 2 months; publ. by Chamber of Commerce of İzmir; Sec.-Gen. Prof. Dr İLTER AKAT; Man. ÜMIT ALEMDAROĞLU.

Konya

Çağrı Dergisi: PK 99, Konya; f. 1957; monthly; literary; Editor FEYZI HALICI.

NEWS AGENCIES

Anatolian News Agency: Hanımeli Sok 7, Sihhıye, Ankara; tel. (312) 2317000; telex 42088; fax (312) 2312174; f. 1920; Chair. ALI AYDIN DUNDAR; Gen. Dir BEHIÇ EKŞI.

ANKA Ajansı: Selanık Cad. 417/8, Kızılay, Ankara; tel. (312) 4172500; telex 42809; fax (312) 4180254; Dir-Gen. MÜŞERREF HEKIM-OĞLU.

Bagımsiz Basın Ajansı (BBA): Saglam Fikir Sok 11, Esentepe, İstanbul; tel. (212) 2122936; fax (212) 2122940.

EBA Ekonomik Basın Ajansı (Economic Press Agency): Bestekar Sok 59/3, Kavakıdere, 06680 Ankara; tel. (312) 4685376; telex 46836; fax (312) 4684114; e-mail ebainfo@superonline.com; internet http://www.ebanews.com; f. 1969; private economic news service; Propr MELEK TOLUN; Editor YAVUZ TOLUN.

Hürriyet Haber Ajansı: Hürriyet Medya Towers, Güneşli, İstanbul; tel. (212) 5500050; telex 22249; fax (212) 5223155; f. 1963; Dir-Gen. UĞUR ÇEBECI.

İKA Haber Ajansı (Economic and Commercial News Agency): Atatürk Bul. 199/A-45, Kavaklıdere, Ankara; tel. (312) 1267327; telex 42569; f. 1954; Dir ZIYA TANSU.

Milha News Agency: Doğan Medya Center, Bağcılar, 34554 İstanbul; tel. (212) 5056111; telex 22251; fax (212) 5056233.

Ulusal Basın Ajansı (UBA): Meşrutiyet Cad. 5/10, Ankara; Man. Editor OĞUZ SEREN.

Foreign Bureaux

Agence France-Presse (AFP): And Sok 8/13, Çankaya, Ankara; tel. (312) 4689680; fax (312) 4689683; e-mail afpank@ada.net.tr; Correspondent FLORENCE BIEDERMANN.

Agenzia Nazionale Stampa Associata (ANSA) (Italy): Sedat Simavi Sok 30/5, Ankara; tel. (312) 4406084; telex 44337; fax (312) 4405029; Correspondent ROMANO DAMIANI.

Associated Press (AP) (USA): Tunus Cad. 87/3, Kavaklıdere, Ankara; tel. (312) 4282709; telex 42340; Correspondent EMEL ANIL.

Bulgarska Telegrafna Agentsia (BTA) (Bulgaria): Hatır Sok. 25/6, Gaziosmanpaşa, Ankara; tel. (312) 4273899; Correspondent LUBOMIR GABROVSKI.

Deutsche Presse-Agentur (dpa) (Germany): Yesil Yalı Sok, Liman Apt 6/6 Yesilköy, İstanbul; tel. (212) 5738607; telex 44356; Correspondent BAHADETTIN GÜNGÖR.

Informatsionnoye Telegrafnoye Agentstvo Rossii—Telegrafnoye Agentstvo Suverennykh Stran (ITAR—TASS) (Russia): Romşu Sok 7/7, Ankara; tel. (312) 4405781; fax (312) 4391955; Correspondent ANDREI PALARIA.

Reuters: Emirhan Cad. 145/A, Dikilitaş Beşiktaş, 80700 İstanbul; tel. (212) 2750875; fax (212) 2116794; Gen. Man. SAMEEH EL-DIN.

United Press International (UPI) (USA): Cağaloğlu, İstanbul; tel. (212) 2285238; telex 22350; Correspondent ISMET İMSET.

Xinhua (New China) News Agency (People's Republic of China): Horasan Sok 16/4, Gaziosmanpaşa, Ankara; tel. (312) 4361456; telex 46138; fax (312) 4465229; Correspondent WANG QIANG.

Zhongguo Xinwen She (China News Agency) (People's Republic of China): Nenehatun Cad. 88-2, Ata Apartmanı, Gaziosmanpaşa, Ankara; tel. (312) 4362261; Correspondent CHANG CHILIANG.

AFP also has representatives in İstanbul and İzmir; AP is also represented in İstanbul.

JOURNALISTS' ASSOCIATION

Gazeteciler Cemiyeti: Cağaloğlu, İstanbul; tel. (212) 5138300; telex 23508; fax (212) 5268046; f. 1946; Pres. NECMI TANYOLAÇ; Sec. RIDVAN YELE.

Publishers

Afa Yayıncılık: Istikal Cad., Bekar Sok 17, Beyoğlu, İstanbul; tel. (212) 2453967; fax (212) 2444362; f. 1985; arts, politics, biography; Pres. ATIL ANT.

Alkim Kitapcılık Yayımcılık: Maregal Fevzi Cad. 6/A, 06500 Ankara; tel. (312) 2226075; fax (312) 2151491; non-fiction.

Altın Kitaplar Yayınevi Anonim ŞTİ: Celal Ferdi Gökçay Sok, Nebioğlu Han, Kat. 1, Cağaloğlu, İstanbul; tel. (212) 5268012; telex 22627; fax (212) 5268011; f. 1959; fiction, non-fiction, biography, children's books, encyclopaedias, dictionaries; Publrs FETHI UL, TURHAN BOZKURT; Chief Editor MÜRSIT UL.

Archaeology and Art Publs: Hayriye Cad. 3/4 Gorlu Apt., Beyoğlu, 80060 İstanbul; tel. (212) 2456838; fax (212) 2456877; f. 1978; classical, Byzantine and Turkish studies, art and archaeology, numismatics and ethnography books; Publr NEZIH BASGELEN.

Arkadas-Adas AŞ: Mithatpaşa Cad. 28c, 06441 Yenisehir, Ankara; tel. (312) 4344624; fax (312) 4356057; e-mail arkadas@arkadas .com.tr; internet http://www.arkadas.com.tr; f. 1979; fiction, educational and reference books; Pres. CUMHUR ÖZDEMIR.

Elif Kitabevi: Sahaflar Çarşısı 4, Beyazıt, İstanbul; tel. (212) 5222096; f. 1956; all types of publications, especially historical, literary; political, drama and reference; old Ottoman and Turkish books and periodicals; Publr ARSLAN KAYNARDAĞ.

IKI NOKTA (Research Press & Publications Industry & Trade Ltd): Moda, Cad. 100, 81300 İstanbul; tel. (216) 4180319; fax (216) 3376756; e-mail ikinokta@superonline.com; humanities; Pres. YÜCEL YAMAN.

Iletisim Yayınları: Klodfarer Cd Iletisim Hon 7/2, Cağaloğlu, 34400 İstanbul; f. 1984; arts, humanities, fiction.

Inkilap Kitabevi: Ankara Cad. 95, Sirkeci, İstanbul; tel. (212) 5140610; fax (212) 5140612; f. 1935; general reference and fiction; Man. Dirs N. FIKRI, J. FIKRI, E. FIKRI.

Kabalci Yayınevi: Himaye-i Etfal Sok 8-B, 34410 Cağaloğlu, İstanbul; tel. (212) 5268586; fax (212) 5268495; art, history, literature, social sciences; Pres. SABRI KABALCI.

Karacan Yayınları: Köyaltı Mevki Oruç Reis Sok 10, Yenibosna, Bakırköy, İstanbul; tel. (212) 5038714; fax (212) 5528353; f. 1980; literary books and magazines; subsidiary of Karacan Media AŞ; Gen. Man. ALI NACI KARACAN.

Kök Yayıncılık: Konur Sok. 8/6, 06550 Kızılay, Ankara; tel. (312) 4172868; fax (312) 4315013; f. 1987; childcare, education, health.

Metis Yayınları: Ipek Sok. 9, 80060 Beyoğlu, İstanbul; tel. (212) 2454509; fax (212) 2454519; f. 1982; fiction, literature, non-fiction, social sciences.

Nurdan Yayınları Sanayi ve Ticaret Ltd Sti: Prof. Kazim Ismail Gürkan Cad. 13, Kati 9, 34410 Cağaloğlu, İstanbul; tel. (212) 5225504; fax (212) 5126329; f. 1983; Pres. ÇETIN TÜZÜNER.

Parantez Yayınları AŞ: Istikal Cad. 212 Anzavur Pasaji B Kat 8, Galatasaray, İstanbul; tel. and fax (212) 2528567; f. 1991; Publr METIN ZEYNIOĞLU.

Poyraz Dış Ticaret AŞ: Lalaşahin Sok 107, 80250 Feriköy, İstanbul; tel. (212) 2489383; telex 28040; fax (212) 2345521; business directories; Gen. Man. AHMET ÜNVER.

Remzi Kitabevi AŞ: Selvili Mescit Sok 3, 34440 Cağaloğlu, İstanbul; tel. (212) 5139424; fax (212) 5229055; e-mail post@remzi .com.tr; internet http://www.remzi.com.tr; f. 1927; general and educational; Dirs EROL ERDURAN, ÖMER ERDURAN, AHMET ERDURAN.

Saray Medikal Yayın Tıc Ltd Sti: 168 Sok. 5/1, Bornova, İzmir; tel. (232) 3394969; fax (232) 3733700; e-mail eozkarahan@ novell.cs.eng.dev.edu.tr; f. 1993; medicine, social sciences.

Seckin Yayınevi: Saglik Sok. 19B, 06410 Sihhiye, Ankara; tel. (312) 4353030; fax (312) 4352472; e-mail kotayk@dominet.in.com.tr; f. 1959; accounting, computer science, economics, law.

Türk Dil Kurumu (Turkish Language Institute): Atatürk Bul. 217, 06680 Kavaklıdere, Ankara; tel. (312) 4268124; fax (312) 4285288; e-mail bilgi@tdk.gov.tr; internet http://tdk.gov.tr; f. 1932; non-fiction, research, language; Pres. Prof. Dr AHMET B. ERCILASUN.

Varlık Yayınları: Cağaloğlu Yokuşu 40/2, İstanbul; tel. (212) 5129528; fax (212) 5226924; e-mail varlik@varlik.com.tr; internet http://www.varlik.com.tr; f. 1946; fiction and non-fiction books; Dirs FILIZ NAYIR DENİZTEKİN, OSMAN DENİZTEKİN.

Government Publishing House

Ministry of Culture: Hanimeli Sok. 11, 06430 Sihhiye, Ankara; tel. (312) 2321965; fax (312) 2315036; f. 1973; Vice-Dir PELIN KIRALOĞLU.

PUBLISHERS' ASSOCIATION

Türkiye Yayıncılar Birliği Derneği (The Publishers' Association of Turkey): Kazım Ismail Gürkan Cad. 12, Ortaklar Han Kat 3/17, Cağaloğlu, İstanbul; tel. (212) 5125602; fax (212) 5117794; f. 1985; Pres. ATIL ANT; Sec. METIN CELAL ZEYNIOĞLU; 214 mems.

Broadcasting and Communications

TELECOMMUNICATIONS

General Directorate of Communications: 90 Str. no. 5, 06338 Ankara; tel. (312) 2128088; fax (312) 2121775; regulatory authority; Dir-Gen. HAYRETTIN SOYTAS.

Turk Telekomunikayson AŞ: Ankara; 20% to be privatized in 1998; provides telecoms services throughout Turkey.

Turkcell: Ankara; subsidiary of Turk Telekomunikayson AŞ; provides mobile cellular services.

BROADCASTING

Regulatory Authority

Broadcasting High Council: Ankara; f. 1994; responsible for issuing licences, drafting regulations for cable and satellite transmissions; verifies compliance of broadcasts with the 'public and national interest'.

Radio

Türkiye Radyo Televizyon Kurumu (TRT) (Turkish Radio-Television Corpn): Merkez Kütüphane, Oran, 06450 Ankara; tel. (312) 4901730; telex 46826; fax (312) 4901733; f. 1964; controls Turkish radio and television services incl. three national radio-broadcasting networks; Head of Radio BENGI BAYTUR.

Voice of Turkey; PK 333, 06443 Yenişehir, Ankara; tel. (312) 4909800; fax (312) 4909845; foreign service of the TRT; Man. Dir MEHMET KARABEYOĞLU.

There are also more than 50 local radio stations, an educational radio service for schools and a station run by the Turkish State Meteorological Service. The US forces have their own radio and television service.

Television

Türkiye Radio Television Kurumu (TRT): (See Radio, above); five national channels in 1998; channel one provides 24 hr service; channels two-five provide reduced service; Head of Television ÇETIN IZBUL; Dir. Ankara TV SABAHATTIN ALPDOĞAN.

Finance

(cap. = capital; res = reserves; dep. = deposits; m. = million; brs = branches; amounts in Turkish liras unless otherwise stated)

The Central Bank of the Republic of Turkey was originally founded in 1930, and constituted in its present form in 1970. The central bank is the bank of issue and is also responsible for the execution of monetary and credit policies, the regulation of the foreign and domestic value of the Turkish lira jointly with the government, and the supervision of the credit system. In 1987 a decree was issued to bring the governorship of the Central Bank under direct government control.

Several banks were created by special laws to fulfil specialized services for particular industries. Etibank operates primarily in the extractive industries and electric power industries; the Ziraat Bankası makes loans for agriculture; the Emlâk Bankası participates in industrial undertakings and the construction of all types of building.

The largest of the private sector Turkish banks is the Türkiye İş Bankası, which operates 831 branches.

There are several credit institutions in Turkey, including the Sınai Kalınma Bankası (Industrial Development Bank), which was founded in 1950, with the assistance of the World Bank, to encourage private investment in industry by acting as underwriter in the issue of share capital.

There are numerous co-operative organizations, including agricultural co-operatives in rural areas. There are also a number of savings institutions.

In 1990 the Turkish Government announced plans to establish a structure for offshore banking. A decree issued in October 1990 exempted foreign banks, operating in six designated free zones, from local banking obligations.

BANKING

Central Bank

Türkiye Cumhuriyet Merkez Bankası AŞ (Central Bank of the Republic of Turkey): Head Office, İstiklal Cad. 10, 06100 Ulus, Ankara; tel. (312) 3103646; telex 44033; fax (312) 3107434; f. 1931; bank of issue; cap. 25,000.0m., res 11,178,501.8m., dep. 2,280,785,502.6m. (Dec. 1996); Gov. GAZI ERÇEL; 21 brs.

State Banks

İller Bankası (Municipalities Bank): Atatürk Bul. 21, 06053 Ulus, Ankara; tel. (312) 3103141; telex 42724; fax (312) 3107459; f. 1933;

cap. 10,800,000m., res 143,117m., total assets 38,382,374m. (Dec. 1995); Chair. and Gen. Man. NIHAT BAŞ; 1 br.

Türkiye Cumhuriyeti Ziraat Bankası (Agricultural Bank of the Republic of Turkey): Atatürk Bul. 42, 06107 Ulus, Ankara; tel. (312) 3103750; telex 44004; fax (312) 3101135; f. 1863; cap. 17,088,101m., res 35,507,899m., dep. 1,450,470,243m. (Dec. 1996); Chair. and Gen. Man. SELÇUK DEMIRALP; 1,256 brs.

Türkiye Emlâk Bankası AŞ (Real Estate Bank of Turkey): Büyükdere Cad., Maslak Meydanı 43/45, 80670 Levent, İstanbul; tel. (212) 2761610; telex 27780; fax (212) 2761659; f. 1988 by merger; absorbed Denizcilik Bankası TAŞ in 1992; cap. 7,612,126m., res 22,943,914m., dep. 405,292,114m. (Dec. 1996); Chair. and Pres. ERDIN ARI; 404 brs.

Türkiye Halk Bankası AŞ: İlkiz Sok 1, Sıhhiye, Ankara; tel. (312) 2317500; telex 44201; fax (312) 4274716; f. 1938; absorbed Turkiye Öğretmenler Bankası TAŞ in May 1992; cap. and res 30,917,857m., dep. 607,748,808m. (Dec. 1996); Gen. Man. YENAL ANSEN; 760 brs.

Türkiye İhracat Kredi Bankası AŞ (Türk Eximbank) (Export Credit Bank of Turkey): Milli Müdafa Cad. 20, 06100 Bakanlıklar, Ankara; tel. (312) 4171300; telex 46106; fax (312) 4257896; f. 1987; fmrly Devlet Yatırım Bankası AŞ (f. 1964); cap. 15,000,000m., res 9,762,962m., total assets 312,794,890m. (March 1997); extends credit to exporters, insures and guarantees export transactions; Chair. and CEO H. CAN YEŞILADA.

Türkiye Kalkınma Bankası AŞ (Development Bank of Turkey): İzmir Cad. 35, 06570 Kızılay, Ankara; tel. (312) 4181515; telex 43206; fax (312) 4254896; f. 1976, renamed in 1988 and in 1989 merged with Türkiye Cumhuriyeti Turizm Bankası AŞ; cap. 1,941,771m., dep. 11,735,557.9m. (Dec. 1995); Chair. and Gen. Man. Dr CANDAN KARLITEKIN; 4 brs.

Türkiye Vakıflar Bankası TAO (Foundation Bank of Turkey): Atatürk Bul. 207, 06683 Kavaklıdere, Ankara; tel. (312) 4681160; telex 46023; fax (312) 4684541; f. 1954; cap. 12,000,000m., res 7,543,000m., dep. 436,458,000m. (Dec. 1996); Gen. Man. ALTAN KOÇER; 329 brs.

Principal Commercial Banks

Akbank TAŞ: Sabancı Center, 4 Levent, 80745 İstanbul; tel. (212) 2699041; telex 24134; fax (212) 2818188; f. 1948; cap. 18,000,000m., res 30,682,287m., dep. 340,437,559m. (Dec. 1996); Chair. NAIM TALU; Gen. Man. ÖZEN GÖKSEL; 506 brs.

Bank Ekspres AŞ: Istınye Yokuşu, 80860 Istınye, İstanbul; tel. (212) 2852525; telex 39511; fax (212) 2854646; f. 1992; cap 5,000,000m., dep. 66,747,000m., total assets 93,622,000m. (Dec. 1997); Chair KORKMAZ YIĞIT; Pres. and CEO SAVAŞ ÖZCAN; 20 brs.

Demirbank TAŞ: Büyükdere Cad. 122, Blok B, 80280 Esentepe, İstanbul; tel. (212) 2751900; telex 27368; fax (212) 2731988; f. 1953; cap. 16,500,000m., res 3,704,855m., dep. 371,326,069m. (Dec. 1997); Chair. NURI CINGILLIOGLU; Gen. Man. and CEO SELAHATTIN SERBEST; 71 brs.

Egebank AŞ: Büyükdere Cad. 106, 80280 Esentepe, İstanbul; tel. (212) 2887400; telex 39491; fax (212) 2887316; internet http://www.egebank.com.tr; f. 1928; cap. 8,000,000m., res 14,500,000m., dep. 128,600,000m. (Dec. 1997); Chair. HUSSEIN BAYRAKTAR; Vice Chair. and CEO SAMI ERDEM; 60 brs.

Eskişehir Bankası TAŞ (Esbank): Meşrutiyet Cad. 141, 80050 Tepebaşı, İstanbul; tel. (212) 2517270; telex 24535; fax (212) 2432396; f. 1927; cap. 10,000,000m., res 3,607,724m., dep. 124,765,472m. (April 1997); Chair. MESUT EREZ; Gen. Man. CANKUT LAC; 74 brs.

Etibank AŞ: Tunus Cad. 33, 06680 Kavaklıdere, Ankara; tel. (312) 4194579; telex 46894; fax (312) 4194576; f. 1935; privatized 1998; cap. US $26m., dep. $506m. (Dec. 1994); Chair. DINC BILGIN; Gen. Man. ŞÜKRÜ KARAHASANOĞLU; 140 brs.

Finansbank AŞ: Büyükdere Cad. 123, 80300 Mecidiyeköy, İstanbul; tel. (212) 2752450; telex 39280; fax (212) 2752496; f. 1987; cap. 5,000,000m., res 4,022,959m., dep. 90,056,362m. (Dec. 1996); Man. Dir Dr ÖMER ARAS; 44 brs.

İktisat Bankası TAŞ: Büyükdere Cad. 165, 80504 Esentepe, İstanbul; tel. (212) 2747111; telex 26021; fax (212) 2747028; f. 1927; cap. 10,000,000m.; res 15,715,169m., dep. 132,440,849m. (Dec. 1997); Gen. Man. ISMAIL EMEN; 37 brs.

Interbank (Uluslararası Endüstri ve Ticaret Bankası AŞ): Büyükdere Cad. 108/C, 80496 Esentepe, İstanbul; tel. (212) 2742000; telex 26098; fax (212) 2728422 f. 1888; cap. 8,659,449m., res 1,078,521m., dep. 102,490,595m. (May 1997); specializes in import and export financing; Chair. ERMAN YERDELEN; CEO NEDIM ÖLÇER; 32 brs.

Koçbank AŞ: Barbaros Bul. Mörbasan Sok Koza İş Merkezi, Blok C, 80700 Beşiktaş, İstanbul; tel. (212) 2747777; telex 39069; fax (212) 2889369; f. 1986; cap. 4,000,000m., res 8,640,185m., dep. 33,702,178m. (Dec. 1995); Gen. Man. ENGIN AKÇAKOCA; 59 brs.

Körfezbank AŞ: Büyükdere Cad., Doğus Han 42–44, Kat 3–4, 80290 Mecidiyeköy, İstanbul; tel. (212) 2882000; telex 39714; fax (212) 2881217; f. 1988; cap. 5,000,000m., res 1,229,634m., dep. 105,490,869m. (Dec. 1996); Gen. Man. HÜSNÜ AKHAN; 5 brs.

Osmanli Bankasi AŞ (Ottoman Bank): Voyvoda Cad. 35-37, Karaköy, İstanbul; tel. (212) 2523000; telex 24828; fax (212) 2526138; internet http://www.ottomanbank.com.tr; f. 1863; cap. 15,000,000m., res 5,322,000m., dep. 230,748,000m. (Dec. 1997); Chair. AYHAN ŞAHENK; CEO ACLAN ACAR; 72 brs.

Pamukbank TAŞ: Büyükdere Cad. 82, 80450 Gayrettepe, İstanbul; tel. (212) 2723484; telex 26959; fax (212) 2758217; f. 1955; cap. 30,000,000m., res 16,459,000m., dep. 655,565,000m. (Dec. 1997); Pres. and CEO ORHAN EMIRDAĞ; 170 brs.

Şekerbank TAŞ: Atatürk Bul. 171, 06680 Kavaklıdere, Ankara; tel. (312) 4179120; telex 42679; fax (312) 4257645; f. 1953; cap. 1,300,000m., res 4,770,000m., dep. 55,812,000m. (Dec. 1996); Gen. Man. HASAN BASRİ GÖKTAN; 204 brs.

Sümerbank AŞ: Eski Buyukdere Cad., Ayagaza Ticaret Merkezi 13, Maslak, 80670 Istanbul; tel. (212) 2764363; telex 26939; fax (212) 2766791; f. 1933; cap. 5,500,000., res 2,407,438m., dep. 72,190,989m. (Dec. 1996); Gen. Man. ISMAIL EMEN; 79 brs.

Toprakbank AŞ: Büyükdere Cad. 23, 80220 Şişli, İstanbul; tel. (212) 2415478; telex 26012; fax (212) 2473430; f. 1992; cap. 12,500,000m., res 2,666,000m., dep. 300,801,000m. (Dec. 1997); Gen. Man. VEYSEL BILEN; 95 brs.

Türk Dış Ticaret Bankası AŞ (Turkish Foreign Trade Bank): Yıldız Posta Cad. 54, 80280 Gayrettepe, İstanbul; tel. (212) 2744280; telex 27992; fax (212) 2725278; f. 1964; cap. 3,500,000m., dep. 63,075,612m., total assets 75,820,336m. (Dec. 1996); Gen. Man. HALİL EROĞLU; 37 brs.

Türk Ekonomi Bankası AŞ: Meclisı Mebusan Cad. 35, 80040 Fındıklı, İstanbul; tel. (212) 2512121; telex 25358; fax (212) 2496568; f. 1927; fmrly Kocaeli Bankası TAŞ; cap. 5,500,000m., dep. 106,755,865m. (Dec. 1997); Chair. YAVUZ CANEVİ; Man. Dir. Dr AKIN AKBAYGIL; 10 brs.

Türk Ticaret Bankası AŞ (Türkbank): Yıldız Posta Cad. 2, 80280 Gayrettepe, İstanbul; tel. (212) 2885900; telex 31380; fax (212) 2886123; f. 1913; f. 1913; scheduled for privatization in 1998; cap. 3,000,000m., res 3,628,032m., dep. 83,328,250m. (Dec. 1995); Chair. URAL ŞEKERCI; Gen. Man. ZAFER KÜLTÜRLÜ; 274 brs.

Türkiye Garanti Bankası AŞ: Büyükdere Cad. 63, 80670 Maslak, İstanbul; tel. and fax (212) 2854040; telex 27635; f. 1946; cap. 18,000,000m., dep. 306,521,837m., total assets 599,374,633m. (Dec. 1996); Chair. AYHAN ŞAHENK; 180 brs.

Türkiye İmar Bankası TAŞ: Büyükdere Cad. Doğuş Han. 42-46, 80300 Mecidiyeköy, İstanbul; tel. (212) 2751190; telex 26646; fax (212) 2724720; f. 1928; cap. 7,000,000m., res 184,888m., dep. 125,456,525 (Dec. 1996); Chair. KEMAL UZAN; Gen. Man. HİLMİ BASARAN; 150 brs.

Türkiye İş Bankası AŞ (İşbank): Atatürk Bul. 191, 06684 Kavaklıdere, Ankara; tel. (312) 4139900; telex 46119; fax (312) 4139090; internet http://www.isbank.com.tr; f. 1924; cap. 10,000,000m., res 38,627,589m., dep. 532,236,895m. (Dec. 1996); Chair. BURHAN KARAGÖZ; CEO ÜNAL KORUKÇU; 841 brs.

Türkiye Tütüncüler Bankası Yaşarbank AŞ: Barbaros Bul. 121, 80700 Balmumcu-Beşiktas, İstanbul; tel. (212) 2758400; telex 26000; fax (212) 2724110; f. 1924; cap. 15,955,000m., res 2,319,000m., dep. 251,433,000m. (Dec. 1997); Chair. SELÇUK YAŞAR; CEO and Man. Dir. NADIR TOPÇUOĞLU; 84 brs.

Ulusal Bank TAŞ: Büyükdere Cad., Maslak Plaza 69, Maslak 80670,İstanbul; tel. (212) 2859797; telex 27226; fax (212) 2859930; f. 1985 as Saudi American Bank, renamed Jan. 1997; cap. 5,000,000m., res 625,702m., dep. 2,477,811m. (June 1998); Gen. Man. GÜRHAN BERKER.

Yapı ve Kredi Bankası AŞ: Yapı Kredi Plaza, Blok A, Büyükdere Cad., 80620 Levent, İstanbul; tel. (212) 2801111; telex 25030; fax (212) 2801670; f. 1944; cap. 25,779,600m., res 15,145,554m., dep. 449,296,342m. (Dec. 1996); Chair. RONA YIRCALI; CEO BURHAN KARAÇAM; 414 brs.

Development and Investment Banks

Park Yatırım Bankası AŞ: Büyükdere Cad., Meşeli Sok 9, Kat 4, 80620 Levent, İstanbul; tel. (212) 2814820; telex 27117; fax (212) 2780445; f. 1992; cap. 143,474m., dep. 116,581m. (Dec. 1995); Chair. HASAN KARAMEHMET; Gen. Man. RIZA SUAT GÖKDEL.

Sınai Yatırım Bankası AŞ (Industrial Investment Bank of Turkey): Büyükdere Cad. 129, Esentepe, 80300 İstanbul; tel. (212) 2131600; telex 26263; fax (212) 2131303; f. 1963; cap. 1,000,000m., res 577,771m., dep. 19,766,106m. (Dec. 1996); Chair. CAHİT KOCAÖMER; Gen. Man. AHMET TÜREL AYAYDIN.

Türkiye Sınai Kalkınma Bankası AŞ (Industrial Development Bank of Turkey): PK 17, Karaköyı, 80002 İstanbul; tel. (212) 2512792; telex 24344; fax (212) 2432975; e-mail urasn@tskb.com.br;

internet http://www.tskb.com.tr; f. 1950; cap. 5,000,000m., res 1,185,194m. (Dec. 1997), dep 1,035,020m. (June 1997); Chair. İLHAN EVLİYAOĞLU; Pres. B. SAFA OCAK; 2 brs.

Foreign Banks

ABN AMRO NV (Netherlands): İnönü Cad. 15/17, 80090 Gümüşsuyu, İstanbul; tel. (212) 2938802; telex 24677; fax (212) 2492008; f. 1921; cap. 20,000m., res 1,359m., dep. 54,950m. (Dec. 1991); Gen. Man. JACK GILLESPIE; 1 br.

Arap Türk Bankası AŞ (Arab Turkish Bank): Vali Konağı Cad. 10, PK 380, 80220 Nişantaşı, İstanbul; tel. (212) 2250500; telex 26830; fax (212) 2250526; f. 1977; cap. 1,300,000m., res 258,372m., dep. 12,741,493m. (Dec. 1996); 48% owned by Libyan Arab Foreign Bank; Chair. YENAL CEVHERİOĞLU; Gen. Man. AYAD S. DAHAIM; 6 brs.

Banca di Roma (Italy): Tünel Cad. 18, PK 211, 80000 Karaköy, İstanbul; tel. (212) 2510917; telex 25440; fax (212) 2496289; f. 1911; cap. 26,777m., res 5,868m. (Dec. 1992); Gen. Man. STEFANO GERMINI; 2 brs.

Bank Mellat (Iran): Büyükdere Cad. Binbirçiçek Sok 1, PK 67, 80620 Levent, İstanbul; tel. (212) 2695820; telex 26502; fax (212) 2642895; f. 1982; cap. 420,514m., res 22,680m., dep. 1,863,484m. (April 1997); Chair. MOHAMMAD MATIN FAR; 2 brs.

BNP-Ak-Dresdner Bank AŞ: Taki Zafer Cad., Vakıf Han C Blok Kat. 4, 80090 Taksim, İstanbul; tel. (212) 2938780; telex 25721; fax (212) 2436742; f. 1985; cap. 1,400,000m., dep. 10,366,901m. (Dec. 1996); Chair. EROL SABANCI.

Chase Manhattan Bank (USA): Kat 11, Atakule A Blok, Enurhan Cad. 145, Beşiktaş, 80700 İstanbul; tel. (212) 2279700; fax (212) 2279729; f. 1984; cap. 30,000m., res 1,458m., dep. 72,340m. (Dec. 1991); Gen. Man. ISAK ANTIKA; 1 br.

Citibank (USA): Abdi Ipekci Cad. 65, 80200, İstanbul; tel. (212) 1414300; telex 26277; fax (212) 1415014; f. 1981; cap. 207,537m., res 22,032m., dep. 302,100m. (March 1994); Gen. Man. ANJUM Z. IQBAL; 3 brs.

Habib Bank Ltd (Pakistan): Abide-i Hürriyet Cad. 12, PK 8, 80260 Şişli, İstanbul; tel. (212) 2460220; telex 27849; fax (212) 2340807; f. 1983; cap. 50,000m., res 1,905m., dep. 82,762m. (Dec. 1997); Gen. Man. HAMIDULLAH SAIF; 1 br.

Kuwait Turkish Evkaf Finance House: Büyükdere Cad. 97, Mecidiyekö, 80300 İstanbul; tel. (212) 2752435; telex 39426; fax (212) 2748425; f. 1988; cap. 1,244,726m., res 274,937m., dep. 29,023,718m. (Dec. 1996); Gen. Man. YUNUS NACAR.

Midland Bank AŞ (England) (UK): Cumhuriyet Cad. Elmadağ Han 8, 80200 Elmadağ, İstanbul; tel. (212) 2315560; telex 38385; fax (212) 2305300; f. 1990; cap. 30,000m., res 738,000m., dep. 2,894,916m. (Dec. 1995); Gen. Man. PIRAYE Y. ANTIKA; 1 br.

Société Générale SA (France): Akmerkez E-3, Nispetiye Cad., Blok Kat. 9, Eitler, 80600 İstanbul; tel. (212) 2821942; telex 39454; fax (212) 2821848; f. 1990; cap. 31,340m., res 433m., dep. 44,447m. (Dec. 1991); Gen. Man. M. BRICOUT; 1 br.

Türk Sakura Bank AŞ: Büyükdere Cad. 108/A, 80280 Esentepe, İstanbul; tel. (212) 2752930; telex 27718; fax (212) 2724270; f. 1985 as Türk Mitsui Bank, adopted current name in 1992; cap. 124,500m. res 726,700m., dep. 2,044,450m. (Dec. 1997); Chair. TAMOTSU MINAMIMOTO; Gen. Man. YOSHIAKI KOBAYASHI; 2 brs.

Turkish Bank AŞ ('TRNC'): Valikonağı Cad. 7, 80200 Nişantaşı, İstanbul; tel. (212) 2250330; telex 27359; fax (212) 2250355; f. 1982; cap. 300,000m., res 80,374m., dep. 3,104,295m. (Dec. 1995); Chair. HAMİT B. BELLİ; 15 brs.

Westdeutsche Landesbank Girozentrale (Germany): Nispetiye Cad. 38, 80630 Levent, İstanbul; tel. (212) 2792537; telex 26862; fax (212) 2802941; f. 1990; cap. 30,000m., res 1,512m., dep. 23,017m. (Dec. 1991); Gen. Man. GILLES LÉRAILLÉ; 2 brs.

Banking Organization

Banks' Association of Turkey: Nıspetiye Cad. Akmerkez B3 Blok. Kat 13–14, 80630 Etiler, İstanbul; tel. (212) 2820973; telex 46771; fax (212) 2820946; f. 1958; Chair. VEYSI ORAL (acting); Sec.-Gen. Dr EKREM KESKIN.

STOCK EXCHANGE

İstanbul Menkul Kıymetler Borsası (İMKB): 80860 İstinye, İstanbul; tel. (212) 2982371; telex 27163; fax (212) 2982500; e-mail info@ise.org; internet http://www.ise.org; f. 1866; revived in 1986 after being dormant for about 60 years; 142 mems of stock market, 175 mems of bond and bills market; Chair. and CEO OSMAN BIRSEN; Senior Vice-Chair ARIL SEREN.

INSURANCE

Anadolu Sigorta TAŞ (Anatolia Turkish Insurance Co): Rıhtım Cad. 57, 80030 Karaköy, İstanbul; tel. (212) 2516540; telex 25407; fax (212) 2432690; f. 1925; Chair. BURHAN KARAGÖZ; Gen. Man. AHMET YAVUZ.

Ankara Sigorta TAŞ (Ankara Insurance Co): Bankalar Cad. 80, 80020 Karaköy, İstanbul; tel. (212) 2521010; telex 24394; fax (212) 2524744; f. 1936; Chair. and Gen. Man. Dr SEBAHATTIN BEYAZ.

Destek Reasürans TAŞ: Abdi İpekçi Cad. 75, 80200 Maçka, İstanbul; tel. (212) 2312832; telex 27748; fax (212) 2415704; f. 1945; reinsurance; Pres. ONUR ÖKTEN; Gen. Man. İBRAHIM YAYCIOĞLU.

Doğan Sigorta AŞ: Serdarı Ekrem Sok 48, 80020 Kuledibi, İstanbul; tel. (212) 2516374; telex 25854; fax (212) 2516379; f. 1942; fire, marine, accident; Chair. T. GÜNGÖR URAS.

Güven Sigorta TAŞ: Bankalar Cad. 122–124, 80000 Karaköy, İstanbul; tel. (212) 2547900; telex 24336; fax (212) 2353650; f. 1924; Chair. NAMIK KEMAL SENTÜRK; Gen. Man. EMIN ATASAGUN.

Halk Sigorta TAŞ: Büyükdere Cad. 161, 80506 Zincirlikuyu, İstanbul; tel. (212) 2743940; telex 26438; fax (212) 2751668; f. 1944; Chair. HALUK CILLOV; Gen. Man. ERHAN DUMANLI.

Hür Sigorta AŞ: Büyükdere Cad., Hür Han 15/A, 80260 Şişli, İstanbul; tel. (212) 2322010; telex 27501; fax (212) 2463673; Chair. BÜLENT SEMILER; Gen. Man. GÜNER YALÇINER.

İMTAŞ İttihadı Milli Sigorta TAŞ: Büyükdere Cad. 116, 80300 Zincirlikuyu, İstanbul; tel. (212) 2747000; telex 26404; fax (212) 2720837; f. 1918; Chair. Prof. Dr ASAF SAVAŞ AKAT; Gen. Man. MUSTAFA AKAN.

İstanbul Reasürans AŞ: Halaskargazi Cad. 309, Kat. 4, 80260 Şişli, İstanbul; tel. (212) 2408070; telex 39014; fax (212) 2300464; f. 1979; Chair. CEMAL ZAGRA; Gen. Man. GÜLGÜN ÜNLÜOGLU.

Milli Reasürans TAŞ: Teşvikiye Cad. 43–57, 80200 Teşvikiye, İstanbul; tel. (212) 2314730; telex 26472; fax (212) 2308608; e-mail info@millire.com; internet http://www.millire.com; f. 1929; premium income 37,037,289m., total assets 26,308,087m. (Dec. 1997); Chair. N. YALKUT AYÖZGER; Dir and Gen. Man. CAHİT NOMER.

Şark Sigorta TAŞ: Bağlarbaşı, Kısıklı Cad. 9, 81180 Altunizade, İstanbul; tel. (212) 3101250; telex 29739; fax (212) 3101349; f. 1923; Chair. M. RAHMI KOÇ; Gen. Man. GÜNEL BAŞER.

Şeker Sigorta AŞ: Meclisi Mebusan Cad. 87, Şeker Sigorta Hanı, PK 519, 80040 Fındıklı, İstanbul; tel. (212) 2514035; fax (212) 2491046; f. 1954; Chair. MEHMET SERT; Gen. Man. YURDAL SERT.

Tam Sigorta AŞ: Meclisi Mebusan Cad. 27/1, Setüstü, Kabataş, İstanbul; tel. (212) 2934064; fax (212) 2517181; f. 1964; all types of insurance except life; Chair. REHA BAVBEK; Gen. Man. MEHMET NEZIR UCA.

Türkiye Genel Sigorta AŞ: Meclisi Mebusan Cad. 91, 80040 Salıpazarı, İstanbul; tel. (212) 2520010; telex 24453; fax (212) 2499651; f. 1948; Chair. MEHMET E. KARAMEHMET; Gen. Man. HULUSI TAŞKIRAN.

Trade and Industry

GOVERNMENT AGENCY

Privatization Administration: Hüseyin Rahmi Gürpınar Sok. 2, Çankaya, 06680 Ankara; tel. (312) 4411500; fax (312) 4403271; co-ordinates privatization programme; Pres. UGUR BAYAR.

DEVELOPMENT ORGANIZATIONS

Turkish Atomic Energy Authority: Prime Minister's Office, 06530 Ankara; tel. (312) 2876013; fax (312) 2878761; f. 1956; controls the development of peaceful uses of atomic energy; 11 mems; Pres. Prof. YALÇIN SANALAN; Sec.-Gen. EROL BARUTÇUGIL.

Turkish Electricity Authority (TEAS) (Nuclear Power Plants Department): İnönü Bul. 27, 06440 Ankara; tel. (312) 2229855; telex 42245; fax (312) 2127853; state enterprise to supervise the construction and operation of nuclear power plants; attached to the Ministry of Energy and Natural Resources; Head of Dept NEVZAT ŞAHIN.

CHAMBERS OF COMMERCE AND INDUSTRY

Union of Chambers of Commerce, Industry, Maritime Commerce and Commodity Exchanges of Turkey (UCCET): 149 Atatürk Bul. 149, Bakanlıklar, Ankara; tel. (312) 4184325; fax (312) 4254854; e-mail info@info.tobb.org.tr; f. 1952; represents 335 chambers and commodity exchanges; Pres. FUAT MIRE; Sec.-Gen. ŞEFIK TOKAT.

Ankara Chamber of Commerce: Ato Sarayi Eskişehir Yolu Söğütözü Mahallesi Cad. 5, Ankara; tel. (312) 2857950; fax (312) 2863446.

Ankara Chamber of Industry: Atatürk Bul. 193/4-5, Kavaklıdere, Ankara; tel. (312) 4171200; fax (312) 4172060; e-mail aso@aso.org.tr; internet http://www.aso.org.

İstanbul Chamber of Commerce (ICOC): Ragip Gümüşpala Cad. 84,34378 Eminönü, İstanbul; tel (212) 5114150; telex 31038; fax (212) 5131565; f. 1882; more than 230,000 mems; Chair. MEHMET YILDIRIM.

İstanbul Chamber of Industry: Meşrutiyet Cad. 118, Tepebaşi, İstanbul; tel. (212) 2522900; fax (212) 2493963.

İzmir Chamber of Commerce: Atatürk Cad. 126, 35210 İzmir; tel. (232) 4417777; telex 52331; fax (232) 4837853; f. 1885; Pres. EKREM DEMIRTAŞ; Sec.-Gen. Prof. Dr İLTER AKAT.

EMPLOYERS' ASSOCIATIONS

Türk Sanayicileri ve İşadamları Derneği (TÜSİAD) (Turkish Industrialists' and Businessmen's Association): Meşrutiyet Cad. 74, 80050 Tepebaşı, İstanbul; tel. (212) 2491131; telex 22318; fax (212) 2491350; internet http://www.tusiad.org; f. 1971; 428 mems; Pres. MUHARREM KAYHAN; Sec.-Gen. Dr HALUK R.TÜKEL.

Türkiye İşveren Sendikaları Konfederasyonu (TİSK) (Turkish Confederation of Employers' Associations): Meşrutiyet Cad. 1/4-5, 06650 Kızılay, Ankara; tel. (312) 4183217; telex 46182; fax (312) 4184473; e-mail gensec@tisk.org.tr; internet http://www.tisk.org.tr; f. 1962; represents (on national level) 19 employers' associations with 2,000 affiliated member employers or companies; official representative in labour relations; Pres. REFIK BAYDUR; Sec.-Gen. KUBILAY ATASAYAR.

UTILITIES

Electricity

Türkiye Elektrik Üretim-İletim AŞ (TEAS-Turkish Electricity Authority): İnönü Bul. 27, 06440 Ankara; tel. (312) 2229855; telex 42245; fax (312) 2127853; attached to Ministry of Energy and Natural Resources.

MAJOR COMPANIES

Aksa (Akrilik Kimya San. AŞ): Miralay Şekipbey Sok. Ak Han 15–17, Kat. 5/6, Gumuşsuyu, İstanbul; tel. (212) 2514500; telex 25801; fax (212) 2514507; produces acrylic fibres and general chemical products; Pres. ALI DINÇKÖK; 850 employees.

Alpet (Aliaga Petrokimya San. ve Tic. AŞ): PK 12, Aliaga, İzmir; tel. (232) 6161240; telex 51706; fax (232) 6161248; manufacture and distribution of petrochemicals; Pres. SEYFETTIN BİÇICI; 3,694 employees.

Arçelik AŞ: 41460 Çayırova, İstanbul; tel. (212) 3954515; telex 34138; fax (212) 3952727; turnover TL 2,375,133m. (1990); produces domestic appliances; Pres. SUNA KIRAÇ; 3,434 employees.

Bağfaş (Bandırma Gübre Fabrikaları AŞ): Susam Sok. 26, 80060 Cihangir, İstanbul; tel. (212) 2930885; telex 26185; fax (212) 2499744; produces fertilizers and acids; Pres. RECEP DINÇER; 590 employees.

Barlan Metal Pazarlama, San. ve Tic. AŞ: Dılovasi Mevkii, 41455 Gebze, Kocaeli; tel (212) 7546606; fax (212) 7547284; producers of aluminium sheet, foil and packaging materials.

Beko Elektronic AŞ: Beylik Düzü Mevkii, 34901 Büyükçekmece, İstanbul; tel. (212) 8722000; telex 23506; fax (212) 8722013; e-mail celalk@beko.com.tr; f. 1966; produces electronic consumer goods; Pres. A. İ. ÇUBUKÇU; 2,000 employees.

Boru Hatları ile Petrol Taşıma AŞ (BOTAŞ): Güneş Sok. 11, 06690 Güvenevler, Ankara; tel. (312) 4670150; telex 42898; fax (312) 4282646; state operator of petroleum and gas pipelines; Dir-Gen. MUSTAFA MURATHAN.

Brisa—Bridgestone Sabanci Tire Manufacturing and Trading Co Inc: Sabanci Centre Kule 2, Kat. 7-9, 80745 4 Levent, İstanbul; tel. (212) 2780021; telex 26145; fax (212) 2811681; manufactures tyres; Pres. SAKIP SABANCI; 1,628 employees.

Çolakoğlu Metalurji AŞ: Kemeraltı Cad. Karaköy Ticaret Merkezi 24, Kat. 6, Karaköy, İstanbul; tel. (212) 2520000; telex 25739; fax (212) 2495588; e-mail colmet@superonline.com; manufactures steel wire rod in coils, reinforcing bars, billets; Pres. MEHMET ÇOLAKOĞLU; 1,110 employees.

Çukurova Çelik Endüstrisi AŞ: Meclisi Mebusan Cad. Salıpazarı Yokuşu 1, 80040 Salıpazarı, İstanbul; tel. (212) 2513737; telex 25065; fax (212) 2511286; f. 1978; manufactures steel billets, reinforcing bars and wire rods; Gen. Man. MEHMET KUZEYLI; 796 employees.

Çukurova Elektrik AŞ: PK 239, Adana; tel. (322) 2350681; telex 62735; fax (322) 2350256; manufactures electrical appliances; Pres. KEMAL UZAN; 1,382 employees.

Enka Holding Investment Co Inc: Balmumcu Mahallesi, Bestekar Şevki Bey Cad., ENKA II Binası, Beşiktaş, İstanbul; tel. (212) 2740970; telex 27035; fax (212) 2728869; f. 1957; contracting, industry, trading, tourism, banking and engineering with 44 specialized subsidiaries; Co-founder and Chair. ŞARIK TARA; Man. Dir VAHITTIN GÜLERYÜZ; 18,000 employees.

Ereğli Demir ve Çelik Fabrikalari TAŞ: Uzunkum 7, Karadeniz, 67330 Ereğli; tel. (372) 3232500; telex 48523; fax (372) 3163969; manufactures steel and iron products; Pres. YALÇIN AMANVERMEZ; 7,002 employees.

Goodyear Lastikleri TAŞ: Büyükdere Cad. Maslak Meydanı 41, Alarko İş Merkezi, Levent, İstanbul; tel. (212) 2764693; telex 26491; fax (212) 2764751; manufactures tyres; Pres. J. KAPLAN; 2,000 employees.

Hyder Mühendislik Müşavirlik Ltd Şirketi: İnönü Cad. STFA Blokları, B-4 Blok, Kat 4/21, 81090 Kozyatağı, İstanbul; tel. (216) 4107560; fax (216) 4107563; e-mail hydertur@superonline.com; transport and environmental infrastructure, industrial facilities.

İzmir Pamuk Mensucatı TAŞ: 1201 Sok. 11, PK 106, Halkapınar, İzmir; tel. (232) 4339810; telex 53220; fax (232) 4339782; f. 1914; manufacturers and exporters of cotton goods; Chief Exec. ÇETİN OKTAY.

Koç Holding AŞ: Nakkaştepe Aziz Bey Sok. 1, 80207 Kuzguncuk, İstanbul; tel. (216) 3414650; telex 24218; fax (216) 3431944; f. 1926; construction and engineering with 116 specialized subsidiaries; manufacturers of consumer durables; Chair. RAHMI KOÇ; Vice-Pres. NECATI ARIKAN; 35,530 employees.

Kordsa (Kord Bezi San. ve Tic. AŞ): Sabancı Centre Kule 2, Kat. 5, 80745 4 Levent, İstanbul; tel. (212) 2810012; telex 26181; fax (212) 2810027; manufactures cord fabric; part of Haci Omer Sabanci Holding; Pres. SAKIP SABANCI; 1,200 employees.

Kutlutaş Holding Co: İnönü Cad. 28/5, Taksim, İstanbul; tel. (212) 2512823; telex 24304; fax (212) 2434511; f. 1970; controlling interests in 18 cos engaged in manufacture of cranes, scaffolding elements, chemicals, electrical appliances, large-scale construction, as well as contracting and tourism.

Mercedes-Benz Türk AŞ: Burmalı Çeşme Sok. Askeri Fırın Yolu 2, 34022 Davutpaşa, İstanbul; tel. (212) 5670409; telex 22374; fax (212) 5770402; manufactures civil and military vehicles; Pres. EIKE LIPPOLD; 2,300 employees.

Metaş (İzmir Metalurji Fabrikası TAŞ): Kemalpaşa Cad. Işıkkent Girişi, 35070 İzmir; f. 1958; tel. (232) 4334010; telex 53384; fax (232) 4334041; construction group; steel producers and exporters; Chair. ATTILA ŞNOL; Gen. Man. NIYAZI ALTAN.

Otosan (Otomobil San AŞ): Ankara Asfaltı 4 KM, Uzunçayır Mevkii, 81302 Kadıköy, İstanbul; tel. (216) 3267060; telex 29470; fax (216) 3390861; manufactures passenger cars, trucks and engines; 1,800 employees.

Oyak—Renault Otomobil Fab. AŞ: Emirhan Cad. Barbaros Plaza Blok C 145, Kat. 6, 80700 Dikilitaş, İstanbul; tel. (212) 2270000; telex 27774; fax (212) 2594545; manufactures automobiles; Pres. ALI BOZER; 4,500 employees.

Paşabahçe Cam San. ve Tic. AŞ: Ankara Asfalti İçmeler Mevkii 81700 Tuzla, İstanbul; tel. (216) 3955473; telex 36024; fax (216) 3954128; e-mail ncokal@sisecam.com.tr; f. 1934; glass tableware and gift exporters; Gen. Man. BURAK GÖNENÇ; 15,000 employees.

Peg (Profilo Elektrikli Gereçler San. AŞ): İkinci Tasocaği Sok. 26/28, Mecidiyeköy, İstanbul; tel. (212) 2743300; telex 26171; fax (212) 2116512; manufactures electrical appliances; Pres. JAK KAMHI; 4,600 employees.

Pekim Petrokimya Holding AŞ: PK 12, 35801 Aliağa, İzmit; tel. (262) 6163240; fax (262) 6161248; produces petrochemicals; Pres. MEHMET YILMAZ; 6,000 employees.

Sasa Sun'i ve Sentetik Elyaf San. AŞ: Sabancı Centre Kule 2, 80745 4 Levent, İstanbul; tel. (212) 2785088; fax (212) 2786201; e-mail sasa@sasa.com.tr; manufactures synthetic yarns and fibres; Pres. ÖMER SABANCI; 4,000 employees.

Sevil Giyim İhracat İthalat Sanayi ve Ticaret AŞ: Sanayi Cad. 49, Bornova, İzmir; tel. (232) 4350050; telex 53046; fax (232) 4350633; manufactures and exports ready-made garments.

Söktaş: Cumhuriyet Mah. Karasuluk Mevkii, PK 32, 09201 Söke; tel. (256) 5182255; telex 51308; manufacturers and exporters of raw and finished cotton fabric and thread; Gen. Man. MUHARREM KAYHAN.

Tat Konserve Sanayii A Ş: İstiklal Cad. 347/4, 80050 Beyoğlu, İstanbul. tel. (212) 2523600; telex 24569; fax (212) 2455133; tomato products.

TDÇ Isl. Genel Müd. Karabük D.C. Mües. Müd.: Karabük; tel. (372) 4182001; telex 48522; fax (372) 4182110; manufactures iron, steel, coke and napthalene; Vice-Pres. COŞKUN AKTEM; 9,000 employees.

TDÇ İşl. İskenderun Demir ve Çelik Fabrikaları Mües. Müd.: Isdemir, Hatay; tel. (326) 7556260; telex 68696; fax (326) 6173895; manufactures steel and iron; Pres. SENCER İMER; 14,158 employees.

Tekfen İnsaat ve Tesisat AŞ: Tekfen Sitesi, 80600 Etiler, İstanbul; tel. (212) 2576100; fax (212) 2659869; e-mail tekfen.com.tr; construction; Pres. ERHAN ÖNER.

Tofaş (Türk Otomobil Fab. AŞ): Büyükdere Cad. 145/5, 80300 Zincirlikuyu, İstanbul; tel. (212) 2753390; telex 26451; fax (212) 2753988; manufactures automobiles and automobile parts; Pres. CAN KIRAÇ; 5,263 employees.

Türk Pirelli Lastikleri AŞ: Büyükdere Cad. 117, Gayrettepe, İstanbul; tel. (212) 2752280; telex 26337; fax (212) 2726077; internet http://www.pirelli.com; manufactures and distributes tyres; Pres. BÜLENT ECZACIBAŞI; 1,250 employees.

Turkish Petroleum Corpn (TPAO): Mustafa Kemal Mah. II Cad. 86, 06520 Bakanlıklar, Ankara; tel. (312) 2869100; telex 42624; fax (312) 2869000; f. 1954; f. 1954; Turkey's largest State Economic Enterprise; explores for, drills and produces crude petroleum; Chair. and Gen. Man. SITKI SANCAR; 5,113 employees.

Türkiye Elektrik Kurumu: İnönü Bulvarı 27, Bahçelievler, Ankara; tel. (312) 2126915; fax (312) 2138870; electrical goods; Pres. MUHITTIN BABALIOĞLU; 69,801 employees.

Türkiye Petrol Rafinerileri AŞ (TÜPRAŞ): Körfez, İzmit; tel. (262) 5270600; telex 33152; fax (262) 5270658; refining of crude oil; Gen. Man. M. ERGUN KURAN; 4,480 employees.

Türkiye Şeker Fabrikaları AŞ: Mithatpaşa Cad. 14, 06100 Yenişehir, Ankara; tel. (312) 4359815; telex 46426; fax (312) 4317225; produces sugar and manufactures machinery used in sugar production; Gen. Dir SELAHATTİN HUN; 19,240 employees.

Turyağ AŞ: PK 171, İzmir; tel. (232) 4845320; telex 53448; fax (232) 4844832; f. 1916; manufacturers of detergents and edible oils.

Tütün, Tütün Mamülleri, Tuz ve Alkol İşletmeleri Genel Müdürlüğü (TEKEL): Atatürk Bul. 25, Unkapanı, İstanbul; tel. (212) 5321078; fax (212) 5320527; production and distribution of tobacco products, alcohol and salt; Pres. MEHMET AKBAY; 48,568 employees.

Unilever—İş Ticaret ve San. Türk Ltd Şti: Yıldız Posta Cad. Yener Sok. 3, Beşiktas, İstanbul; tel. (212) 2754545; telex 28548; fax (212) 2754579; produces edible fats; Pres. DEMIR TIRYAKIOĞLU; 1,050 employees.

Uzel Makine Sanayi AŞ: Topçular, Kışla Cad. 5, 34147 Rami, İstanbul; tel. (212) 5670841; telex 23416; fax (212) 5764595; manufactures tractors, wheels, brakes and automobile springs; Pres. AHMET UZEL; 1,767 employees.

Yaşar Holding Corpn: Gaziosmanpaşa Bul., Batı, İ şhanı Kat. 3-4-7, İzmir; tel. (232) 4890121; telex 53407; fax (232) 4256667; f. 1954; 45 member companies with interests in processed food, tourism, paints, chemicals, paper, banking, insurance, commerce and beer; Chair. SELÇUK YAŞAR; Vice-Chair. SELMIN YAŞAR; 8,500 employees.

Zihni Group: Rıhtım Cad. Zihni Han 28/30, 80030 Tophane, İstanbul; tel. (212) 2511515; telex 25227; fax (212) 2435325; f. 1930; integrated sea and land transport company specializing in imports and exports.

TRADE UNIONS

Confederations

DİSK (Türkiye Devrimci İşçi Sendikaları Konfederasyonu) (Confederation of Progressive Trade Unions of Turkey): Merter Sitesi, Ahmet Kutsi Tecer Cad. Sendikalar Binası 12, Kat. 5, 34010 Merter, İstanbul; tel. (212) 5048083; fax (212) 5061079; e-mail diskf@tr-net.net.tr; f. 1967; member of ICFTU, ETUC and TUF; 26 affiliated unions; Pres. RIDVAN BUDAK; Sec.-Gen. MURAT TOKMAK.

Türk-İş (Türkiye İşçi Sendikaları Konfederasyonu Genel Başkanlığı) (Confederation of Turkish Trade Unions): Bayındır Sok 10, Yenişehir, Ankara; tel. (312) 4333125; fax (312) 4336809; f. 1952; member of ICFTU, ETUC, ICFTU-APRO and OECD/TUAC; 32 national unions and federations with 1.7m. mems; Pres. BAYRAM MERAL; Gen. Sec. ŞEMSI DENIZER.

Principal DİSK Trade Unions

Bank-Sen (Türkiye Devrimci Banka ve Sigorta İşçileri Sendikası): Nakiye Elgun Sok 117, Şişli, İstanbul; tel. (212) 2321000; fax (212) 2464112; Pres. HULUSI KARLI; 11,800 mems.

Basın-İş (Türkiye Basın İşçileri Sendikası) (Press Workers' Union): İstanbul; f. 1964; Pres. YILMAZ ÖZDEMIR; Gen. Sec. DERVIŞ BOYOĞLU; 5,000 mems.

Birlesik Metal-İs (Birlesik Metal İşçileri Sendikası): Tünel Yolu Cad. 2, 81110 Bostancı, Kadıköy, İstanbul; tel. (216) 3622091; fax (216) 3736502; Gen. Sec. MUZAFFER ŞAHIN; 58,800 mems.

Demiryol-İş (Türkiye Demiryolu İşçileri Sendikası) (Railway Workers): Necatibey Cad., Sezenler Sok 5, 06430 Yenişehir, Ankara; tel. (312) 2318029; fax (312) 2318032; f. 1952; Pres. ENVER TOÇOĞLU; Gen. Sec. NURETTIN GIRGINER; 25,000 mems.

Deri-İş (Türkiye Deri İşçileri Sendikası) (Leather Industry): Ahmet Kutsi Tecer Cad. 12/6, Merter, İstanbul; tel. (212) 5048083; fax (212) 5061079; f. 1948; Pres. NUSRETTIN YILMAZ; Gen. Sec. ALI SEL; 11,000 mems.

Dev. Sağlık-İş (Türkiye Devrimci Sağlık İşçileri Sendikası) (Health Employees): İstanbul; f. 1961; Pres. DOĞAN HALIS; Gen. Sec. SABRI TANYERI; 15,000 mems.

Genel-İş (Türkiye Genel Hizmet İşçileri Sendikası) (Municipal Workers): Çankırı Cad. 28, Kat 5-9, Ulus, Ankara; tel. (312) 3091547; fax (312) 3091046; f. 1983; Pres. ISMAIL HAKKI ÖNAL; Gen. Sec. ATILA ÖNGEL; 50,000 mems.

Gıda-İş (Türkiye Gıda Sanayii İşçileri Sendikası): Ahmet Kutsi Tecer Cad. 12/3, 34010 Merter, İstanbul; tel. (212) 5751540; fax (212) 5753099; Pres. MEHMET MUHLACI; Gen. Sec. YURDAKUL GÖZDE; 31,000 mems.

Koop-İş (Türkiye Kooperatif ve Büro İşçileri Sendikası) (Cooperative and Office Workers): İzmir Cad. Fevzi Çakmak Sok 15/11–12, Yenişehir, Ankara; tel. (312) 4300855; f. 1964; Pres. AHMET BALAMAN; Gen. Sec. AHMET GÜVEN; 29,000 mems.

Limter-İş (Liman, Tersane Gemi Yapım Onarım İşçileri Sendikası) (Harbour, Shipyard, Ship Building and Repairs): İcmeler Tren İstasyonu Yanı 12/1, Tuzla, İstanbul; tel. (216) 3955271; f. 1947; Pres. EMIR BABAKUŞ; Gen. Sec. ASKER ŞIT; 7,000 mems.

Nakliyat-İş (Nakliye İşçileri Sendikası) (Transportation Workers): Guraba Hüseyin Ağa Mah. Kakmacı Sok 10, Daire 11 Vatan Cad. Tranvay, Durağı Karşısı, Aksaray, İstanbul; tel. (212) 5332069; Pres. ŞEMSI ERCAN; Gen. Sec. NEDIM FIRAT.

OLEYİS (Otel, Lokanta ve Eğlence Yerleri İşçileri Sendikası) (Hotel, Restaurant and Places of Entertainment Workers' Union): Atatürk Bul. 57, Kızılay, Ankara; tel. (312) 4359680; fax (312) 4358654; e-mail oleyis@tr.net.net.tr; f. 1947; Pres. ENVER ÖKTEM; Gen. Sec. VEYSEL ÇUKUR; 25,000 mems.

Petkim-İş (Türkiye Petrol, Kimya ve Lastik Sanayii İşçileri Sendikası): İzmir Cad., Fevzi Çakmak Sok. 7/13, Ankara; tel. (312) 2300861; fax (312) 2299429; Pres. MUSTAFA KARADAYI; 18,000mems.

Sosyal-İş (Türkiye Sosyal Sigortalar, Eğitim, Büro, Ticaret Kooperatif Banka ve Güzel Sanatlar İşçileri Sendikası) (Banking, Insurance and Trading): Necatibey Cad. Sezenler Sok. Lozan Apt. 2/14, Yenişehir, Ankara; tel. (312) 2318178; fax (312) 2294638; Pres. ÖZCAN KESGEÇ; Gen. Sec. H. BEDRI DOĞANAY; 31,000 mems.

Tekstil İşçileri Sendikası: Ahmet Kutsi Tecer Cad. 12/1, Merter, İstanbul; tel. (212) 6429742; fax (212) 5044887; Pres. RIDVAN BUDAK; 45,000 mems.

Tümka-İş (Türkiye Tüm Kağıt Selüloz Sanayii İşçileri Sendikası): Gündoğdu Sok 19/3, Merter, İstanbul; tel. (212) 5750843; Pres. SABRI KAPLAN; 3,000 mems.

Other Principal Trade Unions

Denizciler (Türkiye Denizciler Sendikası) (Seamen): Rıhtım Cad., Denizciler Sok. 7, Tophane, İstanbul; tel. (212) 2430456; fax (212) 2445221; f. 1959; Pres. TURHAN UZUN; Gen. Sec. Capt. HASAN PEKDEMIR; 7,500 mems.

Fındık-İş (Fiskobirlik İşçileri Sendikası) (Hazel-nut producers): Giresun; Pres. AKÇIN KOÇ; Gen. Sec. ERSAIT ŞEN.

Hava-İş (Türkiye Sivil Havacılık Sendikası) (Civil Aviation): İncirli Cad., Volkan Apt., 68/1 Bakırköy, İstanbul; tel. (212) 6601495; fax (212) 5719051; e-mail havais@mail.turk.net; Pres. ATILAY AYÇIN; Gen. Sec. MUSTAFA YAĞCI; 7,000 mems.

Liman-İş (Türkiye Liman ve Kara Tahmil Tahliye İşçileri Sendikası) (Longshoremen): Necatibey Cad., Sezenler Sok 4, Kat. 5, Yenişehir, Ankara; tel. (312) 2317418; fax (312) 2302484; f. 1963; Pres. HASAN BIBER; Gen. Sec. RAIF KILIÇ; 5,000 mems.

Şeker-İş (Türkiye Şeker Sanayii İşçileri Sendikası) (Sugar Industry): Karanfil Sok 59, Bakanlıklar, Ankara; tel. (312) 4184273; fax (312) 4259258; f. 1952; Pres. ÖMER ÇELIK; Gen. Sec. FETHI TEKIN; 35,000 mems.

Tarım-İş (Türkiye Orman, Topraksu, Tarım ve Tarım Sanayii İşçileri Sendikası) (Agricultural Irrigation and Forestry Workers): Bankacı Sok 10, 06700 Kocatepe, Ankara; tel. (312) 4190456; fax (312) 4193113; f. 1961; Pres. SABRI ÖZDEŞ; Gen. Sec. BAKI BAŞDEMIR; 43,500 mems.

Tekgıda-İş (Türkiye Tütün, Müskirat Gıda ve Yardımcı İşçileri Sendikası) (Tobacco, Drink, Food and Allied Workers' Union of Turkey): 4 Levent Konaklar Sok, İstanbul; tel. (212) 2644996; fax (212) 2789534; f. 1952; Pres. ORHAN BALTA; Gen. Sec. HÜSEYIN KARAKOÇ; 176,000 mems.

Teksif (Türkiye Tekstil, Örme ve Giyim Sanayii İşçileri Sendikası) (Textile, Knitting and Clothing): Ziya Gökalp Cad. Aydoğmuş Sok 1, Kurtuluş, Ankara; tel. (312) 4312170; fax (312) 4357826; f. 1951; Pres. ZEKI POLAT; Gen. Sec. HAYRETTIN DEVRIMÖZ; 100,000 mems.

Tez-Koop-İş (Türkiye, Ticaret, Kooperatif, Eğitim, Büro ve Güzel Sanatlar İşçileri Sendikası) (Commercial and Clerical Employees): Üç Yıldız Cad. 29, Subayevleri, Ayınlıkevler, 06130 Ankara; tel. (312) 3183979; fax (312) 3183988; f. 1962; Pres. SADIK ÖZBEN; Gen. Sec. H. FARAK ÜSTÜN; 30,000 mems.

Türk Harb-İş (Türkiye Harb Sanayii ve Yardımcı İşkolları İşçileri Sendikası) (Defence Industry and Allied Workers): İnkılap Sok 20, Kızılay, Ankara; tel. (312) 4175097; fax (312) 4171364; f. 1956; Pres. İZZET CETIN; Gen. Sec. NURI AYCICER; 35,000 mems.

Türk-Metal (Türkiye Metal, Çelik, Mühimmat, Makina ve Metalden Mamul, Eşya ve Oto, Montaj ve Yardımcı İşçileri

Sendikası) (Auto, Metal and Allied Workers): Kızılırmak Mah., Adalararası Sok. 3, Eskişehir Yolu 1 km, 06560 Söğütözü, Ankara; tel. (312) 2844010; fax (312) 2844018; f. 1963; Pres. MUSTAFA ÖZBEK; Gen. Sec. ÖZBEK KARAKUS; 123,000 mems.

Yol-İş (Türkiye Yol, Yapı ve İnşaat İşçileri Sendikası) (Road Construction and Building Workers' Unions): İstanbul Cad. 58, İskitler, Ankara; tel. (312) 3422240; fax (312) 3412705; f. 1963; Pres. BAYRAM MERAL; Gen. Sec. TEVFIK ÖZÇELIK; 170,000 mems.

Transport

RAILWAYS

The total length of the railways operated within the national frontiers is 10,508 km (1997), of which 8,607 km are main lines, 2,065 km are electrified, and 2,453 km are signalled. A new direct rail link between Ankara and İstanbul, cutting the distance from 577 km to 416 km, is expected to be completed by 2000. There are direct rail links with Bulgaria to Iran and Syria. A new line connecting Turkey with Georgia is expected to be completed by 2000. A light railway system for İstanbul, expected to total 109 km in length upon its completion, is currently under construction. A 7.5-km section of a 29-km 'metro' transport system was scheduled for completion in 1995. A 14.6-km initial phase of a planned 76-km 'metro' and light rail transport system in Ankara, was scheduled to open in 1997. An 8.6 km light rail route for the city opened in 1996.

Türkiye Cumhuriyeti Devlet Demiryolları İşletmesi Genel Müdürlüğü (TCDD) (Turkish Republic State Railways): Genel Müdürlük, Talatpaşa Bul., 06330 Gar, Ankara; tel. (312) 3090515; telex 44390; fax (312) 3123215; f. 1924; operates all railways and connecting ports (see below) of the State Railway Administration, which acquired the status of a state economic enterprise in 1953, and a state economic establishment in 1984; 526 main-line diesel locomotives, 60 main-line electric locomotives, 1,059 passenger coaches and 17,138 freight wagons; Chair. of Board and Gen. Dir TEKIN ÇINAR.

ROADS

At 1 January 1996, 1,246 km of motorways were open to traffic and nearly 530 km of motorways were under construction; the total length of the highway network was 61,245 km and the total length of village roads was 320,000 km. In 1996 there were 58,687 km of roads in the maintenance programme with 49,376 km open all year and 7,316 km open, when possible, in winter.

Bayındırlı ve İskan Bakanlığı Karayolları Genel Müdürlüğü (General Directorate of Highways): KGM Sitesi, Yücetepe, 06100 Ankara; tel. (312) 4252343; fax (312) 4172851; f. 1950; Dir-Gen. YAMAN KÖK.

SHIPPING

At the end of 1996 Turkey's merchant fleet comprised 1,114 vessels and had an aggregate displacement of 6.4m. grt.

General-purpose public ports are operated by two state economic enterprises. The ports of Bandırma, Derince, Haydarpaşa (İstanbul), İskenderun, İzmir, Mersin and Samsun, all of which are connected to the railway network, are operated by Turkish State Railways (TCDD) (see above), while the smaller ports of Antalya, Giresun, Hopa, Tekirdağ and Trabzon are operated by the Turkish Maritime Organization (TDI).

Turkish Maritime Organization (TDI): Genel Müdürlüğü, Karaköy, İstanbul; tel. (212) 2515000; telex 24895; fax (212) 2495391.

Port of Bandırma: TCDD Liman İşletme Müdürlüğü, Bandırma; tel. (266) 2234966; fax (266) 2236011; Port Man. HASAN KARAKUŞ; Harbour Master IBRAHIM YALKIRI.

Port of Derince: TCDD Liman İşletme Müdürlüğü, Derince; Port Man. ALI ARIF AYTAÇ; Harbour Master HAYDAR DOĞAN.

Port of Haydarpaşa (İstanbul): TCDD Liman İşletme Müdürlüğü Haydarpaşa, İstanbul; tel. (212) 3379988; telex 29705; fax (212) 3451705; Port Man. ABDULMUSA APAYDIN; Harbour Master ISMAIL SAFAER.

Port of İskenderun: TCDD Liman İşletme Müdürlüğü, İskenderun; tel. (326) 6640047; telex 68109; fax (326) 6632424; Port Man. ABDULMUSA APAYDIN; Harbour Master CEVAT ÇOLAK.

Port of İzmir: TCDD Liman İşletme Müdürlüğü, İzmir; tel. (232) 4632252; fax (232) 4632248; Port Man. GÜNGÖR ERKAYA; Harbour Master MEHMET ONGEL.

Port of Mersin: TCDD Liman İşletme Müdürlüğü, Mersin; tel. (324) 2330687; telex 67279; fax (324) 2311350; Port Man. FAHRI SAYILI; Harbour Master H. TAŞKIN.

Port of Samsun: TCDD Liman İşletme Müdürlüğü, Samsun; tel. (362) 4357616; telex 82172; fax (362) 4317849; Port Man. SAFFET YAMAK; Harbour Master Capt. ARIF H. UZUNOĞLU.

Private Companies

Cerrahgil Denizcilik, Nakliyat ve Ticaret AŞ: Abdi İpekçi Cad. 33, PK 108, 80200 Teşvikiye, İstanbul; tel. (212) 2324700; telex 39091; fax (212) 2310035; f. 1974; shipowners, agents, charterers, brokers, traders; Gen. Man. HOSROF KÖLETAVITOĞLU; 4 vessels; 262,873 dwt (1997).

Cerrahoğulları Umumi Nakliyat, Vapurculuk ve Ticaret AŞ: Buyukdere Cad., Yapı Kredi Plaza C Blok, Kat. 7 No. 21, 80620 Levent, İstanbul; tel. (212) 2825720; fax (212) 2825730; f. 1954; Pres. and Gen. Man. SAEED RABB CERRAHOĞLU.

Deniz Nakliyatı TAŞ (Turkish Cargo Lines): Meclisı Mebusan Cad. 151, 80040 Fındıklı, İstanbul; tel. (212) 2522600; telex 24125; fax (212) 2512696; f. 1955; privatization pending 1997; regular liner services between Turkey and Mediterranean, Adriatic, Red Sea, US Atlantic, and Indian and Far East ports; Gen. Man. NEVZAT BILICAN; 17 general cargo ships, 4 roll-on, roll-off, 8 bulk/ore carriers.

Genel Denizcilik Nakliyati AŞ (Geden Line): Meclisı Mebusan Cad. 91, Kat. 2/3, 80040 Salıpazarı, İstanbul; tel. (212) 2516700; telex 24248; fax (212) 2490479; f. 1975; shipowners, agents, brokers; Man. Dir BÜLENT ERGİN; 5 vessels; 185,595 dwt (1996).

İstanbul Ship Management SA: Rıhtım Cad. Zihni Han 28–30 Kat. 2, PK 390, 80030 Tophane, İstanbul; tel. (212) 2931950; telex 25805; fax (212) 2458024; f. 1993; Chair. AHMET ŞAHAP ÜNLÜ; Man. GÖKALP TUNCER.

Kalkavan, Resit, Denizcilik ve Ticaret AŞ: Barbaros Bul. 36, Huzur Apt., Kat. 1, 80700 Besiktas, İstanbul; tel. (212) 2752985; telex 26997; fax (212) 2753533; Pres. Capt. ÇETIN KALKAVAN.

Koçtuğ Gemi İşletmeciliği ve Ticaret AŞ: Bankalar Cad., Bozkurt Han Kat. 3, PK 884, 80000 Karaköy, İstanbul; tel. (212) 2513380; telex 24512; fax (212) 2515256; f. 1956; cargo services to and from Europe, North Africa and the USA; Pres. A. KOÇMAN; Gen. Man. M. LEBLEBICIOĞLU.

Türkiye Denizcilik İşletmeleri Denizyolları İşletmesi Mudurlugu (TDI): Meclisı Mebusan Cad. 68, 80040 Salıpazarı, İstanbul; tel. (212) 2521700; telex 25962; fax (212) 2515767; ferry company; Chair. KENAN ÖNER; Man. Dir ERDEM OZSAHIN.

Shipping Associations

SS Gemi Armatörleri Motorlu Taşıyıcılar Kooperatifi (Turkish Shipowners' Asscn): Meclisı Mebusan Cad., Dursun Han, Kat. 7, No 89, Salıpazarı İstanbul; tel. (212) 2510945; telex 25553; fax (212) 2492786; f. 1960; Pres. GÜNDÜZ KAPTANOĞLU; Man. Dir A. GÖKSU; 699 vessels; 5,509,112 dwt (1993).

Türk Armatörler Birliği (Turkish Shipowners' Union): Meclisı Mebusan Cad. Dursun Han, Kat. 7 No. 89, Salıpazarı, İstanbul; tel. (212) 2453022; telex 25552; fax (212) 2492786; f. 1972; 460 mems; Pres. ŞADAN KALKAVAN; Co-ordinator HAKAN ÜNSALER; 8,780,436 dwt (1997).

Vapur Donatanları ve Acenteleri Derneği (Turkish Shipowners' and Shipping Agents' Asscn): Mumhane Cad. Emek İş Hanı Kat. 3 No. 31, Karaköy, İstanbul; tel. (212) 2443294; f. 1902; worldwide agency service; Pres. Capt. M. LEBLEBİCİOĞLU; Man. Dir C. KAPLAN.

CIVIL AVIATION

There are airports for scheduled international and internal flights at Atatürk (İstanbul), Esenboğa (Ankara), Adnan Menderes (İzmir and Trabzon), while international charter flights are handled by Adana, Dalaman and Antalya. Fifteen other airports handle internal flights only.

Alfa Hava Yolları AŞ (Alfa Airlines Inc.): Halkalı Asfaltı A Blok 9/2, Florya, İstanbul; tel. (212) 5733535; fax (212) 5733530; f. 1992; charter services; Gen. Man. SÜKRÜ CAN.

GTI Hava Yolları AŞ: Cumhuriyet Cad. 26/4, Harbiye, İstanbul; tel. (212) 2332707; fax (212) 2485859; f. 1996; international charter services; Gen. Man. ABDÜLKADIR KOLOT.

İstanbul Hava Yolları AŞ (İstanbul Airlines): Firuzköy Yolu, Bağlar İçi Mevzii 26, 34850 Avcılar, İstanbul; tel. (212) 5092100; telex 21012; fax (212) 5938742; internet http://www.istanbulairlines.com.tr; f. 1985; charter services from major Turkish cities to European destinations; Gen. Man. SAFI ERGIN.

Kuzey Kıbrıs Hava Yolları Ltd. Sti. (North Cyprus Air. Inc.): Atatürk Hava Limanı A, Kapısı Yanı, Yeşilköy, İstanbul; tel. (212) 6632721; fax (212) 6632722; f. 1994; international and domestic charter services; Gen. Man. AYTEKIN BİLGİ.

Onur Air Taşımacılık AŞ: Senlik Mahallesi, Gatal Sok. 3, 34810 Florya, İstanbul; tel. (212) 6632300; fax (212) 6632319; f. 1992; regional and domestic charter services; Chair. CANKUT BAGANA; Man. Dir SEVINÇ PINAR.

Pegasus Hava Taşımacılığı AŞ: İstasyon Cad. 24, Kat. 1, 34800 Yeşilyurt, İstanbul; tel. (212) 6632934; telex 21117; fax (212) 6635458; f. 1989; charter services; Chair. O. BERKMAN; Gen. Man. L. J. LOWTH.

Sonmez Hava Yolları: 9 km Yakova Yolu, PK 189, Bursa; tel. (224) 2610440; fax (224) 2465445; f. 1984; scheduled flights and dedicated freight; Chair. ALI OSMAN SÖNMEZ.

SunExpress Air: Fener Mahallesi Sinanoghu Cad., Oktay Airport, PK 28, 07100 Antalya; tel. (242) 3234047; fax (242) 3234057; internet http://www.sunexpress.de; f. 1990; charter and dedicated freight; serves European destinations; Man. Dir. FLORIAN HAMM.

Sunways Intersun Havacilik: Caglayan Mahallesi Sok 34, 07100 Antalya; tel. (242) 3232600; fax (242) 3234010; f. 1994; Chair. NEDIM GURBUZ; CEO ADIL CAVAS.

Top Air: Yeni Hangarlar Bölgesi, Atatürk Havalimani, 34630 Yesilköy, İstanbul; tel. (212) 5990227; fax (212) 5997910; f. 1990; scheduled flights.

Türk Hava Yolları AO (THY) (Turkish Airlines Inc.): Atatürk Hava Limanı, 34830 Yeşilköy, İstanbul; tel. (212) 6636300; telex 21198; fax (212) 6634744; internet http://www.turkishairlines.com; f. 1933; majority state-owned; extensive internal network and scheduled and charter flights to 66 destinations in the Middle East, Africa, the Far East, Central Asia, the USA and Europe; Pres. YUSUF BOLAYIRLI; CEO CEM KOZLU.

Tourism

Visitors to Turkey are attracted by the climate, fine beaches and ancient monuments. Tourism is being stimulated by the Government, and the industry is expanding rapidly. In 1997 receipts from tourism reached a record US $7,002m., compared with $5,650m. in 1996, while the number of tourists increased from 8.6m. in that year to 9.7m. in 1997.

Ministry of Tourism: İsmet İnönü Bul. 5, Bahçelievler, Ankara; tel. (312) 2128300; fax (312) 2128391; f. 1963; Dir-Gen. of Establishments NECIP ACAR; Dir-Gen. of Information EROL ÖZÜDOĞRU; Dir-Gen. of Investments HALUK AKAR.

Defence

Chief of General Staff: Gen. HUSEYIN KIVRIKOGLU.

Ground Forces Commander: Gen. ATILLA ATES.

Navy Commander: Adm. SALIM DERVISOGLU.

Air Force Commander: Gen. ILHAN KILIC.

Gendarmerie Commander: Gen. RASIM BETIR.

Defence Budget (1998): estimated at TL 1,223,000,000m.

Military Service: 18 months.

Total Armed Forces (August 1997): 639,000 (including 528,000 conscripts): army 525,000 men, navy 51,000 men, air force 63,000 men.

Paramilitary Forces: 182,200: 180,000 gendarmerie, 2,200 coast guard.

Education

When the Turkish Republic was formed, the Ministry of Education became the sole authority in educational matters, replacing the dual system of religious schools and other schools. One of the main obstacles to literacy was the Arabic script, which required years of study before proficiency could be attained. In 1928, therefore, a Turkish alphabet was introduced, using Latin characters. At the same time the literary language was simplified, and purged of some of its foreign elements. In 1996 the Government's expenditure on education amounted to TL 442,420,000m., or 11.2% of total budget expenditure.

PEOPLE'S SCHOOLS

This change of script created a need for schools in which reading and writing in the new alphabet could be taught to adults. Temporary institutions, known as 'people's schools' or 'national schools', were established throughout Turkey. During the winter months these schools gave instruction in reading and writing and other basic subjects to men and women beyond the normal school age. Between 1928 and 1935 about 2m. people received certificates of proficiency. Since then, education in Turkey has made significant advances. According to estimates by UNESCO, the average rate of adult literacy in 1995 was 82.3% (males 91.7%; females 72.4%).

PRIMARY EDUCATION

Primary education may be preceded by an optional pre-school establishment which serves 3–6 year old children.

According to the 'Basic Law of National Education', the education of children between the ages of six and 14 is compulsory. Basic Education Institutes are organized to provide eight years of education and are essentially a combination of primary school and middle school. Primary education, therefore, comprises two cycles, the first consisting of five years at primary school and the second of three years at middle school.

The transition from a system of primary and middle schools to that of a single eight-year basic education school was introduced throughout the country from September 1997.

Primary education is now entirely free, and co-education is the accepted basis for universal education. The number of schools has risen from 12,511 in 1950 to 49,240 in 1995/96, and the number of teachers from 27,144 to some 232,000. In 1995/96 some 6.4m. children were enrolled at primary schools. In 1994 enrolment at primary schools included 96% of children in the relevant age-group (mlaes 98%; females 94%).

SECONDARY EDUCATION

The reorganization of the system of secondary education began in the early 1920s. This period of education lasts for a minimum of three years after primary education and provides for students who intend to proceed to higher educational institutions. Secondary education encompasses general high schools, or lycées, and vocational and technical high schools. In addition, since 1992/93, 'open' high schools have provided secondary education opportunities to young working people through the media and other new technologies.

The lycée takes the student up to the age of 17 or 18 years, and those who wish to proceed to an institute of higher education must pass the state matriculation examination. The study of a modern language (English, French or German) is compulsory. In 1995/96 there were around 209,000 staff teaching at the secondary level and some 4.8m. pupils were enrolled at an estimated total of 14,367 secondary schools. In 1994 enrolment at secondary schools included 50% of children in the relevant age-group (males 58%; females 41%).

INFORMAL EDUCATION

Informal education comprises teaching and guidance outside of the formal education system, which aims to ensure all citizens obtain reading, writing and other essential skills. Since 1932, reading-rooms have been established in every town and many villages. They are centres of social and cultural life and provide evening classes. Their libraries, meeting-halls and recreational facilities are open to all. In the towns there are also evening trade schools which provide technical training for adults, and travelling courses are sent out to the villages. Other informal education is provided for children of secondary school age through apprenticeship training.

HIGHER EDUCATION

Higher educational institutions in Turkey were founded, and are administered, by the State. These institutions include the universities and the higher professional schools. In 1995/96 there were 817 institutes of higher education (including universities, teacher training colleges and other technical and vocational institutions). The number of students enrolled at universities and equivalent institutes of higher education was 1.2m. in that academic year.

TECHNICAL EDUCATION

The problem of technical education began to be seriously considered first in 1926; specialists were invited from Europe and America, and a plan was drawn up for perfecting the existing vocational schools and for founding new ones to meet the economic needs of each region. In 1995/96 there were 3,678 technical and vocational lycées, giving training to some 1.3m. students. Plans were made for evening schools to train craftsmen and for the founding of teachers' technical training high schools. In addition, there are colleges for commerce, tourism, communication, local administration and secretarial skills.

TEACHERS' TRAINING

In Turkey teachers' training colleges are divided into three basic categories: two-year teacher-training institutes which train teachers for primary schools, three-year teacher-training institutes which train teachers for middle schools and higher teacher-training schools offering a four-year course qualifying teachers for the lycées. Students of the higher teacher-training schools take specialist subject courses in the relevant university faculty and their pedagogy courses in the higher teacher-training schools.

Bibliography

GENERAL

Allen, H. E. *The Turkish Transformation*. Chicago, 1935.

Armstrong, H. C. *Grey Wolf: Mustafa Kemal: an Intimate Study of a Dictator*. London, 1937.

Auboyneau & Fevret. *Essai de bibliographie pour l'Empire Ottomane*. Paris, 1911.

Bahrampour, Firouz. *Turkey, Political and Social Transformation*. New York, Gaus, 1967.

Barkley, Henri J. (Ed.) *Reluctant Neighbour: Turkey's Role in the Middle East*. US Institute of Peace Press, 1997.

Bean, G. E. *Aegean Turkey*. London, Benn, 1966.

Turkey's Southern Shore. London, Benn, 1968.

Berkes, Niyazi. *The Development of Secularism in Turkey*. Montreal, McGill University Press, 1964.

Bisbee, Eleanor. *The New Turks*. Philadelphia, 1951.

The People of Turkey. New York, 1946.

Cohn, Edwin J. *Turkish Economic, Social and Political Change*. New York, Praeger, 1970.

Cooke, Hedley V. *Challenge and Response in the Middle East: The Quest for Prosperity, 1919–1951*. New York, 1952.

Dodd, C. H. *Politics and Government in Turkey*. Manchester University Press, 1969.

Edgecumbe, Sir, C. N. E. *Turkey in Europe*. New York, Barnes and Noble, 1965.

Eren, Nuri. *Turkey Today and Tomorrow*. New York, 1964.

Frey, F. W. *The Turkish Political Elite*. Cambridge, Mass., MIT Press, 1965.

Gökalp, Ziya. *Turkish Nationalism and Western Civilisation*. London, 1960.

Güntekin, Reşat Nuri (trans. Sir Wyndham Deedes). *Afternoon Sun*. London, 1950.

Hale, William. *Aspects of Modern Turkey*. Epping, Bowker Publishing, 1977.

Harris, George S. *The Origins of Communism in Turkey*. Stanford, Calif., Hoover Institution, 1967.

Heyd, Uriel. *Foundations of Turkish Nationalism: the Life and Teachings of Ziya Gökalp*. London, Luzac and Harvill Press, 1950.

Language Reform in Modern Turkey. Jerusalem, 1954.

Hotham, David. *The Turks*. London, John Murray, 1972.

Jackh, Ernest. *The Rising Crescent*. New York, 1950.

Karpat, Kemal. *Turkey's Politics, The Transition to a Multi-Party System*. Princeton, 1959.

Kazamias, A. M. *Education and the Quest for Modernity in Turkey*. London, Allen and Unwin, 1967.

Keyder, Caglar. *State and Class in Turkey*. London, Verso, 1987.

Kinnane, Dirk. *The Kurds and Kurdistan*. Oxford, 1965.

Kinross, Lord. *Within the Taurus*. London, 1954.

Europa Minor: Journeys in Coastal Turkey. London, 1956.

Turkey. London, 1960.

Atatürk. London, Weidenfeld & Nicolson, 1964.

Kişlali, Ahmet Taner. *Forces politiques dans la Turquie moderne*. Ankara, 1967.

Koray, Enver. *Türkiye Tarih Yayınları Bibliografyası 1729–1950; A Bibliography of Historical Works on Turkey*. Ankara, 1952.

Kürger, K. *Die Türkei*. Berlin, 1951.

Lamb, Harold. *Suleiman the Magnificent: Sultan of the East*. New York, 1951.

Lewis, Bernard. *The Emergence of Modern Turkey*. London and New York, Oxford University Press, revised edn 1970.

Lewis, G. L. *Turkey* ('Nations of the Modern World' series). London, 1955; 3rd edn, New York, Praeger, 1965.

Linke, L. *Allah Dethroned*. London, 1937.

Lukach (Luke), Sir Harry Charles. *The Old Turkey and the New*. London, Geoffrey Bles, 1955.

McDowall, David. *A Modern History of the Kurds*. London, I. B. Tauris & Co Ltd, 1996.

Mellaart, James. *Earliest Civilizations of the Near East*. London, Thames and Hudson, 1965.

Çatal Hüyük. London, Thames and Hudson, 1967.

Moorehead, A. *Gallipoli*. New York, Harper, 1956.

Newman, Bernard. *Turkish Crossroads*. London, 1951.

Turkey and the Turks. London, Herbert Jenkins, 1968.

Orga, Irfan and Margarete. *Atatürk*. London, 1962.

Pettifer, James. *The Turkish Labyrinth: Atatürk and the New Islam*. London, Viking, 1997.

Plate, Herbert. *Das Land der Türken*. Graz, Wien, Köln, Verlag Styria, 1957.

Pope, Nicole and Hugh. *Turkey Unveiled: Atatürk and After*. London, John Murray, 1997.

Poulton, Hugh. *Top Hat, Grey Wolf and Crescent: Turkish nationalism and the Turkish Republic*. London, Hurst and Co, 1997.

Robinson, Richard D. *The First Turkish Republic*. Harvard University Press, 1963.

Rugman, Jonathan, and Hutchings, Roger. *Atatürk's Children: Turkey and the Kurds*. London, Cassell, 1996.

Salter, Cedric. *Introducing Turkey*. London, Methuen, 1961.

Stark, Freya. *Ionia*. London, 1954.

Lycian Shore. London, 1951.

Riding to the Tigris. London, 1956.

Steinhaus, Kurt. *Soziologie der turkischen Revolution*. Frankfurt, 1969.

Szyliowicz, Joseph S. *Political Change in Rural Turkey: Erdemli*. The Hague, Mouton, 1966.

Toynbee, A. J. *The Western Question in Greece and Turkey*. London, Constable, 1923.

Toynbee, A. J., and Kirkwood, D. P. *Turkey*. London, 1926.

Lycian Shore. London, 1956.

Tunaya, T. Z. *Atatürk, the Revolutionary Movement and Atatürkism*. Istanbul, Baha, 1964.

Vali, Ferenc A. *Bridge across the Bosphorus: the Foreign Policy of Turkey*. Johns Hopkins Press, 1970.

Ward, Barbara. *Turkey*. Oxford, 1942.

Ward, Robert E., and Rustow, Oankwart A. (Eds). *Political Modernizations in Japan and Turkey*. Princeton University Press, 1964.

Webster, D. E. *The Turkey of Atatürk: Social Progress in the Turkish Reformation*. Philadelphia, 1939.

Yalman, A. E. *Turkey in my Time*. University of Oklahoma Press, 1956.

HISTORY

Ahmad, Feroz. *The Young Turks*. Oxford University Press, 1969.

The Turkish Experiment in Democracy 1950–1975. London, Hurst, for Royal Institute of International Affairs, 1977.

Alderson, A. D. *The Structure of the Ottoman Dynasty*. Oxford, 1956.

Allen, W. E. D., and Muratoff, P. *Caucasian Battlefields: A History of the Wars on the Turco-Caucasian Border, 1828–1921*. Cambridge, 1953.

Barchard, David. *Turkey and the West*. London, Routledge and Kegan Paul, 1985.

Birand, Mehmet Ali. *The Generals' Coup in Turkey: An Inside Story of September 12, 1980*. Oxford, Brassey's, 1987.

Boghossian, Roupen. *Le Conflit Turco-Arménien*. Beirut, Altapress, 1987.

Cahen, Claude. *Pre-Ottoman Turkey*. London, Sidgwick & Jackson, 1968.

Cassels, Lavender. *The Struggle for the Ottoman Empire, 1717–1740*. London, John Murray, 1967.

Coles, Paul. *The Ottoman Impact on Europe*. London, Thames and Hudson, 1968; New York, Brace and World, 1968.

Davidson, Roderic H. *Turkey*. New York, Prentice-Hall, 1968.

Geyikdagi, Mehmet Yaşar. *Political Parties in Turkey: The Role of Islam*. New York, Praeger, 1986.

Gurney, O. R. *The Hittites*. London, 1952.

Hale, William. *The Political and Economic Development of Modern Turkey*. London, Croom Helm, 1981.

Kazancigil, Ali, and Ozbudun, Ergun (Eds). *Atatürk: Founder of a Modern State*. London, Hurst, 1981.

Kedourie, Elie. *England and the Middle East: The Destruction of the Ottoman Empire, 1914–1921*. Cambridge, 1956.

Kushner, David. *The Rise of Turkish Nationalism*. London, Frank Cass, 1980.

Landau, Jacob M. *Pan-Turkism: A Study in Irredentism*. London, Hurst, 1981.

Lewis, Bernard. *Istanbul and the Civilization of the Ottoman Empire*. University of Oklahoma Press, 1963.

Lewis, Geoffrey. *La Turquie, le déclin de l'Empire, les réformes d'Ataturk, la République moderne*. Belgium, Verviers, 1968.

Liddell, Robert. *Byzantium and Istanbul*. London, 1956.

Lloyd, Seton. *Early Anatolia*. London, 1956.

Mantran, Robert. *Histoire de la Turquie*. Paris, 1952.

Miller, William. *The Ottoman Empire and its Successors, 1801–1927*. Cambridge, 1934.

Ostrogorsky, G. *History of the Byzantine State*. Oxford, 1956.

Pfeffermann, Hans. *Die Zusammenarbeit der Renaissance Päpste mit den Türken*. Winterthur, 1946.

Price, M. Philips. *A History of Turkey: From Empire to Republic*. London, 1956.

Ramsaur, E. E. *The Young Turks and the Revolution of 1908*. Princeton University Press, 1957.

Rice, David Talbot. *Art of the Byzantine Era*. New York, Praeger, 1963.

Byzantine Art. London, Penguin, 1962.

Rice, Tamara Talbot. *The Seljuks*. London, 1962.

Runciman, Sir Steven. *The Fall of Constantinople, 1453*. Cambridge University Press, 1965.

Shaw, Stanford. *History of the Ottoman Empire*. Cambridge University Press, 1976.

Sumner, B. H. *Peter the Great and the Ottoman Empire*. Oxford, 1949.

Vaughan, Dorothy. *Europe and the Turk: A Pattern of Alliances, 1350–1700*. Liverpool, 1954.

Vere-Hodge, Edward Reginald. *Turkish Foreign Policy, 1918–1948*. London, 2nd revised edition, 1950.

Walder, David. *The Chanak Affair*. London, Hutchinson, 1968.

ECONOMY

Insel, Ahmet. *La Turquie entre l'Ordre et le Développement*. Paris, l'Harmattan, 1984.

Issawi, Charles. *The Economic History of Turkey*. University of Chicago Press, 1980.

Shorter, Frederic C. (Ed.). *Four Studies on the Economic Development of Turkey*. London, Cass, 1967; New York, Kelley, 1968.

THE UNITED ARAB EMIRATES

ABU DHABI   DUBAI   SHARJAH   RAS AL-KHAIMAH
UMM AL-QAIWAIN   AJMAN   FUJAIRAH

Geography

The coastline of the seven United Arab Emirates (UAE) extends for nearly 650 km (400 miles) from the frontier of the Sultanate of Oman to Khor al-Odaid, on the Qatari peninsula, in the Persian (Arabian) Gulf, interrupted only by an isolated outcrop of the Sultanate of Oman which lies on the coast of the Persian Gulf to the west and the Gulf of Oman to the east at the Strait of Hormuz. Six of the emirates lie on the coast of the Persian Gulf, while the seventh, Fujairah, is situated on the eastern coast of the peninsula, and has direct access to the Gulf of Oman. The area is one of extremely shallow seas, with offshore islands and coral reefs, and often an intricate pattern of sandbanks and small gulfs as a coastline. There is a considerable tide. The waters of the Gulf contain abundant quantities of fish, hence the important role of fishing in local life.

The climate is arid, with very high summer temperatures; and, except for a few weeks in winter, air humidity is also very high. The total area of the UAE has been estimated at 77,700 sq km (30,000 sq miles), relatively small compared with neighbouring Oman and Saudi Arabia, and it has a rapidly growing population, totalling 2,377,453 at the census of December 1995. In 1997 the population was estimated to be 2,580,000. The population is concentrated in the emirates of Abu Dhabi and Dubai, the principal commercial regions of the country. Abu Dhabi is the largest emirate, with an area of about 67,350 sq km (26,000 sq miles) and a population of 928,360 at the December 1995 census. The town of Abu Dhabi is also the capital of the UAE. The most important port is Dubai, the capital of the UAE's second largest state. Its significance derives from its position on one of the rare deep creeks of the area, and it now has a very large transit trade.

Many inhabitants are still nomadic Arabs, and the official language is Arabic, which is spoken by most of the native inhabitants. Arabs are outnumbered, however, by non-Arab immigrant workers. In the coastal towns there are many Iranians, Indians, Pakistanis and Africans. Most of the native inhabitants are Muslims, mainly of the Sunni sect.

History

Revised for this edition by MICHAEL JAMES DEN HARTOG

In the early 16th century the Portuguese commercial monopoly of the Gulf area was challenged by other European traders. The Portuguese ascendency in the East gradually declined, and in 1650 they evacuated Oman, losing their entire hold on the Arabian shore. There followed a period of commercial and political rivalry between the Dutch and the British. The initial Dutch predominance weakened and in 1766 came practically to an end, while the British were consolidating their position in India.

Both European and Arab pirates were very active in the Gulf during the 17th, 18th and early 19th centuries. Attacks on British-flag vessels led to British expeditions against the pirates and eventually, in 1818, against the pirate headquarters at Ras al-Khaimah and other harbours along the 240 km of 'Pirate Coast'. In 1820 a general treaty of peace, for suppressing piracy and slave traffic, was concluded between Great Britain and the Arab tribes of the Gulf. It was signed by the principal sheikhs of the Pirate Coast and Bahrain. A strong British squadron was stationed at Ras al-Khaimah to enforce the treaty.

Piracy persisted and accordingly, in 1835, the sheikhs agreed, in a 'maritime truce', not to engage, under any circumstances, in hostilities by sea during the pearl-diving season. The advantages of this were so noticeable that the sheikhs willingly renewed the truce for increasing periods until, in May 1853, a 'treaty of maritime peace in perpetuity' was concluded, establishing a 'perpetual maritime truce' on the newly-named 'Trucial Coast' (also called Trucial Oman). It was supervised by the British Government, to whom the signatories would refer any breach. The British did not interfere in wars between the sheikhs on land.

Towards the end of the 19th century, France, Germany and Russia showed increasing interest in the Gulf area, and in 1892 Britain entered into separate but identical 'exclusive' treaties with the Trucial rulers, whereby the sheikhs undertook not to cede, mortgage or otherwise dispose of parts of their territories to anyone except the British Government, nor to enter into any relationship with a foreign government, other than the British, without British consent. Britain had already undertaken to protect the states from outside attack in the perpetual maritime treaty of 1853.

In 1820, when the general treaty was signed, there were only five Trucial states. In 1866, on the death of the Chief Sheikh of Sharjah, his domains were divided among his four sons, the separate branches of the family being established at Sharjah, Ras al-Khaimah, Dibba and Kalba. Kalba was incorporated into Sharjah in 1952, when its ruler agreed to accept all existing treaties between the United Kingdom (UK) and the Trucial States, as did the ruler of Fujairah. This involved recognizing the British Government's right to define state boundaries, to settle disputes between the Trucial sheikhdoms and to render assistance to the Trucial Oman Scouts, a force of some 1,600 men, officered and paid for by Britain, which was set up in 1952.

In 1952, on British advice, a trucial council was established, at which all seven rulers met at least twice a year, under the chairmanship of the political agent in Dubai. Its object was to encourage the pursuit of a common policy in administrative matters, possibly leading to a federation of the states.

The advent of the commercial production of petroleum in mid-1962 gave Abu Dhabi a great opportunity for development. A major obstacle to this development was removed in August 1966, when Sheikh Shakhbut bin Sultan an-Nahyan, the ruler of Abu Dhabi since 1928, was deposed. The ruling family replaced Shakhbut by his younger brother, Sheikh Zayed bin Sultan. The subsequent history of Abu Dhabi has been indicative of a society suddenly transformed by the acquisition of immense wealth. Petroleum was discovered in neighbouring Dubai in 1966, and that sheikhdom also benefited greatly from the petroleum boom.

In June 1965 Sheikh Saqr bin Sultan of Sharjah was deposed. In spite of an appeal to the UN Secretary-General, supported by Iraq and the United Arab Republic (now Egypt), the accession of his cousin, Sheikh Khalid bin Muhammad, proceeded without incident.

Intending to relocate its major military base in the Middle East, Britain started work in 1966 on a base in Sharjah, which by 1968 had become the principal base in the Gulf. However, British forces had been withdrawn from the area by the end of 1971. The Trucial Oman Scouts, based in Sharjah, were proposed as the nucleus of a federal security force after the British withdrawal, but some states, notably Abu Dhabi, were already creating their own defence forces.

In order to avoid disputes over the ill-defined state borders, those between Qatar, Abu Dhabi and Dubai were settled early in 1970—although not without objection from Saudi Arabia, whose territorial claims overlapped those of Abu Dhabi to a considerable extent. In late 1974 a border agreement was signed with Saudi Arabia on the Liwa oases, whereupon Saudi Arabia recognized the United Arab Emirates (UAE) and ambassadors were exchanged.

The original proposals for the formation of a federation (after the British had withdrawn) included Bahrain and Qatar, as well as the seven Trucial States, but these larger and more developed states eventually opted for separate independence. On 1 December 1971 Britain terminated all existing treaties with the Trucial States. On the following day Abu Dhabi, Dubai, Sharjah, Umm al-Qaiwain, Ajman and Fujairah formed the UAE, and a treaty of friendship was made with Britain. The federation approved a provisional constitution, which was to expire after five years, when a formal constitution would be drafted. This has not yet happened, however, and the provisional constitution has been repeatedly renewed. In practice this has lent a flexibility to the developing emirates, allowing the process of centralization to follow a gradual course and averting any serious dispute which could arise from an emirate's contravention of formal constitutional decrees. At independence, Sheikh Zayed, the ruler of Abu Dhabi, took office as the first President of the UAE. Sheikh Rashid bin Said al-Maktoum, the ruler of Dubai since 1958, became Vice-President, while his eldest son, Sheikh Maktoum bin Rashid (Crown Prince of Dubai), became Prime Minister. In December 1991 the UAE became a member of both the League of Arab States (Arab League) and the United Nations (UN). In February 1972 Ras al-Khaimah became the seventh member of the federation.

In January 1972 the Ruler of Sharjah, Sheikh Khalid, was killed by rebels under the leadership of his cousin, Sheikh Saqr, who had been deposed in 1965. The rebels were captured, and Sheikh Sultan bin Muhammad succeeded his brother as ruler, confirming a continuation of the late Khalid's relatively liberal principles of government, and Sharjah's membership of the UAE.

Although the UAE remained one of the most conservative Arab states, it gave considerable support to the Arab cause in the October War of 1973 and participated in the associated petroleum cut-backs and boycotts. It was the first state to impose a total ban on exports of petroleum to the USA, and subsequently supported the Arab ostracism of Egypt, which followed the negotiation of the Camp David agreements between Egypt and Israel in 1978 and the subsequent 1979 peace treaty between the two countries.

TOWARDS GREATER CENTRALIZATION

In December 1973 the separate Abu Dhabi Government was disbanded and, in a ministerial reshuffle, some of its members became federal ministers. Most notably, the Abu Dhabi minister responsible for petroleum, Dr Mana bin Said al-Oteiba, became the first federal Minister of Petroleum and Mineral Resources. The government reorganization involved a considerable extension of central authority and was a further step towards the integration of the seven sheikhdoms. In May 1975, at a session of the Supreme Council, the seven emirs gave their consent, in principle, to further steps towards centralization. In November Sharjah merged the Sharjah National Guard with the Union Defence Force, and also granted control of its broadcasting station to the Federal Ministry of Communications, its police to the Ministry of the Interior and its courts to the Ministry of Justice. The Sharjah flag was abolished in favour of the federal tricolour. Fujairah and Abu Dhabi both discontinued the use of their flags.

The merger of the main defence forces (the Union Defence Force, the Abu Dhabi Defence Force and the Dubai Defence Force) was finally agreed in early May 1976, when Gen. Sheikh Khalifa bin Zayed an-Nahyan, the Crown Prince of Abu Dhabi, was made deputy supreme commander (Sheikh Zayed became supreme commander). In November the provisional constitution was amended so that the right to levy armed forces and acquire weapons was placed exclusively in the hands of federal government.

During 1976 Sheikh Zayed, impatient with the slow rate at which the emirates were achieving centralization, threatened not to stand for a second term as President of the UAE in November 1976. In the event, he was re-elected unanimously after the Supreme Council had granted the federal Government greater control over defence, intelligence services, immigration, public security and border control. A reshuffle of the Council of Ministers followed in January 1977, with ministers chosen on the principle of individual merit rather than equitable representation of the seven emirates. The new 40-member Federal National Council, which was inaugurated on 1 March, showed the same spirit of reinvigoration, as only seven members of the first five-year session (1971–76) were included.

Mounting pressure from within the emirates for a more united federation led, in 1978, to the setting up of a joint Cabinet-Federal National Council committee to discuss methods of achieving this. Events in Iran in 1979 and the resultant security threat prompted a full meeting of the Council of Ministers and the Federal National Council in February. The outcome of this was a 10-point memorandum advocating the abolition of all internal borders, the unification of defence forces and the merging of revenues in a federal budget. This plan was subsequently submitted to the Supreme Council.

Despite their widespread support in the emirates, these proposals aggravated the long-standing rivalry between Abu Dhabi, the financial mainstay of the federation, and Dubai, which had become increasingly critical of the centralized federal Government. Dubai rejected the memorandum completely and, together with Ras al-Khaimah, boycotted a Supreme Council meeting in March, 1979.

It was thought that the deadlock had been broken, at least temporarily, when Sheikh Rashid, ruler of Dubai, replaced his son as Prime Minister of the federal Government (while retaining the vice-presidency) in July 1979. A new Council of Ministers was formed, preserving a similar balance of power between the emirates as before. Ras al-Khaimah integrated its defence force with the federal force, and both Abu Dhabi and Dubai pledged to contribute 50% of their revenues from petroleum to the federal budget. Dubai's forces, however, remained, in practice, a separate entity. Further attempts at integration included the construction of national roads, the installation of telecommunications, and the central planning and financing of health, education and agriculture. In November 1981 Sheikh Rashid was re-elected Prime Minister by the Supreme Council, and Sheikh Zayed was re-elected President.

FOREIGN POLICY AND THE IRAN–IRAQ WAR

With the outbreak of war between Iran and Iraq in 1980, the UAE became vulnerable to external forces over which it had no control. Iran's repeated threats to close the Strait of Hormuz to traffic carrying exports of petroleum from Gulf countries represented a grave potential danger to states such as the UAE, which depend on revenues from petroleum. Partly in response to Iranian threats, the UAE joined with five other Gulf states to form the Co-operation Council of the Arab States of the Gulf (Gulf Co-operation Council—GCC) in March 1981 (see p. 246), to work towards economic, political and social integration in the Gulf. The GCC's primary concern initially was to develop greater economic co-operation, but this gave way to concern over the region's ability to defend itself. A bilateral defence agreement was signed with Saudi Arabia in 1982, and, in accordance with GCC policy, the UAE has substantially increased its defence expenditure.

The foreign policy of the UAE is motivated chiefly by its support for Arab unity, especially in the Palestinian cause. In March 1985 President Zayed pledged his country's support for Lebanon in its fight against Israeli occupation forces. In the Iran–Iraq War, it made substantial donations to Iraq, but in 1984 these were reported to have been discontinued, owing to the UAE's financial difficulties. Whether or not this was the case, the report indicated the UAE's desire to maintain some neutrality in the conflict, an attitude which was less clearly perceptible in other GCC states.

In November 1984 the UAE Government held further talks with leaders of other Arab states, in an effort to find a solution to the Iran–Iraq War. During the sixth regional summit meeting of the GCC, which was held in Oman in November 1985, the member states decided to adopt a more neutral stance in the Iran–Iraq War, and to improve relations with Iran. At the seventh GCC summit meeting, held in Abu Dhabi in November 1986, the member states expressed concern over the escalation of the Iran–Iraq War, and discussed the protection of petroleum installations and shipping in the area.

On 11 August 1987 a Panamanian-registered supertanker, the *Texaco Caribbean,* struck a mine 13 km off the coast of the UAE, near the port of Fujairah. This was the first incident of its kind during the Iran–Iraq War involving mines (presumed to be Iranian) laid outside the Persian Gulf. On 13 August the Government of the UAE declared Fujairah port a danger zone and banned all commercial shipping from a surrounding area of 100 sq km, while minesweeping operations were carried out. At the end of August the UAE gave provisional permission for the use of its ports as a base for British minesweeping operations. In April 1988 the Mubarak oilfield, which belongs to the emirate of Sharjah and is located 30 km off the coast of the UAE, was closed for two months, following an attack on its installations by forces involved in the Iran–Iraq War.

The decline in revenues from petroleum in the mid-1980s had little effect on the comfortable lifestyle of the UAE, although certain development plans were postponed or rescheduled. One effect of decreased revenue was a greater commitment to local co-operation both within the UAE and among Gulf countries in general. Thus, bilateral agreements with Oman, Qatar, the People's Democratic Republic of Yemen and Iraq were made for the purpose of mutual aid in educational, scientific and cultural development. In November 1985 diplomatic relations were established between the UAE and the USSR. This was expected to lead to increased bilateral trade between the countries.

In November 1987 the UAE resumed diplomatic relations with Egypt, following the adoption of a resolution at a summit meeting of the League of Arab States, which permitted member states to resume relations with Egypt at their own discretion.

The escalation of tension in the Gulf, exacerbated by the presence of US and Soviet naval forces, had resulted in the adoption of Resolution 598 by the UN Security Council on 20 July 1987, which urged an immediate cease-fire. In November, at an extraordinary meeting of the League of Arab States in Amman, Jordan, representatives of the member states, including the UAE, unanimously condemned Iran for prolonging the war against Iraq, deplored its occupation of Arab (i.e. Iraqi) territory, and urged it to accept Resolution 598 without pre-conditions.

DEVELOPMENTS IN DOMESTIC POLITICS

In October 1986 the provisional federal constitution was renewed for a further five years, and Sheikh Zayed and Sheikh Rashid were unanimously re-elected to the posts of President, and Vice-President and Prime Minister, respectively.

An attempted coup took place in Sharjah in June 1987, when Sheikh Abd al-Aziz, a brother of the ruler (Sheikh Sultan bin Muhammad al-Qasimi), issued a statement, in his brother's absence, which announced the abdication of Sheikh Sultan, on the grounds that he had mismanaged the economy. Since Sheikh Sultan assumed power in 1972, Sharjah had incurred debts estimated at US $920m. in mid-1987, as the result of an extravagant programme of construction ordered by the ruler. However, Dubai intervened and convened a meeting of the Supreme Council of Rulers, which endorsed Sheikh Sultan's claim to be the legitimate ruler of Sharjah, and restored him to power. As a result of the attempted coup, Sheikh Abd al-Aziz was given the title of Crown Prince and granted a seat on the Supreme Council. In July Sheikh Sultan formed an executive council in Sharjah, comprising the heads of local government departments and other individuals selected by him, to assist in the administration of the public affairs of the emirate. Sheikh Sultan also signed an agreement with bank creditors, whereby Sharjah's loan repayments would be rescheduled until 1993. In February

1990, however, Sheikh Sultan removed his brother from the post of Crown Prince and revoked his right to succeed him. In July Sheikh Sultan appointed Sheikh Ahmad bin Muhammad al-Qasimi, the head of Sharjah's petroleum and mineral affairs office, as Deputy Ruler of Sharjah. He was not given the title of Crown Prince. On 7 October the Ruler of Dubai, Prime Minister and Vice-President of the UAE, Sheikh Rashid bin Said al-Maktoum, died. He was succeeded in all of his offices by his eldest son, Sheikh Maktoum bin Rashid al-Maktoum. In November a reorganization of ministerial portfolios took place. The Minister of Petroleum and Mineral Resources, Dr Mana bin Said al-Oteiba, was replaced by Yousuf bin Omeir bin Yousuf, a former executive at the Abu Dhabi Investment Authority. The post of Minister of Foreign Affairs, vacant since 1982, was filled by the Minister of State for Foreign Affairs, Rashid Abdullah an-Nuaimi. One of the President's sons, Sheikh Hamdan bin Zayed an-Nahyan, replaced an-Nuaimi as Minister of State for Foreign Affairs, while another, Sheikh Sultan bin Zayed an-Nahyan, was appointed Deputy Prime Minister. In October 1991 the Supreme Council confirmed Sheikh Zayed and Sheikh Maktoum as, respectively, President and Vice-President, each for a further five-year term. The provisional federal constitution was also renewed for a further period of five years.

In 1991 the UAE became involved in a major international financial scandal, when, in July, the regulatory authorities in seven countries closed down (without warning) the operations of the Bank of Credit and Commerce International (BCCI), in which the Abu Dhabi ruling family and agencies had held a controlling interest (77%) since April 1990. The termination of the bank's activities followed the disclosure by an auditor's report, commissioned by the Bank of England, of systematic, large-scale fraud by BCCI authorities (perpetrated before April 1990). By the end of July 1991 BCCI's activities had been suspended in all 69 countries in which it had operated. Attempts to formulate a restructuring programme for the bank failed, and in February 1992 the bank's majority shareholders offered to pay a maximum of $2,200m. into a fund to compensate BCCI creditors. By October the compensation plan, worth a total of $1,700m., had been approved by more than 90% of BCCI creditors. In that month the settlement received judicial authorization in Luxembourg. None the less, the compensation process was delayed in December, when three prominent creditors, who had objected to a clause that would require recipients of compensation to waive any further claims against Abu Dhabi in respect of the BCCI scandal, initiated appeal proceedings against the Luxembourg ruling. The ruling was overturned in October 1993, and the BCCI's liquidators, Touche Ross, and the bank's majority shareholders were obliged to negotiate a new compensation agreement. In February 1995 a compensation agreement worth a total of $1,800m. received judicial authorization in Luxembourg. In February 1996 the UAE Central Bank formally revoked the licence of the BCCI, and in May the Abu Dhabi authorities made a payment of $1,550m. to Touche Ross (a further $250m. was to be held in an escrow account for release at a later date).

Meanwhile, in February 1994 the Minister of Petroleum and Mineral Resources, Yousuf bin Omeir bin Yousuf, resigned, citing personal reasons. In that month Sheikh Zayed issued a decree whereby a wide range of crimes, including murder, theft, adultery and drugs-related offences, would be tried in *Shari'a* (Islamic religious law) courts rather than in civil courts, and in April 1995 the Council of Ministers approved the introduction of the death penalty for drugs dealers and smugglers. In September a *Shari'a* court sentenced a 16-year-old Filipino woman to death for the murder of her Arab employer following an alleged rape. The sentence provoked public outcry in the Philippines. In mid-October, following appeals to the UAE authorities from the Philippine Government and the subsequent personal intervention of Sheikh Zayed, the family of the deceased agreed to rescind their right to demand the execution of the accused in return for financial compensation. Later in the month the death sentence was commuted by an appeal court, which sentenced the accused to 100 lashes and one year's imprisonment, followed by deportation.

In January 1995 a decree was issued by the Ruler of Dubai, Sheikh Maktoum bin Rashid al-Maktoum, naming Sheikh Muhammad bin Rashid al-Maktoum as Crown Prince. The decree also named Sheikh Hamdan bin Rashid al-Maktoum as Deputy Ruler of Dubai. In June 1996 legislation designed to make the provisional constitution permanent was endorsed by the Federal National Council, following its approval by the Supreme Council of Rulers.

A three-month amnesty for expatriates resident in the UAE in contravention of the country's entry and residency laws was extended by one month at the end of September 1996. Some 200,000 foreign nationals were expected to leave the country by the new 31 October deadline, or risk severe punishment under the terms of a new residency law to be introduced on 1 November.

In late March 1997 there was a cabinet reshuffle—the first for seven years. Thirteen of the 22 cabinet members, including the ministers of finance, defence and foreign affairs, retained their posts, while the new appointments included Sheikh Fahim bin Sultan al-Qasimi as Minister of Economy and Commerce and Sheikh Abdullah bin Zayed an-Nahyan, son of the late UAE President, as Minister of Information and Culture.

FOREIGN RELATIONS

Iraq's occupation of Kuwait, in August 1990, caused political and economic crisis throughout the Gulf region. The UAE responded by supporting resistance to Iraqi aggression, and on 20 August the UAE ordered all nationals to join the armed forces for six weeks' military training. At the same time it was announced that armed forces opposing Iraq's aggression would be granted military facilities in the UAE. Units from the British and French air forces were among those which were subsequently stationed there. In February 1991, after the outbreak of hostilities between Iraq and a US-led multinational force, the UAE air force conducted four raids against Iraqi targets. In March representatives from GCC Chambers of Commerce met in Dubai in order to discuss the role of GCC companies in the reconstruction of Kuwait.

In the aftermath of the war between Iraq and the US-led multinational force, the Ministers of Foreign Affairs of Egypt, Syria and the six GCC states met in Damascus, Syria, in order to discuss regional security arrangements. The meeting resulted in the signing of the 'Damascus declaration' which envisaged, among other things, the formation of an Arab peace-keeping force comprising mainly Egyptian and Syrian troops. At the beginning of May 1991 the Ministers of Foreign Affairs of the GCC states held an emergency meeting in Kuwait to discuss further regional security measures. In early May Egypt announced that it would withdraw its armed forces from Saudi Arabia and Kuwait within three months: an apparent failure to honour its commitment, under the 'Damascus declaration', to participate in the Arab peace-keeping force. At the beginning of April the President of the UAE had discounted the possibility of Iraq's participation in a Gulf security system while Saddam Hussain remained in power there; but he had indicated that the UAE would be prepared, in concert with the other GCC member states, to consider Iranian security proposals. In September 1992 a meeting attended by Egypt, Syria and the GCC states was presented with an Egyptian proposal to create a series of rapid deployment forces. However, the consideration of military co-operation was discontinued, in favour of discussion of political and economic co-ordination.

Tension between the UAE and Iran was not confined to matters relating to the GCC; there was also a territorial dimension. Rival claims to the island of Abu Musa had been made by Sharjah and Iran in 1970, when petroleum exploration began. In 1971 agreement was reached to divide any oil revenues. In August 1992, however, it was reported that Iran had annexed Abu Musa after 20 years of joint control. It was claimed that Iranian authorities had denied landing permission to more than 100 residents of the island who were returning from Sharjah, and that Iran was refusing a compromise agreement. Iran subsequently claimed sovereignty over Abu Musa, together with the Greater Tunb and Lesser Tunb Islands. Discussions between representatives of the countries' Ministers of Foreign Affairs were convened in Abu Dhabi at the end of September, but collapsed almost immediately, with Iran refusing to discuss ownership of two of the three islands. At a GCC summit meeting in Abu Dhabi in December it was demanded that Iran reverse the 'virtual annexation' of the islands. In April 1993 a GCC

statement expressed satisfaction at recent developments and support for bilateral negotiations. In the same month it was reported that all persons who had been expelled from (or refused entry to) Abu Musa in 1992 had been permitted to return. Both the UAE and Iran periodically proclaimed their commitment to direct talks; however, by late 1994 no significant progress had been made towards resolving the conflict, and in December the UAE announced its intention to refer the dispute to the International Court of Justice. In February 1995 it was alleged that Iran had deployed air defence systems on the islands. In November officials from the UAE and Iran, meeting in Qatar, failed to reach agreement on establishing an agenda for ministerial-level negotiations. In March 1996 relations between the two countries deteriorated further when Iran opened an airport on Abu Musa; in the following month Iran established a power station on the island of Greater Tunb. Although talks were held in March 1997, no solution was reached, and in June the UAE protested to the UN about a pier which, it alleged, Iran had constructed on Greater Tunb. The GCC has supported UAE claims to the islands but has also welcomed an Iranian offer to open dialogue. In mid-1998, however, the issue remained unresolved.

In September 1993 the UAE welcomed the successful negotiation of a preliminary Israeli-Palestinian peace accord, and pledged financial support to the Palestinians. The UAE also continued to modernize its defence capability, signing a defence agreement with the USA in July 1994 which extended the agreement signed in 1991 in the aftermath of the Gulf conflict. This coincided with the announcement of plans to reduce the size of the UAE armed forces by 10,000 to 50,000.

In September 1994 the UAE, along with the other GCC member states, agreed to a partial removal of the Arab economic boycott of Israel. In mid-January 1995 the UAE signed a defence agreement with France which provided for 'consultations' in the event of aggression against or threats to UAE territory. A similar agreement was reportedly under negotiation with the UK. However, negotiations stalled for a period, owing to the reluctance of the British Government to accept the extension of UAE jurisdiction over British troops deployed there. A defence agreement was finally signed in November 1996, by which the UK undertook to defend the UAE in the event of an external attack. The UAE is reported to have spent $66,000m. modernizing its defence capacity during 1991–96. In mid-October 1995, while addressing a meeting of the new ambassadors in the UAE, Sheikh Zayed announced that it was 'time for reconciliation' with Iraq and appealed for the easing of UN sanctions against that country to relieve the suffering of the Iraqi people. In January 1997 the UAE sent a shipment of aid containing food and medicine to Iraq to help alleviate the desperate situation of Iraqi children. In March, in protest at Israel's decision to construct a Jewish settlement in a disputed area of East Jerusalem, the League of Arab States voted to suspend negotiations to establish diplomatic links with Israel, close Israeli missions, restore the economic boycott and withdraw from multilateral peace talks. In November the UAE, in common with most other GCC and Arab League member states, did not attend the fourth Middle East and North Africa economic conference in Doha, Qatar: the boycott was widely observed in protest at the attendance of a delegation from Israel, which was regarded as having failed to fulfil its obligations with regard to the Middle East peace process in general, and the Oslo accords in particular. In late 1997, as the crisis developed between Iraq and weapons inspectors of the UN Special Commission on Iraq (UNSCOM) (see Iraq), the UAE persisted in its reconciliatory stance towards Iraq, refusing US requests to allow the deployment of US fighter aircraft in the UAE, and strongly advocating a diplomatic solution. A further shipment of medicine and food aid from the UAE arrived in Iraq in February 1998. In that month a ship transporting illegal Iraqi oil exports sank off the coast of Sharjah causing a major oil spill. The Minister of State for Foreign Affairs announced his intention to prevent a recurrence of this event, and in August an environmental protection law was approved.

The UAE is expanding its air force as part of a 10-year weapons procurement programme, worth an estimated $15,000m. In December 1997 the Government signed a contract for the modernization of its 33 *Mirage* 2000 jets, and for the purchase of 30 new *Mirage* 2000-9 fighter aircraft, and in May 1998 it was announced that 80 US F-16 fighter aircraft had

been ordered (at a cost of at least $6,000m.), representing the largest defence purchase in the country's history.

Economy

Dr P. T. H. UNWIN

Revised for this edition by MICHAEL JAMES DEN HARTOG

INTRODUCTION

Prior to the discovery of petroleum, the economy of the seven sheikhdoms, or emirates, that comprised the Trucial States was based on pearling, fishing, trade and a limited amount of agriculture. In the 19th century, piracy, as defined by the Western powers that became dominant in the area, also formed an important source of income for the coastal tribes. Since 1958, when petroleum was first discovered off Abu Dhabi, and in particular since June 1962, when it was first exported, the economy of the area has undergone dramatic change. The pace of this change increased appreciably following independence in 1971, leading to the creation of the federal state of the United Arab Emirates (UAE), and the increases in the price of oil dictated by the Organization of the Petroleum Exporting Countries (OPEC), of which the UAE is a member. In 1995, according to estimates by the World Bank, the UAE's gross national product (GNP), measured at average 1993–95 prices, was equivalent to US $17,400 per head. During 1985–95, it was estimated GNP per head decreased, in real terms, by an average annual rate of 3.5%.

The UAE covers approximately 77,700 sq km, most of which is either sand desert or *sibakh* (salt flats). At the March 1968 census its population was 179,126. The pace of the UAE's rapid economic change can be seen in the dramatic increase in population during succeeding years: it reached 1,042,099 by the December 1980 census, and results from the December 1985 census indicated that the population had grown by 55.7% in the intervening five years, to 1,622,464, of whom about 670,000 were inhabitants of Abu Dhabi. According to the Ministry of Planning, the population had reached 2.1m. by 1993, although only 20% of the total were UAE nationals, while most of the remaining 80% were originally from the Indian sub-continent. The December 1995 census recorded a population of 2.38m., of whom 928,360 lived in Abu Dhabi, 674,100 in Dubai, 400,400 in Sharjah and the remainder in the other emirates. During 1990–96 the population increased by an annual average of 5.3%. In 1996 the population was officially estimated to be 2,443,000. As in 1985, males comprised about two-thirds of the total population. The largest relative increases in population have been in the smallest emirates, reflecting their policy of economic expansion. The unequal distribution of the sexes (with males accounting for 65% of the total population in 1985) indicates the large amount of immigration that has been necessary to sustain the country's economic growth. There have been strong demands for the redeployment of labour from non-Arab Asians to Arabs. In a government drive against illegal immigrants, up to 200,000 Asian workers were estimated to have left the country by November 1996. Despite a consequent increase in labour costs, the Government justified its actions on the grounds of the need to avoid cultural dilution and political unrest. In 1996 it was estimated the total number of people in employment was 1,050,800, of whom 7.4% were engaged in agriculture and fishing (compared with 21% in 1965), 29.6% in industry (32% in 1965) and 63.0% in services (47% in 1965).

Despite progress in the UAE towards political integration, co-ordination in economic policies has proved to be difficult to accomplish. Abu Dhabi's wealth tends to overshadow the other emirates but, at the same time, it is the main factor which holds the seven emirates together. Apart from the difference between Abu Dhabi and Dubai over participation in the petroleum industry, the two main emirates have tended to pursue independent strategies in developing their various industries. An important instrument of development policy is the federal budget, which is essentially concerned with the implementation of federal

infrastructure policy. Individual emirates also draw up separate budgets for municipal expenditure and local projects. The Constitution provides for social services, such as health and education, to come under federal control. In the 1970s Abu Dhabi contributed more than 90% of the federal budget revenue, but by 1990 its share had fallen to about 80%, with Dubai contributing about 16%. In terms of gross domestic product (GDP), Abu Dhabi continues to dominate the UAE, but its share of total GDP declined from 70% in 1980 to 61% in 1984. Dubai contributed 25% of total GDP, and Sharjah 8%, in 1984. As a result of depressed petroleum prices from 1983, overall GDP declined in some subsequent years, but in 1989 the economic recovery which followed the cease-fire in the Iran–Iraq War enabled a number of industrial projects, postponed in the mid-1980s, to be revived. GDP in that year increased by 15.9%, to AED 100,976m. ($27,506m.), and in 1990 the combination of increased oil production and higher prices produced a massive increase in GDP, to AED 125,266m. ($34,140m.).

Iraq's invasion of Kuwait in August 1990 initially had a destabilizing effect upon the UAE economy. Work on development projects was suspended and banks lost between 15% and 30% of their deposits in August and September. More than 8,000 Kuwaitis fled to the UAE. Higher shipping insurance premiums acted as a restraint on trade. By the end of 1990, however, work on development projects had resumed, and confidence in the economy had revived as a result of the 54% increase in the revenue which the UAE had earned from its sales of petroleum in the course of the year. At $21,100m., the value of these sales was more than sufficient to meet the additional expenses which the UAE incurred as a result of the crisis in the Gulf. A large part of these expenses arose from the financial support it gave to the military operations of the anti-Iraq coalition; and from aid granted to those countries for which the economic effects of the crisis were most severe. (The UAE donated £275m. towards the cost of British and $4,067m. towards the cost of US military operations. It also made a contribution of $1,469m. to the Gulf Financial Crisis Co-ordination Group.) After the liberation of Kuwait in February 1991 the UAE announced ambitious expenditure plans in both the petroleum and non-petroleum sectors. The UAE also benefited from participation in Kuwait's reconstruction programme, in the aftermath of its liberation, and from a revival of regional trade after the war. The UAE placed orders worth an estimated $12,050m. for defence equipment in 1993. Cumulative UAE defence spending during the 1990s was forecast to total about $20,000m. Under the country's 'offset' rules, foreign defence contractors winning orders worth more than $10m. were required to reinvest, over a seven-year period, 60% of the value of such orders in approved projects beneficial to the UAE economy. In 1995 the French company Giat, which had a $3,700m. contract to supply tanks to the UAE, put forward 'offset' proposals which included an offer to buy a 49% stake in a major power station and desalination complex currently under construction in Abu Dhabi. In the weeks preceding the International Defence Exhibition in Abu Dhabi in early 1997, a series of new industrial ventures was announced by the UAE Offsets Group, involving local investors and international defence manufacturers.

The federation's GDP totalled AED 126,264m. in 1991, AED 130,676m. in 1992, AED 132,116m. in 1993, AED 135,065m. in 1994 and AED 143,970m. ($39,197m.) in 1995. GDP increased, in real terms, by an estimated annual average of 0.4% in 1980–93. According to UN estimates, real growth in GDP was recorded at 2.2% in 1995, 5.0% in 1996 and 4.5% in 1997. The non-oil sectors of the economy accounted for two-thirds of GDP in 1996. According to preliminary planning ministry figures, GDP totalled AED 163,750m. in 1996 and was forecast to rise to AED 171,000m. in 1997. Relatively steady revenues from petroleum exports and rapidly growing non-oil trade have provided a strong financial base to support the Government's ambitious plans for industrial expansion and diversification through the 1990s.

PETROLEUM AND GAS

The economy of the UAE is dominated by petroleum. At the end of 1997 the UAE's proven oil reserves totalled 97,800m. barrels (9.4% of world reserves and 12.3% of OPEC reserves). At the end of 1996 the UAE's proven reserves of natural gas totalled 5,800,000m. cu m (4.1% of world reserves and 10.0% of OPEC reserves), of which 5,300,000m. cu m (91.4%) were in Abu Dhabi. Between 1971 and 1980 the UAE's revenue from petroleum increased about 25-fold, and, particularly between 1973 and 1976, the economy expanded very rapidly. In this period, public-sector spending increased at an annual rate of 72%. The second half of the 1970s, however, was a period of retrenchment, and there was a major recession in the mid-1980s. Owing to the surplus of petroleum supplies in the 1980s, government revenue from exports of petroleum was greatly reduced. Japan, which is the largest customer for crude petroleum from the UAE, imported 26.8% of its total crude oil requirements from the UAE in 1995. The petroleum sector's contribution to GDP declined from 63% in 1980 to 34% in 1995. In 1997, as a result of declining petroleum prices, the sector's contribution to GDP decreased further, to 31%.

In 1983 Abu Dhabi produced 69.9% of the UAE's petroleum output, Dubai 29.5% and Sharjah 0.5%. Output rose rapidly, from an average of 14,200 barrels per day (b/d) in 1962 (the first year of production) to 1,059,000 b/d in 1971. Output nearly doubled to 1,998,700 b/d in 1977 before falling gradually to 1,133,743 b/d in 1981—lower than in any year since 1971. Under the terms of an OPEC agreement in March 1983, the UAE was accorded a production quota of 1.1m. b/d.

Towards the end of 1985 it was evident that Abu Dhabi was exceeding its production quota. After the abandonment of oil-pricing agreements at an OPEC meeting held in Vienna in October 1985, the UAE's production rose appreciably. In December OPEC decided to abandon production restraint and to seek a larger share of the market. By March 1986 it was apparent that Abu Dhabi had raised production levels by almost 30%, while, at the same time, halving prices, in an attempt to maintain its revenue. The UAE's total production rose from 805,000 b/d at the end of 1985 to 1.7m. b/d in July 1986. The OPEC decision to seek a larger market share exacerbated the oil glut and precipitated the collapse in prices during 1986. At the beginning of August OPEC agreed to reduce its members' overall production by about 4m. b/d for two months from 1 September in an effort to stabilize prices. This had the effect of setting the UAE's quota at 950,000 b/d, and this level was reaffirmed at an OPEC meeting held in October, when marginally higher collective production levels were established for November and December. The UAE's production quota for the first six months of 1987 was set at 902,000 b/d, with Abu Dhabi assuming 682,000 b/d to be its share of the quota, and Dubai taking 220,000 b/d. In February 1987, however, Abu Dhabi was producing approximately 780,000 b/d, and Dubai about 380,000 b/d, thereby continuing the trend of over-production that has been characteristic of the UAE in recent years. In June, petroleum prices having stabilized at around $18 per barrel, OPEC introduced new production quotas for the second half of 1987, raising collective production to a notional 16.6m. b/d. The UAE was allocated a quota of 948,000 b/d, but in July it was producing at an average rate of 1.35m. b/d. In mid-November the UAE's petroleum production was reported to be about 1.8m. b/d, well above its quota level. In December OPEC members unofficially agreed to maintain the production quotas allocated in June for the first six months of 1988, in an attempt to stabilize petroleum prices at around $18 per barrel. In May 1988 this unofficial agreement was upheld for the remainder of the year. Despite this, the UAE's production increased to about 2m. b/d in September, and general over-production within OPEC caused the price of oil on the 'spot' market to fall to $10.69 per barrel in October. At the November meeting, OPEC members agreed to

form a committee, consisting of representatives of eight member states, to monitor the production quotas of all members and to supervise adherence to the levels allocated. The UAE was widely acknowledged to be the most flagrant over-producer in OPEC and repeatedly rejected the quotas that it had been allocated, claiming that they were inconsistent with the country's large reserves and disproportionate to the quotas allotted to other OPEC member states.

In June 1988 the Supreme Petroleum Council was formed, following the issuing of a presidential decree which proposed the abolition of the Department of Petroleum and the dissolution of the board of directors of the Abu Dhabi National Oil Co (ADNOC), in an attempt to unify the Government's petroleum policy and planning activities. The 11-member Council, headed by Sheikh Khalifa bin Zayed an-Nahyan, assumed the former responsibilities of ADNOC's directors and of the Department of Petroleum, namely the administration and supervision of all the country's petroleum affairs.

In March 1990 the UAE was producing 2.01m. b/d, against its OPEC quota (which it did not recognize) of 1.095m. b/d. By July the price of oil had fallen to $14 per barrel. The UAE agreed to a compromise proposal that its OPEC quota should be revised to 1.5m. b/d. Iraq's invasion of Kuwait in August, however, led to the suspension of OPEC quotas as member states agreed to compensate for the loss of Iraqi and Kuwaiti production of petroleum due to the UN's mandatory trade embargo. The UAE's average output during the 1990–91 Gulf crisis was 2.4m. b/d, 63% more than its quota figure of July 1990. Increased production was accompanied until January 1991 by higher 'spot' prices. UAE oil revenues for 1990 were $15,700m., 54% more than in 1989. With the outbreak of hostilities between the US-led multinational force and Iraq, prices began to decline to pre-conflict levels. Having reached a maximum price of $32 per barrel in October 1990, by February 1991 the 'spot' price of Dubai crude petroleum had fallen to less than $15 per barrel. In March OPEC agreed to lower production levels by 5% in the second quarter of the year. The UAE agreed to reduce its level of production to 2.320m. b/d. In June the UAE made it clear that it was reluctant to return to its 1.5m. b/d quota of July 1990 as part of a stabilization of the world petroleum market. Actual UAE output in 1991 averaged 2.39m. b/d, yielding earnings of some $14,000m., a fall of 11% from the 1990 level. From March 1992 the UAE's OPEC quota was set at 2.244m. b/d, which the UAE appeared to be observing, notwithstanding Abu Dhabi's decision to proceed with a $5,000m. development programme designed to develop an extra 600,000 b/d of oil production capacity by 1996. In 1992 crude oil production averaged 2,283,200 b/d. UAE petroleum production has fluctuated little since 1993, hovering around its OPEC quota (set in April of that year) of 2.161m. b/d.

In November 1997, at a meeting of OPEC members convened in Jakarta, Indonesia, production quotas were increased to reflect actual production (many OPEC members, including the UAE, exceeded their quotas in 1997) and the expected increase in demand in 1998; the UAE's new quota was 2.366m. b/d. However, declining petroleum prices in 1998 led to production cuts. In March both OPEC and non-OPEC members agreed to reduce production, and in June, following a further decrease in prices, the UAE pledged to reduce production to 2.157m. b/d compared with average output of 2.270m. b/d in May. In addition to the declining petroleum prices, the UAE was also more directly affected by the economic crisis in Asia, as more than 50% of its exports in 1996 went to Japan, South Korea and Singapore.

Abu Dhabi

The first company to obtain a concession to explore for petroleum in Abu Dhabi was the Trucial Coast Development Oil Co, which was granted a concession over the entire territory in 1939. In 1962 the consortium was renamed the Abu Dhabi Petroleum Co (ADPC), and during the 1960s it gradually relinquished much of its concession. Agreements made in the early 1970s gave ADNOC, founded in 1971, an eventual 60% share, back-dated to 1 January 1974. ADNOC has a monopoly over distribution and is responsible for all petroleum installations and oil-based industries in the emirate. The second largest oil company in Abu Dhabi was founded in 1954 as Abu Dhabi Marine

Areas Ltd (ADMA), which in 1971 was a consortium of British Petroleum (BP) and Compagnie Française des Pétroles (CFP). In 1972 BP sold 45% of its shares to the Japan Oil Development Co (JODCO) and by 1974 the Abu Dhabi Government, in the form of ADNOC, had acquired a 60% share. In 1977 ADNOC and ADMA agreed to establish a new company, ADMA-OPCO (with the same shareholders as ADMA), for offshore work, and in 1978 the Abu Dhabi Company for Onshore Oil Operations (ADCO) was formed from ADPC for onshore work. These two companies produced 93% of Abu Dhabi's petroleum in 1979, and the remaining four companies operating in the emirate, the Abu Dhabi Oil Company Ltd, the Total Abu al-Bukhoosh Co, the Al-Bunduq Company Ltd and Amerada Hess, produced about 7%. The main onshore oilfields are the Murban, Bu Hasa and Asab fields, while the main offshore ones are Umm Shaif (which produced an average 133,599 b/d in 1983) and Lower Zakum (average 71,912 b/d in 1983). This level was broadly maintained into the 1990s. With the onset of the Gulf crisis in August 1990 and the suspension of OPEC quotas, Abu Dhabi provided 75% of the UAE's expanded production, at levels of up to 1.8m. b/d.

Two new discoveries of petroleum were reported in 1982, and during 1983 ADNOC drilled a total of 16 exploration wells. In 1985 two further offshore oilfields came into operation, with the Sateh field producing at 10,000 b/d and the Umm ad-Dalkh field producing at 25,000 b/d. However, the oil glut and reductions in OPEC production quotas for the UAE led to a fall in output prior to the last quarter of 1985. During the last quarter of 1985, however, Abu Dhabi raised production considerably in order to offset declines in prices, and the unfavourable prospects for the oil industry in the short term also led to the postponement of two schemes to increase the rate of recovery from the Sahil and Bab fields. In August 1986 Abu Dhabi was producing approximately 1.3m. b/d, but during 1987 some rationalization of ADNOC's activities took place. ZADCO and UDECO were merged, and by 1988 ADCO was operating only four rigs, compared with 15 in mid-1986, but exploration drilling increased in 1989. In early 1989 there was an official decrease in production of 20%, but published figures for 1989 revealed that Abu Dhabi's production over the whole year remained at the 1988 level of 1.6m. b/d. In March 1991 Abu Dhabi announced that, as part of a $7,000m. development plan (1991–95), $2,800m. was to be spent on doubling exports of liquefied natural gas (LNG), increasing long-term production capacity from 2m. b/d to 2.6m. b/d and doubling refining capacity to more than 250,000 b/d. Formal approval had been obtained for the release of the estimated $500m. that was needed to expand capacity at the onshore Bab field and the offshore Upper Zakum field. At the Bab field ADCO aimed to increase capacity from 60,000 b/d to 350,000 b/d. The capacity at the Upper Zakum field was to be increased by 200,000 b/d. Small discoveries that had been ignored over the past decade were also to be reappraised. In late 1994 the broad division of crude oil production within Abu Dhabi was 425,000 b/d from ADMA-OPCO offshore fields, 470,000 b/d from the Upper Zakum offshore field and 920,000 b/d from ADCO's onshore fields. At 1 January 1995 proven oil reserves in Abu Dhabi were 92,200m. barrels (92.6% of the UAE total).

The Government has consistently sought to develop its 'downstream' production, and its first refinery, at Umm an-Nar, came 'on stream' in 1976 with a capacity of 15,000 b/d. A second refinery, at Ruwais, went into operation in June 1981. The Ruwais refinery, which after expansion was originally planned to achieve an output of 300,000 b/d, was producing to a capacity of only 71,000 b/d in 1985 and 1986, after declines in demand had led to cut-backs in the scale of expansion. By 1991 its capacity had fallen to 50,000 b/d. As part of the 1991–95 development plan, the intention to increase the capacity of the Ruwais refinery to the long-held target of 300,000 b/d was reaffirmed. Work on a 60,000 b/d extension of the Umm an-Nar refinery was completed in 1984. In 1993 the capacity of the Umm an-Nar refinery was raised to 85,000 b/d, bringing total refining capacity in Abu Dhabi to 215,500 b/d. In 1994 aggregate refinery throughputs in the UAE averaged 226,000 b/d. The longstanding proposal to expand the Ruwais refinery finally received government approval in January 1995, allowing planners to draw up detailed specifications for a major upgrading package which was expected to cost between $1,300m. and $1,900m. As

well as the construction of two condensate processing plant units, the expansion is expected to include a 420–450-MW power plant, a 30,000 cu m-per-day desalination facility and a major seawater system. In early 1988 the Abu Dhabi-based International Petroleum Investment Co (IPIC) began to develop its refinery interests elsewhere, by purchasing a 10% interest in a Madrid-based refinery, Compañía Española de Petróleos, for $123m. This ensured a secure outlet for 60,000 b/d of Abu Dhabi's crude petroleum. The interest was doubled in early 1989. IPIC (which is jointly owned by ADNOC and the Abu Dhabi Investment Authority) announced plans in May 1994 to acquire a 20% interest in the Austrian energy and chemicals group OMV. During the 1970s there were several plans for the development of petrochemical industries in the emirate, but one of the few to come to fruition was the fertilizer complex at Ruwais, Ruwais Fertilizer Industries (FERTIL), of which two-thirds is owned by ADNOC and one-third by Total-CFP. FERTIL produced 600,000 tons of ammonia and urea in 1994. In 1995 ADNOC announced outline proposals for a major new petrochemical development at Ruwais, to be undertaken after the forthcoming expansion of the Ruwais oil refinery. The project, structured as a joint venture, involves the development of a polyethylene complex, an ethylene dichloride plant and an aromatics plant. In September 1997 IPIC and OMV announced plans to acquire a 50% share in Borealis, a Copenhagen-based polyethylene producer. Borealis is the largest European polyethylene producer and is expected to become the world's fourth-largest producer. It has also been involved in the building of a polyethylene complex in the UAE, which is scheduled to commence production by 2000.

Abu Dhabi's exports of petroleum are transported through two main terminals. The Jebel Dhanna terminal was completed in 1963. Additional installations, finished in 1974, increased the export capacity of ADPC's Murban petroleum to 1,280,000 b/d. ADMA-OPCO's Umm Shaif and Zakum petroleum is exported through the Das terminal. Two smaller terminals exist at Abu al-Bukhoosh and Mubarraz. At the beginning of 1980 ADNOC and JODCO began work on a new terminal, costing $750m., on Delma Island. As a result of the onshore petroleum expansion plans announced in March 1991, Jebel Dhanna was also to be expanded. Three new tanks were to be ready for commissioning in late 1992.

During the early 1970s much of the gas produced in association with petroleum was flared off, but in 1977 an LNG plant at Das Island started recovering offshore associated gas, and in 1981 the GASCO plant began onshore gas collection. In 1981 a new gasfield was found underlying the offshore Zakum oilfield, and in 1984 exploration began in Abu Dhabi's share of the Khuff formation, thought to be one of the largest offshore gasfields in the world.

In 1983 the Abu Dhabi Gas Liquefaction Co (ADGAS) borrowed $500m. to upgrade its Das Island complex by building three new LNG storage tanks and four for liquefied petroleum gas (LPG), together with vapour recovery units. The Thamama C Gas project came on stream in 1984, processing gas from the Thamama C foundation of the Bab field. In 1988 Das Island produced 2.48m. tons of LNG, 7.8% above design capacity, for export to ADGAS's sole long-term contract customer for LNG, Japan's Tokyo Electric Power Co. A third LNG production train and 34m. cu m per day of additional gas-gathering facilities were completed in 1994, raising the plant's capacity to 5m. tons per year. In early 1995 ADGAS made several LNG shipments to Belgian, Spanish and French importers under single-cargo sales agreements. It subsequently secured short-term contracts to supply a total of nearly 1m. tons of LNG to the same customers between July 1995 and April 1996.

ADNOC's ambitious plans for the expansion of its 'upstream' gas industry include the Asab field gas development scheme (AGD), phase two of the onshore gas development programme (OGD) and the Khuff reservoir development project.

Dubai

Dubai is the second largest producer of petroleum in the UAE, producing approximately 420,000 b/d during 1991 and 380,000 b/d in 1992. In 1994 crude oil contributed an estimated 20.1% of Dubai's GDP. By early 1994 output was down to an estimated 275,000 b/d, and steps were being taken to slow the rate of decline through increased use of enhanced recovery techniques. Output had risen to an estimated 320,000 b/d by mid-1994 following the drilling of new wells. Two years later, when Dubai's estimated oil output was around 300,000 b/d, independent analysts were forecasting a decline to around 250,000 b/d in 1997 and to less than 200,000 b/d in 1998, as offshore reservoirs approached exhaustion. In 1963 Conoco acquired the earlier petroleum concession, held from 1937 to 1961 by Iraq Petroleum Co, and formed the Dubai Petroleum Co (DPC), concentrating on offshore production. In 1954 CFP and Hispanoil had obtained an onshore concession, and formed Dubai Marine Areas Ltd (DUMA). In 1963 DPC acquired a 50% share in DUMA's concession and then released some of its shares to other companies, so that by the late 1960s CFP, Hispanoil, Continental Oil, Texaco, Sun Oil and Wintershall all had shares in DUMA–DPC's concession. By 1974 the Government of Dubai had acquired a 60% share in participation in DUMA–DPC. Nevertheless, the former concessionaire companies continued to operate under the same conditions until, in 1979, the Government decided to buy back 50% of the production to market it directly.

Although petroleum was first discovered in Dubai in 1966, production did not begin until 1969. Output averaged 34,236 b/d in 1970, rising to 362,346 b/d in 1978. Despite the OPEC quota, which should have restricted Dubai's production in the first half of 1987 to approximately 220,000 b/d, it is estimated that actual levels of production for the first quarter of the year were almost 380,000 b/d. Output is mainly from the two offshore oilfields of Fateh and South West Fateh, but some petroleum is also lifted from the Rashid and Falah offshore fields. In May 1982 a major new onshore discovery was made in the Margham field, and by 1988 production reached 40,000 b/d of condensate from 15 wells. In April 1989 a 59-km pipeline, linking the Margham field with the gas-processing plant at Jebel Ali, was brought into operation. The pipeline has a maximum capacity of 13.5m. cu ft per day. By the end of 1990 Dubai had a total of 341 oil wells. Exploration was not interrupted by the Gulf crisis, and development work at 21 wells was completed in 1990. DPC also installed a $200m. platform to increase capacity at the Fateh field in 1990. DPC's storage capacity stood at 2.3m. barrels at the end of 1990.

During the 1970s Dubai's natural gas was flared off, but in 1980 a gas treatment plant, owned by the Dubai Natural Gas Co (DUGAS), began operations. Dubai's gas reserves are estimated at 125,000m. cu m, and the DUGAS plant, at Jebel Ali, began operations with a treatment capacity of 3m. cu m per day. In 1985 the plant had a production capacity of between 825 and 850 metric tons per day (t/d) of propane, 600 t/d of butane and 850 t/d–900 t/d of condensate. Most of the production from the plant is shipped to Japan. In 1988 DUGAS and two foreign companies, ASCO (of the USA) and BP, signed an agreement to process associated gas from the Margham field at Jebel Ali. Previously this gas had been flared. Construction of a new DUGAS plant to produce methyl-tertiary-butyl ether, a lead substitute in petrol, was completed in February 1995. In July 1997 the Dubai-based Emirates National Oil Corpn awarded a contract for the construction of a condensate processing plant to an Italian company, Technipetrol. The plant is due to be operational by late 1998, and is expected to produce 60,000 b/d of naphtha, jet fuel and diesel for sale in the local market. The installation of an unleaded petrol plant is also planned at Jebel Ali.

Sharjah

Production of petroleum began in Sharjah in 1974, with the Mubarak field producing at the rate of 60,000 b/d. The field lies in a 'protocol area', which is occupied by Iran, and in the north it lies in Iranian territorial concessions for hydrocarbons exploration. Sharjah has production and drilling rights, but shares production and revenue with Iran. This situation caused considerable difficulties following the onset of hostilities between Iran and Iraq, and in 1984 oil exploration was interrupted when Iranian patrol boats arrived near Abu Musa island. The security problems facing Sharjah became more apparent when Iranian naval forces attacked the Mubarak oilfield in April 1988, thereby causing its closure for a period of two months. Of the remaining revenue 20% is shared with Umm al-Qaiwain, and 10% with Ajman. The field has brought Sharjah

revenues of around AED 20m. per year. At the end of 1980 Amoco announced a major new onshore discovery of petroleum and natural gas. Exports of crude petroleum from this Sajaa field started in mid-1982 at a rate of 25,000 b/d. The emirate's total production in 1983 exceeded 50,000 b/d. It is estimated that Sharjah maintained production levels at an average of 65,000 b/d during 1987–90, although in 1991 output was about 25% lower, owing to problems at the Mubarak field. By 1992 output from the Mubarak field had fallen to 8,000 b/d.

Export revenues from Sharjah's two gasfields, Sajaa 1 and Sajaa 2, were expected substantially to reduce Sharjah's international debt, which was estimated at between $600m. and $700m. in 1986, and average production from the Sajaa fields in 1986 reached 16.98m. cu m per day. However, the collapse of the price of petroleum weakened Sharjah's ability to repay its international debt. A pipeline costing $190m. was completed in 1984, to carry gas from the Sajaa fields to power stations in Ras al-Khaimah, Fujairah, Ajman and Umm al-Qaiwain, and in 1985 this pipeline had a capacity of 60,000 b/d of condensate and 1.1m. cu m per day of gas. Following the settlement of the border dispute between Sharjah and Dubai in 1985, a 24-in (60-cm) gas pipeline was built to supply gas from the Sajaa field to the Dubai Electrical Co's power and desalination plant at Jebel Ali. An agreement was also reached in 1983 for Amoco to drill six wells over the ensuing 15 months, to bring the capacity of the Sajaa field to 14.2m. cu m per day. An LPG plant began production in July 1986, with a capacity of 13,000 b/d of mixed LPGs, 7,500 b/d of propane, 6,000 b/d of butane and 6,000 b/d of condensate. In June 1987 the plant was processing 11.32m. cu m of 'wet' gas per day, to produce the equivalent of 7,000 b/d of propane, 5,000 b/d of butane and more than 4,000 b/d of light oil. Many projects were postponed during the recession of the mid-1980s, but the economic revival following the 1990–91 Gulf crisis enabled the Government to revive development plans. In July 1992 the Amoco Sharjah Oil Co (owned 60% by the Sharjah Government and 40% by Amoco Corpn) announced significant new gas discoveries, and in 1993 plans were announced to expand Sharjah's gas-processing capacity by 60% in 1994. A new contract to supply gas to power stations in the northern emirates was awarded by the UAE federal authorities in June 1994. Amoco Sharjah's gas-processing plant operated at or above its nominal design capacity of 19.8m. cu m per day throughout 1995, achieving daily throughputs in excess of 22.7m. cu m during periods of peak demand. In 1996 the plant's capacity was under expansion, in order to meet an anticipated increase in peak demand to 25.5m. cu m per day. It was estimated that 50%–60% of Sharjah's dry gas production was piped to Dubai in 1995, with the remainder going to Sharjah and the northern emirates' power stations. Production of condensates and natural gas liquids was 40,000 b/d–45,000 b/d in 1995. In December 1995 Amoco Corpn signed a memorandum of understanding with the Government of Oman whereby the US company was granted exclusive representation to market Omani gas in the UAE. Amoco's proposal (dependent on the negotiation of appropriate supply contracts with Dubai and the northern emirates) was to build a pipeline from Oman's gas fields to Amoco Sharjah's gas-treatment plant, which would be expanded to handle a greatly increased throughput. (Gas demand in Dubai and the northern emirates was forecast to rise by as much as 34m. cu m per day within six years.)

FAL Petroleum Co (owned by a Sharjah businessman) announced in late 1995 that it had purchased an existing Canadian oil refinery for shipment to Sharjah and reassembly on a free-zone site at Hamriyya, where it was scheduled to begin producing 20,000 b/d of petroleum products in late 1997.

Ajman, Fujairah, Ras al-Khaimah and Umm al-Qaiwain

Of the remaining emirates, Ras al-Khaimah appears to have the largest reserves of petroleum and natural gas. Offshore discoveries, made in 1976 and 1977, proved not to be commercially exploitable, but Gulf Oil made new discoveries off the west coast in 1981. In the same year, an onshore concession was granted to a consortium of Amoco and Gulf Oil, and, following seismic tests, Gulf Oil announced significant discoveries of petroleum and gas in the second offshore test well, Saleh One X, in February 1983. The well started production in February 1984, at 5,000 b/d, followed in April by Saleh Two X at 3,500 b/d, and production there has since increased. At the beginning of 1985, however, Ras al-Khaimah was producing oil at a rate of only between 8,000 b/d and 10,000 b/d. A new well, Saleh Four X, began operating in February 1985, with a production rate of between 7,000 b/d and 8,000 b/d of oil, and a further well, Saleh Five X, was 'spudded' in April. Ras al-Khaimah's overall production has not, however, been as high as was anticipated, and in 1987 production was only 11,000 b/d, most of the revenue from which was used to finance exploration and development. By the end of 1987 a seventh well had been 'spudded' in the Saleh field, and production was reported to be about 12,000 b/d. By mid-1986 the four-stage programme to establish a 'downstream' oil industry in Ras al-Khaimah, at a cost of $45m.–$50m., had been completed. This consists of pipelines from the Saleh field to the mainland, separation and stabilization facilities, onshore storage facilities for 500,000 barrels, and an LPG plant. During 1986, uncertainty over the future of its petroleum industry led the Government of Ras al-Khaimah to relinquish its 50% share in the Saleh field, and in 1987 Chevron sold its 50.5% interest in Ras al-Khaimah's off-shore concession. In 1991 the Omani Government agreed to allow gas from its Bukha offshore field to be processed at Ras al-Khaimah. Output was expected to be limited to around 5,000 b/d of condensate, 800 b/d of LPG and 40 cu ft of 'dry' gas per day. The emirate has been processing gas at Khor Khuwair since 1985, but utilization has been minimal. In January 1996 a new company, Ras al-Khaimah Oil and Gas, whose principal shareholder was a US investor, signed an agreement to undertake onshore and offshore exploration work in the emirate.

Umm al-Qaiwain's first well was 'spudded' in 1981, and a Canadian concession in the emirate was due to start production in 1985. Exploration continues in Umm al-Qaiwain, as it does in Ajman, where drilling for petroleum finally began in 1982. In July 1983 Ajman formed the Ajman National Oil Co (AJNOC), with a capital of $37m. In February 1984 it was announced that two Canadian oil companies had been granted offshore concessions in Fujairah, and in 1988 Broken Hill Petroleum of Australia conducted a seismic survey off shore from the emirate. Further exploration of the northern emirates featured prominently in the UAE's 1991–95 development plan. In late 1995 a 30,000 b/d refinery, purchased second-hand from a major multinational by the Greek company Metro Oil, went into production in Fujairah upon completion of more than 12 months' reassembly work. The refinery's product mix was configured to supply the needs of shipping using Fujairah's bunkering facilities. In 1995 Fujairah's deep-water port was one of the world's largest bunkering stations. It had about 500,000 cu m of product storage capacity and was well placed to act as a bulk oil trade centre for the Gulf and the Indian sub-continent. A major new tank-terminal venture, with a projected initial capacity of 465,000 cu m and a projected final capacity of 700,000 cu m, was under development in Fujairah in 1996 by a consortium led by Royal Van Ommeren (a Dutch company with world-wide oil storage interests).

INDUSTRY

Since the UAE was formed in 1971, the diversification of the economy away from petroleum has been a clearly stated government policy. The development of an integrated infrastructure and extensive construction work took place in the 1970s, and this early industrial development was manned largely by immigrant labour. It is estimated that by 1982 the labour force of the UAE was 559,960, of whom a large majority—in some sectors over 90%—were non-nationals. In the early 1980s, anxiety over the large number of Asian workers and unemployment led to the enforcement of a restrictive labour-law and stricter visa regulations, making it increasingly difficult for overseas casual labourers to settle in the UAE. However, by 1986, when the expatriate work-force in Dubai totalled only 75,070, the decline of the economy had led to a reversal of this policy, and the Government had begun to encourage immigrant labourers earning incomes above a certain level to bring their families with them. In September 1994 the federal authorities increased the qualifying income level from AED 3,000 per month to AED 5,000 per month (or AED 4,000 in the case of an employee living in accommodation provided by the employer). A survey conducted by the UAE Ministry of Economy and Industry in

1988 indicated the poor productivity of capital invested in manufacturing industry in the UAE, a lack of new technology and the low level of wages paid to the mainly Asian work-force. In 1987 non-oil manufacturing industry contributed 11% of GDP (compared with 4% in 1980), but in 1990 the proportion declined to 7.3%, its value being AED 9,300m. In 1994 this sector contributed 8.3% of GDP, with a value of AED 11,160m.

The federal Ministry of Electricity and Water is responsible for 11 power stations: at Umm al-Qaiwain, Falaj al-Mualla, Dhaid, Masfut, Manama, Uzun, Masafi, Fujairah, Qidfa and Dibba. On the east coast a 33-kV overhead transmission system has been installed, and a number of small contracts were issued in 1980 to link the remainder of the power supply system in this area. In Dubai power is generated by the locally-owned Dubai Electricity Co, and in 1980 a steam power station at Jebel Ali was inaugurated with 60-MW generators. Ras al-Khaimah, Sharjah and Abu Dhabi are also responsible for their own power. In addition to the old diesel, gas and steam stations, Abu Dhabi's power is provided by the Umm an-Nar East and West stations, Units 9 and 10, a new 600-MW station at Bani Yas, and stations at Sadiyat and al-Ain. The UAE's installed generating capacity rose from 1,723.9 MW in 1979 to 3,933 MW in 1986. The UAE's output of electric energy increased from 4,991m. kWh in 1979 to 15,419m. kWh in 1989, with energy consumption per caput increasing from 126 kg of oil equivalent in 1965 to 10,874 kg in 1990.

In 1982 the power stations at Qidfa and Ghalilah began operations, resulting in a 97% rise in power output in the northern emirates during the first nine months of the year. In April 1989 it was announced that the Taweela A power station, under construction since 1984, would begin operation in August, supplying Abu Dhabi with 250 MW of power and 20m. gallons of water per day (g/d). The second phase, originally approved in January 1987 and recently completed, entailed the construction of a power station (Taweela B) with a capacity of 732 MW, and a desalination unit with a capacity of 76m. g/d. Work on the Taweela project was interrupted by the Gulf crisis of 1990–91. Further delays were caused by the decision, in March 1991, to invite retenders for construction of Taweela B, with a view to securing a bid closer to the sum allocated for the project. In the event, the 'turnkey' contract was awarded for the Taweela B project in July 1992, to a Zürich-based consortium. It was reported in April 1997 that the Abu Dhabi Government is understood to have approved the $700m. expansion of the Taweela A power and desalination plant to be implemented as an independent power project. Plans have also been announced for the expansion of the Jebel Ali E station by 232 MW to 472 MW, and for the construction of a new power station, Jebel Ali G, with a capacity of 440 MW. There are also plans to build a major station between Mirfa and Ruwais, to supply power and water to a large number of villages and islands in Abu Dhabi. Expenditure on power has often been subject to budgetary constraints, but, with demand rising by about 10% per year, the Government has decided to press rapidly ahead with expansion projects. By 1994 the total installed capacity of the UAE's power stations was 5,000 MW, while the anticipated demand in 2000 was 7,500 MW. At the beginning of 1995 electricity prices were increased from AED 0.07 to AED 0.15 per kWh, leaving them significantly below the estimated production costs of about AED 0.20 per kWh at the most modern power stations and up to AED 0.35 per kWh at older plants. In mid-1995 more than 1,500 MW of new generating capacity was under construction in the UAE, while distribution networks were undergoing major upgrading and expansion.

The lack of water resources has led to much investment in the provision of fresh water, and by 1985 there were 22 desalination plants in the UAE. In 1982 annual water demand was estimated at 565m. cu m, of which agriculture used 410m. cu m. Examples of projects which have been completed are: a 3.3m. g/d desalination plant associated with the power station at Qidfa, in Fujairah, and a reverse osmosis desalination plant, with a capacity of 3.6m. g/d, at Ajman. Four 50 MW steam turbines, and two 18,000-cu m-per-day multi-stage flash desalination units were built at Raafah, in Umm al-Qaiwain. A project to divert water from two Turkish rivers, the Ceyhan and the Seyhan, to the Gulf along two pipelines, totalling 5,000 km in length, has been discussed, but has never come close to implementation. Total UAE water production in 1989 was 85,000m. gallons, compared with 81,000m. gallons in 1987. The range of projects that the Government announced for expanding the UAE's electric power capacity after the end of the Gulf War in February 1991 all envisaged increases in desalination capacity. In January 1995 Abu Dhabi had an installed desalination capacity of 110m. g/d and was currently proceeding with six new projects which would add an additional 84m. g/d of capacity. Of the 81m. g/d of desalinated water supplied to Abu Dhabi city in 1994, 44m. g/d was for domestic use and the remainder for horticultural use. Dubai had 30m. g/d of excess desalination capacity in 1995, the completion of new water plants at power stations having eliminated the water authority's need to purchase up to half of Dubai's fresh water supply from a desalination facility attached to the Dubai Aluminium Co (DUBAL) complex. Plans were announced in 1995 to install a total of about 8m. g/d of new desalination capacity in the northern emirates of Fujairah, Ajman and Ras al-Khaimah. In July 1997 the federal Ministry of Electricity and Water awarded an AED 235m. contract to the local Emirates Trading Agency for the supply and installation of five new desalination units in the northern emirates.

Abu Dhabi

Most of Abu Dhabi's heavy industry is centred on the Jebel Dhanna-Ruwais industrial zone, 250 km west of Abu Dhabi city, which was officially opened by Sheikh Zayed in March 1982. This is mostly oil-related, with a petroleum refinery capable of processing 120,000 b/d at Ruwais and a fertilizer plant forming the central projects (see Petroleum and Gas).

In 1979 the General Industries Corpn (GIC) was set up to co-ordinate non-petroleum development, and by early 1981 it was involved in a paper bag factory, a brick works, a concrete block factory, a steel-rolling mill, and an animal feed plant, all of which had begun production in the preceding two years. An industrial bank, the Emirates Industrial Bank, was founded in 1983 to fund new industrial projects. Light industry is concentrated in the al-Musalah area, just over the bridges joining Abu Dhabi island to the mainland. In 1985 there was a total of 221 industrial units in Abu Dhabi. A bottling plant for Coca-Cola opened in 1989, and the construction of a plant to manufacture 6,000 tons of polyurethane blocks per year has been announced. The government-owned Abu Dhabi Investment Co (ADIC) launched an industrial investment programme in 1993. Proposals under active consideration by ADIC in 1995 included a project to establish a plate glass factory in Abu Dhabi. Meanwhile the GIC was finalizing plans in 1995 to sell five industrial plants with an estimated combined valuation of AED 700m., this being the UAE's first privatization initiative since 1985 and the first in which the intended means of privatization was a series of share offers through the UAE's informal stock market. In February 1996 the GIC announced that shares worth AED 300m. in several of its food processing companies would be distributed to social security recipients, low-income employees and small shareholders. New projects under active evaluation by the GIC in mid-1996 included the construction of a rolling mill at Taweela to manufacture steel bars for the local building industry. In June 1997 it was reported that the GIC had launched an AED 100m. industrial loan fund to support private sector participation in small and medium-sized industrial ventures in the emirate.

A joint-stock company called Abu Dhabi Ship Building (ADSB) was established in 1995 with the US company Newport News (40%) and the Abu Dhabi Government (18.5%) as founding shareholders. The remaining 41.5% of the share capital was raised through a heavily over-subscribed public offering. ADSB's repair and construction facilities for naval and merchant vessels were to be located initially at an established dry dock at Mussafah pending construction of a purpose-built yard with a projected completion date of 1999.

A decree was issued in July 1996 to establish Abu Dhabi's first free zone on Saadiyat Island, east of Abu Dhabi city. It was intended to invest up to $3,000m. to develop storage, transportation and trading facilities for various commodities, from ores, grain and foodstuffs to precious metals and gems. The island was to be linked to Abu Dhabi city by a 6-km bridge. In August 1997 it was announced that both local and international investors would be offered a $1,700m. equity stake in the initial public offering in the Saadiyat Free Zone Authority (SFZA) which will regulate the free zone. A project development company will build and operate the facilities on the island under a 25-year renewable concession agreement.

Dubai

Dubai has taken the lead in developing non-petroleum industry (which could explain how in 1983, when the UAE witnessed a narrowing of its trade surplus, Dubai's increased by 30%, despite a 14% decline in petroleum revenues). This has been centred on the Jebel Ali port and industrial area, 30 km west of Dubai city. The decision to build a new deep-sea port was taken in August 1976, and there were 15 km of quays by mid-1981. A dry dock was developed in the early 1980s, and in 1985 a total of 111 ships, with a combined capacity of 10m. dwt, were repaired. The dock benefited greatly from the Iran–Iraq War, and was fully occupied by damaged vessels in 1988. The port possessed 67 berths by 1988, and is the largest man-made harbour in the world. In 1989 Jebel Ali Port handled 9.97m. tons of cargo. The older Port Rashid had 35 berths by mid-1984. By 1985 there was a total of 305 industrial units in Dubai. Despite a reduction in trade through Dubai's ports in the immediate aftermath of Iraq's invasion of Kuwait in August 1990, owing to raised war risk insurance premiums, shipping container tonnage in 1990 rose by 79% and general cargo tonnage by 61% compared with 1989. In May 1991 a new company, the Dubai Ports Authority (DPA), was established to take over the running of Port Rashid and Jebel Ali. Dubai's ports are playing an important role as transhipment points for Kuwait's reconstruction programme.

The first major plant to begin production was an aluminium smelter, owned by DUBAL, which commenced operations at the end of 1979. It was built at a cost of $800m., and initially had an installed capacity of 135,000 metric tons of aluminium ingots per year. By 1988 production had increased to 163,445 tons, of which Japan purchased 64%. In May 1989 work began on the expansion of the plant by more than 40%, to a capacity of 240,000 tons per year. It was completed in early 1991. In 1992 DUBAL's production of hot metal totalled 244,605 tons, and a total of 250,000 tons of finished metals were sold to 21 countries, the main export markets being Japan (42.5% of sales), Taiwan, South Korea and Thailand. Sales comprised 50% billets, 36% foundry alloys and 14% high-purity ingots. DUBAL's output and sales volumes fell slightly in 1993 because of a temporary production problem, but were targeted to rise in 1994 to meet strong export demand. DUBAL is powered by five 100-MW gas turbines, driven by fuel from the neighbouring gas treatment plant, operated by DUGAS. In 1994 DUBAL produced 246,264 tons of hot metal and a record 273,085 tons of cast metal. Sales in 1994 totalled 268,292 tons (39% of which went to the Japanese market). In January 1995 DUBAL announced plans to expand its production capacity to 372,600 tons per year by early 1997 at a cost of $503m., of which $253m. would be financed out of company resources and the balance through a five-year syndicated bank loan. In 1979 another industrial plant, cable manufacturer DUCAB, came into production. Its sales of cables were worth a record AED 212m. ($57.7m.) in 1993, when it won major new export orders in Asian markets. In 1994 DUCAB produced nearly 20,000 tons of copper and aluminium cable. In 1995 it expanded its product range to include specialist lead-sheathed cables for the oil, gas and petrochemical industries. Initially, DUCAB was jointly owned by BICC of the United Kingdom (UK) and the Dubai Government, but in June 1997 the Abu Dhabi Government bought a 35% share in the company.

In May 1980, in an effort to promote Dubai's industrial development, Sheikh Rashid decreed that Jebel Ali should be a free-trade zone. The Jebel Ali Free Zone Authority, which offers the advantages of duty-free trade, was finally inaugurated, under full foreign ownership, in early 1985 (see Trade, Transport and Tourism). By mid-1994 around 630 companies had set up businesses in the Jebel Ali Free Zone, and new companies were arriving there at an average rate of 15 per month. Major foreign companies locating there included Xerox, Union Carbide, 3M, Black and Decker, Mitsubishi, York International, BP Arabian Agencies and Shell Markets. Local firms at Jebel Ali include Dubai's National Cement Co and the National Flour Mills, which began production in 1987. A new sugar refinery with a daily capacity of 2,400 tons was due to go into production in late 1994. In 1990 a warehouse and distribution facility for the Sony Corpn and a $3m. manufacturing plant for the Kavoos Co of Iran, to make raw materials for paint production, were opened. Jebel Ali Free Zone has become an important distribution point for Kuwait's reconstruction programme. In 1990 investments in the zone reached AED 1,500m., a 50% increase on 1989 levels. A second area for light industry has also been developed around the extended port area of Mina Rashid in Dubai itself. The garment-manufacturing sector has expanded dramatically, with the value of exports rising from an insignificant level in 1985 to $227.1m. in 1993. The industry is concentrated in Jebel Ali, where 25 factories were established by mid-1988, mostly by Indian businessmen. However, punitive quotas, introduced by the USA, have caused some units to close. The economic importance of this sector to the UAE is diminished by the fact that all raw materials and labour are imported, mainly from India.

In 1994 (which saw a marked decline in textile and garment exports) the Jebel Ali Free Zone Authority adopted a policy of not granting new licences to garment manufacturers, on the grounds that it did not wish to encourage labour-intensive industries. By early 1995 the total number of companies using the zone was about 735, drawn from 70 countries in all parts of the world. Distribution and sales operations (often serving markets far beyond the Gulf region) outnumbered manufacturing and assembly operations by about two to one, although manufacturing and assembly accounted for four-fifths of total investment in the zone. Apart from textiles and garments, the major manufactures included building materials, fertilizers and foodstuffs. Investment in 'high-technology' ventures such as computer assembly fell well short of targets set by the Free Zone Authority, which was currently making special efforts to attract this type of venture. An Indian company announced in early 1995 that it was to invest $27m. at Jebel Ali to establish a nylon tyre cord factory with an annual capacity of 18,000 tons. In mid-1996 India's Southern Petroleum Industries Corpn (SPIC) announced plans to locate a fertilizer plant at Jebel Ali to serve the Indian market. At that time more than 1,000 companies were operating in the Jebel Ali Free Zone.

In April 1993 the authorities introduced a new law that explicitly excluded licensed national firms from the 'offshore' provisions of the original free-zone legislation (see Trade, Transport and Tourism, below), confirmed their liability to the provisions of Dubai's standard company laws, and made the granting of a licence subject to proof of at least 51% UAE or GCC ownership of the company concerned and at least 40% locally added value in its products. It was hoped that the removal of former ambiguities would encourage more local companies to take advantage of the infrastructure benefits of manufacturing within the zone. Industrial investment in Dubai in 1993 totalled AED 10,500m. (8% up on 1992), while investment by foreign companies totalled AED 1,800m. (23% up on 1992). Industrial production in 1993 was valued at AED 9,600m. (an increase of 24.8%), including exports worth AED 4,500m. (39.2% more than in 1992).

The Northern Emirates

Industrial development in the remaining emirates has been based largely on the construction industry and port expansion. Two container ports have been developed in Sharjah, where there is also a lubricating oil plant, a rope factory, the Sharjah Oxygen Co, a factory making plastic pipes and a cement plant producing 700 tons per day. The Gulf Industries Complex in Sharjah's industrial zone was opened in 1981, producing furniture and household utensils. In April 1982 a fodder factory at Mina Khaled, operated by the Gulf Company for Agricultural Development, was opened. An LPG plant came into operation on the site in July 1986. According to a study by the Emirates Industrial Bank, Sharjah was the focus of 35% of the UAE's industrial installations in 1987. Total capital investment in Sharjah increased from AED 461m. in 1977 to AED 997m. in 1987, while the number of employees doubled, from 3,173 to 6,840, over the same period. Sharjah's industrial sector registered 48% growth in 1988. In 1996 Sharjah was well established as a centre for light industry and manufacturing and was

developing its fifteenth industrial estate to facilitate further expansion of this sector.

Ras al-Khaimah has developed a valuable export business in aggregate (stones used in making concrete) from the Hajar Mountains. The first explosives factory in the Gulf was opened there in 1980, and a pharmaceutical factory was opened in 1981. The emirate has a cement factory, an asphalt company and a lime kiln, and in 1981 the Ras al-Khaimah Company for White Cement was established to build the Gulf's first white cement factory at Khor Khuwair. This joint Kuwaiti-UAE venture was due to commence operations in March 1986, producing 300,000 tons of white cement per year.

At the end of 1980 the Government of Fujairah established a department of industry and economy to organize industrial development. Fujairah has factories producing marble, tiles, rockwool (asbestos) insulation, concrete blocks, tyres and shoes, and many of these industries use materials from the Hajar mountains, where surveys have indicated significant quantities of copper, chromite, talc and magnesium. Commercial production of 1,600 tons per day began at a new cement plant in Dibba in 1982, when Fujairah's $4.9m. rockwool factory also started operations, with an annual capacity of 5,000 tons. Cement production capacity was due to rise to 2,500 tons per day during 1996. A new port with 11 berths was opened in Fujairah in 1982. Traffic at the port increased after Iraq's invasion of Kuwait in August 1990 as shippers attempted to avoid the war risk insurance premiums levied on the Gulf ports of Abu Dhabi and Dubai. Plans have been revealed to expand Fujairah's dry docking and ship repair facilities. In 1990 traffic at the port of Fujairah increased by 50% compared with 1989. A crushing plant, designed to produce 3m. tons per year of aggregate for cement production, went into production in May 1985. In 1988 plans were revived for the construction of a ferro-silicon plant to supply steel producers in the Gulf. The lack of an indigenous power source will, however, hamper the project. A five-year Development Plan, announced in 1988, included proposals for a $100m. industrial suburb and a $140m. break-shipment warehouse project. Fujairah outlined ambitious development plans in 1991, based on significant investment by the GCC member states. These include a Gulf railway, with the spur of the line connecting with the port of Fujairah, and a petrochemical complex. A free-zone facility in Fujairah was the base for 55 enterprises in mid-1995. Its total trade volume in the first half of 1995 was 6,152m. tons (principally foodstuffs, textiles, electronic goods, medical equipment, packaging and steel commodities) with a value of AED 260m.

Umm al-Qaiwain has concentrated on construction, and the newly-formed Umm al-Qaiwain Cement Industries Co plans to build a cement works producing 1m. tons per year to add to the one already in existence. Currently, however, the UAE's annual cement capacity is 8.4m. tons, which is four times the level of local demand of 2m. tons, and consequently the UAE's eight cement works are seeking to implement a production quota system. Cement production and related activities are likely to remain the dominant sector of the economy of Umm al-Qaiwain. Plans, announced in 1986, for the construction of an aluminium smelter, at a cost of $1,200m., were abandoned in 1988, and the smelter will now be built in Qatar. Umm al-Qaiwain has also followed Dubai's example by establishing a free zone by Amiri Decree in 1987.

Ajman, the smallest emirate, has a cement factory, a dry dock and a ship repair yard. There is a pressing need for improved infrastructure in Ajman. In 1991 the federal Government announced plans for a 240-MW increase in the electricity production capacity of the northern emirates. Contracts to install an extra 210 MW of capacity were awarded in late 1994. Plans were being drawn up in 1995 for new west-coast electricity distribution links between Ras al-Khaimah, Ajman and Umm al-Qaiwain, while a proposal to link the northern emirates to the Abu Dhabi grid was under consideration as a future development option. In January 1997 the federal Ministry of Electricity and Water signed contracts for the interconnection of the west-coast power distribution network in the northern emirates.

AGRICULTURE

Since the establishment by the FAO of an agricultural experimental station at Digdagga (Ras al-Khaimah) in 1955, agriculture in the UAE has undergone a major transformation. Traditionally, agriculture was based on nomadic pastoralism, in association with some oasis cultivation on the east coast and at Liwa, Dhaid, al-Ain and Falaj al-Mualla. This cultivation was totally dominated by dates. Although dates are still the major crop in terms of area cultivated, the production of vegetables has increased dramatically. The UAE continues to import more than 70% of its food requirements, but it is now largely self-sufficient in salad vegetables, eggs and poultry. In April 1984 a ban was announced on imports of those foods in which the UAE is self-sufficient, during growing seasons. One sign of the UAE's increased confidence in its ability to grow its own food was the announcement, in 1984, that the Government would assume responsibility for managing the Digdagga experimental station. Most agriculture takes place on the gravel plains on either side of the Hajar Mountains, at al-Ain or at Liwa. This expansion has been implemented through the creation of a widespread government extension service. In general, agricultural inputs are provided to farmers at about one-half of their real cost, with the Government subsidizing fertilizers, seeds and pesticides at 50% of cost. A central laboratory for the Ministry of Agriculture and Fisheries was officially opened near al-Ain in April 1982. In 1982 official figures stated that total production of fruit and vegetables reached 343,500 tons. In that year the value of vegetable production was AED 773m., of a total GNP of AED 119,700m. Some of this has, in the past, gone to waste, and in 1983 the Government established the Public Corporation for Agricultural Produce to ensure that surplus vegetables are shared between the emirates, and to package and store produce. Agricultural production increased from 39,000 tons in 1972 to more than 600,000 tons per year in the late 1980s, while the area of cultivable land increased from about 48,000 ha to more than 250,000 ha in 1994. Date production rose from 62,000 tons in 1986 to an estimated 240,000 tons in 1996, while tomato production increased from 42,000 tons in 1990 to an estimated 445,000 tons in 1996. Government figures indicate that in al-Ain the number of farms increased from 980 in 1979 to 1,939 in 1983, with an increase in farm area over the same period from 43,000 dunums to 82,668 dunums. The area of forest in the al-Ain region also increased, from 10,617 ha in 1978 to 13,433 ha in 1983.

There are a number of large-scale agricultural enterprises in the UAE. By 1981 there were three private dairy farms, four poultry farms, a French-sponsored fresh vegetable concern at al-Ain, and a government wheat project on 600 ha at al-Oha, near al-Ain. During 1984 the Arab Company for Animal Production's farm in Ras al-Khaimah was reported to be producing 16,000 cartons of milk and yoghurt daily from its 600 cows. A $26m. poultry farm has been built at Fujairah. This will produce 3.5m. birds and 11m. eggs per year. Experiments in hydroponics are being undertaken on Saadiyat Island. The Arab Company for Livestock Development, based in Damascus, Syria, plans to establish a 200-ha dairy farm, at a cost of AED 13m., in Fujairah, where it also operates the poultry farm. In 1989 the UAE produced about 13,000 tons of poultry, making the country 45% self-sufficient. Output of eggs reached 170m. in 1989, satisfying 70% of domestic requirement. A vegetable-canning factory was opened at al-Ain in 1986. In 1996 the UAE produced an estimated 23,000 tons of poultry, and output of eggs totalled 13m. metric tons.

The increased cultivation of vegetables and, in particular, the extensive forestry programme have led to severe problems with the water tables. Between 1976 and 1980, 1,545 new wells were dug by government teams, and it seems that at least this number were also dug privately. The consequent fall in the water table has been dramatic, especially near the coast. In 1980 the water table in Ras al-Khaimah fell by 3.37m. In places this has led to increased salinity of soil and water. Encroachment of seawater was also reported in 1982, when it apparently penetrated as far as 20 km inland in the northern emirates. As a result, several farms are now going out of production. The Government has attempted to alleviate the problem through the construction of desalination plants (see Industry) and catchment dams, such as those opened in 1982 at Wadi Ham and Wadi

Bih. At the end of 1982 the Government barred the drilling of new wells in parts of the northern emirates. In November 1982 the Tebodin Co of the Netherlands began a comprehensive study of the fresh water needs of the four smallest emirates until 2011, to enable the Ministry of Electricity and Water to formulate policies for those emirates. In 1983 a new dam was opened in Fujairah, with a capacity of 10m. cu m of rain-water, and plans were laid for the construction of a 17,000 cu m-per-day desalination plant at Ajman. Despite the problems facing the UAE concerning its water supply, plans were shelved in 1984 for the construction of eight recharge dams. During 1987 Abu Dhabi's Executive Council announced plans to drill a further 200 artesian wells in three parts of the emirate to supply farmers with yet more water for irrigation purposes. Further plans for the western region in 1988 included the construction of small desalination plants to treat brackish water pumped by free pumps, and the cultivation of 600 ha, using sprinklers and drip irrigation. In 1990 Abu Dhabi announced its intention to cultivate 1,300 ha in Abu Dhabi, the western region and al-Khaten. In order to irrigate this land 100 wells were to be sunk and two reservoirs were to be built. A large fossil-water reservoir was discovered at a depth of 70 m in the Liwa area of Abu Dhabi's western region in 1996, prompting the announcement of a 630-well drilling programme.

Total subsidies for farming in the 1983 budget were estimated at AED 35m., and the Ministry of Agriculture and Fisheries projected investments of AED 1,172m. in farm development between 1983 and 1993. The food sector's contribution to GDP increased sixfold, to AED 106.5m., in the nine years to 1984, and during 1980–89 agricultural GDP increased by an annual average of 8.9%. In 1996 agriculture, livestock and fisheries contributed AED 4,310m. (2.6%) to the UAE's total GDP at factor cost. By 2000, the UAE is expected to reach 100% self-sufficiency in wheat, and 95% self-sufficiency in fish, although in 1985 it was reported that over-fishing in breeding areas was beginning to have adverse effects on the fishing industry. The total catch was 95,129 tons in 1990, when there were 10,611 full-time fishermen, compared with about 4,000 in 1980. It was estimated in 1993 that the current annual catch of 97,200 tons exceeded local demand for fish by about 27,200 tons. Part of this surplus was exported and part was returned to the sea (there being no fish-processing industry in the UAE to provide a market for it). In 1996 the total catch was 105,554 tons.

TRADE, TRANSPORT AND TOURISM

During the 1970s the UAE's earnings from exports of petroleum enabled the country to retain a healthy overall balance of trade. In the early 1980s decreases in the levels of the UAE's petroleum production resulted in a relative decline in the country's trade surplus. The Iran–Iraq War brought considerable problems for the economies of other countries in the region, but Dubai continued to benefit from its trade links with Iran. In 1990, as a result of increased oil export volume and firmer oil prices, occasioned by the Gulf crisis, the trade surplus increaed to AED 37,000m., from AED 20,387m. in 1989. In 1993 exports and re-exports totalled AED 86,500m. (including petroleum worth AED 44,500m.), while imports totalled AED 72,000m. (including AED 25,500m. spent on items for re-export). The resulting visible trade surplus was AED 14,500m., although the current-account surplus was just AED 4,522m. in 1993, compared with AED 11,170m. in 1992. In 1994 exports and re-exports totalled AED 97,924m., while imports totalled AED 83,606m. (including AED 31,000m. spent on items for re-export), resulting in a visible trade surplus of AED 14,318m. In 1995 the trade surplus was AED 14,400m. (exports and re-exports AED 105,900m., total imports AED 91,500m.). There were balance-of-payments surpluses of AED 1,218m. in 1994 and AED 1,950m. in 1995. In 1996, according to Central Bank estimates, exports and imports were valued at AED 121,960m. and AED 94,980m. respectively.

The principal commodity groups in the UAE's imports are basic manufactures, machinery and transport equipment, and food and live animals. The leading purchasers of crude petroleum from Abu Dhabi are Japan, Western Europe and the Far East. All of Sharjah's petroleum exports go to the USA. In 1993 the leading suppliers of imports into the UAE were Japan, China, the USA, the United Kingdom and India. The UAE was admitted to GATT membership in March 1994, and to its successor, the World Trade Organization, in February 1996.

One way in which trade has been allocated is through the designation of free trade zones, such as Jebel Ali and Port Zayed. From April 1982 customs duty in Dubai and Sharjah was lowered from 3% to 1%, to bring it in line with Abu Dhabi. In 1983 all the emirates introduced a 4% unified import tariff, following a GCC unified economic agreement, although this tariff was not uniformly applied throughout the federation until August 1994 (when individual emirates formally abandoned inconsistent customs practices). Imports from within the GCC area were exempt from the 4% tariff, as were many industrial raw materials, agricultural inputs, medicines and certain food items. Since the cease-fire in the Gulf War, several lines which had operated to the east coast during the conflict have returned to the Gulf, and investment in the free-trade zones has risen. The Jebel Ali Free Zone offers various incentives to investors, including: the right to 100% foreign ownership; the absence of taxes, import or export duties; and the right to full repatriation of profits and capital, as well as an ample supply of cheap labour.

The modern internal transport system of the UAE was largely developed in the late 1960s and the 1970s, when main roads were constructed to link all the major cities. The petroleum retailer Emarat (formerly known as Emirates General Petroleum Corpn) operated a network of 168 service stations in 1996. One of the characteristics of the country's economy over recent years has been the expansion in the number of major airports. Over 11.6m. passengers and 637,000 tons of cargo passed through the UAE's airports in 1995. There are six international airports in the UAE, the busiest of which is in Dubai. In 1993 Dubai airport handled 5.67m. passengers and 218,264 tons of cargo, and was considering plans to increase its annual cargo-handling capacity from 250,000 to 350,000 tons. In late 1995 plans were announced to expand the airport, which will increase handling capacity to 12m. passengers a year by 2000, and in 1996 some 8.5m. passengers used the airport. Abu Dhabi has two international airports—the main one handled over 3m. passengers in 1995—which are being upgraded and expanded in a five-year, $500m. investment programme, financed by the Abu Dhabi Government. The new Sharjah international airport handles the bulk of the UAE's air-cargo as well as providing up-to-date facilities for passengers. The other UAE airports are in Fujairah and Ras al-Khaimah. In 1985 Dubai founded its own airline, Emirates Airlines, which by late 1995 was flying to 38 destinations. In 1992 Emirates Airlines announced a $1,000m. investment plan to purchase new aircraft over a 10-year period. Contracts have since been signed with Boeing (for seven B777 aircraft) and Airbus Industrie (for 16 A330-200 airliners). In 1997/98 Emirates Airlines carried 3.68m. passengers and 200,138 tons of cargo, achieving net profits of AED 262.4m. There is strong competition from Gulf Air, which enjoys considerable regional superiority.

Port facilities have also been greatly expanded over recent years. The UAE has a total of 15 commercial ports, which between them handle over 33m. tons of cargo a year. Traffic at the UAE's ports increased in 1988 with the end of the Iran–Iraq War. Fujairah port's container throughput rose to a record 202,827 20-foot-equivalent units (TEUs) from 188,129 TEUs in 1987. Container traffic at Mina Rashid was 557,521 TEUs in 1988, while at Mina Jebel Ali the total freight handled was 4,475,175 metric tons. In 1992 the Dubai Ports Authority's area of operations (taking in Mina Rashid and Mina Jebel Ali) was ranked as the world's sixteenth busiest container port, with combined traffic of 1.48m. TEUs, shared almost equally between the two locations. The number of vessels calling at the Dubai ports in 1992 was 8,253, and the amount of general cargo handled, excluding petroleum, totalled 2.8m. tons. Sea-air cargo in 1992 totalled 9.1m. tons. The Dubai Ports Authority reported a 13% increase in container traffic and a 12% increase in overall tonnage handled in 1993. In 1994 there was a further 12% increase in container traffic to 1.88m. TEUs (a throughput exceeded by only 13 other ports in the world in that year). In the first six months of 1995 the Dubai ports handled 4,612 vessels, a total cargo volume of 13.84m. tons and total container traffic of 982,575 TEUs. In the same period the Abu Dhabi port of Mina Zayed handled 1,071 vessels, 936,258 tons of general cargo and 117,644 TEUs of container traffic. Total container

traffic at the UAE's six major ports was some 3.5m. TEUs for 1995 (of which 2.15m. TEUs passed through the Dubai ports). There are plans for a new port at Taweela in Abu Dhabi to serve the proposed industrial zone. Substantial development is planned for the site with a new shipbuilding facility, and a gas processing facility to treat offshore Khuff gas before it is delivered to Jebel Ali in Dubai.

The UAE tourism industry, which in 1993 catered for more than 1m. visitors for the first time, was undergoing rapid expansion in 1995 as several major development schemes neared completion while others were at earlier stages of construction. In Dubai, the principal centre for UAE tourism (with 1,601,000 visitors in 1995), the main emphasis was on diversification into luxury beach and resort developments catering predominantly for holidaymakers rather than the business travellers who constituted the core clientele of many of Dubai's older-established hotels. Promotion of the UAE as a year-round destination for 'sunshine tourism' was aimed in the mid-1990s mainly at the upper end of the European market. Promotional campaigns in Japan and the USA were due to be stepped up in the later 1990s. About 1.92m. tourists visited the UAE in 1994.

BANKING AND FINANCE

The unit of currency in the UAE is the dirham, which was created in 1973 to replace the Bahraini dinar and the Qatar/Dubai riyal, formerly used in the emirates. With effect from March 1996, 'AED' superseded 'Dh' as the Central Bank's official abbreviation for the currency unit. The dirham is linked officially to the IMF's Special Drawing Right but in practice to the US dollar. In 1979 and 1980 the Currency Board revalued the dirham by small amounts (up to 1%) against the dollar in order to try to curb capital outflows from the country (there are no exchange controls), which were attracted by generally higher interest rates elsewhere. The revaluations were also designed to ease the tightness of liquidity in the domestic money market which had been caused by the capital outflows. As a result of maintaining a fixed exchange rate of US $1 = AED 3.671, the dirham lost more than 40% of its value in relation to the major European currencies between February 1985 and February 1987. During 1987 the dirham depreciated by a further 11.3% against an international 'basket' of currencies, as a result of the decline of the dollar.

A central monetary institution, the UAE Currency Board, was established in 1973, but inter-emirate rivalry prevented it from being given full central banking powers. This has led to a rapid multiplication of banks in the country. The Currency Board, managed mainly by expatriates, was able to bring only a little order to the banking free-for-all. A moratorium on the opening of new banks was imposed in 1975, lifted temporarily and then re-imposed with a let-out for international banks of restricted licences (which allow all operations except domestic retail banking), only five of which have opened. In December 1980 the UAE Central Bank replaced the old Currency Board, and the rulers of Abu Dhabi and Dubai agreed to place one-half of their national revenues with the new institution. In April 1981 the moratorium on new banks was lifted again but in May the governor of the Central Bank announced that no foreign banks would be granted new branch licences. In July 1981 the Central Bank became more aggressive and told all foreign banks that they had until 1984 to reduce their operations to eight branches each. One way in which some banks tried to minimize the impact of this legislation was by becoming locally incorporated, with a 60% UAE shareholding. By the end of 1983, however, all foreign banks had complied with the legislation and reduced their number of branches to eight. Early in 1982 the Central Bank again intervened to keep a high level of liquidity in the country by imposing a 30% interest-free reserve requirement on dirham loans placed outside the UAE for less than one year, replacing the former 15% charge, imposed in May 1981, for loans up to three months.

Other disruptions to the banking sector were announced in early 1983. The ruler of Abu Dhabi decided that foreign banks should pay a tax of 20% on profits; and the Central Bank, implementing certain clauses of the 1980 bank law, established an upper limit on borrowing by individual bank directors and boards of directors. Despite this, many banks continued to do well in the early 1980s. In 1982 Umm al-Qaiwain opened its first locally incorporated bank, the National Bank of Umm al-Qaiwain. However, the general 'ceiling' of 5% on loans to individual directors led to the collapse, in 1983, of the Union Bank of the Middle East, which had loaned its Chairman, Abd al-Wahab Galadari, monies representing 25%–30% of the bank's total lending. The Central Bank forced his resignation in November 1983, and established a committee of bankers and businessmen to take over the management of the bank. By mid-1986, Abd al-Wahab Galadari's creditors had received a payment of 75% from the official receivers, which amounted to $321m. Other banks seem to have adopted policies in accordance with the Central Bank's requirements. It was not until the end of 1987, however, that final agreement was reached on loans valued at $68.6m. which were owed by A. R. E. Galadari Brothers to the nine-bank consortium headed by Citibank.

A further development in the banking sector was the establishment, in 1983, of the Emirates Industrial Bank, with an authorized capital of AED 500m., to provide loans to new industries. Towards the end of 1984, in an attempt to discourage capital outflow, the Central Bank announced increases in the percentage of demand deposits accepted by local banks which would have to be placed with the Central Bank. In addition, since October 1984 all banks have had to maintain an interest-free balance with the Central Bank, equal to 30% of any dirham lendings or placements to non-resident banks with a remaining life of less than one year. The Central Bank's concern over the liquidity of many of the country's smaller banks has continued, and in 1985 a Central Bank circular obliged each of the UAE's banks to provide a detailed account of its financial operations, thus proving the existence of its inner reserves. This move was followed by a series of mergers involving the country's smaller banks. By 1988 the various reorganizations had reduced the total number of local banks in the UAE to 17. In 1985 'bad debts' (i.e. debts unlikely to be repaid) increased by 15%–20%. During 1986 the problem of 'bad debts' increased considerably, and many borrowers had recourse to the courts in an attempt to reduce their debts, by arguing that compound interest was illegal. If interest payments were recalculated on the basis of simple interest, the banks would be obliged, in some cases, to return 80% of the total interest that they had received.

The collapse of the price of petroleum in 1986, and the deepening recession of the mid-1980s, caused an increasing number of problems for the majority of the banks in the UAE. In mid-1986 the Central Bank announced several measures that were aimed at imposing restraint in financial matters. The new measures, in particular, prohibited banks operating in the UAE from making unsecured loans. In 1987 provision for loan losses was reduced, and in 1988 the Central Bank announced that UAE banks were in a position to withstand bad debts. During 1987 a presidential decree specified that, in future, all debt cases would be considered by the civil court rather than the *Shari'a* court, and a further decree spread considerable confusion by announcing that in all cases interest should not exceed the amount of the principal debt. Initially Iraq's invasion of Kuwait in August 1990 severely affected confidence in the banking sector. In August and September between 15% and 30% of total customer deposits were estimated to have been transferred out of the UAE. The continuous withdrawal of deposits forced the Central Bank to inject government money into at least two local banks. The bulk of these deposits have not returned to the UAE, although confidence has gradually returned to the banking sector. The outbreak of hostilities between the US-led multinational force and Iraq in January 1991 did not lead to further transfers of deposits out of the UAE banking sector.

According to UAE spokesmen, the banking sector overcame the negative effects of the Gulf crisis by virtue of speedy action by the Central Bank to ensure liquidity and confidence in the 47 existing commercial banks, whose consolidated balance sheet total increased by 9.5%, to $35,300m., in the second half of 1990. However, the effective failure of the National Investments and Security Corpn (NISCORP) in September 1991, after recording losses of $35m., impelled the federal authorities to seek to restore confidence by appointing a new Governor of the Central Bank. Total bank assets rose by 10% in 1991, to AED 142,000m. In 1995, when 19 local and 28 foreign banks were active in the UAE, aggregate bank assets totalled AED

180,892m. (the highest such figure in any Arab state except Saudi Arabia). By September 1996 the total assets of commercial banks had reached AED 186,169m. This increase was almost entirely due to stronger private credit demand.

Inflation and the growth of bank credit have both been reduced since 1980. In mid-1994 the inflation rate was estimated to be around 6.5% per annum. According to planning ministry figures, the inflation rate was 4.4% in 1995 and 4% in 1996. The UAE has been considering the establishment of a stock exchange since 1985. Limited trading in shares has been conducted by a group of five financial institutions. Companies whose shares are being traded include the 10 leading UAE banks, four local insurance companies, the state telecommunications company (Etisalat) and some smaller industrial groups. In May 1997 it was reported that public subscription in the UAE's first mutual fund was to be invited at the beginning of June. Launched and managed by the Emirates Bank Group, the fund would provide the first opportunity for non-UAE nationals to invest in the UAE's equities market. The fund's launch came at a time of increased activity in the UAE stock market. On the informal market, trading volumes had risen by 100% during the previous two years, boosted by the establishment of several new joint stock companies. Several new public offerings are reportedly planned, in advance of the establishment of the long-awaited stock exchange which is expected in 1998. Several banks have diversified their operations in recent years, notably the Abu Dhabi Commercial Bank, which has introduced Islamic banking, and the British Bank of the Middle East, which has established a regional treasury centre.

In many economic matters, the individual emirates tend to pursue their own separate policies, although they rarely publish detailed budgets. Until recently, Abu Dhabi and, to a lesser extent, Dubai were the only two contributors to the federal budget, but by the beginning of 1986 Sharjah was also publicly committed to contributing to the budget. Nevertheless, by mid-1987, following the attempted coup in Sharjah, it became clear that the country's finances were in difficulties, as its total debt burden was in the order of $920m. By the beginning of July, however, loans valued at $130m. had been rescheduled.

Federal expenditure is divided into current expenditure, development and expenditure for investment. It should be noted, however, that the federal budget reflects only part of the country's total expenditure, as the individual emirates also have their own budgets. Figures for these are not always available, but in Abu Dhabi total budget expenditure declined from a record level of AED 7,000m. in 1982 to AED 6,525.4m. in 1983, when there was a deficit of AED 2,900m. In 1984 a deficit of approximately AED 1,487m. was recorded. Abu Dhabi has not published its budgets since 1984, although in 1988 total expenditure of AED 3,600m. was announced. In 1994 the Abu Dhabi Government announced a 20% spending cut-back for the current year, to be followed by a further 20% cut-back in its 1995 budget. It did not, however, specify the amounts involved, and was generally assumed to be indicating broad objectives rather than imposing binding targets.

The 1993 federal budget proposals envisaged expenditure of AED 17,630m. and revenue of AED 15,911m., leaving a deficit of AED 1,719m., which was effectively increased to AED 2,169m. after taking account of a remaining deficit of AED 900m. from the previous fiscal year. The deficit was to be financed by contributions from Abu Dhabi and Dubai and by borrowing from the UAE Central Bank. New projects accounted for AED 1,180m. of the budgeted expenditure for 1993. In July 1993 the federal authorities advised ministries not to propose new projects for inclusion in the 1994 budget until they had completed at least 80% of their current projects. Any increase in federal revenue in 1994 would, it was stated, be used to reduce the size of the budget deficit. In the event, expenditure was marginally trimmed to AED 17,610m. in the 1994 federal budget, leaving a budget deficit of AED 1,410m. after allowing for a 1.8% increase in revenue to AED 16,200m. (80% of which was to come from the oil and gas sector). Spending allocations included AED 5,340m. for federal civil service salaries, AED 2,770m. for education, AED 2,250m. for health services, AED 1,120m. for water and electricity supply and AED 1,200 for development projects. According to a Central Bank report issued in late 1994, the federal accounts for the period January to June 1994 were in surplus by AED 1,160m., and a surplus of AED 1,400m. was in prospect for the full year if all departments maintained disciplined spending patterns. Various fees charged by the federal authorities, including airport tax and charges for visas, were increased in the latter part of 1994. The 1995 federal budget provided for total spending of AED 17,949m. and total revenue of AED 16,903m., leaving a deficit of AED 1,046m. The 1996 federal budget provided for total spending of AED 18,250m. and total revenue of AED 17,400m., resulting in a deficit of AED 850m. The IMF estimated that total public spending in the UAE in 1995 (including the unpublished budgets of individual emirates) amounted to AED 55,900m. (about 40% of GDP). Federal government expenditure is forecast to increase to AED 19,860m. in 1997 according to the budget approved in April. An increase in revenue to AED 18,870m. is also predicted resulting in a deficit of AED 990m. The federal budget for 1998 envisaged revenue of AED 19,635m., and expenditure of AED 21,393m.

In May 1991 the federal Government announced that a study to assess the feasibility of establishing the UAE, and in particular Dubai, as a centre for 'offshore' banking was to be undertaken. On 5 July 1991, however, such considerations were overtaken by the effects of the closure of operations of the Bank of Credit and Commerce International (BCCI) by the regulatory authorities of seven countries in which it had operated. Within days BCCI operations had been suspended in most of the 69 countries in which it had operated.

Sheikh Zayed bin Sultan an-Nahyan, the ruler of Abu Dhabi and President of the UAE, was a founding shareholder of BCCI. In 1988 BCCI became involved in a scandal when two of its US subsidiaries were accused of 'laundering' profits from trade in illegal drugs. With the bank's problems mounting, Sheikh Zayed and Abu Dhabi agencies purchased a 77% stake in BCCI in mid-1990 and sought to formulate a plan for reconstructing BCCI. In September 1990 the headquarters of BCCI were moved from London to Abu Dhabi. The reconstruction plan was thought to involve dividing BCCI into three separately capitalized entities registered in London, Hong Kong and Abu Dhabi, respectively, and with the holding company based in Abu Dhabi. Abu Dhabi invested as much as $1,000m. in BCCI. These plans, however, were pre-empted when BCCI was closed on 5 July 1991 in seven countries after a report by its auditors, Price Waterhouse, commissioned by the Bank of England, alleged major and systematic fraud by the bank. The UAE protested at the lack of prior consultation before BCCI's closure.

The closure of BCCI caused hardship amongst traders, businessmen and shippers in the UAE. Agencies in Abu Dhabi are owed $1,400m. and 35,000 private depositors are owed $600m. The UAE Government has stated that it will compensate these private depositors. Abu Dhabi's intention appeared to be to reconstruct the bank as a Middle East and Asian bank. On 3 August 1991 the Bank of Credit and Commerce (Emirates) changed its name to the Union National Bank. It was intended that BCCI's 40% shareholding should be purchased in order to sever all ties with the parent bank. In mid-1992 the Abu Dhabi-based majority shareholders in the former BCCI warned creditors that their offer of 30% compensation payment was final. Creditors, however, appeared unwilling to accept this and ready to risk litigation. In July Abu Dhabi was criticized, in a draft of the official British report of the BCCI collapse, for withholding information as to the scale of the fraud from the Bank of England. In October it was reported that 90% of BCCI's creditors had voted to accept the joint liquidators' plan, but in mid-1993 the objections of a minority of creditors (who were pursuing their case in the Luxembourg courts) continued to delay acceptance of the plan. The Ministry of Justice in Abu Dhabi stated in July 1993 that 13 senior managers of BCCI would go on trial in October on charges including forgery of documents, concealment of banking losses, and making false loans. All but one of the 13 defendants were convicted at the conclusion of the trials in May 1994 (although two convictions were later overturned on appeal).

In January 1995 a Luxembourg court approved a revised settlement plan (already approved by courts in London and the Cayman Islands) under which the Abu Dhabi Governnment and ruling family would contribute $1,800m. in compensation payments to BCCI creditors world-wide over a period of three

years. In May 1996 the Abu Dhabi Government signed an agreement implementing the settlement plan, whereby $1,550m. was to be paid directly to the liquidators and $250m. was to be paid into an escrow account for later release. The liquidators' stated intention was to pay a first dividend of about 20% of creditors' claims in mid-1996. Subsequent dividends were expected to increase the total compensation paid to 30%–40% of the amount claimed. The UAE Central Bank formally removed BCCI from its banking register in April 1996 (the closing date for compensation claims from UAE depositors). In November 1996 it was announced that the first payments would be made in December of that year.

With effect from July 1993, the UAE Central Bank introduced new banking regulations whereby the minimum ratio for capital adequacy was raised to 10% (2% higher than the internationally recommended minimum). Moreover, the legal definition of a bank's 'core' capital and its 'supplementary' capital was respecified in accordance with current international standards. All on- and off-balance-sheet items were required to be ranked according to a schedule of risk. Banks were required to maintain a minimum level of 10% of total risk-weighted assets relative to their capital base, in which 'core capital' must reach a minimum of 6% of total risk-weighted assets, while 'supplementary capital' would be considered only up to a maximum of 67% of core capital. Banks would henceforth be required to report to the Central Bank every three months.

In October 1993 the Central Bank issued a circular tightening the banking regulations still further from the beginning of 1994 (with provision for deferral on a case-by-case basis until the end of 1995). This circular limited any bank's exposure to the following proportion of its capital base: 25% if the exposure was to a government-owned commercial entity; 5% to a director or board member, and no more than 25% in aggregate to the bank's whole board; 6% in aggregate to bank employees; 7% to one of its shareholders, or a single borrower, or a group of related borrowers; 20% to a subsidiary or affiliate. There were also ceilings on funded inter-bank exposures, letters of credit and guarantee, and other contingent liabilities. Banks were required to report large exposures (including those of subsidiaries) to the Central Bank on a quarterly basis, a large exposure being defined in the circular as all exposures to a single borrower or a group of related borrowers that total 7% or more of a bank's capital base. The Central Bank later agreed to exclude contingent liabilities from its definition of a large exposure, which was to be calculated after deductions for provisions, cash collateral and deposits under lien. The Central Bank also agreed to draw up a list of acceptable securities against which banks would be permitted to lend without reference to the 'large exposure' limits. During 1994 UAE banks increased their capital by more than $200m. to comply with international adequacy standards and UAE banking regulations.

In February 1995 a total of 53 leading corporate and individual members of the Dubai business community and ruling family (including nine financial institutions) announced the establishment of a new joint-stock company, Dubai Investments, in which they would hold 45% of the shares. The remaining 55% of the shares were sold to the public two months later through a heavily over-subscribed flotation (open to all UAE nationals) managed by Emirates Bank International. Dubai Investments had an authorized capital of AED 1,300m. Its stated aims included the establishment and acquisition of interests in a wide range of economic activities, including agricultural, mining, services, insurance and tourism ventures within the UAE and, in the longer term, suitable ventures in other countries. The new company announced its first equity investment (in a fibre-optic manufacturing venture in the Jebel Ali Free Zone) in February 1996. In November 1996 Dubai Investments announced that it had acquired majority stakes in three local companies and that it planned to build a new industrial park close to the Jebel Ali Free Zone and port.

In late 1997 reports of instability were denied by Mashreq Bank. The Central Bank issued a statement affirming the strong position of the bank, which later announced net profits of AED 486m. for 1997, the largest in local banking history. In March 1998 the Central Bank was obliged to intervene and provide short-term liquidity in support of Dubai Islamic Bank. There was some speculation that the discovery of fraudulent practices had prompted the crisis. At that time, legislation was being prepared to strengthen the role of the Central Bank and to enforce stricter regulation of the financial sector.

DEVELOPMENT PLANNING

Until 1981, development expenditure in the UAE came from the annual federal budget, and there was no attempt at detailed long-term integrated economic planning, although Abu Dhabi did have a loose development plan for 1977–79. The end of the 1970s saw a great increase in health facilities in the country, with the number of hospital beds available rising from 1,750 in 1979 to 3,500 in April 1981. This increase was partly brought about through the completion of two major new hospitals at al-Ain. In 1986 the UAE had 28 hospitals and 119 clinics. In 1989 a total of 10 new primary health care centres were planned, at a cost of AED 10m.–12m. each. In 1990 the UAE had one doctor for every 1,040 inhabitants and one nurse for every 500 inhabitants, and in 1994 there was one doctor for every 598 inhabitants. The infant mortality rate in 1995 was 16 per 1,000 live births, compared with 87 per 1,000 in 1970. In 1993 99% of the population had access to public health services. In January 1995 the Government increased the annual fee for a compulsory health card to AED 300 for each adult non-citizen and AED 100 for each adult citizen.

The first Five-Year Plan was intended to have been implemented in 1981, to run until 1985, but the fall in revenues from petroleum severely restricted initial proposals. Overall expenditure was estimated to be AED 16,000m. for the five years, with Abu Dhabi receiving 21%, Fujairah 12.5%, Sharjah 10.8%, Ras al-Khaimah 9.4%, Umm al-Qaiwain 7.7%, Dubai 5.3%, and Ajman 4.4%. The Plan initially predicted an overall increase of 20% in the country's GDP up to 1985. However, in 1983 alone GDP fell by 13.5%, and in 1981–85 GDP, at constant 1990 prices, declined by an annual average of 2.3%. The Plan also allocated AED 3,800m. to the agricultural sector, which was expected to expand at an annual rate of 10.3%. It was hoped, in particular, to improve productivity and marketing services, and to aim for the best possible use of water resources. Of the AED 16,000m. which was to be spent in the Plan, AED 3,500m. was for investment projects and AED 8,400m. for schemes already under construction. The experience of the first five-year plan for the UAE meant that there was little

enthusiasm for a second and the emirates of the UAE returned to a more flexible approach to defining and planning development priorities. In early 1989 Abu Dhabi announced that the emirate planned to spend about AED 14,800m. in the next decade on infrastructure and development. A total of AED 875m. was allocated to the construction of 85 schools (as part of the fifth education plan), of which 41 were scheduled to be completed by the beginning of the 1990/91 academic year.

In November 1996 the Abu Dhabi Government established a consultative committee for the development of the emirate. The committee is to develop and facilitate procedures for businesses seeking to invest in the emirate. Its establishment is in keeping with Abu Dhabi's overall policy of encouraging greater private sector investment, of which the planned privatization of electricity and water installations is a key aspect. In the same month Dubai unveiled its first strategic development plan, setting out an ambitious programme aimed at achieving economic diversification, high non-oil sector growth and increased productivity by 2010. The plan envisages 5% growth per year in GDP, over the next 15 years, fuelled by a 6%–7% annual increase in the non-oil sector contribution to GDP. The plan envisages capital investments of AED 44,500m. over the next five years, with funding for projects proceeding from both the Government and the private sector.

The UAE, however, has not only been concerned with its own development. Abu Dhabi, through its Fund for Arab Economic Development (ADFAED), has been a major source of international aid. ADFAED was set up in 1971 with a capital of $120m.; its commitments up to the end of 1980 totalled $800m. However, in 1982, as a result of declining revenues from petroleum, the UAE reduced its foreign aid budget to AED 6,500m. from AED 9,400m. in 1981. Aid continued to decline during the 1980s, but in 1988 ADFAED signed loans totalling AED 151m. ($41.1m.), compared with AED 15.6m. ($4.2m.) in 1987. The ADFAED was renamed the Abu Dhabi Fund for Development at the end of 1993 (reflecting its involvement in projects in some non-Arab countries).

On 22 April 1991 the UAE agreed, as part of the GCC, to establish a Gulf Development Fund, with a capital of $10,000m. for an initial 10-year period. The fund was to provide new finance for those Middle East countries whose economies are relatively weak. Finance will be aimed at the private sector and will be incorporated into World Bank and IMF programmes.

Statistical Survey

Source (unless otherwise indicated): Central Statistical Department, Ministry of Planning, POB 1134, Sharjah; tel. (6) 22704.

Area and Population

AREA, POPULATION AND DENSITY

Area (sq km)	77,700*
Population (census results)	
December 1985	1,622,464
17 December 1995 (provisional)	
Males	1,579,743
Females	797,710
Total	2,377,453
Population (official estimates at mid-year)	
1995	2,314,000
1996	2,443,000
Density (per sq km) at mid-1996	31.4

* 30,000 sq miles.

POPULATION BY EMIRATE (estimates, mid-1996)

	Area (sq km)	Population	Density (per sq km)
Abu Dhabi	67,350	952,000	14.1
Dubai	3,900	695,000	178.2
Sharjah	2,600	412,000	158.5
Ras al-Khaimah . .	1,700	147,000	86.5
Ajman	250	123,000	492.0
Fujairah	1,150	78,000	67.8
Umm al-Qaiwain . .	750	36,000	48.0
Total	**77,700**	**2,443,000**	**31.4**

PRINCIPAL TOWNS (population at December 1980 census)

Dubai	265,702	Sharjah . . .	125,149
Abu Dhabi (capital)	242,975	Al-Ain . . .	101,663

Source: UN, *Demographic Yearbook*.

BIRTHS AND DEATHS (UN estimates, annual averages)

	1980–85	1985–90	1990–95
Birth rate (per 1,000) . . .	29.5	27.9	23.2
Death rate (per 1,000) . . .	4.0	2.8	2.7

Source: UN, *World Population Prospects: The 1994 Revision.*

1994: 52,629 registered live births; 7,381 registered marriages; 4,597 registered deaths (Source: UN, *Demographic Yearbook*).
1995: 48,567 registered live births (birth rate 21.0 per 1,000); 4,779 registered deaths (death rate 2.1 per 1,000) (Source: UN, *Population and Vital Statistics Report*).

Expectation of life (UN estimates, years at birth, 1990–95): 73.8 (males 72.9; females 75.3) (Source: UN, *World Population Prospects: The 1994 Revision*).

EMPLOYMENT (estimates, '000 persons)

	1994	1995	1996
Agriculture, hunting, forestry and fishing	72.5	74.5	78.2
Mining and quarrying . .	12.1	12.5	13.0
Manufacturing	96.7	104.2	112.4
Electricity, gas and water .	22.3	23.4	24.9
Construction	149.7	154.6	160.7
Trade, restaurants and hotels . .	185.5	197.3	209.2
Transport, storage and communications . . .	85.8	93.6	101.4
Financing, insurance, real estate and business services . .	43.3	46.0	48.6
Community, social and personal services	272.9	288.1	302.5
Total	940.8	994.1	1,050.8

Agriculture

PRINCIPAL CROPS ('000 metric tons)

	1994	1995	1996*
Cereals	7	7	7
Tomatoes	243	443	445
Cucumbers and gherkins . .	13	14	14
Aubergines	67	52	52
Green chillies and peppers .	6	5	7
Watermelons	4	4	5
Melons	10	16	16
Dates	236	237	240
Tobacco (leaves)	1	1	1

* FAO estimates.

Source: FAO, *Production Yearbook.*

LIVESTOCK ('000 head, year ending September)

	1994	1995	1996*
Cattle	65	69	70
Camels	148	158	160
Sheep	333	356	360
Goats	861	921	950

* FAO estimates.

Poultry (FAO estimates, million): 10 in 1994; 10 in 1995; 11 in 1996.

Source: FAO, *Production Yearbook.*

LIVESTOCK PRODUCTS ('000 metric tons)

	1994	1995	1996
Beef and veal*	8	11	9
Mutton and lamb* . . .	31	32	32
Goat meat*	6	6	7
Poultry meat*	22	22	23
Cows' milk	7	7	7*
Sheep's milk	7	7	7*
Goats' milk	20	21	22*
Hen eggs	11	12	13*

* FAO estimate(s).

Source: FAO, *Production Yearbook.*

Fishing

('000 metric tons, live weight)

	1993*	1994	1995
Fishes	94.9	107.9	105.5
Crustaceans and molluscs . .	0.1	0.1	0.1
Total catch	95.0	108.0	105.6

* FAO estimates.

Source: FAO, *Yearbook of Fishery Statistics.*

Mining

('000 metric tons, unless otherwise indicated)

	1993	1994	1995
Crude petroleum	99,058	104,050	103,209
Natural gas (petajoules) . .	895	991	1,113

Source: UN, *Industrial Commodity Statistics Yearbook.*

Industry

SELECTED PRODUCTS ('000 metric tons, unless otherwise indicated)

	1993	1994	1995
Jet fuels*	1,170	1,210	2,585
Motor spirit (petrol) . . .	1,310*	1,410*	1,498
Naphthas*	630	700	700
Kerosene*	78	90	150
Gas-diesel (distillate fuel) oil .	2,750*	3,000*	3,367
Residual fuel oils . . .	3,000*	3,300*	1,962
Liquefied petroleum gas:			
from natural gas plants* .	2,700	3,700	4,137
from petroleum refineries* .	300	400	396
Electric energy (million kWh)*	17,578	18,870	19,070

* Provisional or estimated figure(s).

Source: UN, *Industrial Commodity Statistics Yearbook.*

Finance

CURRENCY AND EXCHANGE RATES

Monetary Units
100 fils = 1 UAE dirham (AED).

Sterling and Dollar Equivalents (31 May 1998)
£1 sterling = 5.9887 dirhams;
US $1 = 3.6725 dirhams;
100 UAE dirhams = £16.70 = $27.23.

Average Exchange Rate (UAE dirhams per US $)
1995	3.6710
1996	3.6710
1997	3.6711

Note: The Central Bank's official rate was set at US $1 = 3.671 dirhams in November 1980. This remained in force until December 1997, when the rate was adjusted to $1 = 3.6725 dirhams.

GENERAL BUDGET (million UAE dirhams)*

Revenue	1992	1993	1994†
Taxation	920	663	826
Social security contributions .	55	60	57
Domestic taxes on goods and services	865	603	769
Other current revenue . .	3,171	2,266	2,450
Capital revenue	19	46	18
Grants from other levels of government . . .	12,511	1,273	12,689
Total	**16,983**	**15,248**	**15,983**

Expenditure	1992	1993	1994†
General public services . .	544	553	695
Defence	5,827	5,827	5,827
Public order and safety . .	2,063	2,134	2,021
Education	2,492	2,587	2,692
Health	1,048	1,141	1,153
Social security and welfare .	527	530	527
Housing and community amenities	147	292	316
Recreational, cultural and religious affairs and services .	491	505	498
Economic affairs and services .	1,269	700	827
Fuel and energy . . .	952	373	498
Agriculture, forestry, fishing and hunting	121	124	111
Other purposes	1,163	1,302	1,137
Total	**15,571**	**15,571**	**15,693**
Current	14,864	14,973	14,963
Capital	707	598	730

* Excluding the operations of the seven emirate Governments.
† Provisional.

Source: IMF, *Government Finance Statistics Yearbook*.

1995 (estimates, million dirhams): Revenue 16,900; Expenditure 17,950.
1996 (estimates, million dirhams): Revenue 17,400; Expenditure 18,250.
1997 (estimates, million dirhams): Revenue 18,870; Expenditure 19,860.

INTERNATIONAL RESERVES (US $ million at 31 December)

	1995	1996	1997
Gold*	181.7	182.8	181.3
IMF special drawing rights . .	83.1	82.8	78.7
Reserve position in IMF . .	276.2	293.9	266.3
Foreign exchange† . . .	7,111.6	7,678.8	8,027.3
Total	**7,652.6**	**8,238.3**	**8,553.6**

* Valued at US $228 per troy ounce.
† Figures exclude the Central Bank's foreign assets and accrued interest attributable to the governments of individual emirates.

Source: IMF, *International Financial Statistics*.

MONEY SUPPLY (million UAE dirhams at 31 December)

	1995	1996	1997
Currency outside banks . . .	6,404	6,767	7,366
Demand deposits at commercial banks	14,420	15,499	18,002
Total money	**20,824**	**22,266**	**25,368**

Source: IMF, *International Financial Statistics*.

COST OF LIVING (Consumer Price Index; base: 1985 = 100)

	1995	1996
Food, beverages and tobacco	122.1	126.2
Clothing and footwear	127.1	133.5
Housing (incl. rent)	167.9	167.5
Furniture, etc.	133.6	138.1
Transport and communications	152.0	160.3
Recreation and education	136.4	141.5
All items (incl. others)	**141.5**	**146.1**

NATIONAL ACCOUNTS (million UAE dirhams at current prices)
National Income and Product

	1988	1989	1990
Compensation of employees . .	25,226	26,769	27,996
Operating surplus	49,193	60,848	81,633
Domestic factor incomes .	**74,419**	**87,617**	**109,629**
Consumption of fixed capital . .	14,382	15,127	16,078
Gross domestic product (GDP) at factor cost . . .	**88,801**	**102,744**	**125,707**
Indirect taxes, *less* subsidies . .	−1,695	−1,768	−1,699
GDP in purchasers' values .	**87,106**	**100,976**	**124,008**
Factor income from abroad . .	9,940	10,600	10,900
Less Factor income paid abroad .	9,690	10,178	12,200
Gross national product . .	**87,356**	**101,398**	**122,708**
Less Consumption of fixed capital .	14,382	15,127	16,078
National income in market prices	**72,974**	**86,271**	**106,630**
Other current transfers from abroad (net)	−1,040	−744	−11,000
National disposable income .	**71,934**	**85,527**	**95,630**

Source: UN, *National Accounts Statistics*.

Expenditure on the Gross Domestic Product*

	1994	1995	1996
Government final consumption expenditure	24,200	25,390	26,150
Private final consumption expenditure	60,690	69,310	74,410
Increase in stocks	2,020	2,140	2,300
Gross fixed capital formation . .	37,500	39,790	40,940
Total domestic expenditure .	**124,410**	**136,630**	**143,800**
Exports of goods and services . .	104,760	109,440	125,800
Less Imports of goods and services	94,560	99,040	105,850
GDP in purchasers' values .	**134,610**	**147,030**	**163,750**

* Figures are rounded to the nearest 10 million dirhams.

Gross Domestic Product by Economic Activity (at factor cost)

	1994*	1995*	1996†
Agriculture, livestock and fishing .	3,890	4,090	4,310
Mining and quarrying . . .	44,780	47,680	57,460
Manufacturing	12,300	13,520	14,860
Electricity and water . . .	3,010	3,230	3,460
Construction	12,910	13,570	14,140
Trade, restaurants and hotels . .	16,840	17,790	18,700
Transport, storage and communications . . .	8,570	10,540	11,500
Finance, insurance and real estate	18,470	20,690	22,030
Government services . . .	15,910	16,710	17,530
Other community, social and personal services . . .	1,480	1,640	1,740
Domestic services of households .	1,010	1,070	1,110
Sub-total	139,170	150,530	166,840
Less Imputed bank service charge	2,900	3,000	3,190
Total	136,270	147,530	163,650

* Estimates.
† Preliminary.

BALANCE OF PAYMENTS (estimates, million UAE dirhams)

	1995	1996*
Exports of goods f.o.b. . . .	107,300	121,960
Imports of goods c.i.f. . . .	−86,200	−94,980
Trade balance	21,100	26,980
Services and other income (net) . .	9,350	9,750
Balance on goods, services and income .	30,450	36,730
Current transfers (net) . . .	−11,790	−12,270
Current balance	18,660	24,460
Official loans and equity participations . .	50	110
Short-term private capital . . .	−3,630	2,730
Other capital	} −12,300	−25,020
Net errors and omissions . . .		
Overall balance	2,780	2,280

* Preliminary.
Source: Central Bank of the United Arab Emirates.

External Trade

PRINCIPAL COMMODITIES (US $ million)

Imports c.i.f.	1991	1992	1993
Food and live animals . . .	996.4	1,213.9	1,204.8
Cereals and cereal preparations .	133.9	316.3	251.9
Vegetables and fruit . . .	264.7	285.6	313.9
Crude materials (inedible) except fuels	259.0	227.8	315.5
Mineral fuels, lubricants, etc. .	249.0	216.9	225.9
Petroleum, petroleum products, etc.	248.5	216.3	225.0
Chemicals and related products	602.1	712.9	726.6
Basic manufactures . . .	2,706.9	3,374.6	3,837.0
Textile yarn, fabrics, etc.. . .	1,242.6	1,549.6	1,764.1
Woven fabrics of man-made fibres	818.6	1,024.6	1,205.8
Non-metallic mineral manufactures . . .	196.6	272.5	319.8
Iron and steel	276.9	300.4	395.7
Non-ferrous metals . . .	243.9	321.8	417.0
Other metal manufactures . .	342.5	474.3	476.1
Machinery and transport equipment	3,345.1	4,552.4	4,439.2
Power-generating machinery and equipment.	204.1	356.3	248.2
Machinery specialized for particular industries . .	310.8	399.1	274.1
General industrial machinery, equipment and parts . .	526.1	652.5	827.8
Telecommunications and sound equipment.	716.1	710.5	846.3
Other electrical machinery, apparatus, etc. . .	470.9	662.6	579.8
Road vehicles and parts* . .	829.4	1,174.9	1,187.3
Passenger motor vehicles (excl. buses)	478.7	705.0	644.5
Other transport equipment* . .	116.6	372.7	228.5
Miscellaneous manufactured articles	2,070.5	2,491.8	2,858.3
Clothing and accessories (excl. footwear)	634.9	734.2	783.1
Photographic apparatus, optical goods, watches and clocks .	260.4	284.5	329.4
Jewellery, goldsmiths' and silversmiths' wares, etc. . .	309.1	385.5	562.6
Total (incl. others) . . .	10,381.3	12,951.9	13,764.8

Exports f.o.b.†	1991	1992	1993
Food and live animals . . .	29.8	50.4	56.6
Beverages and tobacco. . .	17.3	17.1	16.0
Beverages	17.2	17.1	15.9
Crude materials (inedible) except fuels	36.3	40.1	33.5
Metalliferous ores and metal scrap	30.5	33.7	29.5
Mineral fuels, lubricants, etc. .	35.4	52.0	52.9
Chemicals and related products	23.2	45.2	54.3
Basic manufactures . . .	428.6	403.9	391.3
Non-ferrous metals . . .	367.0	328.6	307.1
Machinery and transport equipment	35.8	60.8	98.0
Electrical machinery, apparatus, etc.	13.3	19.7	15.6
Transport equipment* . . .	19.8	39.1	80.2
Miscellaneous manufactured articles	147.2	228.4	257.3
Clothing and accessories (excl. footwear)	121.5	193.9	227.1
Total (incl. others) . . .	758.7	899.3	3,764.2‡

* Data on parts exclude tyres, engines and electrical parts.
† Figures exclude domestic exports of crude petroleum and all re-exports.
‡ Including re-exports (about $2,800 million), not distributed by commodity.
Source: UN, *International Trade Statistics Yearbook*.
Total Imports c.i.f. (million dirhams): 41,111 in 1990; 50,462 in 1991; 63,927 in 1992; 71,658 in 1993; 77,179 in 1994; 77,032 in 1995; 83,104 in 1996; 109,956 in 1997 (Source: IMF, *International Financial Statistics*).
Petroleum Exports (million dirhams): 54,500 in 1990; 52,700 in 1991; 51,600 in 1992.

Total Exports and Re-exports f.o.b. (million dirhams): 79,500 in 1990; 81,300 in 1991; 88,940* in 1992; 86,267* in 1993; 89,050* in 1994.

* Figures from *Middle East Economic Digest*.

Source (unless otherwise indicated): Central Bank of the United Arab Emirates.

PRINCIPAL TRADING PARTNERS (US $ million)

Imports	1991	1992	1993
Australia	242.0	291.6	230.1
China, People's Republic	818.2	1,042.6	1,187.1
France (incl. Monaco)	369.2	684.8	507.0
Germany	588.3	962.8	861.1
India	573.7	745.6	958.3
Indonesia	240.7	282.0	343.2
Italy	370.7	535.4	605.2
Japan	1,724.1	1,977.0	1,922.4
Korea, Republic	618.1	769.0	899.1
Malaysia	237.5	288.6	372.6
Netherlands	189.9	240.2	215.4
Saudi Arabia	90.2	139.6	162.7
Singapore	209.2	220.0	275.6
Thailand	331.0	370.0	390.0
United Kingdom	724.9	926.6	980.7
USA	928.8	1,027.9	1,073.3
Total (incl. others)	10,366.7	12,943.0	13,764.1

Exports*	1991†	1992†	1993
Bahrain	34.7	43.3	147.4
Congo, Republic	17.7	0.0	0.7
France (incl. Monaco)	22.9	20.3	26.2
Germany	45.6	54.2	112.6
India	12.4	22.1	143.8
Japan	244.3	148.7	141.0
Korea, Republic	35.3	42.4	56.7
Kuwait	20.0	36.5	267.0
Netherlands	9.2	35.5	108.6
Oman	70.5	72.9	73.5
Pakistan	15.2	14.9	140.2
Saudi Arabia	19.1	35.0	215.0
Thailand	22.0	19.2	38.9
United Kingdom	28.0	89.9	87.6
USA	26.1	45.7	101.1
Yemen	20.2	35.5	129.7
Total (incl. others)	754.4	899.3	3,764.2

* Excluding crude petroleum.

† Excluding re-exports.

Source: UN, *International Trade Statistics Yearbook*.

Transport

ROAD TRAFFIC ('000 motor vehicles in use)

	1991	1992	1993
Passenger cars	241.3	257.8	297.1
Commercial vehicles	43.4	60.4	72.8

Source: UN, *Statistical Yearbook*.

SHIPPING

Merchant Fleet (registered at 31 December)

	1995	1996	1997
Number of vessels	299	316	349
Total displacement ('000 grt)	961	890	924

Source: Lloyd's Register of Shipping, *World Fleet Statistics*.

International Sea-Borne Shipping
(estimated freight traffic, '000 metric tons)

	1988	1989	1990
Goods loaded	63,380	72,896	88,153
Crude petroleum	54,159	63,387	78,927
Other cargo	9,221	9,509	9,226
Goods unloaded	8,973	8,960	9,595

Source: UN, *Monthly Bulletin of Statistics*.

CIVIL AVIATION (traffic on scheduled services)*

	1993	1994	1995
Kilometres flown (million)	63	67	73
Passengers carried ('000)	2,936	3,369	3,551
Passenger-km (million)	7,794	8,878	9,958
Total ton-km (million)	1,126	1,322	1,517

* Figures include an apportionment (one-quarter) of the traffic of Gulf Air, a multinational airline with its headquarters in Bahrain.

Source: UN, *Statistical Yearbook*.

Tourism

	1993	1994	1995
Tourist arrivals ('000)*	1,088	1,239	1,601

* Dubai only.

Source: UN, *Statistical Yearbook*.

Communications Media

	1993	1994	1995
Radio receivers ('000 in use)	565	580	600
Television receivers ('000 in use)	192	200	230
Telephones ('000 main lines in use)	553	615	672
Telefax stations (number in use)	26,105	30,000*	24,978*
Mobile cellular telephones (subscribers)	70,586	91,488	128,968
Daily newspapers			
Number	n.a.	8	8*
Combined circulation ('000 copies)	n.a.	300	300*
Book production: titles	293†	n.a.	n.a.

* Estimate.

† Data refer only to school textbooks.

Sources: UNESCO, *Statistical Yearbook*, and UN, *Statistical Yearbook*.

Education

(1994/95, unless otherwise indicated)

	Teachers	Pupils/Students		
		Males	Females	Total
Pre-primary	2,886	29,455	26,973	56,428
Primary	15,449	136,933	125,695	262,628
Secondary				
General	12,388	78,245	80,380	158,625
Vocational	189	n.a.	n.a.	1,215
University*	728	1,947	6,721	8,668
Other higher*	354	627	1,110	1,737

* Figures refer to 1991/92.

Source: UNESCO, *Statistical Yearbook*.

Directory

The Constitution

A provisional Constitution for the UAE took effect in December 1971. This laid the foundation for the federal structure of the Union of the seven emirates, previously known as the Trucial States.

The highest federal authority is the Supreme Council of Rulers, which comprises the rulers of the seven emirates. It elects the President and Vice-President from among its members. The President appoints a Prime Minister and a Council of Ministers. Proposals submitted to the Council require the approval of at least five of the Rulers, including those of Abu Dhabi and Dubai. The legislature is the Federal National Council, a consultative assembly comprising 40 members appointed by the emirates for a two-year term.

In July 1975 a committee was appointed to draft a permanent federal constitution, but the National Council decided in 1976 to extend the provisional document for five years. The provisional Constitution was extended for another five years in December 1981, and for further periods of five years in 1986 and 1991. In November 1976, however, the Supreme Council amended Article 142 of the provisional Constitution so that the authority to levy armed forces was placed exclusively under the control of the federal Government. Legislation designed to make the provisional Constitution permanent was endorsed by the Federal National Council in June 1996, after it had been approved by the Supreme Council of Rulers.

The Government

HEAD OF STATE

President: Sheikh ZAYED BIN SULTAN AN-NAHYAN, Ruler of Abu Dhabi (took office as President of the UAE on 2 December 1971; re-elected 1976, 1981 and 1991).

Vice-President: Sheikh MAKTOUM BIN RASHID AL-MAKTOUM, Ruler of Dubai.

SUPREME COUNCIL OF RULERS
(with each Ruler's date of accession)

Ruler of Abu Dhabi: Sheikh ZAYED BIN SULTAN AN-NAHYAN (1966).

Ruler of Dubai: Sheikh MAKTOUM BIN RASHID AL-MAKTOUM (1990).

Ruler of Sharjah: Sheikh SULTAN BIN MUHAMMAD AL-QASIMI (1972).

Ruler of Ras al-Khaimah: Sheikh SAQR BIN MUHAMMAD AL-QASIMI (1948).

Ruler of Umm al-Qaiwain: Sheikh RASHID BIN AHMAD AL-MU'ALLA (1981).

Ruler of Ajman: Sheikh HUMAID BIN RASHID AN-NUAIMI (1981).

Ruler of Fujairah: Sheikh HAMAD BIN MUHAMMAD ASH-SHARQI (1974).

COUNCIL OF MINISTERS
(September 1998)

Prime Minister: Sheikh MAKTOUM BIN RASHID AL-MAKTOUM.

Deputy Prime Minister: Sheikh SULTAN BIN ZAYED AN-NAHYAN.

Minister of the Interior: Lt-Gen. Dr MUHAMMAD SAID AL-BADI.

Minister of Foreign Affairs: RASHID ABDULLAH AN-NUAIMI.

Minister of Finance and Industry: Sheikh HAMDAN BIN RASHID AL-MAKTOUM.

Minister of Defence: Sheikh MUHAMMAD BIN RASHID AL-MAKTOUM.

Minister of Economy and Commerce: Sheikh FAHIM BIN SULTAN AL-QASIMI.

Minister of Information and Culture: Sheikh ABDULLAH BIN ZAYED AN-NAHYAN.

Minister of Communications: AHMAD BIN HUMAID AT-TAYER.

Minister of Public Works and Housing: RAKKAD BIN SALEM BIN RAKKAD.

Minister of Higher Education and Scientific Research: Sheikh NAHYAN BIN MUBARAK AN-NAHYAN.

Minister of Health: HAMAD ABD AR-RAHMAN AL-MADFA.

Minister of Electricity and Water: HUMAID BIN NASSER AL-OWAIS.

Minister of Labour and Social Affairs: MATEER HUMAID AT-TAYER.

Minister of Planning: Sheikh HUMAID BIN AHMAD AL-MU'ALLA.

Minister of Petroleum and Mineral Resources: OBEID BIN SAIF AN-NASIRI.

Minister of Agriculture and Fisheries: SAID MUHAMMAD AR-RAGABANI.

Minister of Education and Youth: ALI ABD AL-AZIZ ASH-SHARHAN.

Minister of Justice, Islamic Affairs and Awqaf (Religious Endowments): MUHAMMAD NAKHIRA ADH-DHAHERI.

Minister of State for Cabinet Affairs: SAID KHALFAN AL-GHAITH.

Minister of State for Finance and Industry: MUHAMMAD KHALFAN BIN KHARBASH.

Minister of State for Foreign Affairs: Sheikh HAMDAN BIN ZAYED AN-NAHYAN.

Minister of State for Affairs of the Supreme Council: Sheikh MAJEED BIN SAID AN-NUAIMI.

FEDERAL MINISTRIES

Office of the Prime Minister: POB 12848, Dubai; tel. (4) 533122; fax (4) 535883.

Office of the Deputy Prime Minister: POB 831, Abu Dhabi; tel. (2) 651881.

Ministry of Agriculture and Fisheries: POB 213, Abu Dhabi; tel. (2) 662781; fax (2) 654787.

Ministry of Communications: POB 900, Abu Dhabi; tel. (2) 651900; telex 22668; fax (2) 661575.

Ministry of Defence: POB 2838, Dubai; tel. (4) 532330; telex 45554; fax (4) 531974.

Ministry of Economy and Commerce: POB 901, Abu Dhabi; tel. (2) 215455; telex 22897; fax (2) 260000.

Ministry of Education and Youth: POB 295, Abu Dhabi; tel. (2) 213800; telex 22581; fax (2) 351164.

Ministry of Electricity and Water: POB 629, Abu Dhabi; tel. (2) 335099; telex 46453; fax (4) 213738.

Ministry of Finance and Industry: POB 433, Abu Dhabi; tel. (2) 726000; telex 22937; fax (2) 773301.

Ministry of Foreign Affairs: POB 1, Abu Dhabi; tel. (2) 652200; telex 22217; fax (2) 653849.

Ministry of Health: POB 848, Abu Dhabi; tel. (2) 330000; telex 22678; fax (2) 313525.

Ministry of Higher Education and Scientific Research: POB 45253, Abu Dhabi; tel. (2) 669422; fax (2) 645277.

Ministry of Information and Culture: POB 17, Abu Dhabi; tel. (2) 453000; telex 22283; fax (2) 451155; e-mail mininfex@emirates.net.ae.

Ministry of the Interior: POB 398, Abu Dhabi; tel. (2) 414666; telex 22398; fax (2) 415780.

Ministry of Justice and Islamic Affairs and Awqaf (Religious Endowments): POB 2272, Abu Dhabi; tel. (2) 212300; fax (2) 316003.

Ministry of Labour and Social Affairs: POB 809, Abu Dhabi; tel. (2) 651890; fax (2) 665889.

Ministry of Petroleum and Mineral Resources: POB 59, Abu Dhabi; tel. (2) 651810; telex 22544; fax (2) 663414.

Ministry of Planning: POB 904, Abu Dhabi; tel. (2) 211699; telex 22920; fax (2) 311375.

Ministry of Public Works and Housing: POB 878, Abu Dhabi; tel. (2) 651778; telex 23833; fax (2) 665598.

Ministry of State for Affairs of the Supreme Council: POB 545, Abu Dhabi; tel. (2) 343921; fax (2) 344137.

Ministry of State for Cabinet Affairs: POB 899, Abu Dhabi; tel. (2) 651113; telex 23245; fax (2) 652184.

Legislature

FEDERAL NATIONAL COUNCIL

Formed under the provisional Constitution, the Council is composed of 40 members from the various emirates (eight each from Abu Dhabi and Dubai, six each from Sharjah and Ras al-Khaimah, and four each from Ajman, Fujairah and Umm al-Qaiwain). Each emirate appoints its own representatives separately. The Council studies laws proposed by the Council of Ministers and can reject them or suggest amendments.

Speaker: HILAL BIN AHMAD LOOTAH.

Diplomatic Representation

EMBASSIES IN THE UNITED ARAB EMIRATES

Afghanistan: POB 5687, Abu Dhabi; tel. (2) 661244; fax (2) 655310; Chargé d'affaires: M. NOORULHUDA.

Algeria: POB 3070, Abu Dhabi; tel. (2) 448943; telex 23414; fax (2) 447068; Ambassador: MUHAMMAD MELLOUH.

Argentina: POB 3325, Abu Dhabi; tel. (2) 436838; fax (2) 431392; e-mail alfb1@emirates.net.ae; Ambassador: MARIO QUADRI CASTILLO.

Austria: POB 3095, Abu Dhabi; tel. (2) 324103; telex 22675; fax (2) 343133; Ambassador: Dr OTTO DITZ.

Bahrain: POB 3367, Abu Dhabi; tel. (2) 312200; fax (2) 311202; Ambassador: ISA MUHAMMAD AL-JAMEA.

Bangladesh: POB 2504, Abu Dhabi; tel. (2) 668375; telex 22201; fax (2) 667324; Ambassador: ZIA-US-SHAMS CHOWDHURY.

Belgium: POB 3686, Abu Dhabi; tel. (2) 319449; telex 22860; fax (2) 319353; Ambassador: HENRY O. LOBERT.

Belize: POB 43432, Abu Dhabi; tel. (2) 333554; fax (2) 330429; Ambassador: ELHAM S. FREIHA.

Bosnia and Herzegovina: POB 43362, Abu Dhabi; tel. (2) 464235; fax (2) 434991; Chargé d'affaires a.i.: SALKO ČANIĆ.

Brazil: POB 3027, Abu Dhabi; tel. (2) 665352; fax (2) 654559; Ambassador: JOSÉ FERREIRA LOPES.

Brunei: POB 5836, Abu Dhabi; tel. (2) 313739; Chargé d'affaires: Haji ADNAN BIN Haji ZAINAL.

Canada: POB 6970, Abu Dhabi; tel. (2) 263655; fax (2) 263424.

China, People's Republic: POB 2741, Abu Dhabi; tel. (2) 434276; telex 23928; fax (2) 435440; Ambassador: ZHU DACHENG.

Croatia: POB 41227, Abu Dhabi; tel. (2) 662878; fax (2) 659193; Chargé d'affaires: PETAR LJUBIČIĆ.

Czech Republic: POB 27009, Abu Dhabi; tel. (2) 782800; fax (2) 795716; Chargé d'affaires: JOSEF KOUTSKY.

Denmark: POB 46666, Abu Dhabi; tel. (2) 325900; telex 23677; fax (2) 351690; Ambassador: JENS OSTENFELD.

Egypt: POB 4026, Abu Dhabi; tel. (2) 445566; telex 22248; fax (2) 449878; Ambassador: BAHAA ELDIN MOSTAFA REDA.

Eritrea: POB 2597, Abu Dhabi; tel. (2) 331838; fax (2) 346451; Ambassador: MUHAMMAD OMAR MAHMOUD.

Finland: POB 3634, Abu Dhabi; tel. (2) 328927; telex 23161; fax (2) 325063; Ambassador: MATTI PULLINEN .

France: POB 4014, Abu Dhabi; tel. (2) 435100; telex 22325; fax (2) 434158; Ambassador: JEAN-FRANÇOIS THIBAULT.

Germany: POB 2591, Abu Dhabi; tel. (2) 435630; telex 22202; fax (2) 435625; Ambassador: Dr MARTIN SCHNELLER.

Greece: POB 5483, Abu Dhabi; tel. (2) 654847; telex 24383; fax (2) 656008; Ambassador: DIMITRIS ILIOPOULOS.

Hungary: POB 44450, Abu Dhabi; tel. (2) 660107; fax (2) 667877; e-mail hungexad@emirates.net.ae; Chargé d'affaires a.i.: JÁNOS TILLY.

India: POB 4090, Abu Dhabi; tel. (2) 664800; telex 22620; fax (2) 651518; Ambassador: MUTHAL MENON.

Indonesia: POB 7256, Abu Dhabi; tel. (2) 454448; telex 22253; fax (2) 455453; Ambassador: ABDULLAH FUAD RACHMAN.

Iran: POB 4080, Abu Dhabi; tel. (2) 447618; telex 22344; fax (2) 448714; Ambassador: HUSSEIN SADEQI.

Italy: POB 46752, Abu Dhabi; tel. (2) 435622; telex 23861; fax (2) 434337; Ambassador: GIOVANNI FERRERO.

Japan: POB 2430, Abu Dhabi; tel. (2) 435969; telex 22270; fax (2) 434219; Ambassador: SHIN WATANABE.

Jordan: POB 4024, Abu Dhabi; tel. (2) 447100; telex 24411; fax (2) 449157; Ambassador: AWAD ABU OBEID.

Kenya: POB 3854, Abu Dhabi; tel. (2) 666300; telex 24244; fax (2) 652827; Ambassador: MUDE DAE MUDE.

Korea, Republic: POB 3270, Abu Dhabi; tel. (2) 435337; telex 24237; fax (2) 435348; e-mail keauhlee@emirates.net.ae; Ambassador: SONG-TUK KIM.

Kuwait: POB 926, Abu Dhabi; tel. (2) 446888; telex 28804; fax (2) 444990; Ambassador: IBRAHIM AL-MANSOUR.

Lebanon: POB 4023, Abu Dhabi; tel. (2) 434722; telex 22206; fax (2) 435553; Ambassador: GEORGES SIAM.

Libya: POB 5739, Abu Dhabi; tel. (2) 450030; fax (2) 450033; Chargé d'affaires: ABDUL HAMID ALI SHAIKHY.

Malaysia: POB 3887, Abu Dhabi; tel. (2) 656698; telex 22630; fax (2) 656697; Ambassador: ZULKIFLY IBRAHIM BIN ABDUL RAHMAN.

Mauritania: POB 2714, Abu Dhabi; tel. (2) 462724; telex 22512; fax (2) 465772; Ambassador: TELMIDI OULD MUHAMMAD AMMAR.

Morocco: POB 4066, Abu Dhabi; tel. (2) 433963; telex 22549; fax (2) 433917; Ambassador: ABD AR-RAHMAN AL-MANSOUR.

Namibia: Abu Dhabi.

Netherlands: POB 46560, Abu Dhabi; tel. (2) 321920; fax (2) 313158; e-mail nlgovabu@emirates.net.ae; Ambassador: HENRY JURIAAN DE VRIES.

Norway: POB 47270, Abu Dhabi; tel. (2) 211221; fax (2) 213313; Ambassador: STEIN VEGARD HAGEN.

Oman: POB 2517, Abu Dhabi; tel. (2) 463333; fax (2) 464633; Ambassador: SULTAN AL-BUSAIDI.

Pakistan: POB 846, Abu Dhabi; tel. (2) 447800; telex 23003; fax (2) 447172; Chargé d'affaires: ABDUL RAZZAK SOOMRO.

Philippines: POB 3215, Abu Dhabi; tel. (2) 345665; telex 23995; fax (2) 313559; Ambassador: JOSEPH GERARD B. ANGELES.

Poland: POB 2334, Abu Dhabi; tel. (2) 465200; fax (2) 462967; e-mail polemb@emirates.net.ae; Chargé d'affaires: KAZIMIERZ MORDASZEUSKI.

Qatar: 26th St, Al-Minaseer, POB 3503, Abu Dhabi; tel. (2) 435900; telex 24466; fax (2) 434800; Ambassador: ABDULLAH M. AL-UTHMAN.

Romania: 9 Sudan St, Sector 2/35, POB 70416, Abu Dhabi; tel. (2) 666346; telex 23546; fax (2) 651598; Ambassador: DUMITRU CHICAN.

Russia: POB 8211, Abu Dhabi; tel. (2) 721797; fax (2) 788731; Ambassador: OLEG DERKOVSKII.

Saudi Arabia: POB 4057, Abu Dhabi; tel. (2) 445700; telex 22670; fax (2) 448491; Ambassador: SALEH MUHAMMAD AL-GHUFAILI.

Slovakia: POB 3382, Abu Dhabi; tel. (2) 321674; fax (2) 315839; e-mail slovemb@emirates.net.ae; Chargé d'affaires: DUSAN HORNIAK.

Somalia: POB 4155, Abu Dhabi; tel. (2) 669700; telex 22624; fax (2) 651580; Ambassador: HUSSEIN MUHAMMAD BULLALEH.

South Africa: 7th Floor, Union National Bank Building, As-Salaam Street, POB 29446, Abu Dhabi; tel. (2) 726200; fax (2) 723883; Chargé d'affaires: MOHAMED RAFIQ A. H. GANGAT.

Spain: POB 46474, Abu Dhabi; tel. (2) 213544; telex 23340; fax (2) 342978; Ambassador: JAVIER NAVARRO.

Sri Lanka: POB 46534, Abu Dhabi; tel. (2) 666688; telex 23333; fax (2) 667921; Chargé d'affaires: TITOUS MILTON KIRUNATILAKE.

Sudan: POB 4027, Abu Dhabi; tel. (2) 666788; telex 22706; fax (2) 654231; Chargé d'affaires: MOHIEDDIN SLAIM AHMED.

Switzerland: POB 46116, Abu Dhabi; tel. (2) 343636; fax (2) 6269627; e-mail swiemadh@emirates.net.ae; Ambassador: KURT W. WELTE.

Syria: POB 4011, Abu Dhabi; tel. (2) 448768; telex 22729; fax (2) 449387; Ambassador: MUSTAFA OMRAN.

Thailand: POB 47466, Abu Dhabi; tel. (2) 770797; fax (2) 786646; e-mail thaiauh@emirates.net.ae; Ambassador: SNANGHART DEVAHASTIN.

Tunisia: POB 4166, Abu Dhabi; tel. (2) 661331; telex 22370; fax (2) 660707; Ambassador: ABDELKRIM MOUSSA.

Turkey: POB 3204, Abu Dhabi; tel. (2) 655466; telex 23037; fax (2) 662691; e-mail tcabudbe@emirates.net.ae; Ambassador: ERCAN OZER.

Ukraine: POB 45714, Abu Dhabi; tel. (2) 327586; fax (2) 327506; e-mail embukr@emirates.net.ae; Ambassador: Dr OLEH SEMENETS.

United Kingdom: POB 248, Abu Dhabi; tel. (2) 326600; fax (2) 318138; Ambassador: PATRICK NIXON.

USA: POB 4009, Abu Dhabi; tel. (2) 436691; fax (2) 434771; e-mail paoabud@usia.gov; internet http://www.usembabu.gov.ae; Ambassador: DAVID C. LITT.

Yemen: POB 2095, Abu Dhabi; tel. (2) 448454; telex 23600; fax (2) 447978; Ambassador: Dr ABDULLAH HUSSAIN BARAKAT.

Zimbabwe: Abu Dhabi.

Judicial System

The 95th article of the Constitution of 1971 provided for the establishment of the Union Supreme Court and Union Primary Tribunals as the judicial organs of State.

The Union has exclusive legislative and executive jurisdiction over all matters that are concerned with the strengthening of the federation, such as foreign affairs, defence and Union armed forces, security, finance, communications, traffic control, education, currency, measures, standards and weights, matters relating to nationality and emigration, Union information, etc.

President Sheikh Zayed signed the law establishing the new federal courts on 9 June 1978. The new law effectively transferred local judicial authorities into the jurisdiction of the federal system.

Primary tribunals in Abu Dhabi, Sharjah, Ajman and Fujairah are now primary federal tribunals, and primary tribunals in other towns in those emirates have become circuits of the primary federal tribunals.

The primary federal tribunal may sit in any of the capitals of the four emirates and have jurisdiction on all administrative disputes between the Union and individuals, whether the Union is plaintiff or defendant. Civil disputes between Union and individuals will be heard by primary federal tribunals in the defendant's place of normal residence.

The law requires that all judges take a constitutional oath before the Minister of Justice and that the courts apply the rules of *Shari'a* (Islamic religious law) and that no judgment contradicts the *Shari'a*.

All employees of the old judiciaries will be transferred to the federal authority without loss of salary or seniority.

In February 1994 President Sheikh Zayed ordered that an extensive range of crimes, including murder, theft and adultery, be tried in *Shari'a* courts rather than in civil courts.

Chief Shari'a Justice: AHMAD ABD AL-AZIZ AL-MUBARAK.

Religion

ISLAM

Most of the inhabitants are Muslims of the Sunni sect. About 16% of the Muslims are Shi'ites.

CHRISTIANITY

Roman Catholic Church

Apostolic Vicariate of Arabia: POB 54, Abu Dhabi; tel. (2) 461895; fax (2) 465177; e-mail apvicar@emirates.net.ae; responsible for a territory covering most of the Arabian peninsula (including Saudi Arabia, the UAE, Oman, Qatar, Bahrain and Yemen), containing an estimated 880,000 Catholics (31 December 1996); Vicar Apostolic Fr GIOVANNI BERNARDO GREMOLI, Titular Bishop of Masuccaba.

The Anglican Communion

Within the Episcopal Church in Jerusalem and the Middle East, the UAE forms part of the diocese of Cyprus and the Gulf. The Anglican congregations in the UAE are entirely expatriate. The Bishop in Cyprus and the Gulf resides in Cyprus.

Chaplain, St Andrew's Church: Rev. A. T. R. GOODE, St Andrew's Church, POB 262, Abu Dhabi; tel. (2) 461631; fax (2) 465869.

The Press

The Ministry of Information and Culture has placed a moratorium on new titles.

Abu Dhabi

Abu Dhabi Magazine: POB 662, Abu Dhabi; tel. (2) 214000; telex 22449; fax (2) 348954; f. 1969; Arabic, some articles in English; monthly; Editor ZUHAIR AL-QADI; circ. 18,000.

Adh-Dhafra: POB 4288, Abu Dhabi; tel. (2) 328103; Arabic; weekly; independent; publ. by Dar al-Wahdah.

Emirates News: POB 791, Abu Dhabi; tel. (2) 451446; telex 22763; fax (2) 453662; e-mail emrtnews@emirates.net.ae; f. 1975; English; daily; publ. by Al-Ittihad Press, Publishing and Distribution Corpn; Chair. Sheikh ABDULLAH BIN ZAYED AN-NAHYAN; Man. Editor PETER HELLYER; circ. 21,150.

Al-Fajr (The Dawn): POB 505, Abu Dhabi; tel. (2) 478300; telex 22834; fax (2) 474326; Arabic; daily; Man. Editor OBEID AL-MAZROUI; circ. 28,000.

Hiya (She): POB 2488, Abu Dhabi; tel. (2) 474121; Arabic; weekly for women; publ. by Dar al-Wahdah.

Al-Ittihad (Unity): POB 791, Abu Dhabi; tel. (2) 452206; telex 22984; fax (2) 455126; f. 1972; Arabic; daily and weekly; publ. by Al-Ittihad Press, Publishing and Distribution Corpn; Man. Editor OBEID SULTAN; circ. 58,000 daily, 60,000 weekly.

Majed: POB 791, Abu Dhabi; tel. (2) 455555; telex 22984; fax (2) 455855; Arabic; weekly; children's magazine; Man. Editor AHMAD OMAR; circ. 145,300.

Ar-Riyada wa-Shabab (Sport and Youth): POB 2710, Dubai; tel. (4) 444400; telex 48734; fax (4) 445973; Arabic; weekly; general interest.

UAE and Abu Dhabi Official Gazette: POB 899, Abu Dhabi; tel. (2) 660604; Arabic; daily; official reports and papers.

UAE Press Service Daily News: POB 2035, Abu Dhabi; tel. (2) 44292; f. 1973; English; daily; Editor RASHID AL-MAZROUI.

Al-Wahdah (Unity): POB 2488, Abu Dhabi; tel. (2) 478400; fax (2) 478937; f. 1973; daily; independent; Man. Editor RASHID AWEIDHA; Gen. Man. KHALIFA AL-MASHWI; circ. 20,000.

Zahrat al-Khaleej (Splendour of the Gulf): POB 791, Abu Dhabi; tel. (2) 461600; telex 22984; fax (2) 451653; f. 1979; Arabic; weekly; publ. by Al-Ittihad Press, Publishing and Distribution Corpn; women's magazine; circ. 10,000.

Dubai

Akhbar Dubai (Dubai News): Department of Information, Dubai Municipality, POB 1420, Dubai; f. 1965; Arabic; weekly.

Al-Bayan (The Official Report): POB 2710, Dubai; tel. (4) 688222; telex 48734; fax (4) 688222; f. 1980; owned by Dubai authorities; Arabic; daily; Editor-in-Chief Sheikh HASHER MAKTOUM; circ. 82,575.

Dubai Annual Trade Review: Department of Ports and Customs, POB 516, Dubai; tel. (4) 531076; telex 47470; fax (4) 531959; English.

Emirates Woman: POB 2331, Dubai; tel. (4) 824060; fax (4) 824436; e-mail motivate@emirates.net.ae; f. 1979; Motivate Publishing; English; monthly; fashion, health and beauty; Editor ELSE POWELL; circ. 18,690.

Gulf News: POB 6519, Dubai; tel. (4) 447100; telex 47030; fax (4) 441627; f. 1978; An-Nisr Publishing; English; daily; two weekly supplements, *Junior News* (Wednesday), *Gulf Weekly* (Thursday); Editor-in-Chief OBAID HUMAID AT-TAYER; Editor FRANCIS MATTHEW; circ. 86,900.

Al-Jundi (The Soldier): POB 2838, Dubai; tel. (4) 451516; telex 4554; fax (4) 455033; f. 1973; Arabic; monthly; military and cultural; Editor ISMAIL KHAMIS MUBARAK; circ. 4,000–7,000.

Khaleej Times: POB 11243, Dubai; tel. (4) 382400; telex 48620; fax (4) 390519; e-mail ktimes@emirates.net.ae; internet http://www.khaleejtimes.com; f. 1978; a Galadari enterprise; English; daily; free weekly supplement, *Weekend* (Friday); Man. Dir QASSIM MUHAMMAD YOUSUF; Editor S. NIHAL SINGH; circ. 70,000.

Trade and Industry: POB 1457, Dubai; tel. (4) 280000; telex 45997; fax (4) 2028597; e-mail dcciinfo@dcci.org; internet http://www.dcci.org; f. 1975; Arabic and English; monthly; publ. by Dubai Chamber of Commerce and Industry; circ. 26,000.

What's On: POB 2331, Dubai; tel. (4) 824060; fax (4) 824436; e-mail motivate@emirates.net.ae; f. 1979; Motivate Publishing; English; monthly; Exec. Editor IAN FAIRSERVICE; circ. 17,905.

Ras al-Khaimah

Akhbar Ras al-Khaimah (Ras al-Khaimah News): POB 87, Ras al-Khaimah; Arabic; monthly; local news.

Al-Ghorfa: POB 87, Ras al-Khaimah; tel. (7) 333511; fax (7) 330233; f. 1970; Arabic and English; free monthly; publ. by Ras al-Khaimah Chamber of Commerce; Editor ZAKI H. SAQR.

Ras al-Khaimah Magazine: POB 200, Ras al-Khaimah; Arabic; monthly; commerce and trade; Chief Editor AHMAD AT-TADMORI.

Sharjah

Al-Azman al-Arabia (Times of Arabia): POB 5823, Sharjah; tel. (6) 356034; telex 68674.

Gulf Today: POB 30, Sharjah; tel. (6) 391390; fax (6) 391139; e-mail tgtmkt@alkhaleej.co.ae; f. 1995; English; daily; circ. 38,000.

Al-Khaleej (The Gulf): POB 30, Sharjah; tel. (6) 625304; telex 68055; fax (6) 598547; f. 1970; Arabic; daily; political, independent; Editor GHASSAN TAHBOUB; circ. 82,750.

Sawt al-Khaleej (Voice of the Gulf): POB 1385, Sharjah; tel. (6) 358003; telex 68551.

Ash-Sharooq (Sunrise): POB 30, Sharjah; tel. (6) 598777; fax (6) 599336; f. 1970; Arabic; weekly; general interest; Editor YOUSUF AL-HASSAN.

At-Tijarah (Commerce): Sharjah Chamber of Commerce and Industry, POB 580, Sharjah; tel. (6) 541444; telex 68205; fax (6) 541119; e-mail adscci@emirates.net.ae; f. 1970; Arabic/English; monthly magazine; circ. 50,000; annual trade directory; circ. 100,000.

UAE Digest: POB 6872, Sharjah; tel. (6) 354633; telex 68715; fax (6) 354627; English; monthly; publ. by Universal Publishing; commerce and finance; Man. Dir FARAJ YASSINE; circ. 10,000.

NEWS AGENCIES

Emirates News Agency (WAM): POB 3790, Abu Dhabi; tel. (2) 454545; telex 22979; fax (2) 454694; f. 1977; operated by the Ministry of Information and Culture; Dir IBRAHIM AL-ABED.

UAE Press Service: POB 2035, Abu Dhabi; tel. (2) 820424; telex 22353.

Foreign Bureaux

Agenzia Nazionale Stampa Associata (ANSA) (Italy): POB 44106, Abu Dhabi; tel. (2) 454545; telex 23823; Correspondent MUHAMMAD WADHA.

Inter Press Service (IPS) (Italy): Airport Rd, near the Radio and Television Bldg, Abu Dhabi; tel. (2) 464200; telex 23823; fax (2) 454846; Correspondent (vacant).

Reuters (UK): POB 7872, Abu Dhabi; tel. (2) 328000; telex 24145; fax (2) 333380; Man. JEREMY HARRIS.

Publishers

Al-Ittihad Press, Publishing and Distribution Corpn: POB 791, New Airport Rd, Abu Dhabi; tel. (2) 455555; telex 22984; fax (2) 451653; Chair. KHALFAN BIN MUHAMMAD AR-ROUMI.

All Prints: POB 857, Abu Dhabi; tel. (2) 338235; telex 22844; publishing and distribution; Partners BUSHRA KHAYAT, TAHSEEN S. KHAYAT.

Motivate Publishing: POB 2331, Dubai; tel. (4) 824060; fax (4) 824436; e-mail motivate@emirates.net.ae; f. 1979; books and magazines; Dirs OBAID HUMAID AT-TAYER, IAN FAIRSERVICE.

Broadcasting and Communications

TELECOMMUNICATIONS

Ministry of Communications: (see Ministries, above); regulatory authority.

Emirates Telecommunications Corpn (Etisalat): POB 3838, Abu Dhabi; tel. (2) 283333; telex 22135; fax (2) 725456; provides telecommunications services throughout the UAE; privatization pending in 1998.

Radio

Abu Dhabi Radio: POB 63, Abu Dhabi; tel. (2) 451000; telex 22557; fax (2) 451155; f. 1968; stations in Abu Dhabi, Dubai, Umm al-Qaiwain and Ras al-Khaimah, all broadcasting in Arabic over a wide area; Abu Dhabi also broadcasts in English, French, Bengali, Filipino and Urdu, Dubai in English and Ras al-Khaimah in Urdu; Dir-Gen. ABD AL-WAHAB RADWAN.

Capital Radio: POB 63, Abu Dhabi; tel. (2) 451000; telex 22557; fax (2) 451155; English-language FM music and news station, operated by the Ministry of Information and Culture; Station Manager AIDA HAMZA.

Dubai Radio and Colour Television: POB 1695, Dubai; tel. (4) 370255; telex 45605; fax (4) 374111; broadcasts domestic Arabic and European programmes; Chair. Sheikh HASHER MAKTOUM; Dir-Gen. ABD AL-GHAFOOR SAID IBRAHIM.

Ras al-Khaimah Broadcasting Station: POB 141, Ras al-Khaimah; tel. (7) 851151; fax (7) 353441; two transmitters broadcast in Arabic and Urdu; Dir Sheikh ABD AL-AZIZ BIN HUMAID.

Sharjah Broadcasting Station: POB 155, Sharjah; broadcasts in Arabic and French.

Umm al-Qaiwain Broadcasting Station: POB 444, Umm al-Qaiwain; tel. (6) 666044; fax (6) 666055; f. 1978; broadcasts music and news in Arabic, Malayalam, Sinhala, Tagalog and Urdu; Gen. Man. ALI JASSEM.

UAE Radio and Television—Dubai: POB 1695, Dubai; tel. (4) 370255; telex 45605; fax (4) 379275; internet http://www.ecssr.ac.ae/05uae.6television.html; broadcasts in Arabic and English to the USA, India and Pakistan, the Far East, Australia and New Zealand, Europe and North and East Africa; Chair. Sheikh HASHEM MAKTOUM; Dir-Gen. AHMED SAEED AL-GAOUD; Controller of Radio HASSAN AHMAD.

Television

Dubai Radio and Colour Television: (see Radio).

UAE Radio and Television-Dubai: (see Radio); Controller of Programmes NASIB BITAR.

UAE TV—Abu Dhabi: POB 637, Abu Dhabi; tel. (2) 452000; telex 22557; fax (2) 451470; internet http://www.ecssr.ac.ae/05uae.6television.html; f. 1968; broadcasts programmes incorporating information, entertainment, religion, culture, news and politics; Dir-Gen. ALI OBAID.

UAE Television—Sharjah: POB 111, Sharjah; tel. (6) 361111; telex 68599; fax (6) 541755; f. 1989; broadcasts in Arabic and Urdu in the northern emirates; Executive Dir MUHAMMAD DIAB AL-MUSA.

Finance

(cap. = capital; dep. = deposits; res = reserves; m. = million;
brs = branches; amounts in dirhams, unless otherwise indicated)

BANKING

Central Bank

Central Bank of the United Arab Emirates: POB 854, Abu Dhabi; tel. (2) 652220; telex 22330; fax (2) 668483; f. 1973; acts as issuing authority for local currency; superseded UAE Currency Board December 1980; auth. cap. 300m.; total assets 32,277m. (April 1998); Chair. MUHAMMAD EID AL-MURAIKHI; Gov. SULTAN NASSER AS-SUWAIDI; 5 brs.

Principal Banks

Abu Dhabi Commercial Bank (ADCB): POB 939, Abu Dhabi; tel. (2) 720000; telex 22244; fax (2) 776499; f. 1985 by merger; 65% govt-owned, 35% owned by private investors; cap. 1,250.0m., res 1,294.2m., dep. 13,043.2m. (Dec. 1997); Acting Chair. FADHEL SAEED AD-DARMAKI; CEO and Man. Dir KHALIFA HASSAN; 35 brs.

Abu Dhabi Islamic Bank: f. 1997; cap. 1,000m. (June 1997); Chair. OBAID SAIF AN-NASIRI; Man. Dir KHALIL MUHAMMAD BIN BROOK.

Arab Bank for Investment and Foreign Trade: POB 2484, Abu Dhabi; tel. (2) 721900; telex 22455; fax (2) 793497; f. 1976; jointly owned by the UAE Govt, the Libyan Arab Foreign Bank and the Banque Extérieure d'Algérie; cap. 570.0m., res 495.8m., dep. 4,133.0m. (Dec. 1997); Chair. Dr ABD AL-HAFID ZLITNI; Gen. Man. HADI M. GITELI; 2 brs in Abu Dhabi, and one each in Dubai and al-Ain.

Arab Emirate Investment Bank Ltd.: POB 5503 Dubai; tel. (4) 222191; telex 46080; fax (4) 274351; Chair. KHALID MUHAMMAD SAEED AL-MULLA; Gen.-Man. SAJJAD AHMAD.

Bank of Sharjah Ltd: POB 1394, Sharjah; tel. (6) 352111; telex 68039; fax (6) 350323; f. 1973; cap. and res 250m., dep. 1,055m., total assets 1,345m. (1997); Chair. AHMAD AN-NOMAN; Gen. Man. VAROUJ NERGUIZIAN; brs in Abu Dhabi and Dubai.

Commercial Bank of Dubai PSC: POB 2668, Deira, Dubai; tel. (4) 523355; telex 49600; fax (4) 520444; f. 1969; cap. and res 853m., dep. 3,597m., total assets 4,757m. (1997); Chair. AHMAD HUMAID AT-TAYER; Gen. Man. OMAR ABD AR-RAHIM LEYAS; 13 brs.

Commercial Bank International PLC: POB 4449, Dubai; tel. (4) 275265; telex 47899; fax (4) 279038; f. 1991; cap. 100m., res 45.3m., dep. 777.1m. (Dec. 1996); Chair. and Man. Dir SALEH AHMAD ASH-SHALL.

Dubai Islamic Bank PLC: POB 1080, Deira, Dubai; tel. (4) 214888; telex 45889; fax (4) 237243; f. 1975; cap. 420.0m., res 123.6m., dep. 6,442.5m. (Dec. 1996); Chair. and Man. Dir SAID AHMAD LOOTAH; 9 brs.

Emirates Bank International PJSC: POB 2923, Dubai; tel. (4) 256256; telex 46426; fax (4) 268005; e-mail ebilitnl@emirates.net.ae; f. 1977 by merger; the Govt of Dubai has a 77% share; cap. 470.2m., res 1,894.2m., dep. 14,182.5m. (Dec. 1997); Chair. AHMAD HUMAID AT-TAYER; Gen. Man. CHARLES NEIL; 18 brs in the UAE.

First Gulf Bank: Al-Ittihad St, POB 414, Ajman; tel. (6) 423450; telex 69510; fax (6) 446503; f. 1979; cap. and res 186.6m., dep. 477.4m., total assets 766.3m. (Dec. 1996); Chair. Sheikh TAHNOON BIN ZAYED AN-NAHYAN; Gen. Man. and CEO YOUSUF A. AL-HUSAINI; 2 brs.

Investbank PLC: Al-Borj Ave, POB 1885, Sharjah; tel. (6) 355391; telex 68576; fax (6) 546683; f. 1975; cap. and res 305m., dep. 1,483m., total assets 1,859m. (1997); Chair. Dr ABDULLAH AOMRAN TARYAM; Gen. Man. AFIF N. SHEHADEH; 4 brs.

Mashreq Bank PSC: POB 1250, Deira, Dubai; tel. (4) 229131; telex 45429; fax (4) 238830; f. 1967 as Bank of Oman; adopted present name 1993; cap. 542.3m., res 561.1m., dep. 14,353.2m. (Dec. 1997); Chair. ABDULLAH AHMAD AL-GHURAIR; CEO ABD AL-AZIZ AL-GHURAIR; 27 brs.

Middle East Bank PJSC: POB 5547, Deira, Dubai; tel. (4) 256256; telex 46074; fax (4) 255322; f. 1976; controlling interest held by EBI; cap. 500.0m., res 83.1m., dep. 1,211.2m. (Dec. 1997); Chair. Dr MUHAMMAD KHALFAN BIN KHARBASH; Gen. Man. IBRAHIM TAHLAK; 11 brs.

National Bank of Abu Dhabi (NBAD): POB 4, Abu Dhabi; tel. (2) 335262; telex 22266/7; fax (2) 336078; f. 1968; owned jointly by Abu Dhabi Investment Authority and UAE citizens; cap. and res 2,307m., dep. 24,601m., total assets 31,135m. (1997); Chair. Sheikh MUHAMMAD HABROUSH AS-SUWAIDI; CEO JOHN S. W. COOMBS; 45 brs in UAE, 11 brs overseas.

National Bank of Dubai PJSC: POB 777, Dubai; tel. (4) 222111; telex 45421; fax (4) 283000; f. 1963; cap. 861.8m., res 2,630.9m., dep. 18,828.8m. (Dec. 1997); Chair. SULTAN ALI AL-OWAIS; Gen. Man. D. F. MCKENZIE; 26 brs.

National Bank of Fujairah: POB 887, Fujairah; tel. (9) 224518; telex 89050; fax (9) 224516; f. 1982; owned jointly by Govt of Fujairah (36.78%), Govt of Dubai (9.78%), and UAE citizens and cos (53.44%); cap. 300.0m., res 123.9m., dep. 1,916.4m. (Dec. 1997); Chair. Sheikh SALEH BIN MUHAMMAD ASH-SHARQI; Gen. Man. MICHAEL J. CONNOR; 4 brs.

National Bank of Ras al-Khaimah PSC: POB 5300, Ras al-Khaimah; tel. (7) 221127; telex 99109; fax (7) 223238; f. 1976; cap. 200.0m., res 138.3m., dep. 1,248.1m. (Dec. 1997); Chair. Sheikh KHALID BIN SAQR AL-QASIMI; Gen. Man. J. G. HONEYBILL; 8 brs.

National Bank of Sharjah: Al-Borj Ave, POB 4, Sharjah; tel. (6) 547745; telex 68085; fax (6) 543483; f. 1976; commercial bank; cap. and res 239m., dep. 825m., total assets 1,121m. (1997); Chair. Sheikh SULTAN BIN MUHAMMAD BIN SULTAN AL-QASSEMI; Gen. Man. ALAN D. WHYTE; 8 brs.

National Bank of Umm al-Qaiwain PSC: POB 800, Umm al-Qaiwain; tel. (6) 655225; telex 69733; fax (6) 655440; e-mail ummbank@emirates.net.ae; f. 1982; cap. and res 369m., dep. 984m., total assets 1,454m. (1997); Chair. Sheikh SAUD BIN RASHID AL-MU'ALLA; Man. Dir and CEO Sheikh NASSER BIN RASHID AL-MU'ALLA; 10 brs.

Union National Bank: POB 3865, Abu Dhabi; tel. (2) 741600; telex 23693; fax (2) 786080; f. 1983; fmrly Bank of Credit and Commerce (Emirates); cap. and res 521.6m., total assets 5,480m. (June 1996); Chair. Sheikh NAHYAN BIN MUBARAK AN-NAHYAN; CEO ANWER QAYUM SHER; Gen. Man. ALFRED CULLEN; 10 brs in Abu Dhabi, 5 brs in Dubai, and one each in al-Ain, Sharjah, Ras al-Khaimah and Fujairah.

United Arab Bank: POB 3562, Abu Dhabi; tel. (2) 325000; telex 22759; fax (2) 338361; f. 1975; affiliated to Société Générale, France; cap. 171.2m., res 85.2m., dep. 1,033.7m. (Dec. 1997); Chair. Sheikh FAISAL BIN SULTAN AL-QASIMI; Gen. Man. BERTRAND GIRAUD; 8 brs.

Development Banks

Emirates Industrial Bank: POB 2722, Abu Dhabi; tel. (2) 339700; telex 23324; fax (2) 326397; f. 1982; offers low-cost loans to enterprises with at least 51% local ownership; 51% state-owned; cap. 200m.; Chair. MUHAMMAD KHALFAN KHIRBASH; Gen. Man. MUHAMMAD ABD AL-BAKI MUHAMMAD.

United Arab Emirates Development Bank: Abu Dhabi; tel. (2) 344986; telex 22427; f. 1974; participates in development of real estate, agriculture, fishery, livestock and light industries; cap. 500m.; Gen. Man. MUHAMMAD SALEM AL-MELEHY.

Foreign Banks

ABN AMRO Bank NV (Netherlands): Istiqlal St, POB 2720, Abu Dhabi; tel. (2) 335400; telex 22401; fax (2) 330182; f. 1974; POB 2567, Deira, Dubai; tel. (4) 512233; telex 45610; fax (4) 511555; POB 1971, Sharjah; tel. (6) 594900; telex 68467; fax (6) 591009; Man. (Abu Dhabi) J. Y. PELISSON.

Al-Ahli Bank of Kuwait KSC: POB 1719, Deira, Dubai; tel. (4) 5088111; telex 45618; fax (4) 5088222; Gen. Man. GARRY TUNSTALL.

ANZ Grindlays Bank Ltd: POB 4166, Deira, Dubai; tel. (4) 285663; telex 45618; fax (4) 222018; Gen. Man. IAN COLLEY.

Arab Bank PLC (Jordan): POB 875, Abu Dhabi; tel. (2) 334111; telex 24195; fax (2) 336433; f. 1970; POB 11364, Dubai; POB 130, Sharjah; POB 4972, Ras al-Khaimah; POB 300, Fujairah; POB 17, Ajman; Man. FATHI M. SKAIK; 8 local brs.

Arab-African International Bank (Egypt): POB 1049, Dubai; tel. (4) 223131; telex 45503; fax (4) 222257; f. 1970; POB 928, Abu Dhabi; tel. (2) 323400; telex 22587; fax (2) 216009; f. 1976; Chair. Dr FAHD AR-RASHID; Deputy Gen. Man. (Dubai) MUHAMMAD FARAMAWI.

Banca Commerciale Italiana: POB 3839, Abu Dhabi; tel. (2) 324330; telex 22817; fax (2) 323709; Gen. Man. PAOLO TESCARI.

Bank of Baroda (India): POB 3162, Dubai; tel. (2) 531955; telex 46931; fax (2) 536962; f. 1974; CEO A. B. CHOPRA; also brs in Abu Dhabi, al-Ain, Deira (Dubai), Sharjah and Ras al-Khaimah; Regional Man. S. N. AMIN.

Bank Melli Iran: Regional Office and Main Branch, POB 1894, Dubai; tel. (4) 216777; telex 46404; fax (4) 219595; e-mail bmirodxb@emirates.net.ae; f. 1969; Regional Dir AZIZ AZIMI NOBAR; brs in Dubai, Abu Dhabi, al-Ain, Sharjah, Fujairah and Ras al-Khaimah.

Bank Saderat Iran: POB 700, Abu Dhabi; tel. (2) 335155; telex 22263; fax (2) 325062; POB 4182, Dubai; also Sharjah, Ajman, Fujairah and al-Ain; Man. SANI MOSTAGHIM.

Banque Banorabe (France): POB 4370, Dubai; tel. (4) 284655; telex 45801; fax (4) 236260; POB 5803, Sharjah; tel. (6) 736100; telex 68512; fax (6) 736080; e-mail banorabe@emirates.net.ae; f. 1974; fmrly Banque de l'Orient Arabe et d'Outre Mer; Chair. and Gen. Man. Dr NAAMAN AZHARI; UAE Regional Man. BASSEM M. AL-ARISS.

Banque du Caire (Egypt): POB 533, Abu Dhabi; tel. (2) 328700; telex 22304; fax (2) 323881; POB 1502, Dubai; POB 254, Sharjah; POB 618, Ras al-Khaimah; Gulf Regional Man. FOUAD ABD AL-KHALEK TAHOON.

Banque Libanaise pour le Commerce SA (France): POB 4207, Dubai; tel. (4) 222291; telex 45671; fax (4) 279861; POB 854, Sharjah; POB 3771, Abu Dhabi; tel. (2) 320920; telex 22862; fax (2) 213851; POB 771, Ras al-Khaimah; UAE Regional Man. ELIE N. SALIBA.

Banque Paribas (France): POB 2742, Abu Dhabi; tel. (2) 267800; telex 22331; fax (2) 268638; POB 7233, Dubai; tel. (4) 525929; telex 45755; fax (4) 521341; Gen. Man. (Abu Dhabi) RAGI BOUSTANY; Gen. Man. (Dubai) GEORGES TABET.

Barclays Bank PLC (UK): POB 2734, Abu Dhabi; tel. (2) 275313; telex 22456; fax (2) 268060; POB 1891, Zabeel, Dubai; tel. (4) 351551; telex 48989; fax (4) 366700; Man. Dir D. G. C. THOMSON (Dubai).

The British Bank of the Middle East (BritishBank) (Jersey): POB 66, Dubai; tel. (4) 332200; telex 22231; fax (4) 331564; f. 1946; total assets £4,365m. sterling (1997); Dep. Chair. AMAN MEHTA; CEO ABDUL JALIL YOUSUF; 8 brs throughout UAE.

Citibank NA (USA): POB 749, Dubai; tel. (4) 522100; telex 45422; fax (4) 524942; f. 1963; POB 346, Sharjah; POB 999, Abu Dhabi; POB 294, Ras al-Khaimah; POB 1430, al-Ain; total assets 1,372.1m. (1988); Man. S. CRABTREE.

Credit Agricole Indosuez (France): POB 9256, Dubai; tel. (4) 314211; telex 45860; fax (4) 313201; f. 1975; POB 46786, Abu Dhabi; tel. (2) 338400; telex 22464; fax (2) 338581; f. 1981; UAE Gen. Man. STANISLAS DE HAUSS.

Habib Bank AG Zurich (Switzerland): POB 2681, Abu Dhabi; tel. (2) 322838; telex 22205; fax (2) 351822; f. 1974; POB 1166, Sharjah;

POB 3306, Dubai; Joint Pres. H. M. HABIB; Vice-Pres. HATIM HUSAIN; 8 brs throughout UAE.

Habib Bank Ltd (Pakistan): POB 888, Dubai; tel. (4) 268423; telex 45430; fax (4) 260198; f. 1967; POB 897, Abu Dhabi; tel. (2) 325665; telex 22332; fax (2) 333620; f. 1975; Vice-Pres. and Chief Man. (Dubai) MUHAMMAD SHAHJAHAN; Vice-Pres. and Chief Man. (Abu Dhabi) GHULAM HUSSAIN; 6 other brs in UAE.

Janata Bank (Bangladesh): POB 2630, Abu Dhabi; tel. (2) 344542; telex 22402; fax (2) 348749; POB 3342, Dubai; tel. (4) 281442; fax (4) 246023; CEO and Gen. Man. MUHAMMAD RUHUL AMIN; Man. K. M. SHAFIQUR RAHMAN; brs in al-Ain, Dubai and Sharjah.

Lloyds Bank PLC (UK): POB 3766, Dubai; tel. (4) 313005; telex 46450; fax (4) 313026; f. 1977; dep. 500.4m., total assets 1,431.3m. (1994); Area Man. J. G. PRINGLE.

National Bank of Bahrain BSC: POB 46080, Abu Dhabi; tel. (2) 335288; telex 24344; fax (2) 333783; Sr Man. FAROUK KHALAF.

National Bank of Oman SAOG: POB 3822, Abu Dhabi; tel. (2) 325354; telex 22866; fax (2) 216153; Man. MIRAJUDDIN AZIZ.

Nilein Industrial Development Bank (Sudan): POB 6013, Abu Dhabi; tel. (2) 326453; telex 22884; Man. ABDULLAH MAHMOUD AWAD.

Rafidain Bank (Iraq): POB 2727, Abu Dhabi; tel. (2) 44882; telex 22522.

Royal Bank of Canada: POB 3614, Dubai; tel. (4) 225226; telex 45926; fax (4) 215687; f. 1976; Regional Gen. Man. ROGER N. J. GARMAN.

Standard Chartered PLC (UK): POB 240, Abu Dhabi; tel. (2) 330077; telex 22274; fax (2) 341511; POB 999, Dubai; tel. (4) 520455; telex 45431; fax (4) 526679; POB 5, Sharjah; tel. (6) 357788; telex 68245; fax (6) 546676; POB 1240, al-Ain; tel. (3) 641253; telex 34082; fax (3) 654824; Gen. Man. JAMES ALLHUSEN.

United Bank Ltd (Pakistan): POB 1367, Dubai; tel. (4) 552020; telex 49226; fax (4) 514525; POB 237, Abu Dhabi; tel. (2) 326597; telex 22272; fax (2) 344090; f. 1959; Sr Vice-Pres. and Zonal Chief S. M. ASGHAR; 7 other brs in UAE.

Bankers' Association

United Arab Emirates Bankers' Association: POB 44307, Abu Dhabi; tel. (2) 272541; telex 22781; fax (2) 274155; e-mail ebauae@emirates.net.ae; f. 1983.

INSURANCE

Abu Dhabi National Insurance Co (Adnic): POB 839, Abu Dhabi; tel. (2) 264000; telex 22340; fax (2) 268600; e-mail adnic@emirates.net.ae; f. 1972; subscribed 25% by the Govt of Abu Dhabi and 75% by UAE nationals; all classes of insurance; Chair. and Gen. Man. KHALAF A. AL-OTAIBA.

Al-Ahlia Insurance Co: POB 128, Ras al-Khaimah; tel. (7) 721749; telex 47677; f. 1977; Gen. Man. T. A. SAID; 3 brs.

Al-Ain Ahlia Insurance Co: POB 3077, Abu Dhabi; tel. (2) 459900; telex 22352; fax (2) 456685; e-mail alainins@emirates.net.ae; internet http://www.alain-ins-uae.com; f. 1975; Chair. HAMIL AL-GAITH; Gen. Man. M. MAZHAR HAMADEH; brs in Dubai, Sharjah, Tarif and al-Ain.

Dubai Insurance Co PSC: POB 3027, Dubai; tel. (4) 693030; telex 45685; fax (4) 693727; f. 1970; Chair. MAJID AL-FUTTAIM; Gen. Man. FAROUK HUWAIDI.

Sharjah Insurance and Reinsurance Co: POB 792, Sharjah; tel. (6) 355090; telex 68060; fax (6) 352545; f. 1970; Gen. Man. Dr DIAB MIHDAWI.

Union Insurance Co: Head Office: POB 460, Umm al-Qaiwain; tel. (6) 666223; POB 4623, Dubai; POB 3196, Abu Dhabi; Gen. Man. L. F. DOKOV.

Trade and Industry

DEVELOPMENT ORGANIZATIONS

Abu Dhabi Development Finance Corpn: POB 30, Abu Dhabi; tel. (2) 22656; telex 820431; fax (2) 728890; purpose is to provide finance to the private sector; Deputy Man. Dir SAID MUHAMMAD.

Abu Dhabi Fund for Development (ADFD): POB 814; tel. (2) 725800; telex 22287; fax (2) 728890; f. 1971; purpose is to offer economic aid to other Arab states and other developing countries in support of their development; cap. AED 4,000m.; Chair. Sheikh KHALIFA BIN ZAYED AN-NAHYAN; Dir-Gen. SAEED BIN KHALFAN AR-ROMAITHI.

Abu Dhabi Investment Authority (ADIA): POB 3600, Abu Dhabi; tel. (2) 213100; telex 22674; f. 1976; responsible for co-ordinating Abu Dhabi's investment policy; Chair. Sheikh KHALIFA BIN ZAYED AN-NAHYAN; Pres. Sheikh MUHAMMAD HABROUSH AS-SUWAIDI; 1 br. overseas.

Abu Dhabi Investment Company (ADIC): POB 46309, Abu Dhabi; tel. (2) 658100; telex 23824; fax (2) 650575; internet http://www.adic.co.ae; f. 1977; investment and merchant banking activities in the UAE and abroad; 98% owned by ADIA and 2% by National Bank of Abu Dhabi; total assets AED 5,947m. (1997); Chair. HAREB MASOOD AD-DARMAKI; Gen. Man. HUMAID DARWISH AL-KATBI.

Abu Dhabi Planning Department: POB 12, Abu Dhabi; tel. (2) 727200; telex 23194; fax (2) 727749; f. 1974; supervises Abu Dhabi's Development Programme; Chair. MUSALLAM SAEED ABDULLAH AL-QUBAISI; Under-Sec. AHMED M. HILAL AL-MAZRUI.

General Industry Corpn (GIC): POB 4499, Abu Dhabi; tel. (2) 214900; telex 22938; fax (2) 325034; f. 1979; responsible for the promotion of non-petroleum-related industry; due for partial privatization in 1996.

International Petroleum Investment Co (IPIC): POB 7528, Abu Dhabi; tel. (2) 336200; telex 22520; fax (2) 216045; f. 1984; cap. $200m.; state-owned venture to develop overseas investments in energy and energy-related projects; Chair. JOUAN SALEM ADH-DHAHIRI; Man. Dir KHALIFA MUHAMMAD ASH-SHAMSI.

Sharjah Economic Development Corpn (SHEDCO): POB 3458, Sharjah; tel. (6) 371212; telex 68789; industrial investment co; jt venture between Sharjah authorities and private sector; auth. cap. AED 1,000m.; Gen. Man. J. T. PICKLES.

CHAMBERS OF COMMERCE

Federation of UAE Chambers of Commerce and Industry: POB 3014, Abu Dhabi; tel. (2) 214144; telex 23883; fax (2) 339210; POB 8886, Dubai; tel. (4) 212977; telex 48752; fax (4) 235498; Pres. SAEED ALI KHAMAS; Sec.-Gen. ABDULLAH SULTAN ABDULLAH.

Abu Dhabi Chamber of Commerce and Industry: POB 662, Abu Dhabi; tel. (2) 214000; telex 22449; fax (2) 215867; e-mail adcci@emirates.net.ae; internet http://www.adcci-uae.com; f. 1969; 45,000 mems; Pres. RAHMAN MUHAMMAD AL-MASOUD; Dir-Gen. MUHAMMAD OMAR ABDULLAH.

Ajman Chamber of Commerce and Industry: POB 662, Ajman; tel. (6) 422177; telex 69523; fax (6) 427591; f. 1977; Pres. HAMAD MUHAMMAD ABU SHIHAB; Dir-Gen. MUHAMMAD BIN ABDULLAH AL-HUMRANI.

Dubai Chamber of Commerce and Industry: POB 1457, Dubai; tel. (4) 280000; telex 45997; fax (4) 211646; e-mail dcci@dcci.gov.ae; internet http://www.dcci.org; f. 1965; 40,000 mems; Pres. SAID JUMA AN-NABOODAH; Dir-Gen. ABD AR-RAHMAN GHANEM AL-MUTAIWEE.

Fujairah Chamber of Commerce, Industry and Agriculture: POB 738, Fujairah; tel. (9) 222400; telex 89077; fax (9) 221464; Pres. SAID ALI KHAMAS; Dir-Gen. SHAHEEN ALI SHAHEEN.

Ras al-Khaimah Chamber of Commerce, Industry and Agriculture: POB 78, Ras al-Khaimah; tel. (7) 333511; telex 99140; fax (7) 330233; f. 1967; 5,220 mems; Pres. ALI ABDULLAH MUSSABEH; Dir-Gen. MUHAMMAD ALI AL-HARANKI.

Sharjah Chamber of Commerce and Industry: POB 580, Sharjah; tel. (6) 541444; fax (6) 541119; e-mail adscci@emirates.net.ae; f. 1970; 25,000 mems; Chair. AHMED MUHAMMAD AL-MIDFA'A; Dir-Gen. SAID OBEID AL-JARWAN.

Umm al-Qaiwain Chamber of Commerce and Industry: POB 436, Umm al-Qaiwain; tel. (6) 656915; fax (6) 657056; Pres. ABDULLAH RASHID AL-KHARJI; Man. Dir SHAKIR AZ-ZAYANI.

STATE HYDROCARBONS COMPANIES

Supreme Petroleum Council: POB 898, Abu Dhabi; tel. (2) 602000; telex 23300; fax (2) 6023389; f. 1988; assumed authority and responsibility for the administration and supervision of all petroleum affairs in Abu Dhabi; Chair. Sheikh KHALIFA BIN ZAYED AN-NAHYAN; Sec.-Gen. YOUSUF BIN OMEIR BIN YOUSUF.

Abu Dhabi

Abu Dhabi National Oil Co (ADNOC): POB 898, Abu Dhabi; tel. (2) 6020000; telex 22215; fax (2) 6023389; f. 1971; cap. AED 7,500m.; state company; deals in all phases of oil industry; owns two refineries: one on Umm an-Nar island and one at Ruwais; Habshan Gas Treatment Plant (scheduled for partial privatization); gas pipeline distribution network; a salt and chlorine plant; holds 60% participation in operations of ADMA-OPCO and ADCO, and 88% of ZADCO; has 100% control of Abu Dhabi National Oil Company for Oil Distribution (ADNOC-FOD), Abu Dhabi National Tanker Co (ADNATCO), National Drilling Co (NDC) and interests in numerous other companies, both in the UAE and overseas; ADNOC is operated by Supreme Petroleum Council, Chair. Sheikh KHALIFA BIN ZAYED AN-NAHYAN; Gen. Man. YOUSUF BIN OMEIR BIN YOUSUF.

Abu Dhabi Co for Onshore Oil Operations (ADCO): POB 270, Abu Dhabi; tel. (2) 6040000; telex 22222; fax (2) 669785; name changed from Abu Dhabi Petroleum Co Ltd (ADPC) in February 1979; shareholders are ADNOC (60%), British Petroleum, Shell and Total (9.5% each), Exxon and Mobil (4.75% each) and Partex (2%); average production (1990): 1.2m. b/d; Chair. YOUSUF BIN OMEIR BIN YOUSUF; Gen. Man. KEVIN DUNNE.

Abu Dhabi Drilling Chemicals and Products Ltd (ADDCAP): POB 46121, Abu Dhabi; tel. (2) 6029000; telex 23267; fax (2) 6029010; f. 1975; manufacture and marketing of drilling chemicals and operation of an offshore supply marine base; wholly-owned subsidiary of ADNOC; Chair. YOUSUF BIN OMEIR BIN YOUSUF; Gen. Man. MAHFOUD A. DARBOUL ASH-SHEHHI.

Abu Dhabi Gas Industries Co (GASCO): POB 665, Abu Dhabi; tel. (2) 6041111; telex 22365; fax (2) 6047414; started production in 1981; recovers condensate and LPG from Asab, Bab and Bu Hasa fields for delivery to Ruwais natural gas liquids fractionation plant; capacity of 22,000 tons per day; ADNOC has a 68% share; Total, Shell Gas and Partex have a minority interest; Chair. YOUSUF BIN OMEIR BIN YOUSUF; Gen. Man. SAIF NASSER AS-SUWAIDI.

Abu Dhabi Gas Liquefaction Co (ADGAS): POB 3500, Abu Dhabi; tel. (2) 6061111; telex 22698; fax (2) 6065456; f. 1973; owned by ADNOC, 51%; the British Petroleum (BP) Co, 16⅓%; Total, 8⅙%; Mitsui and Co, 22¹⁄₂₀%; Mitsui Liquefied Gas Co, 2⁹⁄₂₀%; operates LGSC and the LNG plant on Das Island, which was commissioned in 1977. The plant uses natural gas produced in association with oil from offshore fields and has a design capacity of approx. 2.3m. tons of LNG per year and 1.29m. tons of LPG per year. The liquefied gas is sold to the Tokyo Electric Power Co, Japan. Chair. YOUSUF BIN OMEIR BIN YOUSUF; Gen. Man. CHRISTIAN DE FRAISSINETTE.

Abu Dhabi Marine Operating Co (ADMA-OPCO): POB 303, Abu Dhabi; tel. (2) 6060000; telex 22284; fax (2) 720099; operates a concession 60% owned by ADNOC, POB 898, Abu Dhabi and 40% by Abu Dhabi Marine Areas Ltd, Britannic House, Moor Lane, London, EC2Y 9BU, England (BP Co 14⅔%; Japan Oil Development Co Ltd 12%; Total 13⅓%). The concession lies in the Abu Dhabi offshore area and currently produces oil from Lower Zakum and Umm Shaif fields. ADMA was the first company to produce and export oil from Abu Dhabi in 1962. ADMA-OPCO was created in 1977 as an operator for the concession. Production (1984): 67,884,769 barrels (8,955,721 metric tons); Chair. YOUSUF BIN OMEIR BIN YOUSUF; Gen. Man. MICHEL VIALLARD.

Abu Dhabi National Oil Company for Distribution (ADNOC-FOD): POB 4188, Abu Dhabi; tel. (2) 771300; telex 22358; fax (2) 722322; 100% owned by ADNOC; distributes petroleum products in Abu Dhabi; Chair. YOUSUF BIN OMEIR BIN YOUSUF; Gen. Man. ABDULLAH SAID AL-BADI.

Abu Dhabi National Tanker Co (ADNATCO): (see Shipping).

Abu Dhabi Petroleum Ports Operating Co (ADPPOC): POB 61, Abu Dhabi; tel. (2) 777300; telex 22209; fax (2) 763293; e-mail adppoc@emirates.net.ae; f. 1979; manages Jebel Dhanna, Ruwais, Das Island, Umm an-Nar and Zirku Island SPM terminal, Mubarraz; cap. AED 50m.; of which ADNOC has a 60% share and LAMNALCO Kuwait 40%; Chair. YOUSUF BIN OMEIR BIN YOUSUF; Gen. Man. KHALIFA M. AL-GOBAISI.

The Liquefied Gas Shipping Co Ltd (LGSC): POB 3500, Abu Dhabi; tel. (2) 333888; telex 22698; f. 1972; cap. $1m.; ADNOC holds 51% share, Mitsui 24.5%, Shell 16.3%, BP 8.2%; Gen. Man. TAYA AL-MENHALI.

National Drilling Co (NDC): POB 4017, Abu Dhabi; tel. (2) 316600; telex 22553; fax (2) 317045; drilling operations; Chair. ABDULLAH NASSER AS-SUWAIDI; Gen. Man. NAJEEB HASSAN AZ-ZAABI.

National Petroleum Construction Co Ltd (NPCC): POB 2058, Abu Dhabi; tel. (2) 549000; telex 22638; fax (2) 549111; e-mail npccnet@emirates.net.ae; f. 1973; 'turnkey' construction and maintenance of offshore facilities for the petroleum and gas industries; cap. AED 100m.; Chair. MUHAMMAD KHALIFA AL-KINDI; Gen. Man. FARID B. ASFOUR.

Ruwais Fertilizers Industries Ltd (FERTIL): POB 2288, Abu Dhabi; tel. (2) 6021111; telex 24205; fax (2) 728084; e-mail fertlmcd@emirates.net.ae; 66⅔% owned by ADNOC and 33⅓% by Total; began production of ammonia and urea in 1984; Chair. RASHED AS-SUWAIDI. Gen. Man. ABDUL HAKIM M. AS-SUWAIDI.

Ajman

Ajman National Oil Co (AJNOC): POB 410, Ajman; tel. (6) 421218; f. 1983; 50% govt-owned, 50% held by Canadian and private Arab interests.

Dubai

DUGAS (Dubai Natural Gas Co Ltd): POB 4311, Dubai (Location: Jebel Ali); tel. (4) 46234; telex 45741; fax (4) 46118; wholly owned by Dubai authorities; Dep. Chair. and Dir MIRZA H. AS-SAYEGH.

Dubai Petroleum Co (DPC): POB 2222, Dubai; tel. (4) 846000; telex 45423; fax (4) 846118; holds offshore concession which began production in 1969; wholly owned by Dubai authorities; Pres. JOHN I. HORNING.

Emirates General Petroleum Corpn (Emarat): POB 9400, Dubai; tel. (4) 444444; telex 47980; fax (4) 444292; f. 1981; wholly owned by Ministry of Finance and Industry; distribution of petroleum; Gen. Man. AHMED MUHAMMAD AL-KAMDA.

Emirates National Oil Co (ENOC): POB 6442, Enoc House, 4th Floor, al-Qutaeyat Road, Dubai; tel. (4) 374400; fax (4) 3031206; e-mail webmaster@enoc.co.ae; f. 1993; responsible for management of Dubai-owned cos in petroleum-marketing sector; Chair. Sheikh HAMDAN BIN RASHID AL-MAKTOUM.

Emirates Petroleum Products Co (Pvt.) Ltd: POB 5589, Dubai; tel. (4) 372131; telex 48342; fax (4) 375990; f. 1980; jt venture between Govt of Dubai and Caltex Alkhaleej Marketing; sales of petroleum products, bunkering fuel and bitumen; Chair. Sheikh HAMDAN BIN RASHID AL-MAKTOUM.

Sharjah

Amoco Sharjah Oil Co: POB 1191, Sharjah; tel. (6) 535000; telex 68685; fax (6) 5099-555; holds onshore concession areas.

Petroleum and Mineral Affairs Department: POB 188, Sharjah; tel. (6) 541888; telex 68708; Dir ISMAIL A. WAHID.

Sharjah Liquefied Petroleum Gas Co (SHALCO): POB 787, Sharjah; tel. (6) 543666; telex 68799; fax (6) 548799; f. 1984; gas processing; 60% owned by Sharjah authorities, 25% Sharjah Amoco-Oil Co, 7.5% each Itochu Corpn and Tokyo Boeki of Japan; Gen. Man. SALEH ALI.

Umm al-Qaiwain

Petroleum and Mineral Affairs Department: POB 9, Umm al-Qaiwain; tel. (6) 666034; Chair. Sheikh SULTAN BIN AHMAD AL-MU'ALLA.

Foreign Concessionaires

Abu Dhabi Oil Co Ltd (Japan) (ADOC): POB 630, Abu Dhabi; tel. (2) 661100; telex 22260; fax (2) 665965; consortium of Japanese oil cos, including Cosmo Oil, JNOC and Japan Energy Co; holds offshore concession, extended by 1,582.5 sq km in 1979; export of oil from Mubarraz Island terminal began in June 1973, production 6,332,897 barrels (1985); Gen. Man. Dr TATSUO TANAKA.

Amerada Hess Oil Corpn of Abu Dhabi (AHOC): Abu Dhabi; tel. and fax (2) 779500; telex 22275; operates the Arzanah field; owned 41.25% by AHOC, 31.5% Pan Ocean, Bow Valley 2.5%, Syracuse Oil 7.5%, Wington Enterprises 4.75%, Neste Oy 10%, Sunningdale 2.5%; Gen. Man. M. MURPHY.

Bunduq Oil Co: POB 46015, Abu Dhabi; tel. (2) 779922; telex 23692; fax (2) 779477; f. 1975; production in al-Bunduq oilfield; Gen. Man. Dr T. NEGISHI.

Crescent Petroleum Co International: POB 2222, Sharjah; tel. (6) 543000; telex 68015; fax (6) 542000; subsidiary of BGOI Inc; Chair. and CEO H. D. JAFAR.

Neyrfor UAE: POB 46135; Abu Dhabi; tel. (2) 540723; fax (2) 540732; e-mail neyrfor@emirates.net.ae.

Sedco-Houston Oil Group: POB 702, Dubai; tel. (4) 224141; telex 45469; holds onshore concession of over 400,000 ha as well as the offshore concession formerly held by Texas Pacific Oil; Pres. CARL F. THORNE.

Total Abu al-Bukhoosh Oil Co Ltd: POB 4058, Abu Dhabi; tel. (2) 785000; telex 22347; fax (2) 788477; owned by Total, operator of Abu al-Bukhoosh field; began production from the Abu al-Bukhoosh offshore field in July 1974; average production of 40,000 b/d in 1993; partner in the field is INPEX.

Zakum Development Co (ZADCO): POB 46808, Abu Dhabi; tel. (2) 605000; telex 22948; fax (2) 669448; jt venture between ADNOC (88%) and JODCO (12%); develop and produce from Upper Zakum, Umm ad-Dalkh and Satah fields on behalf of its owners; manages UDECO; Chair. YOUSUF BIN OMEIR BIN YOUSUF; Gen. Man. I. NAHARA.

UTILITIES

Abu Dhabi

A decree issued in late February 1998 restructured the Abu Dhabi utilities sector in preparation for its privatization. The companies listed below were all to be in place by January 1999.

Abu Dhabi Co for Remote Areas Services: Abu Dhabi.

Abu Dhabi Co for Transmission and Control: Abu Dhabi.

Abu Dhabi Distribution Co: Abu Dhabi.

Abu Dhabi Water and Electricity Authority (ADWEA): POB 219, Abu Dhabi; tel. (2) 731100; telex 22369; f. 1998; successor to Water and Electricity Dept; Chair. Sheikh DHIYAB BIN ZAYED AN-NAYHAN.

Al-Ain Distribution Co: POB 1065, al-Ain; tel. (3) 636000.

Bayounah Power Co.: Abu Dhabi; to control Taweelah A power station, al-Ain and Abu Dhabi steam, and gas turbine stations.

Mirfa Power Co: Abu Dhabi; will control Mirfa and Madinat Zayed plants.

Sewerage Projects Committee (SPC): Abu Dhabi.

Taweelah Power Co: Abu Dhabi; will own and run Taweelah B station.

Umm an-Nar Power Co: Abu Dhabi; will own and control the Umm an-Nar and Bani Yas power stations.

Dubai

Dubai Electricity and Water Authority (DEWA): POB 564, Dubai; tel. (4) 348888; telex 45838; fax (4) 348111.

Northern Emirates (Ajman, Fujairah, Ras al-Khaimah)
Ministry of Electricity and Water: (see Ministries, above).

Sharjah
Sharjah Electricity and Water Autority (SEWA): Sharjah.

MAJOR COMPANIES

Abu Dhabi

Admak General Contracting Co: POB 650, Abu Dhabi; tel. (2) 542200; telex 22320; fax (2) 543134; f. 1968 as M. A. Kharafi, in 1981 adopted present name; general civil engineering and road contractors; part of the M. A. Kharafi Group of Kuwait; Man. Dir IBRAHIM SWEIDAN; Exec. Dir MUNIR MUSTAFA; 1,200 employees.

Arabconstruct International Ltd: POB 238, Abu Dhabi; tel. (2) 322668; telex 22558; f. 1967; general civil works, construction, engineering and contracting; cap. AED 12m.; Chair. and Propr ADNAN M. DERBAS; 1,500 employees.

International Aluminium: POB 2329, Abu Dhabi; tel. (2) 325326; telex 22949; specialist contractors, design, manufacture and erection of high-rise applications; Propr HUSSAIN GHULAM HAJIPOUR.

Mechanical and Civil Engineering Contractors (MACE) Ltd: POB 2307, Abu Dhabi; tel. (2) 666462; telex 22816; fax (2) 662616; Chair. and Man. Dir WILLIAM A. T. HADDAD; 1,200 employees.

Nitco Concrete Products: POB 654, Abu Dhabi; tel. (2) 344255; telex 22407; f. 1980; production and supply of ready-mix concrete, concrete fences and paving stones; sales AED 15m. (1981/82); cap. AED 8m.; Chair. FARAH ABD AR-RAHMAN HAMED; Man. Dir ABDULLAHI FARAH.

Pilco (Pipeline Construction Co): POB 2021, Abu Dhabi; tel. (2) 554500; telex 23210; fax (2) 559053; e-mail pilco@emirates.net.ae; f. 1968; fabrication of steel, piping, tanks, pressure vessels and machine components; general services to the oil industry; Gen. Man. E. N. HAWA; 200 employees.

Ash-Shaheen Gypsum Products Est: POB 2618, Abu Dhabi; tel. (2) 554673; telex 22926; fax (2) 662116; f. 1978; fabrication of gypsum blocks for use in dry wall partitioning; Dirs OBAID AL-MANSOURI, FRANÇOIS LAMA.

Ajman

Ajman Mosaic Co: POB 406, Ajman; tel. (6) 422104; production of marble and terrazzo; Chair. Sheikh HUMAID.

Dubai

Al-Ahmadia Contracting and Trading: POB 2596, Dubai; tel. (4) 450900; telex 45703; fax (4) 450327; f. 1970; building and civil engineering contractors; Pres. and Propr Sheikh HASHER MAKTOUM JUMA AL-MAKTOUMI; Vice-Pres. Col MUHAMMAD MUBARAK IESA; Dir S. K. JOSHI; 1,500 employees.

Dubai Aluminium Co (DUBAL): POB 3627, Dubai; tel. (4) 846666; telex 47240; fax (4) 864292; f. 1979; production of primary aluminium; capacity of 30m. gallons of potable water per day; produces about 390,000 tons of cast metal per annum; Chair. Sheikh HAMDAN BIN RASHID AL-MAKTOUM.

Fibroplast Industries Co (PVT) Ltd: POB 10192, Dubai; tel. (4) 257575; telex 46912; f. 1977; manufacture of glass fibre-reinforced polyester pipes, tanks, fittings; sales AED 49.8m. (1982); cap. AED 8m.; Chair. ABD AL-GHAFFAR HUSSAIN; Man. Dir W. NAJARIAN; 187 employees.

Al-Futtaim Tower Scaffolding (PVT) Ltd: POB 5502, Dubai; tel. (4) 858861; telex 46086; fax (4) 858592; f. 1975; manufacture of scaffolding and steel products; general fabrication; Chair. MAJID MUHAMMAD AL-FUTTAIM; Gen. Man. V. M. G. RAMAN; 150 employees.

Al-Ghurair Group of Companies: POB 1, Dubai; tel. (4) 693311; fax (4) 691852; f. 1960/61; general contracting, banking, import and export, aluminium extrusion and manufacture of aluminium doors, windows, etc., PVC pipes, tiles and marbles, cement and mineral waters; gold and exchange dealers, owners of grain silos and flour mills, printing press, packaging factory, real estate dealers; cap.

AED 1,000m.; Chair. Saif Ahmad Majed al-Ghurair; Vice-Chair. Abdullah Ahmad Majed al-Ghurair; 1,600 employees.

Gulf Eternit Industries S.A.: POB 1371, Dubai; tel. (4) 857256; telex 47040; fax (4) 851935; manufacture of Fibrecement and glass reinforced plastic pipes; Pres. Fouad Makhzoumi.

Al-Habtor Engineering Enterprises Co (LLC): POB 320, Dubai; tel. (4) 857551; telex 45603; fax (4) 857479; e-mail heepd@emirates .net.ae; f. 1970; civil and building contracting; Dirs Khalaf A. Al-Habtoor; Riad T. Sadik; about 4,000 employees.

Bin Hussain Aluminium Factories: POB 1535, Dubai; tel. (4) 660643; telex 45947; fax (4) 661567; process and fabrication of aluminium doors, windows, shop fronts, balustrades, rolling shutters, etc.; Chair. Hussain Muhammad bin Hussain.

Bin Ladin Organization for Construction and General Trading: POB 1555, Dubai; tel. (4) 691500; tel. 45991; fax (4) 691350; f. 1967 in UAE; civil engineering, roadworks, piling, ground services and building, electrical contracting; Chair. and Man. Dir Abu Bakr Salim al-Hamid; 4,000 employees.

National Cement Co Ltd: POB 4041, Dubai; tel. (4) 382671; telex 47202; production and sale of cement; Chair. Saif Ahmad al-Ghurair.

Shirawi Contracting and Trading Co: POB 2032, Dubai; tel. (4) 220251; telex 45483; f. 1971; building and civil engineering contractors, supply of building materials; sales AED 290m.; cap. AED 50m; Chair. Abdullah ash-Shirawi; 2,000 employees.

United Foods Ltd: POB 5836, Dubai; tel. (4) 382688; telex 46689; fax (4) 381987; e-mail aseel@emirates.net.ae; f. 1976; manufacture and trading of hydrogenated vegetable oil and cooking oil; Chair. Saeed Muhammad al-Mulla; Gen. Man. M. Tawfiq Baig; 235 employees.

Unity Contracting Co (UNCO) Ltd: POB 16638, Dubai; tel. (4) 667870; telex 46603; fax (4) 661790; f. 1972; building and civil works contracting; Gen. Man. Hrayr Soghomonian; 900 employees.

Fujairah

Fujairah Cement: POB 600, Fujairah; tel. (9) 223111; telex 89047; fax (9) 227718.

Ras al-Khaimah

Alltek Emirates Ltd: POB 1569, Ras al-Khaimah; tel. (7) 668865; telex 99117; fax (7) 668977; manufacture and marketing of spray plasters, decorative paints and limestone powder.

Raknor (PVT) Ltd: POB 883, Ras al-Khaimah; tel. (7) 668351; telex 99251; fax (7) 668910; f. 1976; manufacture of concrete blocks.

Sharjah

CME Contracting Marine Engineering: POB 1859, Sharjah; tel. (6) 354511; telex 68069; turnkey industrial projects, water and electricity plants, construction, building, marine works; joint venture between Chair. and German cos Klaus Stuff, Helma Greuel-Mainz; Chair. Dr F. al-Gawly; 323 employees.

Conforce Gulf Ltd Co: POB 289, Sharjah; tel. (6) 591433; telex 68082; f. 1979; building contractor, exporter of building and electrical materials; Man. Abdullah Muhammad Bukhatir.

Dafco Trading and Industrial Co WLL: POB 515, Sharjah; tel. (6) 593333; telex 68106; fax (6) 596531; f. 1980; general contracting trading company; operates factories producing bricks and concrete; Man. M. al-Farhan.

General Enterprises Co: POB 1150, Sharjah; tel. (6) 331727; telex 68020; fax (6) 336470; general trading and contracting; Gen. Man. Sheikh Ahmad bin Muhammad Sultan al-Qasimi.

Gulf Building Materials Co Ltd (GBM): POB 1612, Sharjah; tel. (6) 354683; telex 68089; production and supply of building materials: cement, marble and aluminium.

Hempel's Paints (Emirates) Ltd: POB 2000, Sharjah; tel. (6) 283307; telex 68197; f. 1977; manufacture and sale of paints for offshore marine, domestic and industrial use; Chair. Sa'ud Abd al-Aziz ar-Rashid; CEO and Gen. Man. John R. Spendlove.

Sharjah Electrodes: POB 2019, Sharjah; tel. (6) 331000; fax (6) 337244; f. 1976; manufacture and distribution of arc welding electrodes and wire nails; Chair. Muhammad Sharif Zaman; 37 employees.

Umm al-Qaiwain

Umm al-Qaiwain Aluminium Co (UMALCO): Umm al-Qaiwain.

Umm al-Qaiwain Asbestos and Cement Industries Co: POB 547, Umm al-Qaiwain; tel. (6) 671772; telex 69711; fax (6) 671011; Chair. Sheikh Sa'ud bin Rashid al-Mu'alla.

Transport

ROADS

Roads are rapidly being developed in the United Arab Emirates, and Abu Dhabi and Dubai are linked by a good road which is dual carriageway for most of its length. This road forms part of a west coast route from Shaam, at the UAE border with the northern enclave of Oman, through Dubai and Abu Dhabi to Tarif. An east coast route links Dibba with Muscat. Other roads include the Abu Dhabi–al-Ain highway and roads linking Sharjah and Ras al-Khaimah, and Sharjah and Dhaid. An underwater tunnel links Dubai Town and Deira by dual carriageway and pedestrian subway. In 1993 there was a total paved network of roads of 4,555 km, of which 1,753 km were main roads.

SHIPPING

Dubai has been the main commercial centre in the Gulf for many years. Abu Dhabi has also become an important port since the opening of the first section of its artificial harbour, Port Zayed. There are smaller ports in Sharjah, Fujairah, Ras al-Khaimah and Umm al-Qaiwain. Work on a dry-dock scheme for Dubai was completed in 1979. It possesses two docks capable of handling 500,000-ton tankers, seven repair berths and a third dock able to accommodate 1,000,000-ton tankers. In 1988 the Dubai port of Mina Jebel Ali, which has the largest man-made harbour in the world, contained 67 berths. Current modernization of Port Khalid in Sharjah was to double its berth capacity, and the two-berth port of Fujairah was opened in 1983.

Abu Dhabi National Tanker Co (ADNATCO): POB 2977, Abu Dhabi; tel. (2) 277733; telex 22747; fax (2) 272940; subsidiary company of ADNOC, operating owned and chartered tankships, and transporting crude petroleum, refined products and sulphur; Chair. Nasser Ahmed as-Suwaidi; Gen. Man. Bader M. as-Suwaidi.

Abu Dhabi Seaport Authority: POB 422, Port Zayed, Abu Dhabi; tel. (2) 730600; fax (2) 731023; administers Port Zayed; handled 236,000 20-ft equivalent units (TEUs) in 1996; Harbour Master Said Darwish.

Ahmad bin Rashid Port and Free Trade Zone: POB 279, Umm al-Qaiwain; tel. (6) 655882; telex 69717; fax (6) 651552; e-mail abrpftz@emirates.net.ae.

Dubai Drydocks: POB 8988, Dubai; tel. (4) 450626; telex 48838; fax (4) 450116; e-mail drydocks@emirates.net.ae; state-owned dry-docks with cleaning facilities, galvanizing plant, transport systems and facilities for maintenance and repair of ships of any size; Chief Exec. E. S. Ware.

Dubai Ports Authority (DPA): POB 17000, Dubai; tel. (4) 815000; telex 47398; fax (4) 816093; offers duty-free storage areas and facilities for loading and discharge of vessels; supervises ports of Mina Jebel Ali and Mina Rashid; handled 2.25m. TEUs in 1996; Chair. Sultan Ahmad bin Sulayem; Exec. Dir David Gibbons.

Fujairah Port: POB 787, Fujairah; tel. (9) 228800; telex 89085; fax (9) 228811; f. 1982; offers facilities for handling full container, general cargo and 'roll on, roll off' traffic; handled 555,586 20-ft equivalent units (TEUs) in 1996; Chair. Sheikh Saleh bin Muhammad ash-Sharqi; Harbour Master Tamer Masoud.

Jebel Ali Free Zone Authority (JAFZ): POB 17000, Dubai; tel. (4) 815000; telex 47398; fax (4) 815001; e-mail jafza@emirates.net.ae; the authority administers a 100 sq km zone, created by the Govt of Dubai in 1985, which includes the 7,500-acre Jebel Ali port and industrial area offering 67 berths; offers facilities for handling container, bulk, general and liquid traffic; warehouse and office facilities; specialized storage incl. cold stores and tank farms; by December 1996 approx. 1,000 companies had established business in the Free Zone; Port Rashid and Jebel Ali port handled more than 30m. metric tons of cargo in 1996; Chair. Sultan Ahmad bin Sulayem.

Jebel Dhanna/Ruwais Petroleum Port: c/o ADCO, POB 270, Abu Dhabi; tel. (2) 666100; telex 22222; fax (2) 669785; facilities include 5 tanker berths, export of crude petroleum, refined products, fertilizers, ammonia and sulphur; Terminal Superintendent J. B. Sheehan.

Mina Saqr Port Authority: POB 5130, Ras al-Khaimah; tel. (7) 668444; telex 99280; fax (7) 668533; Port operators handling bulk cargoes, containers, general cargo and 'roll on, roll off' traffic; govt owned; Chair. Sheikh Muhammad bin Saqr al-Qasimi; Man. David Allan.

Mina Zayed Port: POB 422, Abu Dhabi; tel. (2) 730600; telex 22731; fax (2) 731023; facilities include 21 deep-water berths of up to 15 metres draft; 5 container gantry cranes of 40 tons capacity; specializes in container traffic, general, reefer and bulk cargoes; in 1995 Port Zayed handled 245,952 metric tons of cargo; Chair. Sheikh Said bin Zayed an-Nahyan; Dir Mubarak al-Bu Ainain.

National Marine Services Co (NMS): POB 7202, Abu Dhabi; tel. (2) 339800; telex 22965; fax (2) 211239; operate, charter and lease specialized offshore support vessels; cap. AED 25m.; owned 60% by ADNOC and 40% by Jackson Marine Corpn USA; Chair. Sohail Fares al-Mazrui; Gen. Man. Capt. Hassan A. Shareef.

Sharjah Ports and Customs Department: POB 510, Sharjah; tel. (6) 281666; telex 68138; fax (6) 281425; the authority administers

Port Khalid and Port Khor Fakkan and offers specialized facilities for container and 'roll on, roll off' traffic, reefer cargo and project and general cargo; in 1997 Port Khalid handled 64,564 20-ft. equivalent units (TEUs) of containerized shipping, and Port Khor Fakkan 750,817 TEUs; Chair. (Ports and Customs) Sheikh SAUD BIN KHALID AL-QASIMI; Dir-Gen. ABD AL-AZIZ SULAIMAN AS-SARKAL.

Umm al-Qaiwain Port: POB 225, Umm al-Qaiwain; tel. (6) 666126; telex 69611.

CIVIL AVIATION

There are six international airports at Abu Dhabi, al-Ain (Abu Dhabi), Dubai, Fujairah and Ras al-Khaimah, and a smaller one at Sharjah, which forms part of Sharjah port, linking air, sea and overland transportation services. In 1995 a total of 11.6m. passengers used the six UAE airports, 3.3m. of them passing through Abu Dhabi airports; and in 1996 a record 8.5m. passengers used Dubai airport.

Civil Aviation Department: POB 20, Abu Dhabi; tel. (2) 757500; telex 24406; responsible for all aspects of civil aviation; Chair. HAMDAN BIN MUBARAK AN-NAHYAN.

Abu Dhabi Aviation: POB 2723, Abu Dhabi; tel. (2) 449100; telex 22656; fax (2) 449081; f. 1976; domestic charter flights; Chair. HAMDAN BIN MUBARAK AN-NAHYAN; Gen. Man. MUHAMMAD IBRAHIM AL-MAZROUI.

Emirates Air Service: POB 2723, Abu Dhabi; tel. (2) 757021; telex 22656; fax (2) 449100; f. 1976 as Abu Dhabi Air Services; overhaul, engine and avionics servicing, component repairs and complete refurbishment.

Emirates Airline: POB 686, Dubai; tel. (4) 228151; telex 48085; fax (4) 214560; e-mail corpcom@emirates.com; internet http://www.ekgroup.com; f. 1985; services to 44 destinations world-wide; owned by the Dubai authorities; in 1997/98 the airline carried 3.7m. passengers and 200,138 tons of freight; Chair. Sheikh AHMAD BIN SAID AL-MAKTOUM; Man. Dir. MAURICE FLANAGAN.

Falcon Express Cargo Airlines: World Trade Centre, POB 9372, Dubai; tel. (4) 826886; fax (4) 823125; f. 1995; dedicated freight.

Gulf Air Co GSC (Gulf Air): POB 5015, Sharjah; tel. (6) 356356; fax (6) 354354; f. 1950; jointly owned by Govts of Bahrain, Oman, Qatar and Abu Dhabi since 1974; flights world-wide; Pres. and Chief Exec. SALIM BIN ALI BIN NASSER.

Tourism

Tourism is an established industry in Sharjah, and plans are being implemented to foster tourism in other emirates, notably in Abu Dhabi and Dubai. In 1994 foreign visitors to the UAE totalled more than 1.9m., compared with 616,000 in 1990. In 1995 more than 1.6m. tourists visited Dubai alone.

Department of Tourism and Commerce Marketing: POB 594, Dubai; tel. (4) 511600; fax (4) 511711.

Dubai Information Department: POB 1420, Dubai; Dir OMAR DEESI.

Fujairah Tourism Bureau: Fujairah; Chair. KHALFAN OBEID KHALFAN.

Ras al-Khaimah Information and Tourism Department: POB 141, Ras al-Khaimah; tel. (7) 751151; Chair. Sheikh ABD AL-AZIZ BIN HUMAID AL-QASSIMI.

Sharjah Department of Tourism: POB 8, Sharjah; tel. (6) 581313; telex 68185; fax (6) 581091; f. 1980; Dir. MUHAMMAD SAIF AL-HAJRI.

Defence

The Union Defence Force and the armed forces of the various emirates were formally merged in May 1976, although difficulties have since been experienced (see History). Abu Dhabi and Dubai retain a degree of independence. Military service is voluntary.

Chief of Staff of Federal Armed Forces: Lt-Gen. MUHAMMAD BIN ZAYED AN-NAHYAN.

Total armed forces (August 1997): 64,500 (army 59,000; navy 1,500; air force 4,000).

Defence Budget (1997): AED 8,000m. (US $2,200m.); federal expenditure on defence has been substantially reduced since the early 1980s, but procurement and project costs are not affected, as individual emirates finance these separately. In 1992 a scheme was announced to draft thousands of local men and women into the army, and to replace the estimated 30% expatriate section of the army with nationals.

Education

Primary education is compulsory, beginning at six years of age and lasting for six years. Secondary education, starting at the age of 12, also lasts for six years, comprising two equal cycles of three years. As a proportion of all school-age children, the total enrolment at primary and secondary schools was equivalent to 87% in 1995 (males 87%; females 88%), compared with only 61% in 1970. Secondary enrolment was equivalent to 78% of children in the relevant age-group in 1995 (males 74%; females 81%). The UAE is engaged in expanding education, which is regarded as a unifying force for the future of the federation. As a result, major accomplishments in the provision of education have been achieved within the emirates. By 1985/86 there were an estimated 255,000 students at all stages of education in the country as a whole, compared with 141,424 in 1980/81 and about 109,000 in 1978/79. In 1994/95 a total of 56,428 children attended government kindergartens, and 262,628 attended primary schools in the UAE. At the same time, secondary enrolment totalled 159,840. There are primary and secondary schools in all the emirates, and further education in technical fields is available in the more advanced areas. Teachers from other Arab countries, most notably Kuwait, Egypt and Jordan, supplement the UAE's native teaching staff; of a total of 8,859 teachers in 1983, only 646 were UAE nationals. Many students receive higher education abroad. The UAE has one university, at al-Ain in Abu Dhabi, where 9,394 students were enrolled in 1992/93. The university was being expanded to take 16,000 students by 2000. The four higher colleges of technology (two for male and two for female students) in Abu Dhabi admitted a total of 1,150 students in 1992/93, all of whom were citizens of the UAE. Federal government expenditure in 1995 included AED 2,699m. for education (15.1% of total expenditure by the central Government). Adult illiteracy averaged an estimated 46.5% (males 41.6%; females 61.9%) in 1975, but, according to UNESCO estimates, had decreased to 20.8% (males 21.1%; females 20.2%) by 1995. A literacy and adult education programme is in operation.

Bibliography

Abdullah, M. Morsy. *The Modern History of the United Arab Emirates*. London, Croom Helm, 1978.

Albaharna, H. M. *The Legal Status of the Arabian Gulf States*. Manchester University Press, 1969.

Amni, Sayed Hassan. *International and Legal Problems of the Gulf*. Menas Press, 1981.

Bulloch, John. *The Gulf*. London, Century Publishing.

Busch, B. C. *Britain and the Persian Gulf 1894–1914*. University of California Press, 1967.

Cordesman, Anthony H. *The Gulf and the Search for Strategic Stability*. Mansell, 1984.

Daniels, John. *Abu Dhabi: A Portrait*. London, Longman, 1974.

Fenelon, K. G. *The United Arab Emirates: an Economic and Social Survey*. London, Longman, 1973.

Gabriel, Erhard F. (Ed.). *The Dubai Handbook*. Ahrensburg, Germany, Institute for Applied Economic Geography, 1989.

Hawley, Donald Frederick. *Courtesies in the Trucial States*. 1965.

The Trucial States. London, George Allen and Unwin, 1971.

Hay, Sir Rupert. *The Persian Gulf States*. Washington, DC, Middle East Institute, 1959.

Heard-Bey, Dr Frauke. *From Trucial States to United Arab Emirates*. London, Longman, 1982.

The Arabian Gulf States and the Islamic Revolution. Bonn, German Institute for Foreign Policy Research.

Khalifa, Ali Mohammad. *The United Arab Emirates: Unity in Fragmentation*. London, Croom Helm, 1980.

McLachlan, Keith, and Joffé, George. *The Gulf War—A Survey of Political Issues and Economic Consequences*. London, Economist Intelligence Unit, 1984.

Mann, Clarence. *Abu Dhabi: Birth of an Oil Sheikhdom*. Beirut, Khayats, 1964.

Marlowe, John. *The Persian Gulf in the 20th Century*. London, Cresset Press, 1962.

Miles, S. B. *The Countries and Tribes of the Persian Gulf*. 3rd edn, London, Cass, 1966.

Ministry of Information and Culture. *United Arab Emirates: A Record of Achievement, 1979–81*. Abu Dhabi, 1981.

Oteiba, Mani Said al-. *Petroleum and the Economy of the United Arab Emirates*. London, Croom Helm, 1977.

Essays on Petroleum. London, Croom Helm, 1982.

Peck, M. C. *The UAE—A Venture in Unity*. London, Croom Helm.

Qasimi, Sultan bin. *Myth of Arab Policy in the Gulf*. London, Croom Helm, 1986.

Sadiq, Muhammad T., and Snavely, William P. *Bahrain, Qatar and the United Arab Emirates: Colonial Past, Present Problems, and Future Prospects*. Lexington, Mass., Heath, 1972.

Sakr, Nadwi. *The UAE to 1990–One market or Seven?* (Special Report No. 238). London, Economist Intelligence Unit, 1986.

Taryam, A. O. *The Establishment of the UAE*. London, Croom Helm.

Yorke, V., and Turner, L. *European Interests and Gulf Oil*. Royal Institute of International Affairs/Gower, 1986.

Zahlan, Rosemarie Said. *The Origins of the United Arab Emirates*. London, Macmillan, 1978.

YEMEN

Geography

On 22 May 1990 the Yemen Arab Republic (YAR) and the People's Democratic Republic of Yemen (PDRY) merged to form the Republic of Yemen. Yemen consists of the south-west corner of the Arabian peninsula—the highlands inland, and the coastal strip along the Red Sea; and the former British colony of Aden (195 sq km or 75.3 sq miles) and the Protectorate of South Arabia (about 333,000 sq km or 128,570 sq miles), together with the islands of Perim (13 sq km or 5 sq miles) and Kamaran (57 sq km or 22 sq miles). The Republic of Yemen lies at the southern end of the Arabian peninsula, approximately between longitude 43°E and 56°E, with Perim Island a few km due west, in the strait marking the southern extremity of the Red Sea; and Socotra in the extreme east. Yemen has frontiers with Saudi Arabia and Oman (the former in the process of delimitation in late 1998 and the latter officially demarcated in mid-1995), although atlases still show considerable variation in the precise boundaries of the three countries, or sometimes do not indicate them at all. The capital of the Republic of Yemen is San'a, which lies on the al-Jehal plateau (2,175 m above sea-level).

Physically Yemen comprises the dislocated southern edge of the great plateau of Arabia. This is an immense mass of ancient granites, once forming part of Africa, and covered in many places by shallow, mainly horizontal layers of younger sedimentary rocks. The whole plateau has undergone down-warping in the east and elevation in the west, so that the highest land (over 3,000 m) occurs in the extreme west, near the Red Sea, with a gradual decline to the lowest parts (under 300 m) in the extreme east. The whole of the southern and western coasts of Yemen were formed by a series of enormous fractures, which produced a flat but very narrow coastal plain, rising steeply to the hill country a short distance inland. Percolation of molten magma along the fracture-lines gave rise to a number of volcanic craters, now extinct, and one of these, partly eroded and occupied by the sea, forms the site of Aden port.

An important topographic feature is the Wadi Hadramawt, an imposing valley running parallel to the coast at 160 km–240 km distance inland. In its upper and middle parts, this valley is broad, and occupied by a seasonal torrent; in its lower (eastern) part it narrows considerably, making a sudden turn south-eastwards and reaching the sea. This lower part is largely uninhabited, but the upper parts, where alluvial soil and inter-mittent flood water are available, support a farming population.

Rainfall is generally scarce, but relatively more abundant on the highlands and in the west. The climate of the highlands is considered to be the best in all Arabia since it experiences a regime rather like that of East Africa: a warm, temperate and rainy summer, and a cool, moderately dry winter with occasional frost and some snow. Aden receives 125 mm of rain annually, all of it during winter (December–March), whilst in the lowlands of the extreme east, it may rain only once in five or 10 years. In the highlands a few miles north of Aden, falls of up to 760 mm occur, for the most part during summer, and this rainfall also gradually declines eastwards, giving 380 mm–500 mm in the highlands of Dhofar. As much as 890 mm of rain may fall annually on the higher parts of the interior, off the Red Sea coast, with 400 mm–500 mm over much of the plateau; but the coast receives less than 130 mm generally, often in the form of irregular downpours. There is, therefore, the phenomenon of streams and even rivers flowing perennially in the western highlands but failing to reach the coast.

Ultimately, to the north and east, rainfall becomes almost negligible, as the edges of the Arabian Desert are reached. This unusual situation of a reversal in climatic conditions over a few miles is thought to be the result of two streams of air; an upper one, damp and unstable in summer, and originating in the equatorial regions of East Africa; and a lower current, generally drier and related to conditions prevailing over the rest of the Middle East. In this way the low-lying coastal areas have a maximum of rainfall in winter, and the hills of Yemen a max-imum in summer. Temperatures are everywhere high, particularly on the coastal plain, which has a southern aspect: mean figures of 25°C (January) to 32°C (June) occur at Aden town, but maxima of more than 38°C are common. Owing to this climate gradation from desert temperate conditions, Yemen has a similar gradation of crops and vegetation. In the interior, off the Red Sea coast, the highest parts appear as 'African', with scattered trees and grassland. Crops of coffee, qat, cereals and vegetables are grown, while, lower down, 'Mediterranean' fruits appear, with millet and, where irrigation water is available, bananas. The date palm is the only tree to grow successfully in the coastal region.

To the east, except on the higher parts, which have a light covering of thorn scrub (including dwarf trees which exude a sap from which incense and myrrh are derived), and the restricted patches of cultivated land, the territory is devoid of vegetation. Cultivation is limited to small level patches of good soil on flat terraces alongside the river beds, on the floor and sides of the Wadi Hadramawt, or where irrigation from wells and occasion-ally from cisterns can be practised. The most productive areas are: Lahej, close to Aden town; two districts near Mukalla (about 480 km east of Aden), and parts of the middle Hadramawt. Irrigation from cisterns hollowed out of the rock has long been practised, and Aden town has a famous system of this kind, dating back many centuries. Today, however, the main system of irrigation is provided by floodwater.

The area of Yemen is approximately 536,869 sq km (207,286 sq miles) and its population was 14,587,807 at the census of 16 December 1994.

History

ROBIN BIDWELL

Revised for this edition by RICHARD I. LAWLESS

PRE-ISLAMIC YEMEN

In the millenium before Christ there were three centres of civilization in the Arabian peninsula; one in the north-west around Madain Salih, the second based in Bahrain and in what is now the United Arab Emirates (UAE); and the third, the most advanced, in the Yemen. Traditional Arab genealogists assign to the Yemenis a different ancestor (*Qahtan*) from that of the northern tribes (*Adnan*). Yemen was unique amongst ancient civilizations in that it was not dependent on a great river, but relied upon rainfall to irrigate terraced fields, controlling the waters by a sophisticated system of dams, of which the one at Marib was famous throughout Arabia. In addition to flourishing agriculture, the incense trade and the use of its ports as a link between India, China, Africa and the Mediterranean made it one of the richest regions of the ancient world. References in the Bible and Classical authors and archaeology indicate that it had a social structure that has endured even into this century: towns with an hereditary literate class, trades divided into noble and ignoble, settled agriculturalists and, separate from these, tribesmen who were sometimes soldiers and sometimes predators. The chronology is uncertain, but it is clear that about 110 BC the whole area including what are now parts of Saudi Arabia and Oman came under the domination of the Himyarites whose rule continued almost until the rise of Islam at which time, after half a century of Abyssinian rule, Yemen had recently been conquered by the Persians.

EARLY ISLAMIC YEMEN

The Persian *satrap* appears to have accepted an invitation from the Prophet to adopt Islam and, according to tradition, the whole of the great tribe of Hamdan, the ancestors of the Hashid and Bakil tribes, were converted in a single day by Muhammad's son-in-law Ali; this forged a link between them and the Hashemites which lasted until the Revolution of 1962. Although huge numbers of Yemenis served in the Islamic armies (which conquered territories from the Atlantic to the borders of China), for a while it seemed that Yemeni particularism might prove too strong to accept a religion of foreign origin, and a series of revolts occurred. The Caliphs of Baghdad took little interest in such a remote area and in 822 their local governor, Ibn Ziyad, revolted and reunited most of the old Himyarite state under his own rule from the city of Zabid. Although short-lived, this had the effect of splitting the Yemen away from the main Arab Empire and reasserted its individuality.

The second half of the ninth century was a period of religious strife as the Ismailis attempted to seize control of the Yemen. In 1037, while the Ismailis were ruling in Cairo, a local chieftain conquered most of the old Himyaritic area and ruled it from San'a in their name. The Sulayhid dynasty survived in great prosperity for almost a century, but as it declined local governors asserted their independence. In 1174, the great Saladin (Salah ad-Din al-Ayyubi), who had overthrown the Ismailis in Egypt, sent his brother to destroy their adherents in Yemen and once again most of south-west Arabia was governed by a single ruler. The Ayyubids remained for half a century and left affairs in the hands of an official, ar-Rasul, who later assumed an independent sovereignty.

The Rasulids, from their capital at Taiz, had diplomatic relations with Persia, India and China and were so effective that they were able to organize a trilateral campaign by land and sea against a rebellious vassal in Dhofar. Their state, in turn, disintegrated and the area was totally fragmented when the Portuguese attacked Aden in 1513.

FROM THE SIXTEENTH TO THE EARLY NINETEENTH CENTURY

The fear that the Portuguese might establish a presence in southern Arabia which could serve as a base to attack the Holy Places led to the intervention of the Ottoman Sultan. An army, using firearms for the first time in the area, succeeded in installing a Pasha in San'a who ruled almost all of the historic Yemen. The Zaidis in the mountains remained detached and in the east the Kathiri family established a semi-independent state in Hadramawt, although they acknowledged Ottoman sovereignty. The discovery of the route to India round the Cape practically destroyed the importance of Aden as an entrepôt, but, from c. 1600, British and Dutch traders travelled to Mocha to buy coffee and sell textiles.

At about the same time a new Zaidi Imam launched a guerrilla war against the Turks who, after nine years' fighting, agreed to leave him in control of the area north of San'a. His son launched a religious and national war which, in 1636, led to their departure. He and succeeding Imams brought the whole of South Arabia, including Dhofar and Asir under their rule.

Once more central authority declined and in 1728 the Governor of Lahej and Aden proclaimed himself an independent Sultan and his example was followed in Asir and most of the South. By the time the explorer Niebuhr visited San'a in 1763 the writ of the Imam was only valid in San'a, Taiz and the Tihamah.

In 1804 the Wahhabis occupied Mecca and Medina and also penetrated into the Tihamah. Some years later the Ottoman Sultan, as Protector of the Holy Places, requested his vassal Muhammad Ali, Pasha of Egypt, to expel them. This he did and went on to take over the Tihamah and monopolize the coffee trade; in 1837 he bought control of Taiz.

In 1834, taking advantage of the plundering of an Indian vessel flying the British flag, the Bombay Government sent Captain Haines of the Indian navy to exact restitution and at the same time to negotiate for the purchase of Aden (a valuable fuelling station between Britain and India). The Sultan of Lahej, fearing that it might be seized by the Egyptians, agreed to sell but then reneged on the deal. His son then tried to kidnap Haines in order to repossess the document and this provided a pretext for an attack in which Aden was stormed on 19 January 1839.

In 1841 as part of a general peace settlement Muhammad Ali Pasha evacuated his troops from Yemen. A period of lawlessness ensued, during which the Imam requested a treaty of protection with the British. Haines, who was at that time Political Agent in Aden, was ordered to refuse. The Turks decided to reassert control and in 1849 they occupied Hodeida.

THE BRITISH IN ADEN 1839-1918

At the time of the conquest, Aden was in a state of dilapidation with about 600 inhabitants, but Haines had the vision to realize that it could be built into a great port to serve the hinterland and resume its historic role as an entrepôt. In seven years the population rose to 25,000. After repelling two attempts by the Sultan of Lahej to recapture the town, Haines sought the friendship of the local tribes by giving small subsidies to their leaders, often through the Sultan of Lahej, and by abstaining from interference in their internal affairs. Aden became a free port in 1850 and from 1869 benefited from the substantial increase in shipping that resulted from the opening of the Suez Canal, although until 1881 it was not master of its own water supply. Aden was a military base, secured by the acquisition of Perim Island and Little Aden, which had been sought by the French, and occupation of part of the Somali coast which ensured that no hostile power could dominate the entrance to the Red Sea. The Kuria Muria Islands were a gift to Queen Victoria from Saiyid Said of Oman.

In the early 1870s the Turks in San'a established contact with some of the tribes, including those of Hadramawt, that had been at least nominally subject to the Ottoman Sultan during the first occupation. This alarmed the British who presented Constantinople with a list of nine tribes that they regarded as under their sphere of influence and in which they would oppose Turkish interference. The Turks occupied part of the Sultanate of Lahej, but withdrew in December 1873 after strong diplomatic action in Constantinople. The British then consolidated their position with a series of treaties, similar to the Exclusive Treaties with the Gulf Sheikhdoms, signed with the tribes, who, in return for protection against outside attack and regular subsidies, undertook to refrain from correspondence with foreign powers to whom they were not to cede any territory without approval. These events were significant in Yemeni history because for the first time southern Arabia was formally divided into two distinct territories separated by a boundary which was apparent to the tribes and recognized by international agreement.

Despite proposals by the British Foreign Office that Aden should be taken over by the Colonial Office, it continued to be administered as part of the Bombay presidency. Consequently, Aden began to adopt a distinctly Indian style of government and trade. Despite the emergence of small numbers of educated local Arabs, the increasing use of English and Urdu words and expressions made its colloquial language difficult for outsiders to understand and it took on a cultural identity of its own which was quite different from the traditional Arab background of San'a.

THE TURKS IN YEMEN AND THE FIRST WORLD WAR

The Turks had occupied Hodeida in 1849 and, after concluding a treaty with the Imam, proceeded to settle in San'a but were expelled with heavy casualties by its inhabitants. There followed twenty years of near-anarchy until the opening of the Suez Canal enabled Constantinople to send large reinforcements by sea as part of its general policy of reasserting its position in Arabia. San'a was occupied again in 1871 and while the Zaidis were left alone, the rest of the country was virtually controlled by occupying forces despite frequent skirmishes with the tribes. Yemen was regarded as a place of exile for Ottoman officials whose financial dishonesty and lax morals caused great resentment.

In 1891 Muhammad Hamid ad-Din was elected Imam and, taking the regnal name assumed by the leader of the seventeenth century revolt, he issued a proclamation denouncing the religious unworthiness of the Turks to rule the country, once again showing the symbiosis of Zaidi doctrine and Yemeni nationalism. Soon all the highlands rallied to him but Constantinople retaliated by sending a notoriously ruthless Pasha who crushed the rebellion. The Turks then attempted to modernize their administration, but the secular nature of many of their reforms alienated the Shafai inhabitants of the Tihamah and Hujariyah.

In 1904 Muhammad's son, Yahya, succeeded him as Imam and called for a new uprising. In addition to their immorality and secularization, he was particularly incensed by the Turkish agreement with the British to delimit a frontier which he regarded as recognizing the separation of territory he considered as part of historic Yemen. Despite the deployment of almost 100,000 troops, the Turks were unable to destroy Yahya's tribal levies and in 1911, anxious to redeploy their troops to confront the Italian invasion of Tripoli and imminent war in the Balkans, they concluded with him the treaty of Da'an. Yahya conceded that the Ottoman Sultan was responsible for the defence and foreign affairs of the Islamic community as a whole, including Yemen, in return for non-interference in the religious and legal affairs of the Zaidis: in effect he was left in control of the Highlands while the Turks ruled the Tihamah where unrest continued.

Despite several British efforts to buy his support after the outbreak of war in 1914, Yahya remained loyal to the treaty. The Turks, by exploiting British military incompetence, occupied Lahej and besieged Aden for over three years. Having failed to win over Yahya, the British sought to undermine his position by providing the intensely ambitious *de facto* independent ruler of Asir, Said Muhammad Ali al-Idrisi, with the financial means to subvert the Hashid and Bakil tribes and encouraged plots to overthrow the Imam. Yahya also resented apparent British support for the pretensions of Sharif Hussain of Mecca to be King of the Arabs and the seizure of Kamaran,

just off the Yemeni coast. The Turks occupied the north-western part of the Protectorate, tried unsuccessfully to incite the tribes east of Aden and only withdrew after their Government, defeated elsewhere, sought an armistice.

BRITISH RELATIONS WITH THE IMAM YAHYA

After the war, relations between Yahya and the British Government were extremely uncordial. They deteriorated further when, upon the withdrawal of the Turks from territories within the recognized area of the Aden Protectorate, Yahya sent his troops to replace the Turkish contingent while the British seized Hodeida and encouraged al-Idrisi to extend his influence in the Tihamah where, as a Shafai, he was preferred to the Zaidi Imam. When Hodeida was evacuated, al-Idrisi was allowed to occupy it. The British then attempted to conciliate Yahya in the same way as had been the strategy with other Peninsular rulers, most of whom received subsidies from Britain in return for accepting direction in their foreign affairs. A mission sent for the purpose was detained in Tihamah by Shafai tribesmen opposed to the Imam. Negotiations lingered on because the British wished to discuss details of a frontier which Yahya, claiming by right of inheritance all that had once been ruled by his Himyaritic ancestors, declared had no legal existence. He also denied the right of the authorities in Aden to have relations with the Protectorate chiefs whom he regarded as Yemeni subjects. After a serious incident in 1928 the British bombed Taiz and other cities and Yahya agreed to withdraw his troops.

In 1933 Yahya, aware of the probability of war with Ibn Sa'ud on his northern frontier, settled his dispute with the British. In the Treaty of San'a, signed in February 1934, he tacitly accepted the boundaries agreed between Britain and the Turks, although he considered this as merely permitting Aden to administer part of his territory. In deference to his claims, no further boundary pillars were erected and no further survey carried out. It was agreed that no changes would be made in the boundaries for forty years after which the matter would be discussed again. The British elevated Yahya's status by recognizing him as King. The treaty ushered in a period of generally peaceful coexistence which lasted for the rest of the reign of Imam Yahya. He resented the toleration of his political opponents in Aden while the British were concerned about his apparent friendship with Fascist Italy, although during the Second World War he remained strictly neutral.

POST-WAR ADEN AND THE HINTERLAND

In 1937, in addition to the hinterland, the Colonial Office had taken control of Aden itself. In 1947 a nominated Legislative Council for Aden was established and in 1949 the first elections, for a township authority, were held. Meanwhile, the town was transformed by the construction of a refinery, and the efficient bunkering service that followed ensured that Aden, still a free port, was by 1957 fourth after London, Liverpool and New York in the amount of shipping that it handled. Local industries were created to satisfy the needs of a population which trebled within a few years and increased still further after the British Government's Defence White Paper of 1957 made the Colony the largest British military base outside Europe. The increase in prosperity enabled the Government in Aden to establish what were, at the time, the best social services in the Arab world. Most who came to work in Aden were from the North, and locally-born Arabs were outnumbered by Yemeni immigrants.

There was no evidence of discontent with colonial rule before December 1947, when there was a general strike, followed by riots in which more than 100 people were killed, as a protest against British policy in Palestine. Subsequently three nationalist groups emerged—the Aden Association, which aimed at eventual independence within the Commonwealth, to be achieved by co-operation; the South Arabian League, seeking independence for a united Colony and Protectorate under the Sultan of Lahej; and a radical United National Front, demanding union with Yemen and Muscat as a republic.

These movements were supported by the freest press in the Arab world, but it was the rise of a trade union movement that strengthened their position. At a time when the voice of Nasser could be heard through the newly-invented transistor radios, the Imam's union with Egypt led to the first talk of 'the occupied South', and, when a reform gave the elected members a majority on the Legislative Council, the question arose of votes for immigrants from North Yemen, who constituted the majority of trade unionists. When, in January 1959, voting was held for 12 seats, there was a boycott by many Arabs: nine Arabs, two Somalis and an Indian were elected.

After the Treaty of San'a, the administration in Aden believed that more should be done for the Protectorate, and the first measure was to appoint a political officer and to enlist local tribesmen to police their own areas. There was a considerable increase in security, and progress was made in educational, health and agricultural matters. In 1937 the Qu'aiti Sultan of Mukalla had become the first ruler to bind himself to accept a resident adviser and 'for the welfare of his state to accept his advice in all matters except those concerning Muhammadan religion and custom'. Within five years the area had an effective, locally-run administration, directed by a State Council.

The hinterland was divided into the Eastern and Western Aden Protectorates (the EAP and the WAP, respectively). The EAP comprised the Hadramawt, the coastal strip of Mahra and the associated island of Socotra, and two minor Wahidi sultanates to the west of Mukalla with a total population estimated at 326,000. The WAP consisted of 17 states and various territories where there was no administration of any sort and which were never even visited by government officials, Arab or English.

Advisory treaties were later signed with the other states of the EAP and with many of those of the WAP. Their effect depended upon the working relationship that the adviser could establish with his local ruler for he had no executive powers. A Sultan who rejected 'advice' tendered through the Governor could be deposed, but this needed the approval of the Secretary of State for the Colonies, who often had little time for the misconduct of a minor sheikh. An Arab chief who was knowledgeable about the area and who was liked or feared by the people, could normally impose his views upon a transitory British official. In practice the sultanates were not colonies because they enjoyed a large degree of independence, albeit hampered by financial dependence on the British.

During the Second World War British intervention increased because of the need to maximize local production of food. By 1954 the number of chiefs in relation with Aden had grown to more than 50 and this incensed the Imam who imposed his own interpretation of the Treaty of San'a, which he declared to have been violated. He therefore initiated a determined effort to incite the tribes to revolt against Christian encroachments. This caused the Governor, Sir Tom Hickinbotham, to reverse the old policy of relying on tribal particularism in order to prevent union against the British and to attempt to form a federal union which would create a distinct South Arabian nation. He attempted, but failed, to impose a ready-made formula, which made no mention of eventual independence and was unsuited to local conditions.

The idea of federation, despite its failure, provoked the Imam into intensifying his efforts to arouse subversion. He was assisted by Egyptian and Russian advisers and technicians. Violent incidents culminated in the spring of 1958, when an estimated 1,000 dissidents besieged a British political officer in a fort near the frontier while, at the same time, bombs were being thrown in Aden Colony. The idea of federation also encouraged the Sultan of Lahej to attempt to unite South Arabia under his own rule and consequently began to recruit adherents in other states while at the same time he talked of joining the Arab League and of employing Egyptian advisers. He was deposed.

The double threat from Lahej and Yemen, which would become more dangerous when Badr, known to be pro-Nasser, succeeded his father; the fact that the increase in economic activity made the existence of customs posts every few miles an absurd inconvenience; and the possibility that oil would be discovered in Hadramawt which would be unlikely to share its benefits unless there was some form of unity, revived the idea of federation. The British authorities primed the most trusted amirs with financial rewards and promises and feigned surprise when the rulers of six WAP states, Beihan, Audhali, Fadhli, Dhala, Lower Yafa and the Upper Aulaqi Sheikhdom travelled to Britain to request assistance in forming a federation.

THE MUTAWAKILITE KINGS (1919–1962)

During the war in 1914 Yahya had only exerted authority in the Zaidi areas and after the departure of the Turks, al-Idrisi made a determined effort to assume control of the Shafai areas. In 1920, however, the British discontinued his subsidy and his supporters decreased. He died in 1923, leaving feuding successors and a situation in which both Yahya and Ibn Sa'ud could intervene. Although a certain amount of fighting was involved, Yahya managed to bring both Zaidi and Shafai areas under either his own control or that of friendly chiefs. British officials travelling to San'a to negotiate the treaty of 1934 were astonished at the tranquillity of the country, which contrasted strongly with the insecurity prevailing in the Aden Protectorate.

Yahya managed to retain some Turkish soldiers and officials to form a backbone for his administration but otherwise he relied upon the traditional allies of the Imamate—the Saiyids and the traditional literate class of Qadis and upon the Hashid and the Bakil to comprise an armed force.

Yemen, before the discovery of petroleum in the Peninsula, was practically the only state that was self-supporting and Yahya saw no need for foreigners who might interfere with his independence and corrupt his people. Not even Arab states were permitted to establish embassies in San'a, foreign newspapers were forbidden, prospecting for petroleum or minerals was prohibited and though some weapons were obtained from Italy, Yahya ensured that it exercised no political influence. His determination to reconstitute the Himyarite 'empire' led to maladroit encroachments in Asir and Najran which culminated in a war with Saudi Arabia. An army under the future King Faisal advanced through the Tihamah, capturing Hodeida, but Ibn Sa'ud, unwilling to commit his troops to fighting in the mountains and to risk European intervention, made peace on generous terms, although Yahya had to withdraw his claims to Asir and Najran. Towards the end of his reign, Yahya joined the Arab League and the UN, uniting with other Arabs in opposition to Zionism.

Yahya had allowed young men to study abroad and had even sent some to Baghdad for military training. They returned convinced of the backwardness of Yemen and formed an opposition group, the *Ahrar,* the Free Yemenis, based in Aden where they received support in the local press. They were financed by merchants who wished to end royal monopolies. Yahya had provoked some of the religious leaders by breaking Zaidi tradition in requiring oaths of allegiance to his son Ahmad as Crown Prince. This particularly affronted the influential Saiyid Abd Allah al-Wazir who considered his right to the throne at least equal to that of Ahmad. These dissidents coalesced in a 'Sacred National Pact' which would establish a constitutional Imamate under al-Wazir, and enlisted tribal outlaws who in February 1948 assassinated Yahya in the first post-war coup in the Arab world.

Ahmad, though personally unpopular, managed to rally the tribes because of the shock of the murder, the failure of the new regime to attract support at home or abroad, and a promise that his tribal followers might sack San'a. He moved the capital to Taiz and ruled as autocratically as his father had done, showing the same immense knowledge of the country and intuitive understanding of the causes of local events. He survived a failed military coup and several assassination attempts.

He ended the country's isolation, admitting resident ambassadors, giving concessions to oil prospectors, accepting Soviet aid to develop Hodeida harbour and a Chinese-built road up to San'a. He maintained the claim to rule the whole of South Arabia and his dislike of the British, intensified by suspicions that they had connived at the murder of his father and by their adoption of a forward policy in the Aden Protectorate at a time when imperialism was in retreat elsewhere. In 1953, with the support of other Arab states, he raised the issue with the UN. He feared that the British might formally annex Shabwa, where there was believed to be oil. His officials fomented trouble across the frontier, attracting malcontents with arms and money. In order to acquire arms he signed a treaty in 1955 with Saudi Arabia and Egypt and later made agreements with several Eastern Bloc countries. Criticism grew of his reactionary and arbitrary policies, but he disconcerted his opponents by joining with Egypt and Syria in the United Arab States, which implied the backing of Nasser, the champion of radical Arab nationalism.

In April 1959 Ahmad was the first Imam ever to leave the country, travelling to Rome, Italy, for treatment for morphine addiction. The unnatural union did not survive Egyptian intervention during his absence and he denounced it. Consequently, hostility to Nasser led to a *rapprochement* with the British. He reverted to morphine addicton after another assassination attempt and gradually allowed Badr to assume power before his death in September 1962.

THE FEDERATION OF SOUTH ARABIA

After a treaty in which the British extended to the new entity, as a whole, the Protectorate Treaties previously concluded with its individual members, the federation came into existence in February 1959. The British would continue to meet the cost of its defence. Its ultimate aim, for which the Colonial Secretary pledged help to prepare, was independence. A new capital, al-Ittihad, was built and Sultans, sitting as the Supreme Council, constituted its only political and legislative organ. The ruler of each state, eventually numbering 17, had to be given a cabinet portfolio. The federation, dependent on British officials and British finances, initially appeared to be an instrument for British foreign policy and was never recognized by Arab Governments, many of which worked to destroy it. Nevertheless, considerable economic and some social progress was made, and in 1961 the federation acquired its own armed forces, consisting of five infantry battalions, an armoured car regiment with signals and administrative units.

In 1961 the British Government, believing that the security of the base in Aden was threatened by the turbulence engendered by trade union activists, now calling themselves the People's Socialist Party, decided to overwhelm the nationalists there by merging the Colony into the new federation. Britain would retain sovereignty over the Colony. Many Aden politicians were strongly opposed, but enough were coerced or bribed and some genuinely supported it. A motion to unite was forced through the Legislative Council in September 1962 and took effect from January 1963, but many, particularly the intellectuals, never ceased to resent the way in which merger was brought about. All those with grievances found a ready hearing amongst those in the British Labour Party who were ideologically opposed to a government of Sultans.

Mutual jealousies amongst the rulers meant that the federation had neither a president nor a prime minister and its titular head was the Chairman of the Supreme Council—an office which rotated monthly. The important states of the EAP refused to join and the British declined to coerce them although federal leaders saw their membership as vital. A constitutional conference arranged for December 1963 had to be postponed when a grenade was thrown amongst the rulers assembled at Aden airport, and it did not take place until June 1964. The leaders assembled in London, England, were relentlessly intimidated by the Colonial Secretary, Duncan Sandys, to the extent that one of the founding Sultans defected, joining the nationalist opposition in Cairo, Egypt. It was announced, however, that independence would come in 1968 and that in the interim there would be a president and a prime minister, an elected assembly and complete arabization of the civil service. These reforms were not implemented, for there was no agreement as to who should occupy the principal offices and outside Aden there was still no real administrative structure and no political organization to mobilize the people in support of the federation. The rulers, in offices in the capital, started to lose touch with what was occurring in their home states. Aden remained under a state of emergency imposed after the grenade attack and there was an increasing tendency amongst British officials to see its population as 'disloyal' in comparison with the 'trust-worthy' Sultans.

The Yemeni Revolution had brought bribed Egyptian officers to the frontier to incite subversion. With their encouragement, young men from the Protectorates, inspired by the ideals of Arab nationalism, formed the National Liberation Front (NLF, which was allegedly entirely financed by Egypt) announcing in a declaration of 14 October 1963 that they intended not merely to expel the British from South Arabia, but to make a socialist revolution. Their first triumph was to provoke a tribal revolt in Radfan which was suppressed by the use of British troops, helicopters and even heavy bombers. The campaign attracted wide publicity and led to criticism by left-wingers in Britain and the Arab world which seriously damaged the image of the federation, in whose name it was undertaken. Further denunciation followed the destruction of a Yemeni fort after Egyptian aircraft had dropped bombs on the territory of the federal Government which then invoked the Defence Treaty with Britain. The anti-colonial group at the UN became increasingly interested in the area, passing, in 1963, Resolution 1949 which called for self-determination for South Arabia, elections under UN supervision and the removal of the British base. Doubts about the future of the federation increased after the election of Harold Wilson as the Prime Minister of the British Government in October 1964.

In April 1964, visiting San'a, Nasser had sworn 'by Allah, to expel the British from all parts of the Arabian peninsula' and a campaign of urban terror was launched to make Aden ungovernable. It was estimated that between December 1963 and May 1966, 60 people were killed and 350 injured in Aden alone, one-third of the casualties being British. On joining the federation Aden had been permitted a chief minister and Abd al-Qawi Makkawi, appointed to that post in March 1965, appeared more anxious to appease the terrorists than to collaborate with the British. He denounced the state of emergency and the banning of the NLF. After Makkawi had publicly refused to condemn the murder of a respected official, he was dismissed by the Governor, Sir Richard Turnbull, who suspended the Constitution and imposed direct colonial rule in September 1965. He went into exile, joined soon afterwards by Asnaj and they and the NLF amalgamated, as a result of Egyptian pressure, to form the Front for the Liberation of Occupied South Yemen (FLOSY).

Financial difficulties and the need to conciliate internal party opposition led the Wilson Government, in February 1966, to announce that there was no further need for the Aden base—the defence of which had been the paramount reason for creating the federation. Moreover, there would be no further British military presence in South Arabia after independence in 1968. The federal leaders, realizing that they had isolated themselves from much of the Arab world by supporting the British, felt betrayed and defenceless. Around the same time militants of the NLF became more radical, finding the ideas of Mao and Guevara more to their liking than those of the bourgeois Nasser and of the FLOSY leaders and, by bank robberies and extortion, they freed themselves from financial dependence on Egypt. Assisted by fellow tribesmen in the police force and the federal armed forces, they fought the British and at the same time wrested control of the Aden streets from FLOSY. Aden was still formally a Colony and the British refused to allow the federal Government to use its own forces to improve security there and its members started to lose confidence in their own future and attempted to negotiate on a basis of Resolution 1949. In December 1966 the NLF declared itself the sole representative of the people of South Arabia.

The British Government was now preoccupied with withdrawing from South Arabia with the minimum cost in British lives and with the lesser objective of leaving a stable government behind. Various expedients were tried, including inviting help from Nasser and from the UN, promising a short-term security cover and working for an alliance between the federal Government and the NLF, with which secret contacts were established. It was even hoped that Saudi Arabia might take over responsibility for the area. There was also a desperate attempt to organize a new administration under an Adeni premier, after a brief but bloody military mutiny in June 1967 but this failed owing to the jealousies of the tribal ministers.

The NLF started to take control of state after state in the hinterland and on 4 September 1967 the High Commissioner stated that the federal Government had ceased to exist. Although the NLF was known to have extreme left-wing views, the British preferred it to the pro-Nasser FLOSY and assisted its assumption of power. FLOSY, deprived of external support as a result of the Egyptian withdrawal from Yemen, was defeated with heavy losses after the federal army declared support for the NLF. The handover to the NLF was formalized by a meeting at Geneva, Switzerland, after which force and threats were used by the British to prevent any of the federal rulers from returning home.

REVOLUTION AND EGYPTIAN INTERVENTION IN THE NORTH

The Imam Ahmad died on 19 September 1962 and Badr assumed the throne. Nasser welcomed this development as it seems likely that he had sanctioned a coup against Ahmad but ordered its postponement on his death as he regarded Badr as an ally who would support his version of Arab nationalism. His instructions were, however, disregarded by the Commander-in-Chief, Field Marshal Abd al-Hakim Amer, who was anxious to find an independent and profitable source of revenue for the Egyptian army. With the help of Egyptian officers, Yemeni officers on the night of 26/27 September bombarded the palace of Badr and announced that he had been assassinated. A senior officer, Col Abd Allah Sallal, who does not seem to have been involved in the coup, was proclaimed President in the expectation that he would later be replaced. Within days, in order to 'oppose any foreign intervention', Egyptian troops arrived with such speed that they had clearly been deployed beforehand, in anticipation of the coup.

The Royalists rallied under Badr's uncle, Hassan, who was proclaimed Imam and called for the tribes to rally to him. Although many supported the new Imam, the traditional allies of the Imamate, the Hashid and Bakil, whose chiefs had suffered at the hands of Ahmad, did not. Hassan set up a government in Saudi Arabia and also received help from the federal rulers of the south, with the connivance of the British. In October the Royalists captured Marib in the east but were repelled at Sada in the north. The Egyptians, knowing that this could not have been achieved without Saudi help, bombed Saudi towns and the two countries appeared on the brink of open war. Sallal called for all-out war, proclaimed a republic of the Arabian peninsula and demanded the return of Najran and Asir.

In November 1962 Badr reappeared, gave a press conference, and resumed the Imamate. The Americans, believing that the republic controlled the whole country and anxious to conciliate Nasser, recognized the new regime but the British who were better informed, did not and their legation was closed. The Yemen Arab Republic (YAR) was admitted to the UN.

Sallal promoted himself Field Marshal and was determined to rule. However, despite several attempts to secure constitutional legitimacy, he was never able to do so. Practically without local adherents, he had to rely on the Egyptians, who, though they often treated him with contempt, were unable to find a more convincing representative. The Egyptian forces were increased, in 1963 numbering about 28,000, and in April the UN attempted to bring about the disengagement of Egyptian and Saudi forces by providing an Observer Mission (UNYOM) but as it was not forbidden to contact the royalists, it proved totally futile and was withdrawn in September 1964.

Many Yemenis came to realize that their country was merely providing a battlefield on which Nasser and King Faisal were contesting the leadership of the Arab world. Moderate republicans and moderate royalists therefore attempted to make a peace between Yemenis at a conference at Erkowit in Sudan in October 1964. They agreed that both Badr and Sallal should relinquish power and that Egyptian forces should be asked to leave, but the initiative failed owing to the intransigence of the Egyptians and of Sallal. A cease-fire was proclaimed, but it lasted only a few days and was followed by a series of royalist successes, which left them in control of one-third of the country. The republicans split and the moderates, led by the Prime Minister, Ahmad Nu'man, tried to make peace but were again frustrated by Sallal's belligerence.

Nasser, realizing that he could not win a war which was becoming extremely unpopular at home, tried to end it by negotiating with King Faisal on the basis that he would withdraw his forces, now estimated at 50,000 provided the Saudis stopped supplying the royalists. Negotiations continued until the publication of a British 'white paper' on defence in February 1966, with the statement of the intended departure from Aden by 1968.

For the next year there was a stalemate—which the armed forces, subsidized by at least one side and with unusual opportunities to loot—were in no hurry to end. Egyptian military activity was confined to bombing and poison gas attacks, while the royalists were divided by internal feuds in the absence of Badr through ill-health.

The situation was transformed by the Egyptian defeat, by Israel, in the June War of 1967. At the Khartoum Summit, Nasser, now dependent upon Saudi Arabian financial assistance, agreed to withdraw his troops from Yemen. This was opposed by Sallal who feared for his own position but the withdrawal of Egyptian troops was nevertheless completed by the end of November, by which time he was out of the country on his way to seek alternative support from the Eastern Bloc. No one rallied to his support, there was no bloodshed and he was succeeded by a three-man Council headed by Qadi Abd ar-Rahman al-Iryani who had been one of the old *Ahrar* but had also been an adviser to the Imam Ahmad.

The royalists launched a major offensive and in December they began a three-month siege of San'a. The republicans, led by Gen. Hassan al-Amri, conducted a vigorous defence in which they were supported firstly by Soviet aircraft and secondly by the NLF which had by then taken power in Aden and which sent volunteers who succeeded in opening the road from Hodeida. Al-Amri, without the Egyptian forces previously thought indispensable, succeeded in reconquering much of the country, helped by intensified royalist feuding which led to the brief deposition of Badr by his cousin Muhammad bin Hussain. Many tribal chiefs defected.

By February 1970 King Faisal had decided that he could tolerate the moderate republic of al-Iryani, a pious Muslim, and indeed use it as an ally against the communist South. He therefore terminated all aid to the royalists and 'ordered' them to cease fighting. Nearly all except members of the ruling family returned and were integrated in the new regime which was then recognized by Saudi Arabia and the United Kingdom. It was estimated that during the war 200,000 Yemenis, 4% of the population, had been killed. Although the Egyptians had done some good work in improving education and other social services, they had also installed a ponderous bureaucracy, modelled on the one in Cairo, which was quite unsuitable for Yemeni needs.

THE SOUTH GOES LEFT (1967–1978)

Qahtan ash-Shaabi, the only one amongst the chiefs of the NLF with sufficient seniority to be credible as a statesman, had emerged as their leader at their first Congress at Taiz in 1965. He led the delegation to the Geneva talks and upon the formal take-over of sovereignty on 30 November 1967 he proclaimed himself President, Prime Minister and Commander-in-Chief. He at once declared South Yemen a unitary state, abolished the old sheikhdoms and demanded the abandonment of all tribal bloodfeuds. Other parties were banned, the press was controlled, a State Security Supreme Court was created and quickly established firm control throughout the country by means of a police force trained by East Germans. An uprising amongst the Aulaqis, who had been the greatest beneficiaries of the federation but who also had preferred FLOSY to the NLF, was crushed with such savagery that henceforth they played little part in affairs and an attempt by the Sharif of Beihan, with Saudi backing, to regain his state was defeated.

Relations with the United Kingdom deteriorated rapidly as advisers who had remained to assist in the build-up of new armed forces were expelled and replaced by Soviet advisers who also provided arms. The handing over to Muscat by the British of the Kuria Muria islands caused bitterness in Aden. Although it was believed that the USA had given covert help to the NLF when it was a clandestine anti-British movement, their military attaché was given 24 hours' notice to leave, and the controlled press made much of their connections with Israel and with Saudi Arabia which had emerged as the principal enemy of the new state.

On the day he assumed office ash-Shaabi declared that 'the aim of our Revolution has been since the beginning to unite both parts of Yemen. We are all one people'. He appointed one of the most influential NLF leaders, Abd al-Fattah Ismail, as Minister of Yemeni Unity Affairs; a similar ministry was set up in San'a. No ambassadors were appointed between the two Governments, whose relations were handled by these ministries. North and South helped each other against local opponents and there was talk of a Greater Yemen embracing Asir, Najran and even Muscat.

The country was in a desperate financial plight as a result of the ending of British subsidies and the departure of the large, free-spending expatriate community which coincided with the closure of the Suez Canal which had been Aden's only other source of income. Faced with the problem of actually running the country, ash-Shaabi showed a definite pragmatism by refusing to dismantle working institutions. Although he had been imprisoned by Nasser, ash-Shaabi believed, like the Egyptian leader, in egalitarianism, imposed by firm authority, and was in no way a communist. Opposing him was an extreme left group, under the leadership of Ismail and Ali Salim al-Baid which called for a complete new beginning with 'scientific socialism' based on rural soviets, collectivization of land, a people's militia, nationalization of banks and foreign trade and the export of revolution throughout the Peninsula. These policies divided the party at the Zinjibar Congress of March 1968 and the leftist view prevailed. Ash-Shaabi, however, persuaded the army that its status would be threatened by the proposed militia and, on his behalf, it arrested his leading opponents.

Ash-Shaabi had, however, been alarmed by the strength of the extremists and he moved to the left. He spoke of the socialist path and the redistribution of land. He took control of imports although he was still anxious to encourage the investment of foreign capital. He called on the Saudi people to overthrow their monarch and provided bases for the Dhofari rebels. His numerous visits abroad included Moscow and Pyongyang (North Korea) among the destinations. These moves, at a time when the YAR was moving into the Saudi orbit, led to verbal hostilities between San'a and Aden.

Ash-Shaabi had released his left-wing opponents and even included some of them in his Government. In June 1969 he quarrelled over the posting of an officer with the Minister of the Interior, Muhammad Ali Haitham, a man with very similar political views, and dismissed him. Haitham, who had considerable influence with the army and with the tribes, thereupon joined forces with the left, and later that month, in a bloodless coup, ash-Shaabi and his cousin, Prime Minister Faisal Abd al-Latif, were deposed. He was replaced by a five-man Presidential Council, chaired by Salim Rubai Ali and including Ismail and Haitham, who was appointed Prime Minister. The shift to the left was signalled immediately by the recognition of East Germany by the new Minister of Foreign Affairs, Ali Salim al-Baid. In October, having called on all Arab countries to follow his lead, he severed diplomatic relations with the USA.

There followed a period of harsh repression with constant speeches about conspiracies, mass arrests with special courts untrammelled by ordinary law 'to review anti-state activity'. Large numbers of citizens, some estimated up to a quarter of the population, fled abroad. The army, whose commander escaped to Taiz, and the police, were subjugated through purges and indoctrination. Military training started in schools. Ismail encouraged the spread of party branches throughout the country.

The Government called for revolution in 'the Occupied Gulf' and refused to recognize the independence of Bahrain, Qatar and the UAE. There was a frontier clash with Saudi Arabia at al-Wadiah in November 1969. Such strong support was given to the rebels in Dhofar that they also succeeded in capturing Salala. Haitham, however, worked to improve relations with the YAR and in November 1970 was the first South Yemeni Prime Minister to visit Taiz where he urged unification. A new Constitution, with its adoption of the name People's Democratic Republic of Yemen (PDRY) was announced. Drawn up by an East German and an Egyptian, its commitment to socialism, tolerance of Islam, stress on the rights of women, and vesting of all power in the party differed greatly from the Constitution adopted shortly afterwards in the YAR. This, drawn up after intensive local consultations, was, more than any other recent Arab Constitution, based on Islamic principles, with a constitutional court of *ulama*, empowered to ensure that laws were based on Islamic principles.

Abd al-Fattah Ismail, as Secretary-General, was immersed in party and doctrinal affairs, building a following amongst the urban proletariat. Ali, the Chairman, visited the People's Republic of China, returning inspired by Maoist ideas of spreading the revolution in the countryside by encouraging the seizure of land by the peasants and in 1970 he signed a series

of decrees nationalizing businesses and concentrating most economic activities in the hands of the state. In the same year Aden ceased to be a free port. Aid from the USSR alone kept the country afloat. Facing the problem of actually administering a country in a perpetual economic crisis, Haitham tried to moderate foreign and domestic policies to encourage foreign and local investment. His colleagues, Ali and Ismail, both adopted a more dogmatic approach and conspired against him. He was replaced in August 1971 by Ali Nasser Muhammad, the Minister of Defence. There followed a new wave of purges and arrests.

The Constitutions of 1970 had shown that there was no common ideological grounds between North and South Yemen and the financial dependence of one on Saudi Arabia and the other on the USSR prevented any move towards unity: indeed neither the Cabinet of the PDRY nor that of the YAR contained a Minister of Unity Affairs. The situation was intensified by the presence on Northern territory of thousands of exiles from the South, armed and funded by Saudi Arabia. Border incidents followed their incursions and a leading northern tribal sheikh was lured across the frontier and murdered with 60 of his followers. In San'a, army officers, who were partly funded by Saudi Arabia, called for war to end communism in the South. Each side accused the other of increasingly grave acts of aggression and in September there was widespread fighting which continued for several days, in the course of which the North captured Kamaran. An Arab League mission mediated a cease-fire and then, on 28 October 1972, to general amazement, an agreement was reached in Cairo, Egypt, which provided for a single unified state, with one flag, one capital, one leadership, with single legislative, executive and judicial organs. A formal Treaty of Union was signed between the two Presidents in Tripoli, Libya in November.

Eight committees were set up to discuss the details of unification with instructions to finalize proceedings within a year, after which a new Constitution would be put to a referendum. Saudi Arabia and the USSR both publicly welcomed the union but each feared that its own protégé would be the weaker partner and become submerged beneath the predominance of the opposing camp. Conservatives in San'a, who had contacts with Saudi Arabia, put obstacles in the way of progress and when in May 1973 a leading opponent of unification was murdered, it was generally believed that Aden had been responsible. President al-Iryani personally favoured unification but admitted that little progress had been made by the committees. After his removal from office, prospects for unity seemed to increase, for his successor, Lt-Col Ibrahim al-Hamadi, established cordial personal relations with Ali; each felt the support of the other would be beneficial in internal politics in which each was under threat, and in foreign affairs in weakening dependence on their respective patrons. They agreed on a gradual approach to unity through economic co-operation and in February 1977 they constituted a council of themselves and senior ministers to meet every six months. A joint diplomatic mission toured the oil states. There was speculation that there would be an important announcement concerning unification when al-Hamadi visited Aden in October 1974 but, two days before he was due to arrive, he was murdered. After his death Lt-Col Ahmad ibn Hussein al-Ghashmi, his successor, established closer contacts with the Saudis and relations with Aden deteriorated.

The death of King Faisal enabled the establishment of diplomatic relations with Saudi Arabia and in August 1977 Ali visited Riyadh. A cease-fire was announced with Oman. Kuwait and Abu Dhabi provided aid. Relations with Britain improved and the Aden refinery was taken over by agreement. In October 1977 at the UN Ali made preliminary overtures to the USA. He tried to maintain equal loyalty to the USSR and the People's Republic of China. All these moves angered Ismail who wanted friendship exclusively with the USSR and with Cuba which provided instructors. The foreign policy of the PDRY followed an erratic course as the two leaders struggled for control. Ismail managed to send troops to assist the new revolution in Ethiopia, the success of which was vitally important to the USSR. Ali, meanwhile, had arranged to receive an envoy from the USA.

It seems that at this juncture Ali attempted to establish with al-Ghashmi the same close ties that he had had with al-Hamadi. He sent a special messenger in whose briefcase a bomb, possibly placed by an agent of Ismail, exploded, killing both the YAR

President and the envoy. Fighting immediately broke out in Aden, either because Ali attempted to arrest his opponents or Ismail ordered an attack, in which it is said Soviet and Cuban elements took part, on the presidential palace. Ali was captured, found guilty of numerous crimes and executed.

THE NORTH GOES RIGHT (1970–1978)

Abd ar-Rahman al-Iryani, who had succeeded Sallal, played an indispensable role in national reconciliation after eight years of war. An obviously pious Muslim with a liberal background, he had to take account of a central government weakened by the war, conservative tribal sheikhs and the *ulama*, and young modernisers and townsfolk anxious for reform against a background of financial crisis with an army demanding expensive new equipment. He played a major part in drafting a Constitution which was a real attempt to find a political system suitable to the country. Consequently, the first (indirect) elections in Yemeni history took place in April 1971.

In foreign affairs he succeeded in creating good relations with all the Arab states and with the West without alienating the USSR. The YAR could reasonably be described as a neutral country, despite its government's dependence on Saudi Arabia for financial aid. This largesse was also extended to influential individuals, especially the tribal chiefs whose domination of the Consultative Council hampered moves towards the unity with the South agreed in 1972.

Within a month of its signature, its principal architect, the Prime Minister Mohsin al-Aini, a man of leftist tendencies but influential tribal background, resigned. Al-Iryani appointed a deeply religious conservative, Qadi Abdullah al-Hajari to succeed al-Aini. Al-Hajari immediately went to Riyadh to re-assure the Saudis and received financial aid in return for renouncing the Yemeni claim to Asir and Najran. Al-Hajari made no attempt at administrative reform in a period of inefficiency and corruption and executed several supporters of unification. In August 1973, al-Iryani went into exile to show his discontent but returned to build up support against his Prime Minister whom, in February 1974, he felt strong enough to replace by the more competent and progressive Dr Hassan Makki. In June a plot backed by Iraq to overthrow the regime was discovered and al-Iryani opposed any strong action. When the army and tribal leaders threatened a coup, he resigned and went to live in Syria.

His successor was Lt-Col Ibrahim al-Hamadi, not a tribesman but a member of the Qadi class, who appointed al-Aini as his Prime Minister. He suspended the Constitution and the Consultative Council. Al-Hamadi gradually became immensely popular, with inspiring oratory, evident honesty and sincerity and his youth (he was about 30). He seemed to represent a new generation and engendered new hope after decades of harsh rule and civil war. He and al-Aini made a determined effort to eradicate corruption but in January 1975, feeling the need of a technocrat with financial expertise, al-Hamadi appointed Abd al-Aziz Abd al-Ghani as Prime Minister.

During 1975 al-Hamadi travelled widely, visiting nearly every Arab country, Iran and Europe. He returned with financial aid which would enable him to launch new projects and reduce dependence on Saudi Arabia, thus realizing one of his main objectives. He was concerned to develop rural areas on which he concentrated the ambitious development plan of 1977. He paid special attention to the Shafais and enlisted their help in making the army less a monopoly of Zaidi tribal notables. He aimed at a strong centralized state with wide political participation and he encouraged the emergence of the leftist National Democratic Front (NDF). These moves offended the practically independent northern chiefs, some of whom rebelled and were consequently bombed by the airforce. On the night of 11/12 October 1977 al-Hamadi and his brother were murdered. The assassins were never caught nor were the motives for the crime established. He was succeeded by the Chief of Staff, Ahmad al-Ghashmi, a tribesman of the Hashid confederation. A Shafai officer attempted to incite an uprising in Taiz but al-Ghashmi, with the help of the Zaidi tribes, crushed it and the rebels with other members of the NDF sought refuge in Aden where Ismail hoped to use them to bring about unity by overthrowing the Government in San'a. Al-Ghashmi therefore loosened ties with Aden and strengthened relations with Saudi

Arabia. He spoke of democracy and nominated a 99-man Constitutional Assembly which was to prepare the way for eventual elections. Preoccupied with day-to-day affairs, he had neither the ability nor the time to make a mark on Yemeni history before his murder on 24 June 1978.

ABD AL-FATTAH ISMAIL AND ALI NASSER MUHAMMAD (1979–1986)

After the execution of Ali in July 1978 several days of heavy fighting ensued with a new flood of refugees to the North. Ali Nasser Muhammad became Chairman of the Presidential Council to which were added the communist, Ali Badeeb and the former guerrilla, Ali Antar. Ismail succeeded in his ambition of changing the NLF into a 'Vanguard Party'–the Yemen Socialist Party (YSP)–with stringent rules for admission and discipline and which contained all his close collaborators, including al-Baid. In December Ismail became Head of State.

The YAR, now led by Col Ali Abdullah Saleh, blamed Aden for the murder of al-Ghashmi and prevailed upon the other Arab states to suspend relations with the PDRY. In February 1979 the PDRY launched an attack against the North in an effort to bring about unity by force. In well-planned attacks the main frontier towns were captured and the YAR army appeared to be on the verge of disintegration. Other Arab states intervened and on 30 March in Kuwait the two Presidents signed an agreement to unite, almost identical with that signed nearly seven years before.

In January 1980 it was stated that 134 articles of a constitution had been agreed. Previously, Ismail had visited the USSR where he signed a Treaty of Friendship which appeared more intimate than those with other Arab states. There was general surprise when on 20 April 1980 he resigned on grounds of ill health, was given an honorary title and went into exile in the USSR.

Ali Nasser Muhammad resumed the Presidency and although he still maintained the Soviet alliance he showed that it was not exclusive by visiting Saudi Arabia, where he established his Muslim credentials by performing *umrah*. He also attended the Islamic Summit in Ta'if. Saudi Arabia gave generous help after floods in March 1982 in which it was estimated that 500 people had perished and 64,000 were made homeless. The hostility to Oman which had existed since independence and continued despite the defeat of the Dhofari rebels nearly a decade before finally ended with an agreement to exchange ambassadors, although this did not happen for several years.

The departure of Ismail did not end Aden's support for the NDF which was extremely active in 1980 and 1981. The two Yemens also adopted different stances in the Iran–Iraq War. San'a was, however, angered by not being allowed to join the Co-operation Council of the Arab States of the Gulf (Gulf Co-operation Council—GCC) and drew nearer to Aden. After a visit by Saleh, in December 1981, Muhammad agreed to reduce help to the NDF and the two Presidents laid down common foreign policy goals in which Saleh appeared to make concessions. They constituted themselves the Supreme Yemeni Council, which would hold regular meetings to discuss the practical details of unification. They also set up joint ministerial committees. Sessions in San'a in August 1983 and in Aden in March 1984 showed some co-ordination of foreign policy. In January 1985 the PDRY and the YAR agreed to co-operate in joint exploitation of natural resources.

Local elections were held in 1981 in which the YSP announced that it had received 94.6% support. Despite nearly 20 years of official condemnation of tribalism, it was noticeable that the President entrusted more and more posts to people from his native Dathina and Abyan. However, when in March 1985 Muhammad decided to divest himself of the Premiership, a Saiyid from Hadramawt, Haidar Abu Bakr al-Attas, succeeded him.

In February 1985 Ismail returned from exile and was later given a place on the Politburo. He was clearly concerned that Muhammad regarded the purity of Marxist-Leninist dogma as secondary to the practical needs of the country. In January 1986 Muhammad's attempt to arrest or kill his opponents at a meeting of the Politburo was only partially successful and triggered a brief but intensive civil war in which at least 2,000, including 55 senior party figures, were killed. The tribes of

Dathina rallied to his side while those of the north-west fought to avenge Ali Antar, who had been killed in the Politburo fighting. Ismail disappeared and his body was never found: al-Baid, of whom Muhammad had hoped to rid himself, escaped. Some 6,000 foreigners were evacuated to Djibouti. Muhammad fled to Ethiopia where he was joined by the navy which had remained loyal to him. During the battle Saleh closed the frontier to prevent YAR tribesmen from joining either side.

ALI ABDULLAH SALEH AS PRESIDENT OF THE YAR
(1978–1990)

Evidence that the assassination of al-Ghashmi in October 1974 was plotted from outside the YAR is provided by the fact that no group in San'a was prepared to take advantage of the incident. There was no obvious successor so a temporary Presidential Council was formed in 1978, under the chairmanship of the politically neutral Speaker of the Constitutional Assembly, Qadi Abd al-Karim al-Arshi. Nearly a month later the Assembly, by a large majority, elected as President, Lt-Col Ali Abdullah Saleh, commander of the Taiz military area, who was, like his predecessor, a tribesman of the Hashid. He appointed al-Arshi Vice-President and Abd al-Ghani retained his portfolio as Prime Minister. At first his position was extremely precarious and he was fortunate to escape assassination in September and to survive what appeared to be an attempted military coup, with backing from Aden, in October. The Shafai South, restless since the murder of al-Hamadi, was stirred up by the NDF, based on Aden. There were also reports of fighting in the regions of Sada, Marib and Jawf and the YAR appeared on the point of collapse as Saleh was forced to revert back to the old Imamate policy of relying on the Hashid and Bakil to deal with internal threats. Only the intervention of other Arab states saved the country from complete disaster during the war with the South in September 1979.

Over the next few years Saleh acquired the skills, shown by the old Imams, required to rule an unusually difficult country. He also made a persistent effort to win support by increasing public participation in government. One of his first speeches promised 'real democracy', starting with municipal elections which took place in 1979. Later that year he appointed a 15-man Consultative Council and expanded the membership of the Constituent Assembly. In February 1980 he announced that there would be a general election and in May he set up a 'committee for national dialogue' to prepare for it. He also launched a new party, the Unified Yemeni Organization, with a charter that comprised both the principles of the Revolution and the 'sublime principles of Islam'. In October he called into being a National Assembly of 1,000 representatives, 700 of whom were elected through elections in co-operatives which met in August 1982.

Progress towards elections was disrupted by increased activity by the NDF, whose leader, Sultan Ahmad Omar, stated that he would only participate if the Government committed itself to a series of measures which included land reform, nationalization of industry and less dependence on Saudi Arabia. The NDF overran considerable areas during 1981 but then Aden decreased its support and the Zaidi tribes, worried about the advance of the 'godless', rallied to the support of Saleh. Early in 1982 Saleh ordered a full-scale offensive, defeated the NDF and allowed the survivors to be reintegrated in the North.

In October 1980 there had been a change of Prime Minister when Abd al-Ghani, the Shafai economist, was replaced by another technocrat, an agricultural economist, Dr Abd al-Karim al-Iryani, a member of the Qadi class. In general Saleh's policy was to choose competent officials and not to interfere in administrative matters.

In foreign policy Saleh avoided total commitment either to the East or the West. The Saudis provided enough aid to keep his Government solvent but not enough to permit total economic independence. At the UN, the YAR abstained from voting on the Afghanistan question. Saleh's ministers sought aid and investment from the West but Saleh also needed to obtain Soviet arms and exert pressure on Aden to reduce its backing for the NDF. As a result relations between the YAR and Saudi Arabia were downgraded. Saleh refused to endorse the US Rapid Deployment Force but did not join the Tripartite Pact of Libya, Ethiopia and the PDRY formed to denounce it. The Republic

did not join the GCC but sent volunteers to fight for Iraq against Iran. In December 1982 the YAR provided a base for 2,000 Palestine Liberation Organization (PLO) guerrillas after their expulsion from Beirut.

In 1984 Saleh revisited Moscow and signed a treaty of friendship similar to those concluded by the USSR with Syria and the PDRY, but refused to Libya. About the same time it was announced that although the USSR had failed to find oil in the YAR, the USA had succeeded in doing so. Western help was essential for its exploitation and also in the development of agriculture to which the Government attached almost equal importance. Also, in the same year, the YAR signed a five-year trade and aid agreement with the EC.

In November 1982 an earthquake devastated central Yemen, resulting in the deaths of more than 3,000 people and causing damage worth an estimated US $3,000m. In December al-Iryani was put in charge of reconstruction and Abd al-Ghani replaced him as Prime Minister. In 1985 al-Iryani was given the newly-created post of Chairman of the Supreme Council for Petroleum and Mineral Resources and another well-known economist, Dr Muhammad Said al-Attar was appointed Deputy Prime Minister and Minister of Development. Much of the attention of the Government had to be devoted to economic matters as the country exported less than 1% of the value of its imports. Until its petroleum could be fully exploited, the YAR was dependent upon aid and remittances from citizens working abroad and had to observe the utmost austerity in restricting imports. There was, however, a great improvement in the infrastructure with the spread of roads and electricity. A particularly striking feature of the 1980s was the emergence of educated women, holding responsible posts in business and administration. Central Government control was loose in the tribal areas with the mountain tribes benefiting both from Saudi subsidies and from smuggling goods across its border.

In May 1983 Saleh unexpectedly resigned, announcing that he would not stand for re-election. The Assembly, however, unanimously re-elected him for a further five years. In July 1985 the YAR held its first free elections when 17,500 representatives were elected to local councils working for co-operative development. About one-half of the electorate voted and the polls were seen as a significant development which would eventually bring into political life educated young Yemenis and weaken the powers of the tribal sheikhs. On 5 July 1988 the long-postponed general election took place for 128 seats in the new 159-member Consultative Council which replaced the old Constituent Assembly. The remaining 31 members were appointed by the President. More than a million registered to vote, including 60,000 women, and more than 1,200 candidates stood for election. None of the 15 women candidates was successful. Approximately one-sixth of the elective seats, including all six constituencies in San'a were won by candidates sympathetic to the Muslim Brotherhood and many others to tribesmen of conservative background. The Consultative Council was to have a life of five years and was empowered to legislate, to ratify treaties and supervise the work of government, in which it could request a vote expressing 'no confidence'. Its first action was to re-elect Saleh for another five years by 152 votes to none with two abstentions and five absentees. The post was strengthened by no longer having to share power with the Military Command Council. Saleh announced his aim to achieve democracy without repression, claimed that there were no political prisoners and stated that he would give priority to agriculture and industry making use of local materials. Abd al-Ghani was reappointed as Prime Minister. Subsequent events showed that the Consultative Council operated more freely than almost any other in the Arab world, criticizing government policies despite the intensification of a personality cult of the President.

In foreign policy Saleh aimed at being on good terms with as many states as possible by avoiding involvement in other people's quarrels. The exploitation of petroleum, which was first exported in December 1987, required investment and technology from most major states. In Arab matters the YAR tried to work through bilateral agreements through which joint committees arranged co-operation over a wide range of activities. In November 1987, following an Arab League decision that members might resume diplomatic relations with Egypt, the YAR did so and in mid-1988 President Mubarak visited San'a. The Government tried to maintain good relations with both Iraq and Syria and the Prime Minister negotiated aid agreements with both countries for the development of the petroleum industry. In October 1988 the Organization of the Islamic Council met in San'a, the first time that the city had hosted an international gathering on such a large scale. Saleh visited Pakistan and China, where he obtained aid worth $42m. In January 1989 President Saddam Hussain of Iraq visited San'a in order to thank Yemeni troops for their participation in the war with Iran. In the same year the YAR became a founder-member of the Arab Co-operation Council (ACC), with Jordan, Iraq and Egypt. The ACC was formed with the object of creating an Arab Common Market of those states that were ineligible to join the GCC, allowing free movement of labour and capital within the bloc and hoping to double trade between its members in the next few years.

Despite occasional frontier incidents, the outcome of local rivalries rather than government policies, relations with Saudi Arabia were generally good. The Saudi-Yemeni Co-ordinating Committee, formed in 1975, continued to meet to distribute aid. In May 1989 Saudi Arabia lifted almost all restrictions imposed on Yemeni emigrant workers, giving them almost equal rights with Saudi citizens. At various stages of the process towards unity with the South, Saleh travelled to Saudi Arabia to reassure King Fahd.

The USSR continued to provide training and technical personnel and in January 1990 Saleh visited the USA for the first time and was saluted by President Bush as 'a pillar of stability'. Saleh took every opportunity to put forward the case for the Palestinians and returned with increased aid.

Following a bomb explosion in the Grand Mosque in San'a in March 1989, three alleged members of the Muslim Brotherhood were summarily executed. In August 12 people were killed in the Marib area when tribesmen opposed the introduction of vehicle registration (which made smuggling more difficult). Following reports of unrest amongst Zaidi tribesmen who realized that the Shafais would be a majority in a united Yemen, their leader, the Paramount Sheikh of the Hashid who had been one of the most influential figures in the country for nearly 30 years, claimed that tribesmen should retain their right to bear arms. Religious leaders, too, continued to regard the Southerners as atheistic communists and to oppose unification.

THE PDRY 1986–1990

When Ali Nasser Muhammad attempted his coup in January 1986, the Prime Minister, Haidar Abu Bakr al-Attas, was on a mission to India, which he interrupted by visiting Moscow, USSR, hoping for some intervention to achieve a peace settlement. Upon his return, he assumed Muhammad's posts as President and Secretary-General of the YSP and appointed as Prime Minister the Deputy Prime Minister and Minister of Fisheries, Dr Yasin Said Numan. As a result of casualties and mass arrests of Muhammad's supporters, the Council of Ministers, the Politburo and the Central Committee underwent drastic changes. The first problem of the new regime was to restore a situation of normality. There were reports of three assassination attempts aimed at al-Attas. Muhammad had taken refuge in the North, where he was allegedly joined by numerous armed supporters. It was uncertain whether Saleh would be willing or able to prevent Muhammad and his supporters launching an invasion but, with assistance from the USSR, he managed to counteract any such action. Most of Muhammad's supporters who had been detained were gradually released and al-Attas succeeded, by a series of amnesties, in persuading most of those who had fled to return, including the entire navy which had sailed to Ethiopia. By October it was felt safe to hold the delayed general election in which 176 candidates contested the 111 seats in the Supreme People's Council. Al-Attas was elected President for five years but it became apparent that al-Baid, Secretary-General of the YSP, held an equally important post.

In December 1986 the Supreme Court began the public trial of Muhammad and 93 others (48 of whom, including the ex-President, were tried *in absentia*) on charges of treason and terrorist activities. After a year, death sentences were passed on 35 of the defendants (19, including Muhammad, still *in absentia*). There were international appeals for clemency and

al-Attas commuted 24 of the death sentences to life imprisonment. Only five were actually executed and in May 1988 Muhammad was offered a retrial if he returned voluntarily. Later that year 35 of the remaining 59 prisoners, including three former ministers, were released. In January 1990, prior to unification, there was a general amnesty for all political offenders.

At a time when it was imperative to neutralize Muhammad and his followers, much power appeared to rest with the military, particularly in the hands of his tribal opponents from the north-west, to the extent that the fourth Congress of the YSP in June 1987 expressed concern about 'opportunist rightists' in the armed forces. Despite the glorification of Ismail, Ali Antar and other 'martyrs' of January 1986, there appeared to be little change in either the internal affairs or foreign policy of the new regime. In the same year al-Attas stated that the relationship with the USSR was the 'corner-stone' of government policy and there was close co-operation in trade, petroleum and economic matters. The USSR replaced the weapons destroyed in January 1986 and agreed to continue aid until 2005.

Nevertheless one of the first visits that al-Attas made as President of the PDRY was to assure King Fahd of Saudi Arabia that there would be no further encouragement to incite revolutionary activities against the Saudi Government. It was noticeable that King Fahd did not, unlike his brother Faisal, finance or arm exiled opponents of the Aden regime. A joint ministerial commission was established, several projects were financed, and the Saudis were the first to give aid after disastrous floods in March 1989. The reconciliation with Oman continued and in October 1988 al-Attas became the first PDRY Head of State to visit Muscat. Amidst references to 'brotherhood', several agreements were signed including one to delimit the frontier. Other Gulf states provided aid. Relations with Ethiopia, a supporter of Muhammad during the fighting of January 1986, were restored as were those with Somalia which had been strained since Ismail had sent troops to oppose the advance into the Ogaden in the war of 1977. As part of the PDRY's attempt to present a more moderate image abroad, diplomatic relations were restored with Morocco, and with Egypt as soon the Arab League lifted its veto. Al-Attas visited Baghdad, Iraq, in July 1988, and later there was an agreement to increase the processing of Iraqi petroleum at Aden refinery with Iraqi crude piped across Saudi Arabia to Yanbu. Dr Abd al-Aziz adh-Dhali in 1989 became the first PDRY Minister of Foreign Affairs to visit an EC capital, and also in 1989 William Waldegrave of the British Foreign Office was the first British Minister to visit Aden since independence. Al-Attas stated that the USA had been approached for the resumption of relations, which were, in fact, restored just before unification. The PDRY therefore ended its separate existence with no outstanding feuds and indeed had achieved international recognition by election to the UN Security Council. In January 1990 al-Attas opened a regional peace conference called by the Organization for Afro-Asian Solidarity, attended by 45 states with a call for withdrawal of all fleets from the Red Sea, the Gulf and the Indian Ocean: Western nations, Iran and Israel were not invited.

Meanwhile, the domestic economy had collapsed after two decades of ideologically-led mismanagement and people were on the verge of starvation. Despite some pressure from military leaders, the USSR under the leadership of Gorbachev stated that there was no need for the Aden base after the end of the cold war and Soviet aid declined from $400m. in 1988 to $50m. in 1989. In 1989 the communist regimes of Eastern Europe started to collapse. There changes were set in motion by a popular revolt but in the PDRY they were introduced by the Government. In early July the YSP set up six working parties to study a comprehensive list of changes, including that of its own role and relationship with the state, and concerning economic, administrative and cultural affairs. There had long been a chronic shortage of housing and it was announced that private individuals might build for sale or rent; then private ownership of hotels and factories was permitted. Adenis were encouraged to invest their capital locally with exemptions from taxes and tariffs. Foreign investors might transfer profits abroad. In particular investment was sought in petroleum, tourism and the port of Aden. In December the Government promised to compensate owners of shares in the banks nationalized in 1969. Just before unification the Government announced that the properties of exiles would be restored. The ponderous communist bureaucracy was dismantled and government monopolies, such as that of supplying ships, were ended. In February 1990 plans were published to re-establish Aden as a free zone.

Al-Baid put forward a programme for political *perestroika*, including a rotating presidency, civil rights and correction of 'wrong stands on Arab and Islamic culture and religion'. In October Numan stated that a multi-party system was 'very necessary for democracy' and that the private sector should 'play its true role in economic developments'. Al-Baid said that things had gone wrong because of the 'leftist adventurist tendency rather than right-wing deviationism'. Pluralism and democracy were more important than ideology. The Institute of Scientific Socialism was renamed the Institute of Social Sciences while the two ash-Shaabis and Salim Rubai Ali were rehabilitated as they had been condemned in the 'absence of democratic thought'. Citizens were given the right to travel abroad. There were local elections, the fifth since independence but the first with any real choice of candidates.

In December 1989 the YSP ended its monopoly and the formerly outlawed Nasserist Unionist Organization applied for recognition and was quickly followed by the Yemeni Unity Party (YUP), the first to have members both South and North of the frontier. Even the partisans of former President Muhammad were able to form the Unionist Democratic Party. In January 1990 the ban on foreign publications was lifted and later permits were issued for a range of independent newspapers and journals.

The relaxation of controls triggered inflation which, in turn, provoked an unprecedented series of strikes for higher pay. The first, on 13 January 1990, was at the petroleum refinery and was followed by strikes in the electricity, banking, textile and fishing industries. Workers claimed that the cost of living had risen by 30% and wages had not kept pace. The Government made concessions and the strikes were usually of short duration.

THE ROAD TO UNIFICATION

Presidents Saleh and Ali Nasser Muhammad had established a good working relationship but during the fighting in Aden in January 1986, San'a remained neutral and abstained from commenting upon events in Aden. The new regime of President al-Attas quickly declared its commitment to unity but the situation was complicated by the presence of Muhammad and his followers in camps just north of the frontier. Gradually the conciliatory policy of the Aden Government led many of them to go home and those that remained refrained from provoking any confrontational incidents between the two states.

In July 1986 both Heads of State met for the first time as participants in a summit in Tripoli, Libya. Although an agreement was not reached they consulted again in September and Saleh stated that he would give priority to unity. Although the exiles were inactive, their presence still caused difficulties and after a death sentence had been passed on Muhammad, Aden demanded his extradition which San'a refused. Kuwait tried to mediate a settlement of the refugee problem but it was still a high priority when al-Baid went to San'a in July 1987 in the hope of co-ordinating economic and social policies. Meanwhile, there had been disputes concerning the exact location of the frontier which had never been delimited and was particularly vague in the area of Shabwa where it was anticipated that petroleum would be found. In December 1987 al-Iryani denied that there had been armed clashes but in the following April there were reports that both sides were reinforcing their border troops. Saleh declared that the long-standing dispute could only be resolved through unification and in May al-Baid travelled to San'a and negotiated a series of agreements. The Higher Yemeni Council, the Joint Ministerial Committee and other joint committees were reconstituted. There was a declaration that there should be no recognition of frontiers drawn up during foreign occupation or during the reign of the Imamate, existing border posts would be replaced by new ones, jointly manned, movement between the two states should be unrestricted, troops should be withdrawn from frontier areas and there should be joint exploitation of a zone of 2,200 sq km in the Marib/Shabwa area which would be demilitarized. Saleh travelled to Riyadh, Saudi Arabia, to reassure King Fahd that this *rapprochement* was not directed against Saudi Arabia, while Muhammad declared that

he welcomed the agreement. The first practical results were the abolition of the need for passports for travel between North and South and a meeting of the Ministers of Petroleum who agreed on the establishment of the Yemeni Company for Investment in Oil and Mineral Resources for joint exploitation of Marib/ Shabwa. The head office was in San'a, its capital was $10m. and it was soon able to announce that it had received 45 bids from international oil companies. The Southern Minister of Petroleum said that neither North nor South could develop properly unless they were united while al-Baid spoke of 'creating unified economic interests that would be a material basis for the political success of unity'. A major objective was to revive the port of Aden as a free zone and to provide it with a larger and more prosperous hinterland. It was clear that neither state could finance its own development unilaterally or attract enough outside help but through unification this would be possible. The Arab Fund for Economic and Social Development (AFESD) agreed to provide $18m. and subsequently $63m. to link the two electricity systems. It appeared that the two Yemens were now set upon at least economic integration.

However a financial crisis, leading to *perestroika* started in Aden shortly afterwards and in the general ferment, the stability of the YAR became more attractive. In November 1989 al-Iryani and the Assistant Secretary-General of the YSP, Salim Salih Muhammad spent three days in San'a discussing a 136-article Constitution, based on agreements reached by the constitutional committee established following the war in 1979. It was published while Saleh was in Aden and he proposed that it should be referred to both Legislatures and then be put to a referendum; this set a target date for unification of November 1990. Al-Baid emphasized that unity in Yemen should be seen as a step towards full Arab unity. Delegations were sent to all the Arab countries to inform them of Yemen's intention to form a single state. The PDRY removed obstacles to a joint foreign policy by ending its last diplomatic dispute, including the restoration of relations with the USA and an invitation to Sultan Qaboos of Oman to visit Aden. The ACC had no objection to the adherence of the PDRY. It was agreed that the YSP and the General People's Congress (GPC), which was regarded as its northern equivalent, should preserve their independence and that there should be room for political parties; the YUP, set up in January 1990, was the first to recruit from both North and South. In the same month al-Iryani travelled to Aden to discuss preparations for elections and for merging the Ministries of the Interior. Plans were announced for a merger of the state airlines. A new press law was introduced in both states. A few days later the two Cabinets held a joint meeting in San'a. All political prisoners were released and a joint committee set up to negotiate with other political parties. This led to an agreement concluded in April that there should be no foreign funding nor campaigning in mosques or barracks and Saleh welcomed 'a multi-party system provided that it is of Yemeni origin'. In February there was a second joint Cabinet meeting, in Aden, at which 46 laws were approved on such matters as customs procedures, taxation, trade unions and education. Plans were drawn up for a single currency from a unified central bank and later Aden promised pay rises to ensure parity with wages in the North. After a brief summit in Mukayras, south of the frontier, Saleh visited Riyadh, Saudi Arabia, and announced that King Fahd supported unity 'totally and without limit', although many doubted that he would really welcome a united democratic Yemen on his southern flank. The USSR, USA and the People's Republic of China welcomed the prospect of unity.

In early March 1990 there was a prolonged summit in Taiz, Aden and again in Taiz, which ended without a communiqué, suggesting that problems had arisen. There still appeared to be opposition amongst hard-line communists in Aden while in the North dissatisfaction amongst religious and tribal leaders was more public. There were reports of fighting in the Saada and of tribesmen receiving Saudi arms and money. A leading Muslim Brother attacked 40 articles of the proposed Constitution as unislamic and demanded that the *Shari'a* should be the only source of law. There was concern over Aden's tolerance of alcohol and freedom given to women. In a four-day meeting in San'a in April Saleh and al-Baid decided to pre-empt the opposition by bringing forward the date of unification to 22 May. On 4 May both currencies were declared legal tender. On 21 May the agreement to unite was passed unanimously in Aden but in San'a three Islamic fundamentalist members walked out and five abstained amid demonstrations by their supporters. The following day a joint session of the two Assemblies elected a five-man Presidential Council, headed by Saleh (promoted to the rank of General), al-Baid (Vice-President), Salim Salih Muhammad, Abd al-Ghani and the former Speaker, al-Arshi.

The priorities of the Government of the Republic of Yemen, which were announced in late May 1990, were to develop the country's economic infrastructure and to improve relations with other Arab states. In particular, the Government was committed to resolving long-standing border disputes with neighbouring Saudi Arabia and Oman. In July 1990 both President Mubarak of Egypt and the Chairman of the PLO, Yasser Arafat, visited Yemen and were reported to have discussed regional issues with President Saleh.

In September 1990 it was reported that more than 30 new political parties had been formed in Yemen since unification. The Yemeni Islah Party (YIP), an Islamic party with widespread support in the new House of Representatives, was regarded as the most important of the new parties.

In November 1990 the Government established a Supreme Council for National Defence, which would be responsible for military mobilization and wartime civil defence. The council would be authorized to declare war and states of emergency. It was to be chaired by the President and would comprise the Vice-President and various members of the Council of Ministers.

In mid-May 1991 the people of Yemen voted in a referendum on the Constitution for the unified state. A few days earlier religious fundamentalists and sympathizers, among whom were members of the YIP, demonstrated about the role of Islam under the proposed Constitution, and urged a boycott of the referendum: a clause in the Constitution stated that *Shari'a* law would be the main source of legislation, but the Islamists stipulated that *Shari'a* law should be the only source of legislation. Those who participated in the referendum approved the new Constitution by a large majority, although fewer than 50% of the electorate registered to vote. Members of the YIP and other opposition groups claimed that irregularities in the voting procedure had rendered the result null and void.

YEMEN'S RESPONSE TO THE GULF CRISIS

In August 1990 Iraq's invasion and annexation of Kuwait placed the Government of Yemen in an especially difficult position. The economy of Yemen was heavily dependent on trade with, and aid from, Iraq, and also on aid from Saudi Arabia, which normally hosts very large numbers of Yemeni expatriate workers. Moreover, there was evidence of widespread popular support in Yemen for President Saddam Hussain of Iraq. These factors explained the Government's equivocal response to the Iraqi invasion of Kuwait and to subsequent developments in the Gulf region. In the immediate aftermath of the invasion the Government condemned Iraq, but also criticized the arrival of US and other Western military forces to defend Saudi Arabia. At the summit meeting of leaders of Arab League member states, held in Cairo on 10 August 1990, Yemen voted against the proposal to send Arab forces to Saudi Arabia as part of a multinational force to deter aggression by Iraq. Yemen also abstained in the UN Security Council vote to impose economic sanctions on Iraq. By late August, however, the Government appeared to be committed to implementing the UN sanctions against Iraq, albeit reluctantly. In October the Yemeni Minister of Foreign Affairs, Abd al-Karim al-Iryani, announced that Yemen would support any measures taken to achieve a peaceful withdrawal of Iraqi troops from Kuwait, but that this should result in the withdrawal of all foreign forces from the area.

Yemen's relations with Saudi Arabia deteriorated as a result of Yemen's initial strong opposition to the presence of foreign armed forces in the Gulf and to the ambiguous stance it subsequently adopted in this respect. On 15 September 1990, in what was regarded as a retaliatory action, Saudi Arabia announced that it had withdrawn the privileges which Yemeni workers in Saudi Arabia had previously enjoyed. This resulted in an exodus from Saudi Arabia of an estimated 500,000–800,000 Yemeni workers during October and November, which caused widespread economic and social disruption. The expulsion and return of the Yemeni workers not only caused a reduction in the

country's income from remittances sent home by the expatriates, but also led to a serious increase in unemployment.

In November 1990 the Yemeni Government voted against the UN Security Council resolution to authorize the multinational contingent stationed in the Gulf to use 'all necessary means' against Iraq in order to remove its forces from Kuwait if they had not withdrawn by 15 January 1991. This prompted a visit to Yemen by the US Secretary of State, James Baker, in an attempt to persuade Yemen to modify its position concerning the UN resolution. In late November the Minister of Foreign Affairs, Abd al-Karim al-Iryani, visited France, Germany and Algeria in the hope of gathering support to prevent the UN Security Council resolution from being passed. In December Yemen assumed the chair of the UN Security Council (which rotates on a monthly basis) and the Government increased its efforts to mediate in the Gulf crisis: the Vice-President of Yemen, Ali Salim al-Baid, met King Hussein of Jordan, in Amman, and the Iraqi President, Saddam Hussain, in Baghdad, for talks concerning the crisis. In January 1991 Yemen presented a peace plan in an attempt to prevent war in the Gulf; the plan included an Iraqi withdrawal from Kuwait, the withdrawal of the multinational military force, and the holding of an international conference on the Arab–Israeli conflict. Despite numerous diplomatic initiatives undertaken by the Yemeni Government, prior to the UN deadline of 15 January, the peace plan failed to prevent the outbreak of war in the Gulf on 16–17 January. Following the US-led military offensive against Iraq, Yemen issued a statement in which it condemned the action, and hundreds of thousands of Yemenis demonstrated in support of Iraq. Later in January it was confirmed that US aid to Yemen was to be severely reduced, apparently as a result of Yemen's policy towards Iraq.

POLITICAL AFFAIRS AFTER REUNIFICATION

The two government parties, the Northern GPC and the Southern YSP, had agreed to share power equally until elections were held in November 1992 but within months of the referendum there were reports that extreme members of each were increasing their stocks of weapons for use against the other. Due to the disparity in the population—10m. in the North and two million in the South—posts had to be found in the North for southerners, who were regarded as secularists, indeed as former communists, and whose presence was resented. Northerners were shocked by the unislamic lifestyle of many in Aden and by the enhanced role of women. The deaths and injuries in both cities that attended an Aden–San'a football match were indicative of the mutual animosity.

In September 1991 a YSP official was murdered; in December two more were killed at a party meeting in Ibb, where a fourth was killed in February. Two were later wounded in Sa'ada and another killed in Taiz. In April 1992, the Minister of Justice, Abd al-Wasi Salam, a YSP leader, survived after gunmen opened fire on his car; there was suspicion that the attempt was connected with his imminent departure for Muscat for frontier negotiations. In May the house of Salim Salih Muhammad, a YSP representative on the Presidential Council, was attacked. Only three days later there was a bomb at the house of the Prime Minister who denied that it had any connection with the Oman dispute. In June the YSP claimed, but the Government denied, that there had been an attack on the home of the editor of their newspaper and the brother of the Prime Minister was murdered in the southern port of Shihr: this was seen as an attempt to disrupt the unification process as he had played no part in politics. In July, in circumstances that are disputed, a colonel, a member of the YSP central committee, 'killed himself' after a shootout in which two policemen were also killed: his car which had failed to stop at a road-block was found to be full of weapons. A former Deputy Prime Minister of the PDRY, Anis Hassan Yahya, escaped assassination in Aden and at the beginning of August security forces defused a mine outside the house in San'a of the former Prime Minister Muhammad Ali Haitham. The YSP also claimed that several of their local officials had been shot dead in provincial towns, mainly in the North of the country. However, in September there were reports of bomb attacks on the homes of leading GPC members.

These incidents were only part of the general breakdown of law and order. In August 1991 the Secretary-General of the

GPC, Ahmad al-Asbahi, was seriously wounded in his office by an employee whom he had refused to promote. In September a senior civil servant was killed in an ambush which, it was believed, had been intended for Umar al-Jawi, leader of the National Grouping Party and editor of a strongly anti-Iraqi newspaper which also attacked tribal leaders and Islamic fundamentalists. Shortly afterwards an MP, the son of the paramount chief of the Hashid tribe, survived an ambush which his party blamed on the YSP. In October there were riots in San'a in which public buildings were set on fire, in protest at an incident in which a colonel shot a policeman who had stopped him for driving through a red light; officials stated that two people were killed, while unofficial reports estimated the toll as nine. In December two groups of heavily-armed saboteurs were arrested in Hadramawt. In March 1992 there was a gun-battle in the presidential office when a senior officer killed two guards before being himself killed in a dispute over forged papers. In May the Government outlawed the carrying of firearms in the cities, and there was a possibility that even the *jambiah*, the curved dagger which is the traditional badge of a tribesman, might be banned.

One of the ways in which the YSP could assert its strength was through its control of the trade unions, particularly in Aden. President Saleh declared industrial unrest unpatriotic but in March 1992 100,000 workers in Aden brought everything from the airport to government services and the university to a halt. They threatened a three-day stoppage unless wages were raised by 40%, a job creation scheme for people expelled from Saudi Arabia and a price 'freeze' were implemented but later they settled for 25% backdated to January and a barely credible promise to keep prices at 1991 levels. Different labour grievances then emerged as the staff of the government newspaper in Aden went on strike for parity of wages with their colleagues in the San'a press.

A human rights organization, Amnesty International, asserted that all political prisoners in the South had been released before reunification, although there were possibly 25 in the North. No executions had taken place although there had been five amputations of hands. Much forcibly-nationalized property in the South was restored to its former owners and journalists sacked under Ismail were reinstated. In May 1992 an amnesty was extended to former President Ali Nasser Muhammad and five of his associates.

The Government estimated that the Gulf crisis had cost the Yemeni economy $3,000m., and although some of this was recouped by the sale of petroleum concessions, the economic situation remained serious. Only 20% of debt repayments were met. In March 1992 the budget envisaged a deficit of $1,000m. The general economic conditions and social unrest proved fertile soil for Islamic fundamentalists, who provided education and other services which the state could not. The question of the place of the *Shari'a* in the legal system continued to provoke controversy. The YIP became, after the two government parties, the next strongest and probably displaced the YSP in the North. It seemed, however, likely to split between its religious and its tribal leadership and even within its tribal element. It was also attacked by some religious leaders, such as Sheikh Ahmad ash-Shami (Secretary-General of the al-Haq party), as an instrument of Saudi Arabia and in thrall to old-fashioned tribal sheikhs. President Saleh was said to have guaranteed Vice-President al-Baid that his position would not be affected whatever the result of the elections but that other parties would join the government. Meanwhile, the estimated 30–40 political parties were encouraged to merge in order to reduce electoral confusion.

FOREIGN AFFAIRS AFTER THE GULF WAR

Yemen's stance during the Gulf War was not quickly forgotten in the Arabian peninsula and, one year later, relations with some of its states were still frosty. In the same month the Secretary-General of the Arab League, Dr Ahmad Esmat Abd al-Meguid, on his first visit to San'a, agreed that it would take time for rifts to be healed. On the first anniversary of reunification the only Arab head of state to attend was Yasser Arafat, although Yemen had tried to establish its Arab credentials, by raising the question of Israeli settlements at the UN Security Council and denying that it had approved an Israeli plan to resettle the remaining 1,500 Yemeni Jews. In mid-1992

French, British and US Jewish groups mounted a diplomatic campaign in order to organize the discreet departure from Yemen of the small remaining Jewish community. The Yemeni response was that, whereas emigration was open to all its citizens, emigration to Israel was forbidden by the Constitution. Israel claimed in July 1993 to have secretly airlifted about 250 Yemeni Jews into the country, although the Yemeni Government denied all knowledge of the affair.

In addition to its resentment at Yemen's attitude to the Gulf crisis, Saudi Arabia, which had ceased its financial support of some $600m. per year and had expelled immigrant workers constituting about 8% of the total population of Yemen, disliked Yemen's new political pluralism and free press, and, in any case, can scarcely have been enthusiastic about reunification. Saudi Arabia delayed the sale of its 49% share-holding in the San'a-based airline Yemenia, thus preventing the company's merger with the Adeni airline Alyemda. Contrary to previous practice, Saudi visas were required from Yemeni *Hajj* pilgrims. More seriously, in April 1992, Saudi Arabia warned the four oil companies, including British Petroleum (BP), that were prospecting in the eastern desert in an area where the frontier had not been precisely delimited that they were trespassing on Saudi territory, and, to the great indignation of the Yemenis, the companies ceased work. A similar threat to the US Hunt Oil Co was said to have been withdrawn after an intercession by President Bush. The frontier dispute continued, with the Saudis claiming that the Yemenis were not serious about wanting a settlement while the Yemenis felt that the dispute was being prolonged to sabotage their development. In September 1992, however, a committee of experts assembled in Riyadh to discuss the border dispute. No apparent progress was made, either on this occasion, or at further meetings in October and November. The process was subsequently suspended during Ramadan and the Yemeni elections, but in August 1993, against a background of improved relations between Yemen and Saudi Arabia, the committee assembled for a fifth round of talks aimed at solving the dispute. Little progress had been made by January 1994 when the talks entered their seventh round. Nevertheless, the Minister of Foreign Affairs, Muhammad Salim Basindwa, appointed because of his good relations with the Gulf states, declared that improving relations with Saudi Arabia was his top priority and the eighth round of talks concerning demarcation took place in April.

The Saudis also disapproved of Yemen's increasing friendship with Iran. Both the Iranian Minister of Foreign Affairs, Velayati, and the Speaker of the Majlis, Mahdi Karrubi, visited San'a, and agreements were signed for co-operation in a range of fields. There were proposals for a joint fishing company and for processing Iranian petroleum at Aden refinery. The GCC stopped funding the expansion of Aden port, and Kuwait instructed its airline not to sell tickets to Yemenis. In mid-1993 it was reported that the Ministers of Foreign Affairs of Kuwait and Yemen were to meet in Vienna, Austria, reflecting a gradual improvement in relations between the two states. The meeting was subsequently cancelled, however, following opposition from the Speaker of the Kuwaiti National Assembly. Yemen's one ally in the Arabian peninsula was Oman, with frequent high-level visitors exchanging messages between Sultan and President. In December 1991 President Saleh said that the agreement on frontier delimitation, envisaged in the Oman–PDRY reconciliation of 1988, would be concluded within two weeks. However, opposition arose, as it was believed that Yemen would sign away nearly 6,000 square miles of territory, and the YUP and the local Mahra authorities challenged the Government's right to do so. In October 1992 Yemen and Oman signed an agreement to establish the demarcation of their border. The agreement was officially ratified in December and co-operation between Yemen and Oman in the areas of construction, transport and commerce was subsequently envisaged. In April 1993 the two countries agreed on measures to open border points and increase bilateral trade.

Relations with the three remaining GCC member states also showed signs of gradual improvement. In February 1993 Sheikh Muhammad al-Maktoum, the UAE Minister of Defence, visited Yemen, and in the following month his visit was returned by the Yemeni Minister of Planning and Development. In June 1993 the Yemeni Minister of Foreign Affairs, Muhammad Basindwa, declared that improving relations with the Gulf states was his highest priority, and in the following month he visited Bahrain.

In August 1991 al-Iryani flew to Egypt and relations were repaired, although Cairo later rejected Yemen's proposal for a revival of the ACC, initially without Iraqi participation. Yemen's relations with the other ACC member, Jordan, were cordial, and in September 1991, during a visit to Amman, Prime Minister al-Attas signed a series of agreements for co-operation in trade, agriculture, educational exchanges and tourism. In the same month, Yemen and Iraq signed a cultural agreement, and in May 1992 Iraq undertook to provide teachers to support Yemen's campaign to develop education. Yemen continued to oppose sanctions against Iraq, but in March 1993 Saddam Hussain sent his half-brother to San'a to protest at Yemeni attempts to improve its relations with the Gulf states.

Reconciliation with the Western powers was smoother. The USA, unwilling to offend its more important GCC allies, let it be known that its attitude would depend upon Yemen's actions in the Security Council and over human rights, but in August 1991 it agreed to sell Yemen 300,000 tons of subsidized wheat, more than ever before. Yemen fully supported the US Middle-East peace initiative. US firms were chosen to draw up the master plan for Aden free port and a feasibility study for a gas-fired power station in Marib. In January 1992 the Deputy Secretary of State for Energy, Hanson Moore, visited the country.

The British had been less upset than their allies over Yemen's attitude to the Gulf War, and relations were fully restored in time for a successful visit by al-Iryani to London in February 1992. Al-Baid had already visited Britain in August 1991, followed by a financial team to seek investment in the free port. British firms won various contracts including one to prospect for gold in the Hadramawt and another to print new currency. The cordiality of relations between Britain and Yemen was confirmed by a successful visit of the Yemeni Minister of Planning and Development to London.

In the West there was a growing belief that Yemen had developed into the most genuine democracy in the Arab world—a sentiment articulated by the French Minister of Foreign Affairs on a visit in October 1991. The EC sent a parliamentary delegation to San'a in June 1992 and in the same month the German President, Dr Richard von Weizsäcker, made a state visit during which he promised aid. The Yemeni Chief of Staff, Brig.-Gen. al-Busheiry, also visited Paris. The problems of investment were discussed in July at a conference in Geneva at which the presence of Qatar gratified the Yemenis. The need for aid and also the broad range of the participants in the development of its oil industry—including Japan, Indonesia, Norway and Canada—kept Yemen active diplomatically, although financial difficulties forced the closure of 16 Yemeni embassies at the end of 1992.

Yemen had increasingly been drawn into the affairs of its neighbours across the Red Sea. In July 1991 Yemeni officials collaborated with French diplomats to settle disputes in Djibouti. After the fall of Lt-Col Mengistu, ships of the Ethiopian navy took refuge in Aden: Zimbabwe's Minister of Foreign Affairs helped to mediate and the fleet returned home. More serious was the crisis that arose from the civil war in Somalia, which obliged Yemen to give refuge to more than 60,000 Somali refugees during 1992 and 1993. The Yemeni Government had great problems in accommodating and feeding them. Finally an agreement was reached whereby Yemen would accept further refugees on the understanding that the UN should take responsibility for their welfare.

THE 1993 ELECTIONS AND THE ENSUING POLITICAL CRISIS

In spite of the climate of unrest, voter registration for the legislative elections, scheduled for 27 April 1993, took place between 15 January and 16 February. An outbreak of attacks on expatriate workers prompted a warning, in February, that the Government could not guarantee the safety of expatriate residents owing to the threat of certain hostile Yemeni tribes. There were 3,400 candidates for the 301 seats in the House of Representatives, many standing as independents. Of the major political parties presenting candidates, the GPC, led by the

President, Ali Abdullah Saleh, and the YSP, led by the Vice-President, Ali Salim al-Baid, were the largest. The two other major parties were the YIP, widely reported to have received substantial financial assistance from Saudi Arabia, led by Sheikh Abdullah bin Hussain al-Ahmar, and the Baath (Renaissance) party, led by Mujahid Abu Shuarib. There were also more than 40 smaller parties, but most of them were in alliance with one of the four major parties.

After lively campaigning in the months preceding the elections, the turnout on election day was very high. International observers expressed broad satisfaction with the conduct of the elections, the first nationwide, multi-party elections based on universal suffrage in the Arabian peninsula. Inevitably there were reports of disturbances in several towns and accusations of fraudulent practices by both of the leading parties. When the results were announced the GPC had, not surprisingly, won the majority of the vote and gained 123 of the 301 seats, most of them in the former YAR. The YIP took second place with 62 seats, again mainly in the former YAR, with the YSP relegated to third place with 56 seats, most of them in the former PDRY. The Baath party took seven seats, minor parties five seats and independents 47 seats. Of the 50 women candidates who stood for election, two won seats.

After the election the YIP is reported to have threatened to boycott the new House of Representatives unless it was admitted to government. The three main parties eventually agreed to form a coalition with the GPC and YSP each taking two seats on the Presidential Council and the YIP the one remaining seat. The YIP was also allocated six posts in the Council of Ministers but these did not include the portfolios of education and finance which the party had demanded. However, the leader of the YIP, Sheikh Abdullah bin Hussain al-Ahmar, became Speaker of the House of Representatives. The YSP leadership was disappointed by the election results and became increasingly apprehensive and resentful about the emerging alliance between the GPC and the YIP. The GPC found it easier to co-operate with the YIP on a number of important political issues, especially proposed constitutional changes, than with the YSP; this co-operation was assisted by the fact that the GPC leader's tribe, the Sanhan, belonged to the Hashid tribal federation, of which the YIP leader was the paramount Sheikh. In August 1993 the Vice-President refused to take part in the Government and decided to return to Aden. His departure from San'a marked the official beginning of a political crisis that was to lead to civil war. This crisis intensified following a series of assassinations of YSP officials including the Vice-President's nephew who was shot in Aden on 29 October. It was widely rumoured in San'a that these assassinations were ordered by the President's 'entourage', notably his brother and three half-brothers who commanded key military units and the security services.

In an attempt to put pressure on President Saleh to make concessions that would restore southern influence, the Vice-President had issued an 18-point list of demands in September. They included security and military reforms and decentralization to allow each governorate more freedom in administrative and financial affairs. In November al-Baid declared that the North was attempting to annex the South rather than unifying with it. Efforts to mediate between the two factions by Oman, Jordan, PLO Chairman Arafat, the USA and the *ulama* (religious scholars) failed to resolve the crisis, while the departure of the Vice-President and other southern officials including the Prime Minister, Haidar al-Attas, brought the business of government to a standstill, aggravating already chronic economic problems. Riots in San'a and Taiz in early January 1994 reflected popular discontent at rising prices and the falling value of the Yemeni riyal. Meanwhile the security situation in the country continued to deteriorate. There were more political killings—al-Baid claimed that more than 150 YSP members had been killed since May 1990—and further kidnappings of foreign nationals.

Amidst the deepening political crisis a National Dialogue Committee was formed with representatives from across the political spectrum, to try to work out a formula acceptable to both factions. After months of discussions and deliberations, the committee drew up a 'Document of Pledge and Agreement' on 18 January 1994 which incorporated many of the demands made by al-Baid in his 18-point list. The document proposed major constitutional reform that would clearly define the powers of the Presidential Council, the President and the Vice-President, devolution of power from central government to local and regional assemblies, the restructuring of the armed forces and the arrest and trial of those responsible for the wave of assassinations largely directed at YSP officials. On 20 February the President and Vice-President signed the document at a public ceremony in Amman, Jordan, attended by representatives from Oman, the USA, France, the PLO and the Arab League. There was no reconciliation between the two Yemeni leaders however; they refused to shake hands after signing the document and al-Baid demanded that Saleh order the immediate arrest of his brothers. Al-Baid and his principal lieutenants walked out on follow-up talks and further strained relations with the President by visiting Saudi Arabia and the Gulf states to seek support for their cause. Some analysts argued that President Saleh had no intention of honouring the concessions made in Amman, but only wanted to gain time, having already chosen the military option. The real intentions of the southern leadership were also unclear. Several observers maintained that while some of the YSP leaders wanted secession, the majority had sought to escalate the political crisis in order to topple the President and take over a united Yemen.

The day after the ceremony there were clashes between rival military units in the southern province of Abyan and in other parts of the country. After unification the armed forces of the former YAR and PDRY had not been integrated; the GPC continued to control the northern forces and the YSP those of the south. The fighting that continued sporadically for some months involved not only forces under the command of the GPC and the YSP but also YSP forces loyal to the former South Yemen President, Ali Nasser Muhammad, as well as tribal militias which used the opportunity to promote their own interests. The GPC was reported to have mobilized the powerful Hashid tribal federation, while the YSP called on the support of their traditional rivals, the Bakil tribes. At the beginning of March a joint military committee of northern and southern officers, Jordanian and Omani officers and the US and French military attachés, attempted to disengage the widely dispersed and intermixed rival military units. Jordan, Oman, Egypt and the UAE all made diplomatic efforts to mediate between the two main rival factions but made no progress. In April both Oman and Jordan withdrew from the joint military committee.

THE CIVIL WAR

On 27 April 1994, the anniversary of the general election, a major tank battle took place between rival army units at Amran, some 60 km to the north of San'a. It was the biggest clash between the opposing forces since the crisis began. Some 200 tanks were involved in the fighting; 85 tanks were reported to have been destroyed and more than 400 soldiers killed or wounded. Both sides claimed that the other attacked first. The YSP claimed that the attack was tantamount to a declaration of war, while the President accused al-Baid of secessionism and pledged to fight to defend the unity of the country. During the night of 4 May fighter aircraft under the command of the YSP attacked northern airports at San'a, Taiz and Hodeida, the presidential palace in San'a, the country's two main power stations, Hodeida port, and petroleum storage and pipeline facilities at Marib. Northern aircraft retaliated on 5 May, badly damaging the airport at Aden. The northern military command reported pitched battles in several areas along the old frontier between the YAR and PDRY and claimed that southern forces had suffered heavy losses in seven of the country's 17 provinces. The civil war had begun in earnest. The President declared a 30-day state of emergency and dismissed the Vice-President. France announced that it was evacuating its nationals and the USA advised its citizens to leave. On 10 May Prime Minister al-Attas, a southerner, was dismissed after he appealed for outside forces to help end the civil war. The Minister of Petroleum and Minerals, Hussainoun, was among other YSP members dismissed from their posts in the Council of Ministers. On 21 May al-Baid proclaimed the breakaway 'Democratic Republic of Yemen' (DRY) and began diplomatic efforts to secure recognition of the old frontier. Al-Attas, the former Prime Minister of Yemen, who had joined the secessionist government in Aden, travelled to Egypt to seek the backing of Arab moderates

and called on the West for support and recognition for the southern government. Al-Baid was named President of the new state, with a five-man Presidential Council drawn from a range of political and tribal affiliations, including the opposition League of the Sons of Yemen, the Nasserite Federation for the Liberation of South Yemen, and the wing of the YSP associated with the ex-President of the PDRY, Ali Nasser Muhammad. The breakaway state adopted the same Constitution as the North, and the same legal system, based on Islamic law. President Saleh denounced the secession, offering an amnesty to all those in the former PDRY who rejected it, with the exception of al-Baid and 15 other YSP leaders.

As northern forces advanced on Aden, Saudi Arabia together with Bahrain, Oman, the UAE and Egypt requested a meeting of the UN Security Council to discuss the Yemeni conflict. San'a's UN representative strongly objected to what it considered interference in its internal affairs. Nevertheless, on 1 June the Security Council unanimously adopted Resolution No. 924 appealing for an immediate cease-fire and requesting the dispatch of a UN commission of inquiry to assess prospects for a renewed dialogue between the belligerents. It also urged an immediate cessation of the supply of arms and other materials that might contribute to the conflict. The Resolution, which Prince Bandar bin Sultan, the Saudi Arabian ambassador to Washington, was reported to have played an important role in drafting, deliberately omitted any direct endorsement of Yemeni unity. Two days later the UN Secretary-General, Dr Boutros Boutros-Ghali, appointed the much respected former Algerian Minister of Foreign Affairs, Lakhdar al-Ibrahimi, as his special envoy and head of the fact-finding mission. Spokesmen for the North and South welcomed al-Ibrahimi's appointment and promised their full co-operation. However, before the commission of inquiry began, the Ministers of Foreign Affairs of the GCC meeting on 4–5 June, issued a statement effectively blaming the North for the conflict and implicitly recognizing the DRY. The Ministers warned that continued hostilities would have repercussions for the GCC states, forcing them to adopt appropriate measures against 'the party that does not abide by the cease-fire'. Only Qatar dissented. While Saudi Arabia maintained that its only concern was to prevent the destabilization of the region, many observers argued that the YSP leadership, given the smaller military forces under its command, would not have declared independence unless it had the support of its powerful neighbour. The Government in San'a condemned the GCC statement and Dr Abd al-Karim al-Iryani, the Minister of Planning and Development and principal political counsellor to President Saleh, maintained that they had clear evidence that arms purchased with Saudi funds were being supplied to the South. The North accused Saudi Arabia of encouraging the secessionists in order to create a new petroleum emirate in the Hadramawt under Saudi influence and providing it with an outlet to the Indian Ocean. One of the principal oil concessions in Hadramawt is held by the Nimr company, owned by the Saudi Arabian Ibn Mahfouz family, who were originally from the Hadramawt. Saudi Arabia had not forgiven Yemen for its support for Iraq during the Gulf crisis and feared that a united and democratic Yemen would threaten its supremacy in the Arabian peninsula. Despite official statements of strict neutrality in the conflict, it was widely believed that Egypt was hostile to the North because the GPC leadership had allowed Egyptian Islamist militants to train in camps set up in Yemen under the protection of Sheikh Abd al-Majid az-Zindani, the leading ideologue of the YIP and a member of Yemen's Presidential Council. Sheikh Zindani was reported to have raised 63m. riyals for the northern war effort through collections from mosques and religious associations. Support for the North came from Iraq, Iran and Sudan. The South accused both Iraq and Sudan of providing military assistance to the North, accusations which Iraq and Sudan denied.

By the first week in June northern forces were besieging the southern capital of Aden and there were reports of air attacks on strategic installations and heavy shelling and artillery fire from northern forces. On 6 June, shortly after the arrival of the UN Commission of Inquiry, San'a agreed to observe a cease-fire, as did the South. Al-Ibrahimi managed to secure the agreement of both factions to the formation of a monitoring body to police the truce, but when San'a suggested that the joint military committee should be revived, Aden objected and demanded a full UN multinational peace-keeping force and the withdrawal of northern forces to behind the old frontier between the YAR and the PDRY. The cease-fire lasted only six hours. Talks arranged in Cairo by al-Ibrahimi also collapsed because San'a insisted that it would only negotiate with the YSP in the context of a united Yemen, whereas the South demanded that negotiations should be between two independent states. The southern negotiating team, led by Muhsin bin Farid, the 'Deputy Prime Minister' of the self-proclaimed DRY, walked out of the talks and appealed for UN intervention to enforce a truce and punish the North for continuing its assault on Aden. Southern officials admitted publicly in mid-June that they were being supplied with arms by 'friendly Arab countries'. On 17 June it was reported that military equipment, including 30–40 tanks and more than 100 missiles, had been unloaded at the port of Mukalla in the south over the past two weeks. Later in June there were reports that the South had acquired new MiG-29 fighter planes from Eastern Europe, with Gulf funding, and was using its air power to bomb the Marib oilfields.

At the end of June the UN Secretary-General reported that UN efforts to mediate between the two rival factions had made no progress. He expressed concern that the fighting had not stopped and drew attention to the deteriorating humanitarian situation. The Security Council, meeting on 29 June, adopted Resolution No. 931 which requested that the Secretary-General continue to mediate between the two factions in order to secure a durable cease-fire and called for a monitoring force to supervise the truce. The Resolution was seen as a setback for supporters of the self-proclaimed DRY who had urged the UN to condemn the North for the continued fighting and to initiate moves that might extend to the official recognition of the DRY. Several observers pointed to the critical role of the USA which finally decided to support a unified Yemen and warned Saudi Arabia against interfering. Despite talks in Moscow on 30 June and again in New York on 2 July on implementing and supervising a cease-fire, northern forces continued their advance and by 4 July had entered northern districts of Aden which was without water or electricity. On 7 July Aden surrendered to northern forces and the self-proclaimed DRY collapsed. Al-Baid fled to Oman, and his 'Vice-President', Abd ar-Rahman al-Jifri, to Saudi Arabia, from where he pledged to continue the struggle against the North. President Saleh reported that 931 civilians and soldiers had been killed in the civil war and 5,000 had been wounded, although others claimed that the death toll was much higher. It was estimated that the war against the southern secessionists had cost the central government $8,000m. Saleh estimated that it would cost $7,500m. in post-war reconstruction. Following the announcement of a general amnesty and the termination of the state of emergency, southern Yemeni soldiers began returning to the country. There were reports that during the dismantling of the southern army, irregular tribal forces carried off much of the army's military equipment. Having obtained supplies of heavy weapons for the first time, the tribal levies are now considered a real threat to the central government.

THE AFTERMATH OF THE CIVIL WAR

After the fall of Aden to northern forces, the victorious North pledged to work for national reconciliation. On 7 July 1994 a document was submitted to the UN Secretary-General stating that military operations would cease immediately, a general amnesty would be declared, democracy and political pluralism, together with human rights, freedom of speech and of the press would be respected, and national dialogue within the framework of constitutional legitimacy would be resumed. These statements were reaffirmed during a meeting of the Council of Ministers in Aden on 12 July, in which it was declared that all northern military units would return to barracks. (In August, moreover, President Saleh announced that party membership would no longer be permitted within the armed forces.) A committee was formed to implement the reconstruction of Aden, which was named as the country's economic capital. However, UN attempts to bring the two opposing sides together for talks in Geneva at the end of July failed. Al-Iryani of the GPC, who had been scheduled to meet al-Attas of the YSP for talks in the presence of UN mediator Lakhdar al-Ibrahimi, denied that any negotiations were under way and stated that the UN had no

further role to play as any discussions between the different parties would take place within Yemen itself. After a meeting of the YSP politburo in Damascus, Syria, under Secretary-General Salim Salih Muhammad, a statement was issued condemning the secession and appealing for unity and reconciliation, and a return to the principles incorporated in the Document of Pledge and Agreement signed in Amman earlier in the year. In September the YSP in Yemen elected a new politburo, none of whose members had been involved in the declaration of the DRY. The politburo elected Ali Saleh Obad as the new Secretary-General of the YSP. In the following month remnants of the secessionist administration, now grouped around Abd ar-Rahman al-Jifri in the newly-formed National Opposition Front, also appealed for a settlement on the basis of the Amman agreement, but while declaring that they hoped to achieve their aims through dialogue, they did not preclude resorting to armed struggle. From exile in Oman, al-Baid had declared that he was retiring from politics.

On 28 September 1994 the House of Representatives in San'a adopted a series of constitutional reforms which greatly strengthened the position of the President, including the abolition of the Presidential Council. Following the defeat of the secular YSP and the dispersal of its military and political power base, the Islamist YIP began asserting its authority. As part of the constitutional reforms *Shari'a* (Islamic law) became the only, rather than the principal, source of legislation, and the last references to the specific rights of women were removed from the Constitution. On 1 October Saleh was re-elected President of the Republic and despite much rhetoric about reconciliation, the YSP was excluded from the new Government. During an interview in early 1995 President Saleh stated that he did not preclude the eventual reintegration of the YSP into the power structure, but only after it had reformed and was prepared to 'respect constitutional rules'. In the new Council of Ministers appointed by the President on 6 October, the GPC retained the majority of posts but the YIP increased its membership from six to nine, including the influential portfolios of education and justice. The South was represented in the new Council of Ministers by four ministers, together with Vice-President Maj.-Gen. Abd ar-Rabbuh Mansur Hadi, all of whom were now standing as members of the GPC but were former allies of the Ali Nasser Muhammad faction.

Despite its minority representation in government, the YIP was the most influential party in the country with the best and most dynamic organization. Its officials were active in the towns and even in remote parts of the countryside, and its broad-based constituency included the tribes, the commercial bourgeoisie and the influential Muslim Brotherhood. In September the YIP congress elected members of the Muslim Brotherhood to most of its key posts. Yet despite the ascendancy of its ideologues, the YIP moved cautiously and was careful in its public statements to stress its commitment to political pluralism and to a market economy, while condemning violence and terrorism in all its forms. The YIP Assistant Secretary-General, Abd al-Wahab al-Ansi, interviewed in early 1995, stated that if the party obtained an absolute majority in the next election, it would not monopolize power since it believed it was necessary to have the co-operation of all Yemeni political groupings in order to solve the problems of underdevelopment. However, statements by the party's leader, Sheikh Abdullah bin Hussain al-Ahmar, and the Chairman of its *majlis*, Sheikh Abd al-Majid az-Zindani, contradicted the YIP's stated commitment to a pluralist democratic system. For their part, YIP ministers acted with discretion but determination. The Minister of Education, Abd Ali al-Qubati, for example, did not overturn existing teaching programmes; however, he did increase the hours devoted to Koranic studies at the expense of science teaching, suspend teachers suspected of socialist and secular sympathies and replace them with Islamist teachers recruited from Sudan or Egypt. He also gradually phased out co-educational classes in schools and in the university in the southern provinces, and 'recommended' that female teachers and students observe the proper dress code. The Minister of Justice, Dr Abd al-Wahab Lufti ad-Daylami, dismissed women judges whose appointment had survived from the former PDRY, stating that they were totally incompetent in Islamic law. The YIP and the GPC, meanwhile, co-operated to destroy the YSP and appeared determined to 'Islamize' the southern provinces. The Government seized all properties belonging to the YSP, and thousands of civil servants suspected of socialist sympathies were dismissed. Both parties blamed southern officials and the YSP for widespread corruption despite the complexity of the problem which could not be ascribed to a single party or faction. Nevertheless in early 1995 there were reports of tensions between the GPC and the YIP, which appeared to have become increasingly dissatisfied with its role in government. Differences emerged over economic policy for example, with the GPC apparently accepting as inevitable at least some of the economic reforms recommended by the World Bank and the IMF, whereas the YIP expressed its opposition to the introduction of austerity measures. Some observers argued that the eclipse of the YSP, the only obstacle to the growing influence of the Islamists, could lead to the weakening of political pluralism, the erosion of basic liberties and the eventual emergence of a new single-party dictatorship under the YIP, with or without President Saleh.

In early February 1995 13 opposition parties from across the political spectrum formed a common front to oppose the ruling GPC/YIP coalition. The new Democratic Coalition of Opposition adopted as its platform the Document of Pledge and Agreement signed before the civil war and urged the Government to abide by its terms. The new bloc demanded that the Government act without delay to implement the economic measures endorsed by the House of Representatives at the end of November 1994 and to eradicate corruption in the country's administration. Because of increasing government interference in what had been a free press, with opposition papers being targeted for harassment by the authorities, and widespread illiteracy, the new coalition stated that it would take its campaign to the people by the use of audio-cassettes.

The economic repercussions of the civil war presented additional problems for the Government in the form of a number of popular protests and civil disturbances, particularly in the south. In September 1994 hundreds demonstrated in Abyan province to protest at water and electricity shortages and the price of basic foodstuffs, which in some instances had increased fivefold. In February 1995 more than 150 wholesalers were arrested in San'a for their alleged role in inflating prices. In late March and early April, moreover, following the devaluation of the riyal and the doubling of the price of fuel, demonstrators clashed with police in Aden, San'a and Dhamar, resulting in more than 50 arrests and three deaths. The activities of Islamist militants, meanwhile, posed a potential threat to internal stability. In early September 1994 some 20 people were reported to have been killed in clashes with the security forces in Abyan province, following the destruction of three Muslim saints' shrines by Islamist militants who deemed them idolatrous. In April 1995 Islamist militants were involved in skirmishes in Hadramawt province, resulting in the deaths of two members of the Hussainain tribe, after they levelled similar accusations at the tribe for unislamic burial practices.

In a reorganization of the Council of Ministers in mid-June 1995 the GPC increased its share of portfolios at the expense of independents, with the result that the Council consisted entirely of members of the GPC and the YIP. Later in the month President Saleh was re-elected head of the GPC at the party's first general assembly to be held since 1988, and was given the new title of party Chairman. The Deputy Prime Minister and Minister of Foreign Affairs, Abd al-Karim al-Iryani, assumed Saleh's previous position of Secretary-General, and the post of party Vice-Chairman was taken by the country's Vice-President, Abd ar-Rabbuh Mansur Hadi. In accordance with a decision to rationalize and restructure the party, the permanent committee, elected to represent the constituencies, was reduced to 300 members, and the size of the politburo, elected by the permanent committee, was reduced from 23 to seven members. Meanwhile, the government continued to pursue a policy of decentralization and was reported to have granted the governorates a degree of control over their own budgets and greater freedom in appointing local officials. New provincial governors were appointed, and in April the President announced the demobilization of some 50,000 troops as part of a plan to rationalize the armed forces.

The tensions which had emerged between the GPC and the YIP in early 1995 continued as the year progressed, with differ-

ences over many aspects of policy becoming more pronounced. While some elements in the YIP were keen to further Islamist influence over the country's banking system, the GPC was in favour of its privatization. The YIP, which had established its own system of educational establishments, quite separate from the state-run education system, was also opposed to the GPC's aim of educational integration and unification. During 1994–95 these religious schools enrolled 326,484 pupils, 13% of total school enrolment in that year. The YIP also declared its opposition to the development of the free-trade zone at Aden arguing that it would attract large numbers of non-Yemenis and thereby undermine the country's Islamic identity. In November YIP ministers boycotted the weekly meeting of the Council of Ministers in protest at a newspaper report that claimed the party was colluding with Islamist radicals. Relations between the YIP and the GPC continued to deteriorate. The YIP expressed its opposition to economic reforms recommended by the World Bank, and criticized the GPC for attending an economic summit meeting in Jordan, in October, at which representatives of Israel were present. Moreover, in December the YIP Minister of Trade and Supply, Muhammad Ahmad Afandi, resigned from his post, citing political and economic differences with the GPC. (In January 1996 responsibility for the portfolio was given to a GPC member, Abd ar-Rahman Muhammad Ali Othman.) A new Minister of Education was appointed in October 1996.

The situation in the southern governorates remained tense. There was widespread frustration and resentment in the south that commitments to reconciliation and reconstruction had not been honoured by the Government in San'a since the end of the civil war. With the collapse of the YSP, the southern governorates felt increasingly marginalized and neglected, and reconstruction work in the south has been mainly financed by foreign governments and organizations. Violent outbreaks continued in 1996 with explosions in Aden and other southern towns. In June 19 people died in riots in Mukalla and a bomb attack on the Egyptian embassy in July was blamed on 'separatist elements'. Although the exiled National Opposition Front denied responsibility, the group's leader, former Vice-President al-Baid, issued a statement reaffirming his commitment to a separate southern state and for a referendum to secure better terms for the southern governorates. He warned of further violence if these issues were not addressed. At the end of September new anti-government demonstrations occurred in Hadramawt but were quickly suppressed. Attempts by Islamists to enforce stricter public morality in the southern governorates were believed to have contributed to the continuing unrest. In November Ali Nasser Muhammad (a former President of the PDRY, in exile since 1986) returned to Yemen at the invitation of President Saleh. He insisted that he did not seek a political role, but there was speculation that the GPC might urge him to mediate with the south.

THE 1997 ELECTIONS

Tensions between the GPC and its coalition partner the YIP increased in the weeks preceding Yemen's second multi-party elections. In October 1996 the YIP took part in a press conference organized by six opposition parties which criticized the registration process, demanded a revision of new voter lists and called for changes to the independent committee responsible for organizing the elections. Some parties indicated that they might boycott the elections unless action was taken. The YIP held talks with several opposition parties including the ideologically-opposed YSP. In an earlier interview, the Prime Minister had played down the recent conflicts between the GPC and the YIP arguing that each party merely wished to emphasize its distinct political identity as the elections approached. He also expressed support for the emergence of an effective opposition and for the return of the YSP to an active role, although stipulating that the party should first dissociate itself from the secessionists. In December the GPC announced plans to bring the YIP-controlled religious institutes into the state education system. This was seen as a direct challenge to the YIP, as the institutes are used for Islamic indoctrination and recruitment. Cabinet discussion of the subject prompted YIP, ministers to walk out, but the plan was later approved during a cabinet meeting at which the YIP ministers were not present. Despite their differences the leaders of both parties met in January 1997 and renewed their coalition agreement. Earlier, opposition parties had accused both the GPC and the YIP of monopolizing access to the state-controlled media and using public funds for their election campaigns.

In the elections, held on 27 April 1997, the GPC swept to victory winning 187 of the 301 seats, 64 more than in 1993. With almost two-thirds of all seats, the GPC secured a clear majority in the new parliament. Its only serious rival, the YIP, secured only 53 seats, compared with 62 in 1993. Many candidates from the party's radical Islamist wing were defeated in the elections although the more traditional tribal elements retained their seats. The party leader, Sheikh Abdullah bin Hussain al-Ahmar, the head of the Hasid tribal federation, was re-elected parliamentary speaker. The YSP, which won 56 seats in 1993, boycotted the elections along with several other opposition groupings. They claimed that the elections would not be fair because of irregularities in voter registration. Nevertheless, some YSP members did stand as independents. In total, independent candidates increased their representation from 48 to 54. Of these, 39 declared their support for the GPC and six for the YIP. The GPC increased its representation throughout the country, particularly in the south, which, in 1993, had been dominated by the YSP. Only four parties were represented in the new parliament compared with eight in 1993.

The Government, which for months had mounted a campaign to encourage people to register to vote, estimated that voter turnout on election day was around 80%; foreign observers put the figure at 60%. Some procedural improvements were made such as the introduction of party symbols on ballot slips to aid illiterate voters. However, as in 1993, the election process was characterized by demonstrations and outbreaks of violence in which at least 20 people were reported to have been killed, and all parties except the GPC made accusations of fraudulent practices. International observers, including the US National Democratic Institute and the mainly European Joint International Observer Group in Yemen, were invited by the Government to monitor the elections, and although they were critical of some aspects of the elections, on balance, they pronounced them reasonably free and fair. In May a new Cabinet was named; 25 of the 29 members were GPC members, three were independents and there was one members of al-Haq, a conservative Islamic party which won no seats in the 1997 election. The GPC emphasized that they were 'participants' and not partners in government. An independent, Faraj Said bin Ghanim, was appointed Prime Minister. A number of GPC members retained their portfolios, and among the new appointments was a former Governor of the Central Bank, Alawi Salih as-Salami, who became Minister of Finance. As a result of their move to opposition, the YIP forfeited all its Cabinet seats and consequently its control over the Ministry of Education, and immediately after the election the President confirmed that the YIP's religious institutes would be incorporated in the state education system and their finances and curriculum brought into line with state schools. In a move seen by many as the first step towards the creation of an upper house of parliament, President Saleh appointed 59 members to a new Consultative Council, designed to broaden the base of participation. Although lacking executive or legislative authority, the Council has a committee structure which parallels that of the Cabinet and was given a mandate to draft laws on local administration including the reorganization of provincial boundaries, a politically sensitive issue. In December the House of Representatives approved the promotion of President Saleh from lieutenant-general to the rank of field marshal.

After two bombs exploded in Aden at the end of July 1997 120 people were arrested throughout the southern governorates, mainly members of those opposition parties which had boycotted the 1997 elections. The authorities claimed that the opposition parties were responsible for the bombings, but Abd ar-Rahman al-Jifri, the leader of the League of the Sons of Yemen, insisted that the bombs had been planted by the Yemeni Government in an attempt to discredit the opposition. Later in the year the authorities stated that most of those detained had been released, but the opposition claimed that the majority of the men were still in prison and that two of the detainees had died after being tortured. The arrests provoked demonstrations during August and September in Mukalla, the capital of the Hadramawt, where support for the exiled separatist leader Ali Salim al-Baid

remains strong. The demonstrators were also reacting to a decision by the newly formed Consultative Council to divide the province of Hadramawt into two parts, a move which was interpreted as an attempt to isolate the coastal areas, including the towns of Mukalla and Shihr (where the YSP retains a strong presence) from the interior of the province. At the end of October several car bombs exploded in Aden. No casualties were reported and some 27 men were arrested and charged including a Syrian who was reported to have confessed to working for Saudi Arabia's intelligence services. The Saudi Arabian authorities, however, denied any involvement in the bombing campaign, and the decision by the Yemeni Government to report the confession was interpreted by some as an attempt to divert attention away from mounting popular discontent in the country. In December several members of the YSP and the League of the Sons of Yemen imprisoned in Mukalla staged a hunger strike; after their health deteriorated President Saleh ordered their release.

Elsewhere in the country the Government's economic reforms were provoking widespread and often violent protests. In October 1997 after fuel prices were increased, local people in Dhammar, Marib and Al-Jawf protested by blocking roads to the capital. Tribal leaders supported the protestors' actions and the authorities responded by dispatching troops to reopen the roads. At Dhammar three people died and many were injured in clashes between armed tribesmen and the security forces. Foreigners were no longer considered immune from violent attacks, and there was a sharp increase in the number of kidnappings of foreign residents and tourists, mainly by tribes seeking to extract material benefits from the state or to demonstrate their dissatisfaction with certain government actions. In November 1997 Brig. Hussain Muhammad Arab, the Minister of the Interior, linked the increase in the number of kidnappings with the Aden bombings, describing them as part of a campaign to 'tarnish Yemen's image and shake its stability'. In the same month 31 people alleged to be 'foreign agents' were put on trial in San'a charged with attacking and robbing military posts.

In a report published in March 1997 Amnesty International described Yemen as a 'major violator of human rights' despite having ratified or acceded to most human rights treaties and incorporated many of their safeguards into its domestic legislation. The report criticized the activities of the political branch of the security forces and the dramatic increase in the use of the death penalty since 1990, and alleged the systematic use of torture in prisons and the arbitrary arrest and detention of political opponents. It also listed abuses against women. The Deputy Prime Minister expressed surprise at the criticism but the Government promised to look into the alleged abuses and gave assurances that the political security branch would be brought under judicial control. At the beginning of April the European Parliament urged the European Commission to put pressure on the Yemeni authorities to improve the country's human rights record, and a new co-operation agreement signed with the EU at the end of the month (replacing the 1984 agreement) was made conditional on progress both in human rights and democracy in Yemen. Later in the year Amnesty International deplored the increase in extra-judicial punishments and instances where international standards to ensure fair trials were disregarded. In a number of cases, following lenient sentencing, crowds of armed civilians took the law into their own hands and the authorities made little effort to curb the increase in vigilante activity. In October a formal Yemeni application for membership of the Commonwealth (former British) was rejected on the grounds that Yemen did not meet the required standards in terms of democracy, the rule of law and respect for human rights. In February 1998 Mansur Rajih, who had been adopted as a prisoner of conscience by several human rights organizations, was released after 15 years in prison under threat of execution.

At the end of March 1998 the year-long trial of 15 members of the separatist southern Yemeni leadership during the 1994 civil war finally came to an end. Five of the men, including the former Yemeni Vice-President, Ali Salim al-Baid, and former Prime Minister Haidar al-Attas, were condemned to death, three, including Abd ar-Rahman al-Jifri, were sentenced to 10 years in prison, five received suspended sentences and two were acquitted. All the accused, who fled abroad after the southern secessionists were defeated by northern forces, were tried *in absentia* and it was thought unlikely that they would be extradited. In April it was reported that more than 2,000 people had demonstrated in the southern town of Mukalla in protest at the death sentences and that three people had been killed and several injured. There were further bomb explosions in Aden at the end of May and violent clashes between demonstrators and police in the southern province of Abyan. Kidnapping of foreigners by tribesmen continued; there were 21 actual kidnappings in 1997 and six attempts and 16 kidnappings in the early part of 1998, and little prospect of those involved being arrested. In April 1998 President Salah instructed the Consultative Council to find a way of ending the practice, and later instructed the Council to form a permanent committee to study the issue of vengeance-related violence in Yemeni society. In August a decree was issued whereby the maximum legal penalty imposed against charges of kidnapping was increased to death.

At the end of March 1998 the Prime Minister, Faraj Said bin Ghanim, left for Switzerland, ostensibly for medical treatment, but on his return to Yemen in late April he resigned from the premiership, after only eleven months in office. His resignation appeared to have been prompted by differences with President Saleh over cabinet changes. For some months bin Ghanim had expressed his frustration at the political obstacles that were thwarting his economic reform programme. The President appointed the Minister of Foreign Affairs, Abd al-Karim al-Iryani, to head a caretaker administration, and in mid-May al-Iryani was confirmed in the post when a new Government was announced. There were three newcomers to the enlarged Council of Ministers but apart from bin Ghanim, only one minister, an independent, departed. The most significant change in the new cabinet was the promotion of Abd al-Qadir Bajammal, the former Minister of Planning and Development, to the post of Deputy Prime Minister and Minister of Foreign Affairs. Presenting the new Government's programme to parliament on 1 June, al-Iryani pledged to continue wider-ranging reforms to tackle the country's economic problems and to begin implementing comprehensive administrative, employment and legal reforms. The Government also indicated that it would proceed with efforts to settle the long-standing border dispute with Saudi Arabia (see below). On 7 June the new Government won a vote of confidence from parliament on its policy programme, with 226 members voting in favour, 17 against and 26 abstentions.

The Government's decision in mid-June to increase prices of fuel and some basic foodstuffs by up to 40% with immediate effect led to a week of riots and demonstrations in the capital, San'a, and several other towns including Taiz, Dhammar, Ibb and Marib. Official sources stated that some 34 people had been killed and 102 injured in the violence, but opposition sources abroad claimed that up to 100 people had died in the unrest. Some 21 soldiers were reported to have been killed on 26 June when the security forces tried to reopen the road from Marib to San'a which had been blocked by tribesmen; an estimated 20-30 tribesmen were reported to have died in the clashes around Marib. On 29 June Hunt Oil stated that its oil pipeline from Marib to the Red Sea had been punctured by bullets fired by protestors, but was still operational. The southern provinces were reported to have been relatively quiet but there was a large peaceful demonstration at Mukalla on 30 June urging the President to reverse the price rises. A group of five opposition parties issued a statement blaming the Government for the rioting and calling on it to reverse its 'wrong policies' because they were impoverishing the people. Al-Iryani, however, told parliament that the price rises would stay but that fuel prices would not be increased again for another four years. Officials accused members of the YIP of direct involvement in the disturbances. (The YIP had announced its intention to bring down the al-Iryani Government.) By the end of June the security forces appeared to have brought the disturbances in the towns under control, but in early July there were reports that tribesmen had seriously damaged the oil pipeline from Marib to the Red Sea. According to the *Yemen Times* the cost of repairs would exceed $1m. although both the Government and Hunt Oil played down the seriousness of the incident. At the same time at least two explosions were reported in Aden.

FOREIGN RELATIONS AFTER THE CIVIL WAR

In the aftermath of the civil war President Saleh quickly embarked on a diplomatic offensive to isolate the secessionists and ensure that they could not regroup in neighbouring countries, most of which had supported the South during the two-month conflict. Oman and Djibouti promised the prompt return of military equipment brought there by the fleeing southern forces, and most states, including Egypt, expressed their support for a unified Yemen. Relations with Oman were strengthened further in June 1995 when the demarcation of the Yemeni-Omani border (initiated in 1992) was officially completed. Relations with Sudan also improved and Iran showed growing interest in Yemen and began providing some medical assistance. However, the arrival of militants from Algeria's banned Front islamique du salut (FIS), and later from the extremist Groupe islamique armé (GIA), provoked a strong protest from the Algerian Government and in late January 1995 Algeria recalled its ambassador from San'a. The YIP was known to have provided military training and political indoctrination for Islamist militants from Algeria and also from Egypt, while declaring publicly that the party supported an end to violence in Algeria and dialogue leading to free, multi-party elections. The Yemen Government strongly denied the existence of training camps for militant Islamists until 1995 when President Saleh, on a visit to Cairo, declared that his security forces had discovered a cell of the militant Egyptian group, Islamic Jihad, and offered to exchange members of the group for Yemeni separatists based in Cairo. Towards the end of 1997 the Yemeni authorities were reported to have arrested a number of Yemeni and foreign Islamist militants including the so-called 'Arab Afghans', possibly in a move to curb the activities of the more extremist elements within the YIP.

Long-standing difficulties with Yemen's powerful neighbour, Saudi Arabia, continued to dominate foreign relations. After the civil war ended, Saudi Arabia provided assistance for the reconstruction of Aden hospital, and promises of further assistance for health projects were made during a visit by Saudi Arabia's Deputy Minister of Health in December 1994, the first sign since the end of the Gulf war that Saudi Arabia might begin to resume financial aid to Yemen. Yemen promised to begin a new chapter in its relations with Saudi Arabia based on 'co-operation, security and stability'. However, in late December tensions between the two countries increased over the disputed border, and there were reports of armed clashes between Saudi and Yemeni forces in disputed territory. The Saudi Minister of Defence, Prince Sultan ibn Abd al-Aziz Abd as-Sa'ud, was reported to have told Prime Minister Abd al-Aziz Abd al-Ghani, that the Saudi airforce would bomb Yemen unless it withdrew military units stationed in certain frontier areas. A large Saudi force of 20,000 men, together with 400 tanks, armoured vehicles and pieces of heavy artillery, penetrated some 70 km inside Yemeni territory. The intervention of the Syrian Vice-President, Abd al-Halim Khaddam, defused the situation and produced a compromise in January 1995. After a month of difficult negotiations the two countries signed a memorandum of understanding in Mecca on 26 February, establishing the basis for future discussions. Under the memorandum, Yemen accepted the terms of the 1934 Ta'if agreement, which had lapsed in 1994, thereby effectively conceding sovereignty over the provinces of Najran, Gizan and Asir, which were annexed by Saudi Arabia in 1934. Although the Ta'if agreement dealt principally with the border area in the north-west of the country, Yemen's Minister of Foreign Affairs succeeded in ensuring that future talks would deal with the entire length of the border between the two countries. The memorandum signed in Mecca provided for the establishment of six joint committees to delineate the land and sea borders and develop economic and commercial ties; both sides also agreed that they would not permit their country to become 'a base and centre for aggression' against the other. If the negotiations did not lead to agreement, the memorandum provided for international arbitration, a point initially rejected by Prince Sultan. On 8 March the memorandum was approved by the Yemeni Council of Ministers and later in the month the joint Yemeni-Saudi military committee, established by the memorandum, held its first meeting in Riyadh. In early June President Saleh and a high-ranking delegation visited Saudi Arabia, constituting the first official visit to that country since February 1990. In a joint statement, issued at the end of the visit, the two Governments expressed their satisfaction with the memorandum of understanding and, in addition, pledged their commitment to strengthening economic, commercial and cultural co-operation. Yemen clearly hoped that the memorandum would lead to the normalization of relations with Saudi Arabia and the possibility that negotiations could lead to the return of at least some of the 800,000 Yemeni workers expelled from Saudi Arabia during the Gulf crisis, as well as the resumption of significant Saudi aid. By the end of 1995 some progress had been made in implementing the February memorandum of understanding as the various joint committees, established under the terms of the memorandum, began their work. The military committee produced plans to reduce troop levels in border areas, and border controls between the two countries were relaxed, allowing an increase in trade. Notably, the Saudi Government agreed to allow Yemenis to seek work in the kingdom, declaring that the Saudi Ministry of Labour would begin issuing work permits to Yemenis provided they had a Saudi sponsor. It was assumed that many Yemenis expelled in 1990 would return to their former employers and businesses in the kingdom, although it was thought unlikely that the level of emigration would be as great as before the expulsion. In December reports of armed clashes along the disputed border were denied by Saudi Arabia and early in 1996 the two countries reached a preliminary agreement on their land frontier. Talks also began on the delimitation of the maritime boundary between the two countries. In July, the two countries signed a bilateral security agreement aimed mainly at combating cross-border drugs-trafficking, but also at preventing Yemen from becoming a refuge for radical Saudi dissidents. In the past Yemen had been accused of providing refuge for foreign dissidents, particularly members of Islamist groups, but since mid-1995 the Government has moved to arrest and extradite many such dissidents including the Arab *mujahidin* who fought in Afghanistan against the Soviet occupation. The two countries concluded a new trade agreement in September 1996. During August and September 1996 a number of high-level meetings were held between Saudi and Yemeni officials including a visit to San'a by the Saudi defence minister, responsible for negotiations with Yemen, and the interior minister. After the elections in Yemen, in May 1997, President Saleh stated that he would visit Saudi Arabia in order to seek a settlement of the border issue, as little progress had been made since the signing of the preliminary agreement. However, tensions between the two countries quickly re-emerged. After a visit to Jeddah, the new Minister of Foreign Affairs, Abd al-karim al-Iryani, a noted critic of Saudi Arabia, complained that he had not been treated with the correct diplomatic protocol. The Yemeni press immediately launched a campaign accusing the Saudis of trying to destabilize Yemen in order to strengthen their hand in the border negotiations. After border clashes were reported in late June and early July, the interior ministers of the two countries held urgent talks which both Governments declared would lead to an early and permanent settlement of the border dispute. However, the joint committees set up under the 1995 memorandum of understanding (see above) had failed to reach any common positions and tensions rose again after the Saudi-owned television station in London, the Middle East Broadcasting Corporation, transmitted an interview with the southern Yemeni leader, al-Baid, who was on trial *in absentia* in Yemen. Later in the year, after further high-level meetings between the two sides, including a meeting between President Saleh and Prince Sultan, the Yemeni press suggested that a settlement of the border dispute was imminent. However, in October al-Iryani accused Saudi Arabia of supporting the tribal unrest in Yemen, and the Yemeni authorities also claimed to have evidence that Saudi Arabia was involved in a series of bombings in Aden (see above). Further border clashes occurred in November in which several soldiers were reported to have been killed. At the end of November al-Iryani held talks with King Fahd and Crown Price Abdullah in Riyadh but no progress was made towards a settlement. In early December al-Iryani stated that Yemen might take the dispute to international arbitration if negotiations remained deadlocked. The border dispute flared up again in late May 1998 when it was reported that Saudi forces had occupied several islands in the Red Sea which are also claimed

by Yemen. While this was seen as an attempt by Saudi Arabia to establish its own claim to the area, some also interpreted it as signalling Saudi disapproval of the new Yemen Government headed by al-Iryani. A joint military committee meeting attended by the respective Chiefs of Staff was held in August but only agreements governing 'guarantees and rules' between the two countries were concluded.

The participation of the USA in the negotiations between Yemen and Saudi Arabia was believed to have played an important role in securing at least a provisional agreement between the two countries and was seen as marking another stage in the gradual normalization of relations between Yemen and Western countries. On a visit to San'a in October 1997, the US Assistant Secretary of State for Middle East and Near East Affairs, Martin Indyk, expressed continued US support for all measures to strengthen security and stability in the region and stated that Washington was keen to promote and expand co-operation with Yemen. He praised the Yemeni Government for their 'rational approach' to the border dispute with Saudi Arabia. In late May 1998 the Commander-in-Chief of the US Central Command, Anthony Zinni, visited Yemen for talks with President Saleh on military co-operation. In February 1995 President Saleh visited the Netherlands, Germany and France, concluding a number of new aid agreements and other joint projects. In April the United Kingdom announced that its aid programme for Yemen would be resumed at a modest level, and in June Japan stated that it was prepared to reactivate fully its economic aid programme for Yemen. After the parliamentary elections in May 1997 Saleh again visited a number of European capitals securing promises of increased aid, help with outstanding debts and a new co-operation agreements. In mid-November he made an official visit to the United Kingdom, the first visit by a Yemeni head of state since Britain's evacuation of Aden in 1967. Early in 1998 the President visited Malaysia (a country with which Yemen has long-established links), China and Indonesia. Relations with Oman improved after June 1995, when a border demarcation agreement, initiated in 1992, was completed. By mid-1996 the last remaining troops had been withdrawn from the border area, and agreements on economic co-operation and investment had been signed. Later in the year the two countries agreed to set up a free-trade zone near the border. In early 1997 agreements were signed to improve air and road links between the two countries, and at the end of May final demarcation maps for their joint border were signed. Although Saudi Arabia had not formally opposed the 1992 agreement, it was reported in April 1998 that Saudi Arabia claimed some of the territory covered in the border demarcation agreement between Yemen and Oman. There was speculation that these claims might be linked to Saudi Arabia's ambitions to secure a corridor to the Arabian Sea between Yemen and Oman. In early July 1995, following a statement made in the previous month by Kuwait's Deputy Prime Minister and Minister of Foreign Affairs, Sheikh Sabah al-Ahmad al-Jaber as-Sabah, which stipulated that Yemen would have to officially demand Iraq's implementation of the UN Security Council's resolutions before Yemeni-Kuwaiti relations could be normalized, the GPC issued a policy statement requiring Iraq's implementation of the aforementioned resolutions. In September a delegation of Kuwaiti trade unionists visited Yemen and at the end of the year the Kuwait-based AFESD agreed to support a development project in Yemen. However, relations with Kuwait remained strained. In October Yemen's Minister of Foreign Affairs, Abd al-Karim al-Iryani, had accused Kuwait of supporting the southern separatists in the civil war. In December 1996 Kuwait opposed the Yemeni application for GCC membership, which was rejected two months later. This decision provoked acrimonious exchanges in the Kuwaiti and Yemeni press, although in early 1997 Yemen did succeed in joining the Indian Ocean Rim Association for Regional Co-operation which promotes co-operation in trade, investment and economic development. In June 1998 the Minister of Foreign Affairs Dr Abd al-Qadir Bajammal stated that Yemen would not repeat its request to join the GCC. The Yemen Government continued to express solidarity with Iraq and urged an end to the UN oil embargo on Iraq. A parliamentary delegation and a senior official of the GPC visited Baghdad in October 1995. Although popular feeling in Yemen remains fiercely pro-Iraqi, the Yemeni Government has been careful not to alienate mainstream international opinion. During the crisis in relations between Iraq and the USA in February 1998 President Saleh cut short a visit to Indonesia to attend discussions on the crisis in Abu Dhabi, and security forces in San'a were reported to have dispersed unlicensed demonstrations against the US and British military build-up in the Gulf. In late 1996 a Libyan-sponsored conference of opponents of the Middle East peace process was held in San'a and several GPC members attended. However, in an interview in January 1997, the Minister of Foreign Affairs stated that the Yemen Government was not opposed to the peace process and supported the principle of 'land-for-peace'. Although Yemen traditionally maintains a hard-line stance towards Israel, it agreed to attend the fourth Middle East and North Africa economic conference held in Doha, Qatar, in November 1997 at which an Israeli delegation was present. Leading Arab states, including Egypt and Saudi Arabia. had refused to take part in the summit.

In November 1995 there were reports that Eritrean troops had attempted to land on the Red Sea island of Greater Hanish, one of three islands (the others being Lesser Hanish and Zuqar) claimed by both Yemen and Eritrea. The attempted invasion had apparently been prompted by Yemen's announced intention to develop Greater Hanish as a tourist resort, and its subsequent refusal to comply with an Eritrean demand that the island be evacuated. Negotiations in Yemen and Eritrea in late November and early December failed to defuse the crisis, and on 15

December fighting broke out between the two sides, resulting in the deaths of six Eritrean and three Yemeni soliders. On 17 December Yemen and Eritrea agreed to a cease-fire, to be monitored by a commission comprising a senior official from each country and two US diplomats. None the less, fighting was renewed the following day and Eritrean forces succeeded in occupying Greater Hanish. The cease-fire was subsequently adhered to, and some 180 Yemeni soliders (captured during the fighting) were released at the end of the month. Attempts by the Ethiopian and Egyptian Governments to broker an agreement between the two sides proved unsuccessful. In late January 1996 France assumed the role of mediator. On 21 May representatives of Eritrea and Yemen signed an arbitration accord in Paris, France, whereby the two sides agreed that they were prepared to submit the dispute to an international tribunal. France and the USA subsequently undertook to observe and supervise military movements in the area around the disputed islands. In August, however, Eritrean troops occupied the Lesser Hanish Island and Yemen threatened to send troops to force them to withdraw. After intervention by the UN and France, Eritrea withdrew its forces and in October the two countries reaffirmed their agreement to allow an international arbitration panel to settle the dispute. The five-member panel began work in January 1997 and is expected to make a judgment on the sovereignty of the Hanish islands and the location of the maritime border between Yemen and Eritrea. By July the arbitration had entered its second stage, but relations remained strained.

Economy

ALAN J. DAY

INTRODUCTION

In 1996, according to World Bank estimates, Yemen's GNP, measured at average 1994–96 prices, was $6,016m. GNP per head in 1996 was an estimated $380, placing Yemen in the lower ranges of the world's low-income countries. In 1989, the last year before Yemeni unification, the World Bank had estimated Yemen's GNP per head as $650, based on aggregated data for the then Yemen Arab Republic (YAR or North Yemen) and the People's Democratic Republic of Yemen (PDRY or South Yemen). Although widely varying estimates have been produced by other sources, the World Bank estimates appear to be broadly consistent with the course of events in Yemen in the years following unification in May 1990. Early plans for economic development and integration were quickly disrupted by the Gulf crisis of 1990–91, particularly by the UN trade embargo on Iraq, which Yemen applied with some reluctance in view of its close economic links with that country. Also damaging was the enforced return of up to 1m. Yemeni workers from Saudi Arabia and other Gulf states and the consequential loss of crucial remittance income. Financial difficulties associated with the crisis obliged the Government to adjust economic policy, notably by reducing expenditure and food subsidies, with the result that social unrest increased in 1992. During the following year the Government appeared to be moving towards the introduction of fundamental structural reforms, but in 1994 normal economic planning was again disrupted by a political crisis, associated on this occasion with the onset of civil war.

Unification created a country of 536,869 sq km with a population estimated at 11,282,000 in mid-1990, excluding up to 2.5m. Yemenis working abroad, mainly in Saudi Arabia. Of the two components, the YAR had a population of 9,274,173 (including nationals abroad) in 1986, while the PDRY had a population of 2,345,266 in 1988. The YAR had fared better economically, achieving a GNP per head of $640 by 1988 (according to the World Bank), whereas the PDRY's equivalent statistic was $430. The results of Yemen's first post-unification census, carried out on 16 December 1994, indicated a total population of approximately 14.6m. (25% of whom lived in urban areas). During 1990–96 the population of Yemen increased by an annual average of 4.7%. Other World Bank statistics for 1995 gave the average life expectancy at birth in Yemen as 53 years and the

infant mortality rate as 100 per 1,000 live births, while in 1994 the male literacy rate was 68.6% and the female literacy rate was 23.1%.

In the mid-1980s the economic prospects of both countries were significantly improved by the discovery of hydrocarbons in commercial quantities, and the perceived need for rapid joint development of their oil and gas sectors was a major factor in the two countries' decision to unite. Prior to unification, both countries had sought to promote development by means of three- or five-year plans which called for large inflows of foreign aid, but both had usually failed to achieve their targets. The YAR's second five-year plan had been disrupted in December 1982 by a major earthquake in Dhamar province which killed about 3,000 people and caused an estimated $650m. of damage. In 1983, moreover, there was a slump in earnings from the remittances of North Yemenis working abroad, caused by cut-backs in petroleum production, reduced revenues and, hence, less profitable employment in the petroleum industries of Saudi Arabia and the Gulf States. These factors caused a crisis in the economy of the YAR, leading to the introduction of austerity measures. However, in 1984 the country's prospects improved, following increases in aid for the relief of the earthquake region. In July 1984 petroleum was discovered in the YAR, and was being produced at a rate of 180,000 barrels per day (b/d) by the time of unification in May 1990.

Under British rule, South Yemen was sustained by Aden's position on the main international shipping lanes. The British Petroleum (BP) refinery was the focus of industry and trade. However, the closure of the Suez Canal in 1967, and the withdrawal of British troops in the same year, put an end to Aden's commercial prosperity, making it impossible for the post-independence Government to cover the budget deficit. Seeking new sources of finance and technical aid to assist it in the transition from a service economy to one based on agriculture and manufacturing, the PDRY accepted the favourable terms offered by the Soviet Union and other communist countries. In November 1969 the Government decreed the nationalization of all important foreign assets in the republic, with the exception of the BP refinery, which was not taken over until 1977. Meanwhile, the reopening of the Suez Canal in 1975 had not produced the anticipated revival in Aden's economy. In 1980 the PDRY Government introduced measures of liberalization, aimed mainly at helping farmers, fishermen and merchants. The political turmoil of January 1986, when the regime of Ali Nasser Muhammad was overthrown by an uncompromising Marxist faction, caused considerable economic disruption in the country. The new Government called for international aid to rebuild the city of Aden, large areas of which had been destroyed, and promised to honour its contracts with foreign companies. The discovery of petroleum in commercial quantities in 1983 improved the PDRY's economic prospects, although little headway had been made in developing production by the time of unification in 1990.

The onset of the Gulf crisis in August 1990 seriously disrupted unified Yemen's economy, especially when the Government, after some hesitation, decided to adhere to UN sanctions against Iraq and Iraqi-occupied Kuwait. Prior to the crisis Yemen had been greatly dependent on trade with, and aid from, both Iraq and, to a lesser extent, Kuwait. It had also relied heavily, for balance-of-payments purposes, on hard currency remittances from Yemeni workers in Saudi Arabia and the Gulf States, who returned home in large numbers, especially from Saudi Arabia, which in late September 1990 terminated Yemeni workers' privileges in retaliation for Yemen's opposition to the US-led military build-up in the Gulf. In October 1990 the Government, in support of a request for special aid from the international community, calculated its actual and prospective losses in 1990–91 at $1,686m. Later Yemeni estimates of the overall cost of the crisis included one by President Saleh in May 1991 which put Yemen's total prospective losses, including 1992, at over $3,000m. Moreover, in April 1991 the Government valued property and assets lost by Yemeni nationals forced to leave Saudi Arabia at $7,900m. By then the total number of returnees from Saudi Arabia was estimated by Yemeni officials at up to 1m., representing a 10% increase in the country's population and giving rise to serious social problems and pressure on scarce resources. Against this background, the World Bank co-ordinated international moves to provide emergency aid and credits for Yemen totalling $245m. Aggravating Yemen's problem was a foreign debt said to be in excess of $7,000m.

In November 1991 President Saleh conceded that Yemen was experiencing an economic crisis, with unemployment between 25% and 30%, and lost aid and other negative effects producing a 50% shortfall in government receipts compared with the original 1991 budget. In response, the Government implemented austerity measures, including cuts in food subsidies and defence expenditure, and co-operated informally with the IMF and other international agencies in adjusting short-term economic policy. On the positive side, activity in the oil and gas sectors accelerated sharply in 1991–92, on the strength of discoveries of significant new reserves, although output from existing oilfields declined in 1992, when government oil revenues remained modest in relation to the country's current financial needs. By mid-1993 there were signs that relations with Saudi Arabia and other GCC states were beginning to improve, and in August 1993 oil production started to rise when the first shipments were made from a newly-developed field.

In 1994 political events led once more to deep economic crisis as the armed conflict of May–July further destabilized the deficit-ridden public finances and burdened the country with a costly agenda of post-war repair work to be undertaken before the normal development programme could resume. An initial assessment of civil war damage by the UN Development Programme (UNDP) put the cost of essential repairs to basic infrastructure and services in the Aden area at between $100m. and $200m., and in mid-August the UN launched an appeal for $22m. of emergency aid to cover the immediate needs of the population of the southern war zone for the next six months. The Yemen Government estimated the overall cost of the war at $4,000m., and anticipated a $3,500m. spending requirement for reconstruction work. Widespread shortages of food, water and electricity continued to be reported in many parts of the country in September 1994, when a particular cause of popular discontent was the fivefold rise in prices of some basic foodstuffs since early July. In mid-September the World Bank authorized the expenditure of $35m. on emergency reconstruction work in five sectors of the economy, while the UNDP announced a $4m. distribution of food aid in the war-affected areas over a period of two months. Countries which extended various types of emer-

gency aid through national agencies included Italy, Germany, the Netherlands and the USA. The World Bank package utilized funds which formed part of Yemen's accumulated entitlement to $345m. of International Development Association (IDA) finance for projects whose implementation had been delayed by bureaucratic inefficiencies in Yemen. The package included $21m. for the power sector but only $700,000 for the water sector, which had already secured some bilateral aid. Allocations for health, education, agriculture and fisheries were to be spent mainly on the replacement of looted equipment and supplies.

Prior to the outbreak of civil war, the Yemen Government had discussed the prospects for structural economic reform in some detail with experts from the World Bank, whose primary recommendation was that the Government should curb the fiscal deficit, adjust the currency exchange rate and adopt a disciplined monetary policy as first steps in any reform programme. A delegation of World Bank and IMF officials visited San'a in January 1995 to reassess the situation and draw up proposals for immediate remedial action. It was estimated at this point that prices were rising at an annual rate of 60% despite direct and indirect government subsidies totalling more than $400m. per year, while the unemployment rate was around 30%, despite widespread overmanning throughout the public sector. By late March the inflation rate was reported to have risen to 100%, and the unemployment rate to 50%, as the country awaited a major economic policy initiative by the Government. The main components of this initiative were price increases and other measures to curb the budget deficit; adoption of a more liberal exchange-rate policy; and a commitment to implement wide-ranging structural reforms (to be finalized in consultation with the IMF and World Bank) from 1996 onwards. Implementation of an IMF-approved reform programme began on schedule in January 1996, and in July the Government published a detailed development plan for the remainder of the decade. At the end of 1996 the World Bank congratulated the Yemen Government on its 'remarkable success' in stabilizing the currency and reducing the rate of price inflation (which by November 1996 was less than 10% on an annualized basis). In June 1997 a consultative group of 26 international aid donors met in Brussels to review the implementation of Yemen's structural adjustment programme. The World Bank, the IMF and other major donors agreed that progress to date had exceeded all expectations and expressed their strong confidence in the future of the programme. The meeting pledged a total of $1,800m. of aid to Yemen over the next three years. In mid-1998, against a background of growing public unrest over the more controversial aspects of the IMF-backed reform programme (notably cuts in price subsidies on foodstuffs and fuels), the Government was re-examining its spending priorities in the light of a major revenue shortfall caused by the unforeseen slump in oil export prices since the end of 1997.

AGRICULTURE AND FISHERIES

The agriculture and fisheries sector contributed an estimated 14.7% of GNP in 1995, while agriculture provided 58% of male employment and 95% of female employment among the 77% of Yemen's population who lived in rural areas at the time of the December 1994 census. The average annual growth rate of agricultural production in the decade to 1995 was estimated as 3.7% by FAO. Only 6% of Yemen's land area is categorized by the World Bank as arable (and only one-half of this as 'crop land') while 7% is classed as forest and woodland and 30% as permanent pasture. The remaining 57% is largely desert and scrub.

The greater part of the arable land is in the western part of the country, which is the most fertile area of the Arabian peninsula, with a long tradition of intensive cultivation by smallholders. The wide range of climatic conditions across the hillsides, mountains, valleys, coastal plains and highland plateaus of western Yemen make it possible to cultivate a diversity of crop types, including dates, tobacco and cotton on the drought-prone Tihama plain and in coastal areas further to the south; coffee (at altitudes above 1,300 m); the qat bush (mainly at altitudes between 1,500 m and 2,500 m); sorghum or durra (at altitudes up to 3,000 m); and other cereals including wheat, barley and maize. Traditional fruit and vegetable crops in the highland areas include citrus fruits, apricots, peaches, grapes, tomatoes and potatoes, while newer crops encouraged since the 1970s under agricultural development programmes (often backed by bans on fruit and vegetable imports) include watermelons, cucumbers, peas, cauliflowers and lettuces. Mangoes, bananas and papayas are grown at lower altitudes where subtropical conditions prevail. The less favourable climate and terrain of Yemen's desert interior restrict agricultural production mainly to the wadi areas with sufficient water resources to support farming. The fertile Wadi Hadramawt, extending across 160 km of eastern Yemen, is the largest wadi system in the Arabian peninsula.

Agricultural development projects, mainly financed by foreign aid, featured prominently in the development plans of the former YAR and PDRY and have remained a priority since unification. The Tihama Development Authority (TDA) was set up with aid from IFAD, IDA and other sources to oversee the development of irrigation systems, water storage schemes and ground-water exploitation in the Tihama region. The TDA's Wadi Sihan project is designed to irrigate an initial 5,700 ha of land. The building of a major new Marib dam at Wadi Abida was completed in 1986 with financing from the Abu Dhabi Fund for Arab Economic Development. The dam has a storage capacity of 390m. cu m and is designed to provide perennial irrigation for 6,000 ha of cereal crops, with 5,000 ha of intermittent irrigation. Small-scale dam-building projects have been undertaken in many other wadi areas throughout Yemen. A major scheme was inaugurated in eastern Yemen in the 1980s to increase production on 3,225 ha of agricultural land in Hadramawt. Third-phase work on this scheme—originally scheduled for completion by 1996 as an irrigation project—was to be extended to include flood control systems designed to provide better protection against exceptionally heavy rainfall (the area having suffered extensive flood damage in early 1989).

Livestock farming and animal herding are important activities in most parts of Yemen, supplying much of the local demand for meat and dairy products and providing a small exportable surplus of hides and skins. A Livestock Development Corpn was set up in the former YAR in 1976 to promote new projects and to raise standards throughout the industry. In 1996 Yemen's estimated livestock numbers included 3.9m. sheep, 3.6m. goats, 1.2m. cattle and 22m. poultry. Production of meat (including poultry) in that year totalled around 137,000 tons, production of milk around 183,000 tons and production of hens' eggs around 19,000 tons. The total catch of the Yemeni fishing industry in 1995 was 104,000 tons; this compared with catches of around 50,000 tons in the former PDRY and 21,000 tons in the former YAR in the mid-1980s. It has long been recognized that the Arabian Sea fishing grounds off southern Yemen and, to a lesser extent, the Red Sea grounds off western Yemen, have considerable untapped development potential. Ongoing fisheries expansion schemes at the time of unification in May 1990 included a long-term programme in the south which was then mid-way through its third phase. Fourth-phase funding was subsequently secured in 1991–92 from IDA, IFAD and the EC. Yemen's fish-canning factories at Mukalla and Shukra were in mid-1998 seeking new investment (possibly involving privatization) to double their production capacity.

Yemen's trade in agricultural produce is heavily in deficit, annual production of such exportable cash crops as coffee and cotton having remained at fairly modest levels (around 11,000 tons each in 1996) while local production of staple food crops has supplied a diminishing proportion of local demand. In 1996 an area of 103,000 ha was planted to wheat and 149,000 tons of wheat were harvested (a decrease of 14% compared with the 1994 yield). Yemen's imports of wheat averaged 1.7m. tons per year between 1990 and 1994. Production of sorghum and millet decreased by 2% in 1996 to 411,000 tons. Other major crops in 1996 included tomatoes (221,000 tons), potatoes (183,000 tons), watermelons (105,000 tons) and grapes (98,000 tons). Yemen spent an estimated $595m. (28% of total expenditure on imports) on imported foodstuffs in 1993.

The true balance between food crops and cash crops in the agriculture of Yemen is difficult to assess accurately, because a key crop, qat, is not reliably recorded in official statistics. There is no doubt that the qat bush is by far the most profitable cash crop, although its growers are not eligible for such benefits as concessionary agricultural loans and do not have access to export markets (qat use being banned in neighbouring Arab countries). Inside Yemen, however, the chewing of qat leaves (which contain a mild stimulant) is a regular social ritual for the majority of the adult population. Chewing sessions take place every day from 2 p.m. to sunset, the former PDRY's 'weekend only' restriction having been abolished after Yemeni unification. Qat growing occupies a significant proportion of Yemen's best agricultural land—between 50,000 ha and 70,000 ha in the mid-1980s, and an estimated 120,000 ha in the late 1990s—and entails weekly irrigation, accounting for an estimated 16% of national water usage. Moreover, qat grows year-round, permanently occupying land that might have been used for crop rotation. Qat has no nutritional value. The World Bank has estimated that Yemen's internal trade in qat generates at least 25% of GDP and 16% of employment. A 1998 estimate by Yemeni analysts suggested that qat-chewing sessions occupied up to 20m. man-hours each day and that current spending on qat exceeded the value of the national budget. Many regular users are said to spend 25% to 50% of their total incomes on qat; some users as much as 66% of income.

Critics of qat cultivation in Yemen include experts on water resource depletion. A World Bank study of regional water resources, published in 1997, described Yemen as the most 'water stressed' country in the Middle East and North Africa, with only 176 cu m of water available per head of population per year from renewable underground reserves, compared with a regional average of 1,250 cu m and a world average of 7,500 cu m. ('Availability' in this context is the maximum rate of extraction from aquifers without causing irreversible depletion of reserves.) In 1994, the report said, Yemen pumped an estimated 2,800m. cu m of water from aquifers whose sustainable withdrawal rate was 2,100m. cu m per year. With all available surface water resources in full use, more than 60% of Yemen's total 1994 water supply was from aquifers, and 93% of the withdrawals from aquifers were for agricultural use. Sustainable patterns of water use on farms with traditional terraced irrigation systems had been critically disrupted by the introduction of modern tube-well technology in response to the pressure of rapid population growth over the past 20 years. The San'a basin, containing 10% of Yemen's population, faced complete exhaustion of its aquifers within 10 years if extraction from them continued at its 1994 rate of 224m. cu m per year. There were at least 45,000 groundwater wells in Yemen in 1994, when the depths of some newly drilled wells in the San'a basin exceeded 2,000 m. Underground water levels near Amran (a major centre of the qat trade) fell by 30 m in the first half of the 1990s. The 1997 World Bank report said that the Government had, in effect, contributed to Yemen's water crisis by banning the importation of qat (which is also cultivated in Ethiopia, Somalia and Kenya), banning the importation of fruit and vegetables, and failing to abolish all subsidies on the price of diesel (the main fuel for water pumps). Yemen's new Prime Minister acknowledged in mid-1998 that the water crisis was his country's 'greatest problem'. There was, he said, a case for differential pricing in the agricultural sector to curb wasteful usage by qat growers.

PETROLEUM AND NATURAL GAS

The discovery in July 1984 of significant oil deposits in the Marib/al-Jawf region, in the north-east of the YAR, was followed by discoveries across the border in the neighbouring Shabwa region of the PDRY. Small-scale production of crude oil began in the YAR at the end of 1985 and in the PDRY in mid-1987. Talks between the YAR and PDRY Governments on closer economic co-operation led to the establishment in January 1989 of a joint company to administer oil exploration and development rights in a cross-border area totalling 2,200 sq km. At the time of Yemeni unification in May 1990, aggregate oil output averaged 180,000 b/d, of which less than 10,000 b/d was produced in the former PDRY's Shabwa region. The first-phase development work in Shabwa was carried out by Soviet contractors, who suspended their oilfield production operations in mid-1990 pending completion of a pipeline link to the port of Bir Ali on the Gulf of Aden. The 200-km Bir Ali pipeline was inaugurated in May 1991 with a rated capacity of 100,000 b/d, greatly exceeding the installed output capacity of the Shabwa wells.

Concession rights in the former YAR's Marib/al-Jawf oilfields were held by a US–South Korean consortium whose operating company was Yemen Hunt Oil Co (a subsidiary of Hunt Oil of the USA). Yemen Hunt Oil's annual average production reached nearly 170,000 b/d in 1988 following the completion in 1987 of a 440-km pipeline running west from Marib to a Red Sea export terminal at Ras Isa, offshore from the port of Salif. The rated capacity of the Ras Isa pipeline was 225,000 b/d, expandable to 400,000 b/d if required in the future. Installations on the Alif oilfield (the first of the Marib/al-Jawf fields to go into production) include a 10,000 b/d 'topping' (primary distillation) plant which came on stream in April 1986 to supply gasoline, diesel and fuel oil for local consumption. In an exploration block immediately to the east of the Marib/al-Jawf concession area, the Jannah oilfield was brought into production by a separate Hunt Oil subsidiary (Jannah Hunt Oil Co) as operator for a consortium of US, French, Kuwaiti and Russian oil companies. The Jannah field's output, which is transported to the coast via the Ras Isa pipeline, averaged 15,000 b/d on start-up in October 1996 and was targeted to reach 75,000 b/d by 1999.

After Yemeni unification more than 10 significant oilfields were discovered in the 1,260 sq km Masila exploration block in the eastern Hadramawt region. Canadian Occidental Petroleum (CanOxy), the operating company in this block, made its first oil shipment in August 1993 via a 140-km pipeline built to link the Masila fields to an export terminal west of the port of ash-Shihr on the Gulf of Aden. Yemen's average annual oil output rose from 210,000 b/d in 1993 to 345,000 b/d in 1994 (about 45% of the 1994 total coming from Masila). In the East Shabwa concession area, immediately west of the Masila fields, Total-CFP (the operator for a consortium of French, Kuwaiti, US and Australian oil companies) brought the Kharir oilfield into production at the end of 1997 at an initial rate of 20,000 b/d. Output from East Shabwa, which is transported via CanOxy's Masila export pipeline, was targeted to reach 30,000 b/d by 1999. Expectations of production growth in the main Shabwa exploration areas (situated 200 km west of the East Shabwa block) were not fulfilled in the 1990s despite extensive exploration work. In 1991 Nimir Petroleum (a Cayman-registered company owned by private Saudi Arabian oil interests) paid an exceptionally high premium to obtain the operating licence for the only Shabwa block with established production facilities (in the Ayadh field linked to the Bir Ali pipeline). However, Nimir's output from the Ayadh field did not exceed 5,000 b/d and was around 3,500 b/d when the company suspended production during Yemen's civil war in 1994. Nimir subsequently sought improved financial terms, bringing the Ayadh field back into production in 1997 at an initial rate of 1,500 b/d after the legislature had approved an amended production-sharing agreement.

In mid-1997 a total of 167,602 sq km of Yemeni territory—including some of the least intensively explored parts of the Arabian peninsula—was divided into 56 oil exploration blocks, of which 31 remained open to bids from prospective concession holders. Yemen currently had 4,000m. barrels of proved oil reserves (virtually all of which were in fields discovered between 1984 and 1993). Competition between foreign oil companies for new oil concessions had been strongest in Yemen's 1991–92 licensing round, which included notably Shabwa blocks regarded at that time as prime development sites. Disappointing exploration results in the Shabwa region caused several companies to opt for non-renewal of their agreements in 1994–95, while Nimir Petroleum, as the operator of a producing Shabwa field, suspended production until it secured improved terms (see above). Prior to the start of small-scale production in the East Shabwa block, Total-CFP successfully negotiated for a 70% cost-recovery allowance (compared with a previous government offer of a 40% allowance). There was a general improvement in 1995–96 in the terms offered to new concession-holders, including an increase of 5% in average cost-recovery allowances, and the Government made particular efforts during 1997 to attract new investment in smaller blocks and blocks that had been assessed as marginal on the basis of previous exploration work. Foreign companies signing new oil exploration agreements or renewing existing agreements in 1997–98 included Transglobe Energy, First Calgary Petroleum and Calvalley Petroleum (all of Canada), Kerr McGee Corpn (of the USA),

MOL (of Hungary), Preussag Energie (of Germany) and three British companies, Mayfair Petroleum, Dove Energy and Oil and Gas Mine Co (OGMC, owned by Yemeni interests). In 1997 the state-owned Yemen Oil and Gas Corpn was authorized to acquire minority equity stakes (of 15% to 25%) in newly awarded exploration blocks.

Yemen's total oil output averaged 350,000 b/d in 1995, 355,000 b/d in 1996 and 385,000 b/d in 1997. In April 1998, when production was running at 386,500 b/d, the contributions of the respective producing companies were 200,000 b/d from CanOxy's Masila block, 140,000 b/d from Yemen Hunt's Marib/al-Jawf block, 25,000 b/d from Jannah Hunt's Jannah block, 20,000 b/d from Total-CFP's East Shabwa block and 1,500 b/d from Nimir Petroleum's Shabwa block. The estimated government share of April 1998 oil output was just over 200,000 b/d, of which about 115,000 b/d was exported and the remainder consumed locally. Yemeni crude oil was normally priced with reference to standard international benchmarks—thus in 1997–98 Marib light crude was priced at parity with North Sea Brent crude, while Masila crude was priced at a specified discount relative to Brent. The Government's reported oil export revenue rose from $958m. in 1996 to a record $1,012m. in 1997, reflecting an increase in production during a period of relatively strong export prices. In the first half of 1998, however, a slump in the world oil market cut the average price of Yemen's main export grade by 32% (from $17.27 per barrel in January–June 1997 to $11.80 per barrel in January–June 1998). Over the same period the state share of Yemeni oil output declined by an estimated 20%, resulting in a fall of 45% in the Government's reported oil export revenue (from $464.6m. in January–June 1997 to $254.6m. in January–June 1998). Yemen was one of several non-members of OPEC to make a public pledge of support for OPEC production cutbacks designed to counteract the 1998 price slump. A March 1998 statement from Yemen's Ministry of Oil and Mineral Resources said that a Yemeni oil production cutback of 2% to 3% was to be introduced (although the state oil corporation continued to forecast an 11% production increase by the end of 1998).

At the end of 1997 Yemen had proved reserves of natural gas totalling 480,000m. cu m, discovered both separately and in association with oil by companies drilling in oil concession areas (the main discoveries of non-associated gas having been made in the Marib/al-Jawf and Jannah blocks). Throughout the first half of the 1990s various proposals were put forward for a major gas development project centred on the export of liquefied natural gas. In March 1997 the Yemeni legislature approved the establishment of a consortium to organize the planned project. As constituted in October 1997, the consortium comprised Total-CFP (the project leader, with a 36% interest), the state-owned General Gas Corpn (21%), Hunt Oil (15.1%), Exxon (14.5%) and the South Korean companies Yukong (8.4%) and Hyundai (5%). It was envisaged that gas would be piped from Marib to a liquefaction plant on the Gulf of Aden with an export capacity of 5.3m. tons per year, However, the consortium's sole memorandum of understanding, with the Turkish company Botas, was not renewed on its expiry at the end of 1997, by which time many target markets in Asia were experiencing severe economic downturns. Total-CFP acknowledged in March 1998 that there could be little progress on the project until firm sales agreements were secured. In May 1998 discussions were opened with BG UK Holdings regarding the possible supply of Yemeni LNG to an import terminal under construction on the west coast of India by British Gas International. The Yemen Government was meanwhile awaiting the completion of a feasibility study on the economics of creating a local gas supply grid and of establishing gas-fired power plants in Yemen.

INDUSTRY AND MINING

In 1995 manufacturing's share of GDP was estimated to be 7.1%. The largest industrial plant in Yemen at the time of unification in 1990 was the former BP oil refinery at Aden, opened in 1954 when Aden was among the world's busiest seaports. The Government designated Aden as the 'economic capital' of the unified state, its aim being to re-establish the port as a major regional trading centre incorporating an industrial free-trade zone.

The state-owned Aden Refinery Co, set up by the former PDRY Government when the predominantly export-oriented Aden refinery was nationalized in 1977, obtained crude oil processing contracts from various countries during the 1980s, including India, Saudi Arabia, Libya, Kuwait, Iran, Algeria, Iraq and the Soviet Union. At the time of the Iraqi invasion of Kuwait in August 1990, Iraq (30,000 b/d) and Kuwait (20,000 b/d) were the Aden refinery's principal suppliers of preferentially priced crude oil. Part of unified Yemen's own recently developed crude oil production (which in mid-1990 came wholly from oilfields in the former YAR) was subsequently diverted from its intended export markets in order to cover the refinery's loss of imports resulting from the UN embargo on trade with Iraq and Iraqi-occupied Kuwait. Only about one-third of the refinery's nominal processing capacity of 170,000 b/d was in use in the early 1990s, when the Government of unified Yemen was seeking financing for a two-phase modernization programme to raise that capacity by 80,000 b/d (the first 30,000 b/d at an estimated cost of $150m., and the final 50,000 b/d at an estimated cost of $200m.). The Aden refinery was shut down for some weeks during and immediately following the 1994 civil war after several of its storage tanks were destroyed in the fighting. There was no major damage to the distillation facilities, and the plant was operating at its normal pre-war production volume by early August 1994. In early 1995 the refinery was processing crude oil from Yemen, Malaysia, Iran and Oman and producing an average 95,000 b/d of refined products.

At the end of 1995 the Aden refinery was processing an average 60,000 b/d of domestic crude and 40,000 b/d of imported crude. In 1996 detailed specifications were drawn up for upgrading works which would entail the construction of a new smaller processing facility at Aden to provide some continuity of supply during a shutdown of the existing plant. Having put the upgrading project out to three successive rounds of tendering, the Government decided in late 1997 to seek private investment in the Aden Refinery Co with the aim of financing the upgrading work out of the proceeds of share sales to local and foreign investors. The principle of returning the company to majority private ownership was approved by the Council of Ministers in May 1998. In an unrelated development, a private Yemeni company secured a $300,000 grant from the US Trade and Development Agency in June 1997 towards a feasibility study for a proposed new oil refinery on northern Yemen's Red Sea coast, near the Ras Isa oil export terminal. The scheduled completion date for the study was April 1998.

A plant for blending lubricating oils was opened at Taiz in May 1996. The $20m. plant, with an annual production capacity of 60,000 tons, was 30% owned by Mobil and Royal Dutch/Shell and 70% owned by a Yemeni firm which had previously distributed imported lubricants. In 1993 unified Yemen achieved self-sufficiency in bottled liquefied petroleum gas (LPG, for which there had previously been a $40m. annual import requirement), following the opening of a bottling plant at San'a.

Non-hydrocarbon manufactures in the former PDRY included textiles, agricultural implements, cigarettes, ginned cotton, liquid batteries, animal feedstuffs, construction materials (including cement blocks, tiles and bricks), crystallized sea salt, food and drink products, plastic products and aluminium goods. It was the policy of the post-unification Government that Yemeni businesses affected by the former PDRY's nationalization policies should in due course be returned to their former private owners. The Arabian peninsula's only brewery, in the Aden suburb of Mansura, was forced to close down in 1994 in the aftermath of the civil war. Industrial development in the former YAR was aimed primarily at achieving self-sufficiency in food processing, clothing and construction materials and at developing traditional occupations using local raw materials, including textiles, leather goods, basketry, jewellery and glass making. In the mid-1980s one-third of the loans to YAR businesses by the Industrial Bank of Yemen were for food and drink production. Other sectors of particular interest to the bank were construction materials; light and household chemicals and plastics; light engineering; woodworking; and electrical and mechanical services. The relatively modest scale of unified Yemen's manufacturing base was illustrated by 1997 estimates showing that local flour production was around 210,000 tons per year, while imports of flour were currently around 800,000

tons per year. Contracts were awarded in late 1997 for a 1,500 tons-per-day flour mill and associated silos at Aden (scheduled for completion in 1999) and for a 600 tons-per-day flour mill and associated silos at the Red Sea port of Salif (scheduled for completion in 2000).

Yemen's two state-owned cement works are located in the former YAR, at Bajil (a 350,000 tons-per-year plant built by Soviet contractors) and at Amran (a 500,000 tons-per-year plant built by Japanese contractors). Planning permission was granted in 1998 for the construction of Yemen's first private-sector cement factory, which was reported to have a design capacity of 670,000 tons per year and a target start-up date of 2001. In 1997 a $120m. iron smelter was under construction in Abyan. Its developer, the United Company for Mineral Industries (owned by Bugshan Steel of Saudi Arabia), anticipated that three-fifths of the smelter's raw materials would consist of scrap iron available within Yemen and that the remainder would be imported.

The principal mine and quarry products of Yemen include rock salt, limestone, marble, gypsum, granite, basalt and clay. Deposits of copper, nickel, zinc, lead, coal, iron, sulphur, silver, gold and uranium are also known to exist, and improved mapping and evaluation of mineral resources have been prioritized by the post-unification Government, which has obtained financial assistance from the World Bank, UNDP and IDA for surveying work. Most government interest centres on the possibility of Yemen's becoming a significant producer of gold, which Soviet surveyors had first discovered at Medden (50 km west of Mukalla) in the early 1980s. Gold-prospecting licences were held by Irish, Dutch and British companies in 1992, and in 1993 prospecting rights in a further 30,000 sq km were granted to a Yemeni company. In 1997 a Canadian company, Menora Resources, was carrying out a pre-feasibility drilling programme at Medden, where the measured resource of gold was put at 280,000 oz. In early 1998 the Yemen Government said that five companies were currently engaged in mineral prospecting, including exploration for zinc and lead, and that new gold discoveries had been made by Canadian, US and Indonesian prospecting companies.

The centre-piece of unified Yemen's industrial development strategy is a commercial and industrial free-zone development at Aden, modelled on similar initiatives in other developing countries. Inaugurated in May 1991 (at which time 50 industrial projects had already received outline approval), the zone was to be developed in stages over a period of years. A proposal submitted by US consultants in 1993 recommended total investment of $5,600m. in four phases over a period of 25 years, centred on the development of port infrastructure to take full advantage of Aden's potential as a transhipment centre for the container traffic of regional ports situated further away from the main international shipping lanes. The plan included proposals for new harbour facilities, an airport extension, a new 300-MW gas-turbine power station and new manufacturing infrastructure, and recommended that development be on a fully-privatized basis. The Yemen Free Zones Public Authority (YFZPA) subsequently announced its intention to seek full privatization of all administrative operations at the port and airport, to countenance full private ownership of the proposed extensions, and to open up Aden's existing port and airport facilities to some form of joint-venture participation by private interests.

In March 1996 the YFZPA finalized an agreement whereby a company called Yemen Investment and Development International (Yeminvest) became the concession holder and project co-ordinator for the Aden development programme. Ownership of Yeminvest from October 1997 was 51% by Yemen Holdings (owned by Saudi Arabian private interests) and 49% by PSA Corpn (formerly known as the Port of Singapore Authority). PSA was to manage and operate a new Aden container terminal for 20 years following completion of the first phase of construction, scheduled for March 1999. Costing up to $280m., the first-phase works included dredging harbour channels, building six quays and a new trans-shipment terminal, installing a small power plant, equipping the terminal with cranes and other facilities and providing access roads and other ancillary features. The handling capacity of the terminal would be 500,000 20-foot-equivalent units (TEUs) per year. Work began in 1996 and was 50% complete by mid-1998. It was intended that completion of the port facilities should be followed by the development of a 1,350-ha site for export-oriented industries; modernization and improvement of infrastructure and facilities and expansion of cargo-handling capacity at Khormaksar international airport; construction of a new power station; and (as the final phase of the development programme) construction of a World Trade Centre complex including 100,000 sq m of office space and 9,300 sq m of exhibition space. According to Yeminvest's initial revenue projections, the free-zone development would be self-financing by its seventh year, with the container port playing an important income-generating role. The Yemen Government's entitlement to revenue from free-zone operations was to rise gradually from 25% to 100% over the 25-year life of the concession.

Yemen's General Investment Authority (GIA), established in 1991 to encourage and supervise new investment in Yemen (including investment by Yemenis resident abroad) was in 1998 operating within the framework of recently amended investment laws offering an extensive range of tax and other incentives. Current GIA promotional campaigns placed particular emphasis on investment in labour-intensive export industries, including the manufacture of textiles, for which Yemen offered the advantage of quota-free access to the EU, the USA and other main markets.

INFRASTRUCTURE

In 1997 Yemen had 69,000 km of roads, 12% of which were asphalted and a further 24% of which were classed as paved roads. Some 535,200 road vehicles (55% of them goods vehicles and buses) were in use in 1996. Road-building and maintenance are important development priorities, and have been funded to a large extent by foreign aid donors in recent years. After Yemeni unification in 1990 there was an increased emphasis on the improvement of road links across the former YAR–PDRY border. In 1993 the Government of Oman agreed to finance a highway across Oman's newly opened border with Yemen. Road-building schemes scheduled to go to tender in 1998 included 180 km in the south (between Aden and Mukalla) and 65 km in the west (between Salif and Hodeida), both of which were to be financed by the World Bank. More than 800 km of existing roads were included in upgrading plans under consideration in 1998.

The port of Aden, developed around a natural deep harbour, was ideally placed to benefit from the growth of international Suez Canal traffic during the period of British colonial rule. Its trade was especially hard hit by the closure of the Canal from 1967 to 1975 and the subsequent failure of the PDRY Government to respond adequately to changing shipping patterns (including the rapid growth of containerization). The first phase of a major modernization and expansion of Aden's port facilities was begun in 1996 and was scheduled for completion in 1999 (see 'Industry and Mining' section above). The state transport sector in Aden, including existing port operations, made a net profit of 424m. riyals on a turnover of 1,200m. riyals in 1997. The port's existing freight and distribution services were transferred to seven private contractors in mid-1998 as part of the Government's privatization programme. The main port serving the easternmost region of Yemen is Mukalla, an important fishing centre with deep-water harbour facilities developed during the 1980s. The region's main oil export terminal is situated about 35 km east of Mukalla. The main port on Yemen's Red Sea coast is Hodeida, which was greatly expanded in the 1970s and 1980s in line with the growth in the import trade of the former YAR. The selection of Aden as unified Yemen's commercial capital in 1990 implied some slowdown in the future expansion of port facilities at Hodeida. The port of Mocha, situated south of Hodeida (and therefore closer to Aden) cancelled many of its own expansion plans after unification. In contrast, the port of Salif, north of Hodeida, benefited in the 1990s from its proximity to Yemen's Red Sea oil export terminal at Ras Isa.

Aden's international airport at Khormaksar was extensively upgraded in the late 1980s with Soviet financial assistance. However, its terminal building, capable of handling 250,000 passengers per year, was damaged in the 1994 civil war. Repairs to the terminal, as well as the construction of a new control tower and related technical facilities, were included in a World Bank-supported airport rehabilitation project which was put out to tender at the start of 1998. Yemen's other international airports are at San'a, Hodeida, Taiz and Mukalla. There are 12 main local airports for domestic flights. In total, Yemen had 46 airports and airfields in the mid-1990s, and most towns were linked by internal air services. Yemen's national carrier, Yemen Airways or Yemenia, was established in May 1996 through the merger of the former YAR airline (also called Yemenia) and the former PDRY airline (Al-Yemen, previously known as Alyemda). Saudi Arabian Airlines held a 49% shareholding in the merged airline, which took delivery of two Airbus A310-300 aircraft in March 1997. There were substantial increases in domestic and international air fares from April 1995 onwards as part of the Government's subsidy reduction programme. Yemenia carried about 700,000 passengers in 1997 (an increase of 18% over 1996). A major fleet renewal programme—involving the replacement of four Boeing 737s, three Boeing 727s and four Dash 7s—was under consideration in 1998.

Yemen has modern international telecommunications links via satellite stations and microwave relays, as well as relatively good links between major centres within the country. However, many smaller towns and rural areas still had fairly limited telephone networks in the mid-1990s, while there was a generally inadequate provision of lines within urban centres. Overall, Yemen had only 1.29 fixed telephone lines per 100 inhabitants in 1996. There were 8,800 cellular phone subscribers in the same year (although mobile telecommunications services, suspended during the 1994 civil war, were not restored until September 1996). It was expected that there would be 260,000 fixed telephone lines in Yemen in the year 2000. Contracts worth $3m. were awarded in November 1996 for an expansion of the telephone network within San'a and the upgrading of links between San'a and other population centres. In March 1997 Japan announced a $29m. loan to help finance the installation of more than 50,000 additional telephone lines in Aden. In late 1997 the French company Alcatel (currently working at 45 locations in Yemen) was awarded a $14m. contract to install 82,000 new lines throughout the country.

A main planning priority in the power sector after unification in 1990 was to link the electricity grids of the former YAR and PDRY. This was finally achieved in July 1997 at a total cost of $64m. (of which $54m. was funded by the AFESD). It was estimated that Yemen's nominal electricity generating capacity from all sources (including small public supplies not connected to the national grid, as well as private diesel generators in remote areas) did not exceed 700 MW in 1997. The World Bank estimated that the Public Electricity Corpn's total 1997 installed capacity was a nominal 596 MW, of which only 408 MW was effectively available because of the technical limitations of Yemen's power plants and distribution lines. High growth of energy demand—stimulated partly by subsidized tariffs—had placed Yemen's electricity supply system under severe pressure for some years. San'a had experienced particularly bad power shortages since 1993, and some generating and transmission facilities had suffered damage in the 1994 civil war. In 1997 the Government drew up a $51m. emergency power project to cover Yemen's electricity needs until the year 2001. As submitted to IDA (from which funding was sought) the project called for the rapid installation of 30 MW of additional generating capacity at the Dhahban power plant serving San'a; the rehabilitation of 20 MW of existing diesel generating capacity at the same plant; and the improvement of transmission lines to ensure that the plant's increased output was fully available to the grid.

Major water-supply initiatives in post-unification Yemen included a project to bring drinking water to 45,000 people in over 100 villages to the north of Aden. The first phase of this project, involving the drilling of wells in the coastal Wadi Bani and the construction of the means of raising the water 1,500 m to the Laboos plateau, was under way in late 1991. The Radaa water supply and sanitation project, involving the supply of drinking water to some 30,000 people, was also under way. Aden's water supply system and sewerage facilities were severely disrupted during the civil war in 1994, and serious water shortages continued to be reported three months after the end of the fighting in the city. UN agencies identified an emergency requirement for up to $5m.-worth of essential repairs to water and sewerage infrastructure. New water and sewerage schemes under consideration in 1996 included a pilot project to improve the water supply in Taiz (for which $10m. was to be provided by the World Bank) and the construction of a waste-water treatment plant in San'a (to be financed by the World Bank, the AFESD and the OPEC Fund for International Development).

According to a World Bank study, about 88% of Yemen's urban households had access to piped water supplies in 1997, although such supplies were often erratic and interruptions of up to eight weeks could be experienced in some areas. (See 'Agriculture and Fisheries', above, for details of Yemen's underlying water shortage.) In some large cities, including Taiz and San'a, over one-fifth of the population depended on private-sector water suppliers. It was estimated that two-thirds of all water consumed in San'a in 1997 was provided by these largely unregulated private suppliers. About 90% of Yemen's urban households were estimated to have access to adequate waste-water facilities, although in the majority of cases these took the form of closed pit systems rather than public sewer networks. The disposal of solid waste was a particular problem in urban Yemen in the mid-1990s, as municipal collections tended to be limited to market areas and main streets, leading to accumulations of rubbish in side streets and to uncontrolled dumping of waste outside towns. Laws on environmental protection and waste management were introduced in 1995 to provide a basis for improving this situation.

EXTERNAL TRADE, AID AND PAYMENTS

The official trade and payments statistics for Yemen, before and after unification, provide a broad outline of developments, based on recorded information. There is a deficiency of accurate and detailed information in several key areas, mostly relating to labour migration and workers' remittances, and some official trade figures give unrealistically low import totals (smuggling having been particularly widespread in the former YAR in the late 1970s and early 1980s). The blurring of such statistics reflects the very high levels of economic inter-dependence that developed within the Arabian peninsula in the 1970s and 1980s as Saudi Arabia and other oil-rich Gulf states provided mass employment opportunities for Yemeni workers. Insofar as they were used to offset the large deficits in the Yemeni states' basic commodity trade, the inflows of remittance income from the oil states strengthened the overall balance-of-payments positions of the YAR and PDRY. (In practice, significant amounts of remittance income were spent on imported consumer goods, particularly in the YAR.) However, remittance income did not eliminate either state's heavy dependence on foreign aid to finance development projects and budget deficits, nor did it represent a stable and predictable income source, being highly dependent on fluctuations in the host countries' economic cycles, which were closely linked to swings in world oil prices. In the 1990s, unified Yemen benefited from a stronger export base as it developed its own oilfields. At the same time import demand was boosted, and remittance income cut, as the country absorbed the impact of the large repatriations of Yemeni workers arising out of the 1990–91 Gulf crisis. Having become accustomed to modest rises in export earnings as oil production developed, Yemen was in 1998 adjusting to a major slump in world oil prices. In late 1997 Yemen secured substantial relief in respect of its major arrears of foreign debt (including debt stemming from the former PDRY's heavy reliance on Soviet aid).

Until the late 1980s, the former YAR's merchandise exports covered less than 3% of the value of imports. World Bank statistics showed that in the period 1965–80 exports grew at an annual average rate of only 2.8%, whereas imports grew by 23.3% per year. In the period 1980–88, however, the average annual growth in exports was 35.6%, while imports declined by 10% per year. The improvement in export performance was attributable to the start of crude oil exports at the end of 1987. In 1987 YAR exports were worth only $19m., against imports of $1,311m.; in 1988 exports rose sharply to $485m., against imports of $1,310m. In the early 1980s the YAR's official annual trade deficit ran at around $1,500m., falling to around $1,200m. per year in 1986 and 1987 and to $835m. in 1988. The estimated value of goods smuggled into the former YAR to avoid high import duties was $1,000m. in 1983. According to the World

Bank, oil and other minerals accounted for 88% of YAR exports by value in 1988 (compared with 9% in 1965), manufactured goods for 11% (0% in 1965) and other primary commodities for 1% (91% in 1965). In the same year food accounted for 28% of total imports by value (compared with 41% in 1965), manufactured goods for 55% (47% in 1965), fuels for 8% (6% in 1965) and other primary commodities for 6% (6% in 1965).

According to the World Bank, the former PDRY's exports declined in value in the period 1965–80 by an annual average of 13.7%, while imports fell by 7.5% per year. In the period 1980–88, however, exports increased by an average of 1.9% per year and imports by 4.4% per year. In 1988 exports were worth $80m., while imports reached $598m. The former PDRY's main export commodities (excluding refined petroleum products) were cotton, hides and skins, fish, rice and coffee. The chief imports (excluding crude oil) were manufactured goods for development projects, clothing, foodstuffs and livestock. Fuels and minerals accounted for 90% of total PDRY exports by value in 1988 (against 80% in 1965), other primary commodities for 9% (14% in 1965) and manufactured goods for 1% (8% in 1965).

Following unification, Yemen's external trade was temporarily disrupted by the UN embargo on trade with Iraq and Kuwait, which necessitated a diversion to the Aden refinery of Yemeni crude oil that would otherwise have gone for export (see Industry and Mining, above). Yemen's merchandise exports in 1990 totalled 7,066m. riyals (including 6,188m. riyals from oil), whereas merchandise imports totalled 20,863m. riyals, producing a visible trade deficit of 13,795m. riyals, compared with a combined deficit for the YAR and PDRY in 1989 of 11,533m. riyals (exports 6,765m. riyals, imports 18,298m. riyals). There was a visible trade deficit of 18,238.4m. riyals in 1992 (exports 6,075.9m. riyals, imports 24,314.3m. riyals). The provisional trade figures for 1993 showed a deficit of 25,382.3m. riyals (exports 5,693.3m. riyals, imports 31,075.6m. riyals). The visible trade deficit in 1994 was 13,850m. riyals (exports 9,940m. riyals, imports 23,790m. riyals). The World Bank estimated Yemen's 1995 visible trade deficit to be $284.4m. (exports $2,110.6m., imports $2,395m.), although IMF estimates indicated a much smaller deficit ($11m.) for that year. Preliminary World Bank estimates for 1996 indicated a visible trade deficit of $602.1m. (exports $2,275.1m., imports $2,877.2m.).

Yemen had an overall current-account deficit of 1,711m. riyals in 1990, compared with a combined YAR and PDRY deficit of 9,853m. riyals in 1989. The services account showed receipts of 17,518m. riyals in 1990 (5,519m. riyals in 1989) exceeding payments of 5,432m. riyals (3,839m. riyals in 1989). The strong upturn in private remittances in 1990 was attributable to Yemeni nationals returning from Saudi Arabia because of the Gulf crisis. The World Bank assessed Yemen's net remittance income at $800m. in 1991, and suggested that the current account was $20m. in surplus in that year. Prior to the 1990 Gulf crisis, remittance income had averaged around $2,000m. per year. According to World Bank estimates, a fall in Yemen's net remittance income to $340m. in 1992 was a contributory factor in an overall current-account deficit of $1,582m. in that year. In mid-1994 the Arab Monetary Fund extended a $47m. loan to Yemen to support the financing of the country's 1993 balance-of-payments deficit. Yemen had a current-account deficit of $1,248m. and an overall balance-of-payments deficit of $1,113m. in 1993. In 1994 there was a current-account surplus of $366m. and an estimated overall deficit of $653m. In 1995 Yemen received estimated remittance income of $1,120m. and recorded a surplus of $183m. on the current account. Provisional balance-of-payments data for 1996 indicated a current-account deficit of $192.6m.

Much practical aid in the fields of health, education and social welfare flowed into the former YAR, particularly from oil-rich Arab countries and organizations, China, the USSR, the World Health Organization and UNICEF. Kuwait, Saudi Arabia and the UAE provided schools, hospitals and clinics, and many other Arab countries sent teachers to the YAR. Qatar provided aid for schools, hospitals and roads, and staff training for radio and television productions. Arab aid supported major infrastructural projects, such as the San'a sewerage scheme, the modernization of San'a International Airport and road building schemes. During the first half of the 1980s the USSR spent about $1,000m. to arm and train the army of the YAR. Thereafter, however, military equipment was purchased increasingly from the USA, with finance provided by Saudi Arabia. Although the USSR remained a major aid donor, increasing amounts of aid were provided in the 1980s by OECD members, including the Netherlands, the Federal Republic of Germany, the USA, Japan and Britain. The World Bank was also an important source of loans through the IDA, and UN agencies provided much technical assistance. Overall, the former YAR's receipts of official development aid from all sources totalled $412m. in 1982, $328m. in 1983, $326m. in 1984, $283m. in 1985, $275m. in 1986, $348m. in 1987 and $223m. in 1988. Between 1962 and 1982, it is estimated, the YAR borrowed some $2,325m., of which the USSR lent $819m., and other Arab countries $744m. In September 1987, according to Central Bank figures, the debt to the Soviet Union was $1,064m., almost half of the country's total external debt of $2,136m.

From 1969 onwards, the USSR was the former PDRY's main development partner under a series of economic agreements. In the 1980s Soviet aid financed several major projects, including major Aden port and airport developments, the exploitation of fishery resources, and mineral surveys. The PDRY also benefited from infrastructural work carried out by the USSR in connection with its military facilities in the country. The former PDRY obtained large development loans in 1979 from Bulgaria and Czechoslovakia, while China lent a further $12.5m. for the purchase of industrial goods. In the 1980s Czechoslovakia and the GDR were involved in mineral survey work, Bulgaria undertook to help in the development of tourist facilities, and China continued to finance and to execute road-building schemes. Official grants from Arab aid donors reached a record $126m. in 1982, but declined to an annual average of $40m. in subsequent years. The main sources of multilateral aid were the UN and the World Bank. The former PDRY's receipts of official development aid from all sources totalled $143m. in 1982, $106m. in 1983, $103m. in 1984, $113m. in 1985, $71m. in 1986, $74m. in 1987 and $76m. in 1988.

In June 1990 the World Bank confirmed that Yemen would be entitled to concessionary finance and that loan programmes and development projects under way in the YAR and the PDRY would continue in the unified country. Unified Yemen's receipts of official development aid amounted to $405m. in 1990 and $313m. in 1991 (in which year it represented 3.9% of GNP).

In 1982 the PDRY and YAR Governments established the Yemen Tourism Co to promote 'package' tours to both countries. In 1987 about 28,000 tourists visited the PDRY. In 1989 the YAR was visited by 55,088 tourists who spent an estimated $22m. In 1995 there were 61,000 tourist arrivals in unified Yemen, over half of them from European countries, generating an estimated revenue of $38m. Yemen's largest tourism company, Universal Travel and Tourism, had links with some 300 overseas tour operators in Europe, the USA and Japan in 1995, when several major hotel developments were in progress to cater for a projected rise in visitor numbers. The main developer was the Tourism Investment Co (50% owned by Universal Travel and Tourism). Yemen earned around $55m. from tourism in 1996, when there were 229 registered hotels in the country. Kidnappings of tourists by tribal communities with grievances against the central Government increased from 10 in 1997 to 20 in the first seven months of 1998. Tourist numbers fell from 30,800 in the period January–June 1997 to 24,000 in January–June 1998. An Egyptian-led consortium submitted proposals in mid-1998 for a major tourism resort development on the thinly populated Yemeni island of Socotra.

Figures disclosed in July 1990 showed unified Yemen's total foreign debt as $7,256m., equivalent to about 110% of current GNP and some 50% higher than the previous Western estimate of about $5,000m. Of the total, $4,366m. was debt attributable to the former PDRY (owed mainly to the USSR, China and eastern European countries) and $2,890m. to the former YAR. In September 1990 France agreed to cancel all of Yemen's outstanding debt to it—some $55m.—and Japan also granted debt-relief aid. According to the World Bank, Yemen's external debt totalled $6,598m. at the end of 1992. In December 1994 the Government said that it intended to negotiate with Russia for the cancellation of 90% of Yemen's debt to the former Soviet Union. In mid-1995 Japan's cumulative debt-relief grants to Yemen totalled $68.4m. In September 1996 the 'Paris Club'

group of creditor countries agreed to recommend the rescheduling of about $100m. of Yemen's debt. In April 1997 the USA announced a rescheduling of Yemeni debt over a period of 40 years, including a 20-year exemption period.

Russia, which became a member of the 'Paris Club' in 1997, disclosed that it was owed $400m. of commercial debt by Yemen, three-quarters of which was overdue for repayment. However, the bulk of the former Soviet Union's lending had been on non-commercial terms within the framework of bilateral co-operation agreements with the former PDRY and YAR. The total lending under these agreements was nearly $6,700m., of which $6,500m. (including nearly $2,700m. of arrears) was still outstanding. Loan agreements had been denominated in roubles, with typical repayment periods of between 5 and 15 years and typical interest rates of 2% to 5%, and had usually specified repayment in hard currency by the YAR or 'in the national currency for subsequent purchase of goods' by the PDRY. The former Soviet Union had by 1988 acceded to 19 requests for postponements of debt repayments, the total value of all repayments received being less than 170m. roubles.

At a 'Paris Club' meeting in November 1997, Russia agreed to waive about $5,360m. of Yemeni debt (80% of $6,700m.) and to apply so-called 'Naples conditions' (67% of debt written off and 33% rescheduled over a greatly extended period at very low interest rates) to the remainder. Yemen's debts to the other 'Paris Cub' countries were to be reviewed by each country with a view to rescheduling on Naples terms. Total Yemeni indebtedness to foreign creditors other than Russia was estimated to be about $1,500m. in 1997. Yemen's Prime Minister said after the November 1997 'Paris Club' meeting that creditor countries in two regions—the Arab world and eastern Europe—had not as yet discussed debt rescheduling with Yemen. In the case of eastern Europe, the amounts involved were relatively modest and were not considered a problem by Yemen. In the case of major Arab creditor countries, including Saudi Arabia, Kuwait and Iraq, the Yemen Government had requested rescheduling negotiations with a view to obtaining terms similar to those applied by 'Paris Club' countries. There had, however, been no response from any of the countries concerned, with the result that all debts to other Arab governments remained 'in place and frozen' at the end of 1997.

POST-UNIFICATION BUDGETS AND ECONOMIC POLICY

After unification, the respective currencies of the two former Yemeni states were legal tender in the Republic of Yemen and could be used at a rate of 1 (South) Yemeni dinar = 26 (North) Yemeni riyals until 20 June 1996, when the old dinar was formally abolished and the riyal became the sole currency unit for the unified Yemen. In mid-1993, when the standard official exchange rate was $1 = 12.01 riyals (as it had been since February 1990), the black-market value of the Yemeni currency was approximately $1 = 46 riyals (reflecting, in part, the country's annual inflation rate of about 200% at that time). In 1992 the Government had introduced a 'customs rate' of $1 = 18 riyals for all non-essential imports, and in May 1993 it had introduced an 'incentive rate' of 25 riyals to the US dollar for oil companies and tourists.

In the unified state's first budget, for 1991, expenditure was projected at 50,980m. riyals (compared with an aggregate figure of 46,256m. riyals in 1990) and revenue at 35,218m. riyals (24,704m. in 1990). The resultant forecast deficit of 15,762m. riyals represented a 27% reduction against the 1990 combined deficit of 21,552m. riyals. The biggest allocation in the 1991 budget was for defence (12,700m. riyals), followed by investment and development (11,000m. riyals) and education (8,300m. riyals). The investment and development allocation did not include loans and grants from external sources, which were seen as crucial for offsetting losses attributable to the Gulf crisis.

The 1992 budget provided for estimated revenue of 45,778m. riyals and expenditure of 58,114m. riyals, and thus for a deficit of 12,336m. riyals. The Government's financial projections for the year envisaged: that its foreign exchange resources would total $2,185m. to meet anticipated commitments of $2,349m. (as against resources of $1,836m. and outgoings of $2,212m. in 1991); that imports of wheat, flour, rice and essential drugs would cost $368m.; that all foreign debt obligations would be met in 1992; and that defence spending would be reduced by 12% compared with 1991. The Government did not publish 1993 budget proposals, and was assumed to be organizing its finances on a month-to-month basis, using its 1992 spending as a guideline for the current year. According to press reports (said to be based on internal Finance Ministry records), actual spending in 1992 had totalled 58,060m. riyals (of which 53,637m. riyals was current spending), while actual revenue had amounted to only 32,008m. riyals (about one-third of estimated GNP). The largest single component of expenditure in 1992 was the public-sector salary bill, reported to total 32,735m. riyals. In 1994 the Government again failed to reach any agreement on a national budget, and was assumed to be maintaining a form of month-to-month accounting system until May, when established procedures were disrupted by the onset of civil war.

According to estimates published by independent Yemeni economists in January 1994, the Government spent 74,000m. riyals in 1993 and collected revenue of 32,000m. riyals, leaving a deficit of 42,000m. riyals, equivalent to more than one-third of the current GDP (which was estimated to be between 110,000m. and 120,000m. riyals). It was not known how the budget deficit had been financed. Following the end of the civil war in July 1994, the Government said that it planned to issue bonds to raise funds for post-war reconstruction work. The Yemeni currency's unofficial exchange rate against the US dollar, which had declined to 80 riyals before the outbreak of hostilities, fell below 100 riyals for the first time during June 1994. Retrospective budget statistics for 1994, published long after the end of that year, showed total revenue of 41,384m. riyals and total expenditure of 85,875m. riyals. The overall deficit was 44,491m. riyals.

In 1995 the Government prepared a formal budget (approved by the legislature on 30 April) which provided for total expenditure of 111,128m. riyals and total revenue of 89,646m. riyals, leaving a deficit of 21,482m. riyals. It had previously been announced in December 1994 that capital spending in 1994 would total around 35,000m. riyals, of which 20,000m. riyals would be spent on post-war reconstruction and infrastructural development. The 1995 budget was preceded by a package of economic measures designed to limit the size of the budget deficit (which would otherwise have reached an estimated 60,000m. riyals). On 29 March the prices of a wide range of commodities and services were raised by between 50% and 100% (petrol being one of the items which doubled in price), while public-sector pay and pensions were increased by between 20% for top grades and 50% (or a minimum of 1,000 riyals per month) for lower grades. Flour and wheat prices remained heavily subsidized, while imported medicines, milk and rice were exempted from increases in customs duties. Significant cutbacks were announced in expenditure on Yemen's diplomatic missions and official offices in other countries, while the armed forces were instructed to retire or discharge a total of 50,000 personnel. On 30 March a unified official exchange rate of 50 riyals per US dollar was introduced, and on 7 May local banks were authorized to carry out currency trading at prevailing free-market exchange rates (which remained far weaker than the new official rate).

Following talks with delegations from the World Bank and the IMF, the Government announced in late May 1995 that it was drawing up a five-year plan to restructure the economy over the period 1996–2000. The draft plan envisaged the flotation of the riyal within three years; progressive withdrawal of price subsidies on basic goods, including grain, rice and flour; liberalization of the food distribution system; far-reaching administrative reforms, including some decentralization measures; full harmonization of the northern and southern legal systems; and the introduction of a privatization programme (to be followed by the establishment of a stock market). Joint public-private sector ventures would be encouraged in infrastructural and other projects, and particular efforts would be made to secure high levels of private investment in labour-intensive projects. Seven publicly-owned companies in Aden (five of which were food-processing concerns) were earmarked for early privatization, as were a number of small-scale power generation facilities. The Government was expected to finalize the content of the five-year plan after further consultations with IMF/World Bank representatives, who were understood to favour a 50% cutback

in public-sector employment and a two-year phasing-out period for all government price subsidies. The Yemen Government, for its part, was hoping that IMF/World Bank financial assistance for structural reforms would be complemented by measures to secure a reduction in Yemen's external indebtedness.

In July 1995 the Central Bank of Yemen raised its maximum deposit rate from 9% to 22% to stimulate savings in local currency, and used an estimated $27m. of its foreign assets to support the free-market exchange rate of the riyal, which had declined in late June to its lowest ever level of 165 to the dollar (a level previously reached on the unofficial currency market in April, prior to the authorization of free-market currency dealing through the banking system). In mid-July Yemen's Prime Minister said that the public finances were currently showing a slightly smaller deficit than had been forecast in the 1995 budget, while a senior World Bank official expressed strong confidence in government economic policy and foresaw a tripling of World Bank assistance to Yemen if the Government moved quickly to implement key structural reforms. The free-market exchange rate per dollar strengthened to 55 riyals during August before declining to 114 riyals in November and 130 riyals in December. At the beginning of December the Central Bank held its first ever auction of treasury bills, having announced that it would be issuing short-dated bills with a total face value of 12,000m. riyals over the next six months with the aim of reducing excess liquidity in the country's economy.

In January 1996 the Government announced the immediate abolition of the official exchange rate of 50 riyals per dollar while stating its readiness to intervene in the currency market if the riyal's free-market value weakened beyond 'the real and practical rate'. (At the same time the so-called customs exchange rate—now the main indicator of current government estimates of the 'real and practical' value of the currency—was devalued to 100 riyals per dollar.) The Central Bank was authorized to use up to $480m. of foreign reserves to support the riyal during the first 15 months of the floating exchange rate regime. Intervention by the Central Bank caused the exchange rate to strengthen to 100 riyals per dollar at some points during the first quarter of 1996. In April 1996, when the Central Bank did not intervene in the local currency market, the rate fell back to 134 riyals per dollar.

As well as abolishing the official exchange rate at the beginning of 1996, the Government reduced official price subsidies for many basic foodstuffs. Market prices rose sharply, and some commodities were in short supply for a time, as a result of hoarding prompted by expectations of future price increases. In January 1996 the Government announced that electricity prices were to rise by 50%–100% and water charges by 40%–60%, depending on consumption. Prices of oil products and domestic gas were also increased, although the price increase for diesel (originally 100%) was reduced to 33% after protest action by farmers.

The 1996 budget provided for expenditure of 181,416m. riyals (a 63.2% increase over the previous budget) and revenue of 155,886m. riyals (an increase of 73.9%), resulting in a deficit of 25,530m. riyals (19% less than the 1995 budget deficit). The spending allocations included 1,000m. riyals to alleviate the severity of economic reforms for the most vulnerable sections of the population. A January 1996 meeting of multilateral, regional and bilateral donors commended Yemen's current economic policies and pledged a total of $500m. of new funding in 1996 ($350m. in support of structural reforms and $150m. to finance development projects). The Arab Monetary Fund was to provide $68m. under a loan agreement signed in November 1995. A 15-month stand-by credit of SDR 132m. (about $194m.) was formally approved by the IMF in March 1996, and the World Bank approved an $80m. structural reform programme in April, to be supplemented by further credits for a number of civil works projects designed to provide short-term employment for labourers. It was announced in late June that the Government was to set up a $20m. Social Development and Employment Fund, through which investment in job-creation and related programmes would be channelled.

In July 1996 the Government finalized its development plan for the period 1996–2000, which included a GDP growth target of 7.2% per annum. Oil and gas production was targeted to grow by 55% during the period of the plan. It was envisaged that total investment would amount to 818,000m. riyals (more than $5,800m. at the prevailing exchange rate). Of this, nearly 390,000m. riyals represented foreign investment in the oil and gas sector (three-quarters of which was for the planned LNG export scheme). There were 207,000m. riyals of foreign aid, 121,600m. riyals of public investment and the balance (nearly 100,000m. riyals) came from private-sector investment.

As originally adopted, Yemen's 1997 budget provided for total expenditure of 313,985m. riyals and total revenue of 301,222m. riyals, leaving a deficit of 12,763m. riyals. However, additional expenditure of 12,610m. riyals was approved by the legislature in September 1997, increasing the final 1997 budget deficit to 25,373m. riyals. When capital items were excluded, the revised 1997 budget was in surplus by 2,690m. riyals on current account. The largest revenue sources in the 1997 budget were oil and gas (63%), taxation (11%), customs duties (10%) and foreign aid (6%), while the largest expenditure categories in the revised total were subsidies on food and energy prices (23%), defence (16%), education (16%), new investment (12%) and debt servicing (10%). The Central Bank's foreign exchange reserves increased from $564m. at the end of 1995 to $969m. at the end of 1996 and stood at $1,072m. in mid-1997. The currency exchange rate averaged around 130 riyals to the dollar in the year to mid-1997. The Central Bank's minimum interest rate on riyal bank deposits (which had been 20% in April 1997) was reduced to 12% in August 1997 and 11% in December 1997.

In early June 1997 the UN Development Programme announced an allocation of $200m. to support projects in Yemen over the next five years. The World Bank had previously announced $420m. of new loan allocations over a period of three years. In mid-June 1997 IMF officials held talks with Yemen's new Government to discuss the terms of a proposed three-year extended structural adjustment facility. Later that month a meeting of 26 donor bodies affirmed aid pledges to Yemen totalling $1,800m. over three years. In pursuance of its structural reform programme, the Government introduced substantial price increases for fuel, wheat and flour at the start of July 1997, while at the same time increasing public-sector wages by 10%. In September 1997 the Government announced its intention to establish an official stock exchange in early 1998 and to begin preparations to privatize the National Bank of Yemen (established in 1969 through the nationalization of foreign commercial banks' operations in the PDRY).

At the end of October 1997 the IMF approved a $512m. loan and credit package in support of the Government's economic programme for the period 1997–2000. The package comprised SDR 264.8m. ($366m.) in loans under the IMF's enhanced structural adjustment facility, plus a credit of SDR 105.9m. ($146m.) under the extended fund facility. The objectives of the medium-term strategy for 1997–2000 were to achieve average non-oil GDP growth of 6% per annum in real terms; to keep the core inflation rate at or below 5% per annum; to restrict the external current-account deficit to 2% of GDP; and to maintain sufficient foreign exchange reserves to cover 4.5 months of imports. The budget deficit was to be limited to an average 2% of GDP. The structural adjustment process was to involve

reorienting spending towards social sectors and infrastructure; reforming direct and indirect taxation; eliminating price subsidies; introducing administrative, civil service and financial sector reforms; implementing a 'rapidly moving and broad privatization programme'; and taking steps to 'enhance the competitive environment'. The World Bank approved two new loans in November 1997: SDR 58.9m. ($80m.) to assist the structural reform process in the financial and banking sector and SDR 17.7m. ($24.7m.) to support rural development in southern Yemen.

Yemen's 1998 budget provided for an 11.7% increase in total revenue, to 336,583m. riyals, while expenditure was set at 350,054m. riyals (7% higher than the revised 1997 total). The resultant deficit of 13,471m. riyals was wholly attributable to capital spending, as the current account was expected to show a surplus of 31,028m. riyals. The oil and gas sector was expected to contribute 61% of revenue in 1998, followed by taxation (13%), customs duties (9%) and foreign aid (6%). The main expenditure categories were education (18%), new investment (16%), defence (15%), subsidies on food and energy prices (14%) and debt servicing (10%). The central assumption in the 1998 revenue estimates was that crude oil prices would average $18 per barrel in 1998. In practice, oil prices fell by around one-third in the opening months of 1998 (see Petroleum and Natural Gas section above), with the result that Yemen's budget deficit stood at 36,200m. riyals, instead of an expected 4,400m. riyals, at the end of April 1998.

In April 1998 the Government announced forthcoming 40% increases in wheat and flour prices and said that it intended to phase out all subsidies on these items by the end of the century. In 1997 the annual cost of wheat and flour subsidies was 48,000m. riyals. Further price rises in mid-June 1998, affecting various subsidized commodities including gasoline, kerosene, bottled gas and basic foodstuffs, sparked protest demonstrations in San'a and several other urban centres. At least 34 deaths were reported as protesters clashed with security forces. The Government raised public-sector wages by 15% from the start of July 1998, having secured IMF approval for a higher 1998 budget deficit (5% of GDP) than had originally been targeted. There was an increase in 1998 in kidnappings of foreigners and government officials by armed tribesmen in rural areas, reportedly aimed at publicizing grievances over low levels of development spending. There was also a reported increase in petty damage to oil pipelines by disaffected tribesmen. Within the oil industry, employees of Yemen Hunt Oil threatened to take strike action unless their pay and conditions were improved.

Yemeni officials made it known in 1998 that Saudi Arabia had begun to issue entry visas to Yemeni workers for the first time since the Gulf war, although Yemenis were now required to have Saudi sponsors and to obtain work and residence permits (requirements that had previously been waived for Yemenis). An estimated 400,000 Yemenis were already working in Saudi Arabia in early 1998. There was no expectation of a large-scale influx of Yemenis into Saudi Arabia at this time, not least because the Saudi economy was itself adversely affected by the sharp downturn in world oil prices.

Statistical Survey

Source (unless otherwise indicated): Republic of Yemen Central Statistical Organization, POB 13434, San'a; tel. (1) 250619; telex 2266; fax (1) 250664.

Area and Population

AREA, POPULATION AND DENSITY

Area (sq km)	536,869*
Population (census results)†	
16 December 1994	
Males	7,473,540
Females	7,114,267
Total	14,587,807
Population (official estimates at mid-year)	
1994	14,859,000
1995	15,369,000
1996	15,919,000
Density (per sq km) at mid-1996	29.7

* 207,286 sq miles.

† Excluding adjustment for underenumeration.

PRINCIPAL TOWNS

(estimated population for urban agglomerations at mid-1993)

San'a (capital)	926,595
Aden	400,783
Taiz	290,107
Hodeida	246,068

Source: UN, *Demographic Yearbook*.

BIRTHS AND DEATHS (UN estimates, annual averages)

	1980–85	1985–90	1990–95
Birth rate (per 1,000) . . .	49.7	49.8	49.4
Death rate (per 1,000) . . .	18.7	17.1	15.5

Expectation of life (UN estimates, years at birth, 1990–95): 50.2 (males 49.9; females 50.4).

Source: UN, *World Population Prospects: The 1994 Revision*.

ECONOMICALLY ACTIVE POPULATION

Mid-1996 (estimates in '000): Agriculture 2,786; Total 4,967. Source: FAO, *Production Yearbook*.

Agriculture

PRINCIPAL CROPS ('000 metric tons)

	1994	1995	1996
Wheat	171	171	149
Barley	63	64	54
Maize	69	58	50
Millet	54	53	46
Sorghum	444	464	365
Potatoes.	181	185	183
Pulses	68	70	67
Sesame seed.	12	14	14*
Cottonseed	7	8	11
Tomatoes	182	199	221
Onions (dry)	57	62	67
Other vegetables.	92	97	105
Watermelons	101	94	94
Melons	31	32	33
Grapes	146	151	98
Dates	21	23	24
Bananas	74	77	79
Papayas.	55	57	58
Other fruit	65	94	132
Coffee (green)	8	9	11
Tobacco (leaves)	7	8	9
Cotton (lint)	4	4	5

* FAO estimate.

Source: FAO, *Production Yearbook*.

LIVESTOCK ('000 head, year ending September)

	1994	1995	1996 *
Horses*	3	3	3
Asses	500†	500*	500*
Cattle	1,151	1,174	1,181
Camels	171	175	175*
Sheep	3,677	3,751	3,922
Goats	3,263	3,328	3,558

Poultry* (million): 22 in 1994; 22 in 1995; 22 in 1996.

* FAO estimate(s).   † Unofficial figure.

Source: FAO, *Production Yearbook*.

LIVESTOCK PRODUCTS ('000 metric tons)

	1994	1995	1996*
Beef and veal	40	41	41
Mutton and lamb*	20	20	20
Goat meat*	18	18	18
Poultry meat*	55	55	56
Cows' milk	150	154	154
Sheep's milk*	13	13	13
Goats' milk*	16	16	16
Cheese*	9	9	9
Butter*	4	4	4
Hen eggs	18†	19†	19
Wool:			
greasy.	4	4	4
clean	2	2	2
Cattle hides*	7	8	8

* FAO estimates.   † Unofficial figure.

Source: FAO, *Production Yearbook*.

Forestry

ROUNDWOOD REMOVALS
('000 cubic metres, excluding bark)

	1987	1988	1989
Total (all fuel wood) . . .	306	312	324

1990–96: Annual output as in 1989.

Source: FAO, *Yearbook of Forest Products*.

Fishing

('000 metric tons, live weight)

	1993	1994	1995
Freshwater fishes . . .	0.9	0.9	1.0
Marine fishes . . .	83.5	81.0	100.2
Other marine animals . .	2.5	1.6	2.7
Total catch	86.8	83.5	104.0

Source: FAO, *Yearbook of Fishery Statistics*.

Mining

('000 metric tons)

	1993	1994	1995
Crude petroleum . . .	11,466	16,005	16,716
Gypsum (crude) . . .	102	99	96

Source: UN, *Industrial Commodity Statistics Yearbook*.

Industry

SELECTED PRODUCTS
('000 metric tons, unless otherwise indicated)

	1993	1994	1995
Motor spirit (petrol) . . .	947	700*	990*
Kerosene*	750	240	250
Jet fuels*	375	100	350
Distillate fuel oils . .	1,300	1,000	1,280
Residual fuel oils . .	2,000	1,100	1,300
Liquefied petroleum gas . .	60*	60	100*
Cement	1,000	898	1,100
Electricity (million kWh)* . .	1,953	1,958	1,980

* Provisional.

Source: UN, *Industrial Commodity Statistics Yearbook*.

Finance

CURRENCY AND EXCHANGE RATES

Monetary Units
100 fils = 1 Yemeni riyal.

Sterling and Dollar Equivalents (31 May 1998)
£1 sterling = 218.22 Yemeni riyals;
US $1 = 133.82 Yemeni riyals;
1,000 Yemeni riyals = £4.583 = $7.473.

Average Exchange Rate (Yemeni riyals per US $)
1995   40.839
1996   94.157
1997   129.286

Note: The exchange rate of US $1 = 9.76 Yemeni riyals, established in the YAR in 1988, remained in force until February 1990, when a new rate of $1 = 12.01 riyals was introduced. Following the merger of the two Yemens in May 1990, the YAR's currency was adopted as the currency of the unified country. In March 1995 the official exchange rate was amended from 12.01 to 50.04 riyals per US dollar. The rate has since been adjusted. In addition to the official rate, there is a market-determined exchange rate, applicable to most private transactions.

GENERAL BUDGET (million riyals)

Revenue*	1993	1994	1995
Taxation	22,017	25,356	44,371
Taxes on income, profits, etc. .	8,311	11,963	15,624
Excises . . .	4,229	4,193	9,106
Import duties . . .	7,535	7,328	16,240
Other current revenue . .	14,235	15,773	44,896
Property income . .	12,891	14,483	42,450
Capital revenue . . .	468	255	379
Total	36,720	41,384	89,646

Expenditure†	1993	1994	1995
General public services . . .	7,619	8,756	10,198
Defence	19,752	30,273	35,897
Public order and safety . . .	6,149	7,755	11,332
Education	13,491	16,662	22,465
Health	3,054	2,989	4,231
Housing and community amenities	1,594	1,443	2,449
Recreational, cultural and religious affairs and services .	1,699	2,173	2,588
Economic affairs and services . .	3,708	3,820	5,286
Interest payments . . .	7,229	10,902	15,297
Sub-total	64,295	84,773	109,743
Adjustment to cash basis . .	952	1,102	1,385
Total	64,247	85,875	111,128

* Excluding grants received from abroad (million riyals): 1,201 in 1993; 856 in 1994; 1,620 in 1995.
† Excluding lending minus repayment (million riyals): 1,971 in 1993; 1,153 in 1994; 5,045 in 1995.

Source: IMF, *Government Finance Statistics Yearbook*.

1996 (Budget estimates, million riyals): Revenue 155,886; Expenditure 181,416.
1997 (Budget estimates, million riyals): Revenue 301,000; Expenditure 313,000.

INTERNATIONAL RESERVES (US $ million at 31 December)

	1994	1995	1996
Gold*	2.6	2.6	18.6
IMF special drawing rights . .	48.9	55.0	47.9
Foreign exchange . . .	205.9	564.0	969.3
Total	257.4	621.6	1,035.8

* Valued at market-related prices.

Source: IMF, *International Financial Statistics*.

MONEY SUPPLY (million riyals at 31 December)

	1994	1995	1996
Currency outside banks . . .	111,006	129,114	120,477
Demand deposits at commercial banks . .	25,390	22,985	27,353
Total money (incl. others) . .	139,590	164,019	156,579

Source: IMF, *International Financial Statistics.*

COST OF LIVING (Consumer price index; base: 1990 = 100)

	1995	1996	1997
All items	537	699	737

Source: IMF, *International Financial Statistics.*

NATIONAL ACCOUNTS (million riyals at current prices)
National Income and Product

	1989	1990
Domestic factor incomes*	52,098	66,010
Consumption of fixed capital . . .	2,499	4,202
Gross domestic product (GDP) at factor cost	54,597	70,212
Indirect taxes, *less* subsidies	6,809	6,947
GDP in purchasers' values . . .	61,406	77,159
Net factor income from abroad . . .	1,454	1,658
Gross national product (GNP) . . .	62,860	78,817
Less Consumption of fixed capital . . .	2,499	4,202
National income in market prices . .	60,361	74,615
Other current transfers from abroad (net) . .	3,706	10,875
National disposable income . . .	64,067	85,490

* Compensation of employees and the operating surplus of enterprises.

Expenditure on the Gross Domestic Product

	1995	1996	1997
Government final consumption expenditure . . .	74,017	97,458	120,106
Private final consumption expenditure . . .	363,757	456,266	452,294
Increase in stocks . . .	20,316	29,483	34,862
Gross fixed capital formation . .	93,763	136,498	170,623
Total domestic expenditure	551,853	719,705	777,885
Exports of goods and services . .	111,821	264,202	320,128
Less Imports of goods and services	215,921	328,715	357,377
GDP in purchasers' values . .	447,753	655,192	740,636
GDP at constant 1990 prices .	144,014	152,141	160,044

Source: IMF, *International Financial Statistics.*

Gross Domestic Product by Economic Activity

	1989	1990
Agriculture, hunting, forestry and fishing . .	14,682	16,101
Mining and quarrying	3,912	7,030
Manufacturing	5,861	6,586
Electricity, gas and water	1,191	1,400
Construction	2,838	3,394
Trade, restaurants and hotels	7,784	9,590
Transport, storage and communications . .	5,202	6,015
Finance, insurance, real estate and business services	4,154	4,929
Government services	10,875	18,201
Other community, social and personal services .	483	572
Private non-profit services to households . .	79	95
Sub-total	57,061	73,913
Import duties	5,000	3,996
Less Imputed bank service charge . . .	655	750
GDP in purchasers' values . . .	61,406	77,159

BALANCE OF PAYMENTS (US $ million)

	1993	1994	1995
Exports of goods f.o.b. . . .	1,166.9	1,824.0	1,937.2
Imports of goods f.o.b. . . .	−2,086.9	−1,521.9	−1,948.2
Trade balance	−920.0	302.1	−11.0
Exports of services . . .	177.2	148.0	179.4
Imports of services . . .	−1,094.6	−622.6	−590.5
Balance on goods and services	−1,837.4	−172.5	−422.1
Other income received . . .	22.0	22.0	37.4
Other income paid . . .	−499.5	−600.6	−536.5
Balance on goods, services and income	−2,314.9	−751.1	−921.2
Current transfers received . .	1,092.8	1,133.6	1,120.5
Current transfers paid . . .	−25.5	−16.6	−16.6
Current balance . . .	−1,247.6	365.9	182.7
Direct investment from abroad . .	897.1	10.5	−217.7
Other investment assets . . .	−53.7	71.8	105.7
Other investment liabilities . .	−931.3	−919.8	−707.0
Net errors and omissions . . .	222.4	−181.0	161.8
Overall balance . . .	−1,113.1	−652.6	−474.5

Source: IMF, *International Financial Statistics.*

External Trade

PRINCIPAL COMMODITIES (distribution by SITC, US $ million)

Imports c.i.f.	1992
Food and live animals	728.0
Dairy products and birds' eggs	85.5
Cereals and cereal preparations	310.9
Vegetables and fruit	42.7
Sugar, sugar preparations and honey	138.4
Beverages and tobacco	49.3
Crude materials (inedible) except fuels . . .	93.3
Cork and wood	64.2
Mineral fuels, lubricants, etc.	156.9
Coal, coke and briquetttes	156.6
Animal and vegetable oils and fats . . .	55.5
Chemicals and related products	171.9
Medicinal and pharmaceutical products . . .	53.3
Artificial resins, plastic materials, etc. . .	45.4
Basic manufactures	626.5
Rubber manufactures	49.6
Paper, paperboard and manufactures . . .	57.4
Textile yarn, fabrics, etc. . . .	53.1
Non-metallic mineral manufactures . . .	99.4
Iron and steel	225.4
Machinery and transport equipment . . .	564.5
Machinery specialized for particular industries . . .	81.8
General industrial machinery, equipment and parts .	113.3
Electrical machinery, apparatus, etc.	107.6
Road vehicles and parts (excl. tyres, engines and electrical parts)	182.8
Miscellaneous manufactured articles	140.6
Total (incl. others)	2,587.9

Exports f.o.b.	1992
Food and live animals	36.3
Coffee, tea, cocoa and spices	21.5
Crude materials (inedible) except fuels . . .	33.3
Raw hides, skins and furskins . . .	16.1
Mineral fuels, lubricants, etc.	244.7
Total (incl. others)	329.0

PRINCIPAL TRADING PARTNERS (US $ million)*

Imports c.i.f.	1992	1993	1994
Australia	51.2	43.1	51.5
Belgium-Luxembourg	97.5	103.1	92.5
Brazil	54.3	63.6	17.4
China, People's Republic	76.0	92.4	44.2
Djibouti	21.1	49.0	48.4
Egypt	25.0	34.4	27.0
France (incl. Monaco)	91.6	199.9	123.1
Germany	88.2	108.9	62.0
India	46.3	47.8	29.9
Italy	132.9	95.1	85.7
Japan	180.9	131.5	93.2
Korea, Republic	44.2	43.0	29.6
Malaysia	109.4	141.7	99.1
Netherlands	111.6	125.2	85.5
Saudi Arabia	192.5	196.4	215.6
Singapore	127.7	111.3	74.6
Somalia	49.2	43.8	28.8
Thailand	92.6	30.3	17.6
Turkey	100.4	142.0	95.3
United Arab Emirates	213.1	272.0	219.0
United Kingdom	142.7	147.4	116.4
USA	238.0	270.8	188.6
Total (inc. others)	2,587.9	2,821.3	2,087.5

Exports f.o.b.	1992	1993	1994
Austria	—	19.9	—
Bahrain	5.9	3.9	29.9
Brazil	0.4	0.1	16.5
Bulgaria	—	—	11.6
China, People's Republic	n.a.	52.9	22.9
Egypt	0.2	0.1	64.0
France (incl. Monaco)	4.9	17.0	29.0
Germany	39.2	1.0	0.0
India	0.5	22.5	19.1
Italy	8.3	5.9	22.3
Japan	55.5	98.0	124.0
Korea, Republic	0.5	21.5	195.0
Malaysia	4.3	1.1	25.9
Netherlands	3.3	0.0	10.5
Saudi Arabia	22.4	28.7	37.7
Singapore	7.2	53.6	133.6
Somalia	11.7	14.0	21.7
United Arab Emirates	4.1	7.1	14.0
USA	116.2	3.4	113.4
Total (incl. others)	329.0	374.2	933.9

* Imports by country of first consignment; exports by country of last consignment.

Source: UN, *International Trade Statistics Yearbook.*

Transport

ROAD TRAFFIC (vehicles in use at 31 December)

	1994	1995	1996
Passenger cars	227,854	229,084	240,567
Buses and coaches	2,712	2,835	3,437
Goods vehicles	279,154	279,780	291,149

Source: IRF, *World Road Statistics.*

SHIPPING

Merchant Fleet (registered at 31 December)

	1995	1996	1997
Number of vessels	43	42	45
Total displacement ('000 grt)	26.6	25.1	26.2

Source: Lloyd's Register of Shipping, *World Fleet Statistics.*

International Sea-borne Freight Traffic ('000 metric tons)

	1988	1989	1990
Goods loaded	1,836	1,883	1,936
Goods unloaded	7,189	7,151	7,829

Source: UN, *Monthly Bulletin of Statistics.*

CIVIL AVIATION (traffic on scheduled services)

	1993	1994	1995
Kilometres flown (million)	13	13	6
Passengers carried ('000)	848	791	375
Passenger-km (million)	1,217	1,183	486
Total ton-km (million)	124	119	49

Source: UN, *Statistical Yearbook.*

Tourism

	1993	1994	1995
Tourist arrivals ('000)	70	40	61
Tourist receipts (US $ million)	45	19	38

Source: UN, *Statistical Yearbook.*

Communications Media

	1993	1994	1995
Radio receivers ('000 in use)	400	450	650
Television receivers ('000 in use)	365	390	420
Telephones ('000 main lines in use)	161	173	187
Telefax stations (subscribers)	1,301	1,926	2,000*
Mobile cellular telephones (subscribers)	5,170	8,191	8,250
Daily newspapers			
Number	n.a.	3	3*
Circulation ('000 copies)	n.a.	230	230*

* Estimate.

Sources: UNESCO, *Statistical Yearbook,* and UN, *Statistical Yearbook.*

Education

(1993/94, unless otherwise indicated)

	Schools	Teachers	Students
Pre-primary	62	680	11,999
Primary	11,013	n.a.	2,678,863
Secondary	n.a.	n.a.	212,129
Higher*	n.a.	1,800	53,082

* 1991/92.

Source: UNESCO, *Statistical Yearbook.*

Directory

The Constitution

A draft constitution for the united Republic of Yemen (based on that endorsed by the Yemen Arab Republic (YAR) and the People's Democratic Republic of Yemen (PDRY) in December 1981) was published in December 1989, and was approved by a popular referendum on 15–16 May 1991.

On 29 September 1994 52 articles were amended, 29 added and one cancelled, leaving a total of 159 articles in the Constitution.

As revised in 1994, the Constitution defines the Yemeni Republic as an independent and sovereign Arab and Islamic country. The document states that the Republic 'is an indivisible whole, and it is impermissible to concede any part of it. The Yemeni people are part of the Arab and Islamic nation.' The Islamic *Shari'a* is identified as the basis of all laws.

The revised Constitution provides for the election, by direct universal suffrage, of the President of the Republic; the President is elected for a five-year term, renewable only once.* The President is empowered to appoint a Vice-President. The President of the Republic is, *ex officio*, Commander-in-Chief of the Armed Forces.

Legislative authority is vested in the 301-member House of Representatives, which is elected, by universal suffrage, for a four-year term. The legislature is empowered to debate and approve legislation, to decide general state policy, to supervise public spending, and to ratify international treaties and agreements. The Constitution states that 'the President can dissolve the House of Representatives only when necessary'.

The President of the Republic appoints the Prime Minister and other members of the Government on the advice of the Prime Minister. The Constitution empowers both the President and the legislature to impeach the Prime Minister and other government members 'for crimes committed in the performance of their duties'.

The Constitution delineates the separation of the powers of the organs of State, and guarantees the independence of the judiciary. The existence of a multi-party political system is confirmed, although serving members of the police and armed forces are banned from political activity.

* The amendments to the Constitution enacted in September 1994 provided for the abolition of the Presidential Council, which had previously been empowered to elect the President of the Republic. On 1 October the House of Representatives, meeting as an electoral college, confirmed Ali Abdullah Saleh as President for a five-year term; following the expiry of this mandate, subsequent elections to the presidency would be as defined above.

HEAD OF STATE

President: Field Marshal ALI ABDULLAH SALEH (took office 24 May 1990, re-elected 1 October 1994).

Vice-President: Maj.-Gen. ABD AR-RABBUH MANSUR HADI.

COUNCIL OF MINISTERS
(September 1998)

Prime Minister: Dr ABD AL-KARIM AL-IRYANI.

Deputy Prime Minister and Minister of Foreign Affairs: ABD AL-QADIR BAJAMMAL.

Minister of Petroleum and Mineral Resources: MUHAMMAD AL-KHADIM AL-WAJIH.

Minister of State for Cabinet Affairs: Dr MUTAHAR AS-SAEEDI.

Minister of Planning and Development: AHMAD MUHAMMAD SUFAN.

Minister of Labour and Vocational Training: MUHAMMAD MUHAMMAD AT-TAYYIB.

Minister of Supply and Trade: ABD AL-AZIZ AL-KOMAIM.

Minister of Local Administration: SADIQ AMIN ABU RAS.

Minister of the Interior: Brig.-Gen. HUSSAIN MUHAMMAD ARAB.

Minister of Finance: ALAWI SALIH AS-SALAMI.

Minister of Justice: ISMAIL AHMAD AL-WAZIR.

Minister of Religious Endowments and Guidance: (vacant).

Minister of Information: ABD AR-RAHMAN MUHAMMAD AL-AKWA.

Minister of Culture and Tourism: ABD AL-MALIK MANSUR.

Minister of Transport: Brig.-Gen. ABD AL-MALIK AS-SAYYANI.

Minister of Industry: ABD AR-RAHMAN MUHAMMAD ALI OTHMAN.

Minister of Construction, Housing and Urban Planning: ABDULLAH HUSSAIN AD-DAFI.

Minister of Health: ABDULLAH ABD AL-WALI NASHIR.

Minister of Agriculture and Water Resources: AHMAD SALIM AL-JABALI.

Minister of Fisheries: AHMAD MUSSAID HUSSAIN.

Minister of Defence: Col MUHAMMAD DAYFALLAH MUHAMMAD.

Minister of Social Security and Social Affairs: MUHAMMAD ABDULLAH AL-BATTANI.

Minister of Electricity and Water: ALI HAMID SHARAF.

Minister for Parliamentary and Legal Affairs: ABDULLAH AHMAD GHANIM.

Minister for the Civil Service and Administrative Reform: MUHAMMAD AHMAD AL-JUNAID.

Minister of Communications: AHMAD MUHAMMAD AL-ANISI.

Minister of Youth and Sport: Dr ABD AL-WAHAB RAWIH.

Minister of Education: YAHYA MUHAMMAD ABDULLAH ASH-SHUAIBI.

Minister of Expatriate Affairs: AHMAD ALI AL-BISHARI.

Minister of State: FAISAL MAHMOOD HASSAN ALI.

MINISTRIES

All ministries are in San'a.

Ministry of Communications: Airport Rd, al-Jiraf, POB 25237, San'a; tel. (1) 271272; telex 2340; fax (1) 271131.

Ministry of Economy, Supply and Trade: POB 1704, San'a; tel. (1) 202471.

Ministry of Petroleum and Mineral Resources: POB 81, San'a; tel. (1) 202313.

Ministry of Planning and Development: POB 175, San'a; tel. (1) 250101; fax (1) 251503.

Legislature

THE HOUSE OF REPRESENTATIVES

The House of Representatives has 301 members, elected for a four-year term. It originally comprised the 159 members of the Consultative Council (*Majlis ash-Shura*) of the former YAR; the 111 members of the Supreme People's Council of the former PDRY; and 31 new members nominated by President Saleh. A general election for a new House of Representatives was held on 27 April 1993, and again on the same date in 1997.

Speaker: Sheikh ABDULLAH BIN HUSSAIN AL-AHMAR.

General Election, 27 April 1997

Party	Seats
General People's Congress (GPC)	187
Yemeni Islah Party (YIP)	53
Independents	54
Baathist and Nasserite parties	7
Total	**301**

Political Organizations

In the former PDRY the YSP was the only legal political party until December 1989, when the formation of opposition parties was legalized. There were no political parties in the former YAR. The two leading parties that emerged in the unified Yemen were the GPC and the YSP. During 1990 an estimated 30 to 40 further political parties were reported to have been formed, and in 1995 43 were known to be in existence. Following the civil war from May to July 1994, President Saleh excluded the YSP from the new Government formed in October 1994.

Al-Haq: San'a; conservative Islamic party; Sec.-Gen. Sheikh AHMAD ASH-SHAMI.

Democratic Coalition of Opposition: San'a; f. 1995 as a coalition of 13 political parties and organizations, including a splinter faction of the YSP and the LSY.

General People's Congress (GPC): San'a; a broad grouping of supporters of President Saleh; Chair. Lt-Gen. ALI ABDULLAH SALEH; Vice-Chair. Maj.-Gen. ABD AR-RABBUH MANSUR HADI; Sec.-Gen. Dr ABD AL-KARIM AL-IRYANI.

League of the Sons of Yemen (LSY): Aden; represents interests of southern tribes; Leader ABD AR-RAHMAN AL-JIFRI; Sec.-Gen. MOHSEN FARID.

Nasserite Unionist Popular Organization: Aden; f. 1989 as a legal party.

Yemen Socialist Party (YSP): San'a; f. 1978 to succeed the United Political Organization—National Front (UPO—NF); fmrly Marxist-Leninist 'vanguard' party based on 'scientific socialism'; has Political Bureau and Cen. Cttee; Sec.-Gen. ALI SALEH OBAD.

Yemeni Islah Party (YIP): POB 23090, San'a; tel. (1) 213281; fax (1) 213311; f. 1990 by mems of the legislature and other political figures, and tribal leaders; seeks constitutional reform based on Islamic law; Leader Sheikh ABDULLAH BIN HUSSAIN AL-AHMAR; Sec.-Gen. Sheikh MUHAMMAD ALI AL-YADOUMI.

Yemeni Unionist Rally Party: Aden; f. 1990 by intellectuals and politicians from the fmr YAR and PDRY to safeguard human rights; Leader OMAR AL-JAWI.

Diplomatic Representation

EMBASSIES IN YEMEN

Algeria: POB 509, 67 Amman St, San'a; tel. (1) 209689; fax (1) 209688; Ambassador: BEN HADID CHADLY.

Bulgaria: POB 1518, St No. 22, San'a; tel. (1) 207924; telex 3114; Chargé d'affaires: ALEXI ALAXIEV.

China, People's Republic: Az-Zubairy St, San'a; tel. (1) 275337; Ambassador: LI LIUGEN.

Cuba: POB 15256, St No. 6B, San'a; tel. (1) 217304; fax (1) 217305; Ambassador: HÉCTOR ARGILES PÉREZ.

Czech Republic: POB 2501, Safiya Janoobia, San'a; tel. (1) 247946; fax (1) 244418; Chargé d'affaires: KAROL FISHER.

Egypt: POB 1134, Gamal Abd al-Nasser St, San'a; tel. (1) 275948; fax (1) 274196; Ambassador: ATA'A M. HARDUN.

Eritrea: POB 11040, Western Safia Bldg, San'a; tel. (1) 209422; fax (1) 214088; Ambassador: MAHMOUD ALI JABRA.

Ethiopia: POB 234, Hadda Rd, San'a; tel. (1) 208833; Ambassador: TEKETEL FORSIDO.

France: POB 1286, Cnr Sts 2/21, San'a; tel. (1) 268888; fax (1) 269160; Ambassador: ANDRÉ JANIER.

Germany: POB 41, Hadda Area, opposite Jamaa ar-Rahman, San'a; tel. (1) 413177; telex 2245; fax (1) 413179; Ambassador: Dr HELGA STRACHWITZ.

Hungary: POB 11558, As-Safiya Al-Gharbiyya, St No. 6B, San'a; tel. (1) 216250; fax (1) 216251; Ambassador: (vacant).

India: POB 1154, San'a; tel. (1) 243440; fax (1) 243439; e-mail indiaemb@y.net.ye; Ambassador: (vacant).

Indonesia: POB 19873, No. 15, St No. 16, Sixty Rd, Hadda Area, San'a; tel. (1) 217388; telex 3372; fax (1) 414383; Ambassador: AHMAD NOOR.

Iran: POB 1437, Haddah St, San'a; tel. (1) 206945; telex 2241; Chargé d'affaires: ALI A. NASSERY.

Iraq: POB 498, South Airport Rd, San'a; tel. (1) 244153; telex 2237; Ambassador: MUHSIN KHALIL.

Italy: POB 1152, No. 5 Bldg, St No. 29, San'a; tel. (1) 265616; telex 2560; fax (1) 266137; Ambassador: Dr VITALIANO NAPOLEONE.

Japan: POB 817, San'a; tel. (1) 207356; telex 2345; fax (1) 209531; Ambassador: SUSUMU AKIYAMA.

Jordan: POB 2152, San'a; tel. (1) 413279; telex 2703; Ambassador: Dr FAIZ AR-RABI.

Korea, Democratic People's Republic: POB 1209, al-Hasaba, Mazda Rd, San'a; tel. (1) 232340; telex 2603; Ambassador: CHU WANG CHOL.

Korea, Republic: POB 1234, No. 15, Abu Bakr as-Saddik St, San'a; tel. (1) 245959; Ambassador: PAK HI-JOO.

Kuwait: POB 3746, South Ring Rd, San'a; tel. (1) 268876; fax (1) 268875; Chargé d'affaires: MANSOUR AL-AWADI.

Lebanon: POB 2283, Haddah St, San'a; tel. (1) 203459; telex 2438; fax (1) 201120; Ambassador: HASSAN BERRO.

Libya: POB 1506, Ring Rd, St No. 8, House No. 145, San'a; telex 2219; Secretary of Libyan Brotherhood Office: A. U. HEFIANA.

Mauritania: POB 19383, No. 6, Algeria St, San'a; tel. (1) 216770; fax (1) 215926; Ambassador: AHMED OULD SIDY.

Morocco: POB 10236, West Safiya, San'a; tel. (1) 247964; telex 2299; Ambassador: MUHAMMAD BOUCHENTOUF.

Netherlands: POB 463, Hadda Rd, San'a; tel. (1) 264078; fax 264094; Ambassador: A. J. MEERBURG.

Oman: POB 105, Aser area, Az-Zubairy St, San'a; tel. (1) 208933; telex 2253; Ambassador: AWAD M. BAKTHEER.

Pakistan: POB 2848, Ring Rd, San'a; tel. (1) 248812; fax (1) 248866; e-mail pakemb@y.net.ye; Ambassador: A. J. NAIM.

Poland: POB 16168, Hadda St, San'a; tel. (1) 412243; fax (1) 413647; Ambassador: KRZYSZTOF SUPROWICZ.

Qatar: San'a; Ambassador: MUHAMMAD BIN HAMAD AL-KHALIFA.

Romania: POB 2169, No. 15, St No. 16, San'a; tel. (1) 215579; telex 4034; fax (1) 267728; Chargé d'affaires: TACHE PANAIT.

Russia: POB 1087, 26 September St, San'a; tel. (1) 278719; telex 2952; fax (1) 283142; Ambassador: IGOR G. IVASHENKO.

Saudi Arabia: POB 1184, Zuhara House, Hadda Rd, San'a; tel. (1) 240429; telex 2420; Ambassador: ALI AL-QUFAIDI.

Somalia: POB 12277, Hadda Rd, San'a; tel. (1) 208864; telex 2610; Ambassador: ABD AS-SALLAM MU'ALLIM ADAM.

Sudan: POB 2561, 82 Abou al-Hassan al-Hamadani St, San'a; tel. (1) 265231; fax (1) 265234; Ambassador: OMAR AS-SAID TAHA.

Syria: POB 494, Hadda Rd, St No. 1, San'a; tel. (1) 413153; telex 2335; Ambassador: YOUSUF GMAOTRA.

Tunisia: POB 2561, Diplomatic area, St No. 22, San'a; tel. (1) 240458; telex 2751; Ambassador: ABBÈS MOHSEN.

Turkey: POB 12450, As-Safiya, San'a; tel. and fax (1) 241395; telex 3159; Ambassador: VOLKAN COTUR.

United Arab Emirates: POB 2250, Ring Rd, San'a; tel. (1) 248777; telex 2225; Ambassador: SAIF BIN MAKTOOM AL-MANSOORY.

United Kingdom: POB 1287, 129 Hadda Rd, San'a; tel. (1) 264081; fax (1) 263059; Ambassador: VICTOR HENDERSON.

USA: POB 22347, Sheraton Hotel District, San'a; tel. (1) 238843; telex 2697; fax (1) 251563; Ambassador: BARBARA BODINE (designate).

Viet Nam: POB 15267, St No. 66, San'a; tel. (1) 215985; Ambassador: DO CONG MINH.

Religion

ISLAM

The majority of the population are Muslims. Most are Sunni Muslims of the Shafi'a sect, except in the north-west of the country, where Zaidism (a moderate sect of the Shi'a order) is the dominant persuasion.

CHRISTIANITY

The Roman Catholic Church

Apostolic Vicariate of Arabia: POB 54, Abu Dhabi, United Arab Emirates; responsible for a territory comprising most of the Arabian peninsula (including Saudi Arabia, the UAE, Oman, Qatar, Bahrain and Yemen), containing an estimated 880,000 Roman Catholics (31 December 1996); Vicar Apostolic GIOVANNI BERNARDO GREMOLI, Titular Bishop of Masuccaba (resident in the UAE); Vicar Delegate for Yemen Rev. GEORGE PUDUSSERY.

The Anglican Communion

Within the Episcopal Church in Jerusalem and the Middle East, Yemen forms part of the diocese of Cyprus and the Gulf. The Anglican congregations in San'a and Aden are entirely expatriate; Bishop in Cyprus and the Gulf: Rt Rev. JOHN BROWN (resident in Cyprus); Archdeacon in the Gulf: Ven. MICHAEL MANSBRIDGE (resident in the UAE).

HINDUISM

There is a small Hindu community.

Judicial System*

In the former YAR:

President of the State Security Court: GHALEB MUTAHIR AL-QANISH.

Public Prosecutor: ABD AR-RIZAQ AR-ROQAIHI.

Attorney General: MUHAMMAD AL-BADRI.

Shari'a Court: San'a; deals with cases related to Islamic law.

Central Organization for Supervision and Accountancy: replaces old Disciplinary Court; presides over cases of misappropriation of public funds; Chair. IZZ AD-DIN AL-MOAZEN.

In the former PDRY:

The administration of justice in the PDRY was entrusted to the Supreme Court and Magistrates' Courts. In the former Protectorate states, Islamic (*Shari'a*) law and local common law (*Urfi*) were also applied.

President of the Supreme Court: Dr MUSTAFA ABD AL-KHALIQ.

* In 1994 amendments to the Constitution of the unified Republic of Yemen identified Islamic (*Shari'a*) law as the basis of all laws.

The Press

Legislation embodying the freedom of the press in the unified Republic of Yemen was enacted in May 1990. The lists below include publications which appeared in the YAR and the PDRY prior to their unification in May 1990.

DAILIES

Al-Jumhuriya: Taiz Information Office, Taiz; tel. (4) 216748; Arabic; circ. 100,000.

Ar-Rabi' 'Ashar Min Uktubar (14 October): POB 4227, Crater, Aden; f. 1968; not published on Saturdays; Arabic; Editorial Dir FAROUQ MUSTAFA RIFAT; Chief Editor MUHAMMAD HUSSAIN MUHAMMAD; circ. 20,000.

Ash-Sharara (The Spark): 14 October Corpn for Printing, Publishing, Distribution and Advertising, POB 4227, Crater, Aden; Arabic; circ. 6,000.

Ath-Thawra (The Revolution): POB 2195, San'a; tel. (1) 262626; fax (1) 274139; Arabic; govt-owned; Editor MUHAMMAD AZ-ZORKAH; circ. 110,000.

WEEKLIES AND OTHERS

Attijarah (Trade): POB 3370, Hodeida; tel. (3) 213784; fax (3) 211528; e-mail hodcci@y.net.ye; monthly; Arabic; commercial.

Al-Bilad (The Country): POB 1438, San'a; weekly; Arabic; centre-right.

Al-Fanoon: Ministry of Culture and Toursim, POB 1187, Tawahi 102, Aden; tel. (2) 23831; f. 1980; Arabic; monthly arts review; Editor FAISAL SOFY; circ. 15,500.

Al-Gundi (The Soldier): Ministry of Defence, Madinat ash-Sha'ab; fortnightly; Arabic; circ. 8,500.

Al-Hikma (Wisdom): POB 4227, Crater, Aden; monthly; Arabic; publ. by the Writers' Union; circ. 5,000.

Al-Hares: Aden; fortnightly; Arabic; circ. 8,000.

Al-Ma'in (Spring): Ministry of Information, San'a; monthly; general interest.

Majallat al-Jaish (Army Magazine): POB 2182, San'a; tel. (1) 231181; telex 2215; monthly; publ. by Ministry of Defence.

Al-Maseerah (Journey): Ministry of Information, POB 2182, San'a; tel. (1) 231181; telex 2215; monthly; general interest.

Al-Mithaq (The Charter): San'a; weekly; organ of the General People's Congress.

Qadiyat al-Asr (Issues of the Age): Aden; f. 1981; weekly; Arabic; publ. by Cen. Cttee of YSP.

Ar-Ra'i al-'Am (Public Opinion): POB 293, San'a; tel. (1) 242090; weekly; independent; Editor ALI MUHAMMAD AL-OLAFI.

Ar-Risalah (The Message): 26 September St, San'a; weekly; Arabic.

As-Sahwa (Awakening): San'a; weekly; Islamic fundamentalist; Editor MUHAMMAD AL-YADDOUMI.

As-Salam (Peace): POB 181, San'a; f. 1948; weekly; Arabic; political, economic and general essays; Editor ABDULLAH AS-SAKAL; circ. 7,000.

San'a: POB 193, San'a; fortnightly; Arabic; inclined to left.

Sawt al-'Ummal (The Workers' Voice): POB 4227, Crater, Aden; weekly; Arabic.

Sawt al-Yemen (Voice of Yemen): POB 302, San'a; weekly; Arabic.

Ash-Shura: POB 15114, San'a; tel. (1) 213584; fax (1) 213468; Editor ABDALLAH SA'AD; circ. 15,000.

At-Ta'awun (Co-operation): At-Ta'awun Bldg, Az-Zubairy St, San'a; weekly; Arabic; supports co-operative societies.

Ath-Thaqafat al-Jadida (New Culture): Ministry of Culture and Tourism, POB 1187, Tawahi 102, Aden; tel. (2) 23831; f. 1970; cultural monthly review; Arabic; circ. 3,000.

Ath-Thawri (The Revolutionary): POB 4227, Crater, Aden; weekly; published on Saturday; Arabic; organ of Cen. Cttee of YSP; Editor Dr AHMAD ABDULLAH SALIH.

26 September: 26 September Publishing, POB 17, San'a; tel. (1) 274240; telex 2557; armed forces weekly; circ. 25,000.

Al-Wahda al-Watani (National Unity): Al-Baath Printing House, POB 193, San'a; tel. (1) 77511; f. 1982; fmrly *Al-Omal*; monthly; Editor MUHAMMAD SALEM ALI; circ. 40,000.

Al-Yemen: Yemen Printing and Publishing Co, POB 1081, San'a; tel. (1) 72376; f. 1971; weekly; Arabic; centre-right; Editor MUHAMMAD AHMAD AS-SABAGH.

The Yemen Times: POB 2579, San'a; tel. (1) 268661; fax (1) 268663; independent weekly; English; Editor ABD AL-AZIZ AS-SAQQAF; circ. 20,000.

Yemeni Women: POB 4227, Crater, Aden; monthly; circ. 5,000.

NEWS AGENCIES

Aden News Agency (ANA): Ministry of Culture and Tourism, POB 1187, Tawahi 102, Aden; tel. (2) 24874; telex 2286; f. 1970; govt-owned; Dir-Gen. AHMAD MUHAMMAD IBRAHIM.

Saba News Agency: POB 1475, San'a; tel. (1) 250078; telex 2568; f. 1970; Dir HASSAN AL-ULUFI.

Foreign Bureaux

In the former YAR:

Informatsionnoye Telegrafnoye Agentstvo Rossii—Telegrafnoye Agentstvo Suverennykh Stran (ITAR—TASS) (Russia): San'a; Correspondent VIKTOR LYSSECHKO.

Xinhua (New China) News Agency (People's Republic of China): POB 482, Az-Zubairy St, San'a; tel. (1) 72073; Correspondent CHEN WENRU.

In the former PDRY:

Informatsionnoye Telegrafnoye Agentstvo Rossii—Telegrafnoye Agentstvo Suverennykh Stran (ITAR—TASS) (Russia): POB 1087, Aden; Correspondent VLADIMIR GAVRILOV.

Xinhua (New China) News Agency (People's Republic of China): POB 5213, Aden; tel. (2) 42710; Correspondent FENG ZHERU.

Publishers

Armed Forces Printing Press: POB 17, San'a; tel. (1) 274240; telex 2557.

14 October Corpn for Printing, Publishing, Distribution and Advertising: POB 4227, Crater, Aden; under control of the Ministry of Information; Chair. and Gen. Man. SALIH AHMAD SALAH.

26 September Publishing: POB 17, San'a; tel. (1) 274240; telex 2557.

Ath-Thawrah Corpn: POB 2195, San'a; fax (1) 251505; Chair. M. R. AZ-ZURKAH.

Yemen Printing and Publishing Co: POB 1081, San'a; telex 2363; Chair. AHMAD MUHAMMAD HADI.

Broadcasting and Communications

TELECOMMUNICATIONS

Public Telecommunications Corporation: POB 17045, Airport Rd, al-Jiraf, San'a; tel. (1) 250040; telex 2617; Dir-Gen. MUHAMMAD AL-KASSOUS.

BROADCASTING

Yemen Radio and Television Corpn: POB 2182, San'a; tel. (1) 231181; telex 2645; fax (1) 230761; state-controlled; Dir ALI CALEH ALGAMRAH.

Finance

(cap. = capital;
res = reserves; dep. = deposits; m. = million; brs = branches;
amounts in Yemeni riyals, unless otherwise indicated)

BANKING

Central Bank

Central Bank of Yemen: POB 59, Ali Abd al-Mughni St, San'a; tel. (1) 274371; telex 2280; fax (1) 274131; f. 1971; merged with Bank of Yemen in May 1990; cap. and res 12,414.5m., dep. 249,998.6m., total assets 362,815.9m. (Dec. 1996); Gov. AHMED A. REHMAN AS-SAMAWI; Dep. Gov. SALEM AL-ASHWALI; 16 brs.

Principal Banks

Arab Bank PLC (Jordan): POB 475, az-Zubairy St, San'a; tel. (1) 276585; telex 2239; fax (1) 276583; f. 1972; Man. A. KARIM AZ-ZOURAIQI; brs in Aden, Hodeida and Taiz.

Co-operative and Agricultural Credit Bank: POB 2015, Banks Complex, az-Zubairy St, San'a; tel. (1) 207327; telex 2544; fax (1) 203742; f. 1976; cap. and res 354m., total assets 3,087m. (Dec. 1995); Chair. ABDALLAH AL-BARAKANI; Dir-Gen. HUSSAIN QASSIM AMER; 27 brs.

Credit Agricole Indosuez (France): POB 651, Al-Qasr al-Jumhuriya St, San'a; tel. (1) 272801; telex 2412; fax (1) 274161; Regional Man. JEAN-PIERRE IMBERT; brs in Hodeida, Aden, Taiz and Mukalla.

Industrial Bank of Yemen: POB 323, Banks Complex, az-Zubairy St, San'a; tel. (1) 207381; telex 2580; f. 1976; industrial investment; cap. 100m., total assets 269.8m. (1987); Chair. and Man. Dir ABBAS ABDU MUHAMMAD AL-KIRSHY; Gen. Man. ABD AL-KARIM ISMAIL AL-ARHABI.

International Bank of Yemen YSC: POB 2847, 106 az-Zubairy St, San'a; tel. (1) 273273; telex 2523; fax (1) 274127; f. 1980; commercial bank; cap. 250.0m., res 304.6m., dep. 8,050.2m. (Dec. 1996); Chair. ALI LUTF ATH-THOUR; Gen. Man. MUHAMMAD ABDULLAH M. AL-AMERY; 4 brs.

National Bank of Yemen: POB 5, Arwa Rd, Crater, Aden; tel. (2) 253484; telex 6224; fax (2) 253484; f. 1970 as National Bank of Southern Yemen; reorg. 1971; transfer of govt control to private sector pending in 1998; cap. 250.0m., res 275.0m., dep. 23,722.0m. (Dec. 1996); Chair. and Gen. Man. ABDUL RAHMAN MUHAMMAD AL-KUHALI; 30 brs.

United Bank Ltd (Pakistan): POB 1295, Ali Abd al-Mughni St, San'a; tel. (1) 272427; telex 2228; fax (1) 274168; Vice-Pres. and Gen. Man. INAYATULLAH BUTT; br. in Hodeida.

Yemen Bank for Reconstruction and Development (YBRD): POB 541, 26 September St, San'a; tel. (1) 270481; telex 2291; fax (1) 271684; f. 1962; cap. 300.0m., res 318.7m., dep. 45,695.5m. (Dec. 1996); Chair. ABDULLAH SALIM AL-GIFRI; Gen. Man. HUSSAIN FADHLE MUHAMMAD; 34 brs.

Yemen Commercial Bank: POB 19845, Az-Zubairy St. San'a; tel. (1) 213662; telex 3373; fax (1) 209566; f. 1993; cap. 280.6m., res 258.1m., dep. 10,654.7m. (Dec. 1996); Chair. Sheikh MUHAMMAD BIN YAHYA AR-ROWAISHAN; Gen. Man. SIKANDER MAHMOUD; 8 brs.

INSURANCE

Marib Yemen Insurance Co: POB 2284, Az-Zubairy St, San'a; tel. (1) 206114; telex 2279; fax (1) 206118; f. 1974; all classes of insurance; cap. 100m.; Gen. Man. KASSIM M. AL-SABRI; Deputy Gen. Man. ABD AL-LATIF AL-QUBATI.

National Insurance and Re-insurance Co: POB 456, Aden; tel. (2) 51464; telex 2245; f. 1970; Lloyd's Agents; cap. 5m. Yemeni dinars; Gen. Man. ABUBAKR S. AL-QOTI.

United Insurance Co (YSC): POB 1983, Al-Qasr al-Jumhuriya St, San'a; tel. (1) 272891; telex 2366; fax (1) 272080; f. 1981; all classes of general insurance and life; cap. 20m.; brs in Taiz and Hodeida; Gen. Man. SARGON D. LAZAR.

Yemen General Insurance Co (SYC): POB 2709, YGI Bldg, 25 Al Giers St, San'a; tel. (1) 265191; telex 2451; fax (1) 263109; f. 1977; all classes of insurance; cap. 20m.; brs in Aden, Taiz and Hodeida; Chair. ABD AL-GABBAR THABET; Gen. Man. WAMIDH AL-JARRAH.

Trade and Industry

GOVERNMENT AGENCIES

Foreign Trade Corpn: POB 77, San'a; tel. (1) 72058.

General Board for Agricultural Research: San'a.

General Corpn for Manufacturing and Marketing of Cement: POB 1920; San'a; tel. (1) 215691; fax (1) 263168; Chair. AMIN ABD AL-WAHID AHMED.

General Corpn for Tourism: San'a; tel. (1) 226623; telex 2592; fax (1) 252316.

National Co for Foreign Trade: POB 90, Crater, Aden; tel. (2) 42793; telex 2211; fax (2) 42631; f. 1969; incorporates main foreign trading businesses (nationalized in 1970) and arranges their supply to the National Co for Home Trade; Gen. Man. AHMED MUHAMMAD SALEH (acting).

National Co for Home Trade: POB 90, Crater, Aden; tel. (2) 41483; telex 2211; fax (2) 41226; f. 1969; marketing of general consumer goods, building materials, electrical goods, motor cars and spare parts, agricultural machinery etc.; Man. Dir ABD AR-RAHMAN AS-SAILANI.

National Dockyards Co: POB 1244, Tawahi, Aden; tel. (2) 23837; telex 2217; Man. Dir SALEH AL-MUNTASIR MEHDI.

National Drug Corpn: POB 192, Crater, Aden; tel. (2) 04912; telex 2293; fax (2) 21242; f. 1972; import of pharmaceutical products, chemicals, medical supplies, baby foods and scientific instruments; Chair. and Gen. Man. Dr AWADH SALAM ISSA BAMATRAF.

Public Corpn for Building and Housing: POB 7022, al-Mansoura, Aden; tel. (2) 342296; fax (2) 345726; f. 1973; govt contractors and contractors of private housing projects; Dir-Gen. HUSSAIN MUHAMMAD AL-WALI.

Public Corpn for Maritime Affairs (PCMA): POB 19396; San'a; tel. (1) 414412; telex 4025; fax (1) 414645; f. 1990; protection of the marine environment; registration of ships; implementation of international maritime conventions; Chair. SAEED YAFAI.

Yemen Co for Industry and Commerce Ltd: POB 5302, Taiz; tel. (4) 218058; telex 8804; fax (4) 218054; Chair. ALI MUHAMMAD SAID.

Yemen Co for Investment and Finance Ltd: POB 2789, San'a; tel. (1) 276372; telex 2564; fax (1) 274178; f. 1981; cap. 100m.; Chair. and Gen. Man. ABDULLAH ISHAQ.

Yemen Drug Co for Industry and Commerce: POB 40, San'a; tel. (1) 234250; telex 2289; fax (1) 234290; Chair. MUHAMMAD ALI MUQBIL; Man. Dir ABD AR-RAHMAN A. GHALEB.

Yemen Economical Corpn: POB 1207, San'a; tel. (1) 262501; telex 2244; fax (1) 262508; Commercial Man. A. KARIM SAYAGHI.

Yemen Land Transport Corpn: POB 279, Taiz St, San'a; tel. (1) 262108; telex 2400; f. 1961; Chair. Col ALI AHMAD AL-WASI; Gen. Man. HAMID MUKRID.

Yemen Trading and Construction Co: POB 1092; San'a; tel. (1) 264005; fax (1) 240624; e-mail ytcc@y.net.ye; f. 1979; intial cap. 100m. riyals.

DEVELOPMENT ORGANIZATIONS

General Board for Agricultural Development: San'a.

General Board for Development of Eastern Region: San'a.

General Board for Development of Tihama: San'a.

Yemen Free Zone Public Authority: Aden; tel. (2) 241210; fax (2) 221237; supervises creation of a free zone for industrial investment; Chair. ABD AL-QADIR BA-JAMMAL.

CHAMBERS OF COMMERCE

Aden Chamber of Commerce and Industry: POB 473, Queen Abban St, Crater 101, Aden; tel. (2) 221176; fax (2) 255660; e-mail cciaden@y.net.ye; f. 1886; 5,000 mems; Pres. MUHAMMAD OMER BAMASHMUS; Gen. Man. BADR MUHAMMAD BA-SALMA.

Federation of Chambers of Commerce: POB 16992, San'a; tel. (1) 211765; telex 2229; Dir JAMAL SHARHAN.

Hodeidah Chamber of Commerce: POB 3370, Az-Zubairy St, Hodeida; tel. (3) 217401; telex 5610; fax (3) 211528; f. 1960; over 1,000 mems; cap. 1m. riyals; Dir NABIL AL-WAJIH.

San'a Chamber of Commerce and Industry: Airport Rd, Al-Hasabah St, POB 195, San'a; tel. (1) 232361; telex 2629; fax (1) 232412; f. 1963; Pres. Al-Haj HUSSAIN AL-WATARI; Gen. Man. ABDULLAH H. AR-RUBAIDI.

Taiz Chamber of Commerce: POB 5029, Chamber of Commerce St, Taiz; tel. (4) 210580; telex 8960; fax (4) 212335; Dir MOFID A. SAIF.

Yemen Chamber of Commerce and Industry: POB 16690, San'a; tel. (1) 223539; fax 251555.

STATE HYDROCARBONS COMPANIES

General Corpn for Oil and Mineral Resources: San'a; f. 1990; state petroleum co; Pres. AHMAD BARAKAT.

Ministry of Oil and Mineral Resources, Aden branch: POB 5176, Maalla, Aden; tel. (2) 24542; telex 2215; f. 1969; responsible for the refining and marketing of petroleum products, and for prospecting and exploitation of indigenous hydrocarbons and other minerals; subsidiaries include:

Aden Refinery Co: POB 3003, Aden 110; tel. (2) 76234; telex 2213; fax (2) 76600; f. 1952; operates petroleum refinery; capacity 8.6m. tons per year; output 4.2m. tons (1990); operates 1 oil tanker; Exec. Dir. MUHAMMAD HUSSEIN AL-HAJ; Refinery Man. AHMAD HASSAN AL-GIFRI.

Yemen National Oil Co: POB 5050, Maalla, Aden; sole petroleum concessionaire, importer and distributor of petroleum products; Gen. Man. MUHAMMAD ABD HUSSEIN.

UTILITIES

Electricity

Public Electricity Corporation: POB 11422, Government Complex, Haddah Rd, San'a; tel. (1) 264131; telex 2619; fax (1) 263115; Man. Dir AHMAD AL-AINI.

Water

National Water and Sanitation Authority (NWSA): (Taiz Branch) POB 5283, Taiz; tel. (4) 222628; fax (4) 212323.

TRADE UNIONS

Agricultural Co-operatives Union: POB 649; tel. (1) 270685; fax (1) 274125.

General Confederation of Workers: POB 1162, Maalla, Aden; f. 1956; affiliated to WFTU and ICFTU; 35,000 mems; Pres. RAJEH SALEH NAJI; Gen. Sec. ABD AR-RAZAK SHAIF.

Trade Union Federation: San'a; Pres. ALI SAIF MUQBIL.

Transport

RAILWAYS

There are no railways in Yemen.

ROADS

In 1995 Yemen had a total road network of 64,605 km, including 5,097 km of main roads and 2,491 km of secondary roads. An estimated 8% of the road network was paved in 1995.

General Corporation for Roads and Bridges: POB 1185, Zubeiri St, Asir Rd, San'a; tel. (1) 202278; telex 2208; fax (1) 209571; responsible for maintenance and construction.

Yemen Land Transport Co: Aden; telex 2307; f. 1980; incorporates fmr Yemen Bus Co and all other public transport of the fmr PDRY; Chair. ABD AL-JALIL TAHIR BADR; Gen. Man. SALIH AWAD AL-AMUDI.

SHIPPING

Aden is the main port. In 1986 the port handled vessels with a combined displacement of 8.3m. net registered tons. Aden Main Harbour has 28 first-class berths. In addition there is ample room to accommodate vessels of light draught at anchor in the 18-foot dredged area. There is also 800 feet of cargo wharf accommodating vessels of 300 feet length and 18 feet draught. Aden Oil Harbour accommodates four tankers of 57,000 tons and up to 40 feet draught. A new port at Nishtun was opened in 1984 to assist in the exploitation of the rich fishing grounds nearby. A multi-purpose port terminal at Maalla was opened in 1993. During the mid-1990s work was proceeding on a US $580m. programme to expand container handling facilities at Aden, with the aim of establishing the port as a major transhipment centre. Completion of the main terminal was scheduled for March 1999.

There were three ports in the former YAR: Hodeida, Mocha and Salif. Hodeida is a Red Sea port of some importance, which has been considerably extended with Soviet aid. The Yemen Navigation Line, which is based in Aden, operates passenger and cargo services to many parts of the Middle East and Africa.

At 31 December 1996 Yemen's merchant fleet comprised 42 vessels, amounting to 25,084 grt.

Hodeida Port Authority: POB 3183, Hodeida; tel. (3) 75057; telex 5565.

Yemen Ports Authority: POB 1316, Steamer Point, Aden; tel. (2) 204953; telex 6278; fax (2) 213805; f. 1888; Harbour Master Capt. BARAKAT ALI DARWISH.

Principal Shipping Companies

Aden Refinery Co: POB 3003, Aden 110; tel. (2) 376234; telex 6213; fax (2) 376600; Exec.-Dir MUHAMMAD HUSSAIN AL-HAJ.

Arabian Gulf Navigation Co (Yemen) Ltd: POB 3740, Hodeida; tel. (3) 2442; telex 5507.

Elkirshi Shipping and Stevedoring Co: POB 3813, Al-Hamdi St, Hodeida; tel. (3) 224263; telex 5569; operates at ports of Hodeida, Mocha and Salif.

Hodeida Shipping and Transport Co Ltd: POB 3337, Hodeida; tel. (3) 238130; telex 5510; fax (3) 211533; cargo, container and ro-ro handling.

Middle East Shipping Co Ltd: POB 3700, Hodeida; tel. (3) 217276; telex 5505; fax (3) 211529; f. 1962; Chair. ABD AL-WASA HAYEL SAEED; Gen. Man. ABD AR-RAHIM ABD AL-GHAFUR; brs in Mocha, Aden, Taiz, Mukalla, San'a and Salif.

National Shipping Co: POB 1228, Steamer Point, Aden; tel. (2) 204861; telex 6217; fax (2) 202644; shipping, bunkering, clearing and forwarding, and travel agents; Gen. Man. MUHAMMAD OTHMAN.

Yemen Navigation Line: POB 4190, Aden; tel. (2) 24861; telex 295; fleet of 3 general cargo vessels.

Yemen Shipping Development Co Ltd: POB 3686, Hodeida; tel. (3) 239252; telex 5530; fleet of 4 general cargo vessels.

CIVIL AVIATION

There are six international airports—San'a International (13 km from the city), Aden Civil Airport (at Khormaksar, 11 km from the port of Aden), al-Ganad (at Taiz), Mukalla (Riyan), Seyoun and Hodeida Airport. In 1994 a total of 791,000 passengers travelled on scheduled services in the Republic of Yemen.

A merger of the former national carriers of the YAR and the PDRY (see below) took effect in May 1996.

Yemen Airways (Yemenia): POB 1183, Airport Rd, San'a; tel. (1) 232380; telex 2204; fax (1) 252991; f. 1963 as Yemen Airlines; nationalized as Yemen Airways Corpn 1972; present name adopted 1978; merged with airlines of fmr PDRY in 1996; owned 51% by Yemeni Govt and 49% by Govt of Saudi Arabia; supervised by a ministerial cttee under the Ministry of Transport; internal services and external services to destinations in the Middle East, Asia, Africa and Europe; Chair. HASSAN ABDO SOHBI.

Tourism

The former YAR formed a joint tourism company with the PDRY in 1980. In 1994 some 40,000 tourists visited Yemen, and tourists receipts for that year were estimated at US $41m.

Yemen Tourist Co: POB 1526, San'a; Chair. ABD AL-HADI AL-HAMDANI.

Defence

The armed forces of the former YAR and the PDRY were officially merged in May 1990, but by early 1994 the process had not been completed and in May civil war broke out between the forces of the two former states, culminating in victory for the North. In October President Saleh announced plans for the modernization of the armed forces, which would include the banning of party affiliation in the security services and armed forces, and in March 1995 the full merger of the armed forces was announced.

Supreme Commander of the Armed Forces: Lt-Gen. ALI ABDULLAH SALEH.

Chief of Staff of the Armed Forces: (vacant).

Chief of the General Staff: Brig.-Gen. ABDULLAH ALI ULAYWAH.

Estimated defence budget (1997): US $400m.

Military Service: conscription, 3 years.

Total Armed Forces (August 1997): 66,300: army 61,000; navy 1,800; air force 3,500. Reserves 40,000 (army).

Paramilitary Forces: an estimated 60,000-strong Ministry of National Security Force, and at least 20,000 tribal levies.

Education

Primary education in the Yemen is compulsory between the ages of six and 15. Secondary education, beginning at 15, lasts for a further three years. In 1993 enrolment at primary schools was equivalent to 83% of children in the relevant age-group (boys 118%; girls 47%). Enrolment at secondary schools in that year was equivalent to just 23% of students in the appropriate age-group (males 37%; females 9%). In the 1993/94 academic year, 11,999 pupils were in pre-primary education and 2,678,863 pupils attended 11,013 primary institutions. There were 212,129 pupils in secondary education in that year. In the 1991/92 academic year, 53,082 students went on to higher education, with some 15,000 students enrolled at universities in San'a and Aden. The average rate of adult illiteracy, according to unofficial sources, is 68% (males 62%; females 74%). In 1993 public expenditure on education was estimated at 13,491m. riyals, equivalent to 20.6% of total government spending.

Bibliography

Amin, Dr S. H. *Law and Justice in Contemporary Yemen.* Glasgow, Royston, 1987.

Ansaldi, C. *Il Yemen nella storia e nella leggenda.* Rome, 1933.

Attar, Mohamed Said El-. *Le sous-développement economique et social du Yémen.* Algiers, Editions Tiers-Monde, 1966.

Badeeb, Said M. *The Saudi–Egyptian Conflict over North Yemen 1962–70.* Colorado, Westview Press, 1986.

Balsan, François. *Inquiétant Yémen.* Paris, 1961.

Behbehari, Hashim, S. H. *China and the People's Democratic Republic of Yemen,* London, KP1, 1985.

Bethmann, E. W. *Yemen on the Threshold.* American Friends of the Middle East, Washington, 1960.

Bidwell, Robin. *The Two Yemens.* London, Longman, 1983.

Brinton, J. Y. *Aden and the Federation of South Arabia.* Washington, DC, American Society of International Law, 1964.

Burrowes, Robert D. *The Yemen Arab Republic: The Politics of Development 1962–1986.* London, Croom Helm, 1987.

Historical Dictionary of Yemen. London, Scarecrow Press, 1995.

Central Office of Information. *Aden and South Arabia.* London, HMSO, 1965.

Chelhod, Joseph. *L'Arabie du Sud. Histoire et civilisation.* 3 vols, Editions Maisonneuve et Larose; Vol. I: *Le peuple yéménite et ses racines;* Vol. II: *La société yéménite de l'hégire aux idéologies modernes;* Vol. III: *Culture et institutions du Yémen* (1985).

Colonial Office. *Accession of Aden to the Federation of South Arabia.* London, HMSO, 1962.

   Aden and the Yemen. London, HMSO, 1960.

   Treaty of Friendship and Protection between the United Kingdom and the Federation of South Arabia. London, HMSO, 1964.

Deutsch, Robert. *Der Yemen.* Vienna, 1914.

Doe, Brian. *Southern Arabia.* London, Thames and Hudson, 1972.

Federation of South Arabia. *Conference on Constitutional Problems of South Arabia.* HMSO, 1964.

Gavin, R. J. *Aden 1839–1967.* London, Hurst, 1973.

Gehrke, Dr Ulrich. *Südarabien, Südarabische Föderation oder Süd-Jemen?* Hamburg, Orient Magazine, German Near and Middle East Association, 1967.

Helfritz, H. *The Yemen: A Secret Journey.* London, Allen and Unwin, 1958.

Heyworth-Dunne, G. E. *Al-Yemen: Social, Political and Economic Survey.* Cairo, 1952.

Hickinbotham, Sir Tom. *Aden.* London, Constable, 1959.

Ingrams, Doreen. *A Survey of the Social and Economic Conditions of the Aden Protectorate.* London.

Ingrams, Doreen, and Ingrams, Leila (Eds), *The Records of Yemen 1798–1960.* London, Archive Editions, 1995.

Ingrams, Harold. *The Yemen; Imams, Rulers and Revolutions.* London, 1963.

Ingrams, W. H. *A Report on the Social, Economic and Political Conditions of the Hadhramaut, Aden Protectorate.* London, 1936.

   Arabia and the Isles. London, Murray, 1947.

Ismail, Tareq Y. and Jacqueline S. *The People's Democratic Republic of Yemen. Politics, Economics and Society.* London, Pinter, 1986.

Jacob, Harold F. *Kings of Arabia.* London, 1923.

Jenner, Michael. *Yemen Rediscovered.* London, Longman, 1983.

Johnston, Charles. *The View from Steamer Point.* London, Collins, 1964.

King, Gillian. *Imperial Outpost – Aden.* New York, Oxford University Press, 1964.

Knox-Mawer, June. *The Sultans Came to Tea.* London, Murray, 1961.

Kostiner, Joseph. *Yemen: The Tortuous Quest for Unity 1990–94.* London, The Royal Institute of International Affairs, 1996.

Kour, Z. H. *The History of Aden, 1839–1972.* London, Frank Cass, 1980.

Lackner, Helen. *The People's Democratic Republic of Yemen: Outpost of Socialist Development in Arabia.* London, Ithaca Press, 1985.

Ledger, David. *Shifting Sands: the British in South Arabia.* London, Peninsula Publishing, 1983.

Little, Tom. *South Arabia.* London, Pall Mall Press, 1968.

Macro, Eric. *Bibliography of the Yemen, with Notes on Mocha.* University of Miami Press, 1959.

   Yemen and the Western World since 1571. London, C. Hurst, and New York, Praeger, 1968.

Mallakh, Ragaie El-. *The Economic Development of the Yemen Arab Republic.* London, Croom Helm, 1986.

Naval Intelligence Division. *Western Arabia and the Red Sea.* (Admiralty Handbook) 1946.

O'Ballance, Edgar. *The War in the Yemen.* London, Faber, 1971.

Page, Stephen. *The Soviet Union and the Yemens: Influence in Assymetrical Relationships.* New York, Praeger, 1985.

Paget, Julian. *Last Post: Aden 1964–67.* London, Faber and Faber, 1969.

Pawelke, Gunther. *Der Yemen: Das Verbotene Land.* Düsseldorf, Econ. Verlag., 1959.

Peterson, J. E. *Yemen, the Search for a Modern State.* London, Croom Helm, 1981.

Pieragostini, Karl. *Britain, Aden and South Arabia.* London, Macmillan, 1992.

Pridham, B. R. (Ed.) *Contemporary Yemen: Politics and Historical Background.* London, Croom Helm, 1984.

   Economy and Society and Culture in Contemporary Yemen. London, Croom Helm, 1985.

Qat Commission of Inquiry. *Report.* Aden, 1958.

Rouaud, Alain. *Le Yémen.* Brussels, Editions Complexe, 1979.

Schmidt, Dana Adams. *Yemen, the Unknown War.* London, Bodley Head, 1968.

Scott, H. *In the High Yemen.* London, Murray, 1942.

Serjeant, R. B. *The Portuguese off the South Arabian Coast.* Oxford, Clarendon, 1963; reprinted Beirut, 1974.

Serjeant, R. B., and Lwecokc, Ronald. *San'a: an Arabian Islamic City.* London, 1983.

Smith, G. Rex. *The Yemens.* Oxford, World Bibliographical Series, Clio Press, 1984.

Stookey, Robert W. *Yemen: The Politics of the Yemen Arab Republic.* Westview Press, 1978.

al-Suwaidi, Jamal S. (Ed.) *The Yemeni War of 1994: Causes and Consequences.* Saqi Books, 1995.

Trevaskis, Sir Kennedy. *Shades of Amber, A South Arabian Episode.* London, Hutchinson, 1967.

Van der Meulen, Daniel. *Hadhramaut: Some of Its Mysteries Unveiled.* Leiden, 1932, reprinted 1964.

Waterfield, Gordon. *Sultans of Aden.* London, Murray, 1968.

Wenner, Manfred W. *Yemen: a selected Bibliography of Literature since 1960.* Washington, DC, Library of Congress Legislative Reference Service, 1965.

   Modern Yemen, 1918–1966. Baltimore, Johns Hopkins Press, 1967.